Full pronunciation key

The pronunciation of each word is shown just after the word, in this way: **ab·bre·vi·ate** (ə brē′vē āt).

The letters and signs used are pronounced as in the words below.

The mark ′ is placed after a syllable with primary or heavy accent, as in the example above.

The mark ′ after a syllable shows a secondary or lighter accent, as in **ab·bre·vi·a·tion** (ə brē′vē ā′shən).

a	hat, cap	**p**	paper, cup
ā	age, face	**r**	run, try
â	care, fair	**s**	say, yes
ä	father, far	**sh**	she, rush
b	bad, rob	**t**	tell, it
ch	child, much	**th**	thin, both
d	did, red	**ŦH**	then, smooth
e	let, best	**u**	cup, butter
ē	equal, be	**ů**	full, put
ėr	term, learn	**ü**	rule, move
f	fat, if	**v**	very, save
g	go, bag	**w**	will, woman
h	he, how	**y**	young, yet
i	it, pin	**z**	zero, breeze
ī	ice, five	**zh**	measure, seizure
j	jam, enjoy	**ə**	represents:
k	kind, seek		a in about
l	land, coal		e in taken
m	me, am		i in pencil
n	no, in		o in lemon
ng	long, bring		u in circus
o	hot, rock		
ō	open, go		
ȯ	all, caught		
ô	order, all		
oi	oil, voice		
ou	house, out		

Thorndike-Barnhart

Junior Dictionary

by E. L. Thorndike / Clarence L. Barnhart

HarperCollins*Publishers*

This dictionary is also published under the title *ScottForesman Intermediate Dictionary*.

This dictionary includes a few entries that are registered trademarks in the United States at the time of this book's copyright; the entries are so identified, as a fact of reference. No judgment should be made or understood, however, as to the actual legal status of any word in the dictionary.

THORNDIKE-BARNHART JUNIOR DICTIONARY. Copyright © 1997 by Scott, Foresman and Company. All rights reserved. Printed in the United States of America. No part of this book may be used or reproduced in any manner whatsoever without written permission except in the case of brief quotations embodied in critical articles and reviews. For information regarding permission, please write to: Scott, Foresman and Company, 1900 East Lake Avenue, Glenview, Illinois 60025.

HarperCollins books may be purchased for business or sales promotional use. For information, please write to: Special Markets Department, HarperCollins Publishers, Inc., 10 East 53rd Street, New York, New York 10022.

Feature Design
Curtis Design / Chicago

First HarperCollins edition 1997.
Picture credits appear on pages 1006-1008.
ISBN 0-06-270161-4

Library of Congress Cataloging-in-Publication Data available upon request

1 2 3 4 5 6 7 8 9 DR 99 98 97 96

Table of Contents

Spellings of English Sounds   *ii*

Parts of an Entry   *iv*

How to Use This Dictionary   *v*

Your Dictionary A to Z   1–1005

Special Information Pages

The Atmosphere	53A–B
China and the Silk Road	153A–B
Dinosaurs	247A–B
Ecosystems	279A–B
Knights and Castles	485A–B
Marine Life	535A–B
Painting	625A–B
Ranks in the U.S. Military	712
Rome: Life in Ancient Rome	747A–B
Sculpture	773A–B
Space	828A–B
Volcanoes	963A–B
Weights and Measures	975A–B
Art Credits	1006–1008

Student Reference Section

Table of Contents	1009
World: Focus on the Atlantic	1010
Physical Features of the World	1012
These United States	1014
Presidents of the United States	1016
Table of Chemical Elements	1020
Geological Time	1021
Mathematical Formulas	1022
Proofreader's Marks	1024

Spellings of English Sounds

This chart shows all the sounds of the English language, and it lists the ways in which each sound may be spelled. It can help you find words you can say but do not know how to spell.

The pronunciation symbols used in this dictionary are shown in the colored boxes. Each symbol represents a different sound.

Following each symbol are words showing different ways the sound may be spelled. The letters used to spell the sound are printed in red type. Common spellings are listed first.

Some of the words used as examples are in more than one list. This is because the words are pronounced in more than one way.

Sound	Spelling and examples
a	at, plaid, half, laugh, baa
ā	age, aid, say, suede, eight, vein, they, break, bouquet, straight, gauge, éclair, eh, matinee
â	care, air, aerial, ere, prayer, their, pear, heir
ä	father, heart, sergeant, ah, calm, guard, bazaar, yacht, baa
b	bad, rabbit
ch	child, future, watch, question, righteous, cello, Czech
d	did, filled, add
e	end, bread, any, said, friend, leopard, says, heifer, bury
ē	equal, happy, each, bee, ski, believe, ceiling, key, algae, phoenix, people, quay, buoy
ėr	stern, turn, first, word, earth, journey, myrtle, err, whirr, purr, myrrh, herb, worry, colonel

Sound	Spelling and examples
f	fat, effort, phrase, laugh
g	go, egg, league, guest, ghost
gz	exact, exhibit
h	he, who
i	in, enough, hymn, manage, ear, build, sieve, busy, marriage, been, women, weird, Aegean
ī	ice, sky, lie, high, rye, eye, island, stein, height, buy, bayou, aisle, aye, geyser, coyote
j	gem, large, jam, bridge, region, gradual, badger, soldier, exaggerate
k	coat, kind, back, chemist, account, excite, quit, antique, liquor, acquire, khaki, saccharin, biscuit, ache
ks	tax, tactics
l	land, tell, kiln

Sound	Spelling and examples	Sound	Spelling and examples
m	me, common, climb, solemn, phlegm	TH	then, breathe
n	no, manner, knife, gnaw, pneumonia	u	under, other, trouble, flood, does
ng	ink, long, tongue, handkerchief	u̇	full, good, detour, wolf, should, pleurisy
o	odd, honest, knowledge	ü	food, rule, move, soup, threw, blue, fruit, shoe, maneuver, through, lieutenant, buoy
ō	old, oak, own, soul, toe, brooch, though, folk, beau, oh, chauffeur, owe, sew, yeoman		
ȯ	all, auto, awful, ought, walk, taught, cough, awe, Utah	v	very, have, of, Stephen, divvy
ô	order, oar, mourn	w	will, wheat, quick, bivouac, choir
oi	oil, boy, buoy	wu	one
ou	out, owl, bough, hour	y	opinion, yes, hallelujah, azalea
p	pay, happy	yü	use, few, feud, cue, view, beauty, adieu, yule, queue
r	run, carry, wrong, rhythm	yu̇	uranium, Europe
s	say, cent, tense, dance, miss, scent, listen, psychology, waltz, sword, schism	z	has, zero, buzz, scissors, xylophone, discern, raspberry, asthma, czar
sh	nation, she, special, mission, tension, machine, conscience, issue, ocean, schwa, sugar, nauseous, pshaw, crescendo	zh	division, measure, garage, azure, regime, equation, jabot, brazier
t	tell, button, stopped, doubt, two, Thomas, receipt, indict, pizza	ə	occur, about, April, essential, cautious, circus, oxygen, bargain, gaiety, dungeon, tortoise, pageant, authority
th	thin		

The Parts of a Dictionary Entry

1. The **entry word** is printed in dark type. It shows how the word is spelled and how it may be divided in writing.

2. The **homograph number** appears when two or more entry words are spelled the same way.

3. The **pronunciation** is in parentheses. Letters in the pronunciation stand for special sounds. These are explained in the pronunciation key at the bottom of every right-hand page.

4. The **part-of-speech label** is an abbreviation in slanting type naming the function of the entry word. When a word may function as more than one part of speech, a label appears after each definition number.

5. The **usage label** shows that use of a word or meaning is limited.

6. The **definition** of a word tells what it means. A word with several meanings has numbered definitions, one for each meaning.

7. The **example** is printed in slanting type after the definition. It shows how the entry word may be used with that particular meaning.

8. The **inflected forms**, in small dark type, are shown whenever their spelling or form might give you trouble.

9. The **homophone note**, with a color square, comes toward the end of an entry. It tells you what words sound the same as the entry word but are spelled differently, so that you can look them up if you need to.

10. The **variant spelling**, beginning with "Also," tells you other correct ways of spelling an entry word.

11. The **run-on entry**, in small dark type, is an undefined word. Its meaning combines the meaning of the entry word with a familiar ending. Each run-on entry has a part-of-speech label.

12. The **idiom**, in dark pink type, follows the rest of an entry. An idiom is a phrase with a special definition.

13. The **feature**, with a color stripe and a title, comes toward the end of an entry. It tells you more information about the entry word: its history, or its synonyms, or how to use it. If the history of the word is short, it appears without the stripe or the title, in blue type within square brackets.

① ③ ⑥

ba·by-sit (bā′bē sit′), *v.* to take care of a child or children while the parents are away for a while. ❑ *v.* **ba·by-sat** (bā′bē sat′), **ba·by-sit·ting.** —**ba′by-sit′ter,** *n.*

⑪ ⑧

④ ⑥ ⑦

bare (bâr), **1** *adj.* without covering; not clothed; naked: *The sun burned her bare shoulders.* **2** *adj.* with the head uncovered; bareheaded. **3** *adj.* not furnished; empty: *a room bare of furniture.* **4** *adj.* plain; not adorned: *a bare little cabin in the woods.* **5** *adj.* just enough and no more; mere: *She earns only a bare living by her work.* **6** *v.* to make bare; uncover; reveal: *to bare your feelings. The dog bared its teeth.* ❑ *adj.* **bar·er, bar·est;** *v.* **bared, bar·ing.** ■ Another word that sounds like this is **bear.** —**bare′ness,** *n.*

lay bare, to uncover; expose; reveal: *The police laid bare the plot to rob the bank.*

⑫

⑨ ⑧ ⑪

②

bark¹ (bärk), **1** *n.* the tough outside covering of the trunk and branches of trees. **2** *v.* to scrape the skin from: *I fell down the steps and barked my shins.*

bark² (bärk), **1** *n.* the short, sharp sound that a dog makes. **2** *n.* a sound like this: *the bark of a fox, the bark of a gun.* **3** *v.* to make this sound: *The dog barked. Rifles barked.* **4** *v.* to speak gruffly or sharply: *The police barked out orders.*

bark³ (bärk), *n.* **1** ship with three masts, square-rigged on the first two masts and fore-and-aft-rigged on the other. **2** OLD USE. boat; ship. Also, **barque.**

⑩ ⑤

⑧

batch (bach), *n.* **1** quantity of bread, cookies, etc., made at one baking. ■ See Synonym Study at **group.** **2** quantity of anything made as one lot or set: *Our second batch of candy was better than the first.* **3** number of persons or things taken together: *We caught a fine batch of fish.* ❑ *n., pl.* **batch·es.**

WORD STORY   **Batch** comes from an old English word meaning "to bake." The same way that you do a deed, think a thought, or see a sight, you would bake a batch. Now the word is used about other things, too.

⑬

How to Use the Dictionary

Dictionary Entries

Dictionary information is divided into sections called entries. A dictionary entry includes spelling, syllable spacing, pronunciation, meaning, usage, and history. A dictionary entry begins with an entry word, written in dark type. It may be a word, a phrase, a prefix or suffix, an abbreviation, a chemical symbol, an acronym, or a proper name. Syllable division of an entry, shown by dots between syllables, indicates where hyphens may be placed when a word needs to be written on on two lines. (Usually one-letter syllables are not hyphenated when writing.) An entry may include inflected forms of nouns, pronouns, adjectives, and verbs, or suffixal forms. All entries are in a single alphabetical list.

Words that Aren't Entry Words

Some words are other forms of base words, and are included in the entries for those base words. **Echoes, echoed,** and **echoing** are other forms of the noun and verb entry word **echo. Edgier** and **edgiest** are other forms of the adjective **edgy.** Other words are suffixal compounds formed from base words. **Eagerly** and **eagerness** are adverb and noun suffixal forms made from the base word **eager.** Extra words like these are in dark type at or near the end of the entry for the base word.

Alphabetical Order

Words are listed in a dictionary in alphabetical order. Spaces between word phrases are ignored for alphabetical purposes: **sea lion** comes after **sealing wax.** Sometimes, two or more words have the same spelling, for historical reasons. Such words have little numbers at the end. To find your word, you need to look at all the words spelled alike.

Guide Words

Guide words at the top of every page show what words are on the page. All words on the page come between the guide words in alphabetical order.

Pronunciations

Pronunciations are provided for every entry word that is not pronounced somewhere else in the dictionary. They consist of symbols that are mainly English letters, with a few marks above some letters. There is a single symbol for each separate sound in English. A short key to these marks appears at the bottom of every right-side page. A complete table of all symbols appears at the very beginning and at the very end of the book. Key words are shown with each pronunciation symbol. Each symbol should be pronounced as it is in its key word: a as in **hat,** zh as in **vision,** etc.

A symbol that is not a letter is the schwa (ə), pronounced like uh, or the *a* in **about.** Pronunciations are divided into syllables. Syllable stress, or accent, is shown by the marks ′ (primary accent) or ′ (secondary accent), as in **butter** (but′ər), or **buttermilk** (but′ər milk′).

All pronunciations listed in this dictionary are considered correct by educated speakers. Some words have more than one acceptable pronunciation wherever you live in this country; other words have different pronunciations in different parts of the country.

Definitions

The meanings of entry words are given in clear, easy-to-understand definitions. A definition is sometimes followed by a semicolon and a synonym. Example sentences or phrases sometimes follow a definition; they are written in slanted, or italic, type.

An entry word may have more than one meaning; if so, the definitions are numbered separately. Or an entry word may be used as more than one part of speech; in this case, a part-of-speech label accompanies each definition number.

Sometimes a phrase that includes an entry word does not mean what it appears to mean, from the words that it contains. "To pull someone's leg" does not mean what it literally says. A phrase like this, called an idiom, is listed near the end of the entry for the main word in the phrase, or **leg**, in this case.

Usage

Some words have limits on their use. The dictionary includes labels on these words. The word **ere** bears the label OLD USE, indicating that the word is old-fashioned. The label INFORMAL goes with the word **lazybones**, indicating that the word is used in everyday talk and casual writing, but not in formal writing or speeches. The label SLANG means that a word such as **wacky** is used in talk among friends, but not in writing except to imitate talk.

A brief note accompanies some entry words, such as **squaw** and **between**. These notes are printed at the end of the entry, and give other kinds of information about word usage.

Word Histories

Every word in English has a history. The word either is native to English, having been used since the earliest stage of English, or it was borrowed from another language, or it arose in one of a number of other ways. This dictionary includes word histories for many words that have especially interesting stories to tell about how they came to be. Brief histories appear in colored type at the end of entries; if the story is not so short, it has its own title and a color background to emphasize it.

Because of the number of words that English has borrowed from other languages,

there are lists of words given at the entries for many names of languages. This information has a color background and a title of its own.

Some groups of words are closely related, coming as they do from a common source. The dictionary includes some of these word families.

Some Other Features

There are three other kinds of information about words given in the dictionary, printed also over patches of color to make them stand out. They are included to give help in choosing the best word for an idea when you are writing something.

A Synonym Study is a list of two or more words with similar meanings. It explains some differences between the meanings. A Synonym Study gives an example sentence for each word's particular sense. Like a Synonym Study, a Word Bank can help you find words for your ideas. A Word Bank is a list of several words, all with meanings connected to one main subject.

Word Power is a feature that gives you added information about taking words apart and putting them together. With the prefixes and suffixes listed in the Word Powers, it is easy to recognize ideas when you see them as word parts.

Illustrations

Illustrations accompany many dictionary entries. They supply graphic details to the verbal definitions, as a help to understanding. Sizes of animals are included.

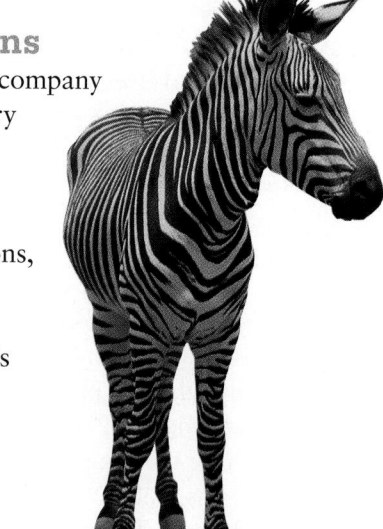

A or **a**¹ (ā), *n.* the first letter of the English alphabet. ❑ *n., pl.* **A's** or **a's.**

A, 1 acre or acres. **2** ampere or amperes.

a² (ə; *stressed* ā), *indefinite article.* **1** any: *A tree has leaves.* **2** one: *Buy a dozen eggs, a loaf of bread, and a pound of butter, please.* **3** every: *Thanksgiving comes once a year.* **4** one kind of: *Chemistry is a science.*

a., 1 acre or acres. **2** ampere or amperes.

AA, 1 Alcoholics Anonymous. **2** antiaircraft.

AAA or **A.A.A.,** Automobile Association of America.

aard·vark (ärd′värk), *n.* a burrowing African mammal with a piglike snout, a long, sticky tongue, and very strong claws. It feeds on ants and termites.

WORD STORY   **Aardvark** comes from Dutch words meaning "earth pig." Dutch settlers in South Africa gave the aardvark this name because it lives in a hole in the ground and has a snout like that of a pig.

Aar·on (âr′ən), *n.* (in the Bible) the brother of Moses and the first high priest of the Hebrews. [**Aaron** comes from a Hebrew word meaning "lofty mountain."]

Aar·on (âr′ən), *n.* **Hank** (hangk), born 1934, American baseball player. ■ **Hank Aaron** hit 755 home runs during his career. His lifetime batting average was .305.

A.B., Bachelor of Arts. Also, **B.A.**

a·back (ə bak′), *adv.* **taken aback,** surprised; confused: *I was taken aback by my friend's angry reply.*

ab·a·cus (ab′ə kəs), *n.* frame with rows of counters or beads that slide back and forth. Abacuses are used in China, Japan, Korea, etc., for adding and other tasks in arithmetic. ❑ *n., pl.* **ab·a·cus·es, ab·a·ci** (ab′ə sī).

a·baft (ə baft′), *adv.* at or toward the back of a ship; aft.

ab·a·lo·ne (ab′ə lō′nē), *n.* shellfish that can be eaten, with a large, rather flat shell lined with mother-of-pearl.

a·ban·don (ə ban′dən), **1** *v.* to give up entirely: *We abandoned the idea of a picnic because of the rain.* **2** *v.* to leave without intending to return to; desert: *The crew abandoned the ship before it sank.* **3** *v.* to give yourself up completely to a feeling or impulse: *When her father died, she abandoned herself to grief.* **4** *n.* freedom from restraint; wild enthusiasm: *The students on the winning side began to cheer with abandon, waving and yelling.* **—a·ban′don·er,** *n.* **—a·ban′don·ment,** *n.*

a·ban·doned (ə ban′dənd), *adj.* **1** deserted: *an old, abandoned house.* **2** wicked; immoral: *an abandoned life.* **3** unrestrained: *abandoned glee.* **—a·ban′doned·ly,** *adv.*

a	hat	ė	term	ô	order	ch	child		a in about
ā	age	i	it	oi	oil	ng	long		e in taken
ä	far	ī	ice	ou	out	sh	she	ə	i in pencil
â	care	o	hot	u	cup	th	thin		o in lemon
e	let	ō	open	ů	put	ᵺ	then		u in circus
ē	equal	ȯ	saw	ü	rule	zh	measure		

a·base (ə bās′), *v.* to make lower in rank, condition, or character; degrade: *Public officials who take bribes abase themselves.* ❏ *v.* **a·based, a·bas·ing.** —**a·base′ment,** *n.*

a·bash (ə bash′), *v.* to make uneasy, shy, and somewhat ashamed; embarrass and confuse: *I was abashed by the laughter of my classmates.* —**a·bash′ment,** *n.*

a·bate (ə bāt′), *v.* to make or become less; decrease; diminish: *Her confidence helped to abate my fear. Although the rain has abated, it is still very windy.* ❏ *v.* **a·bat·ed, a·bat·ing.** —**a·bat′er,** *n.*

a·bate·ment (ə bāt′mənt), *n.* **1** a decrease; lessening. **2** amount abated; reduction.

ab·bess (ab′is), *n.* woman who is the head of an abbey of nuns. ❏ *n., pl.* **ab·bess·es.**

ab·bey (ab′ē), *n.* **1** the building or buildings where monks or nuns live, ruled by an abbot or abbess; monastery or convent. **2** church or building that was once an abbey or part of an abbey: *Westminster Abbey.* ❏ *n., pl.* **ab·beys.**

abbey (def. 2)

ab·bot (ab′ət), *n.* man who is the head of an abbey of monks.

abbrev. or **abbr.,** abbreviation.

ab·bre·vi·ate (ə brē′vē āt′), *v.* **1** to make a word or phrase shorter so that a part stands for the whole: *We abbreviate "hour" as "hr."* ■ See Synonym Study at **shorten. 2** to make briefer. ❏ *v.* **ab·bre·vi·at·ed, ab·bre·vi·at·ing.**

ab·bre·vi·a·tion (ə brē′vē ā′shən), *n.* **1** a shortened form of a word or phrase standing for the whole: *"Dr." is an abbreviation for "Doctor."* **2** act of making briefer.

ABC, American Broadcasting Company.

ABC's, *n.pl.* **1** the alphabet. **2** facts or skills to be learned first; basic principles: *We learned the ABC's of swimming at camp this summer.*

ab·di·cate (ab′də kāt), *v.* to give up or formally renounce office, power, or authority; resign: *When the king abdicated his throne, his brother became king.* ❏ *v.* **ab·di·cat·ed, ab·di·cat·ing.** —**ab′di·ca′tion,** *n.* —**ab′di·ca′tor,** *n.*

ab·do·men (ab′də mən *or* ab dō′mən), *n.* **1** the part of the body containing the stomach, the intestines, and other important organs; belly. **2** the last of the three parts of the body of an insect or a crustacean. —**ab·dom·i·nal** (ab dom′ ə nəl), *adj.*

ab·duct (ab dukt′), *v.* to carry off a person by force or by trickery; kidnap. —**ab·duc′tion,** *n.* —**ab·duc′tor,** *n.*

a·beam (ə bēm′), *adv.* opposite the middle of a ship's side: *They came abeam of the lighthouse.*

a·bed (ə bed′), *adv.* in bed.

A·bel (ā′bəl), *n.* (in the Bible) the second son of Adam and Eve. Abel was killed by his older brother Cain. [Abel comes from a Hebrew word meaning "breath" or "vanity."]

Ab·e·na·ki (ab nä′kē), *n.* member of a tribe of American Indians who live mainly in southern Quebec and Maine. ❏ *n., pl.* **Ab·e·na·ki** or **Ab·e·na·kis.** [Abenaki comes from a word in the language of a neighboring people meaning "easterners." The neighbors, of course, lived to the west.]

Ab·er·deen (ab′ər dēn′), *n.* **1** city in NE South Dakota. **2** port in E Scotland.

Aberdeen An·gus (ang′gəs), any of a breed of small, black, hornless cattle raised for beef, originally bred in Scotland. ❏ *pl.* **Aberdeen An·gus·es.**

ab·er·rant (ab er′ənt), *adj.* different from what is regular, normal, or right. —**ab·er′rant·ly,** *adv.*

ab·er·ra·tion (ab′ə rā′shən), *n.* **1** act of wandering from the normal or right practice: *A lie is an aberration from the truth.* **2** a disordering of the mind: *His peculiarities are no more than harmless aberrations.* **3** failure of a lens or mirror to bring to a single focus the rays of light coming from one point: *Aberration in the mirror caused a blurred and crooked image.* **4** a slight repeated change in the apparent position of a star, planet, etc., seen through a telescope, caused by the movement of the earth.

a·bet (ə bet′), *v.* to encourage or help, especially in doing something wrong: *The thief was abetted in the robbery by two accomplices.* ❏ *v.* **a·bet·ted, a·bet·ting.** —**a·bet′tor** or **a·bet′ter,** *n.*

a·bey·ance (ə bā′əns), *n.* **in abeyance,** in a state of delay; postponed until some later time: *Plans for the new light-rail system were held in abeyance until a budget was prepared.*

ab·hor (ab hôr′), *v.* to shrink away from with horror; feel disgust or hate for; detest: *Most people abhor the thought of war.* ❏ *v.* **ab·horred, ab·hor·ring.** [Abhor comes from Latin words meaning "from" and "to shudder."] —**ab·hor′rer,** *n.*

ab·hor·rence (ab hôr′əns), *n.* a feeling of very great hatred; horror; disgust: *I have an abhorrence of snakes.*

ab·hor·rent (ab hôr′ənt), *adj.* causing horror; disgusting; hateful: *Lying and stealing are abhorrent to someone who is honest.* —**ab·hor′rent·ly,** *adv.*

a·bide (ə bīd′), *v.* **1** to put up with; endure: *I can't abide their always being late.* **2** to stay; remain: *Abide with me for a time.* **3** to dwell; reside. **4** OLD USE. to wait for. ❏ *v.* **a·bode** or **a·bid·ed, a·bid·ing.** —**a·bid′er,** *n.*

abide by, 1 to accept and carry out; obey: *Both teams will abide by the umpire's decision.* **2** to remain faithful to; fulfill: *You must abide by your promise.*

a·bid·ing (ə bī′ding), *adj.* permanent; lasting: *The old sailor had an abiding love of the sea.* —**a·bid′ing·ly,** *adv.*

Ab·i·djan (ab′i jän′), *n.* port and largest city in Côte d'Ivoire, in the SE part.

Ab·i·lene (ab′ə lēn′), *n.* **1** city in central Texas. **2** town in central Kansas.

a·bil·i·ty (ə bil′ə tē), *n.* **1** power to do or act: *Dogs have the ability to hear sounds that people cannot.* **2** power to do some special thing; skill: *He has great ability in making jewelry.* **3** special natural gift; talent: *Musical ability often shows itself early in life.* ❏ *n., pl.* **a·bil·i·ties.**

-ability, *suffix.* quality, condition, or fact of being ___able: *readability = quality or condition of being readable.*

a·bi·ot·ic (ā′bī ot′ik), *adj.* not living and not made by a living thing; inorganic: *Rocks are an abiotic part of the environment.*

ab·ject (ab′jekt), *adj.* **1** so unhappy as to be hopeless; miserable: *Many people live in abject poverty.* **2** deserving contempt; lacking in self-respect: *abject fear, abject flattery.* —**ab·ject′ly,** *adv.* —**ab·ject′ness,** *n.*

ab·jure (ab jūr′), *v.* to swear publicly to give up: *An alien must abjure foreign citizenship before becoming an American citizen.* ❏ *v.* **ab·jured, ab·jur·ing.** —**ab′ju·ra′tion,** *n.* —**ab·jur′er,** *n.*

ab·la·tion (ab lā′shən), *n.* destruction by melting, vaporizing, etc., of part of the nose cone of a missile or spacecraft when it reenters the atmosphere.

a·blaze (ə blāz′), *adj.* **1** on fire: *The forest was set ablaze by lightning.* **2** shining brightly: *The hotel was ablaze with lights.*

a·ble (ā′bəl), *adj.* **1** having enough power, skill, or means to do something; capable: *A cat is able to see in the dark.* **2** having more power or skill than usual; skillful: *She is an able teacher.* **3** done with skill: *The audience applauded her able speech.* ❏ *adj.* **a·bler, a·blest.**

SYNONYM STUDY **Able, capable,** and **competent** all mean having the ability or skill to do something. **Able** suggests the general ability to do or act: *He is now able to earn a living.* **Capable** suggests special fitness for a task: *She is a capable teacher.* **Competent** suggests having enough skill to do something in a satisfactory way: *A competent driver is not necessarily a competent mechanic.*

-able, *suffix.* able to be ___ed: *enjoyable = able to be enjoyed.*

a·ble-bod·ied (ā′bəl bod′ēd), *adj.* strong and healthy; physically fit.

able-bodied seaman or **able seaman,** an experienced seaman who can perform all the duties required of a seaman.

a·bloom (ə blüm′), *adj.* in bloom; blossoming.

ab·lu·tions (ab lü′shənz), *n.pl.* act of washing or cleansing the body, especially as part of a religious ceremony.

a·bly (ā′blē), *adv.* in an able manner; with skill; capably.

-ably, *suffix.* in a ___ manner: *peaceably = in a peaceable manner; pleasurably = in a pleasurable manner.*

ABM, antiballistic missile.

ab·ne·ga·tion (ab′nə gā′shən), *n.* act of giving up your own interests and desires; self-denial; self-sacrifice: *to lead a life of abnegation.*

ab·nor·mal (ab nôr′məl), *adj.* different from the usual, ordinary, or expected conditions; unusual: *an abnormal amount of rain.* **—ab·nor′mal·ly,** *adv.*

ab·nor·mal·i·ty (ab′nôr mal′ə tē), *n.* **1** an abnormal thing or happening. **2** an abnormal condition. ❑ *n., pl.* **ab·nor·mal·i·ties.**

a·board (ə bôrd′), *adv., prep.* on board; in or on a ship, train, bus, airplane, etc.: *"All aboard!" shouted the conductor, and everyone rushed for the train. We had to be aboard the ship by noon.*

a·bode (ə bōd′), **1** *n.* place to live in; dwelling; house: *A simple hut was their abode.* **2** *v.* a past tense and a past participle of **abide:** *She abode there one year.*

a·bol·ish (ə bol′ish), *v.* to do away with completely; put an end to: *Many people wish that nations would abolish war.* **—a·bol′ish·a·ble,** *adj.* **—a·bol′ish·er,** *n.* **—a·bol′ish·ment,** *n.*

ab·o·li·tion (ab′ə lish′ən), *n.* act of putting an end to something: *The abolition of slavery in the United States occurred in 1865.*

ab·o·li·tion·ist (ab′ə lish′ə nist), *n.* person who wishes to put an end to something. People who worked during the early 1800s to end slavery in the United States were called **Abolitionists.**

A-bomb (ā′bom′), *n.* an atomic bomb.

a·bom·i·na·ble (ə bom′ə nə bəl), *adj.* **1** arousing disgust and hatred; loathsome: *Kidnapping is an abominable act.* **2** very unpleasant; disagreeable. **—a·bom′i·na·bly,** *adv.*

Abominable Snowman, an apelike creature supposed to inhabit the higher parts of the Himalayas; yeti.

a·bom·i·nate (ə bom′ə nāt), *v.* **1** to feel disgust and hatred for; loathe: *I abominate cruelty.* **2** to dislike strongly: *She abominates hot, humid weather.* ❑ *v.* **a·bom·i·nat·ed, a·bom·i·nat·ing.**

a·bom·i·na·tion (ə bom′ə nā′shən), *n.* **1** a disgusting or loathsome thing. **2** a feeling of disgust; loathing.

ab·o·rig·i·nal (ab′ə rij′ə nəl), *adj.* **1** existing from the beginning; original; native: *the aboriginal inhabitants of a continent.* **2** of the earliest known inhabitants: *an aboriginal custom.* **—ab′o·rig′i·nal·ly,** *adv.*

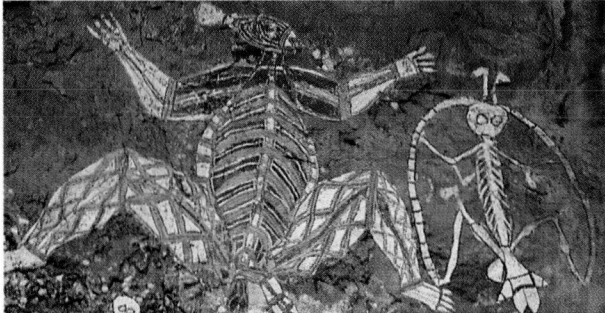
aborigine (def. 2)—art by Aborigines

ab·o·rig·i·ne (ab′ə rij′ə nē), *n.* **1** one of the earliest known inhabitants of a country or area. **2** Aborigine, one of the earliest known inhabitants of Australia. ❑ *n., pl.* **ab·o·rig·i·nes** for 1, **Ab·o·rig·i·nes** for 2.

WORD STORY **Aborigine** comes from a Latin phrase meaning "from the beginning." This is what the Romans called the people who lived in Italy before them.

a·bort (ə bôrt′), *v.* **1** to fail to develop or come to completion: *The rocket flight aborted.* **2** to cause to fail to come to completion: *abort a mission.* **3** to give birth before a fetus can live; miscarry. **4** to remove from the uterus or cause to be born prematurely: *abort a fetus.*

a·bor·tion (ə bôr′shən), *n.* **1** the removal or birth of a developing embryo before it is able to live outside the mother's body. **2** failure to develop or to be completed.

a·bor·tive (ə bôr′tiv), *adj.* **1** unsuccessful; fruitless *An attempt to build a computer in the early 1800s proved abortive.* **2** born too early to live. **—a·bor′tive·ly,** *adv.* **—a·bor′tive·ness,** *n.*

a·bound (ə bound′), *v.* **1** to be plentiful: *Fish abound in the ocean.* **2** to be well supplied; be filled; be rich: *The ocean abounds with fish.*

WORD STORY **Abound** and **abundance** both come from a Latin word meaning "a wave." When things abound, they overflow like waves. An abundance of something is so much that it overflows.

a·bout (ə bout′), **1** *prep.* concerning; having something to do with: *"Black Beauty" is a story about a horse.* **2** *prep.* approximately; roughly: *He weighs about 100 pounds.* **3** *prep.* approximately at: *We arrived about 6:00 p.m.* **4** *adv.* nearly; almost: *I have about finished my work.* **5** *prep., adv.* all around; around: *A collar goes about the neck. Look about and tell me what you see.* **6** *adv.* in the opposite direction: *You are going the wrong way. Face about!* **7** *adv.* one after another; by turns: *Turn about is fair play.* **8** *adj.* moving around; active: *He is able to be up and about.* **9** *adj.* ready; going: *The plane is about to take off.*

a·bout-face (ə bout′fās′ for noun; ə bout′fās′ for verb), **1** *n.* act of turning or going in the opposite direction. **2** *n.* a shift to the opposite attitude or opinion. **3** *v.* to turn or go in the opposite direction. ❑ *v.* **a·bout-faced, a·bout-fac·ing.**

a·bove (ə buv′), **1** *adv.* in or at a higher place; overhead: *The sky is above.* **2** *prep.* to or in a higher place than: *Birds fly above the trees.* **3** *prep.* higher than; over: *A captain is above a sergeant.* **4** *prep.* more than: *Our club has above thirty members—thirty-five, to be exact.* **5** *prep.* beyond: *Turn at the first corner above the school.* **6** *prep.* too great in importance for; superior to: *be above acting in such a childish manner.* **7** *adv., adj.* earlier in a book or article: *See what is written above. The above definition contains six words.* **8** *adv.* above zero: *The temperature is five above.*

a·bove·board (ə buv′bôrd′), *adj., adv.* in open sight; without tricks or concealment: *Everything that the mayor did was open and aboveboard. Her campaign was run aboveboard.*

ab·ra·ca·dab·ra (ab′rə kə dab′rə), *n.* **1** word supposed to have magic power. **2** meaningless talk; senseless chatter.

a·brade (ə brād′), *v.* to wear down by rubbing or scraping: *Glaciers abrade rocks.* ❑ *v.* **a·brad·ed, a·brad·ing.** **—a·brad′er,** *n.*

A·bra·ham (ā′brə ham), *n.* (in the Bible) the ancestor of the Hebrews. [**Abraham** comes from a Hebrew word that may mean "exalted father."]

a·bra·sion (ə brā′zhən), *n.* **1** place where the skin has been scraped or rubbed away: *He had an abrasion on his knee from falling on gravel.* **2** act of wearing down by rubbing or scraping: *Coins become thinner by constant abrasion.*

a·bra·sive (ə brā′siv), **1** *n.* substance that erodes, grinds, or polishes a surface by friction. Sandpaper, pumice, and emery are abrasives. **2** *adj.* wearing down by rubbing; causing abrasion. **3** *adj.* harsh or crude in manner: *an abrasive person.* **—a·bra′sive·ly,** *adv.* **—a·bra′sive·ness,** *n.*

a·breast (ə brest′), **1** *adv., adj.* side by side: *The soldiers marched four abreast. The airplane had four seats per row, two abreast on each side of the aisle.* **2** *adv.* up with; alongside of; even with: *I watch the news to keep abreast of what is going on.*

a	hat	ė	term	ô	order	ch	child		
ā	age	i	it	oi	oil	ng	long		a in about
ä	far	ī	ice	ou	out	sh	she		e in taken
â	care	o	hot	u	cup	th	thin	ə {	i in pencil
e	let	ō	open	ů	put	ŦH	then		o in lemon
ē	equal	ò	saw	ü	rule	zh	measure		u in circus

a·bridge (ə brij′), v. **1** to make shorter, especially by using fewer words: *A long story can be abridged by leaving out unimportant parts.* ■ See Synonym Study at **shorten**. **2** to make less: *The rights of citizens must not be abridged without proper cause.* ❑ v. **a·bridged, a·bridg·ing.** —**a·bridg′er,** n.

a·bridg·ment or **a·bridge·ment** (ə brij′mənt), n. **1** a shortened form of a book, long article, etc.: *That one book is an abridgment of a three-volume history.* **2** act of making shorter.

a·broad (ə brôd′), **1** adv. outside your country; to a foreign land: *I am going abroad next year to study in Italy.* **2** adv. far and wide; widely: *The news that the circus was coming spread abroad quickly.* **3** adj. going around; in motion; current: *A rumor is abroad that school will close early today.*

ab·ro·gate (ab′rə gāt), v. to do away with; repeal; cancel: *When war broke out, the enemy countries abrogated their trade agreements.* ❑ v. **ab·ro·gat·ed, ab·ro·gat·ing.** —**ab′ro·ga′tion,** n.

a·brupt (ə brupt′), adj. **1** sudden; unexpected: *I made an abrupt turn to avoid another car.* **2** very steep: *The road made an abrupt rise up the hill.* **3** short, sudden, or blunt in speech or manner: *a gruff, abrupt way of speaking.* [**Abrupt** comes from a Latin word meaning "broken off."] —**a·brupt′ly,** adv. —**a·brupt′ness,** n.

ab·scess (ab′ses), n. a collection of pus in the tissues of some part of the body. An abscess results from an infection and is usually painful. ❑ n., pl. **ab·scess·es.**

ab·scessed (ab′sest), adj. having an abscess: *an abscessed tooth.*

ab·scis·sa (ab sis′ə), n. the distance of a point on a graph to the left or right of the vertical axis, measured on a line parallel to the horizontal axis. ❑ n., pl. **ab·scis·sas, ab·scis·sae** (ab sis′sē).

ab·scond (ab skond′), v. to go away suddenly and secretly, especially to avoid punishment; go off and hide: *An employee absconded with $50,000 of the bank's money.* —**ab·scond′er,** n.

ab·sence (ab′səns), n. **1** condition of being away: *Her absence from school was excused.* **2** time of being away: *I returned to school after an absence of two days.* **3** condition of being without; lack: *Darkness is the absence of light.*

ab·sent (ab′sənt), adj. **1** away; not present: *Three members of the class are absent today.* **2** lacking; not existing: *In certain fishes the ribs are entirely absent.* **3** absent-minded: *I knew you were daydreaming from your absent look.*

ab·sen·tee (ab′sən tē′), **1** n. person who is away or remains away. **2** adj. of or about an absentee or absentees: *absentee ownership of land.* ❑ n., pl. **ab·sen·tees.**

absentee ballot, ballot of or for a voter who is permitted to vote by mail.

ab·sen·tee·ism (ab′sən tē′iz′əm), n. **1** the practice or habit of being an absentee. **2** number of people who are absent: *During the flu season, absenteeism increases.*

ab·sent·ly (ab′sənt lē), adv. in an absent-minded manner; inattentively.

ab·sent-mind·ed (ab′sənt mīn′did), adj. not paying attention to what is going on around you; forgetful; inattentive: *The absent-minded man put salt in his coffee and sugar on his egg.* —**ab′sent-mind′ed·ly,** adv. —**ab′sent-mind′ed·ness,** n.

ab·so·lute (ab′sə lüt), adj. **1** free from any imperfection or lack; complete; whole; entire: *That is the absolute truth.* **2** with no limits or restrictions: *The dictator had absolute power.* **3** certain; positive: *I had absolute proof that the witness was lying.* —**ab′so·lute′ness,** n.

ab·so·lute·ly (ab′sə lüt′lē or ab′sə lüt′lē), adv. **1** completely; entirely: *My broken bicycle was absolutely useless.* **2** without doubt; certainly: *She is absolutely the finest person I know.*

absolute magnitude, a measure of how bright a star is.

absolute value, the value of a real number, disregarding any arithmetical sign. The absolute value of +5, or of −5, is 5.

absolute zero, the lowest possible temperature. At this temperature, atoms and molecules have the least possible energy. In theory, it is −273.16 degrees Celsius or −459.69 degrees Fahrenheit.

ab·so·lu·tion (ab′sə lü′shən), n. forgiveness for sin, guilt, or blame.

ab·so·lut·ism (ab′sə lü′tiz′əm), n. a system or form of government in which there are no limits or restrictions on the ruler's power; despotism.

ab·solve (ab solv′), v. **1** to declare free from sin, guilt, or blame: *The judge absolved the accused of the crime.* **2** to set free; release: *I absolve you from your promise.* ❑ v. **ab·solved, ab·solv·ing.** —**ab·solv′er,** n.

ab·sorb (ab sôrb′), v. **1** to take in or suck up liquids or gases: *The sponge absorbed the spilled milk.* **2** to take in and make part of itself; assimilate: *The United States has absorbed millions of immigrants. Digested food is absorbed into the bloodstream in the intestines.* **3** to take in without reflecting: *Rugs absorb sounds and make a house quieter.* **4** to take up all the attention of; interest very much: *Building a dam in the brook absorbed them for hours.*

ab·sorbed (ab sôrbd′), adj. very much interested; completely occupied: *I was so absorbed that I did not hear the bell ring.* —**ab·sorb′ed·ly,** adv. —**ab·sorb′ed·ness,** n.

ab·sorb·ent (ab sôr′bənt), adj. able to absorb moisture, light, heat, etc.: *Absorbent paper towels are used to dry the hands.*

ab·sorb·ing (ab sôr′bing), adj. extremely interesting: *an absorbing book.* —**ab·sorb′ing·ly,** adv.

ab·sorp·tion (ab sôrp′shən), n. **1** act or process of absorbing: *A sponge picks up spilled water by absorption.* **2** great interest: *The children's absorption in their game was so complete that they did not hear the doorbell.*

ab·sorp·tive (ab sôrp′tiv), adj. able to absorb.

ab·stain (ab stān′), v. **1** to do without something; hold yourself back; refrain: *To lose weight, abstain from eating rich foods.* **2** to refrain from voting: *Six members voted in favor of the motion, five voted against it, and four abstained.* —**ab·stain′er,** n.

ab·ste·mi·ous (ab stē′mē əs), adj. sparing in eating, drinking, etc.; moderate; temperate: *She was abstemious in her eating habits.* —**ab·ste′mi·ous·ly,** adv. —**ab·ste′mi·ous·ness,** n.

ab·sten·tion (ab sten′shən), n. **1** act of abstaining; abstinence. **2** fact of not voting: *There were five votes in favor, four against, and three abstentions.*

ab·sti·nence (ab′stə nəns), n. partly or entirely giving up certain pleasures, food, drink, etc.: *abstinence from tobacco.*

abstract (def. 3)—abstract painting

ab·stract (ab′strakt or ab strakt′ for adj.; ab strakt′ for verb; ab′strakt for noun), **1** adj. considered apart from any particular object or real thing; not concrete: *Sweetness is abstract; a lump of sugar is concrete.* **2** v. to think of a quality apart from any object or real thing having that quality: *We can abstract the idea of redness from the color of all red objects.* **3** adj. not representing any actual object; having little or no resemblance to real things: *We saw many abstract paintings at the new art museum.* **4** adj. hard to understand; difficult: *The quantum theory of matter is so abstract that it can be fully understood only by advanced students.* **5** v. to take away; remove: *Iron is abstracted from ore.* **6** n. a brief statement of the main ideas in an article, book, case in court, etc.; summary. —**ab·stract′er** or **ab·strac′tor,** n. —**ab′stract·ly,** adv. —**ab·stract′ness,** n.

ab·stract·ed (ab strak′tid), *adj.* absent-minded. **—ab·stract′ed·ly,** *adv.* **—ab·stract′ed·ness,** *n.*

ab·strac·tion (ab strak′shən), *n.* **1** the idea of a quality thought of apart from any particular object or real thing having that quality; abstract idea or term: *Hardness, bravery, and length are all abstractions.* **2** condition of being lost in thought; absent-mindedness. **3** a work of abstract art.

ab·struse (ab strüs′), *adj.* hard to understand: *an abstruse riddle.* **—ab·struse′ly,** *adv.* **—ab·struse′ness,** *n.*

ab·surd (ab sèrd′), *adj.* plainly not true or sensible; foolish; ridiculous: *The idea that the number 13 brings bad luck is absurd.* [Absurd comes from a Latin word meaning "out of tune" or "senseless."] **—ab·surd′ly,** *adv.* **—ab·surd′ness,** *n.*

ab·surd·i·ty (ab sèr′də tē), *n.* **1** absurd quality or condition; lack of sense; foolishness: *the absurdity of superstition.* **2** something absurd; something unreasonable or ridiculous: *Your explanation is an absurdity.* ❑ *n., pl.* **ab·surd·i·ties** for 2.

A·bu Dha·bi (ä′bü dä′bē), port and capital of the United Arab Emirates.

A·bu·ja (ä bü′jä), *n.* capital of Nigeria, in the central part.

a·bun·dance (ə bun′dəns), *n.* quantity that is a lot more than enough: *There is an abundance of apples this year.* [See Word Story at **abound.**]

a·bun·dant (ə bun′dənt), *adj.* **1** more than enough; very plentiful: *an abundant supply of food.* ■ See Synonym Study at **plentiful.** **2** having more than enough; abounding: *a river abundant in salmon.* **—a·bun′dant·ly,** *adv.*

a·buse (ə byüz′ *for verb;* ə byüs′ *for noun*), **1** *v.* to make wrong or bad use of: *The senator abused his office by doing favors for those who paid him.* **2** *n.* a wrong or bad use: *abuse of privileges.* **3** *v.* to treat roughly or cruelly: *to abuse an animal by beating it.* **4** *n.* rough or cruel treatment: *abuse of a helpless animal.* **5** *n.* a bad practice or custom: *Slavery is a terrible abuse.* **6** *v.* to use harsh and insulting language about or to; scold severely: *Instead of debating the issues the candidates abused each other.* **7** *n.* harsh and insulting language; severe scolding. ❑ *v.* **a·bused, a·bus·ing.** **—a·bus′er,** *n.*

a·bu·sive (ə byü′siv), *adj.* **1** using harsh and insulting language; scolding severely. **2** treating roughly or cruelly. **—a·bu′sive·ly,** *adv.* **—a·bu′sive·ness,** *n.*

a·but (ə but′), *v.* to touch at one end or edge; border; end: *Our property abuts on the street. The garden shed abuts a stone wall.* ❑ *v.* **a·but·ted, a·but·ting.** **—a·but′ter,** *n.*

a·but·ment (ə but′mənt), *n.* a support for an arch or bridge.

a·bys·mal (ə biz′məl), *adj.* very bad: *their abysmal ignorance.* **—a·bys′mal·ly,** *adv.*

a·byss (ə bis′), *n.* **1** a bottomless or very great depth; a very deep crack in the earth: *The mountain climber stood at the edge of a cliff overlooking an abyss four thousand feet deep.* **2** anything too deep or great to be measured; lowest depth: *an abyss of despair.* ❑ *n., pl.* **a·byss·es.** [Abyss comes from a Latin word meaning "without bottom."]

Ab·ys·sin·i·a (ab′ə sin′ē ə), *n.* former name of **Ethiopia.** **—Ab′ys·sin′i·an,** *adj., n.*

Abyssinian cat, a kind of domestic cat with a long, tapering tail and short, silky hair with dark tips.

Ac, symbol for actinium.

a.c., A.C., or **a-c,** alternating current.

a·ca·cia (ə kā′shə), *n.* **1** tree or bush with finely divided leaves that grows in tropical or warm regions. Acacias are related to peas and beans, and some are used in making perfume, gum, and dyes. **2** a locust tree of North America. ❑ *n., pl.* **a·ca·cias.**

abyss (def. 1)

ac·a·dem·ic (ak′ə dem′ik), *adj.* **1** of schools, colleges, and their studies: *The academic year begins when school opens in September.* **2** concerned with general education rather than commercial, technical, or professional education: *History and French are academic subjects; typewriting and bookkeeping are commercial subjects.* **3** theoretical; not practical: *"Which came first, the chicken or the egg?" is an academic question.* **—ac′a·dem′i·cal·ly,** *adv.*

a·cad·e·my (ə kad′ə mē), *n.* **1** place for instruction. **2** a private high school. **3** school where some special subject can be studied: *West Point is a military academy.* **4** group of authors, scholars, scientists, artists, etc., organized to encourage literature, science, or art. ❑ *n., pl.* **a·cad·e·mies.**

Academy Award, one of the awards given each year by the Academy of Motion Picture Arts and Sciences for excellence in movie directing, acting, script writing, etc.; Oscar. [See Word Story at **Oscar.**]

A·ca·di·a (ə kā′dē ə), *n.* former French colony, from 1604 until 1713, in SE Canada, including what is now Nova Scotia. **—A·ca′di·an,** *adj., n.*

Acadia National Park, a national park located on an island off the coast of Maine, containing forests, lakes, and seacoast.

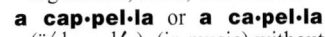

Acadia (about 1700)

NEWFOUNDLAND

CANADA

ACADIA

NEW ENGLAND COLONIES

ATLANTIC OCEAN

St. Lawrence River

N

a cap·pel·la or **a ca·pel·la** (ä′ kə pel′ə), (in music) without instrumental accompaniment.

ac·cede (ak sēd′), *v.* **1** to give in; agree: *Finally I acceded to their requests.* **2** to take office: *When the king died, his daughter acceded to the throne.* ❑ *v.* **ac·ced·ed, ac·ced·ing.**

ac·cel·e·ran·do (ak sel′ə rän′dō), *adv., adj.* (in music) gradually increasing in speed. [Accelerando was borrowed from an Italian word that means "getting quicker."]

ac·cel·e·rate (ak sel′ə rāt′), *v.* **1** to go or cause to go faster; increase in speed: *The car accelerated as it went down the steep hill.* **2** to cause to happen sooner; hasten: *Rest often accelerates recovery from sickness.* ❑ *v.* **ac·cel·e·rat·ed, ac·cel·e·rat·ing.**

ac·cel·e·ra·tion (ak sel′ə rā′shən), *n.* **1** act of speeding up or hastening. **2** (in physics) any change in speed.

ac·cel·e·ra·tor (ak sel′ə rā′tər), *n.* **1** pedal or lever that controls the speed of an engine by controlling the flow of fuel. **2** particle accelerator. **3** anything that causes an increase in speed.

ac·cel·e·rom·e·ter (ak sel′ə rom′ə tər), *n.* device for measuring the acceleration of an aircraft, a rocket, etc.

ac·cent (ak′sent *for noun;* ak′sent *or* ak sent′ *for verb*), **1** *n.* greater force or stronger tone of voice used in pronouncing some syllables or words: *In "letter," the accent is on the first syllable.* **2** *n.* a mark (′) written or printed to show the spoken force of a syllable, as in *to·day* (tə dā′); stress mark; accent mark. Some words have two accents, a primary or stronger accent (′) and a secondary or weaker accent (′), as in *ac·cel·e·ra·tor* (ak sel′ə rā′tər). **3** *v.* to pronounce or mark with an accent: *Is "acceptable" accented on the first or second syllable?* **4** *n.* a characteristic manner of pronunciation heard in a particular section of a country, or in the speech of a person speaking a language not his or her own: *My father was born in Germany and still speaks English with a German accent.* **5** *n.* emphasis on certain musical notes or chords. **6** *v.* to emphasize; accentuate.

WORD STORY Accent comes from a Latin word meaning "song added." An accent changes the way a word is said by adding force or by changing the highness or lowness of sounds, as in songs.

accent mark, accent (def. 2).

a	hat	ė	term	ô	order	ch	child		
ā	age	i	it	oi	oil	ng	long		a in about
ä	far	ī	ice	ou	out	sh	she	ə	e in taken
â	care	o	hot	u	cup	th	thin		i in pencil
e	let	ō	open	ů	put	ŦH	then		o in lemon
ē	equal	ò	saw	ü	rule	zh	measure		u in circus

ac·cen·tu·ate (ak sen′chü āt), v. 1 to call special attention to; emphasize: *Her black hair accentuated the whiteness of her skin.* 2 to pronounce with an accent. 3 to mark with an accent. ❑ v. **ac·cen·tu·at·ed, ac·cen·tu·at·ing.** —**ac·cen′tu·a′tion,** n.

accentuate (def. 1)—eyes and mouth accentuated by makeup

ac·cept (ak sept′), v. 1 to take what is offered or given to you; agree to take: *She accepted the job.* 2 to agree to; consent to: *The United States accepted Japan's proposal for a conference on fishing rights.* 3 to say yes to an invitation, offer, etc.: *They asked me to go along and I accepted.* 4 to take as true or satisfactory; believe: *The teacher accepted our excuse.* 5 to receive with liking and approval; approve: *The design of the new car was not accepted by the public.* —**ac·cept′er** or **ac·cep′tor,** n.

USAGE NOTE **Accept** and **except** are often confused because they sound very much the same. **Accept** is always a verb, and means "to receive": *He accepted the gift.* **Except** can be a verb or a preposition. As a verb, **except** means either "to omit" or "to exclude": *He had a great game if you except that one fumble.* As a preposition, **except** means "but": *Everyone except us went home.*

ac·cept·a·ble (ak sep′tə bəl), adj. 1 likely to be well received; agreeable: *Flowers are an acceptable gift.* 2 good enough but not outstanding; satisfactory: *I received an acceptable grade on the test.* —**ac·cept′a·bil′i·ty,** n. —**ac·cept′a·bly,** adv.

ac·cept·ance (ak sep′təns), n. 1 act of taking something offered or given: *the acceptance of added responsibility.* 2 favorable reception; approval: *the acceptance of a story for publication.* 3 act of taking something as true and satisfactory; belief: *The acceptance of quantum theory led to many scientific discoveries.*

ac·cess (ak′ses), 1 n. right to approach, enter, or use; admittance: *All students have access to the library during the afternoon.* 2 n. approach to places, persons, or things; accessibility: *Access to mountain towns is often difficult because of poor roads.* 3 n. way or means of approach; entrance: *A ladder was the only access to the attic.* 4 v. to make information available by putting into or retrieving from a computer memory: *access a list of names.*

ac·ces·si·ble (ak ses′ə bəl), adj. 1 easy to get at; easy to reach or enter: *A telephone should be put where it will be accessible.* 2 able to be entered or reached. 3 able to be obtained: *Not many facts about the kidnapping were accessible.* —**ac·ces′si·bil′i·ty,** n. —**ac·ces′si·bly,** adv.

ac·ces·sion (ak sesh′ən), n. 1 act of attaining to a right, office, etc.: *The king's death was followed by the princess's accession to the throne.* 2 addition: *The accession of forty new pupils overcrowded the school.*

ac·ces·so·ry (ak ses′ər ē), 1 n. an extra thing added to help something of more importance; less important part or detail: *Her new car has many accessories, including an air conditioner.* 2 adj. added; extra: *His tie supplied an accessory bit of color.* 3 n. person who has helped in a crime or who has helped to hide it: *By not reporting the theft he became an accessory.* ❑ n., pl. **ac·ces·so·ries.** —**ac·ces′so·ri·ly,** adv.

ac·ci·dent (ak′sə dənt), n. 1 something harmful or unlucky that happens unexpectedly: *a car accident.* 2 something that happens without being planned, intended, wanted, or known in advance: *A series of lucky accidents led them to the discovery.*
by accident, by chance; not on purpose: *I met her by accident.*

ac·ci·den·tal (ak′sə den′tl), 1 adj. happening by accident; not planned; unexpected: *Our accidental meeting led to our becoming friends.* 2 n. a sign used in music to show a change of pitch. —**ac′ci·den′tal·ly,** adv.

ac·claim (ə klām′), 1 v. to welcome with loud approval; praise highly; applaud: *The crowd acclaimed the winning team.* 2 n. a shout or show of approval; applause: *His new symphony was received with great acclaim.*

ac·cla·ma·tion (ak′lə mā′shən), n. a shout of welcome or show of approval by a crowd; applause: *The candidate was greeted by the acclamation of the crowd.*
   with an overwhelming oral vote of approval in which the votes are not counted: *All the club members said "Aye," and so the officers were elected by acclamation.*

ac·cli·mate (ə klī′mit or ak′lə māt), v. to accustom or become accustomed to a new climate, surroundings, or conditions: *People from warm climates acclimate slowly to the Arctic.* ❑ v. **ac·cli·mat·ed, ac·cli·mat·ing.** —**ac·cli·ma′tion** (ak′lə mā′shən), n.

ac·cli·ma·tize (ə klī′mə tīz), v. to acclimate. ❑ v. **ac·cli·ma·tized, ac·cli·ma·tiz·ing.** —**ac·cli′ma·ti·za′tion,** n.

ac·cliv·i·ty (ə kliv′ə tē), n. an upward slope of ground. ❑ n., pl. **ac·cliv·i·ties.**

ac·co·lade (ak′ə lād), n. something awarded as an honor; praise or recognition.

ac·com·mo·date (ə kom′ə dāt), v. 1 to have room for; hold comfortably. ■ See Synonym Study at **contain.** 2 to help out; oblige: *I needed change for a ten-dollar bill, but the cashier couldn't accommodate me.* 3 to supply with a place to sleep or live for a time: *Tourists are accommodated here.* 4 to make fit or suitable; adjust: *My eyes soon accommodated themselves to the darkness.* ❑ v. **ac·com·mo·dat·ed, ac·com·mo·dat·ing.**

ac·com·mo·dat·ing (ə kom′ə dā′ting), adj. willing to do favors; obliging: *My teacher was accommodating enough to lend me a dollar.* —**ac·com′mo·dat′ing·ly,** adv.

ac·com·mo·da·tion (ə kom′ə dā′shən), n. 1 Often, **accommodations,** pl. a place to stay, and often a place to eat: *Can we find accommodations at a motel for tonight?* 2 anything that supplies a want or gives aid; a help, favor, or convenience: *It will be an accommodation to me if you will meet me tomorrow instead of today.* 3 the fitting of something to a purpose or situation; adjustment: *The accommodation of our desires to a smaller income took some time.* 4 the automatic adjustment of the lens of the eye to see objects at various distances.

ac·com·pa·ni·ment (ə kum′pə nē mənt), n. 1 anything that goes along with something else: *The ferocious downpour was a very unpleasant accompaniment to our ride.* 2 a part in music that helps or enriches the main part: *We sang with piano accompaniment.*

ac·com·pa·nist (ə kum′pə nist), n. person who plays a musical accompaniment.

ac·com·pa·ny (ə kum′pə nē), v. 1 to go along with: *May we accompany you on your walk?* 2 to be or happen in connection with: *A high wind accompanied the rain and sleet.* 3 to play a musical accompaniment for: *She's such a fine musician that several professional singers want her to accompany them on the piano.* ❑ v. **ac·com·pa·nied, ac·com·pa·ny·ing.**

SYNONYM STUDY **Accompany, attend,** and **escort** all mean to go with someone. **Accompany** suggests going with someone as a companion: *My daughter accompanied me to the store.* **Attend** suggests going with someone as a subordinate: *My assistant attended the meeting with me.* **Escort** suggests special attention, courtesy, or protection: *He escorted her to the dance.*

ac·com·plice (ə kom′plis), n. person who knowingly aids another in committing a crime or other wrong act: *The thief had an accomplice inside the building who unlocked the door.*

ac·com·plish (ə kom′plish), *v.* to succeed in completing; carry out; finish: *Did you accomplish your purpose? She can accomplish more in a day than anyone else in class.* ■ See Synonym Study at **do**[1]. —**ac·com′plish·a·ble**, *adj.* —**ac·com′plish·er**, *n.*

ac·com·plished (ə kom′plisht), *adj.* **1** carried out; completed; done: *Space travel is an accomplished fact.* **2** expert; skilled: *Only an accomplished dancer can perform with this ballet company.* ■ See Synonym Study at **expert.**

ac·com·plish·ment (ə kom′plish mənt), *n.* **1** something that has been done with knowledge, skill, or ability; achievement: *The teachers were proud of their pupils' accomplishments.* **2** skill in some social art or grace: *She was a woman of many accomplishments; she was a respected composer, a fine painter, and an excellent teacher.* **3** act of carrying out; completion: *The accomplishment of that project took two months.*

ac·cord (ə kôrd′), **1** *v.* to be in harmony; agree: *Her account of the accident accords with yours.* **2** *n.* agreement; harmony: *Most people are in accord in their desire for peace.* **3** *v.* to grant a favor, request, etc.: *accord praise for good work.*
of your own accord or **on your own accord**, without being asked; without suggestion from another: *We didn't ask for their help; they helped of their own accord.*

ac·cord·ance (ə kôrd′ns), *n.* agreement; harmony: *to play the game in accordance with the rules.*

ac·cord·ing·ly (ə kôr′ding lē), *adv.* **1** in a way that agrees with what is expected or stated: *These are the rules; you can act accordingly or leave the club.* **2** therefore; for this reason: *I was told to speak briefly; accordingly I cut short my talk.*

ac·cord·ing to (ə kôr′ding), **1** in agreement with: *He paid his debt according to his promise.* **2** in proportion to; on the basis of: *You will be paid according to the work you do.* **3** on the authority of: *According to this prediction we will have a hard winter.*

ac·cor·di·on (ə kôr′dē ən), **1** *n.* a portable musical wind instrument with a bellows, metallic reeds, and keys. **2** *adj.* having folds like the bellows of an accordion: *a skirt with accordion pleats.*

ac·cost (ə kòst′), *v.* to approach and speak to someone in an unpleasant way: *The building guard accosted the boys and demanded that they leave at once.*

ac·count (ə kount′), **1** *n.* statement telling in detail about an event or thing; explanation: *We gave them an account of everything that had happened.* **2** *n.* value or importance: *She thought their ideas were very out-of-date and of little account.* **3** *n.* statement of money received and spent: *I keep a written account of the way I spend my money.* **4** *n.* record of business dealings: *Businesses and factories keep accounts.* **5** *n.* statement of money due: *The office settles its accounts on the tenth of each month.* **6** *v.* to believe to be; consider: *Solomon was accounted wise.*
account for, **1** to tell what has been done with; answer for: *The treasurer of the club had to account for all the dues paid.* **2** to explain: *Can you account for your absence from class?* **3** be the cause of: *Heavy frosts accounted for the poor fruit crop.*
call to account, **1** to demand an explanation of: *The treasurer was called to account for the shortage of funds.* **2** to scold; rebuke; reprimand: *We were called to account for our bad behavior.*
on account, as part payment: *I bought my new camera by paying $10 a week on account.*
on account of, because of: *The game was postponed on account of rain.*
on any account, under any conditions; for any reason: *We were brought up not to lie on any account.*
on no account, under no conditions; for no reason: *On no account should you swim alone.*

accordion (def. 1)

on your account, for your own sake: *Don't wait on my account.*
on your own account, for your own purposes and at your own risk: *She left the firm to go into business on her own account.*
take into account or **take account of**, to make allowance for; consider: *You must take their wishes into account.*
turn to account, to get advantage or profit from: *The rookie turned the coach's advice to good account in the next game.*

ac·count·a·ble (ə koun′tə bəl), *adj.* liable to be called to account; responsible: *You are accountable for your own actions.* —**ac·count′a·bil′i·ty**, *n.* —**ac·count′a·bly**, *adv.*

ac·count·ant (ə koun′tənt), *n.* person who examines or manages business accounts.

ac·count·ing (ə koun′ting), *n.* **1** system or practice of keeping, analyzing, and interpreting business accounts. **2** statement of accounts.

ac·cou·ter (ə kü′tər), *v.* to furnish with clothing or equipment; equip; outfit: *Knights were accoutered in armor.*

ac·cou·ter·ments (ə kü′tər mənts), *n.pl.* **1** a soldier's equipment other than weapons and clothing. A blanket and knapsack are parts of a soldier's accouterments. **2** clothes; outfit.

ac·cou·tre (ə kü′tər), *v.* to accouter. ❑ *v.* **ac·cou·tred, ac·cou·tring.**

ac·cou·tre·ments (ə kü′tər mənts), *n.pl.* accouterments.

Ac·cra (ə krä′), *n.* port and capital of Ghana.

ac·cred·it (ə kred′it), *v.* **1** to give authority to: *to accredit someone as a representative of the government.* **2** to recognize as coming up to an official standard: *to accredit a college.* **3** to accept as true; believe; trust. —**ac·cred′i·ta′tion,** *n.*

ac·cred·it·ed (ə kred′ə tid), *adj.* recognized as coming up to an official standard: *Some colleges will accept without examination the graduates of accredited high schools.*

ac·cre·tion (ə krē′shən), *n.* **1** process of growing together of separate things: *A glacier is formed by the accretion of many particles of frozen packed snow.* **2** something formed in this way.

ac·cru·al (ə krü′əl), *n.* **1** act of accruing: *Savings accounts grow by the accrual of interest.* **2** amount that has accrued.

ac·crue (ə krü′), *v.* **1** to gain little by little: *accrue interest on savings, accrue vacation days.* **2** to grow little by little: *interest accruing on savings.* ❑ *v.* **ac·crued, ac·cru·ing.** —**ac·crue′ment,** *n.*

acct., **1** account. **2** accountant.

ac·cu·mu·late (ə kyü′myə lāt), *v.* to collect little by little; pile up; gather: *They accumulated enough money to buy a car. Dust had accumulated in the empty house.* ❑ *v.* **ac·cu·mu·lat·ed, ac·cu·mu·lat·ing.**

SYNONYM STUDY **Accumulate** and **amass** both mean to collect a large amount. **Accumulate** suggests heaping up little by little over a period of time: *He accumulated a large collection of baseball cards by the time he was twelve.* **Amass** suggests the idea of gathering a large amount in a relatively short time: *She amassed enough votes to win the election for class president.*

ac·cu·mu·la·tion (ə kyü′myə lā′shən), *n.* **1** material collected; mass: *An accumulation of old papers filled the attic.* **2** act of collecting or amassing: *the accumulation of knowledge.*

ac·cu·ra·cy (ak′yər ə sē), *n.* condition of being without errors or mistakes; correctness; exactness: *I question the accuracy of that report.*

ac·cu·rate (ak′yər it), *adj.* without errors or mistakes; precisely correct; exact: *an accurate report, an accurate watch.* ■ See Synonym Study at **correct.** [Accurate comes from a Latin word meaning "done with care."] —**ac′cu·rate·ly,** *adv.* —**ac′cu·rate·ness,** *n.*

ac·curs·ed (ə kėr′sid *or* ə kėrst′), *adj.* **1** annoying and troublesome; detestable; hateful. **2** under a curse; doomed. —**ac·curs·ed·ly** (ə kėr′sid lē), *adv.* —**ac·curs·ed·ness** (ə kėr′sid nis), *n.*

ac·cu·sa·tion (ak′yə zā′shən), *n.* a charge of having done something wrong, or of having broken the law: *The accusation against him was that he had stolen $350 from the store.*

a	hat	ė	term	ô	order	ch	child		a in about
ā	age	i	it	oi	oil	ng	long		e in taken
ä	far	ī	ice	ou	out	sh	she	ə	i in pencil
â	care	o	hot	u	cup	th	thin		o in lemon
e	let	ō	open	ů	put	ŦH	then		u in circus
ē	equal	ò	saw	ü	rule	zh	measure		

ac·cuse (ə kyüz′), *v.* to charge with having done something wrong, or with having broken the law: *The President accused Congress of delaying the passage of his program. The driver was accused of speeding.* ■ See Synonym Study at **blame**. ❑ *v.* **ac·cused, ac·cus·ing. —ac·cus′er,** *n.* **—ac·cus′ing·ly,** *adv.*

ac·cused (ə kyüzd′), *n.sing. or pl.* **the accused,** the person or persons formally charged with an offense or a crime in a court of law.

ac·cus·tom (ə kus′təm), *v.* to make familiar by use or habit; get used to: *When traveling you can accustom yourself to almost any kind of food.*

ac·cus·tomed (ə kus′təmd), *adj.* usual; customary: *By Monday I was well again and was back in my accustomed seat in class.*
accustomed to, used to; in the habit of: *I am accustomed to getting up early.*

ace (ās), **1** *n.* a playing card or domino having one spot. **2** *n.* (in tennis, handball, etc.) a point won on a serve which the opponent fails to return. **3** *n.* person expert at something: *She is an ace at basketball.* **4** *adj.* very skilled; expert. **5** *n.* a combat pilot who has shot down five or more enemy planes.
within an ace of, on the very point of.

ac·e·tate (as′ə tāt), *n.* **1** a chemical substance formed from acetic acid. **2** fabric or other product made from cellulose acetate.

a·ce·tic acid (ə sē′tik), a very sour, colorless acid present in vinegar. It is a compound of hydrogen, carbon, and oxygen, used in making acetates, in drugs, etc.

a·cet·y·lene (ə set′l ēn′), *n.* a colorless gas that burns brightly, with a very hot flame. It is used for lighting, for making plastics, and, when combined with oxygen, for welding metals.

a·ce·tyl·sal·i·cyl·ic acid (ə sē′tl sal′ə sil′ik), aspirin.

ache (āk), **1** *n.* a dull, continuous pain: *Muscular aches often follow hard exercise.* ■ See Synonym Study at **pain**. **2** *v.* to suffer continuous pain; be in pain; hurt: *My arm aches.* **3** *v.* to be eager; wish very much: *During the hot days of August we all ached to go swimming.* ❑ *v.* **ached, ach·ing. —ach′ing·ly,** *adv.*

a·chieve (ə chēv′), *v.* **1** to carry out to a successful end; accomplish; do: *Did you achieve your purpose?* **2** to reach by your own efforts; get by effort: *achieve high grades in mathematics.* ❑ *v.* **a·chieved, a·chiev·ing. —a·chiev′a·ble,** *adj.* **—a·chiev′er,** *n.*

a·chieve·ment (ə chēv′mənt), *n.* **1** thing achieved; some plan or action carried out with courage or unusual ability; accomplishment; feat: *Landing astronauts on the moon was a great achievement.* **2** act of achieving: *the achievement of success.*

A·chil·les (ə kil′ēz), *n.* (in Greek legends) a hero of the Greeks at the siege of Troy.

Achilles' heel, a weak point. No weapon could injure Achilles anywhere, except in the heel.

Achilles tendon, tendon at the back of the leg that connects the muscles in the calf to the bone of the heel.

ach·ro·mat·ic (ak′rə mat′ik), *adj.* **1** refracting white light without breaking it up into the colors of the spectrum: *an achromatic lens.* **2** colorless.

ach·y (ā′kē), *adj.* full of aches. ❑ *adj.* **ach·i·er, ach·i·est. —ach′i·ness,** *n.*

ac·id (as′id), **1** *n.* any compound that yields hydrogen ions when dissolved in water. Acids turn blue litmus paper red and usually react with a base to form a salt. Hydrochloric acid and sulfuric acid are two common acids. **2** *adj.* of or containing acid: *an acid solution.* **3** *adj.* sharp or biting to the taste; sour: *Lemons are an acid fruit.* **4** *adj.* sharp in manner or temper: *an acid comment.* [*Acid* comes from a Latin word meaning "sour."] **—ac′id·ly,** *adv.* **—ac′id·ness,** *n.*

a·cid·ic (ə sid′ik), *adj.* **1** forming acid. **2** containing or being an acid: *an acidic liquid.*

a·cid·i·fy (ə sid′ə fī), *v.* **1** to make or become sour. **2** to change into an acid. ❑ *v.* **a·cid·i·fied, a·cid·i·fy·ing. —a·cid′i·fi·ca′tion,** *n.* **—a·cid′i·fi′er,** *n.*

a·cid·i·ty (ə sid′ə tē), *n.* acid quality or condition; sourness.

acid rain, rain containing a weak solution of sulfuric acid and nitric acid, created by pollutants produced during the burning of fossil fuels.

acid test, a decisive test.

ac·knowl·edge (ak nol′ij), *v.* **1** to admit to be true: *to acknowledge your own faults.* ■ See Synonym Study at **admit**. **2** to recognize the authority or claims of; accept: *Parliament acknowledged Elizabeth I as queen.* **3** to make known that you have received something: *I acknowledged her letter at once.* ❑ *v.* **ac·knowl·edged, ac·knowl·edg·ing. —ac·knowl′edge·a·ble,** *adj.*

ac·knowl·edg·ment or **ac·knowl·edge·ment** (ak nol′ij·mənt), *n.* **1** something given or done to show that you have received a service, favor, gift, message, etc.: *The winner waved in acknowledgment of the cheers.* **2** act of admitting that something is true: *acknowledgment of a mistake.* **3** recognition of authority, claims, or merit.

ACLU, American Civil Liberties Union (a membership organization that protects legal rights under the U.S. Constitution, such as freedom of speech and due process of law).

ac·me (ak′mē), *n.* the highest point: *The acme of the development of spaceships probably lies in the future.*

ac·ne (ak′nē), *n.* a skin disease in which the oil glands in the skin become clogged and inflamed, often causing pimples.

ac·o·lyte (ak′ə līt), *n.* person who helps a priest, deacon, etc., during certain religious services: *The acolyte lit the candles on the altar.*

A·con·ca·gua (ä′kəng kä′gwə), *n.* mountain in the Andes, in W Argentina, 22,834 feet (6960 meters) high. It is the highest mountain in the Western Hemisphere.

a·corn (ā′kôrn), *n.* the nut of an oak tree.

acorns of various kinds of oak trees

a·cous·tic (ə kü′stik), *adj.* **1** of or about the sense or the organs of hearing. **2** of or about music or a musical instrument with sound that is not electrically amplified: *an acoustic guitar.* **3** acoustical. **—a·cous′ti·cal·ly,** *adv.*

a·cous·ti·cal (ə kü′stə kəl), *adj.* of or about the science of sound.

a·cous·tics (ə kü′stiks), *n.* **1** *pl.* the qualities of a room, hall, auditorium, etc., that determine how well sounds can be heard in it: *The acoustics were so good that people in the last row could hear the speaker well.* **2** *sing.* the science of sound.

ac·quaint (ə kwānt′), *v.* to make aware; let know; inform: *Let me acquaint you with your new duties.* ■ See Synonym Study at **tell**.
be acquainted with, to have personal knowledge of; know: *I have heard about your friend, but I am not acquainted with him.*

ac·quaint·ance (ə kwān′təns), *n.* **1** person known to someone, but not a close friend: *We have many acquaintances in our apartment building.* **2** partial knowledge gained from experience: *I have a slight acquaintance with computers.*
make the acquaintance of, to get to know someone: *We soon made the acquaintance of our new neighbors.*

ac·quaint·ance·ship (ə kwān′təns ship), *n.* **1** relation between acquaintances: *Their acquaintanceship lasted many years.* **2** personal knowledge; acquaintance.

ac·qui·esce (ak′wē es′), *v.* to give consent by keeping silent or by not making objections; agree or submit quietly: *We acquiesced in their plan because we could not suggest a better one.* ❑ *v.* **ac·qui·esced, ac·qui·esc·ing.**

ac·qui·es·cence (ak′wē es′ns), *n.* act of agreeing or submitting quietly; consent given without objections.

ac·qui·es·cent (ak′wē es′nt), *adj.* quietly consenting or agreeing; acquiescing. **—ac′qui·es′cent·ly,** *adv.*

ac·quire (ə kwīr′), *v.* to come to have; get as your own: *I acquired that chair at a yard sale.* ■ See Synonym Study at **get.** ❑ *v.* **ac·quired, ac·quir·ing.** —**ac·quir′a·ble,** *adj.*

ac·quire·ment (ə kwīr′mənt), *n.* **1** act of acquiring: *the acquirement of wealth.* **2** something acquired; attainment: *Her musical acquirements are remarkable for a girl of her age.*

ac·qui·si·tion (ak′wə zish′ən), *n.* **1** something acquired: *The gallery's new acquisitions included two paintings by Picasso.* **2** act of acquiring; getting as your own: *the acquisition of skill by practicing.*

ac·quis·i·tive (ə kwiz′ə tiv), *adj.* fond of acquiring; eager to get wealth, power, knowledge, etc.: *My acquisitive friend is too fond of money.* —**ac·quis′i·tive·ly,** *adv.* —**ac·quis′i·tive·ness,** *n.*

ac·quit (ə kwit′), *v.* to declare not guilty; set free: *The accused bank robber was acquitted.* ❑ *v.* **ac·quit·ted, ac·quit·ting.**
acquit yourself, to do your part; behave: *He acquitted himself well during the debate.*

ac·quit·tal (ə kwit′l), *n.* act of setting free by declaring not guilty; release: *The jury brought in a verdict of acquittal.*

a·cre (ā′kər), *n.* **1** a unit of area equal to 160 square rods or 43,560 square feet, used to measure land. **2** acres, *pl.* land; property.

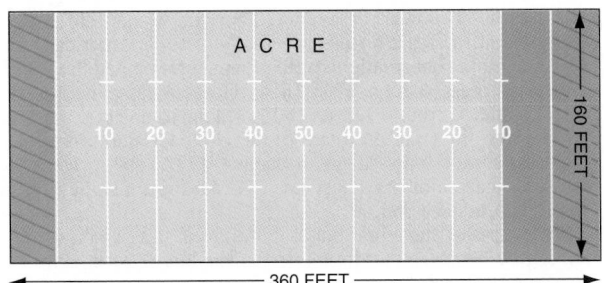

acre shown on a football field

a·cre·age (ā′kər ij), *n.* number of acres.

ac·rid (ak′rid), *adj.* **1** sharp, bitter, or stinging to the mouth, eyes, skin, or nose: *Acrid coal smoke made my eyes water.* **2** irritating in manner; sharp in temper: *The quarrelsome man made acrid comments.* —**ac′rid·ly,** *adv.* —**ac′rid·ness,** *n.*

ac·ri·mo·ni·ous (ak′rə mō′nē əs), *adj.* sharp or bitter in temper, language, or manner: *An acrimonious dispute broke out between the drivers who had the accident.* —**ac′ri·mo′ni·ous·ly,** *adv.* —**ac′ri·mo′ni·ous·ness,** *n.*

ac·ri·mo·ny (ak′rə mō′nē), *n.* sharpness or bitterness in temper, language, or manner.

ac·ro·bat (ak′rə bat), *n.* person who can swing on a trapeze, walk a tightrope, do handsprings, etc. [**Acrobat** is from a French word, which came from a Greek word meaning "walking on tiptoe" or "climbing high," as acrobats do.]

ac·ro·bat·ic (ak′rə bat′ik), *adj.* **1** of an acrobat: *Walking a tightrope is an acrobatic feat.* **2** like an acrobat's: *an acrobatic leap.* —**ac′ro·bat′i·cal·ly,** *adv.*

ac·ro·bat·ics (ak′rə bat′iks), *n.pl.* **1** tricks or performances of an acrobat. **2** tricks or performances like those of an acrobat: *a monkey's acrobatics.*

ac·ro·nym (ak′rə nim), *n.* word formed from the first letters or syllables of other words. EXAMPLE: *scuba* (self-contained *u*nder-water *b*reathing *a*pparatus).

WORD SOURCE **Acronym** comes from Greek words meaning "tip" and "name." Many acronyms started as regular abbreviations, then developed pronunciations of their own. The words below are acronyms. See also Word Source at **initial.**

ASCII	NAFTA	radar	UNESCO
BASIC	NASA	RIF	UNICEF
FORTRAN	NATO	scuba	VISTA
laser	OPEC	sonar	ZIP (Code)

a·crop·o·lis (ə krop′ə lis), *n.* the high, fortified part of an ancient Greek city. The Parthenon was built on the **Acropolis** of Athens. ❑ *n., pl.* **a·crop·o·lis·es.**

a·cross (ə krôs′), **1** *prep.* from one side to the other of; over: *The cat walked across the street.* **2** *adv.* from one side to the other: *What is the distance across?* **3** *prep.* on the other side of; beyond: *The woods are across the river.* **4** *adv.* on or to the other side: *When are you going across?*

a·cros·tic (ə krôs′tik), *n.* composition in verse or arrangement of words in which the first, last, or certain other letters in each line, taken in order, spell a word or phrase.

a·cryl·ic (ə kril′ik), **1** *n.* a durable plastic used to make fabrics, optical lenses, taillights, etc. **2** *adj.* made of such plastic. **3** *n.* paint made from a liquid plastic and used with water.

act (akt), **1** *n.* something done; deed: *Sharing your candy was a generous act.* **2** *n.* process of doing: *I was caught in the act of hiding the gifts.* **3** *v.* to do something: *The fire department acted promptly and saved the burning house.* **4** *v.* to have effect: *The medicine failed to act.* **5** *v.* to behave: *I apologize for acting badly.* **6** *v.* to behave like: *Most people act the fool now and then.* **7** *v.* to pretend to be: *She's just acting angry to make you feel bad.* **8** *n.* a display of pretended behavior: *His illness is just an act.* **9** *v.* to perform on the stage, in movies, on TV, or over the radio; play a part: *He acts the part of the district attorney. She acts very well.* **10** *n.* a main division of a play or opera: *Most modern plays have three acts.* **11** *n.* one of several performances on a program: *We stayed to see the comedian's act.* **12** *n.* a legislative decision; decree. An act of Congress is a bill that has been passed by Congress. **13** *n.* a false display; pretense: *He's not really angry; it's just an act.* —**act′a·ble,** *adj.*
act as, to do the work of: *act as editor of a magazine.*
act for, to take the place of: *Her assistant acted for her during her absence.*
act on or **act upon, 1** to follow; obey: *I will act on your suggestion.* **2** to have an effect or influence on: *Yeast acted on the dough and made it rise.*
act up, to behave badly: *The children began to act up when company came.*

ACTH, 1 a hormone produced by the pituitary gland that stimulates the adrenal cortex to produce other hormones. **2** this hormone obtained from animals, used in the treatment of arthritis and rheumatic fever.

act·ing (ak′ting), *adj.* taking the place of another; serving temporarily as: *While the principal was sick, one of the teachers was acting principal.*

ac·tin·i·um (ak tin′ē əm), *n.* a radioactive chemical element somewhat like radium, found in pitchblende. *Symbol:* Ac

ac·tion (ak′shən), *n.* **1** process of acting; doing something: *The quick action of the firemen saved the building from being burned down. The situation called for immediate action.* **2** something done; act: *Helping a small child to cross the street was a kind action.* **3** actions, *pl.* conduct; behavior: *Her actions revealed her thoughtfulness.* **4** effect or influence of one thing on another: *the action of wind on a ship's sails.* **5** way of moving or working; movement: *a pulley with an easy action.* **6** battle; part of a battle: *to be wounded in action.* **7** series of events in a story or play. **8** lawsuit. —**ac′tion·less,** *adj.*
take action, 1 to begin to do something; start working: *The government decided to take action to prevent a flu epidemic.* **2** to start a lawsuit; sue: *The people hurt in the accident have taken action to obtain payment for their injuries.*

ac·tion·a·ble (ak′shə nə bəl), *adj.* giving cause for a lawsuit: *Deliberate damage of property is actionable behavior.* —**ac′tion·a·bly,** *adv.*

ac·ti·vate (ak′tə vāt), *v.* to make active. ❑ *v.* **ac·ti·vat·ed, ac·ti·vat·ing.** —**ac′ti·va′tion,** *n.* —**ac′ti·va′tor,** *n.*

ac·tive (ak′tiv), **1** *adj.* showing much action; moving rather quickly much of the time; lively: *The baby is very active.* ■ See Synonym Study at **lively.** **2** *adj.* acting; working: *An active vol-*

a	hat	ė	term	ô	order	ch	child		a in about
ā	age	i	it	oi	oil	ng	long		e in taken
ä	far	ī	ice	ou	out	sh	she	ə	i in pencil
â	care	o	hot	u	cup	th	thin		o in lemon
e	let	ō	open	u̇	put	ŦH	then		u in circus
ē	equal	ò	saw	ü	rule	zh	measure		

cano may erupt at any time. **3** *adj.* working hard or with energy; busy and energetic: *We took an active part in organizing the club.* **4** *adj.* (in grammar) showing the subject of a verb as acting. In "She broke the window," *broke* is in the active voice. **5** *n.* a verb form that does this. **—ac′tive·ly,** *adv.* **—ac′tive·ness,** *n.*

active immunity, immunity to a disease because of antibodies produced by the immune person or animal.

ac·ti·vist (ak′tə vist), *n.* person in favor of direct and vigorous action to support a political cause. An activist may break the law and even commit violence: *an activist for animal rights.*

ac·tiv·i·ty (ak tiv′ə tē), *n.* **1** condition of being active; use of power; movement: *physical activity, mental activity.* **2** action; doing: *the activities of enemy spies.* **3** vigorous action; liveliness: *The activity of the children disturbed my sleep.* **4** thing to do: *Students who have too many outside activities may find it hard to keep up with their studies.* ❏ *n., pl.* **ac·tiv·i·ties** for 2,4.

ac·tor (ak′tər), *n.* person who acts on the stage, in movies, on TV, or for radio.

ac·tress (ak′tris), *n.* girl or woman who acts on the stage, in movies, on TV, or for radio. ❏ *n., pl.* **ac·tress·es.**

Acts, *n.* the fifth book of the New Testament. Acts tells about the beginnings of the Christian church.

Acts of the Apostles, Acts.

ac·tu·al (ak′chü əl), *adj.* existing as a fact; real: *What he told us was not a dream but an actual happening.*

ac·tu·al·i·ty (ak′chü al′ə tē), *n.* an actual thing; fact; reality: *A trip to the moon is now an actuality.* ❏ *n., pl.* **ac·tu·al·i·ties.**

ac·tu·al·ize (ak′chü ə līz), *v.* to put a plan or idea into effect. ❏ *v.* **ac·tu·al·ized, ac·tu·al·iz·ing. —ac′tu·al·i·za′tion,** *n.*

ac·tu·al·ly (ak′chü ə lē), *adv.* really; in fact: *Are you actually going to camp this summer or just wishing to go?*

ac·tu·ar·y (ak′chü er′ē), *n.* person who figures risks, rates, premiums, etc., for insurance companies. ❏ *n., pl.* **ac·tu·ar·ies.**

ac·tu·ate (ak′chü āt), *v.* to put into action: *This pump is actuated by a belt driven by an electric motor.* ❏ *v.* **ac·tu·at·ed, ac·tu·at·ing. —ac′tu·a′tion,** *n.* **—ac′tu·a′tor,** *n.*

a·cu·men (ə kyü′mən), *n.* sharpness and quickness in seeing and understanding; keen insight; discernment.

ac·u·punc·ture (ak′yu̇ pungk′chər), *n.* an ancient Chinese practice of inserting needles into certain parts of the body. Acupuncture is used to treat some diseases and to relieve pain.

a·cute (ə kyüt′), *adj.* **1** sharp and severe: *A toothache can cause acute pain.* **2** threatening; critical: *The long drought caused an acute shortage of water in the city.* **3** quick in perceiving and responding to impressions; keen: *Dogs have a very acute sense of smell.* ■ See Synonym Study at **sharp. 4** brief and severe: *an acute disease.* **—a·cute′ly,** *adv.* **—a·cute′ness,** *n.*

adaptation (def. 3)—The development of seals' legs into flippers is an adaptation to life in the water.

acute accent, mark (′) placed over a vowel letter to show the kind of sound, as in French *attaché,* or place of the accent, as in Spanish *Asunción.*

acute angle, angle less than a right angle. See picture at **angle**[1].

acute triangle, a triangle with three acute angles.

ad (ad), *n.* advertisement. ■ Another word that sounds like this is **add.**

A.D., after the birth of Jesus. From 63 B.C. to A.D. 14 is 77 years. [The abbreviation A.D. stands for the Latin phrase *anno domini,* meaning "in the year of the Lord."]

ad·age (ad′ij), *n.* a wise saying that has been much used; proverb. "Haste makes waste" is a well-known adage.

a·da·gio (ə dä′jō), in music: **1** *adj.* slow. **2** *n.* a slow part. **3** *adv.* slowly. ❏ *n., pl.* **a·da·gios.** [**Adagio** comes from an Italian phrase meaning "at ease."]

Ad·am (ad′əm), *n.* (in the Bible) the first man, the husband of Eve. [**Adam** is a Hebrew name that means "man of red earth."]

ad·a·mant (ad′ə mənt), *adj.* not willing to give in; firm and unyielding: *Columbus was adamant in refusing the requests of his sailors to turn back.* [See Word Story at **diamond.**] **—ad′a·mant·ly,** *adv.*

Ad·ams (ad′əmz), *n.* **1 Ab·i·gail** (ab′i gāl′), 1744-1818, American First Lady and writer. ■ **Abigail Adams** wrote a letter to her husband John Adams, asking him and other members of the Continental Congress to "Remember the Ladies. . . (we) will not hold ourselves bound by any Laws in which we have no voice, or Representation." However, they ignored her and women did not get the vote until 1922. **2 An·sel** (an′səl), 1902-1984, American photographer and conservationist. He often photographed the American wilderness. **3 John,** 1735-1826, the second president of the United States, from 1797 to 1801. **4 John Quin·cy** (kwin′zē), 1767-1848, the sixth president of the United States, from 1825 to 1829, son of John Adams. **5 Samuel,** 1722-1803, a leader of the American colonists' resistance to Great Britain at the time of the Revolutionary War.

Adam's apple, the slight bulge in the front of a person's throat caused by cartilage that forms part of the larynx. It is more noticeable in men than in women.

a·dapt (ə dapt′), *v.* **1** to change to fit different conditions; adjust: *Can you adapt your way of working to the new job?* ■ See Synonym Study at **adjust. 2** to change so as to make suitable for a different use: *The story was adapted for the movies from a novel by Jane Austen.* **3** to change yourself; get used to something: *Most students adapt to a new school with no problem.*

USAGE NOTE **Adapt** looks like **adopt,** but they have different meanings. **Adapt** means to change something so that it becomes suitable. **Adopt** means to take as your own. If you think a plan needs changing, you adapt it. If you like the plan, you adopt it.

a·dapt·a·ble (ə dap′tə bəl), *adj.* easily changed or changing easily to fit different conditions: *an adaptable person. My schedule is adaptable; I can see you anytime.* **—a·dapt′a·bil′i·ty,** *n.*

ad·ap·ta·tion (ad′ap tā′shən), *n.* **1** act of changing to fit different conditions: *He made a good adaptation to high school.* **2** something made by adapting: *A movie is often an adaptation of a novel.* **3** (in biology) a change in structure, form, or habits to suit conditions, inherited within a species and increasing rates of reproduction and survival.

a·dapt·ed (ə dap′tid), *adj.* fitted; suitable.

a·dapt·er (ə dap′tər), *n.* **1** device that adapts different-sized parts to each other or adapts a machine to a different use. **2** person who adapts. Also, **adaptor.**

a·dap·tive (ə dap′tiv), *adj.* able to adapt; showing adaptation. **—a·dap′tive·ly,** *adv.* **—a·dap′tive·ness,** *n.*

a·dap·tor (ə dap′tər), *n.* adapter.

ADD, attention deficit disorder.

add (ad), *v.* **1** to find the sum of: *Add 73 and 27 and you have 100.* **2** to say further; go on to say or write: *They said good-by and added that they had had a pleasant visit.* **3** to join one thing to another: *I tasted the lemonade, then added more sugar.* ■ Another word that sounds like this is **ad. —add′er,** *n.*

add to, to make greater; increase: *The fine day added to our pleasure.*

add up, to make the correct total: *These figures don't add up.*

add up to, to amount to: *What do the profits add up to?*

Ad·dams (ad′əmz), *n.* **Jane** (jān), 1860-1935, American social and peace worker. ■ **Jane Addams** founded Hull House, a settlement house in Chicago, in 1899, and shared the Nobel Peace Prize in 1931. She also helped found the ACLU.

ad·dend (ad′end *or* ə dend′), *n.* a number or quantity to be added to another: *In 2 + 3 + 4 = 9, the addends are 2, 3, and 4.*

ad·den·dum (ə den′dəm), *n.* thing added; appendix. □ *n., pl.* **ad·den·da** (ə den′də).

ad·der (ad′ər), *n.* **1** a small, poisonous snake of Europe. **2** hog-nose snake. **3** puff adder. [**Adder** was once spelled *nadder,* but people changed *a nadder* to *an adder* by misdivision.]

ad·dict (ad′ikt), *n.* person who has lost control of a habit, especially the use of a drug.

ad·dict·ed (ə dik′tid), *adj.* uncontrollably following a habit or practice; strongly inclined: *addicted to drugs.*

ad·dic·tion (ə dik′shən), *n.* condition of following a habit uncontrollably.

ad·dic·tive (ə dik′tiv), *adj.* causing or tending to cause addiction: *Alcohol can be addictive.*

Ad·dis Ab·a·ba (ad′is ab′ə bə), capital of Ethiopia, in the central part.

ad·di·tion (ə dish′ən), *n.* **1** an adding of one number or quantity to another: *2 + 3 = 5 is a simple addition.* **2** an adding of one thing to another: *The addition of flour will thicken gravy.* **3** thing added: *Cream is a tasty addition to many desserts.* **4** part added to a building: *We hope to put on a new addition.*

in addition or **in addition to,** besides; also: *In addition to her work as a composer, she is a music critic.*

ad·di·tion·al (ə dish′ə nəl), *adj.* added; extra; more: *I need some additional information.* **—ad·di′tion·al·ly,** *adv.*

ad·di·tive (ad′ə tiv), **1** *n.* substance added to another substance to preserve it, increase its effectiveness, etc. **2** *adj.* involving addition. **—ad′di·tive·ly,** *adv.*

additive inverse, either of two numbers that add up to zero. The additive inverse of +5 is −5, and that of −5 is +5.

ad·dled (ad′ld), *adj.* **1** muddled; confused: *an addled brain.* **2** rotten: *addled eggs.*

ad·dress (ə dres′; *also* ad′res *for 1,3*), **1** *n.* the place to which your mail is directed; place of residence or of business: *Write your name and address on this envelope.* **2** *v.* to write on a letter or package the place where it is to be sent: *to address envelopes for greeting cards.* **3** *n.* numbers and letters identifying the place where certain information is stored in a computer memory. **4** *v.* to retrieve or store information by means of a computer address. **5** *n.* a speech, especially a formal one: *The President gave an address to the nation on TV.* ■ See Synonym Study at **speech. 6** *v.* to make an address to: *The speaker addressed the organization on the subject of ecology.* **7** *v.* to speak to or write to: *The king is addressed as "Your Majesty."* **8** *v.* to apply or devote yourself; direct your energies: *She addressed herself to the task of learning French.* □ *n., pl.* **ad·dress·es. —ad·dress′er,** *n.*

ad·dress·ee (ə dre sē′), *n.* person to whom a letter, package, etc., is addressed. □ *n., pl.* **ad·dress·ees.**

ad·duce (ə düs′), *v.* to offer as a reason; give as proof or evidence; bring up as an example: *The scientist adduced the results of several experiments to prove his point.* □ *v.* **ad·duced, ad·duc·ing. —ad·duc′er,** *n.*

Ad·e·laide (ad′l ād), *n.* capital of South Australia.

A·den (äd′n *or* ād′n), **1** port in Yemen. **2 Gulf of,** part of the Arabian Sea between S Arabia and E Africa.

ad·e·nine (ad′n ēn), *n.* substance present in nucleic acid. It is one of the compounds that form the genetic code in DNA and RNA.

ad·e·noids (ad′n oidz), *n.pl.* growths of glandular tissue in the upper part of the throat, just back of the nose. Adenoids can swell up and make breathing and speaking difficult.

a·dept (ə dept′), *adj.* thoroughly skilled; expert: *She is adept at skiing.* **—a·dept′ly,** *adv.* **—a·dept′ness,** *n.*

ad·e·qua·cy (ad′ə kwə sē), *n.* condition of being adequate; as much as is needed for a particular purpose; sufficiency.

ad·e·quate (ad′ə kwit), *adj.* **1** as much as is needed for a particular purpose; sufficient; enough: *To be healthy you must have an*

adequate diet. **2** suitable; competent: *He is barely adequate for the job.* **—ad′e·quate·ly,** *adv.* **—ad′e·quate·ness,** *n.*

ad·here (ad hir′), *v.* **1** to stick tight; remain attached: *Mud often adheres to your shoes.* ■ See Synonym Study at **stick**[2]. **2** to hold closely or firmly: *The principal adhered to the plan for dropping Latin in spite of teacher opposition.* **3** to be a follower or upholder; give allegiance: *adhere to a political party.* □ *v.* **ad·hered, ad·her·ing. —ad·her′er,** *n.*

ad·her·ence (ad hir′əns), *n.* act of holding to and following closely; faithfulness: *rigid adherence to the rules.*

ad·her·ent (ad hir′ənt), **1** *n.* a faithful supporter; follower: *He was an adherent of the conservative party.* **2** *adj.* sticking fast; attached. **—ad·her′ent·ly,** *adv.*

ad·he·sion (ad hē′zhən), *n.* **1** condition of sticking fast; attachment. **2** act of growing together of body tissues that are normally separate, especially after surgery.

ad·he·sive (ad hē′siv), **1** *n.* glue, paste, or other substance for sticking things together. **2** *n.* adhesive tape. **3** *adj.* sticking easily; sticky. [See Word Story at **hesitate.**] **—ad·he′sive·ly,** *adv.* **—ad·he′sive·ness,** *n.*

adhesive tape, a narrow strip of cloth or plastic that is sticky on one side, used to hold bandages in place.

ad hoc (ad hok′), for a specific purpose; special: *an ad hoc committee to settle this one problem.*

a·dieu (ə dyü′), *interj., n.* good-by. □ *n., pl.* **a·dieus** or **a·dieux** (ə-dyüz′). [**Adieu** comes from French words meaning "to God."]

ad in·fi·ni·tum (ad in′fə nī′təm), LATIN. without limit; endlessly.

a·di·os (ä′dē ōs′ *or* ad′ē ōs′), *interj., n.* good-by. [**Adios** comes from Spanish words meaning "to God."]

ad·i·pose (ad′ə pōs), *adj.* of or resembling fat; fatty: *adipose tissue.* **—ad′i·pose′ness,** *n.*

Ad·i·ron·dack Mountains (ad′ə ron′dak), mountains of a large area in NE New York State.

Ad·i·ron·dacks (ad′ə ron′daks), *n.pl.* Adirondack Mountains.

adj., adjective.

ad·ja·cent (ə jā′snt), *adj.* lying near or close; adjoining; next: *The house adjacent to ours has been sold.* **—ad·ja′cent·ly,** *adv.*

adjacent angles, two angles that have the same tip and one side in common.

ad·jec·ti·val (aj′ik tī′vəl), *adj.* **1** of an adjective. **2** used as an adjective. **—ad′jec·ti·val·ly,** *adv.*

ad·jec·tive (aj′ik tiv), **1** *n.* one of a class of words that qualify, limit, or add to the meaning of a noun or pronoun. In "a tiny brook," "The day is warm," "great happiness," and "this pencil," *tiny, warm, great,* and *this* are adjectives. **2** *adj.* adjectival.

WORD POWER **ADJECTIVES** ■ The quickest way to create a new word is to change an old word. The fastest way to change words is with prefixes and suffixes. Many adjectives are just nouns and verbs with suffixes added. Then you see these suffixes, think about the meaning of the word's main part. Then think "like a ___" or "having ___," "that ___s" or "tending to ___."

-able	-ary	-ian	-ical	-like	-ous
-an	-ent	-ible	-ish	-old	-some
-ant	-ese	-ic	-ive	-ory	-y

ad·join (ə join′), *v.* to be next to; be close to; be side by side: *Canada adjoins the United States.*

ad·join·ing (ə joi′ning), *adj.* being next to or in contact with; bordering: *The twins have adjoining rooms.*

ad·journ (ə jėrn′), *v.* **1** to put off until a later time; postpone: *The members of the club voted to adjourn the meeting until two o'clock.* **2** to stop activity for a time: *The court adjourned from Friday until Monday.* **3** to go to another place: *After the meeting we adjourned to the cafeteria to eat.*

a	hat	ė	term	ô	order	ch	child		a in about
ā	age	i	it	oi	oil	ng	long		e in taken
ä	far	ī	ice	ou	out	sh	she	ə	i in pencil
â	care	o	hot	u	cup	th	thin		o in lemon
e	let	ō	open	u̇	put	ᴛʜ	then		u in circus
ē	equal	ò	saw	ü	rule	zh	measure		

ad·journ·ment (ə jėrn′mənt), *n.* **1** act of adjourning or condition of being adjourned. **2** time during which a court, lawmaking group, etc., is adjourned.

ad·judge (ə juj′), *v.* **1** to decree or decide by law: *The accused was adjudged guilty.* **2** to award by law: *The property was adjudged to the rightful owner.* ❑ *v.* **ad·judged, ad·judg·ing.**

ad·ju·di·cate (ə jü′də kāt), *v.* to decide or settle by law or as an authority: *Dad adjudicated our argument.* ❑ *v.* **ad·ju·di·cat·ed, ad·ju·di·cat·ing.** —**ad·ju′di·ca′tion,** *n.* —**ad·ju′di·ca′tor,** *n.*

ad·junct (aj′ungkt), *n.* something added that is less important or not necessary, but helpful: *A greenhouse formed an adjunct to the back porch.*

ad·jure (ə jůr′), *v.* to ask earnestly or solemnly: *I adjure you on your honor to tell the truth.* ❑ *v.* **ad·jured, ad·jur·ing.**

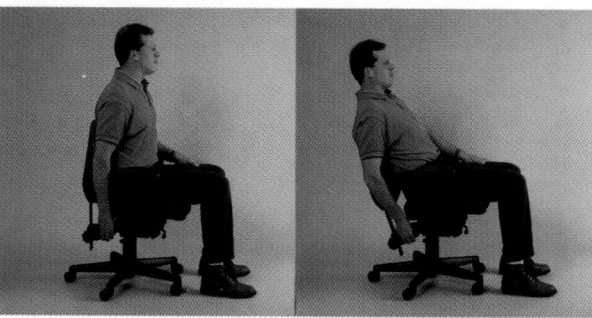

adjust (def. 1)—adjusting a chair

ad·just (ə just′), *v.* **1** to change to make fit: *These desks and seats can be adjusted to the height of any child.* **2** to put in proper order, position, or relation; arrange: *Please adjust the TV so that the picture doesn't jump.* **3** to arrange satisfactorily; set right; settle: *The girls adjusted their difference of opinion and were friends again.* **4** to adapt to; get used to: *Some wild animals never adjust to life in a zoo.* —**ad·just′a·ble,** *adj.* —**ad·just′a·bly,** *adv.* —**ad·just′er** or **ad·jus′tor,** *n.*

SYNONYM STUDY **Adjust** and **adapt** both mean to fit one thing or person to another. **Adjust** suggests matching one thing to another: *The mother adjusted the seat to the height of the child.* **Adapt** suggests making small changes: *I adapted the pattern to the material.*

ad·just·ment (ə just′mənt), *n.* **1** act or process of adjusting: *The adjustment of seats to the right height for children is necessary for their comfort.* **2** a means of adjusting: *All TVs have an adjustment for volume control.* **3** the act of getting used to something: *They were pleased with their daughter's adjustment to the new school.* **4** settlement of a dispute, a claim, etc.

ad·ju·tant (aj′ə tənt), *n.* **1** an army officer who assists a commanding officer by sending out orders, writing letters, etc. **2** assistant.

ad·lib (ad lib′), **1** *v.* to make up as you go along; improvise: *The actor forgot some of his lines and had to adlib.* **2** *adv.* on the spur of the moment; freely: *The jazz band played adlib.* **3** *n.* music or words made up as you go along. ❑ *v.* **ad·libbed, ad·lib·bing.**

Adm., **1** Admiral. **2** Admiralty. **3** Administrator.

ad·min·is·ter (ad min′ə stər), *v.* **1** to manage the affairs of; direct: *The mayor administers the city government.* **2** to give out; apply: *administer first aid to an injured person. Judges administer justice.* **3** to offer formally: *The witness could not testify until the oath had been administered.* **4** to settle or take charge of an estate. **5** to be helpful; contribute: *The government administered to the needs of the flood victims.*

ad·min·is·tra·tion (ad min′ə strā′shən), *n.* **1** the managing of the affairs of a business, an office, etc.: *The administration of a big business requires skill in dealing with people.* **2** group of persons in charge: *The principal and teachers of a school are part of the administration of the school.* **3** management of public affairs by government officials: *She is experienced in city administration.* **4** officials as a group; the government. **5 the Administration,** the President of the United States, the cabinet appointed by the President, and the departments of the government headed by cabinet members or other appointees. **6** the period of time during which a government holds office: *The Liberal administration in Canada lasted many years.* **7** act of giving out or applying: *The Red Cross handled the administration of aid to the flood victims.*

ad·min·is·tra·tive (ad min′ə strā′tiv), *adj.* of or dealing with administration; executive. —**ad·min′is·tra′tive·ly,** *adv.*

ad·min·is·tra·tor (ad min′ə strā′tər), *n.* **1** person who administers; manager. **2** person appointed to settle or take charge of an estate.

ad·mir·a·ble (ad′mər ə bəl), *adj.* worth admiring; very good; excellent: *She has an admirable character.* —**ad′mir·a·ble·ness,** *n.* —**ad′mir·a·bly,** *adv.*

ad·mir·al (ad′mər əl), *n.* **1** a military rank. See chart on page 712. **2** any of several colorful butterflies, especially one kind having reddish streaks on its wings.

WORD STORY **Admiral** comes from an Arabic word meaning "commander." **Emir,** an Arabian chief, comes from the same word. Definition 2 comes from the fact that the streaks on the butterfly's wings look like the stripes on an admiral's uniform.

ad·mir·al·ty (ad′mər əl tē), *n.* branch of law dealing with affairs of the sea and of ships.

ad·mi·ra·tion (ad′mə rā′shən), *n.* **1** a feeling of wonder, pleasure, and approval: *The beauty of the performance excited admiration.* **2** person or thing that is admired: *a spectacular painting that was the admiration of all who viewed it.*

ad·mire (ad mīr′), *v.* **1** to regard with wonder, pleasure, and approval: *We admired the beautiful painting.* **2** to think highly of; respect: *I admire your courage.* ❑ *v.* **ad·mired, ad·mir·ing.** —**ad·mir′er,** *n.* —**ad·mir′ing·ly,** *adv.*

ad·mis·si·ble (ad mis′ə bəl), *adj.* **1** capable or worthy of being admitted: *Any student is admissible to this club.* **2** permitted by a person in authority or by the rules; allowable: *Is it admissible to practice here?* —**ad·mis′si·bil′i·ty,** *n.* —**ad·mis′si·bly,** *adv.*

ad·mis·sion (ad mish′ən), *n.* **1** entrance; permission to enter: *apply for admission into a college.* **2** price paid for the right to enter: *Admission to the show is one dollar.* **3** act of admitting to be true; confession: *Their admission that they were to blame kept others from being punished.*

ad·mit (ad mit′), *v.* **1** to say something is real or true; confess: *She admits now that she made a mistake. His opponent had to admit defeat.* **2** to allow to enter; let in: *He was admitted to a trade school. Windows admit light and air.* **3** to have room for; be large enough for: *This garage door will admit two cars abreast.* ❑ *v.* **ad·mit·ted, ad·mit·ting.**

SYNONYM STUDY **Admit, acknowledge,** and **confess** all mean to say that something is true. **Admit** suggests accepting the truth of something, often after hesitating: *I admit that you were right and I was wrong.* **Acknowledge** suggests declaring knowledge of the existence or truth of something, sometimes reluctantly: *The losing party acknowledged defeat in the election.* **Confess** suggests admitting something about yourself that is not good or is criminal: *The burglar confessed to the robbery.*

ad·mit·tance (ad mit′ns), *n.* right to enter; permission to enter: *She had admittance to the theater free of charge.*

ad·mit·ted·ly (ad mit′id lē), *adv.* without denial; by general consent: *Admittedly the rules are strict.*

ad·mix·ture (ad miks′chər), *n.* **1** act of mixing. **2** mixture: *An admixture of soap and water makes bubbles.* **3** anything added in mixing; ingredient.

ad·mon·ish (ad mon′ish), *v.* **1** to advise someone against something in order to encourage improvement; warn: *The policeman admonished him not to drive so fast.* **2** to scold gently; reprove: *The teacher admonished the student for careless work.* —**ad·mon′ish·er,** *n.* —**ad·mon′ish·ment,** *n.*

ad·mo·ni·tion (ad′mə nish′ən), *n.* a gentle reproof or warning: *They received an admonition from their parents for being late.*

a·do (ə dü′), *n.* **1** noisy activity; stir; fuss: *There was much ado about the party by all the family.* **2** trouble; difficulty.

a·do·be (ə dō′bē), **1** *n.* brick made of clay baked in the sun. **2** *adj.* built or made of adobe. **3** *n.* a building made of adobe. ❏ *n., pl.* **a·do·bes** for 3. [**Adobe** comes from an Arabic word meaning "the brick."]

ad·o·les·cence (ad′l es′ns), *n.* period of growth from childhood to adulthood; youth.

ad·o·les·cent (ad′l es′nt), **1** *n.* person growing up from childhood to adulthood, especially a person from about 12 to about 20 years of age. **2** *adj.* growing up from childhood to adulthood; youthful: *the adolescent stage of development.* **3** *adj.* of adolescents; characteristic of adolescents: *adolescent interests.*

WORD STORY   **Adolescent** comes from a Latin word meaning "growing up." **Adult** comes from another form of this word and means "finished growing up." So an adolescent becomes an adult.

A·don·is (ə don′is *or* ə dō′nis), *n.* **1** (in Greek and Roman myths) a handsome young man who was loved by Aphrodite (Venus). **2** any handsome young man.

a·dopt (ə dopt′), *v.* **1** to take as your own choice: *I liked your idea and adopted it. Few Americans would find it easy to adopt Japanese customs.* **2** to accept formally; approve: *The club adopted the motion by a vote of 20 to 5.* **3** to take a child of other parents and bring up as your own child: *The judge permitted the family to adopt both of the children.* ■ See Usage Note at **adapt.** —**a·dopt′a·ble,** *adj.* —**a·dopt′er,** *n.*

a·dop·tion (ə dop′shən), *n.* **1** act of adopting: *Our club voted for the adoption of some new rules.* **2** condition of being adopted: *The children were offered for adoption.*

a·dop·tive (ə dop′tiv), *adj.* related by adoption: *an adoptive daughter.*

a·dor·a·ble (ə dôr′ə bəl), *adj.* **1** worthy of being adored. **2** attractive; delightful: *What an adorable kitten!* —**a·dor′a·ble·ness,** *n.* —**a·dor′a·bly,** *adv.*

ad·o·ra·tion (ad′ə rā′shən), *n.* **1** devoted love and admiration. **2** worship.

a·dore (ə dôr′), *v.* **1** to love and admire very greatly: *They adore their grandchildren.* **2** to like very much: *I adore that song!* **3** to worship: *"O! Come, let us adore Him," sang the choir at Christmas.* ❏ *v.* **a·dored, a·dor·ing.** —**a·dor′er,** *n.* —**a·dor′ing·ly,** *adv.*

a·dorn (ə dôrn′), *v.* to add beauty to; put ornaments on; decorate: *She adorned her hair with flowers.* ■ See Synonym Study at **decorate.** —**a·dorn′er,** *n.*

a·dorn·ment (ə dôrn′mənt), *n.* **1** something that adds beauty; ornament; decoration: *The park is an adornment to the neighborhood.* **2** act of adorning.

ad·re·nal gland (ə drē′nl), one of the two glands, one on the upper part of each kidney, that secrete adrenaline.

ad·ren·a·line (ə dren′l ən), *n.* hormone produced by the adrenal glands; epinephrine. Adrenaline speeds up the heartbeat and increases bodily energy and resistance to fatigue.

A·dri·at·ic Sea (ā′drē at′ik), sea between Italy and the Balkan Peninsula. It is an arm of the Mediterranean.

a·drift (ə drift′), *adj.* **1** floating without being guided; drifting: *During the storm our boat was adrift on the lake.* **2** without guidance or direction; aimless: *He quit school, but without an education or special talents he found himself adrift.*

a·droit (ə droit′), *adj.* **1** having or showing skill in using the hands or the body; skillful: *Monkeys are adroit climbers.* **2** having or showing skill in using the mind; clever: *A good teacher is adroit in asking questions.* —**a·droit′ly,** *adv.* —**a·droit′ness,** *n.*

ad·sorb (ad sôrb′), *v.* to hold a gas, liquid, or dissolved substance spread out on a surface in a thin layer of molecules: *Dyes are adsorbed on fibers of cloth.*

Adriatic Sea *(map)*

N

ITALY

Adriatic Sea

Tyrrhenian Sea

Sicily

Mediterranean Sea

1 | 2
3 | 4
5
6

1=Slovenia   4=Serbia
2=Croatia   5=Albania
3=Bosnia and Herzegovina   6=Greece

---

adobe (def. 2)—adobe houses

ad·sorp·tion (ad sôrp′shən), *n.* condensation of gases, liquids, or dissolved substances on the surface of solids.

ad·u·la·tion (aj′ə lā′shən), *n.* too much praise; excessive flattery.

a·dult (ə dult′ *or* ad′ult), **1** *adj.* having full size and strength; fully developed; grown-up; mature: *an adult person.* **2** *n.* person who has reached full growth and development; grown-up person. **3** *n.* person who has reached a legal age of maturity, usually the age of 18, but sometimes 21. **4** *n.* a living thing grown to full size and development. **5** *adj.* of, for, or by adults: *adult education, adult behavior.* ■ See Word Story at **adolescent.** —**a·dult′ness,** *n.*

a·dul·te·rate (ə dul′tə rāt′), *v.* to make lower in quality by adding an inferior, impure, or improper substance: *It is against the law to adulterate milk with water.* ❏ *v.* **a·dul·te·rat·ed, a·dul·te·rat·ing.** —**a·dul′te·ra′tion,** *n.* —**a·dul′te·ra′tor,** *n.*

a·dul·ter·er (ə dul′tər ər), *n.* person who commits adultery.

a·dul·ter·ous (ə dul′tər əs), *adj.* of or about adultery. —**a·dul′ter·ous·ly,** *adv.*

a·dul·ter·y (ə dul′tər ē), *n.* unfaithfulness of one spouse to the other by having sexual intercourse with another person.

a·dult·hood (ə dult′hùd), *n.* condition or time of being an adult.

adv., **1** adverb. **2** advertisement.

ad·vance (ad vans′), **1** *v.* to move forward; push forward: *The troops advanced. The general advanced the troops.* **2** *n.* movement forward; progress: *The project's advance was very slow. We have made great advances in airplane design.* **3** *adj.* ahead of time: *The teacher gave advance notice of the change of the date of our test.* **4** *v.* to help forward; further: *The President's speech advanced the cause of peace.* **5** *v.* to put forward; suggest: *advance an opinion.* **6** *v.* to raise to a higher rank; promote: *The teacher was advanced to principal.* **7** *v.* to raise in price or value; increase: *Stock prices advanced several points last week.* **8** *n.* a rise in price or value: *There was an advance of seven cents a quart in the price of milk.* **9** *v.* to pay money before it is due or as a loan: *The company advanced the salesman funds for expenses.* **10** *n.* money paid before it is due or as a loan: *May I have an advance on next week's allowance?* **11** *n.pl.* **advances,** attempts or offers to another or others to settle a difference, to make an acquaintance, etc.: *She made the first advances toward making up her quarrel with me.* ❏ *v.* **ad·vanced, ad·vanc·ing.** —**ad·vanc′er,** *n.* **in advance, 1** in front; ahead: *The leader of the band marched in advance.* **2** ahead of time: *I paid for my ticket in advance.*

SYNONYM STUDY   **Advance** and **proceed** both mean to move forward. **Advance** suggests moving forward toward a definite end or destination: *With today's win, the team advanced to the finals.* **Proceed** suggests continuing to move forward from a definite point, such as a temporary stopping place: *After leaving the candy store, we proceeded to the movies.*

ad·vanced (ad vanst′), *adj.* **1** in front of others; forward: *Our army is in an advanced position.* **2** ahead of most others in

---

a	hat	ė	term	ô	order	ch	child		
ā	age	i	it	oi	oil	ng	long		a in about
ä	far	ī	ice	ou	out	sh	she		e in taken
â	care	o	hot	u	cup	th	thin	ə	i in pencil
e	let	ō	open	ù	put	ᴛʜ	then		o in lemon
ē	equal	ò	saw	ü	rule	zh	measure		u in circus

knowledge, skill, progress, ideas, etc.: *an advanced class in science, an advanced aircraft design.* **3** far along in development; not basic or early: *We are at an advanced stage in the project.* **4** far along in life; very old: *the advanced age of 90.*

ad·vance·ment (ad vans′mənt), *n.* **1** act or process of moving forward; improvement: *Advancements in the science of medicine have saved many lives.* **2** promotion: *Good work won her advancement to a higher position.*

ad·van·tage (ad van′tij), *n.* anything that is in your favor, or is a benefit; a help in getting something desired: *He had the advantage of a good education.*

take advantage of, 1 to use to help or benefit yourself: *take advantage of a beautiful day by working in the garden.* **2** to use unfairly; impose upon: *She was so good-natured that people often took advantage of her.*

to advantage, to a good effect; with a useful effect; favorably: *That frame sets off the painting to advantage.*

to your advantage, to your benefit or help: *It will be to his advantage to study Spanish before he visits Mexico.*

SYNONYM STUDY **Advantage** and **benefit** both mean good things to have or to get. **Advantage** suggests a superiority over others: *In wrestling, sheer strength is often an advantage.* **Benefit** suggests personal or social improvement: *An increase in knowledge is one of the benefits of reading.*

ad·van·ta·geous (ad′vən tā′jəs), *adj.* giving a benefit; favorable; helpful: *The agreement was advantageous to both sides.* —**ad′van·ta′geous·ly,** *adv.* —**ad′van·ta′geous·ness,** *n.*

ad·vent (ad′vent), *n.* **1** arrival or appearance, especially of someone or something seldom seen or unusually important. **2 Advent, a** the season including the four Sundays before Christmas. **b** the coming of Jesus into the world.

ad·ven·ture (ad ven′chər), **1** *n.* an unusual or exciting experience: *The trip to Alaska was quite an adventure for her.* **2** *n.* a bold and difficult undertaking, usually exciting and dangerous. **3** *n.* readiness to take part in exciting or dangerous undertakings: *An explorer must have a spirit of adventure.* **4** *v.* to dare to do; risk. ❑ *v.* **ad·ven·tured, ad·ven·tur·ing.**

adventure (def. 2)—Going through a rapids is a real adventure.

ad·ven·tur·er (ad ven′chər ər), *n.* **1** person who has or seeks adventures. **2** person who schemes to obtain money or social position by pretending to have them already.

ad·ven·ture·some (ad ven′chər səm), *adj.* bold and daring; adventurous.

ad·ven·tur·ous (ad ven′chər əs), *adj.* **1** fond of adventures; ready to take risks; daring: *an adventurous explorer.* **2** full of risk; dangerous: *an adventurous expedition to the North Pole.* —**ad·ven′tur·ous·ly,** *adv.* —**ad·ven′tur·ous·ness,** *n.*

ad·verb (ad′vėrb′), *n.* any word that adds to the meaning of verbs (They sing *well*), adjectives (She is *very* intelligent), or other adverbs (They sing *quite* well), usually to express time, place, way, amount, or circumstance.

WORD POWER **ADVERBS ■** The quickest way to create a new word is to change an old one. The fastest way to change words is with prefixes and suffixes. Many adverbs are just adjectives and nouns with suffixes added. The most common suffix forming adverbs is **-ly**. Added to adjectives, **-ly** means "in a ___ way." Other adverb suffixes are **-ward** and **-wards**, meaning "on the way to ___," and **-wise**, meaning "in the way of ___." This is a way to change words quickly, adverbwards, suffixwise.

ad·ver·bi·al (ad vėr′bē əl), *adj.* **1** used as an adverb. In the sentence, "I worked as quickly as possible," *as quickly as possible* is an adverbial phrase. **2** of an adverb; forming adverbs: *"-ly" is an adverbial suffix.* —**ad·ver′bi·al·ly,** *adv.*

ad·ver·sar·y (ad′vər ser′ē), *n.* **1** person or group opposing or hostile to another person or group; enemy: *The two countries were adversaries in World War II.* **2** person or group on the other side in a game or contest; opponent. ❑ *n., pl.* **ad·ver·sar·ies.**

ad·verse (ad′vèrs′ *or* ad vèrs′), *adj.* **1** unfriendly in purpose; hostile: *Adverse criticism discouraged me.* **2** acting against your interests; unfavorable; harmful: *adverse circumstances.* **3** coming from or acting in a contrary direction; opposing: *adverse winds.* —**ad·verse′ly,** *adv.* —**ad·verse′ness,** *n.*

ad·ver·si·ty (ad vėr′sə tē), *n.* **1** condition of unhappiness, misfortune, or distress. **2** stroke of misfortune; unfavorable or harmful thing or event. ❑ *n., pl.* **ad·ver·si·ties** for 2.

ad·ver·tise (ad′vər tīz), *v.* **1** to praise the good qualities of something in order to create a demand and promote sales: *Manufacturers advertise products that they wish to sell.* **2** to seek to sell goods, etc., by advertising: *It pays to advertise.* **3** to give public notice of in a newspaper, on the radio or TV, etc.: *When people lose something valuable, they advertise it in the newspaper.* **4** to ask for by public notice: *He advertised for a job.* ❑ *v.* **ad·ver·tised, ad·ver·tis·ing.** —**ad′ver·tis·er,** *n.*

WORD STORY **Advertise** comes from Latin words meaning "to turn toward." It used to mean "to notice something." Later, it came to mean "to cause others to notice something."

ad·ver·tise·ment (ad′vər tīz′mənt *or* ad vėr′tis mənt), *n.* a public notice or announcement recommending some product or service, or telling about some need: *The furniture store has an advertisement in the newspaper of a special sale.*

ad·ver·tis·ing (ad′vər tī′zing), *n.* **1** business of preparing, publishing, or circulating advertisements. **2** advertisements: *Billboards carry advertising.* **3** act of bringing to public notice by radio or TV announcements, published notices, posters, or other means: *The store attracted many customers by advertising.*

ad·vice (ad vīs′), *n.* opinion about what should be done; suggestion: *My advice is that you study more.*

ad·vis·a·ble (ad vī′zə bəl), *adj.* to be advised or recommended; wise; sensible; suitable: *It is not advisable for you to go to school while you are still sick.* —**ad·vis′a·bil′i·ty,** *n.* —**ad·vis′a·bly,** *adv.*

ad·vise (ad vīz′), *v.* **1** to give advice to; offer an opinion to; counsel: *Advise them to be cautious. I shall act as you advise.* **2** to give notice; inform: *We were advised that a storm was approaching, so we didn't go sailing.* ❑ *v.* **ad·vised, ad·vis·ing.**

ad·vis·ed·ly (ad vī′zid lē), *adv.* after careful consideration; deliberately.

ad·vise·ment (ad vīz′mənt), *n.* careful consideration: *The lawyer took our case under advisement and said she would give us an answer in two weeks.*

ad·vis·er *or* **ad·vi·sor** (ad vī′zər), *n.* **1** person who gives advice. **2** teacher appointed to advise students.

ad·vi·sor·y (ad vī′zər ē), **1** *adj.* having power to advise: *an advisory committee.* **2** *adj.* containing advice: *an advisory opinion.* **3** *n.* bulletin or report to advise of developments: *An advisory by the Weather Bureau warned of a storm.* ❑ *n., pl.* **ad·vi·sor·ies.**

ad·vo·ca·cy (ad′və kə sē), *n.* act or process of speaking or writing in favor of something; public recommendation; support: *The senator's advocacy of the plan won votes for it.*

ad·vo·cate (ad′və kāt *for verb;* ad′və kit *or* ad′və kāt *for noun*), **1** *v.* to speak or write in favor of; recommend publicly; support: *He advocates building more public housing.* **2** *n.* person who pleads or argues for; supporter: *She is an advocate of lower property taxes.* **3** *n.* lawyer who pleads in a court of law. ❑ *v.* **ad·vo·cat·ed, ad·vo·cat·ing.** —**ad′vo·ca′tion,** *n.* —**ad′vo·ca′tor,** *n.*

advt., advertisement.

adz or **adze** (adz), *n.* a cutting tool for shaping heavy timbers. It is something like an ax but with a blade set across the end of the handle and curving inward. ❑ *n., pl.* **adz·es.**

Ae·ge·an Sea (i jē′ən), sea between Greece and Turkey. It is an arm of the Mediterranean. See **Balkan States** for map.

Ae·ne·as (i nē′əs), *n.* (in Roman legends) a Trojan hero who after the fall of Troy and years of wandering reached Italy, where his descendants supposedly founded Rome.

Ae·ne·id (i nē′id), *n.* a long poem by Virgil telling the story of the wanderings of Aeneas.

aer·ate (âr′āt), *v.* **1** to expose to and mix with air: *Water in this reservoir is aerated and purified by being sprayed high into the air.* **2** to fill with a gas: *Soda water is water that has been aerated with carbon dioxide.* **3** to expose to chemical action with oxygen: *Blood is aerated in the lungs.* ❑ *v.* **aer·at·ed, aer·at·ing.** —**aer·a′tion,** *n.* —**aer′a·tor,** *n.*

aer·i·al (âr′ē əl), **1** *n.* antenna (def. 2). **2** *adj.* of or with aircraft: *aerial photography.* **3** *adj.* growing in air instead of in soil. **4** *adj.* of or about the air; atmospheric: *aerial currents.* —**aer′i·al·ly,** *adv.*

aer·i·al·ist (âr′ē ə list), *n.* acrobat who performs on a trapeze, tightrope, etc.

aer·ie (âr′ē *or* ir′ē), *n.* the lofty nest of an eagle, hawk, or other bird of prey. Also, **eyrie** or **eyry.** ▪ Other words that can sound like this are **airy** and **eerie.**

aero-, *prefix.* **1** air or other gas: *aerosol = fine particles in air or other gas.* **2** atmosphere: *aerospace = the earth's atmosphere and outer space.*

aer·obe (âr′ōb), *n.* any living thing that needs oxygen to live.

aer·o·bic (âr′ō′bik), *adj.* **1** living or growing only where there is oxygen: *aerobic bacteria.* **2** of or caused by aerobic bacteria. **3** of or involving aerobics: *aerobic exercise.* —**aer′o′bi·cal·ly,** *adv.*

aer·o·bics (âr′ō′biks), *n.* **1** *pl.* exercises that increase the body's consumption of oxygen and improve the functioning of the circulatory system. Aerobics include jogging, bicycling, rapid walking, and other similar activities. **2** *sing.* the practice or art of such exercises: *Aerobics has helped him control his weight.*

aerobics (def. 1)

aer·o·dy·nam·ics (âr′ō dī nam′iks), *n.* branch of physics that deals with the forces exerted by air or other gases in motion on flying or windblown objects.

aer·o·nau·tic (âr′ə nò′tik), *adj.* aeronautical.

aer·o·nau·ti·cal (âr′ə nò′tə kəl), *adj.* of aeronautics. —**aer′o·nau′ti·cal·ly,** *adv.*

aer·o·nau·tics (âr′ə nò′tiks), *n.* science of the design, manufacture, and operation of aircraft.

aer·o·plane (âr′ə plān), *n.* airplane.

aer·o·sol (âr′ə sol), *n.* **1** very fine particles of a solid or liquid substance suspended in the air or in some other gas. Smoke and fog are aerosols. **2** product packaged under pressure to be released as a spray or mist.

aer·o·space (âr′ō spās), **1** *n.* the earth's atmosphere and nearby outer space. **2** *adj.* of aircraft or spacecraft: *the aerospace industry.*

Ae·sop (ē′sop), *n.* Greek writer of fables who lived about 600 B.C. He often used animals in his stories to show how people should behave.

aes·thet·ic (es thet′ik), *adj.* **1** of or about the artistic or beautiful rather than the useful or practical. **2** having an appreciation of beauty in nature or art: *an aesthetic person.* **3** showing good taste; artistic: *an aesthetic wallpaper.* —**aes·thet′i·cal·ly,** *adv.*

aes·thet·ics (es thet′iks), *n.* the study of beauty.

AF, Air Force.

A.F. or **a.f.,** audio frequency.

a·far (ə fär′), *adv.* **from afar,** from a distance: *I saw him from afar.*

AFDC, Aid to Families with Dependent Children (a welfare program for needy families with children).

af·fa·ble (af′ə bəl), *adj.* courteous and pleasant; friendly: *Our principal is very affable.* [Affable comes from a Latin word meaning "easy to speak to."] —**af′fa·bil′i·ty,** *n.* —**af′fa·bly,** *adv.*

af·fair (ə fâr′), *n.* **1** matter of business; job; task: *Such a large project is a time-consuming affair.* **2** any thing or matter or happening: *The party was a delightful affair.*

af·fect[1] (ə fekt′), *v.* **1** to have an effect on; influence: *The small amount of rain last year affected the growth of crops. The disease affected her eyesight.* **2** to touch the heart of; stir the feelings of: *The sad story affected me deeply.*

USAGE NOTE Affect[1] and **effect** are easily confused because they sound alike and their meanings are related. **Affect** means to influence someone or something: *The change in the law affected all dog owners in the city.* **Effect** means to make something happen: *A recently effected change in the law requires people to leash their dogs.*

af·fect[2] (ə fekt′), *v.* **1** to pretend to have or feel: *He affected ignorance of the fight, but we knew that he had seen it.* **2** to use because you prefer to; choose: *affect carelessness in dress.* ▪ Another word that sounds like this is **effect.**

af·fec·ta·tion (af′ek tā′shən), *n.* an artificial way of talking or acting put on to impress others; pretense: *Her roughness is an affectation; she really is a quiet, gentle girl.*

af·fect·ed[1] (ə fek′tid), *adj.* **1** acted upon; influenced: *Everyone felt affected by the war.* **2** influenced injuriously: *She froze her feet and the affected toes were numb.*

af·fect·ed[2] (ə fek′tid), *adj.* put on for effect; not natural; artificial: *an affected voice.* —**af·fect′ed·ly,** *adv.* —**af·fect′ed·ness,** *n.*

af·fect·ing (ə fek′ting), *adj.* touching the heart; moving the feelings: *The refugee told an affecting story of hunger and suffering.* —**af·fect′ing·ly,** *adv.*

af·fec·tion (ə fek′shən), *n.* friendly feeling; fondness; love: *the affection of parents for their children.* ▪ See Synonym Study at **love.**

af·fec·tion·ate (ə fek′shə nit), *adj.* showing or having affection; loving and tender: *an affectionate letter, an affectionate farewell.* —**af·fec′tion·ate·ly,** *adv.*

affection

af·fer·ent (af′ər ənt), *adj.* leading inward to a central organ or point. Afferent nerves carry feelings from the nerve endings to the spinal cord.

a	hat	ė	term	ô	order	ch	child		
ā	age	i	it	oi	oil	ng	long	ə	a in about
ä	far	ī	ice	ou	out	sh	she		e in taken
â	care	o	hot	u	cup	th	thin		i in pencil
e	let	ō	open	u̇	put	ŦH	then		o in lemon
ē	equal	ò	saw	ü	rule	zh	measure		u in circus

af·fi·ance (ə fī′əns), *v.* to promise in marriage: *After months of dating they are now affianced.* ❑ *v.* **af·fi·anced, af·fi·anc·ing.**

af·fi·da·vit (af′ə dā′vit), *n.* statement written down and sworn to be true. An affidavit is usually made before a judge or notary public.

af·fil·i·ate (ə fil′ē āt *for verb;* ə fil′ē it *or* ə fil′ē āt *for noun*), **1** *v.* to join in close association; connect: *That TV station recently affiliated with a national network.* **2** *n.* organization or group associated with another or larger organization or group: *Our local automobile club is an affiliate of the national automobile club.* ❑ *v.* **af·fil·i·at·ed, af·fil·i·at·ing.** [**Affiliate** comes from a Latin word meaning "adopted." Becoming an affiliate of a larger organization is like being adopted by a big family.] **—af·fil′i·a′tion,** *n.*

af·fin·i·ty (ə fin′ə tē), *n.* **1** a natural attraction to a person or liking for a thing: *She has an affinity for science.* **2** relationship; connection: *There is an affinity between smallpox and cowpox, which are caused by similar viruses.* ❑ *n., pl.* **af·fin·i·ties.**

af·firm (ə fėrm′), *v.* **1** to declare to be true; say firmly; assert: *The prisoner affirmed his innocence.* **2** to confirm; ratify: *The higher court affirmed the lower court's decision.*

af·fir·ma·tion (af′ər mā′shən), *n.* positive statement; assertion.

af·firm·a·tive (ə fėr′mə tiv), **1** *adj.* stating that a fact is so; saying yes: *His answer to my question was affirmative.* **2** *n.* word or statement that says yes or agrees: *"I will" is an affirmative.* **3** *n.* the side arguing in favor of a question being debated: *The affirmative presented a strong argument.* **—af·firm′a·tive·ly,** *adv.*
in the affirmative, expressing agreement by saying yes: *She answered my question in the affirmative.*

affirmative action, a program that encourages the employment of women and minorities in order to make up for past discrimination.

af·fix (ə fiks′ *for verb;* af′iks *for noun*), **1** *v.* to stick on; fasten; attach: *She affixed a stamp to her letter.* **2** *v.* to add at the end: *The President affixed his signature to the bill.* **3** *n.* a sound or group of sounds added to a word to change its meaning or use. Affixes are either prefixes like *un-* and *re-* or suffixes like *-ly, -ness, -s,* or *-ed.* ❑ *n., pl.* **af·fix·es. —af′fix·a′tion,** *n.* **—af·fix′er,** *n.*

af·flict (ə flikt′), *v.* to cause pain to; trouble greatly; distress: *trees afflicted by parasites and disease.*

af·flic·tion (ə flik′shən), *n.* **1** a cause of pain, trouble, or distress; misfortune: *Poverty is an affliction.* **2** state of pain, trouble, or distress; misery: *the affliction of war.*

af·flu·ence (af′lü əns), *n.* wealth; riches: *The United States is a country of great affluence.*

af·flu·ent (af′lü ənt), *adj.* **1** having wealth; rich. **2** abundant; plentiful. **—af′flu·ent·ly,** *adv.*

> **WORD STORY** **Affluent** comes from a Latin word meaning "to flow towards." **Affluent** used to mean "flowing in great amount," and later on developed the meaning "overflowing in riches, wealthy."

af·ford (ə fôrd′), *v.* **1** to have or spare the money for: *Can we afford a new car?* **2** to manage to give, spare, or have: *A busy person cannot afford delay. He cannot afford to waste so much time.* **3** to be able without difficulty or harm: *I can't afford to take the chance.* **4** to give as an effect or a result; provide; yield: *Reading a good book affords real pleasure.* **—af·ford′a·ble,** *adj.*

af·fray (ə frā′), *n.* a noisy quarrel; public fight; brawl.

af·fright (ə frīt′), *v.* OLD USE. to excite with sudden fear; frighten.

af·front (ə frunt′), **1** *n.* word or act intended to show disrespect; deliberate insult: *To be called a coward is an affront.* **2** *v.* to insult deliberately; offend purposely: *The boy affronted his sister by calling her names.*

> **WORD STORY** **Affront** comes from a French word meaning "to strike on the forehead." At one time, people thought the forehead was the center of feelings.

Af·ghan (af′gan), **1** *n.* person born or living in Afghanistan. **2** *adj.* of Afghanistan or its people. **3** *n.* **afghan,** blanket or shawl made of knitted or crocheted wool, nylon, etc. **4** *n.* Afghan hound.

Afghan hound, a large, swift hunting dog with a narrow head and silky hair.

Af·ghan·i·stan (af gan′ə stan), *n.* country in SW Asia, between Pakistan and Iran. *Capital:* Kabul.

a·fi·cio·na·do (ə fis′yə nä′dō *or* ə fish′ē ə nä′dō), *n.* person who is devoted to some sport, hobby, or special interest: *a baseball aficionado.* ❑ *n., pl.* **a·fi·cio·na·dos.**

a·field (ə fēld′), *adv.* **1** away from home; away: *She wandered far afield in foreign lands.* **2** out of the right way; astray: *We seem to have gone far afield; we are lost.*

a·fire (ə fīr′), *adj.* **1** on fire; burning. **2** enthusiastic.

a·flame (ə flām′), *adj.* **1** in flames; on fire. **2** in a glow; glowing.

AFL-CIO, American Federation of Labor and Congress of Industrial Organizations (a national organization for cooperation among labor unions).

a·float (ə flōt′), *adj.* **1** floating on the water or in the air. **2** on shipboard; at sea. **3** flooded. **4** being spread; going around: *Many rumors were afloat.*

a·flut·ter (ə flut′ər), *adj.* **1** fluttering or waving: *The flags were aflutter in the breeze.* **2** in a flutter; excited: *The town was aflutter at the news.*

aflutter (def. 1)

a·foot (ə fút′), **1** *adv., adj.* on foot; by walking. **2** *adj.* going on; in progress: *There is mischief afoot.*

a·fore·men·tioned (ə fôr′men′shənd), *adj.* spoken of before; mentioned earlier.

a·fore·said (ə fôr′sed′), *adj.* aforementioned.

a·fore·thought (ə fôr′thôt′), *adj.* thought out beforehand; deliberately planned: *The evil deed was planned with malice aforethought.*

a·foul (ə foul′), *adj.* in a tangle; in a collision; entangled: *Raising the sail was impossible with the lines afoul.*
run afoul of, to get into trouble with: *A person who steals may run afoul of the law.*

a·fraid (ə frād′), *adj.* **1** feeling fear; frightened: *afraid of the dark.* **2** sorry to have to say: *I'm afraid you are wrong about that.* ■ **Afraid** is never used directly before the noun or pronoun.

a·fresh (ə fresh′), *adv.* once more; again.

Af·ri·ca (af′rə kə), *n.* continent south of Europe. It is the second largest continent.

Af·ri·can (af′rə kən), **1** *adj.* of Africa or its people. **2** *n.* person born or living in Africa.

African American, **1** an American of African descent. **2** of or about African Americans.

Af·ri·can-A·mer·i·can (af′rə kən ə mer′ə kən), *adj.* African American.

Af·ri·can·ized honeybee (af′rə kə nīzd′), killer bee.

African violet, a tropical plant with violet, white, or pink flowers, often grown as a houseplant.

Af·ri·kaans (af′rə käns′ *or* af′rə känz′), *n.* language spoken in South Africa which developed from the Dutch spoken by colonists who came to the area in the 1600s; South African Dutch.

> **WORD SOURCE** **Afrikaans** has given a number of words to the English language, including the words below.
>
> | | | | |
> |---|---|---|---|
> | aardvark | commando | spoor | veld |
> | apartheid | eland | springbok | wildebeest |
> | commandeer | kraal | trek | |

Af·ri·ka·ner (af′rə kä′nər), *n.* person born in South Africa whose native language is Afrikaans and who is of European, especially Dutch, descent; Boer.

Af·ro (af′rō), *n.* a bushy hairdo like that worn in parts of Africa. ❑ *n., pl.* **Af·ros.**

Af·ro-A·mer·i·can (af′rō ə mer′ə kən), *n., adj.* African American.

aft (aft), **1** *adv.* at or toward the stern of a ship, boat, or aircraft; abaft. **2** *adj.* in or near the stern of a ship, boat, or aircraft.

af·ter (af′tər), **1** *prep.* later in time than: *After dinner we can go.* **2** *adv., adj., prep.* following: *I ran so hard I panted for five minutes after. In after years she did not come to see us so often. Day after day I hoped to get a letter from my friend.* **3** *conj.* later than the time that: *After he goes, we shall eat.* **4** *prep., adv.* behind: *You come after me in the line. He ran off and the dog ran after me.* ∎ See Synonym Study at **behind. 5** *prep.* in search of; in pursuit of: *The dog ran after the rabbit.* **6** *prep.* about; concerning: *Your aunt asked after you.* **7** *prep.* because of; as a result of: *After such a big dinner, I couldn't finish my dessert.* **8** *prep.* in spite of: *After all their success, they still live humbly.* **9** *prep.* in honor of; for: *She is named after her grandmother.* **10** *adj.* nearer or toward the stern of a ship: *the after sails.* [**After** comes from an old English word meaning "farther to the back" or "later."]

af·ter·birth (af′tər bėrth′), *n.* the placenta and membranes that come out of the uterus shortly after birth.

af·ter·burn·er (af′tər bėr′nər), *n.* a jet-engine device that supplies additional fuel to the engine exhaust and burns the combination, thus increasing engine power and the speed of the plane.

af·ter·deck (af′tər dek′), *n.* part of a deck at or near the stern of a ship.

af·ter·ef·fect (af′tər i fekt′), *n.* result or effect that follows later: *The aftereffect of the explosion was a great fire.*

af·ter·glow (af′tər glō′), *n.* **1** glow remaining after something bright has gone. **2** glow in the sky after sunset. **3** a pleasurable feeling following something greatly enjoyed.

af·ter·im·age (af′tər im′ij), *n.* a visual effect that lingers on after the cause of the effect has disappeared: *an afterimage of a bright light.*

af·ter·life (af′tər līf′), *n.* life after death.

af·ter·math (af′tər math), *n.* a result or consequence, especially of something destructive: *The aftermath of war is hunger and disease.*

af·ter·noon (af′tər nün′), *n.* the part of the day between noon and evening.

af·ter·shock (af′tər shok′), *n.* a lesser shock, often one of several, that follows the main shock of an earthquake.

af·ter·taste (af′tər tāst′), *n.* a taste that is noticed in the mouth after eating or drinking: *This lemonade has a sour aftertaste.*

af·ter·thought (af′tər thôt′), *n.* a second or later thought or explanation.

af·ter·ward (af′tər wərd), *adv.* afterwards.

af·ter·wards (af′tər wərdz), *adv.* later: *Afterwards I regretted what I had said.*

Ag, symbol for silver.

a·gain (ə gen′), *adv.* **1** another time; once more: *Come again to play. Say that again.* **2** on the other hand; yet: *It may rain, and again it may not.* **3** moreover; besides: *Again, I must say that you are wrong.*

again and again, many times over; often: *I telephoned again and again before I finally reached him.*

a·gainst (ə genst′), *prep.* **1** in opposition to; contrary to: *Our team will debate against yours. It is against the rules of the game.* **2** in the opposite direction to, so as to meet; upon or toward: *We will sail against the wind. Rain beat against the window.* **3** in contact with: *The ladder is leaning against the wall.* **4** in preparation for: *Squirrels store up nuts against the winter.* **5** so as to defend or protect from: *An umbrella is a protection against rain.*

Ag·a·mem·non (ag′ə mem′non), *n.* (in Greek legends) the leader of the Greeks in the Trojan War, murdered by his wife Clytemnestra after he returned.

A·ga·ña (ä gä′nyä), *n.* port and capital of Guam.

a·gape (ə gāp′), *adj.* with the mouth wide open in wonder or surprise; gaping.

a·gar (ä′gər), *n.* a jellylike extract obtained from certain seaweeds, used in making cultures of bacteria and fungi.

ag·ate (ag′it), *n.* **1** variety of quartz with colored stripes or clouded colors. **2** a playing marble that looks like this.

agate (def. 1)—from several locations

a·ga·ve (ə gä′vē), *n.* an American desert plant which has a dense cluster of rigid, fleshy leaves with spines along the edges and at the tips.

WORD STORY   You might think that the **agave** has an American Indian or Spanish name. But its name comes from a Greek word meaning "noble," probably in praise of its flowers.

age (āj), **1** *n.* time of life: *He has reached the age of 14.* **2** *n.* length of life; time anything has existed: *A species of pine in California is said to have the greatest age of any living thing.* **3** *n.* a particular period or stage in life: *old age, middle age.* **4** *n.* the latter part of life; old age: *the wisdom of age.* **5** *n.* period in history: *the Bronze Age. This is the age of supersonic jets.* **6** *n.pl.* **ages, a** a long time: *I haven't seen him for ages.* **b** hundreds of years: *the work of ages.* **7** *v.* to grow old: *to age fast.* **8** *v.* to make old: *Worry can age you.* **9** *v.* to bring or come to full growth; mature: *This cheese must be aged for a year. Wine is put in casks to age.* ❑ *v.* **aged, ag·ing** or **age·ing.**

of age, at the time of life when a person is considered ready for adult rights and responsibilities, usually 18 years old.

-age, *suffix.* **1** act of ___ing: *marriage = act of marrying.* **2** condition or rank of ___s: *shortage = condition of being short of something.* **3** amount of ___: *wattage = amount of watts.*

a·ged (ā′jid *for 1;* ājd *for 2,3*), *adj.* **1** having lived a long time; old: *The aged couple lived on a small pension.* **2** having the age of: *She was aged six when she first went to school.* **3** improved by aging: *aged cheese.* **—a·ged·ly** (ā′jid lē), *adv.* **—a·ged·ness** (ā′jid nis), *n.*

age·ism (ā′jiz əm), *n.* discrimination against a certain age group, especially against the elderly with regard to jobs and housing.

age·less (āj′lis), *adj.* never growing old; never coming to an end: *the ageless wisdom of the Bible.* **—age′less·ly,** *adv.*

a·gen·cy (ā′jən sē), *n.* **1** a person or company that has the authority to act for another: *An agency rented our house for us. Employment agencies help people to get jobs.* **2** office of such a person or company. **3** a special department of the government concerned with the administration of affairs within a specific field: *The agency which deals with pollution in the United States is the Environmental Protection Agency.* ❑ *n., pl.* **a·gen·cies.**

a·gen·da (ə jen′də), *n.* list of things to be dealt with or done: *The agenda for today's club meeting includes reading of committee reports and admission of new members.* ❑ *n., pl.* **a·gen·das.**

a·gent (ā′jənt), *n.* **1** person or company having the authority to act for another: *She is a real-estate agent and can help you sell your house.* **2** a law enforcement officer. **3** secret agent. **4** any power or cause that produces an effect by its action: *Yeast is an important agent in causing bread to rise.*

age-old (āj′ōld′), *adj.* having existed for a very long time; very old; ancient: *age-old customs.*

ag·glu·ti·nate (ə glüt′n āt), *v.* to stick together; join together. ❑ *v.* **ag·glu·ti·nat·ed, ag·glu·ti·nat·ing.**

a	hat	ė	term	ô	order	ch	child		a in about
ā	age	i	it	oi	oil	ng	long		e in taken
ä	far	ī	ice	ou	out	sh	she	ə	i in pencil
â	care	o	hot	u	cup	th	thin		o in lemon
e	let	ō	open	ů	put	ŦH	then		u in circus
ē	equal	ò	saw	ü	rule	zh	measure		

17

ag·glu·ti·na·tion (ə glüt′n ā′shən), *n.* process of sticking to-gether, especially the clumping together of bacteria or blood cells, usually caused by contact with antibodies.

ag·gran·dize (ə gran′dīz *or* ag′rən dīz), *v.* to make greater or larger in power; increase the rank or wealth of: *The dictator sought to aggrandize himself at the expense of his people.* ❑ *v.* **ag·gran·dized, ag·gran·diz·ing.** —**ag·gran′dize·ment,** *n.* —**ag·gran′diz·er,** *n.*

ag·gra·vate (ag′rə vāt), *v.* **1** to make worse or more severe: *His headache was aggravated by all the noise.* **2** to annoy; irritate; exasperate: *She aggravated me by asking so many questions.* ❑ *v.* **ag·gra·vat·ed, ag·gra·vat·ing.** —**ag′gra·vat′ing·ly,** *adv.* —**ag′gra·va′tor,** *n.*

ag·gra·va·tion (ag′rə vā′shən), *n.* **1** annoyance; irritation. **2** something that aggravates. **3** act of making worse.

ag·gre·gate (ag′rə git *or* ag′rə gāt *for noun;* ag′rə gāt *for verb*), **1** *n.* total amount; sum: *The aggregate of all the gifts was over $100.* **2** *v.* to amount to; come to; total: *The money collected will aggregate $1000.* **3** *n.* mass of separate things joined together: *A lump of sugar is an aggregate of sugar crystals.* **4** *v.* to gather into one mass or whole; unite: *Granite is made of small particles aggregated together.* ❑ *v.* **ag·gre·gat·ed, ag·gre·gat·ing.** —**ag′gre·gate·ly,** *adv.*

ag·gre·ga·tion (ag′rə gā′shən), *n.* **1** act of collecting separate things into one mass or whole. **2** the group or mass collected.

ag·gres·sion (ə gresh′ən), *n.* **1** the first step in an attack or a quarrel; unprovoked attack: *A country that sends its army to oc-cupy another country is guilty of aggression.* **2** practice of mak-ing assaults or attacks on the rights or territory of others as a method or policy.

ag·gres·sive (ə gres′iv), *adj.* **1** taking the first step in an attack or a quarrel; ready to attack others: *a warlike and aggressive na-tion.* ■ See Synonym Study at **hostile. 2** very active; energetic: *They organized an aggressive campaign against pollution.* **3** too confident and certain; assertive: *An aggressive manner can be irritating to others.* —**ag·gres′sive·ly,** *adv.* —**ag·gres′sive·ness,** *n.*

ag·gres·sor (ə gres′ər), *n.* one that begins an attack or a quarrel, especially a nation that starts a war.

ag·grieved (ə grēvd′), *adj.* **1** feeling injured or wronged: *to make amends to an aggrieved person.* **2** feeling troubled or distressed: *I was aggrieved at having lost their friendship.*

a·ghast (ə gast′), *adj.* struck with surprise or horror; filled with terror: *I was aghast when I saw the destruction caused by the earthquake.*

WORD STORY Aghast comes from an old English word mean-ing "to frighten." That word is related to an old English word mean-ing "ghost" or "spirit."

agile (def. 1)—an agile gibbon

Life Nature Library/The Primates, Published by Time-Life Books, Inc.

ag·ile (aj′əl), *adj.* **1** moving quickly and easily; nimble: *as agile as a cat.* **2** quick in thinking; alert: *You need an agile mind to solve puzzles.* —**ag′ile·ly,** *adv.*

a·gil·i·ty (ə jil′ə tē), *n.* ability to move quickly and easily; nim-bleness: *He has the agility of a monkey.*

ag·i·tate (aj′ə tāt), *v.* **1** to move or shake violently: *A sudden wind agitated the surface of the river.* **2** to disturb or upset very much: *He was agitated by the unexpected news of his friend's ill-ness.* **3** to argue about or discuss a matter vigorously to arouse public interest and feeling: *agitate for a shorter working day.* ❑ *v.* **ag·i·tat·ed, ag·i·tat·ing.** [Agitate comes from a Latin word meaning "moved back and forth."] —**ag′i·tat′ed·ly,** *adv.*

ag·i·ta·tion (aj′ə tā′shən), *n.* **1** a disturbed, upset, or troubled state: *Because of her agitation over losing her job, she could not sleep.* **2** argument or discussion to arouse public interest and feeling: *There was much agitation for and against gun control.* **3** act of violent moving or shaking: *The agitation of the sea almost turned the little boat over.*

ag·i·ta·tor (aj′ə tā′tər), *n.* **1** person who stirs up public feeling for or against something. **2** device or machine for shaking or stirring.

a·gleam (ə glēm′), *adj.* gleaming.

a·glit·ter (ə glit′ər), *adj.* glittering.

a·glow (ə glō′), *adj.* glowing: *The baby's cheeks were aglow with health.*

ag·nos·tic (ag nos′tik), *n.* person who believes that nothing is known or can be known about the existence of God. —**ag·nos′ti·cal·ly,** *adv.*

a·go (ə gō′), **1** *adj.* gone by; past: *I met her two years ago.* **2** *adv.* in the past: *He lived here long ago.*

a·gog (ə gog′), *adj.* full of expectation or excitement; eager: *The children were all agog to see their presents.*

ag·o·nize (ag′ə nīz), *v.* to feel great pain; suffer agony: *The lost skiers agonized in the freezing cold for hours.* ❑ *v.* **ag·o·nized, ag·o·niz·ing.**

ag·o·niz·ing (ag′ə nī′zing), *adj.* causing very great suffering. —**ag′o·niz′ing·ly,** *adv.*

ag·o·ny (ag′ə nē), *n.* very painful suffering; great anguish: *the agony of a severe toothache. The loss of their child filled them with agony.* ■ See Synonym Study at **misery.** ❑ *n., pl.* **ag·o·nies.**

WORD STORY Agony comes from a Greek word meaning "public gatherings." Greeks held frequent outdoor celebrations that featured games and contests. Athletes struggled to win these con-tests. Later, the word's meaning was extended to include any strug-gle. And later yet, it came to mean "pain."

a·gou·ti (ə gü′tē), *n.* rodent of the tropical Americas about the size of a rabbit and usually gray. ❑ *n., pl.* **a·gou·tis** *or* **a·gou·ties.**

a·grar·i·an (ə grâr′ē ən), *adj.* **1** of or about farming land, its use, or its ownership: *Most old countries had agrarian disputes be-tween tenants and landlords.* **2** for the support and advancement of farmers or farming: *an agrarian movement.*

a·gree (ə grē′), *v.* **1** to have the same feeling or opinion: *We all agree on that subject. I agree that we should try to be more care-ful.* **2** to be in harmony; correspond: *All accounts of the accident seem to agree.* **3** to get along well together: *My cousin and I don't always agree.* **4** to say that you are willing; consent: *He agreed to go with us.* **5** to come to an understanding, especially in set-tling a dispute: *The workers and employers agreed on the terms of the contract.* **6** to say something is real or true; admit: *We agreed that we had been late.* **7** (in grammar) to have the same number, case, gender, or person. In the sentences "The woman is going," and "All the women are going," the subjects and the verbs agree in person and number. ❑ *v.* **a·greed, a·gree·ing.**
agree with, to have a good effect on; suit: *This food does not agree with me; it makes me sick.*

WORD STORY Agree comes from Latin words meaning "pleas-ing to" someone. **Grateful** comes from the same Latin word mean-ing "pleasing" plus **-ful.** If something pleases you, you'll probably agree to it gratefully.

a·gree·a·ble (ə grē′ə bəl), *adj.* **1** giving pleasure; pleasing: *She had an agreeable manner.* **2** ready to agree; willing: *If you are agreeable we can see the show together this afternoon.* —**a·gree′a·ble·ness,** *n.* —**a·gree′a·bly,** *adv.*

A

a·gree·ment (ə grē′mənt), *n.* **1** an understanding reached by two or more persons, groups of persons, or nations among themselves. Nations make treaties and individuals make contracts; both are agreements. **2** act of coming to an understanding, especially in settling a dispute: *Every obstacle to agreement has been removed.* **3** harmony in feeling or opinion: *The coaches are in complete agreement that she will be a superb gymnast.* **4** (in grammar) correspondence of words in number, case, gender, or person. There is number agreement in "that man" but lack of agreement in "those man."

ag·ri·busi·ness (ag′rə biz′nis), *n.* the business of producing, processing and distributing farm products, especially as carried on by large corporations. ❑ *n., pl.* **ag·ri·busi·ness·es.**

ag·ri·cul·tur·al (ag′rə kul′chər əl), *adj.* of or about farming; of agriculture: *The Middle West is an important agricultural region.* **—ag′ri·cul′tur·al·ly,** *adv.*

ag·ri·cul·ture (ag′rə kul′chər), *n.* science or art of cultivating the soil, including the production of crops and the raising of livestock; farming. **—ag′ri·cul′tur·ist** or **ag′ri·cul′tur·al·ist,** *n.*

a·gron·o·my (ə gron′ə mē), *n.* science of managing farmland; branch of agriculture that deals with crop production. **—a·gron′o·mist,** *n.*

a·ground (ə ground′), *adv., adj.* stranded on the shore or on the bottom in shallow water.

A·guas·ca·lien·tes (ä′gwäs kä lyen′tes), *n.* a state in central Mexico.

ah (ä), *interj.* exclamation of pain, sorrow, regret, pity, admiration, surprise, joy, dislike, contempt, etc.

a·ha (ä hä′), *interj.* exclamation of triumph, satisfaction, surprise, joy, etc.

a·head (ə hed′), *adv.* **1** in front; before: *Walk ahead of me.* **2** forward; onward: *Go ahead with this work for another week.* **3** in advance; earlier: *Leonardo Da Vinci was ahead of his time when he drew plans for a flying machine and a parachute.* **4** into the future; for the future: *Are you planning ahead?* **5** to a later time: *Set the clocks ahead an hour.*

be ahead, 1 be winning: *Our team is ahead by six points.* **2** to have more than is needed or expected: *We're ahead $50 on the budget.*

get ahead, to succeed: *I worked hard at my job in the hope that I would get ahead.*

get ahead of, to do or be better than; surpass: *She worked hard trying to get ahead of the others in the class.*

a·hem (ə hem′), *interj.* a sound made by coughing or clearing the throat, sometimes used to attract attention, express doubt, or gain time.

a·hold (ə hōld′), *n.* INFORMAL. **get ahold of,** to get; acquire: *I need to get ahold of some information.*

a·hoy (ə hoi′), *interj.* call used by sailors to attract the attention of persons at a distance: *The sailors in the lifeboat shouted "Ship ahoy!" to the passing freighter.*

AI, artificial intelligence.

aid (ād), **1** *v.* to give support to; help: *The Red Cross aids flood victims.* ■ See Synonym Study at **help. 2** *n.* a help; assistance: *When my arm was broken, I could not dress without aid.* **3** *n.* person or thing that helps; helper: *A dishwasher is an aid to housework.* **—aid′er,** *n.*

aide (ād), *n.* **1** helper; assistant. **2** aide-de-camp.

aide-de-camp (ād′də kamp′), *n.* a military officer who acts as an assistant to a superior officer by taking and sending messages and acting as a secretary. ❑ *n., pl.* **aides-de-camp.**

AIDS (ādz), *n.* a deadly disease caused by a kind of virus which attacks the immune system, resulting in the body's inability to resist other serious infections.

WORD STORY AIDS is an acronym for **A**cquired **I**mmuno**d**eficiency **S**yndrome. When scientists first recognized this new disease, they did not know what caused it. All they knew was that patients' immune systems were losing proper effect because of something that changed bodily functions. So they named the disease for what they could recognize. Later they discovered HIV, the virus that causes AIDS, and gave it a name of its own.

ai·ki·do (ī kē′dō), *n.* a Japanese self-defense technique using no weapons. It uses various holds and movements to offset an attacker's strength, causing the attacker to lose balance. [Aikido comes from Japanese words meaning "together," "spirit," and "way." In Japan, studying a martial art is considered to be a spiritual way of life and not just a hobby.]

ail (āl), *v.* **1** to be the matter with; trouble: *What ails the child?* **2** to be ill; feel sick: *Our new kitten is still ailing.* ■ Another word that sounds like this is **ale.**

aikido

ai·lan·thus (ā lan′ thəs), *n.* tree originally found in Asia but growing in many parts of North America. It has paired leaves on long, thin branches and small greenish flowers that smell bad. ❑ *n., pl.* **ai·lan·thus·es.**

WORD STORY Ailanthus comes from East Indian words meaning "tree" and "sky." It is sometimes called the tree of heaven in English. The reason is not clear. Because it grows on rough ground where other trees do not grow, people may have thought that it came down from above. Because it can grow tall, people may have been used to seeing it against the sky.

ai·le·ron (ā′lə ron′), *n.* a hinged, movable part on the rear edge of an airplane wing, used for tilting the airplane.

ail·ment (āl′mənt), *n.* disorder of the body or mind; illness: *He has a serious heart ailment.*

aim (ām), **1** *v.* to point or direct something, such as a gun or blow, in order to hit a target: *She aimed carefully at the target.* **2** *n.* act of pointing or directing at something: *Take careful aim.* **3** *n.* ability to point or direct: *She hit the target because her aim was good.* **4** *v.* to direct words or acts at someone or something: *The teacher's talk was aimed at the students who cheated on the test.* **5** *v.* to direct your efforts; try: *He aimed to please his friends.* **6** *v.* to have in mind as a purpose; intend: *I aim to go.* **7** *n.* purpose; intention: *Her aim was to become a lawyer.* [Aim comes from a Latin word meaning "to estimate." Estimate comes from the same Latin word. An estimate is a careful guess, and so is an aim, really.]

aim·less (ām′lis), *adj.* without purpose; pointless: *aimless wandering around.* **—aim′less·ly,** *adv.* **—aim′less·ness,** *n.*

ain't (ānt), **1** am not; is not. **2** are not. **3** have not; has not. ■ Careful speakers and writers do not use **ain't.**

USAGE NOTE Ain't was freely used in the 1600s and 1700s. During the 1800s it was criticized. Today, **ain't** is no longer acceptable in formal English. Even in informal speech, its use is not approved. However, it is often heard, especially in very casual speech.

Ai·nu (ī′nü), *n.* member of a group of people living in northern Japan, believed to have been Japan's original inhabitants. ❑ *n., pl.* **Ai·nu** or **Ai·nus.**

air (âr), **1** *n.* the mixture of gases that surrounds the earth; atmosphere. Air has no smell, taste, or color. It contains mostly nitrogen and oxygen, along with argon, carbon dioxide, hydrogen, and small quantities of neon, helium, and other gases. **2** *n.* space overhead; sky: *Birds fly in the air.* **3** *v.* to put out in the air: *We aired the sleeping bags in the backyard.* **4** *n.* fresh air: *He opened the window to let some air into the overheated room.* **5** *v.* to let fresh air in: *Open the windows and air the room.* **6** *n.* airline; airplane: *We traveled by air on our vacation.* **7** *v.* to make known: *Don't air your troubles too often.* **8** *n.* a simple melody or tune:

a	hat	ė	term	ô	order	ch	child		a in about
ā	age	i	it	oi	oil	ng	long		e in taken
ä	far	ī	ice	ou	out	sh	she	ə	i in pencil
â	care	o	hot	u	cup	th	thin		o in lemon
e	let	ō	open	ù	put	ᴛʜ	then		u in circus
ē	equal	ò	saw	ü	rule	zh	measure		

an old Scottish air. **9** *n.* an imaginary medium through which radio and television waves are said to travel. **10** *n.* general character or appearance of a person or thing: *An air of mystery surrounds the deserted house.* **11** *n.pl.* **airs,** unnatural or showy manners: *Just act naturally; don't put on airs.* **12** *adj.* of or about aviation or aircraft: *air safety.* ■ Other words that can sound like this are **ere, err,** and **heir.**

clear the air, to lessen anger, emotional tension, or misunderstanding by admitting and discussing it: *The sisters' frank talk helped clear the air between them.*

in the air, being spread; going around: *Reports of rebellion were in the air.*

off the air, 1 not broadcasting: *This station is off the air from midnight to six in the morning.* **2** not being broadcast: *We used to watch that show, but it's off the air now.*

on the air, 1 broadcasting: *This station has been on the air since 1958.* **2** being broadcast: *Is that show still on the air?*

up in the air, uncertain or unsettled: *Our plans are still up in the air.*

walk on air, be very happy or pleased: *She has been walking on air since the band recorded her song.*

air bag, an inflatable bag that prevents a person from being thrown forward in the event of a traffic accident. It inflates instantaneously upon impact.

air base, headquarters and airfield for military aircraft.

air·boat (âr′bōt′), *n.* a small flat-bottomed boat driven by an airplane propeller, used for travel in flooded areas, such as the Everglades.

air·borne (âr′bôrn′), *adj.* **1** supported by the air; off the ground: *airborne.* **2** carried in aircraft: *airborne troops.* **3** carried by air: *airborne dust, airborne pollen.*

air bags

air brake, brake operated by forcing compressed air against a piston.

air·brush (âr′brush′), **1** *n.* device that uses compressed air to spray a mist of paint on a surface. **2** *v.* to paint, touch up, etc., with an airbrush: *The artist airbrushed the photo to make the colors brighter.* ❑ *n., pl.* **air·brush·es.**

air-con·di·tion (âr′kən dish′ən), *v.* **1** to supply with air conditioning. **2** to treat air by means of air conditioning. —**air-con·di′-tioned,** *adj.*

air conditioner, device used to air-condition a building, room, motor vehicle, etc.

air conditioning, means of controlling the temperature and humidity of air and of cleansing it of dust.

air-cooled (âr′küld′), *adj.* cooled by air forced onto or around the cylinders of an internal-combustion engine: *This car has no radiator because the engine is air-cooled.*

air·craft (âr′kraft′), *n.* machine for flying in the air. Airplanes, airships, helicopters, and balloons are aircraft. ❑ *n., pl.* **air·craft.**

aircraft carrier, warship designed as a base for aircraft, with a large, flat deck on which to land or take off.

air·drome (âr′drōm′), *n.* airport.

air·drop (âr′drop′), **1** *n.* delivery of food, supplies, or persons by parachute from aircraft in flight. **2** *v.* to deliver by parachute from aircraft in flight. ❑ *v.* **air-dropped, air-drop·ping.**

Aire·dale (âr′dāl), *n.* a large terrier having a wiry brown or tan coat with dark markings.

air element, the branch of the Canadian armed forces that uses aircraft.

air·field (âr′fēld′), *n.* the landing area of an airport or air base.

air·foil (âr′foil′), *n.* a wing, aileron, rudder, or other surface designed to lift or control an aircraft.

air force, 1 branch of the military forces that uses aircraft. **2 Air Force,** branch of the armed forces of the United States that includes aviation personnel, equipment, etc.

air gun, 1 air rifle. **2** device that uses compressed air to force grease, putty, etc., into or onto something.

air·ing (âr′ing), *n.* **1** exposure to air for drying, warming, etc.: *Give the rug a thorough airing.* **2** a walk, ride, or drive outdoors. **3** exposure to public notice or discussion: *The new bill is due for an airing in Congress.*

air lane, a regular route used by aircraft; airway.

air·less (âr′lis), *adj.* **1** without fresh air; stuffy. **2** without a breeze; still.

air·lift (âr′lift′), **1** *n.* system of using aircraft to transport passengers and freight to a place when existing land routes are closed or inadequate: *Medical supplies were brought by airlift to the flooded villages.* **2** *v.* to transport by airlift: *Enough planes were provided to airlift two army divisions.*

air·line (âr′lin′), *n.* company that carries passengers and freight by aircraft from one place to another.

air·lin·er (âr′li′nər), *n.* a large passenger airplane.

air·lock (âr′lok′), *n.* an airtight compartment that allows workers underwater to go between places where there is a difference in air pressure. The pressure in an airlock can be raised or lowered.

air·mail (âr′māl′), **1** *n.* mail sent by aircraft. **2** *adj.* sent or to be sent by aircraft: *an airmail package.* **3** *n.* system for carrying mail by aircraft. **4** *v.* to send by airmail.

air·man (âr′mən), *n.* **1** any of several military ranks. See chart on page 712. **2** pilot of an aircraft; aviator. ❑ *n., pl.* **air·men.**

air mass, a large body of air within the atmosphere that has the same temperature and humidity throughout any particular level and moves great distances horizontally without changing.

air·plane (âr′plān′), *n.* aircraft heavier than air, supported in flight by the action of air on its fixed wings and driven by propeller, jet propulsion, etc.

airplane

air plant, a plant that grows on another plant and is not connected to the ground; epiphyte. Air plants draw nourishment from the air and rain.

air·play (âr′plā′), *n.* act of playing a piece of recorded music on TV or radio: *The song got a lot of airplay.*

air pocket, a downward current of air that causes an aircraft to lose altitude suddenly.

air pollution, the contamination of the air by waste gases from industry, fuel exhaust, etc.

air·port (âr′pôrt′), *n.* area used regularly by aircraft to land or take off. An airport usually has buildings for passengers and aircraft and equipment for repairing and servicing aircraft.

air pressure, pressure caused by the weight of the air; atmospheric pressure. At sea level this pressure is 14.7 pounds per square inch (1.03 kilograms per square centimeter).

air pump, device for forcing air into something or drawing air out of something.

air raid, attack by enemy aircraft, especially by bombers.

air rifle, gun that uses compressed air to shoot a single pellet or dart; air gun.

air sac, 1 one of the tiny pouches in the lungs through which oxygen passes into the blood and carbon dioxide is removed; alveolus. **2** any of several air-filled spaces in the bodies of birds, connected with the lungs.

air·ship (âr′ship′), *n.* a kind of balloon that can be steered. Airship usually have propellers and rudders. Dirigibles and blimps are airships.

air·sick (âr′sik′), *adj.* sick as a result of the motion of aircraft. —**air′sick·ness**, *n.*

air·space (âr′spās′), *n.* the region of the atmosphere above a country or other section of land: *The plane entered Canadian airspace.*

air speed, speed of an aircraft measured in relation to the speed of the air through which it moves.

air·strip (âr′strip′), *n.* a paved or cleared runway, often temporary, on which aircraft land and take off; landing strip.

air·tight (âr′tīt′), *adj.* **1** so tight that no air or other gases can get in or out. **2** having no weak points open to an opponent's attack: *an airtight alibi.*

air·waves (âr′wāvz′), *n.pl.* radio or television broadcasting.

air·way (âr′wā′), *n.* **1** route for aircraft; air lane. **2** passage for air.

air·wor·thy (âr′wėr′ᵀHē), *adj.* fit and safe for service in the air. —**air′wor·thi·ness**, *n.*

air·y (âr′ē), *adj.* **1** light as air; graceful: *an airy tune.* **2** lighthearted and happy: *airy laughter.* **3** open to currents of air; breezy: *a large, airy room.* **4** of air; in the air; aerial: *birds and other airy creatures.* **5** like air; not solid or substantial: *Such airy plans will fail.* ❑ *adj.* **air·i·er, air·i·est.** ■ Other words that can sound like this are **aerie, eyrie,** and **eyry.** —**air′i·ly,** *adv.* —**air′i·ness,** *n.*

aisle (īl), *n.* **1** passage between rows of seats in a hall, theater, school, etc. **2** passage on either side of a church, often set off by pillars. **3** any long, narrow passage. ■ Other words that sound like this are **I'll** and **isle.**

a·jar (ə jär′), *adj.* slightly open: *Please leave the door ajar.*

A·jax (ā′jaks), *n.* (in Greek legends) a Greek hero at the siege of Troy, second only to Achilles in strength and courage.

AK, Alaska (used with postal Zip Code).

aka or **a.k.a.,** also known as: *William Johnson aka Robert Johns.*

A·ke·la (ə kē′lə *or* ə kā′lə), *n.* in Canada, a cubmaster. ❑ *n., pl.* **A·ke·las.**

A·ki·hi·to (ä′kē hē′tō), *n.* born 1933, emperor of Japan since 1989. ■ Japanese emperors choose names for their reigns. Akihito chose *Heisei,* which means "achieving peace." Akihito was the first emperor to marry a woman not of royal birth. [Akihito comes from Japanese words meaning "bright peak of virtue."]

a·kim·bo (ə kim′bō), *adj.* with the hands on the hips and the elbows bent outward.

a·kin (ə kin′), *adj.* **1** of the same kind; similar: *His tastes in music seem akin to mine.* **2** of the same family; related: *Your cousins are akin to you.*

A·ki·ta (ə kē′tə), *n.* a medium-sized dog, originally from Japan, with a sharp nose, pointed ears, and short, rough fur. ❑ *n., pl.* **A·ki·tas.**

Ak·ron (ak′rən), *n.* city in NE Ohio.

-al[1], *suffix.* of; like; as: *ornamental = as ornament.*

-al[2], *suffix.* act of ___ing: *refusal = act of refusing.*

Al, symbol for aluminum.

AL, Alabama (used with postal Zip Code).

Ala., Alabama.

Al·a·bam·a (al′ə bam′ə), *n.* **1** one of the south central states of the United States. *Abbreviation:* AL or Ala. *Capital:* Montgomery. **2** river in Alabama, flowing from central Alabama SW to the Mobile River. —**Al′a·bam′an** or **Al′a·bam′i·an,** *n.*

WORD STORY **Alabama** comes from the name of an American Indian tribe that once lived in the area. The tribe's name came from Indian words meaning "I clear the thicket."

al·a·bas·ter (al′ə bas′tər), **1** *n.* a smooth, white or delicately shaded, translucent mineral, often carved into ornaments and vases. **2** *adj.* smooth and white like alabaster.

à la carte (ä′ lə kärt′ *or* al′ ə kärt′), with a stated price for each dish instead of one price for the whole meal.

a·lack (ə lak′), *interj.* OLD USE. alas.

a·lac·ri·ty (ə lak′rə tē), *n.* brisk and eager action; liveliness: *She began making the arrangements for her trip with alacrity.*

A·lad·din (ə lad′n), *n.* a youth in one of the tales in *The Arabian Nights,* who found a magic lamp and a magic ring. By rubbing either one of them he could call either of two powerful spirits to do whatever he asked.

Al·a·mo (al′ə mō), *n.* a mission building in San Antonio, Texas, used as a fort by a band of Texas rebels fighting for independence from Mexico. Besieged by an army of Mexicans, the Texans were overwhelmed and killed on March 6, 1836.

a la mode or **à la mode** (ä′ lə mōd′ *or* al′ ə mōd′), **1** in style; fashionable. **2** served with ice cream: *pie a la mode.*

a·larm (ə lärm′), **1** *n.* sudden fear of danger; fright: *The deer darted off in alarm.* ■ See Synonym Study at **fear. 2** *v.* to fill with sudden fear; frighten: *The breaking of a branch under my foot alarmed the deer.* ■ See Synonym Study at **scare. 3** *n.* a warning of approaching danger: *This is no false alarm.* **4** *n.* signal giving such a warning: *a fire alarm.* **5** *n.* bell or other device that makes noise to warn or awaken people: *a burglar alarm.* **6** *n.* call to arms or action: *Paul Revere gave the alarm to the towns near Boston.* [Alarm comes from an Italian exclamation meaning "to arms!"]

alarm clock, clock that can be set to ring or sound at any fixed time.

a·larm·ing (ə lär′ming), *adj.* causing alarm and fear; frightening. —**a·larm′ing·ly,** *adv.*

a·larm·ist (ə lär′mist), *n.* person who is easily alarmed or alarms others needlessly or on very slight grounds.

a·las (ə las′), *interj.* exclamation of sorrow, grief, regret, or pity. [Alas comes from a French word meaning "ah, miserable."]

Alas., Alaska.

A·las·ka (ə las′kə), *n.* **1** one of the Pacific states of the United States, in the NW part of North America. *Abbreviation:* AK or Alas. *Capital:* Juneau. **2** Gulf of, arm of the Pacific, off S Alaska. [Alaska comes from an Aleut word meaning "great land" or "mainland."] —**A·las′kan,** *adj., n.*

Alaska Highway, highway that extends from northern British Columbia to Fairbanks, Alaska; Alcan Highway.

Alaskan malamute, a large, strong dog with a gray or black and white coat, commonly used for pulling sleds in Alaska. Also, **malamute** or **malemute.**

Alaska Pipeline, pipeline that carries oil across Alaska from Prudhoe Bay on the Arctic Ocean south to Valdez on the Gulf of Alaska. Its official name is the **Trans Alaska Pipeline.** It is 800 miles (1287 kilometers) long.

Alaska Standard Time, the standard time in central Alaska and all of Hawaii, two hours behind Pacific Standard Time; Hawaii Standard Time.

alb (alb), *n.* a white linen robe worn by Roman Catholic and some Anglican priests at the Communion service.

al·ba·core (al′bə kôr), *n.* a large tuna with long fins and light-colored flesh valued for canning. ❑ *n., pl.* **al·ba·core** or **al·ba·cores.**

Al·ba·ni·a (al bā′nē ə), *n.* country in SE Europe on the Adriatic, north of Greece. *Capital:* Tirana. —**Al·ba′ni·an,** *adj., n.*

Al·ba·ny (ôl′bə nē), *n.* capital of New York, on the Hudson River.

al·ba·tross (al′bə tròs), *n.* **1** a very large web-footed seabird, related to petrels, that can fly long distances. **2** a guilty reminder; burden: *This terrible defeat was an albatross that the general was never allowed to forget.* ❑ *n., pl.* **al·ba·tross** or **al·ba·tross·es.**

WORD STORY **Albatross** comes from an Arabic word meaning "sea eagle." Definition 2 comes from "The Rime of the Ancient Mariner," a poem by Samuel Taylor Coleridge, in which the mariner kills an albatross and has to wear it around his neck as punishment.

al·be·it (ôl bē′it), *conj.* even though; even if; although: *Albeit we are late, we may still be able to catch the bus.*

Al·ber·ta (al bėr′tə), *n.* province in W Canada. *Capital:* Edmonton. [Alberta comes from the name of a daughter of Queen Victoria.] —**Al·ber′tan,** *adj., n.*

a	hat	ė	term	ô	order	ch	child		a in about
ā	age	i	it	oi	oil	ng	long		e in taken
ä	far	ī	ice	ou	out	sh	she	ə	i in pencil
â	care	o	hot	u	cup	th	thin		o in lemon
e	let	ō	open	ů	put	ᵀH	then		u in circus
ē	equal	ò	saw	ü	rule	zh	measure		

al·bi·nism (al′bə niz′əm), *n.* condition of being an albino.

al·bi·no (al bī′nō), *n.* **1** person who has extremely white or pale skin and hair, and pink eyes with red pupils. **2** animal or plant that is similarly white or pale. □ *n., pl.* **al·bi·nos.**

albino (def. 2)

Al·bi·on (al′bē ən), *n.* England.

al·bum (al′bəm), *n.* **1** book with blank pages for holding photographs, stamps, autographs, etc. **2** case for or containing a phonograph record or records. **3** one or more phonograph records packaged together: *Have you heard that singer's new album?* **4** a single long-playing phonograph record.

al·bu·men (al byü′mən), *n.* the white of an egg, consisting mostly of albumin dissolved in water.

al·bu·min (al byü′mən), *n.* protein found in the white of an egg, milk, blood serum, lymph, and other animal and plant tissues and juices.

Al·bu·quer·que (al′bə kėr′kē), *n.* city in central New Mexico.

Al·can Highway (al′kan′), Alaska Highway.

al·che·mist (al′kə mist), *n.* person who studied or practiced a combination of chemistry and magic in the Middle Ages. Alchemists tried to find a way to turn cheaper metals into gold and silver and to produce a substance which would prolong human life.

al·che·my (al′kə mē), *n.* combination of chemistry and magic studied and practiced in the Middle Ages.

al·co·hol (al′kə hȯl), *n.* **1** the colorless liquid in whiskey, gin, wine, beer, etc., that makes them intoxicating; grain alcohol; ethyl alcohol. Alcohol is used in medicines, in manufacturing, and as a fuel. **2** whiskey, gin, or any other intoxicating liquor containing this liquid. **3** any of a group of similar organic compounds, reacting with certain acids to form esters. Wood alcohol is very poisonous.

al·co·hol·ic (al′kə hȯ′lik), **1** *adj.* consisting of alcohol: *alcoholic fumes.* **2** *adj.* containing alcohol: *alcoholic drinks.* **3** *n.* person who suffers from alcoholism. **4** *adj.* suffering from alcoholism. —**al′co·hol′i·cal·ly,** *adv.*

al·co·hol·ism (al′kə hȯ liz′əm), *n.* disease in which a person feels a physical and psychological craving for alcohol.

Al·cott (ȯl′kət), *n.* **Lou·i·sa May** (lü′ē zə mā′), 1832-1888, American author. ■ **Louisa May Alcott** wrote many books for children, including *Little Women* and *Little Men. Little Women* is based on her own childhood.

al·cove (al′kōv), *n.* **1** a small room opening out of a larger room. **2** recess or large, hollow space in a wall.

al·der (ȯl′dər), *n.* tree or bush that usually grows in wet land and has clusters of catkins that develop into small, woody cones.

al·der·man (ȯl′dər mən), *n.* person elected to represent a certain district on a council that governs a city. □ *n., pl.* **al·der·men.**

ale (āl), *n.* a bitter alcoholic beverage fermented from malt and flavored with hops. Ale is similar to beer but contains more alcohol. ■ Another word that sounds like this is **ail.**

a·lee (ə lē′), *adv.* on or toward a ship's side that is away from the wind.

a·lert (ə lėrt′), **1** *adj.* keen and watchful; wide-awake: *A good hunting dog is alert to every sound and movement in the field.* **2** *adj.* quick in action; nimble: *A sparrow is very alert in its movements.* **3** *n.* signal warning of an attack by approaching enemy aircraft, a hurricane, or other threatening danger. **4** *n.* period of time after this warning until the attack is over or the danger has passed: *The hurricane alert is over.* **5** *v.* to warn against an attack by aircraft, a hurricane, or other threatening danger. **6** *v.* to notify troops to get ready for action. **7** *v.* to make aware of; arouse: *to alert people to the dangers of smoking cigarettes.* [**Alert** comes from Italian words meaning "on watch." Soldiers who keep watch have to stay alert.] —**a·lert′ly,** *adv.* —**a·lert′ness,** *n.*

on the alert, ready at any instant for what is coming; watchful: *A driver must be on the alert.*

Al·e·ut (al′ē üt), *n.* **1** person born or living in the Aleutian Islands. **2** the language spoken there, related to Eskimo.

A·leu·tian Islands (ə lü′shən), chain of about 150 small islands in the N Pacific, part of Alaska and extending southwest from the mainland for 1200 miles.

ale·wife (āl′wīf′), *n.* fish found in great numbers along the U.S. Atlantic coast and in the Great Lakes. It is related to the herring. □ *n., pl.* **ale·wives.**

Al·ex·an·der the Great (al′ig zan′dər), 356-323 B.C., king of Macedonia from 336 to 323 B.C. ■ **Alexander** conquered the Greek city-states and the whole Persian empire, from the coasts of Asia Minor and Egypt to India. [**Alexander** comes from a Greek word meaning "helper of men."]

Al·ex·an·dri·a (al′ig zan′drē ə), *n.* port in N Egypt, on the Mediterranean. Alexandria was famous in ancient times for its library and scholars.

al·fal·fa (al fal′fə), *n.* plant somewhat like clover, with deep roots and bluish purple flowers. It is grown as food for horses and cattle. □ *n., pl* **al·fal·fas.** [**Alfalfa** comes from an Arabic word meaning "the best kind of animal food."]

Al·fred the Great (al′frid), A.D. 849-899, king of England from A.D. 871 to 899. ■ **Alfred** defeated the Danes, united southern England, and led a revival of learning and literature. [**Alfred** comes from old English words meaning "elf" and "counsel."]

al·ga (al′gə), *n.* one of the algae. □ *n., pl.* **al·gae.**

al·gae (al′jē), *n.pl.* group of related living things, mostly living in water. Algae contain chlorophyll but lack true stems, roots, or leaves. Some algae are one-celled and form scum on rocks; others, such as the seaweeds, are very large. Some algae are able to move about. Some algae are monerans, and others are classed as protists or plants. —**al′gal,** *adj.*

al·ge·bra (al′jə brə), *n.* branch of mathematics which deals with the relations and properties of quantities. In algebra quantities are denoted by letters, negative numbers as well as ordinary numbers are used, and problems are solved in the form of equations. $x + y = x^2$ is a way of stating, by algebra, that the sum of two numbers equals the square of one of them.

al·ge·bra·ic (al′jə brā′ik), *adj.* of or used in algebra: *The equation $(a+b)\ (a-b) = a^2-b^2$ is an algebraic statement.* —**al′ge·bra′i·cal·ly,** *adv.*

Al·ger·i·a (al jir′ē ə), *n.* country in N Africa, on the Mediterranean, which became independent of France in 1962. *Capital:* Algiers. —**Al·ger′i·an,** *adj., n.*

Al·giers (al jirz′), *n.* port and capital of Algeria, on the Mediterranean.

Al·gon·qui·an (al gong′kē ən *or* al gong′kwē ən), **1** *n.* family of North American Indian languages, including the languages of the Arapaho, Blackfoot, Cheyenne, Ojibwa, Delaware, and Shawnee tribes. **2** *adj.* of this family of languages. **3** *n.* person speaking a language of this family. ❏ *n., pl.* **Al·gon·qui·an** or **Al·gon·qui·ans** for 3.

WORD SOURCE   **Algonquian** has given a number of words to the English language. Other words that are known to have come from American Indian languages are listed at **American Indian.**

caribou	moccasin	raccoon	toboggan
caucus	moose	skunk	tomahawk
hickory	opossum	squash²	totem
hominy	powwow	terrapin	wigwam

Al·gon·quin (al gong′kən *or* al gong′kwən), *n.* member of a tribe of American Indians tribes living in eastern Canada. ❏ *n., pl.* **Al·gon·quin** or **Al·gon·quins.**

al·go·rithm (al′gə riŦH′əm), *n.* a set of steps for a mathematical operation: *the division algorithm.*

Al·ham·bra (al ham′brə), *n.* palace of the Moorish kings at Granada, Spain. The Alhambra was the last stronghold of the Moors in Europe and was conquered in 1492.

A·li (ä lē′), *n.* **Muhammad,** born 1942, American boxer. He won the world heavyweight title three separate times. His original name was Cassius Clay. ■ **Muhammad Ali** was an entertaining champion who often made up poems about his fighting. Sometimes he even predicted which round of a fight he would win in.

a·li·as (ā′lē əs), **1** *n.* name other than a person's real name used to hide who he or she is; assumed name: *The spy's real name was Harrison, but he used the alias of Johnson.* **2** *adv.* otherwise called: *The thief's name was Jones, alias Williams.* ❏ *n., pl.* **a·li·as·es.**

A·li Ba·ba (ä′lē bä′bə *or* al′ē bab′ə), a poor woodcutter in one of the tales in *The Arabian Nights.* He uses the magic words "Open sesame" to open the door to a cave and discovers the treasure hidden there by 40 thieves.

al·i·bi (al′ə bī), **1** *n.* the statement that an accused person was somewhere else when an offense was committed: *Immediately after the robbery the gang scattered to establish alibis.* **2** *v.* to provide an alibi for someone: *His friends alibied him for the time of the break-in.* **3** *n.* INFORMAL. an excuse: *What is your alibi for failing to do your homework?* **4** *v.* INFORMAL. to make an excuse. ❏ *n., pl.* **al·i·bis;** *v.* **al·i·bied, al·i·bi·ing.** [**Alibi** comes from a Latin word meaning "elsewhere."]

al·ien (ā′lyən), **1** *n.* person who is not a citizen of the country in which he or she lives. **2** *adj.* of another country; foreign: *an alien language, alien conquerors.* **3** *adj.* entirely different; not in agreement; strange: *Cruelty is alien to his nature.* **4** *n.* an imaginary creature from outer space.

al·ien·ate (ā′lyə nāt), *v.* **1** to turn from affection to indifference, dislike, or hatred; make unfriendly: *The colonies were alienated from England by disputes over trade and taxation.* **2** to cause to become emotionally withdrawn; isolate: *She refuses to let age and illness alienate her from her friends.* ❏ *v.* **al·ien·at·ed, al·ien·at·ing.** —**al′ien·a′tor,** *n.*

alien (def. 4)—as imagined by an artist

al·ien·a·tion (ā′lyə nā′shən), *n.* **1** condition of being alienated; not feeling interested in or involved with your family, associates, or society: *Her comments led to the alienation of her political supporters.* **2** act of alienating; making unfriendly.

a·light¹ (ə līt′), *v.* **1** to get down; get off; dismount: *She alighted from the bus.* **2** to come down from the air and lightly settle: *The bird alighted on a branch.* ❏ *v.* **a·light·ed** or **a·lit, a·light·ing.**

a·light² (ə līt′), *adj.* **1** on fire; lighted: *Is the kindling alight?* **2** lighted up; aglow: *Her face was alight with happiness.*

a·lign (ə līn′), *v.* **1** to bring into line; arrange in a straight line: *to align the front wheels of a car.* **2** to join with others for or against a cause: *Germany was aligned with Japan in World War II.*

a·lign·ment (ə līn′mənt), *n.* **1** arrangement in a straight line: *The pictures were in perfect alignment.* **2** act of joining with others for or against a cause: *The establishment of the Common Market resulted in a new European alignment.*

a·like (ə līk′), **1** *adv.* in the same way; similarly: *She and her sister think alike.* **2** *adj.* like one another; similar: *These twins are very much alike.* —**a·like′ness,** *n.*

al·i·men·tar·y (al′ə men′tər ē), *adj.* of or about food and nutrition: *alimentary tract.*

alimentary canal, the parts of the body through which food passes in eating, digestion, and elimination.

al·i·mo·ny (al′ə mō′nē), *n.* the money paid in regular installments for support, to one spouse from the other, after a divorce or legal separation. The amount of alimony is fixed by a court.

a·lit (ə līt′), *v.* a past tense and a past participle of **alight¹:** *The bird alit upon a branch.*

a·live (ə līv′), *adj.* **1** having life; living: *Was the snake alive or dead?* **2** in continued activity; in full force; active: *We celebrate Memorial Day to keep alive the memory of those who have died for their country.* **3** of all living: *I was the happiest person alive.* **4** full of energy; lively. —**a·live′ness,** *n.*
alive to, awake to; sensitive to: *Are you alive to what is going on?*
alive with, full of; swarming with: *The streets were alive with people.*

al·ka·li (al′kə lī), *n.* **1** any of many chemical compounds that are soluble in water, neutralize acids and form salts with them, and turn red litmus paper blue. Lye and ammonia are alkalis. **2** any salt or salts found in dry soils. ❏ *n., pl.* **al·ka·lis** or **al·ka·lies.**

al·ka·line (al′kə lin), *adj.* **1** of or like an alkali: *an alkaline reaction.* **2** containing alkali. —**al·ka·lin·i·ty** (al′kə lin′ə tē), *n.*

al·ka·loid (al′kə loid), *n.* any of a group of chemical compounds that contain nitrogen and carbon and are alkalis. Most alkaloids are taken from plants. Drugs such as caffeine, nicotine, and quinine are alkaloids, and some alkaloids are very poisonous.

all (ȯl), **1** *adj.* every one of: *All the children came.* **2** *pron.* everyone: *All of us are going.* **3** *pron.* everything: *All is well.* **4** *adj.* the whole of: *The mice ate all the cheese.* **5** *pron.* the whole amount: *All of the bread has been eaten.* **6** *adv.* wholly; entirely: *The cake is all gone.* **7** *adj.* the greatest possible: *I made all haste to reach home in time.* **8** *adj.* nothing but; only: *This plane carries all cargo and no passengers.* **9** *adv.* each; apiece: *The score was even at 40 all.* ■ Another word that sounds like this is **awl.**
above all, before everything else: *Above all, she loves to travel.*
after all, when everything has been considered; nevertheless: *I see that you came after all.*
all but, nearly; almost: *This job is all but done.*
all in, worn out; weary: *After the race, I was all in.*
all in all, when everything has been taken into account.
all over, 1 everywhere: *I looked all over for your glasses.* **2** done with; finished: *The game is all over.*
at all, 1 under any conditions: *Maybe I won't be able to go at all.* **2** in any way: *I was not at all surprised.*
in all, counting every person or thing; altogether: *There were five of us in all.*

Al·lah (al′ə *or* ä′lə), *n.* the Muslim name for God.

all-A·mer·i·can (ȯl′ə mer′ə kən), **1** *adj.* chosen as the best at a particular position in one year, from among all high school, or collegiate, players of a team sport in the United States. **2** *n.* player so chosen: *an all-American in two sports.*

all-a·round (ȯl′ə round′), *adj.* able to do many things; not limited or specialized: *She is an all-around athlete—she plays tennis, golfs, and swims well.*

al·lay (ə lā′), v. **1** to put at rest; quiet: *The parents' fears were allayed by the news that their children were safe.* **2** to make less; weaken or relieve: *Her fever was allayed by the medicine.* ❑ v. **allayed, al·lay·ing. —al·lay′er,** *n.*

all clear, signal indicating the end of an air raid or other danger.

al·le·ga·tion (al′ə gā′shən), *n.* a positive statement, especially one without proof; assertion: *Everyone knows better than to believe the allegations made against you.*

al·lege (ə lej′), v. **1** to state positively; assert: *Although he has no proof, this man alleges that the janitor stole his watch.* **2** to give or bring forward as a reason, excuse, or argument: *Alleging illness, the mayor retired from office.* ❑ v. **al·leged, al·leg·ing. —al·lege′a·ble,** *adj.* **—al·leg′er,** *n.*

al·leged (ə lejd′), *adj.* **1** stated positively to be, but without proof: *The alleged burglar was held for trial.* **2** doubtful: *an alleged cure for cancer.*

al·leg·ed·ly (ə lej′id lē), *adv.* according to what is alleged.

Al·le·ghe·nies (al′ə gā′nēz), *n.pl.* the Allegheny Mountains.

Al·le·ghe·ny (al′ə gā′nē), *n.* river in W Pennsylvania. It joins the Monongahela at Pittsburgh to form the Ohio River.

Allegheny Mountains, mountain range of the Appalachian Mountain system, in Pennsylvania, Maryland, Virginia, and West Virginia.

al·le·giance (ə lē′jəns), *n.* **1** the loyalty owed to your country or government: *I pledge allegiance to the flag.* **2** loyalty to any person or thing: *We owe allegiance to our friends.*

allegiance (def. 1)—pledging allegiance

al·le·gor·i·cal (al′ə gôr′ə kəl), *adj.* explaining or teaching something by a story; using allegory. **—al′le·gor′i·cal·ly,** *adv.*

al·le·go·ry (al′ə gôr′ē), *n.* a story that is told to explain and teach something. The parables in the Bible are allegories. ❑ *n., pl.* **al·le·go·ries.**

al·le·gret·to (al′ə gret′ō), in music: **1** *adj.* quick, but not as quick as allegro. **2** *adv.* in allegretto time. **3** *n.* an allegretto part in a piece of music. ❑ *n., pl.* **al·le·gret·tos.**

al·le·gro (ə leg′rō *or* ə lā′grō), in music: **1** *adj.* quick; lively. **2** *adv.* in quick time. **3** *n.* a quick, lively part in a piece of music. ❑ *n., pl.* **al·le·gros.** [**Allegro** comes from a Latin word meaning "brisk."]

al·lele (ə lēl′), *n.* any of several forms that a particular gene can take, such as forms of the gene leading to blue or brown eyes.

al·le·lu·ia (al′ə lü′yə), *interj., n.* hallelujah. ❑ *n., pl.* **al·le·lu·ias.**

Al·len (al′ən), *n.* E·than (ē′thən), 1738-1789, American officer in the Revolutionary War. He and his troops helped capture an important fort from the British in 1775.

al·ler·gen (al′ər jən), *n.* any substance that causes an allergy.

al·ler·gic (ə lėr′jik), *adj.* **1** having an allergy: *Some people who are allergic to eggs cannot eat them without breaking into a rash.* **2** of or caused by allergy: *Hay fever is an allergic reaction.* **3** having a strong dislike: *She is allergic to physical exercise.* **—al·ler′gi·cal·ly,** *adv.*

al·ler·gist (al′ər jist), *n.* doctor who specializes in treating allergies.

al·ler·gy (al′ər jē), *n.* an unusual bodily reaction to certain substances such as particular kinds of pollen, food, hair, or cloth. Hay fever, asthma, headaches, and hives are common signs of allergy. ❑ *n., pl.* **al·ler·gies.**

al·le·vi·ate (ə lē′vē āt), v. to make easier to endure; relieve; lessen: *Heat often alleviates pain.* ❑ v. **al·le·vi·at·ed, al·le·vi·at·ing. —al·le·vi·a′tion** (ə lē′vē ā′shən), *n.*

al·ley (al′ē), *n.* **1** a narrow street behind buildings in a city or town; alleyway. **2** path in a park or garden, bordered by trees. **3** a long, narrow wooden floor along which the ball is rolled in bowling. ❑ *n., pl.* **al·leys.**

al·ley·way (al′ē wā), *n.* **1** alley (def. 1). **2** a narrow passageway.

All Fools' Day, April 1; April Fools' Day.

All·hal·lows (ȯl′hal′ōz), *n.* November 1; All Saints' Day.

al·li·ance (ə lī′əns), *n.* a union of persons, groups, or nations formed by agreement for some special purpose or benefit. An alliance may be a joining of national interests by treaty or a joining of family interests by marriage.

al·lied (ə līd′ *or* al′īd), *adj.* **1** united by agreement: *allied nations, allied armies.* **2** similar in some way; related; connected: *Painting, drawing, and sculpture are allied arts.*

al·lies (al′īz *or* ə līz′), **1** *n.* plural of **ally. 2** *v.* a present tense of **ally. 3** Allies, *n.pl.* **a** the countries that fought against Germany, Austria-Hungary, Turkey, and Bulgaria in World War I. **b** the countries that fought against Germany, Italy, and Japan in World War II.

al·li·ga·tor (al′ə gā′tər), *n.* **1** a large reptile with thick skin, related and similar to the crocodile but with a shorter and flatter head.

alligator (def. 1)—up to 12 ft. (3.7 m) long

Alligators live in the rivers and marshes of the warm parts of the United States and China. **2** leather prepared from its skin.

WORD STORY **Alligator** comes from Spanish words meaning "the lizard." When Spanish explorers came to America and saw alligators for the first time, they thought the animals looked like big lizards.

alligator pear, avocado.

all-im·por·tant (ȯl′im pôrt′nt), *adj.* very important; vital: *an all-important mission.*

al·lit·er·a·tion (ə lit′ə rā′shən), *n.* repetition of a consonant sound in a group of words, especially a line of poetry. EXAMPLE: *Peter Piper picked a peck of pickled peppers.*

all-night (ȯl′nīt′), *adj.* **1** open all night: *an all-night drugstore.* **2** lasting all night: *an all-night card game.*

al·lo·cate (al′ə kāt), v. to set or lay aside for a special purpose; allot: *The federal government allocated millions of dollars for cancer research.* ❑ v. **al·lo·cat·ed, al·lo·cat·ing.**

al·lo·ca·tion (al′ə kā′shən), *n.* **1** share, portion, or thing allocated. **2** act of allocating; allotment.

al·lo·saur (al′ə sôr′), *n.* a large meat-eating dinosaur that lived about 140 million years ago, in the Jurassic period.

al·lot (ə lot′), v. **1** to divide and distribute in parts or shares: *The profits have been allotted among the owners of the company.* **2** to give to as a share; assign: *The principal allotted each class a part in the school program.* ❑ v. **al·lot·ted, al·lot·ting.**

al·lot·ment (ə lot′mənt), *n.* **1** division and distribution in parts or shares: *The allotment of profits was made Monday.* **2** share allotted: *Your allotment was four dollars.*

all-out (ȯl′out′), **1** *adj.* greatest possible; complete: *an all-out effort to win.* **2** *adv.* to the utmost extent: *go all-out to win.*

all·o·ver (ȯl′ō′vər), *adj.* covering the whole surface.

al·low (ə lou′), v. **1** to let someone do something; permit something to be done or happen: *They do not allow swimming at this beach.* **2** to let have; give: *My parents allowed me five dollars to spend as I wish.* **3** to accept as true; acknowledge; recognize: *The judge allowed the claim of the person whose property was damaged.* **4** to add or subtract to make up for something: *The trip will cost you only $200, but you ought to allow $50 more for extras,*

such as magazines and snacks. **–al·low′a·ble,** *adj.* **–al·low′a·bly,** *adv.*
allow for, to take into consideration; provide for: *I buy my jeans a little large to allow for shrinking.*

al·low·ance (ə lou′əns), *n.* **1** a sum of money given or set aside for expenses: *a household allowance for groceries of $125 a week. My weekly allowance is $5.* **2** amount subtracted to make up for something; discount: *The salesman offered us an allowance of $1500 on our old car when we bought a new one.*
make allowance for or **make allowances for,** to take into consideration; allow for: *We made allowance for the heavy traffic by leaving half an hour early.*

al·loy (al′oi *or* ə loi′ *for noun;* ə loi′ *for verb*), **1** *n.* metal made by melting and mixing two or more metals or a metal and another substance. An alloy may be harder, lighter, and stronger than the metals of which it is composed. Brass is an alloy of copper and zinc. **2** *v.* to make into an alloy. **3** *n.* an inferior metal mixed with a more valuable one: *This ring is not pure gold; there is some alloy in it.* **4** *v.* to make lower or less valuable by mixing with something bad: *Two days of rain somewhat alloyed their enthusiasm for camping.*

all-pur·pose (ȯl′pėr′pəs), *adj.* able to be used for any purpose: *all-purpose flour, all-purpose tools.*

all right, 1 without error; correct: *The answers were all right.* **2** satisfactory: *The work was not done very well, but it was all right.* **3** in a satisfactory way: *The engine seemed to be working all right.* **4** in good condition; free from harm: *I dropped the bag, but the eggs are all right.* **5** in good health: *The doctor says I am all right.* **6** yes: *"Will you come with me?" "All right."* **7** without doubt; certainly: *I am tired, all right!*

all-round (ȯl′round′), *adj.* all-around.

All Saints' Day, November 1, a church festival honoring all the saints; Allhallows.

All Souls' Day, November 2, a day when Roman Catholics hold services and say prayers for all the souls in purgatory.

all·spice (ȯl′spis′), *n.* spice having a flavor suggesting a mixture of cinnamon, nutmeg, and cloves, made from the berry of a tropical American tree.

all-star (ȯl′stär′), *adj.* made up of the best players or performers: *Two of our players have been named to the all-star team.*

all-ter·rain vehicle (ȯl′te rān′), a lightweight motorized vehicle designed for use on rough or marshy terrain; ATV.

all-time (ȯl′tīm′), *adj.* of the entire past; for all time until now: *the all-time best-selling book.*

al·lude (ə lüd′), *v.* to refer indirectly to something; mention slightly in passing: *Don't tell them of our decision; don't even allude to it.* ❑ *v.* **al·lud·ed, al·lud·ing.**

al·lure (ə lür′), **1** *v.* to tempt or attract very strongly; fascinate; charm: *City life allured her with its action and excitement.* **2** *n.* attractiveness; fascination; charm: *The allure of the sea.* ❑ *v.* **al·lured, al·lur·ing. –al·lure′ment,** *n.*

al·lur·ing (ə lür′ing), *adj.* very attractive; tempting: *an alluring advertisement.* **–al·lur′ing·ly,** *adv.*

al·lu·sion (ə lü′zhən), *n.* slight mention made in passing; indirect reference: *Don't make any allusion to the surprise party while they are present.*

al·lu·sive (ə lü′siv), *adj.* containing an allusion; full of allusions. **–al·lu′sive·ly,** *adv.* **–al·lu′sive·ness,** *n.*

al·lu·vi·al (ə lü′vē əl), *adj.* made of or formed by sand or mud left by flowing water. A delta is an alluvial deposit at the mouth of a river.

al·lu·vi·um (ə lü′vē əm), *n.* sand, silt, or mud left by flowing water, in a floodplain, delta, etc.

alluvial land in a delta

al·ly (al′ī *or* ə lī′ *for noun;* ə lī′ *for verb*), **1** *n.* person, group, or nation united with another for some special purpose: *England*

and France were allies in some wars and enemies in others. See also **Allies. 2** *n.* helper; supporter. **3** *v.* to combine for some special purpose; unite by agreement. Small nations sometimes ally themselves with larger ones for protection. ❑ *n., pl.* **al·lies;** *v.* **al·lied, al·ly·ing.**

-ally, *suffix.* in a ___ic way: *tragically = in a tragic way.*

Al·ma-A·ta (äl′mə ä′tə), *n.* the capital of Kazakhstan.

al·ma ma·ter or **Al·ma Ma·ter** (al′mə mä′tər *or* äl′mə mä′tər), person's school, college, or university.

al·ma·nac (ȯl′mə nak), *n.* **1** a booklike calendar published every year that also gives information about the sun, moon, stars, tides, church days, and other facts, sometimes with weather predictions. **2** reference book published yearly, with tables of facts and figures and information on many subjects. [**Almanac** comes from a Greek word meaning "calendar." Almanacs began as calendars of events for the coming year.]

al·might·y (ȯl mī′tē), **1** *adj.* having supreme power; omnipotent. **2** *n.* **the Almighty,** God. **–al·might′i·ly,** *adv.* **–al·might′i·ness,** *n.*

al·mond (ä′mənd *or* am′ənd), *n.* the oval-shaped nut of the peachlike fruit of a tree growing in warm regions.

al·most (ȯl′mōst), *adv.* very near to; all but; nearly: *It is almost ten o'clock. I almost missed the train.*

alms (ämz), *n.pl. or sing.* money or gifts to help the poor. [**Alms** comes from a Greek word meaning "pity."]

alms·house (ämz′hous′), *n.* home for very poor persons supported at public expense or by private charity. ❑ *n., pl.* **alms·hous·es** (ämz′hou′ziz).

al·ni·co (al′nə kō), *n.* alloy of iron containing aluminum, nickel, cobalt, and other metals, used as a magnet.

al·oe (al′ō), *n.* **1** any of many related plants that grow in warm regions. Aloes have thick, narrow, fleshy leaves and flowers at the end of a tall stalk. **2 aloes,** *sing.* a bitter drug made from the leaves of one kind of aloe and used as a laxative.

aloe ver·a (ver′ə), an aloe that produces a juice used in cosmetics and for treating burns. Aloe vera is also grown as a houseplant.

a·loft (ə lȯft′), *adv.* **1** far above the earth; up in the air; high up: *Some birds fly thousands of feet aloft.* **2** high up among the sails, rigging, or masts of a ship: *The sailor went aloft to get a better view of the distant shore.*

a·lo·ha (ə lō′ə *or* ä lō′hä), *interj., n.* **1** greetings; hello. **2** goodby; farewell. ❑ *n., pl.* **a·lo·has.** [**Aloha** comes from a Hawaiian word meaning "love."]

a·lone (ə lōn′), **1** *adj., adv.* without other persons or things: *After my friends left, I was alone. One tree stood alone on the hill.* **2** *adv.* without help from others: *I solved the problem alone.* **3** *adj.* not anyone else; only: *She alone can do this work.* **4** *adj.* without anything more: *Bread alone is not enough for lunch.* **5** *adv.* and nothing more; only; merely: *I did the job for money alone.*
leave alone, not bother; not meddle with: *She's busy with her homework; you'd better leave her alone.*
let alone, 1 not bother; not meddle with: *If everyone will let him alone, he will get his work done.*

alone (def. 1)

2 not to mention: *It would have been a hot day for summer, let alone early spring.*

a·long (ə lȯng′), **1** *prep.* from one end to the other end of: *Trees are planted along the street.* **2** *adv.* from one end to the other;

a	hat	ė	term	ô	order	ch	child		
ā	age	i	it	oi	oil	ng	long	a	in about
ä	far	ī	ice	ou	out	sh	she	e	in taken
â	care	o	hot	u	cup	th	thin	i	in pencil
e	let	ō	open	u̇	put	ᵺ	then	o	in lemon
ē	equal	ȯ	saw	ü	rule	zh	measure	u	in circus

lengthwise: *Cars are parked along by the stadium.* **3** *adv.* forward; onward: *Let's walk along quickly.* **4** *adv.* together with someone or something: *We took our dog along.* **5** *adv.* INFORMAL. sometime: *Be ready along about one o'clock.*

all along, all the time: *He knew the answer all along.*

along with, in company with; together with: *Will you come along with me, or will you come later?*

a·long·side (ə lông′sīd′), **1** *adv.* at the side; side by side: *As we sat in the truck, a car pulled up alongside.* **2** *prep.* by the side of; side by side with: *The boat was alongside the wharf.*

a·loof (ə lüf′), **1** *adv.* at a distance or apart: *One boy stood aloof from all the others.* **2** *adj.* tending to keep to yourself; reserved. **—a·loof′ly,** *adv.* **—a·loof′ness,** *n.*

a·loud (ə loud′), *adv.* loud enough to be heard; not in a whisper: *The book I was reading was so funny I laughed aloud. The teacher read the story aloud to the class.*

alp (alp), *n.* a high mountain. See **Alps.**

al·pac·a (al pak′ə), *n.* **1** a domesticated animal of South America with long, silky wool. It is closely related to the llama, but smaller. **2** cloth made from this wool. **3** a glossy, wiry cloth made of sheep's wool and cotton. ❑ *n.,* *pl.* **al·pac·as** or **al·pac·a.**

al·pen·stock (al′pən stok′), *n.* a strong wooden stick with an iron point, used in mountain climbing.

al·pha (al′fə), *n.* **1** the first letter of the Greek alphabet (A, α). **2** the first of a series. ❑ *n.,* *pl.* **al·phas.**

al·pha·bet (al′fə bet), *n.* **1** the letters of a language arranged in a fixed order, not as they are in words. **2** set of letters or characters representing sounds, used in writing a language. The English alphabet has only 26 letters to represent more than 40 sounds. [**Alphabet** comes from the names of the first two letters of the Greek alphabet: *alpha* (A) and *beta* (B).]

al·pha·bet·ic (al′fə bet′ik), *adj.* alphabetical.

al·pha·bet·i·cal (al′fə bet′ə kəl), *adj.* **1** arranged by letters in the order of the alphabet: *Dictionary entries are listed in alphabetical order.* **2** of the alphabet. **—al′pha·bet′i·cal·ly,** *adv.*

al·pha·bet·ize (al′fə bə tīz′), *v.* to arrange in alphabetical order: *The names in a telephone book have been alphabetized.* ❑ *v.* **al·pha·bet·ized, al·pha·bet·iz·ing. —al′pha·bet′i·za′tion,** *n.*

al·pha·nu·mer·ic (al′fə nü mer′ik), *adj.* using both letters and numbers: *an alphanumeric computer.* [**Alphanumeric** is a blend of the words **alphabetic** and **numerical.**]

alpha particle, a positively charged particle containing two protons and two neutrons, released at very high speed in the disintegration of radium and other radioactive substances.

alpha ray, a stream of alpha particles.

al·pine (al′pīn), *adj.* **1** of or like high mountains: *alpine plants, alpine terrain.* **2** **Alpine,** of or like the Alps.

Alps (alps), *n.pl.* mountain system in S Europe, with ranges in France, Switzerland, Germany, Italy, Austria, Slovenia, and Croatia.

al·read·y (ôl red′ē), *adv.* before this time; by this time; even now: *You are half an hour late already.*

ALS, amyotrophic lateral sclerosis.

Al·sace-Lor·raine (al sâs′lə rân′), *n.* Alsace and Lorraine, region in NE France, on the border with Germany. It formed a German province from 1871 to 1919 and from 1940 to 1945.

Al·sa·tian (al sā′shən), **1** *adj.* of Alsace or its people. **2** *n.* person born or living in Alsace. **3** *n.* a German shepherd dog.

> **WORD STORY** In World War I, Britain was at war with Germany. People in Britain who had German shepherd dogs no longer wanted to call them "German." So they decided to call them **Alsatians.**

al·so (ôl′sō), *adv.* in addition; besides; too: *That car is the latest model; it is also very expensive.*

al·so-ran (ôl′sō ran′), *n.* **1** an unsuccessful contestant; loser. **2** any horse that finishes behind the first three horses in a race, and thus wins nothing.

Alta., Alberta.

Al·tai Mountains (al′tī *or* äl′tī), a mountain range in NW China and SW Mongolia.

al·tar (ôl′tər), *n.* **1** table or stand used in religious worship in a church or temple: *The worshipers received Communion from the priest at the altar.* **2** block of stone, mound of turf, etc., on which to place sacrifices or burn offerings to a god. ■ Another word that sounds like this is **alter.**

altar (def. 2)

altar boy, man or boy who helps a priest during certain religious services; acolyte.

al·ter (ôl′tər), *v.* **1** to make or become different; change; vary: *The coat can be altered to fit you. Since her summer on the farm, her whole outlook has altered.* ■ See Synonym Study at **change.** **2** to perform surgery on an animal to make it unable to have young: *We had our cat altered before she had kittens.* ■ Another word that sounds like this is **altar. —al′ter·a·ble,** *adj.*

al·ter·a·tion (ôl′tə rā′shən), *n.* **1** change in the appearance or form of anything; altered or changed condition: *My coat fit better after the alterations were made.* **2** act of altering: *The alteration of our house took three months.*

al·ter·ca·tion (ôl′tər kā′shən), *n.* an angry dispute; noisy quarrel: *The two teams had an altercation over the umpire's decision.*

al·ter e·go (ôl′tər ē′gō), a very intimate friend; close associate. [**Alter ego** comes from Latin words meaning "other I" or "other self."]

al·ter·nate (ôl′tər nāt *for verb;* ôl′tər nit *for adj., noun*), **1** *v.* to happen or be arranged by turns. Plus signs and minus signs alternate in this row: + − + − + −. **2** *v.* to arrange by turns: *We alternated work and pleasure.* **3** *v.* to take turns: *The two of us will alternate in setting the table.* **4** *adj.* first one and then the other by turns: *The U.S. flag has alternate stripes of red and white.* **5** *adj.* every other: *My friends and I go bowling on alternate Fridays.* **6** *adj.* in place of another: *If it rains tomorrow, the fair will be held on an alternate day.* **7** *n.* person appointed to take the place of another if it should be necessary; substitute: *We have several alternates on our debating team.* ❑ *v.* **al·ter·nat·ed, al·ter·nat·ing. —al·ter·na·tion** (ôl′tər nā′shən), *n.*

alternate angles, two angles formed when one line crosses two other lines. These angles are both inside the two lines or both outside the two lines, but not touching each other.

al·ter·nate·ly (ôl′tər nit lē), *adv.* by turns.

alternating current, an electric current in which the electricity flows in one direction and then the other, reversing regularly, usually 120 times per second.

al·ter·na·tive (ôl tér′nə tiv), **1** *n.* choice from among two or more things: *She had the alternative of going to summer school or finding a summer job.* **2** *n.* one of the things to be chosen: *She chose the first alternative and went to summer school.* **3** *adj.* giving or requiring a choice from among two or more things: *I offered the alternative suggestions of having a picnic or taking a trip on a boat.* **—al·ter′na·tive·ly,** *adv.* **—al·ter′na·tive·ness,** *n.*

> **USAGE NOTE** **Alternative** comes from a Latin word meaning "other" or "the second of two." Because of the word's original meaning, some people believe it should only be used to mean one of two possibilities. However, it is generally used to mean one of several possibilities.

A

al·ter·na·tor (ȯl′tər nā′ tər), *n.* an electrical generator that produces alternating current.

al·though or **al·tho** (ȯl т͟hō′), *conj.* in spite of the fact that; though: *Although it rained all morning, they went on the hike.*

al·tim·e·ter (al tim′ə tər), *n.* device for measuring altitude. Altimeters are used in aircraft.

al·ti·tude (al′tə tüd), *n.* **1** height above the earth's surface: *What altitude did the airplane reach?* **2** height above sea level: *The altitude of Denver is one mile.* **3** a high place: *At some altitudes snow never melts.* **4** the vertical distance from the base of a geometrical shape to its highest point. **5** the angular distance of a star, planet, etc., above the horizon.

al·to (al′tō), **1** *n.* the lowest singing voice in women and boys. **2** *n.* singer with such a voice. **3** *n.* part in music for such a voice or for an instrument of similar range. **4** *n.* instrument playing such a part. **5** *adj.* of or for an alto. ❑ *n., pl.* **al·tos.**

WORD STORY Alto comes from a Latin word meaning "high." Originally, it meant the highest man's singing voice. Later, it was applied to the lowest woman's singing voice, which sounds about the same.

alto clef, the C clef when the clef symbol is placed on the third line of the staff. See picture at **clef.**

al·to·cu·mu·lus (al′tō kyü′myə ləs), *n.* cloud formation containing heaps or patches of white or grayish clouds like cotton, often partly in shadow. The formation usually occurs about 7000 feet to 18,000 feet (2100 meters to 5500 meters) above ground. ❑ *n., pl.* **al·to·cu·mu·li** (al′tō kyü′myə lī).

al·to·geth·er (ȯl′tə geт͟h′ər), *adv.* **1** to the whole extent; completely; entirely: *The house was altogether destroyed by fire.* **2** on the whole; considering everything: *Altogether, he was well pleased.* **3** all included: *Altogether there were 14 books.*

al·to·stra·tus (al′tō strā′təs), *n.* cloud formation spreading as a bluish gray sheet across the sky, often thin enough to show the sun. The formation usually occurs about 7000 to 18,000 feet (2100 meters to 5500 meters) above the ground. ❑ *n., pl.* **al·to·stra·ti** (al′tō strā′tī).

al·tru·ism (al′trü iz′əm), *n.* unselfish devotion to the welfare of others; unselfishness.

al·tru·ist (al′trü ist), *n.* person who works for the welfare of others; unselfish person.

al·tru·is·tic (al′trü is′tik), *adj.* thoughtful of the welfare of others; unselfish. —**al′tru·is′ti·cal·ly,** *adv.*

al·um (al′əm), *n.* **1** a white mineral substance used in medicine and in dyeing. Alum is sometimes used to stop the bleeding of a small cut. **2** a colorless, crystalline substance used in fire extinguishers, water purification, etc.

a·lu·mi·num (ə lü′mə nəm), *n.* a very lightweight, silver-white, metallic element which does not readily tarnish. Aluminum is one of the most abundant metals, but it occurs only in combination with other elements. These aluminum compounds make up more than 15 percent of the earth's crust. Aluminum is used in alloys, as foil, and to make utensils, beverage cans, tools, aircraft parts, etc. *Symbol:* Al

a·lum·na (ə lum′nə), *n.* a woman graduate or former student of a school, college, or university. ❑ *n., pl.* **a·lum·nae** (ə lum′nē).

a·lum·ni (ə lum′nī), *n.* the plural of **alumnus.** ■ **Alumni** may mean either men graduates or both men and women graduates.

a·lum·nus (ə lum′nəs), *n.* graduate or former student of a school, college, or university. ❑ *n., pl.* **a·lum·ni.**

al·ve·o·lus (al vē′ə ləs), *n.* **1** a small cavity or pit. **2** air sac (def. 1). **3** socket of a tooth. ❑ *n., pl.* **al·ve·o·li** (al vē′ə lī).

al·ways (ȯl′wiz or ȯl′wāz), *adv.* **1** every time; in each case: *Night always follows day.* **2** all the time; continually: *Their home is always open to their friends.* **3** forever: *There will always be stars in the sky.* [**Always** comes from old English words meaning "all the way."]

Alz·heim·er's disease (älts′hī mərz), disease of the brain that causes confusion and gradual loss of memory.

am (am), *v.* form of the verb **be** used with *I* in the present tense: *I am twelve years old. I am going to school. I am frightened by loud noises.*

Am, symbol for americium.

Am., **1** America. **2** American.

AM or **A.M.,** amplitude modulation.

a.m. or **A.M.,** the time from midnight to noon: *School begins at 9 a.m.* [This abbreviation stands for the Latin phrase *ante meridiem,* meaning "before noon."]

A.M., Master of Arts. Also, **M.A.**

A.M.A., American Medical Association.

a·mal·gam (ə mal′gəm), *n.* **1** an alloy of mercury with some other metal or metals: *The dentist used silver amalgam to fill one of my teeth.* **2** mixture or blend of different things.

a·mal·gam·ate (ə mal′gə māt), *v.* to combine so as to form a whole; unite: *The two stores amalgamated to form one big store. The company amalgamated its three sales offices.* ❑ *v.* **a·mal·gam·at·ed, a·mal·gam·at·ing.** —**a·mal′gam·a′tion,** *n.*

am·a·ni·ta (am′ə nī′tə *or* am′ə nē′tə), *n.* any of a group of fungi including mainly very poisonous mushrooms. ❑ *n., pl.* **am·a·ni·tas.**

am·a·ranth (am′ə ranth′), *n.* any of several related plants with showy purple, greenish, or crimson flowers. The seeds of one amaranth were an important food for the Aztec and Inca peoples.

Am·a·ril·lo (am′ə ril′ō), *n.* city in NW Texas.

am·a·ryl·lis (am′ə ril′is), *n.* a lilylike plant with very large red, white, purple, or pink flowers. ❑ *n., pl.* **am·a·ryl·lis·es.**

amaryllis

a·mass (ə mas′), *v.* to heap together; pile up; accumulate: *She invested her money wisely and amassed a fortune.* ■ See Synonym Study at **accumulate.**

am·a·teur (am′ə chər *or* am′ə tər), **1** *n.* person who does something for pleasure, not for money or as a profession: *Only amateurs can compete in Olympic games.* **2** *n.* person who does something unskillfully or in an inexpert way: *This painting is obviously the work of an amateur.* **3** *adj.* of or by amateurs: *an amateur orchestra.* **4** *adj.* being an amateur: *an amateur golfer.* [**Amateur** comes from a Latin word meaning "lover."]

am·a·teur·ish (am′ə chür′ish *or* am′ə tyür′ish), *adj.* done as an amateur might do it; not expert; not very skillful. —**am′a·teur′ish·ly,** *adv.* —**am′a·teur′ish·ness,** *n.*

am·a·to·ry (am′ə tôr′ē), *adj.* of love; expressing love: *Valentine cards often have amatory verses on them.*

a·maze (ə māz′), *v.* to surprise greatly; strike with sudden wonder; astound: *He was amazed at how different the strand of hair looked under a microscope.* ❑ *v.* **a·mazed, a·maz·ing.**

a·maz·ed·ly (ə mā′zid lē), *adv.* with wonder or astonishment.

a·maze·ment (ə māz′mənt), *n.* great surprise; sudden wonder; astonishment: *I was filled with amazement when I saw the ocean for the first time.*

a·maz·ing (ə mā′zing), *adj.* very surprising; wonderful; astonishing. —**a·maz′ing·ly,** *adv.*

Am·a·zon (am′ə zon), *n.* **1** largest river in the world, in N South America. The Amazon flows from sources in the Andes Mountains of Peru across Brazil into the Atlantic. **2** (in Greek legend) one of a race of women warriors. **3 amazon,** a tall, strong, aggressive woman.

Am·a·zo·ni·an (am′ə zō′nē ən), *adj.* **1** of the Amazon River or the region it drains. **2** of the Amazons.

am·bas·sa·dor (am bas′ə dər), *n.* **1** a representative of highest rank sent by one government or ruler to another: *The U.S. am-*

---

a	hat	ė	term	ȯ	order	ch	child		
ā	age	i	it	oi	oil	ng	long		a in about
ä	far	ī	ice	ou	out	sh	she		e in taken
â	care	o	hot	u	cup	th	thin	ə	i in pencil
e	let	ō	open	ů	put	т͟h	then		o in lemon
ē	equal	ȯ	saw	ü	rule	zh	measure		u in circus

bassador to France lives in Paris and speaks and acts for the government of the United States. **2** any messenger with a special errand; agent: *The famous musician was welcomed abroad as an ambassador of goodwill.*

am·ber (am′bər), **1** *n.* a hard, clear, yellow or brown substance, used for jewelry, in making pipe stems, etc. Amber is the fossil resin of pine trees. **2** *n.* a yellow or yellowish brown. **3** *adj.* yellow or yellowish brown: *a black cat with amber eyes.*

am·ber·gris (am′bər grēs′ *or* am′bər gris), *n.* a waxlike, grayish substance produced in the intestines of the sperm whale. Ambergris was formerly used in making perfumes.

am·bi·ance (am′bē əns), *n.* surroundings and special mood: *The restaurant offers good food and a romantic ambiance.* Also, **ambience.**

am·bi·dex·trous (am′bə dek′strəs), *adj.* able to use the left hand and the right hand equally well. —**am′bi·dex′trous·ly,** *adv.* —**am′bi·dex′trous·ness,** *n.*

am·bi·ence (am′bē əns), *n.* ambiance.

am·bi·ent (am′bē ənt), *adj.* of the surroundings; all around: *ambient temperature, ambient sound.*

am·bi·gu·i·ty (am′bə gyü′ə tē), *n.* **1** possibility of two or more meanings: *The ambiguity of the speaker's statement made it hard to tell which side she was on.* **2** word or expression that can have more than one meaning: *Answer me without ambiguities.* □ *n., pl.* **am·bi·gu·i·ties** for 2.

am·big·u·ous (am big′yü əs), *adj.* having more than one possible meaning. The sentence "After John hit Charles he ran away" is ambiguous because we cannot tell which boy ran away. —**am·big′u·ous·ly,** *adv.* —**am·big′u·ous·ness,** *n.*

am·bi·tion (am bish′ən), *n.* **1** a strong desire for fame, honor, wealth, etc.; a longing for a high position or great power: *Because he was filled with ambition, he worked very hard.* **2** thing strongly desired: *Her ambition is to be an oceanographer.*

WORD STORY **Ambition** comes from a Latin word meaning "to go around." Roman politicians eager for fame used to go around looking for votes and money, as politicians do today.

am·bi·tious (am bish′əs), *adj.* **1** having or guided by ambition; desiring strongly: *She is ambitious to get through high school in three years.* **2** showing or arising from ambition: *an ambitious plan.* —**am·bi′tious·ly,** *adv.* —**am·bi′tious·ness,** *n.*

am·biv·a·lence (am biv′ə ləns), *n.* condition of being ambivalent.

am·biv·a·lent (am biv′ə lənt), *adj.* acting in opposite ways; having or showing conflicting feelings: *He has an ambivalent attitude toward his friend; he likes him but always quarrels with him.* —**am·biv′a·lent·ly,** *adv.*

am·ble (am′bəl), **1** *n.* an easy, slow pace in walking. **2** *v.* to walk at an easy, slow pace. □ *v.* **am·bled, am·bling.** —**am′bler,** *n.*

am·bro·sia (am brō′zhə), *n.* **1** (in Greek and Roman myths) the food of the gods. **2** anything especially delicious. [**Ambrosia** comes from Greek words meaning "not mortal." It was believed that the food of the gods gave immortality.] —**am·bro′sial,** *adj.* —**am·bro′sial·ly,** *adv.*

am·bu·lance (am′byə ləns), *n.* a vehicle equipped to carry and care for sick, injured, or wounded persons. [**Ambulance** comes from French words meaning "walking hospital," because it brings medical care where it is needed.]

am·bu·la·to·ry (am′byə lə tôr′ē), *adj.* capable of walking; not bedridden: *an ambulatory patient.*

am·bush (am′bush), **1** *n.* a surprise attack on an approaching enemy from a hiding place. **2** *n.* a secret or hidden place where soldiers or others lie in wait to make such an attack: *The troops lay in ambush, waiting for the signal to open fire.* **3** *v.* to attack unexpectedly from a hidden position: *The bandits ambushed the stagecoach.* □ *n., pl.* **am·bush·es.** —**am·bush·er,** *n.*

a·me·ba (ə mē′bə), *n.* a tiny one-celled living thing that moves by constantly changing its shape. Amebas are so small that they can be examined only with a microscope. Many amebas live in water; others live as parasites in animals. □ *n., pl.* **a·me·bas.** [**Ameba** comes from a Greek word meaning "a change," because its shape is always changing.]

a·me·bic (ə mē′bik), *adj.* **1** of or like an ameba or amebas. **2** caused by amebas: *amebic dysentery.*

a·mel·io·rate (ə mē′lyə rāt′), *v.* to make or become better; improve: *Stricter control of air pollution ameliorated living conditions in the city.* □ *v.* **a·mel·io·rat·ed, a·mel·io·rat·ing.** —**a·mel·io·ra·tion** (ə mē′lyə rā′shən), *n.* —**a·mel·io·ra·tive** (ə mē′lyə rə tiv), *adj.*

a·men (ā′men′ *or* ä′men′), *interj.* so be it; may it become true. *Amen* is said after a prayer, a wish, or a statement with which you agree. [**Amen** comes from a Hebrew word meaning "certainly" or "surely." It was used to express agreement.]

A·men (ä′mən), *n.* Egyptian god of breath and fertility, shown as a man with a ram's head. Amen was later combined with Ra as a supreme god. Also, **Amon.**

a·me·na·ble (ə mē′nə bəl *or* ə men′ə bəl), *adj.* open to influence, suggestion, advice, etc.; responsive: *I am amenable to your plan.* —**a·me′na·bil′i·ty,** *n.* —**a·me′na·ble·ness,** *n.* —**a·men′a·bly,** *adv.*

a·mend (ə mend′), *v.* **1** to change a law, bill, or motion by addition, omission, or alteration of language: *The Constitution of the United States was amended so that no one can be elected President more than twice.* **2** to change for the better; improve: *make efforts to amend conditions in an overcrowded city.* —**a·mend′a·ble,** *adj.* —**a·mend′er,** *n.*

a·mend·ment (ə mend′mənt), *n.* **1** change made in a law, bill, or motion by addition, omission, or alteration of language: *The Constitution of the United States has over twenty amendments.* **2** a change for the better; improvement.

a·mends (ə mendz′), *n.pl.* **make amends,** to make up for a wrong or an injury done by giving or paying something; payment for loss; compensation: *I bought my friend a new book to make amends for the one I lost.*

a·men·i·ty (ə men′ə tē), *n.* **1** **amenities,** *pl.* pleasant ways; polite acts. Saying "thank you" and holding the door open for a person to pass through are amenities. **2** quality of being pleasant; agreeableness: *We are enjoying the amenity of a warm climate.*

Amer., **1** America. **2** American.

A·mer·i·ca (ə mer′ə kə), *n.* **1** the United States of America. **2** North America. **3** Often, **the Americas,** *pl.* North America and South America; the Western Hemisphere.

WORD STORY **America** is named after **Amerigo Vespucci.** A German map maker, believing that Vespucci was the first European to reach America, gave it his name in 1507.

A·mer·i·can (ə mer′ə kən), **1** *adj.* of or in the United States: *an American citizen.* **2** *n.* person born or living in the United States. **3** *adj.* native only to the Western Hemisphere: *Corn and tobacco are American plants.* **4** *adj.* of or in the Western Hemisphere: *the Amazon and other American rivers.* **5** *n.* person born or living in the Western Hemisphere: *The citizens of Mexico, Canada, and Argentina are Americans.*

American cheese, a deep yellow cheese made in America, similar to Cheddar.

American eagle

American eagle, bald eagle. The coat of arms of the United States has a design of the American eagle on it.

American English, the form of English spoken and written in the United States.

American Indian, one of the people who have lived in North or South America from long before the time of the first European settlers. ■ See Usage Note at **Native American.**

> **WORD SOURCE** **American Indian** languages have given many words to English, because American Indians were the first to invent or see and name many things unknown to Europeans. The words below are some of the words that came into English from American Indian languages. See also Word Sources at **Algonquian, Nahuatl, Quechua,** and **Tupi.**
>
> | | | | |
> |---|---|---|---|
> | barbecue | hammock | pecan | potato |
> | bayou | hurricane | peccary | tobacco |
> | cannibal | iguana | petunia | woodchuck |
> | canoe | maize | poncho | |

A·mer·i·can·ism (ə mer′ə kə niz′əm), *n.* **1** devotion or loyalty to the United States and to its customs and traditions. **2** word, phrase, or meaning originating in the United States. **3** custom or trait peculiar to the United States.

A·mer·i·can·ize (ə mer′ə kə niz), *v.* to make or become American in habits, customs, or character: *Although she has lived in the United States only briefly, she is already Americanized.* ❑ *v.* **A·mer·i·can·ized, A·mer·i·can·iz·ing.** —**A·mer′i·can·i·za′tion,** *n.*

American Revolution, Revolutionary War.

American Samoa, group of island in Samoa that belong to the United States. *Capital:* Pago Pago.

American Sign Language, the system of communication by gestures used by many hearing-impaired people in North America.

am·e·ri·ci·um (am′ə rish′ē əm), *n.* a radioactive metallic element produced from plutonium. *Symbol:* Am

am·e·thyst (am′ə thist), *n.* **1** a purple or violet variety of quartz, used for jewelry. **2** a purple or violet color.

a·mi·a·ble (ā′mē ə bəl), *adj.* having a good-natured and friendly disposition; pleasant and agreeable: *She is an amiable person who gets along with almost everyone she meets.* —**a′mi·a·bil′i·ty,** *n.* —**a′mi·a·ble·ness,** *n.* —**a′mi·a·bly,** *adv.*

am·i·ca·ble (am′ə kə bəl), *adj.* having or showing a friendly attitude; peaceable: *Instead of fighting, the company and the union settled their quarrel in an amicable way by arbitration.* —**am′i·ca·bil′i·ty,** *n.* —**am′i·ca·ble·ness,** *n.* —**am′i·ca·bly,** *adv.*

a·mid (ə mid′), *prep.* amidst.

a·mid·ships (ə mid′ships), *adv.* in or toward the middle of a ship; halfway between the bow and stern.

a·midst (ə midst′), *prep.* in the middle of; surrounded by; among: *Amidst numerous foes, the knight fought bravely.*

a·mi·go (ə mē′gō), *n.* INFORMAL. friend. ❑ *n., pl.* **a·mi·gos.**

a·mi·no acid (ə mē′nō), any of a group of complex organic compounds of nitrogen, hydrogen, carbon, and oxygen that combine in various ways to form the proteins that make up living matter.

Am·ish (ā′mish *or* am′ish), **1** *n.pl.* members of a very strict Mennonite sect. **2** *adj.* of this sect. [**Amish** comes from the name Jacob *Amman.* Amman, a Swiss pastor of the 1600s, founded this sect.]

a·miss (ə mis′), *adv., adj.* not the way it should be; out of order; wrong: *Everything has gone amiss today. It would not be amiss to offer an apology, even though you didn't intend harm.*

take something amiss, be offended at something not intended to offend: *Don't take it amiss if I correct your grammar.*

am·i·ty (am′ə tē), *n.* peace and friendship; friendly relations: *If there were amity between nations, there would be no wars.*

Am·man (ā′mān *or* ä män′), *n.* capital of Jordan, in the NW part.

am·me·ter (am′ē′tər), *n.* device for measuring the amount of an electric current in amperes.

am·mo (am′ō), *n.* INFORMAL. ammunition.

am·mo·ni·a (ə mō′nyə), *n.* **1** a colorless gas, a compound of nitrogen and hydrogen, that has a sharp, suffocating smell and a strong alkaline reaction. Ammonia is used in making fertilizers and plastics. **2** this gas dissolved in water. Ammonia is very useful for cleaning.

am·mo·ni·um (ə mō′nē əm), *n.* a group of atoms, four hydrogen combined with one nitrogen.

am·mu·ni·tion (am′yə nish′ən), *n.* **1** bullets, shells, grenades, bombs, etc., that can be exploded or fired from guns or other weapons; military explosives and missiles. **2** any means of attack or defense: *Her speech gave fresh ammunition to her opponents.*

am·ne·sia (am nē′zhə), *n.* loss of memory caused by injury to the brain, or by disease or shock. [See Word Story at **mnemonic.**]

am·nes·ty (am′nə stē), *n.* a general pardon for past offenses against a government. ❑ *n., pl.* **am·nes·ties.**

am·ni·o·cen·te·sis (am′nē ō sen′tē sis), *n.* puncture of an amnion with a hollow needle to obtain amniotic fluid. The fluid contains cells from the embryo or fetus, which are examined for defects.

am·ni·on (am′nē ən), *n.* a membrane forming the inner sac which encloses the embryos of reptiles, birds, and mammals.

am·ni·ot·ic (am′nē ot′ik), *adj.* of or inside the amnion.

a·moe·ba (ə mē′bə), *n.* ameba. ❑ *n., pl.* **a·moe·bas, a·moe·bae** (ə-mē′bē).

a·moe·bic (ə mē′bik), *adj.* amebic.

a·mok (ə muk′ *or* ə mok′), *adv.* **run amok,** to run about in a frenzy; behave wildly: *He ran amok, screaming and throwing things around the room.* Also, **amuck.** [**Amok** comes from a Malay word meaning "in a murderous frenzy."]

A·mon (ā′mən), *n.* Amen.

a·mong (ə mung′), *prep.* **1** one of: *The United States is among the largest countries in the world.* **2** in the company of; with: *to spend time among friends.* **3** surrounded by: *a house among the trees.* **4** with a portion for each of: *Divide the fruit among all of us.* **5** by the combined action of: *You have, among you, done a good job.* **6** by, with, or through the whole of: *There was political unrest among the people.* **7** throughout: *Talk of revolution spread among the crowd.* ■ See Usage Note at **between.**

among ourselves, among yourselves, *or* among themselves, each with all the others; as a group: *They agreed among themselves to have a party.*

a·mongst (ə mungst′), *prep.* among.

a·mo·ral (ā môr′əl *or* a môr′əl), *adj.* not knowing right from wrong or caring about the difference. —**a·mo·ral·i·ty** (ā′mə ral′ə-tē *or* am′ə ral′ə tē), *n.*

am·or·ous (am′ər əs), *adj.* **1** inclined to love; loving; fond: *an amorous disposition.* **2** of love or courtship. —**am′or·ous·ly,** *adv.* —**am′or·ous·ness,** *n.*

a·mor·phous (ə môr′fəs), *adj.* **1** having no definite form; shapeless. **2** not made of crystals: *Glass is amorphous; sugar is crystalline.* —**a·mor′phous·ly,** *adv.* —**a·mor′phous·ness,** *n.*

am·or·tize (am′ər tiz), *v.* to set money aside regularly in a special fund for the future paying or settling of a debt. ❑ *v.* **am·or·tized, am·or·tiz·ing.** —**am′or·ti·za′tion,** *n.*

A·mos (ā′məs), *n.* **1** a Hebrew prophet. **2** book of the Bible. [**Amos** comes from a Hebrew word meaning "a burden bearer."]

a·mount (ə mount′), **1** *n.* the total of two or more numbers or quantities taken together; sum: *What is the amount of the bill for the groceries?* **2** *n.* the full value or extent: *The amount of evidence against them is great.* **3** *n.* quantity: *No amount of coaxing would make the dog leave its owner.* **4** *v.* to add up; reach: *The loss from the flood amounts to ten million dollars.* **5** *v.* to be equal: *Keeping what belongs to another amounts to stealing.*

> **USAGE NOTE** Many people feel that **amount** should be used only to mean how much there is: *a greater amount of traffic.* Some people, however, also use **amount** to mean how many there are: *a greater amount of cars than yesterday.*

a·mour (ə mur′), *n.* a love affair, especially a secret love affair.

amp (amp), *n.* **1** INFORMAL. amplifier. **2** ampere. ❑ *n., pl.* **amps** (or **amp** for 2).

am·per·age (am′pər ij), *n.* amount of an electric current measured in amperes.

am·pere (am′pir), *n.* unit for measuring the amount of an electric current. It is the amount of current one volt can send through

a	hat	ė	term	ô	order	ch	child		
ā	age	i	it	oi	oil	ng	long		a in about
ä	far	ī	ice	ou	out	sh	she		e in taken
â	care	o	hot	u	cup	th	thin	ə	i in pencil
e	let	ō	open	ù	put	ŦH	then		o in lemon
ē	equal	ȯ	saw	ü	rule	zh	measure		u in circus

a resistance of one ohm. Ordinary light bulbs use ½ to 1 ampere. [**Ampere** comes from André M. Ampère, a French scientist who made many discoveries about electricity in the early 1800s.]

am·per·sand (am′pər sand), *n.* the sign (&) meaning "and."

am·phet·a·mine (am fet′ə mēn), *n.* drug that stimulates the central nervous system. It is used to combat fatigue, reduce appetite, and relieve depression.

amphibian (def. 1)—a frog

am·phib·i·an (am fib′ē ən), **1** *n.* any of many cold-blooded animals with backbones and moist, scaleless skins. Their young usually have gills and live in water until they develop lungs for living on land. Frogs, toads, newts, and salamanders are amphibians. **2** *n.* plant that grows on land or in water. **3** *adj.* able to live both on land and in water. **4** *n.* aircraft that can take off from and land on either land or water. **5** *adj.* able to start from, travel across, or land on either land or water. **6** *n.* tank, truck, or other vehicle able to travel across land or water.

WORD STORY **Amphibian** comes from a Greek word meaning "living in two ways." Amphibians live in water when young and on land when older.

am·phib·i·ous (am fib′ē əs), *adj.* **1** able to live both on land and in water: *Frogs are amphibious.* **2** able to travel across land or water: *Some tanks are amphibious.* **3** by the combined action of land, sea, and air forces: *The enemy launched an amphibious attack.* **—am·phib′i·ous·ly,** *adv.* **—am·phib′i·ous·ness,** *n.*

am·phi·the·a·ter (am′fə thē′ə tər), *n.* **1** a circular or oval building with rows of seats around a central open space. Each row is higher than the one in front of it. **2** something like an amphitheater in shape: *The town was set in an amphitheater of hills.* [**Amphitheater** comes from a Greek word meaning "theater on all sides." The ancient Greeks built large public theaters in this shape.]

am·phor·a (am′fər ə), *n.* an oval jug with two handles used by the ancient Greeks and Romans. ❑ *n., pl.* **am·phor·ae** (am′fə rē′), **am·phor·as.**

am·ple (am′pəl), *adj.* **1** more than enough; abundant: *We needn't hurry; there's ample time to catch our bus.* ■ See Synonym Study at **plentiful. 2** as much as is needed; enough; sufficient: *My allowance is ample for carfare and lunches.* **3** having plenty of room; large; roomy: *A well-designed house has ample closets.* ❑ *adj.* **am·pler, am·plest. —am′ple·ness,** *n.* **—am′ply,** *adv.*

am·pli·fi·ca·tion (am′plə fə kā′shən), *n.* **1** act of making greater, stronger, or more extensive: *the amplification of knowledge.* **2** detail or example that amplifies: *Your argument needs amplification before I can understand it.*

am·pli·fi·er (am′plə fi′ər), *n.* a device in a radio, stereo, etc., for strengthening electrical signals.

am·pli·fy (am′plə fi), *v.* **1** to make greater; make stronger: *When sound is amplified, it is louder.* **2** to add to; expand; enlarge: *Please amplify your description of the accident by giving us more details.* ❑ *v.* **am·pli·fied, am·pli·fy·ing.**

am·pli·tude (am′plə tüd), *n.* **1** one half the distance of a regular swinging movement or vibration. The distance between the bottom and the highest position in the arc of a pendulum is its amplitude. **2** the peak strength of an alternating current in one cycle. **3** quantity that is more than enough; abundance: *an amplitude of money.*

amplitude modulation, a controlled changing of the amplitude of radio waves in order to transmit signals. Broadcasting that uses amplitude modulation is called AM.

am·poule (am′pül *or* am pül′), *n.* a small, sealed container, usually holding one dose of a drug for a hypodermic injection.

am·pu·tate (am′pyə tāt), *v.* to cut off all or part of a leg, arm, etc., by surgery. ❑ *v.* **am·pu·tat·ed, am·pu·tat·ing.** [**Amputate** comes from a Latin word meaning "cut" or "pruned."] **—am′pu·ta′tion,** *n.* **—am′pu·ta′tor,** *n.*

am·pu·tee (am′pyə tē′), *n.* person who has had all or part of a leg or arm amputated. ❑ *n., pl.* **am·pu·tees.**

Am·ster·dam (am′stər dam), *n.* port and official capital of the Netherlands, on the North Sea. The unofficial capital is The Hague.

amt., amount.

Am·trak (am′trak), *n.* a public corporation that receives financial support from the federal government to provide railroad passenger service on selected routes in the United States.

a·muck (ə muk′), *adv.* amok.

am·u·let (am′yə lit), *n.* some object worn as a magic charm against evil or harm.

A·mund·sen (ä′mən sən), *n.* **Ro·ald** (rō′äl), 1872-1928, Norwegian explorer who was the first to reach the South Pole in 1911.

a·muse (ə myüz′), *v.* **1** to cause to laugh or smile: *The clown's jokes and antics amused everyone.* **2** to keep pleasantly interested; cause to feel cheerful or happy; entertain: *The new toys amused the children.* ❑ *v.* **a·mused, a·mus·ing. —a·mus′a·ble,** *adj.* **—a·mus′er,** *n.*

SYNONYM STUDY **Amuse** and **entertain** both mean to keep someone pleasantly interested. **Amuse** suggests keeping someone's attention with something that is pleasing: *The toys amused the children.* **Entertain** is used when effort and planning are involved: *He entertained his friends with magic tricks.*

a·mus·ed·ly (ə myü′zid lē), *adv.* in an amused manner.

a·muse·ment (ə myüz′mənt), *n.* **1** condition of being amused: *The boy's amusement was so great that we all had to laugh with him.* **2** anything that amuses, such as an entertainment or sport.

amusement park, an outdoor place of entertainment with booths for games, various rides, and other amusements.

a·mus·ing (ə myü′zing), *adj.* **1** causing laughter or smiles: *an amusing joke.* ■ See Synonym Study at **funny. 2** entertaining: *an amusing book.* **—a·mus′ing·ly,** *adv.*

am·yl·ase (am′ə lās), *n.* an enzyme in saliva and digestive fluid that helps to change starch into sugar in digestion.

a·my·o·tro·phic lateral scle·ro·sis (ā′mī ə trō′fik; skli rō′sis), a disease of the nervous system in which nerve cells of the spinal cord weaken and die, causing muscular weakness and paralysis; Lou Gehrig's disease; ALS.

an (an), *indefinite article.* **1** any: *Is there an apple in the box?* **2** one: *I'll have an egg for breakfast.* **3** every; each: *The job pays $6 an hour.* ■ **An** is used instead of **a** before words that begin, or that sound as if they begin, with vowels.

-an, *suffix.* **1** of someplace or its people: *African = of Africa or its people.* **2** person born or living somewhere: *American = person born or living in America.* **3** of ___: *Lutheran = of Luther.*

a·nach·ro·nism (ə nak′rə niz′əm), *n.* **1** act of placing anything in some time where it does not belong. It would be an anachronism to show Abraham Lincoln in an automobile. **2** something placed or occurring out of its proper time. A famous anachronism in Shakespeare's *Julius Caesar* is a striking clock. The Romans had no such clocks.

WORD STORY **Anachronism** comes from Greek words meaning "back" and "time." Anachronisms usually involve showing something too early in time, in a period before it existed.

a·nach·ro·nis·tic (ə nak′rə nis′tik), *adj.* having or involving an anachronism. **—a·nach′ro·nis′ti·cal·ly,** *adv.*

an·a·con·da (an′ə kon′də), *n.* a very large South American snake that kills its prey by squeezing and is related to the boa constrictor. Anacondas live in tropical forests and rivers and are the longest snakes in America, sometimes more than 30 feet (9 meters) long. ❑ *n., pl.* **an·a·con·das.**

WORD STORY Anaconda comes from a mistake. About 300 years ago, European scientists learned this local name for a large snake of southeast Asia. About 200 years ago, a French scientist gave the name to a large snake he was studying, but his snake came from South America! So the name traveled thousands of miles and changed snakes in the process.

an·aer·obe (an′ə rōb), *n.* any living thing that can live without oxygen. Anaerobes are all very small.

an·ae·ro·bic (an′ə rō′bik), *adj.* **1** living or growing where there is no oxygen: *anaerobic bacteria.* **2** of or caused by anaerobic bacteria. **−an′ae·ro′bi·cal·ly,** *adv.*

an·a·gram (an′ə gram), *n.* **1** word or phrase formed from another by rearranging the letters. EXAMPLE: roved—drove. **2 anagrams,** *sing.* game in which the players make words by changing and adding letters: *Anagrams is an interesting game.*

a·nal (ā′nl), *adj.* **1** of the anus. **2** at or near the anus. **−a′nal·ly,** *adv.*

an·al·ge·sic (an′l jē′zik), **1** *n.* drug that relieves or lessens pain. **2** *adj.* relieving pain.

an·a·log computer (an′l òg), computer that processes data in the form of physical quantities, such as speed, length, voltage, etc., rather than as a numerical code.

a·nal·o·gous (ə nal′ə gəs), *adj.* alike in some way; similar in the quality or feature that is being thought of; comparable: *The heart is analogous to a pump.* **−a·nal′o·gous·ly,** *adv.* **−a·nal′o·gous·ness,** *n.*

a·nal·o·gy (ə nal′ə jē), *n.* **1** likeness in some ways between things that are otherwise unlike; similarity: *There is an analogy between the heart and a pump.* **2** a comparison between two parts that are related in the same way, such as, "*More is to less as loud is to soft.*" ❑ *n., pl.* **a·nal·o·gies.**

a·nal·y·sis (ə nal′ə sis), *n.* **1** separation of anything into its parts or elements to find out what it is made of. A chemical analysis of ordinary table salt shows that it is made up of two elements, sodium and chlorine. **2** an examination made carefully and in detail. An analysis can be made of a book, a person's character, etc. **3** psychoanalysis. ❑ *n., pl.* **a·nal·y·ses** (ə nal′ə sēz′).

an·a·lyst (an′l ist), *n.* **1** person who analyzes. **2** psychoanalyst.

an·a·lyt·ic (an′l it′ik), *adj.* analytical.

an·a·lyt·i·cal (an′l it′ə kəl), *adj.* separating a whole into its parts; using analysis: *The methods of science are analytical. The detective had an analytical mind.* **−an′a·lyt′i·cal·ly,** *adv.*

an·a·lyze (an′l īz), *v.* **1** to separate anything into its parts or elements to find out what it is made of: *The chemistry teacher analyzed water into two colorless gases, oxygen and hydrogen.* **2** to examine carefully and in detail: *analyze a situation. The newspaper analyzed the results of the election.* ❑ *v.* **an·a·lyzed, an·a·lyz·ing. −an′a·lyz′a·ble,** *adj.* **−an′a·lyz′er,** *n.*

An·an·si or **An·an·se** (ä nän′sē), *n.* (in west African mythology) hero and trickster, often thought of as a spider, sometimes as a person.

an·a·pest (an′ə pest), *n.* a measure or foot in poetry, made up of three syllables, two unaccented syllables followed by one accented syllable. EXAMPLE: In Octo′ | ber the gold′ | of the trees′ | overwhelms′. |

an·a·phase (an′ə fāz), *n.* the stage in cell division when chromosomes move to opposite ends of the dividing cell.

an·ar·chic (a när′kik), *adj.* favoring anarchy; lawless: *an anarchic age.* **−an·ar′chi·cal·ly,** *adv.*

an·ar·chism (an′ər kiz′əm), *n.* the political theory that all systems of government are harmful.

an·ar·chist (an′ər kist), *n.* **1** person who wants to destroy governments and laws. **2** person who promotes disorder and stirs up revolt.

an·ar·chy (an′ər kē), *n.* **1** absence of a system of government and law. **2** disorder and confusion; lawlessness. [Anarchy comes from Greek words meaning "without" and "ruler."]

A·na·sa·zi (ä′nə sä′zē), *n.* member of a tribe of American Indians who lived in the southwestern United States between about A.D. 1000 and 1300. The Anasazi were ancestors of the modern Pueblo. ❑ *n., pl.* **A·na·sa·zi.**

Anasazi—ruins of Anasazi buildings

a·nath·e·ma (ə nath′ə mə), *n.* **1** a solemn curse by church authorities excommunicating some person from the church. **2** person or thing that has been cursed. **3** person or thing that is detested or condemned. ❑ *n., pl.* **a·nath·e·mas.**

a·nath·e·ma·tize (ə nath′ə mə tiz), *v.* to pronounce an anathema against; denounce; curse. ❑ *v.* **a·nath·e·ma·tized, a·nath·e·ma·tiz·ing. −a·nath′e·ma·ti·za′tion,** *n.*

An·a·to·li·a (an′ə tō′lē ə), *n.* Asia Minor. **−An′a·to′li·an,** *adj., n.*

an·a·tom·i·cal (an′ə tom′ə kəl), *adj.* of anatomy. **−an′a·tom′i·cal·ly,** *adv.*

a·nat·o·my (ə nat′ə mē), *n.* **1** science of the structure of living things. **2** structure of a living thing: *the anatomy of an earthworm.* ❑ *n., pl.* **a·nat·o·mies. −a·nat′o·mist,** *n.*

-ance, *suffix.* **1** act or fact of ___ing: *avoidance = act of avoiding; resemblance = fact of resembling.* **2** condition of being ___ed: *annoyance = condition of being annoyed.* **3** condition of being ___ant: *importance = condition of being important.*

an·ces·tor (an′ses′tər), *n.* **1** person from whom you are descended, such as your great-grandparents: *Their ancestors came to the United States in 1812.* **2** the early form from which a species or group is descended: *Dinosaurs and snakes have the same ancestor.* [Ancestor comes from a Latin word meaning "to go before." Our ancestors are those people who went before us.]

an·ces·tral (an ses′trəl), *adj.* of or from ancestors: *his ancestral home.* **−an·ces′tral·ly,** *adv.*

an·ces·try (an′ses′trē), *n.* **1** ancestors: *Many early settlers in California had Spanish ancestry.* **2** line of descent from ancestors; lineage: *The king was of noble ancestry.* ❑ *n., pl.* **an·ces·tries.**

an·chor (ang′kər), **1** *n.* a heavy, shaped piece of iron or steel or other heavy weight, attached to a chain or rope and dropped into the water to hold a ship or boat in place: *The anchor kept the boat from drifting.* **2** *v.* to hold in place with an anchor: *Can you anchor the boat in this storm?* **3** *v.* to stay in place by using an anchor: *The ship anchored in the bay.* **4** *v.* to set in place; attach firmly: *The campers anchored the tent to the ground.* **5** *n.* something that makes a person feel safe and secure: *The weekly talks with an understanding counselor were an anchor to the troubled student.* **6** *n.* thing for holding something else in place: *The anchors of the cables of this suspension bridge are set in concrete.* **7** *n.* a person on a TV or radio program who announces news and coordinates reports from correspondents.

at anchor, held by an anchor: *The ship was at anchor.*

cast anchor, to drop the anchor: *The boat cast anchor near the shore.*

an·chor·age (ang′kər ij), *n.* **1** place to anchor. **2** something on which to depend.

An·chor·age (ang′kər ij), *n.* port and largest city, in S Alaska.

a	hat	ė	term	ô	order	ch	child		
ā	age	i	it	oi	oil	ng	long		a in about
ä	far	ī	ice	ou	out	sh	she		e in taken
â	care	o	hot	u	cup	th	thin	ə	i in pencil
e	let	ō	open	ů	put	₮H	then		o in lemon
ē	equal	ò	saw	ü	rule	zh	measure		u in circus

an·cho·rite (ang′kə rīt′), *n.* person who lives alone in a solitary place for religious meditation; hermit.

an·chor·man (ang′kər man′), *n.* **1** the last person to run or swim on a relay team. **2** anchor (def. 7). ◻ *n., pl.* **an·chor·men.**

an·chor·per·son (ang′kər pėr′sən), *n.* anchor (def. 7).

an·chor·wom·an (ang′kər wu̇m′ən), *n.* anchor (def. 7). ◻ *n., pl.* **an·chor·wom·en.**

an·cho·vy (an′chō vē), *n.* a very small fish that looks something like a herring. Anchovies may be packed in oil or made into a paste. ◻ *n., pl.* **an·cho·vies.**

an·cient (ān′shənt), **1** *adj.* of times long past: *In Egypt, we saw the ruins of an ancient temple built 6000 years ago.* **2** *n.pl.* **the ancients,** people who lived long ago, such as the ancient Greeks, Romans, and Egyptians. **3** *adj.* of great age; very old: *Rome is an ancient city.* **4** *n.* a very old person. —**an′cient·ly,** *adv.* —**an′cient·ness,** *n.*

ancient history, **1** history from the earliest times to the fall of the western part of the Roman Empire in A.D. 476. **2** a recent fact or event that no longer seems interesting or important: *We've made up, and our quarrel is ancient history now.*

an·cil·lar·y (an′sə ler′ē), *adj.* **1** subordinate; dependent. **2** assisting; auxiliary: *an ancillary engine in a boat.*

-ancy, *suffix.* a form of **-ance,** as in *buoyancy.*

and (and), *conj.* **1** as well as: *You can come and go in the car.* **2** added to; with: *4 and 2 make 6. She likes ham and eggs.* **3** in addition; then; while: *I washed the dishes and my brother dried them.* **4** as a result: *The sun came out and the grass dried.* **5** IN-FORMAL. to: *Try and do better.* ▪ This use of *and* is considered incorrect by many people.

An·da·lu·sia (an′də lü′zhə), *n.* region in S Spain. —**An′da·lu′sian,** *adj., n.*

an·dan·te (än dän′tā *or* an dan′tē), in music: **1** *adj., adv.* moderately slow. **2** *n.* a moderately slow movement in a piece of music. ◻ *n., pl.* **an·dan·tes.** [Andante comes from an Italian word meaning "going" or "walking."]

An·de·an (an′dē ən *or* an dē′ən), *adj.* of or in the Andes.

An·der·sen (an′dər sən), *n.* **Hans Christian** (hanz), 1805-1875, Danish writer of fairy tales, including "The Ugly Duckling."

An·der·son (an′dər sən), *n.* **Mar·i·an** (mâr′ē ən), 1902-1993, American concert singer. She was the first African American soloist to sing at New York's Metropolitan Opera.

An·des (an′dēz), *n.pl.* mountain range in W South America. It is the longest continuous mountain system in the world. The highest peak is Aconcagua.

and·i·ron (and′ī′ərn), *n.* one of a pair of metal supports for wood in a fireplace; firedog.

and/or, both or either. "To earn money from stocks and/or bonds" means to earn it from both stocks and bonds or from either stocks or bonds.

An·dor·ra (an dôr′ə), *n.* **1** small country between France and Spain. **2** its capital. —**An·dor′ran,** *adj., n.*

An·drew (an′drü), *n.* (in the Bible) one of Jesus' twelve apostles. He is the patron saint of Greece, Russia, and Scotland. [Andrew comes from a Greek word meaning "manly."]

an·dro·gen (an′drə jən), *n.* any hormone, especially testosterone, that helps produce masculine characteristics.

an·droid (an′droid), *n.* robot that resembles a human being.

an·ec·dot·al (an′ik dō′tl *or* an′ik dō′tl), *adj.* containing or consisting of anecdotes: *an anecdotal book.* —**an′ec·dot′al·ly,** *adv.*

an·ec·dote (an′ik dōt), *n.* a short account of some interesting incident or event, often humorous or biographical. ▪ See Synonym Study at **story¹**. [Anecdote comes from a Greek word meaning "unpublished." People usually share anecdotes in conversation.]

a·ne·mi·a (ə nē′mē ə), *n.* a lack of hemoglobin or red corpuscles in the blood. Anemia causes people to be pale, weak, and tired. [Anemia comes from Greek words meaning "without blood."]

a·ne·mic (ə nē′mik), *adj.* **1** of anemia; having anemia: *an anemic patient.* **2** lacking in strength, energy, or spirit: *an anemic defense.*

an·e·mom·e·ter (an′ə mom′ə tər), *n.* device for measuring the speed of wind.

a·nem·o·ne (ə nem′ə nē), *n.* **1** plant with a slender stem and white or colored cup-shaped flowers; windflower. It often blooms early in the spring. **2** the sea anemone, a flowerlike sea animal.

an·e·roid barometer (an′ə roid′), barometer worked by the pressure of air on the elastic lid of an airtight metal box from which the air has been pumped out.

an·es·the·sia (an′əs thē′zhə), *n.* entire or partial loss of the feeling of pain, touch, cold, etc.

an·es·the·si·ol·o·gy (an′əs thē′zē ol′ə jē), *n.* science of giving anesthetics. —**an′es·the′si·ol′o·gist,** *n.*

an·es·thet·ic (an′əs thet′ik), **1** *n.* substance that causes entire or partial loss of the feeling of pain, touch, cold, etc. Anesthetics are given by doctors so that patients will feel no pain. **2** *adj.* causing anesthesia: *anesthetic gas.* —**an′es·thet′i·cal·ly,** *adv.*

an·es·the·tist (ə nes′thə tist), *n.* person specially trained to give anesthetics.

an·es·the·tize (ə nes′thə tīz), *v.* to make unable to feel pain, touch, cold, etc.; make insensible. ◻ *v.* **an·es·the·tized, an·es·the·tiz·ing.** —**an·es′the·ti·za′tion,** *n.*

a·new (ə nü′), *adv.* once more; again: *I made so many mistakes I had to begin the work anew.*

an·gel (ān′jəl), *n.* **1** messenger from God. **2** person as good, kind, or beautiful as an angel.

Angel Falls, waterfall in SE Venezuela, the highest in the world.

an·gel·fish (ān′jəl fish′), *n.* any of several colorful tropical fishes with long spiny fins. ◻ *n., pl.* **an·gel·fish** *or* **an·gel·fish·es.**

angel food cake, a fluffy white cake made with beaten egg whites, flour, and sugar.

an·gel·ic (an jel′ik), *adj.* **1** of angels; heavenly: *an angelic vision.* **2** like an angel; good, kind, or beautiful: *an angelic child.* —**an·gel′i·cal·ly,** *adv.*

An·gel·ou (an′jə lō), *n.* **Ma·ya** (mī′ə), born 1928, American writer and poet. Her first book, an autobiography, was *I Know Why the Caged Bird Sings.*

an·ger (ang′gər), **1** *n.* the feeling that you have toward someone or something that hurts, or annoys; a strong dislike or wish to harm: *In a moment of anger, I hit my brother.* **2** *v.* to feel or cause to feel this way: *The girl's rudeness angered her parents. He angers easily.* [Anger comes from an Icelandic word meaning "grief" or "trouble." People in trouble or grieving often feel anger, too.]

an·gi·na (an jī′nə), *n.* a sudden, acute pain in the chest, and a feeling of suffocation, caused by too little blood reaching the heart muscle.

an·gi·o·sperm (an′jē ə spėrm′), *n.* any plant with seeds enclosed in an ovary or fruit; a flowering plant. Grasses, beans, strawberries, and oaks are angiosperms.

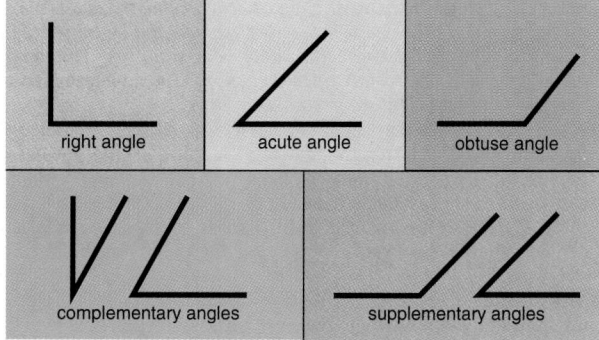

angle¹ (def. 2)—kinds of angles

an·gle¹ (ang′gəl), **1** *n.* the space between two lines or surfaces that meet. **2** *n.* the figure formed by two such lines or surfaces. **3** *n.* the difference in direction between two such lines or surfaces: *The two roads lie at an angle of about 45 degrees.* **4** *v.* to move, turn, or bend at an angle: *The road angles to the right here.* **5** *n.* corner: *the northeast angle of a building.* **6** *n.* point of view: *We are treating the problem from a new angle.* ◻ *v.* **an·gled, an·gling.**

an·gle² (ang′gəl), *v.* **1** to fish with a hook and line. **2** to try to get something by using tricks or schemes: *He angled for an invitation to the party by flattering her.* ❑ *v.* **an·gled, an·gling.**

An·gle (ang′gəl), *n.* member of a Germanic tribe that, with the Jutes and Saxons, conquered England in the A.D. 400s and 500s.

angle of incidence, the angle that energy or objects hitting a surface make with a line perpendicular to the surface.

angle of reflection, the angle that energy or objects reflected from a surface make with a line perpendicular to the surface.

angle of refraction, the angle that a ray of light makes, after being refracted at a surface, with a line perpendicular to the surface.

an·gler (ang′glər), *n.* person who fishes with a hook and line, especially someone who does so often and for sport.

an·gler·fish (ang′glər fish′), *n.* any of many ocean fishes of deep water that have a movable lure growing over the mouth to attract prey. ❑ *n., pl.* **an·gler·fish** or **an·gler·fish·es.**

an·gle·worm (ang′gəl wėrm′), *n.* earthworm.

An·gli·can (ang′glə kən), **1** *adj.* of the Church of England or other churches of the same faith elsewhere. **2** *n.* member of an Anglican church.

An·gli·cize (ang′glə sīz), *v.* to make or become English in form, pronunciation, habits, customs, or character. *Cajole, lace,* and *cousin* are French words that have been Anglicized. ❑ *v.* **An·gli·cized, An·gli·ciz·ing.**

An·glo-Ca·na·di·an (ang′glō kə nā′dē ən), **1** *n.* Canadian whose native language is English. **2** *adj.* of or for Anglo-Canadians.

An·glo·phone or **an·glo·phone** (ang′glə fōn′), *n.* an English-speaking person in a country where two or more languages are spoken.

An·glo-Sax·on (ang′glō sak′sən), **1** *n.* member of the Germanic tribes that invaded England in the A.D. 400s and 500s and ruled most of England until the Norman Conquest in 1066. **2** *n.* the language of these tribes; Old English. **3** *adj.* of the Anglo-Saxons or their language. **4** *n.* person of English descent.

An·go·la (ang gō′lə), *n.* country in SW Africa. *Capital:* Luanda. —**An·go′lan,** *adj., n.*

An·go·ra (ang gôr′ə), *n.* **1** Angora cat. **2** Angora goat. **3** Angora rabbit. **4 angora, a** mohair. **b** a very fluffy yarn made from the hair of Angora goats or Angora rabbits. ❑ *n., pl.* **An·go·ras** for 1-3.

Angora cat, cat with long, silky hair.

Angora goat, goat with long, silky hair. This hair is used for wool and made into a cloth called mohair.

Angora rabbit, rabbit with long, soft hair. This hair is used in making a very fluffy yarn.

Angora rabbit—about 20 in. (50 cm) long

an·gry (ang′grē), *adj.* **1** feeling or showing anger: *I was very angry when you disobeyed. My friend's angry words hurt my feelings.* **2** stormy; threatening: *Angry waves pounded the beach.* **3** red, painful, and often swollen: *An infected cut looks angry.* ❑ *adj.* **an·gri·er, an·gri·est.** —**an′gri·ly,** *adv.* —**an′gri·ness,** *n.*

ang·strom (ang′strəm), *n.* unit for measuring the wavelength of light, equal to one ten-millionth of a millimeter.

an·guish (ang′gwish), *n.* very great pain or grief; great distress: *He was in anguish until the doctor set his broken leg.* [Anguish comes from a Latin word meaning "narrow." A feeling of very great pain often causes a narrow, choking feeling in the throat.]

an·guished (ang′gwisht), *adj.* full of grief or distress; showing anguish: *We saw the anguished faces of the lost child's parents.*

an·gu·lar (ang′gyə lər), *adj.* **1** having angles; having sharp corners: *an angular piece of rock.* **2** somewhat thin and bony; not plump: *Many basketball players have tall, angular bodies.* **3** measured by an angle: *angular distance.*

an·gu·lar·i·ty (ang′gyə lar′ə tē), *n.* condition of having sharp or prominent corners.

an·i·line (an′l ən), *n.* a colorless, oily liquid, obtained from coal tar. It is a compound of carbon, nitrogen, and hydrogen and is used in making dyes, medicines, plastics, etc.

an·i·mal (an′ə məl), **1** *n.* any living thing that contains many cells and that can move about. Most animals feed upon other living things, inhale oxygen and exhale carbon dioxide, and have a digestive cavity and a nervous system. Dogs, birds, fish, snakes, flies, and worms are animals. **2** *n.* an animal other than a human being; beast. **3** *adj.* of animals: *the animal world.* **4** *adj.* like that of animals: *animal cunning.* **5** *n.* person who acts more like a beast than like a human being. [Animal comes from a Latin word meaning "a living being," which comes from another Latin word meaning "life" or "breath."]

animal husbandry, the breeding and care of domestic animals, especially on a farm.

animal kingdom, all animals.

an·i·mate (an′ə māt *for verb;* an′ə mit *for adj.*), **1** *v.* to make lively or vigorous: *Her arrival animated the whole party.* **2** *v.* to be a motive or a reason for; inspire: *Love for her job animated her work.* **3** *v.* to cause to move as if alive: *Wind animated the scarecrow, which appeared to wave at us.* **4** *adj.* living; having life. Animate nature means all living things. ❑ *v.* **an·i·mat·ed, an·i·mat·ing.**

an·i·mat·ed (an′ə mā′tid), *adj.* **1** lively; vigorous: *We had an animated discussion about yesterday's field trip.* **2** made to move or appear to move: *animated dolls.* —**an′i·mat′ed·ly,** *adv.*

animated cartoon, series of drawings arranged to be photographed and shown as a movie. Each drawing shows a slight change from the one before it, so that when projected in rapid sequence the figures appear to move.

an·i·ma·tion (an′ə mā′shən), *n.* **1** the production of an animated cartoon. **2** liveliness; vigor: *The boy acted his part as a pirate with great animation.*

an·i·ma·tor (an′ə mā′tər), *n.* an artist who designs and draws animated cartoons.

an·i·mism (an′ə miz′əm), *n.* belief that there are living souls in trees, stones, stars, etc.

an·i·mist (an′ə mist), *n.* believer in animism.

an·i·mos·i·ty (an′ə mos′ə tē), *n.* violent hatred; active dislike: *What have I done to earn your animosity?* ❑ *n., pl.* **an·i·mos·i·ties.**

an·i·on (an′ī′ən), *n.* a negatively charged ion.

an·ise (an′is), *n.* plant related to parsley, grown especially for its fragrant seeds which are used as a flavoring.

an·i·seed (an′ə sēd), *n.* the seed of the anise, used as a flavoring.

An·jou (an′jü), *n.* region in W France. See **Normandy** for map.

An·kar·a (ang′kər ə), *n.* capital of Turkey, in the central part.

an·kle (ang′kəl), *n.* **1** joint that connects the foot with the leg; tarsus. **2** the slender part of the leg between this joint and the calf.

an·klet (ang′klit), *n.* **1** a short sock. **2** band or bracelet worn around the ankle. An anklet may be an ornament, a brace, or a fetter.

an·ky·lo·saur (ang′kə lō sôr′), *n.* any of numerous dinosaurs with bony plates and spikes covering their bodies. They had short legs and ate plants.

an·nals (an′lz), *n.pl.* **1** historical records; history: *Marie Curie holds an important place in the annals of science.* **2** a written account of events year by year.

An·na·po·lis (ə nap′ə lis), *n.* **1** port and capital of Maryland. **2** the U.S. Naval Academy, located there. [Annapolis comes from the name of Queen Anne of England and a Greek word meaning "city."]

a	hat	ė	term	ô	order	ch	child		a in about
ā	age	i	it	oi	oil	ng	long		e in taken
ä	far	ī	ice	ou	out	sh	she	ə	i in pencil
â	care	o	hot	u	cup	th	thin		o in lemon
e	let	ō	open	ů	put	ŦH	then		u in circus
ē	equal	ò	saw	ü	rule	zh	measure		

33

Anne (an), *n.* 1665-1714, queen of Great Britain from 1702 to 1714. [**Anne** comes from a Hebrew word meaning "grace."]

an·neal (ə nēl′), *v.* to make glass, metals, etc., less brittle by heating and then gradually cooling. —**an·neal′er**, *n.*

an·ne·lid (an′l id), *n.* worm with a body formed of many similar ringlike segments. Earthworms, leeches, and various sea worms are annelids.

Anne of Cleves (klēvz), 1515-1557, German princess and queen of England, fourth wife of Henry VIII. He ended the marriage after six months because he found her unattractive.

an·nex (ə neks′ *for verb;* an′eks *for noun*), **1** *v.* to join or add a smaller thing to a larger thing: *The United States annexed Texas in 1845.* **2** *n.* something annexed; an added part, especially to a building: *We are building an annex to the school.* ❑ *n., pl.* **an·nex·es.** —**an′nex·a′tion**, *n.*

an·ni·hi·late (ə nī′ə lāt), *v.* to destroy completely; wipe out of existence: *An avalanche annihilated the village.* ❑ *v.* **an·ni·hi·lat·ed, an·ni·hi·lat·ing.** [**Annihilate** comes from two Latin words meaning "to nothing."] —**an·ni′hi·la′tion**, *n.*

an·ni·ver·sar·y (an′ə vėr′sər ē), **1** *n.* the yearly return of a special date: *Your birthday is an anniversary you like to have remembered.* **2** *n.* celebration of the yearly return of a special date. **3** *adj.* having to do with an anniversary: *an anniversary dinner.* ❑ *n., pl.* **an·ni·ver·sa·ries.**

an·no Dom·i·ni (an′ō dom′ə nī), LATIN. in the year of the Lord; in the specified year since the birth of Jesus; A.D.

an·no·tate (an′ə tāt), *v.* **1** to provide with notes or comments: *The Bible is often annotated to explain the meaning of certain words and events.* **2** to write or insert notes or comments. ❑ *v.* **an·no·tat·ed, an·no·tat·ing.** —**an′no·ta′tor**, *n.*

an·no·ta·tion (an′ə tā′shən), *n.* **1** note added to explain or criticize: *The editor's annotations were printed in small type at the bottom of the page.* **2** act of providing with notes or comments: *The annotation of this Shakespearean play required the explanation of many words no longer used.*

an·nounce (ə nouns′), *v.* **1** to give public or formal notice of: *The teacher announced that there would be no school tomorrow.* **2** to make known the presence or arrival of: *The loudspeaker announced each airplane as it landed at the airport.* **3** to introduce programs, read news, etc., on the radio or TV. ❑ *v.* **an·nounced, an·nounc·ing.**

an·nounce·ment (ə nouns′mənt), *n.* **1** act of announcing or making known. We speak of the announcement of a speaker, a meeting, a wedding, a concert, etc. **2** what is announced or made known: *The principal made two announcements. The announcement was published in the newspapers.*

an·nounc·er (ə noun′sər), *n.* person who makes announcements, introduces programs, reads news, or describes sports events on radio or TV.

an·noy (ə noi′), *v.* to make somewhat angry; disturb; trouble; vex: *I turned off the radio because it was annoying me.* [**Annoy** comes from Latin words meaning "in hatred." People still say they hate things which are really only annoying.]

an·noy·ance (ə noi′əns), *n.* **1** a feeling of anger, impatience, or the like: *He showed his annoyance at us by slamming the door.* **2** something that annoys; nuisance: *The heavy traffic on our street is an annoyance.*

an·noy·ing (ə noi′ing), *adj.* disturbing; troublesome. —**an·noy′ing·ly**, *adv.*

an·nu·al (an′yü əl), **1** *adj.* coming once a year: *Your birthday is an annual event.* **2** *adj.* in a year; for a year: *For the last two years her annual salary has been $27,000.* **3** *adj.* lasting for a whole year: *The earth makes an annual course around the sun.* **4** *adj.* living only one year or season: *Corn and beans are annual plants.* **5** *n.* plant that lives only one year or season. **6** *n.* book, journal, etc., published once a year. —**an′nu·al·ly**, *adv.*

annual rate, amount of interest charged or earned in a year.

annual ring, any one of the rings of wood seen when the stem of a tree or bush is cut across. Each ring shows one year's growth.

an·nu·i·ty (ə nü′ə tē), *n.* **1** sum of money paid every year or at certain regular times: *Many businesses provide annuities for em-*

ployees after they retire. **2** an investment that provides a fixed yearly income during your lifetime or for a specified time. ❑ *n., pl.* **an·nu·i·ties.**

an·nul (ə nul′), *v.* to do away with; destroy the force of; make void; cancel: *annul a contract, annul a marriage.* ❑ *v.* **an·nulled, an·nul·ling.** —**an·nul′ment**, *n.*

an·nu·lar (an′yə lər), *adj.* of or like a ring; ring-shaped.

annular eclipse, an eclipse of the sun in which the moon does not cover the sun completely, leaving a narrow, bright ring which surrounds the dark moon.

An·nun·ci·a·tion (ə nun′sē ā′shən), *n.* **1** (in the Bible) the announcement by the angel Gabriel to the Virgin Mary that she was to be the mother of Jesus. **2** a church festival held on March 25 in memory of the Annunciation.

an·ode (an′ōd), *n.* electrode by which electricity flows out of a device. The anode is the negative electrode of a battery but is the positive electrode of most other devices.

an·o·dyne (an′ə dīn), *n.* **1** medicine or drug that reduces pain. **2** anything that soothes or relieves.

a·noint (ə noint′), *v.* **1** to put oil on a person as part of a ceremony: *The bishop anointed the new king.* **2** to put oil on; rub with a healing ointment; smear: *He anointed his sunburned skin with aloe.* —**a·noint′ment**, *n.*

a·nom·a·lous (ə nom′ə ləs), *adj.* departing from the common rule; irregular: *It would be anomalous for a principal to have no authority.* —**a·nom′a·lous·ly**, *adv.*

a·nom·a·ly (ə nom′ə lē), *n.* **1** something abnormal: *A dog with six legs would be an anomaly.* **2** departure from the common rule; irregularity: *"A lamb in school is an anomaly," said the teacher to Mary.* ❑ *n., pl.* **a·nom·a·lies.**

an·o·mie (an′ə mē), *n.* lack of standards, values, and goals in an individual or society; aimlessness; alienation: *The congressman blamed a nationwide anomie for the decline in test scores.*

a·non (ə non′), *adv.* OLD USE. **1** in a little while; soon. **2** at another time; again.

anon., anonymous.

an·o·nym·i·ty (an′ə nim′ə tē), *n.* condition of being anonymous.

a·non·y·mous (ə non′ə məs), *adj.* **1** by or from a person whose name is not known or given: *An anonymous letter is one which does not give the name of the writer.* **2** unknown: *This book was written by an anonymous author.* —**a·non′y·mous·ly**, *adv.*

a·noph·e·les (ə nof′ə lēz), *n.* any of several mosquitoes that transmit malaria to human beings with their bite. ❑ *n., pl.* **a·noph·e·les.**

a·no·rak (ä′nə räk′), *n.* a heavy jacket with a fur hood, worn in arctic regions.

an·o·rec·tic (an′ə rek′tik), *adj.* anorexic.

an·o·rex·i·a ner·vo·sa (an′ə rek′sē ə nər vō′sə), condition in which a person deliberately eats very little, usually caused by emotional problems and producing extreme thinness and even starvation.

an·o·rex·ic (an′ə rek′sik), **1** *adj.* having anorexia nervosa. **2** *n.* person who has anorexia nervosa.

annual rings

an·oth·er (ə nuŦH′ər), **1** *adj., pron.* one more: *Have another glass of milk. I ate a candy bar and then asked for another.* **2** *adj.* a different: *Show me another kind of hat.* **3** *pron.* a different one: *I don't like this book; give me another.*

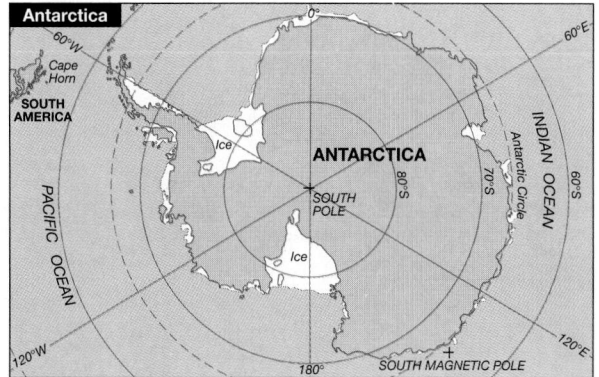

Antarctica

an·ox·i·a (ə nok′sē ə), *n.* a shortage of oxygen in the tissues of the body. It is caused by failure of the lungs to oxygenate the blood, failure of the blood to absorb oxygen, or a slowdown in blood flow.

an·swer (an′sər), **1** *v.* to speak or write in return to a question: *I asked them a question, but they would not answer. He finally answered my question.* **2** *n.* words spoken or written in return to a question: *The girl gave a quick answer.* **3** *n.* gesture or act done in return: *A nod was her only answer.* **4** *v.* to act in return to a call, signal, etc.; respond: *I knocked on the door, but no one answered. She answered the doorbell.* **5** *n.* solution to a problem: *What is the correct answer to this arithmetic problem?* **6** *v.* to be responsible: *The bus driver must answer for the safety of the children in the bus.* **7** *v.* to be similar to; agree with; correspond: *The dog we found answers to your description.* **8** *v.* to meet or satisfy a requirement, wish, etc.; serve: *On the picnic, a newspaper answered for a tablecloth.* [**Answer** comes from old English words meaning "against" and "to swear." Originally, an answer was a reply in a law court, sworn under oath.]

answer back, to reply in a rude, impertinent way: *When the teacher scolded the pupil he answered back.*

an·swer·a·ble (an′sər ə bəl), *adj.* **1** responsible: *The club treasurer is held answerable to the club for the money collected or spent.* **2** able to be answered: *That question is easily answerable.*

answering machine, a device that answers telephone calls automatically, records messages, and plays messages back later.

ant (ant), *n.* any of many small crawling insects living in large colonies either in the ground or in wood. Ants are black, brown, reddish, or yellowish. [**Ant** comes from an old English word meaning "to cut off." Ants cut leaves or other food into pieces they can carry.] ■ Another word that sounds like this is **aunt.** **—ant′like′,** *adj.*

-ant, *suffix.* someone or something that ___s: *assistant = a person that assists; pollutant = something that pollutes.*

ant., antonym.

ant·ac·id (ant′as′id), *n.* substance that neutralizes acids. Baking soda is an antacid.

an·tag·o·nism (an tag′ə niz′əm), *n.* active opposition; hostility: *During the argument, the boy's antagonism showed plainly in his face.*

an·tag·o·nist (an tag′ə nist), *n.* person who fights, struggles, or contends against another in a combat or contest of any kind; adversary; opponent: *The knight defeated each antagonist who came against him.*

an·tag·o·nis·tic (an tag′ə nis′tik), *adj.* acting against each other; opposing; hostile: *Cats and dogs are antagonistic.* **—an·tag′o·nis′ti·cal·ly,** *adv.*

an·tag·o·nize (an tag′ə nīz), *v.* to make an enemy of; arouse dislike in: *Her unkind remarks antagonized people who had been her friends.* ❑ *v.* **an·tag·o·nized, an·tag·o·niz·ing.**

An·ta·na·na·ri·vo (än′tä nä′nä rē′vō), *n.* capital of Madagascar, in the central part.

ant·arc·tic (ant′ärk′tik *or* ant′är′tik), **1** *adj.* at or near the South Pole; of the south polar region. **2** *n.* **the Antarctic,** the south polar region. [**Antarctic** comes from Greek words meaning "the opposite of" and "northern." See Word Story at **arctic.**]

Ant·arc·ti·ca (ant′ärk′tə kə *or* ant′är′tə kə), *n.* continent around or near the South Pole. It is almost totally covered by ice and lies within the antarctic circle.

antarctic circle or **Antarctic Circle,** the imaginary boundary of the south polar region. It runs parallel to the equator at 23 degrees 30 minutes (23°30′) north of the South Pole. See **Antarctica** for map.

ant bear, a large South American anteater with long front claws, a very slender head, and a shaggy, gray coat with a black band on the chest.

ant·eat·er (ant′ē′tər), *n.* any of various mammals that eat ants and termites, which they catch with their long, sticky tongues.

anteater—about 3 ft. 6 in. (1.1 m) long, with tail

an·te·bel·lum (an′ti bel′əm), *adj.* **1** before the war. **2** before the American Civil War.

an·te·ced·ent (an′tə sēd′nt), **1** *n.* the noun or noun phrase to which a pronoun refers. In "The dog which killed the rat is brown," *dog* is the antecedent of *which.* **2** *adj.* coming or happening before; previous: *Cave dwellers lived in a period of history antecedent to written records.* **3** *n.* a previous happening or event. **4** *n.pl.* **antecedents, a** past life or history: *No one knew the antecedents of the mysterious stranger.* **b** ancestors: *She has Polish antecedents.*

an·te·cham·ber (an′ti chām′bər), *n.* anteroom.

an·te·date (an′ti dāt), *v.* **1** to be or happen before; precede: *Radio antedated TV.* **2** to give an earlier date to something. ❑ *v.* **an·te·dat·ed, an·te·dat·ing.**

an·te·di·lu·vi·an (an′ti də lü′vē ən), *adj.* **1** very old; old-fashioned. **2** before the Flood.

an·te·lope (an′tl ōp), *n.* **1** any of numerous hoofed mammals of Africa and Asia that are related to the goat and cow but resemble the deer. Antelopes chew the cud and usually have a single pair of hollow horns that curve backward and do not fork or branch. **2** pronghorn. ❑ *n., pl.* **an·te·lope** or **an·te·lopes.**

an·te me·rid·i·em (an′tē mə rid′ē əm), LATIN. before noon; A.M.

an·ten·na (an ten′ə), *n.* **1** one of the long, slender feelers on the head of an insect, lobster, etc. **2** device used in television or radio for sending out or receiving sounds and pictures; aerial. Antennas may be large dish-shaped structures, sets of narrow rods, or simple lengths of wire. ❑ *n., pl.* **an·ten·nae** (an ten′ē) or **an·ten·nas** for 1, **an·ten·nas** for 2.

an·te·ri·or (an tir′ē ər), *adj.* **1** more to the front; fore: *The anterior part of a fish contains the head and gills.* **2** going before; earlier: *events anterior to the last war.*

an·te·room (an′ti rüm′), *n.* a small room leading to a larger one; waiting room; antechamber.

an·them (an′thəm), *n.* **1** song of praise, devotion, or patriotism: *"The Star-Spangled Banner" is the national anthem of the United States.* **2** piece of sacred music, usually with words from some passage in the Bible.

an·ther (an′thər), *n.* the part of the stamen of a flower that bears the pollen.

a	hat	ė	term	ô	order	ch	child		
ā	age	i	it	oi	oil	ng	long		a in about
ä	far	ī	ice	ou	out	sh	she	ə	e in taken
â	care	o	hot	u	cup	th	thin		i in pencil
e	let	ō	open	u̇	put	ŦH	then		o in lemon
ē	equal	ô	saw	ü	rule	zh	measure		u in circus

ant·hill (ant'hil'), *n.* heap of earth piled up by ants around the entrance to their tunnels.

an·thol·o·gy (an thol'ə jē), *n.* collection of poems or prose selections, usually from various authors. □ *n., pl.* **an·thol·o·gies.** [**Anthology** comes from a Greek word meaning "collection of flowers."]

An·tho·ny (an'thə nē), *n.* **Su·san B.** (sü'zn), 1820-1906, American leader in the women's rights movement. ■ **Susan B. Anthony** worked for laws to give married women the right to own property, keep their own wages, and have custody of their children after a divorce. She was the first woman to have her picture on a U.S. coin.

an·thra·cite (an'thrə sīt), *n.* coal that burns with very little smoke and flame; hard coal. It is almost pure carbon.

an·thrax (an'thraks), *n.* an often fatal disease of cattle, sheep, etc., that may be caught by human beings.

an·thro·poid (an'thrə poid), **1** *adj.* resembling a human being. Anthropoid apes have no tail and lack cheek pouches. **2** *n.* ape that resembles a human being. Gorillas, chimpanzees, orangutans, and gibbons are anthropoids.

an·thro·pol·o·gy (an'thrə pol'ə jē), *n.* the science or study of human beings, dealing especially with their fossil remains, physical characteristics, cultures, customs, and beliefs. [**Anthropology** comes from Greek words meaning "study of a human being."] —**an'thro·po·log'i·cal,** *adj.* —**an'thro·pol'o·gist,** *n.*

an·thro·po·mor·phism (an'thrə pə môr'fiz'əm), *n.* idea that animals or things have human qualities or thoughts, as in fables.

anti-, *prefix.* **1** against ___: *antiaircraft = against aircraft.* **2** preventing or counteracting ___: *antifreeze = preventing water from freezing.*

an·ti·air·craft (an'tē âr'kraft'), *adj.* used in defense against enemy aircraft.

an·ti·bal·lis·tic mis·sile (an'ti bə lis'tik), a guided missile able to seek, hit, and destroy a ballistic missile already in flight.

an·ti·bi·ot·ic (an'ti bī ot'ik), *n.* substance produced by a living thing, especially a bacterium or mold, that destroys or weakens germs. Penicillin is an antibiotic. Antibiotics are prescribed to treat bacterial infections.

an·ti·bod·y (an'ti bod'ē), *n.* any of many proteins produced in the blood that destroy or weaken bacteria and help prevent infection. □ *n., pl.* **an·ti·bod·ies.**

an·tic (an'tik), **1** *n.* Usually, **antics,** *pl.* funny gestures or actions; silly tricks: *The clown's antics amused us.* **2** *adj.* odd, strange; fantastic: *antic behavior.*

WORD STORY **Antic** comes from a Latin word meaning "ancient." **Antique** comes from the same Latin word. Some ancient Roman buildings had odd, fantastic drawings on the walls. When these were discovered centuries later, people used "old drawings" to mean "odd drawings." Because the two meanings are really so different, they developed different spellings and pronunciations.

an·ti·christ (an'ti krīst'), *n.* **1** a person who opposes Jesus. **2 Antichrist,** an expected powerful enemy of Jesus and his church, predicted to wage war against the church and to be defeated.

an·tic·i·pate (an tis'ə pāt), *v.* **1** to look forward to; expect: *We are anticipating a good time at your party.* ■ See Synonym Study at **expect. 2** to do before others do; be ahead of in doing: *The Chinese anticipated the European discovery of gunpowder.* **3** to take care of ahead of time; consider in advance: *We anticipated hot weather and brought our bathing suits.* □ *v.* **an·tic·i·pat·ed, an·tic·i·pat·ing.** —**an·tic'i·pa'tor,** *n.*

an·tic·i·pa·tion (an tis'ə pā'shən), *n.* act of anticipating; looking forward to; expectation: *In anticipation of a cold winter, they cut extra firewood.*

an·ti·cli·mac·tic (an'ti klī mak'tik), *adj.* of or like an anticlimax. —**an'ti·cli·mac'ti·cal·ly,** *adv.*

an·ti·cli·max (an'ti klī'maks), *n.* **1** an abrupt descent from the important to the trivial or unimportant. **2** a thing or event that is much less important or interesting than what has gone before: *After all the publicity, the movie itself was an anticlimax.* □ *n., pl.* **an·ti·cli·max·es.**

an·ti·cline (an'ti klīn), *n.* (in geology) a fold of rock layers that bends down on both sides from the center. —**an'ti·cli'nal,** *adj.*

anticline

an·ti·cy·clone (an'ti sī'klōn), *n.* winds moving around and away from a center of high pressure, which also moves.

an·ti·dote (an'ti dōt), *n.* **1** medicine or remedy that counteracts the harmful effects of a poison: *Milk is an antidote for some poisons.* **2** remedy for anything that is harmful: *Education is an antidote for ignorance.*

An·tie·tam (an tē'təm), *n.* small creek in NW Maryland. A major battle of the Civil War was fought near it in 1862 between Lee and McClellan which resulted in Lee's retreat.

an·ti·freeze (an'ti frēz'), *n.* substance added to a liquid to lower its freezing point. The antifreeze in a car's radiator prevents the water from freezing.

an·ti·gen (an'tə jən), *n.* any foreign substance, such as a protein or carbohydrate, that causes the body to produce antibodies to counteract it.

An·ti·gua and Bar·bu·da (an tē'gwə ənd bär bü'də *or* an tē'gə ənd bär bü'də), island country in the West Indies. *Capital:* St. John's.

an·ti·his·ta·mine (an'ti his'tə mēn'), *n.* medicine that helps to relieve the symptoms of colds and allergies.

an·ti·knock (an'ti nok'), *n.* substance added to the fuel of an internal-combustion engine to reduce noise caused by too rapid combustion.

An·til·les (an til'ēz), *n.pl.* chain of islands in the West Indies. The **Greater Antilles** are Cuba, Hispaniola, Puerto Rico, and Jamaica; the **Lesser Antilles** are smaller islands southeast of Puerto Rico, including the Windward and Leeward Islands.

an·ti·lock brakes (an'ti lok), brakes that help keep a car or truck from skidding. They are made so that brake pressure is applied to the wheels very briefly, over and over. Such pressure keeps the brakes and wheels from sticking in one position and causing a skid.

an·ti·lo·ga·rithm (an'ti lo'gə riŧH əm), *n.* a number that goes with a logarithm of a certain base. It is the base raised to the power shown by the logarithm. If the base is 10, the antilogarithms of the logarithms 1, 2, and 3 are 10, 100, and 1000.

an·ti·mat·ter (an'ti mat'ər), *n.* (in physics) matter made of subatomic particles that have ordinary mass but the opposite of ordinary electric charge. When antimatter comes in contact with ordinary matter, both disappear and much energy is released.

an·ti·mis·sile (an'ti mis'əl), *adj.* used in defense against ballistic missiles, rockets, etc.: *antimissile missiles.*

an·ti·mo·ny (an'tə mō'nē), *n.* a brittle, silver-white, metallic element. It occurs chiefly in combination with other elements. Antimony is used to make alloys harder and its compounds are used to make medicines, pigments, and glass. *Symbol:* Sb

an·ti·neu·tron (an'ti nü'tron), *n.* antiparticle of the neutron.

an·ti·par·ti·cle (an'ti pär'tə kəl), *n.* a subatomic particle with the same mass as another particle, but with the opposite electrical charge. When antiparticles collide, they disappear, and their mass becomes energy.

an·tip·a·thy (an tip′ə thē), *n.* **1** a strong dislike; a feeling against: *He felt an antipathy to snakes.* **2** anything that arouses such a feeling. ❑ *n., pl.* **an·tip·a·thies** for 2.

an·ti·per·spir·ant (an′ti pėr′spər ənt), *n.* a chemical preparation that is applied to the skin to decrease perspiration and control body odor.

an·tip·o·des (an tip′ə dēz′), *n.pl.* **1** two places on directly opposite sides of the earth: *The North Pole and the South Pole are antipodes.* **2** two complete opposites: *Forgiveness and revenge are antipodes.*

an·ti·pol·lu·tion (an′ti pə lü′shən), *adj.* designed to reduce or prevent pollution: *antipollution clean-air laws.*

an·ti·pro·ton (an′ti prō′ton), *n.* antiparticle of the proton.

an·ti·quar·i·an (an′tə kwer′ē ən), **1** *adj.* of antiques or antiquaries: *the antiquarian section of a museum.* **2** *n.* antiquary.

an·ti·quar·y (an′tə kwer′ē), *n.* student or collector of relics from ancient times. ❑ *n., pl.* **an·ti·quar·ies.**

an·ti·quat·ed (an′tə kwā′tid), *adj.* **1** that has grown old but is no longer valued; old-fashioned; out-of-date: *Most science books written 20 years ago are now antiquated.* **2** too old for work or service.

an·tique (an tēk′), **1** *adj.* of times long ago; from times long ago: *This antique chair was made in 1750.* **2** *n.* something made long ago: *This carved chest is a genuine antique.* [See Word Story at **antic**.] —**an·tique′ly,** *adv.* —**an·tique′ness,** *n.*

antique (def. 1)—antique stove

an·tiq·ui·ty (an tik′wə tē), *n.* **1** great age; oldness: *This vase is of such antiquity that it is priceless.* **2** times long ago, especially the period of history between 5000 B.C. and A.D. 476: *Troy was a city of antiquity.* **3** the people of ancient times. **4** **antiquities,** *pl.* things from times long ago: *antiquities in a museum.*

an·ti-Se·mit·ic (an′ti sə mit′ik), *adj.* prejudiced against Jews.

an·ti-Sem·i·tism (an′ti sem′ə tiz′əm), *n.* dislike or hatred for Jews; prejudice against Jews.

an·ti·sep·tic (an′tə sep′tik), **1** *n.* substance that prevents the growth of germs that cause infection. Iodine, peroxide, alcohol, and boric acid are antiseptics. **2** *adj.* preventing infection. [**Antiseptic** is from **anti-** and **septic.** **Septic** comes from a Greek word meaning "to rot."] —**an′ti·sep′ti·cal·ly,** *adv.*

an·ti·slav·er·y (an′ti slā′vər ē), *adj.* opposed to slavery; against slavery.

an·ti·so·cial (an′ti sō′shəl), *adj.* **1** opposed to the principles upon which society is based: *Stealing is an antisocial act.* **2** opposed to friendly relationship and normal companionship with others: *Hermits are antisocial.*

an·tith·e·sis (an tith′ə sis), *n.* **1** the direct opposite: *Hate is the antithesis of love.* **2** opposition; contrast: *the antithesis between theory and fact.* ❑ *n., pl.* **an·tith·e·ses** (an tith′ə sēz′).

an·ti·tox·in (an′ti tok′sən), *n.* **1** antibody formed in response to the presence of a toxin to prevent or reduce the effects of that toxin. **2** serum containing antitoxin, injected to create immunity to disease.

an·ti·trust (an′ti trust′), *adj.* opposed to large corporations that stifle competition and so control the trade practices of certain kinds of businesses.

ant·ler (ant′lər), *n.* **1** bony, horn-like growth on the head of a male deer, elk, or moose, usually growing in pairs and having one or more branches. Antlers are shed once a year and grow back again during the next year. **2** branch of such a horn. [**Antler** comes from Latin words meaning "in front of" and "eye." **Antler** used to mean the branch of a horn closest to the animal's eye.]

antler (def. 1)

ant lion, insect whose larva digs a pit, where it waits to catch ants and other insects as they fall in.

Antoinette, Marie. See **Marie Antoinette.**

An·to·ny (an′tə nē), *n.* **Mark,** 83?-30 B.C., Roman general and political leader. ■ **Mark Antony** is a character in two of Shakespeare's plays, *Antony and Cleopatra* and *Julius Caesar.* In *Julius Caesar,* he makes a famous speech that begins, "Friends, Romans, countrymen, lend me your ears."

an·to·nym (an′tə nim), *n.* word that means the opposite of another word. "True" is the antonym of "false"; "up" is the antonym of "down." [**Antonym** comes from Greek words meaning "opposite" and "name."]

Ant·werp (ant′wərp), *n.* port in NW Belgium.

A·nu·bis (ə nyü′bis), *n.* Egyptian god of the dead, shown as a man with a jackal's head.

a·nus (ā′nəs), *n.* the opening at the lower end of the alimentary canal, through which solid waste material passes from the body ❑ *n., pl.* **a·nus·es.**

an·vil (an′vəl), *n.* **1** an iron or steel block on which metals are hammered and shaped. **2** the central bone of three small bones in the middle ear of human beings and other mammals. It is shaped something like an anvil. See picture at **ear**[1].

anx·i·e·ty (ang zī′ə tē), *n.* **1** uneasy thoughts or fears about what may happen; troubled; worried, or uneasy feeling: *We all felt anxiety when the airplane was caught in the storm.* **2** eager desire: *Her anxiety to succeed led her to work hard.* ❑ *n., pl.* **anx·i·e·ties** for 1.

anx·ious (angk′shəs *or* ang′shəs), *adj.* **1** uneasy because of thoughts or fears of what may happen; troubled; worried: *I felt very anxious about my final exams last year.* **2** causing uneasy feelings or troubled thoughts; distressing: *The week of the flood was an anxious time for all of us.* **3** wishing very much; eager: *He was anxious for a bicycle. She was anxious to learn to play chess.* ■ See Synonym Study at **eager.** —**anx′ious·ly,** *adv.* —**anx′ious·ness,** *n.*

WORD STORY **Anxious** comes from a Latin word meaning "to choke" or "to cause distress." Fear and pain can cause a choking feeling. We may say today, if we are too anxious to do well in a game or performance, that we choked.

an·y (en′ē), **1** *adj.* one out of many: *Choose any book you like from the books on the shelf.* **2** *adj., pron.* some: *Have you any fresh fruit? I need more ink; have you any?* **3** *adj.* every: *Any child knows that.* **4** *adj.* even a little; even one or two: *Because of an allergy, I can't eat any chocolate.* **5** *adv.* to some extent or degree; at all: *Have I improved any?*

an·y·bod·y (en′ē bod′ē), **1** *pron.* any person; anyone: *Has anybody been here?* **2** *n.* an important person: *Everybody who's anybody stays at that hotel.*

an·y·how (en′ē hou), *adv.* **1** in any case; at least: *I can see as well as you can, anyhow.* **2** in any way whatever: *The answer is wrong anyhow you look at it.*

an·y·more (en′ē môr′), *adv.* at present; now; currently: *We seldom see them anymore.* ■ See Usage Note at **anyone.**

a	hat	ė	term	ô	order	ch	child		
ā	age	i	it	oi	oil	ng	long		a in about
ä	far	ī	ice	ou	out	sh	she		e in taken
â	care	o	hot	u	cup	th	thin	ə	i in pencil
e	let	ō	open	ů	put	ᵫ	then		o in lemon
ē	equal	ô	saw	ü	rule	zh	measure		u in circus

an·y·one (en′ē wun), *pron.* any person; anybody: *Can anyone go to this movie or is it just for adults?*

USAGE NOTE People sometimes confuse **anyone** and the two-word phrase **any one**. Anyone is written as one word when the accent is on **any**: *Can anyone tell me where they went?* It is written as two words when the accent is on **one**: *I'd like any one of those shirts.* The same is true of other words and phrases with **any**, including **anymore, anyplace, anything, anytime,** and **anyway.**

an·y·place (en′ē plās), *adv.* anywhere. ■ See Usage Note at **anyone.**

an·y·thing (en′ē thing), **1** *pron.* any thing: *Do you have anything to eat?* ■ See Usage Note at **anyone.** **2** *n.* a thing of any kind whatever: *My dog will eat almost anything.* **3** *adv.* in any way; at all: *My bike isn't anything like yours.*

anything but, not at all: *This old shack is anything but warm.*

an·y·time (en′ē tim), *adv.* at any time; no matter when: *You are welcome to visit us anytime.* ■ See Usage Note at **anyone.**

an·y·way (en′ē wā), *adv.* **1** in any case; at least: *I am coming anyway, no matter what you say.* ■ See Usage Note at **anyone.** **2** in any way whatever; carelessly; anyhow: *She stacked the books on the floor just anyway.*

government. **2** lack of feeling: *She reacted to her former friend's troubles with apathy.* [**Apathy** comes from Greek words meaning "without feeling."]

a·pat·o·saur·us (ə pat′ə sôr′əs), *n.* a huge plant-eating dinosaur with a very long neck and tail; brontosaurus. ❑ *n., pl.* **a·pat·o·saur·us·es, a·pat·o·saur·i** (ə pat′ə sôr′ī).

WORD STORY **Apatosaurus** comes from Greek words meaning "to deceive" and "lizard," because its fossil bones look like the bones of another dinosaur, and scientists were deceived when they first identified it. **Brontosaurus** comes from Greek words meaning "thunder" and "lizard," because people imagined the sound of this giant's footsteps being as loud as thunder. **Apatosaurus** is the scientific name because it was given by the first discoverer. **Brontosaurus** was given later and was more common for a long time.

ape (āp), **1** *n.* any large, tailless monkey with long arms, able to stand almost erect and walk on two feet. **2** *n.* any monkey. **3** *v.* to imitate; mimic: *They aped the mannerisms of their favorite TV stars.* **4** *n.* person who imitates or mimics. ❑ *v.* **aped, ap·ing.** —**ape′like′,** *adj.* —**ap′er,** *n.*

ape (def. 1)—Chimpanzees, gorillas, orangutans, and gibbons are apes.

an·y·where (en′ē wâr), *adv.* in, at, or to any place: *I'll meet you anywhere you say.*

an·y·wise (en′ē wiz), *adv.* in any way; to any degree; at all.

An·zi·o (an′zē ō), *n.* port in central Italy, on the Tyrrhenian Sea. Allied troops made an amphibious landing there in 1944.

A-OK (ā′ō′kā′), *adj., adv., interj.* INFORMAL. OK.

A one or **A-one,** INFORMAL. first-class; excellent: *an A one job of cleaning the garage.*

a·or·ta (ā ôr′tə), *n.* the main artery that carries the blood from the left side of the heart to all parts of the body except the lungs. ❑ *n., pl.* **a·or·tas, a·or·tae** (ā ôr′tē′).

a·pace (ə pās′), *adv.* very soon; swiftly; fast: *The summer flew by, and the time for school was coming on apace.*

A·pach·e (ə pach′ē), *n.* member of a tribe of American Indians living in Arizona, New Mexico, and Oklahoma. ❑ *n., pl.* **A·pach·e** or **A·pach·es.**

a·part (ə pärt′), *adv.* **1** to pieces; in pieces; in separate parts: *They took the watch apart to see how it runs.* **2** away from each other: *Keep the dogs apart.* **3** to one side; aside: *I set some money apart for a vacation each year.* **4** away from others; separately; independently: *View each idea apart.* —**a·part′ness,** *n.*

apart from, besides: *Apart from that, it was a good plan.*

tell apart, to see any difference between: *I can't tell the twins apart.*

a·part·heid (ə pärt′hāt or ə pärt′hīt), *n.* racial segregation as formerly officially practiced in South Africa. [**Apartheid** comes from a Dutch word meaning "apart" or "separate."]

a·part·ment (ə pärt′mənt), *n.* **1** room or group of rooms to live in; flat. **2** apartment house.

apartment house, building with a number of apartments in it.

ap·a·thet·ic (ap′ə thet′ik), *adj.* **1** with little interest or desire for action; indifferent: *The student's apathetic attitude toward schoolwork annoyed the teacher.* **2** lacking in feeling; unemotional. —**ap′a·thet′i·cal·ly,** *adv.*

ap·a·thy (ap′ə thē), *n.* **1** lack of interest or desire for action; indifference: *The citizens' apathy to local affairs resulted in poor*

Ap·en·nines (ap′ə nīnz), *n.pl.* the chief mountain range in Italy, extending north and south.

ap·er·ture (ap′ər chər), *n.* an opening; gap; hole. A diaphragm regulates the size of the aperture through which light passes into a camera. [See Word Story at **overture.**]

a·pex (ā′peks), *n.* **1** the highest point; tip: *The apex of a triangle is the point opposite the base.* **2** climax: *Her role in that film was the apex of her career.* ❑ *n., pl.* **a·pex·es** or **ap·i·ces.**

a·pha·sia (ə fā′zhə), *n.* a complete or partial loss of the ability to speak or understand words. ❑ *n., pl.* **a·pha·sias.**

a·phe·lion (ə fē′lyən), *n.* the point farthest from the sun in the orbit of a planet or comet. ❑ *n., pl.* **a·phe·lia** (ə fē′lyə).

a·phid (ā′fid or af′id), *n.* a very small insect that lives by sucking juices from plants; plant louse.

aph·o·rism (af′ə riz′əm), *n.* a short sentence expressing a general truth or some practical wisdom; maxim; proverb. EXAMPLE: "Live and let live."

aph·ro·dis·i·ac (af′rə dē′zē ak), **1** *adj.* increasing sexual desire. **2** *n.* any food or drug that increases sexual desire.

Aph·ro·di·te (af′rə dī′tē), *n.* Greek goddess of love and beauty. The Romans called her Venus.

A·pi·a (ä pē′ə or ä′pē ə), *n.* port and capital of Western Samoa.

a·pi·ar·y (ā′pē er′ē), *n.* place where bees are kept; group of beehives. ❑ *n., pl.* **a·pi·ar·ies.**

ap·i·ces (ap′ə sēz′ or ā′pə sēz′), *n.* a plural of **apex.**

a·piece (ə pēs′), *adv.* for each one; each: *These apples cost 25 cents apiece.*

ap·ish (ā′pish), *adj.* **1** foolish; silly: *I hid my embarrassment with an apish grin.* **2** like an ape. —**ap′ish·ly,** *adv.* —**ap′ish·ness,** *n.*

a·plomb (ə plom′), *n.* self-possession; assurance; poise.

APO or **A.P.O.,** Army Post Office.

A·poc·a·lypse (ə pok′ə lips), *n.* the last book of the New Testament; the book of Revelation.

A·poc·ry·pha (ə pok′rə fə), *n.pl.* fourteen books included in the Roman Catholic Bible but not generally found in Jewish or Protestant Bibles.

a·poc·ry·phal (ə pok′rə fəl), *adj.* **1** of doubtful genuineness; false: *apocryphal stories about a gigantic ape living in the hills.* **2 Apocryphal,** of or from the Apocrypha. —**a·poc′ry·phal·ly,** *adv.*

ap·o·gee (ap′ə jē), *n.* the point farthest from Earth in the orbit of the moon or any other Earth satellite. ❑ *n., pl.* **ap·o·gees.**

A·pol·lo (ə pol′ō), *n.* Greek and Roman god of the sun, poetry, music, prophecy, and healing; Phoebus.

a·pol·o·get·ic (ə pol′ə jet′ik), *adj.* **1** making an excuse; expressing regret: *He sent an apologetic note saying he could not attend the party.* **2** defending by speech or writing. —**a·pol′o·get′i·cal·ly,** *adv.*

a·pol·o·gist (ə pol′ə jist), *n.* person who defends an idea, belief, religion, etc., in speech or writing.

a·pol·o·gize (ə pol′ə jiz), *v.* **1** to make an apology; say you are sorry; offer an excuse: *I apologized for being so late.* **2** to defend an idea, argument, belief, etc., in speech or writing. ❑ *v.* **a·pol·o·gized, a·pol·o·giz·ing.** —**a·pol′o·giz′er,** *n.*

a·pol·o·gy (ə pol′ə jē), *n.* **1** words saying you are sorry for an offense, fault, or accident; explanation asking pardon: *Will you accept my apology for yelling at you?* **2** explanation of the truth or justice of something; defense: *Thomas Paine's "Common Sense" is an apology for American independence.* **3** a poor substitute; makeshift: *One piece of toast is a skimpy apology for a breakfast.* ❑ *n., pl.* **a·pol·o·gies.**

ap·o·plec·tic (ap′ə plek′tik), *adj.* **1** of or causing apoplexy. **2** suffering from apoplexy. **3** showing symptoms of a tendency to apoplexy. —**ap′o·plec′ti·cal·ly,** *adv.*

ap·o·plex·y (ap′ə plek′sē), *n.* stroke[1] (def. 4).

a·pos·tle or **A·pos·tle** (ə pos′əl), *n.* **1** one of the twelve disciples, **the Apostles,** chosen by Jesus to preach the gospel to all the world. **2** any early Christian leader or missionary: *Paul was frequently called the "Apostle to the Gentiles."* [**Apostle** comes from a Greek word meaning "messenger."]

ap·os·tol·ic or **Ap·os·tol·ic** (ap′ə stol′ik), *adj.* **1** of the Apostles. **2** of the pope; papal.

a·pos·tro·phe (ə pos′trə fē), *n.* sign (') used: **1** to show the omission of one or more letters in contractions, as in *isn't* for *is not, thro'* for *through.* **2** to show the possessive forms of nouns or indefinite pronouns, as in *Lee's book, the lions' den,* and *everybody's business.* **3** to form plurals of letters and numbers: *There are two o's in apology and four 9's in 959,990.*

apothecaries' measure, system of units used to measure volume in mixing and dispensing liquid drugs.

apothecaries' weight, system of weights used in mixing drugs and filling prescriptions.

a·poth·e·car·y (ə poth′ə ker′ē), *n.* OLD USE. person who prepares and sells drugs and medicines; pharmacist. ❑ *n., pl.* **a·poth·e·car·ies.**

WORD STORY **Apothecary** comes from a Greek word meaning "storehouse." The words **bodega** and **boutique** also come from this Greek word. These are all words for a person or place with many things to sell.

Ap·pa·la·chia (ap′ə lā′chə), *n.* region in the E United States covering parts of 11 states from N Pennsylvania to N Alabama.

Ap·pa·la·chian Mountains (ap′ə lā′chən), the chief mountain system in E North America, extending from Quebec Province in Canada to central Alabama.

Ap·pa·la·chians (ap′ə lā′chənz), *n.pl.* Appalachian Mountains.

ap·pall (ə pol′), *v.* to fill with horror or fear; dismay; terrify: *The thought of war appalled us.*

ap·pall·ing (ə po′ling), *adj.* causing horror; dismaying; terrifying. —**ap·pall′ing·ly,** *adv.*

Ap·pa·loo·sa (ap′ə lü′sə), *n.* a horse with dark spots, usually on the rump, on a roan background ❑ *n., pl.* **Ap·pa·loo·sas.**

Appaloosa

ap·pa·ra·tus (ap′ə rā′təs or ap′ə rat′əs), *n.* **1** the tools, machines, or other equipment necessary to carry out a purpose or for a particular use. Test tubes, beakers, and a Bunsen burner are part of the apparatus used in chemistry. **2** the organs of the body which together perform a particular function. The stomach and intestines are part of our digestive apparatus. ❑ *n., pl.* **ap·pa·ra·tus** or **ap·pa·ra·tus·es.**

ap·par·el (ə par′əl), **1** *n.* clothing; dress: *Does this store sell women's apparel?* **2** *v.* to clothe; dress up: *The circus performers were gaudily appareled.* ❑ *v.* **ap·par·eled, ap·par·el·ing** or **ap·par·elled, ap·par·el·ling.**

ap·par·ent (ə par′ənt), *adj.* **1** plain to see or understand; so plain that you cannot help seeing or understanding it: *It was apparent from the way she walked that she was very tired. It is apparent that she enjoys her work.* **2** appearing to be; seeming: *With over half the votes counted, he was the apparent winner.* —**ap·par′ent·ly,** *adv.*

apparent magnitude, a measure of how bright a star appears to be from Earth.

ap·pa·ri·tion (ap′ə rish′ən), *n.* **1** ghost or phantom: *The apparition, clothed in white, glided through the wall.* **2** the appearance of something strange, remarkable, or unexpected.

ap·peal (ə pēl′), **1** *v.* to make an earnest request; ask for help, sympathy, etc.: *When the children were in trouble they appealed to their parents for help.* **2** *n.* a call for help, sympathy, etc.; earnest request: *an appeal for forgiveness, an appeal for money for the poor.* **3** *v.* to call on some person to decide a matter in your favor: *When one of my parents says "No," I appeal to the other.* **4** *n.* a call on some person to decide a matter in your favor: *an appeal for another chance.* **5** *v.* to ask that a case be taken to a higher court or judge to be heard again. **6** *n.* a request to have a case heard again before a higher court or judge. **7** *v.* to be attractive, interesting, or enjoyable: *The blue and red wallpaper appeals to me.* **8** *n.* attraction or interest: *Television has a great appeal for most young people.*

ap·peal·ing (ə pē′ling), *adj.* having great appeal; attractive. —**ap·peal′ing·ly,** *adv.*

ap·pear (ə pir′), *v.* **1** to be seen; come in sight: *One by one the stars appear.* **2** to seem; look as if: *The apple appeared sound on the outside, but it was rotten inside.* **3** to be published: *Her latest book appeared a year ago.* **4** to come before the public as a performer or author: *The singer will appear on TV today.* **5** to become known to the mind; be plain: *It appears that we were mistaken.* **6** to present yourself formally before an authority: *A person accused of a crime must appear in court.*

ap·pear·ance (ə pir′əns), *n.* **1** act of coming in sight: *His sudden appearance in the doorway startled me.* **2** act of coming before the public as a performer or author: *a singer's first appearance.* **3** outward look: *a pleasing appearance.* **4** outward show; pretense: *They buy things they can't afford in order to keep up an appearance of wealth.*

ap·pease (ə pēz′), *v.* **1** to put an end to by satisfying an appetite or desire: *A good dinner will appease your hunger.* **2** to make calm or quiet; pacify: *We tried to appease the crying child by giving her candy.* **3** to give in to the demands of: *The boy appeased his parents and returned to finish school.* ❑ *v.* **ap·peased, ap·peas·ing.** —**ap·peas′er,** *n.*

SYNONYM STUDY **Appease** and **pacify** both mean to make calm. **Appease** means to calm someone by giving in to him or her: *The decision to appease Hitler only put off the start of World War II.* **Pacify** means to quiet someone who is angry or unhappy: *Cuddling will often pacify a crying baby.*

ap·pease·ment (ə pēz′mənt), *n.* **1** act of appeasing or the condition of being appeased; pacification; satisfaction. **2** policy of yielding to the demands of potential enemies, as a means of keeping peace.

a	hat	ė	term	ô	order	ch	child		
ā	age	i	it	oi	oil	ng	long		a in about
ä	far	ī	ice	ou	out	sh	she		e in taken
â	care	o	hot	u	cup	th	thin	ə	i in pencil
e	let	ō	open	ù	put	ŦH	then		o in lemon
ē	equal	ò	saw	ü	rule	zh	measure		u in circus

ap·pel·late court (ə pel′it), court having the power to examine again and reverse the decisions of a lower court.

ap·pel·la·tion (ap′ə lā′shən), *n.* name or title describing some quality. In "Richard the Lion-Hearted" the appellation of *Richard* is *the Lion-Hearted.*

ap·pend (ə pend′), *v.* to add to a larger thing; attach as a supplement: *The amendments to the Constitution of the United States are appended to it.*

ap·pend·age (ə pen′dij), *n.* thing attached to something larger or more important; addition. Arms, tails, fins, legs, etc., are appendages.

ap·pen·dec·to·my (ap′ən dek′tə mē), *n.* removal of the appendix by a surgical operation. ❏ *n., pl.* **ap·pen·dec·to·mies.**

ap·pen·di·ces (ə pen′də sēz′), *n.* a plural of **appendix.**

ap·pen·di·ci·tis (ə pen′də sī′tis), *n.* inflammation of the appendix.

ap·pen·dix (ə pen′diks), *n.* **1** addition at the end of a book or document, usually giving further details. **2** a small functionless sac attached to the large intestine; vermiform appendix. ❏ *n., pl.* **ap·pen·dix·es** or **ap·pen·di·ces.**

ap·per·tain (ap′ər tān′), *v.* to belong as a part; be connected; relate: *Forestry appertains to geography, to botany, and to agriculture.*

ap·pe·tite (ap′ə tīt), *n.* **1** desire for food: *Swimming increases my appetite.* **2** desire: *My grandparents have a great appetite for adventure.* [**Appetite** comes from a Latin word meaning "to long for" or "to seek."]

ap·pe·tiz·er (ap′ə tī′zər), *n.* something that arouses the appetite, usually served before a meal. Pickles and olives are appetizers.

ap·pe·tiz·ing (ap′ə tī/zing), *adj.* arousing or exciting the appetite: *Appetizing food always smells delicious.* ■ See Synonym Study at **tasty.** —**ap′pe·tiz′ing·ly,** *adv.*

ap·plaud (ə plôd′), *v.* **1** to show approval by clapping hands, shouting, etc.: *The audience applauded with great enthusiasm at the end of the play.* **2** to be pleased with; approve of: *My parents applauded my decision to stay in school.* —**ap·plaud′a·ble,** *adj.* —**ap·plaud′er,** *n.*

ap·plause (ə plôz′), *n.* **1** approval shown by clapping the hands, shouting, etc.: *Applause for the singer's good performance rang out from the audience.* **2** approval; praise.

ap·ple (ap′əl), *n.* the firm, fleshy, round fruit of a tree widely grown in temperate regions. Apples have red, yellow, or green skin, and are eaten either raw or cooked. —**ap′ple·like′,** *adj.*

apple of someone's eye, person or thing that is cherished or valued: *His granddaughter is the apple of his eye.*

apple butter, a dark brown, heavy jam, made by cooking apples and sugar.

ap·ple·sauce (ap′əl sôs′), *n.* apples cut in pieces and cooked with sugar, spices, and water until soft.

ap·pli·ance (ə plī′əns), *n.* device or machine designed for a particular purpose or operation. Vacuum cleaners, blenders, and refrigerators are household appliances.

ap·pli·ca·ble (ap′lə kə bəl), *adj.* capable of being applied; able to be put to practical use; appropriate; suitable: *The rule "Look before you leap" is almost always applicable.*

ap·pli·cant (ap′lə kənt), *n.* person who applies for something, such as a loan, a job, or admission to a school.

ap·pli·ca·tion (ap′lə kā′shən), *n.* **1** a request for something, such as employment, an award, a loan, etc.: *I filled out an application for a job at the supermarket.* **2** act of putting to use; use: *The application of what you know will help you solve new problems.* **3** way of using: *"Freedom" is a word of many applications.* **4** act of applying; putting on: *The painter's careless application of paint spattered the floor.* **5** something applied. Cold cream and ointments are applications. **6** continued effort; close attention: *Application to her work got her a promotion.*

ap·pli·ca·tor (ap′lə kā′tər), *n.* tool or device for applying something, such as a medicine, cosmetic, paint, etc.

ap·plied (ə plīd′), *adj.* put to practical use; used to solve actual problems: *The engineer used applied mathematics to solve the practical problems in building a bridge.*

ap·pli·qué (ap′lə kā′), **1** *n.* ornament made of one material sewed or otherwise fastened on another. **2** *v.* to trim or ornament with appliqué. ❏ *n.* **ap·pli·qués;** *v.* **ap·pli·quéd, ap·pli·qué·ing.**

appliqué (def. 1)

ap·ply (ə plī′), *v.* **1** to put on; lay on or in contact with: *She applied two coats of paint to the table. He applied a wet cloth to the bump on my head.* **2** to put to practical use; put into effect; use: *I know the rule but I don't know how to apply it.* **3** to use a word or expression to refer to a person or object: *They applied the nickname "Slowpoke" to the pet turtle.* **4** to be useful or suitable; fit: *When does this rule apply?* **5** to make a request; ask: *She is applying for a summer job.* **6** to set to work and stick to it: *He applied himself to learning to play the piano.* ❏ *v.* **ap·plied, ap·ply·ing.** —**ap·pli′er,** *n.*

ap·point (ə point′), *v.* **1** to name to an office or position; choose: *The class president appointed five students to the cleanup committee.* **2** to decide on; set: *to appoint a time for the meeting.* —**ap·point′er,** *n.* —**ap·point′ive,** *adj.*

ap·point·ee (ə poin′tē′), *n.* person who is appointed to an office or position. ❏ *n., pl.* **ap·point·tees.**

ap·point·ment (ə point′mənt), *n.* **1** act of naming to an office or position; choosing: *The President announced the appointment of his cabinet.* **2** office or position: *She has a government appointment.* **3** a meeting with someone at a certain time and place; engagement: *an appointment to see the doctor at four o'clock.* **4** **appointments,** *pl.* furniture; equipment: *an old hotel with shabby appointments.*

Ap·po·mat·tox (ap′ə mat′əks), *n.* town in central Virginia. Nearby, at **Appomattox Courthouse,** Lee surrendered to Grant on April 9, 1865. A national historical park commemorates this event.

ap·por·tion (ə pôr′shən), *v.* to divide and give out in fair shares; distribute according to some rule: *Their property was to be apportioned among their children.* —**ap·por′tion·ment,** *n.*

ap·po·site (ap′ə zit), *adj.* suitable; appropriate.

ap·po·si·tion (ap′ə zish′ən), *n.* the relationship to a noun of another noun or noun phrase which is placed after the first noun in order to explain it. In the sentence, "Mr. Brown, our next-door neighbor, has a new car," *Mr. Brown* and *our next-door neighbor* are in apposition.

ap·pos·i·tive (ə poz′ə tiv), *n.* a noun or noun phrase placed after another noun in order to explain the first noun. In the sentence, "Mr. Brown, our next-door neighbor, has a new car," *our next-door neighbor* is an appositive.

ap·prais·al (ə prā′zəl), *n.* estimate of value, amount, quality, etc.: *The bank's new appraisal of the worth of our house was $130,000. The coach gave a frank appraisal of her abilities as a gymnast.*

ap·praise (ə prāz′), *v.* **1** to estimate the value, amount, quality, etc., of: *An employer should be able to appraise an employee's work.* **2** to set a price on; fix the value of: *Property is appraised for taxation.* ❏ *v.* **ap·praised, ap·prais·ing.** —**ap·prais′er,** *n.* —**ap·prais′ing·ly,** *adv.*

ap·pre·ci·a·ble (ə prē′shē ə bəl), *adj.* enough to be felt or estimated; noticeable: *The slight hill made an appreciable difference in the ease of walking.* —**ap·pre′ci·a·bly,** *adv.*

ap·pre·ci·ate (ə prē′shē āt), *v.* **1** to think highly of; recognize the worth or quality of; value; enjoy: *Almost everybody appreciates good food.* **2** to be thankful for: *We appreciate your help.* **3** to have an opinion of the value, worth, or quality of; estimate: *Most people can appreciate the contributions of medical research to good health.* **4** to be fully aware of; recognize: *A musician is able to appreciate small differences in sounds.* **5** to rise in value: *This land will appreciate greatly as soon as good roads are built.* ❏ *v.* **ap·pre·ci·at·ed, ap·pre·ci·at·ing.** —**ap·pre′ci·a′tor,** *n.*

ap·pre·ci·a·tion (ə prē′shē ā′shən), *n.* **1** thankfulness; gratitude: *They showed their appreciation by sending flowers to their host-*

ess the next day. **2** understanding of the worth of something; recognition of something's value: *She has no appreciation of modern art.* **3** a rise in value: *She was pleased by the appreciation of her investments.*

ap·pre·ci·a·tive (ə prē′shə tiv *or* ə prē′shē ā′tiv), *adj.* having or showing appreciation; recognizing the value: *The appreciative audience applauded the performer.* **—ap·pre′ci·a·tive·ly,** *adv.*

ap·pre·hend (ap′ri hend′), *v.* **1** to arrest; seize. **2** to grasp with the mind; understand: *Though I couldn't hear him, I could apprehend his meaning from his gestures.*

ap·pre·hen·sion (ap′ri hen′shən), *n.* **1** fear; dread: *The roar of the hurricane filled us with apprehension.* **2** act of seizing; arrest: *The appearance of the suspect's picture in all the papers led to her apprehension.* **3** knowledge; understanding: *I have no apprehension of nuclear physics.*

ap·pre·hen·sive (ap′ri hen′siv), *adj.* feeling alarm; afraid, anxious, or worried: *I felt apprehensive before taking my first airplane trip.* **—ap′pre·hen′sive·ly,** *adv.* **—ap′pre·hen′sive·ness,** *n.*

ap·pren·tice (ə pren′tis), **1** *n.* person learning a trade or art. In return for instruction the apprentice agrees to work for the employer a certain length of time with little or no pay. **2** *v.* to place or take as an apprentice: *Benjamin Franklin's father apprenticed him to a printer.* **3** *n.* beginner; learner. ❑ *v.* **ap·pren·ticed, ap·pren·tic·ing.**

ap·pren·tice·ship (ə pren′tis ship), *n.* **1** condition of being an apprentice. **2** time during which a person is an apprentice.

ap·prise (ə prīz′), *v.* to give notice to; let know; inform: *Our teacher apprised us that there would be a test on Monday.* ❑ *v.* **ap·prised, ap·pris·ing.**

ap·proach (ə prōch′), **1** *v.* to come near or nearer to: *Walk softly as you approach the baby's crib. Winter is approaching. The wind was approaching a gale.* **2** *n.* act of coming near or nearer: *Sirens warned us of the approach of the fire truck. Sunset announces the approach of night.* **3** *n.* way by which a place or person can be reached; access: *The approach to the house was a narrow path. Our best approach to the senator lay through a mutual friend.* **4** *n.* method of starting work on a task or problem: *She seems to have a good approach to the problem.* **5** *v.* to make advances or overtures to: *He approached his boss for a raise.* ❑ *n., pl.* **ap·proach·es. —ap·proach′er,** *n.*

ap·proach·a·ble (ə prō′chə bəl), *adj.* **1** able to be approached; accessible: *The house on the mountain is approachable only on foot.* **2** easy to approach and talk to; friendly and sociable: *No matter how busy she was, our principal was always approachable.* **—ap·proach′a·bil′i·ty,** *n.*

ap·pro·ba·tion (ap′rə bā′shən), *n.* favorable opinion; approval; praise: *The play received the approbation of many critics.*

ap·pro·pri·ate (ə prō′prē it *for adj.;* ə prō′prē āt *for verb*), **1** *adj.* right for the occasion; suitable; proper: *Plain, simple clothes are appropriate for school wear.* **2** *v.* to set apart for some special use: *The state government appropriated money for a new road into our town.* **3** *v.* to take for yourself; use as your own: *You should not appropriate other people's belongings without my permission.* ❑ *v.* **ap·pro·pri·at·ed, ap·pro·pri·at·ing. —ap·pro′pri·ate·ly,** *adv.* **—ap·pro′pri·ate·ness,** *n.* **—ap·pro′pri·a′tive,** *adj.*

ap·pro·pri·a·tion (ə prō′prē ā′shən), *n.* **1** sum of money or other thing set apart: *Our town received a state appropriation of $20,000 for a new playground.* **2** act of setting apart for some special use: *The appropriation of land made it possible to have a park.*

ap·prov·al (ə prü′vəl), *n.* **1** favorable opinion; praise: *We all like others to show approval of what we do.* **2** permission; consent: *I have my parents' approval to go on the trip.*

on approval, so that the customer can inspect the item and decide whether to buy or return it: *We took home the TV set on approval, but brought it back because it didn't work properly.*

ap·prove (ə prüv′), *v.* **1** to think or speak well of; give a favorable opinion: *The teacher read my report and approved it.* **2** to authorize or make legal; consent to: *The school board approved the budget.* ❑ *v.* **ap·proved, ap·prov·ing. —ap·prov′ing·ly,** *adv.*

ap·prox·i·mate (ə prok′sə mit *for adj.;* ə prok′sə māt *for verb*), **1** *adj.* nearly correct: *The approximate length of a meter is 40 inches; the exact length is 39.37 inches.* **2** *v.* to come near to; approach: *Your account of what happened approximates the truth, but there are several small errors.* ❑ *v.* **ap·prox·i·mat·ed, ap·prox·i·mat·ing. —ap·prox′i·mate·ly,** *adv.*

ap·prox·i·ma·tion (ə prok′sə mā′shən), *n.* **1** a nearly correct amount; close estimate: *25,000 miles is an approximation of the circumference of the earth.* **2** version; approach: *Her story was a close approximation to the truth.*

ap·pur·te·nance (ə pėrt′n əns), *n.* addition to something more important; accessory. A radio in a car is an appurtenance; an engine is a necessity.

Apr., April.

a·pri·cot (ā′prə kot *or* ap′rə kot), **1** *n.* the round pale orange fruit of a tree grown in mild climates. Apricots have a downy skin and a large pit something like that of a peach, but are smaller. **2** *n.* a pale orange yellow. **3** *adj.* pale orange-yellow.

A·pril (ā′prəl), *n.* the fourth month of the year. It has 30 days. [**April** may come from the Latin name of the Greek goddess of love and beauty.]

April fool, person who gets fooled on April Fools' Day.

April Fools' Day, April 1, a day on which tricks and jokes are played on people; All Fools' Day.

a·pron (ā′prən), *n.* **1** item of clothing worn over the front part of the body to cover or protect clothes: *a carpenter's apron.* **2** area in front of an airport terminal or hangar on which to park aircraft. **3** area of a stage in front of the curtain. **—a′pron·like′,** *adj.*

ap·ro·pos (ap′rə pō′), *adj.* to the point; fitting; suitable: *Your remark is certainly apropos to what we are discussing.* [**Apropos** comes from French words meaning "to the purpose."]

apropos of, with regard to: *Apropos of the party, what are you going to wear?*

apse (aps), *n.* a semicircular or many-sided recess in a church, usually at the east end. The roof of an apse is arched or vaulted.

apt (apt), *adj.* **1** fitted by nature; likely: *A careless person is apt to make mistakes.* **2** right for the occasion; suitable; fitting: *His apt reply to the question showed that he had understood it very well.* **3** quick to learn: *She is an apt student and did well in school.* **—apt′ly,** *adv.* **—apt′ness,** *n.*

apt., apartment. ❑ *pl.* **apts.**

ap·ti·tude (ap′tə tüd), *n.* **1** natural tendency or talent; ability; capacity. **2** readiness in learning; quickness to understand: *She is a pupil of great aptitude.*

aq·ua (ak′wə), **1** *n.* a light bluish green. **2** *adj.* light bluish green.

aq·ua·cul·ture (ak′wə kul′chər), *n.* the science or business of growing plants, fish, or shellfish in water.

a	hat	ė	term	ô	order	ch	child		
ā	age	i	it	oi	oil	ng	long	ə	a in about
ä	far	ī	ice	ou	out	sh	she		e in taken
â	care	o	hot	u	cup	th	thin		i in pencil
e	let	ō	open	ů	put	ŦH	then		o in lemon
ē	equal	ò	saw	ü	rule	zh	measure		u in circus

Aqua-Lung (ak′wə lung′), *n.* trademark for an underwater breathing device used in skin diving; scuba.

aq·ua·ma·rine (ak′wə mə rēn′), **1** *n.* a transparent, blue-green, semiprecious stone that is a variety of beryl. **2** *n.* a light bluish green. **3** *adj.* light blue-green.

aq·ua·naut (ak′wə nòt), *n.* an underwater explorer.

aq·ua·plane (ak′wə plān′), **1** *n.* a wide board on which a person rides as it is towed by a speeding motorboat. **2** *v.* to ride on an aquaplane. ❑ *v.* **aq·ua·planed, aq·ua·plan·ing. —aq′ua·plan′er,** *n.*

a·quar·i·um (ə kwâr′ē əm), *n.* **1** tank or glass bowl in which fish or other water animals and water plants are kept in water. **2** building used for showing collections of live fish, water animals, and water plants. ❑ *n., pl.* **a·quar·i·ums, a·quar·i·a** (ə kwâr′ē ə). [**Aquarium** comes from a Latin word meaning "a watering place."]

A·quar·i·us (ə kwâr′ē əs), *n.* **1** group of stars shaped something like a person carrying a jar of water. **2** the eleventh sign of the zodiac, associated with the period from mid-January to mid-February.

a·quat·ic (ə kwat′ik *or* ə kwot′ik), *adj.* **1** growing or living in water: *Water lilies are aquatic plants.* **2** taking place in or on water: *Swimming and sailing are aquatic sports.*

aq·ue·duct (ak′wə dukt), *n.* **1** an artificial channel or large pipe for bringing water from a distance. **2** structure that supports such a channel or pipe.

aqueduct (def. 2)

a·que·ous (ā′kwē əs), *adj.* **1** of or made with water: *The druggist put the medicine in an aqueous solution.* **2** like water; watery: *Aqueous matter ran from the sore.*

aqueous humor, the watery liquid which fills the space in the eye between the cornea and the lens.

aq·ui·fer (ak′wə fər), *n.* a wide layer of underground earth or rock that contains water.

aq·ui·line (ak′wə lin *or* ak′wə lən), *adj.* curved like an eagle's beak; hooked.

WORD STORY **Aquiline** comes from a Latin word meaning "eagle." The word first came into English to describe a nose that is hooked or curved like an eagle's beak.

A·qui·nas (ə kwī′nəs), *n.* Saint **Thomas,** 1225?-1274, Italian philosopher and Roman Catholic theologian.

A·qui·no (ä kē′nō), *n.* **Cor·a·zón** (kôr ä zōn′), born 1933, Philippine political leader, president of the Philippines from 1986 to 1992.

Ar, symbol for argon.

AR, Arkansas (used with postal Zip Code).

Ar·ab (ar′əb), **1** *n.* person born or living in Arabia. **2** *n.* member of a Semitic people now widely scattered over southwestern and southern Asia and northern Africa. **3** *adj.* of the Arabs or Arabia.

ar·a·besque (ar′ə besk′), **1** *n.* an elaborate and fanciful design of flowers, leaves, geometrical figures, etc. **2** *adj.* carved or painted in arabesque. **3** *n.* a ballet pose in which the dancer stands on one leg, with the other at right angles to it, and with the arms held away from the body.

A·ra·bi·a (ə rā′bē ə), *n.* large peninsula in SW Asia.

A·ra·bi·an (ə rā′bē ən), **1** *adj.* of Arabia or the Arabs. **2** *n.* person born or living in Arabia; Arab.

Arabian Desert, desert in N Arabia.

Arabian horse, a swift, graceful saddle horse originally developed by the Arabs for use in the deserts.

Arabia

Arabian Nights, The, collection of old tales from Arabia, Persia, and India, dating from the A.D. 900s. It contains tales of Ali Baba, Aladdin, and many others.

Arabian Sea, part of the Indian Ocean between Arabia and India.

Ar·a·bic (ar′ə bik), **1** *n.* the Semitic language of the Arabs, related to Hebrew. Arabic is spoken chiefly in Arabia, Iraq, Syria, Jordan, Lebanon, and North Africa. **2** *adj.* of the language of the Arabs. **3** *adj.* of the Arabs or Arabia; Arabian.

WORD SOURCE **Arabic** has given a number of words to the English language, including the words below.

admiral	coffee	magazine	sequin
albatross	crimson	mask	sofa
alfalfa	ghoul	massage	spinach
algebra	giraffe	mattress	syrop
artichoke	hazard	safari	tambourine
assassin	lilac	satin	zero

Arabic numerals or **Arabic figures,** the figures 1, 2, 3, 4, 5, 6, 7, 8, 9, 0; Hindu-Arabic numerals. They are called Arabic because they were introduced into western Europe by Arabian scholars, but most probably they were derived from India.

ar·a·ble (ar′ə bəl), *adj.* fit for plowing: *There is not much arable land on the side of a rocky mountain.*

a·rach·nid (ə rak′nid), *n.* any of a large group of animals that includes spiders, scorpions, mites, ticks, and daddy-longlegs. Though they resemble insects, arachnids differ in having four pairs of legs, no wings, and a body usually divided into only two parts.

Ar·a·fat (är′ə fat′), *n.* **Yas·ir** (yä′sir), born 1929, Palestinian Arab political leader. He became chairman of the PLO in 1969.

Ar·a·gon (ar′ə gon), *n.* region in NE Spain, formerly a kingdom. See **Castile** for map.

Ar·al Sea (ar′əl), inland sea in Kazakhstan and Uzbekistan, east of the Caspian Sea.

Ar·a·ma·ic (ar′ə mā′ik), *n.* a Semitic language in which much Jewish and early Christian literature was written.

A·rap·a·ho (ə rap′ə hō), *n.* member of a tribe of North American Indians living formerly in Colorado and now in Wyoming, Montana, and Oklahoma. ❑ *n., pl.* **A·rap·a·ho** or **A·rap·a·hos.** [**Arapaho** comes from a Crow word meaning "many tattoos."]

Ar·a·rat (ar′ə rat′), *n.* mountain in E Turkey, 16,900 feet (5151 meters) high. Noah's Ark is said to have grounded there after the Flood.

A·rau·ca·ni·an (ə rou′kä′nē ən), *n.* member of a group of American Indian tribes living in southern Chile and nearby parts of Argentina.

Ar·a·wak (ar′ə wak), *n.* member of a tribe of American Indians formerly living in the West Indies. A few Arawak now live along the Amazon in Brazil. ❑ *n., pl.* **Ar·a·wak** or **Ar·a·waks.**

ar·bi·ter (är′bə tər), *n.* **1** person with full power to judge or decide: *an arbiter of good taste.* **2** person chosen to decide or settle a dispute; arbitrator.

ar·bi·trar·y (är′bə trer′ē), *adj.* **1** based on your own wishes, notions, or will; not going by any rule or law: *The judge tried to be fair and avoided arbitrary decisions.* **2** fixed or determined by chance: *an arbitrary choice.* **3** using or abusing unlimited power; tyrannical: *an arbitrary king.* **—ar′bi·trar′i·ly,** *adv.* **—ar′bi·trar′i·ness,** *n.*

ar·bi·trate (är′bə trāt), *v.* **1** to give a decision in a dispute; act as arbitrator; mediate: *The teacher arbitrated between the two girls* *in their quarrel.* **2** to settle by arbitration; submit to arbitration: *The two nations finally agreed to arbitrate their dispute and war was avoided.* ❏ *v.* **ar·bi·trat·ed, ar·bi·trat·ing.**

ar·bi·tra·tion (är′bə trā′shən), *n.* settlement of a dispute by the decision of a judge, umpire, or committee.

ar·bi·tra·tor (är′bə trā′tər), *n.* **1** person chosen to decide or settle a dispute. **2** person with full power to judge or decide; arbiter.

ar·bor (är′bər), *n.* a shaded place formed by trees or bushes or by vines growing on a wooden frame.

> **WORD STORY** **Arbor** comes from a Latin word meaning "herb" or "grass." In the next entry, **Arbor Day**, the word **arbor** comes from a different Latin word meaning "tree."

Arbor Day, day set aside in many states of the United States and other countries for planting trees. The date varies in different states. [See Word Story at **arbor**.]

ar·bo·re·al (är bôr′ē əl), *adj.* **1** living in or among trees. A squirrel is an arboreal animal. **2** of trees; like trees.

ar·bo·re·tum (är′bə rē′təm), *n.* place where trees and bushes are grown and exhibited for scientific and educational purposes. ❏ *n., pl.* **ar·bo·re·tums, ar·bo·re·ta** (är′bə rē′tə).

ar·bor·vi·tae (är′bər vī′tē), *n.* any of several evergreen trees with small scaly leaves, often planted for ornament and for hedges.

ar·bu·tus (är byü′təs), *n.* a trailing plant of eastern North America that has clusters of fragrant, pink or white flowers that bloom very early in the spring; mayflower. ❏ *n., pl.* **ar·bu·tus·es.**

arc (ärk), **1** *n.* any part of the circumference of a circle. **2** *n.* any part of any curved line. **3** *n.* a curved stream of brilliant light or sparks formed when a strong electric current jumps across a space from one conductor to another. **4** *v.* to form an electric arc. **5** *v.* to take or follow a curved path. ❏ *v.* **arced** (ärkt), **arc·ing** (är′king), or **arcked, arck·ing.** [**Arc** comes from a Latin word meaning "an arch" or "a bow." The words **arch**[1] and **archery** also come from this Latin word.] ■ Another word that sounds like this is **ark.**

ARC, (ā′är′sē′ *or* ärk), AIDS-related complex (a syndrome caused by the AIDS virus, which often develops into AIDS).

ar·cade (är kād′), *n.* **1** passageway with an arched roof. **2** any covered passageway: *This building has an arcade with small stores along either side.* **3** row of arches supported by columns. **4** a store in which customers pay to play games, especially video games.

Ar·ca·di·a (är kā′dē ə), *n.* **1** mountainous district in the S part of ancient Greece. It was famous for the simple, contented life of its people. **2** Also **arcadia,** any region of simple, quiet contentment. —**Ar·ca′di·an,** *adj., n.*

arch[1] (ärch), **1** *n.* a curved structure capable of bearing the weight of the material above it. Arches often form the tops of doors, windows, and gateways. **2** *n.* monument in the form of an arch or arches. **3** *v.* to bend into an arch; curve: *The cat arched its back and hissed at the barking dog.* **4** *v.* to form an arch over; span: *A bridge arched the stream.* **5** *n.* archway. **6** *n.* the lower part of the foot which makes a curve between the heel and the toes: *Fallen arches cause flat feet.* ❏ *n., pl.* **arch·es.** [See word history information at **arc**.]

arch[2] (ärch), *adj.* **1** playfully mischievous: *The girl gave her mother an arch look and left the room giggling.* **2** chief; principal; leading: *He was the arch rebel of them all.* —**arch′ly,** *adv.* —**arch′ness,** *n.*

> **WORD STORY** **Arch**[2] comes from a Greek word meaning "to be first" or "to lead." Because it was so often used about leading in bad behavior, it got a second meaning, "mischievous," which then grew milder and suggested playfulness.

arcade (def. 1)

arch-, *prefix.* main; most important ___: *archenemy = most important enemy.*

arch., **1** archipelago. **2** architecture.

ar·chae·ol·o·gy (är′kē ol′ə jē), *n.* the scientific study of the people, customs, and life of ancient times. Archaeologists study buildings, tools, pottery, weapons, and other objects in order to find out how people lived in the past when there were few or no written records. Also, **archeology.** —**ar′chae·o·log′i·cal,** *adj.* —**ar′chae·ol′o·gist,** *n.*

ar·chae·op·ter·yx (är′kē op′tər iks), *n.* the oldest known fossil bird, from the Jurassic. It was like a reptile because it had teeth and a bony tail. ❏ *n., pl.* **ar·chae·op·ter·yx·es.** [**Archaeopteryx** comes from Greek words meaning "ancient" and "wing."]

ar·cha·ic (är kā′ik), *adj.* **1** no longer in general use. The words *argosy* and *methinks* are archaic. **2** of an earlier time; out-of-date or ancient. —**ar·cha′i·cal·ly,** *adv.*

archaeopteryx—18 in. (46 cm) long

ar·cha·ism (är′kē iz′əm), *n.* word or expression no longer in general use.

arch·an·gel (ärk′ān′jəl), *n.* angel of high rank.

Arch·an·gel (ärk′ān′jəl), *n.* port in NW Russia, on the White Sea.

arch·bish·op (ärch′bish′əp), *n.* bishop having the highest rank.

arch·di·o·cese (ärch′dī′ə sis *or* ärch′dī′ə sēs′), *n.* a church district governed by an archbishop.

arch·duch·ess (ärch′duch′is), *n.* **1** wife or widow of an archduke. **2** princess of Austria-Hungary. ❏ *n., pl.* **arch·duch·ess·es.**

arch·duke (ärch′dük′), *n.* prince of Austria-Hungary.

arched (ärcht), *adj.* having an arch or arches.

arch·en·e·my (ärch′en′ə mē), *n.* a principal enemy. ❏ *n., pl.* **arch·en·e·mies.**

ar·che·ol·o·gy (är′kē ol′ə jē), *n.* archaeology. —**ar′che·o·log′i·cal,** *adj.* —**ar′che·o·log′i·cal·ly,** *adv.* —**ar′che·ol′o·gist,** *n.*

Arch·e·o·zo·ic (är′kē ə zō′ik), *n.* (in geology) time from about 3½ billion to 2 billion years ago. During this time, life first appeared on Earth.

arch·er (är′chər), *n.* person who shoots with a bow and arrow; bowman.

arch·er·y (är′chər ē), *n.* practice or sport of shooting with a bow and arrow. [See word history information at **arc**.]

Arches National Park, a national park in SE Utah, containing many large naturally formed sandstone arches.

ar·che·type (är′kə tīp), *n.* an original model or pattern from which copies are made, or out of which later forms develop; prototype: *Last year's fall festival will serve as the archetype for this year's.*

Ar·chi·me·des (är′kə mē′dēz), *n.* 287?-212 B.C., Greek mathematician, physicist, and inventor, who discovered the principles of the pulley and the lever. ■ **Archimedes** once made an important scientific discovery while taking a bath. He was so excited that he jumped out and ran down the street, shouting "Eureka!" a Greek word meaning "I have found it."

ar·chi·pel·a·go (är′kə pel′ə gō *or* är′chə pel′ə gō), *n.* **1** group of many islands. The islands between southeast Asia and Australia form the Malay Archipelago. **2** sea having many islands in it. ❏ *n., pl.* **ar·chi·pel·a·gos** or **ar·chi·pel·a·goes.**

ar·chi·tect (är′kə tekt), *n.* **1** person who designs and makes plans for buildings and sees that these plans are followed by the people who put up the buildings. **2** maker; creator: *The architects of the United Nations hoped for lasting world peace.*

a	hat	ė	term	ô	order	ch	child		a in about
ā	age	i	it	oi	oil	ng	long		e in taken
ä	far	ī	ice	ou	out	sh	she	ə {	i in pencil
â	care	o	hot	u	cup	th	thin		o in lemon
e	let	ō	open	ù	put	ŦH	then		u in circus
ē	equal	ò	saw	ü	rule	zh	measure		

ar·chi·tec·ture (är′kə tek′chər), *n.* **1** science or art of planning and designing buildings. **2** style or special manner of building: *Greek architecture made much use of columns.* **3** construction: *the massive architecture of the Pyramids.* —**ar′chi·tec′tur·al,** *adj.* —**ar′chi·tec′tur·al·ly,** *adv.*

WORD BANK   Architecture has its own vocabulary. If you want to learn more about it, you can start by looking up these words in this dictionary. See also the Word Bank at **building.**

apse	cornice	mezzanine
arch	cupola	minaret
atrium	dome	nave
attic	dormer	pediment
balcony	facade	pillar
bay window	flying buttress	portico
buttress	gable	Romanesque
canopy	gargoyle	spire
cloister	Gothic	tower
colonnade	keystone	transept
column	lintel	vault

ar·chi·trave (är′kə trāv), *n.* the main beam resting on the top of a column or row of columns.

ar·chives (är′kīvz), *n.pl.* **1** place where public records or historical documents are kept. **2** the public records or historical documents kept in such a place.

arch·way (ärch′wā′), *n.* **1** entrance or passageway with an arch above it. **2** arch covering a passageway.

arc lamp, an electric lamp in which the light comes from an arc.

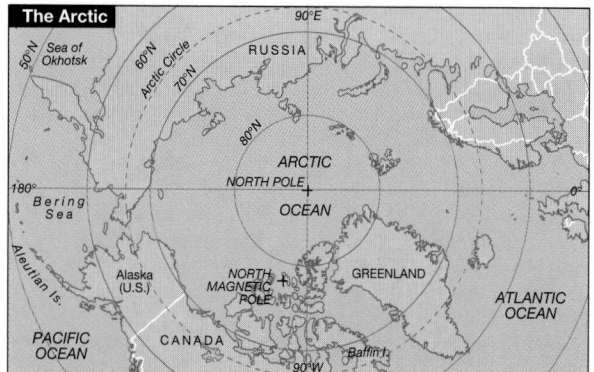

arc·tic (ärk′tik *or* är′tik), **1** *adj.* at or near the North Pole; of the north polar region: *They explored the great arctic wilderness of northern Canada.* **2** *n.* **the Arctic,** the north polar region. The Arctic has an extremely cold winter. **3** *adj.* extremely cold; frigid. —**arc′ti·cal·ly,** *adv.*

WORD STORY   Arctic comes from a Greek word meaning "a bear." The Bear is the constellation Ursa Major, which contains the Big Dipper. It is the most visible northern constellation. The farther north ancient Greeks traveled, the more clearly they saw the Bear.

Arctic Archipelago, a large group of islands in the Arctic Ocean, part of Northwest Territories, Canada.

arctic circle or **Arctic Circle,** the imaginary boundary of the north polar region. It runs parallel to the equator at 66 degrees 30 minutes (66°30′) north latitude. See **arctic** for map.

Arctic Ocean, ocean of the north polar region.

Arc·tur·us (ärk tür′əs), *n.* a very bright star in the northern sky.

ar·dent (ärd′nt), *adj.* full of enthusiasm; eager: *an ardent believer in the benefits of health foods.* [Ardent comes from a Latin word meaning "to burn." An enthusiastic person can be thought of as burning to do something.] —**ar′dent·ly,** *adv.*

ar·dor (är′dər), *n.* great enthusiasm; eagerness; zeal: *The senator spoke with ardor about the need for gun control.*

ar·du·ous (är′jü əs), *adj.* **1** hard to do; requiring much effort; difficult: *an arduous lesson.* **2** using up much energy; strenuous: *She enjoys an arduous workout in the gym.* —**ar′du·ous·ly,** *adv.* —**ar′du·ous·ness,** *n.*

are (är), *v.* form of the verb **be** used with *we, you,* and *they* or with any plural noun in the present tense: *We are ready. You are next. They are waiting. Teachers are impressed by curious students. Bees are insects.*

ar·e·a (âr′ē ə), *n.* **1** amount or extent of surface, especially the measure in square units: *The area of this floor is 600 square feet.* **2** region or district: *The Rocky Mountain area is very scenic.* **3** a level, open space: *a playground area.* **4** range of knowledge or interest; sphere of activity; field: *I took many courses in the areas of physics, chemistry, and related sciences.* ❏ *n., pl.* **ar·e·as.**

area code, combination of three numerals used to dial directly by telephone from one region of the United States and Canada to another.

ar·e·a·way (âr′ē ə wā′), *n.* **1** a sunken area or court at the entrance to a cellar or basement. **2** area used as a passageway between buildings.

a·re·na (ə rē′nə), *n.* **1** a space, surrounded by seats, used for contests or shows: *a boxing arena.* **2** building in which indoor sports are played. **3** space in an ancient Roman amphitheater in which contests or shows took place: *Gladiators fought with lions in the arena at Rome.* **4** any place of conflict and trial: *The United Nations is an arena for world debate.* **5** field of endeavor: *the political arena.* ❏ *n., pl.* **a·re·nas.** [Arena comes from a Latin word meaning "sand." The floors of ancient Roman arenas were covered with sand.]

aren't (ärnt), **1** are not. **2** am not. In this meaning, *aren't* is used only in questions: *Why aren't I allowed to stay?*

Ar·es (âr′ēz), *n.* Greek god of war. The Romans called him Mars.

Ar·gen·ti·na (är′jən tē′nə), *n.* country in S South America. *Capital:* Buenos Aires. —**Ar·gen·tin·e·an** or **Ar·gen·tin·i·an** (är′jən tin′ē ən), *adj., n.*

WORD STORY   Argentina comes from a Latin word meaning "silver." The first European settlers came to Argentina in search of silver and gold during the 1500s.

Ar·gen·tine (är′jən tēn′ *or* är′jən tin), **1** *adj.* of Argentina or its people. **2** *n.* person born or living in Argentina.

Ar·go (är′gō), *n.* (in Greek legends) the ship in which Jason and the Argonauts sailed.

ar·gon (är′gon), *n.* a colorless, odorless, element which is a gas that forms a very small part of the air. Argon is used in electric light bulbs and in welding. *Symbol:* Ar

Ar·go·naut (är′gə nòt), *n.* (in Greek legends) any of the men who sailed with Jason in search of the Golden Fleece.

ar·go·sy (är′gə sē), *n.* OLD USE. **1** a large merchant ship. **2** fleet of such ships. ❏ *n., pl.* **ar·go·sies.**

ar·got (är′gət *or* är′gō), *n.* the specialized speech of a group of people, which people outside the group often find difficult to understand.

ar·gue (är′gyü), *v.* **1** to discuss with someone who disagrees: *He argued with his sister about who should wash the dishes.* **2** to give reasons for or against something: *One side argued for building a new school and the other side argued against it.* **3** to persuade by giving reasons: *They argued me into going along on the trip.* **4** to try to prove by reasoning; maintain: *Scientists argue that the oceans are endangered by pollution.* ❏ *v.* **ar·gued, ar·gu·ing.** —**ar′gu·a·ble,** *adj.* —**ar′gu·a·bly,** *adv.* —**ar′gu·er,** *n.*

ar·gu·ment (är′gyə mənt), *n.* **1** discussion by persons who disagree; dispute: *She won the argument by producing facts to prove her point.* **2** reason or reasons offered for or against something: *His arguments in favor of a new school building are very convincing.*

SYNONYM STUDY   Argument and dispute both mean a discussion of different opinions by persons who disagree. **Argument** suggests the use of facts and reason: *The argument was settled by looking up the record of last year's sale.* **Dispute** suggests angry and lengthy disagreement: *The dispute over the property was settled in court.*

ar·gu·men·ta·tive (är′gyə men′tə tiv), *adj.* fond of arguing; quarrelsome: *an argumentative disposition.* —**ar′gu·men′ta·tive·ly,** *adv.* —**ar′gu·men′ta·tive·ness,** *n.*

a·ri·a (är′ē ə), *n.* song for a single voice, with accompaniment, in an opera, oratorio, or cantata. ❑ *n., pl.* **a·ri·as.**

Ar·i·ad·ne (ar′ē ad′nē), *n.* (in Greek legends) the daughter of Minos, king of Crete. She fell in love with Theseus and helped him escape from Crete after he killed the Minotaur.

Ar·i·as (ä′rē äs), *n.* **Os·car Sán·chez** (ōs′kär sän′chäs), born 1941, president of Costa Rica since 1986. He won the Nobel Peace Prize in 1987 for his Central American peace plan.

ar·id (ar′id), *adj.* **1** having very little rainfall; dry and barren: *Desert lands are arid.* ■ See Synonym Study at **dry. 2** uninteresting and empty; dull: *an arid, boring speech.* —**a·rid′i·ty,** *n.* —**ar′·id·ly,** *adv.* —**ar′id·ness,** *n.*

arid (def. 1)—arid ground

Ar·ies (ar′ēz), *n.* **1** a group of stars shaped something like a ram. **2** the first sign of the zodiac, associated with the period from mid-March to mid-April.

a·right (ə rīt′), *adv.* correctly; rightly: *If I heard you aright, you said you would go.*

a·rise (ə rīz′), *v.* **1** to rise up; get up: *They arose to greet us when we came in.* **2** to move upward; ascend: *Smoke arises from the chimney.* **3** to come into being; come about: *A great wind arose. Accidents often arise from carelessness.* ❑ *v.* **a·rose, a·ris·en** (ə riz′n), **a·ris·ing.**

ar·is·toc·ra·cy (ar′ə stok′rə sē), *n.* **1** class of people having a high position in society because of birth, rank, or title; nobility. Earls, duchesses, etc., belong to the aristocracy. **2** class of people considered superior because of intelligence, culture, or wealth; upper class. **3** government in which the nobility or any privileged upper class rules. ❑ *n., pl.* **ar·is·toc·ra·cies.**

a·ris·to·crat (ə ris′tə krat), *n.* **1** person who belongs to the aristocracy; noble. **2** person like an aristocrat in tastes, opinions, and manners.

a·ris·to·crat·ic (ə ris′tə krat′ik), *adj.* **1** belonging to the upper classes; considered superior because of birth, intelligence, culture, or wealth. **2** of or like the aristocracy or aristocrats. —**a·ris′·to·crat′i·cal·ly,** *adv.*

Ar·is·to·te·li·an (ar′ə stə tē′lē ən *or* ə ris′tə tē′lyən), **1** *adj.* of Aristotle or his philosophy. **2** *n.* follower or student of Aristotle or his philosophy.

Ar·is·tot·le (ar′ə stot′l), *n.* 384-322 B.C., Greek philosopher and scientist, a pupil of Plato. ■ **Aristotle** wrote about logic, physics, ethics, and tragedy. He was one of the most influential Greek thinkers. Alexander the Great was his student.

a·rith·me·tic (ə rith′mə tik), *n.* **1** branch of mathematics that deals with adding, subtracting, multiplying, and dividing numbers. **2** the act of adding, subtracting, multiplying, or dividing numbers; calculation: *There is a mistake in your arithmetic in that problem.* —**ar′ith·met′i·cal,** *adj.* —**ar′ith·met′i·cal·ly,** *adv.*

ar·ith·met·ic mean (ar′ith met′ik), an average.

arithmetic progression, series of numbers in which there is always the same difference between a number and the one next after it. 2, 4, 6, 8, 10, 12 form an arithmetical progression; so do 8, 5, 2, −1, −4.

Ariz., Arizona.

Ar·i·zo·na (ar′ə zō′nə), *n.* one of the southwestern states of the United States. *Abbreviation:* AZ or Ariz. *Capital:* Phoenix. [**Arizona** comes from an American Indian word that may mean "place of the small spring."] —**Ar′i·zo′nan** or **Ar′i·zo′ni·an,** *n.*

ark (ärk), *n.* **1** in the Bible: **a** the large boat in which Noah saved himself, his family, and a pair of each kind of animal from the Flood. **b** **Ark,** the chest or box in which the Hebrews kept the two stone tablets containing the Ten Commandments. **2** a cabinet in a synagogue for housing scrolls of the Torah when they are not being used in worship. [**Ark** comes from a Latin word meaning "chest" or "box."] ■ Another word that sounds like this is **arc.**

Ark., Arkansas.

Ar·kan·sas (är′kən sò; *also* är kan′zəs *for* 2), *n.* **1** one of the south central states of the United States. *Abbreviation:* AR or Ark. *Capital:* Little Rock. **2** river flowing from central Colorado southeast into the Mississippi. [**Arkansas** comes from an American Indian word meaning "land of downstream people."] —**Ar·kan·san** (är kan′zən), *n.*

Ar·ling·ton (är′ling tən), *n.* **1** the largest national cemetery in the United States, in NE Virginia, across the Potomac from Washington, D.C. **2** city in NE Virginia.

arm[1] (ärm), *n.* **1** forelimb of a person or animal. **2** something shaped or used like an arm: *the arm of a chair, an arm of the sea.* **3** a division or branch: *an arm of the U.S. government.* **4** power; authority: *The strong arm of the law keeps order in the city.* —**arm′less,** *adj.* —**arm′like′,** *adj.*

arm in arm, with arms linked: *She walked arm in arm with her sister.*

with open arms, in a warm, friendly way; cordially: *Her friends welcomed her with open arms.*

arm[2] (ärm), **1** *n.pl.* **arms,** weapons of any kind. Guns, swords, axes, or sticks might be arms for defense or attack. **2** *v.* to supply with weapons: *During the American Revolutionary War the French helped arm the colonists.* **3** *v.* to supply with any means of defense or attack: *The lawyer entered court armed with the evidence he planned to use to support his case.* **4** *v.* to take up weapons; prepare for war: *The soldiers armed for battle.* **5** *n.* a combat branch of one of the armed forces, such as the infantry or artillery. —**arm′er,** *n.*

ar·ma·da (är mä′də), *n.* **1** a large fleet of warships. **2** the Armada, the Spanish fleet sent to attack England in 1588. It was defeated in the English Channel. ❑ *n., pl.* **ar·ma·das** for 1.

ar·ma·dil·lo (är′mə dil′ō), *n.* any of several small, burrowing mammals with protective shells of bony plates. Armadillos are found in South America and southern North America. ❑ *n., pl.* **ar·ma·dil·los.**

armadillo—total length 30 in.(76 cm)

WORD STORY **Armadillo** comes from a Spanish word meaning "armed." Early Spanish settlers thought the animal's hard shell of bony plates looked like and served as a kind of armor.

ar·ma·ment (är′mə mənt), *n.* **1** the weapons, ammunition, and equipment used by the military; war equipment and supplies. **2** the military forces of a country, including equipment and people. **3** act or process of arming.

ar·ma·ture (är′mə chər), *n.* a revolving part of an electric motor or dynamo, consisting of wire wound around an iron core placed between opposite poles of a magnet.

arm·band (ärm′band′), *n.* band of cloth worn around the upper arm as a symbol or badge: *a mourning armband of black.*

a	hat	ė	term	ô	order	ch	child		
ā	age	i	it	oi	oil	ng	long		a in about
ä	far	ī	ice	ou	out	sh	she	ə	e in taken
â	care	o	hot	u	cup	th	thin		i in pencil
e	let	ō	open	u̇	put	ŦH	then		o in lemon
ē	equal	ò	saw	ü	rule	zh	measure		u in circus

arm·chair (ärm′châr′), *n.* chair with sidepieces to support a person's arms or elbows.

armed forces, a nation's military, naval, and air forces.

Ar·me·ni·a (är mē′nē ə), *n.* **1** a country in SW Asia. *Capital:* Yerevan. **2** a former country of SW Asia, now divided among Armenia, Turkey, and Iran. —**Ar·me′ni·an,** *adj., n.*

arm·ful (ärm′fŭl), *n.* as much as one arm or both arms can hold: *an armful of groceries.* ❏ *n., pl.* **arm·fuls.**

arm·hole (ärm′hōl′), *n.* hole for the arm or sleeve in a garment.

arm·i·stice (är′mə stis), *n.* a stop in warfare; temporary peace; truce. [**Armistice** comes from Latin words meaning "weapons" and "to stop."]

Armistice Day, November 11, the anniversary of the end of World War I, in 1918. As an official holiday it is now called Veterans Day.

arm·load (ärm′lōd′), *n.* armful.

ar·mor (är′mər), *n.* **1** a covering, usually of metal or leather, worn to protect the body in fighting. **2** any kind of protective covering. The steel plates of a warship and the bony shell of an armadillo are armor. **3** the armored forces and equipment, such as the tanks, of a military unit.

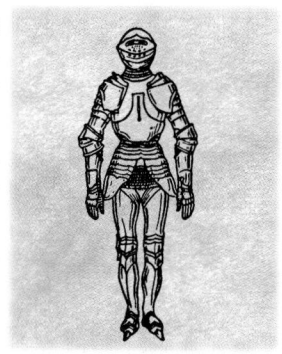
armor (def.1)

ar·mored (är′mərd), *adj.* **1** covered or protected with armor: *an armored car.* **2** using or equipped with armored vehicles: *He served in an armored division.*

ar·mor·er (är′mər ər), *n.* **1** (long ago) a person who made or repaired armor. **2** person in the armed forces who takes care of revolvers, pistols, rifles, and other firearms.

ar·mor·ies (är′mər ēz), *n.* CANADIAN. armory (def. 2). ❏ *n., pl.* **ar·mor·ies.**

armor plate, steel or iron plating to protect warships, tanks, forts, etc. Armor plate is now usually a specially toughened alloy of steel.

ar·mor·y (är′mər ē), *n.* **1** place where weapons are kept or manufactured; arsenal. **2** a building with a drill hall, offices, etc., for militia. ❏ *n., pl.* **ar·mor·ies.**

arm·pit (ärm′pit′), *n.* the hollow place under the arm at the shoulder.

arm·rest (ärm′rest′), *n.* a support for the arm on an armchair, sofa, etc.

arms (ärmz), *n.pl.* **1** arm² (def. 1). **2** fighting; war: *The colonists were quick to answer the call to arms.* **3** symbols and designs used in heraldry; coat of arms.

bear arms, to serve as a soldier; fight: *The soldier bore arms for his country.*

take up arms, to arm for attack or defense: *take up arms against an enemy.*

up in arms, very angry; in rebellion: *The students were up in arms when their after-school activities were canceled.*

arms race, competition among nations for superiority in quality and quantity of weapons.

Arm·strong (ärm′strông′), *n.* **1 Louis** (lü′ē), 1901-1971, American jazz trumpeter. ■ **Louis Armstrong** was called "Satchmo," short for "satchelmouth," his nickname as a child. People thought his big, happy smile looked like the open mouth of a satchel. **2 Neil** (nēl), born 1930, American astronaut. He was the first human being to walk on the surface of the moon, on July 20, 1969.

ar·my (är′mē), *n.* **1** a large, organized group of soldiers trained and armed for war. **2** Often, **Army,** the military land forces of a nation, in some countries including also the air forces. **3** military unit made up of two or more corps plus supporting troops, commanded by a general. It is the largest tactical military unit. **4** any group of people organized for a purpose: *an army of research scientists, the Salvation Army.* **5** a very large number; multitude: *an army of ants.* ❏ *n., pl.* **ar·mies.**

ar·ni·ca (är′nə kə), *n.* **1** a healing liquid used on bruises and sprains, prepared from a European plant. **2** the plant itself, which has showy yellow flowers like daisies. ❏ *n., pl.* **ar·ni·cas** for 2.

Ar·nold (är′nld), *n.* **Ben·e·dict** (ben′ə dikt), 1741-1801, American general in the Revolutionary War who became a traitor. ■ **Benedict Arnold** planned to surrender a fort and supply of arms at West Point to the British, but the plot was discovered when his accomplice was captured.

a·ro·ma (ə rō′mə), *n.* spicy odor; fragrance: *Just smell the aroma of the cake baking in the oven.* ❏ *n., pl.* **a·ro·mas.** ■ See Synonym Study at **smell.**

ar·o·mat·ic (ar′ə mat′ik), *adj.* spicy; fragrant: *The cinnamon tree has an aromatic inner bark.* —**ar′o·mat′i·cal·ly,** *adv.*

a·rose (ə rōz′), *v.* past tense of **arise:** *She arose about 7 A.M.*

a·round (ə round′), **1** *prep.* in a circle about: *She has traveled around the world.* **2** *adv.* in a circle: *The top spun around.* **3** *adv.* in circumference: *The tree measures four feet around.* **4** *prep.* on all sides of: *Woods lay around the house.* **5** *adv.* on all sides; in every direction: *A dense fog lay around.* **6** *prep.* on the far side of; so as to round: *The store is just around the corner. I drove too fast around the curve.* **7** *adv., prep.* here and there; about: *We walked around to see the town. She leaves her books around the house.* **8** *adv., prep.* somewhere about; near: *I waited around for an hour. Stay around the house.* **9** *prep.* near in amount, number, or time to; approximately; about: *That blouse cost around $25. I'll be home around six o'clock.* **10** *adv.* in the opposite direction: *Turn around! You are going the wrong way.* **11** *adv.* from one to another: *I passed my yearbook around for everyone to sign.* **12** *adv.* through a round of time: *Summer will soon come around again.*

a·rous·al (ə rou′zəl), *n.* act of arousing or condition of being aroused.

a·rouse (ə rouz′), *v.* **1** to stir to action; excite: *The mystery story aroused my imagination.* **2** to awaken: *The barking dog aroused me from my sleep.* ❏ *v.* **a·roused, a·rous·ing.**

ar·peg·gi·o (är pej′ē ō *or* är pej′ō), *n.* in music: **1** the sounding of chord notes rapidly one after the other, instead of all at once. **2** a chord sounded in this way. ❏ *n., pl.* **ar·peg·gi·os.**

ar·que·bus (är′kwə bəs), *n.* harquebus. ❏ *n., pl.* **ar·que·bus·es.**

ar·raign (ə rān′), *v.* **1** to bring before a court of law to answer a charge: *The cashier was arraigned on a charge of theft.* **2** to find fault with; accuse. —**ar·raign′ment,** *n.*

ar·range (ə rānj′), *v.* **1** to put in a certain order: *Please arrange the books on the library shelf. I arranged my time so that I could work at my hobbies.* **2** to form plans; prepare beforehand: *Can you arrange to meet me this evening?* **3** to reach an understanding about; settle a dispute: *The two neighbors have now arranged their differences.* **4** to adapt a piece of music to voices or instruments for which it was not written: *This music for cello is also arranged for the piano.* ❏ *v.* **ar·ranged, ar·rang·ing.** —**ar·rang′er,** *n.*

ar·range·ment (ə rānj′mənt), *n.* **1** act of putting or condition of being put in proper order: *Careful arrangement of books in a library makes them easier to find.* **2** way or order in which things or persons are put: *You can make six arrangements of the letters A, B, and C.* **3** something arranged in a particular way: *a beautiful flower arrangement.* **4** adjustment, settlement, or agreement: *No arrangement of the dispute could possibly please everybody.* **5** **arrangements,** *pl.* plans; preparations: *All arrangements have been made for our trip to Chicago.* **6** adaptation of a piece of music to voices or instruments for which it was not written.

arrangement (def. 3)

ar·rant (ar′ənt), *adj.* thoroughgoing; downright: *Nobody will believe such an arrant liar.* —**ar′rant·ly,** *adv.*

ar·ray (ə rā′), **1** *n.* proper order; regular arrangement: *The troops marched in battle array.* **2** *v.* to put in order for some purpose: *The general arrayed his troops for the battle.* **3** *n.* display or collection of persons or things: *The team had an impressive array of fine players.* **4** *n.* clothes, especially for some special occasion: *bridal array.* **5** *v.* to dress in fine clothes; adorn: *He was arrayed in medieval costume for his role as King Richard the Lion-Hearted.* **6** *n.* (in mathematics) an orderly arrangement of objects or symbols in rows and columns. —**ar·ray′er,** *n.*

ar·rears (ə rirz′), *n.pl.* money due but not paid; debts.
in arrears, behind in payments, work, etc.: *She is in arrears with her car payments.*

ar·rest (ə rest′), **1** *v.* to seize and take to jail or court by authority of the law: *A policeman arrested the woman for shoplifting.* **2** *n.* act of seizing of a person by authority of the law; taking to jail or court: *We saw the arrest of the burglary suspect.* **3** *v.* to stop; check: *Filling a tooth arrests decay.* **4** *n.* act of stopping or condition of being stopped: *A heart attack may lead to cardiac arrest.* **5** *v.* to catch and hold: *Our attention was arrested by the unusual sound.* —**ar·rest′er,** *n.*
under arrest, held by the police: *He was under arrest on suspicion of stealing.*

ar·rest·ing (ə res′ting), *adj.* catching and holding the attention; striking. —**ar·rest′ing·ly,** *adv.*

ar·riv·al (ə rī′vəl), *n.* **1** act of arriving: *She is waiting for the arrival of the plane.* **2** person or thing that arrives: *We greeted the new arrivals at the door.*

ar·rive (ə rīv′), *v.* **1** to reach the end of a journey; come to a place: *We arrived in Boston a week ago.* **2** to come; occur: *Summer vacation finally arrived.* **3** to be successful: *He finally arrived as a fashion designer.* ❑ *v.* **ar·rived, ar·riv·ing.**
arrive at, to come to; reach: *You should arrive at school before nine o'clock. We must arrive at a decision soon.*

WORD STORY **Arrive** comes from Latin words meaning "to the shore." If you are crossing a river, when you reach the shore you have arrived at your goal.

ar·ro·gance (ar′ə gəns), *n.* too great pride with contempt of others; haughtiness: *He was a talented actor, but his arrogance made him unpopular.*

ar·ro·gant (ar′ə gənt), *adj.* too proud and contemptuous of others; haughty. —**ar′ro·gant·ly,** *adv.*

ar·row (ar′ō), *n.* **1** a slender, pointed shaft or stick which is shot from a bow. **2** anything like an arrow in shape or speed. **3** a sign (→) used to show direction or position in maps, on road signs, and in writing.

ar·row·head (ar′ō hed′), *n.* head or tip of an arrow. An arrowhead is usually shaped like a wedge and made of harder material than the shaft.

ar·row·root (ar′ō rüt′), *n.* an easily digested starch made from the roots of a tropical American plant.

ar·roy·o (ə roi′ō), *n.* in southwestern United States: **1** the dry bed of a stream; gully. **2** a small river. ❑ *n., pl.* **ar·roy·os.** [**Arroyo** comes from a Latin word meaning "mine shaft." A gully without water looks as if someone had been digging there.]

ar·se·nal (är′sə nəl), *n.* **1** a building for storing or manufacturing military weapons and ammunition. **2** storehouse.

ar·se·nic (är′sə nik), *n.* **1** a very brittle element which has the properties of both a metal and a nonmetal and occurs chiefly in combination with other elements. It forms poisonous compounds with oxygen and is used to make insecticides, weed killers, certain medicines, etc. *Symbol:* As **2** a very strong, tasteless poison that is a compound of this element.

ar·son (är′sən), *n.* the crime of intentionally setting fire to a building or other property.

art[1] (ärt), *n.* **1** a branch or division of learning. History is usually considered one of the arts; chemistry is one of the sciences. **2** a branch of learning that depends more on special practice than on general principles. Writing compositions is an art; grammar is a science. The fine arts include painting, drawing, sculpture, architecture, music, and dancing. **3** painting, drawing, and sculp-

ture: *I am studying both art and music.* **4** paintings, sculptures, and other works of art: *We went to an exhibit at the new museum of art.* **5** working principles; methods: *She understands the art of making friends.* **6** some kind of skill or practical application of skill. Cooking, sewing, and housekeeping are household arts. **7** human skill or effort: *This well-kept garden owes more to art than to nature.* **8** skillful act; cunning; trick: *The magician's arts deceived the audience.*

art[2] (ärt), *v.* OLD USE. are. "Thou art" means "You are."

art deco or **Art Deco** (dek′ō), a decorative style of the 1920s and 1930s that used bright colors, bold outline, and geometric forms.

Ar·te·mis (är′tə mis), *n.* Greek goddess of the hunt and of the moon and twin sister of Apollo. The Romans called her Diana.

ar·te·ri·al (är tir′ē əl), *adj.* **1** of or in an artery or the arteries: *arterial blood.* **2** serving as a major route of transportation, supply, or access: *an arterial highway.* —**ar·te·ri·al·ly,** *adv.*

ar·te·ri·ole (är tir′ē ōl), *n.* a small artery, especially one leading into capillaries.

ar·te·ri·o·scle·ro·sis (är tir′ē ō sklə rō′sis), *n.* an abnormal thickening and hardening of the walls of the arteries, causing a decrease or loss of circulation. Arteriosclerosis occurs chiefly in old age.

ar·ter·y (är′tər ē), *n.* **1** one of the blood vessels that carry blood from the heart to all parts of the body. **2** a main road; important channel: *Main Street and Broadway are the two arteries of traffic in our city.* ❑ *n., pl.* **ar·ter·ies.**

ar·te·sian well (är tē′zhən), a deep, drilled well, especially one from which water gushes up without pumping.

art·ful (ärt′fəl), *adj.* **1** slyly clever; crafty; deceitful: *A swindler uses artful tricks to get people's money away from them.* **2** skillful; clever: *The teacher's artful handling of the situation won the approval of the class.* —**art′ful·ly,** *adv.,* —**art′ful·ness,** *n.*

ar·thrit·ic (är thrit′ik), *adj.* **1** of arthritis. **2** caused by arthritis.

ar·thri·tis (är thrī′tis), *n.* inflammation of a joint or joints of the body.

ar·thro·pod (är′thrə pod), *n.* any animal without a backbone having a jointed body and jointed legs. Insects, spiders, and lobsters are three kinds of arthropods. [**Arthropod** comes from Greek words meaning "jointed foot." In fact, however, it is the legs, not the feet, that are jointed.]

Ar·thur (är′thər), *n.* (in legends of the Middle Ages) king of ancient Britain who gathered around him the knights of the Round Table. The real Arthur was probably a British chieftain about A.D. 500. [**Arthur** comes from a Celtic word that may mean "bear chief."]

Ar·thur (är′thər), *n.* **Ches·ter A.** (ches′tər), 1830-1886, the 21st president of the United States, from 1881 to 1885. He was vice-president and became president when President James Garfield died.

ar·ti·choke (är′tə chōk), *n.* the flower bud of a thistlelike plant with large prickly leaves. Artichokes are cooked and eaten as a vegetable.

ar·ti·cle (är′tə kəl), *n.* **1** a written composition on a special subject, complete in itself, but forming part of a magazine, newspaper, or book: *This newspaper has a good article on gardening.* **2** a clause in a contract, treaty, statute, etc.: *The original Constitution of the United States had*

artichoke

seven articles. **3** a particular thing; item: *Bread is an important article of food.* **4** one of the words *a, an,* or *the,* as in *a book, an egg, the boy. A* and *an* are indefinite articles; *the* is the definite article.

a	hat	ė	term	ô	order	ch	child	ə {	a in about
ā	age	i	it	oi	oil	ng	long		e in taken
ä	far	ī	ice	ou	out	sh	she		i in pencil
â	care	o	hot	u	cup	th	thin		o in lemon
e	let	ō	open	ù	put	ŦH	then		u in circus
ē	equal	ò	saw	ü	rule	zh	measure		

Articles of Confederation, the constitution adopted by the thirteen original states of the United States in 1781, replaced by the present Constitution in 1789.

ar·tic·u·late (är tik′yə lit *for adj.;* är tik′yə lāt *for verb*), **1** *adj.* spoken in distinct syllables or words: *A baby cries and gurgles, but does not use articulate sounds.* **2** *v.* to speak distinctly; express in clear sounds and words: *The speaker was careful to articulate his words so that everyone in the room could understand him.* **3** *adj.* able to put your thoughts into words easily and clearly: *She is the most articulate of the sisters.* **4** *adj.* having joints; jointed. The backbone is an articulate structure. **5** *v.* to fit together in a joint. The leg bones articulate at the knee. ❑ *v.* **ar·tic·u·lat·ed, ar·tic·u·lat·ing. —ar·tic·u·late·ly** (är tik′yə lit lē), *adv.* **—ar·tic′u·la·tor,** *n.*

ar·tic·u·la·tion (är tik′yə lā′shən), *n.* **1** way of speaking; enunciation: *If you speak slowly, your articulation will improve.* **2** a joint. **3** act or manner of connecting by a joint or joints: *The articulation of the bones of the hand is quite complex.*

ar·ti·fact (är′tə fakt), *n.* anything made by human skill or work, especially a tool or weapon.

artifact

ar·ti·fice (är′tə fis), *n.* **1** a clever device; trick; ruse: *The child used every artifice to avoid going to the dentist.* **2** trickery; craft: *Her conduct is free from artifice.*

ar·tif·i·cer (är tif′ə sər), *n.* a skilled worker; craftsman.

ar·ti·fi·cial (är′tə fish′əl), *adj.* **1** made by human skill or labor; not natural: *Plastics are artificial substances that do not occur in nature.* **2** made as a substitute or imitation; not real: *We made artificial paper flowers.* **3** put on for effect; affected; pretended: *When nervous, he had an artificial laugh.* **—ar′ti·fi′cial·ly,** *adv.* **—ar′ti·fi′cial·ness,** *n.*

SYNONYM STUDY **Artificial** and **synthetic** both mean made by people. **Artificial** often means something made by people that is like something found in nature: *The wounded soldier was fitted with an artificial leg.* **Synthetic** describes substances made in a laboratory by combining chemicals: *Nylon is a synthetic fiber.*

artificial intelligence, ability of a computer to do things that require intelligence when done by human beings, such as playing chess.

artificial respiration, method of restoring normal breathing to a person who has stopped breathing by forcing air alternately into and out of the lungs.

ar·til·ler·y (är til′ər ē), *n.* **1** large guns or rocket launchers operated by a crew. **2** the part of an army that uses and manages such guns.

ar·ti·san (är′tə zən), *n.* person skilled in some industry or trade; craftsman. Carpenters, masons, plumbers, and electricians are artisans.

art·ist (är′tist), *n.* **1** person who paints pictures. **2** person who is skilled in any of the fine arts, such as sculpture, music, or literature. **3** a public performer, especially an actor or singer. **4** person who does work with skill and good taste.

ar·tis·tic (är tis′tik), *adj.* **1** of art or artists: *That museum has many artistic treasures.* **2** done with skill and good taste: *an artistic performance.* **3** having good color and design; pleasing to the senses: *an artistic wallpaper.* **4** having or showing appreciation of beauty: *You have an artistic way of arranging flowers.* **—ar·tis′ti·cal·ly,** *adv.*

art·ist·ry (är′tə strē), *n.* artistic work; workmanship of an artist.

art·less (ärt′lis), *adj.* **1** made or done without knowledge of social customs; simple and natural: *Small children ask many artless questions, such as, "Mom, did you want these people to come to see you?"* **2** without art; unskilled; ignorant. **—art′less·ly,** *adv.* **—art′less·ness,** *n.*

art·work (ärt′wėrk′), *n.* **1** a work of art or craft object. **2** production of works of art or craft objects.

A·ru·ba (ə rü′bə), *n.* island country in the Caribbean off the NW coast of Venezuela.

-ary, *suffix.* of or as ___: *legendary = of or as a legend.*

as (az), **1** *adv.* to the same degree or extent; equally: *I am as tall as you.* **2** *prep.* in the character of; doing the work of: *Who will act as teacher?* **3** *conj.* during the time that; while: *As they were walking, it began to rain.* **4** *conj.* in the same way that: *Treat others as you wish them to treat you.* **5** *adv.* for example: *Some animals, as dogs and cats, eat meat.* **6** *conj.* because: *As she was a skilled worker, she received good wages.* **7** *prep.* like: *They treat him as an equal.* **8** *conj.* though: *Brave as they were, the danger made them afraid.* **9** *pron.* that: *Do the same thing as I do.* **10** *pron.* a fact that: *As you know, he is not here today because he is sick.*

as for, about; concerning; referring to: *As for politics, I am indifferent.*

as if, similar to what it would be if.

as is, in the present condition; without a guarantee of good or perfect quality: *If you buy the car as is, it won't cost much.*

as of, beginning on or at a certain date or time: *The new contract becomes effective as of January 1.*

as though, similar to what it would be if: *It looks as though it might rain.*

as to, about; concerning; referring to.

as yet, up to this time; so far.

As, symbol for arsenic.

ASAP (ā′es′ā′pē′ *or* ā′sap), as soon as possible.

as·bes·tos (as bes′təs), *n.* **1** mineral that does not burn or conduct heat and that usually comes in fibers. **2** a fireproof fabric made of these fibers. Asbestos is used to make insulating and roofing materials, brake linings, and fire-resistant clothing.

as·cend (ə send′), *v.* to go up; rise; climb: *She watched the airplane ascend quickly. A group of climbers is planning to ascend Mount Everest.* ■ See Synonym Studies at **climb** and **rise. —as·cend′a·ble** or **as·cend′i·ble,** *adj.*

as·cend·an·cy (ə sen′dən sē), *n.* controlling influence; rule; domination: *to gain ascendancy in a group.*

as·cend·ant (ə sen′dənt), *adj.* rising to a position of power and dominant rule: *an ascendant political figure.*

as·cen·sion (ə sen′shən), *n.* **1** act of rising; ascent. **2 the Ascension,** (in the Bible) the ascent of Jesus from Earth to heaven after the Resurrection.

as·cent (ə sent′), *n.* **1** act of going up; upward movement; rising: *The sudden ascent of the elevator made us dizzy.* **2** act of climbing: *The ascent of Mount Everest is difficult.* **3** place or way that slopes up: *The gradual ascent of the hill made it easy to climb.* ■ Another word that sounds like this is **assent.**

ascension (def. 2)
the Ascension as imagined
by an artist

as·cer·tain (as′ər tān′), *v.* to find out; make sure of; determine: *The detective tried to ascertain the facts about the robbery.* —**as′cer·tain′a·ble,** *adj.* —**as·cer·tain′ment,** *n.*

as·cet·ic (ə set′ik), **1** *n.* person who practices unusual self-denial or self-discipline, especially for religious reasons. Fasting is a common practice of ascetics. **2** *adj.* refraining from pleasures and comforts; practicing unusual self-denial. [**Ascetic** comes from a Greek word meaning "hermit" or "monk." Hermits and monks live lives of self-denial and discipline.] —**as·cet′i·cal·ly,** *adv.*

as·cet·i·cism (ə set′ə siz′əm), *n.* unusual self-denial.

ASCII (as′kē), *n.* American Standard Code for Information Interchange (a system for coding letters, numbers, and other characters into groups of binary digits. It is widely used for passing information between computers, or between a computer and devices used with it.)

a·scor·bic acid (ə skôr′bik), vitamin C.

as·cot (as′kət or as′kot), *n.* a necktie with broad ends, like a scarf, tied so that the ends lie flat and fill the open shirt or jacket collar.

as·cribe (ə skrib′), *v.* to think of as caused by or coming from; attribute: *The police ascribed the car accident to fast driving. The author of this tale is unknown, but it is ascribed to the brothers Grimm.* ❏ *v.* **as·cribed, as·crib·ing.**

a·sep·tic (ə sep′tik), *adj.* free from the living germs causing infection: *Surgical tools can be made aseptic by boiling them.* —**a·sep′ti·cal·ly,** *adv.*

a·sex·u·al (ā sek′shü əl), *adj.* **1** having no sex. **2** independent of sexual processes. The division into two parts by an ameba is a form of asexual reproduction. —**a·sex′u·al·ly,** *adv.*

As·gard (as′gärd), *n.* (in Norse myths) home of gods and heroes.

ash¹ (ash), *n.* what remains of a thing after it has been thoroughly burned: *He flicked his cigarette ash into the fireplace.* See also **ashes.** ❏ *n., pl.* **ash·es.**

ash² (ash), *n.* **1** any of several related timber or shade trees with leaves grouped on stalks, winged seedcases, and hard, strong wood. **2** the tough, springy wood used in baseball bats and elsewhere. ❏ *n., pl.* **ash·es.**

a·shamed (ə shāmd′), *adj.* **1** feeling shame; disturbed or uncomfortable because you have done something wrong, bad, or silly: *I was ashamed because I forgot her birthday.* **2** unwilling because of fear of shame: *I failed math and was ashamed to tell my parents.* —**a·sham·ed·ly** (ə shā′mid lē), *adv.*

> **SYNONYM STUDY** **Ashamed, humiliated,** and **mortified** all mean with a sense of embarrassment and disgrace. **Ashamed** suggests a feeling of disgrace for having done something wrong, improper, or foolish: *I was ashamed when I realized that I had hurt her feelings.* **Humiliated** suggests a painful feeling that you have been lowered in the eyes of others: *The team felt humiliated at losing so badly.* **Mortified** suggests a feeling of great embarrassment and shame: *He was mortified when he forgot his lines in the middle of the play.*

Ashe (ash), *n.* **Arthur,** 1943-1994, American tennis player. He was the first African American to win the U.S. Open singles championship and the Wimbledon singles title.

ash·en (ash′ən), *adj.* **1** like ashes; pale as ashes. **2** of ashes.

ash·es (ash′iz), *n.pl.* **1** what remains of a thing after it has thoroughly burned: *Ashes have to be removed from the fireplace to make room for more wood.* **2** what remains of a dead body when burned. **3** a dead body; corpse.

Ash·kha·bad (äsh kä bäd′), *n.* capital of Turkmenistan.

a·shore (ə shôr′), *adv.* **1** to the shore; to land: *The ship's passengers went ashore.* **2** on the shore; on land: *The sailor had been ashore for months.*

ash·tray (ash′trā′), *n.* a flat holder to put tobacco ashes in.

Ash Wednesday, the first day of Lent; the seventh Wednesday before Easter.

ash·y (ash′ē), *adj.* **1** pale as ashes; ashen. **2** made of or covered with ashes.

A·sia (ā′zhə), *n.* the largest continent, extending eastward from Europe and Africa to the Pacific Ocean. China, India, and much of Russia are in Asia.

Asia Minor, peninsula of SW Asia, between the Black Sea and the Mediterranean Sea; Anatolia. It includes most of Asian Turkey.

A·sian (ā′zhən), **1** *n.* person born or living in Asia. **2** *adj.* of Asia or its people.

A·si·at·ic (ā′zhē at′ik), *adj., n.* Asian. ■ The word **Asian** should be used when referring to the people of Asia, because the word **Asiatic** is sometimes considered offensive.

a·side (ə sid′), **1** *adv.* on one side; to one side; away: *I stepped aside to let them pass.* **2** *adv.* out of your thoughts or consideration: *Swimming is easier if you can put your fears aside.* **3** *n.* remark that others who are present are not supposed to hear. An actor's asides are usually spoken to the audience.

aside from, except for: *Aside from arithmetic, I have finished my homework.*

As·i·mov (az′ə mof), *n.* **Isaac,** 1920-1992, American author and scientist, born in Russia. ■ **Isaac Asimov** wrote almost 500 books for adults and children, including science fiction, mysteries, and nonfiction books about Shakespeare, science, and the Bible.

as·i·nine (as′n in), *adj.* obviously silly; foolish and stupid. [**Asinine** comes from a Latin word meaning "donkey" or "fool."] —**as′i·nine·ly,** *adv.*

ask (ask), *v.* **1** to try to find out by words; inquire: *Why don't you ask? She asked about our health. Ask the way.* **2** to seek the answer to: *Ask any questions you wish.* **3** to put a question to; inquire of: *Ask him how old he is.* **4** to try to get by words; request: *Ask them to sing. Ask for help if you need it.* **5** to invite: *She asked ten guests to the party.* **6** to demand: *They were asking too high a price for their house.*

> **SYNONYM STUDY** **Ask** and **request** both mean to try to get something by saying that you want it. **Ask** is the general word: *They asked us to leave.* **Request** suggests extra politeness: *The store requests that customers not smoke.*

a·skance (ə skans′), *adv.* **1** with suspicion or disapproval: *The students looked askance at the plan to have classes on Saturday.* **2** to one side; sideways.

a·skew (ə skyü′), *adv., adj.* to one side; turned or twisted the wrong way; out of the proper position: *The wind blew her hat askew. Isn't that picture askew?*

ASL, American Sign Language.

a·slant (ə slant′), **1** *adv.* in a slanting direction. **2** *prep.* slantingly across. **3** *adj.* slanting.

a·sleep (ə slēp′), **1** *adj.* not awake; sleeping: *The cat is asleep.* **2** *adv.* into a state of sleep: *The tired boy fell asleep.* **3** *adj.* having lost the power of feeling; numb: *My foot is asleep.*

A·sma·ra (ä smär′ə), *n.* capital of Eritrea.

asp (asp), *n.* any of several small, poisonous snakes of Africa and Europe.

as·par·a·gus (ə spar′ə gəs), *n.* **1** plant with scalelike leaves. **2** its green, tender shoots, eaten as a vegetable.

as·pect (as′pekt), *n.* **1** one of the ways in which a subject or situation may be looked at or thought about: *We must consider each aspect of this plan before we decide.* **2** look; appearance: *Before the storm, the sky had a gray, gloomy aspect.* **3** side fronting or facing in a given direction: *The southern aspect of the house is the warmest in winter.*

as·pen (as′pən), *n.* any of several poplar trees of North America and Europe whose leaves tremble and rustle in the slightest breeze.

as·per·sion (ə spėr′zhən), *n.* a damaging or false statement; slander: *She was accused of casting aspersions on the reputation of an innocent person.*

as·phalt (as′fôlt), *n.* **1** a dark substance much like tar, found in various parts of the world or obtained by refining petroleum. **2** a mixture of this substance with crushed rock or sand. Asphalt is used in surfacing roads.

a	hat	ė	term	ô	order	ch	child		
ā	age	i	it	oi	oil	ng	long	ə	a in about
ä	far	ī	ice	ou	out	sh	she		e in taken
â	care	o	hot	u	cup	th	thin		i in pencil
e	let	ō	open	u̇	put	ŧʜ	then		o in lemon
ē	equal	ȯ	saw	ü	rule	zh	measure		u in circus

as·phyx·i·ate (a sfik′sē āt), v. to suffocate because of lack of oxygen in the blood: *The trapped miners were almost asphyxiated before help reached them.* ❑ v. **a·sphyx·i·at·ed, a·sphyx·i·at·ing.** —**a·sphyx′i·a′tion,** n.

as·pic (as′pik), n. kind of jelly made from meat or fish stock, tomato juice, etc., used as a garnish or in salads.

as·pir·ant (as′pər ənt *or* ə spi′rənt), n. person who aspires; person who seeks a position of honor: *There were many aspirants to the office of class president.*

as·pi·rate (as′pə rāt′ *for verb;* as′pər it *for adj., noun*), **1** v. to begin a word or syllable with a breathing or *h*-sound. *Hot* is aspirated; *honor* is not. **2** v. to pronounce with such a sound. The *h* in *hot* is aspirated. **3** adj. pronounced with a breathing or *h*-sound. The *h* in *here* is aspirate. **4** n. the sound of *h* in *hot*. **5** v. to draw by suction. ❑ v. **as·pi·rat·ed, as·pi·rat·ing.**

as·pi·ra·tion (as′pə rā′shən), n. **1** earnest desire; longing; ambition: *She had aspirations to be a doctor.* **2** act of aspirating: *Many people pronounce "herb" with no aspiration.* **3** act of drawing air into the lungs; breathing.

as·pi·ra·tor (as′pə rā′tər), n. a suction device, especially a medical device used to suck fluids from a body opening or cavity.

as·pire (ə spīr′), v. to have an ambition for something; desire earnestly; seek: *aspire to be captain of the team, aspire after knowledge.* ❑ v. **as·pired, as·pir·ing.** —**as·pir′er,** n.

as·pir·in (as′pər ən), n. drug used to relieve pain or fever in headaches, colds, etc.

ass (as), n. **1** donkey. **2** a stupid, silly, or stubborn person; fool. ❑ n., pl. **ass·es.** —**ass′like′,** adj.

as·sail (ə sāl′), **1** to set upon with violence; attack: *The soldiers assailed the fort.* **2** to set upon vigorously with arguments or abuse: *The senators assailed the President on the subject of the treaty.* —**as·sail′a·ble,** adj.

as·sail·ant (ə sā′lənt), n. person who attacks: *The injured man did not know who his assailant was.*

as·sas·sin (ə sas′n), n. someone who kills a well-known person, especially a political leader, by a sudden or secret attack; murderer.

WORD STORY **Assassin** comes from an Arabic word meaning "hashish eaters." In the 1100s, a group of Muslims in the Middle East were believed to use this drug and to commit murders.

as·sas·si·nate (ə sas′n āt), v. to murder, especially a well-known person, by a sudden or secret attack: *President Kennedy was assassinated in 1963.* ❑ v. **as·sas·si·nat·ed, as·sas·si·nat·ing.** —**as·sas′si·na′tion,** n. —**as·sas′si·na′tor,** n.

as·sault (ə sôlt′), **1** n. a sudden, vigorous attack: *The soldiers made an assault on the fort.* **2** v. to make an attack on: *He fled from the gang that tried to assault him.* **3** n. (in law) a threat or attempt to strike or otherwise harm a person. —**as·sault′er,** n.

assault and battery, an illegal fulfillment of a physical threat, by striking or beating another person.

as·say (ə sā′), **1** v. to analyze an ore or alloy to find out the quantity of gold, silver, or other metal in it. **2** n. an analysis to find out the amount of metal in an ore or alloy or of an ingredient in a drug. ❑ v. **as·sayed, as·say·ing.** —**as·say′er,** n.

as·sem·blage (ə sem′blij), n. **1** group of persons or things collected or gathered together; assembly. **2** process of putting together; fitting together: *the assemblage of parts of an engine.*

as·sem·ble (ə sem′bəl), v. **1** to gather together; bring together: *The principal assembled all the students in the auditorium.* **2** to come together; meet: *Congress assembles in January.* **3** to put together; fit together: *Will you help me assemble my model airplane?* ❑ v. **as·sem·bled, as·sem·bling.** —**as·sem′bler,** n.

as·sem·bly (ə sem′blē), n. **1** a gathering of people for some purpose; meeting: *The principal addressed the school assembly.* **2** a meeting of lawmakers. **3** **Assembly,** the lower branch of the state legislature of some states of the United States. **4** act of coming together: *unlawful assembly.* **5** act of putting together; fitting together: *the assembly of parts to make a car.* **6** all the parts necessary to put something together: *a complicated bicycle gear assembly.* ❑ n., pl. **as·sem·blies** for 1,2, **As·sem·blies** for 3.

assembly language, computer programming language that uses numbers and letter codes, including shortened words, to control computer functions. Each small group of letters and numbers stands for a single data processing step.

assembly line, row of workers and machines along which work is passed until the final product is made: *Most cars are made on an assembly line.*

assembly line

as·sent (ə sent′), **1** v. to agree; consent: *Everyone assented to the plan.* **2** n. acceptance of a proposal, statement, etc.; agreement: *She gave her assent to the plan.* ■ Another word that sounds like this is **ascent.** —**as·sent′er** or **as·sen′tor,** n.

as·sert (ə sėrt′), v. **1** to state positively; declare firmly: *She asserts that her story is true.* **2** to defend or insist on a right or a claim: *It is necessary to assert your independence.* —**as·sert′er** or **as·ser′tor,** n.

assert yourself, to insist on your rights; demand recognition: *Her salary was not raised until she asserted herself and demanded a promotion.*

as·ser·tion (ə sėr′shən), n. **1** a positive statement; firm declaration: *His assertion of innocence was believed by the jury.* **2** act of insisting on a right, a claim, etc.

as·ser·tive (ə sėr′tiv), adj. confident and certain; positive: *He is an assertive boy, always insisting on his rights and opinions.* —**as·ser′tive·ly,** adv. —**as·ser′tive·ness,** n.

as·sess (ə ses′), v. **1** to estimate the value of property or income for taxation; value: *The town clerk has assessed our house at $85,000.* **2** to fix the amount of a tax, fine, damages, etc.: *Damages from last week's flood have been assessed at $30,000,000.* **3** to put a tax on or call for a contribution from a person, property, etc.: *Each member of the club will be assessed $75 to pay for the trip.* **4** to examine carefully and evaluate the value or quality of: *The school board met to assess the idea of a recycling program.* —**as·sess′a·ble,** adj.

as·sess·ment (ə ses′mənt), n. **1** act of assessing. **2** amount assessed.

as·ses·sor (ə ses′ər), n. person who estimates the value of property or income for taxation.

as·set (as′et), n. **1** something having value: *Ability to get along with people is an asset in business.* **2 assets,** pl. **a** things of value; property, such as a house, a car, stocks, bonds, jewelry, etc. **b** property that can be used to pay debts. [**Asset** comes from a Latin word meaning "enough."]

as·sid·u·ous (ə sij′ü əs), adj. careful and attentive; diligent. —**as·sid′u·ous·ly,** adv. —**as·sid′u·ous·ness,** n.

as·sign (ə sīn′), v. **1** to give as a share; allot: *The teacher has assigned the next ten problems for today.* **2** to appoint to a post or duty: *We were assigned to decorate the room for the party.* **3** to name definitely; fix; set: *The judge assigned a day for the trial.* **4** to give out; distribute: *The scoutmasters assigned a different tent area to each troop.* —**as·sign′a·ble,** adj. —**as·sign′er,** n.

as·sign·ment (ə sīn′mənt), *n.* **1** something assigned, especially a piece of work to be done: *Today's assignment in arithmetic consists of ten examples.* **2** act of assigning; appointment: *Home-room assignment is done before school starts.*

assortment

as·sim·i·late (ə sim′ə lāt), *v.* **1** to take in and make part of yourself; absorb; digest: *to assimilate what you read. The body assimilates sugars rapidly.* **2** to become absorbed; be digested: *Fats assimilate slowly.* **3** to make or become like the people of a nation in customs, viewpoint, character, etc.: *The United States has assimilated immigrants from many lands.* □ *v.* **as·sim·i·lat·ed, as·sim·i·lat·ing. —as·sim′i·la′tor,** *n.*

as·sim·i·la·tion (ə sim′ə lā′shən), *n.* **1** act of making or becoming like the people around you. **2** act of absorbing or condition of being absorbed: *assimilation of food.*

As·sin·i·boin (ə sin′ə boin), *n.* member of a tribe of American Indians that live in northeastern Montana and southern Saskatchewan. □ *n., pl.* **As·sin·i·boin** or **As·sin·i·boins.**

WORD STORY **Assiniboin** comes from an Ojibwa word meaning "rocks." They were given this name because the Assiniboin heated stones in fires, then dropped the heated stones into cooking pots or baskets full of water to boil food.

as·sist (ə sist′), **1** *v.* to give aid to; help: *She assisted the science teacher with the experiment.* ■ See Synonym Study at **help. 2** *n.* act of assistance; aid; help: *If you give me an assist I think I can reach the branch.* **3** *n.* (in sports) a play that directly helps a teammate to score, such as a pass in basketball or hockey, or a throw to put a runner out in baseball. **—as·sist′er** or **as·sis′tor,** *n.*

as·sist·ance (ə sis′təns), *n.* aid; help: *I need your assistance.*

as·sist·ant (ə sis′tənt), **1** *n.* person who assists another; aid; helper: *He was my assistant in the library for a time.* **2** *adj.* assisting; helping: *an assistant teacher.*

assn., ass'n, or **Assn.,** association.

assoc., **1** associate. **2** association.

as·so·ci·ate (ə sō′shē āt *or* ə sō′sē āt *for verb;* ə sō′shē it *or* ə sō′sē it *for adj., noun),* **1** *v.* to connect in thought: *We associate turkey with Thanksgiving.* **2** *adj.* joined with another or others: *I am an associate editor of the school paper.* **3** *v.* to join as a companion, partner, or friend: *She is associated with her brothers in business.* **4** *v.* to be friendly; keep company: *He associated with interesting people.* **5** *n.* companion, partner, or friend: *She is an associate in a law firm.* **6** *adj.* admitted to some, but not all, rights and privileges: *After being an associate member of the glee club for a year I became a full member.* □ *v.* **as·so·ci·at·ed, as·so·ci·at·ing.** [**Associate** comes from a Latin word meaning "companion."] **—as·so·ci·a′tor** (ə sō′shē ā′tər *or* ə sō′sē ā′tər), *n.*

as·so·ci·a·tion (ə sō′sē ā′shən *or* ə sō′shē ā′shən), *n.* **1** group of people joined together for some purpose; society: *Will you join the young people's association at our church?* **2** condition of being associated: *Her association with that firm ended several years ago.* **3** companionship or friendship: *They had enjoyed a close association over many years.* **4** idea connected with another idea in thought: *Some people make the association of the color red with anger.* **5** act of associating: *association of ideas.*

as·so·ci·a·tive (ə sō′shē ā′tiv), *adj.* **1** tending to associate. **2** of or about association. **3** of or about a rule that the combinations by which numbers are added or multiplied will not change their sum or product. By this rule, $(2 \times 3) \times 5$ will give the same product as $2 \times (3 \times 5)$. **—as·so·ci·a′tive·ly,** *adv.*

as·so·nance (as′n əns), *n.* repetition of a vowel sound in a group of words, especially a line of poetry. EXAMPLE: "The far stars glimmer in the darkling sky."

as·sort·ed (ə sôr′tid), *adj.* **1** selected so as to be of different kinds; various: *She served assorted vegetables.* **2** arranged by kinds; classified: *There were socks assorted by size on the shelf.*

as·sort·ment (ə sôrt′mənt), *n.* collection of various kinds: *These scarfs come in an assortment of colors.*

asst. or **Asst.,** assistant.

as·suage (ə swāj′), *v.* **1** to calm or soothe: *Her words assuaged their fear.* **2** to make milder or easier; appease: *Aspirin assuages pain.* **3** to satisfy; appease; quench: *She drank some water to assuage her thirst.* □ *v.* **as·suaged, as·suag·ing. —as·suage′ment,** *n.*

as·sume (ə süm′), *v.* **1** to take for granted without proof; suppose: *He assumed that the train would be on time.* **2** to take upon yourself; undertake: *She assumed the leadership of the project.* **3** to take on; put on: *The problem has assumed a new form.* **4** to pretend: *Although she was afraid, she assumed an air of confidence.* **5** to take for yourself; appropriate; usurp: *The king's brother tried to assume the throne.* □ *v.* **as·sumed, as·sum·ing.**

as·sumed (ə sümd′), *adj.* false; not real; pretended: *an assumed name.* **—as·sum·ed·ly** (ə sü′mid lē), *adv.*

as·sump·tion (ə sump′shən), *n.* **1** thing assumed: *His assumption that he would win proved incorrect.* **2** act of assuming: *The nation celebrated the new president's assumption of office.*

as·sur·ance (ə shùr′əns), *n.* **1** statement intended to make a person more sure or certain: *We gave her our assurance that we would not play in her yard again.* **2** security, certainty, or confidence: *We have the assurance of final victory.* **3** confidence in your own ability: *The actor's careful preparation gave him assurance in performing.*

as·sure (ə shùr′), *v.* **1** to tell positively: *They assured me that they would be on time.* **2** to make sure or certain; convince: *She assured herself that the bridge was safe before she crossed it.* **3** to make safe; secure: *Victory was assured when the team scored in the final seconds of the game.* **4** to give or restore confidence to; encourage: *The father assured his frightened son.* □ *v.* **as·sured, as·sur·ing. —as·sur′er,** *n.*

as·sur·ed·ly (ə shùr′id lē), *adv.* **1** surely; certainly: *I will assuredly come.* **2** confidently; boldly: *I spoke more assuredly than I felt.*

As·syr·i·a (ə sir′ē ə), *n.* ancient country in SW Asia, once a great empire. The capital was Nineveh. **—As·syr′i·an,** *adj., n.*

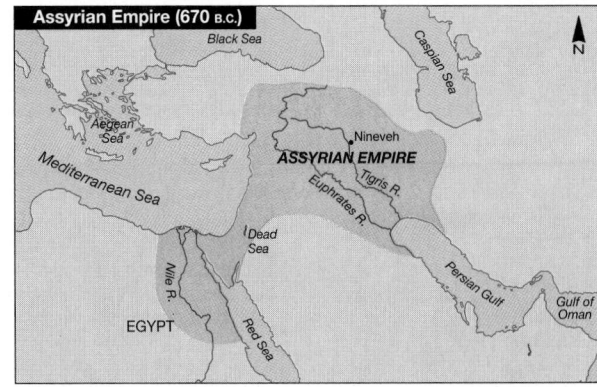

Assyrian Empire (670 B.C.)

As·taire (ə stâr′), *n.* **Fred** (fred), 1899-1987, American dancer. He starred in many musical comedy movies, often with Ginger Rogers.

a	hat	ė	term	ô	order	ch	child		
ā	age	i	it	oi	oil	ng	long		a in about
ä	far	ī	ice	ou	out	sh	she		e in taken
â	care	o	hot	u	cup	th	thin	ə	i in pencil
e	let	ō	open	ù	put	ŦH	then		o in lemon
ē	equal	ȯ	saw	ü	rule	zh	measure		u in circus

as·ta·tine (as′tə tēn′), *n.* a radioactive nonmetallic element produced artificially from bismuth. *Symbol:* At

as·ter (as′tər), *n.* any of many common plants with daisylike flowers that have white, pink, or purple petals around a yellow center. [Aster comes from a Greek word meaning "star." The flower has a starlike appearance.] —**as′ter·like**, *adj.*

as·ter·isk (as′tə risk′), *n.* a star-shaped mark (*) used in printing and writing to call attention to a footnote, indicate the omission of words or letters, etc. [Asterisk comes from a Greek word meaning "small star," which is just what it looks like.]

a·stern (ə stėrn′), *adv.* 1 at or toward the rear of a ship, boat, or aircraft; aft: *The captain went astern.* 2 backward: *The boat moved slowly astern.* 3 behind: *The yacht towed a small boat astern.*

as·ter·oid (as′tə roid′), *n.* any of thousands of rocky objects smaller than 620 miles (1000 kilometers) across, orbiting the sun mainly between the orbits of Mars and Jupiter; planetoid.

asth·ma (az′mə), *n.* a chronic disease causing difficulty in breathing accompanied by wheezing, a feeling of suffocation, and coughing.

asth·mat·ic (az mat′ik), 1 *adj.* suffering from asthma. 2 *n.* person who has asthma.

> **USAGE NOTE** Definition 2 of **asthmatic** is sometimes considered offensive, because it is thought to identify the person with the disease. "A person who has asthma" avoids the problem.

a·stig·ma·tism (ə stig′mə tiz′əm), *n.* defect of an eye or of a lens that makes objects look indistinct or that gives imperfect images, because light is not focused at one point.

a·stir (ə stėr′), *adj.* in motion; up and about: *The whole town was astir.*

as·ton·ish (ə ston′ish), *v.* to surprise greatly; amaze: *We were astonished by the child's remarkable memory.*

> **WORD STORY** **Astonish** comes from a Latin word meaning "thunder." **Astound** comes from the same Latin word. Someone who is totally astonished and astounded may be described in English as *thunderstruck.* The idea is probably that a sudden loud sound is the biggest kind of surprise.

as·ton·ish·ing (ə ston′i shing), *adj.* very surprising; amazing. —**as·ton′ish·ing·ly**, *adv.*

as·ton·ish·ment (ə ston′ish mənt), *n.* great surprise; sudden wonder; amazement.

as·tound (ə stound′), *v.* to surprise greatly; amaze: *She was astounded by the news that she had won the contest.* [See Word Story at **astonish**.]

as·tound·ing (ə stound′ing), *adj.* amazing.

a·strad·dle (ə strad′l), *adv.* astride.

as·tra·khan (as′trə kən), *n.* 1 the curly furlike wool on the skin of some young lambs. 2 a rough cloth that looks like this wool.

a·stray (ə strā′), *adj., adv.* 1 out of the right way or place; off: *The hiker was astray in the woods. The cows have gone astray.* 2 in or into error: *Your reasoning on that subject is astray. We reached the theater late because a mistake in the newspaper ad led us astray.*

a·stride (ə strīd′), 1 *prep.* with one leg on each side of: *She sat astride her horse.* 2 *adv.* with one leg on each side: *The knight sat astride on his horse.*

as·trin·gen·cy (ə strin′jən sē), *n.* quality of being astringent.

as·trin·gent (ə strin′jənt), 1 *n.* substance that contracts body tissues and thus checks the flow of blood or other secretions. Alum is an astringent. 2 *adj.* having the property of contracting tissues. —**as·trin′gent·ly**, *adv.*

astro-, *prefix.* star or space: *astronomy = science of stars and outer space.*

as·tro·labe (as′trə lāb′), *n.* an astronomical device used long ago for measuring the altitude of the sun or stars. It has been replaced by the sextant.

as·trol·o·gy (ə strol′ə jē), *n.* study of the influence that some people believe the sun, moon, stars, and planets have on lives and events here on Earth. —**as·trol′o·ger**, *n.* —**as′tro·log′i·cal**, *adj.* —**as′tro·log′i·cal·ly**, *adv.*

as·tro·naut (as′trə nȯt), *n.* pilot or member of the crew of a spacecraft. [Astronaut comes from Greek words meaning "star sailor."] —**as′tro·naut′ic** or **as′tro·naut′i·cal**, *adj.* —**as′tro·naut′i·cal·ly**, *adv.*

astronaut

as·tro·naut·ics (as′trə nȯ′tiks), *n.* 1 science or art having to do with the design, manufacture, and operation of spacecraft. 2 space travel.

as·tron·o·mer (ə stron′ə mər), *n.* an expert in astronomy.

as·tro·nom·ic (as′trə nom′ik), *adj.* astronomical.

as·tro·nom·i·cal (as′trə nom′ə kəl), *adj.* 1 of astronomy: *astronomical calculations.* 2 enormous; very great: *The government has astronomical expenses.* —**as′tro·nom′i·cal·ly**, *adv.*

astronomical unit, the average distance to the sun from Earth, about 93 million miles (150 million kilometers), used as a unit of measurement of astronomical distances.

as·tron·o·my (ə stron′ə mē), *n.* science that deals with the sun, moon, planets, stars, etc. It studies their motions, positions, distances, sizes, etc. [Astronomy comes from Greek words meaning "star" and "law."]

as·tro·phys·i·cal (as′trō fiz′ə kəl), *adj.* of astrophysics.

as·tro·phys·ics (as′trō fiz′iks), *n.* branch of astronomy that deals with the physical and chemical characteristics of stars, planets, etc. —**as′tro·phys′i·cist**, *n.*

As·tro·Turf (as′trō tėrf′), *n.* trademark for a synthetic material made of nylon and plastic. It is used instead of grass on playing fields and lawns.

as·tute (ə stüt′), *adj.* shrewd with regard to your own interests; clever: *He was an astute businessman.* —**as·tute′ly**, *adv.* —**as·tute′ness**, *n.*

A·sun·ción (ä sün′syōn′), *n.* port and capital of Paraguay, on the Paraguay River.

a·sun·der (ə sun′dər), *adv.* in pieces; into separate parts: *Lightning split the tree asunder.*

As·wan Dam (ä swän′), large dam in SE Egypt, built on the Nile for irrigation and flood control.

a·swarm (ə swôrm′), *adj.* filled up with; overrun with: *On sunny summer days, the park is aswarm with with picnickers.*

a·sy·lum (ə sī′ləm), *n.* 1 institution for the support and care of the mentally ill or other people who need care. 2 refuge; shelter. In olden times a church might be an asylum for a debtor or a criminal, since no one was allowed to drag a person from the altar. Now asylum is sometimes given by one nation to persons of another nation who are accused of political crimes.

a·sym·me·try (ā sim′ə trē), *n.* lack of symmetry. —**a′sym·met′ric** or **a′sym·met′ri·cal**, *adj.* —**a′sym·met′ri·cal·ly**, *adv.*

at (at), *prep.* 1 in; on; by; near: *There is someone at the front door. I will be at home.* 2 in the direction of; to; toward: *The dog ran at the cat.* 3 on or near the time of: *She goes to bed at nine o'clock.* 4 in a place or condition of: *England and France were at war.* 5 doing; trying to do; engaged in: *He is at work on a new project.* 6 for: *We bought two books at a dollar each.* 7 because of; with: *My friends were happy at my success.* 8 according to: *She can wiggle her ears at will.*

At, symbol for astatine.

A·ta·ca·ma Desert (ä tä kä′mä), desert in N Chile.

At·a·hual·pa (ä′tə wäl′pə), *n.* 1502?-1533, thirteenth and last Inca emperor. ▪ Atahualpa was captured and held for ransom by Francisco Pizarro. Although the ransom was received, Pizarro decided to kill him anyway, and gave Atahualpa the choice between being burnt at the stake or converting to Christianity and being strangled. Atahualpa chose to convert.

ate (āt), *v.* past tense of **eat**: *The boy ate his dinner.* ▪ Another word that sounds like this is **eight**.

-ate, *suffix.* **1** having ___: *compassionate = having compassion.* **2** of or like something: *palmate = like a palm.* **3** to make ___ or become ___: *activate = to make or become active.*

at·el·ier (at′l yā), *n.* workshop, especially an artist's studio.

a tem·po (ä tem′pō), (in music) in time; returning to the former speed.

Ath·a·bas·can (ath′ə bas′kən), **1** *n.* family of North American Indian languages, including the languages of the Apache, Dogrib, Navajo, Ojibwa, Sarcee, and Slave tribes. **2** *adj.* of this family of languages. **3** *n.* person speaking a language of this family.

> **WORD STORY** **Athabascan** comes from a Cree word meaning "many reeds." The name was given to a marshy area, a river, a lake, the people nearby, their language, and related languages.

a·the·ism (ā′thē iz′əm), *n.* belief that there is no God.

a·the·ist (ā′thē ist), *n.* person who believes that there is no God.

a·the·is·tic (ā′thē is′tik), *adj.* of atheism or atheists. **—a′the·is′-ti·cal·ly,** *adv.*

A·the·na (ə thē′nə), *n.* Greek goddess of wisdom. The Romans called her Minerva.

A·the·ni·an (ə thē′nē ən), **1** *adj.* of Athens (especially ancient Athens) or its people. **2** *n.* person having the right of citizenship in ancient Athens. **3** *n.* person born or living in Athens.

Ath·ens (ath′ənz), *n.* capital of Greece, in the SE part. Athens was famous in ancient times for its art and literature. See **Sparta** for map.

ath·er·o·scle·ro·sis (ath′ər ō sklə rō′sis), *n.* a disease in which fatty material narrows the inside of the arteries.

a·thirst (ə thėrst′), *adj.* **1** thirsty. **2** eager: *They were athirst for new experiences.*

ath·lete (ath′lēt′), *n.* person trained in sports and exercises of physical strength, speed, and skill. Baseball players, runners, boxers, and swimmers are athletes. [See word history information at **decathlon**.]

athlete

athlete's foot, a very contagious skin disease of the feet, caused by a fungus; ringworm of the feet.

ath·let·ic (ath let′ik), *adj.* **1** of or suited to an athlete. **2** having to do with active games and sports: *an athletic association.* **3** strong and active: *an athletic girl.* **—ath·let′i·cal·ly,** *adv.*

ath·let·ics (ath let′iks), *n.* **1** *pl.* exercises of physical strength, speed, and skill; active games and sports. Athletics include baseball and basketball. **2** *sing.* the practice and principles of physical training: *Athletics is recommended for every student.*

athletic supporter, a kind of underwear for men, worn during sports. It has an elastic waistband and a pouch.

at-home (ət hōm′), *n.* (earlier) an informal reception, usually in the afternoon.

-athon, *suffix.* event such as a race, contest, or project having to do with ___: *bikeathon = a contest using bikes.* These events usually involve endurance and often are used to raise money for a charity. [See Word Story at **marathon**.]

a·thwart (ə thwôrt′), **1** *adv.* across from side to side; crosswise. **2** *prep.* across. **3** *prep.* across the line or course of: *The tug steamed athwart the ship.* **4** *prep.* in opposition to; against.

-ation, *suffix.* act, condition, or result of ___ing: *preparation = act or process of preparing; creation = result of creating.*

At·lan·ta (at lan′tə), *n.* capital of Georgia, U.S.A., in the NW part.

At·lan·tic (at lan′tik), **1** *n.* ocean east of North and South America, west of Europe and Africa. **2** *adj.* of the Atlantic Ocean. **3** *adj.* on, in, over, or near the Atlantic Ocean: *Atlantic air routes.* **4** *adj.* of or on the Atlantic coast of the United States: *New Jersey is one of the Atlantic states.*

Atlantic Provinces, provinces of Canada along the Atlantic coast: New Brunswick, Newfoundland, Nova Scotia, and Prince Edward Island.

Atlantic Standard Time, the standard time in the easternmost part of Canada. It is four hours behind Greenwich time.

At·lan·tis (at lan′tis), *n.* legendary island in the Atlantic Ocean, said to have sunk beneath the sea.

at·las (at′ləs), *n.* **1** book of maps. **2 Atlas,** (in Greek legends) a giant who supported the heavens on his shoulders. ❑ *n., pl.* **at·las·es** for 1. [A book of maps is called an **atlas** because early map makers often put pictures of Atlas on the front pages of their books.]

Atlas Mountains, mountain range in NW Africa, extending from Morocco to Tunisia.

ATM, automated teller machine, an electronic machine that dispenses cash and takes deposits; cash machine: *There is an ATM next to the grocery store.*

atm., atmosphere.

at·mo·sphere (at′mə sfir), *n.* **1** air that surrounds the earth. **2** mass of gases that surrounds, or may surround, any planet, star, etc.: *the cloudy atmosphere of Venus.* **3** air in any given place: *the damp atmosphere of a cellar.* **4** general character or mood of your surroundings; surrounding influence: *a religious atmosphere.* **5** unit of pressure equal to 14.7 pounds per square inch (1.03 kilograms per square centimeter). **—at·mo·spher·ic** (at′mə sfir′ik *or* at′mə sfer′ik), *adj.* **—at′mo·spher′i·cal·ly,** *adv.*

atmospheric pressure, pressure caused by the weight of the air; barometric pressure. The normal atmospheric pressure on the earth's surface at sea level is 14.7 pounds per square inch (1.03 kilograms per square centimeter).

at·oll (at′ol *or* ə tol′), *n.* a ring-shaped coral island or group of islands enclosing or partly enclosing a lagoon.

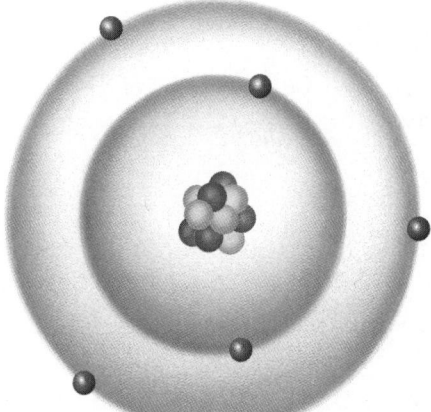
atom (def. 1)—diagram of boron atom

at·om (at′əm), *n.* **1** the smallest particle of any chemical element. An atom can take part in a chemical reaction without being changed. An atom is made up of protons and neutrons in a central nucleus surrounded by electrons. A molecule of water contains two atoms of hydrogen and one atom of oxygen. **2** a very small particle; tiny bit: *There is not an atom of truth in the whole story.*

> **WORD STORY** **Atom** comes from a Greek word meaning "indivisible." It was first used in English to mean the smallest possible part of any substance. Although atoms were later split, the original name is still used.

atom bomb, atomic bomb.

a·tom·ic (ə tom′ik), *adj.* **1** of atoms: *atomic research.* **2** using atomic energy: *an atomic submarine.* **3** extremely small; minute. **—a·tom′i·cal·ly,** *adv.*

a	hat	ė	term	ô	order	ch	child		
ā	age	i	it	oi	oil	ng	long		a in about
ä	far	ī	ice	ou	out	sh	she		e in taken
â	care	o	hot	u	cup	th	thin	ə	i in pencil
e	let	ō	open	ù	put	ᴛʜ	then		o in lemon
ē	equal	ò	saw	ü	rule	zh	measure		u in circus

Atmosphere

Sunset
Sunset is red because the sky is blue. Air scatters light, and blue light most of all, so we see blue all over the sky. When the sun is setting, its light passes through more air to reach us than earlier in the day. More air scatters more blue light in other directions, until the light left to see is mostly red light.

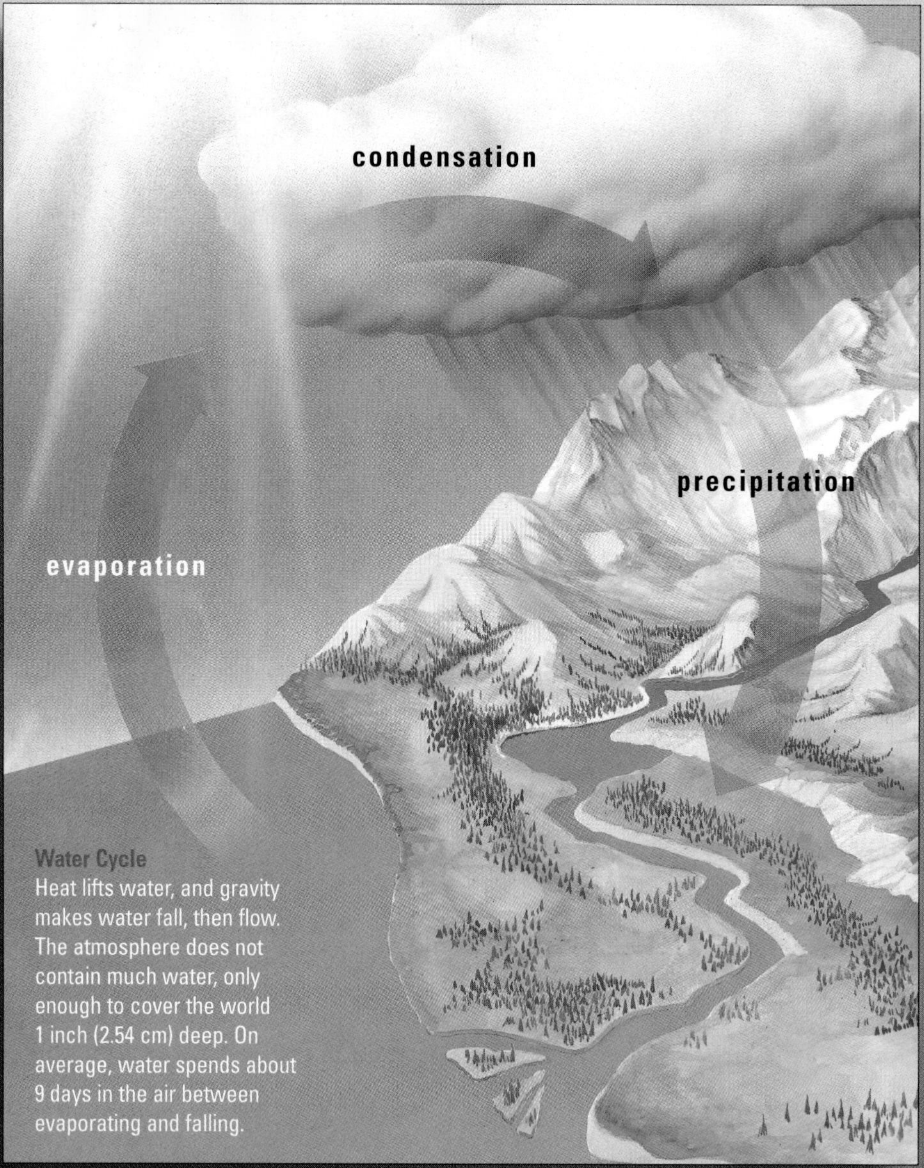

condensation

precipitation

evaporation

Water Cycle
Heat lifts water, and gravity makes water fall, then flow. The atmosphere does not contain much water, only enough to cover the world 1 inch (2.54 cm) deep. On average, water spends about 9 days in the air between evaporating and falling.

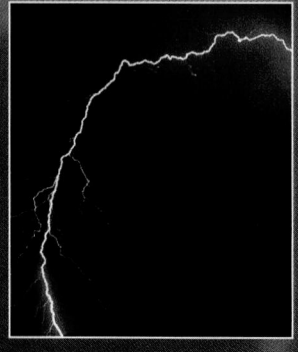

Lightning
Lightning flashes from the sky, carrying 100,000,000 volts of electricity. Water and ice inside storm clouds build up huge electrical charges as tiny droplets and crystals bounce off one another. The gathered electricity bursts out in a giant spark—nearly 10 miles (16 km) long from a cloud to the ground, and possibly 10 times that size between the clouds. Heated air snaps away with the crash of thunder.

Rainbow
Rainbows form when tiny drops of airborne water break sunlight into a spectrum of colors, then reflect the colors down to the ground. Some light gets reflected back and forth inside the drops before it reaches the ground. That light forms a second rainbow, with the colors in reverse order.

Parts of the Atmosphere
The troposphere is what we breathe, and where weather happens. But higher levels of atmosphere are also important to our lives. Between the stratosphere and the mesosphere is the ozone layer, which protects Earth's life from dangerous ultraviolet sunlight. A part of the thermosphere called the ionosphere contains electrically charged particles that reflect or absorb radio waves, helping or hindering broadcast communications.

Stratosphere—10 to 35 miles (16 to 56 km) high

Exosphere—section of thermosphere above 300 miles (480 km) high

Thermosphere/Ionosphere—from 50 miles (80 km) high to outer space

Mesosphere—35 to 50 miles (56 to 80 km) high

Troposphere—to 10 miles (16 km) high

Weather Balloon
Balloons carry scientific equipment high into the atmosphere. A radio transmitter in the equipment reports temperature, humidity, and air pressure at various heights above ground. This information is used in forecasting the weather. When the balloon has completed its mission, it bursts. A parachute carries the equipment safely back to the ground.

Tornado
A tornado forms when air rushing up into a thundercloud begins to spin. With a roar like a railroad train, winds whirl at speeds sometimes reaching 500 miles (800 km) per hour. The tornado may race across the ground at 60 miles (100 km) per hour, destroying everything in its way.

atomic bomb, bomb in which the splitting of atomic nuclei results in an explosion of tremendous force and heat, accompanied by a blinding light; A-bomb.

atomic clock, clock that uses the vibrations of atoms to measure time with extreme accuracy.

atomic energy, energy that exists inside the nucleus of an atom. Some atoms can be made to release some of their energy, either slowly in a reactor or very suddenly in a bomb, by the splitting or the fusion of their nuclei.

atomic mass, the mass of an atom, compared to the mass of the most common form of carbon atom, which is set at 12.

atomic number, the number of protons in the nucleus of an atom of a chemical element: *The atomic number of hydrogen is 1, of uranium 92.*

atomic theory, theory that all matter is composed of small particles called atoms.

atomic weight, the weight of an atom of a chemical element compared to the weight of the most common form of carbon atom, which is set at 12.

at·om·iz·er (at′ə mī′zər), *n.* apparatus used to blow a liquid in a spray of tiny drops: *a perfume atomizer.*

a·ton·al (ā tō′nl), *adj.* (in music) having no key. —**a·ton′al·ly,** *adv.*

a·tone (ə tōn′), *v.* to make up; make amends: *He atoned for his unkindness to his sister by sharing his candy.* ❑ *v.* **a·toned, a·ton·ing.**

a·tone·ment (ə tōn′mənt), *n.* **1** act of making up for something; giving satisfaction for a wrong, loss, or injury; amends. Yom Kippur is the Jewish Day of Atonement. **2 the Atonement,** the reconciliation of God with sinners through the sufferings and death of Jesus.

a·top (ə top′), *prep.* on the top of: *He had a hat atop his head.*

ATP, a chemical compound found in living cells, important for releasing energy necessary for muscle contraction and other bodily activities.

a·tri·um (ā′trē əm), *n.* **1** one of the two chambers of the heart that receive blood from the veins and force it into a ventricle; auricle. See picture at **heart. 2** in a modern building, a large room that is two or more stories tall, often containing trees and other plants. **3** the open-roofed entry room of a house in ancient Rome. ❑ *n., pl.* **a·tri·a** (ā′trē ə), **a·tri·ums.**

a·tro·cious (ə trō′shəs), *adj.* **1** very wicked or cruel; savage or brutal: *Murder is an atrocious crime.* **2** very bad or unpleasant: *atrocious weather.* —**a·tro′cious·ly,** *adv.* —**a·tro′cious·ness,** *n.*

a·troc·i·ty (ə tros′ə tē), *n.* **1** very great wickedness or cruelty: *acts of atrocity committed in war.* **2** a very cruel or brutal act: *the atrocities of war.* ❑ *n., pl.* **a·troc·i·ties** for 2.

at·ro·phy (at′rə fē), **1** *n.* process of wasting away: *Some diseases cause atrophy of the muscles in the legs.* **2** *v.* to waste away: *An ability may atrophy if not used.* ❑ *v.* **at·ro·phied, at·ro·phy·ing.**

at·ro·pine (at′rə pēn′), *n.* a poisonous drug that is used in medicine to help relax muscles and dilate the pupil of the eye. It comes from belladonna and similar plants.

at·tach (ə tach′), *v.* **1** to fix in place; fasten: *We can attach the trailer to our car.* **2** to add at the end; affix: *The signers attached their names to the Constitution.* **3** to bind by affection: *She is very attached to her cousin.* **4** to fasten itself; belong: *The blame for this accident attaches to the driver who did not stop.* **5** to give to; think of as belonging to: *The world at first attached little importance to rockets.* **6** to assign a military unit, soldiers, etc., for a short time to an organization or commander. **7** to take property, etc., by order of a court of law: *If you don't pay them the money you owe, they can attach your salary.* —**at·tach′a·ble,** *adj.*

at·ta·ché (at′ə shā′), *n.* person on the official staff of an ambassador or minister to a foreign country: *a naval attaché.* ❑ *n., pl.* **at·ta·chés.** [*Attaché* comes from a French word meaning "attached." People assigned to an official staff are said to be attached to it.]

attaché case, briefcase.

at·tach·ment (ə tach′mənt), *n.* **1** act of attaching or condition of being attached; connection: *The attachment of the trailer to the car took half an hour.* **2** thing attached, such as an additional device. Some sewing machines have attachments for making buttonholes.

3 means of attaching; fastening. **4** affection that binds a person to someone or something; devotion: *My child has a great attachment to her dog.* **5** the legal taking of property or wages.

at·tack (ə tak′), **1** *v.* to use force or weapons against; set upon to hurt; begin fighting: *The dog attacked the cat. The enemy attacked at dawn.* **2** *v.* to talk or write against: *The candidate angrily attacked his opponent's record as mayor.* **3** *v.* to go at with vigor: *attack a hard lesson.* **4** *n.* an attacking: *The attack took them by surprise.* **5** *v.* to act harmfully on: *Locusts attacked the crops.* **6** *n.* a sudden occurrence of illness, discomfort, etc.: *an attack of flu.* —**at·tack′er,** *n.*

at·tain (ə tān′), *v.* **1** to arrive at; come to; reach: *Grandfather has attained the age of 80.* **2** to gain by effort; accomplish: *She attained her goal.* —**at·tain′a·bil′i·ty,** *n.* —**at·tain′a·ble,** *adj.*

at·tain·der (ə tān′dər), *n.* loss of property and civil rights as the result of being sentenced to death or being outlawed.

at·tain·ment (ə tān′mənt), *n.* **1** act of attaining; achievement: *Her main goal was the attainment of a medical degree.* **2** accomplishment; ability: *Benjamin Franklin was a man of varied attainments; he was a diplomat, statesman, writer, and inventor.*

at·tar (at′ər), *n.* perfume made from the petals of roses or other flowers.

at·tempt (ə tempt′), **1** *v.* to make an effort; try: *attempt to answer the question.* ■ See Synonym Study at **try. 2** *n.* act of making an effort; endeavor: *an attempt to climb Mount Everest.* ■ See Synonym Study at **effort. 3** *n.* an attack: *an attempt upon his life.*

at·tend (ə tend′), *v.* **1** to be present at: *My big sister attends high school.* **2** to give care and thought; pay attention to: *Attend to the instructions.* **3** to go with as a servant: *Noble ladies attended the queen.* ■ See Synonym Study at **accompany. 4** to go with as a result: *Success often attends hard work.* **5** to wait on; care for; tend: *Nurses attend the sick.*

at·tend·ance (ə ten′dəns), *n.* **1** act of being present at a place; an attending: *Our class had perfect attendance today.* **2** number of people present; persons attending: *The attendance at the meeting last night was over 200.*

take attendance, to check names on a list to find out who is present.

at·tend·ant (ə ten′dənt), **1** *n.* person who waits on another: *The airliner had several flight attendants to care for the passengers.* **2** *n.* employee who waits on customers. **3** *adj.* waiting on another to help or serve: *An attendant nurse is at the patient's bedside.* **4** *adj.* going with as a result; accompanying: *Coughing and sneezing are some of the attendant discomforts of a cold.*

at·ten·tion (ə ten′shən), *n.* **1** careful thinking, looking, or listening: *Give me your attention while I explain this math problem.* **2** power of attending; notice: *She called my attention to the problem.* **3** care and thoughtfulness; consideration: *Your letter will receive early attention.* **4** position of standing very straight with the arms at the sides, the heels together, and the eyes looking ahead: *The soldiers stood at attention during the inspection.* **5 attentions,** *pl.* acts of courtesy or devotion: *She received many attentions, such as invitations to parties, candy, and flowers.*

attention (def. 4)

attention deficit disorder, a condition that includes difficulty in paying attention and impulsive behavior. Many people with this condition are also hyperactive.

at·ten·tive (ə ten′tiv), *adj.* **1** paying attention; observant: *an attentive pupil.* **2** courteous; polite: *They were attentive to their guests.* —**at·ten′tive·ly,** *adv.* —**at·ten′tive·ness,** *n.*

at·ten·u·ate (ə ten′yü āt), *v.* **1** to make thin or slender: *attenuated by hunger.* **2** weaken; reduce: *attenuated power.* ❑ *v.,* **at·ten·u·at·ed, at·ten·u·at·ing.**

at·test (ə test′), *v.* **1** to give proof of; certify: *Your good work attests the care you have taken.* **2** to bear witness; testify: *The handwriting expert attested to the genuineness of the signature.* —**at·tes·ta·tion** (at′ə stā′shən), *n.*

at·tic (at′ik), *n.* space in a house just below the roof; garret.

> **WORD STORY** Attic comes from the words *attic story*, meaning the top story of a building. It was called this because, at one time in England, people built houses with rows of pillars along the top so that this part of the house looked like the buildings of Attica.

At·ti·ca (at′ə kə), *n.* district in SE Greece. Its chief city is Athens. Attica was famous in ancient times for its literature and art.

At·ti·la (ə til′ə), *n.* A.D. 406?-453, leader of the Huns in their invasions of Europe. He was defeated by the Romans and Goths in A.D. 451.

at·tire (ə tīr′), **1** *n.* clothing or dress: *The queen wore rich attire to her coronation. The invitation suggested formal attire for the party.* **2** *v.* to clothe or dress; array: *The king was attired in a robe trimmed with ermine.* ❑ *v.* **at·tired, at·tir·ing.**

attire

at·ti·tude (at′ə tüd), *n.* **1** way of thinking, acting, or feeling: *As I got to know him better, my attitude towards him changed.* **2** position of the body suggesting an action, purpose, emotion, etc.: *He raised his fists in the attitude of a boxer ready to fight.* **3** personality combining conceit, rudeness, and readiness to quarrel; cockiness: *He has so much attitude that people avoid him.*

at·tor·ney (ə tėr′nē), *n.* **1** lawyer. **2** person who has power to act for another in business or legal matters. ❑ *n., pl.* **at·tor·neys.**

attorney at law, lawyer. ❑ *pl.* **attorneys at law.**

attorney general, 1 the chief law officer of a country, state, or province. **2 Attorney General, a** the head of the United States Department of Justice and the chief legal adviser of the President. **b** the chief legal officer in Canada. ❑ *pl.* **attorneys general** or **attorney generals.**

at·tract (ə trakt′), *v.* **1** to draw in or draw together; gather: *The magnet attracted the iron filings. The famous musician attracted a crowd.* **2** to be pleasing to; win the attention and liking of: *Bright colors attract children.* —**at·trac′tor** or **at·tract′er,** *n.*

at·trac·tion (ə trak′shən), *n.* **1** thing that delights or attracts people: *The elephants were the chief attraction at the circus.* **2** act or power of attracting: *the attraction of a magnet for iron filings. Sports have no attraction for him.*

at·trac·tive (ə trak′tiv), *adj.* **1** winning attention and liking; pleasing: *an attractive young couple.* **2** attracting: *the attractive power of a magnet.* —**at·trac′tive·ly,** *adv.* —**at·trac′tive·ness,** *n.*

attrib., 1 attribute. **2** attributive.

at·trib·ute (ə trib′yüt *for verb;* at′rə byüt *for noun*), **1** *v.* to regard as an effect of: *She attributes her good health to a carefully planned diet.* **2** *v.* to think of as belonging to or appropriate to: *We attribute courage to the lion and cunning to the fox.* **3** *n.* a quality thought of as belonging to a person or thing; characteristic: *Patience is an attribute of a good teacher.* ❑ *v.* **at·trib·ut·ed, at·trib·ut·ing.** —**at·trib·ut·a·ble** (ə trib′yə tə bəl), *adj.* —**at·trib′ut·er** or **at·trib′u·tor,** *n.* —**at·tri·bu·tion** (at′rə byü′shən), *n.*

at·trib·u·tive (ə trib′yə tiv), **1** *adj.* expressing a quality or attribute. An adjective used before or immediately after a noun is an attributive adjective, as in "a *white* shirt," "the ocean *blue.*" A noun placed immediately before another noun and serving as a modifier is an attributive noun, as in "*highway* patrol." **2** *n.* an attributive word. —**at·trib′u·tive·ly,** *adv.*

at·tri·tion (ə trish′ən), *n.* act of gradually wearing away or wearing down: *Pebbles become smooth by attrition. The long war of attrition exhausted the strength of both countries.*

At·tucks (at′əks), *n.* **Cris·pus** (kris′pəs), 1723?-1770, American patriot. ■ **Crispus Attucks** was one of five Americans killed when British soldiers fired on protesters in Boston in 1770. Historians believe he may have escaped from slavery.

at·tune (ə tün′), *v.* to make used to: *Our ears became attuned to the noise of the city after several months.* ❑ *v.* **at·tuned, at·tun·ing.**

atty., attorney.

ATV, all-terrain vehicle.

a·twit·ter (ə twit′ər), *adj.* excited; nervous: *The whole school was atwitter about the Vice-President's visit.*

at. wt., atomic weight.

a·typ·i·cal (ā tip′ə kəl), *adj.* not typical; irregular. —**a·typ′i·cal·ly,** *adv.*

Au, symbol for gold.

au·burn (ò′bərn), **1** *n.* a reddish brown. **2** *adj.* reddish brown.

Auck·land (òk′lənd), *n.* port on North Island, New Zealand.

au courant (ō kü rä′), well-informed about current happenings or events; up-to-date.

auc·tion (òk′shən), **1** *n.* a public sale in which each thing is sold to the person who offers the most money for it: *a baseball cared auction.* **2** *v.* to sell at an auction: *He auctioned off his baseball card collection.*

> **WORD STORY** Because Latin had no letter *w*, the Romans spelled the sound ò as *au*. When *w* came into English, about 1000 years ago, it was combined with *a* to spell the sound ò, but mostly in words from German, Dutch, Icelandic, and other northern languages. The spelling with *a* and *u* was kept for words from Latin and related languages.

auc·tion·eer (òk′shə nir′), *n.* person whose business is conducting auctions.

au·da·cious (ò dā′shəs), *adj.* **1** having the courage to take risks; bold; daring: *an audacious explorer.* **2** rudely bold; impudent: *The audacious waiter demanded a larger tip.* —**au·da′cious·ly,** *adv.* —**au·da′cious·ness,** *n.*

au·dac·i·ty (ò das′ə tē), *n.* **1** boldness; reckless daring: *The highest trapeze could not daunt the acrobat's audacity.* **2** rude boldness; impudence: *They had the audacity to go to the party without being invited.*

au·di·ble (ò′də bəl), *adj.* able to be heard; loud enough to be heard: *Without a microphone the speaker was barely audible.* —**au·di·bil·i·ty** (ò′də bil′ə tē), *n.* —**au′di·bly,** *adv.*

au·di·ence (ò′dē əns), *n.* **1** group of people gathered to hear or see something: *The audience at the theater enjoyed the play.* **2** any persons within hearing: *That TV show has an audience of over 10 million people.* **3** the readers of a book, newspaper, or magazine. **4** chance to be heard; hearing: *The committee will give you an audience so you may present your plan.* **5** formal interview with a person of high rank: *The queen granted an audience to the ambassador.*

audience share, the number of households with a TV set tuned to a station or in use during a certain period of time.

a	hat	ė	term	ô	order	ch	child		
ā	age	i	it	oi	oil	ng	long		a in about
ä	far	ī	ice	ou	out	sh	she		e in taken
â	care	o	hot	u	cup	th	thin	ə	i in pencil
e	let	ō	open	ù	put	₮H	then		o in lemon
ē	equal	ò	saw	ü	rule	zh	measure		u in circus

au·di·o (ô′dē ō), **1** *adj.* using or involving sound or hearing: *audio equipment.* **2** *adj.* involving or used in transmitting or receiving sound in television. An audio problem is a sound problem; a video problem is a problem with the picture. **3** *n.* sound reproduction: *Some of the audio for this film was very bad.*

WORD FAMILY Audio and the words below are related. They all come from a Latin word meaning "to hear."

| audible | audit | auditorium | obeisance |
| audience | audition | obedient | obey |

audio frequency, a sound wave frequency that can be heard. For human beings this is any frequency from about 15 to about 20,000 hertz.

au·di·om·e·ter (ô′dē om′ə tər), *n.* device for measuring the keenness and range of hearing.

au·di·o·vis·u·al (ô′dē ō vizh′ü əl), *adj.* of hearing and sight. Schools use movies, slides, recordings, and other devices as audiovisual aids in teaching. **—au′di·o·vis′u·al·ly,** *adv.*

au·dit (ô′dit), **1** *v.* to examine and check business accounts. **2** *n.* an examination and check of business accounts. **3** *n.* statement of an account that has been examined and checked.

au·di·tion (ô dish′ən), **1** *n.* act of hearing to test the ability, quality, or performance of a singer, actor, or other performer. **2** *v.* to give a singer, actor, or other performer such a hearing. **3** *v.* to sing, act, or perform at such a hearing.

au·di·tor (ô′də tər), *n.* **1** person who audits business accounts. **2** hearer; listener.

au·di·to·ri·um (ô′də tôr′ē əm), *n.* **1** large room for an audience in a church, theater, school, etc. **2** a building especially designed for public meetings, concerts, lectures, etc. ❑ *n., pl.* **au·di·to·ri·ums, au·di·to·ri·a** (ô′də tôr′ē ə).

au·di·to·ry (ô′də tôr′ē), *adj.* of hearing or the organs of hearing. The **auditory nerve** carries impulses from the ear to the brain.

Au·du·bon (ô′də bon), *n.* **John James,** 1785-1851, American painter who made a study of birds. ■ **John James Audubon** painted and published pictures of all the species of birds known in North America in his time.

Audubon painting

auf Wie·der·seh·en (ouf vē′dər zā′ən), GERMAN. good-by; till we see each other again.

Aug., August.

au·ger (ô′gər), *n.* **1** tool for boring holes in wood. **2** a large tool for boring holes in the earth. ■ Another word that sounds like this is **augur.**

aught[1] (ôt), *pron.* OLD USE. anything: *Has she done aught to help you?* ■ Another word that sounds like this is **ought.**

aught[2] (ôt), *n.* zero; cipher; nothing. ■ Another word that sounds like this is **ought.**

aug·ment (ôg ment′), *v.* to make or become greater in size, number, amount, or degree; increase: *He augmented his income by working overtime three nights a week.* **—aug·ment′a·ble,** *adj.* **—aug·men·ta·tion** (ôg′mən tā′shən), *n.*

au grat·in (ō grat′n *or* ō grät′n), topped with a layer of bread crumbs or grated cheese that is then broiled or baked to make a crust: *au gratin potatoes.*

au·gur (ô′gər), *n.* **1** *v.* to be a sign or promise of: *Those storm clouds augur ill for our picnic.* **2** *n.* priest in ancient Rome who foretold future events and gave advice on the course of public business by interpreting such signs or omens as the flight of birds, thunder and lightning, etc. ■ Another word that sounds like this is **auger.**

au·gust (ô gust′), *adj.* **1** inspiring respect and admiration; majestic; sublime: *an august royal funeral procession.* **2** dignified; eminent; venerable. **—au·gust′ness,** *n.*

Au·gust (ô′gəst), *n.* the eighth month of the year. It has 31 days. [**August** was named in honor of the Roman emperor Augustus. During his reign it was also lengthened to 31 days.]

Au·gus·ta (ô gus′tə), *n.* **1** capital of Maine, in the SW part. **2** city in E Georgia, U.S.A.

Au·gus·tine (ô′gə stēn′), *n.* **Saint,** A.D. 354-430, a theologian and leader in the early Christian church.

Au·gus·tus (ô gus′təs), *n.* 63 B.C.-A.D. 14, the first emperor of Rome, from 27 B.C. to A.D. 14. He was the grandnephew and heir of Julius Caesar.

auk (ôk), *n.* any of several seabirds found in arctic regions, with legs set so far back that they stand like penguins. Auks have short wings used chiefly as paddles in swimming, but they can fly. One kind, the **great auk,** could not fly and was hunted until extinct.

aunt (ant), *n.* **1** sister of your father or mother. **2** wife of your uncle. ■ Another word that sounds like this is **ant.**

aunt·ie or **aunt·y** (an′tē), *n.* INFORMAL. aunt. ❑ *n., pl.* **aunt·ies.**

au pair (ō pâr′), a young woman, often from another country, who lives with a family and carries out various housekeeping duties and child care in return for room, board, and a small salary.

au·ra (ôr′ə), *n.* something that seems to come from or surround a person or thing as an atmosphere: *There was an aura of mystery about the stranger.* ❑ *n., pl.* **au·ras.**

au·ral (ôr′əl), *adj.* of or perceived by the ear. ■ Another word that sounds like this is **oral.** **—au′ral·ly,** *adv.*

au·re·ole (ôr′ē ōl), *n.* ring of light surrounding a figure or object.

Au·re·o·my·cin (ôr′ē ō mī′sn), *n.* trademark for an antibiotic derived from a soil microorganism, used to check or kill certain bacterial infections and viruses.

au re·voir (ō rə vwär′), FRENCH. good-by; till we see each other again.

au·ri·cle (ôr′ə kəl), *n.* **1** the outer part of the ear. **2** atrium (def. 1). ■ Another word that sounds like this is **oracle.**

au·rochs (ôr′oks), *n.* **1** bison of Europe that is now almost extinct. **2** an extinct wild ox of Europe. ❑ *n., pl.* **au·rochs.**

Au·ro·ra (ô rôr′ə), *n.* **1** Roman goddess of the dawn. **2 aurora,** streamers or bands of light that appear in the sky at night, especially in polar regions. **3** city in central Colorado.

au·ro·ra aus·tra·lis (ô strā′lis), streamers or bands of light appearing in the sky at night in southern regions of the Southern Hemisphere; southern lights.

aurora bo·re·al·is (bôr′ē al′is), streamers or bands of light appearing in the sky at night in the northern regions of the Northern Hemisphere; northern lights.

Ausch·witz (oush′vits), *n.* city in SW Poland, site of a Nazi concentration camp where millions were killed during World War II.

aus·pic·es (ô′spə siz), *n.pl.* **1** helpful influence; support; patronage: *The school fair was held under the auspices of the Parents' Association.* **2** omens; signs.

WORD STORY Auspices comes from Latin words meaning "bird watching." The ancient Romans believed that the flight of birds was a sign of future events.

aus·pi·cious (ô spish′əs), *adj.* with signs of success; favorable: *The popularity of her first book was an auspicious beginning for a new author.* **—aus·pi′cious·ly,** *adv.*

Aus·ten (ô′stən), *n.* **Jane** (jān), 1775-1817, English novelist. ■ **Jane Austen** wrote about young women, their families, and middle-class English life. She is considered the first great woman novelist who wrote in English.

aus·tere (ô stir′), *adj.* **1** stern in manner or appearance; harsh: *My father was a silent, austere man, very strict with us.* **2** strict in morals: *Some ideas of the Puritans seem too austere to us.* **3** severely simple: *The tall, plain columns stood against the sky in austere beauty.* **—aus·tere′ly,** *adv.* **—aus·tere′ness,** *n.*

aus·ter·i·ty (ô ster′ə tē), *n.* **1** sternness in manner or appearance; harshness; severity. **2** moral strictness. **3** severe simplicity.

Aus·tin (o'stən), *n.* **1 Ste·phen Fuller** (stē'vən), 1793-1836, Texan patriot. ▪ **Stephen Austin** worked to make Texas a state of Mexico and later to make Texas an independent republic. The city of Austin, Texas, is named for him. **2** capital of Texas, in the central part.

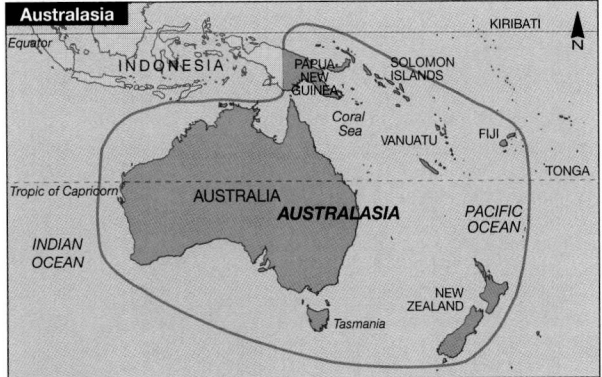

Aus·tral·a·sia (o'strə lā'zhə), *n.* a region made up of the countries of Australia, New Zealand, Papua New Guinea, Fiji, Solomon Islands, and Vanuatu. **—Aus'tral·a'sian,** *adj., n.*

Aus·tral·ia (o strā'lyə), *n.* **1** continent southeast of Asia. **2** Commonwealth of, country that includes this continent and Tasmania. *Capital:* Canberra. [**Australia** comes from a Latin word meaning "the south wind." The continent was originally called "Southern Land."]

Aus·tral·ian (o strā'lyən), **1** *adj.* of Australia or its people. **2** *n.* person born or living in Australia.

Aus·tri·a (o'strē ə), *n.* country in central Europe. Before World War I it was an empire. *Capital:* Vienna. **—Aus'tri·an,** *adj., n.*

Aus·tri·a-Hun·gar·y (o'strē ə hung'gər ē), *n.* monarchy in central Europe from 1867 to 1918, composed of the Austrian empire and the kingdom of Hungary.

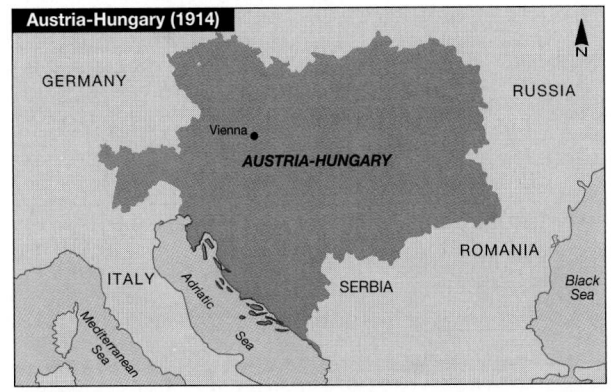

au·teur (o tèr'), *n.* a movie director who, because of a very personal and creative style, is considered the true author of a film.

au·then·tic (o then'tik), *adj.* **1** worthy of trust or belief; reliable: *We heard an authentic account of the wreck, given by one of the ship's passengers.* **2** genuine; real: *That is her authentic signature, not a forgery.* **—au·then'ti·cal·ly,** *adv.*

au·then·ti·cate (o then'tə kāt), *v.* to establish the truth of; show to be valid or genuine: *Handwriting experts authenticated the signature on the will.* ❑ *v.* **au·then·ti·cat·ed, au·then·ti·cat·ing.** **—au·then'ti·ca'tion,** *n.* **—au·then'ti·ca'tor,** *n.*

au·then·tic·i·ty (o then tis'ə tē), *n.* **1** reliability: *The value of the evidence depends on its authenticity.* **2** genuineness: *The lawyer questioned the authenticity of the signature.*

au·thor (o'thər), **1** *n.* person who writes books, poems, stories, or articles; writer. **2** *n.* person who creates or begins anything: *Are you the author of this scheme?* **3** *v.* to be the writer of; compose: *Dr. Seuss authored many books for young children.*

au·thor·i·tar·i·an (ə thôr'ə ter'ē ən), *adj.* favoring obedience to authority instead of individual freedom: *An authoritarian government will often censor newspapers.*

au·thor·i·tar·i·an·ism (ə thôr'ə ter'ē ə niz'əm), *n.* system of government in which the people do not get to choose their leaders but are required to obey and lack individual freedom.

au·thor·i·ta·tive (ə thôr'ə tā'tiv), *adj.* **1** having authority; officially ordered: *Authoritative orders came from the general.* **2** commanding: *In authoritative tones the policeman told us to keep back.* **3** having the authority of expert knowledge: *an authoritative article by a well-known scientist.* **—au·thor'i·ta'tive·ly,** *adv.* **—au·thor'i·ta'tive·ness,** *n.*

au·thor·i·ty (ə thôr'ə tē), *n.* **1** power to enforce obedience; right to command or act: *Parents have authority over their children. The police have the authority to arrest speeding drivers.* ▪ See Synonym Study at **control.** **2** person or group who has such power or right. **3 the authorities,** *pl.* the officials in control: *The authorities at city hall received many complaints about unpaved streets.* **4** source of correct information or wise advice: *A good dictionary is an authority on words.* **5** an expert on some subject: *She is an authority on China.* ❑ *n., pl.* **au·thor·i·ties** for 2-5.

au·thor·i·za·tion (o'thər ə zā'shən), *n.* **1** legal right; official permission: *I have the authorization of the owner to fish in this pond.* **2** act of authorizing; giving legal power to: *The authorization of the police to give tickets to jaywalkers cut down on the number of accidents.* ▪ See Synonym Study at **permission.**

au·thor·ize (o'thə rīz'), *v.* **1** to give power or right to: *The committee authorized her to proceed.* **2** to give formal approval to; approve: *Congress authorized the spending of money for a new post-office building.* ❑ *v.* **au·thor·ized, au·thor·iz·ing.** **—au'thor·iz'er,** *n.*

au·thor·ship (o'thər ship), *n.* origin as to author: *What is the authorship of that novel?*

au·tism (o'tiz'əm), *n.* a mental disorder in which someone lacks normal social and emotional responses and appears to be completely self-absorbed.

au·tis·tic (o tis'tik), *adj.* suffering from a condition in which a person is withdrawn, uncommunicative, and seems to be entirely absorbed with the self.

au·to (o'tō), *n.* automobile. ❑ *n., pl.* **au·tos.**

auto-, *prefix.* **1** by itself: *automatic = moving or acting by itself.* **2** of or to yourself: *autobiography = biography of yourself.*

au·to·an·ti·bod·y (o'tō an'ti bod'ē), *n.* antibody that attacks the body's own cells and tissues. ❑ *n., pl.* **au·to·an·ti·bod·ies.**

au·to·bi·og·ra·phy (o'tə bī og'rə fē), *n.* story of a person's life written by that person. ❑ *n., pl.* **au·to·bi·og·ra·phies.** **—au'to·bi'o·graph'ic** or **au'to·bi'o·graph'i·cal,** *adj.* **—au'to·bi'o·graph'i·cal·ly,** *adv.*

au·to·clave (o'tə klāv), *n.* a strong, closed container that develops steam under pressure, used for sterilizing medical and dental equipment.

au·toc·ra·cy (o tok'rə sē), *n.* **1** government by a single person having unlimited power. **2** absolute authority. ❑ *n., pl.* **au·toc·ra·cies** for 1.

au·to·crat (o'tə krat), *n.* **1** ruler having unlimited power. **2** person who uses power over others in a harsh way: *A good teacher is never an autocrat.*

au·to·crat·ic (o'tə krat'ik), *adj.* of or like an autocrat; having absolute power or authority; ruling without checks or limitations: *The principal's autocratic manner made him unpopular.* **—au'to·crat'i·cal·ly,** *adv.*

au·to·graph (o'tə graf), **1** *n.* a person's signature: *Many people collect the autographs of celebrities.* **2** *v.* to write your name in or on: *The movie star autographed my program.*

Au·to·harp (o'tō härp'), *n.* trademark for a musical instrument similar to the zither, that produces chords. A set of keys presses down on all strings except those required for the chord.

a	hat	ė	term	ô	order	ch	child		⟨a in about
ā	age	i	it	oi	oil	ng	long		e in taken
ä	far	ī	ice	ou	out	sh	she	ə ⟨	i in pencil
â	care	o	hot	u	cup	th	thin		o in lemon
e	let	ō	open	ù	put	ᴛʜ	then		u in circus
ē	equal	ò	saw	ü	rule	zh	measure		

au·to·im·mune (ȯ′tō i myün′), *adj.* caused by an immune system attack against the body's own cells and tissues: *an autoimmune disease.*

Au·to·mat (ȯ′tə mat), *n.* trademark for a self-service cafeteria in which food is obtained from compartments that open when coins are inserted in slots.

au·to·mate (ȯ′tə māt), *v.* to convert to automation; operate by automation. ❏ *v.* **au·to·mat·ed, au·to·mat·ing.**

au·to·mat·ic (ȯ′tə mat′ik), **1** *adj.* moving or acting by itself: *Our apartment house has an automatic elevator.* **2** *adj.* done without thought or attention: *Breathing and swallowing are usually automatic.* **3** *n.* gun that throws out the empty shell and reloads by itself. An automatic continues to fire until the trigger is released. **—au′to·mat′i·cal·ly,** *adv.*

> **SYNONYM STUDY** **Automatic** and **involuntary** both mean not done by free will. **Automatic** means done without thought or attention: *In a restaurant, her automatic choice is always a hamburger.* **Involuntary** means done without will or choice: *He gave an involuntary jump when I shouted "boo!"*

au·to·ma·tion (ȯ′tə mā′shən), *n.* the use of automatic controls in the operation of a machine or group of machines. In automation, electronic or mechanical devices do many of the tasks formerly performed by people.

au·tom·a·ton (ȯ tom′ə ton), *n.* **1** person or animal whose actions are entirely mechanical. **2** machine or toy that moves by itself. ❏ *n., pl.* **au·tom·a·tons, au·tom·a·ta** (ȯ tom′ə tə).

au·to·mo·bile (ȯ′tə mə bēl′), **1** *n.* car. **2** *adj.* of or for automobiles: *automobile mechanics.*

> **WORD STORY** **Automobile** comes from a Greek word meaning "self" and a Latin word meaning "moving." It was called this because it could move itself without horses to pull it.

au·to·mo·tive (ȯ′tə mō′tiv), *adj.* **1** of cars, trucks, and other motor vehicles. Automotive engineering deals with the design and construction of motor vehicles. **2** furnishing its own power; moving by itself: *many types of automotive vehicles.*

au·to·nom·ic nervous system (ȯ′tə nom′ik), the part of the nervous system in animals with backbones that controls involuntary actions such as digestion and breathing.

au·ton·o·mous (ȯ ton′ə məs), *adj.* self-governing; independent: *an autonomous nation.* **—au·ton′o·mous·ly,** *adv.*

au·ton·o·my (ȯ ton′ə mē), *n.* self-government; independence: *Algeria achieved autonomy in 1962.*

au·to·pi·lot (ȯ′tə pī′lət), *n.* a device that automatically steers an airplane without human assistance except to set course: *flying on autopilot.*

au·top·sy (ȯ′top sē), *n.* medical examination of a dead body to find the cause of death; post-mortem: *The autopsy revealed that the patient died of a heart attack.* ❏ *n., pl.* **au·top·sies.**

au·to·troph (ȯ′tə trof), *n.* any living thing that can produce its own food from nonliving substances. All green plants and some bacteria are autotrophs.

au·to·troph·ic (ȯ′tə trof′ik), *adj.* **1** able to produce food from nonliving substances: *autotrophic bacteria.* **2** of an autotroph or autotrophs: *an autotrophic environment.*

au·tumn (ȯ′təm), **1** *n.* season of the year between summer and winter; fall. **2** *adj.* of autumn; coming in autumn: *autumn flowers.* **—au·tum·nal** (ȯ tum′ nəl), *adj.* **—au·tum′nal·ly,** *adv.*

aux·il·iar·y (ȯg zil′yər ē), **1** *adj.* giving help or support; assisting: *Some sailboats have auxiliary engines.* **2** *n.* person or thing that helps; aid: *The microscope is a useful auxiliary to the human eye.* **3 auxiliaries,** *n.pl.* foreign or allied troops that help the army of a nation at war. **4** *adj.* additional: *The main library has several auxiliary branches.* **5** *n.* auxiliary verb. ❏ *n., pl.* **aux·il·iar·ies.**

auxiliary verb, verb used to form the tenses, moods, or voices of other verbs; helping verb. *Be, can, do, have, may, must, shall,* and *will* are auxiliary verbs. EXAMPLES: I *am* going; she *will* go; it *can* happen; we *must* leave; they *had* come.

aux·in (ȯk′sən), *n.* any of several plant hormones that control growth and development.

av., **1** avenue. **2** average. **3** avoirdupois.

a·vail (ə vāl′), **1** *v.* to be of use or value to; help: *Money will not avail you after you are dead.* **2** *v.* to be of use or value: *Talk will not avail without work.* **3** *n.* use; help; benefit: *Crying is of no avail now. I complained about his rudeness, but to no avail.*
avail yourself of, to take advantage of; profit by; make use of: *He availed himself of the opportunity to learn French.*

a·vail·a·ble (ə vā′lə bəl), *adj.* **1** able to be used: *She is not available for the job; she is out of town.* **2** able to be had: *All available tickets were sold.* **—a·vail′a·bil′i·ty,** *n.* **—a·vail′a·ble·ness,** *n.* **—a·vail′a·bly,** *adv.*

av·a·lanche (av′ə lanch), *n.* **1** a large mass of snow and ice, sometimes mixed with dirt and rocks, rapidly sliding or falling down the side of a mountain. **2** anything like an avalanche: *The reporters asked the governor an avalanche of questions.*

a·vant-garde (ä′vänt gärd′), **1** *n.* group of people, especially in the arts, who are ahead of all others in using or creating new ideas, methods, designs, etc. **2** *adj.* of or about the avant-garde.

av·ar·ice (av′ər is), *n.* too great a desire to acquire money or property; greed for wealth.

avalanche (def. 1)

av·a·ri·cious (av′ə rish′əs), *adj.* greatly desiring money or property; greedy for wealth. **—av′a·ri′cious·ly,** *adv.* **—av′a·ri′cious·ness,** *n.*

a·vast (ə vast′), *interj.* stop! stay! *"Avast there!"* shouted the sailor.

a·va·tar (av′ə tär′), *n.* (in Hindu mythology) an appearance of a god or goddess on earth in bodily form; incarnation.

a·vaunt (ə vȯnt′), *interj.* OLD USE. begone! get out! go away!

Ave. or **ave.,** Avenue; avenue.

A·ve Ma·ri·a (ä′vā mə rē′ə), **1** "Hail Mary!", the first words of the Latin form of a prayer of the Roman Catholic Church. **2** this prayer.

a·venge (ə venj′), *v.* to get revenge for: *avenge an insult. They fought to avenge the enemy's invasion of their country.* ❏ *v.* **a·venged, a·veng·ing.** **—a·veng′er,** *n.*

av·e·nue (av′ə nü *or* av′ə nyü), *n.* **1** a wide street. **2** road or walk bordered by trees. **3** way of approach: *Hard work is one avenue to success.*

a·ver (ə vėr′), *v.* to state positively to be true; assert: *They averred that they had nothing to do with breaking into the parked car.* ❏ *v.* **a·verred, a·ver·ring.**

autumn (def. 2)—autumn leaves

av·er·age (av′ər ij), **1** *n.* quantity found by dividing the sum of all the quantities by the number of quantities. The average of 3 and 5 and 10 is 6 (3 + 5 + 10 = 18; 18 ÷ 3 = 6). **2** *v.* to find the average of: *Will you average those numbers for me?* **3** *adj.* obtained by averaging; being an average: *The average temperature for the week was 82°.* **4** *v.* to have as an average; amount on the average to: *The cost of our lunches at school averaged $6 a week.* **5** *n.* usual sort or amount: *The amount of rain this year has been below average.* **6** *adj.* usual; ordinary: *a person of average intelligence.* **7** *v.* to do, get, yield, etc., on an average: *She averages six hours of work a day. The farmer averaged 40 bushels of wheat to the acre.* □ *v.* **av·er·aged, av·er·ag·ing. —av′er·age·ly,** *adv.* **—av′er·age·ness,** *n.*

on the average or **on an average,** considered on the basis of the average: *I work six hours a day on the average. The farm produces, on an average, 40 bushels to the acre.*

WORD STORY **Average** comes from an Arabic word meaning "goods damaged by seawater." Merchants shared the cost of such damage in equal ways. This sharing gave the word its modern meaning.

a·verse (ə vėrs′), *adj.* having a strong or fixed dislike; opposed or unwilling: *I am extremely averse to smoking.* **—a·verse′ly,** *adv.* **—a·verse′ness,** *n.*

a·ver·sion (ə vėr′zhən), *n.* **1** a strong or fixed dislike: *I have an aversion to beef liver.* **2** thing or person disliked: *Impoliteness is his special aversion.*

a·vert (ə vėrt′), *v.* **1** to keep from happening; prevent; avoid: *The driver averted an accident by a quick turn of the steering wheel.* **2** to turn away; turn aside: *I averted my eyes from the accident.* **—a·vert′i·ble** or **a·vert′a·ble,** *adj.*

a·vi·an (ā′vē ən), *adj.* of or relating to birds: *avian anatomy.*

a·vi·ar·y (ā′vē er′ē), *n.* house, enclosure, or large cage in which many birds, especially wild birds, are kept. □ *n., pl.* **a·vi·ar·ies.**

a·vi·a·tion (ā′vē ā′shən), *n.* **1** science or art of operating and navigating aircraft. **2** the design and manufacture of aircraft, especially airplanes.

a·vi·a·tor (ā′vē ā′tər *or* av′ē ā′tər), *n.* person who flies an aircraft; pilot.

aviator glasses, eyeglasses with lightweight metal frames and large, tinted lenses, shaped to resemble fliers′ goggles.

av·id (av′id), *adj.* extremely eager or enthusiastic: *an avid defender of human rights. She is an avid golfer.* **—av′id·ly,** *adv.* **—av′id·ness,** *n.*

a·vid·i·ty (ə vid′ə tē), *n.* **1** great eagerness: *Our suggestion that they visit us was seized upon with avidity.* **2** greed or wealth; avarice.

a·vi·on·ics (ā′vē on′iks), *n.* the development, production, and use of electronic control and sensing devices for aviation, rocketry, and astronautics.

av·o·ca·do (av′ə kä′dō), *n.* the dark green, pear-shaped fruit of a tree that grows in warm regions; alligator pear. Avocados have a large seed surrounded by yellow-green pulp which is used in salads, dips, etc. □ *n., pl.* **av·o·ca·dos.**

avocado

av·o·ca·tion (av′ə kā′shən), *n.* something that a person likes to do in addition to a regular job; hobby: *He is a lawyer, but writing stories is his avocation.* [Avocation comes from a Latin word meaning "to call away." An avocation "calls away" someone from his or her regular job or duties.]

a·void (ə void′), *v.* to keep away from; keep out of the way of: *We avoided driving through large cities on our trip.* **—a·void′a·ble,** *adj.* **—a·void′a·bly,** *adv.*

SYNONYM STUDY **Avoid, evade,** and **shun** all mean to get away or keep away from someone or something. **Avoid** means to keep away: *The kids avoided that gloomy old house.* **Evade** means to get away: *The butterfly evaded our nets.* **Shun** suggests strong dislike and careful effort to keep away: *He is shy and shuns attention.*

a·void·ance (ə void′ns), *n.* act of avoiding; keeping away from: *His avoidance of me made me think he was angry with me.*

av·oir·du·pois weight (av′ər də poiz′), system of weights in which a pound containing 16 ounces is used. Once common, it is now used mostly in the United States. See table on page 975A.

A·von (ā′vən), *n.* name of several rivers in central and southern England.

a·vow (ə vou′), *v.* to declare frankly or openly; admit; acknowledge: *The senator avowed that he had never favored higher taxes for low-income people.* **—a·vow′a·ble,** *adj.*

a·vow·al (ə vou′əl), *n.* a frank or open declaration; admission; acknowledgment: *She made a plain avowal of her opinions even though they were unpopular.*

a·vowed (ə voud′), *adj.* openly declared; admitted: *The governor was an avowed candidate for the presidency.* **—a·vow·ed·ly** (ə-vou′id lē), *adv.*

a·wait (ə wāt′), *v.* **1** to wait for; look forward to: *I shall await your answer to my letter with eagerness.* **2** to be ready for; be in store for: *Many pleasures await you on your trip.*

a·wake (ə wāk′), **1** *v.* to wake up; arouse: *I awoke from a sound sleep. The alarm clock awoke me.* **2** *adj.* roused from sleep; not asleep: *She is always awake early.* **3** *v.* to stir up: *My words awoke his anger.* **4** *adj.* on the alert; watchful: *All during the long journey they were awake to possible danger.* □ *v.* **a·woke, a·wo·ken** or **a·waked, a·wak·ing.**

a·wak·en (ə wā′kən), *v.* to wake up; stir up; arouse: *The sun was shining when he awakened. I was awakened late this morning.* **—a·wak′en·er,** *n.*

a·wak·en·ing (ə wā′kə ning), *n.* act of waking up; arousing.

a·ward (ə wôrd′), **1** *v.* to give after careful consideration; grant: *A medal was awarded to the best speller in the class.* **2** *n.* something given after careful consideration; prize: *The athlete received an award for his performance.* ■ See Synonym Study at **prize**[1]. **3** *v.* to decide upon by law; adjudge: *The court awarded damages of $5000 to the injured man.* **4** *n.* decision by a judge: *We all thought the award was fair.* **—a·ward′a·ble,** *adj.* **—a·ward′er,** *n.*

a·ware (ə wâr′), *adj.* having knowledge; realizing; conscious: *I was too sleepy to be aware how cold it was. She was not aware of her danger.* **—a·ware′ness,** *n.*

a·wash (ə wäsh′), *adj.* **1** covered with water: *The beach was awash with the flowing tide.* **2** carried about by water; floating: *The rising water set everything awash.*

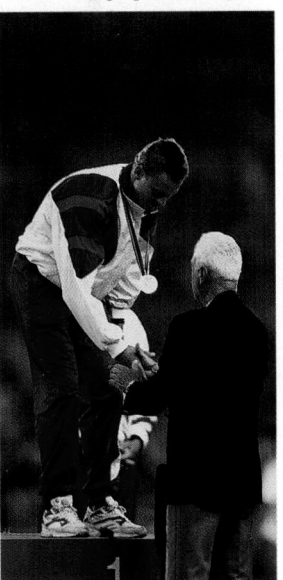

award (def. 2)

a·way (ə wā′), **1** *adv.* from a place; to a distance: *drive away, sail away.* **2** *adj., adv.* at a distance; a way off: *The sailor was far away from home. His home is miles away.* **3** *adj.* absent; gone: *My friend is away today.* **4** *adv.* out of your possession, notice, or use: *He gave his boat away.* **5** *adv.* out of existence: *The sounds died away.* **6** *adv.* in another direction; aside: *She turned her car away to avoid an accident.* **7** *adv.* without stopping; continuously: *work away at a job.* **8** *adv.* without delay; at once: *Fire away!*

do away with, 1 to put an end to; get rid of: *The United States did away with slavery in 1865.* **2** to kill: *They had to do away with the sick animal.*

a	hat	ė	term	ô	order	ch	child
ā	age	i	it	oi	oil	ng	long
ä	far	ī	ice	ou	out	sh	she
â	care	o	hot	u	cup	th	thin
e	let	ō	open	u̇	put	ᵮH	then
ē	equal	ȯ	saw	ü	rule	zh	measure

ə { a in about / e in taken / i in pencil / o in lemon / u in circus }

awe (ȯ), **1** *n.* great fear and wonder; fear and great respect: *The sight of the great waterfall filled us with awe.* **2** *v.* to cause to feel awe; fill with awe: *The majesty of the mountains awed us.* ❏ *v.* **awed, aw·ing.**

awe·some (ȯ′səm), *adj.* **1** causing awe: *The great fire was an awesome sight.* **2** INFORMAL. exceptionally good, desirable, or remarkable; terrific: *Where did you get those awesome shoes?* **—awe′some·ness,** *n.*

awe·struck (ȯ′struk′), *adj.* filled with awe: *She was awestruck by the mountain's grandeur.*

aw·ful (ȯ′fəl), **1** *adj.* causing fear; dreadful; terrible: *an awful storm with thunder and lightning.* **2** *adj.* deserving great respect and reverence: *He felt the awful power of God.* **3** *adj.* filling with awe; impressive: *The mountains rose to awful heights.* **4** *adj.* very bad, great, ugly, etc.: *an awful mess, an awful nuisance.* **5** *adv.* INFORMAL. very: *She was awful mad.* **—aw′ful·ness,** *n.*

> **USAGE NOTE** The widespread use of **awful** as a word of disapproval (def. 4) has made the more literal definitions (defs. 1-3) difficult to understand. It is wise to use *awe-inspiring* or *awesome* when those meanings are meant.

aw·ful·ly (ȯ′flē *or* ȯ′fə lē), *adv.* **1** dreadfully; terribly: *The burn hurt awfully.* **2** very: *I'm awfully sorry.*

a·while (ə wīl′), *adv.* for a short time: *Stay awhile.*

> **USAGE NOTE** People sometimes confuse **awhile** and the two-word phrase **a while. Awhile** is written as one word when used as an adverb: *We talked awhile and then left for home.* **A while,** written as two words, is used when **while** is a noun in a prepositional phrase: *We read for a while and then went to sleep.*

awk·ward (ȯk′wərd), *adj.* **1** not graceful or skillful in movement or shape; clumsy: *Seals are very awkward on land, but graceful in the water.* **2** not easily used: *The handle of this jug has an awkward shape.* **3** not easily managed: *This is an awkward corner to turn.* **4** inconvenient or embarrassing: *an awkward situation. He asked me such an awkward question that I did not know what to reply.* **—awk′ward·ly,** *adv.* **—awk′ward·ness,** *n.*

> **SYNONYM STUDY Awkward** and **clumsy** both mean not graceful. **Awkward** suggests a lack of quickness and skill: *With an awkward motion, she got off the crowded bus.* **Clumsy** suggests stiff and heavy motion, likely to bump into things or drop them: *Heavy gloves made his fingers clumsy, and the key slipped.*

awl (ȯl), *n.* a pointed tool used for making small holes in leather or wood. ■ Another word that sounds like this is **all.**

awn·ing (ȯ′ning), *n.* piece of canvas, metal, wood, or plastic that forms a rooflike covering over a door, window, porch, patio, etc., for protection from the sun or rain.

a·woke (ə wōk′), *v.* past tense of **awake:** *I awoke late.*

a·wo·ken (ə wō′kən), *v.* a past participle of **awake:** *He has awoken late every day this week.*

AWOL or **A.W.O.L.** (ā′wȯl′), *adv., adj.* absent without leave: *Homesick, the soldier went AWOL. He was AWOL for two and a half months.*

a·wry (ə rī′), *adv.* **1** with a twist or turn to one side: *My hat was blown awry by the wind.* **2** wrong; out of order: *Our plans have gone awry.*

ax or **axe** (aks), *n.* tool with a flat, sharp blade fastened on a handle, used for chopping, splitting, and shaping wood. ❏ *n., pl.* **ax·es. —ax′like′** or **axe′like′,** *adj.*

ax·es[1] (ak′siz), *n.* plural of **ax.**

ax·es[2] (ak′sēz′), *n.* plural of **axis.**

ax·i·al (ak′sē əl), *adj.* of or forming an axis.

ax·il (ak′səl), *n.* angle between the upper side of a leaf or stem

and the supporting stem or branch. A bud is usually found in the axil. ■ Another word that sounds like this is **axle.**

ax·i·om (ak′sē əm), *n.* **1** statement taken to be true without proof; self-evident truth: *It is an axiom that if equals are added to equals the results will be equal.* **2** a well-established principle; rule or law.

ax·i·o·mat·ic (ak′sē ə mat′ik), *adj.* accepted without proof; self-evident: *It is axiomatic that a whole is greater than any of its parts.* **—ax′i·o·mat′i·cal·ly,** *adv.*

ax·is (ak′sis), *n.* **1** a straight line around which an object turns or seems to turn. The axis of the earth is an imaginary line through the North Pole and the South Pole. **2** a central or principal line around which parts are arranged regularly. The axis of a cone is a straight line going from the center of its base to its peak. **3** one of the lines along which the coordinates of a point are measured. **4 the Axis,** Germany, Italy, Japan, and their allies, during World War II. ❏ *n., pl.* **ax·es** for 1-3.

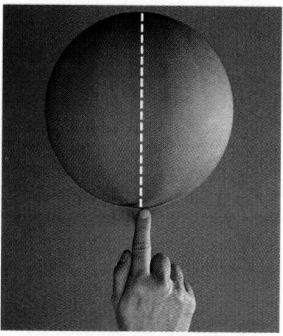
axis (def. 1)—extends upward from the finger

ax·le (ak′səl), *n.* **1** bar or shaft on which a wheel turns. Some axles turn with the wheel. **2** axletree. ■ Another word that sounds like this is **axil.**

ax·le·tree (ak′səl trē′), *n.* a fixed crossbar supporting a cart or other vehicle. The wheels turn around its ends. ❏ *n., pl.* **ax·le·trees.**

ax·o·lotl (ak′sə lot′l), *n.* any of several salamanders, common in lakes and lagoons in Mexico and the southwestern United States, that usually keep their gills and tadpole body for life.

ax·on (ak′son), *n.* the long extension of a neuron that carries nerve impulses away from the body of the cell.

a·ya·tol·lah (ä′yä tō′lə), *n.* **1** a Muslim religious leader. **2** any leader. [*Ayatollah* comes from Arabic words meaning "sign" and "Allah." Allah is the Muslim name of God.]

aye or **ay** (ī), **1** *adv.* yes: *Aye, aye, sir.* **2** *n.* a vote or voter in favor of something: *The ayes won the vote.* ■ Other words that sound like this are **eye** and **I.**

Ayr·shire (âr′shər), *n.* any of a breed of dairy cattle that are red and white or brown and white, originating in Scotland.

AZ, Arizona (used with postal Zip Code).

a·zal·ea (ə zā′lyə), *n.* any of several bushes with showy pink, white, yellow, and purple flowers, growing mainly in northeast North America and in China. Azaleas are related to rhododendrons. ❏ *n., pl.* **a·zal·eas.**

A·zer·bai·jan (ä′zər bī jän′), *n.* country in SE Europe, on the Caspian Sea. *Capital:* Baku.

A·zores (ə zôrz′ *or* ā′zôrz), *n.pl.* group of islands in the Atlantic, west of and belonging to Portugal.

Az·tec (az′tek), *n.* member of a tribe of American Indians of central Mexico. The Aztecs had a highly developed culture, and ruled a large empire during the 1400s, which fell to the Spanish in 1521. ❏ *n., pl.* **Az·tec** or **Az·tecs.**

az·ure (azh′ər), **1** *n.* the blue color of a cloudless sky. **2** *adj.* having this color; sky-blue.

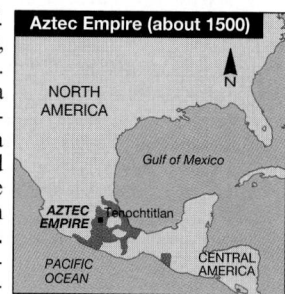
Aztec Empire (about 1500)

NORTH AMERICA

Gulf of Mexico

AZTEC EMPIRE — Tenochtitlan

PACIFIC OCEAN

CENTRAL AMERICA

B or **b** (bē), *n.* the second letter of the English alphabet. ❑ *n., pl.* **B's** or **b's.**

B, symbol for boron.

Ba, symbol for barium.

B.A., Bachelor of Arts. Also, **A.B.**

baa (bä *or* ba), **1** *n.* the sound a sheep makes; bleat. **2** *v.* to make this sound; bleat. ❑ *n., pl.* **baas;** *v.* **baaed, baa·ing.** ■ Another word that can sound like this is **bah.**

bab·ble (bab′əl), **1** *v.* to make sounds like a baby: *The baby was babbling.* **2** *n.* talk that cannot be understood: *confused babble.* **3** *v.* to talk foolishly: *They babbled on without saying anything serious.* **4** *n.* foolish talk. **5** *v.* to talk too much; tell secrets. **6** *v.* to make a murmuring sound: *a babbling brook.* **7** *n.* a murmuring sound: *the babble of the brook.* ❑ *v.* **bab·bled, bab·bling.**

babe (bāb), *n.* baby.

Ba·bel (bā′bəl *or* bab′əl), *n.* **1** (in the Bible) a city where a high tower was built to reach heaven. God punished its builders by changing their language into several new and different languages. Because they could not understand each other, they had to leave the tower unfinished. **2 babel,** noise; confusion.

ba·boon (ba bün′), *n.* any of several large, fierce monkeys with doglike faces and short tails. Baboons live in the rocky hills of Africa and Arabia in large groups. [**Baboon** comes from a French word meaning "stupid person." People thought the animal looked like someone being silly.]

ba·bush·ka (bə bûsh′kə), *n.* scarf worn on the head and tied under the chin. ❑ *n., pl.* **ba·bush·kas.**

WORD STORY **Babushka** comes from a Russian word meaning "grandmother." This word comes in turn from a Russian word meaning "old woman." Russian women, especially older ones, often wear these scarves.

ba·by (bā′bē), **1** *n.* child too young to walk or speak; infant. **2** *n.* the youngest of a family or group. **3** *adj.* young: *a baby lamb.* **4** *adj.* small for its kind; small: *my baby finger.* **5** *adj.* of or for a baby: *baby shoes.* **6** *adj.* childish: *baby talk.* **7** *n.* person who acts like a baby; childish person: *Don't be a baby.* **8** *v.* to treat as a baby; pamper: *You are too old to be babied.* ❑ *n., pl.* **ba·bies;** *v.* **ba·bied, ba·by·ing.**

baby bonus, CANADIAN INFORMAL. Family Allowance.

baby boom, a sudden increase in the number of births. The United States had a baby boom from 1946 to 1964.

baby boomer (bü′mər), person born during a baby boom, especially someone born in the United States between 1946 and 1964.

ba·by·hood (bā′bē hůd), *n.* condition or time of being a baby.

a	hat	ė	term	ô	order	ch	child		a in about
ā	age	i	it	oi	oil	ng	long		e in taken
ä	far	ī	ice	ou	out	sh	she	ə	i in pencil
â	care	o	hot	u	cup	th	thin		o in lemon
e	let	ō	open	ů	put	ŦH	then		u in circus
ē	equal	ò	saw	ü	rule	zh	measure		

ba·by·ish (bā′bē ish), *adj.* like a baby; childish: *His round face and bald head gave him a babyish appearance.* —**ba′by·ish·ly**, *adv.* —**ba′by·ish·ness**, *n.*

Bab·y·lon (bab′ə lən), *n.* capital of ancient Babylonia, on the Euphrates. It was noted for its wealth, power, magnificence, and the wickedness of its people. See **Babylonia** for map.

Bab·y·lo·ni·a (bab′ə lō′nē ə), *n.* ancient empire in SW Asia which reached its peak about 1800 B.C. The capital was Babylon. —**Bab′y·lo′ni·an**, *adj.*, *n.*

Babylonian Empire (1800 B.C.)

ba·by·sit (bā′bē sit′), *v.* to take care of a child or children while the parents are away for a while. ❑ *v.* **ba·by·sat** (bā′bē sat′), **ba·by·sit·ting.** —**ba′by·sit′ter**, *n.*

Bach (bäk), *n.* **Jo·hann Se·bas·tian** (yō′hän sə bas′chən), 1685-1750, German composer and organist. He is one of the greatest composers of classical music.

bach·e·lor (bach′ə lər), *n.* **1** man who has not married. **2** person who has a four-year degree from a college or university.

bach·e·lor's-but·ton or **bach·e·lor's button** (bach′ə lərz but′n), *n.* plant with a single, small, button-shaped flower that is blue, violet, pink, or white; cornflower.

ba·cil·lus (bə sil′əs), *n.* **1** any of the rod-shaped bacteria, especially one that forms spores: *the typhoid bacillus.* **2** any type of bacteria. ❑ *n.*, *pl.* **ba·cil·li** (bə sil′ī). [See Word Story at **bacteria**.]

back (bak), **1** *n.* the part of a person's body opposite the front part of the body or the face. **2** *n.* the upper part of an animal's body from the neck to the end of the backbone. **3** *n.* the backbone; spine. **4** *n.* the side of anything away from the front; rear, upper, or farther part: *I had a bruise on the back of my hand.* **5** *n.* the reverse, under, or wrong side: *the back of a rug, the back of a medal.* **6** *adj.* at the back: *The box is in the back seat of the car.* **7** *n.* part of a chair, couch, or bench that supports the back of a person sitting down. **8** *v.* to support or help: *Many of her friends backed her plan.* **9** *v.* to move or cause to move backward or in the opposite direction: *I backed the car out of the driveway. We backed away from the dog.* **10** *adj.*, *adv.* behind in space or time: *Have you read the back issues of this magazine? Please walk back three steps. Some years back this land was all farms.* **11** *adj.* in distant or frontier regions: *back country.* **12** *adv.* in return: *They paid back what they borrowed.* **13** *adv.* in the place from which something or someone came: *Put the books back.* **14** *adv.* under control; away: *The police held the crowd back.* **15** *n.* a football player whose position is behind the line of scrimmage.
back and forth, first one way and then the other: *The dog ran back and forth across the field.*
back down, to give up an attempt or claim; withdraw: *I said I would go swimming, but I backed down when I found out how cold the water was.*
back of, in the rear of; behind: *The barn is back of the house.*
back out or **back out of,** to withdraw from an undertaking or promise: *The village backed out of building a pool when the cost got too high.*
back up, 1 to move backward: *The freight train backed up to the factory loading dock.* **2** to support or help: *Most of the neighborhood backed up the city's plan for new streetlights.*
behind someone's back, without the person's knowing it; secretly: *The cashier of the store stole money behind the owner's back.*
get off someone's back, to leave a person alone and stop bothering her or him.
go back on, to break a promise to.

back·ache (bak′āk′), *n.* a continuous pain in the back.

back·bite (bak′bīt′), *v.* to say mean or spiteful things about; slander an absent person. ❑ *v.* **back·bit** (bak′bit′), **back·bit·ten** (bak′bit′n), **back·bit·ing.** —**back′bit′er**, *n.*

back·board (bak′bôrd′), *n.* (in basketball) the upright, rectangular surface of wood, glass, or plastic to which the basket is fastened; board. Bank shots are bounced off the backboard.

back·bone (bak′bōn′), *n.* **1** the main bone along the middle of the back in human beings and other mammals, birds, reptiles, amphibians, and fishes; spine. The backbone contains many separate bones, called vertebrae, held together by muscles and tendons. **2** the most important part; chief support; basis: *The Constitution is the backbone of our legal system.* **3** strength of character; firmness: *Although she is criticized, she has the backbone to stand up for her beliefs.*

back·break·ing (bak′brā′king), *adj.* very exhausting; demanding great effort: *Shoveling snow all day is backbreaking work.*

back country, a rural area where few people live, far away from bigger towns or cities.

back·drop (bak′drop′), *n.* curtain at the back of a stage, often painted and used as part of the scenery.

back·er (bak′ər), *n.* person who supports another person, a plan, or an idea.

back·field (bak′fēld′), *n.* the football players whose positions are behind the line of scrimmage.

back·fire (bak′fīr′), **1** *n.* explosion of gas occurring at the wrong time or in the wrong place in a gasoline engine. **2** *v.* to be the location of such an explosion: *The engine backfired.* **3** *n.* a fire deliberately started to control a forest or prairie fire by burning off the space in front of

backdrop

it. **4** *v.* to have a result opposite to the expected result: *His scheme backfired, and instead of getting rich he lost all his money.* ❑ *v.* **back·fired, back·fir·ing.**

back-for·ma·tion (bak′fôr mā′shən), *n.* word formed by dropping an ending from another word that existed first. The longer, older word looks as though it came from the shorter new word, but the facts are the other way round. EXAMPLES: *burgle* from *burglar; greed* from *greedy.*

WORD SOURCE **Back-formations** have been common in English for a long time. Many recent back-formations are verbs, and many are used informally. The words below all came into English as back-formations.

WORD	FROM	WORD	FROM
atone	atonement	escalate	escalator
burgle	burglar	greed	greedy
diagnose	diagnosis	pea	pease
edit	editor	peddle	peddler
enthuse	enthusiasm	peeve	peevish

back·gam·mon (bak′gam′ən), *n.* game for two played on a special board with 12 spaces on each side. Each player has 15 pieces, which are moved according to the throw of the dice.

WORD STORY **Backgammon** probably comes from the English word **back** and an old form of the English word **game**. It may have gotten its name because pieces are removed from the board and put back on it during the game.

back·ground (bak′ground′), *n.* **1** the part of a picture or scene toward the back: *The cottage stands in the foreground with the mountains in the background.* **2** surface against which a thing or person is placed or shown: *Her dress had pink flowers on a white background.* **3** earlier conditions or events that help to explain some later condition or event: *This book gives the background of the Revolutionary War.* **4** past experience, knowledge, and training: *His early background included living on a farm.*
in the background, out of the way; not involved: *A shy person often prefers to stay in the background.*

background music, 1 recorded music played softly in a public area, meant to be soothing and pleasant. **2** any music used to set a mood, especially in a movie.

back·hand (bak′hand′), **1** *n.* stroke in tennis and other games made with the back of the hand turned outward. **2** *n.* handwriting in which the letters slope to the left. **3** *adj.* backhanded.

back·hand·ed (bak′han′did), *adj.* **1** done or made with the back of the hand turned outward: *a backhanded stroke.* **2** indirect: *She means to help, even though she offers to do so in a backhanded way.* **3** sounding like praise but actually an insult; insincere: *a backhanded compliment.* **4** slanting to the left: *backhanded writing.* **−back′hand′ed·ly,** *adv.* **−back′hand′ed·ness,** *n.*

back·hoe (bak′hō′), *n.* machine for digging, having a large scoop attached to a long arm which pulls the scoop back toward the machine.

back·ing (bak′ing), *n.* **1** support or help: *The candidate had the backing of several newspapers in the state.* **2** something placed at the back of anything to support or strengthen it: *a quilt with new backing.*

back·lash (bak′lash′), *n.* **1** a sudden negative reaction caused by fear or anger. **2** a sudden backward movement of a machine or mechanical device. ❑ *n., pl.* **back·lash·es.**

back·log (bak′lôg′), *n.* **1** an accumulation of orders, duties, etc., that have not yet been carried out: *After my illness I had a large backlog of work.* **2** a large log at the back of a wood fire.

back·pack (bak′pak′), **1** *n.* a pack, often supported by a frame, that is worn on the back by hikers and campers to carry food, clothes, and equipment. **2** *v.* to go hiking or camping while carrying a backpack. **−back′pack′er,** *n.*

back·rest (bak′rest′), *n.* a support for the back.

back seat, place of inferiority.

back·seat driver (bak′sēt′), person who gives unwanted advice or criticism, especially a passenger talking to the driver.

back·side (bak′sīd′), *n.* rump; buttocks.

back·slash (bak′slash′), *n.* mark (\) used especially with computer programs. ❑ *n., pl.* **back·slash·es.**

back·slide (bak′slīd′), *v.* to slide back into wrong ways, error, etc.; gradually return to old ways and practices. ❑ *v.* **back·slid** (bak′slid′), **back·slid·ing. −back′slid′er,** *n.*

back·spin (bak′spin′), *n.* spin given to a ball to stop or reverse its forward motion when it strikes the ground or an object.

back·stage (bak′stāj′), *adv., adj.* in the part of a theater not seen by the audience; behind a backdrop, in the wings, or in a dressing room: *to go backstage, a backstage interview.*

back·stop (bak′stop′), *n.* **1** wall, fence, or screen used in various sports to keep the ball in the area of play. **2** catcher in baseball. **3** anything that supports.

back·stroke (bak′strōk′), *n.* **1** a swimming stroke made while lying on your back. **2** a backhanded stroke.

back talk, rude or bold answers, especially by a younger person to an older one.

back·track (bak′trak′), *v.* **1** to go back over a course or path. **2** to withdraw from an undertaking, position, etc.: *He backtracked on the promise he made last week.*

back·up (bak′up′), **1** *n.* reserve: *a backup of troops.* **2** *n.* accumulation: *a backup of traffic.* **3** *adj.* kept in readiness or reserve: *a backup pilot.*

back·ward (bak′wərd), **1** *adv.* with the back first: *He tumbled over backward.* **2** *adv., adj.* toward the back: *He looked backward as she left the room.* **3** *adv.* opposite to the usual way: *Can you read backward?* **4** *adv.* from better to worse: *In some towns living conditions improved; in some they went backward.* **5** *adv.* toward the past: *She looked backward 40 years and talked about her childhood.* **6** *adj.* slow in development: *a backward country, a backward child.* ■ This meaning of **backward** is often considered offensive. **7** *adj.* shy; bashful: *Shake hands with her; don't be backward.* **−back′ward·ly,** *adv.* **−back′ward·ness,** *n.*

back·wards (bak′wərdz), *adv.* backward (defs. 1-5).

back·wash (bak′wäsh′), *n.* **1** water thrown back by oars, a passing ship, etc. **2** a backward current of water.

back·wa·ter (bak′wô′tər), *n.* **1** stretch of water that is held, thrown, or pushed back. **2** a place that is not culturally or economically developed. ■ This meaning of **backwater** is often considered offensive.

back·woods (bak′wüdz′), *n.sing.* or *pl.* **1** uncleared forests or wild regions far away from towns. **2** a remote area.

back·woods·man (bak′wüdz′mən), *n.* person who lives in the backwoods. ❑ *n., pl.* **back·woods·men.**

back·yard (bak′yärd′), *n.* yard behind a house or building.

ba·con (bā′kən), *n.* salted and smoked meat from the back and sides of a hog.

Ba·con (bā′kən), *n.* **Francis,** 1561-1626, English essayist, politician, and philosopher. ■ **Francis Bacon** was one of the earliest supporters of the scientific method. He believed that people could find out the truth more easily if they based theories on careful observation of facts, instead of forming theories based on previous beliefs.

bac·te·ri·a (bak tir′ē ə), *n.pl.* very tiny and simple living things, so small that they can usually be seen only through a microscope. They are single cells, rod-shaped, spherical, or spiral, with no chlorophyll. Some bacteria cause diseases such as pneumonia and typhoid fever; others do useful things, such as turning cider into vinegar. ❑ *n., sing.* **bac·te·ri·um. −bac·ter′i·al,** *adj.* **−bac·ter′i·a·like′,** *adj.*

WORD STORY **Bacteria** is the plural of **bacterium,** which comes from a Greek word meaning "little rod." Scientists who discovered bacteria saw mostly the rod-shaped kind and named them after their shape. **Bacillus,** another word for a bacterium, comes from a Latin word meaning "little rod."

bac·te·ri·o·log·i·cal (bak tir′ē ə loj′ə kəl), *adj.* **1** of or about bacteriology. **2** using bacteria: *bacteriological warfare.* **−bac·ter′i·o·log′i·cal·ly,** *adv.*

bac·te·ri·ol·o·gy (bak tir′ē ol′ə jē), *n.* science that deals with bacteria. **−bac·ter′i·ol′o·gist,** *n.*

bac·te·ri·um (bak tir′ē əm), *n.* singular of **bacteria.**

Bac·tri·an camel (bak′trē ən), camel with two humps and long hair, found in central Asia.

bad (bad), **1** *adj.* not good; not as it ought to be: *It was hard to read in the bad light.* **2** *adj.* evil; wicked: *Only someone bad would hurt a helpless person.* **3** *adj.* not friendly; cross; unpleasant: *a bad temper.* **4** *adj.* causing pain and sorrow: *bad news.* **5** *adj.* naughty; not behaving well: *The child was bad when she hit her playmate.* **6**

Bactrian camel

adj. unfavorable: *a bad time.* **7** *adj.* severe: *A bad thunderstorm delayed the airplane.* **8** *adj.* harmful; unhealthful: *Smoking is bad for you.* **9** *adj.* rotten; spoiled: *Don't use that egg; it's bad.* **10** *adj.* sorry: *I feel bad about losing your baseball.* **11** *adj.* sick: *Her cold made her feel bad.* **12** *adj.* incorrect: *a bad guess.* **13** *adv.* INFORMAL. badly. ■ See Usage Note at **badly. 14** *n.* something that is bad; bad condition or quality. ❑ *adj.* **worse, worst.** ■ Another word that sounds like this is **bade. −bad′ness,** *n.*

be in bad, INFORMAL. be out of favor: *I'm in bad with the teacher because I lost my homework.*

not bad, not so bad, or **not half bad,** fairly good; rather good.

WORD POWER **BAD** ■ One reason that language has prefixes and suffixes is that some ideas are very common. People want a short way of saying the idea, because they say it often, about many things. Prefixes and suffixes are that short way. For example, many things can be good or bad, done well or done badly. So English has two prefixes meaning "badly, poorly, wrong." They are **mal-** and **mis-.** Sometimes one is used, sometimes the other, sometimes even both:

maltreat = to treat badly
mistreat = to treat badly

a	hat	ė	term	ô	order	ch	child		a in about
ā	age	i	it	oi	oil	ng	long		e in taken
ä	far	ī	ice	ou	out	sh	she	ə	i in pencil
â	care	o	hot	u	cup	th	thin		o in lemon
e	let	ō	open	ů	put	ᵺ	then		u in circus
ē	equal	ò	saw	ü	rule	zh	measure		

bad blood, unfriendly feeling; hate: *There is bad blood between the rival gangs.*

bade (bad), *v.* a past tense of **bid:** *The captain bade the soldiers go on.* ■ **Bade** is used in very formal English and in stories: *The king bade her remain.* ■ Another word that sounds like this is **bad.**

Ba·den-Pow·ell (bād′n pō′əl), *n.* Sir **Rob·ert** (rob′ərt), 1857-1941, English general who founded the Boy Scouts in 1908.

badge (baj), *n.* **1** something worn to show that someone belongs to a certain occupation, school, class, club, society, etc.: *The Red Cross badge is a red cross on a white background.* **2** symbol or sign: *Chains are a badge of slavery.*

badg·er (baj′ər), **1** *n.* any of eight kinds of hairy gray mammals that feed at night and dig holes in the ground to live in. Badgers are related to weasels but are larger and more heavily built. They usually have some white and black fur on their head and face. **2** *n.* their fur. **3** *v.* to keep on annoying or teasing; bother or question persistently: *That salesman has been badgering us for the last two weeks to buy a new car.* [**Badger** probably comes from **badge,** because the white fur on the animal's forehead is like an identification mark.]

Bad·lands (bad′landz′), **1** *n.sing* or *n.pl.* rugged, barren region in SW South Dakota and NW Nebraska in which erosion has produced unusual land formations. **2** *n.pl.* **badlands,** any similar region.

Badlands National Park

Badlands National Park, a national park in SW South Dakota, containing scenic eroded landforms.

bad·ly (bad′lē), **1** *adv.* in a bad manner: *She sings badly.* **2** *adj.* IN-FORMAL. bad. **3** *adv.* very much: *He needs help badly.*
badly off, in a condition of poverty or distress.

USAGE NOTE In formal English **badly** is used only to modify action verbs. SAY: *She sings badly.* NOT: *She sings bad.* In formal English, **badly** is not used as an adjective: SAY: *She feels bad.* NOT: *She feels badly.*

bad·min·ton (bad′min tən), *n.* game played by two or four players on a rectangular court, in which a shuttlecock is hit back and forth over a high net with a lightweight racket. [**Badminton** was named after a nobleman's estate where the game was first played in England. The British had learned it in India.]

bad-mouth (bad′mouth′ or bad′mouṯẖ′), *v.* SLANG. to say bad or cruel things about someone; insult: *bad-mouth an enemy.*

bad-tem·pered (bad′tem′pərd), *adj.* having a bad temper; cross; irritable.

Baf·fin Island (baf′ən), a large island between Greenland and Hudson Bay, part of the Canadian Arctic Archipelago.

baf·fle (baf′əl), **1** *v.* to hinder someone by being too hard to understand or solve; bewilder: *The absence of clues baffled the police.* ■ See Synonym Study at **confuse. 2** *n.* device for hindering or changing the flow of air, water, or sound waves: *a baffle to shield a microphone from wind.* ❏ *v.* **baf·fled, baf·fling.**

bag (bag), **1** *n.* container made of paper, cloth, leather, etc.: *Fresh vegetables are sometimes sold in plastic bags.* **2** *n.* amount that a bag holds: *She ate a bag of chips.* **3** *n.* something like a bag in its use or shape; handbag, suitcase, etc.: *Mother calls her purse her*

bag. **4** *v.* to put into a bag or bags: *We bagged the cookies we had baked so we could sell them.* **5** *v.* to hang loosely: *These pants bag at the knees.* **6** *n.* game killed or caught at one time by a hunter. **7** *v.* to kill in hunting: *The hunter bagged many large ducks.* **8** *n.* base in baseball. **9** *n.* SLANG. something for which you have an interest, an ability, or a liking: *Tennis is my bag.* ❏ *v.* **bagged, bag·ging. —bag′like′,** *adj.*
be left holding the bag, 1 be the person who takes the blame in the end. **2** to end up empty-handed.

ba·gel (bā′gəl), *n.* a hard roll made of raised dough shaped into a ring.

bag·gage (bag′ij), *n.* **1** trunks, bags, suitcases, etc., packed for traveling; luggage. **2** equipment that an army takes with it, such as tents, blankets, and dishes.

Bag·gie (bag′ē), *n.* trademark for a small square bag made of transparent plastic, used to keep food in.

bag·gy (bag′ē), *adj.* hanging loosely; baglike: *baggy trousers.* ❏ *adj.* **bag·gi·er, bag·gi·est. —bag′gi·ly,** *adv.* **—bag′gi·ness,** *n.*

Bagh·dad (bag′dad), *n.* capital of Iraq, on the Tigris in SW Asia. Baghdad is an ancient city mentioned many times in *The Arabian Nights.*

bag·pipe (bag′pīp′), *n.* Often, **bagpipes,** *pl.* a musical instrument made of a tube to blow through, a leather bag for air, and four sounding pipes. Bagpipes produce shrill tones and are used especially in Scotland and Ireland.

bag·pip·er (bag′pī′pər), *n.* person who plays a bagpipe.

bah (bä), *interj.* exclamation used to express scorn, dislike, or impatience. ■ Another word that can sound like this is **baa.**

Ba·hai or **Ba·ha'i** (bä hī′ or bə hī′), **1** *n.* person who believes in Bahaism. **2** *n.* Bahaism. **3** *adj.* of a Bahai or Bahaism. ❏ *n., pl.* **Ba·hais** or **Ba·ha'is** for 1.

Ba·ha·ism (bä hī′iz′əm or bə hī′iz′əm), *n.* religion founded in Iran in 1863 that teaches belief in one god and the unity of all people and all religions. Bahaism has no official clergy.

Ba·ha·mas (bə hä′məz), *n.pl.* **the,** country consisting of more than 700 islands in the West Indies, SE of Florida. *Capital:* Nassau. **—Ba·ha·mi·an** (bə hä′mē ən), *adj., n.*

Bah·rain or **Bah·rein** (bä rān′), *n.* island country in the Persian Gulf. *Capital:* Manama.

Bai·kal (bī käl′), *n.* **Lake,** lake in S Siberia. It is the deepest freshwater lake in the world.

bail¹ (bāl), **1** *n.* guarantee of money necessary to release someone under arrest from jail or prison until a trial is held: *They put up bail for their friend who was arrested for speeding.* **2** *n.* amount of money guaranteed. **3** *v.* to obtain the release of someone under arrest by supplying bail: *They bailed their friend out of jail.* ■ Another word that sounds like this is **bale.**
go bail for, to supply bail for.

bail² (bāl), *v.* to throw water out of a boat, using a bucket, pail, or any other container: *She bailed out the canoe.* ■ Another word that sounds like this is **bale.**
bail out, 1 to jump from an airplane by parachute: *When the plane caught fire, the pilot bailed out.* **2** to help someone who is in trouble.

bail·iff (bā′lif), *n.* officer of a court of law who has charge of jurors and guards prisoners while they are in the courtroom.

bail·i·wick (bā′lə wik), *n.* someone's field of knowledge, work, or authority.

bail·out (bāl′out′), *n.* a financial rescue from a failing business situation: *the savings-and-loan bailout.*

bairn (bârn), *n.* SCOTTISH. child.

bait (bāt), **1** *n.* anything, especially food, used to attract fish or other animals so that they may be caught. **2** *v.* to put bait on a hook or in a trap: *I baited the hook.* **3** *n.* thing used to tempt or attract. **4** *v.* to set dogs to attack: *People used to bait bulls and bears for sport.* **5** *v.* to torment or worry by unkind or annoying remarks: *A group of troublemakers kept baiting the speaker.* **—bait′er,** *n.*

baize (bāz), *n.* a thick woolen or cotton cloth like felt, used for the playing surface of pool and billiard tables.

Ba·ja Cal·i·for·nia Nor·te (bä′hä kä lē fôr′nyä nôr′tä), a state in NW Mexico.

Baja California Sur (sür), a state in NW Mexico.

bake (bāk), v. **1** to cook food by dry heat without exposing it directly to the fire: *I am baking a cake in the oven. I bake every Saturday.* **2** to dry or harden by heat: *Clay pots are baked in a special oven called a kiln.* **3** to become baked: *Cookies bake quickly.* ❑ v. **baked, bak·ing.**

bak·er (bā′kər), n. person who makes or sells bread, pies, cakes, and the like.

baker's dozen, a dozen plus one; thirteen.

bak·er·y (bā′kər ē), n. a place where bread, pies, cakes, etc., are made or sold. ❑ n., pl. **bak·er·ies.**

baking powder, mixture of sodium bicarbonate and cream of tartar, used instead of yeast to cause biscuits, cakes, etc., to rise.

baking soda, sodium bicarbonate.

ba·kla·va (bä′klə vä′), n. a Middle Eastern dessert made from layers of thin pastry, chopped nuts, spices, and honey. ❑ n., pl. **ba·kla·va** or **ba·kla·vas.**

Ba·ku (bä kü′), n. port and capital of Azerbaijan, on the Caspian Sea.

bal·a·lai·ka (bal′ə lī′kə), n. a Russian musical instrument somewhat like a guitar, with a triangular body and usually with three strings. ❑ n., pl. **bal·a·lai·kas.**

bal·ance (bal′əns), **1** n. device for weighing. **2** v. to weigh two things against each other on scales, in your hands, or in your mind to see which is heavier or more important: *She balanced a trip to the mountains against a chance to go to a summer camp.* **3** n. condition of being equal in weight, amount, etc.: *The two sides of the scale were in balance.* **4** n. good proportion in design; harmony: *The artist's work shows balance and grace.* **5** n. steady condition or position: *The diver had an impressive sense of balance.* **6** v. to put or keep in a steady condition or position: *to balance a coin on its edge.* **7** v. to be equal or equivalent in weight, amount, force, effect, etc.: *These weights balance.* **8** n. steadiness of character: *His balance kept him from losing his temper very often.* **9** v. to make up for the effect, influence, etc., of; counteract. **10** n. amount you owe to an account or amount you have in an account: *I have a balance of $200 in the bank.* **11** v. to add up money paid, money due, and money owned and compare the sums: *balance a checkbook, balance an account.* **12** n. part that is left over; remainder: *I will be away for the balance of the week.* **13** n. balance wheel. ❑ v. **bal·anced, bal·anc·ing.**

in the balance, undecided: *The outcome of the baseball game was in the balance until the last inning.*

balance (def. 5)

balance beam, a narrow, wooden bar set horizontally about 4 feet (1.2 meters) above the floor, on which gymnasts perform balancing exercises; beam.

bal·anced (bal′ənst), adj. **1** showing equal attention to all sides of a question; fair; unbiased: *a balanced report of the city council meeting.* **2** stable: *a balanced economy.*

balance of trade, the difference between the total values of the imports and the exports of a country in a certain time.

balance wheel, wheel for controlling motion. A clock or watch has a balance wheel that controls the movement of the hands.

Bal·an·chine (bal ən shēn′), n. George, 1904-1983, American choreographer, born in Russia. He choreographed more than 400 ballets.

Bal·bo·a (bal bō′ə), n. **Vas·co de** (väs′ko тнä), 1475?-1517, Spanish explorer who was the first European to see the Pacific Ocean, in 1513.

bal·co·ny (bal′kə nē), n. **1** an outside platform enclosed by a railing, that juts out from an upper floor of a building. **2** upper floor in a theater, hall, or church that sticks partway over the other floor; gallery. ❑ n., pl. **bal·co·nies.**

bald (bold), adj. **1** wholly or partly without hair on the head. **2** without its natural covering: *A mountaintop with no trees or grass is bald.* **3** obvious; plain: *the bald truth, a bald lie.* —**bald′ly,** adv. —**bald′ness,** n.

bald eagle, a large, powerful, North American eagle with white feathers on its head, neck, and tail; American eagle. It is the national emblem of the United States.

bal·der·dash (bol′dər dash), n. nonsense; foolishness.

bal·dric (bol′drik), n. belt for a sword, horn, etc., hung from one shoulder to the opposite side of the body.

Bald·win (bold′win), n. **James,** 1924-1987, African American author. ■ **James Baldwin** wrote essays, novels, and plays. He often wrote about racial injustice and the civil rights movement.

bale (bāl), **1** n. a large bundle of merchandise or material securely wrapped or bound for shipping or storage: *a bale of cotton.* **2** v. to make into bales: *That big machine bales hay.* ■ Another word that sounds like this is **bail.** ❑ v. **baled, bal·ing.** —**bal′er,** n.

Bal·e·ar·ic Islands (bal′ē ar′ik), group of Spanish islands in the W Mediterranean. See **Castile** for map.

ba·leen (bə lēn′), n. whalebone.

baleen whale, any of several whales having strips of whalebone attached to the roof of their mouths that strain the water from the tiny animals they eat. Humpback whales are baleen whales.

bale·ful (bāl′fəl), adj. hostile; menacing: *The stranger gave the dog a baleful look.* —**bale′ful·ly,** adv.

Ba·li (bä′lē), n. island in Indonesia, east of Java.

Ba·li·nese (bä′lə nēz′), **1** n. person born or living in Bali. **2** adj. of Bali or its people. ❑ n., pl. **Ba·li·nese.**

balk (bok), **1** v. to stop short and stubbornly refuse to go on: *My horse balked at the fence.* **2** v. to prevent from going on; hinder: *The police balked the robber's plans.* **3** n. hindrance. **4** in baseball: **a** n. an illegal motion made by a pitcher, especially one in which a throw that has been started is not completed. **b** v. to make a balk. —**balk′er,** n.

Bal·kan (bol′kən), **1** n.pl. **Balkans,** Balkan States. **2** adj. of the people living in the Balkan States. **3** adj. of the Balkan Peninsula or the countries on it.

Balkan Peninsula, peninsula in SE Europe.

Balkan States, countries on the Balkan Peninsula: Slovenia, Croatia, Serbia, Bosnia and Herzegovina, Macedonia, Romania, Bulgaria, Albania, Greece, and European Turkey.

balk·y (bo′kē), adj. stopping short and stubbornly refusing to go on; likely to balk: *Mules are balky animals.* ❑ adj. **balk·i·er, balk·i·est.** —**balk′i·ness,** n.

Balkan States

Key: 1=Slovenia 4=Serbia
2=Croatia 5=Macedonia
3=Bosnia and 6=Albania
Herzegovina

a	hat	ė	term	ô	order	ch	child	(a in about
ā	age	i	it	oi	oil	ng	long	e in taken
ä	far	ī	ice	ou	out	sh	she	ə { i in pencil
â	care	o	hot	u	cup	th	thin	o in lemon
e	let	ō	open	ù	put	ŦH	then	(u in circus
ē	equal	ò	saw	ü	rule	zh	measure	

ball¹ (bȯl), **1** *n.* a round or somewhat oval object that is thrown, hit, batted, kicked, rolled, or carried in various games. Different sizes and types of balls are used in tennis, golf, baseball, football, and soccer. **2** *n.* game in which some kind of ball is used, especially baseball. **3** *n.* anything round or roundish; something that is somewhat like a ball: *a ball of string.* **4** *n.* a rounded part that sticks out of the body: *the ball of the thumb, the ball of the foot.* **5** *n.* baseball pitched too high, too low, or not over the plate, that the batter does not swing at. **6** *n.* a round, solid object shot from a gun or cannon. **7** *v.* to form into a ball: *to ball string or yarn.* **—ball′·like′,** *adj.*

on the ball, alert to what is going on and to what may need to be done.

SYNONYM STUDY **Ball¹, globe,** and **sphere** all mean something round. **Ball** is a general word: *She crumpled the paper into a ball.* **Globe** and **sphere** suggest something perfectly round or thought of as perfectly round: *The principal uses a glass globe as a paperweight. The moon is a sphere.*

ball² (bȯl), *n.* a large, formal party with dancing.

bal·lad (bal′əd), *n.* **1** a simple song. **2** poem that tells a story in a simple verse form, especially one that tells a popular legend. Ballads are often sung. **3** a romantic popular song. **4** a folk song.

ball-and-sock·et joint (bȯl′ən sok′it), joint formed by a ball or knob fitting into a socket, permitting circular motion. The shoulder and hip joints are ball-and-socket joints.

bal·last (bal′əst), **1** *n.* something heavy carried in a ship to steady it. **2** *n.* weight carried in a balloon or dirigible to steady it or control its rise: *The balloon used bags of sand for ballast.* **3** *n.* gravel or crushed rock used in making the base for a road or railroad track. **4** *v.* to furnish or steady with ballast.

ball bearing, 1 a part of a machine in which a metal bar turns upon a number of freely moving steel balls. Ball bearings are used to reduce friction. **2** one of these steel balls.

bal·le·ri·na (bal′ə rē′nə), *n.* a woman who dances in a ballet. ❑ *n., pl.* **bal·le·ri·nas.**

bal·let (bal′ā *or* ba lā′), *n.* **1** an elaborate dance by a group on a stage. A ballet tells a story through the movements of the dancing and is accompanied by music often written especially for it. **2** a dance company that performs ballet.

ball·game (bȯl′gam′), *n.* **1** any game played with a ball, especially baseball. **2** situation or set of circumstances: *Since the twins were born, life at our house is a whole new ballgame.*

ballerina

bal·lis·tic (bə lis′tik), *adj.* of or about the motion of something that is shot or thrown. **—bal·lis′ti·cal·ly,** *adv.*

WORD FAMILY **Ballistic** and the words below are related. They all come from a Greek word meaning "to throw."

antiballistic	hyperbole	parable	parlor
diabolic	hyperbolic	parabola	parole
emblem	metabolism	parley	problem
embolism	palaver	parliament	symbol

ballistic missile, missile aimed at or before the time of launching. It differs from a guided missile, which can be aimed during flight.

bal·lis·tics (bə lis′tiks), *n.* science that deals with the motion of projectiles, such as bullets, shells, or bombs, and also rockets and missiles after thrust has ended.

bal·loon (bə lün′), **1** *n.* an airtight bag filled with some gas lighter than air so that it will rise and float in the air. Some balloons have a basket or container for carrying persons or devices high up in the air. **2** *n.* a child's toy made of thin rubber that may be blown up by mouth or filled with some gas lighter than air. **3** *v.* to ride in a balloon. **4** *v.* to swell out like a balloon: *The sails of the boat ballooned in the wind.* **—bal·loon′like′,** *adj.*

bal·loon·ist (bə lü′nist), *n.* **1** person who goes up in balloons. **2** pilot of a dirigible.

bal·lot (bal′ət), **1** *n.* piece of paper or other object used in voting: *cast a ballot.* **2** *n.* the total number of votes cast. **3** *n.* method of secret voting that uses paper slips, voting machines, etc. **4** *v.* to vote or decide by using ballots: *to ballot for president of the club.*

WORD STORY **Ballot** comes from an Italian word meaning "ball." In old times, small balls of different colors were used in voting as a form of secret ballot. **Blackball** comes from the same voting custom. One black ball was enough to veto the question being voted on.

ball·park (bȯl′pärk′), **1** *n.* a baseball field. **2** *adj.* approximate: *a ballpark estimate.*

ball·play·er (bȯl′plā′ər), *n.* person who plays ball, especially baseball.

ball·point pen (bȯl′point′), pen that writes with a small metal ball at the point. It turns inside the end of a cartridge that holds the ink.

ball·room (bȯl′rüm′), *n.* a large room for dancing.

bal·ly·hoo (bal′ē hü), **1** *n.* sensational or noisy advertising. **2** *n.* uproar; outcry. **3** *v.* to make exaggerated or false statements. ❑ *n., pl.* **bal·ly·hoos;** *v.* **bal·ly·hooed, bal·ly·hoo·ing. —bal′ly·hoo′er,** *n.*

balm (bäm), *n.* **1** a fragrant, oily, sticky substance obtained from certain kinds of trees, used to heal or to relieve pain. **2** an ointment or similar preparation that heals or soothes. **3** anything that heals or soothes: *Your kindness was balm to my hurt feelings.*

balm·y (bä′mē), *adj.* **1** mild; gentle; soothing: *A balmy breeze blew across the lake.* **2** fragrant. ❑ *adj.* **balm·i·er, balm·i·est. —balm′i·ly,** *adv.* **—balm′i·ness,** *n.*

ba·lo·ney (bə lō′nē), *n.* **1** SLANG. nonsense. **2** INFORMAL. bologna. ❑ *n., pl.* **ba·lo·neys.**

bal·sa (bȯl′sə), *n.* **1** a tropical tree of the Americas with strong wood which is very light in weight. **2** its wood, used in making rafts, toy airplanes, etc. ❑ *n., pl.* **bal·sas** for 1.

WORD STORY **Balsa** comes from a Spanish word meaning "raft." Because balsa wood is so light and floats well, Indians in Central and South America used it to make rafts.

bal·sam (bȯl′səm), *n.* **1** balsam fir. **2** balm.

balsam fir, 1 an evergreen tree of North America, related to the pine, with resin that is used in making varnish and turpentine. Balsam firs are much used as Christmas trees. **2** its wood, used for lumber and in making paper.

Bal·tic (bȯl′tik), *adj.* **1** of the Baltic Sea: *the Baltic coasts.* **2** of the Baltic States.

Baltic Sea, sea in N Europe, north of Poland and southeast of Sweden.

Baltic States, Estonia, Latvia, and Lithuania.

Bal·ti·more (bȯl′tə môr), *n.* port and largest city in Maryland.

Baltimore oriole, a North American songbird, the male of which has bright orange and black feathers.

Baltimore oriole—about 8 in. (20 cm) long

bal·us·ter (bal′ə stər), *n.* one of the short posts or columns that support the railing of a staircase, balcony, etc.

bal·us·trade (bal′ə strād), *n.* row of balusters and the railing on them.

Bam·a·ko (bam′ə kō), *n.* capital of Mali, in the SW part.

bam·bi·no (bam bē′nō), *n.* **1** baby. **2** a little child. ❑ *n., pl.* **bam·bi·nos.**

bam·boo (bam bü′), *n.* any of many woody, treelike grasses with very tall, stiff, hollow stems that have hard, thick joints. Bamboos grow in warm regions. Their stems are used for making canes, fishing poles, furniture, and even houses. ❑ *n., pl.* **bam·boos.**

bam·boo·zle (bam bü′zəl), *v.* INFORMAL. **1** to cheat or trick someone. **2** to puzzle; perplex. ❑ *v.* **bam·boo·zled, bam·boo·zling. —bam·boo′zle·ment,** *n.* **—bam·boo′zler,** *n.*

ban (ban), **1** v. to forbid by law or authority; prohibit: *Swimming is banned in this lake.* **2** n. the forbidding of an act or speech by authority: *The city has a ban on parking cars in this busy street.* ❏ v. **banned, ban·ning.**

ba·nal (bā′nl or bə nal′), adj. not new or interesting; commonplace; trite: *Their conversation was banal, full of uninteresting remarks such as "nice weather."* —**ba′nal·ly,** adv.

ba·nal·i·ty (bə nal′ə tē), n. **1** commonplaceness; triteness. **2** a banal remark, idea, etc. ❏ n., pl. **ba·nal·i·ties** for 2.

ba·nan·a (bə nan′ə), n. **1** a slightly curved, yellow tropical fruit with firm, creamy pulp. Bananas grow in clusters on treelike plants with great, long leaves. **2** any of several related fruits. ❏ n., pl. **ba·nan·as.**

go bananas, SLANG. to become very excited.

band¹ (band), **1** n. number of persons or animals joined or acting together: *a band of robbers, a band of coyotes.* **2** v. to unite in a group: *The children banded together to buy a present for their teacher.* **3** n. group of musicians performing together, especially on wind and percussion instruments: *The school band played several marches.* **4** n. CANADIAN. a group of American Indian people of a specific area or reserve, identified by the federal government as an administrative unit.

band² (band), **1** n. a thin, flat strip of material for binding, trimming, or some other purpose: *The oak box was strengthened with bands of iron.* **2** v. to put a band on: *Students of birds often band them in order to identify them later.* **3** n. a stripe: *The white cup has a gold band.* **4** n. a particular range of wavelengths or frequencies, especially of electromagnetic waves such as radio or television signals. —**band′er,** n.

band·age (ban′dij), **1** n. strip of cloth or other material used to wrap or cover a wound or injury. **2** v. to wrap or cover with a bandage. ❏ v. **band·aged, band·ag·ing.** —**band′ag·er,** n.

Band-Aid (band′ād′), n. trademark for a small adhesive bandage, used to cover and protect minor wounds.

ban·dan·na (ban dan′ə), n. a large handkerchief, often worn on the head or neck. ❏ n., pl. **ban·dan·nas.**

WORD STORY   **Bandanna** comes from a Hindustani word meaning "a way of tying cloth so that dyeing the cloth produces designs." We call this **tie-dyeing.** In India, these handkerchiefs were often dyed this way.

Ban·dar Se·ri Be·ga·wan (bän där′ se′rē be gä′ wän), capital of Brunei, in the N part.

band·box (band′boks′), n. a light cardboard box to put hats, collars, etc. in. ❏ n., pl. **band·box·es.**

ban·deau (ban dō′), n. a narrow band worn about the head. ❏ n., pl. **ban·deaux** or **ban·deaus** (ban dōz′).

ban·di·coot (ban′də küt), n. **1** a burrowing, ratlike mammal of Australia and New Guinea, with a narrow head and sharp teeth. The females carry their young in a pouch. **2** either of two large, destructive rats of southern Asia.

ban·dit (ban′dit), n. robber or thief, especially one of a gang of outlaws.

ban·dit·ry (ban′də trē), n. **1** the work of bandits. **2** bandits.

band·lead·er (band′lē′ dər), n. leader of a dance band or jazz band.

band·mas·ter (band′mas′tər), n. leader of a band of musicians.

ban·do·leer or **ban·do·lier** (ban′dl ir′), n. a broad belt worn over the shoulder and across the breast, often with loops for carrying cartridges or with small cases for bullets, gunpowder, etc.

band saw, saw in the form of an endless steel belt running over two pulleys.

band·stand (band′stand′), n. an outdoor platform for band concerts. It usually has a roof.

band·wag·on (band′wag′ən), n. wagon that carries a musical band in a parade.

climb on the bandwagon, to join what appears to be a winning or successful group, movement, etc.

ban·dy (ban′dē), v. to give and take; exchange: *bandy insults.* ❏ v. **ban·died, ban·dy·ing.**

ban·dy-leg·ged (ban′dē leg′id), adj. having legs that curve outward like a bow; bowlegged.

bane (bān), n. cause of death, ruin, or harm: *Attacks by bandits were the bane of the mountain village.*

WORD STORY   **Bane** comes from an old English word meaning "murderer." People borrowed the idea of murder to represent the ruin or end of anything.

bane·ful (bān′fəl), adj. causing harm or destruction: *Air pollution has a baneful effect on trees in cities.* —**bane′ful·ly,** adv. —**bane′ful·ness,** n.

bang (bang), **1** n. a sudden, loud noise or blow: *the bang of firecrackers.* **2** v. to make or cause to make a sudden, loud noise: *The door banged as it blew shut. He banged the door.* **3** n. a violent, noisy blow: *She gave the drum a bang.* **4** v. to strike noisily or violently: *The baby was banging the pan with a spoon.* **5** adv. violently and suddenly: *The bicyclist ran bang into a telephone pole.* **6** n. a thrill: *I get a bang out of riding the roller coaster.* **bang up,** to damage: *My car was banged up in the crash.*

Bang·kok (bang′kok), n. port and capital of Thailand.

Ban·gla·desh (bäng′glə desh′), n. country in S Asia, on the Bay of Bengal. *Capital:* Dhaka.

ban·gle (bang′gəl), n. **1** a small ornament suspended from a bracelet. **2** bracelet or anklet.

Ban·gor (bang′gôr or bang′gər), n. city in SE Maine.

bangs (bangz), n.pl. fringe of hair cut short and worn over the forehead.

Ban·gui (bäng′gē), n. capital of the Central African Republic, in the SW part.

bang-up (bang′up′), adj. extremely good or effective; first-rate: *a bang-up job.*

ban·ish (ban′ish), v. **1** to force someone to leave a country; exile: *The king banished some of his enemies.* **2** to force to go away; drive away; expel: *The twins were banished from the dinner table.* —**ban′ish·ment,** n.

SYNONYM STUDY   **Banish, exile,** and **deport** all mean to cause someone to leave a country. **Banish** means to require someone to go by legal power: *The new government banished the old dictator.* **Exile** can mean to banish someone, or to leave by your own choice: *The Pilgrims exiled themselves to America.* **Deport** means to banish a person who is not a citizen: *The illegal aliens were deported.*

ban·is·ter (ban′ə stər), n. Often, **banisters,** pl. handrail of a staircase, balcony, etc., and its row of supports.

ban·jo (ban′jō), n. a musical instrument having four or five strings, played by plucking the strings with the fingers or a pick. ❏ n., pl. **ban·jos** or **ban·joes.**

Ban·jul (bän′jül), n. capital of The Gambia, in the W part.

bank¹ (bangk), **1** n. a long pile or heap: *a bank of snow over ten feet deep.* **2** v. to pile up; heap up: *The tractors banked the snow by the side of the road.* **3** n. ground bordering a river, lake, etc.; shore: *We fished from the bank.* **4** n. a shallow place in a body of water; shoal: *the fishing banks of Newfoundland.* **5** v. to cause to slope: *The bulldozers banked the curves of the new expressway.* **6** v. to make an airplane tilt to one side when making a turn. **7** n. a tilt like this. **8** v. to bounce a basketball off the backboard into the basket. **9** v. to cover a fire with ashes or fresh fuel so that it will burn slowly: *to bank the fire at night.*

bank² (bangk), **1** n. place of business for keeping, lending, exchanging, and issuing money: *Banks pay interest on money in savings accounts.* **2** v. to keep or put money in a bank: *I bank the money I earn baby-sitting.* **3** n. a small container with a slot through which coins can be dropped to save money. **4** n. any place where reserve supplies are kept: *a bank for blood plasma.* **bank on,** to depend on: *I can bank on my teacher to help me.*

bank³ (bangk), n. **1** row or close arrangement of things: *a bank of machines.* **2** row of keys on an organ, typewriter, etc. **3** row or tier of oars.

a	hat	ė	term	ô	order	ch	child		
ā	age	i	it	oi	oil	ng	long	ə	a in about
ä	far	ī	ice	ou	out	sh	she		e in taken
â	care	o	hot	u	cup	th	thin		i in pencil
e	let	ō	open	ů	put	₮H	then		o in lemon
ē	equal	ò	saw	ü	rule	zh	measure		u in circus

bank account, money deposited in a bank that can be withdrawn by a depositor.

bank barn, CANADIAN. a barn with two floors built into a hill so that each floor can be entered at ground level.

bank·book (bangk′bùk′), *n.* book in which a record of someone's account at a bank is kept; passbook.

bank·card (bangk′kärd′), *n.* a credit card or cash machine card issued by a bank.

bank·er (bang′kər), *n.* person or company that manages a bank.

bank·ing (bang′king), *n.* business of keeping, lending, exchanging, and issuing money.

banyan

bank·roll (bangk′rōl′), *n.* amount of money a person has on hand.

bank·rupt (bang′krupt), **1** *n.* person who is declared by a court of law to be unable to pay his or her debts, and whose property is distributed as far as it will go among the people who are owed money. **2** *adj.* unable to pay your debts. **3** *v.* to make bankrupt: *Foolish expenditures will bankrupt the company.*

WORD STORY   **Bankrupt** comes from Italian words meaning "broken" and "bench." In old times, people did business in public places, using benches as their offices. If a business could not pay its debts, the bench was said to be broken. Today, people who have no money may say they are broke.

bank·rupt·cy (bang′krupt sē), *n.* bankrupt condition.

bank shot, shot in basketball in which a player bounces the ball off the backboard into the basket.

Ban·ne·ker (ban′ə kər), *n.* **Ben·ja·min** (ben′jə mən), 1731-1806, African American astronomer, mathematician, surveyor, and almanac author. ▪ **Benjamin Banneker** assisted the surveyor who laid out the boundaries of the District of Columbia. He was recommended for the job by Thomas Jefferson.

ban·ner (ban′ər), **1** *n.* flag: *The banners of many countries fly outside the headquarters of the United Nations.* **2** *n.* piece of cloth with some design or words on it: *The banner our school displays in parades is blue and white.* **3** *adj.* leading or outstanding: *This has been a banner year for apple growers.* **4** *n.* a newspaper headline extending across the top of a page.

ban·nock (ban′ək), *n.* a flat cake, made of oatmeal or barley flour.

banns (banz), *n.pl.* notice given three separate times in church that a certain man and woman are to be married.

ban·quet (bang′kwit), **1** *n.* a large meal with many courses, prepared for a special occasion or for many people; feast: *a wedding banquet.* **2** *n.* a formal dinner with speeches. **3** *v.* to take part in a banquet; feast: *We banqueted on roast beef and duck.* **—ban′quet·er,** *n.*

ban·shee or **ban·shie** (ban′shē), *n.* (in Irish and Scottish folklore) a female spirit whose wail means that there will soon be a death in the family she visits. ❏ *n., pl.* **ban·shees** or **ban·shies.**

ban·tam or **Ban·tam** (ban′təm), *n.* any quite small breed of chicken. The roosters are often spirited fighters.

ban·tam·weight (ban′təm wāt′), *n.* boxer who weighs more than 112 pounds (51 kilograms) and less than 118 pounds (54 kilograms).

ban·ter (ban′tər), **1** *n.* playful teasing; joking: *There was much banter going on at the party.* **2** *v.* to tease playfully; talk in a joking way. **—ban′ter·er,** *n.* **—ban′ter·ing·ly,** *adv.*

Ban·tu (ban′tü), **1** *n.* member of a large group of peoples living in central and southern Africa. **2** *n.* any of the languages of these peoples. Swahili is a Bantu language. **3** *adj.* of these peoples or their languages. ❏ *n., pl.* **Ban·tu** or **Bantus** for 1.

WORD SOURCE   **Bantu** and other African languages have given a number of words to the English language. From Bantu languages come **chimpanzee, gumbo, Kwanzaa, tsetse fly,** and **zombie.** From Khoikhoi languages come **gnu** and **kudu.** Words from other African languages include the following:

banana	goober	okra
banjo	jazz	voodoo
buckaroo	jukebox	yam

ban·yan (ban′yən), *n.* an East Indian fig tree with branches that have hanging roots. The roots grow down to the ground and start new trunks. One tree may cover several acres.

ban·zai (bän′zi′), *interj.* a Japanese greeting, patriotic cheer, or battle cry. It means "May you live ten thousand years!"

ba·o·bab (bā′ō bab), *n.* a tall tree of tropical Africa, with a very thick trunk and a woolly fruit like a gourd.

bap·tism (bap′tiz əm), *n.* **1** rite or ceremony in which someone is dipped in water or sprinkled with water, as a sign of washing away sin and admission to the Christian church. **2** an experience that tests a person or initiates someone into a new kind of life. **—bap·tis′mal,** *adj.* **—bap·tis′mal·ly,** *adv.*

Bap·tist (bap′tist), *n.* **1** member of a Christian church that believes in baptizing by dipping the whole person in water. **2 the Baptist,** John the Baptist.

bap·tis·ter·y (bap′tə stər ē), *n.* building or part of a church where baptism is performed. ❏ *n., pl.* **bap·tis·ter·ies.**

bap·tis·try (bap′tə strē), *n.* baptistery. ❏ *n., pl.* **bap·tis·tries.**

bap·tize (bap tīz′ or bap′tīz), *v.* **1** to dip someone into water or sprinkle with water as a sign of washing away sin and admission into the Christian church. **2** to give a first name to someone at baptism; christen: *The baby was baptized Maria.* ❏ *v.* **bap·tized, bap·tiz·ing. —bap·tiz′er,** *n.*

bar (bär), **1** *n.* an evenly shaped piece of some solid, longer than it is wide or thick: *a bar of iron, a bar of soap, a bar of chocolate.* **2** *n.* pole or rod put across a door, gate, window, or across any opening to close it off: *The windows of the prison have iron bars.* **3** *v.* to put bars across; fasten or shut off: *Bar the door.* **4** *n.* anything that blocks the way or prevents progress: *Shyness can be a bar to making friends.* **5** *v.* to block; obstruct: *Fallen trees bar the road.* **6** *v.* to exclude or forbid: *All talking is barred during a study period.* **7** *prep.* except; excluding: *He is the best student, bar none.* **8** *n.* band of color; stripe: *a dark bar of cloud across the setting sun.* **9** *v.* to mark with stripes. **10** *n.* unit of rhythm in music. The regular accent falls on the first note of each bar. **11** *n.* the vertical line between two such units on a musical staff, dividing a composition into measures. A **double bar** marks the end of a movement or of an entire piece of music. **12** *n.* counter or place where drinks, usually alcoholic, and sometimes food are served to customers. **13** *n.* place where a prisoner stands in a court of law: *After you have passed your law examinations, you will be admitted to the bar.* **15** *n.* lawyers as a group: *Judges are chosen from the bar.* **16** *n.* court of law. ❏ *v.* **barred, bar·ring.**

barb (bärb), *n.* **1** point sticking out and curving backward from the main point of an arrow, fishhook, etc. **2** something that wounds or stings: *the barb of sarcasm.* [**Barb** comes from a Latin word meaning "beard." The shape of a curving point looks like the shape of some beards.]

Bar·ba·dos (bär bā′dōz), *n.* island country in the West Indies. *Capital:* Bridgetown. **—Bar·ba·di·an** (bär bā′dē ən), *adj., n.*

bar·bar·i·an (bär bâr′ē ən), **1** *n.* member of a primitive, uncivilized people. **2** *adj.* not civilized; without writing, cities, etc. ▪ See Synonym Study at **barbaric. 3** *n.* person who rejects or lacks interest in literature, the arts, etc. ▪ This meaning of **barbarian** is considered offensive. **4** *adj.* of barbarians: *barbarian customs.* [**Barbarian** comes from a Latin word meaning "foreigner." Some people think that foreigners are less civilized because they are different.]

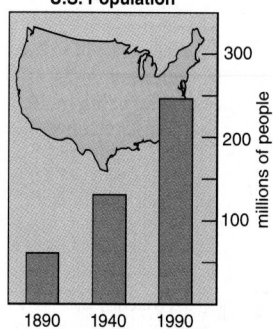

B

bar·bar·ic (bär bar′ik), *adj.* **1** like barbarians; suited to an uncivilized people; primitive; simple; rough. **2** brutal or inhuman. **3** rich or splendid in a crude way: *barbaric color, barbaric music.* —**bar·bar′i·cal·ly,** *adv.*

SYNONYM STUDY **Barbaric, barbarian,** and **barbarous** all mean "not civilized." **Barbaric** suggests lack of gentleness and love of display: *His paintings are bright and cheerful in a barbaric way.* **Barbarian** suggests the lack of civilized things: *The barbarian people had no system of writing.* **Barbarous** suggests fierceness and cruelty: *The town was shocked by the barbarous murder.*

bar·ba·rism (bär′bə riz′əm), *n.* **1** condition of uncivilized people. **2** word or expression not in accepted use.

bar·bar·i·ty (bär bar′ə tē), *n.* **1** brutal or inhuman cruelty. **2** a cruel act. **3** barbaric manner or style; gaudy taste. ❑ *n., pl.* **bar·bar·i·ties** for 2.

bar·ba·rize (bär′bə rīz′), *v.* to make or become barbarous. ❑ *v.* **bar·ba·rized, bar·ba·riz·ing, bar·ba·ri·za′tion,** *n.*

bar·bar·ous (bär′bər əs), *adj.* **1** not civilized; primitive. **2** savagely cruel; brutal: *Torturing prisoners is barbarous.* **3** rough and rude; coarse; unrefined: *barbarous manners.* ■ See Synonym Study at **barbaric.** —**bar′bar·ous·ly,** *adv.* —**bar′bar·ous·ness,** *n.*

Bar·ba·ry (bär′bər ē), *n.* (earlier) region on the N coast of Africa that included the **Barbary States,** Algeria, Tunisia, Morocco, and Tripoli.

bar·be·cue (bär′bə kyü), **1** *n.* an outdoor meal in which meat is roasted over an open fire. **2** *n.* grill or open fireplace for cooking meat, usually over charcoal. **3** *n.* meat roasted over an open fire. **4** *v.* to roast over an open fire. **5** *v.* to cook in a highly flavored sauce. **6** *n.* an outdoor feast at which animals are roasted whole. **7** *n.* animal roasted whole. ❑ *v.* **bar·be·cued, bar·be·cu·ing.** Also, **barbeque.**

WORD STORY **Barbecue** comes from a Caribbean Indian word meaning "a framework of sticks." The Indians used this framework as an outdoor cooking device.

barbed (bärbd), *adj.* **1** having a barb or barbs: *A fishhook is barbed.* **2** sharply critical; cutting: *a barbed remark.*

barbed wire, wire with sharp points on it every few inches, used for fences.

bar·bel (bär′bəl), *n.* a long, thin, fleshy growth on the mouths or nostrils of some fishes, such as catfishes.

bar·bell (bär′bel′), *n.* device like a dumbbell but with a much longer bar, to which weights may be added.

bar·be·que (bär′bə kyü), *n., v.* barbecue. ❑ *v.* **bar·be·qued, bar·be·que·ing.**

bar·ber (bär′bər), *n.* person whose business is cutting hair and shaving or trimming beards.

bar·ber·ry (bär′ber′ē), *n.* any of various related low, thorny bushes with small yellow flowers and sour red berries. ❑ *n., pl.* **bar·ber·ries.**

bar·ber·shop (bär′bər shop′), *n.* place where a barber works.

bar·bi·can (bär′bə kən), *n.* tower for defense built over a gate or bridge to a castle or city.

bar·bit·ur·ate (bär bich′ər it *or* bär bich′ə rāt′), *n.* drug used in medicine to produce sleep.

Bar·ce·lo·na (bär′sə lō′nə), *n.* port in NE Spain, on the Mediterranean.

bar code, a set of short vertical lines that have differing amounts of space between them, differing widths, and sometimes differing lengths. Printed on any item, these lines can be read by a machine which turns them into numbers that stand for a price, an address, or similar information. The Universal Product Code is a bar code.

Barcelona

bard (bärd), *n.* **1** poet and singer of long ago: *The bard sang his own poems to the music of his harp.* **2** any poet.

bard·ic (bär′dik), *adj.* **1** of or about a bard or bards.

bare (bâr), **1** *adj.* without covering; not clothed; naked: *The sun burned her bare shoulders.* **2** *adj.* with the head uncovered; bareheaded. **3** *adj.* not furnished; empty: *a room bare of furniture.* **4** *adj.* plain; not adorned: *a bare little cabin in the woods.* **5** *adj.* just enough and no more; mere: *She earns only a bare living by her work.* **6** *v.* to make bare; uncover; reveal: *to bare your feelings. The dog bared its teeth.* ❑ *adj.* **bar·er, bar·est;** *v.* **bared, bar·ing.** ■ Another word that sounds like this is **bear.** —**bare′ness,** *n.*

lay bare, to uncover; expose; reveal: *The police laid bare the plot to rob the bank.*

bare·back (bâr′bak′), *adv., adj.* without a saddle; on a horse's bare back: *She likes to ride bareback. He is a bareback rider.*

bare·bones (bâr′bōnz′), *adj.* limited to essentials; basic; fundamental: *provide bare-bones services.*

bare·faced (bâr′fāst′), *adj.* shameless; impudent: *a barefaced lie.* —**bare′fac·ed·ly,** *adv.*

bare·foot (bâr′fût′), *adj., adv.* without shoes and stockings on: *A barefoot child played in the puddles. If you go barefoot, watch out for broken glass.*

bare·foot·ed (bâr′fût′id), *adj., adv.* barefoot.

bare·hand·ed (bâr′han′did), *adj., adv.* **1** without any covering on the hands. **2** with no aid but your own hands.

bare·head·ed (bâr′hed′id), *adj., adv.* without a hat or other covering on the head: *You shouldn't be bareheaded in such cold weather.* —**bare′head·ed·ness,** *n.*

bare·knuck·le (bâr′nuk′əl), *adj.* **1** Also, **bareknuckled,** (of a fight or fighter) without boxing gloves; fighting with bare fists: *Professional boxers no longer fight bareknuckle.* **2** without ordinary courtesy or politeness; tough: *bareknuckle negotiations.*

bare·leg·ged (bâr′leg′id), *adj., adv.* without stockings on.

bare·ly (bâr′lē), *adv.* **1** with nothing to spare; only just; scarcely: *I have barely enough money to live on.* **2** poorly: *The room was furnished barely.*

bar·gain (bär′gən), **1** *n.* agreement to trade or exchange; deal: *You can't back out on our bargain.* **2** *n.* something offered for sale cheap or bought cheap: *This hat is a bargain.* **3** *v.* to try to get good terms; try to make a good deal: *I bargained with the owner and bought the baseball card for $5 instead of $8.* —**bar′gain·er,** *n.*

bargain for, be ready for; expect: *I hadn't bargained for rain and have left my umbrella at home.*

into the bargain, besides; also: *My new sweater shrank and it faded into the bargain.*

strike a bargain, to make or reach an agreement: *They finally struck a bargain: a mitt for two baseballs and a bat.*

barge (bärj), **1** *n.* a large, strongly built, flat-bottomed boat for carrying freight on rivers, canals, etc.: *a grain barge.* **2** *n.* a large boat used for excursions, pageants, and special occasions. **3** *v.* to move clumsily like a barge: *He barged into the table and knocked the lamp over.* ❑ *v.* **barged, barg·ing.**

barge in, to enter or intrude rudely: *I'm sorry to barge in, but I really need help with this assignment.*

bar graph, graph representing different quantities by rectangles of different lengths.

U.S. Population

300

200

100

millions of people

1890 1940 1990

bar graph

a	hat	ė	term	ô	order	ch	child	ə	a in about
ā	age	i	it	oi	oil	ng	long		e in taken
ä	far	ī	ice	ou	out	sh	she		i in pencil
â	care	o	hot	u	cup	th	thin		o in lemon
e	let	ō	open	u̇	put	ŦH	then		u in circus
ē	equal	ȯ	saw	ü	rule	zh	measure		

bar·i·tone (bar′ə tōn), **1** *n.* a male voice between tenor and bass. **2** *n.* singer with such a voice. **3** *n.* part to be sung by such a voice. **4** *n.* a brass wind musical instrument that has the quality or range of this voice. **5** *adj.* of or for a baritone.

WORD STORY Baritone comes from Greek words meaning "heavy" and "sound." If something heavy is dropped or tapped, it makes a lower noise than something light.

bar·i·um (bâr′ē əm), *n.* a soft, silvery white metallic element which occurs only in combination with other elements. Barium compounds are used in making pigments, safety matches, vacuum tubes, etc. *Symbol:* Ba

bark[1] (bärk), **1** *n.* the tough outside covering of the trunk and branches of trees. **2** *v.* to scrape the skin from: *I fell down the steps and barked my shins.*

bark[2] (bärk), **1** *n.* the short, sharp sound that a dog makes. **2** *n.* a sound like this: *the bark of a fox, the bark of a gun.* **3** *v.* to make this sound: *The dog barked. Rifles barked.* **4** *v.* to speak gruffly or sharply: *The police barked out orders.*

bark[3] (bärk), *n.* **1** ship with three masts, square-rigged on the first two masts and fore-and-aft-rigged on the other. **2** OLD USE. boat; ship. Also, **barque.**

bar·keep (bär′kēp′), *n.* barkeeper.

bar·keep·er (bär′kē′pər), *n.* bartender.

bark·er (bär′kər), *n.* person who stands in front of a store, show, etc., urging people to go in.

bar·ley (bär′lē), *n.* a cereal grass that has compact spikes of flowers and grows in cool climates. Its grain is used for food and for making malt.

bar magnet, magnet in the shape of a bar or rod, usually made of steel. A bar magnet suspended from a string will serve as a simple compass.

bar·maid (bär′mād′), *n.* woman who serves alcoholic drinks to customers at a bar.

bar·man (bär′mən), *n.* man who serves alcoholic drinks to customers at a bar; bartender. ❑ *n., pl.* **bar·men.**

bar mitz·vah (bär mits′və), **1** ceremony or celebration held when a Jewish boy becomes thirteen years old to affirm that he has reached the age of religious responsibility. **2** the boy himself.

barn (bärn), *n.* building for storing hay, grain, or other farm produce, and for sheltering farm animals and farm machinery. —**barn′like′,** *adj.*

bar·na·cle (bär′nə kəl), *n.* any of various small saltwater shellfish that attach themselves to rocks, the bottoms of ships, the timbers of wharves, etc.

barn dance, 1 an informal party for square dancing, formerly often held in a barn. **2** a lively square dance resembling a polka.

barn owl, a large owl with a heart-shaped face and no ear tufts. It often nests in barns or abandoned buildings and eats small rodents.

barn·storm (bärn′stôrm′), *v.* to travel from one small town or district to another, acting in plays, making political speeches, etc. —**barn′storm′er,** *n.*

barn swallow, swallow with a reddish breast and a long, forked tail. It often nests in barns.

Bar·num (bär′nəm), *n.* **P. T.,** 1810-1891, American showman. ▪ P.T. Barnum sometimes showed fake monsters or curiosities in his shows. He is supposed to have said, when questioned about this practice, "There's a sucker born every minute." He helped found the Ringling Brothers and Barnum & Bailey circus in 1871.

barn·yard (bärn′yärd′), *n.* yard around or next to a barn for livestock.

bar·o·graph (bar′ə graf), *n.* device that automatically records changes in air pressure.

ba·rom·e·ter (bə rom′ə tər), *n.* **1** device for measuring air pressure, used in determining height above sea level and in predicting probable changes in the weather. **2** something that indicates changes: *Newspapers are called barometers of public opinion.*

WORD STORY Barometer comes from a Greek word meaning "weight," and the English word *meter,* meaning "device that measures." When air is under more pressure, it weighs more.

bar·o·met·ric (bar′ə met′rik), *adj.* of a barometer. —**bar′o·met′ri·cal·ly,** *adv.*

barometric pressure, atmospheric pressure.

bar·on (bar′ən), *n.* **1** nobleman of the lowest hereditary rank. In Great Britain, a baron ranks next below a viscount and has "Lord" before his name instead of "Baron." In other European countries "Baron" is used before his name. **2** an English nobleman during the Middle Ages who held his lands directly from the king. **3** a powerful person in industry or business: *a beef baron, a coal baron.* ▪ Another word that sounds like this is **barren.**

bar·on·ess (bar′ə nis), *n.* **1** wife or widow of a baron. **2** woman whose rank is equal to that of a baron. ❑ *n., pl.* **bar·on·ess·es.**

bar·on·et (bar′ə nit), *n.* man in Great Britain ranking next below a baron and next above a knight.

ba·ro·ni·al (bə rō′nē əl), *adj.* **1** of a baron or barons: *a ring with a baronial crest on it.* **2** suitable for a baron; splendid, stately, and grand.

bar·on·y (bar′ə nē), *n.* **1** lands of a baron. **2** rank or title of a baron. ❑ *n., pl.* **bar·on·ies.**

ba·roque (bə rōk′), *adj.* **1** of or about a style of art or architecture that uses curved forms and lavish ornamentation. **2** of or about a style of music with complex rhythms and melodic ornamentation. **3** tastelessly odd; grotesque. **4** irregular in shape: *baroque pearls.*

barque (bärk), *n.* bark[3].

bar·racks (bar′əks), *n.* **1** *pl. or sing.* a building or group of buildings for soldiers to live in, usually in a fort or camp. **2** *sing.* (in Canada) a building where local groups of Royal Canadian Mounted Police are housed.

bar·ra·cu·da (bar′ə kü′də), *n.* any of several saltwater fishes with long, narrow bodies, sharp teeth, and jutting lower jaws. They sometimes attack swimmers. ❑ *n., pl.* **bar·ra·cu·da** or **bar·ra·cu·das.**

bar·rage (bə räzh′), **1** *n.* heavy artillery fire to check the enemy or to protect your own soldiers when advancing or retreating. **2** *n.* a large number of words, blows, etc., coming quickly one after the other: *The reporters kept up a barrage of questions.* **3** *v.* to subject to a barrage. ❑ *v.* **bar·raged, bar·rag·ing.**

barre (bär), *n.* the handrail used by ballet dancers to support themselves while exercising.

barred (bärd), *adj.* **1** having bars: *a barred window.* **2** marked with stripes: *a chicken with barred feathers.*

bar·rel (bar′əl), **1** *n.* container with a round, flat top and bottom and sides that curve out slightly. Barrels are usually made of boards held together by hoops. **2** *n.* amount that a barrel can hold. **3** *n.* unit of capacity for measuring for liquids and dry things. Its exact amount is not the same for all goods, and is often fixed by law. **4** *v.* to put in barrels: *to barrel cider.* **5** *n.* the metal tube of a gun through which a bullet is fired. **6** *n.* INFORMAL. a great deal: *a barrel of fun.* **7** *v.* INFORMAL. to move very rapidly: *The car barreled down the road.* ❑ *v.* **bar·reled, bar·rel·ing** or **bar·relled, bar·rel·ling.**

barrel organ, hand organ.

bar·ren (bar′ən), **1** *adj.* not able to produce offspring: *a barren fruit tree, a barren animal.* **2** *adj.* not able to produce much: *a barren desert.* **3** *adj.* without interest; unattractive; dull. **4** *adj.* unprofitable: *the barren victories of war.* **5** *n.pl.* **barrens,** a barren stretch of land. ▪ Another word that sounds like this is **baron.** —**bar′ren·ly,** *adv.* —**bar′ren·ness,** *n.*

Barren Ground or **Barren Land,** CANADIAN. a treeless, lightly inhabited part of Canada, between Hudson Bay, Great Slave Lake, and Great Bear Lake; Barrens.

Bar·rens (bar′ənz), *n.* CANADIAN. Barren Ground.

bar·rette (bə ret′), *n.* pin with a clasp for holding the hair in place.

bar·ri·cade (bar′ə kād or bar′ə kād′), **1** *n.* a rough, hastily made barrier for defense: *The soldiers cut down trees to make a barricade across the road.* **2** *n.* any barrier or obstruction. **3** *v.* to block or obstruct with a barricade: *The road was barricaded by fallen trees.* ❑ *v.* **bar·ri·cad·ed, bar·ri·cad·ing.** [Barricade comes from a French word meaning "barrel." In old times, barricades were often made of barrels filled with dirt.]

bar·ri·er (bar′ē ər), *n.* **1** something that stands in the way; something that stops progress or prevents approach; obstacle: *A dam is a barrier holding back water. Lack of water was a barrier to settling much of New Mexico.* ■ See Synonym Study at **obstacle**. **2** something that separates or keeps apart: *The Isthmus of Panama forms a barrier between the Atlantic and Pacific oceans.*

barrier reef, ridge of coral just beneath the surface of the sea along a tropical coast. It is separated from land by a deep lagoon.

bar·ring (bär′ing), *prep.* leaving out of consideration; excepting: *Barring poor weather, the plane will leave Chicago at twelve.*

bar·ri·o (bär′ē ō *or* bar′ē ō), *n.* part of a city where mainly Spanish-speaking people live. ❑ *n., pl.* **bar·ri·os.**

bar·ris·ter (bar′ə stər), *n.* lawyer in England who can argue cases in any court.

bar·room (bär′rüm′), *n.* room with a bar for the sale of alcoholic drinks.

bar·row[1] (bar′ō), *n.* **1** frame with two short handles at each end, used for carrying a load. **2** wheelbarrow.

bar·row[2] (bar′ō), *n.* mound of earth or stones over an ancient grave.

Bar·row (bar′ō), *n.* **Point,** the northern tip of Alaska. It is the northernmost point of land in the United States.

bar·tend·er (bär′ten′dər), *n.* person who serves alcoholic drinks to customers at a bar.

bar·ter (bär′tər), **1** *v.* to trade by exchanging one kind of goods for other goods without using money; exchange: *barter furs for supplies.* **2** *n.* trading by exchanging goods. **—bar′ter·er,** *n.*

Bar·thol·o·mew (bär thol′ə myü), *n.* (in the Bible) one of Jesus' twelve apostles.

Bar·tók (bär′tok), *n.* **Bé·la** (bā′lə), 1881-1945, Hungarian composer and pianist. He collected and studied folk music in Europe and North Africa.

Bar·ton (bärt′n), *n.* **Cla·ra** (klâ′rə), 1821-1912, American nurse who organized the American Red Cross in 1881.

Bar·uch (bâr′ək *or* bə rük′), *n.* **1** a Hebrew prophet. **2** a book of the Bible.

Ba·rysh·ni·kov (ba rish′nə kof), *n.* **Mik·hail** (mē′kil), born 1948, American dancer, born in Soviet-controlled Latvia. He dances in both classical ballets and modern works.

bas·al (bā′səl), *adj.* fundamental; basic. **—bas′al·ly,** *adv.*

basal metabolism, amount of energy used by an animal or plant simply by being alive.

ba·salt (bə sôlt′), *n.* a hard, dark-colored rock of volcanic origin. It often occurs in a form resembling a group of columns. **—ba·sal′tic,** *adj.*

basalt

base[1] (bās), **1** *n.* the part on which anything stands or rests; bottom: *This big machine has a wide steel base.* **2** *n.* a starting place; headquarters: *The base for our hiking trip was a camp beside a brook.* **3** *n.* place from which an army, air force, or navy operates and from which it gets its supplies; headquarters. **4** *n.* main or supporting part; basis; foundation: *The new law was a base on which to build needed reforms.* **5** *n.* the most important element of anything; essential part: *This paint has an oil base.* **6** *v.* to find a base or basis for: *This novel is based on a true story.*

7 *n.* place that is a station or goal in certain games, such as baseball or hide-and-seek: *A home run doesn't count if you fail to touch a base.* **8** *n.* any chemical compound that turns red litmus paper blue. A base usually reacts with an acid to form a salt. Many bases dissolve in water and yield ions composed of paired hydrogen and oxygen atoms. Ammonia is a base. **9** *n.* (in biology) any of the five chemical compounds that form the structure of genes in DNA and RNA molecules. **10** *n.* line or surface on which a geometric shape is supposed to rest. Any side of a triangle can be its base. **11** *n.* the number that needs two number places to write in a counting system, and that names that counting system. The base of the decimal system is 10. The base of the binary system is 2, written as 10. **12** *n.* the number that is used to calculate a logarithm of a stated number. The logarithm of 16 to the base 2 is 4. **13** *n.* the form of a word to which prefixes and suffixes can be attached; root. ❑ *v.* **based, bas·ing.**

off base, incorrect; wrong.

> **SYNONYM STUDY** **Base**[1], **basis,** and **foundation** all mean the part on which something stands for support. **Base** usually means a real thing: *The base of the lamp is chipped.* **Basis** usually means an idea. It suggests how important the support is: *The basis for his report is a careful outline.* **Foundation** is used about real things and about ideas. It suggests firmness and solidity: *The foundation for the house is made of thick concrete.*

base[2] (bās), *adj.* **1** morally low or mean; selfish and cowardly: *Betraying a friend is a base action.* **2** having little value when compared with something else; inferior: *Iron and lead are base metals; gold and silver are precious metals.* ❑ *adj.* **bas·er, bas·est. —base′ly,** *adv.* **—base′ness,** *n.*

> **SYNONYM STUDY** **Base**[2] and **vile** both mean bad and nasty. **Base** suggests selfishness and cowardice: *Their base treachery yielded the fort to the enemy.* **Vile** suggests something evil and horrid: *This vile pollution has poisoned the entire lake.*

base·ball (bās′bôl′), *n.* **1** game played with bat and ball by two teams of nine players each, on a field with four bases. A player who touches all the bases, under the rules, scores a run. **2** ball used in this game.

base·board (bās′bôrd′), *n.* line of boards around the inside walls of a room, next to the floor.

base hit, a hit in baseball that allows a batter to reach at least first base without a defensive error and without a force play on a base runner.

base·less (bās′lis), *adj.* without foundation; groundless: *a baseless rumor.*

base·line (bās′līn′), *n.* **1** line used as a starting place: *establish a baseline for a land survey.* **2** (in baseball) the path connecting one base with the next.

base·man (bās′mən), *n.* a baseball player guarding first, second, or third base. ❑ *n., pl.* **base·men.**

base·ment (bās′mənt), *n.* the lowest story of a building, partly or wholly below ground.

ba·sen·ji (bə sen′jē), *n.* a small, silky-haired, curly-tailed hunting dog somewhat like a terrier, first bred in Africa. Basenjis are unable to bark. ❑ *n., pl.* **ba·sen·jis.**

base on balls, (in baseball) a walk.

base runner, baseball player on the team at bat who is on base or running between two bases.

bas·es[1] (bā′siz), *n.* plural of **base**[1].

ba·ses[2] (bā′sēz′), *n.* plural of **basis.**

bash (bash), **1** *v.* to strike with a smashing blow. **2** *n.* a smashing blow. **3** *n.* SLANG. a big party or meal. ❑ *n., pl.* **bash·es.**

bash·ful (bash′fəl), *adj.* uneasy in the presence of others; easily embarrassed; shy: *The child was too bashful to greet us.* ■ See Synonym Study at **shy**[1]. **—bash′ful·ly,** *adv.* **—bash′ful·ness,** *n.*

a	hat	ė	term	ô	order	ch	child	
ā	age	i	it	oi	oil	ng	long	(a in about
ä	far	ī	ice	ou	out	sh	she	(e in taken
â	care	o	hot	u	cup	th	thin	ə (i in pencil
e	let	ō	open	ů	put	ŦH	then	(o in lemon
ē	equal	ò	saw	ü	rule	zh	measure	(u in circus

ba·sic (bā′sik), *adj.* **1** forming the basis or main part; fundamental: *Addition, subtraction, multiplication, and division are the basic processes of arithmetic.* ■ See Synonym Study at **elementary. 2** (in chemistry) being, having the properties of, or containing a base; alkaline. —**ba′si·cal·ly,** *adv.*

BASIC (bā′sik), *n.* computer programming language that uses English words and algebraic notation. It is a simple language often used with smaller computers.

Bas·ie (bā′sē), *n.* **Count,** 1904-1984, African American jazz musician. ■ Famous for his work as a bandleader, **Count Basie** was also a talented pianist.

bas·il (bā′zəl *or* baz′əl), *n.* a sweet-smelling plant related to mint, used in cooking.

ba·sil·i·ca (bə sil′ə kə), *n.* **1** an oblong hall with a row of columns at each side and a structure in the shape of a half circle at one end. The Romans used such buildings for courts of law and public meetings. **2** church built in this form. ❑ *n., pl.* **ba·sil·i·cas.**

ba·sin (bā′sn), *n.* **1** a wide, shallow bowl for holding liquids. **2** amount that a basin can hold: *They have used up a basin of water already.* **3** a shallow area containing water: *Part of the harbor is a basin for yachts.* **4** all the land drained by a river and the streams that flow into it: *The Mississippi basin extends from the Appalachians to the Rockies.* —**ba′sin·like′,** *adj.*

ba·sis (bā′sis), *n.* **1** thing or part on which anything is established or supported; foundation: *The basis of their friendship was a common interest in sports.* **2** the main part; base: *The basis of this medicine is an oil.* ■ See Synonym Study at **base**[1]. ❑ *n., pl.* **ba·ses.**

bask (bask), *v.* **1** to warm yourself pleasantly: *The cat basks before the fire.* **2** to feel great pleasure: *The author basked in the praise of the critics.*

bas·ket (bas′kit), *n.* **1** container made of twigs, grasses, fibers, strips of wood, etc., woven together. **2** amount that a basket holds: *We ate a basket of peaches.* **3** anything that looks like or serves as a basket: *a metal wastepaper basket.* **4** a metal hoop with an open net hanging from it, used as a goal in basketball. **5** score made in basketball by tossing the ball through the basket. —**bas′ket·like′,** *adj.*

bas·ket·ball (bas′kit bôl′), *n.* **1** game played with a large, round ball by two teams of five players each. The players try to toss the ball through baskets hanging at either end of the court. **2** ball used in this game.

bas·ket·ry (bas′kə trē), *n.* **1** art of making baskets. **2** baskets.

bas mitz·vah (bäs mits′və), bat mitzvah.

Basque (bask), **1** *n.* member of a people living in the Pyrenees region of northern Spain and southern France. **2** *n.* the language of the Basques. **3** *adj.* of the Basques or their language.

bas·re·lief (bä′ri lēf′), *n.* carving or sculpture in which the figures stand out only slightly from the background.

bass[1] (bās), **1** *n.* the lowest male voice in music. **2** *n.* singer with such a voice. **3** *n.* part in music for such a voice. **4** *n.* instrument playing such a part. **5** *adj.* having a deep, low sound. ❑ *n., pl.* **bass·es.**

bass[2] (bas), *n.* **1** any of several North American freshwater fishes related to sunfish, popular as game and food. **2** any of numerous similar food fishes living mostly in saltwater, but some in North American freshwater. ❑ *n., pl.* **bass** or **bass·es.**

bass clef (bās), symbol in music showing that the pitch of the notes on a staff is below middle C; F clef. See picture at **clef.**

bass drum (bās), a large drum that makes a deep, low sound when struck on one or both of its heads.

bass drum

Basse·terre (bäs′ter′), *n.* capital of St. Kitts and Nevis.

Basse-Terre (bäs′ter′), *n.* capital of Guadeloupe.

bas·set hound (bas′it), dog with short legs, long ears, and a long body, like a dachshund, but larger and heavier. [**Basset** comes from a French word meaning "low." A basset hound is short-legged and stands very low to the ground.]

bass horn (bās), tuba.

bas·si·net (bas′n et′), *n.* a baby's basketlike cradle, usually with a hood over one end.

bas·so (bas′ō), *n.* singer with a bass voice. ❑ *n., pl.* **bas·sos.**

bas·soon (bə sün′), *n.* a deep-toned wind instrument with a doubled wooden body and a curved metal pipe to which a double reed is attached.

bass viol (bās), double bass.

bass·wood (bas′wùd′), *n.* linden.

bast (bast), *n.* the tough fiber in the inner bark of certain trees, used in making rope, matting, etc.

bas·tard (bas′tərd), *n.* child born of parents who are not married to each other.

baste[1] (bāst), *v.* to drip or pour melted fat or butter on food while roasting it: *Baste the turkey to keep it from drying out.* ❑ *v.* **bast·ed, bast·ing.** —**bast′er,** *n.*

baste[2] (bāst), *v.* to sew with long, loose stitches. These stitches are usually removed after the final sewing. ❑ *v.* **bast·ed, bast·ing.** —**bast′er,** *n.*

Bas·tille (ba stēl′), *n.* an old fort in Paris used as a prison for enemies of the king. A mob captured and destroyed it on July 14, 1789, at the beginning of the French Revolution.

bas·tion (bas′chən), *n.* **1** a part of a fortification that sticks out so that the defenders can fire at attackers from as many angles as possible. **2** stronghold; center of defense.

bat[1] (bat), **1** *n.* a stout wooden or metal club, used to hit the ball in baseball, cricket, etc. **2** *v.* to hit with a bat; hit: *She bats well. I batted the balloon with my hand.* **3** *n.* a turn at batting: *Who goes to bat first?* **4** *n.* a stroke; blow. ❑ *v.* **bat·ted, bat·ting.**
at bat, having a turn at batting: *Our side is at bat.*
go to bat for, to champion the cause of.
right off the bat, without hesitation; immediately.

bat[2] (bat), *n.* any of many flying mammals with mouselike bodies and wings made of thin skin supported by the long, slim bones of the forelimbs. Bats fly at night. There are over 1000 species, with bodies varying in size from 1½ inches to 12 inches (3.8 to 30.5 centimeters). Most of them eat insects, but some live on fruit and a few suck the blood of other mammals. —**bat·like′,** *adj.*

bat[3] (bat), *v.* to wink: *The ball nearly hit her, but she didn't bat an eye.* ❑ *v.* **bat·ted, bat·ting.**

Ba·taan (bə tan′), *n.* peninsula near Manila in the Philippines, where U.S. and Philippine troops surrendered to the Japanese in 1942.

bat·boy (bat′boi′), *n.* boy who takes care of the bats and equipment of a baseball team.

batch (bach), *n.* **1** quantity of bread, cookies, etc., made at one baking. ■ See Synonym Study at **group. 2** quantity of anything made as one lot or set: *Our second batch of candy was better than the first.* **3** number of persons or things taken together: *We caught a fine batch of fish.* ❑ *n., pl.* **batch·es.**

ba·teau (ba tō′), *n.* a lightweight, flat-bottomed boat with pointed ends, used on rivers and lakes in Canada and Louisiana. ❑ *n., pl.* **ba·teaux** (ba tōz′).

bat·ed (bā′tid), *adj.* **with bated breath,** holding your breath in great fear, wonder, interest, etc.: *We listened with bated breath to the exciting story.* ❑ *v.* **bat·ed, bat·ing.**

Bates (bāts), *n.* **Kath·ar·ine Lee** (kath′ər ən), 1859-1929, American poet. She wrote the words to the song "America the Beautiful."

bat·girl (bat′gėrl′), *n.* girl who takes care of the bats and equipment of a baseball team.

bath (bath), *n.* **1** act of washing the body: *I took a hot bath.* **2** water in a tub for a bath: *Your bath is ready.* **3** tub, room, or other place for bathing. In ancient Rome, baths were often elaborate public buildings, which were also used as clubs. **4** liquid in which something is washed or dipped: *a bath for developing photographic film.* **5** container holding the liquid. ❑ *n., pl.* **baths** (baᴛнz). **–bath′less,** *adj.*

bathe (bāᴛн), *v.* **1** to take a bath: *We wash our hair and bathe regularly.* **2** to give a bath to: *She is bathing the dog.* **3** to apply water to; wash or moisten with any liquid: *He bathed his swollen ankle.* **4** to go swimming; go into a river, lake, ocean, etc., for pleasure or to get cool. **5** to cover or surround: *The valley was bathed in sunlight.* ❑ *v.* **bathed, bath·ing. –bath′er,** *n.*

bath·house (bath′hous′), *n.* **1** (earlier) house or building equipped for bathing. **2** building containing dressing rooms for swimmers. ❑ *n., pl.* **bath·hous·es** (bath′hou′ziz).

bathing suit, clothing worn for swimming.

bath·robe (bath′rōb′), *n.* a long, loose garment worn to and from a bath or when resting or lounging.

bath·room (bath′rüm′), *n.* **1** room for taking baths, usually equipped with a sink and a toilet. **2** a room containing a toilet.

bath·tub (bath′tub′), *n.* tub to bathe in, especially one permanently fixed in a bathroom.

bath·y·scaph or **bath·y·scaphe** (bath′ə skaf′), *n.* a diving craft for deep-sea exploration consisting of a round steel chamber suspended from a large, cigar-shaped float.

bath·y·sphere (bath′ə sfir′), *n.* a large, watertight, hollow, steel ball with observation windows, lowered by cables from a ship to study the depths of the sea.

batik

ba·tik (bə tēk′), *n.* **1** method of making designs on cloth by covering the material with wax in a pattern, dyeing the parts left exposed, and then removing the wax. **2** cloth dyed in this way. [Batik comes from a Javanese word meaning "paint" or "tattoo." The dyed cloth has bright designs with small details like paintings or tattoos.]

ba·tiste (bə tēst′), *n.* a fine, thin cloth made of cotton, rayon, or wool.

bat mitz·vah (bät′ mits′və), **1** ceremony or celebration held when a Jewish girl becomes thirteen years old to affirm that she has reached the age of religious responsibility. **2** the girl herself. Also, **bas mitzvah.**

ba·ton (ba ton′), *n.* **1** the light stick or wand used by the leader of an orchestra, chorus, or band to indicate the beat and direct the performance. **2** staff or stick used as a symbol of office or authority. **3** a stick passed from runner to runner in a relay race. **4** a light, hollow metal rod twirled by a drum major or majorette.

Bat·on Rouge (bat′n rüzh′), port and capital of Louisiana, on the Mississippi River.

bats·man (bats′mən), *n.* player whose turn it is to bat in cricket. ❑ *n., pl.* **bats·men.**

bat·tal·ion (bə tal′yən), *n.* **1** military unit made up of two or more companies or batteries, usually commanded by a major or a lieutenant colonel. It is usually part of a group or a regiment. **2** any large group organized to act together: *A battalion of volunteers helped to rescue the flood victims.*

bat·ten (bat′n), **1** *n.* strip of wood or steel used on shipboard to fasten tarpaulins over hatchways to keep out water. **2** *v.* to fasten down with, or as if with, such strips. **3** *n.* narrow strip of wood or plastic inserted into a sail to keep it flat.

bat·ter[1] (bat′ər), *v.* to strike with repeated blows so as to bruise, break, or get out of shape; pound: *They battered down the door with a heavy ax. Violent storms battered the coast for days.* ■ See Synonym Study at **beat.** [See Word Story at **debate.**]

bat·ter[2] (bat′ər), *n.* a liquid mixture of flour, milk, eggs, etc., that becomes solid when cooked. Batter is used to make cakes, pancakes, and muffins, and to coat foods before frying them.

bat·ter[3] (bat′ər), *n.* player whose turn it is to bat in baseball or softball.

bat·tered (bat′ərd), *adj.* **1** damaged by hard use: *I found a battered old bookcase in the office.* **2** beaten; struck with repeated blows: *battered children, battered spouses.*

battering ram, a heavy wooden beam with metal at one end. Battering rams were used in ancient and medieval warfare for battering down walls, gates, etc.

bat·ter·y (bat′ər ē), *n.* **1** container holding materials that produce electricity by chemical action; a single electric cell: *Most flashlights work on two batteries.* **2** set of two or more electric cells that produce electric current: *a car battery.* **3** any set of things similar or connected to each other: *a battery of microphones, a battery of tests.* **4** set of similar pieces of equipment, such as mounted guns, searchlights, mortars, etc., used as a unit. **5** military unit of artillery, usually commanded by a captain. A battery corresponds to a company or troop in other branches of the army. **6** a baseball pitcher and catcher together. **7** the unlawful beating of another person or any threatening touch to another person's clothes or body. ❑ *n., pl.* **bat·ter·ies.**

bat·ting (bat′ing), *n.* cotton, wool, or synthetic material pressed into thin layers, used for padding or filling.

bat·ting average, a three-digit decimal that shows the percentage of a batter's hits compared with the number of times at bat. 40 hits in 120 times at bat is a batting average of .333.

bat·tle (bat′l), **1** *n.* a fight between opposing armies, air forces, or navies: *The battle for the island lasted six months.* **2** *n.* fighting or warfare: *The soldier received his wounds in battle.* **3** *n.* any fight or contest: *The candidates fought a battle of words during the campaign.* **4** *v.* to take part in a battle; fight; struggle; contend: *The swimmer had to battle a strong current. Our team is battling for first place.* ❑ *v.* **bat·tled, bat·tling. –bat′tler,** *n.*

battle-ax

join battle, to begin to fight.

bat·tle-ax or **bat·tle-axe** (bat′l aks′), *n.* (in the Middle Ages) ax with a broad blade, used as a weapon. ❑ *n., pl.* **bat·tle-ax·es.**

battle cry, **1** shout of soldiers rushing into or engaged in battle. **2** motto or slogan in any contest.

bat·tle·dore (bat′l dôr), *n.* a small racket used in the game of badminton to hit the shuttlecock back and forth.

bat·tle·field (bat′l fēld′), *n.* place where a battle is fought or has been fought.

bat·tle·front (bat′l frunt′), *n.* place where the fighting between armies takes place; front.

a	hat	ė	term	ô	order	ch	child		a	in about
ā	age	i	it	oi	oil	ng	long		e	in taken
ä	far	ī	ice	ou	out	sh	she	ə	i	in pencil
â	care	o	hot	u	cup	th	thin		o	in lemon
e	let	ō	open	ù	put	ᴛн	then		u	in circus
ē	equal	ò	saw	ü	rule	zh	measure			

bat·tle·ment (bat′l mənt), *n.* **1** a low wall for defense at the top of a tower or wall in which solid parts alternate with openings. Soldiers of ancient and medieval times stood on a platform behind the wall and shot through the openings. **2** wall built like this for ornament.

battle royal, 1 fight in which several take part; riot. **2** a long, hard fight. ❑ *pl.* **battles royal.**

bat·tle·ship (bat′l ship′), *n.* type of warship having the heaviest armor and the most powerful guns. The last battleships were built during World War II.

bat·ty (bat′ē), *adj.* SLANG. mentally ill. ■ The word **batty** is often considered offensive. ❑ *adj.* **bat·ti·er, bat·ti·est.**

bau·ble (bȯ′bəl), *n.* a showy trifle having no real value; trinket.

baud (bȯd), *n.* unit for measuring the rate of data transmission, usually equal to one bit of information per second.

WORD STORY Baud comes from the name of Jean Maurice Baud, a French engineer who invented a telegraph code. The baud was used about telegraph transmissions before it was used about computer modems.

Baum (bäm), *n.* **L. Frank,** 1856-1919, American writer. He wrote *The Wonderful Wizard of Oz* and thirteen other Oz books.

baux·ite (bȯk′sīt), *n.* a claylike mineral from which aluminum is obtained.

Ba·var·i·a (bə vâr′ē ə), *n.* state in S Germany. In the past it has been a duchy, a kingdom, and a republic. —**Ba·var′i·an,** *n., adj.*

bawd·y (bȯ′dē), *adj.* not decent; lewd; obscene. ❑ *adj.* **bawd·i·er, bawd·i·est.** —**bawd′i·ly,** *adv.* —**bawd′i·ness,** *n.*

bawl (bȯl), **1** *v.* to weep loudly. **2** *v.* to shout or cry out in a noisy way: *a lost calf bawling for its mother.* **3** *n.* a shout at the top of your voice. —**bawl′er,** *n.*

bawl out, to scold loudly; reprimand: *She bawled me out for denting her bicycle.*

bay¹ (bā), *n.* part of a sea or lake extending into the land, usually smaller than a gulf and larger than a cove.

bay² (bā), **1** *n.* a long, deep barking, especially by a large dog: *The hunters heard the distant bay of the hounds.* **2** *v.* to bark with long, deep sounds: *Dogs sometimes bay at the moon.* **3** *n.* position of a hunted animal that turns to face its pursuers when escape is impossible: *The stag stood at bay against the hounds on the edge of the cliff.* **4** *n.* position of an enemy or pursuers that are faced or kept off: *The stag held the hounds at bay.*

bay³ (bā), *n.* a small evergreen tree with smooth, shiny leaves used in cooking; laurel.

bay⁴ (bā), **1** *adj.* reddish brown: *a bay horse.* **2** *n.* a reddish brown horse with black mane and tail. **3** *n.* a reddish brown.

bay⁵ (bā), *n.* **1** space or division of a wall or building between columns, pillars, buttresses, etc. **2** bay window. **3** compartment in an airplane, especially for bombs.

bay·ber·ry (bā′ber′ē), *n.* a North American bush with clusters of grayish white berries coated with wax. Candles made from this wax burn with a pleasant fragrance. ❑ *n., pl.* **bay·ber·ries.**

bay leaf, the dried leaf of a bay tree, used as a flavoring for foods.

Bay of Pigs, bay in W central Cuba. It was the site of an invasion in 1961 by forces trained by the CIA attempting to overthrow the regime of Fidel Castro. The attempt was unsuccessful.

bay·o·net (bā′ə nit *or* bā′ə net′), **1** *n.* knife attached to the front end of a rifle. It may be detached and used as a hand weapon. **2** *v.* to pierce or stab with a bayonet. ❑ *v.* **bay·o·net·ed, bay·o·net·ing.**

bay·ou (bī′ü), *n.* a marshy, slow-moving stream that flows into or out of a lake, river, or gulf in the south central United States.

bay rum, a fragrant liquid used as a soothing skin lotion, made from the leaves of a West Indian tree.

bay window, window or set of windows that sticks out beyond an outside wall to form a small space in a room.

ba·zaar (bə zär′), *n.* **1** street or streets full of small shops and booths, especially in Middle Eastern countries. **2** place for the sale of many kinds of goods. **3** sale of things contributed by various people, held for some charity or other special purpose. ■ Another word that sounds like this is **bizarre.**

ba·zoo·ka (bə zü′kə), *n.* a portable weapon used to fire rockets at tanks. ❑ *n., pl.* **ba·zoo·kas.**

BB (bē′bē′), *n.* **1** a standard, small size of shot, about .18 inch (.46 centimeter) in diameter. **2** shot of this size, used especially in an air rifle. ❑ *n., pl.* **BBs** or **BB's.**

BBC, British Broadcasting Corporation.

BB gun, air rifle.

bbl., barrel. ❑ *pl.* **bbls.**

B.C., 1 before Christ. B.C. is used for times before the birth of Christ. A.D is used for times after the birth of Christ. 350 B.C. is 100 years earlier than 250 B.C. From 20 B.C. to A.D. 50 is 70 years. **2** British Columbia.

B complex, vitamin B complex.

bd., 1 board. **2** bond. **3** bound.

bd. ft., board foot or board feet.

bdl., bundle. ❑ *pl.* **bdls.**

be (bē), *v. Be* is a very common verb that has several different forms. We say: I *am,* you (we, they) *are,* he (she, it) *is,* I (he, she, it) *was,* you (we, they) *were.* **1** to live; exist: *Could there be tigers in this forest?* **2** to have a place or position: *The new bookcase is going to be in the bedroom.* **3** to happen; take place: *Will the meeting be at your house?* **4** to go or come: *Has he ever been to New York?* **5** to belong to the group of: *Whales are mammals.* **6** *Be* is used as a linking verb: *Can this jacket be yours? No, mine is yellow. Who is the librarian?* **7** *Be* is used to begin a request or a question: *Be careful. Is that so?* **8** *Be* is used as a helping verb to show that action is taking place: *Can he be sleeping this late? We are leaving.* **9** *Be* is used as a helping verb to show that action is happening to someone or something: *Can he be coaxed to join us? The room was painted last year.* ❑ *v.* **am, are, is; was, were; been; be·ing.** ■ Another word that sounds like this is **bee.**

Be, symbol for beryllium.

beach (bēch), **1** *n.* an almost flat shore of sand or pebbles along the edge of a sea, lake, or big river. **2** *v.* to go or bring onto a beach; strand: *The damaged ship was beached to avoid being sunk in the storm.* ❑ *n., pl.* **beach·es.** ■ Another word that sounds like this is **beech.** —**beach′less,** *adj.*

beach ball, a large, lightweight ball that is filled with air, often used at the beach.

beach buggy, dune buggy.

beach·comb·er (bēch′kō′mər), *n.* wanderer or loafer, especially on islands of the Pacific.

beach·head (bēch′hed′), *n.* the first position established by an invading military force on an enemy beach or shore to make possible the landing of troops and supplies.

bea·con (bē′kən), *n.* **1** fire or light used as a signal to guide or warn. **2** marker, signal light, or radio station that guides aircraft and ships through fogs, storms, etc. **3** a tall tower for a signal; lighthouse.

bead (bēd), **1** *n.* a small ball or bit of glass, metal, etc., with a hole through it, so that it can be strung on a thread with others like it. **2** *n.pl.* **beads, a** a string of beads. **b** string of beads for keeping count in saying prayers; rosary. **3** *v.* to put beads on; ornament with beads. **4** *n.* any small, round object like a drop or bubble: *Beads of sweat covered her forehead.* **5** *n.* piece of metal at the front end of a gun to aim by. —**bead′like′,** *adj.*

draw a bead on, to aim a gun at; take aim at: *The sheriff drew a bead on the rustler and said, "Drop your gun!"*

say your beads, tell your beads, or **count your beads,** to say prayers, using a rosary.

bead·ed (bē′did), *adj.* **1** trimmed with beads: *a beaded dress.* **2** like beads.

bead·ing (bē′ding), *n.* **1** trimming made of beads. **2** pattern or edge on woodwork, silver, etc., made of small beads.

bea·dle (bē′dl), *n.* a minor parish officer whose duties include helping members of the clergy and keeping order.

bead·work (bēd′werk′), *n.* beading.

bead·y (bē′dē), *adj.* small, round, and shiny: *The parakeet has beady eyes.* ❑ *adj.* **bead·i·er, bead·i·est.**

bea·gle (bē′gəl), *n.* a small dog with smooth hair, short legs, and drooping ears, bred for hunting.

beak (bēk), *n.* **1** bill of a bird. Eagles and hawks have hooked beaks useful for tearing. **2** a similar part in other animals. Turtles and octopuses have beaks. **3** anything shaped like a beak, such as the prow of an ancient warship or the spout of a pitcher, jug, etc. **—beak′like′,** *adj.*

beak·er (bē′kər), *n.* **1** a large cup

beagle—about 14 in. (36 cm) high at the shoulder

or drinking glass with a wide mouth. **2** a thin glass or metal container used in laboratories. A beaker has a flat bottom, no handle, and a small lip for pouring.

bear² (def. 1)—up to 8 ft. (2.4 m) long

beam (bēm), **1** *n.* a large, long piece of timber, iron, or steel, for use in building. **2** *n.* the main horizontal support of a building or ship. **3** *n.* any long piece or bar: *The beam of a balance supports a pair of scales.* **4** *n.* balance beam. **5** *n.* ray or rays of light: *the beam from a flashlight.* **6** *v.* to send out rays of light; shine: *The sun was beaming brightly.* **7** *n.* a bright look or smile. **8** *v.* to look or smile brightly: *Her face beamed with delight.* **9** *n.* a radio signal directed in a straight line, used to guide aircraft, ships, etc. **10** *v.* to direct a broadcast: *A message was beamed to the spacecraft.* **11** *n.* the widest part of a ship.

SYNONYM STUDY **Beam** and **ray**¹ both mean a line of light. **Beam** suggests a long and fairly wide line coming from something that gives light: *The beam of the spotlight moved across the sky.* **Ray** suggests a thin line of light, one of many coming out all around something bright: *There was not a ray of moonlight in the forest.*

beam·ing (bē′ming), *adj.* **1** shining; bright. **2** looking or smiling brightly; cheerful. **—beam′ing·ly,** *adv.*

bean (bēn), *n.* **1** the smooth, flat seed of many related bushes and vines, eaten as a vegetable, such as lima beans, kidney beans, and navy beans. **2** the long pod containing such seeds. The green or yellow pods of some varieties are also eaten as a vegetable. **3** any seed shaped like a bean. Coffee beans are seeds of the coffee plant. **—bean′like′,** *adj.*

spill the beans, to reveal a secret.

bean·bag (bēn′bag′), *n.* a small bag partly filled with dried beans, used to toss in play.

bean curd, tofu.

bean·ie (bē′nē), *n.* **1** a small, close-fitting cap. **2 propeller beanie,** a small, close-fitting cap with a propeller attached to the top. This propeller is usually not motorized.

bean sprouts, seedling growths of beans, eaten as a vegetable.

bean·stalk (bēn′stȯk′), *n.* stem of a bean plant.

bear¹ (bâr), *v.* **1** to carry or support; hold up: *The ice is too thin to bear your weight.* **2** to put up with; endure: *She can't bear the*

noise. **3** to bring forth; produce: *This tree bears fine apples.* **4** to give birth to: *Our cat will soon bear kittens.* ■ See Usage Note at **borne.** **5** to act in a certain way; behave; conduct: *The famous actor bore himself with great dignity.* **6** to hold in mind; hold: *bear a grudge, bear affection.* **7** to move; go: *The ship bore north.* **8** to take on yourself as a duty: *bear the cost, bear the responsibility.* ❑ *v.* **bore, borne** or **born, bear·ing.** ■ Another word that sounds like this is **bare.**

bear down or **bear down on, 1** to put pressure on; press down: *The lead will break if you bear down too hard on your pencil.* **2** to put all your efforts on; try hard: *I bore down on my homework and got it done on time.* **3** to move toward; approach: *The wolves bore down on the exhausted deer.*

bear on, to have something to do with: *Your story does not bear on the question.*

bear out, to support; prove: *The facts bear out our claim.*

bear up, to keep your courage; not lose hope or faith: *bear up under troubles.*

bear with, to put up with; be patient with: *Please bear with me while I ask some questions.*

SYNONYM STUDY **Bear**¹, **endure,** and **stand** all mean to put up with pain or discomfort. **Bear** suggests only waiting until something ends: *He is bearing his grief very well.* **Endure** suggests bearing something for a long time by strength of mind or body: *The pioneers endured many hardships in settling the West.* **Stand** is more informal than **bear:** *My father can't stand this TV show.*

bear² (bâr), *n.* **1** any of seven kinds of large mammals with thick, coarse fur and very short tails. A bear walks flat on the soles of its feet. The black bear, brown bear, grizzly bear, and polar bear are four kinds of bears. **2** a gruff or bad-tempered person. ■ Another word that sounds like this is **bare. —bear′like′,** *adj.*

bear·a·ble (bâr′ə bəl), *adj.* able to be endured. **—bear′a·bly,** *adv.*

beard (bird), **1** *n.* the hair growing on a man's chin and cheeks. The long hair on the chin of a goat is a beard; so are the stiff hairs on the heads of plants like oats, barley, and wheat. **2** *n.* something resembling or suggesting this. **3** *v.* to face boldly; defy: *beard the lion in its den.* **—beard′less,** *adj.*

beard·ed (bir′did), *adj.* having a beard.

beard·less (bird′lis), *adj.* **1** without a beard. **2** young or immature; youthful.

bear·er (bâr′ər), *n.* **1** person or thing that carries. **2** person who holds or presents a check, draft, or note for payment.

bear·ing (bâr′ing), *n.* **1** way of standing, sitting, walking, and behaving; manner: *He has the easy bearing of a man used to public attention.* **2** connection in thought or meaning; relation: *Do not ask questions that have no bearing on our discussion.* **3 bearings,** *pl.* knowledge of where you are in relation to other things: *After missing the turn in the trail, we completely lost our bearings and had to retrace our steps.* **4** part of a machine on which another part moves. A bearing supports the moving part and reduces friction by turning with the motion.

SYNONYM STUDY **Bearing** and **posture** both mean the way a person stands and moves. **Bearing** suggests everything that a person does with the body, and the way it expresses character: *The detective's modest bearing concealed her brilliant mind.* **Posture** suggests only the position of the body: *Grandmother's posture shows her years as a ballet dancer.*

bear·ish (bâr′ish), *adj.* like a bear in manner or temper; rough or surly. **—bear′ish·ly,** *adv.* **—bear′ish·ness,** *n.*

bear·skin (bâr′skin′), *n.* **1** the skin of a bear with the fur on it. **2** rug, blanket, or the like made from this. **3** a tall, black fur cap worn by some soldiers, especially in the British army, and drum majors.

beast (bēst), *n.* **1** any four-footed animal. Lions, bears, cows, and horses are beasts. **2** a brutal person.

a	hat	ė	term	ȯ	order	ch	child			a in about
ā	age	i	it	oi	oil	ng	long			e in taken
ä	far	ī	ice	ou	out	sh	she	ə		i in pencil
â	care	o	hot	u	cup	th	thin			o in lemon
e	let	ō	open	u̇	put	ᴛʜ	then			u in circus
ē	equal	ȯ	saw	ü	rule	zh	measure			

beast·ly (bēst′lē), *adj.* **1** like a beast; cruel; brutal. **2** very bad or irritating; unpleasant: *I have a beastly headache.* ❑ *adj.* **beast·li·er, beast·li·est.** —**beast′li·ness,** *n.*

beast of burden, animal used for carrying or pulling heavy loads.

beat (bēt), **1** *v.* to strike again and again: *The baby beat the floor with the toy hammer.* **2** *n.* stroke or blow made again and again: *the beat of a drum.* **3** *v.* to make a sound by being struck: *The drums beat loudly.* **4** *v.* to get the better of; defeat; overcome: *Their team beat ours by a huge score.* **5** *v.* to outdo; surpass: *This new bicycle sure beats my old one.* **6** *v.* to make flat: *The jeweler beat gold into thin strips with a hammer.* **7** *v.* to mix by stirring rapidly with a fork, spoon, or other utensil: *I helped make the cake by beating the eggs.* **8** *v.* to throb: *Her heart beat fast with joy.* **9** *n.* a throb: *the beat of the heart.* **10** *v.* to move up and down; flap: *The bird beat its wings.* **11** *n.* unit of time or accent in music: *three beats to a measure.* **12** *n.* stroke of the hand, baton, etc., showing musical time. **13** *v.* to mark time with drumsticks or by tapping with the hands, fingers, or feet. **14** *n.* a regular round or route taken by a police officer or guard. **15** *v.* to move against the wind by a zigzag course: *The sailboat beat along the coast.* **16** *adj.* INFORMAL. worn out; tired; exhausted: *I was beat after the race.* ❑ *v.* **beat, beat·en** or **beat, beat·ing.** ▪ Another word that sounds like this is **beet.**

beat back, to force or push back: *Cops beat back the rioting crowd.*

beat down, INFORMAL. to force to set a lower price.

beat it, INFORMAL. to go away.

beat up, INFORMAL. to thrash soundly.

SYNONYM STUDY **Beat, pound**[2], and **batter**[1] all mean to hit over and over. **Beat** does not suggest how hard or with what: *The moth beat on the window with its wings.* **Pound** means to hit hard: *"Quiet!" called the chairman, pounding on his desk with a gavel.* **Batter** means to hit hard enough to cause damage: *Storms battered the town.*

beat·en (bēt′n), **1** *adj.* whipped; struck: *The beaten dog ran away from its owner.* **2** *adj.* much walked on or traveled: *a beaten path across the grass.* **3** *adj.* defeated; overcome: *a beaten army.* **4** *adj.* exhausted. **5** *adj.* shaped by blows of a hammer: *This bowl is made of beaten silver.* **6** *v.* a past participle of **beat:** *Our team was beaten in basketball on Saturday.*

beat·er (bē′tər), *n.* **1** device or utensil for beating eggs, cream, etc. **2** person or thing that beats: *a rug beater.*

be·a·tif·ic (bē′ə tif′ik), *adj.* showing very great happiness; blissful. —**be′a·tif′i·cal·ly,** *adv.*

be·at·i·fy (bē at′ə fī), *v.* **1** to make very happy; bless. **2** to declare by a decree of the pope that a dead person is among the blessed in heaven. ❑ *v.* **be·at·i·fied, be·at·i·fy·ing.** —**be·at′i·fi·ca′tion,** *n.*

beat·ing (bē′ting), *n.* **1** process or act of striking something over and over. **2** punishment by blows; whipping; thrashing. **3** a defeat or loss. **4** throbbing.

be·at·i·tude (bē at′ə tüd), *n.* **1** supreme happiness; bliss. **2** a blessing. **3 the Beatitudes,** *pl.* (in the Bible) the eight verses in the Sermon on the Mount which begin with "Blessed," as "Blessed are the poor in spirit."

Beat·les (bē′tlz), *n.pl.* English rock group. Its members were George Harrison, John Lennon, Paul McCartney, and Ringo Starr. In addition to their best-selling albums, the Beatles starred in two movies, *A Hard Day's Night* and *Help!* and a full-length cartoon, *Yellow Submarine.*

Be·a·trix (bā′ə trēks), *n.* born 1938, queen of the Netherlands since 1980.

beat-up (bēt′up′), *adj.* INFORMAL. worn out from long or hard use: *a beat-up car.*

beau (bō), *n.* **1** a young man courting a young woman; suitor or lover. **2** OLD USE. man who pays much attention to the way he dresses and to the fashion of his clothes; dandy. ❑ *n., pl.* **beaus** or **beaux.** ▪ Another word that sounds like this is **bow**[2].

Beau·fort scale (bō′fərt), scale of wind speeds, ranging from 0 (calm) to 17 (hurricane), used in weather maps.

beaut (byüt), *n.* INFORMAL. something that is extremely beautiful, remarkable or outstanding: *That last touchdown pass was a beaut.* ▪ Another word that sounds like this is **butte.**

beau·te·ous (byü′tē əs), *adj.* beautiful. —**beau′te·ous·ly,** *adv.* —**beau′te·ous·ness,** *n.*

beau·ti·cian (byü tish′ən), *n.* someone who is skilled in the use of cosmetics, especially someone who works in a beauty shop.

beau·ti·ful (byü′tə fəl), *adj.* very pleasing to see or hear; delighting the mind or senses. —**beau′ti·ful·ly,** *adv.* —**beau′ti·ful·ness,** *n.*

beau·ti·fy (byü′tə fī), *v.* to make beautiful; make more beautiful: *Flowers beautify a room.* ❑ *v.* **beau·ti·fied, beau·ti·fy·ing.** —**beau′ti·fi·ca′tion,** *n.*

beau·ty (byü′tē), *n.* **1** good looks: *The child had beauty and intelligence.* **2** quality that pleases in flowers, pictures, music, etc. **3** something beautiful: *the beauties of nature.* **4** a beautiful woman. **5** act, achievement, or example of superior or excellent quality: *a beauty of a high dive.* ❑ *n., pl.* **beau·ties** for 3,4.

beauty shop, beauty parlor, or **beauty salon,** place where women have their hair, skin, and nails cared for.

Beau·voir (bō′vwär′), *n.* **Si·mone de** (sē mōn′ də), 1908-1986, French author. Her most famous book is *The Second Sex,* about women in the modern world.

beaux (bōz), *n.* a plural of **beau.**

bea·ver[1] (bē′vər), *n.* **1** a large rodent with soft fur, a broad, flat tail, webbed hind feet for swimming, and large front teeth. Beavers live both in water and on land and build dams across streams. **2** its fur. —**bea′ver·like′,** *adj.*

bea·ver[2] (bē′vər), *n.* the movable lower part of a helmet, protecting the chin and mouth.

bea·ver·board (bē′vər bôrd′), *n.* a building material made of compressed wood fibers, used for wall partitions and ceilings.

be·calmed (bi kämd′ *or* bi kälmd′), *adj.* kept from moving because there is no wind: *The sailboat lay becalmed on the lake.*

be·came (bi kām′), *v.* past tense of **become:** *The seed became a plant.*

be·cause (bi kôz′), *conj.* for the reason that; since: *Because we were late, we ran the whole way home.*

because of, by reason of; on account of: *The game was called off because of rain.*

beck (bek), *n.* **at someone's beck and call, 1** ready whenever wanted. **2** under someone's complete control.

Beck·et (bek′it), *n.* Saint **Thomas à** (ə), 1118?-1170, archbishop of Canterbury. He was murdered in the cathedral there for resisting Henry II's attempts to control the church in England.

beck·on (bek′ən), *v.* to signal by motion of the head or hand: *He beckoned me to follow him.*

be·cloud (bi kloud′), *v.* **1** to hide by a cloud or clouds. **2** to make obscure; hide: *Too many big words becloud the meaning.*

be·come (bi kum′), *v.* **1** to come to be; grow to be: *It is becoming colder. I became tired and fell asleep.* **2** to seem proper or fitting for: *It does not become them to brag about their furniture.* **3** to look well on; suit: *That blue sweater becomes you.* ❑ *v.* **be·came, be·come, be·com·ing.**

become of, to happen to: *What has become of the box of candy?*

be·com·ing (bi kum′ing), *adj.* **1** fitting; suitable: *the high moral character becoming to a judge.* **2** pleasant to look at; attractive: *a very becoming new suit.* —**be·com′ing·ly,** *adv.*

Bec·quer·el (bek rel′), *n.* **An·toine-Hen·ri** (an twon′ on rē′), 1852-1908, French physicist who discovered radioactivity. He shared the 1903 Nobel Prize for physics with the Curies.

bed (bed), **1** *n.* anything to sleep or rest on. A bed is usually a wooden or metal frame that supports a mattress covered with sheets and blankets. **2** *n.* any place where people or animals sleep or rest: *The cat made its bed by the fireplace.* **3** *v.* to provide with a bed; put to bed; go to bed: *She bedded down her horse in the barn.* **4** *n.* a flat base on which anything rests; foundation: *The tall flagpole was set in a bed of concrete.* **5** *n.* the ground under a body of water: *The river bed was soft and muddy.* **6** *n.* piece of ground in a garden in which plants are grown: *a bed of tulips.* **7** *v.* to plant in a garden: *These tulips should be bedded in rich soil.* **8** *n.* layer; stratum: *a bed of coal deep in the earth.* ❑ *v.* **bed·ded, bed·ding.**

bed down, to go to bed; lie down to sleep: *to bed down for the night.*

get up on the wrong side of the bed, be bad-tempered or irritable.

be·daz·zle (bi daz′əl), *v.* to dazzle completely; confuse by dazzling. ❑ *v.* **be·daz·zled, be·daz·zling.** —**be·daz′zle·ment,** *n.*

bed·bug (bed′bug′), *n.* a small, wingless, reddish brown insect that sucks blood, found in houses and especially in beds. Its bite can be painful.

bed·cham·ber (bed′chām′bər), *n.* bedroom.

bed·clothes (bed′klōz′ *or* bed′klōᴛʜz′), *n.pl.* sheets, blankets, quilts, etc.

bed·ding (bed′ing), *n.* **1** bedclothes. **2** material for beds: *Straw is used as bedding for cows and horses.*

be·deck (bi dek′), *v.* to adorn; decorate: *The actor's magnificent costume was bedecked with jewels and fine lace.*

bedeck—royal robes richly bedecked

be·dev·il (bi dev′əl), *v.* **1** to trouble greatly; torment: *Biting flies bedeviled the horses.* **2** to confuse completely; bewilder. ❑ *v.* **be·dev·iled, be·dev·il·ing** *or* **be·dev·illed, be·dev·il·ling.** —**be·dev′il·ment,** *n.*

be·dew (bi dü′ *or* bi dyü′), *v.* to wet with dew or drops like dew: *cheeks bedewed with tears.*

bed·fel·low (bed′fel′ō), *n.* **1** a person who shares your bed. **2** associate.

be·dim (bi dim′), *v.* to make dim; darken; obscure. ❑ *v.* **be·dimmed, be·dim·ming.**

be·di·zen (bi dī′zn *or* bi diz′n), *v.* OLD USE. to dress or ornament with showy finery.

bed·lam (bed′ləm), *n.* noisy confusion; uproar: *When our team won, there was bedlam in the gym.*

WORD STORY **Bedlam** comes from the name of an asylum for the mentally ill in London, England. The asylum's full name was the Hospital of St. Mary of Bethlehem. People shortened this to Bethlehem and pronounced that as Bedlam.

Bed·ou·in (bed′ü ən), *n.* **1** member of certain tribes of Arab nomads who live in the deserts of Arabia, Syria, and northern Africa. **2** any wanderer or nomad. ❑ *n., pl.* **Bed·ou·in** *or* **Bed·ou·ins.** [**Bedouin** comes from an Arabic word meaning "desert dweller."]

bed·pan (bed′pan′), *n.* pan used as a toilet by sick people in bed.

be·drag·gled (bi drag′əld), *adj.* **1** wet or soiled, and hanging limp: *She tried to comb her bedraggled hair.* **2** soiled by being dragged in the dirt.

bed·rid·den (bed′rid′n), *adj.* compelled to stay in bed for a long time because of sickness or weakness.

bed·rock (bed′rok′), *n.* **1** the solid rock under the soil and under looser rocks. **2** a firm foundation: *The bedrock of our business is our lifetime guarantee.* **3** the lowest level; bottom.

bed·roll (bed′rōl′), *n.* blankets or a sleeping bag that can be rolled up and tied for carrying.

bed·room (bed′rüm′), *n.* a room to sleep in.

bed·side (bed′sīd′), *n.* area by the side of a bed: *The nurse sat by the patient's bedside.*

bed·sore (bed′sôr′), *n.* sore caused by lying too long in the same position.

bed·spread (bed′spred′), *n.* cover for a bed that is spread over the blankets.

bed·spring (bed′spring′), *n.* set of springs forming part of a bed and supporting a mattress.

bed·stead (bed′sted′), *n.* the wooden or metal framework of a bed that supports the springs and mattress.

bed·time (bed′tīm′), *n.* time to go to bed: *My regular bedtime is nine o'clock.*

bee (bē), *n.* **1** insect with four wings that gathers nectar and pollen from flowers and makes honey from the nectar; honeybee. These bees live in large, permanent colonies and produce wax. The colonies contain a queen, many workers, and drones. Only the queen and the workers have stings. **2** a related insect. There are more than 20,000 species of bees in the world. **3** a gathering for work or amusement: *a spelling bee, a quilting bee.* ❑ *n., pl.* **bees.** ∎ Another word that sounds like this is **be.**

bee (def. 1)

bee·bread (bē′bred′), *n.* a brownish, bitter substance containing pollen, or pollen mixed with honey, used by bees as food for their larvae or young.

beech (bēch), *n.* **1** any of several related European and North American trees with smooth, gray bark and glossy leaves. They bear small, sweet nuts that are good to eat. **2** their wood. ❑ *n., pl.* **beech·es** *or* **beech** for 1. ∎ Another word that sounds like this is **beach.**

beech·nut (bēch′nut′), *n.* the small, triangular nut of a beech tree.

beef (bēf), **1** *n.* meat from a steer, cow, or bull. **2** *n.* steer, cow, or bull when full-grown and fattened for food. **3** *v.* SLANG. to complain. **4** *n.* SLANG. complaint. ❑ *n., pl.* **beefs** for 4. [See Word Story at **meat.**]

beef up, INFORMAL. to make greater; enlarge; strengthen: *The company plans to beef up its research staff.*

beef cattle, cattle raised for meat.

beef·steak (bēf′stāk′), *n.* steak.

beef·y (bē′fē), *adj.* strong, solid, and heavy. ❑ *adj.* **beef·i·er, beef·i·est.** —**beef′i·ness,** *n.*

bee·hive (bē′hīv′), *n.* **1** hive or house for bees. **2** a busy, swarming place: *The school was a beehive of activity on visiting day.*

bee·keep·er (bē′kē′pər), *n.* person who raises bees for their honey.

bee·line (bē′līn′), *n.* the straightest way between two places, like the flight of a bee to its hive.

Be·el·ze·bub (bē el′zə bub), *n.* **1** the Devil; Satan. **2** a devil.

been (bin), *v.* past participle of **be**: *I have been sick. The books have been read by everyone in the room.* ∎ Another word that sounds like this is **bin.**

beep (bēp), **1** *n.* a sharp, short sound. **2** *v.* to cause to make sharp, short sounds: *The taxi driver beeped his horn when he pulled up in front of the house.*

beep·er (bē′pər), *n.* an electronic radio device that signals with a beeping sound; pager. A portable beeper signals a person to telephone his or her home or office.

beer (bir), *n.* **1** an alcoholic drink made from malted barley flavored with hops. **2** a soft drink with the flavor of roots or plants, such as root beer. ∎ Another word that sounds like this is **bier.**

beer·y (bir′ē), *adj.* of or caused by beer: *a beery odor.* ❑ *adj.* **beer·i·er, beer·i·est.**

bees·wax (bēz′waks′), *n.* wax given out by bees, from which they make their honeycomb.

beet (bēt), *n.* the thick, fleshy root of a kind of plant grown in gardens and on farms. Red beets and their green leaves are eaten as vegetables. Sugar is made from white beets. ∎ Another word that sounds like this is **beat.** —**beet′like′,** *adj.*

a	hat	ė	term	ô	order	ch	child		a in about
ā	age	i	it	oi	oil	ng	long		e in taken
ä	far	ī	ice	ou	out	sh	she	ə	i in pencil
â	care	o	hot	u	cup	th	thin		o in lemon
e	let	ō	open	u̇	put	ᴛʜ	then		u in circus
ē	equal	ȯ	saw	ü	rule	zh	measure		

Bee·tho·ven (bā′tō vən), *n.* **Lud·wig van** (lüd′vig vän), 1770-1827, German composer. ■ Ludwig van Beethoven is one of the greatest composers who has ever lived. Although without hearing for many years, he wrote great symphonies, string quartets, piano music, and an opera.

bee·tle¹ (bē′tl), *n.* **1** any of many insects with two hard, shiny front wings that cover and protect the delicate rear wings when not flying. There are more than 300,000 species of beetles. **2** any insect resembling a beetle. ■ Another word that sounds like this is **betel**.

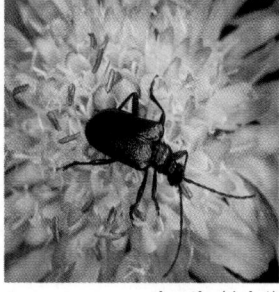
beetle (def. 1)

bee·tle² (bē′tl), *v.* to project or overhang. □ *v.* **bee·tled, bee·tling.** ■ Another word that sounds like this is **betel**.

bee·tle-browed (bē′tl broud′), *adj.* **1** having overhanging eyebrows. **2** scowling; sullen.

be·fall (bi fôl′), *v.* **1** to happen to: *I hope no harm befalls you.* **2** to happen: *Whatever befell, the family held together.* □ *v.* **be·fell, be·fall·en, be·fall·ing.**

be·fall·en (bi fô′lən), *v.* past participle of **befall:** *An accident must have befallen us.*

be·fell (bi fel′), *v.* past tense of **befall:** *Evil befell them.*

be·fit (bi fit′), *v.* to be suitable for; be proper for; suit: *He always wears clothes that befit the occasion.* □ *v.* **be·fit·ted, be·fit·ting.** —**be·fit′ting·ly,** *adv.*

be·fog (bi fog′), *v.* **1** to surround with fog; make foggy. **2** to make obscure; confuse. □ *v.* **be·fogged, be·fog·ging.**

be·fool (bi fül′), *v.* to deceive; fool.

be·fore (bi fôr′), **1** *prep.* earlier than: *Come before five o'clock.* **2** *adv.* earlier: *Come at five o'clock, not before.* **3** *adv.* until now; in the past: *You were never late before.* **4** *prep.* in front of; ahead of: *Walk before me.* **5** *adv.* in front; ahead: *She went before to see if the road was safe.* **6** *prep., conj.* rather than; sooner than: *I will starve before giving in. I will starve before I give in.* **7** *conj.* earlier than the time when: *I would like to talk to her before she goes.*

be·fore·hand (bi fôr′hand′), *adv., adj.* ahead of time; in advance: *Get everything ready beforehand. Aren't you a little beforehand with your request for your allowance?*

be·foul (bi foul′), *v.* make dirty; cover with filth: *The overflow from the garbage cans befouled the floor.*

be·friend (bi frend′), *v.* to act as a friend to; help: *The children befriended the lost dog.*

be·fud·dle (bi fud′l), *v.* to confuse; bewilder. □ *v.* **be·fud·dled, be·fud·dling.** —**be·fud′dle·ment,** *n.*

beg (beg), *v.* **1** to ask for free food, money, clothes, etc.: *The poor woman had to beg for food.* **2** to ask a favor; ask earnestly or humbly: *I beg you to forgive me. The children begged to go to the zoo.* **3** to ask politely and courteously: *I beg your pardon.* □ *v.* **begged, beg·ging.**

beg off, to make an excuse for not being able to keep a promise: *Although he had promised to come to my party, he begged off because of a headache.*

be·gan (bi gan′), *v.* past tense of **begin:** *Snow began to fall.*

be·gat (bi gat′), *v.* OLD USE. a past tense of **beget.**

be·get (bi get′), *v.* **1** to be the father of. **2** to cause to be; produce: *Hate begets hate and love begets love.* □ *v.* **be·got, be·got·ten, be·get·ting.** —**be·get′ter,** *n.*

beg·gar (beg′ər), **1** *n.* person who lives by begging. **2** *n.* a very poor person; pauper. **3** *v.* to bring to poverty: *Your reckless spending will beggar your family.* **4** *v.* to go beyond; outdo: *The grandeur of Niagara Falls beggars description.*

beg·gar·ly (beg′ər lē), *adj.* fit for a beggar; poor. —**beg′gar·li·ness,** *n.*

beg·gar·y (beg′ər ē), *n.* very great poverty.

be·gin (bi gin′), *v.* **1** to do the first part; make a start: *begin on your work. Begin at the third chapter.* **2** to come or bring into being: *Five people began the club two years ago.* **3** to be near; come near: *Your brother's suit wouldn't even begin to fit you.* □ *v.* **be·gan, be·gun, be·gin·ning.**

Be·gin (bā′gin), *n.* **Men·a·chem** (mə nä′kem), 1913-1992, Israeli political leader, prime minister of Israel from 1977 to 1983. ■ Menachem Begin shared the 1978 Nobel Peace Prize with Anwar Sadat, then president of Egypt, for their efforts to bring peace to the Middle East.

be·gin·ner (bi gin′ər), *n.* person who is doing something for the first time; person who lacks skill and experience: *You skate well for a beginner.*

be·gin·ning (bi gin′ing), **1** *n.* a start: *Make a good beginning.* **2** *n.* time when anything begins: *The beginning of winter is usually on December 21st.* **3** *n.* first part: *I enjoyed this book from beginning to end.* **4** *n.* source; origin: *The idea of the airplane had its beginning in the flight of birds.* **5** *adj.* that begins: *This is the beginning lesson of the spelling book.*

beginning—the beginning of the race

be·gone (bi gôn′), **1** *interj.* go away! *"Begone!" said the prince.* **2** *v.* to go away: *The prince bade him begone.*

be·go·nia (bi gō′nyə), *n.* any of numerous related tropical plants often grown for their large, richly colored leaves and waxy flowers. □ *n., pl.* **be·go·nias.** [Begonia comes from Michel Begon. He gave money to help people study plants, so this one was named in his honor.]

be·got (bi got′), *v.* past tense of **beget:** *He begot a son.*

be·got·ten (bi got′n), *v.* past participle of **beget:** *He has begotten a daughter.*

be·grudge (bi gruj′), *v.* **1** to give or allow something unwillingly; grudge: *She is so stingy that she begrudges her dog a bone.* **2** to envy: *The neighbors begrudge us our swimming pool.* □ *v.* **be·grudged, be·grudg·ing.**

be·guile (bi gīl′), *v.* **1** to trick or mislead someone; deceive; cheat: *His flattery beguiled me into thinking that he was my friend.* **2** to win the attention of; entertain; amuse: *The playful puppies beguiled the children with their antics.* □ *v.* **be·guiled, be·guil·ing.** —**be·guile′ment,** *n.* —**be·guil′er,** *n.*

be·gun (bi gun′), *v.* past participle of **begin:** *It has begun to rain.*

be·half (bi haf′), *n.* side, interest, or favor: *I acted in her behalf.*

in behalf of or **on behalf of,** in the interest of; for: *I am speaking in behalf of my friend.*

be·have (bi hāv′), *v.* **1** to manage, handle, or conduct yourself; act: *He behaved himself well during the whole trip.* **2** to act properly; do what is right: *If you behave today, we can come here again.* ❑ *v.* **be·haved, be·hav·ing.**

be·hav·ior (bi hā′vyər), *n.* manner of behaving; way of acting: *Her sullen behavior showed that she was angry.*

be·hav·ior·al (bi hā′vyər əl), *adj.* of or about behavior: *Sociology and psychology are behavioral sciences.* —**be·hav′ior·al·ly,** *adv.*

be·head (bi hed′), *v.* to cut off the head of.

be·held (bi held′), *v.* past tense and past participle of **behold:** *We beheld the beautiful sunset.*

be·he·moth (bi hē′məth), *n.* **1** (in the Bible) a huge and powerful animal shown to Job by God. It may have been the hippopotamus. **2** anything very large and powerful.

be·hest (bi hest′), *n.* command; order: *I am ready to act at your behest.*

be·hind (bi hīnd′), **1** *prep.* at the back of; in the rear of: *Stand behind me.* **2** *adv.* at the back; in the rear: *The dog's tail hung down behind.* **3** *prep.* in support of; supporting: *Don't give up, we're all behind you.* **4** *adv.* farther back: *The rest of the hikers are still quite a way behind.* **5** *prep.* later than: *The mail carrier is behind his usual time today.* **6** *adv.* not on time; late: *The class is behind in its work.* **7** *prep.* inferior to; less advanced than: *If you miss too much school you will be behind your classmates.* **8** *adv.* in the place that has been or is being left: *When my family went to New York, I stayed behind.*

be·hind·hand (bi hīnd′hand′), *adj., adv.* behind time; late: *They are behindhand with their rent.*

be·hold (bi hōld′), **1** *v.* to look at; see; observe: *to behold a beautiful sunset.* **2** *interj.* look! see! *Behold! the king!* ❑ *v.* **be·held, be·hold·ing.** —**be·hold′er,** *n.*

be·hold·en (bi hōl′dən), *adj.* under obligation; in debt: *I am much beholden to you for your help.*

be·hoove (bi hüv′), *v.* to be necessary or proper for: *It behooves you to work harder if you want a raise.* ❑ *v.* **be·hooved, be·hoov·ing.**

beige (bāzh), **1** *adj.* pale brown. **2** *n.* a pale brown.

bei·gnet (ben yā′), *n.* a fritter or square doughnut, coated with powdered sugar, popular in New Orleans.

Bei·jing (bā′jing′), *n.* capital of China, in the NE part. Formerly called **Peking.**

be·ing (bē′ing), **1** *n.* person; living creature: *a human being.* **2** *n.* life; existence: *The world came into being long ago.* **3** *v.* present participle of **be:** *The dog is being fed.*

Bei·rut (bā rüt′), *n.* port and capital of Lebanon, on the Mediterranean.

be·jew·el (bi jü′əl), *v.* to adorn with jewels, or as if with jewels. ❑ *v.* **be·jew·eled, be·jew·el·ing** or **be·jew·elled, be·jew·el·ling.**

be·la·bor (bi lā′bər), *v.* **1** to go over something in too much detail: *belabor a point.* **2** to beat vigorously; thrash: *The rider belabored the tired horse with a stick.*

Bel·a·rus (bel′ə rüs′), *n.* country in E Europe, east of Poland. *Capital:* Minsk. Also, **Byelarus.** Formerly, **White Russia.**

be·lat·ed (bi lā′tid), *adj.* happening or coming late; delayed: *Your belated letter has arrived at last.* —**be·lat′ed·ly,** *adv.* —**be·lat′ed·ness,** *n.*

Be·lau (bā lou′), *n.* Palau.

be·lay (bi lā′), *v.* **1** to fasten a rope by winding it around a pin or cleat. **2** to stop: *"Belay there!" said the captain.* ❑ *v.* **be·layed, be·lay·ing**

belaying pin, sturdy metal or wooden pin in a rail of a ship around which ropes can be wound and fastened.

belch (belch), **1** *v.* to throw out gas noisily from the stomach through the mouth. **2** *v.* to throw out with force: *The volcano belched fire, smoke, and ashes.* **3** *n.* act of belching. ❑ *n., pl.* **belch·es.** —**belch′er,** *n.*

be·lea·guer (bi lē′gər), *v.* **1** to surround with troops; besiege: *The fort was beleaguered.* **2** to surround; beset: *Our cities are beleaguered by problems.*

Be·lém (bə lem′), *n.* port in N Brazil, near the Amazon.

Bel·fast (bel′fast), *n.* port and capital of Northern Ireland, on the Irish Sea.

bel·fry (bel′frē), *n.* **1** tower for a bell or bells. **2** space in a tower in which a bell or bells may be hung. ❑ *n., pl.* **bel·fries.**

Belg., **1** Belgian. **2** Belgium.

Bel·gian (bel′jən), **1** *n.* person born or living in Belgium. **2** *adj.* of Belgium or its people.

Belgian hare, a large, reddish brown, domestic rabbit. It is not really a hare.

Bel·gium (bel′jəm), *n.* country in W Europe, north of France. *Capital:* Brussels.

Bel·grade (bel′grād), *n.* capital of Serbia, on the Danube.

Be·li·al (bē′lē əl), *n.* the Devil.

be·lie (bi lī′), *v.* **1** to give a false idea of; misrepresent: *Her frown belied her usual good nature.* **2** to fail to come up to; disappoint: *The failure of their new business belied their expectations.* ❑ *v.* **be·lied, be·ly·ing.** —**be·li′er,** *n.*

Belgium

be·lief (bi lēf′), *n.* **1** what is held to be true or real; thing believed; opinion: *It was once a common belief that the earth is flat.* **2** acceptance as true or real: *His belief in ghosts makes him afraid of the dark.* **3** confidence in any person or thing; faith; trust: *He expressed his belief in his friend's honesty.* **4** religious faith; creed: *Most children follow the belief of their parents.*

be·liev·a·ble (bi lē′və bəl), *adj.* able to be believed: *His excuse for being late was not believable.* —**be·liev′a·bly,** *adv.*

be·lieve (bi lēv′), *v.* **1** to think something is true or real: *Who doesn't believe that the earth is round?* **2** to think somebody tells the truth: *Her friends believe her.* **3** to have faith; trust: *We believe in our friends.* **4** to think; suppose: *I believe I will go.* ❑ *v.* **be·lieved, be·liev·ing.** —**be·liev′er,** *n.*

be·lit·tle (bi lit′l), *v.* to cause to seem little or unimportant; make less important: *They belittled your success because they were jealous.* ❑ *v.* **be·lit·tled, be·lit·tling.** —**be·lit′tle·ment,** *n.* —**be·lit′tler,** *n.*

Be·lize (be lēz′), *n.* country in Central America. *Capital:* Belmopan.

bell (bel), **1** *n.* a hollow metal cup that makes a musical sound when struck by a clapper or hammer. **2** *n.* anything that makes a ringing sound as a signal: *Did I hear the bell at the front door?* **3** *n.* stroke or sound of a bell: *Our teacher dismissed us before the bell.* **4** *n.* stroke of a bell used on shipboard to indicate a half hour of time. 1 bell = 12:30, 4:30, or 8:30; 2 bells = 1:00, 5:00,

a	hat	ė	term	ȯ	order	ch	child		
ā	age	i	it	oi	oil	ng	long		a in about
ä	far	ī	ice	ou	out	sh	she		e in taken
â	care	o	hot	u	cup	th	thin	ə	i in pencil
e	let	ō	open	ù	put	ᴛʜ	then		o in lemon
ē	equal	ȯ	saw	ü	rule	zh	measure		u in circus

or 9:00; and so on up to 8 bells = 4:00, 8:00, or 12:00. **5** *v.* to put a bell on: *We belled the cat.* **6** *n.* anything shaped like a bell. The flaring end of a funnel or of a musical wind instrument is a bell. **7** *v.* to swell out like a bell. ■ Another word that sounds like this is **belle.** —**bell′like′**, *adj.*

saved by the bell, freed from trouble or difficulty by the sudden end of a situation: *I didn't know what to tell her, but just then we reached my bus stop, so I was saved by the bell.*

Bell (bel), *n.* **Alexander Graham,** 1847-1922, American scientist who invented the telephone.

bel·la·don·na (bel′ə don′ə), *n.* **1** a poisonous plant of Europe with black berries and purplish red, bell-shaped flowers; deadly nightshade. **2** drug made from this plant. ❑ *n., pl.* **bel·la·don·nas** for 1.

bell-bot·tom (bel′bot′əm), *adj.* with the bottom of the legs flared.

bell-bottoms (bel′bot′əmz), *n.pl.* bell-bottom trousers.

bell·boy (bel′boi′), *n.* person whose work is carrying baggage and doing errands for the guests of a hotel or club; bellhop.

belle (bel), *n.* **1** a beautiful woman or girl. **2** the prettiest or most admired woman or girl: *She was the belle of the ball.* ■ Another word that sounds like this is **bell.**

Belle·vue (bel′vū) *n.* city in E Nebraska.

bell·flow·er (bel′flow′ər), *n.* plant with bell-shaped purple, pink, or white flowers, such as the bluebell.

bell·hop (bel′hop′), *n.* bellboy.

bel·li·cose (bel′ə kōs), *adj.* fond of fighting; warlike. —**bel·li·cos·i·ty** (bel′ə kos′ə tē), *n.* —**bel′li·cose·ly**, *adv.*

bel·lig·er·ence (bə lij′ər əns), *n.* **1** fondness for fighting; being warlike. **2** act of fighting; being at war.

bel·lig·er·en·cy (bə lij′ər ən sē), *n.* belligerence.

bel·lig·er·ent (bə lij′ər ənt), **1** *adj.* fond of fighting; quarrelsome: *a belligerent neighborhood gang.* **2** *adj.* at war; engaged in war; fighting: *Great Britain and Germany were belligerent powers in 1941.* **3** *n.* nation or state engaged in war: *France and Germany were belligerents in World War II.* **4** *n.* person engaged in fighting with another person. —**bel·lig′er·ent·ly**, *adv.*

bell jar, a bell-shaped container or cover made of glass, used in laboratories.

bel·low (bel′ō), **1** *v.* to make a loud, deep noise; roar: *The bull bellowed.* **2** *n.* a loud, deep noise; roar. **3** *v.* to shout loudly, angrily, or with pain: *He bellowed at the children who were trampling his flowers.* —**bel′low·er**, *n.*

bel·lows (bel′ōz), *n. sing. or pl.* **1** device for producing a strong current of air, used for making fires burn hotter or sounding an organ, accordion, etc. **2** the folding part of some cameras, behind the lens.

bell·weth·er (bel′weᴛʜ′ər), *n.* a male sheep that leads the flock, wearing a bell.

bel·ly (bel′ē), **1** *n.* the lower part of the human body, which contains the stomach and intestines; abdomen. **2** *n.* the underpart of an animal's body. **3** *n.* stomach. **4** *n.* bulging part of anything, or the hollow in it: *the belly of a sail.* **5** *v.* to swell out; bulge: *The sails bellied in the wind.* ❑ *n., pl.* **bel·lies;** *v.* **bel·lied, bel·ly·ing.**

bel·ly·ache (bel′ē āk′), **1** *n.* pain in the abdomen; stomachache. **2** *v.* INFORMAL. to complain or grumble about small problems. ❑ *v.* **bel·ly·ached, bel·ly·ach·ing.**

bel·ly·band (bel′ē band′), *n.* a strap around an animal's body to keep a saddle, harness, etc., in place.

bel·ly·but·ton (bel′ē but′n), *n.* navel.

bel·ly·flop (bel′ē flop′), *v.* **1** to dive into the water so that the chest and belly take the shock. **2** to dive face down onto a sled before coasting down a slope. ❑ *v.* **bel·ly·flopped, bel·ly·flop·ping.**

bel·ly·land (bel′ē land′), *v.* to land an airplane with the wheels up. —**belly landing.**

belly laugh, a hearty, unrestrained fit of laughter.

Bel·mo·pan (bel′mō pan′), *n.* capital of Belize, in the central part.

be·long (bi lóng′), *v.* to have a usual proper place: *That book belongs on this shelf.*

belong to, 1 be the property of: *Does this cap belong to you?* **2** be a part of: *That top belongs to this box.* **3** be a member of: *She belongs to the Girl Scouts.*

be·long·ings (bi lóng′ingz), *n.pl.* things that someone owns; possessions.

be·lov·ed (bi luv′id *or* bi luvd′), **1** *adj.* dearly loved; dear: *our beloved homeland.* **2** *n.* person who is loved; darling.

be·low (bi lō′), **1** *adv.* in a lower place; to a lower place: *From the airplane we could see the fields below.* **2** *adv.* on a lower floor or deck; downstairs: *The ship's cargo is stored below.* **3** *prep.* lower than; under: *The dining room is below my bedroom.* ■ See Synonym Study at **under.** **4** *prep.* less than: *four degrees below zero.* **5** *prep.* unworthy of: *below contempt.* **6** *adv.* after or later in a book or article: *See the note below.* **7** *adv.* below zero: *The temperature was five below last night.*

belt (belt), **1** *n.* strip of leather, cloth, etc., fastened around the waist to hold in clothes or support weapons. **2** *v.* to put a belt around: *I belted my jeans.* **3** *v.* to fasten on with a belt: *to belt on a hunting knife.* **4** *v.* to beat with a belt. **5** *v.* to hit suddenly and hard: *The hitter belted the ball over the fence.* **6** *n.* any broad strip or band: *A belt of trees grew between the two fields.* **7** *n.* region having distinctive characteristics: *The cotton belt is the region where cotton is grown.* **8** *n.* an endless band that transfers motion from one wheel or pulley to another: *A belt connected to the engine moves the fan in a car.*

be·lu·ga (bə lü′gə), *n.* **1** a small, white whale of arctic seas. **2** a large, white sturgeon of the Black Sea and the Caspian Sea, valued as a source of caviar. ❑ *n., pl.* **be·lu·gas.**

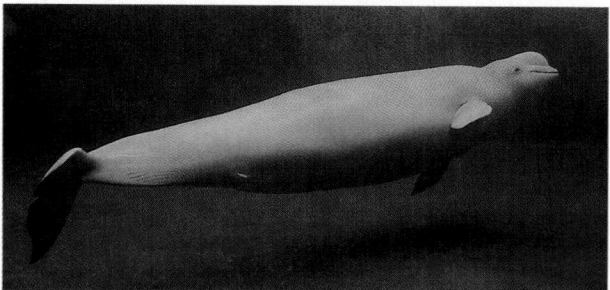

beluga (def. 1)—up to 14 ft. (4.3 m) long

be·moan (bi mōn′), *v.* to moan about; weep for; bewail.

be·mused (bi myüzd′), *adj.* **1** confused; bewildered. **2** absorbed in thought or daydreaming.

bench (bench), **1** *n.* a long seat, usually of wood or stone. **2** *n.* a strong, heavy table used by a carpenter, or by anyone who works with tools and materials. **3** *n.* seat where judges sit in a court of law. **4** *n.* judge or group of judges sitting in a court of law: *Bring the prisoner before the bench.* **5** *n.* position as a judge: *He was appointed to the bench last year.* **6** *v.* to take a player out of a game. ❑ *n., pl.* **bench·es** for 1,2.

bench mark, 1 a surveyor's mark made on an object lying in a fixed position at a known elevation. It is a reference point in measuring differences in elevation. **2** any standard for comparison: *Her playing is a bench mark for tennis everywhere.*

bend (bend), **1** *n.* part that is not straight; curve; turn: *There is a sharp bend in the road here.* **2** *v.* to make or become crooked; curve: *bend a wire. The branch began to bend as I climbed along it.* **3** *v.* to turn or move in a certain direction; direct: *His steps were bent toward home. She bent her mind to her homework.* **4** *v.* to stoop; bow: *She bent down and picked up a stone.* **5** *v.* to submit: *A stubborn person will not bend to the will of others.* **6** *v.* to force to submit: *Her spirit could not be bent.* **7** *n.pl.* **the bends,** cramps caused by changing too suddenly from an environment of high pressure to ordinary air pressure. ❑ *v.* **bent, bend·ing.** —**bend′a·ble**, *adj.*

be·neath (bi nēth′), **1** *adv., prep.* in a lower place; below; underneath; under: *The apple fell to the ground beneath. The dog sat beneath the tree.* ■ See Synonym Study at **under.** **2** *prep.* not even worthy of: *Your insulting remarks are beneath notice.*

Ben·e·dic·tine (ben′ə dik′tēn′), **1** *n.* monk or nun following the rules of the order founded by Saint Benedict (A.D. 480?-543?). **2** *adj.* of Saint Benedict or his order.

be·ne·dic·tion (ben′ə dik′shən), *n.* **1** the asking of God's blessing at the end of a religious service. **2** blessing.

ben·e·fac·tor (ben′ə fak′tər), *n.* person who has given money or kindly help.

be·nef·i·cent (bə nef′ə sənt), *adj.* doing good; kind. —**be·nef′i·cent·ly,** *adv.*

ben·e·fi·cial (ben′ə fish′əl), *adj.* producing good; favorable; helpful: *Daily exercise is beneficial to your health.* —**ben′e·fi′·cial·ly,** *adv.* —**ben′e·fi′cial·ness,** *n.*

ben·e·fi·ci·ar·y (ben′ə fish′ē er′ē), *n.* **1** person who receives benefit: *All the children are beneficiaries of the new playground.* **2** person who receives money or property from an insurance policy, a will, etc. □ *n., pl.* **ben·e·fi·ci·ar·ies.**

ben·e·fit (ben′ə fit), **1** *n.* anything which is for the good of someone or something; advantage: *Good roads are of great benefit to travelers.* ■ See Synonym Study at **advantage. 2** *v.* to do good to; be good for: *Rest will benefit a sick person.* **3** *v.* to receive good; profit: *I benefited from the medicine.* **4** *n.* performance at the theater, a game, etc., to raise money for a worthy cause. **5** *n.pl.* **benefits, a** anything provided by a company to its employees in addition to wages, such as vacation, retirement pension, medical insurance, etc. **b** money paid to a sick or disabled person by an insurance company, government agency, etc.

be·nev·o·lence (bə nev′ə ləns), *n.* **1** desire to promote the happiness of others; goodwill; kindly feeling. **2** act of kindness; something good that is done.

be·nev·o·lent (bə nev′ə lənt), *adj.* having a desire to promote the happiness of others; kindly; charitable. —**be·nev′o·lent·ly,** *adv.*

Ben·gal (beng gȯl′), **1** *n.* former province of India, in the NE part. Bengal is now divided into **West Bengal,** a part of India, and **East Bengal,** the country of Bangladesh. **2** *adj.* of or from Bengal: *a Bengal tiger.* **3** *n.* **Bay of,** bay between India and Myanmar, part of the Indian Ocean.

Ben·gha·zi (ben gä′zē), *n.* port in Libya, on the Mediterranean.

Ben-Gur·i·on (ben′gŭr′ ē ən), *n.* **David,** 1886-1973, the first prime minister of Israel from 1949 to 1953, and again from 1955 to 1963.

be·night·ed (bi nī′tid), *adj.* not knowing right from wrong; ignorant. —**be·night′ed·ness,** *n.*

be·nign (bi nīn′), *adj.* **1** having a kind disposition; gracious: *a benign neighbor with a friendly smile.* **2** favorable; mild: *Hawaii is a popular vacation spot because of its benign climate and wonderful scenery.* **3** not dangerous to health; not malignant: *a benign tumor.* —**be·nign′ly,** *adv.*

Be·nin (be nēn′), *n.* country in W Africa, site of historic Benin Kingdom. *Capital:* Porto-Novo.

[Map caption: Benin Kingdom (about 1000–1700); Niger R.; Lagos; BENIN; ATLANTIC OCEAN; Niger Delta; N]

bent (bent), **1** *adj.* not straight; crooked; curved: *It is hard to hammer a bent nail into wood.* **2** *adj.* determined: *She is bent on being a doctor.* **3** *n.* a natural inclination; tendency: *He has a decided bent for drawing.* **4** *v.* past tense and past participle of **bend:** *I bent the wire. Trees were bent over by the high winds.*

ben·thos (ben′thos), *n.* **1** bottom of the ocean. **2** things that live at the bottom of the ocean.

ben·ton·ite (ben′tə nīt), *n.* a soft, absorbent clay formed from volcanic ash.

be·numb (bi num′), *v.* to make numb; deaden: *fingers benumbed by the cold, an actor benumbed with fright.*

Ben·ze·drine (ben′zə drēn′), *n.* trademark for a drug that causes wakefulness.

ben·zene (ben′zēn′), *n.* a colorless liquid easily set on fire, obtained mainly from coal tar; benzol. It is used for removing grease stains and in making dyes. ■ Another word that sounds like this is **benzine.**

ben·zine (ben′zēn′), *n.* a colorless liquid easily set on fire, obtained in distilling petroleum. It is used in cleaning and dyeing and as a motor fuel. ■ Another word that sounds like this is **benzene.**

ben·zo·ic acid (ben zō′ik), acid present in cranberries and some trees of Asia. It is used in medicine and as a food preservative.

ben·zol (ben′zȯl), *n.* benzene.

be·queath (bi kwēṮḤ′ *or* bi kwēth′), *v.* **1** to give or leave by means of a will when you die: *He bequeathed his fortune to his children.* **2** to hand down; pass along: *One age bequeaths its knowledge to the next.* —**be·queath′er,** *n.*

be·queath·al (bi kwē′ṮḤəl *or* bi kwē′thəl), *n.* bequest.

be·quest (bi kwest′), *n.* **1** something bequeathed; legacy: *When she died she left a bequest of ten thousand dollars to her niece.* **2** act of bequeathing.

be·rate (bi rāt′), *v.* to scold sharply. □ *v.* **be·rat·ed, be·rat·ing.**

Ber·ber (bėr′bər), *n.* **1** member of a group of Muslim tribes living in northern Africa, west of Egypt. **2** their language.

be·reave (bi rēv′), *v.* to leave desolate and alone; deprive: *The family was bereaved by the death of the father.* □ *v.* **be·reaved** or **be·reft, be·reav·ing.**

be·reave·ment (bi rēv′mənt), *n.* **1** loss of a relative or friend by death. **2** bereaved condition; great loss: *We sympathized with the family in their bereavement.*

be·reft (bi reft′), **1** *adj.* deprived: *The refugees were homeless and bereft.* **2** *v.* a past tense and a past participle of **bereave:** *They were bereft by the loss of their child.*

be·ret (bə rā′), *n.* a soft, flat, round cap without a visor.

berg (bėrg), *n.* iceberg. ■ Another word that sounds like this is **burg.**

Ber·gen (bėr′gən), *n.* port in SW Norway, on the Atlantic.

ber·i·ber·i (ber′ē ber′ē), *n.* disease affecting the nervous system, accompanied by weakness and extreme loss of weight. It is caused by lack of vitamin B$_1$ in the diet. [**Beriberi** comes from a word in the main language of Sri Lanka meaning "weakness." It was in Asia that Europeans first met this disease and learned its name.]

Bering Sea, (bir′ing *or* ber′ing), N portion of the Pacific, between Alaska and Siberia.

Bering Strait, strait between the Bering Sea and the Arctic Ocean. During the Ice Age, it dried up as sea level fell, and people are thought to have entered the Americas by walking across from Asia.

ber·kel·i·um (bėr′klē əm), *n.* a metallic element produced artificially from americium, curium, or plutonium. *Symbol:* Bk

Ber·lin (bər lin′), *n.* the capital of Germany. From 1949 to 1990 Berlin was divided into West Berlin, a part of West Germany, and East Berlin, the capital of East Germany.

Berlin (bər lin′), *n.* **Irving,** 1888-1989, American composer. ■ **Irving Berlin** wrote the music and words of many popular American songs, including "White Christmas" and "There's No Business Like Show Business."

Ber·li·oz (ber′lē ōz), *n.* **Hector,** 1803-1869, French composer. He wrote symphonies and operas and was a talented conductor.

berm (berm), *n.* **1** unpaved edge of a road; shoulder. **2** mound of earth built up against a building for protection or insulation. **3** ledge or ridge of earth, sand, or rocks.

Ber·mu·da (bər myü′də), *n.* group of British islands off the coast of the United States, in the N Atlantic.

Bermuda shorts, short trousers that end an inch or two above the knee.

Bermuda shorts

Bermuda Triangle, a roughly triangular area of the North Atlantic Ocean in which airplanes and ships seem to have mysteriously disappeared.

a	hat	ė	term	ô	order	ch	child		
ā	age	i	it	oi	oil	ng	long		a in about
ä	far	ī	ice	ou	out	sh	she	ə	e in taken
â	care	o	hot	u	cup	th	thin		i in pencil
e	let	ō	open	ů	put	ṮḤ	then		o in lemon
ē	equal	ȯ	saw	ü	rule	zh	measure		u in circus

Bern or **Berne** (bėrn), *n.* capital of Switzerland, in the W part.

Bern·stein (bėrn′stīn), *n.* **Leo·nard** (len′ərd), 1918-1990, American composer and conductor. He composed the music for *West Side Story.*

Ber·ra (ber′ə), *n.* **Yo·gi** (yō′gē), born 1925, American baseball player and manager. ■ **Yogi Berra** is famous for his sayings, which are often unintentionally funny, such as "It ain't over 'til it's over."

ber·ry (ber′ē), **1** *n.* any small, juicy fruit with many seeds. Strawberries and raspberries are berries by this definition. **2** *n.* a simple fruit having a skin or rind surrounding the seeds in the pulp. Botanists classify grapes, tomatoes, currants, and bananas as berries, but not strawberries or raspberries. **3** *v.* to gather berries: *During our vacation in Maine we went berrying one day.* ❑ *n., pl.* **ber·ries;** *v.* **ber·ried, ber·ry·ing.** ■ Another word that sounds like this is **bury.** —**ber′ry·like′,** *adj.*

ber·serk (bər sėrk′ or bėr′sėrk′), *adv.* **go berserk,** to be carried away by madness or wild fury; become violently angry: *The sick dog went berserk and tried to bite everyone in its way.*

WORD STORY **Berserk** comes from an Icelandic word meaning "wild warrior." That word came from two others meaning "bear" and "shirt." Berserkers, some of whom wore bears' hides, were the cruelest and most feared Viking warriors. In battle, they acted wild with rage.

berth (bėrth), **1** *n.* place to sleep on a ship or train. **2** *n.* a ship's place at a wharf. **3** *n.* place for a ship to anchor conveniently or safely. **4** *n.* position; job: *My sister has a berth as lifeguard for the summer.* **5** *v.* to provide with a berth; have a berth. ■ Another word that sounds like this is **birth.**

give a wide berth to, to keep well away from: *Give a wide berth to her when she is angry.*

ber·yl (ber′əl), *n.* a very hard mineral, usually green or blue-green, used as a gem and as a source of beryllium. The emerald is a variety of beryl.

be·ryl·li·um (bə ril′ē əm), *n.* a hard, light, metallic element found in various minerals. Beryllium is used in various alloys and in controlling the speed of neutrons in atomic reactors. *Symbol:* Be

be·seech (bi sēch′), *v.* to ask earnestly; beg; implore: *I beseech you to listen to me.* ❑ *v.* **be·sought** or **be·seeched, be·seech·ing.** —**be·seech′ing·ly,** *adv.*

be·set (bi set′), *v.* to attack from all sides; surround or hem in: *beset by mosquitoes in the swamp.* ❑ *v.* **be·set, be·set·ting.**

be·set·ting (bi set′ing), *adj.* always present: *Constantly putting things off is her besetting sin.*

be·side (bi sīd′), *prep.* **1** by the side of; close to; near: *Grass grows beside the fence.* **2** compared with: *My troubles seem small beside yours.* **3** in addition to; besides: *He has other hobbies beside reading.*

beside yourself, very upset; greatly distressed: *They were beside themselves with worry over their lost child.*

be·sides (bi sīdz′), **1** *adv.* more than that; moreover: *I don't want to go shopping; besides, I have no money.* **2** *prep.* in addition to; over and above: *Others came to the school picnic besides our own class.* **3** *adv.* in addition; also: *We tried two other ways besides.* **4** *prep.* other than; except: *They spoke of no one besides you.*

be·siege (bi sēj′), *v.* **1** to surround and try to capture: *Enemy soldiers besieged the fortified town.* **2** to crowd around: *Admirers besieged the famous singer.* **3** to overwhelm with requests, questions, etc.: *During the flood, the Red Cross was besieged with calls for help.* ❑ *v.* **be·sieged, be·sieg·ing.** —**be·sieg′er,** *n.*

be·smirch (bi smėrch′), *v.* to make dirty; soil; stain: *Crime and dishonesty will besmirch your good name.*

be·sought (bi sôt′), *v.* a past tense and a past participle of **be·seech:** *She besought them to listen to her.*

be·span·gle (bi spang′gəl), *v.* to adorn with spangles. ❑ *v.* **be·span·gled, be·span·gling.**

be·spat·ter (bi spat′ər), *v.* to spatter all over; soil by spattering.

be·speak (bi spēk′), *v.* to be a sign of; show; indicate: *The neat appearance of the house bespeaks care.* ❑ *v.* **be·spoke** (bi spōk′), **be·spo·ken** or **be·spoke, be·speak·ing.**

be·spec·ta·cled (bi spek′tə kəld), *adj.* wearing glasses.

be·sprin·kle (bi spring′kəl), *v.* to sprinkle all over. ❑ *v.* **be·sprin·kled, be·sprin·kling.**

Bessemer process, method of making steel by forcing a blast of air through molten iron in order to burn out carbon and other impurities.

best (best), **1** *adj.* of the most desirable, valuable, or superior quality: *My work is good; yours is better; but hers is best. We have the best food to eat. I want to be one of the best students in the class.* **2** *adv.* in the most excellent way: *Who reads best?* **3** *adv.* in or to the greatest degree: *I like this book best.* **4** *n.* person or thing that is best: *Most parents want the best for their children. He is the best in the class.* **5** *adj.* largest: *the best part of the day.* **6** *n.* the most that is possible; utmost: *I did my best to finish on time.* **7** *v.* to outdo; defeat: *Our team was bested in the final game.* ❑ *adj., superlative of* **good;** *adv., superlative of* **well**[1].

all for the best, not so bad as it seems.

at best, under the most favorable circumstances: *Summer is at best very short.*

get the best of, to defeat.

had best, ought to; will be wise to; should: *You had best leave before the storm breaks.*

make the best of, to do as well as possible with: *We didn't enjoy the weather, but we tried to make the best of it.*

bes·tial (bes′chəl), *adj.* like a beast; brutal. —**bes′tial·ly,** *adv.*

bes·ti·al·i·ty (bes′chē al′ə tē), *n.* bestial conduct.

be·stir (bi stėr′), *v.* to rouse to action; stir up; exert: *If we want to win this game we'll have to bestir ourselves.* ❑ *v.* **be·stirred, be·stir·ring.**

best man, the chief attendant of the bridegroom at a wedding.

be·stow (bi stō′), *v.* to give something as a gift; give: *The millionaire bestowed a large sum of money on the university.*

be·stow·al (bi stō′əl), *n.* act of bestowing: *the bestowal of a large sum of money.*

be·strew (bi strü′), *v.* **1** to strew; scatter; sprinkle: *The park was bestrewed with litter.* **2** to lie scattered over: *Papers bestrewed the park.* ❑ *v.* **be·strewed, be·strewed** or **be·strewn** (bi strün′), **be·strew·ing.**

be·stride (bi strīd′), *v.* to get on, sit on, or stand over something with one leg on each side; straddle. You can bestride a horse, a chair, or a fence. ❑ *v.* **be·strode** (bi strōd′), **be·strid·ing.**

best·sel·ler (best′sel′ər), *n.* anything, especially a book, that has a very large sale.

bet (bet), **1** *n.* a promise between two people or groups that the one who guesses wrong will give something of value to the one who guesses right; wager: *We made a 25-cent bet on who would win the game.* **2** *v.* to promise something of value to another if you are wrong; wager: *I bet her a candy bar that my team would win.* **3** *n.* the money or thing promised: *My bet on the game was 25 cents.* **4** *v.* to make a bet: *Which team did you bet on?* **5** *v.* to be very sure: *I bet you are wrong about that.* **6** *n.* thing to bet on: *Which team is a good bet?* ❑ *v.* **bet** or **bet·ted, bet·ting.**

you bet, INFORMAL. you can be certain: *You bet we had fun.*

be·ta (bā′tə), *n.* the second letter of the Greek alphabet (B, β). ❑ *n., pl.* **be·tas.**

be·take (bi tāk′), *v.* OLD USE. **betake yourself,** to go: *The queen and her ladies betake themselves to the mountains every summer.* ❑ *v.* **be·took, be·tak·en** (bi tā′kən), **be·tak·ing.**

beta particle, electron released by the nucleus of a radioactive element in the process of disintegration.

beta ray, stream of beta particles.

be·ta·tron (bā′tə tron), *n.* particle accelerator that greatly increases the speed of electrons.

Be·tel·geuse (bē′tl jüz), *n.* a red supergiant star in the constellation Orion.

be·tel nut (bē′tl), the orange nut of a tropical Asian palm tree. It is chewed for its stimulating effect. ■ Another word that sounds like this is **beetle.**

be·think (bi thingk′), *v.* OLD USE. **bethink yourself of,** to think about; consider; remember: *The knight bethought himself of the wizard's warning: "Avoid the troll!"* ❑ *v.* **be·thought** (bi thôt′), **be·think·ing.**

Beth·le·hem (beth′lə hem), *n.* town in Jordan, the birthplace of Jesus.

Be·thune (bə thün′), *n.* **Mary Mc·Leod** (mə kloud′), 1875-1955, African American educator. ■ **Mary McLeod Bethune** originally studied to be a missionary but wasn't sent overseas because of her race. Instead, she spent her life increasing educational opportunities for African Americans. She founded Bethune-Cookman College in Florida and the National Council of Negro Women.

be·tide (bi tid′), *v.* **1** to happen to: *Woe betide you if you dare break your promise.* **2** to happen: *No matter what betides, the family will hold together.* ❑ *v.* **be·tid·ed, be·tid·ing.**

be·times (bi timz′), *adv.* OLD USE. early.

be·to·ken (bi tō′kən), *v.* to be a sign of; show: *His smile betokens his satisfaction.*

be·took (bi tùk′), *v.* past tense of **betake:** *The queen betook herself to her summer palace.*

be·tray (bi trā′), *v.* **1** to hand over or expose to the power of an enemy by being disloyal: *The traitor betrayed his country.* **2** to be unfaithful to: *She betrayed her promise.* **3** to mislead; deceive: *He was betrayed by his own enthusiasm.* **4** to show signs of; reveal: *The girl's wet shoes betrayed the fact that she had walked through puddles.* **—be·tray′er,** *n.*

be·tray·al (bi trā′əl), *n.* act of betraying; violation of trust or confidence.

be·troth (bi trōᴛʜ′ *or* bi tròth′), *v.* to promise in marriage; engage.

be·troth·al (bi trō′ᴛʜəl *or* bi trò′thəl), *n.* engagement to be married.

be·trothed (bi trōᴛʜd′ *or* bi tròtht′), **1** *n.* person engaged to be married: *My sister introduced me to her betrothed.* **2** *adj.* engaged to be married: *He and my sister are now betrothed.*

bet·ter[1] (bet′ər), **1** *adj.* more desirable, useful, or suitable than another: *She left her old job for a better one.* **2** *adv.* in a more satisfactory way: *Try to read better next time.* **3** *adv.* in a greater degree; more completely: *I know my old friend better than I know anyone else.* **4** *adv.* more: *It is better than a mile to town.* **5** *n.* person or thing that is better: *Which is the better of these two coats?* **6** *n.pl.* **betters,** your superiors: *Listen to the advice of your betters.* **7** *v.* to make better; improve: *We can better that work by being more careful next time.* **8** *v.* to do better than; surpass: *The other team could not better our score.* **9** *adj.* larger: *Four days is the better part of a week.* **10** *adj.* improved in health: *The sick child is better today.* ❑ *adj.,* comparative of **good;** *adv.,* comparative of **well**[1].

better off, in a better condition: *He is better off now that he has a new job.*

for the better, toward improvement or recovery: *The patient took a turn for the better.*

get the better of or **have the better of,** be superior to; defeat: *Their team got the better of our team in yesterday's game.*

had better, ought to; will be wise to; should: *I had better go before it rains.*

think better of, to think over and change your mind about: *In the morning you will think better of your decision to go on such a long hike.*

bet·ter[2] (bet′ər), *n.* bettor.

bet·ter·ment (bet′ər mənt), *n.* act of making better; improvement: *to work for the betterment of living conditions.*

bet·tor (bet′ər), *n.* person who bets. Also, **better.**

be·tween (bi twēn′), **1** *prep., adv.* in the space or time separating two points, objects, places, etc.: *Many cities lie between New York and Chicago. She should arrive between 2 and 3 P.M. The bus from Main Street to Broadway stops at every corner between.* **2** *prep.* in the range of: *She earned between ten and twelve dollars.* **3** *prep.* connecting; joining: *There is a good highway between Chicago and Detroit.* **4** *prep.* of; involving; that concerns: *A war between two countries can affect the whole world.* **5** *prep.* either one or the other of: *We must choose between the two books.* **6** *prep.* by the joint action of: *They caught twelve fish between them.*

between you and me, as a secret; in confidence: *This is between you and me; don't tell anyone else.* ■ *Between you and I* is not correct in standard English.

in between, 1 in the middle: *He studies either very hard or not at all, never anything in between.* **2** in the midst of; among: *In between the rows of corn there was a scarecrow.*

USAGE NOTE **Between** is always used when there are only two of something: *The waitress divided the cake between the two girls.* **Among** is used when there are more than two of anything: *There were three children among the injured.*

be·twixt (bi twikst′), *prep., adv.* between.

betwixt and between, in the middle; neither one nor the other.

BeV, bev, or **Bev** (bev), *n.* a billion electron volts, a unit for measuring in nuclear physics. ❑ *n., pl.* **BeV, bev,** or **Bev.**

bev·el (bev′əl), **1** *n.* a sloping edge. There is often a bevel on the frame of a picture, on a mirror, or on a piece of plate glass. **2** *v.* to cut a square edge to a sloping edge; make slope: *The edges of the board have been beveled with a plane.* **3** *n.* tool or device for drawing or measuring angles. ❑ *v.* **bev·eled, bev·el·ing** or **bev·elled, bev·el·ling.**

bevel (def. 1)

bev·er·age (bev′ər ij), *n.* liquid used or prepared for drinking. Milk, fruit juice, coffee, and tea are beverages.

bev·y (bev′ē), *n.* a small group or flock: *a bevy of quail.* ❑ *n., pl.* **bev·ies.**

be·wail (bi wāl′), *v.* to mourn for; weep for; complain of: *The children bewailed the loss of their cat.* **—be·wail′ing·ly,** *adv.*

be·ware (bi wâr′), *v.* to be on your guard against; be careful: *Beware! There is a deep hole here. You must beware of swimming in a strong current.* ■ **Beware** is used only in the present tense as a command or with helping verbs. This is why no forms of the verb are listed here.

be·wil·der (bi wil′dər), *v.* to confuse completely; puzzle: *bewildered by the confusing instructions.* ■ See Synonym Study at **confuse. —be·wil′der·ing·ly,** *adv.* **—be·wil′der·ment,** *n.*

be·witch (bi wich′), *v.* **1** to put under a spell; use magic on: *The wicked fairy bewitched the princess and made her fall into a long sleep.* **2** to charm; fascinate; enchant: *We were all bewitched by our bright little cousin.* **—be·witch′ing·ly,** *adv.* **—be·witch′ment,** *n.*

bey (bā), *n.* governor of a Turkish province or district. ❑ *n., pl.* **beys.**

be·yond (bi yond′), **1** *prep.* on or to the farther side of: *He lives beyond those tall trees.* **2** *prep.* farther on than: *I fell asleep on the bus and rode beyond my stop.* **3** *adv.* farther away: *Beyond were the hills.* **4** *prep.* later than; past: *I stayed up beyond my usual bedtime.* **5** *prep.* out of the limit, range, or understanding of: *This shirt is so worn that it is beyond repair. The meaning of this poem is beyond me.* **6** *prep.* more than: *The price of the suit was beyond what I could pay. The day at the beach was beyond all we had hoped.* **7** *n.* **the beyond** or **the great beyond,** life after death: *He has gone to the great beyond.*

Bha·ga·vad-Gi·ta (bug′ə vəd gē′tä), *n.* a sacred Hindu text in which the god Krishna discusses the nature and meaning of existence.

Bhu·tan (bü tän′), *n.* country between Tibet and NE India. Bhutan's foreign affairs are partly under Indian control. *Capital:* Thimphu.

Bhut·to (bü′tō), *n.* **Ben·a·zir** (ben ə zir′), born 1953, prime minister of Pakistan from 1988 to 1990, and since 1993. She was the first woman to serve as prime minister of a Muslim country.

bi-, *prefix.* **1** twice a ___: *biannual = twice a year.* **2** every two ___: *bimonthly = every two months.* **3** two ___: *bicoastal = of or between two coasts.*

a	hat	ė	term	ȯ	order	ch	child		a in about
ā	age	i	it	oi	oil	ng	long		e in taken
ä	far	ī	ice	ou	out	sh	she	ə	i in pencil
â	care	o	hot	u	cup	th	thin		o in lemon
e	let	ō	open	ù	put	ᴛʜ	then		u in circus
ē	equal	ò	saw	ü	rule	zh	measure		

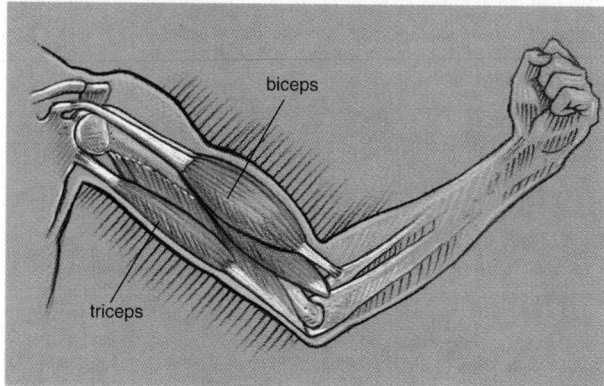

biceps

Bi, symbol for bismuth.

bi·a·ly (bē ä′lē), *n.* a round roll, flattened in the center, often sprinkled with onion flakes. ❑ *n., pl.* **bi·a·lies.**

bi·an·nu·al (bī an′yü əl), *adj.* occurring twice a year: *Our doctor recommends a biannual visit to the dentist.* —**bi·an′nu·al·ly,** *adv.*

bi·as (bī′əs), **1** *n.* a slanting or diagonal line. **2** *n.* tendency to favor or oppose someone or something without real cause; prejudice: *An umpire should have no bias.* **3** *v.* to influence, usually unfairly; prejudice: *Judges cannot let their feelings bias their decisions.* ❑ *n., pl.* **bi·as·es;** *v.* **bi·ased, bi·as·ing** or **bi·assed, bi·as·sing.**
on the bias, diagonally across the weave.

bi·ased (bī′əst), *adj.* favoring or opposing someone or something without real cause; prejudiced: *Parents are often biased concerning their children.*

bi·ath·lon (bī ath′lon), *n.* an Olympic contest combining a cross-country ski race and rifle target shooting.

bib (bib), *n.* **1** cloth worn under the chin, especially by babies and small children, to protect clothing during meals. **2** part of an apron or overalls above the waist.

Bib., **1** Bible. **2** Biblical.

Bi·ble (bī′bəl), *n.* **1** the book of sacred writings of the Christian religion, including the Old Testament and the New Testament. **2** the Hebrew Scripture. **3** book of the sacred writings of any religion. The Koran is the Islamic Bible. **4** **bible,** any book accepted as an authority.

WORD STORY Bible comes from a Greek word meaning "book." In old times, the Bible was the only book most people ever saw. Today it is still sometimes called "The Good Book." The Greek word originally meant "papyrus," the material on which people wrote before paper was invented. The same Greek word also turned into the prefix **biblio-**. So when you see **biblio-**, think "book."

bib·li·cal or **Bib·li·cal** (bib′lə kəl), *adj.* **1** of the Bible: *biblical literature.* **2** according to the Bible: *biblical history.* **3** in the Bible: *a biblical reference to David.* —**bib′li·cal·ly** or **Bib′li·cal·ly,** *adv.*

biblio-, *prefix.* of books: *bibliography = list of books.* [See Word Story at **Bible.**]

bib·li·o·graph·i·cal (bib′lē ə graf′ə kəl), *adj.* of or about bibliography. —**bib·li·o·graph′i·cal·ly,** *adv.*

bib·li·og·ra·phy (bib′lē og′rə fē), *n.* list of books or articles by a certain author or about a particular subject or person. ❑ *n., pl.* **bib·li·og·ra·phies.**

bi·cam·er·al (bī kam′ər əl), *adj.* having two legislative chambers. The Congress of the United States is a bicameral legislature; it consists of the Senate and the House of Representatives.

WORD STORY Bicameral comes from Latin words meaning "two" and "room." Because bicameral legislatures meet in different rooms, their two groups are called chambers.

bi·car·bo·nate of soda (bī kär′bə nit), sodium bicarbonate.

bi·cen·ten·ni·al (bī′sen ten′ē əl), **1** *adj.* of a period of 200 years or its anniversary. **2** *n.* a 200th anniversary: *The town is celebrating its bicentennial.* **3** *n.* celebration of the 200th anniversary.

bi·ceps (bī′seps), *n.* the large muscle in the front part of the upper arm. If you move your fist up to your shoulder, the biceps will stick out. ❑ *n., pl.* **bi·ceps** or **bi·ceps·es.**

bi·chlo·ride (bī klôr′id), *n.* dichloride.

Bi·chon Fri·se (bē shòn′ frē zā′), a small dog with a thick, curly white coat and long ears. ❑ *pl.* **Bi·chons Fri·ses** (bē shòn′ frē zā′).

bick·er (bik′ər), **1** *v.* to take part in a petty, noisy quarrel; squabble: *The children bickered about which TV program to watch.* **2** *n.* a petty, noisy quarrel.

bi·coast·al (bī kō′stl), *adj.* of or between two coasts, especially the Atlantic and Pacific coasts of the United States: *bicoastal commuting.*

bi·con·cave (bī kon′kāv *or* bī′kon kav′), *adj.* concave on both sides: *a biconcave lens.*

bi·con·vex (bī kon′veks *or* bī′kon veks′), *adj.* convex on both sides: *a biconvex seed.*

bi·cus·pid (bī kus′pid), *n.* a double-pointed tooth that tears and grinds food. Adult human beings have eight bicuspids.

bi·cy·cle (bī′sik′əl), **1** *n.* a lightweight vehicle with two wheels, one behind the other, that support a metal frame on which there is a seat. The rider pushes two pedals to turn the back wheel and steers with handlebars. **2** *v.* to ride a bicycle. ❑ *v.* **bi·cy·cled, bi·cy·cling.** —**bi′cy·cler,** *n.*

WORD STORY Bicycle comes from Greek words meaning "two" and "wheel." Of course, the ancient Greeks did not have bicycles. When bicycles were invented in the 1800s, people wanted a name for them that sounded important.

bi·cy·clist (bī′sik/list), *n.* person who rides a bicycle.

bid (bid), **1** *v.* to tell someone what to do, where to go, etc.; command: *We were bidden to assemble in the gym. Do as I bid you.* **2** *v.* to say; tell: *My friends bade me good-by.* **3** *v.* to state the number of tricks or points you propose to win, in some card games. **4** *n.* amount bid in a card game. **5** *n.* turn of a player to bid. **6** *v.* to offer to pay a certain price: *She bid $15 for the table. He then bid $17.* **7** *n.* an offer to pay a certain price: *She made a bid on the table.* **8** *v.* to state your price for doing a certain piece of work: *to bid for a contract.* **9** *n.* amount offered or stated: *My bid for the table was $18. The contractor's bid for building the new bridge was $3,000,000.* **10** *v.* to invite: *The king bade the nobles stay for the feast.* **11** *n.* invitation: *a bid to join the honor society.* **12** *n.* an attempt to secure, achieve, or win something: *a bid for reelection.* ❑ *v.* **bade** or **bid, bid·den** or **bid, bid·ding** (for 1,2,10); **bid, bid·ding** (for 3,6,8). —**bid′da·ble,** *adj.*
bid fair, to seem likely; have a good chance.

bid·den (bid′n), *v.* a past participle of **bid:** *The class was bidden to remain seated until the bell rang.*

bid·der (bid′ər), *n.* person who bids. The highest bidder at an auction is the person who offers to pay the highest price for something.

bid·ding (bid′ing), *n.* **1** command; order: *The servant awaited the queen's bidding.* **2** invitation: *He joined the club at my bidding.* **3** act of offering a price for something: *The bidding at the auction was very slow at first.*
do someone's bidding, to obey someone: *I don't have to do his bidding.*

bid·dy (bid′ē), *n.* hen. ❑ *n., pl.* **bid·dies.**

bide (bid), *v.* **bide your time,** to wait for a good chance: *If you cannot find a camera at the price you want, bide your time until they go on sale.* ❑ *v.* **bid·ed** or **bode, bid·ing.**

bi·en·ni·al (bī en′ē əl), **1** *adj.* living two years or two growing seasons. A biennial plant begins its growth in the first growing season, then flowers, produces fruit, and dies in the second growing season. **2** *n.* plant that lives two years or two growing seasons. Carrots and onions are biennials. **3** *adj.* occurring every two years: *a biennial celebration.* **4** *n.* event that occurs every two years. —**bi·en′ni·al·ly,** *adv.*

bier (bir), *n.* a movable stand or framework on which a coffin or dead body is placed before burial. ■ Another word that sounds like this is **beer.**

bilateral symmetry

bi·fo·cal (bī'fō'kəl *or* bī fō'kəl), **1** *adj.* having two focuses. The lenses of bifocal glasses have two sections with different focal lengths, the upper part for distant vision, the lower for close vision. **2** *n.pl.* **bifocals,** pair of glasses having bifocal lenses.

big (big), **1** *adj.* great in amount or size; large: *a big room, a big book. The growth and distribution of food is a big business. An elephant is a big animal.* **2** *adj.* grown up: *You are a big girl now.* **3** *adj.* important; great: *The election of the President is big news.* **4** *adj.* full; loud: *a big voice.* **5** *adj.* generous: *His brother had a big heart and forgave him for breaking the model airplane.* **6** *adj.* boastful: *big talk.* **7** *adv.* INFORMAL. boastfully: *She talks big.* ❑ *adj.* **big·ger, big·gest.** —**big'ness,** *n.*

big·a·mist (big'ə mist), *n.* person married to more than one person at a time.

big·a·my (big'ə mē), *n.* condition of having two wives or two husbands at the same time. Bigamy is unlawful in most countries.

big bang theory, theory that the universe began in a cosmic explosion of particles of matter, which joined to form hydrogen and helium that became condensed into galaxies.

Big Bear, Ursa Major.

Big Bend National Park, a national park in SW Texas, containing mountains, canyons, desert, and miles of the Rio Grande.

big deal, INFORMAL. an important person or thing.

Big Dipper, group of seven bright stars shaped like a ladle, in the constellation Ursa Major.

Big·foot (big'fùt'), *n.* a large, hairy humanoid creature believed to live in the mountainous parts of the western United States.

big·gish (big'ish), *adj.* somewhat big.

big·heart·ed (big'här'tid), *adj.* kindly; generous.

big·horn (big'hôrn'), *n.* a wild, gray-brown sheep of the Rocky Mountains and Sierra Nevada, with large, curving horns; mountain sheep. ❑ *n., pl.* **big·horn** or **big·horns.**

big·no·ni·a (big nō'nē ə), *n.* a woody vine with clusters of large, orange-red flowers shaped like trumpets; trumpet creeper; trumpet vine. ❑ *n., pl.* **big·no·ni·as.**

big·ot (big'ət), *n.* an intolerant, prejudiced person.

big·ot·ed (big'ə tid), *adj.* sticking to an opinion, belief, party, etc., without reason and not tolerating other views; intolerant; prejudiced. —**big'ot·ed·ly,** *adv.*

big·ot·ry (big'ə trē), *n.* bigoted conduct or attitude; intolerance; prejudice.

big shot, INFORMAL. an important person.

big top, circus.

big·wig (big'wig'), *n.* INFORMAL. an important person.

bike (bīk), **1** *n.* a bicycle. **2** *n.* a motorcycle. **3** *v.* to ride a bicycle or motorcycle. ❑ *v.* **biked, bik·ing.** —**bik'er,** *n.*

bike·way (bīk'wā'), *n.* path or designated route through an urban area, to be used by bicyclists only.

bi·ki·ni (bə kē'nē), *n.* a very scanty bathing suit in two pieces for women and girls. ❑ *n., pl.* **bi·ki·nis.**

Bi·ki·ni (bə kē'nē), *n.* atoll in the Marshall Islands. It was the site of some nuclear bomb tests.

Bi·ko (bē'kō), *n.* **Ste·phen** (stē'vən), 1946-1977, South African reformer. ■ **Stephen Biko** was killed while being held by the South African security police.

bi·lat·er·al (bī lat'ər əl), *adj.* **1** on or having two sides. **2** binding both sides or parties: *The two nations signed a bilateral treaty.* —**bi·lat'er·al·ly,** *adv.*

bilateral symmetry, an exact likeness in size, shape, and arrangement of parts on opposite sides of a line or plane.

bile (bīl), *n.* **1** a bitter, greenish yellow liquid produced by the liver and stored in the gall bladder; gall. It aids in the digestion of fats in the small intestine. **2** ill humor; anger.

bilge (bilj), *n.* **1** the lowest part of a ship's hold; bottom of a ship's hull. **2** bilge water. **3** nonsense.

bilge water, dirty water that collects in the bottom of a ship's hold.

bi·lin·gual (bī ling'gwəl), *adj.* **1** able to speak another language as well or almost as well as your own; knowing two languages. **2** using two languages: *a bilingual dictionary.* —**bi·lin'gual·ly,** *adv.*

bi·lin·gual·ism (bī ling'gwəl iz'əm), *n.* **1** ability to speak and read two languages well. **2** use of two languages.

bil·ious (bil'yəs), *adj.* **1** suffering from or caused by some trouble with bile or the liver: *a bilious headache.* **2** cross; bad-tempered: *a bilious person.* —**bil'ious·ly,** *adv.* —**bil'ious·ness,** *n.*

bilk (bilk), *v.* to cheat; swindle. —**bilk'er,** *n.*

bill[1] (bil), **1** *n.* statement of money owed for work done or things supplied: *I received a $150 bill for clothing I had charged.* **2** *v.* to send a bill to: *The telephone company bills us on the first of each month.* **3** *n.* piece of paper money: *Do you have change for a five-dollar bill?* **4** *n.* a written or printed public notice, such as an advertisement, poster, or handbill: *Post no bills on this fence.* **5** *v.* to announce by bills or public notice: *Many interesting TV programs are billed for next week.* **6** *n.* a written or printed statement; list of items. **7** *n.* a proposed law presented to a lawmaking group for its approval: *This bill for gun control will be voted on by the Senate today.* —**bill'er,** *n.*

fill the bill, to satisfy requirements.

bill[2] (bil), **1** *n.* the horny, exposed part of the jaws of a bird; beak. **2** *n.* anything shaped somewhat like a bird's bill: *the bill of a turtle.*

bill and coo, to kiss and murmur, as pigeons touch bills and coo.

bill·board (bil'bôrd'), *n.* a large board, usually outdoors, on which to display advertisements or notices.

bil·let (bil'it), **1** *n.* a written order to provide board and lodging for a soldier. **2** *n.* place where a soldier is lodged. **3** *v.* to assign to quarters by billet: *Soldiers were billeted in all the houses of the village.*

bill·fold (bil'fōld'), *n.* a small, flat case for carrying paper money, cards, etc., in your pocket or handbag; wallet.

bil·liards (bil'yərdz), *n.* game played with three hard balls on a special table, called a **billiard table,** with a raised, cushioned edge. A long stick called a **billiard cue** is used to hit the **billiard balls.**

Bil·lings (bil'ingz), *n.* city in S Montana.

bil·lion (bil'yən), *n., adj.* **1** (in the United States and Canada) one thousand millions; 1,000,000,000. **2** (in Great Britain, France, and Germany) one million millions; 1,000,000,000,000.

bil·lion·aire (bil'yə nâr'), *n.* an extremely wealthy person who has a billion or more dollars, francs, marks, pounds, etc.

bil·lionth (bil'yənth), *adj., n.* **1** last in a series of a billion. **2** one of a billion equal parts.

bill of fare, menu.

bill of goods, a shipment of merchandise.

sell a bill of goods, to mislead.

Bill of Rights, **1** the first ten amendments to the Constitution of the United States, adopted in 1791, which include a declaration of fundamental rights held by United States citizens. **2** any statement of the fundamental rights of the people of a state or nation.

a	hat	ė	term	ô	order	ch	child		a in about
ā	age	i	it	oi	oil	ng	long		e in taken
ä	far	ī	ice	ou	out	sh	she	ə	i in pencil
â	care	o	hot	u	cup	th	thin		o in lemon
e	let	ō	open	ù	put	ŦH	then		u in circus
ē	equal	ò	saw	ü	rule	zh	measure		

bill of sale, a written statement transferring ownership of something from the seller to the buyer.

bil·low (bil′ō), **1** *n.* a great, swelling wave or surge of the sea. **2** *n.* any great wave or swelling mass of smoke, flame, sound, or the like: *Billows of smoke rose from the chimney.* **3** *v.* to rise or roll in big waves; surge: *The waves billowed toward the shore.* **4** *v.* to swell out; bulge: *The sheets on the clothesline billowed in the wind.*

billow (def. 2)

bil·low·y (bil′ō ē), *adj.* **1** rising or rolling in big waves; surging. **2** swelling out; bulging. ❑ *adj.* **bil·low·i·er, bil·low·i·est.**

bil·ly·club (bil′ē klub′), *n.* nightstick.

billy goat, a male goat.

Bi·lox·i (bi luk′sē *or* bə lok′sē), *n.* port in SE Mississippi, on the Gulf of Mexico.

bi·met·al (bī met′l), **1** *n.* a material made by attaching two different metals together. **2** *adj.* bimetallic.

bi·me·tal·lic (bī′mə tal′ik), *adj.* **1** made of or using two metals. **2** of or based on bimetallism.

bi·met·al·lism (bī met′l iz′əm), *n.* the use of both gold and silver as the basis of the money system of a nation.

bi·month·ly (bī munth′lē), **1** *adj., adv.* once every two months: *A bimonthly magazine is issued six times a year. The magazine is issued bimonthly.* **2** *adj., adv.* twice a month: *The bimonthly meetings are on the first and third Wednesdays of each month. The meetings are held bimonthly.* **3** *n.* newspaper or magazine published bimonthly. ❑ *n., pl.* **bi·month·lies.**

bin (bin), *n.* box or enclosed place for holding or storing grain, coal, etc. ■ Another word that sounds like this is **been.**

bi·nar·y (bī′nər ē), *adj.* made up of two; involving two.

binary star, pair of stars that revolve around a common center of gravity.

binary system, system of numeration which counts only from 0 to 1 and then moves to a new number place, so that each place represents a quantity double that of the previous place. In this system, the decimal number 1 is written as 1, but the decimal number 2 is written as 10 (1 in the twos place, 0 in the ones place), while 5 is written as 101 (1 in the fours place, 0 in the twos place, 1 in the ones place). The binary system is used by electronic devices because 1 and 0 can easily be represented by the presence or absence of electric charge.

bin·au·ral (bī nôr′əl), *adj.* **1** having two ears. **2** of or used with both ears: *a binaural stethoscope.* **3** having or using two sound speakers, in order to give a more realistic quality to what is heard: *binaural reception.* **−bin·au′ral·ly,** *adv.*

bind (bīnd), **1** *v.* to tie together; hold together; fasten: *bind a package with string.* **2** *v.* to stick together: *Gravel in a roadway may be bound by tar.* **3** *v.* to hold by some force; restrain: *Vines are binding the flowers and choking their growth.* **4** *v.* to fasten sheets of paper into a cover; put a cover on a book: *The loose pages were bound into a small book.* **5** *v.* to hold by a promise, duty, law, etc.; oblige: *Bound by his promise not to be home late, he left the party early.* **6** *v.* to put a bandage on: *bind up a wound.* **7** *v.* to put a border or edge on to strengthen or ornament: *The sleeves were bound with leather.* **8** *v.* to fit too tightly: *This new shirt binds across the shoulders.* **9** *n.* a situation that binds or restricts: *We were in a bind when we were invited to two parties in the same evening.* ❑ *v.* **bound, bind·ing.**

bind·er (bīn′dər), *n.* **1** person or business that binds books. **2** anything that ties or holds something together. **3** cover for a loose-leaf notebook. **4** machine that cuts stalks of grain and ties them in bundles.

bind·er·y (bīn′dər ē), *n.* place where books are bound. ❑ *n., pl.* **bind·er·ies.**

bind·ing (bīn′ding), **1** *n.* the covering of a book. **2** *n.* strip protecting or ornamenting an edge. **3** *adj.* having force or power to hold to a promise, duty, law, etc.; obligatory: *a binding agreement.* **−bind′ing·ly,** *adv.*

binge (binj), **1** *n.* time of doing too much of something, especially eating or drinking. **2** *v.* to do too much of something for a time. ❑ *v.* **binged, binge·ing** *or* **bing·ing. −bing′er,** *n.*

bin·go (bing′gō), *n.* game in which each player covers the numbers on a card as they are called out. The first player to cover a column of numbers is the winner.

bin·na·cle (bin′ə kəl), *n.* box or stand that contains a ship's compass. The binnacle is placed near the helm.

bi·noc·u·lar (bə nok′yə lər), *adj.* **1** for both eyes at once: *a binocular microscope.* **2** using both eyes at once: *Most animals have binocular vision.* [See Word Story at **binoculars.**]

bi·noc·u·lars (bə nok′yə lərz), *n.pl.* a double telescope joined as a unit for use with both eyes.

WORD STORY **Binoculars** comes from Latin words meaning "two at a time" and "eye." Originally, the word was used in the phrase "binocular telescope." People shortened this to the noun **binocular,** and because this device has two parts, they made the word for it a plural, **binoculars.**

bi·no·mi·al (bī nō′mē əl), **1** *n.* expression in algebra containing two terms connected by a plus or minus sign. $8a + 2b$ is a binomial. **2** *n.* the scientific name of a living thing, made up of two words. *Homo sapiens* is a binomial. **3** *adj.* made up of two terms or words. **−bi·no′mi·al·ly,** *adv.*

bio-, *prefix.* life and living things: *biochemistry = biological chemistry; biodegradable = able to be broken down by living things.*

bi·o·chem·i·cal (bī′ō kem′ə kəl), *adj.* of or about biochemistry. **−bi′o·chem′i·cal·ly,** *adv.*

bi·o·chem·ist (bī′ō kem′ist), *n.* an expert in biochemistry.

bi·o·chem·is·try (bī′ō kem′ə strē), *n.* science that deals with the chemical processes of living animals and plants.

bi·o·de·grad·a·ble (bī′ō di grā′də bəl), *adj.* able to be eaten or otherwise broken down by bacteria or other living things: *a biodegradable detergent.* **−bi′o·de·grad′a·bil′i·ty,** *n.*

bi·o·de·grade (bī′ō di grād′), *v.* to break down by bacteria or other living things. ❑ *v.* **bi·o·de·grad·ed, bi·o·de·grad·ing.**

bi·o·di·ver·si·ty (bī′ō di vėr′sə tē), *n.* a wide variety of different species living together in one place.

biodiversity

bi·o·en·gi·neer·ing (bī′ō en′jə nir′ing), *n.* branch of engineering which designs and produces replacement devices such as artificial arms, legs, and organs for the human body.

bi·o·eth·ics (bī′ō eth′iks), *n.* the study of ethical questions in the fields of biology and medicine. Bioethics has been especially concerned with such applications of modern technology as genetic engineering and human organ transplants.

bi·o·feed·back (bī/ō fēd/bak), *n.* process in which someone learns to exert some conscious control over bodily conditions such as pulse rate and blood pressure. Information on these conditions, obtained by using a monitoring device, is reported constantly during the process to indicate success or failure.

bi·og·ra·pher (bī og/rə fər), *n.* person who writes a biography.

bi·o·graph·i·cal (bī/ə graf/ə kəl), *adj.* **1** of someone's life: *biographical details.* **2** of or about biography. —**bi/o·graph/i·cal·ly,** *adv.*

bi·og·ra·phy (bī og/rə fē), *n.* an account of someone's life. ❑ *n., pl.* **bi·og·ra·phies.**

bi·o·haz·ard (bī/ō haz/ərd), *n.* a living thing, especially a germ produced in a laboratory, which would be a health threat if released into the environment.

bi·o·log·ic (bī/ə loj/ik), *adj.* biological.

bi·o·log·i·cal (bī/ə loj/ə kəl), *adj.* **1** of living things; connected with the processes of life: *biological studies.* **2** of or for biology: *a biological laboratory.* —**bi/o·log/i·cal·ly,** *adv.*

biological clock, system of parts and processes in a living thing controlling the time of its activities. An animal's biological clock controls when it sleeps, has young, etc., and a plant's biological clock controls when it flowers.

biological control, the control of garden or farm pests by natural means, not by artificial chemicals. Methods include bringing in a natural enemy and spreading a disease that kills pests.

biological warfare, warfare in which disease germs are used against persons, animals, or crops.

bi·ol·o·gy (bī ol/ə jē), *n.* **1** the scientific study of living things, including their origins, structure, activities, and distribution. Botany, zoology, and ecology are branches of biology. **2** the living things of a particular area or region. **3** the biological facts about a particular living thing. —**bi·ol/o·gist,** *n.*

bi·o·lu·mi·nes·cence (bī/ō lü/mə nes/ns), *n.* act of giving off light from the body by living things, such as fireflies.

bi·o·lu·mi·nes·cent (bī/ō lü/mə nes/nt), *adj.* showing bioluminescence.

bi·o·mass (bī/ō mas/), *n.* **1** total weight of all living things in a given space. **2** organic material, especially from plants, considered as a source of energy.

bi·ome (bī/ōm), *n.* a major ecological system, having its own kind of climate, plants, animals, and other living things. Desert and rain forest are two kinds of biome.

bi·o·med·i·cal (bī/ō med/ə kəl), *adj.* **1** of or about biomedicine. **2** of or about both biology and medicine.

bi·o·med·i·cine (bī/ō med/ə sən), *n.* branch of medicine concerned with the ability of human bodies to adapt to an abnormal environment, especially outer space.

bi·on·ic (bī on/ik), *adj.* **1** of or about bionics. **2** having both biological and electronic parts. **3** artificial; contrived.

bi·on·ics (bī on/iks), *n.* study of the anatomy and physiology of animals as a basis for designing new or improved electronic devices or systems. [**Bionics** is a blend of **biology** and **electronics.**]

bi·o·phys·ics (bī/ō fiz/iks), *n.* study of biology in relation to the laws of physics. —**bi·o·phys·i·cist** (bī/ō fiz/ə sist), *n.*

bi·op·sy (bī/op sē), *n.* the removal of cells or tissue from a living body for medical examination. ❑ *n., pl.* **bi·op·sies.**

bi·o·sphere (bī/ə sfir), *n.* the region on and surrounding the earth that can support life, including the atmosphere, water, and soil.

bi·o·tech·nol·o·gy (bī/ō tek nol/ə jē), *n.* the industrial use of living things, such as microorganisms, or other biological substances to manufacture products and carry out services. Biotechnology is used to manufacture drugs and to recycle waste.

bi·ot·ic (bī ot/ik), *adj.* of or about life or living things.

bi·o·tin (bī/ə tən), *n.* vitamin that promotes growth, found in liver, eggs, and yeast. It is one member of the vitamin B complex.

bi·par·ti·san (bī pär/tə zən), *adj.* representing or supported by two political parties: *a bipartisan foreign policy.*

bi·par·tite (bī pär/tīt), *adj.* **1** made or shared by two peoples, nations, etc.: *a bipartite treaty between the United States and Canada.* **2** having two parts: *bipartite shells.* —**bi·par/tite·ly,** *adv.*

bi·ped (bī/ped), **1** *n.* animal with two feet. Birds and human beings are bipeds. **2** *adj.* having two feet. —**bi·ped/al,** *adj.*

bi·plane (bī/plān/), *n.* airplane with two wings on each side, one above the other.

biplane

bi·po·lar disorder (bī pō/lər), manic-depressive mental illness.

bi·ra·cial (bī rā/shəl), *adj.* of, for, or made up of two races: *biracial heritage.*

birch (bėrch), *n.* **1** any of various slender, hardy trees with smooth bark that peels off in thin layers. **2** the hard wood of some birches, often used in making furniture. **3** a birch stick used for whipping. ❑ *n., pl.* **birch·es** for 1,3.

bird (bėrd), **1** *n.* any of many warm-blooded animals with wings and feathers. All birds lay eggs. Most birds can fly. **2** *v.* to watch birds. **3** *n.* INFORMAL. person: *He's an odd bird.* **4** *n.* shuttlecock. [See Word Story at **curl.**] —**bird/er,** *n.* —**bird/ing,** *n.* —**bird/like/,** *adj.*

bird·bath (bėrd/bath/), *n.* a shallow basin raised off the ground and filled with water for birds to bathe in or drink. ❑ *n., pl.* **bird·baths** (bėrd/baŦHz/).

bird·brain (bėrd/brān/), *n.* INFORMAL. a silly, foolish person.

bird·call (bėrd/kȯl/), *n.* **1** sound that a bird makes. **2** device for imitating that sound.

bird dog, any dog trained or bred to find birds or bring back birds shot by hunters.

bird-hipped (bėrd/hipt/), *adj.* with a pelvic structure like a bird's: *bird-hipped dinosaurs.*

bird·house (bėrd/hous/), *n.* a small box with a roof and one or more openings, raised off the ground for birds to nest in. ❑ *n., pl.* **bird·hous·es** (bėrd/hou/ziz).

bird·ie (bėr/dē), **1** *n.* a little bird. **2** *n.* score of one stroke less than par for any hole on a golf course. **3** *v.* to make such a score. ❑ *v.* **bird·ied, bird·y·ing.**

bird of paradise, any of several birds of New Guinea and northern Australia, noted for magnificent plumage.

bird of passage, any bird that flies from one region to another as the seasons change.

bird of prey, any of numerous birds, including eagles, hawks, and owls, that hunt animals.

bird·seed (bėrd/sēd/), *n.* mixture of small seeds often fed to caged birds.

bird's-eye (bėrdz/ī/), *adj.* **1** seen from above or from a distance; general: *a bird's-eye view of the city from an airplane.* **2** having markings somewhat like birds' eyes. **Bird's-eye maple** is a wood used in furniture.

bird of paradise—about 18 in. (46 cm) long

a	hat	ė	term	ô	order	ch	child		a in about
ā	age	i	it	oi	oil	ng	long		e in taken
ä	far	ī	ice	ou	out	sh	she	ə {	i in pencil
â	care	o	hot	u	cup	th	thin		o in lemon
e	let	ō	open	u̇	put	ŦH	then		u in circus
ē	equal	ȯ	saw	ü	rule	zh	measure		

bird watcher, person who observes and classifies wild birds in their natural environment. **–bird watching.**

bi·ret·ta (bə ret′ə), *n.* a stiff, square cap worn by Roman Catholic or Episcopal clergy on certain occasions. ❑ *n., pl.* **bi·ret·tas.**

Bir·ming·ham (bėr′ming ham), *n.* **1** city in central Alabama, on the Alabama River. **2** city in central England.

birth (bėrth), *n.* **1** act of coming into life; being born: *the birth of a baby.* **2** act of beginning; origin: *the birth of a nation.* **3** act of bringing forth: *the birth of a plan, the birth of a new age.* **4** family; descent: *of noble birth.* ■ Another word that sounds like this is **berth.**

　give birth to, 1 to bring forth; bear: *The dog gave birth to four puppies.* **2** be the origin or cause of: *The scientist's experiments gave birth to a new drug.*

birth control, 1 use of contraceptive methods or devices. **2** control of the birthrate by artificial means.

birth·day (bėrth′dā′), *n.* **1** day on which a person was born. **2** day on which something began: *July 4, 1776, was the birthday of the United States.* **3** anniversary of the day on which a person was born, or on which something began: *Tomorrow is my birthday; I'll be ten.*

birth defect, abnormality or disease of a newborn child, either hereditary or acquired during the pregnancy.

birth·mark (bėrth′märk′), *n.* mark on the skin that was there at birth.

birth·place (bėrth′plās′), *n.* **1** place where a person was born. **2** place in which something began; place of origin: *Philadelphia is the birthplace of the United States.*

birth·rate (bėrth′rāt′), *n.* relationship of the number of births in a year to the total population.

birth·right (bėrth′rīt′), *n.* right or privilege that someone is entitled to by birth.

birth·stone (bėrth′stōn′), *n.* gem identified with a certain month of the year. A birthstone is supposed to bring good luck when worn by a person born in its month.

Bis·cay (bis′kā), *n.* **Bay of,** bay north of Spain and west of France. It is part of the Atlantic.

Bis·cayne National Park (bis′kān *or* bis kān′), a national park in S Florida near Miami, containing islands, surrounding waters and sea bottom, and a rare coral reef.

bis·cuit (bis′kit), *n.* **1** soft bread dough baked in small portions. **2** BRITISH. cracker. ❑ *n., pl.* **bis·cuits** *or* **bis·cuit.**

WORD STORY　**Biscuit** comes from a French word meaning "cooked twice." This was a method of making small cakes, which today's biscuits look like.

bi·sect (bī′sekt), *v.* to divide into two equal parts: *You can bisect a 90-degree angle into two 45-degree angles.*

bi·sec·tor (bī sek′tər), *n.* line that bisects something.

bi·sex·u·al (bī sek′shü əl), **1** *adj.* sexually attracted to both sexes. **2** *adj.* of both sexes. **3** *adj.* having both male and female reproductive organs in one plant or animal. **4** *n.* plant or animal that is bisexual. **–bi·sex′u·al′i·ty,** *n.*

Bish·kek (bish kek′), *n.* capital of Kyrgyzstan.

bish·op (bish′əp), *n.* **1** high-ranking member of the clergy in some Christian churches. **2** one of the pieces in the game of chess that move diagonally.

bish·op·ric (bish′əp rik), *n.* **1** position, office, or rank of bishop. **2** church district under the charge of a bishop; diocese.

Bis·marck (biz′märk), *n.* **1 Otto von** (ot′ō fon), 1815-1898, German political leader who created the German empire. **2** capital of North Dakota, in the S part.

bis·muth (biz′məth), *n.* a brittle, reddish white metallic element, used in making medicine and in alloys. *Symbol:* Bi

bi·son (bī′sn), *n.* a large, wild animal of North America with a large shaggy head and a large hump over the shoulders; buffalo. Bison are related to cattle. ❑ *n., pl.* **bi·son.**

bisque (bisk), *n.* a rich, thick soup.

Bis·sau (bi sou′), *n.* capital of Guinea-Bissau.

bis·tro (bis′trō *or* bē′strō), *n.* bar or nightclub. ❑ *n., pl.* **bis·tros.**

bit[1] (bit), *n.* **1** a small piece; small amount: *bits of broken glass. A pebble is a bit of rock.* **2** a short time: *Stay a bit.*

a bit, 1 a little; slightly: *I am a bit tired.* **2** somewhat: *That barking dog is a bit of a nuisance.*
bit by bit, little by little.
do your bit, to do your share: *She did her share of the work, now you do your bit.*

WORD STORY　**Bit**[1] comes from an old English word meaning "to bite." A bit was the amount bitten. People began using **bit** to mean any amount of food, and then just any small amount. But a bit of soap or a bit of steel is not something you are likely to want to bite.

bit[2] (bit), *v.* past tense and a past participle of **bite:** *Our dog bit the dog next door. He was bit by a rat.*

bit[3] (bit), *n.* **1** tool for boring or drilling that fits into a brace, electric drill, etc. **2** the biting or cutting part of a tool. **3** the part of a bridle that goes in a horse's mouth.

bit[4] (bit), *n.* the basic unit of information in an electronic computer. It is the same as a choice between two possibilities, such as "yes" or "no."

bitch (bich), *n.* a female dog, wolf, fox, etc. ❑ *n., pl.* **bitch·es.**

bite (bīt), **1** *v.* to seize, cut into, or cut off with the teeth: *She bit into the apple.* **2** *n.* act of biting: *The dog gave a bite or two at the bone.* **3** *n.* a piece bitten off; mouthful: *Eat the whole apple, not just a bite.* **4** *n.* a light meal; snack: *Have a bite with me now or you'll get hungry later.* **5** *v.* to wound with teeth, fangs, a sting, etc.: *My dog never bites.* **6** *n.* a wound made by biting or stinging: *Mosquito bites itch.* **7** *n.* a sharp, smarting pain: *We felt the bite of the cold wind.* **8** *v.* to cause a sharp, smarting pain to: *Her fingers are bitten by frost.* **9** *v.* to take a tight hold of; grip: *The jaws of a vise bite the wood they hold.* **10** *v.* to take a bait; be caught: *The fish are biting well today.* **11** *n.* way in which the teeth in the upper and lower jaws meet. ❑ *v.* **bit, bit·ten** *or* **bit, bit·ing.** ■ Another word that sounds like this is **byte. –bit′er,** *n.*

bit·ing (bī′ting), *adj.* **1** causing sharp pain or distress: *Dress warmly before you go out in that biting wind.* **2** sarcastic; sneering: *Biting remarks hurt people's feelings.* **–bit′ing·ly,** *adv.*

bit·ten (bit′n), *v.* a past participle of **bite:** *Finish the apple, now that you have bitten into it.*

bit·ter (bit′ər), *adj.* **1** having a sharp, harsh, unpleasant taste: *This coffee is so strong that it tastes bitter.* **2** causing pain or grief; hard to admit or bear: *a bitter defeat. His father's death was a bitter loss.* **3** showing pain or grief: *bitter tears.* **4** harsh or cutting: *a bitter remark, bitter enemies.* **5** very cold: *The bitter winter killed our apple tree.* **–bit′ter·ly,** *adv.* **–bit′ter·ness,** *n.*
to the bitter end, until the very last.

bit·tern (bit′ərn), *n.* any of several small herons that live in marshes and have a peculiar booming cry.

bit·ter·root (bit′ər rüt′), *n.* a small plant with fleshy roots and pink flowers, found in the northern Rocky Mountains.

bit·ter·sweet (bit′ər swēt′), **1** *n.* a climbing plant with purple flowers and poisonous, scarlet berries. **2** *n.* a climbing vine of North America with greenish flowers and orange seedcases that open and show red seeds. **3** *adj.* sweet and bitter mixed: *bittersweet chocolate.* **4** *adj.* pleasant and painful at once: *The movie had a bittersweet ending which left her laughing and crying at once.*

bittern—about 30 in. (76 cm) long

bit·ty (bit′ē), *adj.* very small; tiny. ❑ *adj.* **bit·ti·er, bit·ti·est.**

bi·tu·men (bə tü′mən), *n.* any of a number of minerals that will burn, such as asphalt, petroleum, and naphtha.

bi·tu·mi·nous coal (bə tü′mə nəs), coal that burns with much smoke and flame; soft coal.

bi·valve (bī′valv′), *n.* any mollusk whose shell has two parts hinged together so that it will open and shut like a book. Oysters and clams are bivalves.

biv·ouac (biv′wak *or* biv′ü ak), **1** *n.* a temporary, outdoor camp usually without tents or with very small tents: *The soldiers made a bivouac for the night in a field.* **2** *v.* to camp outdoors in this way: *They bivouacked there until morning.* ❑ *v.* **biv·ouacked, biv·ouack·ing.**

bi·week·ly (bī wēk′lē), **1** *adj., adv.* once every two weeks: *This magazine is a biweekly publication. The group meets biweekly.* **2** *adj., adv.* twice a week: *The teachers have a biweekly conference.* ■ See Usage Note at **first-degree. 3** *n.* newspaper or magazine published biweekly. ❑ *n., pl.* **bi·week·lies.**

bi·zarre (bə zär′), *adj.* strikingly odd or queer in appearance or style; fantastic; grotesque: *The frost made bizarre figures on the windowpanes.* ■ See Synonym Study at **peculiar.** ■ Another word that sounds like this is **bazaar. —bi·zarre′ly,** *adv.* **—bi·zarre′ness,** *n.*

Bi·zet (bē zā′), *n.* Georges (zhôrzh), 1838-1875, French composer of *Carmen* and other operas.

Bk, symbol for berkelium.

blab (blab), *v.* to tell secrets; talk too much. ❑ *v.* **blabbed, blab·bing.**

blab·ber (blab′ər), **1** *n.* person who blabs. **2** *n.* foolish talk. **3** *v.* to blab.

black (blak), **1** *adj.* having the color of coal: *a black sweater.* **2** *n.* the color of coal. This sentence is printed in black. **3** *n.* a black paint, dye, or pigment. **4** *v.* to make black; blacken: *I blacked my shoes before going to the party.* **5** *adj.* without any light; very dark: *The room was black as night.* **6** *adj.* served without cream or milk: *black coffee.* **7** *adj.* dirty; filthy: *Her hands were black with soot.* **8** *adj.* dismal; gloomy: *a black day.* **9** *adj.* sullen; angry: *She gave her brother a black look.* **10** *adj.* wicked: *black deeds.* **11** Also, **Black, a** *n.* person whose ancestors belonged to the group of people who live in Africa south of the Sahara; in the United States, African American. **b** *adj.* of or about people of this background. **—black′ly,** *adv.* **—black′ness,** *n.*

black out, 1 to become temporarily blind or unconscious: *Her pain was so intense that she blacked out for several minutes.* **2** to darken completely: *black out the stage.* **3** to suppress; withhold: *to black out the news of a battle.*

> **USAGE NOTE** **Black** had negative meanings ("dirty," "dismal," "wicked") in English long before English people had much contact with people from Africa. Negative meanings of **black** are also found in many other languages, including some African and Native American languages. Because **black** has been so commonly used with a racial meaning in recent times, careful writers and speakers now avoid using negative meanings of this word.

Black (blak), *n.* **Shir·ley Tem·ple** (shėr′lē tem′pəl), born 1928, American child movie star and diplomat. She won a Special Academy Award in 1934. She has been the U.S. ambassador to Ghana and to Czechoslovakia.

black-and-blue (blak′ən blü′), *adj.* discolored from a bruise.

black·ball (blak′bȯl′), **1** *v.* to vote against; turn down as a candidate for membership: *One member of the club blackballed him, so he could not become a member.* **2** *n.* a vote against someone or something. [See Word Story at **ballot.**] **—black′ball′er,** *n.*

black bear, a large North American bear that has dense black fur.

black belt, 1 the rank of expert in judo and karate. **2** the black waistband or sash that symbolizes this rank. **3** someone who holds this rank.

black·ber·ry (blak′ber′ē), *n.* any of several similar small, dark purple fruits growing on related thorny bushes and vines. They are sweet and juicy. ❑ *n., pl.* **black·ber·ries.**

black·bird (blak′bėrd′), *n.* any of various birds, the male of which is mostly black. The cowbird, grackle, and redwing are blackbirds.

black·board (blak′bôrd′), *n.* a smooth piece of slate, glass, or painted wood on which to write with chalk.

black·bod·y (blak′bod′ē), *n.* a theoretical surface or object capable of completely absorbing all the radiation falling on it and of emitting radiation in forms and amounts directly related to its temperature. ❑ *n., pl.* **black·bod·ies.**

Black Death, the bubonic plague that spread through Europe in the 1300s and destroyed one fourth of its population.

black·en (blak′ən), *v.* **1** to make black: *Soot blackened the snow.* **2** to become black: *The sky blackened and soon it began to rain.* **3** to speak evil of: *Enemies blackened his character with false rumors.* **—black′en·er,** *n.*

Black English, any of several varieties of English spoken by some African Americans, differing from other varieties of English in some features of speech sounds and syntax.

black eye, 1 a bruise around an eye. **2** cause of disgrace or discredit.

black-eyed pea (blak′īd′), seed of a vine related to peas and beans, widely grown in the southern United States for use as a vegetable; cowpea.

black-eyed Su·san (sü′zn), a yellow daisylike flower with a black center.

black·fly (blak′flī′), *n.* a small fly of Canada and the northern United States, with a black body. The female's bite is very painful. ❑ *n., pl.* **black·flies.**

Black·foot (blak′fut′), *n.* member of a tribe of American Indians living in Montana and Alberta. ❑ *n., pl.* **Black·feet** (blak′fēt′), **Black·foot.** [Blackfoot comes from the custom in this tribe of staining moccasins with ashes.]

black-eyed Susan

black-foot·ed ferret (blak′fut′id), ferret (def. 1).

Black Forest, mountains covered with forests in SW Germany.

black·guard (blag′ärd), *n.* OLD USE. a rude, contemptible person; scoundrel.

Black Hawk, 1767-1838, Sauk Indian leader. ■ Black Hawk fought on the side of the British in the War of 1812. He also fought unsuccessfully to prevent settlers from moving further into Illinois.

black·head (blak′hed′), *n.* a small black-tipped lump of dead cells and oil plugging a pore of the skin.

Black Hills, group of mountains in W South Dakota and NE Wyoming.

black hole, a theoretical heavenly body whose mass is so great for its size that its extreme gravity keeps light from escaping and changes the basic properties of time and space in its area.

black hole—as imagined by an artist

black·ing (blak′ing), *n.* a black polish used on shoes, stoves, etc.

black·jack (blak′jak′), **1** *n.* a small, weighted leather-covered weapon with a flexible handle, used for striking someone. **2** *v.* to hit with a blackjack. **3** *n.* the black flag of a pirate. **4** *n.* a card game in which the players draw cards face down from the dealer, trying for a score of not more than 21 points.

a	hat	ė	term	ô	order	ch	child		
ā	age	i	it	oi	oil	ng	long		a in about
ä	far	ī	ice	ou	out	sh	she	ə {	e in taken
â	care	o	hot	u	cup	th	thin		i in pencil
e	let	ō	open	ù	put	ᴛʜ	then		o in lemon
ē	equal	ȯ	saw	ü	rule	zh	measure		u in circus

black light, invisible infrared or ultraviolet rays, used for night-time photography and to make things glow by fluorescence.

black·list (blak′list′), **1** *n.* list of persons who are believed to deserve punishment, blame, suspicion, etc.: *That store keeps a blacklist of persons who do not pay their bills.* **2** *v.* to put on a blacklist.

black lung disease, hardening of lung tissue in coal miners caused by long-term breathing of coal dust. It can cause difficulty in breathing and chest pain.

black magic, evil magic; sorcery; witchcraft.

black·mail (blak′māl′), **1** *n.* money gotten from someone by threatening to tell or reveal something bad about him or her. **2** *v.* to get or try to get blackmail from. **3** *n.* an attempt to get money by threats. —**black′mail·er,** *n.*

black mark, mark of criticism or punishment made against someone.

black market, 1 the selling of goods at unlawful prices or in unlawful quantities. **2** place where such selling is done.

Black Muslim, member of the Nation of Islam, or of a related group. ■ Members of these groups prefer the groups' formal names to **Black Muslim.**

black·out (blak′out′), *n.* **1** act of turning off or going out of all the lights of a city, district, etc., as a protection against an air raid or as the result of power failure. **2** temporary blindness or loss of consciousness resulting from lack of blood circulation in the brain. **3** act of withholding of information usually printed or broadcast: *a news blackout.*

Black Power, power of collective action by African Americans, used to gain equality.

Black Sea, large sea bordered by Turkey, Bulgaria, Romania, Ukraine, Russia, and Georgia.

black sheep, person considered by his or her group or family to be a disgrace.

black·smith (blak′smith′), *n.* person who makes things out of iron by heating it in a forge and hammering it into shape on an anvil. Blacksmiths mend tools and shoe horses.

black·snake (blak′snāk′), *n.* **1** a harmless dark or black snake of North America. **2** a heavy whip made of braided leather.

black·strap molasses (blak′strap′), a dark, thick molasses produced in the final step of making sugar from sugarcane juice. It contains less sugar than ordinary molasses.

Black Studies, a program of courses in African American history, literature, and culture.

black·top (blak′top′), **1** *n.* asphalt used as a pavement for highways, roads, and other surfaces. **2** *n.* surface covered with this substance. **3** *v.* to surface or pave a road with blacktop. ❏ *v.* **black·topped, black·top·ping.**

Black·well (blak′wel), *n.* **Elizabeth,** 1821-1910, first American woman to receive a medical degree. ■ **Elizabeth Blackwell** was rejected from 29 medical schools because she was a woman. She and her sister Emily, who also became a doctor, founded a hospital and a medical school to train other women.

black widow, a small North American spider, the female of which is poisonous and has a shiny black body with a reddish mark in the shape of an hourglass on the underside.

blad·der (blad′ər), *n.* **1** a soft, thin bag in the body that stores urine from the kidneys until it is discharged from the body. **2** anything like this. A football has a hollow rubber bladder that can be blown up with air.

blade (blād), *n.* **1** the cutting part of anything like a knife or sword: *A carving knife should have a sharp blade. He sharpened the blades of his skates.* **2** sword. **3** a smart, dashing fellow. **4** leaf of grass. **5** the flat, wide part of a leaf. **6** the flat, wide part of anything: *the blade of an oar, the shoulder blade.* —**blade′like′,** *adj.*

blah (blä), INFORMAL. **1** *adj.* without spirit; dull; uninteresting: *a blah performance.* **2** *n.pl.* **the blahs,** a general feeling of discomfort or dissatisfaction.

Blake (blāk), *n.* **William,** 1757-1827, English poet and artist. ■ **William Blake's** writing and art were inspired by visions he had. He often illustrated and printed his own books.

blame (blām), **1** *v.* to hold responsible for something bad or wrong: *The driver blamed the fog for his accident.* **2** *n.* responsibility for something bad or wrong: *Carelessness deserves the blame for many mistakes.* **3** *v.* to find fault with: *The teacher will not blame us if we do our best.* **4** *n.* act of finding fault; reproof. ❏ *v.* **blamed, blam·ing.** —**blam′a·ble,** *adj.* —**blam′a·bly,** *adv.*
be to blame, to deserve to be blamed: *Each person said somebody else was to blame.*

SYNONYM STUDY **Blame** and **accuse** both mean to hold someone responsible for something wrong. **Blame** suggests a feeling: *Mom said nothing, but we knew she blamed Dad for the delay.* **Accuse** suggests a statement: *The newspaper accused the factory of polluting the lake.*

blame·less (blām′lis), *adj.* not deserving blame; faultless. —**blame′less·ly,** *adv.* —**blame′less·ness,** *n.*

blame·wor·thy (blām′wėr′THē), *adj.* deserving blame; faulty. —**blame′wor′thi·ness,** *n.*

blanch (blanch), *v.* **1** to make white; bleach. We blanch almonds by soaking off their skins in boiling water. **2** to turn white; become pale: *We blanched with fear when we saw the bear coming.*

bland (bland), *adj.* **1** gentle; soothing: *a bland smile.* **2** smoothly agreeable and polite: *a bland manner.* **3** mild; not irritating: *a bland diet of baby food.* —**bland′ly,** *adv.* —**bland′ness,** *n.*

blan·dish (blan′dish), *v.* to persuade by gentle ways; coax; flatter. —**blan′dish·ment,** *n.*

blank (blangk), **1** *n.* space left empty or to be filled in: *Leave a blank if you can't answer the question.* **2** *adj.* not written or printed on: *blank paper.* ■ See Synonym Study at **empty. 3** *n.* a paper with spaces to be filled in: *Fill out this application blank and return it at once.* **4** *adj.* with spaces left for filling in: *a blank check, a blank form for you to fill in.* **5** *n.* an empty or vacant place: *When he read the hard questions his mind became a complete blank.* **6** *adj.* empty; vacant: *There was a blank look on his face.* **7** *n.* cartridge containing gunpowder but no bullet. **8** *v.* to keep from scoring. —**blank′ly,** *adv.* —**blank′ness,** *n.*
draw a blank, be unsuccessful: *I drew a blank when I tried to recall her name.*

blank check, 1 a signed check with the money amount left blank. The person holding the check may write in any amount. **2** freedom or permission to do as you please; carte blanche.

blan·ket (blang′kit), **1** *n.* a soft, heavy covering woven from wool, cotton, nylon, or other material, used to keep people or animals warm. **2** *n.* anything like a blanket: *A blanket of snow covered the ground.* **3** *v.* to cover with a blanket or anything like a blanket: *The snow blanketed the ground.* **4** *adj.* covering several or all: *a blanket guarantee to repair defects of any kind.*

blank verse, unrhymed poetry having five iambic feet in each line. EXAMPLE: What's in| a name?| that which| we call| a rose
By an|y oth|er name| would smell| as sweet.

blare (blâr), **1** *v.* to make a loud, harsh sound: *The trumpets blared.* **2** *n.* a loud, harsh sound. ❏ *v.* **blared, blar·ing.**

blar·ney (blär′nē), **1** *n.* flattering, coaxing talk. **2** *v.* to flatter; coax. ❏ *v.* **blar·neyed, blar·ney·ing.**

Blarney Stone, a stone in a castle near Cork, Ireland. Anyone who kisses it is supposed to become skillful in flattering and coaxing people.

bla·sé (blä zā′), *adj.* tired of pleasures; bored.

blas·pheme (bla sfēm′), *v.* to speak about God or sacred things with abuse or contempt. ❏ *v.* **blas·phemed, blas·phem·ing.** —**blas·phem′er,** *n.*

blas·phe·mous (blas′fə məs), *adj.* speaking about God or sacred things with abuse or contempt. —**blas′phe·mous·ly,** *adv.* —**blas′phe·mous·ness,** *n.*

blas·phe·my (blas′fə mē), *n.* abuse or contempt for God or sacred things. ❏ *n., pl.* **blas·phe·mies.**

blast (blast), **1** *n.* a strong, sudden rush of wind or air: *the icy blasts of winter.* **2** *n.* the blowing of a trumpet, horn, whistle, etc.: *The warning blast of a bugle aroused the camp.* **3** *n.* sound made by blowing a trumpet, horn, whistle, etc. **4** *n.* current of air used in smelting, etc. **5** *v.* to blow up rocks, earth, etc., with dynamite or other explosives: *Boulders were blasted to clear the way for the new road.* **6** *n.* a blasting; explosion: *We heard the blast a mile away.* **7** *n.* charge of dynamite, gunpowder, etc., that blows up rocks, earth, etc. **8** *v.* to cause to wither; blight; destroy: *The bad news blasted our hopes.* **—blast′er,** *n.*

blast off, to take off into flight propelled by rockets: *The spacecraft blasts off tomorrow morning.*

full blast, in full operation: *The party was going full blast.*

blast furnace, furnace in which ores are smelted by forcing a strong current of air into the furnace from the bottom to make a very great heat.

blast·off (blast′ôf′), *n.* act of launching or taking off into rocket-propelled flight.

blas·tu·la (blas′chə lə), *n.* an early stage in the development of an embryo of an animal. It is a sphere, formed by a single layer of cells around a fluid-filled cavity. ❏ *n., pl.* **blas·tu·las, blas·tu·lae** (blas′chə lē).

bla·tan·cy (blāt′n sē), *n.* noisy or unpleasant intrusion: *Viewers object to the blatancy of some television commercials.*

bla·tant (blāt′nt), *adj.* **1** noisy; offensive: *a blatant fool.* **2** obvious; flagrant: *a blatant lie, blatant disregard.* **—bla′tant·ly,** *adv.*

blaze¹ (blāz), **1** *n.* a bright flame or fire: *We could see the blaze of the campfire across the beach.* **2** *v.* to burn with a bright flame: *A fire was blazing in the fireplace.* **3** *n.* a glow of brightness; intense light; glare: *the blaze of the noon sun.* **4** *v.* to show bright colors or lights: *On New Year's Eve the big house blazed with lights.* **5** *n.* bright display: *The tulips made a blaze of color in the garden.* **6** *v.* to burst out in anger or excitement: *She blazed up at the insult.* **7** *n.* a sudden or violent outburst: *a blaze of temper.* ❏ *v.* **blazed, blaz·ing.**

blaze away, to fire a gun continuously.

blaze¹ (def. 2)—blazing forest fire

blaze² (blāz), **1** *n.* mark made on a tree by cutting off a piece of bark, to indicate a trail or boundary in a forest. **2** *v.* to mark a tree, trail, or boundary by cutting off a piece of bark. **3** *n.* a white spot on the face of a horse, cow, etc. ❏ *v.* **blazed, blaz·ing.**

blaze³ (blāz), *v.* to make known; proclaim. ❏ *v.* **blazed, blaz·ing.**

blaz·er (blā′zər), *n.* a distinctively colored or decorated jacket. Blazers are sometimes worn as part of the uniform of a team or school.

bla·zon (blā′zn), **1** *v.* to make known; proclaim: *Big posters blazoned the wonders of the coming circus.* **2** *v.* to decorate with designs, names, colors, etc. **3** *n.* coat of arms.

bldg., building. *pl.* **bldgs.**

bleach (blēch), **1** *v.* to whiten by exposing to sunlight or by using chemicals: *animal skulls bleached by the desert sun. We bleached the linen napkins in the wash.* **2** *n.* any chemical used in bleaching. ❏ *n., pl.* **bleach·es.**

bleach·ers (blē′chərz), *n.pl.* **1** section of wooden or plastic benches for spectators at baseball or other outdoor events. Bleachers are not roofed, and are the lowest priced seats. **2** similar bench seating for spectators in a gymnasium.

bleak (blēk), *adj.* **1** swept by winds; bare: *The rocky peaks of high mountains are bleak.* **2** chilly; cold: *The bleak winter wind made us shiver.* **3** cheerless and depressing; dismal: *A prisoner's life is bleak.* **—bleak′ly,** *adv.* **—bleak′ness,** *n.*

blear (blir), *v.* to make dim or blurred: *The old dog's eyes were bleared by age.*

blear·y (blir′ē), *adj.* dim; blurred: *Her eyes were bleary from lack of sleep.* ❏ *adj.* **blear·i·er, blear·i·est. —blear′i·ly,** *adv.*

blear·y-eyed (blir′ē īd′), *adj.* having eyes dim with water, tears, etc.

bleat (blēt), **1** *n.* cry made by a sheep, goat, or calf. **2** *n.* a sound like this: *a bleat of terror.* **3** *v.* to make the cry of a sheep, goat, or calf. **4** *v.* to make a sound like this.

bled (bled), *v.* past tense and past participle of **bleed:** *The cut bled for ten minutes.*

bleed (blēd), *v.* **1** to lose blood: *The cut on your leg is bleeding.* **2** to suffer wounds or death: *They fought and bled for their country.* **3** to take blood from: *Doctors used to bleed sick people as a method of treating diseases.* **4** to feel pity, sorrow, or grief: *My heart bleeds for the earthquake victims.* ❏ *v.* **bled, bleed·ing.**

bleed·er (blē′dər), *n.* person who bleeds excessively when injured, because the blood fails to clot.

blem·ish (blem′ish), **1** *n.* something that spoils beauty; defect; flaw: *A pimple is a blemish on a person's skin.* **2** *v.* to injure; mar: *Scandal blemished the mayor's good reputation.* ❏ *n., pl.* **blem·ish·es. —blem′ish·er,** *n.*

blench (blench), *v.* to draw back; shrink away; flinch.

blend (blend), **1** *v.* to mix or become mixed so thoroughly that the things mixed cannot be distinguished or separated; mix together: *Blend the butter and the sugar before adding the other ingredients of the cake.* ■ See Synonym Study at **mix. 2** *v.* to shade into each other, little by little; merge: *The colors of the rainbow blend into one another.* **3** *v.* to go well together; harmonize. **4** *n.* a mixture of several kinds: *This coffee is a blend.* **5** *n.* word made by combining two words, often with a syllable in common. EXAMPLE: *Motel* is a blend of *motor* and *hotel.* **6** *n.* two or more consonants that begin a syllable. *Sp* in *spell* and *pl* in *replace* are blends.

WORD SOURCE **Blends** were very uncommon before 1800, but many have come into English since then. In the list below, the blend at the left was formed by combining the words at the right.

BLEND	FORMED BY COMBINING	
bionics	biology	electronics
bit⁴	binary	digit
brunch	breakfast	lunch
chortle	chuckle	snort
infomercial	information	commercial
infotainment	information	entertainment
meld²	melt	weld
modem	modulator	demodulator
moped	motor	pedal
motel	motor	hotel
pennant	pennon	pendant
pulsar	pulse¹	quasar
quasar	quasi	stellar
simulcast	simultaneous	broadcast
smog	smoke	fog
squiggle	squirm	wriggle

---

blend·er (blen′dər), *n.* an electric kitchen appliance for grinding, mixing, or beating various foods.

bless (bles), *v.* **1** to make holy or sacred: *The bishop blessed the new church.* **2** to ask God's favor for: *Bless these little children.* **3** to wish good to; feel grateful to: *I bless her for her kindness.* **4** to make happy or fortunate: *I have always been blessed with good health.* **5** to praise; glorify: *to bless the Lord.* ❏ *v.* **blessed** or **blest, bless·ing.**

bless·ed (bles′id *or* blest), *adj.* **1** holy; sacred: *a blessed sacrament.* **2** happy; fortunate: *The birth of a baby is often called a blessed event.* **—bless′ed·ly,** *adv.* **—bless′ed·ness,** *n.*

bless·ing (bles′ing), *n.* **1** prayer asking God's favor; benediction: *A religious service often ends with a blessing.* **2** a wish for hap-

---

a	hat	ė	term	ô	order	ch	child		a in about
ā	age	i	it	oi	oil	ng	long		e in taken
ä	far	ī	ice	ou	out	sh	she	ə	i in pencil
â	care	o	hot	u	cup	th	thin		o in lemon
e	let	ō	open	ù	put	ŦH	then		u in circus
ē	equal	ò	saw	ü	rule	zh	measure		

piness or success: *When I left home, I received my family's blessing.* **3** anything that makes someone happy and contented; benefit: *A good temper is a great blessing.* **4** consent or approval: *The committee's proposal has my blessing.*

blest (blest), **1** *v.* a past tense and a past participle of **bless:** *He was blest with good health.* **2** *adj.* blessed.

blew (blü), *v.* past tense of **blow**². *All night long the wind blew.* ∎ Another word that sounds like this is **blue.**

blight (blīt), **1** *n.* any disease that causes plants or parts of plants to wither and die: *The apple crop was wiped out by blight.* **2** *n.* bacterium, fungus, or virus that causes such a disease. **3** *n.* anything that causes destruction or ruin: *The garbage dump is a blight on the neighborhood.* **4** *v.* to cause to wither and die: *Mildew blighted the June roses.* **5** *v.* to destroy; ruin: *Rain blighted our hopes for a picnic.*

blimp (blimp), *n.* an airship without a rigid framework. It is filled with gas that is lighter than air.

WORD STORY **Blimp** comes from "type-B limp," an early name for this kind of aircraft. Unlike dirigibles, blimps do not have stiff frames, and so they are limp until filled with gas.

blind (blīnd), **1** *adj.* not able to see: *a blind person.* **2** *v.* to make unable to see: *He was accidentally blinded in one eye.* **3** *adj.* hard to see; hidden: *Several accidents took place at that blind curve because the drivers could not see the oncoming traffic.* **4** *v.* to make temporarily unable to see: *The bright lights blinded me.* **5** *adj., adv.* without the help of sight; by means of guidance systems: *We flew blind through the storm.* **6** *adj.* without thought, judgment, or good sense: *I made a blind guess.* **7** *v.* to take away the power to understand or judge: *Her prejudices blinded her.* **8** *n.* something that keeps out light or hinders sight. A window shade or shutter is a blind. **9** *n.* anything that conceals an action or purpose: *The shop was a blind for an illegal betting ring.* **10** *adj.* with only one opening. A blind alley is a passageway closed at one end. **11** *adj.* without an opening: *a blind wall.* **12** *n.* a hiding place for a hunter. **—blind′ly,** *adv.* **—blind′ness,** *n.*
blind to, unable to understand or appreciate.

USAGE NOTE **Blind** is not the only word to describe people who cannot see or who do not see well. Some people prefer to use **visually impaired,** and it is wise to be careful. If in doubt, ask!

blind date, 1 date between two people who have not met before. **2** either of the two people.

blind·er (blīn′dər), *n.pl.* **blinders,** leather flaps on a horse's bridle to keep it from seeing sideways; blinkers.

blind·fold (blīnd′fōld′), **1** *v.* to cover the eyes of: *We blindfolded her for a game of blindman's buff.* **2** *n.* thing covering the eyes: *I put on the blindfold.*

blind·man's buff (blīnd′manz), game in which a blindfolded person tries to catch and name one of the other players. Also, **blindman's bluff.**

blinders

blind spot, a point on the retina that is not sensitive to light. The optic nerve enters the eye there.

blink (blingk), **1** *v.* to close the eyes and open them again quickly: *She blinked at the sudden light.* **2** *v.* to shut the eyes to; look with indifference; ignore: *You cannot blink at this terrible injustice.* **3** *v.* to shine with an unsteady light: *A little lantern blinked through the darkness.* **4** *n.* a sudden flash of light; gleam.
on the blink, INFORMAL. not working properly: *My radio is on the blink.*

blink·er (bling′kər), *n.* **1** a device with flashing lights used as a warning signal. **2 blinkers,** *pl.* blinders.

blintz (blints), *n.* a thin, rolled pancake filled with cheese or fruit.

blin·tze (blin′tsə), *n.* blintz.

blip (blip), *n.* a small dot of light on a radar screen, showing the location of an object within its range.

bliss (blis), *n.* great happiness; perfect joy: *What bliss it is to plunge into the cool waves on a hot day!* ∎ See Synonym Study at **joy.**

bliss·ful (blis′fəl), *adj.* very happy; joyful: *blissful memories of a summer vacation.* **—bliss′ful·ly,** *adv.*

blis·ter (blis′tər), **1** *n.* a small swelling in the skin filled with watery liquid. Blisters are often caused by burns or rubbing. *My new shoes have made blisters on my heels.* **2** *n.* a similar swelling on the surface of a plant, on metal, on painted wood, or in glass. **3** *v.* to form or cause to form blisters: *Sunburn has blistered my back.* **4** *v.* to become covered with blisters; have blisters.

blithe (blīᴛʜ or blīth), *adj.* happy and cheerful; joyful: *a blithe spirit.* ☐ *adj.* **blith·er, blith·est. —blithe′ly,** *adv.* **—blithe′ness,** *n.*

blithe·some (blīᴛʜ′səm or blīth′səm), *adj.* OLD USE. blithe.

blitz (blits), **1** *n.* a sudden, violent attack using many airplanes and tanks. **2** *n.* any sudden, violent attack. **3** *v.* to attack or overcome by a blitz. ☐ *n., pl.* **blitz·es.** [See Word Story at **blitzkrieg.**]

blitz·krieg (blits′krēg′), *n.* a sudden, rapid attack by armored forces and aircraft, which is hard to defend against.

WORD STORY **Blitzkrieg** comes from German words meaning "lightning" and "war." It is meant to be as unpredictable and quick as lightning. **Blitz** is short for blitzkrieg.

bliz·zard (bliz′ərd), *n.* a blinding snowstorm with a very strong wind and very great cold.

bloat (blōt), *v.* to swell up; puff up: *Overeating bloated their stomachs.*

blob (blob), *n.* a small, soft drop; sticky lump: *blobs of wax.*

bloc (blok), *n.* group of persons, companies, or nations combined for a purpose: *The farm bloc in Congress is a group from different political parties that favors laws to help farmers.* ∎ Another word that sounds like this is **block.**

block (blok), **1** *n.* a solid piece of wood, stone, metal, ice, etc., usually with one or more flat sides. **2** *v.* to fill up so as to prevent passage or progress: *The country roads were blocked with snow.* **3** *v.* to put things in the way of; obstruct; hinder: *Illness blocked our vacation plans.* **4** *v.* (in sports and games) to hinder an opponent's play. **5** *n.* anything or any group of persons that keeps something from being done; obstruction; hindrance: *A block in traffic kept our car from moving on. Ever since the fire, she has had a block about remembering how it began.* **6** *n.* space in a city or town enclosed by four streets; square. **7** *n.* length of one side of a block in a city or town: *Walk one block east.* **8** *n.* number of buildings close together. **9** *n.* group of things of the same kind: *We bought a block of ten tickets for a play.* **10** *n.* platform where things are put up for sale at an auction. **11** *n.* holder with a hook or eye in which a pulley or pulleys are mounted. **12** *v.* to shape with a mold: *Sweaters are sometimes blocked after washing.* ∎ Another word that sounds like this is **bloc.**
block in or **block out,** to plan or sketch roughly without filling in the details; outline: *The artist blocked in parts of a portrait. The committee blocked out its plan.*
on the block, up for sale: *A collection of paintings will go on the block at the auction.*

block·ade (blo kād′), **1** *n.* act of blocking a place by military means to control who or what goes into or out of it. **2** *v.* to put under blockade. **3** *n.* anything that blocks or obstructs. **4** *v.* to block; obstruct. ☐ *v.* **block·ad·ed, block·ad·ing. —block·ad′er,** *n.*

block·age (blok′ij), *n.* **1** something that blocks a pipe, highway, vein, artery, etc. **2** condition of being blocked.

block and tackle, combination of pulleys and ropes to lift or pull something.

block·bust·er (blok′bus′tər), *n.* **1** anything very large, forceful, or overwhelming: *Her new movie was a real blockbuster.* **2** a very destructive aerial bomb.

block·er (blok′ər), *n.* an offensive player in football whose purpose is to block any opponent who might tackle the player with the ball.

block·head (blok′hed′), *n.* a stupid person; fool.

block·house (blok′hous′), *n.* a small fort or building with small openings to shoot from. ☐ *n., pl.* **block·hous·es** (blok′hou′ziz).

Bloem·fon·tein (blüm′fon tān′), *n.* judicial capital of South Africa.

blond or **blonde** (blond), **1** *adj.* light in color: *blond hair, blond furniture.* **2** *adj.* having yellow or light brown hair and usually blue or gray eyes and fair skin. **3** *n.* person with such hair, eyes, and skin. ▪ A man or boy of this sort is usually referred to as a **blond.** A woman or girl of this sort is usually referred to as a **blonde.**

blood (blud), *n.* **1** the red liquid in the veins, arteries, and capillaries of human beings and some other animals; the red liquid that flows from a cut. Blood is pumped by the heart, carrying oxygen and digested food to all parts of the body and carrying away waste materials. **2** the liquid having the same functions in other animals. It may be colored or colorless. **3** relationship by descent from a common ancestor; family; parentage: *We are connected by blood.* **4** temper; passionate feeling or emotion: *He's nobody to fool with when his blood is up.*

curdle your blood, to frighten very much; horrify; terrify: *The piercing scream curdled my blood.*

draw blood, to inflict damage or pain.

in cold blood, without feeling; cruelly and deliberately: *a murder committed in cold blood.*

blood bank, 1 place for storage of blood to be used in transfusions. **2** the blood kept in storage.

blood-brain barrier (blud/brān/), layer of cells in the capillaries of the brain which completely or partially prevents many substances in the blood from entering brain tissue.

blood count, a count of the number of red and white blood cells in a sample of someone's blood, to see if the blood is normal.

blood·cur·dling (blud/kẻr/ling), *adj.* terrifying; horrible: *a bloodcurdling shriek.*

blood·ed (blud/id), *adj.* coming from good stock; of good breed: *a blooded stallion.*

blood group, any one of the groups into which human blood may be divided on the basis of the presence or absence of certain substances that cause red cells to clump together; blood type.

blood·hound (blud/hound/), *n.* a large, powerful dog with a keen sense of smell.

bloodhound—about 26 in. (66 cm) high at the shoulder

blood·less (blud/lis), *adj.* **1** without bloodshed: *a bloodless victory.* **2** without blood; pale: *a bloodless face.* **3** without energy; spiritless. **–blood/less·ly,** *adv.* **–blood/less·ness,** *n.*

blood·line (blud/līn/), *n.* **1** a list of someone's ancestors; family tree. **2** pedigree or family, especially of animals.

blood·mo·bile (blud/mə bēl/), *n.* a large motor vehicle with medical equipment and staff for collecting blood for transfusions.

blood money, 1 money paid to have someone killed. **2** compensation paid to the family of someone who has been killed. **3** money gained at the cost of someone else's life, freedom, welfare, etc.

blood poisoning, a diseased condition of the blood caused by germs or their poisons in the blood; septicemia.

blood pressure, pressure of the blood against the inner walls of the arteries. Blood pressure varies with exertion, excitement, health, and age.

blood·root (blud/rüt/), *n.* a North American wildflower that has a red root, red sap, and a white flower.

blood·shed (blud/shed/), *n.* the shedding of blood; slaughter: *They captured the escaped convict without bloodshed.*

blood·shot (blud/shot/), *adj.* red and inflamed from broken or swollen blood vessels: *bloodshot eyes.*

blood·stained (blud/stānd/), *adj.* stained with blood: *a bloodstained bandage.*

blood·stream (blud/strēm/), *n.* blood as it flows through the body.

blood·suck·er (blud/suk/ər), *n.* leech or other animal that sucks blood. **–blood/suck/ing,** *adj.*

blood test, examination of a sample of someone's blood, either to determine the type of blood or to diagnose illness.

blood·thirst·y (blud/thẻr/stē), *adj.* eager for bloodshed; cruel and murderous: *a bloodthirsty pirate.* **–blood/thirst/i·ly,** *adv.* **–blood/thirst/i·ness,** *n.*

blood type, blood group.

blood-type (blud/tīp/), *v.* to classify blood or people according to blood group. ❑ *v.* **blood-typed, blood-typ·ing.**

blood vessel, any tube in the body through which blood flows. Arteries, veins, and capillaries are blood vessels.

blood·y (blud/ē), **1** *adj.* covered with blood; bleeding: *He came home with a bloody nose.* **2** *adj.* accompanied by much killing: *It was a bloody battle.* **3** *v.* to cause to bleed. **4** *v.* to stain with blood: *Her knee was bloodied by her fall.* **5** *adj.* stained with blood: *The sword was bloody.* **6** *adj.* eager for bloodshed; cruel. ❑ *adj.* **blood·i·er, blood·i·est;** *v.* **blood·ied, blood·y·ing.** **–blood/i·ly,** *adv.* **–blood/i·ness,** *n.*

bloom (blüm), **1** *v.* to have flowers; open into flowers; blossom: *Many plants bloom in the spring.* **2** *n.* a flower; blossom. **3** *n.* condition or time of flowering: *violets in bloom.* **4** *n.* condition or time of greatest health, vigor, or beauty: *in the bloom of youth.* **5** *v.* to be in the condition or time of greatest health, vigor, or beauty; flourish: *children blooming with youth.* **6** *n.* glow of health and beauty. **7** *n.* the powdery coating on some fruits and leaves. There is a bloom on grapes and plums. **–bloom/er,** *n.*

bloom·ers (blü/mərz), *n.pl.* **1** loose trousers, gathered at the knee or ankle, formerly worn by women and girls for physical training. **2** (earlier) underwear like these trousers.

WORD STORY **Bloomers** were named for Amelia J. Bloomer, an American magazine publisher. During the 1800s, she urged women to wear such trousers to increase their freedom to move about.

Bloom·ing·ton (blü/ming tən), *n.* city in SE Minnesota.

bloop (blüp), in baseball: **1** *v.* to hit as a blooper. **2** *n.* blooper.

bloop·er (blü/pər), *n.* **1** INFORMAL. a foolish mistake; goof; blunder. **2** (in baseball) a fly ball that goes just beyond the infield.

blos·som (blos/əm), **1** *n.* flower, especially of a plant that produces fruit: *apple blossoms.* **2** *n.* condition or time of flowering: *The cherry trees are in blossom.* **3** *v.* to have flowers; open into flowers: *All the orchards blossom in spring.* **4** *v.* to open out; develop: *The shy child blossomed into an outgoing teenager.*

blot (blot), **1** *n.* a spot of ink or stain of any kind. ▪ See Synonym Study at **stain.** **2** *v.* to make blots on; stain; spot: *My pen slipped and blotted the paper.* **3** *v.* to dry something written in ink with absorbent paper: *He wrote with a fountain pen, and was careful to blot each page.* **4** *n.* blemish; disgrace: *The field of rusting cars was a blot on the landscape.* ❑ *v.* **blot·ted, blot·ting.**

blot out, 1 to cover up entirely; hide: *I blotted out the mistake with ink.* **2** to wipe out; destroy: *When the dam broke, a village was blotted out by the violently rushing waters.*

blotch (bloch), **1** *n.* a large, irregular spot or stain. **2** *n.* place where the skin is red or broken out: *Too much sun can cause blotches on the skin.* **3** *v.* to cover or mark with spots or stains. ❑ *n., pl.* **blotch·es.**

blotch·y (bloch/ē), *adj.* having blotches. ❑ *adj.* **blotch·i·er, blotch·i·est.**

blot·ter (blot/ər), *n.* **1** piece of blotting paper. **2** book for recording happenings or transactions. A police station blotter is a record of arrests.

a	hat	ė	term	ô	order	ch	child		a in about
ā	age	i	it	oi	oil	ng	long		e in taken
ä	far	ī	ice	ou	out	sh	she	ə	i in pencil
â	care	o	hot	u	cup	th	thin		o in lemon
e	let	ō	open	ů	put	ŦH	then		u in circus
ē	equal	ò	saw	ü	rule	zh	measure		

blotting paper, a soft paper used to dry writing by soaking up ink.

blouse (blous), *n.* **1** a loose upper garment worn by women and children as a part of their outer clothing. **2** a loosely fitting garment for the upper part of the body: *The sailor wore a wool blouse as a part of his uniform.* **3** a short, fitted coat worn as part of a military uniform.

blowhole

blow[1] (blō), *n.* **1** a hard hit; knock; stroke: *strike a blow with the fist, strike a blow with a hammer.* **2** a sudden happening that causes misfortune or loss; severe shock: *His mother's death was a great blow to him.* **3** a sudden attack or assault: *The army struck a swift blow at the enemy.*

at one blow, by one act or effort.

come to blows, to start fighting.

SYNONYM STUDY **Blow**[1] and **stroke**[1] both mean a sudden hard hit. **Blow** suggests force and heaviness: *With a mighty blow, the boxer knocked out his opponent.* **Stroke** suggests an accurate or unexpected hit: *A stroke of lightning damaged the tree.*

blow[2] (blō), **1** *v.* to send forth a strong current of air: *Blow on the fire or it will go out.* **2** *v.* to move in a current; move rapidly or with power: *The wind blew in gusts.* **3** *v.* to drive or carry by a current of air: *The wind blew the curtain open.* **4** *v.* to force a current of air into, through, or against: *The bellows blew the coals into flames.* **5** *v.* to empty or clear by forcing air through: *He sneezed twice, then blew his nose.* **6** *v.* to form or shape by air; swell with air: *blow glass, blow bubbles.* **7** *v.* to make a sound by a current of air or steam: *The whistle blows at noon.* **8** *v.* to break by an explosion: *The dynamite blew the wall to bits.* **9** *v.* to melt: *The short circuit caused the fuse to blow.* **10** *n.* act of blowing. **11** *n.* gale of wind: *Last night's big blow brought down several trees.* **12** *v.* to expose; reveal: *The spy's alias was blown.* **13** *v.* to spout water in the air: *"There she blows!" was the sailor's cry when he spotted the whale.* **14** *v.* INFORMAL. to spoil; ruin; lose; do or get wrong: *The umpire blew the call at second base, and then our team blew its chance to win the game.* ❑ *v.* **blew, blown, blow·ing.**

blow in, INFORMAL. to arrive: *What time did you blow in last night?*

blow into, INFORMAL. to arrive at a place: *We blew into Reno at noon.*

blow it, INFORMAL. be unsuccessful; do wrong; fail: *The team was winning until they blew it in the last quarter by fumbling twice.*

blow out, 1 to put out or be put out by a current of air: *I blew out the candle. The candle blew out.* **2** to have or cause a blowout in: *The worn tire blew out.*

blow over, 1 to pass by or over: *The storm has blown over.* **2** be forgotten: *In time the scandal blew over.*

blow up, 1 to explode: *The ammunition ship blew up and sank.* **2** to fill with air: *blow up a bicycle tire.* **3** to become very angry: *I blew up at my sister for leaving our room in a mess.* **4** to become stronger; arise: *A storm blew up suddenly.* **5** to enlarge a photograph or image.

blow your stack or **blow your top,** INFORMAL. to become extremely angry; lose your temper.

blow-dry (blō′drī′), **1** *v.* to dry hair with a blow dryer. **2** *adj.* prepared with or dried by a blow dryer: *a blow-dry haircut.* ❑ *v.* **blow-dried, blow-dry·ing.**

blow dryer, an electric hair dryer that dries the hair by a directed jet of warm air.

blow·er (blō′ər), *n.* **1** person or thing that blows: *a glass blower.* **2** fan or other machine for forcing air into a building, furnace, mine, or other enclosed area.

blow·fly (blō′flī′), *n.* any of various two-winged flies that lay their eggs on meat or in wounds. ❑ *n., pl.* **blow·flies.**

blow·gun (blō′gun′), *n.* tube through which a person blows something, such as darts or dried beans; blowpipe.

blow·hard (blō′härd′), *n.* INFORMAL. a noisy boaster; bragger.

blow·hole (blō′hōl′), *n.* hole for breathing, in the top of the head of a whale, porpoise, or dolphin.

blown (blōn), *v.* past participle of **blow**[2]: *My hat was blown away by the wind.*

blow·out (blō′out′), *n.* **1** the bursting of a tire. **2** a sudden or violent escape of air, steam, or the like. **3** INFORMAL. a large, impressive party or banquet. **4** SLANG. (in sports) a loss by a large difference in scores: *It was a close game at halftime, but it turned into a blowout by the end.*

blow·pipe (blō′pīp′), *n.* **1** tube for blowing air or gas into a flame to increase the heat. **2** blowgun.

blow·torch (blō′tôrch′), *n.* a small torch that shoots out a very hot flame under pressure. A blowtorch is used to melt metal and burn off paint. ❑ *n., pl.* **blow·torch·es.**

blow·up (blō′up′), *n.* **1** explosion. **2** outburst of anger. **3** an enlargement of a photograph.

blow·y (blō′ē), *adj.* windy: *a blowy autumn day.* ❑ *adj.* **blow·i·er, blow·i·est.**

blowz·y (blou′zē), *adj.* lacking neatness; untidy. ❑ *adj.* **blowz·i·er, blowz·i·est.** —**blowz′i·ly,** *adv.* —**blowz′i·ness,** *n.*

BLT, bacon, lettuce, and tomato sandwich.

blub·ber (blub′ər), **1** *n.* fat of whales and some other sea animals. The oil obtained from whale blubber was formerly burned in lamps. **2** *v.* to weep noisily.

bludg·eon (bluj′ən), **1** *n.* a short, heavy club. **2** *v.* to strike with a bludgeon. **3** *v.* to bully or threaten.

blue (blü), **1** *n.* the color of the clear sky in daylight. **2** *adj.* having this color. **3** *n.* something having this color. **4** *n.* **the blue, a** the sky. **b** the sea. **5** *adj.* having a dull bluish color; livid: *Her hands were blue from cold.* **6** *adj.* sad; gloomy; discouraged: *She felt blue when her best friend moved away.* See also **blues.** **7** *v.* to use bluing on. ❑ *adj.* **blu·er, blu·est;** *v.* **blued, blu·ing** or **blue·ing.** ■ Another word that sounds like this is **blew.** —**blue′ness,** *n.*

out of the blue, completely unexpectedly: *His visit came out of the blue.*

blue baby, infant born with a bluish skin, indicating a shortage of oxygen in the blood, caused by a defective heart.

blue·bell (blü′bel′), *n.* any plant with blue bell-shaped flowers.

blue·ber·ry (blü′ber′ē), *n.* any of several similar small, sweet blue berries growing on various related bushes. They are good to eat. ❑ *n., pl.* **blue·ber·ries.**

blue·bird (blü′bėrd′), *n.* any of three small songbirds of North America, related to the robin. The males have bright blue backs, wings, and tails, and males of two kinds have reddish breasts.

blue blood, aristocrat.

blue-blood·ed (blü′blud′id), *adj.* aristocratic.

blue·bon·net (blü′bon′it), *n.* a prairie plant with bright blue flowers resembling hats.

blue·bot·tle (blü′bot′l), *n.* a large blowfly with a blue abdomen and a hairy body.

blue cheese, a cheese made from cow's milk, with blue mold allowed to grow in it. The mold gives the cheese a strong flavor.

blue-col·lar (blü′kol′ər), *adj.* of or about industrial or factory work or workers.

blue·fish (blü′fish′), *n.* a saltwater food fish, bluish or greenish above and silvery below, of the Atlantic coast of the Americas. ❑ *n., pl.* **blue·fish** or **blue·fish·es.**

blue flag, kind of iris with blue flowers.

blue·grass (blü′gras′), *n.* **1** a kind of grass with blue-green stems. It is valuable as food for horses and cattle and is used for lawns. **2** any related grass. **3** a kind of country music, usually played on unamplified stringed instruments, especially the fiddle and banjo. ❑ *n., pl.* **blue·grass·es** for 2.

blue-green algae (blü′grēn′), tiny living things that are like algae but are now considered to be bacteria. Large numbers of them form a blue-green layer on rocks or water.

blue jay, a North American bird with a crest and a blue tail.

blue jay—about 1 ft.
(30 cm) long

blue jeans, jeans, usually made of blue denim.

blue law, any very strict law regulating personal conduct. Laws prohibiting entertainment on Sunday are blue laws.

blue line, (in hockey) either of two lines located 30 feet from the red line, one on each side.

blue·print (blü′print′), *n.* **1** a photographic print that shows white outlines on a blue background. The process of making blueprints is used to copy original drawings of building plans, maps, etc. **2** a detailed plan for doing anything.

blue ribbon, the first prize; highest honor: *That sheep won a blue ribbon for best entry in its class at the fair.*

Blue Ridge, a range of the Appalachian Mountains, extending from NW Maryland to N Georgia.

blues (blüz), **1** *n.* a slow, melancholy song with jazz rhythm. **2** *n.pl.* **the blues,** low spirits: *Rainy days give me the blues.*

blu·et (blü′it), *n.* a small plant of North America, with pale blue flowers.

blue whale, a blue-gray whale with yellowish underparts, sometimes growing to be 100 feet (30 meters) in length. It is the largest living animal.

bluff¹ (bluf), **1** *n.* a high, steep slope or cliff. **2** *adj.* abrupt, frank, and hearty in manner. **–bluff′ly,** *adv.* **–bluff′ness,** *n.*

bluff² (bluf), **1** *v.* to fool or mislead, especially by pretending confidence: *She bluffed the robbers by convincing them that the police were on the way.* ■ See Synonym Study at **pretend. 2** *n.* something said or done to fool or mislead others in this way. Pretending to have better cards in a card game than you actually have is a bluff. **–bluff′er,** *n.*

call someone's bluff, to ask for proof or for action when pretense is suspected.

blu·ing (blü′ing), *n.* a blue liquid or powder put in the rinse water when doing laundry. It keeps white fabric from turning yellow.

blu·ish (blü′ish), *adj.* somewhat blue.

blun·der (blun′dər), **1** *n.* a stupid mistake: *Misspelling the title of a book is a silly blunder to make in a book report.* ■ See Synonym Study at **mistake. 2** *v.* to make a stupid mistake: *Someone blundered in sending you to the wrong address.* **3** *v.* to move clumsily or blindly; stumble: *I blundered through the dark house.* **–blun′der·er,** *n.* **–blun′der·ing·ly,** *adv.*

blun·der·buss (blun′dər bus), *n.* a short gun with a wide muzzle and large bore, formerly used to shoot at very close range. ❑ *n., pl.* **blun·der·buss·es.**

blunt (blunt), **1** *adj.* without a sharp edge or point; dull: *He sharpened the blunt knife.* **2** *v.* to make less sharp; make less keen: *Cutting wire blunted my scissors. A cold blunted my sense of smell.* **3** *adj.* saying what you think very frankly, without trying to be polite; outspoken: *When I asked if she liked my vase, her blunt answer was "No."* ■ See Synonym Studies at **rude** and **frank**¹. **–blunt′ly,** *adv.* **–blunt′ness,** *n.*

blur (blėr), **1** *v.* to make less clear in form or outline: *Mist blurred the hills.* **2** *v.* to dim: *Tears blurred my eyes. My eyes blurred with tears.* **3** *n.* thing seen dimly or indistinctly: *When I don't have my glasses on, your face is just a blur.* **4** *v.* to smear; smudge: *You blurred the picture by touching it before the paint was dry.* **5** *n.* a smear; smudge: *The old letter had many blurs.* ❑ *v.* **blurred, blur·ring.**

blurb (blėrb), *n.* advertisement or description, usually on the jacket of a book, album, etc., full of high praise. [**Blurb** is one of the few words that someone simply made up. Gelett Burgess, an American humorist, coined this word in 1907.]

blur·ry (blėr′ē), *adj.* **1** dim; indistinct: *The blurry outline of the tall building could barely be seen through the fog.* **2** full of smears and smudges. ❑ *adj.* **blur·ri·er, blur·ri·est. –blur′ri·ness,** *n.*

blurt (blėrt), *v.* to say suddenly or without thinking: *In my excitement I blurted out the secret.*

blush (blush), **1** *v.* to become red in the face because of shame, confusion, or excitement: *The boy blushed when we laughed at his mistake.* **2** *n.* a reddening of the face caused by shame, confusion, or excitement. **3** *v.* to be ashamed: *I blushed at my sister's bad table manners.* **4** *n.* a rosy color: *The blush of dawn showed in the east.* **5** *v.* to be or become red or rosy. ❑ *n., pl.* **blush·es.**

at first blush, on first glance; at first thought: *At first blush, I thought the job would be easy.*

blush·er (blush′ər), *n.* **1** a pink or rosy cosmetic used to give color to the face. **2** person who blushes readily.

blus·ter (blus′tər), **1** *v.* to storm noisily; blow violently: *The wind blustered around the corner of the house.* **2** *n.* stormy noise and violence: *We heard the bluster of the wind and rain.* **3** *v.* to talk noisily and violently: *They were very excited and angry, and blustered for a while.* **4** *n.* noisy and violent talk with empty threats or protests: *angry bluster.* **–blus′ter·er,** *n.*

blus·ter·y (blus′tər ē), *adj.* blustering.

blvd., boulevard.

Bly (blī), *n.* **Nel·lie** (nel′ē), 1867?-1922, American journalist. ■ Nellie Bly wrote newspaper stories exposing the conditions inside prisons and mental hospitals, but she is most famous for traveling around the world in 72 days, six hours, and 11 minutes, beating the hero of Jules Verne's novel *Around the World in Eighty Days.*

boa constrictor (bō′ə), a large nonpoisonous snake of the tropical parts of America, growing up to 15 feet (4.5 meters) long. It kills animals for food by squeezing them to death.

boar (bôr), *n.* **1** a male pig or hog. **2** wild boar. ❑ *n., pl.* **boars** or **boar.** ■ Another word that sounds like this is **bore.**

board (bôrd), **1** *n.* a broad, thin piece of wood for use in building, etc.: *We used boards 10 inches wide, 1 inch thick, and 3 feet long for shelves in our new bookcase.* **2** *v.* to cover with boards: *We board up the windows of our summer cottage in the fall.* **3** *n.* a flat piece of wood or other material used for one special purpose: *an ironing board, a drawing board.* **4** *n.* group of persons related to something; council: *a school board, a board of directors.* **5** *v.* to get on a ship, train, bus, airplane, etc.: *We board the school bus at the corner.* **6** *n.* meals provided for pay: *The cost of going away to college includes room and board.* **7** *v.* to get meals, or room and meals, for pay: *When she was at college, my sister boarded with a family in town.* **8** *n.* (in basketball) backboard. **9** *n.pl.* **boards,** the low wooden fence around the edge of a hockey rink.

board (def. 5)

on board, on a ship, train, bus, airplane, etc.: *When everybody was on board, the ship sailed.*

board·er (bôr′dər), *n.* person who pays for meals, or for room and meals, at another's house. ■ Another word that sounds like this is **border.**

board foot, unit of measure equal to a board one foot square and one inch thick; 144 cubic inches. It is used for measuring logs and lumber.

board·ing (bôr′ding), *n.* **1** boards. **2** CANADIAN. (in hockey) illegally checking an opponent into the boards surrounding the rink.

a	hat	ė	term	ô	order	ch	child		
ā	age	i	it	oi	oil	ng	long		a in about
ä	far	ī	ice	ou	out	sh	she		e in taken
â	care	o	hot	u	cup	th	thin	ə {	i in pencil
e	let	ō	open	ů	put	ŧH	then		o in lemon
ē	equal	ò	saw	ü	rule	zh	measure		u in circus

board·ing·house (bôr′ding hous′), *n.* house where meals, or room and meals, are provided for pay. ❑ *n., pl.* **board·ing·hous·es** (bôr′ding hou′ziz).

boarding school, school with buildings where the pupils live during the school term.

board·sail·ing (bôrd′sā′ling), *n.* the sport of riding a sailboard; windsurfing.

boardsailing

board·walk (bôrd′wȯk′), *n.* a wide sidewalk usually made of boards, along the beach at a shore resort.

boast (bōst), **1** *v.* to speak too highly of yourself or what you own; brag: *He boasts about his grades.* **2** *n.* statement speaking too highly of yourself or what you own; bragging words: *I don't believe her boast that she can run faster than I can.* **3** *n.* something to be proud of: *The town's boast is its outstanding school system.* **4** *v.* to have something to be proud of: *Our town boasts many fine parks.* —**boast′er,** *n.* —**boast′ing·ly,** *adv.*

SYNONYM STUDY **Boast** and **brag** both mean to praise yourself. **Boast** is a somewhat formal word, suggesting controlled pride: *The governor boasts of the state's good schools.* **Brag** suggests open pride and exaggerated praise for yourself: *She brags that she is stronger than anyone else in sixth grade.*

boast·ful (bōst′fəl), *adj.* fond of bragging; boasting: *It is hard to listen very long to a boastful person.* ■ See Synonym Study at **proud.** —**boast′ful·ly,** *adv.* —**boast′ful·ness,** *n.*

boat (bōt), **1** *n.* a small, open vessel for traveling on water, such as a motorboat or a rowboat. **2** *n.* a large vessel, such as a freighter, passenger liner, or oil tanker; ship. **3** *v.* to go in a boat. **4** *n.* dish shaped somewhat like a boat for gravy or sauce.
in the same boat, in the same position or condition; taking the same chances.
miss the boat, INFORMAL. to lose an opportunity.
rock the boat, INFORMAL. to disturb or upset an accepted situation or arrangement: *If the mayor doesn't rock the boat by raising taxes, his supporters will vote for him again.*

boat·house (bōt′hous′), *n.* house or shed for sheltering a boat or boats. ❑ *n., pl.* **boat·hous·es** (bōt′hou′ziz).

boat·ing (bō′ting), *n.* act or sport of going by boat, as in rowing or sailing.

boat·man (bōt′mən), *n.* person who rents out, operates, works on, or takes care of boats. ❑ *n., pl.* **boat·men.**

boat people, refugees who flee by boat, often by small fishing boats, to any country that will allow them to enter.

boat·swain (bō′sn), *n.* a ship's officer in charge of the anchors, ropes, and rigging. Also, **bo's'n** or **bosun.**

bob[1] (bob), **1** *v.* to move up and down, or to and fro, with short, quick motions: *The pigeon bobbed its head as it picked up crumbs.* **2** *n.* a short, quick motion up and down, or to and fro. ❑ *v.* **bobbed, bob·bing.**
bob up, to appear suddenly or unexpectedly.

bob[2] (bob), **1** *n.* a child's or woman's haircut that is fairly short all around the head. **2** *v.* to cut hair short. **3** *n.* plumb bob; plumb. **4** *n.* a float for a fishing line. ❑ *v.* **bobbed, bob·bing.**

bob[3] (bob), *n.* BRITISH SLANG. shilling. ❑ *n., pl.* **bob.**

bob·bin (bob′ən), *n.* reel or spool for holding thread, yarn, etc. Bobbins are used in spinning, weaving, machine sewing, and making lace.

bob·ble (bob′əl), *v.* to fumble a ball. ❑ *v.* **bob·bled, bob·bling.**

bob·by (bob′ē), *n.* BRITISH INFORMAL. policeman. ❑ *n., pl.* **bob·bies.** [**Bobby** comes from the nickname of Sir Robert Peel, who founded the London police force in the early 1800s.]

bobby pin, a metal hairpin whose prongs close on and hold tightly to the hair.

bob·by·socks or **bob·by·sox** (bob′ē soks′), *n.pl.* socks reaching just above the ankle, worn especially by girls.

bob·cat (bob′kat′), *n.* a small, fierce cat of North America, having a reddish brown coat with black spots.

bob·o·link (bob′ə lingk), *n.* a North American songbird that lives in fields and meadows. In summer, the male is black with white on its head, back, and wings.

bob·sled (bob′sled′), **1** *n.* a long sled with two sets of runners and a continuous seat. It has a steering wheel and brakes. **2** *v.* to ride or coast on a bobsled. ❑ *v.* **bob·sled·ded, bob·sled·ding.** —**bob′sled′der,** *n.*

bobsled

bob·tail (bob′tāl′), **1** *n.* a short tail, or a tail cut short. **2** *n.* horse or dog with its tail cut short. **3** *adj.* having such a tail.

bob·white (bob′wit′), *n.* a North American quail with brown and white feathers. Its name imitates the sound of its call.

bode[1] (bōd), *v.* to be a sign of; indicate beforehand; foreshadow: *The rumble of thunder boded rain.* ❑ *v.* **bod·ed, bod·ing.**
bode ill, be a bad sign: *The dark clouds boded ill for our picnic.*
bode well, be a good sign: *The good weather bodes well for our trip to the zoo.*

bode[2] (bōd), *v.* a past tense of **bide.**

bo·de·ga (bō dā′gə), *n.* a grocery store in a Spanish-speaking neighborhood. ❑ *n., pl.* **bo·de·gas.** [See Word Story at **apothecary.**]

bod·i·less (bod′ē lis), *adj.* without a body; not having material form: *Spirits are bodiless.*

bod·i·ly (bod′l ē), **1** *adj.* of the body; in the body: *bodily pain.* **2** *adv.* in person: *She cannot be with us bodily, but is here in spirit.* **3** *adv.* as a whole; altogether; entirely: *The audience rose bodily to cheer the great pianist.*

bod·kin (bod′kən), *n.* **1** a large, blunt needle. **2** a pointed tool for making holes.

bod·y (bod′ē), *n.* **1** the whole physical structure of a person or animal: *I exercise to keep my body strong and healthy.* **2** the main part or trunk of an animal, apart from the head, limbs, or tail. **3** the main or central part of anything, such as the hull of a ship or the part of a vehicle that holds the passengers or the load. **4** group of persons or things: *The student body of our school gathered for an assembly.* **5** a dead person or animal; corpse. **6** portion of matter; mass: *A lake is a body of water. The moon, the sun, and the stars are heavenly bodies.* **7** substance; density: *Pea soup has more body than chicken broth.* ❑ *n., pl.* **bod·ies.**

bod·y·build·er (bod′ē bil′dər), *n.* person who develops muscles through exercise and weightlifting.

bod·y·build·ing (bod′ē bil′ding), *n.* developing muscles through exercise and weightlifting.

body check, (in hockey or lacrosse) the bumping of a player to block or hinder him or her. **–body-check,** v.

bod·y·guard (bod′ē gärd′), n. person or group of persons who guards someone: *A bodyguard accompanies the President at all public appearances.*

body language, way a person moves and stands and the expression on a person's face, which give clues to what a person is thinking and feeling.

body stocking, a lightweight, tight-fitting, one-piece undergarment for women that covers most of the body.

Boer (bôr), **1** n. person of Dutch descent living in South Africa. **2** adj. of or about the Boers.

bog (bog), **1** n. area of soft, wet, spongy ground; marsh; swamp. **2** v. **bog down,** to make little or no progress; become unable to proceed: *I am bogged down with my homework.* ❏ v. **bogged, bog·ging.**

Bo·gart (bō′gärt), n. **Hum·phrey** (hum′frē), 1899-1957, American actor. ■ **Humphrey Bogart** played detectives, gangsters, and adventure heroes in such movies as *Casablanca* and *The African Queen.*

bo·gey (bō′gē or bug′ē for 1; bō′gē for 2), n. **1** score of one stroke over par for any hole on a golf course. **2** bogy. ❏ n., pl. **bo·geys.**

bo·gey·man (bō′gē man′ or bug′ē man′), n. a frightening imaginary monster. ❏ n., pl. **bo·gey·men.**

bog·gle (bog′əl), v. **1** to hold back; hesitate: *My parents boggled at my request for a pet snake.* **2** to overwhelm or be overwhelmed with wonder, shock, etc.: *The vastness of the universe boggles the imagination.* ❏ v. **bog·gled, bog·gling.**

bog·gy (bog′ē), adj. soft and wet like a bog; marshy; swampy: *boggy ground.* ❏ adj. **bog·gi·er, bog·gi·est.**

bo·gie (bō′gē or bug′ē), n. bogy.

Bo·go·tá (bō′gə tä′), n. capital of Colombia, in the central part.

bo·gus (bō′gəs), adj. not genuine; counterfeit; sham: *a bogus $10 bill.*

bo·gy (bō′gē or bug′ē), n. person or thing, usually imaginary, that is feared without reason; bugbear; bugaboo. ❏ n., pl. **bo·gies.** Also, **bogey** or **bogie.**

Bo·he·mi·a (bō hē′mē ə), n. former country in central Europe, now a region of the Czech Republic.

Bo·he·mi·an (bō hē′mē ən), **1** adj. of Bohemia, its people, or their language. **2** n. person born or living in Bohemia. **3** n. language of Bohemia; Czech. **4** Also, **bohemian, a** adj. carefree and unconventional. **b** n. artist, writer, etc., who lives an unconventional, carefree sort of life.

Bohr (bôr), n. **Niels** (nēls), 1885-1962, Danish physicist. ■ **Niels Bohr** won the Nobel Prize in physics in 1922 for his work on the structure of the atom. His son, **Aage** (ô′gə) **Neils Bohr,** born 1922, shared a Nobel Prize in physics in 1975.

boil[1] (boil), **1** v. to bubble up and give off steam or vapor: *Water at sea level boils when heated to 212 degrees Fahrenheit or 100 degrees Celsius.* **2** v. to cause a liquid to boil by heating it: *Boil some water for tea.* **3** v. to cook by boiling: *We boil eggs four minutes.* **4** v. to have its contents boil: *The pot is boiling.* **5** v. to be very excited; be stirred up: *I boiled with anger.* **6** n. a boiling condition: *Bring the water to a boil.*

boil down, 1 to make less by boiling: *Boil down the sauce to half the amount.* **2** to shorten by getting rid of unimportant parts: *The notes for her report were so long that the teacher asked her to boil them down.*

boil over, 1 to come to the boiling point and overflow: *While I was answering the telephone, the soup boiled over.* **2** be unable to control anger: *I boiled over when someone took my bicycle without asking me first.*

boil[2] (boil), n. a painful, red swelling on the skin, formed by pus around a hard core. Boils are often caused by infection.

boil·er (boi′lər), n. **1** tank for making steam to heat buildings or drive engines. **2** tank for heating and holding hot water. **3** container for heating liquids.

boiling point, temperature at which a liquid boils. The boiling point of water at sea level is 212 degrees Fahrenheit or 100 degrees Celsius.

Boi·se (boi′sē), n. capital of Idaho, in the SW part.

bois·ter·ous (boi′stər əs), adj. **1** noisily cheerful: *The room was filled with boisterous laughter.* **2** rough and noisy: *a boisterous child.* **–bois′ter·ous·ly,** adv. **–bois′ter·ous·ness,** n.

bo·la (bō′lə), n. weapon made of stone or metal balls tied at the ends of long cords. South American cowboys throw it so that it winds around and entangles the animal aimed at. ❏ n., pl. **bo·las.**

bold (bōld), adj. **1** without fear; brave: *Lancelot was a bold knight.* **2** showing or requiring courage: *A circus lion tamer must be bold and fearless.* **3** too free in manner; impudent: *The bold child made faces at us as we passed.* **4** sharp and clear to the eye; striking: *The mountains stood in bold outline against the sky.* **–bold′ly,** adv. **–bold′ness,** n.

bold·face (bōld′fās′), n. a heavy printing type that stands out clearly. **This sentence is in boldface.**

bole (bōl), n. stem or trunk of a tree. ■ Other words that sound like this are **boll** and **bowl.**

bo·ler·o (bə ler′ō), n. **1** a lively Spanish dance in ¾ time. **2** music for it. **3** a short, loose jacket coming barely to the waist. ❏ n., pl. **bo·ler·os.**

Bo·leyn (bù lin′), n. **Anne,** 1507-1536, English queen, second wife of Henry VIII, mother of Elizabeth I. She was beheaded for adultery.

Bo·lí·var (bō lē′vär or bō′lə vär), n. **Si·món** (sē mōn′), 1783-1830, Venezuelan general and politician. ■ **Simón Bolívar** led revolts against Spanish rule in South America. Bolivia is named after him.

Simón Bolívar

Bo·liv·i·a (bə liv′ē ə), n. country in W South America. *Capitals:* La Paz and Sucre. **–Bo·liv′i·an,** adj., n.

boll (bōl), n. the rounded seed pod of a plant, especially of cotton or flax. ■ Other words that sound like this are **bole** and **bowl.**

boll weevil, a small North American beetle that does great damage to the cotton crop by eating young bolls.

bo·lo (bō′lō), n. a long, heavy knife, used in the Philippines. ❏ n., pl. **bo·los.**

Bo·lo·gna (bə lō′nē or bə lō′nə), n. a large sausage usually made of beef, veal, and pork. ❏ n., pl. **bo·lo·gnas.**

Bo·lo·gna (bə lō′nyə), n. city in N Italy.

Bol·she·vik (bōl′shə vik), **1** n. member of a radical political party in Russia that seized power in November 1917. The Bolsheviks became the Communist Party in 1918. **2** n. member of any Communist Party. **3** adj. of the Bolsheviks or Bolshevism. **4** Also, **bolshevik, a** n. any extreme radical. **b** adj. very radical.

Bol·she·vism (bōl′shə viz′əm), n. **1** doctrines and methods of the Bolsheviks. **2** Also, **bolshevism,** extreme radicalism.

Bol·she·vist or **bol·she·vist** (bōl′shə vist), n., adj. Bolshevik.

bol·ster (bōl′stər), **1** n. a long pillow or cushion for a couch or bed. **2** v. to keep from falling; support; prop: *The walls of the church are bolstered with buttresses. Her encouragement bolstered my confidence.* **–bol′ster·er,** n.

bolt (bōlt), **1** n. a metal rod with a head at one end and a screw thread for a nut at the other. Bolts are used to fasten things together or hold something in place. **2** n. bar slid or dropped into a bracket to lock a door, gate, etc. **3** n. part of a lock moved by a key. **4** v. to fasten with a bolt: *Bolt the doors.* **5** n. a short arrow with a thick head. Bolts are shot from crossbows. **6** n. flash of lightning. **7** n. a sudden start; a running away: *When the rabbit saw us, it made a bolt for safety.* **8** v. to dash off; run away: *The*

a	hat	ė	term	ô	order	ch	child		
ā	age	i	it	oi	oil	ng	long		a in about
ä	far	ī	ice	ou	out	sh	she		e in taken
â	care	o	hot	u	cup	th	thin	ə {	i in pencil
e	let	ō	open	u̇	put	ᴛʜ	then		o in lemon
ē	equal	ȯ	saw	ü	rule	zh	measure		u in circus

horse bolted at the sight of the car. **9** *v.* to break away from your party or its candidates. **10** *n.* roll of cloth or wallpaper. **11** *v.* to swallow food quickly without chewing: *The dog bolted its food.*

bolt upright, stiff and straight: *A noise in the middle of the night made me sit bolt upright in bed.*

> **WORD STORY** Bolt comes from an old English word meaning "arrow." This is still one of its meanings (def. 5). Arrows for crossbows are short, strong rods somewhat like the bolt of a door.

bomb (bom), **1** *n.* container filled with an explosive; bombshell. A bomb is set off by a fuse, a timing device, or by the force with which it hits something. **2** *n.* a similar device filled with gas, smoke, or other material: *a tear gas bomb.* **3** *v.* to attack with bombs; hurl bombs at; drop bombs on. **4** *n.* INFORMAL. a failure; flop. **5** *v.* INFORMAL. Also, **bomb out,** to fail; flop: *The movie bombed.*

> **WORD STORY** Bomb comes from a Greek word meaning "a booming sound." That word was probably created to sound like the noise it named. **Boom**[1] is another word created to sound like that noise. When a bomb explodes, the boom is the first thing you notice.

bom·bard (bom bärd′), *v.* **1** to attack with bombs or heavy artillery fire from big guns: *The artillery bombarded the enemy all day.* **2** to keep attacking forcefully: *The lawyer bombarded the witness with one question after another.* **3** to strike the nucleus of an atom with a stream of fast-moving particles to change the structure of the nucleus.

bom·bar·dier (bom′bər dir′), *n.* member of the crew of a bomber who aims and releases the bombs over a target.

bom·bard·ment (bom bärd′mənt), *n.* **1** an attack with bombs or with heavy artillery fire. **2** any vigorous attack. **3** the process of striking the nucleus of an atom with a stream of fast-moving particles.

bom·bas·tic (bom bas′tik), *adj.* using many showy or high-flown words with too little thought: *The speaker used bombastic language to cover up almost total ignorance of the subject.* —**bom·bas′ti·cal·ly,** *adv.*

> **WORD STORY** Bombastic comes from a Greek word meaning "cotton." From the idea of stuffing something with cotton came the idea of padding language with long, fancy words.

Bom·bay (bom bā′), *n.* port in W India, on the Arabian Sea.

bomb bay, compartment in the fuselage of a bomber in which bombs are carried and from which they are dropped.

bomb·er (bom′ər), *n.* airplane used to drop bombs on enemy troops, factories, cities, etc.

bomb·proof (bom′prüf′), *adj.* strong enough to be safe from the effects of bombs and shells.

bomb·shell (bom′shel′), *n.* **1** bomb (def. 1). **2** a sudden, unexpected happening; disturbing surprise: *The news of his accident was a bombshell to the family.*

bomb·sight (bom′sīt′), *n.* device in a combat aircraft for determining when to release a bomb so that it will hit a target.

bo·na fide (bō′nə fīd′ *or* bō′nə fī′dē), in good faith; without make-believe or fraud; genuine: *a bona fide offer.*

bo·nan·za (bə nan′zə), *n.* **1** a rich mass of ore in a mine. **2** any rich source of profit: *Their farm turned out to be a bonanza when they sold it for a housing development.* □ *n., pl.* **bo·nan·zas.**

Bo·na·parte (bō′nə pärt), *n.* Napoleon. See **Napoleon I.**

bon·bon (bon′bon′), *n.* piece of candy, usually soft and often having a fancy shape.

bond (bond), **1** *n.* anything that ties, binds, or unites: *a bond of affection.* **2** *n.pl.* **bonds,** chains; shackles: *the bonds of slavery.* **3** *n.* certificate issued by a government or private company which promises to pay back with interest the money borrowed from the buyer of the certificate: *The city issued bonds to raise money for new parks.* **4** *n.* a written agreement by which a person agrees to pay a certain sum of money if he or she does not perform certain duties properly. **5** *v.* to agree to pay a certain sum of money if a person does not perform certain duties properly: *An insurance company has bonded the city treasurer for one million dollars.* **6** *v.* to bind together. **7** *n.* (in chemistry) an amount of force holding atoms or groups of atoms together. —**bond′a·ble,** *adj.* —**bond′er,** *n.*

bond·age (bon′dij), *n.* condition of being held against your will under the control or influence of some person or thing; lack of freedom; slavery.

bond·man (bond′mən), *n.* **1** (in the Middle Ages) a man who belonged with the land and was sold with it; serf. **2** man who has been enslaved. □ *n., pl.* **bond·men.**

bonds·man (bondz′mən), *n.* **1** person who becomes responsible for another by giving a bond. **2** bondman. □ *n., pl.* **bonds·men.**

bond·wom·an (bond′wum′ən), *n.* **1** (in the Middle Ages) a woman who belonged with the land and was sold with it; serf. **2** woman who has been enslaved. □ *n., pl.* **bond·wom·en.**

bone (bōn), **1** *n.* one of the pieces of the skeleton of an animal: *the bones of the hand, a beef bone for soup.* **2** *v.* to take bones out of: *I boned the fish before eating it.* **3** *n.* the hard substance of which bones are made. □ *v.* **boned, bon·ing.** —**bone′like′,** *adj.*

make no bones about, to show no hesitation about; acknowledge readily: *The tired children made no bones about wanting to go home.*

bone-dry (bōn′drī′), *adj.* very dry.

bone·less (bōn′lis), *adj.* **1** without bones. **2** without courage; cowardly.

bone marrow, the soft tissue that fills the hollow central part of most bones; marrow. Bone marrow produces both the red and the white blood cells.

bon·fire (bon′fīr′), *n.* a large fire built outdoors. [Bonfire comes from *bone-fire,* a fire to burn dead bodies. Such a fire had to be very large and therefore had to burn outside.]

bon·go (bong′gō), *n.* a small drum played with flattened hands, especially in Latin-American and African music. Bongos usually come in pairs and are held between the knees. □ *n., pl.* **bon·gos** or **bon·goes.**

bongo drum, bongo.

bo·ni·to (bə nē′tō), *n.* any of several large saltwater fishes related to mackerel. □ *n., pl.* **bo·ni·to, bo·ni·tos,** or **bo·ni·toes.**

Bonn (bon), *n.* city in W Germany, on the Rhine.

bon·net (bon′it), *n.* **1** a covering for the head usually tied under the chin with strings or ribbons, worn by women and children. **2** cap worn by men and boys in Scotland. **3** headdress of feathers worn by North American Indians.

bon·ny or **bon·nie** (bon′ē), *adj.* fair to see; rosy and pretty: *a bonny baby.* □ *adj.* **bon·ni·er, bon·ni·est.** —**bon′ni·ness,** *n.*

bo·no·bo (bə nō′bō), *n.* an ape of tropical Africa, closely related to chimpanzees but somewhat smaller and more slender; pygmy chimpanzee. □ *n., pl.* **bo·no·bos.**

bonsai (def. 1)

bon·sai (bon′sī), *n.* **1** a tree, kept very small by limiting its root area and its food supply, used for decoration. **2** the art of growing very small plants in this way. □ *n., pl.* **bon·sais** for 1.

bon·spiel (bon′spēl′), *n.* a curling tournament.

bo·nus (bō′nəs), *n.* something extra, given in addition to what is due: *The company gave each worker a vacation bonus.* □ *n., pl.* **bo·nus·es.**

> **WORD FAMILY** Bonus and the words below are related. They all come from a Latin word meaning "good."
>
> | bona fide | bonny | bounteous | bounty |
> |---|---|---|---|
> | bonanza | bon voyage | bountiful | debonaire |
> | bonbon | boon[2] | | |

bon vo·yage (bon′ voi äzh′ *or* bon′ vwä yäzh′), good-by; good luck; pleasant trip.

bon·y (bō′nē), *adj.* **1** of bone. **2** like bone. **3** full of bones: *bony fish.* **4** having big bones that stick out; very thin: *bony hands.* ❑ *adj.* **bon·i·er, bon·i·est. −bon′i·ness,** *n.*

boo (bü), **1** *interj., n.* sound made to show dislike or to frighten: *Boos came from those who didn't like the concert.* **2** *v.* to make such a sound; shout "boo" at: *He sang so badly that the audience booed him.* ❑ *n., pl.* **boos;** *v.* **booed, boo·ing.**

boob (büb), *n.* SLANG. a stupid person; fool; dunce.

boo-boo (bü′bü′), *n.* INFORMAL. a foolish mistake. ❑ *n., pl.* **boo·boos.**

boob tube, SLANG. a TV set.

boo·by (bü′bē), *n.* **1** a stupid person; dunce. **2** any of several kinds of large tropical seabirds. Some have brightly colored feet. ❑ *n., pl.* **boo·bies.**

booby (def. 2)—about 2 ft. (61 cm) long

booby prize, prize given to the person or team that does the worst in a game or contest.

booby trap, 1 bomb arranged to explode when a harmless-looking object to which it is attached is touched or moved. **2** trick arranged to annoy some unsuspecting person.

boo·by-trap (bü′bē trap′), *v.* to catch with or in a booby trap. ❑ *v.* **boo·by-trapped, boo·by-trap·ping.**

boog·ie (bủg′ē), **1** *n.* a lively dance, with rapid, rhythmic movements, to the accompaniment of rock'n'roll music. **2** *v.* to dance the boogie. ❑ *v.* **boog·ied, boog·ie·ing.**

boog·ie-woog·ie (bủg′ē wủg′ē), *n.* form of blues music played especially on the piano. Boogie-woogie has a repeating bass pattern and a varied melody.

boo-hoo (bü′hü′), **1** *v.* to weep or sob loudly. **2** *n.* a loud sob. ❑ *v.* **boo·hooed, boo·hoo·ing;** *n., pl.* **boo·hoos.**

book (bủk), **1** *n.* a written or printed work of considerable length, especially on sheets of paper bound together between covers: *She read that book to me.* **2** *n.* blank sheets bound together: *You can keep a record of what you spend in this book.* **3** *n.* a main division of a book: *Genesis is the first book of the Bible.* **4** *n.* something fastened together like a book: *a book of matches.* **5** *n.* **the Book,** the Bible. **6** *v.* to make reservations to get tickets or to engage service: *He booked two tickets to Los Angeles.* **7** *v.* to enter a charge against someone in a police record: *An officer booked the suspect at the police station.* **−book′like,** *adj.*

by the book, by rule; accurately: *She didn't play by the book.*

keep books, to keep a record of business accounts: *An accountant keeps books for the grocer.*

like a book, with fullness or accuracy; completely: *We are best friends; we know each other like a book.*

book·case (bủk′kās′), *n.* piece of furniture with shelves for holding books.

book club, a company that regularly supplies selected books to subscribers, usually at a reduced rate.

book·end (bủk′end′), *n.* a prop or support placed at the end of a row of books to hold them upright.

book·ie (bủk′ē), *n.* bookmaker.

book·ish (bủk′ish), *adj.* **1** fond of reading or studying; studious: *The bookish boy spent many hours in the library.* **2** knowing books better than real life: *The scholar was a bookish man who did not know the world of business.* **3** stiffly dignified or formal; scholarly in a dull and narrow way: *Her conversation was filled with bookish phrases.* **−book′ish·ly,** *adv.* **−book′ish·ness,** *n.*

book·keep·er (bủk′kē′pər), *n.* person who keeps a record of business accounts.

book·keep·ing (bủk′kē′ping), *n.* work of keeping a record of business accounts.

book·let (bủk′lit), *n.* a little book, often with paper covers.

book·mak·er (bủk′mā′kər), *n.* person whose business is taking bets on horse races or other contests.

book·mark (bủk′märk′), *n.* strip of cloth, paper, etc., put between the pages of a book to mark the reader's place.

book·mo·bile (bủk′mə bēl′), *n.* bus or truck that serves as a traveling branch of a library.

book·sell·er (bủk′sel′ər), *n.* person whose business is selling books.

book·shelf (bủk′shelf′), *n.* shelf for holding books. ❑ *n., pl.* **book·shelves.**

book·store (bủk′stôr′), *n.* store where books are sold.

book·worm (bủk′wėrm′), *n.* **1** person who is very fond of reading and studying. **2** any insect larva that eats the bindings or pages of books.

Bool·e·an algebra (bü′lē ən), a mathematical system dealing with the relationships between sets, used to solve problems in logic, data processing, etc.

boom[1] (büm), **1** *n.* a deep hollow sound like the roar of cannon or of big waves: *The big bell tolled with a loud boom.* **2** *v.* to make a deep hollow sound: *The big man's voice boomed out above the rest.* **3** *n.* a sudden activity and increase in business, prices, or values of property; rapid growth: *Our town is having such a boom that it is likely to double its size in two years.* **4** *v.* to increase suddenly in activity; grow rapidly: *Business is booming.* [See Word Story at **bomb.**]

boom[2] (büm), *n.* **1** a long pole or beam, used to extend the bottom of a sail. **2** the lifting and guiding pole of a derrick. **3** a long metal arm for holding and guiding a microphone while filming movies or TV shows. **4** chain, cable, or line of timbers that keeps logs from floating away.

boom box, SLANG. a large portable radio and cassette player combination.

boo·me·rang (bü′mə rang′), **1** *n.* a curved piece of wood, used as a weapon by the original people of Australia. Certain boomerangs can be thrown so that they return to the thrower. **2** *n.* anything that recoils or reacts to harm the doer or user. **3** *v.* to act as a boomerang: *His scheme to win boomeranged and they lost.*

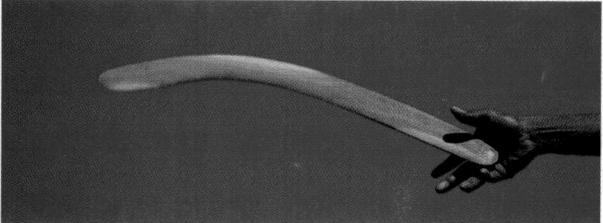

boomerang (def. 1)

boom·town (büm′toun′), *n.* town that has grown up suddenly, usually as a result of an increase in economic activity.

boon[1] (bün), *n.* **1** a great benefit; blessing: *Those warm boots were a boon to me in the cold weather.* **2** something asked for or granted as a favor.

boon[2] (bün), *adj.* jolly; cheerful; merry: *boon companions.*

boon·docks (bün′doks′), *n.pl.* **1** area outside or distant from a city, thought of as lacking culture and excitement. **2** a rough backwoods area.

WORD STORY **Boondocks** comes from a word in Tagalog, a language of the Philippines, meaning "mountain." The mountains of the Philippines are thickly forested and have few villages.

boon·dog·gle (bün′dog′əl), **1** *n.* useless work, done to keep busy or be paid. **2** *v.* to do useless work. **3** *n.* a project or activity organized to create useless work: *The committee is a boondoggle for friends of the mayor.* ❑ *v.* **boon·dog·gled, boon·dog·gling.**

Boone (bün), *n.* **Daniel,** 1734-1820, American frontiersman who explored Kentucky. ■ **Daniel Boone** left Kentucky and went to Missouri when he was 65 years old. He felt that Kentucky had become too crowded and he wanted more "elbow room."

a	hat	ė	term	ô	order	ch	child		
ā	age	i	it	oi	oil	ng	long		a in about
ä	far	ī	ice	ou	out	sh	she		e in taken
â	care	o	hot	u	cup	th	thin	ə	i in pencil
e	let	ō	open	ủ	put	ŦH	then		o in lemon
ē	equal	ò	saw	ü	rule	zh	measure		u in circus

Boones·bor·ough (bünz′ber′ō), *n.* former settlement in central Kentucky. It was the site of a fort founded in 1775 by Daniel Boone.

boon·ies (bü′nēz), *n.pl.* INFORMAL. boondocks.

boor (bur), *n.* a rude person.

boor·ish (bur′ish), *adj.* having bad manners; rude. **—boor′ish·ly,** *adv.* **—boor′ish·ness,** *n.*

boost (büst), **1** *n.* a push or shove that helps someone up or over something: *Give me a boost over the fence.* **2** *v.* to lift or push from below: *Her friend boosted her to the lowest branch of a peach tree.* **3** *v.* to help by speaking well of: *The manufacturers are boosting the new cereal in a series of TV ads.* ▪ See Synonym Study at **promote. 4** *n.* an increase in degree, amount, price, pay, etc.: *a boost in food prices.* **5** *v.* to raise; increase: *The supermarket has boosted its prices.*

boost·er (bü′stər), *n.* **1** person or thing that boosts. **2** rocket or engine that provides part of the thrust to a spacecraft, missile, etc., especially at the first stage of liftoff. **3** a booster shot. **4** any of various devices for increasing the power of an electric circuit.

booster shot, an additional inoculation of a vaccine to continue the effectiveness of a previous inoculation.

booster (def. 2)

boot[1] (büt), **1** *n.* a leather or rubber covering for the foot and lower part of the leg. **2** *v.* to put boots on; supply with boots: *The horseback rider was booted and spurred.* **3** *n.* a kick: *He gave the ball a boot.* **4** *v.* to give a kick to: *She booted the ball.* **5** *n.* **the boot,** INFORMAL. a discharge from a job or position; dismissal: *He got the boot for being late every day.* **6** *n.* BRITISH. an automobile trunk.

boot[2] (büt), *n.* **to boot,** in addition; besides: *For my knife she gave me a compass and a dime to boot.*

boot[3] (büt), *v.* to put into operation by means of a computer program that instructs the computer to load other programs or information: *boot a computer, boot a disk.*

boot·black (büt′blak′), *n.* person whose work is shining shoes and boots.

boot camp, camp at which U.S. Coast Guard, Marine Corps, or Navy recruits are trained.

boot·ee (bü′tē), *n.* a baby's soft shoe, often knitted. ❑ *n., pl.* **boot·ees.** ▪ Another word that sounds like this is **booty.**

booth (büth), *n.* **1** a covered stall or similar place where goods are sold or shown at a fair, market, convention, etc. **2** a small, enclosed place for a telephone, movie projector, etc. **3** a small, enclosed place for voting at elections. **4** a partly enclosed space in a restaurant or café, containing a table and seats for a few persons. ❑ *n., pl.* **booths** (büтнz *or* büths).

Booth (büth), *n.* **1** **John Wilkes** (wilks), 1838-1865, American actor who assassinated President Lincoln. ▪ **John Wilkes Booth** shot Lincoln in Ford's Theatre in Washington, D.C. on April 14, 1865. He escaped, but was caught and killed days later. **2 William,** 1829-1912, English clergyman who founded the Salvation Army.

boot·leg (büt′leg′), **1** *v.* to sell, transport, or make unlawfully: *Some people were bootlegging cigarettes into the state to avoid paying a tax.* **2** *adj.* sold, transported, or made unlawfully. ❑ *v.* **boot·legged, boot·leg·ging. —boot′leg′ger,** *n.*

boot·less (büt′lis), *adj.* of no benefit or profit; useless.

boo·ty (bü′tē), *n.* **1** things taken from the enemy in war. **2** things seized by violence and robbery; plunder: *The pirates fought over how to divide the booty from the captured ship.* ▪ Another word that sounds like this is **bootee.**

booze (büz), INFORMAL. **1** *n.* any intoxicating liquor. **2** *v.* to drink a lot of intoxicating liquor. ❑ *v.* **boozed, booz·ing. —booz′er,** *n.*

bop[1] (bop), INFORMAL. **1** *n.* a blow or punch with the hand, a club, etc. **2** *v.* to hit; punch; strike. ❑ *v.* **bopped, bop·ping.**

bop[2] (bop), *v.* INFORMAL. to move, go, or dance in a quick, spirited way: *bopped around the neighborhood all morning, bopping to the song on the radio.* ❑ *v.* **bopped, bop·ping.**

Bo·phu·tha·tswa·na (bō pü′tä tswä′nä), *n.* former part of South Africa. Now a self-governing homeland, it is recognized as an independent country by South Africa, but not by any other country. *Capital:* Mmabatho.

bo·rax (bôr′aks), *n.* a white, crystalline powder used as an antiseptic, as a cleansing substance, in fusing metals, and in making heat-resistant glass.

Bor·deaux (bôr dō′), *n.* **1** port in SW France. **2** a red or white wine made near Bordeaux.

bor·der (bôr′dər), **1** *n.* the side, edge, or boundary of anything, or the part near it: *We pitched our tent on the border of the lake.* ▪ See Synonym Study at **edge. 2** *v.* to form a boundary to; bound: *The Rio Grande borders part of Texas.* **3** *n.* line which separates one country, state, or province from another; frontier: *We crossed the border between France and Germany.* **4** *n.* a strip on the edge of anything for strength or ornament: *The front walk had a border of flowers.*

border (def. 4)

5 *v.* to put a border on; edge: *We bordered our lawn with flowering bushes.* ▪ Another word that sounds like this is **boarder.**

border on or **border upon, 1** to touch at the border; be next to: *Canada borders on the United States.* **2** be close to; resemble: *Such silly behavior borders on the ridiculous.*

bor·der·land (bôr′dər land′), *n.* **1** land forming, or next to, a border. **2** an uncertain range, extent, or region: *the borderland between sleeping and waking.*

bor·der·line (bôr′dər lin′), **1** *n.* a dividing line; boundary. **2** *adj.* on a border or boundary. **3** *adj.* in between; uncertain: *a borderline case of pneumonia.*

bore[1] (bôr), **1** *v.* to make a hole by means of a revolving tool: *Bore through the handle of this brush so we can hang it up.* **2** *v.* to make a hole, passage, etc., by digging, chewing, or pushing: *A mole has bored its way under the hedge.* **3** *n.* hole made by a revolving tool. **4** *n.* the hollow space inside a pipe, tube, or gun barrel. **5** *n.* the distance across the inside of a hole or tube: *The bore of this pipe is two inches.* ❑ *v.* **bored, bor·ing.** ▪ Another word that sounds like this is **boar.**

bore[2] (bôr), **1** *v.* to make weary by being uninteresting: *This book bores me, so I shall not finish it.* **2** *n.* a dull, tiresome person or thing: *It is a bore to have to wash dishes three times a day.* ❑ *v.* **bored, bor·ing.** ▪ Another word that sounds like this is **boar.**

bore[3] (bôr), *v.* past tense of **bear**[1]: *She bore her loss bravely.* ▪ Another word that sounds like this is **boar.**

bore·dom (bôr′dəm), *n.* a bored condition; weariness caused by uninteresting people or events.

bor·er (bôr′ər), *n.* **1** any insect or worm that bores into wood, fruit, etc. **2** tool for boring holes.

Bor·ges (bôr′hās), *n.* **Jor·ge Lu·is** (hôr′hä lü ēs′), 1899-1986, Argentine writer, known especially for his short stories.

bo·ric acid (bôr′ik), a white, crystalline substance used as a mild antiseptic.

bor·ing (bôr′ing), *adj.* not interesting; dull; tiresome. ▪ See Synonym Study at **dull.**

born (bôrn), **1** *adj.* brought into life; brought forth: *a recently born calf.* **2** *adj.* by birth; by nature: *a born athlete.* **3** *v.* a past participle of **bear**[1]: *He was born on December 30, 1960.* ▪ See Usage Note at **borne.** ▪ Other words that sound like this are **borne** and **bourn.**

be born again, to have a spiritual experience that gives you a new spiritual life.

born-a·gain (bôrn′ə gen′), *adj.* having been born again: *a born-again Christian.*

borne (bôrn), *v.* a past participle of **bear**[1]: *I have borne the pack for three miles. She has borne three children.* ▪ Other words that sound like this are **born** and **bourn**.

USAGE NOTE The past participle of **bear**[1] is spelled **born** only when used in the passive about birth: *They were born last year. I was born in July.* It is spelled **borne** for all other meanings.

Bor·ne·o (bôr′nē ō), *n.* large island in the East Indies, between Java and the Philippines. Borneo is divided among Brunei, Malaysia, and Indonesia.

bo·ron (bôr′on), *n.* a nonmetallic element which occurs only in borax and other compounds. Boron is used in alloys, nuclear reactors, etc. *Symbol:* B

bor·ough (bėr′ō), *n.* **1** an incorporated town with certain privileges, smaller than a city. **2** one of the five divisions of New York City. **3** a district in Alaska similar to a county. ▪ Other words that can sound like this are **burro** and **burrow**.

bor·row (bor′ō), *v.* **1** to get something from another person with the understanding that it must be returned: *I borrowed his book.* **2** to take and use as your own; adopt; take: *The English word for the vegetable "squash" was borrowed from a Native American word.* **3** regroup (def. 2). **—bor′row·er,** *n.*

borscht (bôrsht), *n.* a Russian soup made of meat juice, cabbage, and onions, colored red with beet juice, served with sour cream.

bor·zoi (bôr′zoi), *n.* a tall, slender, swift dog with silky hair; Russian wolfhound. ❑ *n., pl.* **bor·zois.**

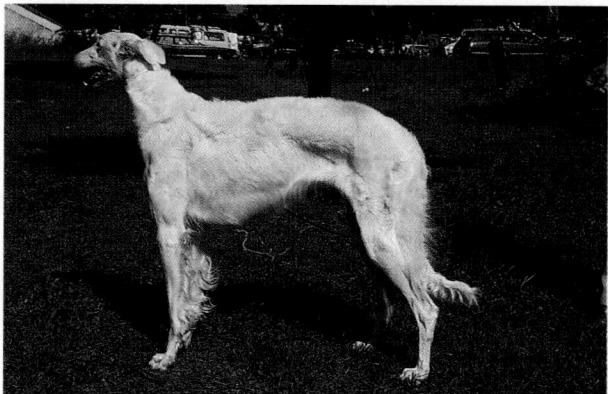
borzoi—about 30 in. (76 cm) high at the shoulder

bosh (bosh), *n., interj.* INFORMAL. nonsense: *She thought the new theories were bosh. "Bosh," he said, when asked for an opinion.*

WORD STORY **Bosh** comes from a Turkish word meaning "empty" or "worthless." At first, people used it about anything worthless. Then it came to mean "empty words" or "nonsense."

bo's'n (bō′sn), *n.* boatswain.

Bos·ni·a and Her·ze·go·vi·na (boz′nē ə and hėr′tsə gə vē′nə), country in SE Europe. *Capital:* Sarajevo.

bos·om (bùz′əm), **1** *n.* the upper, front part of the human body; breast. **2** *n.* part of a garment that covers the bosom: *the bosom of a dress.* **3** *n.* heart or feelings: *He kept the secret in his bosom.* **4** *n.* center or inmost part: *in the bosom of your family.* **5** *adj.* close and trusted: *bosom friends.*

Bos·por·us (bos′pər əs), *n.* strait connecting the Black Sea and the Sea of Marmara. See **Dardanelles** for map.

boss[1] (bòs), **1** *n.* person who hires workers or tells them what to do; foreman; manager. **2** *n.* person who controls a political organization. **3** *v.* to be the boss of; direct; control: *He complained that you were trying to boss him.* ❑ *n., pl.* **boss·es.**

WORD STORY **Boss**[1] comes from a Dutch word meaning "master." Originally, the Dutch word meant "uncle." People often hope their boss will treat them like one of the family. They are often disappointed.

boss[2] (bòs), **1** *n.* a raised ornament on a flat surface. **2** *v.* to decorate with ornamental nails, knobs, or studs. ❑ *n., pl.* **boss·es.**

boss·y (bò′sē), *adj.* fond of telling others what to do and how to do it. ❑ *adj.* **boss·i·er, boss·i·est.**

Bos·ton (bò′stən), *n.* port and capital of Massachusetts. **—Bos·to·ni·an** (bò stō′nē ən), *n.*

Boston Massacre, the killing of six Boston citizens in 1770 by British troops sent to keep order at a demonstration. Two British soldiers were tried, found guilty, and discharged from the army.

bo·sun (bō′sn), *n.* boatswain.

bo·tan·ic (bə tan′ik), *adj.* botanical.

bo·tan·i·cal (bə tan′ə kəl), *adj.* **1** of plants and plant life. **2** of botany. **—bo·tan′i·cal·ly,** *adv.*

botanical garden

botanical garden, garden where many kinds of plants are grown, for public display and for scientific study.

bot·a·nist (bot′n ist), *n.* an expert in botany.

bot·a·ny (bot′n ē), *n.* science of plants; study of plants and plant life. Botany deals with the structure, growth, classification, diseases, etc., of plants.

botch (boch), **1** *v.* to spoil by poor work; bungle: *I botched my math test.* **2** *n.* a poor piece of work. ❑ *n., pl.* **botch·es.**

both (bōth), **1** *adj.* the two; the one and the other: *Both houses are white.* **2** *pron.* the two together: *Both belong to her.* **3** *adv., conj.* together; alike; equally: *He sings and dances both at once. He is both strong and healthy.*

both·er (boŦH′ər), **1** *n.* much fuss or worry about small matters; trouble: *What a lot of bother about nothing!* **2** *v.* concern yourself; make an effort or take time: *Don't bother about my breakfast; I'll eat later.* **3** *n.* person or thing that causes worry, fuss, or trouble: *A door that will not shut is a bother.* **4** *v.* to annoy; irritate: *Hot weather bothers me.*

both·er·some (boŦH′ər səm), *adj.* causing worry or fuss; troublesome: *Losing the car keys was bothersome.*

Bot·swa·na (bot swä′nə), *n.* country in S Africa. *Capital:* Gaborone.

bot·tle (bot′l), **1** *n.* container for holding liquids, made of glass or plastic. Bottles often have narrow necks fitted with caps or stoppers. **2** *n.* amount that a bottle can hold: *We drank a bottle of ginger ale at lunch.* **3** *v.* to put into bottles: *Wine makers bottle wine for sale.* ❑ *v.* **bot·tled, bot·tling. —bot′tler,** *n.*

bottle up, to hold in; keep back; control: *I managed to bottle up my anger.*

WORD STORY **Bottle** comes from a Latin word meaning "barrel." People used that word to mean any container of wine, and gradually bottles of wine became more common than barrels of wine.

bot·tle·neck (bot′l nek′), *n.* person, thing, or condition that hinders progress: *The bridge was a bottleneck during heavy traffic.*

bot·tle-nosed dolphin (bot′l nōzd′), any of several kinds of dolphin with snouts shaped somewhat like a bottle, including the kind most often seen in captivity.

a	hat	ė	term	ô	order	ch	child	ə {	a in about
ā	age	i	it	oi	oil	ng	long		e in taken
ä	far	ī	ice	ou	out	sh	she		i in pencil
â	care	o	hot	u	cup	th	thin		o in lemon
e	let	ō	open	ù	put	ŦH	then		u in circus
ē	equal	ò	saw	ü	rule	zh	measure		

bot·tom (bot′əm), **1** *n.* the lowest part: *These berries at the bottom of the basket are crushed.* **2** *n.* part on which anything rests; base: *The bottom of that glass is wet.* **3** *n.* ground under water: *Many wrecks lie at the bottom of the sea.* **4** *n.* **bottoms, a** *pl.* pajama trousers. **b** *sing.* the low land along a river: *The bottoms has rich soil.* **5** *n.* seat: *This chair needs a new bottom.* **6** *n.* basis; foundation; origin: *We will get to the bottom of the mystery.* **7** *n.* keel or hull of a ship. **8** *adj.* lowest or last: *I see a robin on the bottom branch of that tree.* **9** *n.* the buttocks. **10** *n.* (in baseball) the second half of an inning.

bottom out, to reach a low point and then level off: *The stock market bottomed out yesterday.*

bot·tom·less (bot′əm lis), *adj.* **1** without a bottom. **2** so deep that the bottom cannot be reached; extremely deep: *the bottomless depths of the sea.*

bottom line, 1 the most important point or points; the deciding factor or factors: *The bottom line in choosing a school is a good education.* **2** the final decision. **3** the last line in an earnings report, which shows total profit.

bot·u·lism (boch′ə liz′əm), *n.* poisoning caused by certain bacteria sometimes present in foods not properly canned or preserved.

bou·doir (bü′dwär), *n.* a lady's private bedroom, dressing room, or sitting room.

WORD STORY Boudoir comes from a French word meaning "a place to sulk in." In former times, when a lady was not happy, she often went to her private room to be alone.

bouf·fant (bü fänt′), *adj.* puffed out: *a bouffant hairdo.*

bough (bou), *n.* one of the main branches of a tree. ■ Other words that sound like this are **bow**[1] and **bow**[3].

bought (bôt), *v.* past tense and past participle of **buy:** *We bought apples at the market. I have bought a new pen.*

bouil·la·baisse (bü′lyə bäs′), *n.* a fish chowder highly seasoned with white wine, saffron, herbs, etc.

bouil·lon (bul′yon), *n.* a clear, thin soup or broth.

boul·der (bōl′dər), *n.* a large rock, rounded or worn by the action of water and weather. [**Boulder** comes from a Scandinavian word meaning "rumbling noise." If a stone is large enough, water flowing past it makes noise.]

Boulder Dam, Hoover Dam.

boul·e·vard (bul′ə värd), *n.* **1** a broad street or avenue, often planted with trees. **2** (especially in Canada) a narrow strip of grass between a sidewalk and a paved street.

bounce (bouns), **1** *v.* to spring into the air like a ball: *The baby likes to bounce up and down on the bed.* **2** *v.* to cause to bounce: *Bounce the ball to me.* **3** *n.* act of springing back; bound: *I caught the ball on the first bounce.* **4** *n.* energy; spirit: *I was sick, but now I have my old bounce back.* **5** *v.* (of a check) to be returned uncashed by the bank on which it was drawn due to lack of funds in the account of the person who signed it. **6** *v.* INFORMAL. to throw out; eject. ❑ *v.* **bounced, bounc·ing.**

bounce back, to return to enthusiasm or vigor.

bounc·er (boun′sər), *n.* **1** person hired by a nightclub or bar to throw out disorderly persons. **2** anything that bounces.

bounc·ing (boun′sing), *adj.* **1** that bounces: *a bouncing ball.* **2** vigorous; healthy: *a bouncing baby.* **—bounc′ing·ly,** *adv.*

bounc·y (boun′sē), *adj.* **1** lively; eager: *She was bouncy and full of life.* **2** bouncing back; springy: *He walks with a bouncy step.* ❑ *adj.* **bounc·i·er, bounc·i·est.**

bound[1] (bound), **1** *adj.* under some obligation; obliged: *I feel bound by my promise.* **2** *adj.* certain; sure: *Everyone is bound to make a mistake sooner or later.* **3** *adj.* with your mind firmly made up; determined; resolved: *He was bound to go, though we tried to stop him.* **4** *v.* past tense and past participle of **bind:** *I bound the package with string.* **5** *adj.* put in a cover: *bound books.*

bound up with, closely connected with: *The price of meat is bound up with the price of feed. Her success is bound up with that of the play.*

bound[2] (bound), **1** *v.* to spring back; bounce: *The ball bounded from the wall.* **2** *n.* act of springing back; bounce: *I caught the ball on the first bound.* **3** *v.* to leap or spring lightly along; jump: *Mountain goats can bound from rock to rock.* **4** *n.* act of leaping or springing lightly along; jump: *With one bound the deer went into the woods.*

bound[3] (bound), *v.* to form the boundary of; limit: *Canada bounds the United States on the north.*

out of bounds, outside the area allowed by rules, custom, or law: *I kicked the ball out of bounds. The attic closet is out of bounds at Christmastime.*

bound[4] (bound), *adj.* on the way; going: *I am bound for home.*

bound·ar·y (boun′dər ē), *n.* a limiting line or thing; limit; border: *Lake Superior forms part of the boundary between Canada and the United States.* ❑ *n., pl.* **bound·ar·ies.**

bound·en (boun′dən), *adj.* required: *It is our bounden duty as citizens to obey the laws.*

bound·less (bound′lis), *adj.* **1** not limited; infinite: *Outer space is boundless.* **2** vast: *the boundless ocean. She has boundless energy.* **—bound′less·ly,** *adv.* **—bound′less·ness,** *n.*

bounds (boundz), *n.pl.* **1** limits; control; restraint: *Keep your hopes within bounds.* **2** area included within boundaries.

boun·te·ous (boun′tē əs), *adj.* **1** given freely; generous: *The rich man gave bounteous gifts to the poor.* **2** plentiful; abundant: *a bounteous crop.* **—boun′te·ous·ly,** *adv.* **—boun′te·ous·ness,** *n.*

boun·ti·ful (boun′tə fəl), *adj.* **1** giving freely; generous: *the help of bountiful friends.* **2** more than enough; plentiful; abundant: *We put in so many plants that we have a bountiful supply of tomatoes.* **—boun′ti·ful·ly,** *adv.* **—boun′ti·ful·ness,** *n.*

boun·ty (boun′tē), *n.* **1** whatever is given freely; generous gift. **2** generosity in bestowing gifts and favors: *the bounty of nature.* **3** reward; premium: *The state government used to give a bounty for killing coyotes.* ❑ *n., pl.* **boun·ties** for 1,3.

bou·quet (bō kā′ *or* bü kā′), *n.* **1** bunch of flowers. **2** fragrance; aroma: *the bouquet of a wine.*

bour·bon (bėr′bən), *n.* kind of whiskey, distilled from a fermented grain mash containing at least 51 percent corn.

Bour·bon (bur′bən), *n.* member of the royal family that ruled France from 1589 to 1792, and from 1814 to 1848. The Bourbons also ruled in Spain, Naples, and Sicily.

bour·geois (bur zhwä′), **1** *n.* person of the middle class, such as a merchant or professional person. **2** *adj.* of the middle class. **3** *adj.* like the middle class in way of thinking, appearance, etc.; ordinary: *bourgeois taste.* ❑ *n., pl.* **bour·geois.**

bour·geoi·sie (bur′zhwä zē′), *n.* the middle class; people between the very wealthy class and the working class.

Bourke-White (bėrk′ wīt′), *n.* **Mar·ga·ret** (mär′gə rit), 1906-1971, American photographer. ■ Margaret Bourke-White photographed machines, factories, combat in World War II, German concentration-camp prisoners, and workers in South Africa.

Bourke-White photograph

bourn or **bourne** (bôrn), *n.* OLD USE. **1** boundary; limit. **2** goal. ■ Other words that sound like this are **born** and **borne**.

bout (bout), *n.* **1** trial of strength; contest: *Those are the two boxers who will appear in the main bout.* **2** period spent in some particular way; spell: *I have just had a long bout of illness.*

bou·tique (bü tēk′), *n.* a small shop that specializes in stylish clothes and accessories, especially for women. [See Word Story at **apothecary**.]

bou·ton·niere (büt′n ir′ *or* büt′n yer′), *n.* flower or flowers worn in a buttonhole.

bo·vine (bō′vīn), **1** *n.* ox or cow. **2** *adj.* like an ox or cow; without emotion; dull: *a bovine nature.* **3** *n.* any animal that chews the cud, including domestic cattle, bison, water buffaloes, and the like. **4** *adj.* belonging to this group.

bow¹ (bou), **1** *v.* to bend the head or body in greeting, respect, worship, or obedience: *The people bowed before the queen. Let us bow our heads in prayer.* **2** *n.* act of bending the head or body in this way: *The men made a bow to the queen.* **3** *v.* to show by bowing: *The actors bowed their thanks at the end of the play.* **4** *v.* to cause to stoop; bend: *The old man was bowed by age.* **5** *v.* to give in; yield: *She bowed to her parents' wishes.* ■ Another word that sounds like this is **bough.**

bow out, to withdraw: *When her mother became so ill, she bowed out of the mayoral race.*

take a bow, to accept praise or applause for something done.

bow² (bō), **1** *n.* weapon for shooting arrows. A bow usually consists of a strip of flexible wood bent by a string. **2** *n.* a slender rod with horsehairs stretched on it, for playing a violin, cello, etc. **3** *v.* to play a violin, cello, etc., with a bow. **4** *v.* to curve; bend. **5** *n.* something curved; curved part: *A rainbow is a bow.* **6** *n.* a looped knot: *The gift had a bow on top.* ■ Another word that sounds like this is **beau.** **–bow′like′,** *adj.*

bow³ (bou), *n.* the forward part of a ship, boat, or aircraft. ■ Another word that sounds like this is **bough.**

bow·el (bou′əl), *n.* **1** part of the bowels; intestine. **2** bowels, *pl.* **a** the tube in the body into which food passes from the stomach; intestines. **b** the inner part of anything: *Miners dig for coal in the bowels of the earth.*

bow·er (bou′ər), *n.* **1** shelter of leafy branches. **2** arbor.

bow·ie knife (bō′ē *or* bü′ē), a long, single-edged hunting knife carried in a sheath.

WORD STORY The **bowie knife** is named for Colonel James Bowie, an American pioneer who is believed to have designed it. Bowie made this kind of knife widely known.

bowl¹ (bōl), *n.* **1** a hollow, rounded dish, usually without handles: *Cake batter was in the mixing bowl.* **2** amount that a bowl can hold: *a bowl of soup.* **3** the hollow, rounded part of anything: *The bowl of a pipe holds the tobacco.* **4** structure shaped somewhat like a bowl: *The college holds football games in its bowl.* **5** a special football game played when the season is over: *the Orange Bowl.* ■ Other words that sound like this are **bole** and **boll.** **–bowl′like′,** *adj.*

bowl² (bōl), *v.* **1** to play the game of bowling or lawn bowling. **2** to roll or throw the ball in bowling: *First Jeff bowls, then you, and I go last.* **3** to roll or move along rapidly and smoothly: *The new bus bowled along on the highway.* ■ Other words that sound like this are **bole** and **boll.**

bowl over, 1 to knock over: *The force of the wind nearly bowled me over.* **2** to make helpless and confused: *I was bowled over by the bad news.*

bow·leg·ged (bō′leg′id), *adj.* having the legs curved outward: *a bowlegged cowboy.*

bowl·er (bō′lər), *n.* **1** person who bowls. **2** BRITISH. a derby hat.

bow·line (bō′lən *or* bō′lin), *n.* knot used to tie a loop that does not slip.

bowl·ing (bō′ling), *n.* game played indoors, in which balls are rolled down an alley at bottle-shaped wooden pins; tenpins.

bowling alley, 1 a long, narrow lane for rolling the balls in bowling; alley. **2** building having a number of lanes for bowling.

bowline

bowling green, a smooth, flat stretch of grass for playing the game of bowls.

bowls (bōlz), *n.* lawn bowling.

bow·man (bō′mən), *n.* person who shoots with a bow and arrow; archer. ❑ *n., pl.* **bow·men.**

bow·sprit (bou′sprit′), *n.* pole or spar projecting forward from the bow of a ship. Ropes attached to the bowsprit help to steady sails and masts and hold the jib.

bow·string (bō′string′), *n.* a strong cord stretched from the ends of a bow, pulled back by the archer and then released to send the arrow forward.

bow tie (bō), a small necktie tied in a bow.

box¹ (boks), **1** *n.* container, usually with four sides, a bottom, and a lid, to pack or put things in: *We packed the boxes full of books.* **2** *n.* amount that a box can hold: *a box of soap.* **3** *v.* to pack in a box; put into a box: *She boxed the candy before she sold it.* **4** *n.* a small enclosed space with chairs in a theater, stadium, etc. **5** *n.* an enclosed space in a courtroom for a jury, witnesses, reporters, etc. **6** *n.* the driver's seat on a coach, carriage, etc. **7** *n.* a small shelter: *a box for a sentry.* **8** *n.* (in baseball) one of several places assigned for a player or coach to stand in during play: *the batter's box.* ❑ *n., pl.* **box·es.** **–box′like′,** *adj.*

box in or **box up,** to close in or surround; keep from getting out: *The soldiers had the enemy boxed in between the river and the hills.*

box² (boks), **1** *n.* a blow with the open hand or fist: *A box on the ear hurts.* **2** *v.* to strike with such a blow: *I will box your ears if you yell at me again.* **3** *v.* to fight with the fists as a sport: *He had not boxed since he left school.* ❑ *n., pl.* **box·es.**

box³ (boks), *n.* any of several evergreen bushes or small, bushy trees, much used for hedges, borders, etc.; boxwood. ❑ *n., pl.* **box·es.**

box·car (boks′kär′), *n.* an enclosed railroad freight car, loaded and unloaded through a sliding door on each side.

box elder, a North American maple tree, often grown for shade or ornament.

box·er (bok′sər), *n.* **1** person who fights with the fists as a sport, wearing padded gloves and following special rules. **2** a medium-sized short-haired dog with a smooth brown coat, related to the bulldog and terrier.

box·ing (bok′sing), *n.* act or sport of fighting with the fists.

boxing gloves, padded leather gloves worn when boxing.

box office, office or booth in a theater, hall, etc., where tickets of admission are sold.

box seat, chair in a box of a theater, stadium, or auditorium.

box·wood (boks′wud′), *n.* box³.

boy (boi), *n.* **1** a male child from birth to about eighteen. **2** a male servant. ■ This meaning of **boy** is often considered offensive. ■ Another word that can sound like this is **buoy.**

boy·cott (boi′kot), **1** *v.* to join with others and agree not to buy from, sell to, or associate with a person, business, or nation in order to force a change or to punish. **2** *v.* to refuse to buy or use a product or service. **3** *n.* act of boycotting.

WORD STORY **Boycott** comes from Captain Charles Boycott, an Irish land manager who refused to lower rents in hard times during the 1800s. His tenants got back at him by refusing to have anything to do with him.

boy·friend (boi′frend′), *n.* a girl's sweetheart or steady male companion.

boy·hood (boi′hud), *n.* time of being a boy.

boy·ish (boi′ish), *adj.* **1** of a boy. **2** like a boy. **3** like a boy's; suitable for a boy. **–boy′ish·ly,** *adv.* **–boy′ish·ness,** *n.*

Boyle (boil), *n.* **Rob·ert** (rob′ərt), 1627-1691, Irish scientist. ■ **Robert Boyle** created the modern study of chemistry. He is best known for his experiments with gases. One of his discoveries is now known as Boyle's law.

Boyle's law (boilz), (in physics) a law stating that the volume of a gas grows less when the amount of pressure on the gas grows greater, and vice versa, so long as the temperature of the gas does not change.

boy scout, member of the Boy Scouts.

Boy Scouts, organization for boys that seeks to develop character, citizenship, usefulness to others, and outdoor skills.

boy·sen·ber·ry (boi′zn ber′ē), *n.* a purple fruit like a blackberry in size and shape, and like a raspberry in flavor. Boysenberries grow on trailing, thorny plants and are good to eat. ❑ *n., pl.* **boy·sen·ber·ries.**

a	hat	ė	term	ô	order	ch	child		
ā	age	i	it	oi	oil	ng	long		a in about
ä	far	ī	ice	ou	out	sh	she		i in taken
â	care	o	hot	u	cup	th	thin	ə	i in pencil
e	let	ō	open	ů	put	ŦH	then		o in lemon
ē	equal	ȯ	saw	ü	rule	zh	measure		u in circus

Br, symbol for bromine.

Br., 1 Britain. 2 British.

bra (brä), *n.* brassiere. ❑ *n., pl.* **bras.**

brace (brās), 1 *n.* thing that holds parts together or in place, such as a timber used to strengthen a building or to support a roof. 2 *n.* a device used to support a part of the body, such as a knee or wrist. 3 *n.pl.* **braces, a** metal wires and bands used to straighten crooked teeth. **b** BRITISH. suspenders. 4 *v.* to give strength or firmness to; support: *We braced the roof with four poles.* 5 *v.* to prepare yourself: *I braced myself for the crash.* 6 *v.* to give strength and energy to; refresh: *bracing mountain air.* 7 *n.* a pair; couple: *a brace of ducks.* 8 *n.* handle for a tool or drill used for boring. 9 *n.* either of these signs { }, used to enclose words, figures, staffs in music, or a set in arithmetic. ❑ *v.* **braced, brac·ing.**

brace up, to gather your strength or courage anew: *He braced up after his defeat and decided to run again in the next election.*

brace·let (brās′lit), *n.* band or chain worn for ornament around the wrist or arm.

brach·i·o·pod (brak′ē ə pod′ *or* brä′kē ə pod′), *n.* any of many ocean shellfish that look like clams but have one shell larger than the other and a pair of feeding feelers like tiny arms.

brach·i·o·sau·rus (brak′ē ə sôr′əs *or* brä′kē ə sôr′əs), *n.* a giant plant-eating dinosaur with a very long neck and front legs longer than its back legs. ❑ *n., pl.* **brach·i·o·sau·rus·es, brach·i·o·sau·ri** (brak′ē ə sôr′ī *or* brä′kē ə sôr′ī).

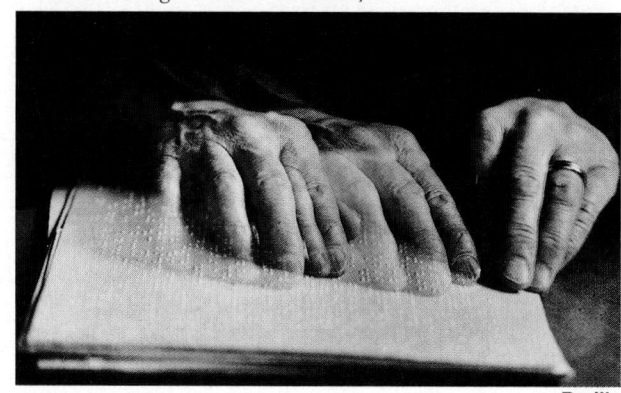
bracelets

brac·ing (brā′sing), *adj.* giving strength and energy; refreshing. **—brac′ing·ly,** *adv.*

brack·en (brak′ən), *n.* 1 a large, coarse fern common on hillsides, in woods, etc. 2 thicket of these ferns.

brack·et (brak′it), 1 *n.* a flat piece of stone, wood, or metal attached to a wall to hold up a shelf, a statue, etc. 2 *v.* to support with a bracket: *She bracketed the shelves to make them stronger.* 3 *n.* shelf supported by brackets. 4 *n.* either of these signs [ ], used to enclose words or figures. The word histories in this dictionary are enclosed in brackets. 5 *v.* to enclose within brackets: *The teacher bracketed the mistakes in my homework.* 6 *v.* to think of or mention together; group in the same class or category. 7 *n.* any group thought of or mentioned together; class or category: *a family in a low income bracket.*

brack·ish (brak′ish), *adj.* 1 slightly salty. Coastal marshes often have brackish waters. 2 bad-tasting. **—brack′ish·ness,** *n.*

bract (brakt), *n.* a small leaf growing at the base of a flower or on a flower stalk, sometimes brightly colored.

brad (brad), *n.* a small, thin nail with a small head.

Brad·ford (brad′fərd), *n.* **William,** 1590-1657, Pilgrim leader. ■ **William Bradford** was the second governor of Plymouth Colony. He was the colony's governor or assistant governor from 1621 to his death.

Brad·ley (brad′lē), *n.* **O·mar** (ō′mär), 1893-1981, American general. ■ **Omar Bradley** commanded more than a million soldiers in World War II. His troops liberated France from the Nazis.

Brad·street (brad′strēt), *n.* **Anne,** 1612?-1672, American poet. ■ **Anne Bradstreet** was the first American poet. Her poetry was written in the Colonies and published in London.

Bra·dy (brā′dē), *n.* **Math·ew B.** (math′yü), 1823?-1896, American photographer. He and his assistants took more than 3500 pictures of battlegrounds and camps during the Civil War.

brae (brā), *n.* SCOTTISH. hillside.

brag (brag), 1 *v.* to praise yourself or what you have; boast: *They bragged about their new car.* ■ See Synonym Study at **boast.** 2 *n.* a boast. 3 *n.* boasting talk. ❑ *v.* **bragged, brag·ging. —brag′ger,** *n.*

brag·gart (brag′ərt), *n.* person who brags; boaster.

Brahe (brä), *n.* **Ty·cho** (tē′kō), 1546-1601, Danish astronomer.

Brah·ma (brä′mə *for 1;* brä′mə *or* brä′mə *for 2), n.* 1 Hindu god of creation. 2 Brahman (def. 2). ❑ *n., pl.* **Brah·mas** *or* **Brah·ma** for 2.

Brah·man (brä′mən), *n.* 1 member of the priestly caste, the highest caste in India; Brahmin. 2 kind of beef cattle with a hump, originally imported from India; Brahma.

Brah·min (brä′mən), *n.* 1 Brahman (def. 1). 2 a cultured, intellectual person of the upper class.

Brahms (brämz), *n.* **Jo·han·nes** (yō hä′nəs), 1833-1897, German composer. He combined classical musical forms with romantic energy and feeling.

braid (brād), 1 *n.* band formed by weaving together three or more strands of hair, ribbon, yarn, etc.: *She wore her hair in braids.* 2 *v.* to weave or twine together three or more strands of hair, ribbon, yarn, etc.: *We braided strips of wool and made a rug.* 3 *v.* to make by weaving such strands together: *to braid a rug.* 4 *n.* a narrow band of fabric used to trim or bind clothing: *a uniform trimmed with gold braid.* **—braid′er,** *n.*

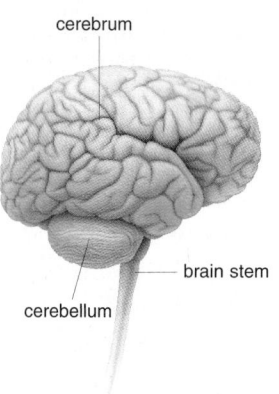
Braille

Braille or **braille** (brāl), *n.* system of reading and writing for people who cannot see. In Braille, letters and numbers are represented by different arrangements of raised dots and are read by touching them.

WORD STORY **Braille** comes from Louis Braille, a visually impaired French 15-year-old student who invented this system in the 1800s. He got the idea from a similar code used by soldiers at night.

brain (brān), 1 *n.* the part of the central nervous system in humans and many other animals that is enclosed in the head and consists of a soft mass of nerve cells. The brain controls almost all the functions of the body, and with it we can learn, think, and remember. 2 *v.* to hit on the head: *If you don't return my bike, I'll brain you.* 3 *v.* to kill by smashing the skull. 4 *n.* a computer or other electronic device to control some mechanism. 5 *n.pl.* **brains, a** intelligence: *It takes brains to get into that university.* **b** person who is the intellectual leader or planner of a group: *She was the brains of the operation.* 6 *n.* INFORMAL. a very intelligent person.

cerebrum

brain stem

cerebellum

brain (def. 1)

rack your brains, to try very hard to think: *He racked his brains for his friend's phone number, but he couldn't remember it.*

brain·child (brān′child′), *n.* any idea, composition, invention, or discovery.

brain·less (brān′lis), *adj.* without brains; stupid; foolish. **—brain′less·ly,** *adv.* **—brain′less·ness,** *n.*

brain stem, the base of the brain, which connects the spinal cord with the front part of the brain. Part of the brain stem controls breathing and heart rate. See picture at **brain.**

brain·storm (brān′stôrm′), 1 *n.* a sudden idea or inspiration. 2 *v.* to participate in brainstorming; consider or produce by brainstorming: *The staff sat around a table and brainstormed. We brainstormed a new advertising slogan.* —**brain′storm·er,** *n.*

brain·storm·ing (brān′stôr′ming), *n.* way of solving problems by group discussion in which all members contribute ideas freely and search for every possible solution to a problem.

brain·wash (brān′wäsh′), *v.* to destroy or weaken a person's beliefs and ideas through torture or other methods, so that the person becomes willing to accept different or opposite beliefs and ideas.

brain·y (brā′nē), *adj.* INFORMAL. intelligent; clever. ❑ *adj.* **brain·i·er, brain·i·est.** —**brain′i·ness,** *n.*

braise (brāz), *v.* to brown food quickly in fat and then cook it long and slowly in a covered pan with very little water. ❑ *v.* **braised, brais·ing.**

brake[1] (brāk), **1** *n.* device used to slow or stop the motion of a wheel or vehicle by friction. **2** *v.* to slow or stop by using a brake: *The driver braked the speeding car and it slid to a stop.* ❑ *v.* **braked, brak·ing.** ■ Another word that sounds like this is **break.** —**brake′less,** *adj.*

brake[2] (brāk), *n.* a thick growth of bushes; thicket. ■ Another word that sounds like this is **break.**

brake·man (brāk′mən), *n.* member of a train crew who helps the conductor; trainman. ❑ *n., pl.* **brake·men.**

bram·ble (bram′bəl), *n.* bush related to the rose, with slender, drooping branches covered with little thorns that prick. Blackberry and raspberry plants are brambles.

bram·bly (bram′blē), *adj.* **1** full of brambles: *a brambly field.* **2** like brambles; prickly: *a brambly bush.* ❑ *adj.* **bram·bli·er, bram·bli·est.**

bran (bran), *n.* the outer covering of the grains of wheat, rye, etc., which is often separated from the inner part in the process of milling flour. Bran is used in cereal and bread, and as food for farm animals.

branch (branch), **1** *n.* part of a tree growing out from the trunk; any wood part of a tree above the ground except the trunk. A bough is a large branch. A twig is a very small branch. **2** *n.* division; part: *a branch of a river, a branch of a family. Biology is a branch of science.* **3** *n.* a local office: *a branch of a bank, a branch of a library.* **4** *v.* to divide into branches: *The road branches there.* ❑ *n., pl.* **branch·es.** —**branch′less,** *adj.*

branch off, to go off a main road or route in a different direction: *The alley branches off to the left.*

branch out, 1 to put out branches. **2** to extend business interests or activities: *They used to be only printers; now they are branching out into publishing books.*

brand (brand), **1** *n.* a certain kind, grade, or make: *Do you like this brand of flour?* **2** *n.* a name or mark that a company uses to distinguish its goods from the goods of others; trademark. **3** *n.* an iron stamp for burning a mark. **4** *n.* a mark made by burning the skin with a hot iron: *The cattle on this big ranch are identified by a brand which shows who owns them.* **5** *v.* to mark by burning the skin with a hot iron. In former times criminals were often branded. **6** *n.* a mark of disgrace: *He could never rid himself of the brand of coward.* **7** *v.* to put a mark of disgrace on: *She has been branded as a traitor.* **8** *n.* piece of wood that is burning or partly burned. —**brand′er,** *n.*

brand·ing iron, an iron tool that is used to burn a mark on cattle or other animals.

bran·dish (bran′dish), *v.* to wave or shake in a threatening manner: *The knight brandished his sword at his enemy.*

brand name, **1** a distinctive name or symbol identifying a particular manufacturer's product; trade name; trademark. **2** product with a well-known trade name; name brand.

brand-new (brand′nü′), *adj.* very new; entirely new.

Bran·do (bran′dō), *n.* **Mar·lon** (mär′lən), born 1924, American stage and movie actor. He has won two Academy Awards for best actor, for *On the Waterfront* and *The Godfather.*

bran·dy (bran′dē), **1** *n.* a strong alcoholic liquor distilled from wine or fermented fruit juice. **2** *v.* to mix, flavor, or preserve with brandy. ❑ *n., pl.* **bran·dies;** *v.* **bran·died, bran·dy·ing.** [Brandy comes from a Dutch word meaning "burned wine." Brandy is made by heating wine until the alcohol boils.]

brant (brant), *n.* either of two small, dark, North American geese. They breed in arctic regions and migrate south in the autumn. ❑ *n., pl.* **brant** or **brants.**

brash (brash), *adj.* **1** showing lack of respect; impudent; saucy: *The brash boy contradicted his parents all the time.* **2** hasty; rash: *When I got over being angry, I regretted my brash act.* —**brash′ly,** *adv.* —**brash′ness,** *n.*

Bra·sí·lia (brə zē′lyə), *n.* capital of Brazil since 1960, in the central part.

brass (bras), **1** *n.* a yellowish metal that is an alloy of copper and zinc. **2** *adj.* made of brass: *brass candlesticks.* **3** *n.pl.* **brass** or **brasses,** brass instruments. **4** *n.* rude boldness; impudence: *She had the brass to go to the party uninvited.* **5** *n.pl.* SLANG. military officers of high rank.

bras·siere (brə zir′), *n.* a woman's undergarment worn to support the breasts; bra.

brass instrument, a musical instrument made of metal. The trumpet, trombone, French horn, and tuba are brass instruments.

brass·y (bras′ē), *adj.* **1** like brass: *a brassy green sky.* **2** loud and harsh: *The brassy music soon gave me a headache.* **3** shameless; impudent: *a loud and brassy manner.* ❑ *adj.* **brass·i·er, brass·i·est.** —**brass′i·ly,** *adv.* —**brass′i·ness,** *n.*

brat (brat), *n.* a rude, annoying, or unpleasant child.

Bra·ti·sla·va (brat′ə slä′və), *n.* capital of Slovakia, in the SW part, on the Danube.

brat·ty (brat′ē), *adj.* disobedient; impudent. ❑ *adj.* **brat·ti·er, brat·ti·est.** —**brat′ti·ness,** *n.*

bra·va·do (brə vä′dō), *n.* a great show of boldness without much real courage or real desire to fight.

brave (brāv), **1** *adj.* without fear; having or showing courage: *The brave girl went into the burning house to save a baby.* **2** *n.pl.* **the brave,** brave people: *The United States has been called "the land of the free and the home of the brave."* **3** *v.* to meet without fear; defy: *The early settlers braved the hardships of life in a new land.* **4** *n.* an American Indian warrior. ❑ *adj.* **brav·er, brav·est;** *v.* **braved, brav·ing.** —**brave′ly,** *adv.* —**brave′ness,** *n.*

SYNONYM STUDY **Brave** and **courageous** both mean showing no fear. **Brave** suggests being able to face danger or difficulty: *The brave athletes pushed their wheelchairs through the rain.* **Courageous** suggests having the strength to do what is right: *It takes a courageous person to admit a bad mistake.*

brav·er·y (brā′vər ē), *n.* quality of being brave; fearlessness; courage: *They owed their lives to the bravery of the firefighters.*

bra·vo (brä′vō), **1** *interj.* well done! fine! excellent! **2** *n.* a cry of "bravo!" ❑ *n., pl.* **bra·vos.**

bra·vur·a (brə vyur′ə), *n.* display of daring; dash; spirit.

brawl (brôl), **1** *n.* a noisy and disorderly quarrel. **2** *v.* to quarrel in a noisy and disorderly way. —**brawl′er,** *n.*

brawn (brôn), *n.* **1** firm, strong muscles; muscle. **2** muscular strength: *Football requires brains as well as brawn.*

brawn·y (brô′nē), *adj.* strong; muscular. ❑ *adj.* **brawn·i·er, brawn·i·est.** —**brawn′i·ness,** *n.*

bray (brā), **1** *n.* the loud, harsh cry or noise made by a donkey. **2** *n.* a sound like this. **3** *v.* to make this sound: *The trumpets brayed.*

bra·zen (brā′zn), *adj.* having no shame; shameless: *The brazen thief told lie after lie.* —**bra′zen·ly,** *adv.* —**bra′zen·ness,** *n.*

brazen it out or **brazen it through,** to act as if you did not feel ashamed: *Although we caught him lying, he tried to brazen it out by claiming it was a joke.*

bra·zier (brā′zhər), *n.* a large, metal pan or tray to hold burning charcoal or coal.

Bra·zil (brə zil′), *n.* largest country in South America. *Capital:* Brasília.

Bra·zil·ian (brə zil′yən), **1** *adj.* of Brazil or its people. **2** *n.* person born or living in Brazil.

a	hat	ė	term	ô	order	ch	child		ə {	a in about
ā	age	i	it	oi	oil	ng	long			e in taken
ä	far	ī	ice	ou	out	sh	she			i in pencil
â	care	o	hot	u	cup	th	thin			o in lemon
e	let	ō	open	ů	put	ŦH	then			u in circus
ē	equal	ȯ	saw	ü	rule	zh	measure			

Brazil nut, a large nut of a tall tree growing in Brazil. It is good to eat.

Bra·zos (brä′zōs or braz′əs), *n.* river in Texas, flowing SE to the Gulf of Mexico.

Braz·za·ville (braz′ə vil), *n.* capital of Congo, in the S part.

breach (brēch), **1** *n.* an opening made by breaking down something solid; gap: *Cannon fire had made a breach in the wall of the fort.* **2** *v.* to break through; make an opening in: *The wall had been breached in several places.* **3** *n.* act of breaking or neglect of a law, trust, obligation, etc.; violation: *For the guard to leave now would be a breach of duty.* **4** *n.* act of breaking friendly relations; quarrel: *There was never a breach between the two friends.* ❑ *n., pl.* **breach·es.** ■ Another word that sounds like this is **breech. —breach′er,** *n.*

bread (def. 1)—of all sorts

bread (bred), **1** *n.* food made of flour or meal mixed with milk or water and usually shortening and yeast. Bread is kneaded, set to rise, and baked in a loaf. **2** *n.* means of keeping alive; food; livelihood: *How will you earn your daily bread?* **3** *v.* to cover with bread crumbs before cooking: *breaded chicken.* **4** *n.* SLANG. money. ■ Another word that sounds like this is **bred.**

break bread, to share a meal.

WORD BANK   There are many different kinds of bread. If you want to know more about them, you can start by looking up these words in this dictionary.

bagel	croissant	muffin	scone
bialy	crouton	pita	sourdough
biscuit	hallah	pumpernickel	toast[1]
bun	hardtack	roll	tortilla
cornbread	matzo	rusk	zwieback

bread and butter, things necessary to live; a living: *He earns his bread and butter by selling cars.*

bread·bas·ket (bred′bas′kit), *n.* **1** basket or tray for bread. **2** region that is a chief source of grain: *The Midwest is the breadbasket of the United States.*

bread·fruit (bred′früt′), *n.* the large, round, starchy fruit of a tropical tree. When baked, its fruit tastes somewhat like bread. ❑ *n., pl.* **bread·fruit** or **bread·fruits.**

bread·stick (bred′stik′), *n.* bread baked in the shape of a stick.

bread·stuff (bred′stuf′), *n.* **1** Also **breadstuffs,** *pl.* grain, flour, or meal for making bread. **2** bread.

breadth (bredth), *n.* **1** how broad a thing is; distance across; width: *He has traveled the length and the breadth of this land.* **2** freedom from narrowness in outlook: *A tolerant person usually has breadth of mind.*

bread·win·ner (bred′win′ər), *n.* person who earns a living and supports a family.

break (brāk), **1** *v.* to come apart or make come apart; smash: *The plate broke into pieces when it fell on the floor. I broke the window with a ball.* **2** *n.* a broken place; crack: *a break in the wall. The X*

ray showed a break in my leg. **3** *v.* to damage; injure: *She broke her watch by winding it too tightly.* **4** *v.* to crack or split the bone of: *to break your arm.* **5** *v.* to fail to keep; act against: *to break a promise. People who break the law are punished.* **6** *v.* to force your way: *The lion broke out of its cage.* **7** *n.* act of forcing your way out: *The prisoners made a break for freedom.* **8** *v.* to come suddenly: *The storm broke within ten minutes.* **9** *v.* to change suddenly: *The spell of rainy weather has broken. His voice broke with emotion.* **10** *n.* an abrupt or marked change: *a break in the weather.* **11** *n.* a short interruption in work, athletic practice, etc.: *a five-minute break between classes.* **12** *v.* to decrease the force of; lessen: *The bushes broke my fall from the tree.* **13** *v.* to become weak; give way; fail: *Glenn's heart broke when his pony died.* **14** *v.* to dawn; appear: *The day is breaking.* **15** *v.* to put an end to; stop: *It's hard to break the habit of smoking.* **16** *v.* to train to obey; tame: *break a colt.* **17** *v.* to go beyond; exceed: *The speed of the new train has broken all records.* **18** *v.* to dig or plow: *to break ground for a new building.* **19** *v.* to make known; reveal: *Someone must break the news of the girl's accident to her parents.* **20** *n.* INFORMAL. stroke of luck; fortune; chance: *Finding that money was a lucky break.* **21** *v.* (in baseball) to curve or swerve abruptly: *The pitcher threw a ball that broke over the plate.* **22** *n.* act of breaking. ❑ *v.* **broke, bro·ken, break·ing.** ■ Another word that sounds like this is **brake. —break′a·ble,** *adj.*

break away, 1 to start before the signal: *The excited horse broke away at a gallop.* **2** to pull or run away from; escape: *The rabbit broke away from my arms.*

break down, 1 to go out of order; stop working: *The school bus broke down.* **2** to become weak; fail suddenly; collapse: *Her health broke down.* **3** to begin to cry: *He broke down when he heard the bad news.* **4** to separate or divide into parts, steps, etc.: *When food is digested, it is broken down into simpler forms that the body can use.*

break in, 1 to prepare for work or duty; train: *to break in a new salesperson.* **2** to wear for a short period of time until comfortable: *Let's go for a walk so I can break in my new shoes.* **3** to enter by force: *The thieves broke in through the cellar.* **4** to interrupt: *She broke in with a funny remark.*

break into, 1 to enter by force: *A robber broke into the house.* **2** to begin suddenly: *She broke into a run.* **3** to interrupt: *He broke into their conversation.*

break off, 1 to stop suddenly: *He broke off in the middle of his speech to clear his throat.* **2** to stop being friends: *She broke off with the old crowd when she went away to college.*

break out, 1 to start suddenly; begin: *War broke out. A fire broke out in the garage.* **2** to have pimples, rashes, etc., appear on the skin: *The child broke out with measles.* **3** to burst out: *A cry of horror broke out among the spectators when someone yelled "Fire!"* **4** to leave by force; escape: *The thief broke out of jail.*

break up, 1 to scatter: *The fog is breaking up.* **2** to come or bring to an end: *The committee broke up its meeting early. Their marriage is breaking up.* **3** to disturb greatly; upset: *The news of his sister's death broke him up.* **4** to laugh or cause to laugh, especially in a hearty or an uncontrollable manner: *The audience broke up at the comedian's jokes. The clown's antics broke us up.*

break with, to stop being friends with: *I broke with him after our fight.*

SYNONYM STUDY   **Break, shatter,** and **smash** all mean to come apart or go to pieces. **Break** is a general word: *The handle broke off the cup in the dishwasher.* **Shatter** means to break suddenly into many pieces: *The plate shattered when I dropped it.* **Smash** means to break forcefully: *The falling tree smashed through the roof.*

break·age (brā′kij), *n.* **1** number or quantity of things broken. **2** damage or loss caused by breaking.

break·a·way (brāk′ə wā′), *n.* (in hockey) a breaking away from the defense in a rush toward the goal.

break·dance or **break-dance** (brāk′dans′), *v.* to perform break dancing. ❑ *v.* **break·danced, break-danced** or **break-danced, break·danc·ing. —break′danc′er** or **break′-danc′er,** *n.*

break dancing or **break·danc·ing** (brāk′dans′ing), *n.* acrobatic, highly energetic dancing performed alone or with others to popular music with a strong beat.

break·down (brāk′doun′), *n.* **1** failure to work: *Lack of oil caused a breakdown in the motor.* **2** failure of health; collapse: *If you don't stop worrying, you will have a nervous breakdown.* **3** separation or division of anything into parts, steps, etc.

break·er (brā′kər), *n.* **1** wave that breaks into foam on the beach or on rocks; comber. **2** someone or something that breaks.

break·fast (brek′fəst), **1** *n.* the first meal of the day. **2** *v.* to eat breakfast: *I like to breakfast alone.*

WORD STORY **Breakfast** comes from the phrase "to break fast." A fast is a period of not eating, and we usually don't eat between dinner and breakfast.

break·in (brāk′in′), *n.* burglary.

break·neck (brāk′nek′), *adj.* likely to cause a broken neck; very dangerous: *The car traveled at breakneck speed.*

break·out (brāk′out′), *n.* **1** act of escaping from a prison. **2** breakthrough (def. 1).

break·through (brāk′thrü′), *n.* **1** a military attack that gets through the enemy defense system into the area in the rear; breakout. **2** a discovery that solves some baffling or technical problem: *an important breakthrough in medical research.*

break·up (brāk′up′), *n.* **1** act of scattering; separation. **2** act of stopping; end.

break·wa·ter (brāk′wô′tər), *n.* wall or barrier built to break the force of waves.

breakwater

bream (brēm *or* brim), *n.* any of many medium-sized fishes including carp of inland European waters and the common North American freshwater sunfish. ❑ *n., pl.* **bream** or **breams.**

breast (brest), **1** *n.* the upper, front part of the body between the shoulders and the stomach; chest. **2** *n.* gland that gives milk. **3** *n.* heart or feelings: *Pity tore his breast.* **4** *v.* to struggle with; face or oppose: *He breasted the waves with powerful strokes.*

make a clean breast of, to confess completely: *When shown proof that he broke the window, he made a clean breast of it.*

breast·bone (brest′bōn′), *n.* the thin, flat bone in the front of the chest to which the ribs are attached by cartilage; sternum.

breast-feed (brest′fēd′), *v.* to feed milk to a baby at the breast; nurse. ❑ *v.* **breast·fed** (brest′fed′), **breast·feed·ing.**

breast·plate (brest′plāt′), *n.* piece of armor worn over the chest.

breast·stroke (brest′strōk′), *n.* stroke in swimming in which the swimmer lies face downward, draws both arms at one time from in front of the head to the sides, and kicks like a frog.

breast·work (brest′wėrk′), *n.* a low, sometimes hastily built wall for defense.

breath (breth), *n.* **1** air drawn into and forced out of the lungs. **2** act of breathing: *Hold your breath a moment.* **3** vapor in the air when a person breathes out: *You can see your breath on a very cold day.* **4** ability to breathe easily: *Running so fast made me lose my breath.* **5** a slight movement in the air; light breeze: *Not a breath was stirring.* **6** a slight trace or suggestion; hint: *a breath of scandal.*

below your breath, in a whisper.

catch your breath, 1 to gasp; pant: *The dogs were catching their*

breath after a long chase. **2** to stop for breath; rest: *The hikers sat down to catch their breath.*

in the next breath or **in the same breath,** at the same time.

out of breath, breathing hard because of effort; winded; breathless: *At the end of the race the winner was out of breath.*

under your breath, in a whisper: *She was talking under her breath so no one could hear.*

waste your breath, to say something with no effect: *He has made up his mind, so you're wasting your breath arguing with him.*

Breath·a·lyz·er (breth′ə lī′zər), *n.* trademark for one kind of device that measures the amount of alcohol present in the blood by analyzing someone's breath.

breathe (brēᴛʜ), *v.* **1** to draw air into the lungs and force it out. A person breathes through the nose or through the mouth. **2** to stop for breath; rest; allow to rest and breathe: *At last there is time to breathe. At the top of the hill the rider breathed his horse.* **3** to say softly; whisper; utter: *Don't breathe a word of this to anyone.* **4** to be alive; live: *As long as I breathe, I will remember your kindness.* **5** to send out; give: *Her enthusiasm breathed new life into our club.* ❑ *v.* **breathed, breath·ing.** —**breath′a·ble,** *adj.*

breath·er (brē′ᴛʜər), *n.* a short stop for breath; rest.

breath·less (breth′lis), *adj.* **1** out of breath: *Running upstairs very fast made me breathless.* **2** holding your breath because of fear, amazement, excitement, etc.: *The beauty of the scenery left us breathless.* —**breath′less·ly,** *adv.* —**breath′less·ness,** *n.*

breath·tak·ing (breth′tā′king), *adj.* thrilling; exciting: *We took a breathtaking ride on a roller coaster.* —**breath′tak′ing·ly,** *adv.*

bred (bred), *v.* past tense and past participle of **breed:** *Our neighbors have bred many prize-winning dogs.* ■ Another word that sounds like this is **bread.**

breathtaking
a breathtaking view

breech (brēch), *n.* **1** part of a gun behind the barrel. **2** the lower part; back part. ❑ *n., pl.* **breech·es.** ■ Another word that sounds like this is **breach.**

breech·cloth (brēch′klôth′), *n.* loincloth. ❑ *n., pl.* **breech·cloths** (brēch′klôᴛʜz′ *or* brēch′klôths′).

breech·es (brich′iz *or* brē′chiz), *n.pl.* **1** short trousers fastened below the knees. **2** trousers.

breeches buoy, pair of short canvas trousers fastened to a belt or life preserver. A breeches buoy slides along a rope on a pulley and is used to rescue people from sinking ships or to transfer people from one ship to another.

breed (brēd), **1** *v.* to produce young: *Rabbits breed rapidly.* **2** *v.* to raise or grow, especially to get new or improved kinds: *to breed new varieties of corn, to breed cattle for market.* **3** *v.* to be the cause of; produce: *Careless driving breeds accidents.* **4** *v.* to bring up; train: *The princess was born and bred to be queen one day.* **5** *n.* group of animals or plants looking much alike and having the same ancestry: *Collies and German shepherds are breeds of dogs.* **6** *n.* kind; sort: *The people of the early West were a hardy breed.* ❑ *v.* **bred, breed·ing.** —**breed′a·ble,** *adj.*

breed·er (brē′dər), *n.* person who breeds animals or plants: *a dog breeder.*

breeder reactor, any reactor that produces at least as much fissionable material as it uses. One kind consumes uranium and produces plutonium.

breed·ing (brē′ding), *n.* **1** act of producing animals or new types of plants, especially to get improved kinds: *Breeding has produced*

a	hat	ė	term	ô	order	ch	child		a in about
ā	age	i	it	oi	oil	ng	long		e in taken
ä	far	ī	ice	ou	out	sh	she	ə	i in pencil
â	care	o	hot	u	cup	th	thin		o in lemon
e	let	ō	open	u̇	put	ᴛʜ	then		u in circus
ē	equal	ò	saw	ü	rule	zh	measure		

types of wheat which can be grown in the far North. **2** upbringing; training; manners: *Politeness is a sign of good breeding.*

Breed's Hill (brēdz), hill near Boston, Massachusetts. The Battle of Bunker Hill actually took place here.

breeze (brēz), **1** *n.* a light, gentle wind. **2** *v.* to move easily or briskly: *She breezed through her homework.* **3** *n.* anything that is easily done: *The exam was a breeze.* ❑ *v.* **breezed, breez·ing.**

breeze·way (brēz′wā′), *n.* a roofed passage open at the sides between a house and a garage.

breez·y (brē′zē), *adj.* **1** having many breezes; with light winds blowing: *It was a breezy day.* **2** lively and jolly: *We like her breezy, joking manner.* ❑ *adj.* **breez·i·er, breez·i·est. —breez′i·ly,** *adv.* **—breez′i·ness,** *n.*

br'er (brér), *n.* DIALECT. brother: *Br'er Rabbit.*

breth·ren (breᴛʜ′rən), *n.pl.* **1** the fellow members of a church, society, or religious order. **2** OLD USE. brothers.

Bret·on (bret′n), **1** *n.* person born in Brittany. **2** *n.* language of Brittany. **3** *adj.* of Brittany, its people, or their language: *Breton folklore.*

bre·vi·ar·y (brē′vē er′ē), *n.* book of prayers, ceremonies, and hymns used daily by Roman Catholic and Anglican clergy. ❑ *n., pl.* **bre·vi·ar·ies.**

brev·i·ty (brev′ə tē), *n.* shortness; briefness: *The brevity of the speech was appreciated by the audience.*

brew (brü), **1** *v.* to make beer or ale by soaking, boiling, and fermenting malt, hops, etc. **2** *v.* to make a drink by soaking or boiling in water: *Tea is brewed in boiling water.* **3** *n.* a drink that is brewed: *The last brew of beer tasted bad.* **4** *v.* to bring about; plan; plot: *The group whispering in the corner is brewing some mischief.* **5** *v.* to begin to form; gather: *Dark clouds show that a storm is brewing.*

brew·er (brü′ər), *n.* person who brews beer, ale, etc.

brew·er·y (brü′ər ē), *n.* place where beer, ale, etc., is brewed. ❑ *n., pl.* **brew·er·ies.**

Brezh·nev (brezh′nef), *n.* **Le·o·nid** (lā ə nēd′), 1906-1982, Russian political leader, general secretary of the Soviet Communist party from 1964 to 1982, and president of the Soviet Union from 1977 to 1982.

bri·ar¹ (brī′ər), *n.* brier¹.

bri·ar² (brī′ər), *n.* brier².

bribe (brīb), **1** *n.* money or other reward given or offered to someone to do something dishonest, unlawful, etc.: *The driver who caused the accident offered the police officer a bribe to let her go.* **2** *n.* a reward for doing something that someone does not want to do: *The stubborn child needed a bribe to go to bed.* **3** *v.* to give or offer a bribe to: *A gambler bribed one of the boxers to lose the fight.* ❑ *v.* **bribed, brib·ing. —brib′a·ble,** *adj.* **—brib′er,** *n.*

brib·er·y (brī′bər ē), *n.* **1** act of giving or offering a bribe. **2** act of taking a bribe: *The dishonest judge was arrested for bribery.*

bric-a-brac (brik′ə brak′), *n.* interesting or curious trinkets used as decorations; small ornaments, such as vases, old china, or small statues.

brick (brik), **1** *n.* block of clay baked by sun or fire. Bricks are used to build walls or houses, pave walks, etc. **2** *n.* these blocks used as building material: *Chimneys are usually built of brick.* **3** *adj.* made of bricks: *a brick house.* **4** *n.* anything shaped like a brick: *Ice cream is often sold in bricks.* **5** *v.* to build or pave with bricks; cover or fill in with bricks: *The old window had been bricked up for many years.*

brick·bat (brik′bat′), *n.* **1** piece of broken brick: *The speaker was injured by brickbats hurled from the crowd.* **2** an insult.

brick·lay·er (brik′lā′ər), *n.* person whose work is building with bricks.

brick·lay·ing (brik′lā′ing), *n.* act or work of building with bricks.

brick·work (brik′wėrk′), *n.* wall, foundation, or other structure made of bricks.

brid·al (brī′dl), *adj.* for a bride or a wedding: *a bridal veil, the bridal cake.* ■ Another word that sounds like this is **bridle.** [Bridal comes from old English words meaning "bride" and "ale." In old times, ale was the favorite drink at wedding feasts.]

bride (brīd), *n.* woman just married or about to be married.

bride·groom (brīd′grüm′), *n.* man just married or about to be married; groom.

brides·maid (brīdz′mād′), *n.* a young woman who attends the bride at a wedding.

bridge¹ (brij), **1** *n.* something built over a river, road, railroad, or other obstacle, so that people, cars, trains, etc., can get across. **2** *v.* to build a bridge over; make or form a bridge over: *The engineers bridged the river.* **3** *n.* platform above the deck of a ship for the officer in command: *The captain directed the course of his ship from the bridge.* **4** *n.* the upper, bony part of the nose. **5** *n.* the curved part of a pair of eyeglasses that rests on the nose. **6** *n.* false tooth or teeth in a mounting fastened to nearby natural teeth. **7** *n.* a thin, arched piece over which the strings of a violin or other stringed instrument are stretched. ❑ *v.* **bridged, bridg·ing. —bridge′a·ble,** *adj.*

bridge¹ (def. 1)

bridge² (brij), *n.* a card game for two pairs of players, played with 52 cards.

bridge·head (brij′hed′), *n.* position obtained and held by troops within enemy territory, used as a starting point for further attack.

Bridge·port (brij′pôrt′), *n.* port in SW Connecticut. [Bridgeport was named in 1800, in honor of the first drawbridge to cross the river in the city.]

Bridge·town (brij′toun), *n.* capital of Barbados.

bridge·work (brij′wėrk′), *n.* false teeth in a mounting fastened to real teeth nearby.

bri·dle (brī′dl), **1** *n.* the part of a harness that fits around a horse's head, including the bit and reins which control the animal. **2** *v.* to put a bridle on: *I saddled and bridled my horse.* **3** *n.* anything that holds back or controls; curb. **4** *v.* to hold back; bring under control; check: *Bridle your temper.* **5** *v.* to hold the head up high with the chin drawn back to show pride, scorn, or anger: *She bridled when we criticized her ideas.* ❑ *v.* **bri·dled, bri·dling.** ■ Another word that sounds like this is **bridal.**

bridle path, path for people riding horses.

brief (brēf), **1** *adj.* lasting only a short time: *The meeting was brief. A brief shower fell in the afternoon.* **2** *adj.* using few words: *She made a brief announcement. Be as brief as you can.* **3** *n.* a short statement; summary: *The lawyer prepared a brief of the facts and the points of law in the case.* **4** *v.* to give detailed information to: *The park ranger briefed the campers on fire prevention.* **—brief′ly,** *adv.* **—brief′ness,** *n.*

in brief, in a few words: *Let me give you the facts in brief.*

brief·case (brēf′kās′), *n.* a flat container for carrying loose papers, books, drawings, etc.; attaché case. A briefcase is often made of leather, plastic, or cloth and has a handle.

bri·er¹ (brī′ər), *n.* any bush with a thorny, woody stem. The blackberry plant and the wild rose are often called briers. Also, **briar.**

bri·er² (brī′ər), *n.* **1** a kind of heath bush found in southern Europe. Its root is used in making tobacco pipes. **2** a tobacco pipe made of this root. Also, **briar.**

brig (brig), *n.* **1** ship with two masts and square sails set at right angles across the ship. **2** prison on a ship. **3** military prison.

Brig., **1** brigade. **2** Brigadier.

bri·gade (bri gād′), *n.* **1** part of an army made up of two or more regiments or groups, commanded by a brigadier general or a colonel. **2** any group of people organized for some purpose. A fire brigade puts out fires.

brig·a·dier (brig′ə dir′), *n.* brigadier general.

brigadier general, a military rank. See chart on page 712.

brig·and (brig′ənd), *n.* person who robs travelers on the road, especially one of a gang of robbers in mountain or forest regions; robber; bandit.

brig·an·tine (brig′ən tēn′), *n.* ship with two masts. The foremast is square-rigged; the mainmast is fore-and-aft-rigged.

bright (brit), **1** *adj.* giving much light; shining: *The stars are bright, but sunshine is brighter.* **2** *adj.* very light or clear: *It is a bright day. Dandelions are bright yellow.* **3** *adj.* clever; intelligent; quick-witted: *A bright student learns quickly.* **4** *adj.* lively or cheerful: *There was a bright smile on his face.* **5** *adj.* likely to turn out well; favorable: *There is a bright outlook for the future.* **6** *adv.* in a bright manner: *The fire shines bright.* —**bright′ly,** *adv.* —**bright′ness,** *n.*

SYNONYM STUDY **Bright, brilliant,** and **radiant** all mean shining. **Bright** means giving much light: *Do your homework at the desk, where there's a bright lamp.* **Brilliant** means extremely bright: *The snow is brilliant in the sunlight.* **Radiant** means full of light inside: *The radiant windows showed holiday toys.*

bright·en (brit′n), *v.* to make or become bright or brighter: *Wild flowers brighten the fields in the spring. The sky brightened after the storm.*

bril·liance (bril′yəns), *n.* **1** great brightness; radiance; sparkle: *the brilliance of a fine diamond.* **2** splendor; magnificence: *the brilliance of the royal court.* **3** great ability: *His brilliance as a pianist was soon recognized.*

bril·liant (bril′yənt), **1** *adj.* shining brightly; sparkling: *brilliant jewels, brilliant sunshine.* ■ See Synonym Study at **bright. 2** *adj.* splendid; magnificent: *The singer gave a brilliant performance.* **3** *adj.* having great ability: *a brilliant musician.* **4** *n.* diamond or other gem cut to sparkle brightly. —**bril′liant·ly,** *adv.*

brim (brim), **1** *n.* edge of a cup, bowl, etc.: *a glass filled to the brim.* **2** *n.* edge or border of anything; rim: *Don't go near the brim of the canyon.* **3** *v.* to fill to the brim; be full to the brim: *The pond was brimming with water after the heavy rain.* **4** *n.* an edge that sticks out from the bottom of a hat: *The hat's wide brim shaded my eyes from the sun.* ❑ *v.* **brimmed, brim·ming.** —**brim′-less,** *adj.*

brim·ful (brim′fúl′), *adj.* full to the brim; full to the very top.

brim·stone (brim′stōn′), *n.* sulfur.

brin·dle (brin′dl), **1** *adj.* brindled. **2** *n.* a brindled color. **3** *n.* a brindled animal.

brin·dled (brin′dld), *adj.* gray, tan, or tawny with darker streaks and spots.

brine (brin), *n.* **1** very salty water. Some pickles are kept in brine. **2** a salt lake, sea, or ocean.

bring (bring), *v.* **1** to come with or carry a thing or person from another place; take along to a place or person: *The bus brought us home. Bring me a clean plate.* **2** to cause to come: *What brings you into town today?* **3** to win over to a belief or action; influence; persuade; convince: *Our arguments finally brought them to agree with us.* **4** to sell for: *Tomatoes bring a high price in winter.* **5** to present before a court of law: *He brought a lawsuit against us.* ❑ *v.* **brought, bring·ing.** —**bring′er,** *n.*

bring about, to cause; cause to happen: *The flood was brought about by a heavy rain.*

bring around or **bring round, 1** to restore to consciousness: *None of the doctor's efforts could bring him around.* **2** to win over to a belief or action; convince; persuade: *At first my parents refused to let me go to the party, but I was able to bring them around.*

bring forth, 1 to give birth to; bear: *In spring ewes bring forth young.* **2** to make known something that was hidden; reveal; show: *New evidence was brought forth by the lawyer.*

bring forward, 1 to reveal; show: *The judge ordered the prisoner to be brought forward.* **2** (in accounting or bookkeeping) to carry over from one page to another.

bring off, to carry out successfully: *They brought off the deal.*

bring on, to cause; cause to happen: *My headache was brought on by a cold.*

bring out, 1 to reveal; show: *The lawyer brought out new evidence at the trial.* **2** to offer to the public: *The company is bringing out a new product.*

bring over, to win over to do or believe; persuade: *Try to bring her over to our way of thinking.*

bring to, 1 to restore to consciousness: *The swimmer was unconscious when the lifeguards rescued her, but they finally brought her to.* **2** to stop; check: *The captain brought the ship to.*

bring up, 1 to care for in childhood: *My grandparents brought up four children.* **2** to educate or train, especially in behavior or manners: *His good manners showed he was well brought up.* **3** to suggest for action or discussion; mention: *Please bring your plan up at the meeting.*

USAGE NOTE **Bring** is used when something is carried toward the person speaking: *Please bring me the can opener.* **Take,** not **bring,** is used when something is carried away from the speaker: *Take the dress to the cleaners.*

bring·ing-up (bring′ing up′), *n.* care and training given to a child when growing up; upbringing.

brink (bringk), *n.* **1** edge at the top of a steep place: *the brink of the cliff.* **2** edge: *The business is on the brink of ruin.*

brink·man·ship (bringk′mən ship), *n.* the maintaining or urging of a policy to the limits of safety before giving ground.

brinks·man·ship (bringk′smən ship), *n.* brinkmanship.

brin·y (brī′nē), *adj.* of or like brine; very salty: *Too much salt gives a briny taste.* ❑ *adj.* **brin·i·er, brin·i·est.** —**brin′i·ness,** *n.*

bri·oche (brē′ōsh *or* brē′osh), *n.* a very light roll raised with yeast, rich in butter and eggs.

bri·quette or **bri·quet** (bri ket′), *n.* a molded block of coal dust or charcoal used for fuel.

Bris·bane (briz′bən *or* briz′bān), *n.* port and capital of Queensland, Australia.

brisk (brisk), *adj.* **1** quick and active; lively: *Grandmother likes to take a brisk walk every morning.* **2** keen; sharp: *A brisk wind was blowing from the north.* —**brisk′ly,** *adv.* —**brisk′ness,** *n.*

bris·ket (bris′kit), *n.* meat from the breast of an animal.

bris·tle (bris′əl), **1** *n.* one of the short, stiff hairs of some animals or plants. Brushes are often made of the bristles of hogs. **2** *v.* to stand up straight: *The dog growled and its hair bristled.* **3** *v.* to make fur stand up straight: *The kitten bristled when it saw the dog.* **4** *v.* to show that you are aroused and ready to fight: *The insult made her bristle.* **5** *v.* to be thickly set: *The harbor bristled with boats and ships.* ❑ *v.* **bris·tled, bris·tling.** —**bris′tle·like′,** *adj.*

bris·tle·cone pine (bris′əl kōn′), either of two bushy pines with cones that bear long bristles. Bristlecone pines are found in the western United States, and are the oldest trees known.

bris·tly (bris′lē), *adj.* **1** rough with bristles or hair like bristles: *The trapper had a bristly chin after a week in the woods.* **2** like bristles: *bristly hair.* **3** likely to bristle: *a bristly temper.* ❑ *adj.* **bris·tli·er, bris·tli·est.**

Brit., 1 Britain. **2** British.

Brit·ain (brit′n), *n.* England, Scotland, and Wales; Great Britain.

Bri·tan·ni·a (bri tan′ē ə), *n.* Great Britain.

britch·es (brich′iz), *n.pl.* INFORMAL. breeches.

too big for your britches, too proud of yourself; arrogant; conceited.

Brit·i·cism (brit′ə siz′əm), *n.* word or phrase used especially by the British. *Lift* meaning *elevator* and *petrol* meaning *gasoline* are Briticisms.

Brit·ish (brit′ish), **1** *adj.* of Great Britain or its people. **2** *n.pl.* the people of Great Britain. **3** *n.* the English language as it is spoken in Great Britain.

British Columbia, province in SW Canada, on the Pacific. *Capital:* Victoria.

a	hat	è	term	ô	order	ch	child		
ā	age	i	it	oi	oil	ng	long	ə	a in about
ä	far	ī	ice	ou	out	sh	she		e in taken
â	care	o	hot	u	cup	th	thin		i in pencil
e	let	ō	open	ú	put	ᴛʜ	then		o in lemon
ē	equal	ò	saw	ü	rule	zh	measure		u in circus

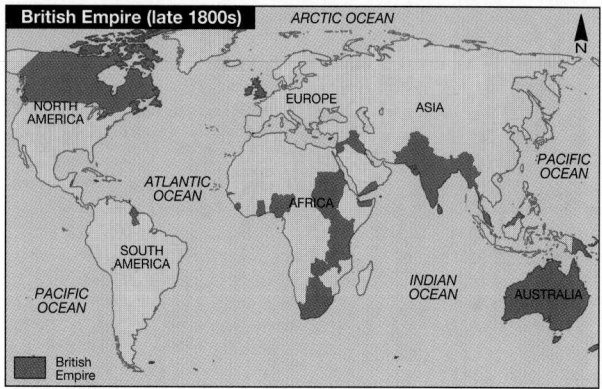

British Empire (late 1800s)

British Empire, former empire consisting of all the countries and colonies owing allegiance to the British crown. At its height, in the late 1800s and early 1900s, it was the largest empire in the history of the world.

British Honduras, former name of **Belize.**

British Isles, Great Britain, Ireland, the Isle of Man, and other nearby islands.

British Isles

British thermal unit, unit for measuring heat. It is the amount of heat necessary to raise the temperature of a pound of water one degree Fahrenheit.

British West Indies, British islands in the West Indies.

Brit·on (brit′n), n. **1** person born or living in Great Britain. **2** one of the Celtic people who inhabited southern Britain before the Roman conquest of Britain.

Brit·ta·ny (brit′n ē), n. **1** region in NW France. See **Burgundy** for map. **2** a kind of spaniel with an orange and white coat or brown and white coat.

brit·tle (brit′l), adj. very easily broken; breaking with a snap; apt to break: *Thin glass is brittle.* ❑ adj. **brit·tler, brit·tlest. —brit′tle·ness,** n.

bro. or **Bro.,** brother.

broach (brōch), **1** v. to begin to talk about: *She broached the subject of a raise in her allowance.* **2** n. a pointed tool to make and shape holes with. **3** v. to open by making a hole: *We broached a barrel of cider.* ❑ n., pl. **broach·es.** ■ Another word that can sound like this is **brooch. —broach′er,** n.

broad (brôd), adj. **1** large across; wide: *a broad road.* **2** having wide range; extensive: *Our librarian has had broad experience with books.* **3** not limited or narrow; liberal: *The police took a broad view of the children's prank and sent them home with only a warning.* **4** including only the most important parts; not detailed; general: *Give the broad outlines of today's lesson.* **5** clear; full: *The theft was made in broad daylight.* **6** plain; plain-spoken: *He gave his parents broad hints of what he wanted for his birthday.* **—broad′ly,** adv. **—broad′ness,** n.

broad·ax or **broad·axe** (brôd′aks′), n. ax with a broad blade. ❑ n., pl. **broad·ax·es.**

broad·cast (brôd′kast′), **1** n. something sent out by radio or television; a radio or television program of speech, music, etc.: *The broadcast was televised from Washington, D.C.* **2** v. to send out by radio or television: *His speech was broadcast at 9 P.M. Some stations broadcast twenty-four hours a day.* **3** n. act of sending out by radio or television: *a nationwide broadcast.* **4** adj. sent out by radio or television. **5** v. to scatter or spread widely: *broadcast seed.* **6** v. to make widely known: *Don't broadcast gossip.* **7** n. act of scattering or spreading far and wide: *nature's broadcast of seed.* **8** adj. scattered widely. **9** adv. over a wide surface: *The seed was sown broadcast.* ❑ v. **broad·cast** or **broad·cast·ed** for 2,6, **broad·cast** for 5, **broad·cast·ing. —broad′cast′er,** n.

broad·cloth (brôd′klôth′), n. **1** a closely woven cotton, silk, or synthetic cloth with a smooth finish, used in making shirts, dresses, pajamas, etc. **2** a closely woven woolen cloth with a smooth finish, used in making suits, coats, etc.

broad·en (brôd′n), v. to become or make broad or broader; widen: *The river broadens at its mouth. Travel broadens a person's experience.*

broad jump, long jump. **—broad jumper.**

broad·leaf (brôd′lēf′), adj. broad-leaved.

broad·leaved (brôd′lēvd′), adj. having wide, flat leaves rather than needles. Oaks, elms, and maples are broad-leaved trees.

broad·loom (brôd′lüm′), **1** adj. woven on a wide loom: *a broadloom carpet.* **2** n. material woven in this way: *gray broadloom.*

broad·mind·ed (brôd′mīn′did), adj. not prejudiced or bigoted; liberal; tolerant: *He tried to be broad-minded, but did not always succeed.* **—broad′-mind′ed·ly,** adv. **—broad′-mind′ed·ness,** n.

broad·side (brôd′sīd′), **1** n. the whole side of a ship above the water. **2** n. act of firing all the guns on one side of a ship at the same time: *The broadside sank the pirate ship.* **3** adv. with the side turned: *The ship drifted broadside to the wharf.*

broad·sword (brôd′sôrd′), n. sword with a broad, flat cutting blade.

Broad·way (brôd′wā′), n. street running northwest and southeast through New York City. Part of Broadway lies in the main theater district.

bro·cade (brō kād′), **1** n. an expensive cloth woven with raised designs on it, used for clothing or upholstery: *silk brocade, velvet brocade.* **2** v. to weave or decorate with raised designs. ❑ v. **bro·cad·ed, bro·cad·ing.**

broc·co·li (brok′ə lē), n. a garden vegetable with green branching stems and flower heads. It is related to cabbage. ❑ n., pl. **broc·co·li.** [**Broccoli** comes from an Italian word meaning "sprouts." Broccoli is eaten while still sprouting, before the flowers bloom.]

bro·chure (brō shùr′), n. pamphlet.

bro·gan (brō′gən), n. a strong work shoe made of heavy leather.

brogue¹ (brōg), n. a strongly marked pronunciation or accent peculiar to a dialect: *She speaks English with an Irish brogue.*

brogue² (brōg), n. a shoe made for comfort and long wear, often with decorative perforations.

broil (broil), v. **1** to cook by putting or holding directly over the fire or heat on a rack, or under it in a pan; grill: *We often broil steaks.* **2** to be or make very hot: *You will broil in this bright sunlight.*

broil·er (broi′lər), n. **1** pan or rack for broiling. **2** a young chicken for broiling.

broke (brōk), **1** v. past tense of **break:** *I broke my watch.* **2** adj. without money.

bro·ken (brō′kən), **1** v. past participle of **break:** *The window was broken by a ball.* **2** adj. separated into parts by a break; in pieces: *a broken cup.* **3** adj. not in working condition; damaged: *a broken watch.* **4** adj. rough; uneven: *broken ground.* **5** adj. acted against; not kept: *a broken promise.* **6** adj. spoken slowly and with mistakes: *The French girl speaks broken English.* **7** adj. weakened in strength, spirit, etc.; tamed; crushed: *broken by failure.* **—bro′ken·ly,** adv. **—bro′ken·ness,** n.

bro·ken-down (brō′kən doun′), adj. **1** shattered; ruined: *broken-down health.* **2** unfit for use: *broken-down furniture.*

bro·ken-heart·ed (brō′kən här′tid), adj. crushed by sorrow or grief; heartbroken. **—bro′ken-heart′ed·ly,** adv.

broken home, a family in which one parent is absent, usually because of divorce or separation.

bro·ker (brō′kər), n. person who buys and sells stocks, bonds, grain, cotton, etc., for other people.

WORD STORY **Broker** comes from a French word meaning "to open a barrel by making a hole in it." People who sold wine did this. Later the word was used for merchants of many sorts.

bro·ker·age (brō′kər ij), n. **1** business of a broker. **2** money charged by a broker for services.

bro·me·li·ad (brō mē′lē ad′), n. any of a group of tropical American plants that includes the pineapple, Spanish moss, and a common house plant. Many bromeliads are air plants.

bro·mide (brō′mīd), *n.* drug containing bromine, used to calm nervousness, cause sleep, etc.

bro·mine (brō′mēn′), *n.* a dark, brownish red, nonmetallic, liquid element. Bromine is somewhat like chlorine and iodine and gives off an irritating vapor. It is used in antiknock compounds for gasoline, in drugs, and in photography. *Symbol:* Br

bron·chi (brong′kī), *n.pl.* **1** the two large, main branches of the windpipe, one going to each lung. **2** the smaller branching tubes in the lungs. ❑ *n., sing.* **bron·chus.**

bron·chi·al (brong′kē əl), *adj.* of or in the bronchi. —**bron′chi·al·ly,** *adv.*

bronchial tubes, bronchi and their branching tubes.

bron·chi·tis (brong kī′tis), *n.* inflammation of the mucous membrane that lines the bronchial tubes. Bronchitis is usually accompanied by a deep cough and may be acute or chronic.

bron·cho·scope (brong′kə skōp′), *n.* a long, flexible tube that can be put into the windpipe and bronchi to examine them or to remove objects that have been breathed in.

bron·chus (brong′kəs), *n.* one of the bronchi. ❑ *n., pl.* **bron·chi.**

bron·co (brong′kō), *n.* a wild or partly tamed horse of the western United States. ❑ *n., pl.* **bron·cos.**

Bron·të (bron′tē), *n.* **1** Char·lotte (shär′lət), 1816-1855, English author. **2** her sister, Em·i·ly (em′ə lē), 1818-1848, English author. ■ The **Brontë** sisters lived in a lonely, isolated part of England. Charlotte's *Jane Eyre* and Emily's *Wuthering Heights* both describe love affairs between a brooding, passionate man and a strong, willful woman. They are the first great romance novels.

bron·to·saur (bron′tə sôr), *n.* brontosaurus; apatosaurus.

bron·to·sau·rus (bron′tə sôr′əs), *n.* apatosaurus. ❑ *n., pl.* **bron·to·sau·rus·es, bron·to·sau·ri** (bron′tə sôr′ī). [See Word Story at apatosaurus.]

Bronx (brongks), *n.* **The,** borough of New York City, the only one on the mainland.

bronze (bronz), **1** *n.* a dark yellow-brown alloy of copper and tin. **2** *n.* a similar alloy of copper and zinc or another metal. **3** *n.* a statue, medal, disk, etc., made of bronze: *A bronze went to the swimmer who came in third.* **4** *n.* color of bronze; a dark yellow-brown. **5** *adj.* dark yellow-brown. **6** *v.* to make or become a dark yellow-brown: *a lifeguard bronzed by the sun.* ❑ *v.* **bronzed, bronz·ing.**

Bronze Age, period after the Stone Age when bronze tools and weapons were used. It was followed by the Iron Age.

bronz·y (bron′zē), *adj.* **1** tinged with bronze color. **2** like bronze.

brooch (brōch *or* brüch), *n.* an ornamental pin having the point fastened by a catch. ❑ *n., pl.* **brooch·es.** ■ Another word that can sound like this is **broach.**

brood (brüd), **1** *n.* the young birds hatched at one time in the nest or cared for together: *a brood of chicks.* **2** *v.* to sit on eggs; incubate. Hens and birds brood till the young are hatched. **3** *n.* young animals or humans who share the same mother or are cared for by the same person: *That father and mother have a brood of four children.* **4** *v.* to think or worry a long time about something: *She brooded over her mistake.* —**brood′ing·ly,** *adv.*

brood·er (brü′dər), *n.* **1** a closed place that can be heated, used in raising chicks, etc. **2** person who tends to worry a long time about some one thing.

brood·y (brü′dē), *adj.* **1** brooding: *broody hens.* **2** apt to worry; moody. ❑ *adj.* **brood·i·er, brood·i·est.** —**brood′i·ness,** *n.*

brook¹ (brük), *n.* a small stream; creek.

brook² (brük), *v.* to put up with; endure; tolerate: *I will not brook any more of your insults.*

brook·let (brük′lit), *n.* a little brook.

Brook·lyn (brük′lən), *n.* borough of New York City, on Long Island. —**Brook′lyn·ite,** *n.*

Brooks (brüks), *n.* Gwen·do·lyn (gwen′dl in), born 1917, American poet. ■ **Gwendolyn Brooks** was the first African American poet to win the Pulitzer Prize. She is the poet laureate of Illinois.

Brook·side (brük′sīd), *n.* city in N Delaware.

broom (brüm), *n.* **1** brush with a long handle for sweeping. **2** any of numerous bushes, especially one kind with slender branches, small leaves, and yellow flowers. Broom plants are related to the pea.

broom·ball (brüm′bôl′), *n.* CANADIAN. a version of hockey, played with brooms and a volleyball, without skates.

broom·stick (brüm′stik′), *n.* the long handle of a broom.

bros. or **Bros.,** brothers.

broth (brôth), *n.* a thin soup made from water in which meat, fish, or vegetables have been boiled. ❑ *n., pl.* **broths** (brôths *or* brôŦHz).

broth·er (bruŦH′ər), *n.* **1** son of the same parents. A boy is a brother to the other children of his parents. **2** a close friend or companion. **3** a male member of the same club, union, religious organization, etc. **4** member of a religious order who is not a priest: *a lay brother.* ❑ *n., pl.* **broth·ers** (or **brethren** for 3,4).

broth·er·hood (bruŦH′ər hud), *n.* **1** bond between brothers; feeling of brother for brother. **2** persons joined as brothers; association of men with some common aim, interest, or profession.

broth·er·in·law (bruŦH′ər in lô′), *n.* **1** brother of your husband or wife. **2** husband of your sister. ❑ *n., pl.* **brothers-in-law.**

broth·er·ly (bruŦH′ər lē), *adj.* **1** of a brother: *brotherly traits.* **2** like a brother; kindly: *brotherly advice.* —**broth′er·li·ness,** *n.*

brought (brôt), *v.* past tense and past participle of **bring:** *I brought my lunch yesterday. They were brought to school by bus.*

brou·ha·ha (brü hä′hä), *n.* a confused uproar; hullabaloo: *The snake getting loose in the classroom certainly created a brouhaha!* ❑ *n., pl.* **brou·ha·has.**

brow (brou), *n.* **1** part of the face above the eyes; forehead: *a wrinkled brow.* **2** arch of hair over the eye; eyebrow. **3** edge of a steep place; top of a slope: *Our house is on the brow of a hill.*

brow·beat (brou′bēt′), *v.* to frighten into doing something by overbearing looks or threats; bully. ❑ *v.* **brow·beat, brow·beat·en, brow·beat·ing.**

brown (broun), **1** *n.* the color of toast and coffee. **2** *adj.* having this color: *Many people have brown hair.* **3** *v.* to make or become brown: *The cook browned the onions in hot butter.* —**brown′ness,** *n.*

Brown (broun), *n.* **1** John, 1800-1859, American Abolitionist. ■ **John Brown** attacked a government armory at Harper's Ferry to get weapons with which he planned to start a slave rebellion. Captured and hanged, he became a hero to Northern Abolitionists and to Union soldiers in the Civil War. **2** Jim (jim), born 1936, American football player. He played nine years for the Cleveland Browns, and led the league in rushing for eight of those years.

brown-bag (broun′bag′), *v.* to carry lunch to work or school, usually in a brown paper bag. ❑ *v.* **brown-bagged, brown-bag·ging.** —**brown′-bag′ger,** *n.*

brown bear, bear with brown fur. It lives in northern Europe and Asia and in North America, especially Alaska.

brown·ie (brou′nē), *n.* **1** a good-natured elf, especially one supposed to help people secretly at night. **2** Brownie, member of the junior division of the Girl Scouts. **3** a small, flat, sweet chocolate cake, often containing nuts.

Brown·ing (brou′ning), *n.* **1** Elizabeth Bar·rett (bar′it), 1806-1861, English poet. **2** Rob·ert (rob′ərt), 1812-1889, English poet. ■ **Elizabeth Barrett Browning** lived an unhappy life as an invalid in the house of her strict father, who didn't allow her to move to Italy for her health. She married **Robert Browning** secretly in 1846, and they left for Italy the next week. Her father never forgave her, but her health improved dramatically.

brown·ish (brou′nish), *adj.* somewhat brown.

brown·out (broun′out′), *n.* a partial lowering of electric power that causes lights to dim.

brown rice, rice that has not had the outer covering of bran removed.

brown·stone (broun′stōn′), *n.* **1** a reddish brown sandstone, used as a building material. **2** house with exterior walls built of this material.

brown sugar, sugar that is only partly refined.

a	hat	ė	term	ô	order	ch	child		
ā	age	i	it	oi	oil	ng	long		a in about
ä	far	ī	ice	ou	out	sh	she	ə	e in taken
â	care	o	hot	u	cup	th	thin		i in pencil
e	let	ō	open	ù	put	ŦH	then		o in lemon
ē	equal	ò	saw	ü	rule	zh	measure		u in circus

browse (brouz), *v.* **1** to feed on growing grass or the leaves and shoots of trees and bushes by nibbling and eating here and there; graze. **2** to read here and there in a book, library, etc. ❑ *v.* browsed, brows·ing. —brows′er, *n.*

bru·in (brü′ən), *n.* bear² (def. 1).

bruise (brüz), **1** *n.* injury to the body, caused by a fall or a blow, that breaks blood vessels without breaking the skin: *The bruise on my arm turned black and blue.* **2** *n.* injury to the outside of a fruit, vegetable, plant, etc. **3** *v.* to injure the outside of: *Rough handling bruised the apples before they could be sold.* **4** *v.* to hurt; injure: *Your harsh words bruised my feelings.* **5** *v.* to become bruised: *My flesh bruises easily.* ❑ *v.* bruised, bruis·ing.

brunch (brunch), *n.* meal taken late in the morning and intended to combine breakfast and lunch. ❑ *n., pl.* brunch·es. [Brunch is a blend of **breakfast** and **lunch.**]

Bru·nei (brü nī′), *n.* country in N Borneo. *Capital:* Bandar Seri Begawan.

bru·nette or **bru·net** (brü net′), **1** *adj.* dark in color: *brunette hair.* **2** *adj.* having dark brown or black hair and usually brown or black eyes and dark skin. **3** *n.* person, especially a woman, with such hair, eyes, and skin.

brunt (brunt), *n.* the main force or violence; hardest part: *The island felt the brunt of the hurricane.*

brush¹ (brush), **1** *n.* a set of bristles, hair, or wires set in a stiff back or fastened to a handle. Brushes are used for sweeping, scrubbing, smoothing, or painting. **2** *v.* to sweep, scrub, smooth or paint with a brush; use a brush on: *I brushed my hair.* **3** *n.* act of brushing; a rub with a brush: *I gave my hair a good brush.* **4** *v.* to wipe away; remove: *The child brushed the tears from his eyes.* **5** *v.* to touch lightly in passing: *No harm was done—your bumper just brushed our fender.* **6** *n.* a light touch in passing: *Give the desk a brush with the cloth.* **7** *n.* a short, brisk fight or quarrel: *After one brush with the police, she has stayed out of trouble.* **8** *n.* the bushy tail of an animal, especially of a fox. **9** *n.* piece of carbon, copper, etc., used to carry the electricity from the revolving part of an electric motor or generator to the outside circuit. ❑ *n., pl.* brush·es. —brush′like, *adj.*

brush aside, to dismiss; refuse to consider: *She brushed aside their criticisms and continued her work.*

brush off, **1** to refuse to see or listen to: *The mayor brushed off the committee.* **2** to dismiss as unimportant; make light of: *The mayor brushed off the reporter's question with a joke.*

brush up or brush up, to refresh your knowledge of: *I brushed up on decimals before the math test.*

brush² (brush), *n.* **1** branches broken or cut off; brushwood. **2** bushes, shrubs, and small trees growing thickly; brushwood. **3** thinly settled country; backwoods.

brush·off (brush′ôf′), *n.* refusal or dismissal of a request, person, etc.: *The reporter got a polite brushoff when she asked the company president for an interview.*

brush·wood (brush′wùd′), *n.* brush² (defs. 1 and 2).

brush·y (brush′ē), *adj.* covered with bushes, shrubs, etc. ❑ *adj.* brush·i·er, brush·i·est.

brusque (brusk), *adj.* abrupt in manner or speech; blunt: *A brusque wave of the hand was her only reply to my question.* —brusque′ly, *adv.* —brusque′ness, *n.*

Brus·sels (brus′əlz), *n.* capital of Belgium, in the central part.

Brussels sprouts, a garden vegetable that looks like small heads of cabbage. The heads grow along the stalk of a plant related to cabbage.

bru·tal (brü′tl), *adj.* savagely cruel; inhuman: *a brutal beating.* ■ See Synonym Study at **cruel.** —bru′tal·ly, *adv.*

bru·tal·i·ty (brü tal′ə tē), *n.* **1** brutal conduct; cruelty. **2** a brutal act. ❑ *n., pl.* bru·tal·i·ties for 2.

bru·tal·ize (brü′tl īz), *v.* to make brutal: *War brutalizes many people.* ❑ *v.* bru·tal·ized, bru·tal·iz·ing. —bru′tal·i·za′tion, *n.*

brute (brüt), **1** *n.* an animal without power to reason. **2** *adj.* like an animal; without power to reason. **3** *n.* a cruel or coarse person. **4** *adj.* without feeling: *the brute forces of nature.*

brut·ish (brü′tish), *adj.* like a brute; cruel or coarse. —brut′ish·ly, *adv.* —brut′ish·ness, *n.*

Bru·tus (brü′təs), *n.* **Mar·cus Ju·ni·us** (mär′kəs jün′yəs), 85-42 B.C., Roman politician. He was the leader of the plot to kill Julius Caesar. Brutus and others stabbed Caesar to death in 44 B.C.

Bry·an (brī′ən), *n.* **William Jen·nings** (jen′ingz), 1860-1925, American politician and public speaker. ■ William Jennings Bryan ran for president three times but was never elected. He opposed Clarence Darrow in the Tennessee evolution trial of 1925.

Bryce Canyon National Park

Bryce Canyon National Park (brīs), a national park in S Utah, with brilliantly colored sandstone canyons and towers.

bry·o·phyte (brī′ə fīt), *n.* any of many plants that have no flowers, roots, stems, or leaves. Mosses and liverworts are bryophytes.

b.s., bill of sale.

B.S., Bachelor of Science.

btl., bottle.

btry., battery.

Btu, B.t.u., or **B.T.U.,** British thermal unit or units.

bu., bushel or bushels.

bub·ble (bub′əl), **1** *n.* a spherical film of liquid enclosing air or gas: *soap bubbles.* **2** *n.* a space filled with air or gas in a liquid or solid. Sometimes there are bubbles in ice or in glass. **3** *v.* to have bubbles; make bubbles; send up or rise in bubbles: *Boiling water bubbles in the pot.* **4** *v.* to make sounds like water boiling; gurgle: *The baby bubbled and cooed.* **5** *n.* a sound like water boiling. **6** *n.* plan or idea that looks good, but soon falls apart. ❑ *v.* bub·bled, bub·bling.

bubble over, **1** be very full and hot; overflow when heated: *The teakettle bubbled over on the stove.* **2** be very enthusiastic: *The children bubbled over at the idea of a camping trip.*

bubble bath, a bath with a mass of bubbles on the surface, formed by adding a certain kind of soap.

bubble chamber, a container of a special liquid through which electrically charged particles make bubbly tracks. The tracks help scientists examine and identify the particles.

bubble gum, a chewing gum that can be blown out through the lips so as to form a large bubble.

bub·bly (bub′lē), *adj.* full of bubbles: *bubbly soda pop.* ❑ *adj.* bub·bli·er, bub·bli·est.

bu·bon·ic plague (byü bon′ik), a very dangerous contagious disease, accompanied by fever, chills, and swelling of the lymph glands. It is carried to human beings by fleas from infected rats.

buc·ca·neer (buk′ə nir′), *n.* pirate.

WORD STORY Buccaneer comes from a Tupi word meaning "a frame for preserving meat." Early Caribbean pirates preserved meat in this way, which they learned from Indians of the region.

Bu·chan·an (byü kan′ən), *n.* **James,** 1791-1868, the 15th president of the United States, from 1857 to 1861.

Bu·cha·rest (bü′kə rest), *n.* capital of Romania, in the S part.

buck¹ (buk), **1** *n.* a male deer, goat, hare, rabbit, antelope, or sheep. **2** *v.* to jump into the air with the back curved and come down with the front legs stiff: *My horse began to buck violently, but I managed to stay on.* **3** *v.* to throw by bucking: *The cowboy was bucked off the bronco.* **4** *n.* a throw or attempt to throw by bucking. **5** *v.* to fight against; work against: *The swimmer bucked the current with strong strokes.* **—buck′er,** *n.*

buck for, to work hard for: *bucking for a promotion.*

buck up, to cheer up; be brave or energetic: *Buck up; everything will be all right.*

buck² (buk), *n.* INFORMAL. dollar.

Buck (buk), *n.* Pearl S. (pėrl), 1892-1974, American novelist. ■ **Pearl S. Buck** won the Nobel Prize for literature in 1938. She grew up in China, where her parents were missionaries and she returned there after college to teach. Her novels were often about peasant life in China.

buck·a·roo (buk′ə rü′ *or* buk′ə rü′), *n.* cowboy. ❑ *n., pl.* **buck·a·roos.**

> **WORD STORY**   **Buckaroo** probably comes from a west African word meaning "white man." People changed the end of that word so that it sounded like *vaquero,* a Spanish word meaning "cowboy."

buck·board (buk′bôrd′), *n.* (earlier) an open four-wheeled carriage with the seat fastened to a platform of long, springy boards.

buck·et (buk′it), *n.* **1** container of wood, metal, or plastic for carrying liquids, sand, etc.; pail. **2** bucketful: *Pour in about four buckets of water.*

buck·et·ful (buk′it fül), *n.* amount that a bucket can hold. ❑ *n., pl.* **buck·et·fuls** or **buck·ets·ful.**

bucket seat, a single seat with a rounded back, used in cars, small airplanes, etc.

buck·eye (buk′ī′), *n.* **1** any of several North American trees or bushes closely related to the horse chestnut, with showy clusters of small flowers, large divided leaves, and large brown seeds. **2** a seed from one of these.

Buck·ing·ham Palace (buk′ing əm), official London residence of all British sovereigns since 1837.

Buckingham Palace

buck·le (buk′əl), **1** *n.* catch or clasp used to hold together the ends of a belt, strap, or ribbon. **2** *v.* to fasten together with a buckle: *buckle your belt.* **3** *n.* a metal, plastic, etc., ornament for a shoe. **4** *v.* to bend out of shape; bulge, kink, or wrinkle: *The heavy snowfall caused the roof of the shed to buckle.* **5** *n.* a bend, bulge, kink, or wrinkle. ❑ *v.* **buck·led, buck·ling.**

buckle down, to work hard: *I buckled down to work before the test.*

buck·ler (buk′lər), *n.* a small, round shield.

buck·min·ster·ful·ler·ene (buk′min stər fül′ə rēn′), *n.* a molecule of carbon containing 60 atoms, shaped like a soccer ball and with links resembling a geodesic dome's; buckyball. [Buckminsterfullerene comes from the name of the American designer who developed the geodesic dome.]

buck·ram (buk′rəm), *n.* a coarse cloth made stiff with glue or something like glue.

buck·saw (buk′sò′), *n.* saw set in a light frame and held with both hands.

buck·shot (buk′shot′), *n.* a large lead shot used to shoot large game, such as deer.

buck·skin (buk′skin′), *n.* **1** a strong, soft leather, yellowish or grayish in color, made from the skins of deer or sheep. **2 buck·skins,** *pl.* clothing made of buckskin.

buck·tooth (buk′tüth′), *n.* an upper front tooth that sticks out beyond the other teeth. ❑ *n., pl.* **buck·teeth.**

buck·toothed (buk′tütht′), *adj.* having upper front teeth that stick out beyond the other teeth.

buck·wheat (buk′wēt′), *n.* **1** any of several related plants with black or gray, triangular seeds and fragrant white or pink flowers. **2** their seeds, used as food for animals or ground into flour for pancakes or other foods.

buck·y·ball (buk′ē bòl′), *n.* buckminsterfullerene.

bu·col·ic (byü kol′ik), *adj.* **1** of shepherds; pastoral. **2** rustic; rural. **—bu·col′i·cal·ly,** *adv.*

bud (bud), **1** *n.* a small swelling that will grow into a flower, leaf, or branch: *Buds on the trees are a sign of spring.* **2** *n.* a partly opened flower or leaf. **3** *v.* to put forth buds: *The trees are budding.* **4** *v.* to begin to grow or develop. **5** *n.* a small swelling on certain plants and animals that grows into a whole new plant or animal. ❑ *v.* **bud·ded, bud·ding. —bud′der,** *n.*

in bud, budding: *In the spring the pear tree is in bud.*

nip in the bud, to stop at the very beginning: *I tried to nip their argument in the bud before it became a fight.*

Bu·da·pest (bü′də pest), *n.* capital of Hungary, on the Danube.

Bud·dha (bü′də *or* bůd′ə), *n.* 563?-483? B.C., religious teacher of northern India, founder of Buddhism. ■ **Buddha** believed that people could escape lives of suffering by ending their attachment to worldly things. Then they would feel peace and happiness. [Buddha comes from a Sanskrit word meaning "awake."]

Bud·dhism (bü′diz əm *or* bůd′iz əm), *n.* religion based on the teachings of Buddha. It developed during his lifetime in northern India and spread widely after his death over central, southeastern, and eastern Asia.

Bud·dhist (bü′dist *or* bůd′ist), **1** *n.* person who believes in and follows the teachings of Buddha. **2** *adj.* of Buddha, his followers, or the religion founded by him: *a Buddhist temple.*

bud·ding (bud′ing), *adj.* showing signs of becoming; developing: *She is a budding scientist.*

bud·dy (bud′ē), *n.* INFORMAL. a close friend; comrade; pal. ❑ *n., pl.* **bud·dies.**

buddy system, an arrangement in which two people taking part in the same activity work as a pair, stay together, and are responsible for each other's safety.

budge (buj), *v.* to move even a little: *The stone was so heavy that we could not budge it. I was too tired to budge from my chair.* ❑ *v.* **budged, budg·ing.**

budg·et (buj′it), **1** *n.* estimate of the amount of money that will probably be received and spent for various purposes in a given time. Governments, companies, schools, families, etc., make budgets. **2** *v.* to make a plan for spending: *She budgeted her allowance so that she could save some money each week for a new tennis racket. Budget your time.* **3** *v.* to put in a budget: *He budgeted six dollars a week for snacks.* **4** *adj.* cheap; not expensive: *a budget vacation.*

> **WORD STORY**   **Budget** comes from a French word meaning "small leather bag." The word **bulge** comes from this same word. In old times, people carried money in small leather bags, often attached to their belts. The more money, the more the bag bulged.

budg·et·ar·y (buj′ə ter′ē), *adj.* of a budget.

bue·no (bwā′nō), *adj.* SPANISH. good.

Bue·nos Ai·res (bwā′nəs ī′rēz *or* bwā′nəs ar′ēz), port and capital of Argentina, in the E part.

buff (buf), **1** *adj.* dull yellow. **2** *n.* a dull yellow. **3** *n.* a strong, soft, dull yellow leather. Buff was formerly made from the skin of buffalo and is now made from the skin of oxen. **4** *v.* to polish with a wheel or stick covered with leather. **5** *v.* to polish; shine: *I buffed my shoes to make them shine.* **6** *n.* a polishing wheel or stick covered with leather. **7** *n.* a fan or devotee: *a model-train buff.*

a	hat	ė	term	ò	order	ch	child		a in about
ā	age	i	it	oi	oil	ng	long		e in taken
ä	far	ī	ice	ou	out	sh	she	ə	i in pencil
â	care	o	hot	u	cup	th	thin		o in lemon
e	let	ō	open	ů	put	ŦH	then		u in circus
ē	equal	ò	saw	ü	rule	zh	measure		

buf·fa·lo (buf′ə lō), *n.* **1** any of several kinds of large animals related to cattle, such as the water buffalo. **2** bison. ❑ *n., pl.* **buf·fa·lo, buf·fa·loes,** or **buf·fa·los.**

Buf·fa·lo (buf′ə lō), *n.* port in W New York State, on Lake Erie.

Buffalo Bill (bil), 1846-1917, American frontier scout and showman. His last name was **Cody** (kō′dē).

buff·er[1] (buf′ər), *n.* **1** anything that helps to soften the shock of a blow or to balance the effect of opposing forces: *He acted as a buffer between the quarreling children.* **2** area in the memory of a computer used to store information temporarily until it can be processed further.

buff·er[2] (buf′ər), *n.* **1** stick or pad having a soft cloth or leather surface for polishing. **2** person who polishes.

buffer state, a small country between two larger countries that are enemies or competitors.

buffer zone, a neutral area used as a barrier between two enemy areas.

buf·fet[1] (buf′it), **1** *v.* to knock about, strike, or hurt: *The waves buffeted the small boat.* **2** *n.* a knock, stroke, or hurt: *The boat withstood the buffets of the waves.* —**buf′fet·er,** *n.*

buf·fet[2] (bu fā′ *or* bù fā′), *n.* **1** a low cabinet with a flat top for dishes and with shelves or drawers for silver and table linen; sideboard. **2** counter where food and drinks are served. **3** restaurant with a counter like this. **4** meal at which guests serve themselves from food laid out on a table or sideboard.

buf·foon (bu fün′), *n.* **1** person who amuses people with tricks, pranks, and jokes; clown. **2** person who makes undignified or rude jokes.

buf·foon·er·y (bu fü′nər ē), *n.* **1** tricks, pranks, and jokes of a clown. **2** undignified or rude joking.

bug (bug), **1** *n.* insect without wings or with a front pair of wings thickened at the base, and a pointed beak for piercing and sucking. Bedbugs, lice, and chinch bugs are true bugs. **2** *n.* any insect or other animal something like a true bug. Ants, spiders, beetles, and flies are often called bugs. **3** *n.* INFORMAL. a disease germ: *the flu bug.* **4** *n.* mechanical defect or difficulty: *The engine needed repair because of a bug in the design of the fuel system.* **5** *n.* a mistake in the instructions given to a computer: *It took all day to find the bugs that kept the program from working.* **6** *n.* a very small microphone hidden within a room, a telephone, etc., for overhearing conversation. **7** *v.* to hide a small microphone within a room, telephone, etc.: *The spy bugged enemy headquarters.* **8** *v.* INFORMAL. to annoy; irritate: *His constant grumbling bugs me.* ❑ *v.* **bugged, bug·ging.** —**bug′like′,** *adj.*

bug·a·boo (bug′ə bü), *n.* an imaginary or real thing that is feared; bogy. ❑ *n., pl.* **bug·a·boos.**

bug·bear (bug′bâr′), *n.* **1** bugaboo. **2** a difficulty, problem, or obstacle.

bug-eyed (bug′īd′), *adj.* SLANG. having eyes wide open and bulging, especially from wonder or excitement.

bug·gy (bug′ē), *n.* **1** a light carriage with a single large seat, with or without a top, pulled by one horse. **2** a baby carriage. ❑ *n., pl.* **bug·gies.**

bu·gle (byü′gəl), *n.* a musical instrument like a small trumpet, made of brass or copper, and sometimes having keys or valves. Bugles are used in the armed forces for sounding calls and orders, and for playing band music. [**Bugle** comes from a Latin word meaning "ox." The first musical horns were made from the horns of oxen.]

bu·gler (byü′glər), *n.* person who plays a bugle.

build (bild), **1** *v.* to make by putting materials together; construct: *People build houses and machines. Birds build nests.* **2** *v.* to form or produce gradually; develop: *The lawyer built her case on facts.* **3** *n.* a bodily shape: *a person with a heavy build.* ❑ *v.* **built, build·ing.**

build up, 1 to strengthen or develop: *When sick you must rest to build up your health.* **2** to fill with houses: *The hill overlooking the town has been built up in the last five years.*

build·er (bil′dər), *n.* **1** person whose business is constructing buildings. **2** person or animal that builds.

build·ing (bil′ding), *n.* **1** thing built. Barns, factories, stores, houses, and hotels are all buildings. **2** business, art, or process of making houses, stores, bridges, ships, etc.

WORD BANK **Buildings** are put up by many people with many different jobs. If you want to learn more about these jobs, you can start by looking these up in this dictionary.

architect	designer	ironworker	plasterer
bricklayer	draftsman	laborer	plumber
cabinetmaker	electrician	locksmith	roofer
carpenter	engineer	mason	stonemason
contractor	glazier	painter[1]	welder

---

build·up (bild′up′), *n.* **1** an increase in the strength or size of: *a military buildup, a buildup of pressure.* **2** promotion, especially by the use of publicity: *The play has had a big buildup in the press.*

built (bilt), *v.* past tense and past participle of **build**: *The bird built a nest. It was built of twigs.*

built-in (bilt′in′), *adj.* put in as part of something; not movable: *a built-in bookcase.*

Bu·jum·bu·ra (bü jəm bùr′ə), *n.* capital of Burundi.

bulb (bulb), *n.* **1** a round, underground part from which certain plants grow. Onions, tulips, and lilies grow from bulbs. **2** a thick part of an underground stem resembling a bulb; tuber: *a crocus bulb.* **3** any object with a rounded end or swelling part: *a light bulb, the bulb of a thermometer.* —**bulb′like′,** *adj.*

bulb·ous (bul′bəs), *adj.* **1** shaped like a bulb; rounded and swelling: *The clown had a bulbous red nose.* **2** having bulbs.

Bul·gar·i·a (bul gâr′ē ə), *n.* country in SE Europe, on the Black Sea. *Capital:* Sofia. —**Bul·gar′i·an,** *adj., n.*

bulge (bulj), **1** *v.* to swell outward: *My pockets bulged with candy.* ▪ See Synonym Study at **expand. 2** *n.* an outward swelling: *The wallet made a bulge in his pocket.* **3 Bulge, Battle of the,** the December 1944 counterattack by German forces against U.S. troops in Belgium, resulting in a large temporary bulge in the front lines, before reinforcements turned back the Germans. ❑ *v.* **bulged, bulg·ing.** [See Word Story at **budget.**]

bulge (def. 1)—chipmunk with bulging cheek pouches

bul·gur (bùl′gùr), *n.* the cracked kernels of wheat that has been boiled and dried again, used as a food. Bulgur originated in the Middle East.

bulg·y (bul′jē), *adj.* having a bulge or bulges. ❑ *adj.* **bulg·i·er, bulg·i·est.** —**bulg′i·ness,** *n.*

bu·lim·i·a (bü lē′mē ə), *n.* an eating disorder in which a person sometimes eats very large amounts and may then force vomiting.

WORD STORY **Bulimia** comes from Greek words meaning "cow" or "ox" and "hunger." A person with bulimia sometimes eats enough food to feed a large animal.

---

bulk (bulk), *n.* **1** size, especially large size: *An elephant has great bulk.* **2** the largest part of: *The oceans cover the bulk of the earth's surface.*

in bulk, 1 lying loose in heaps, not in packages: *beans sold in bulk.* **2** in large quantities: *ore shipped in bulk.*

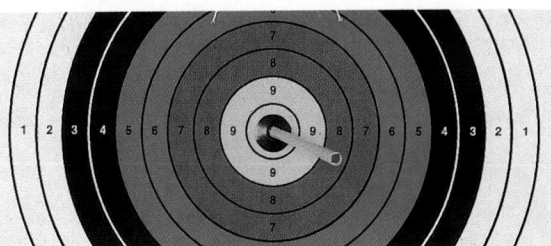

bull's-eye (def. 2)

bulk·head (bulk′hed′), *n.* **1** one of the upright partitions dividing a ship into compartments. **2** wall or partition built in a tunnel to hold back water, earth, rocks, gas, etc.

bulk·y (bul′kē), *adj.* **1** large in size or space: *Bulky shipments are often sent in freight cars.* **2** hard to handle; clumsy: *a bulky package.* ❑ *adj.* **bulk·i·er, bulk·i·est. –bulk′i·ly,** *adv.* **–bulk′i·ness,** *n.*

bull[1] (bul), **1** *n.* the full-grown male of cattle. **2** *n.* the male of the whale, elephant, seal, and other large mammals. **3** *adj.* male: *a bull moose.* **–bull′-like′,** *adj.*

bull[2] (bul), *n.* a formal announcement or official order from the pope.

bull·dog (bul′dog′), **1** *n.* a heavy, muscular dog of medium height with a large head, very short nose, strong jaws, and short hair. **2** *adj.* like a bulldog's: *a bulldog grip.* **3** *v.* to bring a steer to the ground by grasping its horns and twisting its neck. ❑ *v.* **bull·dogged, bull·dog·ging.**

bull·doze (bul′dōz′), *v.* **1** to frighten, sometimes by violence or threats; bully: *The chairman bulldozed the whole committee into voting for his proposal.* **2** to move, clear, dig, or level with a bulldozer. ❑ *v.* **bull·dozed, bull·doz·ing.**

bull·doz·er (bul′dō′zər), *n.* a powerful crawler tractor with a wide steel blade that pushes rocks and earth and knocks down small trees, used for grading, road building, etc.

bul·let (bul′it), *n.* piece of lead, steel, or other metal shaped to be fired from a pistol, rifle, or other small gun.

bul·le·tin (bul′ə tən), *n.* **1** a short statement of news: *Sports bulletins and weather bulletins are published in most newspapers.* **2** magazine or newspaper appearing regularly, especially one published by a club or society for its members.

bulletin board, 1 board on which notices are posted. **2** a computer service that enables users to leave and read messages for all other users. Messages are stored in a central computer, to which users may be connected by telephone line and modems.

bul·let·proof (bul′it prüf′), *adj.* made so that a bullet cannot go through; resistant to bullets: *a bulletproof vest.*

bullet train, a high-speed passenger train.

bull·fight (bul′fīt′), *n.* a public entertainment in which people perform a series of complex, dangerous acts with a bull, usually killing him at last with a sword. Bullfights are popular especially in Spain, Mexico, and parts of South America.

bull·fight·er (bul′fī′tər), *n.* person who fights a bull in an arena.

bull·fight·ing (bul′fī′ting), *n.* act or sport of fighting a bull in an arena.

bull·frog (bul′frog′), *n.* a large North American frog that makes a loud, croaking noise.

bull·head (bul′hed′), *n.* any of various North American catfish with large, broad heads.

bull·head·ed (bul′hed′id), *adj.* stupidly stubborn; obstinate; headstrong. **–bull′head′ed·ness,** *n.*

bull·horn (bul′hôrn′), *n.* a megaphone that has been electrically amplified.

bul·lion (bul′yən), *n.* gold or silver in the form of lumps or bars.

bull·ish (bul′ish), *adj.* like a bull in manner or temper. **–bull′ish·ly,** *adv.* **–bull′ish·ness,** *n.*

bull·ock (bul′ək), *n.* ox; steer.

bull·pen (bul′pen′), *n.* **1** in baseball: **a** a place where relief pitchers warm up during a game. **b** *pl.* relief pitchers as a group. **2** a large business office not divided into individual spaces.

bull·ring (bul′ring′), *n.* arena for bullfights.

Bull Run, stream in NE Virginia where two Civil War battles took place in 1861 and 1862.

bull's-eye (bulz′ī′), *n.* **1** center of a target. **2** shot that hits it. **3** a thick piece of dome-shaped glass in the deck or side of a ship to let in light. **4** (earlier) a small lantern with a dome-shaped lens in its side to focus light.

bull terrier, a strong, active, short-haired dog, originally bred by crossing bulldogs and terriers.

bul·ly (bul′ē), **1** *n.* person who teases, frightens, threatens, or hurts smaller or weaker people. **2** *v.* to frighten someone into doing something by noisy talk or threats: *Stop trying to bully me into doing what you want.* ❑ *n., pl.* **bul·lies;** *v.* **bul·lied, bul·ly·ing.**

bul·rush (bul′rush′), *n.* any of various tall, slender plants that grow in wet places. ❑ *n., pl.* **bul·rush·es.**

bul·wark (bul′wərk), *n.* **1** person, thing, or idea that is a defense or a protection: *A free press and free speech are bulwarks of democracy.* **2** wall of earth or other material for defense against the enemy. **3** breakwater for protection against the force of the waves. **4** Usually, **bulwarks,** *pl.* side of a ship above the deck.

bum (bum), INFORMAL. **1** *n.* an idle person; tramp. **2** *v.* to get food, money, etc., by sponging on others; beg: *bum a ride.* **3** *v.* to loaf around; idle about. **4** *adj.* not working well; injured or damaged: *a bum knee.* ❑ *v.* **bummed, bum·ming;** *adj.* **bum·mer, bum·mest.**
bum steer, bad advice.

bum·ble (bum′bəl), *v.* to act or do something in a clumsy or awkward way: *I forgot his name and bumbled the introduction.* ❑ *v.* **bum·bled, bum·bling. –bum′bling·ly,** *adv.*

bum·ble·bee (bum′bəl bē′), *n.* any of numerous large bees with thick, hairy bodies, usually banded with gold. Bumblebees make a loud, buzzing sound. They live in small colonies in underground nests, old logs, etc. ❑ *n., pl.* **bum·ble·bees.**

bum·mer (bum′ər), *n.* SLANG. any very unpleasant thing, happening, or experience.

bump (bump), **1** *v.* to hit or strike against something large or solid: *She bumped against the table in the dark. That truck bumped our car.* **2** *n.* a heavy blow or knock: *The bump knocked our car forward a few feet.* **3** *v.* to move by bumping against things: *Our car bumped along the dirt road.* **4** *n.* a swelling caused by a bump: *He has a bump on his head from getting hit by a baseball.* **5** *n.* any swelling or lump: *Avoid the bump in the road.*

bump·er (bum′pər), **1** *n.* bar or bars of metal, rubber, or plastic across the front and back of a car or truck that protect it from being damaged if bumped. **2** *adj.* unusually large: *The farmer raised a bumper crop of wheat last year.*

bumper car, a small electric car with large rubber bumpers, driven in an enclosure in an amusement park. The drivers of the bumper cars purposely run into the cars of others.

bump·kin (bump′kən), *n.* an awkward or simple person from the country.

bump·y (bum′pē), *adj.* **1** having bumps; full of bumps: *a bumpy road.* **2** causing bumps; rough: *a bumpy ride.* ❑ *adj.* **bump·i·er, bump·i·est. –bump′i·ly,** *adv.* **–bump′i·ness,** *n.*

bun (bun), *n.* **1** bread or cake in small portions. Buns are often slightly sweetened and may contain spice, raisins, etc. **2** hair coiled at the back of the head in a knot.

bunch (bunch), **1** *n.* group of things of the same kind growing, fastened, placed, or thought of together: *a bunch of grapes, a bunch of flowers.* **2** INFORMAL. group of people: *They are a friendly bunch.* **3** *v.* to come together in one place: *The sheep were all bunched in the shed to keep warm.* **4** *v.* to bring together and make into a bunch: *We have bunched the flowers for you to carry home.* ❑ *n., pl.* **bunch·es. –bunch′er,** *n.*

USAGE NOTE Formal English uses **bunch** only for objects growing together or fastened together: *a bunch of radishes, a bunch of keys.* Informal English, however, uses **bunch** for a small group of anything, including people: *A bunch of us meet at the gym every Tuesday evening for basketball practice.*

a	hat	ė	term	ô	order	ch	child		a in about
ā	age	i	it	oi	oil	ng	long		e in taken
ä	far	ī	ice	ou	out	sh	she	ə	i in pencil
â	care	o	hot	u	cup	th	thin		o in lemon
e	let	ō	open	u̇	put	ŦH	then		u in circus
ē	equal	ò	saw	ü	rule	zh	measure		

bunting² —about 5 in. (13 cm) long

Bunche (bunch), *n.* **Ralph** (ralf), 1904-1971, American educator and diplomat. He won the Nobel Peace Prize in 1950 for his work toward Arab-Israeli peace.

bunch·y (bun′chē), *adj.* **1** having bunches. **2** growing in bunches. □ *adj.* **bunch·i·er, bunch·i·est.**

bun·dle (bun′dl), **1** *n.* number of things tied or wrapped together: *bundles of old newspapers.* **2** *n.* package; parcel: *My arms were so full of bundles that I had trouble opening the door.* **3** *v.* to tie or wrap together; make into a bundle. **4** *v.* to send or go in a hurry; hustle: *The children were bundled off to school.* □ *v.* **bun·dled, bun·dling. —bun′dler,** *n.*

bundle up, to dress warmly: *Bundle up! It's cold.*

bung (bung), *n.* **1** stopper for closing the hole in the side or end of a barrel, keg, or cask. **2** bunghole.

bun·ga·low (bung′gə lō), *n.* a small one-story house. [Bungalow comes from a Hindustani word meaning "of Bengal." Bengal is a warm country, now called Bangladesh, where people need only small, lightly built houses.]

bun·gee (bun′jē), *n.* an elastic cord. Bungee cords with hooks are used to attach things. Long bungee cords are used in recreation. □ *n., pl.* **bun·gees.**

bung·hole (bung′hōl′), *n.* hole in the side or end of a barrel, keg, or cask through which it is filled and emptied.

bun·gle (bung′gəl), **1** *v.* to do or make in a clumsy, unskilled way: *I tried to make a birdhouse but bungled the job.* **2** *n.* a clumsy, unskilled performance or piece of work. □ *v.* **bun·gled, bun·gling. —bun′gler,** *n.* **—bun′gling·ly,** *adv.*

bun·ion (bun′yən), *n.* a painful, inflamed swelling on the foot, especially on the first joint of the big toe.

bunk¹ (bungk), **1** *n.* a narrow bed, often stacked one above another: *My sister sleeps in the top bunk.* **2** *v.* to sleep in a bunk; occupy a bunk. **3** *n.* any place to sleep. **4** *v.* to sleep in rough quarters: *We bunked in a barn.*

bunk² (bungk), *n.* insincere talk; nonsense; humbug.

WORD STORY Bunk² is short for Buncombe County, North Carolina. A local congressman in the early 1800s made so many long-winded speeches in Washington "for Buncombe" that people used the name for any empty talk.

bunk·er (bung′kər), *n.* **1** place or bin for coal or oil on a ship. **2** sandy hollow or mound of earth on a golf course, used as an obstacle. **3** a fortified shelter built partly or entirely below ground.

Bunker Hill, hill near Boston, Massachusetts. An early battle of the Revolutionary War was fought near there on June 17, 1775.

bunk·house (bungk′hous′), *n.* a rough building with sleeping quarters or bunks, especially one provided for workers on a ranch. □ *n., pl.* **bunk·hous·es** (bungk′hou′ziz).

bun·ny (bun′ē), *n.* a rabbit. □ *n., pl.* **bun·nies.**

Bun·sen burner (bun′sən), a gas burner with a very hot, blue flame, used in laboratories.

bunt (bunt), **1** *v.* to tap a baseball lightly with a bat so that the ball goes to the ground and rolls only a short distance. **2** *n.* act of bunting a baseball. **3** *n.* baseball that is bunted. **—bunt′er,** *n.*

bun·ting¹ (bun′ting), *n.* **1** a thin cloth used for flags. **2** long pieces of cloth having the colors and designs of a flag, used to decorate buildings and streets on holidays and special occasions. **3** a baby's warm, hooded, outer garment closed at the bottom.

bun·ting² (bun′ting), *n.* any of various small, usually brightly colored, seed-eating birds with stout bills.

Bun·yan (bun′yən), *n.* **Paul,** (in American folklore) a giant lumberjack with amazing strength.

buoy (bü′ē *or* boi), **1** *n.* an anchored object floating on the water to warn against hidden rocks or shallows or to show the safe part of a channel. **2** *n.* ring, belt, or vest used as a life preserver. **3** *v.* **buoy up, a** to hold up; keep from sinking: *Life jackets buoyed them up until rescuers came.* **b** to support or encourage: *Hope can buoy you up, even when something goes wrong.* □ *v.* **buoyed, buoy·ing.** ■ Another word that can sound like this is **boy.**

buoy·an·cy (boi′ən sē *or* bü′yən sē), *n.* **1** tendency to float: *Wood has more buoyancy than iron, since it is less dense.* **2** power to keep things afloat: *Salt water has greater buoyancy than fresh water.* **3** tendency to be hopeful and cheerful: *Her buoyancy keeps her from being downhearted.*

buoy·ant (boi′ənt *or* bü′yənt), *adj.* **1** tending to float: *Wood and cork are buoyant in water; iron and lead are not.* **2** able to keep things afloat: *Salt water is more buoyant than fresh water.* **3** cheerful and hopeful: *I was in a buoyant mood on that sunny morning.* **—buoy′ant·ly,** *adv.*

bur (bėr), **1** *n.* a prickly, clinging seedcase or flower of some plants. Burs stick to cloth and fur. **2** *n.* plant or weed that has burs. **3** *v.* to remove burs from. □ *v.* **burred, bur·ring.** Also, **burr.**

bur·den¹ (bėrd′n), **1** *n.* something carried; load of things, care, work, duty, or sorrow: *Everyone in my family shares the burden of housework.* **2** *n.* a load too heavy to carry easily; heavy load: *His debts are a burden that will bankrupt him.* **3** *v.* to put a load on; weigh down: *I don't want to burden you with my troubles.* **4** *n.* quantity of freight that a ship can carry; weight of a ship's cargo.

bur·den² (bėrd′n), *n.* the main idea or message: *The need for more pollution control was the burden of her speech.*

bur·den·some (bėrd′n səm), *adj.* hard to bear; very heavy; oppressive: *burdensome duties.* **—bur′den·some·ness,** *n.*

bur·dock (bėr′dok′), *n.* a coarse weed with burs and broad leaves.

bur·eau (byür′ō), *n.* **1** piece of furniture with drawers for clothes and usually a mirror; dresser. **2** a business office, especially one at which facts of various kinds are available: *We asked about the bus fares at the travel bureau.* **3** Usually, **Bureau,** a division within a government department: *Bureau of Land Management, Bureau of Indian Affairs.* □ *n., pl.* **bur·eaus** or **bur·eaux.** [Bureau comes from a French word meaning "coarse woolen cloth." Early desks were covered with this material.]

bu·reauc·ra·cy (byü rok′rə sē), *n.* **1** system of government by groups of officials, each dealing with its own kind of business. **2** the officials running government bureaus. **3** too much insistence on rigid routine, resulting in delay in making decisions; red tape. □ *n., pl.* **bu·reauc·ra·cies** for 2.

bur·eau·crat (byür′ə krat), *n.* **1** official in a bureaucracy. **2** a government official who insists on rigid routine. **—bur′eau·crat′ic,** *adj.* **—bur′eau·crat′i·cal·ly,** *adv.*

bur·eaux (byür′ōz), *n.pl.* a plural of **bureau.**

burg (bėrg), *n.* INFORMAL. town or city. ■ Another word that sounds like this is **berg.**

bur·geon (bėr′jən), *v.* to grow or shoot forth; sprout: *New suburbs have burgeoned all around the city.*

burg·er (bėr′gər), *n.* hamburger. ■ Another word that sounds like this is **burgher.**

Bur·ger (bėr′gər), *n.* **Warren,** 1907-1995, chief justice of the U.S. Supreme Court from 1969 to 1986.

bur·gess (bėr′jis), *n.* member of the lower house of the colonial legislature in Virginia or Maryland. □ *n., pl.* **bur·gess·es.**

burgh·er (bėr′gər), *n.* citizen of a town; citizen. ■ Another word that sounds like this is **burger.**

bur·glar (bėr′glər), *n.* person who breaks into a house or other building to steal something.

116

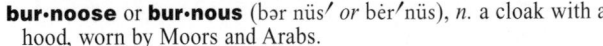

bur·glar·ize (bėr′glə rīz′), *v.* to break into a building to steal. ❑ *v.* **bur·glar·ized, bur·glar·iz·ing.**

bur·glar·y (bėr′glər ē), *n.* act of breaking into a house or other building to steal something. ❑ *n., pl.* **bur·glar·ies.**

bur·gle (bėr′gəl), *v.* to burglarize. ❑ *v.* **bur·gled, bur·gling.**

Bur·gun·di·an (bər gun′dē ən), **1** *adj.* of Burgundy or its people. **2** *n.* person born or living in Burgundy.

Bur·gun·dy (bėr′gən dē), *n.* **1** region in E France. Once an independent kingdom, it became a duchy and later a province of France. **2** a wine first made there. ❑ *n., pl.* **Bur·gun·dies** for 2.

> **Burgundy (1477)**
> ENGLAND
> N
> FLANDERS
> LUXEMBOURG
> *English Channel*
> HOLY ROMAN EMPIRE
> Brittany FRANCE
> BURGUNDY
> ☐ Burgundy
> ■ Burgundian Empire, 1477

bur·i·al (ber′ē əl), *n.* act of putting a dead body in a grave, in a tomb, or in the sea; burying: *a burial at sea.*

bur·ied (ber′ēd), *v.* past tense and past participle of **bury:** *The dog buried a bone. Nuts were buried under the tree.*

Bur·ki·na Fa·so (bur′kē′nä fä′sō), country in W Africa, north of Ghana. *Capital:* Ouagadougou.

bur·lap (bėr′lap), *n.* a coarse fabric made from jute or hemp, used to make bags.

bur·lesque (bər lesk′), **1** *n.* a story, play, etc., that treats a serious subject ridiculously or a trivial subject as if it were important: *Mark Twain's story, "A Connecticut Yankee in King Arthur's Court," is a burlesque of the legends about King Arthur.* **2** *v.* to imitate so as to make fun of. **3** *n.* a ridiculous imitation of something worthy or dignified. ❑ *v.* **bur·lesqued, bur·les·quing.**

Bur·ling·ton (bėr′ling tən), *n.* city in NW Vermont.

bur·ly (bėr′lē), *adj.* big and strong; sturdy: *a burly wrestler.* ❑ *adj.* **bur·li·er, bur·li·est. —bur′li·ness,** *n.*

Bur·ma (bėr′mə), *n.* former name of **Myanmar.**

Bur·mese (bėr′mēz′), **1** *n.* person born or living in Burma. **2** *n.* language of Burma. **3** *adj.* of Burma, its people, or their language. ❑ *n., pl.* **Bur·mese** for 1.

Burmese cat, a kind of pet cat with brown fur, a small body, and yellow eyes.

burn[1] (bėrn), **1** *v.* to be on fire; be very hot: *The campfire burned all night.* **2** *v.* to set on fire; cause to burn: *They burned wood in the fireplace to keep warm.* **3** *v.* to use to produce heat: *Our furnace burns oil.* **4** *v.* to destroy or be destroyed by fire: *Please burn those old papers.* **5** *v.* to injure or be injured by fire, heat, or acid: *The flame from the candle burned her finger.* **6** *n.* injury caused by fire, heat, or acid; burned place: *I got a burn on my hand when I touched the hot pan.* **7** *v.* to make by fire, heat, acid, etc.: *The cigarette burned a hole in the rug.* **8** *v.* to feel hot; give a feeling of heat to: *The child's forehead burned with fever.* **9** *v.* to be full of anger, passion, etc.: *She burned with fury at the unkind remarks.* **10** *v.* to give light: *Lamps were burning in every room.* **11** *v.* to change in chemical form by combining with oxygen: *The body burns food to produce heat and energy.* **12** *v.* (of a rocket engine) to begin consuming fuel and producing power. ❑ *v.* **burned** or **burnt, burn·ing.** ■ See Usage Note at **burnt. —burn′a·ble,** *adj.* **—burn′ing·ly,** *adv.*

burn out, 1 to cease to burn: *The fire has burned out.* **2** to destroy; consume: *During the long race he burned out his brakes.* **3** to use up all energy or enthusiasm, often as a result of stress.

> **SYNONYM STUDY** **Burn**[1], **singe,** and **scorch** mean to damage by heat. **Burn** is the general word: *I burned the toast.* **Singe** means to burn slightly: *He singed his fingers on the pan.* **Scorch** means to burn a surface enough to leave a mark: *The iron scorched his shirt.*

burn[2] (bėrn), *n.* SCOTTISH. a small stream; brook.

burn·er (bėr′nər), *n.* **1** part of a lamp, stove, furnace, etc., where the flame is produced. **2** thing or part that burns or works by heat: *Our furnace is an oil burner.*

bur·nish (bėr′nish), **1** *v.* to make shiny; polish: *burnish copper.* **2** *n.* a polish; shine. **—bur′nish·er,** *n.*

bur·noose or **bur·nous** (bər nüs′ *or* bėr′nüs), *n.* a cloak with a hood, worn by Moors and Arabs.

burn·out (bėrn′out′), *n.* exhaustion of energy or enthusiasm, often as the result of stress or pursuing unreasonably high goals.

Burns (bėrnz), *n.* **Rob·ert** (rob′ərt), 1759-1796, Scottish poet. ■ Robert Burns often wrote in the language and images of Scottish farmers, as in his famous poems "Auld Lang Syne" and "Coming Thro' the Rye."

burnt (bėrnt), **1** *v.* a past tense and a past participle of **burn**[1]. **2** *adj.* injured or scorched by fire, heat, or acid: *burnt toast.*

> **USAGE NOTE** The past tense and past participle of **burn**[1] are **burned** or **burnt. Burnt** is used as an adjective: *The burnt papers could not be read.* **Burned** is used as a verb: *She burned his letters in anger.*

burp (bėrp), **1** *n.* a belch. **2** *v.* to belch. **3** *v.* to help a baby belch by patting it on the back.

burr[1] (bėr), **1** *n., v.* bur. **2** *n.* a rough ridge or edge left by a tool on metal, wood, etc., after cutting or drilling it.

burr[2] (bėr), **1** *n.* a rough pronunciation of *r*: *a Scottish burr.* **2** *n.* a whirring sound. **3** *v.* to make a whirring sound.

Burr (bėr), *n.* **Aaron,** 1756-1836, American political leader, vice-president of the United States from 1801 to 1805. ■ Aaron Burr killed Alexander Hamilton, his political rival, in a duel in New Jersey in 1804. This act ruined his political career. He was charged with murder, but he returned to Washington, D.C., and continued to work there until his term as vice-president ended.

bur·ri·to (bu rē′tō), *n.* tortilla rolled around a seasoned filling, usually of beef, chicken, or beans. ❑ *n., pl.* **bur·ri·tos.**

> **WORD STORY** Burrito comes from a Mexican Spanish word and originally meant "little burro." People may have thought it was like a burro because the tortilla carries other food, or because its shape is like a burro's body.

bur·ro (bėr′ō *or* bur′ō), *n.* donkey used to carry loads or packs in the southwestern United States. ❑ *n., pl.* **bur·ros.** ■ Other words that can sound like this are **borough** and **burrow.**

burro—about 4 ft. (1.2 m) high at the shoulder

bur·row (bėr′ō), **1** *n.* hole dug in the ground by an animal for shelter or protection. Rabbits live in burrows. **2** *v.* to dig a hole in the ground: *The mole quickly burrowed out of sight.* **3** *v.* to search: *She burrowed in the back files for a missing report.* ■ Other words that can sound like this are **borough** and **burro. —bur′row·er,** *n.*

bur·sa (bėr′sə), *n.* sac of the body, especially one containing a lubricating fluid. ❑ *n., pl.* **bur·sas, bur·sae** (bėr′sē′).

bur·sar (bėr′sər), *n.* treasurer, especially of a college.

a	hat	ė	term	ô	order	ch	child		
ā	age	i	it	oi	oil	ng	long		a in about
ä	far	ī	ice	ou	out	sh	she		e in taken
â	care	o	hot	u	cup	th	thin	ə	i in pencil
e	let	ō	open	u̇	put	ŦH	then		o in lemon
ē	equal	ȯ	saw	ü	rule	zh	measure		u in circus

bur·si·tis (bər sī′tis), *n.* inflammation of a bursa, usually near the shoulder or hip.

burst (bėrst), **1** *v.* to break open; break out suddenly: *They burst the lock. The trees had burst into bloom.* **2** *v.* to fly apart or cause to fly apart suddenly with force; explode: *The balloon burst when he stuck a pin into it.* **3** *v.* to go, come, do, etc., by force or suddenly: *Don't burst into the room without knocking.* **4** *v.* to act or change suddenly in a way suggesting a break or explosion: *She burst into laughter.* **5** *v.* to be very full: *The barn was bursting with grain. She was bursting with enthusiasm.* **6** *n.* a sudden release; outbreak: *a burst of laughter.* **7** *n.* a sudden display of activity or energy: *In a burst of speed, she won the race at the last minute.* ❑ *v.* **burst, burst·ing.**

Bu·run·di (bụ̇ rün′dē), *n.* country in central Africa. *Capital:* Bujumbura.

bur·y (ber′ē), *v.* **1** to put a dead body in the earth, in a tomb, or in the sea: *We buried the dead bird.* **2** to cover up; hide: *The squirrels buried many nuts under the dead leaves.* **3** to put or sink deeply: *I buried myself in an interesting book.* **4** to put far from your mind: *I long ago buried any resentment caused by our argument.* ❑ *v.* **bur·ied, bur·y·ing.** ■ Another word that sounds like this is **berry.**

bus (bus), **1** *n.* a large motor vehicle with seats inside. Buses are used to carry many passengers between fixed stations along a set route. **2** *v.* to take or go by bus: *The city bused the children to school.* **3** *n.* an electrical conductor or set of conductors to which several circuits are connected. **4** *n.* a computer circuit that carries data between any of various parts of the computer. ❑ *n., pl.* **bus·es** or **bus·ses;** *v.* **bused, bus·ing** or **bussed, bus·sing.** [**Bus** is short for **omnibus,** which came from a Latin word meaning "for all." Anyone who has the fare may ride a bus.] ■ Another word that sounds like this is **buss.**

bus·boy (bus′boi′), *n.* a waiter's assistant, who brings bread and butter, fills glasses, and carries off empty dishes.

bush (bụsh), *n.* **1** a woody plant smaller than a tree, often with many separate branches starting from or near the ground; shrub. Some bushes are used as hedges; others are cultivated for their fruit. **2** open forest or wild, unsettled land: *the Australian bush.* **3** CANADIAN. **a** bush lot. **b** woods on the edge of plains. ❑ *n., pl.* **bush·es.**

beat around the bush, to avoid coming straight to the point: *Tell me the truth now; don't beat around the bush.*

Bush (bụsh), *n.* **George Her·bert Walk·er** (her′bərt wȯ′kər), born 1924, the 41st president of the United States, from 1989 to 1993.

bush., bushel.

bushed (bụsht), *adj.* very tired; exhausted: *The hikers were bushed after being out on the trail all day.*

bush·el (bụsh′əl), *n.* **1** unit of volume for measuring grain, fruit, vegetables, and other dry things. It is equal to 4 pecks or 32 quarts. **2** container that holds a bushel.

bush·ing (bụsh′ing), *n.* a removable metal lining used to protect parts of machinery from wear.

bush line, CANADIAN. an airline that carries freight and passengers over wild, unsettled land.

bush lot, CANADIAN. an uncleared part of a farm, where trees remain to provide firewood; bush.

Bush·man (bụsh′mən), *n.* San. ❑ *n., pl.* **Bush·men.** ■ **Bushman** is now considered offensive.

bush·mas·ter (bụsh′mas′tər), *n.* the largest poisonous snake of Central and South America. It may grow to 11 feet (3.4 meters) long.

bush pilot, pilot who flies a small plane over unsettled country, such as parts of Alaska.

bush·whack (bụsh′wak′), *v.* to ambush or raid.

bush·y (bụsh′ē), *adj.* **1** spreading out like a bush; growing thickly: *a bushy beard.* **2** overgrown with bushes: *a bushy ravine.* ❑ *adj.* **bush·i·er, bush·i·est.** —**bush′i·ness,** *n.*

bus·i·ly (biz′ə lē), *adv.* in a busy manner; actively: *Bees were busily collecting nectar in the clover.*

busi·ness (biz′nis), **1** *n.* work done to earn a living; occupation: *A carpenter's business is building.* **2** *n.* matter; affair; concern: *I am tired of the whole business.* **3** *n.* buying and selling; commercial dealings; trade: *This hardware store does a big business*

in tools. **4** *adj.* of or about business: *A business office usually has computers, photocopiers, and other business machines.* **5** *n.* a store, factory, or other place that makes or sells goods and services; industrial establishment: *They own a bakery business.* **6** *n.* right to act; responsibility: *That is not your business.* ❑ *n., pl.* **busi·ness·es** for 5.

mean business, be in earnest; be serious: *When I say I'll do something, I mean business.*

busi·ness·like (biz′nis līk′), *adj.* having system and method; well-managed; practical: *They ran a prosperous store in a businesslike manner.*

busi·ness·man (biz′nis man′), *n.* man who is in business or who runs a business. ❑ *n., pl.* **busi·ness·men.**

busi·ness·wom·an (biz′nis wùm′ən), *n.* woman who is in business or who runs a business. ❑ *n., pl.* **busi·ness·wom·en.**

bus·ing or **bus·sing** (bus′ing), *n.* transportation of students by bus from one residential area to another in order to achieve racial balance in schools.

buss (bus), *v., n.* OLD USE. kiss. ❑ *n., pl.* **buss·es;** *v.* **bussed, bus·sing.** ■ Another word that sounds like this is **bus.**

bus·ses (bus′iz), *n.* a plural of **bus.**

bust[1] (bust), *n.* **1** statue of someone's head, shoulders, and upper chest. **2** a woman's breasts.

bust[2] (bust), INFORMAL. **1** *v.* to burst; break. **2** *v.* to punch; hit. **3** *v.* to arrest or put in jail. **4** *v.* to reduce in rank, especially as a punishment; demote: *The corporal was busted to private.* **5** *n.* a total failure: *The movie was a bust.* —**bust′er,** *n.*

go bust, INFORMAL. to become bankrupt: *Much to our dismay, our restaurant went bust within a year.*

bus·tle[1] (bus′əl), **1** *v.* to be noisily busy and in a hurry: *The children bustled to get ready for the party.* **2** *n.* noisy or excited activity: *There was a great bustle as the children got ready for the party.* ❑ *v.* **bus·tled, bus·tling.**

bust[1] (def. 1)

bus·tle[2] (bus′əl), *n.* pad formerly used to puff out the upper back part of a woman's skirt.

bus·y (biz′ē), **1** *adj.* having plenty to do; working; active; not idle: *a busy person.* **2** *adj.* full of work or activity: *Main Street is a busy place. Holidays are a busy time.* **3** *v.* to make busy; keep busy: *The children busied themselves at drawing pictures.* **4** *adj.* in use: *I tried to call you, but your phone was busy.* ❑ *adj.* **bus·i·er, bus·i·est;** *v.* **bus·ied, bus·y·ing.** —**bus′y·ness,** *n.*

SYNONYM STUDY **Busy** and **industrious** both mean working steadily. **Busy** suggests having much to do: *She is such a busy person that it is hard to arrange a meeting with her.* **Industrious** suggests being ready and willing to work hard: *The store rewards industrious employees.*

bus·y·bod·y (biz′ē bod′ē), *n.* person who pries into the affairs of others; meddler. ❑ *n., pl.* **bus·y·bod·ies.**

bus·y·work (biz′ē wėrk′), *n.* work assigned or done merely for someone to appear to be busy.

but (but), **1** *conj.* on the other hand; yet: *You may go, but you must come home soon.* **2** *prep.* except; save: *I worked every day last week but Sunday.* **3** *conj.* unless; except that: *It never rains but it pours.* **4** *conj.* nevertheless; yet: *I wanted to go but I couldn't.* **5** *adv.* no more than; only; merely: *He is but a small boy.* **6** *conj.* other than; otherwise than: *We cannot choose but listen.* **7** *conj.* that: *I don't doubt but she will come.* **8** *adv.* yet: *The story was strange but true.* ■ Another word that sounds like this is **butt.**

USAGE NOTE **But** and **however** both show contrast. **But** states the contrast sharply by putting two ideas side by side: *He is sick, but he can eat.* **However** is more formal, and it suggests that the second idea changes the first: *We have not yet reached a decision; our opinion of your plan is favorable, however.*

bu·tane (byü′tān), *n.* a colorless gas, a hydrocarbon, much used as a fuel.

butch·er (bůch′ər), **1** *n.* person who cuts up and sells meat. **2** *n.* person whose work is killing animals for food. **3** *v.* to kill animals for food. **4** *v.* to kill people, wild animals, or birds needlessly, cruelly, or in large numbers. **5** *n.* a brutal killer; murderer. **6** *v.* to spoil by poor work: *Don't butcher that song by singing off-key.* [**Butcher** comes from a French word meaning "male goat." Goats were eaten so often that the word came to mean any meat cutter.]

butch·er·bird (bůch′ər bėrd′), *n.* any of several shrikes that fasten their prey on thorns.

butch·er·y (bůch′ər ē), *n.* brutal killing; murder in large numbers.

but·ler (but′lər), *n.* the head male servant in a household, in charge of the pantry and table service.

butt[1] (but), *n.* **1** the thicker end of a tool, weapon, ham, etc.: *the butt of a gun.* **2** end that is left; stub; stump: *a cigar butt.* ■ Another word that sounds like this is **but**.

butt[2] (but), *n.* **1** object of ridicule or scorn: *The new boy in school was the butt of jokes for several weeks.* **2** target. ■ Another word that sounds like this is **but**.

butt[3] (but), **1** *v.* to strike or push by knocking hard with the head or horns: *A goat butts.* **2** *n.* a push or blow with the head or horns. ■ Another word that sounds like this is **but**.

butt in, INFORMAL. to busy yourself with or in someone else's affairs, activities, or conversation without being asked.

butte (byüt), *n.* a steep hill that has a flat top and stands alone. Buttes are found in the western United States. ■ Another word that sounds like this is **beaut**.

but·ter (but′ər), **1** *n.* the solid yellowish fat separated from cream by churning. **2** *v.* to put butter on: *Please butter my bread.* **3** *n.* food that is cooked or ground fine so that it spreads like butter: *apple butter, peanut butter.*

butter up, to flatter.

WORD STORY **Butter** comes from Greek words meaning "cow" and "cheese." Ancient Greeks probably ate a lot more cheese than butter, if they had no name for butter except to call it cheese. And they probably kept more goats and sheep than cows, if the only "cow cheese" they knew was butter. So words can tell you how people lived.

butter bean, kind of lima bean grown in the southern United States.

but·ter·cup (but′ər kup′), *n.* any of various related common plants with bright yellow flowers shaped like cups.

but·ter·fat (but′ər fat′), *n.* fat in milk. It can be churned into butter.

but·ter·fin·gers (but′ər fing′gərz), *n.* a careless or clumsy person who often drops things.

but·ter·fish (but′ər fish′), *n.* a small, silvery food fish of the Atlantic coast of North America, with slippery skin, an oval body, and spiny fins. ❑ *n., pl.* **but·ter·fish** or **but·ter·fish·es.**

butterflies (def. 1)

but·ter·fly (but′ər flī′), *n.* **1** any of many insects with slender bodies and two pairs of large, often brightly colored, overlapping wings. Butterflies fly mostly in the daytime. **2** butterflies, *pl.* feelings of nervousness or sickness, especially in the stomach, because of fear, worry, or anticipation. ❑ *n., pl.* **but·ter·flies.**

but·ter·milk (but′ər milk′), *n.* the sour liquid left after butter has been separated from cream. Milk can also be changed to buttermilk artificially.

but·ter·nut (but′ər nut′), *n.* a North American walnut tree bearing oily nuts that are good to eat.

but·ter·scotch (but′ər skoch′), **1** *n.* candy or flavoring made from brown sugar and butter. **2** *adj.* flavored with brown sugar and butter: *butterscotch pudding.*

but·ter·y (but′ər ē), *adj.* **1** like butter. **2** containing or spread with butter.

but·tock (but′ək), *n.* **1** the fleshy part of the upper back leg. **2** buttocks, *pl.* the part of the body on which a person sits; rump.

but·ton (but′n), **1** *n.* a round, flat piece of plastic, metal, wood, etc., sewn onto clothes for decoration or as fasteners. **2** *v.* to fasten the buttons of; close with buttons: *Button your coat.* **3** *n.* knob or disk pushed, turned, etc., to cause something to work: *Push the button of the elevator to make it go up.*

but·ton-down (but′n doun′), *adj.* having buttonholes so that the tips of the collar can be buttoned to the front of the garment.

but·ton·hole (but′n hōl′), **1** *n.* hole or slit through which a button is passed. **2** *v.* to make buttonholes in. **3** *v.* to hold in conversation or force to listen, as if holding someone by his or her coat. ❑ *v.* **but·ton·holed, but·ton·hol·ing. —but′ton·hol′er,** *n.*

but·ton·wood (but′n wůd′), *n.* sycamore (def. 1).

but·tress (but′ris), **1** *n.* a support built against a wall or building to strengthen it. **2** *n.* a support like this; prop. **3** *v.* to support and strengthen: *She buttressed her report with facts and figures.* ❑ *n., pl.* **but·tress·es.**

bux·om (buk′səm), *adj.* plump and large-breasted. **—bux′om·ness,** *n.*

buy (bī), **1** *v.* to get by paying money; purchase: *You can buy a pencil for 25 cents.* **2** *n.* a bargain: *That book was a real buy.* **3** *v.* to bribe: *It was charged that two members of the jury had been bought by the defendant.* **4** *v.* INFORMAL. to believe or accept: *The jury didn't buy the witness's story.* ❑ *v.* **bought, buy·ing.** ■ Another word that sounds like this is **by. —buy′a·ble,** *adj.*

buy off, to control by paying money to; bribe: *The crook tried to buy off the judge.*

buy out, to buy all the shares, rights, merchandise, etc., of: *buy out a business.*

buy up, to buy all that you can: *People bought up the new toy, and now it's hard to find in the stores.*

SYNONYM STUDY **Buy** and **purchase** both mean to get something by paying for it. **Buy** is a general word: *She has saved enough money to buy those fancy shoes.* **Purchase** is more formal and suggests buying after careful planning: *The bank has purchased land on which to put up a new building.*

buy·er (bī′ər), *n.* **1** person who buys. **2** person whose work is buying goods for a department store or other business.

buy·out (bī′out′), *n.* act of buying all the shares of a company, or of enough shares to control it.

buzz (buz), **1** *n.* the humming sound made by flies, mosquitoes, or bees. **2** *n.* the low, humming sound of many people talking quietly: *The buzz of whispers stopped when the teacher entered the room.* **3** *v.* to make a steady, humming sound; hum loudly: *The radio should be fixed; it buzzes when you turn it on.* **4** *v.* to talk excitedly: *The whole class buzzed with the news of the holiday.* **5** *v.* to fly an airplane very fast and low over a place or person: *The pilot buzzed the treetops.* **6** *v.* to signal with a buzzer: *The editor buzzed her secretary.* **7** *n.* SLANG. the latest news about something.

buzz about, to move about busily: *The children buzzed about the stage, getting ready to perform the play.*

buz·zard (buz′ərd), *n.* any American vulture.

a	hat	ė	term	ô	order	ch	child		a in about
ā	age	i	it	oi	oil	ng	long		e in taken
ä	far	ī	ice	ou	out	sh	she	ə	i in pencil
â	care	o	hot	u	cup	th	thin		o in lemon
e	let	ō	open	ů	put	ŦH	then		u in circus
ē	equal	ò	saw	ü	rule	zh	measure		

buzz·er (buz′ər), *n.* an electrical device that makes a buzzing sound as a signal.

buzz saw, circular saw.

buzz·word (buz′wėrd′), *n.* a familiar, often technical-sounding word or phrase, used frequently by a particular group or profession.

B.W.I., British West Indies.

bx., box.

by (bī), **1** *prep.* at the side or edge of; near; beside: *The garden is by the house. Sit by me.* **2** *prep.* along; over; through: *They went by the main road.* **3** *prep.* through the means, use, or action of: *We traveled by airplane. The house was destroyed by fire.* **4** *prep.* in the measure of: *They sell eggs by the dozen.* **5** *prep.* as soon as; not later than: *Try to be here by six o'clock.* **6** *prep.* during: *The sun shines by day.* **7** *adv., prep.* past: *The Pilgrims lived in days gone by. A car raced by. They walked by our house.* **8** *adv.* aside or away: *She puts money by every week to save for a new bicycle.* **9** *prep.* according to: *to play by the rules.* **10** *prep.* combined with in arithmetic or measurement: *a room 4 feet by 9 feet.* **11** *prep.* taken as steps in a series: *week by week, month by month.* **12** *prep.* with a difference of: *We won the game by ten points.* **13** *prep.* in relation to; concerning: *They did well by their children.* ▪ Another word that sounds like this is **buy.**

by and by, after a while; before long; soon: *Summer vacation will come by and by.*

by and large, for the most part: *By and large it is a good book.*

by-the-by, by the way; incidentally.

by-and-by (bī′ən bī′), *n.* the future.

Byel·a·rus (byel′ə rüs′), *n.* Belarus.

by·gone (bī′gon′), **1** *adj.* gone by; past; former: *The ancient Romans lived in bygone days.* **2** *n.pl.* **bygones,** what is gone by and past: *Let bygones be forgotten.*

by·law (bī′lò′), *n.* law made by a city, company, club, etc., for the control of its own affairs.

by·line (bī′līn′), *n.* line at the beginning of a newspaper or magazine article giving the name of the writer.

by·pass (bī′pas′), **1** *n.* road, channel, pipe, etc., providing a secondary passage to be used instead of the main passage: *Drivers use the bypass to avoid the city when there is a lot of traffic.* **2** *v.* to go around: *The new highway bypasses the entire city.* **3** *n.* act of grafting a section of blood vessel onto a blocked or narrowed blood vessel, usually a coronary artery, to carry blood around the obstruction. ❏ *n., pl.* **by·pass·es.**

by·path (bī′path′), *n.* a side path; byway. ❏ *n., pl.* **by·paths** (bī′paᴛнz′ *or* bī′paths′).

by·play (bī′plā′), *n.* action that is not part of the main action, especially on the stage.

by-prod·uct (bī′prod′əkt), *n.* something of value produced as the result of making something else; a secondary product: *Kerosene is a by-product of petroleum refining.*

Byrd (bėrd), *n.* **Richard E.,** 1888-1957, American naval officer, aviator, and Antarctic explorer. He was one of the first men to fly to the North Pole and the South Pole.

by·road (bī′rōd′), *n.* a side road.

By·ron (bī′rən), *n.* **George Gor·don** (gȯr′dn), Lord, 1788-1824, English poet. ▪ **Lord Byron's** life and works made people think of him as a great romantic hero. His troubled marriage and other relationships were scandals in England. He went to Greece to fight in a revolt against Turkish rule, and died there.

by·stand·er (bī′stan′dər), *n.* person who stands near or looks on but does not take part; onlooker.

byte (bīt), *n.* unit of computer information equal to eight bits. ▪ Another word that sounds like this is **bite.**

by·way (bī′wā′), *n.* a side path or road.

by·word (bī′wėrd′), *n.* **1** a common saying; proverb. **2** object of contempt; thing scorned: *Her cheating in class made her a byword to her classmates.*

Byz·an·tine (biz′n tēn′), *adj.* **1** of the Byzantine Empire or Byzantium. **2** of or like a style of architecture developed in the Byzantine Empire, often using circular domes over square spaces, and rich mosaics and frescoes.

Byzantine Empire, E part of the Roman Empire after its division in A.D. 395. The Byzantine Empire ended with the capture of its capital, Constantinople, by the Turks in 1453.

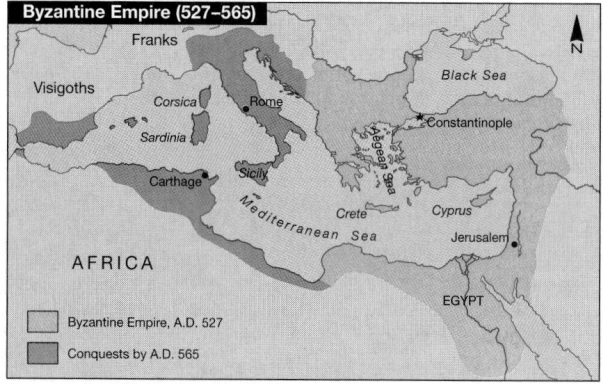

Byzantine Empire (527–565)

By·zan·ti·um (bi zan′shē əm *or* bi zan′tē əm), *n.* ancient city where Istanbul (Constantinople) now is. It became the capital of the Roman Empire in A.D. 330.

C or **c** (sē), *n.* **1** the third letter of the English alphabet. **2** the Roman numeral for 100. □ *n., pl.* **C's** or **c's.**

C, symbol for carbon.

c or **c.,** **1** centimeter. **2** cubic.

c. or **c,** **1** about; approximately. **2** cent or cents. **3** cup or cups.

C or **C.,** Celsius.

Ca, symbol for calcium.

CA, California (used with postal Zip Code).

cab (kab), *n.* **1** car that can be hired with driver; taxicab. **2** carriage that can be hired with driver, usually pulled by one horse: *We rode through the park in a cab.* **3** the enclosed part of a locomotive where the engineer sits. **4** the enclosed part of a truck, crane, or other machine, where the driver or operator sits.

WORD STORY **Cab** comes from a Latin word meaning "goat." **Caper**[1] comes from the same word. The first cabs were horse-drawn carriages with no springs. They bounced, people thought, like a jumping goat.

cab·al·ler·o (kab′ə ler′ō *or* kab′ə yer′ō), *n.* **1** (in Spain) a gentleman. **2** in the southwestern United States: **a** horseman. **b** an ardent admirer. □ *n., pl.* **cab·al·ler·os.** [See Word Story at **chivalry.**]

ca·ban·a (kə ban′ə), *n.* shelter like a small tent or cabin, used on a beach or near a swimming pool for dressing or to provide shade. □ *n., pl.* **ca·ban·as.**

cab·a·ret (kab′ə rā′), *n.* restaurant offering singing and dancing as entertainment.

cab·bage (kab′ij), *n.* vegetable with thick, green or reddish purple leaves closely folded into a round head that grows on a short stem. Cabbage is eaten either cooked or raw.

cab·bie or **cab·by** (kab′ē), *n.* INFORMAL. driver of a cab, especially a taxicab. □ *n., pl.* **cab·bies.**

cab·driv·er (kab′drī′vər), *n.* person who drives a cab.

cab·in (kab′ən), *n.* **1** a small, roughly built house; hut: *Last summer we stayed in a cabin in the Maine woods.* ■ See Synonym Study at **hut.** **2** a private room in a ship. **3** a room on a small boat containing the bunks. **4** place for passengers, crew, or cargo in an aircraft or spacecraft.

cabin boy, boy or man whose work is waiting on the officers and passengers on a ship.

cab·i·net (kab′ə nit), *n.* **1** piece of furniture with shelves or drawers, used to hold articles for use or display: *a medicine cabinet, a filing cabinet. We keep our very best dishes in the china cabinet.* **2** Also, **Cabinet,** group of advisers chosen by the head of a nation, usually to administer particular departments of the government. The Attorney General and the Secretary of Defense are members of the cabinet of the President of the United States.

a	hat	ė	term	ô	order	ch	child		
ā	age	i	it	oi	oil	ng	long		a in about
ä	far	ī	ice	ou	out	sh	she	ə	i in pencil
â	care	o	hot	u	cup	th	thin		o in lemon
e	let	ō	open	ù	put	ŦH	then		u in circus
ē	equal	ò	saw	ü	rule	zh	measure		

cab·i·net·mak·er (kab′ə nit mā′kər), *n.* person whose work is making fine furniture and woodwork.

ca·ble (kā′bəl), **1** *n.* a strong, thick rope, usually made of wires twisted together: *A suspension bridge hangs from strong steel cables.* **2** *n.* an insulated bundle of wires that carries an electric current or electric signals. **3** *n.* bundle of glass fibers that carries signals in the form of light. **4** *n.* cable TV: *We watched a movie on cable.* **5** *n.* cablegram. **6** *v.* (earlier) to send a message across the ocean by underwater cable: *They cabled us from Paris.* ❑ *v.* ca·bled, ca·bling. —ca′ble·like′, *adj.*

cable car, a public passenger vehicle pulled along a moving cable that is operated by an engine.

ca·ble·gram (kā′bəl gram), *n.* message sent across the ocean by underwater cable.

cable TV, a system for direct transmission to subscribers by coaxial cable of television programs that are not available by ordinary broadcast transmission.

ca·boose (kə büs′), *n.* **1** (earlier) a small car attached to a freight train, in which certain members of the train crew worked, rested, and slept. It was usually the last car. **2** CANADIAN. **a** a movable bunkhouse. **b** a horse-drawn cabin on sled runners, for local travel.

Cab·ot (kab′ət), *n.* **John**, 1450?-1498?, English explorer, born in Italy. He reached what is now Canada in 1497.

Ca·bri·ni (kə brē′nē), *n.* Saint **Fran·ces Xa·vi·er** (fran′sis zā′vē-ər), 1850-1917, American nun, born in Italy. ■ **Saint Cabrini** founded many orphanages and schools in the United States. She was the first U.S. citizen to be made a Roman Catholic saint.

ca·ca·o (kə kā′ō *or* kə kä′ō), *n.* **1** the seeds from which cocoa and chocolate are made. **2** the small, tropical American evergreen tree that they grow on. ❑ *n., pl.* **ca·ca·os.** [See Word Story at **cocoa**.]

cache (kash), **1** *n.* a hiding place to store food or other things: *The explorers dug a hole to serve as a cache for the supplies needed on the return trip.* **2** *n.* a hidden store of food or supplies: *Squirrels make caches of nuts for winter food.* **3** *v.* to put in a cache; hide: *The robber had cached the jewels in a cave.* ❑ *v.* cached, cach·ing. ■ Another word that sounds like this is **cash.**

cack·le (kak′əl), **1** *v.* to make the loud clucking sound that a hen makes, especially after laying an egg: *Hens cackled, and the farmer awoke.* **2** *n.* such a sound. **3** *n.* shrill, harsh, or broken laughter: *Before the comedian finished the joke, there were a few cackles from the audience.* **4** *v.* to laugh in a loud, harsh way: *The old man cackled at his own joke.* ❑ *v.* cack·led, cack·ling.

cac·o·mis·tle (kak′ə mis′əl), *n.* a catlike meat-eating mammal, related to the raccoon. It has a long ringed tail and lives in areas from Oregon to Mexico.

WORD STORY Cacomistle comes from Mexican Indian words meaning "half" and "mountain lion." People may have thought that the animal was part mountain lion and part raccoon.

ca·coph·o·ny (kə kof′ə nē), *n.* series of harsh, clashing sounds; discord. —ca·coph′o·nous, *adj.* —ca·coph′o·nous·ly, *adv.*

cac·tus (kak′təs), *n.* plant with a thick, fleshy stem that usually has spines but no leaves. Cactuses grow mostly in very hot, dry regions of the Americas and often have brightly colored flowers. ❑ *n., pl.* **cac·tus·es, cac·ti** (kak′tī).

cactus

cad (kad), *n.* boy or man who does not act like a gentleman. —**cad′dish,** *adj.* —**cad′dish·ly,** *adv.*

ca·dav·er (kə dav′ər), *n.* a dead body; corpse.

ca·dav·er·ous (kə dav′ər əs), *adj.* **1** pale and ghastly. **2** thin and worn. —**ca·dav′er·ous·ly,** *adv.*

cad·die (kad′ē), **1** *n.* person who helps a golf player by carrying golf clubs, finding a lost ball, etc. **2** *v.* to help a golf player in this way. ❑ *v.* cad·died, cad·dy·ing.

cad·dis fly (kad′is), insect something like a moth. A caddis fly larva lives under water and forms for itself a case of sand, bits of leaves, or the like.

Cad·do (kad′ō), *n.* member of a group of American Indian tribes formerly living in Louisiana, Texas, and Arkansas, now living in Oklahoma. ❑ *n., pl.* **Cad·do** *or* **Cad·dos.** [Caddo comes from a word in the language of these people, meaning "real chiefs."]

Cad·do·an (kad′ō ən), **1** *n.* family of North American Indian languages, including the languages of the Pawnee and Caddo tribes. **2** *adj.* of this family of languages. **3** *n.* person speaking a language of this family.

cad·dy (kad′ē), *n.* a small box, can, or chest, often used to hold tea. ❑ *n., pl.* **cad·dies.**

ca·dence (kād′ns), *n.* **1** the measure or beat of music, dancing, marching, or any movement regularly repeating itself; rhythm: *The cadence of the surf lulled us to sleep.* **2** fall of the voice: *the cadence at the end of a sentence.* **3** a rising and falling sound: *She speaks with a pleasant cadence.* **4** series of chords bringing part of a piece of music to an end.

ca·den·za (kə den′zə), *n.* flourish or showy passage, often improvised, usually near the end of a section of a musical composition. ❑ *n., pl.* **ca·den·zas.**

ca·det (kə det′), *n.* **1** a young person in training for service as an officer in one of the armed forces: *The cadets from West Point will graduate next week.* **2** student in a high school or grade school military academy.

Ca·dette (kə det′), *n.* member of the Girl Scouts who is from 12 to 14 years old, or in the seventh, eighth, or ninth grade.

cad·mi·um (kad′mē əm), *n.* a soft, bluish white, metallic element resembling tin, used in plating to prevent corrosion and in making alloys. *Symbol:* Cd

cad·re (kad′rē), *n.* an experienced staff that can set up, train, and form the core of an organization.

ca·du·ce·us (kə dü′sē əs), *n.* rod of Mercury with two snakes twined around it and a pair of wings on top. The caduceus is often used as an emblem of the medical profession. ❑ *n., pl.* **ca·du·ce·i** (kə dü′sē ī).

Cae·sar (sē′zər), *n.* **1 Ju·lius** (jü′lyəs), 102?-44 B.C., Roman general, political leader, and historian. ■ **Julius Caesar** was murdered on March 15, 44 B.C., by Roman leaders who were afraid that he would make himself the king of Rome. **2** title of the Roman emperors from 27 B.C. to 117 A.D., and later of the heir to the throne. **3** emperor. **4** dictator or tyrant.

Cae·sar·e·an section (si zâr′ē ən), operation in which a baby is taken out of the mother's uterus through an incision in her abdomen.

cae·su·ra (si zhur′ə), *n.* a pause in a line of verse, often shown by a vertical line. EXAMPLE: "To be or not to be, | that is the question." ❑ *n., pl.* **cae·su·ras, cae·su·rae** (si zhur′ē).

ca·fé *or* **ca·fe** (ka fā′), *n.* place to buy and eat a meal; restaurant. ❑ *n., pl.* **ca·fés** *or* **ca·fes.**

WORD STORY Café comes from an Arabic word meaning "coffee." **Coffee** and **caffeine** come from the same word. When Europeans first learned about coffee, they drank it in special restaurants.

caf·e·te·ri·a (kaf′ə tir′ē ə), *n.* restaurant where people serve themselves. ❑ *n., pl.* **caf·e·te·ri·as.**

caf·feine (kaf′ēn′ *or* ka fēn′), *n.* a slightly bitter, stimulating drug found in coffee and tea. [See Word Story at **café**.]

caf·tan (kaf′tən *or* kaf tan′), *n.* **1** a long-sleeved, ankle-length gown, worn under the coat by men in countries such as Turkey and Egypt. **2** a similar garment, worn especially by women in Western countries. Also, **kaftan.**

cage (kāj), **1** *n.* frame or place closed in with wires, strong iron bars, or wood. Birds and wild animals are kept in cages. **2** *n.* thing shaped or used like a cage. Movie cashiers sometimes work in cages. **3** *v.* to put or keep in a cage: *After the lion was caught, it was caged.* ❑ *v.* caged, cag·ing. [See Word Story at **jail**.]

Cage (kāj), *n.* **John**, 1912-1992, American composer. ■ **John Cage** wrote music for "prepared pianos." A prepared piano has objects such as pieces of rubber or metal stuck between the piano strings, so that it makes interesting and unusual noises.

cage·y or **cag·y** (kā′jē), *adj.* shrewd and cautious; sharp and wary: *The cagey fox escaped from the farmer's trap.* ❑ *adj.* **cag·i·er, cag·i·est.** —**cag′i·ly,** *adv.* —**cag′i·ness,** *n.*

Cag·ney (kag′nē), *n.* James, 1899-1986, American movie actor.
■ James Cagney's role in *Public Enemy* was the first of many in which he played gangsters. He won an Academy Award in 1942 for *Yankee Doodle Dandy,* in which he played the well-known entertainer George M. Cohan.

Ca·ho·ki·a (kə hō′kē ə), *n.* town in SW Illinois. Near this town are the **Cahokia Mounds,** containing the largest known Mound Builder structure.

ca·hoots (kə hüts′), *n.* INFORMAL. **in cahoots,** in partnership: *Several local residents were in cahoots with the smugglers.*

cai·man (kā′mən), *n.* a large reptile of tropical America, similar to an alligator. ❑ *n., pl.* **cai·mans.** Also, **cayman.**

Cain (kān), *n.* **1** (in the Bible) the oldest son of Adam and Eve. He killed his brother Abel. **2** murderer.
raise Cain, INFORMAL. to make a great disturbance: *When the teacher left the room, the students raised Cain.*

cairn (kârn), *n.* pile of stones heaped up as a memorial, tomb, or landmark.

cairn terrier, a small, long-haired terrier, originally from Scotland. It has a wiry coat.

Cai·ro (kī′rō), *n.* capital of Egypt, in the NE part.

cais·son (kā′son), *n.* **1** a watertight room in which people can work under ground or water to make tunnels, foundations for buildings, etc. **2** a watertight float used in raising sunken ships. **3** wagon to carry ammunition. **4** box for ammunition.

cairn terrier—about 10 in. (25 cm) high at the shoulder

ca·jole (kə jōl′), *v.* to persuade by pleasant words, flattery, or false promises; coax: *He cajoled his friends into deciding in his favor.* ❑ *v.* **ca·joled, ca·jol·ing.** —**ca·jol′er,** *n.* —**ca·jol′ing·ly,** *adv.*

ca·jol·er·y (kə jō′lər ē), *n.* persuasion by pleasant words, flattery, or false promises; coaxing.

Ca·jun (kā′jən), *n.* person who is a descendant of the French-speaking people who came to Louisiana after leaving the colony of Acadia in eastern Canada in the mid-1700s. [**Cajun** comes from a casual pronunciation of **Acadian.**]

cake (kāk), **1** *n.* a baked mixture of flour, sugar, flavoring, and sometimes eggs, shortening and other things: *We baked a chocolate cake with white frosting for Mother's birthday.* **2** *n.* pancake. **3** *n.* a shaped mass of food or other substance: *a fish cake, a cake of soap.* **4** *v.* to form into a solid mass; harden: *Mud cakes as it dries.* ❑ *v.* **caked, cak·ing.**
piece of cake, INFORMAL. something very easy: *She had studied hard, and found the exam a piece of cake.*
take the cake, INFORMAL. **1** to win first prize. **2** to excel.

cake·walk (kāk′wȯk′), **1** *n.* a dance with prancing high steps that developed from an earlier march or promenade for couples. A cake was the prize for the most original steps. **2** *v.* to do a cakewalk. **3** *n.* something that is very easy to do: *He studied so hard that the test was a cakewalk.*

cal or **cal.,** **1** caliber. **2** small calorie or calories.

Cal., **1** California. **2** large calorie or calories.

cal·a·bash (kal′ə bash), *n.* **1** gourd or gourdlike fruit whose dried shell is used to make bottles, bowls, drums, pipes, etc. **2** the tropical plant or tree that it grows on. **3** bottle, bowl, drum, pipe, etc., made from such a dried shell. ❑ *n., pl.* **cal·a·bash·es.**

Cal·ais (ka lā′), *n.* port in N France, on the English Channel. It is the closest spot in France to England.

cal·a·mine (kal′ə mīn), *n.* compound of zinc oxide and iron oxide used in lotions to relieve skin irritations or sunburn.

ca·lam·i·tous (kə lam′ə təs), *adj.* causing calamity; disastrous. —**ca·lam′i·tous·ly,** *adv.* —**ca·lam′i·tous·ness,** *n.*

ca·lam·i·ty (kə lam′ə tē), *n.* **1** a great misfortune such as a flood, a fire, the loss of sight or hearing, or the loss of much money or property; disaster. **2** serious trouble; misery: *Many people still suffer from the calamity of war.* ❑ *n., pl.* **ca·lam·i·ties.**

Calamity Jane (jān), 1852?-1903, American frontierswoman.
■ Calamity Jane grew up in mining camps in the West. She usually wore men's clothes and was an expert with a rifle. She may have worked as a scout for George Custer.

cal·ci·fi·ca·tion (kal′sə fə kā′shən), *n.* **1** process of calcifying. **2** a calcified part.

cal·ci·fy (kal′sə fī), *v.* to make or become hard or bony by the deposit of calcium salts: *Cartilage often calcifies in older people.* ❑ *v.* **cal·ci·fied, cal·ci·fy·ing.**

cal·ci·mine (kal′sə mīn), **1** *n.* a white or tinted lime solution used as a wash for walls, ceilings, etc. **2** *v.* to cover with calcimine. ❑ *v.* **cal·ci·mined, cal·ci·min·ing.**

cal·cine (kal′sīn), *v.* to burn something to ashes or powder: *calcine bones.* ❑ *v.* **cal·cined, cal·cin·ing.**

cal·cite (kal′sīt), *n.* mineral made up of calcium carbonate. It is the chief substance in limestone, chalk, and marble.

cal·ci·um (kal′sē əm), *n.* a soft, silver-white metallic element. It is a part of limestone, chalk, milk, bone, shells, teeth, etc. Calcium is used in alloys and its compounds are used in making plaster, in cooking, and as a bleaching agent. *Symbol:* Ca

calcium carbonate, compound of calcium occurring in rocks such as marble and limestone, in animals' bones, shells, and teeth, and to some extent in plants.

calcium hydroxide, slaked lime.

calcium oxide, lime[1].

cal·cu·la·ble (kal′kyə lə bəl), *adj.* able to be calculated. —**cal′cu·la·bly,** *adv.*

cal·cu·late (kal′kyə lāt), *v.* **1** to find out by adding, subtracting, multiplying, or dividing; compute: *They calculated the cost of building a house.* **2** to find out beforehand by any process of reasoning: *Calculate the day of the week on which New Year's Day will fall.* **3** to plan or intend: *That remark was calculated to make me angry.* **4** INFORMAL. to think; suppose. ❑ *v.* **cal·cu·lat·ed, cal·cu·lat·ing.** —**cal′cu·lat′ed·ly,** *adv.*

WORD STORY Calculate comes from a Latin word meaning "pebble." In old times, people did arithmetic using piles of stones. If you have counted seventy stones into fourteen equal piles, you have calculated 70 ÷ 14 = 5.

cal·cu·lat·ed (kal′kyə lā′tid), *adj.* **1** figured out by mathematical calculation. **2** planned or intended: *a calculated attempt to cheat.* —**cal′cu·lat′ed·ly,** *adv.* —**cal′cu·lat′ed·ness,** *n.*

cal·cu·lat·ing (kal′kyə lā′ting), *adj.* **1** able to calculate: *a calculating machine.* **2** shrewd and careful. **3** scheming and selfish. —**cal′cu·lat′ing·ly,** *adv.*

cal·cu·la·tion (kal′kyə lā′shən), *n.* **1** act or process of adding, subtracting, multiplying, or dividing to find a result; computation. **2** result found by calculating. **3** careful thinking; deliberate planning: *The success of the expedition was the result of much calculation.*

cal·cu·la·tor (kal′kyə lā′tər), *n.* **1** an electronic device that can do arithmetic and can solve some types of mathematical problems. A calculator has buttons with numbers and symbols on them and a display screen that shows the numbers entered and the answers. **2** person who calculates.

cal·cu·lus (kal′kyə ləs), *n.* **1** system of calculation in advanced mathematics, using algebraic symbols to solve problems dealing with changing quantities. **2** crust that forms on teeth when a layer of food and saliva builds up; tartar.

Cal·cut·ta (kal kut′ə), *n.* port in E India, near the Bay of Bengal.

a	hat	ė	term	ȯ	order	ch	child	ə	a in about
ā	age	i	it	oi	oil	ng	long		e in taken
ä	far	ī	ice	ou	out	sh	she		i in pencil
â	care	o	hot	u	cup	th	thin		o in lemon
e	let	ō	open	u̇	put	ŦH	then		u in circus
ē	equal	ȯ	saw	ü	rule	zh	measure		

Calder sculpture

Cal·der (kȯl′dər), *n.* **Alexander,** 1898-1976, American sculptor. ■ In 1932, **Alexander Calder** began creating mobiles, which are sculptures that move in air currents. He also made sculptures that look like mobiles but do not move.

cal·dron (kȯl′drən), *n.* a large kettle or boiler. Also, **cauldron.**

cal·en·dar (kal′ən dər), *n.* **1** a chart showing the months, weeks, and days of the year. A calendar shows the day of the week on which each day of the month falls. *The calendar shows that Memorial Day will fall on a Monday.* **2** system by which the beginning, length, and divisions of the year are fixed: *The Julian calendar was established during the reign of Julius Caesar.* **3** a list or schedule; register: *The clerk of the court announced the next case on the calendar.*

calf[1] (kaf), *n.* **1** a young cow or bull. **2** a young elephant, whale, deer, or seal. **3** calfskin: *The gloves are made of calf.* ❑ *n., pl.* **calves** for 1,2. —**calf′like′,** *adj.*

calf[2] (kaf), *n.* the thick, muscular part of the back of the leg below the knee. ❑ *n., pl.* **calves.**

calf·skin (kaf′skin′), *n.* **1** skin of a calf. **2** leather made from it.

Cal·gar·y (kal′gər ē), *n.* city in S Alberta, Canada.

Cal·houn (kal hün′), *n.* **John C.,** 1782-1850, American political leader, vice-president of the United States from 1825 to 1832. ■ **John Calhoun** resigned as vice-president in 1832 because he had advised the people of his home state, South Carolina, not to obey those federal laws that they believed were unconstitutional.

cal·i·ber (kal′ə bər), *n.* **1** the inside diameter of the barrel of a gun. A .45-caliber revolver has a barrel with an inside diameter of $^{45}/_{100}$ of an inch. **2** the diameter of a bullet or shell fired from a particular gun. **3** amount of ability: *a person of high caliber.* **4** quality: *improve the caliber of our schools.*

cal·i·brate (kal′ə brāt), *v.* to mark, check, or adjust the scale of a thermometer, gauge, or other measuring device. Calibrating is usually done by comparison with a standard device. ❑ *v.* **cal·i·brat·ed, cal·i·brat·ing.** —**cal′i·bra′tion,** *n.* —**cal′i·bra′tor,** *n.*

cal·i·co (kal′ə kō), **1** *n.* a cotton cloth that usually has colored patterns printed on one side. **2** *adj.* made of calico: *a calico dress.* **3** *adj.* spotted in colors, especially used about cats. ❑ *n., pl.* **cal·i·coes** or **cal·i·cos.**

Calif., the official abbreviation of California.

Cal·i·for·nia (kal′ə fôr′nyə), *n.* **1** one of the Pacific states of the United States. *Abbreviation:* CA or Calif. *Capital:* Sacramento. **2 Gulf of,** arm of the Pacific between Lower California and the mainland of Mexico. —**Cal′i·for′nian,** *n.*

cal·i·for·ni·um (kal′ə fôr′nē əm), *n.* a radioactive metallic element, produced artificially from curium, plutonium, or uranium. *Symbol:* Cf

Ca·lig·u·la (kə lig′yə lə), *n.* 12-41 A.D., Roman emperor. ■ Believed to have been insane, **Caligula** claimed to be all of the gods at once, and was said to have made his horse a member of the Roman Senate.

cal·i·pers (kal′ə pərz), *n.pl.* tool used to measure the diameter or thickness of something.

ca·liph (kā′lif), *n.* the former title of religious and political heads of some Islamic states.

cal·iph·ate (kal′ə fāt), *n.* rank, reign, government, or territory of a caliph.

cal·is·then·ics (kal′is then′iks), *n.* **1** *pl.* exercises to develop a strong and graceful body. Calisthenics are carried out simply by moving the body, without the use of special equipment. **2** *sing.* the practice or art of such exercises: *Calisthenics is his favorite way to start the day.* [Calisthenics comes from Greek words meaning "beauty" and "strength."]

call (kȯl), **1** *v.* to speak or say in a loud voice; shout or cry out: *The nurse called the names of the next three patients.* **2** *n.* a loud sound uttered by a person so as to be heard from a distance; shout: *I heard the swimmer's call for help.* **3** *n.* the special noise or cry an animal or bird makes: *The call of a moose came from the forest.* **4** *v.* to make this noise or cry: *The crows called to each other from the trees around the meadow.* **5** *v.* to give a signal to; arouse: *The bugle called the group to assemble. Call me at seven o'clock.* **6** *v.* to command or ask to come; summon: *He called his dog with a loud whistle.* **7** *n.* invitation or summons: *Every farmer in the area answered the firefighters' call for volunteers.* **8** *v.* to give a name to; name: *They called the new baby "Ruth."* **9** *v.* to read over aloud: *The teacher called the class roll.* **10** *v.* to talk to by telephone: *Did anyone call today? Call me at the office.* **11** *n.* a telephone call: *Will you answer that call?* **12** *v.* to make a short visit or stop: *Our pastor called yesterday.* **13** *n.* a short visit or stop: *We paid a call on our new neighbors.* **14** *v.* to consider; estimate: *Everyone called the party a success.* **15** *n.* a claim; demand: *I cannot rest with all these calls on my time.* **16** *n.* need; occasion: *You have no call to meddle in other people's business.* **17** *v.* (in sports) to end; stop: *The ball game was called on account of rain.* **18** *v.* to demand payment of: *The bank called their loan.* **19** *v.* (in sports) to make a spoken judgment about: *The umpire called the long drive a foul ball.* **20** *n.* a decision or ruling by a referee or umpire: *The batter was enraged at the umpire's call of strike three.* **21** *v.* to predict; foretell: *The newspaper called the outcome of the election exactly.*

call down, to scold: *Most people dislike being called down in front of others.*

call for, 1 to go and get; stop and get: *The cab called for her at the hotel.* **2** to need; require: *This recipe calls for two eggs.* **3** to request; demand: *The mayor called for an investigation of the warehouse fire.*

call in, 1 to summon for advice or consultation: *When our furnace shut off, we called in a heating contractor.* **2** to withdraw: *The library calls in books that are damaged.*

call off, 1 to cancel: *We called off our trip.* **2** to say or read over aloud in succession: *The teacher called off the names on the roll.* **3** to order to withdraw: *Call off your dog.*

call on or **call upon, 1** to pay a short visit to: *We must call on our new neighbors.* **2** to appeal to: *He called on his friends for help.*

call out, 1 to say in a loud voice; shout: *She called out to the boys to stop quarreling.* **2** to summon into service: *The governor called out the National Guard during the flood.*

call up, 1 to telephone: *He called me up at work.* **2** to draft into military service: *The army called him up when he finished school.*

on call, ready or available: *Doctors are on call day and night.*

within call, near enough to hear a call: *We are supposed to stay within call since supper is almost ready.*

cal·la (kal′ə), *n.* plant with a large, white leaf like a petal around a thick spike of small yellow flowers. ❑ *n., pl.* **cal·las.**

calla lily, calla.

Cal·las (kal′əs), *n.* **Ma·ri·a** (mə rē′ə), 1923-1977, Greek opera singer, born in the United States. She was known as much for her dramatic abilities and temper as for her beautiful voice.

call·er (kô′lər), *n.* **1** person who makes a short visit: *The doctor said that the patient was now able to receive callers.* **2** person who calls out names, steps at a square dance, etc.

cal·lig·ra·phy (kə lig′rə fē), *n.* **1** beautiful handwriting: *Calligraphy is considered an art in China.* **2** handwriting.

call·ing (kô′ling), *n.* **1** occupation, profession, or trade: *He chose to follow the calling of a teacher while his sister chose medicine as her calling.* **2** urge or summons: *She felt an inner calling to be a social worker.*

cal·li·o·pe (kə lī′ə pē), *n.* a musical instrument having a series of steam whistles played by pressing keys on a keyboard.

calligraphy (def. 1)

cal·lis·then·ics (kal′is then′iks), *n.pl.* calisthenics.

call number, number put on a library book to enable the user to identify and find it.

cal·los·i·ty (kə los′ə tē), *n.* **1** callus. **2** lack of feeling or sensitivity. ❑ *n., pl.* **cal·los·i·ties** for 1.

cal·lous (kal′əs), *adj.* **1** having a callus; hard: *callous feet, callous skin.* **2** unfeeling; not sensitive: *a callous indifference to human suffering.* ■ Another word that sounds like this is **callus.** —**cal′lous·ly,** *adv.* —**cal′lous·ness,** *n.*

cal·loused (kal′əst), *adj.* unfeeling; not sensitive; without compassion: *She became calloused by continual exposure to unpleasant situations.*

cal·low (kal′ō), *adj.* not fully grown or developed; immature: *a callow youth.* —**cal′low·ness,** *n.*

call-up (kôl′up′), *n.* an official order calling citizens to military duty.

cal·lus (kal′əs), *n.* a hard, thickened place on the skin. ❑ *n., pl.* **cal·lus·es.** ■ Another word that sounds like this is **callous.**

call waiting, a telephone service that alerts the user to an incoming call while a call is already going on. The user may ignore the signal, or place the current call on hold to accept the new call. Afterward, the first call can be continued.

calm (käm), **1** *adj.* not stormy or windy; not stirred up; quiet; still: *In fair weather, the sea is usually calm.* **2** *adj.* not excited; peaceful: *Although she was frightened, she answered with a calm voice.* **3** *n.* absence of wind or motion; quietness; stillness: *There was a sudden calm as the wind dropped.* **4** *n.* absence of excitement; peacefulness: *The activity of the game was followed by an unusual calm.* **5** *v.* to make or become calm: *I rocked the cradle to calm the crying baby.* —**calm′ly,** *adv.* —**calm′ness,** *n.*

SYNONYM STUDY **Calm** and **collected** both mean not excited or upset. **Calm** suggests showing no sign of excitement: *Mother's calm behavior impressed the police.* **Collected** suggests self-control and common sense, especially when in danger or in an emergency: *My brother was the only one collected enough to call 911 when we realized that the house was on fire.*

cal·o·mel (kal′ə mel), *n.* a white, tasteless, crystalline powder, formerly used in medicine as a laxative. It is a compound of mercury and chlorine.

ca·lor·ic (kə lôr′ik), *adj.* of or about heat or calories. —**ca·lo′ri·cal·ly,** *adv.*

cal·or·ie (kal′ər ē), *n.* **1** unit for measuring heat. It is the quantity of heat needed to raise by one degree centigrade the temperature of either a gram of water (**small calorie**) or a kilogram of water (**large calorie**). **2** unit of the energy supplied by food, corresponding to the large calorie. An ounce of sugar will produce about one hundred food calories.

cal·o·rif·ic (kal′ə rif′ik), *adj.* caloric.

cal·o·rim·e·ter (kal′ə rim′ə tər), *n.* device that measures the amount of heat flowing from an object or heat resulting from a chemical reaction.

cal·u·met (kal′yə met), *n.* a long, ornamented tobacco pipe smoked by the American Indians in ceremonies as a symbol of peace.

cal·um·ny (kal′əm nē), *n.* a false statement made on purpose to do harm to someone; slander. ❑ *n., pl.* **cal·um·nies.**

Cal·var·y (kal′vər ē), *n.* (in the Bible) a place near Jerusalem where Jesus died on the Cross; Golgotha.

calve (kav), *v.* to give birth to a calf. ❑ *v.* **calved, calv·ing.**

Cal·vert (kal′vərt), *n.* Sir **George** (Lord Baltimore), 1580?-1632, English nobleman. He founded the colony of Maryland.

calves (kavz), *n.* plural of **calf**[1] (defs. 1 and 2) and **calf**[2].

Cal·vin (kal′vən), *n.* **John,** 1509-1564, French leader of the Protestant Reformation at Geneva.

Cal·vin·ism (kal′və niz′əm), *n.* the religious teachings of Calvin and his followers.

Cal·vin·ist (kal′və nist), **1** *n.* person who follows the teachings of Calvin. **2** *adj.* of or about Calvinism or Calvinists.

ca·lyp·so (kə lip′sō), *n.* type of improvised song, usually about some matter of current interest, that originated in the West Indies. ❑ *n., pl.* **ca·lyp·sos.**

ca·lyx (kā′liks *or* kal′iks), *n.* the outer leaves that surround the unopened bud of a flower. The calyx is made up of sepals. ❑ *n., pl.* **ca·lyx·es, cal·y·ces** (kal′ə sēz′ *or* kā′lə sēz′).

cam (kam), *n.* a wheel that is not circular, mounted on a shaft so that it changes circular motion into back-and-forth motion. Cams are used to vary the speed of some mechanisms or change the direction of their movement.

ca·ma·ra·der·ie (kä′mə rä′dər ē), *n.* friendliness and loyalty among comrades; comradeship: *the camaraderie of school days.*

cam·bi·um (kam′bē əm), *n.* **1** layer of soft growing tissue between the bark and the wood of trees and bushes. New bark and new wood grow from it. **2** a similar layer in plants without bark.

Cam·bo·di·a (kam bō′dē ə), *n.* country in SE Asia. *Capital:* Phnom Penh. Also, **Kampuchea.** —**Cam·bo′di·an,** *adj., n.*

Cam·bri·an (kam′brē ən), *n.* (in geology) time between about 600 million and 500 million years ago. During this time, living things became much more complex than before, first having hard shells, joints, jaws, and legs.

cam·bric (kām′brik), *n.* a fine, thin linen or cotton cloth.

cambric tea, drink made of hot water, milk, and sugar, sometimes flavored with a little tea.

Cam·bridge (kām′brij), *n.* **1** city in SE England. **2** the old and famous English university located there.

cam·cor·der (kam′kôr′dər), *n.* a hand-held combination of a camera and a video recorder.

Cam·den (kam′dən), *n.* city in SW New Jersey, on the Delaware River.

came (kām), *v.* past tense of **come:** *I came home late.*

cam·el (kam′əl), *n.* either of two large, four-footed, cud-chewing mammals with long necks and cushioned feet. They are used as beasts of burden in the deserts of northern Africa and central Asia because they can go for a long time without drinking water. The dromedary, the camel of northern Africa, has one hump; the Bactrian camel of central Asia has two humps.

ca·mel·lia (kə mē′lyə), *n.* bush or tree with glossy, evergreen leaves and waxy white, red, pink, or spotted flowers shaped like roses. ❑ *n., pl.* **ca·mel·lias.**

Cam·e·lot (kam′ə lot), *n.* (in legends of the Middle Ages) place in England where King Arthur had his palace.

Cam·em·bert (kam′əm ber), *n.* a rich, soft cheese.

cam·e·o (kam′ē ō), *n.* a semiprecious stone carved so that there is a raised design on a background, usually of a different color. ❑ *n., pl.* **cam·e·os.**

a	hat	ė	term	ô	order	ch	child		
ā	age	i	it	oi	oil	ng	long		a in about
ä	far	ī	ice	ou	out	sh	she		e in taken
â	care	o	hot	u	cup	th	thin	ə	i in pencil
e	let	ō	open	ů	put	ŦH	then		o in lemon
ē	equal	ô	saw	ü	rule	zh	measure		u in circus

cam·er·a (kam′ər ə), *n.* **1** device for taking photographs, making movies, or recording images on videotape. **2** device that converts images into electronic signals for television broadcasting. ❑ *n., pl.* **cam·er·as.**

cam·er·a·man (kam′ər ə man′), *n.* person who operates a movie, TV, or video camera. ❑ *n., pl.* **cam·er·a·men.**

cam·er·a·wom·an (kam′ər ə wûm′ən), *n.* woman who operates a movie, TV, or video camera. ❑ *n., pl.* **cam·er·a·wom·en.**

Cam·er·oon (kam′ə rün′), *n.* country in W central Africa. *Capital:* Yaoundé. —**Cam′er·oon′i·an,** *adj., n.*

WORD STORY   Cameroon comes from a Portuguese word meaning "shrimp." Portuguese explorers found shrimplike animals in one of Cameroon's rivers.

cam·i·sole (kam′ə sōl), *n.* a woman's undergarment that is like the top part of a slip.

cam·o·mile (kam′ə mīl), *n.* chamomile.

cam·ou·flage (kam′ə fläzh), **1** *n.* a disguised appearance that makes a person or animal look much like its surroundings. The white fur of a polar bear is a natural camouflage, for it prevents the bear's being easily seen against the snow. **2** *n.* the act of giving soldiers or equipment an appearance that helps hide them from view. **3** *n.* materials or other means by which this is done: *The guns were hidden by a camouflage of earth and branches.*

camouflage

4 *v.* to give something or someone an appearance that makes it difficult to see: *The hunters wore camouflaged clothing so that they blended with the trees.* ❑ *v.* **cam·ou·flaged, cam·ou·flag·ing.** —**cam′ou·flag′er,** *n.*

camp (kamp), **1** *n.* a place where a person or group lives outdoors, in a tent or tents or other shelter: *The travelers set up camp near the river.* **2** *v.* to live away from home for a time outdoors or in a tent or hut: *The scout troop camped at the foot of the mountain for two weeks.* **3** *n.* a place where people, especially children, live and play outdoors for a time: *summer camp, day camp.* **4** *n.* area where an army sets up temporary shelter. **5** *n.* persons living in a camp: *The camp was awakened by the bugler.* **6** *v.* to live simply, as you would in a tent: *We camped in the empty house until our furniture arrived.* **7** *n.* group of people who agree or work together: *The election of a new president divided the club into two opposing camps.*

break camp, to pack up tents and equipment: *We broke camp early in the morning to return home.*

camp out, to spend the night outdoors.

cam·paign (kam pān′), **1** *n.* series of related military operations in a war which are aimed at some special purpose: *The general planned a campaign to capture the enemy's most important city.* **2** *n.* series of connected activities to do or get something: *Our town had a campaign to raise money for a new hospital.* **3** *v.* to take part or serve in a campaign: *She campaigned for mayor by giving speeches.* —**cam·paign′er,** *n.*

cam·pa·ni·le (kam′pə nē′lē), *n.* tower built to contain a bell or bells. It may be a separate building. ❑ *n., pl.* **cam·pa·niles, cam·pa·ni·li** (kam′pə nē′lē).

Camp·bell (kam′bəl), *n.* **Kim** (kim), born 1947, Canadian prime minister in 1993. She was Canada's first woman prime minister.

Camp David, a private, rural residence in W Maryland, for the use of the President, his family, and guests.

Cam·pe·che (käm pā′chā), *n.* a state in SE Mexico.

camp·er (kam′pər), *n.* **1** person who camps. **2** trailer or vehicle equipped for camping.

cam·pe·si·no (käm pā sē′ nō), *n.* SPANISH. farmer or peasant. ❑ *n., pl.* **cam·pe·si·nos.**

camp·fire (kamp′fīr′), *n.* **1** fire in a camp for cooking or warmth. **2** a social gathering of soldiers, scouts, etc.

Camp Fire, organization formerly called the **Camp Fire Girls,** now for both girls and boys, to help them develop character, health, and responsibility for service to others.

camp·ground (kamp′ground′), *n.* **1** place for camping, especially a public park with campsites, fireplaces for cooking, etc. **2** place where a camp meeting is held.

cam·phor (kam′fər), *n.* a white, crystalline substance with a strong odor, usually obtained from a laurel tree in eastern Asia. Camphor is used in medicine and to protect clothes from moths.

camp·ing (kam′ping), *n.* the practice or recreation of living outdoors in a temporary shelter or vehicle.

camp meeting, a religious gathering held outdoors or in a tent, sometimes lasting several days.

camp·site (kamp′sīt′), *n.* place where people camp.

cam·pus (kam′pəs), *n.* the buildings and grounds of a college, university, school, hospital, business corporation, or the like. ❑ *n., pl.* **cam·pus·es.**

Ca·mus (ka mü′), *n.* **Al·bert** (al bâr′), 1913-1960, French writer and playwright. He won the 1957 Nobel Prize for literature.

can[1] (kan), *v.* **1** to be able to: *He can run fast.* **2** to know how to: *She can speak Spanish.* **3** to have the right to: *Anyone can cross the street here.* **4** to be allowed to; may: *Can I go now? You can go if you want to.* ❑ *v.,* past tense **could.**

USAGE NOTE   Can is used in everyday speech and writing for both permission and ability: *Can I go now? They can run faster than I can.* In formal English, however, **can** means "to be able to" and **may** means "to have permission to": *He can walk with crutches. May I please speak with her?*

can[2] (kan), **1** *n.* an airtight metal container in which food is stored: *a can of peaches.* **2** *n.* a container of metal, usually with a cover or lid: *a trash can, a paint can.* **3** *n.* amount that a can holds: *Add three cans of water to make the orange juice.* **4** *v.* INFORMAL. to dismiss from a job; fire: *I was canned for being late too often.* **5** *v.* to put in an airtight can or jar to preserve: *We are going to can tomatoes.* ❑ *v.* **canned, canning.**

Can., **1** Canada. **2** Canadian.

Ca·naan (kā′nən), *n.* a region in Palestine between the Jordan River and the Mediterranean.

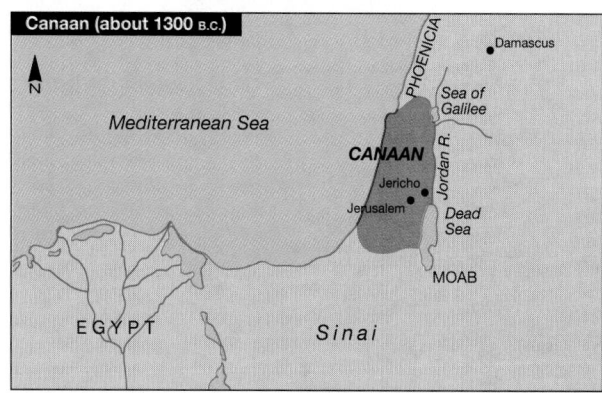
Canaan (about 1300 B.C.)

Ca·naan·ite (kā′nə nīt), *n.* inhabitant of Canaan before it was conquered by the Hebrews.

Can·a·da (kan′ə də), *n.* country in the N part of North America, consisting of ten provinces and two territories and extending from the Atlantic to the Pacific and from the United States to the Arctic Ocean. *Capital:* Ottawa. [Canada probably comes from an Iroquois word meaning "town" or "settlement."]

Canada Day, July 1, celebrated as a holiday in Canada to commemorate the formation of the Dominion of Canada on that date in 1867. Formerly, Dominion Day.

Canada goose, a large, wild goose of North America, with a black head and neck, white throat, and a brownish gray body.

Canada jay, gray jay.

Ca·na·di·an (kə nā′dē ən), **1** *adj.* of Canada or its people. **2** *n.* person born or living in Canada.

Canadian Forces, the armed forces of Canada, including land, sea, and air elements.

Ca·na·di·an·ism (kə na′dē ə niz′əm), *n.* **1** word or expression that originated in Canada, or is used only or mainly in Canada. *Broomball* and *muskeg* are Canadianisms. **2** loyalty to Canada, its customs, and its traditions.

Ca·na·di·an·ize (kə nā′dē ə nīz′), *v.* **1** to make Canadian in character or habit. **2** to change the content of printed or broadcast material so as to portray Canadian viewpoints or attitudes. **3** to bring a business, etc., under Canadian control. ❑ *v.* **Ca·na·di·an·ized, Ca·na·di·an·iz·ing.**

Canadian Shield, a huge area of very old rock that curves around Hudson Bay in a U-shape. It covers about half of Canada, from the Arctic Ocean to the Great Lakes.

Ca·na·di·en (kə nā′dē ən *or* kä nä dyen′), *n.* a French Canadian.

Ca·na·di·enne (kə nā′dē en′ *or* kä nä dyen′), *n.* a French Canadian girl or woman.

ca·nal (kə nal′), *n.* **1** waterway dug across land for small ships or boats to travel through, or to carry water for irrigation. **2** tube in the body of a person or an animal carrying food, liquid, air, etc. The food that a person eats goes through the alimentary canal. **3** one of the long, dark, narrow markings seen on the planet Mars. Scientists once suggested that these were artificial waterways but no longer think so.

Canal Zone, the Panama Canal and the land five miles (eight kilometers) on each side, governed by the United States from 1903 to 1979, and now governed by Panama. Also, **Panama Canal Zone.**

can·a·pé (kan′ə pā *or* kan′ə pē), *n.* cracker or thin piece of toast or bread spread with olives, meat, fish, cheese, etc., and served as an appetizer. ❑ *n., pl.* **can·a·pés.**

ca·nar·y (kə ner′ē), **1** *n.* a small, yellow songbird. It is a kind of finch often kept as a pet, and bred for its beautiful singing. **2** *n.* a light yellow. **3** *adj.* light yellow. ❑ *n., pl.* **ca·nar·ies.**

WORD STORY **Canary** comes from a Latin word meaning "dog." The Canary Islands, where these birds were first found, were named for the large dogs also found there. You may have heard of bird dogs, and now you know that there are "dog" birds.

Canary Islands, group of Spanish islands in the Atlantic, near the NW coast of Africa.

canary yellow, a light yellow.

Can·ber·ra (kan′ber ə), *n.* capital of Australia, in the SE part.

can·cel (kan′səl), *v.* **1** to put an end to, set aside, or withdraw; do away with: *The teacher canceled his order for the books. She canceled her appointment with the doctor.* **2** to make up for; offset; balance: *If I vote "Yes" and you vote "No," we shall cancel out each other's vote.* **3** to cross out; mark, stamp, or punch so that it cannot be used again: *The post office cancels the stamp on a letter.* **4** in mathematics: **a** to reduce a fraction by dividing both the numerator and the denominator by the same quantity. **b** to reduce an equation by dividing both members by a common factor. ❑ *v.* **can·celed, can·cel·ing** or **can·celled, can·cel·ling.**

can·cel·la·tion (kan′sə lā′shən), *n.* **1** act of canceling or condition of being canceled: *cancellation of a baseball game because of rain.* **2** marks made when something is canceled or crossed out: *cancellation of a postage stamp.* **3** something that is canceled.

can·cer (kan′sər), *n.* **1** a very harmful growth in the body; malignant tumor. Cancer tends to spread and to destroy the healthy tissues and organs of the body. **2** an evil or harmful thing that tends to spread: *Slums are a cancer in many a large city.* **3 Cancer, a** tropic of Cancer. **b** a group of stars shaped something like a crab. **c** the fourth sign of the zodiac, associated with the period from mid-June to mid-July.

can·cer·ous (kan′sər əs), *adj.* **1** like cancer: *a cancerous tumor.* **2** having cancer: *a cancerous liver.*

can·de·la (kan dē′lə *or* kan del′ə), *n.* unit for measuring the strength of light; candle. ❑ *n., pl.* **can·de·las.**

can·de·la·bra (kan′dl ä′brə), *n.* candelabrum. ❑ *n., pl.* **can·de·la·bras.**

can·de·la·brum (kan′dl ä′brəm), *n.* an ornamental candlestick with several branches for candles. ❑ *n., pl.* **can·de·la·bra** or **can·de·la·brums.**

can·did (kan′did), *adj.* **1** saying openly what you really think or feel; frank and sincere; outspoken: *a candid reply. Please be candid with me.* **2** fair; impartial: *a candid decision.* **3** not posed: *a candid photograph of children playing.* **–can′did·ly,** *adv.* **–can′did·ness,** *n.*

can·di·da·cy (kan′də də sē), *n.* fact or condition of being a candidate: *Please support my candidacy for class treasurer.*

can·di·date (kan′də dāt), *n.* person who seeks, or is suggested by others for some office or honor: *There are three candidates for president of the club.*

WORD STORY **Candidate** comes from a Latin word meaning "dressed in white." In ancient Rome, men trying to get elected wore white clothes to show their spotless records.

can·died (kan′dēd), *adj.* **1** cooked in sugar; glazed with sugar: *candied sweet potatoes.* **2** preserved or encrusted with sugar: *candied ginger.*

can·dle (kan′dl), **1** *n.* a stick of wax or tallow with a wick in it, burned to give light: *There are 15 candles on the birthday cake.* **2** *v.* (earlier) to test eggs for freshness by holding them in front of a light: *The farmer candled the eggs before he sold them.* **3** *n.* candela. ❑ *v.* **can·dled, can·dling. –can′dler,** *n.*
burn the candle at both ends, to use up your strength and resources rapidly.
not hold a candle to, not be nearly as good as: *The cake from the bakery did not hold a candle to the homemade one.*

can·dle·light (kan′dl līt′), *n.* **1** light of a candle or candles. **2** time when candles are lighted; dusk; twilight; nightfall.

Can·dle·mas (kan′dl məs), *n.* February 2, a church festival in honor of the purification of the Virgin Mary. It is celebrated with lighted candles.

candle (def. 1)

can·dle·pow·er (kan′dl pou′ər), *n.* strength of light, measured in candelas.

can·dle·stick (kan′dl stik′), *n.* holder for a candle, to make it stand up straight.

can·dor (kan′dər), *n.* **1** honesty in giving your view or opinion; frankness: *She expressed her views with great candor.* **2** fairness: *We must weigh each argument with candor before coming to a decision.*

can·dy (kan′dē), **1** *n.* a sweet food made of sugar or syrup, often mixed with chocolate, fruit, nuts, or flavorings. **2** *n.* piece of this: *Take a candy from the box.* **3** *v.* to turn into sugar: *This honey has candied.* **4** *v.* to cook something in sugar; preserve by boiling in sugar: *She candied the peaches before canning them.* ❑ *n., pl.* **can·dies;** *v.* **can·died, can·dy·ing. –can′dy·like′,** *adj.*

WORD STORY **Candy** comes from a Persian word meaning "sugar." Long ago, Europeans had no sugar. They bought sweet foods from Asia and used an Asian name for them.

candy strip·er (strī′pər), INFORMAL. person who works as a volunteer at a hospital. [**Candy striper** comes from volunteers' uniforms with red and white stripes.]

cane (kān), **1** *n.* a slender stick used as an aid in walking: *On long walks the old woman took along her cane.* **2** *n.* stick used to beat with: *A blow with a cane was an old form of punishment.* **3** *v.* to beat with a cane: *Some schoolmasters used to cane boys when they did not obey.* **4** *n.* a long, jointed stem, such as that of the bamboo. **5** *n.* any plant having such stems. Sugarcane, bamboo,

a	hat	ė	term	ô	order	ch	child
ā	age	i	it	oi	oil	ng	long
ä	far	ī	ice	ou	out	sh	she
â	care	o	hot	u	cup	th	thin
e	let	ō	open	ů	put	ᴛʜ	then
ē	equal	ò	saw	ü	rule	zh	measure

ə { a in about / e in taken / i in pencil / o in lemon / u in circus

and rattan are canes. **6** *n.* material made of such stems, used for furniture, chair seats, etc.: *Our porch chairs have cane seats.* **7** *v.* to make or repair with this material: *We are having all our porch furniture caned.* ❑ *v.* **caned, can·ing.**

cane·brake (kān′brāk′), *n.* thicket of cane plants.

cane sugar, sugar made from sugarcane.

ca·nine (kā′nīn), **1** *n.* dog. **2** *adj.* of or like a dog: *canine faithfulness.* **3** *n.* any of various animals related to dogs, including foxes, wolves, etc. **4** *adj.* belonging to this group. The coyote is a canine animal. **5** *n.* canine tooth. [See word history information at **kennel.**]

canine tooth, one of the four pointed teeth next to the incisors; cuspid.

can·is·ter (kan′ə stər), *n.* a small box or can, especially for tea, coffee, flour, or sugar.

can·ker (kang′kər), *n.* **1** a spreading sore, especially one in the mouth. **2** anything that causes rot or decay or destroys by a slow eating away: *a neighborhood ruined by the canker of poverty.*

can·ker·ous (kang′kər əs), *adj.* **1** of or like a canker. **2** causing a canker.

can·ker·worm (kang′kər wèrm′), *n.* any of several caterpillars that eat away the leaves of trees and plants.

can·na (kan′ə), *n.* any of various tropical plants with large, pointed leaves and large red, pink, or yellow flowers. ❑ *n., pl.* **can·nas.**

can·na·bis (kan′ə bis), *n.* **1** hemp plant. **2** marijuana or hashish.

canned (kand), *adj.* **1** put in a can; preserved by being put in airtight cans or jars: *canned peaches.* **2** preserved on a phonograph record or on tape; recorded: *canned music.*

can·ner (kan′ər), *n.* person who cans food.

can·ner·y (kan′ər ē), *n.* factory where food is canned. ❑ *n., pl.* **can·ner·ies.**

Can·nes (kan), *n.* resort in SE France, on the Mediterranean.

can·ni·bal (kan′ə bəl), **1** *n.* person who eats human flesh. **2** *n.* animal that eats others of its own kind: *Many fishes are cannibals.* **3** *adj.* of or like cannibals: *Cannibal ants help control ants that destroy crops.*

can·ni·bal·ism (kan′ə bə liz′əm), *n.* act or habit of eating the flesh of your own kind: *Few animals practice cannibalism.*

can·ni·bal·is·tic (kan′ə bə lis′tik), *adj.* of or like cannibals.

can·ni·bal·ize (kan′ə bə liz), *v.* to take usable parts from a machine to build or repair another: *My brother cannibalized a model car to get its wheels for his robot.* ❑ *v.* **can·ni·bal·ized, can·ni·bal·iz·ing.** —**can′ni·bal·i·za′tion,** *n.*

can·ning (kan′ing), *n.* the preserving of meat, fish, fruit, etc., by cooking it and sealing it in airtight cans or jars.

can·non (kan′ən), *n.* **1** a big gun, especially one that is mounted on a base or wheels. The old-fashioned cannon that fired cannonballs was much used during the Civil War. **2** an automatic gun that fires shells from a tank or an airplane. ❑ *n., pl.* **can·non** or **can·nons.** ■ Another word that sounds like this is **canon.**

Can·non (kan′ən), *n.* **An·nie Jump** (an′ē jump), 1863-1941, American astronomer. She discovered five new stars, 300 variable stars, and a double star.

can·non·ade (kan′ə nād′), **1** *n.* heavy cannon fire. **2** *v.* to attack with cannons. ❑ *v.* **can·non·ad·ed, can·non·ad·ing.**

can·non·ball (kan′ən bȯl′), *n.* a large iron or steel ball, formerly fired from cannons.

can·non·eer (kan′ə nir′), *n.* gunner.

can·not (kan′ot *or* ka not′), *v.* can not.

can·ny (kan′ē), *adj.* shrewd and cautious in dealing with others: *The canny trader made a large profit by buying goods when they were plentiful and selling them when they became scarce.* ❑ *adj.* **can·ni·er, can·ni·est.** —**can′ni·ly,** *adv.* —**can′ni·ness,** *n.*

ca·noe (kə nü′), **1** *n.* a light, narrow boat pointed at both ends and moved with a paddle. **2** *v.* to paddle a canoe; go in a canoe. ❑ *v.* **ca·noed, ca·noe·ing.**

ca·noe·ist (kə nü′ist), *n.* person who paddles a canoe.

ca·no·la (kə nō′lə), *n.* a plant related to mustard and cabbage plants, grown as animal feed and for the oil from its seeds. **Canola oil** is low in many kinds of fat and is used in preparing food.

can·on[1] (kan′ən), *n.* **1** rule by which a thing is judged; standard: *the canons of good taste.* **2** law of a church. **3** a list of the books of the Bible accepted by the Christian church as genuine and inspired. ■ Another word that sounds like this is **cannon.**

can·on[2] (kan′ən), *n.* member of the clergy belonging to a cathedral. ■ Another word that sounds like this is **cannon.**

ca·ñon (kan′yən), *n.* canyon. ❑ *n., pl.* **ca·ñons.**

ca·non·i·cal (kə non′ə kəl), *adj.* **1** according to church laws: *canonical dress.* **2** in the canon of the Bible. —**ca·non′i·cal·ly,** *adv.*

can·on·ize (kan′ə nīz), *v.* to declare a dead person to be a saint; place in the official list of saints: *Joan of Arc was canonized by the Roman Catholic Church in 1920.* ❑ *v.* **can·on·ized, can·on·iz·ing.** —**can′on·i·za′tion,** *n.* —**can′on·iz′er,** *n.*

can·o·py (kan′ə pē), **1** *n.* a covering fixed over a bed, throne, entrance, etc., or carried on poles over a person: *There is a striped canopy over the entrance to the hotel.* **2** *n.* a rooflike covering; shelter or shade: *The trees formed a canopy over the old road.* **3** *v.* to cover with a canopy. **4** *n.* the sliding, clear cover of the cockpit of a small airplane. **5** *n.* the uppermost layer of branches in forest trees. ❑ *n., pl.* **can·o·pies;** *v.* **can·o·pied, can·o·py·ing.**

WORD STORY **Canopy** comes from a Greek word meaning "gnat." Before window screens, people slept under coverings of light cloth to keep insects off them.

canst (kanst), *v.* OLD USE. can[1]. "Thou canst" means "you can."

cant[1] (kant), *n.* **1** talk that is not sincere; moral or religious statements that many people make, but few really believe or act upon. **2** the peculiar language of a special group, using many strange words; jargon: *"Jug" is a word for "jail" in thieves' cant.*

cant[2] (kant), **1** *v.* to give a slant or slope to; bevel: *He canted the edges of the board.* **2** *v.* to put into a slant; tip; tilt: *The wind canted the ship to port.* **3** *n.* a sloping, slanting, or tilting; inclination: *The ship took on a dangerous cant to starboard.*

can't (kant), cannot or can not.

can·ta·loupe or **can·ta·loup** (kan′tl ōp), *n.* muskmelon with a hard, rough rind and sweet, juicy, orange flesh.

can·tan·ker·ous (kan tang′kər əs), *adj.* ready to make trouble and oppose anything suggested; ill-natured; quarrelsome. —**can·tan′ker·ous·ly,** *adv.* —**can·tan′ker·ous·ness,** *n.*

can·ta·ta (kən tä′tə), *n.* musical composition consisting of a story or play which is sung by a chorus and soloists, but not acted. ❑ *n., pl.* **can·ta·tas.**

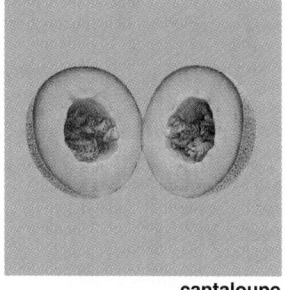
cantaloupe

can·teen (kan tēn′), *n.* **1** a small container for carrying water or other drinks. **2** a store in a school, camp, factory, hospital, etc., where food, drinks, and other articles are sold, often from vending machines. **3** recreation hall for members of the armed forces.

can·ter (kan′tər), **1** *n.* a gait of a horse, like a slow gallop. **2** *v.* to ride at a canter: *I cantered my horse down the road.*

Can·ter·bur·y (kan′tər ber′ē), *n.* city in SE England. Many pilgrims traveled there during the Middle Ages to visit the shrine of Saint Thomas à Becket.

can·ti·cle (kan′tə kəl), *n.* a short song, hymn, or chant with words from the Bible, used in church services.

can·ti·lev·er (kan′tl ev′ər *or* kan′tl ē′vər), *n.* a large, projecting beam or structure that is supported at one end only.

cantilever bridge, bridge made of two cantilevers whose projecting ends meet but do not support each other.

can·to (kan′tō), *n.* one of the main divisions of a long poem. A canto of a poem is like a chapter of a novel. ❑ *n., pl.* **can·tos.**

can·ton (kan′tən *or* kan′ton), *n.* a small part or political division of a country. Switzerland is made up of 22 cantons.

Can·ton (kan ton′), *n.* former name of **Guangzhou.**

Can·ton·ese (kan′tə nēz′), **1** *n.* person born or living in Canton. **2** *n.* the Chinese dialect spoken in or near Canton. **3** *adj.* of Canton, its people, or their dialect. ❑ *n., pl.* **Can·ton·ese** for 1.

can·ton·ment (kan ton′mənt), *n.* place where soldiers live; temporary quarters for soldiers.

can·tor (kan′tər), *n.* **1** person who leads the services in a Jewish religious service. **2** person who leads the singing of a choir or congregation.

Ca·nuck (kə nuk′), *n.* CANADIAN INFORMAL. **1** Canadian. **2** French Canadian. ■ **Canuck** is sometimes considered offensive, especially if used by a non-Canadian.

can·vas (kan′vəs), **1** *n.* a strong cloth with a coarse weave made of cotton, flax, or hemp, used to make tents, sails, certain articles of clothing, etc., and for painting on. **2** *adj.* made of canvas: *The boat had canvas sails.* **3** *n.* something made of canvas: *The artist prepared a canvas for painting on the next day.* **4** *n.* picture painted on canvas; oil painting: *A valuable canvas was stolen from the art gallery.* ❏ *n., pl.* **can·vas·es.** ■ Another word that sounds like this is **canvass.** —**can′vas·like′,** *adj.*

under canvas, 1 in tents: *The circus was held under canvas in an open field.* **2** with sails spread: *The schooner left the harbor under full canvas.*

can·vas·back (kan′vəs bak′), *n.* a large wild duck of North America with grayish feathers on its back. ❏ *n., pl.* **can·vas·backs** or **can·vas·back.**

can·vass (kan′vəs), **1** *v.* to go through a city, district, etc., asking for votes, orders, donations, etc.: *Volunteers canvassed the whole city for the candidate.* **2** *n.* act of asking for votes, orders, donations, etc.: *During his canvass of the neighborhood, my father collected $200 for the cancer fund.* **3** *v.* to examine the parts of carefully; inspect: *He canvassed the papers, hunting for notices of after-school jobs.* **4** *v.* to discuss: *The city council canvassed the mayor's plan thoroughly.* ❏ *n., pl.* **can·vass·es.** ■ Another word that sounds like this is **canvas.** —**can′vass·er,** *n.*

can·yon (kan′yən), *n.* a narrow valley with high, steep sides, usually with a stream at the bottom. Also, **cañon.**

Can·yon·lands National Park (kan′yən landz′), a national park in SE Utah, containing extensive canyons of the Colorado and other rivers.

canyon

cap (kap), **1** *n.* a soft, close-fitting covering for the head, with little or no brim, but often with a visor. **2** *n.* a special head covering worn to show your rank or occupation: *a student's cap and gown.* **3** *n.* anything that covers or forms the top of something. The stopper or top of a jar, bottle, tube, or fountain pen is a cap. The top of a mushroom is called a cap. **4** *n.* the highest part; top: *the polar cap at the North Pole.* **5** *v.* to put a cap on; cover the top of: *I capped the bottle. Snow capped the mountain peak.* **6** *n.* an artificial crown fastened to a tooth. **7** *v.* to fasten an artificial crown to a tooth. **8** *v.* to do or follow up with something as good or better: *Each of the two clowns capped the other's last joke.* **9** *n.* a small amount of explosive in a wrapper or covering: *They shot off caps in their toy guns.* ❏ *v.* **capped, cap·ping.**

cap., capital letter.

ca·pa·bil·i·ty (kā′pə bil′ə tē), *n.* **1** ability to learn or do; power or fitness; capacity: *With her background in Latin, she has the capability to learn French.* **2 capabilities,** *pl.* undeveloped properties; potential uses: *Atomic energy has many unexplored capabilities.* ❏ *n., pl.* **ca·pa·bil·i·ties.**

ca·pa·ble (kā′pə bəl), *adj.* having fitness, power, or ability; able; efficient; competent: *He was such a capable student that everyone had great hopes for his future.* ■ See Synonym Study at **able.** —**ca′pa·bly,** *adv.*

capable of, 1 having ability, power, or fitness for: *Some airplanes are capable of going 1000 miles an hour.* **2** open to; ready for: *a statement capable of being misunderstood.*

ca·pa·cious (kə pā′shəs), *adj.* able to hold much; large and roomy; spacious: *a capacious closet.* —**ca·pa′cious·ly,** *adv.* —**ca·pa′cious·ness,** *n.*

ca·pac·i·tance (kə pas′ə təns), *n.* quality of a capacitor that determines the amount of electrical charge it can receive and store; capacity.

ca·pac·i·tor (kə pas′ə tər), *n.* device for receiving and storing a charge of electricity; condenser.

ca·pac·i·ty (kə pas′ə tē), *n.* **1** amount of space inside; largest amount that can be held by a container: *This can has a capacity of four quarts.* **2** ability to receive and hold: *the capacity of a metal for retaining heat. The theater has a seating capacity of 400.* **3** ability to learn or do; power or fitness: *an intelligent student with a capacity for learning.* **4** position or relation. A person may act in the capacity of guardian, trustee, voter, friend, etc. **5** capacitance. ❏ *n., pl.* **ca·pac·i·ties.**

cap and gown, a flat cap and loose gown, worn by teachers and students on certain occasions, especially at commencement exercises.

ca·par·i·son (kə par′ə sən), **1** *n.* an ornamental covering for a horse. **2** *n.* any rich dress or outfit. **3** *v.* to dress richly.

cape¹ (kāp), *n.* a piece of outer clothing, without sleeves, worn falling loosely from the shoulders and often fastened at the neck.

cape² (kāp), *n.* point of land extending into the water.

Cape Breton Island, island off the E coast of Canada, part of Nova Scotia.

Cape Ca·nav·er·al (kə nav′ər əl), cape in E Florida from which NASA launches rockets.

Cape Cod, hook-shaped peninsula in SE Massachusetts. [**Cape Cod** was named by the first Europeans to see it, sailors who were glad because they caught many cod there.]

Cape Horn, cape which forms the S tip of South America. See **Patagonia** for map.

Cape of Good Hope, cape near the S tip of Africa.

ca·per¹ (kā′pər), **1** *v.* to leap or jump about playfully: *The children capered and laughed in the park.* **2** *n.* a playful leap or jump: *the shouts and capers of children playing tag.* **3** *n.* prank; trick: *The child's capers made us laugh.* **4** *n.* INFORMAL. a crime, especially a burglary: *The jewel thieves pulled off a big caper at the art museum.* [See Word Story at **cab.**]

cut a caper or **cut capers, 1** to play or do a trick. **2** to leap about playfully.

ca·per² (kā′pər), *n.* **1** a low, prickly bush of the Mediterranean region. **2 capers,** *pl.* the green flower buds and berries of this bush, pickled and used for seasoning.

Cape Town, port and legislative capital of South Africa. It is located at the S tip of Africa.

Cape Verde, country consisting of a group of islands west of Senegal. *Capital:* Praia. [**Cape Verde** comes from Portuguese words meaning "green cape."]

cap·il·lar·y (kap′ə ler′ē), **1** *n.* a blood vessel with a very slender, hairlike opening. Capillaries join the end of an artery to the beginning of a vein. **2** *n.* any of very narrow tubes. **3** *adj.* like a hair; very slender. ❏ *n., pl.* **cap·il·lar·ies.**

capillary attraction, the force that causes a liquid to rise in a narrow tube or when in contact with a porous substance. A plant draws up water from the ground and a paper towel absorbs water by means of capillary attraction.

cap·i·tal¹ (kap′ə təl), **1** *n.* city where the government of a country, state, or province is located. Lincoln is the capital of Nebraska. ■ See Usage Note at **Capitol.** **2** *n.* capital letter. **3** *adj.* very important; leading; chief: *The invention of the telephone was a capital advance in communication.* **4** *adj.* punishable by death: *Murder is a capital crime in many countries.* **5** *n.* money or property that companies or individuals use to increase their wealth:

a	hat	ė	term	ô	order	ch	child		a in about
ā	age	i	it	oi	oil	ng	long		e in taken
ä	far	ī	ice	ou	out	sh	she	ə {	i in pencil
â	care	o	hot	u	cup	th	thin		o in lemon
e	let	ō	open	u̇	put	ŦH	then		u in circus
ē	equal	ȯ	saw	ü	rule	zh	measure		

The Smith Company has capital amounting to $3,000,000. [See Word Story at **cattle**.]

make capital of, to take advantage of: *He made capital of his father's fame to get the job.*

cap·i·tal² (kap'ə təl), *n.* the top part of a column or pillar. ■ Another word that sounds like this is **capitol**.

cap·i·tal·ism (kap'ə tə liz'əm), *n.* an economic system in which private individuals or groups of individuals own land, factories, and other means of production. They compete with one another, using the hired labor of other persons, to produce goods and services for profit.

cap·i·tal·ist (kap'ə tə list), *n.* **1** person whose money and property are used in carrying on business. **2** a wealthy person. **3** person who favors or supports capitalism.

capital²

cap·i·tal·is·tic (kap'ə tə lis'-tik), *adj.* **1** of capitalism or capitalists: *capitalistic production.* **2** favoring or supporting capitalism: *capitalistic policies.* —**cap'i·tal·is'ti·cal·ly**, *adv.*

cap·i·tal·i·za·tion (kap'ə tə lə zā'shən), *n.* **1** act of capitalizing or being capitalized. **2** amount at which a company is capitalized; capital stock of a business: *The company increased its capitalization to $10 million.*

cap·i·tal·ize (kap'ə tə liz), *v.* **1** to write or print with a capital letter: *You always capitalize the first letter of your name.* **2** to turn into capital; use as capital: *The company capitalized its reserve funds.* **3** to provide or furnish with capital. ❏ *v.* **cap·i·tal·ized, cap·i·tal·iz·ing.** —**cap'i·tal·iz'a·ble,** *adj.*

capitalize on, to take advantage of; use to your own advantage: *capitalize on someone else's mistake.*

capital letter, the large form of a letter; A, B, C, D, etc., as distinguished from a, b, c, d, etc.

USAGE NOTE **Capital letters** are used at the beginnings of sentences or of proper names: *The girl's name is Jill.* Capital letters are sometimes used at the beginnings of words naming public officials. These words are capitalized when they are used as titles of address: *"What are your plans for the state, Governor?" asked a reporter.* They are also capitalized as part of a person's name: *Tonight's speaker will be Congresswoman Pat Pierce.* These words are usually not capitalized when they are used by themselves: *The mayor praised the district attorney for her work against crime.* A few of these words (especially *president* and *vice-president*) are always capitalized when they refer to the person currently in office: *The President asked the senators to support his policies. The Vice-President cut the ribbon in front of the new library. The Pope gave the crowd his blessing.*

capital punishment, the death penalty for a crime.

capital ship, a large warship, such as a battleship.

Cap·i·tol (kap'ə təl), *n.* **1** the building at Washington, D.C., in which Congress meets. **2 capitol,** the building in which a state legislature meets.

USAGE NOTE **Capitol** and **capital¹** are often confused. **Capitol** is a building. **Capital¹** is a city: *There is a dome on the Capitol in Washington, D.C., the capital of the United States.*

Capitol Hill, 1 hill in Washington, D.C., on which the U.S. Capitol stands. **2** the U.S. Congress: *Capitol Hill is debating the President's bill.*

Capitol Reef National Park, a national park in S Utah, containing an impressive ridge with a white top that is shaped like the dome of a capitol.

ca·pit·u·late (kə pich'ə lāt), *v.* to surrender on certain terms or conditions: *The men in the fort capitulated on condition that they be allowed to go away unharmed.* ❏ *v.* **ca·pit·u·lat·ed, ca·pit·u·lat·ing.** —**ca·pit·u·la'tion,** *n.*

cap·let (kap'lit), *n.* trademark for a smooth, oval medicine tablet. It is covered with gelatin to make it easy to swallow. [**Caplet** is a blend of the words **capsule** and **tablet**.]

ca·pon (kā'pon), *n.* rooster specially raised to be eaten. It is castrated and fattened.

Ca·pone (kə pōn'), *n.* **Al** (al), 1899-1947, American gangster. ■ **Al Capone** was also known as "Scarface," because his left cheek was scarred from a fight. He was blamed for many murders but was eventually jailed for income tax evasion.

Ca·po·te (kə pō'tē), *n.* **Truman,** 1924-1984, American writer. ■ **Truman Capote** blended fact and fiction in *In Cold Blood,* which tells the story of two men who murder a family in Kansas.

Cap·ra (kap'rə), *n.* **Frank,** 1897-1991, American movie director, born in Italy. His best-known film is *It's a Wonderful Life.*

Ca·pri (kə prē'), *n.* small island in W Italy, near Naples.

ca·price (kə prēs'), *n.* a sudden change of mind without reason; unreasonable notion or desire; whim: *The child's refusal to wear red clothes was pure caprice.*

ca·pri·cious (kə prish'əs), *adj.* likely to change suddenly without reason; changeable; fickle: *capricious weather.* —**ca·pri'cious·ly,** *adv.* —**ca·pri'cious·ness,** *n.*

Cap·ri·corn (kap'rə kôrn), *n.* **1** tropic of Capricorn. **2** group of stars shaped something like a goat. **3** the tenth sign of the zodiac, associated with the period from mid-December to mid-January.

caps., capital letters.

cap·size (kap sīz' *or* kap'sīz), *v.* to turn bottom side up; upset; overturn: *The sailboat nearly capsized in the squall.* ❏ *v.* **cap·sized, cap·siz·ing.**

cap·stan (kap'stən), *n.* machine for lifting or pulling that revolves on an upright shaft or spindle. Sailors on old sailing ships hoisted the anchor by turning the capstan.

cap·su·lar (kap'sə lər), *adj.* **1** of a capsule. **2** shaped like a capsule.

cap·sule (kap'səl), **1** *n.* a tiny container. Medicine is often given in capsules made of gelatin, which dissolve easily. **2** *n.* the enclosed front section of a rocket made to carry instruments, astronauts, etc., into space. In flight the capsule can separate from the rest of the rocket and go into orbit or be directed back to Earth. **3** *n.* a dry seedcase that opens when ripe. **4** *n.* membrane enclosing an organ of the body. **5** *adj.* very short; concise: *a capsule account of the accident.*

Capt., Captain.

cap·tain (kap'tən), **1** *n.* head of a group; leader or chief: *the captain of a basketball team.* **2** *n.* commander of a ship. **3** *n.* a military rank. See chart at page 712. **4** *n.* a police officer or fire department officer ranking below a chief and above a lieutenant. **5** *v.* to lead or command as captain: *She will captain the debating team next year.*

cap·tain·cy (kap'tən sē), *n.* rank or authority of a captain. ❏ *n., pl.* **cap·tain·cies.**

cap·tion (kap'shən), **1** *n.* title or heading at the beginning of a page, article, chapter, etc., or under a picture explaining it. **2** *n.* a movie subtitle. **3** *v.* to put a caption on.

cap·tious (kap'shəs), *adj.* **1** hard to please; faultfinding. **2** confusing in a subtle way: *a captious question.* —**cap'tious·ly,** *adv.* —**cap'tious·ness,** *n.*

cap·ti·vate (kap'tə vāt), *v.* to hold captive by beauty or interest; charm; fascinate: *The children were captivated by the story.* ❏ *v.* **cap·ti·vat·ed, cap·ti·vat·ing.** —**cap'ti·va'tion,** *n.* —**cap'ti·va'tor,** *n.*

cap·tive (kap'tiv), **1** *n.* person or animal captured and held against his or her will; prisoner: *The pirates took many captives during raids along the coast.* **2** *adj.* made a prisoner; held against your will: *The enemy released the captive soldiers.*

cap·tiv·i·ty (kap tiv'ə tē), *n.* **1** condition of being in prison. **2** condition of being held against your will: *Some animals cannot bear captivity, and die after a few weeks in a cage.*

cap·tor (kap'tər), *n.* person who takes or holds a prisoner or a captured animal.

cap·ture (kap′chər), **1** *v.* to make a prisoner of; take by force, skill, or trickery; seize: *We captured butterflies with a net.* ■ See Synonym Study at **catch. 2** *n.* person or thing taken in this way: *Captain Jones's first capture was an enemy ship.* **3** *n.* act of capturing or being captured: *The capture of this ship took place on July 6.* **4** *v.* to attract and hold; catch and keep: *The story "Alice in Wonderland" captures the imagination.* **5** *v.* to represent: *The artist captured the power of the ocean in her painting.* ❑ *v.* **cap·tured, cap·tur·ing.**

cap·u·chin (kap′yə shən), *n.* **1** any of four kinds of South American monkeys with black hair on their heads that looks like a hood. **2** Capuchin, a Franciscan monk belonging to an order that wears a long, pointed hood or cowl.

cap·y·ba·ra (kap′ə bär′ə or kap′ə bar′ə), *n.* a tailless rodent of South America. It is the world's largest rodent, growing up to two feet (61 centimeters) high and four feet (1.2 meters) long. ❑ *n., pl.* **cap·y·ba·ras.**

capuchin (def. 1)—about 3 ft. (91 cm) long with the tail

car (kär), *n.* **1** a motor vehicle, for passengers, powered by an internal-combustion engine; automobile: *They made the trip by car.* **2** a railroad car or streetcar. **3** the part of an elevator, balloon, or airship for carrying passengers or cargo. [See word history information at **cargo.**]

ca·ra·ba·o (kär′ə bä′ō), *n.* water buffalo of the Philippines. ❑ *n., pl.* **ca·ra·ba·os** or **ca·ra·ba·o.**

car·a·cal (kar′ə kal′), *n.* a small wildcat of Asia and Africa, related to the lynx. It has reddish brown fur and a tuft of long, black hair at the tip of each ear.

Ca·ra·cas (kə rä′kəs or kə rak′əs), *n.* capital of Venezuela, near the Caribbean.

ca·rafe (kə raf′), *n.* a glass bottle for holding water, wine, coffee, etc.

car·a·mel (kar′ə məl or kär′məl), *n.* **1** sugar browned or burned over heat, used for coloring and flavoring food. **2** a small block of chewy candy flavored with this sugar.

car·a·pace (kar′ə pās), *n.* shell or bony covering on the back of a turtle, armadillo, lobster, crab, etc.

car·at (kar′ət), *n.* **1** unit of weight for precious stones, equal to 200 milligrams. **2** karat. ■ Other words that sound like this are **caret** and **carrot.**

car·a·van (kar′ə van), *n.* (earlier) group of merchants, pilgrims, etc., traveling together for safety through difficult or dangerous country.

car·a·van·sar·y (kar′ə van′sər ē), *n.* Near Eastern or Far Eastern inn where caravans stop to rest. ❑ *n., pl.* **car·a·van·sar·ies.**

car·a·vel (kar′ə vel), *n.* a small, fast sailing ship of the type used by Columbus, with a broad bow and a high stern.

car·a·way (kar′ə wā), *n.* the fragrant, spicy seed of a plant related to parsley, used to flavor bread, rolls, or cakes.

Car·a·way (kar′ə wā), *n.* **Hat·tie Wy·att** (hat′ē wi′ət), 1878-1950, American political leader. ■ Hattie Wyatt Caraway was the first woman elected to the U.S. Senate. She was elected for a one-year term in 1932 to replace her husband, who had died while in office. Then she was elected for a full six-year term.

car·bide (kär′bīd), *n.* compound of carbon with another element.

car·bine (kär′bin or kär′bēn′), *n.* a short, light rifle.

car·bo·hy·drate (kär′bō hī′drāt), *n.* any of many related substances made from carbon dioxide and water by green plants in sunlight. Carbohydrates are made of carbon, hydrogen, and oxygen. Sugar and starch are carbohydrates.

car·bo·lat·ed (kär′bə lā′tid), *adj.* containing carbolic acid.

car·bol·ic acid (kär bol′ik), a very poisonous acid obtained from coal tar, used in solution as a disinfectant and antiseptic; phenol.

car·bon (kär′bən), *n.* **1** a very common nonmetallic element that occurs in combination with other elements in all living things. Diamonds and graphite are pure carbon in the form of crystals; coal and charcoal are mostly carbon in uncrystallized form. *Symbol:* C **2** copy made with carbon paper: *I kept a carbon of each letter I typed.* **3** piece of carbon paper: *I put a carbon between the two sheets of paper.* —**car′bon·less,** *adj.*

carbon 12, the most common isotope of carbon, now used as the standard for measuring atomic weights.

carbon 14, a radioactive form of carbon produced in the atmosphere by cosmic rays; radiocarbon. Scientists are able to find out the age of many ancient remains that once were alive by measuring the amount of carbon 14 in them. After death, carbon 14 vanishes from remains at a known rate, so the amount that is left tells the time since death.

car·bo·na·ceous (kär′bə nā′shəs), *adj.* of, like, or containing carbon.

car·bon·ate (kär′bə nāt), **1** *v.* to saturate with carbon dioxide. Soda water is carbonated to make it bubble and fizz. **2** *n.* a chemical substance formed from carbonic acid. ❑ *v.* **car·bon·at·ed, car·bon·at·ing.** —**car′bon·a′tion,** *n.*

car·bon·at·ed (kär′bə nā′tid), *adj.* saturated with carbon dioxide. Soda water is carbonated water.

carbon copy, 1 copy made with carbon paper. **2** anything that appears to be exactly like something else: *His laugh is a carbon copy of his father's.*

carbon dioxide, a colorless, odorless gas, present in the atmosphere and formed when any fuel containing carbon is burned. The air that is breathed out of an animal's lungs contains carbon dioxide. Plants absorb it from the air and use it to make plant tissue. Carbon dioxide is a greenhouse gas.

carbonic acid (kär bon′ik), acid made when carbon dioxide is dissolved in water. It gives the sharp taste to soda water.

car·bon·if·er·ous (kär′bə nif′ər əs), **1** *adj.* containing or producing coal. **2** *n.* **Carboniferous,** (in geology) time between about 350 million and 260 million years ago. During this time, large forests grew that became the earth's major coal beds.

car·bon·ize (kär′bə nīz), *v.* **1** to change into carbon by burning; char. **2** to cover or combine with carbon. ❑ *v.* **car·bon·ized, car·bon·iz·ing.** —**car′bon·i·za′tion,** *n.*

carbon monoxide, a colorless, odorless, very poisonous gas, formed when carbon burns with an insufficient supply of air. It is part of the exhaust gases of automobile engines.

carbon paper, a thin paper having carbon or some other inky substance on one surface. It is used between sheets of paper to make a copy of what is written or typed on the upper sheet.

carbon tet·ra·chlo·ride (tet′rə klôr′īd), a colorless liquid which does not burn, often used in fire extinguishers and in cleaning fluids. Its fumes are very dangerous if inhaled.

car·bun·cle (kär′bung kəl), *n.* **1** a smooth, round garnet or other deep red jewel. **2** a painful, infected swelling under the skin, larger than a boil and more serious in its effects. —**car·bun·cu·lar** (kär bung′kyə lər), *adj.*

car·bu·re·tor (kär′bə rā′tər), *n.* device for mixing air with a liquid fuel to produce a mixture that burns easily. The gasoline engine of a lawn mower contains a carburetor, and the engines of cars used to have carburetors, now replaced by fuel injection.

car·ca·jou (kär′kə zhü), *n.* CANADIAN. wolverine. ❑ *n., pl.* **car·ca·jous.**

car·cass (kär′kəs), *n.* **1** body of a dead animal. **2** INFORMAL. a human body. ❑ *n., pl.* **car·cass·es.**

car·cin·o·gen (kär sin′ə jən), *n.* any substance that produces cancer. —**car·cin·o·gen·ic** (kär′sin ə jen′ik), *adj.*

car·ci·no·ma (kär′sə nō′mə), *n.* cancer of the skin or of the tissue that lines body organs. ❑ *n., pl.* **car·ci·no·mas.**

a	hat	ė	term	ô	order	ch	child		
ā	age	i	it	oi	oil	ng	long	ə	a in about
ä	far	ī	ice	ou	out	sh	she		e in taken
â	care	o	hot	u	cup	th	thin		i in pencil
e	let	ō	open	ù	put	ᴛʜ	then		o in lemon
ē	equal	ò	saw	ü	rule	zh	measure		u in circus

card¹ (kärd), *n.* **1** a flat piece of stiff paper, thin cardboard, or plastic, usually small and rectangular: *a birthday card, a credit card, a library card.* **2** a playing card. **3 cards,** *pl.* **a** a pack of playing cards. **b** game or games played with a pack of playing cards. **c** act of playing such a game or games: *Many people at the party were busy at cards.* **4** INFORMAL. an odd or amusing person.
in the cards, likely to happen.
put your cards on the table, to show what your have or can do; be frank about something.

WORD STORY **Card¹** comes from a Greek word meaning "leaf." **Chart** comes from the same word. In old times, people used the leaves of certain plants to draw or write on. *Leaf* still means "a sheet of paper" in English.

card² (kärd), **1** *n.* a toothed tool or wire brush used to separate, clean, and straighten the fibers of wool, cotton, flax, etc., before spinning. **2** *v.* to clean or comb with such a tool: *She carded wool for spinning.* **—card′er,** *n.*

card·board (kärd′bôrd′), *n.* a stiff material made of layers of paper pulp pressed together, used to make cards, boxes, etc.

card catalog, list of items in a library, entered on cards arranged alphabetically and filed in a set of drawers.

car·di·ac (kär′dē ak), *adj.* of the heart: *cardiac arteries.*

Car·diff (kär′dif), *n.* port and capital of Wales, in the SE part.

car·di·gan (kär′də gən), *n.* a knitted jacket or sweater that buttons down the front.

car·di·nal (kärd′n əl), **1** *n.* one of the high officials of the Roman Catholic Church, appointed by the pope as his advisers, and ranking next below him. Cardinals wear red robes and red hats. **2** *n.* a colorful songbird of North America. The male has bright red feathers marked with a little gray and black. It is a kind of finch. **3** *adj.* of first importance; chief; principal: *The cardinal value of his plan is that it is simple.* **—car′di·nal·ly,** *adv.*

cardinal (def. 2)—about 9 in. (23 cm) long

WORD STORY **Cardinal** comes from a Latin word meaning "hinge." Hinges are of first importance to a door. The church officials were named for their importance, and the bird was named for the officials' red robes.

cardinal flower, the bright red flower of a North American plant.

cardinal number, number which shows how many are meant. One, two, three, etc., are cardinal numbers.

cardinal points, the four main directions of the compass; north, south, east, and west.

car·di·o·gram (kär′dē ə gram), *n.* electrocardiogram.

car·di·o·graph (kär′dē ə graf), *n.* electrocardiograph.

car·di·ol·o·gy (kär′dē ol′ə jē), *n.* branch of medicine that deals with the heart and the diagnosis and treatment of its diseases. **—car′di·ol′o·gist,** *n.*

car·di·o·pul·mo·nar·y (kär′dē ō pul′mə ner′ē), *adj.* of or affecting both the heart and the lungs.

cardiopulmonary resuscitation. See CPR.

car·di·o·vas·cu·lar (kär′dē ō vas′kyə lər), *adj.* of or affecting both the heart and the blood vessels.

care (kãr), **1** *v.* to be concerned; feel interest: *Musicians care about music.* **2** *n.* a troubled state of mind because of fear of what may happen; worry: *Few people are completely free from care.* **3** *n.* serious attention; heed: *A pilot's work requires great care.* **4** *n.* object of worry, concern, or attention: *The sick puppy was a care to its owners.* **5** *n.* watchful keeping; charge: *The little girl was left in her older brother's care.* **6** *n.* food, shelter, and protection: *While you're away, we will give your pets the best of care.* **7** *v.* to like; want; wish: *A cat does not care to be washed.* **8** *v.* to mind; object to: *Do you care if I leave early?* ❑ *v.* **cared, car·ing.**

care for, 1 be fond of; like: *I don't care for her friends.* **2** to want; wish: *I don't care for any dessert tonight.* **3** to take charge of; attend to: *The nurse will care for him now.*

in care of, at the address of: *All mail for the governor should be sent in care of the statehouse.*

take care, be careful: *Take care to be accurate.*

take care of, 1 to take charge of; attend to: *Grandfather will take care of the children.* **2** be careful with: *Take care of your money.*

SYNONYM STUDY **Care** and **concern** both mean a worried state of mind. **Care** suggests great worries and fears: *The life of a homeless person is full of care.* **Concern** suggests an uneasy feeling about someone or something: *The team's poor play is causing the coach to feel concern.*

CARE (kãr), *n.* Cooperative for American Relief Everywhere. CARE is a general charitable organization based in the United States.

ca·reen (kə rēn′), *v.* to lean to one side or sway sharply; tilt; tip: *The speeding car careened around the corner.*

ca·reer (kə rir′), **1** *n.* a general course of action or progress through life: *It is interesting to read of the careers of great men and women.* **2** *n.* way of living; occupation or profession: *I plan to make law my career.* **3** *v.* to rush along wildly; dash: *A runaway horse careered down the street.*

care·free (kãr′frē′), *adj.* without worry; happy: *The children spent a carefree summer sailing and swimming at the seashore.*

care·ful (kãr′fəl), *adj.* **1** thinking about what you say or do; taking pains; watchful; cautious: *She is a very careful driver. Please be careful with my new bicycle!* **2** showing care; done with thought or effort; exact; thorough: *Arithmetic requires careful work.* **3** full of care or concern; attentive: *Try to be careful of the feelings of others.* **—care′ful·ly,** *adv.* **—care′ful·ness,** *n.*

SYNONYM STUDY **Careful, cautious,** and **wary** all mean paying close attention to what you say or do. **Careful** suggests being watchful so as not to make mistakes: *I'm always careful when measuring ingredients.* **Cautious** suggests being very careful to avoid danger: *She is cautious when riding her bike in traffic.* **Wary** suggests being distrustful and alert for danger: *Cats are usually wary of dogs.*

care·giv·er (kãr′giv′ər), *n.* person who cares for children, the elderly, or people with illnesses or disabilities: *My sister is the caregiver for a man who had a heart attack.*

care·less (kãr′lis), *adj.* **1** not thinking about what you say or do; not careful: *I was careless and broke the cup.* **2** done without enough thought or effort; not exact or thorough: *careless work.* **3** not caring; indifferent: *Some people are careless about their appearance.* **4** without worry; happy: *the careless feeling of summer vacation.* **—care′less·ly,** *adv.* **—care′less·ness,** *n.*

ca·ress (kə res′), **1** *n.* a touch showing affection; tender embrace or kiss. **2** *v.* to touch or stroke tenderly; embrace or kiss. ❑ *n.,* *pl.* **ca·ress·es. —ca·ress′a·ble,** *adj.* **—ca·ress′er,** *n.* **—ca·ress′ing·ly,** *adv.*

car·et (kar′ət), *n.* a mark (^) to show where something should be put in, used in writing or printing. ■ Other words that sound like this are **carat, carrot,** and **karat.**

care·tak·er (kãr′tā′kər), *n.* person who takes care of someone else's house or other property.

care·worn (kãr′wôrn′), *adj.* showing signs of worry; tired or weary from care: *the careworn look on an old person's face.*

car·fare (kär′fãr′), *n.* money paid for riding on a bus, subway, or streetcar.

car·go (kär′gō), *n.* load of goods carried by a ship, plane, or truck: *The freighter had docked to unload a cargo of wheat.* ❑ *n.,* *pl.* **car·goes** or **car·gos.** [Cargo comes from a Latin word meaning "wagon." **Car** comes from the same word.]

car·hop (kär′hop′), *n.* person who serves customers in their cars at a drive-in restaurant.

Car·ib (kar′ib), *n.* member of a group of American Indian tribes living in northeastern South America and the Caribbean islands.

Car·ib·be·an (kar′ə bē′ən or kə rib′ē ən), *adj.* of the Caribbean Sea or the islands in it.

Caribbean Sea, sea bordered by Central America, the West Indies, and South America.

car·i·bou (kar′ə bü), *n.* a large deer with branching antlers that lives in northern North America. Caribou living in Europe and Asia are called reindeer. ❑ *n., pl.* **car·i·bou** or **car·i·bous**.

car·i·ca·ture (kar′ə kə chùr′), **1** *n.* picture, cartoon, or description that exaggerates the peculiarities of a person or the defects of a thing. **2** *n.* art of making such pictures, cartoons, or descriptions: *A person needs a good eye for detail to become a master of caricature.* **3** *v.* to make a caricature of: *The artist caricatured the mayor.* ❑ *v.* **car·i·ca·tured, car·i·ca·tur·ing.**

car·i·ca·tur·ist (kar′ə kə chùr′ist), *n.* person who makes caricatures.

car·ies (kâr′ēz), *n.* **1** decay of teeth or bones. **2** cavity formed in a tooth by such decay. ❑ *n., pl.* **car·ies** for 2.

car·il·lon (kar′ə lon), *n.* set of bells arranged for playing melodies. A carillon is usually played by a person sitting at a keyboard. [**Carillon** comes from a Latin word meaning "four." Early carillons contained only four bells.]

car·jack (kär′jak′), *v.* to steal someone's car by force or the threat of force against the driver.

car·jack·ing (kär′jak′ing), *n.* the act of stealing a car by forcing the driver to hand over the keys and get out.

car·load (kär′lōd′), *n.* as much as a car can hold or carry.

Carls·bad Caverns National Park (kärlz′bad), a national park in SE New Mexico, containing one of the largest caves in the world.

Carlsbad Caverns National Park

car·mak·er (kär′mā kər), *n.* automobile manufacturer.

car·mine (kär′mən), **1** *n.* a deep red with a tinge of purple. **2** *adj.* deep red with a tinge of purple. **3** *n.* a light crimson. **4** *adj.* light crimson.

car·nage (kär′nij), *n.* slaughter of a great number of people.

car·nal (kär′nl), *adj.* of or connected with bodily pleasures; sensual. —**car′nal·ly,** *adv.*

car·na·tion (kär nā′shən), **1** *n.* a red, white, or pink flower with a spicy fragrance, grown in gardens and greenhouses. **2** *adj.* rosy pink.

Car·ne·gie (kär nā′gē *or* kär′nə gē), *n.* **1 Andrew,** 1835-1919, American steel manufacturer, born in Scotland. Famous for his donations to good causes, he founded more than 2500 public libraries in the United States and around the world. **2 Dale** (dāl), 1888-1955, American public speaker and self-help teacher. ■ **Dale Carnegie's** famous book, *How to Win Friends and Influence People,* has sold over ten million copies.

car·nel·ian (kär nē′lyən), *n.* a red or reddish brown stone used in jewelry. Also, **cornelian.**

car·ni·val (kär′nə vəl), *n.* **1** place of amusement or a traveling show having merry-go-rounds, games, sideshows, etc. **2** an organized program of events involving a particular sport, institution, etc.: *a water carnival, a school carnival.* **3** feasting and merrymaking; noisy and unrestrained revels. **4** time of feasting and merrymaking just before Lent.

WORD STORY **Carnival** comes from an Italian word meaning "taking away meat." Traditionally, people ate no meat during Lent and celebrated carnival just before Lent.

car·ni·vore (kär′nə vôr), *n.* any animal that feeds chiefly on flesh. Carnivores have large, strong teeth with sharp cutting edges.

car·niv·or·ous (kär niv′ər əs), *adj.* feeding chiefly on flesh; meat-eating. Cats, dogs, lions, tigers, and sharks are carnivorous animals. —**car·niv′or·ous·ly,** *adv.* —**car·niv′or·ous·ness,** *n.*

car·ob (kar′əb), **1** *n.* powder made by grinding the sweet pulp from the seed pods of a tree grown in warm regions. The powder is used as a flavoring, especially in place of chocolate. **2** *adj.* made of or flavored with carob: *carob ice cream.*

car·ol (kar′əl), **1** *n.* song of joy. **2** *n.* hymn of joy sung at Christmas. **3** *v.* to sing joyously; sing: *The birds carol in the early morning.* **4** *v.* to sing carols: *to go caroling at Christmastime.* ❑ *v.* **car·oled, car·ol·ing** or **car·olled, car·ol·ling.** —**car′ol·er** or **car′ol·ler,** *n.*

Car·o·li·na (kar′ə lī′nə), *n.* **1** either North Carolina or South Carolina. **2 the Carolinas,** *pl.* North Carolina and South Carolina. —**Car·o·lin·i·an** (kar′ə lin′ē ən), *adj., n.*

Car·o·line Islands (kar′ə lin), group of over 500 islands in the W Pacific, east of the Philippines.

car·om (kar′əm), **1** *v.* to hit and bounce off: *The car went out of control and caromed off the wall.* **2** *n.* act of hitting and bouncing off.

car·o·tene (kar′ə tēn), *n.* a red or orange pigment found in carrots and other plants, and in animal tissue. Carotene is changed by the body into vitamin A.

ca·rot·id (kə rot′id), *n.* either of two large arteries that carry blood to the head.

ca·rous·al (kə rou′zəl), *n.* a noisy feast or drinking party.

ca·rouse (kə rouz′), **1** *v.* to drink heavily; take part in noisy feasts or merrymaking. **2** *n.* a noisy feast or drinking party. ❑ *v.* **ca·roused, ca·rous·ing.** —**ca·rous′er,** *n.*

car·ou·sel (kar′ə sel′ *or* kar′ə sel), *n.* merry-go-round. Also, **carrousel.**

carp[1] (kärp), *v.* to find fault; complain. —**carp′er,** *n.*

carp[2] (kärp), *n.* any of various large freshwater fishes that live in ponds and slow streams and feed mostly on plants. One kind is sometimes raised for food. ❑ *n., pl.* **carp** or **carps.**

car·pal (kär′pəl), **1** *adj.* of the carpus. **2** *n.* bone of the carpus.

Car·pa·thi·an Mountains (kär pā′thē ən), Carpathians.

Car·pa·thi·ans (kär pā′thē·ənz), *n.pl.* mountains in central Europe, extending in a curve from Slovakia to SW Romania.

car·pel (kär′pəl), *n.* a modified leaf which forms a pistil or part of a pistil of a flower.

car·pen·ter (kär′pən tər), *n.* person whose work is building and repairing the wooden parts of houses, ships, etc.

carpenter

WORD STORY **Carpenter** comes from a Latin word meaning "carriage." Carriages were built of wood and had to be made very skillfully. So people used the word for a carriage-maker to mean any skilled worker with wood.

car·pen·try (kär′pən trē), *n.* trade or work of a carpenter.

car·pet (kär′pit), **1** *n.* a heavy, woven fabric for covering floors and stairs. **2** *n.* anything like a carpet: *a carpet of grass.* **3** *v.* to cover with a carpet: *In the fall, the ground was carpeted with leaves.* **on the carpet,** being scolded or rebuked: *I was on the carpet for being tardy too often.*

car·pet·bag (kär′pit bag′), *n.* (earlier) a traveling bag made of carpet.

a	hat	ė	term	ô	order	ch	child		
ā	age	i	it	oi	oil	ng	long	ə	a in about
ä	far	ī	ice	ou	out	sh	she		e in taken
â	care	o	hot	u	cup	th	thin		i in pencil
e	let	ō	open	ủ	put	ŦH	then		o in lemon
ē	equal	ò	saw	ü	rule	zh	measure		u in circus

car·pet·bag·ger (kär′pit bag′ər), *n.* Northerner who went to the South to get political or other advantages during the time of disorganization that followed the American Civil War.

carpet beetle or **carpet bug,** a small beetle with larvae that destroy carpets, other fabrics, and furs.

car·pet·ing (kär′pə ting), *n.* **1** fabric for carpets. **2** carpets: *The carpeting was worn and frayed in spots.*

car phone, cellular phone for use in a motor vehicle.

car·pool (kär′pül′), **1** *n.* arrangement made by a group of people to take turns driving themselves and others to and from a place: *The parents formed a carpool to take their children to school.* **2** *n.* such a group: *Our carpool takes a different route to work every day.* **3** *v.* to take part in a carpool: *We carpool twice a week during the school year.*

car·port (kär′pôrt′), *n.* shelter for cars, usually attached to a house and open on at least one side.

car·pus (kär′pəs), *n.* **1** wrist. **2** bones of the wrist. ❑ *n., pl.* **car·pi** (kär′pī).

car·riage (kar′ij), *n.* **1** a four-wheeled vehicle that is pushed or pulled. Some carriages are pulled by horses and are used to carry people. **Baby carriages** are small and light, and can often be folded. **2** frame on wheels that supports a gun. **3** a moving part of various machines.

car·ri·er (kar′ē ər), *n.* **1** person or thing that carries something: *a mail carrier.* Railroads, airlines, bus systems, and truck companies are **common carriers. 2** person or thing that carries or transmits a disease. Carriers are often healthy people who are immune to a disease, but who carry its germs. **3** aircraft carrier. **4** a radio wave or electric current that is varied so as to carry information such as radio and TV broadcasts, telephone calls, and telegraph messages; carrier wave. **5** individual who carries one gene for a certain characteristic, but who does not have the characteristic. Two carriers can produce offspring who have the characteristic.

carrier pigeon, homing pigeon.

carrier wave, carrier (def. 4).

car·ri·on (kar′ē ən), *n.* dead and decaying flesh.

Car·roll (kar′əl), *n.* **Lewis,** 1832-1898, English writer, author of *Alice in Wonderland.* His real name was Charles L. Dodgson.

car·rot (kar′ət), *n.* the long, tapering, orange-red root of a garden plant, eaten cooked or raw as a vegetable. ■ Other words that sound like this are **carat, caret,** and **karat.**

car·rou·sel (kar′ə sel′ *or* kar′ə sel), *n.* **1** carousel. **2** a circular conveyor belt, especially for the delivery of luggage at an airport.

car·ry (kar′ē), **1** *v.* to take from one place to another: *The man carried the child home.* **2** *v.* to bear or have with you: *carry an umbrella in case of rain.* **3** *v.* to transmit from one to another; spread: *Rats carry disease.* **4** *v.* to hold up; support; sustain: *Rafters carry the weight of the roof.* **5** *v.* to hold your body and head in a certain way: *The dancer carried herself gracefully.* **6** *v.* to capture or win: *Our side carried the election.* **7** *v.* to continue; extend: *He carries his practical jokes too far.* **8** *v.* to get a motion or bill passed or adopted: *The motion to adjourn the meeting was carried.* **9** *v.* to cover the distance: *The opera singer's voice carried clear to the back rows of the theater.* **10** *v.* to have as a result; involve: *The expert's judgment carried great weight.* **11** *v.* to keep in stock: *This store carries toys and games.* **12** *v.* to print an article: *Today's paper carried a story about the circus.* **13** *v.* to transfer a number from one place or column in the sum to the next. **14** *n.* (in football) act of running with the ball from scrimmage: *In three carries the speedy running back made nearly 30 yards.* ❑ *v.* **car·ried, car·ry·ing;** *n., pl.* **car·ries.** [See Word Story at **charge.**]

carry a tune, to sing a melody, theme, or part with correct pitch: *I can't carry a tune.*

carry away, to arouse strong feeling in; influence beyond reason: *I was carried away by the sad movie, so I cried.*

carry off, 1 to win a prize, an honor, etc.: *The champion swimmer carried off two gold medals at the Olympic games.* **2** be the death of; kill: *Pneumonia carried him off.*

carry on, 1 to do; manage; conduct: *She carried on a successful business.* **2** to keep going; not stop; continue: *We must carry on in our effort to establish world peace.* **3** to behave wildly or foolishly: *The children carried on at the party.*

carry out, to get done; do; accomplish; complete: *He carried out his job well.*

SYNONYM STUDY **Carry, convey,** and **transport** all mean to take or bring from one place to another. **Carry** suggests holding something while moving it from one place to another: *The cat carried its kittens away.* **Convey** is more formal and suggests getting a person or thing to a place: *Elevators convey people from floor to floor in tall buildings.* **Transport** suggests moving something in a ship, plane, or other vehicle: *Trucks transport all kinds of goods.*

car·ry·all (kar′ē ôl′), *n.* a large bag or basket.

car·ry·out (kar′ē out′), **1** *n.* food that is packaged to be taken away from its place of sale rather than eaten on the premises. **2** *adj.* of or about such food or the place where it is sold.

car seat, infant's portable seat for use in automobile travel. A seat belt attaches it to the seat of the car.

car·sick (kär′sik′), *adj.* nauseated as a result of the motion of a car, train, etc. —**car′sick′ness,** *n.*

Car·son (kär′sən), *n.* **1** **John·ny** (jon′ē), born 1925, American entertainer. He hosted "The Tonight Show" from 1962 to 1993. **2** **Kit** (kit), 1809-1868, American frontiersman, scout, and guide in the Far West. **3** **Rachel,** 1907-1964, American marine biologist and writer and a pioneer in the environmental movement. Her book *The Silent Spring* documented the hazards of pesticides.

Carson City, capital of Nevada, in the W part.

cart (kärt), **1** *n.* vehicle with two wheels, formerly used in farming and for carrying heavy loads. Horses, donkeys, and oxen are used to pull carts. **2** *n.* a light passenger vehicle for short trips, usually battery-powered: *a golf cart.* **3** *n.* a small vehicle on wheels, moved by hand: *a grocery cart.* **4** *v.* to carry in or as if in a cart: *Cart away this rubbish.* —**cart′er,** *n.*

put the cart before the horse, to reverse the usual or logical order of things.

carte blanche (kärt′ blänch′), freedom to use your own judgment; full authority. ❑ *n., pl.* **cartes blanches** (kärts′ blänch′).

WORD STORY **Carte blanche** comes from French words meaning "blank" and "paper." If a queen or king signed a blank piece of paper and gave it to someone, that person was free to write any instructions on the paper. The instructions would become royal commands.

car·tel (kär tel′), *n.* a large group of business firms that agree to operate as a monopoly, especially to regulate prices and production.

Car·ter (kär′tər), *n.* **Jim·my** (jim′ē), born 1924, the 39th president of the United States, from 1977 to 1981. His full name is James Earl Carter, Jr.

Car·te·sian coordinate (kär tē′zhən), coordinate (def. 6).

Car·thage (kär′thij), *n.* ancient port in N Africa, founded by the Phoenicians. It was destroyed by the Romans in 146 B.C., rebuilt in 29 B.C., and finally destroyed by the Arabs in A.D. 698. See **Byzantine Empire** for map. —**Car·tha·gin·i·an** (kär′thə jin′ē ən), *adj., n.*

Car·tier (kär tyā′), *n.* **Jacques** (zhäk), 1491-1557, French explorer. He led the first European expedition up the St. Lawrence River.

car·ti·lage (kär′tl ij), *n.* a tough, white elastic connective tissue forming parts of the skeleton of vertebrates. Cartilage is more flexible than bone and not as hard. The external ear consists of cartilage and skin.

car·ti·lag·i·nous (kär′tl aj′ə nəs), *adj.* **1** of or like cartilage; gristly. **2** having the skeleton formed mostly of cartilage: *Sharks are cartilaginous.*

Cart·land (kärt′lənd), *n.* **Bar·ba·ra** (bär′brə), born 1901, English writer. She has written more than 400 books, most of them romance novels.

car·tog·ra·pher (kär tog′rə fər), *n.* maker of maps or charts.

car·tog·ra·phy (kär tog′rə fē), *n.* the making or study of maps or charts.

car·ton (kärt′n), *n.* **1** box made of pasteboard or cardboard: *Pack the books in large cartons.* **2** amount that a carton holds: *a carton of milk.*

car·toon (kär tün′), *n.* **1** sketch or drawing showing persons, things, or events in an amusing way: *Political cartoons often represent the United States as a tall man with chin whiskers, called Uncle Sam.* **2** animated cartoon. **3** comic strip. **4** a full-size drawing of a design or painting, used as a model for another work.

car·toon·ist (kär tü′nist), *n.* person who draws cartoons.

car·tridge (kär′trij), *n.* **1** case made of metal, plastic, or cardboard for holding gunpowder and a bullet or shot. **2** a small container which holds a supply of material, made to be easily put into a larger device. Film, ink, and magnetic tape come in cartridges. **3** a small device with a plastic case containing electronic circuits. A cartridge put into a computer, a calculator, or a video game machine allows these machines to work in particular ways. **4** a device that transforms vibrations into electrical current, especially vibrations in a phonograph needle caused by variations in the grooves of a record; pickup.

cart·wheel (kärt′wēl′), *n.* **1** wheel of a cart. **2** a sideways handspring with the legs and arms kept straight.

Ca·ru·so (kə rü′sō), *n.* **En·ri·co** (en rē′kō), 1873-1921, Italian operatic tenor. He made many recordings and was one of the most famous stars of his time.

carve (kärv), *v.* **1** to cut into slices or pieces: *I carved the meat at the dinner table.* **2** to make by cutting; cut: *Statues are often carved from marble, stone, or wood.* **3** to decorate with figures or designs cut on the surface: *The oak chest was carved with flowers.* ❑ *v.* **carved, carv·ing.** **−carv′er,** *n.*

Car·ver (kär′vər), *n.* **George Washington,** 1864?-1943, American botanist and chemist. ■ **George Washington Carver** made more than 300 products from the peanut plant and gained national recognition for his research.

carv·ing (kär′ving), *n.* carved work: *a wood carving.*

car·y·at·id (kar′ē at′id), *n.* statue of a woman used as a column.

ca·sa·ba (kə sä′bə), *n.* kind of winter muskmelon with a yellow rind. ❑ *n., pl.* **ca·sa·bas.**

Cas·a·blan·ca (kas′ə blang′kə), *n.* port in N Morocco, on the Atlantic.

Ca·sals (kə sälz′), *n.* **Pab·lo** (päb′lō), 1876-1973, Spanish cellist. He was also a conductor, composer, and teacher.

cas·cade (ka skād′), **1** *n.* a small waterfall. **2** *n.* anything like this: *A cascade of ivy hung from the flower box.* **3** *v.* to fall, pour, or flow in a cascade: *The water cascaded off the roof in the thunderstorm.* ❑ *v.* **cas·cad·ed, cas·cad·ing.**

Cascade Range, mountain range in NW United States, extending from N California to British Columbia.

Cas·cades (ka skādz′), *n.pl.* Cascade Range.

case¹ (kās), *n.* **1** an example or instance: *A case of chicken pox kept me away from school.* **2** the actual condition; real situation; true state: *She said the work was done, but that was not the case.* **3** person who has an injury or illness; patient: *Hospitals had many cases of polio each summer before a vaccine to prevent it was developed.* **4** matter for a court of law to decide: *The case will be brought before the court tomorrow.* **5** a convincing argument: *The agent made a good case for buying insurance.* **6** a situation that needs investigation, especially by an official person or group: *Two detectives were assigned to the murder case.* **7** (in grammar) one of the forms of a noun, pronoun, or adjective used to show its relation to other words. *I* is in the nominative case; *me* is in the objective case; *my* is in the possessive case.

in any case, no matter what happens; anyhow: *In any case, you should prepare for the worst.*

in case, if it should happen that; if; supposing: *What would you do in case fire broke out?*

in case of, if there should be: *In case of fire walk quietly to the nearest door.*

case² (kās), **1** *n.* thing to hold or cover something: *a typewriter case. Put the knife back in its case.* **2** *n.* box: *a big case full of books.* **3** *n.* amount that a case can hold: *The children drank a case of ginger ale at the party.* **4** *n.* frame. A window fits in a case. **5** *v.* to put in a case; cover with a case: *He cased the books for shipping.* **6** *v.* to look over carefully; inspect or examine: *The thieves cased the bank before the robbery.* ❑ *v.* **cased, cas·ing.**

ca·sein (kā′sēn′), *n.* protein present in milk, used in making plastics, adhesives, and certain kinds of paints. Cheese is mostly casein.

case·ment (kās′mənt), *n.* window which opens on hinges like a door.

case·work (kās′wèrk′), *n.* social work involving a thorough study of the problems of an individual or family as a basis for help or guidance.

cash (kash), **1** *n.* money in the form of coins and bills. **2** *n.* money paid at the time of buying something: *Do you want to pay with cash or credit card?* **3** *v.* to give cash for: *The bank will cash your check.* **4** *v.* to get cash for: *I cashed a check at the bank.* ■ Another word that sounds like this is **cache. −cash′a·ble,** *adj.*

cash in, to change into cash: *I cashed in my savings bonds at the bank.*

cash in on, INFORMAL. **1** to make a profit from: *After holding the land till the city needed it, we finally cashed in on our real estate investment.* **2** to take advantage of; use to your advantage: *She cashed in on her love of travel by becoming a tour guide.*

Cash (kash), *n.* **John·ny** (jon′ē), born 1932, American guitarist, singer, and songwriter. He is called "The Man in Black" after his 1971 hit song of the same name.

cash·ew (kash′ü), *n.* the small, kidney-shaped nut of a tropical American tree. Cashews are good to eat.

cash·ier¹ (ka shir′), *n.* person who has charge of money in a bank, or in any business.

cash·ier² (ka shir′), *v.* to dismiss from service; discharge in disgrace: *The dishonest officer was deprived of his rank and cashiered.*

cash machine. See ATM.

cash·mere (kash′mir *or* kazh′mir), *n.* **1** a fine, soft wool, used in making sweaters, coats, etc., obtained from a breed of long-haired goats of Tibet and Kashmir. **2** a fine, soft wool from sheep.

cash register, machine which records and shows the amount of a sale. It usually has a drawer to hold money.

cas·ing (kā′sing), *n.* **1** thing put around something; covering; case. The outermost part of a tire and the skin of a sausage are kinds of casings. **2** frame. A window fits in a casing.

ca·si·no (kə sē′nō), *n.* **1** building or room for public shows, dancing, gambling, etc. **2** cassino. ❑ *n., pl.* **ca·si·nos.**

cask (kask), *n.* **1** barrel. A cask may be large or small, and is usually made to hold liquids. **2** amount that a cask holds. ■ Another word that sounds like this is **casque.**

cas·ket (kas′kit), *n.* **1** coffin. **2** a small box or chest used to hold jewels, letters, or other valuables.

Cas·per (kas′pər), *n.* city in E central Wyoming. [Casper was named for Caspar Collings, a cavalry lieutenant killed while fighting bravely in a battle near here in 1865.]

Cas·pi·an Sea (kas′pē ən), an inland sea between Europe and Asia north of Iran, east of the Black Sea.

casque (kask), *n.* OLD USE. helmet. ■ Another word that sounds like this is **cask.**

Cas·san·dra (kə san′drə), *n.* (in Greek legends) a princess of Troy. Apollo gave her the power to foretell the future, but later punished her by commanding that no one should believe her prophecies. [Cassandra comes from a Greek word meaning "helper of men."]

Cas·satt (kə sat′), *n.* **Mary,** 1844-1926, American painter. ■ **Mary Cassatt** belonged to the impressionist movement. Born in Pennsylvania, she moved to France in 1866 and spent the rest of her life there.

Cassatt painting

a	hat	ė	term	ô	order	ch	child		a in about
ā	age	i	it	oi	oil	ng	long		e in taken
ä	far	ī	ice	ou	out	sh	she	ə {	i in pencil
â	care	o	hot	u	cup	th	thin		o in lemon
e	let	ō	open	ù	put	ᴛʜ	then		u in circus
ē	equal	ȯ	saw	ü	rule	zh	measure		

cas·sa·va (kə sä′və), *n.* either of two tropical plants with starchy roots; manioc. Tapioca is made from one kind of cassava root. ❑ *n., pl.* **cas·sa·vas.**

cas·se·role (kas′ə rōl′), *n.* **1** a covered baking dish in which food can be both cooked and served. **2** food cooked and served in such a dish.

cas·sette (ka set′), *n.* **1** container holding magnetic tape for recording and playing back pictures, sound, or computer information. **2** cartridge for film.

cas·sia (kash′ə), *n.* any of numerous related trees and bushes, including a Chinese tree with spicy bark that is sometimes used as a substitute for cinnamon. Other kinds of cassias have leaves and pods that are used in making senna. ❑ *n., pl.* **cas·sias.**

cas·si·no (kə sē′nō), *n.* a card game in which cards in the hand are matched with cards on the table. Also, **casino.**

cas·sock (kas′ək), *n.* a long outer garment, usually black, worn by a clergyman.

cas·so·war·y (kas′ə wer′ē), *n.* any of three kinds of large birds of Australia and New Guinea something like ostriches. Cassowaries run swiftly but cannot fly. ❑ *n., pl.* **cas·so·war·ies.**

cast (kast), **1** *v.* to throw; fling or hurl: *cast a stone, cast a fishing line. The criminal was cast into jail.* **2** *v.* to throw off; let fall; shed: *The snake cast its skin.* **3** *n.* the distance a thing is thrown; throw: *The fisherman made a long cast with his line.* **4** *v.* to direct or turn: *She cast a glance of surprise at me.* **5** *v.* to cause to fall onto something or in a certain direction: *cast a shadow.* **6** *v.* to deposit a ballot; give or record a vote: *Voters cast their ballots for President of the United States in an election held every four years.* **7** *v.* to shape by pouring or squeezing into a mold to harden. Metal is first melted and then cast. **8** *n.* thing shaped in a mold: *The sculptor made a cast of an antelope.* **9** *n.* mold used to shape or support: *Her broken arm is in a plaster cast.* **10** *v.* to select for a part in a play: *The director cast her in the role of the heroine.* **11** *n.* the actors in a play: *The cast was listed on the program.* **12** *n.* outward form or look; appearance: *His face had a gloomy cast.* **13** *n.* a slight amount of color; tinge: *a white shirt with a pink cast.* **14** *n.* a slight squint. ❑ *v.* **cast, cast·ing.** ■ Another word that sounds like this is **caste.**

cast about, to search; look: *The company cast about for a long time until it found a good site for its new factory.*

cast aside, to throw away; discard: *cast aside an old hat.*

cast down, 1 to turn downward; lower: *He cast down his eyes to avoid looking at me.* **2** to make sad or discouraged: *She was cast down by the bad news.*

cast off, 1 to let loose; set free: *cast off a boat from its moorings.* **2** to abandon or discard: *He cast off his old friends as soon as he left the old neighborhood.*

cas·ta·net (kas′tə net′), *n.* one of a pair of instruments held in the hand and clicked together to beat time for dancing or music. Castanets are made of hard wood, ivory, or plastic. [Castanet comes from a Latin word meaning "chestnut," because it looks like one.]

cast·a·way (kast′ə wā′), **1** *adj.* thrown away; cast adrift. **2** *n.* a shipwrecked person: *The castaways swam to the island.* **3** *adj.* outcast; rejected. **4** *n.* an outcast.

caste (kast), *n.* **1** one of the social classes into which Hindus are divided. By tradition, a Hindu is born into a caste and cannot rise above it. **2** an exclusive social group; distinct class: *The priestly caste in ancient Egypt had great power.* **3** a social system having distinct classes separated by differences of rank, wealth, or position. ■ Another word that sounds like this is **cast.**

lose caste, to lose social rank or position: *They had a fear of losing caste among their neighbors.*

cast·er (kas′tər), *n.* **1** a small wheel on a swivel set into the base of a piece of furniture or other heavy object to make it easier to move. **2** shaker or bottle containing seasoning for table use: *a pepper caster.* **3** stand or rack for such bottles. **4** person or thing that casts. Also, **castor** for 2,3.

cas·ti·gate (kas′tə gāt), *v.* to criticize severely or punish. ❑ *v.* **cas·ti·gat·ed, cas·ti·gat·ing. —cas′ti·ga′tion,** *n.* **—cas′ti·ga′tor,** *n.*

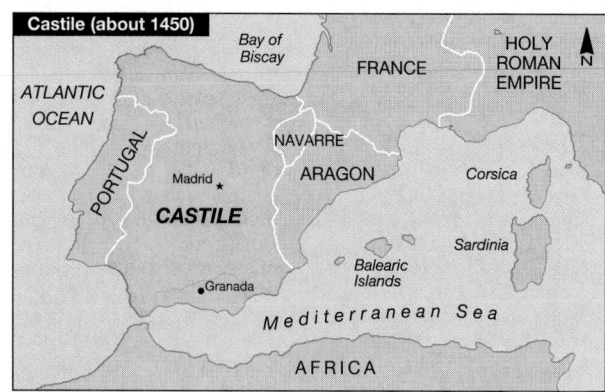

Castile (about 1450)

Cas·tile (ka stēl′), *n.* region in N and central Spain, formerly a kingdom.

Castile soap, a pure, hard soap made from olive oil and sodium hydroxide.

Cas·til·ian (ka stil′yən), **1** *adj.* of Castile, its people, or their language. **2** *n.* Castilian Spanish. **3** *n.* person born or living in Castile.

Castilian Spanish, Spanish as spoken in Castile. It is the standard language of Spain.

cast·ing (kas′ting), *n.* **1** thing shaped by being poured into a mold to harden. **2** act or process of shaping things by pouring into a mold: *Casting in bronze was practiced in ancient Greece.*

cast iron, a hard, brittle form of iron made by casting.

cast-i·ron (kast′ī′ərn), *adj.* **1** made of cast iron: *He fried ham and eggs in a cast-iron skillet.* **2** not yielding; hard: *It took cast-iron control to keep from losing my temper.* **3** hardy; strong: *Her cast-iron stomach could digest almost anything.*

cas·tle (kas′əl), *n.* **1** a large building or group of buildings with thick walls, turrets, battlements, and other defenses against attack: *The knight rode over the drawbridge into the castle.* **2** a large and stately residence. **3** rook².

castle in the air, something imagined but not likely to come true; daydream.

cast·off (kast′ôf′), **1** *adj.* thrown away; abandoned; discarded: *castoff clothes.* **2** *n.* person or thing that has been cast off.

cas·tor (kas′tər), *n.* caster (defs. 2 and 3).

Cas·tor (kas′tər), *n.* (in Greek and Roman myths) one of the twin sons of Zeus. Castor was mortal; his brother, Pollux, was immortal.

castor oil, a thick, yellow oil obtained from the beans of a tall, tropical plant, used as a lubricant for machines.

cas·trate (kas′trāt), *v.* to remove the testicles of; neuter; emasculate. An ox is a castrated bull. ❑ *v.* **cas·trat·ed, cas·trat·ing. —cas·tra′tion,** *n.*

Cas·tries (ka strē′), *n.* capital of St. Lucia.

Cas·tro (kas′trō), *n.* **Fi·del** (fē del′), born 1926, premier of Cuba since 1959.

cas·u·al (kazh′ü əl), *adj.* **1** happening by chance; not planned or expected; accidental: *Our long friendship began with a casual meeting at a party.* **2** without plan or method; careless: *She gave the note a casual glance and then threw it away.* **3** informal in manner; offhand: *Some people mistook his casual behavior for rudeness.* ■ See Synonym Study at **informal. 4** designed for informal wear: *We dressed in casual clothes for the picnic.* **5** occasional or temporary: *a casual hunter.* **—cas′u·al·ly,** *adv.* **—cas′u·al·ness,** *n.*

WORD STORY **Casual** comes from a Latin word meaning "to fall." **Chance** comes from the same word. Usually, when something falls, where it ends up is a matter of chance.

cas·u·al·ty (kazh′ü əl tē), *n.* **1** member of the armed forces who has been wounded, killed, or captured as a result of enemy action: *The war produced many casualties.* **2** person injured or killed in an accident: *If drivers were more careful, there would be fewer casualties on the highways.* ❑ *n., pl.* **cas·u·al·ties.**

cat (kat), *n.* **1** a small, furry, flesh-eating mammal, often kept as a pet or for catching mice and rats. **2** any animal of the group that includes house cats, lions, tigers, leopards, and jaguars. **3** SLANG. fellow; person. —**cat′like′**, *adj.*

let the cat out of the bag, to tell a secret: *It was supposed to be a surprise party, but he let the cat out of the bag.*

rain cats and dogs, to pour down rain very hard.

WORD BANK   There are many different kinds of **cats**, large and small, wild and domestic. If you are interested in learning more, you can start by looking up these words in this dictionary.

Abyssinian	cougar	Manx cat	Siamese cat
bobcat	jaguar	mountain lion	snow leopard
calico	leopard	ocelot	tiger
caracal	lion	panther	tomcat
cheetah	lynx	puma	wildcat

cat., catalog.

cat·a·clysm (kat′ə kliz′əm), *n.* **1** a great flood, earthquake, or any sudden, violent change in the earth. **2** any violent change or upheaval: *Atomic warfare between nations would be a cataclysm for the human race.* —**cat·a·clys·mal** (kat′ə kliz′məl) or **cat·a·clys·mic** (kat′ə kliz′mik), *adj.*

cat·a·combs (kat′ə kōmz), *n.pl.* an underground network of tunnels used as a burial place with holes dug into the walls in which to place the dead.

Cat·a·lan (kat′l ən), **1** *adj.* of Catalonia, its people, or their language. **2** *n.* person born or living in Catalonia. **3** *n.* language spoken in Catalonia.

cat·a·log (kat′l ôg), **1** *n.* list of items in some collection. A library has a catalog of its books, arranged in alphabetical order. Some companies print catalogs with pictures and prices of the things they have for sale. **2** *v.* to make a catalog of; put in a catalog: *to catalog an insect collection.* Also, **catalogue.** □ *v.* **cat·a·loged, cat·a·log·ing.** —**cat′a·log′er,** *n.*

cat·a·logue (kat′l ôg), *n., v.* catalog. □ *v.* **cat·a·logued, cat·a·logu·ing.** —**cat′a·logu′er,** *n.*

Cat·a·lo·ni·a (kat′l ō′nē ə), *n.* region in NE Spain.

ca·tal·pa (kə tal′pə), *n.* any of several trees of North America and Asia with large, heart-shaped leaves, clusters of bell-shaped flowers, and long pods. □ *n., pl.* **ca·tal·pas.** [Catalpa comes from a Creek word meaning "head with wings." The tree was called this because of the shape of its flowers.]

ca·tal·y·sis (kə tal′ə sis), *n.* the causing or speeding up of a chemical reaction by the presence of a catalyst. □ *n., pl.* **ca·tal·y·ses** (kə tal′ə sēz′).

cat·a·lyst (kat′l ist), *n.* **1** substance that causes or speeds up a chemical reaction while remaining practically unchanged itself. Enzymes are important catalysts in digestion. **2** anything that brings about some change or changes without being directly affected itself: *The first successful heart transplant was the catalyst that sparked widespread scientific work in this field.*

cat·a·lyt·ic (kat′l it′ik), *adj.* **1** of catalysis. **2** causing catalysis.

catalytic converter, an emission control device in the exhaust system of a motor vehicle. It contains a catalyst which causes carbon monoxide and hydrocarbons to be converted to carbon dioxide and water vapor.

cat·a·lyze (kat′l īz), *v.* to act upon by catalysis. □ *v.* **cat·a·lyzed, cat·a·lyz·ing.**

cat·a·ma·ran (kat′ə mə ran′), *n.* boat with two hulls fitted side by side.

cat·a·mount (kat′ə mount), *n.* wildcat, such as a cougar or lynx.

cat·a·pult (kat′ə pult), **1** *n.* weapon used in ancient times for shooting stones, arrows, etc. **2** *n.* device for launching an airplane from the deck of a ship. **3** *v.* to throw; hurl: *He stopped his bicycle so suddenly that he was catapulted over the handlebars.* **4** *v.* to shoot up suddenly; spring: *The frightened cat catapulted from the chair when the big dog came in.*

cat·a·ract (kat′ə rakt′), *n.* **1** a large, steep waterfall. **2** a violent rush or downpour of water; flood: *Cataracts of rain flooded the streets.* **3** disease of the eye in which the lens develops a cloudy film, making a person partly or entirely blind.

ca·tas·tro·phe (kə tas′trə fē), *n.* a sudden, widespread, or extraordinary disaster; great calamity or misfortune. An earthquake, flood, or fire is a catastrophe. —**cat·a·stroph·ic** (kat′ə strof′ik), *adj.* —**cat·a·stroph′i·cal·ly,** *adv.*

cat·a·ton·ic (kat′ə ton′ik), *adj.* being or appearing to be in a kind of stupor in which rigid physical positions are held for a long time.

cat·bird (kat′bėrd′), *n.* a grayish North American songbird related to the mockingbird. A catbird can make a sound like a cat mewing.

catbird seat, a position of advantage or power: *When he was put in charge of casting the school play, he felt he was in the catbird seat.*

cat·boat (kat′bōt′), *n.* sailboat with one mast set far forward and no jib.

cat burglar, burglar who enters by skillful climbing, especially in tall buildings.

cat·call (kat′kôl′), *n.* a shrill cry or whistle to express disapproval. Actors who perform poorly are sometimes greeted by catcalls from the audience.

catch (def. 11)

catch (kach), **1** *v.* to take and hold something or someone trying to escape; seize; capture: *The children chased the puppy and caught it.* **2** *v.* to take by trapping or with a hook: *I caught three fish.* **3** *v.* to grab or seize a moving thing: *Catch the ball with both hands.* **4** *v.* to attract and hold the attention of: *The bright display caught my attention.* **5** *v.* to take or get: *Paper catches fire easily. Put on a warm coat or you will catch cold. She caught a glimpse of her friend in the crowd.* **6** *v.* to reach or get to in time: *You have just five minutes to catch your train.* **7** *v.* to see, hear, or understand: *He spoke so rapidly that I didn't catch the meaning of what he said.* **8** *v.* to become hooked or fastened: *My coat caught in the door.* **9** *v.* to entangle or grip: *A nail caught her sleeve.* **10** *v.* to come upon suddenly; surprise: *Mother caught me just as I was hiding her birthday present.* **11** *v.* to act as catcher in baseball. **12** *n.* act of catching: *She made a fine catch with one hand.* **13** *n.* thing that fastens: *The catch on that door is broken.* **14** *n.* thing caught: *A dozen fish is a good catch.* **15** *v.* to reach with a blow; hit; strike: *The stone caught her on the leg.* **16** *n.* game of throwing and catching a ball: *The children played catch on the lawn.* **17** *v.* to check suddenly: *She caught her breath in surprise.* **18** *n.* act of choking or stoppage of the breath: *He had a catch in his voice.* **19** *n.* a hidden or tricky condition in a plan, etc.: *There is a catch to that question.* □ *v.* **caught, catch·ing;** *n., pl.* **catch·es.** [See Word Story at **chase**.]

catch on, 1 to get the idea; understand: *The second time the teacher explained the problem, I caught on.* **2** to become popular; be widely used or accepted: *The theme song from that popular new movie caught on quickly.*

catch up, to come from behind and be even with.

catch up on, to bring up to date: *She caught me up on all the neighborhood news.*

catch up with, to come up even with a person or thing while going the same way; overtake: *I ran to catch up with my friends.*

SYNONYM STUDY   **Catch** and **capture** both mean to get hold of someone or something. **Catch** suggests taking something that is moving: *The boy caught the ball.* **Capture** suggests taking by force: *The enemy captured the fort.*

a	hat	ė	term	ô	order	ch	child		
ā	age	i	it	oi	oil	ng	long		a in about
ä	far	ī	ice	ou	out	sh	she		e in taken
â	care	o	hot	u	cup	th	thin	ə	i in pencil
e	let	ō	open	u̇	put	ŦH	then		o in lemon
ē	equal	ȯ	saw	ü	rule	zh	measure		u in circus

catch·all (kach'ôl'), *n.* container for odds and ends.

catch·er (kach'ər), *n.* **1** a baseball player behind home plate who catches balls thrown by the pitcher that are not hit by the batter. **2** person or thing that catches.

catch·ing (kach'ing), *adj.* **1** spread by infection; contagious: *Colds are catching.* **2** likely to spread from one person to another: *Enthusiasm is catching.*

catch phrase, phrase intended to draw attention to something and to be easily remembered.

catch·up (kech'əp *or* kach'əp), *n.* ketchup.

catch·word (kach'werd'), *n.* word or phrase used again and again for effect; slogan: *"No taxation without representation" was a political catchword during the Revolutionary War.*

catch·y (kach'ē), *adj.* **1** pleasing and easy to remember: *The new musical has several catchy tunes.* **2** tricky; misleading; deceptive: *The third question on the test was catchy; everyone in the class gave the wrong answer.* ❑ *adj.* **catch·i·er, catch·i·est.**

cat·e·chism (kat'ə kiz'əm), *n.* **1** book of questions and answers about religion, used for teaching religious doctrine. **2** any long set of questions and answers about a subject.

cat·e·chize (kat'ə kīz), *v.* **1** to teach by questions and answers. **2** to question closely. ❑ *v.* **cat·e·chized, cat·e·chiz·ing.**

cat·e·gor·i·cal (kat'ə gôr'ə kəl), *adj.* without conditions or qualifications; positive: *His categorical answer left no doubt about his opinion.* —**cat'e·gor'i·cal·ly,** *adv.*

cat·e·go·rize (kat'ə gə rīz'), *v.* to put in a category. ❑ *v.* **cat·e·go·rized, cat·e·go·riz·ing.** —**cat'e·go·ri·za'tion,** *n.*

cat·e·go·ry (kat'ə gôr'ē), *n.* group or general division in classification; class: *The library arranges books according to categories.* ❑ *n., pl.* **cat·e·go·ries.**

ca·ter (kā'tər), *v.* **1** to provide food and supplies, and sometimes service: *They run a restaurant and also cater for weddings and parties.* **2** to provide what is needed or wanted: *The new magazine caters to campers by printing stories about camping, hiking, and nature.*

cat·er-cor·ner (kat'ər kôr'nər), **1** *adj.* diagonal: *a cater-corner walk across the park.* **2** *adv.* diagonally: *My friend moved cater-corner across from our house.* Also, **catty-corner** or **kitty-corner.**

cat·er-cor·nered (kat'ər kôr'nərd), *adj., adv.* cater-corner. Also, **catty-cornered** or **kitty-cornered.**

ca·ter·er (kā'tər ər), *n.* person who provides food and supplies, and sometimes service, for parties, weddings, etc.

cat·er·pil·lar (kat'ər pil'ər), *n.* the wormlike larvae of insects such as butterflies and moths.

WORD STORY **Caterpillar** comes from Latin words meaning "hairy cat." Many caterpillars have fuzz. No one knows for sure why they are named after cats—perhaps because some caterpillars arch their backs the way an angry cat does.

cat·er·waul (kat'ər wôl), **1** *v.* to howl like a cat; screech: *The bagpipes caterwauled.* **2** *n.* such a howl or screech.

cat·fish (kat'fish'), *n.* any of many fishes without scales and with long, slender feelers around the mouth that look something like a cat's whiskers. ❑ *n., pl.* **cat·fish** or **cat·fish·es.**

cat·gut (kat'gut'), *n.* a tough string made from the dried and twisted intestines of sheep or other animals, used to string violins and tennis rackets. It was formerly used by surgeons for stitching wounds.

ca·thar·tic (kə thär'tik), **1** *n.* a strong laxative. Epsom salts and castor oil are cathartics. **2** *adj.* strongly laxative.

Ca·thay (ka thā'), *n.* OLD USE. China.

ca·the·dral (kə thē'drəl), *n.* **1** the official church of a bishop. The bishop of a district or diocese has a throne in the cathedral. **2** a large or important church. [See Word Story at **chair.**]

Cath·er (kaтн'ər), *n.* **Wil·la** (wil'ə), 1876-1947, American writer. Her novels were usually set in the American West.

Cath·er·ine of Aragon (kath'ər ən), 1485-1536, the first wife of Henry VIII of England. ■ **Catherine of Aragon** and Henry VIII had only one living child, Mary. Henry wanted the marriage annulled so that he could marry again and perhaps have a male heir. When the Roman Catholic Church refused, Henry founded the Anglican Church, divorced Catherine, and married Anne Boleyn. [**Catherine** comes from a Greek word meaning "pure."]

Cath·er·ine the Great, 1729-1796, empress of Russia from 1762 to 1796.

cath·e·ter (kath'ə tər), *n.* a slender tube for inserting into a body passage for medical purposes, such as removal of fluid or insertion of dye for X rays.

cath·ode (kath'ōd), *n.* electrode by which electrons flow into an electrical device. In a battery the cathode is the positive terminal; in most other electrical devices the cathode is the negative terminal.

cathode rays, the invisible streams of electrons released by the cathode in a vacuum tube. When cathode rays strike the screen of a CRT, they cause it to light up. By controlling the rays, the CRT forms pictures and text on the screen.

cath·ode-ray tube (kath'ōd rā'). See **CRT.**

Cath·o·lic (kath'ə lik), **1** *adj.* of the Christian church governed by the pope; Roman Catholic. **2** *adj.* of the ancient, undivided Christian church, or of its present representatives, including the Anglican, Orthodox, and Roman Catholic churches. **3** *n.* member of a Catholic church, especially the Roman Catholic. **4** *adj.* **catholic,** of interest or use to all people; broad; universal: *Music has a catholic appeal.*

Ca·thol·i·cism (kə thol'ə siz'əm), *n.* the faith, doctrine, and organization of the Roman Catholic Church.

cat·i·on (kat'ī'ən), *n.* a positively charged ion.

cat·kin (kat'kən), *n.* the soft, downy, drooping thin cluster of flowers, without petals, which grows on willows, birches, and some other trees. [**Catkin** comes from a Dutch word meaning "kitten." It was called this because it is soft and downy and looks like a kitten's tail.]

cat·nap (kat'nap'), **1** *n.* a short nap. **2** *v.* to take a short nap or doze: *We found Mom catnapping in the den.*

cat·nip (kat'nip'), *n.* plant something like mint, with strongly scented leaves that cats like.

cat-o'-nine-tails (kat'ə nīn'tālz'), *n.* whip consisting of nine pieces of knotted cord fastened to a handle. It was formerly used as a means of punishment in the navy. ❑ *n., pl.* **cat-o'-nine-tails.**

CAT scan (kat), a kind of X-ray photography in which X rays are passed from many angles through a cross section of the body. A computer combines the results into one picture.

cat's cradle, a child's game played with a string looped over the fingers of both hands.

Cats·kill Mountains (kats'kil), Catskills.

Cats·kills (kats'kilz), *n.pl.* range of Appalachian Mountains in SE New York State.

cat's-paw or **cats·paw** (kats'pô'), *n.* person used by someone else to do something unpleasant or dangerous.

cat·sup (kech'əp, kach'əp, *or* kat'səp), *n.* ketchup.

Catt (kat), *n.* **Car·rie Chapman** (kar'ē), 1859-1947, American political reformer who worked for voting rights for women. She founded the League of Women Voters.

cat·tail (kat'tāl'), *n.* any of various related tall marsh plants, each with a long, furry, brown spike and long, pointed leaves.

cat·tle (kat'l), *n.pl.* animals related to the ox that chew their cud, have hoofs, and are raised for meat, milk, hides, etc.; cows, bulls, and steers.

WORD STORY **Cattle** comes from a Latin word meaning "head." **Capital** comes from the same word. Because the head is one of the body's most important parts, *head* was used to mean "important" or "leading." Cattle were a very important part of a Roman farmer's property.

cat·tle·man (kat'l mən), *n.* person who raises or takes care of cattle. ❑ *n., pl.* **cat·tle·men.**

cat·ty (kat'ē), *adj.* mean and spiteful: *Catty comments about your classmates will not help you make friends.* ❑ *adj.* **cat·ti·er, cat·ti·est.** —**cat'ti·ly,** *adv.* —**cat'ti·ness,** *n.*

cat·ty-cor·ner (kat'ē kôr'nər), *adj., adv.* cater-corner.

cat·ty-cor·nered (kat'ē kôr'nərd), *adj., adv.* cater-cornered.

CATV, cable TV.

cat·walk (kat′wòk′), *n.* a narrow place to walk on a bridge, near the ceiling of a stage, and the like.

Cau·ca·sia (kò kā′zhə), *n.* region in SE Europe, between the Black and Caspian seas.

Caucasia

Cau·ca·sian (kò kā′zhən), **1** *n.* person whose ancestors belonged to the group of people living in Europe, northern Africa, and southwestern Asia as far as India. **2** *adj.* of or from this background. **3** *n.* person born or living in the Caucasus. **4** *adj.* of the Caucasus or its inhabitants.

Cau·ca·soid (kò′kə soid), *n., adj.* Caucasian (defs. 1 and 2).

Cau·ca·sus (kò′kə səs), *n.* **1** mountain range in SE Europe, extending from the Black Sea to the Caspian Sea. **2** Caucasia.

cau·cus (kò′kəs), **1** *n.* meeting of members or leaders of a political party to make plans, choose candidates, or decide how to vote. **2** *v.* to hold such a meeting. ❑ *n., pl.* **cau·cus·es.**

cau·dal (kò′dl), *adj.* **1** of, at, or near the tail. **2** like a tail.

caught (kòt), *v.* past tense and past participle of **catch:** *I caught the ball. He has caught three passes in the first half.*

caul·dron (kòl′drən), *n.* caldron.

cau·li·flow·er (kò′lə flou′ər), *n.* vegetable having a solid, white head with a few leaves around it. It is related to the cabbage.

caulk (kòk), *v.* to fill up a seam, crack, or joint so that it will not leak; make watertight. Sailors caulk wooden boats with oakum and tar. Plumbers caulk joints in pipe with lead. **—caulk′er,** *n.*

caus·al (kò′zəl), *adj.* of a cause; acting as a cause: *a causal relationship between clean water and good public health.* **—caus′al·ly,** *adv.*

cause (kòz), **1** *n.* person, thing, or event that makes something happen: *The flood was the cause of much damage.* **2** *v.* to make happen; make do; bring about: *The fire caused much damage. A loud noise caused me to jump.* **3** *n.* reason or occasion for action: *The Olympic winner's return was a cause for celebration. You have no cause to complain.* **4** *n.* subject or movement in which many people are interested and to which they give their support: *World peace is the cause she works for.* ❑ *v.* **caused, caus·ing.**

SYNONYM STUDY **Cause, reason,** and **occasion** all mean a reason that something happens. **Cause** suggests making something happen: *Heavy road traffic is one cause of air pollution.* **Reason** suggests an explanation of why something happened: *What is your reason for being late?* **Occasion** suggests a single event or thing that makes something happen right away: *Her excellent report card was an occasion for celebration.*

cause·way (kòz′wā′), *n.* a raised road or path, usually built across wet ground or shallow water.

caus·tic (kò′stik), **1** *n.* substance that burns or destroys flesh; corrosive substance: *My warts were burned away by the caustic put on them.* **2** *adj.* burning or destroying flesh; corrosive. Lye is a caustic material. **3** *adj.* very critical or sarcastic; stinging; biting: *The coach's caustic remarks made the football players angry.* **—caus′ti·cal·ly,** *adv.*

caustic potash, potassium hydroxide.

caustic soda, sodium hydroxide.

cau·ter·ize (kò′tə rīz′), *v.* to burn with heat, electric current, or a caustic substance. Doctors sometimes cauterize wounds to prevent bleeding or infection. ❑ *v.* **cau·ter·ized, cau·ter·iz·ing. —cau′ter·i·za′tion,** *n.*

cau·tion (kò′shən), **1** *n.* great care; regard for safety; unwillingness to take chances: *Always use caution when crossing streets.* **2** *v.* to urge to be careful; warn: *I cautioned them against playing in the street.* **3** *n.* a warning: *A sign with "Danger" on it is a caution.*

cau·tious (kò′shəs), *adj.* very careful; taking care to be safe; not taking chances: *Cautious drivers don't speed.* ▪ See Synonym Study at **careful. —cau′tious·ly,** *adv.* **—cau′tious·ness,** *n.*

cav·al·cade (kav′əl kād′), *n.* **1** procession of persons riding on horses, in carriages, or in cars. **2** series of scenes or events: *a cavalcade of sports.*

cav·a·lier (kav′ə lir′), **1** *n.* horseman, mounted soldier, or knight. **2** *n.* a courteous gentleman. **3** *n.* a courteous escort for a lady. **4** *adj.* careless in manner; free and easy; offhand: *She did not take me seriously and gave a cavalier reply.* **5** *adj.* proud and scornful; haughty; arrogant: *People were often irritated by his cavalier attitude towards them.* **6** *n.* **Cavalier,** person who supported Charles I of England in his struggle with Parliament from 1640 to 1649. [See Word Story at **chivalry.**] **—cav′a·lier′ly,** *adv.* **—cav′a·lier′ness,** *n.*

cav·al·ry (kav′əl rē), *n.* **1** (earlier) soldiers who fought on horseback. **2** soldiers who fight from armored vehicles. [See Word Story at **chivalry.**]

cav·al·ry·man (kav′əl rē mən), *n.* soldier in the cavalry. ❑ *n., pl.* **cav·al·ry·men.**

cave (kāv), **1** *n.* a hollow space underground, especially one with an opening in the side of a hill or mountain. **2** *v.* **cave in,** to fall in; sink: *The weight of the snow caused the roof of the cabin to cave in.* ❑ *v.* **caved, cav·ing.**

cave-in (kāv′in′), *n.* **1** act of caving in; collapse: *a tunnel cave-in, the cave-in of a mine.* **2** place where something has caved in.

cave·man (kāv′man′), *n.* person who lived in a cave in prehistoric times. ❑ *n., pl.* **cave·men.**

cav·ern (kav′ərn), *n.* a large cave.

cav·ern·ous (kav′ər nəs), *adj.* **1** like a cavern; large and hollow: *a cavernous cellar, cavernous eyes.* **2** full of caverns: *cavernous mountains.* **—cav′ern·ous·ly,** *adv.*

cave·wo·man (kāv′wü′mən), *n.* woman who lived in a cave in prehistoric times. ❑ *n., pl.* **cave·wo·men.**

cav·i·ar (kav′ē är′), *n.* the salted eggs of sturgeon or of certain other large fish, eaten as an appetizer.

cav·il (kav′əl), **1** *v.* to find fault without good reason; raise trivial objections: *He cavils about minor points in the rules of the game.* **2** *n.* a trivial objection; petty criticism. ❑ *v.* **cav·iled, cav·il·ing** or **cav·illed, cav·il·ling. —cav′il·er** or **cav′il·ler,** *n.*

cav·i·ty (kav′ə tē), *n.* **1** hollow place; hole. Cavities in teeth are caused by decay. **2** an enclosed space inside the body: *the abdominal cavity.* ❑ *n., pl.* **cav·i·ties.**

ca·vort (kə vôrt′), *v.* to prance about; jump around: *The children cavorted about the field, racing and tumbling.*

Ca·vour (kä vür′), *n.* **Ca·mil·lo Ben·so di** (kä mē′lō ben′sō dē), 1810-1861, Italian political leader. He worked for Italian freedom from Austrian control.

caw (kò), **1** *n.* the harsh cry made by a crow or raven. **2** *v.* to make this cry.

cay (kē *or* kā), *n.* a low island; reef; key. ▪ Other words that can sound like this are **key** and **quay.**

Cay·enne (kī en′ *or* kā en′), *n.* port and capital of French Guiana, on the Atlantic.

cay·enne pepper (kī en′ *or* kā en′), a very hot, biting powder made from the seeds or fruit of a pepper plant; red pepper.

cay·man (kā′mən), *n.* caiman. ❑ *n., pl.* **cay·mans.**

Ca·yu·ga (kī yü′gə), **1** *n.* member of a tribe of American Indians formerly living in New York State and southern Ontario. **2** *adj.* of this tribe. ❑ *n., pl.* **Ca·yu·ga** or **Ca·yu·gas.**

cay·use (kī yüs′ *or* kī′üs), *n.* in the western United States: **1** a pony raised by American Indians. **2** any pony or horse.

CB, citizens band (radio).

CBC, Canadian Broadcasting Corporation.

CBS, Columbia Broadcasting System.

cc, cc., or **c.c.,** cubic centimeter or cubic centimeters.

CCD, charge-coupled device.

C clef, symbol in music that shows the position of middle C. It is called the alto clef when placed on the third line of the staff, and the tenor clef when placed on the fourth line of the staff. See picture at **clef.**

a	hat	è	term	ô	order	ch	child		
ā	age	i	it	oi	oil	ng	long		a in about
ä	far	ī	ice	ou	out	sh	she	ə	e in taken
â	care	o	hot	u	cup	th	thin		i in pencil
e	let	ō	open	u̇	put	ŦH	then		o in lemon
ē	equal	ò	saw	ü	rule	zh	measure		u in circus

celebrate (def.1)—celebrating Kwanzaa

Cd, symbol for cadmium.

CD, compact disc.

CDC, Centers for Disease Control (a U.S. government agency that works to prevent or control all sorts of disease).

CD-ROM (sē′dē′rom′), *n.* compact disc read-only memory (a compact disc for use with a computer, containing information that the computer can display, together with programs that the computer uses to retrieve and process this information; such a disc can store information that produces text, pictures, movies, and sound).

CDT, Central Daylight Time.

Ce, symbol for cerium.

cease (sēs), *v.* to come to an end; put an end to; stop: *The music ceased suddenly. Cease trying to do more than you can.* ◻ *v.* **ceased, ceas·ing.**

cease-fire (sēs′fir′), *n.* a halt in military operations, especially for the purpose of discussing peace.

cease·less (sēs′lis), *adj.* going on all the time; never stopping; continual: *the ceaseless roar of the falls.* —**cease′less·ly,** *adv.* —**cease′less·ness,** *n.*

ce·cro·pi·a moth (sə krō′pē ə), a large silkworm moth of the eastern United States, with red, black, and white markings on brown wings.

ce·dar (sē′dər), *n.* **1** any of several evergreen trees with small flat leaves like scales and fragrant, durable, reddish wood used for lining clothes closets and making chests, pencils, posts, and shingles. **2** any of four evergreen trees related to pines, growing in Mediterranean and Himalayan regions. ■ Another word that sounds like this is **seeder.**

Cedar Rapids, city in E Iowa.

cede (sēd), *v.* to hand over to another; give up; surrender: *Spain ceded the Philippines to the United States in 1898.* ◻ *v.* **ced·ed, ced·ing.** ■ Another word that sounds like this is **seed.**

ce·dil·la (sə dil′ə), *n.* a mark something like a comma (‚) put under *c* before *a, o,* or *u* in certain words to show that it has the sound of *s.* EXAMPLE: façade. ◻ *n., pl.* **ce·dil·las.** [Cedilla comes from the Spanish name of the letter **Z.** This mark used to be written as a little **z** under the **c.**]

ceil·ing (sē′ling), *n.* **1** the inside, top covering of a room; surface opposite the floor. **2** the greatest height to which an airplane can go: *That plane has a ceiling of more than 100,000 feet.* **3** distance between the earth and the lowest clouds: *The weather report said that the ceiling was only 300 feet.* **4** an upper limit set for prices, wages, rents, etc.: *There is a ceiling on the amount rents can be raised in the city.*

Cel·e·bes (sel′ə bēz′), *n.* large island in Indonesia, between Borneo and New Guinea. Also, **Sulawesi.**

cel·e·brant (sel′ə brənt), *n.* **1** person who performs a ceremony or rite. **2** priest who performs Mass.

cel·e·brate (sel′ə brāt), *v.* **1** to observe a special time or day with the proper ceremonies or festivities: *We celebrated her birthday with cake, ice cream, and presents.* **2** to perform publicly with the proper ceremonies and rites: *The priest celebrates Mass in church.* **3** to praise; honor: *Her books are celebrated all over the world.* ◻ *v.* **cel·e·brat·ed, cel·e·brat·ing.** —**cel′e·bra′tor,** *n.*

cel·e·brat·ed (sel′ə brā′tid), *adj.* much talked about; famous; well-known: *a celebrated author.*

cel·e·bra·tion (sel′ə brā′shən), *n.* **1** special services or activities in honor of a particular person, act, time, or day: *A Fourth of July celebration often includes a display of fireworks.* **2** act of celebrating: *celebration of a birthday.*

ce·leb·ri·ty (sə leb′rə tē), *n.* **1** a famous person; person who is well known or much talked about: *Astronauts are celebrities around the world.* **2** condition of being well known or much talked about; fame: *Her celebrity brought her riches.* ◻ *n., pl.* **ce·leb·ri·ties** for 1.

ce·ler·i·ty (sə ler′ə tē), *n.* swiftness; speed.

cel·er·y (sel′ər ē), *n.* vegetable with long, crisp stalks. Celery is eaten raw or cooked.

ce·les·ta (sə les′tə), *n.* a musical instrument resembling a small, upright piano. Its bell-like tones are made by hammers hitting steel plates. ◻ *n., pl.* **ce·les·tas.**

ce·les·tial (sə les′chəl), *adj.* **1** of the sky or outer space: *The sun, moon, planets, and stars are celestial bodies.* **2** of or belonging to heaven; heavenly; divine: *celestial joy.* —**ce·les′tial·ly,** *adv.*

celestial equator, an imaginary circle in the sky, above the Earth's equator, used by astronomers as a method to describe the locations of planets and stars.

celestial navigation, method of navigation in which the position of a ship or aircraft is calculated from the position of stars and planets.

celestial sphere, an imaginary sphere around the universe. To an observer on earth, the visible sky forms half of the celestial sphere.

cel·i·ba·cy (sel′ə bə sē), *n.* **1** the condition of not being sexually active. **2** the condition of being unmarried.

cel·i·bate (sel′ə bit), **1** *n.* person who decides not to be sexually active. **2** *adj.* not sexually active. **3** *n.* an unmarried person. **4** *adj.* unmarried; single: *a celibate life.*

cell (sel), *n.* **1** a small room in a prison, convent, or monastery. **2** any small, hollow place: *Bees store honey in the cells of a honeycomb.* **3** the basic unit of living matter, of which all living things are made. Cells vary in size and shape but are generally microscopic. The cells of animals and plants have a nucleus near the center and are enclosed by a cell membrane or cell wall. The body has blood cells, nerve cells, muscle cells, etc. **4** electric cell. ■ Another word that sounds like this is **sell.** —**cell′-like′,** *adj.*

cel·lar (sel′ər), *n.* an underground room or rooms, usually under a building and often used for storage. ■ Another word that sounds like this is **seller.**

cell division, process by which a cell divides to form two cells of about equal size.

cel·list (chel′ist), *n.* person who plays the cello; violoncellist.

cell membrane, the thin membrane that forms the outer surface of the protoplasm of a cell.

cel·lo (chel′ō), *n.* a musical instrument like a violin, but very much larger and with a lower tone; violoncello. It is held between the knees while it is played. ◻ *n., pl.* **cel·los.**

cel·lo·phane (sel′ə fān), *n.* a transparent paperlike material made from cellulose. It is used as a wrapping to keep things fresh.

cel·lu·lar (sel′yə lər), *adj.* **1** of or about cells: *cellular biology.* **2** made of cells. All animal and plant tissue is cellular. **3** of or referring to a communication system that uses low-power radio receivers and transmitters located in areas called cells. As a user travels about, the radio signal is transferred automatically from cell to cell.

cellular phone, a portable phone, part of a cellular telephone system, for use in a motor vehicle or while walking around.

cellular respiration, process by which a cell breaks down food molecules and obtains energy from them, using oxygen and releasing carbon dioxide.

Cel·lu·loid (sel′yə loid), *n.* trademark for a hard, transparent substance made from cellulose. It catches fire easily. Combs, toilet articles, film, etc., were formerly made of Celluloid.

cel·lu·lose (sel′yə lōs), *n.* substance that forms the walls of plant cells; the stiff or fibrous part of trees and plants. Wood, cotton, flax, and hemp are largely cellulose. Cellulose is used to make paper, rayon, plastics, explosives, etc.

cell wall, the hard outer covering of a cell, found in plants, bacteria, fungi, or algae, made mostly of cellulose and surrounding the cell membrane.

Cel·si·us (sel′sē əs), **1 An·ders** (an′dərz), *n.* 1701-1744, Swedish astronomer. He created the Celsius scale. **2** *adj.* of, based on, or according to the Celsius scale; centigrade.

Celsius scale, a scale for measuring temperature on which 0 degrees marks the freezing point of water and 100 degrees marks the boiling point.

Celt (selt *or* kelt), *n.* member of a people to which the Irish, Scottish Highlanders, Welsh, Bretons, and Manx belong. The ancient Gauls and Britons were Celts.

Celt·ic (sel′tik *or* kel′tik), **1** *adj.* of the Celts or their language. **2** *n.* the group of languages spoken by the Celts, including Irish, Gaelic, Welsh, Breton, and Manx.

WORD SOURCE   **Celtic** languages have given a number of words to the English language, including the words below.

banshee	druid	penguin	slogan
bard	galore	piece	smithereens
blarney	glen	plaid	trousers
bog	league²	shamrock	truant
crag	leprechaun	slob	whiskey

ce·ment (sə ment′), **1** *n.* a fine, gray powder made by burning clay and limestone. Cement is mixed with water to make concrete and mortar. **2** *n.* anything applied soft which hardens to make things stick together: *rubber cement.* **3** *n.* substance used to fill cavities in teeth. **4** *v.* to fasten or repair with cement: *A broken plate can be cemented.* **5** *v.* to spread cement over: *The workmen were cementing the floor.* **6** *v.* to join firmly; unite: *The marriage of our son to their daughter cemented the friendship of our two families.* **—ce·ment′er,** *n.*

ce·men·tum (sə men′təm), *n.* the bony tissue that forms the outer crust of the root of a tooth.

cem·e·ter·y (sem′ə ter′ē), *n.* place for burying the dead; graveyard. □ *n., pl.* **cem·e·ter·ies.** [Cemetery comes from a Greek word meaning "to sleep."]

Cen·o·zo·ic (sen′ə zō′ik), *n.* (in geology) time from about 70 million years ago to the present time. During this time, mammals have been plentiful, mostly dominating the earth.

cen·ser (sen′sər), *n.* container in which incense is burned, especially during religious ceremonies. ■ Other words that sound like this are **censor** and **sensor.**

cen·sor (sen′sər), **1** *n.* person who examines and, if necessary, changes letters, books, newspapers, plays, movies, etc., so as to make their content satisfactory to the government or to some institution or organization. **2** *v.* to examine or change as a censor; make changes in; take out part of news reports, books, letters, movies, etc.: *Letters from the battlefield were censored to make sure military information did not fall into enemy hands. Two scenes in the movie had been censored for having too much violence.* ■ Other words that sound like this are **censer** and **sensor.**

WORD STORY   **Censor** comes from a Latin word meaning "evaluate." **Census** comes from the same word. The ancient Roman officials who counted the citizens also evaluated people's property for taxes. The same officials crossed criminals' names off the census lists.

cen·so·ri·ous (sen sôr′ē əs), *adj.* too ready to find fault; severely critical. **—cen·so′ri·ous·ly,** *adv.* **—cen·so′ri·ous·ness,** *n.*

cen·sor·ship (sen′sər ship), *n.* act or system of censoring: *Censorship of news is common in time of war.*

cen·sure (sen′shər), **1** *n.* expression of disapproval; unfavorable opinion; criticism: *Censure is sometimes harder to bear than punishment.* **2** *v.* to find fault with; criticize: *I was censured by the club for not paying my dues.* □ *v.* **cen·sured, cen·sur·ing. —cen′sur·er,** *n.*

cen·sus (sen′səs), *n.* an official count of the people of a country or district. It is taken to find out the number of people, their age, sex, what they do to make a living, and many other facts about them. □ *n., pl.* **cen·sus·es.** [See Word Story at **censor.**]

cent (sent), *n.* coin of the United States and Canada, usually an alloy of copper; penny. 100 cents make one dollar. ■ Other words that sound like this are **scent** and **sent.**

cent., **1** centigrade. **2** central. **3** century.

cen·taur (sen′tôr), *n.* (in Greek myths) a creature with the head, arms, and chest of a man, and the body and legs of a horse.

cen·ta·vo (sen tä′vō), *n.* **1** coin used in many Latin-American countries and the Philippines. 100 centavos make one peso. **2** coin used in Portugal. 100 centavos make one escudo. □ *n., pl.* **cen·ta·vos.**

cen·te·nar·i·an (sen′tə ner′ē ən), *n.* person who is 100 years old or more.

cen·ten·ar·y (sen ten′ər ē *or* sen′tə ner′ē), **1** *n.* a 100th anniversary: *The town was bustling with plans for its centenary.* **2** *n.* period of 100 years; century. **3** *adj.* of or for 100 years or a 100th anniversary: *a centenary celebration.* □ *n., pl.* **cen·ten·ar·ies.**

cen·ten·ni·al (sen ten′ē əl), **1** *adj.* of or for 100 years or a 100th anniversary. **2** *adj.* 100 years old: *centennial pines.* **3** *n.* a 100th anniversary: *The town is celebrating its centennial.* **4** *n.* celebration of the 100th anniversary: *I hope there will be a fair during our centennial.* **—cen·ten′ni·al·ly,** *adv.*

cen·ter (sen′tər), **1** *n.* point within a circle or sphere equally distant from all points of the circumference or surface. **2** *n.* the middle point, place, or part: *the center of a room.* **3** *n.* person, thing, or group that is the central point of attraction: *The Egyptian mummy was the center of the exhibit.* **4** *n.* place to which people or things go for a particular purpose: *The family went skating at the recreation center.* **5** *v.* to place in or at a center: *A bowl of fruit was centered on the kitchen table.* **6** *v.* to concentrate; rest: *All his hopes are centered on being promoted.* **7** *v.* to collect at a center: *The guests centered around the table.* **8** *n.* player in the middle of a forward line in football, basketball, hockey, etc.

cen·ter·board (sen′tər bôrd′), *n.* a movable keel of a sailboat. It is lowered through a slot in the bottom of a boat to prevent drifting to leeward.

center field, in baseball: **a** the section of the outfield between left field and right field. **b** position of the player in this area. **—center fielder.**

center ice, in hockey: **1** the area of rink ice between the two blue lines. **2** the middle of the rink ice, where play begins at the start of each period.

center of gravity, point in an object around which its weight is evenly balanced.

cen·ter·piece (sen′tər pēs′), *n.* an ornamental piece of glass, lace, etc., or an arrangement of flowers for the center of a dining table, buffet, mantel, etc.

centi-, *prefix.* one hundredth part of: *centimeter = one hundredth part of a meter.*

cen·ti·grade (sen′tə grād), *adj.* Celsius.

cen·ti·gram (sen′tə gram), *n.* ¹/₁₀₀ of a gram.

cen·ti·li·ter (sen′tə lē′tər), *n.* ¹/₁₀₀ of a liter.

cen·time (sän′tēm′), *n.* coin used in France, Belgium, Switzerland, Mali, Niger, Congo, and other countries. 100 centimes make one franc.

cen·ti·me·ter (sen′tə mē′tər), *n.* ¹/₁₀₀ of a meter.

cen·ti·mo (sen′tə mō), *n.* coin used in Spain and various Latin-American countries. 100 centimos make one peseta. □ *n., pl.* **cen·ti·mos.**

a	hat	ė	term	ô	order	ch	child		a in about
ā	age	i	it	oi	oil	ng	long		e in taken
ä	far	ī	ice	ou	out	sh	she	ə	i in pencil
â	care	o	hot	u	cup	th	thin		o in lemon
e	let	ō	open	ù	put	ŦH	then		u in circus
ē	equal	ò	saw	ü	rule	zh	measure		

cen·ti·pede (sen′tə pēd′), *n.* any of many flat, wormlike animals with many pairs of legs, the front pair of which are clawlike and contain poison glands.

cen·tral (sen′trəl), *adj.* **1** being or forming the center: *a central point, the central part of a wheel.* **2** at the center; near the center: *The park is in the central part of the city.* **3** equally distant from all points; easy to get to or from: *We shop at a central market.* **4** main; chief; principal: *What is the central idea in this story?* —**cen·tral·i·ty** (sen tral′ə tē), *n.* —**cen′tral·ly,** *adv.*

Central African Republic, country in central Africa, south of Chad. *Capital:* Bangui.

Central America, part of North America between Mexico and South America. Guatemala, El Salvador, Honduras, Belize, Nicaragua, Costa Rica, and Panama are the countries in Central America. —**Central American.**

central angle, an angle that has its meeting point at the center of a circle.

central city, the center or core of a metropolitan area, often densely populated.

central heat·ing (hēt′ing), a system that provides heat for an entire building from one source through pipes or ducts.

cen·tral·ize (sen′trə līz), *v.* **1** to bring to or toward a center; locate in a center. **2** to gather together in a center; concentrate. **3** to bring or come under the control of a single authority. ❑ *v.* **cen·tral·ized, cen·tral·iz·ing.** —**cen′tral·i·za′tion,** *n.*

central nervous system, part of the nervous system of vertebrates that consists of the brain and spinal cord.

Central Powers, the nations that fought against the Allies in World War I; Germany, Austria-Hungary, Bulgaria, and Turkey.

central processing unit. See CPU.

Central Standard Time, the standard time in the central part of the United States and Canada. It is six hours behind Greenwich Time.

cen·tre (sen′tər), *n., v.* BRITISH. center. ❑ *v.* **cen·tred, cen·tring.**

cen·trif·u·gal (sen trif′yə gəl), *adj.* moving away from the center. —**cen·trif′u·gal·ly,** *adv.*

centrifugal force, the apparent force that seems to cause a revolving object to move away from the point that it revolves around. Centrifugal force actually results from the revolving object's tendency to keep moving in the direction it last moved. This tendency is inertia.

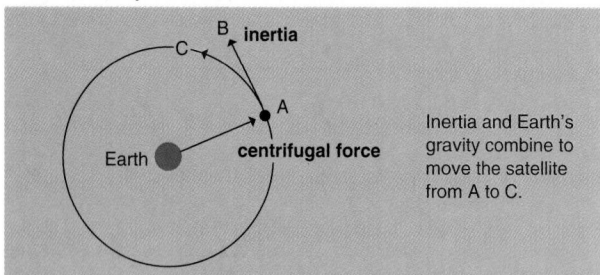

centrifugal force—The apparent force pushing the satellite outward is the centrifugal force.

cen·tri·fuge (sen′trə fyüj), *n.* machine that turns and separates two substances with different densities, such as cream from milk or bacteria from a fluid, by means of centrifugal force.

cen·tri·ole (sen′trē ōl), *n.* one of several tiny structures in a living cell, important to cell division.

cen·trip·e·tal (sen trip′ə təl), *adj.* moving toward the center. —**cen·trip′e·tal·ly,** *adv.*

centripetal force, any force that tends to move things toward the center around which they are turning. Earth's gravity applies a centripetal force on an orbiting satellite and keeps it from flying off into space.

cen·tro·some (sen′trə sōm), *n.* the small part of a living cell that contains the centrioles. —**cen′tro·som′ic,** *adj.*

cen·tur·i·on (sen tùr′ē ən), *n.* leader of about 100 soldiers in the ancient Roman army.

cen·tur·y (sen′chər ē), *n.* **1** each 100 years, counting from some special time, such as the birth of Jesus. The first century is 1 through 100; the nineteenth century is 1801 through 1900; the twentieth century is 1901 through 2000. **2** period of 100 years. From 1824 to 1924 is a century. ❑ *n., pl.* **cen·tur·ies.**

century plant, a large plant with thick leaves, a kind of agave, growing in Mexico and the southwestern United States. It may reach 30 feet (9 meters) in height and is often wrongly supposed to bloom once every 100 years.

ce·phal·ic (sə fal′ik), *adj.* **1** of the head. **2** near or toward the head. —**ce·phal′i·cal·ly,** *adv.*

ceph·a·lo·pod (sef′ə lə pod), *n.* any of many sea animals including octopuses and squids, with large heads and eyes, tentacles like arms around the mouth, and sharp beaks. Many cephalopods can squirt a dark fluid like ink to avoid attack.

ce·ram·ic (sə ram′ik), **1** *n.* any of various materials, such as brick, cement, or glass, that are made by heating nonmetallic minerals. **2** *n.* an item made of baked clay, such as pottery, earthenware, or porcelain. **3** *adj.* of or about such a material or item.

ce·ram·ics (sə ram′iks), *n.* art or science of making items or materials out of heated nonmetallic minerals, especially clay.

Cer·ber·us (sèr′bər əs), *n.* (in Greek myths) a three-headed dog that guarded the entrance to Hades, the home of the dead.

cer·e·al (sir′ē əl), **1** *n.* any grass that produces grain which is used as a food. Wheat, rice, corn, oats, and barley are cereals. **2** *n.* the grain. **3** *n.* food made from the grain. Oatmeal and corn meal are cereals. **4** *adj.* of or from grain or the grasses producing it: *cereal crops.* ■ Another word that sounds like this is **serial.**

cer·e·bel·lum (ser′ə bel′əm), *n.* the part of the brain that controls the coordination of the muscles. See picture at **brain.** ❑ *n., pl.* **cer·e·bel·lums, cer·e·bel·la** (ser′ə bel′ə).

ce·re·bral (sə rē′brəl *or* ser′ə brəl), *adj.* **1** of the brain. **2** of the cerebrum. **3** using or requiring thought and reason rather than emotion or action: *Chess is a cerebral game.* —**ce·re′bral·ly,** *adv.*

cerebral palsy, paralysis caused by damage to the brain before or at birth. Persons suffering from cerebral palsy have trouble coordinating their muscles.

cer·e·bro·spi·nal (sə rē′brō spi′nl *or* ser′ə brō spi′nl), *adj.* of or involving both the brain and the spinal cord.

ce·re·brum (sə rē′brəm *or* ser′ə brəm), *n.* the part of the human brain that controls thought and voluntary muscular movements. See picture at **brain.** ❑ *n., pl.* **ce·re·brums, ce·re·bra** (sə rē′brə *or* ser′ə brə).

cer·e·mo·ni·al (ser′ə mō′nē əl), **1** *adj.* of or for ceremony: *ceremonial costumes.* **2** *adj.* very formal: *The queen receives guests in a ceremonial way.* **3** *n.* the formal actions proper to an occasion. Bowing the head and kneeling are ceremonials of religion. —**cer′e·mo′ni·al·ly,** *adv.* —**cer′e·mo′ni·al·ness,** *n.*

cer·e·mo·ni·ous (ser′ə mō′nē əs), *adj.* **1** full of ceremony: *There was a ceremonious unveiling of the statue.* **2** very formal; extremely polite: *a ceremonious bow.* —**cer′e·mo′ni·ous·ly,** *adv.* —**cer′e·mo′ni·ous·ness,** *n.*

cer·e·mo·ny (ser′ə mō′nē), *n.* **1** a special act or set of acts to be done on special occasions such as weddings, funerals, graduations, or holidays: *The graduation ceremony was held in the gymnasium.* **2** very polite conduct; way of conducting yourself that follows the rules of polite social behavior: *The old gentleman showed us to the door with a great deal of ceremony.* **3** attention to forms and customs; formality: *The princess disliked the traditional court ceremony.* ❑ *n., pl.* **cer·e·mo·nies** for 1.
stand on ceremony, be too polite; be very formal: *We don't stand on ceremony here.*

Cézanne painting

Cer·es (sir′ēz), *n.* Roman goddess of agriculture. The Greeks called her Demeter.

ce·rise (sə rēs′), **1** *adj.* bright pinkish red. **2** *n.* a bright pinkish red. [See Word Story at **cherry**.]

cer·i·um (sir′ē əm), *n.* a soft, grayish metallic element. Cerium is used in porcelain, glass, and alloys. *Symbol:* Ce

cer·tain (sèrt′n), *adj.* **1** without a doubt; sure: *I am certain that these are the facts.* ■ See Synonym Study at **sure**. **2** known but not named; some; particular: *Certain plants will not grow in this country.* **3** settled; fixed: *I earn a certain amount of money each week.* **4** known to be true; reliable: *I have certain information that school will end a day earlier this year.* **5** sure to happen; inevitable: *My mother says that I will meet certain success in my life.* **6** not much; some: *There's a certain amount of truth in what they are saying.*
for certain, without a doubt; surely: *She will be here for certain.*

cer·tain·ly (sèrt′n lē), *adv.* without a doubt; surely: *I will certainly be at the party.*

cer·tain·ty (sèrt′n tē), *n.* **1** condition of being certain; freedom from doubt: *The man's certainty was amusing, for we could all see that he was wrong.* **2** something certain; a sure fact: *The coming of spring is a certainty.* □ *n., pl.* **cer·tain·ties** for 2.

cer·tif·i·cate (sər tif′ə kit), *n.* an official written or printed statement that declares something to be a fact. A birth certificate gives the date and place of a person's birth.

cer·ti·fied (sèr′tə fīd), *adj.* **1** guaranteed: *certified Grade A milk.* **2** having a certificate: *a certified teacher.*

cer·ti·fy (sèr′tə fī), *v.* **1** to declare something true or correct by an official spoken, written, or printed statement: *This diploma certifies that you have completed high school.* **2** to guarantee the quality or value of: *The fire inspector certified the school building as fireproof.* □ *v.* **cer·ti·fied, cer·ti·fy·ing.** —**cer′ti·fi·ca′tion,** *n.* —**cer′ti·fi′er,** *n.*

ce·ru·le·an (sə rü′lē ən), **1** *adj.* sky-blue. **2** *n.* a sky-blue color.

Cer·van·tes (sər van′tēz′), *n.* Mi·guel de (mē gel′ dā), 1547-1616, Spanish writer, author of *Don Quixote.* ■ **Miguel de Cervantes** was a soldier in his youth and was captured by pirates and held for ransom in Algiers. He remained a captive for five years, during which he made four escape attempts, until his family ransomed him.

cer·vi·cal (sèr′və kəl), *adj.* **1** of the cervix of the uterus. **2** of the neck.

cer·vix (sèr′viks), *n.* **1** a necklike part of an organ of the body, such as the end of a woman's uterus. **2** the neck, especially the back of the neck. □ *n., pl.* **cer·vix·es, cer·vi·ces** (sèr′və sēz).

Ce·sar·e·an section (si zâr′ē ən), Caesarean section.

ce·si·um (sē′zē əm), *n.* a soft, silvery, highly reactive metallic element, used in photoelectric cells. *Symbol:* Cs

ces·sa·tion (se sā′shən), *n.* act of ceasing; stopping: *The warring armies agreed on a cessation of the fighting.*

ces·sion (sesh′ən), *n.* act of handing something over to someone else; surrender: *cession of territory to avoid war.* ■ Another word that sounds like this is **session**.

cess·pool (ses′pül′), *n.* a pool or pit for house sewer pipes to empty into.

ce·ta·cean (sə tā′shən), *n.* any mammal living always in water and belonging to one of numerous related species, including whales, dolphins, and porpoises.

Cey·lon (si lon′), *n.* former name of **Sri Lanka.**

Cey·lo·nese (sē′lə nēz′), **1** *adj.* of Ceylon or its people. **2** *n.* person born or living in Ceylon. □ *n., pl.* **Cey·lo·nese.**

Cé·zanne (sā zän′), *n.* **Paul,** 1839-1906, French painter. ■ **Paul Cézanne** is often considered the first modern artist. His paintings developed from impressionist methods toward a much more abstract style.

Cf, symbol for californium.

CF, cystic fibrosis.

cf., compare.

CFC, chlorofluorocarbon.

cg., centigram or centigrams.

C.G., Coast Guard.

ch., **1** chapter. **2** church.

Chad (chad), *n.* country in central Africa south of Libya. *Capital:* N'Djamena.

chafe (chāf), *v.* **1** to rub so as to wear away, scrape, or make sore: *The stiff collar chafed my neck.* **2** to make or become angry: *His big sister's teasing chafed him. He chafed under his big sister's teasing.* □ *v.* **chafed, chaf·ing.**

chaff[1] (chaf), *n.* **1** the tough, outer skin of wheat, oats, rye, etc., especially when separated from grain by threshing. **2** worthless stuff; rubbish.

chaff[2] (chaf), **1** *v.* to tease or make fun of someone in a good-natured way: *Her friends chaffed the girl about her inability to sing on key.* **2** *n.* good-natured joking about a person to his or her face: *She did not mind her friend's chaff.*

chaf·ing dish (chā′fing), pan with a flame under it, used to cook food at the table or to keep it warm.

Cha·gall (shə gäl′), *n.* **Marc** (märk), 1887-1985, Jewish painter born in Russia, who lived in France. ■ **Marc Chagall's** work often showed subjects from his childhood and his own dreams.

cha·grin (shə grin′), **1** *n.* a feeling of disappointment, failure, or humiliation: *I felt chagrin because I did not pass the test.* **2** *v.* to cause to feel chagrin: *She was chagrined by her failure.*

chain (chān), **1** *n.* series of links joined together: *The dog is fastened to a post by a chain.* **2** *n.* series of things linked together: *a chain of mountains, a chain of restaurants, a chain of events.* **3** *v.* to join together with a chain; fasten with a chain: *The dog was chained to a post.* **4** *n.* anything that binds or restrains: *the chains of duty.* **5** *v.* to bind; restrain: *Work chained him to his desk.* **6** *v.* to keep in prison; enslave. **7** *n.pl.* **chains, a** bonds; fetters: *The rebels were brought back in chains.* **b** imprisonment or bondage: *Enemies of the government spent many years in chains.* —**chain′like′,** *adj.*

chain mail, (long ago) kind of flexible armor, made of metal rings linked together.

chain reaction, 1 process of releasing atomic energy by a series of nuclear fissions that continues automatically once it has been started. In a chain reaction, some of the neutrons from a split nucleus collide with other nuclei, which split and give off more neutrons that collide with more nuclei. **2** any series of events, each caused by the preceding one or ones.

chain saw, a portable power saw with a loop of chain with teeth, used to cut tree limbs, cut down small trees, etc.

chain-smoke (chān′smōk′), *v.* to smoke cigarettes, cigars, etc., one right after another, using one to light the next. □ *v.* **chain-smoked, chain-smok·ing.**

chain store, one of a group of stores owned and managed by the same company.

a	hat	è	term	ô	order	ch	child		
ā	age	i	it	oi	oil	ng	long		a in about
ä	far	ī	ice	ou	out	sh	she		e in taken
â	care	o	hot	u	cup	th	thin	ə	i in pencil
e	let	ō	open	ù	put	ᴛʜ	then		o in lemon
ē	equal	ò	saw	ü	rule	zh	measure		u in circus

chair (châr), **1** *n.* seat that has a back, legs, and, sometimes, arms, usually for one person. **2** *n.* seat of rank, dignity, or authority. **3** *n.* position or authority of a person who has such a seat: *Professor Smith has the chair of astronomy at this college.* **4** *n.* chairman or chairwoman: *The chair called the meeting to order.* **5** *v.* to conduct as chairman or chairwoman: *chair a meeting.*

> **WORD STORY** **Chair** comes from a Greek word meaning "chair." **Cathedral** comes from the same word. A cathedral is the official church of a bishop and contains the bishop's throne, an important symbol of office.

chair·lift (châr′lift′), *n.* a series of chairs or seats, attached to an overhead cable. Skiers ride a chairlift to the top of a slope.

chair·man (châr′mən), *n.* **1** person who is in charge of a meeting. **2** person at the head of a committee. ❑ *n., pl.* **chair·men.**

chair·man·ship (châr′mən ship′), *n.* position, duties, or term of office of a person who chairs a meeting or committee.

chair·per·son (châr′per′sən), *n.* **1** person who is in charge of a meeting. **2** person at the head of a committee.

chair·wom·an (châr′wum′ən), *n.* **1** woman in charge of a meeting. **2** woman at the head of a committee. ❑ *n., pl.* **chair·wom·en.**

chairlift

chaise (shāz), *n.* chaise longue.

chaise longue (shāz′ lông′), chair with a long seat and a back at one end, something like a couch. [See Word Story at **chaise lounge.**]

chaise lounge (shāz′ lounj′), chaise longue.

> **WORD STORY** **Chaise longue** looks like **chaise lounge,** and a person in a chaise longue often sits in a lounging way. For these reasons, people who do not know French often use the phrase **chaise lounge,** and it has become a part of the English language.

chal·ced·o·ny (kal sed′n ē *or* kal′sə dō′nē), *n.* a kind of quartz with very small crystals that often has layers or sections of various colors and a waxy or milky shine. Agate and onyx are chalcedony.

Chal·chi·uht·li·cue (chäl′chē ùt′lē kwā), *n.* Aztec goddess of fresh and running water, wife of Tlaloc.

Chal·de·a (kal dē′ə), *n.* an ancient region in SW Asia, on the Tigris and Euphrates rivers. See **Babylonia** for map. —**Chal·de′an,** *adj., n.*

cha·let (sha lā′), *n.* **1** a herdsman's hut or cabin in the Alps. **2** a Swiss house with wide, overhanging eaves. **3** any house like this.

chal·ice (chal′is), *n.* **1** cup or goblet. **2** cup that holds the wine used in the Communion service.

chalk (chôk), **1** *n.* a soft, white or gray limestone, formed mostly of very small fossil seashells. Chalk is used for making lime and for writing or drawing. **2** *n.* a white or colored substance like chalk, used for writing or drawing on a blackboard or chalkboard. **3** *v.* to mark, write, or draw with chalk. —**chalk′like′,** *adj.*
chalk up, 1 to credit: *chalk up success to good advice.* **2** to consider as a gain for: *chalk up a lesson to experience.* **3** to score: *Our team chalked up 12 points.*

chalk·board (chôk′bôrd′), *n.* a smooth, hard surface, used for writing or drawing on with crayon or chalk.

chalk·y (chô′kē), *adj.* **1** of chalk; containing chalk. **2** like chalk; white as chalk. ❑ *adj.* **chalk·i·er, chalk·i·est.** —**chalk′i·ness,** *n.*

chal·lah (hä′lə), *n.* hallah.

chal·lenge (chal′ənj), **1** *n.* a call or invitation to a game or contest: *The champions accepted our team's challenge.* **2** *v.* to call or invite to a game or contest; dare: *The champion swimmer challenged anyone in the world to beat her.* **3** *v.* to call to fight: *The*

knight challenged his rival to a duel. **4** *n.* a call to fight: *His rival accepted the challenge.* **5** *n.* a call to answer and explain: *"Who goes there?" was the challenge of the soldier on guard.* **6** *v.* to stop and question a person about an action: *When I tried to enter the building, the guard at the door challenged me.* **7** *v.* to call in question; doubt; dispute: *The teacher challenged my statement that Montana is a coastal state.* **8** *n.* a demand for proof of the truth of a statement; a doubting or questioning of the truth of a statement: *His challenge led me to read widely about Montana.* **9** *n.* anything that claims or commands effort, interest, feeling, etc.: *Fractions are a real challenge to her.* **10** *v.* to claim or command effort, interest, feeling, etc.: *How to prevent disease is a problem that challenges everyone's attention.* **11** *v.* to object to: *The attorney for the defense challenged the juror.* **12** *n.* objection: *The judge upheld the challenge and dismissed the juror from duty.* ❑ *v.* **chal·lenged, chal·leng·ing.** —**chal′leng·er,** *n.*

chal·lenged (chal′ənjd), *adj.* having special difficulties to overcome: *He is verbally challenged and works hard on his reading skills. Wheelchair access for the mobility-challenged is important for all public buildings.* ■ See Usage Note at **disabled.**

cham·ber (chām′bər), *n.* **1** a room, especially a bedroom. **2** hall where lawmakers meet: *the council chamber.* **3** group of lawmakers: *The Congress of the United States has two chambers, the Senate and the House of Representatives.* **4** an enclosed space in the body of a living thing, or in some kinds of machinery. The heart has four chambers. The part of a gun that holds the bullet is called the chamber. **5 chambers,** *pl.* **a** office of a lawyer or judge: *The judge met the two lawyers in her chambers.* **b** set of rooms in a building arranged for living or for offices.

cham·ber·lain (chām′bər lən), *n.* (long ago) a person who managed the household of a king, queen, or great noble.

cham·ber·maid (chām′bər mād′), *n.* maid who takes care of bedrooms in a hotel or motel.

chamber music, music suited for performance in a room or small hall, such as music for a trio or quartet.

chamber of commerce, group of people in business organized to protect and promote the business interests of a city, state, or country.

cham·bray (sham′brā), *n.* a cotton cloth woven from white and colored threads, used for dresses and men's shirts.

cha·me·le·on (kə mē′lē ən), *n.* **1** any of numerous small lizards that can change the color of their skin to blend with the surroundings. **2** a changeable or fickle person.

> **WORD STORY** **Chameleon** comes from Greek words meaning "lion on the ground." Like a lion, a chameleon hunts other animals for food. The Greeks used "on the ground" to mean "low" or "small." In fact, most chameleons live in trees or bushes.

cham·ois (sham′ē), *n.* **1** a small, goatlike antelope that lives in the high mountains of Europe and southwestern Asia. **2** a soft leather made from its skin or the skin of sheep, goats, or deer. ❑ *n., pl.* **cham·ois.**

chamois (def. 1)—about 30 in. (76 cm) high at the shoulder

cham·o·mile (kam′ə mīl), *n.* any of various plants with daisylike flowers. The flowers and leaves of some kinds are sometimes dried and used as a medicine. Also, **camomile.**

champ[1] (champ), *v.* to bite and chew noisily: *champ food. The racehorse champed its bit.*

champ at the bit, be impatient or restless: *The children were champing at the bit as the parade approached.*

champ[2] (champ), *n.* INFORMAL. champion.

cham·pagne (sham pān′), *n.* **1** a sparkling, bubbling white wine made in Champagne, a region in northern France. **2** any similar wine made elsewhere.

cham·pi·on (cham′pē ən), **1** *n.* person, animal, or thing that wins first place in a game or contest: *He is the swimming champion of our school.* **2** *adj.* having won first place; ahead of all others: *a champion runner.* **3** *n.* person who fights or speaks for another; person who defends a cause: *That writer is a great champion of peace.* **4** *v.* to fight for; speak in behalf of; defend: *All his life he has championed freedom.*

cham·pi·on·ship (cham′pē ən ship), *n.* **1** position of a champion; first place: *Our school won the championship in baseball.* **2** defense; support: *She undertook the championship of our cause.*

Cham·plain (sham plān′), *n.* **1 Samuel de** (də), 1567-1635, French explorer who founded Quebec city. **2 Lake,** a long, narrow lake between New York and Vermont.

chance (chans), **1** *n.* favorable time; opportunity: *Now is your chance.* **2** *n.* likelihood of anything happening; possibility or probability: *The chances are against snow in May.* **3** *n.* fate, fortune, or luck: *Chance led to the finding of gold in California.* ■ See Synonym Study at **luck. 4** *v.* to have the fortune; happen: *I chanced to meet an old friend today.* ■ See Synonym Study at **happen. 5** *n.* a risk; gamble: *He took a big chance when he swam the wide river.* **6** *v.* to take the risk of: *I will not chance driving in this awful blizzard.* **7** *adj.* not expected or planned; accidental: *We had a chance visit from Grandmother.* ■ See Synonym Study at **random. 8** *n.* ticket in a raffle or lottery: *She bought two chances in the car raffle at the fair.* ❑ *v.* **chanced, chanc·ing.** [See Word Story at **casual.**]

by chance, accidentally: *It was only by chance that I found you.*

chance upon or **chance on,** to happen to find or meet: *I chanced upon an old friend.*

on the off chance, depending on luck.

stand a chance, to have favorable prospects.

chan·cel·lor (chan′sə lər), *n.* **1** the prime minister or other very high official of some European countries. **2** the chief judge of a chancery. **3** head or president of some universities.

Chan·cel·lors·ville (chan′sə lərz vil′), *n.* town in NE Virginia. It was the site of a Union defeat in May 1863. The Confederate general "Stonewall" Jackson was killed in this battle.

chan·cer·y (chan′sər ē), *n.* court of law dealing with cases in which justice requires a settlement not covered by either common law or statute law. ❑ *n., pl.* **chan·cer·ies.**

chanc·y (chan′sē), *adj.* uncertain; risky: *a chancy undertaking.* ❑ *adj.* **chanc·i·er, chanc·i·est.** **—chan′ci·ness,** *n.*

chan·de·lier (shan′də lir′), *n.* fixture with branches for lights that hangs from the ceiling.

Chand·ler (chand′lər), *n.* **Ray·mond** (rā′mənd), 1888-1959, American writer. He wrote detective novels, including *The Big Sleep.* Many of his novels were made into movies.

Cha·nel (shə nel′), *n.* **Co·co** (kō′kō), 1883-1971, French fashion designer. ■ **Coco Chanel** was one of the first designers to make women's clothes that were both stylish and comfortable.

change (chānj), **1** *v.* to make or become different: *She changed the decoration of the room. The wind changed from east to west.* **2** *v.* to put or take something in place of another; substitute or exchange: *I changed seats with my brother.* **3** *v.* to take in place of: *change a dollar bill for ten dimes.* **4** *n.* act of changing; a passing from one form or place to another: *Vacationing in the country is a pleasant change from city life.* **5** *n.* variety; difference; alteration: *Let me pitch for a change.* **6** *n.* a changed condition: *Do you see any change in his behavior?* **7** *n.* thing to be used in place of another: *He brought along a change of clothes.* **8** *n.*

money returned to a person who has paid a larger amount than the price of what is purchased. **9** *v.* to put on different clothes: *After swimming we went to the cabin and changed.* **10** *v.* to transfer from one aircraft, train, bus, etc., to another: *Passengers must change here for Chicago.* **11** *n.* money of smaller denomination given in place of money of larger denomination: *Can you give me change for a dollar?* **12** *n.* coins of small denomination: *She was carrying a dollar and some change.* ❑ *v.* **changed, chang·ing.**

SYNONYM STUDY **Change** and **alter** both mean to make or become different. **Change** suggests that the difference is complete: *I change my underwear every day.* **Alter** suggests a slight or limited difference: *The pilot altered her flight plan to avoid a bad storm.*

change·a·ble (chān′jə bəl), *adj.* **1** able or likely to change; varying; fickle: *April weather is changeable.* **2** having a color or appearance that changes. Silk is called changeable when it shows different colors in different lights. **—change′a·ble·ness,** *n.* **—change′a·bly,** *adv.*

change·ful (chānj′fəl), *adj.* full of changes; likely to change; changing. **—change′ful·ly,** *adv.* **—change′ful·ness,** *n.*

change·less (chānj′lis), *adj.* not changing; not likely to change; constant. **—change′less·ly,** *adv.* **—change′less·ness,** *n.*

change·ling (chānj′ling), *n.* **1** child secretly left in the place of another. **2** (in fairy tales) a child left by fairies in place of a child carried off by them.

change·o·ver (chānj′ō′vər), *n.* **1** a shift to the manufacture of a new product, model, etc. **2** a transfer of ownership or control.

chang·er (chān′jər), *n.* person or thing that changes something, especially a device in a record player which automatically changes records.

Chang Jiang (chäng jyäng), river flowing from Tibet through China. Formerly, **Yangtze.**

Chang Jiang

chan·nel (chan′l), **1** *n.* a TV station: *If you don't like this program, change to another channel.* **2** *n.* a narrow band of frequencies that carries the programs of a television or radio station. **3** *n.* the means by which something moves or is carried: *The information came through secret channels.* **4** *n.* body of water joining two larger bodies of water: *The English Channel lies between the North Sea and the Atlantic Ocean.* **5** *n.* the deeper part of a waterway: *There is shallow water on both sides of the channel in this river.* **6** *n.* the bed of a stream, river, etc.: *Rivers cut their own channels to the sea.* **7** *v.* to form a passage: *The river had channeled its way through the rocks.* **8** *n.* passage for liquids; groove or canal; duct: *the poison channel in a snake's fangs.* **9** *n.* course of action; field of activity: *She tried to find a suitable channel for her abilities.* **10** *v.* to direct into a particular course of action: *Channel all your efforts into this one project, and you will succeed.* ❑ *v.* **chan·neled, chan·nel·ing** or **chan·nelled, chan·nel·ling.** **—chan′nel·er** or **chan′nel·ler,** *n.*

a	hat	ė	term	ô	order	ch	child		a in about
ā	age	i	it	oi	oil	ng	long		i in taken
ä	far	ī	ice	ou	out	sh	she	ə	i in pencil
â	care	o	hot	u	cup	th	thin		o in lemon
e	let	ō	open	u̇	put	ŦH	then		u in circus
ē	equal	ȯ	saw	ü	rule	zh	measure		

Channel Islands, British islands near the NW coast of France.

Channel Islands National Park, a national park consisting of five islands off the coast of S California, where many sea lions and seabirds live.

channel surfing, INFORMAL. act or process of switching quickly through TV channels to see what is on each: *She was just channel surfing, not watching anything in particular.*

chant (chant), **1** *n.* a short, simple song in which several syllables or words are sung in one tone. Chants are sometimes used in religious services. **2** *v.* to sing in this way. A choir chants psalms or prayers. **3** *v.* to sing: *chant a melody.* **4** *n.* act of calling or shouting words again and again. **5** *v.* to call over and over again: *The football fans chanted, "Go, team, go!"* —**chant′er,** *n.*

chan·tey (shan′tē *or* chan′tē), *n.* song formerly chanted by sailors in rhythm with the motions of their work. □ *n., pl.* **chan·teys.** Also, **chanty.** ■ Another word that can sound like this is **shanty.**

chan·ti·cleer (chan′tə klir), *n.* (in the Middle Ages) rooster.

chan·ty (shan′tē *or* chan′tē), *n.* chantey. □ *n., pl.* **chan·ties.** ■ Another word that can sound like this is **shanty.**

Cha·nu·kah (hä′nə kə), *n.* Hanukkah.

cha·os (kā′os), *n.* very great confusion; complete disorder: *The tornado left the town in chaos.*

cha·ot·ic (kā ot′ik), *adj.* very confused; completely disordered: *The town was in a chaotic condition after the flood.* —**cha·ot′i·cal·ly,** *adv.*

chap[1] (chap), *v.* to crack open; make or become rough: *A person's lips often chap in cold weather.* □ *v.* **chapped, chap·ping.**

chap[2] (chap), *n.* BRITISH. fellow; man or boy.

chap. or **Chap.,** **1** chapter. **2** chaplain.

chap·ar·ral (shap′ə ral′), *n.* a dense, often thorny thicket of low, brushy vegetation, found in the southwestern United States.

chap·book (chap′bùk′), *n.* (earlier) a small book or pamphlet of popular stories, ballads, poems, etc., sold on the street.

chap·eau (sha pō′), *n.* hat. □ *n., pl.* **chap·eaux** or **chap·eaus.**

chap·el (chap′əl), *n.* **1** a building for worship, not as large as a church. **2** a small place for worship in a larger building: *a hospital chapel.* **3** a religious service in a chapel, especially in a school or college: *There is chapel today.* [Chapel comes from a Latin word meaning "cloak." One early chapel contained the cloak of the patron saint of France.]

chap·e·ron or **chap·e·rone** (shap′ə rōn′),′ **1** *n.* an older person who is present at a party or other social activity of young people and is responsible for their behavior. **2** *n.* a person, especially a married or an older woman, who accompanies a young unmarried woman in public for the sake of her safety and reputation. **3** *v.* to act as a chaperon to. □ *v.* **chap·e·roned, chap·e·ron·ing.**

chap·lain (chap′lən), *n.* member of the clergy authorized or appointed to perform religious functions for a family, court, society, public institution, or unit in the armed forces: *a prison chaplain, an army chaplain.*

Chap·lin (chap′lin), *n.* **Char·lie** (chär′lē), 1889-1977, British movie star. ■ Charlie Chaplin's most famous character is "the Tramp," a cheerful man with badly fitting clothes, a bowler hat, and a cane.

Charlie Chaplin

chaps (shaps *or* chaps), *n.pl.* strong leather trousers without a back, worn over other trousers by cowhands.

chap·ter (chap′tər), *n.* **1** a main division of a book or other writing, dealing with a particular part of the story or subject. **2** anything like a chapter; part; section: *The first moon flight is an interesting chapter in space travel.* **3** a local division of an organization, which holds its own meetings; branch of a club, society, etc.

chapter house, house of a college fraternity or sorority.

Cha·pul·te·pec (chə pul′tə pek), *n.* fort on a rocky hill in SW Mexico City. U.S. troops captured the fort in 1847 during the Mexican War.

char (chär), *v.* **1** to burn to charcoal. **2** to burn enough to blacken; scorch: *After the fire a carpenter replaced the badly charred floor.* □ *v.* **charred, char·ring.**

char., **1** character. **2** charter.

char·ac·ter (kar′ik tər), *n.* **1** all the qualities or features of anything; kind; sort; nature: *The soil on the prairies is of a different character from that in the mountains.* **2** personality; the special way in which any person feels, thinks, and acts: *She has an honest, dependable character.* **3** moral firmness, self-control, or integrity: *It takes character to endure hardship for very long.* **4** person or animal in a play, poem, story, book, or movie: *His favorite character in "Charlotte's Web" is Wilbur, the pig.* **5** person who attracts attention because he or she is different or odd: *Ever since he painted his house in stripes, people have thought of him as a real character.* **6** letter, mark, or sign used in writing or printing: *There are 52 characters in our alphabet, consisting of 26 small letters and 26 capital letters.*

in character, as expected; natural or usual: *It is in character for them to be late.*

out of character, not as expected; not natural or usual: *It is out of character for her to be so rude.*

char·ac·ter·is·tic (kar′ik tə ris′tik), **1** *adj.* distinguishing one person or thing from others; special: *Bananas have their own characteristic smell.* **2** *n.* a special quality or feature; whatever distinguishes one person or thing from others; trait: *Cheerfulness is a characteristic that we admire. An elephant's trunk is its most noticeable characteristic.* —**char′ac·ter·is′ti·cal·ly,** *adv.*

char·ac·ter·i·za·tion (kar′ik tər ə zā′shən), *n.* **1** the methods an author uses to develop the qualities and personalities of people in a story, play, book, or poem. **2** act of characterizing; description of characteristics.

char·ac·ter·ize (kar′ik tə rīz′), *v.* **1** to describe the special qualities or features of: *The story of "Red Riding Hood" characterizes the wolf as a cunning and savage beast.* ■ See Synonym Study at **describe. 2** to be a characteristic of; distinguish: *A camel is characterized by the hump or humps on its back and its ability to go without water for several days.* □ *v.* **char·ac·ter·ized, char·ac·ter·iz·ing.** —**char′ac·ter·iz′er,** *n.*

cha·rade (shə rād′), *n.* Often, **charades,** *pl.* game in which one player acts out a word or phrase and the others try to guess what it is. If the word is *penmanship,* the player might act out "pen," "man," and "ship."

char·broil (chär′broil′), *v.* to broil over charcoal.

char·coal (chär′kōl′), *n.* a black, brittle form of carbon made by partly burning wood in a place where there is no air. Charcoal is used as fuel, in filters, and for drawing.

chard (chärd), *n.* kind of beet whose large leaves are eaten as a vegetable; Swiss chard.

charge (chärj), **1** *v.* to ask as a price; demand in payment: *The store charges 99 cents a dozen for eggs.* **2** *n.* price asked for or put on something: *The charge for delivery is $5.* **3** *v.* to ask to pay; request payment from: *A doctor charges a patient for treatment.* **4** *v.* to put down as a debt to be paid later: *We charged the table, so the store will send a bill for it.* **5** *n.* a debt to be paid: *"Cash or charge?" asked the clerk.* **6** *v.* to load or fill: *charge a gun with powder and shot.* **7** *n.* amount needed to load or fill something. A gun is fired by exploding the charge of powder in the shell. **8** *v.* to put an amount of electricity in: *charge a battery.* **9** *n.* amount of electricity in a battery, capacitor, etc. **10** *v.* to give a task, duty, or responsibility to: *My parents charged me to take good care of the baby.* **11** *n.* task; duty; responsibility: *The committee's charge is to select a name for the park.* **12** *n.* care; management: *Doctors and nurses have charge of sick people.* **13** *n.* person or thing under someone's care or management: *Sick people are the charges of doctors and nurses.* **14** *v.* to give an order or command to; direct: *The judge charged the jury to come to a fair decision.* **15** *n.* an order; command; direction: *a judge's charge to the jury to arrive at a verdict.* **16** *v.* to accuse: *The driver was charged with speeding.* **17** *n.* accusation: *He admitted the truth of the charge and paid a fine.* **18** *v.* to rush with force; attack: *The captain gave the order to charge.* **19** *n.* an attack: *The charge drove the enemy back.* ❑ *v.* **charged, charg·ing.**

charge off, 1 to subtract as a loss: *The store owner charged off all debts over three years old.* **2** to put down as belonging: *A bad mistake must be charged off to experience.*

in charge, having the care or management: *The mate is in charge when the captain leaves the ship.*

in charge of, having the care or management of: *My sister-in-law is in charge of the book department of the store.*

take charge, take command; assume responsibility: *She took charge of the planning for the bazaar.*

charge (def. 18)
charging elephant

WORD STORY **Charge** comes from a Latin word meaning "wagon." **Carry** comes from the same word. Long ago, **charge** and **carry** were one word, a Latin verb meaning "to load" or "to move in a wagon." When this verb passed into French, it was pronounced and spelled in different ways for the different meanings. So it became two words with one story.

charge·a·ble (chär′jə bəl), *adj.* **1** capable of being charged: *The salesman's travel expenses are chargeable to the company.* **2** liable to be charged. **—charge′a·ble·ness,** *n.*

charge account, record kept at a store of things bought by a person on credit. A customer with a charge account receives and uses what he or she purchases and pays for it later.

charge card, credit card.

charge-cou·pled device (chärj′kup′əld), a small electronic device used to detect light in video systems and to control electric currents in computers; CCD.

charg·er (chär′jər), *n.* **1** device that gives an electrical charge to storage batteries. **2** (long ago) a warhorse.

char·i·ot (char′ē ət), *n.* (long ago) a two-wheeled carriage pulled by horses. The chariot was used for fighting, for racing, and in processions.

char·i·ot·eer (char′ē ə tir′), *n.* person who drives a chariot.

cha·ris·ma (kə riz′mə), *n.* a power to fascinate and attract; great personal magnetism or glamor: *the charisma of a popular leader.*

char·is·mat·ic (kar′iz mat′ik), *adj.* **1** having the power to fascinate and attract: *a charismatic personality.* **2** of or about Christian worship that involves powers such as healing and prophecy.

char·i·ta·ble (char′ə tə bəl), *adj.* **1** generous in giving to poor, sick, or helpless people; benevolent and kind: *He was a charitable man who used his wealth to help others.* ■ See Synonym Study at **generous.** **2** of or for charity: *The Salvation Army is a charitable organization.* **3** kindly in judging people and their actions; lenient: *Grandparents are usually charitable toward the mistakes of their grandchildren.* **—char′i·ta·ble·ness,** *n.* **—char′i·ta·bly,** *adv.*

char·i·ty (char′ə tē), *n.* **1** generous giving to the poor, or to organizations which look after the sick, the poor, and the helpless: *The charity of our citizens enabled the hospital to purchase new beds.* **2** fund or organization for helping the sick, the poor, and the helpless: *She gives money regularly to the Red Cross and to other charities.* **3** kindness in judging people's faults. **4** love of other human beings. ❑ *n., pl.* **char·i·ties** for 2.

char·la·tan (shär′lə tən), *n.* person who pretends to have expert knowledge or skill; quack.

Char·le·magne (shär′lə mān), *n.* 742-814, ruler of most of Europe. He made many reforms in government and education. His name means "Charles the Great."

Charles (chärlz), *n.* born 1948, Prince of Wales and heir to the British throne. [Charles comes from a word meaning "man" in an old language related to German.]

Charles I, 1600-1649, king of England from 1625 until he was convicted of treason and executed in 1649.

Charles II, 1630-1685, king of England from 1660 to 1685. He was the son of Charles I.

Charles·ton (chärlz′tən), *n.* **1** capital of West Virginia, in the W part. **2** port in SE South Carolina, on the Atlantic. **3** a lively ballroom dance, especially popular in the 1920s.

char·ley horse (chär′lē), stiffness or cramp in a muscle, especially of the leg or arm.

Char·lotte (shär′lət), *n.* city in S central North Carolina. [Charlotte was named for Queen Charlotte, wife of King George III of Great Britain.]

Charlotte A·ma·lie (ə mal′ē), port and capital of the Virgin Islands that belongs to the United States.

Char·lotte·town (shär′lət toun), *n.* capital of Prince Edward Island, Canada.

charm (chärm), **1** *n.* power of delighting or fascinating; attractiveness: *Our grandmother's house never lost its charm for our family.* **2** *n.* a pleasing quality or feature: *The book has many charms; the chief one is its delightful humor.* **3** *v.* to please greatly; delight; fascinate; attract: *The children were charmed by the pet raccoon.* **4** *n.* a small ornament or trinket worn on a bracelet, watch chain, etc. **5** *n.* word, verse, act, or thing supposed to have magic power to help or harm people. **6** *v.* to affect or overcome by the power to please: *She charmed her grandparents into letting her stay with them for another week.* **—charm′er,** *n.*

WORD STORY **Charm** comes from a Latin word meaning "to sing." **Enchant** comes from the same word. In old times, people who believed in magic would often sing the words that they thought had special power, to try to make them work.

charmed (chärmd), *adj.* protected as by a charm: *The pilot led a charmed life in which he narrowly survived many accidents.*

charm·ing (chär′ming), *adj.* very pleasing; delightful; fascinating; attractive: *We saw a charming play. They are a charming couple.* **—charm′ing·ly,** *adv.*

Char·on (kâr′ən), *n.* (in Greek myths) the boatman who ferried the spirits of the dead to Hades.

chart (chärt), **1** *n.* map used by sailors to show the coasts, rocks, and shallow places of the sea. The course of a ship is marked on a chart. **2** *n.* an outline map showing special conditions or facts: *This weather chart shows where rain fell over the United States yesterday.* **3** *n.* sheet of information arranged in lists, pictures, tables, or

a	hat	ė	term	ô	order	ch	child		a in about
ā	age	i	it	oi	oil	ng	long		e in taken
ä	far	ī	ice	ou	out	sh	she	ə	i in pencil
â	care	o	hot	u	cup	th	thin		o in lemon
e	let	ō	open	u̇	put	ᵀʜ	then		u in circus
ē	equal	ȯ	saw	ü	rule	zh	measure		

diagrams: *a chart of the major scientific discoveries of the last 200 years.* **4** *v.* to make a chart of; show on a chart: *The navigator charted the course of the ship.* [See Word Story at **card**[1].]

char·ter (chär′tər), **1** *n.* a written grant by a government to a colony, a group of citizens, a corporation, etc., giving the right of organization, with other privileges, and specifying the form of organization. **2** *n.* a written order from the authorities of a society, giving to a group of persons the right to organize a new chapter, branch, or lodge. **3** *n.* document setting forth aims and purposes of a group of nations, organizations, or individuals in a common undertaking: *the Charter of the United Nations.* **4** *v.* to give a charter to: *to charter a new airline.* **5** *v.* to hire: *Our school chartered a bus to take the class to the zoo.* **6** *n.* a contract to rent an airplane, boat, car, or other vehicle. —**char′ter·er,** *n.*

Char·tres (shär′trə), *n.* city in N France. Its Gothic cathedral is over 700 years old.

Chartres cathedral

char·treuse (shär trüz′), **1** *n.* a light, yellowish green. **2** *adj.* light yellowish green.

char·y (châr′ē), *adj.* **1** showing caution; careful; wary: *The cat was chary of getting its paws wet.* **2** sparing; stingy: *A jealous person is chary of praising those who do well.* ❑ *adj.* **char·i·est.** —**char′i·ly,** *adv.* —**char′i·ness,** *n.*

Cha·ryb·dis (kə rib′dis), *n.* **1** whirlpool supposedly located between Sicily and Italy, opposite the rock Scylla. **2** (in Greek myths) a monster living there that sucked down ships.

chase (chās), **1** *v.* to run or follow after to catch or kill: *The cat chased the mouse.* **2** *v.* to drive away: *The bird chased the squirrel from its nest.* **3** *v.* to run after; follow; pursue: *I chased the ball as it rolled downhill.* **4** *n.* act of chasing: *The police caught up with the fleeing robbers after a long chase.* **5** *n.* **the chase,** hunting as a sport; hunt: *The fox hunter was devoted to the chase.* **6** *n.* a hunted animal: *The chase escaped the hunter.* ❑ *v.* **chased, chas·ing.** —**chase′a·ble** or **chas′a·ble,** *adj.* —**chas′er,** *n.*

give chase, to run after; pursue: *The fox gave chase as soon as it spotted the rabbit.*

> **WORD STORY** **Chase** comes from a Latin word meaning "to grab at something." **Catch** comes from the same word. At one time, long ago, **chase** and **catch** were one French word. People in different areas pronounced it in different ways, and gradually the different ways got different meanings.

chasm (kaz′əm), *n.* **1** a deep opening or crack in the earth; abyss. **2** a wide difference of feelings or interests between two persons or groups: *The chasm between England and the American colonies finally led to the Revolutionary War.*

Chas·si·dim (hä sē′dim), *n.pl.* Hasidim.

chas·sis (chas′ē *or* shas′ē), *n.* **1** the frame, wheels, and machinery of a motor vehicle that support the body. **2** the base or frame for the parts of a radio or TV set. ❑ *n., pl.* **chas·sis** (chas′ēz *or* shas′ēz).

chaste (chāst), *adj.* **1** pure; virtuous. **2** decent; modest. **3** simple in taste or style; not overly ornamented. —**chaste′ly,** *adv.* —**chaste′ness,** *n.*

chas·ten (chā′sn), *v.* **1** to punish to improve; discipline: *chasten a child.* **2** to restrain from excess or crudeness; moderate. —**chas′ten·er,** *n.*

chas·tise (cha stīz′ *or* chas′tīz), *v.* **1** to inflict punishment or suffering on to improve; punish. **2** to criticize or rebuke severely. ❑ *v.* **chas·tised, chas·tis·ing.** —**chas·tise′ment,** *n.*

chas·ti·ty (chas′tə tē), *n.* **1** purity; virtue. **2** decency; modesty. **3** simplicity of style or taste; absence of too much decoration.

chat (chat), **1** *n.* easy, friendly talk: *The two friends had a pleasant chat about old times.* **2** *v.* to talk in an easy, friendly way: *We sat chatting by the fire after supper.* ■ See Synonym Study at **speak. 3** *n.* any of several birds with a chattering cry. ❑ *v.* **chat·ted, chat·ting.**

cha·teau or **châ·teau** (sha tō′), *n.* **1** a large country house in France or elsewhere in Europe. **2** a French castle. ❑ *n., pl.* **cha·teaus** or **châ·teaux** (sha tōz′).

Chat·ta·noo·ga (chat′n ü′gə), *n.* city in SE Tennessee.

chat·tel (chat′l), *n.* piece of property that is not real estate; any movable possession. Furniture, cars, and animals are chattels.

chat·ter (chat′ər), **1** *v.* to talk constantly and quickly about unimportant things: *The children chattered about the circus.* **2** *n.* constant, quick talk about unimportant things: *The pupils' chatter disturbed the classroom.* **3** *v.* to make quick, indistinct sounds: *Monkeys chatter.* **4** *n.* quick, indistinct sounds: *the chatter of sparrows.* **5** *v.* to rattle together: *Cold can make your teeth chatter.* **6** *n.* sound of rattling together: *the chatter of typewriters.* —**chat′ter·er,** *n.*

chat·ter·box (chat′ər boks′), *n.* person who chatters. ❑ *n., pl.* **chat·ter·box·es.**

chat·ty (chat′ē), *adj.* **1** fond of friendly, familiar talk about unimportant things. **2** having the style or manner of friendly, familiar talk: *a chatty newspaper article about gardening.* ❑ *adj.* **chat·ti·er, chat·ti·est.** —**chat′ti·ly,** *adv.* —**chat′ti·ness,** *n.*

Chau·cer (chô′sər), *n.* **Geof·frey** (jef′rē), 1340?-1400, English poet, author of *The Canterbury Tales.*

chauf·feur (shō′fər *or* shō fėr′), **1** *n.* person whose work is driving a car. **2** *v.* to act as a chauffeur for; drive around. ■ Another word that can sound like this is **shofar.**

chau·vin·ism (shō′və niz′əm), *n.* **1** boastful, warlike patriotism; extreme enthusiasm for the military glory of your country. **2** an excessive enthusiasm for your group: *male chauvinism.*

chau·vin·ist (shō′və nist), *n.* **1** a boastful, warlike patriot. **2** person excessively enthusiastic about his or her sex, race, or group: *a male chauvinist.* —**chau′vin·is′tic,** *adj.*

Cha·vez (shä′vez), *n.* **Ce·sar** (sē′zər), 1927-1993, American labor organizer. ■ **Cesar Chavez** helped to found the United Farm Workers and led national boycotts of grapes and other produce from nonunion farms.

cheap (chēp), **1** *adj.* costing little: *Eggs are cheap out in the country.* **2** *adj.* costing less than it is worth: *My new sweater will be cheap, because I am going to buy the yarn and knit it myself.* **3** *adj.* charging low prices: *He bought that suit at a very cheap department store.* **4** *adj.* of low value; worth little: *My shoes were so cheap they wore out in just a few weeks.* **5** *adj.* unwilling to spend money; stingy: *Although he had the money, he was too cheap to replace his worn suit with a new one.* **6** *adj.* costing little effort; easily obtained: *He thinks that the cheapest way to make friends is to give them presents.* **7** *adj.* of little value; not worth respect; common: *cheap jokes.* **8** *adv.* at a low price; at small cost: *I sold my magazine collection cheap to get rid of it.* ■ Another word that sounds like this is **cheep.** —**cheap′ly,** *adv.* —**cheap′ness,** *n.*

feel cheap, to feel inferior and ashamed: *I felt cheap about forgetting my best friend's birthday.*

> **SYNONYM STUDY** **Cheap** and **inexpensive** both mean low in price. **Cheap** suggests low quality: *I won't buy cheap shoes.* **Inexpensive** usually suggests acceptable quality: *We had dinner at an inexpensive restaurant.*

cheap·en (chē′pən), *v.* **1** to make or become cheap; lower the price of. **2** to cause to be thought little of. —**cheap′en·er,** *n.*

cheap·skate (chēp′skāt′), *n.* INFORMAL. person who is very stingy.

cheat (chēt), **1** *v.* to play or do business in a way that is not honest; deceive or trick: *I hate to play games with a person who cheats.* **2** *n.* person who is not honest and does things to deceive or trick others. **3** *n.* fraud; trick. —**cheat′er**, *n.* —**cheat′ing·ly**, *adv.*

> **SYNONYM STUDY** **Cheat** and **trick** both mean to gain an advantage in a dishonest way. **Cheat** means to do so hoping that others won't notice: *Anyone who cheats on a test will get a failing grade.* **Trick** means to do so by fooling someone: *They tricked him out of his lunch money.*

check (chek), **1** *v.* to stop suddenly: *The tennis player checked her swing as the ball went out of bounds.* **2** *n.* a sudden stop: *The storm warning put a check to our plans for a picnic.* **3** *v.* to hold back; control; restrain: *checked her anger, check a forest fire.* **4** *n.* act of holding back; control; restraint: *Keep a check on your appetite.* **5** *n.* any person, thing, or event that controls or holds back action. **6** *v.* to prove true or right by comparing or examining: *Check your watch with the school clock.* **7** *v.* to match when compared, usually with a duplicate or the original: *The two copies check.* **8** *n.* examination or comparison to prove something true or right: *My work will be a check on yours.* **9** *v.* to seek information and advice from; consult: *I checked the dictionary to find out what the word meant.* **10** *n.* a mark (✓) to show that something has been examined or compared. Often it shows that the thing looked at was found to be true or right. *I put a check beside the correct answer.* **11** *v.* to mark something examined or compared with a check: *How many answers did the teacher check as wrong?* **12** *n.* ticket or token given in return for a coat, hat, baggage, package, etc., left for safekeeping, to show ownership or the right to claim again later: *Give your check to the man in the checkroom when you want your coat.* **13** *v.* to leave or take for safekeeping: *He checked his hat at the door of the club. The hotel checked our baggage.* **14** *n.* a written order directing a bank to pay money to the person named; cheque: *My parents pay most of their bills by check.* **15** *n.* a written statement of the amount owed in a restaurant: *After our meal the waitress brought the check to our table.* **16** *v.* to mark in a pattern of squares. **17** *n.* a pattern made of squares: *Do you want a check or a stripe for your new suit?* **18** *n.* a single one of these squares: *The checks in this dress are big.* **19** *v.* (in hockey) to block a player on the other team. **20** in chess: **a** *n.* position of an opponent's king when it is in danger. **b** *v.* to put an opponent's king in this position. **21** *n.* (in hockey) act of blocking a player on the other team.

check in, to arrive and register at a hotel, motel, etc.: *We checked in and were then shown to our rooms.*

check out, 1 to pay your bill at a hotel, motel, etc., when leaving: *They loaded the car while I checked out at the desk.* **2** to inspect or examine to see if in proper order, condition, etc.: *The mechanic checked out the plane before takeoff.* **3** to prove true or true: *check out a fact or statement.* **4** to borrow from a library: *check out several books about camping.* **5** to add up the prices of purchases in a supermarket or discount store and accept payment for them.

check up on, to examine or compare to prove true or correct: *If you are not sure, you ought to check up on the facts.*

in check, held back; controlled: *He kept his temper in check.*

> **WORD STORY** **Check** comes from a Persian word meaning "king." **Checkers** and **chess** come from the same word. The oldest meaning of **check** is definition 20a. All other meanings developed from that one.

check·book (chek′bùk′), *n.* book of blank checks from a bank.

checked (chekt), *adj.* having a pattern of squares: *a checked shirt.*

check·er[1] (chek′ər), **1** *v.* to mark in a pattern of squares of different colors. **2** *n.* pattern made of such squares. **3** *n.* one of these squares. **4** *n.* one of the flat, round pieces used in the game of checkers. [See Word Story at **check.**]

check·er[2] (chek′ər), *n.* cashier in a self-service store or market.

check·er·board (chek′ər bôrd′), *n.* board marked in a pattern of 64 squares of two alternating colors, used in playing checkers or chess; chessboard.

check·ered (chek′ərd), *adj.* **1** marked in a pattern of squares of different colors: *a checkered tablecloth.* **2** often changing; varied; irregular: *a checkered career.*

check·ers (chek′ərz), *n.* game played by two people, each with 12 round, flat pieces to move on a checkerboard. The object of the game is to capture all the opponent's pieces or to prevent them from being able to move. [See Word Story at **check.**]

checking account, bank account from which checks may be written, directing the bank to pay money to the person named.

check·list (chek′list′), *n.* list of names, titles, jobs, etc., arranged to form a ready means of reference, comparison, or checking: *The pilot went over the flight checklist before takeoff.*

check·mate (chek′māt′), **1** in chess: **a** *v.* to put an opponent's king in check from which there is no escape, and so win the game. **b** *n.* a move that ends the game by putting the opponent's king in check so that there is no way to escape. **2** *v.* to defeat completely. **3** *n.* a complete defeat. ❑ *v.* **check·mat·ed, check·mat·ing.**

check·out (chek′out′), *n.* **1** act of checking out: *Careful checkouts were made on the new equipment. The time for checkout at the motel was 10 a.m.* **2** a place to pay for purchases, such as at a supermarket.

checkout counter, a counter in a store where a cashier collects payment for purchases.

check·point (chek′point′), *n.* place of inspection on a road, at a border, etc.

check·room (chek′rüm′), *n.* place where coats, hats, baggage, etc., can be left for safekeeping until called for later.

check·up (chek′up′), *n.* **1** a careful inspection or examination. **2** a thorough physical examination: *a medical checkup.*

Ched·dar or **ched·dar** (ched′ər), *n.* kind of hard, white or yellow cheese.

chee·cha·ko (chē chä′ko), *n.* (especially in Canada) a newcomer or tenderfoot. ❑ *n., pl.* **chee·cha·kos.**

cheek (chēk), *n.* **1** side of the face below either eye. **2** INFORMAL. rude talk or behavior; impudence: *They had the cheek to barge into line ahead of everyone.*

cheek·bone (chēk′bōn′), *n.* bone just below either eye.

cheek·y (chē′kē), *adj.* rude; impudent. ❑ *adj.* **cheek·i·er, cheek·i·est.** —**cheek′i·ly**, *adv.* —**cheek′i·ness**, *n.*

cheep (chēp), **1** *v.* to make a short, sharp sound such as a young bird makes; chirp; peep. **2** *n.* a young bird's cry. ■ Another word that sounds like this is **cheap.** —**cheep′er**, *n.*

cheer (chir), **1** *n.* a shout of encouragement, approval, praise, etc.: *Give three cheers for the winners.* **2** *v.* to shout encouragement or praise to: *Everyone cheered our team. We all cheered loudly.* **3** *n.* joy or gladness; comfort: *The warmth of the fire and a good meal brought cheer to our hearts again.* **4** *v.* to give joy to; make glad; comfort: *It cheered our sick friend to have us visit him.* **5** *n.* state of mind; condition of feeling: *We encouraged him to be of good cheer.* —**cheer′er**, *n.* —**cheer′ing·ly**, *adv.*

cheer up, to brighten up; be or make glad; raise someone's spirits: *The sick girl said that our visit cheered her up. Cheer up, perhaps we'll win the next game.*

> **WORD STORY** **Cheer** comes from a Greek word meaning "a head." Its first meaning in English was "face" or "expression." **Good cheer** meant a happy face, then the good mood that the face showed. Later people used **cheer** by itself to mean "joy."

cheer·ful (chir′fəl), *adj.* **1** full of cheer; joyful; glad: *She is a smiling, cheerful girl.* ■ See Synonym Study at **happy. 2** filling with cheer; pleasant; bright: *This is a cheerful, sunny room.* **3** willing: *I appreciate a cheerful helper.* —**cheer′ful·ly**, *adv.* —**cheer′ful·ness**, *n.*

cheer·lead·er (chir′lē′dər), *n.* person who leads a group in organized cheering, especially at school or athletic events.

a	hat	ė	term	ô	order	ch	child		⟨ a in about
ā	age	i	it	oi	oil	ng	long		e in taken
ä	far	ī	ice	ou	out	sh	she	ə	i in pencil
â	care	o	hot	u	cup	th	thin		o in lemon
e	let	ō	open	ù	put	ŦH	then		⟨ u in circus
ē	equal	ò	saw	ü	rule	zh	measure		

cheer·less (chir′lis), *adj.* without joy or comfort; gloomy; dreary. —**cheer′less·ly**, *adv.* —**cheer′less·ness**, *n.*

cheer·y (chir′ē), *adj.* cheerful; pleasant; bright: *a cheery smile.* ❏ *adj.* **cheer·i·er, cheer·i·est.** —**cheer′i·ly**, *adv.* —**cheer′i·ness**, *n.*

cheese (chēz), *n.* a solid food made from the curds of milk. Most cheeses are salted, colored, and pressed or molded into a shape. —**cheese′like**, *adj.*

cheese·burg·er (chēz′bėr′gər), *n.* a hamburger sandwich with a slice of melted cheese on top of the meat.

cheese·cake (chēz′kāk′), *n.* kind of cake or pie made of cottage cheese or cream cheese, cream, eggs, sugar, and flavoring.

cheese·cloth (chēz′klôth′), *n.* a thin, loosely woven cotton cloth, first used for wrapping cheese. ❏ *n., pl.* **cheese·cloths** (chēz′klôṫHz′ *or* chēz′klôths′).

chees·y (chē′zē), *adj.* **1** of or like cheese. **2** INFORMAL. of low quality; inferior. ❏ *adj.* **chees·i·er, chees·i·est.** —**chees′i·ly**, *adv.* —**chees′i·ness**, *n.*

chee·tah (chē′tə), *n.* a large, fierce cat something like a leopard, found mainly in Africa. Cheetahs run very fast.

chef (shef), *n.* **1** a head cook, especially in a restaurant. **2** any cook.

Che·khov (chek′ôf), *n.* **An·ton** (an′ton), 1860-1904, Russian writer of short stories and plays.

che·la (kē′lə), *n.* claw of a lobster, crab, scorpion, etc. ❏ *n., pl.* **che·lae** (kē′lē).

chem., **1** chemical. **2** chemist. **3** chemistry.

chem·i·cal (kem′ə kəl), **1** *adj.* of, about, or in chemistry: *Chemical research has made possible many new products.* **2** *n.*

chef (def. 1)

any substance obtained by or used in a chemical process. Sulfuric acid, sodium bicarbonate, and borax are chemicals. **3** *adj.* working, operated, or done by using chemicals: *a chemical fire extinguisher.* —**chem′i·cal·ly**, *adv.*

chemical change, a change in which the nature of a substance is made different from what it was. In a chemical change, atoms are rearranged into new molecules. Burning is a process of chemical change in which the oxygen of the air unites with wood or coal to give ashes, light, and heat.

chemical element, element (def. 1).

chemical engineering, science or profession of using chemistry for industrial purposes.

chemical warfare, the use of poison gas or other chemicals as weapons.

che·mise (shə mēz′), *n.* **1** a loose, shirtlike undergarment worn by women and girls. **2** a loosely fitting dress without a belt.

chem·ist (kem′ist), *n.* **1** an expert in chemistry. **2** BRITISH. druggist.

chem·is·try (kem′ə strē), *n.* **1** science that deals with the characteristics of elements, the changes that take place when they combine to form substances, and the laws of their behavior under various conditions. **2** the application of this science to a certain subject: *the chemistry of foods.*

che·mo·ther·a·py (kē′mō ther′ə pē), *n.* the treatment of disease by chemicals that kill diseased cells or germs. Chemotherapy is often used against cancer.

che·nille (shə nēl′), *n.* **1** a velvety cord, used in embroidery, fringe, etc. **2** fabric woven from this cord, used for rugs, bedspreads, etc.

Che·ops (kē′ops), *n.* 2600? B.C., king of Egypt who built the largest of the Pyramids.

cheque (chek), *n.* BRITISH. check (def. 14).

cher·ish (cher′ish), *v.* **1** to care for tenderly; treat with affection; aid or protect: *Parents cherish their children.* **2** to keep in mind; cling to: *We all cherished the hope of their safe return from the dangerous journey.* —**cher′ish·a·ble**, *adj.*

Cher·no·byl (chėr nō′bəl), *n.* a city in Ukraine north of Kiev. In 1986, a nuclear reactor there exploded and burned, releasing large amounts of radioactive material.

Cher·o·kee (cher′ə kē′), *n.* member of a tribe of American Indians formerly living in the southern Appalachians, now living in Oklahoma and western North Carolina. ❏ *n., pl.* **Cher·o·kee** or **Cher·o·kees.**

cher·ry (cher′ē), **1** *n.* any of several kinds of small, round fruit with a stone or pit in it. Cherries are eaten raw or cooked. **2** *n.* any of the trees that these fruits grow on. **3** *n.* the wood of these trees. **4** *n.* a bright red. **5** *adj.* bright red. ❏ *n., pl.* **cher·ries.**

WORD STORY **Cherry** comes from a French word meaning "cherry." **Cerise** comes from the same word. Originally, since the English name for the fruit, *cherise*, ended in the -s sound, people thought that -s must mean more than one, and left it off. Sometimes a word changes just by mistake, like this one.

cherry tomato, a small red or yellow tomato similar to a cherry in size and shape.

cher·ub (cher′əb), *n.* **1** angel. **2** picture or statue of a child with wings, or of a child's head with wings. **3** a beautiful, innocent, or good child. ❏ *n., pl.* **cher·u·bim** for 1,2, **cher·ubs** for 3. —**che·ru·bic** (chə rü′bik), *adj.* —**che·ru′bi·cal·ly**, *adv.*

cher·u·bim (cher′ə bim), **1** *n.pl.* a plural of **cherub** (defs. 1 and 2). **2** *n.sing.* (formerly) cherub.

Ches·a·peake Bay (ches′ə pēk′), bay of the Atlantic, in Maryland and Virginia.

Chesh·ire cat (chesh′ər), the grinning cat in *Alice in Wonderland.* It faded away until finally only its grin was left.

Ches·nutt (ches′nət), *n.* **Charles Wad·dell** (wä del′), 1858-1932, American writer. He was the first well-known African American novelist.

chess (ches), *n.* game played by two people, each with 16 pieces to move on a checkerboard. The object of the game is to checkmate the other's king. [See Word Story at **check.**]

chess·board (ches′bôrd′), *n.* checkerboard.

chess·man (ches′man′), *n.* one of the pieces used in playing chess. ❏ *n., pl.* **chess·men.**

chest (chest), *n.* **1** front part of the body between the neck and the stomach. **2** a large box with a lid, used for holding things: *a linen chest, a medicine chest, a tool chest.* **3** piece of furniture with drawers. **4** place where money is kept; treasury.

ches·ter·field (ches′tər fēld′), *n.* **1** a single-breasted overcoat with the buttons hidden and a velvet collar. **2** (in Canada) a couch.

chest·nut (ches′nut), **1** *n.* any of several large trees that bear nuts in prickly burs. Chestnuts are related to beeches. **2** *n.* the sweet nut of such trees. **3** *n.* the wood of these trees. **4** *n.* a reddish brown. **5** *adj.* reddish brown. **6** *n.* a reddish brown horse.

chev·i·ot (shev′ē ət), *n.* **1** a rough, woolen cloth. **2** a cotton cloth like it.

chev·ron (shev′rən), *n.* a cloth design shaped like ∧ or ∨, worn on the sleeve by noncommissioned officers, police officers, and the like, to show rank or length of service.

chew (chü), **1** *v.* to crush or grind with the teeth: *We chew food before swallowing it.* **2** *n.* act of chewing: *The puppy gave the rag a good chew.* **3** *n.* thing chewed; piece for chewing. —**chew′a·ble**, *adj.* —**chew′er**, *n.*

chew out, INFORMAL. to criticize severely; scold: *The sergeant chewed out the new recruit for not keeping his equipment clean.*

chewing gum, gum for chewing. It is usually chicle that has been sweetened and flavored.

chewing tobacco, tobacco prepared to be chewed rather than smoked.

chew·y (chü′ē), *adj.* requiring much chewing: *chewy caramels.* ❏ *adj.* **chew·i·er, chew·i·est.** —**chew′i·ness**, *n.*

Chey·enne (shī an′ *or* shī en′ *for 1,2;* shī en′ *for 3*), *n.* **1** capital of Wyoming, in the SE part. **2** river flowing from E Wyoming into the Missouri River in South Dakota. **3** member of a tribe of American Indians of the Great Plains, now living in Montana and Oklahoma. ❏ *n., pl.* **Chey·enne** or **Chey·ennes** for 3.

Chiang Kai-shek (chang′ kī′shek′), 1887-1975, Chinese general and political leader. He was the president of Nationalist China from 1948 to 1975.

Chi·a·pas (chē ä′päs), *n.* a state in E Mexico.

chic (shēk), **1** *adj.* up-to-date in fashion; stylish: *a chic new suit.* **2** *n.* style: *She is famous for her chic.* ■ Another word that can sound like this is **sheik**.

Chi·ca·go (shə kȯ′gō *or* shə kä′gō), *n.* port in NE Illinois, on Lake Michigan. Chicago is the third largest city in the United States. —**Chi·ca′go·an**, *n.*

Chicago

Chi·ca·na (chi kä′nä), *n.* a female American of Mexican descent. ❑ *n., pl.* **Chi·ca·nas.** ■ See Usage Note at **Chicano.**

chi·can·er·y (shi kā′nər ē), *n.* clever trickery; unfair practice: *He used chicanery to outwit his partner and take over the business.* ❑ *n., pl.* **chi·can·er·ies.**

Chi·ca·no (chi kä′nō), *n.* an American of Mexican descent; Mexican American. ❑ *n., pl.* **Chi·ca·nos.**

USAGE NOTE Some Americans of Mexican descent prefer the words **Chicano** and **Chicana** to other ways of referring to them. Others with the same background prefer that these words not be used about them. If you are writing or speaking about people or to people with this background, it is a good idea to think about the words used in your sources and by your audience. If you have doubts, ask!

chick (chik), *n.* **1** a young chicken. **2** a young bird.

chick·a·dee (chik′ə dē′), *n.* any of several small North American birds with black, white, and gray feathers, and dark heads. Their calls sound something like their name. ❑ *n., pl.* **chick·a·dees.**

Chick·a·saw (chik′ə sȯ), *n.* member of a tribe of American Indians formerly living in the southeast United States and now living in western Oklahoma. ❑ *n., pl.* **Chick·a·saw** or **Chick·a·saws.**

chick·en (chik′ən), **1** *n.* a common domestic bird raised for food; hen or rooster. **2** *n.* flesh of a chicken used for food: *fried chicken.* **3** *adj.* INFORMAL. afraid of risk; cowardly. [See Word Story at **meat.**]
chicken out, INFORMAL. to fail to do something because of fear.

chick·en·heart·ed (chik′ən här′tid), *adj.* timid; cowardly. —**chick′en·heart′ed·ness**, *n.*

chicken pox, a mild, contagious disease of children, accompanied by a rash on the skin; varicella.

chicken wire, lightweight wire fencing, often used to enclose chickens or to surround gardens.

chick·pea (chik′pē′), *n.* the seed of a plant related to the pea, used as a vegetable; garbanzo. ❑ *n., pl.* **chick·peas.**

chick·weed (chik′wēd′), *n.* a common weed with small white flowers. The leaves and seeds are eaten by birds.

chic·le (chik′əl), *n.* a tasteless, gummy substance used in making chewing gum. It is the dried milky juice of a tree of tropical America.

chic·o·ry (chik′ər ē), *n.* **1** plant with bright blue flowers and leaves that are used for salad. **2** its root, roasted and used as a substitute for coffee or for mixing with coffee.

chide (chīd), *v.* to find fault with; blame; scold: *My uncle chided me for playing in his flower garden.* ❑ *v.* **chid·ed** or **chid** (chid), **chid·ing.** —**chid′er**, *n.* —**chid′ing·ly**, *adv.*

chief (chēf), **1** *n.* head of a group; person highest in rank or authority; leader: *a police chief.* **2** *adj.* at the head; in authority; leading: *the chief engineer of a building project.* **3** *adj.* most important; main: *The chief thing on my mind was dinner.*
in chief, at the head; of the highest rank or authority: *editor in chief of a book.*

WORD FAMILY **Chief** and the words below are related. They all come from a Latin word meaning "head."

achieve	capitalize	chapter	handkerchief
biceps	capitol	chef	mischief
caddie	capitulate	corporal²	precipitation
cadet	captain	decapitate	recapitulate
capital	cattle		

chief executive, 1 head of the executive branch of a government. **2 Chief Executive,** the President of the United States or the governor of a state.

chief justice, 1 judge who acts as chairman of a group of judges in a court. **2 Chief Justice,** the presiding judge of the U.S. Supreme Court.

chief·ly (chēf′lē), *adv.* **1** for the most part; mainly; mostly: *This juice is made up chiefly of tomatoes.* **2** first of all; especially: *We visited Washington chiefly to see the Capitol and the White House.*

Chief of Staff, the senior officer of the Army or Air Force of the United States.

chief·tain (chēf′tən), *n.* **1** chief of a clan or tribe: *a Highland chieftain.* **2** head of a group; leader.

chif·fon (shi fon′), **1** *n.* a very thin silk or rayon cloth, used for dresses. **2** *adj.* whipped light and fluffy: *lemon chiffon pie.*

chif·fo·nier (shif′ə nir′), *n.* a high chest of drawers, often having a mirror.

chig·ger (chig′ər), *n.* larva of certain mites. Chiggers stick to the skin and suck blood, causing severe itching.

chi·gnon (shē′nyon), *n.* knot or roll of hair worn at the back of the head by women.

chi·hua·hua (chi wä′wä), *n.* Chihuahua (def. 1). ❑ *n., pl.* **chi·hua·huas.**

Chi·hua·hua (chi wä′wä), *n.* **1** a very small dog, short-haired or long-haired, of an ancient Mexican breed. **2** a state in N Mexico. ❑ *n., pl.* **Chi·hua·huas** for 1.

chil·blain (chil′blān′), *n.* Usually, **chilblains,** *pl.* an itching sore or redness on the hands or feet caused chiefly by exposure to cold.

child (chīld), *n.* **1** a young boy or girl: *games for children.* **2** son or daughter: *Parents love their children.* **3** baby; infant. **4** descendant; offspring: *the child of four generations of musicians.* ❑ *n., pl.* **chil·dren.** —**child′less**, *adj.*
with child, pregnant.

Chihuahua (def. 1)—about 5 in (13 cm) high at the shoulder

child abuse, physical or emotional violence against a child by an adult, especially a parent.

child·birth (chīld′bėrth′), *n.* act of giving birth to a child.

child·hood (chīld′hùd′), *n.* **1** condition of being a child. **2** time during which a person is a child.

child·ish (chīl′dish), *adj.* **1** of a child. **2** like a child. **3** not suitable for a grown person; weak; silly: *Crying for things you can't have is childish.* —**child′ish·ly**, *adv.* —**child′ish·ness**, *n.*

child·like (chīld′līk′), *adj.* like a child; innocent; frank; simple.

child·proof (chīld′prüf′), *adj.* not able to be opened, used, or damaged by a child because of its design: *childproof containers.*

a	hat	ė	term	ȯ	order	ch	child		a in about
ā	age	i	it	oi	oil	ng	long		e in taken
ä	far	ī	ice	ou	out	sh	she	ə	i in pencil
â	care	o	hot	u	cup	th	thin		o in lemon
e	let	ō	open	ù	put	ŦH	then		u in circus
ē	equal	ȯ	saw	ü	rule	zh	measure		

chil·dren (chil′drən), *n.* plural of **child**.

child's play, something very easy to do: *That puzzle was child's play.*

chil·e (chil′ē), *n.* chili. ■ Another word that sounds like this is **chilly**.

Chil·e (chil′ē), *n.* country in SW South America, on the Pacific coast. *Capital:* Santiago. [Chile probably comes from a word in the language of American Indians living there, meaning "end of the land."] **—Chil′e·an,** *adj., n.*

chil·i (chil′ē), *n.* **1** a hot-tasting pod of a red pepper, used for seasoning. **2** a highly seasoned Mexican dish of chopped meat cooked with red peppers and, usually, kidney beans. ❑ *n., pl.* **chil·ies** or **chil·is** for 1, **chil·is** for 2. Also, **chile** or **chilli**. ■ Another word that sounds like this is **chilly**.

chili con car·ne (chil′ē kon kär′nē), a highly seasoned Mexican dish of chopped meat cooked with red peppers and, usually, kidney beans.

chili dog, a hot dog topped with chili con carne and served on a roll or bun.

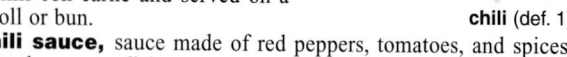
chili (def. 1)

chili sauce, sauce made of red peppers, tomatoes, and spices, used on meat, fish, etc.

chill (chil), **1** *n.* unpleasant coldness: *feel a sudden chill. There was a chill in the air.* **2** *adj.* unpleasantly cold: *A chill wind blew across the lake.* **3** *v.* to make or become cold: *The icy wind chilled us to the bone. Her blood chilled as she read the horror story.* **4** *n.* a sudden coldness of the body with shivering: *I caught a chill yesterday and today I have a fever.* **5** *adj.* cold in manner; unfriendly: *a chill greeting.* **6** *n.* a loss of spirit or joy; discouraging feeling: *The news of the bus accident sent a chill through the school.* **7** *v.* to depress; discourage: *hopes chilled by failure.* **—chill′er,** *n.* **—chill′ness,** *n.*

chill out, INFORMAL. to relax; reduce your stress: *I told him to stop worrying and chill out.*

chill factor, wind chill or wind chill factor.

chil·li (chil′ē), *n.* chili. ❑ *n., pl.* **chil·lies.** ■ Another word that sounds like this is **chilly**.

chill·ing (chil′ing), *adj.* causing a chill: *a chilling wind.* **—chill′ing·ly,** *adv.*

chill·y (chil′ē), *adj.* **1** unpleasantly cool; rather cold: *It is a rainy, chilly day. You'll feel chilly if you don't wear a coat.* ■ See Synonym Study at **cold**. **2** cold in manner; unfriendly: *We gave a chilly reception to the people who came to our party uninvited.* ❑ *adj.* **chill·i·er, chill·i·est.** ■ Other words that sound like this are **chile, chili,** and **chilli**. **—chill′i·ness,** *n.*

chime (chīm), **1** *n.* set of bells tuned to a musical scale and played by hammers or simple machinery. **2** *n.* the musical sound made by a set of tuned bells. **3** *v.* to ring out musically: *The bells of the town clock chime on the hour.* **4** *v.* to tell by ringing out: *The clock chimed midnight.* ❑ *v.* **chimed, chim·ing. —chim′er,** *n.*

chime in, 1 be in harmony; agree: *Her ideas chimed in perfectly with mine.* **2** to break into a conversation, especially to express your agreement: *I said I would like to go to the circus and my brother chimed in.*

WORD STORY **Chime** comes from a Greek word meaning "hollow part." **Cymbal** comes from the same word. Hollow things like bells or bowls make a ringing noise if they are tapped. Solid things usually don't ring so well.

chi·mer·a (kə mir′ə *or* kī mir′ə), *n.* **1** Also, **Chimera**, (in Greek legends) a monster with a lion's head, a goat's body, and a serpent's tail, supposed to breathe out fire. **2** an absurd or impossible idea; wild fancy: *The hope of changing lead to gold was a chimera.* ❑ *n., pl.* **chi·mer·as.**

chi·mer·i·cal (kə mer′ə kəl), *adj.* **1** unreal; imaginary. **2** wildly fanciful; absurd; impossible: *chimerical schemes for getting rich quick.* **—chi·mer′i·cal·ly,** *adv.*

chim·i·chan·ga (chim′ē chäng′gə), *n.* a tortilla rolled around a filling, such as chopped meat, cheese, or chicken, then fried and served with guacamole, salsa, etc. ❑ *n., pl.* **chim·i·chan·gas.**

chim·ney (chim′nē), *n.* **1** an upright structure of brick or stone, connected with a fireplace, furnace, etc., to make a draft and carry away smoke through the roof: *We could see the town's chimneys from afar.* **2** a glass tube placed around the flame of a lamp. ❑ *n., pl.* **chim·neys.**

chimney sweep, person whose work is cleaning out chimneys.

chimney swift, a swift that usually builds its nests in chimneys.

chimp (chimp), *n.* INFORMAL. chimpanzee.

chim·pan·zee (chim′pan zē′ *or* chim pan′zē), *n.* a highly intelligent ape of Africa, smaller than a gorilla. ❑ *n., pl.* **chim·pan·zees.**

chin (chin), **1** *n.* the front of the lower jaw below the mouth. **2** *v.* **chin yourself,** to hang by the hands from an overhead bar and pull up until your chin reaches the bar. ❑ *v.* **chinned, chin·ning.**

Chin., Chinese.

chi·na (chī′nə), *n.* **1** a fine, white pottery baked by a special process, first used in China; porcelain. Colored designs can be baked into china. **2** dishes, vases, or other things made of china. **3** pottery dishes of any kind.

Chi·na (chī′nə), *n.* **1 People's Republic of,** large country in E Asia. *Capital:* Beijing (Peking). **2** country consisting of the island of Taiwan; Nationalist China. *Capital:* Taipei. [China may come from the name of the family who were the first Chinese emperors.]

China Sea, part of the Pacific Ocean, east and southeast of Asia. It is divided into the South China Sea and the East China Sea by the island of Taiwan.

Chi·na·town (chī′nə toun′), *n.* section of a city where Chinese people live.

chi·na·ware (chī′nə wâr′), *n.* china.

chinch bug (chinch), a small, black and white bug that does much damage to grain in dry weather.

chin·chil·la (chin chil′ə), *n.* **1** any of several South American rodents that look something like a squirrel. **2** their very valuable soft, bluish gray fur. **3** a thick woolen fabric woven in small, closely set tufts, used for overcoats. ❑ *n., pl.* **chin·chil·las.**

Chi·nese (chī nēz′), **1** *adj.* of China, its people, or their language. **2** *n.* person born or living in China. **3** *n.* person of Chinese descent. **4** *n.* language of China. ❑ *n., pl.* **Chi·nese** for 2,3.

WORD SOURCE **Chinese** has given few words to the English language, probably because contact between people using these two languages has been limited until recently. The words below are from Chinese.

chop suey	ginseng	kumquat	tea
chow[1]	kaolin	kung fu	tycoon
chow[2]	ketchup	sampan	typhoon
chow mein	kowtow	soy	wok

Chinese checkers, game for two to six players using marbles on a star-shaped board with small holes in which the marbles rest. The object is to move all your marbles by steps or jumps to the opposite side of the board.

Chinese lantern, lantern of thin colored paper that can be folded up like an accordion.

chink[1] (chingk), **1** *n.* a narrow opening; crack: *Wind and snow came through the chinks between the logs of the cabin.* **2** *v.* to fill up the chinks in: *He chinked the cracks in the walls with mud.*

chink[2] (chingk), **1** *n.* a short, sharp, ringing sound like coins or drinking glasses hitting together. **2** *v.* to make or cause to make such a sound.

chi·no (chē′nō), *n.* **1** a strong cotton fabric, used especially in making trousers. **2 chinos,** *pl.* trousers made of this fabric.

chi·nook (shə nůk′ *or* chə nůk′), *n.* **1** a warm, moist wind blowing from the sea to the land in winter and spring in the northwestern United States. **2** a warm, dry wind that comes down the eastern slope of the Rocky Mountains.

Chi·nook (shə nůk′ *or* chə nůk′), *n.* member of a group of American Indian tribes that lived along the Columbia River in Washington. ❑ *n., pl.* **Chi·nook** or **Chi·nooks.**

chinook salmon, a very large, commercially important Pacific salmon.

chintz (chints), *n.* a cotton cloth printed in patterns of various colors and often glazed.

chintz·y (chint′sē), *adj.* **1** of or like chintz. **2** INFORMAL. cheap and showy. ❑ *adj.* **chintz·i·er, chintz·i·est.**

chin-up (chin′up′), *n.* the exercise of chinning yourself.

chip (chip), **1** *n.* a small, thin piece cut or broken off: *They used chips of wood to light a fire.* **2** *n.* place where a small, thin piece has been cut or broken off: *This plate has a chip on the edge.* **3** *v.* to cut or break off in small, thin pieces: *She chipped off the old paint. These cups chip if they are not handled carefully.* **4** *v.* to shape by cutting at the surface or edge: *chipped flint arrowheads.* **5** *n.* a small, thin piece of food or candy. Potato chips are fried slices of potatoes. **6** *n.* a round, flat piece used for counting or to represent money in games: *poker chips.* **7** *n.* a small piece of a semiconductor, usually silicon, that holds an integrated circuit; microchip. ❑ *v.* **chipped, chip·ping.**

chin-up

chip in, to join with others in giving money or help: *We all chipped in to buy our teacher a gift.*

chip off the old block, child who is much like his or her parents.

have a chip on your shoulder, INFORMAL. be ready to quarrel or fight.

chip·munk (chip′mungk), *n.* any of several small, striped, North American rodents related to the squirrel; ground squirrel. Chipmunks live in burrows in the ground.

WORD STORY The Algonquian name for this animal was spelled several ways by European settlers, including *chitamon.* This became *chitmunk,* and later on *chipmunk.* That's what it sounded like, so that's how it came to be spelled.

chipped beef, dried beef, smoked and cut in very thin slices.

chip·per (chip′ər), *adj.* lively and cheerful.

Chip·pe·wa (chip′ə wä *or* chip′ə wā), *n.* Ojibwa. ❑ *n., pl.* **Chip·pe·wa** or **Chip·pe·was.** [See Word Story at **Ojibwa.**]

Chi·rac (shə räk′), *n.* **Jacques** (zhäk), born 1932, president of France since 1995.

chi·rop·o·dist (kə rop′ə dist), *n.* podiatrist.

chi·rop·o·dy (kə rop′ə dē *or* ki rop′ə dē), *n.* podiatry.

chi·ro·prac·tor (kī′rə prak′tər), *n.* person who treats diseases by manipulating parts of the body, especially the spine.

chirp (chėrp), **1** *n.* a short, sharp sound made by some small birds and insects: *the chirp of a sparrow.* **2** *v.* to make a chirp: *The crickets chirped outside the house.*

chir·rup (chir′əp *or* chėr′əp), **1** *v.* to chirp again and again: *She chirruped to her horse to make it go faster.* **2** *n.* the sound of chirruping.

chis·el (chiz′əl), **1** *n.* a cutting tool with a sharp edge at the end of a strong blade, used to cut or shape wood, stone, or metal. **2** *v.* to cut or shape with a chisel: *The sculptor was at work chiseling a statue.* **3** *v.* INFORMAL. to cheat or swindle. ❑ *v.* **chis·eled, chis·el·ing** or **chis·elled, chis·el·ling.** —**chis′el·er** or **chis′el·ler,** *n.* —**chis′-el·like′,** *adj.*

Chis·holm (chiz′əm), *n.* **Shir·ley** (shėr′lē), born 1924, American political leader. She was the first African American woman to serve in the U.S. Congress, from 1969 to 1983.

Chis·holm Trail (chiz′əm), famous western cattle trail from San Antonio, Texas, to Abilene, Kansas.

WORD STORY **Chisholm Trail** is named for Jesse Chisholm, a trader of Cherokee and English ancestry, who created this route when he drove his wagon along it in 1866. Cowboys gave it his name when they began using it.

chit·chat (chit′chat′), **1** *n.* friendly, informal talk; chat. **2** *v.* to talk in a friendly, informal way. **3** *n.* idle talk; gossip. ❑ *v.* **chit·chat·ted, chit·chat·ting.**

chi·tin (kit′n), *n.* a horny substance forming the hard outer covering of beetles, lobsters, crabs, and the like.

chi·tin·ous (kit′n əs), *adj.* of or like chitin.

chit·lings or **chit·lins** (chit′linz), *n.pl.* chitterlings.

chit·ter·lings (chit′linz), *n.pl.* parts of the small intestines of pigs, cooked as food.

chiv·al·rous (shiv′əl rəs), *adj.* **1** having the qualities of an ideal knight; brave, courteous, helpful, and honorable. **2** following the rules and customs of knights in the Middle Ages. —**chiv′al·rous·ly,** *adv.* —**chiv′al·rous·ness,** *n.*

chiv·al·ry (shiv′əl rē), *n.* **1** the qualities of an ideal knight in the Middle Ages; bravery, honor, courtesy, protection of the weak, respect for women, and fairness to enemies. **2** rules and customs of knights in the Middle Ages. **3** knights as a group.

WORD STORY Chivalry, cavalry, cavalier, and **caballero** all come from a Latin word meaning "horse." In old times, only knights rode horses. Common people went on foot.

chive (chīv), *n.* **1** plant related to the onion, having a very small bulb. **2 chives,** *pl.* its long, slender leaves, used as seasoning.

chla·myd·i·a (klə mid′ē ə), *n.* a sexually transmitted disease, caused by a bacterialike living thing. Chlamydia can cause sterility if it is not treated.

chlo·ride (klôr′īd), *n.* compound of chlorine with another element or radical. Sodium chloride is a compound of sodium and chlorine.

chlo·rin·ate (klôr′ə nāt), *v.* to combine or treat with chlorine, especially to disinfect: *chlorinate water in a swimming pool.* ❑ *v.* **chlo·rin·at·ed, chlo·rin·at·ing.** —**chlo′ri·na′tion,** *n.*

chlo·rine (klôr′ēn′), *n.* a greenish yellow, bad-smelling, poisonous gas. It is a chemical element which occurs mainly in combination with sodium as common salt. Chlorine is very irritating to the nose, throat, and lungs. It is used in bleaching and disinfecting, and in making plastics, explosives, and dyes. *Symbol:* Cl

chlo·ro·fluor·o·car·bon (klôr′ə flür′ə kär′bən), *n.* a kind of gas once used widely as the spray in spray cans and in a variety of other products. It is thought that use of these gases weakens the ozone layer.

chlo·ro·form (klôr′ə fôrm), **1** *n.* a colorless liquid with a sharp, sweetish smell and taste. Once a common anesthetic, it is now used to dissolve rubber, resin, wax, and many other substances. **2** *v.* to make unconscious or kill with chloroform.

chlo·ro·phyll (klôr′ə fil), *n.* the green coloring matter of plant cells. In the presence of light it makes carbohydrates, such as starch and sugar, from carbon dioxide and water.

chlo·ro·plast (klôr′ə plast), *n.* a tiny object that contains chlorophyll, found in the cells of green plants.

chock (chok), **1** *n.* block or wedge put under a barrel or wheel to keep it from rolling or under a boat to keep it in place. **2** *v.* to provide or fasten with chocks: *chock a boat on a ship's deck.*

chock-full (chok′fúl′), *adj.* as full as can be; stuffed full: *The closet was chock-full of clothing and shoes.*

choc·o·late (chôk′lit *or* chôk′ə lit), **1** *n.* substance made by roasting and grinding cacao beans. It has a strong, rich flavor and much value as food. **2** *n.* drink made of chocolate with hot milk or water and sugar. **3** *n.* candy made of chocolate. **4** *adj.* made of or flavored with chocolate: *chocolate cake.* **5** *n.* a dark brown. **6** *adj.* dark brown. [See Word Story at **cocoa.**]

Choc·taw (chok′tò), *n.* member of a tribe of American Indians formerly living in the southeast United States, now living mostly in Oklahoma. ❑ *n., pl.* **Choc·taw** or **Choc·taws.**

a	hat	ė	term	ô	order	ch	child			a in about
ā	age	i	it	oi	oil	ng	long			e in taken
ä	far	ī	ice	ou	out	sh	she	ə	{	i in pencil
â	care	o	hot	u	cup	th	thin			o in lemon
e	let	ō	open	ù	put	ŦH	then			u in circus
ē	equal	ȯ	saw	ü	rule	zh	measure			

China and the Silk Road

Silk was discovered in China about 4500 years ago. The Chinese guarded their discovery as a secret, on penalty of death. For 3000 years, only they knew how to make silk; whoever wanted this beautiful fabric had to buy theirs. The demand was so great, the profits so high, that traders risked fortunes traveling on the 5000 miles (8000 km) of the Silk Road between East and West. By this trade, Europe was brought into regular contact with the great civilizations of Asia.

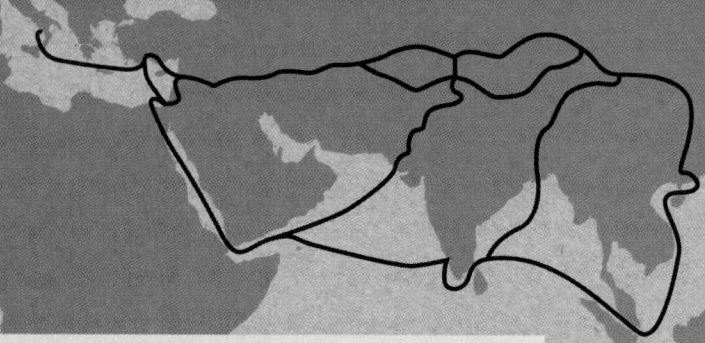

The Road Ahead
Caravans of merchants and soldiers, camels and donkeys and horses, crossed the mountains of Afghanistan and the vast Gobi desert. Food and water were scarce, bandits plentiful.

Fruits and Vegetables
A merchant sells her wares at a market in India. The eggplants, onions, and ginger roots seen here were all first grown in Asia. They came to Europe along the Silk Road. So did oranges, peaches, and pears. Grapes, cucumbers, figs, and walnuts went the other way.

Settlements Ruins in western China mark the site of an inn where caravans stopped for rest and supplies. Travelers meeting in such inns exchanged more than trade goods. Ideas, inventions, and religions passed through the ancient world along this route.

In Exchange
Europe and western Asia had goods that the Chinese valued, especially the beautiful glass that was their people's secret. Incense, purple dye, and woolen cloth also loaded the eastbound pack animals. Amber from Northern Europe reached the Silk Road at the Mediterranean Sea.

choice (chois), **1** *n.* act of choosing; selection: *She was careful in her choice of friends.* **2** *n.* power or chance to choose: *I have my choice between a radio and a camera for my birthday.* **3** *n.* person or thing chosen: *This camera is my choice.* **4** *n.* thing among several things to be chosen; alternative: *Their action left no choice but to adjourn the meeting.* **5** *n.* quantity and variety to choose from: *We found a wide choice of vegetables in the market.* **6** *adj.* of fine quality; excellent; superior: *The choicest fruit had the highest price.* **7** *adj.* indicating a U.S. government grade of meat between prime and good. ❑ *adj.* **choic·er, choic·est.** —**choice′ly,** *adv.* —**choice′ness,** *n.*

choir (kwīr), *n.* **1** group of singers who sing together, often in a church service. **2** part of a church set apart for such a group. **3** any group of singers; chorus.

choir·boy (kwīr′boi′), *n.* boy who sings in a choir; chorister.

choke (chōk), **1** *v.* to stop the breath of an animal or person by squeezing or blocking up the throat; strangle: *She hugged me so tightly that she nearly choked me.* **2** *v.* to be unable to breathe: *I choked when a piece of meat stuck in my throat.* **3** *v.* to fill up or block; clog: *Sand is choking the river.* **4** *n.* valve that reduces the supply of air to an internal-combustion engine. **5** *v.* Often, **choke up,** to become too nervous to do something well; fail because of anxiety: *We had a big lead, but we choked, and we lost.* ❑ *v.* **choked, chok·ing.** —**choke′a·ble,** *adj.* —**chok′ing·ly,** *adv.*

choke back, to hold back, control, or suppress: *I choked back a sharp reply.*

choke off, to put an end to; stop: *The break in the water main choked off the neighborhood's supply of water.*

choke up, **1** to block up; fill up; clog up: *A traffic jam choked up the highway.* **2** to fill with emotion; be or cause to be on the verge of tears: *I was choked up by the movie's sad ending.*

choke·cher·ry (chōk′cher′ē), *n.* bitter wild cherry of North America. ❑ *n., pl.* **choke·cher·ries.**

chok·er (chō′kər), *n.* **1** person or thing that chokes. **2** something fitting tightly around the neck, such as a necklace or high collar.

chol·er (kol′ər), *n.* an irritable disposition; anger. ■ Another word that sounds like this is **collar.**

chol·er·a (kol′ər ə), *n.* an acute, infectious disease of the stomach and intestines, in which the symptoms are vomiting, cramps, and diarrhea.

chol·er·ic (kol′ər ik), *adj.* having an irritable disposition; easily made angry.

cho·les·te·rol (kə les′tə rol′), *n.* a white, fatty substance, found in the blood and tissues of the body and also in foods such as eggs and meat. It is important in metabolism. Too much cholesterol in the body may endanger health.

cho·lla (choi′yə), *n.* a spiny, treelike cactus of Mexico and the southwestern United States. ❑ *n., pl.* **cho·llas.**

chomp (chomp), *v.* to bite and chew noisily: *The horse chomped the carrots.*

Chom·sky (chom′skē), *n.* **Noam** (nōm), born 1928, American linguist and political activist. ■ **Noam Chomsky** argues that every person is born with a natural ability to understand the general principles of language, and that these general principles are the same for every language.

Chong·qing (chông′ching′), *n.* official spelling of **Chungking.**

choose (chüz), *v.* **1** to pick out; select from a group: *to choose a book.* **2** to prefer and decide; think fit: *The cat did not choose to go out in the rain.* ❑ *v.* **chose, cho·sen, choos·ing.** —**choos′er,** *n.*

choose up, to select the team members in a game or contest: *The captains of the softball teams began choosing up sides.*

SYNONYM STUDY **Choose, pick**[1], and **select** all mean to decide what to take or do. **Choose** is a general word: *She chose to stay home.* **Pick** means to choose from many things just what you want: *The children picked the smallest of the puppies.* **Select** suggests picking after careful thought: *Which coat did he finally select?*

choos·y or **choos·ey** (chü′zē), *adj.* particular or fussy: *They are so choosy about their food that no one invites them to dinner.* ❑ *adj.* **choos·i·er, choos·i·est.** —**choos′i·ness,** *n.*

chop[1] (chop), **1** *v.* to cut by hitting with something sharp: *You can chop wood with an ax. We chopped down the dead tree.* **2** *v.* to cut into small pieces: *chop up cabbage for coleslaw.* **3** *n.* a cutting blow or stroke: *I split the log with one chop of the ax.* **4** *n.* slice of meat, especially of lamb, pork, or veal that usually contains a piece of rib bone. **5** *v.* (in tennis, cricket, etc.) to swing at or hit with a downward stroke: *The batter chopped at the ball.* **6** *v.* to make by cutting: *The hikers had to chop their way through the bushes.* ❑ *v.* **chopped, chop·ping.**

chop[2] (chop), *v.* to change suddenly; shift quickly; veer. ❑ *v.* **chopped, chop·ping.**

Cho·pin (shō′pan), *n.* **Fré·dé·ric Fran·çois** (frā dā rēk′ frän swä′), 1810-1849, Polish pianist and composer who lived in France. He wrote brilliant, often difficult compositions for solo piano.

chop·per (chop′ər), *n.* **1** person, tool, or machine that chops: *a wood chopper.* **2** INFORMAL. helicopter.

chop·py[1] (chop′ē), *adj.* **1** making quick, sharp movements; jerky: *The speaker made nervous, choppy gestures.* **2** moving in short, irregular, broken waves: *The wind made the water choppy.* ❑ *adj.* **chop·pi·er, chop·pi·est.** —**chop′pi·ness,** *n.*

chop·py[2] (chop′ē), *adj.* changing suddenly; shifting quickly: *A choppy wind tossed the ship about.* ❑ *adj.* **chop·pi·er, chop·pi·est.**

chops (chops), *n.pl.* jaws or cheeks: *The cat is licking the milk off its chops.*

chop·sticks (chop′stiks′), *n.pl.* pair of small, slender sticks used by Chinese, Japanese and other Asians to raise food to the mouth.

chop su·ey (chop′ sü′ē), fried or stewed meat and vegetables cut up and cooked together in a sauce. It is usually served with rice. [**Chop suey** comes from Chinese words meaning "odds and ends."]

cho·ral (kôr′əl), *adj.* **1** of a choir or chorus: *Our choral society meets on Wednesdays.* **2** sung by a choir or chorus: *a choral hymn.* ■ Another word that sounds like this is **coral.** —**cho′ral·ly,** *adv.*

cho·rale (kə ral′), *n.* **1** a simple hymn sung in unison. **2** chorus or choir. ■ Another word that sounds like this is **corral.**

chord[1] (kôrd), *n.* combination of two or more musical notes sounded together in harmony. ■ Another word that sounds like this is **cord.**

chord[2] (kôrd), *n.* **1** a straight line segment connecting two points on a curve. **2** feeling or emotion: *The stray puppy touched a tender chord in us.* ■ Another word that sounds like this is **cord.**

chor·date (kôr′dāt), *n.* any of very many animals including human beings, all other animals with backbones, and some animals with body parts resembling backbones.

chord[2] (def. 1)

chore (chôr), *n.* **1** a small task or easy job, usually done regularly: *Feeding the dog is my daily chore.* ■ See Synonym Study at **job.** **2** a difficult or disagreeable thing to do: *Painting the house is a real chore.*

cho·re·o·graph (kôr′ē ə graf), *v.* to arrange or design dancing for.

cho·re·og·ra·pher (kôr′ē og′rə fər), *n.* a person who plans, creates, or directs dances in a ballet, movie, musical, etc.

cho·re·og·ra·phy (kôr′ē og′rə fē), *n.* art of planning or creating the dances in a ballet, movie, or musical play. —**cho′re·o·graph′ic,** *adj.* —**cho′re·o·graph′i·cal·ly,** *adv.*

cho·ris·ter (kôr′ə stər), *n.* **1** singer in a choir. **2** leader of a choir.

cho·ri·zo (chə rē′zō), *n.* sausage strongly flavored with garlic and hot spices. ❑ *n., pl.* **cho·ri·zos.**

chor·tle (chôr′tl), **1** *v.* to chuckle or snort with glee: *He chortled at the joke.* **2** *n.* a gleeful chuckle or snort. ❑ *v.* **chor·tled, chor·tling.** —**chor′tler,** *n.*

cho·rus (kôr′əs), **1** *n.* group of singers who sing together, such as a choir: *Our school chorus gave a concert at the town hall.* **2** *n.* a musical composition to be sung by all singers together. A chorus is often a part of an opera or oratorio. **3** *n.* the repeated part of a song coming after each stanza: *Everybody knew the chorus by heart.* **4** *v.* to sing or speak all at the same time: *The audience* *chorused its approval by loud cheering.* **5** *n.* anything sung by many people at once: *The children greeted the teacher with a chorus of "Happy Birthday."* **6** *n.* act of saying all together at the same time: *My question was answered by a chorus of no's.* **7** *n.* group of singers and dancers: *the chorus in a musical comedy.* ❑ *n., pl.* **cho·rus·es.**

in chorus, all together at the same time: *The whole class replied in chorus to the teacher's questions.*

chose (chōz), *v.* past tense of **choose:** *I chose the red shirt.*

cho·sen (chō′zn), **1** *v.* past participle of **choose:** *Have you chosen a book from the library?* **2** *adj.* picked out; selected from a group: *Six chosen scouts marched at the front of the parade.*

Chou En-lai (jō′ en′lī′), 1898-1976, premier of the People's Republic of China from 1949 to 1976. Also, **Zhou Enlai.**

chow[1] (chou), *n.* dog of medium size, first bred in China, with a short, compact body, large head, and thick coat of one color. Chows have a black tongue and a tail that curls over the back.

chow[2] (chou), *n.* INFORMAL. food.

chow·der (chou′dər), *n.* a thick soup or stew usually made of clams or fish with potatoes, onions, etc., and milk.

chow mein (chou′ mān′), a thickened stew of onions, celery, meat, etc., served with fried noodles.

Chré·tien (krā tyan′), *n.* **Jean** (zhän), born 1934, prime minister of Canada since 1993.

Christ (krīst), *n.* Jesus, the founder of the Christian religion.

WORD STORY **Christ** comes from a Greek word meaning "anointed," that is, touched with special oil as a sign of deep respect, as for royal majesty. **Messiah** comes from a Hebrew word with the same meaning.

chris·ten (kris′n), *v.* **1** to give a first name to a person at baptism: *The child was christened Maria.* **2** to give a name to: *The new ship was christened "Waverunner."* **3** to baptize as a Christian.

Chris·ten·dom (kris′n dəm), *n.* **1** Christian countries; the Christian part of the world: *Many of the monarchs of Christendom took part in the Crusades.* **2** all Christians: *Christendom everywhere celebrates Christmas.*

chris·ten·ing (kris′n ing), *n.* act or ceremony of baptizing and naming; baptism.

Chris·tian (kris′chən), **1** *n.* person who believes in and follows the teachings of Jesus. **2** *adj.* believing in or belonging to the religion of Jesus: *the Christian church, the Christian gospel.* **3** *adj.* showing a gentle, humble, helpful spirit: *Christian kindness.* **4** *adj.* of Christians or Christianity: *the Christian faith.*

Chris·ti·an·i·ty (kris′chē an′ə tē), *n.* **1** the religion based on the teachings of Jesus as they appear in the Bible; Christian religion. **2** condition of being a Christian. **3** all Christians; Christendom.

Chris·tian·ize (kris′chə nīz), *v.* to make Christian; convert to Christianity. ❑ *v.* **Chris·tian·ized, Chris·tian·iz·ing.** —**Chris′tian·i·za′tion,** *n.*

Christian name, first name; given name.

Christian Science, religion and system of healing founded by Mary Baker Eddy in 1866. It treats disease by mental and spiritual means. —**Christian Scientist.**

Chris·tie (kris′tē), *n.* **Ag·a·tha** (ag′ə thə), 1890-1976, English mystery writer. She created the detectives Hercule Poirot and Miss Jane Marple.

Christ·like (krīst′līk′), *adj.* like Christ; like that of Christ; showing the spirit of Jesus.

Christ·mas (kris′məs), *n.* the yearly celebration of the birth of Jesus; December 25. ❑ *n., pl.* **Christ·mas·es.**

Christ·mas·time (kris′məs tīm′), *n.* the Christmas season.

Christmas tree, an evergreen or artificial tree hung with decorations at Christmastime.

Chris·to·pher (kris′tə fər), *n.* **Saint,** died A.D. 250?, legendary Christian martyr. He is the patron saint of travelers. [Christopher comes from Greek words meaning "carrier of Christ."]

chro·mat·ic (krō mat′ik), *adj.* **1** of color or colors. **2** progressing only by half steps instead of by the regular intervals of the musical scale. There are twelve chromatic tones in an octave. —**chro·mat′i·cal·ly,** *adv.*

chromatic scale, a musical scale that progresses by half steps.

chro·ma·tin (krō′mə tən), *n.* substance composed of protein and nucleic acid, found throughout the nucleus of a cell. Chromatin draws together to form chromosomes during cellular division.

chro·ma·tog·ra·phy (krō′mə tog′rə fē), *n.* a method for separating chemical compounds from one another. The compounds are passed through paper or gelatin, and different compounds stick to different places.

chrome (krōm), *n.* chromium.

chro·mi·um (krō′mē əm), *n.* a grayish, hard, brittle metallic element that does not rust or become dull easily when exposed to air. Chromium occurs in compounds that are used as plating, as part of stainless steel and other alloys. *Symbol:* Cr

chro·mo·some (krō′mə sōm), *n.* any of the rod-shaped chromatin objects that appear in the nucleus of a cell during cell division. Chromosomes contain DNA molecules that carry the genes that determine heredity.

chron·ic (kron′ik), *adj.* **1** lasting a long time: *a chronic disease.* **2** never stopping; constant; habitual: *a chronic tease.* [See Word Story at **crony.**] —**chron′i·cal·ly,** *adv.*

chron·i·cle (kron′ə kəl), **1** *n.* record of events in the order in which they took place; history; story: *Columbus kept a chronicle of his voyages.* **2** *v.* to write the history of; tell the story of: *Many of the old monks chronicled the Crusades.* ❑ *v.* **chron·i·cled, chron·i·cling.** —**chron′i·cler,** *n.*

Chron·i·cles (kron′ə kəlz), *n.* two books of the Bible, called I and II Chronicles.

chron·o·log·i·cal (kron′ə loj′ə kəl), *adj.* arranged in the order in which things happened: *In telling a story a person usually follows chronological order.* —**chron′o·log′i·cal·ly,** *adv.*

chro·nol·o·gy (krə nol′ə jē), *n.* **1** science of measuring time and determining the proper order and dates of events. **2** table or list that gives the exact dates of events arranged in the order in which they happened. ❑ *n., pl.* **chro·nol·o·gies** for 2.

chro·nom·e·ter (krə nom′ə tər), *n.* clock or watch that keeps very accurate time. A ship's chronometer is used in determining longitude.

chrys·a·lis (kris′ə lis), *n.* the stage in the development of butterflies between the larva and the adult; pupa. ❑ *n., pl.* **chrys·a·lis·es, chry·sal·i·des** (krə sal′ə dēz′).

chrysanthemums

chry·san·the·mum (krə san′thə məm), *n.* the round flower of related plants that bloom in the fall. Chrysanthemums have many petals and various colors, especially white, yellow, red, and purple.

chub (chub), *n.* any of various small, freshwater fishes of central and eastern United States and Canada. ❑ *n., pl.* **chub** or **chubs.**

chub·by (chub′ē), *adj.* round and plump: *Most babies have chubby cheeks.* ❑ *adj.* **chub·bi·er, chub·bi·est.** —**chub′bi·ness,** *n.*

a	hat	ė	term	ô	order	ch	child		a in about
ā	age	i	it	oi	oil	ng	long		e in taken
ä	far	ī	ice	ou	out	sh	she	ə	i in pencil
â	care	o	hot	u	cup	th	thin		o in lemon
e	let	ō	open	ů	put	ŦH	then		u in circus
ē	equal	ȯ	saw	ü	rule	zh	measure		

chuck¹ (chuk), **1** *v.* to give a slight blow or tap; pat: *He chucked the baby under the chin.* **2** *n.* a slight blow or tap: *He gave the baby a chuck under the chin.* **3** *v.* to throw or toss: *She chucked the stones into the pond.* **4** *n.* a throw or toss. **5** *v.* INFORMAL. to throw away; discard: *Why don't you chuck those smelly sneakers?*

chuck² (chuk), *n.* **1** device for holding a tool or piece of work in a machine. **2** cut of beef between the neck and the shoulder.

chuck³ (chuk), *n.* CANADIAN. a large body of water, especially the Pacific Ocean: *logs floating in the chuck.*

chuck·le (chuk′əl), **1** *v.* to laugh softly or quietly: *She kept chuckling to herself throughout the funny movie.* ∎ See Synonym Study at **laugh.** **2** *n.* a soft laugh; quiet laughter. ❑ *v.* **chuck·led, chuck·ling.** —**chuck′ler,** *n.*

chuck wagon, a wagon or truck that carries food and cooking equipment for cowhands or harvest workers.

chuck·wal·la (chuk′wäl′ə), *n.* a large, brownish lizard of the desert areas of the Southwest. ❑ *n., pl.* **chuck·wal·las.**

chug (chug), **1** *n.* a short, loud burst of sound: *the chug of a steam engine.* **2** *v.* to make such sounds. **3** *v.* to go or move with such sounds: *The old truck chugged along.* ❑ *v.* **chugged, chug·ging.**

chum (chum), *n.* OLD USE. a very close friend.

chum·my (chum′ē), *adj.* very friendly; intimate. ❑ *adj.* **chum·mi·er, chum·mi·est.** —**chum′mi·ly,** *adv.* —**chum′mi·ness,** *n.*

chump (chump), *n.* INFORMAL. a foolish or stupid person; blockhead.

Chung·king (chùng′king′), *n.* city in central China, on the Chang Jiang River. Its official name is **Chongqing.**

chunk (chungk), *n.* a thick piece or lump: *Here's a chunk of wood for the fire.*

chunk·y (chung′kē), *adj.* **1** short and thick or stout: *She threw a chunky log on the fire.* **2** stocky: *The child had a chunky build.* ❑ *adj.* **chunk·i·er, chunk·i·est.** —**chunk′i·ly,** *adv.* —**chunk′i·ness,** *n.*

Chun·nel (chun′l), *n.* a railroad tunnel beneath the English Channel, connecting England and France.

church (chėrch), *n.* **1** building for public Christian worship. **2** public worship of God in a church: *Don't be late for church.* **3** Usually, **Church,** group of Christians with the same beliefs and under the same authority; denomination: *the Methodist Church, the Presbyterian Church.* **4** group of people gathered together for religious worship or instruction; congregation. **5 the Church,** all Christians. **6** profession of a clergyman: *He is going into the church as a career.* ❑ *n., pl.* **church·es.** —**church′like′,** *adj.*

church·go·er (chėrch′gō′ər), *n.* one who goes to church regularly.

Church·ill (chėr′chil), *n.* Sir **Win·ston** (win′stən), 1874-1965, British political leader and writer, prime minister of Great Britain from 1940 to 1945 and from 1951 to 1955. He won the 1953 Nobel Prize for literature.

church·man (chėrch′mən), *n.* **1** member of the clergy. **2** member of a church. ❑ *n., pl.* **church·men.**

Church of England, the Episcopal Church in England that is recognized as a national institution by the government; Anglican Church.

Church of Jesus Christ of Latter-day Saints, the official name of the Mormon Church.

church·ward·en (chėrch′wôrd′n), *n.* a lay official in the Church of England or the Protestant Episcopal Church who manages the business, property, and money of a church.

church·wom·an (chėrch′wùm′ən), *n.* a woman member of a church. ❑ *n., pl.* **church·wom·en.**

church·yard (chėrch′yärd′), *n.* the ground around a church. Part of a churchyard is sometimes used as a burial ground.

churl·ish (chėr′lish), *adj.* rude or surly; bad-tempered. —**churl′ish·ly,** *adj.* —**churl′ish·ness,** *n.*

churn (chėrn), **1** *n.* container or machine in which butter is made from cream or milk by beating and shaking. **2** *v.* to beat and shake cream or milk in a churn. **3** *v.* to stir violently; make or become foamy: *The ship's propeller churned the waves.* **4** *v.* to move as if beaten and shaken: *The water churns in the rapids.* —**churn′er,** *n.*

chute (shüt), *n.* **1** a steep slide for dropping or sliding things down to a lower level; shoot. There are chutes for mail, soiled clothes, coal, etc. **2** rapids in a river; waterfall. **3** INFORMAL. parachute.

chut·ney (chut′nē), *n.* a spicy sauce or relish made of fruits, herbs, pepper, etc. ❑ *n., pl.* **chut·neys.**

chutz·pah (hùts′pə), *n.* INFORMAL. bold and impudent self-confidence; gall: *She couldn't believe he had the chutzpah to ask her for a ride after breaking their date.*

chyme (kīm), *n.* a pulpy mass into which food is changed by the action of the stomach. Chyme passes from the stomach into the small intestine.

CIA, Central Intelligence Agency (an agency of the U.S. government that deals with matters involving national security).

ci·ca·da (sə kā′də), *n.* any of several large insects with two pairs of thin, transparent wings; locust. The male makes a shrill sound in hot, dry weather. ❑ *n., pl.* **ci·ca·das.**

cicada—up to 2 in. (5 cm) long

Cic·e·ro (sis′ə rō′), *n.* **Mar·cus Tul·li·us** (mär′kəs tul′ē əs), 106-43 B.C., Roman orator, writer, and political leader.

cich·lid (sik′lid), *n.* any of numerous tropical freshwater fishes resembling sunfishes and often brightly colored. Cichlids are popular aquarium fishes.

Cid (sēd), *n.* **El** (el), 1043?-1099, national hero of Spain. ∎ **El Cid** led an army against the Muslims who then ruled southern Spain. His life has been the subject of Spanish epic poetry and French plays. [**El Cid** comes from two Arabic words meaning "the lord."]

-cide, *suffix.* **1** act of killing: *homicide = act of killing a person.* **2** person or thing that kills: *pesticide = substance that kills pests.*

ci·der (sī′dər), *n.* juice pressed out of apples, used as a drink and in making vinegar.

ci·gar (sə gär′), *n.* a tight roll of tobacco leaves for smoking.

cig·a·rette (sig′ə ret′ *or* sig′ə ret′), *n.* a small roll of finely cut tobacco enclosed in a thin sheet of paper for smoking.

ci·lan·tro (si lan′trō), *n.* leaves of an herb related to carrot and parsley, used to flavor salads and cooked foods.

cil·i·a (sil′ē ə), *n.pl.* very small, hairlike parts growing from certain cells. Cilia in the nose, throat, and lungs help move mucus, dust, and germs away from the lungs. Some microscopic living things use cilia to move around. ❑ *n., sing.* **cil·i·um** (sil′ē əm).

cinch (sinch), **1** *n.* a strong strap for fastening a saddle or pack on a horse. **2** *v.* to fasten on with a cinch; bind firmly. **3** *n.* INFORMAL. something sure and easy: *It's a cinch to ride a bike once you know how.* ❑ *n., pl.* **cinch·es.**

cin·cho·na (sing kō′nə *or* sin kō′nə), *n.* any of several evergreen trees originally found in the Andes Mountains, now also grown in the East Indies. They are valuable for their bark, from which quinine and other drugs are obtained. ❑ *n., pl.* **cin·cho·nas.**

Cin·cin·nat·i (sin′sə nat′ē), *n.* city in SW Ohio, on the Ohio River.

WORD STORY **Cincinnati** comes from the name of a Roman farmer famous for serving as a general only during national emergencies. Veterans of the American Revolutionary War formed a society named for him and the city was named in their honor.

Cin·co de May·o (sin′kō də mī′ō), a holiday celebrated on May 5 in Mexico and by Mexican Americans to celebrate the defeat of French invaders at a battle in Mexico in 1862.

cinc·ture (singk′chər), **1** *n.* belt or girdle. **2** *v.* to encircle; surround. ❑ *v.* **cinc·tured, cinc·tur·ing.**

cin·der (sin′dər), *n.* **1** piece of wood or coal that has burned up. **2 cinders,** *pl.* wood or coal partly burned but no longer flaming. Cinders are made up of larger and coarser pieces than ashes are.

cinder block, a building block of cement and pressed coal cinders, usually hollow. It is used in walls and partitions.

Cin·der·el·la (sin/də rel/ə), *n.* **1** girl in a fairy tale who is cruelly overworked by her stepmother but is rescued by her fairy godmother, and later marries a prince. **2** person or group suddenly successful and famous after being little known. ❑ *n., pl.* **Cin·der·el·las** for 2.

cin·e·ma (sin/ə mə), *n.* **1** a movie theater. **2 the cinema,** movies. ❑ *n., pl.* **cin·e·mas** for 1.

cin·e·ma·tog·ra·pher (sin/ə mə tog/rə fər), *n.* a person in charge of photographing a movie.

cin·e·ma·tog·ra·phy (sin/ə mə tog/rə fē), *n.* art and science of photographing movies.

cin·na·bar (sin/ə bär), *n.* a reddish or brownish mineral that is the chief source of mercury.

cin·na·mon (sin/ə mən), **1** *n.* spice made from the dried inner bark of a small tree of the East Indies. **2** *adj.* light reddish brown: *a cinnamon horse.* **3** *n.* a light, reddish brown.

CIO or **C.I.O.,** Congress of Industrial Organizations. It merged with the AFL in 1955. See **AFL-CIO.**

ci·pher (sī/fər), **1** *n.* secret writing; code: *Part of his letter is in cipher.* **2** *v.* to write a message using secret code: *The spy ciphered a report containing the whole plan.* **3** *n.* zero; 0. **4** *n.* person or thing of no importance. **5** *v.* to do arithmetic: *She can read, write, and cipher.* [See Word Story at **zero.**]

cir·ca (sèr/kə), *prep.* about; approximately: *Muhammad was born circa* A.D. *570.*

cir·ca·di·an (sèr/kā/dē ən), *adj.* repeating in a daily pattern, the way sleep and wakefulness do in human beings: *circadian rhythm.*

Cir·ce (sèr/sē), *n.* (in Greek legends) an enchantress. Ulysses resisted her spell and forced her to free his companions, whom she had changed to pigs.

cir·cle (sèr/kəl), **1** *n.* a round line. Every point on a circle is the same distance from the center. **2** *n.* a plane figure bounded by such a line. **3** *n.* anything shaped like a circle; ring: *We sat in a circle around the teacher.* **4** *v.* to go around in a circle; revolve around: *The moon circles the earth. The airplane circled before it landed.* **5** *v.* to form or make a circle around; surround; encircle: *I circled the wrong answer.* **6** *n.* group of people held together by the same interests: *a circle of friends.* ❑ *v.* **cir·cled, cir·cling.** −**cir/cler,** *n.*

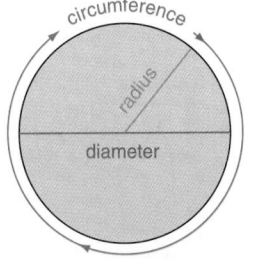

circle (def. 1)

circle graph, circular drawing that compares the parts of anything to the whole; pie chart.

cir·clet (sèr/klit), *n.* **1** a small circle. **2** a round ornament worn on the head, neck, arm, or finger.

cir·cuit (sèr/kit), *n.* **1** act of going around: *It takes a year for the earth to make its circuit of the sun.* **2** route over which a person or group makes repeated journeys at certain times: *In old days, some judges made a circuit, holding court in towns along the way.* **3** the district through which such journeys are made. **4** the complete path over which an electric current flows. **5** arrangement of wiring, transistors, etc., forming electrical connections. **6** number of theaters under the same management and presenting the same shows. **7** (in sports) a series of games or tournaments with the same group of players: *the North American golf circuit.*

circuit breaker, switch that automatically interrupts an electric circuit when the current gets too strong.

cir·cu·i·tous (sər kyü/ə təs), *adj.* not direct; roundabout: *We took a circuitous route home to avoid poor roads.* −**cir·cu/i·tous·ly,** *adv.* −**cir·cu/i·tous·ness,** *n.*

circuit rider, (earlier) a preacher who rode from place to place over a circuit to preach.

cir·cuit·ry (sèr/kə trē), *n.* **1** design or plan of an electric circuit. **2** parts making up an electric circuit.

cir·cu·lar (sèr/kyə lər), **1** *adj.* round like a circle: *The full moon has a circular shape.* **2** *adj.* moving in a circle; going around a circle: *A merry-go-round makes a circular trip.* **3** *adj.* of a circle. **4** *n.* letter, notice, or advertisement sent to each of a number of people. −**cir/cu·lar·ly,** *adv.*

cir·cu·lar·ize (sèr/kyə lə rīz/), *v.* to send circulars to. ❑ *v.* **cir·cu·lar·ized, cir·cu·lar·iz·ing.** −**cir/cu·lar·i·za/tion,** *n.*

circular saw, saw that is a large, thin disk with teeth in its edge, turned at a high speed by machinery; buzz saw.

cir·cu·late (sèr/kyə lāt), *v.* **1** to go around; pass from place to place or from person to person: *Open windows allowed air to circulate through the building.* **2** to send around from person to person or from place to place: *A memo was circulated to the whole staff.* **3** (of the blood) to flow from the heart through the arteries and veins back to the heart. ❑ *v.* **cir·cu·lat·ed, cir·cu·lat·ing.** −**cir/cu·la/tive,** *adj.* −**cir/cu·la/tor,** *n.*

circulating library, library whose books can be rented or borrowed.

cir·cu·la·tion (sèr/kyə lā/shən), *n.* **1** act or process of going around; act of circulating: *Open windows increase the circulation of air in a room.* **2** the flow of the blood from the heart through the arteries and veins back to the heart. **3** the number of copies of a newspaper or magazine that are sent out during a certain time: *That newspaper has a daily circulation of 500,000.* **4** act of sending around of books, papers, news, etc., from person to person or from place to place.

cir·cu·la·to·ry (sèr/kyə lə tôr/ē), *adj.* of circulation. Arteries and veins are parts of the circulatory system of the human body.

circum-, *prefix.* around; in a circle: *circumnavigate = navigate around.*

cir·cum·cise (sèr/kəm sīz), *v.* to cut off the foreskin of. ❑ *v.* **cir·cum·cised, cir·cum·cis·ing.**

cir·cum·ci·sion (sèr/kəm sizh/ən), *n.* act of circumcising.

cir·cum·fer·ence (sər kum/fər əns), *n.* **1** the boundary line of a circle or of certain other surfaces. Every point in the circumference of a circle is at the same distance from the center. **2** the distance around: *The circumference of the earth at the equator is almost 25,000 miles.*

cir·cum·flex (sèr/kəm fleks), *n.* **1** (in the pronunciations in this book) a mark (^) used over *o* to show that it is pronounced as in *order* (ôr/dər) or over the *a* to show that it is pronounced as in *care* (kâr). **2** mark (^) placed over a vowel in certain foreign languages, as in the French word *fête.* ❑ *n., pl.* **cir·cum·flex·es.**

cir·cum·lo·cu·tion (sèr/kəm lō kyü/shən), *n.* **1** the use of several or many words instead of one or a few. **2** a roundabout expression: *"The wife of your father's brother" is a circumlocution for "Your aunt."*

cir·cum·nav·i·gate (sèr/kəm nav/ə gāt), *v.* to sail around: *Magellan's ship circumnavigated the earth.* ❑ *v.* **cir·cum·nav·i·gat·ed, cir·cum·nav·i·gat·ing.** −**cir/cum·nav/i·ga/tion,** *n.*

cir·cum·scribe (sèr/kəm skrib/), *v.* **1** to draw a line around; mark the boundaries of; bound: *The horizon circumscribed my view of the sea.* **2** to put limits on; restrict: *Poor health circumscribes a person's activities.* **3** to draw or be drawn around a geometrical figure so as to touch as many points as possible: *A circle that circumscribes a square touches the four corners of the square.* ❑ *v.* **cir·cum·scribed, cir·cum·scrib·ing.**

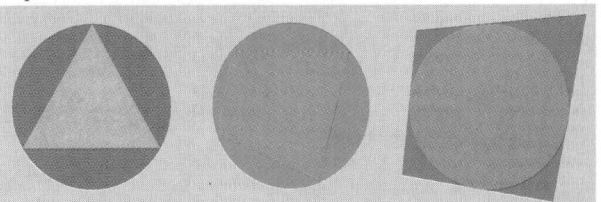

circumscribe (def. 3)—circumscribed figures

a	hat	ė	term	ô	order	ch	child		
ā	age	i	it	oi	oil	ng	long		a in about
ä	far	ī	ice	ou	out	sh	she		e in taken
â	care	o	hot	u	cup	th	thin	ə {	i in pencil
e	let	ō	open	ù	put	ŦH	then		o in lemon
ē	equal	ȯ	saw	ü	rule	zh	measure		u in circus

cir·cum·spect (sėr′kəm spekt), *adj.* watchful on all sides; careful; cautious; prudent: *circumspect actions.* —**cir′cum·spect′ly**, *adv.* —**cir′cum·spect′ness**, *n.*

cir·cum·spec·tion (sėr′kəm spek′shən), *n.* circumspect action or conduct; care; caution; prudence.

cir·cum·stance (sėr′kəm stans), *n.* **1** condition that accompanies an act or event: *Unfavorable circumstances such as fog and rain often delayed us on our trip to the mountains.* **2** fact or event: *It was a lucky circumstance that I found my money.* **3** **circumstances,** *pl.* **a** financial condition: *A rich person is in good circumstances; a poor person is in bad circumstances.* **b** the existing condition or state of affairs: *He was forced by circumstances to resign.* **4** ceremony; display: *The royal procession advanced with pomp and circumstance.*

under no circumstances, never: *Under no circumstances should you reveal that we are planning a surprise party.*

under the circumstances, because of these conditions: *The road was closed; under the circumstances we had no choice but to go home.*

cir·cum·stan·tial (sėr′kəm stan′shəl), *adj.* **1** depending on or based on circumstances: *Stolen jewels found on a person are circumstantial evidence that the person stole them.* **2** not essential; not important *Minor details are circumstantial compared with the main fact.* **3** giving full and exact details; complete: *a circumstantial report of an accident.* —**cir′cum·stan′tial·ly**, *adv.*

cir·cum·vent (sėr′kəm vent′), *v.* **1** to get the better of or defeat by trickery; outwit: *The dishonest official was always trying to circumvent the law.* **2** to go around: *He took a roundabout route to circumvent the traffic.* —**cir′cum·ven′tion**, *n.*

cir·cus (sėr′kəs), *n.* **1** a traveling show of acrobats, clowns, horses, riders, and wild animals. **2** the performers who give this show or the performances they give. **3** (in ancient Rome) an arena with seats around it in rows, each row higher than the one in front of it. ❑ *n., pl.* **cir·cus·es.**

WORD STORY Circus comes from a Latin word meaning "a ring." Today we have three-ring circuses presented by ringmasters. When you see a word with the letters *circ* in it, a ring or circle is probably part of the meaning. **Search** comes from the same Latin word, and a person looking for something tends to wander in circles.

cir·rho·sis (sə rō′sis), *n.* a chronic disease of the liver marked by the breakdown of liver cells and formation of too much connective tissue between cells.

cir·ro·cu·mu·lus (sir′ō kyü′myə ləs), *n.* cloud formation of small, round, white, fluffy clouds in rows or groups, occurring at heights of 20,000 feet (6100 meters) and above. ❑ *n., pl.* **cir·ro·cum·u·li** (sir′ō kyü′myə lī).

cir·ro·stra·tus (sir′ō strā′təs), *n.* a thin, hazy layer of cloud occurring at heights of 20,000 feet (6100 meters) and above. ❑ *n., pl.* **cir·ro·stra·ti** (sir′ō strā′tī).

cir·rus (sir′əs), *n.* a cloud formation of thin, featherlike white clouds at heights of 20,000 feet (6100 meters) and above. ■ Another word that sounds like this is **serous.** ❑ *n., pl.* **cir·ri** (sir′ī). [*Cirrus* comes from a Latin word meaning "a curl."]

cirrus

cis·co (sis′kō), *n.* any of several kinds of whitefish found in the lakes of the northeastern United States and Canada, valuable as a food fish. ❑ *n., pl.* **cis·coes.**

cis·tern (sis′tərn), *n.* an artificial reservoir for storing water, especially a tank below ground.

cit·a·del (sit′ə dəl), *n.* **1** fortress, especially one in a city. **2** a strongly fortified place; stronghold.

ci·ta·tion (sī tā′shən), *n.* **1** quotation or reference given as an authority for facts or opinions. **2** act of citing. **3** honorable mention for bravery in war: *the soldier received a citation from the President.* **4** summons to appear before a court of law.

cite (sīt), *v.* **1** to quote a passage, book, or author, especially as an authority: *She cited the U.S. Constitution to prove her statement.* **2** to refer to; mention as an example: *The lawyer cited a similar case.* **3** to give honorable mention for bravery in war. **4** to summon to appear before a court of law. ❑ *v.* **cit·ed, cit·ing.** ■ Other words that sound like this are **sight** and **site.**

cit·i·zen (sit′ə zən), *n.* **1** person who by birth or by choice is a member of a nation. A citizen owes loyalty to that nation and is given certain rights by it. *Many immigrants have become citizens of the United States.* **2** inhabitant of a city or town.

cit·i·zen·ry (sit′ə zən rē), *n.* citizens as a group.

citizens band, one of two bands of radio frequencies available for the use of private citizens, especially for communications over a short distance.

cit·i·zen·ship (sit′ə zən ship), *n.* **1** the duties, rights, and privileges of a citizen. **2** condition of being a citizen: *Voting is a right of citizenship.*

cit·rate (sit′rāt *or* sī′trāt), *n.* a chemical substance formed from citric acid.

cit·ric (sit′rik), *adj.* of or from citrus fruits, such as lemons and oranges.

cit·ric acid (sit′rik), a white, odorless acid with a sour taste, found in the juice of oranges, lemons, etc. It is used as a flavoring, as a medicine, and in making dyes.

cit·ron (sit′rən), *n.* **1** a pale yellow fruit something like a lemon but larger, with less acid and a thicker rind. **2** the bush or small tree that it grows on. **3** its rind, candied and used in fruit cakes, plum pudding, candies, etc.

cit·ro·nel·la (sit′rə nel′ə), *n.* oil obtained from a fragrant grass of Asia and Central America. It is used in making perfume, soap, liniment, etc., and for keeping mosquitoes away.

cit·rus (sit′rəs), *n.* any tree bearing lemons, grapefruit, limes, oranges, or similar fruits. Citrus fruits contain much vitamin C. Citruses usually grow in warm climates. ❑ *n., pl.* **cit·rus·es.**

cit·y (sit′ē), **1** *n.* a large and important center of population and business activity. New York, Buenos Aires, London, Cairo, and Shanghai are major cities of the world. **2** *n.* division of local government in the United States having a charter from the state that fixes its boundaries and powers. A city is usually governed by a city council and a city manager or mayor. **3** *n.* people living in a city: *The whole city was alarmed by the great fire.* **4** *adj.* of or in a city. ❑ *n., pl.* **cit·ies** for 1,2.

city hall

city hall, 1 the headquarters of the officials, bureaus, etc., of a city government: *The mayor's office is in city hall.* **2** the officials of a city government as a group: *With city hall on her side, she was able to save the old building.*

city manager, person appointed by a city council or commission to manage the government of a city.

cit·y-state (sit′ē stāt′), *n.* an independent state consisting of a city and the territories depending on it. Athens was a city-state in ancient Greece.

civ·et (siv′it), *n.* **1** a yellowish substance produced by glands of the civet cat. It has a musky odor and is used in making perfume. **2** civet cat.

civet cat, any of several small, spotted mammals living in Africa and Asia, with glands that produce civet. They are not cats.

civ·ic (siv′ik), *adj.* **1** of a city: *She is interested in civic affairs and will be a candidate for mayor.* **2** of citizens or citizenship. A person's civic duties include such things as obeying the laws, voting, and paying taxes. **—civ′i·cal·ly,** *adv.*

civ·ics (siv′iks), *n.* study of the duties, rights, and privileges of citizens.

civ·il (siv′əl), *adj.* **1** of a citizen or citizens: *Voting and paying taxes are civil duties.* **2** of the government, state, or nation: *Police departments are civil institutions to protect local citizens.* **3** occurring among citizens of one community, state, or nation: *civil war.* **4** of a citizen or the public; not connected with the armed forces or the church: *The accused soldier was tried in a military rather than in a civil court. The couple had both a civil and a religious marriage ceremony.* **5** polite; courteous: *I pointed out the way in a very civil manner.* **6** having to do with the private rights of individuals and with laws protecting these rights. Civil lawsuits deal with such things as contracts, ownership of property, and payment for personal injury.

civil defense, a civilian emergency program for protecting people and property from disasters such as fire, flood, or enemy attack.

civil disobedience, deliberate, public refusal to obey a law that one considers unjust. Civil disobedience is often used as a form of peaceful protest.

civil engineer, person whose profession is civil engineering.

civil engineering, the planning and directing of the construction of bridges, roads, airports, dams, and other public works.

ci·vil·ian (sə vil′yən), **1** *n.* person who is not enrolled in any of the armed forces. **2** *n.* person who does not serve as a police officer or firefighter. **3** *adj.* of civilians; not of the armed forces: *civilian clothes.*

ci·vil·i·ty (sə vil′ə tē), *n.* **1** polite behavior; courtesy: *Thank you for your civility in replying to my letter so promptly.* **2** act or expression of politeness or courtesy. ❑ *n., pl.* **ci·vil·i·ties** for 2.

civ·i·li·za·tion (siv′ə lə zā′shən), *n.* **1** nations and peoples that have reached advanced stages in social development: *All civilization should be aroused against war.* **2** the ways of living of a people or nation: *The civilizations of ancient Egypt and ancient Greece had many contacts over the centuries.* **3** civilized condition; advanced stage in social development. **4** act of becoming civilized: *The civilization of human society began with the development of cities and writing.*

civ·i·lized (siv′ə līzd), *adj.* **1** advanced in social customs, art, and science: *The ancient Egyptians were a civilized people.* **2** showing culture and good manners; well-bred; refined: *civilized behavior, a civilized attitude.*

civil liberty, the freedom of a person to enjoy the rights guaranteed by the laws or constitution of a country without any undue restraint or interference by the government.

civ·il·ly (siv′ə lē), *adv.* politely; courteously.

civil rights, the rights of a citizen, especially the rights guaranteed to all U.S. citizens, regardless of race, color, religion, or sex.

civil servant, person who is employed in the civil service.

civil service, branch of government service concerned with affairs not military, naval, legislative, or judicial. Forest rangers and postal service employees belong to the U.S. civil service.

civil war, **1** war between opposing groups of citizens of one nation. **2 Civil War,** war between the northern and southern states of the United States from 1861 to 1865; War Between the States.

Cl, symbol for chlorine.

cl., **1** centiliter. **2** class.

clab·ber (klab′ər), **1** *n.* thick, sour milk. **2** *v.* to become thick in souring; curdle.

clack (klak), **1** *v.* to make or cause to make a short, sharp sound: *The train clacked over the rails.* **2** *n.* a short, sharp sound: *the clack of typewriters.* **—clack′er,** *n.*

clad (klad), *v.* a past tense and past participle of **clothe.**

claim (klām), **1** *v.* to demand as your own or your right: *The settlers claimed the land beyond the river as theirs.* **2** *n.* a demand as your own or your right: *Both drivers filed claims for repairs to their cars after the accident.* **3** *n.* a right or title to something; right to demand something: *He has a legal claim to the property.* **4** *n.* something that is claimed, such as a piece of public land which a settler or prospector marks out for possession. **5** *v.* to require; call for; deserve: *Practicing the horn claims his full attention.* **6** *v.* to say strongly; declare as a fact; maintain: *She claimed that her answer was correct.* **7** *n.* declaration of something as a fact: *Careful study showed that the claims that Salk vaccine prevented polio were correct.* **—claim′a·ble,** *adj.* **—claim′er,** *n.*

lay claim to, to assert your right to; claim: *The settlers laid claim to the piece of land they occupied.*

claim·ant (klā′mənt), *n.* person who makes a claim.

clair·voy·ance (klâr voi′əns), *n.* the supposed power of seeing or knowing about things that are out of sight.

clair·voy·ant (klâr voi′ənt), **1** *adj.* supposedly having the power of seeing or knowing about things that are out of sight. **2** *n.* person who has, or claims to have, such power: *The clairvoyant claimed to be able to locate lost articles and to give news of faraway people.* **—clair·voy′ant·ly,** *adv.*

clam (klam), **1** *n.* any of numerous shellfish something like oysters, with soft bodies and shells in two hinged halves. Clams burrow in sand along the seashore or at the edges of rivers, lakes, etc. Many kinds are good to eat. **2** *v.* to go out after clams; dig for clams. ❑ *v.* **clammed, clam·ming. —clam′like,** *adj.*

clam up, INFORMAL. to stop talking.

clam·bake (klam′bāk′), *n.* picnic where clams are baked or steamed.

clam·ber (klam′bər), *v.* to climb, using both hands and feet; climb awkwardly or with difficulty; scramble: *The children clambered up the cliff.*

clam·my (klam′ē), *adj.* cold and damp: *The walls of the cellar were clammy.* ■ See Synonym Study at **damp.** ❑ *adj.* **clam·mi·er, clam·mi·est. —clam′mi·ly,** *adv.* **—clam′mi·ness,** *n.*

clam·or (klam′ər), **1** *n.* a loud noise, especially of voices; continual uproar: *The clamor of the crowd filled the air.* **2** *v.* to make a loud noise or continual uproar; shout. **3** *n.* a noisy demand. **4** *v.* to demand noisily: *The children were clamoring for candy.*

clam·or·ous (klam′ər əs), *adj.* making loud and noisy demands or complaints: *The mayor gave in to the clamorous parents and agreed to discuss building a new school with them.* **—clam′or·ous·ly,** *adv.*

clamp (klamp), **1** *n.* device for holding things tightly together: *She used a clamp to hold the arm on the chair until the glue dried.* **2** *v.* to fasten together with a clamp; put in a clamp; strengthen with a clamp: *A picture frame must be clamped together while the glue is drying.*

clamp down, to become more strict; impose strict control: *The police clamped down on speeders.*

clan (klan), *n.* **1** group of related families that claim to be descended from a common ancestor. **2** group of people closely joined together by some common interest: *The whole clan of jazz fans was at the concert.* [**Clan** comes from a Latin word meaning "plant." People in a clan share a family tree.]

clan·des·tine (klan des′tən), *adj.* arranged or made in a stealthy or underhanded manner; secret; concealed: *The spy's clandestine plans to enter the country went undetected.* **—clan·des′tine·ly,** *adv.* **—clan·des′tine·ness,** *n.*

clang (klang), **1** *n.* a loud, harsh, ringing sound like metal being hit: *The clang of the fire bell aroused the town.* **2** *v.* to make or cause to make such a sound: *The fire bell clanged. The firemen clanged the bell.*

clan·gor (klang′ər or klang′gər), *n.* **1** a continued clanging. **2** clang.

clan·gor·ous (klang′ər əs or klang′gər əs), *adj.* clanging.

clank (klangk), **1** *n.* a sharp, harsh sound like the rattle of a heavy chain: *The clank of heavy machinery filled the factory.* **2** *v.* to

a	hat	ė	term	ȯ	order	ch	child
ā	age	i	it	oi	oil	ng	long
ä	far	ī	ice	ou	out	sh	she
â	care	o	hot	u	cup	th	thin
e	let	ō	open	u̇	put	ŦH	then
ē	equal	ȯ	saw	ü	rule	zh	measure

ə { a in about / e in taken / i in pencil / o in lemon / u in circus

make or cause to make such a sound: *The old bridge rattled and clanked as we drove over it.*

clan·nish (klan′ish), *adj.* closely united; not liking outsiders: *The older settlers were clannish and avoided their new neighbors.* —**clan′nish·ness**, *n.*

clans·man (klanz′mən), *n.* member of a clan. ❑ *n., pl.* **clans·men.**

clap (klap), **1** *v.* to strike together loudly: *clap the cymbals, clap your hands.* **2** *v.* to applaud by striking the hands together: *When the show was over, we all clapped.* **3** *n.* a sudden noise, such as a single burst of thunder, the sound of the hands struck together, or the sound of a loud slap. **4** *v.* to strike with a quick blow; slap: *I clapped my friend on the back.* **5** *n.* a loud, quick blow; slap: *a clap on the shoulder.* **6** *v.* to put or place quickly and effectively: *The police clapped the escaped prisoner back into jail.* ❑ *v.* **clapped, clap·ping.**

clap·board (klab′ərd *or* klap′bôrd′), **1** *n.* a thin board, thicker along one edge than along the other. Clapboards are used to cover the outer walls of wooden buildings. **2** *v.* to cover with clapboards.

clap·per (klap′ər), *n.* the movable part inside a bell that strikes against and rings the outer part.

clar·et (klar′ət), **1** *n.* kind of red wine. **2** *n.* a dark purplish red. **3** *adj.* dark purplish red: *a claret coat.*

clar·i·fy (klar′ə fī), *v.* **1** to make clearer; explain: *The teacher's explanation clarified the difficult instructions.* **2** to make or become clear; purify: *The cook clarified the fat by heating it with a little water and straining it through cloth.* ❑ *v.* **clar·i·fied, clar·i·fy·ing.** —**clar′i·fi·ca′tion**, *n.*

clar·i·net (klar′ə net′), *n.* a woodwind instrument, having a mouthpiece with a single reed and played by means of holes and keys.

clar·i·net·ist (klar′ə net′ist), *n.* person who plays a clarinet.

clar·i·on (klar′ē ən), **1** *n.* a trumpet with clear, shrill tones. **2** *n.* sound made by this trumpet or a sound like it. **3** *adj.* clear and shrill: *a clarion call.*

clar·i·ty (klar′ə tē), *n.* clearness: *He writes with great clarity.*

Clark (klärk), *n.* **1 George Rog·ers** (roj′ərz), 1752-1818, American soldier and frontiersman. **2** his brother, **William**, 1770-1838, American soldier and explorer of the American northwest together with Meriwether Lewis.

clash (klash), **1** *n.* a loud, harsh sound like that of two things running into each other, of striking metal, or of bells rung together but not in tune: *He heard the clash of cymbals.* **2** *v.* to make or cause to make a loud, harsh sound: *The metal gate clashed shut.* **3** *n.* a strong disagreement; conflict: *There are many clashes of opinion between the opposing candidates.* **4** *v.* to come into conflict; disagree strongly: *The freshmen clashed with the sophomores.* **5** *v.* to fail to harmonize: *Those colors clash.* ❑ *n., pl.* **clash·es.**

clasp (klasp), **1** *n.* thing to fasten two parts or pieces together. A buckle on a belt is one kind of clasp. **2** *v.* to fasten together with a clasp. **3** *v.* to hold closely with the arms; embrace: *I clasped the kitten.* **4** *n.* a close hold with the arms: *The dog escaped from the clasp of the bear.* **5** *v.* to grip firmly with the hand; grasp: *I clasped the railing as I climbed the stairs.* **6** *n.* a firm grip with the hand: *She gave my hand a warm clasp.*

class (klas), **1** *n.* group of persons or things alike in some way; kind; sort: *That magazine has an intelligent class of readers.* **2** *n.* group of students taught together: *The art class meets in room 202.* **3** *n.* a meeting of such a group: *When I was absent I missed a great many classes.* **4** *n.* all pupils entering a school together and graduating in the same year: *The class of 2007 graduates in 2007.* **5** *n.* rank or division of society: *the upper class, the middle class, the lower class.* **6** *v.* to put or be in a class or group; classify: *She is classed with the best swimmers in the school.*

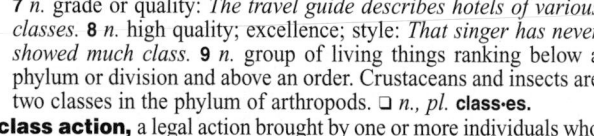
clarinet

7 *n.* grade or quality: *The travel guide describes hotels of various classes.* **8** *n.* high quality; excellence; style: *That singer has never showed much class.* **9** *n.* group of living things ranking below a phylum or division and above an order. Crustaceans and insects are two classes in the phylum of arthropods. ❑ *n., pl.* **class·es.**

class action, a legal action brought by one or more individuals who represent the whole class of persons directly affected by the case.

clas·sic (klas′ik), **1** *n.* work of literature or art of the highest rank or quality: *Louisa May Alcott's book "Little Women" is a classic.* **2** *n.* author or artist of acknowledged excellence whose works serve as a standard, model, or guide: *Shakespeare is a classic.* **3** *adj.* of the highest rank or quality; serving as a standard, model, or guide: *The "Mona Lisa" is a classic work of art.* **4** *adj.* simple and fine in form: *the classic design of a Greek temple.* **5** *n.* contest of great importance: *The World Series is a baseball classic.* **6** *adj.* of the literature, art, and life of ancient Greece and Rome. **7** *n.pl.* **the classics,** the literature of ancient Greece and Rome.

clas·si·cal (klas′ə kəl), *adj.* **1** of or about the literature, art, and life of ancient Greece and Rome: *Classical languages include ancient Greek and the Latin of the ancient Romans.* **2** excellent; first-class. **3** simple and fine in form. **4** of high musical quality and enjoyed especially by serious students of music. Symphonies, concertos, and operas are considered classical music.

clas·si·fi·ca·tion (klas′ə fə kā′shən), *n.* **1** category; class: *Three classifications of cloud are high, middle, and low.* **2** arrangement in classes or groups; grouping according to some system: *the classification of books in a library.*

clas·si·fied (klas′ə fīd), *adj.* **1** sorted or arranged in classes. A classified telephone directory lists names according to classes of business, services, and professions. **2** having a government classification as secret, confidential, or restricted: *classified documents.* **3** secret: *The airplane was on a classified flight.*

classified ad, want ad.

clas·si·fy (klas′ə fī), *v.* to arrange in classes or groups; group according to some system: *Botanists have attempted to classify all plants.* ❑ *v.* **clas·si·fied, clas·si·fy·ing.** —**clas′si·fi′a·ble**, *adj.*

class·mate (klas′māt′), *n.* member of the same class in school.

class·room (klas′rüm′), *n.* room in which classes are held; schoolroom.

clas·tic (klas′tik), *adj.* (of rock or sediment) formed from particles eroded from older rocks. Sandstone is a clastic rock.

clat·ter (klat′ər), **1** *n.* a confused noise like that of many plates being struck together: *The clatter in the cafeteria made it hard for us to hear one another talk.* ■ See Synonym Study at **noise.** **2** *v.* to move or fall with confused noise; make a confused noise: *The horse's hoofs clattered over the stones.* —**clat′ter·er**, *n.*

clause (klôz), *n.* **1** part of a sentence having a subject and predicate. In "He came before we left," "He came" is a main clause that can stand alone as a sentence, and "before we left" is a subordinate clause that depends upon the main clause for completion of its meaning. **2** a single paragraph or division of a contract, deed, will, or any other written agreement: *A clause in our lease says we may not keep a dog in this building.*

claus·tro·pho·bi·a (klô′strə fō′bē ə), *n.* an abnormal fear of enclosed spaces: *Elevators give me claustrophobia.*

clav·i·chord (klav′ə kôrd), *n.* a musical instrument with strings and a keyboard. The piano developed from it.

clav·i·cle (klav′ə kəl), *n.* collarbone.

cla·vier (klə vir′), *n.* **1** keyboard or set of keys of a piano, organ, etc. **2** any musical instrument with a keyboard. The harpsichord and piano are two kinds of claviers.

claw (klô), **1** *n.* a sharp, hooked nail on a bird's or animal's foot. **2** *n.* the pincers of a lobster, crab, etc. **3** *n.* anything like a claw. The part of a hammer used for pulling nails is the claw. **4** *v.* to scratch, tear, seize, or pull with claws or hands: *The kitten was clawing the rug.* —**claw′like′**, *adj.*

clay (klā), *n.* a stiff, sticky kind of earth, that can be easily shaped when wet and hardens when it is dried or baked. Bricks, dishes, and vases may be made from clay. —**clay′like′**, *adj.*

Clay (klā), *n.* Henry, 1777-1852, American political leader. ■ Henry Clay ran for president in 1832 and 1844. He once said "I'd rather be right than be president."

clay·ey (klā′ē), *adj.* **1** of, like, or containing clay. **2** covered or smeared with clay. ❑ *adj.* **clay·i·er, clay·i·est.**

clay pigeon, a saucerlike clay target thrown in the air or released from the trap in trapshooting.

clean (klēn), **1** *adj.* free from dirt or filth; not soiled or stained: *clean clothes.* **2** *adj.* guiltless; free from wrong: *a politician with a clean record.* **3** *adj.* having clean habits: *Cats are clean animals.* **4** *v.* to make clean: *clean a room.* **5** *v.* to do cleaning: *I am going to clean this morning.* **6** *adj.* clear, even, or regular: *a clean cut with no ragged edges.* **7** *adj.* well-shaped; trim: *an airplane with clean, sleek lines.* **8** *adj.* clever; skillful: *a clean performance.* **9** *adj.* complete; entire; total: *After leaving the company, she made a clean break with everyone she had known there.* **10** *adv.* completely; entirely; totally: *The horse jumped clean over the brook.* **11** *adv.* by the rules; in a fair way: *Both teams played the game clean, despite their fierce rivalry.* —**clean′ness,** *n.*

clean out, 1 to make clean by emptying: *Clean out your desk.* **2** to empty; use up: *The children cleaned out a whole box of cookies.* **3** INFORMAL. to deprive of money: *cleaned out in a card game.*

clean up, 1 to make clean by removing dirt, rubbish, etc.: *clean up a campsite.* **2** to put in order: *clean up a cluttered drawer.* **3** to finish; complete: *Let's clean up this work.*

clean-cut (klēn′kut′), *adj.* **1** having clear, sharp outlines; distinct; definite: *a clean-cut profile.* **2** having a neat and wholesome look: *a clean-cut young man.*

clean·er (klē′nər), *n.* **1** person whose work is keeping buildings, windows, or other objects clean. **2** anything that removes dirt, grease, or stains. **3** dry cleaner.

clean·ly[1] (klen′lē), *adj.* clean: *Our cat is a cleanly animal.* ❑ *adj.* **clean·li·er, clean·li·est.** —**clean′li·ness,** *n.*

clean·ly[2] (klēn′lē), *adv.* in a clean manner: *The butcher's knife cut cleanly through the meat.*

cleanse (klenz), *v.* **1** to make clean: *cleanse a wound before bandaging.* **2** to make pure: *cleanse the soul.* ❑ *v.* **cleansed, cleans·ing.** —**cleans′a·ble,** *adj.*

cleaner (def. 1)

cleans·er (klen′zər), *n.* substance for cleaning, especially a powder for scrubbing.

clean·up (klēn′up′), **1** *n.* act of cleaning up: *The cleanup of the school auditorium took an hour.* **2** *adj.* batting fourth in a baseball lineup: *the cleanup hitter.*

clear (klir), **1** *adj.* not cloudy, misty, or hazy; bright; light: *A clear sky is free of clouds.* **2** *adj.* easy to see through; transparent: *clear glass.* **3** *adj.* easily heard, seen, or understood; plain; distinct: *a clear voice, a clear view, a clear account of the accident.* **4** *adj.* free from blemishes: *a clear skin.* **5** *adj.* sure; certain: *It is clear that it is going to rain.* **6** *adj.* open; not blocked: *When the snowplows come, the road will soon be clear.* **7** *v.* to make clear: *The wind cleared the sky of clouds.* **8** *v.* to become clear: *It rained and then it cleared.* **9** *v.* to remove something to make a space clear: *clear the dishes from the table.* **10** *v.* to pass by or over without touching: *The horse cleared the fence.* **11** *adj.* free from blame or guilt; innocent: *a clear conscience.* **12** *v.* to make free from blame or guilt; prove to be innocent: *The jury's verdict cleared the accused.* **13** *adj.* free from debts or charges: *He made a clear profit of $400 after expenses.* **14** *v.* to make as profit free from debts or charges: *The company cleared three million dollars last year.* **15** *v.* to empty data from the temporary memory or the screen of a computer or calculator: *She cleared the total and added the numbers again.* **16** *adv.* in a clear manner; completely; entirely: *We could see clear to the bottom of the lake.* **17** *v.* to get

approval: *I cleared my project topic with the teacher.* —**clear′er,** *n.* —**clear′ly,** *adv.* —**clear′ness,** *n.*

clear away or **clear off, 1** to remove something to make a space clear: *I cleared away the snow with a shovel.* **2** to disappear; go away: *The fog cleared away.*

clear out, 1 to clean up by throwing out or emptying: *clear out trash, clear out a closet.* **2** to go away; leave: *The audience cleared out of the theater quickly.*

clear up, 1 to make or become clear: *Stay indoors until the weather clears up.* **2** to settle; solve: *She cleared up the misunderstanding by explaining what she meant to say.*

in the clear, free of guilt or blame; innocent: *The testimony of the witness puts the suspect in the clear.*

SYNONYM STUDY **Clear, plain,** and **obvious** all mean easy to see, hear, or understand. **Clear** is a general word: *A good definition is short and clear.* **Plain** suggests no questions or doubts: *It is plain that she likes him.* **Obvious** means very plain: *His obvious musical talent should be encouraged.*

clear·ance (klir′əns), *n.* **1** act of clearing away anything no longer wanted where it is: *slum clearance.* **2** a clear space; distance between things that pass by each other without touching: *There was only a foot of clearance between the top of the truck and the roof of the tunnel.* **3** certification that a person considered for a position of trust is reliable. **4** permission or authorization for a vehicle to go forward, or do some other action: *The pilot circled the airfield, waiting for clearance to land.* **5** sale of goods at reduced prices.

clear-cut (klir′kut′), **1** *adj.* having clear, sharp outlines: *a face with clear-cut features.* **2** *adj.* clear; definite; distinct: *She had clear-cut ideas about what she wanted.* **3** *n.* Also, **clear cutting,** a section of forest where all the trees have been cut down. **4** *v.* to cut down all the trees in a section of forest.

clear-cut (def. 3)

clear·head·ed (klir′hed′id), *adj.* having or showing a clear understanding; reasonable.

clear·ing (klir′ing), *n.* an open space of land in a forest or in an area of dense undergrowth.

cleat (klēt), *n.* **1** piece of metal, wood, or stiff leather attached to the sole or heel of a shoe to prevent slipping. **2** strip of wood or iron fastened across anything for support or for sure footing: *The gangway had cleats to keep the passengers from slipping.* **3** piece of wood or iron used for securing ropes or lines to a flagpole, a mast, a dock, etc.

cleav·age (klē′vij), *n.* **1** act of cleaving or condition of being cleft; split; division. **2** the property of a crystal or rock of splitting along planes: *Slate shows a marked cleavage and can easily be separated into layers.*

a	hat	ė	term	ȯ	order	ch	child		
ā	age	i	it	oi	oil	ng	long		a in about
ä	far	ī	ice	ou	out	sh	she		e in taken
â	care	o	hot	u	cup	th	thin	ə	i in pencil
e	let	ō	open	u̇	put	ᴛʜ	then		o in lemon
ē	equal	ȯ	saw	ü	rule	zh	measure		u in circus

cleave¹ (klēv), v. **1** to cut, divide, or split open: *A blow of the whale's tail cleaved the whaling boat in two.* **2** to pass through; pierce; penetrate: *The airplane swept across the sky, cleaving the clouds.* ❑ v. **cleaved** or **cleft** or **clove, cleaved** or **cleft** or **cloven, cleav·ing.** —**cleav′a·ble,** *adj.*

cleave² (klēv), v. to hold fast; cling; adhere: *cleave to an old-fashioned idea.* ❑ v. **cleaved, cleav·ing.**

cleav·er (klē′vər), n. a cutting tool with a heavy blade and a short handle. A butcher uses a cleaver to chop through meat or bone.

clef (klef), n. a sign in music indicating the pitch of the notes on a staff.

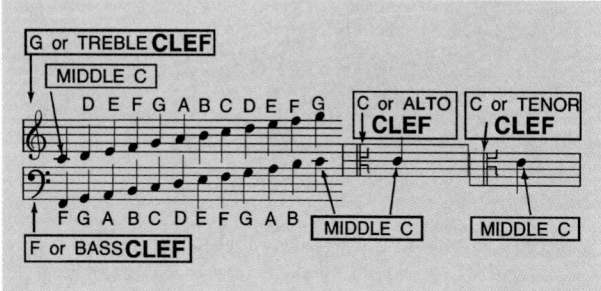

clef

cleft (kleft), **1** v. a past tense and a past participle of **cleave¹**: *A blow of the ax cleft the log in two.* **2** adj. split; divided: *a cleft stick.* **3** n. space or opening made by splitting; crack: *a cleft in the rocks.*

cleft palate, a narrow opening running lengthwise in the roof of the mouth, caused by failure of the two parts of the palate to join. Cleft palate is a birth defect.

clem·a·tis (klem′ə tis), n. any of several climbing vines with clusters of white, red, pink, blue, or purple flowers. ❑ n., pl. **clem·a·tis·es** or **clem·a·tis.**

clem·en·cy (klem′ən sē), n. **1** gentleness in the use of power or authority; mercy: *The government showed clemency to the defeated rebels.* **2** mildness: *The clemency of the weather allowed them to live outdoors.*

Clem·ens (klem′ənz), n. **Samuel Lang·horne** (lang′hôrn), the real name of **Mark Twain.**

clem·ent (klem′ənt), adj. **1** merciful toward those in your power. **2** mild: *Hawaii has clement weather.* —**clem′ent·ly,** *adv.*

Cle·men·te (klə men′ tē), n. **Ro·ber·to** (rō ber′tō), 1934-1972, American baseball player, born in Puerto Rico. ■ Roberto Clemente had a lifetime batting average of .317. He was elected to the National Baseball Hall of Fame in 1973. He died in a plane crash on his way to help earthquake victims in Nicaragua.

clench (klench), **1** v. to close tightly together: *clench your teeth, clench your fist.* **2** v. to grasp firmly: *I clenched the bat and swung at the ball.* **3** n. a firm grasp; tight grip: *the clench of a hand.* **4** v. to clinch a nail, staple, etc. ❑ n., pl. **clench·es.** —**clench′er,** n.

Cle·o·pat·ra (klē′ə pat′rə), n. 69?-30 B.C., last queen of ancient Egypt, from 47 to 30 B.C.

cler·gy (klėr′jē), n.pl. persons appointed to do religious work, such as ministers, pastors, priests, and rabbis.

cler·gy·man (klėr′jē mən), n. member of the clergy; a minister, pastor, priest, or rabbi. ❑ n., pl. **cler·gy·men.**

cler·gy·per·son (klėr′jē pėr′sən), n. member of the clergy; a minister, pastor, priest, or rabbi.

cler·gy·wom·an (klėr′jē wům ən), n. a woman member of the clergy. ❑ n., pl. **cler·gy·wom·en.**

cler·ic (klėr′ik), n. a member of the clergy.

cler·i·cal (kler′ə kəl), adj. **1** of a clerk or clerks; for clerks: *Keeping records and typing letters are clerical jobs in an office.* **2** of the clergy: *clerical duties, clerical robes.* —**cler′i·cal·ly,** *adv.*

clerk (klėrk), **1** n. person employed in a store to sell goods; salesperson in a store. **2** n. person employed in an office to file records, type letters, or keep accounts. **3** v. to work as a clerk: *I clerk in a drugstore after school.* **4** n. a public official who keeps the records and superintends the routine business of a court of law, legislature, town or county government, etc.

Cleve·land (klēv′lənd), n. **1** port in NE Ohio, on Lake Erie. **2 Gro·ver** (grō′vər), 1837-1908, the 22nd and 24th president of the United States, from 1885 to 1889 and from 1893 to 1897.

clev·er (klev′ər), adj. **1** having a quick mind; bright; intelligent: *a clever student.* ■ See Synonym Study at **smart. 2** skillful in doing some particular thing: *clever at working with wood.* **3** showing skill or intelligence: *The magician did a clever trick. Her answer to the riddle was clever.* —**clev′er·ly,** *adv.* —**clev′er·ness,** n.

cli·ché (klē shā′), n. expression or idea worn out by long use. ❑ n., pl. **cli·chés.**

click (klik), **1** n. a short, sharp sound like that of a key turning in a lock: *We heard a click as the dime went down the coin slot.* **2** v. to make or cause to make such a sound: *The key clicked in the lock. I clicked my tongue.* **3** v. INFORMAL. to come to an understanding; be in harmony: *I clicked with them from the start.* **4** v. INFORMAL. to be successful: *The new play clicked with the critics.* **5** v. to press and release a button on a computer mouse, in order to give an instruction to the computer.

cli·ent (klī′ənt), n. **1** person for whom a lawyer, accountant, or other professional person acts. **2** customer.

cli·en·tele (klī′ən tel′), n. **1** clients as a group. **2** customers.

cliff (klif), n. a very steep rock slope. —**cliff′like′,** *adj.*

cliff dweller, member of a group of prehistoric people who lived in the southwestern United States in caves or houses built in a cliff. The cliff dwellers were ancestors of the Pueblos.

cliff·hang·er (klif′hang′ər), n. story, movie, etc., based on very strong and prolonged suspense.

cli·mac·tic (klī mak′tik), adj. of or forming a climax: *the climactic scene of a play.*

cli·mate (klī′mit), n. **1** the kind of weather a place has, year after year. Climate includes heat and cold, moisture and dryness, clearness and cloudiness, wind and calm. **2** region with certain conditions of heat and cold, rainfall, wind, sunlight, etc.: *to live in a dry climate.* **3** condition or feeling that exists at some time: *The climate of public opinion favored tax reforms.* —**cli·mat′ic,** *adj.* —**cli·mat′i·cal·ly,** *adv.*

cli·ma·tol·o·gy (klī′mə tol′ə jē), n. science that deals with climate. —**cli′ma·tol′o·gist,** n.

cli·max (klī′maks), **1** n. the highest point of interest; most exciting part: *A visit to the Grand Canyon was the climax of our vacation.* **2** v. to bring or come to a climax: *Her election to the Senate climaxed a long career in politics.* **3** adj. (in ecology) very well adapted to an environment and likely to continue as a common inhabitant. Climax species and climax communities usually appear after others that are less well adapted and do not continue as inhabitants. ❑ n., pl. **cli·max·es.**

climb (klīm), **1** v. to go up, especially by using the hands or feet, or both; ascend: *She climbed the stairs quickly.* **2** v. to go in any direction, especially with the help of the hands: *climb over a fence, climb down a ladder.* **3** v. to move upward; rise: *The price of gasoline has climbed during the past year.* **4** v. to grow upward by holding on or twining around: *Ivy and honeysuckle climbed over the wall.* **5** n. act of climbing: *Our climb up the mountain took ten hours.* **6** n. place to be climbed: *The path ended in a difficult climb.* ■ Another word that sounds like this is **clime.** —**climb′a·ble,** *adj.*

climb·er (klī′mər), *n.* **1** person or thing that climbs. **2** a climbing plant; vine. **3** INFORMAL. person who is always trying to get ahead socially.

clime (klīm), *n.* OLD USE. **1** region. **2** climate. ■ Another word that sounds like this is **climb.**

clinch (klinch), **1** *v.* to fasten a driven nail, a bolt, etc., firmly by bending over the point that sticks out. **2** *v.* to settle decisively: *A deposit of fifty dollars clinched our bargain.* **3** *v.* to grasp one another tightly in boxing or wrestling; grapple. **4** *n.* act of clinching in boxing or wrestling. □ *n., pl.* **clinch·es.**

clinch·er (klin′chər), *n.* a decisive argument, statement, etc.

climber (def. 1)

cling (kling), *v.* to stick or hold fast; adhere: *Wet clothes cling to the body.* ■ See Synonym Study at **stick**². □ *v.* **clung, cling·ing.**

cling·stone (kling′stōn′), **1** *n.* peach, plum, etc., with a stone that clings to the pulp. **2** *adj.* having a fruit stone that is not easily separated from the pulp.

clin·ic (klin′ik), *n.* **1** place connected with a hospital or medical school where people can receive medical treatment, sometimes at a reduced cost. **2** place for medical treatment or study of certain people or diseases: *The children's clinic is open during school hours.* **3** place where practical instruction on any subject is given: *a football clinic, a reading clinic.* **4** practical instruction of medical students by examining or treating patients in the presence of the students.

clin·i·cal (klin′ə kəl), *adj.* **1** of or about a clinic. **2** used or performed in a sickroom: *Doctors learn clinical procedure.* —**clin′i·cal·ly,** *adv.*

cli·ni·cian (kli nish′ən), *n.* doctor who practices or teaches in a clinic.

clink (klingk), **1** *n.* a light, sharp, ringing sound like that of drinking glasses hitting together. **2** *v.* to make or cause to make this sound: *The spoon clinked in the glass.*

clink·er (kling′kər), *n.* a large, rough cinder.

Clin·ton (klin′tən), *n.* **Bill** (bil), born 1946, the 42nd president of the United States, since 1993. His full name is William Jefferson Clinton.

clip¹ (klip), **1** *v.* to trim with shears, scissors, or clippers; cut short; cut: *A sheep's fleece is clipped off to get wool.* **2** *v.* to trim: *The hedge in front of the house needs to be clipped.* **3** *n.* act of clipping: *My hair needs a clip around the back of my neck.* **4** *v.* to cut out of a magazine, newspaper, etc.: *She clipped the cartoon and passed it around the class.* **5** *n.* piece clipped from a reel of film or videotape, a newspaper, magazine, etc. **6** *n.* a fast speed: *Our bus passed through the village at quite a clip.* **7** *v.* to hit or punch sharply: *The boxer clipped his opponent on the jaw.* □ *v.* **clipped, clip·ping.**

clip² (klip), **1** *v.* to hold tight; fasten: *The teacher clipped the papers together.* **2** *n.* something used for clipping things together. A paper clip is made of a piece of bent wire. **3** *n.* a metal holder for cartridges used in some firearms. **4** *n.* piece of jewelry fastened by means of a hinged clasp; brooch. □ *v.* **clipped, clip·ping.** [Clip² comes from an old English word meaning "to encircle" or "to embrace."]

clip art, simple drawings or pictures copied as illustrations in documents. Clip art is usually not copyrighted.

clip·board (klip′bôrd′), *n.* board with a heavy spring clip at one end for holding papers while writing.

clip·per (klip′ər), *n.* **1** person who clips or cuts. **2** Often, **clippers,** *pl.* tool for cutting: *hair clippers, a nail clipper.* **3** a large sailing ship built and rigged for speed.

clip·ping (klip′ing), *n.* **1** article, picture, or advertisement cut out of a newspaper, magazine, etc. **2** piece cut off or out of something else.

clique (klēk *or* klik), **1** *n.* a small, exclusive group of people within a larger group. **2** *v.* to form or associate in a clique. □ *v.* **cliqued, cli·quing.**

cli·quish (klē′kish *or* klik′ish), *adj.* **1** like a clique. **2** tending to form a clique. —**cli′quish·ness,** *n.*

clit·or·is (klit′ər is), *n.* a small organ of the female of most mammals located at the front of the sex organs.

clo·a·ca (klō ā′kə), *n.* the rear body cavity of birds, reptiles, amphibians, and most fishes. Solid waste, liquid waste, and reproductive material all empty into and from the cloaca. □ *n., pl.* **clo·a·cas, clo·a·cae** (klō ā′sē). [Cloaca comes from a Latin word meaning "sewer."]

cloak (klōk), **1** *n.* long, loose piece of clothing for outdoor wear, usually without sleeves. **2** *v.* to cover with a cloak. **3** *n.* anything that covers or conceals: *They hid their dislike of us behind a cloak of friendship.* **4** *v.* to cover up; conceal: *I tried to cloak my fear by whistling and pretending to be unafraid.*

cloak·room (klōk′rüm′), *n.* room where coats, hats, etc., can be left for a time; coatroom.

clob·ber (klob′ər), *v.* INFORMAL. **1** to hit hard or beat severely. **2** to defeat severely.

clock (klok), **1** *n.* device for measuring and showing time. **2** *v.* to measure or record the time or speed of; time: *I clocked the runners with a stopwatch to see who was the fastest.*

WORD STORY **Clock** comes from a Latin word meaning "bell." The first mechanical clocks were invented in the Middle Ages and had only bells to mark the hours, no numbers or hands.

clock radio, radio with a built-in clock that can be set to turn on or turn off the radio, an alarm, or both.

clock·wise (klok′wīz′), *adv., adj.* in the direction in which the hands of a clock move; from left to right: *Turn the key clockwise to unlock the door. He opened the faucet with a clockwise turn.*

clock·work (klok′wėrk′), *n.* **1** the machinery by which a clock is run. **2** any similar machinery, consisting of gears, wheels, and springs. Mechanical toys are run by clockwork.
like clockwork, with great regularity and smoothness: *The launching of the rocket went off like clockwork.*

clod (klod), *n.* **1** lump of earth. **2** a stupid person; blockhead.

clod·dish (klod′ish), *adj.* like a clod; stupid.

clog (klog), **1** *v.* to fill up; choke up: *Grease clogged the drain.* **2** *v.* to hinder; hold back: *An accident clogged traffic.* **3** *n.* anything that hinders. **4** *n.* shoe with a thick, wooden sole. □ *v.* **clogged, clog·ging.**

clog dance, dance in which a dancer wears clogs to keep time while dancing. —**clog dancer.** —**clog dancing.**

clois·ter (kloi′stər), **1** *n.* a covered walk, often along the wall of a building, with a row of pillars on the open side or sides. A cloister is sometimes built around the courtyard of a monastery, church, or college building. **2** *n.* place of religious retirement; convent or monastery. **3** *n.* a quiet place shut away from the world. **4** *v.* to shut away in a quiet place: *He cloistered himself in his room to work.*

clomp (klomp), *v.* to walk heavily and clumsily; clump.

clone (klōn), **1** *n.* group of plants or animals produced from a single ancestor without sexual reproduction. **2** *n.* a living being with the same genes as another, from which it has been produced asexually. **3** *v.* to reproduce without sexual reproduction. **4** *n.* person or thing almost identical to another: *His new novel is a clone of his last book.* □ *v.* **cloned, clon·ing.**

WORD STORY **Clone** comes from a Greek word meaning "twig." All the twigs of a plant have the same genes in their cells, and living things with a single ancestor are like twigs of one plant.

clop (klop), **1** *n.* a sharp, hard sound like that of a horse's hoof on a paved road. **2** *v.* to make such a sound. □ *v.* **clopped, clop·ping.**

a	hat	ė	term	ô	order	ch	child		a in about
ā	age	i	it	oi	oil	ng	long		e in taken
ä	far	ī	ice	ou	out	sh	she	ə	i in pencil
â	care	o	hot	u	cup	th	thin		o in lemon
e	let	ō	open	u̇	put	ŦH	then		u in circus
ē	equal	ȯ	saw	ü	rule	zh	measure		

close¹ (klōz), **1** *v.* to bring together or move the parts of so as to leave no opening; shut: *Close the door. Close your eyes.* **2** *v.* to stop up; fill; block: *close a crack in the wall with plaster.* **3** *v.* to bring together; come together: *His arms closed around the sobbing child.* **4** *v.* to bring or come to an end; finish: *The meeting closed with refreshments. I closed my speech with a plea for donations.* **5** *v.* to not be open for business any longer: *The bank closes at 2:30 on Wednesdays.* **6** *n.* an end; finish: *She spoke at the close of the meeting.* ❑ *v.* **closed, clos·ing.** ∎ Another word that can sound like this is **clothes.** —**clos′er,** *n.*

close down, to shut completely; stop: *The factory closed down because it had no orders from customers.*

close in on, to come near and shut in on all sides: *The zoo keepers closed in on the escaped tiger.*

close out, to sell in order to get rid of: *The store closed out the old models in a special sale.*

close ranks, to show unity and loyalty, especially in reaction to opposition or difficulty: *After the mayor criticized the principal, the students and faculty closed ranks and showed their support.*

close up, 1 to shut completely; stop up; block: *Workers closed up the old well.* **2** to bring or come nearer together: *She needs to close up her letters when writing in cursive.*

close² (klōs), **1** *adj.* with little space between; near together; near: *These two houses are close.* **2** *adj.* fitting tightly; tight; narrow: *They live in very close quarters.* **3** *adj.* having its parts near together; compact: *This sweater has a close weave.* **4** *adj.* known very well; intimate; dear: *We are close friends.* **5** *adj.* careful; exact: *You need to take closer measurements before ordering the lumber.* **6** *adj.* thorough; strict: *Pay close attention.* **7** *adj.* having little fresh air; stuffy: *With the windows shut, the room was hot and close.* **8** *adj.* near the surface; short: *a close haircut.* **9** *adj.* stingy: *He is as close as a miser with his money.* **10** *adj.* nearly equal: *The last game was a close contest.* **11** *adj.* not fond of talking; not open; reserved: *She is very close about her own affairs.* **12** *adv.* near: *The two farms lie close together. The end of the year is drawing close.* ❑ *adj.* **clos·er, clos·est.** —**close′ly,** *adv.* —**close′ness,** *n.*

close call (klōs), a narrow escape; close shave.

closed captioning, a system of captions that accompany some TV shows in order to aid the hearing-impaired, visible on TV sets equipped with a special device. —**closed-captioned,** *adj.*

closed captioning

closed-cir·cuit (klōzd′sėr′kit), *adj.* of or about television transmission by cable to a limited audience, as in a group of theaters or classrooms, or for security purposes: *Closed-circuit TV cameras watch the back door of the jewelry store.*

closed-door, (klōzd′dôr′), *adj.* private; not open to the public or the press: *a closed-door meeting of the school board.*

closed shop, factory or business that employs only members of labor unions.

close·fist·ed (klōs′fis′tid), *adj.* stingy; miserly.

close-knit (klōs′nit′), *adj.* strongly held together by affection or common interests: *a close-knit family.*

close-mouthed (klōs′mouŦHd′ *or* klōs′moutht′), *adj.* not fond of talking; reserved; reticent.

close-out (klōz′out′), *n.* sale held to get rid of some or all of the goods handled by a business.

close quarters, 1 fighting or struggling close together. **2** place or position with little space.

close shave (klōs), INFORMAL. close call.

clos·et (kloz′it), **1** *n.* a small room for storing clothes or household supplies. **2** *v.* to shut up in a private room for a secret talk: *We were closeted with our lawyer for over an hour.*

close-up (klōs′up′), *n.* **1** picture taken with a camera at close range. **2** a close view.

clos·ing (klō′zing), *n.* **1** word or words that come before the signature at the end of a letter. **2** meeting for final arrangements between buyer and seller at the time property is sold and title of ownership is transferred.

clo·sure (klō′zhər), *n.* **1** act of closing or being closed: *the closure of a shop.* **2** thing that closes. **3** cloture.

clot (klot), **1** *n.* a half-solid lump; thickened mass: *A blood clot formed in the cut and stopped the bleeding.* **2** *v.* to form into clots; coagulate: *Blood clots when it is exposed to the air.* ❑ *v.* **clot·ted, clot·ting.**

cloth (klóth), *n.* **1** material made from wool, cotton, silk, rayon, linen, or other fiber, by weaving, knitting, or rolling and pressing. **2** piece of this material used for a special purpose: *a cloth for the table.* **3 the cloth,** the clergy. ❑ *n., pl.* **cloths** (klóŦHz *or* klóths) for 2.

clothe (klōŦH), *v.* **1** to put clothes on; cover with clothes; dress: *We clothed the child warmly in a heavy sweater and pants.* **2** to provide with clothes: *It costs quite a bit to clothe a family of six.* **3** to cover: *The sun clothes the earth with light.* **4** to provide; furnish; equip: *Congress is clothed with the authority to make laws.* **5** to express: *Her ideas are clothed in simple words.* ❑ *v.* **clothed** or **clad, cloth·ing.**

clothes (klōz *or* klōŦHz), *n.pl.* **1** coverings for a person's body: *I bought some new clothes for my trip.* **2** bedclothes. ∎ Another word that can sound like this is **close¹.**

SYNONYM STUDY Clothes, clothing, and dress all mean covering for a person's body. **Clothes** is a general word: *Their clothes were new.* **Clothing** suggests a large amount: *This store sells children's clothing.* **Dress** suggests clothing of a particular type: *It's a picnic dinner, so casual dress will be fine.*

clothes·line (klōz′līn′), *n.* rope or wire to hang clothes on to dry or air them.

clothes·pin (klōz′pin′), *n.* a wooden or plastic clip to hold clothes on a clothesline.

cloth·ier (klō′ŦHyər), *n.* **1** seller or maker of clothing. **2** seller of cloth.

cloth·ing (klō′ŦHing), *n.* **1** clothes. ∎ See Synonym Study at **clothes. 2** covering.

clo·ture (klō′chər), *n.* act of limiting debate by a legislature in order to get an immediate vote on the question being discussed; closure.

cloud (kloud), **1** *n.* many tiny drops of water or tiny ice particles floating together in the air. Clouds may be white, rounded heaps or fleecy streamers, or dull, dark layers. **2** *n.* mass of smoke or dust in the air. **3** *v.* to cover with a cloud or as if with a cloud: *Mist clouded our view.* **4** *v.* to grow or become cloudy: *The sky clouded over.* **5** *n.* a great number of things moving close together through the air: *a cloud of locusts.* **6** *n.* anything that darkens or dims: *A cloud of disappointment settled on his face.* **7** *v.* to darken; dim; make or become gloomy: *a face clouded with anger.* [**Cloud** comes from an old English word meaning "hill." Clouds often look like big hills.] —**cloud′like′,** *adj.*

in the clouds, 1 unrealistic or fanciful; not practical. **2** daydreaming; absent-minded.

under a cloud, under suspicion.

cloud·burst (kloud′bėrst′), *n.* a sudden, heavy rain.

cloud chamber, a container of a special cloudy vapor through which electrically charged atomic particles make visible tracks. The tracks help scientists to examine and identify the particles.

cloud·less (kloud′lis), *adj.* without a cloud; clear and bright; sunny: *a cloudless sky.* —**cloud′less·ness,** *n.*

cloud·y (klou′dē), *adj.* **1** covered with clouds; having clouds in it: *a cloudy sky.* **2** not clear: *The stream is cloudy with mud.* **3** not carefully thought out; confused; indistinct: *cloudy ideas.* **4** gloomy; frowning: *The unhappy child had a cloudy expression.* ❑ *adj.* **cloud·i·er, cloud·i·est.** —**cloud′i·ly,** *adv.* —**cloud′i·ness,** *n.*

clout (klout), **1** *v.* to hit with the hand; rap; knock. **2** *n.* a rap or knock; cuff. **3** *n.* political force, power, or influence: *The builder has a lot of clout, so the building permit was granted quickly.*

clove¹ (klōv), *n.* Usually, **cloves,** *pl.* the dried flower bud of a tropical tree, used as a strong, fragrant spice.

clove² (klōv), *n.* a small, separate section of a bulb: *a clove of garlic.*

clove³ (klōv), *v.* a past tense of **cleave¹.**

clo·ven (klō′vən), **1** *v.* a past participle of **cleave¹. 2** *adj.* split; divided. Cows and sheep have cloven hoofs.

clo·ver (klō′vər), *n.* any of numerous low plants related to the pea, with leaves having three leaflets and sweet-smelling rounded heads of small red, white, yellow, or purple flowers. Clover is grown as food for horses and cattle and to improve the soil.
in clover, enjoying a life of pleasure without work or worry.

clo·ver·leaf (klō′vər lēf′), *n.* intersection of two highways, with one passing over the other. A series of curving ramps in the shape of a four-leaf clover lets traffic move from one highway to the other without having to cross in front of other traffic.

clown (kloun), **1** *n.* performer in a circus, carnival, etc., who makes people laugh by wearing funny costumes and makeup and by playing tricks and jokes. **2** *v.* to act like a clown; play tricks and jokes; act silly. **3** *n.* person who acts like a clown; silly person. **4** *n.* a rude, bad-mannered person.

clown (def. 1)

clown·ish (klou′nish), *adj.* like a clown; like a clown's: *clownish behavior.* —**clown′ish·ly,** *adv.* —**clown′ish·ness,** *n.*

cloy (kloi), *v.* to make or become weary by too much of anything pleasant: *Her appetite was cloyed with too much holiday food.* —**cloy′ing·ly,** *adv.* —**cloy′ing·ness,** *n.*

club (klub), **1** *n.* a heavy stick of wood, thicker at one end, used as a weapon. **2** *n.* a wooden or metal stick with a long handle, used in some games to hit a ball: *golf clubs.* **3** *v.* to beat or hit with a club or something similar. **4** *n.* group of people joined together for some special purpose: *a tennis club, a yacht club, a nature-study club.* **5** *n.* building or rooms used by a club. **6** *v.* to join together for some special purpose: *The neighborhood children clubbed together to put on a show.* **7** *n.* figure shaped like this: ♣. **8** *n.* a playing card with one or more black, club-shaped figures. **9** *n.pl.* **clubs,** suit of such playing cards. ❑ *v.* **clubbed, club·bing.**

club·foot (klub′fut′), *n.* **1** birth defect in which the foot is twisted out of shape and is shorter than normal. **2** foot that is shaped in this way. ❑ *n., pl.* **club·feet** (klub′fēt′) for 2.

club·house (klub′hous′), *n.* **1** building used by a club. **2** locker room of an athletic team. ❑ *n., pl.* **club·hous·es** (klub′hou′ziz).

club moss, any of several low flowerless plants with upright stems that look like vines covered with pine needles; ground pine.

club sandwich, sandwich made with tomatoes, lettuce, and two kinds of meat, usually on three pieces of bread.

club soda, soda water.

cluck (kluk), **1** *n.* the sound that a hen makes in calling to her chicks. **2** *v.* to make this sound.

clue (klü), **1** *n.* something which helps to solve a mystery or problem: *The police could find no fingerprints or other clues to help them solve the robbery.* **2** *v.* to give a clue to: *The note clued us to what was going on.* ❑ *v.* **clued, clue·ing** or **clu·ing.**

clue·less (klü′lis), *adj.* SLANG. ignorant; foolish; without a clue how to behave or what to do: *She pretends to understand computers, but she's really clueless.*

clump (klump), **1** *n.* number of things of the same kind growing or grouped together; cluster: *The girl hid in a clump of bushes.*

2 *n.* lump or mass: *a clump of earth.* **3** *n.* sound of heavy, clumsy walking. **4** *v.* to walk with a heavy, clumsy, noisy tread; clomp: *The weary hikers clumped along in their heavy boots.* **5** *v.* to form a clump; form into a clump.

clump·y (klum′pē), *adj.* full of clumps.

clum·sy (klum′zē), *adj.* **1** awkward in moving; not graceful or skillful: *The cast on my foot made me walk in a clumsy manner.* ■ See Synonym Study at **awkward. 2** awkwardly done; tactless: *a clumsy reply.* **3** not well shaped or well made: *The stage for the puppet show was a clumsy structure made out of old boxes.* ❑ *adj.* **clum·si·er, clum·si·est.** —**clum′si·ly,** *adv.* —**clum′si·ness,** *n.*

clung (klung), *v.* past tense and past participle of **cling:** *The child clung to his sister. Mud had clung to my boots.*

clunk (klungk), *n.* a dull sound like that of something hard striking the ground; thump.

clus·ter (klus′tər), **1** *n.* number of things of the same kind growing or grouped together: *a cluster of grapes.* **2** *n.* any group of persons or things: *Protesters stood in a cluster before the mayor's house.* **3** *v.* to form into a cluster; gather in a group: *The students clustered around their teacher.*

clutch¹ (kluch), **1** *v.* to grasp tightly: *I clutched the railing to keep my balance.* **2** *n.* a tight grasp; hold: *I lost my clutch on the rope and fell.* **3** *v.* to seize eagerly; snatch: *clutch at an opportunity.* **4** *n.pl.* **clutches,** control; power: *That country is in the clutches of a dictator.* **5** *n.* device in a machine for transmitting motion from one shaft to another or for disconnecting related moving parts. The clutch in motor vehicles with a stick shift is used to connect or disconnect the engine and the transmission. **6** *n.* lever or pedal that operates this device. **7** *adj.* in a tense, important, or critical situation: *She made the clutch winning goal.* ❑ *n., pl.* **clutch·es.**
in the clutch, in a critical situation: *That baseball player can usually be counted on to get a hit in the clutch.*

clutch² (kluch), *n.* nest of eggs. ❑ *n., pl.* **clutch·es.**

clut·ter (klut′ər), **1** *n.* number of things scattered or left in disorder; litter: *It was hard to find the lost pen in the clutter of his room.* **2** *v.* to litter with things in confusion: *Her desk drawer was cluttered with old papers.*

Cly·tem·nes·tra (klī′təm nes′trə), *n.* (in Greek legends) the wife of Agamemnon. She killed him on his return from Troy and was afterwards slain by their son Orestes.

Cm, symbol for curium.

cm or **cm.,** centimeter or centimeters.

CO or **C.O.,** Commanding Officer.

c/o or **c.o.,** in care of.

co-, *prefix.* with; together: *coexist = exist together; copilot = pilot with another pilot.*

Co, symbol for cobalt.

CO, Colorado (used with postal Zip Code).

Co., **1** Company. **2** County.

coach (kōch), **1** *n.* person who teaches or trains athletic teams, singers, etc.: *a swimming coach, a drama coach.* **2** *v.* to teach or train: *She coaches Olympic swimmers.* **3** *n.* a private teacher who helps someone learn a certain subject; tutor. **4** *v.* to help someone learn a certain subject; tutor. **5** *n.* a low-priced class of passenger tickets on a train or aircraft that costs less than first class. **6** *n.* a railroad car with seats for passengers. **7** *n.* bus. **8** *n.* (earlier) a large, usually closed carriage with seats inside and often on top, pulled by horses. Coaches carried passengers along a regular route, stopping for meals and fresh horses. ❑ *n., pl.* **coach·es.**

coach (def. 8)

a	hat	ė	term	ô	order	ch	child		a in about
ā	age	i	it	oi	oil	ng	long		e in taken
ä	far	ī	ice	ou	out	sh	she	ə	i in pencil
â	care	o	hot	u	cup	th	thin		o in lemon
e	let	ō	open	ů	put	ŦH	then		u in circus
ē	equal	ò	saw	ü	rule	zh	measure		

coach dog, Dalmatian. [See Word Story at **dalmatian**.]

coach·man (kōch′mən), *n.* person whose work is driving a coach or carriage. ❑ *n., pl.* **coach·men.**

co·ag·u·late (kō ag′yə lāt), *v.* to change from a liquid to a thickened mass; thicken: *Blood coagulates when it is exposed to the air.* ❑ *v.* **co·ag·u·lat·ed, co·ag·u·lat·ing. —co·ag′u·la′tion,** *n.*

Coa·hui·la (kwä wē′lä), *n.* a state in N Mexico.

coal (kōl), **1** *n.* a black mineral that burns and gives off heat, containing mostly carbon. It is formed from partly decayed plants under great pressure in the earth. **2** *n.* piece or pieces of this mineral for burning: *a bag of coal.* **3** *v.* to supply or be supplied with coal: *The ship stopped just long enough to coal.* **4** *n.* piece of burning wood, coal, etc.; ember: *The big log had burned down to a few glowing coals.*

co·a·lesce (kō′ə les′), *v.* **1** to grow together. **2** to unite into one group, mass, party, etc.; combine: *The thirteen colonies coalesced to form a nation.* ❑ *v.* **co·a·lesced, co·a·lesc·ing.**

co·a·les·cence (kō′ə les′ns), *n.* **1** act or process of growing together. **2** union; combination.

coal gas, 1 gas made from coal, used for heating and lighting. **2** gas given off by burning coal.

co·a·li·tion (kō′ə lish′ən), *n.* **1** union; combination. **2** alliance of statesmen, political parties, etc., for some special purpose. In wartime several countries may form a temporary coalition against a common enemy.

coal oil, kerosene.

coal scuttle, bucket for holding or carrying coal.

coal tar, a black, sticky substance left after coal has been distilled to make coal gas. Coal tar is used to make paving materials and is a source of chemicals used in dyes, medicines, paints, perfumes, and the like.

coarse (kôrs), *adj.* **1** made up of fairly large parts; not fine: *coarse sand.* **2** heavy or rough in looks or texture: *The old fisherman had coarse, weathered features. Burlap is a coarse cloth.* **3** common; poor; inferior: *coarse food.* **4** not delicate or refined; crude; vulgar: *coarse manners.* ❑ *adj.* **coars·er, coars·est.** ■ Another word that sounds like this is **course. —coarse′ly,** *adv.* **—coarse′ness,** *n.*

coars·en (kôr′sən), *v.* to make or become coarse: *Her skin was coarsened by wind and sun.*

coast (kōst), **1** *n.* land along the sea; seashore: *Maine has a rocky coast.* **2** *v.* to sail along or near the coast of: *The disabled ship coasted the island, looking for a harbor to make repairs.* **3** *v.* to ride or slide without the use of effort or power: *You can coast downhill on a sled.* **4** *v.* to move or advance with little effort: *The test was so easy that I coasted through it.* [Coast comes from a Latin word meaning "rib." Your ribs are in your side, and the coast is like the land's side.]

coast·al (kō′stl), *adj.* of the coast; near or along a coast: *The Coast Guard patrols coastal waters.*

coast·er (kō′stər), *n.* **1** a little tray for holding a glass or bottle, used to protect furniture from getting wet. **2** person or thing that coasts. **3** ship that sails or trades along a coast. **4** sled to coast on.

coast guard, 1 group whose work is protecting lives and property and preventing smuggling along the coast of a country. **2** member of any such group. **3 Coast Guard,** the government organization whose work is protecting lives and property and preventing smuggling along the coasts of the United States. It is under the Navy Department in wartime and under the Department of Transportation in peacetime.

coast·line (kōst′līn′), *n.* outline of a coast.

Coast Ranges, mountain system along the Pacific coast of North America, from Alaska to S California.

coat (kōt), **1** *n.* a piece of outer clothing with long sleeves: *a winter coat.* **2** *n.* a natural outer covering: *the silky coat of a kitten.* **3** *n.* a thin layer covering a surface: *a coat of paint.* **4** *v.* to cover with a thin layer: *a floor coated with varnish.* **—coat′less,** *adj.*

co·a·ti (kō ä′tē), *n.* any of several small mammals with long bodies and tails and flexible snouts, something like a raccoon. Coatis live in the southwestern United States, Mexico, and Central and South America. ❑ *n., pl.* **co·a·tis** or **co·a·ti.**

coat·ing (kō′ting), *n.* layer covering a surface: *A coating of dust lay on the furniture.*

Co·at·li·cue (kwät lē′kwä), *n.* Aztec goddess, mother of Huitzilopochtli, and protector of the people.

coat of arms, a design or pattern, usually on a shield, that in former times was a symbol for a knight or lord. Some families, schools, and other groups now have coats of arms. ❑ *n., pl.* **coats of arms.**

coat of arms

coat of mail, clothing made of metal rings or plates, worn as armor. ❑ *n., pl.* **coats of mail.**

coat·room (kōt′rüm′), *n.* cloakroom.

co·au·thor (kō o′thər), *n.* a joint author.

coax (kōks), *v.* **1** to persuade by soft words; influence by pleasant ways: *She coaxed me into letting her borrow my bicycle.* ■ See Synonym Study at **urge. 2** to get by coaxing: *The baby-sitter coaxed a smile from the baby.* **—coax′er,** *n.* **—coax′ing·ly,** *adv.*

co·ax·i·al (kō ak′sē əl), *adj.* having a common axis.

coaxial cable (kō ak′sē əl), an electric cable made of a tube of conducting materials surrounding an insulated central conductor. It is used for transmitting many television, telephone, or telegraph signals at the same time.

cob (kob), *n.* **1** corncob. **2** a male swan.

co·balt (kō′bölt), *n.* a hard, silver-white metallic element with a pinkish tint, which occurs only in combination with other elements. It is used in making alloys and ceramics. *Symbol:* Co

Cobb (kob), *n.* **Ty** (tī), 1886-1961, American baseball player. ■ Ty Cobb is the all-time leading hitter, with a lifetime batting average of .367. He was one of the first five players elected to the National Baseball Hall of Fame. Born in Georgia, he was nicknamed "The Georgia Peach."

cob·ble (kob′əl), *v.* **1** to mend shoes, boots, etc.; repair; patch. **2** to put together clumsily. ❑ *v.* **cob·bled, cob·bling.**

cob·bler[1] (kob′lər), *n.* person whose work is mending or making shoes.

cob·bler[2] (kob′lər), *n.* a fruit pie baked in a deep dish, usually with a crust only on top.

cob·ble·stone (kob′əl stōn′), *n.* a naturally rounded stone formerly much used in paving roads.

CO·BOL (kō′bòl), *n.* language for programming computers, especially to process business data.

co·bra (kō′brə), *n.* any of several very poisonous snakes of Asia and Africa. When excited, a cobra flattens its neck so that its head seems to have a hood. ❑ *n., pl.* **co·bras.**

cob·web (kob′web′), *n.* **1** a spider's web, or the stuff it is made of. **2** anything thin and slight or entangling like a spider's web: *caught in a cobweb of lies.*

co·ca (kō′kə), *n.* **1** a large tropical bush growing in South America. Its dried leaves are used to make cocaine and other drugs. **2** the dried leaves of this plant. ❑ *n., pl.* **co·cas** for 1.

co·caine (kō kān′ *or* kō′kān), *n.* drug formerly used to deaden pain, now used as a stimulant. It is obtained from coca. When used in excess, it can cause addiction and poisoning.

coc·cyx (kok′siks), *n.* a small triangular bone forming the lower end of the backbone in human beings. ❑ *n., pl.* **coc·cy·ges** (kok-si′jēz′), **coc·cyx·es.**

Co·chise (kō chēs′), *n.* 1815?-1874, Apache leader. ■ Cochise had peaceful relationships with settlers in Arizona and New Mexico until he was falsely accused of kidnapping a settler's child in 1861. The U.S. Army and Cochise both took hostages, and war broke out. The war ended in 1869, and Cochise moved his band to a reservation in Arizona.

coch·le·a (kok′lē ə), *n.* a spiral-shaped cavity of the inner ear, containing the nerve endings that transmit sound impulses along the auditory nerve. See picture at **ear**[1]. ❑ *n., pl.* **coch·le·as, coch·le·ae** (kok′lē ē′).

cock[1] (kok), **1** *n.* a male chicken; rooster. **2** *n.* the male of other birds: *a turkey cock.* **3** *n.* faucet used to turn the flow of a liquid or gas on or off. **4** *n.* hammer of a gun. **5** *n.* the position of the hammer or firing pin of a gun when it is pulled back ready to fire. **6** *v.* to pull back the hammer or firing pin of a gun, so that it is ready to fire. **7** *v.* to draw back or pull back your fist before hitting someone or something: *The boxers cocked their fists.*

cock[2] (kok), **1** *v.* to turn or stick up, especially in a carefree, defiant, or inquiring manner: *The dog cocked its ears when it heard the approaching footsteps.* **2** *n.* an upward turn or bend of the eye, ear, hat, etc.

cock[3] (kok), **1** *n.* a small, cone-shaped pile of hay, turf, etc., in a field. **2** *v.* to pile in cocks.

cock·ade (ko kād′), *n.* knot of ribbon or a rosette worn on the hat as a badge.

cock-a-doo·dle-doo (kok′ə dü′dl dü′), *n.* imitation of the loud cry of a rooster. ❑ *n., pl.* **cock-a-doo·dle-doos.**

cock·a·too (kok′ə tü *or* kok′ə tü′), *n.* any of several large parrots of Australia, the East Indies, etc., some white, some black, some brightly colored. A cockatoo has a crest that it can raise and lower. ❑ *n., pl.* **cock·a·toos.**

cocked hat, 1 hat with the brim turned up in three places. **2** hat pointed in front and in back.

cock·er·el (kok′ər əl), *n.* a young rooster, less than one year old.

cock·er spaniel (kok′ər), a small dog with long, silky hair and drooping ears.

cocker spaniel—about 15 in. (38 cm) high at the shoulder

cock·eyed (kok′īd′), *adj.* **1** cross-eyed. **2** tilted or twisted to one side. **3** INFORMAL. foolish; silly.

cock·le (kok′əl), *n.* **1** any of several kinds of saltwater clams with two ridged, heart-shaped shells. **2** cockleshell.

warm the cockles of your heart, to make you feel much pleased and encouraged: *The friendly welcome into the new neighborhood warmed the cockles of her heart.*

cock·le·bur (kok′əl bėr′), *n.* any of several weeds with spiny burs.

cock·le·shell (kok′əl shel′), *n.* **1** shell of a cockle. **2** a small, light, shallow boat.

cock·ney (kok′nē), **1** *n.* person born or living in the eastern section of London who speaks a particular dialect of English. **2** *n.* this dialect. **3** *adj.* of cockneys or their dialect. ❑ *n., pl.* **cock·neys.**

cock·pit (kok′pit′), *n.* **1** place where the pilot sits in an airplane. **2** the open place in a boat where the pilot and passengers sit.

cock·roach (kok′rōch′), *n.* **1** any of several small, brownish or yellowish insects often found in kitchens and around water pipes, usually feeding at night. **2** any of many insects related to these familiar kinds and found worldwide. ❑ *n., pl.* **cock·roach·es.**

WORD STORY The Spanish name for the **cockroach** is *cucaracha* (kü′kä rä′chä). English settlers kept the consonants, but changed the vowels, so that the spelling *cockroach* emerged. Both **cock** and **roach** already existed in English, but had nothing to do with the insect.

cocks·comb (koks′kōm′), *n.* **1** the fleshy, red part on the top of a rooster's head. **2** a garden plant with crested or feathery clusters of red or yellow flowers. ■ Another word that sounds like this is **coxcomb.**

cock·sure (kok′shur′), *adj.* **1** too sure; overly confident. **2** perfectly sure; absolutely certain.

cock·tail (kok′tāl′), *n.* **1** a chilled alcoholic drink of gin, vodka, whiskey, rum, etc., mixed with tonic, fruit juices, sugar, etc. **2** drink served just before a meal: *a tomato juice cocktail.* **3** shellfish or mixed fruits served as an appetizer: *a shrimp cocktail.*

cock·y (kok′ē), *adj.* conceited or swaggering; cocksure: *He was a cocky fellow who thought he knew everything.* ❑ *adj.* **cock·i·er, cock·i·est.** —**cock′i·ly,** *adv.* —**cock′i·ness,** *n.*

co·co (kō′kō), *n.* coconut palm. ❑ *n., pl.* **co·cos.**

co·coa (kō′kō), **1** *n.* powder made by roasting and grinding the kernels of cacao seeds, and removing some of the fat. **2** *n.* drink made of this powder with milk or water and sugar. **3** *n.* a dull brown color, lighter than chocolate. **4** *adj.* dull brown.

WORD STORY Cocoa comes from the Aztec name for the tree on which cacao seeds grow. **Cacao** and **chocolate** come from the same word. Spanish explorers learned the word from the Aztecs, and English people learned it from the Spanish. By then the word had developed several different spellings and pronunciations, and these became different modern words.

co·co·nut (kō′kə nut′), *n.* the large, round, hard-shelled fruit of the coconut palm. It contains a sweet, white liquid called **coconut milk,** which is used as a drink. Coconuts have a brown shell with a sweet, white, pulpy meat that is often shredded for use in cakes, puddings, and pies.

WORD STORY Coconut comes from adding the English word **nut** to a Portuguese word meaning "a grinning face." Portuguese explorers saw coconuts in India and thought that the base of the shell looked like a funny face.

coconut oil, oil obtained from coconuts, used for making soap, candles, etc.

coconut palm, a tall, tropical palm tree on which coconuts grow.

co·coon (kə kün′), *n.* **1** case of silky thread spun by the larvae of various insects, to live in while they are developing into adults. Most moth larvae form cocoons. Silk is obtained from the cocoons of silkworms. **2** any similar protective case or covering.

cod (kod), *n.* any of several related important food fishes found in the cold parts of northern oceans; codfish. ❑ *n., pl.* **cod** or **cods.**

c.o.d. or **C.O.D.,** cash on delivery; collect on delivery.

co·da (kō′də), *n.* (in music) a section that comes after the main parts of a musical piece or movement, in order to form a more definite and satisfactory ending. ❑ *n., pl.* **co·das.** [Coda comes from a Latin word meaning "a tail."]

cod·dle (kod′l), *v.* **1** to treat tenderly; pamper: *coddle a sick child.* **2** to cook in hot water without boiling: *coddle an egg.* ❑ *v.* **cod·dled, cod·dling.**

code (kōd), **1** *n.* system of secret writing; arrangement of words, figures, etc., to keep a message short or secret: *The message was sent in code to keep it safe from the enemy.* **2** *v.* to change into a

a	hat	ė	term	ô	order	ch	child		⟨ a in about
ā	age	i	it	oi	oil	ng	long		e in taken
ä	far	ī	ice	ou	out	sh	she	ə ⟨	i in pencil
â	care	o	hot	u	cup	th	thin		o in lemon
e	let	ō	open	ù	put	ŦH	then		⟨ u in circus
ē	equal	ò	saw	ü	rule	zh	measure		

code: *The spy coded a message to headquarters.* **3** *n.* a collection of laws arranged according to a system so that they can be understood and used: *The punishments for robbery and murder are found in the penal code.* **4** *n.* any set of accepted manners or rules. A moral code is the notions of right and wrong held by a person, a group, or a society. **5** *n.* system of signals for sending messages by telegraph, flags, etc. **6** *n.* any set of signals or symbols used with computers or other machines. ❑ *v.* **cod·ed, cod·ing.**

co·deine (kō′dēn′), *n.* a white, crystalline drug obtained from opium, used to relieve pain and to stop coughs.

cod·fish (kod′fish′), *n.* cod. ❑ *n., pl.* **cod·fish** or **cod·fish·es.**

codg·er (koj′ər), *n.* INFORMAL. an odd or peculiar person, especially an old one. ■ **Codger** is often considered offensive.

cod·i·fy (kod′ə fī or kō′də fī), *v.* to arrange laws, regulations, etc., according to a system: *The laws of France were codified by order of Napoleon I.* ❑ *v.* **cod·i·fied, cod·i·fy·ing.** —**cod′i·fi·ca′tion,** *n.* —**cod′i·fi·er,** *n.*

cod·ling moth (kod′ling), a small moth whose larvae destroy apples, pears, and other tree crops.

cod-liv·er oil (kod′liv′ər), oil extracted from the liver of cod or of related species, used in medicine as a source of vitamins A and D.

co·ed or **co-ed** (kō′ed′), **1** *adj.* coeducational. **2** *adj.* for both men and women or both girls and boys. **3** *n.* (earlier) a girl or woman student at a coeducational school.

co·ed·u·ca·tion (kō′ej ə kā′shən), *n.* education of boys and girls or men and women together in the same school or classes.

co·ed·u·ca·tion·al (kō′ej ə kā′shə nəl), *adj.* educating boys and girls or men and women together in the same school or classes. —**co′ed·u·ca′tion·al·ly,** *adv.*

co·ef·fi·cient (kō′ə fish′ənt), *n.* number or symbol put with and multiplying another. In "3*x*," "3" is the coefficient of *"x,"* and *"x"* is the coefficient of "3."

coe·la·canth (sē′lə kanth), *n.* any of several large fishes with rounded scales and fins, very like fishes of 300 million years ago. Coelacanths were once thought to be extinct.

coe·len·te·rate (si len′tə rāt′), *n.* any of very many round, soft-bodied water animals, including jellyfish, sea anemones, and corals.

co·erce (kō ers′), *v.* to compel; force: *The prisoner was coerced into confessing the crime.* ❑ *v.* **co·erced, co·erc·ing.** —**co·erc′er,** *n.* —**co·erc′i·ble,** *adj.* —**co·er′cion** (kō er′shən or kō er′zhən), *n.*

co·er·cive (kō er′siv), *adj.* using force; compelling. —**co·er′cive·ly,** *adv.* —**co·er′cive·ness,** *n.*

co·ex·ist (kō′ig zist′), *v.* **1** to exist together or at the same time. **2** to live in peace with others in spite of differences: *Our cats and dogs coexist happily.*

co·ex·ist·ence (kō′ig zis′təns), *n.* existence together or at the same time.

cof·fee (kô′fē), **1** *n.* a dark brown drink made from the roasted and ground beans of a tall, tropical bush. **2** *n.* coffee beans. **3** *n.* the color of coffee; a dark brown, darker than chocolate. **4** *adj.* having the color of coffee; dark brown. [See Word Story at **café.**]

coffee bean, seed of the coffee plant. Coffee beans are roasted and ground to make coffee.

coffee break, a pause in work, usually midmorning and midafternoon, for coffee or other refreshments and for a few minutes of relaxation.

cof·fee·cake (kô′fē kāk′), *n.* a cake containing or topped with fruit, raisins, or nuts, and often coated with melted sugar.

cof·fee·house (kô′fē hous′), *n.* place where fancy coffee and other refreshments are served, and people spend time talking, reading, or listening to musical performances. ❑ *n., pl.* **cof·fee·hous·es** (kô′fē hou′ziz).

cof·fee·pot (kô′fē pot′), *n.* container for making or serving coffee.

cof·fee·shop (kô′fē shop′), *n.* a small restaurant, often in a hotel or office building, that serves coffee and light meals quickly.

coffee table, a low table for serving coffee and other refreshments. It is often placed in front of a sofa or chair.

cof·fer (kô′fər), *n.* **1** box, chest, or trunk, especially one used to hold money or other valuable things. **2 coffers,** *pl.* treasury; funds: *The revenue from the sales tax goes into the city's coffers.*

cof·fin (kô′fən), *n.* box into which a dead person is put to be buried; casket.

cog (kog), *n.* **1** one of a series of teeth on the edge of a gear. **2** wheel with teeth on the edge of its rim for sending or receiving motion; cogwheel. **3** person or thing that is a small but necessary part of a system or organization.

co·gen·cy (kō′jən sē), *n.* forcible quality; power of convincing: *The cogency of her argument helped her win the debate.*

co·gen·er·a·tion (kō′jen ə rā′shən), *n.* the production of electricity from steam that is not completely used in an industrial process.

co·gent (kō′jənt), *adj.* having the power to convince; forcible or convincing: *The lawyer used cogent arguments to persuade the jury that his client was innocent.* —**co′gent·ly,** *adv.*

cog·i·tate (koj′ə tāt), *v.* to think over; consider with care; ponder; meditate: *The judge cogitated a long time before making any decision.* ❑ *v.* **cog·i·tat·ed, cog·i·tat·ing.** —**cog′i·ta′tion,** *n.*

co·gnac (kō′nyak), *n.* a French brandy of superior quality.

cog·nate (kog′nāt), **1** *adj.* related by family or origin. English, Dutch, and German are cognate languages. **2** *n.* anything related to another by having a common source. The Spanish word *señor* and the English word *senior* are cognates.

cog·ni·tion (kog nish′ən), *n.* act or process of knowing.

cog·ni·tive (kog′nə tiv), *adj.* of or about knowing. Cognitive psychology studies perception, thinking, and memory.

cog·ni·zance (kog′nə zəns), *n.* knowledge obtained by observation or information; perception; awareness.

cog·ni·zant (kog′nə zənt), *adj.* aware: *When the queen became cognizant of the plot against her, she acted swiftly to crush it.*

cog·wheel (kog′wēl′), *n.* cog (def. 2).

co·hab·it (kō hab′it), *v.* to live together as husband and wife do. —**co·hab′i·ta′tion,** *n.*

Co·han (kō han′), *n.* **George M.,** 1878-1942, American actor, director, producer, songwriter, and playwright. ■ **George M. Cohan** wrote many popular songs, including "I'm a Yankee Doodle Dandy," "Give My Regards to Broadway," and "Over There."

co·here (kō hir′), *v.* **1** to stick together; hold together: *Brick and mortar cohere.* **2** to be well connected; be consistent: *The various details of the witness's story failed to cohere.* ❑ *v.* **co·hered, co·her·ing.**

co·her·ence (kō hir′əns), *n.* **1** logical connection; consistency: *The excited girl's story lacked coherence.* **2** condition of sticking together; tendency to hold together: *the coherence of atoms of the same element.*

co·her·ent (kō hir′ənt), *adj.* **1** logically connected; consistent: *He could not give a coherent account of the accident.* **2** sticking together; holding together. —**co·her′ent·ly,** *adv.*

co·he·sion (kō hē′zhən), *n.* **1** tendency to stick together: *Wet sand has more cohesion than dry sand.* **2** attraction between molecules of the same kind: *Drops of water are held together by cohesion.*

co·he·sive (kō hē′siv), *adj.* sticking together; tending to hold together: *The members of a family are a cohesive unit in our society.* —**co·he′sive·ly,** *adv.* —**co·he′sive·ness,** *n.*

co·ho (kō′hō), *n.* a salmon of the Pacific coast of North America, recently introduced into fresh waters, especially the Great Lakes. ❑ *n., pl.* **co·ho** or **co·hos.**

co·hort (kō′hôrt), *n.* companion; associate; follower.

coif (koif), *n.* cap or hood that fits closely around the head.

coif·fure (kwä fyur′), *n.* style or manner of arranging a woman's hair.

coil (koil), **1** *v.* to wind around and around in a circular or spiral shape: *The snake coiled around a branch. The sailor coiled the rope evenly.* **2** *n.* anything that is coiled: *a coil of rope.* **3** *n.* one wind or turn of a coil. **4** *n.* series of connected pipes arranged in a coil or row: *the coils in a radiator.* **5** *n.* wire wound into a spiral for concentrating electric current, as in an electromagnet.

coin (koin), **1** *n.* piece of metal issued by a government for use as money. Pennies, nickels, dimes, and quarters are coins. **2** *n.* metal money. A government makes coin by stamping metal. **3** *v.* to make money by stamping metal: *The mint coins millions of nickels and dimes each year.* **4** *v.* to make metal into money: *to coin* *copper and zinc into pennies.* **5** *v.* to make up; invent: *We often coin new words or phrases to name new products.* **–coin′er,** *n.*

coin·age (koi′nij), *n.* **1** act of making up; inventing: *Travel in outer space has led to the coinage of many new words.* **2** word, phrase, etc., invented: *"Biodiversity" and "modem" are fairly new coinages.* **3** the making of coins. The U.S. mint is in charge of coinage. **4** metal money; coins.

WORD SOURCE Coinages are words that people make up. Some coinages are related to earlier words. Alfred Nobel created the word **dynamite** from a Greek word meaning "force." Other coinages are completely made up. There are not many of these, but here are some: **blatant, blurb, gas, gnome, googol, hobbit,** and **serendipity.**

co·in·cide (kō′in sīd′), *v.* **1** to occupy the same place in space: *If these two triangles (△△) were placed one on top of the other, they would coincide.* **2** to occupy the same time: *The working hours of the two friends coincide.* **3** to be alike; correspond; agree: *Her opinion coincides with mine.* ■ See Synonym Study at match². ❑ *v.* **co·in·cid·ed, co·in·cid·ing.**

co·in·ci·dence (kō in′sə dəns), *n.* **1** the happening by chance of two things at the same time or place in such a way as to seem remarkable or planned: *It is a coincidence that my cousin and I were born on the very same day.* **2** act of coinciding: *the coincidence of two triangles.*

co·in·ci·dent (kō in′sə dənt), *adj.* **1** happening at the same time: *My cousin's birthday is coincident with mine.* **2** in exact agreement: *Our views were often coincident.* **–co·in′ci·dent·ly,** *adv.*

co·in·ci·den·tal (kō in′sə den′tl), *adj.* showing coincidence; occurring by chance. **–co·in′ci·den′tal·ly,** *adv.*

coin-op·e·ra·ted (koin op′ə rā′tid), *adj.* made to work by putting a coin or coins into a slot: *a coin-operated car wash.*

coke (kōk), *n.* fuel made from coal that has been heated in an oven from which most of the air has been removed. Coke burns with much heat and little smoke, and is used in furnaces, for melting metal, etc.

col-, *prefix.* form of **com-.**

col., column.

Col., Colonel.

co·la (kō′lə), *n.* a soft drink flavored with a nut from a tropical evergreen tree. ❑ *n., pl.* **co·las.**

col·an·der (kul′ən dər *or* kol′ən dər), *n.* a wire or metal dish full of small holes for draining off liquids from foods.

cold (kōld), **1** *adj.* much less warm than the body: *Snow and ice are cold.* **2** *adj.* less warm than usual: *The weather is cold for April.* **3** *adj.* feeling cold or chilly: *Put on a sweater, or you will be cold.* **4** *n.* coldness; being cold: *Warm clothes protect against the cold of winter.* **5** *n.* a common illness that causes a runny nose, a sore throat, coughing, and sneezing. **6** *adj.* lacking in feeling; unfriendly: *Since our argument she has remained cold and aloof.* **7** *adj.* faint; weak: *The hunting dogs could not trail the cold scent of the fox.* **8** *adj.* (in games, treasure hunts, etc.) far from what you are searching for. **9** *adj.* suggesting coolness. Blue, green, and gray are called cold colors. **10** *adj.* INFORMAL. unconscious: *The falling branch knocked him cold.* **–cold′ly,** *adv.* **–cold′ness,** *n.*

catch cold or **take cold,** to become ill with a cold: *I caught cold and stayed home from school.*

in the cold or **out in the cold,** all alone; neglected.

SYNONYM STUDY **Cold, cool,** and **chilly** all mean having or feeling no warmth. **Cold** can suggest a good or bad condition: *A cold drink would be wonderful. My soup is cold.* **Cool** means pleasantly cold: *After the long walk, we rested in the cool shade.* **Chilly** means unpleasantly cold: *Without his coat he was too chilly to enjoy the game.*

cold-blood·ed (kōld′blud′id), *adj.* **1** having blood that is about the same temperature as the air or water around the animal. The blood of such animals is colder in winter than in summer. Turtles, snakes, and many other animals are cold-blooded; birds and mammals are warm-blooded. **2** lacking in feeling; cruel: *a cold-blooded murder.* **3** feeling the cold because of poor circulation. **–cold′-blood′ed·ly,** *adv.* **–cold′-blood′ed·ness,** *n.*

cold cream, a creamy, soothing salve for the skin.

cold cuts, slices of cooked meat, such as corned beef, salami, bologna, and ham, served cold.

cold front, the advancing edge of a cold air mass as it overtakes and passes under a warmer one. Showers usually form along a cold front.

Cold Harbor, locality in central Virginia. It was the site of Civil War battles in June 1862 and June 1864. Lee led Confederates to victories both times.

cold-heart·ed (kōld′här′tid), *adj.* lacking in feeling; unkind. **–cold′-heart′ed·ly,** *adv.* **–cold′-heart′ed·ness,** *n.*

cold shoulder, unfriendly treatment; avoidance; refusal to respond: *He tried to apologize, but she gave him the cold shoulder.* **–cold-shoul·der** (kōld′shōl′dər), *v.*

cold snap, a short spell of cold weather.

cold sore, blister near or on the mouth, caused by a virus which infects the skin; fever blister.

cold war, 1 a prolonged contest between nations or groups of nations, conducted by political, economic, and other means rather than by direct military action. **2 Cold War,** the contest for world leadership between the communist and democratic nations that began after World War II.

cold wave, period of very cold weather.

Cole·ridge (kōl′rij), *n.* **Samuel Taylor,** 1772-1834, English poet. His poems, including "The Rime of the Ancient Mariner," often have supernatural themes or elements.

cole·slaw (kōl′slô′), *n.* salad made of finely shredded raw cabbage; slaw.

co·le·us (kō′lē əs), *n.* any of numerous small plants grown for their showy, colorful leaves. ❑ *n., pl.* **co·le·us·es.**

col·ic (kol′ik), *n.* severe pains in the stomach and intestines.

col·ick·y (kol′i kē), *adj.* having colic.

Co·li·ma (kō lē′mä), *n.* a state in SW Mexico.

col·i·se·um (kol′ə sē′əm), *n.* a large building or stadium for games, contests, etc.

co·li·tis (kə lī′tis), *n.* inflammation of the colon, often causing severe abdominal pain.

col·lab·o·rate (kə lab′ə rāt′), *v.* **1** to work together: *The two authors collaborated in writing a history of the United States.* **2** to aid or cooperate with enemies of your country: *The traitor collaborated with the enemy.* ❑ *v.* **col·lab·o·rat·ed, col·lab·o·rat·ing.** **–col·lab′o·ra′tion,** *n.* **–col·lab′o·ra′tor,** *n.*

col·lage (kə läzh′), *n.* picture made by pasting on a background such things as parts of photographs and newspapers, fabric, and string. [**Collage** comes from a Greek word meaning "glue."]

col·lapse (kə laps′), **1** *v.* to fall down or cave in: *The wreckers' hard work finally made the building collapse.* **2** *n.* act of falling down or caving in: *A heavy flood caused the collapse of the bridge.* **3** *v.* to break down; fail: *The business collapsed because it was run poorly.* **4** *n.* breakdown; failure: *Overwork can cause the collapse of a person's health.* **5** *v.* to fold or push together: *The table collapses so that it can be stored easily.* ❑ *v.* **col·lapsed, col·laps·ing.** **–col·laps′i·ble,** *adj.*

col·lar (kol′ər), **1** *n.* the part of a coat, dress, or shirt that makes a band around or just below the neck. **2** *n.* a separate band of linen, lace, or other material worn

collapse (def. 1)

a	hat	ė	term	ô	order	ch	child		
ā	age	i	it	oi	oil	ng	long	ə	a in about
ä	far	ī	ice	ou	out	sh	she		e in taken
â	care	o	hot	u	cup	th	thin		i in pencil
e	let	ō	open	ů	put	ŦH	then		o in lemon
ē	equal	ô	saw	ü	rule	zh	measure		u in circus

around the neck: *a fur collar.* **3** *n.* a leather or plastic band or metal chain for the neck of a dog or other pet animal. **4** *n.* a padded, leather, oval ring that fits over the neck of a horse as part of the harness. It bears the weight of the loads the horse pulls. **5** *n.* any of various kinds of rings, bands, or pipes in machinery. A collar on a shaft is a metal ring that keeps the shaft from moving sideways. **6** *v.* to seize by the collar; capture: *The police collared the thief after a long chase.* ■ Another word that sounds like this is **choler.**

col·lar·bone (kol′ər bōn′), *n.* the bone connecting the breastbone and the shoulder blade; clavicle.

col·lard (kol′ərd), *n.* Usually, **collards,** *pl.* a kind of kale with fleshy leaves, cooked as greens.

col·late (kə lāt′ *or* kol′āt), *v.* to arrange in order; put together. ❑ *v.* **col·lat·ed, col·lat·ing. —col′la·tor,** *n.*

col·lat·er·al (kə lat′ər əl), **1** *adj.* aside from the main thing; secondary: *The teacher listed ten books about explorers as collateral reading for the chapter on exploring America.* **2** *n.* stocks, bonds, etc., pledged as security for a loan: *The bank will not make a loan without collateral.* **—col·lat′er·al·ly,** *adv.*

col·league (kol′ēg′), *n.* fellow worker; associate.

col·lect (kə lekt′), **1** *v.* to bring or come together; gather together: *We collected sticks of wood to make a fire. A crowd soon collected at the scene of the accident.* ■ See Synonym Study at **gather. 2** *v.* to gather together for a set: *I collect stamps as a hobby.* **3** *v.* to pick up; remove: *The city trucks collect the garbage.* **4** *v.* to heap up; accumulate: *Dust is collecting under the bed.* **5** *v.* to ask for and receive payment for something: *My scout troop collects dues each week.* **6** *adj., adv.* to be paid for at the place of delivery: *a collect telephone call. Telephone me collect.* **7** *v.* to regain control of: *We soon collected ourselves after the slight accident.*

col·lect·a·ble (kə lek′tə bəl), *n.* collectible.

col·lect·ed (kə lek′tid), *adj.* not confused or disturbed; calm: *Throughout all the excitement she remained cool and collected.* ■ See Synonym Study at **calm. —col·lect′ed·ly,** *adv.* **—col·lect′ed·ness,** *n.*

col·lect·i·ble (kə lek′tə bəl), *n.* anything that is collected or might be collected, especially an unusual or out-of-date object.

col·lec·tion (kə lek′shən), *n.* **1** group of things gathered from many places and belonging together: *Our library has a large collection of books.* **2** act or process of bringing together; coming together: *The collection of these stamps took ten years.* **3** money gathered from people: *A church takes up a collection to help pay its expenses.* **4** a large quantity; mass or heap: *There is a collection of dust in the attic.*

collective bargaining, negotiation about wages, hours, and working conditions between workers organized as a group and their employer or employers.

collective noun, noun that names a group made up of individual people or things. In *The crowd was restless,* the word *crowd* is a collective noun.

USAGE NOTE **Collective nouns** are used with either singular or plural verbs, depending on the meaning of the sentence. If the sentence treats the group as one thing, use a singular verb: *A group of lions is called a pride.* If the sentence treats the members of a group as many individuals, use a plural verb: *A group of lions hunt together and share the prey.*

col·lec·tiv·ize (kə lek′ti vīz), *v.* to transfer ownership of, from an individual to the state. ❑ *v.* **col·lec·tiv·ized, col·lec·tiv·iz·ing. —col·lec′tiv·i·za′tion,** *n.*

col·lec·tor (kə lek′tər), *n.* **1** person or thing that collects: *I am a stamp collector.* **2** person hired to collect money owed: *He works for the government as a tax collector.* **3** solar collector.

col·lege (kol′ij), *n.* **1** school of higher learning that gives degrees or diplomas. A college is often a part of a university. **2** school for special training: *a business college.* **3** group of persons with the same duties and privileges: *Many large hospitals have a college of surgeons.*

College, city in central Alaska.

col·le·gian (kə lē′jən), *n.* a college student.

col·le·giate (kə lē′jit), *adj.* **1** of or like a college: *a collegiate library.* **2** of or like college students: *She enjoyed collegiate life.*

col·lide (kə līd′), *v.* **1** to hit or strike violently together; crash: *Two ships collided in the harbor and sank.* **2** to clash; conflict. ❑ *v.* **col·lid·ed, col·lid·ing.**

col·lid·er (kə lī′dər), *n.* a subatomic particle accelerator in which beams of particles with opposite charge strike each other, used to create and identify new particles and study their behavior.

col·lie (kol′ē), *n.* a large, intelligent, long-haired dog used for tending sheep and as a pet.

col·lier (kol′yər), *n.* **1** ship for carrying coal. **2** a coal miner.

col·lier·y (kol′yər ē), *n.* a coal mine and its buildings and equipment. ❑ *n., pl.* **col·lier·ies.**

col·li·sion (kə lizh′ən), *n.* **1** act of hitting or striking violently together; crash: *The car was badly damaged in the collision.* **2** a clash; conflict: *There was a collision of interests on how to spend the city's gasoline tax money.*

col·loid (kol′oid), *n.* any material made of extremely small particles of one substance evenly spread through another substance but not dissolved in it. Paint, milk, and gelatin are colloids.

collection (def. 2)

col·lec·tive (kə lek′tiv), **1** *adj.* of a group; as a group; taken all together: *Our fifth-grade class made a collective decision to write to a similar class in Italy.* **2** *adj.* owned, worked, and managed by a group: *a collective farm.* **3** *n.* farm, factory, or other organization operated and worked by a group cooperatively: *There were many collectives in the Soviet Union.* **4** *n.* collective noun. **—col·lec′tive·ly,** *adv.*

col·lo·qui·al (kə lō′kwē əl), *adj.* used in common talk; belonging to everyday, familiar talk; informal. Such expressions as *chimp* for *chimpanzee* and *close shave* for *narrow escape* are colloquial. **—col·lo′qui·al·ly,** *adv.*

col·lo·qui·al·ism (kə lō′kwē ə liz′əm), *n.* a colloquial word or phrase.

col·lo·quy (kol′ə kwē), *n.* conversation; conference; meeting. ❑ *n., pl.* **col·lo·quies.**

col·lu·sion (kə lü′zhən), *n.* secret agreement for some wrong or harmful purpose; secret or crafty understanding for the purposes of trickery or fraud.

Colo., Colorado.

co·logne (kə lōn′), *n.* a fragrant liquid, not so strong as perfume.

Co·logne (kə lōn′), *n.* city in W Germany, on the Rhine.

Co·lom·bi·a (kə lum′bē ə), *n.* country in NW South America. *Capital:* Bogotá. [**Colombia** comes from the name of Christopher Columbus.] **—Co·lom′bi·an,** *adj., n.*

Co·lom·bo (kə lum′bō), *n.* port and capital of Sri Lanka, on the W coast. [**Colombo** comes from a local word meaning "a port."]

co·lon[1] (kō′lən), *n.* mark (:) of punctuation used before lists, explanations, long quotations, etc., to set them off from the rest of the sentence.

co·lon[2] (kō′lən), *n.* the lower part of the large intestine. ❑ *n., pl.* **co·lons, co·la** (kō′lə).

colo·nel (kėr′nl), *n.* a military rank. See chart on page 712. ■ Another word that sounds like this is **kernel.**

> **WORD STORY** **Colonel** comes from an Italian word meaning "column," because this officer commands a column of soldiers. For a while, hundreds of years ago, it was spelled *coronel* by mistake, and people pronounced it with *r* even after the spelling changed back to *l*.

co·lo·ni·al (kə lō′nē əl), **1** *adj.* of a colony or colonies. **2** *adj.* of the thirteen British colonies which became the United States of America. **3** *n.* person who lives in a colony. **—co·lo′ni·al·ly,** *adv.*

co·lo·ni·al·ism (kə lō′nē ə liz′əm), *n.* policy of a nation that rules or seeks to rule weaker or dependent nations.

co·lo·ni·al·ist (kə lō′nē ə list), **1** *n.* person or nation that favors or practices colonialism. **2** *adj.* favoring colonialism or colonialists: *colonialist policies.*

col·o·nist (kol′ə nist), *n.* **1** person who lives in a colony; settler: *Early colonists in New England suffered from cold and hunger.* **2** person who helped to found a colony.

col·o·nize (kol′ə nīz), *v.* to establish a colony or colonies in: *The English colonized New England.* ❑ *v.* **col·o·nized, col·o·niz·ing.** **—col′o·ni·za′tion,** *n.* **—col′o·niz′er,** *n.*

col·on·nade (kol′ə nād′), *n.* series of columns set the same distance apart.

col·o·ny (kol′ə nē), *n.* **1** group of people who leave their own country and go to settle in another land, but who still remain citizens of their own country: *The Pilgrim colony left England in 1620.* **2** the settlement made by such a group of people: *The Pilgrims founded a colony at Plymouth, Massachusetts.* **3 the Colonies,** *pl.* the thirteen British colonies that became the United States of America: New Hampshire, Massachusetts, Rhode Island, Connecticut, New York, New Jersey, Pennsylvania, Delaware, Maryland, Virginia, North Carolina, South Carolina, and Georgia. **4** territory distant from the country that governs it: *Hong Kong has been a British colony since 1842.* **5** group of people having the same background or occupation who live together in a certain place or area: *a colony of artists.* **6** group of living things of the same kind, living or growing together: *a colony of ants, a coral colony.* ❑ *n., pl.* **col·o·nies.**

col·or (kul′ər), **1** *n.* sensation produced by the effect of waves of light striking the retina of the eye. Different colors are produced by rays of light having different wavelengths. **2** *n.* any color except black, white, or gray; red, yellow, blue, or any combination of them. The color green is a mixture of yellow and blue. **3** *n.* any color including black, white, or gray. The color gray is a mixture of black and white. **4** *v.* to give color to; put color on; change the color of: *I colored the picture with crayons.* **5** *n.* a paint; dye; pigment: *Sunlight faded the colors of the bedspread.* **6** *n.* appearance of the skin; complexion: *She has a healthy color.* **7** *n.* skin coloring other than white: *people of color.* **8** *v.* to become or make red in the face; blush: *He colored when I teased him.* **9** *n.* an outward appearance; show: *Though imaginative, his plays always have the color of truth.* **10** *v.* to change to give a wrong idea; distort: *The fisherman colored the facts to make his catch seem the biggest of all.* **11** *n.* distinguishing quality; vividness: *That young author's gift for description adds color to her stories.*

12 *v.* to give a distinguishing or vivid quality to: *A love of nature colored the author's works.* **13** *n.pl.* **the colors,** the flag of a nation, regiment, etc.: *Salute the colors.* **—col′or·er,** *n.*

change color, 1 to turn pale. **2** to blush.

show your true colors, to show yourself as you really are: *When he saw that he was losing, he showed his true colors and gave up.*

with flying colors, successfully; victoriously: *He passed the test with flying colors.*

> **SYNONYM STUDY** **Color, hue,** and **shade** all mean the sensation produced in the eye by light. **Color** is a general word: *Her dress is the color of the sky.* **Hue** is used in poems and stories: *Jewels of many hues spilled from the treasure chest.* **Shade** means a color like another except for darkness or lightness: *The many shades of green in plants all show the presence of chlorophyll.*

Col·o·rad·o (kol′ə rad′ō *or* kol′ə rä′dō), *n.* **1** one of the western states of the United States. *Abbreviation:* CO or Colo. *Capital:* Denver. **2** river flowing from N Colorado through Utah, Arizona, Nevada, California, and NW Mexico into the Gulf of California. **—Col′o·rad′an,** *n.*

> **WORD STORY** **Colorado** comes from a Spanish word meaning "colored red." The Colorado River runs through canyons of red stone and carries red mud in the water. The state was named for the river.

Colorado Plateau, a large area of high plateaus, deep canyons, and flat-topped hills called mesas, in Colorado, Utah, Arizona, and New Mexico. The Grand Canyon is part of this region.

Colorado Springs, city in central Colorado.

col·or·a·tion (kul′ə rā′shən), *n.* way in which someone or something is colored; coloring: *The coloration of some animals is like that of their surroundings.*

col·or-blind (kul′ər blīnd′), *adj.* unable to tell certain colors apart; unable to perceive certain colors. **—col′or blind′ness.**

col·or-code (kul′ər kōd′), *v.* to color something according to a system for easy identification: *The manufacturer color-coded the wires in the instrument panel.* ❑ *v.,* **col·or-cod·ed, col·or-cod·ing.**

col·ored (kul′ərd), *adj.* **1** having color: *This book has colored pictures.* **2** having a certain kind of color: *a green-colored leaf.* **3** of the black race or any race other than white. ■ This meaning of **colored** is often considered offensive. **4** tinged by prejudice, emotion, or desire for effect; biased: *She gave a highly colored description of the size of the fish she had caught.*

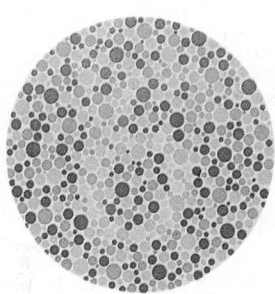

color-blind
Some color-blind people cannot see the number.

col·or·fast (kul′ər fast′), *adj.* resistant to loss or change of color: *colorfast cloth.*

col·or·ful (kul′ər fəl), *adj.* **1** having excitement, variety, or interest; picturesque; vivid: *Her letters give colorful descriptions of her travels abroad.* **2** full of color: *a colorful scarf.* **—col′or·ful·ly,** *adv.* **—col′or·ful·ness,** *n.*

col·or·ing (kul′ər ing), *n.* **1** way in which someone or something is colored; coloration: *Our cat has a tan coloring.* **2** substance used to color: *food coloring.* **3** an outward or false appearance: *Her story had the coloring of truth, but we could not believe her.*

col·or·ize (kul′ə rīz), *v.* to add color to black-and-white images, especially old movies, by using a computer. ❑ *v.* **col·or·ized, col·or·iz·ing.** **—col′or·i·za′tion,** *n.* **—col′or·iz′er,** *n.*

a	hat	ė	term	ô	order	ch	child		a in about
ā	age	i	it	oi	oil	ng	long		e in taken
ä	far	ī	ice	ou	out	sh	she	ə {	i in pencil
â	care	o	hot	u	cup	th	thin		o in lemon
e	let	ō	open	ů	put	ᴛʜ	then		u in circus
ē	equal	ò	saw	ü	rule	zh	measure		

col·or·less (kul'ər lis), *adj.* **1** without color: *Pure water is colorless.* **2** without excitement or variety; uninteresting: *a colorless description.* —**col'or·less·ly,** *adv.* —**col'or·less·ness,** *n.*

co·los·sal (kə los'əl), *adj.* of huge size; gigantic; vast: *Skyscrapers are colossal structures.* —**co·los'sal·ly,** *adv.*

Col·os·se·um (kol'ə sē'əm), *n.* a large amphitheater in Rome, completed in A.D. 80. It was used for games and contests.

co·los·sus (kə los'əs), *n.* **1** a huge statue. The **Colossus of Rhodes** was a huge statue of Apollo made at Rhodes about 280 B.C. It was one of the seven wonders of the ancient world. **2** anything huge; gigantic person or thing. ❑ *n., pl.* **co·los·sus·es, co·los·si** (kə los'ī).

colt (kōlt), *n.* a young horse, donkey, zebra, etc., especially a male less than four or five years old.

colt·ish (kōl'tish), *adj.* like a colt; lively and frisky. —**colt'ish·ly,** *adv.* —**colt'ish·ness,** *n.*

Col·trane (kōl'trān), *n.* **John,** 1926-1967, American musician and composer. ■ **John Coltrane** was an influential jazz musician. He worked at various times with Dizzy Gillespie, Miles Davis, and Thelonious Monk.

Co·lum·bi·a (kə lum'bē ə), *n.* **1** capital of South Carolina, in the central part. **2** river flowing from British Columbia through E Washington and between Washington and Oregon into the Pacific. **3** city in N Maryland. **4** a name for the United States of America. Columbia is often represented as a woman dressed in red, white, and blue. —**Co·lum'bi·an,** *adj.*

Columbia Plateau, a large region of rough land, mountains, and deep canyons, stretching across E Oregon and into Idaho and Washington.

Columbia Plateau

col·um·bine (kol'əm bīn), *n.* any of several plants having flowers with petals shaped like hollow spurs. Wild columbines have red and yellow or blue and white flowers.

Co·lum·bus (kə lum'bəs), *n.* **1 Christopher,** 1451?-1506, Italian explorer in the service of Spain who sailed to the Americas in 1492, making their existence known to Europeans. **2** capital of Ohio, in the central part. **3** city in W Georgia.

Columbus Day, October 12, the anniversary of Columbus's landfall. It is observed as a legal holiday on the second Monday in October in most states of the United States.

col·umn (kol'əm), *n.* **1** a slender, upright structure; pillar. Columns are usually made of stone, wood, or metal, and are used as supports or ornaments to a building. Sometimes a column stands alone as a monument. **2** anything that seems slender and upright like a column: *a column of smoke, a column of figures.* **3** soldiers or ships following one another in a single line. **4** a narrow division of a page reading from top to bottom, kept separate by lines or by blank spaces. Some newspapers have eight columns on a page. **5** part of a newspaper used for a special subject or written by a special writer: *the sports column.*

col·umn·ist (kol'əm nist), *n.* person who writes a special column in a newspaper or magazine.

com-, *prefix.* with; together: *commingle = mingle with another; compress = press together.*

com., **1** commerce. **2** common.

Com., **1** Commissioner. **2** Committee.

co·ma[1] (kō'mə), *n.* a prolonged unconsciousness caused by disease, injury, or poison. ❑ *n., pl.* **co·mas.**

co·ma[2] (kō'mə), *n.* a cloud of gas and dust around the center of a comet. ❑ *n., pl.* **co·mae** (kō'mē).

Co·man·che (kə man'chē), *n.* member of a tribe of American Indians formerly living from Nebraska south to Mexico, now living in Oklahoma. ❑ *n., pl.* **Co·man·che** or **Co·man·ches.**

comb (kōm), **1** *n.* piece of plastic, metal, or other material with teeth, used to arrange the hair or to hold it in place. **2** *n.* anything shaped or used like a comb, especially a tool for combing wool or flax. **3** *v.* to arrange with a comb. **4** *v.* to take out tangles in wool, flax, etc., with a comb. **5** *v.* to search through; look everywhere in: *We had to comb the neighborhood before we found our lost dog.* **6** *n.* the red, fleshy piece on top of the head of chickens and some other fowl. **7** *n.* honeycomb.

com·bat (kəm bat' *or* kom'bat *for verb;* kom'bat *for noun*), **1** *v.* to fight against; struggle with: *Doctors combat disease.* **2** *n.* armed fighting between opposing forces; battle. **3** *n.* any fight or struggle; conflict. ❑ *v.* **com·bat·ed, com·bat·ing** *or* **com·bat·ted, com·bat·ting.**

com·bat·ant (kəm bat'nt *or* kom'bə tənt), *n.* one that takes part in combat; fighter.

com·bat·ive (kəm bat'iv), *adj.* ready to fight; fond of fighting: *A good football team has a combative spirit.* —**com·bat'ive·ly,** *adv.* —**com·bat'ive·ness,** *n.*

comb·er (kō'mər), *n.* **1** breaker (def. 1). **2** person or thing that combs.

com·bi·na·tion (kom'bə nā'shən), *n.* **1** one whole made by combining two or more different things: *The color purple is a combination of red and blue.* **2** series of numbers or letters dialed in opening a certain kind of lock: *Do you know the combination of the safe?* **3** act of combining or being combined; union: *The combination of flour and water makes paste.* **4** (in mathematics) one or more items from a group of items, arranged in any order. From the group ABC, possible two-item combinations are AB, AC, and BC. AB and BA are the same combination.

combination lock, lock that opens only when a dial has been turned to certain numbers or letters.

com·bine (kəm bīn' *for verb;* kom'bīn *for noun*), **1** *v.* to join two or more things together; unite: *Our club combined the offices of secretary and treasurer.* **2** *v.* to unite to form a chemical compound: *Two atoms of hydrogen combine with one of oxygen to form water.* **3** *n.* group of persons joined together for business or political purposes. **4** *n.* machine for harvesting and threshing grain. ❑ *v.* **com·bined, com·bin·ing.** —**com·bin'a·ble,** *adj.* —**com·bin'er,** *n.*

com·bo (kom'bō), *n.* a small group of jazz musicians that play together regularly. ❑ *n., pl.* **com·bos.**

com·bus·ti·ble (kəm bus'tə bəl), **1** *adj.* capable of taking fire and burning: *Gasoline is highly combustible.* **2** *n.* a combustible substance. Wood and coal are combustibles. —**com·bus'ti·bly,** *adv.*

com·bus·tion (kəm bus'chən), *n.* act or process of burning. Many houses are heated by the rapid combustion of coal, oil, or gas. By slow combustion, the cells of the body transform food into energy and heat.

come (kum), *v.* **1** to move toward: *Come this way.* **2** to arrive: *The train comes at noon.* **3** to reach; extend: *The drapes come to the floor.* **4** to take place; happen: *Snow comes in winter.* **5** to be born; descend: *come from a musical family.* **6** to be from: *The word "collage" comes from a French word.* **7** to turn out to be; become: *My wish came true.* **8** to be available or be sold: *This soup comes in a can.* **9** to be equal; amount: *The bill comes to $45.* **10** to be more important than; have priority; rank: *Health comes before pleasure.* **11** to be caused; happen as a result: *Many good things come of hard work.* **12** to arrive at a condition: *come to a decision.* ❑ *v.* **came, come, com·ing.**

come about, 1 to take place; happen: *Many changes have come about in the past year.* **2** to turn around; change direction: *The* *sailboat came about, heading back to the dock.*

come across, to meet or find by chance: *I came across my old fielder's glove while cleaning my closet.*

come around or **come round, 1** to return to consciousness or health; recover. **2** to change direction or opinion.

come at, to rush toward; attack: *The barking dog came at me.*

come back, to return: *Come back home.*

come by, to get; obtain; acquire: *They came by the money honestly.*

come down, 1 to be handed down: *Many fables have come down through the ages.* **2** to lose position, rank, money, etc.

come down on, INFORMAL. to scold; blame.

come down with, to become ill with: *She came down with a flu.*

come forward, to offer yourself for work or duty; volunteer.

come in, 1 to arrive: *When did you come in this morning?* **2** to enter: *Come in, please.*

come in for, to get; receive; acquire.

come into, to inherit: *She came into a lot of money when her aunt died.*

come off, 1 to take place; happen; occur: *The shuttle launching comes off next week.* **2** to turn out to be: *The steering committee meeting did not come off as I had expected.* **3** to finish in a certain way: *Our team came off with a victory in last week's game.*

come on, 1 to find or meet by chance. **2** to improve; progress: *She is coming on well and will be out of the hospital next week.* **3** INFORMAL. to have an effect; give an impression: *Some people come on very strong when you first meet them.* **4** please; if you don't mind: *Come on now, pick up all this stuff on the floor.*

come out, 1 to be revealed or shown: *The sun came out from behind the clouds.* **2** to take place in the end; result: *The ballgame came out in our favor.* **3** to be offered to the public: *The singer's new recording will come out next fall.* **4** to put in an appearance: *How many people came out to cheer the team?* **5** to declare yourself in favor of: *One candidate came out for lower taxes.* **6** to make a debut.

come to, to become conscious again: *He came to slowly after the accident.*

come up, to come into being; arise: *That question won't come up.*

come upon, to find or meet by chance: *We came upon a rabbit in the woods.*

come up with, to think of; create; invent: *He came up with a clever name for our magazine.*

come·back (kum′bak′), *n.* **1** return to a former condition or position: *The team made a comeback after several losses.* **2** INFORMAL. a clever answer; sharp reply.

co·me·di·an (kə mē′dē ən), *n.* **1** actor in comedies. **2** person who amuses other people with funny talk and actions.

co·me·di·enne (kə mē′dē en′), *n.* woman who acts in comedies or who amuses people with funny talk and actions.

come·down (kum′doun′), *n.* loss of position, rank, money, etc.

com·e·dy (kom′ə dē), *n.* **1** an amusing play or show having a happy ending. **2** an amusing happening. ❑ *n., pl.* **com·e·dies.**

come·ly (kum′lē), *adj.* pleasant to look at; attractive: *a comely girl.* ❑ *adj.* **come·li·er, come·li·est.** **—come′li·ness,** *n.*

come-on (kum′on′), *n.* INFORMAL. something offered as an inducement to buy, lease, etc.

com·er (kum′ər), *n.* **1** person who arrives or comes. **2** INFORMAL. person who seems likely to succeed or who shows promise.

com·et (kom′it), *n.* a bright astronomical object that looks like a star with a cloudy tail of light. Comets contain ice and dust, and they shine by reflecting sunlight. Comets move around the sun like planets, but in long oval orbits. [**Comet** comes from a Greek word meaning "hair," which is what a comet's tail looked like to the Greeks.]

comet

com·fort (kum′fərt), **1** *v.* to ease the grief or sorrow of; cheer: *comfort a crying child.* **2** *n.* anything that makes trouble or sorrow easier to bear: *Your friendship brought me comfort while I was in the hospital.* **3** *n.* person or thing that makes life easier or takes away hardship: *The warm bonfire was a comfort to the cold campers.* **4** *n.* freedom from hardship; ease: *live in comfort.* **—com′fort·ing·ly,** *adv.*

SYNONYM STUDY **Comfort** and **console**[1] both mean to ease sorrow, trouble, or pain. **Comfort** means to make someone feel better who is in pain or upset: *I comforted my baby brother when he fell down.* **Console** is a more formal word meaning to comfort at a time of sadness: *We tried to console her over the loss of her cat.*

com·fort·a·ble (kum′fər tə bəl), *adj.* **1** giving comfort: *A soft, warm bed is comfortable.* **2** in comfort; at ease: *We felt comfortable in the warm house after a cold day outdoors.* **3** enough for someone's needs: *a comfortable income.* **—com′fort·a·bly,** *adv.*

com·fort·er (kum′fər tər), *n.* **1** person or thing that gives comfort. **2** a padded or quilted covering used on a bed for warmth.

com·fy (kum′fē), *adj.* INFORMAL. comfortable. ❑ *adj.* **com·fi·er, com·fi·est.**

com·ic (kom′ik), **1** *adj.* causing laughter or smiles; amusing; funny. ■ See Synonym Study at **humorous. 2** *n.* comedian. **3** *adj.* of comedy; in comedies: *a comic actor.* **4** *adj.* containing comic strips: *the comic page of a newspaper.* **5** *n.pl.* **comics,** comic strips; funnies. **6** *n.* comic book.

com·i·cal (kom′ə kəl), *adj.* amusing; funny: *You look comical in that battered old hat.* **—com′i·cal·ly,** *adv.*

comic book, magazine containing comic strips.

comic strip, series of drawings that tell a funny story, a series of happenings, or a story of adventure.

com·ing (kum′ing), **1** *n.* approach; arrival: *the coming of summer.* **2** *adj.* approaching; next: *this coming spring.*

com·ma (kom′ə), *n.* mark (,) of punctuation, usually used where a pause would be made in speaking the sentence aloud. Commas are used to separate ideas, parts of a sentence, the parts of an address, a date, or other series of words or numbers. ❑ *n., pl.* **com·mas.**

com·mand (kə mand′), **1** *v.* to give an order to; direct: *The queen commanded the admiral to set sail at once.* **2** *n.* an order; direction: *The admiral obeyed the queen's command.* **3** *v.* to be in authority over; have power over; be master of: *A captain commands a ship.* **4** *n.* possession of authority; power; control: *She took command and led everyone from the burning building.* **5** *n.* soldiers, ships, or region over which an officer has control or authority: *The captain knew everyone in his command.* **6** *n.* position of control or authority: *The general has held several commands.* **7** *v.* to control by position; rise high above; overlook: *The castle stands on a hill that commands the entire valley.* **8** *v.* to be able to have and use: *That lawyer commands a high fee for his services.* **9** *n.* ability to have and use: *A good speaker has an excellent command of words.* **10** *v.* to deserve and get: *a person who commands our respect.*

SYNONYM STUDY **Command, direct,** and **order** all mean to tell someone to do something. **Command** means to tell someone officially: *The sentry commanded him to halt.* **Direct** suggests giving instructions: *The police officer directed the traffic to halt.* **Order** means to tell someone strongly: *Mom ordered me to behave.*

com·man·dant (kom′ən dant′ or kom′ən dänt′), *n.* **1** commander. **2** officer in command of a military base, district, school, etc.

com·man·deer (kom′ən dir′), *v.* to seize private property for military or public use: *The police commandeered a taxi to chase the bank robber.*

com·mand·er (kə man′dər), *n.* **1** person who commands: *The commander of the rebel forces was captured just before dawn.* **2** a military rank. See chart on page 712.

a	hat	ė	term	ô	order	ch	child		
ā	age	i	it	oi	oil	ng	long		a in about
ä	far	ī	ice	ou	out	sh	she	ə	e in taken
â	care	o	hot	u	cup	th	thin		i in pencil
e	let	ō	open	u̇	put	ᴛʜ	then		o in lemon
ē	equal	ȯ	saw	ü	rule	zh	measure		u in circus

com·mand·er in chief, **1** person who has complete command of the armed forces of a country. In the United States, the President is the commander in chief. **2** officer in command of part of an army or navy. ❑ *pl.* **commanders in chief.**

com·mand·ing (kə man′ding), *adj.* **1** in command: *a commanding officer.* **2** controlling; powerful: *commanding forces.* **3** authoritative; impressive: *a commanding voice.* **—com·mand′ing·ly,** *adv.*

command key, a key on a computer keyboard that is held down in combination with other keys to give instructions to the computer.

com·mand·ment (kə mand′mənt), *n.* **1** one of the ten rules for living and for worship, given by God to the Jews; one of the Ten Commandments. **2** any law or command.

com·man·do (kə man′dō), *n.* **1** soldier trained to make brief, daring, surprise raids upon enemy territory. **2** group of such soldiers. ❑ *n., pl.* **com·man·dos** or **com·man·does.**

com·mem·o·rate (kə mem′ə rāt′), *v.* to honor the memory of: *a stamp commemorating the landing of the Pilgrims.* ❑ *v.* **com·mem·o·rat·ed, com·mem·o·rat·ing. —com·mem′o·ra·tor,** *n.*

com·mem·o·ra·tion (kə mem′ə rā′shən), *n.* **1** service or celebration in memory of some person or event. **2** act of commemorating.

com·mem·o·ra·tive (kə mem′ər ə tiv), *adj.* honoring the memory of some person or event.

com·mence (kə mens′), *v.* to begin; start: *The play commenced at eight o'clock.* ❑ *v.* **com·menced, com·menc·ing.**

com·mence·ment (kə mens′mənt), *n.* **1** a beginning; start. **2** day when a school or college gives diplomas and degrees to students who have completed the required course of study. **3** ceremonies on this day.

commencement (def. 3)

com·mend (kə mend′), *v.* **1** to speak well of; praise: *The teacher commended the pupils who did well on the test.* **2** to hand over for safekeeping; entrust: *The child's parents commended her to her aunt's care for a few days.*

com·mend·a·ble (kə men′də bəl), *adj.* deserving praise or approval. **—com·mend′a·bly,** *adv.*

com·men·da·tion (kom′ən dā′shən), *n.* **1** praise; approval. **2** something that shows praise, especially an official award: *The girl received a commendation from the mayor for her bravery.*

com·men·sal·ism (kə men′sə liz′əm), *n.* relationship between living things in which one benefits from the relationship while the other neither benefits nor is harmed by it.

com·men·sur·ate (kə men′sər it *or* kə men′shər it), *adj.* **1** in the proper proportion: *The pay should be commensurate with the work.* **2** of the same size or extent; equal: *commensurate amounts.* **—com·men′sur·ate·ly,** *adv.*

com·ment (kom′ent), **1** *n.* a short statement, note, or remark that explains, praises, or finds fault with something that has been written, said, or done: *The teacher made some helpful comments about my work.* **2** *v.* to make a comment or comments: *Everyone commented on my new coat.* **3** *n.* talk; gossip: *The scandal has been causing much comment.*

com·men·ta·ry (kom′ən ter′ē), *n.* **1** series of notes explaining the hard parts of a book; explanation. **2** series of comments: *a news commentary.* ❑ *n., pl.* **com·men·ta·ries.**

com·men·ta·tor (kom′ən tā′tər), *n.* **1** person who reports and comments on news, sporting events, plays, concerts, etc.: *a TV commentator, a sports commentator.* **2** writer of comments.

com·merce (kom′ərs), *n.* the buying and selling of goods, especially in large amounts between different places; business; trade.

com·mer·cial (kə mėr′shəl), **1** *adj.* of or about trade or business: *a store or other commercial establishment.* **2** *adj.* made to be sold for a profit: *Anything you can buy in a store is a commercial product.* **3** *adj.* supported by an advertiser or sponsor: *a commercial TV program.* **4** *n.* an advertising message on radio or TV, broadcast between or during programs. **—com·mer′cial·ly,** *adv.*

com·mer·cial·ize (kə mėr′shə līz), *v.* to make a matter of business or trade: *Charging admission to church services would commercialize religion.* ❑ *v.* **com·mer·cial·ized, com·mer·cial·iz·ing. —com·mer′cial·i·za′tion,** *n.*

com·min·gle (kə ming′gəl), *v.* to mingle with one another; blend. ❑ *v.* **com·min·gled, com·min·gling.**

com·mis·e·rate (kə miz′ə rāt′), *v.* to feel or express sorrow for another's suffering or trouble; pity; sympathize. ❑ *v.* **com·mis·e·rat·ed, com·mis·e·rat·ing.**

com·mis·e·ra·tion (kə miz′ə rā′shən), *n.* pity; sympathy.

com·mis·sar (kom′ə sär), *n.* a head of a government department in the former Soviet Union.

com·mis·sar·y (kom′ə ser′ē), *n.* **1** a store that sells food and supplies in a mining camp, lumber camp, army camp, etc. **2** lunchroom; cafeteria. ❑ *n., pl.* **com·mis·sar·ies.**

com·mis·sion (kə mish′ən), **1** *n.* a written order giving certain powers, rights, and duties: *She held a commission as U.S. ambassador to Italy.* **2** *v.* to give someone the power, right, or duty to do something; give authority to: *They commissioned a real estate agent to sell their house.* **3** *n.* a written order giving rank or authority in the armed forces: *A captain in the U.S. Army has a commission signed by the President.* **4** *v.* to give such a rank or authority to. **5** *n.* group of people appointed or elected with authority to do certain things: *A commission was appointed to investigate the assassination of the President.* **6** *n.* act of committing; doing; performance: *People are punished for the commission of crimes.* **7** *n.* a percentage of the amount of business done, paid to the agent who does it: *She gets a commission of 10 percent on all the sales that she makes.* **8** *n.* working order; service; use: *A flat tire has put my bicycle out of commission.* **9** *v.* to put into active service; make ready for use. A new warship is commissioned when it has the officers, sailors, and supplies needed for a sea trip.

commissioned officer, officer holding the rank of second lieutenant or above in the U.S. Army, Air Force, or Marine Corps, or of ensign or above in the U.S. Navy.

com·mis·sion·er (kə mish′ə nər), *n.* **1** member of a commission. **2** official in charge of some department of a government: *a health commissioner.*

com·mit (kə mit′), *v.* **1** to do or perform something, usually something wrong: *commit a crime.* **2** to put under the care or control of another: *Mentally ill people are sometimes committed to mental hospitals.* **3** put in; transfer in order to preserve: *commit a poem to memory.* **4** to decide firmly that you will do something, especially in a public way; promise: *I have committed myself and must do what is expected of me.* ❑ *v.* **com·mit·ted, com·mit·ting. —com·mit′ta·ble,** *adj.*

com·mit·ment (kə mit′mənt), *n.* **1** a pledge; promise. **2** feeling of dedication to or involvement with something: *a strong commitment to justice.* **3** act of committing or being committed: *the commitment of a prisoner to jail.*

com·mit·tee (kə mit′ē), *n.* group of persons appointed or elected to do some special thing: *Our teacher appointed a committee to plan the class picnic.* ❑ *n., pl.* **com·mit·tees.**

com·mode (kə mōd′), *n.* **1** chest of drawers. **2** washstand. **3** toilet.

com·mo·di·ous (kə mō′dē əs), *adj.* having plenty of room; spacious; roomy. **—com·mo′di·ous·ly,** *adv.*

com·mod·i·ty (kə mod′ə tē), *n.* anything that is bought and sold; article of trade or commerce: *Groceries are commodities.* ❑ *n., pl.* **com·mod·i·ties.**

com·mo·dore (kom′ə dôr′), *n.* **1** a military rank. See chart on page 712. **2** title given to the president of a yacht club.

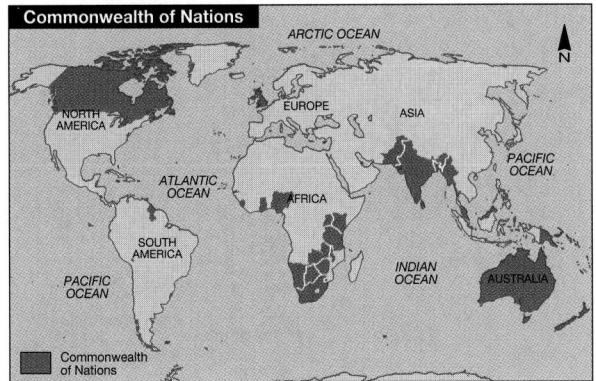

Commonwealth of Nations

ARCTIC OCEAN

N

NORTH AMERICA

EUROPE

ASIA

PACIFIC OCEAN

ATLANTIC OCEAN

AFRICA

SOUTH AMERICA

PACIFIC OCEAN

INDIAN OCEAN

AUSTRALIA

Commonwealth of Nations

com·mon (kom′ən), **1** *adj.* belonging equally to all; joint: *common property.* **2** *adj.* of all; from all; by all; to all; general: *By common consent of the class, she was chosen president.* **3** *adj.* often met with; ordinary; usual: *Snow is common in cold climates.* **4** *adj.* having no special rank or position: *the common people. A common soldier is a private.* **5** *adj.* having poor quality; inferior: *cloth of a common sort.* **6** *adj.* coarse; vulgar: *His speech was very common.* **7** *adj.* belonging to or representing the entire community; public: *A common council of twelve persons governs our city.* **8** *n.* Also, **commons,** *pl.* land owned or used by all the people of a town, village, etc. **—com′mon·ness,** *n.*

in common, equally with another or others; owned, used, or done by both or all: *They have many interests in common.*

SYNONYM STUDY **Common** and **ordinary** both mean usual. **Common** means often met with because shared by many people or things: *Colds are common in winter.* **Ordinary** means like most others: *It was an ordinary summer day, sunny and warm.*

common cold, a cold.

common denominator, a common multiple of the denominators of a group of fractions. 15 is a common denominator of ⅗ and ⅔ because these fractions can be expressed as ⁹⁄₁₅ and ¹⁰⁄₁₅.

common divisor, number that will divide a group of two or more other numbers without a remainder: *2 is a common divisor of 4, 6, 8, and 10.*

com·mon·er (kom′ə nər), *n.* one of the common people; person who is not a noble.

common factor, number that will divide each of two or more other numbers without a remainder: *A common factor of 9 and 12 is 3.*

common fraction, fraction expressed as the ratio of two whole numbers. ½ and ⅞ are common fractions.

common law, law based on custom and usage.

com·mon·ly (kom′ən lē), *adv.* usually; generally: *Arithmetic is commonly taught in elementary schools.*

Common Market, an association established in 1958 to promote free trade among its members; European Economic Community.

common multiple, number that can be divided by two or more other numbers without a remainder: *12 is a common multiple of 2, 3, 4, and 6.*

common name, name by which something is ordinarily known. Animals have scientific names and common names. The common name of sodium chloride is salt.

common noun, name for any one of a class or group of persons, places, or things. *Boy* and *city* are common nouns.

com·mon·place (kom′ən plās′), **1** *adj.* not new or interesting; everyday; ordinary: *The plots of movies made for TV are often commonplace.* **2** *n.* an ordinary or everyday thing: *TV was a novelty 50 years ago; now it is a commonplace.* **3** *n.* an obvious remark: *boring talk full of commonplaces about the weather.* **—com·mon·place·ness,** *n.*

com·mons (kom′ənz), *n.* **1** a dining hall or building where food is served to many at large tables. **2 the Commons,** *pl.* House of Commons. **3** common (def. 8).

common sense, good sense in everyday affairs; practical intelligence.

com·mon·weal (kom′ən wēl′), *n.* the general welfare; public good.

com·mon·wealth (kom′ən welth′), *n.* **1** the people who make up a nation; citizens of a state. **2** nation in which the people have the right to make the laws; republic. Brazil, Australia, and the United States are commonwealths. **3** any state of the United States, especially Kentucky, Massachusetts, Pennsylvania, and Virginia. **4 the Commonwealth,** the Commonwealth of Nations.

Commonwealth of Nations, association of the United Kingdom, the independent member states (such as Canada, Australia, New Zealand, India, Sri Lanka, Ghana, Nigeria, and Cyprus), and various associated states, dependent territories, protectorates, and protected states; the Commonwealth.

com·mo·tion (kə mō′shən), *n.* violent movement; confusion; disturbance; tumult: *Their fight caused quite a commotion in the hall.* ▪ See Synonym Study at **excitement.**

com·mu·nal (kə myü′nl or kom′yə nəl), *adj.* **1** of a community; public: *communal property.* **2** of or in a commune: *communal living.* **—com·mu′nal·ly,** *adv.*

com·mune¹ (kə myün′), *v.* **1** to talk intimately. **2** to receive Holy Communion. **3** to be close to and intimate with: *commune with nature.* ❑ *v.* **com·muned, com·mun·ing.**

com·mune² (kom′yün), *n.* **1** the smallest division for local government in France, Belgium, and several other European countries. **2** group of people living together.

com·mu·ni·ca·ble (kə myü′nə kə bəl), *adj.* that can be transferred or passed along to others: *Chicken pox is a communicable disease. Ideas are communicable by words.* **—com·mu·ni·ca·bil′i·ty,** *n.* **—com·mu·ni·ca·bly,** *adv.*

com·mu·ni·cate (kə myü′nə kāt), *v.* **1** to give or exchange information or news by speaking, writing, etc.; send and receive messages: *She communicated her ideas to her friend.* **2** to pass along; transfer: *communicate a disease.* **3** to be connected: *The dining room communicates with the kitchen.* ❑ *v.* **com·mu·ni·cat·ed, com·mu·ni·cat·ing.** **—com·mu′ni·ca′tor,** *n.*

com·mu·ni·ca·tion (kə myü′nə kā′shən), *n.* **1** act of giving or exchanging information or news by speaking, writing, etc.; communicating: *Sign language is a means of communication.* **2** information or news given; letter, message, etc., which gives information or news: *Your communication came in time to change my plans.* **3 communications,** *pl.* **a** system of communicating by telephone, radio, television, etc.: *A network of communications links all parts of the civilized world.* **b** system of routes or facilities for transporting military supplies, vehicles, and troops.

communications satellite, an artificial satellite that relays radio, telephone, and television signals so that the signals can travel between places far apart, even around the earth.

com·mu·ni·ca·tive (kə myü′nə kə tiv), *adj.* ready to give information; talkative. **—com·mu′ni·ca′tive·ness,** *n.*

com·mun·ion (kə myü′nyən), *n.* **1** exchange of thoughts and feelings; fellowship. **2** group of people having the same religious beliefs. **3 Communion, a** Holy Communion. **b** the part of Mass or other service in which Holy Communion is received. **4** act or condition of having in common; sharing: *The partners had a communion of interests.*

com·mu·ni·qué (kə myü′nə kā′), *n.* an official bulletin, statement, or other communication.

com·mu·nism (kom′yə niz′əm), *n.* **1** an economic and social system in which most or all property is owned by the state or community as a whole and is shared by all. **2 Communism,** the principles and practices of members of a Communist party.

com·mu·nist (kom′yə nist), **1** *n.* person who favors or supports communism. **2** *adj.* communistic. **3** *n.* **Communist,** member of a Communist party. **4** *adj.* **Communist,** of a Communist party.

a	hat	ė	term	ô	order	ch	child		
ā	age	i	it	oi	oil	ng	long		a in about
ä	far	ī	ice	ou	out	sh	she		e in taken
â	care	o	hot	u	cup	th	thin	ə	i in pencil
e	let	ō	open	ů	put	ŦH	then		o in lemon
ē	equal	ò	saw	ü	rule	zh	measure		u in circus

com·mu·nis·tic (kom′yə nis′tik), *adj.* **1** of communists or communism. **2** favoring communism.

com·mu·ni·ty (kə myü′nə tē), *n.* **1** all the people living in the same place and subject to the same laws; people of any district or town: *This lake provides water for six communities.* **2** a neighborhood; the place, district, or area where people live: *There are a few stores and a post office in our community, but not a theater.* **3** group of people living together or sharing common interests: *a monastery and its community of monks, the scientific community.* **4 the community,** the public: *To be successful a new product needs the approval of the community.* **5** ownership together; sharing together: *community of food supplies.* **6** group of living things in any one place. **7** likeness; similarity: *community of interests.* ❑ *n., pl.* **com·mu·ni·ties** for 1-3,6.

community center, building where the people of a community meet for recreation or social and educational purposes.

community chest, fund of money given voluntarily by people to support charity and welfare in their community.

community college, junior college serving the needs of local students, usually supported by public funds.

com·mu·ta·tion (kom′yə tā′shən), *n.* **1** regular travel to and from work by train, bus, car, etc. **2** act of changing a penalty, obligation, etc., to a less severe one: *The prisoner obtained a commutation of his sentence from death to life imprisonment.*

com·mu·ta·tive (kom′yə tā′tiv), *adj.* of or being a rule in mathematics that the order in which numbers are added or multiplied will not change the result. EXAMPLE: $2 + 3$ will give the same result as $3 + 2$.

com·mu·ta·tor (kom′yə tā′tər), *n.* device for controlling the direction of an electric current, used in direct current motors and generators.

com·mute (kə myüt′), **1** *v.* to travel regularly to and from work by train, bus, car, etc. **2** *n.* the distance or trip ordinarily traveled by a commuter: *a long commute, an easy commute.* **3** *v.* to change a penalty, obligation, etc., to a less severe one: *The governor commuted the prisoner's sentence from death to life imprisonment.* ❑ *v.* **com·mut·ed, com·mut·ing. —com·mut′a·ble,** *adj.*

WORD STORY A person who commutes by train may buy a regular ticket at a reduced price. This change to a less severe cost is the connection between the definitions of **commute.**

com·mut·er (kə myü′tər), *n.* person who travels regularly to and from work by train, bus, car, etc.

Com·o·ros (kom′ə rōz), *n.* country consisting of a group of islands in the Indian Ocean, east of N Mozambique. *Capital:* Moroni.

com·pact[1] (kəm pakt′ *or* kom′pakt *for adj.;* kəm pakt′ *for verb;* kom′pakt *for noun*), **1** *adj.* firmly packed together, closely joined: *Cabbage leaves are folded into a compact head.* ■ See Synonym Study at **thick. 2** *adj.* having the parts neatly or tightly arranged within a small space: *a compact stereo.* **3** *v.* to pack firmly together; compress. **4** *adj.* using few words; brief: *a compact report.* **5** *n.* a small case containing face powder or rouge. **6** *n.* car smaller than most models. **—com·pact′ly,** *adv.* **—com·pact′ness,** *n.*

com·pact[2] (kom′pakt), *n.* agreement; contract: *The United Nations is a result of a compact among nations.*

com·pact disk (kom′pakt), a small, thin plastic-coated metal disk, on which is recorded music or computer information. It is a form of optical disk.

com·pac·tor (kəm pak′tər *or* kom′pak tər), *n.* an electrically powered device that compacts or crushes garbage and rubbish to a fraction of its original volume.

com·pan·ion (kəm pan′yən), *n.* **1** person who goes along with or accompanies another; person who shares in what another is doing; comrade: *The twin sisters were companions in work and play.* **2** person paid to live or travel with another as a friend and helper. **3** anything that matches or goes with another in kind, size, and color: *I can't find the companion to this shoe.* [**Companion** comes from Latin words meaning "bread" and "together." Sharing food is a symbol of friendship and loyalty.]

com·pan·ion·a·ble (kəm pan′yə nə bəl), *adj.* pleasant as a companion; agreeable; friendly. **—com·pan′ion·a·bly,** *adv.*

com·pan·ion·ship (kəm pan′yən ship), *n.* friendly feeling between companions; fellowship.

com·pan·ion·way (kəm pan′yən wā′), *n.* stairway from the deck of a ship down to the rooms or area below.

com·pa·ny (kum′pə nē), *n.* **1** a business firm: *He works for a company that makes software.* **2** group of people, especially a group joined together for some purpose: *a company of actors.* **3** one or more guests or visitors: *Are you expecting company for dinner?* **4** companionship: *I've greatly enjoyed your company.* **5** companion or companions: *You are known by the company you keep.* **6** a military unit made up of two or more platoons, usually commanded by a captain. **7** a ship's crew. ❑ *n., pl.* **com·pa·nies** for 1,2,6,7.

keep company, 1 to go with; remain with for companionship: *My dog kept me company on the hike.* **2** to go together; date regularly.

part company, 1 to end a friendship: *They parted company forever.* **2** to go separate ways: *They parted company at the gate.*

com·par·a·ble (kom′pər ə bəl), *adj.* **1** able to be compared: *two actors of comparable ability.* **2** fit to be compared: *A small car is not comparable to a larger one for comfort.* ■ See Synonym Study at **similar. —com′par·a·bly,** *adv.*

com·par·a·tive (kəm par′ə tiv), **1** *adj.* based on comparison; involving comparison: *She made a comparative study of the habits of bees and wasps.* **2** *adj.* measured by comparison with something else; relative: *Although next-door neighbors, they are comparative strangers.* **3** *n.* the second of three degrees of comparison of an adjective or adverb. *Fairer* is the comparative of *fair. More slowly* is the comparative of *slowly.* **4** *adj.* showing the second degree of comparison of an adjective or adverb. *Better* is the comparative form of *good.*

com·par·a·tive·ly (kəm par′ə tiv lē), *adv.* by comparison; relatively; somewhat: *Mountains are comparatively free of mosquitoes.*

com·pare (kəm pâr′), *v.* **1** to find out or point out how persons or things are alike and how they are different: *I compared my answers with the teacher's and found I had made a mistake.* **2** to say two things are alike; consider as similar; liken: *The fins of a fish may be compared to the wings of a bird; both are used in moving.* **3** to be considered like or equal: *Canned fruit cannot compare with fresh fruit.* **4** to name the positive, comparative, and superlative degrees of an adjective or adverb. ❑ *v.* **com·pared, com·par·ing.**

beyond compare, without an equal; most excellent: *The food at this restaurant is beyond compare.*

com·par·i·son (kəm par′ə sən), *n.* **1** act or process of comparing; finding the likenesses and differences: *The teacher's comparison of the heart to a pump helped the students to understand how the heart works.* **2** likeness; similarity: *There is no comparison between these two cameras; one is much better than the other.* **3** change in an adjective or adverb to show degrees. The three degrees of comparison are positive, comparative, and superlative. EXAMPLES: cold, colder, coldest; helpful, more helpful, most helpful; good, better, best.

in comparison with, compared with: *Even a large lake is small in comparison with an ocean.*

com·part·ment (kəm pärt′mənt), *n.* a separate division or section of anything; part of an enclosed place set off by walls or partitions: *Many refrigerators have separate compartments for vegetables and fruit.*

com·pass (kum′pəs), *n.* **1** device for showing directions, having a needle that points to the North Magnetic Pole. **2** tool consisting of two legs hinged together at one end, used for drawing circles and curved lines and for measuring distances. **3** boun-

compass (def. 1)

dary; circumference: *within the compass of four walls.* **4** space within limits; extent; range: *There have been many scientific discoveries within the compass of her lifetime.* **5** range of a voice or musical instrument. ❏ *n., pl.* **com·pass·es** for 1,2.

com·pas·sion (kəm pash′ən), *n.* a feeling for someone else's sorrow or hardship, with a desire to help; sympathy; pity: *Compassion for the earthquake victims brought a flood of contributions.* ■ See Synonym Study at **pity.**

com·pas·sion·ate (kəm pash′ə nit), *adj.* wishing to help those that suffer; sympathetic; pitying.

com·pat·i·ble (kəm pat′ə bəl), *adj.* **1** able to exist or get on well together; agreeing; in harmony: *My new roommate and I are quite compatible.* **2** (in electronics) able to be used with another item or items: *a printer compatible with several computers.* **3** making combination possible without loss of effectiveness or danger to health: *a compatible bone marrow donor.* **—com·pat·i·bil′i·ty,** *n.* **—com·pat′i·bly,** *adv.*

com·pa·tri·ot (kəm pā′trē ət), *n.* person born or living in your own country; fellow citizen.

com·pel (kəm pel′), *v.* **1** to drive or urge with force; force: *Rain compelled us to stop our ballgame.* **2** to bring about by force; command: *A policeman can compel obedience to the law.* ❏ *v.* **com·pelled, com·pel·ling. —com·pel′ling·ly,** *adv.*

com·pen·di·ous (kəm pen′dē əs), *adj.* giving a lot of information in a brief, direct way.

com·pen·di·um (kəm pen′dē əm), *n.* summary that gives much information in little space. ❏ *n., pl.* **com·pen·di·ums, com·pen·di·a** (kəm pen′dē ə).

com·pen·sate (kom′pən sāt), *v.* **1** to give something to someone in order to make up for something lost or taken away: *The children mowed our lawn to compensate us for the window they broke playing ball.* **2** to balance by equal weight or power; make up: *Skill sometimes compensates for lack of strength.* **3** to pay: *The company compensated her for much of her extra work.* ■ See Synonym Study at **pay.** ❏ *v.* **com·pen·sat·ed, com·pen·sat·ing. —com′pen·sa′tor,** *n.*

com·pen·sa·tion (kom′pən sā′shən), *n.* **1** pay: *Equal compensation should be given for equal work.* **2** something given to make up for something else; something which makes up for a loss, injury, etc.: *I was given a day off as compensation for working overtime.*

com·pete (kəm pēt′), *v.* **1** to try hard to win or gain something wanted by others; be rivals; contend: *She competed against many fine athletes for the gold medal. It is difficult for a small grocery store to compete with a supermarket.* **2** to take part in a contest: *Will you compete in the final race?* ❏ *v.* **com·pet·ed, com·pet·ing.**

com·pe·tence (kom′pə təns), *n.* condition of being competent; ability: *No one doubted the guide's competence.*

com·pe·ten·cy (kom′pə tən sē), *n.* competence.

com·pe·tent (kom′pə tənt), *adj.* properly qualified; able: *She is a competent driver who has never caused an accident.* ■ See Synonym Study at **able. —com′pe·tent·ly,** *adv.*

com·pe·ti·tion (kom′pə tish′ən), *n.* **1** act of trying hard to win or gain something wanted by others; rivalry: *competition among stores for customers.* **2** contest: *She won first place in the swimming competition.* **3** a competitor or competitors: *Our company's competition has come out with an exciting new product.*

com·pet·i·tive (kəm pet′ə tiv), *adj.* **1** decided by competition; using competition: *Tennis and soccer are competitive sports.* **2** eager to compete: *athletes full of competitive spirit.* **—com·pet′i·tive·ly,** *adv.*

com·pet·i·tor (kəm pet′ə tər), *n.* person who competes; rival.

com·pi·la·tion (kom′pə lā′shən), *n.* **1** book, list, table, etc., that has been compiled. **2** act of compiling.

com·pile (kəm pīl′), *v.* **1** to collect and bring together in one list or account: *I compiled a list of the supplies and equipment we needed.* **2** to make a book, a report, etc., out of various materials: *It takes many experts to compile an encyclopedia.* ❏ *v.* **com·piled, com·pil·ing.**

com·pil·er (kəm pī′lər), *n.* **1** person who compiles. **2** computer program that converts programs written in normal words, num-

bers, and mathematical symbols into programs in the machine language that a computer can use directly.

com·pla·cence (kəm plā′sns), *n.* complacency.

com·pla·cen·cy (kəm plā′sn sē), *n.* condition of being pleased with yourself or what you have; self-satisfaction: *She solved the difficult puzzle easily and smiled with complacency.*

com·pla·cent (kəm plā′snt), *adj.* pleased with yourself or what you have; self-satisfied: *The winner's complacent smile annoyed the loser.* **—com·pla′cent·ly,** *adv.*

com·plain (kəm plān′), *v.* **1** to say that something is wrong, troublesome, or painful; find fault: *We complained that the room was too cold.* **2** to talk about your pain, troubles, etc.: *He is always complaining.* **3** to make an accusation or charge: *I complained to the police about the barking of my neighbor's dog.* **—com·plain′er,** *n.* **—com·plain′ing·ly,** *adv.*

SYNONYM STUDY **Complain** and **grumble** both mean to express unhappiness with something. **Complain** means to say that something is not the way it should be: *Shoppers complained when the store raised prices.* **Grumble** means to complain in a growling, angry way: *After grumbling for weeks about the extra work, the miners went on strike.*

com·plain·ant (kəm plā′nənt), *n.* person who brings a lawsuit against another.

com·plaint (kəm plānt′), *n.* **1** statement of dissatisfaction; finding fault: *His letter is filled with complaints about the food at camp.* **2** a cause for complaining: *Her main complaint is that she has too much work to do.* **3** accusation; charge: *The judge heard the complaint and ordered an investigation.* **4** illness; disease: *A cold is a very common complaint.*

com·plai·sance (kəm plā′sns), *n.* act of being complaisant or obliging; graciousness.

com·plai·sant (kəm plā′snt), *adj.* inclined to do what is asked; obliging; gracious. **—com·plai′sant·ly,** *adv.*

com·ple·ment (kom′plə ment′ *for verb;* kom′plə mənt *for noun*), **1** *v.* to supply a lack of any kind; complete: *The salty flavor of the olives and pickles complemented the blandness of the cheese.* **2** *n.* something that completes or makes perfect: *The teacher considers homework a necessary complement to classroom work.* **3** *n.* number required to complete or make perfect: *The plane had its full complement of passengers; all seats were taken.* **4** *n.* word or group of words completing a predicate. In "The bus is late" *late* is a complement. **5** *n.* amount needed to make an angle or an arc equal to 90 degrees. ■ See Usage Note at **compliment.**

com·ple·men·tar·y (kom′plə men′tər ē), *adj.* forming a complement; completing: *The four seasons are complementary parts of a year.* ■ Another word that sounds like this is **complimentary.**

complementary angle, either of two angles which together form an angle of 90 degrees. See picture at **angle¹.**

complementary colors, two colors that produce white or gray when combined. Red and green are complementary colors.

com·plete (kəm plēt′), **1** *adj.* with all the parts; whole; entire: *We have a complete set of garden tools.* **2** *v.* to make whole or entire; make up the full number or amount of: *I completed the set of dishes by buying the cups and saucers.* **3** *adj.* perfect; thorough: *a complete surprise.* **4** *v.* to make perfect or thorough: *The good news completed his happiness.* **5** *adj.* finished; done: *My homework is complete.* **6** *v.* to get done; finish: *She completed her homework before dinner.* ❏ *v.* **com·plet·ed, com·plet·ing. —com·plete′ly,** *adv.* **—com·plete′ness,** *n.*

com·ple·tion (kəm plē′shən), *n.* **1** act of completing; finishing: *After the completion of the job, the workers went home.* **2** condition of being completed: *The work is near completion.* **3** (in football) a pass caught by a receiver.

a	hat	ė	term	ô	order	ch	child		ə { a in about
ā	age	i	it	oi	oil	ng	long		e in taken
ä	far	ī	ice	ou	out	sh	she		i in pencil
â	care	o	hot	u	cup	th	thin		o in lemon
e	let	ō	open	ù	put	ŦH	then		u in circus
ē	equal	ò	saw	ü	rule	zh	measure		

com·plex (kəm pleks′ *or* kom′pleks *for adj.;* kom′pleks *for noun*), **1** *adj.* made up of a number of parts: *A watch is a complex device.* **2** *adj.* hard to understand: *The instructions for building the radio were so complex they were hard to follow.* **3** *n.* group of related or connected buildings, structures, units, etc.: *The new cultural complex built in our city includes a library, a museum, and a concert hall.* **4** *n.* a strong prejudice; unreasonable dislike or fear: *He has a complex about cats.* ❑ *n., pl.* **com·plex·es.** —**com·plex′ly,** *adv.* —**com·plex′ness,** *n.*

complex fraction, fraction having a fraction in the numerator, in the denominator, or in both; compound fraction.

EXAMPLES: $\dfrac{1\,3/4}{3}$, $\dfrac{1}{3\,3/4}$, $\dfrac{3/4}{1\,7/8}$.

com·plex·ion (kəm plek′shən), *n.* **1** color, quality, and general appearance of the skin, particularly of the face. **2** general appearance of anything; nature; character: *The complexion of the little farm town was changed when two big factories were built nearby.*

com·plex·i·ty (kəm plek′sə tē), *n.* **1** a complex quality or condition; intricacy: *The complexity of the road map caused me to get thoroughly lost.* **2** something complex; complication. ❑ *n., pl.* **com·plex·i·ties** for 2.

complex sentence, sentence having one main clause and one or more subordinate clauses. EXAMPLE: When the traffic light turns red, traffic must stop.

com·pli·ance (kəm plī′əns), *n.* **1** act of complying; yielding to a request or command: *I appreciated the clerk's ready compliance with my request to exchange the sweater.* **2** tendency to yield to others: *His refusal was all the more surprising in view of his usual compliance.*

in compliance with, complying with; according to: *She sent the package by airmail in compliance with my request.*

com·pli·an·cy (kəm plī′ən sē), *n.* compliance.

com·pli·ant (kəm plī′ənt), *adj.* complying; yielding; obliging. —**com·pli′ant·ly,** *adv.*

com·pli·cate (kom′plə kāt), *v.* **1** to make hard to understand or settle; mix up; make complex; confuse: *Too many rules complicate a game.* **2** to make worse or more mixed up: *Headaches can be complicated by eye trouble.* ❑ *v.* **com·pli·cat·ed, com·pli·cat·ing.** [Complicate comes from a Latin word meaning "to fold together."]

com·pli·cat·ed (kom′plə kā′tid), *adj.* **1** hard to understand; involved: *These directions are too complicated.* **2** made up of many parts; complex: *A jet engine is a complicated machine.* —**com′pli·cat′ed·ly,** *adv.* —**com′pli·cat′ed·ness,** *n.*

com·pli·ca·tion (kom′plə kā′shən), *n.* **1** a complex or confused condition that is hard to understand or settle: *Various complications delayed the start of our camping trip.* **2** something that makes matters worse or harder to untangle or settle: *Infection was the complication we feared most after the operation.* **3** act of complicating.

com·plic·i·ty (kəm plis′ə tē), *n.* involvement or partnership in wrongdoing: *Knowingly receiving stolen goods is complicity in theft.*

com·pli·ment (kom′plə mənt *for noun;* kom′plə ment *for verb*), **1** *n.* something good said about someone; something said in praise of someone's work: *She received many compliments on her science project.* ■ See Synonym Study at **praise.** **2** *n.* a courteous act: *The town paid the old artist the compliment of a large attendance at his exhibit.* **3** *v.* to pay a compliment to; congratulate: *The coach complimented the winner of the race.* **4** *n.pl.* **compliments,** greetings: *In the box of flowers was a card saying "With the compliments of a friend."*

People often confuse **compliment** and **complement** because they sound alike. **Compliment** means to praise: *She complimented his singing.* **Complement** means to complete. It suggests making something better: *This scarf complements the dress.*

com·pli·men·ta·ry (kom′plə men′tər ē), *adj.* **1** expressing a compliment; praising: *a complimentary remark.* **2** given free: *a complimentary ticket to the circus.* ■ Another word that sounds like this is **complementary.** —**com′pli·men·tar′i·ly,** *adv.*

com·ply (kəm plī′), *v.* to act in agreement with a request or a command: *I will comply with their wishes.* ❑ *v.* **com·plied, com·ply·ing.** —**com·pli′er,** *n.*

com·po·nent (kəm pō′nənt), **1** *n.* a necessary or essential part: *Quartz and feldspar are the chief components of granite.* **2** *adj.* forming a necessary part; making up; constituent: *component parts.*

com·port (kəm pôrt′), *v.* to conduct yourself in a certain manner; behave: *Judges should comport themselves with dignity.*

com·port·ment (kəm pôrt′mənt), *n.* behavior.

com·pose (kəm pōz′), *v.* **1** to make up; form: *The ocean is composed of salt water.* **2** to put together. To compose a story or poem is to construct it from words. To compose a piece of music is to invent the tune and write down the notes. To compose a picture is to arrange the things in it artistically. **3** to make calm: *Stop crying and compose yourself.* **4** to settle; arrange: *The union and the company composed their differences and agreed on a contract.* ❑ *v.* **com·posed, com·pos·ing.**

People often confuse **compose** and **comprise.** **Compose** means to form: *Ten hundreds compose a thousand.* **Comprise** means to include: *A thousand comprises ten hundreds.*

com·posed (kəm pōzd′), *adj.* calm; quiet. —**com·pos′ed·ly,** *adv.* —**com·pos′ed·ness,** *n.*

com·pos·er (kəm pō′zər), *n.* **1** person who composes. **2** writer of music.

com·pos·ite (kəm poz′it), **1** *adj.* made up of various parts; compound: *She made a composite photograph by putting together parts of several others.* **2** *adj.* belonging to a group of plants with flower heads consisting of many very tiny flowers. Daisies and dandelions are composite flowers. **3** *n.* any composite thing. **4** *n.* a kind of material composed of two or more different substances combined together. The combined substances have more strength, flexibility, etc., than the substances have separately. A composite of carbon fiber and plastic is used in making some new aircraft.

composite number, number exactly divisible by some counting number other than itself or one. 4, 6, and 9 are composite numbers; 2, 3, 5, and 7 are prime numbers.

com·po·si·tion (kom′pə zish′ən), *n.* **1** the makeup of anything; what is in it: *The composition of this candy includes sugar, chocolate, and milk.* **2** thing composed. A symphony, poem, or painting is a composition. A school paper or report is also a composition. **3** act of putting together of a whole. Writing sentences, writing music, and making pictures are all forms of composition. **4** mixture of substances; compound.

com·post (kom′pōst), *n.* mixture of decaying leaves, grass, manure, etc., for fertilizing soil.

com·po·sure (kəm pō′zhər), *n.* calmness; quietness; self-control: *She always keeps her composure, even during a crisis.*

com·pote (kom′pōt), *n.* **1** stewed fruit: *apple compote.* **2** dish with a long supporting stem, for fruit, candy, etc.

com·pound¹ (kom′pound *for adj., noun;* kom pound′ *for verb*), **1** *adj.* having more than one part: *a compound medicine.* **2** *n.* something made by combining parts; mixture: *Many medicines are compounds.* **3** *n.* word made up of two or more words which keep their separate forms. *Steamship* is a compound made up of the two words *steam* and *ship. Raindrop* is a compound made up of the the the two words *rain* and *drop.* **4** *n.* substance formed by chemical combination of two or more elements in definite proportions: *Water is a compound of hydrogen and oxygen.* **5** *v.* to mix; combine: *The druggist compounded several medicines to fill the prescription.* **6** *v.* to add to; increase; multiply: *I compounded my troubles by forgetting to bring my homework to school.* —**com·pound′a·ble,** *adj.* —**com·pound′er,** *n.*

com·pound² (kom′pound), *n.* an enclosed yard with residences or other buildings in it.

compound eye, the eye of some insects and crustaceans. It is composed of many tiny units, each of which receives an image.

compound fraction, complex fraction.

compound fracture, fracture in which a broken bone cuts through the flesh.

compound interest, interest paid on both the original sum of money borrowed or invested and the interest added to it.

compound leaf, leaf composed of two or more leaflets on a single stalk.

compound machine, machine made up of many simple machines, usually powered by electricity or fuel.

compound sentence, sentence made up of two or more main clauses. EXAMPLE: The winds blew, the rains fell, and the water covered the earth.

com·pre·hend (kom′pri hend′), v. **1** to understand the meaning of: If you can use a word correctly, you comprehend it. **2** to include; contain: Your report comprehended all the facts. —**com′·pre·hend′i·ble,** adj. —**com′pre·hend′ing·ly,** adv.

com·pre·hen·si·ble (kom′pri hen′sə bəl), adj. understandable. —**com′pre·hen′si·bil′i·ty,** n. —**com′pre·hen′si·bly,** adv.

com·pre·hen·sion (kom′pri hen′shən), n. act or power of understanding: Arithmetic is beyond the comprehension of a baby.

com·pre·hen·sive (kom′pri hen′siv), adj. covering a broad range or extent; including much: The month's schoolwork ended with a comprehensive review. —**com′pre·hen′sive·ly,** adv. —**com′pre·hen′sive·ness,** n.

com·press (kəm pres′ for verb; kom′pres for noun), **1** v. to squeeze together; make smaller by pressure: Cotton is compressed into bales. Can you compress the story into a few short sentences? **2** n. pad of cloth applied to some part of the body to prevent bleeding, reduce inflammation, etc.: I put a cold compress on my forehead to relieve my headache. ❑ n., pl. **com·press·es.** —**com·press′i·bil′i·ty,** n. —**com·press′i·ble,** adj.

compressed air, air kept under high pressure so that it has a great deal of force when released, used to operate brakes, drills, etc., or to inflate tires.

com·pres·sion (kəm presh′ən), n. **1** act or process of compressing. **2** a compressed condition. **3** reduction under pressure of the volume of fuel vapor in a cylinder of an internal-combustion engine, before ignition.

com·pres·sor (kəm pres′ər), n. machine for compressing air, gas, etc.

computer graphics

com·prise (kəm prīz′), v. to be made up of; consist of; include: The United States comprises 50 states. ❑ v. **com·prised, com·pris·ing.** ■ See Usage Note at **compose.**

com·pro·mise (kom′prə mīz), **1** v. to settle a quarrel or difference of opinion by agreeing that each will give up a part of what the other person demands: A good politician knows how to compromise. **2** n. settlement of a quarrel or difference of opinion in which both sides agree to give up a part of what each demands: They both wanted the apple; their compromise was to share it. **3** n. result of any such settlement. **4** v. to put under suspicion; put in danger: You will compromise your reputation if you go around with such a bad crowd. ❑ v. **com·pro·mised, com·pro·mis·ing.** —**com′pro·mis′er,** n.

comp·trol·ler (kən trō′lər), n. person employed to look after expenditures and accounts; controller.

com·pul·sion (kəm pul′shən), n. **1** act of compelling or condition of being compelled; use of force; force: A contract signed under compulsion is not legal. **2** impulse that is hard to resist: Some people have a compulsion to gamble.

com·pul·sive (kəm pul′siv), adj. of or caused by an impulse that is hard to resist: a compulsive desire for neatness. —**com·pul′sive·ly,** adv.

com·pul·sor·y (kəm pul′sər ē), adj. **1** compelled; required: Attendance at school is compulsory for children over seven years old. **2** compelling; using force.

com·punc·tion (kəm pungk′shən), n. uneasiness of the mind because of wrongdoing; regret; remorse: She had no compunction about copying her friend's work.

com·pu·ta·tion (kom′pyə tā′shən), n. **1** act of computing; calculation. Addition and subtraction are forms of computation. **2** amount computed; result.

com·pute (kəm pyüt′), v. to find out by arithmetical or other mathematical work; calculate: Mother computed the cost of our trip. ❑ v. **com·put·ed, com·put·ing.**

com·put·er (kəm pyü′tər), n. an electronic machine that can store, recall, or process information. A computer performs these tasks according to instructions which can easily be changed, so it is able to do many different kinds of work. Computers keep files, solve mathematical problems, play games, and control the operations of other machines.

WORD BANK **Computers** have their own vocabulary, much of it very new. If you want to learn more about computers, you can start by looking up these words in this dictionary.

ASCII	DOS	microprocessor
BASIC	download	modem
baud	e-mail	monitor
bit⁴	floppy disk	mouse
boot³	gigabyte	operating system
buffer¹	hard disk	PC
bug	home page	RAM
CD-ROM	hypertext	ROM
CPU	Internet	scroll
chip	kilobyte	software
cursor	laptop	supercomputer
database	laser disk	trackball
desktop	megabyte	World Wide Web

computer graphics, **1** the use of computers to produce pictures, diagrams, and other artwork. **2** images produced by computers.

com·put·er·ize (kəm pyü′tə rīz′), v. **1** to adapt to a computer; operate by means of a computer. **2** to equip with computers: Our school library has been computerized. ❑ v. **com·put·er·ized, com·put·er·iz·ing.** —**com·put′er·i·za′tion,** n.

computer language, any system of words, numbers, and symbols used for programming a computer.

computer literacy, an understanding of the basic concepts of computer use and operation; knowledge of computers equivalent to the knowledge of language necessary to read and write.

computer literate, knowing how to use computers and how they work: The store wants to hire someone who is computer literate to help with the inventory and tax records.

com·rade (kom′rad), n. **1** a close companion and friend. **2** fellow worker; partner. [**Comrade** comes from a Spanish word meaning "roommate." Close friends often choose to be roommates.] —**com′rade·ship,** n.

con¹ (kon), **1** adv. against: The two groups argued the question pro and con. **2** n. a reason against: The pros and cons of a question are the arguments for and against it.

con² (kon), INFORMAL. **1** v. to swindle someone after gaining his or her trust: They were conned into investing money in a company that did not exist. **2** n. a swindle. **3** adj. swindling: a con game. ❑ v. **conned, con·ning.** [**Con²** is short for **confidence.** Swindlers try to win people's confidence—and then get their money.]

con³ (kon), n. INFORMAL. a convict.

a	hat	ė	term	ô	order	ch	child		a in about
ā	age	i	it	oi	oil	ng	long		e in taken
ä	far	ī	ice	ou	out	sh	she	ə	i in pencil
â	care	o	hot	u	cup	th	thin		o in lemon
e	let	ō	open	ú	put	ᴛʜ	then		u in circus
ē	equal	ò	saw	ü	rule	zh	measure		

con-, *prefix.* form of **com-**.

Con·a·kry (kon′ə krē), *n.* capital of Guinea, in the W part.

con·cave (kon kāv′ or kon′kāv), *adj.* hollow and curved like the inside of a circle or sphere. **—con·cave′ly,** *adv.*

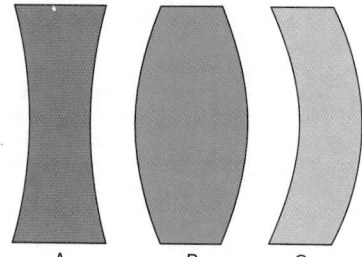

concave and **convex**
A. both concave
B. both convex
C. concave and convex

concave

con·cav·i·ty (kon kav′ə tē), *n.* **1** a concave condition. **2** a concave surface or thing. □ *n., pl.* **con·cav·i·ties** for 2.

con·ceal (kən sēl′), *v.* **1** to put out of sight; hide: *He concealed the surprise gift in the closet.* ■ See Synonym Study at **hide**[1]. **2** to keep secret: *They concealed their identities by wearing masks.* **—con·ceal′a·ble,** *adj.*

con·ceal·ment (kən sēl′mənt), *n.* **1** act of concealing or keeping secret: *The witness's concealment of facts prevented a fair trial.* **2** means or place for concealing.

con·cede (kən sēd′), *v.* **1** to admit as true; acknowledge: *The candidate conceded defeat in the election.* **2** to allow someone to have; grant: *They conceded us the right to use their driveway.* □ *v.* **con·ced·ed, con·ced·ing. —con·ced′er,** *n.*

con·ceit (kən sēt′), *n.* too high an opinion of yourself or of your ability; vanity.

con·ceit·ed (kən sē′tid), *adj.* having too high an opinion of yourself or of your ability; vain. ■ See Synonym Study at **proud**.

con·ceive (kən sēv′), *v.* **1** to form in the mind; think up; imagine: *She conceived a plan for earning some spending money.* **2** to have an idea or feeling; think: *It is difficult to conceive of life without conveniences such as cars and telephones.* **3** to become pregnant with: *conceive a child.* □ *v.* **con·ceived, con·ceiv·ing. —con·ceiv′a·ble,** *adj.* **—con·ceiv′a·bly,** *adv.* **—con·ceiv′er,** *n.*

con·cen·trate (kon′sən trāt), **1** *v.* to bring or come together in one place: *A magnifying glass can concentrate enough sunlight to scorch paper.* **2** *v.* to pay close attention; focus the mind: *He concentrated on his reading so that he would understand the story.* ■ See Synonym Study at **think**. **3** *v.* to make stronger. An acid solution is concentrated when it has a lot of acid in it. **4** *n.* something that has been concentrated: *Lemon juice with the water removed is a concentrate.* □ *v.* **con·cen·trat·ed, con·cen·trat·ing.**

con·cen·tra·tion (kon′sən trā′shən), *n.* **1** act or process of concentrating or condition of being concentrated. **2** close attention: *When she gave the problem her full concentration, she figured out the answer.* **3** a group brought together in one place: *There is a large concentration of fish in the lake.* **4** (of a chemical solution) strength: *The acid solution was of weak concentration because so much water had been added.*

concentration camp, a prison camp where political enemies, prisoners of war, or members of minority groups are held by government order.

con·cen·tric (kən sen′trik), *adj.* having the same center.

con·cept (kon′sept), *n.* idea of a thing or class of things; general notion; idea: *the concept of equal treatment under law.*

con·cep·tion (kən sep′shən), *n.* **1** idea; thought; notion: *Her conception of the problem was dif-*

concentric circles

ferent from mine. **2** act of forming an idea or thought. **3** act of becoming pregnant.

con·cep·tu·al·ize (kən sep′chü ə līz), *v.* to form concepts or ideas about. □ *v.* **con·cep·tu·al·ized, con·cep·tu·al·iz·ing. —con·cep′tu·al·i·za′tion,** *n.*

con·cern (kən sėrn′), **1** *v.* to be about; be the business or affair of; belong to; interest: *The school play concerns every member of the class.* **2** *n.* anything that relates to your work or your interests; business; affair: *The party decorations are my concern; you pay attention to refreshments.* **3** *n.* troubled interest; worry; anxiety: *Their concern over their sick child kept them awake all night.* ■ See Synonym Study at **care**. **4** *v.* to make anxious; cause to worry; trouble: *We didn't want to concern you with the bad news.* **5** *n.* a business company; firm: *We wrote to two big concerns for their catalogs.*

con·cerned (kən sėrnd′), *adj.* **1** worried; anxious: *His parents are quite concerned about his poor health.* **2** interested: *Concerned citizens exercise their right to vote.*

con·cern·ing (kən sėr′ning), *prep.* about; relating to: *The reporter asked many questions concerning the accident.*

con·cert (kon′sərt), *n.* a musical performance in which one or more musicians take part: *The school orchestra gave a concert.* **in concert,** all together; in agreement: *The class worked in concert to put on the play.*

con·cert·ed (kən sėr′tid), *adj.* arranged by agreement; combined: *a concerted effort.* **—con·cert′ed·ly,** *adv.*

con·cer·ti·na (kon sər tē′nə), *n.* a small musical instrument somewhat like an accordion. □ *n., pl.* **con·cer·ti·nas.**

con·cer·to (kən cher′tō), *n.* a long musical composition for one or more principal instruments, such as a violin or piano, with the accompaniment of an orchestra. It usually has three movements. □ *n., pl.* **con·cer·tos, con·cer·ti** (kən cher′tē).

con·ces·sion (kən sesh′ən), *n.* **1** act of conceding; granting: *As a concession to their pleas, the children were allowed to stay up past bedtime.* **2** anything granted or yielded: *The teacher made a special concession and postponed the test.* **3** something conceded or granted by a government or controlling authority; grant. Land or privileges given by a government to a business company are called concessions. **4** the right or space leased for a specific use: *the hot-dog concession at the amusement park.* **5** CANADIAN. **a** (in Ontario and Quebec) one of the areas of land into which townships are divided. **b** concession road.

concession road, (in Ontario) a rural road, usually running east to west between concessions.

conch (kongk or konch), *n.* **1** any of numerous soft-bodied sea animals of tropical waters with a large, spiral shell. **2** a shell of such an animal. □ *n., pl.* **conchs** (kongks) or **conch·es** (kon′chiz). ■ Another word that can sound like this is **conk**.

con·cil·i·ate (kən sil′ē āt), *v.* **1** to win over; soothe: *She conciliated her angry little sister with a candy bar.* **2** to bring into harmony; reconcile. □ *v.* **con·cil·i·at·ed, con·cil·i·at·ing. —con·cil′i·a′tion,** *n.* **—con·cil′i·a′tor,** *n.*

con·cil·i·a·to·ry (kən sil′ē ə tôr′ē), *adj.* tending to win over, soothe, or reconcile: *Shaking hands after a fight is a conciliatory gesture.*

con·cise (kən sīs′), *adj.* expressing much in few words; brief but full of meaning: *He gave a concise report of the meeting.* **—con·cise′ly,** *adv.* **—con·cise′ness,** *n.*

con·clave (kon′klāv), *n.* a private meeting.

con·clude (kən klüd′), *v.* **1** to come or bring to an end; finish: *The play concluded with a happy ending and the curtain came down.* **2** to reach certain decisions or opinions by reasoning; infer: *From its tracks, we concluded that the animal must have been a bear.* **3** to arrange; settle: *The two countries concluded a trade agreement.* □ *v.* **con·clud·ed, con·clud·ing. —con·clud′er,** *n.*

con·clu·sion (kən klü′zhən), *n.* **1** final part; end: *The end of each chapter in our science book has a conclusion summing up all the important facts.* **2** decision or opinion reached by reasoning; inference: *Researchers came to the conclusion that the disease was caused by a virus.* **3** arrangement; settlement: *the conclusion of a peace treaty between two countries.* **4** a final result;

outcome: *bring work to a good conclusion.*

in conclusion, finally; lastly; to conclude: *I will say, in conclusion, that it was an honor to be the speaker at this meeting.*

con·clu·sive (kən klü′siv), *adj.* settling something beyond question; convincing; final: *The evidence against the suspect was conclusive.* —**con·clu′sive·ly,** *adv.* —**con·clu′sive·ness,** *n.*

con·coct (kon kokt′), *v.* **1** to prepare: *He concocted a drink made of grape juice and ginger ale.* **2** to make up; think up; invent: *They concocted an excuse for being late to school.* —**con·coct′er,** *n.*

con·coc·tion (kon kok′shən), *n.* **1** something concocted. **2** act or process of concocting: *The concoction of the milk shake took several minutes.*

con·cord (kon′kôrd *or* kong′kôrd), *n.* agreement; harmony; peace: *concord achieved between historic enemies.* [Concord comes from Latin words meaning "together" and "heart." Today we say that people who agree are "of one mind."]

> **WORD FAMILY** Concord and the following words are related: **accordion, cordial, courage, discord, encourage,** and **record.** They all come from a Latin word meaning "heart."

Con·cord (kong′kərd), *n.* **1** town in E Massachusetts. The second battle of the Revolutionary War was fought there on April 19, 1775. **2** capital of New Hampshire, in the S part.

con·cord·ance (kon kôrd′ns), *n.* an alphabetical list of the principal words of a book with references to the passages in which they occur.

con·course (kon′kôrs), *n.* a place where crowds come: *the main concourse of the railroad station.*

con·crete (kon′krēt′ *or* kon krēt′), **1** *n.* mixture of crushed stone or gravel, sand, cement, and water that hardens as it dries. Concrete is used for foundations, buildings, sidewalks, roads, dams, and bridges. **2** *adj.* made of this mixture: *a concrete sidewalk.* **3** *adj.* existing as an actual object, not merely as an idea or as a quality; real: *A painting is concrete; its beauty is not.* **4** *adj.* specific; particular; not general: *A daisy is a concrete example of a composite flower.* —**con·crete′ly,** *adv.* —**con·crete′ness,** *n.*

con·cu·bine (kong′kyə bīn), *n.* **1** woman who lives with a man without being legally married to him. **2** (in countries where one man can legally have many wives) a wife having inferior rank or rights.

con·cur (kən kėr′), *v.* **1** to be of the same opinion; agree: *The contest judges all concurred in giving her the prize.* **2** to happen at the same time; coincide: *Two weeks of rain concurred with high tides, causing coastal flooding.* ❑ *v.* **con·curred, con·cur·ring.**

con·cur·rence (kən kėr′ns), *n.* **1** agreement. **2** occurrence at the same time.

con·cur·rent (kən kėr′ənt), *adj.* **1** happening at the same time: *concurrent events.* **2** agreeing; harmonious: *concurrent ideas.* **3** coming together; meeting at a point. —**con·cur′rent·ly,** *adv.*

con·cus·sion (kən kush′ən), *n.* **1** injury to the brain caused by a blow, fall, etc. **2** a sudden, violent shaking; shock: *The concussion caused by the explosion broke many windows.*

con·demn (kən dem′), *v.* **1** to express strong disapproval of: *We condemn cruelty to animals.* ∎ See Synonym Study at **criticize. 2** to declare guilty of crime or wrong: *The accused was condemned by the jury.* **3** to give a punishment to; sentence: *The spy was condemned to death.* **4** to declare not sound or suitable for use: *This bridge was condemned as unsafe.* **5** to take for public use under special provision of the law: *Two neighborhood streets have been condemned to make room for the new expressway.* [See Word Story at **mnemonic.**] —**con·dem·na′tion,** *n.*

con·den·sa·tion (kon′den sā′shən), *n.* **1** something condensed; condensed mass. A cloud is a condensation of water vapor in the atmosphere. **2** something that has been shortened: *The magazine printed a condensation of the book.* **3** act or process of condensing or condition of being condensed: *the condensation of milk, the condensation of steam into water.*

con·dense (kən dens′), *v.* **1** to make or become denser or more compact: *Milk is condensed by removing much of the water from it.* **2** to change from a gas or vapor to a liquid. If steam touches cold surfaces, it condenses or is condensed into water. **3** to put

into fewer words; say briefly: *A long story can sometimes be condensed into a few sentences.* ❑ *v.* **con·densed, con·dens·ing.** —**con·den′sa·ble,** *adj.*

condensed milk, a thick, sweetened, canned milk, prepared by evaporating some of the water from ordinary milk.

con·dens·er (kən den′sər), *n.* **1** person or thing that condenses something. **2** capacitor. **3** apparatus for changing gas or vapor into a liquid.

con·de·scend (kon′di send′), *v.* **1** to grant a favor with a haughty or patronizing attitude: *The little boy's older sister finally condescended to take him to the movies.* **2** to act in a way that shows you think you are superior to other people: *He tries never to condescend to children.* —**con′de·scend′ing·ly,** *adv.*

con·de·scen·sion (kon′di sen′shən), *n.* a haughty or patronizing attitude.

con·di·ment (kon′də mənt), *n.* something used to give extra flavor to food, such as mustard and spices.

con·di·tion (kən dish′ən), **1** *n.* state in which someone or something is: *The condition of the house is better than when I bought it.* **2** *n.pl.* **conditions,** set of circumstances: *Icy roads make for poor driving conditions.* **3** *n.* good condition; good health: *People who take part in sports must keep in condition.* **4** *v.* to put in good condition: *Exercise conditions your muscles.* **5** *n.* social position; rank: *Lincoln's parents were poor settlers of humble condition.* **6** *n.* thing on which something else depends; thing without which something else cannot be: *One of the conditions of the peace treaty was the return of all prisoners.* **7** *v.* to cause a living thing to react in a particular way every time that some event happens: *The cat is conditioned to meow for food when it hears my alarm clock.* **8** *n.* sickness; illness: *a heart condition.* **9** *n.* a requirement that is expressed by an open mathematical sentence. The equation $3 + x = 5$ expresses the condition that a number you are to find, added to 3, must equal 5.

on condition that, with the understanding that; if: *I'll go on condition that you will go, too.*

con·di·tion·al (kən dish′ə nəl), *adj.* **1** depending on something else; limited. "You may go if the sun shines" is a conditional promise. **2** expressing or containing a condition: *Conditional statements in the sales agreement limited the use of the land.* —**con·di′tion·al·ly,** *adv.*

con·di·tion·er (kən dish′ə nər), *n.* **1** device or substance that maintains or improves the quality of something: *water conditioner.* **2** air conditioner.

con·do (kon′dō), *n.* condominium. ❑ *n., pl.* **con·dos.**

con·dole (kən dōl′), *v.* to express sympathy; grieve: *Friends condoled with the family at the funeral.* ❑ *v.* **con·doled, con·dol·ing.**

con·do·lence (kən dō′ləns), *n.* expression of sympathy: *Their friends sent the family many condolences.*

con·dom (kon′dom), *n.* a thin rubber or latex covering worn over the penis or within the vagina during sexual intercourse in order to prevent pregnancy and sexually transmitted disease.

con·do·min·i·um (kon′də min′ē əm), *n.* **1** an apartment house in which each apartment is owned rather than rented. **2** apartment in a building like this.

> **WORD STORY** Condominium comes from Latin words meaning "lordship" and "together." The word used to describe an arrangement where two countries shared rule of a colony. Now it means a building in which many people are landlords together.

con·done (kən dōn′), *v.* to forgive or overlook: *Good friends will condone each other's faults.* ❑ *v.* **con·doned, con·don·ing.** —**con′do·na′tion,** *n.* —**con·don′er,** *n.*

con·dor (kon′dər), *n.* either of two large vultures with ruffed necks and bare heads. Condors live on high mountains in South America and California, where they are very rare.

a	hat	ė	term	ô	order	ch	child		
ā	age	i	it	oi	oil	ng	long	ə	a in about
ä	far	ī	ice	ou	out	sh	she		e in taken
â	care	o	hot	u	cup	th	thin		i in pencil
e	let	ō	open	ů	put	ŦH	then		o in lemon
ē	equal	ò	saw	ü	rule	zh	measure		u in circus

con·du·cive (kən dü′siv), *adj.* favorable; helpful: *Exercise is conducive to good health.* **–con·du′cive·ness,** *n.*

con·duct (kon′dukt *for noun;* kən dukt′ *for verb*), **1** *n.* way of acting; behavior thought of as good or bad: *Her conduct was rude and inexcusable.* **2** *v.* to act in a certain way; behave: *When company came, the children were expected to conduct themselves properly.* **3** *v.* to direct; manage: *The president conducts the country's foreign affairs.* ■ See Synonym Study at **manage. 4** *n.* direction; management. **5** *v.* to direct an orchestra, choir, etc., as leader: *He conducts the Civic Orchestra.* **6** *v.* to go along with as a leader; guide: *She conducts tours through the museum.* **7** *v.* to transmit; be a channel for: *Metals conduct heat and electricity.*

con·duc·tion (kən duk′shən), *n.* transmission of heat, sound, electricity, etc., by the transfer of energy between particles of a substance or substances.

con·duc·tiv·i·ty (kon′duk tiv′ə tē), *n.* power of conducting heat, electricity, sound, etc.

con·duc·tor (kən duk′tər), *n.* **1** a railroad worker in charge of a train and its crew. On a passenger train, the conductor may also collect tickets. **2** director of an orchestra, chorus, etc. **3** person who conducts; leader or guide: *the conductor of a tour.* **4** thing that transmits heat, electricity, light, sound, etc. Copper is a good conductor of heat and electricity.

con·du·it (kon′dü it *or* kon′dwit), *n.* **1** channel or pipe for carrying liquids long distances; aqueduct or canal. **2** pipe or underground passage for electric wires or cables.

cone (kōn), *n.* **1** a solid object with a flat, round base that narrows to a point at the top. **2** anything shaped like a cone: *an ice-cream cone, the cone of a volcano.* **3** a cone-shaped, scaly growth that bears the seeds on pine, cedar, fir, and many other evergreen trees. **4** a kind of cell in the retina of the eye that responds to bright light and color.

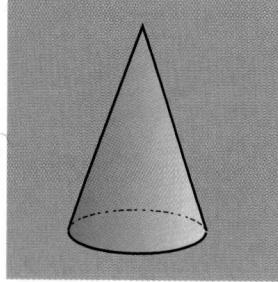

cone (def. 1)

Con·es·to·ga wagon (kon′ə stō′gə), a covered wagon with broad wheels, used by American pioneers. [See Word Story at **stogie.**]

con·fec·tion (kən fek′shən), *n.* piece of candy, a pastry, jam, etc.

con·fec·tion·er (kən fek′shə nər), *n.* person who makes or sells candies, ice cream, and cakes.

con·fec·tion·er·y (kən fek′shə ner′ē), *n.* **1** candies or sweets; confections. **2** place where confections, ice cream, and cakes are made or sold. ❑ *n., pl.* **con·fec·tion·er·ies** for 2.

con·fed·er·a·cy (kən fed′ər ə sē), *n.* **1** union of countries or states; group of people joined together for a special purpose; league. **2 the Confederacy,** group of 11 southern states that seceded from the United States in 1860 and 1861: Virginia, North Carolina, South Carolina, Georgia, Florida, Alabama, Mississippi, Tennessee, Arkansas, Louisiana, and Texas. ❑ *n., pl.* **con·fed·er·a·cies** for 1.

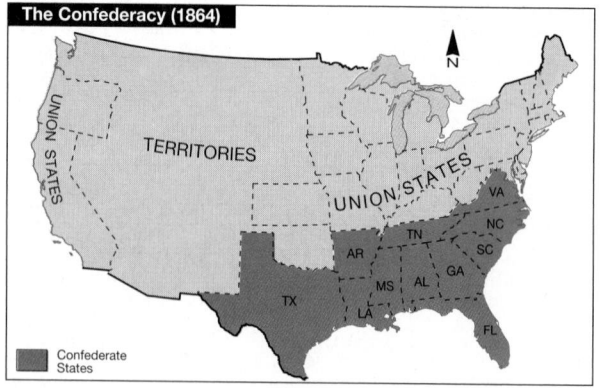

The Confederacy (1864)

N

TERRITORIES

UNION STATES

UNION STATES

VA

AR · TN · NC
· SC
MS · AL · GA
TX
LA
FL

■ Confederate States

con·fed·er·ate (kən fed′ər it *for noun, adj.;* kən fed′ə rāt′ *for verb*), **1** *n.* country, person, etc., joined with another for a special purpose; ally: *The hijacker told his confederate to guard the passengers.* **2** *adj.* joined together for a special purpose; allied. **3** *v.* to join together for a special purpose; ally: *When the Civil War began in 1861, only six states had confederated.* **4 Confederate,** **a** *adj.* of or belonging to the Confederacy. **b** *n.* person who lived in, supported, or fought for the Confederacy. ❑ *v.* **con·fed·er·at·ed, con·fed·er·at·ing.**

Confederate States of America, the Confederacy.

con·fed·er·a·tion (kən fed′ə rā′shən), *n.* **1** league; confederacy; alliance: *The United States was originally a confederation of 13 colonies.* **2 the Confederation,** union of the 13 American states from 1781 to 1789 under the Articles of Confederation. **3 Confederation,** the union of Ontario, Quebec, Nova Scotia, and New Brunswick in 1867. Six other Canadian provinces joined later. **4** act of joining together in a league or alliance: *The conference devised a plan for a confederation of the colonies.*

con·fer (kən fèr′), *v.* **1** to talk things over; consult together; exchange ideas: *The Secretary of State often confers with advisers.* **2** to give; bestow: *to confer a medal on a hero.* ❑ *v.* **con·ferred, con·fer·ring. –con·fer′rer,** *n.*

con·fer·ence (kon′fər əns), *n.* **1** a meeting of interested persons to discuss a particular subject: *A conference was called to discuss the fuel shortage.* **2** act of consulting together: *The teacher was in conference with parents after school.* **3** association of athletic teams, churches, etc., joined together for some special purpose.

con·fess (kən fes′), *v.* **1** to own up; acknowledge; admit: *I confess you are right on one point.* ■ See Synonym Study at **admit. 2** to admit your guilt: *The thief decided to confess.* **3** to tell your sins to a priest in order to obtain forgiveness. **4** to hear someone tell his or her sins in order to obtain forgiveness, as a priest does.

con·fes·sion (kən fesh′ən), *n.* **1** act of confessing; owning up; telling your mistakes or sins: *The burglary suspect made a full confession.* **2** act of telling your sins to a priest in order to obtain forgiveness.

con·fes·sion·al (kən fesh′ə nəl), *n.* a small booth in which a priest hears confessions.

con·fes·sor (kən fes′ər), *n.* **1** person who confesses. **2** priest who has the authority to hear confessions.

con·fet·ti (kən fet′ē), *n.* bits of colored paper thrown about at carnivals, weddings, or parades.

WORD STORY   **Confetti** comes from an Italian word meaning "candies." Italians used to celebrate carnivals by throwing candies wrapped in colored paper. In other countries, people threw just the paper.

con·fi·dant (kon′fə dant *or* kon′fə dänt), *n.* person trusted with your secrets or private affairs; close friend.

con·fide (kən fid′), *v.* **1** to tell as a secret: *He confided his troubles to his brother.* **2** to show trust by telling secrets: *She always confided in her friend.* ❑ *v.* **con·fid·ed, con·fid·ing. –con·fid′er,** *n.*

con·fi·dence (kon′fə dəns), *n.* **1** firm belief or trust: *I have complete confidence in his honesty.* **2** firm belief in yourself; self-confidence: *Years of experience at her work have given her great confidence.* **3** trust that someone will not tell others what is said: *The secret was told to me in strict confidence.* **4** thing told as a secret: *She would never reveal a confidence.*

con·fi·dent (kon′fə dənt), *adj.* having confidence; firmly believing; certain; sure: *I feel confident that our team will win.* ■ See Synonym Study at **sure. –con′fi·dent·ly,** *adv.*

con·fi·den·tial (kon′fə den′shəl), *adj.* **1** told or written as a secret: *a confidential report.* ■ See Synonym Study at **secret. 2** showing confidence or intimacy: *She spoke in low, confidential tones.* **3** trusted with secrets or private affairs: *a confidential secretary.*

WORD STORY   **Confidential** comes from Latin words meaning "with" and "faith." If you tell someone something confidential, you tell it with faith that it will be kept secret. **–con′fi·den′ti·al′i·ty,** *n.* **–con′fi·den′tial·ly,** *adv.*

con·fid·ing (kən fi′ding), *adj.* trustful; trusting: *a confiding nature.* **–con·fid′ing·ly,** *adv.*

con·fig·u·ra·tion (kən fig′yə rā′shən), *n.* manner of arrangement; form; shape; outline: *Geographers study the configuration of the surface of the earth.*

con·fine (kən fīn′ *for verb;* kon′fīn *for noun*), **1** *v.* to keep within limits; restrict: *She confined her reading to biography.* **2** *v.* to keep in; shut in: *A cold confined him to the house.* **3** *n.pl.* **con·fines,** boundary; border; limit: *I have never been beyond the confines of my own state.* ❑ *v.* **con·fined, con·fin·ing.** —**con·fin′er,** *n.*

con·fine·ment (kən fīn′mənt), *n.* **1** act of confining or condition of being confined. **2** period of childbirth and bed rest following a birth.

con·firm (kən fėrm′), *v.* **1** to prove to be true or correct; make certain: *The mayor confirmed the report that taxes would be increased.* **2** to make more certain; place beyond all doubt; verify: *The airline office telephoned to confirm an airplane reservation that I had requested last week.* **3** to make firmer; strengthen: *A sudden storm confirmed my decision not to leave.* **4** to approve by formal consent; ratify: *The Senate confirmed the President's appointments to the Cabinet.* **5** to admit to full membership in a church or synagogue after required study and preparation. —**con·firm′a·ble,** *adj.*

con·fir·ma·tion (kon′fər mā′shən), *n.* **1** act of making certain by more information or evidence: *She telephoned the store for confirmation that it was open evenings.* **2** thing that confirms; proof: *Don't believe rumors that lack confirmation.* **3** ceremony of admitting someone to full membership in a church or synagogue after required study and preparation.

con·firmed (kən fėrmd′), *adj.* **1** firmly established; proved: *a confirmed rumor.* **2** settled; habitual: *a confirmed bachelor.*

con·fis·cate (kon′fə skāt), *v.* **1** to seize for the public treasury: *The traitor's property was confiscated.* **2** to seize by authority; take and keep: *The teacher confiscated my comic book.* ❑ *v.* **con·fis·cat·ed, con·fis·cat·ing.** —**con′fis·ca′tion,** *n.* —**con′fis·ca′tor,** *n.*

con·fla·gra·tion (kon′flə grā′shən), *n.* a big and destructive fire.

con·flict (kon′flikt *for noun;* kən flikt′ *for verb*), **1** *n.* a fight or struggle, especially a long one: *The United Nations General Assembly discussed the conflict in the Middle East.* **2** *n.* a strong disagreement; clash: *A conflict of opinion arose over the need for a new highway.* **3** *v.* to disagree strongly; differ in thought or action; clash: *The testimony of the witnesses conflicted on whether the robber had blond or dark hair.*

con·flu·ence (kon′flü əns), *n.* **1** act or place of flowing together: *the confluence of two streams to form a river.* **2** act of coming together of people or things; throng.

con·form (kən fôrm′), *v.* **1** to act according to law or rule; be in agreement with generally accepted standards: *Members must conform to the rules of our club.* **2** to agree; be the same as: *Her symptoms conform to the usual pattern of flu.* —**con·form′a·ble,** *adj.* —**con·form′er,** *n.*

con·for·ma·tion (kon′fôr mā′shən), *n.* manner in which a thing is formed; structure; form: *the conformation of a flower.*

con·form·ist (kən fôr′mist), *n.* person who conforms.

con·form·i·ty (kən fôr′mə tē), *n.* **1** action in agreement with generally accepted standards. **2** likeness; similarity; agreement.

con·found (kon found′), *v.* to confuse; perplex: *I was confounded by their rude behavior.* —**con·found′er,** *n.*

con·found·ed (kon foun′did *or* kon′foun′did), *adj.* **1** confused; bewildered. **2** very dislikable; cursed; horrible.

con·front (kən frunt′), *v.* **1** to meet face to face; stand facing. **2** to face boldly; oppose: *Once she confronted her problems, she was able to solve them easily.* ■ See Synonym Study at **meet¹.** **3** to bring face to face; place before: *The teacher confronted the student with his failing grade.*

con·fron·ta·tion (kon′frən tā′shən), *n.* act of confronting or condition of being confronted.

Con·fu·cian·ism (kən fyü′shə niz′əm), *n.* the teachings of Confucius and his followers.

Con·fu·cius (kən fyü′shəs), *n.* 551?-479 B.C., Chinese philosopher and moral teacher. [**Confucius** comes from a Chinese phrase meaning "great master Kong." Kong was the philosopher's family name.]

con·fuse (kən fyüz′), *v.* **1** to throw into disorder; mix up; bewilder: *So many people talking to me at once confused me.* **2** to be unable to tell apart; mistake one thing or person for another: *People often confuse this girl with her twin sister.* ❑ *v.* **con·fused, con·fus·ing.** —**con·fus′ing·ly,** *adv.*

con·fu·sion (kən fyü′zhən), *n.* **1** a confused or disordered condition of things: *In the confusion after the collision, I forgot to get the name of the witness.* **2** act of mistaking one thing or person for another: *Words like "believe" and "receive" sometimes cause confusion in spelling.* **3** condition of being perplexed or bewildered: *His confusion over the exact address caused him to go to the wrong house.*

con·fute (kən fyüt′), *v.* **1** to prove an argument, testimony, etc., to be false or incorrect: *The lawyer confuted the testimony by showing actual photographs of the accident.* **2** to prove someone to be wrong: *The speaker confuted her opponent by facts and logic.* ❑ *v.* **con·fut·ed, con·fut·ing.** —**con·fut′er,** *n.*

con·ga (kong′gə), *n.* a fast ballroom dance with a kick on every fourth beat, often performed in a line. ❑ *n., pl.* **con·gas.**

con·geal (kən jēl′), *v.* **1** to harden or make solid by cold; freeze. **2** to thicken; coagulate: *The pudding congealed as it cooled.* —**con·geal′ment,** *n.*

con·gen·ial (kən jē′nyəl), *adj.* **1** having similar tastes and interests; getting on well together: *Congenial companions made the trip pleasant.* **2** agreeable; suitable: *The young scientist found laboratory work more congenial than teaching science.* —**con·gen′ial·ly,** *adv.*

con·gen·i·tal (kən jen′ə təl), *adj.* present at birth: *a congenital defect.* —**con·gen′i·tal·ly,** *adv.*

con·ger (kong′gər), *n.* any of various large ocean eels caught for food along the coasts of Europe.

conger eel, conger.

con·gest·ed (kən jes′tid), *adj.* **1** overcrowded; filled with too many people, vehicles, and so on: *congested streets.* **2** too full of blood or mucus: *congested nasal passages.*

con·ges·tion (kən jes′chən), *n.* **1** an overcrowded or congested condition: *Many drivers were caught in Sunday's traffic congestion and got home late.* **2** too much blood or mucus in one part of the body: *nasal congestion.*

congestion (def. 1)

con·ges·tive (kən jes′tiv), *adj.* of or about congestion; caused by congestion.

con·glom·er·ate (kən glom′ər it *for adj., noun;* kən glom′ə rāt′ *for verb*), **1** *adj.* made up of various parts or materials gathered into a mass: *a conglomerate rock.* **2** *n.* mass formed of fragments. **3** *n.* rock formed of pebbles, gravel, etc., held together by a cementing material. **4** *n.* a group of unrelated corporations operating under a single ownership. **5** *v.* to gather parts in a mass; collect together. ❑ *v.* **con·glom·er·at·ed, con·glom·er·at·ing.**

con·glom·er·a·tion (kən glom′ə rā′shən), *n.* a mixed-up mass of various things or persons; mixture.

a	hat	ė	term	ô	order	ch	child		
ā	age	i	it	oi	oil	ng	long		a in about
ä	far	ī	ice	ou	out	sh	she		e in taken
â	care	o	hot	u	cup	th	thin	ə	i in pencil
e	let	ō	open	ú	put	ŦH	then		o in lemon
ē	equal	ò	saw	ü	rule	zh	measure		u in circus

Con·go (kong′gō), *n.* **1 People's Republic of,** country in central Africa, on the Atlantic. *Capital:* Brazzaville. **2** Also, **Zaïre,** river in central Africa, flowing from SE Zaïre to the Atlantic. **3** former name of **Zaïre.**

con·grat·u·late (kən grach′ə lāt), *v.* to express your pleasure at the happiness or good fortune of: *The judge congratulated the winner of the race.* ❑ *v.* **con·grat·u·lat·ed, con·grat·u·lat·ing.**

con·grat·u·la·tion (kən grach′ə lā′shən), *n.* **1** Often, **congratulations,** *pl.* **a** pleasure at another person's happiness or good fortune: *The spectators shouted their congratulations to the winning team.* **b** word used to express such pleasure: *Congratulations on your high grades on the exam.* **2** act of congratulating; wishing a person joy.

con·gre·gate (kong′grə gāt), *v.* to come together into a crowd or mass; assemble: *They congregated around the campfire.* ❑ *v.* **con·gre·gat·ed, con·gre·gat·ing.** —**con′gre·ga·tor,** *n.*

con·gre·ga·tion (kong′grə gā′shən), *n.* **1** group of people gathered together for religious worship or instruction: *The congregation joined together in prayer.* **2** a gathering of people or things; assembly. **3** act of coming together into a crowd or mass; an assembling.

con·gre·ga·tion·al (kong′grə gā′shə nəl), *adj.* **1** of a congregation: *congregational singing.* **2 Congregational,** of a form of church government in which each individual church governs itself.

Con·gre·ga·tion·al·ist (kong′grə gā′shə nə list), *n.* member of a Congregational church.

con·gress (kong′gris), *n.* **1** the lawmaking group of a nation, especially of a republic. **2 Congress,** the national lawmaking group of the United States, consisting of the Senate and the House of Representatives, with members elected from every state. **3** a meeting of representatives for the discussion of some subject; conference: *Doctors came from all over the world to the medical congress on heart transplants.* ❑ *n., pl.* **con·gress·es** for 1,3.

con·gres·sion·al (kən gresh′ə nəl), *adj.* **1** of or about a congress. **2** Often, **Congressional,** of or about the U.S. Congress. —**con·gres′sion·al·ly,** *adv.*

con·gress·man (kong′gris mən), *n.* member of Congress, especially of the House of Representatives. ■ See Usage Note at **capital letter.** ❑ *n., pl.* **con·gress·men.**

con·gress·wom·an (kong′gris wùm′ən), *n.* a woman member of Congress, especially of the House of Representatives. ■ See Usage Note at **capital letter.** ❑ *n., pl.* **con·gress·wom·en.**

con·gru·ence (kən grü′əns *or* kong′grü əns), *n.* condition of being congruent.

con·gru·ent (kən grü′ənt *or* kong′grü ənt), *adj.* exactly coinciding: *Congruent triangles have the same size and shape.* —**con·gru·ent′ly,** *adv.*

con·ic (kon′ik), *adj.* conical.

con·i·cal (kon′ə kəl), *adj.* **1** shaped like a cone: *Volcanic mountains are conical.* **2** of a cone. —**con′i·cal·ly,** *adv.*

conic section, a curve produced by passing a plane through a cone. Circles, ellipses, and parabolas are conic sections.

con·i·fer (kon′ə fər *or* kō′nə fər), *n.* tree or bush that bears cones. The pine, fir, spruce, hemlock, and larch are conifers.

co·nif·er·ous (kō nif′ər əs), *adj.* **1** bearing cones. **2** belonging to the conifers.

conj., conjunction (def. 1).

con·jec·tur·al (kən jek′chər əl), *adj.* involving a guess; depending on conjecture: *His statement was merely conjectural, not proved.* —**con·jec′tur·al·ly,** *adv.*

con·jec·ture (kən jek′chər), **1** *n.* conclusion reached by guessing: *Her estimate of the height of that mountain is only conjecture, not fact.* **2** *v.* to make a conjecture; guess: *Weather forecasters often have to conjecture about the next day's weather conditions.* ❑ *v.* **con·jec·tured, con·jec·tur·ing.**

con·join (kən join′), *v.* to join together; unite; combine.

con·joint (kən joint′), *adj.* united; combined. —**con·joint′ly,** *adv.*

con·ju·gal (kon′jə gəl), *adj.* **1** of or about marriage: *conjugal life.* **2** of husband and wife: *conjugal love.* —**con′ju·gal·ly,** *adv.*

con·ju·gate (kon′jə gāt *for verb;* kon′jə git *or* kon′jə gāt *for adj.*), **1** *v.* to give the forms of a verb in order. The past tense of the verb "to be" is conjugated "I was, you were, he, she, or it was; we were, you were, they were." **2** *v.* to join: *Some one-celled living things conjugate and exchange genetic material.* **3** *adj.* joined together in a pair or pairs; coupled. ❑ *v.* **con·ju·gat·ed, con·ju·gat·ing.**

con·ju·ga·tion (kon′jə gā′shən), *n.* **1** a systematic arrangement of the forms of a verb. **2** act of joining together; fusion; coupling. Some one-celled animals reproduce by the conjugation of one cell with another.

con·junc·tion (kən jungk′shən), *n.* **1** word that connects words, phrases, clauses, or sentences. *And, but, or, though,* and *if* are conjunctions. **2** act of joining together; union; combination: *Our school, in conjunction with two other schools, will hold a large bazaar next week.*

con·junc·ti·va (kon′jungk ti′və), *n.* the lining that forms the inner surface of the eyelids and the front part of the eyeball. ❑ *n., pl.* **con·junc·ti·vas, con·junc·ti·vae** (kon′jungk ti′vē).

con·junc·ti·vi·tis (kən jungk′tə vi′tis), *n.* inflammation of the conjunctiva.

con·jure (kon′jər *or* kun′jər), *v.* **1** to compel a spirit, devil, etc., to appear or disappear by saying certain words. **2** to cause to appear as if by magic: *To our delight, Grandmother conjured up a bag of old-fashioned toys from the attic.* **3** to perform tricks by very quick, deceiving movements of the hands. ❑ *v.* **con·jured, con·jur·ing.**

con·jur·er *or* **con·jur·or** (kon′jər ər *or* kun′jər ər), *n.* **1** person who performs tricks with quick, deceiving movements of the hands; juggler. **2** magician.

conk (kongk), INFORMAL. **1** *v.* to hit, especially on the head. **2** *n.* a blow on the head. ■ Another word that can sound like this is **conch.**

conk out, INFORMAL. to break down; stall: *The old car conked out three blocks from home.*

Conn., Connecticut.

con·nect (kə nekt′), *v.* **1** to join one thing to another; link two things together; join: *connect a hose to a faucet. The telephone operator connected us. These two rooms connect.* **2** to think of one thing with another: *We usually connect spring with sunshine and flowers.* **3** to join with others in some business or interest; bring into some relation: *This store is connected with a chain of stores.* **4** to plug into an electrical or telephone circuit: *the speaker doesn't work because it's not connected.* **5** (in sports) to hit a ball or throw a ball to someone: *She connected with the receiver for a 20-yard pass.* —**con·nec′tor** *or* **con·nect′er,** *n.*

Con·nect·i·cut (kə net′ə kət), *n.* one of the NE states of the United States. *Abbreviation:* CT or Conn. *Capital:* Hartford.

WORD STORY **Connecticut** comes from an Algonquian word meaning "on the long tidal river." The Connecticut River runs through the center of the state into Long Island Sound. Where it meets the sea, its water rises and falls with the tides.

con·nec·tion (kə nek′shən), *n.* **1** thing that connects; connecting part: *The connection between the radiator and the furnace is a pipe that comes through the floor.* **2** any kind of relation; association: *I had no connection with that prank.* **3** condition of being joined together or connected; link: *His connection with our firm has lasted over 30 years.* **4** act of connecting: *The connection of our telephone took several hours.* **5** an influential, wealthy, or prominent associate or friend: *I got a summer job through my family's connections.* **6** the meeting of trains, ships, etc., at definite times so that passengers can change from one to the other without delay: *Our flight arrived late at the airport, and we missed our connection.* **7** a related person; relative: *My sister-in-law is a connection of mine by marriage.*

in connection with, in relation with; in regard to: *He read a biography of Booker T. Washington in connection with his study of American history.*

con·nec·tive (kə nek′tiv), **1** *adj.* connecting. **2** *n.* anything that connects. Conjunctions and relative pronouns are connectives that join together words, phrases, or clauses. —**con·nec′tive·ly,** *adv.*

connective tissue, tissue that connects, supports, or encloses other tissues and organs in the body.

conning tower

con·ning tower (kon′ing), tower on the deck of a submarine, used as an entrance and as a place for observation.

con·niv·ance (kə ni′vəns), *n.* pretended ignorance or secret encouragement of wrongdoing.

con·nive (kə nïv′), *v.* 1 to cooperate secretly: *connive with the enemy.* 2 to avoid noticing what you might have to condemn; pretend not to see something wrong; give aid to wrongdoing by not telling of it: *The dishonest sheriff connived at gambling.* ❑ *v.* **con·nived, con·niv·ing. —con·niv′er,** *n.* **—con·niv′ing·ly,** *adv.*

con·nois·seur (kon′ə sėr′), *n.* person able to give critical judgments in art or in matters of taste; expert: *a connoisseur of antique furniture.*

con·no·ta·tion (kon′ə tā′shən), *n.* what is suggested in addition to the simple or literal meaning. When Elaine is described in legends about King Arthur as "the lily maid," the connotation is that she was pale, delicate, and pure.

con·note (kə nōt′), *v.* to suggest in addition to the simple or literal meaning; mean besides; imply. The color red can connote feelings of passion, anger, or hatred. ❑ *v.* **con·not·ed, con·not·ing.**

con·nu·bi·al (kə nü′bē əl), *adj.* of marriage; conjugal. **—con·nu′bi·al·ly,** *adv.*

con·quer (kong′kər), *v.* 1 to get by fighting; win in war: *The Romans conquered much of the ancient world.* 2 to overcome; get the better of: *conquer a bad habit.* 3 to be victorious; be the conqueror: *The general said he would conquer or die.* **—con′quer·a·ble,** *adj.* **—con′quer·ing·ly,** *adv.* **—con′quer·or,** *n.*

SYNONYM STUDY **Conquer, overpower,** and **overwhelm** all mean to defeat someone or something completely. **Conquer** suggests great effort: *He has conquered his shyness.* **Overpower** suggests great force: *Mexican soldiers finally overpowered the defenders of the Alamo.* **Overwhelm** suggests total defeat: *The mayor overwhelmed her opponent with 80 percent of the votes.*

con·quest (kon′kwest *or* kong′kwest), *n.* 1 act of conquering: *the conquest of a country, the conquest of disease.* ■ See Synonym Study at **victory.** 2 thing conquered; land, people, etc., conquered: *The city was an easy conquest for the invaders.*

con·quis·ta·dor (kon kē′stə dôr *or* kon kwis′tə dôr), *n.* 1 a Spanish conqueror in North or South America during the 1500s. 2 conqueror. ❑ *n., pl.* **con·quis·ta·dors, con·quis·ta·do·res** (kon-kē′stə dôr′ez).

Con·rad (kon′rad), *n.* **Joseph,** 1857-1924, English author, born in Poland. ■ **Joseph Conrad** did not begin to learn English until he was 20 years old. His intense novels are often set on the sea, using his experiences as a sailor and captain.

con·science (kon′shəns), *n.* sense of right and wrong; ideas and feelings within you that tell you when you are doing right and warn you of what is wrong.

con·sci·en·tious (kon′shē en′shəs), *adj.* 1 careful to do what you know is right; controlled by conscience. 2 done with care to make it right: *Conscientious work is careful and exact.* **—con′-sci·en′tious·ly,** *adv.* **—con′sci·en′tious·ness,** *n.*

conscientious objector, person with moral or religious objections to serving in the armed forces or to taking up arms in warfare.

con·scious (kon′shəs), *adj.* 1 having experience; aware; knowing: *I was conscious of a sharp pain.* 2 aware of what you are doing; awake: *About five minutes after fainting he became conscious again.* 3 known to yourself; felt: *The young woman had a conscious desire to see her family again.* 4 done on purpose; intentional: *She told a conscious lie when she denied that she had broken the vase.* **—con′scious·ly,** *adv.*

con·scious·ness (kon′shəs nis), *n.* 1 condition of being conscious; awareness: *The injured woman did not regain consciousness for two hours.* 2 all the thoughts and feelings of someone.

con·script (kən skript′ *for verb;* kon′skript *for noun, adj.*), 1 *v.* to force by law to serve in the armed forces; draft. 2 *n.* a conscripted soldier or sailor. 3 *adj.* forced to serve; drafted: *conscript troops.*

con·scrip·tion (kən skrip′shən), *n.* forced service in the armed forces; the draft.

con·se·crate (kon′sə krāt), *v.* 1 to set apart as sacred; make holy: *The new chapel in the church was consecrated by the bishop.* 2 to devote to a purpose; dedicate: *The doctor consecrated her life to helping the sick.* ❑ *v.* **con·se·crat·ed, con·se·crat·ing. —con′se·cra′tor,** *n.*

con·se·cra·tion (kon′sə krā′shən), *n.* 1 ordination to a sacred office, especially that of bishop. 2 act of consecrating or condition of being consecrated.

con·sec·u·tive (kən sek′yə tiv), *adj.* following one right after another; successive: *Monday, Tuesday, and Wednesday are consecutive days of the week.* **—con·sec′u·tive·ly,** *adv.* **—con·sec′u·tive·ness,** *n.*

con·sen·sus (kən sen′səs), *n.* general agreement; opinion of all or most of the people consulted: *After much debate, the club members reached a consensus about adopting the proposal.* ❑ *n., pl.* **con·sen·sus·es.**

con·sent (kən sent′), 1 *v.* to give approval or permission; agree: *My father would not consent to my staying up past 10 p.m.* 2 *n.* agreement; approval; permission: *We have mother's consent to go swimming.*

con·se·quence (kon′sə kwens), *n.* 1 a result or effect: *The consequence of the fall was a broken leg.* 2 importance: *The loss of her ring is a matter of great consequence to her.*

take the consequences, to accept what happens because of your action: *She felt that she had to admit her mistake and take the consequences.*

consequence (def. 1)—As a consequence of the fire, the forest was destroyed.

con·se·quent (kon′sə kwent), *adj.* following as an effect; resulting: *His long illness and consequent absence put him far behind in his work.*

con·se·quen·tial (kon′sə kwen′shəl), *adj.* 1 following as an effect; resulting; consequent. 2 important: *a consequential decision.* **—con′se·quen′tial·ly,** *adv.* **—con′se·quen′tial·ness,** *n.*

con·se·quent·ly (kon′sə kwent′lē), *adv.* as a result; therefore: *He overslept and, consequently, he was late.*

a	hat	ė	term	ô	order	ch	child		a in about
ā	age	i	it	oi	oil	ng	long		e in taken
ä	far	ī	ice	ou	out	sh	she	ə	i in pencil
â	care	o	hot	u	cup	th	thin		o in lemon
e	let	ō	open	u̇	put	ŦH	then		u in circus
ē	equal	ȯ	saw	ü	rule	zh	measure		

con·ser·va·tion (kon⁄sər vā⁄shən), *n.* **1** preservation from harm or decay; protection from loss or from being used up: *Conservation of energy saves fuel.* **2** the official protection and care of forests, rivers, and other natural resources.

con·ser·va·tion·ist (kon⁄sər vā⁄shə nist), *n.* person who wants to preserve and protect the forests, rivers, and other natural resources of a country.

con·serv·a·tism (kən sėr⁄və tiz⁄əm), *n.* inclination to keep things as they are or were in the past; opposition to abrupt change, especially any major change in established traditions.

con·serv·a·tive (kən sėr⁄və tiv), **1** *adj.* inclined to keep things as they are or were in the past; opposed to abrupt change, especially any major change in established traditions. **2** *n.* person opposed to change. **3** *adj.* not inclined to take risks; cautious; moderate: *This old, reliable company has conservative business methods.* **4** Often, **Conservative,** *a adj.* of a political party that favors the preservation of established traditions and opposes major changes in national institutions. **b** *n.* member of a conservative political party. **5** *adj.* free from novelties and fads; traditional: *conservative styles in clothing.* **6** *adj.* **Conservative,** of or having to do with a modern branch of Judaism that modifies many traditional practices and rituals but also keeps many others as in the past. **—con·serv⁄a·tive·ly,** *adv.* **—con·serv⁄a·tive·ness,** *n.*

con·serv·a·to·ry (kən sėr⁄və tôr⁄ē), *n.* **1** school for instruction in music. **2** greenhouse for growing and displaying plants and flowers. ❑ *n., pl.* **con·serv·a·to·ries.**

con·serve (kən sėrv⁄ *for verb;* kon⁄sėrv⁄ *for noun*), **1** *v.* to keep from harm or decay; keep from loss or from being used up; preserve: *The runner conserved her strength for the end of the race.* **2** *n.* Often, **conserves,** *pl.* fruit preserved in sugar, often as jam. ❑ *v.* **con·served, con·serv·ing. —con·serv⁄er,** *n.*

con·sid·er (kən sid⁄ər), *v.* **1** to think about in order to decide; think about carefully: *Before you answer, take time to consider the problem.* **2** to think to be; regard as: *I consider him a very able student.* **3** to allow for; take into account: *This watch runs very well, when you consider how old it is.* **4** to be thoughtful of: *A kind person considers others' feelings.* [**Consider** comes from Latin words meaning "with" and "stars." People who believed that the stars could tell the future would use them to make decisions.]

SYNONYM STUDY **Consider, study,** and **weigh** all mean to think about something in order to decide. **Consider** is a general word: *I am considering going to camp.* **Study** means to consider something fully and in detail: *The city is studying plans for a new hospital.* **Weigh** means to consider as thoroughly as possible. This is a formal meaning: *The jury weighed the evidence before reaching a verdict.*

con·sid·er·a·ble (kən sid⁄ər ə bəl), *adj.* **1** worth thinking about; important: *Pollution is a considerable problem.* **2** large; important: *$500 is a considerable sum of money.*

con·sid·er·a·bly (kən sid⁄ər ə blē), *adv.* a good deal; much: *The boy was considerably older than he looked.*

con·sid·er·ate (kən sid⁄ər it), *adj.* thoughtful of others and their feelings: *She is considerate enough to tell her parents where she is going and when she will be back.* ■ See Synonym Study at **thoughtful. —con·sid⁄er·ate·ly,** *adv.* **—con·sid⁄er·ate·ness,** *n.*

con·sid·er·a·tion (kən sid⁄ə rā⁄shən), *n.* **1** careful thought about things in order to decide: *Before writing your answers please give careful consideration to the questions on the test.* **2** something thought of as a reason: *Price and quality are two considerations in buying anything.* **3** thoughtfulness for others and their feelings: *Playing the radio loud at night shows a lack of consideration for the neighbors.* **4** money or other payment: *I will do the work for you for a small consideration.*

in consideration of, 1 because of: *In consideration of my bad cold, the teacher let me leave school early.* **2** in return for: *The neighbor gave the girl a present in consideration of her help.*

take into consideration, to allow for; take into account; consider: *The teacher took my week's absence into consideration in grading my test.*

under consideration, being thought about: *Her request for a higher salary is under consideration.*

con·sid·ered (kən sid⁄ərd), *adj.* carefully thought out: *That is my considered opinion.*

con·sid·er·ing (kən sid⁄ər ing), *prep.* taking into account; making allowance for: *Considering her age, the little girl reads well.*

con·sign (kən sīn⁄), *v.* **1** to hand over; deliver: *His will consigned his property to his sister.* **2** to send: *We will consign the goods to him by overnight express delivery.* **—con·sign⁄a·ble,** *adj.*

con·sign·ment (kən sīn⁄mənt), *n.* **1** act of consigning: *The Red Cross ordered the consignment of food and clothing to the flooded area.* **2** something consigned: *The store received a consignment of fall clothing.*

con·sist (kən sist⁄), *v.* to be made up; be formed: *A week consists of seven days.*

consist in, be contained in; be made up of: *He believes that happiness consists in being easily pleased or satisfied.*

con·sist·en·cy (kən sis⁄tən sē), *n.* **1** degree of firmness or stiffness: *Frosting for a cake must be of the right consistency to spread easily without dripping.* **2** similarity or logical connection between ideas, rules, actions, etc.: *The consistency of her free-throw shooting makes her a valuable basketball player.* ❑ *n., pl.* **con·sist·en·cies** for 1.

con·sist·ent (kən sis⁄tənt), *adj.* **1** thinking or acting today in agreement with what you thought yesterday; keeping to the same principles and habits. **2** in agreement; in accord: *Driving at high speed on a rainy night is not consistent with safety.* **—con·sist⁄ent·ly,** *adv.*

con·sis·tor·y (kən sis⁄tər ē), *n.* court of clergymen to decide church matters; church council. ❑ *n., pl.* **con·sis·tor·ies.**

con·so·la·tion (kon⁄sə lā⁄shən), *n.* **1** a comforting person, thing, or event. **2** act of consoling; comfort.

con·sole¹ (kən sōl⁄), *v.* to ease the grief or sorrow of; comfort. ❑ *v.* **con·soled, con·sol·ing.** ■ See Synonym Study at **comfort. —con·sol⁄er,** *n.* **—con·sol⁄ing·ly,** *adv.*

con·sole² (kon⁄sōl), *n.* **1** part of an organ containing the keyboard, stops, and pedals. **2** (earlier) a radio, TV, or phonograph cabinet standing on the floor. **3** rows of buttons, switches, dials, etc., used to control electrical or electronic equipment in a computer, missile, etc.

con·sol·i·date (kən sol⁄ə dāt), *v.* **1** to combine into one; unite; merge: *The three banks consolidated, forming a single large bank.* **2** to make solid or firm; strengthen: *The political party consolidated its power by winning many state elections.* ❑ *v.* **con·sol·i·dat·ed, con·sol·i·dat·ing. —con·sol⁄i·da⁄tion,** *n.*

con·som·mé (kon⁄sə mā⁄), *n.* a clear soup made by boiling meat in water. ❑ *n., pl.* **con·som·més.**

con·so·nance (kon⁄sə nəns), *n.* **1** agreement; accordance. **2** harmony of sounds.

con·so·nant (kon⁄sə nənt), *n.* **1** a speech sound formed by completely or partially stopping the breath. The two consonants in *ship* are spelled by the letters *sh* and *p.* **2** any letter or combination of letters that stands for such a sound. All the letters that are not vowels (*b, c, d, f,* etc.) are consonants. [**Consonant** comes from Latin words meaning "sound" and "with." Consonants are sounds made with vowels, not by themselves.]

con·sort (kon⁄sôrt *for noun;* kən sôrt⁄ *for verb*), **1** *n.* husband or wife. The husband of a queen is sometimes called the prince consort. **2** *v.* to keep company; associate: *The soldier was jailed for consorting with the enemy.*

con·spic·u·ous (kən spik⁄yü əs), *adj.* **1** easily seen: *A traffic light should be placed where it is conspicuous.* **2** attracting notice; remarkable: *conspicuous bravery.* **—con·spic⁄u·ous·ly,** *adv.* **—con·spic⁄u·ous·ness,** *n.*

con·spir·a·cy (kən spir⁄ə sē), *n.* secret planning with others to do something unlawful or wrong; plot: *The leaders of the conspiracy against the government were caught.* ■ See Synonym Study at **plot.** ❑ *n., pl.* **con·spir·a·cies.**

WORD STORY **Conspiracy** comes from Latin words meaning "to breathe" and "together." It suggests close cooperation and perhaps careful whispering.

con·spir·a·tor (kən spir′ə tər), *n.* person who conspires; plotter: *A group of conspirators planned to overthrow the government.*

con·spire (kən spir′), *v.* **1** to plan secretly with others to do something unlawful or wrong; plot: *The spies conspired to steal secret government documents.* **2** to act together, as if by plan: *All things conspired to make her birthday a happy one.* ❑ *v.* **con·spired, con·spir·ing.**

Con·sta·ble (kon′stə bəl), *n.* **John,** 1776-1837, English painter. He painted realistic landscapes of English farmland and beaches, paying special attention to light and shadow.

con·sta·ble (kon′stə bəl), *n.* BRITISH. a police officer.

WORD STORY **Constable** comes from Latin words meaning "lord" and "a stable." These words were used as a title for the person in charge of a king's horses, who enforced the king's laws.

con·stan·cy (kon′stən sē), *n.* firmness in belief or feeling; steadfastness: *the constancy of friendship.*

con·stant (kon′stənt), **1** *adj.* going on without stopping; continual: *Three days of constant rain caused flooding.* **2** *adj.* continually happening; repeated again and again: *a constant ticking sound.* **3** *adj.* always the same; not changing: *The ship held a constant course due north.* **4** *n.* thing that is always the same; value or quantity that does not change: *The speed of light is an important constant in physics.* **5** *adj.* faithful; loyal; steadfast: *a constant friend.*

Con·stan·tine the Great (kon′stən tēn′ *or* kon′stən tīn), A.D. 275?-337, Roman emperor who granted freedom of worship to Christians and established the city of Constantinople.

Con·stan·ti·no·ple (kon′stan tə nō′pəl), *n.* former name of **Istanbul.** It was the capital of the Byzantine Empire and later the capital of Turkey. See **Byzantine Empire** for map.

con·stant·ly (kon′stənt lē), *adv.* **1** in every case; always: *He is constantly late.* **2** without stopping: *If a clock is kept wound it runs constantly.* **3** often; again and again: *She has to be reminded constantly to clean her room.*

con·stel·la·tion (kon′stə lā′shən), *n.* any of 88 groups of stars having recognized shapes. Orion is a constellation of the winter sky.

con·ster·na·tion (kon′stər nā′shən), *n.* great surprise or shock; dismay: *To his consternation he realized that he had locked his keys in the car.*

con·sti·pa·tion (kon′stə pā′shən), *n.* a condition in which it is difficult to discharge intestinal waste.

con·stit·u·en·cy (kən stich′ü ən sē), *n.* **1** the voters in a district; constituents: *The congresswoman was reelected to office by her constituency.* **2** a district represented by an elected official. ❑ *n., pl.* **con·stit·u·en·cies.**

con·stit·u·ent (kən stich′ü ənt), **1** *adj.* forming a necessary part: *Carbon is a constituent element in all living cells.* **2** *n.* part of a whole; necessary part: *Sugar is the main constituent of candy.* **3** *n.* one of the voters represented by an elected official: *A senator receives many letters from constituents.*

con·sti·tute (kon′stə tüt), *v.* **1** to make up; form: *Seven days constitute a week.* **2** to set up; establish: *Schools are constituted by law to teach children.* **3** to appoint; elect: *The group constituted one member as its leader.* ❑ *v.* **con·sti·tut·ed, con·sti·tut·ing.**

con·sti·tu·tion (kon′stə tü′shən), *n.* **1** system of fundamental principles according to which a nation, state, or group is governed: *The United States has a written constitution.* **2** the **Constitution,** the written set of fundamental principles by which the United States is governed. **3** way in which someone or something is organized; nature; makeup: *A person with a good constitution is strong and healthy.*

con·sti·tu·tion·al (kon′stə tü′shə nəl), **1** *adj.* of, in, or according to the constitution of a nation, state, or group: *The Supreme Court must decide whether this law is constitutional.* **2** *adj.* of or in the constitution of someone or something: *A constitutional weakness makes him catch a cold easily.* **3** *n.* OLD USE. a walk taken for your health: *After Sunday dinner my grandparents always take a constitutional.* —**con′sti·tu′tion·al·ly,** *adv.*

con·sti·tu·tion·al·i·ty (kon′stə tü′shə nal′ə tē), *n.* accordance with the constitution of a nation, state, or group: *The constitutionality of freedom of speech has been upheld in the courts many times.*

constitutional monarchy, monarchy in which the ruler has only those powers granted by the constitution and laws of the nation, usually with many other powers held by the people and their elected government. Denmark and the United Kingdom are constitutional monarchies.

con·strain (kən strān′), *v.* **1** to force to do something; compel: *The evidence constrained me to question them further.* **2** to confine; restrain: *The wild animal was constrained.*

con·straint (kən strānt′), *n.* **1** act of holding back your natural feelings; embarrassment: *They felt a little constraint with the new teacher for the first day or so.* **2** force; compulsion: *The witness testified under constraint.*

con·strict (kən strikt′), *v.* to make smaller by squeezing; contract; compress: *A tourniquet stops the flow of blood by constricting the blood vessels.* —**con·stric′tive,** *adj.*

con·stric·tion (kən strik′shən), *n.* **1** act of constricting; compression. **2** a feeling of tightness; constricted condition: *He coughed and complained of a constriction in his chest.* **3** a constricted part.

con·stric·tor (kən strik′tər), *n.* snake that kills its prey by squeezing it with its coils, such as the boa constrictor.

con·struct (kən strukt′), *v.* to put together; fit together; build: *construct a bridge.*

con·struc·tion (kən struk′shən), *n.* **1** act of constructing; building: *The city council provided funds for the construction of a new gym.* **2** way in which a thing is constructed: *Cracks and leaks are signs of poor construction.* **3** thing built or put together; structure: *The dollhouse was a construction of wood and cardboard.* **4** arrangement or relation of words in a sentence, phrase, clause, etc. **5** art, trade, or business of building: *My father works in construction.* **6** meaning; interpretation: *You put an unfair construction on what I said.*

construction paper, a kind of heavy paper, often brightly colored, used to make things, especially artwork in schools.

con·struc·tive (kən struk′tiv), *adj.* **1** helping to improve; useful: *During my report the teacher gave some constructive suggestions that helped me think of ideas I had overlooked.* **2** having to do with construction; structural. —**con·struc′tive·ly,** *adv.* —**con·struc′tive·ness,** *n.*

con·strue (kən strü′), *v.* to show the meaning of; explain; interpret: *We construed her nod as permission to go.* ❑ *v.* **con·strued, con·stru·ing.** —**con·stru′a·ble,** *adj.* —**con·stru′er,** *n.*

con·sul (kon′səl), *n.* **1** official appointed by a government to live in a foreign city in order to look after its business interests and to protect its citizens who are traveling or living there. **2** either of two chief magistrates of the ancient Roman republic.

con·su·lar (kon′sə lər), *adj.* **1** of a consul. **2** serving as a consul: *the consular representative of the United States at Frankfurt.*

con·su·late (kon′sə lit), *n.* the official residence or the offices of a consul: *the Canadian consulate in New York.*

con·sult (kən sult′), *v.* **1** to seek information or advice from; refer to: *You can consult travelers, books, or maps for help in planning a trip abroad.* **2** to exchange ideas; talk things over: *He consulted with his lawyer before signing the contract.* **3** to take into consideration; have regard for: *A good teacher consults the interests of the class.* —**con·sult′er,** *n.*

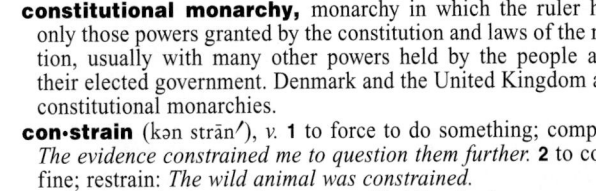

constellation—Orion

a	hat	ė	term	ô	order	ch	child		a in about
ā	age	i	it	oi	oil	ng	long		e in taken
ä	far	ī	ice	ou	out	sh	she	ə	i in pencil
â	care	o	hot	u	cup	th	thin		o in lemon
e	let	ō	open	ů	put	ŦH	then		u in circus
ē	equal	ò	saw	ü	rule	zh	measure		

con·sult·ant (kən sult′nt), *n.* **1** person who gives professional or technical advice. **2** person who consults another.

con·sul·ta·tion (kon′səl tā′shən), *n.* **1** a meeting to exchange ideas or talk things over: *The three doctors held a consultation to discuss the patient.* **2** act of consulting; seeking information or advice.

con·sum·a·ble (kən sü′mə bəl), **1** *adj.* able to be consumed: *consumable products.* **2** *n.* something meant to be consumed or used up: *Some workbooks are consumables.*

con·sume (kən süm′), *v.* **1** to use up; spend: *Rockets consume large quantities of fuel when they take off.* **2** to eat or drink up: *We will each consume at least two sandwiches on our hike.* **3** to destroy; burn up: *A huge fire consumed the entire forest.* ❑ *v.* con·sumed, con·sum·ing. —con·sum′ing·ly, *adv.*
consumed with, absorbed by curiosity, envy, etc.: *She was consumed with the desire to travel.*

con·sum·er (kən sü′mər), *n.* **1** person who buys and uses food, clothing, or anything grown or made by producers: *A low price for wheat should reduce the price of flour to the consumer.* **2** any living thing that has to eat in order to stay alive. Animals are consumers, but plants make their own food.

con·sum·er·ism (kən sü′mə riz′əm), *n.* trend toward increased protection of consumers from unsafe manufacturing processes and from misleading labeling, packaging, and advertising practices, and toward protection of the environment.

con·sum·mate (kon′sə māt *for verb;* kən sum′it *for adj.*), **1** *v.* to bring to completion; realize; fulfill: *My ambition was consummated when I won the first prize.* **2** *adj.* in the highest degree; complete; perfect: *consummate skill.* ❑ *v.* con·sum·mat·ed, con·sum·mat·ing. —con·sum′mate·ly, *adv.* —con′sum·ma′tion, *n.*

con·sump·tion (kən sump′shən), *n.* **1** act or process of using up; use: *We took along some food for consumption on our trip.* **2** amount used up: *The consumption of fuel oil is much greater in winter than in summer.* **3** OLD USE. tuberculosis of the lungs.

con·sump·tive (kən sump′tiv), OLD USE. **1** *adj.* having or likely to have tuberculosis of the lungs. **2** *n.* person who has tuberculosis of the lungs.

cont., continued.

con·tact (kon′takt), **1** *n.* condition of touching; a touching together: *A magnet will draw iron filings into contact with it.* **2** *n.* condition of being in communication: *The control tower lost radio contact with the airplane pilot.* **3** *n.* a powerful or helpful friend or acquaintance; connection: *The reporter had several important contacts in the government.* **4** *v.* to get in touch with: *I've been trying to contact you for two days.* **5** *v.* to put or bring into contact. **6** *n.* connection between two things through which an electric current can pass. **7** *n.* contact lens.

contact lens, a very small, thin, plastic lens fitted on the front of the eyeball to improve vision, worn instead of eyeglasses.

con·ta·gion (kən tā′jən), *n.* **1** the spreading of disease by infection: *Contagion is hard to prevent in crowded areas.* **2** disease spread in this way. **3** the spreading of a harmful influence from one person to another: *At the cry of "Fire!" a contagion of fear swept through the audience.*

con·ta·gious (kən tā′jəs), *adj.* **1** spreading by infection; catching: *Mumps is a contagious disease.* **2** easily spreading from one person to another: *Yawning is often contagious.* —con·ta′gious·ly, *adv.* —con·ta′gious·ness, *n.*

con·tain (kən tān′), *v.* **1** to have within itself; hold as contents: *Books contain information.* **2** to be capable of holding: *That pitcher will contain a quart of milk.* **3** to be equal to: *A pound contains 16 ounces.* **4** to control your feelings; hold back; restrain: *She could not contain her excitement over winning the contest.* —con·tain′ment, *n.*

SYNONYM STUDY **Contain, hold**[1], and **accommodate** all mean to have something inside. **Contain** can be used about ideas or things: *His paper contains three spelling errors. The room contains many books.* **Hold** is used about things or people, sometimes to show possibilities, not facts: *The stadium holds almost 55,000 people.* **Accommodate** means to hold comfortably: *Will the boat accommodate seven of us?*

con·tain·er (kən tā′nər), *n.* box, can, jar, carton, etc., used to hold or contain something.

con·tam·i·nant (kən tam′ə nənt), *n.* something that contaminates; pollutant.

con·tam·i·nate (kən tam′ə nāt), *v.* to make impure by contact or by mixing; pollute: *The water had been contaminated by sewage.* ■ See Synonym Study at **pollute.** ❑ *v.* con·tam·i·nat·ed, con·tam·i·nat·ing. —con·tam′i·na′tion, *n.* —con·tam′i·na′tor, *n.*

con·tem·plate (kon′təm plāt), *v.* **1** to look at or think about for a long time; study carefully: *We contemplated the beautiful mountain landscape.* **2** to have in mind; consider, intend, or expect: *She is contemplating a trip to Europe.* ❑ *v.* con·tem·plat·ed, con·tem·plat·ing. —con′tem·pla′tor, *n.*

con·tem·pla·tion (kon′təm plā′shən), *n.* **1** act of looking at or thinking about something for a long time; deep thought: *I was lost in contemplation and did not hear the doorbell.* **2** expectation or intention: *We are buying tents and other equipment in contemplation of a camping trip next summer.*

con·tem·pla·tive (kon′təm plā′tiv *or* kən tem′plə tiv), *adj.* deeply thoughtful; meditative: *The monks lived a quiet, contemplative life in the monastery.* —con′tem·pla′tive·ly, *adv.* —con′tem·pla′tive·ness, *n.*

con·tem·po·ra·ne·ous (kən tem′pə rā′nē əs), *adj.* belonging to the same period of time; contemporary: *contemporaneous eighteenth-century composers.* —con·tem′po·ra′ne·ous·ly, *adv.* —con·tem′po·ra′ne·ous·ness, *n.*

con·tem·po·rar·y (kən tem′pə rer′ē), **1** *adj.* belonging to or living in the same period of time: *The telephone and the phonograph were contemporary inventions.* **2** *n.* person living in the same period of time: *Abraham Lincoln and Robert E. Lee were contemporaries.* **3** *adj.* of the present time; modern: *The book had contemporary children's stories in addition to the old fairy tales.* ❑ *n., pl.* con·tem·po·rar·ies.

con·tempt (kən tempt′), *n.* **1** the feeling that a person, act, or thing is shameful and disgraceful; scorn: *feel contempt for a cheat.* ■ See Synonym Study at **scorn.** **2** condition of being despised or scorned; disgrace: *The traitor was held in contempt.* **3** disobedience to or open disrespect for the rules or decisions of a court of law or a lawmaking group. A person can be put in jail for contempt of court.

con·tempt·i·ble (kən temp′tə bəl), *adj.* deserving contempt or scorn: *Cruelty is contemptible.* —con·tempt′i·ble·ness, *n.* —con·tempt′i·bly, *adv.*

con·temp·tu·ous (kən temp′chü əs), *adj.* showing contempt; scornful: *a contemptuous look.* —con·temp′tu·ous·ly, *adv.* —con·temp′tu·ous·ness, *n.*

con·tend (kən tend′), *v.* **1** to work hard against difficulties; fight; struggle: *The first settlers in New England had to contend with harsh winters, sickness, and lack of food.* **2** to take part in a contest; compete: *Five runners were contending in the first race.* **3** to declare to be true; state: *Doctors contend that cigarette smoking is dangerous to your health.* —con·tend′er, *n.*

con·tent[1] (kon′tent), *n.* **1** Often, **contents,** *pl.* **a** what is contained in anything; all things inside: *An old chair, a desk, and a bed were the only contents of the room.* **b** chapters or sections in a book. A **table of contents** gives a list of these. **2** facts and ideas stated; what is written in a book or said in a speech: *I didn't understand the content of her speech.* **3** any sort of information that can be broadcast, transmitted by cable or computer network, etc. Movies, TV shows, musical recordings, and computer databases may be called content. **4** amount contained: *Maple syrup has a high sugar content.*

con·tent[2] (kən tent′), **1** *v.* to give satisfaction; please; make easy in mind: *Nothing contents me when I'm in a bad mood.* **2** *adj.* satisfied; pleased; easy in mind; contented: *Will you be content to wait until tomorrow?* **3** *n.* contentment; satisfaction; ease of mind: *The cat lay stretched out beside the fire in complete content.*

con·tent·ed (kən ten′tid), *adj.* satisfied; pleased; easy in mind. —con·tent′ed·ly, *adv.* —con·tent′ed·ness, *n.*

con·ten·tion (kən ten′shən), *n.* **1** statement or point that you have argued for; statement maintained as true: *Galileo's con-*

tention that the earth goes around the sun proved to be true. **2** act of arguing; disputing; quarreling: *There was some contention about the choice of a new captain of the baseball team.* **3** argument; dispute; quarrel.

con·ten·tious (kən ten′shəs), *adj.* fond of arguing; given to disputing; quarrelsome: *A contentious person argues about trifles.* —**con·ten′tious·ly,** *adv.* —**con·ten′tious·ness,** *n.*

con·tent·ment (kən tent′mənt), *n.* happiness; satisfaction; ease of mind.

con·test (kon′test *for noun;* kən test′ *for verb*), **1** *n.* trial of skill to see which can win. A game or race is a contest; so is a debate. **2** *n.* a fight, struggle, or dispute. **3** *v.* to fight for; struggle for: *The blackbirds contested the nesting territory with one another.* **4** *v.* to argue against; dispute about: *The lawyer contested the claim and tried to prove that it was false.*

> **WORD STORY** **Contest** comes from a Latin word meaning "to be a witness." The first use of *contest* in English was about legal struggles, but soon people used it to mean any kind of competition with rules.

con·test·ant (kən tes′tənt), *n.* person who takes part in a contest: *My sister was a contestant in the 100-yard dash.*

con·text (kon′tekst), *n.* the parts directly before and after a word or sentence that influence its meaning. You can often tell the meaning of a word from its use in context.

> **WORD STORY** **Context** comes from Latin words meaning "to weave together." A word, phrase, or sentence is connected to its context like a thread to a fabric.

con·tig·u·ous (kən tig′yü əs), *adj.* **1** in actual contact; touching: *contiguous farms.* **2** near in time or order: *contiguous events.* **3** connected in a continuous series: *contiguous row houses.* —**con·tig′u·ous·ly,** *adv.*

con·ti·nence (kon′tə nəns), *n.* control of your actions and feelings; self-restraint; moderation.

con·ti·nent[1] (kon′tə nənt), *n.* **1** one of the seven great masses of land on the earth. The continents are North America, South America, Europe, Africa, Asia, Australia, and Antarctica. **2 the Continent,** the mainland of Europe. It does not include the British Isles. [**Continent** comes from Latin words meaning "to hold together." **Contain** comes from the same words. Continents contain countries.]

con·ti·nent[2] (kon′tə nənt), *adj.* having good control of bodily functions and urges. —**con′ti·nent·ly,** *adv.*

con·ti·nent·al (kon′tə nen′tl), **1** *adj.* of or like a continent. **2 Continental, a** *adj.* of or like the mainland of Europe: *Continental customs differ from those of England and Ireland.* **b** *n.* person living on the Continent; European. **c** *adj.* of the American colonies at the time of the Revolutionary War: *The Second Continental Congress adopted the Declaration of Independence in 1776.* **d** *n.* soldier of the American army during the Revolutionary War.

continental divide, 1 long mountain ridges that determine the directions a continent's rivers will flow. **2 Continental Divide,** ridge in W North America that separates streams flowing toward the Pacific Ocean from those flowing toward the Atlantic or Arctic Oceans; Great Divide. The Rocky Mountains form a major part of the Continental Divide.

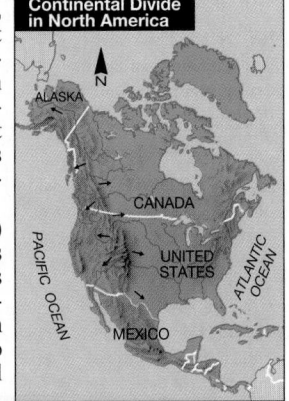

Continental Divide in North America

continental drift, (in geology) theory that the earth's continents and other great land regions slowly move, changing locations and distances from each other. This motion is thought to be caused by the earth's internal heat.

continental shelf, the shallow portion of sea bottom that slopes gradually down from a continent's shoreline to a depth of about 600 feet (180 meters). It ends in a steep slope to deeper water.

continental slope, the edge of a continental shelf sloping steeply toward the deeper ocean bottom.

con·tin·gen·cy (kən tin′jən sē), *n.* **1** a happening or event depending on something that is uncertain; possibility: *The explorer carried supplies for every contingency.* **2** an accidental happening; chance. ❑ *n., pl.* **con·tin·gen·cies.**

con·tin·gent (kən tin′jənt), **1** *n.* share of soldiers, laborers, etc., to be furnished: *The United States sent a large contingent of troops to Europe in World War II.* **2** *n.* group that is part of a larger group: *The New York contingent sat together at the national convention.* **3** *adj.* depending on something not certain; conditional: *Our plans for a picnic are contingent upon fair weather.* **4** *adj.* liable to happen or not to happen; possible; uncertain: *The traveler set aside five dollars a day for contingent expenses.* **5** *adj.* happening by chance; accidental; unexpected.

con·tin·u·al (kən tin′yü əl), *adj.* **1** never stopping: *the continual flow of the river.* **2** repeated many times; very frequent: *continual interruptions.* —**con·tin′u·al·ly,** *adv.*

con·tin·u·ance (kən tin′yü əns), *n.* **1** act or fact of continuing; going on: *the continuance of a friendship.* **2** act of remaining; stay: *The senator's continuance in office depends on the voters.* **3** postponement of legal proceedings until a later date.

con·tin·u·a·tion (kən tin′yü ā′shən), *n.* **1** act of going on with a thing after stopping; beginning again: *Club members voted for a continuation of the discussion at the next meeting.* **2** anything by which a thing is continued; added part: *The continuation of the story will be seen on next week's program.* **3** act or fact of not stopping.

con·tin·ue (kən tin′yü), *v.* **1** to keep up; keep on; go on; go on with: *The rain continued all day.* **2** to go on after stopping; take up; carry on: *The class begged the teacher to continue with the reading.* **3** to last: *The queen's reign continued for 20 years.* **4** to stay; remain: *The children must continue in school till the end of June.* **5** to cause to stay; maintain: *The club members voted to continue the president in office for another term.* **6** to put off until a later time; postpone; adjourn: *The judge continued the case for a month.* ❑ *v.* **con·tin·ued, con·tin·u·ing.** —**con·tin′u·a·ble,** *adj.*

> **SYNONYM STUDY** **Continue** and **last**[2] both mean to go on for a long time. **Continue** suggests steady activity: *Road repair will continue all summer.* **Last** suggests not coming to an end for a while: *The rainbow lasted for half an hour.*

con·ti·nu·i·ty (kon′tə nü′ə tē), *n.* act or process of going on without stopping; continuing without interruption: *The continuity of her story was broken when the telephone rang.*

con·tin·u·ous (kən tin′yü əs), *adj.* without a stop or break; connected; unbroken: *a continuous sound, a continuous line of cars.* —**con·tin′u·ous·ly,** *adv.* —**con·tin′u·ous·ness,** *n.*

con·tort (kən tôrt′), *v.* to twist or bend out of shape; distort: *The clown contorted his face.*

con·tor·tion (kən tôr′shən), *n.* **1** twisted condition: *The acrobat went through various contortions.* **2** act of twisting or bending out of shape.

con·tor·tion·ist (kən tôr′shə nist), *n.* person who can twist or bend his or her body into extremely odd positions.

con·tour (kon′tür), **1** *n.* outline of a figure: *The contour of the coast of Maine is very irregular.* **2** *adj.* following natural ridges and furrows to avoid erosion. **3** *adj.* shaped to fit the outline of a particular object: *a contour chair, contour sheets.*

contour line, line on a map, showing height above sea level. All points on a contour line have the same elevation. The closer the contour lines, the steeper the slope. See picture at **contour map.**

a	hat	ė	term	ô	order	ch	child	
ā	age	i	it	oi	oil	ng	long	a in about
ä	far	ī	ice	ou	out	sh	she	e in taken
â	care	o	hot	u	cup	th	thin	ə {i in pencil
e	let	ō	open	u̇	put	ŦH	then	o in lemon
ē	equal	ò	saw	ü	rule	zh	measure	u in circus

189

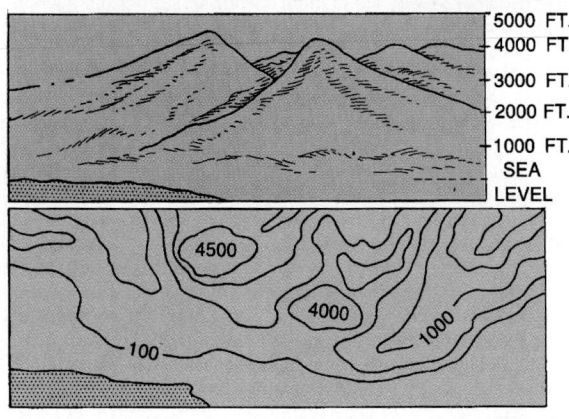

contour map

contour map, map showing heights above sea level by means of contour lines.

con·tra·band (kon′trə band), **1** *n.* goods imported or exported contrary to law; smuggled goods: *Customs officials went through each bag looking for contraband.* **2** *adj.* against the law; prohibited: *to smuggle contraband drugs into a country.*

con·tra·bass (kon′trə bās′), *n.* **1** the lowest bass instrument. **2** double bass. ◻ *n., pl.* **con·tra·bass·es.**

con·tra·bas·soon (kon′trə bə sün′), *n.* a large bassoon, lower in pitch than the ordinary bassoon; double bassoon.

con·tra·cep·tion (kon′trə sep′shən), *n.* prevention of conception or becoming pregnant.

con·tra·cep·tive (kon′trə sep′tiv), **1** *n.* means or device for preventing pregnancy. **2** *adj.* about or used for contraception: *contraceptive information, contraceptive device.*

con·tract (kon′trakt *for 1-4;* kon′trakt *for 5,6;* kon′trakt *or* kən trakt′ *for 7*), **1** *v.* to draw together; make shorter: *The earthworm contracted its body.* **2** *v.* to become shorter or smaller; shrink: *Wool fibers contract in hot water.* **3** *v.* to shorten a word or phrase by omitting some of the letters or sounds: *In talking and writing we often contract "do not" to "don't."* **4** *v.* to bring on yourself; get; form: *Bad habits, once contracted, are hard to get rid of. She contracted a cold.* **5** *n.* agreement. In a contract two or more people agree to do or not to do certain things. **6** *n.* a written agreement that can be enforced by law. **7** *v.* to make a contract: *The builder contracted to build the new house.*

con·trac·tile (kən trak′təl), *adj.* **1** able to become shorter or smaller: *Muscle is contractile tissue.* **2** producing a decrease in size: *Cold has a contractile effect.*

con·trac·tion (kən trak′shən), *n.* **1** something contracted; shortened form: *"Can't" is a contraction of "cannot."* **2** act of contracting: *Cold causes the contraction of substances; heat causes their expansion.* **3** condition of being contracted; decrease in size or volume: *The contraction of mercury by cold makes it go down in thermometers.*

con·trac·tor (kon′trak tər *or* kən trak′tər), *n.* person who agrees to supply materials or to do a piece of work for a certain price: *My family hired a contractor to build our new house.*

con·trac·tu·al (kən trak′chü əl), *adj.* of or like a contract: *a contractual arrangement.* **—con·trac′tu·al·ly,** *adv.*

con·tra·dict (kon′trə dikt′), *v.* **1** to say that a statement is not true; deny: *The company contradicts the government report and says it does not pollute the river.* ◼ See Synonym Study at **deny.** **2** to say the opposite of what another person has said: *I seldom contradict my parents.* **3** to be opposite to; disagree with: *Your story and her story contradict each other.* **—con′tra·dict′a·ble,** *adj.* **—con′tra·dic′tor,** *n.*

con·tra·dic·tion (kon′trə dik′shən), *n.* **1** act of denying what has been said; saying the opposite: *The expert spoke without fear of contradiction by his listeners.* **2** statement or act that contradicts another; denial. **3** disagreement.

con·tra·dic·tor·y (kon′trə dik′tər ē), *adj.* in disagreement; contradicting; contrary: *First reports of the election results were so contradictory we could not tell who won.* **—con′tra·dic′tor·i·ly,** *adv.* **—con′tra·dic′tor·i·ness,** *n.*

con·trail (kon′trāl′), *n.* a narrow white streak of water vapor left by an airplane flying at a high altitude; vapor trail.

con·tral·to (kən tral′tō), **1** *n.* the lowest singing voice of a woman; alto. **2** *n.* singer with such a voice. **3** *n.* part in music for such a voice. **4** *adj.* of or for a contralto. ◻ *n., pl.* **con·tral·tos.**

con·trap·tion (kən trap′shən), *n.* device or gadget; contrivance. ◼ See Synonym Study at **gadget.**

con·tra·ri·wise (kon′trer ē wīz′), *adv.* **1** in the opposite way or direction. **2** on the contrary.

con·tra·ry (kon′trer ē *for 1,2;* kən trer′ē *for 3*), **1** *adj.* completely different; opposed; opposite: *Your taste in music is contrary to mine.* **2** *n.* the opposite: *After promising to come early, she did the contrary and came late.* **3** *adj.* opposing others; stubborn: *The contrary boy often refused to do what was asked of him.* **—con·tra′ri·ly,** *adv.* **—con·tra′ri·ness,** *n.*

on the contrary, exactly opposite to what has been said: *He is not stingy; on the contrary, no one could be more generous.*

to the contrary, with the opposite effect.

con·trast (kon′trast *for noun;* kən trast′ *for verb*), **1** *n.* a great difference; striking difference: *the contrast between night and day.* **2** *n.* person, thing, event, etc., that shows differences when compared with another: *Her dark hair is a sharp contrast to her sister's light hair.* **3** *v.* to compare two things so as to show their differences: *to contrast birds with fishes.* **4** *v.* to show differences when compared or put side by side: *The black and the gold contrast well in that design.* **—con·trast′a·ble,** *adj.* **—con·trast′ing·ly,** *adv.*

in contrast, by comparison; considered in relation: *In contrast to yours, my grades are not good.*

WORD STORY **Contrast** comes from an Italian word meaning "to fight against." Things that are strongly different, if put together, seem to be struggling for attention or effect.

con·trib·ute (kən trib′yüt), *v.* **1** to give money or help along with others: *Everyone was asked to contribute suggestions.* **2** to write articles, stories, etc., for a newspaper or magazine. ◻ *v.* **con·trib·ut·ed, con·trib·ut·ing.** **—con·trib′u·tor,** *n.*

contribute to, to help bring about: *A poor diet contributed to the child's bad health.*

con·tri·bu·tion (kon′trə byü′shən), *n.* **1** money or help contributed; gift: *Our contribution to the picnic was the lemonade.* **2** act of contributing; giving of money or help along with others: *Contribution to worthy causes is her favorite activity.* **3** article, story, etc., written for a newspaper or magazine.

con·trib·u·to·ry (kən trib′yə tôr′ē), *adj.* helping to bring about; contributing: *The worker's own carelessness was a contributory cause of the accident.*

con·trite (kən trīt′ *or* kon′trīt), *adj.* **1** sorry for doing something wrong; repentant: *I felt contrite after losing my temper and yelling.* **2** showing deep regret and sorrow: *I wrote a contrite apology.* [**Contrite** comes from a Latin word meaning "crushed." It feels that way.] **—con·trite′ly,** *adv.* **—con·trite′ness,** *n.*

con·tri·tion (kən trish′ən), *n.* **1** sorrow for your sins or guilt; being contrite; repentance. **2** deep regret.

con·tri·vance (kən trī′vəns), *n.* **1** thing invented; mechanical device: *A can opener is a handy contrivance.* **2** act or manner of contriving: *By careful contrivance she repaired the old clock and made it go.*

con·trive (kən trīv′), *v.* **1** to plan with cleverness or skill; invent; design: *The inventor had contrived a new kind of engine.* **2** to plan; scheme; plot: *to contrive a robbery.* **3** to arrange to have something happen; manage: *Because he was still mad at his former girlfriend, he contrived to arrive at the party after she had left.* ◻ *v.* **con·trived, con·triv·ing.** **—con·triv′er,** *n.*

con·trived (kən trīvd′), *adj.* produced as a result of obvious planning; not natural; artificial: *The novel has a good beginning and middle but an ending that seems contrived.*

con·trol (kən trōl′), **1** *v.* to have power or authority over; direct: *The government controls the printing of money.* **2** *n.* power to direct or guide; authority: *Children are under their parents' control.* **3** *v.* to hold back; keep down; restrain: *I was so upset by the accident that I couldn't control my tears.* **4** *n.* ability to keep back or hold down; restraint: *to lose control of one's temper.* **5** *n.* means of restraint; check: *The President's power to veto is a control over the legislation passed by Congress.* **6** *n.* device on or connected to a machine, that starts, stops, or adjusts its operation: *This control starts the dishwasher. There is a control for the furnace in our kitchen.* **7** *n.pl.* **controls,** the devices by which an aircraft, car, or other machine is operated. **8** *n.* individual or group serving as a standard of comparison for testing the results of a scientific experiment performed on a similar individual or group. ❑ *v.* **con·trolled, con·trol·ling.** [Control comes from French words meaning "against" and "the roll," as in a roll call. A person who has a list copied and checked against the roll can also be in charge of whatever is listed.] —**con·trol′la·ble,** *adj.*

SYNONYM STUDY Control and authority both mean the ability to make things happen. **Control** is a general word and suggests all sorts of events: *The movie director has control of actors, cameras, lights, scenery, and sound effects.* **Authority** suggests an official power of a certain kind: *The Coast Guard has authority over lighthouses.*

con·trol·ler (kən trō′lər), *n.* **1** person employed to supervise expenditures; comptroller: *The mayor directed the city controller to examine the expenses of the fire department.* **2** person who controls, directs, or restrains: *air traffic controller.*

controller (def. 2)

control tower, tower at an airfield for controlling the traffic of aircraft taking off and landing.

con·tro·ver·sial (kon′trə vèr′shəl), *adj.* **1** of or marked by controversy: *controversial writing.* **2** open to controversy; debatable; disputed: *a controversial question.* —**con′tro·ver′sial·ly,** *adv.*

con·tro·ver·sy (kon′trə vèr′sē), *n.* act of arguing a question about which differences of opinion exist; debate; dispute; argument: *The long controversy over slavery was one of the causes of the Civil War.* ❑ *n., pl.* **con·tro·ver·sies.**

con·tu·sion (kən tü′zhən), *n.* a bruise.

co·nun·drum (kə nun′drəm), *n.* **1** riddle whose answer involves a pun or play on words. EXAMPLE: "When is a door not a door?" "When it's ajar." **2** any puzzling problem.

con·va·lesce (kon′və les′), *v.* to recover health and strength after illness: *I convalesced at home for three weeks after my operation.* ❑ *v.* **con·va·lesced, con·va·lesc·ing.**

con·va·les·cence (kon′və les′ns), *n.* **1** the gradual recovery of health and strength after illness. **2** time during which you are convalescing: *The doctor prescribed a three-week convalescence at home for her patient.*

con·va·les·cent (kon′və les′nt), **1** *adj.* recovering health and strength after illness. **2** *adj.* of or for recovering after illness: *a convalescent home.* **3** *n.* person recovering after illness.

con·vec·tion (kən vek′shən), *n.* the transmission of heat from one place to another by the movement of heated particles of a gas or liquid.

con·vene (kən vēn′), *v.* **1** to meet for some purpose; gather together; assemble: *Congress convenes in the Capitol at Washington, D.C., at least once a year.* **2** to call together: *Any member may convene our club in an emergency.* ❑ *v.* **con·vened, con·ven·ing.** —**con·ven′er** or **con·ven′or,** *n.*

con·ven·ience (kən vē′nyəns), *n.* **1** fact or quality of being convenient: *The convenience of packaged meats and other foods helps to increase their sales.* **2** comfort; advantage: *Many stores have a delivery service for the convenience of shoppers.* **3** anything handy or easy to use; thing that saves trouble or work: *A folding table is a convenience in a small room.*

at your convenience, when it is convenient for you; at a suitable time or place, or under suitable conditions: *Come by to pick me up at your convenience.*

convenience store, a small store, usually open many hours a day, that sells basic groceries, snacks, and sometimes gas.

con·ven·ient (kən vē′nyənt), *adj.* **1** saving trouble; well arranged; easy to use: *It's convenient to have running water instead of a well.* ■ See Synonym Study at **useful.** **2** easily done; not troublesome; suitable: *Will it be convenient for you to meet me?* **3** within easy reach; handy: *Would my house be a convenient place to meet?* —**con·ven′ient·ly,** *adv.*

con·vent (kon′vent), *n.* **1** group of nuns living together according to fixed rules and under religious vows. **2** building or buildings in which they live.

con·ven·tion (kən ven′shən), *n.* **1** a meeting arranged for some particular purpose; gathering; assembly: *The Democratic and Republican parties hold conventions every four years to choose candidates for President.* **2** general agreement; common consent; custom: *Convention influences how we dress.* **3** custom or practice approved by general agreement: *Using the right hand to shake hands is a convention.* **4** agreement signed by two or more countries about matters less important than those in a treaty.

con·ven·tion·al (kən ven′shə nəl), *adj.* **1** according to conventions; customary: *"Good morning" is a conventional greeting.* **2** acting or behaving according to commonly accepted and approved ways: *Our neighbors are quiet, conventional people.* **3** of the usual type or design; commonly used or seen: *conventional furniture.* **4** (in the arts) following custom and traditional models; formal: *The ode and the sonnet are conventional forms of English poetry.* —**con·ven′tion·al·ly,** *adv.*

con·ven·tion·al·i·ty (kən ven′shə nal′ə tē), *n.* conventional quality or character; adherence to custom: *His conventionality made his reaction quite predictable.*

con·verge (kən vèrj′), *v.* **1** to tend to meet in a point. **2** to turn toward each other: *If you look at the end of your nose, your eyes converge.* **3** to come together; center: *A large group converged on the city hall. The attention of all the children converged upon the kitten.* ❑ *v.* **con·verged, con·verg·ing.**

con·ver·gence (kən vèr′jəns), *n.* **1** act or process of converging; tendency to meet in a point. **2** point of converging.

con·ver·gent (kən vèr′jənt), *adj.* converging.

con·ver·sant (kən vèr′sənt), *adj.* familiar by use or study; acquainted: *Our music teacher is conversant with all the instruments of the orchestra.* —**con·ver′sant·ly,** *adv.*

con·ver·sa·tion (kon′vər sā′shən), *n.* friendly talk; exchange of thoughts by talking informally together.

con·ver·sa·tion·al (kon′vər sā′shə nəl), *adj.* **1** of conversation. **2** fond of conversation; good at conversation. —**con′ver·sa′tion·al·ly,** *adv.*

con·ver·sa·tion·al·ist (kon′vər sā′shə nə list), *n.* person who is fond of or who is good at conversation.

con·verse[1] (kən vèrs′), *v.* to talk together in an informal way. ❑ *v.* **con·versed, con·vers·ing.** —**con·vers′er,** *n.*

con·verse² (kən vėrs′ *or* kon′vėrs′ *for adj.;* kon′vėrs′ *for noun*), **1** *n.* thing that is turned around, opposite, or contrary to something else: *The converse of a hamburger without onions is onions without a hamburger.* **2** *adj.* reversed in order; turned about: *The converse order of the alphabet is from "z" to "a."* **3** *adj.* opposite or contrary in direction or action: *A converse wind slowed down the airplane.* —**con·verse′ly,** *adv.*

con·ver·sion (kən vėr′zhən), *n.* **1** act or process of changing or turning; change: *Heat causes the conversion of water into steam.* **2** a change from unbelief to faith; change from one religion, party, etc., to another. **3** (in football) one or two extra points scored after a touchdown.

con·vert (kən vėrt′ *for verb;* kon′vėrt′ *for noun*), **1** *v.* to turn to another or a particular use or purpose; change: *The generators at the dam convert water power into electricity.* **2** *v.* to cause to change from one belief to another or from lack of belief to faith: *Missionaries tried to convert the villagers.* **3** *n.* person who has been converted to a different belief or faith. **4** *v.* to exchange for an equivalent: *She converted her dollars into pounds upon arriving in London.* **5** *v.* (in football) to score a conversion: *convert after a touchdown.*

con·vert·er (kən vėr′tər), *n.* person or thing that converts.

con·vert·i·ble (kən vėr′tə bəl), **1** *n.* car with a folding top. **2** *adj.* able to be converted. —**con·vert′i·bil′i·ty,** *n.*

convertible (def. 1)

con·vex (kon veks′ *or* kon′veks), *adj.* curved out like the outside of a circle or sphere; curving out: *The lens of an car headlight is convex on the outside.* See picture at **concave.** —**con·vex′ly,** *adv.*

con·vex·i·ty (kon vek′sə tē), *n.* **1** a convex condition. **2** a convex surface or thing. ◻ *n., pl.* **con·vex·i·ties** for 2.

con·vey (kən vā′), *v.* **1** to take from one place to another; carry: *A bus conveyed the passengers from the city to the airport.* ∎ See Synonym Study at **carry. 2** to transmit; conduct: *A wire conveys an electric current.* **3** to make known; communicate: *convey meaning* **4** to transfer ownership of; hand over; give: *convey property by a will.* ◻ *n., pl.* **con·veyed, con·vey·ing.**

con·vey·ance (kən vā′əns), *n.* **1** act of carrying; transmission: *Freighters engage in the conveyance of goods from one port to another.* **2** thing that carries people and goods; vehicle: *Trains and buses are public conveyances.* **3** transfer of property from one person to another.

con·vey·or *or* **con·vey·er** (kən vā′ər), *n.* **1** person or thing that conveys. **2** conveyor belt.

conveyor belt *or* **conveyer belt,** a mechanical device that carries things from one place to another by means of a moving, endless belt.

con·vict (kən vikt′ *for verb;* kon′vikt *for noun*), **1** *v.* to prove, find, or declare guilty: *The jury convicted the accused woman of stealing.* **2** *n.* person serving a prison sentence for some crime.

con·vic·tion (kən vik′shən), *n.* **1** act of proving or declaring guilty: *The trial resulted in the conviction of the accused man.* **2** condition of being proved or declared guilty: *The thief's conviction meant a year in prison.* **3** firm belief: *It often takes courage to act according to your convictions.*

con·vince (kən vins′), *v.* to make someone feel sure; cause to believe; persuade by argument or proof: *The mistakes she made convinced me she had not studied her lesson.* ∎ See Synonym Study at **persuade.** ◻ *v.* **con·vinced, con·vinc·ing.** —**con·vinc′er,** *n.* —**con·vin′ci·ble,** *adj.*

con·vinc·ing (kən vin′sing), *adj.* able to convince; persuasive: *The lawyer's convincing argument influenced the jury.* —**con·vinc′ing·ly,** *adv.*

con·viv·i·al (kən viv′ē əl), *adj.* **1** fond of eating and drinking with friends; sociable: *They were a convivial couple who enjoyed having friends drop in.* **2** festive: *a convivial party.* —**con·viv′i·al·i·ty,** *n.* —**con·viv′i·al·ly,** *adv.*

con·vo·ca·tion (kon′və kā′shən), *n.* **1** assembly: *The convocation of clergymen passed a resolution condemning violence.* **2** act of calling together.

con·voke (kən vōk′), *v.* to call together; notify to assemble. ◻ *v.* **con·voked, con·vok·ing.** —**con·vok′er,** *n.*

con·vo·lut·ed (kon′və lü′tid), *adj.* **1** complicated; intricate: *a convoluted story.* **2** tangled; winding: *a convoluted vine.*

con·vo·lu·tion (kon′və lü′shən), *n.* **1** action of coiling, winding, or twisting together: *the convolutions of a snake slithering through the grass.* **2** an irregular fold or ridge on the surface of the brain.

con·voy (kən voi′ *or* kon′voi *for verb;* kon′voi *for noun*), **1** *v.* to go with in order to protect; escort: *Warships convoy unarmed merchant ships during time of war.* **2** *n.* an escort; protection: *The gold was moved from the truck to the bank's vault under convoy of armed guards.* **3** *n.* warships, soldiers, etc., that escort. **4** *n.* group of ships or motor vehicles traveling together for protection or convenience.

con·vulse (kən vuls′), *v.* **1** to shake violently: *An earthquake convulsed the island, damaging many buildings.* **2** to cause violent disturbance in: *to be convulsed with rage.* **3** to throw into convulsions; shake with muscular spasms. **4** to throw into fits of laughter; cause to shake with laughter: *The clown's funny antics convulsed the audience.* ◻ *v.* **con·vulsed, con·vuls·ing.**

con·vul·sion (kən vul′shən), *n.* **1** Often, **convulsions,** *pl.* a violent, involuntary contracting and relaxing of the muscles; spasm; fit: *We called the veterinarian when our dog had convulsions.* **2** a fit of laughter. **3** a violent disturbance: *An earthquake is a convulsion of the earth.*

con·vul·sive (kən vul′siv), *adj.* **1** violently disturbing. **2** having convulsions. —**con·vul′sive·ly,** *adv.*

coo (kü), **1** *n.* the soft, murmuring sound made by doves or pigeons. **2** *v.* to make this sound. **3** *v.* to murmur in a soft, loving manner: *to coo to a baby.* ◻ *n., pl.* **coos;** *v.* **cooed, coo·ing.** ∎ Another word that sounds like this is **coup.** —**coo′er,** *n.*

cook (kůk), **1** *v.* to prepare food by using heat. Boiling, frying, broiling, roasting, and baking are forms of cooking. **2** *v.* to undergo cooking; be cooked: *Let the meat cook slowly.* **3** *n.* person who cooks. [See Word Story at **kitchen.**]

cook up, to make up or prepare, especially falsely: *We cooked up an excuse for being late.*

Cook (kůk), *n.* James, 1728-1779, English explorer. ∎ **James Cook** made voyages to the southern Pacific and the coasts of Australia and New Zealand. He sailed around the world twice, and led the first European expedition to visit Hawaii.

cook·book (kůk′bůk′), *n.* book of directions for cooking various kinds of food; book of recipes.

cook·er (kůk′ər), *n.* apparatus or container to cook things in.

cook·er·y (kůk′ər ē), *n.* **1** art or occupation of cooking. **2** CANADIAN. a place for cooking at a lumber camp, mine, etc.

cook·ie (kůk′ē), *n.* a small, flat, sweet cake. Also, **cooky.**

cook·out (kůk′out′), *n.* meal where the food is cooked and eaten outdoors.

cook·y (kůk′ē), *n.* cookie. ◻ *n., pl.* **cook·ies.**

cool (kül), **1** *adj.* somewhat cold; more cold than hot: *a cool, cloudy day.* ∎ See Synonym Study at **cold. 2** *adj.* allowing or giving a cool feeling: *a cool, thin dress.* **3** *adj.* not excited; calm: *Everyone kept cool when paper in the wastebasket caught fire.* **4** *adj.* having little enthusiasm or interest; not cordial: *My former*

C

friend gave me a cool greeting. **5** *n.* something cool; cool part, place, or time: *in the cool of the evening.* **6** *v.* to make or become cool: *Ice cools water. The ground cools off after the sun goes down.* **7** *adj.* bold or impudent in a calm way. **8** *adj.* INFORMAL. without exaggeration: *a cool million dollars.* **9** *adj.* INFORMAL. admirable; excellent. **10** *n.* INFORMAL. calm restraint; presence of mind: *Don't lose your cool.* **11** *adj.* (of colors) having a blue, green, or gray tint, not a red or yellow one: *cool purple tones.* **12** *interj.* INFORMAL. excellent; wonderful: *Cool! It's snowing!* —**cool′ly,** *adv.* —**cool′ness,** *n.*

cool out, INFORMAL. to relax: *He likes to cool out after work by listening to music.*

cool·ant (kü′lənt), *n.* a cooling substance, used to reduce heat in machinery.

cool·er (kü′lər), *n.* container that cools foods or drinks, or keeps them cool.

cool·head·ed (kül′hed′id), *adj.* not easily excited; calm. —**cool′-head′ed·ly,** *adv.* —**cool′-head′ed·ness,** *n.*

Coo·lidge (kü′lij), *n.* **Calvin,** 1872-1933, the 30th president of the United States, from 1923 to 1929.

coo·lie (kü′lē), *n.* formerly, an unskilled laborer in China, India, etc., hired for very low wages. ■ Another word that sounds like this is **coulee.**

coon (kün), *n.* raccoon.

coop (küp), **1** *n.* a small cage or pen for chickens, rabbits, etc. **2** *v.* to keep or put in a coop. **3** *v.* to confine, especially in a small space: *The children were cooped up indoors by the rain.* ■ Another word that sounds like this is **coupe.**

co-op (kō′op), *n.* INFORMAL. cooperative.

coop·er (kü′pər), *n.* (earlier) person who makes or repairs barrels, casks, etc.

Coo·per (kü′pər), *n.* **1 Gary,** 1901-1961, American actor. He won Academy awards as the heroes of the movies *Sergeant York* and *High Noon.* **2 James Fen·i·more** (fen′ə môr′), 1789-1851, American writer. He wrote novels about American Indians and frontier life and about the sea.

co·op·e·rate (kō op′ə rāt′), *v.* to work together: *Everyone cooperated in helping to clean up after the class party.* ❑ *v.* **co·op·e·rat·ed, co·op·e·rat·ing.** —**co·op′e·ra′tor,** *n.*

co·op·e·ra·tion (kō op′ə rā′shən), *n.* act or process of working together; united effort or labor.

co·op·e·ra·tive (kō op′ər ə tiv), **1** *adj.* wanting or willing to work together with others: *Most of the pupils were helpful and cooperative.* **2** *n.* store where merchandise is sold to members who share in the profits and losses according to the amounts they buy. **3** *n.* union of farmers for buying and selling their produce at the best price. **4** *n.* an apartment house owned and operated by the tenants. **5** *n.* apartment in such a building. —**co·op′er·a·tive·ly,** *adv.* —**co·op′er·a·tive·ness,** *n.*

co·or·di·nate (kō ôrd′n āt *for verb;* kō ôrd′n it *for adj., noun),* **1** *v.* to work or cause to work together in the proper way; fit together: *Coordinating the movements of the arms and legs is the hardest part of learning to swim.* **2** *adj.* equal in importance; of equal rank. **3** *v.* to make equal in importance. **4** *n.* a coordinate person or thing; an equal. **5** *adj.* joining words, phrases, or clauses of equal grammatical importance. *And* and *but* are coordinate conjunctions. **6** *n.* any of a set of numbers that give the position of a point by reference to fixed lines; Cartesian coordinates. ❑ *v.* **co·or·di·nat·ed, co·or·di·nat·ing.** —**co·or′di·nate·ly,** *adv.* —**co·or′di·na′tor,** *n.*

co·or·di·na·tion (kō ôrd′n ā′shən), *n.* **1** ability to use the senses together with body parts or to use two or more body parts together: *Playing catch improves hand-eye coordination.* **2** arrangement in proper order or proper relation: *An outline often helps in the coordination of ideas.*

coot (küt), *n.* any of nine wading and swimming birds with short wings and webbed feet.

coot·ie (kü′tē), *n.* SLANG. louse.

cop[1] (kop), *n.* INFORMAL. a police officer.

cop[2] (kop), *v.* SLANG. to take; steal. ❑ *v.* **copped, cop·ping.**

cop out, SLANG. to refuse to become involved; back out.

---

cope[1] (kōp), *v.* to struggle with some degree of success; struggle on even terms; deal successfully: *She was busy but able to cope with extra work.* ❑ *v.* **coped, cop·ing.**

cope[2] (kōp), *n.* a long cape worn by priests during certain religious rites.

Co·pen·ha·gen (kō′pən hā′gən), *n.* port and capital of Denmark, on the Baltic Sea. [**Copenhagen** comes from Danish words meaning "merchant's harbor." It has been a trading port for hundreds of years.]

Copenhagen

cop·e·pod (kō′pə pod), *n.* any of very many very small animals that live in great numbers in fresh and salt water. They are an important source of food for other water animals.

Co·per·ni·can (kə pėr′nə kən), *adj.* of Copernicus or his system of astronomy.

Co·per·ni·cus (kə pėr′nə kəs), *n.* **Nik·o·la·us** (nik′ə lā′əs), 1473-1543, Polish astronomer. He argued that Earth rotates on its axis and that the planets revolve around the sun.

cop·i·er (kop′ē ər), *n.* **1** machine that makes copies. **2** person who copies; imitator. **3** person who makes written copies.

co·pi·lot (kō′pī′lət), *n.* the assistant or second pilot in an aircraft.

cop·ing (kō′ping), *n.* the top layer of a brick or stone wall. It is usually built with a slope to shed water.

coping saw, a narrow saw in a U-shaped frame, used to cut curves.

co·pi·ous (kō′pē əs), *adj.* more than enough; plentiful; abundant: *a copious harvest.* —**co′pi·ous·ly,** *adv.* —**co′pi·ous·ness,** *n.*

WORD STORY **Copious** comes from a Latin word meaning "plenty." **Copy** comes from the same Latin word. When all books were written by hand, centuries ago, the only way to have plenty of books was to make copious copies. This is why a single book or magazine is still called a copy.

Cop·land (kō′plənd), *n.* **Aaron,** 1900-1990, American composer. ■ **Aaron Copland** composed movie scores, operas, and symphonies, but his best-known music is for the ballets *Billy the Kid* and *Appalachian Spring.*

cop·out (kop′out′), *n.* SLANG. **1** act of refusing to become involved; a backing out. **2** person who cops out.

cop·per (kop′ər), **1** *n.* a tough, reddish brown metallic element which occurs in various ores. Copper resists rust and is easily shaped into thin sheets or fine wire. It is an excellent conductor of heat and electricity. **2** *n.* coin made of copper or bronze, especially a penny. **3** *adj.* of copper: *a copper kettle.* **4** *v.* to cover or coat with copper. **5** *adj.* reddish brown. **6** *n.* a reddish brown. *Symbol:* Cu [See Word Story at **Cyprus.**]

Copper Age, the prehistoric period of human culture after the Stone Age and before the Bronze Age, when copper tools were used.

a	hat	ė	term	ô	order	ch	child		
ā	age	i	it	oi	oil	ng	long		a in about
ä	far	ī	ice	ou	out	sh	she	ə	e in taken
â	care	o	hot	u	cup	th	thin		i in pencil
e	let	ō	open	u̇	put	∓H	then		o in lemon
ē	equal	ò	saw	ü	rule	zh	measure		u in circus

cop·per·head (kop′ər hed′), *n.* **1** a poisonous snake with a copper-colored head, found in the eastern United States. It is a pit viper, related to the water moccasin and the rattlesnake. **2** Copperhead, person in the North who sympathized with the South during the Civil War.

cop·per·y (kop′ər ē), *adj.* **1** of or containing copper. **2** like copper: *a coppery sky at sunset.*

co·pra (kō′prə), *n.* the dried meat of coconuts. Coconut oil is obtained from copra.

copse (kops), *n.* a number of small trees or bushes growing together.

cop·ter (kop′tər), *n.* INFORMAL. helicopter.

cop·u·la (kop′yə lə), *n.* a linking verb, often a form of the verb *be.* EXAMPLE: John *is* a boy. ❑ *n., pl.* **cop·u·las.**

cop·u·late (kop′yə lāt), *v.* to have sexual intercourse; mate. ❑ *v.* **cop·u·lat·ed, cop·u·lat·ing.**

cop·u·la·tion (kop′yə lā′shən), *n.* sexual intercourse.

cop·y (kop′ē), **1** *n.* thing made to be just like another; thing made on the pattern or model of another. A written page, a picture, a dress, or a piece of furniture can be an exact copy of another. **2** *v.* to make a copy of: *Copy this page.* **3** *v.* to be a copy of; follow as a model or example; imitate: *to copy someone's way of dressing.* **4** *n.* one of a number of books, newspapers, magazines, pictures, etc., made at the same printing: *six copies of today's paper.* **5** *n.* written material ready to be set in print in a newspaper, magazine, or book: *advertising copy, newspaper copy.* ❑ *n., pl.* **cop·ies** for 1,4; *v.* **cop·ied, cop·y·ing.** [See Word Story at **copious.**]

> **SYNONYM STUDY** **Copy** and **imitation** both mean something made to look like another thing. **Copy** suggests a close likeness: *Give a copy of the map to everyone who will be at the picnic.* **Imitation** suggests something not as good as the thing it is like: *These shoes are only imitations of a famous brand.*

cop·y·book (kop′ē bůk′), *n.* book with models of handwriting to be copied, formerly used in learning to write.

cop·y·cat (kop′ē kat′), *n.* person who imitates someone else.

cop·y·right (kop′ē rit′), **1** *n.* the exclusive right to publish or sell a certain book, picture, etc., granted by a government for a certain number of years. **2** *v.* to protect by getting a copyright. Books, pieces of music, plays, software, etc., are usually copyrighted.

co·py·writ·er (kop′ē ri′tər), *n.* writer of advertising copy or publicity copy.

co·que·try (kō′kə trē *or* kō ket′rē), *n.* flirting.

co·quette (kō ket′), *n.* woman who tries to attract men; flirt.

co·qui·na (kō kē′nə), *n.* a soft, porous, light-colored limestone formed of bits of seashell and coral.

co·ra·cle (kôr′ə kəl), *n.* a small round boat made by covering a light wooden frame with waterproof material.

co·ral (kôr′əl), **1** *n.* a stony substance made of the skeletons of some tiny sea animals called polyps. Reefs and small islands formed of coral are common in tropical seas and oceans. Red, pink, and white coral is often used for jewelry. **2** *n.* a tiny sea animal that secretes a skeleton of coral and forms large branching colonies by budding. **3** *adj.* deep pink or red. **4** *n.* a deep pink or red. ■ Another word that sounds like this is **choral. —cor′al·like′,** *adj.*

coral reef, a ridge of coral at or near the surface of the sea.

Coral Sea, part of the Pacific Ocean off northeast Australia.

coral snake, any of several small, poisonous American snakes with bodies banded by alternating rings of red, yellow, and black.

cord (kôrd), **1** *n.* a thick string; very thin rope: *She tied the package with a cord.* **2** *v.* to fasten or tie up with a cord: *They corded bundles of papers.* **3** *n.* anything resembling a cord, such as an insulated cable fitted with a plug to connect a lamp or other electrical appliance to an electrical outlet. **4** *n.* nerve, tendon, or other structure in an animal body that is something like a cord. The spinal cord is in the backbone. The vocal cords are in the throat. **5** *n.* ridge or ridged pattern on cloth. **6** *n.* cloth with such ridges on it, especially corduroy. **7** *n.* measure of quantity for cut wood, equal to 128 cubic feet. A pile of wood 4 feet wide, 4 feet high, and 8 feet long is a cord. **8** *v.* to pile wood in cords. ■ Another word that sounds like this is **chord.**

cord·age (kôr′dij), *n.* **1** cords or ropes: *Most of the cordage on a sailing ship is in its rigging.* **2** quantity of wood measured in cords.

cord·ed (kôr′did), *adj.* **1** having ridges on it; ribbed: *corded cloth.* **2** fastened with a cord; bound with cords: *corded bundles of newspaper.*

cor·dial (kôr′jəl), **1** *adj.* warm and friendly in manner; hearty: *a cordial welcome.* **2** *n.* liqueur. **—cor′dial·ly,** *adv.*

cor·di·al·i·ty (kôr′jē al′ə tē), *n.* cordial quality or feeling; heartiness: *The cordiality of our host's welcome made us feel at home.*

cor·dil·ler·a (kôr′də lyer′ə), *n.* a system of parallel mountain ranges; chain of mountains. ❑ *n., pl.* **cor·dil·ler·as.**

cord·less (kôrd′lis), *adj.* without a cord, especially a cord that supplies electricity; powered by batteries: *a cordless telephone.*

Cór·do·ba (kôr′də bə), *n.* **1** city in S Spain. **2** city in central Argentina.

cor·don (kôrd′n), **1** *n.* line or circle of soldiers, policemen, forts, etc., enclosing or guarding a place: *A cordon of troops surrounded the dictator's headquarters.* **2** *n.* a cord, braid, or ribbon worn as an ornament or as a badge of honor. **3** *v.* to put a cordon around: *The police cordoned off the area near the fire.*

cor·do·van (kôr′də vən), *n.* **1** kind of soft leather. **2** shoe made from this leather.

cor·du·roy (kôr′də roi′), **1** *n.* a thick, cotton cloth with close, velvetlike ridges. **2** *adj.* made of corduroy: *a corduroy jacket.* **3** *n.pl.* **corduroys** or **cords,** corduroy trousers. **4** *n.* CANADIAN. corduroy road.

corduroy road, road made of logs laid crosswise, usually across low, wet land.

cord·wood (kôrd′wůd′), *n.* **1** wood sold by the cord. **2** firewood piled in cords.

core (kôr), **1** *n.* the hard, central part containing the seeds of fruits like apples and pears. **2** *n.* the central or most important part: *The core of her argument against the plan is its costliness.* **3** *n.* the central or innermost part of the earth lying below the mantle. **4** *v.* to take out the core of fruit: *I cored the apples before baking them.* ❑ *v.* **cored, cor·ing.** ■ Another word that sounds like this is **corps. —cor′er,** *n.*

> **WORD STORY** **Core** probably comes from a Latin word meaning "body." **Corps** and **corpse** come from the same Latin word. People may have thought of the core of a fruit as a body dressed in the outer soft part. A corps moves and works together like a single body.

CORE (kôr), *n.* Congress of Racial Equality (a civil rights organization for African Americans).

Cor·inth (kôr′inth), *n.* port in S Greece. See **Sparta** for map.

Co·rin·thi·an (kə rin′thē ən), **1** *adj.* of Corinth or its people. **2** *n.* person born or living in Corinth. **3** *adj.* of or in the most elaborate style of Greek architecture.

Co·rin·thi·ans (kə rin′thē ənz), *n.* either of two books of the New Testament, consisting of letters written by Saint Paul to the Christians of Corinth.

Cor·i·o·lis effect (kôr′ē ō′lis), the effect of the earth's rotation on the flow of wind currents, objects in flight, etc. It causes wind and water to shift direction clockwise in the Northern Hemisphere and counterclockwise in the Southern Hemisphere.

cork (kôrk), **1** *n.* the light, thick, outer bark of the cork oak. Cork is used for bottle stoppers, floats for fishlines, filling for life preservers, and floor coverings. **2** *n.* a bottle stopper made of cork or other material. **3** *v.* to plug with a cork: *Fill these bottles and cork them tightly.* **—cork′like′,** *adj.*

cork oak, the oak tree of the Mediterranean area, from which cork is obtained.

cork·screw (kôrk′skrü′), **1** *n.* tool used to pull corks out of bottles. **2** *adj.* shaped like a corkscrew; spiral: *corkscrew curls.*

cork·y (kôr′kē), *adj.* of or like cork. ❑ *adj.* **cork·i·er, cork·i·est. —cork′i·ness,** *n.*

cor·mor·ant (kôr′mər ənt), *n.* any of numerous very large seabirds with pouches under their beaks for holding caught fish.

corn[1] (kôrn), **1** *n.* kind of grain that grows on large ears; maize; Indian corn. **2** *n.* plant, a kind of cereal grass, that it grows on.

3 *v.* to preserve meat with strong salt water or with dry salt: *corned beef.* **4** *n.* INFORMAL. something trite, outdated, or sentimental.

corn² (kôrn), *n.* a small, hard, shiny thickening of the outer layer of the skin, caused by pressure or rubbing.

corn·bread (kôrn′bred′), *n.* bread made of corn meal.

corn·cob (kôrn′kob′), *n.* the central, woody part of an ear of corn, on which the kernels grow; cob.

cornucopia

corn·crib (kôrn′krib′), *n.* bin or small, ventilated building for storing corn that has not been shelled.

cor·ne·a (kôr′nē ə), *n.* the transparent part of the outer coat of the eyeball. The cornea covers the iris and the pupil. See picture at **eye.** ❑ *n., pl.* **cor·ne·as.**

corned (kôrnd), *adj.* preserved with strong salt water or with dry salt: *corned beef.* [**Corned** comes from an old English word meaning "formed into lumps," like the lumps of salt used to preserve beef.]

cor·nel·ian (kôr nē′lyən), *n.* carnelian.

cor·ner (kôr′nər), **1** *n.* place where two lines or surfaces meet: *the corner of a room.* **2** *n.* the place where two streets meet: *There is a traffic light at the corner.* **3** *adj.* at or on a corner: *a corner lot.* **4** *adj.* for a corner: *a corner cupboard.* **5** *n.* piece to form, protect, or decorate a corner: *The leather box has gold corners.* **6** *n.* place away from crowds; secret place: *Her money was hidden in odd corners all over the house.* **7** *n.* place that is far away; distant region or quarter: *People have searched in all corners of the earth for gold.* **8** *n.* an awkward or difficult position; place from which escape is impossible: *His enemies had driven him into a corner.* **9** *v.* to force into an awkward or difficult position; drive into a corner. **10** *n.* act of buying up large amounts of some stock or article to raise its price: *a corner in wheat.* **11** *v.* to buy up large amounts of some stock or article to raise its price: *Some speculators have tried to corner wheat.* **12** *v.* (of a car) to round sharp corners at relatively high speeds without swaying. [**Corner** comes from a Latin word meaning "a horn." The angle of two walls is like the bend in some animal horns.]

cut corners, to save money by reducing effort, time, labor, etc.

turn the corner, to pass the worst or most dangerous point.

cor·ner·back (kôr′nər bak′), *n.* (in football) a defensive back who plays behind the linebackers and defends against offensive plays toward the sidelines.

cor·nered (kôr′nərd), *adj.* without hope of escape or relief: *A cornered animal will fight.*

cor·ner·stone (kôr′nər stōn′), *n.* **1** stone at the corner of two walls that holds them together. **2** such a stone built into the corner of a building as its formal beginning. The laying of a cornerstone is often accompanied by a ceremony. **3** something of fundamental importance; foundation; basis: *The cornerstone of most religions is the belief in a creator.*

cor·net (kôr net′), *n.* a wind instrument somewhat like a trumpet, usually made of brass. It has three valves that control the pitch.

cor·net·ist or **cor·net·tist** (kôr net′ist), *n.* person who plays a cornet.

corn·field (kôrn′fēld′), *n.* field in which corn is grown.

corn·flakes (kôrn′flāks′), *n.pl.* crisp toasted flakes of corn, eaten as a breakfast cereal.

corn·flow·er (kôrn′flou′ər), *n.* bachelor's-button.

corn·husk (kôrn′husk′), *n.* husk of an ear of corn.

cor·nice (kôr′nis), *n.* **1** an ornamental molding along the top of a wall, pillar, or side of a building. **2** a molding around the walls of a room just below the ceiling.

Cor·nish (kôr′nish), **1** *adj.* of Cornwall, its people, or the language formerly spoken by them. **2** *n.* a Celtic language spoken as a native language in Cornwall until the late 1700s.

corn·meal (kôrn′mēl′), *n.* coarsely ground dried corn.

corn pone, cornbread shaped into a small flat loaf, and cooked in a frying pan, as in the southern United States.

corn·stalk (kôrn′stȯk′), *n.* stalk of corn.

corn·starch (kôrn′stärch′), *n.* a starchy flour made from corn, used to thicken puddings, custard, etc.

corn syrup, syrup made from cornstarch.

cor·nu·co·pi·a (kôr′nə kō′pē ə or kôr′nyə kō′pē ə), *n.* horn-shaped container represented in art as overflowing with fruits, vegetables, and flowers; horn of plenty. It is a symbol of fruitfulness and plenty. ❑ *n., pl.* **cor·nu·co·pi·as.**

Corn·wall (kôrn′wȯl), *n.* county in SW England.

Corn·wal·lis (kôrn wä′lis), *n.* Lord **Charles,** 1738-1805, British general who surrendered to Washington at Yorktown on October 19, 1781.

corn·y (kôr′nē), *adj.* INFORMAL. trite, outdated, or sentimental: *corny jokes, corny music.* ❑ *adj.* **corn·i·er, corn·i·est.**

co·rol·la (kə rol′ə or kə rō′lə), *n.* the petals of a flower. The petals forming the corolla may be separate or joined together at their edges. ❑ *n., pl.* **co·rol·las.**

co·rol·lar·y (kôr′ə ler′ē), *n.* **1** something proved by inference from something else already proved. **2** a natural consequence or result: *Crop failure was a corollary of the drought.* ❑ *n., pl.* **co·rol·lar·ies.**

co·ro·na (kə rō′nə), *n.* **1** outermost and hottest part of the atmosphere of the sun, visible only as a ring of light during a full solar eclipse. **2** any ring of light seen around the sun, moon, or other luminous body, usually because of cloud. ❑ *n., pl.* **co·ro·nas.**

Co·ro·na·do (kôr′ə nä′dō), *n.* **Fran·cis·co Vás·quez de** (frän sēs′kō väs′kes тнä), 1510-1554, Spanish explorer of the southwestern part of what is now the United States.

co·ro·nar·y (kôr′ə ner′ē), **1** *adj.* of or about either of the two arteries (**coronary arteries**) that supply blood to the muscular tissue of the heart. **2** *n.* coronary thrombosis. ❑ *n., pl.* **co·ro·nar·ies.**

coronary thrombosis, the blocking of a coronary artery or one of its branches by a blood clot.

co·ro·na·tion (kôr′ə nā′shən), *n.* ceremony of crowning a king, queen, emperor, etc.

co·ro·ner (kôr′ə nər), *n.* official of a local government who investigates any death not clearly due to natural causes. [**Coroner** comes from a Latin word meaning "a crown." The first coroners were royal officers, appointed to represent a king or queen.]

co·ro·net (kôr′ə net′), *n.* **1** a small crown indicating a rank of nobility below that of a king or queen. **2** a circle of gold, jewels, or flowers worn around the head as an ornament.

Corp., **1** Corporal. **2** Corporation.

cor·po·ral¹ (kôr′pər əl), *adj.* of the body: *Spanking someone is corporal punishment.* —**cor′po·ral·ly,** *adv.*

WORD FAMILY Corporal and the words below are related. They all come from a Latin word meaning "body."

core	corpse	corset
corporation	corpuscle	habeas corpus
corps	corsage	incorporate

a	hat	ė	term	ô	order	ch	child		a in about
ā	age	i	it	oi	oil	ng	long		e in taken
ä	far	ī	ice	ou	out	sh	she	ə	i in pencil
â	care	o	hot	u	cup	th	thin		o in lemon
e	let	ō	open	ů	put	тн	then		u in circus
ē	equal	ȯ	saw	ü	rule	zh	measure		

cor·por·al² (kôr′pər əl), *n.* a military rank. See chart on page 712.

cor·po·rate (kôr′pər it), *adj.* **1** forming a corporation; incorporated: *Most car manufacturers are corporate companies.* **2** of a corporation: *corporate property.* **3** united; combined: *The corporate will of the majority prevailed.* —**cor′po·rate·ly,** *adv.*

cor·po·ra·tion (kôr′pə rā′shən), *n.* group of persons who obtain a charter giving them as a group the right to buy and sell, own property, manufacture and ship products, etc., as if it were one person.

corps (kôr), *n.* **1** group of soldiers, trained for specialized military service: *the Medical Corps, the Signal Corps.* **2** a military unit made up of two or more divisions plus supporting troops, usually commanded by a lieutenant general. **3** group of people with special training, organized for working together: *A large hospital has a corps of nurses.* ❑ *n., pl.* **corps** (kôrz). [See Word Story at **core.**] ■ Another word that sounds like this is **core.**

corpse (kôrps), *n.* a dead human body. [See Word Story at **core.**]

corps·man (kôr′mən), *n.* an enlisted person in the armed forces who performs medical duties or helps with the wounded. ❑ *n., pl.* **corps·men.**

cor·pu·lence (kôr′pyə ləns), *n.* large or bulky body size; fatness.

cor·pu·lent (kôr′pyə lənt), *adj.* large or bulky in body size; fat.

cor·pus·cle (kôr′pus′əl), *n.* any of the cells that form a large part of the blood and lymph. Red corpuscles carry oxygen to the tissues and remove carbon dioxide; some white corpuscles destroy disease germs.

cor·ral (kə ral′), **1** *n.* pen for horses, cattle, etc. **2** *v.* to drive into or keep in such a pen: *The cowhands corralled the herd of wild ponies.* **3** *v.* to hem in; surround; capture: *The reporters corralled the candidate and asked for a statement.* **4** *n.* a circular camp formed by wagons for defense against attack. **5** *v.* to form wagons into such a circular camp. ❑ *v.* **cor·ralled, cor·ral·ling.** ■ Another word that sounds like this is **chorale.**

cor·rect (kə rekt′), **1** *adj.* free from mistakes; right: *give the correct answer.* **2** *adj.* agreeing with an accepted standard of good behavior; proper: *correct manners.* **3** *v.* to change to what is right; remove mistakes or faults from: *Correct any misspellings that you find.* **4** *v.* to change to a better condition or to what agrees with some standard: *Braces will correct crooked teeth.* **5** *v.* to point out or mark the errors of; check: *The teacher corrected our tests and returned them to us.* **6** *v.* to find fault with in order to improve; punish: *correct a child for misbehaving.* —**cor·rect′a·ble,** *adj.* —**cor·rect′ly,** *adv.* —**cor·rect′ness,** *n.*

SYNONYM STUDY Correct, accurate, and **exact** all mean having the facts and without mistakes. **Correct** means just as it should be: *I got the correct information from our encyclopedia.* **Accurate** suggests careful attention to details: *She gave an accurate account of the accident.* **Exact** suggests matching in every way: *The painting is an exact copy of the original.*

cor·rec·tion (kə rek′shən), *n.* **1** a change to correct an error or mistake: *Write in your corrections neatly.* **2** act of correcting; setting right: *The correction of all my mistakes took nearly an hour.* **3** punishment. A prison is sometimes called a house of correction. —**cor·rec′tion·al,** *adj.*

cor·rec·tive (kə rek′tiv), **1** *adj.* tending to correct; setting right; making better: *Corrective exercises can make weak muscles strong.* **2** *n.* something that corrects.

cor·re·late (kôr′ə lāt), *v.* **1** to put in relation: *Try to correlate your knowledge of history with your knowledge of geography.* **2** to be related one to the other: *Increasing cancer rates appear to correlate with rising pollution levels.* ❑ *v.* **cor·re·lat·ed, cor·re·lat·ing.**

cor·re·la·tion (kôr′ə lā′shən), *n.* **1** the mutual relation of two or more things: *the correlation between annual rainfall and crop yield.* **2** act or process of correlating. —**cor′re·la′tion·al,** *adj.*

cor·rel·a·tive (kə rel′ə tiv), **1** *adj.* having a mutual relation. Conjunctions used in pairs, such as *either...or,* are correlative. **2** *n.* either of two things having a mutual relation and commonly used together. Pairs of words like *husband* and *wife, mother* and *father,* are correlatives. —**cor·rel′a·tive·ly,** *adv.*

cor·re·spond (kôr′ə spond′), *v.* **1** to be the same as; agree: *The answers she got on the test correspond with those I got.* **2** to be

similar or alike: *The fins of a fish correspond to the wings of a bird. The angles of the two triangles correspond.* ■ See Synonym Study at **match².** **3** to exchange letters; write letters to each other: *Will you correspond with me while I am away?*

cor·re·spond·ence (kôr′ə spon′dəns), *n.* **1** harmony; agreement: *Your account of the accident has little correspondence with the story the other driver told.* **2** similarity: *There is a correspondence of form in the skeletons of most mammals.* **3** exchange of letters; practice of letter writing: *The boy kept up a correspondence with his friend in Europe.* **4** letters: *Bring me the correspondence concerning that order.*

cor·re·spond·ent (kôr′ə spon′dənt), *n.* **1** person who exchanges letters with another: *My cousin and I are correspondents.* **2** person employed by a newspaper, magazine, radio or TV network, etc., to send news from a particular place or region: *reports from correspondents in China and Great Britain.*

cor·re·spond·ing (kôr′ə spon′ding), *adj.* similar: *The wings of a bird and the fins of a fish have corresponding functions.* ■ See Synonym Study at **similar.** —**cor′re·spond′ing·ly,** *adv.*

cor·ri·dor (kôr′ə dər), *n.* a long hallway; passage in a large building into which rooms open: *Our classroom is at the end of a corridor.* [**Corridor** comes from a Latin word meaning "to run." In English we still say that a hall runs from one end of a building to the other.]

cor·rob·o·rate (kə rob′ə rāt′), *v.* to make more certain; confirm: *Eyewitnesses corroborated her testimony in court.* ❑ *v.* **cor·rob·o·rat·ed, cor·rob·o·rat·ing.** —**cor·rob′o·ra′tion,** *n.* —**cor·rob′or·a·tive,** *adj.* —**cor·rob′o·ra′tor,** *n.*

cor·rode (kə rōd′), *v.* to wear or eat away gradually: *Acid caused the pipes to corrode.* ❑ *v.* **cor·rod·ed, cor·rod·ing.**

cor·ro·sion (kə rō′zhən), *n.* **1** act or process of corroding. **2** a corroded condition.

cor·ro·sive (kə rō′siv), **1** *adj.* eating away gradually; tending to corrode: *Most acids are corrosive.* **2** *n.* substance that corrodes. —**cor·ro′sive·ly,** *adv.* —**cor·ro′sive·ness,** *n.*

cor·ru·gat·ed (kôr′ə gā′tid), *adj.* bent or shaped into wavy folds or ridges; wrinkled: *corrugated paper.*

cor·ru·ga·tion (kôr′ə gā′shən), *n.* one of a series of wavy folds or ridges; wrinkle.

cor·rupt (kə rupt′), **1** *adj.* influenced by bribes; dishonest: *a corrupt judge.* ■ See Synonym Study at **dishonest.** **2** *v.* to influence by bribes; make dishonest: *That judge cannot be corrupted.* **3** *adj.* morally bad; evil; wicked: *to lead a corrupt life.* **4** *v.* to make evil or wicked: *Bad companions may corrupt a person.* **5** *v.* to make or become rotten or decayed. **6** *adj.* rotten; decayed. —**cor·rupt′er** or **cor·rup′tor,** *n.* —**cor·rupt′ly,** *adv.* —**cor·rupt′ness,** *n.*

cor·rupt·i·ble (kə rup′tə bəl), *adj.* able to be corrupted. —**cor·rupt′i·bil′i·ty,** *n.* —**cor·rupt′i·bly,** *adv.*

cor·rup·tion (kə rup′shən), *n.* **1** the act of causing someone to do wrong, especially by bribery: *The police force must be kept free from corruption.* **2** evil conduct; wickedness. **3** rot; decay.

cor·sage (kôr säzh′), *n.* a small bouquet to be worn on the waist or shoulder of a woman's clothes, or on her wrist.

cor·sair (kôr′sâr), *n.* **1** pirate. **2** a pirate ship.

corse·let (kôrs′lit), *n.* armor for the upper part of the body.

cor·set (kôr′sit), *n.* a close-fitting piece of underwear worn about the waist and hips to support or shape the body.

Cor·si·ca (kôr′sə kə), *n.* island in the Mediterranean, southeast of and belonging to France. See **Castile** for map. —**Cor′si·can,** *adj., n.*

Cor·tés or **Cor·tez** (kôr tez′), *n.* **Her·nan·do** (hər nan′dō), 1485-1547, Spanish military leader who conquered Mexico. ■ **Hernando Cortés** destroyed the Aztec city of Tenochtitlan in 1521 and built Mexico City in its place. He was later buried there.

cor·tex (kôr′teks), *n.* **1** the layer of gray matter which covers most of the surface of the brain. **2** the outer layer of an internal organ: *the cortex of the kidney.* **3** the thin layer of plant tissue growing just under the outer covering of some stems or branches. ❑ *n., pl.* **cor·ti·ces** (kôr′tə sēz′), **cor·tex·es.**

cor·ti·cal (kôr′tə kəl), *adj.* of or about a cortex, especially of the brain or kidneys.

cor·ti·sone (kôr′tə sōn), *n.* hormone produced by the cortex of the adrenal glands or produced synthetically, used in the treatment of arthritis and other diseases.

co·run·dum (kə run′dəm), *n.* an extremely hard mineral. The dark-colored variety is used for polishing and grinding. Sapphires and rubies are transparent varieties of corundum.

cor·vette (kôr vet′), *n.* **1** gunboat used against submarines and in convoy work. **2** a former warship with sails and only one tier of guns.

cos, cosine.

Cos·by (koz′bē), *n.* **Bill** (bil), born 1937, American comedian and actor. ■ **Bill Cosby's** comedy albums have won eight Grammy awards, and his TV series, *The Cosby Show,* was a leader in the ratings.

co·sign (kō′sīn′), *v.* **1** to sign a document, treaty, contract, loan, etc., jointly with another person. Someone who cosigns a document assumes full responsibility if the other signer fails to fulfill the terms of the document. **2** to sign jointly. **—co′sign′er,** *n.*

co·sine (kō′sīn), *n.* the ratio of the length of the side next to an acute angle of a right triangle to the length of the hypotenuse.

cos·met·ic (koz met′ik), **1** *n.* preparation for beautifying the skin, hair, nails, etc. Powder, rouge, lipstick, and face creams are cosmetics. **2** *adj.* beautifying the skin, hair, nails, etc.: *a cosmetic cream.* **3** *adj.* done to restore or correct a physical appearance: *The badly broken nose required cosmetic surgery.* **—cos·met′i·cal·ly,** *adv.*

cos·me·tol·o·gist (koz′mə tol′ə jist), *n.* person who works at the art of applying cosmetics; beautician.

cos·me·tol·o·gy (koz′mə tol′ə jē), *n.* work of a beautician; art of applying cosmetics.

Cos·sack (kos′ak), *n.* one of a people who lived in southwestern Russia, Ukraine, and Poland, noted for their skill as horsemen.

cost (kôst), **1** *n.* price paid: *The cost of this watch was $75.* **2** *v.* to be obtained at the price of: *This watch costs $75.* **3** *n.* loss or sacrifice: *The poor fox escaped from the trap at the cost of a leg.* **4** *v.* to cause the loss or sacrifice of: *A thoughtless remark almost cost me a friend.* **5** *n.pl.* **costs,** expenses of a lawsuit or case in court: *The guilty party was ordered to pay a $1000 fine and $500 in costs.* ❑ *v.* **cost, cost·ing.**

at all costs or **at any cost,** regardless of expense; by all means; no matter what must be done: *Let's catch that bus at all costs; it's the last one today.*

Cos·ta Ri·ca (kos′tə rē′kə), country in Central America, NW of Panama. *Capital:* San José. [**Costa Rica** is Spanish for "rich coast." Spanish explorers hoped to find gold there.] **—Costa Rican.**

cost-ef·fec·tive (kôst′ə fek′tiv), *adj.* economical in terms of the value of goods, services, or results compared to the money spent for them. **—cost′-ef·fec′tive·ly,** *adv.* **—cost′-ef·fec′tive·ness,** *n.*

cost·ly (kôst′lē), *adj.* **1** of great value: *costly jewels.* **2** costing much: *a costly error.* ❑ *adj.* **cost·li·er, cost·li·est. —cost′li·ness,** *n.*

cost of living, the average price paid for food, rent, clothing, transportation, and other necessities by a person, family, etc., within a given period.

costume (def. 1)—costumes of several lands

cos·mic (koz′mik), *adj.* **1** having to do with the whole universe: *Cosmic forces produce galaxies.* **2** vast: *the cosmic amounts of money spent each day.* **—cos′mi·cal·ly,** *adv.*

cosmic dust, fine particles of matter in outer space.

cosmic rays, rays of highly energetic subatomic particles that come to the earth from outer space.

cos·mol·o·gy (koz mol′ə jē), *n.* science or theory of the universe, its parts, and its natural laws. **—cos·mol′o·gist,** *n.*

cos·mo·naut (koz′mə nôt), *n.* a Soviet astronaut.

cos·mo·pol·i·tan (koz′mə pol′ə tən), **1** *adj.* free from national or local prejudices; feeling at home in all parts of the world: *Diplomats are usually cosmopolitan people.* **2** *n.* person who feels at home in all parts of the world. **3** *adj.* belonging to all parts of the world; not limited to any one country or its inhabitants; widely spread: *Music is a cosmopolitan art.*

cos·mos (koz′məs *or* koz′mōs), *n.* **1** universe. **2** any complete, orderly system. **3** any of several tall tropical American plants with showy flowers of many colors, that bloom in the fall or late summer. ❑ *n., pl.* **cos·mos·es** for 1,2; **cos·mos** or **cos·mos·es** for 3.

cos·tume (kos′tüm), **1** *n.* way of dressing, including the way the hair is worn, kind of jewelry worn, etc.: *a hunting costume, the national costume of Japan.* **2** *n.* dress belonging to another time or place, worn on the stage, at masquerades, etc.: *The actors wore colonial costumes.* **3** *v.* to provide a costume for; dress: *costumed in red satin.* ❑ *v.* **cos·tumed, cos·tum·ing.**

costume jewelry, inexpensive imitation jewelry, usually showy or colorful.

cos·tum·er (ko stü′mər), *n.* person who makes, sells, or rents costumes.

a	hat	ė	term	ô	order	ch	child		
ā	age	i	it	oi	oil	ng	long		a in about
ä	far	ī	ice	ou	out	sh	she	ə {	e in taken
â	care	o	hot	u	cup	th	thin		i in pencil
e	let	ō	open	u̇	put	ŦH	then		o in lemon
ē	equal	ȯ	saw	ü	rule	zh	measure		u in circus

co·sy (kō′zē), *adj., n.* cozy. ❏ *adj.* **co·si·er, co·si·est;** *n., pl.* **co·sies.** —**co′si·ly,** *adv.* —**co′si·ness,** *n.*

cot¹ (kot), *n.* a narrow bed, sometimes made of canvas stretched on a frame that folds together.

cot² (kot), *n.* cottage.

Côte d'Iv·oire (kōt′də vwär′), country in W Africa, on the Atlantic. *Capital:* Yamoussoukro. Formerly called **Ivory Coast.**

co·ter·ie (kō′tər ē), *n.* set or circle of close acquaintances; group of people who often meet socially.

co·til·lion (kə til′yən), *n.* **1** a dance with complicated steps and much changing of partners, led by one couple. **2** any large, formal party for dancing.

Co·to·pax·i (kō′tə pak′sē), *n.* volcano in the Andes Mountains in N Ecuador, the highest active volcano in the world, 19,347 feet (5897 meters) high.

cot·tage (kot′ij), *n.* **1** a small house. **2** house at a summer resort.

cottage cheese, a soft, white cheese made from the curds of sour skim milk.

cotter pin (kot′ər), a split pin inserted through a slot to hold small parts of machinery together. The ends are bent back to keep it in the slot.

cot·ton (kot′n), **1** *n.* the soft, white fibers growing in a fluffy mass around the seeds of certain tall plants, used in making fabrics, thread, etc. **2** *n.* any of the plants that produce these fibers. **3** *n.* thread or cloth made of cotton.

cotton candy, a light, fluffy candy made by spinning melted sugar.

cotton gin, machine for separating the fibers of cotton from the seeds; gin.

cot·ton·mouth (kot′n mouth′), *n.* water moccasin. ❏ *n., pl.* **cot·ton·mouths** (kot′n mouᵗʜz′).

cot·ton·seed (kot′n sēd′), *n.* seed of cotton, used for making cottonseed oil, fertilizer, cattle fodder, etc. ❏ *n., pl.* **cot·ton·seeds** or **cot·ton·seed.**

cottonseed oil, oil pressed from cottonseed, used for cooking, for making soap, cosmetics, and the like.

cot·ton·tail (kot′n tāl′), *n.* any of several common American wild rabbits with fluffy white tails.

cot·ton·wood (kot′n wúd′), *n.* **1** any of several North American poplar trees with cottonlike tufts on the seeds. **2** their soft wood.

cot·ton·y (kot′n ē), *adj.* **1** of cotton. **2** like cotton; soft; fluffy; downy.

cot·y·le·don (kot′l ēd′n), *n.* the first leaf, or one of the first pair of leaves, growing from a seed; an embryo leaf in the seed of a plant.

couch (kouch), **1** *n.* a long seat, usually upholstered and having a back and arms; sofa. **2** *n.* any place for rest or sleep: *The deer sprang up from its grassy couch.* **3** *v.* to put in words; express: *thoughts couched in beautiful language.* ❏ *n., pl.* **couch·es.**

cou·gar (kü′gər), *n.* mountain lion.

cough (kôf), **1** *v.* to force air from the lungs with sudden effort and noise. **2** *n.* act of coughing. **3** *n.* sound of coughing. **4** *n.* condition or symptom of repeated coughing: *He had a bad cough.* **5** *v.* to expel from the throat by coughing: *I coughed up the candy that was stuck in my throat.* **6** *v.* to make a noise something like a cough: *The airplane engine coughed before starting.*

cough drop, a tablet containing medicine, held in the mouth and sucked to relieve coughs or hoarseness.

could (kúd), *v.* **1** past tense of **can**¹: *Years ago she could sing beautifully.* **2** might be able to: *Perhaps I could go with you.*

could·n't (kúd′nt), could not.

couldst (kúdst), *v.* OLD USE. could. "Thou couldst" means "You could."

could've (kúd′əv), could have.

cou·lee (kü′lē), *n.* a deep ravine or gulch, usually dry in summer. ❏ *n., pl.* **cou·lees.** [See Word Story at **Grand Coulee.**] ■ Another word that sounds like this is **coolie.**

cou·lomb (kü′lom), *n.* unit for measuring electrical charge, equal to the amount provided by one ampere in one second.

coun·cil (koun′səl), *n.* **1** group of people called together to give advice and to discuss or settle questions. **2** group of persons elected by citizens to make laws for and manage a city or town. ■ Another word that sounds like this is **counsel.**

coun·cil·man (koun′səl mən), *n.* member of the council of a city or town. ❏ *n., pl.* **coun·cil·men.**

coun·ci·lor or **coun·cil·lor** (koun′sə lər), *n.* member of a council.

coun·cil·wo·man (koun′səl wú′mən), *n.* woman member of the council of a city or town. ❏ *n., pl.* **coun·cil·wo·men.**

coun·sel (koun′səl), **1** *n.* act of exchanging ideas; talking things over; consultation: *We benefited from our frequent counsel.* **2** *n.* advice: *A wise person gives good counsel.* **3** *n.* lawyer or group of lawyers: *Each side of a case in a court of law has its own counsel.* **4** *v.* to give advice to; advise: *She counsels sophomores to help them choose their courses.* **5** *v.* to recommend: *The doctor counseled operating at once.* ❏ *v.* **coun·seled, coun·sel·ing** or **coun·selled, coun·sel·ling.** ■ Another word that sounds like this is **council.**

coun·se·lor or **coun·sel·lor** (koun′sə lər), *n.* **1** person who gives advice; adviser. **2** adviser (def. 2). **3** lawyer. **4** instructor or leader in a summer camp.

count¹ (kount), **1** *v.* to name numbers in order: *to count from one to ten.* **2** *v.* to add up; find the number of: *I counted the books and found there were 50.* **3** *n.* act of adding up; a finding out how many: *The count showed that more than 5000 votes had been cast.* **4** *n.* the total number; amount: *The exact count was 5170 votes.* **5** *v.* to include or be included in the total number; take or be taken into account: *Your first race is only for practice; it won't count.* **6** *v.* to have an influence; be of account or value: *Every vote counts in an election.* **7** *v.* to think of as; consider: *Count yourself lucky in having good health!* **8** *n.* (in law) each charge in a formal accusation: *The accused was found guilty on all counts.*
count for, be worth.
count in, to include: *Count me in on the picnic.*
count off, to divide into equal groups by counting: *For the spelling bee, you may count off from the left.*
count on, **1** to expect; allow for: *I hadn't counted on your coming so early; I'm not ready yet.* **2** to depend; rely: *You can count on me for help.*
count out, **1** to fail to consider or include: *If you go skiing, count me out.* **2** to declare (a fallen boxer) the loser for failing to rise after 10 seconds have been counted.

WORD POWER **COUNTING** ■ Unicorn, bicycle, triangle, quadruped, quintuplet. Congratulations! You have just counted from 1 to 5 in prefixes. People say and write so many counting numbers that it is often quicker to make the number part of the word.

uni- (one)	**tri-** (three)	**quint-** (five)	**oct-** (eight)
mono- (one)	**quadr-** (four)	**sext-** (six)	**non-**² (nine)
bi- (two)	**tetra-** (four)	**sept-** (seven)	**deca-** (ten)
di- (two)			

For more number prefixes, see the Word Power at **size**¹.

count² (kount), *n.* a European nobleman having a rank about the same as that of an English earl.

count·a·ble (koun′tə bəl), *adj.* able to be counted: *countable objects.*

count·down (kount′doun′), *n.* **1** the calling out in order of the minutes or seconds left until an event, such as the launching of a rocket. **2** period of time during which this calling out occurs.

coun·te·nance (koun′tə nəns), **1** *n.* expression of the face. **2** *n.* face; features: *a person with a noble countenance.* **3** *v.* to approve; support; encourage: *I will not countenance such rude behavior.* **4** *n.* approval; support; encouragement: *I gave countenance to the plan, but no active help.* ❏ *v.* **coun·te·nanced, coun·te·nanc·ing.** —**coun′te·nanc·er,** *n.*

count·er¹ (koun′tər), *n.* **1** a long, flat, raised surface in a store, restaurant, bank, etc., on which money is counted out, and across which goods, food, or drinks are given to customers. **2** a flat space in a kitchen, usually over a cabinet, used to prepare food on. **3** thing used for counting. The beads on an abacus are counters.

count·er² (koun′tər), *n.* person or thing that counts.

coun·ter³ (koun′tər), **1** *adv., adj.* opposed; opposite; contrary: *He acted counter to his promise. Your plans are counter to ours.* **2** *v.* to act or go against; oppose: *She countered my plan with one of her own.* **3** *v.* to give a blow while receiving or blocking an opponent's blow: *The boxer countered with a right to the jaw.* **4** *n.* blow given while receiving or blocking an opponent's blow.

counter–, *prefix.* against; in opposition to: *counteract = act against. counterattack = attack in opposition to another attack.*

coun·ter·act (koun′tər akt′), *v.* to act against; neutralize the action or effect of: *A hot bath will sometimes counteract a chill.*

coun·ter·at·tack (koun′tər ə tak′), **1** *n.* attack made to counter another attack. **2** *v.* to make an attack in return.

coun·ter·bal·ance (koun′tər bal′əns *for noun;* koun′tər bal′-əns *for verb*), **1** *n.* weight balancing another weight; counterweight. **2** *n.* influence or power balancing or offsetting another: *The captain's coolness was a counterbalance to the crew's panic in the gale.* **3** *v.* to act as a counterbalance to; offset: *Her determination counterbalanced her natural shyness.* ❑ *v.* **coun·ter·bal·anced, coun·ter·bal·anc·ing.**

coun·ter·claim (koun′tər klām′), *n.* an opposing claim; claim made by a person to offset a claim made against him or her: *A counterclaim for damages was filed by the other driver.*

coun·ter·clock·wise (koun′tər klok′wīz′), *adv., adj.* in the direction opposite to that in which the hands of a clock go; from right to left.

coun·ter·es·pi·o·nage (koun′tər es′pē ə- näzh′), *n.* measures taken to prevent or confuse enemy espionage.

coun·ter·feit (koun′tər fit), **1** *v.* to copy money, handwriting, pictures, etc., in order to deceive or defraud: *They were arrested for counterfeiting twenty-dollar bills.* **2** *n.* a copy made to deceive or defraud and passed as genuine: *This twenty-dollar bill looks genuine, but it is a counterfeit.* **3** *adj.* not genuine; fake: *a counterfeit coin.* ■ See Synonym Study at **false. 4** *v.* to pretend: *She counterfeited interest to be polite.* **5** *adj.* pretended but not real: *counterfeit enthusiasm.* **–coun′ter·feit′er,** *n.*

coun·ter·in·tel·li·gence (koun′tər in tel′ə jəns), *n.* system or activity of counteracting the intelligence or spy activities of an enemy.

coun·ter·mand (koun′tər mand), *v.* to withdraw or cancel an order or command.

coun·ter·of·fen·sive (koun′tər ə fen′siv), *n.* an attack by a defending force against an attacking force.

coun·ter·pane (koun′tər pān′), *n.* an outer covering for a bed; bedspread.

coun·ter·part (koun′tər pärt′), *n.* **1** person or thing closely resembling another: *She is the counterpart of her twin sister.* **2** person or thing that complements or corresponds to another: *Night is the counterpart of day.*

coun·ter·point (koun′tər point′), *n.* **1** melody added to another as an accompaniment. **2** art of adding melodies to a given melody according to fixed rules.

coun·ter·pro·duc·tive (koun′tər prə duk′tiv), *adj.* producing results opposite to the desired ones: *The dog caught up with the skunk, but the result was counterproductive.*

coun·ter·rev·o·lu·tion (koun′tər rev′ə lü′shən), *n.* revolution against a government established by a previous revolution.

coun·ter·sign (koun′tər sin′), **1** *n.* a secret signal; password; watchword: *The spy was caught when he could not give the countersign to the sentry.* **2** *v.* to sign something already signed by another to confirm it: *The check was signed by the treasurer and countersigned by the president.*

coun·ter·sink (koun′tər singk′), *v.* **1** to enlarge the upper part of a hole to make room for the head of a screw or bolt. **2** to sink the head of a screw or bolt into such a hole so that it is even with or below the surface. ❑ *v.* **coun·ter·sunk** (koun′tər sungk′), **coun·ter·sink·ing.**

coun·ter·spy (koun′tər spi′), *n.* spy who works to uncover or oppose the activities of enemy spies. ❑ *n., pl.* **coun·ter·spies.**

coun·ter·ten·or (koun′tər ten′ər), *n.* **1** an adult male voice that is higher than a tenor. **2** singer with such a voice.

coun·ter·weight (koun′tər wāt′), *n.* counterbalance (def. 1).

count·ess (koun′tis), *n.* **1** wife or widow of a count or an earl. **2** woman whose rank is equal to that of a count or an earl. ❑ *n., pl.* **count·ess·es.**

count·ing·house (koun′ting hous′), *n.* (long ago) a building or office used for keeping accounts and doing business. ❑ *n., pl.* **count·ing·hous·es** (koun′ting hou′ziz).

count·less (kount′lis), *adj.* too many to count; very many; innumerable: *countless stars spread out against the night sky.* ■ See Synonym Study at **numerous.**

count noun, a noun which may form a plural, and may be preceded by *a* or *an. Log* is a count noun; *butter* is not.

coun·tri·fied (kun′tri fid), *adj.* looking or acting like someone from the country.

coun·try (kun′trē), **1** *n.* land, region, or district: *There are many cities and highways in the country along the river.* **2** *n.* the land of a group of people united under the same government and usually speaking the same language: *France is a country in Europe.* **3** *n.* land where someone was born or where he or she is a citizen: *The United States is my country.* **4** *n.* people of a nation: *The country rejoiced when the war ended.* **5** *n.* land outside of cities and towns: *the farms and fields of the country.* **6** *adj.* of the country; in the country; rural: *hearty country meals and fresh country air.* ❑ *n., pl.* **coun·tries** for 2,3.

country and western, country music.

country club, club on open land near a city, offering social and sports activities.

coun·try·man (kun′trē mən), *n.* person of your own country. ❑ *n., pl.* **coun·try·men.**

country music, folk music that originated in the southern United States, played with a guitar and other stringed instruments.

coun·try·side (kun′trē sid′), *n.* land outside of cities and towns; country.

countryside

coun·try·wom·an (kun′trē wùm′ən), *n.* woman of your own country. ❑ *n., pl.* **coun·try·wom·en.**

coun·ty (koun′tē), *n.* **1** one of the districts into which a state, country, province, or other large political unit is divided for purposes of local government. The county officers collect taxes, hold court, keep county roads in repair, and maintain county schools. **2** people of a county: *The whole county voted against the plan.* **3** the officials of a county. ❑ *n., pl.* **coun·ties.**

county agent, a U.S. government specialist who informs and advises farmers and rural communities about agriculture and home economics.

county seat, town or city where the county government is located.

coup (kü), *n.* **1** a sudden, brilliant action; unexpected, clever move; master stroke. **2** coup d'état. ❑ *n., pl.* **coups** (küz). ■ Another word that sounds like this is **coo.**

coup d'é·tat (kü′ dā tä′), a sudden, decisive act in politics, usually bringing about a change in government unlawfully or by force. ❑ *n., pl.* **coups d'état** (kü′ dā tä′).

coupe (küp), *n.* a closed, two-door car, usually seating two to six people. ■ Another word that sounds like this is **coop.**

a	hat	ė	term	ô	order	ch	child		a in about
ā	age	i	it	oi	oil	ng	long		e in taken
ä	far	ī	ice	ou	out	sh	she	ə	i in pencil
â	care	o	hot	u	cup	th	thin		o in lemon
e	let	ō	open	ù	put	ŦH	then		u in circus
ē	equal	ȯ	saw	ü	rule	zh	measure		

cou·pé (kü pā′), *n.* **1** coupe. **2** (earlier) a four-wheeled, closed carriage with a seat for two people inside and a seat for the driver outside. ❑ *n., pl.* **cou·pés.**

cou·ple (kup′əl), **1** *n.* two things of the same kind that go together; pair: *I bought a couple of tires for my bicycle.* **2** *n.* a small number; a few: *Give me a couple of those apples—about four of them.* **3** *n.* man and woman who are married, engaged, partners in a dance, etc. **4** *v.* to join together: *Two extra cars were coupled to the crowded commuter train.* ❑ *v.* **cou·pled, cou·pling.**

cou·pler (kup′lər), *n.* **1** person or thing that couples. **2** device used to join two railroad cars; coupling.

cou·plet (kup′lit), *n.* two successive lines of poetry, especially two that rhyme and have the same number of feet.

> EXAMPLE: You may think that toads look horrible,
> But toads find other toads adorable.

cou·pling (kup′ling), *n.* **1** device for joining together parts of machinery. **2** coupler. **3** act of joining together.

cou·pon (kü′pon), *n.* **1** a small piece of paper or part of a package or an advertisement that gives the person who holds it certain rights: *If she saves the coupons that come with each box of soap, she can get a free camera.* **2** a printed statement of interest due on a bond, which can be cut from the bond and presented for payment.

WORD STORY   Coupon comes from a French word meaning "to cut." People cut coupons from newspapers, magazines, or packages to get lower prices. Originally, coupons were cut off bonds and turned in for money.

cour·age (kėr′ij), *n.* bravery; mental ability to meet danger without fear; fearlessness: *The pioneers faced the hardships of the westward trek with courage.*

WORD STORY   Courage comes from a Latin word meaning "heart." People today still say that someone "has a lot of heart" when they mean that person has courage.

cou·ra·geous (kə rā′jəs), *adj.* full of courage; brave; fearless. ■ See Synonym Study at **brave.** —**cou·ra′geous·ly,** *adv.* —**cou·ra′geous·ness,** *n.*

cou·reur de bois (kü rėr′ də bwä′), (long ago) a hunter and trapper in French Canadian settlements and nearby parts of North America. ❑ *n., pl.* **cou·reurs de bois** (kü rėr′ də bwä′).

cour·i·er (kėr′ē ər *or* kür′ē ər), *n.* messenger that carries important documents.

course (kôrs), **1** *n.* onward movement; forward progress; advance: *Our history book traces the course of human development from the cave to modern city living.* **2** *n.* direction taken: *Our course was straight to the north.* **3** *n.* line of action; way of doing: *The only sensible course was to go home.* **4** *n.* way, path, track, or channel: *the winding course of the stream.* **5** *n.* number of like things arranged in some regular order: *a course of lectures.* **6** *n.* regular order: *the course of nature.* **7** *n.* series of studies in a school, college, or university. A student must complete a certain course in order to graduate. **8** *n.* one of the studies in such a series: *Each course in history lasts one year.* **9** *n.* part of a meal served at one time: *Soup was the first course and dessert was the last course.* **10** *n.* area marked out for races or games: *a golf course, a race course.* **11** *v.* to run: *tears coursing down the cheeks, blood coursing through his veins.* ❑ *v.* **coursed, coursing.** ■ Another word that sounds like this is **coarse.**

in due course, in the right order; at the proper time: *I'll attend to that business in due course.*

in the course of, during; in the process of: *He mentioned you a few times in the course of our discussion.*

of course, 1 surely; certainly: *Of course you can go!* **2** naturally; as should be expected: *She gave me a gift, and, of course, I accepted it.*

on course, moving in the right direction: *a spaceship on course for Mars.*

course·ware (kôrs′wâr′), *n.* lessons written for use on a computer or with a computer: *The algebra courseware includes a computer game and a book of problems.*

court (kôrt), **1** *n.* place where justice is administered; court of law: *The case will be heard in court next week.* **2** *n.* persons who are chosen to administer justice; judge or judges: *The court found her guilty.* **3** *n.* assembly of such persons to administer justice: *Court is now in session.* **4** *n.* household and followers of a king, queen, or other ruler: *The court of King Solomon was noted for its splendor.* **5** *n.* assembly held by a king, queen, or other ruler: *The queen held court to hear from her advisers.* **6** *n.* ruler and his or her advisers as a ruling group or power: *"By order of the Court of St. James's" is by order of the British government.* **7** *n.* space partly or wholly enclosed by walls or buildings: *The four apartment houses were built around a central grass court.* **8** *n.* a short street. **9** *n.* place marked off for a game: *a tennis court, a basketball court.* **10** *n.* place where a king, queen, or other ruler lives; royal palace. **11** *v.* to seek the favor of; try to please: *The nobles courted the king to gain power.* **12** *v.* to pay loving attention to in order to marry; woo: *The young man courted the young woman by bringing her flowers every day.* **13** *v.* to try to get; seek: *It is foolish to court danger.*

pay court to, to pay attention to someone to get favor; try to please: *pay court to a high official.*

cour·te·ous (kėr′tē əs), *adj.* thoughtful of others; polite: *The clerks are always courteous at this store.* ■ See Synonym Study at **polite.** —**cour′te·ous·ly,** *adv.* —**cour′te·ous·ness,** *n.*

cour·te·sy (kėr′tə sē), *n.* **1** polite behavior; thoughtfulness for others: *It is a sign of courtesy to give your seat to an old person on a crowded bus.* **2** a courteous act or expression: *Thanks for all your courtesies.* ❑ *n., pl.* **cour·te·sies** for 2.

WORD STORY   Courtesy comes from an old form of **court.** It described the kinds of polite good manners suitable for a royal court. Curtsy comes from **courtesy.** At first it meant any good manners, but later it was used about one special way to show respect.

court·house (kôrt′hous′), *n.* **1** building in which courts of law meet. **2** building used for the government of a county. ❑ *n., pl.* **court·hous·es** (kôrt′hou′ziz).

cour·ti·er (kôr′tē ər), *n.* **1** person often present at a royal court; court attendant. **2** person who tries to win the favor of another through flattery.

court·ly (kôrt′lē), *adj.* having manners fit for a royal court; polite, elegant, or polished: *The courtly gentleman was a favorite with the ladies.* ❑ *adj.* **court·li·er, court·li·est.** —**court′li·ness,** *n.*

courthouse (def. 1)

court–mar·tial (kôrt′mär′shəl), **1** *n.* a military court for trying offenders against the laws of the armed forces. **2** *n.* trial by a military court. **3** *v.* to try by a military court. ❑ *n., pl.* **courts-mar·tial** or **court-martials;** *v.* **court-mar·tialed, court·mar·tialled, court·mar·tial·ing** or **court·mar·tial·ling.**

court of law, place where justice is administered; law court.

court·room (kôrt′rüm′), *n.* room in which courts of law meet.

court·ship (kôrt′ship), *n.* condition or time of courting in order to marry; wooing: *Their brief courtship was a very happy one.*

court·yard (kôrt′yärd′), *n.* space enclosed by walls, in or near a large building.

cous·in (kuz′n), *n.* **1** son or daughter of an uncle or aunt. First cousins have the same grandparents; second cousins have the same great-grandparents; and so on for third and fourth cousins, etc. **2** a distant relative. **3** citizen of a related nation. [Cousin comes from a Latin word meaning "mother's sister's child." Many languages have words for this kind of very specific relationship, but English uses more general words.] ■ Another word that sounds like this is **cozen.**

Cous·teau (kü stō′), *n.* **Jacques-Yves** (zhäk′ ēv′), born 1910, French author and undersea explorer. ■ Jacques Cousteau helped invent the Aqua-Lung, and three of his films about sea life have won Academy awards.

co·va·lent bond (kō vā′lənt), a chemical bond in which two atoms share electrons.

cove (kōv), *n.* **1** a small, sheltered bay; inlet on the shore. **2** a sheltered place among hills or woods.

cov·e·nant (kuv′ə nənt), *n.* a solemn agreement between two or more persons or groups: *The rival nations signed a covenant to reduce their armaments.*

cov·er (kuv′ər), **1** *v.* to put something over: *I covered the child with a blanket.* **2** *v.* to be over; occupy the surface of; spread over: *Snow covered the ground.* **3** *n.* anything that is put over, protects, or hides. Books have covers. A box, can, or jar usually has a cover. A blanket is a cover. **4** *v.* to hide: *She tried to cover her mistake.* **5** *v.* to defend from attack; protect: *One soldier ran for the trench, while the others covered him by firing at the enemy.* **6** *v.* to protect against financial loss: *Our insurance covers our belongings against fire and theft.* **7** *n.* protection; shelter: *We took cover in an old shed during the storm. The burglar escaped under cover of darkness.* **8** *v.* to go over; travel: *The travelers covered 400 miles a day by car.* **9** *v.* to take in; include: *The math review covers everything we studied.* **10** *v.* to be enough for; provide for: *My allowance covers my lunch at school.* **11** *v.* (in sports) to protect defensively: *The shortstop covered second base on all throws from right field.* **12** *v.* to report or photograph events, meetings, etc.: *A reporter covered the fire for the newspaper.* **13** *v.* to aim straight at: *cover a target with a rifle.* —**cov′er·a·ble,** *adj.* —**cov′er·er,** *n.* —**cov′er·less,** *adj.*

cover up, 1 to cover completely. **2** to hide; conceal.

under cover, 1 hidden; secret: *He kept his activities under cover.* **2** secretly: *Spies work under cover.*

cov·er·age (kuv′ər ij), *n.* **1** risks covered by an insurance policy: *She has fire coverage on her belongings.* **2** way of presenting information by a reporter, newspaper, etc.: *The President's inauguration got broad coverage on radio and TV.*

cov·er·alls (kuv′ər ôlz), *n.pl.* a one-piece work garment that includes shirt and trousers.

covered wagon, wagon having a canvas cover that can be taken off.

cov·er·ing (kuv′ər ing), *n.* thing that covers: *bed coverings.*

cov·er·let (kuv′ər lit), *n.* a covering, especially a covering for a bed.

cov·ert (kō′vèrt′ *or* kuv′ərt), *adj.* kept from sight; secret; hidden: *The children cast covert glances at the box of candy they were told not to touch.* —**cov′ert·ly,** *adv.*

cov·er-up (kuv′ər up′), *n.* something that covers up or hides an evil or criminal act: *Legally, a cover-up of a crime is itself a crime.*

cov·et (kuv′it), *v.* to desire eagerly something that belongs to another: *Her friends coveted her new bicycle.*

cov·et·ous (kuv′ə təs), *adj.* desiring things that belong to others. —**cov′et·ous·ly,** *adv.* —**cov′et·ous·ness,** *n.*

cov·ey (kuv′ē), *n.* **1** a small flock of partridges, quail, etc. **2** a small group; band; set. ❑ *n., pl.* **cov·eys.**

cow[1] (kou), *n.* **1** the full-grown female of domestic cattle, which gives milk. **2** female of the buffalo, moose, and other large mammals: *an elephant cow.* —**cow′like′,** *adj.*

cow[2] (kou), *v.* to make afraid; frighten: *I was cowed by their threats and stayed out of their sight.*

cow·ard (kou′ərd), *n.* person who lacks courage or is easily made afraid; person who runs from danger, trouble, etc. [Coward comes from a Latin word meaning "a tail." A frightened animal tucks its tail between its legs.]

cow·ard·ice (kou′ər dis), *n.* lack of courage; being easily made afraid: *to be guilty of cowardice in the presence of danger.*

cow·ard·ly (kou′ərd lē), **1** *adj.* lacking courage. **2** *adj.* of a coward; suitable for a coward. **3** *adv.* in a cowardly manner. —**cow′ard·li·ness,** *n.*

cow·bell (kou′bel′), *n.* bell hung around a cow's neck so that she can be found.

cow·bird (kou′bèrd′), *n.* either of two small North American blackbirds that lay their eggs in the nests of other birds.

cow·boy (kou′boi′), *n.* man who works on a cattle ranch or at rodeos.

cow·catch·er (kou′kach′ər), *n.* (earlier) a metal frame on the front of a steam locomotive, streetcar, etc., to clear the tracks of anything in the way; fender.

cow·er (kou′ər), *v.* to crouch or draw back in fear or shame: *The dog cowered under the table after being scolded.*

cow·girl (kou′gèrl′), *n.* woman who works on a cattle ranch or at rodeos.

cow·hand (kou′hand′), *n.* person who works on a cattle ranch.

cow·herd (kou′hèrd′), *n.* person whose work is looking after cattle that are grazing.

cow·hide (kou′hīd′), **1** *n.* leather made from the hide of a cow. **2** *n.* the hide of a cow. **3** *n.* a strong, heavy whip made of rawhide or braided leather. **4** *v.* to whip with a cowhide; flog. ❑ *v.* **cow·hid·ed, cow·hid·ing.**

cowgirl

cowl (koul), *n.* **1** a monk's cloak with a hood. **2** the hood itself. **3** the part of an car body that includes the windshield, the dashboard, and sometimes the hood. **4** cowling.

cow·lick (kou′lik′), *n.* a small tuft of hair that will not lie flat.

cowl·ing (kou′ling), *n.* a metal covering over the engine of an airplane; cowl.

cow·man (kou′mən), *n.* **1** owner of cattle. **2** cowboy. ❑ *n., pl.* **cow·men.**

co·work·er (kō′wèr′kər), *n.* person who works with another.

cow·pea (kou′pē′), *n.* **1** plant related to the pea plant, grown in the southern United States for cattle feed and soil improvement. **2** seed of this plant, used as food for humans; black-eyed pea. ❑ *n., pl.* **cow·peas.**

cow·poke (kou′pōk′), *n.* INFORMAL. cowboy.

cow pony, a pony used in herding cattle.

cow·pox (kou′poks′), *n.* a contagious disease of cows. Vaccine for smallpox is obtained from cows that have cowpox.

cow·punch·er (kou′pun′chər), *n.* INFORMAL. cowboy.

cow·rie *or* **cow·ry** (kou′rē), *n.* the brightly colored, smooth shell of a tropical mollusk, used as money in some parts of Africa and Asia. ❑ *n., pl.* **cow·ries.**

cow·slip (kou′slip′), *n.* any of various unrelated wildflowers, including the marsh marigold.

cox (koks), *n.* INFORMAL. person who steers a rowboat, racing boat, or the like. ❑ *n., pl.* **cox·es.**

cox·comb (koks′kōm′), *n.* a vain man; conceited dandy. ∎ Another word that sounds like this is **cockscomb.**

cox·swain (kok′sən *or* kok′swān′), *n.* cox.

coy (koi), *adj.* **1** acting more shy than you really are. **2** shy or modest; bashful. [Coy comes from a Latin word meaning "quiet." Pretending to be shy often means being quiet, in hope that someone will urge you to speak.] —**coy′ly,** *adv.* —**coy′ness,** *n.*

coy·o·te (kī ō′tē *or* ki′ōt), *n.* **1** a small wolflike mammal living in many parts of North America. It is noted for loud howling at night. **2** Coyote, (in American Indian myths) a supernatural being, often described as a trickster, linked in stories with the creation of the world and human beings and with providing such human necessities as fire. ❑ *n., pl.* **coy·o·tes** *or* **coy·o·te** for 1.

coy·pu (koi′pü), *n.* nutria (def. 1). ❑ *n., pl.* **coy·pus** *or* **coy·pu.**

coz·en (kuz′n), *v.* OLD USE. to deceive or trick; cheat. ∎ Another word that sounds like this is **cousin.** —**coz′en·er,** *n.*

co·zy (kō′zē), **1** *adj.* warm and comfortable; snug: *The cat lay in a cozy corner near the fireplace.* **2** *n.* a padded cloth cover to keep a teapot warm. ❑ *adj.* **co·zi·er, co·zi·est;** *n., pl.* **co·zies.** Also, **cosy.** —**co′zi·ly,** *adv.* —**co′zi·ness,** *n.*

cp., compare.

c.p., candlepower.

a	hat	ė	term	ô	order	ch	child		
ā	age	i	it	oi	oil	ng	long		a in about
ä	far	ī	ice	ou	out	sh	she	ə	i in taken
â	care	o	hot	u	cup	th	thin		i in pencil
e	let	ō	open	ů	put	₮H	then		o in lemon
ē	equal	ò	saw	ü	rule	zh	measure		u in circus

C.P., Communist Party.

C.P.A., Certified Public Accountant.

cpd., compound.

Cpl., corporal.

CPR, cardiopulmonary resuscitation (technique used to revive victims of heart attack, drowning, etc., involving mouth-to-mouth breathing and rhythmical pressure on the breastbone which forces the heart to pump).

cps, cycles per second.

CPU, central processing unit (the part of a computer that carries out instructions and processes data).

Cr, symbol for chromium.

C.R., Costa Rica.

crab[1] (krab), **1** *n.* any of very many broad, flat shellfish with four pairs of legs and one pair of claws. Many kinds of crabs are good to eat. **2** *v.* to catch crabs for eating. **3** *n.* a cross, sour person. **4** *v.* INFORMAL. to find fault; criticize: *Don't crab so much.* ❏ *v.* **crabbed, crab·bing.** —**crab′ber,** *n.* —**crab′like′,** *adj.*

crab[2] (krab), *n.* crab apple.

crab apple, 1 a small, sour apple, used to make jelly. **2** any of numerous small trees bearing such fruit.

crab·bed (krab′id), *adj.* **1** hard to read or decipher because irregular: *crabbed handwriting.* **2** crabby. —**crab′bed·ly,** *adv.* —**crab′bed·ness,** *n.*

crab·by (krab′ē), *adj.* bad-tempered or ill-natured; crabbed. ❏ *adj.* **crab·bi·er, crab·bi·est.**

crab·grass (krab′gras′), *n.* a kind of coarse grass that spreads rapidly and spoils lawns.

crack (krak), **1** *n.* split or opening made by breaking without separating into parts: *There is a crack in this cup.* **2** *v.* to break without separating into parts: *You have cracked the mirror.* **3** *n.* a narrow opening: *I can see between the cracks in the old floorboards.* **4** *n.* a sudden, sharp noise like that made by something breaking, by a whip, or by loud thunder. **5** *v.* to make or cause to make a sudden, sharp noise: *The stagecoach driver cracked the whip.* **6** *v.* to break with a sudden, sharp noise: *The tree cracked and fell. We cracked the nuts.* **7** *n.* a hard, sharp blow: *The falling branch gave me a crack on the head.* **8** *v.* to hit with a hard, sharp blow: *The falling branch cracked me on the head.* **9** *v.* to make or become harsh, broken, or shrill: *His voice cracked with emotion.* **10** *v.* to give way; break down: *His mind cracked under the strain of working for three days without sleep.* **11** *v.* to break into: *The burglar cracked the safe.* **12** *adj.* INFORMAL. excellent; first-rate: *She was a crack shot.* **13** *n.* INFORMAL. a try; effort: *She took a crack at the job and succeeded.* **14** *n.* a funny or clever remark, especially an insulting one: *If you make another crack about my singing, you'll be sorry.* **15** *v.* INFORMAL. to tell or say something funny or clever: *She cracked a joke.* **16** *v.* to figure out the meaning of a code; decipher: *In wartime each enemy tries to crack the other's code.* **17** *n.* Also, **crack cocaine,** a very dangerous, potent form of cocaine. **18** *v.* to separate petroleum into various substances for refining.

crack a book, to open a schoolbook; begin to study: *She hasn't cracked a book yet, although the test is tomorrow.*

crack a smile, to smile, usually unwillingly: *I thought the cartoon was funny, but my brother barely cracked a smile.*

crack down, to take stern measures: *The police intend to crack down on speeders.*

crack of dawn, very early time of day.

crack up, 1 to crash; smash: *The driver skidded off the road and cracked up his car against a tree.* **2** to suffer a mental or physical collapse: *She was in danger of cracking up under the strain of overwork.* **3** to burst out laughing.

cracked up to be, believed or stated to be: *That book is not what it is cracked up to be.*

crack·down (krak′doun′), *n.* act of taking stern measures or swift disciplinary action: *a crackdown on speeders.*

cracked (krakt), *adj.* **1** broken without separating into parts: *a cracked cup.* **2** broken into parts: *cracked ice.* **3** having harsh notes; uneven; broken: *a cracked voice.* **4** INFORMAL. mentally ill.

■ This use of **cracked** is considered offensive.

crack·er (krak′ər), *n.* **1** a thin, crisp wafer. **2** firecracker.

crack·er·jack (krak′ər jak′), INFORMAL. **1** *n.* person or thing of superior ability or grade: *She is a crackerjack at dominoes.* **2** *adj.* of superior ability or grade: *a crackerjack motorboat.*

crack·ing (krak′ing), *n.* process of changing petroleum and other oils into products such as gasoline and jet fuel, by heat, pressure, and a catalyst.

get cracking, to start working; get going: *I'd better get cracking on that report.*

crack·le (krak′əl), **1** *v.* to make slight, sharp sounds: *A fire crackled in the fireplace.* **2** *n.* a slight, sharp sound, such as paper makes when crushed. **3** *n.* very small cracks made in the surface of some kinds of china or glass. ❏ *v.* **crack·led, crack·ling.**

crack·ling (krak′ling), *n.* the crisp, browned skin of roasted pork.

crack·pot (krak′pot′), INFORMAL. **1** *n.* a very eccentric or strange person. **2** *adj.* eccentric or impractical.

crack·up (krak′up′), *n.* **1** a crash; smash-up: *That reckless driver has been in more than one car crackup.* **2** INFORMAL. a mental or physical collapse; breakdown.

cra·dle (krā′dl), **1** *n.* a small bed for a baby, usually mounted on rockers. **2** *v.* to hold as if in a cradle: *She cradled the baby in her arms.* **3** *n.* place where anything begins its growth: *The sea is thought to have been the cradle of life.* **4** *n.* frame to support a ship or other large object while it is being built, repaired, or lifted. **5** *n.* the part of the telephone that supports the receiver. **6** *n.* box on rockers to wash earth from gold or other metals. **7** *v.* to wash earth from gold or other metals in a cradle. ❏ *v.* **cra·dled, cra·dling.** —**cra′dle·like′,** *adj.*

cra·dle·board (krā′dl bôrd′), *n.* a small, portable wooden frame used by North American Indians for carrying an infant.

craft (kraft), **1** *n.* special skill: *The expert carpenter shaped and fitted the wood with great craft.* **2** *n.* trade or art requiring skilled work: *Carpentry is a craft.* **3** *v.* to work, make, or finish with skill or art: *woodwork crafted by expert cabinetmakers.* **4** *n.* skill in deceiving others; slyness; trickiness: *By craft the swindler tricked them out of all their money.* **5** *n.pl.* boats or ships: *Craft of all kinds come into New York every day.* **6** *n.* a boat or ship: *A strange craft sailed into the harbor.* ❏ *n., pl.* **crafts** for 2,6, **craft** for 5.

crafts·man (krafts′mən), *n.* **1** person skilled in a craft or trade. **2** artist. ❏ *n., pl.* **crafts·men.**

crafts·man·ship (krafts′mən ship), *n.* work or skill of a craftsman.

crafts·wo·man (krafts′wu̇ mən), *n.* **1** woman skilled in a craft or trade. **2** artist. ❏ *n., pl.* **crafts·wo·men.**

craft union, a labor union made up of persons in the same craft. Unions of carpenters, plumbers, or bricklayers are craft unions.

craft·y (kraf′tē), *adj.* skillful in deceiving others; sly; tricky: *a crafty schemer.* ■ See Synonym Study at **sly.** ❏ *adj.* **craft·i·er, craft·i·est.** —**craft′i·ly,** *adv.* —**craft′i·ness,** *n.*

crag (krag), *n.* a steep, rugged rock rising above others. —**crag′like′,** *adj.*

crag·gy (krag′ē), *adj.* **1** having many crags; steep and rugged: *The craggy hill was difficult to climb.* **2** rough; uneven: *The old fisherman had a craggy, weathered face.* ❏ *adj.* **crag·gi·er, crag·gi·est.** —**crag′gi·ness,** *n.*

cram (kram), *v.* **1** to force into; force down; stuff: *I crammed all my books and papers into my locker.* **2** to fill too full; crowd: *The bus was crammed, with many people standing.* **3** to eat too fast or too much: *She felt ill after she crammed down her lunch.* **4** to try to learn a lot in a short time: *Having studied very little during the year, he has to cram for his finals.* ❏ *v.* **crammed, cram·ming.** —**cram′mer,** *n.*

cramp (kramp), **1** *v.* to shut into a small space; limit: *In only three rooms, the family was cramped.* **2** *n.* a sudden, painful contracting or pulling together of muscles, often from chill or strain: *The swimmer was seized with a cramp and had to be helped from the pool.* **3** *n.pl.* **cramps,** very sharp pains in the abdomen. **4** *v.* to cause to have a cramp: *The green apples she ate cramped her stomach.* **5** *n.* a metal bar bent at both ends. It is used for holding together blocks of stone, timbers, etc. **6** *v.* to turn sharply to one side or the other; steer: *The driver had to cramp the front wheels to get out of the tight parking space.*

crater (def. 2)

cran·ber·ry (kran′ber′ē), *n.* a firm, sour, dark red berry, used for sauce, juice, and jelly. It grows on several kinds of low bushes found in marshes or bogs. □ *n., pl.* **cran·ber·ries.**

crane (krān), **1** *n.* machine with a long, swinging arm, for lifting and moving heavy weights. **2** *n.* any of several large wading birds with long legs, necks, and bills. **3** *v.* to stretch the neck as a crane does, in order to see better: *The little girl craned her neck to see the parade over the heads of the crowd.* □ *v.* **craned, cran·ing.**

crane (def. 2)—about 4 ft. (1.2 m) long

Crane (krān), *n.* **Steph·en** (stē′vən), 1871-1900, American writer. He wrote *The Red Badge of Courage,* short stories, and poems.

cra·ni·al (krā′nē əl), *adj.* of or about the skull: *cranial nerves.* —**cra′ni·al·ly,** *adv.*

cra·ni·um (krā′nē əm), *n.* **1** the skull of any animal that has a backbone. **2** the part of the skull that encloses the brain. □ *n., pl.* **cra·ni·ums, cra·ni·a** (krā′nē ə).

crank (krangk), **1** *n.* part or handle of a machine connected at right angles to a shaft to set it in motion. **2** *v.* to work or start by means of a crank: *Car engines used to be cranked by hand.* **3** *n.* INFORMAL. person who has strange ideas or habits; odd person.

crank·case (krangk′kās′), *n.* a heavy, metal case forming the bottom of an internal-combustion engine. It contains lubricating oil and encloses the crankshaft.

crank·shaft (krangk′shaft′), *n.* shaft turning or turned by a crank. The crankshaft of an internal-combustion engine is connected to the pistons by piston rods.

crank·y (krang′kē), *adj.* cross; irritable. □ *adj.* **crank·i·er, crank·i·est.** ■ See Synonym Study at **cross.** —**crank′i·ly,** *adv.* —**crank′i·ness,** *n.*

cran·ny (kran′ē), *n.* a small, narrow opening; crack; crevice: *She looked in all the nooks and crannies of the house for the misplaced book.* □ *n., pl.* **cran·nies.**

Crans·ton (kranz′tən), *n.* city in NE Rhode Island.

crap·pie (krap′ē), *n.* either of two small freshwater fishes of North America, used for food. □ *n., pl.* **crappies** or **crappie.**

crash (krash), **1** *n.* a sudden, loud noise like many dishes falling and breaking: *a crash of thunder.* **2** *v.* to make a sudden, loud noise: *The cymbals crashed.* **3** *v.* to fall, hit, or break with force and a loud noise: *The plate crashed to the floor.* **4** *n.* the violent striking of one thing against another; collision: *a two-car crash.* **5** *v.* to strike violently and shatter: *The baseball crashed through the window.* **6** *v.* to fall to the earth in such a way as to be damaged or wrecked: *The airplane went out of control and crashed.* **7** *n.* such a fall or landing: *an airplane crash.* **8** *n.* sudden ruin; severe failure in business: *the stock market crash.* **9** *v.* to go to a

party or dance without being invited. **10** *v.* (of a computer or computer part) to stop functioning because of a problem in the equipment or an error in the computer program. □ *n., pl.* **crash·es.** —**crash′er,** *n.*

crash helmet, a heavily padded head covering worn by racecar drivers, motorcyclists, etc.

crash landing, an emergency landing of an aircraft, so that a crash results. —**crash-land,** *v.*

crass (kras), *adj.* gross or stupid; extremely insensitive: *crass ignorance.* —**crass′ly,** *adv.* —**crass′ness,** *n.*

crate (krāt), **1** *n.* a large frame or box made of strips of wood. Crates are often used to pack furniture, glass, china, or fruit for shipping or storage. **2** *v.* to pack in a crate: *crate a mirror for moving.* □ *v.* **crat·ed, crat·ing.** [See Word Story at **grill.**]

cra·ter (krā′tər), *n.* **1** a bowl-shaped hole around the opening of a volcano. **2** a bowl-shaped hole on the surface of the earth, moon, etc.: *The meteorite crashed to earth, forming a huge crater.* —**cra′ter·like′,** *adj.*

Crater Lake National Park, a national park in SW Oregon, including volcanic **Crater Lake,** the deepest lake in the United States, 1932 feet (589 meters) deep.

cra·vat (krə vat′), *n.* necktie, especially a wide one.

crave (krāv), *v.* **1** to long for greatly; desire strongly: *The thirsty hiker craved water.* ■ See Synonym Study at **want. 2** to ask earnestly for; beg: *He craved a favor of the king.* □ *v.* **craved, crav·ing.**

cra·ven (krā′vən), **1** *adj.* cowardly. **2** *n.* coward. —**cra′ven·ly,** *adv.* —**cra′ven·ness,** *n.*

crav·ing (krā′ving), *n.* a strong desire; great longing; yearning: *a craving for fresh fruit.*

craw (krò), *n.* **1** crop of a bird or insect. **2** stomach of any animal.

craw·fish (krò′fish′), *n.* crayfish. □ *n., pl.* **craw·fish** or **craw·fish·es.**

Craw·ford (krò′fərd), *n.* **Joan,** 1906-1977, American movie star. She won an Academy Award in 1945 for the movie *Mildred Pierce.*

crawl (kròl), **1** *v.* to move slowly with the body close to the ground: *Babies crawl before they begin to walk. Worms and snakes crawl.* **2** *v.* to move on hands and knees: *We crawled through a hole in the fence.* **3** *v.* to move slowly: *The heavy traffic crawled through the narrow tunnel.* **4** *n.* act of crawling; slow movement: *Traffic had slowed to a crawl.* **5** *v.* to swarm with crawling things: *The ground under the garbage can was crawling with ants.* **6** *v.* to feel as if things were creeping over the skin: *My flesh crawled when I saw a big snake.* **7** *n.* a fast way of swimming by overarm strokes and rapid kicking of the feet; freestyle. **8** *v.* to swim this way.

crawler tractor, tractor that can travel over very rough ground on its two endless tracks.

crawl·y (krò′lē), *adj.* **1** feeling as if things were crawling over your skin; creepy: *Just looking at a spider makes me feel crawly.* **2** crawling: *Some people hate spiders and other crawly things.* □ *adj.* **crawl·i·er, crawl·i·est.**

cray·fish (krā′fish′), *n.* any of numerous freshwater shellfish that look much like small lobsters. □ *n., pl.* **cray·fish** or **cray·fish·es.** Also, **crawfish.**

WORD STORY **Crayfish** comes from a French word spelled *crevice* (krə vēs′). Because the animal lives in water, people in England spelled and pronounced *-vice* as *fish.*

Cray·o·la (krā′ō′lə), *n.* trademark for a brand of crayons.

cray·on (krā′on *or* krā′ən), **1** *n.* stick or pencil of chalk, charcoal, or a waxlike, colored substance, used for drawing or writing. **2** *v.* to draw with a crayon or crayons. **3** *n.* drawing made with a crayon or crayons.

craze (krāz), **1** *n.* a short-lived, eager interest in doing some one thing; fad: *The craze for flying kites was soon replaced by another for skateboards.* **2** *v.* to make or become unreasonable or

a	hat	ė	term	ô	order	ch	child		ə { a in about
ā	age	i	it	oi	oil	ng	long		e in taken
ä	far	ī	ice	ou	out	sh	she	ə { i in pencil
â	care	o	hot	u	cup	th	thin		o in lemon
e	let	ō	open	ù	put	ŦH	then		u in circus
ē	equal	ò	saw	ü	rule	zh	measure		

uncontrolled: *to be crazed with pain.* **3** *v.* to make very small cracks on the surface of pottery during the glazing process. ❑ *v.* **crazed, craz·ing.**

cra·zy (krā′zē), *adj.* **1** mentally ill; mad; insane. **2** greatly distressed or shaken by strong emotion: *The parents of the kidnapped child were crazy with worry.* **3** unwise or senseless; foolish: *It was a crazy idea to jump out of such a high tree.* **4** very eager or enthusiastic: *She is so crazy about cats that she has 15 of them.* **5** not strong or sound; shaky: *That crazy light blinks on and off whenever anyone slams the door.* ❑ *adj.* **cra·zi·er, cra·zi·est. —cra′zi·ly,** *adv.* **—cra′zi·ness,** *n.*

like crazy, furiously; very hard, fast, etc.: *We rehearsed like crazy to get ready for the show.*

> **USAGE NOTE** **Crazy** is not a polite word to describe a person with mental illness. Careful writers and speakers do not use *crazy, lunatic, mad,* and similar words except to mean "very foolish or unreasonable."

crazy bone, funny bone.

Crazy Horse, 1844?-1877, American Indian leader. ■ Crazy Horse was a leader of the Lakota Sioux. When the U.S. government ordered the Sioux to go to a reservation, they refused and fought. Crazy Horse led Sioux and Cheyenne warriors to victory over George Custer in 1876. He was killed by a soldier after he surrendered in 1877.

crazy quilt, quilt made of pieces of cloth of various shapes, colors, and sizes, sewed together with no definite pattern.

crazy quilt

creak (krēk), **1** *v.* to squeak loudly: *The hinges on the door creaked because they needed oiling.* **2** *n.* a loud squeaking noise: *The creak of the stairs in the old house was spooky.* ■ Another word that can sound like this is **creek.**

creak·y (krē′kē), *adj.* likely to squeak; squeaking: *a creaky floor.* ❑ *adj.* **creak·i·er, creak·i·est. —creak′i·ly,** *adv.*

cream (krēm), **1** *n.* the oily, yellowish part of milk. Cream rises to the top when milk that is not homogenized is allowed to stand. Butter is made from cream. **2** *n.* a fancy sweet dessert or candy made of cream: *chocolate creams.* **3** *v.* to cook with cream, milk, or a sauce made of cream or milk with butter and flour. **4** *v.* to make into a smooth mixture like cream: *I creamed the butter and sugar together for a cake.* **5** *n.* any preparation like cream that is put on the skin: *shaving cream.* **6** *n.* a yellowish white. **7** *adj.* yellowish white: *cream lace.* **8** *n.* the best or choicest part of anything: *the cream of the crop.* **9** *v.* SLANG. to defeat completely.

cream cheese, a soft, white cheese made from cream, or milk and cream.

cream·er (krē′mər), *n.* **1** a small pitcher for holding cream. **2** a nondairy substitute for cream, used especially in coffee or tea.

cream·er·y (krē′mər ē), *n.* **1** place where butter and cheese are made. **2** place where cream, milk, and butter are bought and sold. ❑ *n., pl.* **cream·er·ies.**

cream of tartar, a white powder obtained from the deposit in wine casks, used in baking powder and in medicine.

cream·y (krē′mē), *adj.* **1** like cream; smooth and soft. **2** having much cream in it: *pie with a rich, creamy filling.* ❑ *adj.* **cream·i·er, cream·i·est. —cream′i·ness,** *n.*

crease (krēs), **1** *n.* line made by folding or pressing cloth, paper, etc.; ridge; fold: *She likes a sharp crease in her slacks.* **2** *n.* a wrinkle: *The creases on his face showed that he was very old.* **3** *v.* to make a crease or creases in: *Mother creased the pleats in her skirt with an iron.* **4** *v.* to become creased: *Some cloth is too thick to crease well.* ❑ *v.* **creased, creas·ing.** [**Crease** comes from **crest.** The fold line looks like a ridge on a hill.]

cre·ate (krē āt′), *v.* **1** to make a thing which has not been made before; cause to be; bring into being; make: *Composers create music.* **2** to be the cause of; cause: *The noise created a disturbance.* ❑ *v.* **cre·at·ed, cre·at·ing.**

> **SYNONYM STUDY** **Create, invent,** and **devise** all mean to bring something into being. **Create** is a general word: *He has created a study area in his room.* **Invent** means to think of something new, especially a device or product: *I wish someone would invent a machine to make things cold as fast as a microwave makes them hot.* **Devise** means to invent in a clever way, especially for immediate use: *She devised a sun hat from folded newspaper.*

cre·a·tion (krē ā′shən), *n.* **1** act of creating; act of making a thing which has not been made before: *The gasoline engine led to the creation of the automobile.* **2** all things created; the world and everything in it; the universe: *They thought their house by the ocean was the nicest spot in all creation.* **3** the Creation, (in Christian and some other religious uses) the creating of the universe by God: *The Bible says the Creation took six days.* **4** thing produced by intelligence or skill, usually something important or original: *Art, drama, and music are creations of the imagination.*

cre·a·tion·ism (krē ā′shə niz əm), *n.* belief that the Biblical version of creation is as scientifically valid as the theory of evolution. **—cre·a′tion·ist,** *adj., n.*

cre·a·tive (krē ā′tiv), *adj.* having the power to create; inventive: *A creative person has a lot of new ideas.* **—cre·a′tive·ly,** *adv.* **—cre·a′tive·ness,** *n.*

cre·a·tiv·i·ty (krē′ā tiv′ə tē), *n.* creative ability; the fact of being creative.

cre·a·tor (krē ā′tər), *n.* **1** person who creates: *Leonardo da Vinci was the creator of many ideas for inventions.* **2** the Creator, God.

crea·ture (krē′chər), *n.* **1** any living thing. **2** anything created: *Ghosts are creatures of the imagination.* **3** person who is strongly influenced or controlled by another person or thing: *I am a creature of habit.*

crèche (kresh), *n.* model of Jesus in the manger, with attending figures, often displayed at Christmas. ❑ *n., pl.* **crèch·es** (kresh′iz).

cre·dence (krēd′ns), *n.* belief: *Don't give credence to that gossip.*

cre·den·tials (kri den′shəlz), *n.pl.* letters of introduction; references: *The new ambassador from England presented his credentials to the President.*

cre·den·za (kri den′zə), *n.* sideboard; buffet. ❑ *n., pl.* **cre·den·zas.**

cred·i·ble (kred′ə bəl), *adj.* worthy of belief; believable: *Her excuse for being absent was hardly credible.* **—cred′i·bil′i·ty,** *n.* **—cred′i·ble·ness,** *n.* **—cred′i·bly,** *adv.*

cred·it (kred′it), **1** *n.* belief in the truth of something; faith; trust: *I know he is sure of his facts and put great credit in what he says.* **2** *v.* to believe in the truth of something; have faith in; trust: *I can credit your story because I had a similar experience.* **3** *n.* a trust in someone's ability and intention to pay: *This store will extend credit to customers.* **4** *n.* amount of money in someone's account: *When I deposit this check, I will have a credit of $50.* **5** *v.* to add to someone's credit in a bank account, business record, etc.: *The bank credited $50 to my account.* **6** *n.* delayed payment; time allowed for delayed payment: *The store allowed us six months' credit on our purchase.* **7** *n.* reputation in money matters: *If you pay your bills on time, your credit will be good.* **8** *n.* good reputation: *The mayor is a man of credit in the community.* **9** *n.* honor; praise: *The person who does the work should get the credit.* **10** *n.* person or thing that brings honor or praise: *A brilliant swimmer, she's a credit to her team.* **11** *n.* entry on a student's record showing that he or she has passed a course of study: *You must pass the examination to get credit for the course.* **12** *n.* unit of work entered in this way: *She needs three credits to graduate.* **13** *n.pl.* **credits,** a listing of those who have worked on the movie, TV show, etc.

credit with, to think that someone has; attribute to: *I credit you with the ability to do well.*

do credit to, to bring honor or praise to: *The winning team did credit to the school.*

on credit, on a promise to pay later: *buy a car on credit.*

cred·it·a·ble (kred′ə tə bəl), *adj.* bringing credit or honor: *She has a creditable record as a senator.* —**cred′it·a·ble·ness,** *n.* —**cred′i·ta·bly,** *adv.*

credit card, a plastic card that allows someone to charge the cost of goods or services instead of paying cash; charge card.

cred·i·tor (kred′ə tər), *n.* person to whom a debt is owed.

credit union, a cooperative association that makes loans to its members at low rates of interest. The money for loans comes from savings paid in by members, who receive interest.

cre·do (krē′dō *or* krā′dō), *n.* creed. □ *n., pl.* **cre·dos.**

cre·du·li·ty (krə dü′lə tē), *n.* great readiness to believe something, even without proof.

cred·u·lous (krej′ə ləs), *adj.* ready to believe something, even without proof: *She was so credulous that the other children could easily fool her.* —**cred′u·lous·ly,** *adv.* —**cred′u·lous·ness,** *n.*

Cree (krē), *n.* member of a tribe of American Indians living in central and southern Canada and in Montana. □ *n., pl.* **Cree** or **Crees.**

creed (krēd), *n.* **1** a brief statement of the main points of religious belief of some church. **2** any statement of faith, belief, or opinions: *"Honesty is the best policy" was his business creed.*

creek (krēk *or* krik), *n.* **1** a small stream. **2** a narrow bay, running inland for some distance. ■ Other words that can sound like this are **creak** and **crick.**

Creek (krēk), *n.* member of a group of American Indian tribes formerly living in Alabama and Georgia, and now living mostly in Oklahoma. □ *n., pl.* **Creek** or **Creeks.** [**Creek** comes from this people's custom of building villages on the banks of creeks.]

creel (krēl), *n.* basket for holding fish that have been caught.

creep (krēp), **1** *v.* to move slowly with the body close to the ground or floor; crawl: *Babies creep on their hands and knees before they begin to walk.* **2** *v.* to move slowly or little by little: *The traffic crept over the narrow bridge.* **3** *v.* to move in a timid or stealthy way: *They didn't see me creeping up on them.* ■ See Synonym Study at **sneak. 4** *v.* to grow along the ground or over a wall by means of clinging stems: *Ivy had crept up the wall of the old house.* **5** *v.* to feel as if things were creeping over the skin: *It made my flesh creep to hear the wolves howl.* **6** *n.* act of creeping; slow movement. **7** *n.pl.* **the creeps,** INFORMAL. a feeling of horror or fear: *Movies about ghosts give me the creeps.* **8** *n.* INFORMAL. an unpleasant or annoying person. □ *v.* **crept, creep·ing.**

creep·er (krē′pər), *n.* **1** person or thing that creeps. **2** any plant that grows along a surface, sending out rootlets from the stem, such as the Virginia creeper and ivy. **3** a small North American bird that creeps around on trees and bushes looking for insects.

creep·y (krē′pē), *adj.* **1** having a feeling of horror, as if things were creeping over your skin; frightened: *The ghost stories made the children creepy.* **2** causing such a feeling: *The wind howling through the old house was creepy.* □ *adj.* **creep·i·er, creep·i·est.** —**creep′i·ly,** *adv.* —**creep′i·ness,** *n.*

cre·mate (krē′māt), *v.* to burn a dead body to ashes. □ *v.* **cre·mat·ed, cre·mat·ing.** —**cre·ma′tion,** *n.* —**cre′ma·tor,** *n.*

cre·ma·to·ri·um (krē′mə tôr′ē əm), *n.* **1** furnace for cremating. **2** building having such a furnace. □ *n., pl.* **cre·ma·to·ri·ums, cre·ma·to·ri·a** (krē′mə tôr′ē ə).

cre·ma·to·ry (krē′mə tôr′ē), *n.* crematorium. □ *n., pl.* **cre·ma·to·ries.**

Cre·ole or **cre·ole** (krē′ōl), **1** *n.* descendant of the early French or Spanish settlers in Louisiana. **2** *n.* the French language as spoken in Louisiana. **3** *n.* a French or Spanish person born in Latin America or the West Indies. **4** *adj.* of or about the Creoles: *Creole customs, Creole cooking.* **5** *adj.* cooked in sauce made of stewed tomatoes, peppers, etc.

cre·o·sote (krē′ə sōt), **1** *n.* a poisonous, oily liquid, made by distilling coal tar. It is used to preserve wood. **2** *n.* a similar liquid made by distilling wood tar. It is used as an antiseptic. **3** *v.* to treat with creosote. □ *v.* **cre·o·sot·ed, cre·o·sot·ing.**

crepe or **crêpe** (krāp), *n.* **1** a thin, light cloth with a finely crinkled surface. **2** crepe paper. **3** a very thin pancake, usually served folded around a filling. [See Word Story at **crisp.**]

crepe paper, a thin, crinkled paper that looks like crepe, used for making decorations.

crepe rubber, a crude rubber with a crinkled surface, used for the soles of shoes.

crept (krept), *v.* past tense and past participle of **creep:** *We crept up on them from behind. We had crept up on them without their seeing us.*

cre·scen·do (krə shen′dō), **1** *adj., adv.* (in music) with a gradual increase in force or loudness. **2** *n.* a gradual increase in force or loudness, especially in music. □ *n., pl.* **cre·scen·dos.**

cres·cent (kres′nt), **1** *n.* shape of the moon in its first or last quarter. **2** *n.* anything that curves in a similar way. **3** *adj.* shaped like the moon in its first or last quarter: *a crescent pin.*

crescent (def. 1)

cress (kres), *n.* any of various plants, especially watercress, having leaves with a peppery taste that are used as a garnish or in salad. □ *n., pl.* **cress·es.**

crest (krest), **1** *n.* the top part; peak; summit: *the crest of a wave, the crest of the hill.* **2** *v.* to reach the crest or summit of a hill, a wave, etc. **3** *n.* tuft or comb on the head of a bird or other animal. **4** *n.* decoration of plumes or feathers worn on the top of a helmet. **5** *n.* decoration at the top of a coat of arms. A family crest is sometimes put on silverware, dishes, or letter paper. **6** *v.* to decorate with a crest. **7** *v.* (of waves) to form or rise into a crest. —**crest′like′,** *adj.*

crest·ed (kres′tid), *adj.* having a crest: *a crested bird, a crested shield.*

crest·fall·en (krest′fô′lən), *adj.* feeling great disappointment; discouraged: *Several students went home crestfallen because they had failed the examination.*

Cre·ta·ceous (kri tā′shəs), *n.* (in geology) time between about 135 million and 70 million years ago. During this time, flowering plants began to appear and dinosaurs became extinct.

Cret·an (krēt′n), **1** *adj.* of Crete or its inhabitants. **2** *n.* person born or living in Crete.

Crete (krēt), *n.* Greek Island in the Mediterranean, southeast of Greece. See **Troy** for map.

cre·vasse (krə vas′), *n.* a deep crack or split in the ice of a glacier, or in the ground after an earthquake.

crev·ice (krev′is), *n.* a narrow split or crack; fissure: *Tiny ferns grew in crevices in the stone wall.*

crew (krü), *n.* **1** the sailors who work aboard a ship. **2** the group of persons who fly and work on an aircraft. **3** any group of people working or acting together: *a logging crew, a railroad maintenance crew.* **4** the members of a rowing team. **5** a group or band; crowd; gang. [**Crew** comes from a Latin word meaning "to grow." If the number of people on a job grows, soon there is a whole crew at work.]

crew cut, kind of very short haircut, usually for men and boys.

crew·el (krü′əl), *n.* **1** a loosely twisted, woolen yarn, used for embroidery. **2** embroidery done with this yarn. ■ Another word that sounds like this is **cruel.**

crew·man (krü′mən), *n.* member of a crew. □ *n., pl.* **crew·men.**

a	hat	ė	term	ô	order	ch	child		a in about
ā	age	i	it	oi	oil	ng	long		e in taken
ä	far	ī	ice	ou	out	sh	she	ə	i in pencil
â	care	o	hot	u	cup	th	thin		o in lemon
e	let	ō	open	ù	put	ᴛʜ	then		u in circus
ē	equal	ò	saw	ü	rule	zh	measure		

crib (krib), **1** *n.* a small bed with high barred sides to keep a baby from falling out. **2** *n.* box or trough for horses and cows to eat from; manger. **3** *n.* building or bin for storing grain: *Rats damaged much of the corn in the crib.* **4** *n.* framework of logs or timbers used in building. The wooden lining inside a mine shaft is a crib. **5** *v.* INFORMAL. to use someone else's words or ideas as your own: *She cribbed from the encyclopedia to write her report.* **6** *n.* INFORMAL. notes or helps that are unfair to use in doing schoolwork. **7** *v.* INFORMAL. to use notes or helps unfairly in doing schoolwork. ❑ *v.* **cribbed, crib·bing.**

crib·bage (krib′ij), *n.* a card game for two, three, or four people. The players keep score by moving pegs along a narrow board.

crib death, sudden infant death syndrome.

crick (krik), *n.* a muscular cramp; painful stiffness of muscles: *I got a crick in my neck from sleeping in the chair.* ■ Another word that can sound like this is **creek.**

Crick (krik), *n.* **Francis,** born 1916, British scientist. ■ **Francis Crick** shared the 1962 Nobel Prize in physiology or medicine with James Watson and Maurice Wilkins for creating the double helix model of DNA.

cricket[1]—about 1 in. (2.5 cm) long

crick·et[1] (krik′it), *n.* any of numerous insects related to and resembling grasshoppers. A male cricket makes a chirping noise by rubbing its front wings together.

WORD STORY **Cricket**[1] and **cricket**[2] both come from French words that were imitations of sounds. One was an imitation of the insect's chirping noise, and the other was an imitation of a ball hitting a wooden post. These two sounds aren't much alike, but both imitations worked well enough for people to keep using them.

crick·et[2] (krik′it), *n.* **1** an outdoor game played by two teams of eleven players each, with a ball, bats, and wickets. Cricket is very popular in England. **2** INFORMAL. fair play; good sportsmanship: *It's not cricket to push ahead of others in line.* [See Word Story at **cricket**[1].]

cried (krīd), *v.* past tense and past participle of **cry:** *He cried when he fell down. The baby has cried all day.*

cri·er (krī′ər), *n.* **1** official who shouts out public announcements. **2** person who cries or shouts.

cries (krīz), **1** *n.* plural of **cry. 2** *v.* a present tense of **cry:** *The baby cries when she is hungry.*

crime (krīm), *n.* **1** a harmful or grave offense against the law. Theft, kidnapping, murder, and arson are crimes. **2** activity of criminals; violation of law: *Police forces combat crime.* **3** an evil or wrong act: *It is a crime to ignore suffering.*

SYNONYM STUDY **Crime, offense,** and **sin** all mean an act that people agree is wrong. **Crime** means an act that breaks a law: *Arson is a serious crime.* **Offense** can mean a legal crime, or it can mean an act that isn't illegal but is disliked by many people: *Their offenses included talking during the movie and littering the theater.* **Sin** means an act against a religious law: *We pray for forgiveness of our sins.*

Cri·me·a (krī mē′ə), *n.* peninsula in S Ukraine, on the north coast of the Black Sea. See **Caucasia** for map. —**Cri·me′an,** *adj., n.*

crim·i·nal (krim′ə nəl), **1** *n.* person who has committed a crime: *The criminal was sentenced to prison for theft.* **2** *adj.* guilty of

wrongdoing: *a criminal person.* **3** *adj.* of or about crime or its punishment: *A criminal court hears criminal cases.* **4** *adj.* like crime; wrong: *It is criminal to neglect a pet.* —**crim′i·nal·ly,** *adv.*

crim·i·nal·ist (krim′ə nəl ist), *n.* police employee who collects and prepares evidence for criminal trials.

crim·i·nol·o·gy (krim′ə nol′ə jē), *n.* the scientific study of crime and its prevention and of criminals and their treatment. —**crim′i·no·log′i·cal,** *adj.* —**crim′i·nol′o·gist,** *n.*

crimp (krimp), **1** *v.* to press into small, regular, narrow folds; make wavy: *The children crimped tissue paper to make paper flowers.* **2** *n.* something crimped; fold or wave. —**crimp′er,** *n.*

crimp·y (krim′pē), *adj.* having small, narrow folds; wavy. ❑ *adj.* **crimp·i·er, crimp·i·est.**

crim·son (krim′zən), **1** *n.* a deep red. **2** *adj.* deep red. **3** *v.* to turn deep red: *He crimsoned with shame.* [**Crimson** comes from the Arabic name of a kind of insect. In old times it was used to make red dye for cloth.]

cringe (krinj), **1** *v.* to shrink from danger or pain; crouch in fear: *The kitten cringed when it saw the dog come into the yard.* **2** *n.* act of cringing. ❑ *v.* **cringed, cring·ing.** —**cring′er,** *n.*

crin·kle (kring′kəl), **1** *v.* to wrinkle or ripple: *Crepe paper is crinkled.* **2** *v.* to rustle: *Paper crinkles when it is crushed.* **3** *n.* a wrinkle or ripple: *There is a crinkle in the tablecloth.* **4** *n.* a rustle. ❑ *v.* **crin·kled, crin·kling.**

crin·kly (kring′klē), *adj.* full of crinkles. ❑ *adj.* **crin·kli·er, crin·kli·est.**

cri·noid (krī′noid), *n.* any of numerous small sea animals with cup-shaped bodies having five branched feathery arms, including sea lilies.

crin·o·line (krin′l ən), *n.* **1** a stiff cloth used as a lining to hold a skirt out, make a coat collar stand up, etc. **2** petticoat of crinoline. **3** a hoop skirt.

crip·ple (krip′əl), **1** *n.* person or animal that cannot use an arm or leg properly because of injury or deformity; lame person or animal. **2** *v.* to make a cripple of; make lame. **3** *v.* to damage; disable; weaken: *a ship crippled by the storm.* ❑ *v.* **crip·pled, crip·pling.**

USAGE NOTE Many people object to the use of **cripple** to describe a person. Careful writers and speakers avoid this use of the word. It is wise to use **disabled,** or to give details. There are those who feel that the word should not be used to describe anything at all, since it bothers some people.

cri·sis (krī′sis), *n.* **1** an important or deciding event; point at which a change must come, either for the better or for the worse: *The election was a crisis in the senator's career.* **2** time of difficulty, lack of security, and of anxious waiting: *A scarcity of oil could produce an energy crisis.* **3** the turning point in a disease, toward life or death: *After his fever broke, the doctor said he had passed the crisis and would recover.* ❑ *n., pl.* **cri·ses** (krī′sēz′).

crisp (krisp), **1** *adj.* hard and thin; breaking easily with a snap: *Dry toast and fresh celery are crisp.* **2** *v.* to make or become crisp: *Crisp the lettuce in cold water.* **3** *adj.* sharp and clear; bracing: *The fresh air was cool and crisp.* **4** *adj.* short and decisive; clear-cut: *a crisp manner.* —**crisp′ly,** *adv.* —**crisp′ness,** *n.*

WORD STORY **Crisp** comes from a Latin word meaning "curled." When something is cooked long enough to be crisp, the edges usually curl up. **Crepe,** a rolled pancake, comes from the same Latin word.

crisp·y (kris′pē), *adj.* crisp. ❑ *adj.* **crisp·i·er, crisp·i·est.** —**crisp′i·ness,** *n.*

criss·cross (kris′krôs′), **1** *v.* to mark or cover with crossed lines: *Little cracks crisscrossed the wall.* **2** *v.* to come and go across: *Buses and cars crisscross the city.* **3** *adj.* made or marked with crossed lines; crossed; crossing: *Plaids have a crisscross pattern.* **4** *n.* a mark or pattern of crossed lines: *The messy paper was a crisscross of lines and scribbles.* ❑ *n., pl.* **criss·cross·es.** [**Crisscross** comes from "Christ's cross."]

cri·ter·i·a (krī tir′ē ə), *n.* a plural of **criterion.**

cri·ter·i·on (krī tir′ē ən), *n.* rule or standard for making a judgment; test: *Wealth is only one criterion of success.* ❑ *n., pl.* **cri·ter·i·a** or **cri·ter·i·ons.**

crit·ic (krit′ik), *n.* **1** person who makes judgments of the good and bad points of books, music, pictures, plays, acting, etc.: *We went to see the movie because we read that the critics liked it.* **2** person who disapproves or finds fault; faultfinder.

crit·i·cal (krit′ə kəl), *adj.* **1** inclined to find fault or disapprove: *a critical disposition.* **2** coming from someone who is skilled as a critic: *a critical judgment, critical essays.* **3** of a crisis; being important to the outcome of a situation: *Help arrived at the critical moment.* **4** full of danger or difficulty: *The patient was in a critical condition.* **5** involving reasoning, judgment, comparison, logic, evaluation, etc.: *Her essay shows excellent critical thinking.* —**crit′i·cal·ly,** *adv.* —**crit′i·cal·ness,** *n.*

crit·i·cism (krit′ə siz′əm), *n.* **1** unfavorable remarks or judgments; finding fault: *I could not let their rudeness pass without criticism.* **2** act of making judgments; analysis of merits and faults: *literary criticism, drama criticism.*

crit·i·cize (krit′ə sīz), *v.* **1** to find fault with; disapprove of; blame: *Do not criticize him until you know all the circumstances.* **2** to judge or speak as a critic: *The editor criticized the author's new novel, comparing it with her last one.* ❏ *v.* **crit·i·cized, crit·i·ciz·ing.** —**crit′i·ciz′er,** *n.*

crit·ter (krit′ər), *n.* DIALECT. creature.

croak (krōk), **1** *n.* the deep, hoarse sound made by a frog, crow, or raven. **2** *v.* to make this sound. **3** *v.* to utter in a deep, hoarse voice: *to croak a reply.* —**croak′er,** *n.*

Cro·at (krō′at), *n.* person born or living in Croatia.

Cro·a·tia (krō ā′shə), *n.* country in SE Europe. *Capital:* Zagreb. —**Cro·a′tian,** *adj., n.*

cro·chet (krō shā′), **1** *v.* to make sweaters, lace, etc., by looping thread or yarn into links with a single hooked needle. **2** *n.* needlework done in this way. ❏ *v.* **cro·cheted** (krō shād′), **cro·chet·ing** (krō shā′ing).

crock (krok), *n.* pot or jar made of baked clay.

crock·er·y (krok′ər ē), *n.* earthenware.

Crock·ett (krok′it), *n.* **Davy,** 1786-1836, American frontiersman and congressman, killed at the Alamo.

croc·o·dile (krok′ə dīl), *n.* any of several large, lizardlike reptiles with thick skin, long narrow heads, and webbed feet. Crocodiles live in rivers and marshes of warm regions.

crocodile tears, pretended or insincere grief. [Crocodile tears are called this because of an old belief that crocodiles shed tears while eating their victims.]

cro·cus (krō′kəs), *n.* any of numerous small plants that grow from bulblike bases and have white, yellow, or purple flowers. Some crocuses bloom very early in the spring. ❏ *n., pl.* **cro·cus·es, cro·cus, cro·ci** (krō′sī).

Croe·sus (krē′səs), *n.* **1** king in Asia Minor from 560 to 546 B.C., famous for his great wealth. **2** any very rich person.

crois·sant (krə sänt′ *or* kwä sänt′), *n.* a small roll of bread shaped like a crescent.

Cro-Mag·non (krō mag′nən), **1** *adj.* belonging to a group of prehistoric people who lived in southwestern Europe. They used stone and bone implements, and some of them were skilled artists. **2** *n.* person of this group.

Crom·well (krom′wel), *n.* **Ol·i·ver** (ol′ə vər), 1599-1658, English general and political leader. He ruled England after leading the overthrow of Charles I.

crone (krōn), *n.* a withered old woman. ■ The word **crone** is often considered offensive.

cro·ny (krō′nē), *n.* a very close friend. ❏ *n., pl.* **cro·nies.**

crook (krük), **1** *v.* to make a hook or curve in; bend: *I crooked my leg around the branch to keep from falling.* **2** *n.* a hooked, curved,* or bent part: *the crook of the elbow. There is a crook in the stream.* **3** *n.* a shepherd's hooked staff. Its upper end is curved or bent into a hook. **4** *n.* a dishonest person; thief or swindler.

crook·ed (krük′id), *adj.* **1** not straight; bent; curved; twisted: *The crooked road twisted and turned through the hills.* **2** dishonest: *a crooked scheme.* —**crook′ed·ly,** *adv.* —**crook′ed·ness,** *n.*

croon (krün), *v.* **1** to hum, sing, or murmur in a low tone: *I crooned a lullaby to the baby.* **2** to sing in a low voice with exaggerated emotion. —**croon′er,** *n.*

crop (krop), **1** *n.* plants grown or gathered by people for their use, especially as food or fiber: *Wheat, corn, and cotton are three main crops of the United States.* **2** *n.* the amount of any grain, fruit, or vegetable which is grown in one season: *The drought made the potato crop very small this year.* **3** *v.* to plant, cultivate, or yield a crop or crops. **4** *n.* anything like a crop; group; collection: *a crop of great stories.* **5** *v.* to cut or bite off the top of: *Sheep had cropped the grass.* **6** *v.* to cut short; clip: *to crop a horse's tail.* **7** *n.* act or result of cropping. A short haircut is a crop. **8** *n.* a baglike swelling of a bird's or insect's food passage where food is prepared for digestion; craw. **9** *n.* a short whip with a loop instead of a lash: *a riding crop.* ❏ *v.* **cropped, crop·ping.**
crop up, to turn up unexpectedly: *Unless you plan carefully, all sorts of difficulties may crop up.*

crop-dust·ing (krop′dus′ting), *n.* act of spraying or spreading powdered insecticides from an airplane onto growing crops.

crop-dusting

crop rotation, the practice of growing different crops on the same ground each year. Crop rotation helps conserve the productivity of the soil and also helps control insect pests.

cro·quet (krō kā′), *n.* an outdoor game played by knocking wooden balls through small wire arches with mallets.

cro·quette (krō ket′), *n.* a small mass of chopped meat, fish, or vegetables, coated with crumbs and fried.

Cros·by (krôz′bē), *n.* **Bing** (bing), 1903-1977, American singer and movie star. His most famous performance is of "White Christmas."

cross (krôs), **1** *v.* to go or move across: *Let's cross the street. The bridge crosses the river.* **2** *v.* to lie across; intersect: *Main Street crosses Market Street. Parallel lines cannot cross.* **3** *n.* stick or post with another across it like a T, an X, or a +. **4** *n.* **the Cross,** the cross on which Jesus died. **5** *n.* thing, design, or mark shaped like a cross. A cross is the symbol of the Christian religion. **6** *v.* to draw a line across: *In writing you cross the letter "t."* **7** *v.* to cancel by marking with a cross or by drawing a line or lines across: *cross off a name on a list.* **8** *v.* to put or lay one over another: *He crossed his arms.* **9** *v.* to meet and pass: *My letter to her and hers to me crossed in the mail.* **10** *adj.* lying or going across; crossing: *We stood at the intersection of the cross streets.* **11** *v.* to make the sign of the cross on or over: *She crossed herself as she*

a	hat	ė	term	ô	order	ch	child		a	in about
ā	age	i	it	oi	oil	ng	long		e	in taken
ä	far	ī	ice	ou	out	sh	she	ə	i	in pencil
â	care	o	hot	u	cup	th	thin		o	in lemon
e	let	ō	open	ủ	put	ŦH	then		u	in circus
ē	equal	ò	saw	ü	rule	zh	measure			

went into the church. **12** *v.* to act against; get in the way of; oppose: *If anyone crosses him, he gets very angry.* **13** *adj.* in a bad temper; complaining: *People are often cross when they don't feel well.* **14** *n.* burden of duty or suffering; trouble: *bear one's cross without complaining.* **15** *v.* to mix kinds or breeds of: *A new plant is sometimes made by crossing two others.* **16** *n.* a mixing or mixture of kinds or breeds: *A mule is a cross between a horse and a donkey.* ❑ *n., pl.* **cross·es** for 3,5,14,16. [See Word Story at **cruise.**] —**cross′ly,** *adv.* —**cross′ness,** *n.*

SYNONYM STUDY **Cross, cranky,** and **disgruntled** all mean in a bad mood. **Cross** is a general, mild word: *The baby is tired and cross.* **Cranky** suggests irritation and grumbling: *I know you don't want to come along, but try not to be cranky.* **Disgruntled** means in a bad mood because of discontent: *Annoyed by poor service, the disgruntled customer left no tip.*

cross·bar (kròs′bär′), *n.* bar, line, or stripe going crosswise.

cross·bones (kròs′bōnz′), *n.pl.* two bones placed crosswise, usually below a skull, to mean death: *Poisonous medicines were sometimes marked with a skull and crossbones.*

cross·bow (kròs′bō′), *n.* (in the Middle Ages) a weapon for shooting arrows, stones, etc., consisting of a bow fixed across a wooden stock, with a groove in the middle to direct the arrows, stones, etc.

cross·breed (kròs′brēd′), **1** *v.* to breed by mixing kinds or breeds: *You crossbreed a female horse and a male donkey to get a mule.* **2** *n.* individual or breed produced by crossbreeding. The loganberry is a crossbreed of the dewberry and the red raspberry. ❑ *v.* **cross·bred** (kròs′bred′), **cross·breed·ing.**

cross·coun·try (kròs′kun′trē), *adj.* **1** across fields or open country instead of by road: *cross-country skiing.* **2** across an entire country, not just a part: *a cross-country flight from N.Y.C. to L.A.*

cross·cut (kròs′kut′), **1** *n.* a cut, course, or path going across. **2** *adj.* used or made for cutting across. **3** *v.* to cut across. ❑ *v.* **cross·cut, cross·cut·ting.**

crosscut saw, saw made for cutting across the grain of wood.

cross·ex·am·i·na·tion (kròs′eg zam′ə nā′shən), *n.* examination to check a previous examination, especially the questioning of a witness by the lawyer of the opposing side to test the truth of the witness's testimony.

cross·ex·am·ine (kròs′eg zam′ən), *v.* to question closely a witness for the opposing side of a case in court, in order to cast doubt on his or her testimony. ❑ *v.* **cross·ex·am·ined, cross·ex·am·in·ing.** —**cross′-ex·am′in·er,** *n.*

cross·eyed (kròs′īd′), *adj.* having both eyes turned toward the nose, and unable to focus on the same point.

cross·fer·ti·lize (kròs′fèr′tl īz), *v.* to fertilize a flower on one plant with the pollen from a flower on another plant; cross-pollinate. ❑ *v.* **cross·fer·ti·lized, cross·fer·ti·liz·ing.**

cross·fire (kròs′fīr′), *n.* **1** gunfire crossing from two or more directions. **2** a verbal attack from two or more sources or directions.

cross·grained (kròs′grānd′), *adj.* having the grain arranged in crossing directions, or irregularly, instead of running straight: *cross-grained wood.*

cross·ing (kró′sing), *n.* **1** place where lines, tracks, etc., cross: *a railroad crossing.* **2** place at which a street, river, etc., may be crossed: *White lines mark the crossing.* **3** act of going across, especially a voyage across water: *The ocean liner made a crossing from New York to England every two weeks.*

cross·leg·ged (kròs′leg′id *or* kròs′legd′), *adj.* **1** with one leg over the other and the knees crossed. **2** with the ankles crossed and the knees apart. **3** with one ankle resting on the other leg's thigh.

cross·ov·er (kròs′ōv ər), *adj.* popular and successful in a second category after success in a first category: *a jazz singer with a crossover rock hit.*

cross·piece (kròs′pēs′), *n.* piece of wood, metal, etc., that is placed across something.

cross·pol·li·nate (kròs′pol′ə nāt), *v.* to cross-fertilize. ❑ *v.* **cross·pol·li·nat·ed, cross·pol·li·nat·ing.**

cross·pol·li·na·tion (kròs′pol′ə nā′shən), *n.* transfer of pollen from the anther of one flower to the stigma of another, by insects, birds, bats, or currents of air.

cross·prod·uct (kròs′prod′əkt), *n.* (in a mathematical proportion) the product of the first number of one ratio and the second number of the other ratio. For ¾ and ⁹⁄₁₂, the cross-products are 3×12 and 9×4, both of which equal 36.

cross·pur·pose (kròs′pèr′pəs), *n.* an opposing or contrary purpose. **at cross-purposes,** misunderstanding each other's purpose: *We cannot accomplish anything while we are at cross-purposes.*

cross·ques·tion (kròs′kwes′chən), *v.* to question closely; cross-examine.

cross·re·fer (kròs′ri fèr′), *v.* to refer from one part to another. ❑ *v.* **cross·re·ferred, cross·re·fer·ring.**

cross·ref·er·ence (kròs′ref′ər əns), *n.* reference from one part of a book, index, etc., to another. The sentence "See picture at **angle**¹." located at the entry **complementary angle,** is a cross-reference.

cross·road (kròs′rōd′), *n.* **1** road that crosses another. **2** road that connects main roads. **3** **crossroads,** *pl.* place where roads cross: *At the crossroads we stopped and read the signs.* **at the crossroads,** in a situation where an important choice must be made.

cross section, 1 act of cutting anything across: *I sliced the tomatoes by making a series of cross sections.* **2** piece cut in this way. **3** *n.* a picture of a thing as it would appear if cut straight through. **4** small selection of people, things, etc., with the same qualities as the entire group; sample: *They interviewed a cross section of the population in their survey of public opinion.*

cross section (def. 3)

cross·town (kròs′toun′), **1** *adj.* going or running across town: *a crosstown bus.* **2** *adv.* across town: *I walk crosstown to work whenever the weather is good.*

cross·trees (kròs′trēz′), *n.pl.* two horizontal bars of wood or metal near the top of a ship's mast.

cross·walk (kròs′wòk′), *n.* area marked with lines, used by pedestrians in crossing a street.

cross·way (kròs′wā′), *n.* crossroad.

cross·ways (kròs′wāz′), *adv.* crosswise.

cross·wise (kròs′wīz′), *adv.* **1** so as to cross; across: *The tree fell crosswise over the stream.* **2** in the form of a cross: *The streets come together crosswise at the intersection.*

cross·word puzzle (kròs′wèrd′), puzzle with sets of numbered squares to be filled in with words, one letter in each square, so that the words may be read both across and down. Synonyms, definitions, or other clues are given with numbers corresponding to the numbers in the squares.

crotch (kroch), *n.* **1** place where a tree, bough, etc., divides into two limbs or branches: *The bird's nest was in the crotch of a tree.* **2** place where the human body divides into the two legs. ❑ *n., pl.* **crotch·es.**

crotch·et·y (kroch′ə tē), *adj.* full of odd notions or unreasonable whims. —**crotch′et·i·ness,** *n.*

Croton bug (krōt′n), a small, pale yellowish brown cockroach, commonly found in houses near damp places; water bug.

WORD STORY **Croton bug** may come from the Croton River, near New York City. When water from the river was sent to the city, in the mid-1800s, the number of bugs in New York City apartments is supposed to have grown.

crouch (krouch), **1** *v.* to stoop low with bent legs as though ready to spring: *The cat crouched in the corner, waiting for the mouse to come out of its hole.* **2** *v.* to shrink down in fear. **3** *n.* a crouching position: *From his crouch, the baseball catcher signaled for a curve.* ❑ *n., pl.* **crouch·es.**

croup (krüp), *n.* a children's disease of the throat and windpipe that causes a hoarse cough and difficult breathing.

croup·y (krü′pē), *adj.* sick with croup: *the wheeze of a croupy baby.* ❑ *adj.* **croup·i·er, croup·i·est.**

crou·ton (krü′ton), *n.* a small piece of toasted or fried bread, often served in soup or salad.

crow[1] (krō), **1** *n.* the loud cry of a rooster. **2** *v.* to make this cry: *The cock crowed as the sun rose.* **3** *n.* a happy sound made by a baby. **4** *v.* to make this sound. **5** *v.* to show your happiness and pride; boast: *The winning team crowed over its victory.* ❑ *v.* **crowed, crowed, crow·ing.**

crow[2] (krō), *n.* **1** a large, glossy black bird of North America that has a harsh cry or caw. **2** any of several birds related to and resembling this one.

as the crow flies, in a straight line; in or by the shortest way: *The distance is exactly one mile as the crow flies.*

eat crow, be forced to do something extremely disagreeable and humiliating.

Crow (krō), *n.* member of a tribe of American Indians living in Montana. ❑ *n., pl.* **Crow** or **Crows.** [Crow is an English translation of the Indian name. The people named themselves after the bird.]

crow·bar (krō′bär′), *n.* a strong iron or steel bar, used to lift things or pry them apart.

crowd (kroud), **1** *n.* a large number of people together: *A crowd gathered at the scene of the fire.* **2** *n.* people in general; the masses: *Advertisements seek to appeal to the crowd.* **3** *n.* group; set: *Our crowd wasn't invited to the party.* **4** *v.* to collect in large numbers: *crowd around a TV star.* **5** *v.* to fill; fill too full: *Christmas shoppers crowded the store.* **6** *v.* to push; shove: *The big man crowded the child out of his way.* **7** *v.* to press forward; force your way: *She crowded into the subway car.*

SYNONYM STUDY **Crowd, throng,** and **swarm** all mean a large number of people together. **Crowd** suggests a large number of people close together: *A crowd was waiting to get into the movie.* **Throng** suggests a greater number of people, with moving and pushing around: *Throngs of excited fans tried to get close to the basketball team.* **Swarm** suggests a large crowd moving in a particular direction: *A swarm of students headed for the cafeteria.*

crown (kroun), **1** *n.* a head covering of precious metal and jewels, worn by a king or queen. **2** *n.* **the Crown,** the governing power and authority in a monarchy; royal power: *The Crown granted lands to William Penn.* **3** *n.* a king or queen: *Always address the crown respectfully.* **4** *v.* to make king or queen: *The princess was crowned in London.* **5** *adj.* of a crown: *the crown jewels.* **6** *n.* wreath for the head: *The winner of the race received a crown.* **7** *n.* an honor; reward: *He won the amateur boxing crown in his last bout.* **8** *v.* to honor; reward: *Her hard work was crowned with success.* **9** *n.* head: *"Jack fell down and broke his crown."* **10** *n.* the highest part; top: *the crown of the head, the crown of a hat. The Olympic victory was the crown of her athletic career.* **11** *v.* to be on top of; cover the highest part of: *A fort crowns the hill.* **12** *v.* to hit someone on the head. **13** *v.* to make perfect or complete; add the finishing touch to: *Success crowned her efforts.* **14** *n.* part of a tooth which appears beyond the gum, or an artificial substitute for it. **15** *v.* to put an artificial crown on a tooth. **16** *n.* a former coin of Great Britain, which was equal to 5 shillings. It was replaced by the 25 new pence piece.

Crown corporation, CANADIAN. a private company that is owned by the federal government or a provincial government.

crown prince, the oldest living son of a king or queen; the male heir to a throne.

crown princess, 1 wife of a crown prince. **2** the female heir to a throne.

crow's-feet (krōz′fēt′), *n.pl.* the tiny wrinkles at the outer corners of the eyes.

crow's-nest (krōz′nest′), *n.* a small, enclosed platform near the top of a ship's mast, used by the lookout.

CRT, cathode-ray tube (a vacuum tube in which a beam of high-speed electrons controlled by magnetic fields causes pictures or text to appear on a shining screen, used in television sets and some computers).

cru·cial (krü′shəl), *adj.* very important or decisive; critical: *This is a crucial game, for it will decide the championship.* —**cru′cial·ly,** *adv.*

cru·ci·ble (krü′sə bəl), *n.* container in which metals, ores, etc., can be melted.

cru·ci·fix (krü′sə fiks), *n.* cross with a figure of the crucified Jesus on it. ❑ *n., pl.* **cru·ci·fix·es.**

cru·ci·fix·ion (krü′sə fik′shən), *n.* **1** act of crucifying or of being crucified. **2 Crucifixion, a** the crucifying of Jesus on the Cross. **b** picture, statue, etc., of this.

cru·ci·form (krü′sə fôrm), *adj.* shaped like a cross.

cru·ci·fy (krü′sə fī), *v.* **1** to put to death by nailing or binding the hands and feet to a cross. **2** to persecute or torture. ❑ *v.* **cru·ci·fied, cru·ci·fy·ing.**

crud (krud), *n.* SLANG. **1** a layer of dirty matter; filth. **2** trash; rubbish.

crude (def. 1)

crude (krüd), *adj.* **1** in a natural or raw state; unrefined: *crude oil, crude rubber.* **2** rough; coarse. **3** lacking finish, grace, taste, or refinement: *crude manners.* ❑ *adj.* **crud·er, crud·est.** —**crude′ly,** *adv.* —**crude′ness,** *n.*

cru·di·ty (krü′də tē), *n.* **1** condition of being crude; lack of finish; roughness: *The crudity of the homemade furniture fit in with the rustic charm of the summer cabin.* **2** a crude action or thing. ❑ *n., pl.* **cru·di·ties** for 2.

cru·el (krü′əl), *adj.* **1** ready to give pain to others or to delight in their suffering; hardhearted: *The cruel man kicked his dog.* **2** showing a cruel nature: *cruel acts.* **3** causing pain and suffering: *a cruel war.* ■ Another word that sounds like this is **crewel.** —**cru′el·ly,** *adv.* —**cru′el·ness,** *n.*

SYNONYM STUDY **Cruel, vicious,** and **brutal** all mean willing to give pain. **Cruel** is a general word: *She was so angry that she made a cruel remark to her friend.* **Vicious** means cruel on purpose: *The gang gave the boy a vicious beating.* **Brutal** means very cruel, without human feeling: *Brutal acts are all too common in war.*

cru·el·ty (krü′əl tē), *n.* **1** readiness to give pain to others or to delight in their suffering. **2** a cruel act or acts: *an organization that seeks to prevent cruelty to animals.* ❑ *n., pl.* **cru·el·ties** for 2.

cru·et (krü′it), *n.* a glass bottle to hold vinegar, oil, etc., for the table.

a	hat	ė	term	ô	order	ch	child		a in about
ā	age	i	it	oi	oil	ng	long		e in taken
ä	far	ī	ice	ou	out	sh	she	ə	i in pencil
â	care	o	hot	u	cup	th	thin		o in lemon
e	let	ō	open	u̇	put	ᴛʜ	then		u in circus
ē	equal	ò	saw	ü	rule	zh	measure		

cruise (krüz), **1** *v.* to sail about from place to place on pleasure or business; sail over or about: *The coast guard cruised along the shore.* **2** *n.* a voyage from place to place for pleasure: *We went for a cruise on the Great Lakes last summer.* **3** *v.* to travel or journey from place to place: *The taxicab cruised the city streets in search of passengers.* **4** *v.* to travel in a car, airplane, boat, etc., at the speed at which it operates best. ❑ *v.* **cruised, cruis·ing.**

WORD STORY **Cruise** comes from a Latin word meaning "a cross." **Cross** comes from the same Latin word. The reason they have different meanings and spellings is that **cruise** came into English from Dutch, while **cross** came into English from Irish.

cruis·er (krü′zər), *n.* **1** warship with less armor and greater speed than a battleship. **2** motorboat having a cabin and equipped with facilities for living on board. **3** a police car used for patrolling streets and highways.

crul·ler (krul′ər), *n.* piece of rich, sweet dough fried brown in deep fat. The dough is usually shaped in twists and cut in short pieces. [**Cruller** comes from a Dutch word meaning "to curl." See Word Story at **curl**.]

crumb (krum), **1** *n.* a very small piece of bread, cake, etc., broken from a larger piece: *I fed crumbs to the birds.* **2** *v.* to break into crumbs; crumble. **3** *v.* to cover with crumbs for frying or baking. **4** *n.* a little bit: *a crumb of comfort.*

crum·ble (krum′bəl), *v.* **1** to break into very small pieces or crumbs: *I crumbled the bread for the birds.* **2** to fall to pieces; decay: *The old wall was crumbling away at the edges.* ❑ *v.* **crumbled, crum·bling.**

crum·bly (krum′blē), *adj.* tending to crumble; easily crumbled. ❑ *adj.* **crum·bli·er, crum·bli·est.** —**crum′bli·ness,** *n.*

crum·my (krum′ē), *adj.* INFORMAL. **1** disgusting; dirty; filthy: *a crummy neighborhood.* **2** having little quality or value; poor: *a crummy movie, a crummy idea.* ❑ *adj.* **crum·mi·er, crum·mi·est.**

crum·ple (krum′pəl), *v.* **1** to crush together; wrinkle: *She crumpled the paper into a ball.* **2** to fall down: *He crumpled to the floor in a faint.* ❑ *v.* **crum·pled, crum·pling.**

crunch (krunch), **1** *v.* to crush noisily with the teeth: *He was crunching celery.* **2** *v.* to make or move with a crunching noise: *The children crunched through the snow.* **3** *n.* act or sound of crunching. **4** *n.* a critical time or situation; crisis: *The crunch came when we ran out of food on our camping trip.* ❑ *n., pl.* **crunch·es.**

crunch·y (krun′chē), *adj.* brittle and crackling: *crunchy candy.* ❑ *adj.* **crunch·i·er, crunch·i·est.** —**crunch′i·ness,** *n.*

crup·per (krup′ər), *n.* **1** strap fastened to the back of a harness and passed under a horse's tail to prevent the harness from slipping forward. **2** rump of a horse.

cru·sade (krü sād′), **1** *n.* Often, **Crusade,** any one of the Christian military expeditions between the years 1096 and 1272 to recover the Holy Land from the Muslims. **2** *n.* a vigorous campaign against a public evil or in favor of some new idea: *We all joined the crusade against cancer.* **3** *v.* to take part in a crusade: *We crusaded against smoking.* ❑ *v.* **cru·sad·ed, cru·sad·ing.**

cru·sad·er (krü sā′dər), *n.* person who takes part in a crusade. The **Crusaders** of the Middle Ages tried to recover the Holy Land from the Muslims.

crush (krush), **1** *v.* to squeeze together violently so as to break or bruise: *The car door slammed and crushed his fingers.* **2** *v.* to wrinkle or crease by pressure or rough handling: *My suitcase was so full that my clothes were crushed.* **3** *v.* to break into fine pieces by grinding, pounding, or pressing: *The ore is crushed between steel rollers.* **4** *n.* act of crushing; violent pressure like grinding or pounding: *She pushed her way through the crush of the crowd.* **5** *n.* mass of people crowded close together: *There was a crush at the narrow exits after the football game.* **6** *v.* to subdue; conquer; overcome: *The revolt was crushed, and its leaders were imprisoned. He was crushed when he failed to get a part in the play.* **7** *n.* a sudden, strong liking for someone: *I used to have a crush on my fifth-grade teacher.* ❑ *n., pl.* **crush·es.** —**crush′er,** *n.*

Crusoe, *n.* Robinson. See **Robinson Crusoe.**

crust (krust), **1** *n.* the hard, outside part of bread. **2** *n.* piece of this. **3** *n.* any hard, dry piece of bread. **4** *n.* rich dough rolled out thin and baked for pies. **5** *n.* any hard outside covering: *The frozen crust on the snow was thick enough for us to walk on it.* **6** *v.* to cover or become covered with a crust; form into a crust: *By the next day the snow had crusted over.* **7** *n.* the solid outside part of the earth: *Heat below the crust of the earth causes volcanoes to form.* —**crust′like′,** *adj.*

crus·ta·cean (krus tā′shən), *n.* any of many animals with hard shells and jointed bodies and legs, living mostly in the water. Crabs, lobsters, shrimps, and crayfish are crustaceans.

crust·y (krus′tē), *adj.* **1** of or like a crust; having a crust; hard: *crusty bread.* **2** harsh in manner or speech: *The crusty sea captain has a quick temper.* ❑ *adj.* **crust·i·er, crust·i·est.** —**crust′i·ly,** *adv.* —**crust′i·ness,** *n.*

crutch (kruch), *n.* **1** a support to help a lame or injured person walk. It is a stick with a padded crosspiece at the top that fits under a person's arm and supports part of the weight in walking. **2** something or someone used like a crutch; support; prop: *She must learn to make her own decisions and not to lean on her friend as a crutch.* ❑ *n., pl.* **crutch·es.**

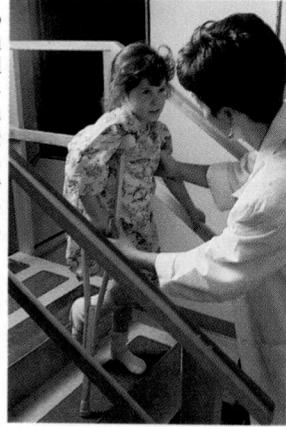

crutch (def. 1)

crux (kruks), *n.* **1** the essential part; most important point: *the crux of an argument.* **2** a puzzling or perplexing question; difficult point to explain. ❑ *n., pl.* **crux·es.**

cry (krī), **1** *v.* to call loudly; shout: *"Wait!" she cried from behind me.* **2** *n.* a loud call; shout: *We heard his cry for help.* **3** *v.* to shed tears; weep: *The child cried when he fell and hurt his knee.* **4** *n.* spell of shedding tears; fit of weeping: *I feel better now that I have had a good cry.* **5** *n.* noise or call of an animal: *the cry of hounds.* **6** *v.* to make such a noise: *The crows cried to one another from the treetops.* **7** *n.* a call to action; slogan: *"Forward" was the army's cry as it attacked.* **8** *n.* a call for help; appeal. ❑ *v.* **cried, cry·ing;** *n., pl.* **cries.**

cry for, to ask earnestly for; beg for: *The captives cried loudly for mercy.*

cry out for, to need very much: *The run-down old house cried out for a coat of paint.*

in full cry, in close pursuit: *The hounds were in full cry after the fox.*

SYNONYM STUDY **Cry, weep,** and **sob** all mean to shed tears. **Cry** is a general word: *Sad movies make him cry.* **Weep** means to cry. It is a somewhat formal word: *The beauty of the music caused the audience to weep.* **Sob** means to cry with quick, short breaths: *The little girl sobbed with rage when her mother would not pick her up.*

cry·ba·by (krī′bā′bē), *n.* person who cries easily or pretends to be hurt. ❑ *n., pl.* **cry·ba·bies.**

cry·ing (krī′ing), *adj.* demanding attention; very bad: *The slums in that city are a crying shame.*

cry·o·gen·ics (krī′ō jen′iks), *n.* branch of physics that deals with substances at extremely low temperatures.

crypt (kript), *n.* an underground room or vault. The crypt beneath the main floor of a church was formerly often used as a burial place. [**Crypt** comes from a Greek word meaning "to hide." So do **cryptic** and **cryptogram.** An underground room is a good place to hide something that you want to keep secret.]

cryp·tic (krip′tik), *adj.* having a hidden meaning; secret; mysterious: *We could not fully understand his cryptic remark.* [See word history information at **crypt.**] —**cryp′ti·cal·ly,** *adv.*

cryp·to·gram (krip′tə gram), *n.* something written in secret code or cipher. [See word history information at **crypt.**]

cryp·tog·ra·pher (krip tog′rə fər), *n.* an expert in creating or figuring out secret codes.

cryp·tog·ra·phy (krip tog′rə fē), *n.* art or process of creating or figuring out secret codes.

crys·tal (kris′tl), **1** *n.* a regularly shaped piece with angles and flat surfaces, into which many substances solidify. The atoms of a crystal form the same pattern over and over throughout it. Crystals of sugar are different in form from crystals of snow. **2** *n.* a fine, transparent glass from which drinking glasses, serving dishes, etc., are made: *goblets of crystal.* **3** *adj.* clear and transparent like glass: *crystal spring water.* **4** *n.* a clear, transparent mineral that looks like ice. It is a kind of quartz. **5** *n.* piece of such quartz cut into forms. Crystals may be hung around lights or worn as beads. **6** *n.* the transparent glass or plastic cover over the face of a watch. —**crys′tal·like′**, *adj.*

crys·tal·line (kris′tl ən), *adj.* **1** made of crystals: *Sugar and salt are crystalline.* **2** made of crystal. **3** clear and transparent like crystal: *A crystalline sheet of ice covered the pond.*

crystalline lens, lens of the eye.

crys·tal·li·za·tion (kris′tl ə zā′shən), *n.* **1** act of crystallizing or condition of being crystallized: *the crystallization of water by freezing.* **2** a crystallized substance or formation. **3** the taking on of a real, concrete, or permanent form: *The meeting resulted in the crystallization of our plans.*

crys·tal·lize (kris′tl īz), *v.* **1** to form into crystals; solidify into crystals: *Water crystallizes to form snow.* **2** to form into definite shape: *After much thought her ideas crystallized into a clear plan.* ❑ *v.* **crys·tal·lized, crys·tal·liz·ing.** —**crys′tal·liz′a·ble**, *adj.*

crys·tal·log·ra·pher (kris′tl og′rə fər), *n.* an expert in crystallography.

crys·tal·log·ra·phy (kris′tl og′rə fē), *n.* science that deals with the form, structure, and qualities of crystals.

Cs, symbol for cesium.

CST or **C.S.T.,** Central Standard Time.

CT, Connecticut (used with postal Zip Code).

ct., **1** cent. **2** court.

Cu, symbol for copper.

cu. or **cu,** cubic.

cub (kub), *n.* **1** a young bear, fox, lion, etc. **2** a young or inexperienced person. **3** a cub scout.

Cu·ba (kyü′bə), *n.* country on the largest island in the West Indies, south of Florida. *Capital:* Havana. —**Cu′ban**, *adj., n.*

WORD STORY Cuba comes from an American Indian word recorded by Christopher Columbus. No one knows if it was actually the name of the island or if it meant something else.

cub·by·hole (kub′ē hōl′), *n.* a small, enclosed space.

cube (kyüb), **1** *n.* a solid object with six square faces or sides, all equal. **2** *n.* anything shaped like a cube: *ice cubes, a cube of sugar.* **3** *v.* to make or form into the shape of a cube: *The beets we had for supper were cubed instead of sliced.* **4** *v.* to use a number three times as a factor: *5 cubed is 125, because 5 × 5 × 5 = 125.* **5** *n.* product obtained when a number is cubed: *The cube of 4 is 64.* ❑ *v.* **cubed, cub·ing.** —**cube′like′**, *adj.*

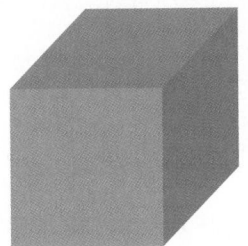

cube (def. 1)

cube root, number that produces a given number when multiplied twice by itself: *The cube root of 27 is 3.*

cu·bic (kyü′bik), *adj.* **1** shaped like a cube: *the cubic form of a block of ice.* **2** of or for cubic measure. A cubic foot is the volume of a cube with edges that are each one foot long. Any other cubic unit is the volume of a cube with each side of the length named. **3** having length, breadth, and thickness. The cubic content of a room is its entire space in three dimensions. **4** of or involving the cubes of numbers.

cu·bi·cal (kyü′bə kəl), *adj.* shaped like a cube; cubic. —**cu′bi·cal·ly**, *adv.*

cu·bi·cle (kyü′bə kəl), *n.* a very small room or compartment.

cubic measure, system of units such as cubic feet or cubic centimeters, used for measuring volume. See table on page 975A.

cub·ism (kyü′biz′əm), *n.* style of painting, drawing, and sculpture in which objects are represented by cubes and other geometric forms rather than by realistic details.

cub·ist (kyü′bist), *n.* artist or sculptor whose art is based on cubism.

cu·bit (kyü′bit), *n.* an ancient measure of length, about 18 to 24 inches (46 to 61 centimeters). Once a cubit meant the length from the elbow to the tip of the middle finger.

cub·mas·ter (kub′mas′tər), *n.* man in charge of a group of Wolf Cubs.

cubism

Cub Scout, member of the junior division of the Boy Scouts. Cub Scouts are seven or eight to ten years of age.

cuck·oo (kü′kü *or* kůk′ü), **1** *n.* any of numerous birds with a call much like their name. The common European cuckoo lays its eggs in the nests of other birds instead of hatching them itself. American cuckoos build their own nests and have calls less like the name. **2** *n.* the call of the cuckoo. **3** *v.* to make this call. **4** *adj.* INFORMAL. silly; foolish. ❑ *n., pl.* **cuck·oos;** *v.* **cuck·ooed, cuck·oo·ing.**

cuckoo clock, clock with a little toy bird that appears and cuckoos to tell the time.

cu·cum·ber (kyü′kum bər), *n.* the fruit of a garden vine related to the squash. It is a long, green vegetable with firm flesh, used in salads and for pickles.

cool as a cucumber, **1** very cool. **2** calm; not excited.

cud (kud), *n.* mouthful of food brought back from the first stomach of cattle or similar animals for a slow, second chewing in the mouth.

cud·dle (kud′l), *v.* **1** to hold closely and lovingly in your arms or lap; hug tenderly: *The child cuddled the kittens.* **2** to lie close and comfortably; curl up: *The two puppies cuddled together near the radiator.* ❑ *v.* **cud·dled, cud·dling.**

cud·dly (kud′lē), *adj.* **1** given to cuddling. **2** pleasing to cuddle. ❑ *adj.* **cud·dli·er, cud·dli·est.**

cudg·el (kuj′əl), **1** *n.* a short, thick stick used as a weapon; club. **2** *v.* to beat with a cudgel. ❑ *v.* **cudg·eled, cudg·el·ing** or **cudg·elled, cudg·el·ling.**

cue[1] (kyü), **1** *n.* action, word, or last part of a speech by an actor which serves as the signal for another actor to come on the stage or begin speaking. **2** *n.* a signal like this to a singer or musician. **3** *n.* hint or suggestion as to what to do or when to act: *Take your cue from me at the party about when it is time to leave.* **4** *v.* to provide someone with a cue or hint: *During the rehearsal the director cued the actors.* ❑ *v.* **cued, cu·ing** or **cue·ing.** ■ Another word that sounds like this is **queue.**

cue[2] (kyü), *n.* **1** a long, tapering stick used for striking the ball in the game of billiards or pool. **2** queue.

cuff[1] (kuf), *n.* **1** band of material attached to a sleeve and worn around the wrist. **2** a turned-up fold around the bottom of the legs of trousers. **3** handcuff. **4** an inflatable band wrapped around the upper arm, used when blood pressure is measured. [**Cuff**[1] comes from an old English word meaning "glove." Most gloves cover at least part of the wrist.]

cuff[2] (kuf), **1** *v.* to hit with the hand; slap. **2** *n.* a hit with the hand; slap.

cuff link, link for the cuff of a shirt.

cu. ft., cubic foot or cubic feet.

cu. in., cubic inch or cubic inches.

a	hat	ė	term	ȯ	order	ch	child		
ā	age	i	it	oi	oil	ng	long	ə	a in about
ä	far	ī	ice	ou	out	sh	she		e in taken
â	care	o	hot	u	cup	th	thin		i in pencil
e	let	ō	open	ů	put	ŦH	then		o in lemon
ē	equal	ȯ	saw	ü	rule	zh	measure		u in circus

cui·rass (kwi ras′), *n.* **1** piece of armor for the body made of a breastplate and a plate for the back fastened together. **2** the breastplate alone. ❑ *n., pl.* **cui·rass·es.**

cui·sine (kwi zēn′), *n.* **1** style of cooking or preparing food; cooking; cookery: *Italian cuisine.* **2** food: *The cuisine is excellent at that restaurant.*

cul-de-sac (kul′də sak′), *n.* street or passage open at one end only; dead end. ❑ *n., pl.* **culs-de-sac** (kulz′də sak′), **cul-de-sac.**

cu·li·nar·y (kyü′lə ner′ē *or* kul′ə ner′ē), *adj.* of or about cooking or the kitchen: *We praised the cook's culinary skill.*

cull (kul), **1** *v.* to pick out; select: *The lawyer culled important facts from the mass of evidence.* **2** *v.* to pick over; make selections from: *We culled the berries, discarding the bad ones.* **3** *n.* something picked out as inferior or worthless. Poor fruit and vegetables as well as animals not up to standard are called culls.

cul·mi·nate (kul′mə nāt), *v.* to reach its highest point; reach a climax: *Weeks of unsuccessful bargaining for wage increases culminated in a strike.* ❑ *v.* **cul·mi·nat·ed, cul·mi·nat·ing.**

cul·mi·na·tion (kul′mə nā′shən), *n.* **1** the highest point; climax: *The fireworks display was the culmination of the Fourth of July celebration.* **2** act of reaching the highest point.

cu·lottes (kü′lots), *n.pl.* a woman's skirt divided and sewed like trousers, but cut so full as to look like a skirt.

cul·pa·ble (kul′pə bəl), *adj.* deserving blame: *The policeman was dismissed for culpable neglect of duty.* —**cul′pa·bil′i·ty,** *n.* —**cul′pa·bly,** *adv.*

cul·prit (kul′prit), *n.* **1** person guilty of a fault or crime; offender: *Someone broke the window; are you the culprit?* **2** prisoner in court accused of a crime.

cult (kult), *n.* **1** system of religious worship. **2** great admiration for a person, thing, or idea; worship. **3** group showing such admiration; worshipers.

cul·ti·vate (kul′tə vāt), *v.* **1** to prepare and use land to raise crops by plowing it, planting seeds, and taking care of the growing plants; till. **2** to help plants grow by labor and care. **3** to loosen the ground around growing plants to kill weeds, etc. **4** to improve or develop by study or training: *cultivate your mind, cultivate good manners.* **5** to seek the friendship of: *She cultivated people who could help her.* ❑ *v.* **cul·ti·vat·ed, cul·ti·vat·ing.** —**cul′ti·vat′a·ble,** *adj.*

cul·ti·vat·ed (kul′tə vā′tid), *adj.* **1** prepared and used to raise crops: *A field of wheat is cultivated land; a pasture is not.* **2** produced by cultivation; not wild: *a cultivated flower.* **3** improved or developed. **4** cultured; refined: *cultivated tastes.*

cul·ti·va·tion (kul′tə vā′shən), *n.* **1** act of preparing land and growing crops by plowing, planting, and necessary care: *Better cultivation of soil will result in better crops.* **2** condition of being prepared by plowing, planting, etc.: *Only half the farm was under cultivation.* **3** act of improving or developing by study or training: *The cultivation of good study habits can lead to better grades.* **4** result of improvement or growth through education and experience; culture.

cul·ti·va·tor (kul′tə vā′tər), *n.* **1** tool or machine used to loosen the ground and destroy weeds. A cultivator is pulled or pushed between rows of growing plants. **2** person or thing that cultivates.

cul·tur·al (kul′chər əl), *adj.* of about culture: *We both enjoy going to symphony concerts, ballets, the theater, and other cultural events.* —**cul′tur·al·ly,** *adv.*

cul·ture (kul′chər), **1** *n.* fineness of feelings, thoughts, tastes, manners, etc.; refinement: *A person of culture appreciates art, music, and literature.* **2** *n.* the customs, arts, and conveniences of a nation or people at a given time: *The culture of the ancient Inca is noted for its art, its fine buildings, and its religion.* **3** *n.* development of the mind or body by education or training: *a course in physical culture.* **4** *n.* preparation of land and producing of crops; cultivation. **5** act or process of cultivating or breeding animals or plants, especially to get new or improved kinds: *bee culture.* **6** *n.* growth of bacteria or other tiny living things in a laboratory for medical or scientific use. **7** *v.* to grow bacteria or other tiny living things in a laboratory for medical or scientific use. ❑ *v.* **cul·tured, cul·tur·ing.**

cul·tured (kul′chərd), *adj.* **1** having a good education and fine manners: *a cultured person.* **2** produced or raised by culture: *cultured pearls.*

cul·vert (kul′vərt), *n.* a small pipe or channel for water crossing under a road, railroad, etc.

Cum·ber·land (kum′bər lənd), *n.* river flowing from SE Kentucky through N Tennessee and W Kentucky into the Ohio River. [**Cumberland** probably comes from a Welsh word meaning "Welsh." The American river and mountains are named for a part of Britain.]

Cumberland Mountains *or* **Cumberland Plateau,** plateau of the Appalachian Mountains, extending from S West Virginia to N Alabama.

cum·ber·some (kum′bər səm), *adj.* hard to manage; clumsy, unwieldy, or burdensome: *The armor worn by knights was often so cumbersome they had to be helped onto their horses.* —**cum′ber·some·ly,** *adv.* —**cum′ber·some·ness,** *n.*

cum·brous (kum′brəs), *adj.* cumbersome. —**cum′brous·ly,** *adv.* —**cum′brous·ness,** *n.*

cu·min (kum′ən), *n.* a small herb related to parsley. Its seedlike fruits are used in cooking.

cum lau·de (kùm lou′dē *or* kùm lò′dē), with honors: *She graduated cum laude with a major in engineering.*

Cum·mings (kum′ingz), *n.* E. E., 1894-1962, American poet and playwright. He often spelled his name *e e cummings.*

cu·mu·la·tive (kyü′myə lə tiv), *adj.* increasing or growing by additions; accumulated: *The cumulative effects of many illnesses made the patient weak.* —**cu′mu·la·tive·ly,** *adv.* —**cu′mu·la·tive·ness,** *n.*

cu·mu·lo·nim·bus (kyü′myə lō nim′bəs), *n.* a very large cloud formation with very tall peaks that sometimes flatten at the top; thundercloud; thunderhead. ❑ *n., pl.* **cu·mu·lo·nim·bus·es, cu·mu·lo·nim·bi** (kyü′myə lō nim′bī).

cu·mu·lus (kyü′myə ləs), *n.* cloud formed of rounded heaps, rising from a low, flat bottom to as high as 60,000 feet (18,000 meters). Cumuli are seen in fair weather. ❑ *n., pl.* **cu·mu·li** (kyü′myə lī).

cumulus

cu·ne·i·form (kyü nē′ə fôrm), **1** *n.* the wedge-shaped characters used in the writing of ancient Babylonia, Assyria, Persia, etc. **2** *adj.* composed of cuneiform inscriptions: *cuneiform tablets.*

cun·ning (kun′ing), **1** *adj.* clever in deceiving; sly: *The cunning fox outwitted the dogs and got away.* ■ See Synonym Study at **sly. 2** *n.* slyness in getting what you need or want or in deceiving your enemies: *The fox has a great deal of cunning.* **3** *adj.* clever; skillful: *With cunning hand the sculptor shaped the little statue.* **4** *n.* skill; cleverness: *The old sculptor's hand never lost its cunning.* **5** *adj.* INFORMAL. pretty and dear; cute: *What a cunning baby!* [See Word Story at **pretty.**] —**cun′ning·ly,** *adv.*

cup (kup), **1** *n.* container to drink from. Most cups have handles. **2** *n.* as much as a cup holds; cupful: *He drank a cup of milk.* **3** *n.*

unit of volume for liquids, equal to eight fluid ounces. **4** *n.* thing shaped like a cup. The petals of some flowers form a cup. **5** *v.* to shape like a cup: *She cupped her hands to catch the ball.* **6** *v.* to take or put in a cup: *I cupped the flour from the bag.* **7** *n.* an ornamental cup, vase, etc., given to the winner of a contest. **8** *n.* (in golf) hole. ❑ *v.* **cupped, cup·ping.** —**cup′like′**, *adj.*

cup·board (kub′ərd), *n.* **1** closet or cabinet with shelves, especially for dishes and food supplies. **2** any small closet.

cup·cake (kup′kāk′), *n.* a small cake about the same size as a cup.

cup·ful (kup′fùl), *n.* as much as a cup holds. In cooking, a cupful equals a half pint. ❑ *n., pl.* **cup·fuls.**

Cu·pid (kyü′pid), *n.* **1** Roman god of love, son of Mercury and Venus. The Greeks called him Eros. Cupid is usually shown as a winged boy with bow and arrows. **2 cupid**, a winged boy used as a symbol of love: *a valentine covered with little cupids.*

cu·pid·i·ty (kyü pid′ə tē), *n.* eager desire to possess something; greed.

cu·po·la (kyü′pə lə), *n.* **1** a rounded roof; dome: *The Capitol at Washington, D.C., has a cupola.* **2** a small dome or tower on a roof. ❑ *n., pl.* **cu·po·las.**

cur (kėr), *n.* **1** dog of mixed breed; mongrel. **2** a bad-tempered, contemptible person.

cur·a·ble (kyùr′ə bəl), *adj.* able to be cured: *With proper care and medicine tuberculosis is a curable disease.* —**cur′a·bil′i·ty**, *n.* —**cur′a·bly**, *adv.*

cu·rar·e (kyù rä′rē or kù rä′rē), *n.* a poisonous extract of some tropical plants, used on arrows by some South American Indians. Curare is used in medicine to help relax muscles.

cur·ate (kyùr′it), *n.* member of the clergy who assists a pastor, rector, or vicar.

cur·a·tive (kyùr′ə tiv), **1** *adj.* having the power to cure; tending to cure; curing. **2** *n.* means of curing; remedy. —**cur′a·tive·ly**, *adv.*

cu·ra·tor (kyù rā′tər), *n.* person in charge of all or part of a museum, library, art gallery, zoo, etc.

curb (kėrb), **1** *n.* a raised border of concrete or stone along the edge of a pavement or sidewalk: *Park the car close to the curb.* **2** *v.* to hold back; check; restrain: *I curbed my hunger by eating a piece of cheese.* **3** *n.* act of holding back; check; restraint: *Put a curb on your temper.* **4** *n.* chain or strap fastened to a horse's bit and passed under its lower jaw. When the reins are pulled tight, the curb checks the horse. **5** *v.* to lead a dog to the curb, gutter, or other place where it may defecate.

curb·ing (kėr′bing), *n.* **1** material for making a curb. **2** a curb.

curb·stone (kėrb′stōn′), *n.* stone or stones forming a curb along the edge of a pavement or sidewalk.

curd (kėrd), *n.* **1** Often, **curds**, *pl.* the thick part of milk that separates from the watery part when milk sours. Cheese is made from curds. **2** any food that resembles this: *lemon curd.* [See Word Story at **curl**.]

cur·dle (kėr′dl), *v.* **1** to form into curds: *Milk curdles when kept too long.* **2** to thicken. ❑ *v.* **cur·dled, cur·dling.**

cure (kyùr), **1** *v.* to make well; bring back to health: *The medicine cured the sick child.* **2** *v.* to get rid of: *Only great determination can cure a bad habit like smoking.* **3** *n.* means of curing; treatment intended to relieve or remove disease or any bad condition: *a cure for polio, a cure for laziness.* **4** *n.* medicine that is a means of curing; remedy: *Quinine is a cure for malaria.* **5** *n.* a successful medical treatment; restoration to health. **6** *v.* to preserve bacon, fish, etc., by drying, salting, smoking, pickling, etc. **7** *v.* to be or become cured: *Tobacco leaves are often hung in barns to cure.* ❑ *v.* **cured, cur·ing.** —**cur′er**, *n.*

cure-all (kyùr′ôl′), *n.* remedy supposed to cure all diseases or ills; panacea.

cur·few (kėr′fyü), *n.* **1** rule requiring certain persons to be off the streets or at home before a fixed time: *There is a 10 P.M. curfew for children in our city.* **2** formerly, the ringing of a bell at a

fixed time every evening as a signal. In the Middle Ages, it was a signal to put out lights and cover fires. **3** time when a curfew begins: *The curfew at our summer camp is 10 o'clock.*

Cur·ie (kyùr′ē or kyù rē′), *n.* **1 Marie**, 1867-1934, French physicist and chemist, born in Poland. She and her husband Pierre discovered radium in 1898. **2 Pierre** (pyer), 1859-1906, French physicist and chemist. ■ **Marie** and **Pierre Curie** shared the Nobel Prize for physics in 1903 with Antoine Becquerel. Marie Curie won another Nobel Prize, for chemistry, in 1911. Their daughter and son-in-law, Irène and Frédéric Joliot-Curie, shared the Nobel Prize for chemistry in 1935.

cur·ie (kyùr′ē or kyù rē′), *n.* unit for measuring the amount of radioactivity. [The **curie** is named for Pierre Curie, who was killed in a traffic accident soon after he and Marie won the Nobel Prize.]

cur·i·o (kyùr′ē ō), *n.* object valued as a curiosity: *a curio from the Orient.* ❑ *n., pl.* **cur·i·os.**

cur·i·os·i·ty (kyùr′ē os′ə tē), *n.* **1** an eager desire to know: *She satisfied her curiosity about animals by visiting the zoo every week.* **2** condition of being too eager to know; inquisitiveness: *Curiosity got the better of me, and I opened the box.* **3** a strange, rare, or novel object: *One of the curiosities we saw was a basket made from an armadillo's shell.* ❑ *n., pl.* **cur·i·os·i·ties** for 3.

cur·i·ous (kyùr′ē əs), *adj.* **1** eager to know: *Small children are very curious and they ask many questions.* **2** too eager to know; inquisitive: *Some people are always curious about their neighbors' business.* **3** strange, odd, or unusual: *I found a curious old box in the attic.* —**cur′i·ous·ly**, *adv.* —**cur′i·ous·ness**, *n.*

cur·i·um (kyùr′ē əm), *n.* a radioactive metallic element produced artificially from plutonium or americium. *Symbol:* Cm

curl (kėrl), **1** *v.* to twist into ringlets; roll into coils: *My hair curls naturally.* **2** *v.* to twist out of shape; bend into a curve: *Paper curls as it burns.* **3** *v.* to rise in rings: *Smoke is curling slowly from the chimney.* **4** *n.* a curled lock of hair. **5** *n.* anything curled or bent into a curve: *Wood shavings form curls.*
curl up, to draw up your legs: *I curled up on the sofa.*

curl·er (kėr′lər), *n.* device on which hair is twisted or wound to make it curl.

cur·lew (kėr′lü), *n.* any of eight large wading birds with long, thin bills curved downward. ❑ *n., pl.* **cur·lews** or **cur·lew.**

curl·i·cue (kėr′lə kyü), *n.* a fancy twist, curl, or flourish: *Curlicues in handwriting.*

curl·ing (kėr′ling), *n.* game in which large, smooth, rounded stones with handles are slid over ice at a target.

curlew—about 20 in. (51 cm) long

curl·y (kėr′lē), *adj.* **1** curling or tending to curl; wavy: *curly hair.* **2** having curls or curly hair: *a curly head.* ❑ *adj.* **curl·i·er, curl·i·est. —cur′li·ness,** *n.*

cur·rant (kėr′ənt), *n.* **1** a small raisin without seeds made from small, sweet grapes grown mostly in the countries on the eastern Mediterranean Sea. Currants are used in puddings, cakes, and buns. **2** a small, sour, red, black, or white berry that grows on any of numerous bushes and is used for jelly and preserves. ■ Another word that sounds like this is **current.**

cur·ren·cy (kėr′ən sē), *n.* **1** money in actual use in a country: *Coins and paper money are currency in the United States.* **2** general use or acceptance; common occurrence: *Words such as "couldst" and "thou" have little currency now.* ❑ *n., pl.* **cur·ren·cies** for 1.

cur·rent (kėr′ənt), **1** *n.* a flow of water, air, or any fluid; running stream: *The current swept the stick down the river.* **2** *n.* flow of electricity through a wire or other conductor: *The current failed when wind knocked down the power lines.* **3** *n.* rate or amount of electrical flow, usually expressed in amperes. **4** *n.* course or movement of events or of opinions: *Newspapers influence the current of public opinion.* **5** *adj.* of the present time. The current issue of a magazine is the latest one published. *We discuss current events in social studies class.* **6** *adj.* widespread and generally accepted: *Long ago the belief was current that the earth was flat.* **7** *adj.* going around; passing from person to person: *A rumor is current that school will close a week early this year.* ■ Another word that sounds like this is **currant. —cur′rent·ness,** *n.*

WORD FAMILY Current and the words below are related. They all come from a Latin word meaning "to run."

concur	curriculum	excursion	occur
corridor	cursive	incur	precursor
courier	cursor	intercourse	recur
course	discourse		

---

cur·rent·ly (kėr′ənt lē), *adv.* at the present time; now: *The flu is currently going around school.*

cur·ric·u·lar (kə rik′yə lər), *adj.* of or for a curriculum.

cur·ric·u·lum (kə rik′yə ləm), *n.* course of study: *At our school the curriculum in sixth grade includes mathematics, science, social studies, reading, and spelling.* ❑ *n., pl.* **cur·ric·u·lums, cur·ric·u·la** (kə rik′yə lə).

cur·ry[1] (kėr′ē), *v.* to rub and clean a horse with a currycomb. ❑ *v.* **cur·ried, cur·ry·ing. —cur′ri·er,** *n.*

cur·ry[2] (kėr′ē), **1** *n.* a peppery sauce or powder made from a mixture of spices, seeds, and vegetables. Curry is a popular seasoning in India. **2** *n.* food flavored with it. **3** *v.* to prepare or flavor food with curry. ❑ *n., pl.* **cur·ries;** *v.* **cur·ried, cur·ry·ing.**

cur·ry·comb (kėr′ē kōm′), *n.* a comb or brush with metal teeth for rubbing and cleaning a horse.

curse (kėrs), **1** *v.* to ask God or a powerful spirit to bring evil or harm on: *The evil witch cursed the prince.* **2** *n.* the words that someone says when cursing in this way: *to utter a curse against an enemy.* **3** *v.* to bring evil or harm on; trouble greatly; torment: *The farmers were cursed with dry weather and dust storms.* **4** *n.* trouble; harm: *My quick temper has been a curse to me all my life.* **5** *v.* to use profane language; swear. **6** *v.* to swear at. **7** *n.* words used in swearing: *Their talk was full of curses.* ❑ *v.* **cursed, curs·ing.**

USAGE NOTE Curse words are almost always meaningless in the situation where they are used. Their effect comes only from the custom of not using them in polite language. Old curse words, such as **zounds,** seem strange, because no one minds them.

Cursing is a way of trying to get attention by bothering people. Those who can use language well are able to get attention in more interesting ways. So cursing is mostly a sign of limited vocabulary and lack of imagination.

---

curs·ed (kėr′sid *or* kėrst), *adj.* **1** under a curse. **2** deserving a curse; evil; hateful. **—curs′ed·ly,** *adv.*

cur·sive (kėr′siv), *adj.* written with the letters joined together. Ordinary handwriting is cursive.

cur·sor (kėr′sər), *n.* a movable mark on a computer screen. It shows the point at which the displayed data may be altered or processed, or at which new data may be inserted.

cur·sor·y (kėr′sər ē), *adj.* without attention to details; hasty and superficial: *She gave the lesson a cursory glance, expecting to study it later.* **—cur′sor·i·ly,** *adv.* **—cur′sor·i·ness,** *n.*

curt (kėrt), *adj.* rudely brief; short; abrupt: *The impatient clerk gave a curt reply.* **—curt′ly,** *adv.* **—curt′ness,** *n.*

cur·tail (kėr tāl′), *v.* to cut short; cut off part of; reduce; lessen: *During the drought it was necessary to curtail the use of water.* **—cur·tail′er,** *n.* **—cur·tail′ment,** *n.*

cur·tain (kėrt′n), **1** *n.* cloth hung across a window or other space to shut out light, give privacy, or for decoration. **2** *n.* the drapery or hanging screen which separates the stage of a theater from the part where the audience sits. **3** *n.* the fall or closing of the curtain at the end of an act or scene. **4** *v.* to provide or shut off with a curtain or curtains: *They took two sheets and curtained off a space in the corner.* **5** *v.* to cover; hide: *Darkness curtained the entire winter countryside.* **6** *n.* thing that covers or hides: *A curtain of fog fell over the harbor.*

curt·sey (kėrt′sē), *n., v.* curtsy. ❑ *n., pl.* **curt·seys;** *v.* **curt·seyed, curt·sey·ing.** [See Word Story at **courtesy.**]

curt·sy (kėrt′sē), **1** *n.* bow of respect or greeting by women and girls, made by bending the knees and lowering the body slightly. **2** *v.* to make a curtsy: *The actress curtsied when the audience applauded.* ❑ *n., pl.* **curt·sies;** *v.* **curt·sied, curt·sy·ing.** [See Word Story at **courtesy.**]

curtsy

cur·va·ture (kėr′və chər), *n.* **1** a curved condition: *curvature of the spine.* **2** act of curving.

curve (kėrv), **1** *n.* line that has no straight part. A circle is a closed curve. **2** *n.* something having the shape of a curve; bend: *The car had to slow down to go around the curves in the road.* **3** *v.* to bend so as to form a curve; bend in a curve: *The highway curved sharply to the right.* **4** *v.* to cause to curve or bend: *He curved his fingers around the peach.* **5** *n.* baseball thrown to swerve just before it reaches the batter. ❑ *v.* **curved, curv·ing.**

throw someone a curve, to take someone by surprise by doing something unexpected: *The crooks threw the detective a curve by hiding their stolen money in her office.*

cush·ion (kush′ən), **1** *n.* a soft pillow or pad used to sit, lie, or kneel on: *The couch has cushions on the seat and along the back.* **2** *n.* anything that makes a soft place: *a cushion of moss under a tree.* **3** *v.* to put or rest on a cushion: *The nurse cushioned the patient's head.* **4** *v.* to provide with a cushion: *cushion a chair with foam rubber.* **5** *n.* anything that softens, lessens, or protects from a shock, jar, or jolt. Air or steam forms a protective cushion in some machines. *The bush acted as a cushion to my fall.* **6** *v.* to soften or ease the effects of: *Nothing could cushion the shock of my friend's death.*

cusp (kusp), *n.* **1** a pointed end; point: *A crescent has two cusps.* **2** a pointed end on the crown of a tooth.

cus·pid (kus′pid), *n.* canine tooth.

cus·pi·dor (kus′pə dôr′), *n.* spittoon.

cuss (kus), INFORMAL. **1** v. to curse. **2** n. an odd or troublesome person: *What a strange cuss he is!* □ n., pl. **cuss·es.**

cus·tard (kus′tərd), n. a baked, boiled, or frozen mixture of eggs, milk, and sugar. Custard is used as a dessert or as a food for sick people.

Cus·ter (kus′tər), n. **George Armstrong,** 1839-1876, U.S. Army officer in the Civil War and in many Indian wars. ■ **George Custer** was defeated by Crazy Horse and Sitting Bull at the Battle of Little Bighorn in 1876. He and every soldier in his command were killed there.

cus·to·di·an (ku stō′dē ən), n. **1** person in charge; guardian; keeper: *He is the custodian of the library's collection of rare books.* **2** person who takes care of a building or offices; janitor: *a school custodian.*

cus·to·dy (kus′tə dē), n. watchful keeping; charge; care: *Parents have the custody of their young children. All the important papers are in the lawyer's custody.*

in custody, in the care of the police; under arrest: *The person accused of the robbery is now in custody.*

take into custody, to arrest: *The suspect was taken into custody by the police.*

cus·tom (kus′təm), **1** n. any usual action or practice; habit: *It was her custom to rise early.* ■ See Synonym Study at **habit. 2** n. a long-established or accepted way of doing things: *The social customs of many countries differ from ours.* **3** adj. made to order; custom-made: *custom clothes.* **4** adj. making things to order: *He had that suit made by a custom tailor.* **5** n.pl. **customs, a** taxes paid to the government on things brought in from foreign countries: *I paid $4 in customs on the $100 Swiss watch.* **b** department of the government that collects these taxes. [See Word Story at **costume.**]

cus·tom·ar·y (kus′tə mer′ē), adj. according to custom; usual: *Ten o'clock is her customary bedtime.* ■ See Synonym Study at **usual.** —**cus′tom·ar′i·ly,** adv. —**cus′tom·ar′i·ness,** n.

customary system, a system for measuring length in inches, feet, yards, and miles; capacity in cups, pints, quarts, and gallons; weight in ounces, pounds, and tons; and temperature in degrees Fahrenheit; now used mostly in the United States. See table on page 975A.

cus·tom·er (kus′tə mər), n. **1** person who buys goods or services. **2** person; individual: *He can be a rough customer when he gets angry.*

cus·tom·house (kus′təm hous′), n. a government building or office, usually at a seaport, airport, or border crossing point, where taxes on things brought into a country are collected. □ n., pl. **cus·tom·hous·es** (kus′təm hou′ziz).

cus·tom·ize (kus′tə mīz), v. to build, alter, or remodel to the desires or requirements of the buyer: *customize a kitchen, customize a car.* □ v. **cus·tom·ized, cus·tom·iz·ing.**

cus·tom-made (kus′təm mād′), adj. made to order; made specially for an individual customer: *a custom-made suit.*

cut (kut), **1** v. to divide, separate, open, or remove with a knife or any tool that has a sharp edge: *I cut the meat with a knife. We cut a branch from the tree.* **2** v. to pierce or wound with something sharp: *She cut her finger on the broken glass.* **3** n. opening made by something sharp: *bandage a cut.* **4** n. passage or channel that has been made by cutting or digging: *The train went through a deep cut in the side of the mountain.* **5** n. piece cut off or cut out: *A leg of lamb is a tasty cut of meat.* **6** v. to make a cut, opening, channel, etc.: *This knife cuts well.* **7** v. to make by cutting: *They cut a hole through the wall with an ax.* **8** v. to be cut: *Cheese cuts easily.* **9** n. way in which a thing is cut; style; fashion: *the narrow, close-fitting cut of his coat.* **10** v. to make a recording on: *cut a record, cut a tape.* **11** v. to have teeth grow through the gums: *The baby is cutting her first tooth.* **12** v. to reduce; decrease: *We must cut our expenses to save money.* **13** n. reduction; decrease: *The store made a cut in prices to attract more customers.* **14** v. to shorten by removing a part or parts; trim: *cut a speech, cut the hedge, cut one's hair.* **15** n. shortcut. **16** v. to go by a shortcut: *She cut across the field to save time.* **17** v. to change direction suddenly; swerve: *The car cut across three lanes toward the high-*

way exit. **18** v. to cross: *A brook cuts through that field.* **19** v. to hit or strike sharply: *The cold wind cut me to the bone.* **20** n. a sharp swing or stroke: *He took a cut at the ball and missed.* **21** v. to hurt the feelings of: *His mean remark cut me.* **22** n. action or speech that hurts the feelings. **23** v. to stop: *cut an engine. The director said, "Cut!"* **24** v. to act as if you do not know someone: *After our fight, she cut me whenever we met.* **25** v. to be absent from a class, lecture, etc.: *cut a history class.* **26** n. an unexcused absence from school or a class. **27** n. block or plate with a picture engraved on it, used in printing. **28** n. a share: *Each partner has a cut of the profits.* **29** v. to divide a deck of cards at random. **30** v. to weaken by mixing; dilute: *Mom cuts bleach with water for cleaning.* □ v. **cut, cut·ting.**

cut and dried, dull; uninteresting: *The speech was cut and dried.*

cut back, to reduce or curtail: *The company had to cut back production because orders fell off.*

cut down, 1 to cause to fall by cutting: *cut down a tree.* **2** to reduce; decrease: *cut down one's allowance.*

cut in, 1 to break in; interrupt: *She cut in suddenly with a remark while I was talking.* **2** to interrupt a dancing couple to take the place of one of them. **3** to move a vehicle suddenly into a line of moving traffic: *The driver cut in, just missing another car.*

cut off, 1 to remove by cutting: *Cut off that branch.* **2** to shut off: *cut off the water.* **3** to stop suddenly: *cut off all hope of success.* **4** to break; interrupt: *cut off a conversation.* **5** to disinherit: *Grandfather cut her off without a cent.* **6** to intercept: *The posse cut off the cattle rustlers near the river.*

cut out, 1 to remove by cutting: *He cut out the picture from a newspaper.* **2** to take out; leave out: *Why did you cut out this part of the play?* **3** to stop doing, using, making, etc.: *Please cut out the noise.*

cut up, 1 to cut to pieces. **2** hurt: *He was cut up by the criticism.* **3** OLD USE. to show off; play tricks.

SYNONYM STUDY **Cut** has many synonyms, each with its own special meaning listed in this dictionary. If you need a synonym for **cut,** try one of the words below:

amputate	cube	prune[2]	slash
butcher	dice	saw[1]	slice
carve	dissect	sever	snip
chop[1]	hack[1]	shave	split
clip[1]	mince	shear	trim

cut·a·way (kut′ə wā′), **1** n. man's formal coat with the lower part cut back in a curve or slope from the waist in front to the tails in back. **2** n. object, or a model or drawing of an object, having part of its covering removed to show a section of its working parts for examination. **3** adj. showing or representing an object in this way: *a cutaway drawing of an engine.*

cut·back (kut′bak′), n. reduction: *a cutback in expenditures, a cutback in production.*

cute (kyüt), adj. **1** pretty and dear: *a cute baby.* **2** handsome; good-looking. **3** clever; shrewd: *a cute trick.* □ adj. **cut·er, cut·est.** —**cute′ly,** adv. —**cute′ness,** n.

WORD STORY **Cute** comes from **acute.** Its oldest meaning is "clever," from which came the meaning "full of clever ideas, attractive," and then our main meaning, "attractive, good-looking." The first letter fell off the word because it is easier to say "very cute" than "very acute."

cu·ti·cle (kyü′tə kəl), n. the hard skin around the sides and base of a fingernail or toenail.

cut·lass (kut′ləs), n. a short, heavy, slightly curved sword, used in former times especially by sailors. □ n., pl. **cut·lass·es.**

cut·ler·y (kut′lər ē), n. **1** cutting tools, such as knives and scissors. **2** knives, forks, and spoons, for table use.

---

a	hat	ė	term	ȯ	order	ch	child		a in about
ā	age	i	it	oi	oil	ng	long		e in taken
ä	far	ī	ice	ou	out	sh	she	ə {	i in pencil
â	care	o	hot	u	cup	th	thin		o in lemon
e	let	ō	open	ů	put	ŦH	then		u in circus
ē	equal	ȯ	saw	ü	rule	zh	measure		

cut·let (kut′lit), *n.* **1** slice of meat cut from the leg or ribs for broiling or frying: *a veal cutlet.* **2** a flat, fried cake of chopped meat or fish.

cut·off (kut′ôf), **1** *n.* a short way across or through; shortcut: *We'll save time if we take the cutoff across the park.* **2** *n.* valve or other device that stops the passage of liquid, gas, etc., through a pipe or opening. **3** *adj.* at or in which anything is cut off: *A cutoff date ends this agreement.*

cut·out (kut′out′), *n.* shape or design to be cut out: *Some books for children have cutouts.*

cut-rate (kut′rāt′), *adj.* **1** offered at reduced rates or prices: *cut-rate merchandise.* **2** offering goods at reduced rates or prices: *cut-rate stores.*

cut·ter (kut′ər), *n.* **1** tool or machine for cutting: *a wire cutter, a cookie cutter.* **2** person who cuts: *A garment cutter cuts out pieces of fabric to be made into clothes.* **3** (earlier) a small, light sleigh, usually pulled by one horse. **4** a small, armed ship used for patrolling by the Coast Guard. **5** boat belonging to a ship, used to carry people and supplies to and from the ship.

cyclone (def. 2)

cut·throat (kut′thrōt′), **1** *n.* person who kills; murderer. **2** *adj.* murderous: *a cutthroat band of pirates.* **3** *adj.* without mercy; relentless or severe: *cutthroat competition.*

cut·ting (kut′ing), **1** *n.* a small shoot cut from a plant to grow a new plant. **2** *n.* a newspaper or magazine clipping. **3** *adj.* able to cut; sharp: *the cutting edge of a knife.* **4** *adj.* hurting the feelings: *a cutting remark.* —**cut′ting·ly,** *adv.*

cutting-edge (kut′ing ej′), *adj.* brand new, using the very latest ideas, technology, etc.: *cutting-edge sports equipment.*

cut·tle·bone (kut′l bōn′), *n.* the hard inside shell of cuttlefish. It is used for making polishing powder and as food for pet birds.

cut·tle·fish (kut′l fish′), *n.* any of numerous saltwater mollusks that have eight short arms, two long tentacles, and a hard internal shell. When threatened, cuttlefishes squirt out an inky fluid. ❑ *n., pl.* **cut·tle·fish** or **cut·tle·fish·es.**

cut·up (kut′up′), *n.* OLD USE. person who shows off or plays tricks.

cut·worm (kut′wėrm′), *n.* any of several caterpillars that cut off the stalks of young plants near or below the ground when feeding on them at night.

-cy, *suffix.* position of or condition of being ___: *captaincy = position of a captain; bankruptcy = condition of being bankrupt.*

cy·an (sī′an), *n.* **1** a greenish blue. **2** a greenish blue ink or dye, used in printing, photography, and other full-color reproduction methods.

cy·a·nide (sī′ə nīd), *n.* any of various metal salts used in making plastics and insecticides, in extracting gold and silver from ores, and in treating metals. Some kinds of cyanide are extremely poisonous.

cyber-, *prefix.* of or about computers: *cyberspace = space created by computers.*

cy·ber·net·ics (sī′bər net′iks), *n.* science which studies and compares systems of communication and control, such as those in the brain and those in electronic or mechanical devices.

cy·ber·space (sī′bər spās), *n.* **1** a three-dimensional visual space created by computer graphics. By giving instructions to the computer, a user can move objects pictured in this space, or change

viewpoint so as to move among the objects. **2** an imaginary space in which computers operate and communicate. Anything done with a computer can be said to happen in cyberspace, such as exchange of messages, playing games, or organization of files: *notes lost in cyberspace, a conference in cyberspace.*

cy·borg (sī′bôrg), *n.* person or animal with many mechanical and electronic body parts. [**Cyborg** is a combination of **cybernetics** and **organism.**]

cy·cad (sī′kad), *n.* any of several large tropical plants with a cluster of long, fernlike leaves that rise from an underground stem or from the top of a thick trunk. Cycads bear cones.

cyc·la·men (sik′lə mən), *n.* any of several plants with heart-shaped leaves and showy white, purple, pink, or deep red flowers, having five petals that bend backward.

cy·cle (sī′kəl), **1** *n.* series of events that repeats itself in the same order again and again. The seasons of the year make a cycle. **2** *n.* a complete set or series: *a cycle of songs.* **3** *n.* all the stories or legends told about a certain hero or event: *There is a cycle of stories about the adventures of King Arthur and his knights.* **4** *n.* bicycle, motorcycle, etc. **5** *v.* to ride a bicycle, motorcycle, etc. **6** *n.* a complete reversal of an alternating electric current in both directions. The number of cycles per second, called hertz, is the frequency of the current. ❑ *v.* **cy·cled, cy·cling.** —**cy′cler,** *n.*

WORD FAMILY Cycle and the words below are related. They all come from a Greek word meaning "wheel."

bicycle	cyclone	motorcycle	tricycle
cyclic	encyclopedia	recycle	unicycle

---

cy·clic (sī′klik), *adj.* **1** of a cycle: *the cyclic motion of a piston.* **2** moving in cycles; coming in cycles: *the cyclic nature of the seasons.* —**cy′cli·cal·ly,** *adv.*

cy·cli·cal (sī′klə kəl), *adj.* cyclic.

cy·clist (sī′klist), *n.* rider of a bicycle, motorcycle, etc.

cy·clone (sī′klōn), *n.* **1** a large area of winds moving around and toward a calm center of low pressure, which also moves. **2** tornado. —**cy·clon′ic,** *adj.*

Cy·clops (sī′klops), *n.* (in Greek legends) one of a race of giants, each having only one eye in the center of the forehead. ❑ *n., pl.* **Cy·clo·pes** (sī klō′pēz).

cy·clo·spo·rine (sī′klə spôr′ēn), *n.* drug that makes organ transplants possible by preventing the body's immune system from attacking and rejecting a heart, kidney, etc., donated from someone else's body.

cy·clo·tron (sī′klə tron), *n.* particle accelerator that forces protons or other subatomic particles to travel at very high speeds in a circular path.

cyg·net (sig′nit), *n.* a young swan. ▪ Another word that sounds like this is **signet.**

cyl·in·der (sil′ən dər), *n.* **1** any long, round object, solid or hollow, with flat ends. Rollers and tin cans are cylinders. **2** a solid bounded by two equal, parallel circles and by a curved surface, formed by moving a straight line of fixed length so that its ends always lie on the two parallel circles. **3** the rotating part of a revolver that contains chambers for cartridges. **4** the piston chamber of a internal-combustion engine.

cygnet

WORD STORY Cylinder comes from a Greek word meaning "to roll." In ancient times, the only way to move heavy objects such as building stones was on rollers, usually wooden ones. Anything shaped like a round log was called a roller too.

---

cy·lin·dri·cal (sə lin′drə kəl), *adj.* shaped like a cylinder; having the form of a cylinder. Silos, candles, and water pipes are often cylindrical. —**cy·lin′dri·cal·ly,** *adv.*

cym·bal (sim′bəl), *n.* one of a pair of brass plates, used as a musical instrument. When cymbals are struck together, they make a loud, ringing sound. [See Word Story at **chime**.] ■ Another word that sounds like this is **symbol**.

cyn·ic (sin′ik), *n.* person inclined to doubt the sincerity and goodness of human motives and to show this doubt by sneers and sarcasm. [**Cynic** comes from a Greek word meaning "dog," probably because a cynic seems like a snarling, unfriendly dog.]

SYNONYM STUDY **Cynic** and **skeptic** both mean a person who doubts usual beliefs. **Cynic** means someone who states that doubt strongly and unpleasantly: *She is such a cynic that she assumes people will always try to cheat her.* **Skeptic** means someone who is hard to convince: *Until I see a UFO myself, I'll stay a skeptic about space aliens.*

cyn·i·cal (sin′ə kəl), *adj.* **1** doubting the sincerity and goodness of others. **2** sneering; sarcastic: *It is hard to befriend someone who is cynical about friendship.* —**cyn′i·cal·ly**, *adv.* —**cyn′i·cal·ness**, *n.*

cyn·i·cism (sin′ə siz′əm), *n.* **1** cynical disposition. **2** a cynical remark.

cy·no·sure (sī′nə shůr), *n.* center of attraction, interest, or attention.

cy·press (sī′prəs), *n.* **1** any of several evergreen trees and bushes with small, dark green leaves like scales. **2** tree of the southern United States, related to the giant sequoia. Its wood is used for boards and shingles. ❑ *n., pl.* **cy·press·es.**

Cyp·ri·ot (sip′rē ət), **1** *n.* person born or living in Cyprus. **2** *adj.* of Cyprus.

Cyp·ri·ote (sip′rē ōt), *n., adj.* Cypriot.

Cy·prus (sī′prəs), *n.* island country in the E Mediterranean, south of Turkey. *Capital:* Nicosia.

WORD STORY **Cyprus** may come from the Greek word for copper, which was plentiful there in old times. Or the Greek word for copper may come from the name **Cyprus**, because it was found there. It's hard to say, but one is named for the other.

Cy·ril (sir′əl), *n.* **Saint**, 827-869, Greek missionary to a region now in the Czech Republic, traditionally thought of as the inventor of the Cyrillic alphabet. [**Cyril** comes from a Greek word meaning "noble."]

ВЕЧЕРИНКА	ЭСКИЗ	ТИШИНЫ!
VECHERINKA	ESKIZ	TISHINY!
PARTY	SKETCH	SILENCE!

Cyrillic alphabet

Cy·ril·lic (si ril′ik), *adj.* of or in the alphabet used for Russian and some other languages.

Cy·rus (sī′rəs), *n.* died 529 B.C., king of Persia and founder of the Persian empire. He was called "Cyrus the Great." ■ **Cyrus** freed the Jews held captive in Babylonia and allowed them to rebuild their temple in Jerusalem. [**Cyrus** comes from a Persian word meaning "throne."]

cyst (sist), *n.* a small, abnormal saclike growth in an animal or plant, sometimes containing diseased matter.

cyst·ic fib·ro·sis (sis′tik fi brō′sis), a disease in which certain cells of the body emit large amounts of thick mucus, usually causing lung infections and other problems. Cystic fibrosis is inherited from parents who usually do not have the disease.

cy·tol·o·gy (sī tol′ə jē), *n.* branch of biology that deals with the structure and function of cells. —**cy·tol′o·gist**, *n.*

cy·to·plasm (sī′tə plaz′əm), *n.* the living substance or protoplasm of a cell, outside of the nucleus.

cy·to·sine (sī′tə sēn′), *n.* substance present in nucleic acid. It is one of the compounds that form the genetic code in DNA and RNA.

cy·to·tox·in (sī′tə tok′sin), *n.* a substance that kills or harms certain cells.

C.Z., Canal Zone.

czar (zär), *n.* **1** emperor. It was the title of the former emperors of Russia. **2** person having absolute power. Also, **tsar** or **tzar**. [See Word Story at **kaiser**.]

czar·das (chär däsh′), *n.* **1** a Hungarian dance made up of a slow beginning section and a fast closing section. **2** the music for it.

cza·ri·na (zä rē′nə), *n.* wife of a czar; Russian empress. ❑ *n., pl.* **cza·ri·nas.** Also, **tsarina** or **tzarina**.

Czech (chek), **1** *n.* member of a branch of the Slavs. Bohemians, Moravians, and Silesians are Czechs. **2** *n.* their language; Bohemian. **3** *n.* Czechoslovak. **4** *adj.* of the Czech Republic, its people, or the language of the Czechs. ❑ *n., pl.* **Czechs** for 1,3.

Czech·o·slo·vak (chek′ə slō′vak *or* chek′ə slō′väk), **1** *adj.* of Czechoslovakia or its people. **2** *n.* person born or living in Czechoslovakia.

Czech·o·slo·va·ki·a (chek′ə slō vä′kē ə), *n.* former country in central Europe. In 1993 it separated into the Czech Republic and Slovakia. *Capital:* Prague. —**Czech′o·slo·va′ki·an**, *adj., n.*

Czech Republic, country in central Europe, surrounded by Germany, Poland, Slovakia, Hungary, and Austria. *Capital:* Prague.

a	hat	ė	term	ô	order	ch	child		a in about
ā	age	i	it	oi	oil	ng	long		e in taken
ä	far	ī	ice	ou	out	sh	she	ə	i in pencil
â	care	o	hot	u	cup	th	thin		o in lemon
e	let	ō	open	ů	put	ᵺ	then		u in circus
ē	equal	ò	saw	ü	rule	zh	measure		

217

D or **d** (dē), *n.* **1** the fourth letter of the English alphabet. **2** the Roman numeral for 500. ❑ *n., pl.* **D's** or **d's.**

D, diameter.

d., 1 date. **2** daughter. **3** day. **4** degree. **5** density. **6** died. **7** dime. **8** dollar.

D., 1 December. **2** Democrat. **3** Dutch.

D.A., District Attorney.

dab (dab), **1** *v.* to touch lightly; pat with something soft or moist; tap: *I dabbed my lips with a napkin.* **2** *n.* a quick, light touch or blow; pat or tap: *The cat made a dab at the moth with its paw.* **3** *v.* to put on with light strokes: *She dabbed paint on the canvas.* **4** *n.* a small, soft or moist mass: *a dab of butter.* **5** *n.* a little bit: *a dab of paint.* ❑ *v.* **dabbed, dab·bing.** —**dab′ber,** *n.*

dab·ble (dab′əl), *v.* **1** to dip in and out of water; splash: *We sat and dabbled our feet in the pool.* **2** to do anything in a slight or superficial manner; work at a little: *He dabbled at painting but soon gave it up.* ❑ *v.* **dab·bled, dab·bling.** —**dab′bler,** *n.*

Dac·ca (dak′ə), *n.* Dhaka.

dace (dās), *n.* any of several small freshwater fishes related to carp. ❑ *n., pl.* **dace** or **dac·es.**

da·cha (dä′chə), *n.* (in Russia) a house in the country or the suburbs. ❑ *n., pl.* **da·chas.**

dachs·hund (däks′hünt′ or daks′hund′), *n.* a small dog with a long body, drooping ears, and very short legs.

Da·cron (dā′kron or dak′ron), *n.* trademark for an artificial fabric that does not wrinkle or fade easily.

dac·tyl (dak′təl), *n.* a measure or foot in poetry consisting of three syllables, the first accented and the next two unaccented.
> EXAMPLE: Mu′sic is | won′derful; | paint′ings are | beau′tiful; Po′ems are | plen′tiful; | why′ not en | joy?′

dad (dad), *n.* INFORMAL. father.

dad·dy (dad′ē), *n.* INFORMAL. father. ❑ *n., pl.* **dad·dies.**

dad·dy-long·legs (dad′ē lông′legz′), *n.* insect that looks much like a spider, but does not bite; harvestman. It has a small body and long, thin legs. ❑ *n., pl.* **dad·dy-long·legs.**

da·do (dā′dō), *n.* the part of a pedestal between the base and the cap. ❑ *n., pl.* **da·does.**

Daed·a·lus (ded′l əs), *n.* (in Greek legends) a skillful craftsman who planned the Labyrinth in Crete and made wings for himself and his son Icarus.

daf·fo·dil (daf′ə dil), *n.* plant with long, slender leaves and yellow flowers that bloom in the spring. It grows from a bulb.

daff·y (daf′ē), *adj.* INFORMAL. daft. ❑ *adj.* **daff·i·er, daff·i·est.**

daft (daft), *adj.* without sense or reason; silly; foolish. —**daft′ly,** *adv.* —**daft′ness,** *n.*

da Gam·a (də gam′ə or də gä′mə), **Vas·co** (väs′kō), 1469?-1524, Portuguese navigator. He discovered a route from Europe to India by sailing around southern Africa.

dag·ger (dag′ər), *n.* **1** a small weapon with a short, pointed blade, used for stabbing. **2** sign (†) used in printing to refer the reader to a note someplace else in the book.
look daggers at, to look angrily or glare at someone.

Dali painting

da·guerre·o·type (də ger′ə tīp), *n.* **1** an early method of photography. The pictures were made on silvered metal plates made sensitive to light. **2** picture made in this way.

dahl·ia (dal′yə), *n.* a tall plant with large, showy flowers of many colors that bloom in autumn. ❏ *n., pl.* **dahl·ias.**

dai·ly (dā′lē), **1** *adj.* done, happening, or appearing every day, or every day but Sunday: *a daily newspaper, a daily visit.* **2** *adj.* by the day or for the day: *the daily cost of renting a car.* **3** *adv.* every day; day by day: *She rides her bike daily.* **4** *n.* newspaper printed every day, or every day but Sunday. ❏ *n., pl.* **dai·lies.**

dain·ty (dān′tē), **1** *adj.* having delicate beauty; fresh and pretty: *The violet is a dainty spring flower.* **2** *adj.* hard to please; particular: *A dainty eater may like only certain foods.* **3** *adj.* good to eat; delicious: *"Wasn't that a dainty dish to set before the king?"* **4** *n.* something very good to eat; delicious bit of food: *Candy and nuts are dainties.* ❏ *adj.* **dain·ti·er, dain·ti·est;** *n., pl.* **dain·ties.** [See Word Story at **dignity.**] —**dain′ti·ly,** *adv.* —**dain′ti·ness,** *n.*

dair·y (der′ē), *n.* **1** *n.* store or company that sells milk, cream, butter, and cheese. **2** *n.* farm where milk and cream are produced and sometimes butter and cheese are made. **3** *n.* room or building where milk and cream are kept and made into butter and cheese. **4** *adj.* of or about milk and milk products: *dairy farming, the dairy industry.* ❏ *n., pl.* **dair·ies.**

dairy cattle, cows bred and kept for the milk they give.

dair·y·maid (der′ē mād′), *n.* (earlier) girl or woman who works in a dairy.

dair·y·man (der′ē mən), *n.* **1** person who owns or manages a dairy. **2** (earlier) man who works in a dairy. ❏ *n., pl.* **dair·y·men.**

da·is (dā′is), *n.* a raised platform at one end of a hall or large room. A throne, seats of honor, a desk, etc., may be set on a dais. ❏ *n., pl.* **da·is·es.**

dai·sy (dā′zē), *n.* any of many plants with white or pink petals around a yellow center. ❏ *n., pl.* **dai·sies.** [Daisy comes from old English words meaning "day's eye." Some daisies have petals that open in the morning and close at night, like an eye.] —**dai′sy·like′,** *adj.*

daisy wheel, a wheel-shaped part of some computer printers and typewriters. It has letters around the edge, and as it turns a tiny rod presses these against an inked ribbon to make marks on paper.

Da·kar (dä kär′), *n.* port and capital of Senegal, on the Atlantic.

Da·ko·ta (də kō′tə), *n.* **1** North Dakota or South Dakota. **2** the former territory of the United States that became North Dakota and South Dakota. **3** Sioux, especially those living in the eastern section of their lands. ■ See Usage Note at **Sioux.** ❏ *n., pl.* **Da·ko·tas** for 1, **Da·ko·ta** for 3. [See word history information at **North Dakota.**] —**Da·ko′tan,** *adj., n.*

Da·lai Lama (dä′ lī), the chief priest of the religion of the lamas, Buddhist priests in Tibet and Mongolia. [Dalai comes from a Mongolian word meaning "ocean." The Dalai Lama is called "ocean of compassion."]

dale (dāl), *n.* valley.

Da·li (dä′lē), *n.* **Sal·va·dor** (sal′və dôr′), 1904-1989, Spanish surrealist artist. ■ **Salvador Dali's** paintings are strange combinations of realistic images.

Dal·las (dal′əs), *n.* city in NE Texas. [Dallas was named for U.S. Vice President (1845-1849) George M. Dallas.]

dalles (dal′əs *or* dalz), *n.pl.* steep, narrow valleys with cliffs on both sides of a rapidly flowing river. ❏ *n., sing.* **dell.**

dal·li·ance (dal′ē əns), *n.* act of dallying; trifling.

dal·ly (dal′ē), *v.* **1** to linger idly; loiter: *They dallied along the way and were late for dinner.* **2** to waste time: *He dallied the afternoon away daydreaming.* **3** to talk, act, or think about without being serious; trifle: *For over a month she dallied with the idea of buying a new car.* ❏ *v.* **dal·lied, dal·ly·ing.** —**dal′li·er,** *n.*

Dal·ma·tia (dal mā′shə), *n.* region in W Croatia, along the Adriatic.

Dal·ma·tian (dal mā′shən), *n.* a large, short-haired dog, usually white with black spots; coach dog.

WORD STORY **Dalmatians** are also called **coach dogs** because they used to run between the wheels of horse-drawn coaches to keep other dogs away from the horses.

dam[1] (dam), **1** *n.* wall built to hold back the water of a stream or any flowing water: *There was a flood when the dam burst.* **2** *v.* to provide with a dam; hold back or block up with anything: *Beavers had dammed the stream.* ❏ *v.* **dammed, dam·ming.** ■ Another word that sounds like this is **damn.**

dam[2] (dam), *n.* the female parent of sheep, cattle, horses, and other four-footed mammals. ■ Another word that sounds like this is **damn.**

dam·age (dam′ij), **1** *n.* harm or injury that lessens value or usefulness: *The accident did some damage to the car.* ■ See Synonym Study at **harm.** **2** *n.* an amount of money lost as a result of some harm or injury: *Damage from the storm totaled more than $2 million.* **3** *v.* to harm or injure so as to lessen value or usefulness: *High winds damaged the wheat crop.* **4** *n.pl.* **damages,** money claimed or paid by law to make up for some harm done to a person or property: *The person who was hit by the car asked for $250,000 in damages.* ❏ *v.* **dam·aged, dam·ag·ing.**

Da·mas·cus (də mas′kəs), *n.* capital of Syria, in the SW part. It is one of the world's oldest cities.

dam·ask (dam′əsk), **1** *n.* a firm, shiny, reversible linen, silk, or cotton fabric with woven designs: *hangings of damask.* **2** *adj.* made of damask: *a damask tablecloth.*

dame (dām), *n.* **1 Dame,** title of honor given in Great Britain to a woman, corresponding to the rank of a knight. **2** (earlier) lady. **3** SLANG. woman. ■ This meaning of **dame** is often considered offensive.

WORD STORY **Dame** comes from a Latin word meaning "house." **Domestic** and **dominate** come from the same word. In old times a woman in charge of a great house was a person of high rank.

damn (dam), **1** *v.* to declare something to be bad or inferior; condemn: *The critics damned the new book.* **2** *v.* to doom to hell. **3** *v.* to swear or swear at by saying "damn"; curse. **4** *n.* act of saying "damn"; curse. **5** *adv.* INFORMAL. very. ■ Another word that sounds like this is **dam.**

dam·na·ble (dam′nə bəl), *adj.* hateful or outrageous; detestable. —**dam′na·bly,** *adv.*

dam·na·tion (dam nā′shən), *n.* act of damning or condition of being damned; condemnation.

damned (damd), **1** *adj.* very dislikable; cursed; horrible. **2** *adv.* INFORMAL. very.

Dam·o·cles (dam′ə klēz′), *n.* (in Greek legends) a man who praised the life of kings. A king in Sicily made Damocles aware of the dangers of a king's life by seating him at a banquet under a sword suspended by a single hair.

a	hat	ė	term	ȯ	order	ch	child		a in about
ā	age	i	it	oi	oil	ng	long		e in taken
ä	far	ī	ice	ou	out	sh	she	ə	i in pencil
â	care	o	hot	u	cup	th	thin		o in lemon
e	let	ō	open	u̇	put	ŦH	then		u in circus
ē	equal	ȯ	saw	ü	rule	zh	measure		

Da·mon (dā′mən), *n.* (in Greek legends) a man who pledged his life for his friend Pythias, who was sentenced to death. Because of his devotion, the lives of both were spared. [**Damon** comes from a Greek word meaning "taming."]

damp (damp), **1** *adj.* slightly wet; moist: *This house is damp in rainy weather.* **2** *n.* moisture: *When it's foggy you can feel the damp in the air.* **3** *v.* to dampen (def. 1). **4** *n.* damper (def. 2). **5** *n.* any poisonous or explosive gas that collects in mines. Firedamp is one kind. **–damp′ly,** *adv.* **–damp′ness,** *n.*

damp down, to slow down the activity of fire in a stove by closing the damper.

> **SYNONYM STUDY** **Damp, moist,** and **clammy** mean slightly wet. **Damp** means slightly wet in an unpleasant way: *The chair was still damp from the spill.* **Moist** means slightly wet in a pleasant way: *The flower shop smells of moist soil.* **Clammy** means slightly wet and cold: *Snakes look clammy, but their skin is as dry as humans'.*

damp·en (dam′pən), *v.* **1** to make or become damp; moisten: *He sprinkled water over the clothes to dampen them before ironing.* **2** to cast a chill over; depress; discourage: *The sad news dampened our spirits.* **–damp′en·er,** *n.*

damp·er (dam′pər), *n.* **1** person or thing that discourages or depresses. **2** a movable plate to control the draft in a stove or furnace; damp.

dam·sel (dam′zəl), *n.* OLD USE. a young girl; maiden.

dam·sel·fly (dam′zəl flī′), *n.* any of many insects that look like dragonflies. Damselflies rest with their wings held up over their backs. ❑ *n., pl.* **dam·sel·flies.**

dance (dans), **1** *v.* to move in rhythm, usually in time with music: *She can dance very well.* **2** *n.* movement in rhythm, usually in time with music. **3** *n.* some special group of steps: *The waltz is a well-known dance.* **4** *n.* party where people dance: *My brother went to the school dance.* **5** *n.* one round of dancing: *May I have this dance?* **6** *v.* to take part in a dance: *They danced a waltz.* **7** *n.* piece of music for dancing. **8** *v.* to jump up and down; move in a lively way: *She danced with delight.* **9** *v.* to cause to dance: *He danced me around the room.* ❑ *v.* **danced, danc·ing.**

> **WORD BANK** **Dance** has many forms. If you want to learn about kinds of dances, you can start by looking up these words in this dictionary.
>
> | | | | |
> |---|---|---|---|
> | ballet | fox trot | minuet | square dance |
> | barn dance | hora | polka | tango |
> | bolero | hula | reel³ | tap dance |
> | breakdancing | jitterbug | rumba | two-step |
> | Charleston | mazurka | salsa | waltz |

danc·er (dan′sər), *n.* **1** person who dances. **2** person whose occupation is dancing.

dan·de·li·on (dan′dl ī′ən), *n.* a common weed with deeply notched leaves and bright yellow flowers that bloom in the spring. [**Dandelion** comes from French words meaning "lion's tooth." The notched leaves were thought to look like a lion's teeth.]

dan·der (dan′dər), *n.* tiny scales from the skin of furry animals. Some people are allergic to dander.

get your dander up, to become angry.

dan·dle (dan′dl), *v.* to move a child up and down on your knees or in your arms. ❑ *v.* **dan·dled, dan·dling.**

dan·druff (dan′drəf), *n.* small flakes of dead skin from the scalp.

dan·dy (dan′dē), **1** *adj.* INFORMAL. excellent; first-rate: *a dandy new bike.* **2** *n.* INFORMAL. an excellent or first-rate thing: *That car is a dandy.* **3** *n.* man who is too concerned about his clothing and appearance. ❑ *n., pl.* **dan·dies;** *adj.* **dan·di·er, dan·di·est.**

Dane (dān), *n.* person born or living in Denmark.

dan·ger (dān′jər), *n.* **1** chance of harm; nearness to harm; risk: *The trip through the jungle was full of danger.* **2** thing that may cause harm: *Hidden rocks are a danger to ships.*

> **SYNONYM STUDY** **Danger** and **peril** both mean a chance of harm or injury. **Danger** is a general word and suggests the possibility, but not the certainty, of harm: *Miners are always in danger.* **Peril** means great danger that is difficult to avoid: *He survived the perils of the storm.*

dan·ger·ous (dān′jər əs), *adj.* likely to cause harm; not safe; risky: *Shooting off firecrackers can be dangerous.* **–dan′ger·ous·ly,** *adv.* **–dan′ger·ous·ness,** *n.*

dan·gle (dang′gəl), *v.* **1** to hang and swing loosely. **2** to hold or carry something so that it swings loosely: *The cat played with the string I dangled in front of it.* ❑ *v.* **dan·gled, dan·gling. –dan′gler,** *n.*

dangling participle, a participle that is not connected with the word it should describe. EXAMPLE: *Flying overhead, I saw a bird.* In this sentence, *flying* is a dangling participle.

Dan·iel (dan′yəl), *n.* **1** a Hebrew prophet whose great faith in God kept him unharmed in a den of lions. **2** book of the Bible. [**Daniel** comes from a Hebrew word meaning "God is my judge."]

Dan·ish (dā′nish), **1** *adj.* of Denmark, its people, or their language. **2** *n.pl.* people of Denmark. **3** *n.* language of Denmark. **4** *n.* kind of rich pastry. ❑ *n., pl.* **Dan·ish** or **Dan·ish·es** for 4.

> **WORD SOURCE** **Danish** has given a number of words to the English language, including the following: **dawn, kilt, nickel, scab, skulk,** and **tern.**

dank (dangk), *adj.* unpleasantly damp or moist: *The cave was dark, dank, and chilly.* **–dank′ly,** *adv.* **–dank′ness,** *n.*

Dan·te (dän′tā), *n.* 1265-1321, Italian poet, author of the *Divine Comedy.* ■ Dante's *Divine Comedy* tells the story of his journeys through hell, purgatory, and finally heaven.

Dan·ube (dan′yüb), *n.* river flowing from S Germany into the Black Sea.

Daph·ne (daf′nē), *n.* (in Greek myths) a nymph pursued by Apollo, from whom she was saved by being changed into a laurel tree. [**Daphne** comes from a Greek word meaning "laurel."]

daph·ni·a (daf′nē ə), *n.* any of several tiny shellfish that look something like a flea, sold for tropical fish food. ❑ *n., pl.* **daph·ni·as.**

dap·per (dap′ər), *adj.* **1** neat, trim, or spruce. **2** small and active. **–dap′per·ly,** *adv.* **–dap′per·ness,** *n.*

dap·ple (dap′əl), **1** *v.* to mark or become marked with spots: *The bleach dappled the dark cloth.* **2** *adj.* dappled. ❑ *v.* **dap·pled, dap·pling.**

dap·pled (dap′əld), *adj.* marked with spots; spotted.

Dar·da·nelles (därd′n elz′), *n.* strait in NW Turkey which connects the Sea of Marmara with the Aegean Sea, and separates European Turkey from Asian Turkey. In ancient times it was called the Hellespont.

dare (dâr), **1** *v.* to have courage; be bold; be bold enough: *The children dared to explore the haunted house.* **2** *v.* to have courage to try; not be afraid of; face or meet boldly: *The pioneers dared the dangers of a strange land.* **3** *v.* to challenge: *I dare you to jump the puddle.* **4** *n.* a challenge: *I took their dare to jump.* ❑ *v.* **dared, dar·ing.**

Dare (dâr), *n.* **Virginia**, 1587-?, the first English child born in the Colonies.

dare·dev·il (dâr′dev′əl), **1** *n.* a reckless person. **2** *adj.* recklessly daring: *The speeder's daredevil driving caused an accident.*

dare·say (dâr′sā′), *v.* to believe: *I daresay you will be late if you don't hurry.* ■ **Daresay** is used only with *I* and only in the present tense. This is why no forms of the verb are listed here.

Dar es Sa·laam (där′ es sə läm′), port in Tanzania, on the Indian Ocean. [**Dar es Salaam** is Arabic for "house of peace."]

dar·ing (dâr′ing), **1** *n.* courage to take risks; boldness: *The lifeguard's daring saved a swimmer's life.* **2** *adj.* bold; fearless; courageous: *Performing on a trapeze high above a crowd is a daring act.* **—dar′ing·ly,** *adv.*

daring (def. 2)

Da·ri·us I (də rī′əs), 550?-486? B.C., Persian emperor. His armies were defeated by the Athenians at Marathon in 490 B.C.

dark (därk), **1** *adj.* without light; with very little light: *A night without a moon is dark.* **2** *adj.* not light-colored; near to black in color: *He has dark brown eyes and dark hair.* **3** *adj.* gloomy; dull; dismal: *It was a dark day, rainy and cold.* **4** *n.* absence of light; darkness: *Don't be afraid of the dark.* **5** *n.* night; nightfall: *The dark comes on early in the winter.* **6** *adj.* secret or hidden: *Her words had a dark meaning we could only guess at.* **7** *adj.* without knowledge or culture; ignorant: *The years after the Roman Empire broke up were dark years for Europe.* **8** *adj.* evil; wicked: *Assassination is a dark deed.* **—dark′ly,** *adv.* **—dark′ness,** *n.*

in the dark, in ignorance; without knowledge or information: *She said nothing, leaving me in the dark about her plans.*

SYNONYM STUDY **Dark** and **dim** both mean with little or no light. **Dark** is a general word: *As winter approaches, the days grow dark earlier.* **Dim** means so dark that things cannot be seen clearly: *She stumbled over the chest in the dim hall.*

Dark Ages, the early part of the Middle Ages, from about A.D. 400 to about A.D. 1000, when learning and culture were in a decline in western Europe.

dark·en (där′kən), *v.* to make or become dark or darker: *As the storm approached, the sky darkened.* **—dark′en·er,** *n.*

dark horse, 1 racehorse, contestant, or the like, about whom little is known or that unexpectedly wins. **2** person who is unexpectedly nominated for a political office.

dark·ish (där′kish), *adj.* somewhat dark.

dark·ling (därk′ling), **1** *adv.* in the dark. **2** *adj.* dark.

dark matter, (in astronomy) a supposed form of matter that emits no light or other radiation detectable by telescopes, but has gravitational effects that can be measured.

dark·room (därk′rüm′), *n.* room for developing photographs. It is cut off from all outside light and has a very dim, colored light.

dar·ling (där′ling), **1** *n.* person or animal very dear to another; person or animal much loved: *You are a darling.* **2** *n.* a favorite: *The baby is everyone's darling.* **3** *adj.* very dear; much loved: *"My darling daughter," his letter began.* **4** *adj.* INFORMAL. pleasing or attractive: *What a darling puppy!*

Dar·ling (där′ling), *n.* river in SE Australia.

darning needle, 1 a large needle used to darn. **2** dragonfly.

Dar·row (dar′ō), *n.* **Clar·ence** (klar′əns), 1857-1938, American lawyer. ■ **Clarence Darrow** was the defense attorney in many important trials, including a number of labor cases and the Tennessee evolution trial of 1925.

dart (därt), **1** *n.* a slender, pointed weapon thrown by hand or shot from a blowgun. **2** *n.pl.* **darts,** game in which darts are thrown at a target. **3** *v.* to move suddenly and swiftly: *The deer saw us and darted away.* **4** *v.* to send suddenly: *She darted an angry glance at her sister.* **—dart′er,** *n.*

Dar·win (där′wən), *n.* **1 Charles,** 1809-1882, English naturalist famous for his theory of evolution. **2** port and capital of Northern Territory, Australia.

dash (dash), **1** *v.* to strike or hurl with force, often so as to break: *I was so angry I dashed the glass to bits against the tile floor. The waves dashed against the rocks.* **2** *v.* to splash: *The car sped by and dashed muddy water all over me.* **3** *n.* a splash: *She was sprayed by a dash of salt water.* **4** *v.* to rush: *They dashed by in a hurry.* **5** *n.* a rush: *We made a dash for safety.* **6** *v.* to ruin or destroy: *Our hopes were dashed by the bad news.* **7** *n.* a small amount: *Put in just a dash of pepper.* **8** *n.* a short race: *the fifty-yard dash.* **9** *n.* energy; spirit; liveliness: *to play with dash.* **10** *n.* a mark (—) used in writing or printing to show a break in thought, omitted letters or words, etc. **11** *n.* a long sound used in sending messages by telegraph. **12** *n.* dashboard. ❑ *n., pl.* **dash·es.**

dash off, to do, make, write, etc., quickly: *He dashed off a letter to his friend.*

dash·board (dash′bôrd′), *n.* panel below the windshield of a motor vehicle or aircraft, containing the speedometer, other indicators, and controls.

dash·er (dash′ər), *n.* CANADIAN. (in hockey) the boards.

dash·ing (dash′ing), *adj.* **1** full of energy and spirit; lively: *a dashing young couple.* **2** showy: *The members of the band wore bright, dashing uniforms.* **—dash′ing·ly,** *adv.*

das·tard·ly (das′tərd lē), *adj.* mean and cowardly: *a dastardly act.* **—das′tard·li·ness,** *n.*

DAT (dē′ā′tē′ or dat), digital audio tape.

da·ta (dā′tə or dat′ə), *n.sing. or pl.* facts from which conclusions can be drawn; things known or admitted; information: *Names, ages, grades, and other data about the class are written in the teacher's notebook.* ■ See Synonym Study at **information.** ❑ *n., sing.* **datum.** [See Word Story at **date[1]**.]

USAGE NOTE **Data** is used as both a singular noun and a plural noun. Because it began as a plural, meaning "facts," many people feel it should be used only as a plural. Because many other people use it as a singular, meaning "information," that use is now gaining acceptance.

da·ta·base (dā′tə bās′ or dat′ə bās′), *n.* a large collection of information, organized and kept and made available by a computer or computers, including such items as newspaper stories, airplane schedules, or inventory lists.

data processing, the handling and storing of data, in coded form, by means of computers.

date[1] (dāt), **1** *n.* time when something happens or happened; a particular day, month, or year: *Give the date of your birth. July 4, 1776, is the date of the signing of the Declaration of Independence.* **2** *n.* statement of time: *There is a date stamped on every piece of U.S. money.* **3** *n.* a day of the month: *Today's date is the 26th.* **4** *v.* to mark the time of; put a date on: *Please date your papers before handing them in.* **5** *v.* to find out the date of; give a date to: *The historian was able to date the letter by its reference to Woodrow Wilson's election.* **6** *n.* period of time: *At that date there were no airplanes.* **7** *v.* to belong to a certain period of time; have its origin: *The oldest house in town dates from the early 1800s.* **8** *v.* to make old-fashioned or out of date: *Grandpa's*

a	hat	ė	term	ô	order	ch	child	
ā	age	i	it	oi	oil	ng	long	⟨a in about
ä	far	ī	ice	ou	out	sh	she	e in taken
â	care	o	hot	u	cup	th	thin	ə ⟨i in pencil
e	let	ō	open	u̇	put	ŦH	then	o in lemon
ē	equal	ȯ	saw	ü	rule	zh	measure	⟨u in circus

long, droopy moustache dates him. **9** *n.* appointment for a certain time: *Don't forget to keep your Monday morning date with the dentist.* **10** *v.* to keep company with someone: visit socially: *They have been dating for months.* **11** *n.* person with whom you keep company: *Will you be my date for the school dance?* ❑ *v.* **dat·ed, dat·ing.** —**dat′a·ble** or **date′a·ble,** *adj.* —**dat′er,** *n.*

out of date, old-fashioned; not in present use: *I refused to wear the suit because it was out of date.*

up to date, 1 according to the latest style or idea; in fashion; modern: *His clothes are always up to date.* **2** up to the present time: *We entered our results in our project log to bring it up to date.*

> **WORD STORY** **Date¹** comes from a Latin word meaning "given." **Data** comes from the same word. Romans put the word with a day and month at the top of a letter to show when it was given to a messenger. Facts are given because they come from outside our control. English still has this idea in phrases such as *a given amount of time.*

date² (dāt), *n.* the oblong, fleshy, sweet fruit of the date palm.
dat·ed (dā′tid), *adj.* **1** marked with or showing a date. **2** out-of-date.
date·less (dāt′lis), *adj.* **1** not dated. **2** endless; unlimited.
date·line (dāt′līn′), *n.* a statement giving the date and often the place that a news report was made.
date line, International Date Line.
date palm, the palm tree on which dates grow.
da·tum (dā′təm *or* dat′əm), *n.* a single fact or piece of information. ❑ *n., pl.* **data.**
daub (dôb), **1** *v.* to coat or cover with plaster, clay, mud, or any greasy or sticky material: *She daubed the cracks in the wall with cement.* **2** *n.* anything daubed on. **3** *v.* to make dirty; soil: *Your skirt is daubed with mud.* **4** *v.* to paint unskillfully: *She is no artist; she just daubs.* **5** *n.* a badly painted picture. —**daub′er,** *n.*
daugh·ter (dò′tər), *n.* **1** a female child. A girl or woman is the daughter of her father and mother. **2** a female descendant.

> **WORD STORY** Words containing the letter combination *-gh,* such as **daughter, enough,** and **through,** look odd today. Long ago, however, *-gh* was pronounced much like the German sound of *-ch* in **Bach.** The spelling has survived in English, but the sound hasn't.

daughter cell, one of the two cells produced by division of a cell.
daugh·ter-in-law (dò′tər in lò′), *n.* wife of your son. ❑ *n., pl.* **daugh·ters-in-law.**
daunt (dônt), *v.* to frighten or discourage: *Rain did not daunt the campers.*
daunt·less (dônt′lis), *adj.* not to be frightened or discouraged; brave: *a dauntless mountain climber.* —**daunt′less·ly,** *adv.* —**daunt′less·ness,** *n.*
dau·phin (dò′fən), *n.* title of the oldest son of the king of France, used from 1349 to 1830.
dav·en·port (dav′ən pôrt), *n.* a long, upholstered sofa, frequently convertible into a bed.
Dav·en·port (dav′ən pôrt), *n.* city in E Iowa.
Da·vid (dā′vid), *n.* 1030?-965? B.C., (in the Bible) Hebrew warrior and poet, and second king of Israel, who organized the Jewish tribes into a national state. According to tradition, he wrote many Psalms of the Bible. [David comes from a Hebrew word meaning "beloved."]
da Vinci, Leonardo. See **Leonardo da Vinci.**
Da·vis (dā′vis), *n.* **1 Bet·te** (bet′ē), 1908-1989, American actress. She played strong independent women and won two Academy awards, in 1935 and 1938. **2 Jefferson,** 1808-1889, president of the Confederacy from 1861 to 1865. **3 Miles** (milz), 1926-1991, American jazz trumpeter. He helped to create several forms of jazz.
dav·it (dav′it *or* dā′vit), *n.* one of a pair of metal or wooden arms at the side of a ship, used to hold or lower a small boat.
Da·vy Jones (dā′vē), spirit of the sea.
Davy Jones's locker, grave of those who die at sea; bottom of the ocean.
daw·dle (dò′dl), *v.* to waste time; idle; loiter: *Don't dawdle so long over your work.* ❑ *v.* **daw·dled, daw·dling.** —**daw′dler,** *n.*
dawn (dòn), **1** *n.* beginning of day; the first light in the east: *The sun rose at dawn.* **2** *n.* beginning: *Dinosaurs roamed the earth*

before the dawn of human life. **3** *v.* to grow light in the morning: *It was dawning when I awoke.* **4** *v.* to grow clear to the eye or mind: *When they didn't leave, it dawned on me that they expected dinner.* **5** *v.* to begin; appear: *Day dawns in the east.*

day (dā), *n.* **1** time of light between sunrise and sunset: *Days are longer in summer than in winter.* **2** the light of day; daylight: *The moon is shining bright as day.* **3** the 24 hours of day and night; time it takes for the earth to make one rotation on its axis. **4** the time it takes a planet to make one rotation on its axis. **5** day or date set aside for a particular purpose or celebration: *a feast day.* **6** hours for work; working day: *Our company has a seven-hour day.* **7** time; period: *In days of old they used candles instead of electric lights.* **8** period of life, activity, power, or influence: *Great Britain has had its day as a great colonial power.* **9** contest; conflict: *Our side won the day.*

call it a day, to stop work: *After rehearsing the play for three hours, the director called it a day.*

Day (dā), *n.* **Dor·o·thy** (dôr′ə thē), 1897-1980, American journalist and reformer. She founded shelters for homeless people across the country during the Depression.
day·break (dā′brāk′), *n.* time when it first begins to get light in the morning; dawn.
day care, 1 a person, place, or business providing care for small children or others while family members are at work. **2** careful supervision of a small child or other person during the day.
day·dream (dā′drēm′), **1** *n.* dreamy thinking about pleasant things. **2** *v.* to think dreamily about pleasant things. ▪ See Synonym Study at **imagine.** **3** *n.* something imagined but not likely to come true. —**day′dream′er,** *n.*
Day-Glo (dā′glō′), *n.* trademark for a kind of paint that gives off a brilliant, fluorescent color.
day·light (dā′līt′), *n.* **1** light of day: *It is easier to read by daylight than by lamplight.* **2** daytime. **3** dawn; daybreak: *We were up at daylight.*

see daylight, 1 to approach the end of a hard or tiresome job. **2** to understand.

day·light-sav·ing time (dā′līt′sā′ving), time that is one hour ahead of standard time. It gives more daylight after working hours.
day·lin·er (dā′lī′nər), *n.* CANADIAN. an express train between cities, or between a city and its suburbs, running only during the day.
Day of Atonement, Yom Kippur.

Day of the Dead, a Mexican and Mexican American holiday, observed every year between October 31 and November 2, honoring and recalling the dead.
day school, 1 school held in the daytime. **2** a private school for students who live at home.
day·star (dā′stär′), *n.* **1** morning star. **2** sun.
day·time (dā′tīm′), *n.* time when it is day and not night: *A baby sleeps even in the daytime.*
day-to-day (dā′tə dā′), *adj.* **1** happening every day or most

Day of the Dead

days: *day-to-day chores, day-to-day shopping.* **2** only for the present day, not for the future: *During our vacation we lived a day-to-day life.*
Day·ton (dāt′n), *n.* city in SW Ohio. [Dayton was named for Jonathan Dayton, youngest signer of the U.S. Constitution.]
daze (dāz), **1** *v.* to make unable to think clearly; bewilder; stun: *A blow on the head dazed him so that he could not keep playing.* **2** *v.* to hurt your eyes with light; dazzle: *I was dazed by the bright sun.* **3** *n.* a dazed condition: *I was in a daze from the accident and could not understand what was happening.* ❑ *v.* **dazed, daz·ing.**
daz·zle (daz′əl), **1** *v.* to hurt the eyes with too bright light or with quick-moving lights: *It dazzles the eyes to look straight at the sun.* **2** *v.* to amaze; impress deeply: *The children were dazzled by the richness of the palace.* **3** *n.* bewildering brightness: *the dazzle of flashbulbs going off.* ❑ *v.* **daz·zled, daz·zling.** —**daz′zler,** *n.*

daz·zling (daz′ling), *adj.* brilliant or splendid: *dazzling lights, a dazzling display of skill.* —**daz′zling·ly,** *adv.*

dB or **db,** decibel or decibels.

DC, 1 District of Columbia (used with postal Zip Code). **2** direct current.

d.c., direct current.

dead heat

D.C., 1 direct current. **2** District of Columbia.

D.D., Doctor of Divinity.

D.D.S., Doctor of Dental Surgery.

DDT or **D.D.T.,** a very powerful insecticide that may endanger animal life.

de-, *prefix.* **1** do the opposite of: *decentralize = do the opposite of centralize.* **2** down; lower: *depress = press down.* **3** take away; remove: *defrost = remove the frost.*

DE, Delaware (used with postal Zip Code).

dea·con (dē′kən), *n.* **1** officer of a church who helps the minister in church duties not connected with preaching. **2** member of the clergy next below a priest or minister in rank. [**Deacon** comes from a Greek word meaning "servant," because a deacon serves a church.]

de·ac·ti·vate (dē ak′tə vāt), *v.* to make inactive. ❑ *v.* **de·ac·ti·vat·ed, de·ac·ti·vat·ing.** —**de·ac′ti·va′tion,** *n.*

dead (ded), **1** *adj.* no longer living: *The flowers in my garden are dead.* **2** *n.pl.* **the dead,** persons no longer living: *We remember the dead of our wars on Memorial Day.* **3** *adj.* without life: *The surface of the moon is dead.* **4** *adj.* like death: *I fell over in a dead faint.* **5** *adj.* not active; dull or quiet: *The summer resort was a dead town in winter.* **6** *adj.* without force, power, or activity: *The car won't start because the battery is dead.* **7** *adj.* no longer in use: *The language of the ancient Romans is a dead language.* **8** *adj.* out of play: *a dead ball.* **9** *adj.* very tired; worn-out: *Dead from exhaustion, the children fell fast asleep.* **10** *adj.* sure: *She was a dead shot with a rifle.* **11** *adj.* complete; absolute: *There was dead silence in the library.* **12** *adv.* completely; absolutely: *You are dead wrong. I was dead tired.* **13** *adv.* directly; straight: *A floating log lay dead ahead of our canoe.* **14** *n.* time when there is the least life stirring: *A strange noise woke us in the dead of night.* —**dead′ness,** *n.*

dead·beat (ded′bēt′), *n.* INFORMAL. **1** person who avoids paying bills. **2** a lazy person; loafer.

dead·bolt (ded′bōlt′), *n.* a kind of strong lock containing a short thick metal bar that has no spring attached to it.

dead·en (ded′n), *v.* **1** to make dull or weak; lessen the force of: *Some medicines deaden pain.* **2** to stop a feeling or keep a part of the body from feeling; make numb: *deaden a toothache, deaden a tooth.* **3** to make soundproof: *The curtains, carpets, and thick walls deadened the room.*

dead end, 1 street, passage, etc., closed at one end. **2** a position from which progress is impossible: *She decided the job was a dead end and went back to school.*

dead·head (ded′hed′), *n.* **1** INFORMAL. person who rides on a train or bus, or sees a game, without paying. **2** train, railroad car, or truck traveling empty.

dead heat, race that ends in a tie.

dead letter, 1 letter that cannot be delivered or returned because of a wrong address, not enough stamps, etc. **2** law or rule that is no longer observed.

dead·line (ded′līn′), *n.* the latest possible time to do something: *The teacher made Friday afternoon the deadline for handing in all book reports.*

dead·lock (ded′lok′), **1** *n.* a complete standstill that occurs when two opposing sides are equally strong and neither one will give in: *Employers and strikers had reached a deadlock in their dispute over wages.* **2** *v.* to bring or come to a complete standstill: *The two groups have been deadlocked for almost a week.*

dead·ly (ded′lē), **1** *adj.* causing or likely to cause death; fatal: *a deadly disease, deadly toadstools.* **2** *adv., adj.* like death; deathly: *deadly pale, deadly stillness.* **3** *adj.* filled with hatred that lasts till death: *deadly enemies.* **4** *adj.* causing death of the soul: *Envy and pride are deadly sins.* **5** *adv.* extremely: *"Washing dishes is deadly dull," she said.* **6** *adj.* dull; boring: *a deadly lecture by a tiresome speaker.* **7** *adj.* absolutely accurate: *The hunter was a deadly shot.* ❑ *adj.* **dead·li·er, dead·li·est.** —**dead′li·ness,** *n.*

deadly nightshade, belladonna.

dead·pan (ded′pan′), **1** *n.* an expressionless face or manner. **2** *adj.* showing no expression or feeling.

dead reckoning, calculation of the position of a ship or aircraft without observations of the sun, stars, etc., by using a compass and studying the navigator's record.

Dead Sea, a salt lake between Israel and Jordan. Its surface is the lowest on earth, almost 1300 feet (400 meters) below sea level. Because it is very salty, it contains few living things.

dead·weight (ded′wāt′), *n.* **1** the weight of anything lifeless, rigid, and heavy. **2** a very great burden.

dead·wood (ded′wüd′), *n.* **1** dead branches or trees. **2** useless people or things.

deaf (def), *adj.* **1** not able, or only partly able, to hear: *Some deaf people use American Sign Language.* **2** not willing to hear: *He is deaf to any criticism of his work.* —**deaf′ness,** *n.*

USAGE NOTE **Deaf** is not the only word to describe people who cannot hear or who do not hear well. Some people prefer to use **hearing-impaired,** and it is wise to be careful. If in doubt, ask!

deaf·en (def′ən), *v.* **1** to make deaf: *A hard blow on the ear can deafen someone for life.* **2** to stun with noise: *A sudden explosion deafened us for a moment.* —**deaf′en·ing·ly,** *adv.*

deaf-mute (def′myüt′), *n.* person who is unable to hear and speak, usually because of deafness from birth or from early childhood. ■ **Deaf-mute** is often considered offensive.

deal (dēl), **1** *v.* to concern; be about: *Arithmetic deals with numbers.* **2** *v.* to act; behave: *Deal kindly with them so you don't hurt their feelings.* **3** *v.* to handle or manage; take action concerning: *When the faucet broke, Mother dealt with it until the plumber came.* **4** *v.* to occupy yourself; take action: *The courts deal with those who break the laws.* **5** *v.* to carry on business; buy and sell: *That store deals in imported fabrics.* **6** *n.* arrangement; plan: *She is proposing that we substitute a new deal for the old one.* **7** *v.* to give or deliver: *One fighter dealt the other a blow.* **8** *v.* to give out among several; distribute: *The Red Cross dealt out food to the victims of the flood.* **9** *n.* a business arrangement; bargain: *If you buy this TV on sale you can get a good deal.* **10** *n.* a secret or underhanded agreement: *The corrupt mayor was caught in a deal*

a	hat	ė	term	ô	order	ch	child		a in about
ā	age	i	it	oi	oil	ng	long		e in taken
ä	far	ī	ice	ou	out	sh	she	ə	i in pencil
â	care	o	hot	u	cup	th	thin		o in lemon
e	let	ō	open	ù	put	₮н	then		u in circus
ē	equal	ȯ	saw	ü	rule	zh	measure		

to take public money. **11** v. to distribute playing cards: *It's your turn to deal.* **12** n. the distribution of playing cards. ❑ v. **dealt, deal·ing.**

a good deal or **a great deal, 1** a large part, portion, or amount: *A great deal of her money goes for rent.* **2** to a great extent or degree; much: *She likes to swim a good deal.*

deal·er (dē′lər), n. **1** person who makes his living by buying and selling: *a dealer in antique furniture.* **2** person who distributes the playing cards in a card game.

deal·er·ship (dē′lər ship′), n. **1** business that sells a certain make or makes of cars. **2** an authorized business, franchise, or agency that markets a product in a specific area.

deal·ing (dē′ling), n. **1** way of doing business: *The auctioneer was respected for his honest dealing.* **2** way of acting; behavior toward others: *The judge is known for her fair dealings.* **3 dealings,** pl. **a** business relations: *That company has dealings with firms all over the world.* **b** friendly relations.

dealt (delt), v. past tense and past participle of **deal:** *The knight dealt his enemy a blow. The cards have been dealt.*

dean (dēn), n. **1** member of the faculty of a school, college, or university who has charge of the behavior or studies of the students: *the dean of women.* **2** head of a division or school in a college or university: *the dean of the law school.* **3** a high official of a church. A dean is often in charge of a cathedral. **4** a respected, longtime member of a group: *the dean of sports writers.*

WORD STORY **Dean** comes from a Latin word meaning "ten." **Decimal** comes from the same Latin word. **Dean** was first used as a name for a man in charge of ten soldiers or monks.

Dean (dēn), n. **James,** 1931-1955, American actor. He played angry, rebellious young men in his movies, including *Rebel Without a Cause.*

dear (dir), **1** adj. much loved; precious: *His sister was very dear to him.* **2** n. dear one; darling: *"Come, my dear," said his grandmother.* **3** adj. much valued; highly esteemed. *Dear* is used as a form of polite address at the beginning of letters: *Dear Sir, Dear Madam.* **4** adj. high in price; costly; expensive: *Fresh strawberries are dear in winter.* **5** adv. at a high price; very much; much: *That mistake will cost you dear.* **6** interj. exclamation of surprise, trouble, etc.: *Oh, dear! I lost my pencil.* ■ Another word that sounds like this is **deer.** **—dear′ness,** n.

dear·ie (dir′ē), n. deary.

dear·ly (dir′lē), adv. **1** fondly: *We love our parents dearly.* **2** at a high price: *She bought her new car quite dearly.* **3** very much: *You will regret your foolish behavior dearly in years to come.*

dearth (dėrth), n. too small a supply; great scarcity or lack: *A dearth of food caused the prices to go up.*

dear·y or **dear·ie** (dir′ē), n. INFORMAL. a dear one; darling. ❑ n., pl. **dear·ies.**

death (deth), n. **1** act or fact of dying; the ending of life: *The old man's death was calm and peaceful.* **2** any ending that is like dying: *the death of their hopes.* **3** condition of being dead: *In death he looked peaceful.* **4** any condition like being dead. **5** cause of dying: *Alcoholism was her death.*

at death's door, dying.

put to death, to kill or execute.

to death, beyond endurance; excessively: *She was bored to death by the long after-dinner speeches.*

death·bed (deth′bed′), **1** n. bed on which someone dies. **2** n. the last hours of life. **3** adj. during the last hours of life: *We tried to honor the patient's deathbed request.*

death·blow (deth′blō′), n. **1** blow that kills: *He received a death-blow early in the battle.* **2** thing that puts an end to something: *My illness was the deathblow to hopes for a trip to Europe.*

death·less (deth′lis), adj. lasting forever; eternal. **—death′less·ly,** adv. **—death′less·ness,** n.

death·like (deth′līk′), adj. like that of death: *There was a death-like silence before the storm.*

death·ly (deth′lē), **1** adj., adv. like death: *Long illness had brought a deathly pallor to his face. The sick woman grew deathly pale.* **2** adv. extremely: *I am deathly afraid of deep water.*

death rate, proportion of the number of deaths per year to the total population.

death row, a row or block of prison cells where criminals condemned to death await execution.

death's-head (deths′hed′), n. a human skull, used as a symbol of death.

death·trap (deth′trap′), n. a building, vehicle, etc., in which unsafe conditions increase the risk of injury or death.

Death Valley, valley in E California. It is the lowest land in the Western Hemisphere.

death's-head

de·ba·cle (di bak′əl or dā bä′-kəl), n. a sudden downfall or collapse; disaster: *The election was a great debacle for the party in power since most of its candidates lost.*

de·bar (di bär′), v. to bar; shut out; prevent; prohibit: *School rules debarred me from playing.* ❑ v. **de·barred, de·bar·ring. —de·bar′ment,** n.

de·bark (di bärk′), v. disembark. **—de·bar·ka′tion,** n.

de·base (di bās′), v. to make low or lower; lessen the value of: *The nation's paper money was debased when the government printed more than it could back with gold.* ❑ v. **de·based, de·bas·ing. —de·base′ment,** n. **—de·bas′er,** n.

de·bat·a·ble (di bā′tə bəl), adj. **1** capable of being debated; open to debate. To be debatable a topic must have at least two sides. **2** not decided; in dispute; questionable: *The results of your experiment are debatable.*

de·bate (di bāt′), **1** v. to consider; think over: *I am debating buying a new car.* **2** n. discussion, often public, for and against: *There has been much debate about the safety of atomic energy.* **3** n. a public argument for and against a question in a meeting. A formal debate is a contest between two sides to see which one has more skill in speaking and reasoning. **4** v. to discuss a question, topic, etc., in a public meeting: *The two candidates debated the right of government employees to go out on strike for higher wages.* ■ See Synonym Study at **discuss.** ❑ v. **de·bat·ed, de·bat·ing. —de·bat′er,** n.

WORD STORY **Debate** comes from a Latin word meaning "to beat." **Batter**[1] comes from the same Latin word. People used to debate with swords; now they debate with words.

de·bauch (di bôch′), **1** v. to lead away from duty, virtue, or morality; corrupt or seduce: *debauched by bad companions.* **2** n. period of excessive eating, drinking, etc.: *a drunken debauch.* ❑ n., pl. **de·bauch·es. —de·bauch′er,** n.

de·bauch·er·y (di bô′chər ē), n. **1** excessive eating, drinking, etc. **2** departure from duty, virtue, or morality.

de·bil·i·tate (di bil′ə tāt), v. to make weak or feeble; weaken: *A hot, wet, tropical climate debilitates those who are not used to it.* ❑ v. **de·bil·i·tat·ed, de·bil·i·tat·ing. —de·bil′i·ta′tion,** n.

de·bil·i·ty (di bil′ə tē), n. weakness; feebleness: *Long illness may cause general debility.*

deb·it (deb′it), **1** n. entry of something owed in an account. **2** v. to charge with or as a debt: *The bank debited her account $500.*

deb·o·nair (deb′ə nâr′), adj. pleasant, courteous, and cheerful: *a carefree and debonair manner.* **—deb′o·nair′ly,** adv. **—deb′o·nair′ness,** n.

Deb·o·rah (deb′ər ə), n. (in the Bible) a judge and prophet. [**Deborah** comes from a Hebrew word meaning "bee."]

de·brief (dē brēf′), v. to question a pilot, astronaut, intelligence officer, etc., after a mission has been completed, in order to record information.

de·bris (də brē′), n. scattered fragments; ruins; rubbish: *The street was covered with broken glass, stone, and other debris from the explosion.*

Debs (debz), n. **Eu·gene** (yü jēn′), 1855-1926, American political leader. ■ **Eugene Debs** ran for president five times as a socialist

D

candidate. In the election of 1920, while in prison for speaking out against war during World War I, he won almost a million votes.

debt (det), *n.* **1** something owed to another: *He paid back all his debts.* **2** condition of owing; indebtedness: *The loan from the bank has put her in debt.*

debt·or (det′ər), *n.* person who owes something to another.

de·bug (dē bug′), *v.* **1** to find and correct the mistakes in a computer program. **2** to find and remove electronic spying devices from: *debug a room.* ❑ *v.* **de·bugged, de·bug·ging.**

de·bunk (dē bungk′), *v.* to expose false or exaggerated claims: *This article debunks the claims of some diet pills.* ❑ *v.* **de·bunked, de·bunk·ing.**

De·bus·sy (də byü′sē), *n.* **Claude** (klȯd), 1862-1918, French composer.

de·but (dā′byü *or* dā byü′), *n.* **1** a first public appearance: *a young actor's debut on the stage.* **2** the first formal appearance of a young woman in society.

dé·but (dā′byü *or* dā byü′), *n.* debut. ❑ *n., pl.* **dé·buts.**

deb·u·tante (deb′yə tänt), *n.* a young woman during her first season in society.

dé·bu·tante (dā′byü tänt *or* deb′yə tänt), *n.* debutante. ❑ *n., pl.* **dé·bu·tantes.**

Dec., December.

deca-, *prefix.* ten: *decaliter = ten liters; decagram = ten grams.*

dec·ade (dek′ād), *n.* period of ten years. From January 1987 through December 1996 is a decade. Two decades ago means twenty years ago.

WORD BANK **Decade** and the words below are related. They all come from Greek and Latin words meaning "ten."

dean	decameter	decibel	decimeter
decaliter	decathlon	decimal	dime
Decalogue	December	decimate	dozen

dec·a·dence (dek′ə dəns), *n.* process of growing worse; decline; decay: *a decadence in literature. The decadence of morals was one of the causes of the fall of Rome.*

dec·a·dent (dek′ə dənt), **1** *adj.* falling off; growing worse; declining; decaying: *a decadent nation.* **2** *n.* a decadent person. **—dec′a·dent·ly,** *adv.*

de·caf·fein·at·ed (di kaf′ə nā′tid), *adj.* without caffeine; treated to remove caffeine: *decaffeinated coffee.*

dec·a·gon (dek′ə gon), *n.* a plane figure having 10 angles and 10 sides.

dec·a·gram (dek′ə gram), *n.* unit of weight or mass equal to 10 grams.

dec·a·he·dron (dek′ə hē′drən), *n.* a solid figure having ten flat surfaces.

de·cal (dē′kal *or* di kal′), *n.* design or picture treated so that it will stick fast when it is put on glass, wood, plastic, or metal.

dec·a·li·ter (dek′ə lē′tər), *n.* unit of volume equal to 10 liters.

Dec·a·logue (dek′ə lȯg), *n.* the Ten Commandments.

dec·a·me·ter (dek′ə mē′tər), *n.* unit of length equal to 10 meters.

de·camp (di kamp′), *v.* **1** to leave quickly and secretly; run away; flee: *The strangers decamped during the night, taking two of our horses.* **2** to leave a camp. **—de·camp′ment,** *n.*

de·cant (di kant′), *v.* **1** to pour gently: *The waiter decanted the wine.* **2** to pour from one container to another.

de·cant·er (di kan′tər), *n.* a glass bottle with a stopper, used for serving wine, liquor, or other liquids.

de·cap·i·tate (di kap′ə tāt), *v.* to cut off the head of; behead. ❑ *v.* **de·cap·i·tat·ed, de·cap·i·tat·ing. —de·cap′i·ta′tion,** *n.*

decanter

de·cath·lon (di kath′lon), *n.* an athletic contest with ten separate track and field events. The person who scores the most points for all ten parts is the winner. [**Decathlon** comes from two Greek words meaning "ten" and "contest." **Athlete** comes from the same Greek word meaning "contest."]

de·cay (di kā′), **1** *v.* to become rotten; rot: *My teeth decayed because I ate too many sweets.* **2** *n.* process of rotting: *The decay in the tree trunk proceeded so rapidly the tree fell over in a year.* **3** *v.* to grow less in power, strength, wealth, or beauty: *Many nations have grown great and then decayed.* **4** *n.* process of growing less in power, strength, wealth, or beauty: *The decay of a nation's strength may be very slow.* **5** *n.* a change in a radioactive substance resulting from the giving off of subatomic particles or rays. **6** *v.* to change from one chemical element to another because the atomic nuclei have given off particles or rays.

SYNONYM STUDY **Decay** and **rot** both mean to change from a healthy condition to an unhealthy one. **Decay** suggests changing little by little through a natural process: *Dentists say this gum won't cause teeth to decay.* **Rot** suggests a disgusting breakdown, especially of plant or animal matter: *The rotting garbage attracted rats.*

Dec·can (dek′ən *or* de kan′), *n.* peninsula that makes up the southern part of India.

de·cease (di sēs′), **1** *n.* act or fact of dying; death: *the unexpected decease of her aunt.* **2** *v.* to die. ❑ *v.* **de·ceased, de·ceas·ing.**

de·ceased (di sēst′), **1** *adj.* no longer living; dead. ■ See Synonym Study at **dead.** **2** *n.sing. or pl.* **the deceased,** a particular dead person or persons: *The deceased had been a famous writer.*

de·ce·dent (di sēd′nt), *n.* (in law) a dead person.

de·ceit (di sēt′), *n.* **1** act of making someone believe as true something that is false; deceiving; lying: *He was a truthful person, incapable of deceit.* **2** a dishonest trick; lie spoken or acted. **3** quality that makes someone tell lies or cheat; deceitfulness: *The dishonest trader was full of deceit.*

de·ceit·ful (di sēt′fəl), *adj.* **1** ready or willing to deceive or lie: *a deceitful person.* **2** meant to deceive; deceiving; misleading: *She told a deceitful story to avoid punishment.* **—de·ceit′ful·ly,** *adv.* **—de·ceit′ful·ness,** *n.*

de·ceive (di sēv′), *v.* **1** to make someone believe as true something that is false; mislead: *His excuse deceived me until I learned the truth.* **2** to use deceit; lie. ❑ *v.* **de·ceived, de·ceiv·ing. —de·ceiv′a·ble,** *adj.* **—de·ceiv′er,** *n.* **—de·ceiv′ing·ly,** *adv.*

SYNONYM STUDY **Deceive** and **fool** both mean to make someone believe something untrue. **Deceive** is a general, serious word: *Criminals deceived her and took her money.* **Fool** suggests harmless play: *The magician fooled us into thinking she could read minds.*

de·cel·e·rate (dē sel′ə rāt′), *v.* to decrease the speed of; slow down: *By firing small rockets the astronauts decelerated the spacecraft.* ❑ *v.* **de·cel·e·rat·ed, de·cel·e·rat·ing. —de·cel′e·ra′tion,** *n.* **—de·cel′e·ra′tor,** *n.*

De·cem·ber (di sem′bər), *n.* the 12th and last month of the year. It has 31 days. [**December** comes from a Latin word meaning "ten." December was the tenth month in the ancient Roman calendar.]

de·cen·cy (dē′sn sē), *n.* **1** quality of being decent; proper behavior: *Common decency requires that you pay for the window you broke.* **2** a regard for modesty or delicacy; respectability. **3** **decencies,** *pl.* **a** suitable acts; proper observances: *courtesy, tolerance, kindness, and other decencies of life.* **b** things required for a proper standard of living.

de·cent (dē′snt), *adj.* **1** proper and right; respectable; modest: *The decent thing to do is to pay for the damage you have done.* **2** good enough; fairly good; adequate: *He is not rich but he earns a decent living.* **3** not severe; rather kind: *It's very decent of you to forgive me.* **4** dressed; not naked: *"Are you decent?" my sister called through the door.* **—de′cent·ly,** *adv.*

a	hat	ė	term	ȯ	order	ch	child		a	in about
ā	age	i	it	oi	oil	ng	long		e	in taken
ä	far	ī	ice	ou	out	sh	she	ə	i	in pencil
â	care	o	hot	u	cup	th	thin		o	in lemon
e	let	ō	open	u̇	put	ŦH	then		u	in circus
ē	equal	ȯ	saw	ü	rule	zh	measure			

de·cen·tral·ize (dē sen′trə līz), v. **1** to spread or distribute authority, power, etc., among more groups or local governments. **2** to spread an organization or activity away from a central location, such as a city: *decentralize industry to the suburbs.* ❑ v. **de·cen·tral·ized, de·cen·tral·iz·ing. –de·cen′tral·i·za′tion,** n.

de·cep·tion (di sep′shən), n. **1** act of misleading; deceiving: *The twins' deception in exchanging places fooled everybody except their parents.* **2** condition of being misled or deceived: *The deception of the magician's audience was almost complete.* **3** trick meant to deceive; fraud; sham: *The scheme is all a deception to cheat people out of their money.*

de·cep·tive (di sep′tiv), adj. tending to deceive; meant to deceive: *the deceptive warmth of winter sunlight, deceptive advertising.* **–de·cep′tive·ly,** adv. **–de·cep′tive·ness,** n.

deci- prefix. one tenth: *decigram = one tenth of a gram.*

dec·i·bel (des′ə bəl), n. unit for measuring the relative loudness of sounds. *Abbreviation:* dB or db

DECIBELS

faintest sound	)
whisper, rustling of leaves	10
quiet conversation	30
quiet radio, average home	50
loud TV, average factory	70
police whistle, heavy traffic	90
very loud factory noise	110
thunder or jet plane nearby	130

decibel—the decibels of various sounds

de·cide (di sīd′), v. **1** to make up your mind; resolve: *She decided to be a scientist.* **2** to settle a question, dispute, etc.: *Fighting is not the best way to decide an argument.* **3** to give judgment or decision: *The jury heard the evidence and decided in favor of the defendant.* **4** to cause someone to reach a decision: *What decided you to vote for him?* ❑ v. **de·cid·ed, de·cid·ing. –de·cid′a·ble,** adj. **–de·cid′er,** n.

SYNONYM STUDY **Decide** and **resolve** both mean to make up your mind. **Decide** is a general word: *Have you decided which book to take?* **Resolve** means to decide very firmly: *They resolved never to eat in that restaurant again.*

de·cid·ed (di sī′did), adj. **1** clear or definite; unquestionable: *There was a decided change in the temperature.* **2** firm; determined; resolute: *I studied hard because I had a decided wish to go to college.* **–de·cid′ed·ness,** n.

de·cid·ed·ly (di sī′did lē), adv. without question; clearly; definitely: *One painting was decidedly better than the others.*

de·cid·u·ous (di sij′ü əs), adj. **1** shedding leaves each year. Maples and elms are deciduous trees. **2** falling off at a particular season or stage of growth: *Maples have deciduous leaves that fall in autumn.* **–de·cid′u·ous·ly,** adv. **–de·cid′u·ous·ness,** n.

dec·i·gram (des′ə gram), n. unit of weight or mass equal to $\frac{1}{10}$ of a gram.

dec·i·li·ter (des′ə lē′tər), n. unit of volume equal to $\frac{1}{10}$ of a liter.

dec·i·mal (des′ə məl), **1** adj. of or based on the number 10; proceeding by tens: *The metric system is a decimal system of measurement.* **2** n. decimal fraction. **3** n. number containing a decimal fraction. EXAMPLES: 75.24, 3.062, .091. **–dec′i·mal·ly,** adv.

decimal fraction, fraction whose denominator is ten or a multiple of ten, expressed by placing a decimal point to the left of the numerator. EXAMPLES: .04 =$\frac{4}{100}$, .2 =$\frac{2}{10}$.

decimal point, period placed before a decimal fraction, as in 2.03, .623.

decimal system, system of numeration which is based on the number 10 and its multiples.

dec·i·mate (des′ə māt), v. to destroy much of; kill a large part of: *War decimated the nation.* ❑ v. **dec·i·mat·ed, dec·i·mat·ing. –dec′i·ma′tion,** n. **–dec′i·ma′tor,** n.

WORD STORY **Decimate** comes from a Latin word meaning "ten." If troops refused orders, the Romans would kill every tenth soldier to frighten the rest.

dec·i·me·ter (des′ə mē′tər), n. unit of length equal to $\frac{1}{10}$ of a meter.

de·ci·pher (di sī′fər), v. **1** to make out the meaning of something that is puzzling or not clear: *I can't decipher this poor handwriting.* **2** to change something in cipher or code to ordinary language; decode: *The spy deciphered the secret message.* **–de·ci′pher·a·ble,** adj. **–de·ci′pher·ment,** n.

de·ci·sion (di sizh′ən), n. **1** act of making up your mind; deciding: *I have not yet come to a decision about buying the property.* **2** judgment reached or given: *The jury brought in a decision of not guilty.* **3** firmness and determination: *She is a woman of decision who makes up her mind what to do and then does it.*

de·ci·sive (di sī′siv), adj. **1** having or giving a clear result; settling something beyond question: *The team won by 20 points, which was a decisive victory.* **2** having or showing decision: *When I asked for a decisive answer, he said flatly, "No."* **–de·ci′sive·ly,** adv. **–de·ci′sive·ness,** n.

deck (dek), **1** n. one of the floors of a ship that divide it into different levels. **2** n. part or floor that resembles a ship's deck: *Carpenters built a deck on the back of our house.* **3** n. a pack of playing cards. **4** n. tape deck. **5** v. to cover, dress, or adorn: *deck the halls with holly.* **6** v. INFORMAL. to knock someone down: *She decked the bully with one punch.* **–deck′er,** n.

on deck, ready to do something.

deck·hand (dek′hand′), n. sailor who works on deck.

de·claim (di klām′), v. **1** to recite in public; make a formal speech. **2** to speak like an orator in a loud and emotional manner; speak for effect: *The politician declaimed against the opposing party.* **–de·claim′er,** n.

dec·la·ma·tion (dek′lə mā′shən), n. **1** act of declaiming; making formal speeches. **2** a formal speech or selection of poetry, prose, etc., for reciting.

dec·la·ra·tion (dek′lə rā′shən), n. **1** thing declared; open or public statement: *The royal declaration was announced in every city and town.* **2** statement of goods, etc., for taxation: *a declaration stating the goods you are bringing into a country.* **3** act of declaring: *The soldiers rejoiced at the declaration of a truce.*

Declaration of Independence, the public statement adopted by the Second Continental Congress on July 4, 1776, in which the American colonies declared themselves free and independent of Great Britain.

Declaration of Independence

de·clar·a·tive (di klar′ə tiv), adj. making a statement; explaining. "I'm eating" and "The dog has four legs" are declarative sentences.

de·clare (di klâr′), v. **1** to say openly; state strongly: *I declared that I would never do anything so foolish again.* ■ See Synonym Study at **say. 2** to announce publicly or formally; make known; proclaim: *Congress has the power to declare war.* **3** to make a statement of purchases for taxation: *Travelers returning to the United States must declare the things which they bought abroad.* **4** to announce a choice or opinion: *The mayor declared against the proposed new law.* ❑ v. **de·clared, de·clar·ing. –de·clar′a·ble,** adj. **–de·clar′er,** n.

de·clas·si·fy (dē klas′ə fī), v. to remove documents, codes, etc., from the list of restricted, confidential, or secret information. ❑ v. **de·clas·si·fied, de·clas·si·fy·ing. —de·clas′si·fi·ca′tion,** n.

de·claw (dē clò′), v. to remove the claws of a cat.

dec·li·na·tion (dek′lə nā′shən), n. **1** deviation of the needle of a compass from true north. **2** a way of describing positions, used in astronomy. The declination of a star or other astronomical object is its distance north or south of an imaginary circle that astronomers draw in the sky, called the celestial equator.

de·cline (di klīn′), **1** v. to turn away from doing; refuse to do or accept something: *The children declined to do as they were told.* **2** v. to refuse politely: *I declined her offer of help.* **3** v. to grow less in power, strength, wealth, beauty, etc.; grow worse; decay: *Great nations have risen and declined. A person's strength declines in old age.* **4** n. process of losing power, strength, wealth, beauty, etc.; growing worse: *Lack of money led to a decline in the condition of the school.* **5** n. act of falling to a lower level; sinking: *a decline in prices, the decline of the sun as it nears the horizon.* **6** n. the last part of anything: *the decline of a person's life.* **7** v. to bend or slope down: *The hill declines to a fertile valley.* **8** n. a downward incline or slope: *The wagon rolled down the decline.* **9** v. to give the different cases or case endings of a noun, pronoun, or adjective. ❑ v. **de·clined, de·clin·ing. —de·clin′a·ble,** adj.

de·cliv·i·ty (di kliv′ə tē), n. a downward slope. ❑ n., pl. **de·cliv·i·ties.**

de·code (dē kōd′), v. to translate secret writing from code into ordinary language. ❑ v. **de·cod·ed, de·cod·ing. —de·cod′er,** n.

de·com·pose (dē′kəm pōz′), v. **1** to rot or become rotten; decay: *Lettuce and oranges decompose quickly in the heat.* **2** to separate a substance into what it is made of: *The prism decomposed the sunlight into its many colors.* ❑ v. **de·com·posed, de·com·pos·ing. —de′com·pos′a·ble,** adj.

de·com·pos·er (dē′kəm pō′zər), n. any living thing that feeds on the wastes or dead bodies of other living things, breaking them down into simpler forms. Many fungi and bacteria are decomposers.

de·com·po·si·tion (dē′kom pə zish′ən), n. **1** process of decay; rot. **2** act or process of decomposing: *the decomposition of water into hydrogen and oxygen.*

de·com·press (dē′kəm pres′), v. **1** to remove pressure from. **2** to change computer data or programs from a very short form to a usable form.

de·com·pres·sion (dē′kəm presh′ən), n. removal or lessening of pressure, especially of air pressure: *Gradual decompression is necessary as deep-sea divers surface.*

de·con·ges·tant (dē′kən jes′tənt), n. drug used to relieve nasal congestion.

de·con·tam·i·nate (dē′kən tam′ə nāt), v. to make safe for use by removing any harmful substances. ❑ v. **de·con·tam·i·nat·ed, de·con·tam·i·nat·ing. —de′con·tam′i·na′tion,** n.

de·con·trol (dē′kən trōl′), v. to remove controls from, especially official controls: *The airline industry changed rapidly after it was decontrolled.* ❑ v. **de·con·trolled, de·con·trol·ling.**

de·cor (dā kôr′), n. the overall arrangement of the decoration and furnishings of a room, house, store, office, etc.

dec·o·rate (dek′ə rāt′), v. **1** to make beautiful; adorn; trim: *We decorated the gymnasium for the dance.* **2** to paint or paper a room, etc.: *The old rooms looked like new after they had been decorated.* **3** to give a medal, ribbon, or badge to someone as an honor: *The general decorated the soldier for bravery.* ❑ v. **dec·o·rat·ed, dec·o·rat·ing.**

SYNONYM STUDY **Decorate, ornament,** and **adorn** all mean to make something look good by adding to it. **Decorate** suggests adding various items for color and cheerfulness: *He decorated the cake with little candies.* **Ornament** suggests something permanent: *Stained glass windows ornament the church.* **Adorn** is a formal word: *The banquet table is adorned with flowers in crystal vases.*

dec·o·ra·tion (dek′ə rā′shən), n. **1** thing used to decorate; ornament: *We put pictures and other decorations up in the classroom.* **2** act of decorating: *Decoration of the gymnasium took most of the day before the dance.* **3** medal, ribbon, or badge given as an honor.

Decoration Day, Memorial Day.

dec·o·ra·tive (dek′ər ə tiv), adj. helping to adorn; ornamental; decorating: *Wallpaper gives a decorative effect to a room.* **—dec′o·ra′tive·ly,** adv. **—dec′o·ra′tive·ness,** n.

dec·o·ra·tor (dek′ə rā′tər), n. **1** person who decorates. **2** interior decorator.

dec·o·rous (dek′ər əs or di kôr′əs), adj. acting properly; in good taste; well-behaved; dignified: *decorous behavior.* **—dec′or·ous·ly,** adv. **—dec′or·ous·ness,** n.

de·co·rum (di kôr′əm), n. proper behavior; good taste in conduct, speech, dress, etc.: *act with decorum, observe decorum in a court of law.*

de·cou·page or **dé·cou·page** (dā′kü päzh′), n. the technique of decorating a surface by gluing down paper cutouts and then coating it all with a finish such as varnish.

decoy (def. 2)

de·coy (di koi′ *for verb;* dē′koi *or* di koi′ *for noun*), **1** v. to lure wild birds, animals, etc., into a trap or near the hunter: *Hunters decoyed the geese into the range of their guns.* **2** n. an artificial bird used to lure birds into a trap or near the hunter: *The duck hunter floated wooden decoys near her.* **3** v. to lead or tempt by trickery; entice: *The bird decoyed us away from her nest by dragging one wing.* **4** n. any person or thing used to lead or tempt into danger; lure. [Decoy may come from Dutch words meaning "the cage." Hunters used to put out a tame bird to attract wild birds into cages.]

de·crease (di krēs′ *for verb;* dē′krēs′ *or* di krēs′ *for noun*), **1** v. to make or become less; lessen: *The driver decreased the speed of the car. Hunger decreases as you eat.* **2** n. a process of becoming less; lessening: *Toward night there was a decrease in temperature.* **3** n. amount by which a thing becomes less or is made less: *The decrease in temperature was 15 degrees.* ❑ v. **de·creased, de·creas·ing.**

on the decrease, decreasing: *Because of the new neighborhood watch program, crime is on the decrease on our block.*

SYNONYM STUDY **Decrease** and **diminish** both mean to make or become less. **Decrease** is a general word: *Her parents decreased her allowance to pay for the broken window.* **Diminish** suggests a gradual taking away: *Every point the other team scored diminished our hopes.*

de·cree (di krē′), **1** n. something ordered by authority; official decision; law: *The new state holiday was declared by a decree of the governor.* **2** v. to order or settle by authority: *The city decreed that all dogs must be licensed.* ❑ n., pl. **de·crees;** v. **de·creed, de·cree·ing.**

de·crep·it (di krep′it), adj. broken down or weakened by old age; old and feeble: *The stairs are decrepit and unsafe.* ■ The use of **decrepit** about people is often considered offensive. **—de·crep′it·ly,** adv.

de·crep·i·tude (di krep′ə tüd), n. feebleness, usually from old age; weakness.

a	hat	ė	term	ô	order	ch	child		
ā	age	i	it	oi	oil	ng	long		a in about
ä	far	ī	ice	ou	out	sh	she		e in taken
â	care	o	hot	u	cup	th	thin	ə	i in pencil
e	let	ō	open	ù	put	ŦH	then		o in lemon
ē	equal	ò	saw	ü	rule	zh	measure		u in circus

de·cre·scen·do (dē′krə shen′dō), in music: **1** *n.* a gradual decrease in force or loudness; diminuendo. **2** *adj., adv.* with a gradual decrease in force or loudness; diminuendo. ❑ *n., pl.* **de·cre·scen·dos.**

de·crim·i·nal·ize (dē krim′ə nə līz), *v.* to make something legal that was once a crime. ❑ *v.* **de·crim·i·nal·ized, de·crim·i·nal·iz·ing.** –**de′crim′i·nal·i·za′tion,** *n.*

de·cry (di krī′), *v.* to express strong disapproval of; condemn: *The taxpayers decried the increase in federal spending.* ❑ *v.* **de·cried, de·cry·ing.** –**de·cri′er,** *n.*

ded·i·cate (ded′ə kāt), *v.* **1** to set apart for a purpose; devote: *The doctor dedicated her life to improving hospital care.* **2** to address a book, poem, etc., to a friend or patron as a mark of affection, respect, or gratitude. ❑ *v.* **ded·i·cat·ed, ded·i·cat·ing.** –**ded′i·ca′tor,** *n.*

ded·i·ca·tion (ded′ə kā′shən), *n.* **1** act of setting apart or condition of being set apart for a purpose: *the dedication of a park.* **2** words dedicating a book, poem, etc., to a friend or patron.

ded·i·ca·to·ry (ded′ə kə tôr′ē), *adj.* of dedication; as a dedication.

de·duce (di düs′), *v.* to reach a conclusion by reasoning; infer: *I deduced from your lack of appetite what had happened to the cookies.* ❑ *v.* **de·duced, de·duc·ing.** –**de·duc′i·ble,** *adj.*

de·duct (di dukt′), *v.* to take away; subtract: *He deducted the cost of the broken dishes from my paycheck.* –**de·duct′i·ble,** *adj.*

de·duc·tion (di duk′shən), *n.* **1** act or process of taking away; subtraction: *No deduction from your pay is made for absence due to illness.* **2** amount deducted: *There was a deduction of $50 from the bill for damage caused by the movers.* **3** act or process of reaching conclusions by reasoning; inference. **4** thing deduced; conclusion: *The detective reached her clever deduction by careful study of the facts.*

> **USAGE NOTE** **Deduction** is often used in mystery stories to mean the process of figuring out the truth by reasoning from details. Experts in logic, however, call that sort of reasoning **induction.** Deduction has been used for centuries to mean reasoning from truths to details, but modern usage may change the word's meaning.

de·duc·tive (di duk′tiv), *adj.* of or using deduction; reasoning by deduction. –**de·duc′tive·ly,** *adv.*

deed (dēd), **1** *n.* something done; act; action: *To feed the hungry is a good deed.* **2** *n.* a written or printed statement of ownership. The buyer of real estate receives a deed to the property. **3** *v.* to transfer by means of a deed: *She deeded the land to her son.* [See Word Story at **batch.**] –**deed′less,** *adj.*

dee·jay (dē′jā′), *n.* disk jockey.

deem (dēm), *v.* to think, believe, or consider: *Doctors prescribe the medicines they deem necessary to cure their patients.*

deep (def. 1)

deep (dēp), **1** *adj.* going a long way down from the top or surface: *a deep well. The pond is deep in the middle.* **2** *adv.* far down or on: *We dug deep before we could find water.* **3** *adj.* far down: *I had a deep cut on my finger.* **4** *adj.* going a long way back from the front: *Our house stands on a deep lot.* **5** *adj.* low in pitch: *a deep voice.* **6** *adj.* hard to understand: *a deep book, deep thoughts.* **7** *adj.* earnest; heartfelt: *Deep feeling is hard to put into words.* **8** *adj.* strong; great; intense; extreme: *I fell into a deep sleep after the hike.* **9** *adj.* strong and dark in color: *a deep red.* **10** *adj.* in depth: *a tank eight feet deep.* **11** *adj.* with the mind fully taken up: *deep in thought.* **12** *adv.* well along in time; far on: *I studied deep into the night.* **13** *n.* the most intense part: *the deep of winter.* **14** *n.* **the deep,** the sea: *Long ago, sailors thought huge monsters lived in the deep.* –**deep′ly,** *adv.* –**deep′ness,** *n.*

deep·en (dē′pən), *v.* to make or become deeper: *We deepened the hole. The water deepened as the tide came in.*

deep-fry (dēp′frī′), *v.* to fry food in enough hot fat to cover it completely. ❑ *v.* **deep-fried, deep-fry·ing.**

deep-root·ed (dēp′rü′tid), *adj.* **1** deeply rooted: *a tall and deep-rooted tree.* **2** firmly instilled: *a deep-rooted fear of snakes.* –**deep′-root′ed·ness,** *n.*

deep-sea (dēp′sē′), *adj.* of or in the deeper parts of the sea: *a deep-sea diver.*

deep-seat·ed (dēp′sē′tid), *adj.* **1** far below the surface. **2** firmly instilled: *She has a deep-seated love of nature.*

deep-set (dēp′set′), *adj.* **1** set deeply: *He has deep-set eyes.* **2** firmly instilled: *deep-set prejudice.*

deer (dir), *n.* any of numerous swift, graceful mammals that have hoofs and chew the cud. All male deer and some female deer have antlers, which are shed and grow again every year. ❑ *n., pl.* **deer.** ■ Another word that sounds like this is **dear.** –**deer′like′,** *adj.*

> **WORD STORY** **Deer** comes from an old English word meaning "beast." That word was used for any kind of animal. Because hunters took more deer than anything else, they began using the word for that kind of animal.

deer mouse, any of numerous small American mice with white feet and large ears.

deer·skin (dir′skin′), *n.* **1** leather made from the skin of a deer. **2** clothing made of this leather. **3** skin of a deer.

def., definition. ❑ *pl.* **defs.**

de·face (di fās′), *v.* to spoil the appearance of; disfigure: *Scribbled notes defaced the pages of the book.* ❑ *v.* **de·faced, de·fac·ing.** –**de·face′a·ble,** *adj.* –**de·face′ment,** *n.* –**de·fac′er,** *n.*

de fac·to (di fak′tō), in fact; in reality; actually existing, whether lawful or not: *de facto racial segregation.*

de·fam·a·to·ry (di fam′ə tôr′ē), *adj.* slanderous or libelous: *defamatory articles.*

de·fame (di fām′), *v.* to attack the good name of; harm the reputation of; speak evil of; slander or libel. ❑ *v.* **de·famed, de·fam·ing.** –**def·a·ma·tion** (def′ə mā′shən), *n.* –**de·fam′er,** *n.*

de·fault (di fôlt′), **1** *n.* failure to do something or to appear somewhere when due; neglect. If, in any contest, one side does not appear, it loses by default. **2** *v.* to fail to do something or appear somewhere when due: *They defaulted in the tennis tournament. She defaulted on her car payment.* **3** *n.* the result or condition that occurs if no other choice is made: *The default for the screen background is blue.* **4** *v.* to set a standard value or condition if no other choice is made: *The printer defaults to one-inch margins all around the page.* –**de·fault′er,** *n.*

de·feat (di fēt′), **1** *v.* to win a victory over; overcome: *defeat an enemy in battle, defeat another softball team.* **2** *v.* to cause to fail; frustrate: *defeat someone's plans.* **3** *n.* act of defeating; an overcoming in a contest: *The crowd cheered their team's defeat of the visiting team.* **4** *n.* condition of being defeated; failing to win: *We were unhappy about our team's defeat.* –**de·feat′er,** *n.*

de·feat·ism (di fē′tiz′əm), *n.* attitude or behavior of a defeatist.

de·feat·ist (di fē′tist), **1** *n.* person who expects or admits defeat. **2** *adj.* expecting or admitting defeat: *defeatist speeches.*

def·e·cate (def′ə kāt), *v.* to discharge intestinal waste from the body. ❑ *v.* **def·e·cat·ed, def·e·cat·ing.** –**def′e·ca′tion,** *n.*

de·fect (dē′fekt or di fekt′ for noun; di fekt′ for verb), **1** *n.* a shortcoming or failing in someone or something; fault or blemish: *The cloth had holes and other defects.* **2** *n.* lack of something necessary for completeness: *an error caused by a defect in reasoning.* **3** *v.* to forsake your own country, group, etc., for another, especially another that is opposed to it: *The traitor defected to the enemy.* –**de·fec′tion,** *n.* –**de·fec′tor,** *n.*

de·fec·tive (di fek′tiv), *adj.* having a flaw or blemish; not perfect; not complete; faulty: *A watch with defective parts will not keep time.* **—de·fec′tive·ly,** *adv.* **—de·fec′tive·ness,** *n.*

de·fend (di fend′), *v.* **1** to guard from attack or harm; keep safe; protect: *defend a fort.* ▪ See Synonym Study at **guard. 2** to act, speak, or write in favor of: *The newspapers defended the governor's action. Lawyers defend people charged with crimes.* **3** to fight or contest a claim or a lawsuit. **—de·fend′er,** *n.*

de·fend·ant (di fen′dənt), *n.* person accused or sued in a court of law: *The defendant is charged with theft.*

de·fense (di fens′ *for 1-3,5,6;* di fens′ *or* dē′fens *for* 4), *n.* **1** thing that defends or protects; thing to guard against attack or harm: *A wall around the city was a defense against enemies.* **2** act of guarding against attack or harm; defending or protecting: *The armed forces are responsible for the defense of the country.* **3** action, speech, or writing in favor of something. **4** team or team members who try to keep their opponents from making points. **5** side that speaks and acts for the accused, or the defendant, in a court of law. **6** an answer of the accused, or defendant, to an accusation or claim in a court of law: *He had no defense against the charge of shoplifting.*

de·fense·less (di fens′lis), *adj.* helpless against attack or harm; having no defense; unprotected: *a defenseless village, a defenseless child.* **—de·fense′less·ly,** *adv.* **—de·fense′less·ness,** *n.*

de·fense·man (di fens′mən), *n.* (in hockey and lacrosse) one of several players assigned to defend the area near the goal. ❑ *n., pl.* **de·fense·men.**

defense mechanism, any mental process that protects someone from guilt, shame, etc. A person who uses a defense mechanism, such as forgetting or denying facts, is often not aware of it.

de·fen·si·ble (di fen′sə bəl), *adj.* able to be defended or justified. **—de·fen′si·bil′i·ty,** *n.* **—de·fen′si·bly,** *adv.*

de·fen·sive (di fen′siv), **1** *adj.* of or for defense; intended to defend: *Knights wore defensive armor in battle.* **2** *n.* position or attitude of defense. **—de·fen′sive·ly,** *adv.* **—de·fen′sive·ness,** *n.*
on the defensive, ready to defend, apologize, or explain: *When his work was criticized, he was put on the defensive.*

de·fer[1] (di fėr′), *v.* to put off; delay: *The test was deferred because so many students were sick.* ❑ *v.* **de·ferred, de·fer·ring. —de·fer′ra·ble,** *adj.* **—de·fer′rer,** *n.*

de·fer[2] (di fėr′), *v.* to yield in judgment or opinion: *The children deferred to their parents' wishes.* ❑ *v.* **de·ferred, de·fer·ring.**

def·er·ence (def′ər əns), *n.* respect for the judgment, opinion, wishes, etc., of another: *He shows deference to his elders.*
in deference to, out of respect for.

def·e·ren·tial (def′ə ren′shəl), *adj.* showing deference; respectful. **—def′e·ren′tial·ly,** *adv.*

de·fer·ment (di fėr′mənt), *n.* act of putting something off; delay.

de·fi·ance (di fi′əns), *n.* act of defying; standing up against authority and refusing to recognize or obey it; open resistance to power: *The colonists' defiance of the king led to war.*
in defiance of, without regard for; in spite of: *The driver failed to stop at the red light in defiance of the law.*

de·fi·ant (di fi′ənt), *adj.* showing defiance; openly resisting: *He told us in a defiant manner that he wouldn't go.* **—de·fi′ant·ly,** *adv.*

de·fi·cien·cy (di fish′ən sē), *n.* lack of something needed or required; incompleteness: *A deficiency of calcium in your diet can cause soft bones and teeth.* ❑ *n., pl.* **de·fi·cien·cies.**

deficiency disease, disease caused by a diet that lacks one or more essential vitamins, minerals, etc.

de·fi·cient (di fish′ənt), *adj.* lacking something needed; not complete; defective: *His knowledge of science is deficient.* **—de·fi′cient·ly,** *adv.*

def·i·cit (def′ə sit), *n.* amount by which a sum of money falls short; shortage: *Since the club owed $15 and had only $10 in the treasury, there was a deficit of $5 to be made up by the members.*

de·fi·er (di fi′ər), *n.* person who defies.

de·file[1] (di fil′), *v.* **1** to make filthy or dirty; make disgusting in any way. **2** to destroy the purity or cleanness of anything sacred; desecrate: *The enemy defiled the church by using it as a stable.* ❑ *v.* **de·filed, de·fil·ing. —de·file′ment,** *n.* **—de·fil′er,** *n.*

de·file[2] (di fil′), **1** *n.* a steep and narrow valley. **2** *v.* to march in single file or a narrow column. ❑ *v.* **de·filed, de·fil·ing.**

de·fine (di fin′), *v.* **1** to make clear the meaning of; explain: *A dictionary defines words.* **2** to make clear; make distinct: *The shape of the building was defined against the dark sky.* **3** to describe in detail; specify: *The powers of the courts are defined by law.* **4** to settle the limits of: *The boundary between the United States and Canada is defined by treaty.* ❑ *v.* **de·fined, de·fin·ing. —de·fin′a·ble,** *adj.* **—de·fin′er,** *n.*

WORD STORY Define comes from a Latin word meaning "an end" or "limit." Final comes from the same Latin word. Defining puts limits on meaning, showing what the meaning of a word includes and where the meaning ends. See also Word Story at **term.**

def·i·nite (def′ə nit), *adj.* **1** clear or exact; not vague: *definite proof. I expect a definite answer, either yes or no.* **2** certain; without doubt: *Is it definite that they are moving?* **3** having settled limits: *a definite boundary line.*

SYNONYM STUDY Definite and distinct both mean clear and exact. Definite suggests something easy to understand: *He made a definite offer of $20 for the lamp.* Distinct suggests something easy to notice: *The kitten has a distinct fondness for that cushion.*

definite article, the article *the.* "A dog" means "any dog"; "the dog" means "a certain or particular dog."

def·i·nite·ly (def′ə nit lē), *adv.* **1** in a definite manner: *Say definitely what you have in mind.* **2** certainly: *I am definitely going.*

def·i·ni·tion (def′ə nish′ən), *n.* **1** statement in which the nature of a thing is explained or the meaning of a word is made clear. One definition of "home" is "the place where a person or family lives." **2** act or process of explaining the nature of a thing or making clear the meaning of a word. **3** clearness; distinctness. *Good photographs have definition.*

de·fin·i·tive (di fin′ə tiv), *adj.* deciding or settling a question; conclusive; final: *The school issued a definitive statement of policy regarding unexcused absences.* **—de·fin′i·tive·ly,** *adv.* **—de·fin′i·tive·ness,** *n.*

de·flate (di flāt′), *v.* **1** to let air or gas out of a balloon, tire, football, etc.: *A nail had deflated the tire.* **2** to reduce inflated prices or currency. **3** to injure or destroy the conceit or confidence of: *I was deflated by their criticisms.* ❑ *v.* **de·flat·ed, de·flat·ing. —de·fla′tor,** *n.*

WORD STORY Deflate comes from **de-** and a Latin word meaning "to blow." It is the opposite of **inflate,** but **inflate** was first used in the 1400s, while **deflate** was not used until 1891. Related words can have very different stories.

de·fla·tion (di flā′shən), *n.* **1** reduction of the amount of available money in circulation so that the value of money increases and prices go down. **2** act or process of letting the air or gas out: *the deflation of a tire.*

de·flect (di flekt′), *v.* to bend or turn aside; change the direction of: *The wind deflected the arrow's flight.* **—de·flec′tor,** *n.*

de·flec·tion (di flek′shən), *n.* **1** act of bending or turning aside: *Strong winds caused some deflection from the plane's charted course.* **2** amount of bending or turning.

De·foe (di fō′), *n.* **Daniel,** 1660?-1731, English author who wrote *Robinson Crusoe.*

de·fo·li·ant (di fō′lē ənt), *n.* any chemical substance used to strip the leaves from trees and other plants.

de·fo·li·ate (di fō′lē āt), *v.* to strip a tree or plant of leaves: *The fire defoliated most of the trees in the forest.* ❑ *v.* **de·fo·li·at·ed, de·fo·li·at·ing. —de·fo′li·a′tion,** *n.*

de·fo·rest (dē fôr′ist), *v.* to remove the trees from; clear of trees: *The land had to be deforested before the settlers could farm it.* **—de·fo′rest·a′tion,** *n.* **—de·fo′rest·er,** *n.*

a	hat	ė	term	ô	order	ch	child	ə	a in about
ā	age	i	it	oi	oil	ng	long		e in taken
ä	far	ī	ice	ou	out	sh	she		i in pencil
â	care	o	hot	u	cup	th	thin		o in lemon
e	let	ō	open	u̇	put	ŧн	then		u in circus
ē	equal	ȯ	saw	ü	rule	zh	measure		

de·form (di fôrm′), v. **1** to spoil the form or shape of: *Wearing shoes that are too tight may deform the feet.* **2** to make ugly: *a face deformed by hate and anger.*

de·for·ma·tion (dē′fôr mā′shən or def′ər mā′shən), n. **1** act of deforming. **2** deformed condition; disfigurement.

de·formed (di fôrmd′), adj. not properly formed: *The baby's deformed foot was corrected by surgery.*

de·form·i·ty (di fôr′mə tē), n. **1** part that is not properly formed. **2** condition of being improperly formed: *Many deformities can be corrected.* ❑ n., pl. **de·form·i·ties.**

de·fraud (di frôd′), v. to take money, rights, etc., away from by fraud; cheat: *The company was accused of defrauding the government of millions of dollars in taxes.* —**de·fraud′er,** n.

de·fray (di frā′), v. to pay costs or expenses: *The expenses of national parks are defrayed by the taxpayers.* —**de·fray′a·ble,** adj. —**de·fray′er,** n. —**de·fray′ment,** n.

de·frost (di frôst′), v. **1** to remove frost or ice from: *defrost the refrigerator.* **2** to thaw out: *Cooking defrosts frozen foods.*

de·frost·er (di frôs′tər), n. device that removes frost or ice.

deft (deft), adj. quick and skillful in action; nimble: *The fingers of a violinist must be deft.* —**deft′ly,** adv. —**deft′ness,** n.

de·funct (di fungkt′), adj. no longer in existence; dead; extinct: *A business that fails is defunct.*

de·fuse (dē fyüz′), v. **1** to remove the fuse from a bomb. **2** to calm or reduce: *Her friendly smile immediately defused the tension in the room.* ❑ v. **de·fused, de·fus·ing.**

de·fy (di fī′), v. **1** to set yourself openly against authority; resist boldly: *defy the law, defy your parents.* **2** to withstand; resist: *The beauty of the forest defies description.* **3** to challenge someone to do or prove something; dare: *I defy you to do that again.* ❑ v. **de·fied, de·fy·ing.** [**Defy** comes from a Latin word meaning "not faithful." Someone who defies authority no longer has faith in that authority.]

De·gas (dā gä′), n. **Ed·gar** (ed·gär′), 1834-1917, French impressionist artist. He painted many scenes from modern life and is best known for paintings of dancers.

de Gaulle (də gōl′), **Charles,** 1890-1970, French general and political leader, president of France from 1959 to 1969.

de·gauss (di gous′ or di gôs′), v. remove magnetism from; demagnetize. Steel ships are degaussed by electric coils so that magnetic mines will not be attracted to the hulls.

de·gen·er·a·cy (di jen′ər ə sē), n. degenerate condition.

de·gen·er·ate (di jen′ə rāt′ for verb; di jen′ər it for adj., noun), **1** v. to grow worse; decline in physical, mental, or moral qualities: *Her health degenerated as the disease progressed.* **2** v. (in biology) to sink to a lower type; lose normal or more highly developed characteristics. **3** adj. showing a decline in physical, mental, or moral qualities: *a degenerate person.* **4** n. person having an evil and unwholesome character. ❑ v. **de·gen·er·at·ed, de·gen·er·at·ing.** —**de·gen′er·ate·ly,** adv.

de·gen·er·a·tion (di jen′ə rā′shən), n. **1** process of degenerating. **2** a degenerate condition.

de·gen·er·a·tive (di jen′ər ə tiv), adj. **1** tending to grow worse in quality. **2** showing steady change to worse: *degenerative muscular disease.*

deg·ra·da·tion (deg′rə dā′shən), n. **1** act or process of degrading: *A poor diet may cause a gradual degradation of health.* **2** condition of being degraded: *an environment's degradation by pollution.*

de·grade (di grād′), v. **1** to make lower in the eyes of others; bring shame upon; dishonor: *Students who cheat degrade them-*

selves. **2** to make worse; spoil; ruin: *degrade a park with trash.* ❑ v. **de·grad·ed, de·grad·ing.** —**de·grad′a·ble,** adj. —**de·grad′er,** n.

de·gree (di grē′), n. **1** a step in a series; stage in a process: *By degrees I improved my ability to swim and dive.* **2** amount; extent: *To what degree are you interested in reading?* **3** unit for measuring temperature: *The freezing point of water is 32 degrees (32°) Fahrenheit, or 0 degrees (0°) Celsius.* **4** unit for measuring an angle or an arc of a circle. A degree is 1/90 of a right angle or 1/360 of the circumference of a circle. 45 degrees (45°) is half a right angle or one eighth of the line bounding a circle. **5** rank: *A noble is a person of high degree.* **6** rank or title given by a college or university to a student whose work fulfills certain requirements, or to a noted person as an honor: *a bachelor's degree.* **7** (in grammar) one of the three stages in the comparison of adjectives or adverbs. The **positive degree** of *fast* is *fast;* the **comparative degree** is *faster;* the **superlative degree** is *fastest.* **8** (in law) a relative measure of the seriousness of a crime: *murder in the first degree.* ❑ n., pl. **de·grees.** —**de·gree′less,** adj.

de·gree-day (di grē′dā′), n. unit that represents a change of one degree below a standard, usually 65 degrees Fahrenheit, in the mean outdoor temperature for one day. Degree-days are used to determine fuel requirements.

de·hu·mid·i·fy (dē′hyü mid′ə fī), v. to remove moisture from. ❑ v. **de·hu·mid·i·fied, de·hu·mid·i·fy·ing.** —**de′hu·mid′i·fi′er,** n.

de·hy·drate (dē hī′drāt), v. **1** to take water or moisture from; dry: *to dehydrate vegetables. High fever dehydrates the body.* **2** to lose water or moisture. ❑ v. **de·hy·drat·ed, de·hy·drat·ing.** —**de′hy·dra′tion,** n. —**de·hy′dra·tor,** n.

de·ice (dē īs′), v. to prevent ice from forming on; remove ice from. ❑ v. **de·iced, de·ic·ing.** —**de′ic′er,** n.

de·i·fy (dē′ə fī), v. **1** to make a god of: *Ancient peoples often deified the sun.* **2** to worship or regard as a god: *Some people deify wealth.* ❑ v. **de·i·fied, de·i·fy·ing.** —**de′i·fi·ca′tion,** n.

deign (dān), v. to choose to do something undignified or unworthy: *So great a novelist would never deign to quarrel with such trifling critics.*

dei·non·y·chus (di non′ə kəs), n. a small, swift, flesh-eating dinosaur with huge claws. It ran upright and resembled a velociraptor. ❑ n., pl. **dei·non·y·chus·es.** [**Deinonychus** comes from Greek words meaning "terrible" and "claw."]

de·i·ty (dē′ə tē), n. **1** god or goddess: *The ancient Romans had many deities.* **2** divine nature; being a god: *Christians believe in the deity of Jesus.* **3 the Deity,** God. ❑ n., pl. **de·i·ties** for 1.

dé·jà vu (dā zhä vü′), illusion of having previously experienced something that you are actually experiencing for the first time.

de·ject·ed (di jek′tid), adj. in low spirits; sad; discouraged: *I was feeling dejected and unhappy until I heard the good news.* —**de·ject′ed·ly,** adv. —**de·ject′ed·ness,** n.

de·jec·tion (di jek′shən), n. sadness; lowness of spirits; discouragement.

deka-, form of **deca-** favored in scientific use of the metric system.

dek·a·gram (dek′ə gram), n. decagram.

dek·a·li·ter (dek′ə lē′tər), n. decaliter.

dek·a·me·ter (dek′ə mē′tər), n. decameter.

deke (dēk), CANADIAN SLANG. in hockey: **1** n. a fake shot or maneuver. **2** v. to lure an opponent out of position by a fake shot or maneuver. ❑ v. **deked, dek·ing.**

de Klerk (də klerk), **F. W.,** born 1936, president of South Africa from 1989 to 1994. He freed Nelson Mandela from prison and began to get rid of the apartheid system.

del., 1 delegate. **2** delete. **3** delivery.

Del., Delaware.

Del·a·ware (del′ə wâr), n. **1** one of the southeastern states of the United States. *Abbreviation:* DE or Del. *Capital:* Dover. **2** river flowing from SE New York State between Pennsylvania and New Jersey into the Atlantic. **3** member of a tribe of American Indians, formerly living in the valley of the Delaware River, now living in Wisconsin, Ontario, and Oklahoma. ❑ n., pl. **Del·a·ware** or **Del·a·wares** for 3. [**Delaware** comes from the title of Lord De La Warr, first governor of England's Virginia colony.]

Degas painting

Delaware Bay, inlet of the Atlantic between Delaware and New Jersey, at the mouth of the Delaware River.

delicate (def. 1)—a delicate web

de·lay (di lā′), **1** v. to put off till a later time: *We will delay the party for a week.* **2** n. act of putting off till a later time: *The delay upset our plans.* **3** v. to make late; keep waiting; hinder the progress of: *The accident delayed the train for two hours.* **4** v. to be late; go slowly; stop along the way: *Do not delay on this errand.* **5** n. period of time that something is put off or held up: *After a delay of one hour, the plane took off.* ❑ v. **de·layed, de·lay·ing. —de·lay′er,** n.

de·lec·ta·ble (di lek′tə bəl), adj. very pleasing; delightful: *the delectable taste of fresh berries.* **—de·lec′ta·bly,** adv.

del·e·gate (del′ə git or del′ə gāt *for noun;* del′ə gāt *for verb*), **1** n. person given power or authority to act for others; representative: *Our club sent two delegates to the meeting.* **2** v. to appoint or send someone as a representative: *The club delegated her to buy the equipment.* **3** v. to give over your power or authority to another so that he or she may act for you: *to delegate a task.* ❑ v. **del·e·gat·ed, del·e·gat·ing. —del′e·ga·tor,** n.

del·e·ga·tion (del′ə gā′shən), n. **1** group of delegates. **2** act of delegating. **3** fact of being delegated.

de·lete (di lēt′), v. to strike out or take out anything written or printed; cross out. ❑ v. **de·let·ed, de·let·ing. —de·le′tion,** n.

del·e·te·ri·ous (del′ə tir′ē əs), adj. causing harm; injurious. **—del′e·te·ri·ous·ly,** adv. **—del′e·te·ri·ous·ness,** n.

delft (delft), n. **1** a kind of glazed earthenware made in the Netherlands, usually decorated in blue on a white background. **2** any pottery like this.

Del·hi (del′ē), n. city in N India, former capital of India.

del·i (del′ē), n. delicatessen. ❑ n., pl. **del·is.**

de·lib·er·ate (di lib′ər it *for adj.;* di lib′ə rāt′ *for verb*), **1** adj. carefully thought out beforehand; made or done on purpose; intended: *Their excuse was a deliberate lie.* **2** adj. slow and careful in deciding what to do: *Deliberate persons do not make up their minds quickly.* ▪ See Synonym Study at **slow. 3** adj. not hurried; slow: *to walk with deliberate steps.* **4** v. to think over carefully; consider: *I am deliberating where to hang my new picture.* **5** v. to talk over reasons for and against; discuss; debate: *Congress deliberated the question of cutting taxes.* ❑ v. **de·lib·er·at·ed, de·lib·er·at·ing. —de·lib′er·ate·ly,** adv. **—de·lib′er·ate·ness,** n.

WORD STORY **Deliberate** comes from a Latin word meaning "to weigh." Careful thinking compares ideas in a way that is like balancing objects on a pair of scales.

de·lib·er·a·tion (di lib′ə rā′shən), n. **1** careful thought: *After long deliberation she decided not to go.* **2** Often, **deliberations,** pl. act or process of talking about reasons for and against something; discussion; debate: *the deliberations of Congress over taxes.* **3** slowness and care: *She drove the car over the icy bridge with great deliberation.*

de·lib·er·a·tive (di lib′ər ə tiv), adj. for deliberation; about deliberation: *Congress is a deliberative group.* **—de·lib′er·a·tive·ly,** adv. **—de·lib′er·a·tive·ness,** n.

del·i·ca·cy (del′ə kə sē), n. **1** fineness of weave, quality, or make; slightness and grace: *the delicacy of lace, the delicacy of a flower, the delicacy of a baby's skin.* **2** fineness of feeling for small differences: *The pianist had great delicacy of touch.* **3** need of care, skill, or tact: *His refusal required great delicacy, because he did not wish to hurt his friend's feelings.* **4** thought for the feelings of others. **5** sensitiveness to what is offensive or not modest. **6** condition of being easily hurt or made ill; weakness: *The parents often worried about their child's delicacy.* **7** a special kind of tasty food; dainty. ❑ n., pl. **del·i·ca·cies** for 7.

del·i·cate (del′ə kit), adj. **1** of fine weave, quality, or make; easily torn; thin: *delicate fabrics.* **2** pleasing to taste or smell; mild or soft: *Roses have a delicate fragrance.* **3** requiring care, skill, or tact: *a delicate situation.* **4** very quickly responding to slight changes of condition; finely sensitive: *Scientists use delicate controls to keep the space telescope precisely aimed.* **5** easily hurt or made ill: *a physically delicate child.* **—del′i·cate·ly,** adv. **—del′i·cate·ness,** n.

del·i·ca·tes·sen (del′ə kə tes′n), n. store that sells prepared foods, such as cooked meats, cheeses, salads, pickles, sandwiches, etc.

de·li·cious (di lish′əs), adj. very pleasing or satisfying, especially to the taste or smell; delightful: *delicious cake.* **—de·li′cious·ly,** adv. **—de·li′cious·ness,** n.

SYNONYM STUDY **Delicious** and **luscious** both mean very good to taste or smell. **Delicious** is a general word: *The ham salad is delicious.* **Luscious** means sweet and rich: *Who made this luscious chocolate pudding?*

de·light (di līt′), **1** n. great pleasure; joy: *The children took delight in their toys.* **2** n. something that gives great pleasure: *Swimming is her delight.* **3** v. to please greatly: *The circus delighted us.* **4** v. to have great pleasure: *Most people delight in fine summer weather.*

WORD STORY **Delight** comes from a Latin word meaning "to attract." It used to be spelled *delite.* Because it is pronounced like *light* and *flight,* people began spelling it that way. **Delicious** comes from the same Latin word. People are usually delighted by delicious food.

de·light·ed (di lī′tid), adj. greatly pleased; very glad: *I am delighted to be here.* **—de·light′ed·ly,** adv. **—de·light′ed·ness,** n.

de·light·ful (di līt′fəl), adj. very pleasing; giving joy: *a delightful concert.* **—de·light′ful·ly,** adv. **—de·light′ful·ness,** n.

De·li·lah (də lī′lə), n. (in the Bible) a Philistine woman who had Samson's hair cut, robbing him of his strength. [Delilah comes from a Hebrew word meaning "dainty."]

de·lin·e·ate (di lin′ē āt), v. **1** to trace the outline of: *The map clearly delineated the boundary between Mexico and Texas.* **2** to draw; sketch. **3** to describe in words; portray: *He delineated his plan in a thorough report.* ❑ v. **de·lin·e·at·ed, de·lin·e·at·ing. —de·lin′e·a·tor,** n.

de·lin·e·a·tion (di lin′ē ā′shən), n. **1** act of delineating. **2** thing delineated; diagram, sketch, portrait, or description.

de·lin·quen·cy (di ling′kwən sē), n. **1** failure in a duty; neglect of an obligation; guilt. **2** condition or habit of behaving unlawfully: *measures to check face delinquency.* **3** juvenile delinquency.

de·lin·quent (di ling′kwənt), **1** adj. failing in a duty; neglecting an obligation: *He was delinquent in paying his overdue taxes.* **2** adj. guilty of a fault or an offense: *The delinquent children had to pay for the windows they broke.* **3** adj. due and unpaid; overdue: *The owner lost her house when it was sold for delinquent taxes.* **4** n. a delinquent person; offender. **5** n. juvenile delinquent. **—de·lin′quent·ly,** adv.

de·lir·i·ous (di lir′ē əs), adj. **1** out of your senses for a short time; wandering in mind; raving: *The patient with the high fever was delirious.* **2** wildly excited: *The students were delirious with joy when their team won the tournament.* ▪ See Synonym Study at **hysterical. —de·lir′i·ous·ly,** adv.

a	hat	ė	term	ô	order	ch	child		
ā	age	i	it	oi	oil	ng	long		a in about
ä	far	ī	ice	ou	out	sh	she		e in taken
â	care	o	hot	u	cup	th	thin	ə	i in pencil
e	let	ō	open	u̇	put	ᴛн	then		o in lemon
ē	equal	ȯ	saw	ü	rule	zh	measure		u in circus

demagogue

de·lir·i·um (di lir′ē əm), *n.* **1** a temporary disorder of the mind that occurs during fevers, insanity, drunkenness, etc. Delirium includes restlessness, excitement, wild talk, and hallucinations. **2** wild excitement.

WORD STORY Delirium comes from Latin words meaning "out of the groove." The Romans compared loss of mental control to loss of control while plowing grooves in a field.

de·liv·er (di liv′ər), *v.* **1** to carry and give out; distribute: *deliver mail.* **2** to hand over; give up: *The defeated army delivered the fort to the enemy.* **3** to give forth in words: *deliver a talk. The jury delivered its verdict.* **4** to strike; throw: *The boxer delivered a blow.* **5** to set free; rescue; save: *A passing ship delivered the shipwrecked crew from certain death.* **6** to help a woman give birth to a child. —**de·liv′er·a·ble,** *adj.* —**de·liv′er·er,** *n.*

de·liv·er·ance (di liv′ər əns), *n.* act of setting free or condition of being set free; rescue; release: *The hostages rejoiced at their deliverance.*

de·liv·er·y (di liv′ər ē), *n.* **1** act of carrying and giving out of letters, goods, etc.: *There is one delivery of mail a day in our city.* **2** act of giving up; handing over: *The captive was released upon the delivery of the ransom.* **3** manner of speaking or singing; way of giving a speech or lecture: *The speaker had an excellent delivery.* **4** act or way of striking, throwing, etc.: *That pitcher has a fast delivery.* **5** a rescue; release. **6** act of giving birth to a child; childbirth. ❑ *n., pl.* **de·liv·er·ies.**

dell[1] (del), *n.* a small, sheltered valley, usually with trees in it.

dell[2] (del), *n.* singular of **dalles.**

Del·mar·va Peninsula (del mär′və), peninsula between Chesapeake Bay and the Atlantic Ocean, made up of Delaware, eastern Maryland, and a small strip of eastern Virginia.

Del·phi (del′fī), *n.* ancient town in Greece where a famous oracle of Apollo was located. See **Sparta** for map.

del·phin·i·um (del fin′ē əm), *n.* larkspur.

del·ta (del′tə), *n.* **1** a deposit of earth and sand that collects at the mouths of some rivers and is usually three-sided. **2** the fourth letter of the Greek alphabet (Δ or δ). **3** anything shaped like Δ. ❑ *n., pl.* **del·tas.**

del·ta-wing (del′tə wing′), *adj.* (of an aircraft) having wings in the shape of a single large triangle.

de·lude (di lüd′), *v.* to mislead the mind or judgment of; trick or deceive: *He deluded me into thinking he was on my side.* ❑ *v.* **de·lud·ed, de·lud·ing.** —**de·lud′er,** *n.*

del·uge (del′yüj), **1** *n.* a great flood: *After the dam broke, the deluge washed away the bridge.* **2** *n.* **the Deluge,** flood (def. 2). **3** *n.* a heavy fall of rain: *We were caught in a deluge on the way home.* **4** *v.* to flood or overflow: *Water deluged our cellar.* **5** *v.* to overwhelm: *The rock star was deluged with requests for her autograph.* **6** *n.* any overwhelming rush: *The post office always has a deluge of mail just before Christmas.* ❑ *v.* **del·uged, del·ug·ing.**

de·lu·sion (di lü′zhən), *n.* **1** a false belief or opinion: *She was under the delusion that she could pass any test without studying for it.* **2** condition of being deluded. —**de·lu′sion·al,** *adj.*

de·lu·sive (di lü′siv), *adj.* misleading the mind or judgment; deceptive; false. —**de·lu′sive·ly,** *adv.*

de·luxe (də luks′), *adj.* of exceptionally good quality; elegant.

delve (delv), *v.* to search carefully for information: *The scholar delved into many books for facts to support her theory.* ❑ *v.* **delved, delv·ing.** —**delv′er,** *n.*

Dem., **1** Democrat. **2** Democratic.

de·mag·net·ize (dē mag′nə tīz), *v.* to deprive of magnetism. ❑ *v.* **de·mag·net·ized, de·mag·net·iz·ing.** —**de·mag′net·i·za′tion,** *n.* —**de·mag′net·iz′er,** *n.*

dem·a·gog or **dem·a·gogue** (dem′ə gog), *n.* a popular leader who stirs up the people by appealing to their emotions and prejudices.

dem·a·gog·uer·y (dem′ə gog/ər ē), *n.* methods or behavior of a demagogue.

de·mand (di mand′), **1** *v.* to ask for as a right: *demand a trial by jury.* **2** *v.* to ask for with authority: *The teacher demanded the name of the student who rang the fire alarm.* **3** *v.* to call for; require; need: *Training a puppy demands patience.* **4** *n.* act of demanding: *a demand for a bigger allowance.* **5** *n.* something demanded; claim: *Parents have many demands upon their time.* **6** *n.* desire and ability to buy: *Because of the large crop, the supply of apples is greater than the demand.* —**de·mand′a·ble,** *adj.* —**de·mand′er,** *n.*

in demand, wanted: *Cabs are much in demand on rainy days.*

de·mand·ing (di man′ding), *adj.* requiring much time, effort, or attention: *a demanding task.*

de·mar·ca·tion (dē′mär kā′shən), *n.* **1** act of setting and marking the limits: *the demarcation of a country's authority.* **2** separation; distinction: *the demarcation of infancy from childhood.*

de·mean (di mēn′), *v.* to lower in dignity or standing; humble; degrade: *Public officials who take bribes demean themselves.*

de·mean·or (di mē′nər), *n.* way someone looks and acts; behavior; manner: *He has a quiet, modest demeanor.*

de·ment·ed (di men′tid), *adj.* extremely mentally ill, especially with loss of memory. ■ The use of **demented** except with this medical meaning is often considered offensive. —**de·ment′ed·ly,** *adv.* —**de·ment′ed·ness,** *n.*

de·mer·it (di mer′it), *n.* **1** fault or defect. **2** a mark against someone's record for bad behavior or poor work.

De·me·ter (di mē′tər), *n.* Greek goddess of agriculture. The Romans called her Ceres.

dem·i·god (dem′i god′), *n.* a being who is partly divine and partly human. Hercules was a demigod.

dem·i·john (dem′i jon), *n.* a large bottle of glass or earthenware enclosed in wicker.

de·mil·i·ta·rize (dē mil′ə tə rīz′), *v.* to free from military control or remove military forces from: *demilitarize a zone or boundary between enemy countries.* ❑ *v.* **de·mil·i·ta·rized, de·mil·i·ta·riz·ing.** —**de·mil′i·tar·i·za′tion,** *n.*

De Mille (də mil′), **1** **Ag·nes** (ag′nis), 1909-1993, American choreographer. She created many ballets and dances with American themes. **2** **Ce·cil B.** (ses′əl), 1881-1959, American movie director and producer. He directed many movies with Biblical themes, including two versions of *The Ten Commandments.*

de·mise (di mīz′), *n.* death.

dem·i·tasse (dem′i tas′), *n.* **1** a very small cup of black coffee. **2** a small cup for serving black coffee.

dem·o (dem′ō), *n.* **1** demonstration or display: *My karate class gave a demo.* **2** a tape recording used to demonstrate a new song, the talent of a musician, etc. ❑ *n., pl.* **dem·os.**

de·mo·bi·lize (dē mō′bə līz), *v.* to remove or dismiss from military service, status, or control: *When a war is over, the soldiers are demobilized and sent home.* ❑ *v.* **de·mo·bi·lized, de·mo·bi·liz·ing.** —**de·mo′bi·li·za′tion,** *n.*

de·moc·ra·cy (di mok′rə sē), *n.* **1** government that is run by the people who live under it. In a democracy the people rule either directly through meetings that all may attend, such as the town meetings in New England, or indirectly through the election of representatives to attend to the business of government. **2** country, state, or community with such a government. **3** treatment of other people as your equals. ❑ *n., pl.* **de·moc·ra·cies** for 2. [**Democracy** comes from Greek words meaning "people" and "rule."]

dem·o·crat (dem′ə krat), *n.* **1** person who believes that a government should be run by the people who live under it. **2** person who treats other people as equals. **3 Democrat,** member of the Democratic Party.

dem·o·crat·ic (dem′ə krat′ik), *adj.* **1** of a democracy; like a democracy. **2** treating other people as your equals: *The queen's democratic ways made her dear to her people.* **3 Democratic,** of the Democratic Party. —**dem′o·crat′i·cal·ly,** *adv.*

Democratic Party, one of the two main political parties in the United States. The other is the Republican Party.

de·moc·ra·tize (di mok′rə tīz), *v.* to make democratic. ❑ *v.* **de·moc·ra·tized, de·moc·ra·tiz·ing.** —**de·moc′ra·ti·za′tion,** *n.*

de·mog·ra·pher (di mog′rə fər), *n.* a scientist who studies human populations.

de·mo·graph·ics (dem′ə graf′iks), *n.pl.* the characteristics of human populations: *The demographics of Florida have changed as many retired people move there.*

de·mog·ra·phy (di mog′rə fē), *n.* science that studies human populations, their size, the number of births, deaths, etc.

de·mol·ish (di mol′ish), *v.* **1** to pull or tear down; destroy: *The old building was demolished to make room for a new one.* ∎ See Synonym Study at **destroy. 2** to put an end to; ruin completely: *Their scorn demolished my self-satisfaction.* —**de·mol′ish·er,** *n.* —**de·mol′ish·ment,** *n.*

dem·o·li·tion (dem′ə lish′ən), *n.* act of destroying something; destruction: *The demolition of several buildings was necessary to clear the land for a new highway.*

de·mon (dē′mən), *n.* **1** an evil spirit; devil; fiend. **2** a very wicked or cruel person. **3** person who has great energy or vigor: *My music teacher is a demon for practicing.* —**de·mon′ic,** *adj.*

de·mo·ni·ac (di mō′nē ak), *adj.* **1** of or like demons. **2** devilish; fiendish: *a demoniac cruelty.* **3** raging; frantic. —**de·mo·ni·a·cal·ly** (dē′mə nī′ik lē), *adv.*

de·mo·ni·a·cal (dē′mə nī′ə kəl), *adj.* demoniac.

de·mon·stra·ble (di mon′strə bəl), *adj.* able to be shown or proved. —**de·mon′stra·bil′i·ty,** *n.* —**de·mon′stra·bly,** *adv.*

dem·on·strate (dem′ən strāt), *v.* **1** to show clearly; prove: *The pianist demonstrated her musical skill.* **2** to explain by carrying out experiments, or by using samples or specimens; show how a thing is done: *The science teacher demonstrated the use of a magnet in class.* **3** to show how something works: *The salesperson demonstrated the vacuum cleaner.* **4** to show feeling openly: *to demonstrate affection by hugging someone.* **5** to take part in a parade or meeting to protest or to make demands: *An angry crowd demonstrated in front of the mayor's office for more police protection.* ❑ *v.* **dem·on·strat·ed, dem·on·strat·ing.**

dem·on·stra·tion (dem′ən strā′shən), *n.* **1** an act of showing or explaining something by carrying out experiments or by using samples or specimens: *A compass was used in a demonstration of the earth's magnetism.* **2** clear proof: *The ease with which she solved the hard problem was a demonstration of her ability in math.* **3** an act of showing the merits of a thing for sale; advertising or making known by carrying out a process in a public place: *the demonstration of a new vacuum cleaner.* **4** parade or meeting to protest or make demands: *The tenants held a demonstration against the raise in rent.* **5** an open show or expression of feeling: *a demonstration of affection.*

de·mon·stra·tive (di mon′strə tiv), *adj.* **1** expressing your affections freely and openly: *a demonstrative greeting.* **2** (in grammar) pointing out the object referred to. *This, that, these,* and *those* are demonstrative pronouns. —**de·mon′stra·tive·ly,** *adv.*

dem·on·stra·tor (dem′ən strā′tər), *n.* **1** someone who takes part in a parade or meeting to protest or make demands. **2** someone who shows a new product: *I worked as a demonstrator in the cosmetics department of a large store.* **3** a new motor vehicle used to demonstrate the vehicle to possible customers.

de·mo·ral·ize (di môr′ə līz), *v.* to lower the morale of; weaken the spirit, courage, or discipline of; dishearten: *The villagers were demoralized by the long famine.* ❑ *v.* **de·mo·ral·ized, de·mo·ral·iz·ing.** —**de·mo′ral·i·za′tion,** *n.* —**de·mo′ral·iz′er,** *n.*

De·mos·the·nes (di mos′thə nēz′), *n.* 384?-322 B.C., the most famous public speaker of ancient Greece. ∎ **Demosthenes** was not always a good speaker. When he was young, he practiced with pebbles in his mouth to improve his speaking.

de·mote (di mōt′), *v.* to put back to a lower grade; reduce in rank: *The soldier was demoted to private.* ❑ *v.* **de·mot·ed, de·mot·ing.** —**de·mo′tion,** *n.*

WORD STORY Demote comes from **de-** and a Latin word meaning "to move." It is the opposite of **promote,** but **promote** was first used in the 1300s, while **demote** was not used until the 1890s. Related words can have very different stories.

de·mur (di mėr′), **1** *v.* to show disapproval or dislike; object: *The clerk demurred at working overtime without extra pay.* **2** *n.* act of demurring; objection; exception: *The clerk's demur was ignored by the boss.* ❑ *v.* **de·murred, de·mur·ring.**

de·mure (di myur′), *adj.* **1** seeming more modest and proper than you really are; coy: *a demure smile.* **2** serious; thoughtful; sober: *their restrained and demure conduct.* ❑ *adj.* **de·mur·er, de·mur·est.** —**de·mure′ly,** *adv.* —**de·mure′ness,** *n.*

den (den), *n.* **1** place where a wild animal lives; lair: *The bear had made her den deep in a snowbank.* **2** place where thieves or the like have their headquarters. **3** a small, dirty room. **4** a private room for reading and work, usually small and cozy. **5** group of two to ten Cub Scouts. —**den′like′,** *adj.*

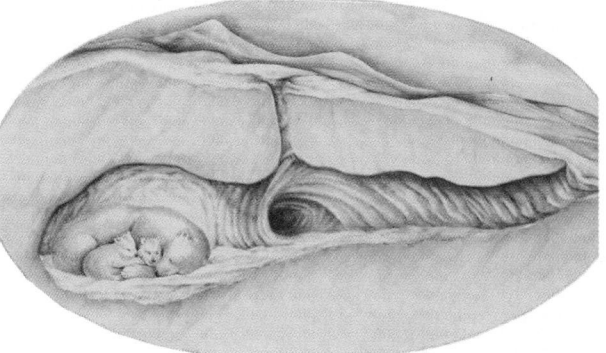

den (def. 1)

Den., Denmark.

De·na·li National Park (də nä′lē), a national park in S central Alaska. Mount McKinley is located here.

den·drite (den′drīt), *n.* the branching part at the receiving end of a neuron. —**den·drit·ic** (den drit′ik), *adj.*

de·ni·al (di nī′əl), *n.* **1** act of saying that something is not true: *a denial of the existence of ghosts.* **2** statement that you do not hold to or accept a belief: *Galileo was forced to make a public denial of his belief that the earth goes around the sun.* **3** act of refusing: *Their quick denial of our request was very unkind.* **4** act of refusing to acknowledge; disowning: *the denial of your family.*

de·ni·er (di nī′ər), *n.* person who denies.

den·im (den′əm), *n.* **1** a heavy, coarse cotton cloth with a diagonal weave, used for overalls, sports clothes, etc. **2 denims,** *pl.* overalls or pants made of this cloth. [See Word Story at **jeans.**]

den·i·zen (den′ə zən), *n.* person or animal that lives in a place; inhabitant; occupant: *Fish are denizens of the sea.*

Den·mark (den′märk), *n.* country in N Europe, between the Baltic Sea and the North Sea. *Capital:* Copenhagen. [Denmark comes from a German word meaning "border with the Danes."]

den mother, woman who supervises a den of cub scouts.

de·nom·i·nate (di nom′ə nāt *for verb;* di nom′ə nit *for adj.*), **1** *v.* to give a name to; name. **2** *adj.* used with a unit of measure-

a	hat	ė	term	ô	order	ch	child		a in about
ā	age	i	it	oi	oil	ng	long		e in taken
ä	far	ī	ice	ou	out	sh	she	ə	i in pencil
â	care	o	hot	u	cup	th	thin		o in lemon
e	let	ō	open	ů	put	ŦH	then		u in circus
ē	equal	ò	saw	ü	rule	zh	measure		

233

ment. 6 feet, 4 ounces, 10 inches, and 9 kilograms are **denomi-nate numbers.** ◻ *v.* **de·nom·i·nat·ed, de·nom·i·nat·ing.**

de·nom·i·na·tion (di nom/ə nā/shən), *n.* **1** name for a group or class of things; name. **2** a religious group or sect: *Methodists and Baptists are two large Protestant denominations.* **3** a kind of unit, especially of numbers or money. Reducing ⁵⁄₁₂, ⅓, and ⅙ to the same denomination gives ⁵⁄₁₂, ⁴⁄₁₂, and ²⁄₁₂.

de·nom·i·na·tion·al (di nom/ə nā/shə nəl), *adj.* of, for, or controlled by some religious denomination: *a denominational school.* **—de·nom/i·na/tion·al·ly,** *adv.*

de·nom·i·na·tor (di nom/ə nā/tər), *n.* the number below or to the right of the line in a fraction. In ¾, 4 is the denominator and 3 is the numerator.

de·no·ta·tion (dē/nō tā/shən), *n.* **1** meaning, especially the exact, literal meaning. The denotation of *home* is "place where you live," but it has many connotations. **2** act of denoting or marking out; indication.

de·note (di nōt/), *v.* **1** to be the sign of; indicate: *If the teacher puts an "A" on your paper, it denotes very good work.* **2** to be a name for; mean: *The word "density" denotes thickness.* ◻ *v.* **de·not·ed, de·not·ing. —de·not/a·ble,** *adj.* **—de·note/ment,** *n.*

de·noue·ment (dā/nü män/), *n.* solution of a plot in a story, play, situation, etc.; outcome; end.

de·nounce (di nouns/), *v.* **1** to speak against; express strong disapproval of: *The mayor denounced crime in the streets.* **2** to give information against; accuse: *denounce someone to the FBI as a spy.* ◻ *v.* **de·nounced, de·nounc·ing. —de·nounce/ment,** *n.* **—de·nounc/er,** *n.*

dense (dens), *adj.* **1** closely packed together; thick: *We could not see through the dense fog.* ■ See Synonym Study at **thick. 2** slow to understand. ■ This meaning of **dense** is often considered offensive. ◻ *adj.* **dens·er, dens·est. —dense/ly,** *adv.* **—dense/ness,** *n.*

den·si·ty (den/sə tē), *n.* **1** condition of being dense; having parts very close together; compactness; thickness: *The density of the forest prevented us from seeing more than a little way ahead.* **2** the quantity of anything in a given area: *Population density in the state is 197 per square mile.* **3** the quantity of matter in a unit of volume or of area: *The density of lead is greater than the density of wood.* **4** stupidity. ◻ *n., pl.* **den·si·ties.**

dent (dent), **1** *n.* a hollow made by a blow or pressure: *When the bike fell over, it put a dent in my fender.* **2** *v.* to make a dent in: *The fall dented my bicycle fender.* **3** *v.* to become dented: *Soft wood dents easily.*

den·tal (den/tl), *adj.* **1** of or for the teeth: *Proper dental care can prevent tooth decay.* **2** of or for a dentist's work: *dental drills.*

dental floss, a strong thread, often waxed, for cleaning between the teeth.

dental hygienist, person who assists a dentist by examining and cleaning a patient's teeth, taking X rays, etc.

den·ti·frice (den/tə fris), *n.* paste, powder, or liquid for cleaning the teeth.

den·tin (den/tən), *n.* the hard, bony material beneath the enamel of a tooth. It forms the main part of a tooth.

den·tine (den/tēn/), *n.* dentin.

den·tist (den/tist), *n.* doctor whose work is the care of teeth. A dentist fills cavities in teeth, cleans, straightens, or pulls them, and supplies caps, crowns, or artificial teeth.

den·tist·ry (den/tə strē), *n.* work, art, or profession of a dentist.

den·ture (den/chər), *n.* Often, **dentures,** *pl.* a partial or complete set of artificial teeth.

de·nude (di nüd/ *or* di nyüd/), *v.* to make bare; strip something of its clothing or covering: *Most trees are denuded of their leaves in winter.* ◻ *v.* **de·nud·ed, de·nud·ing.**

de·nun·ci·a·tion (di nun/sē ā/shən), *n.* **1** expression of strong disapproval; condemnation; denouncing: *the mayor's denunciation of crime.* **2** act of informing against; accusation: *The denunciation of our neighbor as a foreign spy shocked everyone.*

Den·ver (den/vər), *n.* capital of Colorado, in the central part. [**Denver** is named for John W. Denver, governor of the territory when the city was founded.]

de·ny (di nī/), *v.* **1** to say something is not true: *The prisoners denied the charges against them.* **2** to say that you do not hold to or accept: *deny a belief in ghosts.* **3** to refuse to give or grant: *I could not deny the stray cat some milk.* **4** to refuse to acknowledge; disown: *They denied their debts and refused to pay their bills.* ◻ *v.* **de·nied, de·ny·ing.**

deny yourself, to do without the things you want: *Some people deny themselves rich foods in order to lose weight.*

SYNONYM STUDY **Deny** and **contradict** both mean to say that something is not true. **Deny** is used about a general idea or story: *The actor denies that he is going bald.* **Contradict** is used about a specific statement: *The mayor contradicted the newspaper story.*

de·o·dor·ant (dē ō/dər ənt), *n.* a spray, powder, or the like, that prevents or destroys bad odors.

de·o·dor·ize (dē ō/də rīz/), *v.* to destroy the odor of. ◻ *v.* **de·o·dor·ized, de·o·dor·iz·ing. —de·o/dor·iz/er,** *n.*

de·ox·i·dize (dē ok/sə dīz), *v.* to remove oxygen from a chemical compound. ◻ *v.* **de·ox·i·dized, de·ox·i·diz·ing.**

de·ox·y·ri·bo·nu·cle·ic acid (dē ok/sə rī/bō nü klē/ik), See **DNA.**

dep., 1 department. **2** deputy.

de·part (di pärt/), *v.* **1** to go away; leave: *Your flight departs at 6:15.* **2** to turn away; change: *We departed from our usual routine and went out to dinner.*

de·part·ed (di pär/tid), **1** *n.sing. or pl.* **the departed,** a dead person or persons. **2** *adj.* dead. **3** *adj.* gone; past: *departed ages.*

de·part·ment (di pärt/mənt), *n.* a separate part of some whole; special branch; division: *Our city government has a fire department, a police department, and a sanitation department.*

de·part·men·tal (dē/pärt men/tl), *adj.* **1** of or related to a department: *departmental policies.* **2** divided into departments: *Their business is so large that it must be handled on a departmental basis.* **—de/part·men/tal·ly,** *adv.*

department store, a large store that sells many different kinds of articles arranged in separate departments.

de·par·ture (di pär/chər), *n.* **1** act of going away; leaving: *The airplane's departure for New York was delayed by a blizzard.* **2** act of turning away; change: *a departure from our old custom.* **3** act of starting on a course of action or thought: *Attending this dancing class will be a new departure for me, for I have never done anything like it.*

de·pend (di pend/), *v.* **1** to be a result of; be controlled or influenced by something else: *The success of our picnic will depend partly on whether it's sunny.* **2** to get support; rely for help: *Children depend on their parents for food and clothing.* **3** to rely; trust: *I depend on my alarm clock to wake me in time for school.* ■ See Synonym Study at **trust.** [**Depend** comes from Latin words meaning "to hang from." Something you depend on is like a rope you hang from.]

USAGE NOTE People sometimes use **depend** without **on** or **upon:** *It depends how much it costs.* This use is accepted in speech, but not in writing.

de·pend·a·ble (di pen/də bəl), *adj.* reliable; trustworthy: *a dependable person.* **—de·pend/a·bil/i·ty,** *n.* **—de·pend/a·bly,** *adv.*

de·pend·ence (di pen/dəns), *n.* **1** act of trusting or relying on someone or something for support or help: *I am going to work so that I can end my dependence on my parents.* **2** reliance; trust: *I don't put much dependence in the accuracy of that old watch.* **3** fact or condition of being controlled by something else: *the dependence of crops on good weather.*

de·pend·en·cy (di pen/dən sē), *n.* **1** country or territory controlled by another country: *The Virgin Islands is a dependency of the United States.* **2** act of trusting or relying on someone or something for support; dependence. **3** addiction: *drug dependency.* ◻ *n., pl.* **de·pend·en·cies** for 1,3.

de·pend·ent (di pen/dənt), **1** *adj.* trusting to another for support; relying on another for help: *A child is dependent on its parents.* **2** *n.* person who is supported by another. **3** *adj.* possible if something else takes place; depending: *Good crops are dependent on the right amount of rainfall and sunshine.* **—de·pend/ent·ly,** *adv.*

dependent clause, (in grammar) clause in a complex sentence that cannot act alone as a sentence; subordinate clause. In "If I go home, my dog will follow me," *If I go home* is a dependent clause.

de·pict (di pikt′), *v.* to represent by drawing, painting, or describing; portray: *The artist and the poet both tried to depict the splendor of the sunset.* —**de·pic′tion,** *n.*

depict—mural depicting Chinese immigrants' history

de·plete (di plēt′), *v.* to reduce the amount of; empty; exhaust: *Rapid consumption of our natural resources can quickly deplete them.* ❑ *v.* **de·plet·ed, de·plet·ing.** —**de·ple′tion,** *n.*

de·plor·a·ble (di plôr′ə bəl), *adj.* **1** regrettable; lamentable: *a deplorable accident.* **2** wretched; miserable: *deplorable living conditions in slums.* —**de·plor′a·ble·ness,** *n.* —**de·plor′a·bly,** *adv.*

de·plore (di plôr′), *v.* **1** to be very sorry about; express great sorrow for; regret deeply: *We deplore the accident.* **2** to disapprove of; condemn: *She deplores his careless, messy work.* ❑ *v.* **de·plored, de·plor·ing.** —**de·plor′er,** *n.* —**de·plor′ing·ly,** *adv.*

de·ploy (di ploi′), *v.* **1** to spread out troops into position for combat action. **2** to spread out, extend, or place anything, especially in a planned or strategic position: *deploy offensive missiles, deploy actors on a stage.* —**de·ploy′ment,** *n.*

de·pop·u·late (dē pop′yə lāt), *v.* to get rid of the inhabitants of: *The conquerors depopulated the enemy's capital by driving most of the inhabitants away.* ❑ *v.* **de·pop·u·lat·ed, de·pop·u·lat·ing.** —**de·pop′u·la′tion,** *n.* —**de·pop′u·la′tor,** *n.*

de·port (di pôrt′), *v.* **1** to force to leave; banish; expel. Deported aliens are sent out of the country, usually back to their native lands. ■ See Synonym Study at **banish. 2** to behave or conduct yourself in a particular manner: *The children deport themselves well when we have guests.* —**de·port′a·ble,** *adj.*

de·por·ta·tion (dē′pôr tā′shən), *n.* removal from a country by banishment or expulsion: *Deportation of criminals from England to Australia was once common.*

de·port·ment (di pôrt′mənt), *n.* way someone acts; behavior; conduct.

de·pose (di pōz′), *v.* **1** to put out of office or a position of authority, especially a high one like that of king: *The king was deposed by the revolution.* **2** to declare under oath, especially in writing; testify: *The witness deposed that she had seen the accused on the day of the murder.* ❑ *v.* **de·posed, de·pos·ing.** —**de·pos′a·ble,** *adj.* —**de·pos′er,** *n.*

de·pos·it (di poz′it), **1** *n.* money paid as a pledge to do something or to pay more later: *I put down a $25 deposit on the coat, and will pay the balance of $50 on the first of next month.* **2** *v.* to pay as a pledge to do something or to pay more later: *If you deposit part of the price, a store will keep an article for you until you pay the rest.* **3** *n.* something put in a certain place for safekeeping: *Money put in a bank is a deposit.* **4** *v.* to put in a place for safekeeping: *Deposit your money in the bank.* **5** *v.* to put down; lay down; leave lying: *The flood deposited a layer of mud in the streets.* **6** *n.* material laid down or left lying by natural

means: *There is often a deposit of mud and sand at the mouth of a river.* **7** *n.* mass of some mineral in rock or in the ground: *deposits of coal.* —**de·pos′i·tor,** *n.*

on deposit, in a bank.

dep·o·si·tion (dep′ə zish′ən), *n.* **1** testimony, especially a sworn statement in writing: *The prisoner made a deposition to use in appealing his case.* **2** act of putting out of office or a position of authority; removal from power.

de·pos·i·to·ry (di poz′ə tôr′ē), *n.* place where anything is stored for safekeeping; storehouse. ❑ *n., pl.* **de·pos·i·to·ries.**

de·pot (dē′pō *for 1;* dep′ō *for 2,3*), *n.* **1** a railroad or bus station. **2** storehouse; warehouse. **3** place where military supplies are stored.

de·prave (di prāv′), *v.* to make bad; injure morally; corrupt: *Drug addiction can deprave a person's character.* ❑ *v.* **de·praved, de·prav·ing.** —**dep′ra·va′tion,** *n.*

de·praved (di prāvd′), *adj.* morally bad; wicked; corrupt: *The murder was committed by a depraved person.*

de·prav·i·ty (di prav′ə tē), *n.* **1** quality of being depraved; wickedness; corruption. **2** a corrupt act; wicked deed. ❑ *n., pl.* **de·prav·i·ties** for 2.

dep·re·cate (dep′rə kāt), *v.* **1** to express strong disapproval of: *Lovers of peace deprecate war.* **2** to belittle; treat as unimportant: *The manager deprecated the team's losing streak and said it did not matter.* ❑ *v.* **dep·re·cat·ed, dep·re·cat·ing.** —**dep′re·cat′ing·ly,** *adv.* —**dep′re·ca′tion,** *n.*

dep·re·ca·to·ry (dep′rə kə tôr′ē), *adj.* **1** disapproving. **2** apologetic.

de·pre·ci·ate (di prē′shē āt), *v.* **1** to lessen in value: *The government has the power to depreciate currency. The longer a car is driven the more it depreciates.* **2** to speak slightingly of; belittle: *He depreciated the gift I got, saying that his was much nicer.* ❑ *v.* **de·pre·ci·at·ed, de·pre·ci·at·ing.**

de·pre·ci·a·tion (di prē′shē ā′shən), *n.* act of lowering or condition of being lowered in price, value, or estimation.

dep·re·da·tion (dep′rə dā′shən), *n.* act of plundering; robbery; ravaging.

de·press (di pres′), *v.* **1** to make sad or gloomy: *I was depressed by the bad news from home.* **2** to press down; lower: *When you play the piano, you depress the keys.* **3** to make less active; weaken: *Some medicines depress the action of the heart.* —**de·press′i·ble,** *adj.* —**de·press′ing·ly,** *adv.*

de·pres·sant (di pres′nt), *n.* drug or other substance that slows or reduces the body's reactions and relaxes muscles: *Alcohol is a depressant.*

de·pressed (di prest′), *adj.* **1** gloomy; low-spirited; sad. **2** pressed down; lowered. **3** with much poverty, unemployment, etc.: *a depressed region of closed factories.*

de·pres·sion (di presh′ən), *n.* **1** sadness or gloominess; low spirits: *Failure usually brings on a feeling of depression.* **2** act of sinking or lowering: *A rapid depression of the mercury in a barometer usually means a storm is coming.* **3** the **Depression** or the **Great Depression,** the worldwide business depression of the 1930s. **4** a severe slowdown in business activity: *Many people lose their jobs during a depression.* **5** a low place; hollow: *Rain formed puddles in the depressions in the ground.*

dep·ri·va·tion (dep′rə vā′shən), *n.* **1** condition of being deprived; loss; privation. **2** act of depriving.

de·prive (di prīv′), *v.* **1** to take away from by force: *The people deprived the cruel queen of her power.* **2** to keep from having or doing: *Worrying deprived us of sleep.* ❑ *v.* **de·prived, de·priv·ing.**

dept., department.

depth (depth), *n.* **1** distance from top to bottom: *the depth of a hole, the depth of a lake.* **2** distance from front to back: *The depth of our playground is 250 feet.* **3** Often, **depths,** *pl.* the deepest or most central part: *the darkest depth of the jungle, the depths of despair.* **4** deep quality; deepness: *The students admired their*

a	hat	ė	term	ô	order	ch	child	
ā	age	i	it	oi	oil	ng	long	a in about
ä	far	ī	ice	ou	out	sh	she	e in taken
â	care	o	hot	u	cup	th	thin	ə ⟨ i in pencil
e	let	ō	open	u̇	put	ŦH	then	o in lemon
ē	equal	ȯ	saw	ü	rule	zh	measure	u in circus

teacher's depth of understanding. **5** deep understanding; profoundness: *This story has a good plot, but it has no depth at all.* **6** lowness of pitch of a sound.

in depth, in a thorough way: *to study a subject in depth.*

out of your depth, unable to understand or deal with a situation: *I was out of my depth in the advanced class.*

depth charge, an explosive charge dropped from a ship or airplane and set to explode at a certain depth under water. It is used to attack and destroy submarines.

dep·u·ta·tion (dep′yə tā′shən), *n.* group of persons sent to represent others: *The neighborhood sent a deputation of citizens to the meeting of the town council.*

dep·u·tize (dep′yə tīz), *v.* to appoint as deputy. ❑ *v.* **dep·u·tized, dep·u·tiz·ing.**

dep·u·ty (dep′yə tē), *n.* person appointed to do the work of or take the place of another: *A sheriff's deputies help him enforce the law.* ❑ *n., pl.* **dep·u·ties.**

derail—a derailed train

de·rail (di rāl′), *v.* **1** to cause a train to run off the rails. **2** to run off the rails. **—de·rail′ment,** *n.*

de·rail·leur (di rā′lər), *n.* a spring-driven mechanism on a bicycle that changes gears by causing the chain to move from one sprocket wheel to another.

de·range (di rānj′), *v.* to disturb the order or arrangement of something. ❑ *v.* **de·ranged, de·rang·ing. —de·range′ment,** *n.*

de·ranged (di rānjd′), *adj.* unreasonable, strongly excited, and out of control of emotions: *deranged by grief.*

Der·by (der′bē *for 1,3;* där′bē *for 2*), *n.* **1** a race, especially for horses or motor vehicles: *the Kentucky Derby.* **2** a famous horse race run every year near London. **3** **derby,** a stiff hat with a dome-shaped crown and a narrow brim. ❑ *n., pl.* **Der·bies** for 1,2, **der·bies** for 3.

Derby (def. 1)
Soap Box Derby

de·reg·u·late (dē reg′yə lāt), *v.* to remove legal regulation or control of; decontrol: *Gas prices rose quickly after they were deregulated.* ❑ *v.* **de·reg·u·lat·ed, de·reg·u·lat·ing. —de·reg′u·la′tion,** *n.*

der·e·lict (der′ə likt), **1** *adj.* abandoned by its crew, owner, or guardian; forsaken: *a derelict ship.* **2** *n.* ship abandoned at sea. **3** *n.* a penniless person who is homeless, jobless, and abandoned by others. **4** *adj.* failing in your duty; negligent: *The guard was found derelict in letting the prisoner escape.*

der·e·lic·tion (der′ə lik′shən), *n.* failure in your duty; negligence.

de·ride (di rīd′), *v.* to make fun of; laugh at: *They derided me for my fear of the dark.* ❑ *v.* **de·rid·ed, de·rid·ing. —de·rid′er,** *n.* **—de·rid′ing·ly,** *adv.*

de·ri·sion (di rizh′ən), *n.* laughter; ridicule: *Their derision hurt my feelings.*

de·ri·sive (di rī′siv), *adj.* showing ridicule; mocking. **—de·ri′sive·ly,** *adv.* **—de·ri′sive·ness,** *n.*

der·i·va·tion (der′ə vā′shən), *n.* **1** statement of how a word was formed; etymology. **2** system in a language for making new words from old words by adding prefixes and suffixes and by other methods. EXAMPLE: *quickness = quick + suffix -ness.* **3** origin: *The celebration of Halloween is of Scottish derivation.* **4** act or fact of deriving. **—der′i·va′tion·al,** *adj.*

de·riv·a·tive (di riv′ə tiv), **1** *adj.* not original; derived. **2** *n.* something derived: *Many drugs are derivatives of plants.* **3** *n.* word formed by adding a prefix or suffix to another word. *Quickness* and *quickly* are derivatives of *quick.* **—de·riv′a·tive·ly,** *adv.*

de·rive (di rīv′), *v.* **1** to obtain from a source or origin; get; receive: *I derive much enjoyment from reading.* **2** to come from a source or origin; originate: *This story derives from an old legend.* **3** to trace a word, custom, etc., from or to a source or origin: *"December" is ultimately derived from the Latin word "decem," which means "ten."* ❑ *v.* **de·rived, de·riv·ing. —de·riv′a·ble,** *adj.*

der·ma (der′mə), *n.* dermis.

der·ma·tol·o·gy (der′mə tol′ə jē), *n.* branch of medicine that deals with the skin and its diseases. **—der′ma·tol′o·gist,** *n.*

der·mis (der′mis), *n.* the sensitive layer of skin beneath the outer skin; derma.

de·rog·a·to·ry (di rog′ə tôr′ē), *adj.* critical of; belittling; unfavorable: *People resent derogatory remarks about their appearance.* **—de·rog′a·to′ri·ly,** *adv.* **—de·rog′a·to′ri·ness,** *n.*

der·rick (der′ik), *n.* **1** machine for lifting and moving heavy objects. A derrick has a long turning arm attached at its base to the base of an upright post or frame, which supports the weight. **2** a towerlike framework over an oil well that holds the drilling and hoisting machinery.

WORD STORY **Derrick** comes from Godfrey Derrick, an English public executioner in the 1600s. People gave his name to the platform where criminals were hanged, and then to any platform with a rope for lifting heavy objects.

der·ring-do (der′ing dü′), *n.* OLD USE. daring deeds.

der·vish (der′vish), *n.* member of a Muslim religious order that practices unusual self-denial and devotion. Some members dance and spin about violently. ❑ *n., pl.* **der·vish·es.**

de·sal·i·nate (dē sal′ə nāt), *v.* to desalt. ❑ *v.* **de·sal·i·nat·ed, de·sal·i·nat·ing. —de·sal′i·na′tion,** *n.*

de·salt (dē sôlt′), *v.* to remove salt from: *desalt sea water for human use.*

des·cant (des′kant′ *for noun;* des kant′ *for verb*), **1** *n.* tune played or sung at the same time as another tune. **2** *v.* to talk at great length: *She descanted on her problems for hours.*

Des·cartes (dā kärt′), *n.* **Re·né** (rə nā′), 1596-1650, French philosopher and mathematician, inventor of Cartesian coordinates. His most famous saying is, "I think, therefore I am."

de·scend (di send′), *v.* **1** to go or come down from a higher to a lower place: *The river descends from the mountains to the sea. We descended the stairs to get to the basement.* **2** to go or come down from an earlier to a later time: *a superstition descended from the Middle Ages.* **3** to go from larger to smaller numbers; go from higher to lower on any scale: *75-50-25 form a series that descends.* **4** to make a sudden attack or appearance: *Tourists descended on the popular new resort.* **5** to be handed down from parent to child: *This land has descended from my grandfather to my mother and now to me.* **6** to come down or spring from: *He is descended from pioneers.* **7** to lower yourself; stoop: *In order to eat she descended to stealing.* **—de·scend′i·ble,** *adj.*

SYNONYM STUDY **Descend, drop,** and **sink** all mean to go down. **Descend** is a general word: *The elevator descends quickly and smoothly.* **Drop** suggests sudden motion: *The temperature dropped 20 degrees overnight.* **Sink** suggests slow, gradual motion: *The afternoon sun sank toward the hills.*

de·scend·ant (di sen′dənt), *n.* **1** person born of a certain family or group: *a descendant of the Pilgrims.* **2** offspring; child, grandchild, great-grandchild, etc. You are a direct descendant of your parents, grandparents, and earlier ancestors.

de·scent (di sent′), *n.* **1** act of coming or going down from a higher to a lower place: *the descent of a helicopter.* **2** a downward slope: *We climbed down a steep descent.* **3** process of handing down from parent to child: *The descent of certain physical characteristics can sometimes be traced back several generations.* **4** family line; ancestors: *Some of my neighbors are of Spanish descent.* **5** act of sinking to a lower condition; decline; fall. **6** a sudden attack: *The descent of the bandits on the village was unexpected.* ■ Another word that sounds like this is **dissent.**

de·scram·ble (dē skram′bəl), *v.* to restore an electronic signal that has been previously scrambled, so that it can be seen or understood. ❑ *v.* **de·scram·bled, de·scram·bling.** —**de·scram′bler,** *n.*

de·scribe (di skrīb′), *v.* **1** to tell in words how someone looks, feels, or acts, or how a place, a thing, or an event looks: *She described the accident in detail.* ■ See Synonym Study at **report.** **2** to draw the outline of: *The skater described a figure 8.* ❑ *v.* **de·scribed, de·scrib·ing.** —**de·scrib′a·ble,** *adj.* —**de·scrib′er,** *n.*

de·scrip·tion (di skrip′shən), *n.* **1** composition or account that describes or gives a picture in words: *The reporter's vivid description of the hotel fire made me feel as if I were right at the scene.* **2** act of telling or writing how someone looks, feels, or acts or how a place, thing, or event looks. **3** kind; sort: *There were people of every description at the airport.*

de·scrip·tive (di skrip′tiv), *adj.* using description; describing: *A descriptive booklet tells about the tour.* —**de·scrip′tive·ly,** *adv.*

des·e·crate (des′ə krāt), *v.* to treat or use without respect; disregard the sacredness of: *The enemy desecrated the church by using it as a stable.* ❑ *v.* **des·e·crat·ed, des·e·crat·ing.** —**des′e·crat′er** or **des′e·cra′tor,** *n.* —**des′e·cra′tion,** *n.*

de·seg·re·gate (dē seg′rə gāt), *v.* to do away with racial segregation in: *desegregate a public school.* ❑ *v.* **de·seg·re·gat·ed, de·seg·re·gat·ing.** —**de·seg′re·ga′tion,** *n.*

desert[1]

des·ert[1] (dez′ərt), **1** *n.* a dry, barren region that is usually sandy and without trees: *The Sahara is a great desert in northern Africa.* **2** *n.* any region that is not inhabited or cultivated; wilderness. **3** *adj.* dry and barren: *Arabia is largely desert land.* **4** *adj.* not inhabited or cultivated; wild: *They were shipwrecked on a desert island.*

de·sert[2] (di zėrt′), *v.* **1** to go away and leave a person or a place, especially one that should not be left; forsake: *She deserted her old friends when she became famous.* **2** to leave military service without permission and without intending to return: *A soldier who deserts is punished.* ■ Another word that sounds like this is **dessert.**

de·sert·ed (di zėr′tid), *adj.* abandoned; forsaken: *They were afraid to enter the deserted house.*

de·sert·er (di zėr′tər), *n.* member of the armed forces who leaves without permission or intention to return.

de·sert·i·fi·ca·tion (di zėrt′ə fə kā′shən), *n.* the drying up of moist land along the edge of a desert. It is usually caused by a change in climate or by too many people and animals.

de·ser·tion (di zėr′shən), *n.* act of abandoning a responsibility, such as military service or marriage.

de·serts (di zėrts′), *n.* Often, **just deserts,** what you deserve; suitable reward or punishment: *The reckless driver got his just deserts; he was fined and his driver's license was suspended.*

Desert Storm, the Persian Gulf War.

de·serve (di zėrv′), *v.* to have a claim or right to; be worthy of: *A hard worker deserves good pay.* ❑ *v.* **de·served, de·serv·ing.**

de·serv·ed·ly (di zėr′vid lē), *adv.* according to what is deserved; justly; rightly.

de·serv·ing (di zėr′ving), *adj.* worth helping: *The deserving student received a scholarship.* —**de·serv′ing·ly,** *adv.*

des·ic·cat·ed (des′ə kā′tid), *adj.* deprived of moisture or water; dehydrated: *The soil in a desert is desiccated.*

de·sign (di zīn′), **1** *n.* a drawing, plan, or sketch made to serve as a pattern from which to work: *The design showed how to build the machine.* ■ See Synonym Study at **plan.** **2** *n.* arrangement of details, form, and color in painting, weaving, building, etc.: *We chose a wallpaper design with tan and white stripes.* **3** *v.* to make a first sketch of; arrange form and color of; draw in outline: *design a dress.* **4** *v.* to make drawings, sketches, or plans: *He designs for our dress department.* **5** *n.* art of making designs, patterns, or sketches: *Architects study and become skilled in design.* **6** *v.* to plan out; form in the mind: *The author of this detective story has designed an exciting plot.* **7** *n.* purpose; aim; intention: *Whether by accident or design, they always arrived at mealtime.* **8** *v.* to intend to do: *Did you design this result?* **9** *v.* to set apart: *That room was designed to be her studio.*

have designs on or **have designs upon,** a scheme of attack; evil plan: *The thief had designs on the safe.*

des·ig·nate (dez′ig nāt), *v.* **1** to point out; indicate definitely; show: *Red lines designate main roads on this map.* **2** to name: *Historians designate the period A.D. 400 to A.D. 1000, the Dark Ages.* **3** to select for duty, office, etc.; appoint: *She has been designated ambassador to Italy by the president.* ❑ *v.* **des·ig·nat·ed, des·ig·nat·ing.** —**des′ig·na′tor,** *n.*

designated hitter, (in baseball) a player who does not play in the field but is designated at the start of a game to bat in place of the pitcher.

des·ig·na·tion (dez′ig nā′shən), *n.* **1** a descriptive title; name: *"Your honor" is a designation given to a judge.* **2** appointment to an office or position; selection for a duty: *The designation of cabinet officers is one of the powers of the President.* **3** act of marking out; pointing out: *the designation of places on a map.*

de·sign·ed·ly (di zī′nid lē), *adv.* on purpose; intentionally.

de·sign·er (di zī′nər), **1** *n.* person who designs. **2** *adj.* having the name or the mark of some fashion designer: *designer jeans.*

de·sign·ing (di zī′ning), **1** *adj.* scheming; plotting. **2** *adj.* showing plan or forethought. **3** *n.* art of making designs, patterns, sketches, etc. —**de·sign′ing·ly,** *adv.*

de·sir·a·ble (di zī′rə bəl), *adj.* worth wishing for; worth having; pleasing; good: *The valley was a desirable location for a park.* —**de·sir′a·bil′i·ty,** *n.* —**de·sir′a·ble·ness,** *n.* —**de·sir′a·bly,** *adv.*

de·sire (di zīr′), **1** *n.* strong wish: *feel a desire to travel.* **2** *v.* to wish earnestly for; long for: *The people of the warring nations desire peace.* ■ See Synonym Study at **want.** **3** *v.* to express a wish for; ask for: *The principal desires your presence in her office.* **4** *n.* thing wished for: *His greatest desire was a bicycle.* ❑ *v.* **de·sired, de·sir·ing.**

a	hat	ė	term	ô	order	ch	child		a in about
ā	age	i	it	oi	oil	ng	long		e in taken
ä	far	ī	ice	ou	out	sh	she	ə	i in pencil
â	care	o	hot	u	cup	th	thin		o in lemon
e	let	ō	open	u̇	put	ŦH	then		u in circus
ē	equal	ò	saw	ü	rule	zh	measure		

de·sir·ous (di zīˈrəs), *adj.* desiring; wishing; eager: *She is desirous of going to Europe sometime.* —**de·sirˈous·ly**, *adv.* —**de·sirˈous·ness**, *n.*

de·sist (di zistˈ), *v.* to stop doing something; cease.

desk (desk), *n.* **1** piece of furniture with a flat or sloping top on which to write or to rest books for reading. A desk often has drawers. **2** department of work at a certain location or at a desk: *the information desk of a library.* [See Word Story at **dish.**]

desk·top (deskˈtop), **1** *adj.* small enough to fit on a desk: *a desktop copier.* **2** *adj.* done with office computers instead of bigger machines: *desktop publishing.* **3** *n.* a computer small enough to fit on a desk.

Des Moines (də moinˈ), capital of Iowa, in the central part.

des·o·late (desˈə lit *for adj.;* desˈə lāt *for verb*), **1** *adj.* dreary; dismal: *desolate slums.* **2** *adj.* not lived in; deserted: *a desolate house.* **3** *v.* to make unfit to live in; lay waste: *The earthquake desolated the business district.* **4** *adj.* unhappy; forlorn: *The lost child looked very desolate.* **5** *v.* to make unhappy: *We are desolated to hear that you are going away.* ◻ *v.* **des·o·lat·ed, des·o·lat·ing.** —**desˈo·late·ly**, *adv.* —**desˈo·late·ness**, *n.* —**desˈo·lat·er** or **desˈo·la·tor**, *n.*

des·o·la·tion (desˈə lāˈshən), *n.* **1** a ruined, lonely, or deserted condition. **2** lonely sorrow; sadness: *desolation at the loss of loved ones.* **3** a desolate place. **4** destruction; ruin: *the desolation of the country by an invading army.*

De So·to (di sōˈtō), **Her·nan·do** (her nanˈdō), 1500?-1542, Spanish explorer in North America. He was the first European to reach the Mississippi River.

de·spair (di spârˈ), **1** *n.* loss of hope; a hopeless feeling; a dreadful feeling that nothing good can happen: *Despair overcame us as we felt the boat sinking.* **2** *n.* person or thing that causes loss of hope: *Another week without rain was the despair of the farmers.* **3** *v.* to lose hope; be without hope: *The doctors despaired of saving the patient's life.* —**de·spairˈing·ly**, *adv.*

des·per·a·do (desˈpə räˈdō), *n.* a bold, reckless criminal; dangerous outlaw. ◻ *n., pl.* **des·pe·ra·does** or **des·pe·ra·dos.**

des·per·ate (desˈpər it), *adj.* **1** showing recklessness caused by despair: *Suicide is a desperate act.* ∎ See Synonym Study at **hopeless. 2** ready to try anything; ready to run any risk: *He hadn't worked in a year and was desperate for a job.* **3** having little chance for hope or cure; very dangerous: *a desperate illness.* **4**

desperadoes

extremely or hopelessly bad: *People in the slums live in desperate circumstances.* **5** having great desire or need: *The young tennis player was desperate to prove herself in competition.* —**desˈper·ate·ly**, *adv.* —**desˈper·ate·ness**, *n.*

des·pe·ra·tion (desˈpə rāˈshən), *n.* **1** a hopeless and reckless feeling; readiness to try anything: *He jumped out of the window in desperation when he saw that the stairs were on fire.* **2** despair.

des·pi·ca·ble (des pikˈə bəl *or* desˈpi kə bəl), *adj.* to be despised; contemptible: *It is despicable to leave pets to starve.* —**desˈpi·ca·ble·ness**, *n.* —**desˈpi·ca·bly**, *adv.*

de·spise (di spīzˈ), *v.* to feel contempt for; scorn: *They were despised for their dishonesty.* ∎ See Synonym Study at **hate.** ◻ *v.* **de·spised, de·spis·ing.** —**de·spisˈing·ly**, *adv.*

de·spite (di spītˈ), *prep.* in spite of: *We walked despite the rain.*

de·spoil (di spoilˈ), *v.* to strip of possessions; rob; plunder. —**de·spoilˈer**, *n.* —**de·spoilˈment**, *n.*

de·spond·en·cy (di sponˈdən sē), *n.* loss of heart, courage, or hope; discouragement; dejection.

de·spond·ent (di sponˈdənt), *adj.* having lost heart, courage, or hope; discouraged; dejected. —**de·spondˈent·ly**, *adv.*

des·pot (desˈpət), *n.* **1** monarch having unlimited power; absolute ruler. **2** person who does just as he or she likes; tyrant.

des·pot·ic (di spotˈik), *adj.* of a despot; having unlimited power; tyrannical. —**des·potˈi·cal·ly**, *adv.*

des·pot·ism (desˈpə tizˈəm), *n.* **1** government by a monarch having unlimited power. **2** tyranny or oppression.

Des·sa·lines (dā sä lēnˈ), **Jean Jacques** (zhän zhäk), 1758-1806, African-born Haitian leader. He gained Haiti's independence from France in 1804.

des·sert (di zèrtˈ), *n.* course of pie, cake, ice cream, cheese, fruit, etc., served at the end of a meal. ∎ Another word that sounds like this is **desert**[2].

WORD STORY **Dessert** comes from a French word meaning "to clear the table." The dishes from the main meal are usually cleared away before dessert is served.

de·sta·bi·lize (dē stāˈbə līz), *v.* to cause to become unstable: *a government destabilized by economic problems.* ◻ *v.* **de·sta·bi·lized, de·sta·bi·liz·ing.** —**de·staˈbi·li·zaˈtion**, *n.*

des·ti·na·tion (desˈtə nāˈshən), *n.* place to which someone or something is going or is being sent.

des·tine (desˈtən), *v.* **1** to set apart for a particular purpose or use; intend: *The princess was destined from birth to be a queen.* **2** to cause by fate: *My letter was destined never to reach her.* ◻ *v.* **des·tined, des·tin·ing.**

destined for, intended to go to; bound for: *ships destined for England.*

des·ti·ny (desˈtə nē), *n.* **1** what becomes of someone or something; your fate or fortune: *It was young Washington's destiny to become the first president of the United States.* **2** what will happen, believed to be determined beforehand in spite of all later efforts to change or prevent it: *She felt that destiny had been unkind to her in making her poor.* ◻ *n., pl.* **des·ti·nies** for 1.

des·ti·tute (desˈtə tüt), *adj.* lacking necessary things such as food, clothing, and shelter: *Many families were destitute after the earthquake.* —**desˈti·tuˈtion**, *n.*

destitute of, having no; without: *land destitute of trees.*

de·stroy (di stroiˈ), *v.* **1** to break to pieces; make useless; ruin; spoil: *A tornado destroyed the farmhouse.* **2** to put an end to; do away with: *A heavy rain destroyed all hope of a picnic.* **3** to kill: *Fire destroys many trees every year.*

SYNONYM STUDY **Destroy** and **demolish** both mean to put an end to something. **Destroy** is a general word: *The paintings were destroyed in the fire.* **Demolish** means to smash something to pieces, especially something built: *The earthquake demolished the bridge.*

de·stroy·er (di stroiˈər), *n.* **1** person or thing that destroys. **2** a small, fast warship.

de·struct (di struktˈ), **1** *v.* to blow up a rocket or other missile that fails to work properly. **2** *n.* the deliberate blowing up of a rocket or missile.

de·struct·i·ble (di strukˈtə bəl), *adj.* capable of being destroyed. —**de·structˈi·bilˈi·ty**, *n.*

de·struc·tion (di strukˈshən), *n.* **1** a destroying: *A bulldozer was used in the destruction of the old barn.* **2** great damage; ruin: *The storm left destruction behind it.* **3** thing that destroys.

de·struc·tive (di strukˈtiv), *adj.* **1** destroying; causing destruction. **2** tearing down; not helpful; not constructive: *Destructive criticism shows things to be wrong, but does not show how to correct them.* —**de·strucˈtive·ly**, *adv.* —**de·strucˈtive·ness**, *n.*

des·ul·to·ry (desˈəl tôrˈē), *adj.* jumping from one thing to another; without aim or method; unconnected: *He read in a desultory way, skipping pages as he pleased.* —**desˈul·to·ri·ly**, *adv.*

de·tach (di tachˈ), *v.* **1** to loosen and remove; unfasten; separate: *I detached a key from the chain.* **2** to send away on special duty: *One squad of soldiers was detached to guard the road.*

de·tach·a·ble (di tachˈə bəl), *adj.* able to be detached: *A loose-leaf notebook has detachable pages.*

de·tached (di tachtˈ), *adj.* **1** not attached; standing apart; isolated: *A detached house does not touch its neighboring houses.* **2** not taking sides; not influenced by others or by your own interests and prejudices; impartial: *The judge listened to both sides with a detached air.* —**de·tachˈed·ly**, *adv.* —**de·tachˈed·ness**, *n.*

de·tach·ment (di tach′mənt), *n.* **1** lack of interest; aloofness: *He watched the dull movie with detachment.* **2** troops or ships sent away on some special duty. **3** freedom from prejudice or bias; impartial attitude. **4** act of taking apart; separation.

de·tail (di tāl′ *or* dē′tāl), **1** *n.* a small part of a whole thing: *a detail from a painting.* **2** *n.* an unimportant part: *The main idea of her story got lost in the many details.* **3** *n.* the process of dealing with things one by one: *She went into detail about the new science project.* **4** *v.* to tell fully; tell even the small and unimportant parts of: *They detailed to us all the things they had done on their vacation.* **5** *n.* a small group selected for or sent on some special duty: *A detail of six scouts was sent out to find firewood.* **6** *v.* to select for or send on special duty: *Several police officers were detailed to direct traffic after the parade.*
in detail, with all the details; part by part.

> **WORD STORY** **Detail** comes from a French word meaning "to cut." **Tailor** comes from the same French word. Thinking about all the details of something is like cutting it into lots of little bits.

de·tailed (di tāld′ *or* dē′tāld), *adj.* **1** full of details: *The witness gave a detailed account of the accident.* **2** minute: *With a microscope a scientist can make a detailed examination of bacteria.*

de·tain (di tān′), *v.* **1** to keep from going ahead; hold back; delay: *The heavy traffic detained us for almost an hour.* **2** to keep in custody; hold as a prisoner: *The police detained the suspected burglar for further questioning.* —**de·tain′ment,** *n.*

de·tect (di tekt′), *v.* to find out; discover; catch: *Can you detect any odor in the room?* —**de·tect′a·ble,** *adj.* —**de·tec′tion,** *n.*

de·tec·tive (di tek′tiv), **1** *n.* member of a police force or other person whose work is finding information secretly, solving crimes, etc. **2** *adj.* about detectives and their work: *She writes detective stories.* **3** *adj.* used in discovering or finding out: *detective methods, a detective device.*

de·tec·tor (di tek′tər), *n.* **1** person or thing that discovers or detects: *a smoke detector.* **2** the part of a radio that changes radio waves into information used in producing sound.

de·tente (dā tänt′), *n.* an easing of tensions, especially between nations.

de·ten·tion (di ten′shən), *n.* **1** act of keeping in custody; confinement: *A jail is used for the detention of persons who have been arrested.* **2** condition of being held back or delayed: *Detention after hours is a common punishment in school.*

de·ter (di tėr′), *v.* to prevent or keep back; discourage or hinder: *The barking dog deterred me from crossing the neighbor's yard.* ❑ *v.* **de·terred, de·ter·ring.** —**de·ter′ment,** *n.*

de·ter·gent (di tėr′jənt), **1** *n.* substance used for cleansing. **2** *adj.* cleansing. [**Detergent** comes from a Latin word meaning "wiping off." If you wash dishes without detergent, you have to scrub. With detergent, you can just wipe dirt off.]

de·te·ri·o·rate (di tir′ē ə rāt′), *v.* to become lower in quality or value: *Machinery deteriorates rapidly if it is not taken care of.* ❑ *v.* **de·ter·i·o·rat·ed, de·ter·i·o·rat·ing.** —**de·ter′i·o·ra′tion,** *n.* —**de·ter′i·o·ra′tive,** *adj.*

de·ter·mi·nant (di tėr′mə nənt), *adj.* determining; deciding: *Higher pay was the determinant factor in her changing jobs.*

de·ter·mi·na·tion (di tėr′mə nā′shən), *n.* **1** great firmness in carrying out a purpose; fixed purpose: *His determination was not weakened by the difficulties he met.* **2** act of deciding; settling beforehand: *The determination of what things we needed to take on our camping trip took a long time.* **3** process of finding out the exact amount or kind, by weighing, measuring, or calculating: *the determination of the gold in a sample of rock.*

de·ter·mine (di tėr′mən), *v.* **1** to make up your mind very firmly; resolve: *He determined to become the best player on the team.* **2** to find out exactly: *The pilot determined how far she was from the airport.* **3** to be the deciding fact in reaching a certain result: *The number of answers you get right determines your mark on this test.* **4** to decide or settle beforehand; fix: *Can we now determine the date for our next meeting?* **5** to limit; define: *The meaning of a word is partly determined by its use in a particular sentence.* ❑ *v.* **de·ter·mined, de·ter·min·ing.**

de·ter·mined (di tėr′mənd), *adj.* firm; resolute: *Her determined look showed that she had made up her mind.* —**de·ter′mined·ly,** *adv.* —**de·ter′mined·ness,** *n.*

detail (def. 1)

de·ter·min·er (di tėr′mə nər), *n.* a word that points out the thing named, or indicates quantity or number. The words *a* in *a hat,* the *in the big house,* and *every* in *every little thing* are determiners.

de·ter·rence (di tėr′əns), *n.* act or process of discouraging or hindering: *the deterrence of pollution by regulations and penalties.*

de·ter·rent (di tėr′ənt), **1** *n.* something that hinders or discourages. **2** *adj.* hindering or discouraging: *a deterrent influence.*

de·test (di test′), *v.* to dislike very much; hate: *I detest liars.* —**de·test′er,** *n.*

> **WORD STORY** **Detest** comes from a Latin word meaning "a witness." **Testimony** comes from the same Latin word. Ancient Romans would call on their gods to witness when they cursed someone they detested.

de·test·a·ble (di tes′tə bəl), *adj.* deserving to be detested; hateful: *Bombing an office building is a detestable crime.* —**de·test′a·ble·ness,** *n.* —**de·test′a·bly,** *adv.*

de·tes·ta·tion (dē′tes·tā′shən), *n.* very strong dislike; hatred.

de·throne (di thrōn′), *v.* to remove from a throne or a high position; remove from ruling power; depose: *The rebels dethroned the weak king.* ❑ *v.* **de·throned, de·thron·ing.** —**de·throne′ment,** *n.*

det·o·nate (det′n āt), *v.* to explode with a loud noise: *The workers detonated the dynamite.* ❑ *v.* **det·o·nat·ed, det·o·nat·ing.** [**Detonate** comes from a Latin word meaning "thunder." An explosion sounds like thunder.] —**det′o·na′tion,** *n.*

det·o·na·tor (det′n ā′tər), *n.* fuse, percussion cap, or similar device used to set off an explosive.

de·tour (dē′tùr), **1** *n.* road that is used when the main or direct road cannot be traveled. **2** *n.* a roundabout way or course: *I took several detours before I got the right answer.* **3** *v.* to use a detour: *We detoured around the bridge that had been washed out.* **4** *v.* to cause to use a detour: *The police detoured all traffic around the parade.* [**Detour** comes from a French word meaning "to turn away." A detour makes you turn away from your original route.]

de·tox·i·fy (dē tok′sə fī), *v.* to remove poisonous substances from. ❑ *v.* **de·tox·i·fied, de·tox·i·fy·ing.** —**de·tox′i·fi·ca′tion,** *n.*

de·tract (di trakt′), *v.* to take away a part; remove some of the quality or worth: *The ugly frame detracts from the beauty of the picture.* —**de·trac′tion,** *n.* —**de·trac′tor,** *n.*

det·ri·ment (det′rə mənt), *n.* **1** loss, damage, or injury: *She worked her way through college without detriment to her studies.* **2** something that causes loss, damage, or injury: *His poor diet was a detriment to his health.*

det·ri·men·tal (det′rə men′tl), *adj.* harmful; injurious: *Smoking is detrimental to your health.* —**det′ri·men′tal·ly,** *adv.*

a	hat	ė	term	ô	order	ch	child		a in about
ā	age	i	it	oi	oil	ng	long		e in taken
ä	far	ī	ice	ou	out	sh	she	ə	i in pencil
â	care	o	hot	u	cup	th	thin		o in lemon
e	let	ō	open	ù	put	ŦH	then		u in circus
ē	equal	ô	saw	ü	rule	zh	measure		

de·tri·tus (di trī′təs), *n.* particles of rock or other material worn away from a mass.

De·troit (di troit′), *n.* city in SE Michigan. [Detroit comes from a French word meaning "strait." Detroit is on the strait that links Lakes Huron and Ontario.]

deuce (düs *or* dyüs), *n.* **1** a playing card or a side of a die having two spots. **2** (in tennis) a tie score at 40 each in a game, or 5 or more games each in a set. **3** any tie.

deu·ter·i·um (dü tir′ē əm *or* dyü tir′ē əm), *n.* an isotope of hydrogen; heavy hydrogen. Its atoms weigh about twice as much as those of ordinary hydrogen.

Deu·ter·on·o·my (dü′tə ron′ə mē), *n.* book of the Bible.

deut·sche mark or **Deut·sche mark** (doi′chə), the monetary unit of Germany; mark.

de Va·ler·a (dev′ə ler′ə *or* dev′ə lir′ə), **Ea·mon** (ā′mən), 1882-1975, Irish political leader. He was president three times and prime minister three times of the Republic of Ireland between 1932 and 1973.

de·val·u·ate (dē val′yü āt), *v.* to devalue. ❑ *v.* **de·val·u·at·ed, de·val·u·at·ing.**

de·val·ue (dē val′yü), *v.* to reduce the value of; fix a lower legal value on; devaluate: *When a country devalues its money, other countries can buy its products more cheaply.* ❑ *v.* **de·val·ued, de·val·u·ing.** —**de·val′u·a′tion,** *n.*

dev·as·tate (dev′ə stāt), *v.* to lay waste; destroy; make unfit to live in: *A tornado devastated the countryside.* ❑ *v.* **dev·as·tat·ed, dev·as·tat·ing.** —**dev′as·ta′tion,** *n.*

dev·as·tat·ing (dev′ə stā′ting), *adj.* **1** causing much destruction: *a devastating earthquake.* **2** very effective: *devastating criticism.* —**dev′as·tat′ing·ly,** *adv.*

de·vel·op (di vel′əp), *v.* **1** to come into being or activity; grow: *Plants develop from seeds.* ■ See Synonym Study at **grow. 2** to bring into being or activity: *Scientists have developed new drugs to fight disease.* **3** to come to have: *She developed an interest in basketball.* **4** to make or become bigger, better, more useful, etc.: *Exercise develops the muscles. His business developed very slowly.* **5** to work out in greater and greater detail: *Gradually we developed our plans for the club.* **6** to use chemicals on a photographic film or plate to bring out the picture: *We shall print all the films we developed.* **7** to change gradually: *Birds are believed to have developed from the dinosaurs.* **8** (in music) to vary the rhythm, melody, or harmony of a theme. **9** to put up buildings on open land or in an area where old buildings are in poor condition. —**de·vel′op·a·ble,** *adj.*

de·vel·op·er (di vel′ə pər), *n.* **1** person or thing that develops: *a housing developer.* **2** chemical used to bring out the picture on a photographic film or plate.

de·vel·op·ing (di vel′ə ping), *adj.* advancing in production, technology, medicine, and overall standard of living after becoming self-governing: *developing nations.*

de·vel·op·ment (di vel′əp mənt), *n.* **1** process of developing; growth: *We watched the development of the seeds into plants.* **2** outcome; result; new event: *The newspaper described the latest developments in the elections.* **3** group of similar houses or apartment buildings built in one area and usually by the same builder. **4** the condition of being developed: *The singer's voice reached full development when he was 30 years old.* **5** process of working out in greater

devastate
Fire devastated the building.

development (def. 3)

and greater detail: *The development of plans for a flight to the moon took many years.* —**de·vel·op·men·tal,** *adj.* —**de·vel′op·men′tal·ly,** *adv.*

de·vi·ate (dē′vē āt), *v.* to turn aside from a way, course, rule, truth, etc.: *I deviated from my routine and walked to work.* ❑ *v.* **de·vi·at·ed, de·vi·at·ing.** —**de′vi·a′tor,** *n.*

de·vi·a·tion (dē′vē ā′shən), *n.* **1** act of turning aside from a way, course, rule, truth, etc.: *deviation from your usual schedule, a deviation in the needle of a compass.* **2** (in statistics) amount of difference between the average of a set of numbers and one number in the set. This amount is used to measure difference from a normal condition.

de·vice (di vīs′), *n.* **1** something invented or made for a particular use or special purpose: *Our car has a device to control pollution from exhaust.* ■ See Synonym Study at **tool. 2** a plan, scheme, or trick: *Her pen isn't broken; that was a device to borrow your notes.*

leave someone to his or her own devices, to let someone do what seems best: *The teacher left us to our own devices in choosing the books for our reports.*

dev·il (dev′əl), **1** *n.* **the Devil,** (in the Christian, Jewish, and Muslim religions) the supreme evil spirit; Satan. **2** *n.* any evil spirit; fiend; demon. **3** *n.* a wicked or cruel person. **4** *n.* a very clever, energetic, or reckless person: *a mischievous devil.* **5** *n.* an unfortunate or wretched person: *That poor devil hasn't eaten a good meal in weeks.* **6** *n.* (earlier) a young helper in a printing office. **7** OLD USE. *v.* to bother; tease; torment. ❑ *v.* **dev·iled, dev·il·ing** or **dev·illed, dev·il·ling.**

dev·iled (dev′əld), *adj.* chopped fine and highly seasoned: *deviled eggs.*

dev·il·fish (dev′əl fish′), *n.* **1** manta. **2** octopus. ❑ *n., pl.* **dev·il·fish** or **dev·il·fish·es.**

dev·il·ish (dev′ə lish), *adj.* **1** like a devil; worthy of the Devil; very evil: *a devilish temper.* **2** mischievous or daring: *The children played devilish pranks on Halloween.* —**dev′il·ish·ly,** *adv.* —**dev′il·ish·ness,** *n.*

dev·il-may-care (dev′əl mā kâr′), *adj.* careless; reckless.

dev·il·ment (dev′əl mənt), *n.* daring mischief.

devil's advocate, someone who argues with others only for the sake of arguing, not from sincere belief.

devil's food cake, a rich, dark, chocolate cake.

dev·il·try (dev′əl trē), *n.* **1** evil action; wicked or cruel behavior. **2** mischievous, daring behavior: *children full of deviltry.*

de·vi·ous (dē′vē əs), *adj.* **1** out of the direct way; winding; roundabout: *We took a devious route through side streets to avoid the crowded main streets.* **2** straying from the right course; not straightforward: *a devious scheme for finding out the test questions in advance.* —**de′vi·ous·ly,** *adv.* —**de′vi·ous·ness,** *n.*

de·vise (di vīz′), *v.* to think out; plan or contrive; invent: *She devised a way of raising boards up to her tree house by using a pulley.* ■ See Synonym Study at **create.** ❑ *v.* **de·vised, de·vis·ing.** —**de·vis′er,** *n.*

de·void (di void′), *adj.* entirely without; empty; lacking: *A well devoid of water is useless.*

de·volve (di volv′), *v.* **1** to be handed down to someone else; be transferred: *When she resigned as president, her duties devolved upon the vice-president.* **2** to transfer duty, work, etc., to someone else. ❑ *v.* **de·volved, de·volv·ing.** —**de·volve′ment,** *n.*

De·vo·ni·an (də vō′nē ən), *n.* (in geology) time between about 400 million and 350 million years ago. During this time, amphibians, insects, and seed-bearing plants first appeared.

de·vote (di vōt′), *v.* to give money, time, or effort to some person, purpose, or service: *She devoted herself to her studies.* ❑ *v.* **de·vot·ed, de·vot·ing.**

de·vot·ed (di vō′tid), *adj.* very loyal; faithful: *devoted friends.* —**de·vot′ed·ly,** *adv.* —**de·vot′ed·ness,** *n.*

dev·o·tee (dev′ə tē′), *n.* person who is strongly devoted to something: *Many Americans are devotees of golf.* ❑ *n., pl.* **dev·o·tees.**

de·vo·tion (di vō′shən), *n.* **1** deep, steady affection; loyalty; faithfulness: *the devotion of parents to their children.* **2** act of giving up or being given up to some person, purpose, or service:

the devotion of much time to study. **3 devotions,** *pl.* worship, prayers, or praying.

de·vo·tion·al (di vō′shə nəl), *adj.* of or for religious devotion; used in worship: *devotional hymns.* **—de·vo′tion·al·ly,** *adv.*

de·vour (di vour′), *v.* **1** to eat (usually said of animals): *The lion devoured the zebra.* **2** to eat like an animal; eat very hungrily: *The hungry girl devoured her dinner.* **3** to consume, waste, or destroy: *The raging fire devoured the forest.* **4** to take in with eyes or ears in a hungry, greedy way: *He devoured the new book about airplanes.* **5** to absorb wholly: *devoured by curiosity.* [Devour comes from a Latin word meaning "to swallow." People devouring food do a lot of swallowing—but not much chewing.]

diacritical marks

^	circumflex	oar (ôr)
—	macron	team (tēm)
~	tilde	señor
••	dieresis	naïve
ȝ	cedilla	façade
•	single dot	put (pu̇t)
´	acute accent	attaché
`	grave accent	à la carte

de·vout (di vout′), *adj.* **1** active in worship and prayer; religious: *a devout Muslim, a devout Christian.* ■ See Synonym Study at **religious.** **2** earnest; sincere; hearty: *You have our devout thanks for returning our lost child.* **—de·vout′ly,** *adv.* **—de·vout′ness,** *n.*

dew (dü), *n.* **1** moisture from the air that condenses in small drops on cool surfaces during the night: *In the morning there was dew on the grass and flowers.* **2** something fresh or refreshing like dew: *the dew of youth, the dew of sleep.* ■ Other words that sound like this are **do**[1], **'do,** and **due.**

dew·ber·ry (dü′ber′ē), *n.* the sweet, black berry of various trailing vines related to the blackberry. ❑ *n., pl.* **dew·ber·ries.**

dew·drop (dü′drop′), *n.* a drop of dew.

Dew·ey decimal system (dü′ē), system for classifying books, pamphlets, etc., in many libraries. Each subject and its subdivisions are assigned specific three-digit numbers and decimals. Books on language, for example, are numbered in the 400s, on literature, in the 800s.

dew·lap (dü′lap′), *n.* the loose fold of skin under the throat of cattle and some other animals.

dew point, the temperature of the air at which dew begins to form.

dew·y (dü′ē), *adj.* **1** wet with dew. **2** fresh or refreshing like dew. ❑ *adj.* **dew·i·er, dew·i·est. —dew′i·ness,** *n.*

dex·ter·i·ty (dek ster′ə tē), *n.* skill in using the hands, body, or mind: *The jeweler's dexterity was shown in the quick, sure way he repaired the watch.*

WORD STORY Dexterity comes from a Latin word meaning "on the right side." Because the majority of people are right-handed, this is the side on which they are most skillful.

dex·ter·ous (dek′stər əs), *adj.* **1** having skill with the hands: *A typist needs to be dexterous.* **2** quick and skillful in bodily movements: *a dexterous acrobat.* **3** having skill with the mind; clever: *A successful manager must be dexterous in handling people.* **—dex′ter·ous·ly,** *adv.*

dex·trose (dek′strōs), *n.* a crystalline sugar less sweet than cane sugar, occurring in many plant and animal tissues and fluids; grape sugar. It is a form of glucose.

dh or **DH,** designated hitter.

Dha·ka (dak′ə), *n.* the capital of Bangladesh. Also, **Dacca.**

di-, *prefix.* two: *digraph = two letters.*

di·a·be·tes (dī′ə bē′tis *or* dī′ə bē′tēz), *n.* disease in which someone's body cannot properly absorb normal amounts of sugar and starch because the pancreas fails to secrete enough insulin, or because insulin is not used by the body.

di·a·bet·ic (dī′ə bet′ik), **1** *adj.* of or for diabetes. **2** *adj.* having diabetes. **3** *n.* person having diabetes. ■ This meaning of **diabetic** is sometimes considered offensive, because it is thought to identify the person with the disease. "A person who has diabetes" avoids the problem.

di·a·bol·ic (dī′ə bol′ik), *adj.* very cruel or wicked; devilish; fiendish: *The police discovered a diabolic plot to poison the city's drinking water.* **—di′a·bol′i·cal·ly,** *adv.*

di·a·bol·i·cal (dī′ə bol′ə kəl), *adj.* diabolic.

di·a·crit·ic (dī′ə krit′ik), *n.* a diacritical mark.

di·a·crit·i·cal mark (dī′ə krit′ə kəl), a small mark put over, under, or next to a letter to indicate pronunciation, accent, etc. The pronunciation key in this dictionary contains several types of diacritical marks.

di·a·dem (dī′ə dem), *n.* a crown.

di·ag·nose (dī′əg nōs′), *v.* to find out by examination or by tests: *The doctor diagnosed the disease as measles.* ❑ *v.* **di·ag·nosed, di·ag·nos·ing.**

di·ag·no·sis (dī′əg nō′sis), *n.* **1** act or process of finding out what disease a person or animal has by examination and careful study of the symptoms: *The doctors used X rays and blood samples in their diagnosis.* **2** a careful study of the facts about something to find out its essential features, faults, etc.: *The candidate made a diagnosis of the political situation at the start of his campaign.* **3** conclusion reached after a careful study of symptoms or facts: *The doctor's diagnosis was that I had measles.* ❑ *n., pl.* **di·ag·no·ses** (dī′əg nō′sēz).

di·ag·nos·tic (dī′əg nos′tik), *adj.* of, used in, or helping in diagnosis: *diagnostic tests.*

di·ag·nos·ti·cian (dī′əg no stish′ən), *n.* an expert in making diagnoses.

di·ag·o·nal (dī ag′ə nəl), **1** *n.* a line segment connecting two corners that are not next to each other in a four-sided or many-sided figure; line that cuts across in a slanting direction. **2** *adj.* taking the direction of a diagonal; slanting: *My blue tie has red diagonal stripes.* **3** *n.* any slanting part, course, or arrangement of things. **4** *adj.* connecting two corners that are not next to each other in a four-sided or many-sided figure: *a diagonal line.* **—di·ag′o·nal·ly,** *adv.*

di·a·gram (dī′ə gram), **1** *n.* drawing or sketch showing important parts of something. A diagram may be an outline, a plan, a chart, or a combination of any of these, made to show clearly what something is, how it works, or the relation between the parts. Diagrams are used in geometry to help in the proof of the problems. **2** *v.* to put on paper, a blackboard, etc., in the form of a drawing or sketch; make a diagram of: *The teacher diagrammed the math problem on the board.* ❑ *v.* **di·a·gramed, di·a·gram·ing** or **di·a·grammed, di·a·gram·ming.**

di·a·gram·mat·ic (dī′ə grə mat′ik), *adj.* in the form of a diagram: *a diagrammatic sketch.* **—di′a·gram·mat′i·cal·ly,** *adv.*

di·al (dī′əl), **1** *n.* surface of a measuring device with numbers, letters, or marks on it and a pointed indicator that shows amount, time, degree, direction, etc. The face of a clock or of a compass is a dial. A dial may show the amount of water in a tank or the amount of steam pressure in a boiler. **2** *n.* a knob or other device of a radio or TV set with numbers or letters on it for tuning in to a station. **3** *v.* to select a program or station by using a radio or TV dial: *He dials his favorite station every morning.* **4** *n.* a movable disk on some telephones mounted over a larger disk with letters and numbers and used to signal the number being called. **5** *v.* to call by means of a telephone: *She dialed the wrong number.* **6** *n.* plate or disk on a lock, with numbers or letters on it,

a	hat	e	term	ô	order	ch	child		
ā	age	i	it	oi	oil	ng	long		a in about
ä	far	ī	ice	ou	out	sh	she		e in taken
â	care	o	hot	u	cup	th	thin	ə	i in pencil
e	let	ō	open	u̇	put	⟨h	then		o in lemon
ē	equal	ȯ	saw	ü	rule	zh	measure		u in circus

used for opening the lock. **7** *v.* to turn such a dial in order to open a lock: *She dialed the combination to open her locker.* **8** *n.* sundial. ❑ *v.* **di·aled, di·al·ing** or **di·alled, di·al·ling.**

WORD STORY **Dial** probably comes from a Latin word meaning "day." The face of a sundial or clock was called "the wheel of day," and people started using the word for other marked circles.

di·a·lect (dīʹə lekt), *n.* a form of speech spoken in a certain district or by a certain group of people: *The Scottish dialect of English has many words and pronunciations that Americans do not use.*

di·a·lec·tal (dīʹə lekʹtəl), *adj.* of a dialect; like that of a dialect.

di·a·logue or **di·a·log** (dīʹə lòg), *n.* **1** conversation: *Two actors had a dialogue in the middle of the stage.* **2** conversation written out: *That book has a good plot and much clever dialogue.*

dial tone, a humming sound heard on a telephone, which indicates that a number may be dialed.

di·al·y·sis (dī alʹə sis), *n.* process of cleansing the blood artificially for someone whose kidneys do not work properly. Blood is removed from a vein, passed through a membrane that filters out impurities, then returned to the bloodstream. ❑ *n., pl.* **di·al·y·ses** (dī alʹə sēz).

di·am·e·ter (dī amʹə tər), *n.* **1** a line segment passing from one side through the center of a circle, sphere, etc., to the other side. **2** the length of such a line segment; measurement from one side to the other through the center; width; thickness: *The diameter of the earth is about 8000 miles.*

di·a·met·ric (dīʹə metʹrik), *adj.* of or along a diameter.

di·a·met·ri·cal (dīʹə metʹrə kəl), *adj.* diametric.

di·a·met·ri·cal·ly (dīʹə metʹrik lē), *adv.* **1** directly; exactly; entirely: *We have diametrically opposed views.* **2** as a diameter.

di·a·mond (dīʹmənd *or* dīʹə mənd), *n.* **1** a precious stone, usually colorless, that is formed of pure carbon in crystals. Diamond is the hardest substance known. Inferior diamonds are used to cut glass. **2** figure shaped like this: ◇. **3** a playing card marked with one or more red, diamond-shaped figures. **4 diamonds,** *pl.* suit of such playing cards. **5** (in baseball) the area bounded by home plate and the three bases; infield.

WORD STORY **Diamond** comes from Greek words meaning "not conquered." Because it is the hardest substance, it cannot be cut by anything except itself. **Adamant** comes from the same Greek word and means "firm" or "unyielding." A person who is adamant has a mind as hard to change as a diamond is hard to cut.

di·a·mond·back (dīʹmənd bak′ *or* dīʹə mənd bak′), *n.* **1** either of two large rattlesnakes with diamond-shaped markings on their backs, found in the southern and western United States. **2** a turtle living in salt marshes along the Atlantic coast and the Gulf of Mexico. It has diamond-shaped markings on its shell.

Di·an·a (dī anʹə), *n.* Roman goddess of the hunt and of the moon. The Greeks called her Artemis.

dia·per (dīʹpər *or* dīʹə pər), **1** *n.* piece of cloth or other soft material folded and used as underpants for a baby. **2** *v.* to put a diaper on: *diaper the baby after his bath.* [**Diaper** comes from a Greek word meaning "pure white." The word was used for a kind of cloth, and then for a piece of that cloth.]

di·aph·a·nous (dī afʹə nəs), *adj.* nearly transparent: *Gauze is a diaphanous fabric.* —**di·aphʹa·nous·ly,** *adv.*

di·a·phragm (dīʹə fram), *n.* **1** a layer of muscles and tendons separating the cavity of the chest from the cavity of the abdomen. **2** a thin dividing layer. **3** a thin disk that vibrates rapidly when receiving or producing sounds, used in telephones, loudspeakers, microphones, and other devices. **4** disk with a hole in the center for controlling the amount of light entering a camera, microscope, etc.

di·ar·rhe·a (dīʹə rēʹə), *n.* condition of having too many and too loose movements of the bowels.

di·ar·y (dīʹər ē), *n.* **1** account written down each day of what has happened to you, or what you have done or thought, during that day. **2** book for keeping such a daily account. ❑ *n., pl.* **di·ar·ies.** [**Diary** comes from a Latin word meaning "day." A diary is a day-by-day book of your life.]

di·as·to·le (dī asʹtl ē), *n.* the normal, rhythmic expansion of the heart as its chambers fill with blood. —**di·as·tol·ic** (dīʹə stolʹik), *adj.*

di·a·stol·ic pressure (dīʹə stolʹik), the blood pressure measured when the heart is at rest as it refills after pumping blood. Diastolic pressure is lower than systolic pressure.

di·a·tom (dīʹə tom), *n.* any of very many microscopic, one-celled algae that have hard shells.

di·a·ton·ic (dīʹə tonʹik), *adj.* of or using only the eight tones of a standard major or minor musical scale.

di·a·tribe (dīʹə trib), *n.* a speech or discussion bitterly and violently denouncing some person or thing.

dibs (dibz), *n.pl.* INFORMAL. a claim: *I have dibs on the cake.*

dice (dis), **1** *n.pl.* small cubes with a different number of spots (one to six) on each side. Dice are used in playing some games and in gambling. **2** *n.pl.* game played with these. **3** *v.* to cut into small cubes: *Carrots are sometimes diced before they are cooked.* ❑ *n., sing.* **die;** *v.* **diced, dic·ing.**

dic·ey (dīʹsē), *adj.* risky; doubtful; uncertain; chancy: *dicey road conditions during a storm.* ❑ *adj.* **dic·i·er, dic·i·est.**

di·chlo·ride (dī klôrʹid), *n.* chloride with molecules containing two atoms of chlorine; bichloride.

Dick·ens (dikʹənz), *n.* **Charles,** 1812-1870, English novelist. ■ **Charles Dickens** wrote 20 novels, including *A Christmas Carol,* his best-known work. He was the most famous English writer of his time.

dick·er (dikʹər), *v.* to bargain; haggle: *She dickered with the dealer over the price of the antique glasses.* [**Dicker** comes from a Latin word meaning "ten." It used to mean "a set of ten animal skins." Skins were often used in trading.]

dick·ey (dikʹē), *n.* **1** a shirt front that can be detached. **2** an insert at the neck opening of a blouse, jacket, etc. ❑ *n., pl.* **dick·eys.**

Dick·in·son (dikʹən sən), *n.* **Em·i·ly** (emʹə lē), 1830-1886, American poet. ■ Most of **Emily Dickinson's** poems were published after her death. She never married, wore a white dress every day, and after she was 30 years old rarely left her parents' home.

di·cot (dīʹkot), *n.* a flowering plant with seeds that have two seed leaves, called cotyledons. Dicots have petals in groups of four or five. Roses, almonds, peas, and maple trees are dicots.

di·cot·y·le·don (dī kotʹl ēdʹn), *n.* dicot.

dict., dictionary.

dic·ta (dikʹtə), *n.* a plural of **dictum.**

dic·tate (dikʹtāt), **1** *v.* to say or read aloud for another person to write down, or for a machine to record: *The teacher dictated a list of books to the students. She dictates letters to her secretary each morning.* **2** *v.* to speak with authority; give a direction or order that must be carried out or obeyed: *The country that won the war dictated the terms of peace to the country that lost.* **3** *n.* command given with authority; order that must be obeyed: *the dictates of a ruler.* ❑ *v.* **dic·tat·ed, dic·tat·ing.**

dic·ta·tion (dik tāʹshən), *n.* **1** words said or read aloud to another person who writes them down or to a machine that records them: *The secretary took the dictation in shorthand and typed it out later.* **2** the act of saying or reading words aloud to someone who writes them down: *The pupils spelled the words at the teacher's dictation.* **3** act of giving orders or making rules: *She was tired of her sister's constant dictation and refused to obey her.*

dic·ta·tor (dikʹtā tər), *n.* **1** person who uses absolute authority: *The dictator seized control of the government and took complete power over the people of the country.* **2** person who says or reads something aloud for another to write down.

dic·ta·to·ri·al (dikʹtə tôrʹē əl), *adj.* **1** of or like that of a dictator: *That country has a dictatorial government.* **2** fond of commanding and giving orders; domineering; overbearing: *I dislike anyone who has a dictatorial manner.* —**dicʹta·to·ri·al·ly,** *adv.*

dic·ta·tor·ship (dikʹtā tər ship), *n.* **1** position of a dictator. **2** period of time a dictator rules. **3** absolute authority; power that must be obeyed. **4** a country under the rule of a dictator.

dic·tion (dikʹshən), *n.* **1** manner of expressing ideas in words; style of speaking or writing. Good diction involves using words accurately as a speaker or a writer to express your ideas. **2** manner of pronouncing words; enunciation.

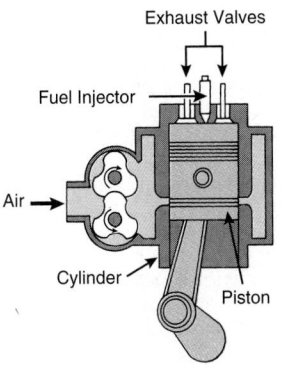

Exhaust Valves

Fuel Injector

Air

Cylinder

Piston

Air entering the cylinder is compressed by the piston and gets very hot. A jet of oil sprayed into the compressed air burns, causing a forceful expansion of the gas, which forces the piston downward.

diesel engine

dic·tion·ar·y (dik′shə ner′ē), *n.* book that explains the words of a language or of some special subject. It is arranged alphabetically. You can use this dictionary to find out the meaning, spelling, or pronunciation of a word. A medical dictionary explains words used in medicine. A German-English dictionary translates German words into English. A biographical dictionary has stories of people's lives arranged alphabetically by name. ❑ *n., pl.* **dic·tion·ar·ies.**

WORD FAMILY Dictionary and the words below are related. They all come from a Latin word meaning "to say."

abdicate	contradict	ditty	jurisdiction
addict	dedicate	edict	predict
benediction	dictator	indict	verdict
condition	ditto	judicious	vindictive

dic·tum (dik′təm), *n.* **1** a formal comment; authoritative opinion: *The dictum of the critics was that the play was excellent.* **2** maxim; saying: *The old dictum says that love is blind.* ❑ *n., pl.* **dic·tums** or **dic·ta.**

did (did), *v.* past tense of **do**[1]: *I did my work yesterday.*

di·dac·tic (di dak′tik), *adj.* **1** meant to instruct: *Aesop's "Fables" are didactic stories; each one has a moral.* **2** inclined to instruct others; teacherlike: *They called their older brother "Professor" because of his didactic manner.* **—di·dac′ti·cal·ly,** *adv.*

did·n't (did′nt), did not.

didst (didst), *v.* OLD USE. did. "Thou didst" means "You did."

die[1] (di), *v.* **1** to stop living; become dead: *The flowers in the garden died from frost.* **2** to lose force or strength; come to an end; stop: *The motor sputtered and died. My anger died.* **3** to want very much: *I'm dying for some ice cream.* ❑ *v.* **died, dy·ing.** ■ Another word that sounds like this is **dye.**

die away or **die down,** to stop or end little by little: *The music died away. The cheers finally died down.*

die off, to die one after another until all are dead: *The entire herd died off during the drought.*

USAGE NOTE **Die** is used mostly with **of:** *She died of old age.* It is sometimes used with **from** to show cause and effect: *He died from his wounds.*

die[2] (di), *n.* **1** tool for shaping, cutting, punching, or stamping things. It is usually a carved metal block or plate. Dies are used for coining money and for raising printing up from the surface of paper. **2** one of a set of dice. ❑ *n., pl.* **dies** for 1, **dice** for 2. ■ Another word that sounds like this is **dye.**

the die is cast, the decision is made and cannot be changed.

die-hard (di′härd′), **1** *adj.* resisting to the very end; refusing to give in: *The senator was a die-hard opponent of any changes in the law.* **2** *n.* person who refuses to give in.

WORD STORY **Die-hard** comes from a battle in 1811, when a British officer urged his soldiers to "fight hard and die hard!" They won the battle and were known afterward as the Die-Hards. People began using the word about others who resist strongly.

di·er·e·sis (di er′ə sis), *n.* two dots (··) placed over the second of two consecutive vowels to indicate that the second vowel is to be

pronounced in a separate syllable. EXAMPLES: naïve, Noël, Zaïre. ❑ *n., pl.* **di·er·e·ses** (di er′ə sēz′).

die·sel or **Die·sel** (dē′zəl), **1** *n.* a diesel engine. **2** *adj.* equipped with or run by a diesel engine: *a diesel locomotive, a diesel tractor.* **3** *n.* truck, locomotive, train, etc., with a diesel engine. **4** *adj.* of or for a diesel engine: *diesel fuel.*

diesel engine, an internal-combustion engine that burns oil with heat produced by compressing air.

di·et[1] (di′ət), **1** *n.* the usual kind of food and drink: *Grass is a large part of a cow's diet.* **2** *n.* special food eaten because you are sick, or to lose or gain weight: *While I was sick I was on a liquid diet.* **3** *v.* to eat special food as a part of a doctor's treatment, or in order to lose or gain weight: *I'm dieting, so don't give me any cake.* **4** *adj.* having fewer calories: *diet sodas.* [**Diet**[1] comes from a Greek word meaning "way of life."] **—di′et·er,** *n.*

di·et[2] (di′ət), *n.* **1** a formal assembly for discussion. **2** the national lawmaking group in certain countries. Switzerland and Japan are governed by diets.

di·e·tar·y (di′ə ter′ē), *adj.* of diet: *Dietary rules tell what foods to eat for healthy living and how to prepare them.*

di·e·tet·ic (di′ə tet′ik), *adj.* **1** of diet or dietetics. **2** specially prepared for people on restricted diets: *Many dietetic foods are without sugar, salt, or fats.*

di·e·tet·ics (di′ə tet′iks), *n.* science that deals with the amount and kinds of food needed by the body.

di·e·ti·tian or **di·e·ti·cian** (di′ə tish′ən), *n.* person trained to plan meals that have the right amount of various kinds of food. Many hospitals and schools employ dietitians.

dif·fer (dif′ər), *v.* **1** to be unlike; be different: *My answer to the arithmetic problem differs from yours.* **2** to have or express a different opinion; disagree: *The two of us differ about how we should spend the money.*

dif·fer·ence (dif′ər əns), *n.* **1** condition of being unlike or different: *There are few differences between baseball and softball.* **2** way of being different; point in which people or things are different: *The only difference between the twins is that Jane weighs five pounds more than Sue.* **3** amount by which one quantity is different from another; what is left after subtracting one number from another: *The difference between 6 and 15 is 9.* **4** condition of having a different opinion; disagreement; quarrel: *The children had a difference over a name for the new puppy.*

make a difference, to have an effect or influence; be important; matter: *Your vote will make a difference in the election.*

dif·fer·ent (dif′ər ənt), *adj.* **1** not alike; not like: *We saw different kinds of animals at the zoo. A boat is different from a car.* **2** not the same; separate; distinct: *I saw her three different times today.* **3** not like others or most others; unusual: *Our teacher is quite different; he never gives us homework.* **—dif′fer·ent·ly,** *adv.*

USAGE NOTE **Different** is used with **from** in writing: *My opinion is different from yours.* In casual speech, **different** is also used with **than,** but some people object to this use.

dif·fe·ren·tial (dif′ə ren′shəl), *adj.* of a difference; showing a difference; depending on a difference: *The differential rates in freight charges are for carrying heavier packages longer distances.* **—dif′fe·ren′tial·ly,** *adv.*

differential gear, arrangement of gears in a car that allows one of the rear wheels to turn faster than the other when going around a corner or a curve.

dif·fe·ren·ti·ate (dif′ə ren′shē āt), *v.* **1** to make different; cause to have differences: *Consideration for others differentiates a thoughtful person from a thoughtless one.* **2** to tell the difference in or between; find or show to be different: *Some color-blind people cannot differentiate red from green.* ❑ *v.* **dif·fe·ren·ti·at·ed, dif·fe·ren·ti·at·ing. —dif′fe·ren′ti·a′tion,** *n.*

a	hat	ė	term	ô	order	ch	child	
ā	age	i	it	oi	oil	ng	long	
ä	far	ī	ice	ou	out	sh	she	
â	care	o	hot	u	cup	th	thin	
e	let	ō	open	ù	put	ᴛʜ	then	
ē	equal	ò	saw	ü	rule	zh	measure	

ə { a in about / e in taken / i in pencil / o in lemon / u in circus }

dif·fi·cult (dif′ə kult), *adj.* **1** hard to do or understand: *Cutting down the tree was difficult. Arithmetic is difficult for some pupils.* ▪ See Synonym Study at **hard. 2** hard to deal with or get along with; not easy to please: *My cousins are difficult and always want their own way.* —**dif′fi·cult·ly,** *adv.*

dif·fi·cul·ty (dif′ə kul′tē), *n.* **1** fact or condition of being difficult; degree to which something is difficult: *The difficulty of the job prevented us from finishing it on time.* **2** hard work; much effort: *I walked with difficulty after I sprained my ankle.* **3** something which stands in the way of getting things done; thing that is hard to do or understand: *Lack of time and money were difficulties we had to overcome.* **4** trouble: *Some children have difficulty learning how to spell. She has been in financial difficulty since she lost her job.* ❑ *n., pl.* **dif·fi·cul·ties.**

dif·fi·dence (dif′ə dəns), *n.* lack of self-confidence; shyness: *His diffidence disappeared after he knew us awhile.*

dif·fi·dent (dif′ə dənt), *adj.* lacking in self-confidence; shy. —**dif′fi·dent·ly,** *adv.*

dif·frac·tion (di frak′shən), *n.* **1** process of the spreading of light around an obstacle into a series of light and dark bands or into the colored bands of the spectrum. **2** a similar process of the spreading of sound waves, radio waves, etc.

dif·fuse (di fyüz′ *for verb;* di fyüs′ *for adj.*), **1** *v.* to spread out or become spread out: *Schools and libraries diffuse knowledge. Heat diffuses from the radiator.* **2** *v.* to mix together by spreading into one another. **3** *adj.* not drawn together at a single point; spread out: *a diffuse light.* **4** *adj.* using many words where a few would do; wordy: *A diffuse book is often boring to read.* ❑ *v.* **dif·fused, dif·fus·ing.** —**dif·fuse′ly,** *adv.* —**dif·fuse′ness,** *n.*

dif·fu·sion (di fyü′zhən), *n.* **1** act or process of spreading or scattering widely: *The invention of printing greatly increased the diffusion of knowledge.* **2** condition of being widely spread or scattered. **3** process of mixing caused by spreading out. If iodine is poured into water, diffusion causes the water to become equally cloudy throughout.

dig (dig), **1** *v.* to use a shovel, spade, hands, claws, or snout to make a hole or to turn over the ground: *Dogs bury bones and dig for them later.* **2** *v.* to make by digging: *dig a well.* **3** *v.* to make a way by digging: *They dug through the mountain to build a tunnel.* **4** *v.* to get by digging: *dig potatoes.* **5** *v.* to make a thrust or stab into: *The cat dug its claws into my hand.* **6** *n.* a thrust or poke: *I gave my friend a dig in the ribs.* **7** *n.* a sarcastic remark: *The candidate made a dig at his opponent.* **8** *n.* a site where fossils or archaeological remains are dug up. **9** *v.* to make a careful search or inquiry: *The writer dug into the family records for the story of her pioneer ancestors.* **10** *v.* to work or study hard. **11** *v.* SLANG. **a** to understand: *I dig what you're saying.* **b** to appreciate: *I dig that group's music.* ❑ *v.* **dug, dig·ging.**

dig in, 1 to begin eating eagerly. **2** to dig trenches for protection. **3** to begin to work or study hard. **4** to take a position firmly: *The school board and teachers have both dug in and a strike seems likely.*

dig up, to get or find, especially by a careful search or study: *You can probably dig up the information you need in the library.*

dig (def. 8)

di·gest (də jest′ *or* dī jest′ *for verb;* dī′jest *for noun*), **1** *v.* to change food in the stomach and intestines so that the body can use it: *The body digests fats slowly.* **2** *v.* to think over something until you understand it clearly, or until it becomes a part of your thoughts: *It can take a long time to digest new ideas.* **3** *n.* a brief statement or a shortened form of what is in a longer book, article, or statement; summary.

di·gest·i·ble (də jes′tə bəl *or* dī jes′tə bəl), *adj.* capable of being digested; easily digested. —**di·gest′i·bil′i·ty,** *n.*

di·ges·tion (də jes′chən *or* dī jes′chən), *n.* **1** process of digesting food: *Proper digestion is necessary for good health.* **2** ability to digest food: *A person's digestion can be affected by illness.*

di·ges·tive (də jes′tiv *or* dī jes′tiv), *adj.* **1** of or for digestion: *The stomach is an important digestive organ.* **2** helping digestion: *digestive tablets.*

digestive system, all the glands and organs of humans and other animals involved in taking in food, digesting it, and absorbing nutrients from it.

dig·ger (dig′ər), *n.* person, tool, or machine that digs.

digger wasp, any of various wasps that dig nests in the ground.

dig·it (dij′it), *n.* **1** any of the figures 0, 1, 2, 3, 4, 5, 6, 7, 8, 9. Sometimes 0 is not called a digit. **2** finger or toe.

dig·it·al (dij′ə təl), *adj.* **1** of or made up of digits: *Digital telephone numbers, such as 555-1212, have replaced most of the old letter and number combinations.* **2** showing time, temperature, or other information by digits, rather than by positions of hands on a dial: *a digital clock.* —**dig′it·al·ly,** *adv.*

digital audio tape, recording tape for sound, specially made to keep information that has been converted into numbers. By measuring sound waves, and recording the measurements, digital systems achieve very good sound reproduction.

digital computer, kind of computer which represents all information and instructions in the form of numbers, usually binary digits.

dig·i·tal·is (dij′ə tal′is), *n.* **1** medicine used for stimulating the heart, obtained from the dried leaves of some varieties of foxglove. **2** foxglove.

dig·i·tize (dij′ə tiz), *v.* to change information, musical sounds, pictures, etc., into numbers for computer processing. ❑ *v.* **dig·i·tized, dig·i·tiz·ing.** —**dig′i·ti·za′tion,** *n.*

dig·ni·fied (dig′nə fid), *adj.* having dignity; noble; stately: *The queen has a dignified manner.*

dig·ni·fy (dig′nə fi), *v.* to give dignity to; make noble, worthwhile, or worthy: *The simple farmhouse was dignified by the great elms around it.* ❑ *v.* **dig·ni·fied, dig·ni·fy·ing.**

dig·ni·tar·y (dig′nə ter′ē), *n.* person who has a position of honor: *We saw several foreign dignitaries when we visited the United Nations.* ❑ *n., pl.* **dig·ni·tar·ies.** [See Word Story at **dignity.**]

dig·ni·ty (dig′nə tē), *n.* **1** proud and self-respecting character or manner: *The candidate maintained her dignity during the heated debate.* **2** degree of worth, honor, or importance: *A judge should maintain the dignity of his or her position.* **3** worth; nobleness: *Honest work has dignity.* **4** a high office, rank, or title: *The candidate hoped to attain the dignity of the presidency.*

> **WORD STORY** **Dignity** comes from a Latin word meaning "worthy." **Dignitary** and **dainty** come from the same Latin word. True dignity is worthy of respect. **Dainty** used to mean "pleasure," especially in the sort of delicate foods worthy of serving to dignitaries. We still call such food "dainties."

di·graph (di′graf), *n.* two letters used together to represent a single sound. EXAMPLES: ea (ē) in *each,* gh (f) in *laugh.*

di·gress (də gres′ *or* dī gres′), *v.* to turn aside from the main subject in talking or writing: *I lost interest in the book because the author digressed too much.* —**di·gres′sion,** *n.*

di·he·dral (dī hē′drəl), **1** *adj.* formed by two intersecting plane surfaces: *a dihedral angle.* **2** *n.* the figure formed by two intersecting plane surfaces.

dike (dik), **1** *n.* a bank of earth or a dam built as a defense against flooding by a river or the sea. **2** *v.* to provide with a dike or dikes. ❑ *v.* **diked, dik·ing.**

di·lap·i·dat·ed (də lap′ə dā′tid), *adj.* falling to pieces; partly ruined or decayed through neglect: *The ghost town was full of dilapidated houses.*

WORD STORY Dilapidated comes from a Latin word meaning "to throw stones." The ancient Romans used the idea of scattering stones to stand for waste and ruin of valuable possessions.

di·lap·i·da·tion (də lap′ə dā′shən), *n.* a partial ruin or decay.

di·late (dī lāt′), *v.* to make or become larger or wider: *When you take a deep breath, you dilate your nostrils. The pupil of the eye dilates in dim light.* ❑ *v.* **di·lat·ed, di·lat·ing.** —**di·la′tion,** *n.*

dil·a·to·ry (dil′ə tôr′ē), *adj.* tending to delay; not prompt: *People who are dilatory in paying their bills are poor customers.* —**dil′a·to′ri·ly,** *adv.* —**dil′a·to′ri·ness,** *n.*

di·lem·ma (də lem′ə), *n.* situation requiring a choice between two evils; difficult choice: *She was faced with the dilemma of either telling a lie or betraying a friend.* ❑ *n., pl.* **di·lem·mas.**

dil·et·tante (dil′ə tänt *or* dil′ə tant), *n.* person who follows some art or science without knowing or learning much about it; dabbler: *He was a dilettante in a dozen fields, an expert in none.*

dil·i·gence (dil′ə jəns), *n.* hard work; careful and steady effort: *The student's diligence was rewarded with high grades.*

dil·i·gent (dil′ə jənt), *adj.* **1** hard-working; industrious: *The diligent student kept on working until he had finished his homework.* **2** careful and steady: *The detective made a diligent search for clues.* —**dil′i·gent·ly,** *adv.*

dill (dil), *n.* **1** plant whose spicy seeds or leaves are used to flavor pickles. **2** its seeds or leaves.

Dil·lin·ger (dil′ən jer), *n.* **John,** 1903-1934, American bank robber. He was shot and killed by federal agents outside a movie theater in Chicago in 1934.

dill pickle, a cucumber pickle flavored with dill.

dil·ly·dal·ly (dil′ē dal′ē), *v.* to waste time; loiter; trifle: *Let's not dillydally over such unimportant matters.* ❑ *v.* **dil·ly·dal·lied, dil·ly·dal·ly·ing.**

di·lute (də lüt′ *or* dī lüt′), **1** *v.* to make weaker or thinner by adding water or some other liquid: *You must dilute the frozen orange juice with several cups of water.* **2** *adj.* weakened or thinned by the addition of water or some other liquid: *a dilute acid, dilute solution.* **3** *v.* to weaken; lessen: *The high price of a new car diluted our enthusiasm for buying one.* ❑ *v.* **di·lut·ed, di·lut·ing.** —**di·lut′er,** *n.*

di·lu·tion (də lü′shən *or* dī lü′shən), *n.* **1** act of diluting or condition of being diluted. **2** something diluted.

dim (dim), **1** *adj.* not bright; without much light; not clear; not distinct: *the dim light of dusk. With the shades drawn, the room was dim.* ■ See Synonym Study at **dark. 2** *adj.* not clearly seen, heard, or understood; faint: *We could see only the dim outline of the mountain in the distance. That happened so long ago that I have only a dim recollection of it.* **3** *adj.* not seeing, hearing, or understanding clearly: *Grandfather's eyesight is getting dim.* **4** *adj.* unfavorable: *She takes a dim view of our chances of winning the game.* **5** *v.* to make or become less bright: *She dimmed the car's headlights as the other car approached. The lights in the house dimmed several times during the storm.* ❑ *adj.* **dim·mer, dim·mest;** *v.* **dimmed, dim·ming.** —**dim′ly,** *adv.* —**dim′ness,** *n.*

dime (dīm), *n.* **1** a copper and nickel coin of the United States, worth 10 cents. **2** a similar coin of Canada, worth 10 cents. [Dime comes from a Latin word meaning "ten."]

di·men·sion (də men′shən), *n.* **1** measurement of length, breadth, or thickness: *I need wallpaper for a room of the following dimensions: 16 feet long, 12 feet wide, 9 feet high.* **2** Also, **dimensions,** *pl.* size; extent: *Building a park in the slum area was a project of large dimensions.* —**di·men′sion·al,** *adj.* —**di·men′sion·al·ly,** *adv.* —**di·men′sion·less,** *adj.*

dime store, store selling a large variety of low-priced things.

di·min·ish (də min′ish), *v.* to make or become smaller; lessen; reduce; decrease: *The poor harvest so diminished the food supply that people were starving. A sound diminishes as you get farther and farther away from it.* ■ See Synonym Study at **decrease.** —**di·min′ish·ment,** *n.*

di·min·u·en·do (də min′yü en′dō), *adj., adv., n.* decrescendo. ❑ *n., pl.* **di·min·u·en·dos.**

dim·i·nu·tion (dim′ə nü′shən), *n.* act of diminishing; lessening; reduction; decrease: *The colonists fought to prevent any diminution of their rights by the king.*

di·min·u·tive (də min′yə tiv), **1** *adj.* very small; tiny; minute: *The dollhouse contained diminutive furniture.* **2** *n.* word or part of a word that expresses the idea of smallness. The endings *-kin, -let, -ette,* and *-ling* are diminutives. **3** *adj.* (in grammar) expressing smallness: *"Droplet" and "lambkin" have diminutive endings.* —**di·min′u·tive·ly,** *adv.* —**di·min′u·tive·ness,** *n.*

dim·i·ty (dim′ə tē), *n.* a thin cotton cloth woven with heavy threads in stripes or checks, used for dresses, curtains, etc.

dim·mer (dim′ər), *n.* device that dims an electric light.

dim·ple (dim′pəl), **1** *n.* a small hollow place in the skin. A dimple is usually in a person's cheek or chin. **2** *n.* any small, hollow place. **3** *v.* to make or show dimples in: *The rain dimpled the surface of the pond.* **4** *v.* to form dimples: *He dimples whenever he smiles.* ❑ *v.* **dim·pled, dim·pling.**

dim sum (dim′sum), small Chinese dumplings filled with mixtures of meat and vegetables and steamed or fried.

din (din), **1** *n.* a loud, confused noise that lasts: *The din of the cheering crowd was deafening.* **2** *v.* to say over and over again; repeat in a tiresome way: *Our boss was always dinning into our ears the importance of hard work.* ❑ *v.* **dinned, din·ning.**

di·nar (di när′), *n.* unit of money in Yugoslavia, Iraq, Bahrain, Jordan, Kuwait, Southern Yemen, Algeria, Libya, and Tunisia.

dine (dīn), *v.* **1** to eat dinner: *We usually dine at six o'clock.* **2** to give dinner to; give a dinner for: *The Chamber of Commerce dined the famous traveler.* ❑ *v.* **dined, din·ing.** ■ Another word that sounds like this is **dyne.**

WORD STORY Dine used to mean "to eat breakfast." It comes from Latin words meaning "not fasting." People probably started using it to mean "to eat," and gradually its meaning moved from one end of the day to the other.

din·er (dī′nər), *n.* **1** person who is eating dinner. **2** a railroad car in which meals are served; dining car. **3** restaurant with booths and a long counter, in a building often shaped like a railroad diner.

di·nette (dī net′), *n.* a small dining room.

ding (ding), **1** *v.* to make the sound of a bell; ring. **2** *n.* this sound.

ding-dong (ding′dông′), *n.* sound made by a ringing bell.

din·ghy (ding′ē), *n.* **1** a small rowboat. **2** a small boat used as a tender by a large boat. ❑ *n., pl.* **din·ghies.**

din·go (ding′gō), *n.* a wolflike wild dog of Australia. ❑ *n., pl.* **din·goes.**

din·gus (ding′əs), *n.* SLANG. thing whose name is unknown, unfamiliar, or forgotten. ❑ *n., pl.* **ding·us·es.**

din·gy (din′jē), *adj.* lacking brightness or freshness; dirty-looking; dull: *Dingy curtains covered the windows of the dusty room.* ❑ *adj.* **din·gi·er, din·gi·est.** —**din′gi·ly,** *adv.* —**din′gi·ness,** *n.*

dingo—2 ft. (61 cm) high at the shoulder

dining car, diner (def. 2).

dining room, room in which dinner and other meals are served.

dink·y (ding′kē), *adj.* small and insignificant. ❑ *adj.* **dink·i·er, dink·i·est.**

din·ner (din′ər), *n.* **1** the main meal of the day: *In the city we have dinner at night, but in the country we have dinner at noon.* **2** a formal meal in honor of some person or occasion: *The city officials gave the mayor a dinner to celebrate his reelection.*

a	hat	ė	term	ô	order	ch	child		a in about
ā	age	i	it	oi	oil	ng	long		e in taken
ä	far	ī	ice	ou	out	sh	she	ə {	i in pencil
â	care	o	hot	u	cup	th	thin		o in lemon
e	let	ō	open	u̇	put	ŦH	then		u in circus
ē	equal	ò	saw	ü	rule	zh	measure		

din·ner·time (din′ər tīm′), *n.* the time at which dinner is served.

din·ner·ware (din′ər wâr′), *n.* dishes, glasses, platters, and utensils used to serve a meal.

di·no (dī′nō), *n.* SLANG. dinosaur. ❑ *n., pl.* **di·nos.**

di·no·flag·el·late (dī′nō flaj′ə lāt), *n.* any of a group of one-celled living things in the ocean, some of which produce a red substance poisonous to fish, called red tide.

di·no·saur (dī′nə sôr′), *n.* any of a group of extinct reptiles that dominated the earth many millions of years ago. Dinosaurs walked on two or four feet. Some dinosaurs were bigger than elephants; others were smaller than cats.

WORD STORY Dinosaur comes from two Greek words meaning "terrible lizard." When scientists first saw dinosaur fossils, the bones looked to them like the bones of lizards—giant lizards.

dint (dint), *n.* **by dint of,** by means of; through: *By dint of hard work we finished the job on time.*

di·o·cese (dī′ə sis *or* dī′ə sēs′), *n.* church district over which a bishop has authority; bishopric; see.

di·ode (dī′ōd), *n.* an electronic device having two connecting points. A diode restricts the flow of an electric current to only one direction.

Di·og·e·nes (dī oj′ə nēz′), *n.* 412?-323 B.C., Greek philosopher who lived in a tub to show his belief in simplicity.

Di·or (dē or′), *n.* **Christian,** 1905-1957, French fashion designer. ■ **Christian Dior's** first popular designs were introduced after World War II. His "New Look" had very full skirts and was a welcome change from the wartime designs that used little fabric because of rationing.

di·o·ram·a (dī′ə ram′ə), *n.* scene or exhibit showing a group of lifelike sculptured figures of animals, people, etc., and surrounding objects against a painted or modeled background. ❑ *n., pl.* **di·o·ram·as.**

di·ox·ide (dī ok′sīd), *n.* oxide having two atoms of oxygen for each molecule.

dip (dip), **1** *v.* to put something under water or any liquid and lift it quickly out again: *She dipped her hand into the pool to see how cold the water was.* **2** *v.* to go under water and come quickly out again. **3** *n.* a quick plunge into and out of a tub of water, the sea, etc.: *She felt refreshed after her dip in the ocean.* **4** *n.* liquid in which to dip something for cleaning, coloring, or other purposes: *The sheep were driven through a dip to disinfect their coats.* **5** *v.* to make a candle by putting a wick into hot tallow or wax over and over. **6** *v.* to take up in the hollow of the hand or with a pail, pan, or other container: *dip water from a bucket, dip up a sample of wheat.* **7** *v.* to put your hand, a spoon, etc., into a container to take out something: *He dipped into the jar and snatched a handful of cookies.* **8** *n.* something that is taken out with a scoop; scoop: *I'd like a cone with two dips of vanilla, please.* **9** *n.* a creamy mixture of foods you eat by dipping crackers, pieces of bread, etc.: *a cheese dip.* **10** *v.* to lower and raise again quickly: *The ship's flag was dipped as a salute.* **11** *v.* to sink or drop down: *The bird dipped low over the water in its flight.* **12** *v.* to slope downward: *The road dips into the valley.* **13** *n.* a sudden drop: *a dip in prices.* ❑ *v.* **dipped, dip·ping.**

dip into, to read or look at briefly; glance at: *dip into a book.*

SYNONYM STUDY Dip and plunge both mean to put something into a liquid. **Dip** means to put something into a liquid and quickly take it out again: *Dip just the tip of your brush in the paint.* **Plunge** means to put something forcefully into a liquid and leave it there for a while: *The diver plunged into the lake and swam away.*

diph·ther·i·a (dif thir′ē ə *or* dip thir′ē ə), *n.* a dangerous, often fatal, infectious disease of the throat caused by bacteria. It is usually accompanied by a high fever and formation of a membrane that makes breathing difficult.

diph·thong (dif′thŏng *or* dip′thŏng), *n.* a vowel sound made up of two vowel sounds pronounced in one syllable, such as *ou* in *house* or *oi* in *noise.*

di·plod·o·cus (di plod′ə kəs), *n.* a long, large, plant-eating dinosaur that lived in western North America. ❑ *n., pl.* **di·plod·o·cus·es.**

di·plo·ma (də plō′mə), *n.* a written or printed paper given by a school, college, or university, which states that someone has completed a certain course of study or has been graduated after a certain amount of work. ❑ *n., pl.* **di·plo·mas.**

WORD STORY Diploma comes from a Greek word meaning "double." In old times, official documents were kept private by folding them double and sealing them. **Diplomat** comes from the same word because diplomats carry official documents.

di·plo·ma·cy (də plō′mə sē), *n.* **1** management of relations between nations. The making of treaties and international agreements is an important part of diplomacy. **2** skill in handling such relations: *The ambassador's diplomacy prevented an outbreak of war between the two countries.* **3** skill in dealing with people; tact: *By using diplomacy we got to use the family car that night.*

dip·lo·mat (dip′lə mat), *n.* **1** person whose work is to manage the relations between his or her nation and other nations. **2** person who is skillful in dealing with others; tactful person. [See Word Story at **diploma.**]

dip·lo·mat·ic (dip′lə mat′ik), *adj.* **1** of or about diplomacy: *Ambassadors are the highest-ranking members of the diplomatic service.* **2** having or showing skill in dealing with others; tactful: *He gave a diplomatic answer to avoid hurting his friend's feelings.* **–dip′lo·mat′i·cal·ly,** *adv.*

dip·per (dip′ər), *n.* **1** a cup-shaped container with a long handle for dipping water or other liquids. **2 Dipper,** either of two groups of stars in the northern sky somewhat resembling the shape of a dipper; Big Dipper or Little Dipper.

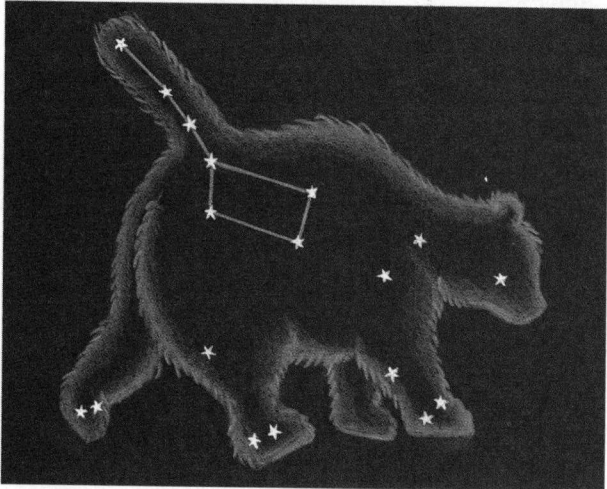

dipper (def. 2)—Big Dipper

dip·stick (dip′stik′), *n.* a slender rod used to measure the level of liquid in a container, such as the oil in a car's crankcase.

dip·ter·an (dip′tər ən), *n.* any of a large group of insects that have one pair of thin wings. Mosquitoes, gnats, and houseflies are dipterans.

dip·ter·ous (dip′tər əs), *adj.* **1** of or belonging to the dipterans. **2** having two wings.

dire (dīr), *adj.* causing great fear or suffering; dreadful: *the dire results of an earthquake, people in dire poverty.* ❑ *adj.* **dir·er, dir·est. –dire′ly,** *adv.* **–dire′ness,** *n.*

di·rect (də rekt′ *or* dī rekt′), **1** *v.* to have authority or control over; manage or guide: *The teacher directs the work of the class.* ■ See Synonym Study at **manage. 2** *v.* to order; command: *The police officer directed the traffic to stop.* ■ See Synonym Study at **command. 3** *v.* to tell or show the way: *Can you direct me to the airport?* ■ See Synonym Study at **guide. 4** *v.* to point or aim: *Direct the hose at the flames. We should be directing our efforts to the problem at hand.* **5** *v.* to put the address on a letter or package. **6** *v.* to address words, statements, etc., to someone: *Direct all your questions to her.* **7** *v.* to conduct a rehearsal or performance of a play, radio or TV show, movie, etc. **8** *adj.* without a stop or turn; straight: *A bee makes a direct flight to the hive.* **9** *adj.* in an unbroken line of descent: *That man is a direct descendant of John Adams.* **10** *adj.* without anyone or anything in between; not through others; immediate: *Selling door to door is direct selling. The new teacher took direct charge of the library.* **11** *adj.* straightforward; frank; plain; truthful: *She gave direct answers to all the questions.* **12** *adj.* exact; absolute: *the direct opposite.* **13** *adj.* in the exact words of a writer or speaker: *a direct quotation.* **14** *adv.* directly: *This plane flies direct from Chicago to Los Angeles without stopping.* **–di·rect′ness,** *n.*

direct address, a name or phrase used when you speak or write to someone. EXAMPLES: *Dear friends,* I hope to see you soon. *Dr. Cortés,* your husband is calling.

direct current, an electric current that flows in one direction only. Batteries produce direct current.

di·rec·tion (də rek′shən *or* dī rek′shən), *n.* **1** any way in which you may face or point. North, south, east, and west are directions. *The school is in one direction from our house and the post office is in another.* **2** order; command: *It was at the teacher's direction that I prepared a report.* **3** Also, **directions,** *pl.* instructions that tell what to do, how to do something, where to go, etc.: *Can you give me directions for driving to Chicago?* **4** course taken by a moving object, such as a ball or a bullet. **5** act of directing; managing or guiding: *the direction of a play or movie. The school is under the direction of the principal.* **6** course along which something moves; way of moving; tendency: *The town shows improvement in many directions.* **–di·rec′tion·less,** *adj.*

WORD POWER **DIRECTIONS** ∎ One of the world's main ideas is direction: up and down, in and out, around and through and between. Many prefixes and suffixes show directions. Often they form words in which the direction is used only as an idea, not as a way to go or point. You don't understand an outcome by getting below it, or overstate an income by getting above it. But you will be able to take in and figure out the meanings of words better if you can follow these directions:

circum-	inter-	sub-	-ward
de-	mid-	super-	-wards
endo-	out-	trans-	-ways
fore-	over-	under-	-wise
in-²	retro-		

di·rec·tion·al (də rek′shə nəl *or* dī rek′shə nəl), *adj.* **1** indicating direction: *the directional signals of a car.* **2** capable of sending or receiving radio, television, or radar signals in or from a particular direction: *a directional antenna.*

di·rec·tive (də rek′tiv *or* dī rek′tiv), *n.* order or instruction telling what to do, how to do something, where to go, etc.: *The principal sent a directive to all the teachers.*

di·rect·ly (də rekt′lē *or* dī rekt′lē), *adv.* **1** in a direct line or manner; straight: *This road runs directly into the center of town.* **2** exactly; absolutely: *That is directly opposite to what I meant.* **3** at once; immediately: *Come home directly!*

direct object, (in grammar) word or words showing the person or thing undergoing the action expressed by the verb. In "The car hit the tree," *tree* is the direct object of the verb *hit.*

di·rec·tor (də rek′tər *or* dī rek′tər), *n.* **1** person who directs; manager. A person who directs the performance of a play, a movie, or a TV or radio show is called a director. **2** one of a group of people who direct the affairs of a company or institution.

di·rec·to·ry (də rek′tər ē *or* dī rek′tər ē), *n.* **1** a book or list of names and addresses, usually in alphabetical order. A telephone book is a directory of people who have published telephone numbers. **2** a list of files in a computer's memory or on a diskette. ❑ *n., pl.* **di·rec·to·ries.**

direct proportion, relationship between two numbers or things in which they change at the same rate in the same way: *a direct proportion between hours of study and grades.*

dirge (dėrj), *n.* a funeral song or tune. **–dirge′like′,** *adj.*

dir·i·gi·ble (dir′ə jə bəl *or* də rij′ə bəl), *n.* an airship made with a rigid framework. It is filled with gas that is lighter than air.

dirk (dėrk), *n.* OLD USE. dagger.

dirt (dėrt), *n.* **1** anything that makes something unclean such as mud, grease, or dust. Dirt soils skin, clothing, houses, or furniture. **2** loose earth or soil. **3** scandal; gossip.

dirt bike, a lightweight motorcycle built especially for travel on trails or dirt roads.

dirt-cheap (dėrt′chēp′), *adj.* very cheap.

dirty (def. 1)

dirt·y (dėr′tē), **1** *adj.* soiled by mud, grease or dirt; not clean: *If you play football, expect to get dirty.* **2** *adj.* indecent; offensive to good taste: *dirty stories.* **3** *adj.* (of weather) stormy or windy; rough. **4** *adj.* not clear or pure in color: *a dirty red.* **5** *adj.* not fair, decent, or acceptable: *To say that you would help me and then not show up was a dirty trick.* **6** *adv.* in an unfair way: *play dirty.* **7** *v.* to make or become dirty; soil: *You will dirty your new clothes if you play in the mud.* ❑ *adj.* **dirt·i·er, dirt·i·est;** *v.* **dirt·ied, dirt·y·ing. –dirt′i·ly,** *adv.* **–dirt′i·ness,** *n.*

dis-, *prefix.* **1** opposite of; lack of; not: *dishonest = not honest; opposite of honest. discomfort = lack of comfort.* **2** to do the opposite of: *disentangle = do the opposite of entangle; disallow = do the opposite of allow.* **3** to deprive of: *disarm = deprive of weapons.* **4** to remove: *dislodge = remove from a position previously occupied.*

dis·a·bil·i·ty (dis′ə bil′ə tē), *n.* **1** lack of ability to do or use something: *disability due to illness.* **2** something that disables: *Severe arthritis can be a disability.* ❑ *n., pl.* **dis·a·bil·i·ties.**

dis·a·ble (dis ā′bəl), *v.* to make unable to use or do something: *A sprained wrist disabled the tennis player for three weeks.* ❑ *v.* **dis·a·bled, dis·a·bling. –dis·a′ble·ment,** *n.*

dis·a·bled (dis ā′bəld), *adj.* not able to perform certain actions that most people can perform.

USAGE NOTE **Disabled** is preferred by many people to **handicapped.** Some people prefer **challenged.** It is wise to consider your audience and subject carefully. If in doubt, ask!

dis·ad·van·tage (dis′əd van′tij), *n.* **1** lack of advantage; unfavorable condition: *Her unfamiliarity with Spanish was a disadvantage in Mexico. Her shyness was a disadvantage in company.* **2** loss or injury: *The candidate's opponents spread rumors that were to his disadvantage.*

dis·ad·van·taged (dis′əd van′tijd), *adj.* lacking advantages; being in an unfavorable condition: *a disadvantaged child.*

dis·ad·van·ta·geous (dis ad′vən tā′jəs), *adj.* causing disadvantage; unfavorable. **–dis·ad′van·ta′geous·ly,** *adv.* **–dis·ad′van·ta′geous·ness,** *n.*

dis·af·fect·ed (dis′ə fek′tid), *adj.* unfriendly, disloyal, or discontented: *The disaffected crew decided to mutiny.* **–dis′af·fect′ed·ly,** *adv.*

dis·af·fec·tion (dis′ə fek′shən), *n.* unfriendliness, disloyalty, or discontent: *Poor working conditions caused disaffection among the employees.*

dis·a·gree (dis′ə grē′), *v.* **1** to fail to agree; be different: *Your account of the accident disagrees with hers.* **2** to have unlike opinions; differ: *Doctors sometimes disagree about the proper method of treating a patient.* **3** to quarrel; dispute: *The two neighbors never spoke to each other again after they disagreed about their boundary line.* **4** to have a bad effect; be harmful: *I can't eat strawberries because they disagree with me.* ❑ *v.* **dis·a·greed, dis·a·gree·ing.**

a	hat	ė	term	ô	order	ch	child		a in about
ā	age	i	it	oi	oil	ng	long		e in taken
â	far	ī	ice	ou	out	sh	she	ə {	i in pencil
â	care	o	hot	u	cup	th	thin		o in lemon
e	let	ō	open	ů	put	ᴛʜ	then		u in circus
ē	equal	ò	saw	ü	rule	zh	measure		

Dinosaurs

Apatosaurus
One of the largest dinosaurs ever, this giant plant-eater browsed across plains and through forests in the late Jurassic, about 140 million years ago. With its long neck, it could eat from the top of trees. Apatosaurus, once known as brontosaurus, was a lizard-hipped dinosaur.

Deinonychus
Its name means "terrible claw." Each hind foot had one hooked talon longer than your fingers. Fast and deadly, this lizard-hipped meat-eater may have hunted in packs about 125 million years ago, in the early Cretaceous.

Eggs and nests
Like other reptiles, dinosaurs laid eggs. Scientists have found fossils of their eggs and nests. This hadrosaur nest was a bowl dug out of the mud. The mother may have sat on the eggs like a hen. When the young hatched, they were about the size of cats. Since there were nests nearby, hadrosaurs may have had breeding colonies like some birds today.

Hadrosaur

Tyrannosaur
As tall and as long as a freight truck, this lizard-hipped hunter tyrannized the late Cretaceous world about 75 million years ago. A few million years later, dinosaurs as a group became extinct.

Rebuilding a dinosaur
Once all the bones of a dinosaur's skeleton have been put together, an attempt at fleshing out the dinosaur can begin. By studying the bones, the muscles can be added as accurately as possible. Finally, the skin is added. A few fossils of dinosaur skin have been found, showing scales and bumps. Color is a matter of guesswork.

Triceratops

Stegosaurus
Big as an elephant, brain small as a walnut, it belonged to the bird-hipped dinosaurs. Like all of that kind, it ate plants. It lived in the late Jurassic, about 140 million years ago.

Ankylosaur

Velociraptor

dis·a·gree·a·ble (dis/ə grē/ə bəl), *adj.* **1** not friendly; bad-tempered; cross: *People often become disagreeable when they're tired.* **2** not to your liking; unpleasant: *a disagreeable smell.* —**dis/a·gree/a·ble·ness,** *n.* —**dis/a·gree/·a·bly,** *adv.*

dis·a·gree·ment (dis/ə grē/mənt), *n.* **1** failure to agree; difference of opinion: *The disagreement that existed between members of the jury led to a new trial.* **2** quarrel; dispute: *Their disagreement led to blows.* **3** difference; lack of agreement: *There is a disagreement between his account of the accident and mine.*

dis·al·low (dis/ə lou/), *v.* to refuse to allow; deny the truth or value of; reject: *The court disallowed my claim to the property.* —**dis/al·low/a·ble,** *adj.*

dis·ap·pear (dis/ə pir/), *v.* **1** to pass from sight; stop being seen: *The car disappeared around the corner.* **2** to pass from existence; stop being: *When spring comes, the snow disappears.* **3** to become lost: *Our dog disappeared for three days.*

> **SYNONYM STUDY** **Disappear** and **vanish** both mean to go from sight. **Disappear** is a general word: *When I turn off the TV, the picture disappears.* **Vanish** suggests sudden, mysterious disappearance: *The magician clapped her hands, and the rabbit vanished.*

dis·ap·pear·ance (dis/ə pir/əns), *n.* act of disappearing: *The disappearance of the airplane led to a search of the entire area.*

dis·ap·point (dis/ə point/), *v.* **1** to fail to satisfy or please: *The circus disappointed me because there were no elephants.* **2** to fail to keep a promise to: *You said you would help; do not disappoint me.* —**dis/ap·point/ing·ly,** *adv.*

dis·ap·point·ment (dis/ə point/mənt), *n.* **1** condition of being disappointed; the feeling you have when you do not get what you expected or hoped for: *When she did not get a new bicycle her disappointment was very great.* **2** person or thing that causes disappointment: *The boring movie was a disappointment.* **3** act or fact of disappointing: *Not having saved enough money led to the disappointment of our hopes for a trip to Europe.*

dis·ap·prov·al (dis/ə prü/vəl), *n.* opinion or feeling against; expression of an opinion against; dislike: *Hisses from the audience showed its disapproval of the speaker's remarks.*

dis·ap·prove (dis/ə prüv/), *v.* **1** to have or express an opinion against; show dislike: *His parents disapprove of rough games.* **2** to refuse consent to; reject: *The mayor disapproved the plan.* ❑ *v.* **dis·ap·proved, dis·ap·prov·ing.** —**dis/ap·prov/ing·ly,** *adv.*

dis·arm (dis ärm/), *v.* **1** to take weapons away from: *The police captured the robbers and disarmed them.* **2** to stop having or reduce the size or amount of a country's armed forces or their weapons: *The nations agreed to disarm.* **3** to remove anger or suspicion from; make friendly: *The little boy's smile could always disarm those who were about to scold him.* **4** to make harmless: *disarm a bomb by removing the fuse.*

dis·ar·ma·ment (dis är/mə mənt), *n.* reduction or removal of a country's armed forces or their weapons.

dis·arm·ing (dis är/ming), *adj.* able to avoid or turn away the anger or hostility of other people; charming: *a disarming manner.* —**dis·arm/ing·ly,** *adv.*

dis·ar·range (dis/ə rānj/), *v.* to disturb the arrangement of; put out of order: *The wind disarranged my hair.* ❑ *v.* **dis·ar·ranged, dis·ar·rang·ing.** —**dis/ar·range/ment,** *n.*

dis·ar·ray (dis/ə rā/), *n.* lack of order; disorder; confusion: *Her room is in such disarray that she can't find anything.*

dis·as·sem·ble (dis/ə sem/bəl), *v.* to take apart: *The mechanic disassembled the motor to repair it.* ❑ *v.* **dis·as·sem·bled, dis·as·sem·bling.**

disarray

dis·as·so·ci·ate (dis/ə sō/shē āt), *v.* to dissociate. ❑ *v.* **dis·as·so·ci·at·ed, dis·as·so·ci·at·ing.** —**dis/as·so·ci·a/tion,** *n.*

dis·as·ter (də zas/tər), *n.* event that causes much suffering or loss; great misfortune such as a destructive fire or an earthquake.

> **WORD STORY** **Disaster** comes from a French word meaning "unfavorable star." Long ago, many people believed that bad events were caused by unfavorable positions of the stars and planets.

dis·as·trous (də zas/trəs), *adj.* bringing disaster; causing much suffering or loss: *A disastrous hurricane struck the city.* —**dis·as/trous·ly,** *adv.* —**dis·as/trous·ness,** *n.*

dis·a·vow (dis/ə vou/), *v.* to deny that you know about, approve of, or are responsible for; disclaim: *The driver disavowed any responsibility for the accident.* —**dis/a·vow/er,** *n.*

dis·a·vow·al (dis/ə vou/əl), *n.* act of disavowing; denial.

dis·band (dis band/), *v.* **1** to break up; dismiss from service: *After peace was declared, the armies were disbanded.* **2** to break ranks; become scattered: *The class disbanded for the summer vacation.* —**dis·band/ment,** *n.*

dis·bar (dis bär/), *v.* to take away from a lawyer the right to practice law. ❑ *v.* **dis·barred, dis·bar·ring.** —**dis·bar/ment,** *n.*

dis·be·lief (dis/bi lēf/), *n.* lack of belief; refusal to believe: *When she heard the shocking rumor she immediately expressed disbelief.* ∎ See Synonym Study at **doubt.**

dis·be·lieve (dis/bi lēv/), *v.* to have no belief in; refuse to believe: *I disbelieved the foolish story.* ❑ *v.* **dis·be·lieved, dis·be·liev·ing.** —**dis/be·liev/er,** *n.*

dis·bur·den (dis bėr/dn), *v.* OLD USE. to relieve of a burden; unburden: *Confession may disburden a conscience of guilt.* —**dis·bur/den·ment,** *n.*

dis·burse (dis bėrs/), *v.* to pay out: *The treasurer is in charge of disbursing money to pay the club's bills.* ❑ *v.* **dis·bursed, dis·burs·ing.** —**dis·burs/er,** *n.*

dis·burse·ment (dis bėrs/mənt), *n.* **1** act of paying out: *Our club treasurer attends to the disbursement of funds.* **2** money paid out: *Disbursements must stay within the budget.*

disc (disk), *n.* disk.

dis·card (dis kärd/ *for verb;* dis/kärd *for noun*), **1** *v.* to give up as useless or not wanted; throw aside: *discard a broken toy, discard a belief.* **2** *n.* thing or things thrown aside as useless or not wanted: *That old book is a discard from the library.* **3** *v.* to get rid of playing cards not wanted by throwing them aside or playing them. **4** *n.* the cards thrown aside or played as not wanted. —**dis·card/a·ble,** *adj.*

disc brake, brake in which flat pads are pressed against both sides of a round, flat part attached to a wheel.

dis·cern (də sėrn/ *or* də zėrn/), *v.* **1** to see, perceive, or recognize: *Through the fog I could discern a person walking toward me.* **2** to tell the difference between things; tell apart; distinguish: *discern modesty from shyness, discern between facts and opinion.* —**dis·cern/i·ble,** *adj.* —**dis·cern/i·bly,** *adv.*

dis·cern·ing (də sėr/ning *or* də zėr/ning), *adj.* keen in seeing and understanding; with good judgment. —**dis·cern/ing·ly,** *adv.*

dis·cern·ment (də sėrn/mənt *or* də zėrn/mənt), *n.* **1** keenness in seeing and understanding; good judgment; shrewdness. **2** act of discerning.

dis·charge (dis chärj/ *for verb;* dis chärj/ *or* dis/chärj *for noun*), **1** *v.* to release; let go; dismiss: *discharge a patient from a hospital, discharge a lazy employee.* **2** *n.* a release; letting go; dismissal: *I expect my discharge from the hospital in a few days.* **3** *n.* writing that shows someone's release or dismissal; certificate of release: *Many members of the armed services got discharges when the war ended.* **4** *v.* to fire off; shoot: *The police officer discharged his gun at the fleeing robbers. The pistol discharged accidentally.* **5** *n.* act of firing off a gun, a blast, etc.: *The discharge of dynamite could be heard for a mile.* **6** *v.* to unload cargo or passengers from a ship, train, bus, etc.: *The ship discharged its passengers at the dock.* **7** *n.* act of unloading: *The discharge of this cargo will not take long.* **8** *v.* to give off; let out: *The infection discharged pus.* **9** *n.* act of giving off; letting out: *Lightning is a discharge of electricity from the clouds.* **10** *n.* thing given off or let out: *a watery discharge from an eye.* **11** *v.* to come or pour forth: *The river discharged into a bay.* **12** *v.* to remove an electric charge; withdraw electricity from. **13** *n.* a transfer or removal of electricity. **14** *v.* to perform or take care of: *I have discharged all the errands I was given.* **15** *n.* performance: *All public officials should be honest in the discharge of their duties.* **16** *v.* to pay: *You discharge a loan when you return the money.* **17** *n.* payment: *Money was set aside for the discharge of the debt.* ❑ *v.* **dis·charged, dis·charg·ing.** —**dis·charge′a·ble,** *adj.* —**dis·charg′er,** *n.*

dis·ci·ple (də sī′pəl), *n.* **1** believer in the thought and teaching of any leader; follower. **2** one of the followers of Jesus. [See Word Story at **discipline.**]

dis·ci·pli·nar·i·an (dis′ə plə ner′ē ən), *n.* person who enforces discipline or who believes in strict discipline.

dis·ci·pli·nar·y (dis′ə plə ner′ē), *adj.* **1** of or about discipline: *The well-behaved children presented no disciplinary problems.* **2** for discipline; intended to improve discipline: *I will have to take disciplinary measures if you continue to come to work late.*

dis·ci·pline (dis′ə plin), **1** *n.* training, especially training of the mind or character: *Children who have had no discipline are often hard to teach.* **2** *n.* a trained condition of order and obedience; order kept among pupils, soldiers, or members of any group: *When the fire broke out, the students showed good discipline.* **3** *v.* to bring to a condition of order and obedience; bring under control; train: *The teacher was unable to discipline the unruly class.* **4** *n.* a particular system of rules for conduct: *The discipline of a military school is usually strict.* **5** *n.* punishment: *A little discipline would do them a world of good.* **6** *v.* to punish: *They have never disciplined their children unfairly.* ❑ *v.* **dis·ci·plined, dis·ci·plin·ing.** —**dis′ci·plin·er,** *n.*

WORD STORY **Discipline** comes from a Latin word meaning "pupil." **Disciple** comes from the same word. Pupils receive training, and disciples are students of a great teacher.

disc jockey, disk jockey.

dis·claim (dis klām′), *v.* **1** to refuse to recognize as your own; deny connection with: *The motorist disclaimed responsibility for the accident.* **2** to give up all claim to: *She disclaimed any share in the inheritance.*

dis·claim·er (dis klā′mər), *n.* act of disclaiming; denial.

dis·close (dis klōz′), *v.* **1** to open to view; reveal: *Raising the curtain disclosed a painting.* **2** to make known: *This letter discloses a secret.* ❑ *v.* **dis·closed, dis·clos·ing.** —**dis·clos′er,** *n.*

dis·clo·sure (dis klō′zhər), *n.* **1** act of disclosing: *disclosure of a secret.* **2** something disclosed: *The newspaper's disclosures shocked the public.*

dis·co (dis′kō), **1** *n.* style of popular music with quick, strong rhythm, especially successful in the late 1970s. **2** *n.* style of dance performed to this music, with showy, complex steps and turns. **3** *n.* nightclub where recorded music is played for dancing; discotheque. **4** *v.* to dance at a disco. ❑ *n., pl.* **dis·cos;** *v.* **dis·coed, dis·coing.**

dis·cog·ra·phy (dis kog′rə fē), *n.* list of music recordings and of comments about them. ❑ *n., pl.* **dis·cog·ra·phies.**

dis·col·or (dis kul′ər), *v.* **1** to change or spoil the color of; stain: *Smoke and grime had discolored the building.* **2** to become changed in color: *Many materials fade and discolor if exposed to bright sunshine.*

dis·col·or·a·tion (dis kul′ə rā′shən), *n.* **1** a stain. **2** act of discoloring or condition of being discolored.

dis·com·bob·u·late (dis′kəm bob′yə lāt), *v.* INFORMAL. to confuse. ❑ *v.* **dis·com·bob·u·lat·ed, dis·com·bob·u·lat·ing.**

dis·com·fit (dis kum′fit), *v.* **1** to defeat the plans or hopes of; frustrate. **2** to embarrass; confuse.

dis·com·fort (dis kum′fərt), *n.* **1** lack of comfort; uneasiness: *Embarrassing questions cause discomfort.* **2** thing that causes discomfort: *Mud and cold were the discomforts the campers minded most.*

dis·com·pose (dis′kəm pōz′), *v.* to disturb the self-control of; make uneasy; confuse: *The grins of his friends discomposed him when he tried to make his report before the class.* ❑ *v.* **dis·com·posed, dis·com·pos·ing.**

dis·com·po·sure (dis′kəm pō′zhər), *n.* condition of being discomposed; confusion; uneasiness.

dis·con·cert (dis′kən sėrt′), *v.* to disturb the self-possession of; embarrass greatly; confuse: *I was disconcerted to find that I was wearing two different shoes.* —**dis′con·cert′ing·ly,** *adv.*

dis·con·nect (dis′kə nekt′), *v.* to undo or break the connection of; separate; unfasten: *I pulled out the plug to disconnect the toaster.* —**dis′con·nec′tion,** *n.*

dis·con·nect·ed (dis′kə nek′tid), *adj.* **1** not connected; separate: *Our house and the garage are entirely disconnected.* **2** without order or connection; incoherent; broken: *I cannot tell from her disconnected account of the accident what really happened.* —**dis′con·nect′ed·ly,** *adv.* —**dis′con·nect′ed·ness,** *n.*

dis·con·so·late (dis kon′sə lit), *adj.* without hope; forlorn; unhappy; cheerless: *disconsolate over the death of a friend.* —**dis·con·so·late·ly,** *adv.* —**dis·con·so·late·ness,** *n.*

dis·con·tent (dis′kən tent′), **1** *n.* a dislike of what you have and a desire for something different; uneasy feeling; dissatisfaction: *Low pay and long hours caused discontent among the workers.* **2** *v.* to dissatisfy; displease. —**dis′con·tent′ment,** *n.*

dis·con·tent·ed (dis′kən ten′tid), *adj.* not contented; not satisfied; displeased and restless: *The discontented workers went on strike.* —**dis′con·tent′ed·ly,** *adv.* —**dis′con·tent′ed·ness,** *n.*

dis·con·tin·ue (dis′kən tin′yü), *v.* to put an end or stop to; give up; stop: *I discontinued my subscription to that magazine.* ❑ *v.* **dis·con·tin·ued, dis·con·tin·u·ing.**

dis·con·tin·u·ous (dis′kən tin′yü əs), *adj.* not continuous; interrupted. —**dis′con·tin′u·ous·ly,** *adv.* —**dis′con·tin′u·ous·ness,** *n.*

dis·cord (dis′kôrd), *n.* **1** difference of opinion; disagreement; disputing: *Constant argument caused angry discord that spoiled the meeting.* **2** (in music) a lack of harmony in notes sounded at the same time. **3** harsh, clashing sounds.

dis·cord·ant (dis kôrd′nt), *adj.* **1** not in agreement; differing; disagreeing: *A quarrel started after several discordant opinions had been expressed.* **2** not in harmony: *a discordant note in music.* **3** harsh; clashing: *The discordant sound of car horns honking in a traffic jam.* —**dis·cord′ant·ly,** *adv.*

dis·co·theque (dis′kə tek), *n.* disco.

discount (def. 4)

dis·count (dis′kount), **1** *v.* to take off a certain amount from a price: *The store discounts all clothes ten percent.* **2** *n.* the amount taken off from a price: *We bought our new TV on sale at a 20 percent discount.* **3** *v.* to allow for exaggeration in; believe only part of: *You must discount some of what he tells you, for he likes to make up stories.* **4** *adj.* selling goods at prices below those suggested by manufacturers: *a discount store.* —**dis′count′a·ble,** *adj.* —**dis′count′er,** *n.*

dis·cour·age (dis kėr′ij), *v.* **1** to take away the courage of; lessen the hope or confidence of; dishearten: *Failing again and again discourages anyone.* **2** to try to prevent by disapproving; frown upon: *All their friends discouraged them from sailing their small*

a	hat	ė	term	ô	order	ch	child	
ā	age	i	it	oi	oil	ng	long	a in about
ä	far	ī	ice	ou	out	sh	she	e in taken
â	care	o	hot	u	cup	th	thin	ə i in pencil
e	let	ō	open	ù	put	ᴛʜ	then	o in lemon
ē	equal	ò	saw	ü	rule	zh	measure	u in circus

boat on the ocean. **3** to prevent or hinder: *Fear that it might rain discouraged us from camping out.* ❏ *v.* **dis·cour·aged, dis·cour·ag·ing.** **—dis·cour′ag·ing·ly,** *adv.*

dis·cour·age·ment (dis kėr′ij mənt), *n.* **1** loss of hope or courage; act or condition of being discouraged: *Discouragement over poor grades sometimes makes students want to drop out of school.* **2** something that discourages.

dis·course (dis′kôrs *for noun;* dis kôrs′ *for verb*), **1** *n.* a formal speech or writing: *Lectures and sermons are discourses.* **2** *n.* talk; conversation. **3** *v.* to talk; converse. ❏ *v.* **dis·coursed, dis·cours·ing.**

dis·cour·te·ous (dis kėr′tē əs), *adj.* not courteous; rude; impolite: *It is discourteous to interrupt someone who is talking.* **—dis·cour′te·ous·ly,** *adv.* **—dis·cour′te·ous·ness,** *n.*

dis·cour·te·sy (dis kėr′tə sē), *n.* **1** lack of courtesy; rudeness; impoliteness: *Their discourtesy in pushing into line ahead of us annoyed me.* **2** a rude or impolite act: *It is a discourtesy to interrupt another person's remarks.* ❏ *n., pl.* **dis·cour·te·sies** for 2.

dis·cov·er (dis kuv′ər), *v.* to see or learn of for the first time; find out: *discover a new drug, discover a secret.* ■ See Synonym Study at **find.** **—dis·cov′er·a·ble,** *adj.* **—dis·cov′er·er,** *n.*

dis·cov·er·y (dis kuv′ər ē), *n.* **1** act of discovering: *Marie and Pierre Curie's discovery of the element radium occurred in 1898.* **2** something discovered: *One of Benjamin Franklin's discoveries was that lightning is electricity.* ❏ *n., pl.* **dis·cov·er·ies.**

dis·cred·it (dis kred′it), **1** *v.* to cast doubt on; destroy belief or trust in: *The lawyer discredited the witnesses by proving they had been bribed.* **2** *n.* loss of belief or trust; doubt: *cast discredit on a theory.* **3** *v.* to refuse to believe: *We discredit her account because she has lied so often.* **4** *v.* to do harm to the good name or standing of; give a bad reputation to: *His cheating discredited him among his classmates.* **5** *n.* loss of good name or standing: *The player who took a bribe brought discredit upon the team.* **6** *n.* person or thing that causes loss of good name or standing: *A dishonest politician is a discredit to all politicians.*

dis·cred·it·a·ble (dis kred′ə tə bəl), *adj.* bringing discredit; disgraceful. **—dis·cred′it·a·bly,** *adv.*

dis·creet (dis krēt′), *adj.* very careful in speech and action; having or showing good judgment; wisely cautious: *a discreet person, a discreet answer.* ■ Another word that sounds like this is **discrete.** **—dis·creet′ly,** *adv.* **—dis·creet′ness,** *n.*

dis·crep·an·cy (dis krep′ən sē), *n.* lack of consistency; difference: *There was a discrepancy in the two reports of the accident.* ❏ *n., pl.* **dis·crep·an·cies.**

dis·crete (dis krēt′), *adj.* distinct from others; separate; individual: *three discrete plans to choose from.* ■ Another word that sounds like this is **discreet.** **—dis·crete′ly,** *adv.* **—dis·crete′ness,** *n.*

dis·cre·tion (dis kresh′ən), *n.* **1** great carefulness in speech or action; good judgment; wise caution: *It requires discretion to criticize others without hurting their feelings.* **2** freedom to decide: *It is within the principal's discretion to punish a pupil.*

dis·cre·tion·ar·y (dis kresh′ə ner′ē), *adj.* with freedom to decide or choose; left to your own judgment: *The law gave the mayor certain discretionary powers.*

dis·crim·i·nate (dis krim′ə nāt), *v.* **1** to make or see a difference; distinguish: *People who are color-blind usually cannot discriminate between red and green.* **2** to show a difference in treatment: *It is wrong to discriminate against people because of their race, religion, or sex.* ❏ *v.* **dis·crim·i·nat·ed, dis·crim·i·nat·ing.**

dis·crim·i·na·tion (dis krim′ə nā′shən), *n.* **1** act of showing an unfair difference in treatment: *Racial or religious discrimination in hiring employees is against the law.* ■ See Synonym Study at **prejudice. 2** the ability to make fine distinctions; good judgment: *I think they showed lack of discrimination when they painted their house a bright purple.*

dis·crim·i·na·to·ry (dis krim′ə nə tôr′ē), *adj.* showing partiality or prejudice: *discriminatory hiring practices.*

dis·cur·sive (dis kėr′siv), *adj.* wandering from one subject to another; rambling: *a long, discursive speech.* **—dis·cur′sive·ly,** *adv.* **—dis·cur′sive·ness,** *n.*

dis·cus (dis′kəs), *n.* a heavy, circular plate of wood with a metal rim. It is used in an athletic contest to see who can throw it farthest. ❏ *n., pl.* **dis·cus·es.**

dis·cuss (dis kus′), *v.* **1** to consider from different points of view; talk over: *The class discussed several problems. Congress is discussing tax rates.* **2** to examine a topic in speech or writing: *This chapter discusses the causes of the Civil War.*

SYNONYM STUDY **Discuss** and **debate** both mean to talk something over. **Discuss** means to consider all sides of a question: *We discussed the problems caused by the vacant buildings.* **Debate** means to discuss something in a formal way, often in public, taking turns to speak: *They debated the idea of a longer school day.*

dis·cus·sion (dis kush′ən), *n.* consideration of something from different points of view; discussing things; talk: *After hours of discussion, we came to a decision.*

dis·dain (dis dān′), **1** *v.* to look down on; scorn: *The policewoman disdained the offer of a bribe. Now that they are rich, they disdain to speak to their old friends.* **2** *n.* scorn; contempt: *The older students tended to treat the younger ones with disdain.*

dis·dain·ful (dis dān′fəl), *adj.* feeling or showing disdain; proud and scornful. **—dis·dain′ful·ly,** *adv.*

dis·ease (də zēz′), *n.* **1** condition of poor health; condition in which an organ, system, or part does not function properly; sickness; illness: *People, animals, and plants are all liable to disease.* **2** any particular illness: *Measles and chicken pox are two diseases of children.*

dis·eased (də zēzd′), *adj.* having a disease; showing signs of sickness: *a diseased lung, a diseased pet.*

dis·em·bark (dis′em bärk′), *v.* to go or put ashore from a ship; land from a ship. **—dis′em′bar·ka′tion,** *n.*

dis·em·bod·ied (dis′em bod′ēd), *adj.* separated from the body: *Ghosts are usually thought of as disembodied spirits.*

dis·em·bow·el (dis′em bou′əl), *v.* to take or rip out the bowels of. ❏ *v.* **dis·em·bow·eled, dis·em·bow·el·ing** or **dis·em·bow·elled, dis·em·bow·el·ling. —dis′em·bow′el·ment,** *n.*

dis·en·chant (dis′en chant′), *v.* to free from enchantment or illusion; disillusion: *I thought that living in the city would be exciting, but I soon became disenchanted.* **—dis′en·chant′ment,** *n.*

dis·en·cum·ber (dis′ən kum′bər), *v.* to free from a burden, annoyance, or trouble.

dis·en·fran·chise (dis′en fran′chīz), *v.* **1** to take the right to vote, hold office, etc., away from. **2** to take any right or privilege away from. Also, **disfranchise.** ❏ *v.* **dis·en·fran·chised, dis·en·fran·chis·ing. —dis′en·fran′chise·ment,** *n.*

dis·en·gage (dis′en gāj′), *v.* **1** to free or release from anything that holds; detach; loosen: *He disengaged his hand from that of the sleeping child. She shifted gears and disengaged the clutch.* **2** to free from an engagement, pledge, or obligation. ❏ *v.* **dis·en·gaged, dis·en·gag·ing. —dis′en·gage′ment,** *n.*

dis·en·tan·gle (dis′en tang′gəl), *v.* to free from tangles or complications; untangle: *disentangle a confusing story, disentangle a fishline.* ❏ *v.* **dis·en·tan·gled, dis·en·tan·gling. —dis′en·tan′gle·ment,** *n.*

dis·fa·vor (dis fā′vər), **1** *n.* a feeling of not liking; dislike or disapproval: *The workers looked with disfavor on any attempt to lower their wages.* **2** *v.* to dislike or disapprove. **3** *n.* condition of having lost favor or trust: *The government was in disfavor with the people.*

dis·fig·ure (dis fig′yər), *v.* to spoil the appearance of; hurt the beauty of: *Large billboards disfigure the countryside. A scar may disfigure a person's face.* ❏ *v.* **dis·fig·ured, dis·fig·ur·ing.**

dis·fig·ure·ment (dis fig′yər mənt), *n.* something that disfigures; defect.

dis·fran·chise (dis′fran′chīz), *v.* to disenfranchise. ❏ *v.* **dis·fran·chised, dis·fran·chis·ing. —dis′fran′chise·ment,** *n.*

dis·gorge (dis gôrj′), *v.* **1** to throw up what has been swallowed. **2** to pour forth; discharge: *Swollen streams disgorged their waters into the river.* **3** to give up unwillingly: *force someone to disgorge secrets.* ❏ *v.* **dis·gorged, dis·gorg·ing.**

dis·grace (dis grās′), **1** *n.* loss of honor or respect; shame: *the disgrace of being sent to jail.* **2** *n.* loss of favor or trust: *The king's former adviser is now in disgrace.* **3** *v.* to cause disgrace to; bring shame upon: *The embezzler disgraced her family.* **4** *n.* person or thing that causes disgrace: *The slums are a disgrace to our city.* ❑ *v.* **dis·graced, dis·grac·ing.** —**dis·grac′er,** *n.*

dis·grace·ful (dis grās′fəl), *adj.* causing loss of honor or respect; shameful. —**dis·grace′ful·ly,** *adv.* —**dis·grace′ful·ness,** *n.*

dis·grun·tled (dis grunt′ld), *adj.* in bad humor; discontented. ■ See Synonym Study at **cross.**

dis·guise (dis gīz′), **1** *v.* to make changes in clothes or appearance so as to look like someone else: *On Halloween I disguised myself as a ghost.* **2** *n.* the use of such changes: *Detectives sometimes depend on disguise.* **3** *n.* clothes, actions, etc., used in making such changes: *Glasses and a wig formed the spy's disguise.* **4** *v.* to hide what something really is; make a thing seem like something else: *She disguised her handwriting by writing with her left hand.* **5** *n.* a false or misleading appearance; deception: *My outward show of indifference was only a disguise for my disappointment.* ❑ *v.* **dis·guised, dis·guis·ing.**

dis·gust (dis gust′), **1** *n.* strong dislike; sickening dislike: *We feel disgust for bad odors or tastes.* ■ See Synonym Study at **dislike.** **2** *v.* to cause to feel disgust: *The smell of rotten eggs disgusts many people.*

dis·gust·ed (dis gus′tid), *adj.* filled with dislike or displeasure. —**dis·gust′ed·ly,** *adv.*

dis·gust·ing (dis gus′ting), *adj.* extremely unpleasant; very distasteful. —**dis·gust′ing·ly,** *adv.*

dish (dish), **1** *n.* anything to serve food in. Plates, platters, bowls, cups, and saucers are all dishes. **2** *n.* amount of food served in a dish: *I ate two dishes of ice cream.* **3** *n.* food served: *Chicken is the dish I like best.* **4** *v.* to put food into a dish for serving at the table: *You may dish up the rice now.* **5** *n.* antenna shaped like a dish or having a dish-shaped reflector. ❑ *n., pl.* **dish·es.**

dish it out, to criticize, attack, or punish someone harshly.

dish out, to give out; distribute: *She dishes out insincere compliments to everyone.*

Dish comes from a Latin word meaning "disk." **Desk** comes from the same word, and so does **disk.** Dishes are usually round and flat. So are some tables, and tables were used as desks when the word was first used in English.

dish·cloth (dish′klȯth′), *n.* a cloth used to wash dishes. ❑ *n., pl.* **dish·cloths** (dish′klȯths or dish′klȯᴛʜs′).

dis·heart·en (dis härt′n), *v.* to cause to lose hope; discourage; depress: *Long illness is disheartening.* —**dis·heart′en·ing·ly,** *adv.* —**dis·heart′en·ment,** *n.*

di·shev·el (də shev′əl), *v.* to disarrange or rumple hair, clothing, etc. ❑ *v.* **di·shev·eled, di·shev·el·ing** or **di·shev·elled, di·shev·el·ling.** —**di·shev′el·ment,** *n.*

di·shev·eled or **di·shev·elled** (də shev′əld), *adj.* not neat; rumpled; mussed; disordered: *a disheveled appearance.*

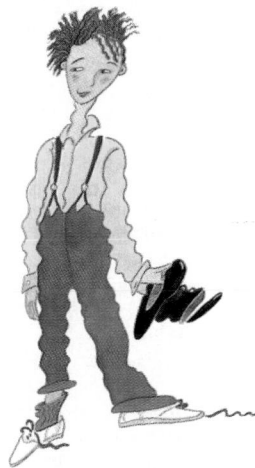

disheveled

dis·hon·est (dis on′ist), *adj.* **1** showing lack of honesty or fair play: *Lying, cheating, and stealing are dishonest.* **2** ready to cheat; not upright: *A person who lies or steals is dishonest.* **3** arranged to work in an unfair way: *dishonest scales weighted to cheat the customer.* —**dis·hon′est·ly,** *adv.*

Dishonest and **corrupt** both mean willing to lie, cheat, and steal. **Dishonest** is a general word: *People distrust him because they know he is dishonest.* **Corrupt** is a formal word suggesting dishonesty in public life: *The corrupt judge took a bribe to let the criminals go free.*

dis·hon·es·ty (dis on′ə stē), *n.* **1** lack of honesty. **2** a dishonest act. ❑ *n., pl.* **dis·hon·es·ties** for 2.

dis·hon·or (dis on′ər), **1** *n.* loss of honor or reputation; shame; disgrace: *Cheating brought dishonor to the team.* **2** *n.* person or thing that causes dishonor: *The team's poor sportsmanship was a dishonor to the school.* **3** *v.* to bring reproach or shame to; cause dishonor to: *The player who cheated dishonored the entire team.*

dis·hon·or·a·ble (dis on′ər ə bəl), *adj.* without honor; disgraceful; shameful. —**dis·hon′or·a·ble·ness,** *n.* —**dis·hon′or·a·bly,** *adv.*

dish·pan (dish′pan′), *n.* pan used to wash dishes.

dish·tow·el (dish′tou′əl), *n.* towel to dry dishes with.

dish·wash·er (dish′wäsh′ər), *n.* **1** machine for washing dishes, pots, glasses, etc. **2** person who washes dishes, especially in a restaurant, etc.

dish·wa·ter (dish′wȯ′tər), *n.* water in which dishes have been or are to be washed.

dis·il·lu·sion (dis′i lü′zhən), **1** *v.* to free from illusion: *Immigrants who expected the United States to have streets of gold were disillusioned.* **2** *n.* freedom from illusion. —**dis′il·lu′sion·ment,** *n.*

dis·in·cli·na·tion (dis in′klə nā′shən), *n.* unwillingness.

dis·in·clined (dis′in klīnd′), *adj.* unwilling: *I was watching TV and was disinclined to clean up my room.*

dis·in·fect (dis′in fekt′), *v.* to destroy the disease germs in or on: *disinfect surgical tools.* —**dis′in·fec′tion,** *n.*

dis·in·fect·ant (dis′in fek′tənt), **1** *n.* substance used to destroy disease germs. Alcohol and iodine are disinfectants. **2** *adj.* used to destroy disease germs: *a disinfectant soap.*

dis·in·her·it (dis′in her′it), *v.* to prevent from inheriting; take away an inheritance from: *She disinherited her son by leaving him out of her will.*

dis·in·te·grate (dis in′tə grāt), *v.* **1** to break up; separate into small parts or bits: *The old papers had disintegrated into a pile of fragments and dust.* **2** (of the nucleus of an atom) to undergo a change in structure by giving off particles or rays. ❑ *v.* **dis·in·te·grat·ed, dis·in·te·grat·ing.** —**dis·in′te·gra′tor,** *n.*

dis·in·te·gra·tion (dis in′tə grā′shən), *n.* **1** act or process of breaking up; separation into small parts or bits: *Rain and frost had caused the gradual disintegration of the rock.* **2** a change in the structure of an atomic nucleus by its giving off particles or rays.

dis·in·ter (dis′in tėr′), *v.* to remove from a grave or tomb; dig up. ❑ *v.* **dis·in·terred, dis·in·ter·ring.** —**dis′in·ter′ment,** *n.*

dis·in·ter·est (dis in′tər ist), *n.* lack or absence of personal interest or bias.

dis·in·ter·est·ed (dis in′tər ə stid), *adj.* free from selfish reasons for acting; impartial; fair: *An umpire makes disinterested decisions.* —**dis·in′ter·est·ed·ly,** *adv.* —**dis·in′ter·est·ed·ness,** *n.*

Disinterested and **uninterested** do not mean the same thing. **Disinterested** means having no personal reason to be unfair. **Uninterested** means not wanting to pay attention. *A judge should be disinterested, but not uninterested.* Some people use both words to mean not interested, but careful writers do not.

dis·joint (dis joint′), **1** *v.* to take apart at the joints: *The butcher disjointed the chicken for me.* **2** *v.* to break up; put out of order: *War disjoints a nation's affairs.* **3** *adj.* (in mathematics) having no common members. (0,1,2) and (3,4,5) are disjoint sets.

dis·joint·ed (dis join′tid), *adj.* broken up; disconnected; incoherent: *I was so nervous that my speech became disjointed.* —**dis·joint′ed·ly,** *adv.* —**dis·joint′ed·ness,** *n.*

disk (disk), *n.* **1** a round, flat, thin object shaped like a coin. **2** a round, flat surface that the sun, moon, and other planets seem to have. **3** a round, flat part of a plant or animal: *The yellow center of a daisy is a disk.* **4** a phonograph record. **5** a round, flat plate, made of metal or plastic and with a magnetic surface, used to

a	hat	ė	term	ô	order	ch	child		
ā	age	i	it	oi	oil	ng	long		a in about
ä	far	ī	ice	ou	out	sh	she	ə	e in taken
â	care	o	hot	u	cup	th	thin		i in pencil
e	let	ō	open	ù	put	ᴛʜ	then		o in lemon
ē	equal	ȯ	saw	ü	rule	zh	measure		u in circus

store information and instructions for computers. The two main kinds are floppy disks and hard disks. Also, **disc.** [See Word Story at **dish.**]

disk drive, an electronic device that transfers information back and forth between a computer and magnetic storage disks.

disk·ette (dis ket′), *n.* floppy disk.

disk harrow, harrow with a row of sharp, revolving disks, used in preparing ground for planting or sowing.

disk jockey, announcer for a radio program that consists mostly of recorded popular music; deejay.

dis·like (dis lik′), **1** *v.* to not like; object to; have a feeling against: *He dislikes studying and would rather play football.* **2** *n.* a feeling of not liking; a feeling against: *I have a dislike of thunder.* ❑ *v.* **dis·liked, dis·lik·ing.** —**dis·lik′a·ble,** *adj.*

SYNONYM STUDY **Dislike** and **disgust** both mean a feeling of not liking someone or something. **Dislike** is a general word: *He enjoys jogging but has a dislike for team sports.* **Disgust** means extreme dislike of something physically unpleasant: *The smell of the garbage filled me with disgust.*

dis·lo·cate (dis′lō kāt), *v.* to put out of joint: *She dislocated her shoulder when she fell down the stairs.* ❑ *v.* **dis·lo·cat·ed, dis·lo·cat·ing.**

dis·lo·ca·tion (dis′lō kā′shən), *n.* act of dislocating or condition of being dislocated.

dis·lodge (dis loj′), *v.* to drive or force out of a place, position, etc.: *She used a crowbar to dislodge a heavy stone. Smoke dislodged the guests from the hotel.* ❑ *v.* **dis·lodged, dis·lodg·ing.** —**dis·lodg′ment,** *n.*

dis·loy·al (dis loi′əl), *adj.* not loyal; unfaithful: *a disloyal friend, a disloyal act.* —**dis·loy′al·ly,** *adv.*

SYNONYM STUDY **Disloyal** and **treacherous** both mean not faithful. **Disloyal** suggests betraying trust: *A disloyal employee revealed the company's secret plan.* **Treacherous** suggests betraying your country: *The spy's treacherous message helped the enemy win the battle.*

dis·loy·al·ty (dis loi′əl tē), *n.* **1** lack of loyalty; unfaithfulness: *The traitor was imprisoned for disloyalty to his country.* **2** a disloyal act: *Revealing a friend's secret is a disloyalty.* ❑ *n., pl.* **dis·loy·al·ties** for 2.

dis·mal (diz′məl), *adj.* **1** dark and gloomy; dreary: *A rainy day is dismal.* **2** depressed; miserable: *Sickness often makes a person feel dismal.* —**dis′mal·ly,** *adv.*

WORD STORY **Dismal** comes from Latin words meaning "evil day." In old times, people thought certain days were unlucky, as some people now think Friday the 13th is unlucky. People expected those days to be dark and gloomy.

dis·man·tle (dis man′tl), *v.* **1** to pull down; take apart: *We had to dismantle the bookcases in order to move them.* **2** to strip of covering, equipment, furniture, guns, rigging, etc.: *The ship was dismantled before the hull was sold for scrap iron.* ❑ *v.* **dis·man·tled, dis·man·tling.** —**dis·man′tle·ment,** *n.*

dis·may (dis mā′), **1** *n.* sudden helpless fear of what is about to happen or what has happened: *I was filled with dismay when the basement began to flood.* **2** *v.* to trouble greatly; make afraid: *The thought that she might fail the test dismayed her.* —**dis·may′ing·ly,** *adv.*

dis·mem·ber (dis mem′bər), *v.* **1** to separate or divide into parts: *After the war the defeated country was dismembered.* **2** to cut or tear the limbs from; divide limb from limb: *The wolves dismembered the deer's carcass.* —**dis·mem′ber·ment,** *n.*

dis·miss (dis mis′), *v.* **1** to send away; allow to go: *At noon the teacher dismissed the class for lunch.* **2** to remove from office or service; not allow to keep a job: *We dismissed the painters because their work was so poor.* **3** to put out of mind; stop thinking about: *Dismiss your troubles and be happy with what you have.* **4** to refuse to consider in a court of law: *The judge dismissed the case because of lack of evidence.*

dis·miss·al (dis mis′əl), *n.* **1** act of dismissing: *The dismissal of those five workers caused a strike.* **2** condition or fact of being dismissed: *The company refused to announce the reason for the workers' dismissal.* **3** a written or spoken order dismissing someone: *The workers received their dismissal last Friday.*

dis·mount (dis mount′), *v.* **1** to get off something, such as a horse or bicycle: *The riders dismounted and led their horses across the stream.* **2** to take something from its setting or support: *The cannons were dismounted for shipping to another fort.*

Dis·ney (diz′nē), *n.* **Walt** (wȯlt), 1901-1966, American movie and television producer and amusement park creator. ∎ **Walt Disney** created Mickey Mouse and many other cartoon characters. He produced the first full-length cartoon film, *Snow White and the Seven Dwarfs.*

Disney movie character

dis·o·be·di·ence (dis′ə bē′dē-əns), *n.* refusal to obey; failure to obey: *The child was punished for disobedience.*

dis·o·be·di·ent (dis′ə bē′dē ənt), *adj.* refusing to obey; failing to obey: *The disobedient child would not do as she was told.* —**dis′o·be·di·ent·ly,** *adv.*

dis·o·bey (dis′ə bā′), *v.* to refuse to obey; fail to obey: *The student who disobeyed the teacher was punished.* ❑ *v.* **dis·o·beyed, dis·o·bey·ing.**

dis·or·der (dis ôr′dər), **1** *n.* lack of order; confusion: *Our whole house was in disorder after the birthday party.* **2** *v.* to put out of order; destroy the order of; throw into confusion: *A series of accidents disordered traffic.* **3** *n.* a public disturbance; riot: *The National Guard was called to put an end to the disorder in the streets.* **4** *n.* sickness; disease: *Eating the wrong food can cause a stomach disorder.* **5** *v.* to cause sickness in: *A severe emotional shock may disorder the mind.*

dis·or·der·ly (dis ôr′dər lē), *adj.* **1** not orderly; in confusion: *I can never find anything in this disorderly closet.* **2** causing disorder; making a disturbance; breaking rules; unruly: *A disorderly mob ran through the streets, shouting and breaking windows.* —**dis·or′der·li·ness,** *n.*

dis·or·gan·ize (dis ôr′gə nīz), *v.* to throw into confusion or disorder; upset the order and arrangement of: *Heavy snowstorms delayed all flights and disorganized the airline schedule.* ❑ *v.* **dis·or·gan·ized, dis·or·gan·iz·ing.** —**dis·or′gan·i·za′tion,** *n.*

dis·o·ri·ent (dis ôr′ē ent), *v.* to cause to lose the sense of direction or position: *The sailors were disoriented by the fog.* —**dis·o′ri·en·ta′tion,** *n.*

dis·own (dis ōn′), *v.* to refuse to recognize as your own; cast off: *They disowned their daughter.*

dis·par·age (dis par′ij), *v.* **1** to speak slightingly of; say something is of less value or importance than it actually is; belittle: *Perhaps you disparage her accomplishments because you are jealous of them.* **2** to lower the reputation of; discredit. ❑ *v.* **dis·par·aged, dis·par·ag·ing.** —**dis·par′ag·ing·ly,** *adv.* —**dis·par′age·ment,** *n.*

dis·par·i·ty (dis par′ə tē), *n.* **1** lack of equality. **2** quality of being unlike; difference: *The disparity in the accounts of the two witnesses puzzled the police.* ❑ *n., pl.* **dis·par·i·ties** for 2.

dis·pas·sion·ate (dis pash′ə nit), *adj.* free from emotion or prejudice; calm and impartial: *To a dispassionate observer, both drivers were to blame for the accident.* —**dis·pas′sion·ate·ly,** *adv.* —**dis·pas′sion·ate·ness,** *n.*

dis·patch (dis pach′), **1** *v.* to send off to some place or for some purpose: *Extra fire trucks were dispatched to the site of the blaze.* **2** *n.* a written message or communication: *a dispatch from the ambassador in France.* **3** *n.* news story: *The correspondent in Paris rushed dispatches to her newspaper in New York.* **4** *n.* act of sending off a letter, a messenger, etc.: *Please hurry the dispatch of this telegram.* **5** *v.* to get done promptly or speedily: *The teacher dispatched the roll call and began the lesson.* **6** *n.* promptness in doing anything; speed: *They work with neatness and dispatch.* **7** *v.* to kill: *dispatch an animal that has rabies.* ❑ *n., pl.* **dis·patch·es** for 2,3.

dis·patch·er (dis pach′ər), *n.* person who dispatches. A train dispatcher is in charge of sending off the trains on schedule.

dis·pel (dis pel′), *v.* to drive away; get rid of: *He helped dispel our fears by explaining what had actually happened.* ❑ *v.* **dis·pelled, dis·pel·ling.**

dis·pen·sa·ble (dis pen′sə bəl), *adj.* able to be done without; un-necessary; unimportant.

dis·pen·sar·y (dis pen′sər ē), *n.* place where medicines, medical care, and medical advice are given out. ❑ *n., pl.* **dis·pen·sar·ies.**

dis·pen·sa·tion (dis′pən sā′shən), *n.* **1** act of giving out; distributing: *the dispensation of food and clothing to the flood victims.* **2** rule; management: *From 1558 to 1603 England was under the dispensation of Elizabeth I.* **3** official permission to disregard a rule.

dis·pense (dis pens′), *v.* **1** to give out; distribute: *The Red Cross dispensed food and clothing to the flood victims.* **2** to carry out; put in force; apply: *Judges and courts of law dispense justice.* **3** to prepare and give out: *Druggists must dispense medicine with the greatest care.* ❑ *v.* **dis·pensed, dis·pens·ing.**

dispense with, to do without; get along without: *I shall dispense with these crutches as soon as my leg heals.*

dis·pens·er (dis pen′sər), *n.* container that is designed to give out in convenient portions some item of general use: *a paper-cup dispenser, a soap dispenser.*

dis·per·sal (dis pèr′səl), *n.* act or process of scattering or condition of being scattered; dispersing: *the dispersal of a crowd.*

dis·perse (dis pèrs′), *v.* **1** to spread in different directions; scatter: *The police dispersed the onlookers. The crowd dispersed when it began raining.* **2** to divide light into rays of different colors. ❑ *v.* **dis·persed, dis·pers·ing.** —**dis·per·sion** (dis pèr′zhən), *n.*

dis·pir·it (dis pir′it), *v.* to lower the spirits of; discourage; depress; dishearten. —**dis·pir′it·ed·ly,** *adv.* —**dis·pir′it·ed·ness,** *n.*

dis·place (dis plās′), *v.* **1** to take the place of; replace: *The car has displaced the horse and buggy.* **2** to remove from a position of authority: *The mayor displaced the police chief.* **3** to move from its usual place or position: *The war displaced thousands of people.* ❑ *v.* **dis·placed, dis·plac·ing.** —**dis·place′a·ble,** *adj.*

displaced person, person forced out of his or her own country by war, famine, political disturbance, etc.

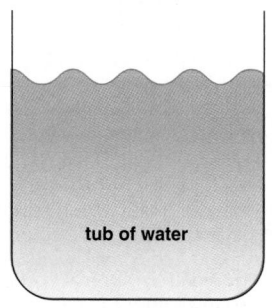
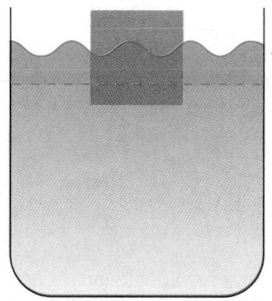

displacement—One pound (0.45 kg) of wood, floating in water, displaces its own weight but not its own volume of water.

tub of water

dis·place·ment (dis plās′mənt), *n.* **1** act of displacing or condition of being displaced. **2** weight of the water displaced by a ship or other floating object. This weight is equal to that of the floating object.

dis·play (dis plā′), **1** *v.* to put on view; show: *The American flag is displayed on the Fourth of July. The lecturer displayed her good nature by patiently answering the same question several times.* **2** *n.* act of showing; exhibition: *a display of bad temper.* **3** *v.* to show without meaning to; reveal: *A person's true nature is often displayed during a crisis.* **4** *v.* to show in a special way, so as to attract attention: *The stores are displaying the new spring clothes in their windows.* **5** *n.* act of showing off; ostentation: *Their fondness for display led them to buy flashy cars.* **6** *n.* a planned showing of a thing, for some special purpose; exhibit: *Grade 6 had two displays of children's drawings.* **7** *n.* information in visual form, as on the screen of a computer or calculator. **8** *v.* to show information on a computer screen or calculator. **9** *n.* device that shows such information.

SYNONYM STUDY **Display** and **exhibit** both mean something meant to be seen. **Display** suggests something of limited size: *The store window has a display of watches.* **Exhibit** means something meant to be seen by many people: *The museum's new dinosaur exhibit is very popular.*

dis·please (dis plēz′), *v.* to annoy or anger somewhat; offend: *The teacher is displeased by students who are late for class.* ❑ *v.* **dis·pleased, dis·pleas·ing.** —**dis·pleas′ing·ly,** *adv.*

dis·pleas·ure (dis plezh′ər), *n.* the feeling of being displeased; annoyance; dislike.

dis·port (dis pôrt′), *v.* to amuse or entertain yourself: *People laughed at the clumsy bears disporting themselves in the water.* [See word history information at **sport.**]

dis·pos·a·ble (dis pō′zə bəl), *adj.* able to be disposed of or thrown away after use: *disposable paper napkins.*

dis·pos·al (dis pō′zəl), *n.* **1** act of getting rid of something: *The city takes care of the disposal of garbage.* **2** act of giving away or selling: *His will provided for the disposal of his property after his death.* **3** act of dealing with; settling: *Her disposal of the difficulty satisfied everybody.* **4** an electric device installed under a sink to grind up kitchen waste and dispose of it down the drain.

at your disposal, ready for your use or service at any time: *His car is at my disposal while he is on vacation.*

dis·pose (dis pōz′), *v.* **1** to put in a certain order or position; arrange: *The flags were disposed in a straight line for the parade.* **2** to make ready or willing; incline: *More pay and a shorter workday disposed him to take the new job.* **3** to make liable or subject: *Getting overly tired disposes you to catching cold.* ❑ *v.* **dis·posed, dis·pos·ing.** —**dis·pos′er,** *n.*

dispose of, **1** to get rid of: *Dispose of that rubbish.* **2** to give away: *The Salvation Army will dispose of this clothing among the poor.* **3** to sell: *The owner disposed of her house for $235,000.* **4** to eat or drink: *They quickly disposed of the picnic lunch.* **5** to arrange; settle: *The committee disposed of all its business in an hour.*

dis·po·si·tion (dis′pə zish′ən), *n.* **1** habitual ways of acting toward others or of thinking about things; nature: *His cheerful disposition made him popular.* **2** tendency; inclination: *A quarrelsome person has a disposition to start trouble.* **3** order or arrangement: *The teacher changed the disposition of the desks in the classroom.* **4** settlement: *What disposition did the court make of the case?* **5** disposal: *She had a lot of money at her disposition.*

dis·pos·sess (dis′pə zes′), *v.* to force to give up the possession of a house, land, etc.: *The tenant was dispossessed for not paying the rent.* —**dis′pos·ses′sion,** *n.*

dis·proof (dis prüf′), *n.* **1** act of disproving; refutation. **2** fact or reason that disproves something.

dis·pro·por·tion (dis′prə pôr′shən), *n.* lack of proper proportion.

dis·pro·por·tion·ate (dis′prə pôr′shə nit), *adj.* out of relation in size, number, etc., to something else; not well proportioned: *A dollar would be disproportionate pay for a day's work.* —**dis′pro·por′tion·ate·ly,** *adv.*

a	hat	ė	term	ô	order	ch	child		a in about
ā	age	i	it	oi	oil	ng	long		e in taken
ä	far	ī	ice	ou	out	sh	she	ə	i in pencil
â	care	o	hot	u	cup	th	thin		o in lemon
e	let	ō	open	ù	put	ŦH	then		u in circus
ē	equal	ò	saw	ü	rule	zh	measure		

dis·prove (dis prüv′), v. to prove false or incorrect: *She disproved her brother's claim that he had less candy by weighing both boxes.* ❑ v. **dis·proved, dis·prov·ing.**

dis·put·a·ble (dis pyü′tə bəl *or* dis′pyə tə bəl), adj. liable to be disputed; uncertain; questionable: *The existence of flying saucers is disputable.* —**dis·put′a·bly,** adv.

dis·pu·tant (dis pyüt′nt), n. person who takes part in a dispute or debate.

dis·pu·ta·tion (dis′pyə tā′shən), n. 1 debate; controversy. 2 dispute.

dis·pute (dis pyüt′), 1 v. to give reasons or facts for or against something; argue; debate; discuss: *Congress disputed over the need for new taxes.* ■ See Synonym Study at **argument.** 2 n. argument; debate: *There is a dispute over where to build the new school.* 3 v. to quarrel: *The children disputed over the last piece of cake.* 4 n. a quarrel: *The dispute between the two neighbors threatened their friendship.* 5 v. to disagree with a statement; declare to be false or wrong; call in question: *The insurance company disputed his claim for damages to his car.* 6 v. to fight for; fight over; contest: *The soldiers disputed every inch of ground when the enemy attacked.* 7 v. to try to win: *The losing team disputed the victory up to the last minute of play.* ❑ v. **dis·put·ed, dis·put·ing.** —**dis·put′er,** n.

dispute

dis·qual·i·fi·ca·tion (dis kwäl′ə fə kā′shən), n. 1 something that disqualifies: *Poor eyesight is a disqualification for many jobs.* 2 act of disqualifying or condition of being disqualified.

dis·qual·i·fy (dis kwäl′ə fī), v. 1 to make unfit; make unable to do something: *Her broken leg disqualified her from all sports.* 2 to declare unfit or unable to do something: *The principal disqualified two members of the school play because they had low grades.* ❑ v. **dis·qual·i·fied, dis·qual·i·fy·ing.**

dis·qui·et (dis kwī′ət), 1 v. to make uneasy or anxious; disturb: *The child's strange actions disquieted the parents.* 2 n. uneasy feelings; anxiety: *Her disquiet made the rest of us uneasy, too.* —**dis·qui′et·ing·ly,** adv.

dis·qui·e·tude (dis kwī′ə tüd), n. uneasiness; anxiety.

dis·re·gard (dis′ri gärd′), 1 v. to pay no attention to; take no notice of: *Disregarding the cold weather, we played outside all day.* 2 n. lack of attention; neglect: *Her disregard for the traffic signs caused her to have an accident.*

dis·re·pair (dis′ri pâr′), n. bad condition; need of repair: *The house was in disrepair.*

dis·rep·u·ta·ble (dis rep′yə tə bəl), adj. 1 having a bad reputation: *Police closed the disreputable barroom.* 2 not fit to be used or seen; in poor condition: *a disreputable old hat.* —**dis·rep′u·ta·ble·ness,** n. —**dis·rep′u·ta·bly,** adv.

dis·re·pute (dis′ri pyüt′), n. disgrace; discredit; disfavor: *Many old remedies for illness have fallen into disrepute.*

dis·re·spect (dis′ri spekt′), n. lack of respect; rudeness; impoliteness: *I meant no disrespect by my remark.*

dis·re·spect·ful (dis′ri spekt′fəl), adj. showing no respect; lacking in courtesy to elders or superiors; rude; impolite: *Making fun of your elders is disrespectful.* —**dis′re·spect′ful·ly,** adv. —**dis′re·spect′ful·ness,** n.

dis·robe (dis rōb′), v. to undress. ❑ v. **dis·robed, dis·rob·ing.**

dis·rupt (dis rupt′), v. to break up or cause disorder in: *The storm disrupted telephone service.* —**dis·rupt′er,** n.

dis·rup·tion (dis rup′shən), n. 1 act of breaking up; splitting: *Arguments led to the disruption of their partnership.* 2 condition of being broken up: *a disruption of telephone service during the storm.*

dis·rup·tive (dis rup′tiv), adj. causing disruption: *Their whispering was a disruptive influence in the library.* —**dis·rup′tive·ly,** adv.

diss (dis), v. SLANG. to show someone disrespect; to insult someone or something.

dis·sat·is·fac·tion (dis′sat i sfak′shən), n. discontent; displeasure: *Poor working conditions caused dissatisfaction among the employees.*

dis·sat·is·fied (dis sat′i sfīd), adj. discontented; displeased: *The dissatisfied workers voted to strike for higher pay.*

dis·sat·is·fy (dis sat′i sfī), v. to fail to satisfy; make discontented; displease: *My teacher was dissatisfied with the paper I wrote.* ❑ v. **dis·sat·is·fied, dis·sat·is·fy·ing.**

dis·sect (di sekt′ *or* dī sekt′), v. 1 to cut apart something that was once alive in order to examine its structure. 2 to examine carefully part by part; analyze: *Let us dissect that statement and find out just what it means.* —**dis·sec′tor,** n.

dis·sec·tion (di sek′shən *or* dī sek′shən), n. 1 act of cutting apart an animal, plant, etc., in order to examine its structure. 2 examination of something in detail or point by point; analysis.

dis·sem·ble (di sem′bəl), v. 1 to hide your real feelings, thoughts, plans, etc.; disguise: *She dissembled her anger with a smile.* 2 to put on the appearance of; pretend; feign: *The bored listener dissembled an interest he didn't feel.* ❑ v. **dis·sem·bled, dis·sem·bling.** —**dis·sem′bler,** n.

dis·sem·i·nate (di sem′ə nāt), v. to scatter widely; spread abroad: *Television and radio stations disseminated news of the hurricane.* ❑ v. **dis·sem·i·nat·ed, dis·sem·i·nat·ing.** —**dis·sem′i·na′tion,** n. —**dis·sem′i·na′tor,** n.

dis·sen·sion (di sen′shən), n. violent disagreement; strong difference of opinion; quarreling; disputing: *The club broke up because of dissension among its members.*

dis·sent (di sent′), 1 v. to differ in opinion; disagree: *Two of the judges dissented from the decision of the other three.* 2 n. difference of opinion; disagreement: *Dissent among the members broke up the club meeting.* ■ Another word that sounds like this is **descent.** —**dis·sent′er,** n.

dis·ser·ta·tion (dis′ər tā′shən), n. a formal oral or written discussion of a subject. A university student who is working for a doctor's degree is required to write a dissertation.

dis·serv·ice (dis sėr′vis), n. bad treatment; harm; injury: *You do a disservice to him when you fail to give him credit for his efforts.*

dis·sev·er (di sev′ər), v. to cut into parts; sever; separate. —**dis·sev′er·ment,** n.

dis·si·dent (dis′ə dənt), 1 adj. disagreeing in opinion; dissenting: *dissident members of a jury.* 2 n. person who disagrees or dissents.

dis·sim·i·lar (di sim′ə lər), adj. not similar; unlike; different. —**dis·sim′i·lar′i·ty,** n. —**dis·sim′i·lar·ly,** adv.

dis·sim·u·late (di sim′yə lāt), v. to disguise or hide under a pretense; hide the truth; dissemble: *She was unable to dissimulate her feelings.* ❑ v. **dis·sim·u·lat·ed, dis·sim·u·lat·ing.** —**dis·sim′u·la′tion,** n. —**dis·sim′u·la′tor,** n.

dis·si·pate (dis′ə pāt), v. 1 to spread in different directions; scatter so as to disappear or cause to disappear; disperse; dispel: *The fog is beginning to dissipate.* 2 to spend foolishly; waste on things of little value: *In a short time she had dissipated her inheritance.* 3 to indulge too much in harmful or foolish pleasures. ❑ v. **dis·si·pat·ed, dis·si·pat·ing.**

dis·si·pat·ed (dis′ə pā′tid), adj. indulging too much in harmful or foolish pleasures; dissolute: *a dissipated life spent drinking and gambling.* —**dis′si·pat′ed·ly,** adv. —**dis′si·pat′ed·ness,** n.

dis·si·pa·tion (dis′ə pā′shən), n. 1 too much indulgence in harmful or foolish pleasures; intemperance. 2 act of wasting time, money, etc. 3 act of scattering in different directions.

dis·so·ci·ate (di sō′shē āt), v. **1** to break the connection or association with; separate: *When the lawyer discovered that his client was lying, he immediately dissociated himself from the case.* **2** (in chemistry) to undergo dissociation. ◻ v. **dis·so·ci·at·ed, dis·so·ci·at·ing.**

dis·so·ci·a·tion (di sō′sē ā′shən), n. (in chemistry) the changing of a substance into two or more simpler substances, by heat or pressure: *the dissociation of water into hydrogen and oxygen.*

dis·so·lute (dis′ə lüt), adj. living an evil life; very wicked; immoral: *dissolute companions with bad reputations.* —**dis′so·lute·ly,** adv. —**dis′so·lute·ness,** n.

dis·so·lu·tion (dis′ə lü′shən), n. **1** act of breaking up; an ending: *The partners arranged for the dissolution of their partnership.* **2** act or process of making or becoming liquid; dissolving.

dis·solve (di zolv′), v. **1** to change from a solid or gas to a liquid; form into a solution in a liquid: *Salt or sugar will dissolve in water.* **2** to break up; end: *The two partners dissolved their partnership because they could not agree on how to conduct the business.* **3** to fade away: *The dream dissolved when she woke up.* **4** to be overcome by emotion: *When they heard the good news, they dissolved into tears of relief.* **5** (in movies and television) to fade gradually from the screen while the next picture or scene slowly appears. ◻ v. **dis·solved, dis·solv·ing.**

> **WORD FAMILY**   Dissolve and the words below are related. They all come from a Latin word meaning "to loosen."
>
> | | | | |
> |---|---|---|---|
> | absolute | insoluble | resolution | solution |
> | absolve | insolvent | resolve | solve |
> | dissolute | resolute | | |

dis·so·nance (dis′n əns), n. **1** harshness and unpleasantness of sound; discord. **2** lack of harmony; disagreement.

dis·so·nant (dis′n ənt), adj. **1** harsh and unpleasant in sound; not harmonious; clashing: *dissonant chords.* **2** out of harmony with other conditions, persons, etc.; disagreeing: *Two dissonant groups caused a split in the political party.* —**dis′so·nant·ly,** adv.

dis·suade (di swād′), v. to persuade not to do something: *I dissuaded her from quitting the play.* ◻ v. **dis·suad·ed, dis·suad·ing.**

dist., **1** distance. **2** district.

dis·taff (dis′taf), n. **1** a stick, split at the tip, to hold wool or flax for spinning by hand. **2** staff on a spinning wheel for holding wool or flax.

distaff side, the mother's side of a family: *My cousin and I are related on the distaff side.*

dis·tance (dis′təns), **1** n. space in between: *The distance from the farm to the town is five miles.* **2** n. condition of being far away: *Because of the lake's distance, we will have to stop overnight on the way.* **3** n. a place far away: *He saw a light in the distance.* **4** v. to leave for behind; do much better than; outdistance: *Well-trained runners quickly distance other runners in a marathon.* **5** v. to put or keep at a distance: *She distanced herself from her friends while she mourned her loss.* ◻ v. **dis·tanced, dis·tanc·ing.**

at a distance, a long way: *The farm is at a distance from the road.*

keep at a distance, to refuse to be friendly or familiar with; treat coldly: *The teacher kept the students at a distance.*

keep your distance, be not too friendly or familiar: *The shy boy kept his distance and did not mingle with his new classmates.*

dis·tant (dis′tənt), adj. **1** far away in space: *The sun is distant from the earth.* **2** away: *The town is three miles distant.* **3** far off in time: *We may take a trip to Europe in the distant future.* **4** not closely related: *A third cousin is a distant relative.* **5** not friendly: *I gave him only a distant nod.* —**dis′tant·ly,** adv. —**dis′tant·ness,** n.

> **SYNONYM STUDY**   Distant and remote both mean far away. Distant can mean somewhat far or very far: *After three days' travel, they reached the distant mountains.* Remote suggests extremely far and hard or impossible to get to: *Light from remote stars takes centuries to reach Earth.*

dis·taste (dis tāst′), n. dislike: *I have always had a distaste for Brussels sprouts.*

dis·taste·ful (dis tāst′fəl), adj. unpleasant; disagreeable; offensive. —**dis·taste′ful·ly,** adv. —**dis·taste′ful·ness,** n.

dis·tem·per (dis tem′pər), n. an infectious disease of dogs and other animals, with fever, a short, dry cough, and a loss of strength.

dis·tend (dis tend′), n. stretch out; swell out; expand: *The balloon was distended almost to the bursting point.*

dis·ten·tion (dis ten′shən), n. condition of being bloated or swollen: *abdominal distention.*

dis·till or **dis·til** (dis til′), v. **1** to heat a liquid or other substance and condense the vapor given off by cooling it into liquid form again. A substance is distilled in order to purify it, to separate its liquid parts from its solid parts, or to break it down into separate substances. **2** to obtain by distilling: *Alcoholic liquor is distilled from mash made from grain.* **3** to get the essential part of something out; extract: *A jury must distill the truth from the testimony of witnesses.* **4** to give off in drops: *These flowers distill a sweet nectar.* ◻ v. **dis·tilled, dis·till·ing.** —**dis·till′a·ble,** adj.

dis·til·late (dis′tl it), n. **1** a distilled liquid; something obtained by distilling. **2** anything concentrated or extracted; essence: *Her speech was a distillate of her years of experience.*

dis·til·la·tion (dis′tl ā′shən), n. **1** act or process of distilling: *Fresh water can be obtained by the distillation of salt water.* **2** something distilled.

dis·till·er (dis til′ər), n. **1** person or company that makes whiskey, rum, brandy, etc. **2** person or thing that distills.

dis·till·er·y (dis til′ər ē), n. place where whiskey, rum, brandy, etc., are made. ◻ n., pl. **dis·till·er·ies.**

dis·tinct (dis tingkt′), adj. **1** not the same; separate: *She asked me about it three distinct times.* **2** different in quality or kind: *Mice are distinct from rats.* **3** easily seen, heard, or understood; clear: *Large, distinct print is easy to read.* **4** unmistakable; definite; decided: *Tall players have a distinct advantage in basketball.* ■ See Synonym Study at **definite.** —**dis·tinct′ly,** adv. —**dis·tinct′ness,** n.

dis·tinc·tion (dis tingk′shən), n. **1** difference: *The distinction between hot and cold is easily noticed.* **2** special quality or feature; point of difference: *He has the distinction of being the best chess player in his school.* **3** honor: *The senator had served his country with distinction.* **4** act of distinguishing from others; making a difference: *They treated all their children alike without distinction.* **5** mark or sign of honor: *The scientist received many awards as distinctions for her achievements.* **6** excellence; superiority: *Prizes were awarded to authors of great distinction.*

dis·tinc·tive (dis tingk′tiv), adj. clearly showing a difference from others; special; characteristic: *Police officers wear a distinctive uniform.* —**dis·tinc′tive·ly,** adv. —**dis·tinc′tive·ness,** n.

dis·tin·guish (dis ting′gwish), v. **1** to see or show the differences in; tell apart: *Can you distinguish silk from nylon?* **2** to see or show the difference: *to distinguish between right and wrong.* **3** to see or hear clearly; make out plainly: *On a clear day you can distinguish things far away.* **4** to make different; be a special quality or feature of: *The elephant's trunk distinguishes it from all other animals.* **5** to make famous or well known: *She distinguished herself by winning two prizes.* —**dis·tin′guish·a·ble,** adj. —**dis·tin′guish·a·bly,** adv.

dis·tin·guished (dis ting′gwisht), adj. **1** famous or well-known because of excellence: *The distinguished artist had paintings displayed in many museums.* **2** looking important or superior: *Your new suit gives you a distinguished look.*

dis·tort (dis tôrt′), v. **1** to pull or twist out of shape; change the normal appearance of: *Rage distorted his face.* **2** to change from the truth; misrepresent: *The driver distorted the facts of the accident to escape blame.* **3** to damage the quality of a radio or television signal: *Turning on the vacuum cleaner distorts the radio program.* —**dis·tort′er,** n.

a	hat	ė	term	ô	order	ch	child		
ā	age	i	it	oi	oil	ng	long		a in about
ä	far	ī	ice	ou	out	sh	she	ə	e in taken
â	care	o	hot	u	cup	th	thin		i in pencil
e	let	ō	open	ů	put	ᴛʜ	then		o in lemon
ē	equal	ò	saw	ü	rule	zh	measure		u in circus

dis·tor·tion (dis tôr′shən), *n.* **1** act of distorting; twisting out of shape: *Exaggeration is a distortion of the truth.* **2** condition of being distorted. **3** anything distorted: *Her story was full of distortions.* **4** damage to the quality of a radio or television signal.

distortion (def. 2)

dis·tract (dis trakt′), *v.* **1** to draw away the mind, attention, etc.: *Noise distracts me when I am trying to study.* **2** to confuse; disturb: *Several people talking at once distract a listener.*

dis·trac·tion (dis trak′shən), *n.* **1** thing that draws away the mind, attention, etc.: *Noise is a distraction when you are trying to study.* **2** relief from continued thought, grief, or effort; amusement: *Movies and TV are popular distractions.* **3** confusion of mind; disturbance of thought: *The parents of the lost child scarcely knew what they were doing in their distraction.* **4** act of drawing away the mind, attention, etc.

dis·traught (dis trôt′), *adj.* in a state of mental conflict and confusion; distracted: *distraught with fear.*

dis·tress (dis tres′), **1** *n.* great pain or sorrow; anxiety; trouble: *The loss of our kitten caused us much distress.* **2** *v.* to cause great pain or sorrow to; make unhappy: *Your tears distress me.* **3** *n.* something that causes distress; misfortune: *The failure of his business was a great distress to him.* **4** *n.* a dangerous condition; difficult situation: *A sinking ship is in distress.* —**dis·tress′ing·ly,** *adv.*

dis·tress·ful (dis tres′fəl), *adj.* causing distress; painful. —**dis·tress′ful·ly,** *adv.* —**dis·tress′ful·ness,** *n.*

dis·trib·ute (dis trib′yüt), *v.* **1** to give some of to each; divide and give out in shares; deal out: *I distributed the candy among my friends.* **2** to spread; scatter: *A painter should distribute the paint evenly over a wall.* **3** to divide or arrange into groups; sort: *The books were distributed into groups according to subject. A mail clerk distributes mail by putting each letter into the proper bag.* ❑ *v.* **dis·trib·ut·ed, dis·trib·ut·ing.**

dis·tri·bu·tion (dis′trə byü′shən), *n.* **1** act of distributing: *After the contest the distribution of prizes to the winners took place.* **2** way of being distributed: *If some get more than others, there is an uneven distribution.* **3** act or process of distributing to consumers of goods grown or made by producers. **4** thing distributed. —**dis′tri·bu′tion·al,** *adj.*

dis·trib·u·tive (dis trib′yə tiv), *adj.* **1** (in grammar) referring to each individual of a group considered separately. *Each, every, and either are distributive pronouns.* **2** (in mathematics) of a rule that multiplication produces the same result when performed on a set of numbers as when performed on the numbers individually. EXAMPLE: $3(4 + 5) = (3 \times 4) + (3 \times 5)$. **3** of or about distribution. —**dis·trib′u·tive·ly,** *adv.*

dis·trib·u·tor (dis trib′yə tər), *n.* **1** person or company that distributes goods to consumers. **2** part of a gasoline engine that distributes electric current to the spark plugs. **3** person or thing that distributes.

dis·trict (dis′trikt), **1** *n.* part of a larger area; region: *The leading farming district of the United States is in the Middle West.* **2** *n.* part of a country, state, or city marked off for a special purpose such as providing schools or courts of law, or electing certain government officials. ■ See Synonym Study at **zone.** **3** *v.* to divide into districts.

district attorney, lawyer who prosecutes cases for the government within a certain district of a state or the country.

District of Columbia, district in E United States between Maryland and Virginia, governed by the Federal government. It is entirely occupied by the national capital, Washington. *Abbreviation:* DC or D.C. [**District of Columbia** comes from the name of Christopher Columbus.]

dis·trust (dis trust′), **1** *v.* to have no confidence in; not trust; be suspicious of; doubt: *Many people distrust statements made in advertisements.* **2** *n.* lack of trust or confidence; suspicion: *I could not explain my distrust of the stranger.*

dis·trust·ful (dis trust′fəl), *adj.* not trusting; suspicious. —**dis·trust′ful·ly,** *adv.* —**dis·trust′ful·ness,** *n.*

dis·turb (dis tėrb′), *v.* **1** to break in upon with noise or change: *Please don't disturb her while she's studying.* **2** to make uneasy; trouble: *He was disturbed to hear of his friend's illness.* **3** to destroy the peace, quiet, or rest of: *Truck traffic disturbed the neighborhood all day long.* **4** to put out of order: *Someone has disturbed my books; I can't find the one I want.* **5** to inconvenience: *Don't disturb yourself; I can do it.* —**dis·turb′er,** *n.*

dis·turb·ance (dis tėr′bəns), *n.* **1** confusion; disorder: *The police were called to quiet the disturbance at the street corner.* **2** thing that disturbs: *Turn off the TV, so it won't be a disturbance.* **3** act of disturbing or condition of being disturbed. **4** uneasiness; trouble; worry.

di·sul·fide (dī sul′fīd), *n.* (in chemistry) compound made of two atoms of sulfur combined with another element.

dis·un·ion (dis yü′nyən), *n.* **1** separation; division. **2** lack of unity; disagreement; unfriendliness.

dis·u·nite (dis′yü nīt′), *v.* to destroy the unity of; cause to disagree or to become unfriendly. ❑ *v.* **dis·u·nit·ed, dis·u·nit·ing.**

dis·u·ni·ty (dis yü′nə tē), *n.* lack of unity; disunion; dissension.

dis·use (dis yüs′), *n.* lack of use; not being used: *The old tools were rusted from disuse.*

ditch (dich), **1** *n.* a long, narrow hole dug in the earth. Ditches are usually used to carry off water. **2** *v.* to dig a ditch in or around. **3** *v.* to drive or throw into a ditch: *The careless driver skidded off the road and ditched the car.* **4** *v.* to make a forced landing or crash-landing in an airplane: *The pilot ditched the plane in the lake.* **5** *v.* INFORMAL. to get rid of: *The robber ditched the gun in a sewer.* ❑ *n., pl.* **ditch·es.**

dith·er (diᴛн′ər), *n.* a confused, excited condition: *He's in a dither about tomorrow's test.*

dit·to (dit′ō), **1** *n.* the same; exactly the same as appeared or was said before. **2** *n.* ditto mark. **3** *n.* a copy; duplicate. **4** *adv.* as said before; likewise. ❑ *n., pl.* **dit·tos.**

WORD STORY Ditto comes from a Latin word meaning "to say." Ditty comes from the same word. **Ditto** is a way not to say something all over again, while a **ditty** is something easy to say.

ditto mark, a small mark (″) used to avoid repeating something written immediately above. Ditto marks are often used on long lists, bills, tables, etc. EXAMPLE:

6 lb. apples at 75¢	. . . .	$4.50
4 ″ grapes ″ ″	. . . .	3.00

dit·ty (dit′ē), *n.* a short, simple song or poem. ❑ *n., pl.* **dit·ties.** [See Word Story at **ditto.**]

di·ur·nal (dī ėr′nl), *adj.* **1** occurring every day; daily: *Sunrise is a diurnal event.* **2** of or belonging to the daytime: *Diurnal temperatures are usually higher than those of the night.* **3** active in the daytime: *Butterflies are diurnal.* —**di·ur′nal·ly,** *adv.*

di·van (dī′van *or* də van′), *n.* a long, low, soft couch or sofa, usually with no arms or back.

dive (dīv), **1** *v.* to plunge headfirst into water. **2** *n.* act of diving: *The crowd applauded the girl's graceful dive.* **3** *v.* to go down or out of sight suddenly: *The gopher dived into its hole and disappeared.* **4** *v.* to plunge the hand suddenly into anything: *He dived into his pockets and brought out a dollar.* **5** *v.* to plunge with the mind; begin with energy and zeal: *She dived into her work with enthusiasm.* **6** *v.* to plunge downward at a steep angle: *The hawk*

dived straight at the field mouse. **7** *n.* a downward plunge at a steep angle: *The submarine made a dive toward the bottom.* **8** *n.* a cheap tavern or nightclub. ❏ *v.* **dived** or **dove, dived, div·ing.**
■ **Dive** has two past forms: **dived** and **dove**². Both are equally correct, and there is no difference in their meaning or use.

dive bomber, bomber that releases its load of bombs just before it pulls out of a dive toward the target.

div·er (dī′vər), *n.* **1** person who dives. **2** person whose occupation is working or diving under water. **3** any diving bird. Loons, penguins, and some ducks are divers.

di·verge (də vėrj′ *or* dī vėrj′), *v.* **1** to move or lie in different directions from the same point; branch off: *Their paths diverged at the fork in the road; he turned left, and she turned right.* **2** to differ; vary; deviate: *Contestants who diverge from the rules will be eliminated from the competition.* ❏ *v.* **di·verged, di·verg·ing.**

di·ver·gence (də vėr′jəns *or* dī vėr′jəns), *n.* difference: *The committee couldn't come to an agreement because of the wide divergence of opinion among its members.*

di·ver·gent (də vėr′jənt *or* dī vėr′jənt), *adj.* diverging; different. —**di·ver′gent·ly,** *adv.*

di·vers (dī′vərz), *adj.* more than one; several different; various: *A well-balanced diet is made up of divers foods.*

di·verse (də vėrs′), *adj.* not alike; different; varied: *Many diverse opinions were expressed at the meeting.* —**di·verse′ly,** *adv.* —**di·verse′ness,** *n.*

di·ver·si·fy (də vėr′sə fī), *v.* **1** to make diverse; give variety to; vary: *diversify your interests. Mountains, plains, trees, and lakes diversify the landscape.* **2** to buy different kinds of investments, in order to reduce risk of loss. **3** to make a business or company larger by making different kinds of products. ❏ *v.* **di·ver·si·fied, di·ver·si·fy·ing.** —**di·ver′si·fi·ca′tion,** *n.*

di·ver·sion (də vėr′zhən), *n.* **1** act of turning aside; a diverting: *A magician's talk creates a diversion of attention so that people do not see how the tricks are done.* **2** distraction from work, care, etc.; amusement; entertainment; pastime: *Golf is my parents' favorite diversion.*

di·ver·si·ty (də vėr′sə tē), *n.* **1** variety: *The diversity of faces in the crowd was fascinating to look at.* **2** unlikeness. **3** differences or variety among living things; biodiversity.

diversity (def. 1)

di·vert (də vėrt′), *v.* **1** to turn aside: *A ditch diverted water from the stream into the fields. The siren of the fire engine diverted the audience's attention from the play.* **2** to amuse; entertain: *Listening to music diverted him after a hard day's work.*

di·vest (də vest′), *v.* **1** to rid or free; strip: *We divested ourselves of our clothes and dived into the water.* **2** to force to give up; deprive: *A person in prison is divested of the right to vote.*

di·vide (də vīd′), **1** *v.* to separate into parts: *A brook divides the field. The path divides at the pond.* ■ See Synonym Study at **separate. 2** *v.* to separate into equal parts: *When you divide 8 by 2, you get 4.* **3** *v.* to give some of to each; share: *They divided the candy.* **4** *v.* to sort out by kinds; classify: *We divided the cards into suits.* **5** *v.* to disagree or cause to disagree; separate in feeling, opinion, etc.: *The school divided on the question of a short-*

er lunch hour. **6** *n.* ridge of land between two regions drained by different river systems: *The Rocky Mountains form part of the Continental Divide.* ❏ *v.* **di·vid·ed, di·vid·ing.**

div·i·dend (div′ə dend), *n.* **1** number or quantity to be divided by another: *In 728 ÷ 16, 728 is the dividend.* **2** money earned by a company and divided among the owners or stockholders as their share of the profits. **3** share of such money.

di·vid·er (də vī′dər), *n.* **1** something that divides: *There is a concrete divider in the center of the parkway.* **2 dividers,** *pl.* compass used for dividing lines, measuring distances, etc.

div·i·na·tion (div′ə nā′shən), *n.* **1** act of foreseeing the future or foretelling the unknown by inspiration, by magic, or by signs and omens. **2** a skillful guess or prediction.

di·vine (də vīn′), **1** *adj.* of God or a god: *The Bible describes the creation of the world as a divine act.* **2** *adj.* given by or coming from God: *The queen believed her power to rule was a divine right.* **3** *adj.* to or for God; sacred; holy: *Services for divine worship were held daily.* **4** *adj.* like God or a god; heavenly. **5** *adj.* INFORMAL. excellent or delightful; unusually good or great: *Oh, what a divine vacation we had!* **6** *n.* member of the clergy who knows a great deal about theology; minister; priest. **7** *v.* to foresee or foretell by inspiration, by magic, or by signs and omens; predict. **8** *v.* to find out without actually knowing; guess correctly: *We divined who had eaten the cake from the guilty looks on the children's faces.* ❏ *v.* **di·vined, di·vin·ing.** —**di·vine′ly,** *adv.* —**di·vine′ness,** *n.*

di·vin·er (də vī′nər), *n.* person who foresees or foretells things; prophet.

diving bell, a large, hollow container filled with air and open at the bottom. People can work in it under water.

diving board, a flexible board attached to the side of a pool and extending out over the water, from which someone can dive.

diving suit, a waterproof suit with a helmet into which air can be pumped through a tube. Diving suits are worn by persons working under water.

di·vin·i·ty (də vin′ə tē), *n.* **1** a divine being; god or goddess. **2 the Divinity,** God. **3** divine nature or quality. **4** study of God, religion, and divine things; theology. ❏ *n., pl.* **di·vin·i·ties** for 1.

di·vis·i·ble (də viz′ə bəl), *adj.* **1** able to be divided. **2** able to be divided without leaving a remainder: *12 is divisible by 1, 2, 3, 4, 6, and 12.* —**di·vis′i·bil′i·ty,** *n.*

di·vi·sion (də vizh′ən), *n.* **1** one of the parts into which a thing is divided; group; section: *the research division of a drug company.* **2** operation of dividing one number by another: *26 ÷ 2 = 13 is a simple division.* **3** act of giving some to each; sharing: *The making of cars in large numbers is made possible by a division of labor, in which each worker has a certain part of the work to do.* **4** act of dividing or condition of being divided: *the division of land into lots for houses.* **5** something that divides: *This fence is the division between your property and mine.* **6** a military unit made up of several brigades or regiments plus supporting troops, usually commanded by a major general. It is smaller than a corps. **7** a difference of opinion, thought, or feeling; disagreement: *There was a division in our class over the date for our spring trip.*

division sign, the symbol ÷ which represents the arithmetic operation of division. The divisor follows the division sign.

di·vi·sive (də vī′siv), *adj.* tending to cause disagreement. —**di·vi′sive·ly,** *adv.* —**di·vi′sive·ness,** *n.*

di·vi·sor (də vī′zər), *n.* number or quantity by which another is to be divided: *In 728 ÷ 16, 16 is the divisor.*

di·vorce (də vôrs′), **1** *n.* the legal ending of a marriage. **2** *v.* to end legally a marriage between: *The judge divorced the husband and wife.* **3** *v.* to separate from by a divorce: *She divorced her husband.* **4** *v.* to separate: *The writers of the Constitution wanted*

a	hat	ė	term	ô	order	ch	child		
ā	age	i	it	oi	oil	ng	long		a in about
ä	far	ī	ice	ou	out	sh	she		e in taken
â	care	o	hot	u	cup	th	thin	ə	i in pencil
e	let	ō	open	ù	put	ᴛʜ	then		o in lemon
ē	equal	ȯ	saw	ü	rule	zh	measure		u in circus

to divorce government and religion in the United States. **5** *n.* separation: *Some people prefer a complete divorce of government and religion.* ❑ *v.* **di·vorced, di·vorc·ing.** —**di·vorce′ment,** *n.*

di·vor·cé (də vôr sā′), *n.* a divorced man. ❑ *n., pl.* **di·vor·cés.**

di·vor·cée (də vôr sā′), *n.* a divorced woman. ❑ *n., pl.* **di·vor·cées.**

div·ot (div′ət), *n.* a small clump of grass or dirt dug up when a golfer's club strikes the ball.

di·vulge (də vulj′ *or* di vulj′), *v.* to make known; tell; reveal: *At the end of the story Sherlock Holmes divulged the name of the murderer.* ❑ *v.* **di·vulged, di·vulg·ing.**

div·vy (div′ē), *v.* INFORMAL. to share or divide: *We divvied up the money we won between us.* ❑ *v.* **div·vied, div·vy·ing.**

Dix (diks), *n.* **Dor·o·the·a** (dôr′ə thē′ə), 1802-1887, American reformer. She worked for better treatment of the mentally ill and for better prison conditions.

Dix·ie (dik′sē), *n.* the southern states of the United States. [No one knows where **Dixie** comes from. Also see Word Story at **Mason-Dixon line.**]

Dix·ie·land (dik′sē land′), *n.* a style of jazz which began in New Orleans, with a strong beat, fast tunes, and a lot of improvising.

diz·zy (diz′ē), **1** *adj.* likely to fall, stagger, or spin around; not steady: *When you spin round and round, and stop suddenly, you feel dizzy.* **2** *adj.* confused; bewildered: *The noise and crowds of the city streets made the boy dizzy.* **3** *v.* to make dizzy: *The ride on the merry-go-round dizzied her.* **4** *adj.* likely to make dizzy; causing dizziness: *The airplane climbed to a dizzy height.* ❑ *adj.* **diz·zi·er, diz·zi·est;** *v.* **diz·zied, diz·zy·ing.** [**Dizzy** comes from an old English word meaning "foolish." When you are very dizzy, you may feel and act foolish.] —**diz′zi·ly,** *adv.* —**diz′zi·ness,** *n.*

DJ *or* **D.J.,** disk jockey.

Dja·kar·ta (jə kär′tə), *n.* Jakarta.

Dji·bou·ti (ji bü′tē), *n.* **1** country in E Africa. **2** its capital, a port on the Gulf of Aden.

D layer, D region.

DMZ, demilitarized zone.

DNA, a large, complex molecule found in the nuclei of all living cells; deoxyribonucleic acid. It is the substance of which genes are made and is chiefly responsible for the transmission of inherited characteristics.

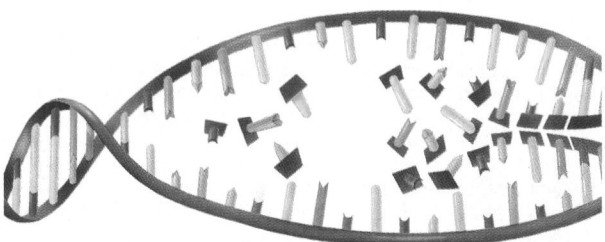

DNA—diagram showing molecular structure

do¹ (dü), *v.* **1** to carry through to an end any action or piece of work; carry out; perform: *Do your work well.* **2** to produce; make: *She did a book on her travels in Africa.* **3** to act; behave: *You did very well in ignoring the insult.* **4** to be the cause of; bring about: *Your work does you credit.* **5** to deal with; take care of: *do the dishes, do your hair.* **6** to get along; manage; fare: *My sister is doing well in her new job.* **7** to be satisfactory: *This hat will do.* **8** to work at; exert yourself: *We did everything we could to help the survivors.* **9** to work out; solve: *do an arithmetic problem.* **10** to go at a speed of: *We did 55 miles an hour all the way to Miami.* **11** to give: *do justice to an innocent victim.* **12** *Do* is used: **a** to ask questions: *Do you like milk?* **b** to make what you say stronger: *I do want to go.* **c** to stand for another verb already used: *My dog goes where I do.* **d** in expressions that contain *not*: *People talk; animals do not.* ❑ *v.* **did, done, do·ing.** ∎ Other words that sound like this are **dew, 'do,** and **due.** —**do′a·ble,** *adj.*

do away with, 1 to put an end to; abolish: *do away with a rule.* **2** to kill: *The trap did away with the rat.*

do for, ruin or damage: *That fire means my business is done for.*

do in, 1 ruin. **2** INFORMAL. kill: *They plotted to do him in.* **3** exhaust: *That hike really did me in.*

do up, 1 to wrap up; tie up: *Please do up this package more securely.* **2** to arrange: *do up your hair.*

do without, to get along without.

SYNONYM STUDY **Do**¹, **accomplish,** and **perform** all mean to carry on an activity to its end. **Do** is a general word: *I did my homework before turning on the TV.* **Accomplish** means to finish something that needs time and effort: *Did you accomplish all those tasks today?* **Perform** means to do something that needs practice: *The doctor performed a difficult operation.*

do² (dō), *n.* (in music) the first and last tone of the scale. *Do, re, mi, fa, sol, la, ti, do* are the names of the tones of the scale. ❑ *n., pl.* **dos.** ∎ Other words that sound like this are **doe** and **dough.**

'do (dü), *n.* SLANG. hairdo. ❑ *n., pl.* **'dos.** ∎ Other words that sound like this are **dew, do**¹, and **due.**

DOA, dead on arrival.

dob·bin (dob′ən), *n.* a slow, gentle, plodding horse.

Do·ber·man pin·scher (dō′bər mən pin′shər), a medium-sized, slender dog with short, dark hair.

do·cent (dō′snt), *n.* **1** a lecturer at a college or university. **2** a guide, especially a person who gives tours of a museum.

doc·ile (dos′əl), *adj.* easily trained or managed; obedient: *a docile horse, a docile student.* —**do·cil′i·ty,** *n.* —**doc′ile·ly,** *adv.*

dock¹ (dok), **1** *n.* platform built on the shore or out from the shore; wharf; pier. Ships load and unload beside a dock. **2** *v.* to come or bring to such a platform: *The ship docked at dawn.* **3** *n.* water between two piers, permitting the entrance of ships. **4** *n.* place where a ship may be repaired, often built watertight so that the water may be kept high or pumped out. **5** *n.* platform for loading and unloading trucks or freight cars. **6** *v.* to join two spacecraft while in space.

dock² (dok), *v.* **1** to cut down; cut some off of: *Workers' wages are docked if they are late.* **2** to cut short; cut off the end of. Horses' and dogs' tails are sometimes docked.

dock³ (dok), *n.* the place where an accused person stands or sits in a court of law.

dock⁴ (dok), *n.* any of several large weeds with sour or bitter leaves and clusters of greenish flowers.

dock·et (dok′it), **1** *n.* list of lawsuits to be tried by a court. **2** *n.* any list of matters to be considered by some person or group. **3** *v.* to enter on a docket. **4** *n.* label or ticket giving the contents of a package, document, etc.

dock·yard (dok′yärd′), *n.* shipyard.

doc·tor (dok′tər), **1** *n.* person trained and licensed to treat diseases or injuries. Physicians, surgeons, dentists, and veterinarians are doctors. **2** *v.* to treat disease in: *My sister doctored me when I had a cold.* **3** *n.* person who has the highest degree given by a university: *a Doctor of Philosophy.* **4** *v.* to falsify; tamper with: *to doctor the books.* —**doc′tor·al,** *adj.*

doc·tor·ate (dok′tər it), *n.* a doctor's degree given by a university.

doc·trine (dok′trən), *n.* **1** what is taught as true by a church, nation, or group of persons; belief: *religious doctrine.* **2** what is taught; teachings. —**doc′tri·nal,** *adj.* —**doc′tri·nal·ly,** *adv.*

doc·u·dra·ma (dok′yə drä′mə *or* dok′yə dram′ə), *n.* a TV show, often broadcast in several parts, that has facts combined with fictional events added for greater interest. ❑ *n., pl.* **doc·u·dra·mas.**

doc·u·ment (dok′yə mənt *for noun,* dok′yə ment *for verb*), **1** *n.* something written or printed that gives information or proof of some fact; any object used as evidence. Letters, maps, and pictures are documents. **2** *v.* to prove or support by means of documents or the like: *Can you document your theory with facts?*

doc·u·men·tar·y (dok′yə men′tər ē), **1** *adj.* consisting of documents; in writing, print, etc.: *The photographs were used as documentary evidence at the trial.* **2** *adj.* presenting or recording factual information in an artistic way: *a documentary film about the history of Boston.* **3** *n.* a documentary movie, book, or radio or TV show. ❑ *n., pl.* **doc·u·men·tar·ies.**

doc·u·men·ta·tion (dok′yə men tā′shən), *n.* **1** preparation and use of documentary evidence. **2** proof or support of a claim or opinion by documentary evidence: *Your essay lacks proper documentation.* **3** instructions and other information explaining how a computer, computer program, or computer accessory machine works. Documentation may be provided in printed or electronic form.

dod·der (dod′ər), *v.* to be unsteady; shake; tremble; totter.

dodge (doj), **1** *v.* to move or jump quickly to one side: *As I looked, they dodged behind a bush.* **2** *v.* to avoid by jumping or moving to one side; get away from by twisting or turning quickly aside: *She dodged the bicycle as it came flying at her.* **3** *n.* a sudden movement to one side. **4** *v.* to avoid by cleverness; get away from by some trick: *She dodged our question by changing the subject.* **5** *n.* a trick intended to cheat someone: *a clever dodge to avoid taxes.* ❑ *v.* **dodged, dodg·ing.** —**dodg′er,** *n.*

dodge·ball (doj′bôl′), *n.* a children's game in which players stand in a circle or in two opposite lines, and try to hit other players inside the circle or in the other line with a large rubber ball.

Dodg·son (doj′sən), *n.* **Charles L.,** the real name of **Lewis Carroll.**

do·do (dō′dō), *n.* a large, clumsy bird that could not fly. Dodos lived on Mauritius in the Indian Ocean until they were hunted to extinction in the 1600s. ❑ *n., pl.* **do·dos** or **do·does.**

dodo—4 ft. (1.2 m) long

WORD STORY   **Dodo** comes from a Portuguese word meaning "a fool." Because the bird was clumsy, could not fly, and did not fear hunters, the hunters thought of it as foolish.

Do·do·ma (dō′dō mä), *n.* capital of Tanzania.

doe (dō), *n.* a female deer, goat, hare, rabbit, or antelope. ◼ Other words that sound like this are **do²** and **dough.**

do·er (dü′ər), *n.* person who does something, especially with energy and drive: *He is a doer, not a dreamer.*

does (duz), *v.* a present tense of **do¹**: *He does all his work.*

doe·skin (dō′skin′), *n.* **1** a soft leather, now usually made from lambskin. **2** a smooth, soft woolen cloth, used for clothing.

does·n't (duz′nt), does not. ◼ See Usage Note at **don't.**

doff (dof), *v.* to take off; remove: *He doffed his hat.*

dog (dȯg), **1** *n.* a four-legged, flesh-eating mammal kept as a pet and used for hunting and for guarding property. Dogs are related to wolves, foxes, and coyotes. **2** *v.* to hunt or follow like a dog: *Bill collectors dogged them for over a month.* ❑ *v.* **dogged, dog·ging.** —**dog′like′,** *adj.*

go to the dogs, be ruined: *The house was not looked after and soon went to the dogs.*

dog·cart (dȯg′kärt′), *n.* **1** a small cart pulled by dogs. **2** a small, open, horse-drawn carriage with two seats that are placed back to back.

dog·catch·er (dȯg′kach′ər), *n.* person whose work is to catch stray dogs.

dog days, period of very hot and uncomfortable weather during July and August.

WORD STORY   **Dog days** comes from a constellation called the Big Dog by the Romans. The very bright star Sirius, called the Dog Star, is in this constellation. During the hottest weeks of summer, Sirius rises when the sun does, and people believed that it added to the sun's heat.

doge (dōj), *n.* the chief magistrate of Venice or Genoa when they were republics.

dog-ear (dȯg′ir′), **1** *n.* a folded-down corner of a page in a book. A dog-ear is often made to mark the page where the reader has stopped. **2** *v.* to fold down the corner of a page in a book.

dog-eared (dȯg′ird′), *adj.* badly worn: *dog-eared carpets.*

dog·fight (dȯg′fit′), *n.* **1** combat between individual fighter planes at close quarters. **2** brawl.

dog·fish (dȯg′fish′), *n.* any of numerous kinds of small shark. ❑ *n., pl.* **dog·fish** or **dog·fish·es.**

dog·ged (dȯ′gid), *adj.* not giving up; stubborn; persistent: *Her dogged determination helped her to win the prize.* —**dog′ged·ly,** *adv.* —**dog′ged·ness,** *n.*

dog·ger·el (dȯ′gər əl), **1** *n.* very poor poetry; poetry that is not artistic. **2** *adj.* crude; poor; not artistic: *doggerel verses.*

dog·gie (dȯ′gē), *n.* **1** a little dog. **2** an affectionate name for a dog whose name you don't know. Also, **doggy.**

dog·gie bag or **dog·gy bag,** a small bag furnished by a restaurant to a customer who has not finished a meal, so that the uneaten food may be carried home.

dog guide, dog that has been trained to lead or guide someone with impaired sight or hearing; guide dog.

dog·gy (dȯ′gē), **1** *adj.* like a dog: *The rug had a doggy smell.* **2** *n.* doggie. ❑ *adj.* **dog·gi·er, dog·gi·est;** *n., pl.* **dog·gies.**

dog·house (dȯg′hous′), *n.* a small house or shelter for a dog. ❑ *n., pl.* **dog·hous·es** (dȯg′hou′ziz).

in the doghouse, out of favor: *I am in the doghouse with my parents for staying out too late last night.*

do·gie (dō′gē), *n.* (in the western United States and Canada) a motherless calf on the range or in a range herd. [No one knows where **dogie** comes from.]

dog·ma (dȯg′mə), *n.* **1** belief taught or held as true, especially by authority of a church; doctrine. **2** opinion stated in a positive manner as if it were of the highest authority. ❑ *n., pl.* **dog·mas.**

dog·mat·ic (dȯg mat′ik), *adj.* **1** positive and emphatic in stating opinions: *The audience disliked the speaker's dogmatic manner in stating his opinions as if they were facts.* **2** of or about dogma; doctrinal. —**dog·mat′i·cal·ly,** *adv.*

dog·ma·tism (dȯg′mə tiz′əm), *n.* positive and emphatic statement of opinion.

dog paddle, a very simple form of swimming by paddling with the arms under water while shoving the legs backward, somewhat as dogs swim. —**dog-pad·dle,** *v.*

Dog·rib (dȯg′rib′), *n.* member of a tribe of American Indians that live in Northwest Territories, Canada. ❑ *n., pl.* **Dog·rib** or **Dog·ribs.**

WORD STORY   **Dogrib** is an English translation of the Indian name. According to a myth of the tribe, the Dogrib began as children of a man who could turn into a dog.

dog·sled (dȯg′sled′), *n.* sled that is pulled by dogs.

Dog Star, Sirius.

dog·trot (dȯg′trot′), *n.* a gentle, easy trot.

dog·wood (dȯg′wud′), *n.* any of several trees or bushes, especially one kind with large white or pinkish flowers in the spring and red berries in the fall. Its flower is the provincial flower of British Columbia.

Do·ha (dō′hə), *n.* port and capital of Qatar, on the Persian Gulf.

doi·ly (doi′lē), *n.* a small piece of linen, lace, paper, or plastic, used under a dish or vase as a decoration or to protect the surface beneath it. ❑ *n., pl.* **doi·lies.**

do·ings (dü′ingz), *n.pl.* **1** activities; actions; events: *There were dances, parties, and lots of doings over the holidays.* **2** behavior; conduct.

do-it-your·self (dü′it yər self′), *adj.* designed for use, construction, or assembly by an amateur. —**do′-it-your·self′er,** *n.*

dol·drums (dol′drəmz or dōl′drəmz), *n.pl.* **1** gloomy feeling; low spirits: *My brother has been in the doldrums since he failed the history test.* **2** region of the ocean near the equator where the wind is very light or constantly shifting. When a sailing ship gets in the doldrums, it makes little headway.

dole (dōl), **1** *n.* portion of money, food, etc., given in charity. **2** *v.* to give out in portions to the poor. **3** *n.* a small portion. **4** *v.* to give in small portions: *Mom doled out a few raisins as a snack.* **5** *n.* money given by a government to unemployed workers. ❑ *v.* **doled, dol·ing.**

a	hat	ė	term	ô	order	ch	child		
ā	age	i	it	oi	oil	ng	long		a in about
ä	far	ī	ice	ou	out	sh	she	ə	e in taken
â	care	o	hot	u	cup	th	thin		i in pencil
e	let	ō	open	u̇	put	ŦH	then		o in lemon
ē	equal	ȯ	saw	ü	rule	zh	measure		u in circus

dole·ful (dōl′fəl), *adj.* very sad or dreary; mournful; dismal. —**dole′ful·ly**, *adv.* —**dole′ful·ness**, *n.*

doll (dol), **1** *n.* a child's toy made to look like a person, usually a baby or child. **2** *n.* a pretty child, girl, or woman. ■ Used about women, this meaning of **doll** is sometimes considered offensive. **3** *v.* INFORMAL. to dress in a stylish or showy way: *They were all dolled up in party clothes.* —**doll′-like′**, *adj.*

> **WORD STORY** **Doll** comes from a nickname for *Dorothy.* Hundreds of years ago, people began using the nickname to mean "girlfriend." Most dolls at that time were made to look like dressed-up young women.

dol·lar (dol′ər), *n.* **1** unit of money in the United States. **2** a similar unit of money in Canada, Australia, and some other countries.

doll·house (dol′hous′), *n.* a toy house for children to use in playing with dolls. ❑ *n., pl.* **doll·hous·es** (dol′hou′ziz).

dol·lop (dol′əp), *n.* portion or serving, either large or small.

doll·y (dol′ē), *n.* **1** a child's name for a doll. **2** a small, low frame on wheels, used to move heavy things: *The refrigerator was moved into the house on a dolly.* ❑ *n., pl.* **doll·ies.**

do·lor (dō′lər), *n.* OLD USE. sorrow; grief.

dol·or·ous (dol′ər əs *or* dō′lər əs), *adj.* **1** full of or expressing sorrow; mournful. **2** causing or giving rise to sorrow; grievous; painful. —**dol′or·ous·ly**, *adv.*

dol·phin (dol′fən), *n.* **1** any of numerous sea mammals related to the whale, but smaller. Dolphins have beaklike snouts and remarkable intelligence. **2** either of two large saltwater fishes that change color when taken from the water.

dolphin (def. 1)—about 10 ft. (3 m) long

dolt (dōlt), *n.* a dull, stupid person.

dolt·ish (dōl′tish), *adj.* like a dolt; dull and stupid. —**dolt′ish·ly**, *adv.* —**dolt′ish·ness**, *n.*

do·main (dō mān′), *n.* **1** territory under the control of one ruler or government. **2** land owned by one person; estate. **3** field of thought or action: *the domain of science, the domain of religion.*

dome (dōm), *n.* **1** a large, rounded roof or ceiling on a circular or many-sided base. **2** something high and rounded: *the dome of a hill.* **3** a large closed sports arena with a curved ceiling. —**dome′-like′**, *adj.*

do·mes·tic (də mes′tik), **1** *adj.* of the home, household, or family affairs: *The roommates shared cooking, cleaning, and other domestic duties.* **2** *adj.* fond of home and family life: *He is a domestic man who enjoys spending time with his children.* **3** *n.* servant in a household. A butler or a maid is a domestic. **4** *adj.* not wild; tame. Cats, dogs, cows, horses, and pigs are domestic animals. **5** *adj.* of or made in your own country; not foreign: *Most newspapers publish both domestic and foreign news.* [See Word Story at **dame**.] —**do·mes′ti·cal·ly**, *adv.*

do·mes·ti·cate (də mes′tə kāt), *v.* **1** to change from a wild to a tame or cultivated state: *People have domesticated many plants and animals.* ■ See Synonym Study at **tame**. **2** to make fond of home and family life. ❑ *v.* **do·mes·ti·cat·ed, do·mes·ti·cat·ing.** —**do·mes′ti·ca′tion**, *n.*

do·mes·tic·i·ty (dō′mes tis′ə tē), *n.* **1** home and family life. **2** fondness for home and family life.

dom·i·cile (dom′ə sil), **1** *n.* a dwelling place; house; home. **2** *n.* place of permanent residence. A person may have several residences, but only one legal domicile at a time. **3** *v.* to settle in a domicile. ❑ *v.* **dom·i·ciled, dom·i·cil·ing.**

dom·i·nance (dom′ə nəns), *n.* controlling influence; supreme authority; rule; control.

dom·i·nant (dom′ə nənt), **1** *adj.* most powerful or influential; controlling; ruling; governing: *She was a dominant figure in local politics.* **2** *adj.* rising high above its surroundings; towering over: *Dominant hills sheltered the bay.* **3** *n.* the fifth note in a musical scale. G is the dominant in the key of C. **4** *n.* dominant gene. —**dom′i·nant·ly**, *adv.*

dominant gene, one of a pair of genes that overcomes the effect of the other. The gene for brown eyes is a dominant gene. If it is paired with a gene for blue eyes, the gene for blue eyes will be overcome.

dom·i·nate (dom′ə nāt), *v.* **1** to control or rule by strength or power: *She has the authority needed to dominate the meeting.* **2** to rise high above; tower over: *The mountain dominates the city and its harbor.* ❑ *v.* **dom·i·nat·ed, dom·i·nat·ing.** [See Word Story at **dame**.] —**dom′i·na′tive**, *adj.* —**dom′i·na′tor**, *n.*

dom·i·na·tion (dom′ə nā′shən), *n.* act of dominating; control; rule: *The champion's long domination of archery ended when the challenger defeated her.*

dom·i·neer (dom′ə nir′), *v.* to rule or assert your authority or opinions in an arrogant way: *The oldest child in a family may sometimes domineer over the younger children.*

dom·i·neer·ing (dom′ə nir′ing), *adj.* inclined to domineer; arrogant; overbearing: *I dislike the domineering attitude of people who always want things done their own way.* —**dom′i·neer′ing·ly**, *adv.*

Do·min·go (dō ming′gō), *n.* **Pla·cid·o** (plä′sĭ dō), born 1941, Spanish opera singer.

Dom·i·nic (dom′ə nik), *n.* **Saint,** 1170-1221, Spanish priest who founded an order of preaching friars, called **Dominicans.** [**Dominic** comes from a Latin word meaning "of the Lord."]

Dom·i·ni·ca (dom′ə nē′kə *or* də min′ə kə), *n.* island country in the Caribbean. *Capital:* Roseau.

Do·min·i·can (də min′ə kən), **1** *adj.* of Saint Dominic or the religious order founded by him. **2** *n.* friar belonging to the Dominican order. **3** *adj.* of or about the Dominican Republic. **4** *n.* person born or living in the Dominican Republic.

Dominican Republic, country in the E part of the island of Hispaniola, in the West Indies. *Capital:* Santo Domingo.

do·min·ion (də min′yən), *n.* **1** power or right of governing and controlling; rule; control: *The ancient Romans had dominion over a large part of the world.* **2** territory under the control of one ruler or government. **3** Dominion, name formerly used for a self-governing country within the British Commonwealth.

Dominion Day, former name of **Canada Day.**

dom·i·no (dom′ə nō), *n.* **1** dominoes, *pl.* game played with flat, oblong pieces of wood or plastic that are either blank or marked with dots. Players try to match pieces having blanks or the same number of dots. **2** one of the pieces used in the game of dominoes. **3** a loose cloak with a small mask covering the upper part of the face. It was formerly worn as a disguise at masquerades. **4** the small mask. ❑ *n., pl.* **dom·i·noes** *or* **dom·i·nos.**

don[1] (don), *v.* to put on (clothing, etc.): *The knight donned his armor.* ❑ *v.* **donned, don·ning.** [**Don**[1] is short for *do on,* meaning "put on."]

don[2] (don), *n.* **1** Don, a Spanish title meaning Mister or Sir: *Don Juan.* **2** a head, fellow, or tutor of a college at Oxford or Cambridge University in England.

Don (don), *n.* river in SW Russia. [**Don** comes from a word meaning "river" in the prehistoric language that Indo-European languages came from.]

do·nate (dō′nāt), *v.* to give money or help, especially to a fund or institution; contribute: *She donated $200 to the community chest.* ❑ *v.* **do·nat·ed, do·nat·ing.** —**do′na·tor**, *n.*

do·na·tion (dō nā′shən), *n.* **1** gift of money or help; contribution: *The class made a donation to UNICEF.* **2** act of giving; donating.

done (dun), **1** *adj.* finished or completed; through: *He is done with his assignments.* **2** *adj.* cooked: *I want my steak well done.* **3** *v.* past participle of **do**¹: *Have you done all your chores?* ■ Another word that sounds like this is **dun**.

done in, exhausted: *After mowing the entire lawn, I was done in.*

Don Juan (don wän´), a legendary Spanish nobleman who had many love affairs.

don·key (dong´kē), *n.* **1** an animal somewhat like a small horse but with longer ears and a shorter mane; ass. **2** a stubborn person. **3** a silly fool; stupid person. ❏ *n., pl.* **don·keys.**

do·nor (dō´nər), *n.* person who donates; giver; contributor. A blood donor is a person who gives blood for a transfusion.

do·noth·ing (dü´nuth´ing), **1** *n.* person who does not act in situations requiring action. **2** *n.* a lazy person. **3** *adj.* refusing to act when action is required: *a do-nothing government.*

Don Qui·xo·te (don ki hō´tē), hero of a famous novel of the same name by the Spanish writer Cervantes. Don Quixote is chivalrous and idealistic, but also foolish and impractical.

don't (dōnt), do not.

Don Quixote—as imagined by an artist

USAGE NOTE **Don't** is sometimes used with *he, she,* or *it* in speech instead of **doesn't.** This use is not accepted in writing or in standard or formal speech. SAY: *She doesn't like our new teacher.* NOT: *She don't like our new teacher.*

do·nut (dō´nut´), *n.* doughnut.

doo·dad (dü´dad), *n.* INFORMAL. **1** a fancy, pointless ornament: *a bike with streamers and other doodads.* **2** doohickey.

doo·dle (dü´dl), **1** *v.* to make drawings or marks absent-mindedly while talking or thinking. **2** *n.* drawing or mark made absent-mindedly. ❏ *v.* **doo·dled, doo·dling. —doo´dler,** *n.*

doo·dle·bug (dü´dl bug´), *n.* larva of the ant lion.

doo·hick·ey (dü´hik´ē), *n.* an object or gadget with a name that is not known or not remembered; doodad. ❏ *n., pl.* **doo·hick·eys.**

doom (düm), **1** *n.* an unhappy or terrible fate; ruin or death: *As the ship sank, the voyagers faced their doom.* **2** *v.* to condemn to an unhappy or terrible fate: *The prisoner was doomed to death. Poor health doomed my cousin to an inactive life.* **3** *n.* judgment; sentence: *The judge pronounced the prisoner's doom.* **4** *v.* to make a bad or unwelcome outcome certain: *The weather doomed our hopes for a picnic.* [**Doom** comes from an old English word meaning "law" or "judgment." Judgment often doomed a prisoner.]

dooms·day (dümz´dā´), *n.* end of the world; Judgment Day.

door (dôr), *n.* **1** barrier that opens and shuts by turning on hinges or sliding on tracks. Doors may be set into the walls of buildings or rooms, into vehicles, upright furniture cabinets, stoves, etc. **2** doorway: *The salesman had a foot in the door.* **3** room, house, or building to which a door belongs: *Her house is three doors down the street from ours.* **4** way to go in or out; way to get something: *The door to knowledge is study.* **—door´·like´,** *adj.*

lay at the door of, to blame for.

out of doors, not in a house or building; outside.

show someone the door, to ask someone to leave: *When the two boys tried to crash the party my father showed them the door.*

door·bell (dôr´bel´), *n.* bell that a caller may ring by pressing a button or pulling a handle on the outside of a door to a house.

door·knob (dôr´nob´), *n.* handle on either side of a door, used for opening or closing the door.

door·man (dôr´mən), *n.* person whose work is opening or guarding the door of a hotel, store, apartment house, etc., for people going in or out. ❏ *n., pl.* **door·men.**

door·mat (dôr´mat´), *n.* mat placed near a door for wiping off the dirt from the bottom of your shoes before entering.

door·nail (dôr´nāl´), *n.* nail with a large head.

dead as a doornail, completely dead.

door·post (dôr´pōst´), *n.* the upright piece forming the side of a doorway.

door·step (dôr´step´), *n.* step leading from an outside door to the ground.

door·stop (dôr´stop´), *n.* **1** a wedge inserted under a door or an object placed against the lower part of a door to keep it open. **2** a small rubber-tipped spike attached to a wall that protects it when a door is opened.

door·way (dôr´wā´), *n.* an opening in a wall where a door is.

door·yard (dôr´yärd´), *n.* yard near the door of a house; yard around a house.

dope (dōp), **1** *n.* INFORMAL. a drug, such as heroin or marijuana. **2** *v.* INFORMAL. to give dope to. **3** *n.* SLANG. information. **4** *n.* INFORMAL. a very stupid person. **5** *n.* a thick varnish or similar liquid applied to a fabric to strengthen or waterproof it. Dope is sometimes used on model airplanes. ❏ *v.* **doped, dop·ing. —dop´er,** *n.*

WORD STORY **Dope** comes from a Dutch word meaning "sauce." **Dope** used to mean "gravy" in English. It became a slang word for any drug, and then for a person made unintelligent by drugs.

dop·ey or **dop·y** (dō´pē), *adj.* INFORMAL. **1** drugged; drowsy. **2** very stupid. ❏ *adj.* **dop·i·er, dop·i·est. —dop´i·ness,** *n.*

Dop·pler effect (dop´lər), (in physics) the apparent change in the frequency of sound waves or light waves when the distance between the source of the waves and the observer changes. Because of the Doppler effect, a car horn on a vehicle approaching you sounds higher in pitch than when it is moving away from you.

Doppler radar, type of radar that measures the speed of moving objects by using the Doppler effect.

Do·ric (dôr´ik), *adj.* of the oldest and simplest kind of Greek architecture.

dork (dôrk), *n.* SLANG. person perceived by others as foolish or ridiculous; jerk; nerd.

dork·y (dôr´kē), *adj.* SLANG. foolish; ridiculous; stupid; unattractive: *He insists on wearing that dorky shirt.* ❏ *adj.* **dork·i·er, dork·i·est. —dork´i·ness,** *n.*

dorm (dôrm), *n.* dormitory.

dor·mant (dôr´mənt), *adj.* **1** sleeping; seeming to sleep; not moving or feeling: *Bears are dormant during the winter.* **2** without activity; inactive: *Many volcanoes are dormant.*

dor·mer (dôr´mər), *n.* **1** an upright window that sticks out from a sloping roof. **2** the part of a roof that sticks out and contains such a window.

dormer

WORD STORY **Dormer** comes from a Latin word meaning "to sleep." **Dormitory** comes from the same word. The window got its name because many bedroom windows have this shape.

dor·mi·to·ry (dôr´mə tôr´ē), *n.* **1** a building with many rooms for sleeping in. Many colleges have dormitories for students whose homes are elsewhere. **2** room for sleeping that has several beds. ❏ *n., pl.* **dor·mi·to·ries.** [See Word Story at **dormer.**]

dor·mouse (dôr´mous´), *n.* a small rodent that looks something like a squirrel and sleeps all winter. ❏ *n., pl.* **dor·mice** (dôr´mis´).

dor·sal (dôr´səl), *adj.* of, on, or near the back: *A shark has a dorsal fin.* **—dor´sal·ly,** *adv.*

a	hat	ė	term	ô	order	ch	child		a in about
ā	age	i	it	oi	oil	ng	long		e in taken
ä	far	ī	ice	ou	out	sh	she	ə	i in pencil
â	care	o	hot	u	cup	th	thin		o in lemon
e	let	ō	open	ù	put	ᵀH	then		u in circus
ē	equal	ò	saw	ü	rule	zh	measure		

do·ry (dôr′ē), *n.* rowboat with a narrow, flat bottom and high sides. It is often used by fishermen. ❑ *n., pl.* **do·ries.**

DOS (dos), disk operating system (a computer operating system designed especially to transfer information to and from computer disks).

dos·age (dō′sij), *n.* **1** amount of a medicine to be given or taken at one time. **2** the giving of medicine in doses.

dose (dōs), **1** *n.* amount of a medicine to be given or taken at one time: *a dose of cough medicine.* **2** *v.* to give medicine to in doses; treat with medicine: *The doctor dosed the sick child with penicillin.* **3** *n.* something unpleasant or disagreeable: *We had a dose of freezing rain this morning.* ❑ *v.* **dosed, dos·ing.**

dost (dust), *v.* OLD USE. do¹. "Thou dost" means "you do" (singular).

Dos·to·ev·ski (dos′tə yef′skē), *n.* Feo·dor (fyô′dər), 1821-1881, Russian novelist. ■ **Feodor Dostoevski** was condemned to death for reading and discussing books banned by the Russian czar but was pardoned just moments before he was to be executed by a firing squad. His most famous works, including *Crime and Punishment* and *The Brothers Karamazov*, examine crime, judgment, forgiveness, and the purpose of life.

dot (dot), **1** *n.* a tiny, round mark; point. There is a dot over each *i* in this line. **2** *n.* a small spot: *a blue necktie with white dots.* **3** *v.* to mark with a dot or dots: *Dot your i's and j's.* **4** *v.* to be here and there in: *Trees and bushes dotted the broad lawn.* **5** *n.* a short sound used in sending messages in Morse code by telegraph or radio. ❑ *v.* **dot·ted, dot·ting.** **–dot′like′,** *adj.* **–dot′ter,** *n.*

on the dot, at exactly the right time: *Our train arrived on the dot.*

dot·age (dō′tij), *n.* a weak-minded and childish condition that sometimes accompanies old age. ■ The word **dotage** is often considered offensive.

dote (dōt), *v.* **dote on** or **dote upon,** to be foolishly fond of; be too fond of: *The parents dote on their only son, giving him everything he wants.* ❑ *v.* **dot·ed, dot·ing.**

doth (duth), *v.* OLD USE. does. "She doth" means "she does."

dot·ing (dō′ting), *adj.* foolishly fond; too fond: *Doting parents see no fault in their children.* **–dot′ing·ly,** *adv.*

dot matrix printer, type of computer printer in which the tips of several narrow wires push an inked ribbon against paper. Each wire prints a dot, and the patterns of dots form letters, numbers, etc.

dot·ty (dot′ē), *adj.* INFORMAL. very silly and forgetful. ❑ *adj.* **dot·ti·er, dot·ti·est.**

dou·ble (dub′əl), **1** *adj.* twice as much, as many, as large, as strong, etc.: *She was given double pay for working on Sunday.* **2** *adv.* twice; doubly: *I was paid double by mistake.* **3** *n.* number or amount that is twice as much: *Four is the double of two.* **4** *v.* to make twice as much or twice as many: *He doubled his money in ten years by investing it wisely.* **5** *v.* to become twice as much or twice as many: *Money left in a bank account can double in less than ten years.* **6** *adj.* made of two like parts; in a pair: *Double doors open wide.* **7** *adj.* having two unlike parts; having two meanings, characters, etc. The spelling *b-e-a-r* has a double meaning: *carry* and *a certain animal.* **8** *adv.* two instead of one: *It is dangerous to ride double on a bicycle.* **9** *adj.* made for two: *a double bed.* **10** *v.* to take the place of another; substitute: *The principal is doubling for the teacher today.* **11** *n.* person or thing just like another. In a movie an actor often has a double to do the dangerous scenes. **12** *v.* to serve two purposes; play two parts: *Our den doubles as a guest bedroom.* **13** *v.* to fold; bend: *She doubled her slice of bread to make a sandwich.* **14** *n.* a fold; bend. **15** *v.* to close tightly together; clench: *He doubled his fists in anger.* **16** *v.* to bend or turn sharply backward: *The fox doubled on its tracks to get away from the dogs.* **17** *v.* to go around: *The ship doubled Cape Horn.* **18** *adj.* having more than one set of petals: *Some roses are double; others are single.* **19** in baseball: **a** *n.* hit by which a batter gets to second base. **b** *v.* to hit a double. **20** *n.pl.* **doubles,** game of tennis, etc., with two players on each side. ❑ *v.* **dou·bled, dou·bling.** **–dou′ble·ness,** *n.*

double back, to go back the same way that you came: *The fox doubled back to avoid capture.*

double up, 1 to bend over: *I doubled up with laughter.* **2** to share a room, bed, or quarters with another: *Since there was only one room left at the hotel, the girls doubled up.*

on the double, quickly: *The teacher warned us to stop talking and get to work on the double.*

see double, to see two images of what you are looking at: *The blow on the head made him see double.*

double bass (bās), a deep-toned stringed instrument shaped like a cello but much larger; bass viol; contrabass.

double bassoon, contrabassoon.

double boiler, a pair of cooking pots, one of which is smaller than the other and fits down into it. Heat caused by boiling water in the lower pot cooks the food in the upper pot.

dou·ble-breast·ed (dub′əl bres′tid), *adj.* (of a jacket or coat) having overlapping front flaps and usually two rows of buttons.

dou·ble-check (dub′əl chek′), **1** *v.* to check twice: *double-check the facts.* **2** *n.* a second check of something: *make a double-check.*

double cross, act of treachery.

dou·ble-cross (dub′əl krôs′), *v.* to promise to do one thing and then do another; be treacherous to. **–dou′ble-cross′er,** *n.*

double date, a date that two couples go on together: *We went on a double date with them last Friday.* **–dou′ble-date′,** *v.*

dou·ble-deal·ing (dub′əl dē′ling), **1** act of pretending to do one thing and then doing another; deceitful action or behavior. **2** *adj.* ready to deceive; deceitful. **–dou′ble-dea′ler,** *n.*

dou·ble-deck·er (dub′əl dek′ər), *n.* **1** bus, railroad car, ship, bed, etc., with two decks, floors, levels, or sections. **2** sandwich with two layers of filling between three slices of bread.

double-decker (def. 1)

dou·ble-dig·it (dub′əl dij′it), *adj.* consisting of a numeral from 10 through 99: *double-digit inflation of 12 percent.*

dou·ble·head·er (dub′əl hed′ər), *n.* two games played one after another on the same day.

dou·ble-joint·ed (dub′əl join′tid), *adj.* having joints that let fingers, arms, legs, etc., bend in unusual ways.

dou·ble-knit (dub′əl nit′), **1** *n.* a knitted fabric with two interlocked layers. **2** *adj.* knitted with two interlocked layers: *doubleknit slacks.*

double negative, statement that has two negative words and a negative meaning. EXAMPLE: I don't have none = I don't have any.

dou·ble-park (dub′əl pärk′), *v.* to park a car beside another car that is occupying a legal parking area.

double play, a play in baseball in which two base runners are put out.

dou·ble-quick (dub′əl kwik′), **1** *adj.* very quick. **2** *n.* double time (def. 2).

dou·blet (dub′lit), *n.* **1** a man's close-fitting jacket. Men in Europe wore doublets from the 1400s to the 1600s. **2** one of two words in one language that both come from the same word in another language, but that have different histories. EXAMPLE: *fragile* and *frail*.

WORD SOURCE As people use words, the words often change spelling and pronunciation. This change is especially likely when a word goes from one language to another. Changes can happen differently in different parts of a country, or at different times. So one word can become two **doublets.** English contains many doublets, including the ones below.

DOUBLETS		**DOUBLETS**	
abbreviate	abridge	glamour	grammar
balm	balsam	guard	ward
chase	catch	hospital	hotel
coy	quiet	royal	regal
cipher	zero	shirt	skirt
diamond	adamant		

double take, a briefly delayed reaction to a comment or situation that was not understood at first.

dou·ble-talk (dub′əl tôk′), *n.* speech that is purposely meaningless, but seems meaningful because normal words and intonations are mixed in.

dou·ble-team (dub′əl tēm′), *v.* (in sports) to guard or defend against an offensive player using two defensive players at once.

double time, 1 double the usual rate of pay. **2** a marching speed of 180 steps per minute; double-quick.

dou·bloon (du blün′), *n.* a former Spanish gold coin.

WORD STORY **Doubloon** comes from a Spanish word meaning "double." The first doubloons were worth twice as much as certain other coins.

dou·bly (dub′lē), *adv.* twice as; twice: *Be doubly careful when driving during a storm.*

doubt (dout), **1** *v.* to not believe or trust; not be sure of; feel uncertain about: *She doubted if we would arrive home on time.* **2** *n.* lack of belief; feeling of uncertainty: *My doubts about her ability to run fast vanished when she won the race.* **3** *n.* an uncertain state of mind: *We were in doubt as to the right road.* **4** *n.* an uncertain condition of affairs: *The ship's fate is still in doubt.* —doubt′er, *n.* —doubt′ing·ly, *adv.*

beyond doubt, certain; certainly.

no doubt or **without doubt,** surely; certainly: *No doubt it will rain today.*

SYNONYM STUDY **Doubt** and **disbelief** both mean a feeling of not believing something. **Doubt** suggests not being certain of what is true: *In spite of her doubt, she decided to accept his excuse.* **Disbelief** means a strong feeling that something is not true: *His disbelief was so obvious that we did not try to persuade him.*

doubt·ful (dout′fəl), *adj.* **1** full of doubt; not sure; uncertain: *We are doubtful about the weather for tomorrow.* **2** causing doubt; open to question or suspicion: *His sly answers made his sincerity doubtful.* —doubt′ful·ly, *adv.* —doubt′ful·ness, *n.*

doubt·less (dout′lis), *adv.* **1** without doubt; surely. **2** probably. —doubt′less·ly, *adv.*

dough (dō), *n.* **1** a soft, thick mixture of flour, milk, fat, and other ingredients for baking. Bread, biscuits, cake, and pie crust are made from dough. **2** INFORMAL. money. ▪ Other words that sound like this are **do²** and **doe.** —dough′like′, *adj.*

dough·nut (dō′nut′), *n.* a small cake of sweetened dough cooked in deep fat. A doughnut is usually made in the shape of a ring. Also, **donut.**

dough·ty (dou′tē), *adj.* strong and bold; stout; brave; hardy: *a doughty knight.* ❑ *adj.* **dough·ti·er, dough·ti·est.** —dough′ti·ly, *adv.* —dough′ti·ness, *n.*

dough·y (dō′ē), *adj.* of or like dough; soft and thick; pale and flabby. ❑ *adj.* **dough·i·er, dough·i·est.**

Doug·las (dug′ləs), *n.* **Steph·en** (stē′vən), 1813-1861, American political leader. ▪ **Stephen Douglas** ran for the Senate in Illinois in 1858. His opponent was Abraham Lincoln, and they held a series of debates about slavery which attracted national attention. Douglas won the Senate race, but he lost to Lincoln in the presidential race of 1860.

Douglas fir, a large evergreen tree, related to the pine, common in the western United States and British Columbia. It is a valuable source of timber.

Doug·lass (dug′ləs), *n.* **Frederick,** 1817-1895, American author, public speaker, and Abolitionist who was once enslaved. ▪ **Frederick Douglass** escaped from slavery when he was about 20 years old. Some people who heard him speak did not believe that such a good speaker could have grown up in slavery, so Douglass wrote his famous autobiography, giving details of his life.

Dou·kho·bor (dü′kə bôr′), *n.* member of a Christian sect that emigrated from Russia to western Canada in the late 1800s.

dour (dur *or* dour), *adj.* **1** gloomy or sullen: *They sulked in dour silence.* **2** stern; severe: *Her dour remarks frightened me.* —dour′ly, *adv.* —dour′ness, *n.*

douse (dous), *v.* **1** to plunge into water or any other liquid. **2** to throw water over; drench: *We quickly doused the flames.* **3** to put out; extinguish: *Douse the lights.* ❑ *v.* **doused, dous·ing.**

dove¹ (duv), *n.* **1** pigeon, especially one of the smaller wild kinds. The dove is often a symbol of peace. **2** someone who supports peaceful solutions instead of conflict.

dove² (dōv), *v.* a past tense of **dive.** ▪ See Usage Note at **dive.**

dove·cote (duv′kōt′), *n.* a small house or shelter for doves or pigeons.

Do·ver (dō′vər), *n.* **1** seaport in SE England, the nearest English port to France. **2 Strait of,** narrow channel or strait between N France and SE England. **3** capital of Delaware, in the central part. [**Dover** may come from a Welsh word meaning "water."]

dove·tail (duv′tāl′), **1** *n.* piece that sticks out at the end of a piece of wood, metal, etc., that can be fitted into a corresponding opening at the end of another piece to form a joint. **2** *n.* the joint formed in this way. **3** *v.* to fasten, join, or fit together with dovetails. **4** *v.* to fit together exactly: *The various pieces of evidence dovetailed so completely that the mystery was solved at once.*

dow·a·ger (dou′ə jər), *n.* **1** woman who has received some title or property from her dead husband: *The queen and her mother-in-law, the queen dowager, were present.* **2** a dignified, elderly woman, usually of high social position.

dow·dy (dou′dē), *adj.* poorly dressed; not stylish; shabby. ❑ *adj.* **dow·di·er, dow·di·est.** —dow′di·ly, *adv.* —dow′di·ness, *n.*

dow·el (dou′əl), **1** *n.* peg on a piece of wood, metal, etc., made to fit into a corresponding hole on another piece, so as to form a joint fastening the two pieces together. **2** *v.* to fasten with dowels. ❑ *v.* **dow·eled, dow·el·ing** or **dow·elled, dow·el·ling.**

dow·er (dou′ər), *n.* a widow's share for life of her dead husband's property.

down¹ (doun), **1** *adv.* from a higher to a lower place or condition: *They ran down from the top of the hill. I put the hammer down.* **2** *adj., adv.* in a lower place or condition: *The sun is down. Down in the valley the fog still lingers.* **3** *adv.* from an earlier to a later time: *The story has come down through many years.* **4** *prep.* down along, through, or in: *ride down a hill, walk down a street, sail down a river.* **5** *adj.* going or pointed down: *the down elevator.* **6** *v.* to put down; throw down; get down: *She downed the medicine with one swallow. I was downed in a fight. Down, Spot!* **7** *adj.* in a flat position: *The robber told all the customers to get down on the floor.* **8** *adv.* from a larger size or amount to a smaller: *The temperature went down.* **9** *adv.* toward the south: *They go down to Florida every winter.* **10** *adj.* sick; ill: *We are both down with colds.* **11** *adj.* sad; discouraged: *I felt down about my grades.* **12** *adj.* out of order: *Our computer is down.* **13** *n.* piece of bad luck: *the ups and downs of life.* **14** *v.* to defeat: *We downed their team in a close game.* **15** *adv.* actually; really: *Stop*

a	hat	ė	term	ô	order	ch	child		a in about
ā	age	i	it	oi	oil	ng	long		e in taken
ä	far	ī	ice	ou	out	sh	she	ə	i in pencil
â	care	o	hot	u	cup	th	thin		o in lemon
e	let	ō	open	ů	put	ŦH	then		u in circus
ē	equal	ò	saw	ü	rule	zh	measure		

263

talking, and get down to work. **16** *adv.* on paper; in writing: *Take down what I say.* **17** *adv., adj.* in cash when bought: *You can pay $10 down and the rest later. We made a down payment on a new car.* **18** in football: **a** *n.* a play from scrimmage. A team has four downs to make at least ten yards. **b** *v.* to put or throw the ball down, so that it is out of play. [**Down** comes from old English words meaning "from the hill." From the top of a hill, every direction is down.]

down and out, completely without health, money, friends, etc.; wretched; forsaken.

down on, angry at; having a grudge against: *The other players were down on him for quitting the game.*

down with, to put down; throw down: *Down with tyranny!*

down² (doun), *n.* **1** soft feathers: *the down of a young bird.* **2** soft hair or fluff: *the down on a boy's chin.*

down³ (doun), *n.* Usually, **downs,** *pl.* rolling, grassy land.

down·beat (doun′bēt′), *n.* (in music) the first beat in a measure.

down·cast (doun′kast′), *adj.* **1** directed downward: *She stood with downcast eyes, avoiding my look.* **2** dejected; sad; discouraged: *After all our plans failed, we felt very downcast.*

down·draft (doun′draft′), *n.* a powerful downward current of air: *The aircraft was caught in a sudden downdraft during a thunderstorm.*

down·er (doun′ər), *n.* INFORMAL. a depressing experience, person, or event.

down·fall (doun′fôl′), *n.* **1** a sudden fall; ruin; overthrow: *the downfall of a government. Lack of practice caused the team's downfall, as they lost the championship game.* **2** a heavy rain or snow.

down·field (doun′fēld′), *adj., adv.* (in football) beyond the line of scrimmage, in the part of the field that the defensive team is protecting: *a downfield pass, to run downfield.*

down·grade (doun′grād′), **1** *n.* a downward slope. **2** *v.* to lower in position, importance, reputation, etc.: *downgrade an employee. He downgrades people he does not like, in spite of their merits.* ❑ *v.* **down·grad·ed, down·grad·ing.**

on the downgrade, growing less in strength, power, etc.

down·heart·ed (doun′här′tid), *adj.* in low spirits; discouraged; dejected; depressed. **–down′heart′ed·ly,** *adv.* **–down′heart′ed·ness,** *n.*

down·hill (doun′hil′), **1** *adv.* down the slope of a hill; downward. **2** *adj.* going or sloping downward: *a downhill race.*

go downhill, to get worse: *Our business has been going downhill since we raised our prices.*

down·load (doun′lōd′), *v.* to transfer computer information from one computer to another smaller one, or from a computer to another device such as a printer.

down payment, payment of a portion of the money that something costs. The rest of the money is to be paid later.

down·play (doun′plā′), *v.* to understate; belittle the importance of: *The newspapers downplayed the effects of road repairs on traffic.*

down·pour (doun′pôr′), *n.* a heavy rain.

down·right (doun′rīt′), **1** *adj.* thorough; complete: *a downright fool, a downright lie.* **2** *adv.* thoroughly; completely: *They were downright rude to me.* **3** *adj.* plain; positive: *Her downright answer left no doubt as to what she thought.*

down·shift (doun′shift′), *v.* to shift from a higher to a lower gear.

down·stage (doun′stāj′), *adv., adj.* toward or at the front of the stage in a theater.

down·stairs (doun′stârz′), **1** *adv.* down the stairs: *I hurried downstairs.* **2** *adv., adj.* on or to a lower floor: *Look downstairs*

downhill skiing

for my glasses. The downstairs rooms are dark. **3** *n.* the lower floor or floors: *The entire downstairs was flooded after the heavy rain.*

down·stream (doun′strēm′), *adv., adj.* with the current of a stream; down a stream: *The raft floated downstream. The downstream current was swift after the flood.*

Down syndrome (doun), a medical condition that causes someone to have a broad, flattened face with eyes that appear to be slanted. The condition, which also causes difficulty in learning, is present at birth and continues throughout life.

down·time (doun′tīm′), *n.* a period of time when a machine, factory, or worker is not working.

down-to-earth (doun′tə ėrth′), *adj.* matter-of-fact; realistic.

down·town (doun′toun′), *adv., adj.* to or in the central or main business section of a town or city: *My parents went downtown shopping. Her office is in downtown Chicago.*

down·trod·den (doun′trod′n), *adj.* trampled upon; oppressed.

down·ward (doun′wərd), **1** *adv., adj.* toward a lower place or position: *The bird swooped downward on its prey. The downward trip on the elevator was very slow.* **2** *adv.* toward a later time: *There has been great progress in science from the 18th century downward.*

down·wards (doun′wərdz), *adv.* downward.

down·wind (doun′wind′), *adj., adv.* in the same direction as the wind: *a downwind drift. The boat glided easily downwind.*

down·y (dou′nē), *adj.* **1** made of soft feathers or hair: *a downy pillow.* **2** covered with soft feathers or hair: *a downy chick.* **3** like down; soft and fluffy: *downy fur.* ❑ *adj.* **down·i·er, down·i·est.**

dow·ry (dou′rē), *n.* money or property that a woman brings to the man she marries. ❑ *n., pl.* **dow·ries.**

dowse (douz), *v.* to use a divining rod to locate water. ❑ *v.* **dowsed, dows·ing. –dows′er,** *n.*

dox·ol·o·gy (dok sol′ə jē), *n.* hymn or statement praising God. One familiar doxology begins: "Praise God from whom all blessings flow." ❑ *n., pl.* **dox·ol·o·gies.**

Doyle (doil), *n.* **Arthur Co·nan** (kō′nən), Sir, 1859-1930, English writer, author of the Sherlock Holmes detective stories. ■ **Sir Arthur Conan Doyle** wrote a story in 1893 in which Holmes died. People were so upset by this that he had to write another story bringing Holmes back to life.

doz., dozen or dozens.

doze (dōz), *v.* to sleep lightly; be half asleep: *After dinner I dozed on the couch.* ■ See Synonym Study at **sleep.** ❑ *v.* **dozed, doz·ing. –doz′er,** *n.*

doze off, to fall into a light sleep: *The cat dozed off by the fire.*

doz·en (duz′n), *n.* group of 12; 12: *We had to have dozens of chairs for the party. We will need three dozen eggs and a dozen rolls.* ❑ *n., pl.* **doz·ens** or (after a number) **doz·en.** [**Dozen** comes from Latin words meaning "two" and "ten."]

DP or **D.P., 1** displaced person. **2** data processing.

dpt., department.

Dr., Doctor.

drab (drab), **1** *adj.* not attractive; dull; monotonous: *the drab houses of the smoky, dingy mining town.* **2** *adj.* dull brownish gray. **3** *n.* a dull brownish gray color. ❑ *adj.* **drab·ber, drab·best.** [See Word Story at **drape.**] **–drab′ly,** *adv.* **–drab′ness,** *n.*

drach·ma (drak′mə), *n.* **1** unit of money of modern Greece. **2** an ancient Greek silver coin. ❑ *n., pl.* **drach·mas.**

draft (draft), **1** *n.* current of air: *I caught cold sitting in a draft.* **2** *n.* a rough copy: *She made two drafts of her book report before she handed in the final form.* **3** *v.* to write out a rough copy of: *Three members of the club drafted a new set of rules to be discussed and voted on by the membership.* **4** *n.* selection of persons for some special purpose. Men needed as soldiers may be supplied to the army by draft. **5** *v.* to select for some special purpose: *If nobody volunteers to help me, I will draft someone.* **6** *adj.* for pulling loads: *A big, strong horse or ox is a draft animal.* **7** *n.* a written order from one person or bank to another, requiring the payment of a stated amount of money. **8** *n.* a single act of drinking: *He emptied the glass at one draft.* **9** *n.* amount taken in a single drink. **10** *n.* device for controlling a current of air: *the draft* *of the furnace.* **11** *n.* depth of water that a ship needs for floating. Also, **draught.** —**draft′er,** *n.*

draft·ee (draf tē′), *n.* person who is drafted for military service. ❑ *n., pl.* **draft·ees.**

drafts·man (drafts′mən), *n.* person who makes plans or sketches. A draftsman draws designs or diagrams from which buildings and machines are made. ❑ *n., pl.* **drafts·men.**

drafts·man·ship (drafts′mən ship), *n.* work of a draftsman.

draft·y (draf′tē), *adj.* **1** in a current of air: *I had a drafty seat near the window.* **2** having many currents of air: *a drafty room.* ❑ *adj.* **draft·i·er, draft·i·est.** —**draft′i·ly,** *adv.* —**draft′i·ness,** *n.*

drag (drag), **1** *v.* to pull or move along heavily or slowly; pull or draw along the ground: *We dragged the heavy crates out of the garage. I dragged along on my sprained ankle.* **2** *v.* to go too slowly: *Time drags when you have nothing to do.* **3** *v.* to pull a net, hook, harrow, etc., over or along for some purpose: *They dragged the lake for fish.* **4** *n.* net, hook, harrow, etc., used in dragging. **5** *n.* anything that holds back; obstruction; hindrance: *If you don't practice, you'll be a drag on the team.* **6** *n.* the force acting on an object in motion through a fluid, in a direction opposite to the object's motion. It is produced by friction. **7** *v.* INFORMAL. to take part in a drag race. **8** *n.* INFORMAL. a boring person or situation. ❑ *v.* **dragged, drag·ging.** —**drag′ger,** *n.*

drag·gy (drag′ē), *adj.* INFORMAL. boring; slow-moving. ❑ *adj.* **drag·gi·er, drag·gi·est.**

drag·net (drag′net′), *n.* **1** net pulled over the bottom of a river, pond, etc., or along the ground. Dragnets are used to catch fish and small game. **2** set of plans for catching or gathering in: *The criminals were caught in a police dragnet.*

drag·on (drag′ən), *n.* (in old stories) a huge, fierce animal supposed to look like a winged snake with claws, which often breathed out fire and smoke.

drag·on·fly (drag′ən flī′), *n.* a large, harmless insect, with a long, slender body and two pairs of gauzy wings, which darts about catching flies, mosquitoes, etc. ❑ *n., pl.* **drag·on·flies.**

dra·goon (drə gün′), **1** *n.* (long ago) a mounted soldier trained to fight on foot or on horseback. **2** *v.* to compel; force: *The prisoner was dragooned into signing a false confession.*

drag race, race between cars to determine which can accelerate faster over a given distance. —**drag racer,** *n.* —**drag racing,** *n.*

drag·ster (drag′stər), *n.* INFORMAL. a car used in a drag race, especially one built with reduced wind resistance and increased engine power.

dragon

drain (drān), **1** *v.* to draw off or flow off slowly: *That ditch drains water from the swamp. The water drains into the river.* **2** *v.* to draw water or other liquid from; empty or dry by draining: *The farmers drained the swamps to get more land for crops. In one drink she drained the cup. Set the dishes here to drain.* **3** *n.* channel or pipe for carrying off water or waste of any kind: *The sink drain is clogged.* **4** *v.* to take away from slowly; use up little by little: *drain a country of its natural resources.* **5** *n.* act of slowly taking away; using up little by little; draining: *A long illness can be a drain on your strength.*

drain·age (drā′nij), *n.* **1** act or process of draining; drawing off or flowing off of water: *The drainage of swamps improved the land.* **2** system of channels or pipes for carrying off water or waste of any kind. **3** what is drained off.

drain·pipe (drān′pīp′), *n.* pipe for carrying off water or other liquid.

drake (drāk), *n.* a male duck.

Drake (drāk), *n.* Sir **Francis,** 1540?-1596, English sea captain. He commanded the first English ship to sail around the world.

dram (dram), *n.* a small weight. In apothecaries' weight, 8 drams make one ounce; in avoirdupois weight, 16 drams make one ounce.

dra·ma (drä′mə *or* dram′ə), *n.* **1** story written to be performed by actors. **2** the art of writing, acting, or producing plays: *He is studying drama.* **3** series of happenings in real life that seem like those of a play, movie, or TV show: *The news program showed the drama of a daring rescue by firefighters.* ❑ *n., pl.* **dra·mas.**

Dram·a·mine (dram′ə mēn′), *n.* trademark for a drug used against nausea caused by motion, especially while traveling.

drama

dra·mat·ic (drə mat′ik), *adj.* **1** like a drama; of or about plays: *a dramatic actor.* **2** seeming like a play; full of action or feeling; exciting: *the dramatic reunion of a family separated during wartime.* **3** striking; impressive: *a dramatic use of color.* —**dra·mat′i·cal·ly,** *adv.*

dra·mat·ics (drə mat′iks), *n.* **1** *sing.* art of acting or producing plays: *Dramatics is taught in some colleges.* **2** *pl.* tendency to show off.

dram·a·tist (dram′ə tist), *n.* writer of plays; playwright.

dram·a·ti·za·tion (dram′ə tə zā′shən), *n.* **1** what is dramatized: *That play is a dramatization of the life of Joan of Arc.* **2** act of dramatizing.

dram·a·tize (dram′ə tīz), *v.* **1** to make a drama of; arrange in the form of a play: *dramatize a novel.* **2** to show or express in a dramatic way; make seem exciting and thrilling: *The speaker dramatized her story with many actions and gestures.* ❑ *v.* **dram·a·tized, dram·a·tiz·ing.**

drank (drangk), *v.* past tense of **drink:** *The hungry cat drank its milk rapidly.*

drape (drāp), **1** *v.* to cover or hang with cloth falling loosely in folds, especially as a decoration: *The buildings were draped with red, white, and blue bunting.* **2** *v.* to arrange clothes, hangings, etc., to hang loosely in folds: *The actor draped the cape over his shoulders.* **3** *n.* cloth hung in folds: *There were heavy drapes at the windows.* ❑ *v.* **draped, drap·ing.**

WORD STORY **Drape** comes from a French word meaning "cloth." **Drab** comes from the same word. Before cloth is dyed, it is a dull brownish color.

dra·per·y (drā′pər ē), *n.* **1** hangings or clothing arranged in folds, especially such hangings hung as curtains: *The bold colors of the drapery made the living room bright and cheery.* **2** cloths or fabrics; dry goods. ❑ *n., pl.* **dra·per·ies.**

dras·tic (dras′tik), *adj.* very forceful or harsh; extreme: *During the drought the city took the drastic step of turning the water off at certain times.* —**dras′ti·cal·ly,** *adv.*

drat (drat), *v.* to damn; condemn: *Drat that dog—he dug another hole in the yard.* ❑ *v.* **drat·ted, drat·ting.**

draught (draft), *n., v., adj.* draft.

draw (drô), **1** *v.* to make a picture or likeness of with pencil, pen, chalk, crayon, etc.: *Draw a circle. He draws very well for a six-year-old.* **2** *v.* to cause to move by the use of force or effort; pull or drag; haul: *The horses drew the wagon.* **3** *v.* to pull out; pull up; cause to come out; take out; get: *Draw a pail of water from the well. She drew ten dollars from the bank. Until you hear both sides of the argument, draw no conclusions.* **4** *n.* act of pulling or taking out: *The cowgirl was skilled with guns and quick on the draw.* **5** *v.* to come or go; move: *We drew near the fire to get warm.* **6** *v.* to attract: *A parade draws a crowd.* **7** *v.* to describe: *The characters in this novel are not fully drawn; they seem unreal.* **8** *v.* to make a current of air to carry off smoke: *The chimney does not draw well.* **9** *v.* to breathe in; inhale; take in: *Draw*

a	hat	ė	term	ô	order	ch	child		a in about
ā	age	i	it	oi	oil	ng	long		e in taken
ä	far	ī	ice	ou	out	sh	she	ə {	i in pencil
â	care	o	hot	u	cup	th	thin		o in lemon
e	let	ō	open	ů	put	ᴛʜ	then		u in circus
ē	equal	ò	saw	ü	rule	zh	measure		

a deep breath. **10** *n.* a tie in a game. If neither side wins, it is a draw. **11** *v.* to stretch: *The girls drew the rope taut.* **12** *v.* to sink to a depth of; need for floating: *A ship draws more water when it is loaded than when it is empty.* **13** *n.* a small land basin into or through which water drains; kind of valley: *We found the stray cattle grazing in a draw.* ❑ *v.* **drew, drawn, draw·ing.**

draw out, 1 to make long or longer: *His speech was too drawn out.* **2** to persuade to talk: *It is hard to draw out a shy person.*

draw up, 1 to arrange in order: *The marchers were drawn up in formation for the parade.* **2** to write out in proper form: *draw up a will.* **3** to stop: *A car drew up in front of the house.*

draw yourself up, to stand up straight: *She drew herself up to her full height.*

draw·back (drȯ′bak′), *n.* something that makes a situation or experience less complete or satisfying; unfavorable condition; disadvantage: *Our trip was interesting but the rainy weather was a drawback.*

draw·bridge (drȯ′brij′), *n.* bridge that can be entirely or partly lifted, lowered, or moved to one side. In old castles, drawbridges were lifted to keep out enemies. A drawbridge over a river is lifted to let boats pass.

drawbridge

drawer (drȯr *for 1,3;* drȯ′ər *for 2*), *n.* **1** box with handles built to slide in and out of a table, desk, or bureau: *He kept his shirts in the dresser drawer.* **2** person or thing that draws. **3 drawers,** *pl.* undergarment fitting over the legs and around the waist.

draw·ing (drȯ′ing), *n.* **1** picture, sketch, plan, or design done with pencil, pen, chalk, crayon, etc. **2** the making of such a picture, sketch, plan, or design; representing objects by lines. **3** the choosing of a ticket that awards the owner a prize: *The drawing for the bicycle will be tonight.*

drawing room, room for entertaining guests; parlor.

drawl (drȯl), **1** *v.* to talk in a slow way, drawing out the vowels: *He drawled his words in imitation of his favorite movie cowboy.* **2** *n.* such a way of talking; speech of someone who drawls: *a southern drawl, a soft-spoken drawl.* [Drawl probably comes from a Dutch word meaning "to linger." People who speak with a drawl seem to linger over the pronunciation of each word.] –drawl′er, *n.* –drawl′ing·ly, *adv.*

drawn (drȯn), **1** *v.* past participle of **draw:** *That old horse has drawn many loads.* **2** *adj.* made tense; strained: *a face drawn and stiff with pain.*

draw·string (drȯ′string′), *n.* string or cord threaded through the folded border of a bag, jacket, etc., so that it can be tightened or loosened.

dray (drā), *n.* (earlier) a low, strong cart for carrying heavy loads.

dread (dred), **1** *v.* to fear greatly; feel terror or uneasiness about: *I dread visits to the dentist.* **2** *n.* great fear; feeling of terror or uneasiness about what may happen. **3** *adj.* causing fear; frightening; terrible: *the dread day of the execution.* **4** *adj.* held in awe; awe-inspiring: *the dread sight of the immense, glowing volcano.*

dread·ful (dred′fəl), *adj.* **1** causing dread; fearful; terrible: *a fairy tale about a dreadful dragon.* **2** very bad; very unpleasant: *I have a dreadful cold.* —**dread′ful·ly,** *adv.* —**dread′ful·ness,** *n.*

dread·nought (dred′nȯt′), *n.* a big, powerful battleship with heavy armor and large guns. [Dreadnought, meaning "fear nothing," comes from the name of the first battleship of this kind, launched by the British in 1906.]

dream (drēm), **1** *n.* images passing through the mind during sleep: *I had a bad dream last night.* **2** *n.* something like a dream; daydream; wish: *Sometimes I sit at my desk and have dreams of becoming a famous writer.* **3** *v.* to imagine with the mind during sleep; have a dream or dreams: *I dreamed that I was flying.* **4** *v.* to have daydreams; form fancies: *For years they dreamed of fame and riches.* **5** *v.* to think of something as possible; imagine: *The day seemed so bright that we never dreamed it would rain.* **6** *n.* something having great beauty or charm: *It was a dream of a vacation.* ❑ *v.* **dreamed** or **dreamt, dream·ing.** —**dream′less,** *adj.* —**dream′like′,** *adj.*

dream up, to create an invention, solution to a problem, etc., by using your imagination.

WORD STORY Dream comes from an old English word meaning "joy" or "music." Clearly, people had good dreams then—and we still call something wonderful "a dream."

dream·er (drē′mər), *n.* **1** someone who dreams or daydreams. **2** someone whose dreams, plans, or ideas are not practical.

dream·land (drēm′land′), *n.* place that exists only in someone's dreams.

dreamt (dremt), *v.* dreamed; a past tense and a past participle of **dream.**

dream·y (drē′mē), *adj.* **1** full of dreams: *a dreamy sleep.* **2** like a dream; vague; dim: *a dreamy recollection.* **3** wonderful; exciting; attractive: *They moved into a dreamy new house with a swimming pool and a tennis court.* **4** fond of daydreaming; fanciful; not practical: *a dreamy person.* **5** causing dreams; soothing: *a dreamy lullaby.* ❑ *adj.* **dream·i·er, dream·i·est.** —**dream′i·ly,** *adv.* —**dream′i·ness,** *n.*

drear (drir), *adj.* dreary.

drear·y (drir′ē), *adj.* **1** without cheer; dull; gloomy: *A cold, rainy day is dreary.* **2** boring; without interest: *a dreary job doing the same things all day.* ❑ *adj.* **drear·i·er, drear·i·est.** —**drear′i·ly,** *adv.* —**drear′i·ness,** *n.*

dredge[1] (drej), **1** *n.* machine with a scoop or a suction pipe for cleaning out or deepening a body of water. **2** *v.* to clean out or deepen with a dredge: *dredge a harbor.* **3** *n.* apparatus with a net, used for gathering oysters, etc. It is dragged along the bottom of a river or the sea. **4** *v.* to bring up or gather with a dredge. **5** *v.* to dig up; collect: *dredge up all the facts.* ❑ *v.* **dredged, dredg·ing.**

dredge[2] (drej), *v.* to sprinkle: *dredge meat with flour.* ❑ *v.* **dredged, dredg·ing.**

D region, region of the atmosphere at the bottom of the ionosphere, which tends to absorb radio signals; D layer.

dregs (dregz), *n.pl.* **1** the solid bits of matter that settle to the bottom of a liquid: *I rinsed the dregs out of the coffeepot.* **2** the least desirable part: *dregs of humanity.*

drei·del or **drei·dl** (drād′l), *n.* **1** a small toy that spins like a top, with four sides marked with Hebrew letters. **2** a children's game of chance played with this toy at Hanukkah.

Drei·ser (drī′zər), *n.* **The·o·dore** (thē′ə dôr), 1871-1945, American author. His novels explore the moral relationships between individuals and society.

drench (drench), *v.* to wet thoroughly; soak: *A sudden heavy rain drenched us.*

WORD STORY Drench comes from an old English word meaning "to drink." When something gets drenched, it appears to have been drinking up liquid.

drenched (drencht), *adj.* completely wet; soaked: *Even though he had his umbrella open, he was drenched to the skin by the time he reached the bus stop.* ■ See Synonym Study at **wet.**

Dres·den (drez′dən), *n.* city in SE Germany, on the Elbe River.

dress (dres), **1** *n.* a piece of clothing worn by women and girls. A dress is a top and skirt made as one piece or sewed together. **2** *n.* clothes; clothing: *casual dress.* ■ See Synonym Study at **clothes. 3** *v.* to put clothes on: *Please dress the baby.* **4** *v.* to wear clothes properly and attractively: *Your dad certainly knows how to dress!* **5** *v.* to wear formal clothes. **6** *v.* to decorate; adorn. **7** *v.* to prepare an animal's body, or a part of it, for sale or cooking: *The butcher dressed the chicken by pulling out the feathers, cutting off the head and feet, and taking out the insides.* **8** *v.* to comb, brush, and arrange hair. **9** *v.* to put medicine, bandages, etc., on a wound or sore. **10** *v.* to form in a straight line: *The soldiers dressed their ranks.* **11** *v.* to smooth; finish: *to dress leather.* ❑ *n., pl.* **dress·es** for 1; *v.* **dressed, dress·ing.**

dress down, to scold; rebuke.

dress up, 1 to put on your best clothes: *dress up for a party.* **2** to put on a costume or unusual clothes: *dress up as a clown for Halloween.*

WORD STORY **Dress** comes from a Latin word meaning "to form a straight line." The word's first meaning in English was "to arrange properly." People used the word so often about arranging clothing that the word got its modern meaning.

dress code, a set of rules designating the kind of clothing that must be worn, especially in a school environment.

dress·er[1] (dres′ər), *n.* person who dresses himself, another person, a shop window, etc.

dress·er[2] (dres′ər), *n.* **1** piece of furniture with drawers for clothes and sometimes a mirror; bureau. **2** piece of furniture with shelves for dishes.

dress·ing (dres′ing), *n.* **1** sauce for salads or other foods. **2** mixture of bread crumbs, seasoning, etc., used to stuff chicken, turkey, etc. **3** medicine or a bandage put on a wound or sore. **4** process or act of putting on clothes, decorating, making ready, etc.

dress·ing-down (dres′ing doun′), *n.* a scolding; rebuke.

dressing gown, a loose robe worn at home while dressing or resting.

dressing table, table with a mirror, at which someone sits to comb the hair, put on makeup, etc.

dress·mak·er (dres′mā′kər), *n.* person whose work is making women's or children's clothing.

dress·mak·ing (dres′mā′king), *n.* the work of making women's or children's clothing.

dress rehearsal, rehearsal of a play with costumes and scenery just as for a regular performance.

dress suit, a man's suit worn on formal occasions.

dress·y (dres′ē), *adj.* **1** fancy and suited to special occasions such as parties and dances: *I'm going to buy something very dressy for the party.* **2** stylish; fashionable. ❑ *adj.* **dress·i·er, dress·i·est.**

drew (drü), *v.* past tense of **draw:** *He drew a picture of his dog.*

Drew (drü), *n.* Charles Richard, 1904-1950, African American doctor and scientist. ■ Charles Richard Drew did much important research on the uses of blood plasma and how to set up blood banks. During the early part of World War II he organized blood plasma drives that saved millions of lives, even though at the time the U.S. government refused to accept plasma from African American donors.

dressy

drib·ble (drib′əl), **1** *v.* to flow or let flow in drops or small amounts; trickle: *Gasoline dribbled from the leak in the tank.* **2** *v.* to let saliva run from the mouth; drool: *Babies dribble on*

their bibs. **3** *n.* a drip; trickle: *There's a dribble of milk running down your chin.* **4** *v.* to move a ball along by bouncing it or giving it short kicks: *dribble a basketball or soccer ball.* **5** *n.* act of dribbling a ball. ❑ *v.* **drib·bled, drib·bling.** —**drib′bler,** *n.*

drib·let (drib′lit), *n.* a small amount: *She paid off her big debt in driblets, a dollar or two a week.*

dried (drīd), *v.* past tense and past participle of **dry:** *I dried my hands. The dishes have already been dried.*

dri·er (drī′ər), **1** *adj.* comparative of **dry. 2** *n.* person or thing that dries. **3** *n.* dryer (def. 2). ■ Another word that sounds like this is **dryer.**

dries (drīz), *v.* a present tense of **dry:** *Dad washes the dishes and Mom dries them.*

dri·est (drī′ist), *adj.* superlative of **dry:** *Which is the driest towel?*

drift (drift), **1** *v.* to carry or be carried along by currents of air or water: *The wind drifted the boat onto the rocks. A raft drifts if it is not steered.* **2** *v.* to move or appear to move aimlessly: *People drifted in and out of the meeting.* **3** *v.* to go along without knowing or caring where you are going: *Some people have a purpose in life; others just drift.* **4** *n.* movement caused by currents of air or water: *the drift of an iceberg.* **5** *n.* direction of such movement: *The drift of the Gulf Stream is to the north.* **6** *n.* tendency or trend: *Many politicians watch the drift of public opinion carefully.* **7** *n.* direction of thought; meaning: *Please explain that again; I did not quite get the drift of your words.* **8** *n.* anything carried along by wind, water, or ice. **9** *v.* to pile or be piled up by the wind: *The strong wind drifted the snow. The snow drifted along the fence.* **10** *n.* snow, sand, etc., heaped up by the wind: *After the heavy snow there were deep drifts in the yard.* **11** *n.* distance that a ship or aircraft is off course because of currents. —**drift′er,** *n.*

drift·wood (drift′wüd′), *n.* wood carried along by water or washed ashore from the water.

drill (dril), **1** *n.* tool or machine for boring holes. **2** *v.* to bore a hole in; pierce with a drill. **3** *v.* to teach by having the learner do a thing over and over: *The sergeant drilled the new soldiers.* **4** *n.* teaching or training by having the learners do a thing over and over for practice: *The teacher gave the class plenty of drill in arithmetic.* ■ See Synonym Study at **practice.** —**drill′er,** *n.*

drink (dringk), **1** *v.* to swallow anything liquid: *Kittens like to drink milk. We drank from paper cups.* **2** *n.* liquid swallowed or to be swallowed: *Water is a good drink to quench your thirst.* **3** *n.* portion of a liquid: *Please give me a drink of milk.* **4** *v.* to suck up; absorb: *The dry soil drank up the rain.* **5** *n.* alcoholic liquor. **6** *v.* to drink alcoholic liquor. ❑ *v.* **drank, drunk, drink·ing.** —**drink′a·ble,** *adj.*

drink in, to take in through the senses with eagerness and pleasure: *Our ears drank in the music.*

drink to, to drink in honor of; drink with good wishes for: *The guests drank to the happiness of the bride and groom.*

SYNONYM STUDY **Drink, guzzle,** and **sip** all mean to swallow liquid. **Drink** is a general word: *The deer drink from the stream.* **Guzzle** means to drink greedily, one swallow right after another: *Hot and thirsty, I guzzled the juice straight from the bottle.* **Sip** means to drink slowly, little by little: *She sipped the hot chocolate.*

drink·er (dring′kər), *n.* **1** person who drinks. **2** person who drinks alcoholic liquor often or too much.

drip (drip), **1** *v.* to fall or let fall in drops: *Rain drips from an umbrella. The awning dripped water onto her head.* **2** *n.* act of falling in drops: *the drip of water from a leaky faucet.* **3** *v.* to be so wet that drops fall: *My forehead was dripping with perspiration.* **4** *n.* liquid that falls in drops. ❑ *v.* **dripped, drip·ping.**

drip-dry (drip′drī′), **1** *v.* to wash and hang to dry without wringing and with little or no ironing: *drip-dry a shirt or blouse.* **2** *adj.* able to be drip-dried; wash-and-wear: *drip-dry fabrics.* ❑ *v.* **drip-dried, drip-dry·ing.**

a	hat	ė	term	ô	order	ch	child		
ā	age	i	it	oi	oil	ng	long		a in about
ä	far	ī	ice	ou	out	sh	she		e in taken
â	care	o	hot	u	cup	th	thin	ə	i in pencil
e	let	ō	open	ủ	put	ʇʜ	then		o in lemon
ē	equal	ȯ	saw	ü	rule	zh	measure		u in circus

drip·pings (drip'ingz), *n.pl.* the melted fat and juice that drip down from meat while it cooks.

drive (drīv), **1** *v.* to make go: *Drive the dog away. Drive the nails into the board. The wind drives the windmill. The noise of the drums almost drove me mad.* **2** *v.* to control the movement of a motor vehicle: *Can you drive a car?* **3** *v.* to go or carry in a motor vehicle: *We want to drive through the mountains on the way home. She drove us to the station.* **4** *n.* trip in a motor vehicle: *On Sunday we took a drive in the country.* **5** *n.* road: *He built a drive from the street to his house.* **6** *v.* to force; urge on: *Hunger drove them to steal.* **7** *n.* a strong force; pressure: *She has a drive to succeed.* **8** *v.* to bring about or obtain by cleverness or force: *He drove a good bargain at the store.* **9** *v.* to cause to happen; give force and direction to: *The existence and spread of deadly diseases drive medical research.* **10** *n.* vigor; energy: *a person with drive.* **11** *n.* a special effort of a group for some purpose; campaign: *The town had a drive to get money for charity.* **12** *n.* (in football) an offensive effort that is kept up, usually resulting in a score: *an eighty-yard drive following the kickoff.* **13** *v.* to work hard or compel to work hard: *They said their boss drove them too hard.* **14** *v.* to dash or rush with force; dash violently: *The ship drove on the rocks.* **15** *v.* (in sports) to hit very hard and fast: *drive a golf ball.* **16** *n.* a very hard, fast hit: *The batter's drive went into deep left field.* **17** *n.* act of driving cattle overland to a shipping point. **18** *n.* the thing or things driven: *a drive of cattle.* **19** *v.* to get or make by drilling, boring, etc.: *drive a well.* **20** *n.* part that drives machinery. **21** *n.* disk drive. **22** *n.* the means by which power is transmitted to the wheels in a motor vehicle: *rear-wheel drive, four-wheel drive.* ❑ *v.* **drove, driv·en, driv·ing.**

drive at, to mean; intend: *What are you driving at?*

let drive, to strike; aim: *The fighter let drive a left to the jaw.*

drive-in (drīv'in'), **1** *adj.* arranged and equipped so that customers may drive in and be served or entertained while remaining seated in their cars: *a drive-in movie, a drive-in bank.* **2** *n.* place arranged and equipped in this way.

driv·el (driv'əl), *n.* silly talk; nonsense.

driv·en (driv'ən), *v.* past participle of **drive:** *Mom has just driven to work.*

-driven, *suffix.* caused or controlled by ___: *market-driven prices = prices controlled by the market.*

driv·er (drī'vər), *n.* **1** person who drives, especially someone who drives a car or other vehicle. **2** person who makes people who are lower in rank work very hard. **3** a golf club with a wide head. It is used in hitting the ball off the tee. **4** a machine part that transmits force or motion.

drive shaft, a shaft that transmits power from an engine to the various working parts of a machine. In a car, a drive shaft connects the transmission to the rear or front axle.

drive·way (drīv'wā'), *n.* a privately owned road to drive on, usually leading from a house or garage to the road.

driz·zle (driz'əl), **1** *v.* to rain gently, in very small drops like mist. **2** *n.* very small drops of rain like mist: *A steady drizzle made it hard to see across the muddy football field.* ❑ *v.* **driz·zled, driz·zling.**

driz·zly (driz'lē), *adj.* drizzling. ❑ *adj.* **driz·zli·er, driz·zli·est.**

droll (drōl), *adj.* odd and amusing; quaint and laughable. **–droll'ness,** *n.* **–drol'ly,** *adv.*

drom·e·dar·y (drom'ə der'ē), *n.* a swift camel with one hump and short hair, found in parts of India, Arabia, and northern Africa and used for riding. ❑ *n., pl.* **drom·e·dar·ies.** [**Dromedary** comes from a Greek word meaning "running." Dromedaries bred for racing may reach speeds of 40 miles per hour.]

dromedary—7 ft. 6 in. (2.3 m) high at the hump

drone (drōn), **1** *n.* a male bee, especially a male honeybee. Drones have no stings and do no work. **2** *v.* to make a deep, continuous humming sound: *The bees droned among the flowers.*

3 *n.* a deep, continuous humming sound: *the drone of mosquitoes. The hikers heard the drone of a far-off motorboat.* **4** *n.* a pilotless aircraft flown by computer program or by remote control. **5** *v.* to talk or say in a monotonous voice: *Several people in the audience fell asleep as the speaker droned on.* **6** *n.* someone who is not willing to work; idler; loafer. **7** *v.* to spend time idly; loaf. ❑ *v.* **droned, dron·ing.**

drool (drül), *v.* **1** to let saliva run from the mouth as a baby does. **2** to show great desire: *drool over a new car.*

droop (drüp), **1** *v.* to hang down; bend down: *His eyelids drooped with fatigue. Flowers soon droop if they are not put in water.* **2** *n.* a bending position; hanging down: *There was a slight droop to his shoulders after the long hike.* **3** *v.* to become weak; lose strength and energy: *The children were drooping by the end of the walk in the hot sun.* **4** *v.* to become discouraged; be sad and gloomy. ▪ Another word that sounds like this is **drupe. –droop'ing·ly,** *adv.*

droop·y (drü'pē), *adj.* **1** hanging down; drooping: *a droopy hat.* **2** discouraged; depressed. ❑ *adj.* **droop·i·er, droop·i·est.**

drop (drop), **1** *v.* to fall or let fall, especially suddenly: *The acrobat dropped from the high rope into the net below. The price of sugar may drop soon.* ▪ See Synonym Study at **descend. 2** *n.* a small amount of liquid in a somewhat round shape: *a drop of rain, a drop of blood.* **3** *n.* a small amount of something shaped like a drop: *a cough drop.* **4** *n.pl.* **drops,** liquid medicine given in drops: *eye drops, nose drops.* **5** *n.* a very small amount of anything: *At the end of the two-mile race, the runners didn't have a drop of strength left.* **6** *v.* to fall or let fall in very small amounts. **7** *n.* a sudden fall: *a drop in temperature, a drop in prices.* **8** *n.* the distance down; a sudden fall in level; length of a fall: *From the top of the cliff to the water is a drop of 200 feet.* **9** *v.* to fall dead, wounded, or tired out: *After working all day I was ready to drop.* **10** *v.* to cause to fall dead; kill: *The hunter dropped the deer with a single shot.* **11** *v.* to go lower; sink: *Her voice dropped to a whisper.* **12** *v.* to make lower: *Drop your voice.* **13** *v.* to let go; dismiss: *Members who do not pay their dues will be dropped from the club.* **14** *v.* to reject; end a relationship with: *drop a friend.* **15** *v.* to leave out; omit: *Drop the "e" in "drive" before adding "ing."* **16** *v.* to stop; end: *The matter is not important; let it drop.* **17** *v.* to send a letter, note, etc.: *While you are away on your trip, drop me a card.* **18** *v.* to give or express: *He dropped a hint that he would like to be invited to the party.* **19** *v.* to go with the current or tide: *The raft dropped down the river.* **20** *v.* to let out of a car or other vehicle: *Drop me at the corner of Main Street.* ❑ *v.* **dropped, drop·ping. –drop'like',** *adj.*

drop in, to visit informally: *Drop in and see me some day.*

drop off, **1** to go to sleep: *I dropped off soon after going to bed.* **2** to become less; fade: *Profits dropped off last year.*

drop out, to quit being a participant or member; withdraw: *drop out of school. Two club members have dropped out.*

drop over, to visit someone casually: *Drop over sometime.*

drop cloth, a large sheet of cloth or plastic used to protect floors and furniture from drips or spills, especially while painting a room.

drop·let (drop'lit), *n.* a tiny drop.

drop·out (drop'out'), *n.* **1** student who leaves school or college before completing a course or a term. **2** person who withdraws or drops out: *a dropout from the Democratic Party, a dropout from middle-class society.*

drop·per (drop'ər), *n.* a narrow glass or plastic tube open at one end with a hollow rubber cap at the other end. It is used to put drops of liquid into the eyes, nose, or throat.

drop·pings (drop'ingz), *n.pl.* bodily waste of animals and birds.

drop·sy (drop'sē), *n.* OLD USE. edema.

dro·soph·i·la (drō sof'ə lə), *n.* any of numerous fruit flies, especially one kind used in gene research. ❑ *n., pl.* **dro·soph·i·lae** (drō sof'ə lē), **dro·soph·i·las.**

dross (drôs), *n.* **1** waste or scum that comes to the surface of melting metals. **2** waste material; rubbish.

drought (drout), *n.* **1** a long period of dry weather; continued lack of rain: *A drought of three months during the summer caused the brooks and streams to dry up.* **2** lack of moisture; dryness.

drums (def. 1)

drove¹ (drōv), *v.* past tense of **drive:** *We drove for six hours today.*

drove² (drōv), *n.* **1** group of cattle, sheep, hogs, etc., moving or driven along together; flock; herd: *The rancher sent a drove of cattle to market.* **2** many people moving along together; crowd: *People rushed to the main square in droves.*

drov·er (drō′vər), *n.* **1** person who drives cattle, sheep, hogs, etc., to market. **2** dealer in cattle.

drown (droun), *v.* **1** to die under water or other liquid because of lack of air to breathe: *We almost drowned when our sailboat suddenly overturned.* **2** to kill by keeping under water or other liquid: *The flood drowned many cattle in the lowlands.* **3** to be stronger or louder than; keep from being heard: *The boat's whistle drowned out what she was trying to tell us.*

drowse (drouz), *v.* to be sleepy; be half asleep: *I drowsed, but did not quite fall asleep.* ❑ *v.* **drowsed, drows·ing.** [**Drowse** comes from an old English word meaning "to fall" or "to sink." We still speak of falling asleep.]

drow·sy (drou′zē), *adj.* **1** half asleep; sleepy: *After a big meal, he often feels drowsy.* **2** making you sleepy: *It was a warm, quiet, drowsy afternoon.* ❑ *adj.* **drow·si·er, drow·si·est.** —**drow′si·ly,** *adv.* —**drow′si·ness,** *n.*

drub (drub), *v.* **1** to beat with a stick; whip soundly; thrash. **2** to defeat by a large margin in a fight, game, contest, etc. ❑ *v.* **drubbed, drub·bing.** [**Drub** may come from an Arabic word meaning "he beat."] —**drub′ber,** *n.*

drudge (druj), *n.* **1** person who does hard, tiresome, or disagreeable work. **2** *v.* to do hard, tiresome, or disagreeable work. ❑ *v.* **drudged, drudg·ing.** —**drudg′er,** *n.*

drudg·er·y (druj′ər ē), *n.* work that is hard, tiresome, or disagreeable: *I think that washing dishes every day is drudgery.*

drug (drug), **1** *n.* substance used as a medicine or in preparing medicines. Drugs are obtained from plants, animals, chemicals, minerals, etc. Penicillin and aspirin are drugs. **2** *n.* substance taken for its effect and not for medical reasons. Such drugs speed up or slow down the activity of the body or affect the senses. Alcohol and heroin are drugs. **3** *v.* to give drugs to, particularly drugs that are harmful or cause sleep: *The spy drugged the guard and then searched for the secret documents.* **4** *v.* to mix harmful drugs with food or drink: *The spy drugged the guard's coffee.* **5** *v.* to affect or overcome the body or the senses in a way that is not natural: *The wine had drugged her.* ❑ *v.* **drugged, drug·ging.**

drug abuse, the use of a drug for nonmedical reasons and in a way that causes harm to health. Drug abuse can lead to addiction.

drug addict, person addicted to drugs.

drug·gist (drug′ist), *n.* (earlier) pharmacist.

drug·store (drug′stôr′), *n.* store that sells drugs and other medicines and often also soft drinks, cosmetics, magazines, etc.

dru·id or **Dru·id** (drü′id), *n.* one of the priests of the ancient Celts of Britain, Ireland, and France. The druids were very powerful leaders and judges until the Christian religion was accepted by the Celts. —**dru·id′ic** or **dru·id′i·cal,** *adj.*

drum (drum), **1** *n.* a musical instrument that makes a sound when it is beaten. A drum is a hollow cylinder with a covering stretched tightly over the ends. **2** *n.* sound made by beating a drum. **3** *n.* any sound like this: *the drum of rain on a roof.* **4** *v.* to beat or play the drum: *I drum in the school band.* **5** *v.* to beat, tap, or strike again and again: *Stop drumming on the table with your fingers.* **6** *v.* to teach or drive into someone's head by repeating over and over: *The importance of being on time was drummed into me.* **7** *n.* container or other thing shaped something like a drum: *an oil drum.* **8** *n.* a thick bar or cylinder in a machine on which something is wound: *a drum of cable.* ❑ *v.* **drummed, drum·ming.** —**drum′like′,** *adj.*

drum out of, to send away from in disgrace: *The corrupt politician was drummed out of office.*

drum up, 1 to call together: *We could not drum up enough players to make a baseball team.* **2** to get by asking again and again; obtain: *The company's advertising campaign drummed up more business.*

drum·beat (drum′bēt′), *n.* sound made by beating a drum.

drum major, person who leads a marching band, often twirling a baton.

drum ma·jor·ette (mā′jə ret′), a girl or woman who leads parades, twirling a baton; majorette.

drum·mer (drum′ər), *n.* person who plays a drum.

drum·stick (drum′stik′), *n.* **1** stick for beating a drum. **2** the lower half of the leg of a cooked chicken, turkey, etc.

drunk (drungk), **1** *adj.* having had too many alcoholic drinks; intoxicated. People who are drunk may have trouble speaking, thinking, or acting normally. **2** *n.* person who is drunk. **3** *n.* someone who suffers from alcoholism. **4** *adj.* very much excited or affected: *drunk with success.* **5** *v.* past participle of **drink:** *I have drunk several glasses of milk already.*

drunk·ard (drung′kərd), *n.* person who is often drunk; person who drinks too much alcoholic liquor.

drunk·en (drung′kən), *adj.* **1** overcome by alcoholic liquor; drunk. **2** caused by being drunk: *a drunken argument.* —**drunk′en·ly,** *adv.* —**drunk′en·ness,** *n.*

drunk·om·e·ter (drung kom′ə tər), *n.* a device that measures the amount of alcohol in someone's blood by testing the breath. A Breathalyzer is one kind of drunkometer.

drupe (drüp), *n.* fruit with a single large seed inside a hard pit surrounded by soft, pulpy flesh. Cherries, plums, and peaches are drupes. ▪ Another word that sounds like this is **droop.**

dry (drī), **1** *adj.* not wet; not moist: *Dust is dry. The paint is dry now.* **2** *v.* to make or become dry: *We washed and dried the dishes after dinner. Clothes dry in the sun.* **3** *adj.* having little or no rain: *Arizona has a dry climate.* **4** *adj.* not giving milk: *That cow has been dry for a month.* **5** *adj.* empty of water or other liquid: *That pond is often dry during the summer.* **6** *adj.* wanting a drink; thirsty: *I'm awfully dry after that hike.* **7** *adj.* not under, in, or on water: *I was glad to be on dry land and away from the swamp.* **8** *adj.* not shedding tears: *After the sad play there wasn't a dry eye in the theater.* **9** *adj.* not fresh: *The cook used dry bread to make turkey stuffing.* **10** *adj.* quietly humorous in a sharp, biting way: *a dry wit, a dry remark.* **11** *adj.* not interesting; dull: *A book full of facts and figures is dry.* **12** *adj.* free from sweetness or fruity flavor: *dry wine.* **13** *adj.* without butter: *dry toast.* **14** *adj.* forbidding the sale of alcoholic drinks: *a dry city, a dry state.* ❑ *adj.* **dri·er, dri·est;** *v.* **dried, dry·ing.** —**dry′ly,** *adv.* —**dry′ness,** *n.*

dry up, INFORMAL. stop talking.

SYNONYM STUDY **Dry** and **arid** both mean without water. **Dry** is a general word: *When the dishes are dry, I'll put them away.* **Arid** means getting little rain. It is used about land: *In arid regions, farmers depend on irrigation.*

a	hat	ė	term	ô	order	ch	child		
ā	age	i	it	oi	oil	ng	long	ə	a in about
ä	far	ī	ice	ou	out	sh	she		e in taken
â	care	o	hot	u	cup	th	thin		i in pencil
e	let	ō	open	ù	put	ℑH	then		o in lemon
ē	equal	ò	saw	ü	rule	zh	measure		u in circus

duck[1] (def. 2)—about 2 ft. (61 cm) long

dry·ad (drī′əd), *n.* (in Greek and Roman myths) a nymph that lives in a tree; wood nymph.

dry cell, an electric cell in which the chemicals producing the current are made into a paste, so that they cannot spill. A flashlight battery is a dry cell.

dry-clean (drī′klēn′), *v.* to clean clothing or fabrics with a chemical cleaning fluid instead of water. **—dry cleaner,** *n.* **—dry cleaning,** *n.*

dry dock, dock built watertight so that the water may be pumped out. Dry docks are used for building or repairing ships.

dry·er (drī′ər), *n.* **1** device or machine that removes water by heat, air, etc.: *a clothes dryer, a hair dryer.* **2** Also, **drier.** substance mixed with paint, varnish, ink, etc., to make it dry more quickly. ■ Another word that sounds like this is **drier.**

dry farming, way of farming in places where there is little rain and no irrigation. Dry farming uses methods that conserve soil moisture to raise crops that can survive long dry periods.

dry goods, cloth, ribbons, laces, etc., and similar textile fabrics.

dry ice, a very cold, white solid formed when carbon dioxide is greatly compressed and then cooled. It is used for keeping ice cream and other things cold because it changes from a solid back to a gas without becoming liquid.

dry measure, system for measuring the volume of such things as grain, vegetables, or fruit, using quarts, bushels, pecks, or liters. See table on page 975A.

dry run, a practice test or session.

dry·wall (drī′wôl′), **1** *n.* wall or part of a wall inside a building made of prepared sections of a dry material, such as wood fiber. **2** *v.* to use these sections to put up a wall.

DST or **D.S.T.,** daylight-saving time.

du·al (dü′əl), *adj.* **1** consisting of two parts; double; twofold: *The car had dual controls, one set for the learner and one for the teacher.* **2** of two; showing two. ■ Another word that sounds like this is **duel.** **—du·al′i·ty,** *n.* **—du′al·ly,** *adv.*

dub[1] (dub), *v.* **1** to give a title, name, or nickname to; name; call: *My sister dubbed our new sailboat "Sea Breeze."* **2** to make someone a knight by striking his shoulder lightly with a sword. ❑ *v.* **dubbed, dub·bing.**

dub[2] (dub), *v.* **1** to add music, voices, or other sounds to a movie, a radio or TV show, a recording, etc.: *The Italian film was dubbed with English dialogue.* **2** to copy a tape or record. ❑ *v.* **dubbed, dub·bing.** [Dub[2] comes from **double,** because the new recording is a second version.]

du·bi·ous (dü′bē əs), *adj.* **1** filled with or being in doubt; doubtful; uncertain: *The senator was dubious about his chances of re-election.* **2** of questionable character; probably bad: *The police are investigating the swindler's dubious schemes for making money.* **—du′bi·ous·ly,** *adv.* **—du′bi·ous·ness,** *n.*

Dub·lin (dub′lən), *n.* capital of the Republic of Ireland, in the E part.

WORD STORY **Dublin** comes from Irish words meaning "black pool." Originally this was the name for part of the river that runs through the city.

Du Bois (dü bois′), **W. E. B.,** 1868-1963, American sociologist and author. W. E. B. stands for William Edward Burghardt. ■ W. E. B. Du Bois helped found the NAACP in 1909.

du·cal (dü′kəl), *adj.* of a duke or dukedom.

duc·at (duk′ət), *n.* any of various gold or silver coins once used in Europe.

Du·champ (dü shän′), *n.* **Mar·cel** (mär sel′), 1887-1968, French artist. ■ Marcel Duchamp often exhibited everyday items as works of art to poke fun at people's ideas of what art should be.

duch·ess (duch′is), *n.* **1** wife or widow of a duke. **2** woman whose rank is equal to that of a duke. ❑ *n., pl.* **duch·ess·es.**

duch·y (duch′ē), *n.* lands ruled by a duke or a duchess. ❑ *n., pl.* **duch·ies.**

duck[1] (duk), *n.* **1** any of numerous swimming birds with short necks, short legs, webbed feet, and broad, flat bills. **2** a female duck. A male is called a drake. **3** flesh of a duck used for food. ❑ *n., pl.* **ducks** or **duck.** **—duck′like′,** *adj.*

duck[2] (duk), **1** *v.* to dip or plunge suddenly under water and out again. **2** *n.* a sudden dip or plunge under water and out again. **3** *v.* to lower the head or bend the body suddenly to keep from being hit, seen, etc.: *She ducked to avoid a low branch.* **4** *n.* a sudden lowering of the head or bending of the body to keep from being hit, seen, etc. **5** *v.* to get or keep away from; avoid; dodge: *duck a blow. He ducked my question.* **6** *v.* to enter or leave quickly: *We ducked into the grocery store for a minute.* **—duck′er,** *n.*

duck[3] (duk), *n.* **1** a strong cotton or linen cloth with a lighter and finer weave than canvas. Duck is used to make small sails, tents, and clothing. **2** ducks, *pl.* trousers made of duck.

duck·bill (duk′bil′), *n.* platypus.

duck·billed dinosaur (duk′bild′), hadrosaur.

duck·billed platypus, platypus.

duck·ling (duk′ling), *n.* a young duck.

duck·weed (duk′wēd′), *n.* a very small plant that has no stem. It grows in water and often forms dense, green floating mats on the surface.

duct (dukt), *n.* **1** tube, pipe, or channel for carrying liquid, air, wires, etc. **2** tube in the body for carrying a bodily fluid: *tear ducts.*

WORD FAMILY Duct and the words below are related. They all come from a Latin word meaning "to lead."

abduct	conduit	duke	reproduce
adduce	deduce	induce	seduce
aqueduct	deduct	introduce	subdue
conducive	duchess	produce	viaduct
conduct	ductile	reduce	

duc·tile (duk′təl), *adj.* **1** capable of being hammered out thin or drawn out into a wire: *Copper is a ductile metal.* **2** capable of being easily molded or shaped; flexible: *Wax is ductile when it is warm.* **3** easily managed or influenced; docile. **—duc·til′i·ty,** *n.*

duct·less (dukt′lis), *adj.* having no duct.

ductless gland, endocrine gland.

duct tape, a wide adhesive tape made to seal joints or holes in ducts. It is often a dull silvery color.

dud (dud), *n.* **1** shell or bomb that fails to explode. **2** failure: *The rocket test was a complete dud.*

dude (düd), *n.* **1** man who pays too much attention to his clothes; dandy. **2** (in the western parts of the United States and Canada) person raised in the city, especially an easterner who vacations on a ranch. **3** SLANG. guy; fellow.

dude ranch, ranch which is run as a tourist resort.

dudg·eon (duj′ən), *n.* **in high dudgeon,** very angry; resentful: *He was in high dudgeon when he found out that we had left without him.*

duds (dudz), *n.pl.* INFORMAL. clothes: *We packed our duds and left the camp.*

due (dü), **1** *adj.* owed as a debt; to be paid as a right; owing: *The money due her for her work was paid today. Respect is due to older people.* **2** *n.* what is owed to someone; someone's right: *Courtesy is their due as long as they are your guests.* **3** *adj.* proper; suitable; rightful: *You will receive a due reward for your good work.* **4** *adj.* as much as needed; enough: *Use due care in crossing streets.* **5** *n.pl.* **dues,** amount of money it costs to be a member of a club; fee or tax for some purpose: *Members who do not pay their dues will be suspended from the club.* **6** *adj.* promised to come or be ready; looked for; expected: *The train is due at noon. Your report is due tomorrow.* **7** *adv.* straight; directly: *The ship sailed due west.* ■ Other words that sound like this are **dew, do**[1], and **'do.**

due to, 1 caused by: *The accident was due to carelessness.* **2** INFORMAL. because of: *The game was called off due to rain.*

USAGE NOTE **Due to** is often used to mean "because of," but some people feel that it is used correctly only to mean "caused by." In formal writing, it is wise to use **due to** only with the meaning that everyone agrees on.

du·el (dü′əl), **1** *n.* a formal fight between two persons armed with pistols or swords. Duels were once fought to settle quarrels, or avenge insults, and took place in the presence of two witnesses called seconds. **2** *n.* any fight or contest between two opponents: *The two opposing lawyers fought a duel of wits.* **3** *v.* to fight a duel. ❑ *v.* **du·eled, du·el·ing** or **du·elled, du·el·ling.** ■ Another word that sounds like this is **dual.** —**du′el·er** or **du′el·ler,** *n.*

du·el·ist (dü′ə list), *n.* person who fights a duel or duels.

du·en·na (dü en′ə), *n.* **1** an elderly woman who is the governess and chaperon of young girls in a Spanish or Portuguese family. **2** governess or chaperon. ❑ *n., pl.* **du·en·nas.**

due process, any established process that protects people's rights during court proceedings and other governmental activities.

du·et (dü et′), *n.* **1** piece of music for two voices or instruments. **2** two singers or players performing together.

duf·fel bag (duf′əl), **1** a large canvas sack for carrying clothing and other belongings, used by campers and soldiers. **2** any small bag made of a tough material.

dug (dug), *v.* past tense and past participle of **dig**: *The dog dug a hole under the fence. The potatoes have all been dug.*

du·gong (dü′gong), *n.* a large, plant-eating sea mammal that lives in the coastal waters of southern Asia and Australia. It is closely related to the manatee.

dug·out (dug′out′), *n.* **1** a rough shelter or dwelling formed by digging into the side of a hill, trench, etc. **2** a small shelter at the side of a baseball field. It is used by players who are not at bat or not in the game. **3** boat made by hollowing out a large log; pirogue.

dugout (def. 3)

DUI, driving under the influence (of alcohol).

duke (dük), *n.* **1** nobleman of the highest title, ranking just below a prince. **2** prince who rules a duchy.

duke·dom (dük′dəm), *n.* **1** lands ruled by a duke; duchy. **2** title or rank of a duke.

dul·ci·mer (dul′sə mər), *n.* **1** a musical instrument with metal strings, played by striking the strings with two hammers. **2** a stringed musical instrument plucked with a goose quill, the fingers, etc. It is used to play folk music in the Appalachian Mountain region. [**Dulcimer** comes from Latin words meaning "sweet song." Dulcimers produce a soft, sweet sound.]

dull (dul), **1** *adj.* not sharp or pointed; blunt: *It is hard to cut with a dull knife.* **2** *adj.* not bright or clear: *dull eyes, a dull day, a dull color.* **3** *adj.* slow in understanding; stupid: *a dull mind. A dull person often fails to get the meaning of a joke.* **4** *adj.* not felt sharply; vague: *the dull pain of a bruise.* **5** *adj.* not clear to the ear; muffled: *a dull thud.* **6** *adj.* not interesting; tiresome; boring: *a dull book.* **7** *adj.* having little life, energy, or spirit; not active: *The fur coat business is usually dull in summer.* **8** *v.* to make or become dull: *Chopping wood dulled the blade of the ax. This cheap knife dulls very easily.* —**dull′ness,** *n.* —**dul′ly,** *adv.*

SYNONYM STUDY **Dull, boring,** and **tiresome** all mean not interesting. **Dull** is a general word: *The TV show was dull, so he turned it off.* **Boring** means so dull that it makes you unhappy: *I can't believe I paid to see this boring movie!* **Tiresome** means dull and making you tired: *She spent a tiresome morning washing windows.*

Du·luth (də lüth′), *n.* city in NE Minnesota, on Lake Superior.

du·ly (dü′lē), *adv.* **1** in a proper way; as due; properly; rightly; suitably: *The documents were duly signed before a lawyer.* **2** when due; at the proper time: *The debt will be duly paid.*

Du·mas (dü mä′), *n.* **1** **A·lex·an·dre** (ă′lek sän′drə), 1802-1870, French novelist and dramatist. ■ **Alexandre Dumas** wrote many adventure novels, including *The Three Musketeers* and *The Count of Monte Cristo.* **2** his son, **Alexandre,** 1824-1895, French dramatist.

dumb (dum), *adj.* **1** not able to speak: *Even intelligent animals are dumb.* **2** silenced for the moment by fear, surprise, shyness, etc.: *When I heard the news, I was struck dumb with astonishment.* **3** unwilling to speak; not speaking; silent. **4** not intelligent; stupid; silly: *Forgetting your homework was a dumb thing to do.* —**dumb′ness,** *n.*

dumb down, to lower the level of difficulty or content of informational material: *to dumb down textbooks.*

USAGE NOTE **Dumb** is not used by careful writers and speakers today to mean "unable to speak," because the word's other meanings have made it sound unfriendly. See the Usage Note at **mute.**

dumb·bell (dum′bel′), *n.* **1** a short bar of wood or iron with large, heavy, round ends. Dumbbells are generally used in pairs and are lifted or swung around to exercise the muscles of the arms, back, etc. **2** INFORMAL. a very stupid person.

WORD STORY **Dumbbell** comes from **dumb,** meaning "silent," and **bell.** Three hundred years ago, dumbbells were machines with ropes like those used to ring church bells. Pulling on the dumbbell's rope provided exercise but produced no sound. Later the name was given to other exercise equipment.

dumb·found (dum′found′), *v.* to amaze and cause someone to be unable to speak; bewilder; confuse. Also, **dumfound.**

dumb show, pantomime.

dumb·wait·er (dum′wā′tər), *n.* a box with shelves that can be pulled up or down a shaft. A dumbwaiter is used to send dishes, food, rubbish, etc., from one floor of a building to another.

dum·found (dum′found′), *v.* to dumbfound.

dum·my (dum′ē), **1** *n.* a life-size figure of a person used in place of a real person. Dummies are used to display clothing in store windows, to shoot at in rifle practice, to tackle in football practice, etc. **2** *n.* INFORMAL. a stupid person with no more sense than such a figure; blockhead. **3** *n.* person who has nothing to say or who takes no active part in affairs. **4** *n.* anything made to resemble a real thing; an imitation. **5** *adj.* made to resemble the real thing; imitation: *We had a sword fight with dummy swords made of wood.* **6** *n.* corporation, person, or group that seems to be acting for itself, but is really acting for another. **7** *n.* a card player whose cards are laid face up on the table and played by his or her partner. ❑ *n., pl.* **dum·mies.**

a	hat	ė	term	ô	order	ch	child			a in about
ā	age	i	it	oi	oil	ng	long			e in taken
ä	far	ī	ice	ou	out	sh	she	ə	{	i in pencil
â	care	o	hot	u	cup	th	thin			o in lemon
e	let	ō	open	ů	put	ŦH	then			u in circus
ē	equal	ò	saw	ü	rule	zh	measure			

dump (dump), **1** v. to empty out; throw down in a heap; unload in a mass: *The truck backed up to the hole and dumped the dirt in it.* **2** n. place for throwing rubbish: *Garbage is taken to the city dump.* **3** n. INFORMAL. a dirty, shabby, or untidy place. **4** v. to get rid of; reject: *The party dumped the unpopular candidate.* **5** v. to sell in large quantities at a very low price or below cost. **6** n. place for storing military supplies: *an ammunition dump.* **7** v. to transfer data in large amounts from a computer memory to some other form of storage, such as a printout. **8** n. a mass transfer of data from a computer memory.

dump·ling (dump′ling), n. **1** a rounded piece of dough, boiled or steamed and usually served with meat. **2** a small pudding made by enclosing fruit in a piece of dough and baking or steaming it.

dumps (dumps), n.pl. **in the dumps**, feeling gloomy or sad: *She was in the dumps because her bike was broken.*

Dump·ster (dump′stər), n. trademark for a large, metal receptacle, often fitted with a lid, for holding garbage and having a means for easy dumping into a truck.

dump truck, truck which can be unloaded of waste, sand, etc., by tipping or by opening downward.

dump·y (dum′pē), adj. short and fat. □ adj. **dump·i·er, dump·i·est. —dump′i·ness,** n.

dun[1] (dun), **1** v. to demand payment of a debt from someone again and again: *The store dunned him until his overdue bills were finally paid.* **2** n. a demand for payment of a debt. □ v. **dunned, dun·ning.** ■ Another word that sounds like this is **done.**

dun[2] (dun), **1** adj. dull, grayish brown. **2** n. a dull, grayish brown. ■ Another word that sounds like this is **done.**

Dun·bar (dun′bär), n. **Paul Laur·ence** (lôr′əns), 1872-1906, African American author. He published 12 books and was nationally popular for his poetry and fiction.

Dun·can (dung′kən), n. **Is·a·dor·a** (iz′ə dôr′ə), 1877-1927, American dancer. ■ **Isadora Duncan's** dances were inspired by poetry, classical music, nature, and the art of Greece. They greatly influenced the development of modern dance.

dunce (duns), n. person who is stupid or slow to learn.

dune (dün), n. mound or ridge of loose sand heaped up by the wind.

dunes

dune buggy, a motor vehicle with very large tires, used to drive on sand; beach buggy.

dung (dung), n. waste matter from the intestines of animals, much used as a fertilizer; manure.

dun·ga·ree (dung′gə rē′), n. **1** a coarse cotton cloth, used for work clothes. **2 dungarees,** pl. trousers, work clothes, or overalls made of this cloth. [See Word Story at **jeans**.]

dun·geon (dun′jən), n. a dark underground room or cell to keep prisoners in.

WORD STORY In the Middle Ages **dungeon** meant "the strong central tower of a castle" or that tower's cellar. Prisoners were kept in both places, but people began using the word mostly about the cellar—perhaps because it was a worse place to be, perhaps because **dungeon** goes so well with *deep* and *dark.*

dung·hill (dung′hil′), n. heap of dung or refuse: *a dunghill in the farmyard.*

Dun·ham (dun′əm), n. **Kath·er·ine** (kath′ər in), born 1912, African American choreographer and anthropologist. ■ **Katherine Dunham** choreographed dances based on dances of black people around the world, and did anthropological research in Jamaica and Haiti.

dunk (dungk), **1** v. to dip something to eat into a liquid: *I like to dunk doughnuts in coffee.* **2** n. a dunk shot. **3** v. (in basketball) to make a dunk shot. **—dunk′er,** n.

dunk shot, a basketball shot made by leaping so that the hands are above the rim of the basket, and throwing the ball down through the netting.

du·o (dü′ō), n. **1** duet. **2** pair. □ n., pl. **du·os.**

du·o·dec·i·mal (dü′ō des′ə məl), **1** adj. of twelves; counting or figuring with twelve as a base: *The duodecimal number system.* **2** n. a number in a system based on twelve.

du·o·de·nal (dü′ō dē′nl), adj. of or about the duodenum: *a duodenal ulcer.*

du·o·de·num (dü′ō dē′nəm), n. the first part of the small intestine, just below the stomach. □ n., pl. **du·o·de·na** (dü′ō dē′nə), **du·o·de·nums.**

dup., duplicate.

dupe (düp), **1** n. person easily deceived or tricked. **2** v. to deceive or trick: *They were dishonest and duped their customers.* □ v. **duped, dup·ing. —dup′er,** n.

du·ple (dü′pəl), adj. **1** double. **2** (in music) having two, or a multiple of two, beats to a measure.

du·plex (dü′pleks), **1** adj. having two parts; double; twofold. A **duplex apartment** has rooms on two floors. A **duplex house** is a house accommodating two families. **2** n. a duplex house or apartment. □ n., pl. **du·plex·es.**

du·pli·cate (dü′plə kit for adj., noun; dü′plə kāt for verb), **1** adj. exactly like something else: *We have duplicate keys for the front door.* **2** n. one of two things exactly alike; an exact copy: *I mailed the letter, but kept a duplicate.* **3** v. to make an exact copy of; repeat exactly: *duplicate a picture.* **4** adj. having two corresponding parts; twofold; double: *A human being has duplicate lungs but only one heart.* □ v. **du·pli·cat·ed, du·pli·cat·ing.**

in duplicate, in two copies exactly alike: *Please fill out the application in duplicate.*

du·pli·ca·tion (dü′plə kā′shən), n. **1** act or process of duplicating or condition of being duplicated: *duplication of effort.* **2** a duplicate copy: *Her answers were a duplication of her sister's.*

du·pli·ca·tor (dü′plə kā′tər), n. machine for making many exact copies of anything that is written, typed, or drawn.

du·plic·i·ty (dü plis′ə tē), n. an acting secretly in one way and openly in another in order to deceive; deceitfulness: *the duplicity of a friend who talks about you behind your back.*

du·ra·ble (dur′ə bəl), adj. **1** able to withstand wear, decay, etc.: *durable fabric.* **2** lasting a long time: *a durable peace.* **—dur′a·bil′i·ty,** n. **—dur′a·ble·ness,** n. **—dur′a·bly,** adv.

dur·ance (dur′əns), n. OLD USE. **durance vile,** imprisonment: *years of durance vile in a foul dungeon.*

Du·ran·go (dù rang′gō), n. a state in NW Mexico.

du·ra·tion (dù rā′shən), n. length of time; time during which anything continues: *The storm was sudden and of short duration.*

Dü·rer (dü′rər), n. **Al·brecht** (äl′brekt), 1471-1528, German painter and engraver.

du·ress (dù res′), n. use of force; compulsion. The law does not require a person to fulfill a contract signed under duress.

dur·ing (dur′ing), prep. **1** through the whole time of; throughout: *The children played inside during the storm.* **2** at some time in; in the course of: *Come to see me during my office hours.*

durst (dėrst), v. OLD USE. a past tense of **dare.**

Du·shan·be (dü shän′bə), n. capital of Tajikistan.

dusk (dusk), n. **1** the darker stage of twilight; time just before dark: *We saw the evening star at dusk.* **2** shade; gloom: *the dusk of a forest.*

dusk·y (dus′kē), adj. somewhat dark; like dusk; dim: *the dusky shadow of the deep woods.* □ adj. **dusk·i·er, dusk·i·est. —dusk′i·ly,** adv. **—dusk′i·ness,** n.

dust (dust), **1** *n.* fine, dry earth: *Dust lay thick on the road.* **2** *n.* any fine powder: *The old papers had turned to dust. The bee is covered with yellow dust from the flowers.* **3** *v.* to brush or wipe the dust from; get dust off: *He dusted the furniture.* **4** *v.* to sprinkle with powder, sugar, insecticide, etc.: *to dust powder over a baby, to dust the crops with pesticides.* **5** *n.* what is left of a dead body after decay: *The tomb contains the dust of royalty.*

bite the dust, 1 to fall dead or wounded. **2** be defeated, dismissed, or eliminated: *The other team bit the dust.*

throw dust in someone's eyes, to deceive or mislead someone.

dust bowl, 1 area, especially in the western plains of the United States and Canada, where dust storms may be frequent and violent. **2 Dust Bowl,** the agricultural region in the south central and southwestern United States that was heavily damaged by dust storms in the 1930s.

Dust Bowl scene

dust·er (dus′tər), *n.* **1** person or thing that dusts. **2** cloth or brush used to get the dust off things. **3** a long, light garment worn over the clothes to keep dust off them. **4** a similar article of clothing worn by women, especially indoors.

dust jacket, an outer paper cover for protecting a book; jacket.

dust·pan (dust′pan′), *n.* a flat, broad pan with a handle, onto which dust can be swept from the floor.

dust storm, a strong wind carrying clouds of dust across or from a dry region.

dust·y (dus′tē), *adj.* **1** covered or filled with dust: *She found some dusty old books in the attic.* **2** like dust; dry and powdery: *dusty chalk.* **3** having the color of dust; grayish: *a dusty brown.* ❑ *adj.* **dust·i·er, dust·i·est. —dust′i·ly,** *adv.* **—dust′i·ness,** *n.*

Dutch (duch), **1** *adj.* of the Netherlands, its people, or their language. **2** *n.pl.* people of the Netherlands. **3** *n.* their language. **4** *n.pl.* OLD USE. Germans: *The ancestors of the Pennsylvania Dutch came from Germany, not from the Netherlands.*

go Dutch, to have each person pay for him- or herself: *Since neither of us could afford to treat the other to dinner, we went Dutch.*

in Dutch, in trouble or disgrace: *I'm in Dutch with my parents for tearing my new jacket.*

Dutch has given a number of words to the English language, including the words below.

bamboo	furlough	sleigh	trigger
brandy	gruff	slim	tub
cookie	iceberg	snoop	wagon
cruller	pickle	spook	walrus
deck	roster	spool	yacht
dope	sled		

Dutch door, door divided in two horizontally, so that one half may be open while the other is closed.

Dutch·man (duch′mən), *n.* **1** person born or living in the Netherlands. **2** OLD USE. a German. ❑ *n., pl.* **Dutch·men.**

Dutch oven, a heavy iron pot with a close-fitting cover. Some Dutch ovens are covered with hot coals and used for baking.

Dutch treat, meal or entertainment at which each person pays for himself or herself.

Dutch·wo·man (duch′wum′ən), *n.* **1** woman born or living in the Netherlands. **2** OLD USE. a German. ❑ *n., pl.* **Dutch·wo·men.**

du·te·ous (dü′tē əs), *adj.* dutiful; obedient. **—du′te·ous·ly,** *adv.*

du·ti·ful (dü′tə fəl), *adj.* doing the duties required of you; obedient: *Dutiful children help their parents.* **—du′ti·ful·ly,** *adv.* **—du′ti·ful·ness,** *n.*

du·ty (dü′tē), *n.* **1** thing that is right to do; what a person ought to do; obligation: *It is your duty to obey the laws.* **2** the binding force of what is right; moral obligation: *a sense of duty.* **3** thing that you must do in your work: *One of the duties of a class treasurer is to keep records of the money in the treasury.* **4** a tax, especially a tax on articles brought into a country. ❑ *n., pl.* **du·ties.**

off duty, not working at your job or position.

on duty, working at your job or position.

dwarf (dwôrf), **1** *n.* person, animal, or plant much smaller than the usual size for its kind. **2** *n.* (in fairy tales) an ugly little man with magic power. **3** *n.* any of a type of star having about the size and brightness of the sun, smaller and less bright than giant stars. **4** *adj.* much smaller than the usual size for its kind; stopped from growing: *dwarf trees.* **5** *v.* to keep from growing large; check the growth of. **6** *v.* to cause to look or seem small. ❑ *n., pl.* **dwarfs, dwarves** (dwôrvz).

USAGE NOTE **Dwarf** and **midget** are both used to mean animals, plants, or people much smaller than the usual size. When used about people, the two words have different meanings, however. A dwarf has a head and body of the usual size but short arms and legs. A midget has a head, body, arms, and legs all smaller than usual. Some people object to the use of **dwarf** and **midget.** It is wise to consider the preferences of your sources and your audience. If in doubt, ask!

dwarf·ish (dwôr′fish), *adj.* like a dwarf; much smaller than usual. **—dwarf′ish·ly,** *adv.* **—dwarf′ish·ness,** *n.*

dwell (dwel), *v.* to make your home; live: *They dwell in the city.* ■ See Synonym Study at **live**[1]. ❑ *v.* **dwelt** or **dwelled, dwell·ing. —dwell′er,** *n.*

dwell on or **dwell upon, 1** to think, write, or speak about for a long time: *Her mind dwelt on the pleasant day she had spent in the country.* **2** to put stress on: *The speaker dwelt especially on the great need for teachers.*

dwell·ing (dwel′ing), *n.* place in which you live; house; residence.

dwelt (dwelt), *v.* a past tense and a past participle of **dwell:** *We dwelt there a long time. We have dwelt in the country for years.*

DWI, driving while intoxicated.

dwin·dle (dwin′dl), *v.* to become smaller and smaller; shrink; diminish: *During the blizzard the campers' supply of food dwindled day by day.* ❑ *v.* **dwin·dled, dwin·dling.**

Dy, symbol for dysprosium.

dye (dī), **1** *n.* a coloring matter used to color cloth, hair, etc. Some dyes are vegetable, others chemical. **2** *n.* a color produced by such coloring matter: *A good dye will not fade or run.* **3** *v.* to color cloth, hair, etc., by dipping in a liquid containing coloring matter: *have a shirt dyed.* **4** *v.* to become colored when treated with a dye: *This material dyes evenly and quickly.* **5** *v.* to color or stain: *Grape juice dyed the tablecloth purple.* ❑ *v.* **dyed, dye·ing.** ■ Another word that sounds like this is **die. —dy′er,** *n.*

dye (def. 3)

a	hat	ė	term	ô	order	ch	child		a in about
ā	age	i	it	oi	oil	ng	long		e in taken
ä	far	ī	ice	ou	out	sh	she	ə	i in pencil
â	care	o	hot	u	cup	th	thin		o in lemon
e	let	ō	open	u̇	put	ᵺ	then		u in circus
ē	equal	ȯ	saw	ü	rule	zh	measure		

dyed–in–the–wool (dīd′in ͭHə wůl′), *adj.* thoroughgoing; complete: *a dyed-in-the-wool conservative in politics.*

dye·ing (dī′ing), *n.* act or process of coloring fabrics with dye.

dye·stuff (dī′stuf′), *n.* substance yielding a dye or used as a dye.

dy·ing (dī′ing), **1** *adj.* about to die: *a dying old man.* **2** *adj.* coming to an end: *the dying year.* **3** *adj.* of death; at death: *his dying words.* **4** *v.* present participle of **die**[1]: *The storm is dying down.*

dyke (dīk), *n., v.* dike. ❑ *v.* **dyked, dyk·ing.**

Dy·lan (dil′ən), *n.* **Bob** (bob), born 1941, American musician. ■ **Bob Dylan** began his career as a folk singer in the 1960s, with protest songs, including "Blowin' in the Wind" and "The Times, They Are A-Changin'." He later wrote and performed songs influenced by country music and rock.

dy·nam·ic (dī nam′ik), *adj.* **1** of energy or force in motion. **2** active; energetic; forceful: *a dynamic personality.* **3** continuously changing or active: *a dynamic situation.* **—dy·nam′i·cal·ly,** *adv.*

dy·nam·ics (dī nam′iks), *n.* **1** branch of physics dealing with the action of forces on objects in motion. **2** the forces at work in any field: *the new dynamics of education.*

dy·na·mite (dī′nə mīt), **1** *n.* a powerful explosive made of nitroglycerin mixed with an absorbent material and pressed into round sticks. It is used in blasting rock, tree stumps, etc. **2** *v.* to blow up or destroy, especially with dynamite. **3** *adj.* INFORMAL. terrific; excellent: *That was a dynamite movie.* ❑ *v.* **dy·na·mit·ed, dy·na·mit·ing. —dy′na·mit′er,** *n.*

WORD STORY **Dynamite** comes from a Greek word meaning "power." The word was made up by Alfred Nobel, the Swedish chemist who invented this explosive and created the Nobel prizes.

dy·na·mo (dī′nə mō), *n.* **1** machine that produces electricity; generator, especially one that produces direct current. **2** a very energetic and forceful person. ❑ *n., pl.* **dy·na·mos.**

dy·nas·ty (dī′nə stē), *n.* **1** succession of rulers who belong to the same family: *The Bourbon dynasty ruled France for more than 200 years.* **2** a powerful family which controls some area of activity, such as a newspaper, passing that control from one generation to the next. ❑ *n., pl.* **dy·nas·ties. —dy·nas′tic,** *adj.* **—dy·nas′ti·cal·ly,** *adv.*

dyne (dīn), *n.* unit of force required to give a mass of one gram an acceleration of one centimeter per second for each second the force is applied. ■ Another word that sounds like this is **dine.**

dys·en·ter·y (dis′n ter′ē), *n.* disease of the intestines, producing diarrhea with blood and mucus.

dys·func·tion (dis fungk′shən), *n.* abnormal or weakened function of a body part, machine, social group, etc. **—dys·func′tion·al,** *n.*

dys·lex·i·a (dis lek′sē ə), *n.* difficulty in reading or in understanding what is read.

dys·lex·ic (dis lek′sik), **1** *adj.* having dyslexia. **2** *n.* person who has dyslexia. ■ This meaning of **dyslexic** is sometimes considered offensive, because it is thought to identify the person with the problem. "A person who has dyslexia" avoids the problem.

dys·pep·si·a (dis pep′sē ə), *n.* poor digestion; indigestion.

dys·pep·tic (dis pep′tik), **1** *adj.* of dyspepsia. **2** *adj.* suffering from dyspepsia. **3** *n.* person who has dyspepsia. **4** *adj.* gloomy; pessimistic. **—dys·pep′ti·cal·ly,** *adv.*

dys·pro·si·um (dis prō′zē əm), *n.* a metallic element found in various minerals which forms highly magnetic compounds. *Symbol:* Dy

dz., dozen or dozens.

E or **e** (ē), *n.* the fifth letter of the English alphabet. ❑ *n., pl.* **E's** or **e's.**

E or **E.,** 1 east. 2 eastern.

each (ēch), 1 *adj.* every one of two or more persons or things considered separately: *Each child has a name.* 2 *pron.* every one: *Each of the students has a parent at the school's open house.* 3 *adv.* for each; apiece: *These apples cost 25 cents each.* ■ See Usage Note at **every.**

each other, 1 each one the other one: *The sisters hugged each other.* 2 one another: *The three gladiators struck at each other with their swords.*

ea·ger (ē′gər), *adj.* wanting very much; desiring strongly: *We are eager to go to the picnic.* —**ea′ger·ly,** *adv.* —**ea′ger·ness,** *n.*

eager beaver, INFORMAL. an overly hard-working, ambitious, or enthusiastic person.

ea·gle (ē′gəl), 1 *n.* any of a group of large birds of prey that are related to hawks and have keen eyesight and powerful wings. There are many kinds of eagles and they live in most parts of the world, but only the bald eagle and golden eagle breed in North America. The bald eagle is the emblem of the United States. 2 (earlier) a gold coin of the United States, worth $10.

ea·gle-eyed (ē′gəl īd′), *adj.* 1 able to see far and clearly: *an eagle-eyed scout.* 2 paying close attention to detail: *Our eagle-eyed accountant found the error.*

Eagle Scout, the highest rank that can be achieved in the U.S. Boy Scouts.

ea·glet (ē′glit), *n.* a young eagle.

Ea·kins (ā′kinz), *n.* **Thomas,** 1844-1916, American artist. He painted portraits and realistic pictures of outdoor life and sporting events.

Eames (ēmz), *n.* **Charles,** 1907-1978, American designer and architect. He designed the **Eames chair,** a comfortable, inexpensive chair that can be stacked.

a	hat	ė	term	ô	order	ch	child		
ā	age	i	it	oi	oil	ng	long		a in about
ä	far	ī	ice	ou	out	sh	she		e in taken
â	care	o	hot	u	cup	th	thin	ə {	i in pencil
e	let	ō	open	ů	put	ŦH	then		o in lemon
ē	equal	ò	saw	ü	rule	zh	measure		u in circus

ear¹ (ir), *n*. **1** part of the body by which people and animals hear. It consists of the outer ear, the middle ear, and the inner ear. **2** the outer part of the ear; auricle. **3** thing shaped like the outer part of the ear. **4** Also, **ears**, *pl*. sense of hearing: *Her voice is pleasing to the ear.* **5** ability to hear small differences in sounds: *I have a good ear for music.* **6** attention: *Please give ear to my request.* **−ear′less**, *adj*. **−ear′like′**, *adj*.

be all ears, to listen eagerly; pay careful attention: *The children were all ears while their teacher read them the exciting story.*

play by ear, to play a piece of music or a musical instrument without using written music.

prick up your ears, **1** to point the ears upward: *The dog pricked up its ears at the sudden noise.* **2** to give sudden attention: *I pricked up my ears when I heard my name mentioned.*

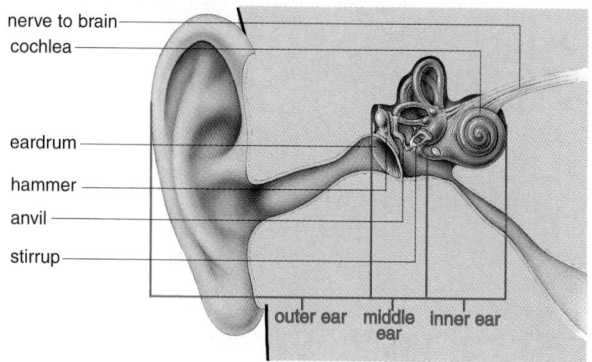

nerve to brain
cochlea
eardrum
hammer
anvil
stirrup
outer ear   middle ear   inner ear

ear¹ (def. 1)

ear² (ir), *n*. the part of certain plants on which grains grow. The grains of corn, wheat, oats, barley, and rye come from ears.

ear·ache (ir′āk′), *n*. pain in the ear.

ear·drum (ir′drum′), *n*. a thin membrane across the middle ear that vibrates when sound waves strike it. See picture at **ear¹**.

ear·ful (ir′fùl), *n*. **1** a severe scolding; rebuke: *She gave us an earful about the mess.* **2** a startling disclosure. ❑ *n*., *pl*. **ear·fuls**.

Ear·hart (âr′härt), *n*. **A·mel·ia** (ə mē′lyə), 1897-1937?, American aviator. ■ **Amelia Earhart** was the first woman to fly solo across the Atlantic Ocean. In 1937 she was attempting to fly around the world when her plane disappeared over the Pacific Ocean.

earl (ėrl), *n*. a British nobleman ranking below a marquis and above a viscount.

earl·dom (ėrl′dəm), *n*. **1** lands ruled by an earl. **2** title or rank of an earl.

ear·lobe (ir′lōb′), *n*. the hanging lower part of the external ear.

ear·ly (ėr′lē), *adv*., *adj*. **1** near the beginning; in the first part: *The sun is not hot early in the day.* **2** before the usual or expected time: *Please come early. We had an early dinner.* **3** before very long: *Spring may come early this year.* **4** earlier, before the present time; used in the past: *"Icebox" is an earlier word for a refrigerator.* ❑ *adj*. **ear·li·er**, **ear·li·est**. **−ear′li·ness**, *n*.

early bird, person who gets up or arrives early.

ear·mark (ir′märk′), **1** *n*. a special mark, quality, or feature that gives information about someone or something; sign: *Truthfulness is an earmark of an honest person.* **2** *v*. to set aside for some special purpose: *This money is earmarked for new books.* **3** *n*. mark made on the ear of an animal to show who owns it.

ear·muffs (ir′mufs′), *n.pl*. pair of coverings worn over the ears in cold weather to keep them warm.

earn (ėrn), *v*. **1** to get in return for work or service; be paid: *She earns $25 a day.* **2** to do enough to get; do good enough work for; deserve: *He earned a vacation.* **3** to bring or get as deserved; win: *Her hard work earned her the respect of her teachers.* **4** to gain as a profit or return: *Money well invested earns good interest.* ■ Another word that sounds like this is **urn**. **−earn′er**, *n*.

ear·nest¹ (ėr′nist), *adj*. strong and firm in purpose; eager and serious: *Earnest pupils try very hard to do their best.* ■ See Synonym Study at **serious**. **−ear′nest·ly**, *adv*. **−ear′nest·ness**, *n*.

in earnest, strong and firm in purpose; eager and serious.

ear·nest² (ėr′nist), *n*. part of the purchase price paid by the buyer to the seller of a house as a pledge to pay the rest.

earn·ings (ėr′ningz), *n.pl*. money earned; wages or profits.

Earp (ėrp), *n*. **Wy·att** (wī′ət), 1848-1929, American lawman. ■ **Wyatt Earp** and his brothers won a famous gunfight with outlaws at the O.K. Corral in Tombstone, Arizona in 1881.

ear·phone (ir′fōn′), *n*. device placed over or in the ear to carry sound directly from a radio, phonograph, stereo, etc.

ear·plug (ir′plug′), *n*. a small, round piece of soft rubber or plastic placed in the ear to keep out noise or water.

ear·ring (ir′ring′), *n*. jewelry for the ear.

ear·shot (ir′shot′), *n*. distance at which a sound can be heard; range of hearing: *We shouted, but he was out of earshot.*

ear·split·ting (ir′split′ing), *adj*. very noisy and loud; deafening: *The bomb exploded with an earsplitting sound.*

earth (ėrth), *n*. **1** Also, **Earth**, the planet on which we live; the globe. Earth is the fifth largest planet in the solar system, and the third in distance from the sun. **2** all the people who live on this planet: *What if the whole earth spoke only one language?* **3** dry land: *Our environment is made up of the earth, the sea, and the sky.* **4** ground; soil; dirt: *The earth in the garden is soft.*

down to earth, seeing things as they are; practical.

> **USAGE NOTE** Some people feel that **Earth** should always be capitalized, but others disagree. Everyone agrees on one rule: when you write about the earth in relation to other planets, you should capitalize it, like the names of the other planets: *Saturn is larger than Earth and smaller than Jupiter.*

earth·en (ėr′thən), *adj*. **1** made of baked clay: *an earthen jug.* **2** made of earth: *The old cabin had an earthen floor.*

earth·en·ware (ėr′thən wâr′), **1** *n*. dishes or containers made of baked clay; crockery. Coarse pottery is earthenware. **2** *adj*. made of baked clay: *an earthenware pot.*

earth·ling (ėrth′ling), *n*. human who lives on the earth.

earth·ly (ėrth′lē), *adj*. **1** on earth; not heavenly: *She left all her earthly goods to her niece.* **2** possible: *That rubbish is of no earthly use.* ❑ *adj*. **earth·li·er**, **earth·li·est**. **−earth′li·ness**, *n*.

earth·quake (ėrth′kwāk′), *n*. a shaking or shifting motion of the earth's surface. It is caused by the sudden breaking of masses of rock along a fault. Some violent earthquakes cause serious damage, but most earthquakes are unimportant.

earth satellite, satellite of the earth made by human beings.

earth science, any of the sciences dealing with the origin, composition, and physical features of the earth. Geology, geography, meteorology, and oceanography are earth sciences.

earth·ward (ėrth′wərd), *adv*., *adj*. toward the earth: *The meteor hurtled earthward. The eagle started its earthward descent.*

earth·wards (ėrth′wərdz), *adv*. earthward.

earth·work (ėrth′wėrk′), *n*. earth piled up for a fortification.

earth·worm (ėrth′wėrm′), *n*. a reddish brown or grayish worm that lives in and loosens the soil; angleworm.

earth·y (ėr′thē), *adj*. **1** of earth or soil: *Potatoes have an earthy smell.* **2** like earth or soil: *The color of the field was a rich, earthy brown.* **3** down to earth; realistic; practical: *an earthy person.* **4** not refined; coarse: *earthy language.* ❑ *adj*. **earth·i·er**, **earth·i·est**. **−earth′i·ness**, *n*.

ear·wig (ir′wig′), *n*. any of several slender insects that look something like a beetle and have large pincers at their back end.

ease (ēz), **1** *n*. freedom from pain or trouble; comfort: *a life of ease.* **2** *v*. to make free from pain or trouble; give comfort to: *Her reassuring words helped ease my worried mind.* **3** *n*. freedom from trying hard: *You can do this lesson with ease.* **4** *n*. freedom from embarrassment; natural or easy manner: *He spoke to the class with ease and humor.* **5** *v*. to loosen: *The belt is too tight; ease it a notch or two.* **6** *v*. to move slowly and carefully: *We eased the big box through the narrow door.* ❑ *v*. **eased**, **eas·ing**.

at ease, **1** free from pain or trouble; comfortable: *The doctor soon made the worried patient feel at ease.* **2** with the body relaxed and the feet apart: *The soldiers stood at ease.*

ease off or **ease up**, to lessen; lighten.

ea·sel (ē′zəl), *n*. a stand for holding a picture, blackboard, etc.

eas·i·ly (ē′zə lē), *adv.* **1** without trying hard; with little effort: *The simple tasks were easily done.* **2** without pain or trouble; comfortably: *The patient was resting easily.* **3** surely; without question: *He is easily the best singer in the choir.* **4** very likely; probably: *She is a good writer and may easily become famous.*

east (ēst), **1** *n.* direction of the sunrise. **2** *adv., adj.* toward the east; farther toward the east: *Take the east road.* **3** *adj.* from the east: *an east wind.* **4** *n.* Also, **East,** the part of any country toward the east. **5** *n.* **the East, a** the eastern part of the United States; region from Maine through Maryland. **b** the countries in Asia; the Orient: *China and Japan are in the East.*

east of, further east than: *Ohio is east of Indiana.*

East Berlin, formerly, the capital of East Germany.

east·bound (ēst′bound′), *adj.* going east: *an eastbound express.*

East China Sea, part of the Pacific Ocean, east of Asia, extending north from Taiwan to Korea and Japan. It is connected to the South China Sea by the Taiwan Strait.

Eas·ter (ē′stər), *n.* the yearly Christian celebration of Jesus' rising from the dead. Easter comes between March 22 and April 25, on the first Sunday after the first full moon on or after March 21.

WORD STORY **Easter** comes from **east.** The old English goddess of the dawn and her holiday were named for the direction where the sun rises. When the Christian celebration replaced this holiday, people kept using the name they were used to.

Easter Island, an island of Chile in the S Pacific. It is famous for the ruins of many large stone heads found there. [Easter Island was discovered by Europeans on Easter in 1722.]

Easter lily, lily with large, white, trumpet-shaped flowers. Easter lilies are often used at Easter to decorate church altars.

east·er·ly (ē′stər lē), **1** *adj., adv.* toward the east: *an easterly exposure.* **2** *adj., adv.* from the east: *an easterly wind.* **3** *n.* wind that blows from the east. □ *n., pl.* **east·er·lies.**

east·ern (ē′stərn), *adj.* **1** toward the east: *an eastern trip.* **2** from the east: *eastern tourists.* **3** of or in the east: *eastern schools.* **4 Eastern, a** of or in the eastern part of the United States. **b** of or in the countries in Asia; Asian: *a blend of Eastern spices.*

Eastern Church, group of Christian churches that give the greatest honor to the patriarch of Constantinople; Greek Orthodox Church; Orthodox Church; Eastern Orthodox Church.

east·ern·er (ē′stər nər), *n.* **1** person born or living in the east. **2 Easterner,** person born or living in the eastern United States.

Eastern Hemisphere, the half of the world that includes Europe, Asia, Africa, and Australia.

east·ern·most (ē′stərn mōst), *adj.* farthest east.

Eastern Orthodox Church, Eastern Church.

Eastern Standard Time, the standard time in the eastern part of the United States and most of eastern Canada.

East Germany, a former country in central Europe, from 1949 to 1990. It is now part of Germany.

East Indian, 1 of the East Indies. **2** person born or living in the East Indies.

East Indies, 1 the islands of the Malay Archipelago. **2** (earlier) these islands, India, and southeastern Asia.

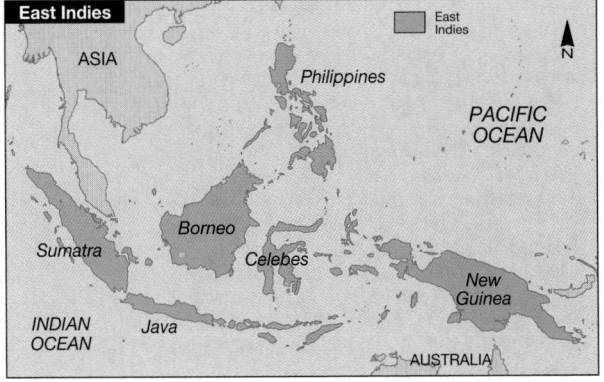

East Indies

ASIA

Philippines

PACIFIC OCEAN

Sumatra

Borneo

Celebes

New Guinea

INDIAN OCEAN

Java

AUSTRALIA

East Indies

N

East·man (ēst′mən), *n.* **George,** 1854-1932, American inventor and businessman. He produced the first lightweight cameras and founded the Kodak corporation.

east·ward (ēst′wərd), **1** *adv., adj.* toward the east; east: *She walked eastward.* **2** *n.* an eastward part, direction, or point.

east·wards (ēst′wərdz), *adv.* eastward.

East·wood (ēst′wůd′), *n.* **Clint** (klint), born 1930, American actor and director. He has played strong, silent heroes in western and action movies, some of which he also directed.

eas·y (ē′zē), **1** *adj.* not hard to do or get: *an easy victory.* **2** *adj.* free from pain, difficulty, or worry; pleasant: *a wealthy person who has an easy life.* **3** *adj.* not strict or harsh: *The new teacher is an easy grader.* **4** *adj.* smooth and pleasant; not awkward: *She has an easy way of speaking to everyone.* **5** *adj.* slow; not fast: *an easy pace.* **6** *adv.* INFORMAL. without much trouble; easily. □ *adj.* **eas·i·er, eas·i·est.** **—eas′i·ness,** *n.*

go easy on, 1 be cautious or sparing of: *The doctor advised me to go easy on sweets.* **2** to treat gently or carefully: *The lawyer went easy on the witness.*

take it easy or **take things easy, 1** to act calmly; move slowly and carefully. **2** to relax.

SYNONYM STUDY **Easy** and **effortless** both mean not hard to do. **Easy** suggests that something is no problem or challenge: *That test was easy.* **Effortless** suggests needing little strength or energy because of skill or practice: *She makes her jump shot look effortless.*

easy chair, a large, comfortable chair, usually with padded arms and cushions.

eas·y·go·ing (ē′zē gō′ing), *adj.* taking matters easily; not worrying: *an easygoing person.*

eat (ēt), *v.* **1** to chew and swallow food: *Cows eat grass and grain.* **2** to have a meal: *Where shall we eat?* **3** to gnaw or devour: *Termites have eaten the posts.* **4** to destroy as if by eating; wear away: *Rust ate away part of the car's fender.* **5** to make by eating: *Moths ate holes in my wool coat.* **6** INFORMAL. to bother; annoy: *What's eating him today?* □ *v.* **ate, eat·en, eat·ing. —eat′er,** *n.*

eat up, to use up; take away: *Medical bills ate up our savings.*

eat·a·ble (ē′tə bəl), *adj.* fit to eat; edible.

eat·en (ēt′n), *v.* past participle of **eat:** *Have you eaten yet?*

eaves (ēvz), *n.pl.* the lower edge of a roof that sticks out over the side of a building.

eaves·drop (ēvz′drop′), *v.* to listen to talk you are not supposed to hear; listen secretly to a private conversation. □ *v.* **eaves·dropped, eaves·drop·ping. —eaves′drop′per,** *n.*

ebb (eb), **1** *n.* flow of the tide away from the shore. **2** *v.* to flow out: *We waded farther out as the tide ebbed.* **3** *n.* a low point; decline: *His fortunes were at an ebb because of his long illness.* **4** *v.* to grow less or weaker; decline: *Her courage ebbed as she climbed to the high diving board.*

ebb tide, process of the tide flowing away from the shore. Ebb tide occurs twice every 24 hours in most parts of the world.

E·bo·la virus (i bō′lə), kind of virus that causes serious or deadly bleeding in human beings. It was identified in 1976 in Africa.

eb·on·y (eb′ə nē), **1** *n.* the hard, black wood of a tropical tree, used for the black keys of a piano and for ornamental woodwork. **2** *adj.* like ebony; black; dark.

e·bul·lient (i bul′yənt), *adj.* overflowing with excitement or liveliness; very enthusiastic. **—e·bul′lient·ly,** *adv.*

EC, European Community.

ec·cen·tric (ek sen′trik), **1** *adj.* out of the ordinary; not usual; odd; peculiar: *Wearing a fur coat in hot weather is eccentric behavior.* **2** *n.* person who behaves in an unusual manner: *The behavior of an eccentric is hard to predict.* **3** *adj.* not having the same center. **4** *adj.* not perfectly circular: *The planets are in eccentric orbits around the sun.* **5** *adj.* off center; having its axis set off center: *an eccentric wheel.* **—ec·cen′tri·cal·ly,** *adv.*

a	hat	ė	term	ô	order	ch	child	
ā	age	i	it	oi	oil	ng	long	ə { a in about
ä	far	ī	ice	ou	out	sh	she	e in taken
â	care	o	hot	u	cup	th	thin	i in pencil
e	let	ō	open	ù	put	ŦH	then	o in lemon
ē	equal	ò	saw	ü	rule	zh	measure	u in circus

ec·cen·tric·i·ty (ek′sen tris′ə tē), *n.* **1** something out of the ordinary; oddity; peculiarity: *It is an eccentricity to carry around an open umbrella on sunny days.* **2** eccentric condition; being unusual or out of the ordinary: *The clock's eccentricity became noticeable when it struck thirteen.* ❑ *n., pl.* **ec·cen·tric·i·ties.**

Ec·cle·si·as·tes (i klē′zē as′tēz), *n.* book of the Bible, supposed to have been written by Solomon.

ec·cle·si·as·tic (i klē′zē as′tik), **1** *n.* member of the clergy. **2** *adj.* ecclesiastical.

ec·cle·si·as·ti·cal (i klē′zē as′tə kəl), *adj.* of the church or the clergy. **—ec·cle′si·as′ti·cal·ly,** *adv.*

ECG, electrocardiogram.

ech·e·lon (esh′ə lon), *n.* arrangement of troops, ships, or planes in a steplike formation, rather than in line.

e·chid·na (i kid′nə), *n.* either of two small, egg-laying, ant-eating mammals of Australia with long snouts, no teeth, and coverings of spines; spiny anteater. ❑ *n., pl.* **e·chid·nas, e·chid·nae** (i kid′nē).

e·chi·no·derm (i kī′nə dėrm′), *n.* any of many small sea animals, including starfish and sea urchins, with body parts arranged like the spokes of a wheel.

ech·o (ek′ō), **1** *n.* repeating of a sound; process or instance of sounding again. You hear an echo when a sound you make bounces back from a distant hill or wall so that you hear it again. **2** *v.* to sound again; repeat or be repeated in sound: *The gunshot echoed through the valley.* **3** *v.* to repeat or imitate what another says or does: *Small children sometimes echo their parents.* ❑ *n., pl.* **ech·oes;** *v.* **ech·oed, ech·o·ing.**

e·cho·ic (e kō′ik), *adj.* like an echo.

ech·o·lo·ca·tion (ek′ō lō kā′shən), *n.* **1** method of locating distant or unseen objects by measuring the time it takes for sound waves echoed off the objects to return to the waves' source. **2** method used by bats, dolphins, and other animals to locate objects by making high-pitched sounds that echo off the objects.

e·clair or **é·clair** (ā klâr′), *n.* an oblong piece of pastry filled with whipped cream or custard and covered with icing. ❑ *n., pl.* **e·clairs** or **é·clairs.**

e·clipse (i klips′), **1** *n.* process of complete or partial blocking of light passing from one heavenly body to another. A **solar eclipse** occurs when the moon passes between the sun and the earth. A **lunar eclipse** occurs when the earth passes between the sun and the moon. **2** *v.* to cut off or dim the light from; darken. **3** *v.* to make dim by comparison; surpass; outshine: *In sports he eclipsed his older brother.* **4** *n.*

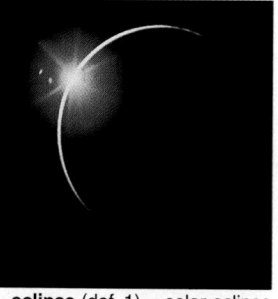

eclipse (def. 1)—solar eclipse

loss of importance or reputation: *The former champion has suffered an eclipse.* ❑ *v.* **e·clipsed, e·clips·ing.**

e·clip·tic (i klip′tik), *n.* path that the sun appears to travel through the stars in one year, because of the earth's movement around the sun.

eco-, *prefix.* of or for ecology or the environment: *ecotourism = tourism for ecology.*

e·co·cide (ē′kō sid *or* ek′ō sid), *n.* destruction of a natural environment, especially by chemical means.

ec·o·log·i·cal (ē′kə loj′ə kəl *or* ek′ə loj′ə kəl), *adj.* of or about ecology: *ecological studies.* **—ec′o·log′i·cal·ly,** *adv.*

e·col·o·gy (ē kol′ə jē), *n.* branch of biology that deals with the relation of living things to their environment and to one another. It studies the distribution of food, living space, and other natural resources. **—e·col′o·gist,** *n.*

WORD STORY **Ecology** comes from Greek words meaning "house" and "the study of." It is the study of things living together in their home. **Economy** comes from Greek words meaning "house" and "to manage." The first economic questions were how to manage a household budget, especially for a palace with dozens of people.

e·co·nom·ic (ē′kə nom′ik *or* ek′ə nom′ik), *adj.* **1** of or about economics. Economic issues have to do with the production, distribution, and consumption of goods and services. **2** of or about the management of the income, supplies, and expenses of a household, government, etc. ■ See Usage Note at **economical.**

e·co·nom·i·cal (ē′kə nom′ə kəl *or* ek′ə nom′ə kəl), *adj.* avoiding waste; saving; thrifty: *We can finish early if we are economical in the use of our time.* **—e′co·nom′i·cal·ly,** *adv.*

USAGE NOTE **Economical** and **economic** look as if they should mean the same thing—but they don't. **Economical** means careful with money: *The smaller car is a more economical choice.* **Economic** means about money or business: *The country is making economic progress.*

e·co·nom·ics (ē′kə nom′iks *or* ek′ə nom′iks), *n.* science of the production, distribution, and consumption of goods and services. Economics studies capital, labor, wages, prices, taxes, etc.

e·con·o·mist (i kon′ə mist), *n.* an expert in economics.

e·con·o·mize (i kon′ə mīz), *v.* to be thrifty; cut down expenses: *We can economize on household expenses by turning off lights when they don't need to be on.* ❑ *v.* **e·con·o·mized, e·con·o·miz·ing. —e·con′o·miz′er,** *n.*

e·con·o·my (i kon′ə mē), *n.* **1** act of making the most of what you have; avoiding waste; thrift: *By using economy in buying food and clothes, we were able to save enough money for our vacation.* **2** business affairs of a country or area: *Under the new administration, the country's economy improved greatly.* ❑ *n., pl.* **e·con·o·mies.** [See Word Story at **ecology.**]

e·co·sys·tem (ē′kō sis′təm *or* ek′ō sis′təm), *n.* a physical environment with its community of living things, considered as an ecological unit. An ecosystem may be a lake, a desert, etc.

e·co·tone (ē′kə tōn *or* ek′ə tōn), *n.* boundary area of two ecosystems, such as a coast or mountain foothills.

e·co·tour·ism (ē′kō tùr′iz əm), *n.* tourism attracted to an area by the area's interesting, endangered, or exotic ecology: *Ecotourism brings much money to the rain forest.*

ec·ru (ek′rü *or* ā′krü), **1** *adj.* pale brown. **2** *n.* a pale brown.

ec·sta·sy (ek′stə sē), *n.* feeling of very great joy; thrilling or overwhelming delight: *She was speechless with ecstasy after winning the gold medal.* ❑ *n., pl.* **ec·sta·sies.**

ec·stat·ic (ek stat′ik), *adj.* very joyful; excited and delighted: *an ecstatic look of pleasure.* **—ec·stat′i·cal·ly,** *adv.*

ec·to·derm (ek′tə dėrm′), *n.* the outer layer of cells formed during the development of animal embryos. Skin, hair, and nails grow from the ectoderm. **—ec′to·der′mal, —ec′to·der′mic,** *adj.*

ec·to·plasm (ek′tə plaz′əm), *n.* the outer section of a cell, just inside the cell's enclosing membrane.

Ec·ua·dor (ek′wə dôr), *n.* country in NW South America. *Capital:* Quito. [**Ecuador** comes from a Spanish word meaning "equator." It was named for its location, which is on the equator.] **—Ec′ua·do′ran, Ec′ua·do′re·an,** or **Ec′ua·do′ri·an,** *adj., n.*

ec·u·men·i·cal (ek′yə men′ə kəl), *adj.* **1** general; universal. **2** of or representing the whole Christian Church: *an ecumenical council stressing Christian unity.* **—ec′u·men′i·cal·ly,** *adv.*

ec·ze·ma (ek′sə mə *or* eg zē′mə), *n.* inflammation of the skin with itching and the formation of scaly, encrusted sores.

ed., **1** edited. **2** edition. **3** editor.

ed·dy (ed′ē), **1** *n.* water, air, smoke, etc., moving against the main current, especially when it has a whirling motion: *An eddy of wind pushed paper from the street against the buildings.* **2** *v.* to move against the main current in a whirling motion; whirl. ❑ *n., pl.* **ed·dies;** *v.* **ed·died, ed·dy·ing.**

Ed·dy (ed′ē), *n.* **Mary Ba·ker** (bā′kər), 1821-1910, American religious thinker who founded Christian Science. She taught that people could be cured of sickness by religious belief.

e·del·weiss (ā′dl vīs), *n.* a small plant that grows in high places. It has very small, white flowers in the center of star-shaped leaf clusters. ❑ *n., pl.* **e·del·weiss** or **e·del·weiss·es.**

e·de·ma (i dē′mə), *n.* accumulation of watery liquid in part of the body of a person, animal, or plant, caused by disease or injury, often shown by swelling.

E·den (ēd′n), *n.* **1** (in the Bible) the garden where Adam and Eve first lived. **2** a delightful place; paradise.

Ed·er·le (ā′dər lē), *n.* **Ger·trude** (gėr′trüd), born 1906, American swimmer. She was the first woman to swim the English Channel, in 1926. ■ Gertrude Ederle swam the 35-mile (56-kilometer) channel in 14 hours and 39 minutes, a time that broke the previous record and remained the women's record for 35 years.

edge (ej), **1** *n.* line or place where something ends or begins; side: *This page has four edges.* **2** *n.* the farthest or outer part: *The stag stood on the edge of the cliff.* **3** *n.* the thin side that cuts: *The knife had a very sharp edge.* **4** *n.* advantage: *The taller player had a slight edge.* **5** *v.* to put an edge on; form an edge on: *a path edged with white stones.* **6** *v.* to move sideways: *She edged through the narrow passageway.* **7** *v.* to move little by little: *The dog edged nearer to the fire.* ❑ *v.* **edged, edg·ing.**

on edge, disturbed; irritated; tense: *My nerves were on edge from the constant noise.*

take the edge off, to take away the force, strength, or pleasure of: *The pitcher's injury took the edge off the team's victory.*

edge·ways (ej′wāz′), *adv.* with the edge forward; in or along the direction of the edge.

edge·wise (ej′wīz′), *adv.* edgeways.

edg·ing (ej′ing), *n.* something forming an edge or put on an edge; border or trimming: *an edging of lace on a tablecloth.*

edg·y (ej′ē), *adj.* impatient; irritable; tense: *The long wait in the dentist's office had made him edgy.* ❑ *adj.* **edg·i·er, edg·i·est.** —**edg′i·ly,** *adv.* —**edg′i·ness,** *n.*

ed·i·ble (ed′ə bəl), *adj.* fit to eat: *Toadstools are not edible.* —**ed′i·bil′i·ty,** *n.*

e·dict (ē′dikt), *n.* a public order or decree by some authority: *The queen issued an edict creating a new national holiday.*

ed·i·fice (ed′ə fis), *n.* a building, especially a large one.

ed·i·fy (ed′ə fi), *v.* to improve morally; benefit spiritually; instruct and uplift. ❑ *v.* **ed·i·fied, ed·i·fy·ing.** [Edify comes from a Latin word meaning "to build." Something edifying has the effect of building character.] —**ed′i·fi·ca′tion,** *n.* —**ed′i·fi′er,** *n.*

Ed·in·burgh (ed′n bėr′ō), *n.* capital of Scotland, in the SE part.

Ed·i·son (ed′ə sən), *n.* **Thomas Al·va** (al′və), 1847-1931, American inventor. ■ Thomas Edison patented 1093 inventions, including the phonograph, the electric light, and improvements to the telephone, the typewriter, and the movies.

ed·it (ed′it), *v.* **1** to prepare for publication by correcting errors and checking facts: *edit a manuscript.* **2** to have charge of a publication and decide what will be printed in it. **3** to put into final form by selecting and reassembling the parts of: *edit a film, edit a tape recording.*

edit., 1 edited. **2** edition. **3** editor.

e·di·tion (i dish′ən), *n.* **1** all the copies of a book, newspaper, etc., printed just alike and issued at or near the same time: *The second edition of the book corrected many errors found in the first edition.* **2** form in which a book is printed or published: *Some books appear in paperback editions.*

ed·i·tor (ed′ə tər), *n.* **1** person who edits: *She is the editor of our school paper.* **2** person who writes editorials.

ed·i·to·ri·al (ed′ə tôr′ē əl), **1** *n.* article in a newspaper or magazine giving the editor's or publisher's opinion on some subject: *Today's editorial was about gun control laws.* **2** *n.* a radio or TV program giving the station manager's opinion on some subject. **3** *adj.* of an editor: *editorial work.* **4** *adj.* of an editorial: *an editorial comment.* —**ed′i·to′ri·al·ly,** *adv.*

ed·i·to·ri·al·ize (ed′ə tôr′ē ə liz), *v.* to include comment and criticisms in a news article, book, etc. ❑ *v.* **ed·i·to·ri·al·ized, ed·i·to·ri·al·iz·ing.** —**ed′i·to′ri·al·i·za′tion,** *n.*

ed·i·tor·ship (ed′ə tər ship), *n.* position or duties of an editor.

Ed·monds (ed′mundz), *n.* **Sarah,** 1841-1898, American soldier, born in Canada. ■ Sarah Edmonds served in the Union Army during the Civil War disguised as a man. She was a nurse, a messenger, and a spy, using the name Frank Thompson.

Ed·mon·ton (ed′mən tən), *n.* capital of Alberta, Canada.

EDT or **E.D.T.,** Eastern daylight time.

ed·u·cate (ej′ə kāt), *v.* **1** to develop in knowledge or skill by teaching, training, or study; teach: *The job of teachers is to educate people.* **2** to send to school: *My cousin is being educated in England.* ❑ *v.* **ed·u·cat·ed, ed·u·cat·ing.** —**ed′u·cat′a·ble,** *adj.*

ed·u·cat·ed (ej′ə kā′tid), *adj.* **1** having an education: *an educated person.* **2** based on facts or training: *The forecaster made an educated guess about next week's weather.*

ed·u·ca·tion (ej′ə kā′shən), *n.* **1** development in knowledge or skill by teaching, training, or study: *In the United States, public schools offer an education to all children.* **2** knowledge or skill developed by teaching, training, or study: *A person with education knows how to speak, write, and read well.* **3** study of the methods, principles, problems, etc., of teaching and learning.

ed·u·ca·tion·al (ej′ə kā′shə nəl), *adj.* **1** of education: *The teachers in our school belong to the state educational associations.* **2** giving education: *an educational movie about wild animals.* —**ed′u·ca′tion·al·ly,** *adv.*

ed·u·ca·tor (ej′ə kā′tər), *n.* **1** person whose profession is education; teacher. **2** leader in education; authority on methods and principles of education.

-ee, *suffix.* **1** person who is ___: *absentee = person who is absent; appointee = person who is appointed.* **2** person who ___s: *escapee = person who escapes.*

EEG, 1 electroencephalogram. **2** electroencephalograph.

eel (ēl), *n.* any of numerous long, slippery fishes shaped like snakes. ❑ *n., pl.* **eel** or **eels.** —**eel′like′,** *adj.*

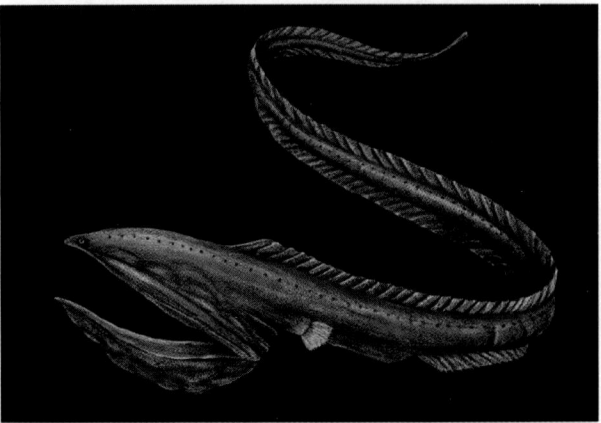

eel—up to 6 ft. (1.8 m) long

eel·grass (ēl′gras′), *n.* a sea plant with long, narrow leaves, growing underwater along the coasts of North America.

e'en (ēn), *adv.* OLD USE. even.

e'er (er), *adv.* OLD USE. ever.

eer·ie (ir′ē), *adj.* causing fear because of strangeness or weirdness: *a dark and eerie old house.* ❑ *adj.* **eer·i·er, eer·i·est.** ■ Other words that can sound like this are **aerie, eyrie,** and **eyry.** [Eerie comes from an old English word meaning "frightened." It shifted from the feeling to whatever causes it.] —**eer′i·ly,** *adv.* —**eer′i·ness,** *n.*

a	hat	ė	term	ô	order	ch	child		
ā	age	i	it	oi	oil	ng	long		a in about
ä	far	ī	ice	ou	out	sh	she		e in taken
â	care	o	hot	u	cup	th	thin	ə	i in pencil
e	let	ō	open	ů	put	ŦH	then		o in lemon
ē	equal	ȯ	saw	ü	rule	zh	measure		u in circus

Ecosystems

A stream, a meadow, a pond—a beautiful mountain scene, and a picture of an ecosystem. The ecosystem includes every living thing here and every part of the non-living environment. The wind, for instance, brings the moisture that falls as snow and forms glaciers on the mountaintops. The sun melts the glaciers and starts the water on its way back down to the sea. The stream supplies water to forests, meadow plants, and all sorts of animals.

One of these animals, the beaver, builds an environment for itself and other living things. The beaver's dam of felled trees turns the stream into a pond, where the beaver lives with its family. Reeds and other tall plants grow in and around the pond. Birds build nests there, and butterflies visit the flowers.

Water flows so slowly through the pond that a surface layer of tiny plants and bacteria can grow there. These are food for insects, tadpoles, and tiny fishes.

And they are food for bigger fishes and for birds. This food web carries energy through the ecosystem, from sunlight through plants and bacteria to animals. And when the plants and animals die, their bodies provide energy to scavengers and enrich the soil.

You can see how many kinds of living things there are in this ecosystem. This richness of life is called biodiversity. You can imagine, if the stream stopped flowing into this valley, how much less biodiversity the valley would have. Other changes might produce the same effect. The swallows, which feed here on pond and meadow insects during the summer, will fly south for the winter. They need two places to live, called habitats. A bad change in either habitat—or in the places the swallows fly through as they migrate back and forth—might threaten their survival. Loss of biodiversity in one place can cause more loss somewhere else. Everything is connected. In ecology, that's Lesson Number One.

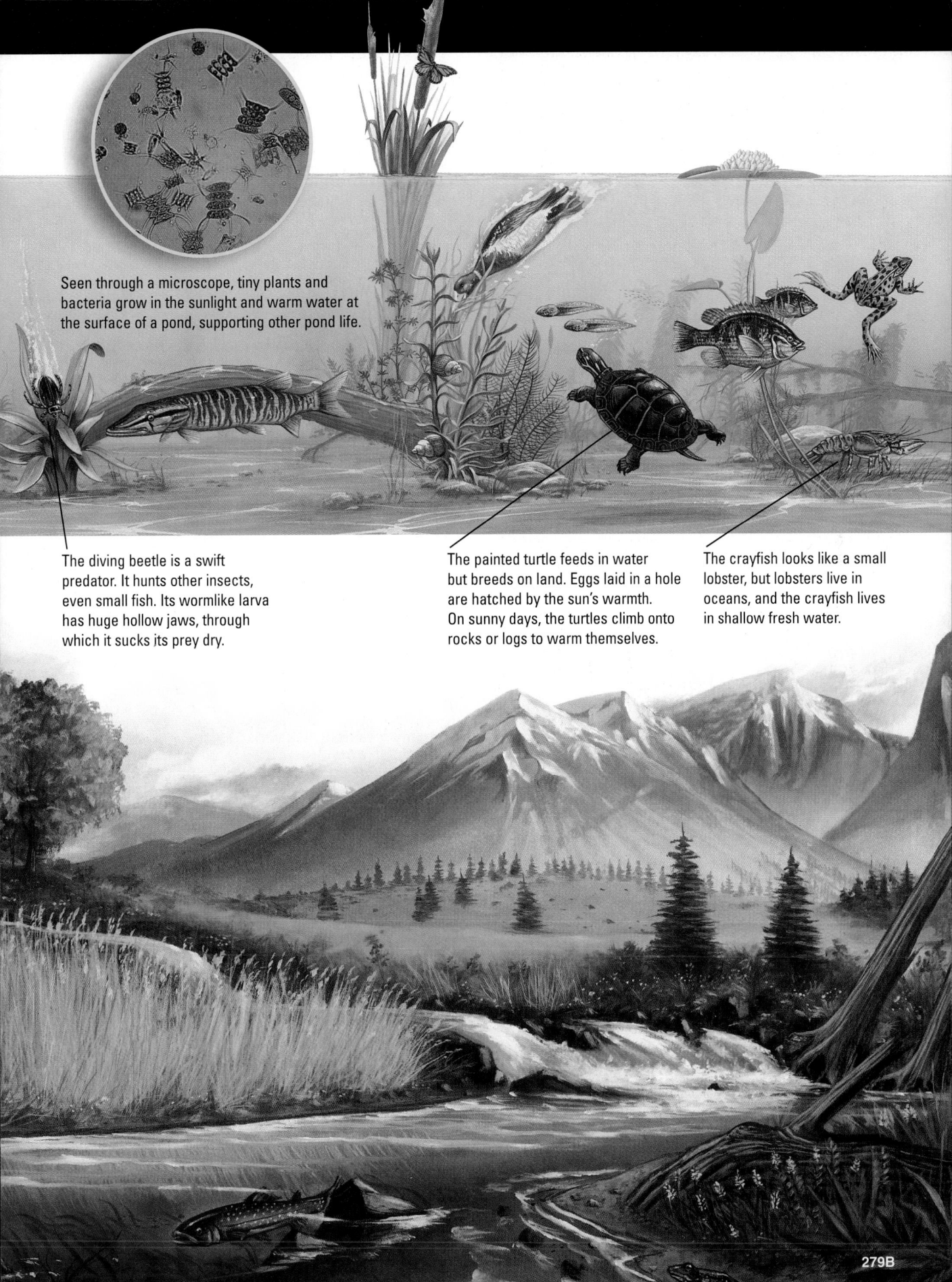

Seen through a microscope, tiny plants and bacteria grow in the sunlight and warm water at the surface of a pond, supporting other pond life.

The diving beetle is a swift predator. It hunts other insects, even small fish. Its wormlike larva has huge hollow jaws, through which it sucks its prey dry.

The painted turtle feeds in water but breeds on land. Eggs laid in a hole are hatched by the sun's warmth. On sunny days, the turtles climb onto rocks or logs to warm themselves.

The crayfish looks like a small lobster, but lobsters live in oceans, and the crayfish lives in shallow fresh water.

ef·face (ə fās′), *v.* **1** to rub out; blot out; do away with; wipe out; destroy: *The inscriptions on many ancient monuments have been effaced by time.* **2** to keep yourself from being noticed; make inconspicuous: *The shy students effaced themselves by staying in the background.* ❑ *v.* **ef·faced, ef·fac·ing.** —**ef·face′a·ble,** *adj.* —**ef·face′ment,** *n.* —**ef·fac′er,** *n.*

efface (def. 1)—partly effaced columns

ef·fect (ə fekt′), **1** *n.* whatever is produced by a cause; something made to happen by a person or thing; result: *The company's new advertising campaign had a positive effect on sales.* ■ See Usage Note at **affect**[1]. **2** *v.* to make happen; bring about: *Computers have effected many changes in the way we live.* **3** *n.* impression produced on the mind or senses: *The room was painted yellow for a light, sunny effect.* **4** *n.* something which produces such an impression: *The movie used many special effects.* **5** *n.pl.* **effects,** belongings; goods: *personal effects.* ■ Another word that sounds like this is **affect.** [See Word Story at **feckless.**]

for effect, for show; in order to impress or influence others: *He said that only for effect; he really didn't mean it.*

in effect, 1 almost the same as; practically; virtually: *By not speaking out against this plan you are saying, in effect, that you approve it.* **2** in force or operation; active: *That law has been in effect for two years.*

take effect, to begin to operate; become active: *That pill takes effect as soon as you swallow it.*

ef·fec·tive (ə fek′tiv), *adj.* **1** producing the desired effect; getting results: *an effective medicine.* **2** in operation; active: *The law passed by Congress became effective as soon as the President signed it.* **3** striking; impressive: *Her skillful use of color resulted in a very effective picture.* —**ef·fec′tive·ly,** *adv.* —**ef·fec′tive·ness,** *n*

ef·fec·tu·al (ə fek′chü əl), *adj.* producing the desired effect; capable of producing the desired effect: *Quinine is an effectual remedy for malaria.* —**ef·fec′tu·al·ly,** *adv.* —**ef·fec′tu·al·ness,** *n.*

ef·fec·tu·ate (ə fek′chü āt), *v.* to make happen; bring about. ❑ *v.* **ef·fec·tu·at·ed, ef·fec·tu·at·ing.**

ef·fem·i·nate (ə fem′ə nit), *adj.* (of a man or boy) having qualities or characteristics traditionally considered to be feminine. —**ef·fem′i·nate·ly,** *adv.* —**ef·fem′i·nate·ness,** *n.*

ef·fer·ent (ef′ər ənt), *adj.* leading away from a central organ or point. Efferent nerves carry impulses from the brain and spinal cord to the muscles.

ef·fer·ves·cence (ef′ər ves′ns), *n.* **1** act or process of giving off bubbles of gas; bubbling. **2** liveliness and happiness.

ef·fer·ves·cent (ef′ər ves′nt), *adj.* **1** giving off bubbles of gas; bubbling: *Ginger ale is effervescent.* **2** lively and happy: *an effervescent personality.* —**ef′fer·ves′cent·ly,** *adv.*

ef·fi·ca·cious (ef′ə kā′shəs), *adj.* producing the desired results; effective: *Vaccination is efficacious in preventing smallpox.* —**ef′fi·ca′cious·ly,** *adv.* —**ef′fi·ca′cious·ness,** *n.*

ef·fi·ca·cy (ef′ə kə sē), *n.* power to produce the effect wanted: *The efficacy of aspirin in relieving headaches is well known.*

ef·fi·cien·cy (ə fish′ən sē), *n.* **1** ability to produce the effect wanted without waste of time, energy, etc.: *The skilled carpenter worked with great efficiency.* **2** efficient operation: *Argument reduces the efficiency of a committee.* **3** ratio of work done to energy used, or ratio of energy produced to energy used. Efficiency compares the output and input of a machine, process, etc. **4** a very small apartment, usually having just one room, a kitchenette, and a bathroom. ❑ *n., pl.* **ef·fi·cien·cies** for 4.

ef·fi·cient (ə fish′ənt), *adj.* able to produce the effect wanted without waste of time, energy, etc.; capable: *An efficient worker makes good use of his or her skills.* —**ef·fi′cient·ly,** *adv.*

ef·fi·gy (ef′ə jē), *n.* image or statue, usually of a person: *The dead woman's monument bore her effigy.* ❑ *n., pl.* **ef·fi·gies.**

burn in effigy or **hang in effigy,** to burn or hang an image of a person to show hatred or contempt.

ef·flu·ent (ef′lü ənt), **1** *n.* outflow of liquid waste such as from a sewer, factory, etc. **2** *n.* stream flowing out of a lake, river, etc. **3** *n.* anything that flows away; outflow. **4** *adj.* flowing out or away.

ef·fort (ef′ərt), *n.* **1** use of energy and strength to do something; trying hard: *Climbing a steep hill takes effort.* **2** a hard try; strong attempt: *He did not win, but at least he made an effort.* **3** result of effort; thing done with effort; achievement: *Works of art are artistic efforts.*

ef·fort·less (ef′ərt lis), *adj.* needing or showing no effort; easy: *The cat jumped to the table with an effortless leap.* ■ See Synonym Study at **easy.** —**ef′fort·less·ly,** *adv.* —**ef′fort·less·ness,** *n.*

ef·fron·ter·y (ə frun′tər ē), *n.* shameless boldness; impudence: *My neighbor had the effrontery to say that I talk too much.*

ef·ful·gent (i ful′jənt), *adj.* shining brightly; radiant.

ef·fu·sion (i fyü′zhən), *n.* an unrestrained expression of feeling, opinion, etc., in talking or writing.

ef·fu·sive (i fyü′siv), *adj.* showing too much feeling; too demonstrative and emotional. —**ef·fu′sive·ly,** *adv.* —**ef·fu′sive·ness,** *n.*

eft (eft), *n.* a young newt. An eft lives on land.

e.g., for example; for instance.

egg[1] (eg), *n.* **1** the round or oval object, covered with a shell or membrane, that is laid by the female of birds, fishes, insects, and some other types of animals. Young animals hatch from the eggs. **2** the contents of an egg, especially a hen's egg, used as food: *She likes two boiled eggs for breakfast.* **3** a female reproductive cell; ovum. —**egg′less,** *adj.* —**egg′like′,** *adj.*

egg[2] (eg), *v.* to urge or encourage: *We egged them on to victory.*

egg·beat·er (eg′bē′tər), *n.* device with revolving blades for beating eggs, cream, etc.

egg cell, a female reproductive cell; ovum.

egg cream, a cold drink made from milk, flavored syrup, and soda water.

egg foo yung (eg′ fü′ yung′), a fried omelet made with bean sprouts, onions, green peppers, shrimp or pork, etc., and usually seasoned with soy sauce.

egg·head (eg′hed′), *n.* INFORMAL. an intellectual.

egg·nog (eg′nog′), *n.* drink made of eggs beaten up with milk and sugar. It often has whiskey, brandy, or wine in it.

egg·plant (eg′plant′), *n.* the large, purple fruit of a garden plant, cooked and eaten as a vegetable.

egg roll, a small tube of egg dough, filled with a mixture of minced vegetables and sometimes shrimp or meat, and fried.

egg·shell (eg′shel′), **1** *n.* shell covering an egg. **2** *n.* a yellowish white. **3** *adj.* yellowish white.

egg white, the white part of an egg; albumen.

e·go (ē′gō), *n.* **1** the individual as a whole with the capacity to think, feel, and act; self. **2** sense of worth; self-esteem: *Their criticism punctured my ego.* **3** conceit; self-importance. ❑ *n., pl.* **e·gos.** [**Ego** comes from a Latin word meaning "I." People with a lot of ego say "I" a lot.]

e·go·ism (ē′gō iz′əm), *n.* **1** seeking the welfare of yourself only; selfishness. **2** conceit.

e·go·ist (ē′gō ist), *n.* **1** person who seeks the welfare of himself or herself only; selfish person. **2** a conceited person.

e·go·tism (ē′gə tiz′əm), *n.* **1** act or habit of thinking or talking too much of yourself; conceit. **2** selfishness.

e·go·tist (ē′gə tist), *n.* **1** person who thinks or talks about himself or herself too much; conceited person. **2** a selfish person.

e·go·tis·tic (ē′gə tis′tik), *adj.* **1** conceited. **2** selfish. —**e′go·tis′·ti·cal·ly,** *adv.*

e·go·tis·ti·cal (ē′gə tis′tə kəl), *adj.* egotistic.

e·gre·gious (i grē′jəs), *adj.* remarkably bad: *an egregious waste of time.* —**e·gre′gious·ly,** *adv.* —**e·gre′gious·ness,** *n.*

WORD STORY **Egregious** comes from Latin words meaning "out of the herd." **Egregious** used to describe things that stand out from the rest, good or bad, but now it describes only bad things.

e·gret (ē′gret), *n.* any of several wading birds with long necks and long bills, especially one kind that is pure white. Egrets are herons.

E·gypt (ē′jipt), *n.* country in NE Africa. *Capital:* Cairo.

E·gyp·tian (i jip′shən), **1** *adj.* of Egypt or its people. **2** *n.* person born or living in Egypt. **3** *n.* language of the ancient Egyptians.

eh (ā *or* e), *interj.* exclamation expressing doubt, surprise, failure to hear exactly, or suggesting "Yes" for an answer: *Eh? What's that you said? That's a good joke, eh?*

ei·der (ī′dər), *n.* **1** any of several large northern sea ducks with very soft feathers on their breasts. The feathers are used by the ducks to keep their eggs warm. **2** eiderdown (def. 1).

ei·der·down (ī′dər doun′), *n.* **1** the soft feathers of eiders, used to stuff pillows and bed quilts; eider. **2** quilt stuffed with these feathers.

eight (āt), *n., adj.* one more than seven; 8. ■ Another word that sounds like this is **ate.**

eight ball, (in pool) a black ball with the number 8 on it. Many versions of pool require that it be the last ball pocketed.

behind the eight ball, INFORMAL. in a very bad position: *Three tests on the same day had me behind the eight ball.*

eight·een (ā′tēn′), *n., adj.* eight more than ten; 18.

eight·eenth (ā′tēnth′), *adj., n.* **1** next after the 17th; last in a series of 18. **2** one of 18 equal parts.

eighth (ātth), *adj., n.* **1** next after the seventh; last in a series of eight. **2** one of eight equal parts.

eighth note, (in music) a note played for one eighth as long a time as a whole note.

eight·i·eth (ā′tē ith), *adj., n.* **1** next after the 79th; last in a series of 80. **2** one of 80 equal parts.

eight·y (ā′tē), *adj., n.* eight times ten; 80. ❑ *n., pl.* **eight·ies.**

Ein·stein (īn′stīn), *n.* **Al·bert** (al′bərt), 1879-1955, American physicist, born in Germany. ■ Albert Einstein created the theory of relativity, which made it possible to develop nuclear energy.

ein·stein·i·um (īn stī′nē əm), *n.* a rare, radioactive element produced artificially from plutonium or uranium. *Symbol:* Es

Eir·e (âr′ə), *n.* Republic of Ireland.

Ei·sen·how·er (ī′zn hou′ər), *n.* **Dwight D.** (dwīt), 1890-1969, American general, the 34th president of the United States, from 1953 to 1961.

eis·tedd·fod (ā steᴛʜ′vod), *n.* a meeting of Welsh poets and musicians. ❑ *n., pl.* **eis·tedd·fods, eis·tedd·fod·au** (ā steᴛʜ vod′ī).

ei·ther (ē′ᴛʜər *or* ī′ᴛʜər), **1** *conj.* one of the possibilities mentioned: *Either you or I will call her.* **2** *adj., pron.* one or the other of two: *You may read either book. Choose either of the candy bars.* **3** *adj., pron.* each of two: *There are cornfields on either side of the river.* **4** *adv.* also; likewise: *If you don't go, I won't go either.*

USAGE NOTE **Either** and **or** may be used with singular nouns, plural nouns, or both. Singular nouns with **either** and **or** take a singular verb: *Either the kitten or the puppy is under the couch.* Plural nouns take a plural verb: *Either parents or teachers give a party every month to raise money for the P.T.A.* The combination of a singular noun and a plural noun sounds best with the plural noun last and a plural verb: *Either toast or muffins are good for breakfast.*

e·jac·u·late (i jak′yə lāt), *v.* **1** to say suddenly; exclaim. **2** to discharge a fluid suddenly. ❑ *v.* **e·jac·u·lat·ed, e·jac·u·lat·ing.**

e·jac·u·la·tion (i jak′yə lā′shən), *n.* **1** something said suddenly and briefly; exclamation. **2** the sudden discharge of a fluid.

e·ject (i jekt′), *v.* to throw out; force out; drive out: *The volcano ejected lava.* ■ See Synonym Study at **evict.** —**e·jec′tor,** *n.*

e·jec·tion (i jek′shən), *n.* act of ejecting or of being ejected: *The audience demanded the ejection of the hecklers. The pilot's life was saved by his automatic ejection from the burning plane.*

ejection seat, an airplane seat that in case of danger can be instantly ejected with its occupant and parachuted to earth.

eke (ēk), *v.* **eke out, 1** to add to; increase: *The clerk eked out her regular wages by working evenings.* **2** to barely manage to make a living, a profit, etc.: *eke out a living doing odd jobs.* ❑ *v.* **eked, ek·ing.**

EKG, electrocardiogram.

el (el), *n.* elevated (def. 3).

El Aai·ún (el′ ä yün′), capital of Western Sahara.

e·lab·or·ate (i lab′ər it *for adj.;* i lab′ə rāt′ *for verb*), **1** *adj.* worked out with great care; having many details; complicated: *The scientists made elaborate plans for launching a new satellite.* **2** *v.* to work out with great care; add details to: *The author spent months elaborating plans for a new book.* **3** *v.* to talk or write in great detail; give added details: *The witness was asked to elaborate on one of his statements.* ❑ *v.* **e·lab·o·rat·ed, e·lab·o·rat·ing.** —**e·lab′or·ate·ly,** *adv.* —**e·lab′or·ate·ness,** *n.* —**e·lab′o·ra′·tion,** *n.* —**e·lab′o·ra′tor,** *n.*

E·laine (i lān′), *n.* (in legends of the Middle Ages) a beautiful maiden who died for love of Lancelot. [**Elaine** comes from a Greek word meaning "light" or "bright."]

é·lan (ā län′), *n.* enthusiasm; liveliness; spirit: *She carried off throwing an impromptu party with great élan.*

e·land (ē′lənd), *n.* either of two large, heavy African antelopes that have twisted horns. ❑ *n., pl.* **e·land** or **e·lands.**

e·lapse (i laps′), *v.* to slip away; glide by; pass: *Many hours elapsed while I slept soundly.* ❑ *v.* **e·lapsed, e·laps·ing.**

e·las·tic (i las′tik), **1** *adj.* able to spring back to its original shape after being stretched, squeezed, bent, etc.: *Rubber bands, sponges, and steel springs are elastic.* **2** *adj.* bouncy; springy: *an elastic step.* **3** *adj.* recovering quickly from weariness, low spirits, or misfortune: *Her elastic spirits kept her from being discouraged for long.* **4** *adj.* easily changed to suit conditions; flexible; adaptable: *I have an elastic schedule.* **5** *n.* tape or cloth woven partly of an elastic material: *My trunks have a band of elastic at the top.* **6** *n.* a rubber band. —**e·las′ti·cal·ly,** *adv.*

eland—5 ft. (1.5 m) high at the shoulder

a	hat	ė	term	ô	order	ch	child		a	in about
ā	age	i	it	oi	oil	ng	long		e	in taken
ä	far	ī	ice	ou	out	sh	she	ə	i	in pencil
â	care	o	hot	u	cup	th	thin		o	in lemon
e	let	ō	open	u̇	put	ᴛʜ	then		u	in circus
ē	equal	ò	saw	ü	rule	zh	measure			

e·las·tic·i·ty (i las tis′ə tē *or* ē′- las tis′ə tē), *n.* elastic quality: *Rubber has elasticity.*

e·las·ti·cized (i las′tə sīzd), *adj.* woven or made with elastic: *an elasticized waistband.*

e·las·to·mer (i las′tə mər), *n.* any of various elastic substances, natural or artificial. Rubber and latex are elastomers.

e·lat·ed (i lā′tid), *adj.* in high spirits; joyful: *She was elated about the good news.* —**e·lat′ed·ly**, *adv.* —**e·lat′ed·ness**, *n.*

elated

Elated comes from a Latin word meaning "carried away." In English today we still use the expression *carried away* to mean full of strong feelings of any kind.

e·la·tion (i lā′shən), *n.* high spirits; joy or pride.

E layer, E region.

El·ba (el′bə), *n.* Italian island between Italy and Corsica. Napoleon I was in exile there from 1814 to 1815.

El·be (el′bə), *n.* river flowing from W Czechoslovakia through Germany into the North Sea.

el·bow (el′bō), **1** *n.* joint between the upper and lower arm. **2** *n.* anything like a bent arm in shape or position. A bent joint for connecting pipes or a sharp turn in a road or river may be called an elbow. **3** *v.* to push with the elbow; make your way by pushing: *Don't elbow me off the sidewalk.*

rub elbows, to mingle.

elbow grease, INFORMAL. hard work.

el·bow·room (el′bō rüm′), *n.* plenty of room; enough room or space to move or work in.

El·brus (el′brüs *or* el′brüz), *n.* **Mount,** mountain in the Caucasus Mountains in Georgia, 18,481 feet (5633 meters) high. It is the highest mountain in Europe.

eld·er[1] (el′dər), **1** *adj.* older; senior: *my elder sister.* **2** *n.* an older person: *An only child, she spent a lot of time with her elders.* **3** *n.* one of the older and more influential members of a tribe or community. **4** *n.* any of various officers in certain churches.

Elder[1] and **eldest** are old-fashioned forms of **older** and **oldest,** used in formal writing. They describe people in a family: *She is the eldest daughter.* They also occur in certain traditional phrases, such as *elder statesman.*

el·der[2] (el′dər), *n.* **1** any of several small trees, especially one with white flowers and black or red berries. **2** its berry, used in wine, pies, etc.

el·der·ber·ry (el′dər ber′ē), *n.* elder[2]. ◻ *n., pl.* **el·der·ber·ries.**

eld·er·ly (el′dər lē), *adj.* somewhat old; beyond middle age. —**el′der·li·ness**, *n.*

elder statesman, an older political leader or politician, usually no longer in office, who is turned to for advice.

eld·est (el′dist), *adj.* oldest. ▪ See Usage Note at **elder**[1].

El·do·ra·do (el′də rä′dō), *n.* El Dorado. ◻ *n., pl.* **El·do·ra·dos.**

El Do·ra·do (el də rä′dō), **1** an imaginary place supposed to be full of treasure, sought by early Spanish explorers in South America. **2** any wealthy place. ◻ *pl.* **El Do·ra·dos** for 2.

El·ean·or of A·qui·taine (el′ə nər əv ak′wi tān), 1122-1204, French and English queen. ▪ **Eleanor of Aquitaine** was married to Louis VII of France and later to Henry II of England. She was the mother of two English kings, Richard the Lion-Hearted and John. [**Eleanor** comes from her mother's name, *Anor,* and a Latin word meaning "another."]

e·lect (i lekt′), **1** *v.* to choose or select for an office by voting: *We elect our class officers every autumn.* **2** *adj.* elected but not yet in office: *the governor-elect.* **3** *v.* to choose; select: *The children elected to play baseball.* **4** *n.pl.* **the elect,** members of any group with special privileges or influence; select few: *She is among the elect who can choose what movies they'll star in.*

e·lec·tion (i lek′shən), *n.* **1** act of choosing or selecting for an office by vote: *an election for mayor.* **2** condition of being chosen or selected for an office by vote: *The candidate's excellent and honest campaign resulted in her election.* **3** choice; selection.

Elections have their own vocabulary with many special words. If you want to know more about them, you can begin by looking up these words in this dictionary.

ballot	district	plebiscite
barnstorm	electoral college	poll
campaign	electorate	precinct
canvass	landslide	primary
caucus	mandate	referendum
constituency	nomination	runoff
convention	PAC	vote
delegation	platform	ward

e·lec·tion·eer (i lek′shə nir′), *v.* to work for the success of a candidate or party in an election.

e·lec·tive (i lek′tiv), **1** *adj.* chosen by an election: *Senators are elective officials.* **2** *adj.* filled by an election: *The office of President of the United States is elective.* **3** *adj.* open to choice; not required: *Spanish is an elective subject in many high schools.* **4** *n.* subject or course of study which may be taken, but is not required. —**e·lec′tive·ly**, *adv.* —**e·lec′tive·ness**, *n.*

e·lec·tor (i lek′tər), *n.* **1** person who has the right to vote in an election. **2** member of the electoral college.

e·lec·tor·al (i lek′tər əl), *adj.* **1** of electors: *electoral votes.* **2** of an election. —**e·lec′tor·al·ly**, *adv.*

electoral college, group of people chosen by the voters to elect the President and Vice-President of the United States.

e·lec·tor·ate (i lek′tər it), *n.* the persons having the right to vote in an election.

e·lec·tric (i lek′trik), *adj.* **1** of or using electricity: *an electric light, an electric current.* **2** producing musical sounds amplified electronically through a speaker: *an electric guitar.* **3** exciting; thrilling: *an electric feeling.*

e·lec·tri·cal (i lek′trə kəl), *adj.* electric: *electrical energy.*

e·lec·tri·cal·ly (i lek′trik lē), *adv.* by electricity.

electric cell, container holding materials that produce electricity by chemical action. A battery consists of one or more electric cells.

electric chair, 1 chair used in electrocuting criminals. **2** sentence of death in such a chair: *The killer got the electric chair.*

electric eel, a large South American freshwater fish resembling an eel, which can give strong electric shocks.

electric eye, photoelectric cell.

e·lec·tri·cian (i lek′trish′ən), *n.* person whose work is installing or repairing electric wiring, lights, motors, etc.

e·lec·tric·i·ty (i lek′tris′ə tē), *n.* **1** form of energy that can produce light, heat, motion, and magnetic force. Electricity comes from generators for people to buy and use, but it can be produced in small amounts by running a comb through your hair or by chemical change in a flashlight battery. Most familiar forms of electricity involve the flow of electrons. **2** electric current: *The storm damaged the wires carrying electricity to the house.*

Electricity comes from a Greek word meaning "amber." If amber is rubbed with a cloth, it becomes charged with electricity and attracts straws or hair. The ancient Greeks were the first to record this fact and give it a name.

e·lec·tri·fy (i lek′trə fi), *v.* **1** to charge with electricity. **2** to equip for the use of electric power: *Some railroads once run by steam are now electrified.* **3** to give an electric shock to. **4** to excite; thrill: *The spectators were electrified by the team's performance.* ◻ *v.* **e·lec·tri·fied, e·lec·tri·fy·ing.** —**e·lec′tri·fi·ca′tion**, *n.*

electro-, *prefix.* **1** electric: *electromagnet = an electric magnet.* **2** electricity: *electrocute = kill by electricity.*

e·lec·tro·car·di·o·gram (i lek′trō kär′dē ə gram), *n.* a chart of information recorded by an electrocardiograph; cardiogram.

e·lec·tro·car·di·o·graph (i lek′trō kär′dē ə graf), *n.* machine that detects and records the electrical impulses produced by the action of the heart with each beat; cardiograph. It is used to diagnose diseases of the heart.

e·lec·tro·cute (i lek′trə kyüt), *v.* to kill or execute by a strong electric shock: *A live wire can electrocute a person who touches it.* ❑ *v.* **e·lec·tro·cut·ed, e·lec·tro·cut·ing.** —**e·lec′tro·cu′tion,** *n.*

WORD STORY Electrocute is a blend of **electric** and **execute.** The word was invented about 100 years ago, when the death penalty was first carried out with electric power.

e·lec·trode (i lek′trōd), *n.* **1** either of the two terminals of a battery or any other source of electricity. The anode and cathode of an electric cell are electrodes. **2** conductor by which a current is brought into or out of any liquid or gas.

e·lec·tro·en·ceph·a·lo·gram (i lek′trō en sef′ə lə gram), *n.* a chart of the measurements made by an electroencephalograph.

e·lec·tro·en·ceph·a·lo·graph (i lek′trō en sef′ə lə graf), *n.* machine for measuring the electrical activity of the brain, used in identifying brain disorders.

e·lec·tro·en·ceph·a·log·ra·phy (i lek′trō en sef′ə log′rə fē), *n.* science or technique of using an electroencephalograph. —**e·lec′tro·en·ceph′a·lo·graph′ic,** *adj.*

e·lec·trol·y·sis (i lek′trol′ə sis), *n.* **1** removal of unwanted hair, moles, etc., from the skin by destruction with an electrified needle. **2** separation of a dissolved chemical compound into its ions by passing an electric current through it.

e·lec·tro·lyte (i lek′trə līt), *n.* a chemical compound whose water solution will conduct an electric current; chemical compound that ionizes. Acids, bases, and salts are electrolytes.

e·lec·tro·mag·net (i lek′trō mag′nit), *n.* piece of soft iron that becomes a strong magnet when an electric current is passing through wire coiled around it.

e·lec·tro·mag·net·ic (i lek′trō mag net′ik), *adj.* **1** of or caused by an electromagnet. **2** of electromagnetism.

electromagnetic spectrum, the entire range of the different types of electromagnetic waves, from the very long, low-frequency radio waves, through infrared and light waves, to the very short, high-frequency X rays and gamma rays.

electromagnetic wave, wave of energy in the form of regularly changing electric and magnetic fields. Light waves and radio waves are electromagnetic waves.

e·lec·tro·mag·net·ism (i lek′trō mag′nə tiz′əm), *n.* **1** magnetism produced by a current of electricity. **2** branch of physics that deals with the relationship between electricity and magnetism.

e·lec·tro·mo·tive force (i lek′trə mō′tiv), the force that causes a flow of electricity. Electromotive force is produced by differences in electrical charge, and is measured in volts.

e·lec·tron (i lek′tron), *n.* a subatomic particle with extremely small mass and an amount of negative electric charge that is the smallest occurring in nature. All atoms have one or more electrons outside a nucleus.

electron gun, device that produces and guides a beam of electrons, especially in a CRT. In a television set, an electron gun directs a beam of electrons to the screen.

e·lec·tron·ic (i lek′tron′ik), *adj.* **1** working by electricity: *an electronic game.* **2** used in or produced by electronics: *an electronic device.* —**e·lec′tron′i·cal·ly,** *adv.*

electronic banking, system of carrying out bank business, such as depositing or transferring funds, with computers linked by telephone wires.

electronic bulletin board, a computer service for sending and receiving messages or computer software. A computer can reach such a service through a modem.

electronic mail, e-mail.

electronic music, music made electronically, especially with a synthesizer.

e·lec·tron·ics (i lek′tron′iks), *n.* branch of physics that deals with the production and effects of electrons in motion through a vacuum, gases, or semiconductors. Electronics has made possible the development of television, radio, and computers.

electron microscope, microscope that uses beams of electrons instead of beams of light, and that has much higher power of magnification than any ordinary microscope.

electron tube, vacuum tube.

electron volt, unit of electrical energy equal to the energy that one electron gains from a force of one volt.

e·lec·tro·plate (i lek′trə plāt), *v.* to cover silverware, printing plates, etc., with a coating of metal by means of electrolysis. ❑ *v.* **e·lec·tro·plat·ed, e·lec·tro·plat·ing.**

e·lec·tro·scope (i lek′trə skōp), *n.* device that indicates the presence of very small charges of electricity and that shows whether they are positive or negative.

el·e·gance (el′ə gəns), *n.* good taste; refined grace and richness; luxurious beauty: *We admired the elegance of the clothes worn to the formal dinner.*

el·e·gant (el′ə gənt), *adj.* having or showing good taste; gracefully and richly refined; beautifully luxurious: *The palace had elegant furnishings.* —**el′e·gant·ly,** *adv.*

el·e·gy (el′ə jē), *n.* a mournful or melancholy poem, usually a lament for the dead. ❑ *n., pl.* **el·e·gies.**

el·e·ment (el′ə mənt), *n.* **1** one of the basic substances from which all other things are made; chemical element. An element cannot be separated into parts by chemical means, and all its atoms are chemically alike. Gold, iron, carbon, sulfur, oxygen, and hydrogen are elements.

elegant—an elegant outfit

There are more than 100 known elements. **2** one of the parts of which anything is made: *I like a story that has an element of surprise to it.* **3** a simple or necessary part to be learned first; first principle: *the elements of arithmetic.* **4** **the elements,** *pl.,* the forces of the atmosphere, especially in bad weather: *The raging storm seemed to be a war of the elements.* **5** environment or activity in which someone feels especially at home and able to do his or her best work or live most fully: *He loves books and is in his element in a library.* **6** member of a set in mathematics. **7** the part of a heat-producing electrical device that actually grows hot.

el·e·men·tal (el′ə men′tl), *adj.* **1** of the forces of the atmosphere, especially of the weather: *The storm showed elemental fury in its violence.* **2** natural; simple but powerful: *Hunger is an elemental feeling.* **3** elementary. —**el′e·men′tal·ly,** *adv.*

el·e·men·ta·ry (el′ə men′tər ē *or* el′ə men′trē), *adj.* of or dealing with the simple, necessary parts to be learned first; about first principles; introductory: *Addition, subtraction, multiplication, and division are taught in elementary arithmetic.*

SYNONYM STUDY **Elementary, primary,** and **basic** all mean first. **Elementary** means first and simplest: *She is learning how to use tools in her elementary carpentry class.* **Primary** means first in time or order: *In the primary grades, children learn to read and write.* **Basic** means first and necessary for everything that follows: *A basic part of judo is learning how to fall.*

elementary particle, one of the basic units that all matter is made of. There are many kinds of elementary particles, including electrons, photons, and quarks.

elementary school, **1** school of usually six grades for pupils from about six to twelve years of age, followed by junior high school. **2** school of eight grades for pupils from about six to fourteen years of age, followed by a four-year high school. **3** school of four or five grades for pupils from about six to nine or ten years of age, followed by middle school.

el·e·phant (el′ə fənt), *n.* either of two huge, heavy mammals, the largest living land animals, with ivory tusks and a long, muscu-

a	hat	ė	term	ô	order	ch	child		a in about
ā	age	i	it	oi	oil	ng	long		e in taken
ä	far	ī	ice	ou	out	sh	she	ə {	i in pencil
â	care	o	hot	u	cup	th	thin		o in lemon
e	let	ō	open	u̇	put	₮H	then		u in circus
ē	equal	ȯ	saw	ü	rule	zh	measure		

lar snout called a trunk. **African elephants** have large ears, and both the males and females have tusks. **Asian** or **Indian elephants** have smaller ears, and the females often have no tusks. ❏ *n., pl.* **el·e·phants** or **el·e·phant.** [See Word Story at **ivory.**]

el·e·phan·tine (el′ə fan′tēn *or* el′ə fan′tin), *adj.* **1** like an elephant; huge, heavy, and clumsy. **2** of elephants.

el·e·vate (el′ə vāt), *v.* to lift up; raise: *The company elevated her to the position of assistant manager.* ❏ *v.* **el·e·vat·ed, el·e·vat·ing.**

el·e·vat·ed (el′ə vā′tid), **1** *adj.* lifted up; raised: *an elevated platform.* **2** *adj.* dignified: *elevated conversation.* **3** *n.* an electric railroad raised above street level on a supporting frame, allowing traffic to pass underneath; el.

el·e·va·tion (el′ə vā′shən), *n.* **1** height above the earth's surface: *The airplane flew at an elevation of 20,000 feet.* **2** height above sea level: *The elevation of Denver is 5280 feet.* **3** a raised place; high place: *A hill is an elevation.* **4** act of elevating or condition of being elevated: *The elevation of a clerk to store manager surprised us.*

el·e·va·tor (el′ə vā′tər), *n.* **1** a moving room, platform, or cage to carry people and things up and down in a building, mine, etc. **2** grain elevator. **3** an adjustable, flat piece on the tail of an airplane to cause it to go up or down.

e·lev·en (i lev′ən), **1** *adj., n.* one more than ten; 11. **2** *n.* a football, soccer, or cricket team.

> **WORD STORY** **Eleven** comes from an old English word meaning "one left." **Twelve** comes from an old English word meaning "two left." Do you think that people in those days counted by tens?

e·lev·enth (i lev′ənth), *adj., n.* **1** next after the 10th; last in a series of 11. **2** one of 11 equal parts.

eleventh hour, the latest possible moment; time just before it is too late.

elf (elf), *n.* a tiny fairy that is full of mischief. ❏ *n., pl.* **elves.**

elf·in (el′fən), *adj.* of or for elves; like an elf's: *an elfin smile.*

elf·ish (el′fish), *adj.* like an elf; elfin; mischievous.

El Grec·o (el grek′ō), 1541?-1614, Spanish painter born in Crete. ▪ **El Greco** did most of his work in Spain. He had a Greek name, and **El Greco,** the name given him by the Spanish, means "the Greek."

El Greco painting

e·lic·it (i lis′it), *v.* to draw forth; bring out: *The comedian's joke elicited laughter from the audience.*

> **USAGE NOTE** **Elicit** and **illicit** are sometimes confused because they sound alike. **Elicit** means to draw out reactions or ideas: *The teacher elicited the students' thoughts about gun control.* **Illicit** means illegal: *A police unit was formed to stop illicit gambling.*

el·i·gi·ble (el′ə jə bəl), *adj.* fit to be chosen; properly qualified: *Pupils had to pass all subjects to be eligible to play sports.* —**el′-i·gi·bil′i·ty,** *n.* —**el′i·gi·bly,** *adv.*

E·li·jah (i lī′jə), *n.* (in the Bible) a Hebrew prophet. [Elijah comes from a Hebrew word meaning "my God."]

e·lim·i·nate (i lim′ə nāt), *v.* **1** to get rid of; remove: *The losing team was eliminated from the semifinals.* **2** to leave out of consideration; omit; disregard: *In choosing a new bike, I decided to eliminate all colors except blue and black.* **3** to expel waste from the body; excrete. ❏ *v.* **e·lim·i·nat·ed, e·lim·i·nat·ing.** —**e·lim′i·na′-tion,** *n.* —**e·lim′i·na′tor,** *n.*

El·i·ot (el′ē ət *or* el′yət), *n.* **1 George,** 1819-1880, pen name of Mary Ann Evans, English novelist. **2 T. S.,** 1888-1965, British poet and essayist, born in the United States. He won the Nobel Prize for literature in 1948.

e·lite or **é·lite** (i lēt′ *or* ā lēt′), *n.pl. or sing.* the choice or distinguished part; those thought of as the best people: *Only the elite attended the reception for the queen.* ❏ *n., pl.* **e·lites** or **é·lites.**

e·lix·ir (i lik′sər), *n.* **1** medicine made of drugs or herbs mixed with alcohol and syrup. **2** (in the Middle Ages) substance supposed to have the power of changing lead into gold or of lengthening life.

E·liz·a·beth I (i liz′ə bəth), 1533-1603, queen of England from 1558 to 1603, daughter of Henry VIII. [Elizabeth comes from a Hebrew word meaning "oath of God."]

Elizabeth II, born 1926, since 1952 queen of Great Britain and Northern Ireland, and head of the Commonwealth of Nations; daughter of George VI.

E·liz·a·be·than (i liz′ə bē′thən *or* i liz′ə beth′ən), **1** *adj.* of the time when Elizabeth I ruled England (1558-1603): *Elizabethan drama.* **2** *n.* an English person, especially a writer, of the time of Elizabeth I: *Shakespeare is a famous Elizabethan.*

elk (elk), *n.* **1** a large reddish deer of North America with long, slender antlers; wapiti. **2** a large deer of northern Europe and Asia. In North America, it is called a moose. ❏ *n., pl.* **elk** or **elks.**

> **WORD STORY** **Elk** is the old English name of the moose, which lives in northern Europe and Asia as well as in America. When English settlers in America saw a large American deer, they named it *elk* after the animal they already knew. Then they needed a new American name for the animal they knew before, so they called it by an American Indian word, *moose.*

El·ling·ton (el′ing tən), *n.* **Duke** (dük), 1899-1974, American jazz composer. He wrote many popular songs, including "Mood Indigo," and many longer jazz pieces.

el·lipse (i lips′), *n.* a figure shaped like an oval with both ends alike.

el·lip·sis (i lip′sis), *n.* **1** marks (… or ***) used to show an omission in writing or printing. **2** omission of a word or phrase needed to complete a sentence grammatically, but not needed to understand its meaning. EXAMPLE: "She is as tall as her brother" instead of "She is as tall as her brother is tall." ❏ *n., pl.* **el·lip·ses** (i lip′sēz′).

el·lip·tic (i lip′tik), *adj.* elliptical.

el·lip·ti·cal (i lip′tə kəl), *adj.* shaped like an ellipse. —**el·lip′ti·cal·ly,** *adv.*

El·lis Island (el′is), a small island in the harbor of New York, just south of Manhattan. From 1891 to 1943 it housed reception facilities for immigrants to the United States. It is part of the Statue of Liberty National Monument.

Ell·i·son (el′ə sən), *n.* **Ralph** (ralf), 1914-1994, American author. ▪ **Ralph Ellison's** most famous work, *The Invisible Man,* deals with an African American man's efforts to find his role in society.

elm (elm), *n.* a tall shade tree with high, spreading branches.

El Ni·ño (el nē′nyō), a rise in the surface temperature of the Pacific Ocean near the coast of Peru and Ecuador, occurring unpredictably every few years. It hurts the local fishing industry and can cause major weather changes around the world. [El Niño comes from Spanish words meaning "the boy," used to mean the baby Jesus, because the rise occurs around Christmastime.]

el·o·cu·tion (el′ə kyü′shən), *n.* art of speaking or reading clearly and effectively in public.

e·lon·gate (i lông′gāt), **1** *v.* to make or become longer; lengthen; extend; stretch: *The balloon elongated as it became filled with air.* **2** *adj.* long and thin: *Earthworms have elongate bodies.* ❏ *v.* **e·lon·gat·ed, e·lon·gat·ing.**

e·lon·ga·tion (ē′lông gā′shən), *n.* a lengthening; extension.

e·lope (i lōp′), *v.* to run away to get married. ❏ *v.* **e·loped, e·lop·ing.** —**e·lope′ment,** *n.* —**e·lop′er,** *n.*

el·o·quence (el′ə kwəns), *n.* **1** flow of speech that has grace and force: *The jury was moved by the eloquence of the lawyer's words.* **2** power to win by speaking; art of speaking so as to stir the feelings.

el·o·quent (el′ə kwənt), *adj.* **1** having the power of expressing feelings or thoughts with grace and force; having eloquence: *an eloquent speaker.* **2** very expressive: *eloquent eyes.* —**el′o·quent·ly,** *adv.*

El Sal·va·dor (el sal′və dôr), country in W Central America. *Capital:* San Salvador. [El Salvador is Spanish for "the Savior."]

else (els), **1** *adj.* other than the person, place, thing, etc., mentioned; different: *Will somebody else speak? What else could I say?* **2** *adj.* in addition; more: *The Browns are here; do you expect anyone else?* **3** *adv.* differently: *How else can it be done?* **4** *adv.* otherwise; if not: *Hurry, or else you will be late.*

else·where (els′wâr), *adv.* in, at, or to some other place; somewhere else.

e·lu·ci·date (i lü′sə dāt), *v.* to make clear; explain: *The scientist was asked to elucidate her theory.* □ *v.* **e·lu·ci·dat·ed, e·lu·ci·dat·ing. —e·lu′ci·da′tion,** *n.* **—e·lu′ci·da′tive,** *adj.* **—e·lu′ci·da′tor,** *n.*

e·lude (i lüd′), *v.* **1** to avoid or escape by cleverness or quickness; slip away from: *The fox eluded the dogs.* ■ See Synonym Study at **escape. 2** to remain undiscovered or unexplained by; baffle: *The answer to the problem eluded me.* □ *v.* **e·lud·ed, e·lud·ing.**

e·lu·sive (i lü′siv), *adj.* **1** hard to describe or understand; baffling: *I had an idea that was too elusive to put in words.* **2** tending to elude or escape: *The elusive fox got away.* ■ Another word that sounds like this is **illusive. —e·lu′sive·ly,** *adv.* **—e·lu′sive·ness,** *n.*

elves (elvz), *n.* plural of **elf.**

E·ly·sian (i lizh′ən), *adj.* **1** of or in Elysium. **Elysian Fields** is another name for Elysium. **2** happy; delightful.

E·ly·si·um (i lizh′e əm *or* i liz′ē əm), *n.* **1** (in Greek myths) a place where heroes and other people favored by the gods lived after death. **2** any place or condition of perfect happiness; paradise.

'em (əm), *pron.pl.* INFORMAL. them.

e·ma·ci·at·ed (i mā′shē ā′tid), *adj.* unnaturally thin and weak.

e·ma·ci·a·tion (i mā′shē ā′shən), *n.* condition of being emaciated.

e-mail (ē′māl), *n.* electronic mail, **a** a system of sending messages using computers linked by telephone wires or radio signals. **b** messages sent by such a system.

em·a·nate (em′ə nāt), *v.* to come forth; spread out: *The story emanated from the mayor's office.* □ *v.* **em·a·nat·ed, em·a·nat·ing.**

em·a·na·tion (em′ə nā′shən), *n.* **1** act or process of coming forth; spreading out. **2** anything that comes forth or spreads out from a source: *Light and heat are emanations from the sun.* **—em′a·na′tion·al,** *adj.*

e·man·ci·pate (i man′sə pāt), *v.* to set free from slavery or restraint; release: *Women have been emancipated from many old restrictions.* □ *v.* **e·man·ci·pat·ed, e·man·ci·pat·ing. —e·man′ci·pa′tor,** *n.*

e·man·ci·pa·tion (i man′sə pā′shən), *n.* act of setting free from slavery or restraint; release: *The discoveries of science have led to people's emancipation from many old superstitions.*

Emancipation Proclamation, proclamation issued by Abraham Lincoln on January 1, 1863, declaring free all persons in slavery in any state rebelling against the United States.

e·mas·cu·late (i mas′kyə lāt), *v.* **1** to remove the testicles of; castrate. **2** to destroy the force of; weaken: *emasculate a speech by cutting out its strongest passages.* □ *v.* **e·mas·cu·lat·ed, e·mas·cu·lat·ing. —e·mas′cu·la′tion,** *n.* **—e·mas′cu·la′tor,** *n.*

em·balm (em bäm′), *v.* to treat a dead body with chemicals to keep it from decaying. **—em·balm′er,** *n.* **—em·balm′ment,** *n.*

em·bank·ment (em bangk′mənt), *n.* a raised bank of earth, stones, etc., used to hold back water, support a road, etc.

em·bar·go (em bär′gō), **1** *n.* an order of a government forbidding ships to enter or leave its ports. **2** *n.* any restriction put on commerce by law. **3** *v.* to put under an embargo; forbid to enter or leave port: *The government embargoed all foreign ships.* □ *n., pl.* **em·bar·goes;** *v.* **em·bar·goed, em·bar·go·ing.**

em·bark (em bärk′), *v.* **1** to go or put on board a ship or an aircraft: *to embark for Europe. The general embarked his troops.* **2** to set out; start: *After leaving college, the young woman embarked upon a business career.* **—em′bar·ka′tion,** *n.*

em·bar·rass (em bar′əs), *v.* to make uneasy and ashamed; make self-conscious: *She embarrassed me by asking me if I really liked her.*

em·bar·rassed (em bar′əst), *adj.* **1** uneasy and ashamed; self-conscious. **2** kept from normal activity, especially financial activity: *The company was financially embarrassed and could not pay its employees.*

em·bar·rass·ing (em bar′ə sing), *adj.* causing embarrassment: *an embarrassing situation.*

em·bar·rass·ment (em bar′əs mənt), *n.* **1** shame; an uneasy feeling: *He blushed in embarrassment at such a stupid mistake.* **2** something that embarrasses: *Forgetting the name of an old friend is a great embarrassment.*

em·bas·sy (em′bə sē), *n.* **1** ambassador and his or her staff of assistants. **2** the official residence and offices of an ambassador. **3** position or duties of an ambassador. □ *n., pl.* **em·bas·sies.**

em·bat·tled (em bat′ld), *adj.* **1** drawn up ready for battle; prepared for battle. **2** fortified.

em·bed (em bed′), *v.* to enclose in a surrounding mass; fasten or fix firmly: *Precious stones are often found embedded in rock.* □ *v.* **em·bed·ded, em·bed·ding.** Also, **imbed.**

em·bel·lish (em bel′ish), *v.* **1** to add beauty to; decorate; adorn; ornament: *He embellished his letters with clever sketches.* **2** to make more interesting by adding details: *The speaker embellished the old stories.*

em·bel·lish·ment (em bel′ish mənt), *n.* **1** decoration; adornment; ornament. **2** detail, often imaginary, added to make a story or account more interesting.

embellishment (def. 1)

em·ber (em′bər), *n.* **1** piece of wood or coal still glowing in the ashes of a fire. **2** embers, *pl.* ashes in which there is still some fire: *She stirred the embers to make them blaze up again.*

em·bez·zle (em bez′əl), *v.* to steal money entrusted to your care: *The cashier embezzled $25,000 from the bank.* □ *v.* **em·bez·zled, em·bez·zling. —em·bez′zle·ment,** *n.* **—em·bez′zler,** *n.*

em·bit·ter (em bit′ər), *v.* to make bitter: *embittered by constant failure.* **—em·bit′ter·ment,** *n.*

em·bla·zon (em blā′zn), *v.* to decorate; adorn: *The shield was emblazoned with a coat of arms.* **—em·bla′zon·er,** *n.* **—em·bla′zon·ment,** *n.*

em·blem (em′bləm), *n.* sign that stands for an idea; symbol; token: *The dove is an emblem of peace. The Stars and Stripes and the eagle are emblems of the United States.*

emblem—UNICEF emblem

em·blem·at·ic (em′blə mat′ik), *adj.* used as an emblem; symbolic: *The lion is emblematic of courage.*

a	hat	ė	term	ô	order	ch	child	
ā	age	i	it	oi	oil	ng	long	(a in about
ä	far	ī	ice	ou	out	sh	she	(e in taken
â	care	o	hot	u	cup	th	thin	ə ⟨ i in pencil
e	let	ō	open	u̇	put	ŦH	then	(o in lemon
ē	equal	ȯ	saw	ü	rule	zh	measure	(u in circus

em·bod·i·ment (em bod′ē mənt), *n.* someone or something symbolizing some idea or quality: *They thought their leader was the embodiment of authority.*

em·bod·y (em bod′ē), *v.* **1** to put into a form that can be seen; express in definite form: *A building embodies the idea of an architect.* **2** to make part of an organized book, law, system, etc.; incorporate: *embody suggestions in a revised plan.* ❑ *v.* **em·bod·ied, em·bod·y·ing.**

em·bold·en (em bōl′dən), *v.* to make bold; encourage.

em·bo·lism (em′bə liz′əm), *n.* act of blocking a blood vessel by a clot, a bit of fat, etc., carried there by the blood.

em·boss (em bòs′), *v.* **1** to decorate with a design or pattern that stands out from the surface. **2** to cause to stand out from the surface: *He ran his finger over the letters on the book's cover to see if they had been embossed.* **—em·boss′er,** *n.* **—em·boss′ment,** *n.*

em·brace (em brās′), **1** *v.* to hold in the arms to show love or friendship; hug: *I embraced my old friend.* **2** *n.* a hug with both arms; *My old friend gave me a fond embrace.* **3** *v.* to take up; take for yourself; accept: *She eagerly embraced the offer of a trip to Europe.* **4** *v.* to include; contain: *The cat family embraces cats, lions, tigers, and similar animals.* **5** *v.* to surround; enclose: *Vines embraced the hut.* ❑ *v.* **em·braced, em·brac·ing.** **—em·brace′a·ble,** *adj.* **—em·brace′ment,** *n.* **—em·brac′er,** *n.*

em·bra·sure (em brā′zhər), *n.* an opening in a wall for a gun, with sides that spread outward to permit the gun to swing.

em·broi·der (em broi′dər), *v.* **1** to ornament cloth, leather, etc., with a raised design or pattern of stitches: *embroider a shirt with a colorful design.* **2** to make an ornamental design or pattern on cloth, leather, etc., with stitches: *I embroidered silver stars on my blue jeans.* **3** to add imaginary details to; exaggerate: *She often embroiders her stories to make them more interesting.* **—em·broi′der·er,** *n.*

em·broi·der·y (em broi′dər ē), *n.* **1** act or art of embroidering. **2** embroidered work or material.

em·broil (em broil′), *v.* to involve in a quarrel: *Even bystanders became embroiled in our argument.* **—em·broil′ment,** *n.*

em·bry·o (em′brē ō), *n.* **1** animal in the earlier stages of its development, before birth or hatching. A human embryo more than three months old is usually called a fetus. **2** an undeveloped plant within a seed. ❑ *n., pl.* **em·bry·os.**

in embryo, in an undeveloped stage: *a plan in embryo.*

em·bry·ol·o·gy (em′brē ol′ə jē), *n.* branch of biology that deals with the formation and development of embryos. **—em′bry·ol′o·gist,** *n.*

em·bry·on·ic (em′brē on′ik), *adj.* **1** of the embryo. **2** not mature; undeveloped: *an embryonic leaf, an embryonic plan.* **—em′bry·on′i·cal·ly,** *adv.*

em·cee (em′sē′), **1** *n.* master of ceremonies. **2** *v.* to act as master of ceremonies. ❑ *n., pl.* **em·cees;** *v.* **em·ceed, em·cee·ing.** [Emcee comes from the pronunciation of the letters *M.C.,* an abbreviation for "Master of Ceremonies."]

e·mend (i mend′), *v.* to free from faults or errors; correct; revise. **—e·men·da·tion** (ē′men dā′shən), *n.*

em·er·ald (em′ər əld), **1** *n.* a clear, hard, deep green precious gem, a variety of beryl. **2** *n.* a bright green. **3** *adj.* bright green.

e·merge (i mėrj′), *v.* **1** to come into view; come out; come up: *The sun emerged from behind a cloud.* **2** to become known: *Important new facts emerged as a result of a second investigation.* ❑ *v.* **e·merged, e·merg·ing.**

e·mer·gence (i mėr′jəns), *n.* act or fact of emerging: *the emergence of a chick from its egg.*

e·mer·gen·cy (i mėr′jən sē), **1** *n.* a sudden need for immediate action: *I keep tools in my car for use in an emergency.* **2** *adj.* for a time of sudden need: *When the other brakes failed, the emergency brake stopped the car.* ❑ *n., pl.* **e·mer·gen·cies.**

e·mer·gent (i mėr′jənt), *adj.* emerging.

e·mer·i·tus (i mer′ə təs), *adj.* retired from active service, but still part of a school or university faculty: *At the age of 70, Professor Arnold became professor emeritus.*

Em·er·son (em′ər sən), *n.* **Ralph Wal·do** (ralf wàl′dō), 1803-1882, American essayist, poet, and philosopher. ■ Well-known phrases from **Ralph Waldo Emerson's** works include "the shot heard 'round the world," "Hitch your wagon to a star," and "The only way to have a friend is to be one."

em·er·y (em′ər ē), *n.* a hard, dark mineral used in powdered form to grind, smooth, and polish metals, stones, etc.

emery board, a thin, flat piece of cardboard with a coating of powdered emery. It is used to file fingernails.

e·met·ic (i met′ik), **1** *adj.* causing vomiting. **2** *n.* medicine that causes vomiting.

em·i·grant (em′ə grənt), *n.* person who leaves his or her own country to settle in another: *My grandparents were emigrants from Japan.*

em·i·grate (em′ə grāt), *v.* to leave your own country to settle in another: *My grandparents emigrated from Ireland to the United States.* ■ See Usage Note at **immigrate.** ❑ *v.* **em·i·grat·ed, em·i·grat·ing.**

em·i·gra·tion (em′ə grā′shən), *n.* **1** act of leaving your own country to settle in another: *There has been much emigration from Italy to the United States.* **2** body of emigrants: *The largest emigration from Europe came to the United States in 1907.*

é·mi·gré (em′ə grā), *n.* **1** emigrant. **2** member of a refugee group. ❑ *n., pl.* **é·mi·grés** (em′ə grāz).

em·i·nence (em′ə nəns), *n.* **1** rank or position above all or most others; high standing; fame: *to achieve eminence in the field of medicine.* **2** a high place; high point of land: *The lighthouse was built on an eminence above the shore.* **3 Eminence,** title of honor given to a cardinal in the Roman Catholic Church.

em·i·nent (em′ə nənt), *adj.* above all or most others; outstanding; famous: *an eminent writer.* **—em′i·nent·ly,** *adv.*

e·mir (ə mir′), *n.* **1** an Arabian chief, prince, or military leader. **2** title of honor of the descendants of Mohammed. [See Word Story at **admiral.**]

em·ir·ate (em′ər it), *n.* **1** rank or authority of an emir. **2** territory governed by an emir.

em·is·sar·y (em′ə ser′ē), *n.* **1** person sent on a mission or errand. **2** a secret agent; spy. ❑ *n., pl.* **em·is·sar·ies.**

e·mis·sion (i mish′ən), *n.* **1** act or fact of emitting: *the emission of light from the sun.* **2** something emitted.

emission control, limitation of polluting gases or particles given off by burning fuels, industrial processes, etc.

e·mit (i mit′), *v.* to give off; send out: *The sun emits light and heat. Volcanoes emit lava. The trapped lion emitted roars of rage.* ❑ *v.* **e·mit·ted, e·mit·ting.** **—e·mit′ter,** *n.*

Em·my (em′ē), *n.* one of several small golden statues awarded each year by the people who work in the television industry, for the best performances, productions, and programs during the year. ❑ *n., pl.* **Em·mys.**

e·mote (i mōt′), *v.* **1** to act or perform, especially in an exaggerated way. **2** to show emotion. ❑ *v.* **e·mot·ed, e·mot·ing.**

e·mo·tion (i mō′shən), *n.* a strong feeling of any kind. Joy, grief, fear, hate, love, anger, and excitement are emotions. ■ See Synonym Study at **feeling.**

e·mo·tion·al (i mō′shə nəl), *adj.* **1** of the emotions: *His constant fears show that he is suffering from a serious emotional illness.* **2** showing or appealing to the emotions: *The speaker made an emotional plea for money to help disabled children.* **3** easily excited: *Emotional people are likely to cry if they hear sad music or read sad stories.* **—e·mo′tion·al·ly,** *adv.*

e·mo·tion·al·ism (i mō′shə nə liz′əm), *n.* tendency to show emotion too easily.

em·pa·na·da (em′pə nä′də), *n.* a turnover filled with meat or vegetables, then baked or fried, commonly eaten in Spanish America. ❑ *n., pl.* **em·pa·na·das.**

em·pa·thize (em′pə thīz), *v.* to feel empathy: *I empathize with his fear of strange dogs.* ❑ *v.* **em·pa·thized, em·pa·thiz·ing.**

em·pa·thy (em′pə thē), *n.* ability to imagine yourself in someone else's situation and to understand that person's feelings.

em·per·or (em′pər ər), *n.* man who is the ruler of an empire.

em·pha·sis (em′fə sis), *n.* **1** special force; stress; importance: *That school puts emphasis on arithmetic and reading.* **2** special force put on particular syllables, words, or phrases. ❑ *n., pl.* **em·pha·ses** (em′fə sēz′).

em·pha·size (em′fə sīz), *v.* **1** to stress; call attention to: *The number of car accidents emphasizes the need for careful driving.* **2** to give extra force to in speaking: *He emphasized her name as he read the list of winners.* ❑ *v.* **em·pha·sized, em·pha·siz·ing.**

em·phat·ic (em fat′ik), *adj.* **1** said or done with force; strongly expressed: *Her answer was an emphatic "No!"* **2** attracting attention; very noticeable; striking: *The club made an emphatic success of its party.* —**em·phat′i·cal·ly,** *adv.*

em·phy·se·ma (em′fə sē′mə), *n.* a diseased increase in size of the air sacs in the lungs. Emphysema makes breathing difficult.

em·pire (em′pīr), *n.* **1** group of countries or states under one ruler or government: *The Roman Empire consisted of many separate territories and different peoples.* **2** country that has an emperor or empress: *the Japanese Empire.* **3** absolute power; supreme authority. **4** a large business or group of businesses under the control of a single person, family, syndicate, etc.

em·pir·i·cal (em pir′ə kəl), *adj.* based on experiment and observation: *empirical knowledge.* —**em·pir′i·cal·ly,** *adv.*

em·place·ment (em plās′mənt), *n.* space or platform for a heavy gun or guns.

em·ploy (em ploi′), **1** *v.* to give work and pay to: *That big factory employs many workers.* ■ See Synonym Study at **hire. 2** *n.* service for pay; employment: *workers in the employ of that big factory.* **3** *v.* to use: *She employs her time wisely.* **4** *v.* to keep busy; occupy: *He employed himself in growing roses after he retired.* —**em·ploy′a·ble,** *adj.*

em·ploy·ee or **em·ploy·e** (em ploi′ē or em′ploi ē′), *n.* person who works for some person or firm for pay. ❑ *n., pl.* **em·ploy·ees** or **em·ploy·es.**

em·ploy·er (em ploi′ər), *n.* person or firm that employs one or more persons.

em·ploy·ment (em ploi′mənt), *n.* **1** work; job: *She had no difficulty finding employment.* **2** act of employing or condition of being employed: *A large office requires the employment of many people.* **3** use: *The painter was clever in his employment of brushes and colors.*

em·po·ri·um (em pôr′ē əm), *n.* **1** (earlier) center of trade; marketplace. **2** a large store selling many different things. ❑ *n., pl.* **em·po·ri·ums, em·po·ri·a** (em pôr′ē ə).

em·pow·er (em pou′ər), *v.* to give power or authority to; authorize: *The secretary was empowered to sign certain contracts.* —**em·pow′er·ment,** *n.*

em·press (em′pris), *n.* **1** woman who is the ruler of an empire. **2** wife of an emperor. ❑ *n., pl.* **em·press·es.**

emp·ty (emp′tē), **1** *adj.* with nothing or no one in it: *The birds had gone and their nest was empty.* **2** *adj.* hungry. **3** *v.* to pour out or take out all that is in something; make empty: *She emptied her glass. He emptied the trash from the wastebasket.* **4** *v.* to become empty: *The hall emptied as soon as the concert was over.* **5** *v.* to flow out: *The Mississippi River empties into the Gulf of Mexico.* **6** *adj.* not real; meaningless: *An empty threat has no force behind it.* **7** *n.* something with nothing in it, such as a container, freight car, etc. ❑ *adj.* **emp·ti·er, emp·ti·est;** *v.* **emp·tied, emp·ty·ing;** *n., pl.* **emp·ties.** [**Empty** comes from an old English word meaning "leisure." Leisure time is time that has no work in it.] —**emp′ti·ly,** *adv.* —**emp′ti·ness,** *n.*

SYNONYM STUDY **Empty, blank,** and **hollow** all mean containing nothing. **Empty** means with nothing or no one in it: *The room was empty.* **Blank** means with nothing on it: *She handed me a blank piece of paper.* **Hollow** means with space inside: *Within the hollow wall was a secret staircase.*

emp·ty-hand·ed (emp′tē han′did), *adj.* having nothing in the hands; bringing or taking nothing of value.

empty set, a set that has no elements; null set.

EMT, emergency medical technician (person who is not a doctor or nurse but has been trained and licensed to provide medical treatment in an emergency, especially while someone with a severe medical problem is being taken to a hospital).

e·mu (ē′myü), *n.* a large, three-toed Australian bird like an ostrich, but smaller. Emus cannot fly, but they can run very fast. ❑ *n., pl.* **e·mus.**

emu—6 ft. (1.8 m) tall

em·u·late (em′yə lāt), *v.* to imitate the achievements or qualities of an admired person: *to try to emulate the style of a famous author.* ❑ *v.* **em·u·lat·ed, em·u·lat·ing.** —**em′u·la·tor,** *n.*

em·u·la·tion (em′yə lā′shən), *n.* imitation of desired achievements or qualities: *deeds done in emulation of heroic ancestors.*

e·mul·si·fy (i mul′sə fī), *v.* to make into an emulsion: *to emulsify oil and water.* ❑ *v.* **e·mul·si·fied, e·mul·si·fy·ing.** —**e·mul′si·fi·er,** *n.* —**e·mul′si·fi·ca′tion,** *n.*

e·mul·sion (i mul′shən), *n.* mixture of liquids that do not dissolve in each other. In an emulsion one of the liquids contains minute droplets of the other evenly distributed throughout.

en-, *prefix.* **1** make ___: *enfeeble = make feeble.* **2** to put in or on ___: *enthrone = put on a throne.*

-en, *suffix.* **1** make or become ___: *blacken = to make black. sicken = to become sick.* **2** to give or gain ___: *strengthen = to give strength; lengthen = to gain length.*

en·a·ble (en ā′bəl), *v.* to give ability, power, or means to; make able: *Airplanes enable people to travel great distances rapidly.* ❑ *v.* **en·a·bled, en·a·bling.** —**en·a′bler,** *n.*

en·act (en akt′), *v.* **1** to make into law: *Congress enacted a bill to lower taxes.* **2** to act out; play: *He enacted the part of Long John Silver very well.* —**en·act′a·ble,** *adj.* —**en·ac′tor,** *n.*

en·act·ment (en akt′mənt), *n.* **1** act or process of enacting or condition of being enacted: *After the House and Senate agreed on a compromise the enactment of the bill followed quickly.* **2** a law.

e·nam·el (i nam′əl), **1** *n.* a glasslike substance melted and then cooled to make a smooth, hard surface. Different colors of enamel are used to cover or decorate metal, glass, pottery, etc. **2** *n.* paint or varnish used to make a smooth, hard, glossy surface. **3** *n.* the smooth, hard, glossy outer layer of the teeth. **4** *v.* to cover or decorate with enamel. ❑ *v.* **e·nam·eled, e·nam·el·ing** or **e·nam·elled, e·nam·el·ling.** —**e·nam′el·er** or **e·nam′el·ler,** *n.*

e·nam·el·ware (i nam′əl wâr′), *n.* pots, pans, etc., made of metal coated with enamel.

en·am·ored (en am′ərd), *adj.* in love: *She was enamored of the young man.*

en·camp (en kamp′), *v.* **1** to make a camp: *It took the soldiers only an hour to encamp.* **2** to live in a camp for a time: *The Girl Scouts encamped all week by the river.*

en·camp·ment (en kamp′mənt), *n.* place where a camp is; camp.

en·case (en kās′), *v.* **1** to put into a case. **2** to cover completely; enclose: *A cocoon encased the caterpillar.* ❑ *v.* **en·cased, en·cas·ing.** —**en·case′ment,** *n.*

-ence, *suffix.* **1** act or fact of ___ing: *dependence = act or fact of depending.* **2** condition of being ___ent: *absence = condition of being absent.*

en·ceph·a·li·tis (en sef′ə lī′tis), *n.* inflammation of the brain caused by injury, infection, poison, etc.

en·chant (en chant′), *v.* **1** to use magic on; put under a spell: *The witch enchanted the princess so that she slept for a month.* **2** to delight greatly; charm: *The music enchanted us all.* [See Word Story at **charm.**] —**en·chant′er,** *n.*

en·chant·ing (en chan′ting), *adj.* very delightful; charming. —**en·chant′ing·ly,** *adv.*

a	hat	ė	term	ô	order	ch	child	
ā	age	i	it	oi	oil	ng	long	⎧ a in about
ä	far	ī	ice	ou	out	sh	she	⎪ e in taken
â	care	o	hot	u	cup	th	thin	ə ⎨ i in pencil
e	let	ō	open	ù	put	ŧн	then	⎪ o in lemon
ē	equal	ò	saw	ü	rule	zh	measure	⎩ u in circus

en·chant·ment (en chant′mənt), *n.* **1** use of magic spells; spell or charm: *In "The Wizard of Oz" Dorothy finds herself at home again by the enchantment of the Good Witch.* **2** delight; rapture. **3** something that delights or charms: *We felt the enchantment of the moonlight on the lake.*

en·chan·tress (en chan′tris), *n.* **1** woman who enchants; witch. **2** a very delightful, charming woman. ❑ *n., pl.* **en·chan·tress·es.**

en·chi·la·da (en′chi lä′də), *n.* tortilla rolled around a filling of meat or cheese and served with a peppery sauce. ❑ *n., pl.* **en·chi·la·das.**

en·cir·cle (en sėr′kəl), *v.* **1** to form a circle around; surround: *Trees encircled the pond.* **2** to go in a circle around: *The moon encircles the earth.* ❑ *v.* **en·cir·cled, en·cir·cling.** **—en·cir′cle·ment,** *n.*

en·clave (en′klāv), *n.* country or district surrounded by territory of a foreign country: *Vatican City is an enclave in Rome, Italy.*

en·close (en klōz′), *v.* **1** to shut in on all sides; surround: *The little park was enclosed by tall apartment buildings.* **2** to put a wall or fence around: *We are going to enclose our backyard to keep dogs out.* **3** to put in an envelope along with a letter, etc.: *He enclosed a check when he mailed his order.* **4** to contain: *a letter enclosing a dollar's worth of stamps.* ❑ *v.* **en·closed, en·clos·ing.**

en·clo·sure (en klō′zhər), *n.* **1** an enclosed place, such as a pen or corral: *At the zoo, the elephants and giraffes were kept in separate enclosures.* **2** something that encloses. A wall or fence is an enclosure. **3** something enclosed: *The envelope contained a card and $5 as an enclosure.*

en·code (en kōd′), *v.* to put into code: *The spy encoded his message and gave it to a courier for delivery.* ❑ *v.* **en·cod·ed, en·cod·ing.** **—en·cod′er,** *n.*

en·co·mi·um (en kō′mē əm), *n.* an elaborate expression of praise. ❑ *n., pl.* **en·co·mi·ums, en·co·mi·a** (en kō′mē ə).

en·com·pass (en kum′pəs), *v.* **1** to go or reach all the way around; encircle: *The atmosphere encompasses the earth.* **2** to include; contain: *Our history book encompasses all the important events in U.S. history since 1607.* **—en·com′pass·ment,** *n.*

en·core (äng′kôr *or* än′kôr), **1** *interj.* once more; again: *The audience liked the song so much they shouted, "Encore! Encore!"* **2** *n.* a demand by the audience, made by shouting "Encore!," for the repetition of a song, etc., or for another appearance of the performer or performers. **3** *n.* an extra song, appearance, etc., by the performer.

en·coun·ter (en koun′tər), **1** *v.* to meet unexpectedly: *What if we should encounter a bear?* ■ See Synonym Study at **meet**[1]. **2** *n.* an unexpected meeting: *The explorers had a surprising encounter with a polar bear.* **3** *v.* to be faced with: *She encountered many difficulties before the job was done.* **4** *v.* to meet as an enemy; meet in a fight or battle: *He encountered the strange knight in direct combat.* **5** *n.* a meeting of enemies; fight; battle: *The two armies had a desperate encounter.*

encounter (def. 2)

en·cour·age (en kėr′ij), *v.* **1** to give courage; increase the hope or confidence of; urge on: *The cheers of their schoolmates encouraged them.* **2** to be favorable to; help; support: *Sunlight encourages plant growth.* ❑ *v.* **en·cour·aged, en·cour·ag·ing.**

en·cour·age·ment (en kėr′ij mənt), *n.* **1** condition of being or feeling encouraged: *The singer drew her encouragement from the audience.* **2** something that encourages. **3** act of encouraging: *Her encouragement was a great help to me.*

en·cour·ag·ing (en kėr′ə jing), *adj.* giving courage, hope, or confidence: *encouraging words.* **—en·cour′ag·ing·ly,** *adv.*

en·croach (en krōch′), *v.* **1** to go beyond proper or usual limits: *The sea encroached upon the shore and submerged the beach.* **2** to trespass upon the property or rights of another; intrude: *Our neighbor's irrigation system is encroaching on our land.* **—en·croach′er,** *n.* **—en·croach′ment,** *n.*

en·crust (en krust′), *v.* to cover with a crust or coating: *The inside of the kettle was encrusted with rust.* Also, **incrust.**

en·cryp·tion (en krip′shən), *n.* process of putting computer files or other information into a secret code, to keep them private.

en·cum·ber (en kum′bər), *v.* **1** to hold back; hinder; hamper: *Heavy shoes encumber a runner in a race.* **2** to burden with weight, difficulties, cares, debt, etc.: *The farm was encumbered with a heavy mortgage.*

en·cum·brance (en kum′brəns), *n.* something useless or in the way; hindrance; burden: *Shoes would be an encumbrance to a swimmer.*

-ency, *suffix.* a form of **-ence,** as in *dependency.*

en·cyc·li·cal (en sik′lə kəl), *n.* letter from the Pope to his bishops, stating the position of the church on important questions.

en·cy·clo·pae·di·a (en sī′klə pē′dē ə), *n.* encyclopedia. ❑ *n., pl.* **en·cy·clo·pae·di·as.**

en·cy·clo·pae·dic (en sī′klə pē′dik), *adj.* encyclopedic.

en·cy·clo·pe·di·a (en sī′klə pē′dē ə), *n.* **1** book or set of books giving information on all branches of knowledge, with its articles arranged alphabetically. **2** book treating one subject very thoroughly, with its articles arranged alphabetically: *an encyclopedia of art.* ❑ *n., pl.* **en·cy·clo·pe·di·as.**

en·cy·clo·pe·dic (en sī′klə pē′dik), *adj.* covering a wide range of subjects; possessing wide and varied information: *encyclopedic knowledge, an encyclopedic mind.*

end (end), **1** *n.* the last part; conclusion: *She read to the end of the book.* **2** *n.* the part where a thing begins or stops: *Drive to the end of this road.* **3** *v.* to bring or come to its last part; stop; finish: *Let us end this fight. The fight ended in a draw.* **4** *v.* to form the end of; be the end of: *This scene ends the play.* **5** *n.* purpose; object: *The end he had in mind was to skip a grade.* **6** *n.* result; outcome: *It is hard to tell what the end will be.* **7** *n.* death; destruction: *He met his end in the accident.* **8** *n.* an offensive or defensive player at either end of the line in football. **—end′er,** *n.*

at loose ends, 1 without something definite to do: *The boy was at loose ends until he was put to work cleaning his room.* **2** in confusion or disorder.

end to end, with the ends placed so that they touch; endways.

end up, to wind up; come out.

in the end, finally; at last: *In the end, he admitted his mistake.*

make ends meet, to spend no more than you have; live within your income: *The family had a hard time making ends meet.*

on end, 1 upright: *Place the log on end. His hair stood on end.* **2** one after another: *It snowed for days on end.*
put an end to, to do away with; stop.

en·dan·ger (en dān′jər), *v.* to cause danger to: *Fire endangered the hotel's guests, but no lives were lost.*

en·dan·gered (en dān′jərd), *adj.* liable to become extinct: *an endangered species.*

en·dear (en dir′), *v.* to make dear: *Her kindness endeared her to all of us.* —**en·dear′ing·ly,** *adv.*

en·dear·ment (en dir′mənt), *n.* act or word showing love or affection.

en·deav·or (en dev′ər), **1** *v.* to make an effort; try hard; attempt strongly: *Each time she endeavored to do better than before.* ■ See Synonym Study at **try. 2** *n.* a serious effort over time. ■ See Synonym Study at **effort.**

en·dem·ic (en dem′ik), *adj.* regularly found among a particular people or in a particular locality: *Cholera is endemic in India.* —**en·dem′i·cal·ly,** *adv.*

end·ing (en′ding), *n.* **1** the last part; end: *The story has a sad ending.* **2** letter or syllable added to a word to change its meaning; suffix. The common plural ending is "s" or "es."

en·dive (en′dīv), *n.* **1** a green plant that looks something like lettuce, used for salad. **2** this same plant, cultivated to form flat, narrow leaves; escarole. [Endive comes from an Egyptian word meaning "January." In Egypt, that is when it grows.]

end·less (end′lis), *adj.* **1** having no end; lasting or going on forever: *the endless rotation of planets around the sun.* **2** seeming to have no end: *an endless scolding.* **3** with the ends joined; without ends. —**end′less·ly,** *adv.* —**end′less·ness,** *n.*

end·most (end′mōst), *adj.* most distant; farthest.

endo-, *prefix.* within; inner: *endoderm = inner layer of cells.*

en·do·crine gland (en′dō krən *or* en′dō krīn), any of various glands that produce secretions that pass directly into the bloodstream or lymph instead of into a duct; ductless gland. The thyroid and the pituitary are endocrine glands, part of the **endocrine system,** which controls growth and many other body activities.

en·do·cri·nol·o·gy (en′dō krə nol′ə je), *n.* branch of medicine dealing with the functions and diseases of the endocrine glands. —**en′do·cri·nol′o·gist,** *n.*

en·do·derm (en′dō dėrm), *n.* the inner layer of cells formed during the development of animal embryos. The linings of the digestive system and respiratory system grow from the endoderm. —**en′do·der′mal,** *adj.* —**en′do·der′mic,** *adj.*

en·dog·a·my (en dog′ə mē), *n.* custom of marrying someone from your own group, clan, or tribe. Some religious groups tend to practice endogamy.

en·dor·phin (en dôr′fin), *n.* any of a group of chemical substances produced in the central nervous system that reduce the feeling of pain.

en·dorse (en dôrs′), *v.* **1** to write your name on the back of a check, note, or other document: *She had to endorse the check before the bank would cash it.* **2** to approve; support: *Parents endorsed the plan for a school playground.* ❑ *v.* **en·dorsed, en·dors·ing.** [Endorse comes from Latin words meaning "on the back." Celebrities who endorse a product or a project give it their backing.] —**en·dors′er,** *n.*

en·dorse·ment (en dôrs′mənt), *n.* **1** person's name or other writing on the back of a check, bill, or other document. **2** approval; support: *endorsement from the dental association.*

en·do·scope (en′də skōp′), *n.* a lighted, often flexible tube used to examine the inside of the body. Many endoscopes are made of optical fibers.

en·do·skel·e·ton (en′dō skel′ə tən), *n.* the internal skeleton that animals with backbones and related animals have.

en·do·sperm (en′dō spėrm′), *n.* food material for the embryo of a plant, enclosed in the seed.

en·do·ther·mic (en′dō thėr′mik), *adj.* warm-blooded.

en·dow (en dou′), *v.* **1** to give money or property to provide an income for: *The rich man endowed the college he had attended.* **2** to give from birth; provide with some ability, quality, or talent: *Nature endowed him with good looks.*

en·dow·ment (en dou′mənt), *n.* **1** money or property given to an institution to provide an income: *This college has a large endowment.* **2** gift from birth; ability; talent: *Artistic ability is a natural endowment.*

end·point (end′point′), *n.* **1** the point where a line segment begins or ends. **2** time or place at which something is completed, especially one planned for: *The opening of the park was the endpoint of years of planning and work.*

end table, a small table placed beside a couch or chair.

en·dur·ance (en dur′əns), *n.* **1** power to last and to withstand hard wear: *It takes great endurance to run a marathon.* **2** power to stand something without giving out; holding out; bearing up: *Her endurance of pain is remarkable.*

endurance (def. 1)

en·dure (en dur′), *v.* **1** to keep on; last: *Metal and stone endure for a long time.* **2** to put up with; bear; stand: *The pioneers endured many hardships.* ■ See Synonym Study at **bear**[1]. ❑ *v.* **en·dured, en·dur·ing.** [Endure comes from a Latin word meaning "to make hard." Hard things usually last longer and stand more use than soft things.] —**en·dur′a·ble,** *adj.* —**en·dur′a·bly,** *adv.*

en·dur·ing (en dur′ing), *adj.* lasting; permanent: *an enduring peace.* —**en·dur′ing·ly,** *adv.*

end·ways (end′wāz′), *adv.* **1** on end; upright. **2** with the end forward; in the direction of the end. **3** lengthwise. **4** with the ends placed so that they touch; end to end.

end·wise (end′wīz′), *adv.* endways.

end zone, the part of a football field between the goal line and the end of the field.

en·e·ma (en′ə mə), *n.* injection of liquid into the rectum to flush the lower intestines. ❑ *n., pl.* **en·e·mas.**

en·e·my (en′ə mē), *n.* **1** person or group that hates and tries to harm another: *They have many friends and few enemies.* **2** force, nation, army, fleet, or air force at war with another; soldier, ship, etc., of a hostile nation. **3** anything harmful: *Drought is an enemy of farmers.* ❑ *n., pl.* **en·e·mies.** [Enemy comes from Latin words meaning "not friendly."]

en·er·get·ic (en′ər jet′ik), *adj.* full of energy; active; vigorous: *I feel energetic in the morning.* —**en′er·get′i·cal·ly,** *adv.*

en·er·gize (en′ər jīz), *v.* to give energy to; make active. ❑ *v.* **en·er·gized, en·er·giz·ing.** —**en′er·giz′er,** *n.*

en·er·gy (en′ər jē), *n.* **1** will to work; vigor: *The boy is so full of energy that he cannot keep still.* **2** power to work or act; force: *All our energies were used in keeping the fire from spreading.* **3** ability to do work, such as lifting or moving an object. Light,

a	hat	ė	term	ô	order	ch	child		
ā	age	i	it	oi	oil	ng	long	ə	a in about
ä	far	ī	ice	ou	out	sh	she		e in taken
â	care	o	hot	u	cup	th	thin		i in pencil
e	let	ō	open	ù	put	ŦH	then		o in lemon
ē	equal	ȯ	saw	ü	rule	zh	measure		u in circus

heat, and electricity are different forms of energy. **4** fuel or power produced from fuel: *The cost of energy continues to increase.* ❑ *n., pl.* **en·er·gies** for 2.

en·er·vate (en′ər vāt), *v.* to reduce the vigor or strength of; weaken: *A hot, damp climate enervates people who are not used to it.* ❑ *v.* **en·er·vat·ed, en·er·vat·ing.** —**en′er·va′tion,** *n.*

en·fee·ble (en fē′bəl), *v.* to make feeble; weaken. ❑ *v.* **en·fee·bled, en·fee·bling.** —**en·fee′ble·ment,** *n.*

en·fold (en fōld′), *v.* **1** to fold in; wrap up: *The old woman was enfolded in a shawl.* **2** to embrace; clasp: *The little boy enfolded the puppy in his arms.* —**en·fold′er,** *n.*

en·force (en fôrs′), *v.* **1** to force obedience to; cause to be carried out: *Monitors help enforce school regulations.* **2** to force; compel: *We have laws to enforce the payment of income taxes.* ❑ *v.* **en·forced, en·forc·ing.** —**en·force′a·ble,** *adj.* —**en·forc′er,** *n.*

en·force·ment (en fôrs′mənt), *n.* act of enforcing; carrying out: *Strict enforcement of the traffic laws will reduce accidents.*

en·fran·chise (en fran′chīz), *v.* **1** to give the right to vote to: *In 1920, the 19th amendment to the Constitution enfranchised American women.* **2** to set free. ❑ *v.* **en·fran·chised, en·fran·chis·ing.** —**en·fran′chise·ment,** *n.*

eng., **1** engineer. **2** engineering.

Eng., **1** England. **2** English.

en·gage (en gāj′), *v.* **1** to keep yourself busy; be occupied; take part: *They engaged in conversation.* **2** to keep busy; occupy: *Work engages much of her time.* **3** to take for use or work; hire: *We engaged two rooms in the hotel.* ■ See Synonym Study at **hire.** **4** to promise or pledge to marry: *He is engaged to my sister.* **5** to catch and hold; attract: *Bright colors engage a baby's attention.* **6** to bind by a promise or contract; pledge: *He engaged himself as an apprentice to a printer.* **7** to fit into; lock together: *The gears engaged, and the car moved forward.* **8** to start a battle with; attack: *They engaged the enemy.* ❑ *v.* **en·gaged, en·gag·ing.**

en·gaged (en gājd′), *adj.* **1** promised or pledged to marry: *A party was given for the engaged couple.* **2** busy; occupied: *Engaged in conversation, they did not see us.*

en·gage·ment (en gāj′mənt), *n.* **1** a promise or pledge to marry: *The young couple announced their engagement.* **2** a meeting with someone at a certain time; appointment: *My parents have a dinner engagement tonight.* **3** a promise; pledge: *She tries to fulfill her engagements.* **4** period of being hired; time of use or work: *The actor had an engagement of three weeks in a play.* **5** a fight; battle.

en·gag·ing (en gā′jing), *adj.* very attractive; pleasing; charming: *an engaging smile.* —**en·gag′ing·ly,** *adv.*

Eng·els (eng′gəlz), *n.* **Fried·rich** (frē′drik), 1820-1895, German scholar and revolutionary. He wrote the *Communist Manifesto* with Karl Marx.

en·gen·der (en jen′dər), *v.* to bring into existence; produce; cause: *Filth engenders disease.*

en·gine (en′jən), *n.* **1** machine that changes energy from fuel, steam, water pressure, etc., into motion and power. An engine is used to apply power to some work, such as running other machines. **2** machine that pulls a railroad train; locomotive.

engine block, the main part of an engine, cast as a single unit, containing the cylinders.

en·gi·neer (en′jə nir′), **1** *n.* person who takes care of or runs engines. The person who runs a locomotive is an engineer. **2** *n.* an expert in engineering: *a mining engineer.* **3** *v.* to plan, build, direct, or work as an engineer. **4** *v.* to manage cleverly; guide skillfully: *She engineered an election victory.*

en·gi·neer·ing (en′jə nir′ing), *n.* science, work, or profession of planning, building, or managing engines, machines, roads, bridges, railroads, mines, electrical systems, chemical plants, etc.: *The Golden Gate bridge is a triumph of engineering.*

Eng·land (ing′glənd), *n.* the largest division of Great Britain, in the S part. *Capital:* London. See **United Kingdom** for map.

WORD STORY **England** comes from old English words meaning "land of the Angles." The Angles settled England from Germany about 1500 years ago, along with the Saxons.

Eng·lish (ing′glish), **1** *adj.* of England, its people, or their language. **2** *n.pl.* the people of England. **3** *n.* the language of England. English is also spoken in the United States, Canada, Australia, New Zealand, the Republic of South Africa, and many other countries. **4** *n.* **english,** a spinning motion given to a ball by hitting, throwing, kicking, etc., on one side of its center.

English Channel, strait between England and France. See **Normandy** for map.

English horn, a woodwind instrument resembling an oboe, but larger and having a lower tone.

Eng·lish·man (ing′glish mən), *n.* man born or living in England. ❑ *n., pl.* **Eng·lish·men.**

English muffin, a flat, round roll baked on a griddle, split and toasted before eating.

English sparrow, house sparrow.

Eng·lish·wom·an (ing′glish wùm′ən), *n.* woman born or living in England. ❑ *n., pl.* **Eng·lish·wom·en.**

en·gorged (en gôrjd′), *v.* thickened with blood.

en·grave (en grāv′), *v.* **1** to cut deeply in; carve in; carve in an artistic way: *The jeweler engraved my initials on the back of the watch.* **2** to cut a picture, design, map, etc., in lines on a metal plate, block of wood, etc., for printing. **3** to fix firmly: *The incident was engraved in her mind.* ❑ *v.* **en·graved, en·grav·ing.** —**en·grav′er,** *n.*

en·grav·ing (en grā′ving), *n.* **1** act or art of an engraver. **2** picture printed from an engraved plate, block, etc.; print.

engraving (def. 2)

en·gross (en grōs′), *v.* to occupy wholly; take up all the attention of: *The artist was so engrossed in his painting that he didn't notice the people watching him.* —**en·gross′ment,** *n.*

en·gulf (en gulf′), *v.* to swallow up; overwhelm: *A wave engulfed the small boat.* —**en·gulf′ment,** *n.*

en·hance (en hans′), *v.* to make greater; add to; heighten: *The gardens enhanced the beauty of the house.* ❑ *v.* **en·hanced, en·hanc·ing.** —**en·hance′ment,** *n.*

e·nig·ma (i nig′mə), *n.* a baffling or puzzling problem, situation, person, etc.; riddle: *How the magician got out of the locked trunk was an enigma to the audience.* ❑ *n., pl.* **e·nig·mas.**

en·ig·mat·ic (en′ig mat′ik), *adj.* like an enigma or riddle; baffling; puzzling: *We could not understand their enigmatic answers to our questions.* —**en′ig·mat′i·cal·ly,** *adv.*

en·ig·mat·i·cal (en′ig mat′ə kəl), *adj.* enigmatic.

en·join (en join′), *v.* **1** to order, direct, or urge: *The father enjoined his children to always be honest.* **2** to forbid; prohibit: *The judge enjoined the contractor from building a factory in an area set aside for homes.* —**en·join′er,** *n.*

en·joy (en joi′), *v.* **1** to have or use with joy; be happy with; take pleasure in: *The children enjoyed their visit to the museum.* **2** to have as an advantage or benefit: *She enjoys good health.* —**en·joy′a·ble,** *adj.* —**en·joy′a·ble·ness,** *n.* —**en·joy′a·bly,** *adv.*

enjoy yourself, to have a good time; be happy: *He enjoyed himself at the party.*

en·joy·ment (en joi′mənt), *n.* **1** pleasure; joy; delight. **2** act of having as an advantage or benefit; possession or use: *the enjoyment of good health. Laws protect the enjoyment of our rights.*

en·large (en lärj′), *v.* to make or become larger; increase in size: *to enlarge a photograph.* ■ See Synonym Study at **increase.** ❑ *v.* **en·larged, en·larg·ing.** —**en·larg′er,** *n.*

enlarge on, to talk or write about in more detail: *The principal enlarged on his plans for a new school.*

en·large·ment (en lärj′mənt), *n.* **1** photograph or other thing which has been made larger. **2** act of enlarging or condition of being enlarged.

en·light·en (en lit′n), v. to give truth and knowledge to; inform; instruct: *The book enlightened me on the subject of medicine.* —**en·light′en·er,** n. —**en·light′en·ment,** n.

en·list (en list′), v. **1** to join some branch of the armed forces: *He enlisted in the Air Force.* **2** to get to join some branch of the armed forces; induct: *Many men were enlisted during the war.* **3** to get to join in some cause or undertaking; get the help or support of: *We enlisted her help in building our clubhouse.* **4** to join in some cause or undertaking; give help or support: *Many members of our class enlist in the Red Cross drive each year.*

enlisted man, person in the armed forces who is not a commissioned officer or warrant officer.

en·list·ment (en list′mənt), n. **1** act of enlisting. **2** time for which someone enlists.

en·liv·en (en li′vən), v. to make lively, active, or cheerful: *enliven a speech with humor.*

en·mesh (en mesh′), v. to catch in a net; entangle.

en·mi·ty (en′mə tē), n. the feeling that enemies have for each other; hostility or hatred. □ n., pl. **en·mi·ties.**

en·no·ble (en nō′bəl), v. **1** to raise the respect of others for; make noble; dignify: *A good deed ennobles the person who does it.* **2** to raise to a noble rank; give a title of nobility to. □ v. **en·no·bled, en·no·bling.** —**en·no′ble·ment,** n. —**en·no′bler,** n.

en·nui (än′wē), n. a feeling of weariness and discontent from having no occupation or interest; boredom.

e·nor·mi·ty (i nôr′mə tē), n. **1** extreme wickedness: *The enormity of the crime made it likely that the criminal was not sane.* **2** an extremely wicked crime. □ n., pl. **e·nor·mi·ties** for 2. ■ **Enormity** does not mean "enormousness," although people use it that way. **Enormity** means wickedness.

e·nor·mous (i nôr′məs), adj. extremely large; huge: *enormous jaws, an enormous task, an enormous appetite.* ■ See Synonym Study at **huge.** [**Enormous** comes from Latin words meaning "out of the pattern." Something that is enormous does not fit the pattern for size.] —**e·nor′mous·ly,** adv. —**e·nor′mous·ness,** n.

enormous jaws

e·nough (i nuf′), **1** adj. as much or as many as needed or wanted; sufficient: *Are there enough seats for all?* ■ **Enough** may be used before or after the noun it describes: *There is enough room for three. There is room enough for three.* **2** n. quantity or number needed or wanted; sufficient amount: *I have had enough to eat.* **3** adv. sufficiently; adequately: *Have you played enough?* **4** adv. quite; fully: *He was willing enough to go.* **5** adv. rather; fairly: *She talks well enough for a baby.*

en·quire (en kwir′), v. to inquire. □ v. **en·quired, en·quir·ing.**

en·quir·y (en kwi′rē or en′kwər ē), n. inquiry. □ n., pl. **en·quir·ies.**

en·rage (en rāj′), v. to make very angry; make furious: *The dog was enraged by the teasing.* □ v. **en·raged, en·rag·ing.**

en·rap·ture (en rap′chər), v. to move to rapture; fill with great delight: *The audience was enraptured by the singer's beautiful voice.* □ v. **en·rap·tured, en·rap·tur·ing.**

en·rich (en rich′), v. to make rich or richer: *Adding vitamins or minerals to food enriches it.* —**en·rich′ment,** n.

en·roll or **en·rol** (en rōl′), v. **1** to become a member; enlist: *Her mother enrolled in a boating class. He enrolled in the navy.* **2** to make someone a member: *He enrolled his daughter and son in a music school.* **3** to write in a list; register: *The secretary enrolled our names.* □ v. **en·rolled, en·roll·ing.**

en·roll·ment or **en·rol·ment** (en rōl′mənt), n. number enrolled: *The school has an enrollment of 200 students.*

en route (än rüt′), on the way: *We shall stop at Philadelphia en route from New York to Washington.*

en·sconce (en skons′), v. **1** to shelter safely; hide: *The family was ensconced in the cellar when the tornado hit.* **2** to settle comfortably and firmly: *The cat ensconced itself in the armchair.* □ v. **en·sconced, en·sconc·ing.**

en·sem·ble (än säm′bəl), n. **1** all the parts of a thing considered together; general effect. **2** group of musicians playing or singing together: *Two violins, a cello, and a harp made up the string ensemble.* **3** a complete, harmonious outfit: *Her dress and coat made an attractive ensemble.* [**Ensemble** comes from a Latin word meaning "at the same time."]

en·shrine (en shrin′), v. **1** to enclose in a shrine: *A statue is enshrined in the cathedral.* **2** to keep sacred; cherish: *happy memories enshrined in your heart.* □ v. **en·shrined, en·shrin·ing.** —**en·shrine′ment,** n.

en·shroud (en shroud′), v. to cover or hide; veil: *Fog enshrouded the ship.*

en·sign (en′sīn or en′sən for 1,3,4; en′sən for 2), n. **1** a flag or banner: *The ensign of the United States is the Stars and Stripes.* **2** a military rank. See chart on page 712. **3** sign of rank, position, or power; symbol of authority: *The ensign of the queen was her crown and scepter.*

en·si·lage (en′sə lij), n. silage.

en·slave (en slāv′), v. to make a slave or slaves of; take away freedom from. □ v. **en·slaved, en·slav·ing.** —**en·slave′ment,** n.

en·snare (en snâr′), v. to catch in a snare; trap. □ v. **en·snared, en·snar·ing.**

en·sue (en sü′), v. **1** to come after; follow. *The ensuing year follows this one.* **2** to happen as a result: *Our talk became heated, and an argument ensued.* □ v. **en·sued, en·su·ing.**

en·sure (en shůr′), v. **1** to make sure or certain: *Careful planning and hard work ensured the success of the party.* **2** to make sure of getting; secure: *A letter of introduction will ensure you an interview.* □ v. **en·sured, en·sur·ing.** ■ See Usage Note at **insure.**

-ent, suffix. **1** ___ing: *absorbent = absorbing.* **2** person who ___s: *president = person who presides.*

en·tail (en tāl′), v. to impose or require: *Owning a car entailed greater expense than we had expected.* —**en·tail′ment,** n.

en·tan·gle (en tang′gəl), v. **1** to get twisted up and caught; tangle: *He entangled his feet in the coil of rope and fell down.* **2** to get into difficulty; involve: *Don't get entangled in their scheme.* □ v. **en·tan·gled, en·tan·gling.**

en·tan·gle·ment (en tang′gəl mənt), n. **1** act of entangling or condition of being entangled: *The new nation avoided an entanglement with foreign countries.* **2** thing that entangles; snare: *The trenches were protected by barbed wire entanglements.*

en·ter (en′tər), v. **1** to go into; come into: *She entered the house.* **2** to go in; come in: *Let them enter.* **3** to pierce; penetrate: *The bullet entered the victim's heart.* **4** to become a part or member of; join: *She entered the contest.* **5** to cause to join or enter; enroll: *Parents enter their children in school.* **6** to begin; start: *After years of training, doctors enter the practice of medicine.* **7** to write or print in a book, list, etc.: *Words are entered alphabetically in a dictionary.* —**en′ter·a·ble,** adj.

enter into, to take part in; join in: *The two speakers entered into a debate.*

enter on or **enter upon,** to begin; start: *She entered on her professional duties as soon as she finished law school.*

en·te·ri·tis (en′tə rī′tis), n. inflammation of the intestines, usually accompanied by diarrhea and fever.

a	hat	ė	term	ô	order	ch	child	
ā	age	i	it	oi	oil	ng	long	ə { a in about
ä	far	ī	ice	ou	out	sh	she	e in taken
â	care	o	hot	u	cup	th	thin	i in pencil
e	let	ō	open	ů	put	ŦH	then	o in lemon
ē	equal	ô	saw	ü	rule	zh	measure	u in circus

en·ter·prise (en′tər prīz), *n.* **1** an important, difficult, or dangerous plan to be tried; great or bold undertaking: *A trip into space is a daring enterprise.* **2** any undertaking; project: *a business enterprise.* **3** readiness to try important, difficult, or dangerous plans; willingness to undertake great or bold projects: *The American pioneers were people of great enterprise.*

en·ter·pris·ing (en′tər prī′zing), *adj.* likely to start projects; ready to face difficulties: *an enterprising young businessman.* —**en′ter·pris′ing·ly,** *adv.*

en·ter·tain (en′tər tān′), *v.* **1** to keep pleasantly interested; please or amuse: *The circus entertained the children.* ■ See Synonym Study at **amuse. 2** to have as a guest: *They entertained ten people at dinner.* **3** to have guests; provide entertainment for guests: *He entertains a great deal.* **4** to take into the mind; consider: *I refuse to entertain such a foolish idea.* [**Entertain** comes from Latin words meaning "to hold between." If a story really holds your interest, you might say that it's gripping, or that you're caught up in it.]

en·ter·tain·er (en′tər tā′nər), *n.* **1** singer, musician, etc., who performs in public. **2** person who entertains.

en·ter·tain·ing (en′tər tā′ning), *adj.* interesting; pleasing or amusing. —**en′ter·tain′ing·ly,** *adv.*

en·ter·tain·ment (en′tər tān′mənt), *n.* **1** something that interests, pleases, or amuses. A show or a circus is an entertainment. **2** act of entertaining: *The host and hostess devoted themselves to the entertainment of their guests.* **3** condition of being entertained; amusement: *He played the piano for our entertainment.*

en·thrall (en thrôl′), *v.* to hold captive by beauty or interest; fascinate; charm. ❑ *v.* **en·thralled, en·thrall·ing.** —**en·thrall′ment,** *n.*

entertainer (def. 1)

en·throne (en thrōn′), *v.* **1** to set on a throne. **2** to place highest of all; exalt. ❑ *v.* **en·throned, en·thron·ing.** —**en·throne′ment,** *n.*

en·thuse (en thüz′), *v.* **1** to show enthusiasm: *She enthused over the idea of going away to college.* **2** to fill with enthusiasm: *Plans for a trip enthused the family.* ❑ *v.* **en·thused, en·thus·ing.**

en·thu·si·asm (en thü′zē az′əm), *n.* eager interest; zeal: *The pep talk filled the team with enthusiasm.*

WORD STORY **Enthusiasm** comes from Greek words meaning "in" and "god." From these came a Greek word meaning "inspired by a god." Eager interest is like an inspiration.

en·thu·si·ast (en thü′zē ast), *n.* person who is filled with enthusiasm: *a football enthusiast.*

en·thu·si·as·tic (en thü′zē as′tik), *adj.* full of enthusiasm; eagerly interested: *My little brother is very enthusiastic about going to kindergarten.* —**en·thu′si·as′ti·cal·ly,** *adv.*

en·tice (en tīs′), *v.* to attract by arousing hopes or desires; tempt: *The smell of food enticed the hungry children into the house.* ❑ *v.* **en·ticed, en·tic·ing.** —**en·tice′ment,** *n.* —**en·tic′ing·ly,** *adv.*

en·tire (en tīr′), *adj.* **1** having all the parts; whole; complete: *The entire class behaved very well on the trip.* **2** not broken; in one piece: *The original property is still entire.* —**en·tire′ly,** *adv.*

WORD STORY **Entire** comes from Latin words meaning "not" and "touch." **Integer** comes from the same Latin words. Something untouched by use or time remains complete and whole, and the idea was borrowed to describe whole numbers also.

en·tire·ty (en tīr′tē), *n.* the whole; completeness.
in its entirety, wholly; completely: *I enjoyed the concert in its entirety.*

en·ti·tle (en tī′tl), *v.* **1** to give someone a claim or right: *The one who wins is entitled to first prize.* **2** to give a book, play, etc., the title of; call by the name of: *I entitled my theme "Looking for Treasure."* ❑ *v.* **en·ti·tled, en·ti·tling.** —**en·ti′tle·ment,** *n.*

en·ti·tle·ment (en tī′tl mənt), *n.* **1** a right to benefits under a government-sponsored program, such as social security, Medicaid, and military pensions. **2** act of entitling or condition of being entitled.

en·ti·ty (en′tə tē), *n.* something that has a real, separate existence. Persons, mountains, and languages are entities. ❑ *n., pl.* **en·ti·ties.**

en·tomb (en tüm′), *v.* to bury in a tomb. —**en·tomb′ment,** *n.*

en·to·mo·log·i·cal (en′tə mə loj′ə kəl), *adj.* of entomology. —**en′to·mo·log′i·cal·ly,** *adv.*

en·to·mol·o·gy (en′tə mol′ə jē), *n.* branch of biology that deals with insects. [See Word Story at **insect.**] —**en′to·mol′o·gist,** *n.*

en·tou·rage (än′tü räzh′), *n.* group of attendants; people usually accompanying a person: *a queen and her entourage.*

en·trails (en′trālz), *n.pl.* the inner parts of the body of a human being or animal, especially the intestines.

en·trance[1] (en′trəns), *n.* **1** act of entering: *The actor's entrance was greeted with applause.* **2** place by which to enter; door, passageway, etc.: *The entrance to the hotel was blocked with baggage.* **3** freedom or right to enter; permission to enter: *Entrance to the exhibit is on weekdays only.*

en·trance[2] (en trans′), *v.* **1** to fill with joy; delight; charm: *From the first note the singer's voice entranced the audience.* **2** to put into a trance. ❑ *v.* **en·tranced, en·tranc·ing.** —**en·trance′ment,** *n.* —**en·tranc′ing·ly,** *adv.*

en·trant (en′trənt), *n.* person who takes part in a contest: *There were many entrants in the spelling contest.*

en·trap (en trap′), *v.* **1** to catch in a trap. **2** to bring into difficulty or danger; trick: *The lawyer entrapped the witness into contradicting himself.* ❑ *v.* **en·trapped, en·trap·ping.** —**en·trap′ment,** *n.*

en·treat (en trēt′), *v.* to keep asking earnestly; beg and pray; implore: *The prisoners entreated the governor to pardon them.* —**en·treat′ing·ly,** *adv.*

en·treat·y (en trē′tē), *n.* an earnest request; prayer. ❑ *n., pl.* **en·treat·ies.**

en·tree (än′trā), *n.* **1** the main dish of food at dinner or lunch: *You can choose chicken or fish for your entree.* **2** freedom or right to enter; access. ❑ *n., pl.* **en·trees** for 1.

en·trée (än′trā), *n.* entree. ❑ *n., pl.* **en·trées.**

en·trench (en trench′), *v.* **1** to surround with a trench; fortify with trenches: *Our soldiers were entrenched opposite the enemy.* **2** to establish firmly: *a custom entrenched by long tradition.* —**en·trench′er,** *n.*

en·trench·ment (en trench′mənt), *n.* **1** defense consisting of a trench and a wide bank of earth or stone. **2** an entrenched position. **3** act of entrenching.

en·tre·pre·neur (än′trə prə nėr′ *or* än′trə prə nùr′), *n.* person who organizes and manages a business or industrial undertaking.

en·tro·py (en′trə pē), *n.* (in physics) the tendency of any system, including the universe, to become steadily more random.

en·trust (en trust′), *v.* **1** to charge with a trust: *We entrusted the class treasurer with all the money for bus fares on our class trip.* **2** to give the care of; hand over for safekeeping: *They entrusted the child to her grandparents for a few days.*

en·try (en′trē), *n.* **1** act of entering: *His sudden entry startled me.* **2** place by which to enter; way to enter: *The entry to the hotel was blocked with luggage.* **3** thing written or printed in a book, list, etc. Each word explained in a dictionary is an entry or **entry word. 4** person or thing that takes part in a contest: *The car race had 30 entries.* ❑ *n., pl.* **en·tries.**

en·twine (en twin′), *v.* to twine together or around: *Vines entwined the cottage.* ❑ *v.* **en·twined, en·twin·ing.**

e·nu·me·rate (i nü′mə rāt′), *v.* **1** to name one by one; list: *She enumerated the capitals of the 50 states.* **2** to find out the number of; count. ❑ *v.* **e·nu·me·rat·ed, e·nu·me·rat·ing.** —**e·nu′me·ra′tion,** *n.* —**e·nu′me·ra′tor,** *n.*

e·nun·ci·ate (i nun′sē āt′), *v.* **1** to speak or pronounce words: *Radio and TV announcers must enunciate very clearly.* **2** to state definitely; announce: *After performing many experiments, the scientist enunciated a new theory.* ❑ *v.* **e·nun·ci·at·ed, e·nun·ci·at·ing.** —**e·nun′ci·a′tion,** *n.* —**e·nun′ci·a′tor,** *n.*

en·vel·op (en vel′əp), v. to wrap, cover, or hide: *The vines grew so rapidly they enveloped the telephone pole.* —**en·vel′op·ment,** n.

envelop—vines enveloping a telephone pole

en·ve·lope (en′və lōp *or* än′və lōp), n. **1** a paper cover in which a letter or anything flat can be mailed. It usually has a flap which can be folded over and sealed. **2** a covering; wrapper.

en·vi·a·ble (en′vē ə bəl), adj. worth having; desirable: *an enviable position.* —**en′vi·a·ble·ness,** n. —**en′vi·a·bly,** adv.

en·vi·ous (en′vē əs), adj. feeling or showing discontent because someone else has what you want; full of envy: *envious of another's good fortune.* —**en′vi·ous·ly,** adv. —**en′vi·ous·ness,** n.

en·vi·ron·ment (en vī′rən mənt), n. **1** all the surrounding things, conditions, and influences affecting the growth of living things: *A child's character is influenced by the environment at home.* **2** surroundings: *an environment of poverty.* **3** condition of the air, water, soil, etc.: *working for a pollution-free environment.* —**en·vi′ron·men′tal,** adj. —**en·vi′ron·men′tal·ly,** adv.

environmental impact statement, an official report describing the likely effects of a plan, a program, or an action on a particular environment. Such a report may be a necessary step in obtaining government approval or permission.

en·vi·ron·men·tal·ist (en vī′rən men′tl ist), n. person involved in trying to solve environmental problems, such as pollution, the improper use of natural resources, and overpopulation.

en·vi·rons (en vī′rənz), n.pl. surrounding districts; suburbs: *We visited Boston and its environs.*

en·vis·age (en viz′ij), v. to form a mental picture of: *The architect looked at the plans and envisaged the finished house.* ❑ v. **en·vis·aged, en·vis·ag·ing.**

en·vi·sion (en vizh′ən), v. to picture in your mind: *I like to envision myself as famous.*

en·voy (en′voi), n. **1** messenger or representative. **2** diplomat ranking next below an ambassador and next above a minister.

en·vy (en′vē), **1** n. feeling of discontent, dislike, or desire because another person has what you want: *The children were filled with envy when they saw her new bicycle.* **2** n. the object of such feeling; person or thing envied: *Their new car was the envy of the neighborhood.* **3** v. to feel envy toward: *Some people envy the rich.* **4** v. to feel envy because of: *He envied his friend's success.* ❑ v. **en·vied, en·vy·ing.** —**en′vi·er,** n. —**en′vy·ing·ly,** adv.

WORD STORY Envy comes from Latin words meaning "against" and "to look." Envy often occurs when a person watches someone else succeed and feels resentment against that success.

en·wrap (en rap′), v. to wrap. ❑ v. **en·wrapped, en·wrap·ping.**

en·zyme (en′zīm), n. any substance produced in living cells that influences a chemical reaction within a living thing without being changed itself. Some enzymes, such as pepsin, help break down food so that it can be digested.

E·o·cene (ē′ə sēn), n. (in geology) time between 60 million and 40 million years ago. During this time, the ancestors of many modern mammals first appeared.

e·o·hip·pus (ē′ō hip′əs), n. an extinct horse that was the ancestor of modern horses. It was about 11 inches (28 centimeters) high at the shoulder and had toes instead of hoofs. ❑ n., pl. **e·o·hip·pus·es.**

e·o·lith·ic (ē′ə lith′ik), adj. of a very early stage in human culture when rough stone tools were used; of the Stone Age.

e·on (ē′ən), n. a very long period of time; many millions of years: *Eons passed before life existed on the earth.*

EPA *or* **E.P.A.,** Environmental Protection Agency (a U.S. government agency for preventing and cleaning up pollution).

ep·au·let *or* **ep·au·lette** (ep′ə let), n. ornament on the shoulder of a uniform, especially a military uniform.

e·phed·rine (i fed′rən), n. drug used to relieve hay fever, asthma, head colds, etc.

e·phem·er·al (i fem′ər el), adj. lasting for only a day; lasting for only a very short time; very short-lived. —**e·phem′er·al·ly,** adv.

E·phe·sians (i fē′zhənz), n. book of the New Testament. It consists of a letter by Saint Paul to the Christians at Ephesus.

Eph·e·sus (ef′ə səs), n. an ancient Greek city in what is now W Turkey.

ep·ic (ep′ik), **1** n. a long poem that tells the adventures of one or more great heroes. It is written in a dignified, majestic style and often shows the ideals of a nation or race. Homer's *Odyssey* is an epic. **2** n. any writing having the qualities of an epic. Some very long novels are sometimes called epics. **3** adj. of or like an epic; grand; heroic: *The first flight over the Atlantic was an epic deed.*

WORD STORY Epic comes from a Greek word meaning "word, song, or story." Before the Greeks had writing, epics such as Homer's poem were memorized and chanted aloud.

ep·i·cen·ter (ep′ə sen′tər), n. **1** point on the earth's surface directly above the true center of an earthquake. **2** any central point.

ep·i·cure (ep′ə kyůr), n. person who enjoys eating and drinking and who is very particular in choosing fine foods, wines, etc.

ep·i·cu·re·an (ep′ə kyů rē′ən), **1** adj. of or fit for an epicure: *an epicurean banquet.* **2** n. person who is fond of pleasure and luxury; epicure.

ep·i·dem·ic (ep′ə dem′ik), **1** n. the rapid spread of a disease so that many people have it at the same time: *an epidemic of measles.* **2** n. the rapid spread of an idea, fashion, etc.: *The city suffered from an epidemic of strikes by different labor unions.* **3** adj. affecting many people at the same time; widespread: *The flu became epidemic last winter.* —**ep′i·dem′i·cal·ly,** adv.

WORD STORY Epidemic comes from Greek words meaning "among" and "people." During an epidemic, disease is widespread, and anyone can catch it.

ep·i·de·mi·ol·o·gy (ep′ə dē′mē ol′ə jē), n. branch of medicine dealing with the causes, pattern, prevention, and control of the spread of diseases in a community. —**ep′i·de′mi·o·log′i·cal,** adj. —**ep′i·de′mi·ol′o·gist,** n.

ep·i·der·mis (ep′ə dėr′mis), n. **1** the outer layer of the skin. **2** a skinlike layer of cells in plants.

ep·i·glot·tis (ep′ə glot′is), n. a thin, triangular plate of cartilage that covers the entrance to the windpipe during swallowing, so that food and drink do not get into the lungs.

ep·i·gram (ep′ə gram), n. **1** a short, pointed or witty saying. EXAMPLE: "The only thing we have to fear is fear itself." **2** a short poem ending in a witty or clever turn of thought.

ep·i·gram·mat·ic (ep′ə grə mat′ik), adj. **1** like an epigram; short and witty. **2** full of epigrams. —**ep′i·gram·mat′i·cal·ly,** adv.

ep·i·lep·sy (ep′ə lep′sē), n. disorder of the nervous system which may cause periods of unconsciousness and convulsions.

ep·i·lep·tic (ep′ə lep′tik), **1** adj. of or having epilepsy. **2** n. person having epilepsy. ∎ This meaning of **epileptic** is sometimes considered offensive, because it is thought to identify the person with the disease. "A person who has epilepsy" avoids the problem.

a	hat	ė	term	ô	order	ch	child		
ā	age	i	it	oi	oil	ng	long	ə	a in about
ä	far	ī	ice	ou	out	sh	she		e in taken
â	care	o	hot	u	cup	th	thin		i in pencil
e	let	ō	open	ů	put	ᴛʜ	then		o in lemon
ē	equal	ò	saw	ü	rule	zh	measure		u in circus

ep·i·logue or **ep·i·log** (ep'ə lòg), *n.* **1** a part added after the end of a novel, poem, etc. **2** speech or poem at the end of a play. It is spoken to the audience by one of the actors.

ep·i·neph·rine (ep'ə nef'rən), *n.* adrenaline.

e·piph·a·ny (i pif'ə nē), *n.* **1** Epiphany, January 6, the anniversary of the Three Wise Men's arrival at Bethlehem to honor the infant Jesus. **2** a moment of enlightenment or realization, when something is suddenly known or made clear: *When I helped the sick dog, I had an epiphany and realized I wanted to be a veterinarian and not a doctor.* ❑ *n., pl.* **e·piph·a·nies** for 2.

ep·i·phyte (ep'ə fīt), *n.* air plant.

e·pis·co·pal (i pis'kə pəl), *adj.* **1** of or governed by bishops. **2** Episcopal, of the Church of England or the Protestant Episcopal Church.

E·pis·co·pa·lian (i pis'kə pā'lyən), **1** *n.* member of the Protestant Episcopal Church. **2** *adj.* Episcopal.

ep·i·sode (ep'ə sōd), *n.* **1** a single happening or group of happenings in real life or in a story: *Being named the best athlete of the year was an important episode in the baseball player's life.* **2** one part of a story that is published or broadcast in several parts, one at a time. **–ep·i·sod·ic** (ep'ə sod'ik), *adj.*

WORD STORY Episode comes from Greek words meaning "in addition" and "on the way." Ancient stories were often about journeys. As people traveled, things happened on the way, and these happenings were called episodes.

e·pis·tle (i pis'əl), *n.* **1** letter, especially one that is long, instructive, and written in formal or elegant language. **2** Epistle, any of the letters written by the Apostles to various churches and individuals. The Epistles make up 21 books of the New Testament.

ep·i·taph (ep'ə taf), *n.* a short statement in memory of a dead person. It is often put on a gravestone or tombstone.

ep·i·the·li·al (ep'ə thē'lē əl), *adj.* of epithelium.

ep·i·the·li·um (ep'ə thē'lē əm), *n.* a thin layer of cells forming a tissue that covers body surfaces and lines hollow organs. ❑ *n., pl.* **ep·i·the·li·ums, ep·i·the·li·a** (ep'ə thē'lē ə).

ep·i·thet (ep'ə thet), *n.* a descriptive expression; word or phrase expressing some quality or attribute. In "Honest Abe" and "Richard the Lion-Hearted" the epithets are "Honest" and "the Lion-Hearted."

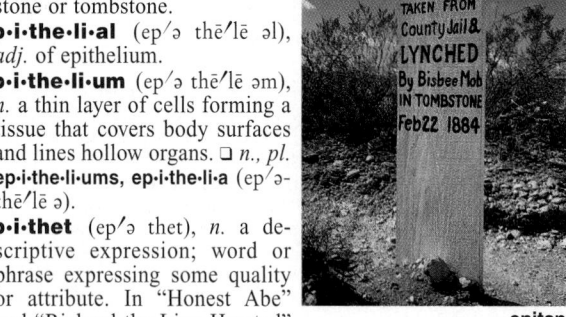
epitaph

e·pit·o·me (i pit'ə mē), *n.* someone or something that is the best or most typical example of something: *Solomon is often spoken of as the epitome of wisdom.*

e·pit·o·mize (i pit'ə mīz), *v.* to be a typical example of: *Helen Keller epitomizes the human ability to overcome overwhelming challenges.* ❑ *v.* **e·pit·o·mized, e·pit·o·miz·ing.**

e plu·ri·bus u·num (ē plür'ə bəs yü'nəm), LATIN. out of many, one. It is the motto inscribed on the official seal of the United States. It was once the official motto of the United States, but since 1956 the official motto has been "In God We Trust."

ep·och (ep'ək), *n.* **1** period of time; era: *There have been few peaceful epochs in the history of our country.* **2** period of time in which striking things happen: *The years of the Civil War were an epoch in the United States.* **3** the starting point of such a period: *The invention of the steam engine marked an epoch in the growth of industry.* **4** one of the divisions of time into which a geological period may be divided. ❑ *n., pl.* **e·pochs. –ep'och·al,** *adj.*

ep·och-mak·ing (ep'ək mā'king), *adj.* beginning an epoch; causing important changes: *the epoch-making arrival in America.*

ep·o·nym (ep'ə nim), *n.* word or name that is based on the name of a real or imaginary person. The begonia, named after Michel Begon and the poinsettia, named after Joel R. Poinsett, are eponyms.

ep·ox·y (e pok'sē), *n.* kind of synthetic resin used in plastics and adhesives. ❑ *n., pl.* **ep·ox·ies.**

WORD STORY Epoxy comes from the Greek word meaning "upon" and the English word **oxygen.** The qualities of epoxy resins depend upon the way they are held together by oxygen atoms.

Ep·som salts (ep'səm), a bitter white powder used as a laxative or mixed with warm water to soak sore parts of the body.

eq·ua·ble (ek'wə bəl), *adj.* changing little; uniform; even; tranquil: *She has an equable disposition.*

eq·ua·bly (ek'wə blē), *adv.* uniformly; evenly: *Laws should be equably enforced.*

e·qual (ē'kwəl), **1** *adj.* the same in amount, size, number, value, or rank: *Ten dimes are equal to one dollar. All persons are considered equal before the law.* ■ See Synonym Study at **same. 2** *v.* to be the same as: *Four times five equals twenty.* **3** *n.* person or thing that is equal: *In spelling she had no equal.* **4** *v.* to make or do something equal to: *Our team equaled the other team's score, and the game ended in a tie.* **5** *adj.* the same throughout; even; uniform: *an equal mixture.* ❑ *v.* **e·qualed, e·qual·ing** or **e·qualled, e·qual·ling.**

equal to, strong enough for: *Our horse is not equal to that load.*

WORD FAMILY Equal and the words below are related. They all come from a Latin word meaning "even" or "just."

adequate	equation	equilibrium	equity
equable	equator	equinox	equivalent
equality	equidistant	equipoise	equivocal
equanimity	equilateral	equitable	iniquity

e·qual·i·ty (i kwol'ə tē), *n.* sameness in amount, size, number, value, rank, etc.; being equal.

e·qual·ize (ē'kwə līz), *v.* **1** to make equal. **2** to make even or uniform. ❑ *v.* **e·qual·ized, e·qual·iz·ing. –e'qual·i·za'tion,** *n.*

e·qual·iz·er (ē'kwə lī'zər), *n.* device in a radio or other electronic music system that corrects poorly reproduced sound.

e·qual·ly (ē'kwə lē), *adv.* in equal shares; in an equal manner; to an equal degree: *Divide the pie equally.*

USAGE NOTE Equally and as should not be used together, because only one of the words is needed: *He is as good a player as his sister. Talent is important, and practice is equally important.* It would be wrong to use *equally as* in either of these sentences.

Equal Rights Amendment, a proposed amendment to the Constitution of the United States, stating that "equality of rights under the law shall not be denied or abridged by the United States or by any state on account of sex."

equal sign, the sign (=), indicating that what follows is the same in value, amount, meaning, etc., as what came before.

e·qua·nim·i·ty (ē'kwə nim'ə tē *or* ek'wə nim'ə tē), *n.* evenness of mind or temper; calmness; composure: *The speaker endured the insults of the heckler with equanimity.*

e·quate (i kwāt'), *v.* to present as equal; treat as equal: *Some people equate thin with pretty.* ❑ *v.* **e·quat·ed, e·quat·ing.**

e·qua·tion (i kwā'zhən), *n.* **1** statement of the equality of two quantities. EXAMPLES: $(4 \times 8) + 12 = 44$; $C = 2\pi r$. **2** expression using chemical formulas and symbols to show the substances used and produced in a chemical change. EXAMPLE: $HCl + NaOH = NaCl + H_2O$. This means that hydrochloric acid and sodium hydroxide combine to form sodium chloride (table salt) and water.

e·qua·tor (i kwā'tər), *n.* an imaginary circle around the middle of the earth, halfway between the North Pole and the South Pole. The equator divides the earth into the Northern Hemisphere and the Southern Hemisphere.

WORD STORY Equator comes from a Latin phrase meaning "equalizer of day and night." At the times when the sun rises and sets right over the equator, the day and night are of equal length.

e·qua·to·ri·al (ē'kwə tôr'ē əl *or* ek'wə tôr'ē əl), *adj.* **1** of, at, or near the equator: *Ecuador is an equatorial country.* **2** like conditions at or near the equator: *The weather was humid and hot enough to be equatorial.*

Equatorial Guinea, country in W Africa consisting of two parts, one on the mainland, **Rio Muni** (rē′o mü′nē), and the other an island, **Bioko** (bē ō′kō). *Capital:* Malabo.

e·ques·tri·an (i kwes′trē ən), **1** *adj.* of or for horseback riding: *equestrian skill.* **2** *adj.* on horseback. An equestrian statue shows a person riding a horse. **3** *n.* rider or performer on horseback.

equestrian (def. 3)

e·ques·tri·enne (i kwes′trē en′), *n.* a woman rider or performer on horseback.

equi-, *prefix.* equal or equally: *equidistant = equally distant; equilateral = having equal sides.*

e·qui·an·gu·lar (ē′kwē ang′gyə lər), *adj.* having all angles equal: *A square is equiangular.*

e·qui·dis·tant (ē′kwə dis′tənt), *adj.* equally distant: *All points of the circumference of a circle are equidistant from the center.* —e′qui·dis′tant·ly, *adv.*

e·qui·lat·er·al (ē′kwə lat′ər əl), *adj.* having all sides equal. —e′qui·lat′er·al·ly, *adv.*

equilateral triangle, triangle that has all three sides equal.

e·qui·lib·ri·um (ē′kwə lib′rē əm), *n.* **1** balance: *Scales are in equilibrium when the weights on each side are equal.* **2** mental poise: *My mother does not let quarrels upset her equilibrium.*

e·quine (ē′kwīn), *adj.* **1** of horses. **2** like a horse.

e·qui·noc·tial (ē′kwə nok′shəl), *adj.* of or occurring at an equinox: *an equinoctial storm.*

e·qui·nox (ē′kwə noks), *n.* either of the two times in the year when day and night are of equal length everywhere on the earth. An equinox occurs when the sun passes directly above the earth's equator, about March 21 (**vernal equinox**) and about September 23 (**autumnal equinox**). ❑ *n., pl.* **e·qui·nox·es.**

e·quip (i kwip′), *v.* to supply with all that is needed; fit out; provide; furnish: *We were equipped for the hike.* ❑ *v.* **e·quipped, e·quip·ping.** [**Equip** comes from an Icelandic word meaning "a ship." Once a ship leaves the land, the crew has only what is on board. It is important to have everything that will be needed.] —**e·quip′per,** *n.*

e·quip·ment (i kwip′mənt), *n.* **1** what someone or something is equipped with; outfit; furnishings; supplies: *camping equipment.* **2** act of equipping; fitting out: *The equipment of the expedition took six months.*

e·qui·poise (ek′wə poiz *or* ē′kwə poiz), *n.* equal distribution of weight or force; even balance.

eq·ui·ta·ble (ek′wə tə bəl), *adj.* fair; just: *It is equitable to pay a person good wages for work well done.* —**eq′ui·ta·bly,** *adv.*

eq·ui·ta·tion (ek′wə tā′shən), *n.* horseback riding.

eq·ui·ty (ek′wə tē), *n.* **1** fairness; justice: *The judge was noted for the equity of her decisions.* **2** amount that a property is worth, minus what is owed on it.

e·quiv·a·lence (i kwiv′ə ləns), *n.* condition of being equivalent.

e·quiv·a·len·cy (i kwiv′ə lən sē), *n.* equivalence. ❑ *n., pl.* **e·quiv·a·len·cies.**

e·quiv·a·lent (i kwiv′ə lənt), **1** *adj.* equal; the same in value, effect, meaning, etc.: *Nodding is equivalent to saying yes.* **2** *n.* something equivalent: *Ten pennies are the equivalent of a dime.* **3** *adj.* (in mathematics) matching one-for-one, as some sets do. —**e·quiv′a·lent·ly,** *adv.*

e·quiv·o·cal (i kwiv′ə kəl), *adj.* **1** having two or more meanings; ambiguous: *an equivocal answer.* **2** undecided; uncertain: *Because so many voters are undecided, the result of the poll is equivocal.* —**e·quiv′o·cal·ly,** *adv.* —**e·quiv′o·cal·ness,** *n.*

e·quiv·o·cate (i kwiv′ə kāt), *v.* to use expressions of double meaning in order to mislead: *When asked if he had finished his arithmetic, he equivocated by saying, "I was working on that an hour ago."* ❑ *v.* **e·quiv·o·cat·ed, e·quiv·o·cat·ing.** —**e·quiv′o·cat′ing·ly,** *adv.* —**e·quiv′o·ca′tor,** *n.*

e·quiv·o·ca·tion (i kwiv′ə kā′shən), *n.* **1** the use of expressions with double meaning in order to mislead. **2** an ambiguous statement or expression.

-er, *suffix.* **1** person or thing that ___s: *admirer = a person who admires; burner = thing that burns.* **2** person living in ___: *New Yorker = a person living in New York.* **3** person who makes or works with ___: *hatter = a person who makes hats.*

Er, symbol for erbium.

er·a (ir′ə), *n.* **1** a period of time or history: *We live in the era of space exploration.* **2** period of time starting from an important or significant happening, date, etc.: *We live in the 20th century of the Christian era.* **3** one of the five very large divisions of time in geological history. ❑ *n., pl.* **er·as.**

ERA, Equal Rights Amendment.

e·rad·i·cate (i rad′ə kāt), *v.* to get rid of entirely; destroy completely: *Smallpox has been eradicated.* ❑ *v.* **e·rad·i·cat·ed, e·rad·i·cat·ing.** —**e·rad′i·ca′tion,** *n.* —**e·rad′i·ca′tor,** *n.*

e·rase (i rās′), *v.* **1** to rub out; remove by rubbing, wiping, or scraping: *She erased the wrong answer and wrote in the right one.* **2** to remove all trace of; blot out: *The blow on his head erased the details of the accident from his memory.* ❑ *v.* **e·rased, e·ras·ing.** —**e·ras′a·ble,** *adj.*

> **WORD STORY** **Erase** comes from Latin words meaning "scrape away." Before Europeans learned about rubber, they erased writing by scraping it off with a sharp knife. Rubbing is easier, and that is how **rubber**[1] got its name.

e·ras·er (i rā′sər), *n.* something used to erase marks made with pencil, ink, chalk, etc.

e·ra·sure (i rā′shər), *n.* **1** act of erasing: *the erasure of a typing error.* **2** place where a word, letter, etc., has been erased.

er·bi·um (ėr′bē əm), *n.* a soft, lustrous, grayish metallic element which occurs as a minute part of various minerals. *Symbol:* Er

ere (âr), *prep., conj.* OLD USE. before. ■ Other words that can sound like this are **air, err,** and **heir.**

e·rect (i rekt′), **1** *adj.* straight up; not bending; not tipping; upright: *erect posture.* **2** *v.* to put straight up; set upright: *They erected a TV antenna on the roof. The mast was erected on a firm base.* **3** *v.* to put up; build: *That house was erected 40 years ago.* —**e·rect′a·ble,** *adj.* —**e·rect′ly,** *adv.* —**e·rect′ness,** *n.* —**e·rect′or,** *n.*

e·rec·tion (i rek′shən), *n.* **1** act of setting up; raising; erecting: *The erection of the tent took only a few minutes.* **2** condition in which a body part, especially the penis, fills with blood and swells up. **3** something erected; building or other structure.

E region, region of the atmosphere, within the ionosphere, that reflects shortwave radio waves; E layer; Kennelly-Heaviside layer.

erg (ėrg), *n.* unit for measuring work or energy. It is the amount of work done by a force of one dyne acting through a distance of one centimeter.

> **WORD FAMILY** **Erg** and the words below are related. They all come from a Greek word meaning "work."
>
> | | | | |
> |---|---|---|---|
> | allergy | energy | liturgy | surgery |
> | argon | lethargy | metallurgy | synergy |

er·go (ėr′gō), *adv.* LATIN. therefore.

Er·ic·son (er′ik sən), *n.* **Leif** (lēf), Viking explorer who probably visited North America about A.D. 1000.

a	hat	ė	term	ô	order	ch	child		
ā	age	i	it	oi	oil	ng	long		a in about
ä	far	ī	ice	ou	out	sh	she	ə	e in taken
â	care	o	hot	u	cup	th	thin		i in pencil
e	let	ō	open	u̇	put	ŦH	then		o in lemon
ē	equal	ȯ	saw	ü	rule	zh	measure		u in circus

Er·ie (ir′ē), *n.* **1 Lake,** one of the five Great Lakes. **2** city in NW Pennsylvania on Lake Erie.

Erie Canal, canal in New York State between Buffalo and Albany, connecting Lake Erie with the Hudson River.

Er·in (er′ən), *n.* Ireland.

Er·i·tre·a (er′ə trē′ə), *n.* country in NE Africa. *Capital:* Asmara.

er·mine (ėr′mən), *n.* **1** weasel of northern regions that is brown in summer but white with a black tip on its tail in winter. **2** its soft, white fur. ❑ *n., pl.* **er·mine** or **er·mines.**

e·rode (i rōd′), *v.* **1** to eat or wear away gradually; eat into: *Running water eroded the soil.* **2** to be worn away: *The stream bank eroded after the rains.* ❑ *v.* **e·rod·ed, e·rod·ing. —e·rod′i·ble,** *adj.*

WORD STORY Erode comes from Latin words meaning "to gnaw" and "away." **Rodent** comes from the Latin word meaning "to gnaw." Rodents are animals that gnaw. Eroded land looks as though it has been chewed on by a gigantic rodent.

Er·os (ir′os *or* er′os), *n.* the Greek god of love, son of Aphrodite. The Romans called him Cupid.

e·ro·sion (i rō′zhən), *n.* **1** process of gradually eating or wearing away by glaciers, running water, waves, or wind: *Trees help prevent the erosion of soil.* **2** condition of being eaten or worn away. **—e·ro′sion·al,** *adj.*

err (ėr *or* âr), *v.* **1** to go wrong; make a mistake: *Everyone errs at some time or other.* **2** to be wrong; be mistaken or incorrect: *to err in an opinion or belief.* **3** to do wrong; sin: *To err is human; to forgive, divine.* ■ Other words that can sound like this are **air, ere,** and **heir.**

erosion (def. 2)

WORD STORY Err and erratic both come from a Latin word meaning "to wander." A person who errs wanders from the truth. An erratic person wanders from regular, normal action.

er·rand (er′ənd), *n.* **1** a trip to do something: *She went on an errand to the store.* **2** what you are sent to do: *I did six errands in one trip.* ■ See Synonym Study at **job.**

er·rant (er′ənt), *adj.* **1** wandering; roving: *an errant knight seeking adventures.* **2** wrong; mistaken: *errant conduct.* **3** doing what is considered wrong; erring: *an errant child.* **—er′rant·ly,** *adv.*

er·rat·ic (ə rat′ik), *adj.* **1** uncertain; irregular: *An erratic alarm clock is not dependable.* **2** strange; odd: *erratic behavior.* [See Word Story at **err.**] **—er·rat′i·cal·ly,** *adv.*

er·ro·ne·ous (ə rō′nē əs), *adj.* not correct; wrong; mistaken: *Years ago many people held the erroneous belief that the earth was flat.* **—er·ro′ne·ous·ly,** *adv.* **—er·ro′ne·ous·ness,** *n.*

er·ror (er′ər), *n.* **1** something done that is wrong; something that is not the way it ought to be; mistake: *I failed my test because of errors in spelling.* **2** condition of being wrong or mistaken: *You are in error.* **3** (in baseball) a fielder's mistake that allows either a batter to reach first or a runner to advance one or more bases. **4** (in mathematics) the difference between an observed or calculated amount and the correct amount. **—er′ror·less,** *adj.*

erst·while (ėrst′wīl′), **1** *adj.* former; past: *their erstwhile companion.* **2** *adv.* OLD USE. in time past; formerly.

er·u·dite (er′ū dīt *or* er′yə dīt), *adj.* having much knowledge; scholarly; learned: *an erudite teacher, an erudite book.* **—er′u·dite′ly,** *adv.* **—er′u·dite′ness,** *n.*

er·u·di·tion (er′ū dish′ən *or* er′yə dish′ən), *n.* scholarship; learning: *The expert's erudition came from years of study.*

e·rupt (i rupt′), *v.* **1** to burst forth: *Hot water erupted from the geyser.* **2** to throw forth: *The volcano erupted lava and ashes.* **3** to break out in a rash: *My skin erupted when I had measles.*

e·rup·tion (i rup′shən), *n.* **1** act or process of bursting or throwing forth: *There was an eruption of glowing melted rock from the mountaintop.* **2** red spots on the skin; rash: *Chicken pox causes an eruption.*

e·rup·tive (i rup′tiv), *adj.* **1** bursting forth. **2** causing the skin to break out: *Measles is an eruptive disease.*

Er·ving (ėr′ving), *n.* **Jul·ius** (jü′lyəs), born 1950, American basketball player. He was nicknamed "Dr. J" and was known for his amazing dunk shots.

-ery, *suffix.* **1** condition of a ___: *slavery = condition of a slave.* **2** group of ___s: *machinery = group of machines.*

e·ryth·ro·cyte (i rith′rō sīt), *n.* red blood cell. **—e·ryth·ro·cyt·ic** (i rith′rō sit′ik), *adj.*

Es, symbol for einsteinium.

E·sau (ē′sò), *n.* (in the Bible) the older son of Isaac and Rebecca, who sold his birthright to his twin brother Jacob.

es·ca·late (es′kə lāt), *v.* to increase or expand rapidly or by stages: *The commotion in the prison almost escalated into a riot. To send in more troops would only escalate the war.* ❑ *v.* **es·ca·lat·ed, es·ca·lat·ing. —es′ca·la′tion,** *n.*

es·ca·la·tor (es′kə lā′tər), *n.* a moving stairway.

es·cal·lop (e skol′əp), *v.* to scallop (def. 2).

es·ca·pade (es′kə pād), *n.* wild prank or adventure that breaks the rules.

es·cape (e skāp′), **1** *v.* to get out and away; get free: *to escape from prison. The bird escaped from its cage.* **2** *v.* to get free from: *He thinks he will never escape hard work.* **3** *v.* to keep free or safe from; avoid: *We all escaped the measles.* **4** *n.* act of escaping: *Their escape was aided by the thick fog.* **5** *n.* way of escaping: *There was no escape from the trap.* **6** *v.* to come out or find a way out from a container; leak: *Gas had been escaping from the cylinder all night.* **7** *v.* to come out of without being intended: *A cry escaped her lips.* **8** *v.* to fail to be noticed or remembered by: *I knew his face, but the name escaped me.* **9** *n.* relief from boredom, trouble, etc.: *Some people find escape in mystery stories.* ❑ *v.* **es·caped, es·cap·ing.** [Escape comes from Latin words meaning "out of" and "cloak." Without a cloak, a person can run faster.] **—es·cap′a·ble,** *adj.* **—es·cap′er,** *n.*

SYNONYM STUDY Escape and elude both mean to get away. **Escape** means to get away or get out: *Everyone escaped from the burning building.* **Elude** means to escape in a clever way: *The fox eluded the hounds by doubling back on its tracks.*

es·cap·ee (e skā′pē′ *or* e skā′pē), *n.* person or animal that has escaped. ❑ *n., pl.* **es·cap·ees.**

escape velocity, the speed that an object such as a rocket must reach to get away permanently from the gravitational pull of the Earth or other heavenly body. Once a rocket's speed reaches 25,000 miles (40,000 kilometers) per hour, it can escape the pull of the earth.

es·cap·ism (e skā′piz′əm), *n.* an avoiding of unpleasant things by daydreaming or by entertainment, such as movies.

es·car·ole (es′kə rōl′), *n.* endive (def. 2).

es·carp·ment (e skärp′mənt), *n.* a steep slope; cliff.

es·chew (es chü′), *v.* to keep away from; avoid; shun: *The doctor advised me to eschew rich foods.* **—es·chew′er,** *n.*

es·cort (es′kôrt *for noun;* e skôrt′ *for verb*), **1** *n.* person or group of persons going with another to give protection, show honor, etc.: *An escort of several city officials accompanied the famous visitor.* **2** *n.* one or more ships or airplanes serving as a guard. **3** *n.* person who goes on a date with another: *Her escort to the party was a tall young man.* **4** *v.* to go with as an escort: *Three police cars escorted the governor's limousine in the parade.* ■ See Synonym Study at **accompany.**

es·crow (es′krō *or* e skrō′), *n.* deed, bond, or other written agreement held by a third person until certain conditions are met by two other parties.

in escrow, held by a third party in accordance with an agreement.

es·cu·do (e skü′dō), *n.* **1** unit of money in Portugal. **2** a former gold or silver coin of Spain, Portugal, and their colonies. ❑ *n., pl.* **es·cu·dos.**

es·cutch·eon (e skuch′ən), *n.* shield on which a coat of arms is put; scutcheon.

-ese, *suffix.* **1** of ___: *Japanese = of Japan.* **2** person born or living in ___: *Portuguese = person born or living in Portugal.* **3** language of ___: *Chinese = language of China.*

es·ker (es′kər), *n.* a trail or ridge or gravel, sand, etc., left by a stream flowing in or under under a melting glacier.

Es·ki·mo (es′kə mō), **1** *n.* member of a people living in the arctic regions of North America and northeastern Asia. **2** *n.* language of the Eskimos. **3** *adj.* of the Eskimos or their language. ❑ *n., pl.* **Es·ki·mo** or **Es·ki·mos** for 1.

> **USAGE NOTE** **Eskimo** is a word disliked by many members of the people who have been called by that name. They prefer **Inuit** or **Inupiaq** as names for themselves and their language. (For more information, see the entries at those words.) Others use these names in respect for this preference. However, **Eskimo** remains common. It is a good idea to follow the preferred usage of your subjects, your sources, and your audience. If in doubt, ask!

Eskimo dog, a strong, broad-chested dog of the arctic regions, used for pulling sleds. Eskimo dogs have furry outer hair with another coat of fine hair near the skin for warmth.

Eskimo dog—2 ft. (61 cm) high at the shoulder

ESL, English as a second language.

e·soph·a·gus (i sof′ə gəs), *n.* passage for food from the throat to the stomach; gullet. ❑ *n., pl.* **e·soph·a·gi** (i sof′ə jī).

es·o·ter·ic (es′ə ter′ik), *adj.* understood only by a select few; intended for an inner circle of disciples, scholars, etc.: *esoteric literature.* **—es′o·ter′i·cal·ly,** *adv.*

ESP, extrasensory perception.

esp., especially.

es·pe·cial (e spesh′əl), *adj.* more than others; special: *my especial friend, of no especial value. Your birthday is an especial day for you.* **—es·pe′cial·ness,** *n.*

es·pe·cial·ly (e spesh′ə lē), *adv.* particularly; principally; chiefly: *This book is designed especially for students.*

> **SYNONYM STUDY** **Especially** and **specifically** both mean one more than others. **Especially** means more, compared to others: *I like that family, especially the younger daughter.* **Specifically** means just that one: *They went to the mall specifically to buy shoes.*

Es·pe·ran·to (es′pə rän′tō *or* es′pə ran′tō), *n.* a simple artificial language for international use, with vocabulary and grammar based on forms common to many European languages.

es·pi·o·nage (es′pē ə näzh *or* es′pē ə nij), *n.* the use of spies; spying. Nations use espionage to find out the military and political secrets of other nations.

es·pla·nade (es′plə näd′ *or* es′plə näd′), *n.* any open level space used for public walks or drives, especially along a shore.

es·pous·al (e spou′zəl), *n.* **1** Also, **espousals,** *pl.* ceremony of becoming engaged or married. **2** act of espousing; adoption of a cause: *The candidate's espousal of the campaign for a new park made her very popular.*

es·pouse (e spouz′), *v.* **1** to marry. **2** to support a cause or project: *She espouses vegetarianism.* ❑ *v.* **es·poused, es·pous·ing.** **—es·pous′er,** *n.*

es·pres·so (e spres′ō), *n.* **1** a very strong coffee made from beans roasted black, brewed under steam pressure, usually in a special machine. **2** cup of this coffee. ❑ *n., pl.* **es·pres·sos** for 2.

es·prit (e sprē′), *n.* FRENCH. lively wit; spirit.

es·prit de corps (e sprē′ də kôr′), FRENCH. group spirit; comradeship: *The club's strong esprit de corps showed itself in the intense loyalty of its members.*

es·py (e spī′), *v.* OLD USE. to see at a distance; catch sight of; spy: *They espied the castle from afar.* ❑ *v.* **es·pied, es·py·ing.**

Esq., Esquire: *Henry Smith, Esq.*

es·quire (es′kwir), *n.* **1** (in the Middle Ages) a knight's attendant; squire. **2** Englishman ranking next below a knight. **3 Esquire,** a formal title placed after someone's last name, especially that of an attorney.

es·say (es′ā *for 1*; e sā′ *for 2*; es′ā *or* e sā′ *for 3*), **1** *n.* a short written composition. **2** *v.* to try; attempt: *The student essayed her first solo flight.* **3** *n.* a try; an attempt. ❑ *v.* **es·sayed, es·say·ing.** **—es·say′er,** *n.*

es·say·ist (es′ā ist), *n.* writer of essays.

es·sence (es′ns), *n.* **1** the most important or characteristic part of something: *Being thoughtful of others is the essence of politeness.* **2** a concentrated substance that has the characteristic flavor, fragrance, or effect of the plant or fruit from which it is taken: *essence of peppermint.* **3** perfume.

es·sen·tial (ə sen′shəl), **1** *adj.* absolutely necessary; very important: *Good food and enough rest are essential to good health.* ■ See Synonym Study at **necessary. 2 essentials,** *n.pl.* absolutely necessary elements or qualities: *Learn the essentials first, then learn the details.* **3** *adj.* of or making up the essence of a substance: *The essential oil of a plant or fruit is what gives it its own peculiar flavor or fragrance.* **—es·sen′tial·ly,** *adv.*

EST or **E.S.T.,** Eastern Standard Time.

es·tab·lish (e stab′lish), *v.* **1** to set up on a firm or lasting basis: *establish a foundation.* **2** to settle in a position; set up in a business: *A new doctor has established herself on our street.* **3** to cause to be accepted and used for a long time: *to establish a custom.* **4** to show beyond any doubt; prove: *He established his innocence to the satisfaction of the jury.* **—es·tab′lish·er,** *n.*

es·tab·lish·ment (e stab′lish mənt), *n.* **1** something established. A household, business, church, or army is an establishment. **2 the Establishment,** group that holds all the positions of influence or authority in a country, society, etc.

es·tan·cia (e stän′syä), *n.* a large ranch or estate in Latin America. ❑ *n., pl.* **es·tan·cias.**

es·tate (e stāt′), *n.* **1** a large piece of land, usually with a large house built on it. **2** money and property that someone owns; possessions: *an estate of $2,000,000.*

es·teem (e stēm′), **1** *v.* to have a very favorable opinion of; think highly of; value: *We esteem courage.* **2** *n.* a very favorable opinion; high regard: *Courage is held in esteem.* **3** *v.* to think; consider: *She esteemed it an honor to be chosen for the award.*

es·ter (es′tər), *n.* compound produced by the reaction of an acid and an alcohol. Animal and vegetable fats and oils are esters.

Es·ther (es′tər), *n.* **1** (in the Bible) the Jewish wife of a Persian king, who saved her people from massacre. **2** book of the Bible that tells her story. [**Esther** comes from a Persian word meaning "star."]

es·thet·ic (es thet′ik), *adj.* aesthetic. **—es·thet′i·cal·ly,** *adv.*

es·thet·ics (es thet′iks), *n.* aesthetics.

es·ti·ma·ble (es′tə mə bəl), *adj.* worthy of esteem; deserving high regard: *Unselfishness is an estimable trait.*

a	hat	ė	term	ô	order	ch	child		
ā	age	i	it	oi	oil	ng	long		a in about
ä	far	ī	ice	ou	out	sh	she		e in taken
â	care	o	hot	u	cup	th	thin	ə	i in pencil
e	let	ō	open	u̇	put	ᴛʜ	then		o in lemon
ē	equal	ȯ	saw	ü	rule	zh	measure		u in circus

es·ti·mate (es′tə mit *or* es′tə māt *for noun;* es′tə māt *for verb*), **1** *n.* judgment or opinion about how much, how many, how good, etc.: *My estimate of the length of the room was 15 feet; it actually measured 14 feet, 9 inches.* **2** *v.* to form a judgment or opinion about how much, how many, how good, etc.: *We estimated that it would take four hours to weed the garden.* **3** *n.* statement of what certain work will cost, made by someone willing to do the work: *The painter's estimate for painting the house was $1500.* ❑ *v.* **es·ti·mat·ed, es·ti·mat·ing.** [See word history information at **aim.**] **—es′ti·ma·tor,** *n.*

SYNONYM STUDY **Estimate** and **evaluate** both mean to form an opinion about something. **Estimate** means to make a careful guess about size, weight, or value: *She estimates that the job will cost $150.* **Evaluate** means to judge quality: *Critics evaluate movies.*

es·ti·ma·tion (es′tə mā′shən), *n.* **1** judgment or opinion: *In my estimation, your plan will not work.* **2** esteem; respect: *The doctor was held in high estimation by the community.*

Es·to·ni·a (e stō′nē ə), *n.* a country in N Europe, on the Baltic Sea. *Capital:* Tallinn. **—Es·to′ni·an,** *adj., n.*

es·trange (e strānj′), *v.* to turn someone from affection to indifference, dislike, or hatred; make unfriendly; keep apart; separate: *A quarrel had estranged him from his family.* ❑ *v.* **es·tranged, es·trang·ing.** **—es·trange′ment,** *n.*

es·tro·gen (es′trə jən), *n.* any of several similar hormones that cause women and female animals to develop female sexual characteristics, and that are important to reproduction.

es·trus (es′trəs), *n.* a condition of sexual excitement that occurs at regular intervals in female mammals other than humans, during which mating may take place; heat.

es·tu·ar·y (es′chü er′ē), *n.* **1** a broad mouth of a river into which the tide flows. **2** inlet of the sea. ❑ *n., pl.* **es·tu·ar·ies.**

etc., et cetera. *Etc.* is usually read "and so forth." The definition of *equality* reads "sameness in amount, size, number, value, rank, etc." *Etc.* in this and other definitions shows that the definition applies to many similar items in addition to the ones mentioned.

et cet·er·a (et set′ər ə), and so forth; and others; and the like: *He collects toy planes, boats, et cetera.* [**Et cetera** comes from Latin words meaning "and all the rest."]

etch (ech), *v.* **1** to engrave a drawing or design on a metal plate, glass, etc., by means of acid that eats away the lines. When filled with ink, the lines of the design will reproduce a copy on paper. **2** to make drawings or designs by this method. **3** to impress deeply: *Her face was etched in my memory.* **—etch′er,** *n.*

WORD STORY **Etch** comes from a German word meaning "to cause to eat," used about feeding animals. The acid burning the metal surface makes the metal disappear as if eaten away.

etch·ing (ech′ing), *n.* **1** picture or design printed from an etched plate. **2** art or process of engraving a drawing or design on a metal plate, glass, etc., by means of acid.

e·ter·nal (i tėr′nl), **1** *adj.* without beginning or ending; lasting throughout all time. **2** *adj.* always and forever the same: *the eternal truths.* **3** *adj.* seeming to go on forever; constant: *When will we have an end to this eternal noise?* **4** *n.* **the Eternal,** God. **—e·ter′nal·ly,** *adv.* **—e·ter′nal·ness,** *n.*

etching (def. 1)

Eternal City, Rome.

e·ter·ni·ty (i tėr′nə tē), *n.* **1** all time; all the past and all the future. **2** the endless period after death. **3** a period of time that seems endless: *I waited in the dentist's office for an eternity.* ❑ *n., pl.* **e·ter·ni·ties** for 3.

-eth, *suffix.* number ___ in a series: *sixtieth = number sixty in a series.*

eth·a·nol (eth′ə nôl), *n.* ethyl alcohol.

e·ther (ē′thər), *n.* **1** a colorless, sweet-smelling liquid that burns and evaporates readily. Its fumes cause unconsciousness when deeply inhaled. **2** OLD USE. regions beyond the earth's atmosphere; outer space.

e·the·re·al (i thir′ē əl), *adj.* light; airy; delicate: *the ethereal beauty of a butterfly, the ethereal music of a harp.* **—e·the′re·al·ly,** *adv.* **—e·the′re·al·ness,** *n.*

eth·i·cal (eth′ə kəl), *adj.* **1** of standards of right and wrong; of ethics or morals. **2** morally right: *ethical conduct.* **3** following formal or professional rules of right and wrong: *It is not ethical for a doctor to gossip about a patient.* **—eth′i·cal·ly,** *adv.*

eth·ics (eth′iks), *n.* **1** *sing.* the study of standards of right and wrong; the part of philosophy dealing with moral conduct, duty, and judgment. **2** *pl.* formal or professional rules of right and wrong: *It is against medical ethics for doctors to repeat a patient's confidences.*

E·thi·o·pi·a (ē′thē ō′pē ə), *n.* **1** country in E Africa. *Capital:* Addis Ababa. **2** ancient region in NE Africa, south of Egypt. [**Ethiopia** comes from Greek words meaning "sunburned face."] **—E′thi·o′pi·an,** *adj., n.*

eth·nic (eth′nik), **1** *adj.* of the various racial or cultural groups of people and the characteristics, language, and customs of each. **2** *n.* member of an ethnic group. **—eth′ni·cal·ly,** *adv.*

eth·nol·o·gy (eth nol′ə jē), *n.* science that deals with the various races or cultural groups of people, their distinctive characteristics, customs, institutions, and culture. **—eth′no·log′i·cal,** *adj.*

eth·yl (eth′əl), *n.* a group of two carbon atoms linked to five hydrogen atoms, present in many organic chemical compounds. Ordinary alcohol contains ethyl.

eth·yl alcohol (eth′əl), ordinary alcohol, made by the fermentation of grain, sugar, etc. It is in alcoholic beverages, and is also used in drugs, dyes, cleaning solutions, etc.

eth·yl·ene (eth′ə lēn′), *n.* a colorless, flammable gas with an unpleasant odor. It is used in the manufacture of ethyl alcohol, plastics, and many other compounds, and to ripen fruit.

ethylene glycol, glycol.

et·i·quette (et′ə ket), *n.* **1** the customary rules for behavior in polite society: *Etiquette requires that we eat peas with a fork, not a knife.* **2** formal rules for governing behavior in a profession, official ceremony, etc.: *Ambassadors observe diplomatic etiquette.*

WORD STORY **Etiquette** comes from a French word meaning "label" or "sign." **Ticket** comes from the same word. In public places, there are often signs telling people how to behave. Drivers who don't obey traffic signs may get tickets.

Et·na (et′nə), *n.* **Mount,** active volcano in NE Sicily, 10,902 feet (3325 meters) high.

E·ton (ēt′n), *n.* an old English school for boys.

E·tru·ri·a (i trür′ē ə), *n.* ancient country in W Italy.

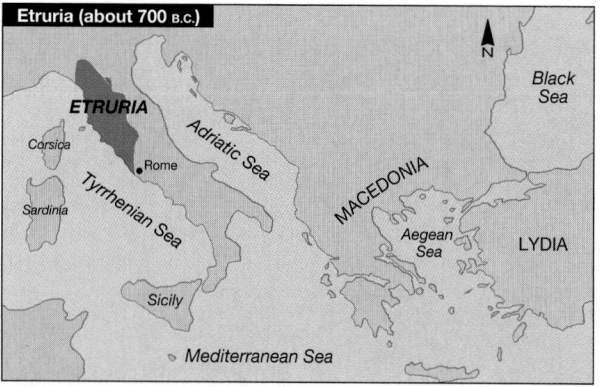

E·trus·can (i trus′kən), **1** *adj.* of Etruria, its people, their language, art, or customs. **2** *n.* person who was born or lived in Etruria. **3** *n.* language of Etruria.

-ette, *suffix.* little ___: *kitchenette = a little kitchen.*

é·tude (ā′tüd), *n.* piece of music intended to develop skill in technique. ❑ *n., pl.* **é·tudes.**

et·y·mol·o·gy (et′ə mol′ə jē), *n.* **1** the history of a word. **2** account or explanation of the origin and history of a word; word story. **3** the study dealing with the origin and history of words. ❑ *n., pl.* **et·y·mol·o·gies** for 1,2. **—et′y·mo·log′i·cal,** *adj.* **—et′y·mol′o·gist,** *n.*

Eu, symbol for europium.

EU, European Union.

eu·ca·lyp·tus (yü′kə lip′təs), *n.* any of numerous evergreen trees that grow mainly in Australia and neighboring islands. They are valued for timber and for a medicinal oil made from the leaves. ❑ *n., pl.* **eu·ca·lyp·tus·es, eu·ca·lyp·ti** (yü′kə lip′tī). [**Eucalyptus** comes from Greek words meaning "well covered." A small cap covers young buds on the tree.]

Eu·cha·rist (yü′kər ist), *n.* **1** sacrament of the Lord's Supper; Holy Communion. **2** the consecrated bread and wine used in this sacrament.

Eu·clid (yü′klid), *n.* Greek mathematician who wrote a famous book on geometry about 300 B.C.

Eu·gene (yü jēn′), *n.* city in W central Oregon.

eu·gen·ic (yü jen′ik), *adj.* of eugenics.

eu·gen·ics (yü jen′iks), *n.sing. or pl.* supposed science of improving the human race by controlled breeding.

eu·gle·na (yü glē′nə), *n.* any of many microscopic, one-celled living things, usually green, that move by means of a whiplike tail in fresh water. Euglenas are protists. ❑ *n., pl.* **eu·gle·nas.**

eu·kar·y·ote (yü′kar′ē ōt), *n.* **1** living cell with a definite nucleus. **2** living thing composed of such cells.

eu·lo·gist (yü′lə jist), *n.* person who eulogizes.

eu·lo·gis·tic (yü′lə jis′tik), *adj.* of or like a eulogy; praising very highly. **—eu′lo·gis′ti·cal·ly,** *adv.*

eu·lo·gize (yü′lə jīz), *v.* to praise very highly. ❑ *v.* **eu·lo·gized, eu·lo·giz·ing. —eu′lo·giz′er,** *n.*

eu·lo·gy (yü′lə jē), *n.* speech or writing in praise of someone or something; high praise: *He delivered the eulogy at the mayor's funeral.* ❑ *n., pl.* **eu·lo·gies.**

eu·nuch (yü′nək), *n.* **1** a castrated man. **2** such a man in charge of a harem or the household of some Asian rulers. ❑ *n., pl.* **eu·nuchs.**

eu·phe·mism (yü′fə miz′əm), *n.* a mild or indirect expression used instead of one that is harsh or unpleasantly direct. "Pass away" is a common euphemism for "die"; "not very well" is a euphemism for "badly."

eu·phe·mis·tic (yü′fə mis′tik), *adj.* using mild or indirect words instead of harsh or unpleasant ones. **—eu′phe·mis′ti·cal·ly,** *adv.*

eu·pho·ni·ous (yü fō′nē əs), *adj.* pleasing to the ear; harmonious: *euphonious door chimes.* **—eu·pho′ni·ous·ly,** *adv.*

eu·pho·ni·um (yü fō′nē əm), *n.* a brass musical instrument like a tuba, but having a mellower, deeper tone.

eu·pho·ny (yü′fə nē), *n.* combination of pleasant, harmonious sounds.

eu·pho·ri·a (yü fôr′ē ə), *n.* a feeling of happiness and bodily well-being. **—eu·phor′ic,** *adj.* **—eu·phor′i·cal·ly,** *adv.*

Eu·phra·tes (yü frā′tēz), *n.* river in SW Asia, flowing from E Turkey through Syria and Iraq into the Persian Gulf. It joins the Tigris River in SE Iraq.

Eur·a·sia (yùr ā′zhə), *n.* Europe and Asia, thought of as a single landmass or continent.

Eur·a·sian (yùr ā′zhən), **1** *n.* person of mixed European and Asian parentage. **2** *adj.* of or about Eurasia or its people. **3** *adj.* of mixed European and Asian parentage.

eu·re·ka (yù rē′kə), *interj.* I have found it! (an exclamation of triumph at any discovery).

Eur·ope (yùr′əp), *n.* continent east of the North Atlantic Ocean and west of Asia. France, Denmark, Poland, and Spain are countries in Europe.

Eur·o·pe·an (yùr′ə pē′ən), **1** *adj.* of Europe or its people. **2** *n.* person born or living in Europe. **3** *n.* person of European descent.

European Community, an organization of 15 European countries with a common market and common economic and social policies, within the European Union. Its members are: Austria, Belgium, Denmark, Finland, France, Germany, Greece, Ireland, Italy, Luxembourg, the Netherlands, Portugal, Spain, Sweden, and the United Kingdom.

European Economic Community, the Common Market.

European Union, an international organization linking countries of the European Community for purposes of foreign policy, defense, and law enforcement. It came into existence in 1993.

eu·ro·pi·um (yù rō′pē əm), *n.* a soft, grayish metallic element found only in combination with other elements. *Symbol:* Eu

Eus·ta·chi·an tube (yü stā′kē ən *or* yü stā′shən), a slender canal between the pharynx and the middle ear. It equalizes the air pressure on the two sides of the eardrum.

eu·tha·na·sia (yü′thə nā′zhə), *n.* a painless killing, or allowing the death of someone, especially to end a painful and incurable disease; mercy killing.

EVA, extravehicular activity (experimentation, repairs, or other activity done outside an orbiting spacecraft).

e·vac·u·ate (i vak′yü āt), *v.* **1** to leave empty; withdraw from: *The tenants evacuated the burning apartment house.* **2** to withdraw; remove: *Efforts were made to evacuate all civilians from the war zone.* **3** to make empty, especially to discharge intestinal waste. ❑ *v.* **e·vac·u·at·ed, e·vac·u·at·ing. —e·vac′u·a′tion,** *n.*

e·vac·u·ee (i vak′yü ē′), *n.* person who is removed to a place of greater safety. ❑ *n., pl.* **e·vac·u·ees.**

e·vade (i vād′), *v.* to get away from by trickery; avoid by cleverness: *The thief evaded the police.* ■ See Synonym Study at **avoid.** ❑ *v.* **e·vad·ed, e·vad·ing. —e·vad′a·ble,** *adj.* **—e·vad′er,** *n.*

e·val·u·ate (i val′yü āt), *v.* to find out the value or the amount of; estimate the worth or importance of; appraise: *An expert will evaluate the paintings you wish to sell.* ❑ *v.* **e·val·u·at·ed, e·val·u·at·ing.** ■ See Synonym Study at **estimate.** **—e·val′u·a′tor,** *n.*

e·val·u·a·tion (i val′yü ā′shən), *n.* **1** act of evaluating: *The jury began its careful evaluation of the evidence.* **2** appraisal or estimation of the quality, importance, value, or progress of your work: *a year-end evaluation.* **3** an estimated value; valuation.

e·van·gel·i·cal (ē′van jel′ə kəl), *adj.* **1** of or according to the four Gospels or the New Testament. **2** of the Protestant churches that emphasize Jesus' atonement and human salvation by faith. Methodists and Baptists are evangelical.

e·van·gel·ism (i van′jə liz′əm), *n.* act of preaching the Gospel; earnest effort for the spread of the Gospel.

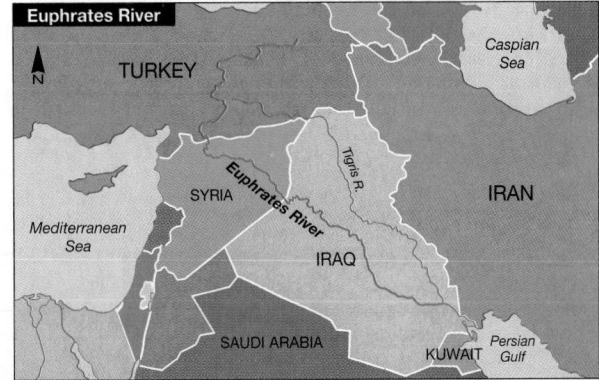
Euphrates River

e·van·gel·ist (i van′jə list), *n.* **1** preacher of the Gospel. **2** a traveling preacher who stirs up religious feeling in revival services. **3 Evangelist,** writer of one of the four Gospels; Matthew, Mark, Luke, or John. [**Evangelist** comes from a Greek word meaning "good news."] **—e·van′gel·is′tic,** *adj.*

Evans (ev′ənz), *n.* **1 Mary Ann** (an), the real name of **George Eliot. 2 Walk·er** (wô′kər), 1903-1975, American photographer. He photographed many poor Southern farmers during the Depression.

a	hat	ė	term	ô	order	ch	child			
ā	age	i	it	oi	oil	ng	long		a in about
ä	far	ī	ice	ou	out	sh	she		e in taken
â	care	o	hot	u	cup	th	thin	ə	i in pencil
e	let	ō	open	ù	put	ᴛʜ	then		o in lemon
ē	equal	ò	saw	ü	rule	zh	measure		u in circus

Ev·ans·ville (ev′ənz vil), *n.* city in SW Indiana.

e·vap·o·rate (i vap′ə rāt′), *v.* **1** to change from a liquid into a gas: *Boiling water evaporates rapidly.* **2** to remove water or other liquid from: *Heat is used to evaporate milk.* **3** to vanish; disappear: *My good resolutions evaporated soon after New Year.* ❑ *v.* **e·vap·o·rat·ed, e·vap·o·rat·ing.** —**e·vap′o·ra′tion,** *n.* —**e·vap′o·ra′tor,** *n.*

evaporated milk, a thick, unsweetened, canned milk, prepared by evaporating some of the water from ordinary milk.

e·va·sion (i vā′zhən), *n.* **1** act of getting away from something by trickery; avoiding by cleverness: *I had no excuse for the evasion of my responsibilities.* **2** an attempt to escape an argument, a charge, a question, etc.: *The prisoner's evasions of the lawyer's questions convinced the jury that he was guilty.*

e·va·sive (i vā′siv), *adj.* tending or trying to evade: *"I really haven't given it much thought" is an evasive answer.* —**e·va′sive·ly,** *adv.* —**e·va′sive·ness,** *n.*

eve (ēv), *n.* **1** the evening or day before a holiday or some other special day: *New Year's Eve.* **2** time just before something happens: *on the eve of the election.* **3** OLD USE. evening.

Eve (ēv), *n.* (in the Bible) the first woman, the wife of Adam. [**Eve** comes from a Hebrew word meaning "life."]

e·ven[1] (ē′vən), **1** *adj.* having the same height everywhere; level; flat; smooth: *The countryside is even, with no hills or slopes.* **2** *adj.* at the same level: *The snow was even with the windowsill.* **3** *adj.* keeping about the same; uniform: *an even motion, an even temperature.* **4** *adj.* owing nothing; square: *He repaid the $5, and they were even.* **5** *adj.* no more or less than; equal: *They divided the money in even shares.* **6** *v.* to make level or equal; make even: *I evened the edges by trimming them.* **7** *adj.* able to be divided by 2 without a remainder: *2, 4, 6, 8, and 10 are even numbers.* **8** *adj.* neither more nor less; exact: *an even dozen.* **9** *adv.* just: *She left even as you came.* **10** *adj.* not easily disturbed or angered; calm: *an even temper.* **11** *adv.* indeed: *I am ready, even eager, to go.* **12** *adv.* though you would not expect it: *Even a child can operate this machine.* **13** *adv.* still; yet: *You can read even better if you try.* —**e′ven·ly,** *adv.* —**e′ven·ness,** *n.*

break even, to have equal gains and losses.

even if, in spite of the fact that; although: *I will come, even if it rains.*

even though, although.

get even, to have revenge.

e·ven[2] (ē′vən), *n.* OLD USE. evening.

e·ven·hand·ed (ē′vən han′did), *adj.* impartial; fair. —**e′ven·hand′ed·ly,** *adv.* —**e′ven·hand′ed·ness,** *n.*

eve·ning (ēv′ning), *n.* the last part of day and early part of night; time between sunset and bedtime.

ev·en·ste·ven (ē′vən stē′vən), *adj.* INFORMAL. **1** with neither side owing the other: *I treated him to ice cream and then we were even-steven.* **2** having an equal score; tied: *The game was even-steven at 23 points.* [**Even-steven** doesn't come from a specific person named Steven. The second part was added for the rhyme.]

e·vent (i vent′), *n.* **1** a happening, especially an important happening: *Newspapers report current events.* **2** one item in a program of sports: *The 100-yard dash was the last event.*

in any event, in any case; whatever happens.

in the event of, if there should be; in case of; if there is: *In the event of rain, the party will be held indoors.*

WORD FAMILY   **Event** and the words below are related. They all come from a Latin word meaning "to come."

adventure	convention	inventory	souvenir
avenue	covenant	prevent	supervene
convenient	intervene	revenue	venture
convent	invent		

e·vent·ful (i vent′fəl), *adj.* **1** full of events; having many unusual events: *The class spent an eventful day touring the new zoo.* **2** having important results; important: *The discovery of atomic energy began an eventful period in history.* —**e·vent′ful·ly,** *adv.* —**e·vent′ful·ness,** *n.*

e·ven·tide (ē′vən tīd′), *n.* OLD USE. evening.

e·ven·tu·al (i ven′chü əl), *adj.* coming in the end; final: *After several failures, their eventual success surprised us.*

e·ven·tu·al·i·ty (i ven′chü al′ə tē), *n.* a possible occurrence or condition; possibility: *They were prepared for the eventuality of a drought.* ❑ *n., pl.* **e·ven·tu·al·i·ties.**

e·ven·tu·al·ly (i ven′chü ə lē), *adv.* in the end; finally: *We waited for them, but eventually we had to leave.*

ev·er (ev′ər), *adv.* **1** at any time: *Is she ever at home?* **2** at all times; always: *She is ever ready to accept a new challenge.* **3** in any way; at all: *How did you ever move the table by yourself?*

ever so, very: *The ocean is ever so deep.*

Ev·er·est (ev′ər ist), *n.* **Mount,** mountain in the Himalayas between Tibet and Nepal, 29,028 feet (8848 meters) high. It is the highest mountain in the world.

Ev·er·glades (ev′ər glādz′), *n.pl.* **the,** a swampy region in S Florida.

WORD STORY   **Everglades** comes from **glade,** which means "forest meadow," and **ever.** The name was probably used to suggest that this region took forever to cross.

Everglades National Park, a national park in S Florida, containing part of one of the world's largest wetlands.

Everglades National Park

evening dress, formal clothes worn in the evening.

evening star, a bright planet seen in the western sky after sunset. Venus is often the evening star.

e·ven·song (ē′vən sòng′), *n.* vespers.

ev·er·green (ev′ər grēn′), **1** *adj.* having green leaves or needles all year round. **2** *n.* an evergreen plant. Pine, ivy, rhododendrons, etc., are evergreens. **3** *n.pl.* **evergreens,** evergreen branches used for decoration, especially at Christmas.

ev·er·last·ing (ev′ər las′ting), **1** *adj.* lasting forever; never stopping: *the everlasting beauty of nature.* **2** *adj.* lasting a long time: *We wished them everlasting happiness.* **3** *adj.* lasting too long; tiresome: *His everlasting complaints annoy me.* **4** *n.* **the Everlasting,** God. **—ev′er·last′ing·ly,** *adv.* **—ev′er·last′ing·ness,** *n.*

ev·er·more (ev′ər môr′), *adv.* always; forever.
for evermore, for all time; for eternity; forever.

Ev·ers (ev′ərs), *n.* **1 Med·gar** (med′gər), 1925-1963, American civil rights leader. ■ **Medgar Evers** encouraged African Americans to register to vote and to boycott businesses that discriminated against them. He was murdered in 1963. **2** his brother, **Charles,** born 1922, American civil rights leader. He has encouraged African Americans to start their own businesses and to register to vote.

Ev·ert (ev′ərt), *n.* **Chris** (kris), born 1954, American tennis champion.

eve·ry (ev′rē), *adj.* **1** each one of the entire number of persons or things: *Read every word on the page. Every student must have a book.* **2** all possible: *We showed them every consideration.*
every now and then, from time to time: *Every now and then we have a frost that ruins the crop.*
every other, every second: *Every other day I wash my hair.*
every which way, in all directions.

It is now common in speech and informal writing to use **their** after **each, every,** and **everyone:** *Every student should write their name on their paper. Does everyone have their lunch? Each passenger must show their ticket.* Many people object to this usage, but it is increasingly frequent. It is wise to consider your audience and the purpose of your speech or writing when thinking about such questions of usage. Often you can find other ways to express yourself. In the sentences above, for example, we might have written: *All students should write their names on their papers. Do all of you have your lunch? All passengers must show their tickets.* Notice how we used **all** in each of the sentences.

eve·ry·bod·y (ev′rē bud′ē), *pron.* every person; everyone: *Everybody likes the new principal.*

eve·ry·day (ev′rē dā′), *adj.* **1** of every day; daily: *Accidents are everyday occurrences.* **2** for every ordinary day; not for Sundays or holidays: *everyday clothes.* **3** not exciting; usual: *He had only an everyday story to tell.* ■ See Usage Note at **everyone.**

eve·ry·one (ev′rē wun′), *pron.* each one; everybody: *Everyone in the class is here.* ■ See also Usage Note at **every.**

USAGE NOTE People sometimes confuse **everyone** and the two-word phrase **every one. Everyone** is written as one word when the accent is on **every:** *Has everyone seen the newspaper?* It is written as two words when the accent is on **one:** *The dog ate every one of the cookies.* The same is true of other words and phrases with *every,* including **everyday** and **everything.**

eve·ry·thing (ev′rē thing′), **1** *pron.* every thing; all things: *She did everything she could to help her friend.* **2** *n.* something extremely important; very important thing: *This news means everything to us.* ■ See Usage Note at **everyone.**

eve·ry·where (ev′rē wâr′), *adv.* in every place; in all places: *We looked everywhere for our lost dog.*

e·vict (i vikt′), *v.* to expel by law from land, a building, etc.; eject: *They were evicted for not paying their rent.* **—e·vic·tion** (i vik′shən), *n.*

SYNONYM STUDY **Evict, expel,** and **eject** all mean to make someone leave. **Evict** means to force someone legally to leave a home or land: *The tenants were evicted for not paying rent.* **Expel** suggests formal punishment: *They were expelled for fighting.* **Eject** suggests rapid action: *Two players and a coach were ejected from the game.*

ev·i·dence (ev′ə dəns), **1** *n.* anything that shows what is true and what is not; facts; proof: *The evidence showed that he had not been there.* **2** *n.* facts established and accepted in a court of law: *The judge heard all the evidence.* **3** *n.* indication; sign: *A smile gives evidence of pleasure.* **4** *v.* to show clearly: *Their smiles evidenced their pleasure.* ❏ *v.* **ev·i·denced, ev·i·denc·ing.**
in evidence, easily seen or noticed: *The damage caused by the flood was in evidence throughout the county.*

ev·i·dent (ev′ə dənt), *adj.* easy to see or understand; clear; plain: *It was evident that the shattered vase could never be repaired.*

ev·i·dent·ly (ev′ə dənt lē), *adv.* plainly; clearly: *If he hasn't arrived yet, he evidently missed his train.*

e·vil (ē′vəl), **1** *adj.* causing harm; bad; wrong; wicked: *an evil plan.* ■ See Synonym Study at **wicked. 2** *n.* bad or evil quality; wickedness: *Their thoughts were full of evil.* **3** *n.* something causing harm: *Crime and poverty are some of the evils of society.* **—e′vil·ly,** *adv.* **—e′vil·ness,** *n.*

e·vil·do·er (ē′vəl dü′ər), *n.* someone who does evil.

e·vil-mind·ed (ē′vəl mīn′did), *adj.* having an evil mind; wicked; malicious. **—e′vil-mind′ed·ly,** *adv.* **—e′vil-mind′ed·ness,** *n.*

e·vince (i vins′), *v.* to show clearly: *The judge evinced his disapproval of the attorney's courtroom antics by fining her for contempt.* ❏ *v.* **e·vinced, e·vinc·ing.**

e·vis·ce·rate (i vis′ə rāt′), *v.* to remove the internal organs, especially the intestines, from: *The butcher eviscerated a chicken.* ❏ *v.* **e·vis·ce·rat·ed, e·vis·ce·rat·ing. —e·vis′ce·ra′tion,** *n.*

e·voc·a·tive (i vok′ə tiv), *adj.* tending to evoke; calling to mind: *photographs evocative of memories.* **—e·voc′a·tive·ly,** *adv.*

e·voke (i vōk′), *v.* to call forth; bring out: *His witty remarks evoked many smiles.* ❏ *v.* **e·voked, e·vok·ing. —e·voc′a·ble,** *adj.*

ev·o·lu·tion (ev′ə lü′shən), *n.* **1** a gradual development: *the evolution of transportation from horse and buggy to jet aircraft.* **2** process in which slight bodily changes are passed from living things to their young, adding up to larger changes over a number of generations. According to Darwin's theory of evolution, all forms of life are the results of evolution from earlier forms, and the changes that adapt a living thing to its environment are the most likely to be passed on. **3** (in mathematics) the calculation of roots from powers.

WORD STORY **Evolution** comes from Latin words meaning "to roll" and "out." The English word was originally used about movements of soldiers marching or riding horses, as they separated from each other and spread out over the land.

ev·o·lu·tion·ar·y (ev′ə lü′shə ner′ē), *adj.* **1** of or about evolution. **2** in accordance with the theory of evolution.

ev·o·lu·tion·ist (ev′ə lü′shə nist), *n.* person who believes in and supports the theory of evolution.

e·volve (i volv′), *v.* **1** to develop gradually: *Buds evolve into flowers.* **2** to develop by a process of slight changes to a more adapted form: *The modern horse has evolved from a small animal like a dog.* ❏ *v.* **e·volved, e·volv·ing.**

ewe (yü), *n.* a female sheep. ■ Other words that sound like this are **yew** and **you.**

ex-, *prefix.* former; formerly: *ex-president = former president.*

Ex., Exodus.

ex·act (eg zakt′), **1** *adj.* without any mistake; correct; accurate; precise: *an exact measurement.* ■ See Synonym Study at **correct. 2** *adj.* with careful attention to detail; strict; rigorous: *the exact discipline of a military commander.* **3** *v.* to demand and get: *If you do the work, you can exact payment for it.* **—ex·act′ness,** *n.*

ex·act·ing (eg zak′ting), *adj.* **1** requiring much; hard to please: *An exacting teacher will not permit careless work.* **2** requiring effort, care, or attention: *Flying an airplane is exacting work.*

ex·act·i·tude (eg zak′tə tüd), *n.* exactness.

ex·act·ly (eg zakt′lē), *adv.* **1** accurately; precisely. **2** just so; quite right.

ex·ag·ge·rate (eg zaj′ə rāt′), *v.* **1** to say or think something is larger or greater than it is; go beyond the truth: *The little boy exaggerated when he said he had a million computer games.* **2** to increase or enlarge beyond what is normal: *The artist exaggerated parts of the drawing to make them clearer.* ❏ *v.* **ex·ag·ge·rat·ed, ex·ag·ge·rat·ing.** [**Exaggerate** comes from Latin words meaning "to pile up high." Someone who exaggerates makes things too big.] **—ex·ag′ge·ra′ted·ly,** *adv.* **—ex·ag′ge·ra′tor,** *n.*

a	hat	ė	term	ô	order	ch	child		a in about
ā	age	i	it	oi	oil	ng	long		e in taken
ä	far	ī	ice	ou	out	sh	she	ə	i in pencil
â	care	o	hot	u	cup	th	thin		o in lemon
e	let	ō	open	ü	put	ᴛʜ	then		u in circus
ē	equal	ò	saw	ü	rule	zh	measure		

ex·ag·ge·ra·tion (eg zaj/ə rā/shən), *n.* **1** an exaggerated statement: *It is an exaggeration to say that you would rather die than touch a snake.* **2** act of exaggerating: *His constant exaggeration made people distrust him.*

ex·alt (eg zôlt/), *v.* **1** to make high in rank, honor, power, character, or quality: *The queen exalted the commoner to the rank of earl.* **2** to fill with pride, joy, or noble feeling: *He was exalted by success.* **3** to praise; honor; glorify: *The worshipers exalted their god.* **—ex·alt/er**, *n.*

ex·alt·ed (eg zôl/tid), *adj.* **1** high in rank, honor, power, character, or quality: *an exalted piece of music, the exalted rank of editor in chief.* **2** very excited; elated. **—ex·alt/ed·ly**, *adv.*

ex·am (eg zam/), *n.* examination.

ex·am·i·na·tion (eg zam/ə nā/shən), *n.* **1** act of examining or condition of being examined: *The doctor made a thorough examination of my eyes.* **2** test of knowledge or qualifications; list of questions; test: *The teacher gave us an examination in arithmetic.*

ex·am·ine (eg zam/ən), *v.* **1** to look at closely and carefully: *The doctor examined the wound.* **2** to test the knowledge or qualifications of; ask questions of; test: *The lawyer examined the witness.* ❑ *v.* **ex·am·ined, ex·am·in·ing. —ex·am/in·er**, *n.*

ex·am·ple (eg zam/pəl), *n.* **1** one thing taken to show what others are like; sample: *New York is an example of a busy city.* **2** person or thing to be imitated; model; pattern: *You are an example to your younger sister.* **3** problem in arithmetic, grammar, etc.: *She wrote the example on the blackboard.*

for example, as an example; for instance: *Many flowers are fragrant: lilacs, for example.* ■ See Usage Note at **e.g.**

make an example of, to use as a warning to others: *The principal made an example of the students who cheated by suspending them for a week.*

set an example, be someone or something to be imitated; be a model or pattern: *Parents set an example for their children.*

> **WORD FAMILY**
> **Example** and the words below are related. They all come from a Latin word meaning "to take" or "to buy."
>
> | | | |
> |---|---|---|
> | exempt | premium | redeem |
> | impromptu | prompt | sample |
> | preempt | ransom | vintage |

ex·as·pe·rate (eg zas/pə rāt/), *v.* to irritate very much; annoy greatly; make angry: *Her continual lateness exasperated me.* ❑ *v.* **ex·as·pe·rat·ed, ex·as·pe·rat·ing.**

ex·as·pe·ra·tion (eg zas/pə rā/shən), *n.* extreme annoyance; irritation; anger.

Ex·cal·i·bur (ek skal/ə bər), *n.* (in legends of the Middle Ages) the magic sword of King Arthur.

ex·ca·vate (ek/skə vāt), *v.* **1** to make hollow; hollow out: *The tunnel was made by excavating the side of a mountain.* **2** to make by digging; dig: *The workers excavated a tunnel for the new subway.* **3** to dig out; scoop out: *Power shovels excavated the dirt and loaded it into trucks.* **4** to uncover by digging: *They excavated an ancient buried city.* ❑ *v.* **ex·ca·vat·ed, ex·ca·vat·ing.**

excavate (def. 2)—excavating a fossil

ex·ca·va·tion (ek/skə vā/shən), *n.* **1** act or process of excavating; a digging out: *The excavation for the basement of our new house took three days.* **2** hole made by digging: *The excavation for the new building was 50 feet across.*

ex·ca·va·tor (ek/skə vā/tər), *n.* person or thing that excavates. A power shovel is an excavator.

ex·ceed (ek sēd/), *v.* **1** to be more or greater than: *Lifting that heavy trunk exceeds my strength.* **2** to do more than; go beyond: *Drivers are not supposed to exceed the speed limit.*

ex·ceed·ing (ek sē/ding), **1** *adj.* very great; unusual: *She is a girl of exceeding talent.* **2** OLD USE. *adv.* exceedingly.

ex·ceed·ing·ly (ek sē/ding lē), *adv.* very greatly; to an unusual degree; very: *Yesterday was an exceedingly hot day.*

ex·cel (ek sel/), *v.* **1** to be better than; do better than: *He excelled his classmates in spelling.* **2** to be better than others; do better than others: *She excels in arithmetic.* ❑ *v.* **ex·celled, ex·cel·ling.**

ex·cel·lence (ek/sə ləns), *n.* unusually good quality; being better than others; superiority: *His teacher praised him for the excellence of his report.*

Ex·cel·len·cy (ek/sə lən sē), *n.* title of honor used in speaking to or of a prime minister, governor, bishop, ambassador, or other high official: *His Excellency, the British Ambassador.* ❑ *n., pl.* **Ex·cel·len·cies.**

ex·cel·lent (ek/sə lənt), *adj.* of unusually good quality; better than others; superior: *Excellent work deserves high praise.* **—ex/cel·lent·ly**, *adv.*

> **SYNONYM STUDY**
> **Excellent, superior,** and **exceptional** all mean of very high quality. **Excellent** is the general word: *These tacos are excellent.* **Superior** means of very high quality compared to others: *All of the VCRs worked well, but this one was clearly superior.* **Exceptional** means outstanding, much better than most others: *She shows exceptional musical talent.*

ex·cept (ek sept/), **1** *prep.* leaving out; other than: *He works every day except Sunday.* ■ After **except**, use an objective pronoun, *me, him, her, us,* or *them: Everyone is going except me. She talked to no one except us.* **2** *v.* to leave out; exclude: *Those who passed the first test were excepted from the second.* ■ See Usage Note at **accept. 3** *conj.* only; but: *I would have had a perfect score, except I missed the last question.*

except for, 1 with the exception of; except: *They all came early except for her.* **2** if it were not for: *We could have gone today except for the rain.*

ex·cept·ing (ek sep/ting), *prep.* leaving out; other than; except; but: *We have school every day excepting Saturday and Sunday.*

ex·cep·tion (ek sep/shən), *n.* **1** someone or something left out: *She praised the pictures, with two exceptions.* **2** act of leaving out; excepting: *I like all my studies, with the exception of math.* **3** objection: *a statement liable to exception.*

take exception, 1 to object: *Several teachers and students took exception to the plan of having classes on Saturdays.* **2** be offended: *I took exception to their rude remarks.*

ex·cep·tion·al (ek sep/shə nəl), *adj.* **1** out of the ordinary; unusual: *This warm weather is exceptional for January.* **2** in need of special training or handling, especially because of below-average mental or physical capabilities: *exceptional children.* ■ See Synonym Study at **excellent. —ex·cep/tion·al·ly**, *adv.*

ex·cerpt (ek/sėrpt/ *for noun;* ek sėrpt/ *for verb*), **1** *n.* passage taken out of a book, etc.; quotation; extract: *The English teacher read the class excerpts from several plays.* **2** *v.* to take out passages from a book, etc.; quote: *In his report on Eleanor Roosevelt, he included some passages excerpted from her speeches.*

ex·cess (ek ses/ *or* ek/ses), **1** *n.* part that is too much; more than enough: *The tailor trimmed off the excess from the cloth being measured for the two sleeves.* **2** *n.* amount by which one thing is greater than another: *The excess of five quarts over a gallon is one quart.* **3** *adj.* beyond the usual amount; extra: *Passengers must pay extra for excess baggage.* ❑ *n., pl.* **ex·cess·es.**

in excess of, more than: *a gift in excess of $5000.*

to excess, too much: *He eats candy to excess.*

ex·ces·sive (ek ses/iv), *adj.* too much; too great; going beyond what is necessary or right: *We moved because the rent was excessive.* —**ex·ces′sive·ly,** *adv.* —**ex·ces′sive·ness,** *n.*

ex·change (eks chānj′), **1** *v.* to give for something else; change: *He exchanged the tight coat for one that was a size larger.* **2** *v.* to give and take things of the same kind: *We exchanged letters. They exchanged blows.* **3** *n.* act of exchanging; giving and taking: *During the truce there was an exchange of prisoners.* **4** *n.* place where people buy, sell, or trade things. A stock exchange is a place to do business in stocks. **5** *n.* a central station or office. A telephone exchange handles telephone calls. ❑ *v.* **ex·changed, ex·chang·ing.** —**ex·change′a·ble,** *adj.* —**ex·chang′er,** *n.*

ex·cheq·uer (eks chek′ər), *n.* **1** treasury, especially of a state or nation. **2 Exchequer,** department of the British government in charge of its finances and the public revenues.

WORD STORY **Exchequer** comes from a Latin word meaning "chess." In old times, tables with tops marked in squares like a chessboard were used to keep track of government finance.

ex·cise[1] (ek′sīz *or* ek′sīs), *n.* tax on the manufacture, sale, or use of certain articles made, sold, or used within a country.

ex·cise[2] (ek sīz′), *v.* to cut out; remove: *The doctor excised some scar tissue.* ❑ *v.* **ex·cised, ex·cis·ing.** —**ex·ci·sion** (ek sizh′ən), *n.*

ex·cit·a·ble (ek sī′tə bəl), *adj.* easily excited. —**ex·cit′a·bil′i·ty,** *n.* —**ex·cit′a·ble·ness,** *n.* —**ex·cit′a·bly,** *adv.*

ex·cite (ek sīt′), *v.* **1** to stir up the feelings of: *I was excited about going to summer camp.* **2** to arouse: *Plans for a field trip excited the students' interest.* **3** to stir to action: *Do not excite the dog; keep away from it.* **4** to raise an electron, atom, etc., to a higher level of energy. ❑ *v.* **ex·cit·ed, ex·cit·ing.** —**ex·cit′er,** *n.*

ex·cit·ed (ek sī′tid), *adj.* stirred up; aroused: *The excited mob rushed into the mayor's office.* —**ex·cit′ed·ly,** *adv.*

ex·cite·ment (ek sīt′mənt), *n.* **1** an excited condition: *Birth of twins caused great excitement in the family.* **2** something that excites: *We enjoyed the excitement of camping out in the mountains.*

SYNONYM STUDY **Excitement, commotion,** and **fuss** all mean strong feelings causing loud noise. **Excitement** means the feelings, often shown by noise: *The fans roared with excitement.* **Commotion** means noisy disturbance: *A commotion outside made us run to the window.* **Fuss** means excitement about something unimportant: *She made a big fuss about the missing cookie.*

ex·cit·ing (ek sī′ting), *adj.* causing excitement; arousing; stirring: *an exciting story about pirates.* —**ex·cit′ing·ly,** *adv.*

ex·claim (ek sklām′), *v.* to speak suddenly in surprise or strong feeling; cry out: *"That's wonderful!" she exclaimed.* —**ex·claim′er,** *n.*

ex·cla·ma·tion (ek′sklə mā′shən), *n.* something said suddenly as the result of surprise or strong feeling.

WORD BANK **Exclamations** express many strong feelings. If you want to know more about exclamations and which feelings they express, you can begin by looking up these words in this dictionary.

aha!	fiddlesticks!	hey!	whoops!
alas!	gee!	hurrah!	wow!
amen!	golly!	oops!	yea!
bravo!	gosh!	ouch!	yippee!
eureka!	ha!	phooey!	yuck!

exclamation point or **exclamation mark,** mark (!) of punctuation used after a word, phrase, or sentence to show that it was exclaimed: *Cool! It's snowing!*

ex·clam·a·to·ry (ek sklam′ə tôr′ē), *adj.* using, containing, or expressing exclamation.

ex·clude (ek sklüd′), *v.* to shut out; keep out: *The club's rules exclude from membership anyone who lives out of town.* ❑ *v.* **ex·clud·ed, ex·clud·ing.** —**ex·clud′a·ble,** *adj.* —**ex·clud′er,** *n.*

ex·clu·sion (ek sklü′zhən), *n.* act of excluding or condition of being excluded: *exclusion of trucks from one-way streets.*

ex·clu·sive (ek sklü′siv), *adj.* **1** not divided or shared with others; single; sole: *exclusive rights to sell a product.* **2** limited to a single object: *exclusive attention to instructions.* **3** very particular about choosing friends, members, etc.: *It is hard to get admitted to an exclusive club.* **4** each shutting out the other. "Tree"

and "animal" are exclusive terms; a thing cannot be both a tree and an animal. —**ex·clu′sive·ly,** *adv.* —**ex·clu′sive·ness,** *n.*

exclusive of, excluding; leaving out; not counting: *There are 26 days in that month, exclusive of Sundays.*

ex·com·mu·ni·cate (ek′skə myü′nə kāt), *v.* to cut off from membership in a church. ❑ *v.* **ex·com·mu·ni·cat·ed, ex·com·mu·ni·cat·ing.** —**ex′com·mu′ni·ca′tor,** *n.*

ex·com·mu·ni·ca·tion (ek′skə myü′nə kā′shən), *n.* **1** act of cutting someone off from membership in a church and from any part in its ceremonies. **2** an official statement announcing this.

ex·cre·ment (ek′skrə mənt), *n.* waste matter that is discharged from the body, especially from the intestines.

ex·cres·cence (ek skres′ns), *n.* an abnormal outgrowth. Warts are excrescences on the skin.

ex·crete (ek skrēt′), *v.* to discharge waste matter from the body: *The sweat glands excrete sweat.* ❑ *v.* **ex·cret·ed, ex·cret·ing.**

ex·cre·tion (ek skrē′shən), *n.* **1** a discharge of waste matter from the body. **2** the waste matter that is separated and discharged.

ex·cre·to·ry (ek′skrə tôr′ē), *adj.* involved in excretion: *The kidneys are excretory organs.*

ex·cru·ci·at·ing (ek skrü′shē ā′ting), *adj.* causing great suffering; very painful. —**ex·cru′ci·at′ing·ly,** *adv.*

ex·cur·sion (ek skėr′zhən), *n.* **1** a short trip taken for interest or pleasure, often by a number of people together: *Our hiking club went on an excursion to the mountains.* **2** trip on a train, ship, or aircraft, at fares lower than those usually charged.

excursion (def. 1)

ex·cuse (ek skyüz′ *for verb;* ek skyüs′ *for noun*), **1** *n.* reason for doing or not doing something: *an excuse for staying home.* **2** *v.* to offer a reason or apology for; try to remove the blame of: *He excused his bad temper as the result of a headache.* **3** *v.* to be a reason or explanation for: *Sickness excuses absence from school.* **4** *v.* to pardon; forgive; overlook: *Excuse me, I have to go now.* ■ See Synonym Study at **pardon. 5** *v.* to free from duty; let off: *Those who passed the first test will be excused from the second one.* **6** *n.* a note saying that someone should be excused for something or from something: *Your parent must write you an excuse.* ❑ *v.* **ex·cused, ex·cus·ing.** —**ex·cus′a·ble,** *adj.* —**ex·cus′er,** *n.*

excuse yourself, 1 to ask to be pardoned: *She excused herself for bumping into me by saying that she was in a hurry.* **2** to ask permission to leave: *I excused myself from the table.*

ex·ec (egs′ek), *n.* INFORMAL. executive.

ex·e·cute (ek′sə kyüt), *v.* **1** to put to death according to law: *The murderer was executed.* **2** to carry out; do: *He executed her instructions.* **3** to put into effect; enforce: *Congress makes the laws; the President executes them.* **4** to make according to a plan or design: *The artist took several months to execute the statue.* ❑ *v.* **ex·e·cut·ed, ex·e·cut·ing.** —**ex′e·cut′er,** *n.*

a	hat	ė	term	ô	order	ch	child		
ā	age	i	it	oi	oil	ng	long		a in about
ä	far	ī	ice	ou	out	sh	she	ə	e in taken
â	care	o	hot	u	cup	th	thin		i in pencil
e	let	ō	open	ů	put	ŦH	then		o in lemon
ē	equal	ò	saw	ü	rule	zh	measure		u in circus

ex·e·cu·tion (ek′sə kyü′shən), *n.* **1** act of putting to death according to law. **2** act or process of carrying out; doing: *She was prompt in the execution of her duties.* **3** act of putting into effect; enforcing: *the execution of a law.* **4** way of carrying out or doing; skill. **5** act of making according to a plan or design.

ex·e·cu·tion·er (ek′sə kyü′shə nər), *n.* person who puts criminals to death according to law.

ex·ec·u·tive (eg zek′yə tiv), **1** *adj.* of or about managing affairs: *A principal has an executive position.* **2** *n.* someone who manages affairs: *The president of a business firm is an executive.* **3** *adj.* having the duty and power of putting laws into effect: *The President of the United States is the head of the executive branch of the government.* **4** *n.* person, group, or branch of government that has the duty and power of putting the laws into effect.

ex·ec·u·tor (eg zek′yə tər), *n.* someone named in a will to carry out the wishes of the person making the will.

ex·em·plar·y (eg zem′plər ē), *adj.* **1** worth imitating: *exemplary conduct.* **2** serving as a warning to others: *exemplary punishment.* **3** serving as an example; typical: *an exemplary case.*

ex·em·pli·fy (eg zem′plə fī), *v.* to show by example; be an example of: *Ballet dancers exemplify grace and skill.* ❑ *v.* **ex·em·pli·fied, ex·em·pli·fy·ing.**

ex·empt (eg zempt′), **1** *v.* to make free from a duty, obligation, rule, etc.; release: *Students who get good grades all year are exempted from final exams.* **2** *adj.* freed from a duty, obligation, rule, etc.; released: *School property is exempt from taxes.*

ex·emp·tion (eg zemp′shən), *n.* **1** freedom from a duty, obligation, rule, etc.; release: *exemption from jury duty.* **2** something which permits such a release. Each person financially supported by a taxpayer is an exemption releasing some income from being taxed. **3** act of exempting.

ex·er·cise (ek′sər sīz), **1** *n.* the active use of the body or mind for its improvement: *Physical exercise is good for the health.* **2** *n.* act of using or practicing: *Safety requires the exercise of caution.* **3** *v.* to make active use of: *When you vote you exercise your right as a citizen.* **4** *n.* something that gives practice and training or causes improvement: *Study the lesson, and then do the exercises at the end.* **5** *v.* to take exercise; go through exercises: *I exercise for 10 minutes each morning.* **6** *v.* to give exercise to; train: *She exercises her horse after school every day.* **7** *v.* to carry out in action; perform: *The mayor exercises the duties and powers of his office.* **8** *n.* Often, **exercises,** *pl.* ceremony: *She gave the farewell address at the graduation exercises.* ❑ *v.* **ex·er·cised, ex·er·cis·ing.** —**ex′er·cis′a·ble,** *adj.* —**ex′er·cis′er,** *n.*

SYNONYM STUDY **Exercise** and **training** both mean physical activity to improve strength and health. **Exercise** means activity for personal reasons: *He gets a lot of exercise from jogging with his dog.* **Training** means activity preparing for a particular event or competition: *Her training for the race is to run four miles every morning.*

ex·ert (eg zėrt′), *v.* to put into use; use fully; use: *A gymnast exerts both strength and skill. A ruler exerts authority.*
exert yourself, to make an effort; try hard; strive: *She'll have to exert herself to make up the work she missed.*

exert—exerting strength

ex·er·tion (eg zėr′shən), *n.* **1** effort: *Our exertions kept the fire from spreading.* **2** act of putting into action; active use; use: *exertion of the mind, exertion of authority.*

ex·ha·la·tion (eks′hə lā′shən), *n.* act of exhaling.

ex·hale (eks hāl′), *v.* to breathe out: *We exhale air from our lungs.* ❑ *v.* **ex·haled, ex·hal·ing.**

ex·haust (eg zȯst′), **1** *v.* to empty completely: *exhaust an oil well.* **2** *v.* to use up: *exhaust the supply of water, exhaust your strength.* **3** *v.* to tire very much: *The long, hard climb up the hill exhausted us.* **4** *v.* to find out or say everything important about: *Her detailed lecture on ways to earn money just about exhausted the subject.* **5** *n.* the escape of burned gases from an engine. **6** *n.* pipe for burned gases to escape from an engine. **7** *n.* the burned gases that escape from an engine: *Automobile exhaust is poisonous.*

ex·haust·ed (eg zȯs′tid), *adj.* **1** worn out; very tired: *The exhausted hikers did not have the energy to go on.* ■ See Synonym Study at **tired. 2** used up: *Our patience was exhausted by everyone's trying to talk at once.*

ex·haus·tion (eg zȯs′chən), *n.* **1** condition of being exhausted. **2** extreme fatigue. **3** act of exhausting.

ex·haus·tive (eg zȯs′tiv), *adj.* tending to exhaust or use up resources, strength, or a subject, etc.; thorough: *The students were given an exhaustive examination covering the major points of the year's work.* —**ex·haus′tive·ly,** *adv.* —**ex·haus′tive·ness,** *n.*

ex·hib·it (eg zib′it), **1** *v.* to show; display: *Both of their children exhibit a talent for music.* **2** *v.* to show publicly; put on display: *She hopes to exhibit her paintings in New York.* **3** *n.* act of exhibiting; public showing: *The village art exhibit drew 10,000 visitors.* ■ See Synonym Study at **display. 4** *n.* thing or things shown publicly. **5** *n.* thing shown in court as evidence: *The defendant's glove was labeled Exhibit A.* —**ex·hib′i·tor,** *n.*

ex·hi·bi·tion (ek′sə bish′ən), *n.* **1** a public show: *The art school holds an exhibition every year.* **2** thing or things shown publicly; exhibit. **3** act of showing; display: *Pushing and shoving in line is an exhibition of bad manners.*

ex·hi·bi·tion·ist (ek′sə bish′ə nist), *n.* person who tends to show off or behave in an unusual way in order to attract attention.

ex·hil·a·rate (eg zil′ə rāt′), *v.* to make lively; stimulate; cheer: *Seeing friends at the holiday season always exhilarates me.* ❑ *v.* **ex·hil·a·rat·ed, ex·hil·a·rat·ing.** —**ex·hil′a·ra·tive,** *adj.*

ex·hil·a·ra·tion (eg zil′ə rā′shən), *n.* high spirits; lively joy.

ex·hort (eg zȯrt′), *v.* to urge strongly; advise or warn earnestly: *The preacher exhorted the congregation to lead good lives.* —**ex·hort′er,** *n.*

ex·hor·ta·tion (eg′zȯr tā′shən *or* ek′sȯr tā′shən), *n.* strong urging; earnest advice or warning.

ex·hume (eg züm′ *or* eks hyüm′), *v.* **1** to remove a buried body from a grave or the ground. **2** to bring to light; reveal: *The librarian exhumed the old book from the archives.* ❑ *v.* **ex·humed, ex·hum·ing.** —**ex·hu·ma·tion** (eks′hyə mā′shən), *n.*

ex·i·gen·cy (ek′sə jən sē), *n.* **1** situation demanding prompt action or attention; emergency: *The fire department measured up to the exigency of two fires within an hour, and put them both out.* **2** Often, **exigencies,** *pl.* an urgent need; demand for prompt action or attention: *The exigencies of business kept them from taking a vacation.* ❑ *n., pl.* **ex·i·gen·cies.**

ex·i·gent (ek′sə jənt), *adj.* demanding prompt action or attention; urgent: *The exigent pangs of hunger sent the bear on a search for food.* —**ex′i·gent·ly,** *adv.*

ex·ile (eg′zil *or* ek′sil), **1** *v.* to force to leave your country or home, often by law as a punishment; banish: *Napoleon was exiled to Elba.* ■ See Synonym Study at **banish. 2** *n.* person who is exiled: *She has been an exile since the end of the war.* **3** *n.* condition of being exiled; banishment: *be sent into exile for life.* ❑ *v.* **ex·iled, ex·il·ing.**

ex·ist (eg zist′), *v.* **1** to have being; be: *Space travel has existed for only a few years.* **2** to be real: *She believes that ghosts exist.* **3** to have life; live: *A person cannot exist without air.* **4** to be found; occur: *The whooping crane exists only in North America.*

ex·ist·ence (eg zis′təns), *n.* **1** condition of being: *Dinosaurs disappeared from existence millions of years ago.* **2** condition of being real: *Most people do not now believe in the existence of ghosts.* **3** life: *Drivers of racing cars lead a dangerous existence.* **4** occurrence: *The newspapers report the existence of many new cases of flu in the city.*

ex·ist·ent (eg zis′tənt), *adj.* **1** existing. **2** now existing; of the present time.

ex·it (eg′zit *or* ek′sit), **1** *n.* way out: *The theater had six exits.* **2** *n.* act of going out; departure: *When the cat came in, the mice made a hasty exit.* **3** *v.* to go out; leave: *Passengers exit the station to the street. We exited quickly.* **4** *n.* act of leaving the stage: *a graceful exit.*

> **WORD STORY** **Exit** comes from a Latin word meaning "he or she goes out." It came into English 500 years ago as a note in scripts of plays, to show that an actor leaves the stage.

ex·o·bi·ol·o·gy (ek′sō bī ol′ə jē), *n.* study of life on other planets. **—ex′o·bi′o·log′i·cal,** *adj.* **—ex′o·bi·ol′o·gist,** *n.*

ex·o·dus (ek′sə dəs), *n.* **1** act of going out; departure: *Every June there is an exodus of students from the colleges.* **2** **the Exodus,** the departure of the Israelites from Egypt under Moses. **3** **Exodus,** book of the Bible, containing an account of this departure. ❑ *n., pl.* **ex·o·dus·es** for 1.

ex of·fi·ci·o (eks ə fish′ē ō), because of your office: *The Vice-President is, ex officio, the presiding officer of the Senate.*

ex·on·e·rate (eg zon′ə rāt′), *v.* to free from blame: *Witnesses to the accident completely exonerated the truck driver.* ❑ *v.* **ex·on·e·rat·ed, ex·on·e·rat·ing.** **—ex·on′e·ra′tion,** *n.*

ex·or·bi·tant (eg zôr′bə tənt), *adj.* much too high; unreasonably excessive: *One dollar is an exorbitant price for a pack of bubble gum.* **—ex·or′bi·tant·ly,** *adv.*

ex·or·cise (ek′sôr sīz), *v.* **1** to drive out an evil spirit by prayers, ceremonies, etc. **2** to free someone or some place from an evil spirit. ❑ *v.* **ex·or·cised, ex·or·cis·ing.** **—ex′or·cis′er,** *n.*

ex·or·cism (ek′sôr siz′əm), *n.* **1** act of exorcising. **2** the prayers, ceremonies, etc., used in exorcising.

ex·or·cist (ek′sôr sist), *n.* someone who exorcises evil spirits.

ex·o·skel·e·ton (ek′sō skel′ə tən), *n.* any hard, external covering which protects or supports an animal body. A turtle shell is an exoskeleton.

exoskeleton

ex·o·sphere (ek′sō sfir), *n.* the outermost region of the atmosphere, beginning about 300 miles (480 kilometers) above the earth's surface.

ex·ot·ic (eg zot′ik), **1** *adj.* foreign; strange; not native: *exotic plants.* **2** *n.* anything exotic. **—ex·ot′i·cal·ly,** *adv.*

> **WORD STORY** **Exotic** comes from a Greek word meaning "outside." Exotic things come from outside the country, or outside people's familiar experience.

ex·pand (ek spand′), *v.* **1** to make or grow larger; increase in size; enlarge: *The balloon expanded as it was filled with air. Heat expanded the metal.* **2** to spread out; open out; unfold: *A bird expands its wings before flying.* **3** to express in fuller form or greater detail: *The writer expanded one sentence into a paragraph.* **4** (in mathematics) to express in a more detailed form, for instance by showing all the factors that multiply to a certain product, or all the amounts that add to a certain sum. **—ex·pand′a·ble,** *adj.* **—ex·pand′er,** *n.*

> **SYNONYM STUDY** **Expand, swell,** and **bulge** all mean to become larger. **Expand** is the general word: *His business is expanding.* **Swell** means to become larger by puffing up: *Her sprained ankle swelled and had to be bandaged.* **Bulge** means to swell and stick out: *The weightlifter's muscles bulged as she raised the heavy load.*

ex·panse (ek spans′), *n.* open or unbroken stretch; wide, spreading surface: *The Pacific Ocean is a vast expanse of water.*

ex·pan·sion (ek span′shən), *n.* **1** act of expanding: *Heat causes the expansion of gas.* **2** condition of being expanded; increase in size, volume, etc.: *The expansion of the factory made room for more machines.* **3** an expanded part or form: *That book is an expansion of a magazine article.* **4** (in mathematics) the more fully detailed expression of a particular operation: *The expansion of* $(a + b)^3$ *is* $a^3 + 3a^2b + 3ab^2 + b^3$.

ex·pan·sive (ek span′siv), *adj.* **1** capable of expanding; tending to expand: *expansive gases.* **2** wide; spreading: *an expansive lake.* **3** taking in much or many things; broad; extensive: *an expansive view of history.* **4** showing feelings freely and openly; demonstrative: *With her expansive personality, she makes friends easily.* **—ex·pan′sive·ly,** *adv.* **—ex·pan′sive·ness,** *n.*

ex·pa·ti·ate (ek spā′shē āt), *v.* to write or talk much: *He expatiated on the thrills of his trip to Hawaii.* ❑ *v.* **ex·pa·ti·at·ed, ex·pa·ti·at·ing.** **—ex·pa′ti·a′tion,** *n.* **—ex·pa′ti·a′tor,** *n.*

ex·pa·tri·ate (ek spā′trē āt *for verb;* ek spā′trē it *or* ek spā′trē·āt *for noun),* **1** *v.* to force someone to leave that person's own country; banish. **2** *v.* to withdraw from your country or citizenship: *Some Americans expatriate themselves and live in Europe.* **3** *n.* anyone living outside his or her own country. ❑ *v.* **ex·pa·tri·at·ed, ex·pa·tri·at·ing.** **—ex·pa′tri·a′tion,** *n.*

ex·pect (ek spekt′), *v.* **1** to think something will probably come or happen; look forward to: *I expect to take a vacation in May.* **2** to count on as necessary or right: *I expect you to keep your promise.* **3** to think; suppose: *I expect you're right about that.*

> **SYNONYM STUDY** **Expect, anticipate,** and **hope** all mean to think that something will happen. **Expect** is the general word: *I expect to see him soon.* **Anticipate** means to expect something pleasing: *She anticipates getting a letter from her pen pal in Australia soon.* **Hope** means to expect and wish for something: *They hope to move into their new house in June.*

ex·pect·an·cy (ek spek′tən sē), *n.* expectation. ❑ *n., pl.* **ex·pect·an·cies.**

ex·pect·ant (ek spek′tənt), *adj.* **1** expecting something; thinking something will come or happen; looking forward: *She opened her package with an expectant smile.* **2** pregnant: *an expectant mother.* **—ex·pect′ant·ly,** *adv.*

ex·pec·ta·tion (ek′spek tā′shən), *n.* **1** good reason for expecting something; prospect: *They have expectations of money from a rich aunt.* **2** act of expecting or condition of being expected; anticipation: *the expectation of a good harvest.*

ex·pec·to·rate (ek spek′tə rāt′), *v.* to cough up and spit out phlegm, etc.; spit. ❑ *v.* **ex·pec·to·rat·ed, ex·pec·to·rat·ing.**

ex·pe·di·ence (ek spē′dē əns), *n.* expediency.

ex·pe·di·en·cy (ek spē′dē ən sē), *n.* **1** desirability under the circumstances: *I enjoy traveling by train, but when I haven't much time I prefer the expediency of air travel.* **2** personal advantage; self-interest: *The salesclerk was influenced more by the expediency of making a sale than by the needs of the buyer.*

a	hat	ė	term	ô	order	ch	child	
ā	age	i	it	oi	oil	ng	long	⎧ a in about
ä	far	ī	ice	ou	out	sh	she	⎪ e in taken
â	care	o	hot	u	cup	th	thin	ə ⎨ i in pencil
e	let	ō	open	ù	put	ᴛʜ	then	⎪ o in lemon
ē	equal	ò	saw	ü	rule	zh	measure	⎩ u in circus

ex·pe·di·ent (ek spē′dē ənt), **1** *adj.* helping to bring about a desired result; desirable under the circumstances: *It is expedient to be friendly and pleasant if you want to have friends.* **2** *n.* means of bringing about a desired result: *When the truth wouldn't convince them I used the expedient of telling a believable lie.* **3** *adj.* giving or seeking personal advantage; based on self-interest. —**ex·pe′di·ent·ly,** *adv.*

ex·pe·dite (ek′spə dit), *v.* to make easy and quick; speed up: *Airplanes expedite travel.* ❏ *v.* **ex·pe·dit·ed, ex·pe·dit·ing.** [See Word Story at **expedition.**]

ex·pe·di·tion (ek′spə dish′ən), *n.* **1** journey for some special purpose, such as exploration, scientific study, or for military purposes. **2** the people, ships, etc., making such a journey.

> **WORD STORY**   **Expedition** comes from Latin words meaning "out" and "foot." **Expedite** comes from the same Latin words. Romans used the idea of releasing feet from a trap or chains as a way to say "speed up." **Expedition,** meaning "a special journey," was first used about military campaigns, for which speed was important.

ex·pe·di·tion·ar·y (ek′spə dish′ə ner′ē), *adj.* of or on an expedition, especially for military purposes: *an expeditionary force.*

ex·pe·di·tious (ek′spə dish′əs), *adj.* efficient and prompt; quick; speedy: *an expeditious method of packing.*

ex·pel (ek spel′), *v.* **1** to drive out with much force; force out; eject: *The army defeated the invaders and expelled them from the country.* ■ See Synonym Study at **evict.** **2** to put someone out; dismiss permanently: *A student caught cheating may be expelled from school.* ❏ *v.* **ex·pelled, ex·pel·ling.** —**ex·pel′la·ble,** *adj.* —**ex·pel′ler,** *n.*

> **WORD FAMILY**   **Expel** and the words below are related. They all come from a Latin word meaning "to drive," "to push," or "to beat."
>
> | | | | |
> |---|---|---|---|
> | appeal | expulsion | propel | repeal |
> | compel | impel | pulse¹ | repel |
> | compulsion | impulse | push | repulsive |
> | dispel | peal | rappel | |

ex·pend (ek spend′), *v.* to use up; spend: *He expended thought, work, and money on his project.* [See Word Story at **spend.**]

ex·pend·a·ble (ek spen′də bəl), *adj.* **1** able to be expended or used up. **2** worth giving up or sacrificing, especially in order to succeed at a plan. —**ex·pend′a·bil′i·ty,** *n.*

ex·pend·i·ture (ek spen′də chər), *n.* **1** amount of money spent; expense: *Her expenditures for Christmas presents were $328 and 14 hours of shopping.* **2** act of using up; a spending: *Building a sailboat requires the expenditure of much money, time, and effort.*

ex·pense (ek spens′), *n.* **1** amount of money spent; cost; charge: *He traveled at his uncle's expense.* ■ See Synonym Study at **cost.** **2** act of expending; a paying out of money; outlay: *The wise expense of a few dollars now will save hundreds later.* **3** cause of spending: *Running a car is an expense.* **4 expenses,** *pl.* money to repay charges brought about by doing a job: *In addition to salary, a salesman receives expenses.* **5** loss; sacrifice: *The town was captured at great expense to the victors.*

ex·pen·sive (ek spen′siv), *adj.* costly; high-priced: *She has an expensive car.* —**ex·pen′sive·ly,** *adv.* —**ex·pen′sive·ness,** *n.*

> **SYNONYM STUDY**   **Expensive** and **overpriced** both mean costly. **Expensive** suggests that something is or should be worth the cost: *Those sneakers are expensive.* **Overpriced** means costing more than it is worth: *The milk at this store is overpriced.*

ex·per·i·ence (ek spir′ē əns), **1** *n.* what happens to someone; what is seen, done, or lived through: *We had several pleasant experiences on our trip. People often learn by experience.* **2** *n.* knowledge or skill gained by seeing, doing, or living through things; practice: *Have you had any experience in this kind of work?* **3** *v.* to have happen to you; feel: *experience great pain.* ❏ *v.* **ex·per·i·enced, ex·per·i·enc·ing.**

> **WORD STORY**   **Experience, experiment,** and **expert** all come from a Latin word meaning "to try out." An experiment is a try that gives experience, and enough experience makes an expert.

ex·per·i·enced (ek spir′ē ənst), *adj.* **1** having experience; taught by experience: *The job calls for a person experienced in teaching children.* **2** skillful or wise because of experience: *an experienced teacher.*

ex·per·i·ment (ek sper′ə ment *for verb;* ek sper′ə mənt *for noun*), **1** *v.* to try in order to find out; make trials or tests: *The painter is experimenting with different paints to get the color she wants.* **2** *n.* trial or test to find out something: *an experiment to learn the weight of the air in a basketball.* ■ See Synonym Study at **trial.** [See Word Story at **experience.**] —**ex·per′i·ment′er,** *n.*

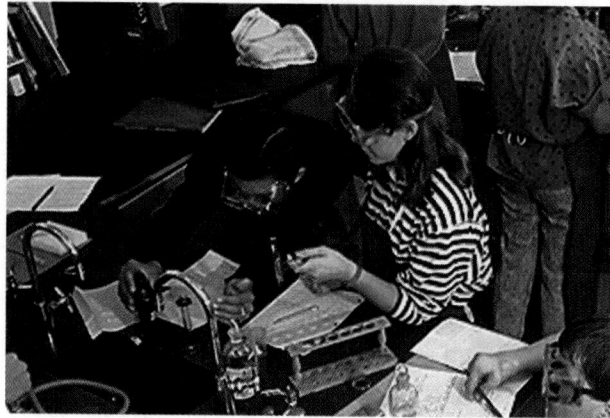

experiment (def. 2)

ex·per·i·men·tal (ek sper′ə men′tl), *adj.* **1** based on experiments: *Chemistry is an experimental science.* **2** used for experiments: *A new variety of wheat was developed at the experimental farm.* **3** for testing or trying out: *The young bird made experimental attempts to fly.* —**ex·per′i·men′tal·ly,** *adv.*

ex·per·i·men·ta·tion (ek sper′ə men tā′shən), *n.* act or process of experimenting.

ex·pert (ek′spėrt′ *for noun;* ek spėrt′ *or* ek′spėrt′ *for adj.*), **1** *n.* a very skillful person; person who knows a great deal about some special thing: *an expert at fishing.* **2** *adj.* very skillful; knowing a great deal about some special thing: *an expert chemist.* **3** *adj.* requiring or showing special skill or knowledge: *We were amazed at the expert workmanship in the fine carving.* [See Word Story at **experience.**] —**ex·pert′ly,** *adv.* —**ex·pert′ness,** *n.*

> **SYNONYM STUDY**   **Expert, accomplished,** and **skilled** all mean good at something. **Expert** means knowing a lot about something: *It takes expert handling to train a dog.* **Accomplished** means expert, especially at a particular thing: *She is an accomplished singer.* **Skilled** means good at something because of knowledge and practice: *After three years on the team, he is a skilled wrestler.*

ex·pert·ise (ek′spər tēz′), *n.* expert skill.

ex·pi·ate (ek′spē āt), *v.* to pay the penalty of; make amends for a wrong, sin, etc.; atone for. ❏ *v.* **ex·pi·at·ed, ex·pi·at·ing.** —**ex′pi·a′tion,** *n.* —**ex′pi·a′tor,** *n.*

ex·pi·ra·tion (ek′spə rā′shən), *n.* **1** an end; conclusion: *We shall move at the expiration of our lease.* **2** act of breathing out; exhalation: *the expiration of air from the lungs.*

ex·pire (ek spīr′), *v.* **1** to come to an end of effectiveness: *Your library card has expired.* **2** to die. **3** to breathe out; exhale: *Air is expired from the lungs.* ❏ *v.* **ex·pired, ex·pir·ing.** —**ex·pir′er,** *n.*

ex·plain (ek splān′), *v.* **1** to make plain or clear; tell the meaning of: *The teacher explained long division to the class.* **2** to give reasons for; state the cause of; account for: *Can you explain your friend's absence?* —**ex·plain′a·ble,** *adj.* —**ex·plain′er,** *n.*

> **WORD STORY**   **Explain** comes from Latin words meaning "out" and "flat." Explaining something is like opening and smoothing it until it can be seen clearly.

ex·pla·na·tion (ek′splə nā′shən), *n.* **1** act of explaining; making clear or giving reasons: *I did not understand the teacher's explanation of long division.* **2** something that explains: *This diagram is a good explanation of how a car engine works.*

ex·plan·a·to·ry (ek splan′ə tôr′ē), *adj.* helping to explain; helping to make clear: *Read the explanatory part of the lesson before you try to do the problem.*

ex·ple·tive (ek′splə tiv), *n.* exclamation or oath. "Damn" and "My goodness!" are expletives.

ex·pli·ca·ble (ek splik′ə bəl *or* ek′splə kə bəl), *adj.* able to be explained.

ex·pli·cate (ek′splə kāt), *v.* to explain. ❏ *v.* **ex·pli·cat·ed, ex·pli·cat·ing. —ex′pli·ca′tion,** *n.* **—ex′pli·ca′tor,** *n.*

ex·plic·it (ek splis′it), *adj.* clearly expressed; distinctly stated; definite: *She gave such explicit directions that everyone understood them.* **—ex·plic′it·ly,** *adv.* **—ex·plic′it·ness,** *n.*

ex·plode (ek splōd′), *v.* **1** to burst with a loud noise; blow up: *The building was destroyed when the defective boiler exploded.* **2** to cause to explode: *Some people explode firecrackers on the Fourth of July.* **3** to burst forth noisily: *The speaker's remark was so funny the audience exploded with laughter.* **4** to increase suddenly: *The urban population in many nations has exploded.* **5** to cause to be rejected; destroy belief in: *Columbus and other navigators helped to explode the theory that the earth is flat.* ❏ *v.* **ex·plod·ed, ex·plod·ing.**

WORD STORY **Explode** comes from Latin words meaning "to clap" and "out." In Roman theater, bad actors were driven off the stage by loud clapping. When something explodes, it vanishes with a loud noise.

ex·ploit (ek′sploit *for noun;* ek sploit′ *for verb*), **1** *n.* a bold, unusual act; daring deed: *This book tells about the exploits of Robin Hood.* **2** *v.* to make use of: *A mine is exploited for its minerals.* **3** *v.* to make unfair or selfish use of: *Nations exploited their colonies, taking as much wealth out of them as they could.* **—ex·ploit′a·ble,** *adj.* **—ex·ploit′er,** *n.*

ex·ploi·ta·tion (ek′sploi tā′shən), *n.* **1** selfish or unfair use: *There are laws against the exploitation of children as workers.* **2** use: *the exploitation of the ocean as a source for food.*

ex·plo·ra·tion (ek′splə rā′shən), *n.* **1** act of traveling in little-known lands or seas or in outer space for the purpose of discovery. **2** act of going over carefully; a looking into closely; examining.

ex·plor·a·to·ry (ek splôr′ə tôr′ē), *adj.* of or done for exploration: *She had exploratory surgery to investigate the tumor.*

explore (def. 1)

ex·plore (ek splôr′), *v.* **1** to travel over little-known lands or seas or in outer space for the purpose of discovery: *explore the ocean's depths.* **2** to go over carefully; look into closely; examine: *explore a possibility.* ❏ *v.* **ex·plored, ex·plor·ing.**

WORD STORY **Explore** comes from Latin words meaning "to call out." In old times, hunters searching for animals would shout if they saw any, to bring other hunters and to make the animals run.

ex·plor·er (ek splôr′ər), *n.* person who explores.

Explorer Scout, person between 14 and 20 years old who is in the exploring program of the Boy Scouts of America, which focuses on vocational or hobby interests.

ex·plo·sion (ek splō′zhən), *n.* **1** act of bursting with a loud noise; a blowing up: *The explosion of the bomb shook the whole* neighborhood. **2** a loud noise caused by this: *People five miles away heard the explosion.* **3** a noisy outburst: *explosions of anger, an explosion of laughter.* **4** a sudden or rapid increase or growth: *The explosion of the world's population has created a shortage of food in many countries.*

ex·plo·sive (ek splō′siv), **1** *adj.* able to explode; tending to explode: *Gunpowder is explosive.* **2** *n.* substance that is able or likely to explode: *Explosives are used in making fireworks.* **3** *adj.* tending to burst forth noisily: *an explosive temper, explosive laughter.* **—ex·plo′sive·ly,** *adv.* **—ex·plo′sive·ness,** *n.*

ex·po (ek′spō), *n.* exposition (def. 1). ❏ *n., pl.* **ex·pos.**

ex·po·nent (ek spō′nənt), *n.* **1** someone or something that explains. **2** someone or something that stands as an example, type, or symbol of something: *Martin Luther King was a famous exponent of civil rights.* **3** a small number written above and to the right of a symbol or quantity to show how many times the symbol or quantity is to be used as a factor. EXAMPLES: $2^2 = 2 \times 2$; $a^3 = a \times a \times a$.

ex·po·nen·tial (ek′spō nen′shəl), *adj.* of algebraic exponents. **—ex′po·nen′tial·ly,** *adv.*

ex·port (ek spôrt′ *or* ek′spôrt *for verb;* ek′spôrt *for noun*), **1** *v.* to send goods out of one country for sale and use in another: *The United States exports corn.* ■ See Usage Note at **import. 2** *n.* article exported: *Cotton is an important export of the United States.* **3** *n.* act or fact of exporting: *the export of oil from the Arab nations.* **—ex·port′a·ble,** *adj.* **—ex′por·ta′tion,** *n.*

ex·port·er (ek spôr′tər *or* ek′spôr tər), *n.* person or company whose business is exporting.

ex·pose (ek spōz′), *v.* **1** to lay open; leave without protection; uncover: *We were exposed to the hot sun all day while fishing. All the children have been exposed to mumps.* **2** to make known; reveal: *She exposed the plot to the police.* **3** to bring someone into contact with something: *expose children to good music.* **4** to allow light to reach and act on a photographic film or plate. ❏ *v.* **ex·posed, ex·pos·ing. —ex·pos′er,** *n.*

ex·po·sé (ek′spō zā′), *n.* public exposure of crime, dishonesty, fraud, etc.: *a newspaper exposé of graft.* ❏ *n., pl.* **ex·po·sés.**

ex·po·si·tion (ek′spə zish′ən), *n.* **1** a public show or exhibition; expo. A world's fair with exhibits from many countries is an exposition. **2** speech or writing explaining a process, thing, or idea. **3** (in music) the first section of a movement, in which the principal themes are presented.

ex·pos·i·tor (ek spoz′ə tər), *n.* someone who explains.

ex·pos·i·to·ry (ek spoz′ə tôr′ē), *adj.* explanatory.

ex·pos·tu·late (ek spos′chə lāt), *v.* to reason earnestly with someone, protesting against something that person means to do or has done: *The teacher expostulated with the student about her poor work.* ❏ *v.* **ex·pos·tu·lat·ed, ex·pos·tu·lat·ing. —ex·pos′tu·la′tion,** *n.*

ex·po·sure (ek spō′zhər), *n.* **1** act of exposing; laying open; making known: *The exposure of the real criminal cleared the innocent suspect.* **2** condition of being exposed: *Exposure to the rain has ruined this machinery.* **3** position in relation to the sun and wind. A house with a southern exposure receives sun and wind from the south. **4** act of allowing light to reach and form a picture on a photographic film or plate. **5** a part of a roll of photographic film that holds one picture.

exposure meter, device for measuring the amount of light and the proper exposure time for taking photographs.

ex·pound (ek spound′), *v.* **1** to make clear; explain: *The teacher expounds each new principle in arithmetic to the class.* **2** to set forth or state in detail: *The Senator expounded her objections to the bill.* **—ex·pound′er,** *n.*

ex·pres·i·dent (eks′prez′ə dənt), *n.* a former president; living person who once was president, but no longer is.

a	hat	ė	term	ô	order	ch	child		a in about
ā	age	i	it	oi	oil	ng	long		e in taken
ä	far	ī	ice	ou	out	sh	she	ə	i in pencil
â	care	o	hot	u	cup	th	thin		o in lemon
e	let	ō	open	ů	put	ᴛʜ	then		u in circus
ē	equal	ò	saw	ü	rule	zh	measure		

ex·press (ek spres′), **1** v. to put into words: *Try to express your ideas clearly.* **2** v. to show by look, voice, or action; reveal: *Your smile expresses joy.* **3** adj. clear and definite: *It was his express wish that we should go without him.* **4** adj. special; particular: *She came for the express purpose of seeing you.* **5** n. a quick or direct means of sending things. Packages and money can be sent by express in trains or airplanes. **6** n. system or company that carries packages, money, etc. **7** v. to send by some quick means: *Express this package to Chicago.* **8** adv. by express; directly: *Please send this package express to Boston.* **9** adj. traveling fast and making few stops: *an express train.* **10** n. train, bus, elevator, etc., traveling fast and making few stops. **11** adj. for fast traveling: *an express highway.* ❑ n., pl. **ex·press·es** for 10. —**ex·press′·er,** n. —**ex·press′i·ble,** adj.

express yourself, to say what you think: *The speaker expressed himself clearly.*

ex·pres·sion (ek spresh′ən), n. **1** act of putting into words: *the expression of an idea.* **2** word or group of words used as a unit: *"Wise guy" is a slang expression.* **3** act of showing by look, voice, or action: *A sigh is often an expression of sadness.* **4** look that shows feeling: *The winners had happy expressions on their faces.* **5** a way of speaking, reading, singing or playing that brings out the meaning or beauty of something: *Try to read with more expression.* **6** any combination of constants, variables, and symbols expressing some mathematical operation or quantity.

ex·pres·sion·less (ek spresh′ən lis), adj. without expression: *an expressionless face, an expressionless voice.*

ex·pres·sive (ek spres′iv), adj. **1** expressing: *"Alas!" is a word expressive of sadness.* **2** full of expression; having much feeling, meaning, etc.: *"The cat's skin hung on its bones" is a more expressive sentence than "The cat was very thin."* —**ex·pres′sive·ly,** adv. —**ex·pres′sive·ness,** n.

ex·press·ly (ek spres′lē), adv. **1** plainly; definitely: *The package is not for you; you are expressly forbidden to touch it.* **2** on purpose; specially: *She came expressly to see you.*

ex·press·way (ek spres′wā′), n. highway built for high-speed, long-distance travel. An expressway has limited access, and a divider between the lanes of traffic going in opposite directions.

ex·pro·pri·ate (ek sprō′prē āt), v. to take land, possessions, etc., from the owner, especially for public use. ❑ v. **ex·pro·pri·at·ed, ex·pro·pri·at·ing.** —**ex·pro′pri·a′tion,** n. —**ex·pro′pri·a′tor,** n.

ex·pul·sion (ek spul′shən), n. **1** act of forcing out: *expulsion of air from the lungs.* **2** condition of being forced out: *expulsion from school for bad behavior.*

ex·punge (ek spunj′), v. to remove completely; erase: *to expunge certain remarks from the record.* ❑ v. **ex·punged, ex·pung·ing.** —**ex·pung′er,** n.

ex·pur·gate (ek′spər gāt), v. to remove objectionable passages or words from a book, letter, etc. ❑ v. **ex·pur·gat·ed, ex·pur·gat·ing.** —**ex′pur·ga′tion,** n. —**ex′pur·ga′tor,** n.

ex·qui·site (ek′skwi zit *or* ek·skwiz′it), adj. **1** very lovely; delicate: *These violets are exquisite.* **2** sharp; intense: *A toothache causes exquisite pain.* **3** of highest excellence; most admirable: *They have exquisite taste and manners.* —**ex′qui·site·ly,** adv. —**ex′qui·site·ness,** n.

exquisite (def. 1)
an exquisite pattern

ex·tant (ek′stənt *or* ek stant′), adj. still existing: *Some of George Washington's letters are extant.*

ex·tem·po·ra·ne·ous (ek stem′pə rā′nē əs), adj. spoken or done without preparation; offhand: *an extemporaneous speech.* [**Extemporaneous** comes from Latin words meaning "out of time." An extemporaneous speech is made with no time to prepare it.] —**ex·tem′po·ra′ne·ous·ly,** adv. —**ex·tem′po·ra′ne·ous·ness,** n.

ex·tend (ek stend′), v. **1** to stretch out: *extend your hand.* **2** to lengthen in time: *I am extending my vacation another week.* ■ See Synonym Study at **lengthen. 3** to continue; go on: *This beach extends for miles in both directions.* **4** to increase or enlarge: *They plan to extend their research in that field.* **5** to offer; give; grant: *This organization extends help to poor people.*

extended family, family consisting of parents, children, and other near relatives of varying generations and relationships, all living together in one household.

ex·tend·er (ek sten′dər), n. something that extends, especially a less expensive ingredient added to increase the bulk of a more expensive substance.

ex·ten·sion (ek sten′shən), n. **1** act of extending: *the extension of a vacation for three more days, the extension of a road.* **2** an extended part; addition: *The new extension to our school will make room for more students.* **3** telephone connected with the main telephone or with a switchboard but in a different location.

extension cord, an electric cord with a plug and a socket, used to connect a short cord to a source of power.

ex·ten·sive (ek sten′siv), adj. far-reaching; large: *an extensive park, extensive changes.* —**ex·ten′sive·ly,** adv. —**ex·ten′sive·ness,** n.

ex·ten·sor (ek sten′sər), n. muscle that straightens a leg, arm, or other part of the body when the muscle is contracted.

ex·tent (ek stent′), n. **1** size, length, amount, or degree to which a thing extends: *The extent of a judge's power is limited by law.* **2** something extended; extended space: *a vast extent of prairie.*

ex·ten·u·ate (ek sten′yü āt), v. to make the seriousness of a fault or an offense seem less; excuse in part. ❑ v. **ex·ten·u·at·ed, ex·ten·u·at·ing.** [**Extenuate** comes from Latin words meaning "to thin out." Extenuating circumstances make a misdeed seem less solid and important.] —**ex·ten′u·a′tion,** n.

ex·ten·u·at·ing (ek sten′yü āt ing), adj. making the seriousness of a fault or an offense seem less; partially excusing: *The teacher realized that there were extenuating circumstances causing the unhappy student's poor schoolwork.*

ex·te·ri·or (ek stir′ē ər), **1** n. outer part; outward appearance; outside: *The exterior of the house was made of brick. The gruff man has a harsh exterior but a kind heart.* **2** adj. on or for the outside; outer: *Exterior paint should be durable.* **3** adj. coming from without: *exterior influences.* —**ex·ter′i·or·ly,** adv.

ex·ter·mi·nate (ek stėr′mə nāt), v. to get rid of; destroy completely; kill: *This poison will exterminate rats.* ❑ v. **ex·ter·mi·nat·ed, ex·ter·mi·nat·ing.** —**ex·ter′mi·na′tion,** n.

ex·ter·mi·na·tor (ek stėr′mə nā′tər), n. someone or something that exterminates, especially someone whose business is exterminating fleas, cockroaches, bedbugs, rats, etc.

ex·ter·nal (ek stėr′nl), **1** adj. on the outside; outer: *An ear of corn has an external husk.* **2** n.pl. **externals,** clothing, manners, or other outward acts or appearances: *Don't judge people by mere externals.* **3** adj. for use only on the outside of the body: *Rubbing alcohol is an external remedy.* **4** adj. easily seen but not essential; superficial: *an external display of concern.* **5** adj. of or about international affairs; foreign: *War affects a nation's external trade.* —**ex·ter′nal·ly,** adv.

external ear, the outer part of the ear, including the passage leading to the middle ear.

ex·tinct (ek stingkt′), adj. **1** no longer existing. ■ See Synonym Study at **dead. 2** no longer active: *an extinct volcano.*

ex·tinc·tion (ek stingk′shən), n. act of bringing to an end; wiping out; destruction: *Physicians are working toward the extinction of many serious diseases.*

ex·tin·guish (ek sting′gwish), v. **1** to put out: *Water extinguished the fire.* **2** to bring to an end; wipe out; destroy: *One failure after another extinguished my hopes.* —**ex·tin′guish·a·ble,** adj.

ex·tin·guish·er (ek sting′gwish ər), n. a device for putting out fires; fire extinguisher.

ex·tir·pate (ek′stər pāt), v. to remove completely; destroy totally: *extirpate disease and poverty.* ❑ v. **ex·tir·pat·ed, ex·tir·pat·ing.** —**ex′tir·pa′tion,** n. —**ex′tir·pa′tor,** n.

ex·tol or **ex·toll** (ek stōl′), *v.* to praise highly; commend: *The newspapers extolled the mayor's plan for a new park.* ❑ *v.* **ex·tolled, ex·tol·ling. —ex·tol′ler,** *n.* **—ex·tol′ment,** *n.*

ex·tort (ek stôrt′), *v.* to obtain money, a promise, etc., by threats, force, fraud, or wrong use of authority: *Blackmailers try to extort money from their victims.* **—ex·tort′er,** *n.*

ex·tor·tion (ek stôr′shən), *n.* act of extorting.

ex·tor·tion·ate (ek stôr′shə nit), *adj.* much too great: *$200 for a softball glove is an extortionate price.*

ex·tor·tion·ist (ek stôr′shə nist), *n.* person guilty of extortion.

ex·tra (ek′strə), **1** *adj.* beyond what is usual, expected, or needed; additional: *extra pay.* **2** *n.* something extra; anything beyond what is usual, expected, or needed: *a new car equipped with many extras.* **3** *n.* a special edition of a newspaper: *The paper published an extra to announce the end of the war.* **4** *n.* person who is employed by the day to play minor parts in a movie: *Two hundred extras were hired for the crowd scene.* **5** *adv.* more than usually: *I am extra busy on Saturdays.* ❑ *n., pl.* **ex·tras.**

SYNONYM STUDY **Extra, spare,** and **surplus** all mean more than usual or necessary. **Extra** is the general word: *I have an extra umbrella if you need one.* **Spare** suggests that something is not usually needed: *There is a spare key for the garage.* **Surplus** suggests much more than is needed: *The restaurant gives surplus food to the shelter for the homeless.*

extra-, *prefix.* outside ___; beyond ___: *extracurricular = outside the curriculum.*

ex·tract (ek strakt′ *for verb;* ek′strakt *for noun*), **1** *v.* to pull out or draw out, usually with some effort: *extract a tooth, extract iron from the earth, extract a confession.* **2** *v.* to obtain by pressing, squeezing, etc.: *extract oil from olives.* **3** *v.* to obtain; derive: *extract comedy from confusion.* **4** *v.* to calculate a root of a number. **5** *v.* to take out a passage from a book, speech, etc.: *He extracted several sections of the article to read at the meeting.* **6** *n.* passage taken out of a book, speech, etc.: *He read several extracts from a book of poems.* **7** *n.* a concentrated preparation of a substance: *Vanilla extract, made from vanilla beans, is used as flavoring.* **—ex·tract′a·ble,** *adj.* **—ex·trac′tor,** *n.*

ex·trac·tion (ek strak′shən), *n.* **1** act of extracting or condition of being extracted: *the extraction of a tooth.* **2** origin; descent: *Miss del Rio is of Spanish extraction; her parents came from Spain.*

ex·tra·cur·ric·u·lar (ek′strə kə rik′yə lər), *adj.* outside the regular course of study: *Football, dramatics, and debating are extracurricular activities in our high school.*

ex·tra·dite (ek′strə dīt), *v.* **1** to give up a fugitive or prisoner to another state or nation: *England extradited the suspect to the United States.* **2** to gain extradition of such a person. ❑ *v.* **ex·tra·dit·ed, ex·tra·dit·ing. —ex′tra·dit′a·ble,** *adj.*

ex·tra·di·tion (ek′strə dish′ən), *n.* delivery of a fugitive or prisoner by one state or nation to another.

ex·tra·ga·lac·tic (ek′strə gə lak′tik), *adj.* outside our own galaxy: *extragalactic distances.*

ex·tra·ne·ous (ek strā′nē əs), *adj.* not essential: *The speaker made many extraneous remarks.*

ex·traor·di·nar·y (ek strôr′də ner′ē), *adj.* beyond what is ordinary; very unusual; very remarkable: *Eight feet is an extraordinary height for a person.* **—ex·traor′di·nar′i·ly,** *adv.*

ex·tra·sen·so·ry perception (ek′strə sen′sər ē), the perceiving of thoughts or actions through something other than the usual five senses.

ex·tra·ter·res·tri·al (ek′strə tə res′trē əl), **1** *adj.* beyond or outside the earth or its atmosphere. **2** *n.* an imaginary creature from outer space.

ex·trav·a·gance (ek strav′ə gəns), *n.* **1** careless and wasteful spending; wastefulness: *Their extravagance kept them in debt.* **2** an extravagant action, idea, purchase, etc.: *A mink coat is an extravagance.*

ex·trav·a·gant (ek strav′ə gənt), *adj.* **1** spending carelessly and wastefully: *An extravagant person has expensive tastes and habits.* **2** beyond the bounds of reason: *an extravagant price, extravagant praise.* **—ex·trav′a·gant·ly,** *adv.*

ex·trav·a·gan·za (ek strav′ə gan′zə), *n.* a very imaginative and complicated stage performance, movie, piece of music, etc. Musical comedies with elaborate scenery and gorgeous costumes are extravaganzas. ❑ *n., pl.* **ex·trav·a·gan·zas.**

extravaganza

ex·tra·ve·hic·u·lar (ek′strə vi hik′yə lər), *adj.* outside a spacecraft.

ex·treme (ek strēm′), **1** *adj.* much more than usual; very great; very strong: *She drove with extreme caution during the snowstorm.* ■ See Synonym Study at **very. 2** *adj.* going to the greatest possible lengths; very severe; very violent; drastic: *extreme measures, an extreme case.* **3** *adj.* at the very end; farthest possible; last: *He lives in the extreme western part of town.* **4** *n.* the first and last term in a proportion or series: *In the proportion, 2 is to 4 as 8 is to 16, 2 and 16 are the extremes.* **5** *n.* something extreme; one of two things as far or as different as possible from each other: *Joy and grief are two extremes of feeling.* **—ex·treme′ly,** *adv.* **—ex·treme′ness,** *n.*

go to extremes, to do or say too much: *A person who has 20 cats is going to extremes.*

in the extreme, to the highest degree.

ex·trem·ist (ek strē′mist), *n.* person who goes to extremes; supporter of extreme doctrines or practices.

ex·trem·i·ty (ek strem′ə tē), *n.* **1** the very end; farthest possible place; last part or point: *Alaska is at the western extremity of North America.* **2 extremities,** *pl.* the hands and feet. **3** very great danger or need: *People on a sinking ship are in extremity.* **4** extreme degree: *Joy is the extremity of happiness.* **5** an extreme action: *The government was forced to the extremity of rationing gas during the fuel shortage.* ❑ *n., pl.* **ex·trem·i·ties** for 1,5.

ex·tri·cate (ek′strə kāt), *v.* to set free from entanglements, difficulties, etc.; release: *I extricated the kitten from the net. He extricated me from a boring conversation.* ❑ *v.* **ex·tri·cat·ed, ex·tri·cat·ing. —ex′tri·ca′tion,** *n.*

ex·trin·sic (ek strin′sik), *adj.* **1** outside of a thing; coming from without; external: *extrinsic influences.* **2** not essential: *extrinsic differences.* **—ex·trin′si·cal·ly,** *adv.*

ex·tro·vert (ek′strə vėrt′), *n.* person who is interested in other people and in events, more than in private thoughts and feelings.

ex·tro·vert·ed (ek′strə vėr′tid), *adj.* interested in other people and in events, more than in private thoughts and feelings.

ex·trude (ek strüd′), *v.* **1** to thrust out; push out: *to extrude toothpaste from a tube.* **2** to shape plastics, rubber, etc., by forcing through dies. ❑ *v.* **ex·trud·ed, ex·trud·ing. —ex·trud′er,** *n.*

ex·tru·sion (ek strü′zhən), *n.* act or process of extruding or condition of being extruded.

ex·u·ber·ance (eg zü′bər əns), *n.* **1** a great abundance: *an exuberance of joy.* **2** high spirits.

a	hat	ė	term	ȯ	order	ch	child		a in about
ā	age	i	it	oi	oil	ng	long		e in taken
ä	far	ī	ice	ou	out	sh	she	ə	i in pencil
â	care	o	hot	u	cup	th	thin		o in lemon
e	let	ō	open	u̇	put	∓H	then		u in circus
ē	equal	ȯ	saw	ü	rule	zh	measure		

ex·u·ber·ant (eg zü′bər ənt), *adj.* abounding in health and high spirits; overflowing with good cheer: *I was in an exuberant mood all day.* —**ex·u′ber·ant·ly,** *adv.*

ex·u·da·tion (ek′syə dā′shən), *n.* **1** act of exuding. **2** something exuded.

ex·ude (eg züd′), *v.* **1** to come or send out in drops; ooze: *The pores in the skin exude sweat.* **2** to give forth: *Some people exude self-confidence.* ❏ *v.* **ex·ud·ed, ex·ud·ing.**

ex·ult (eg zult′), *v.* to be very glad; rejoice greatly: *The winners exulted in their victory.* —**ex·ult′ing·ly,** *adv.*

ex·ult·ant (eg zult′nt), *adj.* rejoicing greatly; exulting; triumphant: *an exultant shout.* —**ex·ult′ant·ly,** *adv.*

WORD STORY **Exultant** comes from Latin words meaning "to jump out." Great joy is so strong that it seems to burst forth, escaping self-control like an animal jumping over a fence.

ex·ul·ta·tion (eg′zul tā′shən *or* ek′sul tā′shən), *n.* great rejoicing; triumph: *There was exultation over our team's victory.*

ex·ur·bi·a (ek sėr′bē ə), *n.* region between a city's suburbs and the country.

eye (ī), **1** *n.* the organ of the body by which people and animals see. **2** *n.* the colored part of the eye; iris: *He has brown eyes.* **3** *n.* region surrounding the eye: *The blow gave her a black eye.* **4** *n.* **eyes,** *pl.* sense of seeing; vision; sight: *A jet pilot must have good eyes.* **5** *n.* ability to see small differences in things: *A good artist must have an eye for color.* **6** *n.* a look; glance: *I cast an eye over the books and quickly found one I liked.* **7** *v.* to look at; watch; observe: *The child eyed the monkey with great interest.* **8** *n.* Often, **eyes,** *pl.* way of thinking or considering; view; opinion; judgment: *In the coach's eyes, missing practice was serious.* **9** *n.* thing shaped like, resembling, or suggesting an eye. The little spots on potatoes, the hole for thread in a needle, and the loop in which a hook fastens are all called eyes. **10** *n.* the relatively calm, clear area at the center of a hurricane. ❏ *v.* **eyed, ey·ing** *or* **eye·ing.** ▪ Other words that sound like this are **ay, aye,** and **I.** —**eye′-less,** *adj.* —**eye′like′,** *adj.*

an eye for an eye, punishment as severe as the injury.

catch someone's eye, to attract someone's attention: *The bright red sign caught my eye.*

in the public eye, 1 often seen in public. **2** widely known.

keep an eye on, to look after; watch carefully: *Keep an eye on the baby while I go to the store.*

lay eyes on *or* **set eyes on,** to look at; see: *I never laid eyes on these people until today.*

make eyes at, to flirt with: *He was making eyes at that girl.*

open someone's eyes, to make someone see what is really happening.

see eye to eye, to agree entirely: *My parents and I do not see eye to eye on my weekly allowance.*

shut your eyes to, to refuse to see or consider; ignore: *We often shut our eyes to the faults of our friends.*

with an eye to, for; considering.

eye·ball (ī′bȯl′), **1** *n.* the eye without the surrounding lids and bony socket. It is shaped like a ball. **2** *v.* INFORMAL. to look at; stare at: *Everyone eyeballed the new kid.*

eye·brow (ī′brou′), *n.* hair that grows along the bony ridge just above the eye.

eye·drop·per (ī′drop′ər), *n.* dropper used to apply liquid medicine to the eyes.

eye·ful (ī′fül), *n.* **1** as much as the eye can see at one time. **2** a good look. **3** INFORMAL. a good-looking person. ❏ *n., pl.* **eye·fuls.**

eye·glass·es (ī′glas′əz), *n.pl.* pair of glass or plastic lenses, mounted in a frame, to correct defective eyesight; glasses; spectacles.

eye·lash (ī′lash′), *n.* **1** one of the hairs on the edge of the eyelid. **2** fringe of such hairs. ❏ *n., pl.* **eye·lash·es.** See picture at **eye.**

eye·let (ī′lit), *n.* **1** a small, round hole for a lace or cord to go through. **2** a metal ring around such a hole to strengthen it. **3** a small, round hole with stitches around it, used to make a pattern in embroidery. ▪ Another word that sounds like this is **islet.**

eye·lid (ī′lid′), *n.* the movable fold of skin, upper or lower, by means of which we can shut and open the eyes.

eye-o·pen·er (ī′ō′pə nər), *n.* a surprising event or discovery.

eye·piece (ī′pēs′), *n.* lens or set of lenses in a telescope, microscope, etc., nearest to the eye of the user.

eye shadow, makeup used to color the eyelids.

eye·sight (ī′sīt′), *n.* **1** power of seeing; sight: *A hawk has keen eyesight.* **2** range of vision; view: *The water was within eyesight.*

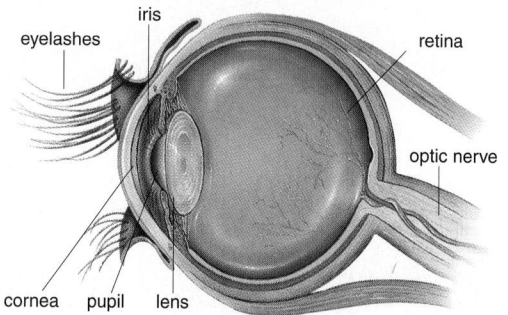

eyelashes · iris · retina · optic nerve · cornea · pupil · lens

eye (def. 1)

eye·sore (ī′sôr′), *n.* something unpleasant to look at: *That garbage heap is an eyesore.*

eye·spot (ī′spot′), *n.* a simple organ for sensing light, found in certain lower animals.

eye·stalk (ī′stȯk′), *n.* stalk on which the eye of a lobster, shrimp, etc., is located.

eye·strain (ī′strān′), *n.* pain or tiredness of the eyes caused by overuse, or the lack of corrective glasses.

eye·tooth (ī′tüth′), *n.* an upper canine tooth. ❏ *n., pl.* **eye·teeth.**

eye·wash (ī′wäsh′), *n.* **1** a liquid preparation to clean or heal the eyes. **2** INFORMAL. deceiving flattery.

eye·wit·ness (ī′wit′nis), *n.* person who actually sees or has seen some act or happening, and thus can give testimony concerning it. ❏ *n., pl.* **eye·wit·ness·es.**

eyr·ie *or* **eyr·y** (âr′ē *or* ir′ē), *n.* aerie. ❏ *n., pl.* **eyr·ies.** ▪ Other words that can sound like this are **airy** and **eerie.**

E·ze·ki·el (i zē′kē əl), *n.* **1** a Hebrew prophet. **2** book of the Bible. [Ezekiel comes from a Hebrew word meaning "God makes strong."]

Ez·ra (ez′rə), *n.* **1** Hebrew scribe who led a revival of Judaism in the 400s or 300s B.C. **2** book of the Bible. [Ezra comes from a Hebrew word meaning "helper."]

F or **f** (ef), *n.* the sixth letter of the English alphabet. ❑ *n., pl.* **F's** or **f's.**

f, focal length.

F, symbol for fluorine.

f., **1** false. **2** female. **3** feminine. **4** forte. **5** franc.

F., **1** February. **2** Friday.

F or **F.,** Fahrenheit.

fa (fä), *n.* the fourth tone of the musical scale. ❑ *n., pl.* **fas.**

FAA or **F.A.A.,** Federal Aviation Agency (an agency of the U.S. Department of Transportation, established to promote the safety and usefulness of airplane traffic, which it controls).

fa·ble (fā′bəl), *n.* **1** story which is made up to teach a lesson. Fables are often about animals who can talk, such as *The Hare and the Tortoise* and *The Fox and the Crow.* **2** legend; myth. **3** an untrue story; falsehood.

fa·bled (fā′bəld), *adj.* told about in fables, legends, or myths.

fab·ric (fab′rik), *n.* **1** woven or knitted material; cloth. Velvet, denim and linen are fabrics. **2** way in which a thing is put together; frame or structure: *the fabric of society.*

fab·ri·cate (fab′rə kāt), *v.* **1** to make by putting parts together; build or manufacture: *Cars are fabricated from parts made in different factories.* **2** to make up; invent a story, lie, excuse, etc. ❑ *v.* **fab·ri·cat·ed, fab·ri·cat·ing. —fab′ri·ca′tor,** *n.*

fab·ri·ca·tion (fab′rə kā′shən), *n.* **1** something fabricated, especially a false story, lie, excuse, etc. **2** manufacture.

fab·u·lous (fab′yə ləs), *adj.* **1** wonderful; exciting. ■ See Synonym Study at **wonderful. 2** not believable; amazing: *The painting was sold at a fabulous price.* **3** of a fable; imaginary: *The centaur is a fabulous monster.* **4** like a fable. **—fab′u·lous·ly,** *adv.* **—fab′u·lous·ness,** *n.*

fa·cade (fə säd′), *n.* **1** the front part of a building, especially the part that faces a street or an open space. **2** outward appearance that is deceptive or misleading. [**Facade** comes from a Latin word meaning "face." A building's facade is the side you usually see first, the side that faces the street.]

fa·çade (fə säd′), *n.* facade. ❑ *n., pl.* **fa·çades.**

face (fās), **1** *n.* the front part of the head. The eyes, nose, and mouth are parts of the face. **2** *n.* look; expression: *There were many sad faces after the test.* **3** *n.* an ugly or funny look made by twisting the face: *We made faces at each other.* **4** *n.* the front or important side of something: *the face of a playing card.* **5** *n.* outward appearance: *The tall buildings changed the face of the city.* **6** *v.* to have the face or front toward; be opposite to: *Please face the camera. The house faces the street.* **7** *v.* to meet bravely or boldly: *face danger.* **8** *v.* to present itself to: *A crisis faced us.*

a	hat	ė	term	ô	order	ch	child		
ā	age	i	it	oi	oil	ng	long		a in about
ä	far	ī	ice	ou	out	sh	she		e in taken
â	care	o	hot	u	cup	th	thin	ə	i in pencil
e	let	ō	open	ù	put	ᵺ	then		o in lemon
ē	equal	ò	saw	ü	rule	zh	measure		u in circus

9 *n.* dignity; self-respect; personal importance: *to lose face.* **10** *v.* to cover with a different material: *A wooden house is sometimes faced with brick.* **11** *v.* to cover the inside or outside edges of cuffs, a collar, etc., with the same or different material for protection or trimming: *The lapels of my jacket are faced with velvet.* **12** *n.* any of the planes or surfaces that bound a solid figure. A cube has six faces. ❑ *v.* **faced, fac·ing.**

face down, to face fearlessly; meet boldly.

face off, (in hockey) to begin or resume play with a faceoff.

face to face, 1 with faces toward each other: *The enemies stood face to face.* **2** in direct awareness of: *Hearing the rattlesnake, we knew we were face to face with danger.*

face up to, to meet boldly; admit and accept.

fly in the face of, to disobey openly; defy.

in someone's face, very competitive; ready to quarrel; aggressive: *I won't play basketball with him because he's always in my face.*

in the face of, 1 in the presence of. **2** in spite of: *He insisted he was right in the face of facts that proved he was wrong.*

to someone's face, in someone's presence; openly; boldly.

face card, king, queen, or jack of playing cards.

face·lift (fās'lift'), *n.* **1** operation to tighten the skin of the face and remove wrinkles. **2** a superficial change to improve your appearance, or to modernize something: *The front of the store got a facelift, but it's the same inside.*

face·off (fās'ôf'), *n.* (in hockey or lacrosse) the act of putting the puck or ball in play when the referee drops it between two opposing players.

fac·et (fas'it), *n.* **1** one of the small, polished surfaces of a cut gem. **2** any one of several sides or views: *Selfishness was a facet of her character that we seldom saw.* **3** the outside part of one of the tiny units of a compound eye in insects and crustaceans.

fa·ce·tious (fə sē'shəs), *adj.* **1** having the habit of joking; being slyly humorous. **2** said in fun; not to be taken seriously: *facetious remarks.* **—fa·ce'tious·ly,** *adv.* **—fa·ce'tious·ness,** *n.*

facet (def. 1)
gem with many facets

face value, 1 value stated on a bond, check, note, bill, etc. **2** apparent worth, meaning, etc.

fa·cial (fā'shəl), **1** *adj.* of or for the face: *facial expressions, a facial tissue.* **2** *n.* massage or treatment of the face. **—fa'cial·ly,** *adv.*

fac·ile (fas'əl), *adj.* **1** easily done or used; taking little effort: *facile tasks, facile methods.* **2** moving, acting, or working easily or rapidly: *a facile tongue for gossip, to write in a facile style.* **3** not carefully thought out; done or made in a careless way: *facile answers.* **—fac'ile·ly,** *adv.* **—fac'ile·ness,** *n.*

fa·cil·i·tate (fə sil'ə tāt), *v.* to make easy; lessen the labor of; help bring about; assist: *Computers facilitate the solving of many problems.* ❑ *v.* **fa·cil·i·tat·ed, fa·cil·i·tat·ing. —fa·cil'i·ta'tion,** *n.* **—fa·cil'i·ta'tor,** *n.*

fa·cil·i·ty (fə sil'ə tē), *n.* **1** Usually, **facilities,** *pl.* something that makes an action easy; aid; convenience: *laundry facilities, research facilities.* **2** power to do anything easily and quickly; skill in using the hands or mind: *His facility with music suggests that he may have a real talent.* **3** absence of difficulty; ease: *He swam the length of the pool with great facility.* ❑ *n., pl.* **fa·cil·i·ties** for 1,2.

fac·ing (fā'sing), *n.* **1** a covering of different material for ornament, protection, etc.: *a wooden house with a brick facing.* **2** material put around the inside or outside edge of cloth to protect or trim it: *a blue coat with red facings on the collar and cuffs.*

fac·sim·i·le (fak sim'ə lē), *n.* **1** an exact copy or likeness. **2** fax. [See word history information at **fax.**]

fact (fakt), *n.* **1** thing known to be true or to have really happened: *It is a fact that the Pilgrims sailed on the Mayflower in 1620.* **2** what is true; truth: *The fact of the matter is, I really did want to go to the dance even though I said I didn't.* **3** thing said or sup-

posed to be true or to have really happened: *We doubted his facts.*
as a matter of fact, in fact.
in fact, truly; really.

fac·tion (fak'shən), *n.* group of persons who stand up for their side or act together for some common purpose against the rest of a larger group: *A faction in our club tried to make the president resign.* **—fac'tion·al,** *adj.*

fac·tious (fak'shəs), *adj.* fond of stirring up disputes. **—fac'tious·ly,** *adv.* **—fac'tious·ness,** *n.*

fac·tor (fak'tər), **1** *n.* any one of the causes that helps bring about a result; one element in a situation: *Price was a factor in my decision to buy this car.* **2** *n.* any of the numbers or expressions which, when multiplied together, form a product: *The numbers 5, 3, and 4 are factors of 60.* **3** *v.* to separate into factors.

fac·to·ri·al (fak tôr'ē əl), in mathematics: **1** *adj.* of or involving a factor. **2** *n.* the product of a number multiplied by all the numbers from that number down to 1. EXAMPLE: The factorial of 4, shown in mathematical symbols as 4!, is $4 \times 3 \times 2 \times 1 = 24$.

fac·to·ri·za·tion (fak'tə rə zā'shən), *n.* (in mathematics) a separating of a number into its factors.

fac·to·ry (fak'tər ē), *n.* building or group of buildings where things are made with machines. ❑ *n., pl.* **fac·to·ries.**

fac·to·tum (fak tō'təm), *n.* person employed to do all kinds of work. [**Factotum** comes from Latin words meaning "to do" and "everything." A factotum has a very broad job description.]

fac·tu·al (fak'chü əl), *adj.* concerned with fact; containing facts: *I wrote a factual account of the field trip for the school newspaper.* **—fac'tu·al·ly,** *adv.*

fac·ul·ty (fak'əl tē), *n.* **1** the teachers of a school, college, or university. **2** **faculties,** *pl.* powers of the mind or body: *Although 100 years old now, she still has all her faculties.* **3** power or ability to do some special thing: *She has a great faculty for arithmetic.* ❑ *n., pl.* **fac·ul·ties.**

fad (fad), *n.* something everybody is very much interested in for a short time; fashion or craze: *No one plays that game anymore; it was only a fad.*

fad·dish (fad'ish), *adj.* **1** inclined to follow fads. **2** like a fad. **—fad'dish·ly,** *adv.* **—fad'dish·ness,** *n.*

fade (fād), *v.* **1** to make or become less bright; lose or cause to lose color: *Sunlight faded the curtains.* **2** to lose freshness or strength; wither: *Our garden flowers faded at the end of the summer.* **3** to die away; disappear little by little: *The sound of the train faded after it went by.* ❑ *v.* **fad·ed, fad·ing.**

fade-in (fād'in'), *n.* in a movie or TV show, the gradual appearance of a new picture on the screen.

fade-out (fād'out'), *n.* **1** the gradual fading from the screen of a scene in a movie or TV show. **2** a gradual disappearance.

fag (fag), *v.* to tire by work: *After climbing to the top of the mountain we were completely fagged out.* ❑ *v.* **fagged, fag·ging.**

fag·ot or **fag·got** (fag'ət), *n.* bundle of sticks or twigs tied together for fuel: *to build a fire with fagots.*

Fahd (fäd), *n.* born 1923, king and prime minister of Saudi Arabia since 1982.

Fahr·en·heit (far'ən hīt), *adj.* of, based on, or according to a scale for measuring temperature on which 32 degrees marks the freezing point of water and 212 degrees marks the boiling point. The **Fahrenheit thermometer** uses this scale.

WORD STORY The **Fahrenheit** scale was named for Gabriel D. Fahrenheit, a German physicist and maker of scientific instruments. In the early 1700s he invented the mercury thermometer and created the scale to use with it.

fail (fāl), *v.* **1** to try but not succeed in doing or becoming something: *He tried hard to learn to skate, but he failed.* **2** to not do; neglect: *She failed to follow our advice.* **3** to be of no use to when needed; abandon; desert: *When I needed their help, they failed me.* **4** to be missing; be not enough: *When our supplies failed, we had no food.* **5** to lose strength; grow weak; die away: *The patient's heart was failing.* **6** to stop working or operating: *It was so cold, the engine failed.* **7** to not be able to pay what you owe; become bankrupt: *The company lost all its money and failed in* *business.* **8** to be unsuccessful in an examination, etc.; receive a failing grade: *You failed the test because you didn't study.* **9** to give a failing grade to a student.

without fail, surely; certainly: *You must do your chores without fail.*

fail·ing (fā′ling), **1** *n.* fault; weakness; defect: *One of his failings is forgetfulness.* **2** *prep.* in the absence of; lacking; without: *Failing good weather, the tennis match will be played indoors.*

fail-safe (fāl′sāf′), *adj.* **1** having or being a built-in safety device that is automatically activated in case of some failure or malfunction: *fail-safe emergency brakes.* **2** guaranteed to be safe from failure; foolproof: *a fail-safe design.*

fail·ure (fā′lyər), *n.* **1** a lack of success: *Her efforts to learn to play the guitar ended in failure.* **2** the act of not doing; neglecting: *Failure to obey orders on a ship is mutiny.* **3** the condition of not being enough: *The failure of the wheat crop caused the price of bread to rise.* **4** the condition of losing strength; becoming weak: *heart failure.* **5** the act of stopping or not operating: *engine failure.* **6** the condition of being unable to pay what you owe; bankruptcy. **7** someone or something that has failed: *The picnic was a failure because it rained.*

faint (fānt), **1** *adj.* not clear or plain; dim: *faint colors, a faint idea.* **2** *adj.* weak; feeble: *a faint voice, a faint attempt.* **3** *v.* to fall into a state of shock, in which someone is unconscious for a short time: *After the car accident the driver fainted.* **4** *n.* a brief loss of consciousness: *As the driver got out of the car after the accident, he collapsed in a faint.* **5** *adj.* about to lose consciousness; dizzy and weak: *I felt quite faint from hunger.* **6** *adj.* lacking courage; cowardly: *a faint heart.* ■ Another word that sounds like this is **feint.** —**faint′ly,** *adv.* —**faint′ness,** *n.*

faint·heart·ed (fānt′här′tid), *adj.* lacking courage; cowardly; timid. —**faint′heart′ed·ly,** *adv.* —**faint′heart′ed·ness,** *n.*

fair[1] (fâr), **1** *adj.* not favoring one more than others; just; honest: *Try to be fair to everyone.* **2** *adj.* according to the rules: *fair play.* **3** *adj.* not good and not bad; average: *That movie wasn't one of my favorites; it was only fair.* **4** *adj.* not dark; light: *A blond person has fair hair and skin.* **5** *adj.* not cloudy or stormy; clear; sunny: *The weather will be fair today.* **6** *adj.* OLD USE. pleasing to see; beautiful: *our fair city.* **7** *adj.* without spots or stains; clean: *He typed a fair copy of the letter.* **8** *adv.* in a just manner; honestly: *to play fair.* **9** *adj.* (in baseball) falling within the base lines; not foul: *The batter hit a fair ball past the first baseman.* ■ Another word that sounds like this is **fare.** —**fair′ness,** *n.*

fair[2] (fâr), *n.* **1** a public show of farm products and goods of a certain region: *Prizes were given for the best livestock at the county fair.* **2** a gathering of buyers and sellers, often held at the same place every year: *a trade fair, an art fair.* **3** sale of articles; bazaar: *Our church held a fair to raise money for charity.* ■ Another word that sounds like this is **fare.**

Fair·banks (fâr′bangks), *n.* city in central Alaska.

fair game, 1 animals or birds that it is lawful to hunt. **2** a suitable object of attack: *The playful puppy thought I was fair game.*

fair·ground (fâr′ground′), *n.* place outdoors where fairs are held.

fair-haired (fâr′hârd′), *adj.* **1** having fair hair; blond or blonde. **2** favorite: *fair-haired boy.*

fair·ly (fâr′lē), *adv.* **1** in a fair manner; justly; honestly: *That salesperson deals fairly with all customers.* **2** moderately; rather: *She is a fairly good pupil, neither bad nor very good.* **3** absolutely; positively: *He was fairly beside himself with anger.*

fair-mind·ed (fâr′mīn′did), *adj.* not prejudiced; just; impartial. —**fair′-mind′ed·ly,** *adv.* —**fair′-mind′ed·ness,** *n.*

fair play, just and honest action.

fair·way (fâr′wā′), *n.* the part of a golf course between the tee and putting green where the grass is kept short.

fair·y (fâr′ē), *n.* (in stories) a tiny being with magic powers. ❑ *n., pl.* **fair·ies.** —**fair′y·like′,** *adj.*

WORD STORY **Fairy** comes from a Latin word meaning "to speak." **Fate** and **fatal** come from the same word. Ancient Romans believed that events were controlled by the three Fates, goddesses who spoke, or made decisions, about the future. These decisions often involved matters of life and death. Fairies, like the Fates, were believed to affect human events in supernatural ways.

fair·y·land (fâr′ē land′), *n.* **1** place where the fairies are supposed to live. **2** a very pleasant or delightful place.

fairy tale, 1 story about fairies. **2** something said that is not true; falsehood; lie.

faith (fāth), *n.* **1** belief without proof; trust: *We have faith in our friends.* ■ See Synonym Study at **belief. 2** belief in God or in God's promises. **3** what someone believes. **4** religion: *the Jewish faith, the Christian faith.* **5** loyalty.

break faith, to break your promise.

in bad faith, dishonestly.

keep faith, to keep your promise.

faith·ful (fāth′fəl), **1** *adj.* worthy of trust; loyal: *a faithful friend. Six workers received awards for long and faithful service.* ■ See Synonym Study at **loyal. 2** *adj.* true to fact; accurate: *The witness gave a faithful account of the event.* **3** *n.pl.* **the faithful, a** loyal followers of a religion. **b** loyal followers or supporters. —**faith′ful·ly,** *adv.* —**faith′ful·ness,** *n.*

faith·less (fāth′lis), *adj.* failing in your duty; breaking your promises; not loyal: *a faithless friend.* —**faith′less·ly,** *adv.* —**faith′less·ness,** *n.*

fa·ji·ta (fä hē′tä), *n.* thin strip of meat soaked in flavoring, then broiled or grilled and served with others like it as a Mexican food. ❑ *n., pl.* **fa·ji·tas.**

fake (fāk), **1** *n.* something false: *The diamond ring was a fake.* **2** *adj.* intended to deceive; not real; false: *a fake fur, fake money.* **3** *v.* to make something false appear real in order to deceive; counterfeit: *to fake someone else's signature.* **4** *v.* to pretend: *to fake illness. I wasn't really crying; I was only faking.* **5** *n.* person who fakes. ❑ *v.* **faked, fak·ing.** —**fak′er,** *n.*

fak·er·y (fā′kər ē), *n.* act or result of making something false: *Mom said I didn't have a cold and could stop my fakery.*

fa·kir (fə kir′ *or* fā′kər), *n.* a Muslim or Hindu holy man who lives by begging. Fakirs sometimes do extraordinary things, such as lying upon sharp knives.

WORD STORY Some people who claim to be fakirs are only fakers. Their amazing feats are often simply a magician's tricks. **Fakir** and **faker** are not related, however. **Fakir** comes from an Arabic word meaning "poor man" because fakirs live by begging. The origin of **faker** is unknown.

fa·la·fel (fə lä′fəl), *n.* **1** a small ball or patty made from ground chickpeas and spices, then fried in oil. **2** sandwich made from these balls or patties and lettuce, tomatoes, etc., in pita bread.

fal·con (fôl′kən *or* fal′kən), *n.* **1** any of various swift-flying hawks with short, curved bills and long claws and wings. **2** any hawk trained to hunt and kill birds and small game. In the Middle Ages, hunting with falcons was a popular sport. [**Falcon** comes from a Latin word meaning "sickle." Like a sickle, the falcon's beak and claws are hooked and sharp.]

falcon (def. 1)—up to 20 in. (51 cm) long

fal·con·er (fôl′kə nər *or* fal′kə nər), *n.* **1** person who hunts with falcons. **2** person who breeds and trains falcons.

a	hat	ė	term	ô	order	ch	child		a in about
ā	age	i	it	oi	oil	ng	long		e in taken
ä	far	ī	ice	ou	out	sh	she	ə	i in pencil
â	care	o	hot	u	cup	th	thin		o in lemon
e	let	ō	open	u̇	put	ᴛʜ	then		u in circus
ē	equal	ȯ	saw	ü	rule	zh	measure		

313

fal·con·ry (fôl′kən rē or fal′kən rē), n. 1 sport of hunting with falcons. 2 the training of falcons to hunt.

Falk·land Islands (fôk′lənd or fôlk′lənd), group of British islands in the S Atlantic, east of the Strait of Magellan, claimed also by Argentina. See **Patagonia** for map.

fall (fôl), 1 v. to drop or come down from a higher place: *The snow falls fast. Leaves fall from the trees.* 2 n. act of dropping from a higher place: *a fall from a horse.* 3 n. amount that comes down: *We had a heavy fall of snow last winter.* 4 n. distance that anything drops or comes down: *The fall of the river here is two feet.* 5 n. Usually, **falls**, pl. fall of water; waterfall: *Niagara Falls. Many tourists come to see the falls.* 6 v. to come down suddenly from a standing position: *A baby who is learning to walk often falls.* 7 n. act of coming down suddenly from a standing position: *The child had a bad fall.* 8 v. to hang down: *The draperies in the living room fall to the floor.* 9 v. to be directed downward: *He blushed, and his eyes fell. She placed the lamp so the light would fall on her book.* 10 n. ruin; destruction; downfall: *the fall of an empire.* 11 n. **the Fall**, (in the Bible) the sin of Adam and Eve in yielding to temptation and eating the forbidden fruit. 12 v. to lose position or power: *The ruler fell from the people's favor.* 13 v. to be captured, overthrown, or destroyed: *The fort fell after the enemy's violent attack.* 14 v. to drop wounded or dead; be killed: *Many fell in the battle.* 15 v. to pass into some condition, position, etc.: *She fell sick. The baby fell asleep. The boy and girl fell in love.* 16 v. to come as if by dropping: *When night falls, the stars appear.* 17 v. to come by chance or lot: *Our choice fell on her.* 18 v. to come to pass; happen; occur: *My birthday falls on Sunday this year.* 19 v. to have proper place or position: *The accent of "over" falls on the first syllable.* 20 n. proper place or position: *The fall of the accent is on the first syllable.* 21 v. to become lower or less: *Prices fell sharply. The water in the river has fallen two feet. When they saw me, their voices fell.* 22 n. act of becoming lower or less: *a fall in prices.* 23 v. to be divided: *The story falls into five parts.* 24 v. to look sad or disappointed: *His face fell at the news.* 25 v. to slope downward: *The land falls gradually to the beach.* 26 n. a downward slope. 27 n. season of the year between summer and winter; autumn. 28 adj. of, for, or coming in the fall: *fall clothes, fall plowing.* 29 n. way of throwing or being thrown to the mat in wrestling. ❏ v. **fell, fall·en, fall·ing.**

fall back, to go toward the rear; retreat: *The enemy fell back as our army advanced.*

fall back on, 1 to go back to for safety. **2** to turn to for help or support.

fall behind, to fail to keep up.

fall in, to take a place in line: *"Fall in!" said the officer to the soldiers.*

fall in with, 1 to meet: *On our trip, we fell in with some interesting people.* **2** to agree with: *They fell in with our plans.*

fall off, to become less; drop: *The profits of the business fell off last month.*

fall on or **fall upon,** to attack: *The invading army fell on the city during the night.*

fall out, 1 to leave a place in line: *"Fall out!" said the officer to the soldiers.* **2** to stop being friends; quarrel: *She has fallen out with her friends.*

fall short of, to fail to equal: *The sale wasn't a failure, but it did fall short of the success we had expected.*

fall through, to fail: *Her plans fell through.*

fall to, 1 to begin: *They fell to and worked with a will.* **2** to begin to attack, eat, etc.: *When food was served, they fell to.*

fall under, to belong under; be classified as: *Whales fall under the class of mammals.*

ride for a fall, to act so as to invite danger or trouble.

fal·la·cious (fə lā′shəs), adj. not logical: *It is fallacious reasoning to base a general rule on just two or three instances.* —**fal·la′cious·ly,** adv. —**fal·la′cious·ness,** n.

fal·la·cy (fal′ə sē), n. 1 a false idea; mistaken belief; error: *It is a fallacy that riches always bring happiness.* 2 mistake in reasoning; misleading or unsound argument. ❏ n., pl. **fal·la·cies.**

fall·en (fô′lən), 1 v. past participle of **fall:** *Much rain has fallen.* 2 adj. dropped: *feet with fallen arches.* 3 adj. face down; down

on the ground; down flat: *a fallen tree.* 4 adj. overthrown; destroyed: *a fallen fortress.* 5 adj. dead: *fallen heroes.*

fall guy, INFORMAL. person left to take the blame for something or face the consequences of something; scapegoat.

fal·li·ble (fal′ə bəl), adj. liable to be deceived or mistaken; liable to make mistakes. —**fal′li·bil′i·ty,** n. —**fal′li·bly,** adv.

fall·ing-out (fô′ling out′), n. disagreement; quarrel. ❏ n., pl. **fall·ings-out** or **fall·ing-outs.**

falling star, meteor.

fall·off (fôl′ôf′), n. decline; decrease: *a falloff in sales.*

Fal·lo·pi·an tubes (fə lō′pē ən), pair of slender tubes through which eggs from the ovaries pass to the uterus.

fall·out (fôl′out′), n. the radioactive particles and dust that fall to the earth after a nuclear explosion.

fal·low (fal′ō), adj. plowed and left unseeded for a season or more; uncultivated: *We shall let the north 40 acres lie fallow next spring.* —**fal′low·ness,** n.

fallow deer, a small European deer with a yellowish coat that is spotted with white in the summer.

false (fôls), 1 adj. not true; not correct; wrong: *false statements.* 2 adj. not truthful; lying: *a false witness.* 3 adj. not loyal; not faithful; deceitful: *A person who tells someone else what you said in secret is a false friend.* 4 adj. used to deceive; deceiving: *false advertising.* A ship sails under **false colors** when it raises the flag of a country other than its own. A **false bottom** in a trunk or drawer is used to form a secret compartment. 5 adj. (in music) not true in pitch: *a false note.* 6 adj. not real; artificial: *false teeth, false diamonds.* 7 adj. based on wrong notions: *False pride kept her from accepting help when she lost her job.* 8 adv. in a false manner. ❏ adj. **fals·er, fals·est.** —**false′ly,** adv. —**false′ness,** n.

play someone false, to deceive, cheat, trick, or betray someone: *He thought they were engaged, but she played him false and married for money.*

SYNONYM STUDY **False** and **counterfeit** both mean not real. **False** does not always suggest deception: *The clown wore a big false nose.* **Counterfeit** always suggests an attempt to deceive: *We found a $50 bill, but it turned out to be counterfeit.*

false arrest, an illegal arrest, such as one for which there is no evidence at all.

false·hood (fôls′hud), n. 1 a false statement; lie. 2 quality of being false.

false step, a mistake; error.

fal·set·to (fôl set′ō), 1 n. an unnaturally high-pitched male voice. 2 adv. in falsetto. ❏ n., pl. **fal·set·tos.**

WORD STORY **Falsetto** comes from a Latin word meaning "to deceive." Adult male singers using a falsetto voice may deceive the ear by sounding like women.

fal·si·fy (fôl′sə fī), v. to make false; change in order to deceive; misrepresent: *He falsified his tax records.* ❏ v. **fal·si·fied, fal·si·fy·ing.** —**fal′si·fi′a·ble,** adj. —**fal′si·fi·ca′tion,** n. —**fal′si·fi′er,** n.

fal·si·ty (fôl′sə tē), n. 1 the fact of being false: *Education often shows the falsity of superstitions.* 2 something false; falsehood. ❏ n., pl. **fal·si·ties** for 2.

Fal·staff (fôl′staf), n. Sir **John**, a fat, jolly, swaggering soldier, impudent and dishonest, in three of Shakespeare's plays.

fal·ter (fôl′tər), v. 1 to lose courage; draw back or hesitate; waver: *I faltered for a moment before I made my decision.* 2 to move unsteadily; stumble: *The horse faltered on the rocky path.* 3 to speak in hesitating or broken words; stammer: *Greatly embarrassed, he faltered out his thanks.* —**fal′ter·er,** n. —**fal′ter·ing·ly,** adv.

fame (fām), n. fact or condition of being very well known; having much said or written about you: *Athletes may win fame at the Olympic games.*

famed (fāmd), adj. famous.

fa·mil·ial (fə mil′ē əl), adj. 1 of or about a family or families: *familial concerns.* 2 occurring more often among people who are related to each other than among the general population: *familial diseases.*

fa·mil·iar (fə mil′yər), *adj.* **1** well-known; common: *a familiar face. French was as familiar to him as English.* **2** well-acquainted: *She is familiar with French and English.* **3** not formal; friendly: *a familiar attitude.* **4** too friendly; presuming; forward: *His manner is too familiar.* —**fa·mil′iar·ly,** *adv.*

fa·mil·iar·i·ty (fə mil′yar′ə tē), *n.* **1** close acquaintance; knowledge: *A cab driver needs great familiarity with the city streets.* **2** thing done or said in a familiar way: *I dislike such familiarities as the use of my nickname by people that I have just met.* **3** lack of formality or ceremony. □ *n., pl.* **fa·mil·iar·i·ties** for 2.

fa·mil·iar·ize (fə mil′yə rīz′), *v.* **1** to make someone well acquainted with something: *Before playing the new game, familiarize yourself with the rules.* **2** to make well known: *Exploration in space has familiarized the word "astronaut."* □ *v.* **fa·mil·iar·ized, fa·mil·iar·iz·ing.** —**fa·mil′iar·i·za′tion,** *n.* —**fa·mil′iar·iz′er,** *n.*

fam·i·ly (fam′ə lē), *n.* **1** parents or a parent and child or children; household: *Our town has about a thousand families.* **2** children of a father and mother; offspring: *bring up a large family.* **3** group of people living in the same house. **4** all of someone's relatives: *His family holds an annual reunion.* **5** group of related people; tribe or clan: *the Roosevelt family.* **6** group of related living things. Lions, tigers, and leopards belong to the cat family. A family ranks below an order and above a genus. **7** any group of related or similar things. □ *n., pl.* **fam·i·lies.**

Family Allowance, (in Canada) an allowance paid by the federal government for children under age 18 who are cared for by parents or guardians.

family name, a last name; surname.

family room, a room in a home used for family activities, such as watching TV, conversation, listening to music, or reading.

family tree, diagram showing how all the members and ancestors of a family are related.

family tree

fam·ine (fam′ən), *n.* a serious lack of food in a place, causing much starvation: *Many people died during the famine in India.*

fam·ished (fam′isht), *adj.* very hungry: *We were famished after not eating anything for ten hours.*

fa·mous (fā′məs), *adj.* very well known; much talked about or written about; noted: *The famous singer was greeted by a crowd.*

fa·mous·ly (fā′məs lē), *adv.* excellently; very well: *The new neighbors are getting along famously with everyone.*

fan¹ (fan), **1** *n.* device made up of blades or vanes attached to a hub and rotated by an electric motor. It is used to stir the air in order to cool a room, an engine, or yourself, or to remove odors. **2** *n.* device made of stiff paper, held in the hand and waved back and forth to stir the air in order to cool your face. **3** *v.* to stir, blow, or move air on or toward: *She fanned herself.* **4** *v.* to stir up;

arouse: *The cheering crowd fanned our enthusiasm.* **5** *n.* anything spread out like an open fan: *The peacock spread out its tail into a beautiful fan.* **6** *v.* to spread out like an open fan: *The campers fanned out across the field, looking for the lost child.* **7** *v.* (in baseball) to strike out. □ *v.* **fanned, fan·ning.** —**fan′like′,** *adj.* —**fan′ner,** *n.*

fan² (fan), *n.* **1** person extremely interested in some sport, the movies, TV, etc.: *A baseball fan would hate to miss the championship game.* **2** admirer of an actor, writer, etc.

fa·nat·ic (fə nat′ik), **1** *n.* person who is very enthusiastic about an activity, belief, way of life, or the like: *My friend is a fanatic about fresh air and refuses to stay in a room with the windows closed.* **2** *adj.* very enthusiastic; extremely zealous: *a fanatic interest in tennis.* [See Word Story at **fan².**] —**fa·nat′i·cal·ly,** *adv.*

fa·nat·i·cal (fə nat′ə kəl), *adj.* fanatic. —**fa·nat′i·cal·ness,** *n.*

fa·nat·i·cism (fə nat′ə siz′əm), *n.* unreasonable enthusiasm.

fan·cied (fan′sēd), *adj.* imagined: *a fancied insult.*

fan·ci·er (fan′sē ər), *n.* person who is especially interested in something: *A dog fancier is interested in breeding show dogs.*

fan·ci·ful (fan′sə fəl), *adj.* **1** imaginary; unreal; suggested by fancy: *I read a fanciful story about talking butterflies.* ■ See Synonym Study at **imaginary.** **2** having a good imagination: *The fanciful author wrote a book of fairy tales.* **3** showing fancy in design; quaint or odd in appearance: *fanciful decorations.* —**fan′ci·ful·ly,** *adv.* —**fan′ci·ful·ness,** *n.*

fan·cy (fan′sē), **1** *adj.* not plain or simple; decorated; ornamental: *a fancy dinner for guests, fancy trimming.* **2** *adj.* requiring much skill: *fancy skating.* **3** *adj.* much too high: *fancy prices.* **4** *adj.* of high quality or of an unusual kind: *fancy fruit.* **5** *v.* to picture to yourself; imagine: *Can you fancy yourself on the moon?* ■ See Synonym Study at **imagine.** **6** *n.* power to imagine; imagination: *Dragons, fairies, and giants are creatures of fancy.* **7** *n.* something imagined or supposed; idea; notion: *I had a sudden fancy to go swimming.* **8** *v.* to have an idea or belief; suppose: *I fancy that is right, but I am not sure.* **9** *n.* a liking; fondness: *They took a great fancy to each other and became close friends.* **10** *v.* to be fond of; like: *Do you fancy the idea of a picnic?* □ *v.* **fan·cied, fan·cy·ing;** *n., pl.* **fan·cies;** *adj.* **fan·ci·er, fan·ci·est.** —**fan′ci·ly,** *adv.* —**fan′ci·ness,** *n.*

fan·fare (fan′fâr), *n.* **1** a short tune or call played on trumpets, bugles, or the like. **2** a loud show of activity, talk, etc.: *The new bridge was opened with great fanfare by city officials.*

fang (fang), *n.* **1** a long, pointed tooth of a dog, wolf, snake, etc. Poisonous snakes have hollow or grooved fangs. **2** something like it. —**fang′like′,** *adj.*

fanged (fangd), *adj.* having fangs.

fan·tail (fan′tāl′), *n.* **1** tail, end, or part spread out like an open fan. **2** pigeon, goldfish, or other animal whose tail spreads out like an open fan.

fan·ta·size (fan′tə sīz), *v.* to have fanciful notions or ideas; daydream: *They fantasized about what they would do if they had six months of vacation time.* □ *v.* **fan·ta·sized, fan·ta·siz·ing.**

fan·tas·tic (fan tas′tik), *adj.* **1** very odd; wild and strange in shape or manner: *People often see fantastic things in their dreams.* **2** very fanciful; imaginary; unreal: *The idea that machines could be made to fly seemed fantastic 200 years ago.* **3** unbelievably good: *The class prepared a fantastic science exhibition.* —**fan·tas′ti·cal·ly,** *adv.*

a	hat	ė	term	ô	order	ch	child		
ā	age	i	it	oi	oil	ng	long	ə	a in about
ä	far	ī	ice	ou	out	sh	she		e in taken
â	care	o	hot	u	cup	th	thin		i in pencil
e	let	ō	open	u̇	put	ᴛʜ	then		o in lemon
ē	equal	ȯ	saw	ü	rule	zh	measure		u in circus

fan·ta·sy (fan′tə sē), *n.* **1** creation or work of the imagination. Many stories, such as *Gulliver's Travels* and *Alice in Wonderland,* are fantasies. **2** picture existing only in the mind; mental image or illusion; daydream: *I have a fantasy in which I win a million dollars.* ❑ *n., pl.* **fan·ta·sies.**

far (fär), **1** *adv.* a long way; a long way off: *She studied far into the night. Far in the past, the Norsemen began sailing westward.* **2** *adj.* not near; distant: *They live in a far country. The moon is far from Earth.* **3** *adj.* more distant: *We live on the far side of the hill.* **4** *adv.* very much: *It is far better to go by train.* ❑ *adv., adj.* **far·ther, far·thest** *or* **fur·ther, fur·thest.**

as far as, to the distance, point, or degree that: *Tall maples lined the road as far as I could see. As far as I'm concerned, we can leave right now.*

by far, very much.

far and away, very much.

far and near, everywhere.

far and wide, everywhere; even in distant parts.

how far, to what distance, point, or degree; how much.

so far, 1 until now: *So far this week we've enjoyed fine weather.* **2** to this or that point: *I had read just so far when the phone rang.*

so far as, to the extent that: *So far as I know, his statement is true.*

far·ad (far′əd), *n.* unit for measuring the ability of a device, such as a capacitor, to store an electric charge.

Far·a·day (far′ə dā), *n.* **Michael,** 1791-1867, English physicist and chemist. He discovered that a magnet in motion generates an electric current.

far·a·way (fär′ə wā′), *adj.* **1** far away; distant; remote: *He read of faraway places in geography books.* **2** dreamy: *A faraway look in her eyes showed that she was thinking of something else.*

farce (färs), *n.* **1** a play full of ridiculous happenings, absurd actions, and unreal situations, meant to be very funny. **2** something that is ridiculous, unorganized, and absurd: *Without rules, the game turned into a farce.*

WORD STORY **Farce** comes from a French word meaning "to stuff." Hundreds of years ago in France, comedy skits were performed between the acts of religious plays. These skits were called stuffing because they filled the interval like bread in a roast chicken.

far·ci·cal (fär′sə kəl), *adj.* of or like a farce; ridiculous; absurd. **—far′ci·cal·ly,** *adv.*

far cry, a long way.

fare (fâr), **1** *n.* the money that someone pays to ride in a taxi, bus, train, airplane, etc. **2** *n.* passenger: *The cabdriver picked up three fares at the airport.* **3** *n.* food: *They dined on plain and simple fare.* **4** *v.* to get along; get on; do: *She is faring well in school.* ❑ *v.* **fared, far·ing.** ■ Another word that sounds like this is **fair.**

Far East, China, Japan, and other parts of E Asia, including Korea and E Siberia. **—Far Eastern.**

fare·well (fâr′wel′), **1** *interj., n.* good-by. **2** *interj., n.* good wishes when saying good-by. **3** *n.* departure; leave-taking. **4** *adj.* parting; last: *a farewell kiss. The singer gave a farewell performance.*

far·fetched (fär′fecht′), *adj.* not likely or probable: *His excuse was too farfetched for anyone to believe.*

far·flung (fär′flung′), *adj.* covering a large area; widely spread: *Many U.S. banks have far-flung operations around the world.*

Far·go (fär′gō), *n.* city in SE North Dakota.

farm (färm), **1** *n.* piece of land which someone uses to raise crops or animals. **2** *v.* to raise crops or animals either to eat or to sell: *Her parents farm for a living.* **3** *v.* to cultivate land: *They farm 50 acres.* **4** *n.* a place where someone raises a certain kind of animal for food or fur: *a fish farm, a mink farm.*

farm out, 1 to rent out: *He farms out the right to pick berries on his land.* **2** to assign to a baseball team in a minor league. **3** to send out work to be done elsewhere: *The company farms out small jobs to free-lance editors and designers.*

WORD STORY **Farm** comes from a Latin word meaning "not changing." **Firm**[1] comes from the same word. **Farm** used to mean "rented land," for which the same money had to be paid every month, a firm price.

farm·er (fär′mər), *n.* person who owns or works on a farm.

farm·hand (färm′hand′), *n.* person who works on a farm.

farm·house (färm′hous′), *n.* house to live in on a farm. ❑ *n., pl.* **farm·hous·es** (färm′hou′ziz).

farm·ing (fär′ming), *n.* business of raising crops or animals on a farm; agriculture.

farm·land (färm′land′), *n.* land used or suitable for raising crops or grazing.

farm·stead (färm′sted), *n.* farm with its buildings.

farm·yard (färm′yärd′), *n.* yard connected with farm buildings or enclosed by them.

farmyard

Far North, the Arctic and nearby regions of Canada.

far-off (fär′ôf′), *adj.* far away; distant.

far-out (fär′out′), *adj.* INFORMAL. **1** very unusual; not at all customary: *a far-out idea.* **2** very difficult to understand: *far-out research.* **3** extreme: *far-out political views.*

far-reach·ing (fär′rē′ching), *adj.* having a wide influence or effect; extending far: *Computers are having far-reaching effects today.*

far·ri·er (far′ē ər), *n.* blacksmith who shoes horses.

far·row (far′ō), *n.* litter of pigs.

far-see·ing (fär′sē′ing), *adj.* **1** able to see far. **2** looking ahead; planning wisely for the future.

Far·si (fär′sē), *n.* Persian (def. 3).

far·sight·ed (fär′si′tid), *adj.* **1** seeing distant things more clearly than near ones; not seeing nearby objects clearly. Farsighted people often wear glasses, especially when they get older. **2** looking ahead; planning wisely for the future; shrewd; prudent: *Farsighted people save money for the future.* **—far′sight′ed·ly,** *adv.* **—far′sight′ed·ness,** *n.*

far·ther (fär′ᴛʜər), **1** *adj.* more distant: *Three miles is farther than two.* **2** *adv.* at or to a greater distance: *We walked farther than we meant to and were very tired by the time we got home.* **3** *adj., adv.* further. ❑ *adj., adv.* **far, far·thest.**

far·ther·most (fär′ᴛʜər mōst′), *adj.* most distant; farthest: *He has traveled to the farthermost points of the earth.*

far·thest (fär′ᴛʜist), **1** *adj.* most distant: *the farthest journey of the space age. Ours is the house farthest down the road.* **2** *adv.* to or at the greatest distance: *She hit the ball farthest.* **3** *adv.* most: *Their ideas were the farthest advanced at that time.* ❑ *adj., adv.* **far, far·ther.**

far·thing (fär′ᴛʜing), *n.* a former British coin equal to a fourth of a British penny.

Far West, the part of the United States between the Rocky Mountains and the Pacific Ocean. **—Far Western.**

fas·ci·nate (fas′n āt), *v.* to interest greatly; attract very strongly; charm: *She was fascinated by the designs and colors in African art.* ❑ *v.* **fas·ci·nat·ed, fas·ci·nat·ing. —fas′ci·nat′ing·ly,** *adv.* **—fas′ci·na′tor,** *n.*

fas·ci·nat·ing (fas′n ā′ting), *adj.* **1** extremely interesting; absorbing: *a fascinating game, a fascinating book.* ■ See Synonym Study at **interesting.** **2** very attractive; enchanting; charming. **—fas′ci·nat′ing·ly,** *adv.*

fas·ci·na·tion (fas′n ā′shən), *n.* **1** the state of being interested greatly in something: *The audience watched the magician in fascination.* **2** very strong attraction; charm; enchantment.

fas·cism or **Fas·cism** (fash′iz′əm), *n.* **1** the form of government in Italy from 1922 to 1943, under Benito Mussolini. **2** the principles or methods of this or any similar government, or of a political party favoring such a government. Under fascism, a country is ruled by a dictator, with strong control of industry and labor by the central government, great restrictions upon the freedom of individuals, and extreme nationalism and militarism.

WORD STORY   Fascism comes from a Latin word meaning "bundle." A bundle of sticks tied around an ax was a symbol of authority in ancient Rome. Italian dictator Benito Mussolini began using this symbol in 1919. You may find pictures of the Roman symbol on public buildings and monuments or even on old U.S. dimes.

fas·cist or **Fas·cist** (fash′ist), **1** *n.* person who favors and supports fascism. **2** *adj.* of or about fascism or fascists.

fash·ion (fash′ən), **1** *n.* way a thing is made, shaped, or done; manner: *to walk in a peculiar fashion.* **2** *n.* custom of a time in dress, manners, speech, etc.; style: *the latest fashion in shoes.* **3** *v.* to make, shape, or form: *to fashion a whistle out of wood.* —**fash′ion·er,** *n.*
after a fashion or **in a fashion**, in some way or other; not very well: *He plays the violin, after a fashion.*

fash·ion·a·ble (fash′ə nə bəl), *adj.* **1** following the fashion; in fashion; stylish: *They replaced their old clothes with fashionable new outfits.* **2** of, like, or used by people who set the styles: *They are members of a fashionable club.* —**fash′ion·a·ble·ness,** *n.* —**fash′ion·a·bly,** *adv.*

fashion (def. 2)
fashion of the middle 1800s

fast¹ (fast), **1** *adj.* moving, acting, or doing with speed; quick; rapid; swift: *She is a fast runner.* ■ See Synonym Study at **quick.** **2** *adv.* quickly; rapidly; swiftly: *Airplanes go fast.* **3** *adj.* showing a time ahead of the correct time: *My watch is fast, which is why I got here so early.* **4** *adj.* concerned only with pleasure; too wild: *lead a fast life of drinking and gambling.* **5** *adj.* firm; secure; tight: *a fast hold on a rope.* **6** *adv.* firmly; securely; tightly: *He held fast as the sled went on down the hill.* **7** *adj.* loyal; faithful: *fast friends.* **8** *adj.* not fading easily: *Good cloth is dyed with fast color.* **9** *adj.* adapted for speed: *a fast track.* **10** *adv.* thoroughly; soundly: *fast asleep.*

fast² (fast), **1** *v.* to go without food; eat little or nothing; go without certain kinds of food: *Some people fast for religious reasons.* **2** *n.* act of fasting. **3** *n.* day or time of fasting.

fast·back (fast′bak′), *n.* car with a roof that slopes down toward the rear in a single curve.

fas·ten (fas′n), *v.* **1** to tie, lock, or make hold together in any way; make stay in place: *fasten a seat belt, fasten a door.* **2** to attach; connect: *try to fasten the blame on others.* **3** to direct; fix: *The dog fastened its eyes on the stranger.*

fas·ten·er (fas′n ər), *n.* **1** person who fastens. **2** attachment or device used to fasten something together. A zipper is a fastener.

fas·ten·ing (fas′n ing), *n.* thing used to fasten something. Locks, bolts, clasps, hooks, buttons, etc., are all fastenings.

fast-food (fast′füd′), *adj.* of or serving food that is prepared quickly, such as hamburgers, pizza, fried chicken, pasta, salads, etc.: *fast-food restaurants.*

fas·tid·i·ous (fa stid′ē əs), *adj.* hard to please; dainty in taste; easily disgusted: *a fastidious dresser, a fastidious eater.* —**fas·tid′i·ous·ly,** *adv.* —**fas·tid′i·ous·ness,** *n.*

fast·ness (fast′nis), *n.* a strong, safe, place; stronghold: *The bandits hid in their mountain fastness.* ❏ *n., pl.* **fast·ness·es.**

fat (fat), **1** *n.* a white or yellow oily substance formed in the bodies of animals. Fat is also found in plants, especially in some seeds. Fats are made up chiefly of carbon, hydrogen, and oxygen. **2** *n.* animal tissue made up mainly of such a substance. **3** *adj.* consisting of or containing fat; oily: *fat meat.* **4** *adj.* having much flesh; fleshy; plump; well-fed: *a nice fat chicken.* **5** *adj.* extremely fleshy and heavy; greatly overweight. ■ This meaning of **fat** is sometimes considered offensive. **6** *adj.* profitable: *a fat government contract.* **7** *v.* to fatten. ❏ *adj.* **fat·ter, fat·test;** *v.* **fat·ted, fat·ting.** —**fat′ness,** *n.*

SYNONYM STUDY   **Fat, stout,** and **portly** all mean having too much body weight. **Fat** means any sort of being overweight—from well-fed to unhealthy excess: *Last winter our dog got much less exercise and grew fat.* **Stout** suggests a thick but firm body and is often used in a kindly way: *She buys her clothes in the Stylishly Stout Shop.* **Portly** suggests dignified stoutness: *The actor's rich, deep voice suited his portly, slow-moving body.*

fa·tal (fā′tl), *adj.* **1** causing death: *a fatal accident.* **2** causing destruction or ruin: *The loss of all our money was fatal to our plans.* **3** important; decisive; fateful: *At last the fatal day for the contest arrived.* [See Word Story at **fairy.**] —**fa·tal′ly,** *adv.*

fa·tal·ism (fā′tl iz′əm), *n.* belief that fate controls everything that happens.

fa·tal·ist (fā′tl ist), *n.* believer in fatalism. —**fa·tal·is′tic,** *adj.* —**fa′tal·is′ti·cal·ly,** *adv.*

fa·tal·i·ty (fā tal′ə tē), *n.* a fatal accident or happening; death: *Careless driving causes thousands of fatalities every year.* ❏ *n., pl.* **fa·tal·i·ties.**

fat·back (fat′bak′), *n.* salt pork from the upper part of a side of pork.

fate (fāt), *n.* **1** power supposed to fix beforehand and control what is to happen. Fate is beyond any person's control. **2** your lot or fortune; what happens to a person, group, etc.: *History shows the fate of many nations.* **3** what becomes of someone or something: *The jury decided the fate of the accused.* **4** Fates, *pl.* (in Greek and Roman myths) the three goddesses who controlled human life. One spun the thread of life, one decided how long it should be, and one cut it off. [See Word Story at **fairy.**] ■ Another word that can sound like this is **fete.**

WORD FAMILY   Fate and the words below are related. They all come from a Latin word meaning "to speak."

affable	fairy	fatal	infantry
fable	fame	infamous	preface
fabulous	famous	infant	

fat·ed (fā′tid), *adj.* controlled or destined by fate: *A fortuneteller told me that I was fated to be a great leader.*

fate·ful (fāt′fəl), *adj.* **1** determining what is to happen; important; decisive: *a fateful battle of the war.* **2** showing what will happen according to fate; prophetic: *fateful words.* **3** causing death, destruction, or ruin; disastrous: *a fateful blow.* —**fate′ful·ly,** *adv.* —**fate′ful·ness,** *n.*

fa·ther (fä′THər), **1** *n.* a male parent. **2** *n.* **Father,** God. **3** *v.* to be the father of: *He fathered four daughters.* **4** *v.* to take care of; act as father to: *father an orphan.* **5** *n.* person who is like a father. **6** *n.* a male ancestor; forefather: *the customs of our fathers.* **7** *n.* man who did important work as a maker or leader: *George Washington is often called the father of our country.* **8** *v.* to be the cause of; make; originate: *Edison fathered many inventions.* **9** *n.* **Father,** title of respect for a priest: *Father Walker.* —**fa′ther·like′,** *adj.*

fa·ther·hood (fä′THər húd), *n.* condition of being a father.

fa·ther-in-law (fä′THər in lô′), *n.* father of your husband or wife. ❏ *n., pl.* **fathers-in-law.**

fa·ther·land (fä′THər land′), *n.* **1** your native country. **2** land of your ancestors.

fa·ther·less (fä′THər lis), *adj.* having no father: *a fatherless child.*

a	hat	ė	term	ô	order	ch	child		⎧ a in about
ā	age	i	it	oi	oil	ng	long		e in taken
ä	far	ī	ice	ou	out	sh	she	ə	i in pencil
â	care	o	hot	u	cup	th	thin		o in lemon
e	let	ō	open	ù	put	ᴛʜ	then		⎩ u in circus
ē	equal	ò	saw	ü	rule	zh	measure		

fa·ther·ly (fä′ᴛʜər lē), *adj.* of or like a father; kindly: *a fatherly person, a fatherly smile.* —**fa′ther·li·ness,** *n.*

Father's Day, the third Sunday in June, set apart in the United States in honor of fathers.

fath·om (faᴛʜ′əm), **1** *n.* unit of measure equal to six feet. It is used mostly in measuring the depth of water and the length of ships' ropes, cables, etc. **2** *v.* to measure the depth of. **3** *v.* to get to the bottom of; understand fully: *I can't fathom what you mean.* ❑ *n., pl.* **fath·oms** or **fath·om.** —**fath′om·a·ble,** *adj.*

fath·om·less (faᴛʜ′əm lis), *adj.* **1** too deep to be measured; bottomless: *The stream disappeared into a fathomless abyss.* **2** impossible to be fully understood: *the fathomless riddle of the origin of the universe.* —**fath′om·less·ness,** *n.*

fa·tigue (fə tēg′), **1** *n.* weariness caused by hard work or effort: *I felt extreme fatigue after studying for four hours.* ■ See Synonym Study at **tired. 2** *v.* to make weary or tired; cause fatigue in: *Getting too little sleep will fatigue a person.* **3** *n.pl.* **fatigues,** work clothes or uniform worn by soldiers for routine work. ❑ *v.* **fa·tigued, fa·ti·guing.**

fat·ten (fat′n), *v.* **1** to make fat: *to fatten beef cattle for market.* **2** to become fat: *The pigs fattened on corn.* —**fat′ten·er,** *n.*

fat·ty (fat′ē), *adj.* **1** of or containing fat. **2** like fat; oily; greasy. ❑ *adj.* **fat·ti·er, fat·ti·est.** —**fat′ti·ness,** *n.*

fatty acid, any of a group of organic acids, many of which are found in animal and vegetable fats and oils.

fat·u·ous (fach′ü əs), *adj.* stupid but self-satisfied; foolish; silly. —**fat′u·ous·ly,** *adv.* —**fat′u·ous·ness,** *n.*

fau·cet (fó′sit), *n.* device having a valve for turning on or off a flow of liquid from a pipe or a container holding it; tap; spigot.

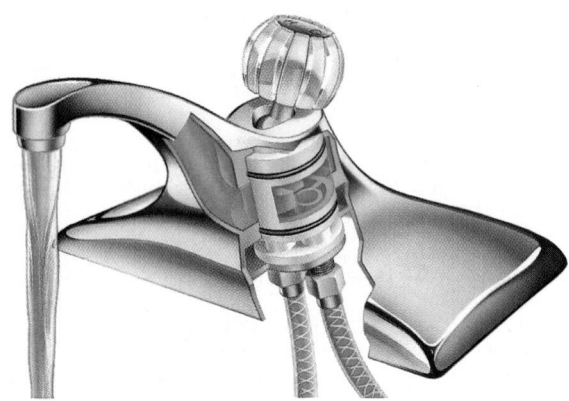

faucet

Faulk·ner (fók′nər), *n.* **William,** 1897-1962, American writer of novels and short stories. He won the 1949 Nobel Prize for literature. ■ Many of **William Faulkner's** novels are set in the same imaginary Southern county and involve the same families.

fault (fólt), **1** *n.* cause for blame; responsibility: *Whose fault was it?* **2** *n.* weakness or defect; a failing: *Carelessness is her greatest fault.* **3** *n.* a break in the earth's crust, with the mass of rock on one side of the break pushed up, down, or sideways. **4** *n.* failure to serve the ball properly or into the right place in tennis and similar games. **5** *v.* to find fault with: *The teacher could not fault us on our math.*

at fault, deserving blame; wrong.

find fault, to find mistakes; complain.

find fault with, to object to; criticize.

to a fault, too much; excessively: *She is generous to a fault.*

fault·find·er (fólt′fin′dər), *n.* someone who finds fault; someone who complains.

fault·find·ing (fólt′fin′ding), **1** *n.* act of finding fault. **2** *adj.* finding fault; complaining.

fault·less (fólt′lis), *adj.* without a single fault or defect; perfect: *The violinist gave a faultless performance.* —**fault′less·ly,** *adv.* —**fault′less·ness,** *n.*

fault·y (fól′tē), *adj.* having faults; wrong; imperfect; defective: *The leak in the faucet was caused by a faulty valve.* ❑ *adj.* **fault·i·er, fault·i·est.** —**fault′i·ly,** *adv.* —**fault′i·ness,** *n.*

faun (fón), *n.* (in Roman myths) a creature like a man, but with the ears, horns, tail, and legs of a goat. ■ Another word that sounds like this is **fawn.**

fau·na (fó′nə), *n.* animals as a group: *The fauna of Australia is unique.* ❑ *n., pl.* **fau·nas.**

Faust (foust), *n.* (in German legends) a man who sold his soul to the devil in return for youth, knowledge, and magic powers.

fave (fāv), *n.* SLANG. favorite.

fa·vor (fā′vər), **1** *n.* act of kindness: *Will you do me a favor?* **2** *v.* to like; approve; prefer: *We favor her plan.* **3** *n.* liking; approval: *They will look with favor on your plan.* **4** *n.* more than fair treatment: *Parents should not show favor toward one of their children.* **5** *v.* to give more than fair treatment to: *The teacher favors you.* **6** *v.* to treat gently; go easy on: *The dog favors its sore foot when it walks.* **7** *n.* a small token given to every guest at a party, dinner, etc.: *Small hats were used as favors at the party.* **8** *v.* to look like: *That girl favors her mother.* —**fa′vor·er,** *n.*

in favor of, 1 on the side of; supporting. **2** to the advantage of; helping.

in someone's favor, to someone's benefit: *The bank made an error in my favor.*

fa·vor·a·ble (fā′vər ə bəl), *adj.* **1** showing approval: *"Yes" is a favorable answer to a request.* **2** pleasing: *a favorable impression.* **3** to your advantage; helping; promising: *A favorable wind made the boat go faster.* —**fa′vor·a·ble·ness,** *n.* —**fa′vor·a·bly,** *adv.*

fa·vor·ite (fā′vər it), **1** *adj.* liked better than others: *What is your favorite flower?* **2** *n.* the one liked better than others; person or thing liked very much: *He is a favorite with everybody.* **3** *n.* person, horse, etc., expected to win a contest.

fa·vor·it·ism (fā′vər ə tiz′əm), *n.* act of giving better treatment to some people than to others; having favorites: *A teacher should try not to show favoritism.*

fawn[1] (fón), **1** *n.* deer less than a year old. **2** *n.* a light, yellowish brown. **3** *adj.* light yellowish brown. ■ Another word that sounds like this is **faun.** —**fawn′like′,** *adj.*

fawn[2] (fón), *v.* **1** to try to win favors by flattery or other insincere behavior toward someone: *Many relatives fawned on the rich old woman.* **2** to show fondness by crouching, wagging the tail, licking the hand, etc., as dogs do. ■ Another word that sounds like this is **faun.** —**fawn′er,** *n.* —**fawn′ing·ly,** *adv.*

fax (faks), **1** *n.* an electronic process for sending printed pages and photographs over telephone lines and reproducing exact copies at the receiving end. **2** *n.* fax machine. **3** *n.* the exact copy made. **4** *v.* to send printed matter and photographs by such a process. ❑ *n., pl.* **fax·es.** [**Fax** is short for **facsimile,** which comes from Latin words meaning "to make" and "similar."]

fax machine, an electronic device for sending and receiving copies over telephone lines.

fay (fā), *n.* fairy.

faze (fāz), *v.* to disturb; worry; bother: *Nothing we said fazed her; she did as she pleased.* ❑ *v.* **fazed, faz·ing.** ■ **Faze** is almost always used negatively: *After years as a criminal lawyer, nothing fazes her.* ■ Another word that sounds like this is **phase.**

FBI or **F.B.I.,** Federal Bureau of Investigation (a bureau of the U.S. Department of Justice, established to investigate violations of federal laws and safeguard national security).

FCC or **F.C.C.,** Federal Communications Commission (an agency of the U.S. government established to regulate communications by telephone, telegraph, radio, and television).

F clef, bass clef.

F.D., Fire Department.

FDA or **F.D.A.,** Food and Drug Administration (an agency of the U.S. Department of Health and Human Services, established to promote the safety of food, cosmetics, and drugs, and to make sure that drugs and other medical products are effective).

Fe, symbol for iron.

fe·al·ty (fē′əl tē), *n.* (in the Middle Ages) loyalty and duty owed by a vassal to his feudal lord: *The nobles swore fealty to the king.*

fear (fir), **1** *n.* a feeling that danger or evil is near; being afraid: *a fear of heights, shake with fear.* **2** *v.* to be afraid of: *Our cat fears big dogs.* **3** *v.* to feel fear; have an uneasy feeling or idea: *I fear that I am late.* **4** *n.* cause for fear; danger; chance: *There is no fear of our losing this game.* **5** *n.* an uneasy feeling: *a fear for your life.* —**fear′er,** *n.*

fear·ful (fir′fəl), *adj.* **1** causing fear; terrible; dreadful: *a fearful dragon.* **2** feeling fear; frightened: *fearful of the dark.* **3** showing fear; caused by fear: *fearful cries.* **4** very bad, unpleasant, ugly, etc.: *I have a fearful cold.* —**fear′ful·ly,** *adv.* —**fear′ful·ness,** *n.*

fear·less (fir′lis), *adj.* without fear; afraid of nothing; brave; daring. —**fear′less·ly,** *adv.* —**fear′less·ness,** *n.*

fear·some (fir′səm), *adj.* causing fear; frightful: *a fearsome sight.* —**fear′some·ly,** *adv.* —**fear′some·ness,** *n.*

fea·si·ble (fē′zə bəl), *adj.* **1** able to be done easily; possible without difficulty or damage: *The committee selected the plan that seemed most feasible.* **2** likely; probable: *The witness's explanation of the accident sounded feasible.* —**fea′si·bil′i·ty,** *n.* —**fea′si·ble·ness,** *n.* —**fea′si·bly,** *adv.*

feast (fēst), **1** *n.* a rich meal prepared for some special occasion, usually a joyous one; banquet: *We went to the wedding feast.* **2** *v.* to eat a rich meal; have a feast: *They feasted on turkey and pumpkin pie at Thanksgiving.* **3** *v.* to provide a rich meal for: *The king feasted his friends.* **4** *v.* to give pleasure or joy to; delight: *We feasted our eyes on the sunset.* **5** *n.* a religious festival or celebration: *Easter is an important Christian feast; Passover is an important Jewish feast.* —**feast′er,** *n.*

feast (def. 1)

feat (fēt), *n.* a great or unusual deed; act showing great skill, strength, or daring. ▪ Another word that sounds like this is **feet.**

feath·er (feᴛн′ər), **1** *n.* one of the light, thin growths that cover a bird's skin. **2** *n.* something like a feather in shape or lightness. **3** *v.* to supply or cover with feathers. **4** *v.* to turn edgeways: *feather an oar.* —**feath′er·less,** *adj.*

feather in your cap, something to be proud of.

feather bed, **1** a very soft, warm mattress filled with feathers. **2** bed with such a mattress.

feath·er·bed·ding (feᴛн′ər bed′ing), *n.* the practice of forcing employers to hire more workers than needed for a particular job.

feathered serpent, Quetzalcoatl.

feath·er·weight (feᴛн′ər wāt′), *n.* boxer who weighs more than 118 pounds (54 kilograms) and less than 126 pounds (57 kilograms).

feath·er·y (feᴛн′ər ē), *adj.* **1** having feathers; covered with feathers. **2** like feathers; soft. **3** light; flimsy. —**feath′er·i·ness,** *n.*

fea·ture (fē′chər), **1** *n.* part of the face. Your eyes, nose, mouth, chin, and forehead are your features. **2** *n.* a distinct part or quality; thing that stands out and attracts attention: *Your plan has many good features.* **3** *n.* a full-length motion picture: *They are showing a good feature this week.* **4** *n.* a special article, comic strip, etc., in a newspaper. **5** *v.* to give special attention to; make a feature of: *The local newspapers featured the mayor's speech.* ❑ *v.* **fea·tured, fea·tur·ing.**

fea·ture·less (fē′chər lis), *adj.* without distinct features.

Feb., February.

Feb·ru·ar·y (feb′rü er′ē *or* feb′yü er′ē), *n.* the second month of the year. It has 28 days except in leap years, when it has 29. ❑ *n., pl.* **Feb·ru·ar·ies.**

fe·cal (fē′kəl), *adj.* of feces.

fe·ces (fē′sēz), *n.pl.* waste matter discharged from the intestines.

feck·less (fek′lis), *adj.* **1** useless; futile. **2** SCOTTISH. spiritless; worthless. —**feck′less·ly,** *adv.* —**feck′less·ness,** *n.*

fe·cund (fē′kənd *or* fek′ənd), *adj.* able to produce much; fruitful; productive; fertile: *a fecund mind.*

fe·cun·di·ty (fi kun′də tē), *n.* fertility; fruitfulness; productiveness.

fed (fed), *v.* past tense and past participle of **feed:** *We fed the birds. Have they been fed today?*

fed up, bored, impatient, or disgusted.

fed., **1** federal. **2** federation.

fed·er·al (fed′ər əl), **1** *adj.* formed by an agreement between states setting up a central government to handle their common affairs while the states keep separate control of local affairs: *Switzerland and the United States both became nations by federal union.* **2** *adj.* of the central government formed in this way: *Congress is the federal lawmaking group of the United States.* **3** *adj.* Also, **Federal,** of the central government of the United States, not of any state or city alone: *Coining money is a federal power.* **4 Federal, a** *adj.* of the Federalist Party. **b** *adj.* supporting the Union during the Civil War. **c** *n.* supporter of the Union during the Civil War. —**fed′er·al·ly,** *adv.*

fed·er·al·ism (fed′ər ə liz′əm), *n.* the federal principle of government.

fed·er·al·ist (fed′ər ə list), *n.* **1 Federalist,** member of the Federalist Party. **2** supporter of the federal principle of government.

Federalist Party, a political party in the United States that favored the adoption of the Constitution and a strong central government. It existed from about 1791 to about 1816.

fed·er·ate (fed′ə rāt′), *v.* to form into a union or federation: *a plan to federate the provinces.* ❑ *v.* **fed·er·at·ed, fed·er·at·ing.**

fed·er·a·tion (fed′ə rā′shən), *n.* union by agreement, often a union of states, nations, groups, etc.; league: *Each member of the federation keeps control over its own affairs.*

fe·do·ra (fi dôr′ə), *n.* a low, soft felt hat with a curved brim, having the crown creased from front to back. ❑ *n., pl.* **fe·do·ras.**

fee (fē), *n.* **1** money asked for or paid for some service or privilege; charge: *entrance fee, legal fees.* **2** (long ago) fief. ❑ *n., pl.* **fees.**

fee·ble (fē′bəl), *adj.* lacking strength; weak: *A sick person is often feeble. A feeble attempt is liable to fail.* ❑ *adj.* **fee·bler, fee·blest.** [Feeble comes from a Latin word meaning "to weep." Crying has been considered a sign of weakness.] —**fee′ble·ness,** *n.* —**fee′bly,** *adv.*

a	hat	è	term	ô	order	ch	child		
ā	age	i	it	oi	oil	ng	long		a in about
ä	far	ī	ice	ou	out	sh	she	ə	e in taken
â	care	o	hot	u	cup	th	thin		i in pencil
e	let	ō	open	u̇	put	ᴛн	then		o in lemon
ē	equal	ò	saw	ü	rule	zh	measure		u in circus

fee·ble-mind·ed (fē′bəl min′did), *adj.* lacking normal intelligence. ■ Feeble-minded is often considered offensive. **—fee′ble-mind′ed·ly,** *adv.* **—fee′ble-mind′ed·ness,** *n.*

feed (fēd), **1** *v.* to give food to: *We feed babies because they cannot feed themselves.* **2** *v.* to give as food: *Feed this grain to the chickens.* **3** *v.* to eat: *Our cows feed in a shed near the barn.* **4** *n.* food for animals: *Give the chickens their feed.* **5** *n.* meal for someone. **6** *v.* to supply with material or something necessary: *Find some dry wood to feed the fire.* ❑ *v.* **fed, feed·ing.**

feed·back (fēd′bak′), *n.* **1** process by which a system, machine, etc., regulates itself by feeding back to itself part of its output. **2** response or reaction, especially when it affects the process causing the response: *She improved the organization of her report after feedback from the teacher.*

feed·er (fē′dər), *n.* **1** a device that supplies food to an animal: *a bird feeder.* **2** person or animal that eats. **3** a branch that supplies something to a main part, such as a river or form of transportation: *a feeder ramp.*

feed·lot (fēd′lot′), *n.* land where animals, especially beef cattle, are fattened before slaughter.

feel (fēl), **1** *v.* to put the hand or some other part of the body on or against; touch: *Feel this cloth.* **2** *n.* quality sensed by touch; way something seems to the touch; feeling: *I like the feel of silk.* **3** *v.* to try to find or make your way by touch: *I felt my way across the room when the lights went out.* **4** *v.* to test or examine by touching: *feel a person's pulse.* **5** *v.* to try to find by touching: *He felt in his pockets for a dime.* **6** *v.* to find out by touching: *Feel how cold my hands are.* **7** *v.* to be aware of: *He felt the cool breeze on his face.* **8** *v.* to have the feeling of being; be: *She feels sure. We felt hot. I feel angry.* **9** *v.* to give the feeling of being; seem: *The air feels cold. Your shirt feels wet.* **10** *v.* to have in your mind; experience: *She felt pain.* **11** *v.* to have a feeling: *Try to feel more kindly toward them. I feel that we shall win.* **12** *v.* to have pity or sympathy: *We feel for those who suffer.* ❑ *v.* **felt, feel·ing.**
feel like, to have a desire or preference for: *Even though it was raining they felt like going out for a walk.*
feel out, to find out from in a cautious way: *Feel them out on this matter.*
feel up to, to think you are capable of: *He doesn't feel up to working just now.*

feel·er (fē′lər), *n.* **1** a special part of an animal's body for sensing by touch. Insects, crabs, lobsters, shrimp, etc., have feelers on their heads. **2** remark, hint, or question made to find out what others are thinking or planning.

feel·ing (fē′ling), **1** *n.* emotion. Joy, sorrow, fear, and anger are feelings. *The loss of the ball game stirred up much feeling.* **2** *n.pl.* **feelings,** the tender or sensitive side of your nature: *You hurt my feelings when you yelled at me.* **3** *n.* awareness; sensation: *I had a feeling that someone was watching me.* **4** *n.* sense of touch. By feeling we tell what is hard from what is soft. **5** *adj.* sympathetic; sensitive: *a feeling heart.* **6** *n.* pity; sympathy: *Have you no feeling for that poor, sick creature?* **7** *n.* opinion; idea: *I have no feeling about the plan, one way or the other.*

SYNONYM STUDY **Feeling, emotion,** and **mood**[1] all mean a pleasant or painful state of mind. **Feeling** can be used about any state of mind: *He had a feeling of hope in spite of the doctor's solemn face.* **Emotion** is used about strong feelings and is a somewhat formal word: *Please try to control your emotions.* **Mood** is used about a feeling that lasts for a while: *He's been in a bad mood all week.*

feel·ing·ly (fē′ling lē), *adv.* with emotion: *She spoke feelingly of her old friend.*

feet (fēt), *n.* plural of **foot**: *A dog has four feet.* ■ Another word that sounds like this is **feat.**

feign (fān), *v.* **1** to put on a false appearance of; make believe; pretend: *feigning illness.* **2** to make up to deceive: *feign an excuse.* **—feign′er,** *n.*

feint (fānt), **1** *n.* movement intended to deceive; sham attack; pretended blow: *The boxer made a feint at his opponent with his right hand and struck with his left.* **2** *v.* to make a feint. ■ Another word that sounds like this is **faint.**

feis·ty (fī′stē), *adj.* **1** full of spirit and energy. **2** quarrelsome; touchy.

WORD STORY **Feisty** comes from an old English word that meant "an unpleasant smell." That word was used to describe a small dog that was unpleasantly nervous and bad-tempered, perhaps as someone today might call a naughty dog a "little stinker."

feld·spar (feld′spär′), *n.* kind of crystalline mineral containing aluminum, silicon, and various other elements. Feldspars are the most abundant minerals in the earth's crust. They are used in making glass and pottery.

fe·lic·i·tate (fə lis′ə tāt), *v.* to express good wishes to formally; congratulate: *The young woman's friends felicitated her upon her promotion.* ❑ *v.* **fe·lic·i·tat·ed, fe·lic·i·tat·ing.**

fe·lic·i·ta·tion (fə lis′ə tā′shən), *n.* Often, **felicitations,** *pl.* a formal expression of good wishes; congratulations.

fe·lic·i·tous (fə lis′ə təs), *adj.* suitable for the occasion; appropriate; apt: *The poem was full of striking and felicitous phrases.* **—fe·lic′i·tous·ly,** *adv.* **—fe·lic′i·tous·ness,** *n.*

fe·lic·i·ty (fə lis′ə tē), *n.* **1** great happiness; bliss. **2** good fortune; blessing. **3** a pleasing ability in expression; appropriateness or gracefulness: *The writer phrased his ideas with felicity.*

fe·line (fē′līn), **1** *n.* cat. **2** *adj.* of a cat: *feline eyes.* **3** *adj.* like that of a cat: *feline stealth.* **4** *n.* any animal belonging to a group of meat-eating animals including domestic cats, lions, tigers, leopards, etc. **5** *adj.* belonging to this group. **—fe′line·ly,** *adv.*

fell[1] (fel), *v.* past tense of **fall**: *Snow fell last night.*

fell[2] (fel), *v.* **1** to cause to fall; knock down: *The blow felled her to the ground.* **2** to cut down a tree. **3** to turn down and stitch one edge of a seam over the other. **—fell′a·ble,** *adj.*

fell[3] (fel), *adj.* **1** extremely bad; cruel; fierce; terrible: *a fell blow.* **2** deadly; destructive: *a fell disease.*

fell[4] (fel), *n.* skin or hide of an animal.

fel·lah (fel′ə), *n.* peasant or laborer in Egypt and other Arabic-speaking countries. ❑ *n.,* *pl.* **fel·la·hin** or **fel·la·heen** (fel′ə hēn′).

fel·low (fel′ō), **1** *n.* a male person; man or boy. **2** *n.* a person; anybody; one: *What can a fellow do?* **3** *n.* companion; comrade: *He was cut off from his fellows.* **4** *adj.* being in a similar situation, group, etc.: *fellow citizens, fellow sufferers.* **5** *n.* person who has a fellowship from a university or college. **6** *n.* member of a learned society.

fellow man, fellow human being.

fel·low·ship (fel′ō ship), *n.* **1** companionship; friendliness. **2** condition of being one of a group: *I enjoy my fellowship with my friends.* **3** group of people having similar tastes, interests, beliefs, aims, etc. **4** position or money given by a university or college to a student to enable him or her to continue studying.

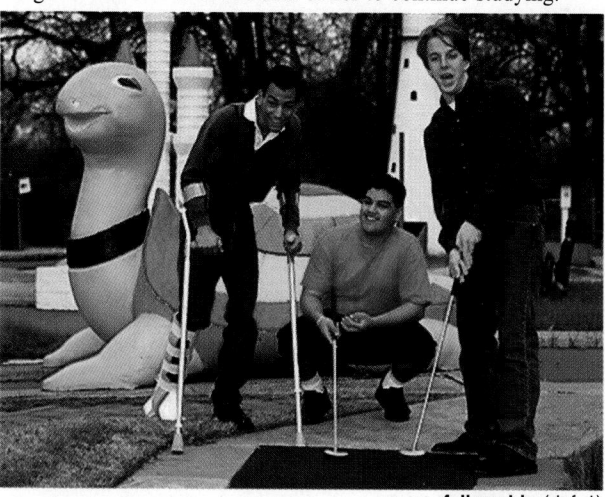

fellowship (def. 1)

fel·on (fel′ən), *n.* person who has committed a felony; criminal. *Murderers and thieves are felons.*

fe·lo·ni·ous (fə lō′nē əs), *adj.* of or involving a felony: *break into a house with felonious intent.* —**fe·lo′ni·ous·ly,** *adv.*

fel·o·ny (fel′ə nē), *n.* crime more serious than a misdemeanor. *Murder and burglary are felonies.* ◻ *n., pl.* **fel·o·nies.**

felony murder, an unintentional killing that is treated as murder, because the killer was committing a felony, such as robbery, at the time.

felt[1] (felt), *v.* past tense and past participle of **feel:** *I felt the cat's soft fur. It was felt the picnic should be postponed.*

felt[2] (felt), **1** *n.* cloth that is not woven, but is made by rolling and pressing together fibers such as wool, nylon, or fur. Felt is used to make hats, slippers, and pads. **2** *adj.* made of felt: *a felt hat.*

felt-tip pen (felt′tip′), pen that writes with a point made of felt saturated with ink.

fe·male (fē′māl), **1** *n.* woman or girl. **2** *adj.* of women or girls. **3** *adj.* belonging to the sex that can give birth to young or lay eggs. *Cows and hens are female animals.* **4** *n.* animal belonging to this sex. **5** *n.* flower having a pistil or pistils but no stamens. **6** *n.* plant bearing only flowers with pistils. —**fe′male·ness,** *n.*

fem·i·nine (fem′ə nən), *adj.* **1** of women or girls. **2** like a woman; womanly. **3** (in grammar) of the gender to which nouns and adjectives referring to females belong. *She is a feminine pronoun; he is a masculine pronoun.* —**fem′i·nine·ly,** *adv.*

fem·i·nin·i·ty (fem′ə nin′ə tē), *n.* feminine quality or condition.

fem·i·nism (fem′ə niz′əm), *n.* **1** belief in increased rights and activities for women in their economic, social, political, and private lives. **2** movement to obtain these rights.

fem·i·nist (fem′ə nist), **1** *n.* person who believes in or favors feminism. **2** *adj.* believing in or favoring feminism.

fe·mur (fē′mər), *n.* thighbone. ◻ *n., pl.* **fe·murs.**

fence (fens), **1** *n.* railing, wall, or similar enclosure put around a yard, garden, field, farm, etc., to show where it ends or to keep people or animals out or in. Most fences are made of wood, wire, or metal. **2** *v.* to put a fence around; keep out or in with a fence. **3** *v.* to fight with long, slender swords or foils. **4** *v.* to buy or sell stolen goods. **5** *n.* person who buys and sells stolen goods. ◻ *v.* **fenced, fenc·ing.** [**Fence** is a shortened form of **defense.** Fences around land and fencing with a sword are two kinds of self-defense.] —**fence′less,** *adj.*

on the fence, uncertain about which side to take; doubtful.

fenc·er (fen′sər), *n.* person who knows how to fight with a sword or foil.

fenc·ing (fen′sing), *n.* **1** art or sport of fighting with swords or foils. **2** material for fences. **3** fences.

fend (fend), *v.* **1 fend for yourself,** to provide for yourself; get along by your own efforts: *While traveling alone she had to fend for herself.* **2 fend off,** to ward off; keep off: *The boxer fended off blow after blow.*

fend·er (fen′dər), *n.* **1** metal frame over the wheel of a car, truck, bicycle, etc., that protects the wheel and reduces splashing in wet weather; mudguard. **2** cowcatcher. **3** bar, frame, or screen in front of a fireplace to keep hot coals and sparks from the room.

fen·nec (fen′ek), *n.* a small fox of North Africa and Arabia.

fen·nel (fen′l), *n.* a tall herb with yellow flowers and fragrant leaves. Its fragrant seeds are used as flavoring.

fer·al (fir′əl), *adj.* gone back to the original wild condition after being domesticated: *feral cats.*

fer-de-lance (fer′də läns′), *n.* a large, very poisonous pit viper of tropical America. It has brown and grayish markings and is related to the rattlesnake.

Fer·di·nand V (ferd′n and), 1452-1516, Spanish king from 1474 to 1516. He and his queen, Isabella I, paid for the voyages of Christopher Columbus. [**Ferdinand** comes from an old German word meaning "a voyage."]

fer·ment (fər ment′ *for verb;* fer′ment *for noun*), **1** *v.* to undergo or produce a gradual chemical change in which yeast, fungi, or bacteria change sugar into alcohol or lactic acid and produce carbon dioxide. Grape juice ferments into wine. Penicillin is produced by some fermenting fungi. **2** *n.* substance that causes others to fer-

ment. Yeast is a ferment. **3** *n.* a chemical change caused by such a substance. **4** *n.* excitement; agitation; unrest: *Rumors of war caused ferment throughout the country.* —**fer·ment′a·ble,** *adj.*

fer·men·ta·tion (fer′men tā′shən), *n.* **1** act or process of fermenting: *Fermentation causes milk to sour and bread to rise.* **2** ferment.

Fer·mi (fer′mē), *n.* **En·ri·co** (en rē′kō), 1901-1954, American physicist, born in Italy. He directed the first controlled nuclear chain reaction in 1942. ■ Enrico Fermi won the 1938 Nobel Prize for physics. He and his Jewish wife emigrated to the United States immediately after the award ceremony, because they were troubled by anti-Semitic laws that had recently been passed in Italy. In the United States, he made important contributions to the creation of the atomic bomb.

fer·mi·um (fer′mē əm), *n.* a radioactive metallic element produced artificially from plutonium or uranium. *Symbol:* Fm

fern (fern), *n.* any of very many plants that have roots, stems, and feathery leaves, but not flowers or seeds. A fern reproduces by means of spores which grow in little brown clusters on the backs of the leaves. —**fern′less,** *adj.* —**fern′like′,** *adj.*

fe·ro·cious (fə rō′shəs), *adj.* **1** very cruel; savage; fierce: *The bear's ferocious growl was terrifying.* **2** intense: *a ferocious headache.* —**fe·ro′cious·ly,** *adv.* —**fe·ro′cious·ness,** *n.*

fe·roc·i·ty (fə ros′ə tē), *n.* great cruelty; savageness; fierceness.

fer·ret (fer′it), **1** *n.* kind of weasel with black feet, found in western North America, now almost extinct; black-footed ferret. **2** *n.* a white or yellowish white, weasellike European animal used for killing rats and driving rabbits from their holes. **3** *v.* to hunt with ferrets. **4** *v.* to find out by searching hard for a long time: *ferret out important evidence.* [**Ferret** comes from a Latin word meaning "thief." The European ferret has long been known for stealing chickens for its dinner.] —**fer′ret·er,** *n.*

Ferris wheel

Fer·ris wheel (fer′is), a large, revolving wheel with hanging seats, used in carnivals, amusement parks, fairs, etc.

WORD STORY The **Ferris wheel** was named for George Ferris, the inventor. Ferris built his first wheel in 1893 for the World's Columbian Exposition in Chicago. Since then, no fair has been complete without a Ferris wheel.

fer·ro·mag·net·ic (fer′ō mag net′ik), *adj.* easily able to become strongly magnetic. Iron, steel, cobalt, and nickel are ferromagnetic substances.

fer·ry (fer′ē), **1** *v.* to carry people, vehicles, and goods across a river, lake, or other narrow stretch of water. **2** *n.* boat that carries people, vehicles, and goods on such a trip; ferryboat. **3** *n.* place where boats make such trips. **4** *v.* to go across in a ferryboat. **5** *v.* to carry back and forth in an airplane. **6** *v.* to fly an airplane to a destination for delivery. ◻ *v.* **fer·ried, fer·ry·ing;** *n., pl.* **fer·ries.**

fer·ry·boat (fer′ē bōt′), *n.* ferry (def. 2).

fer·ry·man (fer′ē man′), *n.* **1** person who owns or is in charge of a ferry. **2** person who works on a ferry. ◻ *n., pl.* **fer·ry·men.**

fer·tile (fer′tl), *adj.* **1** able to bear seeds, fruit, young, etc.: *a fertile animal or plant.* **2** able to develop into a new living thing; fertilized: *Chicks hatch from fertile eggs.* **3** able to produce much; producing crops easily: *fertile soil.* **4** producing ideas; creative: *a fertile mind.* —**fer′tile·ly,** *adv.* —**fer′tile·ness,** *n.*

a	hat	ė	term	ô	order	ch	child		
ā	age	i	it	oi	oil	ng	long	ə	a in about
ä	far	ī	ice	ou	out	sh	she		e in taken
â	care	o	hot	u	cup	th	thin		i in pencil
e	let	ō	open	ù	put	ŦH	then		o in lemon
ē	equal	ò	saw	ü	rule	zh	measure		u in circus

fer·til·i·ty (fər til′ə tē), *n.* **1** condition of being fertile: *The fertility of the soil was increased by the use of manure.* **2** power to produce: *The fertility of her imagination made her a first-class writer of science fiction stories.*

fer·ti·li·za·tion (fėr′tl ə zā′shən), *n.* **1** act or process of making something fertile. **2** union of a male reproductive cell and a female reproductive cell to form a cell that will develop into a new living thing.

fer·ti·lize (fėr′tl īz), *v.* **1** to make fertile; make able to produce much. **2** to unite with an egg cell in fertilization. **3** to put fertilizer on: *fertilize a lawn.* ❑ *v.* **fer·ti·lized, fer·ti·liz·ing.** —**fer′ti·liz′·a·ble,** *adj.*

fer·ti·liz·er (fėr′tl ī′zər), *n.* substance such as manure, chemicals, etc., spread over or put into the soil to make it able to produce more.

fer·ven·cy (fėr′vən sē), *n.* fervor.

fer·vent (fėr′vənt), *adj.* showing great warmth of feeling; very earnest: *She made a fervent plea for more food and medical supplies for the earthquake victims.* —**fer′vent·ly,** *adv.*

fer·vid (fėr′vid), *adj.* full of strong feeling; very emotional; spirited: *The speaker's fervid words stirred the crowd to action.* —**fer′vid·ly,** *adv.* —**fer′vid·ness,** *n.*

fer·vor (fėr′vər), *n.* great strength of feeling; enthusiasm or earnestness: *patriotic fervor.*

> **WORD STORY** **Fervor** comes from a Latin word meaning "to boil" or "to glow with heat." Strong emotions are often compared to physical warmth. People speak of a hot temper and warmest love.

fes·tal (fes′tl), *adj.* of a feast, festival, or holiday; festive: *A wedding is a festal occasion.* —**fes′tal·ly,** *adv.*

fes·ter (fes′tər), *v.* **1** to form pus: *The neglected wound festered and became very painful.* **2** to cause pain or resentment; rankle: *The hurt of the insult festered in her mind.*

fes·ti·val (fes′tə vəl), *n.* **1** day or special time of rejoicing or feasting, often in memory of some great happening: *Christmas is a Christian festival; Hanukkah is a Jewish festival.* **2** program of entertainment, often held annually: *Every September the city has a music festival.*

festival

fes·tive (fes′tiv), *adj.* of or suitable for a feast, festival, or holiday; merry: *A birthday is a festive occasion.* —**fes′tive·ly,** *adv.* —**fes′tive·ness,** *n.*

fes·tiv·i·ty (fe stiv′ə tē), *n.* **1** festive activity; thing done to celebrate: *The festivities on the Fourth of July included a parade and fireworks.* **2** gaiety; merriment. ❑ *n., pl.* **fes·tiv·i·ties** for 1.

fes·toon (fe stün′), **1** *n.* a string or chain of flowers, leaves, ribbons, etc., hanging in a curve between two points: *The bunting was draped on the wall in colorful festoons.* **2** *v.* to decorate with festoons: *The gym was festooned with crepe paper for the dance.*

fe·ta (fet′ə), *n.* a soft, white Greek cheese made from goat's milk or sheep's milk. [**Feta** comes from a Greek word meaning "a slice." The word is commonly used in a Greek phrase meaning "a slice of cheese."]

fe·tal (fē′tl), *adj.* of or for a fetus: *a fetal heartbeat.*

fetch (fech), *v.* **1** to go and get; bring: *Please fetch me my reading glasses.* **2** to cause to come; succeed in bringing: *Her call fetched me at once.* **3** to be sold for: *fetch a good price.* —**fetch′er,** *n.*

fetch·ing (fech′ing), *adj.* attractive; charming: *a fetching new outfit.* —**fetch′ing·ly,** *adv.*

fete or **fête** (fāt *or* fet), **1** *n.* festival or party, especially an elaborate one and often one held outdoors: *A large fete was given for the benefit of the town hospital.* **2** *v.* to honor with a fete; entertain: *My parents were feted by their friends on their twentieth anniversary.* ❑ *n., pl.* **fetes** or **fêtes;** *v.* **fet·ed, fet·ing** or **fêt·ed, fêt·ing.** ■ Another word that can sound like this is **fate.**

fet·id (fet′id), *adj.* smelling very bad; stinking: *a stagnant, fetid pond.* —**fet′id·ly,** *adv.* —**fet′id·ness,** *n.*

fe·tish (fet′ish), *n.* **1** thing supposed to have magic powers: *The tribe worshiped a fetish that was a snake carved out of stone.* **2** any object of excessive concern or unthinking devotion: *Some people make a fetish of stylish clothes.* ❑ *n., pl.* **fe·tish·es.**

fet·lock (fet′lok), *n.* **1** tuft of hair above a horse's hoof on the back part of its leg. **2** the part of a horse's leg where this tuft grows.

fet·ter (fet′ər), **1** *n.* Usually, **fetters,** *pl.* chains or shackles for the feet: *Fetters prevented the prisoner's escape.* **2** *v.* to bind with chains; chain the feet of. **3** *n.* anything that shackles or binds; restraint. **4** *v.* to place restraints on something: *progress fettered by tradition.*

fet·tle (fet′l), *n.* condition; state: *The horse is in fine fettle and should win the race.*

> **WORD STORY** **Fettle** comes from an old English word meaning "belt." In the Middle Ages, a knight's sword hung from his belt. A knight who put on his belt was in a condition or state to engage in battle.

fet·tuc·ci·ne or **fet·tu·ci·ne** (fet′ə chē′nē), *n.* noodles made in long thin flat strips, often served with a sauce of butter, Parmesan cheese, and cream.

fe·tus (fē′təs), *n.* an animal embryo during the later stages of its development in the womb or in the egg, especially a human embryo more than three months old. ❑ *n., pl.* **fe·tus·es.**

feud (fyüd), **1** *n.* a long and deadly quarrel between families or tribes. Feuds are often passed down from generation to generation. **2** *n.* bitter hatred between two persons or groups. **3** *v.* to carry on a long and deadly quarrel. [See Word Story at **feudal.**]

feu·dal (fyü′dl), *adj.* of or about feudalism: *the feudal system, feudal laws.* —**feu′dal·ly,** *adv.*

> **WORD STORY** Although feudal people were often feuding, the words are not related. **Feudal** comes from a Latin word meaning "land that a lord lets a soldier use in return for military service." **Feud** comes from an old German word meaning "enmity" or "hatred." People spelled the words alike because the idea of each involved fighting.

feu·dal·ism (fyü′dl iz′əm), *n.* the social, economic, and political system of Europe in the Middle Ages. Under this system vassals gave military and other services to their lord in return for his protection and the use of land.

fe·ver (fē′vər), *n.* **1** an unhealthy condition in which the body temperature is higher than normal (98.6 degrees Fahrenheit or 37.0 degrees Celsius in human beings). **2** any sickness that causes or is accompanied by fever: *scarlet fever, typhoid fever.* **3** an excited, restless condition; agitation: *a fever of excitement.*

fever blister, cold sore.

fe·vered (fē′vərd), *adj.* **1** having fever. **2** excited; restless.

fe·ver·ish (fē′vər ish), *adj.* **1** having fever. **2** having a slight degree of fever. **3** caused by fever: *a feverish thirst.* **4** causing fever: *a feverish climate.* **5** excited; restless: *I packed in feverish haste.* —**fe′ver·ish·ly,** *adv.* —**fe′ver·ish·ness,** *n.*

fever sore, cold sore.

few (fyü), **1** *adj.* not many: *Few people attended the meeting.* **2** *n.* a small number: *I haven't many friends, only a few.* **3** *n.pl.* **the few,** the minority. —**few′ness,** *n.*

quite a few, a good many: *Quite a few of us went to the game.*

fez (fez), *n.* a felt cap, usually red and ornamented with a long, black tassel. ❑ *n., pl.* **fez·zes.**

ff, fortissimo.

ff., and the following pages, sections, etc.; and what follows.

fi·an·cé (fē′än sā′), *n.* man engaged to be married: *He is her fiancé.* ❑ *n., pl.* **fi·an·cés.**

fi·an·cée (fē′än sā′), *n.* woman engaged to be married: *She is his fiancée.* ❑ *n., pl.* **fi·an·cées.**

fi·as·co (fē as′kō), *n.* a complete or ridiculous failure; humiliating breakdown: *The play was a fiasco and closed after only three performances.* ❑ *n., pl.* **fi·as·cos** or **fi·as·coes.**

> **WORD STORY** Fiasco comes from an Italian word meaning "bottle." In Italian, "to make a bottle" is an idiom that means to fail completely. No one, including the Italians, knows why.

fi·at (fī′ət *or* fī′at), *n.* an authoritative order or command; decree. [Fiat comes from a Latin word meaning "let it be done."]

fib (fib), **1** *n.* a lie about some small matter. **2** *v.* to tell such a lie. ❑ *v.* **fibbed, fib·bing.** —**fib′ber,** *n.*

fi·ber (fī′bər), *n.* **1** a threadlike part; thread. A muscle is made of many fibers. **2** substance made of threads or threadlike parts: *an artificial fiber.* **3** any part of food, such as the cellulose in vegetables, that cannot be digested, and so stimulates the movement of food and waste products through the intestines. **4** character; nature: *a person of strong moral fiber.*

fi·ber·board (fī′bər bôrd′), *n.* a building material made by compressing wood fibers and other material into flat sheets.

fi·ber·fill (fī′bər fil′), *n.* a synthetic fiber used for filling or padding cushions, mattresses, coats, etc.

fi·ber·glass (fī′bər glas′), *n.* thin threads of glass used for insulating materials or to strengthen rigid plastics.

fiber optics, 1 branch of physics that deals with sending sounds, pictures, and computer data by laser light along very thin clear fibers of glass or plastic. The fibers carry much information quickly and can be bent without loss of information. **2** a single bundle of these optical fibers. —**fi·ber-op·tic** (fī′bər op′tik), *adj.*

fiber optics (def. 2)

fi·brin (fī′brən), *n.* a white, tough, elastic substance formed when blood clots.

fi·brin·o·gen (fī brin′ə jən), *n.* a protein from which fibrin is made in the blood.

fi·broid (fī′broid), *adj.* made up of fibers or fibrous tissue: *a fibroid tumor.*

fi·brous (fī′brəs), *adj.* **1** made up of fibers; having fibers. **2** like fiber; stringy.

fib·u·la (fib′yə lə), *n.* the outer and thinner of the two bones in the human lower leg. It extends from knee to ankle. ❑ *n., pl.* **fib·u·lae** (fib′yə lē′), **fib·u·las.** [Fibula comes from the Latin word for the pin on a piece of jewelry. The two leg bones together look like this sort of fastener.]

-fication, *suffix.* act or process of making or doing: *falsification = act or process of making false.*

fick·le (fik′əl), *adj.* likely to change without reason; changing; not constant: *a fickle friend.* —**fick′le·ness,** *n.*

fic·tion (fik′shən), *n.* **1** novels, short stories, and other prose writings that tell about imaginary people and happenings. **2** something imagined or made up: *They exaggerate so much that it is impossible to separate fact from fiction.*

fic·tion·al (fik′shə nəl), *adj.* of fiction: *Dorothy and Toto in "The Wizard of Oz" are fictional characters.* —**fic′tion·al·ly,** *adv.*

fic·tion·al·ize (fik′shə nə līz), *v.* to give a fictional form to; make into fiction. ❑ *v.* **fic·tion·al·ized, fic·tion·al·iz·ing.** —**fic′tion·al·i·za′tion,** *n.*

fic·ti·tious (fik tish′əs), *adj.* **1** not real; imaginary: *a fictitious story.* **2** used in order to deceive; false: *a fictitious name.* —**fic·ti′tious·ly,** *adv.* —**fic·ti′tious·ness,** *n.*

fi·cus (fī′kəs), *n.* any of several trees and bushes that grow in warm regions, especially one kind that bears figs. Some ficus trees are raised as houseplants. ❑ *n., pl.* **fi·cus** or **fi·cus·es.**

fid·dle (fid′l), **1** *n.* violin. **2** *v.* to play on a violin. **3** *v.* to make aimless movements; play nervously; toy: *I fiddled with my pen and paper during the boring lecture.* **4** *v.* to waste: *He fiddled away the whole day doing nothing.* ❑ *v.* **fid·dled, fid·dling.**

fid·dler (fid′lər), *n.* person who plays a violin.

fiddler crab, a small, burrowing crab found along coasts in warm regions. One of the claws of the male is much enlarged.

fid·dle·sticks (fid′l stiks′), *interj.* nonsense! rubbish!

fi·del·i·ty (fi del′ə tē *or* fə del′ə tē), *n.* **1** steadfast faithfulness; loyalty: *a dog's fidelity to its owner.* **2** exactness; accuracy: *She repeated the message with absolute fidelity.* **3** the ability of a radio, CD player, etc., to reproduce sound accurately.

> **WORD FAMILY** Fidelity and the words below are related. They all come from the Latin word meaning "to trust."
>
> | | | | |
> |---|---|---|---|
> | affiance | confident | diffident | fiancée |
> | affidavit | confidential | faith | infidel |
> | bona fide | defiance | fealty | perfidious |
> | confidant | defy | fiancé | |
> | confide | diffidence | | |

fidg·et (fij′it), **1** *v.* to move about restlessly; be uneasy: *Many people fidget if they have to sit still a long time.* **2** *n.pl.* **the fidgets,** a fit of restlessness or uneasiness: *The long speech gave us the fidgets.*

fidg·et·y (fij′ə tē), *adj.* restless; uneasy: *That fidgety child keeps twisting and moving.*

fie (fī), *interj.* OLD USE. for shame!; shame!: *Fie upon you!*

fief (fēf), *n.* piece of land held on condition of giving military and other services to the feudal lord owning it, in return for his protection and the use of the land.

field (fēld), **1** *n.* land with few or no trees; open country: *They drove through the woods until they came to a field covered with wild flowers.* **2** *n.* piece of land used for crops or for pasture: *a soybean field.* **3** *n.* piece of land used for some special purpose: *a baseball field.* **4** *n.* battlefield: *the field of Gettysburg.* **5** *n.* land yielding a natural resource: *oil fields, coal fields.* **6** *n.* a flat space; broad surface: *A field of ice surrounds the North Pole.* **7** *n.* surface on which something is pictured or painted; background: *Their flag shows a red circle on a white field.* **8** *n.* range of opportunity or interest; sphere of activity: *the field of politics, the field of art, the field of science.* **9** *n.* (in physics) the space throughout which a force operates. A magnet has a magnetic field around it. **10** *n.* area that can be seen through a telescope, microscope, etc. **11** *n.* area where contests in jumping, throwing, etc., are held. **12** *n.* all those in a game, contest, or outdoor sport: *She led the field until the last hurdle.* **13** *n.* a single item that is part of a record in a computer database. A record contains related fields. A person's name, address, and Zip Code are fields that form a record in a mailing list database. **14** *v.* (in baseball, cricket, etc.) to stop or catch a batted ball and throw it in. **15** *v.* to send players or a team to the playing area.

take the field, to begin a battle, campaign, game, etc.

field day, 1 day for athletic contests and outdoor sports. **2** day of unusual opportunities for activity or display.

field·er (fēl′dər), *n.* (in baseball, cricket, etc.) a player who fields batted balls. Fielders are stationed around or outside the diamond in baseball.

field glasses, small binoculars for use outdoors.

field goal, 1 a play in football counting three points, made by a place kick through the goalposts. **2** a basket scored in basketball while the ball is in play, counting either two or three points.

field hockey, hockey played on a field.

field house, 1 building near an athletic field, used for storing equipment, for dressing rooms, etc. **2** a large building used for various athletic events.

a	hat	ė	term	ô	order	ch	child		
ā	age	i	it	oi	oil	ng	long	⎧	a in about
ä	far	ī	ice	ou	out	sh	she		e in taken
â	care	o	hot	u	cup	th	thin	ə ⎨	i in pencil
e	let	ō	open	ù	put	ᴛʜ	then		o in lemon
ē	equal	ò	saw	ü	rule	zh	measure	⎩	u in circus

field magnet, magnet used to provide a magnetic field, especially in a generator or electric motor.

field marshal, (in the British, French, German, and some other armies) officer ranking next below the commander in chief.

field mouse, mouse that lives in open fields.

Fields (fēldz), *n.* **W. C.,** 1879-1946, American comedian and movie star. He often played characters who hated children and talked in a fancy way with many long words.

field trip, trip away from school to give students an opportunity to learn by seeing things closely and at first hand.

fiend (fēnd), *n.* **1** an evil spirit; devil. **2** a very wicked or cruel person. **3** person who spends a lot of time in some game or activity: *a tennis fiend.* —**fiend′like′,** *adj.*

fiend·ish (fēn′dish), *adj.* very cruel; wicked; devilish: *fiendish tortures, a fiendish yell.* —**fiend′ish·ly,** *adv.* —**fiend′ish·ness,** *n.*

fierce (firs), *adj.* **1** savagely cruel; ferocious; wild: *A wounded lion can be fierce.* **2** raging; violent: *fierce anger. A fierce wind blows very hard.* **3** very eager or active: *a fierce determination to win.* ❑ *adj.* **fierc·er, fierc·est.** —**fierce′ly,** *adv.* —**fierce′ness,** *n.*

fie·ry (fī′rē), *adj.* **1** containing fire; burning; flaming: *a fiery furnace.* **2** like fire; very hot; glowing: *a fiery red, fiery heat.* **3** full of feeling or spirit: *a fiery speech.* **4** easily aroused or excited: *a fiery temper.* ❑ *adj.* **fie·ri·er, fie·ri·est.** —**fi′er·i·ness,** *n.*

fi·es·ta (fē es′tə), *n.* **1** a religious festival or saint's day, especially in a Spanish-speaking country or area. **2** holiday or festivity. ❑ *n., pl.* **fi·es·tas.**

fife (fīf), *n.* a small, shrill musical instrument like a flute, played by blowing. Fifes are used with drums in marching bands.

fif·teen (fif′tēn′), *n., adj.* five more than ten; 15.

fif·teenth (fif′tēnth′), *adj., n.* **1** next after the 14th; last in a series of 15. **2** one of 15 equal parts.

fifth (fifth), *adj., n.* **1** next after the fourth; last in a series of five. **2** one of five equal parts.

Fifth Amendment, the fifth amendment to the U.S. Constitution, which protects people from having to testify against themselves in criminal cases. It is part of the Bill of Rights.

fifth column, persons living within a country who secretly aid its enemies.

fifth·ly (fifth′lē), *adv.* in the fifth place.

fif·ti·eth (fif′tē ith), *adj., n.* **1** next after the 49th; last in a series of 50. **2** one of 50 equal parts.

fif·ty (fif′tē), *adj., n.* five times ten; 50. ❑ *n., pl.* **fif·ties.**

fif·ty-fif·ty (fif′tē fif′tē), *adj., adv.* in two equal parts; with two equal shares: *a fifty-fifty chance of winning, go fifty-fifty on expenses.*

fig (fig), *n.* a small, soft, sweet fruit of a tree that grows in warm regions. Figs are often dried like dates and raisins.

fig., figure.

fight (fīt), **1** *n.* a violent struggle; combat; contest: *A fight ends when one side gives up.* **2** *n.* an angry dispute; quarrel: *Their fight was over money.* **3** *v.* to take part in a violent struggle, quarrel, combat, etc.; have a fight: *Enemy countries fight with armies.* **4** *v.* to take part in a struggle against; try to overcome: *fight disease.* **5** *v.* to carry on a struggle, conflict, etc.: *fight a duel.* **6** *v.* to get or make by struggling: *She had to fight her way through the crowd.* **7** *n.* power or will to struggle or combat: *There was not much fight in the defeated team.* ❑ *v.* **fought, fight·ing.**

fight it out, to struggle or battle until one side wins.

fight off, to battle or take action against with success: *to fight off an invading army, to fight off the flu.*

fight shy of, to keep away from; avoid.

fight·er (fī′tər), *n.* **1** someone who fights. **2** a boxer. **3** a fast airplane, used mainly for attacking enemy airplanes or for flying low and attacking enemy ground forces.

fig·ment (fig′mənt), *n.* something imagined; made-up story: *I don't believe it; it's just a figment of your imagination.*

fig·ur·a·tive (fig′yər ə tiv), *adj.* **1** using words out of their literal or ordinary meaning to add beauty or force. **2** having many figures of speech. Much poetry is figurative. —**fig′ur·a·tive·ly,** *adv.* —**fig′ur·a·tive·ness,** *n.*

fig·ure (fig′yər), **1** *n.* symbol for a number. 1, 2, 3, 4, etc., are figures. **2** *v.* to use numbers to find out the answer to some problem; calculate: *Can you figure the cost of painting this room?* **3** *n.pl.* **figures,** calculations using figures; arithmetic: *She is very good at figures.* **4** *n.* amount or value given in figures; price: *The figure for that house is very high.* **5** *n.* a form partially or completely enclosing a surface or space: *Circles and cubes are geometric figures.* **6** *n.* someone's body shape: *a slender figure.* **7** *n.* a form or shape: *In the darkness she saw dim figures moving.* **8** *n.* person; character: *Napoleon is a well-known figure in history.* **9** *v.* to stand out; appear: *The names of great leaders figure in the story of human progress.* **10** *n.* picture; drawing; diagram; illustration: *This book has many figures to help explain words.* **11** *n.* a design or pattern: *the figures in the wallpaper.* **12** *n.* outline traced by movements: *figures made by an airplane.* **13** *n.* set of movements in dancing or skating. **14** *n.* figure of speech. **15** *v.* to think; consider: *I figured I should stop where I was.* **16** *v.* INFORMAL. to seem likely; be as expected: *They didn't come to our party; well, it figured.* ❑ *v.* **fig·ured, fig·ur·ing.**

figure on, to depend on; plan on: *I can figure on my parents' help to pay my way through college.*

figure out, to think out; understand: *Even the repairman couldn't figure out what had gone wrong with the washer.*

fig·ured (fig′yərd), *adj.* decorated with a design or pattern; not plain: *figured silk.*

fig·ure·head (fig′yər hed′), *n.* **1** person who is the head of a business, government, etc., in name only, without real authority. **2** ornamental figure on the bow of a ship.

figure of speech, expression in which words are used out of their literal meaning or out of their ordinary use to add beauty or force. Similes and metaphors are figures of speech.

figure skating, **1** ice skating while performing athletic dance movements. **2** competition in this type of skating.

figurehead (def. 2)

fig·u·rine (fig′yə rēn′), *n.* a small, ornamental figure made of stone, pottery, metal, etc.; statuette.

Fi·ji (fē′jē), *n.* island country in the S Pacific, made up of the **Fiji Islands.** *Capital:* Suva. See **Australasia** for map. —**Fi′ji·an,** *adj., n.*

fil·a·ment (fil′ə mənt), *n.* **1** a very fine thread; very slender, threadlike part. The wire that gives off light in a light bulb is a filament. **2** (earlier) the heated wire acting as the negative electrode in a vacuum tube. **3** (in plants) the stalklike part of a stamen that supports the anther.

fil·bert (fil′bərt), *n.* a sweet, thick-shelled kind of cultivated hazelnut. [The **filbert** was named for Saint Philibert. The nuts usually ripen around the time of his feast day, August 20.]

filch (filch), *v.* to steal in small quantities; pilfer: *She filched cookies from the pantry.* —**filch′er,** *n.*

file¹ (fīl), **1** *n.* container, drawer, folder, etc., for keeping memorandums, letters, or other papers in order. **2** *n.* set of papers kept in order: *a file of receipts.* **3** *v.* to put away in order: *Please file* those letters. **4** *n.* information or instructions that a computer keeps together under a single name. A file can be placed in memory, recalled from memory, or processed all at once. **5** *n.* row of persons or things one behind another: *a file of soldiers.* **6** *v.* to march or move in a file: *The pupils filed out of the room during the fire drill.* **7** *v.* to place among the records of a court, public office, etc.: *The deed to our house is filed with the county clerk.* ❑ *v.* **filed, fil·ing.** —**fil′er,** *n.*

in file, one after another: *ships sailing in file.*

file² (fīl), **1** *n.* a steel tool with many small ridges or teeth on it. Its rough surface is used to smooth rough materials or wear away hard substances. **2** *v.* to smooth or wear away with a file. ❑ *v.* **filed, fil·ing.** —**fil′er,** *n.*

fi·let (fi lā′ *or* fil′ā), *n.* fillet (def. 1).

fil·i·al (fil′ē əl), *adj.* due from a son or daughter toward a mother or father: *filial affection.* —**fil′i·al·ly,** *adv.* —**fil′i·al·ness,** *n.*

fil·i·bus·ter (fil′ə bus′tər), **1** *n.* the deliberate hindering of the passage of a bill in a legislature by long speeches or other means of delay. **2** *v.* to deliberately hinder the passage of a bill by such means. —**fil′i·bus′ter·er,** *n.*

fil·i·gree (fil′ə grē), *n.* **1** very delicate, lacelike, ornamental work of gold or silver wire. **2** anything very lacy, delicate, or fanciful: *The frost made a beautiful filigree on the windowpane.* ❑ *n., pl.* **fil·i·grees.**

fil·ings (fī′lingz), *n.pl.* small pieces of iron, wood, etc., which have been removed by a file.

Fil·i·pi·no (fil′ə pē′nō), **1** *n.* person born or living in the Philippines. **2** *adj.* Philippine. ❑ *n., pl.* **Fil·i·pi·nos.**

filigree (def. 1)

fill (fil), **1** *v.* to make full; put into until there is room for nothing more: *Fill this bottle with water. We filled the pots with soil before planting the seeds.* **2** *v.* to become full: *The well filled with water.* **3** *v.* to take up all the space in; spread throughout: *The crowd filled the hall. Smoke filled the room.* **4** *n.* all that is needed or wanted: *There is plenty of food, so eat your fill.* **5** *v.* to supply what is needed or wanted: *The pharmacist filled the doctor's prescription.* **6** *v.* to stop up or close by putting something in: *After the dentist took out the decayed part, he filled my tooth.* **7** *v.* to hold and do the duties of a position, office, etc.; occupy: *We need someone to fill the office of treasurer.* **8** *n.* something that fills. Earth or rock used to make uneven land level is called fill. **9** *v.* (of the wind) to stretch out a sail by blowing fully into it.

fill in, 1 to put in to complete something; insert: *fill in the date of an application.* **2** be a substitute.

fill out, 1 to grow larger; swell: *Her cheeks have filled out.* **2** to supply what is needed in; complete: *My sister filled out an application for a summer job.*

fill up, to fill; fill completely.

fill·er (fil′ər), *n.* thing put in to fill something. A pad of paper for a notebook and a preparation used to fill holes and cracks in wood before painting it are fillers.

fil·let (fi lā′, fil′ā, *or* fil′it), **1** *n.* slice of fish or meat without bones or fat; filet. **2** *v.* to cut fish or meat into such slices.

fill·ing (fil′ing), *n.* thing put in to fill something: *a filling in a tooth.*

filling station, place where gasoline and oil for motor vehicles are sold; gas station; service station.

fil·lip (fil′əp), *n.* thing that rouses, revives, or excites: *The relishes served as a fillip to my appetite.*

Fill·more (fil′môr), **Mil·lard** (mil′ərd), 1800-1874, the 13th president of the United States, from 1850 to 1853, vice-president

from 1849 to 1850. ■ In 1819, **Millard Fillmore** bought his first book—a dictionary.

fil·ly (fil′ē), *n.* a young female horse, donkey, or zebra; mare that is less than four or five years old. ❑ *n., pl.* **fil·lies.**

film (film), **1** *n.* roll or sheet of thin, flexible material covered with a coating that is sensitive to light, used in taking photographs. **2** *n.* a very thin layer, sheet, surface, or coating, often of liquid: *The tanker sank, leaving a film of oil on the water.* **3** *v.* to cover or become covered with a film; dim: *Her eyes filmed over with tears.* **4** *n.* a movie. **5** *v.* to make a movie of: *They filmed "The Wizard of Oz."* **6** *v.* to photograph for a movie: *They filmed the scene three times.* **7** *n.* a thin layer of clear plastic, used for wrapping or packaging something. —**film′like′,** *adj.*

film·strip (film′strip′), *n.* series of still pictures printed on a reel of film.

film·y (fil′mē), *adj.* **1** like a film; very thin. **2** covered with a film. ❑ *adj.* **film·i·er, film·i·est.** —**film′i·ness,** *n.*

fil·ter (fil′tər), **1** *n.* device for straining out substances from a liquid or a gas by slow passage through cloth, paper, sand, charcoal, etc. Filters are used to purify water. **2** *n.* material through which the liquid or gas passes in a filter. **3** *n.* device for allowing only certain light rays, frequencies, etc., to pass while blocking all others. An ultraviolet filter placed in front of a camera lens allows less hazy light to appear in the picture. **4** *v.* to pass or flow very slowly: *Water filters through the sandy soil and into the well.* **5** *v.* to put through a filter; strain: *The city filters its water and then disinfects it.* **6** *v.* to remove by a filter: *Only part of cigarette smoke's dangerous contents can be filtered out.* ■ Another word that sounds like this is **philter.** —**fil′ter·er,** *n.*

fil·ter·a·ble (fil′tər ə bəl), *adj.* capable of passing through a filter that traps bacteria: *a filterable virus.*

filth (filth), *n.* **1** foul dirt: *The alley was filled with garbage and filth.* **2** dirty words or thoughts.

filth·y (fil′thē), *adj.* very dirty; foul: *a filthy shirt.* ❑ *adj.* **filth·i·er, filth·i·est.** —**filth′i·ly,** *adv.* —**filth′i·ness,** *n.*

fil·trate (fil′trāt), *n.* liquid that has been filtered.

fil·tra·tion (fil trā′shən), *n.* act or process of filtering: *air filtration.*

fin (fin), *n.* **1** one of the movable winglike or fanlike parts of a fish's or other sea animal's body. By moving its fins a fish can swim and balance itself in the water. **2** thing shaped or used like a fin. Some aircraft have fins to help balance them in flight. —**fin′less,** *adj.* —**fin′like′,** *adj.*

fi·na·gle (fə nā′gəl), *v.* to get something by trickery or fraud. ❑ *v.* **fi·na·gled, fi·na·gling.** —**fi·na′gler,** *n.*

fi·nal (fī′nl), **1** *adj.* at the end; with no more; coming last: *The book was interesting from the first to the final chapter.* ■ See Synonym Study at **last¹.** **2** *adj.* deciding completely; settling the question: *The one with the highest authority makes the final decisions.* **3** *n.* Often, **finals,** *pl.* the last or deciding set in a series of games or examinations: *If you pass your finals at the end of the term, you will be promoted.* [See Word Story at **define.**]

fi·na·le (fə nä′lē *or* fə nal′ē), *n.* **1** the concluding part of a piece of music or a play. **2** the last part; end.

fi·nal·ist (fī′nl ist), *n.* person who takes part in the last or deciding set in a series of contests.

fi·nal·i·ty (fī nal′ə tē), *n.* condition of being final, finished, or settled: *She refused with finality; we knew that she would not change her mind.*

fi·nal·ize (fī′nl īz), *v.* to make final or conclusive: *finalize an agreement.* ❑ *v.* **fi·nal·ized, fi·nal·iz·ing.** —**fi′nal·i·za′tion,** *n.* —**fi′nal·iz′er,** *n.*

fi·nal·ly (fī′nl ē), *adv.* **1** at the end; at last: *The school bus finally came.* **2** in such a way as to decide or settle the question: *Has Mom finally chosen which computer to buy?*

fi·nance (fə nans′ *or* fī′nans), **1** *n.* management or control over money matters, including banking and investments. **2** *n.* system by which the income of a nation, state, corporation, etc., is raised and managed. **3** *n.pl.* **finances,** financial condition; money; income; funds; revenues: *New taxes were needed to increase the nation's finances.* **4** *v.* to provide money for: *A part-time job helped finance my college education.* ❑ *v.* **fi·nanced, fi·nanc·ing.** [**Finance** comes from a French word meaning "to end a debt."]

fi·nan·cial (fə nan′shəl *or* fī nan′shəl), *adj.* **1** of or about money or the management of money: *Their financial affairs are in bad condition.* **2** of or about the management of large sums of public or private money. —**fi·nan′cial·ly,** *adv.*

fin·an·cier (fin′ən sir′ *or* fī′nən sir′), *n.* **1** person who is skilled in managing and investing money. Bankers are financiers. **2** person who is active in matters involving large sums of money.

finch (finch), *n.* **1** any of various small songbirds with a bill shaped like a cone. Sparrows, buntings, grosbeaks, canaries, and cardinals are finches. **2** any of several such birds that are more closely related than the others. ❑ *n., pl.* **finch·es.**

find (fīnd), **1** *v.* to come upon by chance; happen on; meet with: *He found a dime in the road.* **2** *v.* to look for and get: *Please find my hat for me.* **3** *v.* to discover; learn: *We found that he could not swim.* **4** *v.* to get; get the use of: *Can you find time to do this?* **5** *v.* to arrive at; reach: *Water finds its level.* **6** *v.* to decide and declare: *The jury found them guilty.* **7** *v.* to gain or recover the use of: *find your tongue.* **8** *n.* something found, especially something valuable or important: *a scientific find.* ❑ *v.* **found, find·ing.**

find out, to learn about; come to know; discover.

find yourself, to learn your abilities and how to use them well.

find·er (fīn′dər), *n.* **1** person or thing that finds. **2** viewfinder.

find·ing (fīn′ding), *n.* **1** act of discovery: *The finding of a cure for the disease was a welcome event.* **2** decision reached after an examination or inquiry. The verdict of a jury is its finding. **3** **findings,** *pl.* results of an investigation or inquiry.

fine¹ (fīn), **1** *adj.* of very high quality; very good; excellent: *Everybody praised his fine singing. She is a fine scholar.* **2** *adj.* in good health; well. **3** *adj.* very small or thin: *Thread is finer than rope. Sand is finer than gravel.* **4** *adj.* sharp: *a tool with a fine edge.* **5** *adj.* not coarse or heavy; delicate: *fine linen.* **6** *adj.* refined; elegant: *fine manners.* **7** *adj.* subtle: *The law makes fine distinctions.* **8** *adj.* without impurities. Fine gold is gold not mixed with any other metal. **9** *adv.* very well; excellently: *I'm doing fine.* ❑ *adj.* **fin·er, fin·est.** —**fine′ness,** *n.*

fine² (fīn), **1** *n.* sum of money paid as a punishment for breaking a law or regulation. **2** *v.* to make pay such a sum: *The judge fined her $50.* ❑ *v.* **fined, fin·ing.**

fine arts, arts depending upon taste and appealing to the sense of beauty; painting, drawing, sculpture, and architecture.

fine-drawn (fīn′drôn′), *adj.* **1** drawn out until very small or thin. **2** very subtle: *a fine-drawn distinction.*

fine·ly (fīn′lē), *adv.* **1** in a fine manner. **2** in very small pieces: *finely chopped vegetables.*

fine print, 1 part of a contract which is in smaller type or more difficult language than the main part of the contract. It may include details unfavorable to one party to the contract. **2** details of any agreement, especially details limiting benefits.

fin·er·y (fī′nər ē), *n.* showy clothes or ornaments.

fi·nesse (fə nes′), **1** *n.* great skill or delicacy in doing something: *That young artist shows wonderful finesse.* **2** *n.* the skillful handling of a delicate situation to your advantage: *A successful diplomat must be a master of finesse.* **3** *v.* to use finesse. ❑ *v.* **fi·nessed, fi·ness·ing.**

fine-tune (fīn′tün′), *v.* to make delicate adjustments so as to make something work better: *to fine-tune a TV set.* ❑ *v.* **fine-tuned, fine-tun·ing.**

fin·ger (fing′gər), **1** *n.* one of the five end parts of the hand, especially the four besides the thumb. **2** *n.* part of a glove that covers a finger. **3** *n.* anything shaped or used like a finger: *a long finger of land.* **4** *v.* to touch or handle with the fingers: *He absent-mindedly fingered the paper clip.* **5** *v.* to use the fingers on: *finger the keyboard of a piano.* **6** *v.* to perform or mark a passage of music with a certain fingering. **7** *n.* width of a finger; ¾ inch. —**fin′ger·like′,** *adj.*

put your finger on, to point out exactly: *The inspector was able to put his finger on the weak point in the suspect's alibi.*

fin·ger·board (fing′gər bôrd′), *n.* the strip of wood on the neck of a guitar, violin, or other stringed instrument where the player's fingers press the strings to change the sounds.

finger food, food, especially appetizers or snacks, picked up and eaten with your fingers.

fin·ger·ing (fing′gər ing), *n.* **1** way of using the fingers in playing a musical instrument. **2** signs marked on a piece of music to show how the fingers are to be used in playing it.

fingering (def. 1)

fin·ger·nail (fing′gər nāl′), *n.* a hard layer of horn on the upper side of the end of each finger.

finger painting, 1 method of painting pictures or designs on large sheets of paper, with fingers or hands instead of brushes. **2** picture or design painted in this way.

fin·ger·print (fing′gər print′), **1** *n.* mark made by the lines on the skin of the inner surface of the last joint of a finger or thumb. A person can be identified from fingerprints because everyone's fingerprints are different. **2** *v.* to take the fingerprints of.

fin·ger·tip (fing′gər tip′), *n.* tip of a finger.

fin·i·cal (fin′ə kəl), *adj.* finicky. —**fin′i·cal·ly,** *adv.* —**fin′i·cal·ness,** *n*

fin·ick·y (fin′ə kē), *adj.* too dainty or particular; too precise; fussy. —**fin′ick·ness,** *n.*

fi·nis (fin′is *or* fī′nis), *n.* the end.

fin·ish (fin′ish), **1** *v.* to bring to an end; reach the end of; complete: *finish your dinner, finish sewing a dress.* ■ See Synonym Study at **end. 2** *v.* to come to an end: *There was so little wind that the sailing race didn't finish until after dark.* **3** *n.* an end: *the finish of a race.* **4** *v.* to use up completely: *finish off a bottle of milk.* **5** *n.* way in which the surface is prepared: *a smooth finish on furniture.* **6** *v.* to prepare the surface of in some way: *finish metal with a dull surface.* **7** *v.* to perfect in detail; polish. ❑ *n., pl.* **fin·ish·es.** —**fin′ish·er,** *n.*

finish off, 1 to complete. **2** to overcome completely; destroy; kill.

finish up, 1 to complete: *finish up a job*. **2** to use up completely: *I've finished up all the paint.*

finish with, 1 to complete. **2** to stop being friends with; have nothing to do with.

fin·ished (fin′isht), *adj.* **1** ended or completed. **2** brought to the highest degree of excellence; perfected; polished: *It takes years of study and practice to become a finished musician.*

finish line, line marking the end of a race.

fi·nite (fī′nīt), *adj.* **1** having limits; not infinite: *Human understanding is finite.* **2** in mathematics: **a** able to be reached or passed in counting: *a finite number.* **b** (of a set) having a limited number of elements. **—fi′nite·ly,** *adv.* **—fi′nite·ness,** *n.*

fink (fingk), *n.* SLANG. **1** informer. **2** an undesirable person.

Fink (fingk), *n.* **Mike** (mīk), 1770-1823, American frontiersman and folk hero. ■ Mike Fink was famous for his courage and his skill with a boat or a rifle. Because of his strength and readiness to fight, he was called "half horse, half alligator."

Fin·land (fin′lənd), *n.* **1** country in N Europe, east of Sweden. *Capital:* Helsinki. **2 Gulf of,** part of the Baltic Sea, south of Finland.

Finn (fin), *n.* person born or living in Finland.

fin·nan had·die (fin′ən had′ē), smoked and dried haddock.

Finn·bo·ga·dót·tir (fin′bō′gə dot′ər), *n.* **Vig·dis** (vig′dəs), born 1930, president of Iceland since 1980. She was the first woman in the world to be elected as a head of state.

finned (find), *adj.* having a fin or fins.

Finn·ish (fin′ish), **1** *adj.* of Finland, its people, or their language. **2** *n.pl.* the people of Finland. **3** *n.* language of Finland.

fin·ny (fin′ē), *adj.* **1** filled with fish. **2** having fins. **3** like a fin. ❏ *adj.* **fin·ni·er, fin·ni·est.**

fin whale, a very large baleen whale with a large fin on its back, found throughout the world.

fiord (fyôrd), *n.* fjord.

fir (fėr), *n.* any of several evergreen trees related to the pine, with needles growing evenly around the branch. Some firs are valued for their timber. Small firs are often used for Christmas trees. ■ Another word that sounds like this is **fur.**

fire (fīr), **1** *n.* flame, heat, and light caused by something burning. **2** *n.* something burning: *They had a nice fire in the fireplace.* **3** *n.* destruction by burning: *A cigarette thrown into the woods in dry weather may start a fire.* **4** *v.* to make burn; set on fire. **5** *n.* fuel burning or arranged so that it will burn quickly: *A fire was laid in the fireplace.* **6** *v.* to supply with fuel; tend the fire of: *fire a furnace.* **7** *v.* to dry with heat; bake: *Bricks are fired to make them hard.* **8** *n.* heat of feeling; readiness to act; passion, fervor, enthusiasm, or excitement: *Their hearts were full of patriotic fire.* **9** *v.* to arouse; excite; inflame: *Stories about adventures fire the imagination.* **10** *n.* the shooting of guns or other weapons: *The enemy's fire forced the troops to take shelter in a ravine.* **11** *v.* to shoot: *to fire at the target, to fire a gun.* **12** *v.* to throw: *The shortstop fired the ball to first base.* **13** *v.* to dismiss from a job. ❏ *v.* **fired, fir·ing. —fir′er,** *n.*

catch fire, to begin to burn.

hang fire, be slow in going off or acting; be delayed.

miss fire, 1 to fail to go off. **2** to fail to do what was attempted.

on fire, 1 burning. **2** full of a feeling or spirit like fire; excited.

open fire, to begin shooting.

under fire, 1 exposed to shooting from the enemy's guns. **2** attacked; blamed.

fire ant, any of several ants having painful, burning stings.

fire·arm (fīr′ärm′), *n.* weapon to shoot with. Pistols, rifles, and shotguns are firearms.

fire·ball (fīr′bòl′), *n.* **1** the great, glowing cloud of hot gases, water vapor, and dust produced by a nuclear explosion. **2** anything that looks like a ball of fire, such as a ball of lightning. **3** a large, brilliant meteor. **4** person having great energy.

fire·boat (fīr′bōt′), *n.* boat with equipment for putting out fires.

fire·brand (fīr′brand′), *n.* **1** piece of burning wood. **2** person who arouses angry feelings in others.

fire·break (fīr′brāk′), *n.* a strip of cleared or plowed land created to prevent the spreading of a forest fire or a prairie fire.

fire·bug (fīr′bug′), *n.* INFORMAL. person who purposely sets buildings or property on fire; person who commits arson.

fire·crack·er (fīr′krak′ər), *n.* a paper roll containing gunpowder and a fuse. Firecrackers explode with a loud noise.

fire·dog (fīr′dòg′), *n.* andiron.

fire drill, practice of what to do in case of fire. In a fire drill, people practice leaving a building in an orderly way, and firefighters practice using their equipment.

fire engine, truck with equipment for pumping and spraying water, chemicals, etc., to put out fires; fire truck.

fire escape, stairway or ladder in or on a building, to use when the building is on fire.

fire extinguisher, container filled with chemicals which can be sprayed on a small fire to put it out.

fire·fight·er (fīr′fī′tər), *n.* person who belongs to a fire department, trained to put out fires.

fire·fly (fīr′flī′), *n.* any of many small beetles that give off flashes of light at night; lightning bug. ❏ *n., pl.* **fire·flies.**

fire·house (fīr′hous′), *n.* building where fire trucks are kept; fire station. ❏ *n., pl.* **fire·hous·es** (fīr′hou′ziz).

fire·light (fīr′līt′), *n.* light from a fire.

fire·man (fīr′mən), *n.* **1** firefighter. **2** person whose work is looking after fires in a furnace, boiler, etc. ❏ *n., pl.* **fire·men.**

fire·place (fīr′plās′), *n.* place built to hold a fire. Indoor fireplaces are usually made of brick or stone, with a chimney leading up through the roof or up the outside of an exterior wall.

fire·plug (fīr′plug′), *n.* hydrant.

fire·pow·er (fīr′pou′ər), *n.* amount of ammunition that can be fired by a military unit or a particular weapon.

fire·proof (fīr′prüf′), **1** *adj.* very resistant to fire; almost impossible to burn: *fireproof pajamas.* **2** *v.* to make fireproof.

fire·side (fīr′sīd′), *n.* **1** space around a fireplace or hearth. **2** home; hearth: *We were weary of traveling and longed to be back at our own fireside.* **3** home life: *a happy fireside.*

fire station, firehouse.

fire tower, tower from which forest rangers can watch for forest fires.

fire·trap (fīr′trap′), *n.* building that could burn very easily and would be hard to get out of if it were on fire.

fire truck, fire engine.

fire·wa·ter (fīr′wò′tər), *n.* a strong alcoholic drink.

fire·weed (fīr′wēd′), *n.* any of several kinds of plant that grow quickly in burned areas, especially one kind with white or purple flowers. It is the territorial flower of Canada's Yukon Territory.

fire·wood (fīr′wùd′), *n.* wood to make a fire.

fire tower

fire·work (fīr′wėrk′), *n.* **1** a firecracker, bomb, rocket, etc., that makes a loud noise or a beautiful, fiery display at night. **2 fireworks,** *pl.* a firework display.

firm[1] (fėrm), *adj.* **1** not yielding when pressed; solid; hard: *a firm mattress, firm ground.* **2** not easily moved or shaken; securely in place: *She made the shelf firm by screwing it to the wall.* **3** not easily changed; determined; resolute; positive: *a firm voice, a firm character, a firm belief.* **4** strong: *a firm handshake.* **5** not changing; staying the same; steady: *a firm price.* [See Word Story at **farm.**] **—firm′ly,** *adv.* **—firm′ness,** *n.*

firm[2] (fėrm), *n.* a company or other business organization.

fir·ma·ment (fėr′mə mənt), *n.* OLD USE. the heavens; sky.

a	hat	ė	term	ô	order	ch	child		
ā	age	i	it	oi	oil	ng	long		a in about
ä	far	ī	ice	ou	out	sh	she		e in taken
â	care	o	hot	u	cup	th	thin	ə	i in pencil
e	let	ō	open	ù	put	ŦH	then		o in lemon
ē	equal	ò	saw	ü	rule	zh	measure		u in circus

firm·ware (fẻrm′wâr′), *n.* any computer program that cannot be contacted or changed by the computer user. Firmware is usually built into ROM devices. [**Firmware** got its name to separate it from **software,** programs the user can affect, and **hardware,** unchangeable physical devices.]

first (fẻrst), **1** *adj.* coming before all others: *She is first in her class.* **2** *adv.* before all others; before anything else: *We eat first and then feed the cat.* **3** *n.* person, thing, place, etc., that is first: *We were the first to get here.* **4** *n.* the beginning: *At first I did not like school.* **5** *adv.* for the first time: *When I first met her, she was a child.* **6** *adv.* instead of something else; rather; sooner: *I won't give up; I will die first.* **7** *adj.* (in music) playing or singing the chief part or the part highest in pitch: *first flute, first soprano.* **8** *n.* the first day of the month: *I'll see you on the first.*

first aid, emergency treatment given to an injured or sick person before a doctor sees the person.

first-aid (fẻrst′ād′), *adj.* of or for first aid: *a first-aid kit.*

first-born (fẻrst′bôrn′), **1** *adj.* born first; oldest. **2** *n.* the first-born child.

first class, 1 the best and most expensive passenger seating and service offered for travel by ship, airplane, or train. **2** class of mail that includes letters and post cards.

first-class (fẻrst′klas′), **1** *adj.* of the highest class or best quality; excellent: *a first-class singer.* **2** *adv.* by the best and most expensive passenger seating and service offered by ship, airplane, or train: *We could not afford to travel first-class.*

first cousin, son or daughter of your uncle or aunt.

first-de·gree (fẻrst′də grē′), *adj.* **1** of the worst kind: *First-degree murder is planned murder.* **2** of the least bad kind: *First-degree burns cause only redness and pain, not blistering.*

> **USAGE NOTE** Sometimes a word or phrase has two meanings that are opposites of each other. **First-degree** can mean "most bad" (def. 1) or "least bad" (def. 2). **Scan** can mean to look over something closely (def. 1): *The programmer will scan the computer printout line by line, looking for errors.* **Scan** can also mean to look over something quickly (def. 2): *She scans the whole paper first, then reads some stories carefully.* **Biweekly** can mean happening every two weeks (def. 1), or it can mean happening twice a week (def. 2). And **gauge** can mean to estimate (def. 4), or it can mean to measure carefully (def. 3). If you see a word that seems to be used in a way that doesn't make sense to you, it's always a good idea to check to see if it has meanings other than the ones you know.

first·hand (fẻrst′hand′), *adj., adv.* from the original source; direct: *firsthand information, to get information firsthand.*

first lady, the official hostess, usually the wife, of the President of the United States or of the governor of a state.

first lieutenant, a military rank. See chart on page 712.

first person, form of a pronoun or verb used to refer to the speaker or writer and those with whom he or she is included. *I, me, we,* and *us* are pronouns of the first person.

first quarter, 1 period of time between the new moon and the first half moon. **2** phase of the moon represented by the first half moon after the new moon.

first-rate (fẻrst′rāt′), **1** *adj.* of the highest class; excellent; very good: *a first-rate actor.* **2** *adv.* excellently; very well: *He did first-rate on the test.*

first sergeant, a military rank. See chart on page 712.

firth (fẻrth), *n.* (especially in Scotland) a narrow arm of the sea; estuary of a river.

fis·cal (fis′kəl), *adj.* **1** financial. **2** having to do with public finance: *governmental fiscal policies.* —**fis′cal·ly,** *adv.*

fiscal year, time between one yearly settlement of financial accounts and another. The fiscal year of the U.S. government begins July 1 and ends June 30.

Fisch·er (fish′ər), *n.* **Bob·by** (bob′ē), born 1943, American chess champion. ■ **Bobby Fischer** was the youngest International Grand Master ever at the age of 15, and was the first American to win the world chess championship, in 1972.

fish (fish), **1** *n.* any of a very large group of animals that live in the water and have gills instead of lungs for breathing. Fish have backbones and are usually covered with scales and have fins for swimming. Some kinds of fish lay eggs in the water; others produce living young. **2** *n.* flesh of fish used for food. **3** *v.* to catch fish; try to catch fish. **4** *v.* to try for something as if with a hook: *The boy fished with a stick for his watch which had fallen through a grating.* **5** *v.* to search: *She fished in her purse for a coin.* **6** *v.* to find and pull: *She fished an old map out of a box.* **7** *v.* to try to get in sly, indirect ways: *fish for compliments.* ❑ *n., pl.* **fish** or **fish·es.** —**fish′like′,** *adj.*

> **USAGE NOTE** **Fish** has two plural forms, **fish** and **fishes. Fish** is the usual plural form: *She has a tank of fish in her room.* People have to learn not to use **fishes** in sentences like that one, so it may be a surprise to find **fishes** used in dictionary definitions. **Fishes** is used when more than one kind of fish is involved: *Tuna, salmon, and trout are fishes often used for food.* **Fish** can also be used about several different kinds, if the difference isn't important to your idea: *The lake is full of fish.*

fish and chips, pieces of fried fish and French-fried potatoes.

fish·er (fish′ər), *n.* **1** person or animal that fishes. **2** a slender, meat-eating mammal of North America. It is related to the weasel. **3** its dark brown fur. ■ Another word that sounds like this is **fissure.**

fish·er·man (fish′ər mən), *n.* person who fishes, especially someone who makes a living by catching fish. ❑ *n., pl.* **fish·er·men.**

fish·er·y (fish′ər ē), *n.* place for catching or breeding fish. ❑ *n., pl.* **fish·er·ies.**

fish-eye (fish′ī′), *adj.* covering an extremely wide angle of view. A fish-eye lens distorts what it shows so that straight lines seem to curve.

fish farm, place where fish are raised in tanks or ponds, usually to be sold to markets and restaurants.

fish hawk, osprey.

fish·hook (fish′hůk′), *n.* hook with a barb used for catching fish.

fish·ing (fish′ing), *n.* the catching of fish for a living or for pleasure.

fish-eye—photograph with fish-eye lens

fishing rod, a long, light pole with a line and hook attached to it, and often having a reel, used in catching fish.

fish·line (fish′lin′), *n.* cord used with a fishhook for catching fish.

fish meal, dried fish that have been ground up for use as animal food and fertilizer.

fish·mon·ger (fish′mung′gər), *n.* dealer in fish.

fish stick, a boneless piece of cod, perch, etc., dipped in batter and breaded, usually sold in frozen form.

fish·wife (fish′wīf′), *n.* woman who uses coarse and abusive language. ❑ *n., pl.* **fish·wives** (fish′wīvz′). ■ **Fishwife** is often considered offensive.

fish·y (fish′ē), *adj.* **1** like a fish in smell, taste, or shape. **2** not probable; doubtful; unlikely; suspicious: *Her excuse sounds fishy; I don't believe it.* ❑ *adj.* **fish·i·er, fish·i·est.** —**fish′i·ly,** *adv.* —**fish′i·ness,** *n.*

fis·sion (fish′ən), *n.* **1** act or process of splitting apart; division into parts. **2** method of reproduction in which the body of the parent divides to form two or more independent offspring. Many simple living things reproduce by fission. **3** act of splitting an atomic nucleus into two parts, especially when bombarded by a neutron; nuclear fission. Fission releases huge amounts of energy when the nuclei of heavy elements, especially uranium and plutonium, are split. Fission causes the chain reaction in a nuclear power plant or an atomic bomb.

fis·sion·a·ble (fish′ə nə bəl), *adj.* capable of nuclear fission.

fission bomb, atomic bomb.

fis·sure (fish′ər), *n.* a long, narrow opening; split; crack: *Water dripped from a fissure in the rock.* ■ Another word that sounds like this is **fisher.**

fist (fist), *n.* hand closed tightly with the fingers bent against the palm: *He shook his fist at me.*

fist·i·cuffs (fis′tə kufs′), *n.pl.* OLD USE. a fight with the fists.

fis·tu·la (fis′chə lə), *n.* a deep, tubelike passage connecting the skin with some internal cavity or organ. It is caused by a wound, abscess, disease, etc. ◻ *n.,* pl. **fis·tu·las, fis·tu·lae** (fis′chə lē′).

fit[1] (fit), **1** *adj.* having the necessary qualities; suitable: *Grass is food for cows; it is not fit for people.* **2** *adj.* in good physical condition; healthy and strong: *I am now well and fit for work.* ■ See Synonym Study at **healthy**. **3** *v.* to be right or proper for; be suitable to: *a punishment that fits the crime.* **4** *adj.* right; proper: *It is fit that we give thanks.* **5** *v.* to make right, proper or suitable; suit: *fit the action to the word.* **6** *v.* to have the right size or shape; have the right size or shape for: *Does this glove fit?* **7** *v.* to make the right size or shape; adjust: *I had my new jacket fitted at the store.* **8** *n.* way that something fits: *The coat was not a very good fit; it was too tight.* **9** *v.* to supply with everything needed; equip: *We fitted out our summer cabin with wooden furniture.* ◻ *adj.* **fit·ter, fit·test;** *v.* **fit** or **fit·ted, fit·ting.** —**fit′ly,** *adv.*

fit to be tied, very angry or annoyed: *When I said "I quit!" she was fit to be tied.*

see fit or **think fit,** to prefer and decide; choose.

fit[2] (fit), *n.* **1** a sudden, sharp attack of disease: *a fit of colic.* **2** a violent outburst of feeling: *a fit of anger.* **3** a short period of doing some one thing; spell: *a fit of coughing, a fit of laughter.*

by fits and starts, irregularly; starting, stopping, beginning again, and so on: *He does his homework by fits and starts instead of steadily.*

have a fit or **throw a fit,** to show great anger: *My parents had a fit when I spilled a gallon of paint.* .

fit·ful (fit′fəl), *adj.* going on and then stopping for a while; irregular: *She had a fitful sleep during the storm, waking up every few minutes.* —**fit′ful·ly,** *adv.* —**fit′ful·ness,** *n.*

fit·ness (fit′nis), *n.* the state of being healthy and strong: *physical fitness.*

fitness walking, exercise by rapid walking to improve cardiovascular function.

fit·ter (fit′ər), *n.* person who supplies and fixes anything necessary for some purpose: *a pipe fitter.*

fit·ting (fit′ing), **1** *adj.* proper and right; suitable: *a fitting reward.* **2** *n.* a small part used to connect or adjust things: *a pipe fitting.* —**fit′ting·ly,** *adv.* —**fit′ting·ness,** *n.*

Fitz·ger·ald (fits jer′əld), *n.* **1** **El·la** (el′ə), born 1918, American singer and composer. She is famous for her own songs and for her versions of songs by Cole Porter, Irving Berlin, and others. **2** **F. Scott,** 1896-1940, American writer of novels and short stories. He wrote *The Great Gatsby.*

five (fiv), *n., adj.* one more than four; 5.

Five Nations, group of American Indian tribes that joined together probably before 1500 A.D. and that included the Mohawk, Oneida, Onondaga, Cayuga and Seneca. This group is also called the Iroquois.

five pins, (in Canada) a kind of bowling in which only five pins are used.

fix (fiks), **1** *v.* to put back into good condition; repair; mend: *fix a watch.* ■ See Synonym Study at **repair**[1]. **2** *v.* to put in order; set right; arrange: *fix your hair.* **3** *v.* to prepare a meal or food: *fix dinner.* **4** *v.* to make firm; fasten tightly: *We fixed the post in the ground.* **5** *v.* to settle; set: *Did you fix on a day for the picnic?* **6** *v.* to direct or hold your eyes, attention, etc., steadily. **7** *v.* to make or become stiff or rigid: *eyes fixed in death.* **8** *v.* to put or place definitely: *She fixed the blame on them.* **9** *v.* to treat to prevent fading or other changes: *fix a dye or a photograph with chemicals.* **10** *v.* to bribe someone to decide something favorable to you and unfavorable to your opponents: *fix a jury, fix a game.* **11** *v.* to get revenge upon; get even with; punish. **12** *n.* position hard to get out of; awkward state of affairs: *He got himself into a bad fix.* **13** *n.* SLANG. dose of a narcotic, especially an injection of heroin. ◻ *n.,* pl. **fix·es.** —**fix′a·ble,** *adj.* —**fix′er,** *n.*

fix on or **fix upon,** to choose; select.

fix up, 1 to mend; repair. **2** to put in order; arrange. **3** arrange a date or meeting for someone: *She fixed me up with her cousin.*

fix·a·tion (fik sā′shən), *n.* an extreme or unhealthy interest in something.

fix·a·tive (fik′sə tiv), *n.* substance used to prevent something from fading or otherwise changing.

fixed (fikst), *adj.* **1** not movable; made firm: *Some classrooms have fixed seats.* **2** definitely assigned; settled; set: *fixed charges for taxis.* **3** steady; not moving: *a fixed gaze.*

fix·ed·ly (fik′sid lē), *adv.* in a fixed manner; without change; intently: *She stared fixedly at the ring.*

fixed star, (old use) star that does not appear to move in relation to other stars.

fix·ings (fik′singz), *n.pl.* trimmings: *We had turkey and all the fixings for Thanksgiving dinner.*

fix·ture (fiks′chər), *n.* **1** thing put in place to stay: *a bathroom fixture, light fixtures.* **2** person or thing that stays in one place, job, etc.: *He is a fixture in the office.*

fizz (fiz), **1** *v.* to make a hissing sound. **2** *n.* a hissing sound; bubbling: *the fizz of soda water.* ◻ *n.,* pl. **fizz·es.** [Fizz comes from the sound it names. To imitate the sound, say the word. The process of forming words by imitating sounds is called onomatopoeia.]

fiz·zle (fiz′əl), **1** *v.* to make a hissing sound that dies out weakly: *The firecracker just fizzled instead of exploding.* **2** *v.* to fail or end in failure, especially after a good start: *After three days the strike fizzled.* **3** *n.* failure. ◻ *v.* **fiz·zled, fiz·zling.**

fizzle out, to come to a poor end; fail, especially after a good start: *The picnic fizzled out when it began to rain.*

fizz·y (fiz′ē), *adj.* bubbly; effervescent. ◻ *adj.* **fizz·i·er, fizz·i·est.**

fjord

fjord (fyôrd), *n.* a long, narrow bay of the sea bordered by steep cliffs. Norway has many fjords. Also, **fiord.**

Fl, symbol for fluorine.

FL, Florida (used with postal Zip Code).

fl., 1 florin. **2** flourished. **3** fluid.

Fla., Florida.

flab (flab), *n.* **1** soft flesh; too much weight or fat. ■ This meaning of **flab** is sometimes considered offensive. **2** too much of anything: *cut the flab out of the report.*

flab·ber·gast·ed (flab′ər gas′tid), *adj.* speechless with surprise; greatly astonished.

a	hat	ė	term	ô	order	ch	child		a in about
ā	age	i	it	oi	oil	ng	long		e in taken
ä	far	ī	ice	ou	out	sh	she	ə	i in pencil
â	care	o	hot	u	cup	th	thin		o in lemon
e	let	ō	open	u̇	put	ᴛн	then		u in circus
ē	equal	ȯ	saw	ü	rule	zh	measure		

flab·by (flab′ē), *adj.* lacking firmness or force; soft; weak: *His muscles were flabby after his three-month illness.* ❑ *adj.* **flab·bi·er, flab·bi·est.** —**flab′bi·ly,** *adv.* —**flab′bi·ness,** *n.*

flac·cid (flak′sid), *adj.* limp; weak: *flaccid muscles, a flaccid will.* —**flac·cid′i·ty,** *n.* —**flac′cid·ly,** *adv.*

flag[1] (flag), **1** *n.* piece of cloth, usually with square corners, with a pattern or picture on it that stands for some country, city, etc.: *the Mexican flag.* Flags are hung on poles over buildings, ships, army camps, etc. **2** *n.* cloth or banner, often used as a signal: *a red flag showing danger.* **3** *v.* to stop or signal with or as if with a flag: *We tried to flag a bus at the corner.* ❑ *v.* **flagged, flag·ging.**

flag[2] (flag), *n.* iris with blue, purple, yellow, or white flowers and sword-shaped leaves.

flag[3] (flag), *v.* to get tired; grow weak: *My horse was flagging, but I urged him on.* ❑ *v.* **flagged, flag·ging.**

Flag Day, June 14, the anniversary of the day in 1777 when the Second Continental Congress adopted the Stars and Stripes as the flag of the United States.

flag·el·late (flaj′ə lāt *for verb;* flaj′ə lāt *or* flaj′ə lət *for adj., noun),* **1** *v.* to whip; flog. **2** *adj.* having flagella. **3** *n.* any of a large group of protists that have flagella. ❑ *v.* **flag·el·lat·ed, flag·el·lat·ing.** —**flag′el·la′tion,** *n.*

fla·gel·lum (flə jel′əm), *n.* a long, whiplike tail or part. Certain cells, protists, etc., have flagella with which they move. ❑ *n., pl.* **fla·gel·la** (flə jel′ə), **fla·gel·lums.** [Flagellum comes from a Latin word meaning "a whip." It was called this because of its appearance.]

flag·e·o·let (flaj′ə let′), *n.* a small wind instrument somewhat like a flute, with a mouthpiece at one end, six main finger holes, and sometimes keys. [Flageolet comes from a Latin word meaning "to blow." Flute probably comes from the same Latin word.]

flag·man (flag′mən), *n.* person who signals with a flag or lantern at a railroad crossing, etc. ❑ *n., pl.* **flag·men.**

flag·on (flag′ən), *n.* container for liquids, usually having a handle, a spout, and a cover.

flag·pole (flag′pōl′), *n.* pole from which a flag is flown; flagstaff.

fla·grant (flā′grənt), *adj.* **1** notorious; outrageous; scandalous: *a flagrant crime.* **2** glaring: *a flagrant error.* —**fla′grant·ly,** *adv.*

flag·ship (flag′ship′), *n.* ship that carries the officer in command of a fleet or squadron and displays that officer's flag.

flag·staff (flag′staf′), *n.* flagpole.

flag·stone (flag′stōn′), *n.* a large, flat stone, used for paving paths, terraces, etc.

flail (flāl), **1** *n.* tool for threshing grain by hand. A flail consists of a wooden handle with a short, heavy stick fastened at one end by a strip of leather. **2** *v.* to strike with or as if with a flail: *The rider flailed the horse.* **3** *v.* to wave your arms about wildly: *The campers flailed away at the buzzing mosquitoes.*

flair (flâr), *n.* natural talent: *The poet had a flair for making clever rhymes.* ■ Another word that sounds like this is **flare.**

flak (flak), *n.* **1** shellfire from antiaircraft cannon. **2** criticism.

flake (flāk), **1** *n.* a flat, thin piece, usually not very large: *a flake of snow, flakes of rust, corn flakes.* **2** *v.* to come off in flakes; separate into flakes: *Dirty, gray spots showed where the paint had flaked off.* ❑ *v.* **flaked, flak·ing.**

flak·y (flā′kē), *adj.* **1** consisting of flakes. **2** easily broken or separated into flakes. **3** INFORMAL. very strange or peculiar: *That group has some pretty flaky ideas.* ❑ *adj.* **flak·i·er, flak·i·est.** —**flak′i·ly,** *adv.* —**flak′i·ness,** *n.*

flam·boy·ant (flam boi′ənt), *adj.* **1** gorgeously brilliant; brightly beautiful: *Some flowers have flamboyant colors.* **2** very ornate; much decorated: *flamboyant architecture.* **3** given to display; showy: *a flamboyant person.* —**flam·boy′ant·ly,** *adv.*

flame (flām), **1** *n.* one of the glowing tongues of light, usually red or yellow, that rise when a fire blazes up: *The burning house went up in flames.* **2** *n.* a burning gas or vapor. **3** *v.* to rise up in

flames; blaze; burn: *The dry logs flamed up in the fireplace.* **4** *n.* condition of burning with flames; blaze: *The dying fire suddenly burst into flame.* **5** *v.* to shine brightly; flash: *Her dark eyes flamed with rage.* **6** *n.* a burning feeling; zeal. ❑ *v.* **flamed, flam·ing.** —**flame′like′,** *adj.*

fla·men·co (flə meng′kō), *n.* style of Spanish Gypsy dance performed with castanets to fast, vigorous rhythms. [See Word Story at **flamingo.**]

flame·throw·er (flām′thrō′ər), *n.* weapon that throws a stream of burning fuel through the air.

fla·min·go (flə ming′gō), *n.* any of four tropical wading birds with very long legs and necks, and feathers that vary from pink to scarlet. ❑ *n., pl.* **fla·min·gos** or **fla·min·goes.**

flamingo—up to 5 ft. (1.5 m) tall

flam·ma·ble (flam′ə bəl), *adj.* easily set on fire; inflammable: *Paper is flammable.* —**flam′ma·bil′i·ty,** *n.*

flan (flän *or* flan), *n.* a baked custard dessert with a caramel topping.

Flan·ders (flan′dərz), *n.* region in N Europe. It is now divided among Belgium, France, and the Netherlands. See **Burgundy** for map.

flange (flanj), *n.* a raised edge, collar, or rim on a wheel, pulley, pipe, or other object. It is used to keep an object in place, fasten it to another, strengthen it, etc. Railroad cars have wheels with flanges to keep them on the track.

flank (flangk), **1** *n.* side of an animal or person between the ribs and the hip. **2** *n.* piece of beef cut from this part. **3** *n.* side of a mountain, building, etc. **4** *v.* to be at the side of: *A garage flanked the house.* **5** *n.* the far right or the far left side of an army, fort, fleet, or formation. **6** *v.* to attack or get around the flanks.

flank·er (flang′kər), *n.* **1** person or thing that flanks. **2** (in football) an offensive back who lines up on either the far right or far left of the formation, closer to the sidelines than other members of the team.

flank·er·back (flang′kər bak′), *n.* flanker (def. 2).

flan·nel (flan′l), *n.* **1** a soft, warm, woolen or cotton cloth. **2 flannels,** *pl.* clothes made of flannel.

flan·nel·ette (flan′l et′), *n.* a soft, warm, cotton cloth with a nap that looks like flannel.

flap (flap), **1** *v.* to swing or sway about loosely and with some noise: *The sails flapped in the wind.* **2** *v.* to move wings, arms, etc., up and down: *The goose flapped its wings but could not rise from the ground.* **3** *v.* to fly by flapping the wings: *The bird flapped away.* **4** *n.* a flapping motion; flapping noise: *the flap of a bird's wing.* **5** *v.* to strike noisily with something broad and flat: *The clown's big shoes flapped along the ground.* **6** *n.* piece hanging or fastened at one edge only: *a coat with flaps on the pockets.* **7** *n.* INFORMAL. an excited or disturbed state: *Things were in a terrible flap after the robbery.* ❑ *v.* **flapped, flap·ping.**

flap·jack (flap′jak′), *n.* pancake.

flap·per (flap′ər), *n.* a young woman of the 1920s whose behavior was considered wild.

flare (flâr), **1** *v.* to flame up briefly or unsteadily, sometimes with smoke: *The damp logs flared up briefly; then the fire died out.* **2** *n.* a bright, brief, unsteady flame; blaze: *In the flare of the match I was able to locate the light switch.* **3** *n.* a device that produces a dazzling light that burns for a short time, used for signaling, lighting up an area, or as a warning: *The Coast Guard ship responded to the flare sent up from the lifeboat.* **4** *v.* to burst out into open anger or violence: *Her temper flared at the insult.* **5** *v.* to spread out in the shape of a bell: *These pants flare at the bottom.* **6** *n.* act of spreading out into a bell shape: *the flare of a skirt.* □ *v.* **flared, flar·ing.** ■ Another word that sounds like this is **flair**.

flare up, to burst out into open anger, violence, etc.

flare-up (flâr′up′), *n.* **1** outburst of flame. **2** a sudden outburst of anger or violence.

flash (flash), **1** *n.* a sudden, brief light or flame: *a flash of lightning.* **2** *v.* to give out such a light or flame: *Lightning flashed across the sky.* **3** *v.* to come suddenly; pass quickly: *A thought flashed across my mind.* **4** *n.* a sudden, short feeling or display: *a flash of hope, a flash of wit.* **5** *n.* a very brief time; instant: *It all happened in a flash.* **6** *v.* to give out or send out like a flash: *His eyes flashed defiance.* **7** *v.* to send by computer, satellite, TV, etc.: *flash the news across the country.* **8** *n.* a news report sent by TV, radio, satellite, etc. □ *n., pl.* **flash·es.**

flash·back (flash′bak′), *n.* a break in the continuous series of events of a novel, motion picture, etc., to introduce some earlier event or scene.

flash·bulb (flash′bulb′), *n.* an electric bulb which gives out a brilliant flash of light for a very short time. It is used in taking photographs indoors or at night.

flash·card (flash′kärd′), *n.* card bearing a letter, word, number, simple problem or picture. In drills in elementary reading, arithmetic, etc., the teacher displays a flashcard briefly and the student gives a quick answer.

flash·cube (flash′kyüb′), *n.* device shaped like a cube containing a set of four small flashbulbs. When attached to a camera, it can be used to take several photographs rapidly.

flash flood, a sudden, violent flooding of a river, stream, etc.

flash-for·ward (flash′fôr′wərd), *n.* a break in the continuous series of events of a novel, motion picture, etc., to show some later event or scene.

flash gun, (in photography) a device for holding and setting off a flashbulb.

flash·ing (flash′ing), *n.* pieces of sheet metal used around windows, chimneys, roof joints, etc., to make them watertight.

flash·light (flash′lit′), *n.* a portable electric light, powered by batteries.

flash point, the lowest temperature at which a small flame will set fire to the vapors from a flammable liquid.

flashy (def. 2)

flash·y (flash′ē), *adj.* **1** brilliant or sparkling, especially in a superficial way or for a short time; flashing: *a flashy dance routine.* **2** showy; gaudy: *a flashy new car.* ■ See Synonym Study at **showy.** □ *adj.* **flash·i·er, flash·i·est.** —**flash′i·ly,** *adv.* —**flash′i·ness,** *n.*

flask (flask), *n.* a glass or metal bottle, especially one with a narrow neck.

flat¹ (flat), **1** *adj.* smooth and level; even: *flat land.* ■ See Synonym Study at **level.** **2** *adj.* at full length; horizontal: *The storm left the trees flat on the ground.* **3** *n.* the flat part: *The flat of your hand is the palm.* **4** *n.* Often **flats,** *pl.* land that is flat and level:

mud flats. **5** *adj.* not very deep or thick: *A plate is flat.* **6** *n.* a shallow box or basket: *I started the plants in flats, transplanting them in warm weather.* **7** *adj.* with little air in it: *A nail or sharp stone can cause a flat tire.* **8** *n.* a tire with little air in it. **9** *adj.* not to be changed; absolute: *a flat refusal.* **10** *adj.* not varied; fixed: *a flat rate with no extra charges.* **11** *adj.* without much life, interest, flavor, etc.; dull: *Plain food tastes flat.* **12** *adj.* not shiny or glossy: *a flat yellow.* **13** in music: **a** *adv.* below the true pitch: *sing flat.* **b** *adj.* one half step or half note below natural pitch: *Play a B flat.* **c** *n.* such a tone or note. **d** *n.* sign (♭) that shows such a tone. **e** *adj.* (of a key) having flats in the signature. **f** *v.* to lower in pitch. **14** *adv.* in a flat manner; flatly: *I fell flat on the floor.* **15** *adv.* exactly: *Her time for the race was two minutes flat.* □ *adj.* **flat·ter, flat·test;** *v.* **flat·ted, flat·ting.** —**flat′ly,** *adv.* —**flat′ness,** *n.*

fall flat, to fail completely: *His attempts at clowning fell flat.*

flat² (flat), *n.* BRITISH. apartment or set of rooms on one floor.

flat·bed (flat′bed′), *n.* truck or trailer having a low, shallow floor without sides.

flat·boat (flat′bōt′), *n.* (long ago) a large boat with a flat bottom, much used for carrying goods on a river or canal.

flat·car (flat′kär′), *n.* a railroad freight car without a roof or sides.

flat·fish (flat′fish′), *n.* any of a group of fishes having a flat body, and swimming on one side, with both eyes on the upper side of the head; fluke. Halibut, flounder, and sole are kinds of flatfish. □ *n., pl.* **flat·fish** or **flat·fish·es.**

flat-foot·ed (flat′fùt′id), *adj.* having feet with flattened arches. —**flat′-foot′ed·ly,** *adv.* —**flat′-foot′ed·ness,** *n.*

Flat·head (flat′hed′), *n.* member of an American Indian tribe of the Salish group, now living in Montana.

flat·i·ron (flat′ī′ərn), *n.* iron (def. 7).

flat·land (flat′land′), *n.* level land, without hills and valleys.

flat-out (flat′out′), **1** *adj.* absolute; outright: *flat-out lies.* **2** *adv.* absolutely; entirely; outright: *Your statement is flat-out wrong.*

flat·ten (flat′n), *v.* to make or become flat: *Use a rolling pin to flatten the pie dough.* —**flat′ten·er,** *n.*

flat·ter (flat′ər), *v.* **1** to praise too much or beyond the truth in order to please; praise insincerely: *Were you only flattering me when you said I sang well, or did you mean it?* ■ See Synonym Study at **praise.** **2** to show as more beautiful or better looking than is the truth: *This picture flatters me.* **3** to cause to be pleased or feel honored: *You flatter me with your concern for my welfare.* —**flat′ter·er,** *n.* —**flat′ter·ing·ly,** *adv.*

flat·ter·y (flat′ər ē), *n.* **1** act of flattering. **2** praise that is too much or untrue: *Some people use flattery to get favors.*

flat·tish (flat′ish), *adj.* somewhat flat.

flat·top (flat′top′), *n.* **1** INFORMAL. an aircraft carrier. **2** a very short haircut similar to a crew cut but cut flat on top of the head.

flat·ware (flat′wâr′), *n.* **1** knives, forks, and spoons. **2** plates, platters, saucers, and other flat or nearly flat dishes.

flat·worm (flat′wėrm′), *n.* any of very many worms with thin, flat bodies that live in water or as parasites on some animals. Tapeworms are flatworms.

flaunt (flônt), *v.* to show off to impress others: *flaunt expensive new clothing before your friends.* —**flaunt′er,** *n.* —**flaunt′ing·ly,** *adv.*

a	hat	ė	term	ô	order	ch	child	
ā	age	i	it	oi	oil	ng	long	a in about
ä	far	ī	ice	ou	out	sh	she	e in taken
â	care	o	hot	u	cup	th	thin	ə i in pencil
e	let	ō	open	ù	put	ŦH	then	o in lemon
ē	equal	ò	saw	ü	rule	zh	measure	u in circus

fla·vor (flā′vər), **1** *n.* taste, especially a particular taste: *Chocolate and vanilla have different flavors.* **2** *v.* to give added taste to; season: *The onion flavors the whole stew.* **3** *n.* flavoring. **4** *n.* a special quality: *Stories about ships have a flavor of the sea.* —**fla′vor·less,** *adj.*

fla·vor·ful (flā′vər fəl), *adj.* having flavor and interest. ■ See Synonym Study at **tasty.**

fla·vor·ing (flā′vər ing), *n.* something used to give a particular taste to food or drink: *chocolate flavoring.*

flaw (flô), **1** *n.* a slight defect; fault; blemish: *A flaw in the dish caused it to break. A quick temper is a character flaw.* **2** *v.* to make or become defective: *A tiny chip flawed the diamond.*

flaw·less (flô′lis), *adj.* without a flaw; perfect: *The actor's performance was flawless.* —**flaw′less·ly,** *adv.* —**flaw′less·ness,** *n.*

flax (flaks), *n.* **1** a slender, upright plant with small, narrow leaves, blue flowers, and slender stems. Linseed oil is made from its seeds. **2** the threadlike parts into which the stems of this plant separate. Flax is spun into thread and woven into linen.

flax·en (flak′sən), *adj.* **1** made of flax. **2** like the color of flax; pale yellow: *Flaxen hair is very light.*

flay (flā), *v.* **1** to strip off the skin or outer covering of. **2** to scold severely; criticize without pity or mercy. —**flay′er,** *n.*

F layer, F region.

flea (flē), *n.* any of numerous small, jumping insects without wings. Fleas live on the bodies of dogs, cats, and other animals and feed on their blood. □ *n., pl.* **fleas.** ■ Another word that sounds like this is **flee.**

flea collar, collar for a dog or cat that is treated with a substance to repel or kill fleas.

flea market, an outdoor market dealing in secondhand items, junk, and sometimes antiques.

fleck (flek), **1** *n.* a small spot or patch of color or light; speck; mark: *Freckles are brown flecks on the skin.* **2** *n.* a small particle; flake: *a fleck of dust.* **3** *v.* to mark with spots of color or light; speckle: *The bird's breast is flecked with brown.*

fled (fled), *v.* past tense and past participle of **flee:** *The enemy fled when we attacked. The prisoner has fled.*

fledge (flej), *v.* **1** (of a young bird) to grow the feathers needed for flying. **2** to provide or cover with feathers: *She fledged her arrows carefully.* □ *v.* **fledged, fledg·ing.**

fledg·ling (flej′ling), *n.* **1** a young bird that has just grown feathers needed for flying. **2** a young, inexperienced person.

flee (flē), *v.* **1** to run away; get away by running: *The robbers tried to flee, but they were caught.* **2** to run away from: *They fled the burning house.* **3** to go quickly; move away swiftly: *The summer days were fleeing.* □ *v.* **fled, flee·ing.** ■ Another word that sounds like this is **flea.** —**fle′er,** *n.*

fleece (flēs), **1** *n.* wool that covers a sheep or similar animal. **2** *n.* the amount of wool cut off or shorn from a sheep at one time. **3** *v.* to cut the fleece from. **4** *v.* to strip of money or belongings; rob; cheat: *The gamblers fleeced him of all his money.* □ *v.* **fleeced, fleec·ing.** —**fleec′er,** *n.*

fleec·y (flē′sē), *adj.* **1** like a fleece; soft and white: *fleecy clouds.* **2** covered with or made of fleece. □ *adj.* **fleec·i·er, fleec·i·est.** —**fleec′i·ness,** *n.*

fleet¹ (flēt), *n.* **1** group of ships under one command: *the U.S. fleet.* **2** group of ships sailing together: *a fleet of fishing boats.* **3** group of airplanes, cars, buses, trucks, or the like, moving or working together or having one owner. [**Fleet¹** comes from an old English word meaning "to float."]

fleet² (flēt), *adj.* swiftly moving; rapid: *The fleet horse won the race.* —**fleet′ly,** *adv.* —**fleet′ness,** *n.*

fleet admiral, a military rank. See chart on page 712.

fleet·ing (flē′ting), *adj.* passing swiftly; soon gone: *a fleeting smile.* —**fleet′ing·ly,** *adv.* —**fleet′ing·ness,** *n.*

Flem·ing (flem′ing), *n.* **1** person born or living in Flanders. **2** a Belgian whose native language is Flemish. **3** Sir **Alexander,** 1881-1955, Scottish bacteriologist who discovered penicillin.

Flem·ish (flem′ish), **1** *adj.* of Flanders, its people, or their language. **2** *n.pl.* the people of Flanders. **3** *n.* the language of Flanders.

flesh (flesh), *n.* **1** the soft tissue of the body that covers the bones and is covered by skin. Flesh consists mostly of muscles and fat. **2** meat: *Lions eat the flesh of zebras.* **3** the body, not the soul or spirit. **4** the soft part of fruits or vegetables; the part of fruits that can be eaten: *The flesh of an apple is white.* —**flesh′less,** *adj.*
flesh and blood, family or relatives by birth.
in the flesh, in person; really present.

flesh·ly (flesh′lē), *adj.* **1** of the flesh; bodily. **2** sensual. □ *adj.* **flesh·li·er, flesh·li·est.** —**flesh′li·ness,** *n.*

flesh·y (flesh′ē), *adj.* **1** having much flesh; plump; fat. **2** of flesh; like flesh. □ *adj.* **flesh·i·er, flesh·i·est.** —**flesh′i·ness,** *n.*

fleur-de-lis (flėr′də lē′), *n.* design or image used in heraldry to represent an iris. A fleur-de-lis was used as the coat of arms of the royal family of France. □ *n., pl.* **fleurs-de-lis** (flėr′də lēz′).

flew (flü), *v.* past tense of **fly²:** *The bird flew high in the air.* ■ Other words that sound like this are **flu** and **flue.**

flex (fleks), *v.* to bend: *She flexed her stiff arm slowly.*

flex·i·ble (flek′sə bəl), *adj.* **1** easily bent; not stiff; bending without breaking: *Leather, rubber, and wire are flexible.* **2** able to change easily to fit different conditions: *My mother works from our home and her hours are very flexible.* —**flex′i·bil′i·ty,** *n.* —**flex′i·bly,** *adv.*

fleur-de-lis

flex·or (flek′sər), *n.* any muscle that when contracted bends an arm, leg, or other body part at a joint.

flex·time (fleks′tīm′), *n.* a system of flexible working hours that permits employees to choose what time they will start and finish work each day.

flick¹ (flik), **1** *n.* a quick, light blow; sudden, snapping stroke: *With a flick of his whip, he drove the fly from the horse's head.* **2** *n.* the snapping sound of such a blow or stroke: *the flick of an electric light switch.* **3** *v.* to strike lightly with a quick, snapping blow: *She flicked the dust from her shoes with a handkerchief.* **4** *v.* to make a sudden, snapping stroke with: *The children flicked wet towels at each other.* **5** *v.* to move quickly and lightly; flutter.

flick² (flik), *n.* INFORMAL. **1** movie. **2** the **flicks,** *pl.* the movies.

flick·er¹ (flik′ər), **1** *v.* to shine or burn with a wavering, unsteady light: *The firelight flickered on the walls.* **2** *n.* a wavering, unsteady light or flame: *the flicker of an oil lamp.* **3** *v.* to move quickly and lightly in and out or back and forth: *We heard the birds flicker among the leaves.* **4** *n.* a quick, light movement: *We saw he was not sleeping by the flicker of his eyelids.* **5** *n.* a brief flash; spark: *a flicker of hope.* —**flick′er·ing·ly,** *adv.*

flick·er² (flik′ər), *n.* a large, common woodpecker of North America, with a spotted brown back, spotted white breast, black collar mark, and white rump. The **yellow-shafted flicker,** of eastern North America, has yellow on the underside of its wings. The **red-shafted flicker,** of western North America, has red on the underside of its wings.

flied (flīd), *v.* a past tense and past participle of **fly²** (def. 12): *The batter flied to center field. She has flied out twice.*

fli·er (flī′ər), *n.* **1** someone or something that flies: *That eagle is a high flier.* **2** pilot of an airplane; aviator. **3** a small handbill. Also, **flyer.**

flies¹ (flīz), *n.* plural of **fly¹** and **fly²:** *There are many flies on the window. Both batters hit flies to the outfield.*

flies² (flīz), *v.* a present tense of **fly²:** *A bird flies. He flies a plane.*

flight¹ (flīt), *n.* **1** act or manner of flying: *the flight of a bird across the sky.* **2** distance a bird, bullet, airplane, etc., can fly: *a flight of 500 miles.* **3** group of things flying through the air together: *a flight of pigeons.* **4** trip in an aircraft, especially a scheduled trip on an airline. **5** airplane that makes a scheduled trip: *She took the 3:15 flight to Boston.* **6** act of soaring above or beyond the ordinary: *a flight of the imagination.* **7** set of stairs or steps from one landing or story of a building to the next.

flight² (flit), *n.* act of fleeing; running away; escape: *The flight of the prisoners was discovered.*

put to flight, to force to flee: *They put the enemy to flight.*

flight attendant, someone employed by an airline to look after passengers during an airplane flight.

flight bag, a lightweight piece of baggage designed for carrying personal belongings on board an airplane.

flight·less (flit′lis), *adj.* unable to fly: *Ostriches are flightless.*

flight recorder, a device on an airplane that automatically records the aircraft's speed, course, altitude, etc., and the outside weather conditions.

flight·y (fli′tē), *adj.* likely to be unreliable or fickle; full of whims; frivolous. □ *adj.* **flight·i·er, flight·i·est.** —**flight′i·ly,** *adv.* —**flight′i·ness,** *n.*

flim·sy (flim′zē), *adj.* **1** easily torn or broken; not strongly made: *I accidentally tore the flimsy paper.* **2** unconvincing; shallow: *Their excuse was so flimsy that no one believed it.* □ *adj.* **flim·si·er, flim·si·est.** —**flim′si·ly,** *adv.* —**flim′si·ness,** *n.*

flinch (flinch), **1** *v.* to draw back from difficulty, danger, or pain; shrink: *He flinched when he touched the hot radiator.* **2** *n.* act of drawing back. □ *n., pl.* **flinch·es.** —**flinch′er,** *n.*

fling (fling), **1** *v.* to throw with force; throw: *fling clothes onto the floor, fling herself into a chair.* **2** *n.* a throw. **3** *v.* to move hastily or violently; rush; dash: *fling off in a new direction.* **4** *n.* time of doing as you please: *to have a brief fling before settling down.* **5** *n.* a lively Scottish dance. **6** *n.* a try; attempt: *She had a brief fling at acting after college.* □ *v.* **flung, fling·ing.**

flint (flint), *n.* **1** a very hard, gray or brown stone that makes a spark when struck against steel. It is a kind of quartz. **2** piece of this used with steel to light fires, explode gunpowder, etc.

flint·lock (flint′lok′), *n.* an old-fashioned gun in which a piece of flint striking against steel makes sparks that explode the gunpowder.

flint·y (flin′tē), *adj.* **1** made of flint; containing flint. **2** like flint; very hard; unyielding: *flinty stubbornness.* □ *adj.* **flint·i·er, flint·i·est.** —**flint′i·ly,** *adv.* —**flint′i·ness,** *n.*

flip (flip), **1** *v.* to cause to spin in the air: *to flip a coin. He flipped me over his shoulder, and I landed on my feet.* **2** *n.* act of flipping; a toss: *The winner was picked by the flip of a coin.* **3** *v.* to move with a snap or a jerk: *to flip the pages of a book. Please flip that light switch for me.* **4** *v.* to turn over: *The cook flipped the pancake over in the frying pan.* **5** *n.* a somersault performed in the air. **6** *adj.* not respectful; flippant: *a flip reply.* □ *v.* **flipped, flip·ping.**

flip out, INFORMAL. **1** to get excited; go wild. **2** to become mentally disturbed; become very upset.

flip-flop (flip′flop′), *n.* a change to the opposite opinion or argument; reversal: *He did a complete flip-flop on the question and insists he was wrong before.*

flip·pan·cy (flip′ən sē), *n.* flippant quality or behavior.

flip·pant (flip′ənt), *adj.* not properly serious; not respectful: *Her flippant answer to my question annoyed me.* —**flip′pant·ly,** *adv.*

flip·per (flip′ər), *n.* **1** a broad, flat limb especially adapted for swimming. Seals have flippers. **2** a molded rubber attachment for the human foot, used as an aid to swimming.

flip side, the opposite side of anything: *the flip side of a hit record.*

flirt (flėrt), **1** *v.* to pay attention to someone in a romantic way without being serious about it. **2** *n.* someone who flirts. **3** *v.* to trifle; toy: *He flirted with the idea of going to Europe, even though he couldn't afford it.* **4** *v.* to move quickly; flutter: *The bird flirted from branch to branch.* **5** *n.* a quick movement or flutter: *With a flirt of its tail the squirrel ran off.*

flir·ta·tion (flėr′tā′shən), *n.* **1** act of flirting. **2** a courtship that is not serious.

flir·ta·tious (flėr′tā′shəs), *adj.* **1** inclined to flirt: *a flirtatious teenager.* **2** of or about flirtation: *a flirtatious glance.* —**flir′ta′tious·ly,** *adv.* —**flir′ta′tious·ness,** *n.*

flit (flit), *v.* **1** to fly lightly and quickly: *Birds flitted from tree to tree.* **2** to pass lightly and quickly: *Many thoughts flitted through my mind as I sat daydreaming.* □ *v.* **flit·ted, flit·ting.** —**flit′ting·ly,** *adv.*

float (flōt), **1** *v.* to stay on top of or be held up by air, water, or other liquid. A cork will float, but a stone sinks. **2** *n.* anything that stays up or holds up something else in water. A raft is a float. A cork on a fishline is a float. **3** *v.* to rest or move in a liquid, the air, etc.: *Clouds floated in the sky. The boat floated out to sea.* **4** *v.* to cause to float: *float logs downstream.* **5** *v.* to put up for sale on the stock or bond market: *To get money the government floated an issue of bonds.* **6** *n.* a hollow, metal ball that floats on and regulates the level, supply, or outlet of a liquid in a tank, boiler, etc. **7** *n.* a low, flat car that carries something to be shown in a parade. —**float′a·ble,** *adj.* —**float′er,** *n.*

flock (flok), **1** *n.* group of animals of one kind keeping, feeding, or herded together: *a flock of geese, a flock of birds.* **2** *n.* a large group or number; crowd: *Visitors came in flocks to the zoo to see the new gorilla.* **3** *v.* to go or gather in a flock; come crowding: *Sheep usually flock together. The children flocked around the ice-cream stand.* **4** *n.* people of the same church group.

floe (flō), *n.* field or sheet of floating ice. ■ Another word that sounds like this is **flow.**

flog (flog), *v.* to whip very hard; beat with a whip or stick. □ *v.* **flogged, flog·ging.** —**flog′ger,** *n.*

flood (flud), **1** *n.* a great flow of water over what is usually dry land: *The heavy rains caused a serious flood.* **2** *n.* **the Flood,** (in the Bible) the water that covered the earth in the time of Noah; Deluge. **3** *v.* to flow over; cover or fill with water: *The river flooded our fields.* **4** *n.* a great flow of anything: *a flood of light, a flood of words.* **5** *v.* to fill, cover, or overcome like a flood: *The TV star was flooded with requests for autographs. The room was flooded with moonlight.* **6** *v.* to cause or allow too much fuel to flow into an engine, so that it will not start. **7** *v.* to become covered or filled with water: *During the storm, our cellar flooded.*

flood (def. 1)

flood·gate (flud′gāt′), *n.* gate in a canal, river, stream, etc., to control the flow of water.

flood·light (flud′līt′), **1** *n.* lamp that gives a broad beam of light. **2** *n.* beam of light from such a lamp. **3** *v.* to light with a floodlight: *The baseball field was brightly floodlighted for the night game.* □ *v.* **flood·light·ed** or **flood·lit** (flud′lit′), **flood·light·ing.**

flood·plain (flud′plān′), *n.* plain bordering a river and made of soil deposited during floods.

flood tide, the flowing of the tide toward the shore.

flood·wa·ter (flud′wô′tər), *n.* water flooding dry land.

floor (flôr), **1** *n.* the part of a room to walk on: *The floor of this room is made of wood.* **2** *n.* story of a building: *Five families live on the fourth floor.* **3** *v.* to put a floor in or on: *The carpenter will floor this room with oak.* **4** *n.* a flat surface at the bottom: *They dropped their net to the floor of the ocean.* **5** *n.* right to speak: *"You may have the floor," said the chairman.* **6** *v.* to knock down:

a	hat	ė	term	ô	order	ch	child		a in about
ā	age	i	it	oi	oil	ng	long		e in taken
ä	far	ī	ice	ou	out	sh	she	ə {	i in pencil
â	care	o	hot	u	cup	th	thin		o in lemon
e	let	ō	open	ù	put	ᴛʜ	then		u in circus
ē	equal	ò	saw	ü	rule	zh	measure		

The boxer floored his opponent with one blow. **7** *v.* to confuse; puzzle: *The last question on the exam floored me.*

floor·board (flôr′bôrd′), *n.* **1** one of the strips of wood used in a wooden floor. **2** Usually, **floorboards,** *pl.* the floor of a car.

floor hockey, an indoor game like hockey, in which long sticks are used to hit a plastic puck or a tied circle of rope.

floor·ing (flôr′ing), *n.* **1** floor. **2** floors. **3** material for making or covering floors, such as wood, linoleum, or tile.

floor·walk·er (flôr′wô′kər), *n.* person employed in a large store to direct the work of salesclerks and help customers.

flop (flop), **1** *v.* to move loosely or heavily; flap around clumsily: *The fish flopped helplessly on the deck.* **2** *v.* to fall, drop, throw, or move heavily or clumsily: *The tired girl flopped down into a chair.* **3** *n.* a dull, heavy sound made by flopping. **4** *n.* failure: *His last book was a flop.* **5** *v.* to fail: *Her first business venture flopped.* □ *v.* **flopped, flop·ping.** —**flop′per,** *n.*

flop·py (flop′ē), **1** *adj.* tending to flop; soft and flexible: *a floppy hat.* **2** *n.* floppy disk. □ *adj.* **flop·pi·er, flop·pi·est;** *n., pl.* **flop·pies.** —**flop′pi·ly,** *adv.* —**flop′pi·ness,** *n.*

floppy disk, a small, bendable plastic disk with a magnetic surface, used to store information and instructions for computers; diskette. Some floppy disks are made with unbending cases.

flo·ra (flôr′ə), *n.* plants as a group: *the floras of the two islands.* □ *n., pl.* **flo·ras.**

flo·ral (flôr′əl), *adj.* of or resembling flowers: *floral decorations, floral patterns.* —**flo′ral·ly,** *adv.*

Flo·rence (flôr′əns), *n.* city in central Italy.

Florence

Flo·ren·tine (flôr′ən tēn′), **1** *adj.* of Florence or its people. **2** *n.* person born or living in Florence.

flo·ret (flôr′it), *n.* a small flower.

flo·rid (flôr′id), *adj.* **1** reddish; ruddy: *a florid complexion.* **2** much ornamented; flowery; showy: *florid language, florid architecture.* —**flo′rid·ly,** *adv.* —**flo′rid·ness,** *n.*

Flo·ri·da (flôr′ə də), *n.* one of the southeastern states of the United States. *Abbreviation:* FL or Fla. *Capital:* Tallahassee. —**Flo·rid′i·an** or **Flor′i·dan,** *n.*

WORD STORY **Florida** comes from Spanish words meaning "flowery" and "Easter." Juan Ponce de León, the Spanish explorer, gave the area this name when he first sighted it, on Easter of 1513.

Florida Keys, chain of small coral islands and reefs stretching for about 225 miles off the coast of S Florida into the Gulf of Mexico. They are part of Florida.

flo·rin (flôr′ən), *n.* any of various gold or silver coins used in different countries of Europe, especially a former English silver and nickel coin that was worth ten pence.

flo·rist (flôr′ist), *n.* person who raises or sells flowers.

floss (flôs), **1** *n.* dental floss. **2** *v.* to use dental floss, or use dental floss on: *I flossed my teeth this morning.* **3** *n.* a shiny, untwisted thread made from short, loose, silk fibers. It is used for embroidery. **4** *n.* soft, silky fluff or fibers. Milkweed pods contain white floss.

floss·y (flôs′ē), *adj.* of or like floss. □ *adj.* **floss·i·er, floss·i·est.**

flo·ta·tion (flō tā′shən), *n.* act or process of floating.

flo·til·la (flō til′ə), *n.* **1** a small fleet. **2** fleet of small ships. □ *n., pl.* **flo·til·las.**

flot·sam (flot′səm), *n.* wreckage of a ship or its cargo found floating on the sea.

flounce[1] (flouns), *v.* to go with an angry or impatient fling of the body: *flounce out of the room in a rage.* □ *v.* **flounced, flounc·ing.**

flounce[2] (flouns), **1** *n.* a wide strip of cloth, gathered along the top edge and sewed to a dress, skirt, etc., for trimming; a wide ruffle. **2** *v.* to trim with a flounce or flounces. □ *v.* **flounced, flounc·ing.**

floun·der[1] (floun′dər), *v.* **1** to struggle awkwardly without making much progress: *After the blizzard, we found cattle floundering in snowdrifts.* **2** to be clumsy or confused and make mistakes: *I was so nervous I floundered through my speech.*

floun·der[2] (floun′dər), *n.* any of many saltwater flatfishes used for food. □ *n., pl.* **floun·der** or **floun·ders.**

flour (flour), **1** *n.* the fine meal made by grinding and sifting wheat or other grain. It is used to make bread, rolls, cake, pasta, etc. **2** *v.* to cover or sprinkle with flour.

WORD STORY **Flour** is an early spelling of **flower.** When wheat or other grain is ground, part of the meal is finer than the rest. This was called the "flower of meal," meaning the best part.

flour·ish (flėr′ish), **1** *v.* to grow or develop well; thrive: *Your radishes are flourishing. Our newspaper business flourished.* **2** *v.* to wave in the air: *She flourished the letter when she saw us.* **3** *n.* act of waving about: *The magician removed his cape with a flourish.* **4** *n.* an extra ornament or curve in handwriting. **5** *n.* a showy trill or passage in music: *a flourish of trumpets.* □ *n., pl.* **flour·ish·es.** —**flour′ish·ing·ly,** *adv.*

WORD STORY **Flourish** comes from a Latin word meaning "to bloom." All definitions of this word suggest something as easy to notice as a healthy plant covered with flowers.

flour·y (flou′rē), *adj.* **1** of or like flour. **2** covered with flour.

flout (flout), *v.* to treat with contempt or scorn; scoff at; mock: *You are foolish to flout such good advice.* ■ See Usage Note at **flaunt.** —**flout′er,** *n.* —**flout′ing·ly,** *adv.*

flow (flō), **1** *v.* to run like water; move in a current or stream: *Blood flows through our bodies.* **2** *n.* current; stream: *There is a constant flow of water from the spring.* **3** *v.* to pour out; pour along: *The crowd flowed out of the town hall and down the main street.* **4** *v.* to move easily or smoothly: *Poetry flowed from her pen.* **5** *n.* any smooth and steady movement: *The police officer helped maintain the flow of traffic.* **6** *v.* to hang loose and waving: *The emperor's robes flowed to the floor.* **7** *n.* act of pouring out: *A tight bandage should stop the flow of blood.* **8** *n.* rate of flowing: *a flow of three feet per second.* ■ Another word that sounds like this is **floe.**

SYNONYM STUDY **Flow, gush,** and **stream** all mean to move in a current. **Flow** suggests continuous forward motion: *More than 200 tributaries flow into the Amazon River.* **Gush** suggests a sudden large flow: *The rancher stared in awe as oil gushed from his land.* **Stream** is used for a strong, steady flow from a single source: *Water streamed from the open hydrant.*

flow·chart (flō′chärt), *n.* diagram that shows, step by step, each thing a computer must do to perform a particular task.

flow·er (flou′ər), **1** *n.* part of a plant that produces the seed; blossom. Flowers are often beautifully colored or shaped. **2** *n.* plant grown for its blossoms. **3** *v.* to have or produce flowers: *Many fruit trees flower in the spring.* **4** *n.* the finest part: *the flower of the country's youth.* **5** *n.* time when a thing is at its best: *a person in the flower of life.* **6** *v.* to be at its best: *Her athletic talent flowered early.* —**flow′er·less,** *adj.* —**flow′er·like′,** *adj.*

flow·ered (flou′ərd), *adj.* covered or decorated with flowers: *flowered wallpaper.*

flowering plant, plant that produces flowers, seeds and fruit; angiosperm.

flow·er·pot (flou′ər pot′), *n.* pot for a plant to grow in.

flow·er·y (flou′ər ē), *adj.* **1** having many flowers. **2** full of fine words and fanciful expressions: *a flowery speech.* ❑ *adj.* **flow·er·i·er, flow·er·i·est.** —**flow′er·i·ness,** *n.*

flown (flōn), *v.* past participle of **fly²**: *The bird has flown.*

fl. oz. or **fl oz,** fluid ounce or fluid ounces.

flu (flü), *n.* an acute, contagious disease caused by a virus; influenza. Its symptoms sometimes resemble those of a very bad cold, but it is more dangerous and exhausting. ■ Other words that sound like this are **flew** and **flue.**

WORD STORY Flu is a shortened form of **influenza,** which comes from a Latin word meaning "influence." The disease was thought to occur because of the influence of bad stars on its victims.

flub (flub), INFORMAL. **1** *v.* to do something very clumsily; perform badly; fail: *I really flubbed my lines in the play. Every time he tries that kick, he flubs.* **2** *n.* failure in doing something; blunder. ❑ *v.* **flubbed, flub·bing.**

fluc·tu·ate (fluk′chü āt), *v.* to rise and fall; change continually; waver: *The temperature fluctuates from day to day.* ❑ *v.* **fluc·tu·at·ed, fluc·tu·at·ing.** —**fluc′tu·a′tion,** *n.*

flue (flü), *n.* tube, pipe, or other enclosed passage for smoke or hot air. A chimney often has several flues. ■ Other words that sound like this are **flew** and **flu.**

flu·en·cy (flü′ən sē), *n.* **1** a smooth, easy flow: *The senator had great fluency of speech.* **2** easy, rapid speaking or writing.

flu·ent (flü′ənt), *adj.* **1** flowing smoothly or easily: *to speak fluent French.* **2** speaking or writing easily and rapidly: *She is a fluent lecturer.* —**flu′ent·ly,** *adv.*

fluff (fluf), **1** *n.* soft, light, downy particles: *Woolen blankets often have fluff on them.* **2** *n.* a soft, light, downy mass: *The kitten was a ball of fluff.* **3** *v.* to shake or puff out hair, feathers, etc., into a soft, light, downy mass: *fluff a pillow.* **4** *v.* to make a mistake in reading or speaking: *I fluffed my lines in the play.*

fluff·y (fluf′ē), *adj.* **1** soft and light like fluff: *a fluffy shawl.* **2** covered or filled with fluff; downy: *fluffy baby chicks, a fluffy pillow.* ❑ *adj.* **fluff·i·er, fluff·i·est.** —**fluff′i·ly,** *adv.* —**fluff′i·ness,** *n.*

flu·id (flü′id), **1** *n.* any liquid or gas; something that will flow. Water, mercury, air, and helium are fluids at room temperature. ■ See Synonym Study at **liquid. 2** *adj.* like a liquid or gas; flowing: *She poured the fluid mass of hot metal into a mold to harden.* **3** *adj.* changing easily; not fixed: *The situation on the battlefield was fluid.*

fluffy (def . 2)

fluid dram, one eighth of a fluid ounce.

flu·id·i·ty (flü id′ə tē), *n.* condition or quality of being fluid.

flu·id·ize (flü′ə dīz), *v.* to make fluid. ❑ *v.* **flu·id·ized, flu·id·iz·ing.** —**flu′id·i·za′tion,** *n.*

fluid ounce, unit of volume for liquids. There are 16 fluid ounces in 1 pint.

fluke¹ (flük), *n.* **1** the flat, three-cornered piece at the end of each arm of an anchor, which catches in the ground and holds the anchor fast. **2** the barbed head of an arrow or harpoon. **3** either of the two halves of a whale's tail.

fluke² (flük), *n.* a lucky stroke in games, business, or life.

fluke³ (flük), *n.* **1** flatfish. **2** trematode.

fluk·y (flü′kē), *adj.* **1** obtained by chance rather than by skill. **2** uncertain: *fluky weather.* ❑ *adj.* **fluk·i·er, fluk·i·est.**

flume (flüm), *n.* **1** a deep and very narrow valley with a stream running through it. **2** a large, inclined trough or chute for carrying water. Flumes are used to transport logs or to furnish water for power.

flum·mox (flum′əks), *v.* INFORMAL. to confuse; bewilder.

flung (flung), *v.* past tense and past participle of **fling**: *I flung my coat on the chair. The paper was flung into the fire.*

flunk (flungk), *v.* **1** to fail in schoolwork: *I must study so that I don't flunk the exam.* **2** to give someone a failing grade: *The teacher flunked him.*
flunk out, to dismiss or be dismissed from school or college for failing work.

flunk·ey (flung′kē), *n.* flunky. ❑ *n., pl.* **flunk·eys.**

flunk·y (flung′kē), *n.* **1** a flattering, fawning person; toady. **2** someone who does unskilled tasks. ❑ *n., pl.* **flunk·ies.**

fluo·res·cence (flù res′ns *or* flü′ə res′ns), *n.* **1** act or process of producing light by a substance exposed to X rays, ultraviolet rays, or certain other rays, continuing only as long as exposure to these rays continues. **2** light given off in this way.

fluo·res·cent (flù res′nt *or* flü′ə res′nt), *adj.* able to give off light by fluorescence. Fluorescent substances glow in the dark when exposed to X rays.

fluorescent lamp, an electric lamp consisting of a tube in which a coating of fluorescent powder exposed to ultraviolet rays gives off a light that is cooler and less glaring than incandescent light.

fluor·i·date (flùr′ə dāt), *v.* to add small amounts of a fluorine compound to drinking water to decrease tooth decay. ❑ *v.* **fluor·i·dat·ed, fluor·i·dat·ing.** —**fluor′i·da′tion,** *n.*

fluo·ride (flùr′īd *or* flü′ə rīd′), *n.* compound of fluorine and another element or radical.

fluo·rine (flùr′ēn *or* flü′ə rēn′), *n.* a pale yellow, bad-smelling, poisonous gas. Fluorine is a chemical element that occurs naturally only in combination with certain other elements. It is the most active of all the elements and is used in small amounts in water to prevent tooth decay.

fluor·ite (flùr′īt *or* flü′ə rīt′), *n.* mineral made of calcium and fluorine. Fluorite crystals occur in many colors. Fluorite is used in making steel and aluminum, and as a source of fluorine.

fluor·o·car·bon (flùr′ə kär′bən), *n.* **1** any of a group of compounds of fluorine and carbon used as solvents, lubricants, refrigerator gases, etc. **2** chlorofluorocarbon.

fluor·o·scope (flùr′ə skōp), *n.* device for examining the inner parts of a human body, machine, etc., by placing it between a source of radiation, such as an X-ray machine, and a fluorescent screen. Parts of the object being examined that absorb more radiation cast darker shadows on the screen.

flur·ry (flèr′ē), **1** *n.* a sudden gust: *A flurry of wind upset the small sailboat.* **2** *n.* a light fall of rain or snow. **3** *n.* a sudden commotion: *There was a flurry of alarm when the fire broke out.* **4** *v.* to fluster; excite; agitate: *Noise in the audience flurried the actor so that he forgot his lines.* ❑ *n., pl.* **flur·ries;** *v.* **flur·ried, flur·ry·ing.**

WORD STORY Flurry may be a combination of **flutter** and **hurry.** Or it may be a word that sounds right for the ideas it expresses. People do create and use words for just that reason.

flush¹ (flush), **1** *v.* to become red suddenly; blush; glow: *Her face flushed when they laughed at her.* **2** *v.* to cause to blush or glow: *Exercise flushed her face.* **3** *n.* a rosy glow or blush: *The flush of sunrise was on the clouds.* **4** *v.* to rush suddenly; flow rapidly: *Blood flushed to my cheeks.* **5** *n.* a sudden rush; rapid flow. **6** *v.* to send a sudden flow of water over or through: *The city streets were flushed to make them clean.* **7** *v.* to make joyful and proud; excite: *The team was flushed with its first victory.* **8** *n.* an excited condition or feeling: *the flush of victory.* **9** *n.* glowing vigor; freshness: *the first flush of youth.* **10** *adj.* even; level: *The edge of the new shelf must be flush with the old one.* **11** *adv.* so as to be level; evenly: *The two edges met flush.* **12** *adj.* well supplied; having plenty: *Payday is the only day I am flush with money.* ❑ *n., pl.* **flush·es.**

flush² (flush), *v.* to cause to fly or start up suddenly: *The hunter's dog flushed a partridge in the woods.*

a	hat	ė	term	ô	order	ch	child		a in about
ā	age	i	it	oi	oil	ng	long		e in taken
ä	far	ī	ice	ou	out	sh	she	ə	i in pencil
â	care	o	hot	u	cup	th	thin		o in lemon
e	let	ō	open	ù	put	ᴛʜ	then		u in circus
ē	equal	ò	saw	ü	rule	zh	measure		

flus·ter (flus′tər), **1** *v.* to make nervous and excited; confuse: *The honking of horns flustered the driver, and he stalled his car.* **2** *n.* nervous excitement; confusion: *He was in a fluster before giving his speech.*

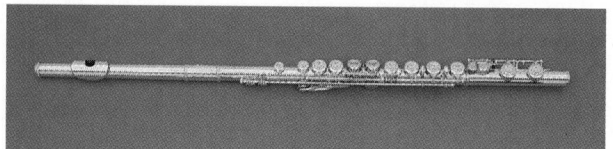

flute (def. 1)

flute (flüt), **1** *n.* a long, slender, pipelike musical instrument, played by blowing across a hole near one end. Different notes are made by opening and closing holes along its side with the fingers or with keys. **2** *v.* to play on a flute. **3** *n.* a long, round groove. Some columns have flutes. ❑ *v.* **flut·ed, flut·ing.** [See word history information at **flageolet**.]

flut·ed (flü′tid), *adj.* having long, round grooves: *fluted columns.*

flut·ing (flü′ting), *n.* decoration made of long, round grooves.

flut·ist (flü′tist), *n.* person who plays a flute.

flut·ter (flut′ər), **1** *v.* to wave back and forth quickly and lightly: *The flag fluttered in the breeze.* **2** *v.* to move or flap the wings rapidly without flying or with short flights: *The chickens fluttered excitedly when they saw the dog.* **3** *v.* to move through the air with a wavy motion: *The falling leaves fluttered to the ground.* **4** *v.* to move restlessly: *They fluttered around making preparations for the party.* **5** *v.* to move quickly and unevenly; tremble: *My heart fluttered when I rose to give my speech.* **6** *n.* a quick, light flapping movement: *the flutter of curtains in a breeze.* **7** *n.* a confused or excited condition: *The appearance of the queen caused a great flutter in the crowd.* **—flut′ter·er,** *n.*

flux (fluks), *n.* **1** continuous change: *New words and meanings keep the English language in a state of flux.* **2** an abnormal discharge of liquid matter from the body. **3** rosin or other substance used in soldering, welding, etc., to clean the surfaces of metals and help them join. ❑ *n., pl.* **flux·es.**

fly[1] (flī), *n.* **1** any of a large group of insects that have two wings, especially the housefly. **2** any insect with transparent wings, such as a mayfly. **3** fishhook with feathers, silk, tinsel, etc., tied on it to make it look like an insect. ❑ *n., pl.* **flies.**

fly in the ointment, something that ruins a plan, event, or occasion: *It's a funny book, but those dumb puns are a fly in the ointment.*

fly[2] (flī), **1** *v.* to move through the air with wings: *These birds fly long distances.* **2** *v.* to float or wave in the air: *Our flag flies every day.* **3** *v.* to cause to float or wave in the air: *The children are flying kites.* **4** *v.* to travel in an aircraft. **5** *v.* to pilot an aircraft. **6** *v.* to carry in an aircraft: *We flew supplies to the flooded city.* **7** *v.* to move swiftly; go rapidly: *When the phone rang, I flew to answer it.* **8** *v.* to run away; flee: *fly from your enemies.* **9** *n.* flap to cover buttons or a zipper on clothing. **10** *n.* piece of canvas, nylon, etc., forming an extra, outer top for a tent. **11** *n.* baseball batted high in the air. **12** *v.* to bat a baseball high in the air. ❑ *v.* **flew, flown, fly·ing** for 1-8, **flied, fly·ing** for 12; *n., pl.* **flies.**

fly at, to attack violently.

fly by the seat of your pants, to work by guessing or from experience instead of from training or rules.

let fly, to shoot or throw: *The archer let fly an arrow.*

on the fly, while still in the air: *He caught the ball on the fly.*

fly ball, baseball batted high in the air.

fly·by (flī′bī′), *n.* flight of a spacecraft close to a planet or other astronomical object. ❑ *n., pl.* **fly·bys.**

fly·catch·er (flī′kach′ər), *n.* any of various birds that catch flies and other insects while flying. Kingbirds and phoebes are flycatchers.

fly·er (flī′ər), *n.* flier.

fly·ing (flī′ing), **1** *adj.* able to fly. **2** *adj.* floating or waving in the air. **3** *adj.* swift. **4** *n.* action of piloting or traveling in an aircraft.

flying boat, seaplane with a watertight boatlike hull and floats under its wings.

flying buttress, an arched support or brace built between the wall of a building and a supporting column to bear some of the weight of the roof.

flying colors, success; victory: *The team finished the tournament with flying colors.*

flying fish, any of numerous tropical sea fish with winglike fins enabling them to leap for some distance through the air.

flying fish—about 18 in. (46 cm) long

flying saucer, UFO.

flying squirrel, any of several squirrels that can make long, gliding leaps through the air. They have winglike folds of skin from their front legs to their hind legs, and they open these folds when in the air.

flying wing, (in Canadian football) player who usually takes a position in the backfield but may also line up as an end.

fly·leaf (flī′lēf′), *n.* a blank sheet of paper at the beginning or end of a book. ❑ *n., pl.* **fly·leaves.**

Flynn (flin), *n.* **Er·rol** (er′əl), 1909-1959, American movie star. He often played heroic men in historical dramas.

fly·pa·per (flī′pā′pər), *n.* paper covered with a sticky or poisonous substance, used to catch or kill flies.

fly·speck (flī′spek′), *n.* **1** a tiny spot left by a fly. **2** any tiny speck.

fly·swat·ter (flī′swot′ər), *n.* a piece of plastic or wire mesh several inches square, attached to a long handle and used to swat flies.

fly·way (flī′wā′), *n.* route usually followed by migrating birds.

fly·weight (flī′wāt′), *n.* boxer who weighs less than 112 pounds (51 kilograms).

fly·wheel (flī′wēl′), *n.* a heavy wheel attached to a machine to keep it and its parts moving at an even speed.

Fm, symbol for fermium.

FM or **F.M.,** frequency modulation.

f-number (ef′num′bər), *n.* (in photography) one of several numbers on an adjustable camera lens, showing changes in the size of the opening that lets light reach the film. Larger f-numbers show a smaller opening. The size of the opening controls which parts of the picture are in sharp focus, and how fast the shutter moves.

foal (fōl), **1** *n.* a young horse, donkey, or zebra; colt or filly. **2** *v.* to give birth to a foal: *Our mare foaled twin colts last spring.*

foam (fōm), **1** *n.* mass of very small bubbles formed in a liquid by agitation, fermentation, boiling, etc. **2** *v.* to form or gather into a mass of bubbles; froth: *The soda foamed over the glass.* **3** *n.* a frothy mass formed in the mouth as saliva or on the skin of animals as sweat: *The dog with foam around its mouth has rabies.* **4** *n.* a spongy, flexible, or stiff material made from plastics, rubber, or the like, by solidification of the material around air bubbles. **—foam′like′,** *adj.*

foam rubber, a soft, spongy rubber used for mattresses, cushions, etc.

foam·y (fō′mē), *adj.* **1** covered with foam; foaming. **2** made of foam. **3** like foam. ❑ *adj.* **foam·i·er, foam·i·est. —foam′i·ly,** *adv.* **—foam′i·ness,** *n.*

fob[1] (fob), *n.* **1** a small pocket for holding a watch, etc. **2** a short watch chain, ribbon, etc., that hangs out of such a pocket. **3** ornament worn at the end of such a chain, ribbon, etc.

fob[2] (fob), *v.* **fob off, 1** to deceive by a trick or an excuse. **2** to get rid of by a trick or an excuse. ❑ *v.* **fobbed, fob·bing.**

f.o.b. or **F.O.B.,** free on board. The price $2500, f.o.b. Detroit, means that the $2500 does not pay for freight or other expenses after the article has been put on board a freight car at Detroit.

fo·cal (fō′kəl), *adj.* of or about a focus. **—fo′cal·ly,** *adv.*

focal length, distance from the surface of a lens or mirror to the point of focus.

fo·ci (fō′sī), *n.* a plural of **focus.**

fo'c'sle (fōk′səl), *n.* forecastle.

fo·cus (fō′kəs), **1** *n.* point at which rays of light, heat, etc., meet after being reflected from a mirror or bent by a lens. **2** *v.* to bring rays of light, heat, etc., to a point: *The lens focused the sun's rays on a piece of paper and burned a hole in it.* **3** *n.* focal length. **4** *n.* the correct adjustment of a lens, the eye, etc., to make a clear image: *If the camera is not brought into focus, the photograph will be blurred.* **5** *v.* to adjust a lens, the eye, etc., to make a clear image: *A nearsighted person cannot focus accurately on distant objects.* **6** *v.* to make an image clear by adjusting a lens, the eye, etc. **7** *n.* (in geometry) a fixed point used in determining a conic section. A parabola has one focus while an ellipse has two focuses. **8** *n.* the central point of attraction, attention, activity, etc.: *The new baby was the focus of attention.* **9** *v.* to concentrate: *When studying, he focused his mind on his lessons.* □ *n., pl.* **fo·cus·es** or **fo·ci;** *v.* **fo·cused, fo·cus·ing** or **fo·cussed, fo·cus·sing.**

> **WORD STORY** **Focus** comes from a Latin word meaning "hearth" or "fireplace." Some lenses can bring light together at a point that becomes hot and catches fire. This is the fireplace of the lens. **Fuel** comes from the same Latin word.

fod·der (fod′ər), *n.* coarse food for horses, cattle, etc. Hay and cornstalks are fodder. [See Word Story at **foray.**]

foe (fō), *n.* enemy.

fog (fog), **1** *n.* cloud of fine drops of water just above the earth's surface; thick mist. **2** *v.* to cover with fog. **3** *v.* to make or become misty or cloudy: *Something fogged six of our photographs. My breath caused the window to fog.* **4** *n.* a confused or puzzled condition: *a fog of ignorance.* **5** *v.* to confuse; puzzle. **6** *v.* to treat or spray with insecticide: *fog a backyard.* □ *v.* **fogged, fog·ging.**

fog bank, a dense mass of fog seen at a distance.

fog·gy (fog′ē), *adj.* **1** having much fog; misty. **2** not clear; dim; blurred: *Their ideas are confused and rather foggy.* □ *adj.* **fog·gi·er, fog·gi·est. —fog′gi·ly,** *adv.* **—fog′gi·ness,** *n.*

fog·horn (fog′hôrn′), *n.* horn that warns ships in foggy weather.

fo·gy (fō′gē), *n.* old-fashioned person; person who is behind the times: *He's sort of an old fogy.* □ *n., pl.* **fo·gies.**

foi·ble (foi′bəl), *n.* a weak point in someone's behavior: *Talking too much is one of my foibles.*

foil[1] (foil), *v.* to prevent from carrying out plans; get the better of; outwit: *Quick thinking by the bank clerk foiled the robbers.*

foil[2] (foil), *n.* **1** metal beaten, hammered, or rolled into a very thin sheet: *Candy is sometimes wrapped in foil to keep it fresh.* **2** anything that makes something else look or seem better by contrast: *The colorful pillows were a perfect foil for the beige couch.*

foil[3] (foil), *n.* a long, narrow sword with a flexible blade and blunted point to prevent injury, used in fencing.

foist (foist), *v.* to palm off as genuine: *The dishonest shopkeeper foisted inferior goods on customers.*

> **WORD STORY** **Foist** comes from a Dutch word meaning "fist." Many kinds of cheating are done by hand—notice the idiom **palm off.** The goal of cheating is to get someone's money into the cheater's fist.

fold[1] (fōld), **1** *v.* to bend or double over on itself: *fold a napkin.* **2** *n.* layer of something folded; pleat: *The kitten played in the folds of the curtain.* **3** *n.* mark or line made by folding: *Cut along the fold.* **4** *v.* to bend until close to the body: *You fold your arms. A bird folds its wings.* **5** *v.* to put the arms around and hold tenderly: *He folded the crying child to him.* **6** *v.* to wrap: *She folded her bathing suit in a towel.* **7** *v.* to fail in business. **—fold′a·ble,** *adj.*

fold[2] (fōld), *n.* **1** pen to keep sheep in. **2** a church group; congregation.

-fold, *suffix.* **1** ___ times as many: *tenfold = ten times as many.* **2** with ___ parts: *twofold plan = plan with two parts.*

fold·a·way (fōld′ə wā′), **1** *adj.* made to be folded and stored out of the way when not in use: *a sofa with a foldaway bed.* **2** *n.* something made this way.

fold·er (fōl′dər), *n.* **1** holder for papers made by folding a piece of stiff paper once. **2** pamphlet made of one or more folded sheets. **3** person or thing that folds.

fo·li·age (fō′lē ij), *n.* leaves of a plant.

fo·li·a·tion (fō′lē ā′shən), *n.* **1** process of putting forth leaves. **2** (in geology) a natural splitting of rock into thin layers.

folic acid (fō′lik), vitamin of the vitamin B complex, found in leaves, liver, and fruit. Folic acid is used in treating anemia.

fo·li·o (fō′lē ō), *n.* **1** a large sheet of paper folded once to make two leaves, or four pages, of a book. **2** a volume consisting of sheets folded in this way; volume having pages of the largest size. **3** the page number of a printed book. □ *n., pl.* **fo·li·os.**

folk (fōk), **1** *n.* people of a certain kind: *Most city folk know very little about farming.* **2** *n.* tribe or nation. **3** *n.pl.* **folks,** a people. **b** INFORMAL. relatives: *How are all your folks?* **c** parents: *My folks aren't home tonight.* **4** *adj.* of the common people, their beliefs, legends, customs, etc.: *folk tunes.* □ *n., pl.* **folk** or **folks** for 1,2.

folk dance, 1 dance originating and handed down among the common people. **2** music for it.

folk dance (def. 1)

folk etymology, popular but mistaken idea of the origin of a word that often results in a change in its sound or spelling. For example, French *crevice* became English *crayfish,* influenced by *fish.*

> **WORD SOURCE** **Folk etymology** is obvious, for instance, when people make up stories to explain where words come from. The most common made-up stories explain words as initials. **Wimp,** for instance, has been said to come from "Weak, Ineffectual, Meaningless Person." It probably didn't.
>
> Folk etymology is less obvious, but more important, in causing a word's spelling to change. Many English words come from other languages, then are changed to look as if they came from other English words. **Crayfish** is one example. Some others are **chipmunk, cockroach, mushroom, muskrat,** and **woodchuck.**

folk·lore (fōk′lôr′), *n.* beliefs, customs, etc., of a people or tribe.

folk music, music originating and handed down among the folk, or the common people.

folk-rock (fōk′rok′), *n.* type of music like folk music with rock-'n'-roll rhythms added.

folk singer, person who sings folk songs.

folk song, 1 song originating and handed down among the common people. **2** song imitating a real folk song: *"Oh! Susannah" is a folk song written by Stephen Foster.*

folk·sy (fōk′sē), *adj.* **1** sociable; friendly. **2** simple; not fancy. □ *adj.* **folk·si·er, folk·si·est. —folk′si·ly,** *adv.* **—folk′si·ness,** *n.*

folk·tale (fōk′tāl′), *n.* story or legend originating and handed down among the common people.

folk·way (fōk′wā′), *n.* custom or habit that is common among the members of an ethnic group or other large group.

a	hat	ė	term	ô	order	ch	child		a in about
ā	age	i	it	oi	oil	ng	long		e in taken
ä	far	ī	ice	ou	out	sh	she	ə	i in pencil
â	care	o	hot	u	cup	th	thin		o in lemon
e	let	ō	open	u̇	put	ŦH	then		u in circus
ē	equal	ò	saw	ü	rule	zh	measure		

fol·li·cle (fol′ə kəl), *n.* a small cavity, sac, or gland in the body. Hair grows from follicles.

fol·low (fol′ō), *v.* **1** to go or come after: *Sheep follow a leader. April follows March.* **2** to pursue: *The dogs followed the fox.* **3** to result from: *Confusion followed the traffic accident.* **4** to go along: *Follow this road to the corner.* **5** to act according to; take as a guide; use; obey: *Follow her advice.* **6** to watch closely; keep in view: *I followed the bird's flight.* **7** to keep the mind on; keep up with and understand: *Try to follow the mayor's speech.* **8** to take as your work: *She expects to follow a career in law.*

follow through, to continue a motion, plan, etc., through to the end.

follow up, 1 to follow closely and steadily. **2** to carry out to the end. **3** to act upon with energy.

fol·low·er (fol′ō ər), *n.* **1** person who follows the ideas or beliefs of another. **2** person or thing that follows.

fol·low·ing (fol′ō ing), **1** *n.* group of followers or fans: *That team has quite a following.* **2** *adj.* next after: *If that was Sunday, then the following day must have been Monday.* **3** *n.pl.* **the following,** persons or things now to be named or described.

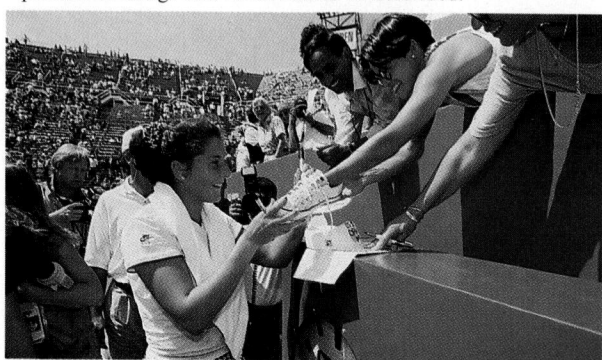

following (def. 1)

fol·low-up (fol′ō up′), *n.* any action or thing, such as a second or third visit, appeal, or letter, designed to be a further effort in achieving some goal.

fol·ly (fol′ē), *n.* **1** lack of sense; failure of wisdom or reason: *Her folly led her deep into debt.* **2** a foolish act, practice, or idea; something silly: *It was a folly to leave your bike unlocked in the street.* ❑ *n., pl.* **fol·lies** for 2.

fo·ment (fō ment′), *v.* to stir up trouble, rebellion, etc.; promote: *Three sailors were fomenting a mutiny on the ship.*

fond (fond), *adj.* **1** loving or liking: *She gave her child a fond look.* **2** cherished: *fond hopes.* **—fond′ly,** *adv.* **—fond′ness,** *n.*

fond of, having a liking for: *I am very fond of my uncle.*

Fon·da (fon′də), *n.* **1** **Henry,** 1905-1982, American stage and movie actor. He won an Academy Award in 1981 for the movie *On Golden Pond,* which also starred his daughter Jane. **2** **Jane** (jān), born 1937, American movie actor and political activist known for her anti-war views. She has won two Academy awards, for *Klute* in 1971 and for *Coming Home* in 1978.

fon·dle (fon′dl), *v.* to handle or treat with fondness; pet; caress: *They fondled the kittens.* ❑ *v.* **fon·dled, fon·dling.**

fon·due (fon′dü *or* fon dü′), *n.* a dish made of melted cheese, eggs, butter, etc., into which crackers or small pieces of bread or toast are dipped and eaten. [See Word Story at **font²**.]

font¹ (font), *n.* **1** basin holding water for baptism. **2** basin for holy water.

font² (font), *n.* (in printing) a complete set of type of any one size and style, or a set of letters and numbers used by a computer printer.

Fon·teyn (fon tān′), *n.* Dame **Mar·got** (mär′gō), 1919-1991, British ballerina. She often danced with Rudolf Nureyev.

food (füd), *n.* **1** anything that living things eat, drink, or take in that makes them live and grow: *Milk and green vegetables are valuable foods for young people.* **2** what is eaten: *Give him food and drink.* **3** anything that causes growth: *Books are food for the mind.* [See Word Story at **foray**.]

food chain, connection including several kinds of living things that are linked because each uses another as food. Cats, birds, caterpillars, and plants are a food chain because each eats the one named next.

food court, group of fast-food stores next to each other in a mall, with common seating for customers.

food poisoning, illness caused by eating foods that contain harmful bacteria or poisonous chemicals.

food processor, a small electric kitchen appliance with a covered plastic container and rotating attachments for quickly chopping, slicing, grating, or mixing foods.

food stamp, stamp given or sold by the U.S. government to persons or families whose income is below a certain amount. The stamps may be used instead of cash to buy food.

food·stuff (füd′stuf′), *n.* material for food. Grain and meat are foodstuffs.

food web, all the food chains in an ecological community.

fool (fül), **1** *n.* person without sense; person who acts unwisely. **2** *n.* clown formerly kept by royalty or nobility to amuse people; jester. **3** *v.* to joke, tease, or pretend: *I'm not really hurt, I was only fooling.* **4** *v.* to deceive; trick: *You can't fool me.* ■ See Synonym Study at **deceive**.

fool with, to meddle foolishly with.

fool·har·dy (fül′här′dē), *adj.* foolishly bold. ❑ *adj.* **fool·har·di·er, fool·har·di·est. —fool′har′di·ly,** *adv.* **—fool′har′di·ness,** *n.*

fool·ish (fü′lish), *adj.* without sense; unwise; silly: *foolish notions.* **—fool′ish·ly,** *adv.* **—fool′ish·ness,** *n.*

fool·proof (fül′prüf′), *adj.* so safe, simple, or well made that anyone can use or do it: *a foolproof device, a foolproof scheme.*

fool's gold, pyrite.

foot (füt), **1** *n.* the end part of a leg; part that a person, animal, or thing stands on. **2** *n.* part opposite the head of something; end toward which the feet are put: *the foot of a bed.* **3** *n.* the lowest part; bottom; base: *the foot of a hill, the foot of a page.* **4** *n.* part of a stocking that covers the foot. **5** *n.* unit of length equal to 12 inches. 3 feet = 1 yard. **6** *n.* one of the units of rhythm into which a line of poetry is divided. This line has four feet: "O beau | ti ful | for spa | cious skies." **7** *v.* to pay a bill: *I'll foot the bill for lunch.* ❑ *n., pl.* **feet.**

on foot, standing or walking.

put your foot down, to make up your mind and act firmly.

under foot, in the way.

foot·age (füt′ij), *n.* length in feet.

foot·ball (füt′bôl′), *n.* **1** game played with an inflated leather ball by two teams of eleven players each, on a field with a goal at each end. A player scores by carrying the ball over the goal line by a run or pass, or by kicking it through the goal posts. **2** BRITISH. **a** soccer. **b** rugby. **3** ball used in any game called football.

foot·board (füt′bôrd′), *n.* **1** board or small platform on which to support the feet. **2** an upright piece across the foot of a bed.

foot·bridge (füt′brij′), *n.* bridge for people on foot only.

foot-can·dle (füt′kan′dl), *n.* unit for measuring illumination. It is the amount of light produced by a standard candle on a surface at a distance of one foot.

–footed, *suffix.* having ____ feet: *four-footed = having four feet.*

foot·fall (fut′fôl′), *n.* OLD USE. sound of a footstep.

foot·hill (fut′hil′), *n.* a low hill at the base of a mountain or mountain range.

foot·hold (fut′hōld′), *n.* **1** place to put your foot; support for the feet: *I climbed the steep cliff by getting footholds in cracks in the rock.* **2** a first connection or position: *She got a foothold in the company by working as an intern.*

foot·ing (fut′ing), *n.* **1** a firm position of the feet: *He lost his footing and fell down on the ice.* **2** place to put a foot; support for the feet: *The steep cliff gave us no footing.* **3** a firm or secure place or position: *The new business has gained a footing in the community and is doing well.* **4** condition; relationship: *The United States and Canada are on a friendly footing.*

foot·lights (fut′līts′), *n.pl.* row of lights at the front of a stage.

foot·lock·er (fut′lok′ər), *n.* a small chest for personal belongings, usually kept at the foot of your bed, as in a barracks.

foot·loose (fut′lüs′), *adj.* free to go anywhere or do anything.

foot·man (fut′mən), *n.* a uniformed male servant who answers the bell, waits on the table, goes with an car or carriage to open the door, etc. □ *n., pl.* **foot·men.**

foot·note (fut′nōt′), *n.* note at the bottom of a page about something on the page.

foot·path (fut′path′), *n.* path for people on foot only. □ *n., pl.* **foot·paths** (fut′paᴛʜz′ or fut′paths′).

foot·pound (fut′pound′), *n.* unit of work done by a force that moves a one-pound object straight ahead one foot.

foot·print (fut′print′), *n.* mark made by a foot.

foot·rest (fut′rest′), *n.* support to rest the feet on.

foot soldier, infantryman.

foot·sore (fut′sôr′), *adj.* having sore feet from much walking: *The hike left us footsore and hungry.*

foot·step (fut′step′), *n.* **1** someone's step. **2** sound of steps. **3** footprint.

follow in someone's footsteps, to do as someone else has done.

foot·stool (fut′stül′), *n.* a low stool on which to place the feet when seated.

foot·wear (fut′wâr′), *n.* anything you wear on your feet, such as shoes, slippers, sandals, and socks.

foot·work (fut′werk′), *n.* way of using the feet: *Footwork is important in boxing and dancing.*

fop (fop), *n.* OLD USE. a vain man who is very fond of fine clothes and has affected manners; dandy.

fop·per·y (fop′ər ē) *n.* behavior or dress of a fop.

fop·pish (fop′ish), *adj.* **1** of a fop; suitable for a fop. **2** vain; affected. **—fop′pish·ly,** *adv.* **—fop′pish·ness,** *n.*

footwork

for (fôr), **1** *prep.* in place of: *We used boxes for chairs.* **2** *prep.* in support of; in favor of: *She is for changing the tax laws.* **3** *prep.* at a price of: *These apples are 12 for a dollar.* **4** *prep.* with the object or purpose of: *She went for a walk.* **5** *prep.* in order to become, have, keep, get to, etc.: *He ran for his life. She is hunting for her cat. He has just left for New York.* **6** *prep.* meant to belong to or be used with; suited to: *a box for gloves, books for children.* **7** *prep.* meant to belong to: *This gift is for you.* **8** *prep.* with a feeling toward: *She has an eye for beauty. We longed for home.* **9** *prep.* with respect or regard to: *It is warm for April. Eating too much is bad for your health.* **10** *prep.* because of; by reason of: *shouted for joy, punished for stealing.* **11** *prep.* in honor of: *A party was given for her.* **12** *conj.* because: *We can't go, for it is raining.* **13** *prep.* as far as: *We walked for a mile.* **14** *prep.* as long as: *She worked for an hour.* **15** *prep.* as being: *They know it for a fact.* **16** *prep.* in spite of: *For all her faults, we still like her.* **17** *prep.* in proportion to: *For one poisonous snake there are many harmless ones.* **18** *prep.* in the amount of: *a check for $20.* ■ Other words that sound like this are **fore** and **four.**

for., **1** foreign. **2** forestry.

fo·rage (fôr′ij), **1** *n.* hay, grain, or other food for horses, cattle, etc. **2** *v.* to hunt or search for food: *Rabbits forage in our garden.* **3** *v.* to get by hunting or searching about. **4** *v.* to search about; hunt: *The boys foraged for lumber to build a tree house.* **5** *v.* to plunder: *The soldiers foraged nearby villages.* □ *v.* **fo·raged, fo·rag·ing.** [See Word Story at **foray.**] **—fo′rag·er,** *n.*

fo·ray (fôr′ā), **1** *n.* a raid for plunder: *Armed bandits made a foray on the village and took the sheep.* **2** *v.* to lay waste; plunder.

WORD STORY **Foray** comes from an old French word meaning "to forage." **Forage** comes from the same word. (**Food** and **fodder** come from related old English words.) Throughout history, armies have searched and raided the areas they were traveling through to feed soldiers and animals.

for·bade or **for·bad** (fər bad′), *v.* past tense of **forbid:** *My parents forbade me to stay out past ten o'clock.*

for·bear[1] (fôr bâr′), *v.* **1** to hold back; keep from doing, saying, using, etc.: *I forbore telling her the truth because I knew it would upset her.* **2** to be patient; control yourself. □ *v.* **for·bore, for·borne, for·bear·ing.** **—for·bear′er,** *n.* **—for·bear′ing·ly,** *adv.*

for·bear[2] (fôr′bâr), *n.* forebear; ancestor.

for·bear·ance (fôr bâr′əns), *n.* **1** act of forbearing. **2** patience; self-control.

for·bid (fər bid′), *v.* to not allow; say you must not do; make a rule against; prohibit: *Mom forbids us to pick her roses.* □ *v.* **for·bade** or **for·bad, for·bid·den, for·bid·ding.**

SYNONYM STUDY **Forbid** and **prohibit** both mean to refuse to allow something. **Forbid** suggests a rule that is personal: *My dad forbids me to ride on motorcycles.* **Prohibit** suggests a law or official rule: *The city prohibits smoking in public buildings.*

for·bid·den (fər bid′n), **1** *adj.* not allowed; against the law or rules: *forbidden activities.* **2** *v.* past participle of **forbid:** *My parents have forbidden me to swim in that river.*

for·bid·ding (fər bid′ing), *adj.* causing fear or dislike; looking dangerous or unpleasant: *The coast was rocky and forbidding.* **—for·bid′ding·ly,** *adv.*

for·bore (fôr bôr′), *v.* past tense of **forbear**[1]: *She forbore from showing her disappointment.*

for·borne (fôr bôrn′), *v.* past participle of **forbear**[1]: *We have forborne from asking nosy questions.*

force (fôrs), **1** *n.* active power; strength: *The falling tree hit the ground with great force.* ■ See Synonym Study at **power.** **2** *n.* strength used against someone or something; violence: *We had to use force to open the locked suitcase.* **3** *n.* power to control, influence, persuade, convince, etc.; effectiveness: *She writes with force.* **4** *v.* to make someone act against his or her will: *Give it to me at once, or I will force you to.* **5** *v.* to get or take by force: *They forced their way in.* **6** *v.* to break open or through by force: *force a lock.* **7** *v.* to make by an unusual or unnatural effort; strain: *The unhappy child forced a smile.* **8** *v.* to hurry the growth or development of flowers, fruits, etc. **9** *n.* group of people working or acting together: *our office force, the police force.* **10** *n.pl.* **forces,** the armed forces: *U.S. forces were stationed on the island during the war.* **11** *n.* cause that produces, changes, or stops the motion of an object: *the force of gravitation, magnetic force.* **12** in baseball: **a** *n.* a force play. **b** *v.* to put out a runner in a force play. □ *v.* **forced, forc·ing.** **—force′a·ble,** *adj.* **—forc′er,** *n.*

in force, **1** in effect or operation: *The old rules are still in force.* **2** with full strength: *The enemy attacked in force.*

forced (fôrst), *adj.* **1** made, compelled, or driven by force: *Some convicts do forced labor.* **2** done by unusual effort: *The soldiers made a forced march of three days.* **3** not natural; strained: *She hid her dislike with a forced smile.*

a	hat	ė	term	ô	order	ch	child		a in about
ā	age	i	it	oi	oil	ng	long		e in taken
ä	far	ī	ice	ou	out	sh	she	ə	i in pencil
â	care	o	hot	u	cup	th	thin		o in lemon
e	let	ō	open	ủ	put	ᴛʜ	then		u in circus
ē	equal	ò	saw	ü	rule	zh	measure		

force·ful (fôrs′fəl), *adj.* having much force; strong; powerful: *a forceful manner.* **–force′ful·ly,** *adv.* **–force′ful·ness,** *n.*

force play, a play in baseball in which a base runner must go to the next base because the batter has hit the ball and it has not been caught for an out. If the ball reaches the base to which the runner must go, before the runner does, the runner is out.

for·ceps (fôr′seps), *n.pl. or sing.* small pincers or tongs used by surgeons, dentists, etc., for grasping and pulling.

WORD STORY Forceps comes from Latin words meaning "hot" and "to take." Perhaps the earliest use of tongs was to take hold of food heated by a fire, or to rearrange burning logs.

for·ci·ble (fôr′sə bəl), *adj.* **1** made or done by force; using force: *a forcible entrance into a house.* **2** having or showing force; strong; powerful; convincing: *a forcible speaker.* **–for′ci·ble·ness,** *n.* **–for′ci·bly,** *adv.*

ford (fôrd), **1** *n.* place where a river or stream is not too deep to cross by walking or driving through it. **2** *v.* to cross a river or stream by walking or driving through it. **–ford′a·ble,** *adj.*

ford

Ford (fôrd), *n.* **1 Gerald R.** (jer′əld), born 1913, the 38th president of the United States, from 1974 to 1977, vice-president from 1973 to 1974. **2 Harrison** (har′ə sən), born 1942, American movie actor. He played Han Solo in the *Star Wars* trilogy and Indiana Jones in three movies. **3 Henry,** 1863-1947, American automobile manufacturer. He pioneered the use of the moving assembly line in mass-production of cars. **4 John,** 1895-1973, American movie director. He won four Academy Awards and directed more than 200 movies, especially westerns.

fore[1] (fôr), **1** *adj.* at the front; toward the front; forward: *The fore wall of a house faces the street.* **2** *adv.* at or toward the bow or front: *Several of the crew went fore.* **3** *n.* the forward part. ■ Other words that sound like this are **for** and **four.**

to the fore, into full view; into a conspicuous place or position: *The question of new taxes will soon come to the fore.*

fore[2] (fôr), *interj.* (in golf) a shout of warning to persons ahead who are liable to be struck by the ball. ■ Other words that sound like this are **for** and **four.**

fore-, *prefix.* in front or before: *forepaw = a front paw; foregoing = going before.*

fore and aft, 1 at or toward both bow and stern of a ship. **2** lengthwise on a ship; from bow to stern; placed lengthwise.

fore-and-aft (fôr′ən aft′), *adj.* lengthwise on a ship; from bow to stern. Fore-and-aft sails are set lengthwise.

fore·arm[1] (fôr′ärm′), *n.* the part of the arm between the elbow and the wrist.

fore·arm[2] (fôr ärm′), *v.* to prepare for trouble ahead of time.

fore·bear (fôr′bâr′), *n.* ancestor; forefather. Also, **forbear**[2].

fore·bode (fôr bōd′), *v.* **1** to give warning of; predict: *Those black clouds forebode a storm.* **2** to have a feeling that something bad is going to happen. ❑ *v.* **fore·bod·ed, fore·bod·ing.**

fore·bod·ing (fôr bō′ding), *n.* **1** prediction; warning. **2** a feeling that something bad is going to happen.

fore·cast (fôr′kast′), **1** *v.* to tell what is coming; prophesy; predict: *Cooler weather is forecast for tomorrow.* **2** *n.* statement of what is coming; prediction: *What is the weather forecast today?* ❑ *v.* **fore·cast** or **fore·cast·ed, fore·cast·ing. –fore′cast′er,** *n.*

fore·cas·tle (fōk′səl or fôr′kas′əl), *n.* **1** the upper deck in front of the foremast. **2** the crew's quarters in the forward part of a merchant ship.

fore·close (fôr klōz′), *v.* **1** to shut out; prevent; exclude: *The club voted to foreclose further discussion of the subject.* **2** to take away the right to redeem a mortgage: *When the conditions of the mortgage were not met, the holder foreclosed and took possession of the house.* ❑ *v.* **fore·closed, fore·clos·ing.**

fore·clo·sure (fôr klō′zhər), *n.* act of foreclosing a mortgage.

fore·doom (fôr düm′), *v.* to doom beforehand: *Their plans were foredoomed to fail.*

fore·fa·ther (fôr′fä′ᴛʜər), *n.* ancestor.

fore·fin·ger (fôr′fing′gər), *n.* finger next to the thumb; index finger.

fore·foot (fôr′füt′), *n.* one of the front feet of an animal having four or more feet. ❑ *n., pl.* **fore·feet.**

fore·front (fôr′frunt′), *n.* place of greatest importance, activity, etc.; foremost part; extreme front: *She was at the forefront of the citizens' campaign for cleaner living conditions.*

fore·go[1] (fôr gō′), *v.* to forgo. ❑ *v.* **fore·went, fore·gone, fore·go·ing. –fore·go′er,** *n.*

fore·go[2] (fôr gō′), *v.* to go before. ❑ *v.* **fore·went, fore·gone, fore·go·ing.**

fore·go·ing (fôr′gō′ing), *adj.* going before; preceding; previous: *There are many pictures in the foregoing pages.*

fore·gone[1] (fôr gon′), *v.* past participle of **forego**[1]: *He has foregone his trip.*

fore·gone[2] (fôr′gon for adj.; fôr gon′ for verb), **1** *adj.* known or decided beforehand; inevitable: *That one of the good students in the class would win the prize was a foregone conclusion.* **2** *adj.* having gone before; previous. **3** *v.* past participle of **forego**[2]: *The tale of his heroic deeds had foregone his arrival.*

fore·ground (fôr′ground′), *n.* the part of a picture or scene nearest the observer; the part in the front: *The cottage stands in the foreground with the mountains in the background.*

fore·hand (fôr′hand′), **1** *n.* stroke in tennis and other games made with the palm of the hand turned forward. **2** *adj.* done or made with the palm of the hand turned forward.

fore·hand·ed (fôr′han′did), *adj.* providing for the future; prudent; thrifty. **–fore′hand′ed·ly,** *adv.* **–fore′hand′ed·ness,** *n.*

fore·head (fôr′id or fôr′hed′), *n.* the part of the face above the eyes.

fo·reign (fôr′ən), *adj.* **1** outside your own country: *He has traveled a lot in foreign countries.* **2** coming from outside your own country: *a foreign language, foreign money.* **3** of or with other countries; carried on or dealing with other countries: *foreign trade, foreign affairs.* **4** not belonging; not related: *Sitting still all day is foreign to my nature.* **–fo′reign·ness,** *n.*

foreign aid, economic, technical, or military help given by one nation to another.

fo·reign·er (fôr′ə nər), *n.* person from another country; alien.

foreign policy, plan of action followed by a country's government in dealings with other nations.

fore·know (fôr nō′), *v.* to know beforehand. ❑ *v.* **fore·knew** (fôr nü′), **fore·known** (fôr nōn′), **fore·know·ing.**

fore·knowl·edge (fôr′nol′ij or fôr nol′ij), *n.* knowledge of a thing before it exists or happens.

fore·leg (fôr′leg′), *n.* one of the front legs of an animal having four or more legs.

fore·limb (fôr′lim′), *n.* one of the front limbs of an animal having four or more limbs.

fore·lock (fôr′lok′), *n.* lock of hair that grows just above the forehead.

fore·man (fôr′mən), *n.* **1** person in charge of a group of workers or of part of a factory. **2** chairman of a jury. ❑ *n., pl.* **fore·men.**

Fore·man (fôr′mən), *n.* **George,** born 1949, American boxer. ■ **George Foreman** won the world heavyweight title in 1973 and in 1994. He is the oldest boxer ever to win the world heavyweight title.

fore·mast (fôr′mast′ *or* fôr′məst), *n.* mast nearest the front of a ship.

fore·most (fôr′mōst), **1** *adv.* first: *He stumbled and fell head foremost.* **2** *adj.* chief; leading: *one of the foremost scientists of this century.*

fore·noon (fôr′nün′), *n.* time between early morning and noon; part of the day from sunrise to noon.

fo·ren·sic (fə ren′sik), *adj.* of or used in a court of law or in public debate: *forensic evidence.* **—fo·ren′si·cal·ly,** *adv.*

fore·or·dain (fôr′ôr dān′), *v.* to ordain beforehand; determine beforehand; predestine: *He felt their success had been foreordained.* **—fore′or·dain′ment,** *n.*

fore·part (fôr′pärt′), *n.* the front part; early part.

fore·paw (fôr′pò′), *n.* a front paw.

fore·quar·ter (fôr′kwôr′tər), *n.* a front leg, shoulder, and nearby ribs of beef, lamb, pork, etc.

fore·run·ner (fôr′run′ər), *n.* **1** person who is sent ahead to prepare for and announce another's coming; herald. **2** sign or warning that something is coming: *Black clouds are forerunners of a storm.* **3** predecessor; ancestor.

fore·sail (fôr′sāl′ *or* fôr′səl), *n.* **1** the principal sail on the foremast of a schooner. **2** the lowest sail on the foremast of a square-rigged ship.

fore·saw (fôr sò′), *v.* past tense of **foresee:** *We foresaw that we would be late and called to tell our friends.*

fore·see (fôr sē′), *v.* to see or know beforehand: *We didn't take our bathing suits, because we could foresee that the water would be cold.* ❏ *v.* **fore·saw, fore·seen, fore·see·ing. —fore·see′a·ble,** *adj.* **—fore·se′er,** *n.*

fore·seen (fôr sēn′), *v.* past participle of **foresee:** *Nobody could have foreseen how cold it would be.*

fore·shad·ow (fôr shad′ō), *v.* to indicate beforehand; be a warning of: *Those clouds foreshadow a storm.* **—fore·shad′ow·er,** *n.*

fore·shad·ow·ing (fôr′shad′ō ing), *n.* the technique in literature and drama of giving the reader, listener, or viewer hints of what is to come: *That mishap is a foreshadowing of the terrible accident that happens to the character later in the novel.*

fore·shock (fôr′shok′), *n.* an earthquake that occurs a few days or weeks before a larger earthquake and begins near the focus of the larger earthquake.

fore·shore (fôr′shôr′), *n.* part of the shore between the high-water mark and the low-water mark.

fore·short·en (fôr shôrt′n), *v.* to shorten lines, objects, etc., in a drawing or painting in order to give the impression of depth and distance to the eye. Foreshortening helps give perspective to a drawing or painting.

fore·sight (fôr′sīt′), *n.* **1** ability to see what is likely to happen and prepare for it: *No one had enough foresight to predict the winner.* **2** careful thought about what is likely to happen in the future; prudence: *A spendthrift does not use foresight.*

foreshorten
foreshortened finger

fore·sight·ed (fôr′sī′tid), *adj.* having or showing foresight. **—fore′sight′ed·ly,** *adv.* **—fore′sight′ed·ness,** *n.*

fore·skin (fôr′skin′), *n.* fold of skin that covers the end of the penis.

fo·rest (fôr′ist), **1** *n.* thick woods that cover a large area. **2** *adj.* of a forest; in a forest: *Help prevent forest fires.* [**Forest** comes from a Latin word meaning "door." In Latin as in English, the natural world was called the outdoors.]

fore·stall (fôr stòl′), *v.* **1** to prevent by acting first: *The mayor forestalled a strike by starting to negotiate early with the union.* **2** to act sooner than and so get the better of; get ahead of: *By settling the deal over the telephone, she had forestalled all her competitors.* **—fore·stall′er,** *n.*

fo·rest·a·tion (fôr′ə stā′shən), *n.* the planting of forests.

fo·rest·ed (fôr′ə stid), *adj.* covered with trees; thickly wooded.

fo·rest·er (fôr′ə stər), *n.* person in charge of planting and taking care of a forest.

forest ranger, person who is in charge of, and who supervises activities in, a national, state, or other public forest.

fo·rest·ry (fôr′ə strē), *n.* science and art of planting and taking care of forests.

fore·taste (fôr′tāst′), *n.* a taste beforehand: *The boy got a foretaste of business life by working during his vacation from school.*

fore·tell (fôr tel′), *v.* to tell or show beforehand; predict; prophesy: *Who can foretell what the future will be?* ❏ *v.* **fore·told, fore·tell·ing.**

fore·thought (fôr′thòt′), *n.* careful thought or planning for the future; foresight: *A great deal of forethought went into their trip.*

fore·told (fôr tōld′), *v.* past tense and past participle of **foretell:** *She foretold the future. The Weather Bureau had foretold the cold wave.*

for·ev·er (fər ev′ər), *adv.* **1** without ever coming to an end; for always; for ever: *Nobody lives forever.* **2** all the time; always: *She is forever telling me that I should exercise more.*

for·ev·er·more (fər ev′ər môr′), *adv.* forever.

fore·warn (fôr wôrn′), *v.* to warn beforehand: *We should have been forewarned of his illness when he began to lose weight.*

fore·went (fôr went′), *v.* past tense of **forego:** *She forewent a second helping.*

fore·wing (fôr′wing′), *n.* one of the front wings of an insect having four wings.

fore·wom·an (fôr′wùm′ən), *n.* **1** woman who supervises a group of workers, as in a factory. **2** chairwoman of a jury. ❏ *n., pl.* **fore·wom·en.**

fore·word (fôr′wèrd′), *n.* a brief introduction or preface to a book, speech, etc. ■ Another word that sounds like this is **forward.**

for·feit (fôr′fit), **1** *v.* to lose or have to give up by your own act, neglect, or fault: *Some of our players didn't show up, so we had to forfeit the game.* **2** *n.* thing lost or given up because of some act, neglect, or fault; penalty; fine: *The forfeit of the game cost us the championship.* **—for′feit·a·ble,** *adj.* **—for′feit·er,** *n.*

for·fei·ture (fôr′fi chər), *n.* **1** loss by forfeiting. **2** something forfeited; penalty; fine.

for·gath·er (fôr gaTH′ər), *v.* **1** to gather together; assemble; meet. **2** to meet by accident. **3** to be friendly; associate.

for·gave (fər gāv′), *v.* past tense of **forgive:** *She forgave my mistake.*

forge[1] (fôrj), **1** *n.* place with a furnace or open fire where metal is heated very hot and then hammered into shape. **2** *n.* a blacksmith's shop; smithy. **3** *v.* to heat metal very hot and then hammer it into shape: *The blacksmith forged a bar of iron into a big, strong hook.* **4** *v.* to make, shape, or form: *forge an agreement to increase trade.* **5** *v.* to make or write something false to deceive; sign falsely: *forge a letter of recommendation, forge checks.* ❏ *v.* **forged, forg·ing. —forge′a·ble,** *adj.*

forge[2] (fôrj), *v.* to move forward slowly but steadily: *She forged ahead and won the race.* ❏ *v.* **forged, forg·ing.**

forg·er (fôr′jər), *n.* **1** person who forges another person's name or makes any fraudulent imitation. **2** person who forges metals.

forg·er·y (fôr′jər ē), *n.* **1** act of forging another person's name or making or writing something false. Forgery is a crime and is punishable by law. **2** something made or written falsely to deceive: *The painting was a forgery. The signature on the check was not mine but a forgery.* ❏ *n., pl.* **forg·er·ies.**

for·get (fər get′), *v.* **1** to be unable to remember; fail to recall: *I forgot the poem which I had memorized.* **2** to fail to remember; fail to do, take, notice, etc.: *I forgot to call the dentist. He had forgotten his umbrella.* ❏ *v.* **for·got, for·got·ten, for·get·ting. —for·get′ta·ble,** *adj.* **—for·get′ter,** *n.*

forget yourself, to forget what you should do or be; say or do something improper: *The angry man forgot himself and started to shout in front of everybody on the bus.*

a	hat	ė	term	ô	order	ch	child		
ā	age	i	it	oi	oil	ng	long		a in about
ä	far	ī	ice	ou	out	sh	she		e in taken
â	care	o	hot	u	cup	th	thin	ə	i in pencil
e	let	ō	open	ù	put	ŦH	then		o in lemon
ē	equal	ò	saw	ü	rule	zh	measure		u in circus

for·get·ful (fər get′fəl), *adj.* apt to forget; having a poor memory: *When I get too tired I become forgetful.* **—for·get′ful·ly,** *adv.* **—for·get′ful·ness,** *n.*

for·get-me-not (fər get′mē not′), *n.* either of two small plants with hairy stems and clusters of small blue, pink, or white flowers.

for·give (fər giv′), *v.* to give up the wish to punish; not have hard feelings at or toward; pardon; excuse: *She forgave me for breaking her tennis racket.* ■ See Synonym Study at **pardon.** ❏ *v.* **for·gave, for·giv·en, for·giv·ing. —for·giv′a·ble,** *adj.* **—for·giv′er,** *n.*

for·giv·en (fər giv′ən), *v.* past participle of **forgive:** *Your mistakes are forgiven, but be more careful.*

for·give·ness (fər giv′nis), *n.* **1** act of forgiving; pardon. **2** willingness to forgive.

for·giv·ing (fər giv′ing), *adj.* willing to forgive. **—for·giv′ing·ly,** *adv.* **—for·giv′ing·ness,** *n.*

for·go (fôr gō′), *v.* to do without; give up: *She decided to forgo the movies and do her lessons.* ❏ *v.* **for·went, for·gone, for·go·ing.** Also, **forego.**

for·gone (fôr gon′), *v.* past participle of **forgo:** *I have forgone dessert for a month in an effort to lose weight.*

for·got (fər got′), *v.* past tense of **forget:** *She was so busy that she forgot to eat her lunch.*

for·got·ten (fər got′n), *v.* past participle of **forget:** *He has forgotten much of what he learned.*

fork (fôrk), **1** *n.* tool with a handle and two or more long, pointed parts at one end. A small fork is used to lift food. A much larger fork, called a pitchfork, is used to lift and throw hay. Another kind is used for digging. **2** *v.* to lift, throw, or dig with a fork: *fork hay into a wagon.* **3** *n.* anything shaped like a fork; any branching. The place where a tree, road, or stream divides into branches is a fork. **4** *n.* one of the branches into which anything is divided: *Take the right-hand fork.* **5** *v.* to divide into forks: *There is a garage where the road forks.* **—fork′like′,** *adj.*

fork out, fork over, or **fork up,** INFORMAL. to hand over; pay out: *He forked over the money.*

fork·ball (fôrk′bôl′), *n.* baseball thrown from between the pitcher's index and middle fingers, causing it to drop just before it reaches home plate.

forked (fôrkt), *adj.* **1** having a fork or forks; divided into branches: *the forked tail of a bird.* **2** zigzag: *forked lightning.*

fork·lift (fôrk′lift′), *n.* device attached to one end of a truck or small vehicle, with horizontal metal arms that can be inserted under a load to lift or lower it.

for·lorn (fôr lôrn′), *adj.* miserable and hopeless from being left alone and neglected: *The lost kitten, a forlorn little animal, was wet and dirty.* **—for·lorn′ly,** *adv.* **—for·lorn′ness,** *n.*

form (fôrm), **1** *n.* kind; sort; variety: *Ice, snow, and steam are forms of water.* **2** *n.* appearance apart from color or materials; shape: *Circles and triangles are simple forms.* **3** *v.* to shape; make: *Bakers form dough into loaves.* ■ See Synonym Study at **make. 4** *v.* to be formed; take shape: *Clouds form in the sky.* **5** *v.* to become: *Water forms ice when it freezes.* **6** *v.* to make up; compose: *Several dozen members form our club.* **7** *v.* to organize; establish: *We formed a committee.* **8** *v.* to develop: *She formed the good habit of doing her homework before watching TV.* **9** *n.* way of doing something; manner; method: *He is a fast runner, but his form is bad.* **10** *n.* set way of behaving according to custom or rule; formality; ceremony: *She said "Good morning" as a matter of form, although she hardly noticed me.* **11** *n.* piece of printed paper with blank spaces to be filled in: *We filled out a form to get a license for our dog.* **12** *n.* arrangement: *In what form was the list of words?* **13** *n.* mold; pattern: *Ice cream is often made in forms.* **14** *n.* good condition of body or mind: *Athletes exercise to keep in form.* **15** *n.* (in grammar) any of the ways in which a word is spelled or pronounced to show its different meanings. *Toys* is the plural form of *toy. Saw* is the past form of *see. My* and *mine* are the possessive forms of *I.*

WORD FAMILY Form and the words below are related. They all come from a Latin word meaning "a shape."

| conform | former | informal | performance |
| format | formula | information | uniform |

for·mal (fôr′məl), **1** *adj.* not familiar and homelike; stiff: *a formal greeting. A judge has a formal manner in a court of law.* **2** *adj.* according to set customs or rules: *The ambassador paid a formal call on the prime minister.* **3** *adj.* done with or having authority; official: *A written contract is a formal agreement to do something.* **4** *adj.* very regular; symmetrical; orderly: *a formal arrangement of furniture, a formal poem.* **5** *adj.* of or about the form, not the content of a thing. **6** *n.* a dance, party, or other social affair at which women often wear long, fancy dresses and men wear elegant suits. **7** *n.* a long, fancy dress worn to such a social affair: *She wore a formal to the dance.* **—for′mal·ly,** *adv.*

for·mal·de·hyde (fôr mal′də hīd), *n.* a colorless gas with a sharp, irritating odor. It is used in a water solution to disinfect and to preserve animal specimens.

for·mal·i·ty (fôr mal′ə tē), *n.* **1** a set way of doing something according to custom; ceremony: *At a wedding there are many formalities.* **2** attention to forms and customs: *The queen received her visitors with much formality.* **3** stiffness of manner, behavior, or arrangement: *The formality of the party made me uneasy.* ❏ *n., pl.* **for·mal·i·ties** for 1.

for·mal·ize (fôr′mə līz), *v.* **1** to make formal. **2** to give a definite form to. ❏ *v.* **for·mal·ized, for·mal·iz·ing.**

for·mat (fôr′mat), **1** *n.* shape, size, and general arrangement of a book, magazine, etc. **2** *n.* the design, plan, arrangement, form, or manner of anything: *the format of a TV show.* **3** *v.* to arrange; put in a format or give a format to: *to format a new magazine.* ❏ *v.* **for·mat·ted, for·mat·ting.**

for·ma·tion (fôr mā′shən), *n.* **1** act or process of forming, making, or shaping something: *Heat causes the formation of steam from water.* **2** way in which something is arranged; arrangement; order: *The planes flew over the fairgrounds in perfect formation.* **3** something that is formed: *Clouds are formations of tiny drops of water in the sky.*

formation (def. 2)

form·a·tive (fôr′mə tiv), *adj.* of or about formation or development; forming; molding: *Home and school are the chief formative influences in a child's life.*

for·mer (fôr′mər), *adj.* **1** the first of two: *When I am offered ice cream or pie, I always choose the former.* **2** earlier; past: *In former times, cooking was done in fireplaces instead of stoves.*

for·mer·ly (fôr′mər lē), *adv.* in the past; some time ago: *Our teacher formerly taught at a different school.*

For·mi·ca (fôr mī′kə), *n.* trademark for a plastic that resists water, heat, and most chemicals. It is used on kitchen and bathroom surfaces, tables and other furniture, etc.

for·mi·da·ble (fôr′mə də bəl), *adj.* **1** hard to overcome; hard to deal with; to be dreaded: *a formidable opponent.* **2** very good; awe-inspiring: *formidable talent.* **—for′mi·da·bly,** *adv.*

form·less (fôrm′lis), *adj.* without definite or regular form; shapeless. **—form′less·ly,** *adv.* **—form′less·ness,** *n.*

form letter, letter copied from a pattern so that copies may be made easily and sent to many different people.

For·mo·sa (fôr mō′sə), *n.* former name of **Taiwan.** —**For·mo′san,** *adj., n.*

for·mu·la (fôr′myə lə), *n.* **1** recipe or prescription: *a formula for making soap.* **2** mixture of milk, water, sugar, and other nutrients for feeding babies that are not nursed. **3** method or way of achieving a desired result: *formula for increasing profits.* **4** combination of symbols used in chemistry to show what is in a compound: *The formula for water is H_2O.* **5** combination of symbols used in mathematics to state a rule or principle. EXAMPLE: $(a + b)^2 = a^2 + 2ab + b^2$ is an algebraic formula. **6** a set form of words, especially one which by much use has partly lost its meaning: *"How do you do?" is a polite formula.* ❏ *n., pl.* **for·mu·las.**

for·mu·late (fôr′myə lāt), *v.* to state definitely or clearly; express in a formula: *The Constitution formulates requirements to be eligible for federal office.* ❏ *v.* **for·mu·lat·ed, for·mu·lat·ing.** —**for′mu·la′tion,** *n.*

for·sake (fôr sāk′), *v.* to give up; leave alone; leave; abandon: *The Pilgrims forsook their homes and friends to settle in North America.* ❏ *v.* **for·sook, for·sak·en, for·sak·ing.**

for·sak·en (fôr sā′kən), **1** *v.* past participle of **forsake:** *That girl has forsaken her old friends now that her parents have become so wealthy.* **2** *adj.* deserted; abandoned: *We found an old, forsaken graveyard out in the country.*

for·sook (fôr súk′), *v.* past tense of **forsake:** *He forsook his family and friends.*

for·sooth (fôr sü̇th′), *adv.* OLD USE. in truth; indeed.

for·swear (fôr swâr′), *v.* **1** to swear solemnly to give up: *The coach asked the team to forswear smoking.* **2** to be untrue to your sworn word or promise; perjure yourself. ❏ *v.* **for·swore, for·sworn, for·swear·ing.**

for·swore (fôr swôr′), *v.* past tense of **forswear:** *The team forswore smoking.*

for·sworn (fôr swôrn′), *v.* past participle of **forswear:** *They have forsworn liquor and cigarettes.*

for·syth·i·a (fôr sith′ē ə), *n.* any of several bushes with many bell-shaped, yellow flowers in early spring before its leaves come out. ❏ *n., pl.* **for·syth·i·as.**

fort (fôrt), *n.* **1** a strong building or place that can be defended against an enemy; fortified place; stronghold. **2** (earlier) trading post. ■ Another word that sounds like this is **forte**[1].

> **WORD FAMILY** **Fort** and the following words are related: **forte**[1], **forte**[2], **fortification, fortify, fortissimo, fortitude,** and **fortress.** They all come from a Latin word meaning "strong."

forte[1] (fôrt), *n.* something someone does very well; strong point: *Bowling is her forte.* ■ Another word that sounds like this is **fort.**

for·te[2] (fôr′tā), *adj., adv.* (in music) loud.

forth (fôrth), *adv.* **1** forward; onward: *From this day forth I'll try to do better.* **2** into view; out: *The sun came forth from behind the clouds.* ■ Another word that sounds like this is **fourth.**

and so forth, and so on; and the like: *This leather case can be used to carry books, papers, drawings, and so forth.*

forth·com·ing (fôrth′kum′ing), *adj.* **1** about to appear; approaching: *The forthcoming week will be busy.* **2** ready when wanted; coming forth: *I needed help, but none was forthcoming.*

forth·right (fôrth′rīt′), *adj.* frank and outspoken; straightforward; direct: *The speaker did not like the plan and made forthright objections to it.* —**forth′right′ly,** *adv.*

forth·with (fôrth′with′ or fôrth′wiᴛʜ′), *adv.* at once; immediately: *The judge's summons ordered the witness to appear forthwith in court.*

for·ti·eth (fôr′tē ith), *adj., n.* **1** next after the 39th; last in a series of 40. **2** one of 40 equal parts.

for·ti·fi·ca·tion (fôr′tə fə kā′shən), *n.* **1** wall or fort built to make a place strong. **2** place made strong by building walls and forts.

for·ti·fy (fôr′tə fī), *v.* **1** to build forts, walls, etc.; protect a place against attack; strengthen against attack. **2** to give support to; strengthen: *They fortified themselves for a busy day by eating a big breakfast.* **3** to enrich with vitamins and minerals: *fortify bread.* ❏ *v.* **for·ti·fied, for·ti·fy·ing.** —**for′ti·fi·er,** *n.*

for·tis·si·mo (fôr tis′ə mō), *adj., adv.* (in music) very loud.

for·ti·tude (fôr′tə tüd), *n.* courage in facing pain, danger, or trouble; firmness of spirit.

Fort Mc·Hen·ry (mək hen′rē), a fort and national monument in N Maryland, at the entrance to the harbor of Baltimore. It was bombarded by British forces in 1814 but resisted the attack. Francis Scott Key wrote "The Star Spangled Banner" during this battle.

fort·night (fôrt′nīt), *n.* two weeks. [**Fortnight** comes from old English words meaning "fourteen nights." Long ago, a week was called a *sennight,* from "seven nights."]

fort·night·ly (fôrt′nīt lē), **1** *adv.* once in every two weeks. **2** *adj.* happening once in every two weeks.

FORTRAN (fôr′tran), *n.* computer programming language that uses algebraic notation, designed for mathematical tasks.

for·tress (fôr′tris), *n.* place built with walls and defenses; large fort or fortification. ❏ *n., pl.* **for·tress·es.**

Fort Smith, city in W Arkansas.

Fort Sum·ter (sump′tər), a fort and national monument in the harbor of Charleston, South Carolina. A Confederate attack on this fort in April 1861 began the Civil War.

for·tu·i·tous (fôr tü′ə təs), *adj.* happening by chance; accidental: *The fortuitous falling of an apple led Newton to formulate the law of gravity.* —**for·tu′i·tous·ly,** *adv.* —**for·tu′i·tous·ness,** *n.*

for·tu·nate (fôr′chə nit), *adj.* **1** having good luck; lucky: *You are fortunate in having such a fine family.* **2** bringing good luck; having favorable results: *a fortunate decision.* —**for′tu·nate·ly,** *adv.*

for·tune (fôr′chən), *n.* **1** a great deal of money or property; riches; wealth: *They made a fortune in oil.* **2** what happens; luck; chance: *Fortune was against us; we lost.* **3** good luck; prosperity; success. ■ See Synonym Study at **luck. 4** what is going to happen to someone; fate: *I know someone who claims to be able to tell people's fortunes.*

fortune cookie, a thin cookie that has been folded and baked with a slip of paper inside on which a prediction or proverb is printed. Fortune cookies are often served in Chinese restaurants.

fortune hunter, person who tries to get rich by marrying someone wealthy.

for·tune·tell·er (fôr′chən tel′ər), *n.* person who claims to be able to tell what is going to happen to people.

Fort Wayne (wān), city in NE Indiana.

Fort Worth (wėrth), city in N Texas.

for·ty (fôr′tē), *adj., n.* four times ten; 40. ❏ *n., pl.* **for·ties.**

for·ty-nin·er (fôr′tē nī′nər), *n.* person who went to California in 1849 to seek gold during the gold rush that had started in 1848.

fo·rum (fôr′əm), *n.* **1** the public square or marketplace of an ancient Roman city. There business was done, and courts and public assemblies were held. **2** a meeting to discuss questions of public interest. **3** court of law; tribunal.

for·ward (fôr′wərd), **1** *adv.* toward the front; onward; ahead: *Forward, march! From this time forward we shall be good friends.* **2** *adv., adj.* to the front; near the front: *come forward, the forward part of a ship.* **3** *adj.* advanced; far ahead: *forward for your age.* **4** *adv.* into view or consideration; out: *In her talk she brought forward several new ideas.* **5** *v.* to help along: *She did everything she could to forward her friend's plan.* **6** *v.* to send on farther: *Please forward my mail to my new address.* **7** *adj.* ready; eager: *He knew his lesson and was forward with his answers.* **8** *adj.* impudent; bold: *Don't be so forward as to interrupt the speaker.* **9** *n.* player whose position is in the front line in games such as basketball, hockey, or soccer. ■ Another word that sounds like this is **foreword.** —**for′ward·er,** *n.* —**for′ward·ly,** *adv.*

for·ward·ness (fôr′wərd nis), *n.* **1** readiness; eagerness. **2** impudence; boldness.

for·wards (fôr′wərdz), *adv.* forward.

for·went (fôr went′), *v.* past tense of **forgo:** *The knight forwent dinner in his haste to begin the quest.*

a	hat	ė	term	ô	order	ch	child		a in about
ā	age	i	it	oi	oil	ng	long		e in taken
ä	far	ī	ice	ou	out	sh	she	ə	i in pencil
â	care	o	hot	u	cup	th	thin		o in lemon
e	let	ō	open	ů	put	ᴛʜ	then		u in circus
ē	equal	ò	saw	ü	rule	zh	measure		

fos·sil (fos′əl), **1** *n.* the hardened remains or traces of something that lived in a former age. Fossils provide our knowledge of dinosaurs and other living things from millions of years ago. **2** *n.* a very old-fashioned person with out-of-date ideas. [**Fossil** comes from a Latin word meaning "to dig." Most fossils are underground. People have to dig them up to see them.]

fossil (def. 1)

fossil fuel, any fuel found in the earth and formed from the remains of things that lived millions of years ago. Coal, oil, and natural gas are fossil fuels.

fos·sil·ize (fos′ə līz), *v.* to change into a fossil. ❏ *v.* **fos·sil·ized, fos·sil·iz·ing. —fos′sil·i·za′tion,** *n.*

fos·ter (fô′stər), **1** *adj.* in the same family, but not related by birth or by law. A **foster child** is a child brought up by a person or persons who are not the parents by birth or adoption. A **foster father, foster mother,** and **foster parent** are persons who bring up the child of another, not legally a member of the family. **2** *v.* to help the growth or development of; encourage: *Our city fosters libraries and parks.* ■ See Synonym Study at **promote. 3** *v.* to care for fondly; cherish. **4** *v.* to bring up; help to grow; make grow; rear. **—fos′ter·er,** *n.*

Fos·ter (fô′stər), *n.* **Ste·phen** (stē′vən), 1826-1864, American composer and songwriter. He wrote "Oh! Susannah," "Camptown Races," and many other popular songs.

foster home, a home in which a child is brought up by people who are not the parents by birth or adoption. A child may be placed in such a home under the supervision of a governmental or social agency, which pays for the cost of the child's care.

fought (fôt), *v.* past tense and past participle of **fight:** *They fought for their rights. A battle was fought there.*

foul (foul), **1** *adj.* very dirty, nasty, or smelly: *We opened the windows to let out the foul air.* **2** *v.* to make or become dirty; soil; defile: *The oil spilled by the damaged ship fouled the harbor.* **3** *adj.* very wicked or cruel: *Murder is a foul crime.* **4** *adj.* offending modesty or decency; obscene; profane: *foul language.* **5** *adj.* done against the rules; unfair. **6** in sports: **a** *n.* an unfair play; thing done against the rules. **b** *v.* to make an unfair play against. **7** in baseball: **a** *n.* ball hit outside the foul lines. **b** *adj.* outside the foul lines. **c** *v.* to hit a ball outside the foul lines. **8** *v.* to hit against: *One boat fouled the other.* **9** *v.* to get tangled up with; catch: *The rope they threw fouled our anchor chain.* **10** *v.* to clog up: *Grease fouled the drain.* **11** *adj.* unfavorable; stormy: *Foul weather delayed us for several days.* ■ Another word that sounds like this is **fowl. —foul′ly,** *adv.*

foul out, 1 (in baseball) to be put out by hitting a ball caught on the fly outside the foul lines. **2** (in basketball) to be put out of a game for committing more fouls than are allowed.

foul up, to make a mess of; botch: *foul up the repairs on a car.*

fou·lard (fu lärd′), *n.* a soft, thin fabric made of silk, rayon, or cotton, usually with a printed pattern. It is used for neckties, dresses, etc.

foul line, 1 (in baseball) either one of two straight lines extending from home plate through first base and third base to the limits of the playing field. **2** (in basketball) line 15 feet (4.5 meters) in front of each basket from which free throws are made.

foul play, 1 unfair play; thing or things done against the rules. **2** treachery; violence.

foul-up or **foul·up** (foul′up′), *n.* state of confusion; mix-up; mess: *a ticket foul-up.*

found[1] (found), *v.* past tense and past participle of **find:** *We found the treasure. The lost child was found.*

found[2] (found), *v.* **1** to set up; establish: *The Pilgrims founded a colony at Plymouth.* **2** to rest for support; base: *He founded his claim on facts.*

foun·da·tion (foun dā′shən), *n.* **1** part on which the other parts rest for support; base: *the foundation of a house.* ■ See Synonym Study at **base**[1]. **2** basis: *This report has no foundation in fact.* **3** a charitable organization that provides money, especially for research.

foun·der[1] (foun′dər), *v.* **1** to fill with water and sink: *The ship foundered in the storm.* **2** to fall down; stumble: *The weary ponies foundered in the swamp.* **3** to break down; fail: *Their business has foundered.*

found·er[2] (foun′dər), *n.* person who founds something.

Founding Father, 1 one of the men who planned and wrote the Constitution of the United States. **2 founding father,** person who sets up a business, company, or institution.

found·ling (found′ling), *n.* baby or little child found by someone after being abandoned.

found·ry (foun′drē), *n.* place where metal is melted and molded; place where things are made of molten metal. ❏ *n., pl.* **found·ries.**

fount (fount), *n.* **1** fountain. **2** source; origin.

foun·tain (foun′tən), *n.* **1** water flowing or rising into the air in a spray. **2** pipes through which the water is forced and the basin built to receive it. **3** spring or source of water. **4** device from which someone can get a drink of water: *The school had a drinking fountain on each floor.* **5** source; origin: *My friend is a fountain of information about football.*

fountain (defs. 1 and 2)

foun·tain·head (foun′tən hed′), *n.* **1** source of a stream. **2** an original source: *She is a fountainhead of fashion designs.*

fountain pen, pen for writing that gives a steady supply of ink from a rubber or plastic tube.

four (fôr), *n., adj.* one more than three; 4. ■ Other words that sound like this are **for** and **fore.**

on all fours, 1 on all four feet. **2** on hands and knees.

four·fold (fôr′fōld′), **1** *adj., adv.* four times as much or as many. **2** *adj.* having four parts.

four-foot·ed (fôr′fut′id), *adj.* having four feet; quadruped: *A dog is a four-footed animal.*

Four-H clubs or **4-H clubs** (fôr′āch′), a national system of clubs to teach agriculture and home economics to children in rural areas.

four-post·er (fôr′pō′stər), *n.* bed with four tall corner posts for supporting a canopy.

four·score (fôr′skôr′), *adj., n.* four times twenty; 80.

four·some (fôr′səm), *n.* **1** group of four people. **2** game played by four people, two on each side. **3** the players.

four·square (fôr′skwâr′), *adj.* **1** square. **2** frank; outspoken.

four·teen (fôr′tēn′), *n., adj.* four more than ten; 14.

four·teenth (fôr′tēnth′), *adj., n.* **1** next after the 13th; last in a series of 14. **2** one of 14 equal parts.

fourth (fôrth), *adj., n.* **1** next after the third; last in a series of four. **2** one of four equal parts; quarter. ■ Another word that sounds like this is **forth.**

fourth dimension, a dimension in addition to length, width, and thickness. Time has been thought of as a fourth dimension.

fourth estate, newspapers or newspaper workers; journalists; the press.

Fourth of July, Independence Day.

four-wheel drive (fôr′wēl′), a motor vehicle drive system in which power goes to all four wheels for better traction in snow or rough terrain.

4WD, four-wheel drive.

fowl (foul), *n.* **1** any of several kinds of large birds used for food. The hen, rooster, and turkey are fowl. **2** flesh of these birds used for food. **3** wild fowl. ❑ *n., pl.* **fowl** or **fowls.** ■ Another word that sounds like this is **foul.**

fowl·er (fou′lər), *n.* person who hunts or traps wild birds.

fowling piece, a lightweight shotgun for shooting wild birds.

fox (foks), *n.* **1** any of several wild animals something like dogs, with pointed muzzles and bushy tails. In many stories the fox gets the better of other animals by its cleverness. **2** its fur. **3** a clever or sly person. ❑ *n., pl.* **fox·es** or **fox** for 1; **fox·es** for 3. —**fox′like′,** *adj.*

fox·glove (foks′gluv′), *n.* any of several plants with tall stalks having many bell-shaped purple or white flowers; digitalis.

fox·hole (foks′hōl′), *n.* hole in the ground, large enough for one or two soldiers, for protection against enemy fire.

fox·hound (foks′hound′), *n.* hound with a keen sense of smell, bred and trained to hunt foxes.

fox terrier, a small, active dog kept as a pet, formerly trained to drive foxes from their holes. Fox terriers are white with brown or black spots and may have smooth or wiry coats.

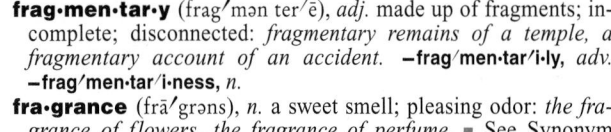

fox terrier—15 in. (38 cm) high at the shoulder

fox trot, 1 dance having short, quick steps. **2** music for it.

fox-trot (foks′trot′), *v.* to dance the fox trot. ❑ *v.* **fox-trot·ted, fox-trot·ting.**

fox·y (fok′sē), *adj.* sly; crafty; as a fox is considered to be. ❑ *adj.* **fox·i·er, fox·i·est.** —**fox′i·ly,** *adv.* —**fox′i·ness,** *n.*

foy·er (foi′ər), *n.* **1** an area where people can sit or wait in a theater, apartment house, or hotel; lobby. **2** an entrance hall.

Foyt (foit), *n.* **A. J.,** born 1935, American race car driver. He is one of the most successful race car drivers ever. He has won the Indianapolis 500 four times.

FPC, Federal Power Commission.

fps or **f.p.s.,** feet per second.

Fr, symbol for francium.

fr., 1 fragment. **2** franc. **3** from.

Fr., 1 Father. **2** France. **3** French. **4** Friar. **5** Friday.

fra·cas (frā′kəs), *n.* a noisy quarrel or fight; disorderly noise; uproar; brawl. ❑ *n., pl.* **fra·cas·es.**

frac·tion (frak′shən), *n.* **1** one or more of the equal parts of a whole. ½, ⅓, and ¾ are fractions; so are ⁴⁄₃ and ¹⁰⁄₆. **2** a very small part, amount, etc.; not all of a thing; fragment: *She has done only a fraction of her homework.*

WORD STORY Fraction comes from a Latin word meaning "to break." A fraction is like a part broken off a larger number. **Fracture, fragile, fragment,** and **frail** all come from the same Latin word. You can find the idea of breaking in their definitions.

frac·tion·al (frak′shə nəl), *adj.* **1** forming a fraction: *440 yards is a fractional part of a mile.* **2** small by comparison; insignificant. —**frac′tion·al·ly,** *adv.*

frac·tious (frak′shəs), *adj.* **1** cross; fretful; peevish. **2** hard to manage; unruly. —**frac′tious·ly,** *adv.* —**frac′tious·ness,** *n.*

frac·ture (frak′chər), **1** *n.* result of breaking a bone or cartilage; break: *She suffered a leg fracture.* **2** *n.* result of breaking; break; crack: *The fracture in the foundation is widening.* **3** *v.* to break; crack: *I fractured my arm.* ❑ *v.* **frac·tured, frac·tur·ing.** [See Word Story at **fraction.**]

frag·ile (fraj′əl), *adj.* easily broken, damaged, or destroyed; delicate; frail: *Be careful; that thin glass is fragile.* [See Word Story at **fraction.**] —**frag′ile·ly,** *adv.* —**fra·gil·i·ty** (frə jil′ə tē), *n.*

frag·ment (frag′mənt), *n.* **1** piece of something broken; part broken off: *After I broke the vase, I tried to put the fragments back together.* **2** an incomplete or disconnected part: *Because of the noise he could hear only fragments of the conversation.* [See Word Story at **fraction.**]

frag·men·tar·y (frag′mən ter′ē), *adj.* made up of fragments; incomplete; disconnected: *fragmentary remains of a temple, a fragmentary account of an accident.* —**frag′men·tar′i·ly,** *adv.* —**frag′men·tar′i·ness,** *n.*

fra·grance (frā′grəns), *n.* a sweet smell; pleasing odor: *the fragrance of flowers, the fragrance of perfume.* ■ See Synonym Study at **smell.**

fra·grant (frā′grənt), *adj.* having or giving off a pleasing odor; sweet-smelling: *fragrant roses.* —**fra′grant·ly,** *adv.*

frail (frāl), *adj.* **1** slender and not very strong; weak: *a frail old man.* **2** easily broken or giving way: *Be careful; those little branches are a very frail support.* [See Word Story at **fraction.**] —**frail′ly,** *adv.* —**frail′ness,** *n.*

frail·ty (frāl′tē), *n.* **1** frail condition; weakness: *We were concerned about his frailty after such a long illness.* **2** fault caused by weakness: *Nobody is perfect; we all have our frailties.* ❑ *n., pl.* **frail·ties** for 2.

frame (frām), **1** *n.* support over which something is stretched or built: *the frame of a house.* **2** *n.* body: *a slender person with a small frame.* **3** *n.* border in which a thing is set: *a window frame, eyeglass frames.* **4** *v.* to put a border around: *frame a picture.* **5** *v.* to put together; plan; make: *It took time to frame an answer to his question. Thomas Jefferson helped to frame the Constitution.* **6** *v.* to make seem guilty by some false arrangement: *frame an innocent person.* **7** *n.* an individual picture on a strip of movie film. **8** *n.* one turn at bowling. ❑ *v.* **framed, fram·ing.** —**fram′er,** *n.*

frame house, house made of a wooden framework covered with boards, shingles, etc.

frame of mind, way you are thinking or feeling; mood.

frame-up (frām′up′), *n.* **1** a secret and dishonest arrangement made beforehand. **2** a scheme to have someone falsely accused.

frame·work (frām′wèrk′), *n.* **1** a structure that gives shape or support: *A bridge often has a steel framework.* **2** way in which a thing is put together; structure; system: *the framework of government.*

franc (frangk), *n.* unit of money in France, Belgium, Switzerland, Mali, Niger, Congo, and some other countries. ■ Another word that sounds like this is **frank.**

France (frans), *n.* country in W Europe. *Capital:* Paris.

fran·chise (fran′chīz), *n.* **1** privilege or right granted by a government: *The city granted the company a franchise to operate its buses.* **2** right to vote: *The United States gave women the franchise in 1920.* **3** privilege of selling the products of a manufacturer in a given area.

Fran·cis·can (fran sis′kən), **1** *adj.* of Saint Francis or the religious order founded by him in 1209. **2** *n.* friar belonging to the Franciscan order.

Fran·cis of As·si·si (fran′sis əv ə sē′zē), **Saint,** 1181?-1226, Italian founder of the Franciscan order of friars. [**Francis** comes from a French word meaning "French."]

fran·ci·um (fran′sē əm), *n.* a radioactive, metallic element produced artificially from actinium or thorium. *Symbol:* Fr

Fran·co (frang′kō), *n.* **Fran·cis·co** (fran sis′kō), 1892-1975, Spanish general, ruler of Spain from 1936 to 1975.

Fran·co·phone or **fran·co·phone** (frang′kə fōn′), *n.* a French-speaking person in a country where two or more languages are spoken.

fran·gi·pan·i (fran′jə pan′ē), *n.* any of several related tropical American plants with large, sweet-smelling, red flowers. ❑ *n., pl.* **fran·gi·pan·i** or **fran·gi·pan·is.**

a	hat	ė	term	ô	order	ch	child	
ā	age	i	it	oi	oil	ng	long	a in about
ä	far	ī	ice	ou	out	sh	she	e in taken
â	care	o	hot	u	cup	th	thin	ə i in pencil
e	let	ō	open	ù	put	₮H	then	o in lemon
ē	equal	ò	saw	ü	rule	zh	measure	u in circus

Fran·glais (fräng′glä *or* fräng glä′), *n.* French that includes many English words and phrases.

frank[1] (frangk), **1** *adj.* free in expressing your real thoughts, opinions, and feelings; not hiding what is in your mind; not afraid to say what you think: *She was frank in telling me that she thought the plan would not work.* **2** *v.* to send a letter or package without charge. **3** *n.* mark to show that a letter or package is to be sent without charge. **4** *n.* right to send letters or packages without charge. ■ Another word that sounds like this is **franc.** **–frank′ly,** *adv.* **–frank′ness,** *n.*

SYNONYM STUDY **Frank**[1] and **blunt** both mean saying just what you think. **Frank** suggests honesty and courage: *She made a frank apology for her mistake.* **Blunt** suggests a plain way of speaking without care for the feelings of other people: *The speaker's blunt answer hurt the questioner's feelings.*

frank[2] (frangk), *n.* frankfurter. ■ Another word that sounds like this is **franc.**

Frank (frangk), *n.* **1** member of the German tribes that conquered Gaul in the A.D. 500s. **2 Anne,** 1929-1945, Dutch writer. Her diary of her Jewish family's experiences hiding from the Nazis was published in 1947. She died in a concentration camp.

Frank·en·stein (frang′kən stīn), *n.* **1** scientist in a novel, written in 1818 by Mary Wollstonecraft Shelley, who creates a monster that he cannot control. **2** the monster itself.

Frank·fort (frangk′fərt), *n.* capital of Kentucky, in the N part.

Frank·furt (frangk′fərt, frängk′-fərt), *n.* Frankfurt am Main.

Frank·furt am Main (frängk′-fürt äm mīn′), city in central Germany.

frank·furt·er (frangk′fər tər), *n.* a reddish sausage made of beef and pork, or of beef alone; wiener; hot dog.

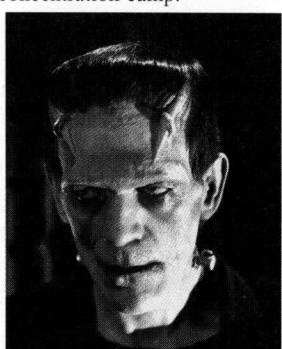

Frankenstein (def. 2)
as played by an actor

frank·in·cense (frang′kən sens), *n.* a fragrant resin from certain Asian or African trees. It gives off a sweet, spicy odor when burned.

Frank·ish (frang′kish), *adj.* of the Franks.

Frank·lin (frang′klən), *n.* **1 A·re·tha** (ə rē′thə), born 1942, American singer and pianist. Nicknamed "Lady Soul" or "The Queen of Soul," she has made many popular and gospel recordings. **2 Ben·ja·min** (ben′jə mən), 1706-1790, American political leader, writer, scientist, printer, and inventor. ■ **Benjamin Franklin** invented bifocal glasses and the lightning rod but never patented his inventions. He wrote and published *Poor Richard's Almanac* from 1733 to 1758. He was a leader in efforts to make the United States independent and to create the Constitution.

fran·tic (fran′tik), *adj.* very much excited; wild with rage, fear, pain, or grief: *The trapped animal made frantic efforts to escape.* ■ See Synonym Study at **wild.** **–fran′ti·cal·ly,** *adv.* **–fran′tic·ness,** *n.*

frappe (frap), *n.* **1** milk shake. **2** frappé.

frap·pé (fra pā′), *n.* fruit juice sweetened and partially frozen, or shaken with finely cracked ice.

fra·ter·nal (frə tėr′nl), *adj.* **1** of brothers or a brother; brotherly. **2** of or about a group organized for mutual fellowship: *a fraternal association.* **–fra·ter′nal·ly,** *adv.*

fraternal twins, twins of the same or opposite sex coming from two separately fertilized egg cells rather than from one egg cell as identical twins do.

fra·ter·ni·ty (frə tėr′nə tē), *n.* **1** club or society of men or boys, especially at a college. **2** group having the same interests, kind of work, etc.: *the musical fraternity.* **3** fraternal feeling; brotherhood. ❑ *n., pl.* **fra·ter·ni·ties** for 1,2.

frat·er·nize (frat′ər nīz), *v.* to associate in a brotherly way; be friendly. ❑ *v.* **frat·er·nized, frat·er·niz·ing.** **–frat′er·ni·za′tion,** *n.* **–frat′er·niz′er,** *n.*

Frau (frou), *n.* GERMAN. **1** Mrs. **2** wife. ❑ *n., pl.* **Frau·en** (frou′ən).

fraud (frôd), *n.* **1** dishonest dealing; trickery; cheating: *obtain a prize by fraud, win an election by fraud.* **2** a dishonest act, statement, etc.; something which is not what it seems to be; trick. **3** person who is not what he or she pretends to be.

fraud·u·lent (frô′jə lənt), *adj.* **1** cheating; dishonest: *a fraudulent dealer at cards.* **2** done by fraud; gotten by trickery: *fraudulent gains.* **–fraud′u·lent·ly,** *adv.*

fraught (frôt), *adj.* filled with something unpleasant: *The attempt to climb Mount Everest was fraught with danger.*

WORD STORY **Fraught** comes from an old German word meaning "freight." Once it was used about ships loaded with cargo. Then people began using the word about other filled things. Today it usually describes actions or situations, not solid objects. It usually suggests something negative, such as danger or tension, in the same way that *heavy* can suggest difficulty or trouble.

Fräu·lein (froi′līn), *n.* GERMAN. **1** Miss. **2** an unmarried woman. ❑ *n., pl.* **Fräu·lein.**

fray[1] (frā), *v.* **1** to separate into threads; make or become ragged or worn along the edge: *Long wear had frayed the collars of his old shirts.* **2** to wear at; irritate: *Constant stress frayed his nerves.*

fray[2] (frā), *n.* a noisy quarrel; fight.

Fra·zier (frā′zhər), *n.* **Joe** (jō), born 1944, American boxer. He was the world heavyweight champion from 1968 to 1973, and he was the first man to beat Muhammad Ali in a professional fight.

fraz·zle (fraz′əl), **1** *v.* to make someone physically and nervously exhausted. **2** *n.* a frazzled condition: *worn to a frazzle.* ❑ *v.* **fraz·zled, fraz·zling.**

freak (frēk), **1** *n.* something very odd or unusual: *Snow in summer would be called a freak of nature.* **2** *n.* a living thing that has developed abnormally. **3** *adj.* very odd or unusual: *a freak storm.* **4** *n.* INFORMAL. someone who is especially interested in or devoted to something: *a movie freak.* **5** *v.* SLANG. Usually, **freak out, a** to make or become very excited, disturbed, or angry. **b** to come under or put under the influence of a drug that distorts reality in a disturbing way.

freak·ish (frē′kish), *adj.* full of freaks; very odd or unusual. **–freak′ish·ly,** *adv.* **–freak′ish·ness,** *n.*

freak·y (frē′kē), *adj.* freakish. ❑ *adj.* **freak·i·er, freak·i·est.** **–freak′i·ly,** *adv.* **–freak′i·ness,** *n.*

freck·le (frek′əl), **1** *n.* a small, light brown spot on the skin, often caused by exposure to the sun. **2** *v.* to become marked or spotted with freckles. ❑ *v.* **freck·led, freck·ling.**

freck·led (frek′əld), *adj.* marked with freckles.

Fred·er·icks·burg (fred′riks bėrg′), *n.* city in NE Virginia. A Union attack on Confederate forces near here in December 1862 resulted in a severe defeat of Union forces.

Fred·er·ick the Great (fred′ər ik), 1712-1786, king of Prussia from 1740 to 1786. [**Frederick** comes from German words meaning "peace" and "lord."]

Fred·er·ic·ton (fred′rik tən), *n.* capital of New Brunswick, Canada.

free (frē), **1** *adj.* not under another's control; not a captive or slave: *a free people, a free nation, free speech.* **2** *adj.* not held back, fastened, or shut up; released; loose: *Once free from the cage, the bear cub ran to its mother's side.* **3** *adj.* not held back from acting or thinking as you please: *She was free to do as she liked.* **4** *adj.* not busy: *The doctor will call you back as soon as she is free.* **5** *v.* to make free; let loose; let go: *We freed the bird from its cage.* **6** *adj.* open to all: *a free port.* **7** *v.* to clear: *The judge freed her of all charges after hearing the testimony.* **8** *adj., adv.* without anything to pay: *These tickets are free. Children under 12 attend free.* **9** *adj.* having no tax or duty: *free trade.* **10** *adj.* not following rules, forms, or words exactly; not literal: *a free translation.* **11** *adj.* not combined with something else: *Oxygen exists free in air.* **12** *adv.* in a free manner; freely: *The animals ran free around the farm.* ❑ *adj.* **fre·er, fre·est;** *v.* **freed, free·ing.** **–free′ly,** *adv.* **–free′ness,** *n.*

free and easy, paying little attention to rules and customs.

free from *or* **free of,** without; having no; lacking: *free from fear, air free of dust.*

-free, *suffix.* without ___: *carefree = without care.*

free agent, a professional athlete who may choose what team to play for, and whose salary is set by negotiations before a contract is signed.

free·bie or **free·bee** (frē′bē), *n.* INFORMAL. something given or received free of charge, such as a ticket to a ball game. ❑ *n., pl.* **free·bies** or **free·bees.**

free·boot·er (frē′bü′tər), *n.* pirate. [See Word Story at **filibuster.**]

freed·man (frēd′mən), *n.* person freed from slavery. ❑ *n., pl.* **freed·men.**

free·dom (frē′dəm), *n.* **1** condition of being free: *The American colonies gained freedom from England.* **2** power to do, say, or think as you please; liberty: *freedom of speech.* **3** free use: *We gave our guest the freedom of the house.* **4** too great liberty; lack of restraint; frankness: *We did not like the freedom of his manner.* **5** ease of movement or action: *A fine athlete performs with freedom.* **6** condition of being released from unfavorable or undesirable conditions: *freedom from fear.*

free enterprise, the right of private business to select and operate undertakings for profit with little control or regulation by the government; private enterprise.

free fall, 1 the motion of an object in flight through space when it is not acted upon by any force except gravity. An object in free fall is not being propelled or braked or guided. **2** the part of a parachute jump before a parachute is opened.

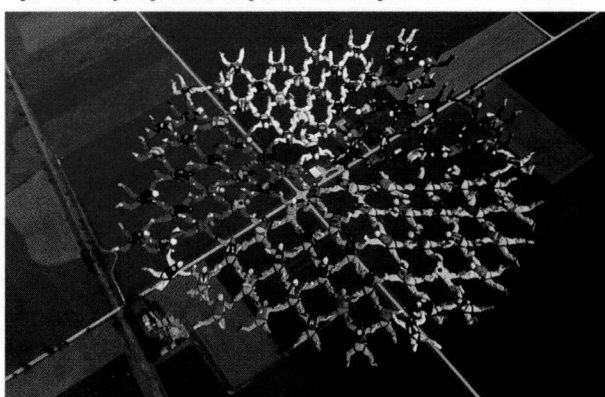

free fall (def. 2)

free-for-all (frē′fər ôl′), *n.* a noisy, disorderly fight or quarrel in which everyone takes part.

free·hand (frē′hand′), *adj.* done by hand without using tools, devices, measurements, etc.: *freehand drawing.*

free·lance (frē′lans′), **1** *v.* to work as an independent, selling your professional skills to whoever will buy them, rather than as an employee of a single firm. **2** *adj.* of such work: *free-lance designers.* ❑ *v.* **free-lanced, free-lanc·ing.** —**free′-lanc′er,** *n.*

WORD STORY **Free-lance** comes from a name given to knights of the Middle Ages who had not promised loyalty to a lord. These knights were free to fight with their lances for anyone who would pay them. Free-lance workers today can also take any jobs that they choose.

free·man (frē′mən), *n.* **1** person who is neither enslaved nor a serf. **2** citizen. ❑ *n., pl.* **free·men.**

Free·ma·son (frē′mā′sn), *n.* member of a worldwide secret society, whose purpose is mutual aid and fellowship; Mason.

free·stone (frē′stōn′), *adj.* having a fruit stone that is easily separated from the pulp: *freestone peaches.*

free·style (frē′stīl′), **1** *adj.* unrestricted as to style or method: *A freestyle swimmer may choose his or her own stroke.* **2** *n.* a freestyle race or figure-skating contest. **3** *n.* crawl (def. 7).

free·think·er (frē′thing′kər), *n.* one who forms religious opinions independently of authority or tradition.

free throw, (in basketball) an unhindered shot while standing at a line about 15 feet (4.5 meters) away from the basket, awarded to a player fouled by a member of the opposing team, and worth one point.

Free·town (frē′toun), *n.* capital of Sierra Leone, on the Atlantic.

free trade, trade between countries that is free from taxes, tariffs, quotas, etc.

free verse, poetry that does not have the usual conventions of meter and rhyme.

free·way (frē′wā′), *n.* a high-speed highway on which no tolls are charged.

free·wheel·ing (frē′wē′ling), *adj.* **1** (of a car, bicycle, etc.) coasting freely. **2** acting freely or without restraint: *freewheeling discussions.*

free·will (frē′wil′), *adj.* of your own accord; voluntary: *a freewill offering to the Red Cross.*

free will, will free from outside restraints; voluntary choice; freedom of decision.

freeze (frēz), **1** *v.* to harden by cold; turn into a solid by removal of heat. Water becomes ice when it freezes. **2** *v.* to make or become very cold: *The north wind froze the spectators.* **3** *v.* to kill or injure by frost; be killed or injured by frost: *This cold weather will freeze the flowers.* **4** *v.* to cover or become covered with ice; clog with ice: *The snow and hail will freeze the pond.* **5** *v.* to fix or become fixed to something by freezing: *His fingers froze to the tray of ice cubes.* **6** *n.* period during which there is freezing weather. **7** *v.* to make or become stiff and unfriendly: *The new boy froze up when I tried to be friendly.* **8** *v.* to chill or be chilled with fear, etc.: *She froze at the sight of the ghostly hand.* **9** *v.* to become motionless: *The baby rabbit froze with fear at the strange sound.* **10** *v.* to set at a definite amount, usually by governmental decree: *freeze prices, freeze rents.* **11** *n.* an act of freezing: *a freeze on prices, a hiring freeze.* ❑ *v.* **froze, fro·zen, freez·ing.** ■ Another word that sounds like this is **frieze.** —**freeze′·a·ble,** *adj.*

freeze-dry (frēz′drī′), *v.* to dry food by freezing and evaporating the liquid content in a vacuum. Freeze-dried food keeps well without being refrigerated. ❑ *v.* **freeze-dried, freeze-dry·ing.**

freeze-frame (frēz′frām′), *n.* (in a movie or television sequence) a single image repeated for some seconds, giving the illusion of a still picture.

freeze-dry—freeze-dried food for astronauts

freez·er (frē′zər), *n.* **1** a refrigerator or part of a refrigerator in which the temperature is well below the freezing point. Foods are frozen and kept from spoiling in freezers. **2** machine that freezes ice cream.

freezer burn, loss of moisture in poorly packaged frozen food, leading to loss of color and flavor.

freezing point, temperature at which a liquid freezes. The freezing point of water at sea level is 32 degrees Fahrenheit or 0 degrees Celsius.

F region, region of the atmosphere, within the ionosphere, that reflects high-frequency radio waves; F layer.

freight (frāt), **1** *n.* goods that a train, truck, ship, or aircraft carries. **2** *n.* system of carrying goods on a train, truck, ship, or aircraft: *She sent the box by freight.* **3** *n.* price paid for carrying goods. **4** *n.* train for carrying goods. **5** *v.* to load with goods. **6** *v.* to carry as goods. **7** *v.* to send as goods.

freight car, a railroad car for carrying goods.

freight·er (frā′tər), *n.* ship that carries goods.

freight train, freight (def. 4).

Fré·mont (frē′mont), *n.* **John Charles,** 1813-1890, American explorer and political leader. He was the first Republican candidate for the U.S. presidency.

a	hat	ė	term	ô	order	ch	child	
ā	age	i	it	oi	oil	ng	long	a in about
ä	far	ī	ice	ou	out	sh	she	e in taken
â	care	o	hot	u	cup	th	thin	ə i in pencil
e	let	ō	open	u̇	put	ᴛʜ	then	o in lemon
ē	equal	ȯ	saw	ü	rule	zh	measure	u in circus

French (french), **1** *adj.* of France, its people, or their language. **2** *n.pl.* the people of France. **3** *n.* their language.

French has given many words to the English language. The words below are some of them.

ambiance	coupon	glacier	picnic
ambulance	croquet	goblet	quiche
baboon	curfew	grudge	sabotage
bribe	dandelion	lawn	supper
budge	deluxe	mascot	turquoise
butcher	detour	pansy	vinegar
café	garage	parachute	zigzag

French and Indian War, war between Great Britain and France, fought in North America from 1754 to 1763. The French were greatly aided by Indian allies.

French Canada, the part of Canada where mainly French Canadians live, especially the province of Quebec.

French Canadian, 1 Canadian whose ancestors came from France. **2** of French Canadians.

French Community, an association formed in 1958 including France, many former French colonies, and French territories overseas.

French doors, pair of doors hinged at both sides and opening in the middle. They have panes of glass like a window from top to bottom.

French fries, potatoes cut into thin strips and fried in deep fat until crisp on the outside.

French-fry (french′frī′), *v.* to fry in deep fat. ❏ *v.* **French-fried, French-fry·ing.**

French Guiana, French territory in N South America. *Capital:* Cayenne.

French horn, a brass wind instrument that has a mellow tone.

French·man (french′mən), *n.* man born or living in France. ❏ *n., pl.* **French·men.**

French Revolution, revolution in France from 1789 to 1799 which ousted the monarchy and set up a republic.

French toast, slices of bread dipped in a mixture of egg and milk and then fried in a small amount of fat.

French·wom·an (french′wùm′ən), *n.* woman born or living in France. ❏ *n., pl.* **French·wom·en.**

fre·net·ic (frə net′ik), *adj.* frenzied. —**fre·net′i·cal·ly,** *adv.*

fren·zied (fren′zēd), *adj.* very much excited; frantic; wild. ■ See Synonym Study at **wild.** —**fren′zied·ly,** *adv.*

fren·zy (fren′zē), *n.* **1** a state of near madness; frantic condition: *They were in a frenzy when they heard that their child was missing.* **2** a condition of very great excitement: *The crowd was in a frenzy after the winning goal was scored.* ❏ *n., pl.* **fren·zies.**

Fre·on (frē′on), *n.* trademark for a group of odorless, colorless gases used especially as refrigerants. These gases are fluorocarbons.

freq., 1 frequent. **2** frequently.

fre·quen·cy (frē′kwən sē), *n.* **1** condition of being frequent: *The baby walks with increasing frequency.* **2** rate of occurrence: *The flashes of light came with a frequency of three per minute.* **3** number of complete cycles per second, called hertz, of an alternating current or electromagnetic wave. Different radio and television stations broadcast at different frequencies so that their signals can be received distinctly. **4** number of complete cycles per second of a sound wave. ❏ *n., pl.* **fre·quen·cies** for 3.

frequency modulation, the deliberate changing of the frequency of radio waves in order to carry signals. Frequency modulation is used for stereo radio broadcasts and to broadcast sound for television.

fre·quent (frē′kwənt *for adj.;* fri kwent′ *for verb*), **1** *adj.* happening often, near together, or every little while: *Storms are frequent in March.* **2** *v.* to go to often; be often in or on: *Fishing boats frequent these waters.* —**fre·quent′er,** *n.*

frequent flyer, person who travels many miles on the airplanes of a particular company or companies, and who is given free tickets or other benefits as a reward.

fre·quent·ly (frē′kwənt lē), *adv.* often; repeatedly; every little while: *The twins are frequently mistaken for each other.*

fresco (def. 2)

fres·co (fres′kō), *n.* **1** act or art of painting with water colors on damp, fresh plaster. **2** picture or design painted in this way: *Beautiful frescoes covered the walls and ceiling of the cathedral.* ❏ *n., pl.* **fres·coes** or **fres·cos.**

Fresco comes from an Italian word meaning "cool" or "fresh." In old times, painters often made pictures on fresh, damp plaster walls. As the plaster dried, the painting became part of it and so would last much longer than a painting done on top of dry plaster.

fresh[1] (fresh), *adj.* **1** newly made, grown, or gathered: *fresh footprints, fresh vegetables.* **2** not known, seen, or used before; new; recent: *Is there any fresh news from home?* **3** additional; further; another: *After her failure she made a fresh start.* **4** not salty: *Rivers are usually fresh water.* **5** not spoiled; not stale: *Is this milk fresh?* **6** clean; not soiled by use: *I put fresh sheets on my bed.* **7** not artificially preserved: *Fresh foods usually have more flavor than canned ones.* **8** not tired out; vigorous; lively: *fresh horses.* **9** not faded or worn; bright: *The long trip abroad was fresh in his memory.* **10** looking healthy or young: *Mother is as fresh in appearance as she was ten years ago.* **11** pure; cool; refreshing: *fresh air.* —**fresh′ly,** *adv.* —**fresh′ness,** *n.*

fresh[2] (fresh), *adj.* too bold; impudent: *a fresh remark.*

fresh·en (fresh′ən), *v.* to make or become fresh: *The rest freshened my spirits.* —**fresh′en·er,** *n.*

fresh·en·er (fresh′ən ər), *n.* device that gives off or sprays a scented aroma, used to overcome bad smells in a space: *an air freshener, a room freshener.*

fresh·et (fresh′it), *n.* **1** flood caused by heavy rains or melted snow. **2** rush of fresh water flowing into the sea.

fresh·man (fresh′mən), *n.* student in the first year of high school or college. ❏ *n., pl.* **fresh·men.**

fresh·wa·ter (fresh′wô′tər), *adj.* of or living in water that is not salty: *a freshwater fish.*

fret[1] (fret), *v.* **1** to be unhappy or worried about something: *The baby frets in hot weather. Don't fret over your mistakes.* **2** to make unhappy or worried: *His failures fretted him.* ❏ *v.* **fret·ted, fret·ting.** —**fret′ter,** *n.*

Fret[1] comes from an old English word that means "to eat" or "to devour." Even today, we may ask a person who frets, "What's eating you?" And if something really were eating you, you'd probably be unhappy about it.

fret[2] (fret), *n.* any of a series of ridges of wood, ivory, or metal on a guitar, banjo, etc., to show where to put the fingers in order to produce certain tones.

fret·ful (fret′fəl), *adj.* unhappy or worried: *Babies are fretful when they are cutting teeth.* —**fret′ful·ly,** *adv.* —**fret′ful·ness,** *n.*

fret·work (fret′werk′), *n.* ornamental openwork or carving.

Freud (froid), *n.* **Sig·mund** (sig′mənd), 1856-1939, Austrian physician who first developed a theory and technique of psychoanalysis. —**Freud·i·an** (froi′dē ən), *n.*

Freudian slip, a mistake, especially in speech, that suggests someone's true feelings or opinions.

Fri., Friday.

fri·a·ble (frī′ə bəl), *adj.* easily crumbled. **–fri′a·ble·ness,** *n.*

fri·ar (frī′ər), *n.* man who belongs to one of certain religious brotherhoods of the Roman Catholic Church. ■ Other words that sound like this are **frier** and **fryer.**

fric·as·see (frik′ə sē′), **1** *n.* meat cut up, stewed, and served in a sauce made with its own gravy. **2** *v.* to prepare meat in this way. ❑ *n., pl.* **fric·as·sees;** *v.* **fric·as·seed, fric·as·see·ing.**

fric·tion (frik′shən), *n.* **1** resistance to motion of surfaces that touch: *A sled moves more easily on smooth ice than on rough ground because there is less friction.* **2** act of rubbing one thing against another: *Matches are lighted by friction.* **3** conflict of differing ideas, opinions, etc.; disagreement; clash: *Constant friction among the players led to our loss.* **–fric′tion·less,** *adj.*

fric·tion·al (frik′shə nəl), *adj.* of or caused by friction: *frictional resistance.* **–fric′tion·al·ly,** *adv.*

friction tape, a cotton adhesive tape treated to repel moisture. It is used to protect electric wires.

Fri·day (frī′dā or frī′dē), *n.* the sixth day of the week, following Thursday.

WORD STORY **Friday** comes from an old English word meaning "Frigg's day." Frigg was the old English goddess of love, and her day was considered the luckiest day of the week.

fridge (frij), *n.* INFORMAL. refrigerator.

fried (frīd), **1** *adj.* cooked in hot fat. **2** *v.* past tense and past participle of **fry**[1]: *I fried the ham. The potatoes had been fried.*

Frie·dan (frē dan′), *n.* **Bet·ty** (bet′ē), born 1921, American feminist. ■ **Betty Friedan's** first book, *The Feminine Mystique,* discusses the pressure that society puts on women to be housewives. She helped found the National Organization for Women in 1966.

friend (frend), *n.* **1** person who knows and likes another person. **2** person who favors and supports: *She was a generous friend to the poor.* **3** person who belongs to the same side or group: *Are you friend or foe?* **4 Friend,** member of the Society of Friends; Quaker. **–friend′less,** *adj.*

be friends with, be a friend of.

make friends with, to become a friend of.

man's best friend, a dog.

friend·ly (frend′lē), *adj.* **1** of a friend; having the attitude of a friend; kind: *a friendly teacher.* **2** like a friend; like a friend's: *a friendly greeting.* **3** on good terms; not hostile: *friendly relations between countries.* **4** favoring and supporting; favorable. ❑ *adj.* **friend·li·er, friend·li·est. –friend′li·ness,** *n.*

friend·ship (frend′ship), *n.* **1** condition of being friends. **2** friendliness.

fri·er (frī′ər), *n.* fryer. ■ Another word that sounds like this is **friar.**

fries (frīz), **1** *n.pl.* French fries. **2** *n.* plural of **fry**[1]. **3** *v.* a present tense of **fry**[1]: *Dad fries a few eggs for breakfast every morning.*

frieze (frēz), *n.* a horizontal band of decoration around a room, building, or mantel. ■ Another word that sounds like this is **freeze.**

frig·ate (frig′it), *n.* **1** a fast, three-masted, square-rigged sailing warship of medium size. Frigates were used from 1750 to 1850. **2** a small, modern warship equipped to destroy submarines.

fright (frīt), *n.* **1** sudden and extreme fear; sudden terror or alarm: *The howl filled me with fright.* **2** person or thing that is ugly, shocking, or ridiculous: *You look like a fright in that clown wig!*

fright·en (frīt′n), *v.* **1** to fill with fright; make or become afraid; scare or terrify: *Thunder frightened the puppy.* ■ See Synonym Study at **scare. 2** to drive or force by terrifying: *The sudden noise frightened the deer away.* **–fright′en·ing·ly,** *adv.*

fright·ful (frīt′fəl), *adj.* **1** causing fear or terror: *Being lost in the forest was a frightful experience.* **2** terrible to think about; shocking: *The frightful destruction caused by the fire stretched for blocks.* **3** disagreeable; unpleasant: *There was a frightful smell in the air from the burning tar.* **4** very great: *I'm in a frightful hurry.* **–fright′ful·ly,** *adv.* **–fright′ful·ness,** *n.*

frig·id (frij′id), *adj.* **1** very cold: *Arctic regions have a frigid climate.* **2** cold in feeling or manner; stiff; chilling: *He received a frigid greeting from the man he had insulted.* **–fri·gid′i·ty,** *n.* **–frig′id·ly,** *adv.* **–frig′id·ness,** *n.*

Frigid Zone, either of the two polar regions, north of the arctic circle and south of the antarctic circle.

fri·joles (frē hō′lēz), *n.pl.* beans often used for food in Mexico and the southwestern United States.

frill (fril), *n.* **1** a ruffle. **2** thing added merely for show; useless ornament.

frill·y (fril′ē), *adj.* full of frills; like frills. ❑ *adj.* **frill·i·er, frill·i·est.**

fringe (frinj), **1** *n.* border or trimming made of threads, cords, etc., either loose or tied together in small bunches. **2** *n.* anything like this; border: *A fringe of hair hung over her forehead.* **3** *v.* to make a fringe for. **4** *v.* to be a fringe for: *Bushes fringed the road.* ❑ *v.* **fringed, fring·ing.**

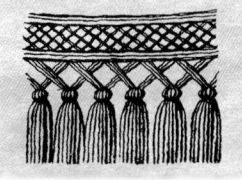
fringe (def. 1)

fringe benefit, any benefit given to employees by their employer in addition to wages and compensations required by law. Medical insurance, pension plans, paid holidays and vacations, and recreational facilities are fringe benefits.

Fris·bee (friz′bē), *n.* trademark for a saucer-shaped disk of colored plastic tossed back and forth in play. ❑ *n., pl.* **Fris·bees.**

frisk (frisk), *v.* **1** to run and jump about playfully; dance and skip joyously: *Our lively puppy frisks all over the house.* **2** to search for concealed weapons or stolen goods by running a hand quickly over someone's clothes. **–frisk′er,** *n.*

frisk·y (fris′kē), *adj.* playful; lively. ❑ *adj.* **frisk·i·er, frisk·i·est. –frisk′i·ly,** *adv.* **–frisk′i·ness,** *n.*

frit·il·lar·y (frit′l er′ē), *n.* **1** any of numerous plants with drooping, bell-shaped flowers spotted with dark green or purple. Fritillaries grow from bulbs. **2** any of several butterflies with spots on both the upper sides and undersides of their wings. ❑ *n., pl.* **frit·il·lar·ies.**

WORD STORY **Fritillary** comes from a Latin word meaning "dice box." The plant's spots resemble the spots on dice, and the butterflies are named after the plant.

frit·ter[1] (frit′ər), *v.* to waste little by little: *fritter away a day watching TV.*

frit·ter[2] (frit′ər), *n.* sliced fruit, vegetables, meat, or fish covered with batter and fried.

fritz (frits), *n.* INFORMAL. **on the fritz,** not working right; out of order: *go on the fritz. My TV is on the fritz.*

fri·vol·i·ty (fri vol′ə tē), *n.* **1** frivolous behavior. **2** a silly thing; frivolous act. ❑ *n., pl.* **fri·vol·i·ties** for 2.

friv·o·lous (friv′ə ləs), *adj.* **1** lacking in seriousness or sense; silly: *Frivolous behavior is out of place in a courtroom.* **2** of little worth or importance; trivial: *Don't waste time on frivolous matters.* **–friv′o·lous·ly,** *adv.* **–friv′o·lous·ness,** *n.*

frizz or **friz** (friz), **1** *v.* to form into small, crisp curls; curl. **2** *n.* hair curled in small, crisp curls or a very close crimp. ❑ *v.* **frizzed, friz·zing;** *n., pl.* **friz·zes.**

friz·zle[1] (friz′əl), **1** *v.* to curl hair in small, crisp curls. **2** *n.* a small, crisp curl. ❑ *v.* **friz·zled, friz·zling.**

friz·zle[2] (friz′əl), **1** *v.* to make a hissing, sputtering noise when cooking; sizzle: *The ham frizzled in the frying pan.* **2** *n.* a hissing, sputtering noise; sizzle. ❑ *v.* **friz·zled, friz·zling.**

friz·zly (friz′lē), *adj.* frizzy. ❑ *adj.* **friz·zli·er, friz·zli·est.**

friz·zy (friz′ē), *adj.* full of small, crisp curls; curly. ❑ *adj.* **friz·zi·er, friz·zi·est.**

fro (frō), *adv.* **to and fro,** first one way and then back again; back and forth: *A rocking chair goes to and fro.*

frock (frok), *n.* **1** OLD USE. a woman's or girl's dress; gown. **2** robe worn by a member of the clergy.

a	hat	ė	term	ȯ	order	ch	child		
ā	age	i	it	oi	oil	ng	long		a in about
ä	far	ī	ice	ou	out	sh	she		e in taken
â	care	o	hot	u	cup	th	thin	ə	i in pencil
e	let	ō	open	u̇	put	ᴛʜ	then		o in lemon
ē	equal	ȯ	saw	ü	rule	zh	measure		u in circus

frog (frog), *n.* any of many small, leaping animals with webbed feet living in or near water. Frogs hatch from eggs as tadpoles and live in the water until they grow legs. **—frog′like′,** *adj.*

frog in your throat, slight hoarseness caused by soreness or swelling in the throat.

frog·man (frog′man′), *n.* scuba diver trained for underwater military or scientific operations. ❑ *n., pl.* **frog·men.**

frol·ic (frol′ik), **1** *n.* a joyous game or party; play; fun. **2** *v.* to play about joyously; have fun together: *The children frolicked with the puppy.* ❑ *v.* **frol·icked, frol·ick·ing. —frol′ick·er,** *n.*

frol·ic·some (frol′ik səm), *adj.* full of fun; playful; merry.

from (frum), *prep.* **1** out of: *I took a quarter from my pocket.* **2** out of the possession of: *Take the book from her.* **3** starting at; beginning with: *a train from New York. Three weeks from today is a holiday.* **4** having its source or origin in: *oil from Alaska, a word from Spanish.* **5** because of; by reason of: *act from a sense of duty. He was suffering from a cold.* **6** given, sent, caused, etc., by: *a letter from Anne. The cut in his finger was from a knife.* **7** as being unlike; as distinguished from: *Anyone can tell apples from oranges.* **8** off: *He took a book from the table.*

frond (frond), *n.* the leaf of a fern or of a palm tree.

front (frunt), **1** *n.* the first part: *The title page is in the front of a book.* **2** *n.* part that faces forward: *the front of a dress.* **3** *n.* thing fastened or worn on the front. **4** *n.* place where fighting is going on; battle front. **5** *n.* land facing a street, river, etc.: *We have a house on the lake front.* **6** *adj.* of, on, in, or at the front: *a front door.* **7** *v.* to have the front toward; face: *Her house fronts the park.* **8** *v.* to meet face to face; meet as an enemy; defy; oppose. **9** *n.* manner of looking or behaving: *a genial front.* **10** *n.* an outward appearance of wealth, importance, etc.: *The newcomer put up an impressive front.* **11** *n.* person or thing that serves as a cover for unlawful activities. **12** *n.* the forward part of a great mass of air: *A cold front is moving toward this area from Canada.*

up front, 1 INFORMAL. honest; open; sincere: *He was up front about not enjoying the movie we recommended.* **2** in advance: *He demanded the money up front.*

front·age (frun′tij), *n.* **1** front of a building or of a lot. **2** length of this front. **3** land facing a street, river, etc. **4** land between a building and a street, river, etc.

fron·tal (frun′tl), *adj.* **1** of, on, in, or at the front: *The soldiers charged ahead and made a frontal attack.* **2** of the forehead: *frontal bones.* **—fron′tal·ly,** *adv.*

fron·tier (frun tir′), *n.* **1** the farthest part of a settled country, where the wilds begin. **2** part of a country next to another country; border. **3** the farthest limits: *explore the frontiers of science.*

fron·tiers·man (frun tirz′mən), *n.* man who lives on the frontier. ❑ *n., pl.* **fron·tiers·men.**

fron·tiers·wo·man (frun tirz′wů mən), *n.* woman who lives on a frontier. ❑ *n., pl.* **fron·tiers·wo·men.**

front-page (frunt′pāj′), *adj.* suitable for the front page of a newspaper; important: *front-page news.*

front-run·ner (frunt′run′ər), *n.* the leader at any particular time in a contest.

front-wheel (frunt′hwēl′), *adj.* acting only on the front wheels of a vehicle: *front-wheel brakes, front-wheel drive.*

frost (frôst), **1** *n.* a freezing condition; temperature below the point at which water freezes: *Frost came early last winter.* **2** *n.* moisture frozen on or in a surface; feathery crystals of ice formed when water vapor in the air condenses at a temperature below freezing: *On cold fall mornings, there is frost on the grass.* **3** *v.* to cover with frost or something that suggests frost. **4** *v.* to cover with frosting: *The cook frosted the cake.* **5** *v.* to kill or injure by frost or freezing: *A sudden drop in temperature frosted the tomato plants.* **—frost′less,** *adj.* **—frost′like′,** *adj.*

Frost (frôst), *n.* **Robert,** 1874-1963, American poet. He read his poem "The Gift Outright" at John F. Kennedy's inauguration.

frost-belt (frôst′belt′), *n.* snowbelt.

frost-bite (frôst′bīt′), **1** *n.* injury to a part of the body caused by freezing. **2** *v.* to injure a part of the body by frost; harm by severe cold: *My ears were frostbitten.* ❑ *v.* **frost·bit** (frôst′bit′), **frost·bit·ten** (frôst′bit′n), **frost·bit·ing.**

frost·ed (frô′stid), *adj.* **1** covered with frost: *a frosted window.* **2** having a surface like frost: *Frosted glass has a rough surface.* **3** covered with frosting; iced: *a frosted cake.* **4** frozen.

frost·ing (frô′sting), *n.* **1** mixture of sugar, butter or margarine, egg whites, etc., used to cover cakes and other baked goods; icing. **2** a dull, rough finish on a glass or metal.

frost·y (frô′stē), *adj.* **1** cold enough for frost; freezing: *a frosty morning.* **2** covered with frost: *The glass is frosty.* **3** cold and unfriendly; with no warmth of feeling: *After our quarrel, she spoke to us in a frosty manner.* ❑ *adj.* **frost·i·er, frost·i·est. —frost′i·ly,** *adv.* **—frost′i·ness,** *n.*

froth (frôth), **1** *n.* mass of very small bubbles formed in liquid; foam: *There was froth at the edge of the wave.* **2** *v.* to give out froth; foam. **3** *n.* something light and trifling; unimportant talk.

froth·y (frô′thē), *adj.* **1** of, like, or having froth; foamy: *frothy soapsuds.* **2** light; trifling; unimportant: *frothy conversation.* ❑ *adj.* **froth·i·er, froth·i·est. —froth′i·ly,** *adv.* **—froth′i·ness,** *n.*

frown (froun), **1** *n.* act of wrinkling the forehead to show disapproval, anger, etc. **2** *v.* to wrinkle the forehead to show disapproval, anger, etc.; look displeased or angry: *The teacher frowned when I came in late.* **3** *v.* to look with disapproval: *The principal frowned on our plan for a class picnic just before finals.* **—frown′ing·ly,** *adv.*

frow·zy (frou′zē), *adj.* **1** dirty and untidy; slovenly. **2** smelling bad; musty. ❑ *adj.* **frow·zi·er, frow·zi·est. —frow′zi·ness,** *n.*

froze (frōz), *v.* past tense of **freeze:** *The water in the pond froze last week.*

fro·zen (frō′zn), **1** *adj.* hardened by cold; turned into ice: *frozen sherbet.* **2** *adj.* very cold: *My hands are frozen; I need some gloves.* **3** *adj.* kept from spoiling by freezing: *frozen foods.* **4** *adj.* killed or injured by frost: *frozen flowers.* **5** *adj.* covered or clogged with ice: *frozen water pipes.* **6** *adj.* cold and without feeling: *a frozen heart, a frozen stare.* **7** *adj.* too frightened or stiff to move: *frozen to the spot in horror.* **8** *v.* past participle of **freeze:** *The water has frozen to ice.*

fruc·tose (fruk′tōs), *n.* sugar present in many fruits and in honey; fruit sugar. It is sweeter than glucose or sucrose.

fru·gal (frü′gəl), *adj.* **1** without waste; saving; using things well: *My parents are frugal—they shop carefully and use only what they need.* **2** costing little; barely enough: *He ate a frugal supper of bread and milk.* **—fru·gal·i·ty** (frü gal′ə tē), *n.* **—fru′gal·ly,** *adv.*

fruit (def. 1)

fruit (früt), **1** *n.* a juicy or fleshy part of a tree, bush, or vine, containing the seed and a covering, usually sweet and good to eat. Apples, pears, oranges, bananas, peaches, and plums are fruits. **2** *n.* part of a seed plant that contains the seeds. Pea pods, acorns, cucumbers, and grains of wheat are fruits. **3** *n.* group or selection of fruits: *Fruit is good for you.* **4** *n.* result of anything; product: *This invention was the fruit of much effort.* **5** *v.* to produce fruit. **—fruit′like′,** *adj.*

fruit·cake (früt′kāk′), *n.* a rich cake usually containing many fruits and sometimes nuts and spices.

fruit fly, any of several small flies having larvae that feed on decaying fruits and vegetables.

fruit·ful (früt′fəl), *adj.* **1** producing much fruit. **2** producing much of anything: *a fruitful mind.* **3** having good results; bringing benefit or profit: *a fruitful idea.* —**fruit′ful·ly,** *adv.* —**fruit′ful·ness,** *n.*

fru·i·tion (frü ish′ən), *n.* **1** condition of having results; fulfillment; attainment: *After years of hard work their plans came to fruition.* **2** condition of producing fruit.

fruit·less (früt′lis), *adj.* **1** having no results; useless; unsuccessful: *Our search was fruitless; we could not find the lost book.* **2** producing no fruit; barren: *fruitless soil.* —**fruit′less·ly,** *adv.* —**fruit′less·ness,** *n.*

fruit sugar, fructose.

fruit·y (frü′tē), *adj.* tasting or smelling like fruit: *the fruity odor of jam.* ◻ *adj.* **fruit·i·er, fruit·i·est.** —**fruit′i·ness,** *n.*

frus·trate (frus′trāt), *v.* **1** to make useless or worthless; block; defeat: *Heavy rain frustrated our plans for a picnic.* **2** to thwart; oppose: *The struggling artist was often frustrated in her ambition to paint.* **3** to cause to feel angry and helpless with lack of success: *Frustrated by refusals to publish his work, he stopped writing and became an editor.* ◻ *v.* **frus·trat·ed, frus·trat·ing.** —**frus′trat·er,** *n.* —**frus′trat·ing·ly,** *adv.*

frus·tra·tion (fru strā′shən), *n.* a feeling of anger and helplessness, caused by bad luck, failure, or defeat.

fry[1] (frī), **1** *v.* to cook in hot fat in a deep or shallow pan, often over a flame: *He is frying potatoes.* **2** *n.* dish of something cooked in this way. **3** *n.* an outdoor social gathering at which food is fried and eaten: *a fish fry.* ◻ *v.* **fried, fry·ing;** *n., pl.* **fries.**

fry[2] (frī), *n.* young fish. ◻ *n., pl.* **fry.**

fry·er (frī′ər), *n.* **1** chicken intended for frying. **2** pan used for frying. Also, **frier.** ■ Another word that sounds like this is **friar.**

frying pan, a shallow pan with a handle, used for frying; skillet. **out of the frying pan into the fire,** from a bad or difficult situation to one that is worse.

ft., **1** foot or feet. **2** fort.

FTC, Federal Trade Commission (a U.S. government agency established to prevent unfair business practices).

fuch·sia (fyü′shə), **1** *n.* any of numerous bushes with handsome pink, red, or purple flowers that droop from the stems. **2** *n.* a purplish red. **3** *adj.* purplish red. ◻ *n., pl.* **fuch·sias** for 1.

fud·dle (fud′l), *v.* **1** to make stupid with liquor; intoxicate. **2** to confuse; muddle. ◻ *v.* **fud·dled, fud·dling.**

fudge[1] (fuj), **1** *n.* a soft candy made of sugar, milk, chocolate, butter, etc. **2** *interj., n.* nonsense.

fudge[2] (fuj), *v.* **1** to put together in a clumsy, makeshift, or dishonest way; fake: *They fudged the repair and tried to hide it with paint.* **2** to avoid doing something; get out of a duty, responsibility, etc.: *to fudge on a promise.* ◻ *v.* **fudged, fudg·ing.**

Fueh·rer (fyür′ər), *n.* Führer.

fu·el (fyü′əl), **1** *n.* anything that can be burned to produce useful heat or power. Coal, wood, and oil are fuels. **2** *n.* atomic matter that can produce heat in a nuclear reactor. **3** *n.* anything that keeps up or increases a feeling: *Her success was fuel to his resentment.* **4** *v.* to supply with fuel. **5** *v.* to get fuel: *The ship will have to fuel at the nearest port.* ◻ *v.* **fu·eled, fu·el·ing,** or **fu·elled, fu·el·ling.** [See Word Story at **focus.**]

fuel cell, device that produces electricity directly from a chemical reaction between oxygen and a gas such as hydrogen or carbon monoxide.

fuel injection, system of pumping vaporized fuel into the cylinders of an internal-combustion engine. Fuel injection has replaced the carburetor in many motor vehicles.

fuel oil, oil used for fuel, refined from petroleum.

Fu·en·tes (fwen′tās), *n.* **Car·los** (kär′lōs), born 1928, Mexican writer. He has written many novels and was Mexico's ambassador to France from 1975 to 1977.

fu·gi·tive (fyü′jə tiv), **1** *n.* person who is running away or who has run away: *The murderer became a fugitive from justice.* **2** *adj.* running away; having run away: *a fugitive serf.* **3** *adj.* lasting only a very short time; passing swiftly: *fugitive thoughts, fugitive moments.* [See Word Story at **fugue.**] —**fu′gi·tive·ly,** *adv.* .

fugue (fyüg), *n.* a musical composition based on one or more short themes in which different voices or instruments repeat the same melody with slight variations.

> **WORD STORY** **Fugue** comes from a Latin word meaning "to flee." **Fugitive** also comes from this word. The repeated tune in a fugue seems to flee from one musical instrument to another as the musicians take turns with it.

Füh·rer (fyür′ər), *n.* a German word meaning leader. It was the title given to Adolf Hitler. Also, **Fuehrer.**

Fu·ji (fü′jē), *n.* **Mount,** Fujiyama.

Fu·ji·ya·ma (fü′jē yä′mə), *n.* extinct volcano in S Japan, 12,395 feet (3780 meters) high. It is the highest mountain in Japan.

Fujiyama

-ful, *suffix.* **1** full of ___: *cheerful = full of cheer.* **2** showing ___: *careful = showing care.* **3** having a tendency to ___: *harmful = having a tendency to harm.* **4** enough to fill a ___: *cupful = enough to fill a cup.*

ful·crum (ful′krəm), *n.* point on which a lever turns and is supported in moving or lifting something. ◻ *n., pl.* **ful·crums, ful·cra** (ful′krə).

ful·fill or **ful·fil** (ful fil′), *v.* **1** to keep or carry out a promise or an agreement: *The mechanic did not fulfill his promise to have our car fixed by Saturday.* **2** to perform or do a duty, command, etc.: *She fulfilled all the teacher's requests.* **3** to satisfy a requirement, condition, etc.: *This diet will fulfill all your needs in food.* **4** to bring to an end; finish or complete a period of time, work, etc.: *fulfill a contract.* ◻ *v.* **ful·filled, ful·fill·ing.**

ful·fill·ment or **ful·fil·ment** (ful fil′mənt), *n.* completion; performance; accomplishment.

full (ful), **1** *adj.* able to hold no more; with no empty space; filled: *a full cup. This suitcase is full.* **2** *adj.* complete; entire: *I ran a full mile.* **3** *adv.* completely: *Fill the pail full.* **4** *n.* completeness; greatest degree: *Her new job satisfies her ambition to the full.* **5** *adj.* more than enough to satisfy; well supplied: *He ate three full meals a day.* **6** *adj.* well filled out; plump; round: *a full face.* **7** *adj.* having wide folds or much cloth: *a full skirt.* **8** *adj.* strong, rich, and distinct: *An orator should have a full voice.* **9** *adv.* straight; directly: *The ball hit me full in the face.* —**full′ness,** *n.* **full of,** filled with: *The child's room is full of toys.* **full well,** very well: *She knew full well that the report was due last Friday.* **in full, 1** to or for the complete amount: *make payment in full.* **2** not abbreviated or shortened: *a document reproduced in full.*

full·back (ful′bak′), *n.* **1** a football player who is a member of the offensive backfield and lines up behind the offensive line. **2** a soccer player who plays near his own goal on defense.

a	hat	ė	term	ô	order	ch	child		
ā	age	i	it	oi	oil	ng	long		a in about
ä	far	ī	ice	ou	out	sh	she		e in taken
â	care	o	hot	u	cup	th	thin	ə	i in pencil
e	let	ō	open	ù	put	℟	then		o in lemon
ē	equal	ô	saw	ü	rule	zh	measure		u in circus

full-blood·ed (fůl′blud′id), *adj.* **1** of pure or unmixed race, breed, or strain; thoroughbred. ■ This meaning of **full-blooded** is sometimes considered offensive if used to describe a person. **2** vigorous; hearty: *full-blooded youth.*

full-blown (fůl′blōn′), *adj.* **1** in full bloom: *a full-blown rose.* **2** completely developed: *a full-blown plan.*

Ful·ler (fůl′ər), *n.* **1** Buck·min·ster (buk′min′ster), 1895-1983, American inventor, architect, and engineer. He invented the geodesic dome. **2** Mar·ga·ret (mar′gə rit), 1810-1850, American journalist and political reformer. Her book *Woman in the Nineteenth Century* discusses the status of women in society.

full-fledged (fůl′flejd′), *adj.* **1** fully developed. **2** of full rank or standing: *He is now a full-fledged doctor.*

full-grown (fůl′grōn′), *adj.* fully grown; mature.

full-length (fůl′lengkth′ *or* fůl′length′), *adj.* **1** showing the entire human body: *a full-length portrait.* **2** of considerable length: *I watched a full-length movie on TV.*

full moon, the moon seen from the earth as a whole circle.

full-scale (fůl′skāl′), *adj.* **1** having the same size and proportions as the original: *a full-scale model of an old sailing ship.* **2** not limited; using all resources; complete; all-out: *a full-scale investigation, a full-scale battle.*

full-service (fůl′sėr′vis), *adj.* providing many related services in addition to the basic services: *a full-service bank.*

full-time (fůl′tīm′), *adj., adv.* for all of the usual time: *She is looking for a full-time job. I work full-time.*

ful·ly (fůl′ē), *adv.* **1** completely; entirely: *The bill is now fully paid.* **2** abundantly; plentifully: *The gym was fully equipped.* **3** at least; no less than: *She has been gone fully an hour.* **4** quite; exactly: *He could not fully describe what he had seen.*

ful·mi·nate (ful′mə nāt), *v.* to criticize loudly with threats; denounce something violently. ❑ *v.* **ful·min·at·ed, ful·min·at·ing.** —ful′mi·na′tion, *n.* —ful′mi·na′tor, *n.*

ful·some (fůl′səm), *adj.* so much as to be excessive and offensive: *fulsome flattery.* —ful′some·ly, *adv.* —ful′some·ness, *n.*

Ful·ton (fůlt′n), *n.* Rob·ert (rob′ərt), 1765-1815, American inventor who built the first successful steamboat in 1803.

fum·ble (fum′bəl), **1** *v.* to feel about clumsily; search awkwardly: *I fumbled in the darkness for the doorknob.* **2** *v.* to handle awkwardly. **3** *v.* to let a ball drop instead of catching and holding it: *The quarterback fumbled the ball, and the other team recovered it.* **4** *n.* an awkward attempt to find or handle something. ❑ *v.* **fum·bled, fum·bling.** —fum′bler, *n.*

fume (fyüm), **1** *n.* Often, **fumes,** *pl.* vapor, gas, or smoke, especially if harmful, strong, or giving out odor: *The fumes from the car exhaust nearly choked me.* **2** *v.* to give off vapor, gas, or smoke: *The candle fumed, sputtered, and went out.* **3** *v.* to let off rage in angry comments: *We fumed about the slowness of the train.* ❑ *v.* **fumed, fum·ing.**

fu·mi·gate (fyü′mə gāt), *v.* to expose to fumes that will kill mice, rats, insects, etc. ❑ *v.* **fu·mi·gat·ed, fu·mi·gat·ing.** —fu′mi·ga′tion, *n.* —fu′mi·ga′tor, *n.*

fun (fun), **1** *n.* playfulness; amusement; joking: *They had a lot of fun at the party.* **2** *adj.* enjoyable; pleasant; entertaining: *We had a fun time at the beach.* ❑ *adj.* **fun·ner, fun·nest.** [See Word Story at **fond.**] ■ Many people consider **funner** and **funnest** to be very informal.

for fun or **in fun,** as a joke; playfully.

make fun of or **poke fun at,** to laugh at; ridicule.

Fu·na·fu·ti (fü′nə fü′tē), *n.* capital of Tuvalu.

func·tion (fungk′shən), **1** *n.* proper work; normal action or use; purpose: *The function of the stomach is to help digest food.* **2** *v.* to work; act: *One of the older students can function as teacher.* **3** *n.* a formal public or social gathering: *The hotel ballroom is often used for weddings and other functions.* **4** *n.* in mathematics: **a** a quantity whose value depends on the value given to another related quantity: *The area of a circle is a function of its radius.* **b** a relationship between two sets such that each element in the first set is associated with exactly one element in the second set. —func′tion·less, *adj.*

func·tion·al (fungk′shə nəl), *adj.* **1** of or for a function. **2** having a function; working; acting: *The functional wings of an insect are those used for flying.* —func′tion·al·ly, *adv.*

functional illiterate, person who reads and writes much less well than an average eighth grader. Such a person has problems functioning in a society based on literacy.

func·tion·ar·y (fungk′shə ner′ē), *n.* an official. ❑ *n., pl.* **func·tion·ar·ies.**

function word, word that mainly expresses a grammatical relationship between other words in a sentence. Prepositions, such as *of* and *to,* conjunctions, such as *and* and *but,* and auxiliary verbs, such as *is* and *have,* are function words.

fund (fund), **1** *n.* sum of money set aside for a special purpose: *The school has a fund of $2000 to buy books with.* **2** *n.pl.* **funds,** **a** money ready to use: *We took $10 from the club's funds to buy a flag.* **b** money: *I used up my allowance and am low on funds.* **3** *n.* stock or store ready for use; supply: *There is a fund of information in our new library.* **4** *v.* to provide money for something: *fund a recreation program.*

fun·da·men·tal (fun′də men′tl), **1** *adj.* of or forming a foundation or basis; essential; basic: *Reading is a fundamental skill.* **2** *n.* something fundamental; essential part: *the fundamentals of grammar.* —fun′da·men′tal·ly, *adv.*

fun·da·men·tal·ism (fun′də men′tl iz′əm), *n.* the belief that the words of the Bible were inspired by God and should be believed and followed literally.

fun·da·men·tal·ist (fun′də men′tl ist), **1** *n.* person who believes in fundamentalism. **2** *adj.* of or about fundamentalism.

fund·rais·er (fund′rā′zər), *n.* an event, such as a special sale, dinner, or performance, put on by or for a nonprofit organization to raise money: *A turkey sale is this year's band fundraiser.* —fund′rais·ing, *adj.*

Fun·dy (fun′dē), *n.* Bay of, an arm of the Atlantic in Canada, between Nova Scotia and New Brunswick.

fu·ner·al (fyü′nər əl), **1** *n.* ceremonies performed when a dead person's body is buried or burned. A funeral usually includes a religious service and the act of taking the body to the place where it is buried or burned. **2** *adj.* of or suitable for a funeral: *a funeral procession. A funeral march is very slow.*

funeral director, person whose work is arranging a funeral service and the burial or cremation of someone who has died; mortician; undertaker.

funeral home or **funeral parlor,** place of business where the dead are prepared for burial or cremation. A funeral home also has rooms for wakes and funeral services.

fu·ner·e·al (fyü nir′ē əl), *adj.* of or like a funeral; gloomy; dismal. —fu·ner′e·al·ly, *adv.*

fun·gal (fung′gəl), *adj.* **1** of or like a fungus or fungi. **2** caused by a fungus: *Wheat rust is a fungal disease.*

fun·gi (fun′jī *or* fung′gī), *n.* a plural of **fungus.**

fun·gi·cide (fun′jə sīd), *n.* any substance that destroys harmful fungi.

fun·gous (fung′gəs), *adj.* fungal.

fun·gus (fung′gəs), *n.* any of many living things that are like plants but have no flowers, leaves, or green coloring matter. Fungi get their nourishment from dead or living organic matter. Yeasts and some mushrooms are useful fungi and can be eaten. Other mushrooms are poisonous. Smuts, rusts, and mildews are harmful fungi. Certain fungi, such as molds, are used in medicine. ❑ *n., pl.* **fun·gi** or **fun·gus·es.**

fungus

funk¹ (fungk), *n.* **1** condition of panic or fear. **2** a depressed mood.

funk² (fungk), *n.* **1** a kind of music that has its origins in African American gospel songs and blues, and that has a strong beat. **2** state of being funky.

funk·y[1] (fung′kē), *adj.* fearful; timid.

funk·y[2] (fung′kē), *adj.* **1** (in music) having a quality or sound like that of the blues or gospel music. **2** down to earth; realistic; unpretentious. **3** INFORMAL. offbeat or unconventional, but stylish: *funky clothes.* **4** having an unpleasant odor; foul-smelling. ❏ *adj.* **funk·i·er, funk·i·est.** —**funk′i·ness,** *n.*

fun·nel (fun′l), **1** *n.* utensil that is like a narrow tube at the bottom and a cone with a wide mouth at the top. A funnel is used to prevent spilling in pouring liquids, powder, grain, etc., into containers with small openings. **2** *n.* anything shaped like a funnel: *a tornado funnel.* **3** *n.* smokestack or chimney on a steamship or steam engine. **4** *v.* to pass or feed through a funnel: *funnel gasoline into a can. The crowd funneled through the gate.* ❏ *v.* **fun·neled, fun·nel·ing** or **fun·nelled, fun·nel·ling.**

fun·nies (fun′ēz), *n.pl.* **1** comic strips; comics. **2** section of a newspaper carrying comic strips.

fun·ny (fun′ē), *adj.* **1** causing laughter; amusing: *The clown's funny jokes and antics kept us laughing.* **2** strange; odd: *It's funny that they are so late.* ❏ *adj.* **fun·ni·er, fun·ni·est.** —**fun′ni·ly,** *adv.* —**fun′ni·ness,** *n.*

get funny with, to become rude or impertinent: *Don't get funny with me, young lady!*

SYNONYM STUDY **Funny, amusing,** and **hilarious** all mean causing people to laugh. **Funny** is the general word: *She told a really funny joke.* **Amusing** means mildly funny: *The play was amusing but not as funny as we expected.* **Hilarious** means very funny: *This book is so hilarious, I laughed till I cried.*

---

funny bone, place at the bend of the elbow over which a nerve passes. When it is struck, a sharp, tingling sensation is felt in the arm and hand; crazy bone.

WORD STORY **Funny bone** probably comes from a pun. Doctors call the upper bone in the arm the **humerus,** which sounds like **humorous.** If you hit it, it feels funny too, but not in a humorous way.

---

fur (fėr), **1** *n.* the soft hair covering the skin of many animals. **2** *n.* skin with such hair on it. **3** *n.* Usually, **furs,** *pl.* clothes made of fur: *dressed in furs.* **4** *adj.* made of fur: *a fur collar.* **5** *n.* a coating of foul or waste matter like fur. A sick person's tongue often has fur on it. ■ Another word that sounds like this is **fir.** —**fur′less,** *adj.* —**fur′like′,** *adj.*

WORD STORY **Fur** comes from an old French word for the case in which a knife or sword was kept. People at that time wore clothes lined with fur. They thought of the fur lining as a case and gave it the same name.

Fur·ies (fyur′ēz), *n.pl.* (in Greek and Roman myths) the three spirits of revenge.

fur·i·ous (fyur′ē əs), *adj.* **1** very angry; full of wild, fierce anger: *The owner of the house was furious when she learned of the broken window.* ■ See Synonym Study at **mad. 2** of unrestrained energy, speed, violence, etc.: *furious activity, a furious gallop, a furious storm.* —**fur′i·ous·ly,** *adv.*

furl (fėrl), *v.* to roll up; fold up: *furl a sail, furl a flag.*

fur·long (fėr′lông), *n.* unit of distance equal to one eighth of a mile; 220 yards.

fur·lough (fėr′lō), **1** *n.* leave of absence: *The soldier has two weeks' furlough.* **2** *v.* to give leave of absence to.

fur·nace (fėr′nis), *n.* an enclosed space to make a very hot fire in. Furnaces are used to heat buildings, melt metals, etc.

fur·nish (fėr′nish), *v.* **1** to supply with something necessary, useful, or wanted; provide: *furnish an army with blankets. The sun furnishes heat.* **2** to supply a room, house, etc., with furniture or equipment. —**fur′nish·er,** *n.*

fur·nish·ings (fėr′ni shingz), *n.pl.* **1** furniture or equipment for a room, house, or office. **2** articles of clothing: *That store sells men's furnishings.*

fur·ni·ture (fėr′nə chər), *n.* movable articles needed in a room, house, or office. Beds, chairs, tables, and desks are furniture.

fur·or (fyur′ôr), *n.* **1** wild enthusiasm or excitement: *The news that the first astronauts had orbited the moon caused great furor everywhere.* **2** a craze; mania. **3** a rage; fury.

fur·ri·er (fėr′ē ər), *n.* **1** dealer in furs. **2** person whose work is preparing furs or making and repairing fur coats, etc.

fur·row (fėr′ō), **1** *n.* a long, narrow groove or track cut in the earth by a plow. **2** *n.* any long, narrow groove or track: *Heavy trucks made deep furrows in the muddy road.* **3** *v.* to make furrows in. **4** *n.* a wrinkle: *a furrow in your brow.* **5** *v.* to make wrinkles in; wrinkle: *The old man's face was furrowed with age.*

fur·ry (fėr′ē), *adj.* **1** of fur; consisting of fur. **2** covered with fur: *furry animals.* **3** soft like fur: *furry moss.* ❏ *adj.* **fur·ri·er, fur·ri·est.** —**fur′ri·ness,** *n.*

fur seal, any of several seals valued for their thick undercoats.

fur·ther (fėr′ฐәr), **1** *adv.* to a more advanced point: *Inquire further into the matter.* **2** *adj.* more: *Do you need further help?* **3** *v.* to help forward; promote: *Let us further the cause of peace.* **4** *adv.* also; in addition: *My teacher told me to study more and said further that I must cut down on sports.* **5** *adj., adv.* farther. ❏ *adj.* **far, fur·thest;** *adv.* **far, fur·thest.**

fur·ther·ance (fėr′ฐәr əns), *n.* act of furthering; helping forward; advancement; promotion.

fur·ther·more (fėr′ฐәr môr), *adv.* in addition; also; besides.

fur·ther·most (fėr′ฐәr mōst), *adj.* furthest.

fur·thest (fėr′ฐist), **1** *adj.* most distant. **2** *adv.* to or at the greatest distance. **3** *adv.* to the greatest degree or extent; most. ❏ *adj., adv.* **far, fur·ther.**

fur·tive (fėr′tiv), *adj.* **1** done quickly and with stealth to avoid being noticed; secret: *a furtive glance into the forbidden room.* **2** sly; shifty; stealthy: *I suspected them because of their furtive manner.* [**Furtive** comes from a Latin word meaning "thief." A person who is stealing usually moves fast and tries not to be noticed.] —**fur′tive·ly,** *adv.* —**fur′tive·ness,** *n.*

fur·y (fyur′ē), *n.* **1** wild, fierce anger; rage: *She was in a fury because I had dropped her camera.* **2** violence; fierceness: *the fury of a battle, the fury of a hurricane.* **3** a raging or violent person. ❏ *n., pl.* **fur·ies** for 2,3.

furze (fėrz), *n.* a low, prickly, evergreen bush with yellow flowers, common in wastelands in Europe; gorse.

fuse[1] (fyüz), *n.* a slow-burning wick or other device used to set off a shell, a bomb, a blast of gunpowder, or other explosive charge. Also, **fuze.**

fury

fuse[2] (fyüz), **1** *n.* wire or strip of metal inserted in an electric circuit that melts and breaks the connection when the current becomes dangerously strong. **2** *v.* to join together by melting; melt: *Copper and zinc are fused to make brass.* **3** *v.* to blend; unite: *Two political parties fused to form a new third party.* ❏ *v.* **fused, fus·ing.**

WORD FAMILY **Fuse**[2] and the words below are related. They all come from a Latin word meaning "to pour" or "to melt."

confound	fondue	fusion	refund
confuse	font[2]	futile	refuse[1]
diffuse	foundry	infuse	refuse[2]
dumfound	funnel	profusion	transfusion

---

fu·see (fyü zē′), *n.* **1** a large-headed match that will burn in a wind. **2** flare that burns with a red light, used as a warning signal to traffic on railroads or highways. ❏ *n., pl.* **fu·sees.**

fu·se·lage (fyü′sə läzh or fyü′sə lij), *n.* body of an airplane, to which the wings, tail, etc., are fastened. The fuselage holds the passengers, crew, and cargo.

a	hat	ė	term	ô	order	ch	child	
ā	age	i	it	oi	oil	ng	long	⟨ a in about
ä	far	ī	ice	ou	out	sh	she	e in taken
â	care	o	hot	u	cup	th	thin	ə ⟨ i in pencil
e	let	ō	open	ů	put	ฐ	then	o in lemon
ē	equal	ò	saw	ü	rule	zh	measure	u in circus

fu·si·ble (fyü′zə bəl), *adj.* able to be fused or melted. **−fu′si·bil′-i·ty**, *n.*

fu·sil·lade (fyü′sə lād′), *n.* **1** a rapid or continuous discharge of many firearms at the same time. **2** any rapid discharge or burst: *The reporters greeted the mayor with a fusillade of questions.*

fu·sion (fyü′zhən), *n.* **1** act of melting together; fusing: *Bronze is made by the fusion of copper and tin.* **2** a blending; union: *A new club was formed by the fusion of two previous clubs.* **3** the combining of two atomic nuclei to produce a nucleus of greater mass; nuclear fusion. *The fusion of atomic nuclei releases tremendous amounts of energy and is used in a hydrogen bomb. Attempts have been made to produce commercial energy by fusion, including an unproven low energy form called* **cold fusion.**

fusion bomb, hydrogen bomb.

fuss (fus), **1** *n.* much bother about small matters; useless talk and worry; attention given to something not worth it. ■ See Synonym Study at **excitement. 2** *v.* to make a fuss: *There's no need to fuss over the broken cup.* ❑ *n., pl.* **fuss·es. −fuss′er**, *n.*

fuss·y (fus′ē), *adj.* **1** hard to please; never satisfied: *A sick person is likely to be fussy about food.* **2** elaborately made: *fussy clothes.* **3** full of details; requiring much care: *a fussy job.* ❑ *adj.* **fuss·i·er, fuss·i·est. −fuss′i·ly**, *adv.* **−fuss′i·ness**, *n.*

fust·y (fus′tē), *adj.* **1** having a stale smell; moldy; stuffy. **2** too old-fashioned; out-of-date. ❑ *adj.* **fust·i·er, fust·i·est. −fust′i·ly**, *adv.* **−fust′i·ness**, *n.*

fu·tile (fyü′tl), *adj.* **1** not successful; useless: *He fell down after making futile attempts to keep his balance.* **2** not important; trifling: *futile tasks.* **−fu′tile·ly**, *adv.*

WORD STORY **Futile**, says the Word Family at **fuse²**, comes from a Latin word meaning "to pour." How? Through another Latin word that first meant "pouring easily" and then came to mean "leaky." Trying to keep water in a leaky pot is a futile business.

---

fu·til·i·ty (fyü til′ə tē), *n.* **1** uselessness. **2** unimportance.

fu·ton (fü′ton), *n.* a padded sleeping mat, often placed directly on the floor, originally used in Japan. ❑ *n., pl.* **fu·tons** or **fu·ton.**

fu·ture (fyü′chər), **1** *n.* time to come; what is to come; what will be: *You cannot change the past, but you can do better in the future.* **2** *adj.* that is to come; that will be; coming: *We hope your future years will be happy.* **3** *n.* chance of success or prosperity: *She has a job with a future.* **4** *adj.* expressing something expected to happen or exist in time to come: *the future tense of a verb.* **5** *n.* the verb form with *shall* or *will* that expresses something taking place in time to come. "I shall go" or "I will go" is the future of "I go."

future perfect, 1 a verb tense that expresses past time with respect to some point in future time. In "By next Saturday he will have left," *will have left* is in the future perfect tense. **2** a verb form in this tense.

fu·tur·is·tic (fyü′chə ris′tik), *adj.* of or like the future; not traditional: *futuristic car design.*

futuristic

fu·tur·i·ty (fyü chûr′ə tē *or* fyü tùr′ə tē), *n.* **1** future. **2** a future state or event. **3** quality of being future.

fuze (fyüz), *n.* fuse¹.

fuzz (fuz), *n.* loose, light fibers or hairs; fine down: *the fuzz on a caterpillar. Peach fuzz washes off easily.*

fuzz·y (fuz′ē), *adj.* **1** of fuzz. **2** like fuzz. **3** covered with fuzz. **4** blurred; indistinct: *This photograph is too fuzzy for me to identify the people in it.* ❑ *adj.* **fuzz·i·er, fuzz·i·est. −fuzz′i·ly**, *adv.* **−fuzz′i·ness**, *n.*

fwd., forward.

FYI, for your information.

G or **g** (jē), *n.* **1** the seventh letter of the English alphabet. **2** unit of force exerted on an object by the pull of gravity. The force exerted on an object at rest on the earth is one G. An accelerating object may experience a force of several G's. ❑ *n., pl.* **G's** or **g's.**

G or **G.,** **1** German. **2** gravity. **3** Gulf.

G, General (a rating for a movie that is recommended for all age groups).

g or **g.,** gram or grams.

Ga, symbol for gallium.

GA, Georgia (used with postal Zip Code).

Ga., Georgia.

G.A., General Assembly.

gab (gab), INFORMAL. **1** *v.* to talk too much; chatter; gabble. **2** *n.* idle talk; chatter. ❑ *v.* **gabbed, gab·bing.**

gab·ar·dine (gab′ər dēn′), *n.* a closely woven wool, cotton, or rayon cloth used for raincoats, suits, etc.

gab·ble (gab′əl), **1** *v.* to talk rapidly and noisily with little or no meaning; jabber. **2** *n.* rapid and noisy talk with little or no meaning. ❑ *v.* **gab·bled, gab·bling. —gab′bler,** *n.*

gab·by (gab′ē), *adj.* INFORMAL. very talkative. ❑ *adj.* **gab·bi·er, gab·bi·est.**

ga·ble (gā′bəl), *n.* the triangular piece of wall between two sloping surfaces of a roof.

Ga·ble (gā′bəl), *n.* **Clark,** 1901-1960, American movie star. ■ **Clark Gable** won an Academy Award in 1934 for *It Happened One Night.* He also played Rhett Butler in *Gone With the Wind.*

Ga·bon (gä bōn′), *n.* country in central Africa, on the Atlantic. *Capital:* Libreville.

WORD STORY **Gabon** comes from a Portuguese word meaning "cabin." Something about the coast here may have reminded sailors of a ship's cabin, but no one really knows.

Ga·bo·ro·ne (gä′bə rō′nä), *n.* capital of Botswana, in the SE part.

Ga·bri·el (gā′brē əl), *n.* (in the Bible) an archangel who acts as God's messenger. He is the angel of good news. [**Gabriel** comes from a Hebrew word meaning "God is my strong one."]

gad (gad), *v.* to move about restlessly; go about looking for pleasure or excitement: *They were out all day gadding about town.* ❑ *v.* **gad·ded, gad·ding. —gad′der,** *n.*

gad·a·bout (gad′ə bout′), *n.* person who moves about restlessly or goes about looking for pleasure or excitement.

gad·fly (gad′flī′), *n.* **1** any fly that bites cattle, horses, and other animals. The horsefly is one kind. **2** person who constantly irritates or annoys others, especially in order to bring about changes in the way things are. ❑ *n., pl.* **gad·flies.**

a	hat	ė	term	ô	order	ch	child		
ā	age	i	it	oi	oil	ng	long	(a in about	
ä	far	ī	ice	ou	out	sh	she	e in taken	
â	care	o	hot	u	cup	th	thin	ə { i in pencil	
e	let	ō	open	ù	put	₮H	then	o in lemon	
ē	equal	ȯ	saw	ü	rule	zh	measure	(u in circus	

gadg·et (gaj′it), *n.* a small tool or device designed to do a certain task: *Can openers and cookie cutters are kitchen gadgets.*

Gadget and **contraption** both mean a device for a special purpose. **Gadget** means a small clever device: *Where is the gadget for flattening cans?* **Contraption** means an odd, complicated device: *She built a contraption to scare rabbits out of her garden.*

Gadhafi. See Qaddafi.

gad·o·lin·i·um (gad′l in′ē əm), *n.* a highly magnetic metallic element which occurs in combination with certain minerals. *Symbol:* Gd

Gads·den Purchase (gadz′dən), a strip of land forming part of southern New Mexico and Arizona. James Gadsden, a U.S. diplomat, arranged the sale by Mexico of the land in 1854.

Gael (gāl), *n.* **1** a Scottish Highlander. **2** Celt born or living in Scotland, Ireland, or the Isle of Man.

Gael·ic (gā′lik), **1** *adj.* of the Gaels or their language. **2** *n.* language of the Gaels. **3** *n.* Irish.

gaff (gaf), **1** *n.* a strong hook on a handle or barbed spear for pulling large fish out of the water. **2** *v.* to hook or pull a fish out of the water with a gaff. **3** *n.* spar or pole used to extend the upper edge of a fore-and-aft sail.

galaxy (def. 1)—distant galaxies

gag (gag), **1** *n.* something put in someone's mouth to prevent talking or crying out. **2** *v.* to stop up someone's mouth with a gag: *The robbers tied their victims' arms and gagged them.* **3** *n.* anything used to silence someone; anything that stops or prevents free speech. **4** *v.* to force to keep silent; stop or prevent from speaking freely. **5** *v.* to choke or strain in an effort to vomit; retch: *Bad-tasting medicines make us gag.* **6** *n.* joke; amusing remark or trick: *The comedian's gags made the audience laugh.* ❏ *v.* **gagged, gag·ging.**

Ga·ga·rin (gə gär′ən), *n.* **Yu·ri** (yür′ē), 1934-1968, Russian cosmonaut. In 1961 he was the first person in outer space.

gage (gāj), *n., v.* gauge. ❏ *v.* **gaged, gag·ing.**

gag·gle (gag′əl), *n.* a group of geese.

gai·e·ty (gā′ə tē), *n.* cheerful liveliness; joyousness: *Her gaiety helped to make the party a success.* Also, **gayety.**

gai·ly (gā′lē), *adv.* **1** merrily; happily: *Excited by the good news, she danced gaily around the room.* **2** brightly; showily: *They were gaily dressed in colorful costumes.* Also, **gayly.**

gain (gān), **1** *v.* to come to have; get; obtain: *The farmer gained possession of more land.* **2** *n.* what is gained; increase, addition, or advantage: *a gain of ten percent over last year's earnings.* **3** *n.pl.* **gains,** profits; earnings; winnings. **4** *v.* to get as an increase, addition, or advantage; profit: *How much did they gain by that?* **5** *v.* to make progress; improve: *The sick child is gaining and will soon be well.* **6** *v.* to be the victor in; win: *The stronger team gained the victory.* **7** *v.* to get to; arrive at; reach: *The swimmer gained the shore.*

gain on, to come closer to; catch up with: *The second runner is gaining on the leader.*

gain·er (gā′nər), *n.* **1** person or thing that gains. **2** dive in which the diver turns a back somersault in the air.

gain·ful (gān′fəl), *adj.* bringing in money or advantage; profitable: *a gainful occupation.* —**gain′ful·ly,** *adv.*

gain·said (gān′sed′), *v.* past tense and past participle of **gainsay:** *Her athletic ability cannot be gainsaid.*

gain·say (gān′sā′), *v.* to deny; contradict; dispute: *We could not gainsay his opinion.* ❏ *v.* **gain·said, gain·say·ing.**

gait (gāt), *n.* the kind of steps used in moving; manner of walking or running: *A gallop is one of the gaits of a horse.* ■ Another word that sounds like this is **gate.**

gal (gal), *n.* INFORMAL. girl.

gal., gallon. ❏ *pl.* **gal.** or **gals.**

ga·la (gā′lə *or* gal′ə), **1** *adj.* of festivity; festive: *In our family, Christmas and the Fourth of July are gala days.* **2** *n.* a festive occasion; festival. ❏ *n., pl.* **ga·las.**

ga·lac·tic (gə lak′tik), *adj.* of or about the Milky Way or other galaxies.

Gal·a·had (gal′ə had), *n.* (in legends of the Middle Ages) the noblest and purest knight of King Arthur's Round Table, who found the Holy Grail.

Ga·lá·pa·gos Islands (gə lä′pə gəs *or* gə lä′pə gōs), group of islands in the Pacific, west of and belonging to Ecuador. [**Galápagos** comes from a Spanish word meaning "turtles." The islands are home to a species of giant turtle.]

Ga·la·tians (gə lā′shənz), *n.* book of the New Testament, written by Saint Paul.

gal·ax·y (gal′ək sē), *n.* **1** group of billions of stars forming one system. Earth and the sun are in the Milky Way galaxy. Many galaxies outside our own can be seen with a telescope. **2 Galaxy,** the Milky Way. **3** a brilliant or splendid group, especially of very attractive or distinguished persons. ❏ *n., pl.* **gal·ax·ies** for 1,3. [**Galaxy** comes from a Greek word meaning "milk." From Earth, the Milky Way looks like a streak of milk on the night sky.]

Gal·braith (gal′brāth), *n.* **John Ken·neth** (ken′əth), born 1908, American economist and diplomat, born in Canada. He has argued that large stores with a lot of buying power and strong unions are necessary to balance the power of large companies.

gale (gāl), *n.* **1** a very strong wind. A gale blows with a velocity of 32 to 63 miles (51 to 101 kilometers) per hour. **2** a noisy outburst: *The joke caused gales of laughter.*

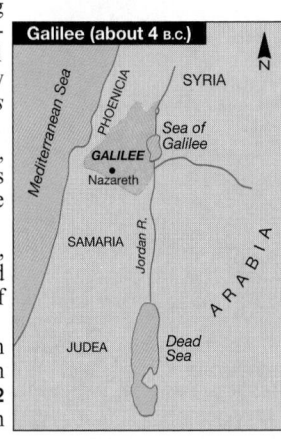

Galilee (about 4 B.C.)

Ga·len (gā′lən), *n.* 129-210? A.D., Greek doctor and writer. He was the first person to state that the heart pumps blood.

ga·le·na (gə lē′nə), *n.* a metallic, gray mineral containing lead and sulfur. It is the chief source of lead.

Gal·i·lee (gal′ə lē′), *n.* **1** region in N Israel that was a Roman province in the time of Jesus. **2 Sea of,** a small freshwater lake in NE Israel.

Galilee comes from a Hebrew word meaning "a circle." Long ago, this region was encircled by areas inhabited by non-Jews and separated from other areas where Jews lived. **Gallery** comes from the same word. In the Middle Ages, a church porch was called "a galilee," perhaps because it was separate from the main part. The name was borrowed for other parts of buildings.

Gal·i·le·o (gal′ə lē′ō), *n.* 1564-1642, Italian astronomer and physicist. ■ Galileo was the first to use the telescope to study the sun, moon, and planets. He discovered the moons of Jupiter.

gall¹ (gôl), *n.* **1** bile (def. 1). **2** anything very bitter or harsh. **3** bitterness; hate. **4** too great boldness; impudence.

gall² (gôl), **1** *v.* to make or become sore by rubbing: *The rough strap galled the horse's skin.* **2** *v.* to annoy; irritate: *It galls me that they are always late for dinner.* **3** *n.* a sore spot on the skin caused by rubbing, especially one on a horse's back.

gall³ (gòl), *n.* lump or ball that forms on the leaves, stems, or roots of plants where they have been injured by insects, bacteria, or fungi.

Gall (gòl), *n.* 1840-1894, a leader of the Lakota Sioux. He led warriors against George Custer at the Battle of Little Bighorn in 1876.

gal·lant (gal′ənt *for adj.;* gal′ənt *or* gə lant′ *for noun*), **1** *adj.* noble in spirit or in conduct; brave: *She was praised for her gallant action in saving the drowning child.* **2** *adj.* grand; fine; stately: *A ship with all of its sails spread is a gallant sight.* **3** *adj.* very polite and attentive to women. **4** *n.* man who is very polite and attentive to women. **5** *n.* man who wears showy, stylish clothes. —**gal′lant·ly,** *adv.* —**gal′lant·ness,** *n.*

gal·lant·ry (gal′ən trē), *n.* **1** noble spirit or conduct; bravery. **2** great politeness and attention to women. **3** a gallant act or speech. ❑ *n., pl.* **gal·lant·ries** for 3.

gall bladder, sac attached to the liver, in which bile is stored until needed.

gal·le·on (gal′ē ən), *n.* a large, high ship with three or four decks, used especially in the 1400s and 1500s.

gal·ler·i·a (gal′ə rē′ə), *n.* an indoor shopping center, especially one with a high glass roof covering a courtyard or a central walk. ❑ *n., pl.* **gal·ler·i·as.**

gal·ler·y (gal′ər ē), *n.* **1** room or building used to show collections of pictures and statues. **2** balcony looking down into a

galleon

large hall or room. **3** the highest balcony of a theater. It contains the cheapest seats. **4** people who sit there. **5** a hall or long, narrow passage, often with windows along one side. **6** room or building used for a particular purpose, such as taking photographs or practicing shooting. ❑ *n., pl.* **gal·ler·ies.** [See Word Story at **Galilee.**]

gal·ley (gal′ē), *n.* **1** (in ancient times and the Middle Ages) a long, narrow ship with oars and sails. Galleys were often rowed by enslaved people or convicts. **2** kitchen of a ship or airplane. **3** (earlier) a long, narrow tray for holding printing type. **4** galley proof. ❑ *n., pl.* **gal·leys.**

galley proof, (in printing) a proof printed as a test sample, so that errors can be corrected before a final printing. Galley proofs used to be printed from type in a galley, but today most are done using computers and photography.

galley slave, 1 enslaved person or convict forced to row a galley. **2** drudge.

gall·fly (gòl′flī′), *n.* any insect that deposits its eggs in plants, causing galls to form. ❑ *n., pl.* **gall·flies.**

Gal·lic (gal′ik), *adj.* **1** of Gaul or its people. **2** French: *Gallic wit.*

Gal·li·cism or **Gal·li·cism** (gal′ə siz′əm), *n.* a French idiom or expression.

gal·li·mau·fry (gal′ə mò′frē), *n.* a confused jumble; hodgepodge. ❑ *n., pl.* **gal·li·mau·fries.**

gall·ing (gò′ling), *adj.* irritating; chafing.

gal·li·um (gal′ē əm), *n.* a grayish white metallic element similar to mercury, with a melting point slightly above room temperature. It is used in thermometers. *Symbol:* Ga

gallium ar·se·nide (är′sə nīd), a crystalline compound of gallium and arsenic. It is used as a semiconductor.

gal·li·vant (gal′ə vant), *v.* to go about seeking pleasure; gad about.

gal·lon (gal′ən), *n.* unit of volume for measuring liquids, equal to four quarts.

gal·lop (gal′əp), **1** *n.* the fastest gait of a horse or of many other four-footed animals. In a gallop, all four feet are off the ground at the same time in each leap. **2** *v.* to ride at a gallop: *The hunters galloped after the hounds.* **3** *v.* to go or cause to go at a gallop: *The wild horse galloped off when it saw us.* **4** *v.* to go very fast; hurry: *gallop through a speech or book.* —**gal′lop·er,** *n.*

gal·lows (gal′ōz), *n.* **1** a wooden frame made of a crossbar on two upright posts, used for hanging criminals by a rope. **2** punishment by hanging: *The judge sentenced the murderer to the gallows.* ❑ *n., pl.* **gal·lows** or **gal·lows·es.**

gallows humor, humor that makes light of a dangerous or bad situation.

gall·stone (gòl′stōn′), *n.* a painful, pebblelike mass of cholesterol, mineral salts, etc., that sometimes forms in the gall bladder or its duct.

Gal·lup (gal′əp), *n.* George, 1901-1984, American statistician and specialist in surveys of public opinion.

ga·loot *n.* SLANG. an awkward or foolish person.

ga·lore (gə lôr′), *adj.* in large amounts or quantities: *This lake has fish galore.* ■ Galore always follows the noun it goes with.

ga·losh·es (gə losh′iz), *n.pl.* rubber or plastic boots worn over the shoes in wet or snowy weather.

ga·lumph (gə lumf′), *v.* to gallop in a clumsy way: *cows galumphing home.* [Galumph was invented by Lewis Carroll. It may be a blend of **gallop** and **triumph,** but only he knows for sure.]

gal·van·ic (gal van′ik), *adj.* of, caused by, or producing an electric current by chemical action.

gal·van·ism (gal′və niz′əm), *n.* electricity produced by chemical action.

gal·va·nize (gal′və nīz), *v.* **1** to arouse suddenly; startle: *The ringing of the alarm bell galvanized the firefighters into rapid action.* **2** to cover iron or steel with a thin coating of zinc to prevent rust. ❑ *v.* **gal·va·nized, gal·va·niz·ing.** —**gal′va·ni·za′tion,** *n.* —**gal′va·niz′er,** *n.*

gal·va·nom·e·ter (gal′və nom′ə tər), *n.* device for detecting, measuring, and telling the direction of a small electric current.

Gal·ves·ton (gal′vəs tən), *n.* port in SE Texas, near the Gulf of Mexico.

Gama. See da Gama.

Gam·bi·a (gam′bē ə), *n.* The, country in W Africa. *Capital:* Banjul. [Gambia comes from a local word meaning "river." A river and the land along its banks form the entire country.] —**Gam′bi·an,** *adj., n.*

gam·bit (gam′bit), *n.* **1** any opening move or action, especially one done to gain some advantage. **2** way of opening a game of chess by purposely sacrificing a piece to gain some advantage.

WORD STORY Gambit comes from an Italian word meaning "leg." Gambol comes from the same word. A gambit reminded people of tripping an opponent by surprise, and gamboling is playing in a way that uses the legs.

gam·ble (gam′bəl), **1** *v.* to play games of chance for money; bet: *Some people gamble on horse races.* **2** *v.* to take a risk; take great risks in business or speculation: *to gamble in stocks and bonds.* **3** *v.* to risk money or other things of value: *The daredevil gambled his life on the chance he could leap the deep canyon.* **4** *n.* a risky act or undertaking: *Putting money into a new business is often a gamble.* ❑ *v.* **gam·bled, gam·bling.** ■ Another word that sounds like this is **gambol.**

gamble away, to lose by gambling: *gamble away a fortune.*

gam·bler (gam′blər), *n.* **1** person who gambles a great deal. **2** person whose occupation is gambling.

gam·bol (gam′bəl), *v.* to run and jump about in play; frolic. [See Word Story at **gambit.**] ■ Another word that sounds like this is **gamble.**

gambrel roof, roof with two slopes on each side. The lower slope is steeper than the upper one.

game¹ (gām), **1** *n.* way of playing; pastime; amusement: *a game of tag, a game with bat and ball.* **2** *n.* contest with certain rules. One person or side tries to win it: *a football game.* **3** *n.* a set of objects, such as dice, cards, round pieces of wood or plastic, and a board, used in playing certain kinds of games, such as checkers, backgammon, etc. **4** *n.* number of points that wins a game:

a	hat	ė	term	ô	order	ch	child		
ā	age	i	it	oi	oil	ng	long	ə	a in about
ä	far	ī	ice	ou	out	sh	she		e in taken
â	care	o	hot	u	cup	th	thin		i in pencil
e	let	ō	open	ů	put	ŦH	then		o in lemon
ē	equal	ò	saw	ü	rule	zh	measure		u in circus

In volleyball, a game is fifteen points. **5** *n.* plan; scheme: *She tried to trick us, but we saw through her game.* **6** *n.* wild animals, birds, or fish hunted or caught for sport or for food. **7** *n.* flesh of wild animals or birds used for food. **8** *adj.* of or about game, hunting, or fishing: *Game laws protect wildlife.* **9** *adj.* brave; courageous: *The losing team put up a game fight.* **10** *adj.* ready; eager: *The children were game for any adventure.* **11** *v.* to gamble. ❑ *adj.* **gam·er, gam·est;** *v.* **gamed, gam·ing.** [**Game¹** comes from an old English word meaning "joy." Joy is what games are for.] **—game′ly,** *adv.* **—game′ness,** *n.*

play the game, be fair; follow the rules; be a good sport.

the game is up, the plan or scheme has failed.

WORD BANK There are many different kinds of **games,** with many different names. If you want to learn more about them, you can begin by looking up these words in this dictionary.

backgammon	hopscotch	poker²
billiards	horseshoes	pool²
bingo	jacks	quoits
bridge²	kickball	rummy
checkers	leapfrog	tag²
chess	mah-jongg	table tennis
Chinese checkers	marbles	tetherball
cribbage	mumblety-peg	tick-tack-toe
croquet	pachisi	tiddlywinks
darts	pinball	tug-of-war
dominoes	pinochle	video game
hide-and-seek		

game² (gām), *adj.* lame; crippled; injured: *a game leg.*

game·cock (gām′kok′), *n.* rooster bred and trained for fighting.

game·keep·er (gām′kē′pər), *n.* person employed to take care of wild animals and birds on a private estate and prevent anyone from stealing them or killing them without permission.

game plan, plan of action; strategy: *The politician has a new game plan for winning the next election.*

game show, a TV or radio show in which people compete for prizes by playing games or answering questions.

games·man·ship (gāmz′mən ship), *n.* skill in using strategy to gain an advantage in games, contests, relationships, etc.

gam·ete (gam′ēt *or* gə mēt′), *n.* a mature reproductive cell that can unite with another to form a fertilized cell able to develop into a new living thing; an egg or sperm cell; germ cell.

ga·me·to·phyte (gə mē′tō fit), *n.* any plant or generation of plants that produces gametes. **—ga·me·to·phyt·ic** (gə mē′tō fit′ik), *adj.*

game warden, official whose duty is to enforce the game laws in a district.

gam·in (gam′ən), *n.* a neglected child who roams the streets.

gam·ing (gā′ming), **1** *n.* the playing of games of chance for money; gambling. **2** *adj.* of or about playing games, especially fantasy, war, or role-playing games: *a gaming magazine, a gaming club.*

gam·ma (gam′ə), *n.* the third letter of the Greek alphabet (Γ, γ). ❑ *n., pl.* **gam·mas.**

gamma glob·u·lin (glob′yə lən), part of the human blood. Gamma globulin contains many antibodies which protect against infectious diseases.

gamma ray, electromagnetic radiation of very high frequency given off by radium and other radioactive substances. Gamma rays are like X rays but have a shorter wavelength and more energy.

gam·ut (gam′ət), *n.* the whole range of anything: *Her feelings about the contest ran the gamut from hope to despair.*

gam·y (gā′mē), *adj.* **1** having a strong taste or smell like the flesh of wild animals or birds. **2** brave; courageous. ❑ *adj.* **gam·i·er, gam·i·est. —gam′i·ly,** *adv.* **—gam′i·ness,** *n.*

gan·der (gan′dər), *n.* a male goose.

Gan·dhi (gän′dē *or* gan′dē), *n.* **1 In·dir·a** (in dir′ə), 1917-1984, prime minister of India from 1966 to 1977 and from 1980 to 1984. **2 Mo·han·das** (mō hän′dəs), 1869-1948, Hindu political, social, and religious leader. **3 Ra·jiv** (rä jēv′), 1944-1991, prime minister of India from 1984 to 1989, son of Indira.

Ga·ne·sha (gə nā′shə), *n.* Hindu god of wisdom, believed to remove obstacles, often shown with a man's body and an elephant's head.

gang (gang), **1** *n.* group of people working or going around together: *A whole gang of us went swimming.* **2** *n.* group engaged in wrongdoing: *A gang of hoodlums broke several windows along our street.* **3** *n.* group of people working together under one foreman: *A gang of workers was mending the road.* **4** *v.* to form a gang: *The boys ganged together to build a raft.*

Ganesha—as imagined by an artist

gang up on, to get together with others to oppose or attack someone: *Some girls ganged up on her and pushed her in the snow.*

Gan·ges (gan′jēz′), *n.* river flowing across N India and Bangladesh into the Bay of Bengal. Hindus regard it as sacred. [**Ganges** comes from a Sanskrit word meaning "a stream."]

gang·li·a (gang′glē ə), *n.* a plural of **ganglion.**

gang·ling (gang′gling), *adj.* awkwardly tall and slender.

gang·li·on (gang′glē ən), *n.* group of nerve cells forming a nerve center, especially outside of the brain or spinal cord. ❑ *n., pl.* **gang·gli·a** *or* **gan·gli·ons.**

gang·gly (gang′glē), *adj.* gangling. ❑ *adj.* **gan·gli·er, gan·gli·est.**

gang·plank (gang′plangk′), *n.* a movable bridge used in getting on and off a ship.

gan·grene (gang′grēn′), **1** *n.* decay of living tissue when its blood supply is interfered with by injury, infection, or freezing. **2** *v.* to be or become affected with gangrene; decay. ❑ *v.* **gan·grened, gan·gren·ing.**

gan·gre·nous (gang′grə nəs), *adj.* having gangrene; decaying: *The gangrenous leg was amputated.*

gang·sta (gang′stə), *adj.* SLANG. **1** of or about street gangs or street violence: *gangsta clothes.* **2 gangsta rap,** rap music about street gangs, criminal activities, or violence.

gang·ster (gang′stər), *n.* member of a gang of criminals.

gang·way (gang′wā′), **1** *n.* passageway. **2** *n.* passageway on a ship: *a gangway between the rail and the cabins.* **3** *n.* gangplank. **4** *interj.* get out of the way! stand aside and make room!

gan·net (gan′it), *n.* a large, fish-eating seabird that resembles a goose but has a sharper bill, long, pointed wings, and a short tail.

gan·try (gan′trē), *n.* **1** a movable framework used for setting up and servicing rockets. **2** a bridgelike framework for supporting a suspended crane or signal lights over railway tracks. ❑ *n., pl.* **gan·tries.**

gap (gap), *n.* **1** a broken place; opening: *The cows got out of the field through a gap in the fence.* **2** an empty part; unfilled space; blank: *The story is not complete; there are several gaps in it.* **3** a wide difference of opinion, character, etc. **4** a lack of trust or understanding: *a credibility gap, a communication gap.* **5** a pass through mountains. **6** space between two electrodes, for example in the spark plug of a gasoline engine, across which an electric spark jumps.

gape (gāp), **1** *v.* to open wide: *A deep hole in the earth gaped before us.* **2** *v.* to open the mouth wide; yawn. **3** *n.* act of opening the mouth wide; yawning. **4** *v.* to stare with the mouth open: *The crowd gaped at the daring tricks performed by the tightrope walkers.* ❑ *v.* **gaped, gap·ing. —gap′er,** *n.* **—gap′ing·ly,** *adv.*

gar (gär), *n.* any of several fish with long, slender bodies covered with hard scales and long narrow jaws. ❑ *n., pl.* **gar** *or* **gars.**

ga·rage (gə razh′ *or* gə räj′), **1** *n.* place where motor vehicles are kept. **2** *n.* shop for repairing motor vehicles. **3** *v.* to put or keep in a garage. ❑ *v.* **ga·raged, ga·rag·ing.**

garage sale, sale of used furniture, clothing, tools, etc., held in the seller's garage, yard, or basement; yard sale.

garb (gärb), **1** *n.* the way you are dressed; kind of clothing: *stylish garb, official garb.* **2** *v.* to clothe: *The bride was garbed in* *white.* [**Garb** comes from an Italian word meaning "elegance." Because clothing is so important to an elegant appearance, that meaning took over the word.]

gar·bage (gär′bij), *n.* scraps of food to be thrown away.

gar·ban·zo (gär bän′zō), *n.* chickpea. ❑ *n., pl.* **gar·ban·zos.**

gar·ble (gär′bəl), *v.* to mix up facts, statements, or the like, often in order to misrepresent; distort: *The paper gave a garbled account of the speech.* ❑ *v.* **gar·bled, gar·bling.**

Gar·bo (gär′bō), *n.* **Gre·ta** (gret′ə), 1905-1990, American movie star, born in Sweden. Noted for her beauty, dignity, and desire for privacy, she played many grand tragic parts.

Gar·cí·a Már·quez (gär sē′ə mär kez′), **Gabriel,** born 1928, Colombian writer. He won the 1982 Nobel Prize for literature.

gar·den (gärd′n), **1** *n.* piece of ground used for growing vegetables, herbs, flowers, or fruits. **2** *v.* to take care of a garden; make a garden; work in a garden: *She liked to garden as a hobby.* **3** *n.* park or place where people go for amusement or to see things that are displayed: *the botanical garden.* —**gar′den·like′,** *adj.*

gar·den·er (gärd′nər), *n.* **1** person employed to take care of a garden, lawn, etc. **2** person who gardens.

gar·de·nia (gär dē′nyə), *n.* an evergreen bush or small tree bearing fragrant, white flowers with smooth, waxy petals. ❑ *n., pl.* **gar·de·nias.**

Gar·field (gär′fēld′), *n.* **James A.,** 1831-1881, the 20th president of the United States. He was assassinated in 1881, his first year in office.

gar·gan·tu·an (gär gan′chü ən), *adj.* enormous; gigantic; huge: *a gargantuan appetite.*

gar·gle (gär′gəl), **1** *v.* to wash or rinse the throat with a liquid kept in motion by the outgoing breath: *He gargled with hot salt water to relieve his sore throat.* **2** *n.* liquid used for gargling. ❑ *v.* **gar·gled, gar·gling.**

gar·goyle (gär′goil), *n.* an ornamental stone carving in the shape of a grotesque animal or human being, often for draining water from the gutter of a building.

Gar·i·bal·di (gar′ə bôl′dē), *n.* **Giu·sep·pe** (jü zep′ā), 1807-1882, Italian patriot and general. He fought for the unification and independence of Italy.

gar·ish (gâr′ish *or* gar′ish), *adj.* unpleasantly bright; glaring; showy; gaudy: *The circus performer was dressed in garish colors.* —**gar′ish·ly,** *adv.* —**gar′ish·ness,** *n*

gargoyle

gar·land (gär′lənd), **1** *n.* wreath or string of flowers, leaves, etc. **2** *v.* to decorate with garlands.

Gar·land (gär′lənd), *n.* **Ju·dy** (jü′dē), 1922-1969, American movie star and singer. Her most famous role was Dorothy in *The Wizard of Oz.*

gar·lic (gär′lik), *n.* plant related to the onion, with a strong-smelling bulb formed of small sections called cloves, which are used to flavor meats, salads, etc.

gar·ment (gär′mənt), *n.* any piece of clothing.

gar·ner (gär′nər), *v.* to gather and store away: *Wheat is cut and garnered at harvest time. Squirrels garner nuts in the fall.*

gar·net (gär′nit), **1** *n.* a hard mineral occurring in many varieties. A deep red, transparent variety is used for jewelry and as an abrasive. **2** *n.* a deep red. **3** *adj.* deep red. —**gar′net·like′,** *adj.*

gar·nish (gär′nish), **1** *n.* something laid on or around food as a decoration: *The turkey was served with a garnish of cranberries and parsley.* **2** *v.* to decorate food. ❑ *n., pl.* **gar·nish·es.**

gar·nish·ee (gär′ni shē′), *v.* to withhold someone's money or property by legal authority to pay a debt. If a creditor garnishees a debtor's salary, a certain portion of the salary is withheld and paid to the creditor. ❑ *n., pl.* **gar·nish·ees;** *v.* **gar·nish·eed, gar·nish·ee·ing.**

gar·ret (gar′it), *n.* space just below a sloping house roof; attic.

Gar·ri·son (gar′ə sən), *n.* **William Lloyd** (loid), 1805-1879, American editor and Abolitionist. He also worked for equal rights for women.

gar·ri·son (gar′ə sən), **1** *n.* group of soldiers stationed in a fort, town, etc., to defend it. **2** *n.* place that has a garrison. **3** *v.* to station soldiers in a fort, town, etc., to defend it.

gar·ru·lous (gar′ə ləs), *adj.* **1** talking too much; talkative. **2** using too many words; wordy: *garrulous comments.*

gar·ter (gär′tər), **1** *n.* an elastic band or strap to hold up a stocking or sock. **2** *v.* to fasten with a garter.

garter snake, any of several small, harmless, brownish or greenish snakes with light stripes that run along their bodies.

Gar·vey (gär′vē), *n.* **Mar·cus** (mär′kəs), 1887-1940, American political reformer, born in Jamaica. ■ **Marcus Garvey** believed that African Americans would never get fair treatment in a country where most of the people were white. He encouraged African Americans to move to Africa.

Gar·y (gâr′ē), *n.* city in NW Indiana, on Lake Michigan.

gas (gas), **1** *n.* substance that is not a solid or a liquid. A gas has no shape or size of its own and can expand without limit. Air is a mixture of gases. **2** *n.* any mixture of gases that can be burned, obtained from coal and other substances. Gas is used for cooking and heating. **3** *n.* any gas used as an anesthetic. Nitrous oxide is such a gas. **4** *n.* substance in the form of a gas that poisons, suffocates, or stupefies. Tear gas is one kind. **5** *v.* to injure or kill by poisonous gas. **6** *n.* gasoline. **7** *v.* to supply with gasoline: *gas up the car.* **8** *v.* SLANG. to talk idly or in a boasting way. ❑ *n., pl.* **gas·es;** *v.* **gassed, gas·sing.**

gas chamber, an airtight room in which a poison gas can be released. It is used in some states to execute criminals sentenced to death.

gas·e·ous (gas′ē əs), *adj.* in the form of gas; of or like a gas: *Steam is water in a gaseous condition.*

gas guz·zler (guz′lər), car or other motor vehicle which gets low gasoline mileage.

gash (gash), **1** *n.* a long, deep cut or wound. **2** *v.* to make a long, deep cut or wound in. ❑ *n., pl.* **gash·es.**

gas·ket (gas′kit), *n.* ring or piece of rubber, plastic, etc., packed around a pipe joint or placed between machine parts to keep a liquid or a gas from escaping.

gas·light (gas′līt′), *n.* **1** light made by burning gas. **2** lamp which burns gas.

gas mask, helmet or mask that covers the mouth and nose and has a filter to prevent your breathing poisonous gas or smoke.

gas·o·hol (gas′ə hòl), *n.* a fuel for internal-combustion engines, composed of ninety percent unleaded gasoline and ten percent ethyl alcohol.

gas·o·line (gas′ə lēn′ *or* gas′ə lēn′), *n.* a colorless, liquid mixture of hydrocarbons which evaporates and burns very easily. It is made from petroleum or from gas formed in the earth. Gasoline is used mostly as a fuel to run motor vehicles.

gasp (gasp), **1** *v.* to try hard to get your breath with open mouth. A person gasps when out of breath or surprised. **2** *n.* act of trying hard to get your breath with your mouth open. **3** *v.* to utter with gasps: *"Help!" gasped the drowning man.* —**gasp′ing·ly,** *adv.*

a	hat	ė	term	ô	order	ch	child		
ā	age	i	it	oi	oil	ng	long		a in about
ä	far	ī	ice	ou	out	sh	she		e in taken
â	care	o	hot	u	cup	th	thin	ə	i in pencil
e	let	ō	open	ù	put	ᴛʜ	then		o in lemon
ē	equal	ò	saw	ü	rule	zh	measure		u in circus

Gas·pé Peninsula (ga spā′), *n.* peninsula in SE Canada, in Quebec province, extending into the Gulf of St. Lawrence. —**Gas·pe·sian** (gas pē′zhən), *adj., n.*

gas station, filling station.

gas·sy (gas′ē), *adj.* 1 full of gas; containing gas: *a gassy atmosphere.* 2 like gas: *a gassy smell.* ❑ *adj.* **gas·si·er, gas·si·est.** —**gas′si·ness,** *n.*

gas·tric (gas′trik), *adj.* of or near the stomach.

gastric juice, the digestive fluid produced by glands in the lining of the stomach. It contains pepsin and other enzymes and hydrochloric acid.

gas·tri·tis (ga strī′tis), *n.* inflammation of the stomach, especially of its lining.

gas·tro·in·tes·ti·nal (gas′trō in tes′tə nəl), *adj.* of the stomach and intestines.

gas·tro·pod (gas′trə pod), *n.* any of many mollusks with eyes and feelers on a distinct head, a muscular foot used for moving, and often a shell that is spiral or cone-shaped. Snails and slugs are gastropods.

gate (gāt), *n.* 1 a movable frame or door to close an opening in a wall or fence. It turns on hinges or slides open and shut. 2 an opening in a wall or fence where a door is; gateway. 3 door or valve to stop or control the flow of water in a pipe, dam, canal, lock, etc. 4 number of people who pay to see a contest, exhibition, etc. 5 the total amount of money received from them: *The two teams divided a gate of $20,000.* ■ Another word that sounds like this is **gait.** —**gate′less,** *adj.* —**gate′like′,** *adj.*

Gauguin painting

-gate, *suffix.* scandal or criminal activity, usually involving government or business: *Scandal about money for the city gardens was called Gardengate in the newspaper.* [-gate comes from Watergate, the name of an office building in Washington, D.C. A burglary there led to a famous political scandal in the 1970s.]

gate·keep·er (gāt′kē′pər), *n.* 1 person who takes care of a gate to control who comes and goes. 2 person who guards; guardian; protector: *a gatekeeper of democracy.*

gate·post (gāt′pōst′), *n.* post on either side of a gate. A swinging gate is fastened to one gatepost and closes against the other.

Gates of the Arctic National Park, a national park in N Alaska, containing mountains and Arctic tundra.

gate·way (gāt′wā′), *n.* 1 an opening in a wall or fence where a gate is. 2 way to go in or out; way to get to something: *A good education can be a gateway to success.*

gateway drug, drug that is not addictive but may lead to use of an addictive drug.

gath·er (gaᴛн′ər), 1 *v.* to bring into one place; collect: *He gathered his books and papers and started to school.* 2 *v.* to come together; assemble: *A crowd gathered at the scene of the accident.* 3 *v.* to pick and collect from the place of growth; glean or pluck: *to gather crops.* 4 *v.* to get or gain little by little: *The train gathered speed as it left the station.* 5 *v.* to put together in the mind; conclude: *I gather from the excitement that something important has happened.* 6 *v.* to pull together in folds: *The dressmaker gathered the skirt at the waist. She gathered her brows in a*

frown. 7 *n.* one of the little folds between stitches when cloth is gathered. —**gath′er·er,** *n.*

gath·er·ing (gaᴛн′ər ing), *n.* a group of people met together; meeting; assembly: *We had a large family gathering at our house on Thanksgiving Day.*

ga·tor (gā′tər), *n.* INFORMAL. alligator.

GATT (gat), *n.* General Agreement on Tariffs and Trade (an international treaty to promote world trade by removing or reducing tariffs, quotas, etc.).

gauche (gōsh), *adj.* awkward; clumsy. —**gauche′ly,** *adv.* —**gauche′ness,** *n.*

gau·cho (gou′chō), *n.* cowboy in the southern plains of South America, usually of mixed Spanish and American Indian descent. ❑ *n., pl.* **gau·chos.**

gaud·y (gô′dē), *adj.* too bright and showy; too cheap to be in good taste: *gaudy jewelry, a gaudy tie.* ■ See Synonym Study at **showy.** ❑ *adj.* **gaud·i·er, gaud·i·est.** —**gaud′i·ly,** *adv.* —**gaud′i·ness,** *n.*

gauge (gāj), 1 *n.* a standard measure; scale of standard measurements; measure. There are gauges of the capacity of a barrel, the thickness of sheet iron, the inside diameter of a shotgun barrel or of a wire, etc. 2 *n.* device for measuring. A steam gauge measures the pressure of steam. 3 *v.* to measure accurately; find out the exact measurement of something with a gauge. 4 *v.* to estimate; judge: *It's difficult to gauge the educational value of TV.* ■ See Usage Note at **first-degree.** 5 *n.* distance between the rails of a railroad. Standard gauge between rails is 56½ inches (1.44 meters). ❑ *v.* **gauged, gaug·ing.** Also, **gage.** —**gauge′a·ble,** *adj.*

Gau·guin (gō gan′), *n.* Paul, 1848-1903, French painter. ■ Paul Gauguin lived in Tahiti for several years. He painted many pictures showing the islanders as peaceful and gentle.

Gaul (gôl), *n.* 1 ancient region of W Europe. It included what is now France, Belgium, Luxembourg, and parts of Switzerland, Germany, the Netherlands, and N Italy. 2 one of the Celtic inhabitants of ancient Gaul. 3 Frenchman.

Gaul (about 300 B.C.)
BRITAIN
N
GERMANY
GAUL
ATLANTIC OCEAN
SPAIN	ITALY
Mediterranean Sea

gaunt (gônt), *adj.* 1 very thin and bony; with hollow eyes and a starved look. 2 gloomy; desolate: *the gaunt slopes of a high mountain in winter.* —**gaunt′ly,** *adv.* —**gaunt′ness,** *n.*

gaunt·let[1] (gônt′lit), *n.* a former punishment or torture in which the offender had to run between two rows of people who struck him or her with clubs or other weapons.

run the gauntlet, 1 to pass between two rows of people each of whom strikes the runner as he or she passes. **2** be exposed to unfriendly attacks or severe criticism.

gaunt·let[2] (gônt′lit), *n.* 1 (in the Middle Ages) a stout, heavy glove with a wide, flaring cuff covering the wrist and lower part of the arm. Gauntlets, usually of leather covered with plates of iron or steel, were part of a knight's armor. 2 a stout, heavy glove with a wide, flaring cuff covering part of the arm.

throw down the gauntlet, to challenge.

gauss (gous), *n.* unit for measuring magnetic induction. ❑ *n., pl.* **gauss** or **gauss·es.**

gauze (gôz), *n.* a very thin, light cloth, easily seen through. Gauze is often used for bandages. —**gauze′like′,** *adj.*

gauz·y (gô′zē), *adj.* like gauze; thin and light as gauze: *a gauzy mist, gauzy wings.* ❑ *adj.* **gauz·i·er, gauz·i·est.**

gave (gāv), *v.* past tense of **give:** *She gave me some of her candy.*

gav·el (gav′əl), *n.* a small wooden hammer used in a meeting or in court to signal for attention or order or by an auctioneer to announce that the bidding is over: *The club's president rapped on the table twice with a gavel.*

ga·vi·al (ga′vē əl), *n.* a large reptile of southern Asia related and similar to the crocodile. It has a very slender long snout.

ga·votte (gə vot′), *n.* **1** an old French dance something like a minuet but much more lively. **2** the music for it.

Ga·wain (gə wān′ *or* gä′win), *n.* (in legends of the Middle Ages) one of the knights of the Round Table and nephew of King Arthur.

gawk (gôk), *v.* to stare idly, rudely, or stupidly.

gawk·y (gô′kē), *adj.* awkward; clumsy. ❑ *adj.* **gawk·i·er, gawk·i·est. –gawk′i·ly,** *adv.* **–gawk′i·ness,** *n.*

gay (gā), **1** *adj.* happy and full of fun; merry: *The children were cheerful and gay on the day of the first snowfall.* **2** *adj.* bright; showy: *a gay red scarf.* **3** *adj.* of or about homosexuals; homosexual. **4** *n.* a homosexual person, especially a male. **–gay′ness,** *n.*

gay·e·ty (gā′ə tē), *n.* gaiety. ❑ *n., pl.* **gay·e·ties.**

gay·ly (gā′lē), *adv.* gaily.

Ga·za Strip (gä′zə), area in W Palestine between Israel and the Mediterranean Sea.

gaze (gāz), **1** *v.* to look long and steadily: *For hours we sat gazing at the stars.* **2** *n.* a long, steady look. ■ See Synonym Study at **watch.** ❑ *v.* **gazed, gaz·ing. –gaz′er,** *n.*

ga·ze·bo (gə zē′bō), *n.* a light, open building, such as a pavilion or summerhouse, that overlooks a fine view. ❑ *n., pl.* **gaz·e·bos.**

ga·zelle (gə zel′), *n.* any of several small, swift, and graceful antelopes of Africa and Asia. ❑ *n., pl.* **ga·zelles** *or* **ga·zelle.**

ga·zette (gə zet′), **1** *n.* name used for certain newspapers: *the "Emporia Gazette."* **2** *n.* an official government journal containing lists of appointments, promotions, etc. [**Gazette** may come from an Italian word meaning "small coin." Gazettes can usually be bought for very little money.]

gaz·et·teer (gaz′ə tir′), *n.* dictionary of geographical names arranged alphabetically.

gaz·pa·cho (gäs pä′chō), *n.* soup made of raw chopped vegetables such as tomatoes, cucumbers, onions, and peppers, mixed with oil, vinegar, and spices, and served cold. ❑ *n., pl.* **gaz·pa·chos.**

G.B., Great Britain.

G clef, treble clef.

Gd, symbol for gadolinium.

Ge, symbol for germanium.

gear (gir), **1** *n.* wheel having teeth that fit into the teeth of another wheel, so that one wheel can turn the other. Gears pass motion from one part of a machine to another. **2** *n.* set of such wheels working together to transmit power or change the direction of motion in a machine. In a car, power is transmitted from the motor to the wheels by means of gears. **3** *v.* to connect by gears: *The motor is geared to the rear wheels of the car.* **4** *n.* any arrangement of gears or moving parts; mechanism; machinery: *The car ran off the road when the steering gear broke.* **5** *n.* equipment needed for some purpose: *camping gear.* **6** *v.* to make fit; adjust; adapt: *Auto production is geared to sales.*

in gear, with the gears connected so that power can be passed from the engine to the wheels of a motor vehicle.

out of gear, disconnected from the motor, etc.

shift gears, to change from one gear to another; connect a motor, etc., to a different set of gears.

gear·ing (gir′ing), *n.* set of gears, chains, or parts of machinery for transmitting motion or power; gear.

gear·shift (gir′shift′), *n.* device for connecting a motor to any of several sets of gears.

gear·wheel (gir′wēl′), *n.* cogwheel; gear.

geck·o (gek′ō), *n.* any of several small, harmless, insect-eating lizards with adhesive pads on their feet for climbing. Geckos can walk up walls and hang from ceilings. ❑ *n., pl.* **geck·os** *or* **geck·oes.**

GED or **GED test,** General Educational Development test (a test given by state departments of education to persons who have not completed high school). Passing this test entitles a person to a certificate of high school equivalency.

gee[1] (jē), **1** *interj.* word of command to horses or oxen directing them to turn to the right. **2** *v.* to turn to the right. ❑ *v.* **geed, gee·ing.**

gee[2] (jē), *interj.* exclamation or mild oath, used to express surprise or enthusiasm: *Gee, it's almost time for dinner.*

geese (gēs), *n.* plural of **goose.**

gee·zer (gē′zər), *n.* SLANG. an odd or strange man, especially an old one.

ge·fil·te fish (gə fil′tə), fish minced with bread crumbs, eggs, and seasoning, formed into balls or cakes and poached. It is usually served cold.

Geh·rig (ger′ig), *n.* **Lou** (lü), 1903-1941, American baseball player. ■ **Lou Gehrig** played 2130 consecutive games for the New York Yankees between 1925 and 1939. In 1939 he retired because of amyotrophic lateral sclerosis, which is often called Lou Gehrig's disease. He was elected to the Baseball Hall of Fame that same year

Gei·ger counter (gī′gər), device that detects and counts ionizing radiation. It is used to measure or detect radioactivity, cosmic-ray particles, etc.

Gei·sel (gī′zəl), *n.* **The·o·dor Seuss** (thē′ə dôr süs). See **Seuss, Dr.**

gei·sha (gā′shə *or* gē′shə), *n.* (in Japan) a young woman trained to be a professional entertainer. ❑ *n., pl.* **gei·sha** *or* **gei·shas.**

WORD STORY **Geisha** comes from Japanese words meaning "art" and "person." Geisha spend years learning the arts of dance, music, and conversation.

gel (jel), **1** *n.* any material that feels like jelly or that is formed like jelly from a substance containing many very tiny particles of another substance. When such materials harden, they may become rubbery, like jelly, or hard, like dried glue. A gel is a solid colloid. **2** *v.* to form a gel. Egg white gels when it is cooked. ❑ *v.* **gelled, gel·ling.** ■ Another word that sounds like this is **jell.**

gel·a·tin or **gel·a·tine** (jel′ə tən), *n.* **1** an odorless, tasteless substance like glue or jelly, obtained by boiling the bones, hoofs, and other tissues of animals. It is used in making jellied desserts, glue, film, etc. **2** any of various vegetable substances like this.

WORD STORY **Gelatin** comes from a Latin word meaning "to freeze." **Gelato** comes from the same word. Gelatin got its name because it grows solid when it gets cold, while gelato really is frozen.

ge·la·to (jə lä′tō), *n.* a soft, creamy, Italian ice cream. ❑ *n., pl.* **ge·la·ti** (jə lä′tē). [See Word Story at **gelatin.**]

geld·ing (gel′ding), *n.* a castrated horse or other animal.

gem (jem), *n.* **1** a precious or semiprecious stone, especially when cut and polished for ornament; jewel. Diamonds, rubies, and opals are gems. **2** someone or something that is very precious, beautiful, etc.: *The gem of the collection was a rare Persian stamp.*

Gem·i·ni (jem′ə nī), *n.* **1** a group of stars shaped something like twin heroes. **2** the third sign of the zodiac, associated with the period from mid-May to mid-June.

gems·bok (gemz′bok), *n.* a large antelope of southwestern Africa, with long, nearly straight horns and a long, tufted tail.

gem·stone (jem′stōn′), *n.* stone that can be cut and polished to make a gem.

Gen., General.

gen·darme (zhän′därm), *n.* member of the police in France and several other European countries who has had military training. ❑ *n., pl.* **gen·darmes** (zhän′därmz).

gemsbok—4 ft. 6 in. (1.4 m) high at the shoulder

gen·der (jen′dər), *n.* **1** a system of grouping words into certain classes, such as masculine, feminine, or neuter. In English, except in pronouns (*him, her, it*) and a few nouns with endings such as *-ess* (*actress*), gender is now indicated only by the meaning of the word: *man—woman, nephew—niece, rooster—hen.* **2** one of such classes. **3** sex: *the female gender.*

a	hat	ė	term	ô	order	ch	child	
ā	age	i	it	oi	oil	ng	long	a in about
ä	far	ī	ice	ou	out	sh	she	e in taken
â	care	o	hot	u	cup	th	thin	ə i in pencil
e	let	ō	open	ù	put	ŦH	then	o in lemon
ē	equal	ò	saw	ü	rule	zh	measure	u in circus

gene (jēn), *n.* a tiny part of a chromosome that controls the inheritance and development of a particular characteristic. Each chromosome contains many genes. The genes inherited from its parents determine what kind of plant or animal will develop from a fertilized egg cell.

WORD STORY **Gene** comes from a Greek word meaning "a breed." **Genealogy** comes from the same word plus **-logy.** Genes make members of a particular breed resemble their ancestors, and genealogy is the study of family ancestors.

ge·ne·a·log·i·cal (jē′nē ə loj′ə kəl), *adj.* of or about genealogy. A genealogical chart is called a family tree.

ge·ne·al·o·gist (jē′nē al′ə jist *or* jē′nē ol′ə jist), *n.* someone who makes a study of or traces genealogies.

ge·ne·al·o·gy (jē′nē al′ə jē *or* jē′nē ol′ə jē), *n.* **1** account of the descent of a person or family from an ancestor or ancestors. **2** descent of a person or family from an ancestor; pedigree. **3** study of family histories. ❑ *n., pl.* **ge·ne·al·o·gies** for 1. [See Word Story at **gene.**]

gene pool, all the genes of a particular species or a particular group within one species.

gen·er·a (jen′ər ə), *n.* a plural of **genus.**

gen·er·al (jen′ər əl), **1** *adj.* common to many or most; not limited to a few; widespread: *In our school there is a general interest in sports.* **2** *adj.* of all; for all; from all: *A government takes care of the general welfare.* **3** *adj.* not detailed: *The teacher gave us only general instructions.* **4** *adj.* not specialized: *The village had a general store that sold food, clothing, and hardware.* **5** *adj.* chief; of highest rank: *The Attorney General is the head of the Justice Department.* **6** *n.* any of several military ranks. See chart on page 712.

in general, for the most part; usually; commonly: *In general I don't like seafood, but this fish tastes very good.*

SYNONYM STUDY **General** and **universal** both mean in all cases. **General** suggests that there are few exceptions: *As a general rule, people wear lighter clothes in summer than in winter.* **Universal** suggests that there are no exceptions: *Doctors recommend universal immunization against many diseases.*

General Assembly, **1** legislature of certain states of the United States. **2** the main group of the United Nations, made up of delegates from every member nation.

general delivery, the part of a post office that handles the delivery of mail addressed to people who pick it up there: *I addressed the letter to Mary Smith, General Delivery, Springfield, Ohio.*

gen·er·al·i·ty (jen′ə ral′ə tē), *n.* **1** a general or vague statement; word or phrase not definite enough to have much meaning or value: *The candidates spoke in generalities; not once did they say what they would do if elected.* **2** a general principle or rule: *"Nothing happens without a cause" is a generality.* ❑ *n., pl.* **gen·er·al·i·ties.**

gen·er·al·i·za·tion (jen′ər ə lə zā′shən), *n.* a general idea, statement, principle, or rule: *"A rainbow appears when the sun shines after a shower" is a generalization.*

gen·er·al·ize (jen′ər ə līz), *v.* **1** to make into a general rule; conclude from particular facts: *If you know that cats, lions, leopards, and tigers eat meat, you can generalize that the cat family eats meat.* **2** to talk or write indefinitely or vaguely; use generalities: *The commentators generalized because they knew no details.* ❑ *v.* **gen·er·al·ized, gen·er·al·iz·ing. —gen′er·al·iz′er,** *n.*

gen·er·al·ly (jen′ər ə lē), *adv.* **1** in most cases; usually: *I am generally on time.* **2** for the most part; widely: *It was once generally believed that the earth is flat.* **3** in a general way; without giving details; not specially: *Generally speaking, it is coldest in January.*

general practitioner, physician who does not specialize in any single field of medicine.

general store, store, especially one in a rural area, that sells a wide variety of goods but is not divided into departments.

gen·er·ate (jen′ə rāt′), *v.* to cause to be; bring into being; produce: *Burning coal can generate steam. I couldn't generate any enthusiasm over the plan.* ❑ *v.* **gen·er·at·ed, gen·er·at·ing.**

gen·er·a·tion (jen′ə rā′shən), *n.* **1** all the people born about the same time. Your parents and their friends belong to one generation; you and your friends belong to the next generation. **2** about thirty years, or the time from the birth of one generation to the birth of the next generation. There are three generations in a century. **3** one step or degree in the descent of a family: *The picture showed four generations—great-grandmother, grandfather, mother, and baby.* **4** act of bringing into being; generating: *Steam and water power are used for the generation of electricity.*

generation gap, differences in attitudes and values between the people of one generation and those of the next.

gen·er·a·tive (jen′ər ə tiv), *adj.* **1** of or about the production of offspring. **2** having the power of producing.

gen·er·a·tor (jen′ər ə rā′tər), *n.* **1** machine that uses flowing water, steam, or other energy sources to produce electricity. It produces either direct or alternating current. **2** person or thing that generates.

ge·ner·ic (jə ner′ik), *adj.* **1** general; not specific or special: *"Liquid" is a generic term, but "milk" is a specific term.* **2** not sold under a trademark or brand name: *generic drugs.* **3** characteristic of a genus, kind, or class: *Cats and lions show generic differences.*

gen·er·os·i·ty (jen′ə ros′ə tē), *n.* **1** willingness to share with others; unselfishness: *That wealthy family is known for its generosity.* **2** nobleness of heart or of mind; willingness to forgive.

gen·er·ous (jen′ər əs), *adj.* **1** willing to share with others; unselfish: *a generous giver. Our teacher is always generous with his time.* **2** noble and forgiving; not mean: *He was generous in accepting their apology.* **3** large; plentiful: *a generous piece of pie.* **—gen′er·ous·ly,** *adv.*

SYNONYM STUDY **Generous** and **charitable** both mean willing to share. **Generous** suggests making personal gifts: *It's generous of her to lend me her bicycle while she's at camp.* **Charitable** suggests organized giving to people in need: *He does charitable work at the shelter for the homeless.*

gen·e·sis (jen′ə sis), *n.* origin; creation; coming into being: *the genesis of an idea.* ❑ *n., pl.* **gen·e·ses** (jen′ə sēz′).

Gen·e·sis (jen′ə sis), *n.* the first book of the Bible. Genesis contains the Bible story of the creation of the world.

gene-splic·ing (jēn′splī′sing), *n.* process or act of inserting a gene or genes from one living thing into the genes of another, so as to change physical characteristics of the second.

ge·net·ic (jə net′ik), *adj.* **1** of or about a gene or genes: *a genetic mutation.* **2** of genetics. **—ge·net′i·cal·ly,** *adv.*

genetic code, the various combinations of chemical compounds in a chromosome that determine the nature and effect of its genes.

genetic engineering, alteration of the genes of a living thing so as to change inherited features.

ge·net·i·cist (jə net′ə sist), *n.* an expert in genetics.

ge·net·ics (jə net′iks), *n.* branch of biology dealing with the principles of heredity and variation in living things.

Ge·ne·va (jə nē′və), *n.* **1** city in SW Switzerland. **2 Lake,** long, narrow lake in SW Switzerland and E France.

Gen·ghis Khan (jeng′gis kän′), 1162-1227, Mongol conqueror of central Asia. ■ **Genghis Khan** created the largest land empire in history. At his death, his empire reached from the Pacific Ocean to the Caspian Sea, and from Siberia to Tibet.

gen·ial (jē′nyəl), *adj.* **1** smiling and pleasant; cheerful and friendly; kindly: *She was glad to see us again and gave us a genial welcome.* **2** helping growth; pleasantly warming; comforting: *The south of France has a warm and genial climate.* **—gen′ial·ly,** *adv.*

Genghis Kahn

ge·ni·al·i·ty (jē′nē al′ə tē), *n.* genial quality or behavior.

ge·nie (jē′nē), *n.* an imaginary spirit that can take human form and do magical things: *When Aladdin rubbed his lamp, the genie came and did what Aladdin asked.*

gen·i·tal (jen′ə tǝl), *adj.* of or about reproduction or the sex organs.

genital herpes, a sexually transmitted disease caused by a virus and producing sores on the genitals.

gen·i·tals (jen′ə tǝlz), *n.pl.* the external sex organs.

gen·ius (jē′nyǝs), *n.* **1** very great natural power of mind: *Important discoveries are usually made by men and women of genius.* **2** person having such power: *Shakespeare was a genius.* **3** great natural ability: *to have a genius for composing music.* **4** person having such natural ability: *She is a genius at playing the violin.* **5** person who powerfully influences another: *Rasputin was Russia's evil genius.* ❑ *n., pl.* **gen·ius·es.**

Gen·o·a (jen′ō ǝ), *n.* port in NW Italy.

gen·o·cide (jen′ə sīd), *n.* the extermination of a cultural or racial group. —**gen′o·cid′al,** *adj.*

WORD STORY **Genocide** comes from Greek words meaning "a kind" and "a killing." The word was created in 1944 to describe Nazi murders of millions of Jews.

Gen·o·ese (jen′ō ēz′), **1** *adj.* of Genoa or its people. **2** *n.* person born or living in Genoa. ❑ *n., pl.* **Gen·o·ese.**

ge·nome (jē′nōm), *n.* the total genetic nature of a cell or living thing.

gen·o·type (jen′ə tīp), *n.* the genetic nature of a living thing, as distinguished from the way it looks.

gen·re (zhän′rǝ), *n.* a kind or sort, especially in art or literature: *Poe was an originator of the detective story genre.*

gent (jent), *n.* man.

gen·teel (jen tēl′), *adj.* **1** belonging or suited to polite society. **2** polite; well-bred; fashionable; elegant. **3** artificially polite and courteous. —**gen·teel′ly,** *adv.*

gen·tian (jen′shǝn), *n.* any of numerous plants with usually blue flowers and stemless leaves.

gen·tile or **Gen·tile** (jen′tīl), **1** *n.* person who is not a Jew. **2** *adj.* not Jewish.

gen·til·i·ty (jen til′ə tē), *n.* **1** gentle birth; being of good family and social position. **2** good manners; politeness; refinement: *The gracious couple greeted us with gentility.*

gen·tle (jen′tl), *adj.* **1** not severe, rough, or violent; mild: *A gentle, rocking motion put the baby to sleep.* **2** soft; low: *the gentle sound of a purring cat.* **3** not too much or too fast; not harsh or extreme; moderate: *gentle heat, a gentle slope.* **4** kindly; friendly: *a gentle disposition.* ■ See Synonym Study at **kind**[1]. **5** easily handled or managed: *a gentle horse.* **6** of good family and social position; wellborn. **7** having or showing good manners; refined; polite. ❑ *adj.* **gen·tler, gen·tlest.** [See word history information at **jaunty.**] —**gen′tle·ness,** *n.*

gen·tle·man (jen′tl mǝn), *n.* **1** man of good family and social position. **2** man having good manners: *A gentleman would not push into line ahead of others.* **3** a polite term for any man: *"Gentlemen" is often used in speaking or writing to a group of men.* ❑ *n., pl.* **gen·tle·men.** —**gen′tle·man·ly,** *adj.*

gentleman's agreement or **gentlemen's agreement,** an informal agreement that is not legally binding. The people or countries that make it are bound only by their promise.

gen·tle·wom·an (jen′tl wùm′ǝn), *n.* **1** woman of good family and social position. **2** a well-bred woman; lady. **3** a woman attendant of a lady of rank. ❑ *n., pl.* **gen·tle·wom·en.**

gent·ly (jent′lē), *adv.* **1** in a gentle way; tenderly; softly: *Handle the baby gently.* **2** gradually: *a gently sloping hillside.*

gen·try (jen′trē), *n.* people of good family and social position. The English gentry are next below the nobility.

gen·u·flect (jen′yǝ flekt), *v.* to bend the knee as an act of reverence or worship. —**gen′u·flec′tion,** *n.*

gen·u·ine (jen′yü ǝn), *adj.* **1** actually being what it seems or is claimed to be; real; true: *genuine leather.* **2** sincere; honest: *We felt genuine regret when our neighbors moved away.* —**gen′u·ine·ly,** *adv.* —**gen′u·ine·ness,** *n.*

ge·nus (jē′nǝs), *n.* group of related living things ranking below a family and above a species. ❑ *n., pl.* **gen·er·a** or **ge·nus·es.**

geo-, *prefix.* earth; of the earth: *geology = science of the earth.*

ge·o·cen·tric (jē′ō sen′trik), *adj.* **1** viewed or measured from the earth's center. **2** having or representing the earth as a center: *a geocentric universe.* —**ge′o·cen′tri·cal·ly,** *adv.*

ge·ode (jē′ōd), *n.* rock containing a cavity lined with crystals or other mineral matter.

ge·o·des·ic (jē′ǝ des′ik), **1** *adj.* geodetic. **2** *adj.* having a curve like the curvature of the earth. **3** *n.* the shortest line between two points on a surface.

geodesic dome, a dome in the shape of half a sphere, held up by a lightweight framework of connected triangles.

geodesic domes

ge·od·e·sy (jē od′ǝ sē), *n.* the part of mathematics that deals with the measurement of the earth and its gravity and with the location of points on the earth's surface.

ge·o·det·ic (jē′ǝ det′ik), *adj.* having to do with geodesy; geodesic. —**ge′o·det′i·cal·ly,** *adv.*

geog., **1** geographer. **2** geography.

ge·og·ra·pher (jē og′rǝ fǝr), *n.* an expert in geography.

ge·o·graph·ic (jē′ǝ graf′ik), *adj.* geographical.

ge·o·graph·i·cal (jē′ǝ graf′ǝ kǝl), *adj.* of geography. —**ge′o·graph′i·cal·ly,** *adv.*

ge·og·ra·phy (jē og′rǝ fē), *n.* **1** study of the earth's surface, climate, continents, countries, peoples, natural resources, industries, and products. **2** the surface features of a place or region: *the geography of New England.*

geol., geology.

ge·o·log·ic (jē′ǝ loj′ik), *adj.* geological.

ge·o·log·i·cal (jē′ǝ loj′ǝ kǝl), *adj.* of geology. —**ge′o·log′i·cal·ly,** *adv.*

ge·ol·o·gy (jē ol′ǝ jē), *n.* **1** science that deals with the composition of the earth or of other solid heavenly bodies, the processes that have formed them, and their history. **2** physical features of an area of the earth or of a solid heavenly body; rocks, rock formation, etc., of a particular area. —**ge·ol′o·gist,** *n.*

geom., **1** geometric. **2** geometry.

ge·o·met·ric (jē ǝ met′rik), *adj.* **1** of geometry; according to the principles of geometry: *geometric proof.* **2** consisting of straight lines, circles, triangles, etc.; regular and symmetrical. —**ge′o·met′ri·cal·ly,** *adv.*

ge·o·met·ri·cal (jē ǝ met′rǝ kǝl), *adj.* geometric.

geometric progression, sequence of numbers in which each number is multiplied by the same factor in order to obtain the following number. 2, 4, 8, 16, and 32 form a geometric progression.

ge·om·e·try (jē om′ǝ trē), *n.* branch of mathematics which studies the relationship of points, lines, angles, and surfaces of figures in space; the mathematics of space. Geometry includes the definition, comparison, and measurement of squares, triangles, circles, cubes, cones, spheres, and other plane and solid figures. [**Geometry** comes from Greek words meaning "earth" and "measure." Geometry developed in connection with surveying land.]

a	hat	ė	term	ô	order	ch	child		a in about
ā	age	i	it	oi	oil	ng	long		e in taken
ä	far	ī	ice	ou	out	sh	she	ǝ	i in pencil
â	care	o	hot	u	cup	th	thin		o in lemon
e	let	ō	open	ù	put	ᴛʜ	then		u in circus
ē	equal	ò	saw	ü	rule	zh	measure		

G

ge·o·phys·i·cal (jē′ō fiz′ə kəl), *adj.* of or concerning geophysics.

ge·o·phys·i·cist (jē′ō fiz′ə sist), *n.* an expert in geophysics.

ge·o·phys·ics (jē′ō fiz′iks), *n.* study of the relations between the features of the earth and the forces that change or produce them. Geophysics includes geology, meteorology, oceanography, and similar sciences.

ge·o·po·lit·i·cal (jē′ō pə lit′ə kəl), *adj.* of geopolitics.

ge·o·pol·i·tics (jē′ō pol′ə tiks), *n.* study of government and its policies as affected by physical geography.

George (jôrj), *n.* Saint, died A.D. 303?, Christian martyr, the patron saint of England.

> **WORD STORY** **George** comes from a Greek word meaning "farmer." **Georgia** (def. 2), the country, comes from the same word, because people there were farmers surrounded by nomadic herders.

George III, 1738-1820, king of Great Britain from 1760 to 1820. The Revolutionary War took place during his reign.

George·town (jôrj′toun′), *n.* port and capital of Guyana, on the Atlantic.

Geor·gia (jôr′jə), *n.* **1** one of the southeastern states of the United States. *Abbreviation:* GA or Ga. *Capital:* Atlanta. **2** country on the Black Sea, south of Russia. *Capital:* Tbilisi. [Georgia (def. 1) comes from George II, king of England when Georgia was founded as a colony.] **—Geor′gian,** *adj., n.*

ge·o·syn·cline (jē ō sing′klīn), *n.* a downward fold in the earth's crust, forming a trough or basin in which deep layers of sediment have accumulated.

ge·o·ther·mal (jē′ō thèr′məl), *adj.* of or produced by the internal heat of the earth: *geothermal energy.*

ge·ot·ro·pism (jē′ō trō′pizm), *n.* response by various parts of plants to gravity.

Ger., **1** German. **2** Germany.

ge·ra·ni·um (jə rā′nē əm), *n.* any of numerous plants with fragrant leaves and large clusters of showy red, pink, or white flowers. Some kinds are grown in pots for window plants.

ger·bil (jèr′bəl), *n.* any of numerous small desert rodents with long hind legs. Gerbils are used in scientific research and are kept as pets.

ger·i·at·ric (jer′ē at′rik), *adj.* of or about elderly people, old age, and geriatrics.

ger·i·at·rics (jer′ē at′riks), *n.* branch of medicine dealing with the study of the process of aging and the diseases and treatment of the aged.

germ (jèrm), *n.* **1** a microscopic living thing that causes disease: *the flu germ.* **2** the earliest form of a living thing; seed or bud; spore. **3** the beginning of anything; origin: *the germ of an idea.* **—germ′like′,** *adj.*

Ger·man (jèr′mən), **1** *adj.* of Germany, its people, or their language: *German culture.* **2** *n.* person born or living in Germany. **3** *n.* language of Germany, Austria, and part of Switzerland.

> **WORD SOURCE** **German** has given a number of words to the English language, including the words below.

accordion	frankfurter	plunder	waltz
blitz	hamster	poodle	wiener
dachshund	hex	poltergeist	yodel
delicatessen	kindergarten	snorkel	zither
fife	nickel		

ger·mane (jər mān′), *adj.* closely connected; to the point; pertinent: *Her statement is not germane to the discussion.*

Ger·man·ic (jər man′ik), *adj.* **1** German. **2** of the people of northwestern Europe, such as the Germans, Scandinavians, and English, and their languages. English, German, Dutch, and Swedish are Germanic languages. **3** Teutonic.

ger·ma·ni·um (jər mā′nē əm), *n.* a brittle, silver-white element which occurs in zinc ores. It has the properties of both a metal and a nonmetal and is used as a semiconductor in transistors. *Symbol:* Ge

German measles, a contagious disease resembling measles, but much less serious except in pregnant women; rubella.

German shepherd, a large, strong, intelligent dog first bred in Germany, often trained to work with soldiers and police or to guide blind persons; Alsatian; police dog.

Ger·ma·ny (jèr′mə nē), *n.* a country in central Europe. From 1949 to 1990 Germany was divided into West Germany and East Germany. *Capital:* Berlin.

German Shepherd—about 2 ft. (61 cm) high at the shoulder

germ cell, **1** an egg or sperm cell; gamete. **2** a cell from which an egg or sperm cell develops.

germ·free (jèrm′frē′), *adj.* free of living germs; sterile.

ger·mi·cide (jèr′mə sīd), *n.* any substance that kills germs. Disinfectants and fungicides are germicides. **—ger′mi·cid′al,** *adj.*

ger·mi·nate (jèr′mə nāt), *v.* to begin to grow or develop; sprout: *Seeds germinate when the soil is warm and moist.* ❑ *v.* **ger·mi·nat·ed, ger·mi·nat·ing. —ger′mi·na′tion,** *n.* **—ger′mi·na′tor,** *n.*

germ plasm, substance in germ cells that transmits hereditary characteristics to the offspring.

germ warfare, the spreading of germs to produce disease among the enemy in time of war.

Ge·ron·i·mo (jə ron′ə mō), *n.* 1829-1909, Apache leader. ■ Geronimo led attacks on soldiers and settlers in the southwestern United States and Mexico in the 1870s and 1880s. He escaped several times from reservations but surrendered in 1886.

ger·ry·man·der (jer′ē man′dər), **1** *v.* to arrange the political divisions of a state, county, etc., to give one political party an unfair advantage in elections. **2** *n.* act of gerrymandering.

> **WORD STORY** **Gerrymander** comes from Elbridge Gerry (ger′ē), an American politician, and **salamander.** While Gerry was governor of Massachusetts, his party changed the boundaries of the voting districts in the state. One district became so oddly shaped that it looked something like a salamander.

Gersh·win (gèrsh′wən), *n.* **George,** 1898-1937, American composer. ■ George Gershwin wrote many musical comedies and the opera *Porgy and Bess.* His best-known symphonic work is *Rhapsody in Blue.*

ger·und (jer′ənd), *n.* a verb form ending in *-ing* and used as a noun. In "Watching them carefully was hard work," *watching* is a gerund used as the subject of *was;* like a verb it takes an object *them* and is modified by an adverb *carefully.*

> **USAGE NOTE** **Gerunds** are forms of verbs that are used as nouns. In careful writing and speaking, gerunds, like nouns, are connected by possessive forms: *I was upset by his leaving early. We can't hear their singing.* In casual speech, possessive forms are often not used.

Ge·sta·po (gə stä′pō *or* gə shtä′pō), *n.* **1** a secret police force in Nazi Germany. **2 gestapo,** any group that is like the Gestapo in ruthless methods and determination. [Gestapo is an acronym formed from German words meaning "secret state police."]

ges·ta·tion (je stā′shən), *n.* **1** process of having young developing in the uterus; pregnancy. **2** period of pregnancy. **3** formation and development of a project, idea, plan, etc.

ges·tic·u·late (je stik′yə lāt), *v.* to make gestures to show ideas or feelings: *The excited speaker gesticulated by raising his arms and waving them.* ❑ *v.* **ges·tic·u·lat·ed, ges·tic·u·lat·ing.**

ges·tic·u·la·tion (je stik′yə lā′shən), *n.* **1** a lively or excited gesture. **2** act of making lively or excited gestures.

ges·ture (jes′chər), **1** *n.* movement of any part of the body to help express an idea or a feeling: *Speakers often make gestures with their hands to stress something that they are saying.* **2** *n.* anything said or done to impress or influence others: *Their refusal was merely a gesture; they really wanted to go.* **3** *v.* to make gestures; use gestures. ❑ *v.* **ges·tured, ges·tur·ing.**

get (get), *v.* **1** to come to have; obtain: *I got a new coat yesterday.* **2** to reach: *I got home early last night.* **3** to catch; get hold of: *I got the cat by one leg.* **4** to cause to be or do: *Get the windows open.* **5** to be; become: *get sick. Don't get nervous when you take the test.* **6** to persuade; influence: *Try to get them to come, too.* **7** to make ready; prepare: *Should I help them get dinner?* **8** to possess: *What have you got in your hand?* **9** to hit; strike: *The ball got the batter on the arm.* **10** to understand: *The teacher explained the math problem, but I still didn't get it.* ❏ *v.* **got, got** or **got·ten, get·ting.**

get about, 1 to go from place to place. **2** to become widely known.

get across, to make clear, understood, or appreciated: *He was a good speaker and got his ideas across quickly to the audience.*

get along with, be friendly with: *She gets along well with her classmates.*

get around, 1 to go from place to place: *The new roads will allow people to get around faster.* **2** to become widely known; spread. **3** to overcome: *He found the problem hard to get around.* **4** to deceive; trick: *You can't get around that child; she's too smart to be fooled.*

get around to, to make the time for: *They finally got around to cleaning the attic.*

get at, 1 to reach: *We could not get at the cat on the tree without a ladder.* **2** to find out.

get away, 1 to go away: *Let's get away from here.* **2** to escape: *The prisoner got away.*

get away with, to take or do something and escape safely: *get away with lying.*

get back, 1 to return. **2** to recover.

get back at, to take revenge on.

get by, 1 to pass: *Let me get by, I'm in a rush.* **2** not be noticed or caught. **3** to manage: *She has just enough money to get by.*

get in, 1 to go in. **2** to put in: *They kept talking, and I couldn't get in a word.* **3** to arrive: *Our train should get in at 9 p.m.*

get it, be scolded or punished.

get nowhere, to have no success in spite of much effort: *I spent all day in the library but got nowhere with my paper.*

get off, 1 to come down from or out of: *She got off the horse.* **2** to take off. **3** to escape punishment. **4** to help to escape punishment. **5** to start.

get off someone's back or **get off someone's case,** leave someone alone; stop criticizing or nagging someone: *I told her to get off my back about the dance decorations.*

get on, 1 to go up on or into: *I got on the train.* **2** to put on: *Get on your boots; it's snowing outside.* **3** to advance: *get on in years.* **4** to manage: *We can't get on without their help.* **5** to succeed: *How are you getting on in your new job?*

get out, 1 to go out: *Let's get out of here!* **2** to take out. **3** to go away. **4** to escape. **5** to help to escape. **6** to become known. **7** to publish.

get out of, 1 to escape. **2** to help to escape.

get over, to recover from.

get there, to succeed.

get through, to finish.

get to, be allowed to: *I got to stay up late last night.*

get together, 1 to bring or come together; meet; assemble. **2** to come to an agreement.

get up, 1 to arise: *They got up at six o'clock.* **2** to stand up.

get·a·way (get′ə wā′), *n.* **1** act of getting away; escape. **2** a start from a complete stop: *a racing car's fast getaway.*

Geth·sem·a·ne (geth sem′ə nē), *n.* (in the Bible) a garden near Jerusalem, the scene of Jesus' agony, betrayal, and arrest.

get-to·geth·er (get′tə geŦʜ′ər), *n.* an informal social gathering or party.

Get·tys·burg (get′ēz bėrg′), *n.* town in S Pennsylvania. An important battle of the Civil War was fought there.

Gettysburg Address, a brief speech given by President Lincoln on November 19, 1863, at the dedication of a national cemetery on the Civil War battlefield at Gettysburg.

get-up (get′up′), *n.* INFORMAL. dress or costume.

get-up-and-go (get′up′ən gō′), *n.* energy; initiative.

gew·gaw (gyü′gö), **1** *n.* a showy trifle; gaudy, useless ornament or toy; bauble. **2** *adj.* showy but trifling.

gey·ser (gī′zər), *n.* a spring that spouts a fountain or jet of hot water and steam into the air at regular intervals. There are many geysers in Yellowstone National Park.

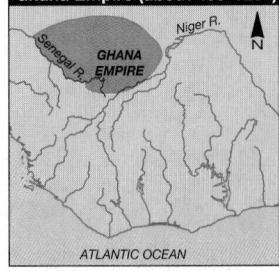
geyser

WORD STORY **Geyser** comes from an Icelandic word meaning "to gush." A well-known gushing spring in Iceland was named Geysir, and all geysers are named for it.

Gha·na (gä′nə), *n.* **1** country in W Africa. *Capital:* Accra. **2** **Ghana Empire,** a commercial empire controlling trade in a region north of modern Ghana, during the years between A.D. 400 and 1235.

Ghana Empire (about 400-1235)

Niger R. | N
Senegal R. | GHANA EMPIRE
ATLANTIC OCEAN

ghast·ly (gast′lē), *adj.* **1** causing terror; horrible; shocking: *Murder is a ghastly crime.* **2** very pale; like a ghost: *The sick man looked ghastly.* **3** very bad: *a ghastly failure.* ❏ *adj.* **ghast·li·er, ghast·li·est.** —**ghast′li·ness,** *n.*

gher·kin (gėr′kən), *n.* a small cucumber often used for pickles.

ghet·to (get′ō), *n.* **1** part of a city where any particular racial group or nationality lives. **2** (earlier) a part of a city in Europe where Jews were required to live. ❏ *n., pl.* **ghet·tos.**

ghost (gōst), *n.* **1** spirit of a dead person, supposed to appear to living people as a pale, dim, shadowy form: *The ghost of the murdered servant was said to haunt the house.* **2** anything pale, dim, or shadowy like a ghost: *Our team didn't have a ghost of a chance to win.* —**ghost′like′,** *adj.*

give up the ghost, to die.

ghost·ly (gōst′lē), *adj.* like a ghost; pale, dim, and shadowy: *A ghostly form.* ❏ *adj.* **ghost·li·er, ghost·li·est.** —**ghost′li·ness,** *n.*

ghost town, a once-flourishing town where nobody lives now.

ghost·writ·er (gōst′rī′tər), *n.* person who writes something for another person who pretends to be the author.

ghoul (gül), *n.* **1** (in Muslim legends) a demon that robs graves and feeds on corpses. **2** person who robs graves or corpses. **3** person who enjoys what is revolting, brutal, and horrible.

ghoul·ish (gü′lish), *adj.* like a ghoul; revolting, brutal, and horrible. —**ghoul′ish·ly,** *adv.* —**ghoul′ish·ness,** *n.*

GI or **G.I.** (jē′ī′), **1** *adj.* government issue: *GI shoes, GI socks.* **2** *adj.* of or for a member of the armed forces: *a GI loan.* **3** *n.* soldier in the U.S. Army; serviceman. ❏ *n., pl.* **GI's** or **G.I.'s** (jē′īz′).

Gi·a·co·met·ti (jä′kō met′ē), *n.* **Al·ber·to** (al bâr′tō), 1901-1966, Swiss sculptor and painter. He made many bronze statues with long, thin arms and legs.

a	hat	ė	term	ô	order	ch	child		
ā	age	i	it	oi	oil	ng	long		a in about
ä	far	ī	ice	ou	out	sh	she		e in taken
â	care	o	hot	u	cup	th	thin	ə	i in pencil
e	let	ō	open	u̇	put	Ŧʜ	then		o in lemon
ē	equal	ȯ	saw	ü	rule	zh	measure		u in circus

gi·ant (jī'ənt), **1** *n.* an imaginary being having human form, but larger and more powerful than a person. **2** *n.* someone or something of great size, strength, or importance. **3** *adj.* like a giant; huge: *a giant potato.*

giant panda, panda (def. 1).

giant sequoia, a very large evergreen tree of California; big tree. Though not as tall as the largest redwoods, giant sequoias are the most massive trees in the world, with trunks up to 100 feet (30 meters) around.

giant star, a very bright star of vast size, about 10 to 100 times as big as the sun.

gib·ber (jib'ər), *v.* to chatter senselessly; talk in a confused, meaningless way: *The monkeys gibbered angrily at each other.*

gib·ber·ish (jib'ər ish), *n.* senseless chatter; confused, meaningless talk or writing.

gib·bet (jib'it), **1** *n.* an upright post with an arm that sticks out at the top, from which the bodies of criminals were hung after execution. **2** *v.* to hang on a gibbet.

giant sequoia

gib·bon (gib'ən), *n.* any of several small apes of southeastern Asia and the East Indies with very long arms and no tail. Gibbons live in trees.

gib·bous (gib'əs), *adj.* (of the moon) more than half full but less than full. **—gib'bous·ly,** *adv.* **—gib'bous·ness,** *n.*

gibe (jīb), **1** *v.* to speak in a sneering way; jeer; scoff; sneer: *My family gibed at my efforts to paint a picture.* **2** *n.* a jeer; taunt; sneer: *Their gibes hurt her feelings.* ❑ *v.* **gibed, gib·ing.** Also, **jibe**[3]. **—gib'er,** *n.* **—gib'ing·ly,** *adv.*

gib·let (jib'lit), *n.* the heart, liver, or gizzard of a fowl.

Gi·bral·tar (jə brôl'tər), *n.* **1** seaport and fortress on the Mediterranean Sea, near the S tip of Spain. It is a British colony. **2 Rock of,** the large rock on which this fortress stands. **3 Strait of,** strait between Africa and Europe, connecting the Mediterranean Sea with the Atlantic.

gid·dap (gi dap' *or* gi dup'), *interj.* go! *"Giddap!" she said to her horse.*

gid·dy (gid'ē), *adj.* **1** having a whirling feeling in one's head; dizzy: *It makes me giddy to go on a merry-go-round.* **2** likely to make dizzy; causing dizziness: *a giddy ride on a roller coaster.* **3** never serious; frivolous; fickle: *That giddy crowd thinks only of parties.* ❑ *adj.* **gid·di·er, gid·di·est. —gid'di·ly,** *adv.* **—gid'di·ness,** *n.*

gid·dy·ap (gid'ē ap), *interj.* giddap.

gid·dy·up (gid'ē əp), *interj.* giddap.

gift (gift), *n.* **1** something given freely; present: *a birthday gift, the gift of a million dollars to a university.* **2** natural ability; special talent: *A great artist must have a gift for painting.*

gift·ed (gif'tid), *adj.* having natural ability or special talent; unusually able: *a gifted musician.*

gift-wrap (gift'rap'), *v.* to wrap a parcel or gift in fancy paper and with decorative trimmings. ❑ *v.* **gift-wrapped, gift-wrap·ping.**

gig[1] (gig), **1** *n.* a fish spear. **2** *v.* to spear fish with a gig. ❑ *v.* **gigged, gig·ging.**

gig[2] (gig), *n.* **1** a period of employment or a single performance of a jazz or rock group or solo entertainer: *Their next gig is Saturday night at Ye Olde Jazze Shoppe.* **2** any habitual work or interest: *She has a regular gig volunteering at the nature center.*

giga-, *prefix.* one billion: *gigabyte = one billion bytes.* [See Word Story at **gigantic**.]

gig·a·bit (gig'ə bit'), *n.* one billion bits, used as a measurement of computer storage capacity.

gig·a·byte (gig'ə bīt'), *n.* one billion bytes, used as a measurement of computer storage capacity. [See Word Story at **gigantic**.]

gi·gan·tic (jī gan'tik), *adj.* like a giant; huge: *An elephant is a gigantic animal.* **—gi·gan'ti·cal·ly,** *adv.*

WORD STORY **Gigantic** comes from a Greek word meaning "giant." **Gigabyte** comes from the same Greek word and **byte.** Science uses *giga-* to mean "a billion" because that amount, like a giant, is very large. **Gigantic** came into English about 400 years ago, and it is pronounced with a *j* sound as it was then. Science words with *giga-* are more commonly pronounced with *g* sounds, because they look as if they should be. In fact, the Greek word was pronounced with *g* sounds, too.

gig·gle (gig'əl), **1** *v.* to laugh in a silly or uncontrolled way. ■ See Synonym Study at **laugh. 2** *n.* a silly or uncontrolled laugh. ❑ *v.* **gig·gled, gig·gling. —gig'gler,** *n.* **—gig'gling·ly,** *adv.*

Gi·la monster (hē'lə), a large, poisonous lizard of the southwestern United States and northern Mexico. It has a thick tail and a heavy, clumsy body, and it is covered with beadlike, orange and black scales.

Gil·bert (gil'bərt), *n.* Sir **William,** 1836-1911, English playwright and poet. He is best known for the comic operettas he created with Sir Arthur Sullivan.

gild (gild), *v.* **1** to cover with a thin layer of gold or similar material; make golden. **2** to make something look bright and pleasing. **3** to make something seem better than it is. ❑ *v.* **gild·ed** or **gilt, gild·ing.** ■ Another word that sounds like this is **guild.**

gill (gil), *n.* an organ in fish, tadpoles, crabs, etc., formed of thin membranes. Oxygen passes in and carbon dioxide passes out through the thin walls of the gills.

Gil·les·pie (gə les'pē), *n.* **Diz·zy** (diz'ē), 1917-1993, American jazz trumpeter, composer, and bandleader.

Gil·man (gil'mən), *n.* **Char·lotte Per·kins** (shar'lət pėr'kənz), 1860-1935, American writer and reformer. She encouraged women to work in offices, stores, and factories.

gilt (gilt), **1** *n.* a thin layer of gold or similar material with which a surface is gilded: *The gilt is coming off this frame.* **2** *adj.* gilded: *a gilt sword.* **3** *v.* a past tense and a past participle of **gild.** ■ Another word that sounds like this is **guilt.**

gim·crack (jim'krak'), *n.* a showy, useless trifle; knickknack.

gim·let (gim'lit), *n.* a small tool with a screw point, for boring holes.

gim·mick (gim'ik), *n.* a clever or tricky idea, stunt, or device.

gin[1] (jin), *n.* a strong alcoholic drink, distilled from grain and usually flavored with juniper berries.

gin[2] (jin), **1** *n.* cotton gin. **2** *v.* to separate cotton from its seeds. ❑ *v.* **ginned, gin·ning. —gin'ner,** *n.*

gin[3] (jin), *n.* gin rummy.

gin·ger (jin'jər), *n.* **1** spice made from the root of a tropical plant. The root is often preserved in syrup or candied. **2** liveliness; energy.

ginger ale, a bubbling nonalcoholic drink flavored with ginger.

ginger beer, drink similar to ginger ale, but made with fermenting ginger.

gin·ger·bread (jin'jər bred'), **1** *n.* cake flavored with ginger and sweetened with molasses. Gingerbread is often made in fancy shapes. **2** *n.* something showy and elaborate; tasteless ornamentation. Cheap carvings glued on furniture are gingerbread.

gin·ger·ly (jin'jər lē), **1** *adv.* with extreme care or caution. **2** *adj.* extremely cautious or wary. **—gin'ger·li·ness,** *n.*

gin·ger·snap (jin'jər snap'), *n.* a thin, crisp cookie flavored with ginger and sweetened with molasses.

ging·ham (ging'əm), *n.* a cotton cloth made from colored threads. Its patterns are usually in stripes, plaids, or checks. [**Gingham** comes from a Malay word meaning "here and there." The word also means "striped," because stripes alternate colors.]

gin·gi·vi·tis (jin'jə vī'tis), *n.* inflammation of the gums.

gink·go (ging'kō), *n.* a large ornamental tree with fan-shaped leaves and nuts that can be eaten. ❑ *n., pl.* **gink·goes.**

gin rummy, a card game like rummy, usually for two players.

Gins·berg (ginz'bėrg), *n.* **Allen,** born 1926, American poet. His two best-known poems are "Kaddish" and "Howl."

Gins·burg (ginz'bėrg'), *n.* **Ruth Ba·der** (bā'dər), born 1933, U.S. Supreme Court justice, appointed in 1993.

gin·seng (jin′seng), *n.* a plant of China and North America, with a thick, branched root much used in Chinese medicine.

Giot·to (jot′ō), *n.* 1266?-1337, Italian painter and architect. His works begin the Renaissance in painting.

Gip·sy or **gip·sy** (jip′sē), *adj., n.* Gypsy. ❑ *n., pl.* **Gip·sies** or **gip·sies**.

gi·raffe (jə raf′), *n.* a large African mammal that chews its cud and has hoofs, a very long neck, long legs, and a spotted skin. Giraffes are the tallest living animals.

gird (gėrd), *v.* **1** to fasten with a belt, cord, etc.: *gird on your sword.* **2** to surround; enclose. **3** to get ready: *She girded herself to face the final examination.* ❑ *v.* **gird·ed** or **girt, gird·ing.**

gird·er (gėr′dər), *n.* a horizontal beam of steel, concrete, or wood, used as a main support. The weight of a floor is usually supported by girders. A tall building or big bridge often has steel girders for its frame.

gir·dle (gėr′dl), **1** *n.* a tight-fitting undergarment covering the waist and hips, which shapes and supports the body. **2** *n.* belt, sash, cord, etc., worn around the waist. **3** *n.* anything that surrounds or encloses: *a girdle of trees around the pond.* **4** *v.* to put a girdle on or around. **5** *v.* to surround; encircle: *Wide roads girdle the city.* **6** *v.* to cut away the bark so as to make a ring around a tree, branch, etc. ❑ *v.* **gir·dled, gir·dling. —gir′dler,** *n.*

girl (gėrl), *n.* **1** a female child from birth to about eighteen. **2** a young, unmarried woman. **3** a female servant. ■ This meaning of **girl** is often considered offensive. **4** sweetheart. **5** INFORMAL. woman.

girl·friend (gėrl′frend′), *n.* **1** sweetheart or steady female companion. **2** a female friend.

Girl Guides, (in Canada) organization for girls to develop character, citizenship, usefulness to others, and various skills.

girl·hood (gėrl′hůd), *n.* time of being a girl.

girl·ish (gėr′lish), *adj.* **1** of a girl. **2** like a girl. **3** like a girl's; suitable for a girl. **—girl′ish·ly,** *adv.* **—girl′ish·ness,** *n.*

girl scout, member of the Girl Scouts.

Girl Scouts, organization for girls to develop character, citizenship, usefulness to others, and various skills.

girt (gėrt), *v.* OLD USE. a past tense and a past participle of **gird.**

girth (gėrth), *n.* **1** the measure around anything: *a man of large girth, the girth of a tree.* **2** strap or band that keeps a saddle, pack, etc., in place on a horse's back.

gist (jist), *n.* the essential meaning; real point; main idea: *The gist of the discussion was that we should build a new school.*

give (giv), **1** *v.* to hand over as a gift; make a present of: *My parents gave me ice skates for my birthday.* **2** *v.* to hand over: *Give me that pencil.* **3** *v.* to hand over in return for something; pay: *She gave three dollars for the wagon.* **4** *v.* to let have; cause to have: *She gave us permission to go. Don't give me any trouble.* **5** *v.* to deal; administer: *give medicine, give hard blows.* **6** *v.* to offer; present: *give a lecture. This newspaper gives a full story of the game.* **7** *v.* to put forth; utter: *He gave a cry of pain.* **8** *v.* to yield; furnish; supply: *Lamps give light.* **9** *v.* to yield to force: *The lock gave when they pushed hard against the door.* **10** *n.* flexibility; yielding to force. ❑ *v.* **gave, giv·en, giv·ing. —giv′er,** *n.*

give away, 1 to give as a present: *He gave away his best toy.* **2** to present a bride to a bridegroom at a wedding. **3** to cause to be known; reveal; betray: *The spy gave away secrets to the enemy.*

give back, to return: *Give back the book.*

give in, to surrender; yield under pressure; admit defeat: *A stubborn person will not give in easily even when wrong.*

give it to, INFORMAL. to punish or scold.

give off, to send out; put forth: *This lamp gives off a bright light.*

give out, 1 to send out; put forth. **2** to distribute: *The supplies will be given out tomorrow.* **3** to make known: *Who has given out this information?* **4** to become used up or worn out: *My strength gave out after the long climb.*

give up, 1 to have no more hope for. **2** to stop having or doing:

We gave up the search when it got dark. **3** to stop trying: *Don't give up so soon.* **4** to hand over; deliver; surrender.

give-and-take (giv′ən tāk′), *n.* **1** an even or fair exchange. **2** good-natured banter; exchange of talk.

give·a·way (giv′ə wā′), *n.* **1** something revealed or made known unintentionally. **2** something given away or sold at a cheap price to promote business or good relations.

giv·en (giv′ən), **1** *adj.* fixed; specified: *You must finish the test in a given time.* **2** *adj.* having a fondness or habit; inclined; disposed: *A braggart is given to boasting.* **3** *v.* past participle of **give:** *That book was given to me.*

given name, name given to a person in addition to a family name. *Judith is the given name of Judith Stein.*

giz·mo (giz′mō), *n.* INFORMAL. a gadget; device. ❑ *n., pl.* **giz·mos.**

giz·zard (giz′ərd), *n.* a bird's second stomach, where the food from the first stomach is ground up. The gizzard usually contains bits of sand or gravel.

Gk., Greek.

gla·cial (glā′shəl), *adj.* **1** of ice or glaciers; having much ice or many glaciers. **2** like ice; very cold; icy. **—gla′cial·ly,** *adv.*

gla·cier (glā′shər), *n.* a great mass of ice moving very slowly down a mountain or along a valley, or spreading very slowly over a land area. Glaciers are formed from snow on high ground wherever winter snowfall exceeds summer melting for many years.

Glacier Bay National Park, a national park in SE Alaska, containing sea and land previously covered by nearby glaciers.

Glacier Bay National Park

Glacier National Park, a national park in NW Montana, containing part of the Rocky Mountains and more than 50 glaciers.

glad (glad), *adj.* **1** feeling joy, pleasure, or satisfaction; happy; pleased: *I am glad to see you.* ■ See Synonym Study at **happy. 2** bringing joy; pleasant: *The glad news pleased us.* **3** willing; ready: *I will be glad to go if you need me.* ❑ *adj.* **glad·der, glad·dest. —glad′ly,** *adv.* **—glad′ness,** *n.*

glad·den (glad′n), *v.* to make or become glad.

glade (glād), *n.* a little open meadow in a wood or forest. [See Word Story at **Everglades.**]

glad·i·a·tor (glad′ē ā′tər), *n.* captive, enslaved person, or professional fighter who fought at the public shows in the arenas in ancient Rome.

glad·i·o·la (glad′ē ō′lə), *n.* gladiolus. ❑ *n., pl.* **glad·i·o·las.**

a	hat	ė	term	ô	order	ch	child		
ā	age	i	it	oi	oil	ng	long		a in about
ä	far	ī	ice	ou	out	sh	she		e in taken
â	care	o	hot	u	cup	th	thin	ə	i in pencil
e	let	ō	open	ů	put	ŦH	then		o in lemon
ē	equal	ò	saw	ü	rule	zh	measure		u in circus

glad·i·o·lus (glad′ē ō′ləs), *n.* any of several plants that grow from bulblike, underground stems and have sword-shaped leaves and spikes of large, handsome flowers in various colors; gladiola. ❑ *n., pl.* **glad·i·o·li** (glad′ē ō′lē *or* glad′ē ō′lī), **glad·i·o·lus**, **glad·i·o·lus·es**. [See Word Story at **gladiator**.]

glam·or (glam′ər), *n.* glamour.

glam·or·ize (glam′ə rīz′), *v.* to make someone or something glamorous. ❑ *v.* **glam·or·ized**, **glam·or·iz·ing**.

glam·or·ous (glam′ər əs), *adj.* full of glamour; fascinating; charming: *a glamorous job in a foreign city.* **—glam′or·ous·ly,** *adv.* **—glam′or·ous·ness,** *n.*

glam·our (glam′ər), *n.* mysterious fascination; alluring charm; magic attraction: *the glamour of circus life.* Also, **glamor.**

WORD STORY **Glamour** is a Scottish pronunciation of **grammar.** During the Middle Ages, few people could read or write, and scholars who understood grammar were suspected of having magical powers.

glance (glans), **1** *n.* a quick look: *She gave him only a glance.* **2** *v.* to look quickly: *He glanced out the window to see if the rain had stopped.* **3** *v.* to hit and go off at a slant: *The spear glanced against the wall and missed the target.* ❑ *v.* **glanced**, **glanc·ing**. [**Glance** comes from a Latin word meaning "ice." When you glance at something, your eyes slide over it, like feet do on ice.]

gland (gland), *n.* any organ in the body that produces a substance for use in the body or to be discharged from the body. The salivary glands make saliva. The liver, the kidneys, the pancreas, and the thyroid are glands. **—gland′like′,** *adj.*

glan·du·lar (glan′jə lər), *adj.* of or like a gland; having glands; made of glands. **—glan′du·lar·ly,** *adv.*

glare (glâr), **1** *n.* a strong, bright light; light that shines so brightly that it hurts the eyes. **2** *v.* to give off a strong, bright light; shine so brightly as to hurt the eyes. **3** *n.* a bright, smooth surface. **4** *adj.* bright and smooth. **5** *n.* a fierce, angry stare. **6** *v.* to stare fiercely and angrily. ❑ *v.* **glared**, **glar·ing**.

glar·ing (glâr′ing), *adj.* **1** very bright; shining so brightly that it hurts the eyes; dazzling. **2** staring fiercely and angrily. **3** too bright and showy: *a shirt with glaring colors.* **4** very easily seen; conspicuous: *a glaring error in spelling.* **—glar′ing·ly,** *adv.*

Glas·gow (glas′gō *or* glas′kō), *n.* port and largest city in Scotland. [**Glasgow** is said to come from a Gaelic word meaning "dear green place."]

glas·nost (glaz′nost *or* gläz′nost), *n.* policy late in the history of the former Soviet Union permitting open public discussion of politics and the economy.

glass (glas), **1** *n.* a hard substance that breaks easily and can usually be seen through. It is made by melting sand with soda, potash, lime, or other substances. Windows are made of glass. **2** *n.* container to drink from made of glass: *I filled the glass with water.* **3** *n.* amount a glass can hold: *drink a glass of water* **4** *n.* mirror: *Look at yourself in the glass.* **5** *n.* lens, telescope, thermometer, windowpane, or other thing made of glass. **6** *n.pl.* **glasses,** eyeglasses. **7** *adj.* made of glass: *a glass dish.* **8** *v.* to cover or protect with glass. ❑ *n., pl.* **glass·es.** **—glass′like′,** *adj.*

glass blowing, art or process of shaping glass objects by blowing air from the mouth through a tube into a blob of molten glass at the other end of the tube. **—glass blower.**

glass·ful (glas′fùl), *n.* as much as a glass holds. ❑ *n., pl.* **glass·fuls.**

glass snake, any of several limbless, snakelike lizards with tails that break off easily.

glass·ware (glas′wâr′), *n.* articles made of glass.

glass·y (glas′ē), *adj.* **1** like glass; smooth; easily seen through: *With no wind, the small pond had a glassy surface.* **2** having a fixed, stupid stare: *glassy eyes.* ❑ *adj.* **glass·i·er**, **glass·i·est.** **—glass′i·ly,** *adv.* **—glass′i·ness,** *n.*

glau·co·ma (glô kō′mə), *n.* disease of the eye common in old age in which increasing internal pressure causes damage resulting in a gradual loss of sight.

glaze (glāz), **1** *v.* to put glass in; cover with glass. Pieces of glass cut to the right size are used to glaze windows and picture frames. **2** *n.* a smooth, glossy surface or coating: *the glaze on a*

china cup. **3** *n.* substance used to make such a surface or coating on things. **4** *v.* to cover with a shiny, smooth coating: *The pottery is glazed at the factory.* **5** *v.* to become shiny: *glazed with fever.* ❑ *v.* **glazed**, **glaz·ing**. **—glaz′er,** *n.*

gla·zier (glā′zhər), *n.* person whose work is putting glass in windows, picture frames, etc.

gleam (glēm), **1** *n.* a flash or beam of light: *We saw the gleam of headlights through the rain.* **2** *v.* to flash or beam with light: *The car's headlights gleamed through the rain.* **3** *n.* a short or faint light: *the gleam of a candle.* **4** *v.* to send out a short or faint light: *A candle gleamed in the dark.* **5** *n.* a short appearance; faint show: *a gleam of hope.*

glean (glēn), *v.* **1** to gather little by little: *I was able to glean some information from each book.* **2** to gather grain left on a field by reapers. **—glean′er,** *n.*

glee (glē), *n.* a feeling of lively joy; great delight: *They laughed with glee at the clown's antics.* ■ See Synonym Study at **joy.**

glee club, group organized for singing songs.

glee·ful (glē′fəl), *adj.* filled with glee; merry; joyous. **—glee′ful·ly,** *adv.* **—glee′ful·ness,** *n.*

glen (glen), *n.* a small, narrow valley.

Glen·dale (glen′dāl), *n.* city in central Arizona.

Glenn (glen), *n.* **John,** born 1921, American astronaut and political leader. He was the first American to orbit the earth, in 1962.

glib (glib), *adj.* speaking or spoken too smoothly and easily, without sufficient thought: *No one believed their glib excuses.* ❑ *adj.* **glib·ber**, **glib·best.** **—glib′ly,** *adv.* **—glib′ness,** *n.*

glide (glīd), **1** *v.* to move along smoothly, evenly, and easily: *Birds, ships, dancers, and skaters glide.* ■ See Synonym Study at **slide.** **2** *n.* a smooth, even, easy movement. **3** *v.* to pass gradually, quietly, or without being noticed: *The years glided past.* **4** *v.* to come down slowly at a slant without using a motor. **5** *n.* act of coming down in this way. ❑ *v.* **glid·ed**, **glid·ing**.

glid·er (glī′dər), *n.* **1** aircraft without an engine. Rising air currents keep it up in the air. **2** a swinging seat suspended on a frame. Gliders are usually placed on porches or outdoors.

glider (def. 1)

glim·mer (glim′ər), **1** *n.* a faint, unsteady light. **2** *v.* to shine with a faint, unsteady light: *The candle glimmered and went out.* **3** *n.* a faint idea or feeling: *a glimmer of hope.*

glimpse (glimps), **1** *n.* a short, quick view or look: *I caught a glimpse of the falls as our train went by.* **2** *v.* to catch a short, quick view of: *I glimpsed the falls as our train went by.* ■ See Synonym Study at **see**[1]. **3** *n.* a short, faint appearance: *There was a glimpse of truth in what they said.* ❑ *v.* **glimpsed**, **glimps·ing**.

glint (glint), **1** *n.* a gleam; flash: *The glint in her eye showed that she was angry.* **2** *v.* to gleam; flash.

glis·san·do (gli sän′dō), *n.* (in music) part performed with a gliding effect. A pianist plays a glissando by running one finger rapidly over the white keys or the black keys on a piano. ❑ *n., pl.* **glis·san·dos**, **glis·san·di** (gli sän′dē).

glis·ten (glis′n), *v.* to shine because wet or as if wet: *stones glistening in the stream, pearls glistening in candlelight.* ■ See Synonym Study at **shine.**

glitch (glich), *n.* any sudden, unexpected malfunction, technical difficulty, or mishap: *a computer glitch.* ❑ *n., pl.* **glitch·es.** [**Glitch** comes from a Yiddish word meaning "a slip" or "a skid." When something develops a glitch, it's as if it slips out of the way.]

glit·ter (glit′ər), **1** *v.* to shine with a bright, sparkling light: *The jewels glittered.* **2** *n.* a bright, sparkling light: *The glitter of the harsh lights hurt my eyes.* **3** *n.* tiny, sparkling objects such as tinsel or spangles, used for decoration. **4** *v.* to be bright and showy. **5** *n.* brightness; showiness.

glitter (defs. 1 and 2)

glit·ter·y (glit′ər ē), *adj.* glittering.

glitz (glits), *n.* showiness; flashiness; glitter: *the glitz of a national beauty contest.*

glitz·y (glit′sē), *adj.* flashy; gaudy; showy: *a glitzy new hotel.*

gloam·ing (glō′ming), *n.* evening twilight; dusk.

gloat (glōt), *v.* to think about or gaze at with great satisfaction: *She gloated over her success. The miser gloated over his gold.* —**gloat′er**, *n.* —**gloat′ing·ly**, *adv.*

glob (glob), *n.* a shapeless mass; blob.

glob·al (glō′bəl), *adj.* of the earth as a whole; worldwide: *the threat of global war.* —**glob′al·ly**, *adv.*

global warming, possible warming of the earth's atmosphere, which could result in worldwide changes in climate. Global warming is believed to be caused by the greenhouse effect.

globe (glōb), *n.* **1** anything round like a ball; sphere. ■ See Synonym Study at **ball**[1]. **2** the earth; world. **3** sphere with a map of the earth or sky on it. **4** anything rounded like a globe. An electric light bulb is a globe.

glob·u·lar (glob′yə lər), *adj.* **1** shaped like a globe or globule; round; spherical. **2** made up of globules.

glob·ule (glob′yül), *n.* a very small sphere or ball; tiny drop: *Globules of sweat stood out on the worker's forehead.*

glob·u·lin (glob′yə lən), *n.* any of several similar proteins found in plant and animal tissue, and in humans mainly in blood. Some globulins are important to the immune system.

glock·en·spiel (glok′ən spēl′), *n.* a percussion instrument made up of a series of tuned metal bells, bars, or tubes mounted in a frame and played by striking with two little hammers. [Glockenspiel comes from German words meaning "bells" and "to play."]

gloom (glüm), *n.* **1** deep shadow; darkness; dimness. **2** dark thoughts and feelings; low spirits; sadness.

gloom·y (glü′mē), *adj.* **1** dark; dim: *a gloomy winter day.* **2** in low spirits; sad; melancholy: *a gloomy mood.* **3** causing low spirits; discouraging; dismal: *a gloomy scene of poverty.* ❑ *adj.* **gloom·i·er, gloom·i·est.** —**gloom′i·ly**, *adv.* —**gloom′i·ness**, *n.*

glop (glop), *n.* INFORMAL. any thick, soft, sloppy, or gluelike substance or material: *We couldn't get all the glop off our shoes.*

Glo·ri·a (glôr′ē ə), *n.* **1** song of praise to God. **2** the music for it. ❑ *n., pl.* **Glo·ri·as.**

glo·ri·fy (glôr′ə fī), *v.* **1** to give glory to; make glorious: *glorify a hero or a saint.* **2** to praise; worship: *singing hymns to glorify God.* **3** to make more beautiful or splendid than it usually appears: *The sunset glorified the valley.* ❑ *v.* **glo·ri·fied, glo·ri·fy·ing.** —**glo′ri·fi·ca′tion**, *n.* —**glo′ri·fi′er**, *n.*

glo·ri·ous (glôr′ē əs), *adj.* **1** having or deserving glory; illustrious. **2** giving glory: *a glorious victory.* **3** magnificent; splendid: *a glorious day.* —**glo′ri·ous·ly**, *adv.* —**glo′ri·ous·ness**, *n.*

glo·ry (glôr′ē), **1** *n.* great praise and honor given to someone or something by others; fame: *The heroic act won her glory.* **2** *n.* something that brings praise and honor; source of pride and joy: *America's great men and women are its glory.* **3** *n.* adoring praise and thanksgiving: *"Glory be to God on high!"* **4** *v.* to be proud; rejoice: *The teachers gloried in their classes' achievements.* **5** *n.* brightness; splendor: *the glory of the royal palace.* **6** *n.* condition of greatest magnificence, splendor, or prosperity: *The British Empire reached its greatest glory in the 1800s, during the reign of Queen Victoria.* **7** *n.* heaven. ❑ *n., pl.* **glo·ries;** *v.* **glo·ried, glo·ry·ing.** —**glo′ry·ing·ly**, *adv.*

in your glory, having your greatest satisfaction or enjoyment: *He is in his glory when he can perform before an audience.*

gloss (glôs), **1** *n.* a smooth, shiny surface; luster: *Varnished furniture has a gloss.* **2** *v.* to put a smooth, shiny surface on. **3** *n.* an outward appearance or surface that covers something bad or wrong underneath. ❑ *n., pl.* **gloss·es.** —**gloss′er**, *n.* —**gloss′less**, *adj.*

gloss over, to make something seem right even though it is really wrong; smooth over: *They tried to gloss over their mistakes.*

glos·sar·y (glos′ər ē), *n.* list of special, technical, or hard words, usually in alphabetical order, with explanations or comments: *a glossary of terms used in chemistry. Textbooks sometimes have glossaries at the end.* ❑ *n., pl.* **glos·sar·ies.**

> **WORD STORY** **Glossary** comes from a Greek word meaning "tongue." As we do now, the Greeks used the word *tongue* to mean "a language." Someone who uses a word from a foreign language needs to explain its meaning, and so the Greek word came to mean "an explanation" of hard words.

gloss·y (glô′sē), *adj.* smooth and shiny. ❑ *adj.* **gloss·i·er, gloss·i·est.** —**gloss′i·ly**, *adv.* —**gloss′i·ness**, *n.*

glove (gluv), **1** *n.* a covering for the hand, usually with separate places for each of the four fingers and the thumb. Gloves are worn to keep the hands warm or clean. Boxers and baseball, handball, and hockey players use specially padded gloves for protection. **2** *v.* to catch a baseball, puck, etc., in a glove. ❑ *v.* **gloved, glov·ing.** —**glove′like′**, *adj.*

glove compartment, small compartment built into a car dashboard, used for storing maps and various small items.

glow (glō), **1** *v.* to shine because of heat; be red-hot or white-hot: *Embers glowed in the fireplace after the fire had died down.* ■ See Synonym Study at **shine**. **2** *n.* the shine from something that is red-hot or white-hot: *the glow of embers in the fireplace.* **3** *n.* a similar shine without heat: *the glow of gold.* **4** *v.* to give off light without heat: *The cat's eyes glowed in the dark.* **5** *n.* a bright, warm color; brightness: *the glow of sunset.* **6** *n.* the warm feeling or color of the body: *the glow of health on her cheeks.* **7** *v.* to show a warm color; look warm; be red or bright: *His cheeks glowed as he skated.* **8** *n.* an eager look on the face: *a glow of excitement.* **9** *v.* to look or be eager: *Their eyes glowed at the thought of a trip.* **10** *n.* warmth of feeling or passion; ardor: *The team was filled with the glow of success.*

glow·er (glou′ər), **1** *v.* to stare angrily; scowl fiercely. **2** *n.* an angry stare; fierce scowl. —**glow′er·ing·ly**, *adv.*

glow·worm (glō′wėrm′), *n.* any insect larva or insect that glows in the dark. Fireflies develop from some glowworms.

glu·cose (glü′kōs), *n.* **1** a kind of sugar found in the tissues of most living things. Blood sugar is mostly glucose. Glucose is not as sweet as table sugar. **2** syrup made from starch. [Glucose comes from a Greek word meaning "sweet wine."]

glue (glü), **1** *n.* substance used to stick things together, made by boiling the hoofs, skins, and bones of animals in water. **2** *n.* any similar sticky substance made of casein, rubber, etc.; adhesive. **3** *v.* to stick together with glue. **4** *v.* to fasten tightly; attach firmly: *Her hands were glued to the steering wheel as she drove down the dangerous mountain road.* ❑ *v.* **glued, glu·ing.** —**glue′like′**, *adj.* —**glu′er**, *n.*

a	hat	ė	term	ô	order	ch	child		a in about
ā	age	i	it	oi	oil	ng	long		e in taken
ä	far	ī	ice	ou	out	sh	she	ə	i in pencil
â	care	o	hot	u	cup	th	thin		o in lemon
e	let	ō	open	ù	put	ŦH	then		u in circus
ē	equal	ò	saw	ü	rule	zh	measure		

glum (glum), *adj.* gloomy; dismal; sullen: *I felt very glum when my friend moved away.* ❑ *adj.* **glum·mer, glum·mest. —glum′ly,** *adv.* **—glum′ness,** *n.*

glut (glut), **1** *v.* to fill full; feed or satisfy fully: *The children glutted themselves with cake.* **2** *v.* to supply more than there is a demand for: *The prices for wheat dropped when the market was glutted with it.* **3** *n.* too great a supply. ❑ *v.* **glut·ted, glut·ting. —glut′ting·ly,** *adv.*

glu·ten (glüt′n), *n.* a tough, sticky protein substance in the flour of wheat and other grains.

glu·ti·nous (glüt′n əs), *adj.* sticky. **—glu′ti·nous·ly,** *adv.* **—glu′ti·nous·ness,** *n.*

glut·ton (glut′n), *n.* **1** a greedy eater; person who eats too much: *Sometimes I go off my diet and eat like a glutton.* **2** person who never seems to have enough of something: *That boxer is a glutton for punishment.*

glut·ton·ous (glut′n əs), *adj.* greedy about food; liking to eat too much. **—glut′ton·ous·ly,** *adv.* **—glut′ton·ous·ness,** *n.*

glut·ton·y (glut′n ē), *n.* habit of eating too much.

glyc·er·in or **glyc·er·ine** (glis′ər ən), *n.* a colorless, syrupy, sweet liquid obtained from fats and oils. Glycerin is used in ointments, lotions, antifreeze solutions, and explosives.

glyc·e·rol (glis′ə rōl′ or glis′ə rol′), *n.* glycerin.

gly·co·gen (glī′kə jən), *n.* a carbohydrate stored in the liver and other animal tissues. It is changed into glucose when needed.

gly·col (glī′kol), *n.* poisonous alcohol used as an antifreeze; ethylene glycol.

gm., gram or grams.

G-man (jē′man′), *n.* (earlier) a special agent of the U.S. Department of Justice; agent of the FBI. ❑ *n., pl.* **G-men.**

GMT or **G.M.T.,** Greenwich mean time.

gnarl (närl), *n.* knot in wood; hard, rough lump: *Wood with gnarls is hard to cut.*

gnarled (närld), *adj.* rough and twisted; having knots: *The farmer's gnarled hands grasped the plow firmly.*

gnarled—gnarled roots

gnash (nash), *v.* to strike or grind together: *I gnashed my teeth in rage.* **—gnash′ing·ly,** *adv.*

gnat (nat), *n.* any of various small, two-winged flies. Most gnats suck blood and give bites that itch. **—gnat′like′,** *adj.*

WORD STORY Gn- is used to spell the beginnings of some English words in which the *g* is not pronounced. Hundreds of years ago, the *g* was pronounced in many of these words. Gnat, for instance, was pronounced (gə nat′).

gnaw (nȯ), *v.* **1** to bite at and wear away: *to gnaw a bone. A mouse has gnawed the cover of this box.* **2** to make by biting: *A rat can gnaw a hole through wood.* **3** to trouble; harass; torment: *A feeling of guilt gnawed at the prisoner's conscience day and night.* ❑ *v.* **gnawed, gnaw·ing. —gnaw′a·ble,** *adj.* **—gnaw′er,** *n.*

gneiss (nīs), *n.* a common kind of rock that occurs in layers. It is metamorphic and contains quartz, feldspar, and various other minerals. ■ Another word that sounds like this is **nice.**

gnome (nōm), *n.* (in folklore) a dwarf supposed to live in the earth and guard treasures of precious metals and stones.

GNP or **G.N.P.,** gross national product.

gnu (nü), *n.* either of two large African antelopes with an oxlike head, curved horns, and a long tail; wildebeest. ❑ *n., pl.* **gnu** or **gnus.** ■ Other words that sound like this are **knew** and **new.**

go (gō), **1** *v.* to move along: *Cars go on the road.* **2** *v.* to move away; leave: *Don't go yet.* **3** *v.* to be in motion or action; act; work; run: *Electricity makes the washing machine go.* **4** *v.* to get to be; become: *go mad.* **5** *v.* to be habitually; be: *go hungry for a week.* **6** *v.* to proceed; advance: *go to New York.* **7** *v.* to take part in the activity of: *go skiing, go swimming.* **8** *v.* to extend; reach:

Does your memory go back that far? **9** *v.* to pass: *Vacation goes quickly.* **10** *v.* to be given: *First prize goes to you.* **11** *v.* to be sold: *The painting goes to the highest bidder.* **12** *v.* to turn out; have a certain result: *How did the ballgame go?* **13** *v.* to have its place; belong: *This book goes on the top shelf.* **14** *v.* to make a certain sound: *The cork went "pop!"* **15** *v.* to have certain words; be said: *How does that song go?* ■ See Usage Note below. **16** *v.* to break down; give way; fail: *My grandfather's eyesight is going. The engine in the old car finally went.* **17** *n.* try; attempt; chance: *Let's have another go at this problem.* **18** *n.* something successful; a success: *She made a go of the new store.* **19** *adj.* in perfect order and ready to proceed: *All systems are go for the rocket launching.* ❑ *v.* **went, gone, go·ing;** *n., pl.* **goes. —go′er,** *n.*

go about, 1 be busy at; work on: *She went about her work with energy.* **2** to turn around; change direction.

go along, to cooperate: *The club members decided to go along with the president's recommendation.*

go around, to satisfy everyone; give some for all: *There were enough apples and nuts to go around.*

go at, 1 to attack: *The dogs don't go at each other now they've become friendly.* **2** to take in hand with energy; work at: *Let's go at this problem in a different way.*

go back on, to be unfaithful or disloyal to; betray: *She went back on her promise.*

go by, 1 to pass: *We went by that store often. He let the insult go by.* **2** be guided by; follow: *Go by what she says.* **3** be known by: *He goes by the name of Smith.*

go down, 1 to descend; decline; sink: *The wrecked ship went down.* **2** be defeated; lose: *Their team went down as a result of our superior playing.*

go for, 1 to try to get: *Our athletes went for the gold medal.* **2** to favor; support: *The public goes for her ideas.* **3** to attack: *That dog goes for anyone who gets near it.*

go in for, INFORMAL. to take part in; spend time and energy at: *Our whole family goes in for touch football.*

go into, 1 to enter into a condition, activity, or occupation: *to go into a rage. She went into law.* **2** be contained in: *How many pints go into a gallon?* **3** to investigate: *The police have gone into the case and made an arrest.*

go off, 1 to leave; depart: *My sister has gone off to college.* **2** be fired; explode: *The pistol went off unexpectedly.* **3** to take place; happen: *The picnic went off as planned.* **4** to start to ring; sound: *The alarm went off at 6:30 A.M.*

go on, 1 to go ahead; continue: *After a pause she went on reading.* **2** to happen: *What goes on here?* **3** to behave: *You shouldn't go on in this manner.*

go out, 1 to go to a party, show, etc.: *We had a very good time when we went out Saturday night.* **2** to stop burning: *Don't let the candle go out.*

go over, 1 to look at carefully: *go over a problem.* **2** to do or read again; repeat: *I went over the explanation several times. Go over the poem till you memorize it.* **3** to succeed: *The play went over very well and became a hit.*

go through, 1 to go to the end of; do all of: *Let's go through the rehearsal without any interruption.* **2** to undergo; experience: *I went through a serious operation.* **3** to search: *Going through his pockets he found the missing key.* **4** be accepted or approved: *The new schedule did not go through.*

go through with, to carry out to the end; complete: *The contractor went through with his bargain to build the house in three months.*

go together, 1 to harmonize; match: *These colors go together.* **2** to keep steady company as sweethearts: *That couple has been going together for a long time.*

go under, be ruined; fail: *Poor management caused the business to go under.*

go up, 1 to rise; ascend: *The thermometer is going up.* **2** to increase: *The price of milk has gone up.*

go with, 1 to belong with; go well together: *Cheese goes with salad.* **2** date: *The girl he had gone with moved out of town.*

go without, to do without; not have: *You can eat what is on the table or go without.*

let go, 1 to allow to escape: *Let me go.* **2** to give up your hold: *Let go of my shirt.*

let yourself go, 1 to give way to your feelings or desires: *He is much too shy to let himself go.* **2** to fail to keep yourself in good condition: *The coach warned the team not to let themselves go during vacation.*

no go, INFORMAL. useless; worthless: *I knew that the idea would be no go from the start.*

on the go, busily occupied; active or restless: *Some people are always on the go.*

to go, to be eaten outside, rather than within, a restaurant: *two pizzas to go.*

USAGE NOTE **Go** is sometimes used in speech to mean "say" before a quotation. This use, which may come from definition 14, is considered unsuitable for writing or for any speech that is not very casual.

goad (gōd), **1** *v.* to drive or urge on; act as a goad or spur to: *Hunger can goad a person to steal.* **2** *n.* a sharp-pointed stick for driving cattle. **3** *n.* anything which drives or urges you on. —**goad′like′,** *adj.*

go·a·head (gō′ə hed′), *n.* permission to go ahead or begin: *The train engineer got the go-ahead from the signal tower.*

goal (gōl), *n.* **1** place where a race ends. **2** place to which players try to advance a ball or puck in certain games in order to make a score. **3** score or points won by reaching this place. **4** something for which an effort is made; something desired: *The goal of her ambition was to be a scientist.* ∎ See Synonym Study at **intention.** —**goal′less,** *adj.*

goal·ie (gō′lē), *n.* (in hockey, soccer, etc.) player who tries to prevent the ball or puck from reaching the goal; goalkeeper.

goal·keep·er (gōl′kē′pər), *n.* goalie.

goal line, line marking a goal in a game.

goalpost (gōl′pōst), *n.* one of a pair of posts with a bar across them, forming a goal in football, soccer, etc.

goat (gōt), *n.* **1** any of several lively, cud-chewing mammals with hollow horns and usually beards. Goats are closely related to sheep but are stronger, less timid, and more active than sheep. They are raised for their milk and their hides. **2** scapegoat. ∎ *n., pl.* **goat·ees. —goat′like′,** *adj.*

get someone's goat, INFORMAL. to make someone angry or annoyed: *He really gets my goat with his silly questions.*

goat·ee (gō tē′), *n.* a pointed beard on a man's chin. ∎ *n., pl.* **goat·ees.**

goat·herd (gōt′hėrd′), *n.* person who tends goats.

goat·skin (gōt′skin′), *n.* **1** skin of a goat. **2** leather made from it.

gob[1] (gob), *n.* SLANG. sailor in the U.S. Navy.

gob[2] (gob), *n.* lump; mass.

gob·ble[1] (gob′əl), *v.* to eat fast and greedily; swallow quickly in big pieces. ∎ *v.* **gob·bled, gob·bling.**

gobble up, to seize eagerly: *Large firms sometimes gobble up small companies.*

gob·ble[2] (gob′əl), **1** *v.* to make the throaty sound of a male turkey or a sound like it. **2** *n.* the throaty sound that a male turkey makes. ∎ *v.* **gob·bled, gob·bling.**

gob·ble·dy·gook or **gob·ble·de·gook** (gob′əl dē gúk′), *n.* speech or writing which is hard to understand because it is full of long, involved sentences and big words.

gob·bler (gob′lər), *n.* a male turkey.

go-be·tween (gō′bi twēn′), *n.* person who goes back and forth between others with messages, proposals, suggestions, etc.

Go·bi (gō′bē), *n.* desert in E Asia. Most of it is in Mongolia.

gob·let (gob′lit), *n.* a drinking glass with a base and stem.

gob·lin (gob′lən), *n.* (in folklore) a dangerous spirit or elf in the form of an ugly dwarf. [**Goblin** comes form the name of a ghost that was thought to haunt a town in France in the 1100s.]

go-cart or **go·cart** (gō′kärt′), *n.* **1** a very small car, big enough for a driver only, with its bottom near the ground and an open framework enclosing its sides and top. Go-carts are used for racing and for entertainment. **2** stroller (def. 1). **3** walker (def. 3).

god (god), *n.* **1** a being thought to have supernatural or superhuman powers and considered worthy of worship. **2** likeness or im-

age of a god; idol. **3** someone or something greatly admired and respected or thought of as very important: *Wealth and power are his gods.*

God (god), *n.* an all-powerful being worshiped in most religions as the maker and ruler of the world.

god·child (god′child′), *n.* child whom a grown-up person sponsors at its baptism. ∎ *n., pl.* **god·chil·dren.**

god·chil·dren (god′chil′drən), *n.* plural of **godchild.**

God·dard (god′ərd), *n.* **Rob·ert** (rob′ərt), 1882-1945, American physicist who pioneered modern rocketry.

god·daugh·ter (god′dò′tər), *n.* a female godchild.

god·dess (god′is), *n.* **1** a female god. **2** a very beautiful or charming woman. ∎ *n., pl.* **god·dess·es.**

god·fa·ther (god′fä′тнər), *n.* man who sponsors a child when it is baptized.

god·head (god′hed′), *n.* **1** divine nature; divinity. **2 Godhead,** God.

god·less (god′lis), *adj.* **1** not believing in God; not religious. **2** ungodly; wicked; evil. —**god′less·ness,** *n.*

god·like (god′līk′), *adj.* **1** like God or a god; divine. **2** suitable for God or a god. —**god′like′ness,** *n.*

god·ly (god′lē), *adj.* obeying, loving, and fearing God; religious; pious. ∎ *adj.* **god·li·er, god·li·est.** —**god′li·ness,** *n.*

god·moth·er (god′muтн′ər), *n.* woman who sponsors a child when it is baptized.

god·par·ent (god′pâr′ənt), *n.* godfather or godmother.

goat (def. 1)—30 in. (76 cm) high at the shoulder

god·send (god′send′), *n.* something unexpected and very welcome, as if sent from God; sudden piece of good luck: *The money I received on my birthday was a godsend.*

god·son (god′sun′), *n.* a male godchild.

God·speed (god′spēd′), *n.* a wish of success to someone starting on a journey or undertaking.

Goeb·bels (gėr′bəlz), *n.* **Joseph,** 1897-1945, German propagandist. ∎ **Goebbels** publicized Nazi philosophy and controlled all media in Germany during World War II. He committed suicide when Germany was defeated.

Goer·ing (gėr′ing), *n.* **Her·mann** (hėr′män), 1893-1946, German military leader. ∎ **Hermann Goering** was Adolf Hitler's second in command and commander of the German air force. He committed suicide before he could be hanged for his war crimes.

goes (gōz), *v.* a present tense of **go:** *He goes to school.*

Goe·the (gėr′tə), *n.* **Johann Wolfgang von** (yō′hän vúlf′gäng fón), 1749-1832, German poet, prose writer, and dramatist.

go·fer (gō′fər), *n.* INFORMAL. person who helps by going for things and running errands. [**Gofer** comes from *go for.* The spelling has changed to imitate a casual pronunciation.] ∎ Another word that sounds like this is **gopher.**

go-get·ter (gō′get′ər), *n.* INFORMAL. an energetic and ambitious person.

gog·gle (gog′əl), **1** *v.* to stare with wide-open eyes: *The children goggled at the magician pulling a rabbit out of the empty hat.* **2**

a	hat	ė	term	ô	order	ch	child		a in about
ā	age	i	it	oi	oil	ng	long		e in taken
ä	far	ī	ice	ou	out	sh	she	ə	i in pencil
â	care	o	hot	u	cup	th	thin		o in lemon
e	let	ō	open	ú	put	тн	then		u in circus
ē	equal	ò	saw	ü	rule	zh	measure		

n.pl. **goggles,** large, close-fitting eyeglasses to protect the eyes from light or dust. ❑ *v.* **gog·gled, gog·gling.**

gog·gle-eyed (gog′əl īd′), *adj.* having eyes staring in surprise.

Gogh. See Van Gogh.

go·ing (gō′ing), **1** *n.* act of going away; leaving: *Her going was very sudden.* **2** *adj.* moving; acting; working; running: *Set the clock going.* **3** *n.* condition of the ground or road for walking or riding: *The going is bad on a muddy road.* **4** *adj.* doing well; operating with success: *Her new business is a going concern.*

be going to, will; be about to: *It is going to rain soon.*

go·ing-o·ver (gō′ing ō′vər), *n.* a thorough, searching inspection: *Police gave the scene of the crime a real going-over.*

go·ings-on (gō′ingz on′), *n.pl.* actions or events: *the goings-on at the convention.*

goi·ter (goi′tər), *n.* enlargement of the thyroid gland which is often seen as a large swelling in the front of the neck. A goiter is usually caused by a diet with too little iodine.

gold (gōld), **1** *n.* a shiny, bright yellow, precious metallic element which resists rust and other chemical changes and can easily be drawn out into fine wire or hammered into thin sheets. Gold is used mostly for making coins and jewelry. *Symbol:* Au **2** *n.* coins made of gold. **3** *n.* money in large sums; wealth; riches. **4** *adj.* made of gold: *a gold watch.* **5** *adj.* of or like gold. **6** *n.* a bright yellow. **7** *adj.* bright yellow.

Gold·berg (gōld′bėrg′), *n.* **Rube** (rüb), 1883-1970, American cartoonist. Many of his cartoons were of ridiculously complicated machines to do very simple jobs, such as opening a door or cutting a piece of cake.

gold·brick (gōld′brik′), INFORMAL. **1** *v.* to avoid duties, especially by pretending to be sick. **2** *n.* person, especially in the armed forces, who avoids duty or shirks work. **–gold′brick′er,** *n.*

Gold Coast, region in W Africa, a former British colony, now largely included in Ghana.

gold·en (gōl′dən), *adj.* **1** made of gold: *The queen wore a golden crown.* **2** shining like gold; bright yellow: *golden hair.* **3** very good; excellent; extremely favorable, valuable, or important: *a golden opportunity.* **–gold′en·ness,** *n.*

golden age, 1 Golden Age, (in Greek and Roman myths) the first and best age of human history, a time of peace, prosperity, and happiness. **2** the period when a nation is most prosperous, or when some art or activity is at its best. **3** the period of someone's life after middle age, thought to be a time of happiness, prosperity, and wisdom.

golden ag·er (ā′jər), someone past middle age, especially an elderly, retired person.

golden eagle, a large eagle of the Northern Hemisphere with golden brown feathers on the top of its head and the back of its neck.

Golden Gate, strait forming the entrance to San Francisco Bay from the Pacific.

golden mean, sensible way of doing things; moderation.

gold·en·rod (gōl′dən rod′), *n.* any of numerous plants with many small, yellow flowers on tall, slender stalks, blooming in late summer or early autumn.

golden rule, rule of conduct which states that you should treat others as you would have them treat you.

gold-filled (gōld′fild′), *adj.* made of cheap metal covered with a layer of gold.

gold·finch (gōld′finch′), *n.* **1** any of three small American songbirds. The male is yellow marked with black. **2** a European songbird with a patch of yellow on its wings. ❑ *n., pl.* **gold·finch·es.**

gold·fish (gōld′fish′), *n.* a small, usually reddish gold fish, kept as pets in garden pools or in glass bowls. It is a kind of carp. ❑ *n., pl.* **gold·fish** or **gold·fish·es.**

gold leaf, gold beaten into very thin sheets, used in gilding.

gold rush, a sudden rush of people to a place where gold has just been found.

gold·smith (gōld′smith′), *n.* person who makes or sells things made of gold.

golf (golf), **1** *n.* game played on an outdoor course with a small, hard ball and a set of golf clubs. The player tries to hit the ball

into each of a series of holes in as few strokes as possible. **2** *v.* to play this game. **–golf′er,** *n.*

golf club, 1 any of several long-handled clubs with metal or wooden heads, used in playing golf. **2** group of people joined together for the purpose of playing golf. **3** buildings and land used by such a group.

golf course or **golf links,** place where golf is played, including tees, greens, and fairways.

Gol·go·tha (gol′gə thə), *n.* (in the Bible) the place where Jesus was crucified; Calvary. [Golgotha comes from an Hebrew word meaning "skull."]

Go·li·ad (gō′lē ad), *n.* city in S Texas. At the start of the revolution of Texas against Mexican rule, a force of more than 300 Texan soldiers was defeated here and then killed after surrendering to Mexican troops, in March 1836.

Go·li·ath (gə lī′əth), *n.* (in the Bible) a giant whom David killed with a stone from a sling.

gol·ly (gol′ē), *interj.* exclamation of wonder, pleasure, joy, etc.

Go·mor·rah (gə môr′ə), *n.* (in the Bible) a wicked city destroyed, together with Sodom, by fire from heaven.

-gon, *suffix.* shape with ___ angles: *polygon = shape with many angles.*

go·nad (gō′nad), *n.* organ in which reproductive cells develop in the male or female. Ovaries and testicles are gonads.

gon·do·la (gon′dl ə), *n.* **1** a long, narrow boat with a high peak at each end, used on the canals of Venice. **2** a railroad freight car that has low sides and no top. **3** car or basket which hangs under an airship or balloon and holds the passengers, equipment, etc. **4** an enclosed car, hung from a cable, that carries passengers up a ski slope or mountain. ❑ *n., pl.* **gon·do·las.**

gondola (def. 1)

gon·do·lier (gon′dl ir′), *n.* person who rows or poles a gondola.

gone (gon), **1** *adj.* away: *The students are gone on their vacation.* **2** *adj.* dead: *Great-grandmother is gone now.* **3** *adj.* used up; consumed: *Is all the candy gone?* **4** *v.* past participle of **go:** *They have gone far away.*

far gone, much advanced; deeply involved: *The business was far gone in debt and could not be saved.*

gon·er (go′nər), *n.* INFORMAL. person or thing that is past help.

gong (gong), *n.* a large piece of metal shaped like a bowl or a saucer which makes a loud noise when struck.

gon·o·coc·cus (gon′ə kok′əs), *n.* bacterium that causes gonorrhea. ❑ *n., pl.* **gon·o·coc·ci** (gon′ə kok′sī).

gon·or·rhe·a (gon′ə rē′ə), *n.* a sexually transmitted disease caused by the gonococcus bacterium, resulting in inflammation of the genital and urinary organs.

goo (gü), *n.* INFORMAL. thick, sticky matter.

goo·ber (gü′bər), *n.* (in the southern United States) a peanut.

good (gùd), **1** *adj.* having high quality; superior: *a good piece of work.* **2** *adj.* as it ought to be; right; proper; satisfactory: *good health, good weather.* **3** *adj.* well-behaved: *a good girl.* **4** *adj.* kind; friendly: *Say a good word for me.* **5** *adj.* desirable: *a good book for children.* **6** *adj.* honorable; worthy: *my good friend, a good reputation.* **7** *adj.* reliable; dependable: *good judgment.* **8** *adj.* real; genuine: *It is hard to tell counterfeit money from good* *money.* **9** *adj.* agreeable; pleasant: *Have a good time.* **10** *adj.* beneficial; advantageous; useful: *medicine good for a fever.* **11** *n.* benefit; advantage; use: *work for the common good.* **12** *adj.* satisfying; enough; full: *a good meal.* **13** *adj.* skillful; clever: *a good manager, be good at arithmetic.* **14** *adj.* fairly great; more than a little: *work a good while.* **15** *n.* that which is good: *find the good in people.* **16** *adj.* indicating a U.S. government grade of meat below choice. **17** *interj.* that is good! ❏ *adj.* **bet·ter, best.**

as good as, almost the same as; almost: *The game was as good as won.*

for good, forever; finally; permanently: *They have moved out for good.*

good and, very: *Get the water good and hot.*

good for, 1 able to do, live, or last: *Our car is good for another year.* **2** able to pay or contribute: *He is good for about $10.*

make good, 1 to make up for; pay for: *The girls made good the damage they had done.* **2** to fulfill; carry out: *Will you make good your promise?* **3** to succeed in doing: *The soldiers made good their retreat.* **4** to succeed: *She made good in business.* **5** to prove: *Can you make good your accusation?*

no good, without worth or value: *This TV show is no good.*

to the good, on the side of profit or advantage; in your favor: *By winning the second game our team is now two games to the good.*

USAGE NOTE **Good** is an adjective, and so it is commonly used with linking verbs such as **feel** and **look**: *After a long vacation, he feels good and he looks good.* It is common in speech to use **good** with other verbs, as if it were an adverb, but careful writers and speakers use **well**[1] instead: *This soap smells good and cleans well.*

Good·all (gùd'òl'), *n.* **Jane** (jān), born 1934, English zoologist known for her close studies of chimpanzees in the wild.

good·by (gùd'bī'), *interj., n.* good-by. ❏ *n., pl.* **good·bys.**

good·by (gùd'bī'), *interj., n.* an expression of good wishes at parting: *He called "Good-by!" as he drove off.* ❏ *n., pl.* **good·bys.**

WORD STORY **Good-by** comes from words of farewell, "God be with you." Because people said this often, they tended to shorten it. Because they also said "good day" and "good evening," they tended to begin this farewell with "good." See also **adieu** and **adios.**

good-bye (gùd'bī'), *interj., n.* good-by. ❏ *n., pl.* **good-byes.**

good day, form of greeting or farewell; hello or good-by.

good evening, form of greeting or farewell in the evening; hello or good-by.

good faith, honesty and sincerity: *act in good faith.*

good-for-noth·ing (gùd'fər nuth'ing), **1** *adj.* worthless; useless. **2** *n.* person who is regarded as worthless or useless.

Good Friday, the anniversary of Jesus' crucifixion, observed on the Friday before Easter.

good-heart·ed (gùd'här'tid), *adj.* kind and generous. **—good'-heart'ed·ly,** *adv.* **—good'heart'ed·ness,** *n.*

good-hu·mored (gùd'hyü'mərd), *adj.* cheerful; pleasant. **—good'-hu'mored·ly,** *adv.* **—good'-hu'mored·ness,** *n.*

good-look·ing (gùd'lùk'ing), *adj.* having a pleasing appearance; handsome or pretty.

good·ly (gùd'lē), *adj.* considerable; rather large; fairly great: *a goodly quantity.* ❏ *adj.* **good·li·er, good·li·est.** **—good'li·ness,** *n.*

Good·man (gùd'mən), *n.* **Ben·ny** (ben'ē), 1909-1986, American clarinetist and bandleader. He was one of the first white bandleaders to hire African American musicians.

good morning, form of greeting or farewell in the morning; hello or good-by.

good-na·tured (gùd'nā'chərd), *adj.* having a pleasant disposition; kindly; cheerful; obliging. ■ See Synonym Study at **kind**[1]. **—good'-na'tured·ly,** *adv.* **—good'-na'tured·ness,** *n.*

good·ness (gùd'nis), **1** *n.* a being good; kindness. **2** *interj.* exclamation of surprise: *My goodness!*

good night, form of farewell said at night.

goods (gùdz), *n.pl.* **1** personal property; belongings: *household goods.* **2** things for sale; wares. **3** material for clothing; cloth.

Good Samaritan, 1 (in the Bible) a traveler who rescued another traveler who had been beaten and robbed by thieves. **2** person who is unselfish in helping others.

good-sized (gùd'sīzd'), *adj.* somewhat large.

good-tem·pered (gùd'tem'pərd), *adj.* easy to get along with; agreeable. **—good'-tem'pered·ly,** *adv.* **—good'-tem'pered·ness,** *n.*

good·will (gùd'wil'), *n.* **1** kindly or friendly feeling. **2** cheerful consent; willingness. **3** the good reputation that a business has with its customers.

good·y (gùd'ē), **1** *n.* Usually, **goodies,** *pl.* something good to eat, such as candy. **2** *interj.* exclamation of pleasure: *Oh, goody!*

good·y-good·y (gùd'ē gùd'ē), **1** *adj.* too concerned with being good; good in an affected or artificial way. **2** *n.* person who is too concerned with being good. ❏ *n., pl.* **good·y-good·ies.**

goo·ey (gü'ē), *adj.* INFORMAL. like goo; sticky. ❏ *adj.* **goo·i·er, goo·i·est.**

goof (güf), INFORMAL. **1** *v.* to make a stupid mistake; blunder. **2** *n.* a blunder. **3** *n.* simpleton; fool.

goof off, INFORMAL. to waste time; avoid work: *They spent the afternoon goofing off.*

goof-off (güf'òf'), *n.* INFORMAL. person who wastes time or avoids work.

goof·y (gü'fē), *adj.* INFORMAL. silly. ❏ *adj.* **goof·i·er, goof·i·est.**

goo·gol (gü'gəl), *n.* the number 1 followed by 100 zeros. [**Googol** is a made-up word, coined by a nine-year-old boy whose uncle, a mathematician, was talking with him about such numbers.]

goon (gün), *n.* INFORMAL. **1** hoodlum or thug hired to frighten your opponents, disrupt labor disputes, etc. **2** a stupid person.

goop (güp), *n.* INFORMAL. a thick, sticky substance; goo.

goose (güs), *n.* **1** any of several swimming birds, like ducks but larger and having longer necks. A goose has webbed feet. **2** a female goose. The male is called a gander. **3** flesh of a goose used for food. **4** a silly person. ❏ *n., pl.* **geese.** **—goose'like',** *adj.*

cook someone's goose, to ruin someone's reputation, chances, etc.

goose (def. 1)—about 3 ft. (91 cm) long

goose·ber·ry (güs'ber'ē), *n.* a small, sour berry something like a currant but larger, that grows on two kinds of thorny bushes. Gooseberries are used to make pies, tarts, jam, etc. ❏ *n., pl.* **goose·ber·ries.**

goose·bumps (güs'bumps'), *n.pl.* gooseflesh.

goose egg, INFORMAL. **1** a zero, indicating a miss or failure to score in a game. **2** a lump on the head from being hit.

goose·flesh (güs'flesh'), *n.* a rough condition of the skin, like that of a plucked goose, caused by cold or fear; goose pimples.

goose·neck (güs'nek'), *n.* something long and curved like a goose's neck, such as a movable support for a lamp or a support for bicycle handlebars.

goose pimples, gooseflesh.

goose step, a marching step in which the leg is swung high with a straight, stiff knee.

G.O.P. or **GOP,** Grand Old Party; the Republican Party in the United States.

go·pher (gō'fər), *n.* **1** any of several burrowing rodents of North America with large cheek pouches and long claws, especially on

a	hat	ė	term	ô	order	ch	child		
ā	age	i	it	oi	oil	ng	long		a in about
ä	far	ī	ice	ou	out	sh	she		e in taken
â	care	o	hot	u	cup	th	thin	ə	i in pencil
e	let	ō	open	ù	put	ŦH	then		o in lemon
ē	equal	ò	saw	ü	rule	zh	measure		u in circus

the front feet. **2** any of several striped ground squirrels of the western plains of the North America. ■ Another word that sounds like this is **gofer.**

Gor·ba·chev (gôr′bə chôf′), *n.* **Mik·hail** (mē′kil′), born 1931, Russian political leader. He was the general secretary of the Soviet Communist Party from 1985 to 1991.

Gor·di·mer (gôr′də mər), *n.* **Na·dine** (nā′dēn), born 1923, South African writer. She won the 1991 Nobel Prize for literature.

Gore (gôr), *n.* **Al·bert** (al′bərt), born 1948, vice president of the United States since 1993.

gore¹ (gôr), *n.* blood that is shed; thick blood; clotted blood: *The battlefield was covered with gore.*

gore² (gôr), *v.* to wound with a horn or tusk: *The angry bull gored the farmer in the leg.* ❏ *v.* **gored, gor·ing.**

gore³ (gôr), **1** *n.* a long, three-sided piece of cloth put or made in a skirt, sail, etc., to give greater width or change the shape. **2** *v.* to put or make a gore in. ❏ *v.* **gored, gor·ing.**

Gore-Tex (gôr′teks), *n.* trademark for a water-repellent material used in clothing and footwear.

gorge (gôrj), **1** *n.* a deep, narrow valley, usually steep and rocky, especially one with a stream. **2** *v.* to eat greedily until full; stuff with food: *I gorged myself with cake at the party.* ❏ *v.* **gorged, gorg·ing. —gorg′er,** *n.*

gor·geous (gôr′jəs), *adj.* **1** richly colored; splendid: *a gorgeous sunset.* **2** very beautiful: *The peacock spread its gorgeous tail.* [Gorgeous may come from a French word meaning "throat." Splendid jewels are often worn as necklaces.] **—gor′geous·ly,** *adv.* **—gor′geous·ness,** *n.*

Gor·gon (gôr′gən), *n.* (in Greek legends) any of three sisters with snakes for hair and faces so horrible that anyone who looked at them turned to stone.

Gor·gon·zo·la (gôr′gən zō′lə), *n.* a white Italian cheese with blue-green veins, usually made with cow's milk. It has a strong flavor.

go·ril·la (gə ril′ə), *n.* the largest and most powerful ape. It is found in the forests of central Africa. ❏ *n., pl.* **go·ril·las.** ■ Another word that sounds like this is **guerrilla.**

WORD STORY **Gorilla** comes from an African word. About 2500 years ago, an explorer from North Africa wrote in Greek about seeing these animals. His report was the only written evidence until a missionary from the United States saw and wrote about them in 1847. The missionary used the word from the earlier explorer's report.

go-round (gō′round′), *n.* INFORMAL. **1** heated discussion; argument: *We had quite a go-round about what to name the kitten.* **2** time: *We have a lot to accomplish this go-round.*

gorp (gôrp), *n.* mixture of nuts, dried fruit, candy, etc., eaten as an energy-producing snack.

gorse (gôrs), *n.* furze.

gor·y (gôr′ē), *adj.* **1** covered with gore; bloody. **2** with much bloodshed: *a gory accident, a gory tale.* ❏ *adj.* **gor·i·er, gor·i·est. —gor′i·ly,** *adv.* **—gor′i·ness,** *n.*

gosh (gosh), *interj.* exclamation or mild oath: *Gosh, it's cold!*

gos·hawk (gos′hôk′), *n.* a powerful, short-winged hawk, formerly much used in falconry.

Gosh·en (gō′shən), *n.* **1** (in the Bible) a fertile part of Egypt where the Israelites lived before the Exodus. **2** any land of plenty and comfort.

gos·ling (goz′ling), *n.* a young goose.

gos·pel (gos′pəl), **1** *n.* the teachings of Jesus and the Apostles. **2** *adj.* in agreement with the gospel; evangelical. **3** *n.* **Gospel, a** any one of the first four books of the New Testament, by Matthew, Mark, Luke, and John. They tell about the life and teachings of Jesus. **b** part of one of these books read during a religious service. **4** *n.* anything earnestly believed or taken as a guide for action: *Drink plenty of water: that is my gospel.* [Gospel comes from an old English word meaning "good news." The teachings of Jesus and the Apostles have often been described this way.]

gospel music, religious music with much emotion and enthusiasm, including features of spirituals and jazz.

gos·sa·mer (gos′ə mər), **1** *n.* any very thin, light cloth or substance. **2** *adj.* very light, thin, and easily seen through.

gos·sip (gos′ip), **1** *n.* idle talk, not always true, about other people and their private affairs. **2** *v.* to repeat what you know or hear about other people and their private affairs: *Don't gossip about the neighbors.* **3** *n.* person who gossips a good deal. **—gos′sip·er,** *n.* **—gos′sip·ing·ly,** *adv.*

gos·sip·y (gos′ə pē), *adj.* **1** fond of gossip. **2** full of gossip: *a gossipy letter.* **—gos′sip·i·ness,** *n.*

got (got), *v.* past tense and a past participle of **get:** *She got the letter yesterday. We had got tired of waiting for it.*

USAGE NOTE **Got** is sometimes used in speech with **have** or **has** where those words make sense without **got.** Careful writers and speakers avoid this use except in the most casual speech. SAY: *I have to study. I have a pen.* NOT: *I have got to study. I have got a pen.*

Goth (goth), *n.* member of a Germanic people who invaded the Roman Empire in the A.D. 200s, 300s, and 400s. The Goths settled mainly in southern and eastern Europe.

Goth·ic (goth′ik), **1** *n.* style of architecture using pointed arches, flying buttresses, and high, steep roofs. It was developed in western Europe during the Middle Ages from about 1150 to 1550. **2** *adj.* of this kind of architecture. **3** *adj.* of the Goths or their language. **4** *n.* language of the Goths. **5** *adj.* of or belonging to a kind of literature interested in the supernatural and the grotesque, usually telling stories about the Middle Ages: *Gothic horror, Gothic novels.*

got·ten (got′n), *v.* a past participle of **get:** *It has gotten cold.*

gouache (gwäsh *or* gü äsh′), *n.* **1** method of painting with opaque watercolors obtained by mixing pigments with water and gum. **2** a color made in this way. **3** a painting made by this method. ❏ *n., pl.* **gouach·es.**

Gou·da (gü′də), *n.* a mild yellow whole-milk cheese made in the shape of a thick, flat disk.

gouge (gouj), **1** *n.* chisel with a curved, hollow blade. Gouges are used for cutting round grooves or holes in wood. **2** *v.* to cut with a gouge. **3** *n.* groove or hole made by gouging. **4** *v.* to trick; cheat; swindle: *The used car dealer gouged me on that car.* ❏ *v.* **gouged, goug·ing. —goug′er,** *n.*

gou·lash (gü′läsh), *n.* stew made of beef or veal and vegetables, usually highly seasoned.

WORD STORY **Goulash** comes from a Hungarian word meaning "herdsman." Probably this stew was easy to make for people out in the country taking care of cattle or sheep.

gourd (gôrd), *n.* **1** any of various fleshy fruits that grow on vines and are related to squash. Gourds have hard rinds and are often dried and hollowed out for use as cups, bowls, and other utensils. **2** cup, bowl, etc., or an ornament, made from the dried shell of a gourd, often decorated. **—gourd′like′,** *adj.*

gourds (def. 2)

gour·mand (gur′mənd), *n.* person who is fond of good eating.

gour·met (gur′mā), *n.* person who is expert in judging and choosing fine foods, wines, etc.

gout (gout), *n.* a painful disease of the joints, especially of the big toe.

gout·y (gou′tē), *adj.* **1** diseased or swollen with gout. **2** of gout; caused by gout. ❏ *adj.* **gout·i·er, gout·i·est.**

gov., **1** government. **2** governor.

Gov., governor.

gov·ern (guv′ərn), *v.* **1** to direct or manage with authority; rule or control: *The election determined which party would govern the United States for four years.* ■ See Synonym Study at **rule. 2** to determine or guide: *What were the motives governing the king's decision to give up his throne?* **3** to hold back; restrain: *Govern your temper.* **—gov′ern·a·ble,** *adj.*

gov·ern·ess (guv′ər nis), *n.* (earlier) woman who teaches and trains children in their home. ❏ *n., pl.* **gov·ern·ess·es.**

gov·ern·ment (guv′ərn mənt), *n.* **1** act or process of ruling a country, state, district, etc.; direction of the affairs of state; rule, control, or management. **2** person or persons ruling a country, state, district, etc., at any time. The government of the United States consists of the President, the cabinet, and administrative assistants appointed by the President. **3** system of ruling: *The United States has a democratic form of government.* **–gov′ern·men′tal,** *adj.* **–gov′ern·men′tal·ly,** *adv.*

WORD BANK There are many words about **government.** Some of them are about local government, some about national government. Some are about the government of the United States, some about governments of many countries. If you want to learn more about government, you can begin by looking up these words in this dictionary, and by seeing the Word Bank at **election.**

absolutism	constitution	parliament
alderman	communism	President
Attorney General	democracy	prime minister
bureau	dictatorship	province
bureaucracy	executive	Representative
cabinet	fascism	republic
Capitol	governor	Senator
Chief Justice	judiciary	socialism
citizen	legislature	state
civil service	lobby	Supreme Court
Congress	mayor	totalitarianism
constituent	monarchy	Vice-President

gov·er·nor (guv′ər nər), *n.* **1** official elected as the executive head of a state of the United States. The governor of a state carries out the laws made by the state legislature. ■ See Usage Note at **capital letter. 2** official appointed to govern a province, colony, city, fort, etc. **3** person who manages or directs a club, society, institution, etc. **4** an automatic device that controls the supply of fuel or power and keeps a machine going at a set speed.

Governor General, (in Canada) the representative of Elizabeth II, Queen of Great Britain and Canada. The Governor General is appointed to a five-year term on the prime minister's advice.

gov·er·nor·ship (guv′ər nər ship), *n.* position, duties, or term of office of governor.

govt. or **Govt.,** government.

gown (goun), *n.* **1** a woman's dress, especially a long, fancy dress worn at parties. **2** nightgown or dressing gown. **3** a loose outer garment worn by college graduates, judges, clergymen, lawyers, and others to show their position, profession, etc.

Go·ya (goi′ə), *n.* **Fran·cis·co** (fränsēs′kō), 1746-1828, Spanish painter and etcher. ■ **Francisco Goya** made many powerful pictures and prints of war during Napoleon's occupation of Spain.

G.P.O. or **GPO, 1** General Post Office. **2** Government Printing Office.

gr. or **gr, 1** grain or grains. **2** gram or grams. **3** gross (12 dozen).

Gr., 1 Grecian. **2** Greece. **3** Greek.

grab (grab), **1** *v.* to seize suddenly; snatch: *I grabbed the child before she fell.* **2** *n.* act of snatching; sudden seizing: *He made a grab at the ball.* **3** *n.* something that is grabbed. ❑ *v.* **grabbed, grab·bing. –grab′ber,** *n.*

Goya painting

grab bag, bag containing various unseen and unknown objects from which a person can take out one.

grab·by (grab′ē), *adj.* wanting more than your share; greedy. ❑ *adj.* **grab·bi·er, grab·bi·est. –grab′bi·ness,** *n.*

grace (grās), **1** *n.* beauty of form, movement, or manner; pleasing or agreeable quality: *The ballerina danced with much grace.* **2** *v.* to give or add grace to: *A vase of flowers graced the room.* **3** *n.* the favor and love of God: *fall from grace.* **4** *n.* a short prayer of

thanks said before or after a meal. **5** *n.* amount of time granted before something has to be done, paid, returned, etc.: *Our library allows three day's grace on overdue books before fines begin.* **6** *v.* to give grace or honor to: *The queen graced the ball with her presence.* **7** *n.* **Grace,** title of a duke, duchess, or archbishop: *May I assist Your Grace?* **8** *n.pl.* **Graces,** (in Greek myths) three sister goddesses who gave beauty, charm, and joy to people and nature. ❑ *v.* **graced, grac·ing.** [Grace comes from a Latin word meaning "pleasing."] **–grace′like′,** *adj.*

in someone's bad graces, disfavored or disliked by.

in someone's good graces, favored or liked by: *I wonder if I am in the teacher's good graces.*

with bad grace, unpleasantly; unwillingly: *The apology was made with bad grace.*

with good grace, pleasantly; willingly: *He obeyed the order with good grace.*

grace·ful (grās′fəl), *adj.* beautiful in form, movement, or manner; pleasing; agreeable: *a graceful dancer.* **–grace′ful·ly,** *adv.* **–grace′ful·ness,** *n.*

grace·less (grās′lis), *adj.* **1** ugly in form, movement, or manner: *awkward, graceless movements.* **2** without any sense of what is right or proper; impolite: *a graceless rascal.* **–grace′less·ly,** *adv.* **–grace′less·ness,** *n.*

grace note, (in music) a note or group of notes not essential to the harmony or melody, added for ornament.

gra·cious (grā′shəs), **1** *adj.* pleasant and kindly; courteous: *He welcomed his guests in such a gracious manner that they felt at home.* **2** *adj.* pleasant and kindly to people of lower social position: *The queen greeted the crowd with a gracious smile.* **3** *interj.* exclamation of surprise. **–gra′cious·ly,** *adv.* **–gra′cious·ness,** *n.*

grack·le (grak′əl), *n.* any of several American blackbirds with shiny, black feathers.

grad., 1 graduate. **2** graduated.

gra·da·tion (grā dā′shən), *n.* **1** one of the steps in a series: *the gradations of color in a rainbow.* **2** a change by steps or stages; gradual change: *A camera lens allows gradation of the light that reaches the film.*

grade (grād), **1** *n.* division of elementary school or high school, arranged according to the pupils' progress and covering a year's work: *the seventh grade.* **2** *n.pl.* **the grades,** elementary school. **3** *n.* degree in rank, quality, or value: *Grade A milk is the best milk.* **4** *n.* group of persons or things having the same rank, quality, or value. **5** *v.* to place in classes; arrange in grades; sort: *These apples are graded by size.* **6** *n.* number or letter that shows how well you have done; mark: *Her grade in English is B.* **7** *v.* to give a grade to: *The teacher graded the papers.* **8** *n.* slope of a road or railroad track: *a steep grade.* **9** *n.* amount of slope. **10** *v.* to make more nearly level: *The road up the steep hill was graded.* ❑ *v.* **grad·ed, grad·ing.**

make the grade, be successful: *It takes a lot of hard work to make the grade in business.*

WORD FAMILY **Grade** and the words below are related. They all come from a Latin word meaning "a step."

biodegradable	gradation	gradual
centigrade	gradient	ingredient
degrading	graduate	retrograde
degree		

grade crossing, place where a railroad crosses a street or another railroad on the same level.

grad·er (grā′dər), *n.* **1** someone or something that grades. **2** person who is in a certain grade at school: *a fifth grader.*

grade school, elementary school; grammar school.

gra·di·ent (grā′dē ənt), *n.* **1** rate of upward or downward slope of a road, railroad track, etc.: *steep gradients.* **2** the sloping part of a road, railroad, etc.; grade.

a	hat	ė	term	ô	order	ch	child		a in about
ā	age	i	it	oi	oil	ng	long		e in taken
ä	far	ī	ice	ou	out	sh	she	ə	i in pencil
â	care	o	hot	u	cup	th	thin		o in lemon
e	let	ō	open	ů	put	ŦH	then		u in circus
ē	equal	ò	saw	ü	rule	zh	measure		

grad·u·al (graj′ü əl), *adj.* happening slowly by small steps or degrees; changing step by step; moving little by little: *This low hill has a gradual slope. A child's growth into an adult is gradual.* —**grad′u·al·ly,** *adv.* —**grad′u·al·ness,** *n.*

grad·u·ate (graj′ü āt *for verb;* graj′ü it *for noun, adj.*), **1** *v.* to finish a course of study at a school, college, or university and be given a diploma or paper saying so: *Her brother will graduate from college soon.* **2** *v.* to give a diploma to for finishing a course of study: *She was graduated with honors.* **3** *n.* person who has graduated and has a diploma. **4** *adj.* that has graduated: *a graduate student.* **5** *adj.* of or for graduates: *A graduate school is for students continuing their studies after college.* **6** *v.* to mark out in equal spaces for measuring: *Rulers are graduated in inches and centimeters.* ❑ *v.* **grad·u·at·ed, grad·u·at·ing.** —**grad′u·a′tor,** *n.*

grad·u·a·tion (graj′ü ā′shən), *n.* **1** act of graduating from a school, college, or university. **2** ceremony of graduating; graduating exercises. **3** division into equal spaces. **4** mark or set of marks to show degrees for measuring.

Graf (gräf), *n.* **Stef·fi** (stef′ē), born 1969, German tennis player. In 1988 she won all four major tennis tournaments.

graf·fi·ti (grə fē′tē), *n.pl.* drawings or writings scratched or scribbled on a wall or other surface. ❑ *n., sing.* **graf·fi·to** (grə fē′tō).

graft[1] (graft), **1** *v.* to transfer a piece of skin, bone, etc., from one part of the body to another, or to another body, so that it will grow there permanently. **2** *n.* piece of skin, bone, etc., so transferred. **3** *v.* to put a shoot, bud, etc., from one tree or plant into a slit in another tree or plant, so it will grow there permanently. **4** *n.* shoot, bud, etc., put into another tree or plant. A graft from a fine apple tree may be put on an inferior one to improve it. **5** *n.* act of grafting. —**graft′er,** *n.*

graft[2] (graft), *n.* **1** act of taking money dishonestly in connection with city or government business: *The crooked inspector was guilty of accepting bribes and other forms of graft.* **2** money dishonestly taken. —**graft′er,** *n.*

Gra·ham (grā′əm), *n.* **1 Bil·ly** (bil′ē), born 1918, American evangelist. **2 Mar·tha** (mär′thə), 1894-1991, American dancer and choreographer. She was a pioneer in modern dance.

gra·ham (grā′əm), *adj.* made from whole-wheat flour, including all the bran: *graham crackers.* [Graham comes from Sylvester Graham, an American minister and dietary reformer, who urged the use of this flour.]

Grail (grāl), *n.* (in legends of the Middle Ages) the cup or dish used by Jesus at the Last Supper, and to catch the last drops of Jesus' blood at the Cross; Holy Grail. The knights of the Round Table vowed to search for the Grail.

grain (grān), *n.* **1** the seed of wheat, corn, oats, and similar cereal grasses. **2** plants that these seeds grow on. **3** one of the tiny bits of which sand, sugar, salt, etc., are made up. **4** a very small unit of weight. One pound avoirdupois equals 7000 grains; one pound troy equals 5760 grains. **5** the smallest possible amount; tiniest bit: *There isn't a grain of truth in the charge.* **6** the little lines and other markings in wood, marble, etc.: *That mahogany table has a fine grain.* **7** natural character; disposition: *Laziness went against his grain.* —**grain′less,** *adj.* —**grain′like′,** *adj.*

with a grain of salt, with some doubt or allowance: *Her story must be taken with a grain of salt.*

grain alcohol, ordinary alcohol, made by the fermentation of grain.

grained (grānd), *adj.* **1** having little lines and markings. **2** painted to look like the grain in wood, marble, etc.

grain elevator, building for storing grain.

grain·y (grā′nē), *adj.* **1** like the grain of wood, marble, etc. **2** made up of grains; granular. ❑ *adj.* **grain·i·er, grain·i·est.** —**grain′i·ness,** *n.*

gram (gram), *n.* unit of weight or mass in the metric system.

-gram, *suffix.* **1** grams: *kilogram = one thousand grams.* **2** part of a gram: *centigram = a hundredth part of a gram.*

gram atom, amount of mass of a chemical element that equals in number of grams the element's atomic weight number. A gram atom of oxygen is 16 grams because oxygen's atomic weight is almost exactly 16.

gram·mar (gram′ər), *n.* **1** the study of the forms and uses of words in sentences in a particular language. **2** rules describing the use of words in a language. **3** the use of words according to these rules: *My teacher's grammar is excellent.* [See Word Story at **glamour.**]

gram·mar·i·an (grə mer′ē ən), *n.* an expert in grammar.

grammar school, 1 (in the United States) an elementary school. **2** (in England) a preparatory school.

gram·mat·i·cal (grə mat′ə kəl), *adj.* **1** according to the rules of grammar: *Our French teacher speaks grammatical English but has a French accent.* **2** of grammar: *"You should have saw it" is a grammatical mistake.* —**gram·mat′i·cal·ly,** *adv.* —**gram·mat′i·cal·ness,** *n.*

gram molecule, mole[3].

Gram·my (gram′ē), *n.* award given each year by the National Academy for Recording Arts and Sciences for the best performances, songwriting, production, etc. ❑ *n., pl.* **Gram·mies.**

Gra·na·da (grə nä′də), *n.* city in S Spain, last stronghold of the Moors till they were driven out of Spain in 1492. See **Castile** for map. [Granada may come from a Spanish word meaning "pomegranate." That fruit is plentiful there.]

Granada—palace in Granada

gran·a·ry (gran′ər ē *or* grā′nər ē), *n.* **1** building where grain is stored. **2** region producing much grain. ❑ *n., pl.* **gran·a·ries.**

grand (grand), **1** *adj.* large and of fine appearance: *The royal family lived in a grand palace.* **2** *adj.* of very high or noble quality; dignified: *grand music, a grand old man.* **3** *adj.* highest or very high in rank; chief: *grand duchess.* **4** *adj.* great; important; main: *The grand prize in the contest was a new car.* **5** *adj.* complete; comprehensive: *grand total.* **6** *adj.* excellent; very good: *We had a grand time at the party last night.* **7** *n.* INFORMAL. a thousand dollars. —**grand′ly,** *adv.* —**grand′ness,** *n.*

SYNONYM STUDY Grand, magnificent, and **majestic** all mean large and fine-looking. **Grand** is a general word: *The new hotel by the river is very grand.* **Magnificent** means impressively splendid: *What a magnificent sunset!* **Majestic** means grand and very dignified: *The eagle is a majestic bird.*

Grand Army of the Republic, 1 organization of men who served in the Union Army or Navy during the Civil War, founded in 1866 and disbanded in 1956, after its last member died.

Grand Banks or **Grand Bank,** shoal off the SE coast of Newfoundland. It is important for cod fishing.

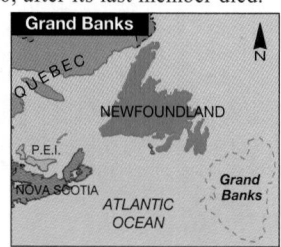

Grand Canyon, deep gorge of the Colorado River, in N Arizona.

Grand Canyon National Park, a national park in NW Arizona, containing the Grand Canyon.

grand·child (grand′child′), *n.* child of your son or daughter. ❑ *n., pl.* **grand·chil·dren** (grand′-chil′drən).

Grand Cou·lee (kü′lē), large dam on the Columbia River, in E Washington.

grand·dad (gran′dad′), *n.* INFORMAL. grandfather.

grand·daugh·ter (gran′dȯ′tər), *n.* daughter of your son or daughter.

gran·dee (gran dē′), *n.* **1** a Spanish or Portuguese nobleman of the highest rank. **2** person of high rank or great importance. ❑ *n., pl.* **gran·dees.**

gran·deur (gran′jər), *n.* greatness; majesty; dignity; splendor.

grand·fa·ther (grand′fä′ᴛʜər), *n.* father of your father or mother.

grandfather clock, clock in a tall, wooden case, which stands on the floor.

grand·fa·ther·ly (grand′fä′ᴛʜər lē), *adj.* like or characteristic of a grandfather.

grandfather's clock, grandfather clock.

Grand Forks, city in E North Dakota.

gran·dil·o·quence (gran dil′ə kwəns), *n.* the use of lofty or pompous words.

gran·dil·o·quent (gran dil′ə kwənt), *adj.* using lofty or pompous words. **—gran·dil′o·quent·ly,** *adv.*

gran·di·ose (gran′dē ōs), *adj.* **1** grand in a showy or pompous way. **2** grand in an imposing or impressive way; magnificent. **—gran′di·ose·ly,** *adv.*

Grand Island, city in S central Nebraska.

grand jury, jury of from 12 to 23 persons chosen to investigate accusations of crime and decide whether there is enough evidence for a trial in court.

grand·ma (grand′mä′ *or* gram′ə), *n.* INFORMAL. grandmother. ❑ *n., pl.* **grand·mas.**

Grandma Moses. See Moses, Grandma.

grand·moth·er (grand′muᴛʜ′ər), *n.* mother of your father or mother.

grand·moth·er·ly (grand′muᴛʜ′ər lē), *adj.* like or characteristic of a grandmother.

grand·neph·ew (grand′nef′yü) *n.* son of your nephew or niece.

grand·niece (grand′nēs′), *n.* daughter of your nephew or niece.

grand·pa (grand′pä′ *or* gram′pə), *n.* INFORMAL. grandfather. ❑ *n., pl.* **grand·pas.**

grand·par·ent (grand′pâr′ənt), *n.* grandfather or grandmother.

grand piano, a large, harp-shaped piano with horizontal strings.

Grand Rapids, city in SW Michigan.

grand slam, 1 (in baseball) a home run with three runners on base. **2** Often, **Grand Slam,** act or fact of winning all the major championships in one season by one golf or tennis player. **3** act of winning all the tricks in a hand of bridge.

grand·son (grand′sun′), *n.* son of your son or daughter.

grand·stand (grand′stand′), **1** *n.* the main seating place for people at an athletic field, racetrack, parade, etc. **2** *v.* to act so as to attract attention to yourself; try to impress those who are watching. **—grand′stand′er,** *n.*

Grand Te·ton National Park (tē′ton), a national park in NW Wyoming, containing a spectacular mountain range.

grange (grānj), *n.* **1** **Grange,** an association of farmers for the improvement of their welfare, founded in 1867. **2** a local chapter of this association.

gran·ite (gran′it), *n.* a very hard gray or pink rock that is formed when lava cools slowly underground. Granite is used for buildings and monuments. **—gran′ite·like′,** *adj.*

gran·ny *or* **gran·nie** (gran′ē), *n.* INFORMAL. **1** grandmother. **2** an old woman. ❑ *n., pl.* **gran·nies.**

granny knot, knot differing from a square knot in having the ends crossed the opposite way.

gra·no·la (grə nō′lə), *n.* a dry breakfast cereal of rolled oats, flavored with other things such as honey, dried fruit, and nuts. ❑ *n., pl.* **gran·olas.**

grant (grant), **1** *v.* to give what is asked; allow: *grant a request, grant permission.* **2** *v.* to admit to be true; accept without proof; concede: *I grant that you are right so far.* **3** *v.* to give or confer a right, privilege, etc., by formal act. **4** *n.* gift, especially land or money given by the government: *a research grant of $80,000.* **—grant′a·ble,** *adj.* **—grant′er,** *n.*

take for granted, 1 to assume to be true; regard as proved or agreed to: *We take the law of gravitation for granted.* **2** to accept as probable: *We took for granted that the sailor could swim.*

Grant (grant), *n.* **1** **Ca·ry** (kâr′ē), 1904-1986, American movie star, born in England. He starred in many comedies and several Alfred Hitchcock thrillers, including *Notorious* and *North by Northwest.* **2** **Ulysses S.,** 1822-1885, Union commanding general during the Civil War, and 18th president of the United States, from 1869 to 1877. ■ **Ulysses S. Grant's** original name was Hiram Ulysses Grant, but his family called him Ulysses. The congressman who recommended him for West Point thought his first name was Ulysses and added his mother's family name, Simpson.

grant·ee (gran′tē′), *n.* person to whom a grant is made. ❑ *n., pl.* **grant·ees.**

grant·or (gran′tər), *n.* (in law) person who makes a grant.

gran·u·lar (gran′yə lər), *adj.* **1** consisting of or containing grains or granules; grainy: *granular stone.* **2** like grains or granules. **—gran′u·lar·ly,** *adv.*

gran·u·lat·ed (gran′yə lā′tid), *adj.* **1** formed into grains or granules: *granulated sugar.* **2** roughened on the surface: *granulated leather.*

gran·u·la·tion (gran′yə lā′shən), *n.* formation into grains or granules.

gran·ule (gran′yül), *n.* a small grain.

grape (grāp), *n.* **1** a small, round fruit, purple, pale green, or red, that grows in bunches on several kinds of vines. Grapes are eaten raw or made into raisins or wine. **2** grapeshot. **—grape′like′,** *adj.*

WORD STORY **Grape** comes from a French word meaning "a hook." **Grapnel** and **grapple** come from the same word. People used sticks with hooks to gather grapes.

grape·fruit (grāp′früt′), *n.* a pale yellow, round, juicy citrus fruit of a tree grown in warm climates. ❑ *n., pl.* **grape·fruit** *or* **grape·fruits.**

grape·shot (grāp′shot′), *n.* cluster of small iron balls formerly fired from a cannon.

grandstand (def. 1)

grape sugar, dextrose.

grape·vine (grāp′vīn′), *n.* **1** vine that grapes grow on. **2** way by which news or rumors are mysteriously spread.

graph (graf), **1** *n.* line or diagram showing how one quantity depends on or changes with another. You could draw a graph to show how your weight has changed each year with your change in age. **2** *n.* a line representing the mathematical relations of the elements in an equation or function. **3** *v.* to make a graph of.

WORD FAMILY **Graph** and the words below are related. They all come from a Greek word meaning "to write" or "to draw."

autograph	geography	lexicography	phonograph
biography	graffiti	mimeograph	photograph
choreography	graphics	paragraph	seismograph

a	hat	ė	term	ô	order	ch	child		ə	a in about
ā	age	i	it	oi	oil	ng	long			e in taken
ä	far	ī	ice	ou	out	sh	she			i in pencil
â	care	o	hot	u	cup	th	thin			o in lemon
e	let	ō	open	u̇	put	ᴛʜ	then			u in circus
ē	equal	ȯ	saw	ü	rule	zh	measure			

G

-graph, *suffix.* device that records, draws, or writes: *seismograph = device that records earthquake data.*

graph·ic (graf′ik), *adj.* **1** producing by words the effect of a picture; lifelike; vivid: *Her graphic description of the English countryside made me feel as though I had been there myself.* **2** shown by a graph: *The school board kept a graphic record of school attendance for a month.* **3** of or about drawing, painting, engraving, etching, etc.: *the graphic arts.* **4** of or using pictures or diagrams. **5** of or used in handwriting: *graphic symbols.* —**graph′i·cal·ly,** *adv.*

graph·i·cal (graf′ə kəl), *adj.* **1** using pictures instead of written words: *a graphical computer interface.* **2** graphic.

graphic arts, the arts or methods of printing, engraving, etching, and lithography, which involve producing multiple copies of pictures made with lines on flat surfaces. Graphic arts may include painting, drawing, and photography.

graph·ics (graf′iks), *n.* **1** pictures or diagrams made by a computer or video game. **2** art or science of drawing, especially by mathematical methods, as in mechanical drawing.

graph·ite (graf′īt), *n.* a soft, black form of carbon used for pencil leads and for greasing machinery.

graph·ol·o·gy (gra fol′ə jē), *n.* the study of handwriting, especially as a way of analyzing someone's character.

graph paper, paper ruled in squares, for making graphs.

-graphy, *suffix.* **1** process of recording, writing, or drawing: *photography = the process of recording with light.* **2** a descriptive science: *geography = the descriptive science of the earth.*

grap·nel (grap′nəl), *n.* **1** tool with one or more hooks for seizing and holding something; grapple; grappling iron. Grapnels thrown by ropes were once used to catch on an enemy's ship. **2** a small anchor with three or more hooks. [See Word Story at **grape.**]

grap·ple (grap′əl), **1** *v.* to seize and hold fast; grip or hold firmly. **2** *n.* act of seizing and holding fast; firm grip or hold. **3** *v.* to struggle; fight: *The wrestlers grappled in the center of the ring. I grappled with the problem for an hour before I solved it.* **4** *n.* grapnel. ❏ *v.* **grap·pled, grap·pling.** [See Word Story at **grape.**]

grappling iron, grapnel.

grasp (grasp), **1** *v.* to seize and hold fast by closing the fingers around: *I grasped the tree limb to keep from falling.* **2** *n.* act of seizing and holding tightly; clasp of the hand: *I almost lost my grasp on the rope.* **3** *n.* power of seizing and holding; reach: *Success is within her grasp.* **4** *n.* control; possession: *The people regained power from the grasp of the dictator.* **5** *v.* to understand: *She grasped my meaning at once.* **6** *n.* understanding: *He has a good grasp of mathematics.* —**grasp′a·ble,** *adj.* —**grasp′er,** *n.*

grasp at, 1 to try to take hold of; try to grasp. **2** to accept eagerly: *She grasped at the opportunity.*

grasp·ing (gras′ping), *adj.* eager to get all that you can; greedy. —**grasp′ing·ly,** *adv.* —**grasp′ing·ness,** *n.*

grass (gras), *n.* **1** any of many plants with green blades which cover fields, lawns, and pastures. Horses, cows, and sheep eat grass. **2** any of many plants that have jointed stems and long, narrow leaves. Wheat, corn, sugar cane, and bamboo are grasses. **3** land covered with grass; lawn: *The children played on the grass.* **4** SLANG. marijuana. ❏ *n., pl.* **grass·es** for 2. —**grass′less,** *adj.* —**grass′like′,** *adj.*

grass hockey, CANADIAN. field hockey.

grass·hop·per (gras′hop′ər), *n.* any of numerous winged insects with strong hind legs for jumping. Locusts are grasshoppers.

grass·land (gras′land′), *n.* land with grass on it.

grass roots, the ordinary citizens of a region, rather than their political party leaders: *The senator is certain to get support from the grass roots.*

grass·y (gras′ē), *adj.* **1** covered with grass; having much grass. **2** of or like grass. ❏ *adj.* **grass·i·er, grass·i·est.**

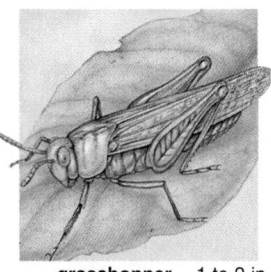
grasshopper—1 to 2 in. (2.5 to 5 cm) long

grate¹ (grāt), *n.* **1** framework of iron bars to hold burning fuel in a furnace, fireplace, etc. **2** fireplace. **3** framework of bars over a window or opening; grating. [See Word Story at **grill.**] ■ Another word that sounds like this is **great.**

grate² (grāt), *v.* **1** to wear down or grind off in small pieces: *The cook grated the cheese before melting it.* **2** to make a harsh, jarring noise by rubbing: *The door grated on its rusty hinges.* **3** to have an annoying or unpleasant effect: *Their loud voices grate on my nerves.* ❏ *v.* **grat·ed, grat·ing.** ■ Another word that sounds like this is **great.**

grate·ful (grāt′fəl), *adj.* feeling kindly because of a favor received; wanting to do a favor in return; thankful: *I am grateful for your help.* [See Word Story at **agree.**] —**grate′ful·ly,** *adv.* —**grate′ful·ness,** *n.*

grat·er (grā′tər), *n.* utensil with a rough, sharp surface used to grate cheese, vegetables, and other food.

grat·i·fi·ca·tion (grat′ə fə kā′shən), *n.* **1** act of gratifying or condition of being gratified: *The gratification of a person's every wish is not always possible.* **2** something that satisfies or pleases: *Your faith in my ability is a gratification to me.*

grat·i·fy (grat′ə fī), *v.* **1** to give pleasure to; please: *Praise gratifies most people.* **2** to give satisfaction to; satisfy; indulge: *gratify a craving for sweets.* ❏ *v.* **grat·i·fied, grat·i·fy·ing.** —**grat′i·fi′a·ble,** *adj.* —**grat′i·fi′er,** *n.* —**grat′i·fy′ing·ly,** *adv.*

grat·ing¹ (grā′ting), *n.* framework of parallel or crossed bars; grate. Windows in a prison, bank, or ticket office usually have gratings over them.

grat·ing² (grā′ting), *adj.* harsh or jarring in sound: *a loud, grating voice.* —**grat′ing·ly,** *adv.*

grat·is (grat′is or grā′tis), *adv., adj.* for nothing; free of charge: *I will give it to you gratis. Parking is gratis for club members.*

grat·i·tude (grat′ə tüd), *n.* kindly feeling because of a favor received; desire to do a favor in return; thankfulness.

gra·tu·i·tous (grə tü′ə təs), *adj.* without reason or cause; unnecessary; uncalled-for: *a gratuitous insult.* —**gra·tu′i·tous·ly,** *adv.* —**gra·tu′i·tous·ness,** *n.*

gra·tu·i·ty (grə tü′ə tē), *n.* present of money in return for service; tip. ❏ *n., pl.* **gra·tu·i·ties.**

grave¹ (grāv), *n.* **1** hole dug in the ground where a dead body is to be buried. **2** any place of burial: *a watery grave.* **3** death. —**grave′like′,** *adj.*

grave² (grāv), *adj.* **1** important; weighty; heavy; momentous: *grave cares, a grave decision.* **2** serious; threatening; critical: *a grave illness, grave news.* **3** sober; dignified; solemn: *a grave face.* ❏ *adj.* **grav·er, grav·est.** [**Grave²** comes from a Latin word meaning "heavy." See also word history information at **grieve.**] —**grave′ly,** *adv.* —**grave′ness,** *n.*

grave accent, mark (`) placed over a vowel to show pitch, quality of sound, etc. The phrase *à la mode* has a grave accent. In English poetry a grave accent may be used to indicate that a word is pronounced with one more syllable than usual, as in *wreathèd* (rē′ᴛHid).

grave·dig·ger (grāv′dig′ər), *n.* person whose work is digging graves.

grav·el (grav′əl), **1** *n.* pebbles and pieces of rock coarser than sand. Gravel is used for roads and paths. **2** *v.* to lay or cover with gravel. ❏ *v.* **grav·eled, grav·el·ing** or **grav·elled, grav·el·ling.**

grav·el·ly (grav′ə lē), *adj.* **1** having much gravel. **2** of or like gravel. **3** rough; rasping; grating: *a gravelly voice.*

grav·en (grā′vən), *adj.* engraved; carved: *graven images.*

grave·stone (grāv′stōn′), *n.* stone that marks a grave.

grave·yard (grāv′yärd′), *n.* cemetery.

graveyard shift, the working hours between midnight and the morning shift.

grav·i·tate (grav′ə tāt′), v. **1** to move or tend to move toward an object by the force of gravity: *The planets gravitate toward the sun.* **2** to settle down; sink; fall: *The dirt in the water gravitated to the bottom of the bottle.* **3** to tend to go; be strongly attracted: *The attention of the audience gravitated to her as she sang.* ❑ *v.* **grav·i·tat·ed, grav·i·tat·ing. —grav′i·tat′er,** *n.*

grav·i·ta·tion (grav′ə tā′shən), *n.* **1** the force or pull that makes all objects in the universe attract one another. Gravitation keeps the planets in their orbits around the sun. **2** a steady tendency toward some point or object of influence: *The gravitation of people to the cities leaves many farms vacant.* **—grav′i·ta′tion·al,** *adj.* **—grav′i·ta′tion·al·ly,** *adv.*

grav·i·ty (grav′ə tē), *n.* **1** the natural force that causes objects to move or tend to move toward the center of the earth. Gravity causes objects to have weight. **2** gravitation. **3** seriousness; earnestness: *The gravity of her expression told us that the news was bad.* **4** critical quality; importance: *The gravity of the situation was greatly increased by threats of war.* [See word history information at **grieve**.]

gra·vy (grā′vē), *n.* **1** juice that comes out of meat in cooking. **2** sauce for meat, potatoes, etc., made from this juice.

gray (grā), **1** *n.* color made by mixing black and white. **2** *adj.* having a color between black and white: *gray hair.* **3** *v.* to make or become gray: *His hair is graying fast.* **4** *adj.* having gray hair. **5** *adj.* dark; gloomy; dismal: *a gray, rainy day.* Also, **grey.** **—gray′ly,** *adv.* **—gray′ness,** *n.*

gray·beard (grā′bird′), *n.* an old man.

gray·ish (grā′ish), *adj.* somewhat gray.

gray jay, a North American jay with gray feathers and no crest; Canada jay; whisky-jack.

gray·ling (grā′ling), *n.* any of several freshwater fishes resembling trout and much valued as food and game fishes.

gray matter, 1 the grayish tissue in the brain and spinal cord that contains nerve cells and some nerve fibers. **2** intelligence; brains.

gray wolf, a large wolf, usually with dark gray fur, of northern North America and Asia. In North America it is sometimes called timber wolf.

graze[1] (grāz), *v.* **1** to feed on growing grass: *Cattle were grazing in the field.* **2** to put cattle, sheep, etc., to feed on growing grass or a pasture: *The farmer grazed his sheep.* ❑ *v.* **grazed, graz·ing. —graze′a·ble** or **graz′a·ble,** *adj.* **—graz′er,** *n.*

graze[2] (grāz), **1** *v.* to touch lightly in passing; rub lightly against: *The car grazed the garage door.* **2** *v.* to scrape the skin from: *She fell and grazed her knee.* **3** *n.* a slight wound made by grazing. ❑ *v.* **grazed, graz·ing.**

grease (grēs *for noun;* grēs *or* grēz *for verb*), **1** *n.* soft, melted animal fat. **2** *n.* any thick, oily substance. **3** *v.* to rub grease on: *grease a cake pan.* **4** *v.* to put grease on; lubricate: *Please grease my bike chain.* ❑ *v.* **greased, greas·ing. —grease′less,** *adj.*

grease·paint (grēs′pānt′), *n.* mixture of tallow or grease and a pigment, used by actors in painting their faces.

greas·y (grē′sē *or* grē′zē), *adj.* **1** smeared with grease; having grease on it: *a greasy rag.* **2** containing much grease; oily: *Greasy food is hard to digest.* **3** like grease; smooth; slippery. ❑ *adj.* **greas·i·er, greas·i·est. —greas′i·ly,** *adv.* **—greas′i·ness,** *n.*

great (grāt), *adj.* **1** large in extent, amount, size, or number; big: *a great crowd.* **2** more than is usual; much: *great kindness.* **3** high in rank; important; remarkable: *a great writer.* **4** much in use; favorite: *Her great sport was tennis.* **5** very much of a: *a great talker.* **6** very good; fine: *We had a great time at the party.* ■ Another word that sounds like this is **grate. —great′ness,** *n.*

great ape, any of the larger apes, including the gorilla, orangutan, and chimpanzee.

great-aunt (grāt′ant′), *n.* aunt of your father or mother.

Great Barrier Reef, the longest coral reef in the world, in the S Pacific along the NE coast of Australia.

Great Basin, region in the W United States with rivers and lakes lacking an outlet to the ocean. It includes most of Nevada and parts of Utah, California, Oregon, Wyoming, and Idaho.

Great Basin National Park, a national park in E Nevada.

Great Bear, Ursa Major.

Great Bear Lake, lake in Northwest Territories, Canada.

Great Britain, England, Scotland, and Wales. Great Britain is the largest island of Europe. See **British Isles** for map.

great circle, any circle on the surface of a sphere with its center at the center of the sphere. The equator is a great circle.

great·coat (grāt′kōt′), *n.* a heavy overcoat.

Great Dane, a very large, thin, powerful, short-haired dog.

Great Divide, Continental Divide.

Great Falls, city in central Montana.

great-grand·child (grāt′grand′child′), *n.* grandchild of your son or daughter. ❑ *n., pl.* **great-grand-chil·dren.**

great-grand·chil·dren (grāt′grand′chil′drən), *n.* plural of great-grandchild.

great-grand·daugh·ter (grāt′gran′dȯ′tər), *n.* granddaughter of your son or daughter.

great-grand·fa·ther (grāt′grand′fä′thər), *n.* grandfather of your father or mother.

great-grand·moth·er (grāt′grand′muᴛH′ər), *n.* grandmother of your father or mother.

great-grand·par·ent (grāt′grand′pâr′ənt), *n.* great-grandfather or great-grandmother.

great-grand·son (grāt′grand′sun′), *n.* grandson of your son or daughter.

great·heart·ed (grāt′här′tid), *adj.* **1** noble; generous. **2** brave; fearless. **—great′heart′ed·ness,** *n.*

great horned owl, a large owl of the Americas with brown and white striped markings and large ear tufts.

Great Lakes, five large lakes between the United States and Ontario, Canada; Lakes Ontario, Erie, Huron, Michigan, and Superior.

great·ly (grāt′lē), *adv.* much: *greatly feared.*

great-neph·ew (grāt′nef′yü), *n.* grandnephew.

great-niece (grāt′nēs′), *n.* grandniece.

Great Plains, region just east of the Rocky Mountains in the United States and SW Canada. It is mostly pasture land.

Great Salt Lake, shallow lake in NW Utah. Its water is much saltier than ocean water.

Great Slave Lake, lake in Northwest Territories, Canada.

Great Smoky Mountains, mountain range in E Tennessee and W North Carolina, part of the Appalachian Mountains.

Great Smoky Mountains National Park, a national park in SE Tennessee and SW North Carolina.

great-un·cle (grāt′ung′kəl), *n.* uncle of your father or mother.

Great Victoria Desert, desert in SW Australia.

Great Wall of China, a stone wall about 4000 miles (6400 kilometers) long between China and Mongolia. It was begun in the 400s B.C. for defense.

Great Wall of China

a	hat	ė	term	ô	order	ch	child		
ā	age	i	it	oi	oil	ng	long	ə	a in about
ä	far	ī	ice	ou	out	sh	she		e in taken
â	care	o	hot	u	cup	th	thin		i in pencil
e	let	ō	open	ù	put	ᴛH	then		o in lemon
ē	equal	ȯ	saw	ü	rule	zh	measure		u in circus

great white shark, a very large shark that sometimes attacks human beings.

greave (grēv), *n.* Often, **greaves,** *pl.* armor for the leg below the knee. ■ Another word that sounds like this is **grieve.**

grebe (grēb), *n.* any of several diving birds something like ducks, but with feet not completely webbed and pointed bills.

Gre·cian (grē′shən), **1** *adj.* Greek. **2** *n.* a Greek.

Greco. See El Greco.

Greece (grēs), *n.* country in SE Europe, on the Mediterranean. *Capital:* Athens.

greed (grēd), *n.* a very strong desire to have a lot of something: *Their greed for money and success was never satisfied.*

greed·y (grē′dē), *adj.* **1** feeling a strong desire to have a lot of something: *greedy for power.* ■ See Synonym Study at **selfish. 2** wanting to eat or drink a great deal in a hurry; ravenous. ❑ *adj.* **greed·i·er, greed·i·est.** —**greed′i·ly,** *adv.* —**greed′i·ness,** *n.*

Greek (grēk), **1** *adj.* of Greece, its people, or their language. **2** *n.* person born or living in Greece. **3** *n.* language of Greece.

WORD SOURCE Greek has given a number of words to the English language, including the words below.

alphabet	electric	hippopotamus	orphan
astronaut	elephant	hyena	panther
Bible	episode	lantern	planet
bishop	galaxy	licorice	rhinoceros
church	govern	marathon	skeleton
comet	graphic	marmalade	telephone
crocodile	gymnasium	melon	zodiac
dinosaur	helicopter	octopus	zone

Greek Orthodox Church, 1 Eastern Church. **2** the part of the Eastern Church forming the established church in Greece.

Gree·ley (grē′lē), *n.* **Hor·ace** (hor′is), 1811-1872, American newspaper publisher, Abolitionist, and presidential candidate. He made the phrase "Go West, young man" popular.

green (grēn), **1** *n.* the color of most growing plants, grass, and the leaves of trees in summer; color in the spectrum between yellow and blue. **2** *adj.* having this color; of this color: *green paint. An emerald is green.* **3** *adj.* covered with growing plants, grass, leaves, etc.: *green fields.* **4** *adj.* not ripe; not fully grown: *Most green fruit is not good to eat.* **5** *adj.* not dried, cured, seasoned, or otherwise prepared for use: *green wood.* **6** *adj.* not trained or experienced: *green players.* **7** *n.* ground covered with grass; grassy land: *the village green.* **8** *adj.* supporting or working for a pollution-free environment. **9** *n.pl.* **greens, a** green leaves and branches used for decoration. **b** leaves and stems of plants used for food: *beet greens,collard greens.* **10** *n.* a putting green of a golf course. —**green′ly,** *adv.* —**green′ness,** *n.*

green·back (grēn′bak′), *n.* piece of U.S. paper money having the back printed in green.

Green Bay, city in NE Wisconsin.

green bean, string bean that has a green pod.

green·belt (grēn′belt′), *n.* section of woods and parks surrounding a town or city, in which building is limited or not permitted.

green card, an identification card issued to people who are living legally in the United States but are not citizens, permitting them to work.

green·er·y (grē′nər ē), *n.* green plants, grass, or leaves. ❑ *n., pl.* **green·er·ies.**

green·horn (grēn′hôrn′), *n.* **1** person without training or experience. **2** person easy to trick or cheat.

green·house (grēn′hous′), *n.* building with a glass or plastic roof and sides kept warm for growing plants; hothouse. ❑ *n., pl.* **green·hous·es** (grēn′hou′ziz).

greenhouse effect, the effect of carbon dioxide, water vapor, and some other gases in the atmosphere. They act to trap heat from the ground, produced by sunlight, much as the glass of a greenhouse does, causing warming. With increasing carbon dioxide from fossil fuels, this effect could cause a change in climate.

greenhouse gas, any of the gases in the atmosphere, such as carbon dioxide, that trap solar heat and cause the greenhouse effect.

green·ish (grē′nish), *adj.* somewhat green.

Green·land (grēn′lənd), *n.* arctic island NE of North America; Kalaallit Nunaat.It is the largest island in the world and belongs to Denmark. [Greenland comes from an Icelandic word meaning "green land." When it was first explored 1000 years ago, its climate was warmer, and the explorers saw fields of green grass.]

green light, 1 a green traffic light used to signal vehicles and pedestrians to go. **2** permission to go ahead with something: *We got a green light on our project.*

green pepper, the unripe fruit of a red pepper plant. It is eaten as a vegetable.

green revolution, an increased production of wheat, rice, and other grain crops in developing countries, beginning in the late 1960s. The increase was achieved by the introduction of new farming methods, new plant varieties, and new chemicals.

Green River, river flowing south from W Wyoming into the Colorado River in Utah.

Greens·bor·o (grēnz′bėr′ō), *n.* city in N central North Carolina.

green thumb, a remarkable ability to grow flowers, vegetables, etc.: *She must have a green thumb to have such a beautiful garden.*

Green·ville (grēn′vəl), *n.* **1** city in NW South Carolina. **2** city in W Mississippi, on the Mississippi River.

Green·wich (gren′ich), *n.* borough in SE London, England. Longitude is measured east and west of Greenwich.

Greenwich Time, the standard time used in England and the basis for setting standard time elsewhere. It sets noon as the time when the sun is directly over the meridian passing through Greenwich, England.

Greer (grir), *n.* **Ger·maine** (jər mān′), born 1939, Australian writer and feminist. She has written about women's problems in male-dominated society.

greet (grēt), *v.* **1** to speak or write to in a friendly, polite way; address in welcome; hail: *She greeted us with a friendly "Hello." 2* to respond to: *His speech was greeted with cheers.* **3** to present itself to; meet: *As we went out, an icy wind greeted us.* —**greet′er,** *n.*

greet·ing (grē′ting), *n.* **1** act or words of a person who greets another; welcome. **2 greetings,** *pl.* friendly wishes on a special occasion: *Season's greetings.*

gre·gar·i·ous (grə gâr′ē əs), *adj.* **1** fond of being with others: *He is not gregarious, and spends most of his time alone.* **2** living in flocks, herds, or other groups: *Sheep are gregarious, raccoons are not.* —**gre·gar′i·ous·ly,** *adv.* —**gre·gar′i·ous·ness,** *n.*

Gre·go·ri·an (grə gôr′ē ən), *adj.* **1** of Pope Gregory I. **2** of Pope Gregory XIII.

Gregorian calendar, calendar now in use in the United States and most other countries, introduced by Pope Gregory XIII in 1582. According to this calendar, an ordinary year has 365 days and leap year has 366 days. It corrects the Julian calendar.

Gregorian chant, a kind of chant introduced by Pope Gregory I and still sometimes used in the Roman Catholic Church.

Greg·or·y I (greg′ər ē), **Saint,** A.D. 540?-604, pope from 590 to 604, called "Gregory the Great." Gregorian chant is named for him. [Gregory comes from a Greek word meaning "watchman."]

greenhouse effect

Gregory XIII, 1502-1585, pope from 1572 to 1585. He introduced the Gregorian calendar.

grem·lin (grem′lən), *n.* an imaginary creature that causes trouble in an aircraft, its engines, parts, etc.

Gre·na·da (grə nā′də), *n.* island country in the West Indies. *Capital:* St. George's.

gre·nade (grə nād′), *n.* a small bomb, which is thrown by hand or fired from a rifle. [Grenade comes from a French phrase meaning "pomegranate." The shape of the bomb resembled the shape of the fruit.]

gren·a·dier (gren′ə dir′), *n.* **1** (formerly) a soldier who threw grenades. **2** (later) a member of a specially chosen unit of foot soldiers. **3** (now) a member of a special regiment of guards in the British army.

Gresh·am (gresh′əm), *n.* city in NW Oregon.

Gretz·ky (grets′kē), *n.* **Wayne** (wān), born 1961, American hockey player. He has scored more goals and made more assists than any other hockey player.

grew (grü), *v.* past tense of **grow:** *It grew colder as the sun set.*

grey (grā), *n., adj., v.* gray. ❑ *n., pl.* **greys;** *v.* **greyed, grey·ing.**

Grey (grā), *n.* **Lady Jane** (jān), 1537-1554, English queen. ■ **Lady Jane Grey** was the great-granddaughter of Henry VII. She ruled as queen for nine days after the death of Edward VI, but then his sister Mary took power. Lady Jane and her husband were beheaded for treason.

Grey Cup, 1 trophy awarded each year to the champion in Canadian professional football. It was first awarded in 1909. **2** game played each year to determine who wins this trophy.

grey·hound (grā′hound′), *n.* a tall, slender dog with a long nose. Greyhounds can run very fast.

grid (grid), *n.* **1** a pattern of evenly spaced lines running both across and up and down. Grids are used on maps to locate places and in mathematics to locate pairs of numbers. **2** framework of parallel iron bars with spaces between them; grating; gridiron. **3** (earlier) electrode in a vacuum tube consisting of wires or a screen to control the flow of electrons from cathode to anode. [See Word Story at **grill.**]

grid·dle (grid′l), *n.* a heavy, flat, metal pan or surface, on which to cook pancakes, hamburgers, bacon, and other fried foods. [See Word Story at **grill.**]

grid·dle·cake (grid′l kāk′), *n.* pancake.

grid·i·ron (grid′ī′ərn), *n.* **1** a football field. **2** grill for broiling. [See Word Story at **grill.**]

grid·lock (grid′lok′), *n.* **1** a complete tie-up of traffic, which prevents vehicles from moving in any direction. **2** any tie-up, blockage or standstill: *an information gridlock.*

grief (grēf), *n.* **1** great sadness caused by trouble or loss; deep sorrow. ■ See Synonym Study at **sorrow. 2** cause of sadness or sorrow. **come to grief,** to have trouble; fail.

griev·ance (grē′vəns), *n.* a real or imagined wrong; reason for being angry or annoyed: *The car owner felt the mechanic did a poor repair job and reported his grievances to the manager.*

grieve (grēv), *v.* **1** to feel grief; be very sad: *The children grieved over their kitten's death.* **2** to cause to feel grief; make very sad: *The news of your illness grieved me.* ❑ *v.* **grieved, griev·ing.** ■ Another word that sounds like this is **greave.** [Grieve comes from a Latin word meaning "heavy." Gravity comes from the same Latin word. People describe grief as a heavy-hearted feeling.] —**griev′er,** *n.* —**griev′ing·ly,** *adv.*

griev·ous (grē′vəs), *adj.* **1** hard to bear; causing great pain or suffering; severe: *Grandfather's death was a grievous loss to all of us.* **2** very evil or offensive; outrageous: *Murder is a grievous crime.* **3** causing grief: *a grievous loss.* **4** full of grief; showing grief: *a grievous cry.* —**griev′ous·ly,** *adv.* —**griev′ous·ness,** *n.*

grif·fin (grif′ən), *n.* an imaginary creature with the head, wings, and forelegs of an eagle, and the body, hind legs, and tail of a lion.

Grif·fith (grif′ith), *n.* **D. W.,** 1875-1948, American movie director and producer. He directed or produced nearly 500 movies, and created many basic techniques, including panning and the use of a moving camera.

grill (gril), **1** *n.* a cooking utensil with parallel iron bars or wires for broiling meat, fish, etc.; gridiron. **2** *v.* to cook by holding near the fire; broil. **3** *n.* dish of broiled meat, fish, etc. **4** *n.* restaurant or dining room that specializes in serving broiled meat, fish, etc. **5** *v.* to question severely and persistently: *The detectives grilled several suspects about the crime.* —**grill′er,** *n.*

WORD STORY **Grill** comes from a Latin word meaning "frame with crossbars." **Crate, grate¹, grid, griddle,** and **gridiron** all come from this word also. Wood set crossways makes a box, and metal set crossways makes a cooking tool.

grille (gril), *n.* an openwork, metal structure or screen, used as a gate, door, window, or to cover the opening in front of the radiator of a car; grating.

grill·work (gril′werk′), *n.* pattern of grilles.

grim (grim), *adj.* **1** without mercy; stern, harsh, or fierce: *grim, stormy weather.* **2** not yielding; not relenting: *Near exhaustion, the runner kept on with grim determination.* **3** looking stern, fierce, or harsh: *My parents were grim when they heard about the broken window.* **4** horrible; frightful; ghastly: *It was my grim task to tell them of their friend's death.* ❑ *adj.* **grim·mer, grim·mest.** —**grim′ly,** *adv.* —**grim′ness,** *n.*

gri·mace (grim′is *or* grə mās′), **1** *n.* a twisted expression of the face; ugly or funny smile: *a grimace caused by pain.* **2** *v.* to make faces: *The clown grimaced at the children.* ❑ *v.* **gri·maced, gri·mac·ing.** —**gri·mac′er,** *n.*

grime (grīm), *n.* dirt rubbed deeply and firmly into a surface.

Grim·ké (grim′kē), *n.* **Sarah,** 1792-1873, and her sister, **An·ge·li·na** (an′jə lē′nə), 1805-1879, American Abolitionists and political reformers. ■ **Sarah** and **Angelina Grimké** became involved in working for rights for women when their antislavery efforts were criticized as "unwomanly."

Grimm (grim), *n.* **Jakob** (yä′kōb), 1785-1863, and his brother, **Wilhelm** (vil′helm), 1786-1859, German dictionary editors and collectors of fairy tales.

grim·y (grī′mē), *adj.* covered with grime; very dirty: *grimy feet.* ❑ *adj.* **grim·i·er, grim·i·est.** —**grim′i·ly,** *adv.* —**grim′i·ness,** *n.*

grin (grin), **1** *v.* to smile broadly. **2** *n.* a broad smile. ❑ *v.* **grinned, grin·ning.** —**grin′ner,** *n.* —**grin′ning·ly,** *adv.*

grind (grīnd), **1** *v.* to crush into bits or powder: *That mill grinds corn into meal and wheat into flour.* **2** *v.* to sharpen, smooth, or wear by rubbing on something rough: *grind an ax on a grindstone.* **3** *v.* to work by turning a handle; produce by turning a crank: *grind a pepper mill.* **4** *v.* to crush by harshness or cruelty: *The serfs were ground down by their lords.* **5** *v.* to make a harsh sound by rubbing; grate: *grind your teeth in frustration.* **6** *v.* to force by rubbing or pressing: *grind one's heel in the dirt.* **7** *n.* something made by grinding: *a fine grind of coffee.* **8** *n.* INFORMAL. long, hard work or study: *To some of the students, mathematics was a grind.* **9** *v.* INFORMAL. to work or study long and hard. **10** *n.* INFORMAL. person who studies long and hard. ❑ *v.* **ground, grind·ing.** —**grind′a·ble,** *adj.* —**grind′ing·ly,** *adv.*

grind·er (grīn′dər), *n.* **1** someone or something that grinds. **2** person or machine that sharpens tools. **3** hero sandwich.

grind·stone (grīnd′stōn′), *n.* a flat, round stone set in a frame and turned by hand, foot, or a motor. It is used to sharpen tools, such as axes and knives, or to smooth and polish things.

grindstone

a	hat	ė	term	ô	order	ch	child		a in about
ā	age	i	it	oi	oil	ng	long		e in taken
ä	far	ī	ice	ou	out	sh	she	ə {	i in pencil
â	care	o	hot	u	cup	th	thin		o in lemon
e	let	ō	open	u̇	put	ŦH	then		u in circus
ē	equal	ȯ	saw	ü	rule	zh	measure		

grin·go (gring′gō), *n.* (in Spain and Spanish America) a term for a foreigner, especially an American or Englishman. ❑ *n., pl.* **grin·gos.** ◼ Gringo is often considered offensive.

WORD STORY   Gringo comes from a Latin word meaning "Greek." People in Spain called any foreigner a Greek, perhaps because the Greek language is much more unlike Spanish than French or Italian are.

gri·ot (grē ō′ *or* grē′ō *or* grē′ot), *n.* person, in some western African tribes and villages, whose inherited responsibility is to keep an oral history of the tribe or village and its traditions.

griot

grip (grip), **1** *n.* a firm hold; seizing and holding tight; tight grasp. **2** *v.* to take a firm hold on; seize and hold tight: *The dog gripped the stick.* **3** *n.* way of gripping a bat, club, or racket. **4** *n.* part to take hold of; handle. **5** *n.* a certain way of gripping the hand as a sign of belonging to some secret society. **6** *n.* (earlier) a small suitcase or handbag. **7** *n.* firm control: *The entire region was in the grip of a severe drought.* **8** *n.* mental grasp; understanding: *She has a grip of the subject.* **9** *v.* to get and keep the interest and attention of: *The exciting story gripped the whole class.* ❑ *v.* **gripped, grip·ping.** —**grip′per,** *n.* —**grip′ping·ly,** *adv.*
come to grips with, 1 to fight hand to hand with; struggle close together: *come to grips with an enemy.* **2** to work hard and seriously; struggle: *come to grips with a problem.*

gripe (grip), **1** *v.* to annoy; irritate. **2** *n.pl.* **gripes,** pain in the intestines. **3** *v.* to complain: *He was always griping about school.* **4** *n.* complaint. ❑ *v.* **griped, grip·ing.** —**grip′er,** *n.*

grippe (grip), *n.* OLD USE. influenza.

gris·ly (griz′lē), *adj.* causing horror; frightful; horrible; ghastly. ❑ *adj.* **gris·li·er, gris·li·est.** ◼ Another word that sounds like this is **grizzly.** —**gris′li·ness,** *n.*

grist (grist), *n.* **1** grain to be ground. **2** grain that has been ground; meal or flour.

gris·tle (gris′əl), *n.* a tough, elastic tissue, such as is found in meat; cartilage.

gris·tly (gris′lē), *adj.* of, containing, or like gristle. ❑ *adj.* **gris·tli·er, gris·tli·est.** —**gris′tli·ness,** *n.*

grist·mill (grist′mil′), *n.* mill for grinding grain.

grit (grit), **1** *n.* very fine bits of gravel or sand. **2** *n.* a coarse sandstone. **3** *n.* courage; bravery; endurance. **4** *v.* to grate; grind: *The swimmer gritted her teeth and plunged into the cold water.* ❑ *v.* **grit·ted, grit·ting.** —**grit′less,** *adj.*

grits (grits), *n.pl.* corn, oats, wheat, etc., husked and coarsely ground. Grits are eaten boiled.

grit·ty (grit′ē), *adj.* **1** of or containing grit; like grit; sandy. **2** courageous; brave. ❑ *adj.* **grit·ti·er, grit·ti·est.** —**grit′ti·ly,** *adv.* —**grit′ti·ness,** *n.*

griz·zled (griz′əld), *adj.* **1** grayish; gray: *a grizzled beard.* **2** gray-haired.

griz·zly (griz′lē), **1** *adj.* grayish; gray. **2** *n.* grizzly bear. ❑ *adj.* **griz·zli·er, griz·zli·est;** *n., pl.* **griz·zlies.** ◼ Another word that sounds like this is **grisly.**

grizzly bear, a large, gray or brownish gray bear of western North America.

groan (grōn), **1** *n.* sound made deep in the throat that expresses grief, pain, or disapproval; deep moan: *We heard the groans of the injured people.* **2** *v.* to give a groan or groans: *The movers groaned as they lifted the piano.* **3** *v.* to make a deep, creaking sound: *The rickety stairs groaned as I climbed them.* **4** *v.* to express by groaning: *He groaned his disapproval.* ◼ Another word that sounds like this is **grown.** —**groan′er,** *n.* —**groan′ing·ly,** *adv.*

gro·cer (grō′sər), *n.* person who sells food and household supplies.

gro·cer·y (grō′sər ē), *n.* **1** store that sells food and household supplies. **2 groceries,** *pl.* articles of food and household supplies sold by a grocer. ❑ *n., pl.* **gro·cer·ies.**

grog (grog), *n.* drink made of rum, or whisky, and water.

grog·gy (grog′ē), *adj.* **1** not steady; shaky: *A blow on the head made me groggy.* **2** not completely awake: *I had just woken up from a nap and still felt groggy.* ❑ *adj.* **grog·gi·er, grog·gi·est.** —**grog′gi·ly,** *adv.* —**grog′gi·ness,** *n.*

groin (groin), *n.* **1** the hollow on either side of the body where the thigh joins the abdomen. **2** the curved edge where two vaults of a roof intersect.

grom·met (grom′it), *n.* **1** a metal eyelet. **2** ring of rope, used as an oarlock, to hold a sail on its stays, etc.

groom (grüm), **1** *n.* bridegroom. **2** *v.* to take care of the appearance of; make neat and tidy: *He was grooming himself for the party.* **3** *v.* to prepare someone for an office: *The lawyer was being groomed as a candidate for mayor.* **4** *n.* person whose work is taking care of horses. **5** *v.* to feed, rub down, brush, and generally take care of horses. —**groom′er,** *n.*

groove (grüv), **1** *n.* a long, narrow channel or furrow, especially one cut by a tool: *My desk has a groove for pencils.* **2** *n.* any similar channel; rut: *Wheels leave grooves in a dirt road.* **3** *v.* to make a groove in. **4** *n.* a fixed way of doing things: *It is hard to get out of a groove.* ❑ *v.* **grooved, groov·ing.** —**groove′like′,** *adj.*

groov·y (grü′vē), *adj.* SLANG. excellent; perfect; just right: *a groovy party.* ❑ *adj.* **groov·i·er, groov·i·est.** —**groov′i·ness,** *n.*

grope (grōp), *v.* **1** to feel about with the hands: *I groped for a flashlight when the lights went out.* **2** to search blindly and uncertainly: *The detectives groped for some clue to the mysterious crime.* **3** to find by feeling about with the hands; feel your way slowly: *She groped her way down the dark, narrow hall.* ❑ *v.* **groped, grop·ing.** —**grop′er,** *n.* —**grop′ing·ly,** *adv.*

gros·beak (grōs′bēk′), *n.* any of several colorful birds with large, stout bills.

gross (grōs), **1** *adj.* with nothing taken out; total; whole; entire. Gross receipts are all the money taken in before costs are deducted. **2** *n.* the whole sum; total amount. **3** *v.* to make a gross profit of; earn a total of: *The company grosses over $2,000,000 per year.* **4** *n.* twelve dozen; 144. **5** *adj.* very easily seen; glaring; flagrant: *gross misconduct, gross superstition.* **6** *adj.* coarse; vulgar; disgusting: *gross manners.* **7** *adj.* too big and fat; overfed. **8** *adj.* INFORMAL. very bad, especially in a disgusting way: *No movie is too gross for my brother.* ❑ *n., pl.* **gross·es** for 2, **gross** for 4. —**gross′ly,** *adv.* —**gross′ness,** *n.*

gross national product, the total money value of all the goods and services produced in a nation during a certain period of time; GNP.

gro·tesque (grō tesk′), *adj.* **1** odd or unnatural in shape, appearance, manner, etc.; fantastic; odd: *a grotesque monster.* **2** ridiculous; absurd: *The monkey's grotesque antics made us laugh.* —**gro·tesque′ly,** *adv.* —**gro·tesque′ness,** *n.*

WORD STORY   Grotesque comes from a Greek word meaning "vault." During the Middle Ages, people discovered underground vaults of ancient buildings, which had been decorated with fantastic pictures.

grot·to (grot′ō), *n.* **1** cave or cavern. **2** an artificial cave made for coolness and pleasure. ❑ *n., pl.* **grot·toes** *or* **grot·tos.**

grouch (grouch), **1** *n.* a surly, ill-tempered person; person who tends to grumble or complain. **2** *n.* a surly, ill-tempered mood; fit of grumbling or complaining. **3** *v.* to grumble or complain in a surly, ill-tempered way. ❑ *n., pl.* **grouch·es.** [See word history information at **grudge.**]

grouch·y (grou′chē), *adj.* tending to grumble or complain; surly; ill-tempered. ❑ *adj.* **grouch·i·er, grouch·i·est. —grouch′i·ly,** *adv.* **—grouch′i·ness,** *n.*

ground[1] (ground), **1** *n.* the solid part of the earth's surface; soil: *A blanket of snow covered the ground.* **2** *n.* Often, **grounds,** *pl.* any piece of land or region used for some special purpose: *The school band practices daily on the parade ground.* **3** *n.pl.* **grounds, a** land, lawns, and gardens around a house, school, etc. **b** small bits that sink to the bottom of a drink such as coffee or tea; dregs; sediment. **4** *adj.* of, on, at, or near the ground: *the ground floor of a building.* **5** *v.* to run aground; hit the bottom or shore: *The boat grounded in shallow water.* **6** *n.* Often, **grounds,** *pl.* basis for what is said, thought, claimed, or done; reason: *What are your grounds for that statement?* **7** *v.* to set firmly; establish: *Their beliefs are grounded on facts.* **8** *v.* to instruct in the first principles or basics: *The class is well grounded in arithmetic.* **9** *n.* underlying surface; background: *The cloth has a blue pattern on a white ground.* **10** *n.* the connection of an electrical conductor with the earth. **11** *v.* to connect an electric wire or other conductor with the earth. **12** *v.* to keep a pilot or an aircraft from flying: *The pilot was grounded by injury.* **13** *v.* to keep a child or teenager from going out of the home for entertainment, as a discipline or punishment. **14** *v.* (in baseball) to hit a ball that rolls or bounces along the ground.

break ground, 1 to turn up soil with a plow, shovel, etc.; dig; plow. **2** to begin building.

cover ground, 1 to go over a certain distance or area: *Did you cover much ground on your hike?* **2** to do a certain amount of work, etc.: *We covered considerable ground in history today.*

gain ground, 1 to go forward; advance; progress. **2** to become more common or widespread: *His ideas are gaining ground.*

give ground, to retreat; yield.

lose ground, 1 to fail to move forward or progress; go backward: *We lost ground because of the storm.* **2** to become less common or widespread: *Superstition loses ground as people become more educated.*

ground[2] (ground), *v.* past tense and past participle of **grind:** *The miller ground the corn into meal. The wheat was ground to make flour.*

ground ball, grounder.

ground·break·ing (ground′brā′king), **1** *n.* the breaking of new ground in order to begin construction of some kind. **2** *adj.* bringing in something new; innovative: *a groundbreaking discovery that changed the course of science.*

ground cover, low plants, bushes, etc., planted for ornament, to enrich the soil, or to prevent eroding of topsoil.

ground crew, mechanics and other nonflying personnel responsible for conditioning and maintenance of aircraft.

ground crew

ground·er (groun′dər), *n.* baseball hit so as to bounce or roll along the ground; ground ball.

ground·hog (ground′hog′), *n.* woodchuck.

Groundhog Day, February 2, the day when groundhogs are believed to come out of their holes. If the sun is shining, and the groundhogs see their shadows, it is believed that they go back in their holes and that winter continues for six more weeks.

ground·less (ground′lis), *adj.* without foundation or basis: *a groundless rumor.* **—ground′less·ly,** *adv.* **—ground′less·ness,** *n.*

ground pine, club moss.

ground rule, one of a basic set of rules regulating an activity, especially certain rules used in baseball. **—ground′-rule′,** *adj.*

ground squirrel, any of several burrowing squirrels, such as the chipmunk.

ground swell, a broad, deep wave or swell of the ocean caused by a distant storm or earthquake.

ground·wa·ter (ground′wô′tər), *n.* water that flows or seeps downward, saturates the rock below the soil, and supplies springs and wells.

ground·work (ground′wėrk′), *n.* foundation; basis.

group (grüp), **1** *n.* number of persons or things together: *A group of children were playing tag.* **2** *n.* number of persons or things belonging or classed together: *Wheat, rye, and oats belong to the grain group.* **3** *v.* to form into a group: *The children grouped themselves at the monkey's cage.* **4** *v.* to put in a group; arrange in groups: *Group the numbers to form three columns.* **5** *n.* a military unit made up of two or more battalions of supporting personnel, usually commanded by a colonel. **6** *n.* an air force unit smaller than a wing and composed of two or more squadrons. ■ See Usage Note at **collective noun.**

> **SYNONYM STUDY** **Group, set,** and **batch** all mean a number of people, animals, or things. **Group** is a general word: *A small group of deer came out of the woods.* **Set** means a number of things that belong together: *These dishes are sold as a set.* **Batch** suggests a number of things made at one time: *We will each bake a batch of cookies for the party.*

group·er (grü′pər), *n.* any of numerous large food fishes of warm seas. ❑ *n., pl.* **group·er** or **group·ers.**

group·ie (grü′pē), *n.* INFORMAL. **1** a young person who is a fan of rock stars or singing groups and follows them wherever they perform. **2** a fan or follower of any famous person: *Politicians, like rock stars, have their groupies.* **3** person strongly devoted to something; devotee: *a literary groupie, a sports groupie.*

group·ing (grü′ping), *n.* **1** act of placing or way of being placed in a group or groups. **2** people or things forming a group.

group insurance, insurance, especially life, medical, dental, and disability insurance, available to a group, such as the employees of a company, under a single contract and at reduced cost. The company may pay all or part of the cost.

group therapy or **group psychotherapy,** treatment of people's mental or emotional problems in small groups under the direction of a therapist.

grouse[1] (grous), *n.* any of several birds that look like plump chickens with feathered legs. Grouse are mostly brown, with some black or white feathers, and are hunted for food. ❑ *n., pl.* **grouse. —grouse′like′,** *adj.*

grouse[2] (grous), *v.* to grumble; complain. ❑ *v.* **groused, grous·ing. —grous′er,** *n.*

grove (grōv), *n.* group of trees standing together. An orange grove is an orchard of orange trees.

grov·el (gruv′əl *or* grov′əl), *v.* **1** to lie face downward; crawl at someone's feet; cringe: *The dog groveled at its master's feet.* **2** to humble yourself: *I will always apologize when I am wrong, but I will grovel before no one.* ❑ *v.* **grov·eled, grov·el·ing** or **grov·elled, grov·el·ling. —grov′el·er** or **grov′el·ler,** *n.* **—grov′el·ing·ly,** *adv.*

grow (grō), *v.* **1** to become bigger by taking in food, as plants and animals do; develop toward full size or age: *Plants grow from seeds.* **2** to exist; thrive: *Few trees grow in the desert.* **3** to become bigger; increase: *Their business has grown fast.* **4** to plant and cause to grow; produce; raise: *We grow cotton here.* **5** to come to be; become: *grow rich.* **6** to become attached or united

a	hat	ė	term	ô	order	ch	child		a in about
ā	age	i	it	oi	oil	ng	long		e in taken
ä	far	ī	ice	ou	out	sh	she	ə	i in pencil
â	care	o	hot	u	cup	th	thin		o in lemon
e	let	ō	open	ů	put	ŦH	then		u in circus
ē	equal	ò	saw	ü	rule	zh	measure		

by growth: *The vine has grown fast to the wall.* ❑ *v.* **grew, grown, grow·ing. —grow′a·ble,** *adj.* **—grow′ing·ly,** *adv.*

grow on, to have an increasing effect or influence on: *The habit grew on me.*

grow out of, 1 to grow too large for; outgrow: *When I grew out of my jacket, I gave it to my little brother.* **2** to result from; develop from: *Several interesting ideas grew out of the discussion.*

grow up, to become full-grown; become an adult: *What will you be when you grow up?*

SYNONYM STUDY **Grow** and **develop** both mean to increase in size or amount. **Grow** is a general word: *She has grown very quickly this year.* **Develop** means to grow gradually to a completed condition: *Flowers develop from buds into full bloom.*

grow·er (grō′ər), *n.* **1** person who grows something: *a fruit grow-er.* **2** plant that grows in a certain way: *a quick grower.*

growl (groul), **1** *v.* to make a deep, low, angry sound: *The dog growled at the stranger.* **2** *n.* a deep, low, angry sound; deep, warning snarl. **3** *v.* to complain angrily; grumble: *The sailors growled about the poor food.* **4** *n.* an angry complaint; grumble. **5** *v.* to rumble: *Thunder growled in the distance.* **6** *n.* a rumble. **—growl′er,** *n.* **—growl′ing·ly,** *adv.*

grown (grōn), **1** *adj.* arrived at full growth. A grown person is an adult. **2** *v.* past participle of **grow:** *This corn has grown very tall.* ■ Another word that sounds like this is **groan.**

grown-up (grōn′up′), **1** *adj.* adult: *a grown-up person.* **2** *adj.* of, like, or suitable for adults: *grown-up manners.* **3** *n.* an adult: *The grown-ups helped the kids inflate the raft.* **—grown′-up′ness,** *n.*

growth (grōth), *n.* **1** process of growing; development. **2** amount grown; increase: *one year's growth.* **3** size, condition, or form produced by growing: *to reach full growth.* **4** what has grown or is growing: *A thick growth of bushes covered the ground.* **5** an abnormal mass of tissue formed in or on the body. A tumor is a growth.

growth hormone, hormone that is formed in the pituitary gland and released into the bloodstream. It controls the growth of the body.

grub (grub), **1** *n.* any soft, thick, wormlike larva of an insect, especially of a beetle. **2** *v.* to root out of the ground; dig up; dig: *Pigs grub for roots.* **3** *v.* to toil; drudge. **4** *n.* SLANG. food. ❑ *v.* **grubbed, grub·bing. —grub′ber,** *n.*

grub·by (grub′ē), *adj.* very dirty; grimy. ❑ *adj.* **grub·bi·er, grub·bi·est. —grub′bi·ly,** *adv.* **—grub′bi·ness,** *n.*

grub·stake (grub′stāk′), **1** *n.* food, equipment, money, etc., supplied to a prospector on the condition of sharing in whatever is found. **2** *v.* to supply with a grubstake. ❑ *v.* **grub·staked, grub·stak·ing. —grub′stak′er,** *n.*

grudge (gruj), **1** *n.* feeling of anger or dislike against because of a real or imaginary wrong; ill will: *She has a grudge against the neighbors who built the fence.* **2** *v.* to feel anger or dislike toward someone because of something; envy the possession of: *He grudged me my little prize even though he had won a bigger one.* **3** *v.* to give or allow unwillingly: *My boss grudged me a small raise.* ❑ *v.* **grudged, grudg·ing.** [**Grudge** comes from a French word meaning "to grumble quietly." **Grouch** comes from the same word. A grouch with a grudge is sure to grumble.] **—grudg′ing·ly,** *adv.*

gru·el (grü′əl), *n.* a thin, almost liquid food made by boiling oatmeal, etc., in water or milk.

gru·el·ing or **gru·el·ling** (grü′ə ling), *adj.* very tiring; exhausting: *Mountain climbing can be grueling.* **—gru′el·ing·ly** or **gru′el·ling·ly,** *adv.*

grue·some (grü′səm), *adj.* causing fear or horror; horrible; revolting. **—grue′some·ly,** *adv.* **—grue′some·ness,** *n.*

gruff (gruf), *adj.* **1** deep and harsh; hoarse: *a gruff voice.* **2** rough, rude, or unfriendly; bad-tempered: *a gruff manner.* **—gruff′ly,** *adv.* **—gruff′ness,** *n.*

grum·ble (grum′bəl), **1** *v.* to mutter in discontent; complain in a bad-tempered way; find fault: *grumbling about the rainy weather.* ■ See Synonym Study at **complain. 2** *n.* a mutter of discontent; bad-tempered complaint. **3** *v.* to make a low, heavy sound like far-off thunder; rumble. **4** *n.* a rumble. ❑ *v.* **grum·bled, grum·bling. —grum′bler,** *n.*

grump (grump), **1** *v.* to sulk. **2** *n.* a grumpy person.

grump·y (grum′pē), *adj.* surly; ill-humored; gruff: *Grumpy people can find fault with almost anything.* ❑ *adj.* **grump·i·er, grump·i·est. —grump′i·ly,** *adv.* **—grump′i·ness,** *n.*

grunt (grunt), **1** *n.* the deep, hoarse sound that a hog makes. **2** *n.* a sound like this: *She picked up the heavy carton with a grunt.* **3** *v.* to make this sound: *He grunted in pain.* **4** *v.* to say with this sound: *He grunted an apology.* **—grunt′er,** *n.* **—grunt′ing·ly,** *adv.*

GSA or **G.S.A.,** Girl Scouts of America.

G-suit (jē′süt′), *n.* suit worn by a pilot or astronaut to prevent blackout, which may be caused by forces greater than the force of gravity.

gt. or **gt,** great.

Gt. Br. or **Gt. Brit.,** Great Britain.

gua·ca·mo·le (gwä′kə mō′lē), *n.* a spread or dip made of mashed avocado, tomato, onion, and seasoning. [**Guacamole** comes from Nahuatl words meaning "avocado" and "sauce."]

Gua·dal·ca·nal (gwä′dl kə nal′), *n.* one of the Solomon Islands, in the W. Pacific. In savage fighting, U.S. forces defeated the Japanese here in 1942-1943.

Gua·da·lupe Mountains National Park (gwä′dl üp′), a national park in W Texas, containing mountains made of stone formerly submerged beneath the sea, containing many fossils.

Gua·de·loupe (gwä′dl üp′), *n.* a group of two islands in the West Indies. They are a part of France. *Capital:* Basse-Terre.

Guam (gwäm), *n.* island in the W Pacific, east of the Philippines. Guam belongs to the United States. *Capital:* Agaña.

gua·na·co (gwä nä′kō), *n.* a wild South American cud-chewing mammal, similar to the llama. ❑ *n., pl.* **guan·a·cos.**

Gua·na·jua·to (gwä′nä hwä′tō), *n.* a state in central Mexico.

Guang·zhou (gwäng′jō′), *n.* city in SE China. It was formerly called **Canton.**

gua·nine (gwä′nēn′), *n.* substance present in nucleic acid. It is one of the compounds that form the genetic code in DNA and RNA.

guanaco—42 in. (1 m) high at the shoulder

gua·no (gwä′nō), *n.* waste matter from seabirds, used as a fertilizer. It is found especially on islands near Peru. ❑ *n., pl.* **guan·os.** [**Guano** comes from a Quechua word meaning "manure."]

Guan·tá·na·mo Bay (gwän tä′nə mō), inlet of the Caribbean Sea in NE Cuba, site of a U.S. naval base.

guar·an·tee (gar′ən tē′), **1** *n.* a promise or pledge to replace or repair a purchased product, return the money paid, etc., if something is not as it should be: *We have a one-year guarantee on our new car.* **2** *v.* to stand back of; give a guarantee for: *This company guarantees its clocks for a year.* ■ See Synonym Study at **promise. 3** *n.* guaranty. **4** *v.* to undertake to secure for another: *The landlady will guarantee us possession of the house by May.* **5** *v.* to make secure; protect: *Our home insurance guarantees us against loss in case of fire or theft.* **6** *v.* to promise to do something; pledge that something has been or will be: *The store guaranteed to deliver my purchase by next Friday.* **7** *n.* something that makes certain something will happen as a result: *Failure to study is practically a guarantee of failure to learn.* ❑ *n., pl.* **guar·an·tees;** *v.* **guar·an·teed, guar·an·tee·ing.**

guar·an·tor (gar′ən tôr), *n.* someone who makes or gives a guarantee.

guar·an·ty (gar′ən tē), **1** *n.* a pledge or promise by which a person gives security for the payment of a debt or the performance of an obligation by another person; guarantee. **2** *n.* property, money, or goods given or taken as security. **3** *n.* act or fact of giving security. **4** *v.* to guarantee. ❑ *n., pl.* **guar·an·ties;** *v.* **guar·an·tied, guar·an·ty·ing.**

guard (gärd), **1** *v.* to watch over; take care of; keep safe; defend; protect: *The dog guarded the child day and night.* **2** *v.* to keep from getting out; hold back; check: *Guard the prisoners.* **3** *n.*

person or group that guards. A soldier or group of soldiers guarding a person or place is a guard. **4** *v.* to take precautions: *Guard against cavities by brushing your teeth regularly.* **5** *n.* anything that gives protection; arrangement to give safety: *A helmet is a guard against head injuries.* **6** *n.* careful watch: *The shepherd kept guard over the sheep.* **7** *v.* to try to keep an opponent from scoring or playing well. **8** *n.* position in which you are ready to defend in boxing, fencing, or cricket. **9** *n.* an offensive player at either side of the center in football. **10** *n.* either of two players in basketball stationed near the center of the court. **–guard′a·ble,** *adj.* **–guard′er,** *n.*

off guard, unprepared for a sudden attack or surprise.

on guard, ready to defend or prevent; watchful.

stand guard, to keep a careful watch: *One goose stands guard while the rest are feeding.*

SYNONYM STUDY **Guard, defend,** and **protect** all mean to keep safe. **Guard** suggests possible danger: *Alarms guard the store against burglars or fire.* **Defend** suggests an attack: *The fort defends the harbor from enemy ships.* **Protect** suggests possible injury: *He always wears a helmet to protect him when riding his bike.*

guard cell, one of the two kidney-shaped cells on each side of the tiny holes in plants that let water and air in and out. Guard cells control the opening and closing of these holes.

guard·ed (gär′did), *adj.* **1** kept safe; carefully watched over; defended. **2** careful; cautious: *"Maybe" was the guarded answer to my question.* **–guard′ed·ly,** *adv.* **–guard′ed·ness,** *n.*

guard·house (gärd′hous′), *n.* **1** building used by soldiers on guard. **2** building used as a jail for soldiers. ❑ *n., pl.* **guard·hous·es** (gärd′hou′ziz).

guard·i·an (gär′dē ən), **1** *n.* someone who takes care of another person or of some special thing. **2** *n.* person appointed by law to take care of the affairs of someone who is young or who cannot take care of his or her own affairs. **3** *adj.* protecting: *guardian angel.* **–guard′i·an·ship,** *n.*

guard·room (gärd′rüm′), *n.* room used by soldiers on guard.

guards·man (gärdz′mən), *n.* **1** guard. **2** soldier who belongs to the National Guard. ❑ *n., pl.* **guards·men.**

Gua·te·ma·la (gwä′tə mä′lə), *n.* country in NW Central America. *Capital:* Guatemala City. **–Gua′te·ma′lan,** *adj., n.*

Guatemala City, capital of Guatemala, in the central part.

gua·va (gwä′və), *n.* a small, yellow or red fruit of any of several tropical American evergreen trees or bushes, used for jelly, jam, etc. ❑ *n., pl.* **gua·vas.**

Gua·ya·quil (gwī′ə kēl′), *n.* port and largest city in Ecuador.

gu·ber·na·to·ri·al (gü′bər nə tôr′ē əl), *adj.* of a governor.

Guern·sey (gėrn′zē), *n.* **1** one of the Channel Islands. **2** one of a breed of tan and white dairy cattle that came from this island. ❑ *n., pl.* **Guern·seys** for 2.

Guer·re·ro (gə rer′ō), *n.* a state in S Mexico.

guer·ril·la (gə ril′ə), *n.* member of an independent band of fighters who harass an enemy by sudden raids, ambushes, robbing supply trains, etc. Guerrillas are not part of a regular army. ❑ *n., pl.* **guer·ril·las.** ■ Another word that sounds like this is **gorilla.**

guess (ges), **1** *v.* to form an opinion of something without really knowing: *Do you know this or are you just guessing?* **2** *n.* opinion formed without really knowing: *My guess is that it will rain tomorrow.* **3** *v.* to get right or find out by guessing: *Can you guess the answer to that riddle?* **4** *v.* to think; believe; suppose: *I guess he was serious after all.* ❑ *n., pl.* **guess·es. –guess′a·ble,** *adj.* **–guess′er,** *n.*

guess·ti·mate (ges′tə mit *or* ges′tə māt *for noun;* ges′tə māt *for verb*), **1** *n.* an estimate based on a guess without having all the facts. **2** *v.* to estimate or make an estimate by guessing. ❑ *v.* **guess·ti·mat·ed, guess·ti·mat·ing.** [Guesstimate is a blend of **guess** and **estimate.**]

guess·work (ges′wėrk′), *n.* work, action, or results based on guessing; guessing.

guest (gest), *n.* **1** person who is received and entertained at someone else's home, club, etc.; visitor. ■ See Synonym Study at **vis-** itor. **2** person staying at a hotel or motel. **3** a well-known person invited to appear at a single performance of a radio or TV show, concert, etc.: *The senator was a guest on the talk show.*

guf·faw (gu fô′), **1** *n.* burst of loud, coarse laughter. **2** *v.* to laugh loudly and coarsely.

guid·ance (gīd′ns), *n.* **1** act or process of guiding; leadership; direction: *Under her mother's guidance, she learned how to swim.* **2** counseling and information given to students to help them solve their problems, plan their education, and choose careers. **3** process of controlling the path of a rocket or other missile in flight by means of radar, computers, radio signals, etc.

guidance counselor, adviser (def. 2).

guide (gīd), **1** *v.* to show the way; lead; direct: *The scout guided us through the pass.* **2** *n.* person or thing that shows the way, leads, or directs: *Tourists sometimes hire guides.* **3** *n.* part of a machine for directing or regulating motion or action. **4** *n.* guidebook. ❑ *v.* **guid·ed, guid·ing. –guid′a·ble,** *adj.* **–guid′er,** *n.*

SYNONYM STUDY **Guide, lead**[1], and **direct** all mean to show or tell the way. **Guide** means to show the way by going along: *The usher guided us to our seats.* **Lead** means to show the way by going in front: *The high school band will lead the parade.* **Direct** means to tell the way: *A police officer can direct you to the library.*

guide·book (gīd′bůk′), *n.* book of directions and information for travelers, tourists, etc.

guided missile, missile that can be guided in flight to its target by means of radio signals from the ground or by automatic devices inside the missile which direct its course.

guide dog, dog guide.

guide·line (gīd′līn′), *n.* Usually, **guidelines,** *pl.* guide, principle, or policy for determining a future course of action: *guidelines for foreign trade.*

guide·post (gīd′pōst′), *n.* post with signs and directions on it. A guidepost where roads meet tells travelers what places each road goes to and how far it is to each place.

guide word, word put at the top of a page as a guide to the contents of the page. The guide words for this page are *guard cell* and *guillotine.*

guild (gild), *n.* **1** association formed by people having the same interests, work, etc., for some useful or common purpose: *The author is a member of the Writers Guild.* **2** (in the Middle Ages) a union of the men in one particular trade or craft, formed to keep its standards high and to protect the interests of its members. ■ Another word that sounds like this is **gild.**

guil·der (gil′dər), *n.* unit of money in the Netherlands.

guild·hall (gild′hôl′), *n.* hall in which a guild meets.

guile (gīl), *n.* crafty deceit; sly tricks; cunning: *The girl got the candy from her younger brother by guile.*

guile·ful (gīl′fəl), *adj.* crafty and deceitful; sly and tricky. **–guile′ful·ly,** *adv.* **–guile′ful·ness,** *n.*

guile·less (gīl′lis), *adj.* without guile; honest; frank; straightforward. **–guile′less·ly,** *adv.* **–guile′less·ness,** *n.*

guil·lo·tine (gil′ə tēn′), **1** *n.* ma- chine for cutting off someone's head by means of a heavy blade that slides down between two grooved posts. **2** *v.* to behead with this machine. ❑ *v.* **guil·lo·tined, guil·lo·tin·ing.**

guillotine

WORD STORY **Guillotine** comes from Joseph-Ignace Guillotine, a French doctor who proposed at the beginning of the French Revolution that such a machine be used in executions.

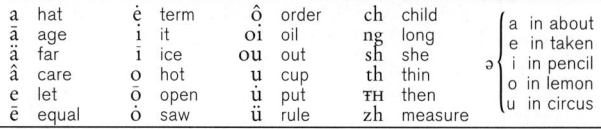

a	hat	ė	term	ô	order	ch	child	
ā	age	i	it	oi	oil	ng	long	(a in about
ä	far	ī	ice	ou	out	sh	she	(e in taken
â	care	o	hot	u	cup	th	thin	ə (i in pencil
e	let	ō	open	ů	put	ŦH	then	(o in lemon
ē	equal	ȯ	saw	ü	rule	zh	measure	(u in circus

guilt (gilt), *n.* **1** fact or condition of having done wrong; being guilty; being to blame: *The evidence proved the accused person's guilt.* **2** guilty action or conduct; crime; offense; wrongdoing. **3** a feeling of having done wrong or being to blame. ■ Another word that sounds like this is **gilt.**

guilt·less (gilt′lis), *adj.* free from guilt; not guilty; innocent. **—guilt′less·ly,** *adv.* **—guilt′less·ness,** *n.*

guilt·y (gil′tē), *adj.* **1** having done wrong; deserving to be blamed and punished: *The jury pronounced the defendant guilty of theft.* **2** knowing or showing that you have done wrong: *a guilty look.* ❑ *adj.* **guilt·i·er, guilt·i·est. —guilt′i·ly,** *adv.* **—guilt′i·ness,** *n.*

guin·ea (gin′ē), *n.* **1** (long ago) a British gold coin worth 21 shillings. **2** (earlier) amount equal to 21 shillings, formerly used in Great Britain in stating prices, fees, etc. ❑ *n., pl.* **guin·eas.**

Guin·ea (gin′ē), *n.* country in W Africa on the Atlantic. *Capital:* Conakry. **—Guin′e·an,** *adj., n.*

Guin·ea-Bis·sau (gin′ē bi sou′), *n.* country in NW Africa. *Capital:* Bissau.

guinea fowl, any of several related domestic fowl something like a pheasant, originally from Africa. Guinea fowl have dark gray feathers with small white spots.

guinea hen, 1 guinea fowl. **2** a female guinea fowl.

guinea pig, 1 any of about 20 kinds of small, fat, harmless rodents with short ears and either short tails or no tail. Guinea pigs make good pets and are often used for laboratory experiments. **2** any person or thing serving as a subject for experiment or observation.

guinea pig (def. 1)
about 6 in. (15 cm) long

Guin·e·vere (gwin′ə vir), *n.* (in legends of the Middle Ages) King Arthur's queen, who was loved by Lancelot. [Guinevere comes from a Celtic word meaning "white."]

guise (gīz), *n.* **1** assumed appearance; pretense: *Under the guise of friendship he plotted treachery.* **2** style of dress; garb: *The spy went in the guise of a nurse and was not recognized by the enemy.*

gui·tar (gə tär′), *n.* a musical instrument usually having six strings, played with the fingers or with a pick.

> **WORD STORY** Guitar comes from the Greek name of a stringed instrument. **Zither** comes from the same word but got its form in German, while **guitar** got its form in Spanish.

gui·tar·ist (gə tär′ist), *n.* person who plays a guitar.

gu·lag or **Gu·lag** (gü′läg), *n.* (in the former Soviet Union) a prison work camp or a political prison.

gulch (gulch), *n.* a very deep, narrow ravine with steep sides, especially one made by a stream. ❑ *n., pl.* **gulch·es.**

gulf (gulf), *n.* **1** a large bay; arm of an ocean or sea with land surrounding most of it: *The Gulf of Mexico is between Florida and Mexico.* **2** separation too great to be closed; wide gap: *The quarrel created a gulf between the old friends.* **—gulf′like′,** *adj.*

Gulf States, Texas, Louisiana, Mississippi, Alabama, and Florida, the states bordering on the Gulf of Mexico.

Gulf Stream, current of warm water in the Atlantic. It flows out of the Gulf of Mexico, north along the East coast of the United States, and then northeast across the Atlantic toward the British Isles.

Gulf War, the Persian Gulf War.

gull[1] (gul), *n.* any of many graceful, gray and white birds living on or near large bodies of water. Gulls have long wings, webbed feet, and thick, strong beaks.

gull[2] (gul), **1** *v.* to deceive; cheat. **2** *n.* person who is easily deceived or cheated.

Gul·lah (gul′ə), *n.* **1** one of a group of African Americans living along the coast of South Carolina and Georgia, and on the islands off the coast. **2** the language spoken by the Gullahs.

gul·let (gul′it), *n.* **1** esophagus. **2** throat.

gul·li·ble (gul′ə bəl), *adj.* easily deceived or cheated. **—gul·li·bil·i·ty** (gul′ə bil′ə tē), *n.*

Gul·li·ver (gul′ə vər), *n.* **Lemuel,** hero of voyages to four imaginary regions in Jonathan Swift's satire, *Gulliver's Travels.*

gul·ly (gul′ē), *n.* a narrow gorge; small ravine; ditch made by heavy rains or running water. ❑ *n., pl.* **gul·lies.**

gulp (gulp), **1** *v.* to swallow eagerly or greedily: *The hungry girl gulped down the bowl of soup.* **2** *n.* act of swallowing: *He ate the cookie in one gulp.* **3** *n.* amount swallowed at one time; mouthful: *I took a gulp of the wine.* **4** *v.* to keep in; choke back: *The disappointed boy gulped down a sob and tried to smile.* **5** *v.* to make a swallowing sound in the throat: *When she saw how high she had climbed, she gulped loudly.* **—gulp′er,** *n.*

gum[1] (gum), **1** *n.* a sticky juice given off by certain trees and plants that hardens in the air and dissolves in water. Gum is used to make candy and medicine, and to make things stick together. **2** *n.* gum tree. **3** *n.* chewing gum. **4** *n.* the sticky substance on the back of a stamp, the flap of an envelope, etc.; mucilage. **5** *n.* rubber. **6** *v.* to coat with gum: *gummed labels.* ❑ *v.* **gummed, gum·ming.**
gum up, to clog with something sticky: *Oil and sawdust have gummed up the power saw chain.*

gum[2] (gum), **1** *n.* Often, **gums,** *pl.* the firm tissue around the teeth. **2** *v.* to chew something with toothless gums: *The baby gummed a piece of zwieback.* ❑ *v.* **gummed, gum·ming.**

gum arabic, gum obtained from acacia trees, used in making candy, medicine, and mucilage.

gum·bo (gum′bō), *n.* **1** soup usually made of chicken and rice and thickened with okra pods. **2** okra plant. **3** its sticky pods. **4** a kind of fine soil that is very sticky when wet. ❑ *n., pl.* **gum·bos.**

gum·drop (gum′drop′), *n.* a stiff, jellylike piece of candy made of gum arabic, gelatin, etc., sweetened and flavored.

gum·my (gum′ē), *adj.* **1** sticky like gum. **2** covered with gum. **3** giving off gum. ❑ *adj.* **gum·mi·er, gum·mi·est. —gum′mi·ness,** *n.*

gump·tion (gump′shən), *n.* initiative; energy.

gum resin, mixture of gum and resin, obtained from certain plants.

gum tree, any of many trees that yield gum. The eucalyptus is one kind of gum tree.

gun (gun), **1** *n.* weapon with a metal tube for shooting bullets or shells. Cannons and pistols are guns. **2** *n.* anything resembling a gun in use or shape: *a spray gun.* **3** *n.* the shooting of a gun as a signal or salute: *a salute of 21 guns.* **4** *v.* to shoot with a gun; hunt with a gun: *gunning for rabbits.* **5** *v.* to increase the speed of; accelerate: *gun an engine.* ❑ *v.* **gunned, gun·ning.** [Gun comes from *Gunnhildr,* an Icelandic woman's name meaning "war." People used to give personal names to cannons, the way they do still to boats.]
stick to your guns, to keep your position; refuse to retreat or yield.

gun·boat (gun′bōt′), *n.* a small warship that can be used in shallow water.

gun·fight (gun′fīt′), *n.* fight in which guns are used.

gun·fire (gun′fīr′), *n.* the shooting of a gun or guns.

gung-ho (gung′hō′), *adj.* INFORMAL. eager; enthusiastic: *a gung-ho student.* [Gung-ho comes from Chinese words meaning "to work together." The Chinese words were used as a slogan by a group of U.S. Marines in the Far East during World War II.]

gun·man (gun′mən), *n.* person who uses a gun to rob or kill. ❑ *n., pl.* **gun·men.**

gun·ner (gun′ər), *n.* **1** member of the armed forces trained to handle and fire large guns. **2** (in the Navy) a warrant officer in charge of a ship's guns.

gun·ner·y (gun′ər ē), *n.* the construction and management of large guns.

gunnery sergeant, either of two military ranks. See chart on page 712.

gun·ny (gun′ē), *n.* **1** a strong, coarse fabric made of jute, used for sacks, bags, etc. **2** gunnysack. ❑ *n., pl.* **gun·nies** for 2.

gun·ny·sack (gun′ē sak′), *n.* sack, bag, etc., made of gunny.

gun·point (gun′point′), *n.* the open end of a gun barrel.
at gunpoint, threatened by a gun.

gun·pow·der (gun′pou′dər), *n.* powder that explodes when brought into contact with fire, used in guns and fireworks.

gun·shot (gun′shot′), *n.* **1** shot fired from a gun. **2** the shooting of a gun: *We heard gunshots.* **3** distance that a gun will shoot: *The deer was within gunshot.*

gun·shy (gun′shī), *adj.* **1** suspicious; wary: *Ever since she lost money in a fake sweepstakes, she's been gun-shy of responding to "you might be a winner" letters.* **2** afraid of the sound of a gun.

gun·smith (gun′smith′), *n.* person whose work is making or repairing small guns.

gun·stock (gun′stok′), *n.* the wooden support or handle to which the barrel of a gun is fastened.

gun·wale (gun′l), *n.* the upper edge of the side of a ship or boat.

gup·py (gup′ē), *n.* a very small, brightly colored fish of tropical fresh water, often kept in aquariums. The female bears live young instead of laying eggs. The male is brightly colored. □ *n., pl.* **gup·pies.** [Guppy comes from R. J. L. Guppy, a clergyman in Trinidad who first brought the fish to scientific attention about 150 years ago.]

gur·gle (gėr′gəl), **1** *v.* to flow or run with a bubbling sound: *Water gurgles over stones.* **2** *n.* a bubbling sound. **3** *v.* to make a bubbling sound: *The baby gurgled.* □ *v.* **gur·gled, gur·gling.**

gur·ney (gėr′nē), *n.* cart for moving patients in a hospital. It has a flat top and movable side rails. □ *n., pl.* **gur·neys.**

gu·ru (gü′rü *or* gù rü′), *n.* **1** a religious teacher or guide in Hinduism. **2** any guide or leader, in the spiritual, political, literary, or musical field.

gush (gush), **1** *v.* to rush out suddenly; pour out: *Oil gushed from the new well.* ■ See Synonym Study at **flow. 2** *n.* rush of water or other liquid from an enclosed space: *If you get a deep cut, there often is a gush of blood.* **3** *v.* to talk in a way that shows too much silly feeling: *The child gushed about the puppy.* □ *n., pl.* **gush·es.**

gush·er (gush′ər), *n.* an oil well which spouts a steady stream of oil without pumping.

gush·y (gush′ē), *adj.* showing too much silly feeling. □ *adj.* **gush·i·er, gush·i·est. –gush′i·ly,** *adv.* **–gush′i·ness,** *n.*

gus·set (gus′it), *n.* a triangular piece of material inserted in an article of clothing to give greater strength or more room.

gust (gust), *n.* **1** a sudden, violent rush of wind: *A gust upset the small sailboat.* **2** a sudden burst of rain, smoke, sound, etc. **3** a sudden bursting forth of anger, enthusiasm, or other feeling: *Gusts of laughter greeted the clown.*

gus·to (gus′tō), *n.* hearty enjoyment; keen relish: *The hungry boy ate his dinner with gusto.*

gust·y (gus′tē), *adj.* coming in gusts; windy; stormy. □ *adj.* **gust·i·er, gust·i·est. –gust′i·ly,** *adv.* **–gust′i·ness,** *n.*

gut (gut), **1** *n.* the whole alimentary canal or one of its parts, such as the intestine or stomach. **2** *n.pl.* **guts, a** intestine. **b** INFORMAL. courage. **3** *n.* catgut. **4** *v.* to remove the intestines of; disembowel. **5** *v.* to destroy the inside of. □ *v.* **gut·ted, gut·ting.**

Gu·ten·berg (güt′n bėrg′), *n.* **Johann** (yō′hän), 1395?-1468?, German printer. He is the first European known to have printed from movable type.

Guth·rie (guth′rē), *n.* **Wood·y** (wùd′ē), 1912-1967, American folk singer and composer. He wrote more than 1000 songs, including "This Land is Your Land."

gut·less (gut′lis), *adj.* lacking courage; cowardly.

guts·y (gut′sē), *adj.* INFORMAL. **1** courageous; bold: *a gutsy fighter.* **2** full of energy; very lively: *a gutsy singer.* □ *adj.* **guts·i·er, guts·i·est.**

gut·ta-per·cha (gut′ə pėr′chə), *n.* substance like rubber, made from the thick, milky juice of certain tropical trees.

gut·ter (gut′ər), **1** *n.* channel or ditch along the side of a street or road to carry off water; low part of a street beside the sidewalk. **2** *n.* channel or trough along the lower edge of a roof to carry off rain water. **3** *n.* a channel; groove: *the gutters on either side of a bowling alley.* **4** *v.* to flow or melt in streams: *The candle guttered when the melted wax ran down its sides.*

gut·tur·al (gut′ər əl), **1** *adj.* formed in the throat; harsh: *a deep, guttural voice.* **2** *adj.* formed between the back of the tongue and the soft palate. The *g* in *go* is a guttural sound. **3** *n.* sound formed between the back of the tongue and the soft palate. The sound *k* is a guttural in the word *cool.* **–gut′tur·al·ly,** *adv.*

guy¹ (gī), **1** *n.* rope, chain, or wire attached to something to steady or secure it. **2** *v.* to steady or secure with a guy or guys: *The mast was guyed by four ropes.* □ *v.* **guyed, guy·ing.**

guy² (gī), *n.* INFORMAL. fellow.

Guy² comes from Guy Fawkes, who plotted to blow up the English government 400 years ago but failed. Every year since, to celebrate his arrest, people have burned dummies called guys. The word came to mean anyone who looked odd, and then anyone at all.

Guy·an·a (gī an′ə), *n.* country in N South America. *Capital:* Georgetown.

guz·zle (guz′əl), *v.* to drink greedily; drink too much: *guzzle soft drinks.* ■ See Synonym Study at **drink.** □ *v.* **guz·zled, guz·zling. –guz′zler,** *n.*

gym (jim), *n.* **1** gymnasium. **2** physical education.

gym·na·si·um (jim nā′zē əm), *n.* room, building, etc., fitted up for physical exercise or training and for indoor athletic sports. □ *n., pl.* **gym·na·si·ums, gym·na·si·a** (jim nā′zē ə). [Gymnasium comes from a Greek word meaning "naked." In ancient times athletes exercised naked.]

gym·nast (jim′nast), *n.* an expert in gymnastics.

gymnast

gym·nas·tic (jim nas′tik), *adj.* of or relating to physical exercises or activities. **–gym·nas′ti·cal·ly,** *adv.*

gym·nas·tics (jim nas′tiks), *n.* **1** *pl.* exercises for developing the muscles and improving physical fitness and health, such as are done in a gymnasium. **2** *sing.* a sport in which very difficult exercises are performed.

gym·no·sperm (jim′nə spėrm′), *n.* any plant having its seeds exposed, not enclosed in an ovary or fruit. The pine, spruce, and ginkgo are gymnosperms.

gy·ne·col·o·gy (gī′nə kol′ə jē), *n.* part of medicine that deals with the bodily functions and diseases of women, especially of the reproductive system. **–gy·ne·co·log·ic** (gī′nə kə loj′ik), **gy·ne·co·log′i·cal,** *adj.* **–gy·ne·col′o·gist,** *n.*

gyp (jip), **1** *v.* to cheat; swindle. **2** *n.* a cheating; swindle. **3** *n.* person who cheats; swindler. □ *v.* **gypped, gyp·ping. –gyp′per,** *n.*

Gyp is used by many people who do not realize that it is an insult. It is short for **Gypsy.** People who did business with Gypsies had a prejudice that the Gypsies would cheat them, and this belief became a word. Careful writers and speakers avoid using it.

gyp·sum (jip′səm), *n.* a soft, white mineral containing calcium, sulfur, oxygen, and water. It is used to make plasterboard.

Gyp·sy (jip′sē), **1** *n.* Also, **gypsy,** person belonging to a wandering group of people who came originally from India. **2** *n.* language of the Gypsies; Romany. **3** *adj.* of Gypsies: *Gypsy music.* **4** *n.* **gypsy,** wanderer: *a musician living as a gypsy from job to job.* □ *n., pl.* **Gyp·sies** or **gyp·sies** for 1, **gyp·sies** for 4. Also, **Gip·sy** or **gipsy.** [Gypsy comes from the word **Egyptian.** It was formerly believed that Gypsies came from Egypt.]

a	hat	ė	term	ô	order	ch	child		
ā	age	i	it	oi	oil	ng	long		a in about
ä	far	ī	ice	ou	out	sh	she		e in taken
â	care	o	hot	u	cup	th	thin	ə	i in pencil
e	let	ō	open	ù	put	ŦH	then		o in lemon
ē	equal	ò	saw	ü	rule	zh	measure		u in circus

gypsy moth, a brownish or white moth brought to the United States from France and accidentally released. Its larvae damage and kill trees by eating their leaves.

gy·rate (jī′rāt), *v.* to move in a circle or spiral; whirl; rotate: *A spinning top gyrates.* ❑ *v.* **gy·rat·ed, gy·rat·ing. —gy·ra′-tion,** *n.*

gyr·fal·con (jėr′fȯl′kən *or* jėr′fal′kən), *n.* a large falcon of the Arctic, with white, black, or gray feathers.

gy·ro (hir′ō *or* gir′ō), *n.* pressed, seasoned lamb and beef formed into a cone on a vertical rotating grill and roasted over a charcoal fire. The crisp crust is cut off for serving, often on round bread. Also, **gyros.** ❑ *n., pl.* **gyr·os.**

gyrfalcon

gy·ro·com·pass (jī′rō kum′pəs), *n.* compass using a gyroscope instead of a magnetic needle. It points to true north instead of to the North Magnetic Pole and is not affected by nearby objects of iron or steel. ❑ *n., pl.* **gy·ro·com·pass·es.**

gyr·os (hir′ōs *or* gir′ōs), *n.* gyro.

gy·ro·scope (jī′rə skōp), *n.* a wheel mounted inside a frame. When the wheel spins, it tends to resist any change in the direction that its axis is pointed. Small gyroscopes are toys. Large gyroscopes help to keep ships, aircraft, and guided missiles steady on course.

gy·ro·scop·ic (jī′rə skop′ik), *adj.* of a gyroscope.

gyroscope

H or **h** (āch), *n.* the eighth letter of the English alphabet. ❑ *n., pl.* **H's** or **h's.**

H, symbol for hydrogen.

ha (hä), *interj.* **1** exclamation of surprise, joy, or triumph: *"Ha! I've caught you!" he shouted.* **2** sound of a laugh: *"Ha! ha! ha!" laughed the boys.* Also, **hah.**

Ha, symbol for hahnium.

Ha·bak·kuk (hab′ə kək), *n.* **1** a Hebrew prophet. **2** book of the Bible.

ha·be·as cor·pus (hā′bē əs kôr′pəs), writ or order requiring that a prisoner be brought before a judge or into court to decide whether he or she is being held lawfully. The right of habeas corpus is a protection against unjust imprisonment.

hab·er·dash·er (hab′ər dash′ər), *n.* dealer in the things men wear, such as hats, ties, shirts, socks, etc.

hab·er·dash·er·y (hab′ər dash′ər ē), *n.* **1** store of a haberdasher. **2** articles sold by a haberdasher. ❑ *n., pl.* **hab·er·dash·er·ies** for 1.

hab·it (hab′it), *n.* **1** tendency to act in a certain way; usual way of acting; custom; practice. **2** addiction, especially to a drug. **3** the clothing worn by members of some religious orders. Monks and nuns often wear habits. **4** the clothing worn for horseback riding: *a black riding habit.*

hab·it·a·ble (hab′ə tə bəl), *adj.* fit to live in; able to be inhabited: *repair an abandoned house to make it habitable.* **—hab′it·a·ble·ness,** *n.* **—hab′it·a·bly,** *adv.*

hab·it·ant (hab′ə tənt *for 1;* hab′ə tənt *or* ä bē tän′ *for 2*), *n.* **1** inhabitant. **2** farmer of French descent in Canada or Louisiana.

hab·i·tat (hab′ə tat), *n.* place where a living thing naturally lives or grows: *The jungle is the habitat of monkeys.*

hab·i·ta·tion (hab′ə tā′shən), *n.* **1** place or building to live in; home; dwelling. **2** act of living in something; inhabiting: *A barn is not fit for human habitation.*

hab·it-form·ing (hab′it fôr′ming), *adj.* tending to cause a craving or addiction, as many drugs do.

ha·bit·u·al (hə bich′ü əl), *adj.* **1** done by habit; caused by habit: *a habitual smile.* **2** being or doing something by habit; regular; steady: *A habitual reader reads a great deal.* **3** often done, seen, or used; usual; customary: *a habitual sight.* **—ha·bit′u·al·ly,** *adv.* **—ha·bit′u·al·ness,** *n.*

ha·bit·u·ate (hə bich′ü āt), *v.* to make used; accustom: *The pioneers were habituated to the hardships of frontier life.* ❑ *v.* **ha·bit·u·at·ed, ha·bit·u·at·ing. —ha·bit′u·a′tion,** *n.*

a	hat	ė	term	ô	order	ch	child		
ā	age	i	it	oi	oil	ng	long		a in about
ä	far	ī	ice	ou	out	sh	she		e in taken
â	care	o	hot	u	cup	th	thin	ə	i in pencil
e	let	ō	open	u̇	put	₮H	then		o in lemon
ē	equal	ȯ	saw	ü	rule	zh	measure		u in circus

Shivering in snow,
sparrow, why will you not come
to my nice warm cage

haiku

ha·ci·en·da (hä′sē en′də), *n.* (in Spanish America) a ranch or country house. ❑ *n., pl.* **ha·ci·en·das.** [Hacienda comes from Latin words meaning "things to be done." On a ranch, there are always things that need doing.]

hack[1] (hak), **1** *v.* to cut roughly: *She hacked the meat into jagged pieces.* **2** *n.* a rough cut. **3** *v.* to give frequent, short, dry coughs. **4** *n.* a short, dry cough. [See word history information at nuthatch.]

hack[2] (hak), **1** *n.* person hired to do routine work, especially literary work; drudge. **2** *adj.* working just for money; hired; drudging: *a hack writer.* **3** *adj.* done just for money: *a hack job.* **4** *n.* taxicab. **5** *n.* carriage for hire: *We rode around the park in a hack.*

hack·ber·ry (hak′ber′ē), *n.* **1** any of numerous trees with small, cherrylike fruit that can be eaten. **2** wood of these trees. ❑ *n., pl.* **hack·ber·ries** for 1.

hack·er (hak′ər), *n.* **1** person who is especially interested in computers and skilled in using them. **2** person who illegally accesses other people's computer systems.

hack·le (hak′əl), *n.* **1** one of the long, slender feathers on the neck of a rooster, pigeon, etc. **2 hackles,** *pl.* hairs on the back of a dog's neck that can become erect.
raise the hackles, to arouse anger; make mad.

hack·neyed (hak′nēd), *adj.* used too often; commonplace: *"White as snow" is a hackneyed comparison.*

hack·saw (hak′sȯ′), *n.* saw for cutting metal, consisting of a narrow, fine-toothed blade fixed in a frame.

had (had), *v.* past tense and past participle of **have:** *She had a party. A fine time was had by all who came.*

had·dock (had′ək), *n.* a food fish of the northern Atlantic, similar to the cod, but smaller. ❑ *n., pl.* **had·dock** or **had·docks.**

Ha·des (hā′dēz′), *n.* **1** (in Greek and Roman myths) the home of the dead, a gloomy place below the earth. **2** Also, **hades,** hell.

had·n't (had′nt), had not.

had·ro·saur (had′rə sȯr), *n.* any of many medium-sized dinosaurs that had bills like a duck's bill and webbed feet; duck-billed dinosaur. They ate plants, and many of them stood upright.

hadst (hadst), *v.* OLD USE. had. "Thou hadst" means "you had."

haf·ni·um (haf′nē əm), *n.* a silvery metallic element which is used to control the rate of reaction in nuclear reactors. *Symbol:* Hf

haft (haft), *n.* handle of a knife, sword, dagger, etc.

hag (hag), *n.* **1** a very ugly old woman, especially one who is vicious or malicious. **2** witch.

hag·fish (hag′fish′), *n.* any of several small, eel-shaped, saltwater fishes that attach themselves by their round mouths to other fishes which they eat.They are related to lampreys. ❑ *n., pl.* **hag·fish** or **hag·fish·es.**

Hag·ga·dah or **Hag·ga·da** (hə gä′də), *n.* **1** the religious text read at the Seder feast on the first two nights of Passover. **2** story or legend in the Jewish Talmud that explains the Jewish law. ❑ *n., pl.* **Hag·ga·dahs** or **Hag·ga·das.**

Hag·ga·i (hag′ē ī), *n.* **1** a Hebrew prophet. **2** book of the Bible.

hag·gard (hag′ərd), *adj.* looking worn from pain, fatigue, worry, hunger, etc.; careworn: *the haggard faces of the rescued miners.* **—hag′gard·ly,** *adv.* **—hag′gard·ness,** *n.*

hag·gle (hag′əl), *v.* to dispute, especially about a price or the terms of a bargain. ❑ *v.* **hag·gled, hag·gling.** [Haggle comes from an old English word meaning "to chop." People haggle in order to chop something off a price.] **—hag′gler,** *n.*

Hague (hāg), *n.* **The,** unofficial capital of the Netherlands, in the SW part. The official capital is Amsterdam. [Hague comes from a Dutch word meaning "a garden." The city grew up around a count's country palace.]

hah (hä), *interj.* ha.

hahn·i·um (hä′nē əm), *n.* proposed name for a radioactive metallic element, produced artificially from californium. *Symbol:* Ha

Hai·da (hi′də), *n.* member of a tribe of American Indians living in northern British Columbia and southern Alaska. ❑ *n., pl.* **Hai·da** or **Hai·das.**

hai·ku (hi′kü), *n.* a three-line poem having five syllables in the first line, seven in the second, and five in the third. ❑ *n., pl.* **hai·ku.** [Haiku comes from Japanese words meaning "joke" and "verse." Many Japanese haiku are funny.]

hail[1] (hāl), **1** *n.* small, round pieces of ice formed in thunderclouds and falling like rain; hailstones: *Hail fell with such violence that it broke windows.* **2** *v.* to fall in balls of ice: *Sometimes it hails during a summer storm.* **3** *n.* a shower like hail: *a hail of bullets.* **4** *v.* to pour down in a shower like hail: *The mob hailed insults at the speaker.* ▪ Another word that sounds like this is **hale.**

hail[2] (hāl), **1** *v.* to shout in welcome to; greet; cheer: *The crowd hailed the winner.* **2** *n.* a shout of welcome; greeting; cheer. **3** *interj.* greetings! welcome!: *Hail to the winner!* **4** *v.* to call out or signal to: *I hailed a taxi to take me to the airport.* ▪ Another word that sounds like this is **hale.** **—hail′er,** *n.*
hail from, to come from: *She hails from Boston.*

Hai·le Se·las·sie I (hi′lē sə las′ē *or* hi′lē sə läs′ē), 1891-1975, emperor of Ethiopia from 1930 to 1974.

Hail Mary, Ave Maria.

hail·stone (hāl′stōn′), *n.* a ball of hail. Hailstones are usually very small, but they can be as big as oranges.

hail·storm (hāl′stôrm′), *n.* storm with hail.

hair (hâr), *n.* **1** a fine, threadlike growth from the skin of mammals. **2** mass of such growths on the human head or forming the coat of a mammal. **3** a fine, threadlike growth from the outer layer of plants. **4** hairbreadth: *The ball missed his head by a hair.* ▪ Another word that sounds like this is **hare.** **—hair′less,** *adj.* **—hair′like′,** *adj.*
get in someone's hair, INFORMAL. to annoy someone.
let your hair down, 1 be frank or candid. **2** be very relaxed and informal.
make someone's hair stand on end, 1 to frighten someone greatly. **2** to horrify someone.
split hairs, to pay too much attention to tiny differences.

hair·breadth (hâr′bredth′), **1** *adj.* very narrow; extremely close: *When the tree fell, we had a hairbreadth escape.* **2** *n.* a very narrow space or distance: *Our team came within a hairbreadth of winning the game.*

hair·brush (hâr′brush′), *n.* a stiff brush for smoothing the hair. ❑ *n., pl.* **hair·brush·es.**

hair·cloth (hâr′klȯth′), *n.* a scratchy fabric made of cotton and horsehair or camel's hair, used to cover furniture or stiffen articles of clothing.

hair·cut (hâr′kut′), *n.* act or manner of cutting the hair.

hair·do (hâr′dü′), *n.* way of arranging the hair. ❑ *n., pl.* **hair·dos.**

hair·dress·er (hâr′dres′ər), *n.* person whose work is arranging or cutting women's hair.

hair·line (hâr′lin′), *n.* **1** a very thin line. **2** the irregular outline where hair growth ends on the head or forehead.

hair·pin (hâr′pin′), **1** *n.* a small, thin piece of metal or plastic, usually shaped like a U, used by women and girls to keep their hair in place. **2** *adj.* shaped like a hairpin: *a hairpin turn.*

hair-rais·ing (hâr′rā′zing), *adj.* making the hair stand on end from fright; terrifying: *a hair-raising ghost story.* **—hair′-rais′ing·ly,** *adv.*

hair·split·ting (hâr′split′ing), **1** *n.* act of making too fine distinctions. **2** *adj.* making too fine distinctions.

hair·spray (hâr′sprā), *n.* a product sprayed on the hair to hold it in place.

hair·spring (hâr′spring′), *n.* a fine, hairlike spring which regulates the motion of the balance wheel in a watch or clock.

hair·style (hâr′stīl′), *n.* way of arranging the hair; hairdo.

hair·styl·ist (hâr′stī′list), *n.* hairdresser.

hair trigger, trigger that operates by very slight pressure.

hair·y (hâr′ē), *adj.* **1** covered with hair; having much hair: *hairy hands, a plant with hairy leaves.* **2** of or like hair. **3** SLANG. **a** frightening or risky: *a hairy undertaking.* **b** difficult: *a hairy problem.* ❑ *adj.* **hair·i·er, hair·i·est.** —**hair′i·ness,** *n.*

Hai·ti (hā′tē), *n.* **1** country in the W part of the island of Hispaniola in the West Indies. *Capital:* Port-au-Prince. **2** former name of Hispaniola. [**Haiti** comes from a local word. It may mean "land of mountains."] —**Hai·tian** (hā′shən), *adj., n.*

hake (hāk), *n.* any of several saltwater fishes that look something like cod but are more slender. ❑ *n., pl.* **hake** or **hakes.**

Hal·as (hal′əs), *n.* **George,** 1895-1983, American football player, team owner, and coach. He played for, coached, and owned the Chicago Bears professional football team.

hal·cy·on (hal′sē ən), *adj.* calm; peaceful; happy: *The elderly couple liked to recall the halcyon days of their youth.*

> **WORD STORY** **Halcyon** comes from a Greek word meaning "kingfisher." The ancient Greeks believed that kingfishers built floating nests on the sea during two weeks of especially calm weather every winter.

hale[1] (hāl), *adj.* **hale and hearty,** strong and well; healthy: *Grandpa is still hale and hearty at 85.* ■ Another word that sounds like this is **hail.**

hale[2] (hāl), *v.* to force to go: *The company was haled into court for polluting the river with chemicals.* ❑ *v.* **haled, hal·ing.** ■ Another word that sounds like this is **hail.**

Hale (hāl), *n.* **Na·than** (nā′thən), 1755-1776, American patriot hanged as a spy by the British. According to tradition, before he was hanged he said, "I only regret that I have but one life to lose for my country."

Ha·le·a·ka·la National Park (hä′le ä′kä lä′), a national park in Hawaii, on the island of Maui, containing a large inactive volcano. The park used to be part of Hawaii Volcanoes National Park.

half (haf), **1** *n.* one of two equal parts: *Half of four is two. Two halves make a whole.* **2** *adj.* making half of; being one of two equal parts: *a half pound.* **3** *adv.* to half of the full amount or degree: *a glass half full of milk.* **4** *n.* one of two nearly equal parts: *the bigger half of a candy bar.* **5** *n.* one of the two equal periods of active play in certain games. **6** *adj.* not complete; being only part of: *A half truth is often no better than a lie.* **7** *adv.* not completely; partly: *The potatoes were half cooked.* ❑ *n., pl.* **halves.**

half past, (in stating the time of day) half an hour past the hour named: *Our school bus leaves at half past seven.*

in half, into two equal parts.

not half bad, fairly good.

half·back (haf′bak′), *n.* (in football) an offensive back who lines up near either flank.

half-baked (haf′bākt′), *adj.* **1** not fully worked out or planned; foolish: *a half-baked scheme for getting rich quick.* **2** not cooked enough.

half-breed (haf′brēd′), *n.* person whose parents are of different races. ■ The word **half-breed** is often considered offensive.

half brother, brother related through one parent only.

half-caste (haf′kast′), *n.* **1** person who has one European parent and one Asian parent. **2** half-breed. ■ The word **half-caste** is often considered offensive.

half dollar, a coin of the United States and Canada, worth 50 cents.

half-heart·ed (haf′här′tid), *adj.* lacking courage, interest, or enthusiasm; not earnest. —**half′heart′ed·ly,** *adv.*

half hour, 1 thirty minutes. **2** the halfway point in an hour: *The train stops here on the half hour.*

half-hour (haf′our′), *adj.* of a half hour; lasting a half hour: *a half-hour trip.* —**half′-hour′ly,** *adv.*

half-life (haf′līf′), *n.* length of time it takes for half the atoms of a particular radioactive substance to break down. The half-life of

each radioactive substance is always the same, so it can be used to identify substances and to date materials, as in carbon 14 dating.

half-line (haf′līn′), *n.* ray[1] (def. 5).

half-mast (haf′mast′), *n.* position halfway or part way down from the top of a mast, staff, etc.; half-staff. A flag is lowered to half-mast as a mark of respect for someone who has died.

half-moon (haf′mün′), *n.* moon when only half of its surface appears bright.

half nelson, hold used in wrestling. It is done by hooking one arm under an opponent's armpit and putting a hand on the back of the opponent's neck.

half note, (in music) a note played for one half as long a time as a whole note.

half·pen·ny (hāp′nē), *n.* a former British coin worth half a penny. ❑ *n., pl.* **half·pence** (hā′pəns), **half·pen·nies.**

half sister, sister related through one parent only.

half sole, sole of a shoe or boot from the toe to the instep.

half-staff (haf′staf′), *n.* half-mast.

half step, difference in pitch between two keys next to each other on a piano; semitone.

half·time (haf′tīm′), *n.* the time between two halves of a game, such as football or basketball.

half tone, half step.

half-track or **half·track** (haf′trak′), *n.* a military motor vehicle with wheels in front and short tracks in the rear, used to carry troops and weapons.

half·way (haf′wā′), **1** *adv.* half the way: *The rope reached only halfway around the tree.* **2** *adv.* not completely; partially: *a job that is halfway finished.* **3** *adj.* midway: *the halfway point.* **4** *adj.* not going far enough; incomplete: *Halfway measures often fail.*

meet halfway or **go halfway,** to do your share to agree or be friendly with someone.

half-wit (haf′wit′), *n.* **1** a feeble-minded person. ■ This meaning of **half-wit** is considered offensive. **2** a stupid, foolish person.

half-wit·ted (haf′wit′id), *adj.* **1** feeble-minded. ■ This meaning of **half-witted** is often considered offensive. **2** very stupid; foolish.

hal·i·but (hal′ə bət), *n.* any of several large flatfishes, much used for food. Halibuts sometimes weigh several hundred pounds. ❑ *n., pl.* **hal·i·but** or **hal·i·buts.** [**Halibut** comes from old English words meaning "holy flatfish." The fish was called this because it was eaten on holy days.]

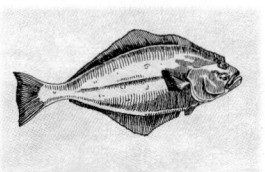

halibut—up to 10 ft. (3 m) long

Hal·i·fax (hal′ə faks), *n.* port and capital of Nova Scotia, Canada, on the Atlantic. —**Hal·i·go·ni·an** (hal′ə gō′nē ən), *adj., n.*

hal·ite (hal′īt *or* hā′līt), *n.* rock salt.

hal·i·to·sis (hal′ə tō′sis), *n.* breath with a foul smell; bad breath.

hall (hol), *n.* **1** way for going through a building; passageway: *A hall ran the length of the upper floor of the house.* **2** passage or room at the entrance of a building: *Leave your umbrella in the hall.* **3** a large room for holding meetings, parties, banquets, etc. **4** building for public business, meetings, etc.: *a village hall.* **5** building of a school, college, or university in which students live or classes are held. **6** house of an English landowner. ■ Another word that sounds like this is **haul.**

hal·lah (hä′lə), *n.* loaf of white bread, usually shaped like a braid, eaten by Jews on the Sabbath and holidays.

hal·le·lu·jah (hal′ə lü′yə), **1** *interj.* praise ye the Lord! **2** *n.* song of praise. Also, **alleluia.**

Hal·ley's comet (hal′ēz *or* hāl′lēz), comet seen about every 76 years. It was last seen in 1986. [**Halley's comet** is named for Edmund Halley, an English astronomer who calculated the comet's return time about 300 years ago.]

a	hat	ė	term	ô	order	ch	child		a in about
ā	age	i	it	oi	oil	ng	long		e in taken
ä	far	ī	ice	ou	out	sh	she	ə	i in pencil
â	care	o	hot	u	cup	th	thin		o in lemon
e	let	ō	open	u̇	put	ᴛʜ	then		u in circus
ē	equal	ȯ	saw	ü	rule	zh	measure		

hall·mark (hôl′märk′), **1** *n.* an official mark indicating standard of purity, put on gold or silver articles. **2** *n.* any mark or sign of genuineness or good quality. **3** *v.* to put a hallmark on. **4** *n.* any distinguishing feature: *Self-control is a hallmark of maturity.*

hal·low (hal′ō), *v.* **1** to make holy; make sacred. **2** to honor as holy or sacred: *"Hallowed be Thy name."*

Hal·low·een or **Hal·low·e'en** (hal′ə wēn′), *n.* evening of October 31, before All Saints' Day. It is observed especially by children, who wear masks and costumes, ask for treats, play pranks, etc. [**Halloween** comes from *All Hallow Eve.* In the past, All Saints' Day was called All Hallow Day because saints are honored as holy.]

hal·lu·ci·nate (hə lü′sn āt), *v.* to have hallucinations. ◻ *v.* **hal·lu·ci·nat·ed, hal·lu·ci·nat·ing.**

hal·lu·ci·na·tion (hə lü′sn ā′shən), *n.* **1** an imaginary thing seen or heard. **2** act of seeing or hearing things that exist only in a person's imagination.

hal·lu·cin·o·gen (hə lü′sn ə jən), *n.* drug that produces or tends to produce hallucinations. LSD and marijuana are hallucinogens. **–hal·lu·cin·o·gen′ic,** *adj.*

hall·way (hôl′wā′), *n.* **1** passage in a building; corridor; hall. **2** passageway or room at the entrance of a building.

ha·lo (hā′lō), *n.* **1** a golden circle or disk of light shown around the head of a holy person or angel in pictures or statues; nimbus. **2** ring of light around the sun, moon, or other shining object, usually caused by clouds. ◻ *n., pl.* **ha·los** or **ha·loes.**

hal·o·gen (hal′ə jən), *n.* any of the chemical elements iodine, bromine, chlorine, fluorine, and astatine, which form salts readily.

halt¹ (hôlt) **1** *v.* to stop for a time: *The hikers halted and rested from their climb. The store halted deliveries during the strike.* **2** *n.* a stop for a time: *During a strike work comes to a halt.*

call a halt, to order a stop.

halt² (hôlt), **1** *v.* to be in doubt; hesitate; waver. **2** *adj.* lame; crippled; limping. **3** *v.* OLD USE. to be lame or crippled; limp.

hal·ter (hôl′tər), *n.* **1** rope or strap with a noose for leading or tying an animal. **2** rope for hanging someone; noose. **3** a blouse worn by women and girls which fastens behind the neck and across the back and leaves the arms and back bare.

halt·ing (hôl′ting), *adj.* slow and uncertain; wavering; hesitating: *to speak in a halting manner.* **–halt′ing·ly,** *adv.*

hal·vah (häl vä′ or häl′vä), *n.* candy made from ground sesame seeds and honey.

halve (hav), *v.* **1** to divide into two equal parts; share equally: *He and I agreed to halve expenses on our trip.* **2** to cut in half; reduce to half: *The new machine will halve the time and cost of doing the work by hand.* ◻ *v.* **halved, halv·ing.** ▪ Another word that sounds like this is **have.**

halves (havz), *n.* plural of **half.**

by halves, 1 not completely; partly. **2** in a halfhearted way.
go halves, to share equally.

hal·yard (hal′yərd), *n.* rope or tackle used on a ship to raise or lower a sail, yard, or flag.

ham (ham), **1** *n.* meat from the upper part of a hog's hind leg, usually salted and smoked. **2** *n.* the back of the thigh; thigh and buttock. **3** *n.* INFORMAL. actor or performer who plays poorly and in an exaggerated manner. **4** *v.* INFORMAL. to play or act a part in this manner. **5** *n.* an amateur radio operator. ◻ *v.* **hammed, ham·ming.**

ham·burg·er (ham′bėr′gər), *n.* **1** ground beef, usually shaped into round, flat cakes and fried or broiled. **2** sandwich made with hamburger, usually in a roll or bun.

Ham·il·ton (ham′əl tən), *n.* **1** **Alexander,** 1755?-1804, American political leader, killed in a duel by Aaron Burr. He was the first Secretary of the Treasury. **2** capital of Bermuda.

ham·let (ham′lit), *n.* a small village.

Ham·let (ham′lit), *n.* **1** play by Shakespeare. **2** the principal character in this play, a prince of Denmark, who avenges his father's murder.

Ham·mar·skjöld (ham′ər shuld′), *n.* **Dag** (däg), 1905-1961, Swedish political leader. He was secretary-general of the United Nations from 1953 to 1961.

ham·mer (ham′ər), **1** *n.* tool with a metal head set crosswise on a handle, used to drive nails and to beat metal into shape. **2** *v.* to drive, hit, or work with a hammer: *I hammered a nail into the wall to hold up a picture.* **3** *v.* to hit again and again: *The teacher hammered on the desk with a ruler to get the class to quiet down.* **4** *v.* to force by repeated efforts: *to hammer common sense into someone's head.* **5** *v.* to beat into shape with a hammer: *The silver was hammered into bowls.* **6** *n.* something shaped or used like a hammer. The hammer of a gun explodes the charge. **7** *n.* a metal ball attached to a wire with a handle on the other end. It is used by athletes, who twirl it and throw it for distance. **8** *n.* the outermost of three small bones in the middle ear of human beings and other mammals. It is shaped something like a hammer. See picture at **ear**¹. **–ham′mer·er,** *n.*

hammer and tongs, with all your force and strength: *The boxers punched at each other hammer and tongs.*
hammer away at, to keep working hard at.
hammer out, to work out with much effort: *to hammer out a new policy.*

ham·mer·head (ham′ər hed′), *n.* any of several sharks with wide heads that look something like double-headed hammers.

hammerhead—up to 15 ft. (4.6 m) long

ham·mer·lock (ham′ər lok′), *n.* a hold in wrestling in which an opponent's arm is forced behind the back and upward.

Ham·mer·stein (ham′ər stīn), *n.* **Os·car** (os′kər), 1895-1960, American writer of scripts and lyrics for musicals.

Ham·mett (ham′it), *n.* **Da·shiell** (də shēl′), 1894-1961, American writer. ▪ **Dashiell Hammett** wrote many detective stories, most of which had heroes who were tough private eyes. His novels include *The Maltese Falcon* and *The Thin Man.*

ham·mock (ham′ək), *n.* a hanging bed or couch made of canvas, cord, etc. It has cords or ropes at each end for hanging it between two trees, posts, etc.

Ham·mu·ra·bi (ham′ü rä′bē), *n.* ?- 1750 B.C., king of Babylon from 1792 B.C. to 1750 B.C. He revised and expanded older law codes to make a new code of laws, called the Code of Hammurabi, for his people.

ham·per¹ (ham′pər), *v.* to hold back; hinder: *Wet wood hampered our efforts to start the campfire.*

ham·per² (ham′pər), *n.* a large container, often a wicker basket, usually having a cover: *a picnic hamper, a laundry hamper.*

ham·ster (ham′stər), *n.* any of several small rodents with short tails and large cheek pouches. Hamsters are used in scientific research and are often kept as pets.

ham·string (ham′string′), **1** *n.* one of the two tendons at the back of the knee in human beings. **2** *n.* the great tendon at the back of the hock in a four-footed animal. **3** *v.* to disable by cutting a hamstring. **4** *v.* to destroy activity or efficiency; disable: *Plans to expand the business were hamstrung by lack of money.* ◻ *v.* **ham·strung** (ham′strung′), **ham·string·ing.**

Han·cock (han′kok), *n.* **John,** 1737-1793, American political leader, the first signer of the Declaration of Independence.

hand (hand), **1** *n.* the end part of the arm, below the wrist, which takes and holds objects. Each hand has four fingers and a thumb. **2** *n.* end of any limb that grasps, holds, or clings. We call a monkey's front feet hands. **3** *n.* something like a hand in appearance or use: *The hands of a clock show the time.* **4** *n.* a hired worker who uses his or her hands: *a factory hand.* **5** *v.* to give with the hand; pass: *Please hand me a spoon.* **6** *v.* to help with the hand: *I handed the old woman into the bus.* **7** *n.pl.* **hands,** possession; control: *The property is no longer in my hands.* **8** *n.* part or share in doing something: *She had no hand in the matter.* **9** *n.* side: *There was a small table at my left hand.* **10** *n.* style of handwriting: *He writes in a clear hand.* **11** *n.* skill; ability: *The artist's work showed a master's hand.* **12** *n.* round of applause: *The crowd gave the winner a big hand.* **13** *n.* promise of marriage. **14** *n.* the breadth of a hand; four inches: *This horse is 18 hands high.* **15** *n.* cards held by a player in one round of a card game. **16** *n.* a single round in a card game. **17** *adj.* of, for, by, or in the hand: *a hand mirror, hand weaving, a hand pump.*

at first hand, from direct knowledge or experience.

at hand, 1 within reach; near. **2** ready.

at second hand, from the knowledge or experience of another; not directly: *He heard the story at second hand.*

at the hand of or **at the hands of,** through the act or deed of: *We have received many favors at the hands of our neighbors.*

by hand, by using the hands, not machinery: *embroidered by hand.*

change hands, to pass from one person to another: *That building changed hands many times.*

from hand to mouth, with nothing in reserve for the future: *Many poor people are forced to live from hand to mouth.*

give someone a hand or **lend someone a hand,** to help someone: *Please give me a hand with this trunk.*

hand down, to pass along: *The family heirloom is handed down to the oldest child in each generation.*

hand in, to give; deliver: *Hand in your test papers now.*

hand in glove or **hand and glove,** in close connection; sharing plans and knowledge: *The city planning commission is hand in glove with major local landowners.*

hand in hand, 1 holding hands. **2** together.

hand on, to pass along.

hand out, to give out; distribute.

hand over, to give to another; deliver.

hands down, easily: *She won the contest hands down.*

hand to hand, close together: *The soldiers fought hand to hand.*

have your hands full, be very busy; be able to do no more; have all you can do: *She has her hands full with a job and school.*

in hand, 1 under control. **2** in your possession; ready: *cash in hand.*

lay hands on, 1 to get hold of; seize. **2** to attack; harm.

off your hands, out of your care or responsibility.

on hand, 1 within reach; near: *Try to be on hand when I need you.* **2** ready: *have cash on hand.* **3** present: *I will be on hand again tomorrow.*

on the one hand, from this point of view: *On the one hand I want to buy this new car.*

on the other hand, from the opposite point of view: *On the other hand, it costs too much money.*

out of hand, out of control: *Your temper is getting out of hand.*

play into the hands of, to act so as to give the advantage to.

the upper hand, a better position; advantage.

turn your hand to, to work at: *Since she turned her hand to photography, she has done little painting.*

wash your hands of, to have no more to do with; refuse to be responsible for: *I washed my hands of that committee when I discovered that no one else would do any work.*

hand·bag (hand′bag′), *n.* **1** a woman's small bag for money, keys, etc.; purse. **2** a small traveling bag to hold clothes, etc.

hand·ball (hand′bôl′), *n.* **1** game played by hitting a small, hard ball against a wall with the hand. **2** ball used in this game.

hand·bill (hand′bil′), *n.* notice or advertisement, usually printed on one page, that is to be handed out to people.

hand·book (hand′buk′), *n.* a small book of directions or reference, especially in some field of study: *a handbook of engineering.*

hand·car (hand′kär′), *n.* (earlier) a light, open car moved by pumping a handle, used on railroads by workmen.

hand·cart (hand′kärt′), *n.* a small cart pulled or pushed by hand.

hand·clasp (hand′klasp′), *n.* the grasp of someone's hand in friendship, agreement, greeting, etc.

hand·craft (hand′kraft′), *v.* to make or work by hand.

hand·cuff (hand′kuf′), **1** *n.* one of a pair of metal rings joined by a short chain and locked around the wrists of a prisoner. **2** *v.* to put handcuffs on: *handcuff a prisoner.*

-handed, *suffix.* having or using a ___ hand or ___ hands: *left-handed = using the left hand; a two-handed stroke = a stroke using two hands.*

Han·del (han′dl), *n.* **George Frederick,** 1685-1759, English composer, born in Germany. His most famous work is his *Messiah* oratorio.

hand·ful (hand′ful′), *n.* **1** as much or as many as the hand can hold: *a handful of candy.* **2** a small number: *Only a handful of football fans sat watching the game in the cold rain.* **3** person or thing that is hard to manage: *That spirited horse is quite a handful.* ❑ *n., pl.* **handfuls.**

hand·gun (hand′gun′), *n.* pistol.

hand-held (hand′held′), **1** *adj.* used while being held in the hand. **2** *n.* a small computer held in the hand while being used.

hand·i·cap (han′dē kap′), **1** *n.* something that puts someone at a disadvantage; something that hinders: *A sore throat was a handicap to the singer.* **2** *v.* to put at a disadvantage; hinder: *A sore arm handicapped our pitcher.* **3** *n.* race, contest, or game in which better contestants are given special disadvantages and the rest are given certain advantages, so that all have an equal chance to win. **4** *n.* the disadvantage or advantage given in such a race, contest, or game: *a runner with a five yard handicap.* **5** *v.* to give a handicap to. ❑ *v.* **hand·i·capped, hand·i·cap·ping.**

hand·i·capped (han′dē kapt′), *adj.* **1** having a physical or mental disability. ∎ See Usage Note at **disabled. 2** having an assigned handicap in a race, contest, etc.

hand·i·craft (han′dē kraft′), *n.* **1** skill with the hands. **2** trade or art requiring skill with the hands. Weaving baskets from willow branches is a handicraft.

handicraft (def. 2)

hand·i·work (han′dē werk′), *n.* **1** work done by someone's hands. **2** work which someone has done personally.

hand·ker·chief (hang′kər chif), *n.* **1** a soft, usually square piece of cloth used for wiping the nose, face, hands, eyes, etc. **2** kerchief.

han·dle (han′dl), **1** *n.* a part of a thing made to be held or grasped by the hand. Spoons, pitchers, hammers, and pails have handles. **2** *v.* to touch, feel, hold, or use with the hand: *I handled the cat gently, feeling its soft fur.* **3** *v.* to manage; direct: *The rider handled the horse well.* **4** *v.* to behave or act when handled: *This car handles easily.* **5** *v.* to deal with; treat: *handle complaints.* **6** *v.* to

a	hat	è	term	ô	order	ch	child		a in about
ā	age	i	it	oi	oil	ng	long		e in taken
ä	far	ī	ice	ou	out	sh	she	ə	i in pencil
â	care	o	hot	u	cup	th	thin		o in lemon
e	let	ō	open	ù	put	ŦH	then		u in circus
ē	equal	ò	saw	ü	rule	zh	measure		

deal in; trade in; buy and sell: *That wholesaler handles meat, poultry, and fish.* ❑ *v.* **han·dled, han·dling.**

fly off the handle, to get angry or excited; lose your temper or self-control.

han·dle·bar (han′dl bär′), *n.* Often, **handlebars,** *pl.* the curved bar on a bicycle, motorcycle, etc., that the rider holds and steers by.

han·dler (han′dlər), *n.* **1** someone who trains or exhibits an animal. **2** someone who helps train or manage a boxer. **3** someone who manages a public figure such as a political candidate.

hand·made (hand′mād′), *adj.* made by hand, not by machine: *handmade pottery.*

hand·maid (hand′mād′), *n.* handmaiden.

hand·maid·en (hand′mād′n), *n.* **1** a female servant. **2** person or thing that serves: *political handmaidens of the rich.* Also, **handmaid.**

hand-me-down (hand′mē doun′), *n.* something handed down from one person to another, such as a used article of clothing.

hand·off (hand′ôf′), *n.* a football play in which a player, usually the quarterback, hands the ball to a teammate, who runs with it.

hand organ, a large, portable music box which is made to play tunes by turning a crank; barrel organ.

hand·out (hand′out′), *n.* **1** portion of food, clothing, or money handed out to someone who needs it. **2** a news story or piece of publicity issued to the press by a business organization, government agency, etc.

hand·pick (hand′pik′), *v.* to select personally and carefully: *handpick a replacement.*

hand·rail (hand′rāl′), *n.* railing used as a guard or as a support to the hand on a stairway, platform, etc.

hand·saw (hand′sò′), *n.* saw used with one hand.

hand·set (hand′set′), *n.* the part of a telephone including the receiver, the mouthpiece, and the handle.

hand·shake (hand′shāk′), *n.* act of clasping and shaking each other's hands in friendship, agreement, greeting, etc.

hands-off (handz′ôf′), *adj.* avoiding involvement or interference: *a hands-off policy toward foreign political issues.*

hand·some (han′səm), *adj.* **1** pleasing in appearance; good-looking. We usually say that a man is handsome, but that a woman is pretty or beautiful. **2** fairly large; considerable: *A thousand dollars is a handsome sum of money.* **3** generous: *a handsome gift.* ❑ *adj.* **hand·som·er, hand·som·est.** ■ Another word that sounds like this is hansom. **—hand′some·ly,** *adv.*

hands-on (handz′on′), *adj.* using or involving personal action or close participation; direct: *hands-on experience with computers.*

hand·spring (hand′spring′), *n.* spring or leap in which someone lands on one or both hands and then back on the feet, making a complete turn of the body.

hand·stand (hand′stand′), *n.* the act of balancing on your hands with your feet in the air.

hand-to-hand (hand′tə hand′), *adj.* close together; at close quarters: *a hand-to-hand fight.*

hand-to-mouth (hand′tə mouth′), *adj.* not providing for the future; having nothing to spare: *a hand-to-mouth existence.*

hand·work (hand′wėrk′), *n.* work done by hand, not by machinery.

hand·writ·ing (hand′rī′ting), *n.* **1** writing by hand; writing with pen, pencil, etc. **2** manner or style of writing: *He recognized his mother's handwriting on the envelope.*

hand·writ·ten (hand′rit′n), *adj.* written by hand.

hand·y (han′dē), *adj.* **1** easy to reach or use; saving work; useful; convenient: *a handy device.* ■ See Synonym Study at **useful.** **2** skillful with the hands: *My aunt is handy with tools.* ❑ *adj.* **hand·i·er, hand·i·est.** **—hand′i·ly,** *adv.* **—hand′i·ness,** *n.*

come in handy, be useful or helpful.

Han·dy (han′dē), *n.* **W. C.,** 1873-1958, American jazz composer and bandleader. His blues songs include "St. Louis Blues" and "Memphis Blues."

hand·y·man (han′dē man′), *n.* person who can do many kinds of odd jobs. ❑ *n., pl.* **hand·y·men.**

hang (hang), **1** *v.* to fasten or be fastened to something above: *Hang your hat on the hook.* **2** *v.* to fasten or be fastened so as to swing or turn freely: *hang a door on its hinges.* **3** *v.* to put to death by hanging with a rope around the neck. **4** *v.* to die by hanging. **5** *v.* to bend down; droop: *He hung his head in shame.* **6** *v.* to cover or decorate with things that are fastened to something above: *The walls were hung with pictures.* **7** *v.* to attach wallpaper to walls. **8** *v.* to depend: *His future hangs on the court's decision.* **9** *v.* to keep a jury from making a decision or reaching a verdict. One member can hang a jury by refusing to agree with the others. **10** *n.* way that a thing hangs: *There is something wrong with the hang of this coat.* **11** *n.* INFORMAL. way of using or doing: *Riding a bicycle is easy after you get the hang of it.* **12** *n.* INFORMAL. idea; meaning: *After studying an hour I finally got the hang of the lesson.* **13** *v.* to loiter; linger: *hang about a place.* ❑ *v.* **hung** (or, usually, **hanged** for 3,4), **hang·ing.**

hang back, be unwilling to go forward; be backward.

hang in there, INFORMAL. to keep on; be unwilling to let go, stop, or leave: *Don't give up now; hang in there.*

hang on, 1 to hold tightly: *Hang on to my hand going down these steep stairs.* **2** to wait for a short time, especially when telephoning: *Please hang on while I check the calendar.*

hang out, 1 to lean out: *hang out of a window.* **2** INFORMAL. to live or stay: *This is the corner where that gang hangs out.*

hang over, be about to happen to; threaten: *The prospect of defeat hangs over that political party.*

hang together, 1 to stick together; support each other. **2** be coherent or consistent: *The story is confusing and does not hang together.*

hang up, 1 to put on a hook, peg, etc. **2** to end a telephone conversation by putting the telephone receiver back in place.

hang with or **hang out with,** INFORMAL. to keep company with; be with often: *None of the people I hang with smoke.*

hang·ar (hang′ər), *n.* building for storing aircraft. ■ Another word that sounds like this is **hanger.**

hang·dog (hang′dòg′), *adj.* ashamed or sneaking: *a guilty, hangdog look.*

hang·er (hang′ər), *n.* **1** thing on which something else is hung: *a coat hanger.* **2** person who hangs things. ■ Another word that sounds like this is **hangar.**

hang·er-on (hang′ər on′), *n.* **1** follower or dependent. **2** an undesirable follower. ❑ *n., pl.* **hang·ers-on.**

hang glider

hang glider, device like a large kite, from which someone hangs in a harness while gliding down from a high place.

hang gliding, act or sport of riding a hang glider.

hang·ing (hang′ing), **1** *n.* death by hanging with a rope around the neck. **2** *n.* Often, **hangings,** *pl.* thing that hangs from a wall, bed, etc. Curtains and draperies are hangings. **3** *adj.* fastened to something above: *a hanging basket of flowers.*

hang·man (hang′mən), *n.* person who puts condemned criminals to death by hanging them. ❑ *n., pl.* **hang·men.**

hang·nail (hang′nāl′), *n.* bit of skin that hangs partly loose near a fingernail.

hang·out (hang′out′), *n.* INFORMAL. place you live in or go to often.

hang·o·ver (hang′ō′vər), *n.* **1** headache, nausea, etc., resulting from drinking too much alcoholic liquor. **2** something that remains from an earlier time or condition.

hang-up (hang′up′), *n.* INFORMAL. problem, worry, etc., that a person cannot get rid of.

hank (hangk), *n.* **1** coil or loop: *a hank of hair.* **2** bundle of yarn containing a specific number of yards.

han·ker (hang′kər), *v.* to have a longing or craving; yearn: *The lonely child hankered for friends.* —**han′ker·er,** *n.*

han·kie or **han·ky** (hang′kē), *n.* handkerchief. ❑ *n., pl.* **han·kies.**

han·ky-pan·ky (hang′kē pang′kē), *n.* INFORMAL. **1** trickery; mischief. **2** questionable or immoral behavior.

Han·ni·bal (han′ə bəl), *n.* 247-183 B.C., general of Carthage who fought the Romans and invaded Italy by crossing the Alps.

Ha·noi (hä noi′), *n.* capital of Vietnam, in the N part. It was formerly the capital of North Vietnam.

Hans·ber·ry (hanz′ber′ē), *n.* **Lor·raine** (lô rān′), 1930-1965, American playwright. Her most famous play is *A Raisin in the Sun.*

Han·sen's disease (han′sənz), leprosy.

han·som (han′səm), *n.* (earlier) a two-wheeled cab for two passengers, pulled by one horse. The driver sat on a seat high up behind the cab, and the reins passed over the roof. ■ Another word that sounds like this is **handsome.**

han·ta·vi·rus (hän′tə vī′rəs), *n.* any of several related viruses, carried by rodents and able to cause serious or deadly illness in human beings, especially one variety that produces flulike symptoms but may progress quickly to a major lung infection. ❑ *n., pl.* **han·ta·vi·rus·es.**

Ha·nuk·kah (hä′nə kə), *n.* a yearly Jewish festival that lasts eight days, mostly in December. It celebrates the rededication of the temple in Jerusalem after a victory over the Syrians in 165 B.C. Candles are lighted on each of the eight days of Hanukkah. Also, **Chanukah.** [Hanukkah comes from a Hebrew word meaning "dedication," which is what is celebrated.]

hap (hap), OLD USE. **1** *n.* chance; luck. **2** *v.* to happen. ❑ *v.* **happed, hap·ping.**

hap·haz·ard (hap haz′ərd), **1** *adj.* not planned; random: *Haphazard answers are often wrong.* **2** *adv.* by chance; at random: *papers scattered haphazard on the desk.* —**hap·haz′ard·ly,** *adv.* —**hap·haz′ard·ness,** *n.*

hap·less (hap′lis), *adj.* unlucky; unfortunate. —**hap′less·ly,** *adv.* —**hap′less·ness,** *n.*

hap·ly (hap′lē), *adv.* OLD USE. by chance; perhaps.

hap·pen (hap′ən), *v.* **1** to come about; take place; occur: *What happened at the party yesterday?* **2** to be or take place by chance: *Accidents will happen.* **3** to have the fortune; chance: *I happened to sit beside him at dinner.* **4** to be done: *What happened to my book? It's all dirty.* [See word history information at **happy.**] **happen on, 1** to meet: *They happened on each other by chance.* **2** to find: *She happened on a dime while looking for her ball.*

hap·pen·ing (hap′ə ning), *n.* something that happens; event; occurrence: *The evening newscast reviewed the happenings of the day.*

hap·pen·stance (hap′ən stans), *n.* a chance occurrence; accident.

hap·pi·ly (hap′ə lē), *adv.* **1** in a happy manner: *The cousins played happily together.* **2** by luck; with good fortune: *Happily, I found my lost wallet.*

hap·pi·ness (hap′ē nis), *n.* **1** condition of being happy; gladness. **2** good luck; good fortune.

hap·py (hap′ē), *adj.* **1** feeling as you do when you are well and are having a good time; glad; pleased; contented: *She is happy in her new work.* **2** showing that you are glad; showing pleasure and joy: *a happy smile, a happy look.* **3** lucky; fortunate: *By a happy chance, I found my book just where I had left it in the theater.* **4** clever and fitting; successful and suitable: *That writer has a happy way of expressing his ideas.* ❑ *adj.* **hap·pi·er, hap·pi·est.** [Happy and happen come from an old English word meaning "chance." If chance happens to favor you, you will probably be happy about that.]

hap·py-go-luck·y (hap′ē gō luk′ē), *adj.* taking things easily as they come; trusting to luck.

Haps·burg (haps′bėrg′), *n.* member of a German princely family, prominent since about 1100. Many rulers of the Holy Roman Empire, Austria, and Spain were Hapsburgs.

har·a-kir·i (har′ə kir′ē), *n.* suicide by ripping open the abdomen with a knife. It was the form of honorable suicide in Japan for the warrior class.

ha·rangue (hə rang′), **1** *n.* a noisy speech. **2** *n.* a long, pompous speech. **3** *v.* to address in a harangue. **4** *v.* to deliver a harangue. ❑ *v.* **ha·rangued, ha·rangu·ing.** —**ha·rangu′er,** *n.*

Ha·ra·re (hä rä′rā), *n.* capital of Zimbabwe, in the NE part.

har·ass (har′əs *or* hə ras′), *v.* **1** to disturb; worry; torment: *Flies harassed the hikers.* **2** to trouble by repeated attacks; harry: *Pirates harassed the villages along the coast.* [Harass may come from a French word meaning "to cause a dog to attack." Dogs attack larger animals by repeatedly biting and jumping away.]

har·ass·ment (har′əs mənt *or* hə ras′mənt), *n.* act of harassing or condition of being harassed; worry.

har·bin·ger (här′bən jər), *n.* something that indicates something else is coming; forerunner: *The robin is a harbinger of spring.*

harbor (def. 1)

har·bor (här′bər), **1** *n.* area of deep water protected from winds, currents, etc., forming a place of shelter for ships and boats: *Many yachts are in the harbor.* **2** *n.* any place of shelter: *The child fled to the harbor of her father's arms.* **3** *v.* to give shelter to; give a place to hide: *The dog's shaggy hair harbors fleas.* **4** *v.* to have and keep in the mind: *Don't harbor a grudge against her; she didn't mean to hurt you.*

a	hat	ė	term	ô	order	ch	child		
ā	age	i	it	oi	oil	ng	long		a in about
ä	far	ī	ice	ou	out	sh	she		e in taken
â	care	o	hot	u	cup	th	thin	ə	i in pencil
e	let	ō	open	ů	put	ᴛʜ	then		o in lemon
ē	equal	ȯ	saw	ü	rule	zh	measure		u in circus

hard (härd), **1** *adj.* like steel, glass, and rock; not yielding to touch; not soft: *a hard nut, hard wood.* **2** *adv.* so as to be hard, solid, or firm: *The river is frozen hard.* **3** *adj.* firm; tight: *a hard knot.* **4** *adv.* firmly; tightly: *Don't hold my hand so hard.* **5** *adv.* with difficulty: *The runner was breathing hard after she finished the race.* **6** *adj.* needing much ability, effort, or time; difficult or troublesome: *a hard problem, a hard person to get along with.* **7** *adj.* acting or done with energy, persistence, etc.: *a hard worker.* **8** *adv.* with steady effort or much energy: *Try hard.* **9** *adj.* vigorous or violent: *a hard run.* **10** *adv.* with vigor or violence: *It is raining hard.* **11** *adj.* causing much pain, trouble, care, etc.; bad; severe: *a hard winter. When my parents were out of work, we had a hard time.* **12** *adv.* so as to cause trouble, pain, care, etc.; severely; badly: *It will go hard with those kidnappers if they are caught.* **13** *adj.* not pleasant; harsh; ugly: *a hard laugh.* **14** *adj.* not yielding to influence; stern; unfeeling: *a hard heart.* **15** *adv.* close; near: *The house stands hard by the bridge.* **16** *adj.* containing mineral salts that keep soap from forming suds: *hard water.* **17** *adj.* containing much alcohol: *hard liquor.* **18** *adj.* causing addiction and damaging your health: *Heroin is a hard drug.* **19** *adj.* sounded like the *c* in *corn* or the *g* in *get,* rather than like the soft *c* and *g* in *city* and *gem.* **—hard′ness,** *n.*

hard and fast, that cannot be changed or broken; strict: *hard and fast rules.*

hard of hearing, somewhat deaf.

hard put, having much difficulty or trouble: *I am hard put to solve this problem.*

hard up, INFORMAL. needing money or anything very badly.

> **SYNONYM STUDY** **Hard, difficult,** and **tough** all mean needing a lot of work. **Hard** is a general word: *Shoveling snow is hard work.* **Difficult** means not easy to do or figure out: *Only two students solved this difficult problem.* **Tough** means very hard: *Floods made this a tough year for farmers.*

hard·ball (härd′bôl′), *n.* baseball.

hard-bit·ten (härd′bit′n), *adj.* stubborn; unyielding.

hard-boiled (härd′boild′), **1** (of an egg) boiled until the white and yolk are firm. **2** not easily moved by your feelings; tough; rough: *a hard-boiled sergeant.*

hard coal, anthracite.

hard copy, copy that can be read or viewed without the use of any special equipment. Computer printouts are hard copy, words on a computer screen are not.

hard core, the firm, unyielding, central part, resistant to pressure or change.

hard-core (härd′kôr′), *adj.* **1** firmly established and hard to get rid of: *hard-core unemployment.* **2** stubborn; thoroughly committed: *hard-core rock music fans.*

hard disk, a disk made of hard material with a magnetic surface, used for storing very large amounts of computer data. Unlike smaller disks, hard disks are not moved in and out of a computer by the user.

hard·en (härd′n), *v.* to make or become hard: *When the candy cooled, it hardened.* **—hard′en·er,** *n.*

hard hat, 1 type of helmet worn by construction workers as protection against falling objects. **2** worker who wears such a helmet, especially a construction worker.

hard·head·ed (härd′hed′id), *adj.* **1** not easily excited or deceived; practical; clever. **2** stubborn; obstinate. **—hard′head′ed·ly,** *adv.* **—hard′head′ed·ness,** *n.*

hard·heart·ed (härd′här′tid), *adj.* without pity; cruel. **—hard′heart′ed·ly,** *adv.* **—hard′heart′ed·ness,** *n.*

hard hat (def. 1)

har·di·hood (här′dē hůd), *n.* boldness; daring.

Har·ding (här′ding), *n.* **Warren Ga·ma·li·el** (gə mā′lē əl), 1865-1923, the 29th president of the United States, from 1921 to 1923.

He was elected in the first presidential election where women could vote.

hard·line (härd′līn′), *adj.* resisting change; firm: *a hardline political stand.*

hard·ly (härd′lē), *adv.* **1** only just; not quite; barely: *We hardly had time to eat breakfast.* **2** probably not: *They will hardly come in all this rain.* ▪ See Usage Note at **double negative.**

hard palate, the bony front part of the roof of the mouth.

hard·pan (härd′pan′), *n.* a hard layer of earth through which roots cannot grow, just below the surface soil; pan.

hard·ship (härd′ship), *n.* something hard to bear; hard condition of living: *Hunger, cold, and sickness were among the hardships of pioneer life.*

hard·tack (härd′tak′), *n.* a very hard, dry biscuit, formerly eaten on shipboard; ship biscuit.

hard·top (härd′top′), *n.* a passenger car with a rigid metal or plastic top but with window space like a convertible.

hard·ware (härd′wâr′), *n.* **1** articles made from metal. Locks, hinges, nails, screws, etc., are hardware. **2** a computer and any machine used with it, such as a disk drive or printer.

hard·wood (härd′wůd′), **1** *n.* the hard, compact wood of such trees as oak, cherry, maple, ebony, or mahogany. **2** *n.* any of these trees, having broad leaves instead of needles. **3** *adj.* made of this wood: *hardwood floors.*

har·dy (här′dē), *adj.* **1** able to bear hard treatment, fatigue, etc.; strong; robust: *Cold weather did not kill the hardy plants.* **2** bold; daring: *hardy mountain climbers.* ❑ *adj.* **har·di·er, har·di·est.** **—har′di·ly,** *adv.* **—har′di·ness,** *n.*

Har·dy (här′dē), *n.* **Thomas,** 1840-1928, English novelist and poet. ▪ **Thomas Hardy** began writing poetry when people objected to his frank descriptions of human relationships in his novels. His novels include *The Return of the Native* and *Tess of the d'Urbervilles.*

hare (hâr), *n.* **1** any of several gnawing mammals that resemble rabbits but are larger, with longer ears and legs, and do not live in burrows. The jack rabbit is a hare; the cottontail is a rabbit. **2** **Hare,** (in African myths) trickster and schemer, quick to take advantage of others and usually able to outwit other characters. ❑ *n., pl.* **hares** or **hare** for 1. ▪ Another word that sounds like this is **hair.**

hare·bell (hâr′bel′), *n.* a wildflower of the Northern Hemisphere with blue, bell-shaped flowers, sometimes known as the bluebell of Scotland.

hare·brained (hâr′brānd′), *adj.* giddy, heedless, or reckless: *a harebrained scheme.*

hare·lip (hâr′lip′), *n.* deformity existing from birth, in which the upper lip is divided. It resembles the lip of a hare.

hare·lipped (hâr′lipt′), *adj.* having a harelip.

har·em (hâr′əm), *n.* **1** the wives, female relatives, and female servants of a Muslim household. **2** part of a Muslim house where the women live.

hark (härk), *v.* **1** to listen; hearken: *"Hark, the Herald Angels Sing."* **2** **hark back,** to go back; turn back: *Those ideas hark back 20 years.*

Har·lem (här′ləm), *n.* part of New York City in N Manhattan.

har·le·quin (här′lə kwən *or* här′lə kən), *n.* **1 Harlequin,** character in comedy and pantomime who is usually masked and wears a costume of varied colors. **2** a mischievous person; buffoon.

har·lot (här′lət), *n.* OLD USE. prostitute.

harm (härm), **1** *n.* something that causes pain, loss, etc.; injury; damage: *He slipped and fell down but suffered no harm.* **2** *n.* evil; wrong: *It was an accident; she meant no harm.* **3** *v.* to damage; injure; hurt: *Do not pick or harm the flowers in the park.*

> **SYNONYM STUDY** **Harm, injure,** and **damage** all mean to cause pain or loss of value. **Harm** is a general word: *The rumors harmed his reputation.* **Injure** means to wound: *They took the injured dog to the animal hospital.* **Damage** means to cause loss of value: *High winds damaged the beach house.*

harm·ful (härm′fəl), *adj.* causing harm; injurious; hurtful: *harmful germs.* **—harm′ful·ly,** *adv.* **—harm′ful·ness,** *n.*

harm·less (härm′lis), *adj.* causing no harm; not harmful: *It's only a harmless spider.* —**harm′less·ly**, *adv.* —**harm′less·ness**, *n.*

har·mon·ic (här mon′ik), **1** *adj.* of or about harmony in music. **2** *n.* overtone. **3** *adj.* of or about such tones. **4** *adj.* musical. —**har·mon′i·cal·ly**, *adv.*

har·mon·i·ca (här mon′ə kə), *n.* a small musical instrument with metal reeds, played by breathing in and out through a set of openings; mouth organ. ❏ *n., pl.* **har·mon·i·cas**.

har·mo·ni·ous (här mō′nē əs), *adj.* **1** agreeing in feelings, ideas, or actions; getting on well together: *harmonious neighbors.* **2** arranged so that the parts are orderly or pleasing; going well together: *A beautiful picture has harmonious colors.* **3** sweet-sounding; musical: *the harmonious sounds of a choir.* —**har·mo′ni·ous·ly**, *adv.* —**har·mo′ni·ous·ness**, *n.*

har·mo·ni·um (här mō′nē əm), *n.* reed organ.

har·mo·nize (här′mə nīz), *v.* **1** to be in harmony or agreement: *The colors in the room harmonized to give a pleasing effect.* **2** to bring into harmony or agreement; make harmonious: *She harmonized the two plans by using parts of each one.* **3** to sing or play in harmony: *We like to get together and harmonize before choir practice.* **4** to add tones to a melody to make chords in music. ❏ *v.* **har·mo·nized**, **har·mo·niz·ing**. —**har′mo·ni·za′tion**, *n.* —**har′mo·niz′er**, *n.*

har·mo·ny (här′mə nē), *n.* **1** agreement of feeling, ideas, or actions; getting on well together: *The two brothers lived and worked in perfect harmony.* **2** an orderly or pleasing arrangement of parts; going well together: *In a beautiful landscape there is harmony of the different colors.* **3** the sounding together of musical tones in a chord. **4** study of chords in music and of relating them to successive chords. **5** sweet or musical sound; music. ❏ *n., pl.* **har·mo·nies** for 2,3.

WORD STORY **Harmony** comes from a Greek word meaning "a joint." In musical harmony, sounds work together in connection, like parts of the body that are joined.

har·ness (här′nis), **1** *n.* the leather straps, bands, and other pieces used to hitch a horse or other animal to a carriage, wagon, plow, etc. **2** *n.* any similar arrangement of straps, bands, etc., especially a combination of straps by which a parachute is attached to someone. **3** *v.* to put harness on: *Harness the horse.* **4** *v.* to control and put to use: *Windmills harness the power of the wind.* ❏ *n., pl.* **har·ness·es**.

in harness, in your regular work: *I was glad to get back in harness again after my long illness.*

harness race, horse race in which a driver is pulled in a light carriage by a trotting or pacing horse.

harp (härp), **1** *n.* a large, stringed musical instrument played by plucking the strings with the fingers. **2** *v.* to play on the harp. —**harp′er**, *n.* —**harp′like′**, *adj.*

harp on, to talk about very much or too much.

Har·pers Ferry (här′pərz), town in NE West Virginia. John Brown's raid on a government arsenal was made there in 1859.

harp·ist (här′pist), *n.* person who plays the harp.

har·poon (här pün′), **1** *n.* a barbed spear with a rope tied to it, used for catching whales and other sea animals. It is thrown by hand or fired from a gun. **2** *v.* to strike, catch, or kill with a harpoon. —**har·poon′er**, *n.*

harp (def. 1)

harp·si·chord (härp′sə kôrd), *n.* a stringed musical instrument like a piano, used especially from about 1550 to 1750. It has a tinkling sound from its strings being plucked by leather or quill points instead of being struck by hammers.

har·ri·er (har′ē ər), *n.* a hound like a large beagle, originally bred to hunt hares.

Har·ris·burg (har′is bėrg′), *n.* capital of Pennsylvania, in the S part, on the Susquehanna River.

Har·ri·son (har′ə sən), *n.* **1 Ben·ja·min** (ben′jə mən), 1833-1901, the 23rd president of the United States, from 1889 to 1893. He was the grandson of President William Henry Harrison. **2 George**, born 1943, English musician, a member of the Beatles. **3 William Henry**, 1773-1841, American general and ninth president of the United States, in 1841. ■ **William Henry Harrison** served the shortest time in office of any president. He caught a cold at his inauguration and died 30 days later.

har·row (har′ō), **1** *n.* a heavy farm tool with iron teeth or upright disks. Harrows are used to break up the soil into fine pieces before planting seeds. **2** *v.* to pull a harrow over land. —**har′row·er**, *n.*

har·row·ing (har′ō ing), *adj.* very painful or distressing: *a harrowing experience.*

har·ry (har′ē), *v.* **1** to raid and rob with violence: *The pirates harried the towns along the coast, burning what they could not carry off.* **2** to keep troubling; worry; torment: *Fear of losing her voice harried the ailing opera singer.* ❏ *v.* **har·ried**, **har·ry·ing**.

harsh (härsh), *adj.* **1** rough to the touch, taste, eye, or ear; sharp and unpleasant: *a harsh voice, a harsh climate.* **2** without pity; unfeeling; cruel; severe: *a harsh judge.* **3** unpleasant but real: *harsh facts.* —**harsh′ly**, *adv.* —**harsh′ness**, *n.*

WORD STORY **Harsh** comes from a Danish word meaning "rotten." Because rotten food looks, tastes, and smells bad, people began using the word to mean "roughly unpleasant."

hart (härt), *n.* a male deer, especially the male red deer after its fifth year. ❏ *n., pl.* **harts** or **hart**. ■ Another word that sounds like this is **heart**.

har·te·beest (här′tə bēst′), *n.* either of two large, swift African antelopes with ringed, curved horns bent backward at the tips. ❏ *n., pl.* **har·te·beests** or **har·te·beest**.

Hart·ford (härt′fərd), *n.* capital of Connecticut, in the central part.

har·um-scar·um (hâr′əm skâr′əm), **1** *adj.* too hasty; reckless; rash: *a harum-scarum decision.* **2** *adv.* recklessly; rashly: *He rushed harum-scarum down the street.*

har·vest (här′vist), **1** *n.* act of reaping and gathering in of grain and other food crops. **2** *n.* time or season of the harvest, usually in the late summer or early autumn. **3** *v.* to gather in and bring home for use: *harvest wheat.* **4** *n.* one season's yield of any natural product; crop: *The oyster harvest was small this year.* **5** *n.* result; consequences: *She is reaping the harvest of her hard work.*

har·vest·er (här′və stər), *n.* **1** machine for harvesting crops, especially grain. **2** person who works in a harvest field; reaper.

har·vest·man (här′vist mən), *n.* **1** daddy-longlegs. **2** person who harvests. ❏ *n., pl.* **har·vest·men**.

harvest moon, the full moon at harvest time, about the beginning of autumn.

Har·vey (här′vē), *n.* **William**, 1578-1657, English physician who discovered that blood circulates through the body.

has (haz), *v.* a present tense of **have**: *Who has my book?*

has-been (haz′bin′), *n.* person or thing whose best days are past.

hash[1] (hash), **1** *n.* mixture of cooked meat, potatoes, and other vegetables, chopped into small pieces and fried or baked. **2** *v.* to chop into small pieces. **3** *n.* mixture. **4** *n.* a mess; muddle: *I made such a hash of the job that I had to do it over.*

hash over, INFORMAL. to discuss or review; reminisce about.

WORD STORY **Hash**[1] comes from a French word meaning "an ax." **Hatchet** comes from the same word. Hash is usually chopped with something smaller, of course.

hash[2] (hash), *n.* INFORMAL. hashish.

hash browns, potatoes that are boiled and then cut into small pieces and fried in fat or oil until browned.

a	hat	ė	term	ȯ	order	ch	child		a in about
ā	age	i	it	oi	oil	ng	long		e in taken
ä	far	ī	ice	ou	out	sh	she	ə	i in pencil
â	care	o	hot	u	cup	th	thin		o in lemon
e	let	ō	open	u̇	put	ᴛʜ	then		u in circus
ē	equal	ȯ	saw	ü	rule	zh	measure		

hash·ish or **hash·eesh** (hash′ēsh′), *n.* a drug prepared from the flowering tops of the hemp plant. Hashish is smoked for its intoxicating effect.

Has·i·dim (hä sē′dim), *n.pl.* members of a Jewish group founded in the 1700s in Poland. Hasidim favor religious piety and devotion over formal learning. ❑ *n., sing.* **Has·id** (has′id). [Hasidim comes from a Hebrew word meaning "pious."]

has·n't (haz′nt), has not.

hasp (hasp), *n.* clasp or fastening for a door, window, trunk, box, etc., especially a hinged metal clasp that fits over a staple or into a hole and is fastened by a peg or padlock.

has·sle (has′əl), INFORMAL. **1** *n.* bother; trouble: *the hassle of fixing a broken bicycle.* **2** *v.* to bother someone; annoy; harass: *He doesn't repay loans unless you hassle him.* **3** *n.* a struggle or contest. **4** *v.* to struggle; tussle. ❑ *v.* **has·sled, has·sling.** [The word *hassle* is only about 50 years old. Even so, nobody knows where it comes from. Sometimes words just appear.]

has·sock (has′ək), *n.* a thick cushion or cushioned footstool to rest the feet on, sit on, or kneel on.

hast (hast), *v.* OLD USE. have. "Thou hast" means "you have."

haste (hāst), *n.* **1** act of hurrying; trying to be quick: *All my haste was of no use; I missed the bus anyway.* **2** quickness without thought or care; rashness: *Haste makes waste.*

make haste, be quick; hurry: *Make haste or you will miss your train.*

has·ten (hā′sn), *v.* **1** to be quick; go fast: *She hastened to explain that she had not meant to be rude.* ■ See Synonym Study at **hur·ry. 2** to cause to be quick; speed; hurry: *Sunshine and rest hastened his recovery.* —**hast′en·er,** *n.*

Has·tings (hā′stingz), *n.* town in SE England, where William I defeated the Saxons to become king of England in 1066.

hast·y (hā′stē), *adj.* **1** done or made in a hurry; quick: *She gave her watch a hasty glance and ran for the train.* **2** not well thought out; rash: *Their hasty decisions caused many mistakes.* ❑ *adj.* **hast·i·er, hast·i·est.** —**hast′i·ly,** *adv.* —**hast′i·ness,** *n.*

hasty pudding, mush made of corn meal.

hat (hat), **1** *n.* a covering for the head when outdoors. A hat usually has a crown and a brim. **2** *v.* to provide with a hat; put a hat on. ❑ *v.* **hat·ted, hat·ting.** —**hat′less,** *adj.*

pass the hat, to ask for contributions; take up a collection.

take off your hat to, to admire; respect; honor.

talk through your hat, to talk foolishly; speak ignorantly.

under your hat, as a secret; to yourself: *Keep this information under your hat; tell it to no one.*

hat·band (hat′band′), *n.* band around the crown of a hat, just above the brim.

hat·box (hat′boks′), *n.* box or case for a hat. ❑ *n., pl.* **hat·box·es.**

hatch¹ (def. 1)

hatch¹ (hach), **1** *v.* to come out of an egg: *One of the chickens hatched today.* **2** *v.* to keep an egg or eggs warm until the young come out: *The heat of the sun hatches turtles' eggs.* **3** *v.* to bring forth young; open: *The eggs will probably hatch tomorrow.* **4** *n.* a group of young from eggs laid together: *There are 12 chickens in this hatch.* **5** *v.* to plan something secretly; plot: *The spies hatched a scheme to steal government secrets.* ❑ *n., pl.* **hatch·es.**

hatch² (hach), *n.* **1** an opening in a ship's deck or in the floor or roof of a building, etc.; hatchway. A ship's cargo is loaded through the hatch. The escape hatch in an airplane permits passengers to get out in an emergency. **2** a trapdoor covering such an opening: *The hatches were closed tightly during the storm.* ❑ *n., pl.* **hatch·es.**

hatch·back (hach′bak′), **1** *adj.* having a sloping rear side that opens upward: *a hatchback coupe.* **2** *n.* a car having this form.

hatch·er·y (hach′ər ē), *n.* place for hatching eggs of fish, hens, etc. ❑ *n., pl.* **hatch·er·ies.**

hatch·et (hach′it), *n.* a small ax with a short handle, for use with one hand. [See Word Story at **hash¹.**] —**hatch′et·like′,** *adj.*

bury the hatchet, to stop quarreling or fighting; make peace.

hatch·way (hach′wā′), *n.* hatch.

hate (hāt), **1** *v.* to dislike intensely; feel hostile towards: *I hated them for hurting my friend.* **2** *n.* a very strong dislike: *feel hate toward an enemy.* **3** *v.* to be very unwilling; dislike: *I hate to study.* ❑ *v.* **hat·ed, hat·ing.** —**hat′er,** *n.*

SYNONYM STUDY **Hate** and **despise** both mean to dislike very much. **Hate** suggests anger: *She hates the way he makes fun of her.* **Despise** means to dislike and look down on someone or something: *Many people despise bullies.*

hate·ful (hāt′fəl), *adj.* **1** showing hate: *a hateful comment.* **2** causing hate: *hateful behavior.* —**hate′ful·ly,** *adv.* —**hate′ful·ness,** *n.*

hath (hath), *v.* OLD USE. has. "He hath" means "he has."

hat·pin (hat′pin′), *n.* a long pin used by women to fasten a hat to their hair.

ha·tred (hā′trid), *n.* very strong dislike; hate.

hat·ter (hat′ər), *n.* person who makes or sells hats.

Hat·ter·as (hat′ər əs), *n.* **Cape,** cape on an island off E North Carolina.

Hat·ties·burg (ha′tēz bėrg), *n.* city in S Mississippi.

hat trick, (in hockey) the scoring by one player of three goals in a single game.

haugh·ty (hô′tē), *adj.* **1** too proud, and full of scorn for others: *A haughty person is often unpopular.* **2** showing too great pride and scorn for others: *a haughty glance, haughty words.* ❑ *adj.* **haugh·ti·er, haugh·ti·est.** [Haughty comes from a Latin word meaning "high." Haughty people have a high opinion of themselves.] —**haugh′ti·ly,** *adv.* —**haugh′ti·ness,** *n.*

haul (hôl), **1** *v.* to pull or drag with force: *We hauled the heavy trunk out of the house.* **2** *n.* act of hauling; hard pull. **3** *v.* to transport; carry: *Trucks, trains, and ships haul freight.* **4** *n.* load hauled: *Powerful trucks are used for heavy hauls.* **5** *n.* distance that a load is hauled: *Long hauls cost more than short ones.* **6** *n.* amount won, taken, etc., at one time; catch: *The fishing boats made a good haul and came back fully loaded.* ■ Another word that sounds like this is **hall.** —**haul′er,** *n.*

in the long haul, in the distant future or for a long time.

in the short haul, in the near future or for a short time.

haul off, to draw back your arm to give a blow.

haunch (hônch), *n.* **1** the fleshy part of the body around the hip; hip. **2 haunches,** *pl.* the hindquarters of an animal: *The dog sat on its haunches.* **3** the leg and loin of an animal, used for food: *a haunch of venison.* ❑ *n., pl.* **haunch·es.**

haunt (hônt), **1** *v.* (of a ghost) to appear or be seen somewhere: *People say ghosts haunt that old house.* **2** *v.* to visit often: *haunt a video arcade.* **3** *n.* place often gone to or visited: *The swimming pool was the children's favorite haunt on hot summer days.* **4** *v.* to be often with; come often to: *Memories of his youth haunted the old man.* —**haunt′ing·ly,** *adv.*

haunt·ed (hôn′tid), *adj.* visited by ghosts: *They were afraid to go into the haunted house.*

hau·teur (hō tėr′), *n.* arrogance; haughtiness.

Ha·van·a (hə van′ə), *n.* port and capital of Cuba, in the NW part, on the Gulf of Mexico. [Havana comes from a Spanish word meaning "haven." It has a fine harbor.]

have (hav *or* əv), *v.* **1** to hold in your hand; hold in your keeping; hold in your possession: *We have a farm. A house has windows. He has a cheerful disposition.* **2** to be forced; be compelled: *All ani-*

mals have to sleep. I have to go now or I'll be late. **3** to cause somebody to do something or something to be done: *Please have the store deliver my order.* **4** to take; get: *Have a seat. You need to have a rest.* **5** to eat or drink: *We always have breakfast in the kitchen.* **6** to experience: *Have a pleasant time. They had trouble with their car.* **7** to engage in; carry on; perform: *Have a talk with him.* **8** to allow; permit: *She won't have any noise while she is reading.* **9** to be ill with; suffer from: *I've had a headache all day.* **10** to hold in the mind: *have an idea.* **11** to give birth to: *She had a girl.* **12** to be in a certain relation to: *She has three brothers.* **13** to be the parent or parents of: *They have three children.* **14** *Have* is used with words like *asked, been, broken, done,* or *called* to express completed action. *They have eaten. She had gone before. I have called her. They will have seen her by Sunday.* ❑ *v.* **had, hav·ing. ■** Another word that sounds like this is **halve.**

have at, to attack; hit.

have done, be through; stop: *Let's have done with this quarreling.*

have had it, to be fed up; to want no more.

have it in for, to have a grudge against; try to get revenge on: *He has it in for me because I won the prize he wanted.*

have it out, to fight or argue until a question is settled: *We have had it out, and now we are friends once more.*

have on, be wearing.

have to do with, to relate to; deal with: *Botany has to do with the study of plants.*

Hav·el (häv′əl), *n.* **Vá·clav** (vät′släf), born 1936, Czech playwright and political leader. ■ **Václav Havel** wrote many plays criticizing totalitarianism, and after the collapse of communism he was the president of Czechoslovakia from 1989 to 1992.

ha·ven (hā′vən), *n.* **1** place of shelter and safety: *The warm cabin was a haven from the storm.* ■ See Synonym Study at **shelter. 2** harbor; port.

have-not (hav′not′), *n.* person, group, or country that has little or no property or wealth.

have·n't (hav′ənt), have not.

hav·oc (hav′ək), *n.* very great destruction or injury: *Tornadoes can create widespread havoc.*

play havoc with, to injure severely; ruin; destroy.

haw[1] (hô), *n.* **1** the red fruit of a hawthorn. **2** hawthorn.

haw[2] (hô), *interj.* word of command to horses, oxen, etc., directing them to turn to the left.

Ha·wai·i (hə wī′ē), *n.* **1** state of the United States in the N Pacific, consisting of the Hawaiian Islands. *Abbreviation:* HI *Capital:* Honolulu. **2** the largest of the Hawaiian Islands.

Ha·wai·ian (hə wī′yən), **1** *adj.* of Hawaii, its people, or their language. **2** *n.* person born or living in Hawaii. **3** *n.* the Polynesian language of Hawaii.

Hawaiian Islands, group of islands in the N Pacific.

Hawaii Standard Time, Alaska Standard Time.

Hawaii Volcanoes National Park, a national park in Hawaii, on the island of Hawaii. The volcanoes Kilauea and Mauna Loa are in this park.

hawk[1] (hôk), **1** *n.* any of numerous birds of prey with strong, hooked beaks, long claws, broad wings, and keen sight. **2** *v.* to hunt with trained hawks. **—hawk′er,** *n.* **—hawk′like′,** *adj.*

hawk[2] (hôk), *v.* to carry goods about and offer them for sale by shouting: *Peddlers hawked their wares in the street.*

hawk[3] (hôk), *v.* to clear the throat noisily.

hawk·er (hô′kər), *n.* person who carries wares around and offers them for sale by shouting; peddler.

hawk-eyed (hôk′īd′), *adj.* having sharp eyes like a hawk.

Hawk·ing (hô′king), *n.* **Ste·phen** (stē′vən), born 1942, English physicist. ■ **Stephen Hawking** has done research on black holes and wrote a best-selling book describing his theories, *A Brief History of Time.* He has amyotrophic lateral sclerosis.

haw·ser (hô′zər), *n.* a large rope or small cable, used for mooring or towing ships.

haw·thorn (hô′thôrn), *n.* any of numerous bushes or trees with many thorns, clusters of fragrant white, red, or pink flowers, and small, red fruit; haw.

Haw·thorne (hô′thôrn), *n.* **Na·than·iel** (nə than′yəl), 1804-1864, American writer of novels and short stories. His novels include *The Scarlet Letter* and *The House of the Seven Gables.*

hay (hā), **1** *n.* grass, alfalfa, clover, etc., cut and dried for use as food for cattle and horses. **2** *v.* to cut and dry grass, alfalfa, clover, etc., for hay: *They are haying in the east field.* ■ Another word that sounds like this is **hey.**

hit the hay, INFORMAL. to go to bed.

Hay·dn (hīd′n), *n.* **Franz Jo·seph** (fränts′ yō′zef), 1732-1809, Austrian composer. He wrote more than 100 symphonies and helped develop the symphony in its modern form.

Hayes (hāz), *n.* **Ruth·er·ford Bir·chard** (ruᴛH′ər férd bér′chərd), 1822-1893, the 19th president of the United States, from 1877 to 1881. ■ **Rutherford B. Hayes** and his wife, Lucy, held the first White House Easter-egg roll for children in 1878.

hay fever, allergy caused by the pollen of ragweed and other plants. It causes itching and fits of sneezing and makes the nose and eyes run.

hay·field (hā′fēld′), *n.* field in which grass, alfalfa, clover, etc., are grown for hay.

hay·fork (hā′fôrk′), *n.* **1** pitchfork. **2** a mechanical device equipped with hooks for moving hay into or out of a hayloft.

hay·loft (hā′lôft′), *n.* place in a barn or stable where hay is stored.

hay·mow (hā′mou′), *n.* **1** hayloft. **2** heap of hay stored in a barn or stable.

hay·rick (hā′rik′), *n.* haystack.

hay·ride (hā′rīd′), *n.* outing in a wagon partly filled with hay.

hay·stack (hā′stak′), *n.* a large pile of hay outdoors.

haystack in a painting

hay·wire (hā′wīr′), **1** *n.* wire used to tie up bales of hay. **2** *adj.* out of order; wrong: *The TV went haywire, jumping from channel to channel.* **3** *adj.* confused or unreasonable: *haywire reasoning, a haywire excuse.*

a	hat	ė	term	ô	order	ch	child		a in about
ā	age	i	it	oi	oil	ng	long		e in taken
ä	far	ī	ice	ou	out	sh	she	ə	i in pencil
â	care	o	hot	u	cup	th	thin		o in lemon
e	let	ō	open	ů	put	ᴛH	then		u in circus
ē	equal	ò	saw	ü	rule	zh	measure		

haz·ard (haz′ərd), **1** *n.* chance of harm; risk; danger; peril: *Mountain climbing is full of hazards.* **2** *n.* a possible source of harm: *a fire hazard.* **3** *v.* to take a chance with; risk; venture: *I won't even hazard a guess.* **4** *n.* any obstruction on a golf course.

haz·ard·ous (haz′ər dəs), *adj.* full of risk; dangerous; perilous: *Flying across the ocean in a small plane was a hazardous undertaking.* —**haz′ard·ous·ly,** *adv.*

> **WORD STORY** **Hazardous** comes from an Arabic word meaning "one of a set of dice." A hazardous situation is as uncertain and uncontrollable as the roll of dice.

haze[1] (hāz), *n.* **1** a small amount of mist, smoke, dust, etc., in the air: *A thin haze veiled the distant hills.* **2** slight confusion; vagueness: *Everything happened so fast that my mind is in a haze.*

haze[2] (hāz), *v.* to force new students, fraternity initiates, etc., to undergo physically abusive harassment. ❑ *v.* **hazed, haz·ing.** —**haz′er,** *n.*

ha·zel (hā′zəl), **1** *n.* any of about 15 small trees or bushes, with light brown nuts that are good to eat. **2** *n.* a light brown. **3** *adj.* light brown.

ha·zel·nut (hā′zəl nut′), *n.* nut of a hazel; filbert.

ha·zy (hā′zē), *adj.* **1** full of haze; misty; smoky: *a hazy sky.* **2** slightly confused; vague; dim; obscure: *It was so long ago, I have only a hazy memory of what happened.* ❑ *adj.* **ha·zi·er, ha·zi·est.** —**ha′zi·ly,** *adv.* —**ha′zi·ness,** *n.*

H-bomb (āch′bom′), *n.* a hydrogen bomb.

hdqrs., headquarters.

HDTV, high-definition television (an advanced television system that can produce pictures with great clearness and sharp detail).

he (hē), **1** *pron.* boy, man, or male animal spoken about or mentioned before: *He works hard, but is paid well.* **2** *n.* a male: *Is your dog a he or a she?* **3** *pron.* anyone: *He who hesitates is lost.*

> **USAGE NOTE** **He** and its forms **him, his,** and **himself** have traditionally been used in English to mean any unnamed individual, in sentences such as: *Everyone should bring his lunch.* Since there are as many women and girls as men and boys, many people now object to this usage. Careful writers and speakers avoid using **he** this way, either by using the plural (*All students should bring their lunches.*) or by *his or her* (*Everyone should bring his or her lunch.*).

He, symbol for helium.

head (hed), **1** *n.* the top part of the human body or the front part of most animal bodies where the eyes, nose, ears, mouth, and brain are. **2** *n.* mind; understanding; intelligence: *She can do that math problem in her head.* **3** *n.* the top part of anything: *the head of a pin, the head of a bed.* **4** *n.* the front part of anything: *the head of a parade, the head of a comet.* **5** *adj.* at the top or front: *the head marchers of a parade.* **6** *v.* to put at the top: *head a letter with a date.* **7** *v.* to be or go at the top or front of: *head a parade.* **8** *v.* to move toward; face toward: *Let's head for home.* **9** *n.* chief person; leader: *a department head.* **10** *adj.* chief; leading: *a head nurse.* **11** *v.* to be the chief of; lead: *head a business.* **12** *n.* one or ones; individual or individuals: *ten head of cattle.* **13** *n.* anything rounded like a head: *a head of cabbage.* **14** *n.* the part of a boil or pimple where pus is about to break through the skin. **15** *n.* the striking or cutting part of a tool: *You hit the nail with the head of a hammer.* **16** *n.* piece of skin stretched tightly over the end of a drum. **17** *n.* topic; subject: *She arranged her speech under four main heads.* **18** *n.* crisis or conclusion; decisive point: *His sudden refusal brought matters to a head.* **19** *n.* pressure of water, gas, etc.: *a full head of steam.* **20** *n.* source of a river or stream. **21** *v.* to hit a soccer ball with the head. **22** *n.* **heads,** the top side of a coin. **23** *n.* part of a tape recorder or disk drive that produces, detects, or erases magnetic signals on the tape or disk. ❑ *n., pl.* **heads** for 1-3,9,13-20,23, but **head** for 12. —**head′like′,** *adj.*

go to your head, **1** to make you dizzy: *The wine went to my head.* **2** to make you conceited: *I'm afraid all this praise will go to his head.*

head off, to get in front of and turn back or aside: *Cowboys tried to head off the runaway cattle.*

keep your head, to stay calm; not get excited.

lose your head, to get excited; lose your self-control.

out of your head, foolish; unreasonable.

over someone's head, **1** too hard for someone to understand: *Einstein's theory of relativity is way over my head.* **2** passing over someone without giving that person a chance to act: *I went over my supervisor's head and complained to the president.*

put heads together or lay heads together, to plan together.

turn someone's head, to make a person conceited.

head·ache (hed′āk′), *n.* **1** pain in the head. **2** something or someone which causes great bother or annoyance.

head·band (hed′band′), *n.* band worn around the head.

head·dress (hed′dres′), *n.* covering or decoration for the head. ❑ *n., pl.* **head·dress·es.**

-headed, *suffix.* having a ___ head or ___ heads: *bald-headed* = having a bald head; *two-headed* = having two heads.

head·er (hed′ər), *n.* a plunge, dive, or fall headfirst: *I slipped and took a header.*

head·first (hed′fėrst′), *adv.* **1** with the head first. **2** hastily; rashly.

head·gear (hed′gir′), *n.* **1** covering for the head; hat, cap, helmet, etc. **2** the parts of a harness which fit around an animal's head.

head·ing (hed′ing), *n.* **1** something written or printed at the top

headdress

of a page or at the beginning of a chapter, section, etc. A letterhead and a chapter title are headings. **2** direction in which an aircraft or ship is moving.

head·land (hed′lənd), *n.* narrow ridge of high land jutting out into water; promontory.

head·less (hed′lis), *adj.* **1** having no head. **2** without a leader.

head·light (hed′līt′), *n.* a bright light at the front of a motor vehicle or railroad engine. A car has two headlights.

head·line (hed′līn′), **1** *n.* words printed in heavy type at the top of a newspaper article telling what it is about. **2** *n.pl.* **headlines,** publicity: *The invention got headlines.* **3** *v.* to furnish with a headline. **4** *v.* to give publicity to: *headline a story.* **5** *v.* to list or be listed as the main attraction: *The circus headlined a famous animal trainer.* ❑ *v.* **head·lined, head·lin·ing.**

head·long (hed′lòng), *adv., adj.* **1** with the head first: *plunge headlong into the sea, a headlong plunge or dive.* **2** with great speed and force: *rush headlong into the crowd, a headlong course.* **3** in too great a rush; without stopping to think: *The boy ran headlong across the busy street. One should not make a headlong decision about something important.*

head·man (hed′man′), *n.* man who is a chief; leader. ❑ *n., pl.* **head·men.**

head·mas·ter (hed′mas′tər), *n.* man in charge of a school, especially of a private school; principal.

head·mis·tress (hed′mis′tris), *n.* woman in charge of a school, especially of a private school; principal. ❑ *n., pl.* **head·mis·tress·es.**

head·note (hed′nōt′), *n.* an explanatory note placed before a chapter, section, article, etc.

head-on (hed′on′), *adj., adv.* with the head or front first: *a head-on collision, collide head-on.*

head·phone (hed′fōn′), *n.* earphone held against one or both ears by a band over the head.

head·piece (hed′pēs′), *n.* **1** helmet worn with a suit of armor. **2** any covering for the head.

head·quar·ters (hed′kwôr′tərz), *n.pl. or sing.* **1** place from which the chief or commanding officer of any army, police force, etc., sends out orders. **2** place from which any organization is controlled and directed; main office: *The headquarters of the company is in Washington.*

head·rest (hed′rest′), *n.* a support for the head, as on a dentist's chair.

head·set (hed′set′), *n.* pair of headphones used by telephone and radio operators, etc.

heads·man (hedz′mən), *n.* (long ago) person who cuts off the heads of people condemned to death. ❑ *n., pl.* **heads·men.**

head·stand (hed′stand′), *n.* act of balancing on the head, with the hands placed in front of the head for support.

head start, 1 an advantage or lead allowed to someone at the start of a race, a course of study, etc. 2 advantage gained by beginning something before somebody else.

head·stone (hed′stōn′), *n.* stone, often carved, set at the head of a grave; gravestone.

head·strong (hed′strông′), *adj.* rashly or foolishly determined to have your own way; hard to control or manage; obstinate.

head·wait·er (hed′wā′tər), *n.* person in charge of the waiters in a restaurant, hotel, etc.

head·wa·ters (hed′wô′tərz), *n.pl.* the sources of a river.

head·way (hed′wā′), *n.* 1 motion forward; progress: *The ship could make no headway against the strong wind and tide.* 2 progress with work, etc.: *Science has made much headway in fighting disease.* 3 a clear space overhead in a doorway or under an arch, bridge, etc.; clearance.

head·wind (hed′wind′), *n.* wind blowing from the direction in which a ship or aircraft is moving.

head·y (hed′ē), *adj.* 1 hasty; rash; headlong. 2 apt to affect the head and make you dizzy; intoxicating: *a heady wine.* ❑ *adj.* **head·i·er, head·i·est.** —**head′i·ness,** *n.*

heal (hēl), *v.* 1 to make healthy, sound, or well; bring back to health; cure. 2 to become healthy or sound; get well; return to health; be cured: *My cut finger healed in a few days.* —**heal′-able,** *adj.* —**heal′er,** *n.* ■ Other words that sound like this are **heel** and **he'll.**

health (helth), *n.* 1 condition of being well; freedom from sickness: *Rest is important to your health.* 2 condition of body or mind: *be in excellent health.* 3 sound condition; well-being; welfare: *We drank a toast to the health of the nation.* 3 a toast drunk in honor of a person with a wish for that person's health and happiness.

WORD POWER   **HEALTH AND MEDICINE** ■ Doctors and other health professionals sometimes seem to have their own language. Medical knowledge has been growing for 2400 years. Because there is so much to learn and tell, medical vocabulary needs to be efficient, and it is full of prefixes and suffixes that save time. Because the history of health studies is so old, most of the prefixes and suffixes come from Greek and Latin. Prefixes and suffixes used in health and medicine and defined in the body of this dictionary include:

anti-	-graphy	hypo-	psycho-
bio-	hemo-	intra-	thermo-
-cide	hyper-	micro-	ultra-
endo-			

health club, a club with exercise equipment and other facilities for those wishing to join for a fee.

health food, food grown without chemicals or prepared without preservatives, selected for its nutritional value and believed to have health-giving properties.

health·ful (helth′fəl), *adj.* 1 giving health; good for the health: *healthful exercise, a healthful diet.* 2 having good health. —**health′ful·ly,** *adv.* —**health′ful·ness,** *n.*

Health Maintenance Organization. See HMO.

health·y (hel′thē), *adj.* 1 having good health: *a healthy baby.* 2 showing good health: *a healthy look.* 3 good for the health; healthful: *healthy exercise, healthy foods.* ❑ *adj.* **health·i·er, health·i·est.** —**health′i·ly,** *adv.* —**health′i·ness,** *n.*

SYNONYM STUDY   **Healthy, well**[1], and **fit**[1] all mean in good condition of body. **Healthy** suggests that everything is as it should be: *The baby was born early, but she's perfectly healthy.* **Well** suggests free of illness: *It took me two weeks to get well again.* **Fit** means healthy and strong: *They keep fit by taking long walks.*

heap (hēp), 1 *n.* pile of many things thrown or lying together in a confused way: *a heap of stones.* 2 *v.* to form into a heap; gather in heaps: *I heaped the dirty clothes beside the washing machine.* 3 *n.* INFORMAL. a large amount: *a heap of trouble.* 4 *v.* to give generously or in large amounts: *to heap praise on someone.* 5 *v.* to fill full or more than full: *to heap a plate with food.*

hear (hir), *v.* 1 to take in a sound or sounds through the ear: *We couldn't hear in the back row.* 2 to find out about something: *I hear there will be an assembly today.* 3 to listen to: *You must hear what I have to say.* 4 to give a formal hearing to: *to hear a complaint.* 5 to receive news or information: *I heard from my parents.* ❑ *v.* **heard, hear·ing.** ■ Another word that sounds like this is **here.** —**hear′a·ble,** *adj.* —**hear′er,** *n.*
will not hear of, will not listen to, agree to, or allow.

heard (hèrd), *v.* past tense and past participle of **hear:** *I heard the noise. The sound was heard a mile away.* ■ Another word that sounds like this is **herd.**

hear·ing (hir′ing), *n.* 1 sense by which sound is perceived: *Please speak up; my hearing is poor.* 2 act or process of taking in sound, listening, or receiving information: *Hearing the good news made her happy.* 3 a formal or official meeting to hear facts or arguments: *The judge gave both sides a hearing.* 4 a chance to be heard: *Give us a hearing.* 5 distance that a sound can be heard; earshot: *be within hearing.*

hearing aid, a small battery-powered device which amplifies sounds, worn by people who cannot hear well.

hear·ing-im·paired (hir′ing im pârd′), *adj.* not able to hear so well as most others can; with a weak sense of hearing; hard of hearing. ■ See Usage Note at **deaf.**

heark·en (här′kən), *v.* OLD USE. to pay attention to what is said; listen attentively; listen.

hear·say (hir′sā′), *n.* common talk; gossip or rumor.

hearse (hèrs), *n.* car, carriage, etc., for carrying a coffin to the cemetery. [See Word Story at **rehearse.**]

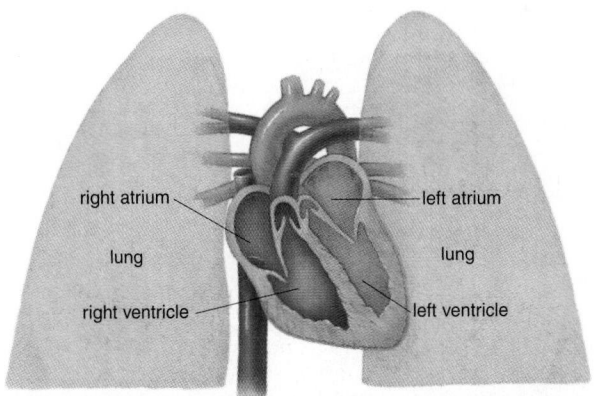

heart (def. 1)

heart (härt), *n.* 1 a hollow, muscular organ which pumps the blood throughout the body by contracting and relaxing. 2 the part that feels, loves, hates, and desires: *a heavy heart, a kind heart.* 3 love; affection: *give your heart to someone.* 4 kindness; sympathy: *a generous heart.* 5 spirit; courage; enthusiasm: *The losing team still had plenty of heart.* 6 the innermost part; middle; center: *in the heart of the forest.* 7 the main part; most important part: *the very heart of the matter.* 8 figure shaped like this: ♥. 9 a playing card marked with one or more red, heart-shaped figures. 10 **hearts,** *pl.* suit of such playing cards. ■ Another word that sounds like this is **hart.**
after your own heart, just as you like it; pleasing you perfectly: *Now that's a meal after my own heart!*

H

a	hat	ė	term	ô	order	ch	child	⟨ a in about
ā	age	i	it	oi	oil	ng	long	e in taken
ä	far	ī	ice	ou	out	sh	she	ə ⟨ i in pencil
â	care	o	hot	u	cup	th	thin	o in lemon
e	let	ō	open	ů	put	ᴛʜ	then	⟨ u in circus
ē	equal	ô	saw	ü	rule	zh	measure	

at heart, in your deepest thoughts or feelings: *He is kind at heart, though he appears to be gruff.*

by heart, 1 by memory: *I learned the poem by heart.* **2** from memory: *She can recite the poem by heart.*

cross your heart, to make a sign of a cross over your heart when swearing that something is true, or when making a solemn promise.

lose your heart to someone, to fall in love with someone.

set your heart on, to want something in a very determined way.

take heart, be encouraged.

take to heart, to think seriously about; be deeply affected by.

with all your heart, 1 sincerely: *He said that he loved her with all his heart.* **2** gladly.

heart·ache (härt′āk′), *n.* great sorrow or grief; deep pain.

heart attack, a sudden failure of the heart to work properly, sometimes resulting in death.

heart·beat (härt′bēt′), *n.* a beat or pulsation of the heart, including one complete contraction and relaxation.

heart·break (härt′brāk′), *n.* a crushing sorrow or grief.

heart·break·ing (härt′brā′king), *adj.* crushing with sorrow or grief. —**heart′break′ing·ly,** *adv.*

heart·bro·ken (härt′brō′kən), *adj.* crushed by sorrow or grief. —**heart′bro′ken·ly,** *adv.*

heart·burn (härt′bėrn′), *n.* a burning feeling in the throat and chest caused by acid flowing up from the stomach.

-hearted, *suffix.* having a ___ heart: *hardhearted = having a hard heart.*

heart·en (härt′n), *v.* to cheer up; encourage: *This good news will hearten you.* ■ See Synonym Study at **encourage.**

heart·felt (härt′felt′), *adj.* with deep feeling; sincere; genuine: *heartfelt sympathy.*

hearth (härth), *n.* **1** stone or brick floor of a fireplace, often extending into the room. **2** fireside; home: *The soldiers longed for their own hearths.* **3** the lowest part of a blast furnace, where the molten metal and slag collects.

hearth (def.1)

hearth·stone (härth′stōn′), *n.* **1** stone forming a hearth. **2** fireside; home.

heart·i·ly (här′tl ē), *adv.* **1** in a warm, friendly way; sincerely: *to express good wishes very heartily.* **2** with courage, spirit, or enthusiasm; vigorously: *set to work heartily.* **3** with a good appetite: *eat heartily.* **4** completely; extremely: *I heartily approve of her decision.*

heart·land (härt′land′), *n.* area in the center of a country, especially where traditional beliefs are strong.

heart·less (härt′lis), *adj.* without kindness or sympathy; unfeeling; cruel: *heartless words.* —**heart′less·ly,** *adv.*

heart·rend·ing (härt′ren′ding), *adj.* causing mental anguish; very distressing: *The loss of their parents in an accident was a heartrending experience.*

heart·sick (härt′sik′), *adj.* sick at heart; very depressed; very unhappy. —**heart′sick′ness,** *n.*

heart·strings (härt′stringz′), *n.pl.* deepest feelings: *The sad story tugged at their heartstrings.*

heart·throb (härt′throb′), *n.* **1** passionate or sentimental emotion. **2** an person who inspires such emotion, especially a man: *He is the new soap-opera heartthrob.*

heart·warm·ing (härt′wôr′ming), *adj.* causing happiness and pleasure: *a heartwarming letter from an old friend.*

heart·wood (härt′wùd′), *n.* the hard, central wood of a tree.

heart·y (här′tē), *adj.* **1** warm and friendly; full of feeling; sincere: *We gave our old friends a hearty welcome.* **2** strong and well; vigorous: *My grandmother was still hale and hearty at eighty.* **3** full of energy and enthusiasm; not restrained: *a hearty laugh.* **4** with plenty to eat; abundant: *a hearty meal.* **5** having a good appetite: *People who work outdoors are usually hearty eaters.* ❑ *adj.* **heart·i·er, heart·i·est.** —**heart′i·ness,** *n.*

heat (hēt), **1** *n.* condition of being hot; hotness; warmth; high temperature: *the heat of a fire.* **2** *n.* a form of energy that passes from one object to another, raising the temperature of the second object. **3** *v.* to make or become warm or hot: *The stove heats the room.* **4** *n.* strength of feeling; violence; excitement: *In the heat of the argument we lost our tempers.* **5** *n.* one trial in a race: *I won the first heat, but lost the final race.* **6** *n.* estrus. —**heat′less,** *adj.*

heat·ed (hē′tid), *adj.* angry, excited, or violent: *a heated argument.* —**heat′ed·ly,** *adv.*

heat engine, any machine designed to change heat into work.

heat·er (hē′tər), *n.* something that gives heat or warmth. A stove, furnace, or radiator is a heater.

heath (hēth), *n.* **1** open wasteland with heather or low bushes growing on it; moor. It has few or no trees. **2** any low plant, such as heather, growing on such land. —**heath′like′,** *adj.*

hea·then (hē′тнən), **1** *n.* person who does not believe in the God of the Bible; person who is not a Christian, Jew, or Muslim; pagan. **2** *n.* people who are heathens. **3** *adj.* of or about heathens; not Christian, Jewish, or Muslim. ❑ *n., pl.* **hea·thens** or **hea·then.**

hea·then·ish (hē′тнə nish), *adj.* like heathens.

heath·er (heтн′ər), *n.* any of numerous low, evergreen bushes with stalks of small, purple or pink, bell-shaped flowers, covering many heaths of Scotland and England, and growing also in Europe and Africa.

heat lightning, lightning in broad flashes seen near the horizon, especially on hot summer evenings; sheet lightning. It is actually a reflection of lightning that occurs beyond the horizon.

heat shield, covering of special material on the nose cone of a missile or spacecraft, to protect against heat caused by friction during reentry into the earth's atmosphere.

heat·stroke (hēt′strōk′), *n.* a sudden illness with fever and dry skin, caused by too much heat.

heat wave, period of very hot weather.

heave (hēv), **1** *v.* to lift with force or effort: *She heaved the heavy box into the station wagon.* **2** *v.* to lift and throw: *We heaved the old carpet out the back door.* **3** *v.* to pull with force or effort; haul: *They heaved on the rope.* **4** *v.* to give a sigh, groan, etc., with a deep, heavy breath: *She heaved a sigh of relief.* **5** *v.* to rise and fall alternately: *The waves heaved in the storm.* **6** *v.* to breathe hard; pant. **7** *v.* to vomit. **8** *v.* (of a ship) to move in some direction. **9** *v.* to rise; swell; bulge: *The ground heaved from the earthquake.* **10** *n.* act of heaving: *With a mighty heave, we pushed the boat into the water.* ❑ *v.* **heaved** (or **hove** for 8), **heav·ing.**

heave ho! sailors' cry when pulling up the anchor, etc.

heave in sight, to come into view.

heave to, to stop a ship; stop.

heav·en (hev′ən), *n.* **1** (in Christian and some other religious use) place where God and the angels live and where the blessed go after death. **2 Heaven,** God; Providence: *It was the will of Heaven.* **3** place or condition of greatest happiness. **4** Usually, **heavens,** *pl.* the upper air; sky: *Millions of stars were shining in the heavens.*

for heaven's sake! or **good heavens!** exclamation of surprise or protest.

heav·en·ly (hev′ən lē), *adj.* **1** of or in heaven; divine: *heavenly angels, heavenly Father.* **2** very happy, beautiful, or excellent: *It was a heavenly day for a hike in the woods.* **3** of or in the heavens: *The sun, moon, and stars are heavenly bodies.* —**heav′en·li·ness,** *n.*

heav·en·ward (hev′ən wərd), *adv., adj.* toward heaven: *The rocket soared heavenward. The spaceship set out on its heavenward course.*

heav·y (hev′ē), **1** *adj.* hard to lift or carry; of great weight: *a heavy load.* **2** *adj.* of more than usual weight for its kind: *heavy silk, heavy bread.* **3** *adj.* of great amount, force, or intensity; greater than usual; large: *a heavy rain, a heavy meal, a heavy vote.* **4** *adj.* hard to bear or endure: *Their troubles became heavier.* **5** *adj.* hard to deal with, manage, etc.; trying or difficult in any way: *heavy soil, a heavy job.* **6** *adj.* hard to digest: *heavy food.* **7** *adj.* weighted down; laden: *air heavy with moisture.* **8** *adj.* sorrowful; gloomy: *His heart was heavy.* **9** *adj.* serious; deep; grave: *a heavy discussion.* **10** *adj.* INFORMAL. unpleasant; troublesome: *My being so late caused a heavy scene at home.* **11** *adj.* cloudy; overcast: *a heavy sky.* **12** *adj.* broad; thick; coarse: *heavy features.* **13** *adj.* clumsy; sluggish; slow: *a heavy walk.* **14** *adj.* uninteresting; dull; ponderous: *heavy reading.* **15** *n.* villain: *the heavy in a play.* **16** *adv.* in a heavy manner; heavily. ❑ *adj.* **heav·i·er, heav·i·est. —heav′i·ly,** *adv.* **—heav′i·ness,** *n.*

hang heavy, to pass slowly and dully: *Time hung heavy on her hands.*

heav·y-du·ty (hev′ē dü′tē), *adj.* made to endure hard use or strain: *heavy-duty tires for rough roads.*

heav·y-hand·ed (hev′ē han′did), *adj.* **1** clumsy; awkward: *heavy-handed humor.* **2** treating others harshly.

heav·y-heart·ed (hev′ē här′tid), *adj.* sad; gloomy.

heavy hydrogen, deuterium.

heavy industry, industry that manufactures basic products, such as machines or steel, for use by other industries.

heavy metal, loud rock music with a very strong beat: *She plays drums in a heavy metal band.*

heav·y·set (hev′ē set′), *adj.* having a heavy body build; stocky.

heavy water, water formed of oxygen and deuterium. Heavy water is much like ordinary water, but is about 1.1 times as heavy and has a higher freezing point. It occurs in very small amounts in ordinary water.

heav·y·weight (hev′ē wāt′), *n.* **1** person or thing of more than average weight. **2** boxer or wrestler who weighs 175 pounds (79 kilograms) or more.

Heb., Hebrew or Hebrews.

He·bra·ic (hi brā′ik), *adj.* of the Hebrews or their language or culture.

He·brew (hē′brü), **1** *n.* the ancient Semitic language of the Jews, in which many books of the Bible were written. Citizens of Israel speak a modern form of Hebrew. **2** *n.* Jew; Israelite. **3** *adj.* Jewish.

WORD SOURCE Hebrew has given a number of words to the English language, including the words below.

amen	kosher	rabbi	schwa
cherub	pita	Sabbath	seraph
Jehovah	leviathan	Satan	Torah

He·brews (hē′brüz), *n.* book of the New Testament.

Hebrew Scripture, sacred writings of the Jewish religion.

Heb·ri·des (heb′rə dēz′), *n.pl.* group of Scottish islands off NW Scotland.

WORD STORY Hebrides comes from a mistake. The Romans called these islands *Hebudes.* Someone copied the name wrong, and people who didn't know better copied the mistake.

He·bron (hē′brən *or* heb′rən), *n.* town in W Jordan, near Jerusalem. [**Hebron** comes from a Hebrew word meaning "friendship."]

heck (hek), **1** *interj.* exclamation or mild oath: *Heck, I forgot my lunch money!* **2** *n.* **the heck,** exclamation or mild oath: *What the heck is that?*

heck·le (hek′əl), *v.* to interrupt and annoy a speaker by asking bothersome questions, jeering, or making loud remarks. ❑ *v.* **heck·led, heck·ling. —heck′ler,** *n.*

hec·tare (hek′tār), *n.* unit of area in the metric system equal to 10,000 square meters.

hec·tic (hek′tik), *adj.* very exciting; feverish: *The children had a hectic time getting to school after the big snowstorm.* **—hec′ti·cal·ly,** *adv.* **—hec′tic·ness,** *n.*

hecto-, *prefix.* hundred: *hectogram = hundred grams.*

hec·to·gram (hek′tə gram), *n.* unit of weight or mass in the metric system, equal to 100 grams.

hec·to·li·ter (hek′tə lē′tər), *n.* unit of volume in the metric system, equal to 100 liters.

hec·to·me·ter (hek′tə mē′tər), *n.* unit of length in the metric system, equal to 100 meters.

hec·tor (hek′tər), **1** *n.* a bragging, bullying fellow. **2** *v.* to bluster; bully. **3** *v.* to tease.

Hec·tor (hek′tər), *n.* (in Greek legends) the bravest of the Trojan warriors. He was killed by Achilles. [**Hector** comes from a Greek word meaning "firm defender." Hector was the chief defender of Troy against the Greeks.]

he'd (hēd), **1** he had. **2** he would. ■ Another word that sounds like this is **heed.**

hedge (hej), **1** *n.* a thick row of bushes or small trees, planted as a fence or boundary. **2** *n.* any barrier or boundary. **3** *v.* to put a hedge around: *hedge a garden.* **4** *v.* to avoid giving a direct answer or taking a definite stand; evade questions. **5** *v.* to bet on both sides in order to reduce your possible losses. ❑ *v.* **hedged, hedg·ing. —hedg′er,** *n.*

hedge in, to hem in; surround on all sides: *The town was hedged in by mountains and a dense forest.*

hedge·hog (hej′hog′), *n.* any of several small, insect-eating mammals of Europe, Asia, and Africa, with spines on their backs. When attacked, a hedgehog rolls up into a bristling ball.

hedge·hop (hej′hop′), *v.* to fly an airplane very low. ❑ *v.* **hedge·hopped, hedge·hop·ping. —hedge′hop′per,** *n.*

hedge·row (hej′rō′), *n.* a thick row of bushes or small trees forming a hedge.

hedgehog—about 9 in. (23 cm) long

heed (hēd), **1** *v.* to give careful attention to; take notice of: *Now heed what I say.* **2** *n.* careful attention: *Pay heed to her instructions.* ■ Another word that sounds like this is **he'd. —heed′er,** *n.*

heed·ful (hēd′fəl), *adj.* careful; attentive. **—heed′ful·ly,** *adv.* **—heed′ful·ness,** *n.*

heed·less (hēd′lis), *adj.* careless; thoughtless. **—heed′less·ly,** *adv.* **—heed′less·ness,** *n.*

hee-haw (hē′hȯ′), **1** *n.* the braying sound made by a donkey. **2** *v.* to make such a sound.

heel¹ (hēl), **1** *n.* the back part of the foot, below the ankle. **2** *n.* the part of a stocking or shoe that covers the heel. **3** *n.* the part of a shoe or boot that is under the heel or raises the heel: *a pair of shoes with high heels.* **4** *n.* the part of the hind leg of an animal that corresponds to a person's heel: *The horse kicked up its heels trying to throw the rider.* **5** *v.* to put a heel or heels on: *heel a pair of shoes.* **6** *v.* to follow closely at your heels: *The dog was trained to heel.* **7** *n.* anything shaped, used, or placed at an end like a heel. The end crust of bread is a heel. **8** *n.* OLD USE. a hateful person. ■ Other words that sound like this are **heal** and **he'll.**

at heel, near the heels; close behind.

down at the heel or **down at the heels, 1** with the heel of a shoe worn down. **2** shabby.

kick up your heels, to have a good time.

take to your heels, to run away.

heel² (hēl), *v.* to lean over to one side; tilt; tip: *The sailboat heeled as it turned.* ■ Other words that sound like this are **heal** and **he'll.**

heft (heft), **1** *n.* weight; heaviness. **2** *v.* to lift; heave. **3** *v.* to judge the weight of something by lifting it.

a	hat	ė	term	ô	order	ch	child		
ā	age	i	it	oi	oil	ng	long		a in about
ä	far	ī	ice	ou	out	sh	she	ə	e in taken
â	care	o	hot	u	cup	th	thin		i in pencil
e	let	ō	open	ù	put	ŦH	then		o in lemon
ē	equal	ȯ	saw	ü	rule	zh	measure		u in circus

heft·y (hef'tē), *adj.* **1** weighty; heavy. **2** big and strong. ❑ *adj.* **heft·i·er, heft·i·est.** —**heft'i·ly,** *adv.*

Hei·del·berg (hī'dl bėrg'), *n.* city in SW Germany. A famous university is located there.

heif·er (hef'ər), *n.* a young cow that has not had a calf.

heigh-ho (hī'hō' *or* hā'hō'), *interj.* sound made to express surprise, joy, sadness, or weariness.

height (hīt), *n.* **1** measurement from top to bottom; how tall or high someone or something is: *the height of a mountain.* **2** quality of being tall: *She used her height to advantage in sports.* **3** a distance up; altitude: *the height of a plane in the sky.* **4** a high point or place: *She stood on a height above the river.* **5** the highest point; greatest degree: *Fast driving on icy roads is the height of folly.*

> **USAGE NOTE** **Height** is often used in sentences with **breadth** and **width.** Some people say **height** as if it also ended in *-th,* but this is not standard.

height·en (hīt'n), *v.* **1** to make or become higher. **2** to make or become stronger or greater; increase: *The wind whistling outside heightened the suspense of the ghost story.*

height of land, CANADIAN. watershed (def. 1).

Heim·lich maneuver (hīm'lik), method used in first aid to save someone who is choking. You grasp the victim from behind, beneath the ribs, and squeeze hard with both hands clasped together. This will clear whatever is stuck in the person's windpipe.

hei·nous (hā'nəs), *adj.* very wicked; hateful. —**hei'nous·ly,** *adv.*

heir (âr), *n.* person who has the right to property or a title after the death of its owner. ■ Other words that can sound like this are **air, ere,** and **err.**

heir apparent, person who will be heir if he or she lives longer than the person holding the property or title: *The king's oldest son is heir apparent to the throne.* ❑ *pl.* **heirs apparent.**

heir·ess (âr'is), *n.* **1** heir who is a woman or girl. **2** woman or girl inheriting great wealth. ❑ *n., pl.* **heir·ess·es.**

heir·loom (âr'lüm'), *n.* possession handed down from generation to generation: *This clock is a family heirloom.*

Hei·sen·berg (hī'zən bėrg), *n.* **Wer·ner** (ver'nər), 1901-1976, German atomic physicist who discovered the uncertainty principle.

heist (hīst), INFORMAL. **1** *v.* to rob or steal. **2** *n.* a robbery or theft.

held (held), *v.* past tense and past participle of **hold**[1]: *I held the kitten gently. The swing is held by strong ropes.*

Hel·e·na (hel'ə nə), *n.* capital of Montana, in the W part.

Hel·en of Troy (hel'ən), (in Greek legends) a very beautiful Greek queen. Her kidnapping by Paris caused the Trojan War. [**Helen** comes from a Greek word meaning "light."]

hel·i·ces (hel'ə sēz'), *n.* a plural of **helix.**

hel·i·cop·ter (hel'ə kop'tər), *n.* aircraft without wings that is lifted from the ground and moves through the air by horizontal propellers.

> **WORD STORY** **Helicopter** comes from Greek words meaning "spiral" and "wing." As a helicopter rises, the propeller blades move upward in a spiral and act as a lifting wing.

he·li·o·cen·tric (hē'lē ō sen'trik), *adj.* with the sun as the center.

he·li·o·trope (hē'lē ə trōp), **1** *n.* any of several plants with clusters of small, sweet-smelling purple or white flowers. **2** *n.* a pinkish purple. **3** *adj.* pinkish purple.

hel·i·pad (hel'ə pad'), *n.* a small area for helicopters to take off from and land on.

hel·i·port (hel'ə pôrt'), *n.* airport designed for use by helicopters. Heliports may be built on the tops of buildings.

he·li·um (hē'lē əm), *n.* a very light, colorless, odorless gas that will not burn. It is a chemical element that occurs in small amounts in the air, in natural gas, etc., and that is also produced artificially. Helium is used to inflate balloons and, in the liquid state, as a refrigerant. *Symbol:* He [**Helium** comes from a Greek word meaning "sun." Scientists discovered this element in the sun before they found it on earth.]

he·lix (hē'liks), *n.* anything having a spiral, coiled form. A screw thread, a watch spring, or a snail shell is a helix. ❑ *n., pl.* **he·lix·es** or **hel·i·ces.**

hell (hel), *n.* **1** (in Christian religious use) place where devils and evil spirits live and where wicked persons are punished after death. **2** any place or condition of wickedness, torment, or misery.

he'll (hēl), **1** he will. **2** he shall. ■ Other words that sound like this are **heal** and **heel.**

hel·le·bore (hel'ə bôr), *n.* **1** any of several European and Asian plants with showy flowers that bloom before spring. Most hellebores are poisonous. **2** any of several unrelated tall plants, **false hellebores,** especially one of North America with large leaves and small greenish flowers. Its root is used in medicine or as a powder to kill insects.

Hel·lene (hel'ēn), *n.* a Greek.

Hel·len·ic (he len'ik), *adj.* **1** Greek. **2** of Greek history, language, or culture from 776 B.C. to the death of Alexander the Great in 323 B.C.

Hel·len·is·tic (hel'ə nis'tik), *adj.* of Greek history, language, or culture after 323 B.C.

Hel·les·pont (hel'i spont), *n.* ancient name for the Dardanelles.

hell·ish (hel'ish), *adj.* fit to have come from hell; devilish; fiendish: *hellish shrieks.* —**hell'ish·ly,** *adv.* —**hell'ish·ness,** *n.*

Hell·man (hel'mən), *n.* **Lil·li·an** (lil'ē ən), 1905-1984, American playwright. Her works include *The Little Foxes* and *The Children's Hour.*

hel·lo (he lō' *or* hə lō'), **1** *interj.* a call or exclamation to attract attention, express greeting, etc. We usually say "hello" when we call or answer a call on the telephone. *"Hello, Mother!" the boy said.* **2** *n.* a call or shout: *She gave a loud hello to let us know where she was.* ❑ *n., pl.* **hel·los.**

helm (helm), *n.* **1** handle or wheel controlling the rudder, by which a ship is steered. **2** position of control or guidance: *Upon the President's death, the Vice-President took the nation's helm.*

hel·met (hel'mit), *n.* covering made of steel, leather, plastic, or some other sturdy material, worn to protect the head. —**hel'met·like',** *adj.*

helms·man (helmz'mən), *n.* person who steers a ship. ❑ *n., pl.* **helms·men.**

helm (def. 1)

help (help), **1** *v.* to give or do what is needed or useful; give aid; assist: *My parents helped me with my homework.* **2** *n.* act of helping; aid; assistance: *I need some help with my work.* **3** *n.* someone or something that helps; helper: *A sewing machine is a help in making clothes.* **4** *n.* a hired helper or group of hired helpers: *The storekeeper treats her help well.* **5** *v.* to make better; relieve: *This medicine will help your cough.* ■ See Synonym Study at **improve. 6** *n.* means of making better; remedy: *The medicine was a help.* **7** *v.* to prevent; stop: *It can't be helped.* **8** *v.* to avoid; keep from: *I can't help yawning.* —**help'er,** *n.*

help out, to help; help in doing or getting: *The children were asked to help out around the house.*

help yourself to, to take for or serve yourself: *They helped themselves to some cake.*

> **SYNONYM STUDY** **Help, aid,** and **assist** all mean to do part of the work that someone else has to do. **Help** is a general word: *She helps her grandparents by mowing their lawn.* **Aid** suggests providing something that someone needs: *The gift of blankets will aid the shelter for the homeless.* **Assist** means to help by working with someone: *Her secretary assists her in preparing reports.*

help·ful (help'fəl), *adj.* giving help; useful. —**help'ful·ly,** *adv.* —**help'ful·ness,** *n.*

help·ing (hel'ping), *n.* portion of food served to a person at one time.

helping verb, auxiliary verb.

help·less (help'lis), *adj.* **1** not able to help yourself: *A little baby is helpless.* **2** without help or protection: *Though alone and helpless, he managed to keep himself afloat until help arrived.* —**help'less·ly,** *adv.* —**help'less·ness,** *n.*

help·mate (help′māt′), *n.* OLD USE. companion and helper, especially a wife or husband.

help·meet (help′mēt′), *n.* OLD USE. helpmate.

Hel·sin·ki (hel′sing kē), *n.* port and capital of Finland, on the Gulf of Finland.

hel·ter-skel·ter (hel′tər skel′tər), **1** *adv.* with headlong, disorderly haste: *The children ran helter-skelter when the dog rushed at them.* **2** *adj.* disorderly; confused: *a helter-skelter way of playing a game.*

hem[1] (hem), **1** *n.* border or edge on a garment; edge made on cloth by folding it over and sewing it down. **2** *v.* to fold over and sew down the edge of cloth: *I hemmed the curtains.* ❏ *v.* **hemmed, hem·ming.** —**hem′mer,** *n.*

hem in, hem around, or hem about, to close in or surround, and not let out.

hem[2] (hem), **1** *interj., n.* sound like clearing the throat, used to attract attention or show doubt or hesitation. **2** *v.* to make this sound. ❏ *v.* **hemmed, hem·ming.**

hem and haw, **1** to hesitate in speaking. **2** to stall or put off.

he-man (hē′man′), *n.* a virile, rugged man. ❏ *n., pl.* **he-men.**

hem·a·tite (hem′ə tīt), *n.* an important iron ore that is reddish brown when powdered.

Hem·ing·way (hem′ing wā), *n.* **Er·nest** (ėr′nəst), 1899-1961, American writer. ■ **Ernest Hemingway** won a Pulitzer Prize in 1953 for his novel *The Old Man and the Sea* and the Nobel Prize for literature in 1954.

hem·i·sphere (hem′ə sfir), *n.* **1** one half of a sphere or globe. **2** one half of the earth's surface. North America and South America are in the Western Hemisphere. Europe, Asia, Africa, and Australia are in the Eastern Hemisphere. All countries north of the equator are in the Northern Hemisphere, and the countries south of it are in the Southern Hemisphere. —**hem′i·spher′ic** or **hem′i·spher′i·cal,** *adj.*

hem·line (hem′līn′), *n.* the lower border of a skirt or coat; hem.

hem·lock (hem′lok), *n.* **1** any of several evergreen trees related to pines, with flat needles, small cones, and reddish bark used in tanning. **2** their wood. **3** a poisonous plant with small white flowers. It looks something like parsley. **4** poison made from it.

hemo-, *prefix.* blood: *hemoglobin = substance in red blood cells.*

he·mo·glo·bin (hē′mə glō′bən), *n.* substance in the red blood cells made up of iron and protein. It carries oxygen from the lungs to the tissues, and carbon dioxide from the tissues to the lungs. Hemoglobin gives blood its red color.

he·mo·phil·i·a (hē′mə fil′ē ə), *n.* an inherited disorder of the blood in males in which clotting does not occur normally, making it difficult to stop bleeding after even the slightest injury.

he·mo·phil·i·ac (hē′mə fil′ē ak), *n.* person who has hemophilia. ■ Some people prefer not to use **hemophiliac,** because they feel the word identifies a person with the disorder. They prefer a *person with hemophilia* instead.

hem·or·rhage (hem′ər ij), **1** *n.* discharge of blood, especially a heavy discharge from a damaged blood vessel. A nosebleed is a mild hemorrhage. **2** *v.* to have a hemorrhage; lose much blood. ❏ *v.* **hem·or·rhaged, hem·or·rhag·ing.**

WORD FAMILY **Hemorrhage** and the following words are related: **anemia, hematite, hemoglobin, hemophilia,** and **leukemia.** They all come from a Greek word meaning "blood."

hem·or·rhoids (hem′ə roidz′), *n.pl.* painful swellings formed by the enlargement of blood vessels near the anus.

hemp (hemp), *n.* **1** a tall plant with tough fibers that are made into heavy string, rope, and coarse cloth. **2** hashish or other drugs obtained from this plant. —**hemp′like′,** *adj.*

hemp·en (hem′pən), *adj.* of or like hemp.

hem·stitch (hem′stich′), **1** *v.* to hem along a line from which threads have been drawn out, gathering the cross threads into a series of little groups. **2** *n.* the stitch used. **3** *n.* ornamental needlework made by hemstitching. ❏ *n., pl.* **hem·stitch·es** for 2. —**hem′stitch′er,** *n.*

hen (hen), *n.* **1** a female chicken: *a hen and her chicks.* **2** female of other birds. —**hen′like′,** *adj.*

hence (hens), *adv.* **1** as a result of this; therefore: *The king died, hence his son became king.* **2** from now; from this time onward: *Football season begins three weeks hence.* **3** from here: *"Go hence, I pray thee."*

USAGE NOTE **Hence** (def. 1) is used mostly in formal writing and speaking. In everyday language, **and so** and **therefore** are much more common.

hence·forth (hens′fôrth′), *adv.* from this time on; from now on.

hence·for·ward (hens′fôr′wərd), *adv.* henceforth.

hench·man (hench′mən), *n.* **1** a trusted attendant or follower. **2** an obedient, unscrupulous follower, especially of a criminal gang leader. ❏ *n., pl.* **hench·men.**

Hen·drix (hen′driks), *n.* **Jim·i** (jim′ē), 1942-1970, American rock guitarist and singer.

hen·house (hen′hous′), *n.* house for chickens. ❏ *n., pl.* **hen·hous·es** (hen′hou′ziz).

hen·na (hen′ə), **1** *n.* a reddish brown dye used on the hair. **2** *n.* a small, thorny tree or bush of Asia and Africa from the leaves of which this dye is made. **3** *n.* a reddish brown. **4** *adj.* reddish brown. **5** *v.* to color with this dye. ❏ *n., pl.* **hen·nas;** *v.* **hen·naed, hen·na·ing.**

hen·pecked (hen′pekt′), *adj.* dominated, ruled, or nagged by your wife. ■ **Henpecked** is often considered offensive.

hen·ry (hen′rē), *n.* unit for measuring the power of an electrical circuit to produce electromotive force in a nearby circuit. This power is called inductance. ❏ *n., pl.* **hen·rys** or **hen·ries.**

Hen·ry (hen′rē), *n.* **1 John,** American folklore hero. ■ **John Henry** was a real person who raced a steam drill. In the legend, John Henry beats the machine but dies from exhaustion. The real John Henry also beat the machine, but the effort didn't kill him. **2 O.,** 1862-1910, American writer. He wrote many short stories with ironic or surprising endings. His real name was William Sydney Porter. **3 Patrick,** 1736-1799, American patriot and political leader. He is remembered for the saying "Give me liberty or give me death."

Henry VIII, 1491-1547, king of England from 1509 to 1547. ■ **Henry VIII** established the Church of England with himself as its head. He married six times. His wives were Catherine of Aragon, Anne Boleyn, Jane Seymour, Anne of Cleves, Catherine Howard, and Catherine Parr.

Hen·son (hen′sən), *n.* **Matthew,** 1867-1955, American explorer. He accompanied Admiral Robert Peary on an expedition to the North Pole.

he·pat·i·ca (hi pat′ə kə), *n.* any of several low plants with delicate purple, pink, or white flowers that bloom early in the spring; liverwort. ❏ *n., pl.* **he·pat·i·cas.**

hep·a·ti·tis (hep′ə tī′tis), *n.* any of several diseases, caused by viruses, that produce inflammation of the liver.

Hep·burn (hep′bərn), *n.* **Kath·er·ine** (kath′rin), born 1909, American actress. She has been nominated for 12 Academy Awards, more than any other performer, and has won four.

hep·ta·gon (hep′tə gon), *n.* a plane figure having seven angles and seven sides.

her (hėr), **1** *pron.* the girl, woman, or female animal spoken about: *She is not here; have you seen her? Find her.* **2** *adj.* of her; belonging to her: *her book, her work.*

Her·a (hir′ə), *n.* Greek goddess of marriage, the wife of Zeus. The Romans called her Juno.

Her·a·cles (her′ə klēz′), *n.* Hercules.

her·ald (her′əld), **1** *n.* someone who carries messages and makes announcements; messenger. In former times, a herald was an official who made public announcements and carried messages between rulers, etc. **2** *v.* to bring news of; announce: *The newspapers heralded the signing of the treaty.* **3** *n.* someone or some-

a	hat	ė	term	ô	order	ch	child	
ā	age	i	it	oi	oil	ng	long	⟨a in about
ä	far	ī	ice	ou	out	sh	she	e in taken
â	care	o	hot	u	cup	th	thin	ə⟨i in pencil
e	let	ō	open	u̇	put	ŦH	then	o in lemon
ē	equal	ȯ	saw	ü	rule	zh	measure	u in circus

thing that goes or is sent before and shows something more is coming; harbinger: *Dawn is the herald of day.*

he·ral·dic (he ral′dik), *adj.* of heraldry or heralds. —**he·ral′di·cal·ly,** *adv.*

her·ald·ry (her′əl drē), *n.* science or art dealing with coats of arms. Heraldry determines a person's right to use a coat of arms, traces family descent, designs coats of arms for new countries, etc.

herb (erb *or* herb), *n.* **1** any plant with leaves or stems used for medicine, seasoning, food, or perfume. Sage, mint, and lavender are herbs. **2** any flowering plant that lives only one season and does not develop a woody stem like the stems of bushes and trees. Lilies, corn, and onions are herbs. —**herb′al,** *adj.* —**herb′less,** *adj.* —**herb′like′,** *adj.*

her·ba·ceous (er′bā′shəs *or* her bā′shəs), *adj.* of or like an herb; containing herbs: *herbaceous borders.*

herb·age (er′bij *or* her′bij), *n.* grass used as food by grazing horses, cattle, etc.

her·bi·cide (her′bə sid *or* er′bə sīd), *n.* a poisonous chemical used to destroy weeds.

her·bi·vore (er′bə vôr *or* her′bə vôr), *n.* any animal that feeds mainly on plants.

her·biv·or·ous (er·biv′ər əs *or* her′biv′ər əs), *adj.* feeding mainly on grass or other plants. Cattle are herbivorous animals.

her·cu·le·an *or* **Her·cu·le·an** (her′kyü′lē ən *or* her′kyə lē′ən), *adj.* **1** of great strength, courage, or size; very powerful: *a herculean warrior.* **2** requiring great strength, courage, or size; very hard to do: *a herculean task.*

Her·cu·les (her′kyə lēz), *n.* **1** (in Greek and Roman myths) a hero famous for his great strength and for the 12 great labors he performed. The Greeks called him Heracles. **2** Also, **hercules,** any person of great strength, courage, or size.

herd (herd), **1** *n.* group of animals of one kind, especially large animals, keeping, feeding, or moving together: *a herd of cows, a herd of elephants.* **2** *n.* a large number of people. **3** *v.* to join or flock together: *We all herded under an awning to get out of the rain.* **4** *v.* to drive or guide a group in a particular direction: *herding cows to the barn door, herding children through a museum.* **5** *v.* to tend or take care of cattle, sheep, etc. ■ Another word that sounds like this is **heard.**

ride herd on, to control strictly.

herd (def. 1)

herd·er (her′dər), *n.* herdsman.

herds·man (herdz′mən), *n.* person who takes care of a herd. ❑ *n., pl.* **herds·men.**

here (hir), **1** *adv.* in this place; at this place: *We will stop here.* **2** *adv.* to this place: *Come here.* **3** *n.* this place: *Where do we go from here?* **4** *adv.* at this time; now: *Here the speaker paused.* **5** *n.* this life: *the here and now.* **6** *interj.* an answer showing that you are present when roll is called. **7** *interj.* exclamation used to call attention to some person or thing: *"Here! take away the dishes."* ■ Another word that sounds like this is **hear.**

here and there, in this place and that; at intervals.

neither here nor there, not to the point; off the subject; unimportant.

here·a·bout (hir′ə bout′), *adv.* about this place; around here.

here·a·bouts (hir′ə bouts′), *adv.* hereabout.

here·af·ter (hir af′tər), **1** *adv.* after this; in the future. **2** *n.* the future. **3** *n.* the life or time after death.

here·by (hir bi′), *adv.* by this; in this way: *The license said, "You are hereby given the right to hunt and fish in Dover County."*

he·red·i·tar·y (hə red′ə ter′ē), *adj.* **1** coming by inheritance: *"Prince" and "Princess" are hereditary titles.* **2** holding a position by inheritance: *The queen of England is a hereditary ruler.* **3** passed on or caused by heredity: *Having brown eyes is hereditary.* **4** taken from your parents or ancestors: *a hereditary custom or belief.* —**he·red′i·tar′i·ly,** *adv.* —**he·red′i·tar′i·ness,** *n.*

he·red·i·ty (hə red′ə tē), *n.* **1** the process in which physical characteristics are passed from parent to offspring by means of genes. **2** characteristics that have come to offspring from parents.

Here·ford (her′fərd), *n.* one of a breed of reddish brown beef cattle with a white face and white markings under the body.

here·in (hir in′), *adv.* **1** in this place. **2** in this matter; in this way.

here·of (hir ov′ *or* hir uv′), *adv.* of this; about this.

here·on (hir on′), *adv.* **1** on this. **2** immediately after this.

here's (hirz), here is.

her·e·sy (her′ə sē), *n.* **1** belief different from the accepted belief of a church or some other group. **2** act of holding such a belief. ❑ *n., pl.* **her·e·sies** for 1.

her·e·tic (her′ə tik), *n.* person who holds a belief that is different from the accepted belief of a church or some other group.

he·ret·i·cal (hə ret′ə kəl), *adj.* **1** of or about heresy or heretics. **2** containing heresy; not accepted. —**he·ret′i·cal·ly,** *adv.* —**he·ret′i·cal·ness,** *n.*

here·to (hir tü′), *adv.* to this place, thing, document, etc.

here·to·fore (hir′tə fôr′), *adv.* before this time; until now.

here·un·to (hir′un tü′), *adv.* to this place, thing, document, etc.; hereto.

here·up·on (hir′ə pon′), *adv.* **1** upon this thing, point, subject, or matter. **2** immediately after this.

here·with (hir wiᴛʜ′ *or* hir with′), *adv.* with this: *I am sending a first-class stamp herewith.*

her·it·a·ble (her′ə tə bəl), *adj.* **1** capable of being inherited: *heritable diseases, heritable tendencies.* **2** capable of inheriting. —**her′it·a·bly,** *adv.*

her·it·age (her′ə tij), *n.* what is handed down from one generation to the next, such as traditions, skills, etc.; inheritance: *Freedom is our most precious heritage.*

her·maph·ro·dite (hər maf′rə dit), *n.* animal or plant having both male and female reproductive organs.

Her·mes (her′mēz), *n.* Greek god of travel and commerce, of science and invention, and of eloquence, luck, and cunning. He was the messenger of Zeus and the other gods. The Romans called him Mercury.

her·met·ic (hər met′ik), *adj.* closed tightly so that air cannot get in or out; airtight: *The bottle has a hermetic seal.* —**her·met′i·cal·ly,** *adv.*

her·met·i·cal (hər met′ə kəl), *adj.* hermetic.

her·mit (her′mit), *n.* person who goes away from others and lives alone. A hermit often lives a religious life. [**Hermit** comes from a Greek word meaning "uninhabited." Hermits live in places where no one else lives.] —**her′mit·like′,** *adj.*

her·mit·age (her′mə tij), *n.* home of a hermit.

hermit crab, any of several crabs with soft bodies that live in the empty shells of snails, whelks, etc., as a means of protection.

hermit thrush, a brown thrush of North America, with spotted breast and reddish tail, noted for its song.

her·ni·a (her′nē ə), *n.* an abnormal bulging out of a part of the intestine or some other organ through a break in its surrounding walls; rupture. ❑ *n., pl.* **her·ni·as, her·ni·ae** (her′nē ē).

her·o (hir′ō), *n.* **1** person admired for bravery, great deeds, or noble qualities: *Daniel Boone and Clara Barton are American heroes.* **2** the most important male person in a story, play, poem, movie, etc. **3** hero sandwich. ❑ *n., pl.* **her·oes.**

Her·od (her′əd), *n.* 73?–4 B.C., king of Judea from 37? to 4 B.C. Jesus was born during his reign.

He·rod·o·tus (hə rod′ə təs), *n.* 484?–425? B.C., Greek historian.

He wrote a history of the world up to his own time and is called "the father of history."

he·ro·ic (hi rō′ik), *adj.* **1** of, like, or suitable for a hero; brave, great, or noble: *the heroic deeds of our firemen.* **2** of or about heroes and their deeds: *The "Iliad" and the "Odyssey" are heroic poems.* **3** unusually daring or bold: *Heroic measures saved the town from the flood.* —**he·ro′i·cal·ly,** *adv.*

he·ro·i·cal (hi rō′ə kəl), *adj.* heroic.

he·ro·ics (hi rō′iks), *n.pl.* words or actions that seem grand or noble, but are only for effect.

her·o·in (her′ō ən), *n.* a poisonous, habit-forming, narcotic drug made from morphine. ■ Another word that sounds like this is **heroine.**

her·o·ine (her′ō ən), *n.* **1** woman or girl admired for her bravery, great deeds, or noble qualities. **2** the most important female person in a story, play, poem, movie, etc. ■ Another word that sounds like this is **heroin.**

her·o·ism (her′ō iz′əm), *n.* actions and qualities of a hero or heroine; great bravery; daring courage.

her·on (her′ən), *n.* any of numerous wading birds with long necks, long bills, and long legs. Herons feed on fish, frogs, and small reptiles.

heron—about 4 ft. (1.2 m) long

hero sandwich, a large roll cut lengthwise and filled with meat, cheese, lettuce, etc.; hoagie; sub.

her·pes (her′pēz), *n.* any of several diseases caused by viruses and producing sores on the skin and mucous membranes. [**Herpes** comes from a Greek word meaning "to creep." The sores seem to creep as they spread over a person's skin.]

her·pe·tol·o·gy (her′pə tol′ə jē), *n.* branch of zoology dealing with reptiles and amphibians. —**her′pe·tol′o·gist,** *n.*

Herr (her), *n.* GERMAN. **1** Mr.; Sir. **2** gentleman. ❑ *n., pl.* **Her·ren** (her′ən).

her·ring (her′ing), *n.* **1** small food fish of the northern Atlantic. The fish are eaten fresh, salted, or smoked. **2** a similar, related fish of the northern Pacific. ❑ *n., pl.* **her·rings** or **her·ring.**

her·ring·bone (her′ing bōn′), **1** *adj.* having a zigzag pattern or arrangement like the spine of a herring. **2** *n.* a zigzag pattern, arrangement, or stitch. **3** *n.* a way of going up a slope on skis by setting the ski tips pointed outward.

herring gull, a large gull, common in the Northern Hemisphere.

hers (herz), *pron.* the one or ones belonging to her: *This money is hers. Your answers are wrong; hers are right.*

Her·schel (her′shəl), *n.* **1 Caroline Lu·cre·tia** (lü krē′shə), 1750-1848, English astronomer, born in Germany. She was the sister of Sir William Herschel. **2** Sir **William,** 1738-1822, English astronomer, born in Germany. He discovered the planet Uranus.

her·self (hər self′), *pron.* **1** form of *she* or *her* used to make a statement stronger: *She did it herself.* **2** form used instead of *she* or *her* in cases like: *She hurt herself.* **3** her real or true self: *She is so tired that she's not herself.*

hertz (herts), *n.* unit of frequency equal to one cycle per second. ❑ *n., pl.* **hertz.**

Herzegovina, *n.* See **Bosnia and Herzegovina.**

Herzl (her′tsəl), *n.* **The·o·dor** (tā′ō dôr′), 1860-1904, Austrian journalist who founded Zionism, born in Hungary.

he's (hēz), **1** he is. **2** he has.

hes·i·tan·cy (hez′ə tən sē), *n.* hesitation; tendency to hesitate.

hes·i·tant (hez′ə tənt), *adj.* hesitating; doubtful; undecided: *At first I was hesitant about accepting the invitation.* ■ See Synonym Study at **reluctant.** —**hes′i·tant·ly,** *adv.*

hes·i·tate (hez′ə tāt), *v.* **1** to fail to act promptly; hold back because you feel doubtful or undecided; show that you have not yet made up your mind: *I hesitated about taking his side until I knew the whole story.* **2** to feel that perhaps you should not; be unwilling; not want: *I hesitated to ask you; you were so busy.* **3** to stop for an instant; pause: *He hesitated before asking the question.* ❑ *v.* **hes·i·tat·ed, hes·i·tat·ing.** —**hes′i·tat′er,** *n.* —**hes′i·tat′ing·ly,** *adv.*

WORD STORY **Hesitate** comes from a Latin word that means "to stick." **Adhesive** comes from the same word. Hesitating is like having your feet stuck with adhesive tape so that you cannot go forward.

hes·i·ta·tion (hez′ə tā′shən), *n.* act of hesitating; doubt; indecision.

Hesse (hes *or* hes′ə), *n.* district in central Germany.

Hes·sian (hesh′ən), **1** *adj.* of Hesse or its people. **2** *n.* person born in or living in Hesse. **3** *n.* a German soldier hired by England to fight against the Americans during the Revolutionary War.

het (het), *adj.* DIALECT. **het up,** heated up; excited; riled.

hetero-, *prefix.* different: *heterogeneous = different in kind.*

het·er·o·ge·ne·ous (het′ər ə jē′nē əs), *adj.* **1** different in kind; unlike; varied: *a heterogeneous group of people.* **2** made up of unlike parts; miscellaneous: *a heterogeneous mass of rubbish.* —**het′er·o·ge′ne·ous·ly,** *adv.* —**het′er·o·ge′ne·ous·ness,** *n.*

het·er·o·sex·u·al (het′ər ə sek′shü əl), **1** *adj.* having or showing sexual feeling for members of the opposite sex. **2** *n.* a heterosexual person. **3** *adj.* (in biology) of the different sexes.

hew (hyü), *v.* **1** to cut with an ax, sword, etc.; chop: *He hewed down the tree.* **2** to cut into shape; form by cutting with an ax, etc.: *hew logs into beams.* ❑ *v.* **hewed, hewed** or **hewn, hew·ing.** ■ Another word that sounds like this is **hue.** —**hew′er,** *n.*

hewn (hyün), *v.* a past participle of **hew.**

hex (heks), **1** *v.* to practice witchcraft on; bewitch. **2** *n.* person or thing that brings bad luck. **3** *n.* a magic spell. ❑ *n., pl.* **hex·es.** [**Hex** comes from a German word meaning "a witch."] —**hex′er,** *n.*

hexa-, *prefix.* six: *hexagon = shape with six angles.*

hex·a·dec·i·mal (hek′sə des′ə məl), *adj.* having to do with a numbering system based on the number 16. Hexadecimal number systems are sometimes used with computers.

hex·a·gon (hek′sə gon), *n.* a plane figure having six angles and six sides.

hex·ag·o·nal (hek sag′ə nəl), *adj.* having the form of a hexagon. —**hex·ag′o·nal·ly,** *adv.*

hex·a·he·dron (hek′sə hē′drən), *n.* a solid figure having six faces. ❑ *n., pl.* **hex·a·he·drons, hex·a·he·dra** (hek′sə hē′drə).

hex·am·e·ter (hek sam′ə tər), *n.* line of poetry having six feet or measures. EXAMPLE: Sev′enteen | sau′sages, | sim′mering | slow′-ly in | soup′ stock, smelled | won′derful.

hey (hā), *interj.* sound made to attract attention, to express surprise or other feeling, or to ask a question: *"Hey! stop!" "Hey? what did you say?"* ■ Another word that sounds like this is **hay.**

hey·day (hā′dā′), *n.* period of greatest strength, vigor, success, prosperity, etc.

HF, H.F., or **h.f.,** high frequency.

Hf, symbol for hafnium.

hf., half.

Hg, symbol for mercury.

hgt., height.

HHS, Health and Human Services (department of the U.S. government).

a	hat	ė	term	ô	order	ch	child	a in about
ā	age	i	it	oi	oil	ng	long	e in taken
ä	far	ī	ice	ou	out	sh	she	ə ⟨ i in pencil
â	care	o	hot	u	cup	th	thin	o in lemon
e	let	ō	open	u̇	put	ẕ	then	u in circus
ē	equal	ȯ	saw	ü	rule	zh	measure	

hi (hī), *interj.* a call of greeting; hello. ∎ Other words that sound like this are **hie** and **high.**

HI, Hawaii (used with postal Zip Code).

H.I., Hawaiian Islands.

hi·a·tus (hī ā′təs), *n.* pause; interruption; gap: *There was a five-year hiatus before we saw one another again.* ❑ *n., pl.* **hi·a·tus·es** or **hi·a·tus.**

Hi·a·wath·a (hī′ə wäth′ə), *n.* the young Ojibwa hero of Longfellow's poem *The Song of Hiawatha.*

hi·ba·chi (hi bä′chē), *n.* a small, cast-iron container covered by a grill, used to burn charcoal for cooking. ❑ *n., pl.* **hi·ba·chis.** [**Hibachi** comes from Japanese words meaning "fire pot."]

hi·ber·nate (hī′bər nāt), *v.* to spend the winter in sleep or in an inactive condition, as woodchucks, prairie dogs, and some other wild animals do. ❑ *v.* **hi·ber·nat·ed, hi·ber·nat·ing.** —**hi′ber·na′tion,** *n.*

hi·bis·cus (hī bis′kəs), *n.* any of several plants, bushes, or trees of warm regions, with large red, pink, or white flowers. ❑ *n., pl.* **hi·bis·cus·es.**

hic·cough (hik′up), *n., v.* hiccup.

hic·cup (hik′up), **1** *n.* an involuntary catching of the breath with a sharp, clicking sound, caused by a muscular spasm of the diaphragm. **2** *n.pl.* hiccups, condition of having one hiccup after another. **3** *v.* to have the hiccups. ❑ *v.* **hic·cupped, hic·cup·ping** or **hic·cuped, hic·cup·ing.** [**Hiccup** comes from an imitation of the sound.]

hick (hik), **1** *n.* person who lives in the country or in a small town. **2** *n.* an ignorant, unsophisticated person. **3** *adj.* of or like a hick: *a hick town.* ∎ **Hick** is often considered offensive.

Hick·ok (hik′ok), *n.* **Wild Bill** (bil), 1837-1876, American frontier scout and marshal.

hick·or·y (hik′ər ē), *n.* **1** any of several North American trees with nuts that are good to eat. **2** their tough, hard wood. ❑ *n., pl.* **hick·or·ies.**

hid (hid), *v.* past tense and a past participle of **hide**¹: *The dog hid the bone. The money was hid in a safe place.*

hi·dal·go (hi dal′gō), *n.* a Spanish nobleman ranking below a grandee. ❑ *n., pl.* **hi·dal·gos.**

Hi·dal·go (ē T͟Häl′gō *or* hi dal′gō), *n.* a state in central Mexico.

hid·den (hid′n), **1** *adj.* put or kept out of sight; concealed; secret: *The story is about hidden treasure.* **2** *v.* a past participle of **hide**¹: *The moon was hidden behind a dark cloud.*

hide¹ (hīd), *v.* **1** to put or keep out of sight; conceal: *Hide it where no one else will ever find it.* **2** to cover up; shut off from sight: *Clouds hide the sun.* **3** to keep secret: *He hid his disappointment.* **4** to hide yourself: *I'll hide, and you find me.* ❑ *v.* **hid, hid·den** or **hid, hid·ing.** —**hid′a·ble,** *adj.*

hide² (hīd), *n.* **1** an animal's skin, either raw or tanned. Leather is made from the hides of cattle. **2** INFORMAL. someone's skin, reputation, or benefit: *He tried to save his own hide by putting the blame on us.*

hide-and-go-seek (hīd′n gō sēk′), *n.* hide-and-seek.

hide-and-seek (hīd′n sēk′), *n.* a children's game in which one player tries to find the players who have hidden.

hide·a·way (hīd′ə wā′), *n.* place for hiding or being alone.

hide·bound (hīd′bound′), *adj.* narrow-minded and stubborn: *Some people are too hidebound to accept new ideas.*

hid·e·ous (hid′ē əs), *adj.* very ugly; frightful; horrible: *a hideous monster, a hideous crime.* [See Word Story at **ugly.**] —**hid′e·ous·ly,** *adv.* —**hid′e·ous·ness,** *n.*

hide·out (hīd′out′), *n.* place for hiding or being alone.

hid·ing¹ (hī′ding), *n.* condition of being hidden; concealment: *The fox remained in hiding.*

hid·ing² (hī′ding), *n.* OLD USE. a beating; thrashing.

hie (hī), *v.* OLD USE. to go quickly; hasten; hurry: *hie yourself to work.* ❑ *v.* **hied, hie·ing** or **hy·ing.** ∎ Other words that sound like this are **hi** and **high.**

hi·e·rar·chy (hī′ə rär′kē), *n.* **1** organization of persons or things arranged one above the other according to rank, class, or grade. **2** group of church officials of different ranks. The church hierarchy is composed of archbishops, bishops, priests, etc. ❑ *n., pl.* **hi·e·rar·chies.**

hi·er·o·glyph (hī′ər ə glif), *n.* hieroglyphic (def. 1).

hi·er·o·glyph·ic (hī′ər ə glif′ik), **1** *n.* picture, character, or symbol standing for a word, idea, or sound. The ancient Egyptians used hieroglyphics instead of an alphabet like ours. **2** *n.pl.* **hieroglyphics,** writing that uses hieroglyphics. **3** *adj.* of or written in hieroglyphics. —**hi′er·o·glyph′i·cal·ly,** *adv.*

hieroglyphics (def. 2)

hi-fi (hī′fī′), **1** *n.* radio or other electronic equipment that reproduces sound very like the original from CDs, tapes, or records. **2** *n.* high fidelity. **3** *adj.* of or for high fidelity. ❑ *n. pl.* **hi-fis** for 1.

hig·gle·dy-pig·gle·dy (hig′əl dē pig′əl dē), **1** *adv.* in jumbled confusion. **2** *adj.* jumbled; confused.

high (hī), **1** *adj.* having height; rising up; tall: *The mountain is over 20,000 feet high.* **2** *adj.* above or far above the ground: *a high leap, a high dive.* **3** *adj.* up above others: *a high official. A general has high rank.* **4** *adj.* greater, stronger, or better than usual; great: *a high price, high winds, high praise.* **5** *adj.* most important; chief; main: *the high altar.* **6** *adj.* extreme of its kind; serious; grave: *high treason, high crimes.* **7** *adj.* not low in pitch; shrill; sharp: *A soprano can sing high notes.* **8** *adj.* happily excited: *high spirits.* **9** *adv.* at or to a high point, place, rank, amount, degree, price, pitch, etc.: *The eagle flies high. Strawberries come high in winter.* **10** *adj.* exhilarated or dazed from taking a drug or intoxicated due to drinking liquor. **11** *n.* a high point, level, position, etc.: *Food prices reached a new high last month.* **12** *n.* arrangement of gears to give the greatest speed. ∎ Other words that sound like this are **hi** and **hie.**

high and dry, 1 up out of water: *The boat ran ashore, high and dry.* **2** all alone; without help; stranded.

high and low, everywhere: *I searched high and low for my pen.*

high beam, beam from a motor vehicle's headlights that is focused high, and so allows a driver to see farther ahead.

high blood pressure, hypertension.

high·born (hī′bôrn′), *adj.* OLD USE. of noble birth.

high·boy (hī′boi′), *n.* a tall chest of drawers on legs.

high·brow (hī′brou′), **1** *n.* person who cares or claims to care a great deal about knowledge and culture. **2** *adj.* of or fit for a highbrow.

high·chair (hī′châr′), *n.* chair with a high seat and a tray, used for feeding babies.

high-def·i·ni·tion television (hī′def′ə nish′ən). See **HDTV.**

higher education, education beyond high school, especially education at a college or university.

high·fa·lu·tin (hī′fə lüt′n), *adj.* INFORMAL. high-sounding; pompous.

high fidelity, reproduction of sound by electronic equipment with very little distortion of the original sound. —**high′-fi·del′i·ty,** *adj.*

high-five (hī′fīv′), INFORMAL. **1** *n.* a gesture in which one person slaps the palm of his or her hand against the upraised palm of another person in congratulation or greeting: *Everyone gave her a* *high-five after she made the winning foul shot.* **2** *v.* to make this gesture: *He high-fived me as he came in.* ❏ *v.* **high-fived, high-fiv·ing.**

high-flown (hī′flōn′), *adj.* **1** aspiring; extravagant: *high-flown ideas.* **2** attempting to be elegant or eloquent: *high-flown compliments.*

high frequency, the band of radio frequencies between 3 and 30 megahertz. —**high-fre·quen·cy,** *adj.*

high-grade (hī′grād′), *adj.* of fine quality; superior: *high-grade oil.*

high-hand·ed (hī′han′did), *adj.* acting or done in a bold, arbitrary way; overbearing: *high-handed methods.* —**high′-hand′ed·ly,** *adv.* —**high′-hand′ed·ness,** *n.*

high-hat (hī′hat′), INFORMAL. **1** *v.* to treat as inferior; snub. **2** *adj.* snobbish. ❏ *v.* **high-hat·ted, high-hat·ting.**

High Holidays, the Jewish holidays of Rosh Hashanah and Yom Kippur.

high jump, 1 an athletic contest or event to determine how high each contestant can jump over a raised crossbar. **2** the jump itself. —**high jumper.**

high·land (hī′lənd), **1** *n.* country or region that is higher and hillier than the neighboring country; land high above sea level. **2** *n.pl.* **Highlands,** a mountainous region in N and W Scotland. **3** *adj.* of or in a highland. **4** *adj.* **Highland,** of or in the Highlands.

high·land·er (hī′lən dər), *n.* **1** person born or living in a highland. **2 Highlander,** person born or living in the Highlands.

Highland fling, a lively dance of the Highlands of Scotland.

high-lev·el language (hī′lev′əl), any computer programming language that is not written entirely in binary numbers, especially any language using common words and mathematical symbols.

high·light (hī′līt′), **1** *v.* to cast a bright light on. **2** *n.* part of a painting, photograph, etc., in which light is represented as falling with greatest intensity. **3** *n.* the most prominent or interesting part, event, scene, etc.: *The highlight of our trip was seeing the Grand Canyon.* **4** *v.* to make prominent. ❏ *v.* **high·light·ed, high·light·ing.**

high·ly (hī′lē), *adv.* **1** in a high degree; very much; very: *highly amusing, highly recommended.* ■ See Synonym Study at **very. 2** very favorably: *He spoke highly of his best friend.* **3** at a high rate or price: *highly paid.* **4** in or to a high position or rank: *a highly placed government official.*

high·mind·ed (hī′mīn′did), *adj.* having or showing high principles; noble. —**high′-mind′ed·ness,** *n.*

high·ness (hī′nis), *n.* **1 Highness,** title of honor given to members of royal families: *The Prince is addressed as "Your Highness."* **2** condition of being high; height. ❏ *n., pl.* **High·ness·es** for 1.

high-oc·tane (hī′ok′tān), *adj.* having a high octane content. High-octane gasoline is more efficient than gasoline with less octane

high-pitched (hī′picht′), *adj.* **1** of high tone or sound; shrill: *a high-pitched voice.* **2** having a steep slope: *a high-pitched roof.*

high-pow·ered (hī′pou′ərd), *adj.* having much power: *a high-powered car.*

high-pres·sure (hī′presh′ər), **1** *adj.* having, using, or resisting more than the usual pressure: *a high-pressure boiler.* **2** *adj.* using strong, vigorous methods: *high-pressure selling.* **3** *v.* to use strong, vigorous methods on, in selling, etc.: *high-pressure a customer.* ❏ *v.* **high-pres·sured, high-pres·sur·ing.**

high-res (hī′rez′), *adj.* high-resolution. Also, **hi-res.**

high-res·o·lu·tion (hī′rez′ə lü′shən), *adj.* forming a very sharp image; showing a large number of pixels: *a high-resolution photograph, a high-resolution computer monitor.*

high-rise (hī′rīz′), **1** *adj.* having many stories; very tall. **2** *n.* a high-rise building.

high school, school attended after elementary school or junior high school; secondary school. High school consists of grades 9 through 12 or 10 through 12.

high seas, the open ocean. The high seas are outside the jurisdiction of any country.

high-sound·ing (hī′soun′ding), *adj.* having an imposing or pretentious sound.

high-spir·it·ed (hī′spir′ə tid), *adj.* **1** proud or courageous: *a high-spirited people.* **2** spirited; fiery: *a high-spirited horse.* —**high′-spir′it·ed·ly,** *adv.* —**high′-spir′it·ed·ness,** *n.*

high-stick·ing (hī′stik′ing), *n.* (in hockey and lacrosse) the act of carrying the stick too high when blocking an opposing player. It is against the rules and may result in a penalty.

high-strung (hī′strung′), *adj.* very nervous; easily excited.

high-tech (hī′tek′), *adj.* made or working by advanced modern technology such as lasers, computer chips, or genetic engineering; very sophisticated in methods and materials: *high-tech toys, high-tech virtual reality systems.*

high-ten·sion (hī′ten′shən), *adj.* having or using a high voltage: *high-tension wires.*

high tide, 1 the highest level of the tide. **2** time when the tide is highest.

high time, time just before it is too late: *It is high time they got here.*

high-water mark (hī′wät′ər), **1** the highest level reached by a body of water, such as a river in flood. **2** any highest point.

high·way (hī′wā′), *n.* **1** a public road. **2** a main road or route.

high·way·man (hī′wā′mən), *n.* (long ago) person who robbed travelers on a public road. ❏ *n., pl.* **high·way·men.**

high wire, a tightrope for acrobats stretched high above the ground, often made of wire cable. —**high′-wire′,** *adj.*

high wire

hi·jack (hī′jak′), *v.* to rob or take by force goods in transit, an airplane in flight, etc. [Hijack looks as if it comes from other English words, but nobody knows. The word just appeared, about 75 years ago.] —**hi′jack′er,** *n.*

hike (hīk), **1** *v.* to take a long walk; tramp or march. **2** *n.* a long walk; tramp or march: *It was a four-mile hike to the camp.* **3** *v.* to raise with a jerk; hitch: *Hike up your socks.* **4** *v.* to raise; increase: *The company is going to hike wages.* ❏ *v.* **hiked, hik·ing.** —**hik′er,** *n.*

hi·lar·i·ous (hə lâr′ē əs), *adj.* very merry; very funny; noisy and cheerful: *a hilarious tale, a hilarious party.* ■ See Synonym Study at **funny.** —**hi·lar′i·ous·ly,** *adv.* —**hi·lar′i·ous·ness,** *n.*

hi·lar·i·ty (hə lar′ə tē), *n.* great merriment; noisy cheerfulness.

hill (hil), *n.* **1** a raised part of the earth's surface, smaller than a mountain. **2** a little heap or pile: *Ants and moles make hills.* **3** a plant with a little heap of soil over and around its roots: *a hill of corn.*

Hil·lar·y (hil′ər ē), *n.* Sir **Ed·mund** (ed′mənd), born 1919, New Zealand mountain climber. He and his Sherpa guide, Tenzing Norgay, climbed Mount Everest in 1953.

hill·bil·ly (hil′bil′ē), *n.* person who lives in the backwoods or a mountain region, especially in the southern United States. ■ The use of this word is often considered offensive. ❏ *n., pl.* **hill·bil·lies.**

hill·ock (hil′ək), *n.* a little hill.

hill·side (hil′sīd′), *n.* side of a hill.

hill·top (hil′top′), *n.* top of a hill.

a	hat	ė	term	ô	order	ch	child		
ā	age	i	it	oi	oil	ng	long	ə	a in about
ä	far	ī	ice	ou	out	sh	she		e in taken
â	care	o	hot	u	cup	th	thin		i in pencil
e	let	ō	open	u̇	put	ŦH	then		o in lemon
ē	equal	ȯ	saw	ü	rule	zh	measure		u in circus

H

hill·y (hil′ē), *adj.* **1** having many hills: *hilly country.* **2** like a hill; steep: *a hilly slope.* ❑ *adj.* **hill·i·er, hill·i·est. —hill′i·ness,** *n.*

Hi·lo (hē′lō), *n.* port on E Hawaii Island.

hilt (hilt), *n.* handle of a sword, dagger, or tool.

to the hilt, thoroughly; completely: *She was in the race to the hilt.*

him (him), *pron.* the boy, man, or male animal spoken about: *Take him home.* ■ Another word that sounds like this is **hymn.**

Him·a·la·yan (him′ə lā′ən), *adj.* of or from the Himalayas.

Him·a·la·yas (him′ə lā′əz *or* hə mä′lyəz), *n.pl.* mountain range along the N borders of India and Pakistan. Mount Everest, the world's highest mountain, is in the Himalayas. [Himalayas comes from Sanskrit words meaning "home of snow." These high mountains are snow-topped all year.]

Himm·ler (him′lər), *n.* **Hein·rich** (hin′rik), 1900-1945, German Nazi leader. ■ Heinrich Himmler was the head of the German police and Gestapo and was responsible for ordering the deaths of millions of people. He committed suicide after being captured by Allied troops.

him·self (him self′ *or* im self′), *pron.* **1** form of *he* or *him* used to make a statement stronger: *He himself did it. Did you see John himself?* **2** form used instead of *he* or *him* in cases like: *He cut himself. He cared more for himself than for anybody else.* **3** his real or true self: *He feels like himself again.*

hind[1] (hind), *adj.* back; rear: *a dog's hind legs.*

hind[2] (hind), *n.* a female deer, especially a female red deer in and after its third year. ❑ *n., pl.* **hinds** or **hind.**

hin·der[1] (hin′dər), *v.* to keep back; hold back; get in the way of; make hard to do; stop: *Deep mud hindered travel.*

hind·er[2] (hin′dər), *adj.* OLD USE. hind; back; rear.

hind·er·most (hin′dər mōst), *adj.* hindmost.

Hin·di (hin′dē), *n.* an official language of India. It is a form of Hindustani.

hind·most (hind′mōst), *adj.* farthest back; nearest the rear; last.

hind·quar·ter (hind′kwôr′tər), *n.* **1** the rear half of a side of beef, veal, lamb, etc., including the leg, loin, and one or more ribs. **2** hindquarters, *pl.* the rear part of an animal's body, including the lower back, buttocks, and thighs; haunches.

hin·drance (hin′drəns), *n.* **1** person or thing that hinders; obstacle: *Noise was a hindrance to our studying.* ■ See Synonym Study at **obstacle. 2** act of hindering.

hind·sight (hind′sīt′), *n.* ability to see, after the event is over, what should have been done.

Hin·du (hin′dü), **1** *n.* person who believes in Hinduism. **2** *n.* person born or living in India. **3** *adj.* of the Hindus, their language, or their religion. ❑ *n., pl.* **Hin·dus.** [Hindu comes from a Persian word meaning "India."]

Hin·du-Ar·a·bic numerals or **Hin·du-Ar·a·bic figures** (hin′dü ar′ə bik), Arabic numerals.

Hin·du·ism (hin′dü iz′əm), *n.* the religion and social system of the Hindus.

Hin·du·stan·i (hin′dü stan′ē), **1** *adj.* of India, its people, or their languages. **2** *n.* the most common language of northern India.

WORD SOURCE Hindustani has given a number of words to the English language, including the words below.

bangle	cowrie	shampoo	veranda
bungalow	dungaree	thug	yoga
chutney	gavial	tom-tom	

hinge (hinj), **1** *n.* joint on which a door, gate, cover, lid, etc., swings back and forth. **2** *v.* to furnish with hinges; attach by hinges. **3** *v.* to hang or turn on a hinge. **4** *v.* to depend: *The success of the picnic hinges on the kind of weather we will have.* ❑ *v.* **hinged, hing·ing. —hinge′less,** *adj.*

hint (hint), **1** *n.* a slight sign; indirect suggestion: *A small black cloud gave a hint of a coming storm.* **2** *v.* to give a slight sign of; suggest indirectly: *She hinted that she was tired by yawning.*

hin·ter·land (hin′tər land′), *n.* **1** land or district behind a coast. **2** region far from towns and cities; thinly settled country.

hip[1] (hip), *n.* **1** the fleshy part that sticks out on each side of the body below the waist, where the leg joins the body. **2** a similar part in animals, where the hind leg joins the body.

hip[2] (hip), *n.* seedcase of a rose.

hip[3] (hip), *adj.* SLANG. having up-to-date knowledge; informed. ❑ *adj.* **hip·per, hip·pest.**

hip·bone (hip′bōn′), *n.* either of the two wide, irregular bones which, with the lower backbone, form the pelvis.

hip-hop (hip′hop′), *n.* **1** the culture of inner-city youth that includes rap music, break dancing, and graffiti art. **2** rap music or similar music.

hip·hug·gers (hip′hug′ərz), *n.pl.* pants that do not come up to the waistline but cling tightly to the hips.

hip·pie (hip′ē), *n.* **1** one of many people, mostly young, who during the late 1960s and the 1970s rejected previous social customs for a way of life that included unusual clothing, long hair, and group living. **2** anyone whose way of life resembles that of these people. Also, **hippy.**

hip·po (hip′ō), *n.* INFORMAL. hippopotamus. ❑ *n., pl.* **hip·pos.**

Hip·poc·ra·tes (hi pok′rə tēz′), *n.* 460?-377? B.C., Greek physician, called "the father of medicine."

hip·po·pot·a·mus (hip′ə pot′ə məs), *n.* a huge, thick-skinned, almost hairless mammal found in and near the rivers of Africa. Hippopotamuses feed on plants and can stay under water for a long time. ❑ *n., pl.* **hip·po·pot·a·mus·es, hip·po·pot·a·mi** (hip′ə pot′ə mī). [Hippopotamus comes from Greek words meaning "river horse." Because it eats plants and walks on four legs, the Greeks thought it was like a horse.]

hippopotamus—about 13 ft. (4 m) long

hip·py (hip′ē), *n.* hippie. ❑ *n., pl.* **hip·pies.**

hire (hir), **1** *v.* to pay for the use of a thing or the work or services of someone: *They hired a car and a driver.* **2** *n.* payment for the use of a thing or the work or services of someone. ❑ *v.* **hired, hir·ing. —hir′a·ble** or **hire′a·ble,** *adj.* **—hir′er,** *n.*

for hire, for use or work in return for payment: *boats for hire.*

hire out, to work in return for payment: *I hired out as a house painter.*

SYNONYM STUDY **Hire, employ,** and **engage** all mean to give someone a job. **Hire** suggests a new job: *He was hired as a secretary last week.* **Employ** suggests a permanent job: *The business employs six people.* **Engage** is used in formal language: *The prince has engaged an architect for his palace.*

hire·ling (hir′ling), *n.* person who works only for money, without interest or pride in the work.

hi-res (hi′rez′), *adj.* high-resolution. Also, **high-res.**

Hir·o·hi·to (hir′ō hē′tō), *n.* 1901-1989, emperor of Japan from 1926 to 1989. ■ Before World War II, Japanese emperors were considered divine beings. Hirohito was the first Japanese emperor to give up claims of divinity.

Hir·o·shi·ma (hir′ō shē′mə), *n.* port in W Japan, target of the first atomic bomb to be used in war, on August 6, 1945.

hir·sute (hėr′süt), *adj.* hairy. **—hir′sute·ness,** *n.*

his (hiz), **1** *adj.* of him; belonging to him: *This is his book.* **2** *pron.* the one or ones belonging to him: *My books are new; his are old.*

His·pan·ic (hi span′ik), **1** *adj.* Spanish. **2** *adj.* of or from South America. **3** *n.* person of Spanish-speaking descent.

USAGE NOTE Hispanic is used by many people and by many official organizations, but a number of people prefer other words, such as **Latina** or **Latino.** It is wise to consider your source and your audience. If in doubt, ask!

His·pan·io·la (his′pə nyō′lə), *n.* the second largest island in the West Indies, between Cuba and Puerto Rico. It is divided into the Dominican Republic and Haiti.

WORD STORY Hispaniola comes from a Spanish word meaning "little Spain." Sailors in Columbus's crew caught fish there that reminded them of Spanish fish.

hiss (his), **1** *v.* to make a sound like *ss,* or like a drop of water on a hot stove: *Geese and snakes hiss.* **2** *n.* a sound like *ss: Hisses were heard from many who disliked what the speaker was saying.* **3** *v.* to show disapproval of by hissing: *The audience hissed the dull play.* **4** *v.* to force or drive by hissing: *They hissed her off the stage.* ❑ *n., pl.* **hiss·es.**

hist., **1** historian. **2** history.

his·ta·mine (his′tə mēn), *n.* a substance released by the body in allergic reactions. It causes widening of blood vessels and increased flow of mucus.

his·to·gram (his′te gram), *n.* a bar graph used to show the frequency of items in a set of data. Items are divided into as many groups as there are bars, and the height of each bar shows how many items are in that group.

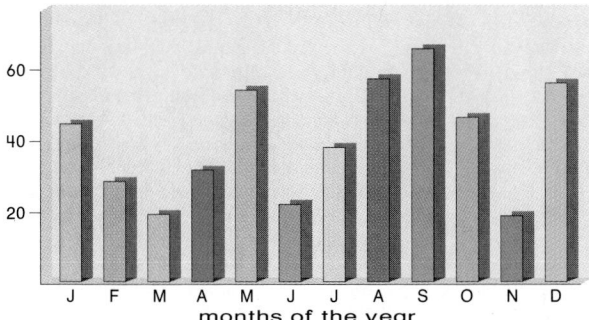

histogram—The bars represent the number of students born each month.

his·to·ri·an (hi stôr′ē ən), *n.* person who writes about history; expert in history.

his·tor·ic (hi stôr′ik), *adj.* **1** famous or important in history: *Plymouth Rock and Bunker Hill are historic spots.* **2** historical.

his·tor·i·cal (hi stôr′ə kəl), *adj.* **1** of or about history: *historical documents.* **2** according to history; based on history: *a historical novel.* **3** known to be real or true; in history, not in legend: *a historical fact.* **4** famous in history; historic: *a historical town.* —**his′to·ri·cal·ly,** *adv.* —**his·to·ri·cal·ness,** *n.*

his·tor·y (his′tər ē), *n.* **1** story or record of important past events connected with a person or a nation: *the history of Mexico.* **2** branch of knowledge that deals with past events: *a class in history.* **3** all past events considered together; course of human affairs: *the lessons of history.* **4** a known past: *This ship has a history.* **5** statement of what has happened; account. ❑ *n., pl.* **his·tor·ies** for 4,5.

his·tri·on·ic (his′trē on′ik), *adj.* **1** of or about actors or acting. **2** theatrical; insincere.

his·tri·on·ics (his′trē on′iks), *n.sing. or pl.* **1** dramatic representation; theatricals; dramatics. **2** a theatrical or insincere manner, expression, etc.

hit (hit), **1** *v.* to give a blow to; strike; knock: *He hit the ball with the bat. The ball hit the window.* **2** *n.* a blow; stroke: *I drove the stake into the ground with one hit.* **3** *v.* to get to what is aimed at: *The second arrow hit the bull's-eye.* **4** *n.* act of striking what is aimed at: *a direct hit.* **5** *v.* to have a painful effect on; affect severely: *They were hard hit by the failure of their business.* **6** *n.* a successful attempt, performance, or production: *The new play is the hit of the season.* **7** *adj.* very successful; extremely popular: *a hit song.* **8** *n.* a successful hitting of the baseball so that the batter gets at least to first base. ❑ *v.* **hit, hit·ting.** —**hit′ter,** *n.*

hit it off, to get along well together; agree: *We hit it off from the start.*

hit on or hit upon, **1** to come upon; meet with: *We hit on the right road in the dark.* **2** to think up: *We hit upon a plan for making money.*

hit or miss, with no plan; at random.

hit-and-run (hit′n run′), *adj.* of or caused by someone hitting a person or vehicle and driving away without stopping to see what happened: *a hit-and-run driver, a hit-and-run accident.*

hitch (hich), **1** *v.* to fasten with a hook, ring, rope, strap, etc.: *She hitched her horse to a post.* **2** *v.* to become fastened or caught; fasten; catch: *A knot made the rope hitch.* **3** *n.* a fastening; catch:

Our car has a hitch for pulling a trailer. **4** *n.* kind of knot used for temporary fastening. **5** *v.* to move or pull with a jerk: *He hitched his chair nearer to the fire.* **6** *n.* a short, sudden pull or jerk: *He gave his pants a hitch.* **7** *n.* obstacle; hindrance; delay: *A hitch in their plans made them miss the train.* **8** *v.* INFORMAL. to get a ride by hitchhiking. **9** *n.* period of time, especially a period of service in the armed forces. ❑ *n., pl.* **hitch·es.**

Hitch·cock (hich′kok), *n.* Sir **Alfred,** 1899-1980, English movie director. He made many suspense movies, including *North by Northwest* and *Psycho.*

hitch·hike (hich′hīk′), *v.* to travel by walking and getting free rides from passing motor vehicles. ❑ *v.* **hitch·hiked, hitch·hik·ing.** —**hitch′hik·er,** *n.*

hith·er (hiᴛʜ′ər), *adv.* to this place; here: *Come hither, child.*

hither and thither, here and there.

hith·er·to (hiᴛʜ′ər tü′), *adv.* until now: *a fact hitherto unknown.*

Hit·ler (hit′lər), *n.* **A·dolf** (ā′dolf), 1889-1945, German dictator, born in Austria, ruler of Nazi Germany from 1933 to 1945. ■ **Adolf Hitler** was responsible for the deaths of six million European Jews and of five million other people, including Gypsies, Poles, and Slavs, during World War II.

hit-or-miss (hit′ər mis′), *adj.* not planned; random.

hit·ter (hit′ər), *n.* someone or something that hits.

Hit·tite (hit′īt), *n.* member of an ancient people in Asia Minor and Syria. Their civilization existed from about 2000 B.C. until about 1200 B.C.

HIV, human immunodeficiency virus (the virus that causes AIDS).

hive (hīv), **1** *n.* house or box for honeybees to live in; beehive. **2** *n.* a large number of bees living in such a place. **3** *v.* to put bees in a hive. **4** *n.* a busy, swarming place full of people or animals: *The kitchen was a hive of activity.* ❑ *v.* **hived, hiv·ing.**

hives (hīvz), *n.pl.* condition in which the skin itches and shows raised patches of red. It is usually caused by an allergy to some food or drug.

WORD STORY **Hives** look like the swelling caused by some stings, and you might expect that **hives** comes from **hive,** but it doesn't. Where does it come from? No one knows.

hl., hectoliter or hectoliters.

hm., hectometer or hectometers.

H.M., **1** Her Majesty. **2** His Majesty.

HMO, health maintenance organization (a medical organization that provides complete services to members for a fixed monthly fee, or a similar organization providing medical services at lowered prices to members, who pay for each service separately).

H.M.S., **1** Her Majesty's Service. **2** Her Majesty's Ship. **3** His Majesty's Service. **4** His Majesty's Ship.

ho (hō), *interj.* **1** exclamation of surprise, joy, or scornful laughter. **2** exclamation to get attention: *Ho! Listen to this!* ■ Another word that sounds like this is **hoe.**

Ho, symbol for holmium.

hoa·gie or **hoa·gy** (hō′gē), *n.* hero sandwich. ❑ *n., pl.* **hoa·gies.**

hoar (hôr), *adj.* hoary. ■ Another word that sounds like this is **whore.**

hoard (hôrd), **1** *v.* to save and store away: *A squirrel hoards nuts for the winter. The wealthy man hoarded his money.* **2** *n.* what is saved and stored away; things stored: *They have a hoard of candy.* ■ Another word that sounds like this is **horde.** —**hoard′er,** *n.*

hoar·frost (hôr′frôst′), *n.* feathery crystals of ice formed when dew freezes; rime.

hoarse (hôrs), *adj.* **1** sounding rough and deep: *the hoarse croak of the bullfrog.* **2** having a rough voice: *A bad cold has made her hoarse.* ❑ *adj.* **hoars·er, hoars·est.** ■ Another word that sounds like this is **horse.** —**hoarse′ly,** *adv.* —**hoarse′ness,** *n.*

hoar·y (hôr′ē), *adj.* **1** white or gray. **2** white or gray with age: *a hoary beard.* **3** old; ancient: *the hoary ruins of a castle.* ❑ *adj.* **hoar·i·er, hoar·i·est.** —**hoar′i·ness,** *n.*

a	hat	ė	term	ô	order	ch	child		a in about
ā	age	i	it	oi	oil	ng	long		e in taken
ä	far	ī	ice	ou	out	sh	she	ə {	i in pencil
â	care	o	hot	u	cup	th	thin		o in lemon
e	let	ō	open	ů	put	ᴛʜ	then		u in circus
ē	equal	ò	saw	ü	rule	zh	measure		

hoax (hōks), **1** *n.* a mischievous trick, especially a made-up story passed off as true: *The report of an attack from Mars was a hoax.* **2** *v.* to play a mischievous trick on; deceive. ❑ *n., pl.* **hoax·es.** [**Hoax** probably comes from *hocus* in **hocus-pocus.** Try saying *hocus* quickly.] —**hoax′er,** *n.*

hob[1] (hob), *n.* shelf at the back or side of a fireplace. Food can be kept warm by placing it on the hob.

hob[2] (hob), *n.* **play hob** or **raise hob,** to cause trouble: *The bad weather played hob with our plans for a picnic.*

hob·bit (hob′it), *n.* an imaginary creature like a human being but smaller and furrier, described as gentle but also brave.

hob·ble (hob′əl), **1** *v.* to walk awkwardly; limp: *hobble around with a broken toe.* **2** *n.* a limping walk. **3** *v.* to tie the legs of a horse or other animal together: *They hobbled the horses at night so that they would not wander away.* **4** *n.* rope or strap used to hobble a horse or other animal. **5** *v.* to hinder. ❑ *v.* **hob·bled, hob·bling.** —**hob′bler,** *n.*

hob·by (hob′ē), *n.* something a person enjoys doing which is not the person's occupation; favorite pastime: *Our teacher's hobby is gardening.* ❑ *n., pl.* **hob·bies.** —**hob′by·less,** *adj.*

hob·by·horse (hob′ē hôrs′), *n.* **1** a long stick with a horse's head, used as a toy horse by children. **2** rocking horse.

hob·by·ist (hob′ē ist), *n.* person who is very interested in a hobby or hobbies.

hob·gob·lin (hob′gob/lən), *n.* **1** goblin; elf. **2** ghost.

hob·nail (hob′nāl′), *n.* a short nail with a large head to protect the soles of heavy boots and shoes.

hob·nob (hob′nob′), *v.* to be on familiar terms; associate intimately: *They hobnob with some important people.* ❑ *v.* **hob·nobbed, hob·nob·bing.** —**hob′nob′ber,** *n.*

ho·bo (hō′bō), *n.* person who wanders about and lives by begging or doing odd jobs; tramp. ❑ *n., pl.* **ho·boes** or **ho·bos.**

Ho Chi Minh (hō′ chē′ min′), 1890?-1969, president of North Vietnam from 1954 to 1969.

Ho Chi Minh City (hō′ chē min′), city in S Vietnam, formerly the capital of South Vietnam. Former name, **Saigon.**

hock[1] (hok), *n.* joint in the hind leg of a horse, cow, etc., corresponding to the human ankle.

hock[2] (hok), *v., n.* INFORMAL. pawn.
in hock, in debt.

hock·ey (hok′ē), *n.* game played by two teams on ice or on a field. The players hit a puck or ball with curved sticks to drive it into the other team's goal.

ho·cus-po·cus (hō′kəs pō′kəs), *n.* **1** a meaningless form of words used in performing magic tricks. **2** trickery.

hod (hod), *n.* **1** trough with a long, straight handle, used for carrying bricks or mortar on the shoulder. **2** coal scuttle.

hodge·podge (hoj′poj′), *n.* a disorderly mixture; mess.

hoe (hō), **1** *n.* tool with a thin blade set across the end of a long handle, used for loosening soil, cutting weeds, etc. **2** *v.* to loosen, dig, or cut with a hoe. **3** *v.* to use a hoe. ❑ *v.* **hoed, hoe·ing.** ■ Another word that sounds like this is **ho.** —**hoe′like′,** *adj.*

hoe·cake (hō′kāk′), *n.* kind of bread made of corn meal.

hoe·down (hō′doun′), *n.* **1** a noisy, lively square dance. **2** music for such a dance.

hog (hog), **1** *n.* pig. **2** *n.* a full-grown pig, raised for its meat. **3** *n.* INFORMAL. a selfish, greedy, or dirty person. **4** *v.* INFORMAL. to take more than your share of something. ❑ *v.* **hogged, hog·ging.** —**hog′like′,** *adj.*

ho·gan (hō′gän′), *n.* dwelling used by the Navajo. Hogans are built with logs and covered with earth.

hog·gish (hog′ish), *adj.* **1** very selfish or greedy. **2** dirty; filthy. —**hog′gish·ly,** *adv.* —**hog′gish·ness,** *n.*

hog (def. 2)—28 in. (71 cm) high at the shoulder

hog·nose snake (hog′nōz′), any of several harmless North American snakes with upturned snouts; adder.

hog-tie (hog′tī′), *v.* **1** to tie all four feet, or the feet and hands, together; tie securely. **2** to hinder; hold back. ❑ *v.* **hog-tied, hog-ty·ing.**

hog·wash (hog′wäsh′), *n.* **1** worthless stuff; nonsense. **2** garbage given to hogs.

Ho·ho·kam (hō′hō käm′), *n.* member of a tribe of American Indians who lived in the southwestern United States between about 300 and 1400 A.D. The Hohokam were the ancestors of the modern Pima. ❑ *n., pl.* **Ho·ho·kam.** [**Hohokam** comes from a Pima word meaning "those who are gone."]

ho-hum (hō′hum′), **1** *interj.* expression of boredom, lack of interest, etc. **2** *adj.* uninteresting; boring: *a ho-hum movie.*

hoist (hoist), **1** *v.* to raise on high; lift up, often with ropes and pulleys: *hoist a flag, hoist sails.* **2** *n.* a push; lift; boost: *She gave me a hoist up the wall.* **3** *n.* elevator or other device for hoisting heavy loads. —**hoist′er,** *n.*

Hok·kai·do (hō kī′dō), *n.* the second largest island of Japan.

hold[1] (hōld), **1** *v.* to grasp and keep: *Please hold my hat.* **2** *n.* a grasp or grip: *Take a good hold of this rope.* **3** *n.* thing to hold by: *The face of the cliff had enough holds for a good climber.* **4** *v.* to keep in some place or position: *Hold the dish level.* **5** *v.* to stay strong or secure; not break, loosen, or give way: *The dike held during the flood.* **6** *v.* to keep from acting; keep back: *Hold your breath.* **7** *v.* to keep from going away; detain: *Police held the burglary suspect for questioning.* **8** *v.* to contain: *This theater holds 500 people.* ■ See Synonym Study at **contain. 9** *v.* to have: *Shall we hold a meeting of the club? She has held the office of mayor for ten years.* **10** *v.* to think; consider: *People once held that the world was flat.* **11** *v.* to be faithful: *I held to my promise.* **12** *v.* to be true; be in force or effect: *Will this rule hold in all cases?* **13** *v.* to keep the same; continue: *The warm weather held all week.* **14** *n.* a controlling force or influence: *A habit has a hold on you.* **15** *n.* sign for a pause in music. ❑ *v.* **held, hold·ing.** —**hold′a·ble,** *adj.*
hold forth, 1 to talk or preach. **2** to offer.
hold in, 1 to keep in; keep back. **2** to restrain yourself.
hold off, 1 to keep at a distance: *hold off the enemy.* **2** to be delayed: *The storm may hold off.*
hold on, 1 to keep your hold. **2** to keep on; continue. **3** stop!
hold out, 1 to continue; last. **2** to keep resisting; not give in.
hold over, 1 to keep for future action or consideration; postpone: *The bill has been held over until next year.* **2** to keep or stay longer than the expected time: *The play was so successful it was held over.*
hold up, 1 to keep from falling; support: *The roof is held up by pillars.* **2** to show; display: *She held up the sign for us to see.* **3** to continue; last; endure: *If this wind holds up, we can go sailing.* **4** to stop; delay: *I don't want to hold you up if you're in a hurry.* **5** to stop by force and rob.
hold with, 1 to side with. **2** to agree with. **3** to approve of.
lay hold of or **take hold of,** to seize; grasp.
on hold, 1 waiting for someone to take part in a telephone conversation: *So many people were calling for tickets that I was on hold for ten minutes.* **2** delayed; suspended; awaiting further developments: *Until we can get the tickets, our plans are on hold.*
take hold, to become attached; take root.

hold[2] (hōld), *n.* the space inside a ship or airplane where the cargo is carried. A ship's hold is below the deck.

hold·er (hōl′dər), *n.* **1** person who holds something. An owner or possessor of property is a holder. **2** thing to hold something else: *a toothbrush holder.*

hold·ing (hōl′ding), *n.* **1** piece of land or property. **2** Often, **holdings,** *pl.* property in stocks or bonds.

holding pattern, 1 a circular or oval flight pattern flown by airplanes waiting for permission to land at an airport. **2** a condition of waiting for something to happen.

hold·out (hōld′out′), *n.* **1** person or group that refuses to accept terms or to comply with a trend or order. **2** a refusal to accept terms or comply.

hold·up (hōld′up′), *n.* **1** act of stopping by force and robbing: *a bank holdup.* **2** a delay; stopping: *I was late because of a holdup in traffic.*

hole (hōl), **1** *n.* an open place; opening: *a hole in a sock.* **2** *n.* a hollow place in something solid: *Swiss cheese has holes in it.* **3** *n.* a hollow place in the earth in which an animal lives; burrow: *a rabbit hole.* **4** *n.* a small, dark, dirty room or place. **5** *n.* flaw; defect: *There's a hole in your argument.* **6** *n.* a small, round, hollow place on a golf course, into which a golf ball is hit. **7** *n.* one of the divisions of a golf course. A regular golf course has 18 holes. **8** *v.* to hit or drive a golf ball into a hole: *She holed out in four strokes.* ❑ *v.* **holed, hol·ing.** ■ Another word that sounds like this is **whole.**

hole up, 1 to go or put into a hole: *In November the badgers all hole up for the winter.* **2** to go or put into hiding.

in the hole, in debt.

pick holes in, to find fault with.

hol·ey (hō′lē), *adj.* full of holes: *holey socks.* ❑ *adj.* **ho·li·er, ho·li·est.** ■ Other words that sound like this are **holy** and **wholly.**

hol·i·day (hol′ə dā), **1** *n.* day when you do not work; day of pleasure and enjoyment: *Labor Day and the Fourth of July are holidays in the United States.* **2** *n.* Often, **holidays,** *pl.* vacation: *We plan to spend our holidays in the mountains.* **3** *adj.* of or suited to a holiday: *holiday traffic.* **4** *n.* holy day; religious festival.

Hol·i·day (hol′ə dā), *n.* **Bill·ie** (bil′ē), 1915-1959, American jazz and blues singer.

ho·li·ness (hō′lē nis), *n.* **1** quality of being holy. **2 Holiness,** title used in speaking to or of the pope: *The pope is addressed as "Your Holiness" and spoken of as "His Holiness."*

ho·lis·tic (hō lis′tik), *adj.* of or concerned with the physical, mental, emotional, and spiritual factors that affect health, rather than with isolated symptoms or diseases: *holistic medicine.*

Hol·land (hol′ənd), *n.* the Netherlands. [**Holland** comes from a Dutch word meaning "land with trees."]

hol·ler (hol′ər), INFORMAL. **1** *v.* to cry or shout loudly. **2** *n.* a loud cry or shout.

hol·low (hol′ō), **1** *adj.* having nothing, or only air, inside; with a hole inside; not solid; empty: *A tube or pipe is hollow. Most rubber balls are hollow.* ■ See Synonym Study at **empty. 2** *adj.* shaped like a bowl or cup: *a hollow spot in the sidewalk.* **3** *n.* a hollow place; hole: *a hollow in the road.* **4** *v.* to make by hollowing; bend or dig out to a hollow shape: *hollow a whistle from a piece of wood.* **5** *v.* to make or become hollow. **6** *n.* a low place between hills; valley: *Rip Van Winkle lived in Sleepy Hollow.* **7** *adj.* as if coming from something hollow; deep and dull: *the hollow boom of a foghorn.* **8** *adj.* deep and sunken: *hollow eyes and cheeks.* **9** *adj.* not real or sincere; false: *hollow promises.* **–hol′low·ly,** *adv.* **–hol′low·ness,** *n.*

hol·ly (hol′ē), *n.* any of numerous evergreen trees or bushes with shiny, sharp-pointed leaves and bright red berries, often used as Christmas decorations. ❑ *n., pl.* **hol·lies.**

hol·ly·hock (hol′ē hok), *n.* a tall garden plant with large, showy flowers that grow along the stem.

Hol·ly·wood (hol′ē wùd), *n.* **1** district of Los Angeles, where many movies and TV shows are filmed. **2** the American movie industry.

Holmes (hōmz), *n.* **Sherlock,** a fictional detective with remarkable powers of observation and reasoning, created by Sir Arthur Conan Doyle.

hol·mi·um (hōl′mē əm), *n.* a metallic element which occurs in combination with certain minerals. Its compounds are highly magnetic. *Symbol:* Ho

hol·o·caust (hol′ə kôst), *n.* **1** complete destruction by fire, especially of animals or human beings. **2** great or wholesale destruction. **3 the Holocaust,** the systematic annihilation by the Nazis of about six million European Jews from 1933 to 1945.

WORD STORY **Holocaust** comes from a Greek word meaning "burned whole." The Greek word described religious sacrifices, and was used to translate a Hebrew word used in the Bible to describe sacrifices, sometimes called "burnt offerings" in English. The English word was already 700 years old when history gave it a new meaning.

Hol·o·cene (hol′ə sēn′), *n.* the present period of geological time.

hol·o·gram (hol′ə gram *or* hō′lə gram), *n.* a kind of photograph showing three dimensions. A hologram is made by exposing film to two sources of light. One source is a laser beam and the other is light reflected from an object lit by the same laser beam. To view a hologram, light is passed through the film, and an image of the object appears, apparently solid.

hol·o·graph (hol′ə graf), *n.* a document, such as a will, written entirely in the handwriting of the person who signs it. **–hol′o·graph′ic,** *adj.*

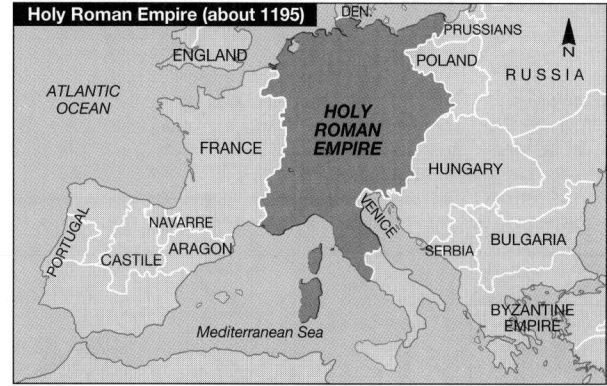
hologram

ho·log·ra·phy (hō log′rə fē), *n.* photography using laser beams to produce holograms.

Hol·stein (hōl′stēn *or* hōl′stīn), *n.* breed of large, black and white dairy cattle.

hol·ster (hōl′stər), *n.* a leather case for a pistol, worn on the belt or under the shoulder. A holster for a rifle may be attached to a saddle.

ho·ly (hō′lē), **1** *adj.* belonging to God; set apart for God's service; coming from God; sacred: *the Holy Bible, holy sacraments.* **2** *adj.* like a saint; spiritually perfect; very good; pure in heart: *a holy missionary.* **3** *adj.* worthy of reverence: *Jerusalem is a holy place to Jews, Christians, and Muslims.* **4** *n.* a holy place. ❑ *adj.* **ho·li·er, ho·li·est;** *n., pl.* **ho·lies.** ■ Other words that sound like this are **holey** and **wholly.**

Holy Communion, 1 a sharing in the Lord's Supper as a part of Christian worship. **2** celebration of the Lord's Supper.

holy day, a religious festival. Good Friday and Ash Wednesday are holy days.

Holy Father, the pope.

Holy Ghost, Holy Spirit.

Holy Grail, Grail.

Holy Land, Palestine.

holy of holies, 1 the holiest place. **2** the inner shrine of the Jewish Tabernacle and Temple.

Holy Roman Empire, empire in western and central Europe. It began in A.D. 962, or, according to some, in A.D. 800, and ended in 1806.

Holy Roman Empire (about 1195)

DEN.
PRUSSIANS
ENGLAND
POLAND
ATLANTIC OCEAN
RUSSIA
N
FRANCE
HOLY ROMAN EMPIRE
HUNGARY
PORTUGAL
NAVARRE
ARAGON
VENICE
SERBIA
BULGARIA
CASTILE
BYZANTINE EMPIRE
Mediterranean Sea

Holy Scriptures, Scripture (def. 2).

Holy See, office or jurisdiction of the pope; the pope's court.

Holy Spirit, spirit of God; third person of the Trinity; Holy Ghost.

holy water, water blessed by a priest.

Holy Week, the week before Easter.

a	hat	ė	term	ô	order	ch	child		a in about
ā	age	i	it	oi	oil	ng	long		e in taken
ä	far	ī	ice	ou	out	sh	she	ə	i in pencil
â	care	o	hot	u	cup	th	thin		o in lemon
e	let	ō	open	ù	put	₮H	then		u in circus
ē	equal	ò	saw	ü	rule	zh	measure		

Holy Writ, the Bible.

hom·age (hom′ij *or* om′ij), *n.* **1** dutiful respect; reverence; honor: *Everyone paid homage to the great leader.* **2** (in the Middle Ages) a pledge of loyalty and service by a vassal to a lord.

hom·bre (òm′brā), *n.* INFORMAL. man; fellow.

home (hōm), **1** *n.* place where a person or family lives; your own house: *Her home is at 25 South Street.* **2** *n.* place where a person was born or brought up; your own town or country: *His home is New York.* **3** *n.* place where a thing is very common: *Alaska is the home of fur seals.* **4** *n.* place where people who are homeless, poor, old, sick, blind, etc., may live: *a nursing home, a home for the aged.* **5** *adj.* of or for your home; domestic: *home cooking.* **6** *adj.* (in sports) played in a team's hometown: *a home game.* **7** *adv.* at or to your own home or country. **8** *n.* goal in many games. **9** *n.* home plate in baseball. **10** *adv.* to the thing aimed at: *The spear hit home. The criticism struck home.* **11** *adv.* to the heart or center; deep in: *drive a nail home.* ❏ *v.* **homed, hom·ing.**

at home, **1** at ease; comfortable: *to make yourself at home in a friend's house.* **2** ready to receive visitors.

bring home, to make clear or emphatic.

hit home, to affect you personally or deeply: *Her criticism of his laziness hit home; he's looking for a job today.*

home in on, **1** to locate a target and move in a straight line toward it. **2** to proceed toward; concentrate on: *The legislature homed in on a bill to strengthen antipollution laws.*

home·bod·y (hōm′bod′ē), *n.* person who prefers the pleasures of home and family to outside attractions. ❏ *n., pl.* **home·bod·ies.**

home·bound (hōm′bound′), *adj.* unable to leave home because of illness, limited mobility, or other conditions.

home·boy (hōm′boi′), *n.* **1** INFORMAL. a boy or man who comes from your own neighborhood or town. **2** SLANG. a fellow member of a gang.

home·com·ing (hōm′kum′ing), *n.* **1** act of coming or returning home. **2** day or weekend of special events at a college or university, during which graduates return.

home computer, a personal computer especially designed for use in the home.

home economics, science and art of managing a household. Home economics includes housekeeping, budgeting of finances, preparation of food, child care, etc.

home·grown (hōm′grōn′), *adj.* **1** grown at home: *homegrown vegetables.* **2** coming from or characteristic of a place: *homegrown talent.*

home·land (hōm′land′), *n.* country that is your home; your native land.

home·less (hōm′lis), *adj.* without a home: *a stray, homeless dog.*

home·like (hōm′līk′), *adj.* familiar or comfortable; like home.

home·ly (hōm′lē), *adj.* **1** not good-looking; ugly; plain. **2** suited to home life; simple; everyday: *homely pleasures.* **3** of plain manners; unpretending: *a simple, homely person.* ❏ *adj.* **home·li·er, home·li·est. —home′li·ness,** *n.*

home·made (hōm′mād′), *adj.* made at home: *homemade bread.*

home·mak·er (hōm′mā′kər), *n.* person who manages a home and its affairs.

home·own·er (hōm′ō′nər), *n.* person who owns a home.

home page, 1 a World Wide Web document. **2** the starting page of a World Wide Web document.

home plate, flat, rubber slab beside which a player stands to bat the ball in baseball. A player must touch the other three bases and then home plate in order to score a run.

hom·er (hō′mər), *n.* a home run in baseball.

Ho·mer (hō′mər), *n.* the great epic poet of ancient Greece. According to legend, Homer lived about the 800s B.C., and was the author of the *Iliad* and the *Odyssey.* [**Homer** comes from a Greek word meaning "something given to strengthen a promise."]

Ho·mer (hō′mər), *n.* **Win·slow** (win′zlō), 1836-1910, American painter. He painted many pictures of the sea, fishermen, and sea captains.

home·room (hōm′rüm′), *n.* **1** classroom where members of a class meet to answer roll call, hear announcements, etc. **2** period during which this class meets.

home rule, management of a country, district, or city by its own people; local self-government.

home run, a hit in baseball which allows the batter to round the bases without a stop and reach home plate to score a run.

home·sick (hōm′sik′), *adj.* very sad because you are far away from home; ill with longing for home. **—home′sick′ness,** *n.*

home·spun (hōm′spun′), **1** *adj.* spun or made at home. **2** *n.* cloth made of yarn spun at home. **3** *n.* a strong, loosely woven cloth similar to it. **4** *adj.* made of homespun cloth. **5** *adj.* not polished; plain; simple: *homespun manners.*

home·stead (hōm′sted′), **1** *n.* house with its buildings and grounds; farm with its buildings. **2** *n.* public land granted to a settler under certain conditions by the U.S. government. **3** *v.* to take and occupy as a homestead: *He homesteaded 160 acres of land.*

home·stead·er (hōm′sted′ər), *n.* **1** person who has a homestead. **2** settler granted a homestead by the U.S. government.

home·stretch (hōm′strech′), *n.* **1** the straight part of a racetrack between the last turn and the finish line. **2** the last part of anything.

home·town (hōm′toun′), *n.* town or city where someone was born or brought up.

home·ward (hōm′wərd), *adv., adj.* toward home: *We turned homeward. The ship is on a homeward course.*

home·wards (hōm′wərdz), *adv.* homeward.

home·work (hōm′wėrk′), *n.* **1** lesson to be studied or prepared outside the classroom. **2** work done at home.

home·y (hō′mē), *adj.* homelike. ❏ *adj.* **hom·i·er, hom·i·est. —hom′ey·ness,** *n.*

hom·i·cid·al (hom′ə sī′dl), *adj.* **1** of or about homicide. **2** murderous. **—hom′i·cid′al·ly,** *adv.*

hom·i·cide (hom′ə sīd), *n.* **1** act of killing one human being by another. **2** person who kills another human being.

homing pigeon, pigeon bred and trained to fly home from great distances carrying written messages; carrier pigeon.

hom·i·nid (hom′ə nid), *n.* any member of the group of primates that includes human beings. Humans are the only hominids now.

hom·i·ny (hom′ə nē), *n.* kernels of corn that are hulled and used whole or coarsely ground, usually eaten boiled.

homo-, *prefix.* same: *homophone = word with the same sound as another word.*

Ho·mo e·rec·tus (hō′mō i rek′təs), an extinct species of human beings that lived from about 1,600,000 years ago to about 300,000 years ago. They had smaller brains than modern human beings but used stone tools and fire.

ho·mo·ge·ne·ous (hō′mə jē′nē əs), *adj.* the same in kind; made up of similar items: *a homogeneous collection of books, all mysteries.* **—ho′mo·ge′ne·ous·ly,** *adv.* **—ho′mo·ge′ne·ous·ness,** *n.*

ho·mog·e·nize (hə moj′ə nīz), *v.* to make homogeneous. In **ho·mogenized milk** the fat is distributed evenly throughout the milk and does not rise to the top as cream. ❏ *v.* **ho·mog·e·nized, ho·mog·e·niz·ing. —ho·mog′e·ni·za′tion,** *n.* **—ho·mog′e·niz′er,** *n.*

hom·o·graph (hom′ə graf), *n.* word having the same spelling as another word, but a different origin and meaning. *Bass* (bas), meaning "a kind of fish," and *bass* (bās), meaning "a male singing voice," are homographs. ■ See Usage Note at **homonym.**

hom·o·nym (hom′ə nim), *n.* word having the same pronunciation and the same spelling as another word, but a different origin and meaning. *Bark,* meaning "the covering of a tree," and *bark,* meaning "the sound a dog makes," are homonyms.

USAGE NOTE **Homonym, homograph,** and **homophone** are words that often get confused. But the differences among them are simple. Homographs, such as **tear**[1] and **tear**[2], are spelled the same but pronounced differently. Homophones, such as **wait** and **weight,** are pronounced the same but spelled differently. Homonyms, such as **bark**[1], **bark**[2], and **bark**[3], are spelled and pronounced the same.

ho·mo·pho·bi·a (hō′mə fō′bē ə), *n.* unreasonable fear of or strong dislike of homosexuals and homosexuality. **—ho′mo·phobe′,** *n.* **—ho′mo·pho′bic,** *adj.*

hom·o·phone (hom′ə fōn), *n.* word having the same pronunciation as another, but a different spelling, origin, and meaning. *Ate* and *eight* are homophones. ■ See Usage Note at **homonym.**

Ho·mo sa·pi·ens (hō′mō sā′pē enz), the species of human beings that all people today belong to. Neanderthal people also belonged to this species, which has replaced every previous species of human being.

ho·mo·sex·u·al (hō′mə sek′shü əl), **1** *adj.* showing sexual feeling for someone of the same sex. **2** *n.* a homosexual person.

ho·mo·sex·u·al·i·ty (hō′mə sek′shü al′ə tē), *n.* **1** sexual feelings for someone of the same sex. **2** sexual activity with someone of the same sex.

ho·mo·zy·gous (hō′mə zī′gəs *or* hom′ə zī′gəs), *adj.* having chromosomes that contain an identical pair of genes for a particular physical feature.

Hon., Honorable.

hon·cho (hon′chō), *n.* INFORMAL. person in charge; boss; chief. ❑ *n., pl.* **hon·chos.** [Honcho comes from Japanese words meaning "crew" and "chief."]

Hon·dur·as (hon dür′əs *or* hon dyür′əs), *n.* country in N Central America. *Capital:* Tegucigalpa. [Honduras comes from a Spanish word meaning "deep." The ocean is deep along much of the coast.] —**Hon·dur′an,** *adj., n.*

hone (hōn), **1** *n.* a whetstone on which to sharpen cutting tools, especially straight razors. **2** *v.* to sharpen on a hone. ❑ *v.* **honed, hon·ing.**

hon·est (on′ist), *adj.* **1** fair and upright; truthful; not lying, cheating, or stealing: *honest people.* **2** without lying, cheating, or stealing: *make an honest profit.* **3** not hiding your real nature; frank; open: *She is honest about her feelings.* **4** not mixed with something of less value; genuine; pure: *Stores should sell honest goods.*

> **SYNONYM STUDY** **Honest, honorable,** and **truthful** all mean not lying, cheating, or stealing. **Honest** is a general word: *I want your honest opinion of my work.* **Honorable** means knowing and doing what is right: *It was honorable of you to return the money you found.* **Truthful** means telling the facts: *The jury believed that the witness was truthful.*

hon·est·ly (on′ist lē), **1** *adv.* in an honest way; with honesty: *The salesclerk dealt honestly with her customers.* **2** *interj.* indeed; really: *Honestly! I never saw such rudeness.*

hon·es·ty (on′ə stē), *n.* quality of being honest; sincerity.

hon·ey (hun′ē), *n.* **1** a thick, sweet, yellow or golden liquid that bees make out of the nectar they collect from flowers. **2** something sweet like honey; sweetness. **3** darling; dear. ❑ *n., pl.* **hon·eys** for 3. —**hon′ey·like′,** *adj.*

hon·ey·bee (hun′ē bē′), *n.* bee that makes honey. ❑ *n., pl.* **hon·ey·bees.**

hon·ey·comb (hun′ē kōm′), **1** *n.* a structure of wax containing rows of six-sided cells made by bees to store honey, pollen, and their eggs. **2** *n.* anything having a structure like this: *The village market was a honeycomb of tiny shops and passageways.* **3** *adj.* like a honeycomb: *a honeycomb pattern in knitting.* **4** *v.* to make like a honeycomb; pierce with many holes: *The old castle was honeycombed with passages.*

hon·ey·dew (hun′ē dü′), *n.* **1** a sweet substance that oozes from the leaves of certain plants in hot weather. **2** a sweet substance on leaves and stems, produced by aphids or other tiny insects. **3** honeydew melon.

honeydew melon, kind of muskmelon with sweet green flesh and a smooth, pale green skin.

hon·ey·moon (hun′ē mün′), **1** *n.* holiday spent together by a newly married couple. **2** *n.* a period of good feeling or good relations. **3** *v.* to spend or have a honeymoon. —**hon′ey·moon′er,** *n.*

hon·ey·suck·le (hun′ē suk′əl), *n.* any of many bushes or climbing vines with fragrant white, yellow, or red flowers; woodbine.

Hong Kong (hong′ kong′), harbor, trade center, and urban area on the SE coast of China. A British territory from 1898 until 1997, when under Chinese rule again. [Hong Kong may come from two Chinese words meaning "sweet-smelling port."]

Ho·ni·a·ra (hō′nē ä′rə), *n.* capital of the Solomon Islands.

honk (hongk), **1** *n.* the cry of a wild goose. **2** *n.* any similar sound: *the honk of a car horn.* **3** *v.* to make or cause to make such a sound: *Stop honking that horn!* —**honk′er,** *n.*

Hon·o·lu·lu (hon′ə lü′lü), *n.* port and capital of Hawaii, in S Oahu. [Honolulu comes from a Hawaiian word meaning "sheltered bay."]

hon·or (on′ər), **1** *n.* a sense of what is right or proper; nobility of mind: *A person of honor always keeps his or her promises.* **2** *v.* to show respect to: *The memorial honors those who died in the war by listing their names.* **3** *n.* source of credit; person or thing that reflects honor: *to be an honor to your family. It is an honor to be chosen class president.* **4** *n.pl.* **honors,** special mention given to a student by a school for having done work much above the average. **5** *n.* credit for acting well; glory,

honor (def. 2)

fame, or reputation; good name: *It was greatly to her honor to be given the scholarship.* **6** *n.* great respect; high regard: *She was held in honor by all who knew her.* **7** *n.* **Honor,** title of respect used in speaking to or of a judge, mayor, or other public official. **8** *n.* act that shows respect or high regard: *funeral honors, military honors.* **9** *v.* to respect highly; think highly of. **10** *v.* to give an honor to; favor: *be honored by a royal visit.* **11** *v.* to accept and pay a check, note, etc., when due. —**hon′or·er,** *n.*

do the honors, to act as host or hostess.

on your honor, acting or expected to act according to what you know is right to do.

hon·or·a·ble (on′ər ə bəl), *adj.* **1** having or showing a sense of what is right and proper; honest; upright: *It is not honorable to lie or cheat.* ■ See Synonym Study at **honest.** **2** causing honor; bringing honor to the person who has it: *honorable wounds.* **3** worthy of honor; noble: *to perform honorable deeds.* **4** showing honor or respect: *honorable burial.* **5** having a title, rank, or position of honor. **6** **Honorable,** title of respect before the names of certain officials. —**hon′or·a·ble·ness,** *n.* —**hon′or·a·bly,** *adv.*

hon·or·ar·y (on′ə rer′ē), *adj.* **1** given or done as an honor: *The university awarded honorary degrees to three well-known scientists.* **2** as an honor only; without pay or regular duties: *That association has an honorary secretary as well as a regular paid secretary who does the actual work.* —**hon′o·rar′i·ly,** *adv.*

honor roll, list of students who have achieved the highest grades during the school term or year.

honor system, system of trusting people in schools and other organizations or activities to obey rules and do their work without being watched or forced.

Hon·shu (hon′shü), *n.* the largest and most important island of Japan.

hood¹ (hud), **1** *n.* a soft covering for the head and neck, either separate or as part of a coat: *My raincoat has a hood.* **2** *n.* anything like a hood in shape or use. **3** *n.* a hinged metal covering over the engine of a car. **4** *v.* to cover with a hood; furnish with a hood. —**hood′less,** *adj.* —**hood′like′,** *adj.*

hood² (hud), *n.* INFORMAL. hoodlum.

-hood, *suffix.* **1** condition of being ___: *childhood = condition of being a child.* **2** group of: *priesthood = the group of priests.*

hood·ed (hud′id), *adj.* **1** having a hood: *He wears a hooded jacket.* **2** shaped like a hood. —**hood′ed·ness,** *n.*

hood·lum (hüd′ləm), *n.* **1** criminal or gangster. **2** a disorderly young person.

hood·wink (hud′wingk), *v.* to mislead by a trick; deceive.

hoof (huf), **1** *n.* a hard, horny covering on the feet of horses, cattle, sheep, pigs, and various other animals. **2** *n.* the whole foot of

a	hat	ė	term	ô	order	ch	child		
ā	age	i	it	oi	oil	ng	long		a in about
ä	far	ī	ice	ou	out	sh	she		e in taken
â	care	o	hot	u	cup	th	thin	ə	i in pencil
e	let	ō	open	u̇	put	ŦH	then		o in lemon
ē	equal	ȯ	saw	ü	rule	zh	measure		u in circus

H

such animals. **3** *v.* OLD USE. to walk or dance. ❑ *n., pl.* **hoofs** or **hooves. —hoof′less,** *adj.* **—hoof′like′,** *adj.*

hoof·beat (hŭf′bēt′), *n.* sound made by an animal's hoof.

hoofed (hŭft), *adj.* having hoofs.

hook (hŭk), **1** *n.* piece of metal, wood, or other stiff material, curved or having a sharp angle, for catching hold of something or for hanging things on. **2** *v.* to catch or take hold of with a hook. **3** *v.* to fasten with a hook or hooks: *Will you hook my dress for me?* **4** *n.* a curved piece of wire, usually with a barb at the end, for catching fish. **5** *v.* to catch fish with a hook. **6** *n.* anything curved or bent like a hook. **7** *v.* to make into the shape of a hook: *I hooked my arm in hers and we started off.* **8** *n.* a sharp bend: *a hook in the river.* **9** *n.* a curved point of land. **10** *v.* to be curved or bent like a hook. **11** *v.* to throw or hit a ball so that it curves. **12** *n.* a curving throw or hit. **13** *n.* (in boxing) a short, swinging blow. **14** *v.* to hit with such a blow. **—hook′less,** *adj.* **—hook′like′,** *adj.*

by hook or by crook, in any way at all; by fair means or foul.

hook up, to arrange and connect the parts of a radio set, telephone, modem, etc.

off the hook, free of responsibility.

hooked (hŭkt), *adj.* **1** curved or bent like a hook. **2** having hooks. **3** made with a hook. A **hooked rug** is made by pulling loops of yarn or strips of cloth through a piece of canvas, burlap, etc., with a hook.

hooked on, SLANG. extremely dependent; addicted.

hook·up (hŭk′up′), *n.* **1** arrangement and connection of the parts of a radio set, telephone, broadcasting facilities, etc.: *a nation-wide television hookup.* **2** connection or combination.

hook·worm (hŭk′wėrm′), *n.* **1** a small roundworm that enters the body through the skin and fastens itself to the walls of the small intestine. **2** disease caused by this worm, in which the symptoms are weakness and apparent laziness.

hook·y (hŭk′ē), *n.* **play hooky,** INFORMAL. stay away from school without permission.

hoo·li·gan (hü′lə gən), *n.* INFORMAL. one of a gang of street hoodlums.

hoop (hŭp *or* hüp), **1** *n.* ring or round, flat band: *a hoop for embroidery, a basketball hoop.* **2** *v.* to bind or fasten together with a hoop or hoops. **3** *n.* a large wooden, iron, or plastic ring used as a toy, especially for spinning around the body at the hips. **4** *n.* a circular frame formerly used to hold out a woman's skirt. ∎ Another word that can sound like this is **whoop. —hoop′like′,** *adj.*

hoop skirt, a woman's skirt worn over a frame of flexible hoops to hold out or expand the skirt; crinoline.

hoo·ray (hù rā′), *interj., n., v.* hurrah.

hoot (hüt), **1** *n.* sound that an owl makes. **2** *v.* to make this sound or one like it. **3** *n.* a shout to show disapproval or scorn. **4** *v.* to make such a shout. **5** *v.* to show disapproval of or scorn for by hooting: *The audience hooted the speaker's plan.* **6** *v.* to force or drive by hooting: *What he said was so foolish that they hooted him off the platform.* **7** *n.* INFORMAL. the smallest thought; trifle: *She doesn't give a hoot about what happens to us.* **—hoot′er,** *n.*

hoop skirt

hoot·e·nan·ny (hüt′n an′ē), *n.* an informal musical gathering featuring folk singing, especially one in which the audience joins in. ❑ *n., pl.* **hoot·e·nan·nies.**

Hoo·ver (hü′vər), *n.* **1 Her·bert Clark** (her′bert), 1874-1964, the 31st president of the United States, from 1929 to 1933. **2 J. Ed·gar** (ed′gər), 1895-1972, American director of the FBI from 1924 to 1972. ∎ **J. Edgar Hoover** made the FBI a model of law enforcement, but he also abused his power by collecting information about people he didn't like or who criticized the government.

Hoover Dam, dam on the Colorado River between Arizona and Nevada; Boulder Dam.

hooves (hùvz), *n.* a plural of **hoof.**

hop[1] (hop), **1** *v.* to jump, or move by jumping, on one foot: *How far can you hop?* **2** *v.* to jump, or move by jumping, with both or all feet at once: *Many birds hop.* **3** *v.* to jump over: *hop a ditch.* **4** *v.* INFORMAL. to jump on a moving train, car, etc. **5** *n.* a jump or a leap. **6** *n.* to take a train, bus, etc.: *Hop a train to Greenville for the weekend.* **7** *v.* to fly in an airplane. **8** *n.* a short airplane flight. **9** *n.* a bounce: *She fielded the grounder on one hop.* ❑ *v.* **hopped, hop·ping.**

hop[2] (hop), *n.* **1** any of several vines with flower clusters that look like small pine cones. **2 hops,** *pl.* the dried flower clusters of a hop vine, used to flavor beer and other malt drinks.

hope (hōp), **1** *n.* a feeling that what you desire will happen: *Your encouragement gave me hope.* **2** *v.* to wish and expect: *I hope to do well in school this year.* ∎ See Synonym Study at **expect. 3** *n.* thing hoped for: *It is our hope that she succeeds.* **4** *n.* a cause of hope; person or thing that gives hope to others or that others have hope in: *With two out, the batter was our last hope of winning the game.* ❑ *v.* **hoped, hop·ing. —hop′er,** *n.*

hope·ful (hōp′fəl), **1** *adj.* feeling or showing hope; expecting to receive what you desire: *a hopeful attitude.* **2** *adj.* giving hope; likely to succeed. **3** *n.* boy or girl thought likely to succeed: *a young hopeful.* **—hope′ful·ness,** *n.*

hope·ful·ly (hōp′fə lē), *adv.* **1** in a hopeful manner: *She smiled hopefully at the audience.* **2** it is hoped that: *Hopefully, business will improve soon.*

> **USAGE NOTE** **Hopefully** is often used to mean "It is to be hoped that": *Hopefully, the weather will stay warm.* Many people object to this use. Many others feel that it is not different from the widely accepted common use of **fortunately** and similar adverbs in similar sentences. Careful writers and speakers avoid the disagreement by avoiding the use of **hopefully** except to describe an action full of hope.

hope·less (hōp′lis), *adj.* **1** feeling no hope: *He was disappointed so often that he became hopeless.* **2** giving no hope: *a hopeless illness.* **—hope′less·ly,** *adv.* **—hope′less·ness,** *n.*

> **SYNONYM STUDY** **Hopeless, pessimistic,** and **desperate** all mean with no feeling that something good will happen. **Hopeless** suggests sadness: *After looking for his bicycle all day, he had a hopeless feeling that it was gone forever.* **Pessimistic** means ready to believe that bad things will happen: *She expects to win, but I am pessimistic.* **Desperate** means reckless because of being without hope: *Desperate people jumped from the burning building.*

Ho·pi (hō′pē), *n.* member of a tribe of American Indians living in adobe villages in northern Arizona. ❑ *n., pl.* **Ho·pi** or **Ho·pis.** [Hopi comes from a word in the Hopi language meaning "peaceful."]

hop·per (hop′ər), *n.* **1** container with a narrow opening at the bottom, used to receive and hold coal, grain, or other material before feeding it into a machine or storage bin. **2** person or thing that hops. **3** grasshopper or other hopping insect.

Hopper painting

Hop·per (hop′ər), *n.* **Ed·ward** (ed′wərd), 1882-1967, American painter.

hop·scotch (hop/skoch/), *n.* a children's game in which the players hop over the lines of a figure drawn on the ground and pick up an object thrown or kicked into one of the numbered squares of the figure.

ho·ra (hôr/ə), *n.* a lively Israeli folk dance performed by couples moving around to the left or right in a circle. ❏ *n., pl.* **ho·ras.**

horde (hôrd), *n.* **1** multitude; crowd; swarm: *Hordes of grasshoppers destroyed the crops.* **2** a wandering tribe or troop: *Hordes of Mongols roamed central Asia.* ■ Another word that sounds like this is **hoard.**

hore·hound (hôr/hound/), *n.* **1** any of several plants related to mint, with woolly, whitish leaves. **2** candy or cough medicine flavored with a bitter extract made from the leaves of these plants.

ho·ri·zon (hə rī/zn), *n.* **1** line where the earth and sky seem to meet; skyline. You cannot see beyond the horizon. **2** limit of your thinking, experience, interest, or outlook.

ho·ri·zon·tal (hôr/ə zon/tl), **1** *adj.* parallel to the horizon; at right angles to a vertical line: *A ceiling is horizontal.* ■ See Synonym Study at **level. 2** *adj.* flat; level: *A table top is a horizontal surface.* **3** *n.* a horizontal line, plane, direction, position, etc. —**ho/ri·zon/tal·ly,** *adv.*

hor·mone (hôr/mōn), *n.* any substance produced in one part of an animal or plant but controlling the activity of another part. In human beings, most hormones are formed in the endocrine glands and move through the bloodstream. Adrenalin and insulin are hormones. —**hor·mo/nal,** *adj.*

horn (hôrn), *n.* **1** a hard, hollow, permanent growth, usually curved and pointed, on the heads of cattle, sheep, goats, and various other animals. **2** the substance of horns; keratin. A person's fingernails, the beaks of birds, the hoofs of horses, and tortoise shells are all made of horn. **3** anything that sticks up on the head of an animal: *a snail's horns, an insect's horns.* **4** a musical instrument shaped something like a horn, sounded by blowing into it. It was once made of horn, but now it is made of brass or other metal. **5** device sounded as a warning signal: *a car horn.* **6** anything that sticks out like a horn or is shaped like a horn: *a saddle horn.* **7** each pointed tip of a new or old moon, or of any crescent. —**horn/less,** *adj.* —**horn/like/,** *adj.*

blow your own horn or **toot your own horn,** INFORMAL. to praise yourself; boast.

draw in your horns or **pull in your horns, 1** to restrain yourself. **2** to back down; withdraw.

horn in, INFORMAL. to meddle or intrude.

Horn (hôrn), *n.* Cape. See **Cape Horn.**

horn·bill (hôrn/bil/), *n.* any of numerous large tropical birds with very large horny bills. Hornbills live in Africa and Asia. They resemble but are not related to toucans, which live in American tropics.

hornbill—4 ft. (1.2 m) long

horn·blende (hôrn/blend/), *n.* a common black, dark green, or brown mineral found in granite and other rocks.

horn·book (hôrn/buk/), *n.* page with the alphabet, etc., on it, covered with a sheet of transparent horn and fastened in a frame with a handle, formerly used in teaching children to read.

horned (hôrnd), *adj.* having a horn, horns, or hornlike growths.

horned lizard, horned toad.

horned owl, any of several owls with hornlike tufts of feathers on their heads.

horned toad, any of several small, harmless lizards with broad, flat bodies, short tails, and many hornlike spines; horned lizard.

hor·net (hôr/nit), *n.* any of several large wasps that can give a very painful sting. Hornets build paper nests from wood and other plant fiber that they chew up.

horn of plenty, cornucopia.

horn·pipe (hôrn/pīp/), *n.* **1** a lively dance done by one person. It was formerly popular among sailors. **2** music for it.

horn·y (hôr/nē), *adj.* **1** made of horn or a substance like it. **2** hard like a horn; calloused: *A farmer's hands are horny from work.* **3** having a horn or horns; horned. ❏ *adj.* **horn·i·er, horn·i·est.** —**horn/i·ness,** *n.*

ho·ro·scope (hôr/ə skōp), *n.* **1** diagram used in telling fortunes according to the relative position of the planets at a particular time, especially at the hour of someone's birth. **2** fortune told by using such a diagram.

Hor·o·witz (hôr/ə vits), *n.* **Vlad·i·mir** (vlad/ə mir), 1904-1989, Russian pianist who lived in the United States.

hor·ren·dous (hô ren/dəs), *adj.* horrible; terrible; frightful. —**hor·ren/dous·ly,** *adv.*

hor·ri·ble (hôr/ə bəl), *adj.* **1** causing horror; terrible; dreadful; frightful; shocking: *a horrible crime.* **2** extremely unpleasant: *a horrible noise.* —**hor/ri·ble·ness,** *n.* —**hor/ri·bly,** *adv.*

hor·rid (hôr/id), *adj.* **1** causing great fear; terrible; frightful. **2** very unpleasant: *a horrid person, a horrid day.* —**hor/rid·ly,** *adv.* —**hor/rid·ness,** *n.*

hor·ri·fy (hôr/ə fī), *v.* **1** to cause to feel horror. **2** to shock very much: *We were horrified by such rude behavior.* ❏ *v.* **hor·ri·fied, hor·ri·fy·ing.** —**hor/ri·fy/ing·ly,** *adv.*

hor·ror (hôr/ər), *n.* **1** a shivering, shaking terror. **2** a very strong dislike: *I have a horror of high places.* **3** thing that causes horror. [**Horror** comes from a Latin word meaning "to stand up," as hair does on a person or animal that is badly frightened.]

hors d'oeuvre (ôr/ dėrv/), relish or light food served as an appetizer before the regular courses of a meal. Olives, cheeses, celery, pickles, etc., are hors d'oeuvres. ❏ *pl.* **hors d'oeuvres** (ôr/ dėrvz/).

horse (def. 1)—about 4 ft. 9 in. (1.4 m) high at the shoulder

horse (hôrs), **1** *n.* a large, four-legged mammal with solid hoofs and a mane and tail of long, coarse hair. Horses are used for riding and for carrying and pulling loads. **2** *n.* a full-grown male horse. **3** *n.* a padded piece of gymnasium equipment, supported by legs, used in jumping exercises and for gymnastics. **4** *n.* a supporting frame with legs: *Five boards laid on two horses made our picnic table.* **5** *v.* INFORMAL. **horse around,** to fool around; get

a	hat	ė	term	ô	order	ch	child		a in about
ā	age	i	it	oi	oil	ng	long		e in taken
ä	far	ī	ice	ou	out	sh	she	ə {	i in pencil
â	care	o	hot	u	cup	th	thin		o in lemon
e	let	ō	open	ů	put	ŦH	then		u in circus
ē	equal	ò	saw	ü	rule	zh	measure		

into mischief. ❑ *n., pl.* **hors·es** or **horse;** *v.* **horsed, hors·ing.**
▪ Another word that sounds like this is **hoarse.**

from the horse's mouth, from a well-informed source.

horse of a different color, something quite different.

horse·back (hôrs′bak′), **1** *n.* the back of a horse. **2** *adv.* on the back of a horse: *ride horseback.*

horse chestnut, any of about 15 shade trees with spreading branches, large leaves, clusters of showy white flowers, and glossy brown nuts, which are bitter and poisonous.

horse·flesh (hôrs′flesh′), *n.* **1** horses for riding, driving, and racing. **2** meat from horses.

horse·fly (hôrs′flī′), *n.* any of numerous large flies that bite animals, especially horses. ❑ *n., pl.* **horse·flies.**

horse·hair (hôrs′hâr′), *n.* **1** hair from the mane or tail of a horse. **2** a stiff fabric made of this hair; haircloth.

horse·hide (hôrs′hīd′), *n.* **1** leather made from the hide of a horse. **2** hide of a horse.

horse latitudes, two regions with usually very light winds or no winds. They extend around the earth at about 30 degrees north and 30 degrees south of the equator.

horse·man (hôrs′mən), *n.* **1** person who rides on horseback. **2** person who is skilled in riding or managing horses. ❑ *n., pl.* **horse·men.**

horse·man·ship (hôrs′mən ship), *n.* skill in riding or managing horses: *She is proud of her horsemanship.*

horse opera, SLANG. a western movie.

horse·play (hôrs′plā′), *n.* rough, boisterous fun.

horse·pow·er (hôrs′pou′ər), *n.* unit for measuring the power of engines, motors, etc. One horsepower is the power to lift 550 pounds one foot in one second.

horse·rad·ish (hôrs′rad′ish), *n.* **1** a tall plant with a white, hot-tasting root. **2** its root, which is ground up and used as a relish with meat, fish, etc.

horse sense, INFORMAL. plain, practical good sense; common sense.

horse·shoe (hôrs′shü′ *or* hôrsh′shü′), *n.* **1** a flat piece of metal shaped like a U, nailed to a horse's hoof to protect it. **2** something shaped like a horseshoe. **3** **horseshoes,** *pl.* game in which the players try to throw horseshoes over or near a stake 40 feet (12 meters) away. —**horse′sho·er,** *n.*

horseshoe crab, any of four kinds of crablike sea animals related to the spiders, with horseshoe-shaped shells and long, spiny tails.

horse·whip (hôrs′wip′), **1** *n.* whip for driving or controlling horses. **2** *v.* to beat with a horsewhip. ❑ *v.* **horse·whipped, horse·whip·ping.**

horse·wom·an (hôrs′wum′ən), *n.* **1** woman who rides on horseback. **2** woman skilled in riding or managing horses. ❑ *n., pl.* **horse·wom·en.**

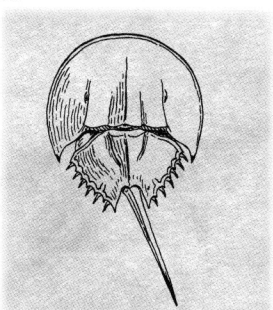

horseshoe crab
up to 20 in. (51 cm) long

hors·y or **hors·ey** (hôr′sē), *adj.* **1** of or like a horse or horses. **2** fond of horses or horse racing. **3** dressing or talking like people who spend much time with horses. ❑ *adj.* **hors·i·er, hors·i·est.** —**hors′i·ness,** *n.*

hor·ti·cul·tur·al (hôr′tə kul′chər əl), *adj.* of or related to the growing of flowers, fruits, vegetables, and plants: *a horticultural exhibit.* —**hor′ti·cul′tur·al·ly,** *adv.*

hor·ti·cul·ture (hôr′tə kul′chər), *n.* **1** science or art of growing flowers, fruits, vegetables, and plants. **2** cultivation of a garden; hobby of gardening.

hor·ti·cul·tur·ist (hôr′tə kul′chər ist), *n.* an expert in horticulture.

Ho·rus (hôr′əs), *n.* the Egyptian god of the sky and the sun, the son of Isis and Osiris, shown as a man with a falcon's head.

ho·san·na (hō zan′ə), *interj.* a shout of praise to God: *The high priest cried, "Hosanna!"* ❑ *n., pl.* **ho·san·nas.**

hose (defs. 1 and 4)

hose (hōz), **1** *n.* a flexible tube of rubber or plastic for carrying a liquid or a gas. A hose is used in pumping gasoline into cars. **2** *n.pl.* stockings or socks. **3** *n.pl.* long, tight breeches formerly worn by men. **4** *v.* to put water on with a hose. ❑ *v.* **hosed, hos·ing.** —**hose′like′,** *adj.*

WORD STORY Hose comes from an old English word meaning "legging." When people first made tubes for carrying liquid, the tubes reminded them of stockings, so that's what they called them.

Ho·se·a (hō zē′ə), *n.* **1** a Hebrew prophet. **2** book of the Bible. [**Hosea** comes from a Hebrew word meaning "salvation."]

ho·sier·y (hō′zhər ē), *n.* hose; stockings or socks.

hos·pice (hos′pis), *n.* **1** nursing home or similar facility where people with terminal illness go to die. **2** (earlier) house where travelers can stop and rest. It was often kept by monks.

hos·pi·ta·ble (hos′pi tə bəl *or* ho spit′ə bəl), *adj.* **1** giving or liking to give a welcome, food and shelter, and friendly treatment to guests or strangers: *a hospitable family, a hospitable reception.* **2** with the mind open or receptive: *a person hospitable to new ideas.* —**hos′pi·ta·bly,** *adv.*

hos·pi·tal (hos′pi təl), *n.* place for the care of the sick or injured.

hos·pi·tal·i·ty (hos′pə tal′ə tē), *n.* the generous treatment of guests or strangers.

hos·pi·tal·ize (hos′pi tə līz), *v.* to put in a hospital for treatment. ❑ *v.* **hos·pi·tal·ized, hos·pi·tal·iz·ing.** —**hos′pi·tal·i·za′tion,** *n.*

host[1] (hōst), **1** *n.* person who receives another person as a guest. **2** *v.* to receive or entertain as a host does: *host a party.* **3** *n.* a living thing in or on which a parasite lives: *The oak tree is the host of the mistletoe that grows on it.*

WORD FAMILY Host[1] and the words below are related. They all come from a Latin word meaning "stranger" or "enemy." In old times, people distrusted strangers, even people whose business was to provide food and shelter to strangers.

hospital	host[2]	hostel	hostile
hospitality	hostage	hostess	hotel

host[2] (hōst), *n.* **1** a large number; multitude: *As it grew dark, a few stars appeared, then a host.* **2** army.

Host (hōst), *n.* Often, **host,** bread or wafer used in the Mass of the Roman Catholic Church.

WORD STORY Host comes from a Latin word meaning "a sacrifice." The Mass recalls the Last Supper before the death of Jesus, regarded as a sacrifice to save the world from sin.

hos·tage (hos′tij), *n.* **1** person held as a prisoner until some demand is agreed to: *The convicts took guards as hostages until they were promised better living conditions.* **2** pledge; security.

hos·tel (hos′tl), *n.* **1** a lodging place; inn; hotel. **2** youth hostel.
▪ Another word that sounds like this is **hostile.**

hos·tel·ry (hos′tl rē), *n.* inn; hotel. ❑ *n., pl.* **hos·tel·ries.**

host·ess (hō′stis), *n.* **1** woman who receives another person as her guest. **2** woman employed in a restaurant, hotel, etc., to greet and attend to customers. **3** woman who works as a flight attendant. ❑ *n., pl.* **host·ess·es.**

hos·tile (hos′tl), *adj.* **1** of or like an enemy or enemies: *the hostile army.* **2** opposed; unfriendly; unfavorable: *a hostile look.* ■ Another word that sounds like this is **hostel.** —**hos′tile·ly,** *adv.*

SYNONYM STUDY **Hostile, aggressive,** and **warlike** all mean likely to fight. **Hostile** means being an enemy: *She gets hostile when she loses.* **Aggressive** suggests being always likely to fight: *That dog is so aggressive that I keep away from it.* **Warlike** means ready and eager for war: *The warlike Vikings raided far and wide.*

hos·til·i·ty (ho stil′ə tē), *n.* **1** the feeling that an enemy has; unfriendliness; dislike: *He showed signs of hostility toward our plan.* **2 hostilities,** *pl.* acts of war; warfare; fighting: *The peace treaty brought hostilities between the two countries to an end.*

hos·tler (os′lər *or* hos′lər), *n.* (earlier) person who takes care of horses at an inn or stable.

hot (hot), **1** *adj.* having much heat; very warm: *Fire is hot.* **2** *adj.* warmer than it usually is: *The weather is hot for April.* **3** *adj.* feeling hot or warm: *That long run made me hot.* **4** *adj.* having a sharp, burning taste: *Pepper and mustard are hot.* **5** *adj.* fiery: *a hot temper, hot with rage.* **6** *adj.* INFORMAL. very eager: *The children were hot to go camping.* **7** *adj.* new; fresh: *I just got some hot news.* **8** *adj.* following closely: *We were in hot pursuit of the runaway horse.* **9** *adj.* (in games, treasure hunts, etc.) very near or approaching what you are searching for. **10** *adj.* radioactive: *the hot debris left by an atomic explosion.* **11** *adj.* INFORMAL. obtained illegally; stolen: *hot diamonds.* **12** *adv.* with much heat: *The sun beats hot upon the sand.* ❑ *adj.* **hot·ter, hot·test.** —**hot′ly,** *adv.* —**hot′ness,** *n.*

hot under the collar, INFORMAL. very angry.

make it hot for, to make trouble for.

SYNONYM STUDY **Hot, sultry,** and **sweltering** all mean having a high temperature. **Hot** is a general word: *In summer even the nights are hot.* **Sultry** means hot and damp: *The afternoon was sultry, so I took a cool bath.* **Sweltering** means very unpleasantly hot: *After hours in the sun, the car was sweltering inside.*

hot air, empty, showy talk or writing.

hot·bed (hot′bed′), *n.* **1** place where anything grows and develops rapidly: *Crowded cities are hotbeds of disease and crime.* **2** bed of earth covered with glass and kept warm for growing plants.

hot-blood·ed (hot′blud′id), *adj.* **1** easily excited or angered. **2** passionate. —**hot′-blood′ed·ness,** *n.*

hot cake, pancake.

go like hot cakes or **sell like hot cakes,** to sell well and rapidly; be in great demand.

hot dog, 1 sandwich made with a hot frankfurter enclosed in a bun. **2** frankfurter. **3** SLANG. an athlete who does stunts, especially while surfing or skiing.

hot-dog (hot′dȯg′), *v.* SLANG. to do stunts, especially while surfing or skiing. ❑ *v.* **hot-dogged, hot-dog·ging.**

ho·tel (hō tel′), *n.* a place where people traveling away from home can rent a room to sleep in.

hot·foot (hot′fůt′), *v.* INFORMAL. to go in great haste; hurry.

hot-head·ed (hot′hed′id), *adj.* **1** having a fiery temper; easily angered. **2** hasty; rash. —**hot′head′ed·ly,** *adv.*

hot·house (hot′hous′), *n.* greenhouse. ❑ *n., pl.* **hot·hous·es** (hot′hou′ziz).

hot line, 1 a direct telephone or teletype line providing immediate communication in an emergency. **2** a telephone connection available to the public, for quick contact with help. Hot lines deal with complaints, personal crises, requests for information, etc.

hot plate, a small, portable electric stove, with one or two burners, for cooking.

hot potato, INFORMAL. situation or issue that is very difficult to deal with.

hot rod, car with a rebuilt motor for faster starts and higher speeds.

hot·shot (hot′shot′), *n.* INFORMAL. person having more than ordinary skill at something and often being conceited about it.

hot spot, 1 area known to be dangerous. **2** area of extreme heat, radiation, etc. **3** a place where molten rock rises from the Earth's mantle to the Earth's crust, creating volcanoes or other geological effects of extreme heat.

hot spring

hot spring, a spring of naturally warm water, especially at a temperature above that of the human body.

Hot Springs National Park, a national park in central Arkansas, containing naturally heated springs of mineral water.

hot-tem·pered (hot′tem′pərd), *adj.* easily made angry; short-tempered.

Hot·ten·tot (hot′n tot), *n.* Khoikhoi. ■ **Hottentot** is now considered offensive.

hot tub, a large tub used for individual or group bathing or soaking in hot water. Hot tubs are made of wood, ceramic, or plastic. —**hot′-tub′ber,** *n.* —**hot′-tub′bing,** *n.*

hot water, trouble: *Telling lies got him into hot water.*

Hou·di·ni (hü dē′nē), *n.* **Har·ry** (har′ē), 1874-1926, American magician and escape artist, born in Hungary. ■ **Harry Houdini** escaped easily from jail cells, ten pairs of handcuffs at once, straitjackets, and even an airtight tank filled with water.

hound (hound), **1** *n.* dog of any of various breeds, most of which hunt by scent and have large, drooping ears and short hair. **2** *n.* any dog. **3** *v.* to keep on chasing or hunting: *The police hounded the criminals and finally caught them.* **4** *v.* to urge on; nag: *The children hounded their parents to buy a swimming pool.*

hour (our), *n.* **1** one of the 12 equal periods of time between noon and midnight, or between midnight and noon; 60 minutes; ¹⁄₂₄ of a day. **2** the time of day: *This clock strikes the hours and the half hours.* **3** a particular or fixed time: *When is lunch hour?* **4** hours, *pl.* time for work, study, etc.: *What are the hours in this office? Our school hours are 9 to 12 and 1 to 4.* **5** distance which can be traveled in an hour: *The concert hall is only an hour away.* ■ Another word that sounds like this is **our.**

hour·glass (our′glas′), *n.* device for measuring time, made up of two glass bulbs connected by a narrow neck. It takes an hour for sand in the top bulb to pass through the neck to the bottom bulb. ❑ *n., pl.* **hour·glass·es.**

hour hand, the shorter hand on a clock or watch that indicates hours. It moves around the whole dial once in 12 hours.

hour·i (hůr′ē), *n.* one of the young, eternally beautiful women of the Islamic paradise. ❑ *n., pl.* **hour·is.**

hour·ly (our′lē), **1** *adj.* done, happening, or counted every hour: *There are hourly reports of the news and weather on this radio station.* **2** *adv.* every hour; hour by hour: *Give two doses of the medicine hourly.* **3** *adj.* coming very often; frequent: *hourly messages.* **4** *adv.* very often; frequently: *Messages were coming from the front hourly.*

house (hous *for noun;* houz *for verb*), **1** *n.* building in which people live. **2** *n.* people living in a house; household: *The noise woke up the whole house.* **3** *n.* building for any purpose: *a tool house, a movie house.* **4** *v.* to take or put into a house; provide with a house; shelter: *Where can we house all these children?* **5** *n.* place

a	hat	ė	term	ô	order	ch	child		
ā	age	i	it	oi	oil	ng	long		a in about
ä	far	ī	ice	ou	out	sh	she		e in taken
â	care	o	hot	u	cup	th	thin	ə	i in pencil
e	let	ō	open	ů	put	ŦH	then		o in lemon
ē	equal	ȯ	saw	ü	rule	zh	measure		u in circus

of business or a business firm: *a publishing house.* **6** *n.* Often, **House,** family with its ancestors and descendants, especially a noble family: *He was a prince of the royal house.* **7** *n.* Often, **House,** assembly for making laws and considering questions of government; lawmaking group. In the United States, the House of Representatives is the lower house of Congress; the Senate is the upper house. **8** *n.* audience: *The singer sang to a large house.* ❑ *n., pl.* **hous·es** (hou′ziz); *v.* **housed, hous·ing.**

keep house, to manage a home and its affairs; do housework.

on the house, paid for by the owner of the business; free.

house·boat (hous′bōt′), *n.* boat fitted out for use as a place to live in.

houseboat

house·break (hous′brāk′), *v.* to train a dog, cat, etc., to have clean habits for living indoors. ❑ *v.* **house·broke** (house′brōk′), **house·bro·ken, house·break·ing.**

house·break·ing (hous′brā′king), *n.* act of breaking into a house to steal or commit some other crime. **—house′break′er,** *n.*

house·bro·ken (hous′brō′kən), *adj.* (of a dog, cat, etc.) trained to have clean habits for living indoors. ■ See Synonym Study at **tame.**

house·coat (hous′kōt′), *n.* a loose, flowing outer garment worn indoors by women and girls.

house·fly (hous′flī′), *n.* a two-winged fly that lives around and in houses in all parts of the world, feeding on food and garbage. Houseflies carry disease germs. ❑ *n., pl.* **house·flies.**

house·hold (hous′hōld′), **1** *n.* all the people living in a house: *Everyone in our household helps with the chores.* **2** *n.* a home and its affairs. **3** *adj.* of a household; domestic: *household chores.*

house·hold·er (hous′hōl′dər), *n.* **1** person who owns or lives in a house. **2** head of a family.

house·hus·band (hous′huz′bənd), *n.* married man who manages a home and its affairs for his family.

house·keep·er (hous′kē′pər), *n.* **1** person who takes care of a household or who does housework. **2** a woman who is hired to manage or do housework in a home, hotel, or motel.

house·keep·ing (hous′kē′ping), *n.* management of a home and its affairs; doing the housework.

house·maid (hous′mād′), *n.* a woman servant who does housework.

house·moth·er (hous′muᴛн′ər), *n.* woman who looks after and takes care of a group of young people living together in a dormitory or similar residence.

House of Commons, the lower house of the Parliament of Great Britain or of Canada, composed of elected representatives; the Commons.

house of correction, place of confinement and reform for persons convicted of minor offenses.

House of Lords, the upper house of the Parliament of Great Britain, composed of nobles and clergymen of high rank; the Lords.

House of Representatives, the lower house of Congress or of the legislature of certain states of the United States.

house·plant (hous′plant′), *n.* any plant in a pot or box, kept inside the house. African violets are popular houseplants.

house·sit (hous′sit′), *v.* to live in and keep watch over a home during the absence of the owner or tenant. ❑ *v.* **house·sat** (hous′-sat′), **house·sit·ting. —house′-sit′ter,** *n.*

house sparrow, a small, brownish gray, European bird, now very common in America, especially in cities and towns; English sparrow. It is a kind of finch.

house·top (hous′top′), *n.* top of a house; roof.

house·warm·ing (hous′wôr′ming), *n.* party given when a family moves into a home for the first time.

house·wife (hous′wīf′), *n.* a married woman who manages a home and its affairs for her family. ❑ *n., pl.* **house·wives** (hous′-wīvz′).

house·wife·ly (hous′wīf′lē), *adj.* of or like a housewife.

house·work (hous′wėrk′), *n.* work to be done in housekeeping, such as washing, ironing, cleaning, and cooking.

hous·ing (hou′zing), *n.* **1** act of sheltering; providing shelter. **2** houses or other places to live in: *There is not enough housing in that city.* **3** frame or plate to hold part of a machine in place.

Hous·ton (hyü′stən), *n.* **1 Sam** (sam), 1793-1863, American general and political leader who was twice president of Texas before it became a state in 1845. **2** port in SE Texas, near the Gulf of Mexico.

hove (hōv), *v.* a past tense and a past participle of **heave.**

hov·el (huv′əl *or* hov′əl), *n.* house that is small, crude, and unpleasant to live in.

hov·er (huv′ər *or* hov′ər), *v.* **1** to stay in or near one place in the air: *The two birds hovered over their nest.* **2** to stay in or near one place; wait nearby: *The dogs hovered around the kitchen door at mealtime.* **3** to be in an uncertain condition; waver: *The patient hovered between life and death.*

hov·er·craft (huv′ər kraft′ *or* hov′ər kraft′), *n.* a vehicle that travels a few feet above the surface of land or water on a cushion of air. The air is created by jets or fans blowing downward.

how (hou), **1** *adv., conj.* in what way; by what means: *Tell me how to do it.* **2** *adv.* to what degree or amount: *How tall are you?* **3** *adv., conj.* in what condition: *How are you today?* **4** *adv.* for what reason; why: *How is it you don't like candy?*

and how!, INFORMAL. absolutely!: *Is it raining hard? And how!*

how come, INFORMAL. why: *How come you didn't call me last night?*

How·ard (hou′ərd), *n.* **Catherine,** 1520?-1542, English queen, fifth wife of Henry VIII. She was beheaded when the king discovered that she had not been a virgin when they married.

how·dah (hou′də), *n.* seat for persons riding on the back of an elephant.

how·dy (hou′dē), *interj.* DIALECT. a call of greeting; hello.

Howe (hou), *n.* **1 E·li·as** (ə lī′əs), 1819-1867, American inventor of the sewing machine. **2 Ju·lia Ward** (jü′lyə wôrd′), 1819-1910, American writer and social reformer. ■ **Julia Ward Howe** wrote the lyrics to "The Battle Hymn of the Republic." She also began the celebration of Mother's Day.

how·ev·er (hou ev′ər), *adv.* **1** in spite of that; nevertheless; yet: *We were very late for dinner; however, there was plenty left for us.* ■ See Usage Note at **but. 2** to whatever extent, degree, or amount; no matter how: *I'll come however busy I am.* **3** in whatever way; by whatever means: *However did you get so dirty?*

how·it·zer (hou′it sər), *n.* a short cannon for firing shells in a high curve, so that they drop on the target.

howl (houl), **1** *v.* to give a long, loud, mournful cry: *Our dog often howls at night.* **2** *n.* a long, loud, mournful cry: *the howl of a wolf.* **3** *v.* to give a long, loud cry of pain or rage. **4** *n.* a loud cry of pain or rage. **5** *n.* a yell or shout: *We heard howls of laughter.* **6** *v.* to yell or shout: *howl with laughter.*

howl·er (hou′lər), *n.* **1** person or thing that howls. **2** any of several tropical American monkeys with long, grasping tails and very loud calls. **3** a ridiculous mistake or blunder.

howl·ing (hou′ling), *adj.* very great: *a howling success.* **—howl′-ing·ly,** *adv.*

how·so·ev·er (hou′sō ev′ər), *adv.* **1** to whatever extent, degree, or amount. **2** in whatever way.

hp., h.p., HP, or **H.P.,** horsepower.

h.q. or **H.Q.,** headquarters.

hr., hour or hours. ❑ *pl.* **hrs.**

H.R., House of Representatives.

H.R.H., **1** Her Royal Highness. **2** His Royal Highness.

ht., height.

Huang He (hwäng′hu′), river in China flowing from central China into the Yellow Sea. Formerly called **Yellow River.** [Huang He comes from Chinese words meaning "yellow river." The river is called this because it is so muddy. The mud is yellow.]

hua·ra·che (wə rä′chē), *n.* a heavy leather sandal with a flat sole. Huaraches are commonly worn in Mexico.

hub (hub), *n.* **1** the central part of a wheel. **2** center of interest, activity, etc.: *Malls are the hubs of suburban life.*

Hub·ble Space Telescope (hub′əl), a large telescope placed in orbit around the earth in order to obtain highly detailed pictures and information from outer space without interference from the atmosphere.

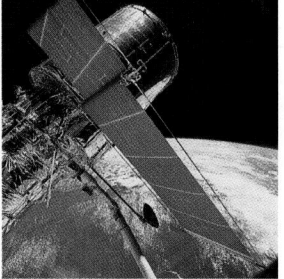
Hubble Space Telescope

hub·bub (hub′ub), *n.* loud, confused noise; uproar: *A fight caused a hubbub on the crowded playground.*

hub·cap (hub′kap′), *n.* a removable, dish-shaped metal piece that covers the outer hub of a motor vehicle wheel.

huck·le·ber·ry (huk′əl ber′ē), *n.* a small berry like a blueberry, but darker and with larger seeds. It grows on any of several North American bushes. ❑ *n., pl.* **huck·le·ber·ries.**

huck·ster (huk′stər), *n.* **1** peddler. **2** person who is in the advertising business.

HUD (hud), Housing and Urban Development (department of the U.S. government).

hud·dle (hud′l), **1** *v.* to crowd close: *The sheep huddled together in a corner.* **2** *v.* to nestle in a heap: *The cat huddled itself on the cushion.* **3** *n.* a closely packed group or crowd. **4** *n.* a grouping of football players behind the line of scrimmage to get ready for the next play. **5** *n.* a secret consultation: *After the meeting, the lawyer went into a huddle with his partner.* **6** *v.* to confer secretly. ❑ *v.* **hud·dled, hud·dling. –hud′dler,** *n.*

Hud·son (hud′sən), *n.* **1** Henry, died 1611, English navigator and explorer in America. The Hudson River and Hudson Bay were named for him. **2** river in E New York State. New York City is at its mouth.

Hudson Bay, large bay in NE Canada. It is an extension of the Atlantic Ocean.

Hudson's Bay Company, company founded in 1670 to carry on trade for furs with North American Indians. It is now a large corporation with retail and wholesale businesses.

hue (hyü), *n.* color or shade of color: *The room was painted in several hues of green.* ■ See Synonym Study at **color.** ■ Another word that sounds like this is **hew.**

hue and cry, shouts of alarm or protest.

huff (huf), **1** *n.* fit of anger or annoyance: *We had a heated argument, and she left in a huff.* **2** *v.* to go while breathing rapidly and loudly: *He huffed up the stairs with the heavy packages.*

huff·y (huf′ē), *adj.* **1** in a huff; offended. **2** easily offended; touchy. ❑ *adj.* **huff·i·er, huff·i·est. –huff′i·ly,** *adv.* **–huff′i·ness,** *n.*

hug (hug), **1** *v.* to put the arms around and hold close, especially to show love or friendship: *The girl hugged her big dog.* **2** *n.* a tight clasp with the arms: *She gave her dog a hug.* **3** *v.* to cling firmly or fondly to: *hug an opinion or belief.* **4** *v.* to keep close to: *The boat hugged the shore.* ❑ *v.* **hugged, hug·ging. –hug′ger,** *n.*

huge (hyüj), *adj.* very big; unusually large or great: *A whale is a huge animal. He won a huge sum of money in the lottery.* ❑ *adj.* **hug·er, hug·est. –huge′ly,** *adv.* **–huge′ness,** *n.*

SYNONYM STUDY Huge, enormous, and immense all mean very big. **Huge** suggests excitement about the size: *These hamburgers are huge.* **Enormous** means much larger than usual: *The town celebrated its hundredth anniversary with an enormous parade.* **Immense** means too big to measure: *An immense flood covered the valley.*

Hughes (hyüz), *n.* **Lang·ston** (lang′stən), 1902-1967, American writer. His works include *The Ways of White Folks* (a collection of short stories), several plays, and many poems.

Hu·go (hyü′gō), *n.* **Vic·tor** (vik′tər), 1802-1885, French writer of poetry, novels, and plays. His novels include *The Hunchback of Notre Dame* and *Les Misérables.*

Hu·gue·not (hyü′gə not), *n.* a French Protestant of the 1500s and 1600s.

huh (hu), *interj.* sound made to express surprise, contempt, etc., or to ask a question.

hui·pil (wē pēl′), *n.* a large blouse with a square neck, pulled over the head. Huipils are worn by women in Mexico and Central America.

Huit·zi·lo·poch·tli (wēt′zē lō poch′tlē), *n.* Aztec supreme god and god of the sun and war.

hu·la (hü′lə), *n.* a native Hawaiian dance. ❑ *n., pl.* **hu·las.**

Hu·la-Hoop (hü′lə hüp′), *n.* trademark for a plastic hoop that is rotated around the body by swinging the hips. Hula-Hoops are used as toys and for exercise.

huipil

hulk (hulk), *n.* **1** a big, clumsy ship. **2** a big, clumsy person or thing.

hulk·ing (hul′king), *adj.* big and clumsy: *a large, hulking boy.*

hull (hul), **1** *n.* body or frame of a ship. **2** *n.* body or frame of a seaplane, airship, etc. **3** *n.* the outer covering of a seed or fruit. **4** *n.* the small leaves around the stem of a strawberry and certain other fruits. **5** *v.* to remove the hull or hulls from.

hul·la·ba·loo (hul′ə bə lü), *n.* a loud noise or disturbance; uproar. ❑ *n., pl.* **hul·la·ba·loos.**

Hull House (hul), a settlement house in Chicago, Illinois, founded in 1899 by Jane Addams.

hum (hum), **1** *v.* to make a continuous murmuring sound like that of a bee or of a spinning top: *The sewing machine hums busily.* **2** *n.* a continuous murmuring sound: *the hum of the bees.* **3** *v.* to sing with closed lips, not sounding words: *hum a tune.* **4** *v.* to put or bring by humming: *The father hummed the baby to sleep.* **5** *v.* to make a low sound like *mm* or *hm* in hesitation, embarrassment, dissatisfaction, etc. **6** *interj.* a low sound like *mm* or *hm* made in hesitation, embarrassment, etc. **7** *v.* to be busy and active: *Things hummed at campaign headquarters just before the election.* ❑ *v.* **hummed, hum·ming. –hum′mer,** *n.*

hu·man (hyü′mən), **1** *adj.* of or relating to people: *Language is a human characteristic.* **2** *adj.* being a person or persons; having the form or qualities of people: *Men, women, and children are human beings.* **3** *adj.* having or showing qualities, good or bad, natural to people: *She is a very human person, warm and understanding but sometimes impatient.* **4** *adj.* for or about people: *human interest, the course of human events.* **5** *n.* a human being; person. **–hu′man·like′,** *adj.* **–hu′man·ness,** *n.*

human being, **1** man, woman, or child; any person; human. **2** an individual: *a wonderful human being.*

hu·mane (hyü mān′), *adj.* not cruel or brutal; kind; merciful: *We believe in the humane treatment of prisoners.* **–hu·mane′ly,** *adv.* **–hu·mane′ness,** *n.*

human immunodeficiency virus. See **HIV.**

hu·man·ism (hyü′mə niz′əm), *n.* **1** any system of thought or action centrally concerned with human interests, values, and reason. **2** the study of the humanities.

hu·man·ist (hyü′mə nist), *n.* **1** person who believes in or practices humanism. **2** student of the humanities. **–hu′man·is′tic,** *adj.*

hu·man·i·tar·i·an (hyü man′ə ter′ē ən), **1** *adj.* helpful to humanity; philanthropic. **2** *n.* person who is devoted to the welfare of all human beings.

a	hat	e	term	ô	order	ch	child		a in about
ā	age	i	it	oi	oil	ng	long		e in taken
ä	far	ī	ice	ou	out	sh	she	ə	i in pencil
â	care	o	hot	u	cup	th	thin		o in lemon
e	let	ō	open	u̇	put	∓H	then		u in circus
ē	equal	ȯ	saw	ü	rule	zh	measure		

hummingbird—about 4 in. (10 cm) long

hu·man·i·ty (hyü man′ə tē), *n.* **1** human beings; people; mankind: *Advances in medicine should help all humanity.* **2** human nature: *Humanity is a mixture of good and bad qualities.* **3** humane treatment; kindness; mercy: *Treat animals with humanity.* **4** the humanities, *pl.* cultural studies as opposed to the sciences, including languages, literature, philosophy, art, etc.

hu·man·ize (hyü′mə nīz), *v.* **1** to make or become human. **2** to make or become humane. ❏ *v.* **hu·man·ized, hu·man·iz·ing.** —**hu′·man·i·za′tion,** *n.* —**hu′man·iz′er,** *n.*

hu·man·kind (hyü′mən kīnd′), *n.* human beings; mankind; people.

hu·man·ly (hyü′mən lē), *adv.* **1** by human means: *The doctor did everything humanly possible to save the patient.* **2** in a human manner: *Even a judge is humanly liable to make a mistake.*

hu·man·oid (hyü′mə noid), **1** *adj.* having human characteristics; of human form. **2** *n.* a being having human characteristics: *Space aliens in the movies are usually humanoids, because they are acted by humans.*

hum·ble (hum′bəl), **1** *adj.* not proud; modest: *a humble heart, to be humble in spite of success.* ■ See Synonym Study at **modest.** **2** *adj.* low in position or condition; not important or grand: *They lived in a humble, one-room cottage.* **3** *v.* to make humble; make lower in position, condition, or pride: *humbled by defeat.* ❏ *adj.* **hum·bler, hum·blest;** *v.* **hum·bled, hum·bling.** —**hum′ble·ness,** *n.* —**hum′bler,** *n.* —**hum′bly,** *adv.*

WORD STORY **Humble** comes from a Latin word meaning "dirt." **Humus** comes from the same word. Proud people look down on humble people, as people look down at the ground.

humble pie, eat humble pie, to be forced to do something very disagreeable and humiliating.

hum·bug (hum′bug′), **1** *n.* person who tries to deceive or cheat; fraud. **2** *n.* deception or pretense: *There's no humbug about her; she speaks her mind straight out.* **3** *v.* to deceive; cheat: *I won't be humbugged into buying inferior goods.* ❏ *v.* **hum·bugged, hum·bug·ging.**

hum·ding·er (hum ding′ər), *n.*INFORMAL. someone or something remarkable for its kind: *His new bike is a real humdinger.*

hum·drum (hum′drum′), *adj.* without variety; commonplace; dull: *a humdrum life.*

hu·mer·us (hyü′mər əs), *n.* the long bone in the upper part of the arm, from the shoulder to the elbow. ❏ *n., pl.* **hu·mer·i** (hyü′mə rī′). ■ Another word that sounds like this is **humorous.**

hu·mid (hyü′mid), *adj.* slightly wet; moist; damp: *The air is very humid near the sea.* —**hu′mid·ly,** *adv.*

hu·mi·dex (hyü′mə deks′), *n.* CANADIAN. a discomfort index based on humidity, temperature, and a dew point that is equal to the temperature.

hu·mid·i·fi·er (hyü mid′ə fī′ər), *n.* device for keeping air moist.

hu·mid·i·fy (hyü mid′ə fī), *v.* to make moist or damp. ❏ *v.* **hu·mid·i·fied, hu·mid·i·fy·ing.**

hu·mid·i·ty (hyü mid′ə tē), *n.* **1** moistness; dampness: *The humidity today is worse than the heat.* **2** amount of moisture in the air: *On a hot, sultry day the humidity is high.* [See Word Story at **humor.**]

hu·mil·i·ate (hyü mil′ē āt), *v.* to lower the pride, dignity, or self-respect of; make ashamed: *They humiliated me by criticizing me in front of my friends.* ■ See Synonym Study at **ashamed.** ❏ *v.* **hu·mil·i·at·ed, hu·mil·i·at·ing.** —**hu·mil′i·a′tion,** *n.*

hu·mil·i·ty (hyü mil′ə tē), *n.* humbleness of mind; lack of pride; meekness.

hum·ming·bird (hum′ing bėrd′), *n.* any of many very small, brightly colored American birds with long, thin bills and narrow wings that move so rapidly they make a humming sound.

hum·mock (hum′ək), *n.* **1** a very small, rounded hill; knoll; hillock. **2** a bump or ridge in a field of ice.

hum·mus (hum′əs *or* hùm′əs), *n.* mixture of chickpeas, boiled to a pulp and then pushed through a sieve, with sesame seed paste, oil, lemon juice, and minced garlic.

hu·mon·gous (hyü mung′gəs *or* hyü mong′gəs), *adj.* INFORMAL. extraordinarily large; huge: *a humongous snow storm that closed all the schools.*

hu·mor (hyü′mər), **1** *n.* funny or amusing quality: *I see no humor in your tricks.* **2** *n.* ability to see or show the funny or amusing side of things: *A sense of humor can help you overcome many problems.* **3** *n.* speech, writing, etc., showing this ability. **4** *n.* state of mind; mood; disposition; temper: *Is the teacher in a good humor this morning?* **5** *v.* to give in to someone's wishes; agree with; indulge: *to humor a sick child.*

out of humor, in a bad mood; angry; displeased; cross.

WORD STORY **Humor** comes from a Latin word meaning "be moist." People used to believe that body fluids controlled mood. Certain fluids, they thought, produced good humor and a sense of fun.

hu·mor·ist (hyü′mər ist), *n.* a humorous talker or writer; person who tells or writes jokes and funny stories.

hu·mor·less (hyü′mər lis), *adj.* without humor. —**hu′mor·less·ly,** *adv.* —**hu′mor·less·ness,** *n.*

hu·mor·ous (hyü′mər əs), *adj.* full of humor; funny; amusing: *I laughed at the humorous story.* ■ Another word that sounds like this is **humerus.** —**hu′mor·ous·ly,** *adv.* —**hu′mor·ous·ness,** *n.*

SYNONYM STUDY **Humorous, witty,** and **comic** all mean funny. **Humorous** is a general word: *It's a mystery story, but a humorous one.* **Witty** means clever and funny, especially with words: *Her witty letters are full of puns.* **Comic** means funny because of the things that happen: *The comic parts of this movie show disguises, mistakes, and accidents.*

hump (hump), **1** *n.* a rounded lump that sticks out: *Some camels have two humps on their backs.* **2** *v.* to raise or bend up into a hump: *The cat humped its back when it saw the dog.* **3** *n.* mound. [See word history information at **hunch.**] —**hump′like′,** *adj.*

hump·back (hump′bak′), *n.* **1** hunchback. **2** a back having a hump on it. **3** humpback whale.

hump·backed (hump′bakt′), *adj.* hunchbacked.

humpback whale, a large whale with a rounded back that has a humplike fin, and with long, narrow flippers. It is known for its songs.

humph (humpf), *interj., n.* exclamation expressing doubt, disgust, contempt, etc.

hu·mus (hyü′məs), *n.* a dark brown or black substance found in soil, formed from decayed living things. Humus holds water and contains valuable nutrients for plants. [See Word Story at **humble.**]

Hun (hun), *n.* **1** member of a warlike Asian people who invaded Europe in the A.D. 300s and 400s. **2** a barbarous, destructive person.

hunch (hunch), **1** *n.* a vague feeling or suspicion: *I had a hunch that it would rain, so I took along an umbrella.* **2** *n.* a hump. **3** *v.* to hump: *hunch your shoulders.* **4** *v.* to draw, bend, or form into a hump: *She sat hunched up with her chin on her knees.* ❏ *n., pl.* **hunch·es.** [**Hunch** and **hump** mean the same thing and sound alike. Do they come from the same word? No one knows. No one knows how either of these words came into English.]

hunch·back (hunch′bak′), *n.* **1** person with a backbone that curves outward, forming a hump on the back; humpback. **2** back having a hump on it.

hunch·backed (hunch′bakt′), *adj.* having a hump on the back; humpbacked.

hun·dred (hun′drəd), *n., adj.* ten times ten; 100. There are one hundred cents in a dollar.

hun·dredth (hun′drədth), *adj., n.* **1** next after the 99th; last in a series of 100. **2** one of 100 equal parts.

hung (hung), *v.* a past tense and a past participle of **hang**: *He hung up his cap. Your coat has hung here all day.* ■ See Usage Note at **hang**.

Hun·gar·i·an (hung gâr′ē ən), **1** *adj.* of Hungary, its people, or their language. **2** *n.* person born or living in Hungary. **3** *n.* language of Hungary.

WORD SOURCE Hungarian has given a number of words to the English language, including **coach, goulash, hussar, paprika, saber,** and **shako.**

Hun·gar·y (hung′gər ē), *n.* country in central Europe. Hungary was formerly a part of the empire of Austria-Hungary. *Capital:* Budapest.

hun·ger (hung′gər), **1** *n.* an uncomfortable or painful feeling in the stomach caused by having had nothing to eat. **2** *n.* desire or need for food: *I ate an apple to satisfy my hunger.* **3** *v.* to feel hunger; be hungry. **4** *n.* a strong desire; craving; longing: *to have a hunger for knowledge.* **5** *v.* to have a strong desire; crave; long: *The neglected child hungered for love and attention.*

hunger strike, refusal to eat until certain demands are granted, or as a protest against certain conditions.

hung jury, jury that cannot reach a unanimous verdict and is dismissed for that reason.

hun·gry (hung′grē), *adj.* **1** feeling a desire or need for food: *I missed breakfast and was hungry all morning.* **2** showing hunger: *The stray cat had a hungry look.* **3** having a strong desire or craving; eager: *Many young people are hungry for knowledge.* ❑ *adj.* **hun·gri·er, hun·gri·est.** —**hun′gri·ly,** *adv.* —**hun′gri·ness,** *n.*

hunk (hungk), *n.* **1** a big lump or piece: *a hunk of cheese.* **2** INFORMAL. a very muscular, good-looking man.

hunt (hunt), **1** *v.* to go after wild birds and other animals to catch or kill them for food or sport. **2** *n.* act of hunting: *They went on a duck hunt in the marsh.* **3** *n.* group of persons hunting together. **4** *v.* to search; seek; look for: *hunt through drawers, hunt for a lost book.* **5** *n.* an attempt to find something; search: *The hunt for the lost child continued until she was found.*

hunt·er (hun′tər), *n.* **1** person who hunts. **2** horse or dog trained for hunting.

hunt·er-gath·er·er (hun′tər gaᴛʜ′ər ər), *n.* member of a group of people who obtain food by hunting, fishing, gathering fruits and nuts, etc., and who grow little or none of their food as crops. Hunter-gatherers often roam the land in search of food.

hunt·ing (hun′ting), *n.* act or sport of chasing game.

Hunt·ing·ton (hunt′ing tən), *n.* city in SW West Virginia.

hunt·ress (hun′tris), *n.* woman who hunts. ❑ *n., pl.* **hunt·ress·es.**

hunts·man (hunts′mən), *n.* **1** hunter. **2** manager of a hunt. ❑ *n., pl.* **hunts·men.**

Hunts·ville (hunts′vil), *n.* city in N Alabama.

hur·dle (hėr′dl), **1** *n.* barrier for people or horses to jump over in a race. **2** *n.pl.* **hurdles,** race in which the runners jump over hurdles. **3** *v.* to jump over: *The horse hurdled both the fence and the ditch.* **4** *n.* something that stands in the way; obstacle, difficulty, etc. **5** *v.* to overcome an obstacle, difficulty, etc. ❑ *v.* **hur·dled, hur·dling.** —**hur′dler,** *n.*

hur·dy-gur·dy (hėr′dē gėr′dē), *n.* hand organ played by turning a handle. ❑ *n., pl.* **hur·dy-gur·dies.**

hurl (hėrl), *v.* **1** to throw with much force; fling: *hurl a spear.* **2** to throw forth words, cries, etc., violently: *They hurled insults at me.* —**hurl′er,** *n.*

hur·ly-bur·ly (hėr′lē bėr′lē), *n.* disorder and noise; commotion.

Hur·on (hyur′ən), *n.* **1** Lake, one of the five Great Lakes. **2** member of a group of American Indian tribes formerly living north of Lake Ontario, now living in Oklahoma and Quebec. ❑ *n., pl.* **Hu·rons** or **Hu·ron** for 2.

hur·rah (hə rä′ *or* hə rô′), **1** *interj., n.* a shout of joy, approval, etc.: *"Hurrah!" they shouted as the team scored again. Give a hurrah for the team!* **2** *v.* to shout hurrahs; cheer. Also, **hooray.**

hur·ray (hə rā′), *interj., n., v.* hurrah.

hur·ri·cane (hėr′ə kān), *n.* storm with violent wind and, usually, very heavy rain. Hurricanes are common in the West Indies and the Gulf of Mexico. The wind in a hurricane blows with a speed more than 75 miles (121 kilometers) per hour.

hurricane

hur·ried (hėr′ēd), *adj.* done or made in a hurry; hasty: *a hurried escape, a hurried reply.* —**hur′ried·ly,** *adv.*

hur·ry (hėr′ē), **1** *v.* to drive, carry, send, or move quickly: *They hurried the sick child to the doctor.* **2** *v.* to move or act with more than an easy or natural speed: *If you hurry, your work may be poor. She hurried to get to work on time.* **3** *n.* a hurried movement or action: *In his hurry he dropped the groceries.* **4** *n.* need to hurry; eagerness to have quickly or do quickly: *She was in a hurry to meet her friends.* **5** *v.* to urge to act soon or too soon: *The salesman hurried the customer to make a choice.* **6** *v.* to urge to great speed or to too great speed: *Don't hurry the driver.* **7** *v.* to make go on or occur more quickly; hasten: *Please hurry dinner.* ❑ *v.* **hur·ried, hur·ry·ing;** *n., pl.* **hur·ries.** —**hur′ri·er,** *n.*

SYNONYM STUDY **Hurry, hasten,** and **speed** all mean to go or do quickly. **Hurry** suggests a need to move fast: *Hurry, or you'll miss the bus.* **Hasten** means to move fast in order to do something: *On festival days, the people hasten to finish their labors so that they may begin celebrations.* **Speed** means to move very fast: *The runners sped toward the finish line.*

Hurs·ton (hėr′stən), *n.* **Zo·ra** Neale (zôr′ə nēl), 1901?-1960, American writer. ■ Zora Neale Hurston's best-known novel is *Their Eyes Were Watching God.* She also collected and published southern U.S. and Caribbean folklore and customs.

hurt (hėrt), **1** *v.* to cause pain to; wound; injure: *The stone hurt my foot.* **2** *n.* a cut, bruise, or fracture; any wound or injury: *A scratch is not a serious hurt.* **3** *v.* to suffer pain: *My hand hurts.* **4** *v.* to have a bad effect on; do damage or harm to: *Large price increases can hurt sales.* **5** *v.* to cause emotional pain to someone: *Did I hurt your feelings?* **6** *n.* a bad effect; damage; harm. ❑ *v.* **hurt, hurt·ing.** —**hurt′er,** *n.*

hurt·ful (hėrt′fəl), *adj.* causing pain, harm, or damage; injurious: *a mean and hurtful remark.* —**hurt′ful·ly,** *adv.* —**hurt′ful·ness,** *n.*

hur·tle (hėr′tl), *v.* to dash or drive violently; rush violently: *The express train hurtled past.* ❑ *v.* **hur·tled, hur·tling.**

hus·band (huz′bənd), **1** *n.* man who has a wife; a married man. **2** *v.* to manage carefully; be saving of: *to husband your strength.*

hus·band·man (huz′bənd mən), *n.* OLD USE. farmer. ❑ *n., pl.* **hus·band·men.**

hus·band·ry (huz′bən drē), *n.* **1** careful management of your affairs or resources; thrift: *To repair a leaking roof is good husbandry.* **2** farming; agriculture.

a	hat	ė	term	ô	order	ch	child	⟨a in about
ā	age	i	it	oi	oil	ng	long	e in taken
ä	far	ī	ice	ou	out	sh	she	ə ⟨i in pencil
â	care	o	hot	u	cup	th	thin	o in lemon
e	let	ō	open	u̇	put	ᴛʜ	then	u in circus
ē	equal	ȯ	saw	ü	rule	zh	measure	

hush (hush), **1** *v.* to stop making a noise; make or become silent or quiet: *The wind has hushed.* **2** *n.* silence; quiet; stillness. **3** *interj.* stop the noise! be silent! keep quiet! ❑ *n., pl.* **hush·es.**

hush up, 1 to keep from being told; stop discussion of: *The facts were hushed up to keep them secret.* **2** hush!

hush puppy, a small ball of fried cornmeal dough. ❑ *n., pl.* **hush pup·pies.**

husk (husk), **1** *n.* the dry outer covering of certain seeds or fruits. An ear of corn has a husk. **2** *n.* the dry or worthless outer covering of anything. **3** *v.* to remove the husk from: *Husk the corn before cooking it.* —**husk′er,** *n.*

husk·y[1] (hus′kē), *adj.* **1** big and strong: *a husky young man.* **2** sounding rough and deep: *A bad cold made her voice husky.* ❑ *adj.* **husk·i·er, husk·i·est.** —**husk′i·ly,** *adv.* —**husk′i·ness,** *n.*

hus·ky[2] or **Hus·ky** (hus′kē), *n.* **1** a strong, medium-sized, arctic sled dog that usually has a thick coat and a bushy tail; Siberian husky. **2** any arctic sled dog. ❑ *n., pl.* **hus·kies** or **Hus·kies.** [**Husky**[2] comes from **Eskimo.** These dogs are sometimes called "Eskimo dogs."]

hus·sar (hu̇ zär′), *n.* a lightly armed cavalry soldier in various European armies.

Hus·sein I (hu̇ sān′), born 1935, king of Jordan since 1952.

hus·sy (hus′ē *or* huz′ē), *n.* **1** an impolite, bad-mannered girl. **2** an immoral or promiscuous woman. ❑ *n., pl.* **hus·sies.** ■ **Hussy** is often considered offensive.

husky[2] (def. 1)—about 23 in. (58 cm) high at the shoulder

hus·tle (hus′əl), **1** *v.* to push or shove roughly or hurriedly; jostle rudely: *Guards hustled the demonstrators away from the mayor's office.* **2** *v.* to go or work quickly or with energy: *He had to hustle to get the lawn mowed before dinner.* **3** *v.* to rush roughly or hurriedly; push your way: *hustle along through the crowd.* **4** *n.* tireless energy. **5** *n.* hurried movement: *It was a hustle to get the dishes washed by seven o'clock.* **6** INFORMAL. *v.* to get or sell in a hurried, rough, or illegal manner: *hustle used cars, hustle stolen goods.* **7** INFORMAL. *n.* business or activity, often one that is illegal: *His hustle is selling fake concert tickets.* ❑ *v.* **hus·tled, hus·tling.** [**Hustle** comes from a Dutch word meaning "to shake." In English, **shake a leg** is another way of telling someone **to hurry.**]

hus·tler (hus′lər), *n.* **1** person who hustles. **2** a very energetic person.

Hus·ton (hüs′tən), *n.* **John,** 1906-1987, American movie director, screenwriter, and actor. He won an Academy Award for his movie *The Treasure of the Sierra Madre.*

hut (hut), *n.* a small, roughly built dwelling or crude shelter.

SYNONYM STUDY **Hut, cabin,** and **shed**[1] all mean a very small building. **Hut** means a small house: *The village huts have mud walls and straw roofs.* **Cabin** means a hut built of wood: *Lincoln was born in a log cabin.* **Shed** means a building smaller than a hut, for keeping things in: *Put the rake in the tool shed.*

hutch (huch), *n.* **1** box or pen for small animals. Rabbits are kept in hutches. **2** hut. **3** box; chest; bin. **4** cupboard with open shelves on the upper part for holding dishes, etc. ❑ *n., pl.* **hutch·es.**

Hut·ter·ite (hut′ə rīt′), *n.* member of a Mennonite sect that lives in Montana, South Dakota, and western Canada.

hutz·pah (hu̇ts′pə), *n.* SLANG. chutzpah.

huz·zah (hə zä′), **1** *interj., n.* a loud shout of joy, encouragement, or applause; hurrah. **2** *v.* to shout huzzahs; cheer.

Hwang Ho (hwäng′hō′), former spelling of **Huang He.**

hwy., highway.

hy·a·cinth (hī′ə sinth), *n.* a spring plant that grows from a bulb and has many small, fragrant flowers along its stem.

hy·brid (hī′brid), **1** *n.* offspring of two living things of different species, varieties, etc. The loganberry is a hybrid because it is a cross between a red raspberry and a blackberry. **2** *adj.* bred from two different species, varieties, etc. A mule is a hybrid animal. **3** *n.* anything of mixed origin. A word formed of parts from different languages is a hybrid. **4** *adj.* of mixed origin.

hy·brid·ize (hī′brə dīz), *v.* to cause to produce hybrids: *Botanists hybridize plants to get new varieties.* ❑ *v.* **hy·brid·ized, hy·brid·iz·ing.** —**hy′brid·i·za′tion,** *n.*

hy·dra (hī′drə), *n.* **1** any of several freshwater polyps with tube-like bodies and stinging tentacles. If a hydra's body is cut into pieces, each piece forms a new individual. **2 Hydra,** (in Greek myths) a monster with many snakelike heads. When one head was cut off, two or three grew in its place. Hercules finally killed it with fire. ❑ *n., pl.* **hy·dras, hy·drae** (hī′drē′).

hy·dran·gea (hī drān′jə), *n.* any of several bushes with large, showy clusters of white, pink, or blue flowers. ❑ *n., pl.* **hy·dran·geas.**

hy·drant (hī′drənt), *n.* a large, upright pipe with a valve for drawing water directly from a water main; hose connection on a street, road, etc.; fireplug. Hydrants are used to get water to put out fires and to wash the streets.

WORD FAMILY **Hydrant** and the words below are related. They all come from a Greek word meaning "water."

carbohydrate	hydra	hydrocarbon	hydroplane
dehydrate	hydrangea	hydroelectric	hydroponics
formaldehyde	hydraulic	hydrogen	

hy·drate (hī′drāt), **1** *n.* any chemical compound made when certain substances chemically unite with water. **2** *v.* to become or cause to become a hydrate; combine with water to form a hydrate. ❑ *v.* **hy·drat·ed, hy·drat·ing.** —**hy·dra′tion,** *n.*

hy·drau·lic (hī drȯ′lik), *adj.* **1** of or about hydraulics. **2** operated by the pressure of water or other liquids in motion: *a hydraulic press.* **3** hardening under water: *hydraulic cement.*

hy·drau·lics (hī drȯ′liks), *n.* science dealing with water and other liquids at rest or in motion, their uses in engineering, and the natural laws of their actions.

hy·dro (hī′drō), **1** *adj.* hydroelectric. **2** *n.* CANADIAN. **a** hydroelectric power. **b** electricity.

hydro-, *prefix.* water: *hydroelectric power = electric power from water.*

hy·dro·car·bon (hī′drō kär′bən), *n.* any of a class of chemical compounds containing only hydrogen and carbon. Gasoline is a mixture of hydrocarbons.

hy·dro·chlo·ric acid (hī′drə klôr′ik), a clear, colorless liquid containing hydrogen and chlorine, with a strong, sharp odor.

hy·dro·e·lec·tric (hī′drō i lek′trik), *adj.* producing electricity by using the power of moving water.

hy·dro·foil (hī′drə foil), *n.* **1** fin just below the water line of a boat that raises the hull out of the water at high speeds, decreasing friction and increasing the speed of the boat. **2** boat with hydrofoils.

hy·dro·gen (hī′drə jən), *n.* a colorless, odorless gas that burns easily. Hydrogen is a chemical element that weighs less than any other element. It combines with oxygen to form water and is present in most organic compounds. *Symbol:* H

hy·dro·gen·ate (hī droj′ə nāt *or* hī′drə jə nāt), *v.* to combine or treat with hydrogen. When vegetable oils are hydrogenated, they become solid fats. ❑ *v.* **hy·dro·gen·at·ed, hy·dro·gen·at·ing.**

hydrogen bomb, bomb that uses the fusion of atoms to cause an explosion of tremendous force; H-bomb; fusion bomb. It is many times more powerful than the atomic bomb.

hydrogen peroxide, a colorless compound of hydrogen and oxygen; peroxide. It is used in water solution as an antiseptic and to bleach hair.

hy·drol·y·sis (hī drol′ə sis), *n.* a chemical process in which a compound is broken down and changed into other compounds by taking up the elements of water.

hy·dro·lyze (hī′drə līz), *v.* to break down by hydrolysis. ❑ *v.* **hy·dro·lyzed, hy·dro·lyz·ing.** —**hy′dro·ly·za′tion,** *n.*

hy·drom·e·ter (hī drom′ə tər), *n.* device for measuring the specific gravity of a liquid.

hy·dro·pho·bi·a (hī′drə fō′bē ə), *n.* rabies.

hy·dro·plane (hī′drə plān), **1** *n.* a fast motorboat that glides on the surface of water. **2** *n.* seaplane. **3** *v.* to slide over the surface of water, for instance on the thin layer of water on a road during rain: *I could barely keep the car from hydroplaning.* ❑ *v.* **hy·dro·planed, hy·dro·plan·ing.**

hy·dro·pon·ics (hī′drə pon′iks), *n.* process or business of growing plants without soil by the use of water containing the necessary nutrients.

hy·dro·sphere (hī′drə sfir), *n.* water on the surface of the earth, sometimes also thought of as including the water vapor in the atmosphere.

hy·dro·ther·mal (hī′drə thèr′məl), *adj.* of or using water heated by the internal heat of the earth. —**hy′dro·ther′mal·ly,** *adv.*

hy·drot·ro·pism (hī drot′rə piz′əm), *n.* a tendency of plants or plant parts to turn or bend toward moisture. Hydrotropism causes roots to grow toward water.

hy·drous (hī′drəs), *adj.* containing water, usually in combination.

hy·drox·ide (hī drok′sīd), *n.* a chemical compound that contains a radical made up of an oxygen and a hydrogen atom.

hy·dro·zo·an (hī′drə zō′ən), **1** *n.* any of a group of sea animals with saclike bodies including hydras and jellyfish. **2** *adj.* of or belonging to this group.

hy·e·na (hī ē′nə), *n.* any of several wild, flesh-eating mammals of Africa and Asia that hunt at night. ❑ *n., pl.* **hy·e·nas.** [Hyena comes from a Greek word meaning "pig." Hyenas have bristles on their necks and backs like the bristles of pigs.]

hy·giene (hī′jēn), *n.* rules of health; science of keeping well.

hy·gien·ic (hī jē′nik *or* hī jen′ik), *adj.* **1** favorable to health; healthful; sanitary. **2** of health or hygiene. —**hy·gien′i·cal·ly,** *adv.*

hy·gien·ist (hī jē′nist), *n.* **1** an expert in hygiene. **2** dental hygienist.

hy·grom·e·ter (hī grom′ə tər), *n.* device for measuring the amount of moisture in the air.

hy·grom·e·try (hī grom′ə trē), *n.* the measurement of the amount of moisture in the air.

hy·gro·scope (hī′grə skōp), *n.* device that shows variations in the amount of moisture in the air.

hy·gro·scop·ic (hī′grə skop′ik), *adj.* **1** having to do with or able to be measured by a hygroscope. **2** absorbing or attracting moisture from the air.

hy·ing (hī′ing), *v.* a present participle of **hie.**

hy·men (hī′mən), *n.* a fold of mucous membrane that partially closes the vagina. —**hy′men·al,** *adj.*

hymn (him), *n.* **1** song in praise or honor of God. **2** any song of praise. ■ Another word that sounds like this is **him.** —**hymn′like′,** *adj.*

> **WORD STORY** **Hymn** comes from a Greek word, *hymnos,* meaning "song of praise." This is why it is spelled with a final *-n,* which people pronounced for hundreds of years—long enough to make the spelling permanent.

hym·nal (him′nəl), *n.* book of hymns.

hymn·book (him′bùk′), *n.* hymnal.

hype (hīp), INFORMAL. **1** *n.* publicity; advertisement: *The hype for the new album began months before it reached the stores.* **2** *v.* to seek favorable widespread attention; advertise; publicize; promote: *hype a new movie.* ❑ *v.* **hyped, hyp·ing.**

hy·per (hī′pər), *adj.* INFORMAL. excessively nervous, jumpy, or irritable: *He's so hyper he can't sit still.*

hyper-, *prefix.* more than usual; extremely: *hypersensitive = extremely sensitive.*

hy·per·ac·tive (hī′pər ak′tiv), *adj.* overactive, especially to an abnormal or unhealthy degree. People with attention deficit disorder are often also hyperactive. —**hy′per·ac·tiv′i·ty,** *n.*

hy·per·bo·la (hī pèr′bə lə), *n.* a curve formed when a cone is cut by a plane that is closer to the vertical than the side of the cone is. ❑ *n., pl.* **hy·per·bo·las.**

hy·per·bo·le (hī pèr′bə lē), *n.* an exaggerated statement used for effect and not meant to be taken literally, such as "I'm so hungry I could eat a horse."

hy·per·bol·ic (hī′pər bol′ik), *adj.* of, like, or using hyperbole; exaggerated; exaggerating.

hy·per·crit·i·cal (hī′pər krit′ə kəl), *adj.* too critical.

hy·per·o·pi·a (hī′pər ō′pē ə), *n.* farsightedness.

hy·per·sen·si·tive (hī′pər sen′sə tiv), *adj.* extremely sensitive: *hypersensitive to the slightest criticism.* —**hy′per·sen·si·tiv′i·ty,** *n.*

hy·per·ten·sion (hī′pər ten′shən), *n.* an abnormally high blood pressure.

hy·per·text (hī′pər tekst′), *n.* a system of storing and retrieving computer data that allows users to move rapidly from any item to a wide variety of related information. Related information may be of many different kinds, including text, sound, graphics, or other programs. The system encourages users to create connections between items, so that the number and form of relationships can change as the system is used.

hy·per·tro·phy (hī pèr′trə fē), **1** *n.* enlargement of a body part or organ. **2** *v.* to grow too big. ❑ *v.* **hy·per·tro·phied, hy·per·tro·phy·ing.**

hy·per·ven·ti·late (hī′pər ven′tl āt), *v.* to breathe in too much air or too often, as when anxious or excited. This lowers the carbon dioxide level of the blood, which produces dizziness, tingling sensations, etc. ❑ *v.* **hy·per·ven·ti·lat·ed, hy·per·ven·ti·lat·ing.** —**hy′per·ven′ti·la′tion,** *n.*

hyena—about 2 ft. (61 cm) high at the shoulder

hy·pha (hī′fə), *n.* one of the long, slender threadlike parts that form the body of most fungi. ❑ *n., pl.* **hy·phae** (hī′fē).

hy·phen (hī′fən), *n.* **1** mark (-) used to show that two or more words have been combined into a single term, as in *hide-and-seek.* A hyphen also shows that a word has been divided at the end of a line. **2** mark (-) used to join groups of numbers: *His Zip Code is 12345-6789.*

> **WORD STORY** **Hyphen** comes from Greek words meaning "under" and "one." The ancient Greeks put a line under parts of a word to show that it was one word. We put a hyphen between parts.

hy·phen·ate (hī′fə nāt), *v.* to join words or to divide a word by using a hyphen. ❑ *v.* **hy·phen·at·ed, hy·phen·at·ing.** —**hy′phen·a′tion,** *n.*

hyp·no·sis (hip nō′sis), *n.* condition resembling deep sleep, but more active, in which a person acts according to the suggestions of the person who brought about the condition.

hyp·not·ic (hip not′ik), **1** *adj.* of hypnosis or hypnotism. **2** *adj.* causing sleep. **3** *n.* drug or other means of causing sleep. —**hyp·not′i·cal·ly,** *adv.*

hyp·no·tism (hip′nə tiz′əm), *n.* **1** act of putting someone into a hypnotic state; a hypnotizing. **2** science dealing with hypnosis.

hyp·no·tist (hip′nə tist), *n.* person who has the ability to hypnotize other people.

a	hat	ė	term	ô	order	ch	child		
ā	age	i	it	oi	oil	ng	long		a in about
ä	far	ī	ice	ou	out	sh	she		e in taken
â	care	o	hot	u	cup	th	thin	ə	i in pencil
e	let	ō	open	ù	put	ᴛʜ	then		o in lemon
ē	equal	ò	saw	ü	rule	zh	measure		u in circus

hyp·no·tize (hip′nə tīz), v. **1** to put someone into a hypnotic state; cause hypnosis in. **2** to dominate or control by suggestion; cast a spell over: *The candidate's speech hypnotized her audience.* ◻ v. **hyp·no·tized, hyp·no·tiz·ing.** —**hyp′no·tiz′a·ble,** adj. —**hyp′no·tiz′er,** n.

hypnotize (def. 1)

hy·po[1] (hī′pō), n. a chemical compound used to treat photographic negatives and prints to keep them from fading. ◻ n., pl. **hy·pos.**

hy·po[2] (hī′pō), n. INFORMAL. hypodermic. ◻ n., pl. **hy·pos.**

hypo-, prefix. under; less than usual: *hypodermic = under the skin.*

hy·po·al·ler·gen·ic (hī′pō al′ər jen′ik), adj. having few or no ingredients that might cause an allergic response if eaten or used: *hypoallergenic cosmetics.*

hy·po·cen·ter (hī′pə sen′tər), n. the underground center of an earthquake, directly below the epicenter.

hy·po·chon·dri·a (hī′pə kon′drē ə), n. abnormal anxiety over your health; imaginary illness.

hy·po·chon·dri·ac (hī′pə kon′drē ak), n. person who imagines feeling ill, is often depressed, and worries unnecessarily about personal health.

hy·po·cot·yl (hī′pə kot′l), n. part of a plant embryo below the cotyledons, between the stem and the roots.

hy·poc·ri·sy (hi pok′rə sē), n. pretending to be what you are not, especially claiming to be very good or religious but not acting that way.

hyp·o·crite (hip′ə krit), n. person who pretends to be what he or she is not, especially someone who claims to be very good or religious but does not act that way. [**Hypocrite** comes from a Greek word meaning "actor." Like actors, hypocrites pretend to be other than who they really are.]

hyp·o·crit·i·cal (hip′ə krit′ə kəl), adj. of or like a hypocrite; insincere. —**hyp′o·crit′i·cal·ly,** adv.

hy·po·der·mic (hī′pə dèr′mik), **1** adj. injected or used to inject under the skin: *The doctor used a hypodermic needle.* **2** n. dose of medicine injected under the skin: *The doctor gave her a hypodermic to make her sleep.* **3** n. a hypodermic syringe.

hypodermic syringe, syringe fitted with a hollow needle, used to inject a dose of medicine beneath the skin, or to take out blood or other bodily fluid.

hy·po·gly·ce·mi·a (hī′pō glī sē′mē ə), n. a condition caused by a lowered level of sugar in the blood, usually because of the presence of too much insulin.

hy·po·ten·sion (hī′pō ten′shən), n. abnormally low blood pressure.

hy·pot·e·nuse (hī pot′n üs), n. the side of a right triangle opposite the right angle.

hy·po·thal·a·mus (hī′pō thal′ə məs), n. the section of the brain beneath the thalamus, controlling temperature, hunger, thirst, the pituitary gland, etc.

hy·po·ther·mi·a (hī′pō thèr′mē ə), n. a lower than normal body temperature, especially one low enough to cause harmful changes in the body. Hypothermia is produced by exposure to cold. —**hy′po·ther′mic,** adj.

hy·poth·e·sis (hī poth′ə sis), n. something assumed because it seems likely to be a true explanation; theory: *We began looking for her glasses with the hypothesis that they were probably in the living room somewhere.* ◻ n., pl. **hy·poth·e·ses** (hī poth′ə sēz′). [See Word Story at **suppose.**]

hy·poth·e·size (hī poth′ə sīz), v. **1** to make a hypothesis. **2** to assume; suppose. ◻ v. **hy·poth·e·sized, hy·poth·e·siz·ing.**

hy·po·thet·i·cal (hī′pə thet′ə kəl), adj. of or based on a hypothesis; assumed; supposed: *a hypothetical case.*

hy·rax (hī′raks), n. any of a group of small mammals of Africa and Asia. Hyraxes look something like woodchucks. ◻ n., pl. **hy·rax·es, hy·ra·ces** (hī′rə sēz′).

hys·te·rec·to·my (his′tə rek′tə mē), n. surgical removal of the uterus. ◻ n., pl. **hys·te·rec·to·mies.**

hys·te·ri·a (hi stir′ē ə or hi ster′ē ə), n. **1** excitement or emotion that is out of control: *When a fire broke out, fear of being trapped caused hysteria in the theater audience.* **2** a mental illness caused by anxiety or worry. Its physical symptoms may include blindness, paralysis, or stomach upsets.

hys·ter·ic (hi ster′ik), adj. hysterical.

hys·ter·i·cal (hi ster′ə kəl), adj. **1** unnaturally excited; emotional: *hysterical weeping.* **2** showing an unnatural lack of self-control; suffering from hysteria: *The hysterical child was unable to stop crying.* **3** of or caused by hysteria: *a hysterical fit.* **4** very funny: *Isn't that cartoon hysterical?* —**hys·ter′i·cal·ly,** adv.

SYNONYM STUDY **Hysterical, raving,** and **delirious** all mean very excited. **Hysterical** means uncontrollably excited: *You couldn't hear the band because of the audience's hysterical shrieking.* **Raving** means excited and talking wildly: *Raving with anger, the manager charged at the umpire.* **Delirious** suggests joyous excitement: *The candidate's supporters are delirious at her victory.*

hys·ter·ics (hi ster′iks), n.pl. fit of hysterical laughing and crying.

I¹ or **i** (ī), *n.* **1** the ninth letter of the English alphabet. **2** the Roman numeral for 1. ❑ *n., pl.* **I's** or **i's.**

I² (ī), *pron.* the person speaking or writing: *John said, "I am happy." I like my dog.* ■ Other words that sound like this are **ay, aye,** and **eye.**

> **WORD STORY** The pronoun **I** is written with a capital because in old handwritten manuscripts a small *i* was likely to get lost or get attached to another word. Using the capital letter helped keep it a separate word.

I, symbol for iodine.

i., **1** intransitive. **2** island.

I., **1** island. **2** isle.

IA, Iowa (used with postal Zip Code).

Ia., Iowa.

i·amb (ī′am *or* ī′amb), *n.* (in poetry) a measure or foot containing two syllables, an unaccented followed by an accented. EXAMPLE: "I think′| therefore′| I am′,"| Descartes′| announced′.

i·am·bic (ī am′bik), *adj.* of or containing iambs. Much English poetry is iambic.

-ian, *suffix.* form of **-an.**

I·ber·i·a (ī bir′ē ə), *n.* peninsula in SW Europe, containing Spain and Portugal.

i·bex (ī′beks), *n.* any of several wild goats of the Alps, mountains of the Middle East and Africa, and the Himalayas. Male ibex have large horns that curve backward. ❑ *n., pl.* **i·bex** or **i·bex·es.**

ibid., in the same place; in the same book, chapter, page, etc. Ibid. is used in footnotes to refer to the work previously mentioned.

-ibility, *suffix.* condition or fact of being ___ible: *defensibility = condition of being defensible.*

i·bis (ī′bis), *n.* any of numerous large, long-legged wading birds of warm regions, having long, downward-curving bills. The ancient Egyptians regarded the ibis as sacred. ❑ *n., pl.* **i·bis** or **i·bis·es.**

-ible, *suffix.* able to be ___ed: *perfectible = able to be perfected.*

ibn-Sa·ud (ib′ən sä üd′), *n.* **Ab·dul-A·ziz** (əb dùl′ a zēz′), 1880-1953, king of Saudi Arabia from 1932 to 1953.

Ib·sen (ib′sən), *n.* **Hen·rik** (hen′rik), 1828-1906, Norwegian playwright. His plays include *A Doll's House* and *Hedda Gabler.*

-ic, *suffix.* **1** of ___: *atmospheric = of the atmosphere.* **2** like ___; like that of ___: *heroic = like a hero.* **3** containing ___: *alcoholic = containing alcohol.*

-ical, suffix meaning the same as **-ic,** as in *historical, geometrical, economical.*

Ic·ar·us (ik′ər əs), *n.* (in Greek legends) the son of Daedalus. Using wings that Daedalus had made, Icarus flew so high that the sun melted the wax attaching his wings. He drowned in the sea.

a	hat	ė	term	ô	order	ch	child		a in about
ā	age	i	it	oi	oil	ng	long		e in taken
ä	far	ī	ice	ou	out	sh	she	ə	i in pencil
â	care	o	hot	u	cup	th	thin		o in lemon
e	let	ō	open	ů	put	ŦH	then		u in circus
ē	equal	ô	saw	ü	rule	zh	measure		

ICBM, intercontinental ballistic missile.

ICC or **I.C.C.,** Interstate Commerce Commission (an agency of the U.S. government to regulate the business of transportation across state borders, especially by road and railroad).

ice skater

ice (īs), **1** *n.* water made solid by cold; frozen water. **2** *n.* layer or surface of ice. **3** *v.* to make cool with ice; put ice in or around: *We iced the punch.* **4** *v.* to cover with ice. **5** *v.* to turn to ice; freeze. **6** *n.* a frozen dessert, usually one made of sweetened fruit juice. **7** *v.* to cover a cake with icing. **8** *v.* (in hockey) to shoot a puck from your own zone past the red line at the other end of the rink, against the rules. ❑ *v.* **iced, ic·ing.** —**ice′less,** *adj.* —**ice′-like′,** *adj.*

break the ice, to overcome first difficulties in talking or meeting.
cut no ice, to have little or no effect.
on thin ice, in a dangerous or difficult position.

ice age, 1 any of the times when large parts of the earth were covered with glaciers. **2** Usually, **Ice Age,** the most recent such time, when much of the Northern Hemisphere was covered with glaciers; Pleistocene.

ice·berg (īs′bėrg′), *n.* a large mass of ice, detached from a glacier and floating in the sea. About 90 percent of its mass is below the surface of the water. [Iceberg comes from a Dutch word meaning "ice mountain." The part of an iceberg above water may be hundreds of feet high.]

ice·boat (īs′bōt′), *n.* **1** a light, narrow frame on runners, fitted with sails for gliding on ice. **2** icebreaker.

ice·bound (īs′bound′), *adj.* **1** held fast by ice; frozen in. **2** shut in or obstructed by ice.

ice·box (īs′boks′), *n.* **1** (earlier) refrigerator. **2** an insulated box in which food is kept cool with ice. ❑ *n., pl.* **ice·box·es.**

ice·break·er (īs′brā′kər), *n.* **1** a strong boat used to break a channel through ice; iceboat. **2** anything that helps overcome first difficulties in talking or getting acquainted.

ice·cap (īs′kap′), *n.* a permanent thick covering of ice over a large area, as in Antarctica or Greenland.

ice-cold (īs′kōld′), *adj.* cold as ice.

ice cream, a smooth, frozen dessert made of various milk products, sweetened and flavored.

ice cube, a small, usually cubical piece of ice used for cooling drinks.

ice hockey, hockey played on ice with a puck.

Ice·land (īs′lənd), *n.* island country in the N Atlantic between Greenland and Norway, formerly a Danish possession. Iceland has been independent since 1944. *Capital:* Reykjavik.

Ice·land·er (īs′lan′dər), *n.* person born or living in Iceland.

Ice·lan·dic (īs lan′dik), **1** *adj.* of Iceland, its people, or their language. **2** *n.* language of Iceland.

Icelandic has given many words to the English language, including the words below.

anger	oaf	sister	ugly
calf²	odd	skirt	Viking
egg¹	outlaw	sky	weak
egg²	ransack	sleuth	wheeze
get	reindeer	tatter	window
leak	scant	tight	wing
loft	scare	trust	wrong

ice·man (īs′man′), *n.* (earlier) a person who sells, delivers, or handles ice. ❑ *n., pl.* **ice·men.**

ice milk, a frozen dessert like ice cream but made of skim milk instead of cream.

ice pack, 1 a large area of masses of ice floating close together in the sea. **2** bag containing ice for placing on a sore or injured body part.

ice pick, a sharp-pointed hand tool for breaking up ice.

ice sheet, a broad, thick sheet of ice covering a very large area for a long time, especially during an ice age.

ice skate, 1 a shoe with a metal runner attached for skating on ice; skate. **2** the metal runner itself.

ice-skate (īs′skāt′), *v.* to skate on ice. ❑ *v.* **ice-skat·ed, ice-skat·ing.**

ice ska·ter (skā′tər), person who ice-skates.

ice storm, a storm in which rain freezes solid on contact with all surfaces, causing widespread breakage of tree branches and utility lines.

ice water, water cooled with ice.

ich·neu·mon (ik nü′mən), *n.* **1** a large, gray mongoose of Africa, Southern Europe, and the Middle East. It somewhat resembles a weasel. **2** ichneumon wasp.

ichneumon wasp, any of many wasplike insects that do not sting. The larvae are parasites of caterpillars and other insects.

ich·thy·ol·o·gy (ik′thē ol′ə jē), *n.* branch of zoology dealing with fishes. —**ich′thy·ol′o·gist,** *n.*

ich·thy·o·saur (ik′thē ə sôr′), *n.* large fishlike reptile, now extinct, that lived in the sea. It had a long beak, paddlelike flippers, and a tail with a large fin.

i·ci·cle (ī′si kəl), *n.* a pointed, hanging stick of ice formed by the freezing of dripping water.

ic·ing (ī′sing), *n.* frosting.

i·con (ī′kon), *n.* **1** a picture; image. **2** a small picture on a computer screen that stands for a file, program, or software command that may be selected with a cursor. **3** a picture or image of Jesus, an angel, or a saint. Icons are sacred in the Eastern Church.

i·con·o·clast (ī kon′ə klast), *n.* **1** someone who attacks cherished beliefs or institutions. **2** someone opposed to worshiping images. —**i·con′o·clas′tic,** *adj.* —**i·con′o·clas′ti·cal·ly,** *adv.*

Iconoclast comes from Greek words meaning "image breaker," which describes someone who actually destroys religious pictures or statues. The meaning of the word was extended to include anyone who tries to break down strongly held beliefs.

ICU, intensive care unit.

i·cy (ī′sē), *adj.* **1** like ice; very cold: *icy fingers.* **2** covered with ice; slippery: *icy streets.* **3** of ice: *an icy snowball.* **4** without warm feeling; cold and unfriendly: *an icy stare.* ❑ *adj.* **i·ci·er, i·ci·est.** —**i′ci·ly,** *adv.* —**i′ci·ness,** *n.*

I'd (īd), **1** I should. **2** I would. **3** I had.

ID or **I.D.,** ID card.

ID, Idaho (used with postal Zip Code).

Id. or **Ida.,** Idaho.

I·da·ho (ī′də hō), *n.* one of the Western states of the United States. *Abbreviation:* ID, Id., or Ida. *Capital:* Boise. [Idaho may have come from an Apache name for the Comanche.] —**I′da·ho′an,** *n.*

Idaho Falls, city in E Idaho.

ID card, card, usually with a photograph attached, issued to someone to prove his or her identity, age, etc.

i·de·a (ī dē′ə), *n.* **1** belief, plan, or picture in the mind: *Swimming is my idea of fun.* **2** thought, fancy, or opinion: *I had no idea that the job would be so difficult.* **3** point or purpose: *The idea of this vacation was to get a rest.* ❑ *n., pl.* **i·de·as.** —**i·de′a·less,** *adj.*

Idea, inspiration, and impression all mean a picture or plan formed in the mind. Idea, the general word, means any mental picture or plan: *She had an idea of where to put the new piano.* Inspiration means a sudden, very good idea: *He had an inspiration for a surprise ending to his story.* Impression suggests an idea that is not very clear: *They had the impression that the clown was watching them.*

i·de·al (ī dē′əl), **1** *n.* a perfect type; model to be imitated; what you would wish to be: *Her mother is her ideal.* **2** *n.* a standard or concept of perfection: *The house was far from their ideal, but it was the best they could afford.* **3** *n.* goal; principle: *a person with high ideals.* **4** *adj.* just as you would wish; perfect: *A warm, sunny day is ideal for a picnic.* ■ See Synonym Study at **perfect.** —**i·de′al·less,** *adj.*

i·de·al·ism (ī dē′ə liz′əm), *n.* **1** practice of acting according to your ideals of what ought to be, regardless of what happens or of what other people may think; a cherishing of fine ideals. **2** act of neglecting practical matters in following ideals; not being practical. **3** belief that reality is made of ideas only and not of material objects.

i·de·al·ist (ī dē′ə list), *n.* **1** person who has high ideals and acts according to them. **2** person who neglects practical matters in following ideals.

i·de·al·is·tic (ī/dē ə lis′tik *or* ī dē′ə lis′tik), *adj.* **1** having high ideals and acting according to them. **2** forgetting or neglecting practical matters in trying to live your ideals; not practical. **3** of idealism or idealists. —**i′de·al·is′ti·cal·ly,** *adv.*

i·de·al·ize (ī dē′ə līz), *v.* to make ideal; think of or represent as perfect rather than as is actually true: *He idealized his older sister and thought that everything she did was right.* ❑ *v.* **i·de·al·ized, i·de·al·iz·ing.** —**i·de′al·i·za′tion,** *n.* —**i·de′al·iz′er,** *n.*

i·de·al·ly (ī dē′ə lē), *adv.* **1** according to an ideal; perfectly. **2** only as an idea or theory; not really.

i·den·ti·cal (ī den′tə kəl), *adj.* **1** the same: *Both events happened on the identical day.* **2** exactly alike: *identical bicycles.* —**i·den′ti·cal·ly,** *adv.* —**i·den′ti·cal·ness,** *n.*

identical twins, twins of the same sex and physical appearance coming from a single fertilized egg cell rather than from two egg cells as fraternal twins do.

identical twins

i·den·ti·fi·ca·tion (ī den′tə fə kā′shən), *n.* **1** act of identifying or condition of being identified. **2** something used to identify someone or something: *He offered his driver's license as identification.*

i·den·ti·fy (ī den′tə fī), *v.* **1** to recognize as being, or show to be, a particular person or thing; prove to be the same: *She identified the wallet as hers by describing it.* **2** to make the same; treat as the same: *The king identified his people's good with his own.* **3** to connect closely; associate: *identify with a political party.* ❑ *v.* **i·den·ti·fied, i·den·ti·fy·ing.** —**i·den′ti·fi′a·ble,** *adj.* —**i·den′ti·fi′a·bly,** *adv.* —**i·den′ti·fi′er,** *n.*

i·den·ti·ty (ī den′tə tē), *n.* **1** who or what you are: *The writer concealed her identity by signing her stories with a pen name.* **2** exact likeness; sameness: *The identity of the two crimes led the police to think that the same person committed them.* **3** condition or fact of being the same one: *The museum established the identity of the painting with one described in an old document.* **4** identity element. **5** (in algebra) an equation that remains true whatever number replaces each letter, as: $(x - y)^2 = x^2 - 2xy + y^2$. ❑ *n., pl.* **i·den·ti·ties.**

identity element, (in mathematics) an element of a set that does not change any other element it is combined with under a specific operation; identity. The identity element for addition is 0. The identity element for multiplication is 1.

id·e·o·gram (id′ē ə gram *or* ī′dē ə gram), *n.* ideograph.

id·e·o·graph (id′ē ə graf *or* ī′dē ə graf), *n.* a graphic symbol that represents a thing or an idea directly, without representing the sounds of the word for the thing or idea. Most Egyptian hieroglyphics and some Chinese characters are ideographs.

i·de·ol·o·gy (ī/dē ol′ə jē *or* id′ē ol′ə jē), *n.* set of doctrines or body of opinions that a group of people have. A political party or movement usually has an ideology. ❑ *n., pl.* **i·de·ol·o·gies.** —**i′de·o·log′i·cal,** *adj.* —**i′de·o·log′i·cal·ly,** *adv.*

ides (īdz), *n.pl. or sing.* (in the ancient Roman calendar) the 15th day of March, May, July, and October, and the 13th day of the other months.

id·i·o·cy (id′ē ə sē), *n.* **1** great stupidity. **2** a foolish act or statement, ❑ *n., pl.* **id·i·o·cies** for 2.

id·i·om (id′ē əm), *n.* **1** phrase or expression whose meaning cannot be understood from the ordinary meanings of the words in it. "Hold your tongue" is an English idiom meaning "keep quiet." **2** the language or dialect of a particular area or group: *the idiom of the French Canadians.* **3** a people's way of expressing themselves: *It is often hard to translate English into the French idiom.*

id·i·o·mat·ic (id′ē ə mat′ik), *adj.* **1** containing an idiom; having or using idioms. **2** showing the individual character of a language; characteristic of a particular language: *The American spoke excellent idiomatic French.* —**id′i·o·mat′i·cal·ly,** *adv.*

id·i·o·syn·cra·sy (id′ē ō sing′krə sē), *n.* a personal peculiarity: *One of his idiosyncrasies was eating a hamburger for breakfast.* ❑ *n., pl.* **id·i·o·syn·cra·sies.**

id·i·o·syn·crat·ic (id′ē ō sin krat′ik), *adj.* of or caused by idiosyncrasy. —**id′i·o·syn·crat′i·cal·ly,** *adv.*

id·i·ot (id′ē ət), *n.* a very stupid or foolish person: *Like an idiot I lost the key.*

WORD STORY Idiot comes from a Greek word originally meaning "private person," used to describe someone who did not take part in government. Because the ancient Greeks believed that any intelligent and informed person was interested in government, the word took on an insulting meaning.

id·i·ot·ic (id′ē ot′ik), *adj.* very stupid or foolish. —**id′i·ot′i·cal·ly,** *adv.*

i·dle (ī′dl), **1** *adj.* doing nothing; not busy; not working: *the idle hours of a holiday, idle hands.* ■ See Synonym Study at **lazy.** **2** *adj.* fond of doing nothing; not willing to work; lazy: *an idle student.* **3** *adj.* not in operation; inactive: *idle factories.* **4** *adj.* without any good reason: *idle rumors.* **5** *v.* to be idle; do nothing: *Are you going to spend your whole vacation just idling?* **6** *v.* to cause someone or something to be idle; take out of work or use: *A strike idled the factory workers.* **7** *v.* to spend or waste time: *She idled away many hours lying in the hammock.* **8** *v.* to run slowly without transmitting power. The motor of a car idles when out of gear and running slowly. ❑ *adj.* **i·dler, i·dlest;** *v.* **i·dled, i·dling.** ■ Other words that sound like this are **idol** and **idyll.** —**i′dle·ness,** *n.* —**i′dly,** *adv.*

i·dler (ī′dlər), *n.* a lazy person.

i·dol (ī′dl), *n.* **1** image or something else worshiped as a god. **2** someone or something that is loved or admired very much. ■ Other words that sound like this are **idle** and **idyll.**

i·dol·a·ter (ī dol′ə tər), *n.* person who worships idols.

i·dol·a·trous (ī dol′ə trəs), *adj.* **1** worshiping idols. **2** of or relating to idolatry. **3** blindly adoring. —**i·dol′a·trous·ly,** *adv.* —**i·dol′a·trous·ness,** *n.*

i·dol·a·try (ī dol′ə trē), *n.* **1** worship of idols. **2** worship of someone or something; extreme devotion: *The queen was adored to the point of idolatry.*

a	hat	ė	term	ô	order	ch	child		
ā	age	i	it	oi	oil	ng	long		a in about
ä	far	ī	ice	ou	out	sh	she		e in taken
â	care	o	hot	u	cup	th	thin	ə	i in pencil
e	let	ō	open	u̇	put	ŧн	then		o in lemon
ē	equal	ȯ	saw	ü	rule	zh	measure		u in circus

i·dol·ize (ī′dl īz), *v.* **1** to love or admire very much; be extremely devoted to: *Some baseball fans idolize their favorite players.* **2** to worship as an idol; make an idol of: *The ancient Hebrews idolized the golden calf.* ❑ *v.* **i·dol·ized, i·dol·iz·ing.** —**i′dol·i·za′tion,** *n.* —**i′dol·iz′er,** *n.*

i·dyll (ī′dl), *n.* **1** description in poetry or prose of a simple and charming scene or event of country life. **2** a simple and charming scene or event suitable for such a description. ■ Other words that sound like this are **idle** and **idol.**

i·dyl·lic (ī dil′ik), *adj.* suitable for an idyll; simple and charming. —**i·dyl′li·cal·ly,** *adv.*

i.e., that is; that is to say; namely. ■ The abbreviation **i.e.** is seldom used except in reference books. Ordinarily the phrase *that is* is used instead.

if (if), *conj.* **1** supposing that; on condition that; in case: *Come if you can. If it rains tomorrow, we shall stay at home.* **2** whether: *I wonder if they will go.* **3** although; even though: *It was a welcome if unexpected holiday.* **4** *If* is used to begin an exclamation of surprise, wishing, etc.: *If I had only known!*

if·fy (if′ē), *adj.* having unknown qualities or conditions; doubtful: *an iffy undertaking.* ❑ *adj.* **if·fi·er, if·fi·est.**

-ify, *suffix.* to make or become ___: *simplify = make simple; solidify = become solid.*

ig·loo (ig′lü), *n.* an Eskimo hut shaped like a dome, often built of blocks of hard snow. ❑ *n., pl.* **ig·loos.**

ig·ne·ous (ig′nē əs), *adj.* formed by the cooling of melted rock either below or on the surface of the earth. *Granite is an igneous rock.*

ig·nite (ig nīt′), *v.* **1** to set on fire: *A spark from the campfire ignited the dry grass.* ■ See Synonym Study at **kindle. 2** to take fire; begin to burn: *Gasoline ignites easily.* ❑ *v.* **ig·nit·ed, ig·nit·ing.** —**ig·nit′a·ble** or **ig·nit′i·ble,** *adj.* —**ig·nit′er** or **ig·nit′or,** *n.*

ig·ni·tion (ig nish′ən), *n.* **1** switch for turning on a vehicle's ignition with a key. **2** apparatus for igniting the fuel vapor in the cylinders of an internal-combustion engine. *Spark plugs are part of the ignition.* **3** act or process of setting something on fire or catching fire.

ig·no·ble (ig nō′bəl), *adj.* without honor; disgraceful; base: *To betray a friend is ignoble.* —**ig′no·bil′i·ty,** *n.* —**ig·no′ble·ness,** *n.* —**ig·no′bly,** *adv.*

ig·no·min·i·ous (ig′nə min′ē əs), *adj.* shameful; disgraceful; dishonorable: *After an ignominious defeat the army surrendered.* —**ig′no·min′i·ous·ly,** *adv.* —**ig′no·min′i·ous·ness,** *n.*

ig·no·min·y (ig′nə min′ē), *n.* public shame and disgrace; dishonor.

ig·no·ra·mus (ig′nə rā′məs), *n.* an ignorant person. ❑ *n., pl.* **ig·no·ra·mus·es.** [**Ignoramus** comes from a Latin word meaning "we do not know."]

ig·no·rance (ig′nər əns), *n.* lack of knowledge; condition of being ignorant.

ig·no·rant (ig′nər ənt), *adj.* **1** knowing little or nothing; without knowledge. *A person who has not had much chance to learn may be ignorant but not stupid: People who live in the city are often ignorant of farm life.* **2** caused by or showing lack of knowledge: *Saying that the earth is flat is an ignorant remark.* **3** uninformed; unaware: *He was ignorant of the fact that Paris is the capital of France.* —**ig′nor·ant·ly,** *adv.*

ig·nore (ig nôr′), *v.* to pay no attention to; disregard: *The driver ignored the traffic light and almost hit another car.* ❑ *v.* **ig·nored, ig·nor·ing.** —**ig·nor′a·ble,** *adj.* —**ig·nor′er,** *n.*

i·gua·na (i gwä′nə), *n.* any of various large tropical American lizards with a spiny crest along the back. ❑ *n., pl.* **i·gua·nas.**

iguana—about 5 ft. (1.5 m) long

IL, Illinois (used with postal Zip Code).

Il·i·ad (il′ē əd), *n.* a Greek epic poem about the siege of Troy. Homer is supposed to be its author.

ilk (ilk), *n.* class; kind; sort: *cattle rustlers, bank robbers, and others of that ilk.*

ill (il), **1** *adj.* in poor health; having some disease; not sound in body or mind; not well; sick: *ill with a fever.* ■ See Synonym Study at **sick[1]. 2** *adj.* bad; evil; harmful: *an ill wind, do a person an ill turn.* **3** *adv.* badly; harmfully: *Strength is ill used in destroying property.* **4** *adj.* not good; not proper; imperfect; faulty: *ill manners.* **5** *adj.* feeling nausea; nauseated. **6** *n.* Often, **ills,** *pl.* evil; harm; trouble: *Poverty and hunger are among the ills of our society.* **7** *n.* something unfavorable or unkind: *I can think no ill of him.* **8** *adv.* in an unkind manner; harshly; cruelly: *He speaks ill of his former friend.* **9** *adv.* with trouble or difficulty; scarcely: *You can ill afford to waste your money.* ❑ *adj., adv.* **worse, worst.**

ill at ease, uncomfortable.

I'll (īl), **1** I shall. **2** I will. ■ Other words that sound like this are **aisle** and **isle.**

ill., **1** illustrated. **2** illustration.

Ill., Illinois.

ill-ad·vised (il′əd vīzd′), *adj.* acting or done without enough thought; unwise.

ill-bred (il′bred′), *adj.* badly brought up; impolite; rude.

il·le·gal (i lē′gəl), *adj.* not lawful; against the law; forbidden by law. —**il·le′gal·ly,** *adv.*

il·le·gal·i·ty (il′ē gal′ə tē), *n.* **1** condition of being illegal; unlawfulness. **2** an illegal act. ❑ *n., pl.* **il·le·gal·i·ties** for 2.

il·leg·i·ble (i lej′ə bəl), *adj.* very hard or impossible to read; not plain enough to read. —**il·leg′i·bil′i·ty,** *n.* —**il·leg′i·ble·ness,** *n.* —**il·leg′i·bly,** *adv.*

il·le·git·i·mate (il′i jit′ə mit), *adj.* **1** not according to the law or the rules. **2** born of parents who are not married to each other. —**il′le·git′i·mate·ly,** *adv.*

ill-fat·ed (il′fā′tid), *adj.* **1** sure to have a bad fate or end. **2** bringing bad luck; unlucky.

ill-fa·vored (il′fā′vərd), *adj.* **1** not pleasant to look at; ugly. **2** unpleasant; offensive.

ill feeling, suspicious dislike; mistrust.

ill-got·ten (il′got′n), *adj.* acquired by evil or unfair means; dishonestly obtained: *ill-gotten gains.*

ill-hu·mored (il′hyü′mərd), *adj.* cross; unpleasant. —**ill′-hu′mored·ly,** *adv.*

il·lib·er·al (i lib′ər əl), *adj.* **1** not liberal; narrow-minded; prejudiced. **2** stingy; miserly. —**il·lib′er·al·ly,** *adv.*

il·lic·it (i lis′it), *adj.* not permitted by law; forbidden. ■ Another word that sounds like this is **elicit.** ■ See Usage Note at **elicit.** —**il·lic′it·ly,** *adv.* —**il·lic′it·ness,** *n.*

il·lim·it·a·ble (i lim′ə tə bəl), *adj.* without limit; boundless; infinite. —**il·lim′it·a·bly,** *adv.*

Il·li·nois (il′ə noi′), *n.* one of the north central states of the United States. *Abbreviation:* IL or Ill. *Capital:* Springfield. [**Illinois** comes from a local Native American word meaning "person" or "man." Members of this tribe called themselves "the people."] —**Il′li·nois′an** (il′ə noi′ən *or* il′ə noiz′ən), *n.*

il·lit·er·a·cy (i lit′ər ə sē), *n.* lack of knowledge of how to read and write.

il·lit·er·ate (i lit′ər it), **1** *adj.* not knowing how to read and write: *People who have never gone to school are usually illiterate.* **2** *n.* person who does not know how to read and write. **3** *adj.* showing a lack of education: *illiterate writing.* **4** *n.* an uneducated person. ■ See Synonym Study at **ignorant.** —**il·lit′er·ate·ly,** *adv.*

ill-man·nered (il/man/ərd), *adj.* having or showing bad manners; impolite; rude. —**ill/-man/nered·ly**, *adv.*

ill-na·tured (il/nā/chərd), *adj.* cross; disagreeable. —**ill/na/-tured·ly**, *adv.*

ill·ness (il/nis), *n.* an abnormal, unhealthy condition; disease; sickness. ❏ *n., pl.* **ill·ness·es.**

il·log·i·cal (i loj/ə kəl), *adj.* **1** contrary to the principles of sound reasoning; not logical: *Your illogical behavior worries me.* **2** not reasonable; foolish: *an illogical fear of the dark.* —**il·log/i·cal·ly**, *adv.* —**il·log/i·cal·ness**, *n.*

ill-starred (il/stärd/), *adj.* unlucky; unfortunate.

ill-suit·ed (il/sü/tid), *adj.* poorly suited; not fit or proper; unsuitable: *ill-suited to the job.*

ill-tem·pered (il/tem/pərd), *adj.* having or showing a bad temper; often angry or annoyed; cross. —**ill/-tem/pered·ly**, *adv.*

ill-timed (il/tīmd/), *adj.* coming at a bad time; not appropriate.

ill-treat (il/trēt/), *v.* to treat badly or cruelly; do harm to; abuse. —**ill-treat/ment**, *n.*

il·lu·mi·nate (i lü/mə nāt), *v.* **1** to light up; make bright: *The room was illuminated by four large lamps.* **2** to make clear; explain: *Our teacher could illuminate almost any subject we studied.* **3** to decorate with gold, colors, pictures, and designs. The letters and pages in some old books and manuscripts were illuminated. ❏ *v.* **il·lu·mi·nat·ed, il·lu·mi·nat·ing.** —**il·lu/mi·na·tive**, *adj.* —**il·lu/mi·na/tor**, *n.*

il·lu·mi·na·tion (i lü/mə nā/-shən), *n.* **1** act of lighting something up or making it bright. **2** amount of light; light. **3** act of

illuminate (def. 3)—illuminated manuscript

making clear; explanation. **4** decoration with many lights. **5** decoration of letters or pages in books with gold, colors, pictures, and designs.

il·lu·mine (i lü/mən), *v.* to make bright; illuminate: *A smile illumined his face.* ❏ *v.* **il·lu·mined, il·lu·min·ing.**

illus., **1** illustrated. **2** illustration.

ill-us·age (il/yü/sij), *n.* bad, cruel, or unfair treatment.

ill-use (il/yüz/ *for verb;* il/yüs/ *for noun*), **1** *v.* to treat badly, cruelly, or unfairly. **2** *n.* bad, cruel, or unfair treatment. ❏ *v.* **ill-used, ill-us·ing.**

il·lu·sion (i lü/zhən), *n.* **1** something that appears to be different from what it actually is: *The highway gave the illusion of becoming narrower in the distance.* **2** a false notion or belief: *They have the illusion that wealth is the chief source of happiness.* [**Illusion** comes from Latin words meaning "at play." Play often includes make-believe and pretending things that are not real.]

il·lu·sive (i lü/siv), *adj.* illusory. ■ Another word that sounds like this is **elusive.** —**il·lu/sive·ly**, *adv.* —**il·lu/sive·ness**, *n.*

il·lu·so·ry (i lü/sər ē), *adj.* due to an illusion; misleading; deceptive.

il·lus·trate (il/ə strāt *or* i lus/trāt), *v.* **1** to make clear or explain by stories, examples, comparisons, etc.: *The way that a pump works is used to illustrate how the heart sends blood around the body.* **2** to provide with pictures, diagrams, maps, etc., that explain or decorate: *This book is well illustrated.* ❏ *v.* **il·lus·trat·ed, il·lus·trat·ing.**

il·lus·tra·tion (il/ə strā/shən), *n.* **1** picture, diagram, map, etc., used to explain or decorate something. **2** story, example, comparison, etc., used to make clear or explain something: *An apple cut into four equal pieces is a good illustration of what ¼ means.* **3** act or process of illustrating: *Her illustration of how to build a bookcase taught us a lot.*

il·lus·tra·tive (i lus/trə tiv *or* il/ə strā/tiv), *adj.* used to illustrate; helping to explain: *A good teacher uses many illustrative examples to explain difficult ideas.* —**il·lus/tra·tive·ly**, *adv.*

il·lus·tra·tor (il/ə strā/tər), *n.* artist who makes pictures to be used as illustrations.

il·lus·tri·ous (i lus/trē əs), *adj.* very famous; great; outstanding: *an illustrious leader.* —**il·lus/tri·ous·ly**, *adv.* —**il·lus/tri·ous·ness**, *n.*

ill will, unkind or unfriendly feeling; dislike; spite: *I bear no ill will toward those who defeated me.*

I'm (īm), I am.

im·age (im/ij), *n.* **1** likeness or copy: *She saw her image in the mirror. She is almost the exact image of her mother.* **2** likeness made of stone, wood, or some other material; statue: *The shelf was full of little images of all sorts of animals.* **3** likeness of an object or person produced by a mirror or through a lens. **4** picture in the mind; idea: *I no longer have a clear image of him.* **5** a comparison, description, or figure of speech that helps the mind to form forceful or beautiful pictures. Poetry often contains images. **6** impression that a person, group, or organization presents to the public.

im·age·ry (im/ij rē), *n.* **1** pictures formed in the mind; things imagined. **2** comparisons, descriptions, and figures of speech that help the mind to form forceful or beautiful pictures. Poetry often contains imagery.

i·mag·i·na·ble (i maj/ə nə bəl), *adj.* able to be imagined; possible: *We had the best time imaginable at the party.* —**i·mag/i·na·bly**, *adv.*

i·mag·i·nar·y (i maj/ə ner/ē), *adj.* existing only in the imagination; not real: *Elves are imaginary. The equator is an imaginary circle around the earth.*

SYNONYM STUDY **Imaginary, unreal,** and **fanciful** all mean existing only in the mind. **Imaginary** means existing in the imagination: *He has an imaginary friend who lives under the stairs.* **Unreal** calls attention to the fact that something does not actually exist: *The talking fish in my dream was unreal but interesting.* **Fanciful** suggests that something shows much imagination: *The fanciful characters in her drawings are the best feature in our school paper.*

imaginary number, the square root or other even root of a negative number, or any expression involving such a root. $\sqrt{-1}$, $3 = \sqrt{-15}$, $\sqrt{-4} = 2\sqrt{-1}$ are imaginary numbers.

i·mag·i·na·tion (i maj/ə nā/shən), *n.* **1** power of forming pictures or images in the mind of things not present to the senses. A poet, artist, or inventor must have imagination to create new things or ideas or to combine old ones in new forms. **2** thing imagined; creation of the mind; fancy.

i·mag·i·na·tive (i maj/ə nə tiv), *adj.* **1** full of imagination; showing imagination: *Fairy tales are imaginative.* **2** having a good imagination; able to imagine well; fond of imagining: *The imaginative child made up stories about life on other planets.* **3** of imagination. —**i·mag/i·na·tive·ly**, *adv.* —**i·mag/i·na·tive·ness**, *n.*

i·mag·ine (i maj/ən), *v.* **1** to picture in your mind; form an image or idea of: *The girl likes to imagine herself a doctor.* **2** to suppose; guess: *I cannot imagine what you mean.* ❏ *v.* **i·mag·ined, i·mag·in·ing.**

SYNONYM STUDY **Imagine, fancy,** and **daydream** all mean to form a mental picture of something. **Imagine,** the general word, means to form a picture in one's mind: *The captain imagined piloting one of the new cargo planes.* **Fancy** suggests imagining something unreal and unlikely to happen: *Short as he is, he likes to fancy himself slam-dunking the basketball.* **Daydream** means to spend time playing with pleasant mental pictures: *I was daydreaming about taking a trip around the world.*

i·ma·go (i mā/gō), *n.* insect in the final adult stage, especially a winged stage. ❏ *n., pl.* **i·ma·goes, i·mag·i·nes** (i maj/ə nēz).

i·mam (i mäm/), *n.* **1** a Muslim leader or chief. **2** a Muslim priest.

im·bal·ance (im bal/əns), *n.* lack of balance.

im·be·cile (im/bə səl), **1** *n.* a very stupid or foolish person. **2** *adj.* very stupid or foolish. —**im/be·cile·ly**, *adv.* —**im·be·cil·ic** (im/bə·sil/ik), *adj.*

a	hat	ė	term	ô	order	ch	child		
ā	age	i	it	oi	oil	ng	long		a in about
ä	far	ī	ice	ou	out	sh	she		e in taken
â	care	o	hot	u	cup	th	thin	ə	i in pencil
e	let	ō	open	ù	put	ŦH	then		o in lemon
ē	equal	ȯ	saw	ü	rule	zh	measure		u in circus

im·be·cil·i·ty (im′bə sil′ə tē), *n.* **1** great stupidity. **2** a very stupid or foolish action, remark, etc. ❑ *n., pl.* **im·be·cil·i·ties** for 2.

im·bed (im bed′), *v.* to embed. ❑ *v.* **im·bed·ded, im·bed·ding.**

im·bibe (im bīb′), *v.* **1** to drink in; drink. **2** to absorb. **3** to take into your mind: *A student imbibes a great deal of information during a school term.* ❑ *v.* **im·bibed, im·bib·ing.** —**im·bib′er,** *n.*

im·bro·glio (im brō′lyō), *n.* a complicated or difficult misunderstanding or disagreement. ❑ *n., pl.* **im·bro·glios.**

> **WORD STORY** **Imbroglio** comes from an Italian word meaning "to tangle up." That word comes from a French word that means "to jumble together." An imbroglio is like a tangled jumble.

im·bue (im byü′), *v.* to fill the mind of; inspire: *They imbued their child with the ambition to succeed.* ❑ *v.* **im·bued, im·bu·ing.**

im·i·tate (im′ə tāt), *v.* **1** to try to be like or act like; follow the example of: *The little boy imitated his older brother.* **2** to make or do something like; copy: *A parrot imitates the sounds it hears.* **3** to act like; make fun of by acting like: *She amused the class by imitating a duck, a monkey, and a bear.* **4** to be like; look like; resemble: *Wood is sometimes painted to imitate stone.* ❑ *v.* **im·i·tat·ed, im·i·tat·ing.** —**im′i·ta·tor,** *n.*

> **SYNONYM STUDY** **Imitate, impersonate,** and **mimic** all mean to try to copy someone or something. **Imitate** is the general word: *She can imitate bird calls.* **Impersonate** means to pretend to be someone by imitating that person's voice, style, and appearance: *He can impersonate the mayor.* **Mimic** means to make fun of someone or something by imitating: *My brother mimics the way I run, and it makes me furious!*

im·i·ta·tion (im′ə tā′shən), **1** *n.* something that imitates something else; likeness; copy: *Give as good an imitation as you can of a rooster crowing.* ■ See Synonym Study at **copy. 2** *adj.* made to look like something better; not real: *The imitation diamond was made of glass.* **3** *n.* act or process of imitating: *We learn many things by imitation.*

im·i·ta·tive (im′ə tā′tiv), *adj.* **1** fond of imitating; likely to imitate others: *Monkeys are imitative.* **2** imitating; showing imitation: *"Whiz" is an imitative word.* —**im′i·ta′tive·ly,** *adv.* —**im′i·ta′tive·ness,** *n.*

> **WORD SOURCE** **Imitative words** come from the sound of the animal, thing or activity they name. The words below are some imitative words.

boom[1]	fizz	moo	thump
bump	giggle	purr	toot
chickadee	gobble[2]	quack[1]	whack
chirp	growl	rustle	whimper
chuckle	gurgle	sizzle	whippoorwill
click	hiccup	snicker	whiz
cluck	honk	spank	zap
coo	jump	splash	zoom
crunch	katydid	squirm	

im·mac·u·late (i mak′yə lit), *adj.* **1** without a spot or stain; absolutely clean: *The newly washed shirts were immaculate.* **2** without errors or flaws. —**im·mac′u·late·ly,** *adv.* —**im·mac′u·late·ness,** *n.*

Immaculate Conception, doctrine of the Roman Catholic Church that the Virgin Mary was conceived free of original sin.

im·ma·ter·i·al (im′ə tir′ē əl), *adj.* **1** not important; insignificant: *This error is immaterial.* **2** not material; spiritual rather than physical. —**im′ma·ter′i·al·ly,** *adv.* —**im′ma·ter′i·al·ness,** *n.*

im·ma·ture (im′ə chur′ *or* im′ə tur′), *adj.* **1** not mature; undeveloped. **2** childish: *A food fight is immature behavior.* **3** acting in a childish way; not showing the good sense expected at your age: *It is immature to expect to get your own way all the time.* ■ See Synonym Study at **young.** —**im′ma·ture′ly,** *adv.* —**im′ma·tur′i·ty,** *n.*

im·meas·ur·a·ble (i mezh′ər ə bəl), *adj.* too large to be measured; very great; boundless: *the immeasurable vastness of the universe.* —**im·meas′ur·a·bly,** *adv.*

im·me·di·a·cy (i mē′dē ə sē), *n.* quality of being immediate.

im·me·di·ate (i mē′dē it), *adj.* **1** coming at once; without delay: *Please send an immediate reply.* **2** with nothing in between; direct: *Things that are touching are in immediate contact.* **3** closest; nearest; next: *Your immediate neighbors live next door.* **4** close; near: *I expect an answer today, tomorrow, or in the immediate future.* **5** of or about the present; current: *What are your immediate plans?* —**im·me′di·ate·ness,** *n.*

> **WORD STORY** **Immediate** comes from Latin words meaning "not in the middle." The word describes things that are as close as possible in time or space, with nothing else coming between.

im·me·di·ate·ly (i mē′dē it lē), *adv.* **1** at once; without delay: *I answered his letter immediately.* **2** with nothing in between; directly.

im·me·mo·ri·al (im′ə môr′ē əl), *adj.* extending back beyond the bounds of memory; extremely old. —**im′me·mo′ri·al·ly,** *adv.*

im·mense (i mens′), *adj.* very large; huge; vast: *An ocean is an immense body of water.* ■ See Synonym Study at **huge.** —**im·mense′ness,** *n.*

im·mense·ly (i mens′lē), *adv.* very greatly: *We enjoyed the party immensely.*

im·men·si·ty (i men′sə tē), *n.* very great size or extent; vastness: *the ocean's immensity.*

im·merse (i mėrs′), *v.* **1** to dip or lower into a liquid until covered by it: *I immersed my aching feet in a bucket of hot water.* **2** to baptize by dipping someone completely under water. **3** to involve deeply; absorb: *The young pianist immersed herself in practice seven days a week.* ❑ *v.* **im·mersed, im·mers·ing.**

im·mer·sion (i mėr′zhən *or* i mėr′shən), *n.* **1** act of immersing or condition of being immersed. **2** baptism by dipping someone completely under water.

im·mi·grant (im′ə grənt), *n.* someone who comes into a country or region to live there: *Canada has many immigrants from Europe.*

immigrants

im·mi·grate (im′ə grāt), *v.* to come into a country or region to live there. ❑ *v.* **im·mi·grat·ed, im·mi·grat·ing.**

> **USAGE NOTE** **Immigrate** and **emigrate** are often confused. **Immigrate** means to come into a country to live. **Emigrate** means to leave a country in order to go live in another country: *They emigrated from India and immigrated to the United States.*

im·mi·gra·tion (im′ə grā′shən), *n.* **1** act of coming into a country or region to live there: *There has been immigration to the United States from many countries.* **2** the persons who immigrate; immigrants: *The immigration of 1956 included many people from Hungary.*

im·mi·nence (im′ə nəns), *n.* quality of being imminent.

im·mi·nent (im′ə nənt), *adj.* likely to happen soon; about to occur: *The black clouds show that a storm is imminent.* —**im′mi·nent·ly,** *adv.*

im·mo·bile (i mō′bəl), *adj.* **1** not movable; firmly fixed. **2** not moving; not changing; motionless. —**im′mo·bil′i·ty,** *n.*

im·mo·bi·lize (i mō′bə līz), *v.* to make immobile. ❑ *v.* **im·mo·bi·lized, im·mo·bi·liz·ing.** —**im·mo′bi·li·za′tion,** *n.*

im·mod·er·ate (i mod′ər it), *adj.* not moderate; going too far; extreme: *A fanatic has immoderate ideas.* —**im·mod′er·ate·ly,** *adv.* —**im·mod′er·ate·ness,** *n.* —**im·mod′er·a′tion,** *n.*

im·mod·est (i mod′ist), *adj.* **1** not modest; bold and rude. **2** indecent; improper. **—im·mod′est·ly,** *adv.*

im·mod·es·ty (i mod′ə stē), *n.* **1** lack of modesty; boldness and rudeness. **2** lack of decency; improper behavior.

im·mo·late (im′ə lāt), *v.* to kill or offer in sacrifice. ❑ *v.* **im·mo·lat·ed, im·mo·lat·ing. —im′mo·la′tion,** *n.* **—im′mo·la′tor,** *n.*

im·mor·al (i môr′əl), *adj.* morally wrong; wicked: *Stealing is immoral.* **—im·mor′al·ly,** *adv.*

im·mo·ral·i·ty (im′ə ral′ə tē), *n.* **1** wickedness; wrongdoing; vice. **2** an immoral act or practice. ❑ *n., pl.* **im·mo·ral·i·ties** for 2.

im·mor·tal (i môr′tl), **1** *adj.* living forever; never dying; everlasting: *Most religions teach that the soul is immortal.* **2** *n.* an immortal being. **3** *adj.* remembered or famous forever: *A great hero is immortal.* **4** *n.* person remembered or famous forever: *Shakespeare is one of the immortals.* **—im·mor′tal·ly,** *adv.*

im·mor·tal·i·ty (im′ôr tal′ə tē), *n.* **1** life without death; a living forever. **2** fame that lasts forever.

im·mor·tal·ize (i môr′tl īz), *v.* **1** to make immortal. **2** to cause to be remembered or famous forever: *Great authors are immortalized by their works.* ❑ *v.* **im·mor·tal·ized, im·mor·tal·iz·ing. —im·mor′tal·i·za′tion,** *n.* **—im·mor′tal·iz′er,** *n.*

im·mov·a·ble (i mü′və bəl), *adj.* **1** not able to be moved; firmly fixed: *immovable mountains.* **2** firm; steadfast; unyielding: *She was immovable in her beliefs.* **—im·mov′a·ble·ness,** *n.* **—im·mov′a·bly,** *adv.*

im·mune (i myün′), *adj.* **1** protected from disease, poison, etc.; having immunity: *Vaccination makes a person practically immune to polio.* **2** free; exempt: *Nobody is immune from criticism.* **3** of or related to the immune system: *immune reaction, immune response.*

WORD STORY Immune comes from a Latin word meaning "free from duties or obligations." In English that was the only meaning until about 100 years ago, when doctors started using the word.

immune serum, serum in which antibodies to a particular disease are present.

immune system, system of antibodies and special white blood cells in a person or animal that recognize, attack, and destroy germs and other foreign material that enter the body.

im·mu·ni·ty (i myü′nə tē), *n.* **1** resistance to disease, poison, etc.: *One attack of measles usually gives a person immunity to that disease.* **2** freedom; exemption: *The law gives schools and churches immunity from taxation.*

im·mu·nize (im′yə nīz), *v.* to protect from disease, poison, etc.; give immunity to; make immune: *Vaccination immunizes people against smallpox.* ❑ *v.* **im·mu·nized, im·mu·niz·ing. —im′mu·ni·za′tion,** *n.* **—im′mu·niz′er,** *n.*

im·mu·no·de·fi·cien·cy (i myü′nō di fish′ən sē), *n.* failure of the immune system to function as it should, causing lowered resistance to diseases, as in people who have AIDS.

im·mu·nol·o·gy (im′yə nol′ə jē), *n.* science dealing with the nature and causes of immunity from diseases and of immune system reactions, such as those involved in allergies.

im·mure (i myür′), *v.* OLD USE. to shut up within walls; put in prison; confine. ❑ *v.* **im·mured, im·mur·ing.**

im·mu·ta·ble (i myü′tə bəl), *adj.* never changing; not changeable. **—im·mu′ta·bil′i·ty,** *n.* **—im·mu′ta·ble·ness,** *n.* **—im·mu′ta·bly,** *adv.*

imp (imp), *n.* **1** a young or small devil or demon. **2** a mischievous child.

WORD STORY Imp comes from an old English word meaning "stalk of a plant." It was applied to young children because they are like new branches on a family tree. Because children can be mischievous, the word came to mean "young devil."

imp., imperative.

im·pact (im′pakt), **1** *n.* action of striking one thing against another; collision: *The impact of the heavy stone against the windowpane shattered the glass.* **2** *n.* a forceful or dramatic effect: *Her speech had a great impact on the audience.* **3** *v.* to hit or strike against something; reach; come to: *The capsule impacted the moon.* **4** *v.* to have an effect on: *choices that impact your life.* **—im·pac′tion,** *n.*

im·pact·ed (im pak′tid), *adj.* **1** firmly wedged in place. **2** (of a tooth) wedged between the jawbone and another tooth.

im·pair (im pâr′), *v.* to make worse; damage; harm; weaken: *Poor eating habits impaired his health.* **—im·pair′er,** *n.* **—im·pair′ment,** *n.*

im·paired (im pârd′), *adj.* **1** having an ability in a form that is distinctly less than usual, or not having some ability in any form; disabled. ■ See Usage Note at **disabled. 2** distinctly less than usual, or not existing: *impaired vision.* **3** (in Canada) driving under the influence of alcohol or narcotic drugs.

im·pa·la (im pä′lə), *n.* a medium-sized reddish brown antelope, found in eastern and southern Africa and noted for its long, graceful leaps. The male impala has long curved horns. *n. pl.* **im·pa·las.**

impala—about 3 ft. (91 cm) high at the shoulder

im·pale (im pāl′), *v.* **1** to pierce through with anything pointed; fasten upon anything pointed: *The dead butterflies were impaled on pins stuck in a sheet of cork.* **2** to torture or punish by thrusting upon a pointed stake. ❑ *v.* **im·paled, im·pal·ing. —im·pale′ment,** *n.* **—im·pal′er,** *n.*

im·pal·pa·ble (im pal′pə bəl), *adj.* **1** not able to be felt by touching; intangible: *Color is impalpable.* **2** very hard to understand; not able to be grasped by the mind: *The impalpable distinctions in your argument only confuse me.* **—im·pal′pa·bly,** *adv.*

im·pan·el (im pan′l), *v.* **1** to put on a list for duty on a jury. **2** to select a jury from the list. ❑ *v.* **im·pan·eled, im·pan·el·ing** or **im·pan·elled, im·pan·el·ling.**

im·part (im pärt′), *v.* **1** to give a part or share of; give: *The new furnishings imparted an air of newness to the old house.* **2** to communicate; tell: *They imparted the news of their engagement to their families.* **—im·part′ment,** *n.*

im·par·tial (im pär′shəl), *adj.* showing no more favor to one side than to the other; fair; just: *A judge should be impartial.* **—im·par′tial·ly,** *adv.* **—im·par′tial·ness,** *n.*

im·par·ti·al·i·ty (im′pär shē al′ə tē), *n.* fairness; justice.

im·pass·a·ble (im pas′ə bəl), *adj.* not passable; not able to be traveled over or across: *Snow and ice made the road impassable.* **—im·pass′a·bil′i·ty,** *n.* **—im·pass′a·ble·ness,** *n.* **—im·pass′a·bly,** *adv.*

im·passe (im′pas), *n.* position or situation from which there is no escape; deadlock.

im·pas·sioned (im pash′ənd), *adj.* full of strong feeling; stirring; rousing: *She gave an impassioned speech in favor of equal rights for all people.* **—im·pas′sioned·ly,** *adv.*

im·pas·sive (im pas′iv), *adj.* **1** without feeling or emotion; unmoved: *Her face was impassive when we told her the news.* **2** not feeling pain or injury; insensible: *The injured man lay as impassive as if he were dead.* **—im·pas′sive·ly,** *adv.* **—im·pas′sive·ness,** *n.* **—im′pas·siv′i·ty,** *n.*

im·pa·tience (im pā′shəns), *n.* **1** lack of patience; being impatient. **2** uneasiness and eagerness; restlessness.

a	hat	ė	term	ô	order	ch	child	
ā	age	i	it	oi	oil	ng	long	a in about
ä	far	ī	ice	ou	out	sh	she	e in taken
â	care	o	hot	u	cup	th	thin	ə { i in pencil
e	let	ō	open	u̇	put	ŦH	then	o in lemon
ē	equal	ȯ	saw	ü	rule	zh	measure	u in circus

im·pa·tiens (im pā′shənz), *n.* any of numerous plants with seed pods that burst open and eject the seeds when ripe.

im·pa·tient (im pā′shənt), *adj.* **1** not patient; not willing to put up with delay, opposition, pain, bother, etc.: *She is impatient with her little sister.* **2** uneasy and eager; restless: *The horses are impatient to start the race.* **3** showing lack of patience; cross: *an impatient answer.* —**im·pa′tient·ly,** *adv.*

im·peach (im pēch′), *v.* **1** to accuse a public official of wrong conduct while in office. Charges are brought before a special kind of court, and the official is removed from office if found guilty. **2** to cast doubt on; call in question: *impeached his honor.* —**im·peach′a·ble,** *adj.*

WORD STORY Impeach comes from Latin words meaning "on" and "foot." Romans chained the feet of prisoners. An accusation is like a chain that holds someone in court. **Impede** and **impediment** come from the same Latin words.

im·peach·ment (im pēch′mənt), *n.* **1** act of impeaching: *The impeachment of the dishonest judge resulted in a verdict of "Guilty."* **2** condition of being impeached: *The verdict resulting from his impeachment destroyed his political career.*

im·pec·ca·ble (im pek′ə bəl), *adj.* faultless: *impeccable manners.* —**im·pec′ca·bil′i·ty,** *n.* —**im·pec′ca·bly,** *adv.*

im·pe·cu·ni·ous (im′pi kyü′nē əs), *adj.* having little or no money; poor. —**im′pe·cu′ni·ous·ly,** *adv.* —**im′pe·cu′ni·ous·ness,** *n.*

im·pede (im pēd′), *v.* to hinder; obstruct: *The deep snow impeded travel.* ❑ *v.* **im·ped·ed, im·ped·ing.** [See Word Story at **impeach.**] —**im·ped′er,** *n.* —**im·ped′ing·ly,** *adv.*

im·ped·i·ment (im ped′ə mənt), *n.* **1** hindrance; obstacle. **2** defect in speech: *Stuttering is a speech impediment.* [See Word Story at **impeach.**]

im·pel (im pel′), *v.* **1** to drive or force; cause: *The cold impelled her to go indoors.* **2** to cause to move; drive forward; push along: *Wind and tide impelled the boat toward the shore.* ❑ *v.* **im·pelled, im·pel·ling.** —**im·pel′ler,** *n.*

im·pend (im pend′), *v.* to be likely to happen soon; be about to happen: *Black clouds are a sign that a storm impends.*

im·pend·ing (im pen′ding), *adj.* likely to happen soon; threatening; about to occur: *an impending storm.*

im·pen·e·tra·ble (im pen′ə trə bəl), *adj.* **1** not able to be penetrated; so dense or well protected that you cannot get into or through: *The thorny branches made a thick, impenetrable hedge.* **2** impossible to explain or understand: *His sudden disappearance was an impenetrable mystery.* —**im·pen′e·tra·bil′i·ty,** *n.* —**im·pen′e·tra·ble·ness,** *n.* —**im·pen′e·tra·bly,** *adv.*

im·pen·i·tence (im pen′ə təns), *n.* lack of any sorrow or regret for doing wrong.

im·pen·i·tent (im pen′ə tənt), *adj.* not penitent; feeling no sorrow or regret for having done wrong. —**im·pen′i·tent·ly,** *adv.*

im·per·a·tive (im per′ə tiv), **1** *adj.* not to be avoided; urgent; necessary: *It is imperative that this very sick child should stay in bed.* **2** *n.* command: *The dog trainer issued sharp imperatives to the dog.* **3** *adj.* (in grammar) of or relating to a verb form which expresses a command, request, or advice. **4** *n.* form of a verb which expresses this. In "Try to be quiet" and "Make up your mind," *try* and *make* are imperatives. **5** *n.* mood of such a verb. —**im·per′a·tive·ly,** *adv.* —**im·per′a·tive·ness,** *n.*

im·per·cep·ti·ble (im′pər sep′tə bəl), *adj.* not able to be perceived or felt; very slight; gradual: *There were imperceptible differences between the original painting and the copy.* —**im′per·cep′ti·bil′i·ty,** *n.* —**im′per·cep′ti·bly,** *adv.*

im·per·cep·tive (im′pər sep′tiv), *adj.* not perceptive.

im·per·fect (im pėr′fikt), *adj.* **1** not perfect; having some defect or fault: *A crack in the cup made it imperfect.* **2** not complete; lacking some part. **3** (in grammar) expressing incompleted, continued, or customary action in the past. English has no imperfect tense, but such constructions as *was studying* and *used to study* are like the imperfect verbs of other languages. —**im·per′fect·ly,** *adv.* —**im·per′fect·ness,** *n.*

im·per·fec·tion (im′pər fek′shən), *n.* **1** lack of perfection; imperfect condition or character. **2** fault; defect.

im·pe·ri·al (im pir′ē əl), **1** *adj.* of or about an empire or its ruler: *the imperial palace.* **2** *adj.* of or related to the rule or authority of one country over other countries and colonies: *England had imperial power over many other countries.* **3** *n.* a small, pointed beard growing beneath the lower lip. —**im·pe′ri·al·ly,** *adv.*

imperial gallon, the British gallon, equal to about 1⅕ U.S. gallons (4.546 liters).

im·pe·ri·al·ism (im pir′ē ə liz′əm), *n.* **1** policy of extending the rule or authority of one country over other countries and colonies. **2** an imperial system of government.

im·pe·ri·al·ist (im pir′ē ə list), *n.* someone who favors imperialism.

im·pe·ri·al·is·tic (im pir′ē ə lis′tik), *adj.* favoring imperialism. —**im·pe′ri·al·is′ti·cal·ly,** *adv.*

im·per·il (im per′əl), *v.* to put in danger: *Children who play with matches imperil their lives.* ❑ *v.* **im·per·iled, im·per·il·ing** or **im·per·illed, im·per·il·ling.** —**im·per′il·ment,** *n.*

im·pe·ri·ous (im pir′ē əs), *adj.* **1** acting in a proud and domineering way: *The nobles treated the common people in an imperious way.* **2** not to be avoided; necessary; urgent: *the imperious demands of hunger.* —**im·pe′ri·ous·ly,** *adv.* —**im·pe′ri·ous·ness,** *n.*

im·per·ish·a·ble (im per′i shə bəl), *adj.* not perishable; unable to be destroyed; lasting forever; enduring. —**im·per′ish·a·bil′i·ty,** **im·per′ish·a·ble·ness,** *n.* —**im·per′ish·a·bly,** *adv.*

im·per·ma·nent (im pėr′mə nənt), *adj.* not permanent; temporary. —**im·per′ma·nent·ly,** *adv.*

im·per·me·a·ble (im pėr′mē ə bəl), *adj.* not allowing the passage of water, gas, etc.: *Gas masks are only impermeable to certain kinds of gas.* —**im·per′me·a·bil′i·ty,** **im·per′me·a·ble·ness,** *n.* —**im·per′me·a·bly,** *adv.*

im·per·son·al (im pėr′sə nəl), *adj.* **1** not referring to any one person in particular; not personal: *History is usually written from an impersonal point of view.* **2** not influenced by human feelings: *large, impersonal business organizations.* **3** without emotion; showing no feelings: *a cold, impersonal response to angry words.* **4** (of a verb) not requiring a subject or having indefinite *it* for a subject, such as *rained* in "It rained yesterday." —**im·per′son·al′i·ty,** *n.* —**im·per′son·al·ly,** *adv.*

im·per·son·ate (im pėr′sə nāt), *v.* **1** to play the part of: *We impersonated Pilgrims in the school play.* **2** to pretend to be; mimic the voice, appearance, and manners of: *He impersonated a popular TV star to amuse us.* ■ See Synonym Study at **imitate.** ❑ *v.* **im·per·son·at·ed, im·per·son·at·ing.** —**im·per′son·a′tion,** *n.*

im·per·son·a·tor (im pėr′sə nā′tər), *n.* **1** person who pretends to be someone else. **2** actor who impersonates particular persons or types; professional mimic.

im·per·ti·nence (im pėr′n əns), *n.* **1** boldness and rudeness; impudence; insolence. **2** an impertinent act or speech. **3** lack of pertinence; irrelevance.

impersonator
Marilyn Monroe look-alike

im·per·ti·nent (im pėr′n ənt), *adj.* **1** rudely bold; impudent; insolent: *Talking back to older people is impertinent.* **2** not pertinent; not to the point; out of place: *His impertinent remarks wasted valuable time.* —**im·per′ti·nent·ly,** *adv.*

im·per·turb·a·ble (im′pər tėr′bə bəl), *adj.* not easily excited or disturbed; calm. —**im′per·turb′a·bil′i·ty,** **im′per·turb′a·ble·ness,** *n.* —**im′per·turb′a·bly,** *adv.*

im·per·vi·ous (im pėr′vē əs), *adj.* **1** not able to be penetrated; allowing no passage: *A coat made of rubber or vinyl is impervious to rain.* **2** not open to argument, suggestions, etc.: *Because they were impervious to our hints, we finally told them it was time to go.* —**im·per′vi·ous·ly,** *adv.* —**im·per′vi·ous·ness,** *n.*

im·pe·ti·go (im′pə tī′gō), *n.* an infectious skin disease in which the symptoms are pimples filled with pus.

im·pet·u·os·i·ty (im pech′ü os′ə tē), *n.* sudden or rash energy; hastiness: *The impetuosity of her temper got her into many arguments.*

im·pet·u·ous (im pech′ü əs), *adj.* acting or done with sudden or rash energy; hasty: *He was so angry that he made an impetuous decision.* —**im·pet′u·ous·ly,** *adv.* —**im·pet′u·ous·ness,** *n.*

im·pe·tus (im′pə təs), *n.* **1** the force with which a moving object tends to maintain its velocity and overcome resistance: *Anything that you can stop easily has little impetus.* **2** a driving force; cause of action or effort; incentive: *Ambition is an impetus to work for success.* ❑ *n., pl.* **im·pe·tus·es.** [Impetus comes from Latin words meaning "in" and "to aim." Things that are aimed, such as darts or arrows, usually move with force and speed.]

im·pi·e·ty (im pī′ə tē), *n.* **1** lack of piety or reverence for God. **2** an impious act. ❑ *n., pl.* **im·pi·e·ties** for 2.

im·pinge (im pinj′), *v.* **1** to trespass; encroach: *to impinge on the rights of other people.* **2** to hit; strike: *Rays of light impinge on the eye.* ❑ *v.* **im·pinged, im·ping·ing.** —**im·pinge′ment,** *n.* —**im·ping′er,** *n.*

im·pi·ous (im′pē əs *or* im pī′əs), *adj.* not pious; not having or not showing reverence for God. —**im′pi·ous·ly,** *adv.* —**im′pi·ous·ness,** *n.*

imp·ish (imp′ish), *adj.* **1** of or like an imp. **2** mischievous. —**imp′ish·ly,** *adv.* —**imp′ish·ness,** *n.*

im·pla·ca·ble (im plak′ə bəl *or* im plā′kə bəl), *adj.* unable to be appeased; refusing to be reconciled; unyielding: *The new nation was constantly threatened by its implacable enemies.* —**im·pla′ca·bil′i·ty, im·pla′ca·ble·ness,** *n.* —**im·pla′ca·bly,** *adv.*

im·plant (im plant′ *for verb;* im′plant *for noun*), **1** *v.* to graft or set a piece of skin, bone, etc., into the body. **2** *n.* organ or tissue grafted or set into the body by surgery; graft. **3** *n.* organ or tissue set into the body by surgery. **4** *v.* to instill; fix deeply: *A good teacher implants high ideals in children.* **5** *v.* to insert: *a steel tube implanted in a socket.* **6** *v.* to set in the ground; plant. —**im·plant′a·ble,** *adj.* —**im′plan·ta′tion,** *n.* —**im·plant′er,** *n.*

im·plau·si·ble (im plȯ′zə bəl), *adj.* not plausible; not having the appearance of truth or reason. —**im·plau′si·bil′i·ty,** *n.* —**im·plau′si·bly,** *adv.*

im·ple·ment (im′plə mənt *for noun;* im′plə ment *for verb*), **1** *n.* a useful piece of equipment; tool; instrument; utensil. Plows and threshing machines are farm implements. An ax, a shovel, and a broom are implements. **2** *v.* to carry out; get done: *Do not undertake a project unless you can implement it.* [Implement comes from Latin words meaning "in" and "to fill." An implement fills a need for help with a job.] —**im′ple·men·ta′tion,** *n.* —**im′ple·ment′er,** *n.*

im·pli·cate (im′plə kāt), *v.* to show to have a part or to be connected; involve: *She confessed to taking part in the theft and implicated two other students.* ❑ *v.* **im·pli·cat·ed, im·pli·cat·ing.**

im·pli·ca·tion (im′plə kā′shən), *n.* **1** something implied; indirect suggestion; hint: *She wouldn't say definitely, but her implication was that she really likes him.* **2** Usually, **implications,** *pl.* something likely to happen as a result of a decision, policy, etc.: *What are the implications of a budget cut now?* **3** involvement: *The suspect denied any implication in the burglary.*

im·plic·it (im plis′it), *adj.* **1** meant, but not clearly expressed; implied: *Her opposition to the present tax laws was implicit in her speech on tax reform.* **2** without doubting, hesitating, or asking questions; absolute: *He had implicit confidence in his friend.* —**im·plic′it·ly,** *adv.* —**im·plic′it·ness,** *n.*

im·plode (im plōd′), *v.* to burst or cause to burst inward. ❑ *v.* **im·plod·ed, im·plod·ing.**

im·plore (im plôr′), *v.* **1** to beg someone to do something: *I implored my parents to let me go on the trip.* **2** to beg earnestly for: *The prisoner implored pardon.* ❑ *v.* **im·plored, im·plor·ing.** [Implore comes from Latin words meaning "to weep" and "toward." A person who implores may do so with tear-filled eyes.] —**im·plor′er,** *n.* —**im·plor′ing·ly,** *adv.*

im·ply (im plī′), *v.* to mean without saying so; express indirectly; suggest: *The teacher's smile implied that she had forgiven us.* ❑ *v.* **im·plied, im·ply·ing.** [Imply comes from Latin words meaning "to fold in." An implied meaning is folded into words or actions.]
■ See Usage Note at **infer.**

im·po·lite (im′pə līt′), *adj.* not polite; having or showing bad manners; rude; discourteous. —**im′po·lite′ly,** *adv.* —**im′po·lite′ness,** *n.*

im·port (im pôrt′ *or* im′pôrt *for verb;* im′pôrt *for noun*), **1** *v.* to bring in from a foreign country for sale or use: *The United States imports coffee from Brazil.* **2** *n.* something imported: *Rubber is a useful import.* **3** *n.* act or fact of importing; importation: *The import of diseased animals was forbidden.* **4** *v.* to mean; signify: *Tell me what your remark imports.* **5** *n.* meaning; significance: *Explain your remark; I do not understand its import.* **6** *n.* importance; consequence: *matters of great import.* —**im·port′a·ble,** *adj.*

USAGE NOTE Import and **export** sometimes get confused. **Import** means to bring something into a country. **Export** means to send something out of a country: *The United States imports bananas and exports corn.*

im·por·tance (im pôrt′ns), *n.* quality of being important; value; significance: *Anybody can see the importance of good health.*

im·por·tant (im pôrt′nt), *adj.* **1** meaning or mattering much; worth noticing or considering; having value or significance: *important business, an important occasion.* **2** having social position or influence: *Our mayor is an important person in our town.* —**im·por′tant·ly,** *adv.*

SYNONYM STUDY **Important, major,** and **significant** all mean mattering a lot. **Important,** the general word, means mattering a lot or making a big difference: *Getting a new job is really important to my mom.* **Major** means more important than others: *The steel industry used to be the major employer in this city.* **Significant** means important in meaning: *Winning the music scholarship was a significant event in his life.*

im·por·ta·tion (im′pôr tā′shən), *n.* **1** act or process of importing; bringing in merchandise from foreign countries. **2** something imported: *This pottery is a recent importation from Mexico.*

im·port·er (im pôr′tər *or* im′pôr tər), *n.* person or company whose business is importing goods.

im·por·tu·nate (im pôr′chə nit), *adj.* asking repeatedly; annoyingly persistent; urgent. —**im·por′tu·nate·ly,** *adv.* —**im·por′tu·nate·ness,** *n.*

im·por·tune (im′pôr tün′), *v.* to ask urgently or repeatedly; annoy with pressing demands. ❑ *v.* **im·por·tuned, im·por·tun·ing.** —**im′por·tun′er,** *n.*

im·por·tu·ni·ty (im′pôr tü′nə tē), *n.* urgent or repeated asking; act of demanding again and again. ❑ *n., pl.* **im·por·tu·ni·ties.**

im·pose (im pōz′), *v.* **1** to put a burden, tax, or punishment on: *The judge imposed fines on each guilty person.* **2** to force or thrust your authority or influence on another or others. **3** to force or thrust yourself or your company on another or others; presume. ❑ *v.* **im·posed, im·pos·ing.** —**im·pos′a·ble,** *adj.* —**im·pos′er,** *n.*
impose on or **impose upon,** to take advantage of; use for selfish purposes: *Do not let them impose on you.*

im·pos·ing (im pō′zing), *adj.* impressive because of size, appearance, dignity, etc. —**im·pos′ing·ly,** *adv.*

im·po·si·tion (im′pə zish′ən), *n.* **1** act of putting a burden, tax, or punishment on: *protest the imposition of heavy taxes.* **2** an unfair burden, tax, or punishment. **3** an imposing by taking advantage of someone's good nature: *Would it be an imposition to ask her to mail this parcel?*

im·pos·si·bil·i·ty (im pos′ə bil′ə tē), *n.* **1** condition of being impossible: *We all realize the impossibility of living long without food.* **2** something impossible. ❑ *n., pl.* **im·pos·si·bil·i·ties** for 2.

a	hat	ė	term	ô	order	ch	child		a in about
ā	age	i	it	oi	oil	ng	long		e in taken
ä	far	ī	ice	ou	out	sh	she	ə	i in pencil
â	care	o	hot	u	cup	th	thin		o in lemon
e	let	ō	open	ů	put	⸬ then			u in circus
ē	equal	ȯ	saw	ü	rule	zh	measure		

im·pos·si·ble (im pos′ə bəl), *adj.* **1** not capable of being, being done, or happening; not possible: *It is impossible for two and two to be six.* **2** not possible to use; not to be done: *He proposed an impossible plan.* **3** known to be not possible; known to be untrue: *an impossible story.* **4** not possible to endure; very objectionable: *an impossible person.* —**im·pos′si·bly**, *adv.*

im·post (im′pōst), *n.* a tax or duty, especially on goods brought into a country: *There is an impost on imported wool.*

im·pos·tor (im pos′tər), *n.* person who pretends to be someone else in order to deceive or defraud others.

im·pos·ture (im pos′chər), *n.* deception; fraud.

im·po·tence (im′pə təns), *n.* lack of power; helplessness; condition or quality of being impotent: *The government was overthrown because of its impotence when the crisis arose.*

im·po·tent (im′pə tənt), *adj.* not having power; helpless: *We were impotent against the force of the tornado.* —**im′po·tent·ly**, *adv.*

im·pound (im pound′), *v.* **1** to shut up in a pen or pound: *The town impounds stray animals.* **2** to put in the custody of a court of law: *The court impounded the documents to use as evidence.* **3** to enclose or confine within limits: *A dam impounds water.* —**im·pound′er**, *n.* —**im·pound′ment**, *n.*

im·pov·er·ish (im pov′ər ish), *v.* **1** to make very poor: *A long war had impoverished the nation's treasury.* **2** to exhaust the strength, richness, or resources of: *Careless farming impoverished the soil.* —**im·pov′er·ish·ment**, *n.*

im·prac·ti·ca·ble (im prak′tə kə bəl), *adj.* not able to be done without greater difficulty, expense, etc., than is wise or sensible; impossible to put into practice: *impracticable suggestions.* ■ See Usage Note at **impractical**. —**im·prac′ti·ca·bly**, *adv.* —**im·prac′ti·ca·bil′i·ty**, *n.*

im·prac·ti·cal (im prak′tə kəl), *adj.* **1** not practical; of or about theory rather than actual practice; not useful. **2** not having good sense. —**im·prac′ti·cal·i·ty** (im prak′tə kal′ə tē), *n.*

> **USAGE NOTE** **Impractical** and **impracticable** are sometimes confused. **Impractical** describes things that are useless or that show little common sense: *Keeping a Great Dane in this small apartment is impractical.* **Impracticable** describes things that would be impossible: *Replacing all the main streets with canals is an impracticable solution to the traffic problem.*

im·pre·ca·tion (im′prə kā′shən), *n.* a curse: *The gardener shouted imprecations at the stray dogs.*

im·pre·cise (im′pri sīs′), *adj.* not precise; lacking precision; inaccurate. —**im′pre·cise′ly**, *adv.* —**im′pre·cise′ness**, *n.*

im·preg·na·ble (im preg′nə bəl), *adj.* able to resist attack; not yielding to force, persuasion, etc.: *an impregnable fortress, an impregnable argument.* —**im·preg′na·bil′i·ty**, *n.* —**im·preg′na·bly**, *adv.*

im·preg·nate (im preg′nāt), *v.* **1** to make pregnant. **2** to spread through the whole of; fill; saturate: *Seawater is impregnated with salt.* ❑ *v.* **im·preg·nat·ed**, **im·preg·nat·ing**. —**im·preg·na′tion**, *n.* —**im·preg′na·tor**, *n.*

im·pre·sa·ri·o (im′prə sär′ē ō), *n.* the organizer, director, or manager of a concert tour, an opera or ballet company, etc. ❑ *n., pl.* **im·pre·sa·ri·os.**

> **WORD STORY** **Impresario** comes from an Italian word meaning "task" or "business." Opera and ballet began in Italy; so did the job of organizing them.

im·press[1] (im pres′ *for verb;* im′pres *for noun*), **1** *v.* to have a strong effect on the mind or feelings of; influence deeply: *The movie impressed those who saw it.* **2** *n.* act of impressing. **3** *v.* to fix firmly in the mind: *She repeated the words to impress them in her memory.* **4** *v.* to make marks on by pressing or stamping: *impress wax with a seal.* **5** *v.* to imprint; stamp.

> **WORD FAMILY** **Impress** and the words below are related. They all come from a Latin word meaning "to press."
>
> | | | | |
> |---|---|---|---|
> | compress | express | misprint | print |
> | compressor | impression | oppress | repress |
> | decompress | imprint | press | reprimand |
> | depress | irrepressible | pressure | suppress |

im·press[2] (im pres′), *v.* press[2].

im·pres·sion (im presh′ən), *n.* **1** idea; notion: *I have a vague impression that I left the front door unlocked.* ■ See Synonym Study at **idea**. **2** effect produced on someone: *Punishment seemed to make little impression on the stubborn child.* **3** imitation; impersonation: *The comedian did impressions of several movie stars.* **4** mark made by pressing or stamping: *A deer had left impressions of its hoofs in the soft dirt.*

im·pres·sion·a·ble (im presh′ə nə bəl), *adj.* sensitive to impression; easily impressed or influenced: *Children are more impressionable than adults.* —**im·pres′sion·a·bil′i·ty**, *n.*

im·pres·sion·ism (im presh′ə niz′əm), *n.* **1** style of painting that conveys the impression of light striking and reflecting from a surface, rather than a photographic reproduction of the surface. **2** style of music that uses unusual and rich harmonies and combinations of instruments to suggest the composer's impressions of a scene, emotion, etc.

im·pres·sion·ist (im presh′ə nist), *n.* artist or composer who works in the manner of impressionism.

im·pres·sion·is·tic (im presh′ə nis′tik), *adj.* of or about impressionism or impressionists. —**im·pres′sion·is′ti·cal·ly**, *adv.*

im·pres·sive (im pres′iv), *adj.* able to impress the mind, feelings, conscience, etc.: *The actors gave an impressive performance.* —**im·pres′sive·ly**, *adv.* —**im·pres′sive·ness**, *n.*

im·print (im′print *for noun;* im print′ *for verb*), **1** *n.* mark made by pressure; print: *Your foot made an imprint in the sand.* **2** *n.* mark; impression: *Suffering left its imprint on her face.* **3** *n.* the printer's or publisher's name, with the place and date of publication, on the title page or at the end of a book. **4** *v.* to mark by pressing or stamping: *imprint a postmark on an envelope, imprint a letter with a postmark.* **5** *v.* to put by pressing: *He imprinted a kiss on his grandmother's cheek.* **6** *v.* to fix firmly in the mind: *His boyhood home was imprinted in his memory.*

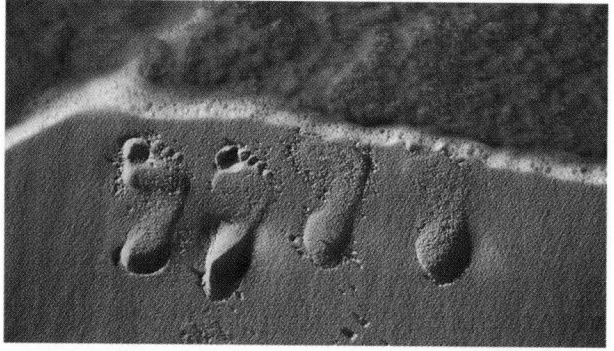

imprint (def. 1)

im·pris·on (im priz′n), *v.* **1** to put in prison; keep in prison. **2** to confine closely; restrain. —**im·pris′on·ment**, *n.*

im·prob·a·bil·i·ty (im prob′ə bil′ə tē), *n.* **1** unlikelihood. **2** something improbable. ❑ *n., pl.* **im·prob·a·bil·i·ties** for 2.

im·prob·a·ble (im prob′ə bəl), *adj.* not probable; not likely to happen; not likely to be true. —**im·prob′a·ble·ness**, *n.* —**im·prob′a·bly**, *adv.*

im·promp·tu (im promp′tü), **1** *adv.* without previous thought or preparation; offhand: *a speech made impromptu.* **2** *adj.* made or done without previous thought or preparation: *He gave an impromptu talk when asked to say a few words.* [Impromptu comes from Latin words meaning "in readiness." A person who does something impromptu had better be ready.]

im·prop·er (im prop′ər), *adj.* **1** wrong; incorrect: *That driver made an improper turn into a one-way street.* **2** not suitable: *A damp basement is an improper place to store books.* **3** not decent: *Reading another person's mail is improper.* —**im·prop′er·ly**, *adv.* —**im·prop′er·ness**, *n.*

> **SYNONYM STUDY** **Improper** and **indecent** both mean not right to do. **Improper** suggests using bad judgment about what is right or wrong: *The company was fined for improper waste disposal.* **Indecent** means morally wrong or socially offensive: *It was indecent of them to read her mail when she was out of the room.*

improper fraction, fraction that is equal to or greater than 1. EXAMPLES: $^3/_2$, $^4/_3$, $^{27}/_4$, $^8/_5$, $^{21}/_{12}$, $^4/_4$, $^{12}/_{12}$.

im·pro·pri·e·ty (im′prə prī′ə tē), *n.* **1** lack of propriety; quality of being improper. **2** an improper act, expression, etc. ❑ *n., pl.* **im·pro·pri·e·ties** for 2.

impure (def. 1)

im·prove (im prüv′), *v.* **1** to make or become better: *Try to improve your spelling.* **2** to increase the value of: *Land is improved by farming it.* ❑ *v.* **im·proved, im·prov·ing. —im·prov′a·ble,** *adj.* **—im·prov′er,** *n.*
improve on, to make better than; do better than: *improve on your earlier work.*

SYNONYM STUDY **Improve, help,** and **reform** all mean to make something better. **Improve** means to increase value, or correct faults: *"This story will be improved if you add some details,"* my writing coach said. **Help** can mean to make a medical problem smaller: *The doctor told her that new glasses would help her headaches.* **Reform** suggests getting rid of faults: *This newspaper article gives suggestions for reforming the town government.*

im·prove·ment (im prüv′mənt), *n.* **1** act of making better or becoming better: *Her schoolwork shows much improvement since last term.* **2** an increase in value. **3** a change or addition that increases value: *The improvements in our house cost over a thousand dollars.* **4** better condition; thing that is better than another; a gain; advance: *The new lighting system is an improvement over the previous one.*

im·prov·i·dence (im prov′ə dəns), *n.* lack of foresight; failure to look ahead; carelessness in providing for the future; lack of thrift.

im·prov·i·dent (im prov′ə dənt), *adj.* lacking foresight; not looking ahead; not careful in providing for the future; not thrifty: *Improvident people spend their money as fast as they can make it.* **—im·prov′i·dent·ly,** *adv.*

im·prov·i·sa·tion (im prov′ə zā′shən), *n.* **1** something improvised. **2** act of improvising.

im·pro·vise (im′prə vīz), *v.* **1** to make up music, poetry, etc., on the spur of the moment; sing, recite, speak, etc., without preparation: *She likes to improvise popular songs on the piano.* **2** to make for the occasion: *The girls improvised a tent out of blankets and long poles.* ❑ *v.* **im·pro·vised, im·pro·vis·ing. —im′pro·vis′er,** *n.*

im·pru·dence (im prüd′ns), *n.* lack of prudence; imprudent behavior.

im·pru·dent (im prüd′nt), *adj.* not prudent; rash; unwise: *It is imprudent to rush into something without thinking what may happen.* **—im·pru′dent·ly,** *adv.*

im·pu·dence (im′pyə dəns), *n.* shameless boldness; great rudeness; insolence.

im·pu·dent (im′pyə dənt), *adj.* shamelessly bold; very rude and insolent: *The impudent child made faces at us.* **—im′pu·dent·ly,** *adv.*

im·pugn (im pyün′), *v.* to call in question; attack by words or arguments; challenge as false, worthless, etc.: *The attorney impugned the witness's testimony.* [**Impugn** comes from Latin words meaning "to fight against." An attack in words is as real as a physical fight.] **—im·pugn′a·ble,** *adj.* **—im·pugn′er,** *n.*

im·pulse (im′puls), *n.* **1** a sudden inclination or urge: *I had a strong impulse to contact my old friend.* **2** a sudden, driving force or influence; thrust; push: *the impulse of hunger, the impulse of curiosity.* **3** stimulus that is transmitted, especially by nerve cells, and influences action in the muscle, gland, or other nerve cells that it reaches. **4** surge of electrical current in one direction.

im·pul·sion (im pul′shən), *n.* **1** driving force: *The impulsion of hunger drove her to steal food.* **2** impulse. **3** impetus.

im·pul·sive (im pul′siv), *adj.* acting or done upon impulse; with a sudden inclination or tendency to act: *Impulsive buyers often buy things they don't need.* **—im·pul′sive·ly,** *adv.* **—im·pul′sive·ness,** *n.*

im·pu·ni·ty (im pyü′nə tē), *n.* freedom from punishment, injury, or other bad consequences: *If laws are not enforced, crimes are committed with impunity.*

im·pure (im pyür′), *adj.* **1** not pure; dirty; unclean: *The air in cities is often impure.* **2** mixed with something of lower value; adulterated: *impure gold ore.* **3** bad; corrupt: *impure thoughts, impure acts.* **—im·pure′ly,** *adv.* **—im·pure′ness,** *n.*

im·pu·ri·ty (im pyür′ə tē), *n.* **1** lack of purity; being impure. **2** Usually, **impurities,** *pl.* things that make something else impure: *Filtering the water removed some of its impurities.*

im·pute (im pyüt′), *v.* to consider as belonging to; attribute; blame: *impute your failures to bad luck.* ❑ *v.* **im·put·ed, im·put·ing. —im·put′a·ble,** *adj.* **—im′pu·ta′tion,** *n.*

in (in). *In* shows position with reference to space, time, state, circumstances, etc. **1** *prep.* inside; within: *in the box.* **2** *prep.* at, during, or after: *I'll be there in ten minutes. You can do this in an hour.* **3** *prep.* into: *Go in the house.* **4** *prep.* using; by means of: *She wrote in pencil. I paid in cash.* **5** *prep.* from among; out of: *one in a hundred.* **6** *prep.* because of; for: *act in self-defense.* **7** *prep.* to or at the position or condition of; affected by: *Is your brother in trouble?* **8** *adv.* in or into some place; on the inside: *Come in. Lock the dog in.* **9** *adv.* present, especially in one's home or office: *The doctor is not in today.* **10** *adj.* having power or influence: *The in party has won another election.* **11** *adj.* coming or leading in: *The train is on the in track.* **12** *adj.* INFORMAL. in style; fashionable: *That's the in thing to do.* **13** *n.* a position of familiarity or influence: *She has an in with the company president.* ■ Another word that sounds like this is **inn.**
in for, unable to avoid; sure to get or have: *We are in for a storm.*
in on, having knowledge of; being a part of: *We are all in on the surprise.*
ins and outs, 1 turns and twists; nooks and corners: *He knows the ins and outs of the road because he has traveled it so often.* **2** different parts; details: *The manager knows the ins and outs of the business better than the owner.*
in that, because.
in with, 1 friendly with. **2** partners with: *She was in with him in the robbery.*

USAGE NOTE **In** is mostly used to show location: *That clinic is in the remodeled building down the street.* **Into** is mostly used to show direction: *They wandered into a strange little pottery shop.*

In, symbol for indium.

IN, Indiana (used with postal Zip Code).

in-[1], *prefix.* not; the opposite of: *inexpensive = not expensive; inattention = the opposite of attention.*

in-[2], *prefix.* in; within; into; toward: *input = to put in; indoors = within doors; inshore = in toward the shore.*

in., inch or inches.

in·a·bil·i·ty (in′ə bil′ə tē), *n.* lack of ability, power, or means; being unable.

in·ac·ces·si·ble (in′ək ses′ə bəl), *adj.* **1** hard to get at; hard to reach or enter: *The house on top of the steep hill is inaccessible.* **2** not accessible; not able to be reached or entered at all. **—in′ac·ces′si·bil′i·ty,** *n.* **—in′ac·ces′si·bly,** *adv.*

a	hat	è	term	ô	order	ch	child		a in about
ā	age	i	it	oi	oil	ng	long		e in taken
ä	far	ī	ice	ou	out	sh	she	ə	i in pencil
â	care	o	hot	u	cup	th	thin		o in lemon
e	let	ō	open	ů	put	ŦH	then		u in circus
ē	equal	ò	saw	ü	rule	zh	measure		

in·ac·cu·ra·cy (in ak′yər ə sē), *n.* **1** lack of accuracy; being inaccurate. **2** error; mistake. ❑ *n., pl.* **in·ac·cur·a·cies** for 2.

in·ac·cur·ate (in ak′yər it), *adj.* not accurate; not exact; containing mistakes. —**in·ac′cur·ate·ly,** *adv.* —**in·ac′cur·ate·ness,** *n.*

in·ac·tion (in ak′shən), *n.* absence of action; idleness.

in·ac·ti·vate (in ak′tə vāt), *v.* to make inactive; destroy the action of: *inactivate a virus.* ❑ *v.* **in·ac·ti·vat·ed, in·ac·ti·vat·ing.** —**in·ac′ti·va′tion,** *n.*

in·ac·tive (in ak′tiv), *adj.* not active; idle; slow: *Bears are inactive during the winter.* —**in·ac′tive·ly,** *adv.* —**in·ac′tive·ness,** *n.*

in·ac·tiv·i·ty (in′ak tiv′ə tē), *n.* absence of activity; idleness; slowness.

in·ad·e·qua·cy (in ad′ə kwə sē), *n.* **1** condition of lacking necessary powers or abilities: *feelings of inadequacy.* **2** shortage; deficiency. ❑ *n., pl.* **in·ad·e·qua·cies** for 2.

in·ad·e·quate (in ad′ə kwit), *adj.* not adequate; not enough; not as much as is needed: *an inadequate amount of food for so many guests.* —**in·ad′e·quate·ly,** *adv.* —**in·ad′e·quate·ness,** *n.*

in·ad·mis·si·ble (in′əd mis′ə bəl), *adj.* not to be permitted; not allowable: *inadmissible evidence.* —**in′ad·mis′si·bil′i·ty,** *n.* —**in′ad·mis′si·bly,** *adv.*

in·ad·vert·ence (in′əd vėrt′ns), *n.* **1** lack of attention; carelessness. **2** an inadvertent act; oversight; mistake.

in·ad·vert·ent (in′əd vėrt′nt), *adj.* **1** not attentive; careless; negligent. **2** not done on purpose; caused by oversight: *I forgave her inadvertent rudeness.* —**in′ad·vert′ent·ly,** *adv.*

in·ad·vis·a·ble (in′əd vī′zə bəl), *adj.* not advisable; unwise; not prudent. —**in′ad·vis′a·bil′i·ty,** *n.*

in·al·ien·a·ble (in ā′lyə nə bəl), *adj.* not able to be given or taken away: *an inalienable right.* —**in·al′ien·a·bil′i·ty,** *n.* —**in·al′ien·a·bly,** *adv.*

in·ane (in ān′), *adj.* silly or foolish; senseless: *an inane question.* —**in·ane′ly,** *adv.* —**in·ane′ness,** *n.*

in·an·i·mate (in an′ə mit), *adj.* **1** lifeless: *Stones are inanimate objects.* **2** without liveliness or spirit; dull: *an inanimate face.* —**in·an′i·mate·ly,** *adv.* —**in·an′i·mate·ness,** *n.*

in·an·i·ty (in an′ə tē), *n.* **1** silliness; lack of sense. **2** a silly or senseless act, remark, etc. ❑ *n., pl.* **in·an·i·ties** for 2.

in·ap·pli·ca·ble (in ap′lə kə bəl *or* in′ə plik′ə bəl), *adj.* not applicable; not suitable. —**in·ap′pli·ca·bil′i·ty,** *n.* —**in·ap′pli·ca·bly,** *adv.*

in·ap·pre·ci·a·ble (in′ə prē′shē ə bəl), *adj.* too small to be noticed or felt; very slight. —**in′ap·pre·ci·a·bly,** *adv.*

in·ap·pro·pri·ate (in′ə prō′prē it), *adj.* not appropriate; not suitable. —**in′ap·pro′pri·ate·ly,** *adv.* —**in′ap·pro′pri·ate·ness,** *n.*

in·apt (in apt′), *adj.* **1** not apt; not suitable; unfit. **2** unskillful; awkward. —**in·apt′ly,** *adv.* —**in·apt′ness,** *n.*

in·ap·ti·tude (in ap′tə tüd), *n.* **1** unfitness. **2** lack of skill.

in·ar·tic·u·late (in′är tik′yə lit), *adj.* **1** not distinct; not like regular speech: *an inarticulate mutter.* **2** unable to speak in words; unable to say what you think; dumb: *inarticulate with grief.* **3** not jointed: *A jellyfish's body is inarticulate.* —**in′ar·tic′u·late·ly,** *adv.* —**in′ar·tic′u·late·ness,** *n.*

in·ar·tis·tic (in′är tis′tik), *adj.* not artistic; lacking good taste. —**in′ar·tis′ti·cal·ly,** *adv.*

in·as·much as (in′əz much′), because; since: *I stayed indoors, inasmuch as it was raining.*

in·at·ten·tion (in′ə ten′shən), *n.* lack of attention; negligence; carelessness: *Her inattention was due to lack of sleep.*

in·at·ten·tive (in′ə ten′tiv), *adj.* not attentive; negligent; careless. —**in′at·ten′tive·ly,** *adv.* —**in′at·ten′tive·ness,** *n.*

in·au·di·ble (in ò′də bəl), *adj.* not able to be heard. —**in·au′di·bil′i·ty,** *n.* —**in·au′di·bly,** *adv.*

in·au·gur·al (in ò′gyər əl), **1** *adj.* of or for an inauguration: *The President gave an inaugural address when he took office.* **2** *n.* the address or speech made by a person when formally admitted to office. **3** *n.* an inaugural ceremony; inauguration.

in·au·gu·rate (in ò′gyə rāt′), *v.* **1** to install in office with a ceremony: *A President of the United States is inaugurated every four years.* **2** to make a formal beginning of; begin: *The invention of the airplane inaugurated a new era in transportation.* **3** to open for public use with a ceremony or celebration: *The new city*

hall was inaugurated with a parade and speeches. ❑ *v.* **in·au·gu·rat·ed, in·au·gu·rat·ing.** [Inaugurate comes from a Latin word meaning "priest." Roman priests conducted a special ceremony installing a public official or another priest.] —**in·au′gu·ra′tor,** *n.*

in·au·gu·ra·tion (in ò′gyə rā′shən), *n.* **1** act or ceremony of installing someone in office. The inauguration of a President of the United States takes place on January 20. **2** a formal beginning; beginning. **3** an opening for public use with a ceremony or celebration: *The inauguration of the new city hall began with a parade.*

in·aus·pi·cious (in′ò spish′əs), *adj.* with signs of failure; unlucky. —**in′aus·pi′cious·ly,** *adv.* —**in′aus·pi′cious·ness,** *n.*

in·board (in′bôrd′), *adj.* inside the hull of a ship or boat: *an inboard motor.*

in·born (in′bôrn′), *adj.* born in a person; instinctive; natural: *The artist had an inborn talent for drawing.*

in·bound (in′bound′), *adj.* inward bound: *an inbound flight.*

in·bred (in′bred′), **1** *adj.* inborn; natural: *an inbred musical ability.* **2** *adj.* produced by breeding between closely related ancestors: *an inbred strain of horses.* **3** *v.* past tense and past participle of **inbreed.**

in·breed (in′brēd′), *v.* to breed closely related living things. ❑ *v.* **in·bred, in·breed·ing.**

inc., incorporated.

In·ca (ing′kə), *n.* member of an American Indian tribe or group of tribes that lived in the Andes Mountains region of South America. The Inca had a highly developed culture, and ruled a large empire in Peru and other parts of South America. This empire fell to the Spaniards in the 1500s. ❑ *n., pl.* **In·ca** or **In·cas.** [Inca comes from a Quechua word meaning "ruler."] —**In′can,** *adj.*

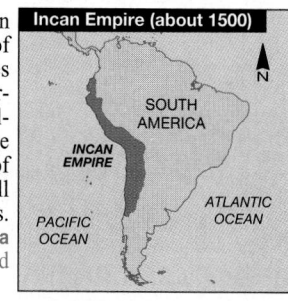

Incan Empire (about 1500)

SOUTH AMERICA

INCAN EMPIRE

PACIFIC OCEAN

ATLANTIC OCEAN

N

in·cal·cu·la·ble (in kal′kyə lə bəl), *adj.* **1** too great in number to be calculated; innumerable: *The sands of the sea are incalculable.* **2** impossible to foretell or reckon beforehand: *A flood in the valley would cause incalculable losses.* —**in·cal′cu·la·bil′i·ty,** *n.* —**in·cal′cu·la·bly,** *adv.*

in·can·des·cence (in′kən des′ns), *n.* a glow produced by heat.

in·can·des·cent (in′kən des′nt), *adj.* **1** glowing with heat; red-hot or white-hot: *Steel comes from the furnace as an incandescent liquid.* **2** shining brightly; brilliant. —**in′can·des′cent·ly,** *adv.*

in·can·ta·tion (in′kan tā′shən), *n.* **1** set of words spoken as a magic charm or to cast a magic spell. "Double, double, toil and trouble, Fire burn and caldron bubble," is an incantation. **2** the use of such words.

in·ca·pa·ble (in kā′pə bəl), *adj.* having very little ability; not capable; not competent: *We cannot afford to hire incapable workers.* —**in·ca′pa·bil′i·ty, in·ca′pa·ble·ness,** *n.* —**in·ca′pa·bly,** *adv.*

incapable of, 1 without the ability, power, or fitness for: *I felt incapable of playing such difficult piano music.* **2** not susceptible to; not open or ready for: *Gold is incapable of rusting.*

in·ca·pac·i·tate (in′kə pas′ə tāt), *v.* to limit in ability, power, or fitness; disable: *Her injury incapacitated her for work.* ❑ *v.* **in·ca·pac·i·tat·ed, in·ca·pac·i·tat·ing.** —**in′ca·pac′i·ta′tion,** *n.*

in·ca·pac·i·ty (in′kə pas′ə tē), *n.* lack of ability, power, or fitness; disability.

in·car·ce·rate (in kär′sə rāt′), *v.* to imprison. ❑ *v.* **in·car·ce·rat·ed, in·car·ce·rat·ing.** —**in·car′ce·ra′tion,** *n.* —**in·car′ce·ra′tor,** *n.*

in·car·nate (in kär′nit *or* in kär′nāt for adj.; in kär′nāt for verb), **1** *adj.* embodied in flesh, especially in human form: *The villain was evil incarnate.* **2** *v.* to make or be incarnate; embody: *Lancelot incarnated the spirit of chivalry.* ❑ *v.* **in·car·nat·ed, in·car·nat·ing.**

in·car·na·tion (in′kär nā′shən), *n.* **1** someone who represents some quality or idea; embodiment: *The miser was an incarna-*

tion of greed. **2** act of taking on human form by a divine being: *the incarnation of an angel.* **3 the Incarnation,** (in Christian theology) the union of divine nature and human nature in the person of Jesus; assumption of human form by the son of God.

in·cau·tious (in kȯ′shəs), *adj.* not cautious; reckless; rash: *In an incautious moment I revealed the secret I had sworn to keep.* —**in·cau′tious·ly,** *adv.* —**in·cau′tious·ness,** *n.*

in·cen·di·ar·y (in sen′dē er′ē), **1** *adj.* causing fires; used to start a fire: *The enemy town was set on fire with incendiary bombs.* **2** *n.* bomb or shell containing chemicals that cause fire. **3** *adj.* of or involving the setting of property on fire intentionally. **4** *n.* person who intentionally sets fire to property. **5** *adj.* deliberately stirring up discontent, violence, or rebellion: *He was arrested for making incendiary speeches.* **6** *n.* person who deliberately stirs up discontent, violence, or rebellion. ❑ *n., pl.* **in·cen·di·ar·ies.**

in·cense[1] (in′sens), *n.* **1** substance giving off a sweet smell when burned. **2** the perfume or smoke from it. **3** something sweet like incense: *the incense of flowers, the incense of flattery.*

in·cense[2] (in sens′), *v.* to make very angry; fill with rage: *Their cruelty incensed me.* ❑ *v.* **in·censed, in·cens·ing.**

in·cen·tive (in sen′tiv), *n.* something that urges someone to do something; cause of action or effort; motive; stimulus: *The fun of playing the game was a greater incentive than the prize.*

in·cep·tion (in sep′shən), *n.* beginning: *the inception of a plan.*

in·ces·sant (in ses′nt), *adj.* never stopping; continual: *The incessant noise of traffic kept me awake all night.* —**in·ces′sant·ly,** *adv.*

incessant traffic

in·cest (in′sest), *n.* a sexual relationship between persons so closely related that their marriage is prohibited by law or custom, as between brother and sister or parent and child.

in·ces·tu·ous (in ses′chü əs), *adj.* **1** involving incest. **2** guilty of incest. —**in·cest′tu·ous·ly,** *adv.* —**in·ces′tu·ous·ness,** *n.*

inch (inch), **1** *n.* unit of length equal to ¹⁄₁₂ of a foot. **2** *n.* the smallest part, amount, or degree; a very little bit. **3** *v.* to move slowly or little by little: *The worm inched along.* ❑ *n., pl.* **inch·es.** [**Inch** comes from a Latin word meaning "one twelfth." Romans measured length in units that they called feet, which in turn were divided in twelfths.]

by inches, by slow degrees; gradually.

every inch, in every way; completely: *every inch a leader.*

inch by inch, little by little; slowly.

within an inch of, very near; very close to: *within an inch of death.*

In·chon (in′chon′), *n.* port in W South Korea, on the Yellow Sea. An amphibious invasion here in September 1950, by U.S. forces commanded by General MacArthur, resulted in the defeat of North Korean troops who had invaded South Korea in June 1950.

inch·worm (inch′wėrm′), *n.* any of several small green or brown caterpillars that move by bringing the rear end of the body forward, forming a loop, and then advancing the front end; measuring worm.

in·ci·dence (in′sə dəns), *n.* **1** rate or frequency with which something happens: *In an epidemic the incidence of a disease is widespread.* **2** the falling or striking of a projectile, ray of light, etc., on a surface.

in·ci·dent (in′sə dənt), **1** *n.* something that happens; event: *an exciting incident.* **2** *n.* event or disturbance that seems to be mi-

nor but which may have serious consequences: *The incident in the street set off a riot.* **3** *adj.* liable to happen; belonging: *Hardships were incident to the lives of the pioneers.* [**Incident** comes from Latin words meaning "to fall on." Something that just happens is like something that falls unexpectedly.]

in·ci·den·tal (in′sə den′tl), **1** *adj.* happening or likely to happen along with something else more important: *Certain discomforts are incidental to camping out.* **2** *adj.* occurring by chance: *an incidental meeting of an old friend on the street.* **3** *n.* Often, **incidentals,** *pl.* something incidental: *On our trip we spent $252 for meals and fare, and $11.50 for incidentals, such as stamps.*

in·ci·den·tal·ly (in′sə den′tl ē), *adv.* **1** by the way: *Incidentally, are you coming to the meeting?* **2** in an incidental manner; as an incident along with something else: *She mentioned incidentally that she hadn't eaten.*

in·cin·er·ate (in sin′ə rāt′), *v.* to burn to ashes. ❑ *v.* **in·cin·er·at·ed, in·cin·er·at·ing.** —**in·cin·er·a′tion,** *n.*

in·cin·er·a·tor (in sin′ə rā′tər), *n.* furnace or other device for burning trash and other things to ashes.

in·cip·i·ent (in sip′ē ənt), *adj.* just beginning; in an early stage: *I hope this incipient cold doesn't become worse.* —**in·cip′i·ent·ly,** *adv.*

in·cise (in sīz′), *v.* **1** to cut into: *incise wood.* **2** to carve; engrave: *incise an inscription.* ❑ *v.* **in·cised, in·cis·ing.**

in·ci·sion (in sizh′ən), *n.* **1** a cut made in something, especially surgically. **2** act of incising.

in·ci·sive (in sī′siv), *adj.* sharp; penetrating; forceful: *Incisive criticism goes directly to the point and uses plain words.* —**in·ci′sive·ly,** *adv.* —**in·ci′sive·ness,** *n.*

in·ci·sor (in sī′zər), *n.* tooth with a sharp edge for cutting; one of the front teeth between the canine teeth in each jaw.

in·cite (in sīt′), *v.* to urge on; stir up; rouse: *The speaker incited the audience to quick action.* ❑ *v.* **in·cit·ed, in·cit·ing.** —**in·cit′er,** *n.*

in·cite·ment (in sīt′mənt), *n.* **1** thing that urges on, stirs up, or rouses: *Poverty can be an incitement to steal.* **2** act of urging on, stirring up, or rousing.

in·clem·ent (in klem′ənt), *adj.* **1** rough or stormy: *inclement weather.* **2** unmerciful: *an inclement ruler.* —**in·clem′ent·ly,** *adv.*

in·cli·na·tion (in′klə nā′shən), *n.* **1** preference; liking: *That family has a strong inclination for sports.* **2** a slope; slant: *That high roof has a sharp inclination.* **3** act of leaning, bending, or bowing: *The inclination of his head showed that he approved.*

in·cline (in klīn′ *for verb;* in′ klīn *or* in klīn′ *for noun*), **1** *v.* to be favorable or willing; tend: *Dogs incline to eat meat as a food.* **2** *v.* to make favorable or willing; influence: *A hobby may incline a person toward a particular career.* **3** *v.* to slope; slant: *This street inclines upward.* **4** *n.* a sloping surface. The side of a hill is an incline. **5** *v.* to lean, bend, or bow: *She inclined her head toward the sound.* ❑ *v.* **in·clined, in·clin·ing.** —**in·clin′er,** *n.*

in·clined (in klīnd′), *adj.* **1** favorable or willing; tending: *I am inclined to agree with you.* **2** sloping; slanting.

inclined plane, plank or other plane surface placed at an angle to a horizontal surface. It is a simple machine used to move heavy weights to a higher level.

inclined plane used in building a pyramid

a	hat	ė	term	ô	order	ch	child		
ā	age	i	it	oi	oil	ng	long		a in about
ä	far	ī	ice	ou	out	sh	she		e in taken
â	care	o	hot	u	cup	th	thin	ə	i in pencil
e	let	ō	open	u̇	put	ŦH	then		o in lemon
ē	equal	ȯ	saw	ü	rule	zh	measure		u in circus

in·cli·nom·e·ter (in′klə nom′ə tər), *n.* device for measuring an angle that an airplane or ship makes with the horizon.

in·clude (in klüd′), *v.* **1** to have within itself; contain; comprise: *Their farm includes 160 acres.* **2** to put in a total, a class, or the like; reckon in a count: *The price includes the land, house, and furniture.* ❑ *v.* **in·clud·ed, in·clud·ing.** —**in·clud′a·ble** or **in·clud′i·ble,** *adj.*

in·clu·sion (in klü′zhən), *n.* **1** act of including or condition of being included. **2** something included.

in·clu·sive (in klü′siv), *adj.* **1** including; taking in; counting in; comprising: *"Read pages 10 to 20 inclusive" means "Begin with page 10 and read through to the very end of page 20."* **2** including everything concerned: *Make an inclusive list of your expenses.* —**in·clu′sive·ly,** *adv.* —**in·clu′sive·ness,** *n.*

in·cog·ni·to (in′kog nē′tō *or* in kog′nə tō), *adj., adv.* with your real name, character, rank, etc., hidden: *A disguise allows you to be incognito. The prince traveled incognito to avoid crowds and ceremonies.*

WORD STORY **Incognito** comes from Latin words meaning "not to get to know." The reason for being incognito is so that people don't get to know the truth.

in·co·her·ence (in′kō hir′əns), *n.* **1** disconnected thought or speech: *After she awoke from the surgery, her speech was marked by some incoherence.* **2** lack of logical connection.

in·co·her·ent (in′kō hir′ənt), *adj.* **1** not coherent; disconnected; confused: *rambling, incoherent talk.* **2** lacking logical connection; illogical: *incoherent policies.* —**in′co·her′ent·ly,** *adv.*

in·com·bus·ti·ble (in′kəm bus′tə bəl), *adj.* not capable of being burned; fireproof. —**in′com·bus′ti·bil′i·ty,** *n.*

in·come (in′kum′), *n.* money that comes in from property, business, work, etc.: *A person's yearly income is all the money earned in a year.*

income tax, tax on a person's or a corporation's income above a certain amount.

in·com·ing (in′kum′ing), *adj.* **1** coming in: *incoming flights.* **2** newly elected: *the incoming president.*

in·com·men·su·rate (in′kə men′shər it *or* in′kə men′sər it), *adj.* **1** not in proportion; not adequate: *Her salary is incommensurate to her ability.* **2** having no common measure; not able to be compared. —**in′com·men′sur·ate·ly,** *adv.* —**in′com·men′sur·ate·ness,** *n.*

in·com·mu·ni·ca·ble (in′kə myü′nə kə bəl), *adj.* not able to be communicated or told.

in·com·mu·ni·ca·do (in′kə myü′nə kä′dō), *adj.* without any way of communicating with others: *The prisoner was held incommunicado.*

WORD STORY **Incommunicado** comes from Latin words meaning "not shared." A person who is incommunicado cannot share information with others.

in·com·par·a·ble (in kom′pər ə bəl), *adj.* **1** without equal; matchless: *incomparable beauty.* **2** not able to be compared; unsuitable for comparison. —**in·com′par·a·bly,** *adv.*

in·com·pat·i·ble (in′kəm pat′ə bəl), *adj.* **1** not able to live or act together peaceably; opposed in character: *My cats and dogs are incompatible.* **2** (in electronics) not able to be used with another item or items: *The two computers have incompatible operating systems and use different programs.* **3** making combination impossible without loss of effectiveness or danger to health: *an incompatible blood donor.* **4** inconsistent: *Bad eating habits are incompatible with good health.* —**in′com·pat′i·bil′i·ty,** *n.* —**in′com·pat′i·bly,** *adv.*

in·com·pe·tence (in kom′pə təns), *n.* lack of ability, power, or fitness: *The worker was discharged for incompetence.*

in·com·pe·tent (in kom′pə tənt), **1** *adj.* not able to do something; without ability or qualifications: *an incompetent mechanic.* **2** *n.* an incompetent person, especially someone suffering from some type of mental deficiency. —**in·com′pe·tent·ly,** *adv.*

in·com·plete (in′kəm plēt′), *adj.* not complete; lacking some part; unfinished. —**in′com·plete′ly,** *adv.* —**in′com·plete′ness,** *n.*

in·com·pre·hen·si·ble (in′kom pri hen′sə bəl), *adj.* impossible to understand. —**in′com·pre·hen′si·bil′i·ty, in′com·pre·hen′si·ble·ness,** *n.* —**in′com·pre·hen′si·bly,** *adv.*

in·com·pre·hen·sion (in′kom pri hen′shən), *n.* lack of comprehension or understanding.

in·com·press·i·ble (in′kəm pres′ə bəl), *adj.* not able to be squeezed into a smaller size. —**in′com·press′i·bil′i·ty,** *n.*

in·con·ceiv·a·ble (in′kən sē′və bəl), *adj.* hard to imagine or believe; incredible: *It is inconceivable that two nations so friendly for centuries should now be at war.* —**in′con·ceiv′a·ble·ness,** *n.* —**in′con·ceiv′a·bly,** *adv.*

in·con·clu·sive (in′kən klü′siv), *adj.* not convincing; not settling or deciding something doubtful; not effective: *The result of my blood test was inconclusive, so I'll have to have another test.* —**in′con·clu′sive·ly,** *adv.* —**in′con·clu′sive·ness,** *n.*

in·con·gru·i·ty (in′kən grü′ə tē), *n.* **1** inappropriateness; unfitness. **2** lack of agreement or harmony; inconsistency. **3** something that is incongruous. ❑ *n., pl.* **in·con·gru·i·ties** for 3.

in·con·gru·ous (in kong′grü əs), *adj.* **1** not appropriate; out of place. **2** lacking in agreement or harmony; inconsistent. —**in·con′gru·ous·ly,** *adv.* —**in·con′gru·ous·ness,** *n.*

in·con·se·quen·tial (in′kon sə kwen′shəl), *adj.* not important; trifling. —**in′con·se·quen′tial·ly,** *adv.*

in·con·sid·er·a·ble (in′kən sid′ər ə bəl), *adj.* not worth consideration; not important; insignificant. —**in′con·sid′er·a·ble·ness,** *n.* —**in′con·sid′er·a·bly,** *adv.*

in·con·sid·er·ate (in′kən sid′ər it), *adj.* not thoughtful of others and their feelings; thoughtless. —**in′con·sid′er·ate·ly,** *adv.* —**in′con·sid′er·ate·ness,** *n.* —**in′con·sid′er·a′tion,** *n.*

in·con·sist·en·cy (in′kən sis′tən sē), *n.* **1** failure to keep to the same principles, course of action, etc.; lack of consistency: *She was accused of inconsistency in now defending what she had previously condemned.* **2** thing, act, etc., that is inconsistent. ❑ *n., pl.* **in·con·sist·en·cies** for 2.

in·con·sist·ent (in′kən sis′tənt), *adj.* **1** not consistent; lacking in agreement with itself or something else: *Your failure to arrive on time is inconsistent with your usual promptness.* **2** failing to keep to the same rules, habits, course of action, etc.; changeable: *An inconsistent person says one thing today and the opposite tomorrow.* —**in′con·sist′ent·ly,** *adv.*

in·con·sol·a·ble (in′kən sō′lə bəl), *adj.* not able to be comforted; broken-hearted: *The girl was inconsolable at the loss of her kitten.* —**in′con·sol′a·ble·ness,** *n.* —**in′con·sol′a·bly,** *adv.*

in·con·spic·u·ous (in′kən spik′yü əs), *adj.* not conspicuous; attracting little or no attention: *They live in a small, inconspicuous house.* —**in′con·spic′u·ous·ly,** *adv.* —**in′con·spic′u·ous·ness,** *n.*

in·con·stant (in kon′stənt), *adj.* not constant; changeable; fickle. —**in·con′stant·ly,** *adv.*

in·con·ti·nent (in kon′tən nt), *adj.* **1** without self-control. **2** lacking control over urination and defecation.

in·con·tro·vert·i·ble (in′kon trə vėr′tə bəl), *adj.* not able to be disputed or denied; too clear or certain to be argued about.

in·con·ven·ience (in′kən vē′nyəns), **1** *n.* a cause of trouble; lack of convenience or ease; bother. **2** *n.* something inconvenient; cause of trouble, difficulty, or bother. **3** *v.* to cause trouble, difficulty, or bother to: *It will not inconvenience me to wait a few minutes.* ❑ *v.* **in·con·ven·ienced, in·con·ven·ienc·ing.**

in·con·ven·ient (in′kən vē′nyənt), *adj.* not convenient; causing trouble, difficulty, or bother; troublesome: *Shelves that are too high to reach easily are inconvenient.* —**in′con·ven′ient·ly,** *adv.*

in·cor·po·rate (in kôr′pə rāt′), *v.* **1** to make something a part of something else; join or combine something with something else: *We will incorporate your suggestion in this new plan.* **2** to make into a corporation: *When the business became large, the owners incorporated it.* ❑ *v.* **in·cor·po·rat·ed, in·cor·po·rat·ing.** —**in·cor′po·ra′tion,** *n.*

WORD STORY **Incorporate** comes from Latin words meaning "into a body." In business, people incorporate by forming a group that has the legal right to operate a company, as if the group were a single person.

incrustation (def. 1)—mineral incrustation

in·cor·po·rat·ed (in kôr′pə rā′tid), *adj.* made into a corporation; chartered as a corporation.

in·cor·po·re·al (in′kôr pôr′ē əl), *adj.* not made of any material substance; spiritual. **—in′cor·po′re·al·ly,** *adv.*

in·cor·rect (in′kə rekt′), *adj.* **1** containing errors or mistakes; not correct; wrong: *The newspaper gave an incorrect account of the accident.* **2** not agreeing with an accepted standard of good behavior; not proper: *incorrect behavior.* **—in′cor·rect′ly,** *adv.* **—in′cor·rect′ness,** *n.*

in·cor·ri·gi·ble (in kôr′ə jə bəl), **1** *adj.* too firmly fixed in bad ways, an annoying habit, etc., to be reformed or changed: *Nothing could break her of her incorrigible habit of interrupting.* **2** *n.* an incorrigible person. **—in·cor′ri·gi·bil′i·ty, in·cor′ri·gi·ble·ness,** *n.* **—in·cor′ri·gi·bly,** *adv.*

in·cor·rupt·i·ble (in′kə rup′tə bəl), *adj.* **1** not to be corrupted; honest: *An incorruptible judge cannot be bribed.* **2** not capable of decay; lasting forever: *Diamonds are incorruptible.* **—in′cor·rupt′i·bil′i·ty,** *n.* **—in′cor·rupt′i·bly,** *adv.*

in·crease (in krēs′ *for verb;* in′krēs *for noun*), **1** *v.* to make greater, more numerous, more powerful, etc.; add to: *The driver increased the speed of the car.* **2** *v.* to become greater; grow in numbers; advance in quality, power, etc.: *My weight has increased by ten pounds.* **3** *n.* a gain in size, numbers, etc.; growth: *There has been a great increase in student enrollment during the past year.* **4** *n.* result of increasing; amount added; addition: *an increase of five cents a gallon in the gasoline tax.* ❑ *v.* **in·creased, in·creas·ing.** **—in·creas′a·ble,** *adj.* **—in·creas′er,** *n.*
on the increase, increasing: *The movement of people from the cities to the suburbs is on the increase.*

SYNONYM STUDY **Increase, enlarge,** and **multiply** all mean to make larger. **Increase** is the general word: *In week three of our experiment, we increased light to half the plants.* **Enlarge** means to make something larger, especially in area: *My cousin enlarged this photo to make a poster for me.* **Multiply** can mean to increase in number or size: *That video chain plans to multiply the number of its stores in the city.*

in·creas·ing·ly (in krē′sing lē), *adv.* to a greater degree; more and more: *As we went south, the weather became increasingly warm.*

in·cred·i·ble (in kred′ə bəl), *adj.* hard to believe; seeming too extraordinary to be possible; unbelievable: *The racing car rounded the curve with incredible speed. Many old superstitions seem incredible to us.* ■ See Usage Note at **incredulous.** **—in·cred′i·bil′i·ty,** *n.* **—in·cred′i·bly,** *adv.*

in·cre·du·li·ty (in′krə dü′lə tē), *n.* lack of belief; doubt.

in·cred·u·lous (in krej′ə ləs), *adj.* **1** not ready to believe; doubting: *Most people nowadays are incredulous about ghosts and witches.* **2** showing a lack of belief: *He listened to the neighbor's story with an incredulous smile.* **—in·cred′u·lous·ly,** *adv.*

USAGE NOTE **Incredulous** and **incredible** are sometimes confused. Some people use **incredulous** as if it meant "unbelievable." This is an error. **Incredulous** means "doubting." It does not mean **incredible.**

in·cre·ment (in′krə mənt), *n.* **1** an increase; growth. **2** amount by which something increases: *The wages are $220 a week with an increment of $25 for each year of service.*

in·crim·i·nate (in krim′ə nāt), *v.* to accuse of a crime; tend to show someone's guilt: *The robber's confession incriminated two others who helped to rob the bank.* ❑ *v.* **in·crim·i·nat·ed, in·crim·i·nat·ing.** **—in·crim′i·na′tion,** *n.*

in·crust (in krust′), *v.* to encrust.

in·crus·ta·tion (in′krus′tā′shən), *n.* **1** crust or hard coating. **2** a decorative layer of costly material.

in·cu·bate (ing′kyə bāt *or* in′kyə bāt), *v.* **1** to sit on eggs in order to hatch them; brood. **2** to keep eggs warm so that they will develop. **3** to cause to grow or develop: *The team is incubating a plan to wash cars for uniform money.* ❑ *v.* **in·cu·bat·ed, in·cu·bat·ing.**

in·cu·ba·tion (ing′kyə bā′shən *or* in′kyə bā′shən), *n.* **1** act of incubating or condition of being incubated. **2** stage of a disease from the time of infection until the first symptoms appear: *The period of incubation for measles is about ten days.*

in·cu·ba·tor (ing′kyə bā′tər *or* in′kyə bā′tər), *n.* **1** box or chamber for hatching eggs by keeping them warm and properly supplied with moisture and oxygen. **2** any similar box or chamber. Very small babies and premature babies are sometimes kept for a time in hospital incubators.

in·cul·cate (in kul′kāt), *v.* to impress on someone by repetition; teach persistently: *Over the years she inculcated a love of books into her pupils.* ❑ *v.* **in·cul·cat·ed, in·cul·cat·ing.** **—in′cul·ca′tion,** *n.* **—in·cul′ca·tor,** *n.*

WORD STORY **Inculcate** comes from Latin words meaning "in" and "heel." These words were combined in a Latin word meaning "trampled in." Teaching by repetition may be like stepping repeatedly on the same spot.

in·cum·ben·cy (in kum′bən sē), *n.* term of office: *During her incumbency as mayor the city thrived.* ❑ *n., pl.* **in·cum·ben·cies.**

in·cum·bent (in kum′bənt), **1** *adj.* currently holding an office, position, etc.: *the incumbent governor.* **2** *n.* person holding an office, position, etc.: *The former incumbent had been very popular in the district.* **3** *adj.* resting on someone as a duty: *She felt it incumbent upon her to answer the letter at once.* **4** *adj.* lying, leaning, or pressing on something. **—in·cum′bent·ly,** *adv.*

in·cur (in kėr′), *v.* to run or fall into something unpleasant or inconvenient; bring on yourself: *incur many expenses. The pioneers incurred great danger when they crossed the Rocky Mountains.* ❑ *v.* **in·curred, in·cur·ring.** **—in·cur′ra·ble,** *adj.*

in·cur·a·ble (in kyùr′ə bəl), **1** *adj.* not able to be cured: *an incurable invalid, an incurable disease.* **2** *n.* someone having an incurable disease: *a home for incurables.* **—in·cur′a·ble·ness,** *n.* **—in·cur′a·bly,** *adv.*

in·cur·i·ous (in kyùr′ē əs), *adj.* lacking curiosity; uninterested; indifferent. **—in·cur′ious·ly,** *adv.*

in·cur·sion (in kėr′zhən), *n.* a sudden attack; invasion; raid: *The pirates made incursions along the coast.*

in·curve (in′kėrv′), **1** *n.* an inward curve. **2** *v.* to curve inward. ❑ *v.* **in·curved, in·curv·ing.**

ind., **1** independent. **2** index.

Ind., Indiana.

in·debt·ed (in det′id), *adj.* owing money or gratitude; in debt; obliged: *We are indebted to science for many of our comforts.*

in·debt·ed·ness (in det′id nis), *n.* **1** condition of being in debt. **2** amount owed; debts.

in·de·cen·cy (in dē′sn sē), *n.* **1** lack of decency; being indecent. **2** an indecent act or word. ❑ *n., pl.* **in·de·cen·cies** for 2.

in·de·cent (in dē′snt), *adj.* **1** not decent; in very bad taste; improper: *They showed an indecent lack of gratitude to those who had helped them.* ■ See Synonym Study at **improper. 2** not modest; morally bad; disgusting; obscene. **—in·de′cent·ly,** *adv.*

a	hat	ė	term	ô	order	ch	child		
ā	age	i	it	oi	oil	ng	long		a in about
â	far	ī	ice	ou	out	sh	she	ə	e in taken
â	care	o	hot	u	cup	th	thin		i in pencil
e	let	ō	open	ù	put	ᵺ	then		o in lemon
ē	equal	ò	saw	ü	rule	zh	measure		u in circus

in·de·ci·pher·a·ble (in/di sī/fər ə bəl), *adj.* not able to be deciphered; impossible to read: *Her handwriting is indecipherable.*

in·de·ci·sion (in/di sizh/ən), *n.* lack of decision; tendency to delay or to hesitate.

in·de·ci·sive (in/di sī/siv), *adj.* **1** having the habit of hesitating and putting off decisions: *an indecisive person.* **2** not deciding or settling the matter; without a clear result: *Neither side wins in an indecisive battle.* —**in/de·ci/sive·ly,** *adv.* —**in/de·ci/sive·ness,** *n.*

in·deed (in dēd/), **1** *adv.* in fact; in truth; really; surely: *She is hungry; indeed, she is starving.* **2** *interj.* expression of surprise, doubt, contempt, etc.: *Indeed! I never would have thought it.*

in·de·fat·i·ga·ble (in/di fat/ə gə bəl), *adj.* never getting tired or giving up; tireless: *An indefatigable worker keeps on working until the work is done.* —**in/de·fat/i·ga·bil/i·ty, in/de·fat/i·ga·ble·ness,** *n.* —**in/de·fat/i·ga·bly,** *adv.*

in·de·fen·si·ble (in/di fen/sə bəl), *adj.* **1** not able to be defended: *an indefensible island.* **2** not justifiable; inexcusable: *an indefensible lie.* —**in/de·fen/si·bly,** *adv.*

in·de·fin·a·ble (in/di fī/nə bəl), *adj.* not able to be defined or described exactly: *It was a place of indefinable beauty.* —**in/de·fin/a·bly,** *adv.*

in·def·i·nite (in def/ə nit), *adj.* **1** not clearly defined; not exact: *indefinite instructions.* **2** undecided; vague: *"Maybe" is an indefinite answer.* **3** not limited: *We have an indefinite time to finish this work.* **4** not naming exactly; not identifying a specific person, thing, time, etc. **Indefinite pronouns** such as *some, many,* and *few* stand for a number of things or people, but the number is not named. —**in·def/i·nite·ly,** *adv.* —**in·def/i·nite·ness,** *n.*

indefinite article, the article *a* or *an.* "A dog" or "an animal" means "any dog" or "any animal"; "the dog" means "a certain or particular dog."

in·del·i·ble (in del/ə bəl), *adj.* **1** not able to be erased or removed; permanent: *indelible ink. Her experiences in India left an indelible impression on her memory.* **2** making an indelible mark: *The papers were graded with an indelible pencil.* —**in·del/i·ble·ness,** *n.* —**in·del/i·bly,** *adv.*

in·del·i·ca·cy (in del/ə kə sē), *n.* lack of delicacy; being indelicate.

in·del·i·cate (in del/ə kit), *adj.* **1** not delicate; coarse; crude: *It is indelicate to talk back rudely to someone.* **2** improper; immodest. —**in·del/i·cate·ly,** *adv.* —**in·del/i·cate·ness,** *n.*

in·dem·ni·fy (in dem/nə fī), *v.* **1** to make up for damage, loss, or hardship; make good; repay: *The railroad indemnified them for their injuries in the train wreck.* **2** to protect against damage or loss; insure. ❑ *v.* **in·dem·ni·fied, in·dem·ni·fy·ing.**

in·dem·ni·ty (in dem/nə tē), *n.* **1** payment for damage, loss, or hardship. Money demanded by a victorious nation at the end of a war as a condition of peace is an indemnity. **2** security against damage or loss; insurance. ❑ *n., pl.* **in·dem·ni·ties** for 1.

in·dent[1] (in dent/), *v.* to begin a line farther from the left margin than the other lines: *The first line of a paragraph is usually indented.*

in·dent[2] (in dent/), *v.* **1** to make a dent in; mark with a dent. **2** to press in; stamp.

in·den·ta·tion (in/den tā/shən), *n.* **1** a dent, notch, or cut. **2** act of indenting or condition of being indented.

in·den·ted (in dent/id), *adj.* having jagged or worn-away edges: *an indented coastline.* [Indented comes from Latin words meaning "in" and "tooth." A notched edge looks as if it has been bitten.]

in·den·tion (in den/shən), *n.* **1** a beginning of a line farther from the left margin than the other lines. **2** the blank space left by doing this. **3** indentation.

in·den·ture (in den/chər), *n.* (long ago) contract by which someone was bound to serve someone else: *An apprentice has an indenture with the master from whom he learned a trade.* ❑ *v.* **in·den·tured, in·den·tur·ing.**

in·den·tured (in den/chərd), *adj.* (long ago) bound by a contract to serve someone else: *Many settlers who came to the American colonies were indentured servants for several years.*

in·de·pend·ence (in/di pen/dəns), *n.* condition of being independent; freedom from the control, influence, support, or help of others: *The American colonies won independence from England.* ∎ See Synonym Study at **liberty.**

In·de·pend·ence (in/di pen/dəns), *n.* city in W Missouri.

Independence Day, holiday in honor of the adoption of the Declaration of Independence on July 4, 1776; Fourth of July.

Independence Day

in·de·pend·ent (in/di pen/dənt), **1** *adj.* not influenced by others; thinking or acting for yourself: *an independent voter, an independent thinker.* **2** *adj.* not under another's rule or control; ruling, guiding, or governing yourself: *The United States is an independent country.* **3** *adj.* not connected with others; separate or distinct: *an independent investigation, independent work.* **4** *adj.* not depending on others for your support: *Now that I have a better-paying job, I can be completely independent.* **5** *adj.* enough to live on without working: *an independent income.* **6** *n.* person who is independent in thought or behavior. **7** *n.* person who votes without regard to party. —**in/de·pend/ent·ly,** *adv.*

independent clause, (in grammar) clause in a complex sentence that can act by itself as a sentence; main clause.

in-depth (in/depth/), *adj.* thorough; detailed: *an in-depth report.*

in·de·scrib·a·ble (in/di skrī/bə bəl), *adj.* not able to be described; beyond description: *a scene of indescribable beauty.* —**in/de·scrib/a·ble·ness,** *n.* —**in/de·scrib/a·bly,** *adv.*

in·de·struct·i·ble (in/di struk/tə bəl), *adj.* not able to be destroyed. —**in/de·struct/i·bil/i·ty, in/de·struct/i·ble·ness,** *n.* —**in/de·struct/i·bly,** *adv.*

in·de·ter·mi·na·ble (in/di tėr/mə nə bəl), *adj.* not able to be settled, decided, or determined exactly. —**in/de·ter/mi·na·bly,** *adv.*

in·de·ter·mi·nate (in/di tėr/mə nit), *adj.* not determined; not fixed; indefinite; vague: *As the floodwaters rose, an indeterminate number of people were stranded.* —**in/de·ter/mi·nate·ly,** *adv.* —**in/de·ter/mi·nate·ness,** *n.*

in·dex (in/deks), **1** *n.* list of what is in a book, telling on what pages to find names, topics, etc. An index is usually put at the end of the book and arranged in alphabetical order. **2** *v.* to put an index in; provide with an index; make an index of: *to index files alphabetically, to index your notes.* **3** *n.* thing that points out or shows; sign: *A person's face is often an index of his or her mood.* **4** *n.* pointer. A dial or scale usually has an index. ❑ *n., pl.* **in·dex·es** or **in·di·ces.** —**in/dex·er,** *n.*

index finger, forefinger.

In·di·a (in/dē ə), *n.* **1** country in S Asia. *Capital:* New Delhi. **2** region and former country in S Asia. It is now chiefly divided into the countries of India, Pakistan, and Bangladesh.

India ink, a black paint or ink.

In·di·an (in/dē ən), **1** *n.* Native American. ∎ See Usage Note at **Native American. 2** *adj.* of or for Native Americans: *an Indian camp, an Indian language.* **3** *n.* INFORMAL. any one of the languages of Native Americans. **4** *adj.* of, living in, or belonging to India or the East Indies: *Indian elephants, Indian temples, Indian costumes.* **5** *n.* someone born or living in India or the East Indies.

In·di·an·a (in/dē an/ə), *n.* one of the north central states of the United States. *Abbreviation:* IN or Ind. *Capital:* Indianapolis. —**In/di·an/an** or **In/di·an/i·an,** *n.*

WORD STORY **Indiana** comes from the word **Indian,** meaning "Native American." When the name was first used, the region was inhabited mostly by American Indians.

In·di·a·nap·o·lis (in′dē ə nap′ə lis), *n.* capital of Indiana, in the central part.

Indian club, a bottle-shaped wooden club swung for exercise.

Indian corn, 1 kind of cereal grass first raised by Native Americans; corn; maize. **2** grain or ears of this plant.

Indian Ocean, ocean south of Asia, east of Africa, and west of Australia.

Indian pipe, a North American and eastern Asian waxy, leafless, white or pinkish plant with a single flower. It looks something like a tobacco pipe.

Indian summer, time of mild, dry, hazy weather in late October or early November, after the first frosts of autumn.

India paper, a thin, tough printing paper.

india rubber or **India rubber,** rubber.

in·di·cate (in′də kāt), *v.* **1** to point out; make known; show: *The arrow on the sign indicates the right way to go.* **2** to give a sign or hint of: *People often indicate their feelings by facial expressions.* **3** to be a sign or hint of: *Fever indicates illness.* ❑ *v.* **in·di·cat·ed, in·di·cat·ing.**

in·di·ca·tion (in′də kā′shən), *n.* **1** act of indicating: *We use different words for the indication of different meanings.* **2** thing that indicates; sign: *There was no indication that the house was occupied.*

in·dic·a·tive (in dik′ə tive), **1** *adj.* pointing out; showing; being a sign; suggestive: *A headache is sometimes indicative of eyestrain.* **2** *adj.* (in grammar) of a verb form which expresses or denotes a state, act, or happening as actual, or which asks a simple question of fact. **3** *n.* form of a verb which expresses this. In "I go" and "Did you win?" *go* and *did win* are indicatives. **4** *n.* mood of such a verb. **−in·dic′a·tive·ly,** *adv.*

in·di·ca·tor (in′də kā′tər), *n.* **1** someone or something that indicates. **2** pointer on the dial of a device that shows the amount of heat, pressure, speed, etc. **3** a measuring or recording device. **4** substance which, by changing color, indicates the chemical condition of a solution. Litmus is an indicator.

in·di·ces (in′də sēz′), *n.* a plural of **index.**

in·dict (in dīt′), *v.* **1** to charge an accused person with a crime and hold him or her for trial on the recommendation of a grand jury which has heard the evidence and considered it sufficient. **2** to charge with an offense or crime; accuse. **−in·dict′a·ble,** *adj.* **−in·dict′er** or **in·dict′or,** *n.*

in·dict·ment (in dīt′mənt), *n.* **1** a formal written accusation, especially on the recommendation of a grand jury: *an indictment for murder.* **2** accusation.

In·dies (in′dēz), *n.pl.* **1** the East Indies. **2** the West Indies.

in·dif·fer·ence (in dif′ər əns), *n.* **1** lack of interest or attention; not caring: *The child's indifference to food worried its parents.* **2** lack of importance: *It is a matter of indifference to me.*

in·dif·fer·ent (in dif′ər ənt), *adj.* **1** not caring one way or the other; having or showing no interest: *I enjoyed the trip but she was indifferent.* **2** impartial; neutral; without preference: *Courts should make indifferent decisions.* **3** neither good nor bad; just fair: *an indifferent player.*

in·dif·fer·ent·ly (in dif′ər ənt lē), *adv.* **1** with indifference. **2** without distinction; equally. **3** poorly; badly.

in·di·gence (in′də jəns), *n.* poverty.

in·dig·e·nous (in dij′ə nəs), *adj.* originating or produced in a particular country; growing or living naturally in a certain region, soil, climate, etc.; native: *Lions are indigenous to Africa.* **−in·dig′e·nous·ly,** *adv.*

> **WORD STORY** **Indigenous** comes from Latin words meaning "in" and "to give birth." Being indigenous to a place means having been born there.

in·di·gent (in′də jənt), *adj.* poor or needy. [**Indigent** comes from Latin words meaning "be in need."] **−in′di·gent·ly,** *adv.*

in·di·gest·i·ble (in′də jes′tə bəl), *adj.* not able to be digested; hard to digest.

in·di·ges·tion (in′də jes′chən), *n.* **1** the feeling of discomfort that people may get from difficulty in digesting food: *The rich food we ate gave us indigestion.* **2** inability to digest food; difficulty in digesting food.

in·dig·nant (in dig′nənt), *adj.* angry at something unworthy, unjust, or mean: *She was indignant when her sister threw cold water at her.* **−in·dig′nant·ly,** *adv.*

in·dig·na·tion (in′dig nā′shən), *n.* the feeling of being angry at something unworthy, unjust, or mean; anger mixed with scorn; righteous anger: *Cruelty to animals aroused his indignation.*

in·dig·ni·ty (in dig′nə tē), *n.* an injury to your dignity; lack of respect or proper treatment; insult: *Bill felt that being called "Willie dear" was an indignity.* ❑ *n., pl.* **in·dig·ni·ties.**

in·di·go (in′də gō), **1** *adj.* deep violet blue. **2** *n.* a deep violet blue. **3** *n.* a blue dye formerly obtained from various plants, but now usually made artificially. **4** *n.* any of various plants from which indigo was made. ❑ *n., pl.* **in·di·gos** or **in·di·goes.** [**Indigo** comes from a Greek word meaning "Indian." The dye came originally from India.]

in·di·rect (in′də rekt′), *adj.* **1** not directly connected; secondary: *An increase in traffic was an indirect result of higher bus fares.* **2** not going straight to the point: *She would not say yes or no but gave an indirect answer to my question.* **3** not direct; not straight: *We walk to town by a road that is indirect, but very pleasant.* **−in·di·rect′ly,** *adv.* **−in·di·rect′ness,** *n.*

indirect object, (in grammar) a word or group of words that usually comes before the direct object and shows the person or thing to which or for which something is done. In "Give me the book," *me* is the indirect object and *book* is the direct object.

in·dis·creet (in′dis krēt′), *adj.* not discreet; not wise and judicious; imprudent: *You were indiscreet to tell them your secret.* **−in·dis·creet′ly,** *adv.* **−in·dis·creet′ness,** *n.*

in·dis·cre·tion (in′dis kresh′ən), *n.* **1** lack of discretion or good judgment: *They were embarrassed at his indiscretion in talking about family matters in front of strangers.* **2** an indiscreet act or remark.

in·dis·crim·i·nate (in′dis krim′ə nit), *adj.* **1** without discrimination; not distinguishing carefully between persons, things, etc.: *an indiscriminate reader.* **2** mixed up; confused: *She tipped everything out of her suitcase in an indiscriminate pile.* **−in·dis·crim′i·nate·ly,** *adv.* **−in·dis·crim′i·nate·ness,** *n.*

in·dis·pen·sa·ble (in′dis pen′sə bəl), *adj.* absolutely necessary: *Air is indispensable to life.* **−in·dis·pen′sa·bil′i·ty, in·dis·pen′sa·ble·ness,** *n.* **−in·dis·pen′sa·bly,** *adv.*

in·dis·posed (in′dis pōzd′), *adj.* **1** slightly ill: *I have been indisposed with a cold.* **2** unwilling; not inclined.

in·dis·po·si·tion (in′dis pə zish′ən), *n.* **1** a slight illness. **2** unwillingness.

in·dis·put·a·ble (in′dis pyü′tə bəl *or* in dis′pyə tə bəl), *adj.* too evident to be disputed; undoubted; certain; unquestionable: *an indisputable fact.* **−in·dis·put′a·ble·ness,** *n.* **−in·dis·put′a·bly,** *adv.*

indigenous produce for sale

a	hat	ė	term	ô	order	ch	child	⟨ a in about
ā	age	i	it	oi	oil	ng	long	e in taken
ä	far	ī	ice	ou	out	sh	she	ə ⟨ i in pencil
â	care	o	hot	u	cup	th	thin	o in lemon
e	let	ō	open	ů	put	ŦH	then	⟨ u in circus
ē	equal	ò	saw	ü	rule	zh	measure	

in·dis·sol·u·ble (in′di sol′yə bəl), *adj.* not able to be dissolved, undone, or destroyed; lasting; firm: *Let us make an indissoluble agreement.* —**in′dis·sol′u·bly,** *adv.*

in·dis·tinct (in′dis tingkt′), *adj.* not clear to the eye, ear, or mind; not distinct; confused: *an indistinct voice. I have an indistinct memory of the accident.* —**in′dis·tinct′ly,** *adv.* —**in′dis·tinct′ness,** *n.*

in·dis·tin·guish·a·ble (in′dis ting′gwi shə bəl), *adj.* not able to be distinguished. —**in′dis·tin′guish·a·bly,** *adv.*

in·di·um (in′dē əm), *n.* a very soft, silvery metallic element found only in combination with other elements. It is used as a coating on bearings. *Symbol:* In

in·di·vid·u·al (in′də vij′ü əl), **1** *n.* person: *an extremely unpleasant individual.* **2** *n.* a single person, animal, or thing. **3** *adj.* for or by one only; single; particular; separate: *Each student was given individual attention.* **4** *adj.* belonging to or marking off one person or thing specially: *an individual style of writing.* [**Individual** comes from Latin words meaning "not" and "divide." Unlike a group, an individual cannot be divided into parts.]

USAGE NOTE **Individual** is used about someone as a particular person rather than as a member of a group: *Every individual should decide how to vote.* It is also used about someone with special qualities: *One dancer stood out as a real individual.* When the meaning is not a particular person, however, **person** or **people** should be used: *Any people who would like to volunteer should leave their names.* Not: *Any individuals who would like to volunteer should leave their names.*

in·di·vid·u·al·ism (in′də vij′ü ə liz′əm), *n.* **1** belief that individual freedom is as important as the welfare of the community or group as a whole. **2** absence of cooperation; wanting a separate existence for yourself.

in·di·vid·u·al·ist (in′də vij′ü ə list), *n.* **1** person who lives independently and does not try to cooperate with or follow others. **2** supporter of individualism.

in·di·vid·u·al·is·tic (in′də vij′ü ə lis′tik), *adj.* of or about individualism or individualists. —**in′di·vid′u·al·is′ti·cal·ly,** *adv.*

in·di·vid·u·al·i·ty (in′də vij′ü al′i tē), *n.* **1** the sum of the qualities which make one object or living thing different from another. **2** condition of being individual; existence as an individual.

in·di·vid·u·al·ly (in′də vij′ü ə lē), *adv.* **1** one at a time; as individuals; personally: *Sometimes our teacher helps us individually.* **2** each from the others: *People differ individually.*

in·di·vis·i·ble (in′də viz′ə bəl), *adj.* **1** not able to be divided: *"One nation under God, indivisible, with liberty and justice for all."* **2** not able to be divided without a remainder: *Any odd number is indivisible by 2.* —**in′di·vis′i·bil′i·ty,** *n.* —**in′di·vis′i·bly,** *adv.*

In·do·chi·na (in′dō chī′nə), *n.* **1** peninsula in SE Asia including Myanmar, Cambodia, Laos, Malaya, Singapore, Thailand, and Vietnam. **2** countries in the E part of this peninsula; Cambodia, Laos, and Vietnam.

In·do·chi·nese (in′dō chī nēz′), *adj.* of or relating to Indochina, the peoples living there, or their languages.

in·doc·tri·nate (in dok′trə nāt), *v.* **1** to teach a particular belief or doctrine so that it is accepted uncritically. **2** to teach; instruct. ❑ *v.* **in·doc·tri·nat·ed, in·doc·tri·nat·ing.** —**in·doc′tri·na′tion,** *n.* —**in·doc′tri·na′tor,** *n.*

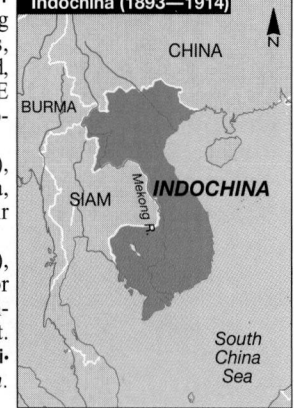

Indochina (1893—1914)

CHINA
N
BURMA
SIAM
Mekong R.
INDOCHINA
South China Sea

In·do-Eur·o·pe·an (in′dō yür′ə pē′ən), *n.* a group of related languages derived from a single prehistoric language, spoken in India, western Asia, and Europe. Indo-European includes English, German, Latin, Greek, Persian, Sanskrit, and other languages.

in·do·lence (in′dl əns), *n.* dislike of work; laziness; idleness.

in·do·lent (in′dl ənt), *adj.* disliking work; lazy. —**in′do·lent·ly,** *adv.*

in·dom·i·ta·ble (in dom′ə tə bəl), *adj.* not able to be discouraged, beaten, or conquered; unyielding: *The team's indomitable spirit was a help in winning a very close game.* —**in·dom′i·ta·bil′i·ty, in·dom′i·ta·ble·ness,** *n.* —**in·dom′i·ta·bly,** *adv.*

In·do·ne·sia (in′də nē′zhə), *n.* **1** country in the East Indies that includes Java, Sumatra, Celebes, parts of Borneo and New Guinea, and over 3000 smaller islands. *Capital:* Jakarta. **2** Malay Archipelago. —**In′do·ne′sian,** *adj., n.*

in·door (in′dôr′), *adj.* done, used, etc., in a house or building: *indoor tennis.*

in·doors (in′dôrz′ *or* in dôrz′), *adv.* in or into a house or building: *Go indoors.*

In·dra (in′drə), *n.* the Hindu god of war, lightning, and thunder.

in·du·bi·ta·ble (in dü′bə tə bəl), *adj.* too evident to be doubted; certain; unquestionable: *It is an indubitable truth that all living matter dies.* —**in·du′bi·ta·ble·ness,** *n.* —**in·du′bi·ta·bly,** *adv.*

in·duce (in düs′), *v.* **1** to lead on; influence; persuade: *Advertisements induce people to buy.* **2** to cause; bring about: *The doctor says that this medicine will induce sleep.* **3** to produce an electric current, electric charge, or magnetic field without direct contact, by a nearby current, charge, or magnetic field. **4** to infer by reasoning from particular facts to a general rule or principle. ❑ *v.* **in·duced, in·duc·ing.** —**in·duc′er,** *n.* —**in·duc′i·ble,** *adj.*

in·duce·ment (in düs′mənt), *n.* **1** something that influences or persuades; incentive: *A new bicycle for the winner was an inducement to try hard to win the contest.* **2** act of influencing or persuading.

in·duct (in dukt′), *v.* **1** to install in an official position: *She was inducted as governor. He was inducted as treasurer of the club.* **2** to bring in; introduce into a place, seat, position, etc. **3** to take into the armed forces.

in·duct·ance (in duk′təns), *n.* the quality of an electric circuit that induces an electromotive force in the circuit itself or any nearby circuit when the current changes.

in·duc·tee (in duk′tē′), *n.* person who has been or soon will be inducted, especially into the armed forces. ❑ *n., pl.* **in·duc·tees.**

in·duc·tion (in duk′shən), *n.* **1** act of inducting; act or ceremony of installing a person in office. **2** enrollment in military service. **3** process by which an electric current, electric charge, or magnetic field induces a current, charge, or field in a nearby object, without direct contact. **4** act or process of reasoning from particular facts to general truths or principles. ■ See Usage Note at **deduction.**

induction coil, device that uses low-voltage direct current to induce high-voltage alternating current. The direct current flows through a wire coil with few loops. Another coil with many more loops runs alongside. When the direct current is repeatedly interrupted, it produces alternating current in the other coil, with increased voltage because of the more numerous loops affected.

in·duc·tive (in duk′tiv), *adj.* **1** of or using induction; reasoning by induction. **2** of or caused by electric or magnetic induction. —**in·duc′tive·ly,** *adv.* —**in·duc′tive·ness,** *n.*

in·dulge (in dulj′), *v.* **1** to give in to your impulse; let yourself have, use, or do what you want: *Every so often he indulges in a chocolate soda.* **2** to give in to the wishes or whims of; humor: *We often indulge a sick person.* ■ See Synonym Study at **gratify.** ❑ *v.* **in·dulged, in·dulg·ing.** —**in·dulg′er,** *n.*

in·dul·gence (in dul′jəns), *n.* **1** act of indulging. **2** something indulged in: *Luxuries are indulgences.* **3** favor; privilege: *Fond parents often allow their children special indulgences.* **4** (in the Roman Catholic Church) act of freeing from the punishment still due for sin after the guilt has been forgiven.

in·dul·gent (in dul′jənt), *adj.* **1** giving in to another's wishes or whims; too kind or agreeable: *Their indulgent parents gave them everything they wanted.* **2** making allowances; not critical; lenient: *Our indulgent teacher praised every poem we wrote.* —**in·dul′gent·ly,** *adv.*

In·dus (in′dəs), *n.* river flowing from W Tibet through Kashmir and Pakistan into the Arabian Sea.

in·dus·tri·al (in dus′trē əl), *adj.* **1** of or produced by industry: *industrial products.* **2** having highly developed industries: *industrial nations.* **3** engaged in or connected with industry: *industri-*

al workers, industrial schools. **4** for use in industry: *industrial diamonds.* —**in·dus′tri·al·ly,** *adv.*

industrial arts, arts and skills taught to students that will help them work with tools and machines in industry.

in·dus·tri·al·ist (in dus′trē ə list), *n.* person who manages or owns an industrial enterprise.

in·dus·tri·al·ize (in dus′trē ə līz), *v.* to make industrial; develop large industries in a country or economic system. ❑ *v.* **in·dus·tri·al·ized, in·dus·tri·al·iz·ing.** —**in·dus′tri·al·i·za′tion,** *n.*

industrial park, an area of a city, suburb, or village planned for industrial buildings, often with landscaping resembling a park.

Industrial Revolution, the change from an agricultural to an industrial society and from home manufacturing to factory production, especially the one that took place in England from about 1750 to about 1850.

in·dus·tri·ous (in dus′trē əs), *adj.* working hard and steadily; diligent: *An industrious student usually has good grades.* ■ See Synonym Study at **busy.** —**in·dus′tri·ous·ly,** *adv.* —**in·dus′tri·ous·ness,** *n.*

in·dus·try (in′də strē), *n.* **1** any form of business, trade, or manufacture: *the automobile industry. Industries dealing with steel, copper, coal, and construction employ millions of people.* **2** all such business, trade, and manufacture taken as a whole: *Chicago is a center of industry.* **3** steady effort; hard work: *She became a lawyer through much industry.* ❑ *n., pl.* **in·dus·tries** for 1.

industry (def. 1)

in·e·bri·ate (in ē′brē āt *for verb;* in ē′brē it *for noun*), **1** *v.* to make drunk; intoxicate. **2** *n.* a drunken person. ❑ *v.* **in·e·bri·at·ed, in·e·bri·at·ing.** —**in·e′bri·a′tion,** *n.*

in·ed·i·ble (in ed′ə bəl), *adj.* not fit to eat: *Poisonous mushrooms are inedible.*

in·ef·fa·ble (in ef′ə bəl), *adj.* not to be expressed in words; too great to be described in words: *the ineffable beauty of a sunset.* —**in·ef′fa·bil′i·ty, in·ef′fa·ble·ness,** *n.* —**in·ef′fa·bly,** *adv.*

in·ef·fec·tive (in′ə fek′tiv), *adj.* **1** not producing the desired effect; of little use: *an ineffective medicine.* **2** not able to do as well as expected; incapable: *Without the proper training, she was an ineffective supervisor.* —**in′ef·fec′tive·ly,** *adv.* —**in′ef·fec′tive·ness,** *n.*

in·ef·fec·tu·al (in′ə fek′chü əl), *adj.* without effect; failing to have the effect wanted; useless: *His attempts to become friends again after the quarrel were ineffectual.* —**in′ef·fec′tu·al·ly,** *adv.* —**in′ef·fec′tu·al·ness,** *n.*

in·ef·fi·cien·cy (in′ə fish′ən sē), *n.* **1** lack of efficiency; wastefulness. **2** inability to get things done.

in·ef·fi·cient (in′ə fish′ənt), *adj.* **1** not able to produce an effect without waste of time or energy; not efficient; wasteful: *A machine that uses too much fuel is inefficient.* **2** not able to get things done; incapable: *an inefficient worker.* —**in′ef·fi′cient·ly,** *adv.*

in·e·las·tic (in′i las′tik), *adj.* not elastic; stiff; inflexible; unyielding.

in·el·e·gant (in el′ə gənt), *adj.* not elegant; in poor taste; crude; vulgar. —**in·el′e·gant·ly,** *adv.*

in·el·i·gi·ble (in el′ə jə bəl), *adj.* not eligible; not suitable or qualified; unfit to be chosen: *A foreign-born citizen of the United States is ineligible for the Presidency.* —**in·el′i·gi·bil′i·ty,** *n.* —**in·el′i·gi·bly,** *adv.*

in·ept (in ept′), *adj.* **1** not suitable; out of place: *Such a poor player would be an inept choice as captain.* **2** awkward; clumsy: *an inept performance.* —**in·ept′ly,** *adv.* —**in·ept′ness,** *n.*

in·e·qual·i·ty (in′i kwol′ə tē), *n.* **1** lack of equality; condition of being unequal in amount, size, value, rank, etc.: *There is a great inequality between the salaries of a bank president and a teller.* **2** lack of evenness, regularity, or uniformity: *There are many inequalities in the New England coastline.* **3** a mathematical expression showing that two quantities are unequal. EXAMPLES: $a > b$ means a is greater than b; $a < b$ means a is less than b; $a \neq b$ means a and b are unequal. ❑ *n., pl.* **in·e·qual·i·ties** for 2,3.

in·eq·ui·ta·ble (in ek′wə tə bəl), *adj.* not equitable; unfair; unjust. —**in·eq′ui·ta·bly,** *adv.*

in·eq·ui·ty (in ek′wə tē), *n.* **1** lack of equity; unfairness; injustice. **2** an unfair or unjust act. ❑ *n., pl.* **in·eq·ui·ties** for 2. [See Word Story at **iniquity.**]

in·e·rad·i·ca·ble (in′i rad′ə kə bəl), *adj.* that cannot be rooted out or got rid of. —**in′e·rad′i·ca·bly,** *adv.*

in·ert (in ėrt′), *adj.* **1** having no power to move or act; lifeless: *A stone is an inert mass of matter.* **2** inactive; slow; sluggish: *He was sleepy and inert.* **3** with few or no active properties; rarely combining with other elements: *Helium and neon are inert gases.* [**Inert** comes from Latin words meaning "without art or skill." Someone who has no skill gets nothing done.] —**in·ert′ly,** *adv.* —**in·ert′ness,** *n.*

in·er·tia (in ėr′shə), *n.* **1** tendency of all objects and matter in the universe to stay still, or if moving, to go on moving in the same direction, unless acted on by some force. **2** tendency to remain as before, and not start changes: *Only inertia, not shyness, keeps him from making new friends.*

in·er·tial guidance (in ėr′shəl), method of guiding a missile or aircraft in flight by automatic electronic equipment using inertia to detect changes of direction and to correct the course.

in·es·cap·a·ble (in′ə skā′pə bəl), *adj.* not able to be escaped or avoided; sure to happen. —**in′es·cap′a·bly,** *adv.*

in·es·ti·ma·ble (in es′tə mə bəl), *adj.* too great to be estimated; priceless; invaluable: *Freedom of speech is an inestimable privilege.* —**in·es′ti·ma·bly,** *adv.*

in·ev·i·ta·ble (in ev′ə tə bəl), *adj.* not to be avoided; sure to happen; certain to come: *Death is inevitable.* —**in·ev′i·ta·bil′i·ty,** *n.* —**in·ev′i·ta·bly,** *adv.*

in·ex·act (in′ig zakt′), *adj.* not exact; with errors or mistakes; not strictly correct; not just right. —**in′ex·act′ly,** *adv.* —**in′ex·act′ness,** *n.*

in·ex·cus·a·ble (in′ik skyü′zə bəl), *adj.* not to be excused; not able to be justified; unpardonable: *The winning team's poor sportsmanship was inexcusable.* —**in′ex·cus′a·ble·ness,** *n.* —**in′ex·cus′a·bly,** *adv.*

in·ex·haust·i·ble (in′ig zò′stə bəl), *adj.* **1** not able to be exhausted; very abundant: *The wealth of our country seems inexhaustible to many people abroad.* **2** tireless: *The new president is a woman of inexhaustible energy.* —**in′ex·haust′i·bil′i·ty,** *n.* —**in′ex·haust′i·bly,** *adv.*

inexhaustible (def. 1)
inexhaustible supply of seeds

a	hat	ė	term	ô	order	ch	child		
ā	age	i	it	oi	oil	ng	long		a in about
ä	far	ī	ice	ou	out	sh	she	ə	e in taken
â	care	o	hot	u	cup	th	thin		i in pencil
e	let	ō	open	ů	put	ŦH	then		o in lemon
ē	equal	ò	saw	ü	rule	zh	measure		u in circus

in·ex·o·ra·ble (in ek′sər ə bəl), *adj.* acting despite any attempt to prevent or avoid; relentless; unyielding: *The forces of nature are inexorable.* —**in·ex′or·a·bil′i·ty, in·ex′or·a·ble·ness,** *n.* —**in·ex′or·a·bly,** *adv.*

WORD STORY Inexorable comes from Latin words meaning "not" and "to pray earnestly." Something inexorable cannot be stopped by pleading, no matter how earnest.

in·ex·pe·di·ent (in′ik spē′dē ənt), *adj.* not expedient; not practicable, suitable, or wise. —**in′ex·pe′di·ent·ly,** *adv.*

in·ex·pen·sive (in′ik spen′siv), *adj.* not expensive; cheap; low-priced. ■ See Synonym Study at **cheap.** —**in′ex·pen′sive·ly,** *adv.* —**in′ex·pen′sive·ness,** *n.*

in·ex·pe·ri·ence (in′ik spir′ē əns), *n.* lack of experience; lack of practice; lack of skill or wisdom gained from experience.

in·ex·pe·ri·enced (in′ik spir′ē ənst), *adj.* not experienced; without practice; lacking the skill and wisdom gained from experience.

in·ex·pert (in′ik spėrt′ *or* in ek′spėrt′), *adj.* not expert; unskilled. —**in′ex·pert′ly,** *adv.* —**in′ex·pert′ness,** *n.*

in·ex·pli·ca·ble (in′ik splik′ə bəl *or* in ek′splə kə bəl), *adj.* not able to be explained; mysterious: *an inexplicable fire.* —**in·ex′pli·ca·bil′i·ty, in′ex·plic′a·ble·ness,** *n.* —**in′ex·plic′a·bly,** *adv.*

in·ex·press·i·ble (in′ik spres′ə bəl), *adj.* not able to be expressed; impossible to express in words; indescribable. —**in′ex·press′i·bil′i·ty, in′ex·press′i·ble·ness,** *n.* —**in′ex·press′i·bly,** *adv.*

in·ex·tin·guish·a·ble (in′ik sting′gwi shə bəl), *adj.* not able to be put out or stopped: *an inextinguishable fire, an inextinguishable desire for knowledge.*

in·ex·tri·ca·ble (in ek′strə kə bəl *or* in′ik strik′ə bəl), *adj.* 1 not able to be gotten out of: *an inextricable maze, inextricable difficulty.* 2 not able to be disentangled or solved: *inextricable confusion.* —**in·ex′tri·ca·bly,** *adv.*

inf., 1 infantry. 2 infinitive.

in·fal·li·ble (in fal′ə bəl), *adj.* 1 free from error; not able to be mistaken: *an infallible authority.* 2 absolutely reliable; sure: *infallible rules.* —**in·fal′li·bil′i·ty,** *n.* —**in·fal′li·bly,** *adv.*

in·fa·mous (in′fə məs), *adj.* 1 having a very bad reputation; notorious: *A traitor's name is infamous.* 2 deserving or causing a very bad reputation; shamefully bad; very wicked: *To betray your country is an infamous deed.* —**in′fa·mous·ly,** *adv.*

in·fa·my (in′fə mē), *n.* 1 a very bad reputation; public disgrace: *Traitors are held in infamy.* 2 shameful badness; extreme wickedness. 3 an infamous or disgraceful act. ❑ *n., pl.* **in·fa·mies** for 3.

in·fan·cy (in′fən sē), *n.* 1 condition or time of being a baby; babyhood; early childhood. 2 an early stage; very beginning of development: *Space travel is still in its infancy.*

in·fant (in′fənt), 1 *n.* a very young child; baby. 2 *adj.* of or for an infant: *an infant blanket, infant food.* 3 *adj.* in an early stage; just beginning to develop: *an infant industry.* 4 *n.* person under the legal age of responsibility; minor. [See Word Story at **infantry.**]

in·fan·ti·cide (in fan′tə sīd), *n.* 1 the killing of a baby. 2 person who kills a baby.

in·fan·tile (in′fən tīl), *adj.* 1 of or related to an infant or infants: *Measles and chicken pox are infantile diseases.* 2 like an infant; babyish; childish: *an infantile display of temper.*

infantile paralysis, polio.

in·fan·try (in′fən trē), *n.* 1 soldiers trained, equipped, and organized to fight on foot. 2 branch of an army consisting of such troops.

WORD STORY Infantry comes from Latin words meaning "not" and "speak." **Infant** comes from the same words. An infant is too young to speak. In old times, many foot soldiers were boys too young to be made knights. They were called "infants," perhaps as a joke. The name stuck, even when most infantry were full-grown men.

in·fan·try·man (in′fən trē mən), *n.* soldier who fights on foot; foot soldier. ❑ *n., pl.* **in·fan·try·men.**

in·fat·u·at·ed (in fach′ü ā′tid), *adj.* having an exaggerated fondness or passion; foolishly in love.

in·fat·u·a·tion (in fach′ü ā′shən), *n.* exaggerated fondness or passion; foolish love.

in·fect (in fekt′), *v.* 1 to cause disease or an unhealthy condition in by introducing germs, viruses, fungi, etc.: *Dirt infects an open cut. Anyone with a bad cold may infect others.* 2 to influence in a bad way: *A noisy pupil may infect the behavior of a whole class.* 3 to influence by spreading from one to another: *Her joy infected the rest of us.*

WORD STORY Infect comes from a Latin word meaning "to dip in stain." Like stain, infection spreads and is hard to stop. Like stain, it may cause damage.

in·fec·tion (in fek′shən), *n.* 1 act or process of causing disease in people and other living things by bringing into contact with germs, viruses, fungi etc. 2 disease caused in this manner, especially one that can spread from one person to another. 3 something that causes a disease. 4 fact or condition of being infected.

in·fec·tious (in fek′shəs), *adj.* 1 spread by germs, viruses, fungi, etc.: *an infectious disease.* 2 causing infection. 3 apt to spread from one to another: *an infectious laugh.* —**in·fec′tious·ly,** *adv.* —**in·fec′tious·ness,** *n.*

in·fer (in fėr′), *v.* to find out by reasoning; come to believe after thinking; conclude: *I inferred from the smoke that something was burning.* ❑ *v.* **in·ferred, in·fer·ring.** —**in·fer′a·ble,** *adj.* —**in·fer′rer,** *n.*

USAGE NOTE Infer and imply are sometimes confused. **Infer** means to get a meaning: *We inferred from our teacher's comment that there will be a test soon.* **Imply** means to give a meaning: *She implied by her grin that she knew something about the joke.*

in·fer·ence (in′fər əns), *n.* 1 the process of inferring; finding out by reasoning: *What happened is only a matter of inference; no one saw the accident.* 2 something that is inferred; conclusion: *What inference do you draw from smelling smoke?*

in·fer·i·or (in fir′ē ər), 1 *adj.* not very good; below most others; low in quality: *an inferior grade of coffee. This cloth is inferior to real silk.* 2 *adj.* lower in position, rank, or importance: *A lieutenant is inferior to a captain.* 3 *n.* person who is lower in rank or station: *A good leader gets on well with inferiors.* 4 *n.* something that is below average. [See Word Story at **inferno.**]

in·fer·i·or·i·ty (in fir′ē ôr′ə tē), *n.* inferior condition or quality.

inferiority complex, an abnormal feeling of being inferior to other people.

in·fer·nal (in fėr′nl), *adj.* 1 of the lower world; of hell. 2 fit to have come from hell; hellish; devilish: *infernal cruelty.* 3 INFORMAL. hateful; shocking; outrageous: *Stop that infernal racket!* —**in·fer′nal·ly,** *adv.*

in·fer·no (in fėr′nō), *n.* place of torment or intense heat like hell: *The firefighters fought their way through a flaming inferno.* ❑ *n., pl.* **in·fer·nos.**

WORD STORY Inferno comes from Latin words meaning "located below." **Inferior** comes from the same words. Hell was believed to be underground and very hot.

in·fer·tile (in fėr′tl), *adj.* not fertile; sterile.

in·fest (in fest′), *v.* to trouble or disturb frequently or in large numbers: *Mosquitoes infest swamps.* —**in′fes·ta′tion,** *n.*

in·fi·del (in′fə dəl), 1 *n.* person who does not believe in religion. 2 *adj.* not believing in religion. 3 *n.* person who does not accept a particular faith. 4 *n.* person who does not accept Christianity.

in·fi·del·i·ty (in′fə del′ə tē), *n.* lack of faithfulness, especially to husband or wife; disloyalty. ❑ *n., pl.* **in·fi·del·i·ties.**

in·field (in′fēld′), *n.* 1 the part of a baseball field that is inside the lines connecting the bases; diamond. 2 first, second, and third basemen and shortstop of a baseball team.

in·field·er (in′fēl′dər), *n.* player in the infield.

in·fil·trate (in fil′trāt *or* in′fil trāt), *v.* 1 to penetrate or slip through an enemy's lines individually or in small groups: *Enemy troops infiltrated the front lines.* 2 to penetrate an organization for the purposes of spying, sabotage, or the like. 3 to pass into or through by filtering. 4 to filter into or through; permeate. ❑ *v.* **in·fil·trat·ed, in·fil·trat·ing.** —**in′fil·tra′tor,** *n.*

in·fil·tra·tion (in′fil trā′shən), *n.* 1 act of infiltrating or condition of being infiltrated. 2 something that infiltrates.

infin., infinitive.

inflate (def. 1)

in·fi·nite (in′fə nit), **1** *adj.* extremely great: *Working a jigsaw puzzle sometimes takes infinite patience.* **2** *adj.* without limits or bounds; endless: *the infinite reaches of outer space.* **3** *n.* that which is infinite. **4** *adj.* in mathematics: **a** greater than can be reached in counting: *an infinite number.* **b** (of a set) having an unlimited number of elements. **5** *n.* **the Infinite,** God. **—in′fi·nite·ly,** *adv.* **—in′fi·nite·ness,** *n.*

USAGE NOTE In science and mathematics, **infinite** cannot be used to compare things, because "more limitless" and "more uncountable" do not make sense. However, in describing experiences, **infinite** may be used with *more* or *most* to describe a very strong feeling or quality: *Music gives me a most infinite joy.*

in·fin·i·tes·i·mal (in′fi nə tes′ə məl), *adj.* so small as to be almost nothing: *Germs are infinitesimal.* **—in′fi·ni·tes′i·mal·ly,** *adv.*

in·fin·i·tive (in fin′ə tiv), *n.* (in grammar) form of a verb not limited by person and number, often preceded by *to.* In "I want to buy a hat," *to buy* is an infinitive. In "We must go now," *go* is an infinitive.

USAGE NOTE The present tense of the **infinitive** is the simple form of the verb, usually with *to: I'd like to go.* Infinitives are used as nouns: *To sail around the world is my ambition;* as adjectives: *They had two hours to kill;* as adverbs: *She went abroad to study;* and as part of verb phrases: *He wants to do more of the work.*

in·fin·i·ty (in fin′ə tē), *n.* **1** condition of having no limits; endlessness: *the infinity of space.* **2** an infinite distance, space, time, or quantity. **3** an infinite extent, amount, or number. **4** an imaginary place infinitely far from everywhere else: *I wish for enough money to reach from here to infinity.*

in·firm (in fėrm′), *adj.* **1** weak; lacking strength or health: *The patient was old and infirm.* **2** without a firm purpose; faltering: *infirm judgment.* **—in·firm′ly,** *adv.*

in·fir·mar·y (in fėr′mər ē), *n.* place for the care of the infirm, sick, or injured; hospital in a school or institution. ❑ *n., pl.* **in·fir·mar·ies.** [Infirmary comes from Latin word words meaning "not" and "firm" or "healthy."]

in·fir·mi·ty (in fėr′mə tē), *n.* **1** weakness; lack of strength or health. **2** sickness; illness: *the infirmities of age.* ❑ *n., pl.* **in·fir·mi·ties** for 2.

in·flame (in flām′), *v.* to make more violent; excite: *Her stirring speech inflamed the crowd.* ❑ *v.* **in·flamed, in·flam·ing.**

in·flamed (in flāmd′), *adj.* unnaturally hot, red, sore, or swollen: *eyes inflamed from smoke.*

in·flam·ma·ble (in flam′ə bəl), *adj.* **1** flammable. **2** easily excited or aroused; excitable: *an inflammable temper.* **—in·flam′ma·bil′i·ty,** *n.*

in·flam·ma·tion (in′flə mā′shən), *n.* a diseased condition of some part of the body, marked by heat, redness, swelling, and pain: *A boil is an inflammation of the skin.*

in·flam·ma·to·ry (in flam′ə tôr′ē), *adj.* **1** tending to excite or arouse: *The crowd was stirred up by the inflammatory speech.* **2** of, causing, or accompanied by inflammation: *An inflammatory condition of the tonsils causes a sore throat.*

in·flate (in flāt′), *v.* **1** to force air or gas into a balloon, tire, ball, etc., causing it to swell. **2** to swell or puff out: *After his success he was inflated with pride.* **3** to increase prices beyond the normal amount. ❑ *v.* **in·flat·ed, in·flat·ing.** [See Word Story at **deflate.**] **—in·flat′a·ble,** *adj.* **—in·flat′er** or **in·fla′tor,** *n.*

in·fla·tion (in flā′shən), *n.* **1** a sharp or steady increase in prices of goods. **2** a swollen state; too great expansion.

in·fla·tion·ar·y (in flā′shə ner′ē), *adj.* of, caused by, or producing inflation: *inflationary prices.*

in·flect (in flekt′), *v.* **1** to vary the form of a word to show case, number, gender, person, tense, mood, voice, or comparison. By inflecting *who* we have *whose* and *whom.* **2** to change the tone or pitch of the voice. **3** to bend; curve. **—in·flec′tor,** *n.*

WORD STORY **Inflect** comes from Latin words meaning "in" and "to bend." The Romans thought of a change in pronunciation as a bending of the voice, and they changed word forms by pronouncing them differently.

in·flec·tion (in flek′shən), *n.* **1** a change in the tone or pitch of the voice: *We usually end questions with a rising inflection.* **2** variation in the form of a word to show case, number, gender, person, tense, mood, voice, or comparison. **3** suffix or ending used for this: *-est* and *-ed* are common inflections in English. **4** act of bending or curving. **5** a bend; curve. **—in·flec′tion·al,** *adj.* **—in·flec′tion·al·ly,** *adv.*

in·flex·i·ble (in flek′sə bəl), *adj.* **1** not yielding; firm; steadfast: *an inflexible decision.* **2** not able to be changed; unalterable. **3** not easily bent; stiff; rigid: *an inflexible rod.* **—in·flex′i·bil′i·ty,** *n.* **—in·flex′i·bly,** *adv.*

in·flict (in flikt′), *v.* **1** to give a blow or wound: *A knife can inflict a bad wound on someone.* **2** to force to endure suffering, punishment, something unwelcome, etc.: *to inflict pain. Our unpleasant neighbors inflicted themselves on us all afternoon.*

in·flic·tion (in flik′shən), *n.* act of inflicting: *the infliction of pain.*

in·flight (in′flīt′), *adj.* within or during flight: *in-flight meals, in-flight movie.*

in·flo·res·cence (in′flôr es′ns), *n.* **1** pattern of flowers on a stem. **2** a flower cluster. **3** flowering time.

in·flow (in′flō′), *n.* **1** act or process of flowing in or into: *an inflow of money.* **2** that which flows in.

in·flu·ence (in′flü əns), **1** *n.* power of acting on others and having an effect without using force: *Use your influence to persuade your friends to join our club.* **2** *n.* person or thing that has such power: *My older sister was a good influence on me.* **3** *v.* to have an influence on: *What we read influences our thinking.* **4** *v.* to use influence on: *We tried to influence the teacher by offering him our suggestions.* **5** *n.* power someone has due to wealth, social status, or position: *use political influence for personal gain.* ❑ *v.* **in·flu·enced, in·flu·enc·ing.**

in·flu·en·tial (in′flü en′shəl), *adj.* **1** having much influence: *Influential friends helped her get a good job.* **2** using influence; producing results. **—in·flu·en′tial·ly,** *adv.*

in·flu·en·za (in′flü en′zə), *n.* flu.

in·flux (in′fluks), *n.* an arrival in great numbers; steady flow: *An influx of immigrants from Europe greatly increased the population of the United States.* ❑ *n., pl.* **in·flux·es.**

in·fo (in′fō), *n.* INFORMAL. information.

in·fo·mer·cial (in′fō mėr′shəl), *n.* a TV commercial made to resemble an informative program but intended to advertise particular products. [Infomercial is a blend of **information** and **commercial.**]

in·form (in fôrm′), *v.* **1** to give knowledge, facts, or news to; tell: *Her letter informed us of how and when she expected to arrive.* ■ See Synonym Study at **tell. 2** to give information about someone's wrongdoing to the police or other authority: *The criminal who was caught informed against the other robbers.*

a	hat	ė	term	ô	order	ch	child		
ā	age	i	it	oi	oil	ng	long	ə	a in about
ä	far	ī	ice	ou	out	sh	she		e in taken
â	care	o	hot	u	cup	th	thin		i in pencil
e	let	ō	open	ù	put	ᴛʜ	then		o in lemon
ē	equal	ò	saw	ü	rule	zh	measure		u in circus

in·for·mal (in fôr′məl), *adj.* **1** not formal; everyday; without ceremony: *an informal party, informal clothes.* **2** used in everyday, common talk, but not used in formal talking or writing; colloquial. An expression like *kids* for *children* is informal. —**in·for′mal·ly,** *adv.*

SYNONYM STUDY **Informal, casual,** and **natural** all mean for everyday use or in an everyday manner. **Informal** means not used on serious or important occasions: *For the family picnic, informal clothes were all we needed.* **Casual** can mean just letting things happen: *He loves playing a casual game with his friends, but he wants to try out for the team too.* **Natural** can mean acting without planning: *Since she retired, our neighbor has become much more relaxed and natural.*

in·for·mal·i·ty (in′fôr mal′ə tē), *n.* **1** lack of ceremony. **2** an informal act or behavior. ❑ *n., pl.* **in·for·mal·i·ties** for 2.

in·form·ant (in fôr′mənt), *n.* someone who gives information to another person: *My informant told me what happened.*

in·for·ma·tion (in′fər mā′shən), *n.* **1** knowledge given or received concerning some fact or circumstance; news: *We have just received information of the astronauts' safe landing. A dictionary contains much information about words.* **2** act of informing: *A guidebook is for the information of travelers.* **3** person or office whose duty is to answer questions. —**in′for·ma′tion·al,** *adj.*

SYNONYM STUDY **Information, data,** and **news** all mean facts or things that are known. **Information** is the general word: *Before she buys the VCR, she needs more information about the guarantee.* **Data** means recorded facts: *For our report on tornadoes, we got data from the weather service.* **News** means information about recent events: *He's eager for news about his friends.*

information highway, information superhighway.

information science, the management of information, especially the collecting, sorting, and recovering of information stored in a computer.

information su·per·high·way (sü′pər hī′wā), a proposed, very large communications network providing many services, including e-mail, interactive entertainment, information databases, etc., used through a computer or television. Also, **information highway.**

in·form·a·tive (in fôr′mə tiv), *adj.* giving information; instructive: *The class trip to see how a newspaper is printed was very informative.* —**in·form′a·tive·ly,** *adv.* —**in·form′a·tive·ness,** *n.*

in·formed (in fôrmd′), *adj.* **1** having information. **2** educated; knowledgeable: *an informed opinion.*

in·form·er (in fôr′mər), *n.* **1** person who tells authorities of violations of the law; person who informs on another: *An informer told the police that the store was selling stolen goods.* **2** informant.

in·fo·tain·ment (in′fō tān′mənt), *n.* information presented in the form of entertainment, such as a TV show or book, in which scenes have been dramatized or reenacted to be more interesting.

in·frac·tion (in frak′shən), *n.* act of breaking a law or obligation; violation: *Reckless driving is an infraction of the law.*

in·fra·red (in′frə red′), *adj.* of or about the invisible rays with wavelengths longer than those of red light. Infrared rays carry heat.

in·fra·son·ic (in′frə son′ik), *adj.* (of sound waves) having a frequency below the range of human hearing.

in·fra·struc·ture (in′frə struk′-chər), *n.* **1** the most important, underlying foundation or basis of any system or structure: *The infrastructure of that business is its experienced sales force.* **2** structures such as roads, bridges, sewers, etc., necessary to a society's function: *The city's crumbling infrastructure will cost many millions to repair.*

infrared—photograph made with infrared film

in·fre·quen·cy (in frē′kwən sē), *n.* scarcity; rarity.

in·fre·quent (in frē′kwənt), *adj.* occurring seldom or far apart; not frequent; scarce; rare: *Her visits are infrequent, so we rarely see her.* —**in·fre′quent·ly,** *adv.*

in·fringe (in frinj′), *v.* **1** to violate a law, obligation, right, etc.: *A false label infringes the food and drug law.* **2** to go beyond the proper or usual limits; trespass; encroach: *Do not infringe upon the rights of others.* ❑ *v.* **in·fringed, in·fring·ing.** —**in·fringe′ment,** *n.* —**in·fring′er,** *n.*

in·fu·ri·ate (in fūr′ē āt), *v.* to fill with wild, fierce anger; make furious; enrage: *Their insults infuriated him.* ❑ *v.* **in·fu·ri·at·ed, in·fu·ri·at·ing.** —**in·fu′ri·at′ing·ly,** *adv.* —**in·fur′i·a′tion,** *n.*

in·fuse (in fyüz′), *v.* **1** to pour in; put in; instill: *She infused her excitement into those who listened to her.* **2** to inspire: *The crowd was infused with her excitement.* **3** to steep or soak a plant or leaves in a liquid to get something out: *Tea leaves are infused in hot water to make tea.* ❑ *v.* **in·fused, in·fus·ing.** —**in·fus′er,** *n.*

in·fu·sion (in fyü′zhən), *n.* **1** act or process of infusing: *The plan was improved by the infusion of new ideas.* **2** a liquid extract obtained by steeping or soaking: *Tea is an infusion of leaves in hot water.*

in·gen·ious (in jē′nyəs), *adj.* **1** skilled in planning or making; clever: *The ingenious boy made a radio set for himself.* **2** cleverly planned and made: *He made an ingenious bird feeder from an old tin can and some wire.* ■ See Usage Note at **ingenuous.** —**in·gen′ious·ly,** *adv.* —**in·gen′ious·ness,** *n.*

WORD STORY **Ingenious** comes from Latin words meaning "born in." People who were clever at designing and making things were thought to be born with a natural talent. **Ingenuous** comes from the same words. The Romans thought that people born in their country had good natures.

in·ge·nue or **in·gé·nue** (an′zhə nü), *n.* **1** a simple, innocent girl or young woman. **2** actress who plays the part of such a girl or young woman. ❑ *n., pl.* **in·ge·nues** or **in·gé·nues.**

in·ge·nu·i·ty (in′jə nü′ə tē), *n.* skill in planning or making; cleverness: *The girl showed ingenuity in making toys out of scraps of wood.*

in·gen·u·ous (in jen′yü əs), *adj.* **1** simple; natural; innocent: *an ingenuous child.* **2** free from restraint or reserve; frank and open; sincere: *He gave an ingenuous account of his acts, concealing nothing.* [See Word Story at **ingenious.**] —**in·gen′u·ous·ly,** *adv.* —**in·gen′u·ous·ness,** *n.*

USAGE NOTE **Ingenuous** and **ingenious** are sometimes confused. **Ingenuous** means frank or sincere: *My ingenuous little brother says exactly what he thinks.* **Ingenious** means clever or skillful: *His sister is so ingenious that we think she will become an inventor.*

in·gest (in jest′), *v.* to take food into the body for digestion. —**in·gest′i·ble,** *adj.* —**in·ges′tion,** *n.*

in·gle·nook (ing′gəl núk′), *n.* nook or corner beside a fireplace. [**Inglenook** comes from a Scottish Gaelic word meaning "fire" and an old English word meaning "nook" or "hidden corner."]

in·glo·ri·ous (in glôr′ē əs), *adj.* bringing no glory; shameful; disgraceful: *an inglorious defeat.* —**in·glo′ri·ous·ly,** *adv.* —**in·glo′ri·ous·ness,** *n.*

in·got (ing′gət), *n.* mass of metal, such as gold, silver, or steel, cast into a block or bar to be recast, rolled, or forged at a later time.

in·grain (in grān′), *v.* to fix deeply and firmly.

in·grained (in grānd′), *adj.* deeply and firmly fixed in your very nature or being: *ingrained honesty.*

in·grate (in′grāt), *n.* an ungrateful person.

in·gra·ti·ate (in grā′shē āt), *v.* to bring yourself into favor; make yourself acceptable: *He tried to ingratiate himself with the teacher by cleaning the blackboards.* ❑ *v.* **in·gra·ti·at·ed, in·gra·ti·at·ing.** —**in·gra′ti·at′ing·ly,** *adv.* —**in·gra′ti·a′tion,** *n.*

ingots of gold

in·grat·i·tude (in grat′ə tüd), *n.* lack of gratitude or thankfulness; being ungrateful.

in·gre·di·ent (in grē′dē ənt), *n.* one of the parts of a mixture: *Cake ingredients usually include eggs, sugar, flour, and flavoring.* [**Ingredient** comes from Latin words meaning "to go in."]

in-group (in′grüp′), *n.* group of people united by the same interests. An in-group often excludes outsiders.

in·grown (in′grōn′), *adj.* grown into the flesh: *an ingrown toenail.*

in·hab·it (in hab′it), *v.* to live in: *Fish inhabit the sea.* —**in·hab′it·a·ble,** *adj.* —**in·hab′i·ta′tion,** *n.* —**in·hab′it·er,** *n.*

in·hab·it·ant (in hab′ə tənt), *n.* person or animal that lives in a place: *Our town has ten thousand inhabitants.*

WORD POWER HOME SWEET HOME ■ Where people live, or where people come from, is usually one of the first things we learn about them. It is also an important part of much history and politics. Imagine if you had to say "people living in or coming from," each time that you mentioned this information. You would probably figure out a shorter way to get the idea across. Prefixes and suffixes meaning "inhabiting, born in, from, or about a place" include:

-an	Chicagoan	-ite	Brooklynite
-er	New Yorker	-man	Irishman
-ese	Chinese	-woman	Frenchwoman
-ian	Hungarian		

in·hal·ant (in hā′lənt), *n.* medicine to be inhaled.

in·ha·la·tor (in′hə lā′tər), *n.* apparatus that helps the body inhale oxygen, used in resuscitation.

in·hale (in hāl′), *v.* to breathe in; draw air, gas, tobacco smoke, etc., into the lungs. □ *v.* **in·haled, in·hal·ing.** —**in′ha·la′tion,** *n.*

in·hal·er (in hā′lər), *n.* **1** device for breathing in medicinal vapor, especially to relieve nasal congestion. **2** a person who inhales.

in·har·mo·ni·ous (in′här mō′nē əs), *adj.* not harmonious; disagreeing; conflicting; discordant. —**in′har·mo′ni·ous·ly,** *adv.* —**in′har·mo′ni·ous·ness,** *n.*

in·her·ent (in hir′ənt), *adj.* belonging to someone or something as a quality or attribute; essential: *Her inherent curiosity about nature led her to study botany.* —**in·her′ent·ly,** *adv.*

in·her·it (in her′it), *v.* **1** to get or have something after the former owner dies; receive as an heir: *After Grandfather's death, Mother inherited all of his property.* **2** to receive from your parents or ancestors through heredity. **3** to receive something by succession from someone who came before: *I inherited this old pen from the person who used to have my desk.* —**in·her′i·tor,** *n.*

in·her·it·ance (in her′ə təns), *n.* **1** anything inherited: *The house was her inheritance.* **2** act or right of inheriting: *He obtained his house by inheritance from an aunt.*

in·hib·it (in hib′it), *v.* to hold back; hinder or restrain; check: *Their aloof reception inhibited his usual friendliness.* —**in·hib′it·a·ble,** *adj.* —**in·hib′i·tor,** *n.*

WORD FAMILY Inhibit and the words below are related. They all come from a Latin word meaning "to have" or "to hold."

able	exhibit	habituate	prohibit
disability	habit	inhabit	rehabilitate

in·hi·bi·tion (in′hə bish′ən), *n.* **1** idea, emotion, attitude, habit, or other inner force holding back or checking your impulses, desires, etc. **2** act of holding back; restraint; checking: *Some drugs can cause the inhibition of normal bodily activity.*

in·hib·i·to·ry (in hib′ə tôr′ē), *adj.* inhibiting; tending to inhibit.

in·hos·pit·a·ble (in′ho spit′ə bəl *or* in hos′pi tə bəl), *adj.* **1** not hospitable; not making visitors comfortable: *That inhospitable man never offers visitors any refreshments.* **2** providing no shelter; barren: *a rocky, inhospitable shore.* —**in′hos·pit′a·bly,** *adv.*

in·hos·pi·tal·i·ty (in hos′pə tal′ə tē), *n.* lack of hospitality.

in·hu·man (in hyü′mən), *adj.* **1** without kindness, mercy, or tenderness; cruel; brutal: *an inhuman lack of concern for the sufferings of others.* **2** not human; not having the qualities natural to a human being: *Some of the Olympic runners seem to have inhuman powers of endurance.* —**in·hu′man·ly,** *adv.*

in·hu·mane (in′hyü mān′), *adj.* not humane; lacking in kindness, mercy, or tenderness. —**in′hu·mane′ly,** *adv.*

in·hu·man·i·ty (in′hyü man′ə tē), *n.* **1** lack of kindness, mercy, or tenderness; cruelty; brutality. **2** an inhuman, cruel, or brutal act. □ *n., pl.* **in·hu·man·i·ties** for 2.

in·im·i·cal (in im′ə kəl), *adj.* **1** unfriendly; hostile: *The townspeople were inimical to strangers.* **2** unfavorable; harmful: *Censorship is inimical to freedom of the press.* —**in·im′i·cal·ly,** *adv.*

in·im·i·ta·ble (in im′ə tə bəl), *adj.* impossible to imitate or copy; matchless. —**in·im′i·ta·bil′i·ty, in·im′i·ta·ble·ness,** *n.* —**in·im′i·ta·bly,** *adv.*

in·iq·ui·tous (in ik′wə təs), *adj.* very unjust; wicked. —**in·iq′ui·tous·ly,** *adv.*

in·iq·ui·ty (in ik′wə tē), *n.* **1** very great injustice; wickedness. **2** a wicked or unjust act: *the many iniquities of slavery.* □ *n., pl.* **in·iq·ui·ties** for 2.

WORD STORY Iniquity comes from Latin words meaning "not" and "level." Inequity comes from the same word. The Latin word for "level" also meant "equal" and "just," because justice and equality mean not treating some people as higher or lower than others.

i·ni·tial (i nish′əl), **1** *adj.* occurring at the beginning; first; earliest: *the initial letter of a word. His initial effort at skating was a failure.* **2** *n.* the first letter of a word: *The initials U.S. stand for United States.* **3** *v.* to mark or sign with initials: *Lee Anne King initialed the note "L.A.K."*

WORD SOURCE Sometimes, phrases in English or foreign languages are shortened by using just their **initial letters.** When these letters are pronounced as new words, they become **acronyms.** (See the Word Source at **acronym.**) Other initials are pronounced as letters, like those below.

A.D.	CD	KO	OK	R.N.
A.M.	GI	M.C.	P.M.	TV
B.C.	ID	MP	Q.E.D.	VCR

i·ni·tial·ly (i nish′ə lē), *adv.* at the beginning.

i·ni·ti·ate (i nish′ē āt *for verb;* i nish′ē it *for noun*), **1** *v.* to be the first one to start; begin: *This year we shall initiate a series of free concerts for the public.* **2** *v.* to admit someone with formal ceremonies into a group or society: *The old members initiated the new members.* **3** *v.* to help to get a first understanding; introduce into the knowledge of some art or subject: *The teacher initiated the class into the theory of continental drift by showing how Africa and South America might fit together.* **4** *n.* someone who is initiated. □ *v.* **i·ni·ti·at·ed, i·ni·ti·at·ing.** —**i·ni′ti·a′tor,** *n.*

i·ni·ti·a·tion (i nish′ē ā′shən), *n.* **1** formal admission into a group or society. **2** ceremonies by which someone is admitted to a group or society: *All the club members attended the initiation.* **3** act or process of being the first one to start something; beginning.

i·ni·ti·a·tive (i nish′ə tiv), *n.* **1** active part in starting any undertaking; lead: *She likes to take the initiative in planning class programs.* **2** readiness and ability to be the one to start something: *A good leader must have initiative.* **3** right or procedure of citizens outside the legislature to introduce or enact a new law by vote: *A statewide initiative to increase the speed limit in rural areas.*

in·ject (in jekt′), *v.* **1** to force liquid into the body through a hollow needle: *inject penicillin into a muscle.* **2** to throw in; insert: *While she and I were talking he injected a remark into the conversation.* —**in·ject′a·ble,** *adj.* —**in·jec′tor,** *n.*

in·jec·tion (in jek′shən), *n.* **1** liquid injected: *A nurse prepared the injection.* **2** act or process of injecting: *The medicine was given by injection rather than by mouth.*

in·ju·di·cious (in′jü dish′əs), *adj.* showing bad judgment; unwise; not judicious: *An injudicious person says or does things without thinking what their results may be.* —**in′ju·di′cious·ly,** *adv.* —**in′ju·di′cious·ness,** *n.*

a	hat	ė	term	ô	order	ch	child		a in about
ā	age	i	it	oi	oil	ng	long		e in taken
ä	far	ī	ice	ou	out	sh	she	ə	i in pencil
â	care	o	hot	u	cup	th	thin		o in lemon
e	let	ō	open	ů	put	ŦH	then		u in circus
ē	equal	ò	saw	ü	rule	zh	measure		

in·junc·tion (in jungk′shən), *n.* **1** a formal order from a court of law requiring a person or group to do or not to do something: *The injunction prohibited the teachers from striking before the end of the school year.* **2** command; order: *The driver obeyed the police officer's injunction to pull over.*

inlet (def. 1)

in·jure (in′jər), *v.* to do damage to; harm; hurt: *I injured my arm while skiing. The misunderstanding injured their friendship.* ■ See Synonym Study at **harm.** ❑ *v.* **in·jured, in·jur·ing.**

in·jur·i·ous (in jŭr′ē əs), *adj.* causing injury; harmful: *Smoking is injurious to health.* —**in·jur′i·ous·ly,** *adv.* —**in·jur′i·ous·ness,** *n.*

in·jur·y (in′jər ē), *n.* hurt or loss caused to or endured by someone or something; harm; damage: *She escaped from the train wreck without injury. You did me an injury when you said I lied.* ❑ *n., pl.* **in·jur·ies.** [**Injury** comes from a Latin word meaning "unjust." Injustice harms victims and damages their rights.]

in·jus·tice (in jus′tis), *n.* **1** lack of justice; being unjust: *We were angry at the injustice of everyone's being punished after just one person misbehaved.* **2** an unjust act: *It is an injustice to send an innocent person to jail.*

ink (ingk), **1** *n.* a colored or black liquid used for writing, printing, or drawing. **2** *v.* to put ink on; mark or stain with ink. **3** *n.* a dark liquid thrown out for protection by cuttlefish, squids, etc. —**ink′er,** *n.* —**ink′like′,** *adj.*

WORD STORY **Ink** comes from Greek words meaning "to burn in." The ancient Greeks used a paint that became permanent when heated. They called the paint "burnt in." Ink with the same color got the same name.

ink·blot (ingk′blot′), *n.* blot made with ink.

ink·horn (ingk′hôrn′), *n.* a small container, often made of horn, formerly used to hold ink.

ink·jet printer (ingk′jet′), a kind of computer printer in which letters, numbers, etc., are formed by ink sprayed onto paper from tiny nozzles.

in·kling (ing′kling), *n.* vague notion; slight suspicion; hint: *give a person an inkling of what is going on.*

ink·stand (ingk′stand′), *n.* **1** stand to hold ink and pens. **2** inkwell.

ink·well (ingk′wel′), *n.* container used to hold ink on a desk or table.

ink·y (ing′kē), *adj.* **1** like ink; dark; black: *inky shadows.* **2** covered with ink; marked or stained with ink. **3** of ink. ❑ *adj.* **ink·i·er, ink·i·est.** —**ink′i·ness,** *n.*

in·laid (in′lād′ *or* in lād′), **1** *adj.* set in the surface as a decoration or design. **2** *adj.* decorated with a design or material set in the surface: *The desk had an inlaid top of silver.* **3** *v.* past tense and past participle of **inlay:** *They inlaid tiles in the kitchen floor. The floor was inlaid with colored tiles.*

in·land (in′lənd), **1** *adj.* away from the coast or the border; situated in the interior: *Illinois is an inland state.* **2** *n.* interior of a country; land away from the border or the coast. **3** *adv.* in or toward the interior: *He traveled inland from New York to Chicago.*

in-law (in′lô′), *n.* person related by marriage.

in·lay (in lā′ *or* in′lā′ *for verb;* in′lā′ *for noun*), **1** *v.* to set in the surface as a decoration or design: *The silversmith inlaid strips of*

gold in the top of the silver box. **2** *v.* to decorate with a design set in the surface: *inlay a wooden box with gold.* **3** *n.* an inlaid decoration, design, or material. **4** *n.* a shaped piece of gold, porcelain, etc., cemented in a tooth as a filling. ❑ *v.* **in·laid, in·lay·ing.** —**in′lay·er,** *n.*

in·let (in′let), *n.* **1** a narrow strip of water running from a larger body of water into the land or between islands: *The fishing village was on a small inlet of the sea.* **2** entrance.

in-line skates (in′līn′), skates with wheels or rollers attached in a single line, instead of in pairs side by side.

in·mate (in′māt), *n.* person kept in a prison, asylum, hospital, etc.

in·most (in′mōst), *adj.* innermost.

inn (in), *n.* **1** place where travelers and others can get meals and a room to sleep in. **2** restaurant or tavern. ■ Another word that sounds like this is **in.**

in-line skates

in·nards (in′ərdz), *n.pl.* INFORMAL. **1** the internal organs of the body. **2** the internal workings or parts of a machine or structure.

in·nate (i nāt′ *or* in′āt), *adj.* **1** born in a person; natural: *an innate talent for drawing.* **2** existing naturally in anything; inherent. —**in·nate′ly,** *adv.* —**in·nate′ness,** *n.*

in·ner (in′ər), *adj.* **1** farther in; inside: *The buildings formed a square surrounding an inner courtyard.* **2** more private; more secret: *He kept his inner thoughts to himself.* **3** of or relating to the mind or soul: *a person's inner life.*

inner city, 1 the central part of a large city or metropolitan area. **2** the crowded, poor, run-down part of a city; the slums.

inner ear, the innermost part of the ear, beyond the middle ear. In human beings it contains the organs of balance and the organs that change sound into nerve messages. See picture at **ear¹.**

in·ner·most (in′ər mōst), *adj.* **1** farthest in; deepest within: *We went down to the innermost depths of the mine.* **2** most private; most secret: *He kept his innermost thoughts to himself.*

inner tube, an inflatable rubber tube placed inside the casing of some tires.

in·ning (in′ing), *n.* **1** division of a baseball game during which each team has a turn at bat. **2** the turn one team or group has to play and score in a game.

inn·keep·er (in′kē′pər), *n.* person who owns or manages an inn.

in·no·cence (in′ə səns), *n.* **1** freedom from sin, wrong, or guilt; being innocent: *The accused woman proved her innocence of the crime.* **2** simplicity; lack of cunning: *"I hope you will buy me a present," he said with the innocence of a child.*

in·no·cent (in′ə sənt), **1** *adj.* doing no wrong or evil; free from sin or wrong; not guilty: *In the United States a person is presumed innocent until proved guilty.* **2** *adj.* doing no harm; harmless: *innocent amusements.* **3** *adj.* having a simple and trusting nature; naive: *It was innocent of you to lend your bike to a stranger.* **4** *n.* an innocent person. —**in′no·cent·ly,** *adv.*

in·noc·u·ous (i nok′yü əs), *adj.* harmless: *She took my innocuous remark as an insult.* —**in·noc′u·ous·ly,** *adv.* —**in·noc′u·ous·ness,** *n.*

in·no·vate (in′ə vāt), *v.* to make changes; bring in something new or new ways of doing things: *It is difficult to innovate when people feel that the old, familiar way of doing something is better.* ❑ *v.* **in·no·vat·ed, in·no·vat·ing.** —**in′no·va′tor,** *n.*

in·no·va·tion (in′ə vā′shən), *n.* **1** change made in the established way of doing things: *The principal made many innovations.* **2** act or process of making changes; bringing in new things or new ways of doing things: *Many people are opposed to innovation.*

in·no·va·tive (in′ə vā′tiv), *adj.* making changes; tending to innovate. —**in′no·va′tive·ness,** *n.*

in·nu·en·do (in′yü en′dō), *n.* an indirect suggestion meant to discredit someone: *He was the victim of a vicious scandal spread by the use of lies and innuendoes.* ❑ *n., pl.* **in·nu·en·dos** *or* **in·nu·en·does.** [**Innuendo** comes from Latin words meaning "in" and "to nod." A nod of the head can suggest an idea or agree to an idea without any direct statement.]

in·nu·mer·a·ble (i nü′mər ə bəl), *adj.* too many to count; very many; countless: *innumerable stars.* ■ See Synonym Study at **numerous.** **—in·nu′mer·a·ble·ness,** *n.* **—in·nu′mer·a·bly,** *adv.*

in·oc·u·late (in ok′yə lāt), *v.* to infect a person or animal with killed or weakened germs or viruses. The infected individual will suffer only a very mild form of the disease. In this way the body builds up protection by strengthening its immune system. Doctors inoculate against diphtheria, typhoid fever, and other diseases. ❑ *v.* **in·oc·u·lat·ed, in·oc·u·lat·ing. —in·oc′u·la′tor,** *n.*

WORD STORY Inoculate comes from a Latin word meaning "to graft." Grafting puts part of one plant into another plant, where it becomes attached and grows, improving the second plant. People have been doing this for thousands of years. When inoculation against disease began, about 300 years ago, people thought it resembled the grafting of plants.

in·oc·u·la·tion (in ok′yə lā′-shən), *n.* **1** act or process of inoculating: *Inoculation has greatly reduced deaths from polio.* **2** bacteria, serums, etc., used in inoculating.

in·of·fen·sive (in′ə fen′siv), *adj.* not offensive; not arousing objections; harmless: *"Please try to be more quiet" is an inoffensive way of telling people to stop their noise.* **—in′of·fen′sive·ly,** *adv.* **—in′of·fen′sive·ness,** *n.*

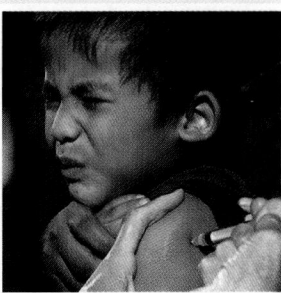
inoculation (def. 1)

in·op·er·a·ble (in op′ər ə bəl), *adj.* **1** not able to be cured by surgery; unsuited for a surgical operation: *an inoperable tumor.* **2** not operable; unworkable: *The plan was so complex that it seemed inoperable.*

in·op·er·a·tive (in op′ər ə tiv), *adj.* not operative; not working; without effect. **—in·op′er·a·tive·ness,** *n.*

in·op·por·tune (in op′ər tün′), *adj.* not opportune; coming at a bad time; unsuitable: *An inopportune telephone call delayed us.* **—in·op′por·tune′ly,** *adv.* **—in·op′por·tune′ness,** *n.*

in·or·di·nate (in ôrd′n it), *adj.* much too great; excessive: *an inordinate desire for sweets.* **—in·or′di·nate·ly,** *adv.* **—in·or′di·nate·ness,** *n.*

in·or·gan·ic (in′ôr gan′ik), *adj.* **1** not organic; not animal, vegetable, or otherwise alive; not having the organized physical structure characteristic of life. Water and minerals are inorganic substances. **2** (in chemistry) not containing organic matter. Chemical compounds without carbon are inorganic. **—in′or·gan′i·cal·ly,** *adv.*

in·pa·tient (in′pā′shənt), *n.* patient who is lodged and fed in a hospital while undergoing treatment.

in·put (in′pu̇t), **1** *v.* to put information or instructions into a computer. **2** *n.* information or instructions put into a computer. **3** *n.* power supplied to a machine. **4** *n.* what is put in or taken in. ❑ *v.* **in·put** (or **in·put·ted), in·put·ting.**

in·quest (in′kwest), *n.* a legal inquiry, especially before a jury: *An inquest was held to determine if his death was the result of a crime.*

in·quire (in kwīr′), *v.* **1** to try to find out by questions; ask: *The detective went from house to house, inquiring whether anyone had seen the lost girl.* **2** to make a search for information, knowledge, or truth: *The scholar pored over old documents while inquiring into the history of the town.* ❑ *v.* **in·quired, in·quir·ing.** Also, **enquire. —in·quir′er,** *n.* **—in·quir′ing·ly,** *adv.*

in·quir·y (in kwī′rē *or* in′kwər ē), *n.* **1** act of inquiring; asking. **2** a search for information, knowledge, or truth: *His inquiry into the town's history led him to many old books and newspapers.* **3** question: *The guide answered all our inquiries.* ❑ *n., pl.* **in·quir·ies.** Also, **enquiry.**

in·qui·si·tion (in′kwə zish′ən), *n.* **1** a thorough investigation; searching inquiry. **2** an official investigation; judicial inquiry. **3** **the Inquisition,** court established by the Roman Catholic Church

in the 1200s to discover and punish heresy. It was abolished in the 1800s.

in·quis·i·tive (in kwiz′ə tiv), *adj.* **1** asking many questions; curious: *an inquisitive person with a good mind.* **2** prying into other people's affairs; too curious: *Our neighbors are very inquisitive about what we do.* ■ See Synonym Study at **curious.** **—in·quis′i·tive·ly,** *adv.* **—in·quis′i·tive·ness,** *n.*

in·quis·i·tor (in kwiz′ə tər), *n.* **1** person who makes an inquisition; official investigator. **2 Inquisitor,** member of the Inquisition.

in·road (in′rōd′), *n.* **1** an attack or raid. **2 inroads,** *pl.* an effect of decreasing or harming; reduction; demand: *The expenses of her trip made inroads into her savings.*

in·rush (in′rush′), *n.* act of rushing in; inflow: *The inrush of water filled the pool.* ❑ *n., pl.* **in·rush·es.**

in·sane (in sān′), *adj.* **1** not sane; mentally ill. ■ **Insane** is now used to mean "mentally ill" only in legal discussions. **2** for mentally ill people: *an insane asylum.* **3** very foolish; completely lacking in common sense: *People used to think that plans for flying machines were insane.* **—in·sane′ly,** *adv.* **—in·sane′ness,** *n.*

in·san·i·tar·y (in san′ə ter′ē), *adj.* not sanitary; not healthful.

in·san·i·ty (in san′ə tē), *n.* **1** madness; mental illness: *The lawyer insisted that the accused had fired the shot during a fit of temporary insanity.* **2** extreme folly; complete lack of common sense: *It is insanity to drive a car without any brakes.*

in·sa·tia·bil·i·ty (in sā′shə bil′ə tē), *n.* insatiable quality.

in·sa·tia·ble (in sā′shə bəl), *adj.* not able to be satisfied; extremely greedy: *The boy had an insatiable appetite for candy.* **—in·sa′tia·bil′i·ty, in·sa′tia·ble·ness,** *n.* **—in·sa′tia·bly,** *adv.*

in·sa·ti·ate (in sā′shē it), *adj.* never satisfied: *A vain person has an insatiate desire for praise.* **—in·sa′ti·ate·ly,** *adv.* **—in·sa′ti·ate·ness,** *n.*

in·scribe (in skrīb′), *v.* **1** to write or engrave words, names, etc., on stone, metal, paper, etc.: *Her name was inscribed on the ring.* **2** to mark stone, metal, paper, etc., with words, names, etc.: *The ring was inscribed with his name.* **3** to address or dedicate a book, picture, etc., informally to someone. **4** to impress deeply: *My father's words are inscribed in my memory.* **5** to put in a list; enroll. ❑ *v.* **in·scribed, in·scrib·ing. —in·scrib′er,** *n.*

in·scrip·tion (in skrip′shən), *n.* **1** something inscribed; words, names, etc., written or engraved on stone, metal, paper, etc. A monument or a coin has an inscription on it. **2** an informal dedication in a book, on a picture, etc. **3** act of writing upon or in something.

in·scru·ta·ble (in skrü′tə bəl), *adj.* not able to be understood; so mysterious or obscure that you cannot make out its meaning. **—in·scru′ta·bil′i·ty, in·scru′ta·ble·ness,** *n.* **—in·scru′ta·bly,** *adv.*

WORD STORY Inscrutable comes from Latin words meaning "not" and "trash." If you have lost something and are looking for it really hard, you will look even in wastebaskets. So the Latin word for "search" or "examine" comes from the word for "trash." So does **scrutiny.**

in·sect (in′sekt), *n.* **1** any of a very large number of small animals with no backbone and with the body divided into three parts: head, thorax, and abdomen. Insects have three pairs of legs, and one or two pairs of wings. Flies, mosquitoes, butterflies, bees, grasshoppers, and beetles are insects. **2** any similar animal, especially a wingless one with four pairs of legs. Spiders, centipedes, mites, and ticks are often called insects. **—in′sect·like′,** *adj.*

WORD STORY Insect comes from a Latin word meaning "divided," because the bodies of insects are divided into three main parts. **Entomology** comes from Greek words meaning "the study of divided animals." This division is the first thing that people notice when they look at bugs.

a	hat	ė	term	ô	order	ch	child		
ā	age	i	it	oi	oil	ng	long		a in about
ä	far	ī	ice	ou	out	sh	she		e in taken
â	care	o	hot	u	cup	th	thin	ə	i in pencil
e	let	ō	open	u̇	put	ᴛʜ	then		o in lemon
ē	equal	ȯ	saw	ü	rule	zh	measure		u in circus

in·sec·ti·cide (in sek′tə sīd), *n.* any substance for killing insects.

in·sec·ti·vore (in sek′tə vôr), *n.* any animal or plant that feeds mainly on insects. Moles and mantises are insectivores.

in·sec·tiv·or·ous (in′sek tiv′ər əs), *adj.* insect-eating; feeding mainly on insects.

in·se·cure (in′si kyùr′), *adj.* 1 not safe from danger, failure, etc.: *During an earthquake, people in tall buildings are in an insecure position.* 2 liable to give way; not firm: *an insecure support, an insecure lock.* 3 lacking self-confidence; not sure of doing well; fearful; timid: *an insecure person.* —in′se·cure′ly, *adv.* —in′se·cure′ness, *n.*

in·se·cur·i·ty (in′si kyùr′ə tē), *n.* 1 lack of security; being insecure; unsafe condition. 2 lack of self-confidence; uncertainty of doing well. ❑ *n., pl.* in·se·cur·i·ties for 2.

in·sem·i·nate (in sem′ə nāt), *v.* to inject semen into; fertilize; impregnate. ❑ *v.* in·sem·i·nat·ed, in·sem·i·nat·ing. —in·sem′i·na′tion, *n.* —in·sem′i·na′tor, *n.*

in·sen·sate (in sen′sāt), *adj.* 1 without sensation; lifeless; inanimate: *insensate stones.* 2 unfeeling; brutal: *insensate cruelty.* 3 senseless; stupid: *insensate folly.* —in·sen′sate·ly, *adv.* —in·sen′sate·ness, *n.*

in·sen·si·bil·i·ty (in sen′sə bil′ə tē), *n.* 1 lack of feeling; unawareness. 2 lack of consciousness; senselessness.

in·sen·si·ble (in sen′sə bəl), *adj.* 1 not sensitive; not able to feel or notice: *She appeared to be insensible to cold.* 2 not aware; unmoved; indifferent: *The swimmers were insensible to the dangers of the high waves.* 3 not able to feel anything; unconscious; senseless: *The man hit by the truck was insensible for four hours.* —in·sen′si·ble·ness, *n.* —in·sen′si·bly, *adv.*

in·sen·si·tive (in sen′sə tiv), *adj.* 1 not sensitive: *an insensitive area of the skin.* 2 slow to feel or notice: *They were insensitive to the needs of others.* —in·sen′si·tive·ly, *adv.* —in·sen′si·tive·ness, in·sen′si·tiv′i·ty, *n.*

in·sep·a·ra·ble (in sep′ər ə bəl), *adj.* not able to be separated; constantly together: *The two friends are inseparable companions.* —in·sep′ar·a·bil′i·ty, in·sep′ar·a·ble·ness, *n.* —in·sep′ar·a·bly, *adv.*

in·sert (in sèrt′ *for verb;* in′sèrt′ *for noun*), 1 *v.* to put or set something in: *He inserted the key into the lock.* 2 *n.* something put or set in: *The newspaper had an insert of several pages of pictures.* —in·sert′a·ble, *adj.* —in·sert′er, *n.*

in·ser·tion (in sèr′shən), *n.* 1 act of inserting: *The insertion of one word can change the meaning of a whole sentence.* 2 something inserted.

in·set (in set′ *for verb;* in′set′ *for noun*), 1 *v.* to set in; insert. 2 *n.* something inserted, such as a small map, picture, etc., set within the border of a larger one. ❑ *v.* in·set, in·set·ting.

in·shore (in′shôr′), 1 *adj.* near the shore: *Inshore fishing is not allowed where people swim.* 2 *adv.* in toward the shore: *The boat was driven inshore by the winds.*

in·side (in′sīd′ *for noun, adj.;* in′sīd′ *for adv., prep.*), 1 *n.* the part within; the inner surface: *The inside of the box was lined with colored paper.* 2 *n.* the contents: *The inside of the book was more interesting than the cover.* 3 *adj.* being on the inside: *an inside seat.* 4 *adv.* on or to the inside; within; in the inner part: *Please step inside.* 5 *prep.* within; in: *The nut is inside the shell.* 6 *prep.* into: *The children went inside the house.* 7 *prep.* within the limits of; in: *We plan to finish the meeting inside an hour.* 8 *adj.* used indoors; indoor. 9 *adj.* done or known by people on the inside of a group, a building, etc.: *The informer had inside information of the gang's plans.*

inside of, within the limits of; in.

inside out, 1 so that what should be inside is outside; with the inside showing: *He turned his pockets inside out.* 2 completely; thoroughly: *She learned her lessons inside out.*

inside job, a crime committed by or in cooperation with a person who knows, works for, or lives with the victim: *The jewel theft was an inside job; the butler let in the burglars.*

in·sid·er (in′sī′dər), *n.* 1 person who belongs to a certain group, club, society, political party, etc. 2 person who has private or secret information about something not known to most others.

insider trading, act of illegally buying or selling stocks, bonds, etc., because of or on the basis of secret information.

in·sides (in′sīdz′), *n.pl.* the soft organs inside the body.

inside track, 1 the lane nearest the inside of the curve on a racetrack. 2 INFORMAL. an advantageous position or situation: *Since she already knew the language, she had the inside track on the overseas internship.*

in·sid·i·ous (in sid′ē əs), *adj.* 1 seeking to entrap or ensnare; sly; crafty; tricky. 2 working secretly or subtly; developing without attracting attention: *Tuberculosis is an insidious disease; you can have it without knowing it.* [Insidious comes from a Latin word meaning "an ambush." The word came to describe any tricky or sly thing.] —in·sid′i·ous·ly, *adv.* —in·sid′i·ous·ness, *n.*

in·sight (in′sīt′), *n.* wisdom and understanding in dealing with people or with facts: *We study science to gain insight into the world we live in.* [See word history information at intuition.]

in·sight·ful (in′sīt′fəl), *adj.* having or showing insight. —in·sight′ful·ly, *adv.*

in·sig·ni·a (in sig′nē ə), *n.* medal, badge, or other distinguishing mark of a rank, an organization, or some honor. ❑ *n., pl.* in·sig·ni·a or in·sig·ni·as.

in·sig·nif·i·cance (in′sig nif′ə kəns), *n.* 1 unimportance; uselessness. 2 meaninglessness.

in·sig·nif·i·cant (in′sig nif′ə kənt), *adj.* 1 having little use or importance; trivial: *A tenth of a cent is an insignificant amount of money.* 2 having little meaning; meaningless: *insignificant chatter.* —in′sig·nif′i·cant·ly, *adv.*

in·sin·cere (in′sin sir′), *adj.* not sincere; not honest or candid; deceitful: *He never intended to keep his insincere promises.* —in′sin·cere′ly, *adv.*

insignia

in·sin·cer·i·ty (in′sin ser′ə tē), *n.* lack of sincerity; hypocrisy.

in·sin·u·ate (in sin′yü āt), *v.* 1 to suggest in an unpleasant, indirect way; hint: *To say "That worker can't do the job; it takes skill" is to insinuate that the worker is not skilled.* 2 to push in or get in by an indirect, subtle way: *The spy insinuated himself into the confidence of important army officers.* ❑ *v.* in·sin·u·at·ed, in·sin·u·at·ing. —in·sin′u·at′ing·ly, *adv.* —in·sin′u·a′tor, *n.*

WORD STORY **Insinuate** comes from Latin words meaning "a curve in." Someone who insinuates is like someone who takes a winding path, not a straight way. Today we may ask someone to be honest by saying, "Be straight with me."

in·sin·u·a·tion (in sin′yü ā′shən), *n.* 1 an indirect suggestion meant to discredit someone: *The student objected strongly to the insinuation of dishonesty.* 2 act or process of insinuating: *the insinuation of oneself into the confidence of others.*

in·sip·id (in sip′id), *adj.* 1 without any particular flavor; tasteless: *A mixture of milk and water is an insipid drink.* 2 lacking interest or spirit; dull, colorless, or weak: *The insipid conversation bored everyone.* —in′si·pid′i·ty, *n.* —in·sip′id·ly, *adv.*

in·sist (in sist′), *v.* to keep firmly to some demand, statement, or position; take a stand and refuse to give in: *After her arrest she insisted on her innocence.* —in·sist′er, *n.* —in·sist′ing·ly, *adv.*

in·sist·ence (in sis′təns), *n.* 1 act of insisting: *At the teacher's insistence the class became quiet.* 2 quality of being insistent.

in·sist·ent (in sis′tənt), *adj.* 1 continuing to make a strong, firm demand or statement; insisting: *In spite of the rain she was insistent on going out.* 2 impossible to overlook or disregard; compelling attention or notice; pressing; urgent: *Her insistent knocking on the door woke us.* 3 persistent; repeated; steady: *The insistent drip has worn a hollow in the stone.* —in·sist′ent·ly, *adv.*

in·so·far as (in′sō fär′), to such an extent or degree as: *Insofar as I can tell, the weather should be nice tomorrow.*

in·sole (in′sōl′), *n.* **1** the inner sole of a shoe or boot. **2** layer of warm or waterproof material put on the sole inside a shoe or boot.

in·so·lence (in′sə ləns), *n.* bold rudeness; insulting behavior or speech; intentional disregard of the feelings of others.

in·so·lent (in′sə lənt), *adj.* boldly rude; intentionally disregarding the feelings of others; insulting: *You were insolent to turn your back on me while I was talking to you.* —**in′so·lent·ly,** *adv.*

in·sol·u·ble (in sol′yə bəl), *adj.* **1** not able to be dissolved: *Fats are insoluble in water.* **2** not able to be solved: *The detective finally gave up, declaring the mystery insoluble.* —**in·sol′u·bil′i·ty, in·sol′u·ble·ness,** *n.* —**in·sol′u·bly,** *adv.*

in·sol·ven·cy (in sol′vən sē), *n.* condition of not being able to pay debts; bankruptcy.

in·sol·vent (in sol′vənt), *adj.* unable to pay debts; bankrupt.

in·som·ni·a (in som′nē ə), *n.* inability to sleep; sleeplessness.

in·som·ni·ac (in som′nē ak), *n.* person who is unable to sleep; person who has insomnia.

in·so·much as (in′sō much′), inasmuch as; since.

in·spect (in spekt′), *v.* **1** to look over carefully; examine: *The engineers inspected the new dam.* **2** to look over officially; examine formally: *Government officials inspect factories and mines to make sure that they are safe for workers.*

in·spec·tion (in spek′shən), *n.* **1** act or process of inspecting; examination: *An inspection of the roof showed no leaks.* **2** a formal or official examination: *The soldiers lined up for their daily inspection by their officers.*

in·spec·tor (in spek′tər), *n.* **1** someone whose job is to inspect something: *The city building inspector told the landlord to fix the fire escape.* **2** a police officer, usually ranking next below a superintendent.

in·spi·ra·tion (in′spə rā′shən), *n.* **1** influence of thought and strong feelings on actions, especially on good actions: *Some people get inspiration from sermons, some from poetry.* **2** someone or something that puts life or force into others and arouses them to do well: *The teacher was an inspiration to her students.* **3** idea that is inspired; sudden, brilliant idea. ■ See Synonym Study at **idea.** **4** act of breathing in; a drawing of air into the lungs. —**in′spi·ra′tion·al,** *adj.* —**in′spi·ra′tion·al·ly,** *adv.*

in·spire (in spīr′), *v.* **1** to fill with a thought or feeling; influence: *A chance to try again inspired her with hope.* **2** to cause a thought or a feeling: *Her courage inspired confidence in others.* **3** to fill with excitement: *His speech inspired the crowd.* **4** to cause; move; impel: *What inspired him to quit his job?* **5** to cause to be told or written; suggest: *Helen Keller's life story inspired a movie.* **6** to draw air into the lungs; breathe in. ❑ *v.* **in·spired, in·spir·ing.** —**in·spir′a·ble,** *adj.* —**in·spir′er,** *n.* —**in·spir′ing·ly,** *adv.*

in·spir·it (in spir′it), *v.* to put spirit into; encourage; hearten; cheer. —**in·spir′i·ter,** *n.* —**in·spir′it·ing·ly,** *adv.*

in·sta·bil·i·ty (in′stə bil′ə tē), *n.* lack of firmness; being unstable; unsteadiness.

in·stall (in stȯl′), *v.* **1** to put in place for use: *The new owner of the house had a security system installed.* **2** to put someone into office with ceremonies: *The new judge was installed without delay.* **3** to put in a place or position; settle: *The cat installed itself in the easy chair.* ❑ *v.* **in·stalled, in·stall·ing.** —**in·stall′er,** *n.*

in·stal·la·tion (in′stə lā′shən), *n.* **1** something installed, especially machinery placed in position for use. **2** act of installing: *Installation of more electric lights made the room brighter.* **3** a military base or camp, including personnel, equipment, buildings, etc. **4** process of being installed: *I attended my mother's installation as president of the P.T.A.*

in·stall·ment[1] (in stȯl′mənt), *n.* **1** part of a sum of money or of a debt to be paid at certain stated times: *The table cost $200; we* paid for it in four monthly installments of $50 each. **2** one of several parts issued at different times as part of a series: *This magazine has a serial story in six installments.*

in·stall·ment[2] (in stȯl′mənt), *n.* act of installing: *the installment of electric lights in a house.*

installment plan, system of paying for goods in regular, usually monthly, installments.

in·stance (in′stəns), **1** *n.* person or thing serving as an example; illustration; case: *Lincoln is an instance of a poor boy who became famous.* **2** *v.* to give as an example; cite. **3** *n.* stage or step in an action; occasion: *I went in the first instance because I was asked to go.* ❑ *v.* **in·stanced, in·stanc·ing.**

for instance, as an example: *Her many different hobbies include, for instance, skating and stamp collecting.*

in·stant (in′stənt), **1** *n.* moment of time: *He paused for an instant.* **2** *n.* particular moment: *Stop talking this instant!* **3** *adj.* coming at once; without delay; immediate: *The medicine gave instant relief from pain.* **4** *adj.* pressing; urgent: *When there is a fire, there is an instant need for action.* **5** *adj.* prepared beforehand and requiring little or no cooking, mixing, or additional ingredients: *instant coffee, instant pudding.*

in·stan·ta·ne·ous (in′stən tā′nē əs), *adj.* coming or done in an instant; happening with no delay: *A flash of lightning is instantaneous.* —**in′stan·ta·ne·ous·ly,** *adv.* —**in′stan·ta·ne·ous·ness,** *n.*

in·stant·ly (in′stənt lē), *adv.* in an instant; at once; immediately.

instant replay, 1 the videotape recording and immediate rebroadcast of a play in a televised sporting event. **2** any immediate repetition of an event.

in·stead (in sted′), *adv.* in another's place; as a substitute: *She stayed home, and her sister went riding instead.*

instead of, rather than; in place of; as a substitute for: *Instead of studying, I watched TV.*

in·step (in′step), *n.* **1** the upper surface of the human foot between the toes and the ankle. **2** the part of a shoe, stocking, etc., over this part of the foot.

instep

instep

in·sti·gate (in′stə gāt), *v.* to urge on; stir up: *The older boy instigated a quarrel between his two younger brothers.* ❑ *v.* **in·sti·gat·ed, in·sti·gat·ing.** —**in′sti·ga′tion,** *n.* —**in′sti·ga′tor,** *n.*

in·still (in stil′), *v.* to put into someone's mind little by little; cause to enter the mind, heart, etc., gradually: *Reading good books instills a love for fine literature.* ❑ *v.* **in·stilled, in·still·ing.** —**in·stil·la′tion,** *n.* —**in·still′er,** *n.* —**in·still′ment,** *n.*

WORD STORY **Instill** comes from Latin words meaning "to drop in." Dropping may not sound gradual, but **instill** used to mean "to put in drop by drop," like medicines.

in·stinct (in′stingkt), *n.* **1** a natural feeling, knowledge, or ability, such as that which guides animals; inborn tendency to act in a certain way: *Birds build their nests by instinct.* **2** a natural talent or gift: *Even as a child the artist had an instinct for drawing.*

in·stinc·tive (in stingk′tiv), *adj.* of or by instinct; caused or done by instinct; born in an animal or person, not learned: *The spinning of webs is instinctive in spiders.* —**in·stinc′tive·ly,** *adv.*

in·sti·tute (in′stə tüt), **1** *n.* organization or society for some special purpose. An art institute teaches or displays art. A technical school or college is often called an institute. **2** *n.* building used by such an organization or society: *We spent the afternoon in the Art Institute.* **3** *v.* to set up; establish; begin; start: *After the accident, the police instituted an inquiry into its causes.* ❑ *v.* **in·sti·tut·ed, in·sti·tut·ing.** —**in′sti·tut′er** or **in′sti·tu′tor,** *n.*

instability

a	hat	ė	term	ȯ	order	ch	child		a in about
ā	age	i	it	oi	oil	ng	long		e in taken
ä	far	ī	ice	ou	out	sh	she	ə	i in pencil
â	care	o	hot	u	cup	th	thin		o in lemon
e	let	ō	open	ů	put	ŦH	then		u in circus
ē	equal	ȯ	saw	ü	rule	zh	measure		

in·sti·tu·tion (in/stə tü/shən), *n.* **1** society, club, college, or any organization established for some public or social purpose. A church, school, university, hospital, asylum, or prison is an institution. **2** a building used for the work of an institution. **3** an established law or custom: *Marriage is an institution among most of the world's people.* **4** act or process of setting up; beginning; starting: *We hope for the institution of hot lunches at school this winter.* —**in/sti·tu/tion·al,** *adj.* —**in/sti·tu/tion·al·ly,** *adv.*

in·sti·tu·tion·al·ize (in/stə tü/shə nə līz), *v.* **1** to make into an institution. **2** to put someone into an institution. ❑ *v.* **in·sti·tu·tion·al·ized, in·sti·tu·tion·al·iz·ing.** —**in/sti·tu/tion·al·i·za/tion,** *n.*

in·struct (in strukt/), *v.* **1** to give knowledge to; show how to do; teach; train; educate: *We have one teacher who instructs us in reading, English, history, and arithmetic.* **2** to give directions to; order: *The owner of the house instructed her agent to sell it.* **3** to inform; tell: *The family lawyer instructed them that the contract would be signed Monday.* [**Instruct** comes from Latin words meaning "to pile on" or "to build on." Knowledge is like a structure built of information.] —**in·struct/i·ble,** *adj.*

in·struc·tion (in struk/shən), *n.* **1** teaching; training; education: *He devoted his life to the instruction of handicapped children.* **2** knowledge or teaching given; lesson. **3 instructions,** *pl.* directions; orders. —**in·struc/tion·al,** *adj.*

in·struc·tive (in struk/tiv), *adj.* useful for instruction; giving knowledge or information: *His confusing directions were not very instructive.* —**in·struc/tive·ly,** *adv.* —**in·struc/tive·ness,** *n.*

in·struc·tor (in struk/tər), *n.* **1** teacher. **2** teacher ranking below professors in American colleges and universities.

in·stru·ment (in/strə mənt), *n.* **1** a mechanical device that is portable, of simple construction, and usually operated by hand; tool: *a dentist's instruments.* ■ See Synonym Study at **tool. 2** device for producing musical sounds: *wind instruments, stringed instruments. A violin, cello, and piano were the instruments in the trio.* **3** device for measuring, recording, or controlling. A thermometer is an instrument for measuring temperature. **4** something with or by which something is done; person made use of by another; means: *The young king's wicked uncle used his influence as an instrument to gain power.* **5** a formal legal document, such as a contract, deed, or grant.

WORD BANK There are many different musical **instruments.** If you want to know more about them, you can begin by looking up these words in this dictionary.

accordion	cymbal	koto	sousaphone
Autoharp	double bass	lute	spinet
bagpipe	drum	lyre	synthesizer
banjo	dulcimer	mandolin	tambourine
bass drum	English horn	maraca	timpani
bassoon	fife	marimba	tom-tom
bongo	flute	oboe	triangle
bugle	French horn	ocarina	trombone
calliope	glockenspiel	organ	trumpet
carillon	guitar	panpipe	tuba
celesta	hand organ	piano[1]	ukulele
cello	harmonica	piccolo	vibraphone
clarinet	harp	pipe	viola
clavichord	harpsichord	recorder	violin
clavier	horn	samisen	virginal
concertina	Jew's harp	saxophone	xylophone
contrabass	kettledrum	sitar	zither
cornet	kazoo	snare drum	

in·stru·men·tal (in/strə men/tl), *adj.* **1** acting or serving as a means; useful; helpful: *A friend was instrumental in getting me a job.* **2** played on or written for musical instruments: *The singer was accompanied by instrumental music.* —**in/stru·men/tal·ly,** *adv.*

in·stru·men·tal·ist (in/strə men/tl ist), *n.* someone who plays a musical instrument.

in·stru·men·tal·i·ty (in/strə men tal/ə tē), *n.* quality or condition of being instrumental; helpfulness; agency; means.

in·stru·men·ta·tion (in/strə men tā/shən), *n.* **1** arrangement or composition of music for instruments. **2** use of instruments; work done with instruments.

in·sub·or·di·nate (in/sə bôrd/n it), *adj.* not submitting to authority; refusing to obey; disobedient; rebellious. —**in/sub·or/di·nate·ly,** *adv.* —**in/sub·or/di·na/tion,** *n.*

in·sub·stan·tial (in/səb stan/shəl), *adj.* **1** frail; flimsy: *A cobweb is very insubstantial.* **2** unreal; not actual; imaginary: *Dreams and ghosts are insubstantial.* —**in/sub·stan/ti·al/i·ty,** *n.*

in·suf·fer·a·ble (in suf/ər ə bəl), *adj.* unbearable; intolerable: *The heat of the desert at noon was insufferable.* —**in·suf/fer·a·ble·ness,** *n.* —**in·suf/fer·a·bly,** *adv.*

in·suf·fi·cien·cy (in/sə fish/ən sē), *n.* too small an amount; lack; deficiency.

in·suf·fi·cient (in/sə fish/ənt), *adj.* not enough; less than is needed: *She was tired because she had had insufficient sleep.* —**in·suf/fi·cient·ly,** *adv.*

in·su·lar (in/sə lər), *adj.* **1** of islands or islanders. **2** living or situated on an island. **3** standing alone like an island; isolated: *No nation can now keep an insular position in world affairs.* **4** narrow-minded; prejudiced. —**in·su·lar/i·ty** (in/sə lar/ə tē), *n.*

in·su·late (in/sə lāt), *v.* **1** to keep something from losing electricity, heat, or sound by lining or surrounding it with a material that does not conduct the kind of energy involved: *Telephone wires are often insulated by a covering of rubber.* **2** to set apart; separate from others; isolate: *Celebrities are insulated from contact with common people.* ❑ *v.* **in·su·lat·ed, in·su·lat·ing.** [**Insulate** comes from a Latin word meaning "island." Insulating makes an "island" of something by surrounding it or setting it apart.]

instruments (def. 2)

in·su·la·tion (in/sə lā/shən), *n.* **1** material used in insulating: *Rubber is a common insulation for electric wires.* **2** act of insulating: *The workers who did the insulation of this house forgot one wall.* **3** condition of being insulated: *The insulation of the outer walls helps keep our house warm in the winter.*

in·su·la·tor (in/sə lā/tər), *n.* something that insulates; something that prevents the passage of electricity, heat, or sound; nonconductor.

in·su·lin (in/sə lən), *n.* **1** hormone secreted by the pancreas that enables the body to use sugar and other nutrients. **2** drug containing insulin, used in treating diabetes. [**Insulin** comes from a Latin word meaning "island." The hormone comes from small glands that look like islands surrounded by the pancreas.]

in·sult (in sult/ *for verb;* in/sult *for noun*), **1** *v.* to say or do something very scornful, rude, or harsh to: *She insulted me by calling me a liar.* **2** *n.* an insulting speech or action: *To be called stupid is an insult.* [**Insult** comes from a Latin word meaning "to jump at." If someone calls you a name, you may feel attacked, as if you'd been pounced on.] —**in·sult/er,** *n.* —**in·sult/ing·ly,** *adv.*

in·su·per·a·ble (in sü/pər ə bəl), *adj.* not able to be passed over or overcome: *an insuperable barrier.* —**in·su/per·a·bly,** *adv.*

in·sup·port·a·ble (in/sə pôr/tə bəl), *adj.* not endurable; unbearable; intolerable. —**in/sup·port/a·ble·ness,** *n.*

in·sur·a·ble (in shúr/ə bəl), *adj.* capable of being insured; fit to be insured.

in·sur·ance (in shùr′əns), *n.* **1** act or business of insuring property, persons, or life. Fire insurance, burglary insurance, accident insurance, life insurance, and health insurance are some of the many kinds. **2** amount of money for which a property, person, or life is insured: *He has $50,000 in life insurance, which his wife will receive if he dies before she does.* **3** amount of money paid for insurance; premium: *The fire insurance on our house is $600 a year.*

in·sure (in shùr′), *v.* **1** to agree to pay money if certain kinds of harm or loss happen to something or someone. An insurance company will insure your property, person, or life. **2** to make safe from financial loss or harm by paying money to an insurance company: *She insured her car against accident, theft, and fire.* **3** to make sure or safe; ensure. ❑ *v.* **in·sured, in·sur·ing.**

USAGE NOTE Insure and ensure look alike because they began as different spellings of the same word. Today they have similar meanings, but there are differences to keep in mind. In general, people mostly use **ensure** when they mean making certain of something: *To ensure that the card arrives by his birthday, mail it early.* **Insure** means to buy or sell protection against financial loss: *They insured the car against accidents and theft.*

in·sured (in shùrd′), *n.* person who is insured.

in·sur·er (in shùr′ər), *n.* person or company that insures.

in·sur·gen·cy (in sėr′jən sē), *n.* a minor revolt; rebellion. ❑ *n., pl.* **in·sur·gen·cies.**

in·sur·gent (in sėr′jənt), **1** *n.* person who rises in revolt; rebel: *The insurgents captured the town.* **2** *adj.* rising in revolt; rebellious: *insurgent peasants.* —**in·sur′gent·ly,** *adv.*

in·sur·mount·a·ble (in′sər moun′tə bəl), *adj.* not able to be overcome. —**in′sur·mount′a·ble·ness,** *n.* —**in′sur·mount′a·bly,** *adv.*

in·sur·rec·tion (in′sə rek′shən), *n.* an uprising against established authority; revolt; rebellion.

in·sur·rec·tion·ist (in′sə rek′shə nist), *n.* person who takes part in or favors an insurrection; rebel.

int., **1** interest. **2** interior. **3** internal.

in·tact (in takt′), *adj.* with nothing missing or broken; whole; untouched; uninjured: *The missing money was found and returned to the bank intact.* —**in·tact′ness,** *n.*

in·take (in′tāk′), *n.* **1** place where water, air, gas, etc., enters a channel, pipe, or other narrow opening. **2** act or process of taking in: *an intake of breath.* **3** amount or thing taken in: *The intake through the pipe was 5000 gallons a day.*

in·tan·gi·ble (in tan′jə bəl), **1** *adj.* not capable of being touched or felt: *Sound and light are intangible.* **2** *adj.* not easily grasped by the mind; vague: *Charm is an intangible quality.* **3** *n.* something intangible. —**in·tan′gi·bil′i·ty, in·tan′gi·ble·ness,** *n.* —**in·tan′gi·bly,** *adv.*

in·te·ger (in′tə jər), *n.* any positive or negative whole number, or zero. [See Word Story at **entire.**]

in·te·gral (in′tə grəl), *adj.* **1** necessary to make something complete; essential: *Steel is an integral part of a modern skyscraper.* **2** entire; complete. **3** of an integer; not fractional. —**in′te·gral·ly,** *adv.*

in·te·grate (in′tə grāt), *v.* **1** to put or bring parts together into a whole: *The committee will try to integrate the different ideas into one uniform plan.* **2** to make public places available to people of all races on an equal basis: *integrate a neighborhood.* ❑ *v.* **in·te·grat·ed, in·te·grat·ing.** —**in′te·gra′tor,** *n.*

integrated circuit, a complex electrical circuit designed for a single function and manufactured as a unit on or in a chip of semiconductor material; chip. An integrated circuit containing thousands of transistors may be less than an inch across.

in·te·gra·tion (in′tə grā′shən), *n.* **1** inclusion of people of all races on an equal basis in schools, parks, neighborhoods, etc. **2** act of integrating: *the integration of activities on a complex project.*

in·te·gra·tion·ist (in′tə grā′shə nist), *n.* person who believes in the integration of people of all races.

in·teg·ri·ty (in teg′rə tē), *n.* **1** honesty or sincerity; uprightness: *A person of integrity is respected.* **2** wholeness; completeness: *to defend the integrity of a country against its enemies.*

in·tel·lect (in′tə lekt), *n.* **1** power of knowing; understanding; intelligence: *To learn spelling or math, you must use your intellect.*

2 great intelligence; high mental ability: *Isaac Newton was a man of intellect.* **3** someone of high mental ability: *Einstein was one of the greatest intellects of his time.*

in·tel·lec·tu·al (in′tə lek′chü əl), **1** *adj.* needing or using intelligence: *Teaching is an intellectual occupation.* **2** *adj.* of the intellect: *Thinking is an intellectual process.* **3** *adj.* having or showing intelligence: *an intellectual person.* **4** *n.* someone who is well informed and intelligent. —**in′tel·lec′tu·al·ly,** *adv.*

in·tel·li·gence (in tel′ə jəns), *n.* **1** ability to learn and know; quickness of understanding; mind: *Many schools give tests to measure intelligence.* **2** knowledge, news, or information, especially secret information, about an enemy: *Spies supply our government with intelligence.* **3** group engaged in obtaining secret information: *Intelligence sent agents to infiltrate the enemy's missile bases.*

intelligence quotient, number that expresses a measure of a person's intelligence. It is found by dividing the mental age shown in tests by the actual age (16 is the largest age used) and multiplying by 100.

intelligence test, any test used to measure mental development.

in·tel·li·gent (in tel′ə jənt), *adj.* **1** having or showing intelligence; able to learn and know; quick to understand. ■ See Synonym Study at **smart.** **2** in data processing: **a** containing a microprocessor and so able to perform functions often requiring a computer: *an intelligent terminal.* **b** having artificial intelligence. —**in·tel′li·gent·ly,** *adv.*

WORD STORY **Intelligent** comes from Latin words meaning "to choose between" or "to gather together." Part of intelligence is seeing differences, and part is seeing how things are alike.

in·tel·li·gent·si·a (in tel′ə jent′sē ə), *n.pl.* persons representing, or claiming to represent, the educated class; the intellectuals.

WORD STORY **Intelligentsia** comes from a Russian word meaning "intellectuals," which came from a Latin word meaning "intelligence." People writing about Russian intellectuals used the Russian word, even though English already had a word for this idea.

in·tel·li·gi·ble (in tel′ə jə bəl), *adj.* capable of being understood; clear. —**in·tel′li·gi·bil′i·ty,** *n.* —**in·tel′li·gi·bly,** *adv.*

in·tem·per·ance (in tem′pər əns), *n.* **1** lack of moderation or self-control; excess: *Intemperance in eating can cause you to become very fat.* **2** too much drinking of intoxicating liquor.

in·tem·per·ate (in tem′pər it), *adj.* **1** not moderate; lacking in self-control; excessive: *intemperate anger.* **2** drinking too much alcoholic liquor. —**in·tem′per·ate·ly,** *adv.* —**in·tem′per·ate·ness,** *n.*

in·tend (in tend′), *v.* **1** to have in mind as a purpose; plan: *I intend to go home soon.* **2** to mean for a particular purpose or use: *That gift was intended for you.* —**in·tend′er,** *n.*

in·tend·ed (in ten′did), **1** *adj.* in mind as a purpose; meant; planned: *The medicine had the intended effect and stopped the pain.* **2** *adj.* going to be; future: *A woman's intended husband is the man she is going to marry.* **3** *n.* an intended husband or wife. —**in·tend′ed·ly,** *adv.* —**in·tend′ed·ness,** *n.*

in·tense (in tens′), *adj.* **1** very much; very great; very strong; extreme: *Intense heat melts iron. A bad burn causes intense pain.* **2** full of vigorous activity, strong feelings, etc. **3** having or showing strong feeling. An intense person is one who feels things very deeply and is likely to be extreme in action. —**in·tense′ly,** *adv.* —**in·tense′ness,** *n.*

USAGE NOTE The meanings of **intense** and **intensive** are sometimes very close, but at times the words are used in different ways. **Intense** is used to describe strong feelings or great activity: *She has an intense love for horses.* **Intensive** is used to describe something that is done in a very thorough way: *Intensive research will be needed to find a cure for this disease.*

a	hat	ė	term	ô	order	ch	child		a in about
ā	age	i	it	oi	oil	ng	long		e in taken
ä	far	ī	ice	ou	out	sh	she	ə	i in pencil
â	care	o	hot	u	cup	th	thin		o in lemon
e	let	ō	open	ù	put	ᴛʜ	then		u in circus
ē	equal	ȯ	saw	ü	rule	zh	measure		

in·ten·si·fi·er (in ten′sə fī/ər), *n.* (in grammar) an intensive.

in·ten·si·fy (in ten′sə fī), *v.* to make or become intense or more intense; strengthen; increase: *My first failure only intensified my desire to succeed.* ❑ *v.* **in·ten·si·fied, in·ten·si·fy·ing.** —**in·ten′si·fi·ca′tion,** *n.*

in·ten·si·ty (in ten′sə tē), *n.* **1** quality of being intense; great strength: *the intensity of tropical sunlight.* **2** extreme energy; great vigor; force: *intensity of thought, intensity of feeling.* **3** amount of strength of electricity, heat, light, sound, etc., per unit of area, volume, etc. ❑ *n., pl.* **in·ten·si·ties** for 3.

in·ten·sive (in ten′siv), **1** *adj.* deep and thorough: *New laws were passed following an intensive study of the causes of pollution.* ■ See Usage Note at **intense. 2** *adj.* (in grammar) giving force or emphasis; expressing intensity. In "I did it myself," *myself* is an intensive pronoun. **3** *n.* word, prefix, etc., that expresses intensity or gives force or emphasis. In "It's terribly late," *terribly* is an intensive. —**in·ten′sive·ly,** *adv.*

intensive care unit, a medical unit specially equipped to provide continuous hospital care for patients who are very seriously ill or emergency care for accident or heart attack victims.

in·tent (in tent′), **1** *adj.* with your mind or attention fixed on a goal; determined; resolute: *be intent on making money. I am intent on doing my best.* **2** *adj.* very attentive; having the eyes or thoughts earnestly fixed on something; earnest: *an intent look. She was intent on a math problem.* **3** *n.* that which is intended; purpose; intention: *I'm sorry I hurt you; that wasn't my intent.* **4** *n.* meaning; significance: *What is the intent of that remark?* —**in·tent′ly,** *adv.* —**in·tent′ness,** *n.*

to all intents and purposes, in almost every way; practically; almost.

in·ten·tion (in ten′shən), *n.* **1** purpose; design; plan: *Our intention is to travel next summer.* **2** meaning.

SYNONYM STUDY **Intention, purpose,** and **goal** all mean what a person has in mind to do. **Intention** does not suggest strong effort: *It was my intention to go, but I forgot.* **Purpose** means a strong intention and suggests making choices: *The purpose of the trip is for students to learn how county government works.* **Goal** can mean something for which a person works, usually with effort: *The team's goal is to win at least two more games than last year.*

in·ten·tion·al (in ten′shə nəl), *adj.* done on purpose; meant; planned; intended: *His lateness was intentional; he wanted to hear just the last two speakers.* —**in·ten′tion·al·ly,** *adv.*

in·ter (in tėr′), *v.* to put a dead body into a grave or tomb; bury. ❑ *v.* **in·terred, in·ter·ring.**

inter-, *prefix.* **1** with or on each other; together: *intercommunicate = communicate with each other.* **2** between or among: *international = between or among nations.*

in·ter·act (in′tər akt′), *v.* to act on each other: *The summer heat and my bad temper interacted, each making the other seem worse.* —**in′ter·ac′tion,** *n.*

in·ter·ac·tive (in′tər ak′tiv), *adj.* **1** acting on each other. **2** (of a computer, cable television system, compact disk, etc.) allowing two-way communication between a user and the device, so that the user can ask and answer questions or make other choices and responses that affect the information shown and heard.

in·ter·breed (in′tər brēd′), *v.* to breed by the mating of different kinds; breed by using different varieties of living things. Many of our cultivated plants are hybrids developed by interbreeding various plants to combine their desirable qualities. ❑ *v.* **in·ter·bred** (in′tər bred′), **in·ter·breed·ing.**

in·ter·cede (in′tər sēd′), *v.* **1** to plead for another; ask a favor from one person for another: *The senator interceded with the governor to help us save the state park.* **2** to mediate in order to bring about an agreement: *The debate between the lawyers became so heated that the judge had to intercede.* ❑ *v.* **in·ter·ced·ed, in·ter·ced·ing.**

in·ter·cel·lu·lar (in′tər sel′yə lər), *adj.* situated between or among cells.

in·ter·cept (in′tər sept′), *v.* **1** to take or seize on the way from one place to another: *intercept a letter, intercept a messenger, intercept a pass in a football game.* **2** (in mathematics) to mark off part of a line or space between points or lines. A diameter of a circle intercepts the circumference at two points. [*Intercept* comes from Latin words meaning "to catch between."]

in·ter·cep·tion (in′tər sep′shən), *n.* **1** act or process of intercepting. **2** something that is intercepted. **3** act of intercepting a football pass: *The interception prevented our team from scoring.* **4** a football pass that is intercepted: *The quarterback threw two touchdowns and three interceptions.*

in·ter·cep·tor or **in·ter·cept·er** (in′tər sep′tər), *n.* **1** a fast-climbing airplane designed to intercept enemy aircraft. **2** someone or something that intercepts.

in·ter·ces·sion (in′tər sesh′ən), *n.* act or fact of pleading for another: *The girl's intercession for her brother won their parents' consent to his request.*

in·ter·ces·sor (in′tər ses′ər), *n.* someone who intercedes.

in·ter·change (in′tər chānj′ *for verb;* in′tər chānj′ *for noun*), **1** *n.* act or process of giving and taking; exchanging. **2** *n.* act or process of putting each of two or more persons or things in the other's place; an exchange: *The word "team" becomes "meat" by the interchange of the first and last letters.* **3** *v.* to put each of two or more persons or things in the other's place; exchange: *If you interchange those two pictures, they'll look better.* **4** *v.* to give and take; exchange: *We interchanged our ideas and opinions before making a decision.* **5** *n.* a point at which a highway, especially an express highway, connects with another main traffic route. ❑ *v.* **in·ter·changed, in·ter·chang·ing.**

interchange (def. 5)

in·ter·change·a·ble (in′tər chān′jə bəl), *adj.* **1** able to be put or used in each other's place: *interchangeable parts.* **2** able to change places. —**in′ter·change′a·bil′i·ty,** *n.* —**in′ter·change′a·bly,** *adv.*

in·ter·cit·y (in′tər sit′ē), *adj.* between cities; from one city to another: *intercity railroad service.*

in·ter·col·le·giate (in′tər kə lē′jit), *adj.* between colleges or universities: *intercollegiate football games.*

in·ter·com (in′tər kom′), *n.* a system of microphones and loudspeakers by which people can talk to each other from different parts of a building, aircraft, ship, tank, etc.

in·ter·com·mu·ni·cate (in′tər kə myü′nə kāt), *v.* to communicate with each other. ❑ *v.* **in·ter·com·mu·ni·cat·ed, in·ter·com·mu·ni·cat·ing.** —**in′ter·com·mu′ni·ca′tion,** *n.*

in·ter·con·nect (in′tər kə nekt′), *v.* to connect with each other. —**in′ter·con·nec′tion,** *n.*

in·ter·con·ti·nen·tal (in′tər kon′tə nen′tl), *adj.* between continents; from one continent to another: *an intercontinental railroad.*

intercontinental ballistic missile, a ballistic missile with a range of more than 5000 miles (8000 kilometers).

in·ter·course (in′tər kôrs′), *n.* **1** dealings between people; exchange of thoughts, services, and feelings; communication: *Airplanes, good roads, and telephones make intercourse with different parts of the country far easier than it was 50 years ago.* **2** sexual intercourse.

in·ter·cul·tur·al (in′tər kul′chər əl), *adj.* between different cultures; involving two or more cultures: *intercultural communication.*

in·ter·de·nom·i·na·tion·al (in′tər di nom′ə nā′shə nəl), *adj.* between different religious denominations.

in·ter·de·pend·ence (in′tər di pen′dəns), *n.* dependence upon each other.

in·ter·de·pend·ent (in′tər di pen′dənt), *adj.* dependent upon each other. —**in′ter·de·pend′ent·ly,** *adv.*

in·ter·dict (in′tər dikt′ *for verb;* in′tər dikt *for noun*), **1** *v.* to prohibit or forbid; restrain. **2** *n.* prohibition based on authority; formal order forbidding something. **3** in the Roman Catholic Church: **a** *v.* to cut off from certain church privileges. **b** *n.* act of cutting off from certain church privileges. —**in′ter·dic′tion,** *n.*

in·ter·est (in′tər ist), **1** *n.* a feeling of wanting to know, see, do, own, share in, or take part in: *He has an interest in reading and in collecting stamps.* **2** *v.* to arouse such a feeling in; make curious and hold the attention of: *An exciting mystery interests most people.* **3** *n.* something in which someone has a share or part. Any business, activity, or pastime can be an interest. **4** *n.* power of arousing such a feeling: *A dull book lacks interest.* **5** *n.* a share or part in property and actions: *She bought a half interest in the business.* **6** *v.* to cause someone to take a share or part in something; arouse the concern, curiosity, or attention of: *The salesperson tried to interest us in buying a TV.* **7** *n.* group of people having the same business, activity, etc.: *the business interests of the town.* **8** *n.* advantage; benefit; profit: *The parents look after the interests of the family.* **9** *n.* money paid for the use of someone else's money, usually a percentage of the amount invested, borrowed, or loaned: *The interest on the loan was 7 percent a year.*
in the interest of, for; to help.

WORD STORY **Interest** comes from a Latin word meaning "it matters." That Latin word comes from Latin words that mean "to be" and "between." Something between you and your goal probably matters to you.

in·ter·est·ed (in′tər ə stid *or* in′tə res′tid), *adj.* **1** feeling or showing interest; with your interest aroused: *an interested spectator.* **2** having an interest or share. —**in′ter·est·ed·ly,** *adv.*

in·ter·est·ing (in′tər ə sting *or* in′tə res′ting), *adj.* arousing interest; holding your attention: *Stories about travel and adventure are interesting to many people.* —**in′ter·est·ing·ly,** *adv.*

SYNONYM STUDY **Interesting, intriguing,** and **fascinating** all mean catching a person's attention. **Interesting** means making a person feel like paying attention and knowing more: *Grandma's stories about the island where she grew up are really interesting.* **Intriguing** means interesting in a way that makes someone curious: *This mystery story is intriguing.* **Fascinating** means so interesting that it is hard to stop doing something: *He finds computers fascinating and sometimes sits at the keyboard for hours.*

in·ter·face (in′tər fās′), **1** *n.* connection linking two or more separate items so they can work together. A computer program can be the interface for other programs. **2** *v.* to connect; join. **3** *n.* surface that forms a border between two objects, spaces, or kinds of matter. ❑ *v.* **in·ter·faced, in·ter·fac·ing.**

in·ter·faith (in′tər fāth′), *adj.* of or for different faiths or religions: *an interfaith chapel, an interfaith conference.*

in·ter·fere (in′tər fir′), *v.* **1** to get in the way of each other; come into opposition; clash: *The two plans interfere; one must be changed.* **2** to mix in the affairs of others; meddle: *That neighbor is always interfering in other people's affairs.* ■ See Synonym Study at **meddle.** ❑ *v.* **in·ter·fered, in·ter·fer·ing.** —**in′ter·fer′er,** *n.*

in·ter·fer·ence (in′tər fir′əns), *n.* **1** act or fact of interfering: *Your interference spoiled our game.* **2** something that interferes. **3** (in radio or television) the interruption of a desired signal by other signals, static, noise, etc., that prevent clear reception. **4** (in football, hockey, and other sports) the obstruction of an opposing player in a way that is against the rules. **5** (in football) protection of the player who has the ball by blocking opposing players.

in·ter·fer·on (in′tər fir′on), *n.* protein produced by animal cells that have been infected by a virus. It protects similar cells from infection by the same or other viruses.

in·ter·ga·lac·tic (in′tər gə lak′tik), *adj.* between galaxies: *intergalactic space.*

in·ter·im (in′tər im), **1** *n.* time between; the meantime. **2** *adj.* for the meantime; temporary: *an interim solution.*

in·ter·i·or (in tir′ē ər), **1** *n.* inner surface or part; inside: *The interior of the house was beautifully decorated.* **2** *adj.* on or for the inside; inner: *The interior walls of the house were painted last year.* **3** *n.* part of a region or country away from the coast or border: *There are deserts in the interior of Asia.* **4** *adj.* away from the coast or border. **5** *n.* affairs within a country, regarded as separate from foreign affairs. In the United States, the Department of the Interior is responsible for managing federal land and the nation's natural resources.

interior decorator, person whose business is planning and arranging the furnishings, decoration, etc., of houses, offices, or public buildings.

interj., interjection (def. 1).

in·ter·ject (in′tər jekt′), *v.* to introduce something suddenly into a conversation or speech: *Every now and then the speaker interjected a joke to keep us interested.*

in·ter·jec·tion (in′tər jek′shən), *n.* **1** an exclamation showing emotion. It is regarded as a part of speech. *Oh! ah! ouch!* and *hurrah!* are interjections. **2** a sudden insertion into a conversation or speech: *The interjection of amusing stories into the speech made it more interesting.* **3** something interjected; remark thrown in; exclamation. —**in′ter·jec′tion·al,** *adj.*

in·ter·lace (in′tər lās′), *v.* to arrange threads, strips, or branches so that they go over and under each other; weave together; intertwine: *Baskets are made by interlacing reeds or fibers.* ❑ *v.* **in·ter·laced, in·ter·lac·ing.** —**in′ter·lace′ment,** *n.*

in·ter·lard (in′tər lärd′), *v.* to give variety to; mix; intersperse: *The speaker interlarded the long speech with amusing stories to keep the listeners interested.*

in·ter·lin·ing (in′tər lī′ning), *n.* an extra lining inserted between the outer cloth and the ordinary lining of a garment.

in·ter·lock (in′tər lok′), *v.* to join or fit tightly together; lock together: *The two stags were fighting with their horns interlocked. The pieces of a jigsaw puzzle interlock.*

in·ter·lop·er (in′tər lō′pər), *n.* person who interferes, unasked and unwanted; intruder.

in·ter·lude (in′tər lüd), *n.* **1** anything thought of as filling the time between two things; interval: *There was an interlude of sunshine between the two showers.* **2** piece of music played between the parts of a song, church service, or drama.

in·ter·lu·nar (in′tər lü′nər), *adj.* of the time when the moon is not seen at night, between the old moon and the new moon.

in·ter·mar·riage (in′tər mar′ij), *n.* marriage between members of different families, tribes, religions, or racial groups.

in·ter·mar·ry (in′tər mar′ē), *v.* **1** (of families, tribes, religions, or racial groups) to become connected by marriage: *The families of this old town have intermarried for generations.* **2** to marry outside your tribe, religion, or racial group. ❑ *v.* **in·ter·mar·ried, in·ter·mar·ry·ing.**

in·ter·me·di·ar·y (in′tər mē′dē er′ē), **1** *n.* someone who acts to bring about an agreement between others; someone who acts for someone else: *The teacher acted as intermediary for the students with the principal.* **2** *adj.* acting between others; acting for another. **3** *adj.* intermediate: *A cocoon is an intermediary stage between caterpillar and butterfly.* ❑ *n., pl.* **in·ter·me·di·ar·ies.**

in·ter·me·di·ate (in′tər mē′dē it), **1** *adj.* being or occurring between others; middle: *Classes are offered in beginning, intermediate, and advanced French. Gray is intermediate between black and white.* **2** *adj.* of or referring to grades six through eight. **3** *n.* something in between.

in·ter·ment (in tėr′mənt), *n.* act of interring; burial.

in·ter·mez·zo (in′tər met′sō *or* in′tər med′zō), *n.* a short musical composition played between the main divisions of an opera, symphony, or other long musical work. ❑ *n., pl.* **in·ter·mez·zos, in·ter·mez·zi** (in′tər met′sē *or* in′tər med′zē). [**Intermezzo** comes from Latin words meaning "between" and "in the middle."]

a	hat	ė	term	ô	order	ch	child		
ā	age	i	it	oi	oil	ng	long	ə	a in about
ä	far	ī	ice	ou	out	sh	she		e in taken
â	care	o	hot	u	cup	th	thin		i in pencil
e	let	ō	open	ù	put	ᴛʜ	then		o in lemon
ē	equal	ò	saw	ü	rule	zh	measure		u in circus

in·ter·mi·na·ble (in tèr′mə nə bəl), *adj.* so long as to seem endless; very long and tiring. **—in·ter′mi·na·bly,** *adv.*

in·ter·min·gle (in′tər ming′gəl), *v.* to mix together; mingle: *The hosts encouraged guests with different interests to intermingle.* ❑ *v.* **in·ter·min·gled, in·ter·min·gling.**

in·ter·mis·sion (in′tər mish′ən), *n.* **1** interval between periods of activity; pause; interruption: *The band played from eight to twelve with a short intermission at ten.* **2** stopping for a time; interruption: *The rain continued all day without intermission.*

SYNONYM STUDY **Intermission, time-out,** and **recess** all mean a pause. **Intermission** means a scheduled pause during a performance: *During the intermission I met my best friend in the lobby.* **Time-out** means a short pause during a game: *With the home team two points behind, the coach called a time-out.* **Recess** means a pause during an official activity: *The trial judge called a recess for lunch.*

in·ter·mit·tent (in′tər mit′nt), *adj.* stopping for a time and beginning again; not continuous: *The pilot watched for an intermittent red light, flashing on and off every 15 seconds.* **—in′ter·mit′tent·ly,** *adv.*

in·ter·mix (in′tər miks′), *v.* to mix together; blend: *Oil and water do not intermix.*

in·tern[1] (in tèrn′), *v.* to confine within a country or place; force to stay in a certain place, especially during wartime. **—in·tern′ment,** *n.*

in·tern[2] (in′tèrn′), **1** *n.* doctor undergoing training in a hospital and acting as an assistant. **2** *n.* student in a professional field who receives work training under experienced supervision. **3** *v.* to be an intern. **—in′tern·ship,** *n.*

in·ter·nal (in tèr′nl), *adj.* **1** on the inside; inner: *The accident caused internal injuries.* **2** to be taken inside the body: *Pills are internal remedies.* **3** of affairs within a country; domestic: *internal politics. Internal revenue is money from taxes on business and income within a country.*

in·ter·nal-com·bus·tion engine (in tèr′nl kəm bus′chən), any engine in which power is produced by burning a mixture of fuel and air inside the engine itself, usually inside cylinders. Gasoline engines and diesel engines are internal-combustion engines; steam engines are not.

in·ter·nal·ly (in tèr′nl ē), *adv.* **1** inside. **2** inside the body: *This ointment must not be taken internally.*

internal rhyme, rhyme of a word within a line of verse with the word at the end of the line. In the lines below, there is internal rhyme in the first line.

> EXAMPLE: We *three* shall *flee* across the *sea*
> And share in new-found *liberty.*

in·ter·na·tion·al (in′tər nash′ə nəl), *adj.* **1** of or referring to two or more countries: *A treaty is an international agreement.* **2** of or referring to the relations between nations: *international law.* **—in′ter·na′tion·al·ly,** *adv.*

International Date Line, an imaginary line agreed to be the place where each new calendar day begins. It runs north and south through the Pacific, mostly along the 180th meridian. When it is Sunday just east of the International Date Line, it is Monday just west of it.

international grand master, a chess player officially ranked among the world's best in tournament play.

in·ter·na·tion·al·ism (in′tər nash′ə nə liz′əm), *n.* principle of international cooperation for the good of all nations.

in·ter·na·tion·a·list (in′tər nash ə nə′list), *n.,* someone who favors internationalism.

in·ter·na·tion·al·ize (in′tər nash′ə nə liz), *v.* to make international; bring under the control of several nations. ❑ *v.* **in·ter·na·tion·al·ized, in·ter·na·tion·al·iz·ing. —in′ter·na′tion·al·i·za′tion,** *n.*

International Joint Commission, commission set up by Canada and the United States in 1909 that rules on potential disputes over boundary waters or elsewhere along their border.

international unit, the smallest amount of a particular substance that will produce an effect on the body. Some vitamins and drugs are measured in international units.

in·ter·ne·cine (in′tər nē′sn *or* in′tər nē′sīn), *adj.* **1** destructive to both sides within a group. **2** deadly; mutually destructive.

in·ter·nee (in′tèr′nē′), *n.* person interned. Prisoners of war, enemy aliens, etc., may be internees. ❑ *n., pl.* **in·ter·nees.**

In·ter·net (in′tər net′), *n.* an extremely large computer network, including many smaller networks of university, government, business, and private computers, linked by telephone lines. Using the Internet, people can exchange messages, data, and electronic services all over the world.

in·tern·ist (in tèr′nist), *n.* doctor who treats internal organs or diseases.

in·ter·per·son·al (in′tər pèr′sə nəl), *adj.* between people: *interpersonal relations.*

in·ter·plan·e·tar·y (in′tər plan′ə ter′ē), *adj.* between the planets: *interplanetary travel.*

in·ter·play (in′tər plā′), *n.* action or influence on each other: *the interplay of light and shadow.*

in·ter·po·late (in tèr′pə lāt), *v.* **1** to alter a book, passage, etc., by putting in new words or groups of words, especially without authorization or deceptively: *So many later writers had interpolated the old manuscript that it was hard to tell what parts were genuine.* **2** (in mathematics) to find or insert a value between two known values by some method. ❑ *v.* **in·ter·po·lat·ed, in·ter·po·lat·ing. —in·ter′po·la′tion,** *n.* **—in·ter′po·la′tor,** *n.*

WORD STORY **Interpolate** comes from Latin words meaning "to make smooth" and "between." Like a patch that fills a hole and makes a surface smooth, new words may fill a gap.

in·ter·pose (in′tər pōz′), *v.* **1** to put between; insert. **2** to come or be between other things. **3** to put forward; break in with; interrupt: *I'd like to interpose an objection at this point.* **4** to interfere in order to help; intervene: *I interposed in the dispute between my friends.* ❑ *v.* **in·ter·posed, in·ter·pos·ing. —in′ter·pos′a·ble,** *adj.* **—in′ter·pos′er,** *n.*

in·ter·po·si·tion (in′tər pə zish′ən), *n.* **1** act of interposing: *the interposition of a remark.* **2** something interposed.

in·ter·pret (in tèr′prit), *v.* **1** to explain the meaning of: *interpret a hard passage in a book, interpret a dream.* **2** to bring out the meaning of a dramatic work, a character, music, etc.: *The actress interpreted the part of the queen with wonderful skill.* **3** to understand: *We interpreted your silence as consent.* **4** to serve as an interpreter; translate. **—in·ter′pret·a·ble,** *adj.*

in·ter·pre·ta·tion (in tèr′prə tā′shən), *n.* **1** act of interpreting; explanation: *People often give different interpretations to the same facts.* **2** act of bringing out the meaning: *The newspapers praised the musician's interpretation of the piece.*

in·ter·pre·ta·tive (in tèr′prə tā′tiv), *adj.* used for interpreting; explanatory. **—in·ter′pre·ta′tive·ly,** *adv.*

in·ter·pret·er (in tèr′prə tər), *n.* someone who interprets, especially someone whose business is translating, especially orally, from a foreign language.

in·ter·pre·tive (in tèr′prə tiv), *adj.* interpretative. **—in·ter′pre·tive·ly,** *adv.*

in·ter·ra·cial (in′tər rā′shəl), *adj.* between or involving different racial groups: *interracial cooperation.*

in·ter·reg·num (in′tər reg′nəm), *n.* time between the end of one ruler's reign and the beginning of the next ruler's reign. ❑ *n., pl.* **in·ter·reg·nums, in·ter·reg·na** (in′tər reg′nə).

in·ter·re·late (in′tər ri lāt′), *v.* to bring into relation to each other. ❑ *v.* **in·ter·re·lat·ed, in·ter·re·lat·ing.**

in·ter·re·lat·ed (in′tər ri lā′tid), *adj.* closely connected with each other; mutually related. **—in′ter·re·lat′ed·ly,** *adv.* **—in′ter·re·lat′ed·ness,** *n.*

in·ter·re·la·tion (in′tər ri lā′shən), *n.* close connection with each other; mutual relationship.

in·ter·re·la·tion·ship (in′tər ri lā′shən ship), *n.* interrelation.

in·ter·ro·gate (in ter′ə gāt), *v.* to ask questions of; examine or get information from by asking questions; question thoroughly: *The lawyer took two hours to interrogate the witness.* ❑ *v.* **in·ter·ro·gat·ed, in·ter·ro·gat·ing.**

interrogation

in·ter·ro·ga·tion (in ter′ə gā′shən), *n.* act of interrogating; a questioning. The formal examination of a witness by asking questions is an interrogation.

interrogation mark or **interrogation point,** question mark; the mark (?).

in·ter·rog·a·tive (in′tə rog′ə tiv), *adj.* **1** asking a question; having the form of a question: *an interrogative sentence.* **2** (in grammar) used in asking a question. *Where, when, why* are interrogative adverbs. *Who* and *what* are interrogative pronouns. **−in′ter·rog′a·tive·ly,** *adv.*

in·ter·ro·ga·tor (in ter′ə gā′tər), *n.* person who interrogates; questioner.

in·ter·rog·a·to·ry (in′tə rog′ə tôr′ē), *adj.* questioning.

in·ter·rupt (in′tə rupt′), *v.* **1** to break in upon talk, work, rest, someone speaking, etc.; keep from going on; stop for a time; hinder: *A fire drill interrupted the lesson.* **2** to cause a break; break in: *It is not polite to interrupt when someone is talking.* **3** to make a break in: *A dam interrupts the flow of the river.* **−in′ter·rupt′er,** *n.* **−in′ter·rupt′i·ble,** *adj.* **−in′ter·rup′tive,** *adj.*

in·ter·rup·tion (in′tə rup′shən), *n.* **1** act of interrupting; breaking in on. **2** a break; stopping: *The rain continued without interruption all day.*

in·ter·scho·las·tic (in′tər skə las′tik), *adj.* between schools: *We won the interscholastic softball competition.*

in·ter·sect (in′tər sekt′), *v.* **1** to cross each other: *Streets usually intersect at right angles.* **2** to cross; cut or divide by passing through or across: *A path intersects the field.* **3** (in geometry) to have one or more points in common: *intersecting circles.*

in·ter·sec·tion (in′tər sek′shən), *n.* **1** point, line, or place where one thing crosses another: *a dangerous intersection.* **2** act of intersecting: *Bridges and underpasses are used to avoid the intersection of a railroad and a highway.* **3** any point that geometric figures or lines have in common. **4** (in mathematics) the set that contains only those elements shared by two or more sets.

in·ter·sperse (in′tər spėrs′), *v.* **1** to vary with something put here and there: *The grass was interspersed with beds of flowers.* **2** to scatter here and there among other things: *Bushes were interspersed among the trees.* ▢ *v.* **in·ter·spersed, in·ter·spers·ing.**

in·ter·state (in′tər stāt′), **1** *adj.* between persons or organizations in different states; between states: *The federal government regulates interstate commerce.* **2** *n.* highway that is part of a system of federal highways connecting most major cities in the United States.

in·ter·stel·lar (in′tər stel′ər), *adj.* between the stars: *interstellar distances.*

in·ter·twine (in′tər twīn′), *v.* to twine, one with another: *Two vines intertwined on the wall.* ▢ *v.* **in·ter·twined, in·ter·twin·ing.** **−in′ter·twine′ment,** *n.*

in·ter·ur·ban (in′tər ėr′bən), *adj.* between cities or towns: *an interurban bus line.*

in·ter·val (in′tər vəl), *n.* **1** period of time between things: *There is an interval of six days between Christmas and New Year's Day.* **2** space between things: *Trees were planted with intervals of 25 feet between each two trees.* **3** the set of all numbers between two stated numbers: *the interval between 2 and 7.* **4** (in music) the difference in pitch between two tones.
at intervals, 1 now and then. **2** here and there.

WORD STORY **Interval** comes from Latin words meaning "between walls." In old times, cities and forts were often built with two walls, inner and outer, and a space between.

in·ter·vene (in′tər vēn′), *v.* **1** to come between persons or groups to help settle a dispute: *The President was asked to intervene in the coal strike.* **2** to happen; take place so as to get in the way: *The parade was fun until bad weather intervened.* **3** to come between; be between: *A week intervenes between my sister's birthday and mine.* **4** to interfere in the affairs of another nation. ▢ *v.* **in·ter·vened, in·ter·ven·ing. −in′ter·ve′nor** or **in′ter·ven′er,** *n.*

in·ter·ven·tion (in′tər ven′shən), *n.* **1** act of intervening: *The strike was settled by the intervention of the President.* **2** interference, especially by one nation in the affairs of another.

in·ter·view (in′tər vyü′), **1** *n.* a meeting, generally of persons face to face, to talk over something special: *a job interview.* **2** *n.* a meeting between a reporter and someone from whom information is sought for publication or broadcast. **3** *n.* newspaper or magazine article, or broadcast containing the information given at such a meeting. **4** *v.* to have an interview with; meet and talk with, especially to obtain information: *Reporters interviewed the mayor.*

in·ter·view·er (in′tər vyü′ər), *n.* person whose business is to visit and talk with other people, and to report the conversation in a newspaper or magazine, or on radio or TV.

in·ter·weave (in′tər wēv′), *v.* **1** to weave together: *interweave bamboo strips to make a basket.* **2** to mix together; blend: *interweave truth with fiction in a story.* ▢ *v.* **in·ter·wove** (in′tər wōv′), **in·ter·wo·ven, in·ter·weav·ing.**

in·ter·wo·ven (in′tər wō′vən), **1** *adj.* woven together. **2** *adj.* mixed together; blended. **3** *v.* past participle of **interweave:** *Various strands were interwoven to create a colorful pattern.*

in·tes·tate (in tes′tāt), *adj.* having made no will: *to die intestate.*

in·tes·ti·nal (in tes′tə nəl), *adj.* of or in the intestine. **−in·tes′ti·nal·ly,** *adv.*

in·tes·tine (in tes′tən), *n.* Also, **intestines,** *pl.* the part of the digestive system extending from the stomach to the anus. Partially digested food passes from the stomach into the **small intestine,** a winding, narrow tube, where digestion is completed and nutrients are absorbed by the blood. The small intestine empties into the **large intestine,** a wide tube, where water is absorbed and wastes are eliminated. In humans, the small intestine is about 20 feet (6 meters) long and the large intestine is about 5 feet (1.5 meters) long.

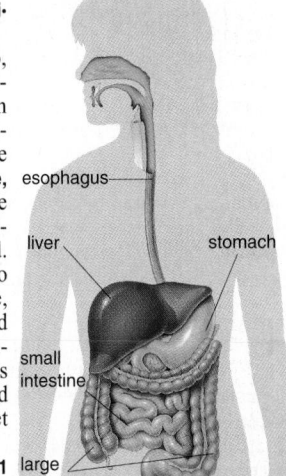

esophagus

liver

stomach

small intestine

large intestine

intestine

in·ti·ma·cy (in′tə mə sē), *n.* **1** condition of being intimate; close acquaintance; closeness. **2** a familiar or intimate act. ▢ *n., pl.* **in·ti·ma·cies** for 2.

in·ti·mate[1] (in′tə mit), **1** *adj.* very familiar; known very well; closely acquainted: *They have been intimate friends since childhood.* **2** *adj.* resulting from close familiarity; close: *intimate*

a	hat	ė	term	ô	order	ch	child		
ā	age	i	it	oi	oil	ng	long		a in about
ä	far	ī	ice	ou	out	sh	she		e in taken
â	care	o	hot	u	cup	th	thin	ə	i in pencil
e	let	ō	open	u̇	put	ᴛʜ	then		o in lemon
ē	equal	ȯ	saw	ü	rule	zh	measure		u in circus

knowledge of something. **3** *adj.* personal; private: *A diary is a very intimate book.* **4** *n.* a close friend. **5** *adj.* deepest; inmost: *a person's intimate thoughts.* **—in′ti·mate·ly,** *adv.*

in·ti·mate² (in′tə māt), *v.* **1** to suggest indirectly; hint: *Her smile intimated that she was pleased.* **2** to make known; announce; notify. ❑ *v.* **in·ti·mat·ed, in·ti·mat·ing. —in′ti·mat′er,** *n.*

in·ti·ma·tion (in′tə mā′shən), *n.* **1** indirect suggestion; hint: *His frown is an intimation of his disapproval.* **2** announcement; notice.

in·tim·i·date (in tim′ə dāt), *v.* to make afraid; frighten; influence by fear: *intimidate a witness.* ❑ *v.* **in·tim·i·dat·ed, in·tim·i·dat·ing. —in·tim′i·da′tion,** *n.* **—in·tim′i·da′tor,** *n.*

in·to (in′tü; *before consonants often* in′tə), *prep.* **1** to the inside of; toward and inside: *Come into the house. We drove into the city.* ■ See Usage Note at **in. 2** so as to become; to the form of: *Divide the apple into three parts. Cold weather turns water into ice.* **3** against: *In the dark, she walked into the closet door.* **4** INFORMAL. involved with; interested in: *They were into rock music.*

in·tol·er·a·ble (in tol′ər ə bəl), *adj.* too much to be endured; unbearable: *The pain of the toothache was intolerable.* **—in·tol′er·a·bil′i·ty, in·tol′er·a·ble·ness,** *n.* **—in·tol′er·a·bly,** *adv.*

in·tol·er·ance (in tol′ər əns), *n.* **1** unwillingness to let others do and think as they choose, especially in religion: *The Pilgrims left England because of intolerance and persecution.* ■ See Synonym Study at **prejudice. 2** inability to tolerate; lack of tolerance: *She developed an intolerance to penicillin.*

in·tol·er·ant (in tol′ər ənt), *adj.* not tolerant; not willing to let others do and think as they choose, especially in religion: *Some Puritans were strict and intolerant.* **—in·tol′er·ant·ly,** *adv.*
intolerant of, not able to endure; unwilling to endure or accept: *intolerant of cold, intolerant of lactose.*

in·to·na·tion (in′tō nā′shən), *n.* **1** manner of sounding words or speaking, especially with regard to the rise and fall of the pitch of the voice. **2** manner of producing musical notes, especially with regard to pitch.

in·tone (in tōn′), *v.* to read or recite in a singing voice: *A cantor intones part of the service.* ❑ *v.* **in·toned, in·ton·ing. —in·ton′er,** *n.*

in·tox·i·cant (in tok′sə kənt), *n.* anything that intoxicates, especially an alcoholic liquor.

in·tox·i·cate (in tok′sə kāt), *v.* **1** to make drunk: *Too much wine intoxicates people.* **2** to excite greatly; exhilarate: *The joy of winning intoxicated the team.* ❑ *v.* **in·tox·i·cat·ed, in·tox·i·cat·ing. —in·tox′i·cat′ing·ly,** *adv.*

in·tox·i·cat·ed (in tok′sə kā′tid), *adj.* **1** drunk: *an intoxicated person.* **2** very much excited. **—in·tox′i·cat′ed·ly,** *adv.*

in·tox·i·ca·tion (in tok′sə kā′shən), *n.* **1** an intoxicated condition; drunkenness. **2** great excitement.

intra-, *prefix.* within; into; inside: *intramuscular = into a muscle.*

in·trac·ta·ble (in trak′tə bəl), *adj.* hard to handle or manage; stubborn. **—in·trac′ta·bil′i·ty,** *n.* **—in·trac′ta·bly,** *adv.*

in·tra·mur·al (in′trə myùr′əl), *adj.* among students of the same school or college: *intramural sports.*

in·tra·mus·cu·lar (in′trə mus′kyə lər), *adj.* within or into a muscle: *an intramuscular injection.* **—in′tra·mus′cu·lar·ly,** *adv.*

in·tran·si·tive (in tran′sə tiv), *adj.* not taking a direct object. The verbs *belong, go,* and *seem* are intransitive. The verb *run* may be transitive or intransitive. In "I run to school" *run* is intransitive. **—in·tran′si·tive·ly,** *adv.*

in·tra·state (in′trə stāt′), *adj.* within a state, especially within a state of the United States: *intrastate commerce.*

in·tra·u·ter·ine (in′trə yü′tər ən), *adj.* within the uterus.

in·tra·ve·nous (in′trə vē′nəs), *adj.* going into someone's body through a vein: *When a person is too ill to digest food, an intravenous feeding is often given.* **—in′tra·ve′nous·ly,** *adv.*

in·trep·id (in trep′id), *adj.* very brave; fearless; courageous: *an intrepid adventurer.* **—in·trep′id·ly,** *adv.* **—in·trep′id·ness,** *n.*

in·tre·pid·i·ty (in′trə pid′ə tē), *n.* great bravery; courage; fearlessness.

in·tri·ca·cy (in′trə kə sē), *n.* **1** an intricate thing or event; complication: *The laws are full of intricacies.* **2** intricate nature or condition; complexity: *The intricacy of the plan made it hard to understand.* ❑ *n., pl.* **in·tri·ca·cies** for 1.

in·tri·cate (in′trə kit), *adj.* **1** with many twists and turns; puzzling, entangled, or complicated: *A mystery story usually has a very intricate plot.* **2** very hard to understand: *The directions were so intricate that I made several errors.* **—in′tri·cate·ly,** *adv.* **—in′tri·cate·ness,** *n.*

in·trigue (in trēg′ *or* in′trēg′ *for noun;* in trēg′ *for verb*), **1** *n.* secret scheming and plotting; crafty dealings: *The royal palace was filled with intrigue.* **2** *n.* a crafty plot; secret scheme: *The king's younger brother took part in the intrigue to make himself king.* **3** *v.* to form and carry out plots; plan in a secret or underhand way: *He pretended to be loyal while he intrigued against the king.* **4** *v.* to excite the curiosity and interest of: *The book's unusual title intrigued me.* **5** *n.* a secret love affair. ❑ *v.* **in·trigued, in·tri·guing. —in·tri′guer,** *n.*

in·tri·guing (in trē′ging), *adj.* exciting the curiosity and interest: *The book's intriguing title caught my attention.* ■ See Synonym Study at **interesting. —in·tri′guing·ly,** *adv.*

in·trin·sic (in trin′zik *or* in trin′sik), *adj.* belonging to a thing by its very nature; essential; inherent: *The intrinsic value of a coin is how much its metal content is worth.* **—in·trin′si·cal·ly,** *adv.*

in·tro (in′trō), *n.* INFORMAL. introduction. ❑ *n., pl.* **in·tros.**

intro. or **introd., 1** introduction. **2** introductory.

in·tro·duce (in′trə düs′), *v.* **1** to bring into acquaintance with; make known: *I introduced my new friend to several of my old friends.* **2** to bring into use, notice, knowledge, etc.: *introduce new products. Television and space travel are introducing many new words into our language.* **3** to bring in: *She introduced a story into the conversation.* **4** to put in; insert: *The doctor introduced a tube into the sick man's throat so he could breathe.* **5** to bring forward for consideration: *introduce a question for debate.* **6** to begin; start: *He introduced his speech by telling a joke.* ❑ *v.* **in·tro·duced, in·tro·duc·ing. —in′tro·duc′er,** *n.*

in·tro·duc·tion (in′trə duk′shən), *n.* **1** process of being introduced: *She was confused by her introduction to so many strangers.* **2** act of introducing: *The introduction of steel made tall buildings easier to build.* **3** first part of a book, speech, piece of music, etc., leading up to the main part. **4** book for beginners in a subject: *an introduction to geometry.* **5** something brought into use: *Television is a later introduction than radio.*

in·tro·duc·to·ry (in′trə duk′tə rē), *adj.* used to introduce; serving as an introduction; preliminary: *The speaker began her talk with a few introductory remarks about her subject.*

in·tro·spec·tion (in′trə spek′shən), *n.* examination of your own thoughts and feelings.

in·tro·spec·tive (in′trə spek′tiv), *adj.* inclined to examine your own thoughts and feelings. **—in′tro·spec′tive·ly,** *adv.*

in·tro·vert (in′trə vèrt′), *n.* person tending to think rather than act. Introverts are more interested in their own thoughts and feelings than in what is going on around them.

in·tro·vert·ed (in′trə vèr′tid), *adj.* having a tendency to think rather than act and to be more interested in your own thoughts and feelings than in what is going on around you.

in·trude (in trüd′), *v.* to force yourself in; come unasked and unwanted: *He intrudes upon the privacy of his neighbors.* ■ See Synonym Study at **enter.** ❑ *v.* **in·trud·ed, in·trud·ing. —in·trud′er,** *n.*

in·tru·sion (in trü′zhən), *n.* **1** act or process of intruding; entry unasked and unwanted: *Excuse my intrusion; I didn't know that you were busy.* **2** in geology: **a** the forcing of molten rock into cracks in other rocks or between layers of other rock. **b** the rock forced in when molten, then cooled and hardened in place.

in·tru·sive (in trü′siv), *adj.* intruding; coming unasked and unwanted. **—in·tru′sive·ly,** *adv.* **—in·tru′sive·ness,** *n.*

in·tu·i·tion (in′tü ish′ən), *n.* **1** immediate perception or understanding of truths, facts, etc., without reasoning: *By experience with many kinds of people the doctor had developed great powers of intuition.* **2** truth, fact, etc., perceived or understood immediately and without reasoning. [**Intuition** comes from Latin words meaning "to look in." The English word **insight** also compares perceptive thought to seeing.] **—in′tu·i′tion·al,** *adj.*

in·tu·i·tive (in tü′ə tiv), *adj.* **1** perceiving or understanding immediately and without reasoning: *an intuitive mind.* **2** acquired by intuition; instinctive; natural: *an artist's intuitive understanding of color.* **—in·tu′i·tive·ly,** *adv.* **—in·tu′i·tive·ness,** *n.*

In·u·it (in′ü it *or* in′yü it), **1** *n.* the people living mainly in the arctic regions of Canada and Greenland; the Eskimo people. **2** *n.* the language of this people; Eskimo. **3** *adj.* of this people or their language: *an Inuit word.* ■ See Usage Note at **Eskimo.**

in·un·date (in′un dāt), *v.* **1** to overflow; flood: *Heavy rains caused the river to rise and inundate the valley.* **2** to overspread as if with a flood; overwhelm: *Requests for free tickets inundated the radio station.* ❑ *v.* **in·un·dat·ed, in·un·dat·ing. —in′un·da′tion,** *n.* **—in′un·da′tor,** *n.*

I·nu·pi·aq (i nü′pē ak′), **1** *n.* the people living mainly in the arctic regions of Alaska; the Eskimo people. **2** *n.* the language of this people; Eskimo. **3** *adj.* of this people or their language: *an Inupiaq story.* ❑ *n., pl.* **I·nu·pi·aq** *or* **I·nu·pi·aqs** for 1. ■ See Usage Note at **Eskimo.**

in·ure (in yür′), *v.* to toughen or harden; accustom: *Nurses become inured to the sight of blood.* ❑ *v.* **in·ured, in·ur·ing. —in·ure′ment,** *n.*

in·vade (in vād′), *v.* **1** to enter with force or as an enemy; attack: *Soldiers invaded the country to conquer it.* **2** to enter as if to take possession: *Tourists invaded the city.* **3** to interfere with; break in on; violate: *The law punishes people who invade the rights of others.* **4** to enter and harm: *Infection invaded the wound.* ❑ *v.* **in·vad·ed, in·vad·ing. —in·vad′er,** *n.*

in·va·lid[1] (in′və lid), **1** *n.* person who is weak because of sickness or injury. An invalid cannot get around and do things. **2** *adj.* weak because of sickness or injury; not well; disabled. **3** *adj.* for the use of invalids: *an invalid chair.* **4** *v.* to make weak or sick; disable.

in·val·id[2] (in val′id), *adj.* not valid; without force or effect; without value; worthless: *Unless a check is signed, it is invalid.* **—in·va·lid·i·ty** (in′və lid′ə tē), *n.* **—in·val′id·ly,** *adv.*

in·val·i·date (in val′ə dāt), *v.* to make valueless; cause to be worthless; deprive of force or effect: *A contract is invalidated if only one party signs it.* ❑ *v.* **in·val·i·dat·ed, in·val·i·dat·ing. —in·val′i·da′tion,** *n.* **—in·val′i·da′tor,** *n.*

in·val·u·a·ble (in val′yü ə bəl *or* in val′yə bəl), *adj.* valuable beyond measure; very precious; priceless: *Good health is an invaluable blessing.* [See Word Story at **valuable.**] **—in·val′u·a·ble·ness,** *n.* **—in·val′u·a·bly,** *adv.*

in·var·i·a·ble (in vâr′ē ə bəl), *adj.* always the same; not changing: *After dinner it was her invariable habit to take a walk.* **—in·var′i·a·bil′i·ty,** *n.* **—in·var′i·a·bly,** *adv.*

in·va·sion (in vā′zhən), *n.* act or process of invading; entering by force or as an enemy; attack.

invasion

in·va·sive (in vā′siv), *adj.* **1** tending to invade; invading. **2** involving or waged by invasion: *invasive war.* **3** requiring that a medical device or tool enter the body: *Surgery is invasive treatment.*

in·vec·tive (in vek′tiv), *n.* a violent attack in words; abusive speech: *His opponents were overcome by the fury of his invective.* [**Invective** and **inveigh** both come from Latin words meaning

"to carry against." The Latin words were used about soldiers and came to mean "attack."]

in·veigh (in vā′), *v.* to make a violent attack in words: *The agitator inveighed against the government.* [See word history information at **invective.**] **—in·veigh′er,** *n.*

in·vei·gle (in vā′gəl), *v.* to get someone to do something by trickery: *The saleswoman inveigled me into buying four magazine subscriptions.* ❑ *v.* **in·vei·gled, in·vei·gling.** [**Inveigle** comes from Latin words meaning "without eyes." A person who is inveigled loses sight of the truth.] **—in·vei′gle·ment,** *n.* **—in·vei′gler,** *n.*

in·vent (in vent′), *v.* **1** to make something for the first time; think up something new: *Alexander Graham Bell invented the telephone.* ■ See Synonym Study at **create.** **2** to make up an excuse, story, etc.: *Since they had no good reason for being late, they invented one.* **—in·ven′tor,** *n.*

invention (def. 1)
a cotton gin

in·ven·tion (in ven′shən), *n.* **1** something invented: *Television is a twentieth-century invention.* **2** act of making something new: *the invention of gunpowder.* **3** power of inventing: *An author must have invention to think up new ideas for stories.* **4** a made-up story; false statement: *That rumor is an invention.*

WORD SOURCE It used to be common for inventors to create names for their **inventions** from Greek or Latin words: **tele** (from a Greek word meaning "far") + **vision** (from a Latin word meaning "sight") or **tele** + **phone** (from a Greek word meaning "sound") or **phone** + **graph** (Greek word meaning "write"). What do you think **telegraph** came from? Today, inventions are often named from initial letters of their descriptions: **radar** = **ra**dio **d**etection **a**nd **r**anging; **CD** = **c**ompact **d**isc; and **VCR** = **v**ideo **c**assette **r**ecorder.

in·ven·tive (in ven′tiv), *adj.* good at inventing; quick to invent things: *An inventive person thinks up ways to save time, money, and work.* **—in·ven′tive·ly,** *adv.* **—in·ven′tive·ness,** *n.*

in·ven·to·ry (in′vən tôr′ē), **1** *n.* a complete and detailed list of articles. An inventory of property or goods tells how many there are of each article and what they are worth. **2** *n.* all the articles listed or to be listed; stock: *The shoe store had a sale to reduce its inventory.* **3** *v.* to make a complete and detailed list of; enter in a list: *Some stores inventory their stock once a month.* ❑ *n., pl.* **in·ven·to·ries;** *v.* **in·ven·to·ried, in·ven·to·ry·ing.**

in·verse (in vėrs′ *or* in′vėrs′), **1** *adj.* exactly opposite; reversed in position, direction, or tendency; inverted: *DCBA is the inverse order of ABCD.* **2** *n.* something reversed: *Subtraction is the inverse of addition. The inverse of ¾ is ⁴/₃.* **3** *n.* direct opposite: *Evil is the inverse of good.* **—in·verse′ly,** *adv.*

in·ver·sion (in vėr′zhən), *n.* **1** act or process of inverting or being inverted. **2** something inverted. **3** an increase in air temperature at higher altitudes, instead of the usual decrease, preventing lower air from rising away: *An inversion caused air pollution to build up over the city.*

in·vert (in vėrt′), *v.* **1** to turn upside down: *I inverted the pan and the cake dropped onto the rack.* ■ See Synonym Study at **reverse.** **2** to turn the other way; change to the opposite; reverse in position, direction, order, etc.: *If you invert "I can," you have "Can I?"* **—in·vert′er,** *n.* **—in·vert′i·ble,** *adj.*

in·ver·te·brate (in vėr′tə brit *or* in vėr′tə brāt), **1** *n.* animal without a backbone. Worms and insects are invertebrates; fishes and mammals are vertebrates. **2** *adj.* without a backbone; spineless: *an invertebrate animal.*

a	hat	ė	term	ô	order	ch	child		a in about
ā	age	i	it	oi	oil	ng	long		e in taken
ä	far	ī	ice	ou	out	sh	she	ə	i in pencil
â	care	o	hot	u	cup	th	thin		o in lemon
e	let	ō	open	u̇	put	ᴛʜ	then		u in circus
ē	equal	ò	saw	ü	rule	zh	measure		

in·vest (in vest′), *v.* **1** to use money to buy something that is expected to produce a profit, or income, or both: *She invested her money in stocks, bonds, and land.* **2** to spend or put in time, energy, etc., for later benefit: *Much time and energy has been invested in the cancer crusade.* **3** to clothe; cover; surround: *The castle was invested with mystery and romance.* **4** to give power, authority, or right to: *I invested my lawyer with power to act for me.* **5** to give a quality or characteristic to: *The author invested the main character with every virtue.* **6** to put in office with a ceremony: *A queen or king is invested by being crowned.* —**in·ves′tor,** *n.*

in·ves·ti·gate (in ves′tə gāt), *v.* to look into thoroughly; search into carefully; examine closely: *Detectives investigate crimes to find out who did them. Scientists investigate nature to learn more about it.* ◻ *v.* **in·ves·ti·gat·ed, in·ves·ti·gat·ing.** —**in·ves′ti·ga·tive,** *adj.* —**in·ves′ti·ga·tor,** *n.*

in·ves·ti·ga·tion (in ves′tə gā′shən), *n.* a careful search; detailed or careful examination: *An investigation of the accident by the police put the blame on the drivers of both cars.*

in·ves·ti·ga·tive (in ves′tə gā′tiv), *adj.* of or relating to investigation: *an investigative reporter.*

in·ves·ti·ture (in ves′tə chŭr), *n.* act of formally investing someone with an office, dignity, power, right, etc.

in·vest·ment (in vest′mənt), *n.* **1** act of investing; a laying out of money: *Getting an education is a wise investment of time and money.* **2** amount of money invested: *Their investments amount to thousands of dollars.* **3** something that is expected to yield money as income or profit or both: *She has a good income from wise investments.*

investment bank, a bank whose main business is underwriting new securities.

in·vet·er·ate (in vet′ər it), *adj.* **1** confirmed in a habit, practice, feeling, etc.; habitual: *It is very hard for an inveterate smoker to give up tobacco.* **2** long and firmly established; deeply rooted: *There was an inveterate distrust of newcomers in the old neighborhood.* —**in·vet′er·ate·ly,** *adv.*

in·vid·i·ous (in vid′ē əs), *adj.* likely to cause ill will or resentment; giving offense because unfair or unjust: *An invidious comparison of the skills of the two players increased the bitter rivalry between them.* —**in·vid′i·ous·ly,** *adv.* —**in·vid′i·ous·ness,** *n.*

in·vig·o·rate (in vig′ə rāt′), *v.* to give vigor to; fill with life and energy: *Exercise invigorates the body.* ◻ *v.* **in·vig·o·rat·ed, in·vig·o·rat·ing.** —**in·vig′o·ra′tion,** *n.* —**in·vig′o·ra′tor,** *n.*

in·vig·o·rat·ing (in vig′ə rā′ting), *adj.* giving vigor to; filling with life and energy: *An invigorating breeze made our hike enjoyable.* —**in·vig′o·rat′ing·ly,** *adv.*

in·vin·ci·ble (in vin′sə bəl), *adj.* impossible to overcome; unconquerable: *The champion team seemed invincible.* —**in·vin′ci·bil′i·ty, in·vin′ci·ble·ness,** *n.* —**in·vin′ci·bly,** *adv.*

in·vi·o·la·ble (in vī′ə lə bəl), *adj.* **1** not to be violated or injured; sacred: *an inviolable vow.* **2** not to be trespassed on: *inviolable boundaries.* —**in·vi′o·la·bil′i·ty,** *n.* —**in·vi′o·la·bly,** *adv.*

in·vi·o·late (in vī′ə lit *or* in vī′ə lāt), *adj.* not violated; uninjured; unbroken: *An inviolate promise is carried out.*

in·vis·i·ble (in viz′ə bəl), *adj.* not visible; not capable of being seen: *Thought is invisible. Germs are invisible to the naked eye.* —**in·vis′i·bil′i·ty, in·vis′i·ble·ness,** *n.* —**in·vis′i·bly,** *adv.*

in·vi·ta·tion (in′və tā′shən), *n.* **1** a polite request to come to some place or to do something: *The children received invitations to the party.* **2** act of inviting.

in·vite (in vīt′), *v.* **1** to ask someone politely to come to some place or to do something: *I invited some friends to a party. We invited them to join our club.* ∎ See Synonym Study at **call.** **2** to make a polite request for: *She invited our opinion of her story.* **3** to give a chance for; tend to cause: *New Year's Day invites resolutions. Carelessness invites trouble.* **4** to attract; tempt; encourage: *The cool water invited us to swim.* ◻ *v.* **in·vit·ed, in·vit·ing.**

in·vit·ing (in vī′ting), *adj.* attractive; tempting: *The cool water looks inviting.* —**in·vit′ing·ly,** *adv.*

in·vo·ca·tion (in′və kā′shən), *n.* **1** prayer appealing for God's blessing, said at the start of public or religious events: *A church service often begins with an invocation to God.* **2** act of calling upon someone or something; appealing for help or protection: *By invocation of the Fifth Amendment, the witness avoided answering the question.* **3** act of calling forth spirits with magic words or charms. **4** set of magic words used to call forth spirits. —**in′vo·ca′tion·al,** *adj.*

in·voice (in′vois), **1** *n.* list of goods sent to a buyer showing prices, amounts, shipping charges, etc. **2** *v.* to make an invoice of; enter on an invoice. ◻ *v.* **in·voiced, in·voic·ing.**

in·voke (in vōk′), *v.* **1** to call on in prayer; appeal to for help or protection: *The Pilgrims invoked God's help in their undertaking.* **2** to call upon someone or something for assistance or protection: *invoke the law.* **3** to call forth with magic words or charms: *Aladdin invoked the powerful genie of the magic lamp.* **4** to ask earnestly for; beg for: *The condemned criminal invoked the judge's mercy.* ◻ *v.* **in·voked, in·vok·ing.** —**in·vok′er,** *n.*

WORD FAMILY Invoke and the following words are related: **advocate, provoke, revoke, vocabulary, vocal, voice,** and **vowel.** They all come from a Latin word meaning "to call" or "voice."

in·vol·un·tar·y (in vol′ən ter′ē), *adj.* **1** not controlled by the will: *Breathing is mainly involuntary.* ∎ See Synonym Study at **automatic.** **2** not voluntary; not done of your own free will; unwilling: *Taking gym was involuntary on my part; the school requires it.* **3** not done on purpose; not intended: *An accident is involuntary.* —**in·vol′un·tar′i·ly,** *adv.*

involuntary muscle, smooth muscle.

in·volve (in volv′), *v.* **1** to have as a necessary part, condition, or result; take in; include: *Housework involves cooking, washing dishes, sweeping, and cleaning.* **2** to bring into difficulty, danger, etc.: *One foolish mistake can involve you in a good deal of trouble.* **3** to entangle; complicate. **4** to take up the attention of; absorb: *She was involved in working out a puzzle.* ◻ *v.* **in·volved, in·volv·ing.** —**in·volve′ment,** *n.* —**in·volv′er,** *n.*

in·volved (in volvd′), *adj.* complicated: *an involved sentence, an involved explanation.*

in·vul·ner·a·ble (in vul′nər ə bəl), *adj.* not able to be wounded or hurt; safe from attack: *The massive fortification was considered invulnerable.* —**in·vul′ner·a·bil′i·ty, in·vul′ner·a·ble·ness,** *n.* —**in·vul′ner·a·bly,** *adv.*

in·ward (in′wərd), **1** *adv.* toward the inside: *a passage leading inward.* **2** *adj.* on the inside; inner; internal: *inward surfaces of a hollow wall.* **3** *adj.* directed toward the inside: *an inward flow of fresh air.* **4** *adv.* into the mind or soul: *to turn your thoughts inward.* **5** *adj.* in mind or soul: *inward peace.*

in·ward·ly (in′wərd lē), *adv.* **1** on the inside; within. **2** toward the inside. **3** in the mind or soul. **4** not aloud or openly.

in·wards (in′wərdz), *adv.* inward.

i·o·dide (ī′ə dīd), *n.* a chemical compound of iodine with another element.

inviting scene

i·o·dine (ī′ə dīn), *n.* **1** a nonmetallic element having the form of grayish black crystals which give off a dense, violet vapor with an irritating odor when heated. Iodine is used in medicine, in making dyes, in photography, etc. *Symbol:* I **2** a brown liquid containing iodine, used as an antiseptic. [Iodine comes from Greek words meaning "violet shape." The name describes the purple gas that forms when iodine is heated.]

i·o·dized salt (ī′ə dīzd), common salt containing iodide as a diet supplement, especially of persons with an iodine deficiency.

i·on (ī′ən), *n.* atom or group of atoms having a negative or positive electric charge as a result of having lost or gained one or more electrons. A cation is a positive ion formed by the loss of electrons; an anion is a negative ion formed by the gain of one or more electrons.

-ion, *suffix.* **1** act of ___ing: *calculation = act of calculating.* **2** result of ___ing: *collection = result of collecting.* **3** condition of being ___ed: *fascination = condition of being fascinated.*

Io·nes·co (yo nes′kō), *n.* **Eu·gène** (ü zhen′), 1912-1994, French playwright, born in Romania. His plays include *The Bald Soprano* and *Rhinoceros.*

I·o·ni·a (ī ō′nē ə), *n.* ancient region on the W coast of Asia Minor, with the islands near it. The Greeks colonized Ionia in very early times.

i·on·ic[1] (ī on′ik), *adj.* of, related to, or present as ions.

I·on·ic[2] (ī on′ik), *adj.* **1** of or related to the order of Greek architecture having scrolls in the capitals of the columns. **2** of or referring to Ionia or its people.

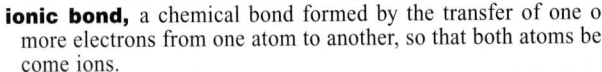

ionic bond, a chemical bond formed by the transfer of one or more electrons from one atom to another, so that both atoms become ions.

i·on·ize (ī′ə nīz), *v.* to separate into ions; produce ions in. Acids, bases, and salts ionize when dissolved in a solution. ❑ *v.* **i·on·ized, i·on·iz·ing.** —**i′on·iz′a·ble,** *adj.* —**i′on·i·za′tion,** *n.* —**i′on·iz′er,** *n.*

ionizing radiation, electromagnetic waves or subatomic particles with enough energy to ionize atoms by removing electrons, dangerous in large amounts.

i·on·o·sphere (ī on′ə sfir), *n.* region of ionized layers of air, extending from about 50 miles (80 kilometers) above the earth's surface out to the edge of the atmosphere. The ionosphere reflects certain radio waves, making transmission over long distances on earth possible.

i·o·ta (ī ō′tə), *n.* **1** a very small part or quantity; bit: *There is not an iota of truth in the story.* **2** the ninth letter of the Greek alphabet (I or ι). ❑ *n., pl.* **i·o·tas.** [See Word Story at **jot.**]

IOU (ī′ō′yü′), *n.* an informal written promise to pay a debt: *Write me your IOU for ten dollars.* ❑ *n., pl.* **IOUs** or **IOU's.** [IOU comes from the pronunciation of the phrase *I owe you.*]

I·o·wa (ī′ə wə), *n.* one of the midwestern states of the United States. *Abbreviation:* IA or Ia. *Capital:* Des Moines. —**I′o·wan,** *n.*

WORD STORY Iowa comes from the name of a Native American tribe. It was the name another tribe used to make fun of them, and meant "the sleepy ones."

IQ or **I.Q.,** intelligence quotient.

Ir, symbol for iridium.

IRA (ī′rə or ī′är′ā′), *n.* individual retirement account (a pension fund in which a person can deposit a certain amount of money each year and defer paying income tax on the savings and interest until after retirement). ❑ *n., pl.* **IRAs** or **IRA's.**

IRA or **I.R.A.,** Irish Republican Army (a group of outlawed Irish nationalists operating secretly by terrorism and other means for a united Irish republic).

I·ran (i ran′ or i rän′), *n.* country in SW Asia, south of the Caspian Sea. *Capital:* Teheran.

I·ra·ni·an (i rā′nē ən), **1** *adj.* of Iran, its people, or their language. **2** *n.* person born or living in Iran. **3** *n.* language of Iran.

I·raq (i rak′ or i räk′), *n.* country in SW Asia, west of Iran. *Capital:* Baghdad.

I·raq·i (i rak′ē or i rä′kē), **1** *adj.* of Iraq, its people, or their language. **2** *n.* person born or living in Iraq. **3** *n.* Arabic as spoken in Iraq. ❑ *n., pl.* **I·raq·is** for 2.

i·ras·ci·ble (i ras′ə bəl), *adj.* easily made angry. —**i·ras′ci·bil′i·ty,** *n.* —**i·ras′ci·bly,** *adv.*

i·rate (ī′rāt or ī rāt′), *adj.* angry. —**i′rate·ly,** *adv.*

ire (īr), *n.* anger; wrath.

Ire·land (īr′lənd), *n.* **1** one of the British Isles, divided into the Republic of Ireland and Northern Ireland. **2 Republic of,** country in NW, central, and S Ireland; Eire. *Capital:* Dublin.

Ir·i·an Jaya (ir′ē än ji′ə), the W part of New Guinea, which is part of Indonesia.

ir·i·des·cence (ir′ə des′ns), *n.* display of changing colors; change of color when moved or turned: *the iridescence of mother-of-pearl.*

ir·i·des·cent (ir′ə des′nt), *adj.* displaying changing colors; changing color when moved or turned: *Soap bubbles are iridescent.* —**ir′i·des′cent·ly,** *adv.*

i·rid·i·um (i rid′ē əm), *n.* a silver-white, hard metallic element which is used as an alloy with platinum for jewelry and the points of fountain pens. *Symbol:* Ir

WORD STORY Iridium comes from the Latin word meaning "rainbow." It gets this name from the changing colors that appear when it is dissolved in a strong acid.

i·ris (ī′ris), *n.* **1** any of numerous related plants with sword-shaped leaves and large flowers that have three upright parts and three drooping parts; fleur-de-lis. **2** the colored part of the eye around the pupil. See picture at **eye.** ❑ *n., pl.* **i·ris·es.**

iris (def. 1)—irises in a painting

I·rish (ī′rish), **1** *adj.* of Ireland, its people, or their language. **2** *n.pl.* the people of Ireland. **3** *n.* the Celtic language spoken by some of the Irish; Gaelic.

I·rish·man (ī′rish mən), *n.* man born or living in Ireland. ❑ *n., pl.* **I·rish·men.**

Irish potato, potato (def. 1).

Irish Sea, part of the Atlantic between Ireland and England. See **British Isles** for map.

Irish setter, a hunting dog with long, silky, reddish brown hair.

Irish terrier, a small dog with reddish brown, wiry hair. It is something like a small Airedale.

Irish wolfhound, a very large and powerful dog, formerly used in hunting wolves and elk.

I·rish·wom·an (ī′rish wum′ən), *n.* woman born or living in Ireland. ❑ *n., pl.* **I·rish·wom·en.**

irk (ėrk), *v.* to cause to feel disgusted, annoyed, or troubled; weary by being tedious or disagreeable; bore: *It irks us to wait for him.*

a	hat	ė	term	ô	order	ch	child		
ā	age	i	it	oi	oil	ng	long		a in about
ä	far	ī	ice	ou	out	sh	she		e in taken
â	care	o	hot	u	cup	th	thin	ə	i in pencil
e	let	ō	open	ù	put	ŦH	then		o in lemon
ē	equal	ò	saw	ü	rule	zh	measure		u in circus

irk·some (ėrk′səm), *adj.* tiresome; tedious; annoying: *Washing dishes all day would be an irksome task.* —**irk′some·ly,** *adv.* —**irk′some·ness,** *n.*

i·ron (ī′ərn), **1** *n.* a silver-gray, easily shaped, heavy metallic element. Iron is the most useful metal and is used to make steel. Iron occurs in the hemoglobin of the red blood cells where it serves to carry oxygen to all parts of the body. *Symbol:* Fe **2** *adj.* made of iron: *an iron fence.* **3** *n.* something made of iron: *a branding iron.* **4** *adj.* like iron; hard and strong; unyielding: *an iron will.* **5** *n.* great hardness and strength; firmness: *muscles of iron.* **6** *n.pl.* **irons,** chains or bands of iron; handcuffs; shackles. **7** *n.* a household appliance with a flat surface which is heated and used for smoothing cloth or pressing clothes; flatiron. **8** *v.* to smooth or press cloth, etc., with a heated iron. **9** *n.* a golf club with an iron or steel head. —**i′ron·like′,** *adj.*

iron out, to smooth away or overcome difficulties, differences, inconsistencies, etc.: *The dispute between the two players was ironed out by the coach.*

irons in the fire, projects or undertakings you are working on at one time: *She had too many irons in the fire, so she gave up working after school.*

pump iron, INFORMAL. to exercise and develop muscles by lifting weights.

strike while the iron is hot, to act while conditions are favorable.

Iron Age, period after the Bronze Age, when people used iron tools, weapons, etc.

i·ron·clad (ī′ərn klad′), **1** *n.* warship of the 1800s, protected with iron plates. **2** *adj.* very hard to change or get out of: *An ironclad agreement must be kept.*

Iron Curtain, an imaginary wall or dividing line separating the Soviet Union and the countries under its control or influence from other nations, following World War II.

iron hand, with complete or harsh control; strict: *He ruled the country with an iron hand.*

i·ron·ic (ī ron′ik), *adj.* **1** expressing one thing and meaning the opposite: *Her ironic laugh showed that she wasn't the least bit amused.* **2** contrary to what would naturally be expected: *It was ironic that the man was run over by his own car.*

i·ron·i·cal (ī ron′ə kəl), *adj.* ironic. —**i·ron′i·cal·ly,** *adv.*

ironing board, a padded board covered with a smooth cloth, used for ironing clothes, pressing seams, etc. It usually has folding legs so that it can be collapsed and put away.

iron lung, (earlier) device which applies periodic pressure on the chest wall in order to force air in and out of the lungs. It was used to enable people to breathe whose chest muscles were paralyzed.

iron oxide, compound of iron and oxygen, used especially as a pigment.

i·ron·wood (ī′ərn wùd′), *n.* any of various trees with hard, heavy wood.

i·ron·work (ī′ərn wėrk′), *n.* things made of iron; work in iron.

i·ron·work·er (ī′ərn wėr′kər), *n.* **1** person whose work is making iron or iron articles. **2** person whose work is building the steel framework of bridges, skyscrapers, etc.

i·ron·works (ī′ərn wėrks′), *n.pl. or sing.* place where iron is made or worked into iron articles.

i·ro·ny (ī′rə nē), *n.* **1** way of speaking or writing in which the ordinary meaning of the words is the opposite of the thought in the speaker's mind: *The tallest person was called "Shorty" in irony.* **2** event or outcome which is the opposite of what would naturally be expected: *By the irony of fate the farmers had rain when they needed sun, and sun when they needed rain.* ❑ *n., pl.* **i·ro·nies** for 2.

Ir·o·quois (ir′ə kwoi), *n.* member of a group of American Indian tribes called the Five Nations or the Six Nations, formerly living in New York and now living in New York, Ontario, and Quebec. ❑ *n., pl.* **Ir·o·quois.**

ir·ra·di·ate (i rā′dē āt), *v.* **1** to expose to radiation; treat with radiation. **2** to shine upon; light up; make bright; illuminate. **3** to radiate; give out. **4** to treat food with electromagnetic rays to kill harmful microorganisms and make the food last longer before spoiling. ❑ *v.* **ir·ra·di·at·ed, ir·ra·di·at·ing.** —**ir·ra′di·a′tion,** *n.*

ir·ra·tion·al (i rash′ə nəl), *adj.* **1** not rational; contrary to reason; unreasonable: *It is irrational to be afraid of the number 13.* **2** unable to think and reason clearly. **3** in mathematics: **a** (of an equation or expression) involving roots or fractional exponents. **b** of or related to an irrational number. —**ir·ra·tion·al′i·ty,** *n.* —**ir·ra′tion·al·ly,** *adv.*

irrational number, any real number that cannot be expressed as an integer or as a ratio between two integers. $\sqrt{2}$ and π are irrational numbers.

ir·re·claim·a·ble (ir′i klā′mə bəl), *adj.* not able to be reclaimed. —**ir′re·claim′a·bly,** *adv.*

ir·rec·on·cil·a·ble (i rek′ən sī′lə bəl), *adj.* not able to be reconciled; opposed: *irreconcilable enemies. Good and evil are irreconcilable.* —**ir·rec′on·cil′a·bly,** *adv.*

ir·re·cov·er·a·ble (ir′i kuv′ər ə bəl), *adj.* not able to be regained: *Wasted time is irrecoverable.* —**ir′re·cov·er·a·bly,** *adv.*

ir·re·deem·a·ble (ir′i dē′mə bəl), *adj.* **1** not able to be exchanged for coin: *irredeemable paper money.* **2** impossible to change; beyond remedy; hopeless: *The auditor's mistake was serious, but not irredeemable.* —**ir′re·deem′a·bly,** *adv.*

ir·re·duc·i·ble (ir′i dü′sə bəl), *adj.* impossible to make less, smaller, simpler, etc. —**ir′re·duc′i·bil′i·ty,** *n.* —**ir′re·duc′i·bly,** *adv.*

ir·ref·u·ta·ble (i ref′yə tə bəl), *adj.* not able to be refuted or disproved; undeniable; unanswerable: *irrefutable arguments.* —**ir·ref′u·ta·bly,** *adv.*

ir·re·gard·less (ir′i gärd′lis), *adj.* regardless. ■ Careful speakers and writers do not use **irregardless.**

ir·reg·u·lar (i reg′yə lər), *adj.* **1** not regular; not according to custom or rule: *irregular behavior.* **2** not in normal timing or rhythm: *The doctor listened carefully to the irregular breathing of the feverish child.* **3** not even; not smooth or straight; broken and rough: *New England has a very irregular coastline.* **4** (of a word) not inflected in the usual way. *Be* is an irregular verb. —**ir·reg′u·lar·ly,** *adv.*

ir·reg·u·lar·i·ty (i reg′yə lar′ə tē), *n.* **1** lack of regularity; being irregular. **2** something irregular. ❑ *n., pl.* **ir·reg·u·lar·i·ties** for 2.

ir·rel·e·vance (i rel′ə vəns), *n.* **1** condition of being irrelevant. **2** something irrelevant.

ir·rel·e·vant (i rel′ə vənt), *adj.* not to the point; off the subject: *A question about arithmetic is irrelevant in a French lesson.* —**ir·rel′e·vant·ly,** *adv.*

ir·re·li·gious (ir′i lij′əs), *adj.* **1** not religious; indifferent to religion. **2** contrary to religious principles; impious. —**ir′re·li′gious·ly,** *adv.* —**ir′re·li′gious·ness,** *n.*

ir·rep·ar·a·ble (i rep′ər ə bəl), *adj.* not able to be repaired or put right: *irreparable damage.* —**ir·rep′ar·a·bly,** *adv.*

ir·re·place·a·ble (ir′i plā′sə bəl), *adj.* not replaceable; impossible to replace with another. —**ir′re·place′a·bly,** *adv.*

ir·re·press·i·ble (ir′i pres′ə bəl), *adj.* not able to be repressed or restrained; uncontrollable: *irrepressible laughter.* —**ir′re·press′i·bil′i·ty,** *n.* —**ir′re·press′i·bly,** *adv.*

ir·re·proach·a·ble (ir′i prō′chə bəl), *adj.* free from blame; faultless: *irreproachable conduct.* —**ir′re·proach′a·bly,** *adv.*

ir·re·sist·i·ble (ir′i zis′tə bəl), *adj.* not able to be resisted; too great to be withstood; overwhelming: *She had an irresistible desire for some ice cream.* —**ir′re·sist′i·bil′i·ty,** *n.* —**ir′re·sist′i·bly,** *adv.*

ir·res·o·lute (i rez′ə lüt), *adj.* not resolute; unable to make up your mind; not sure of what you want; hesitating: *Irresolute persons make poor leaders.* —**ir·res′o·lute·ly,** *adv.* —**ir·res′o·lute·ness,** *n.* —**ir·res′o·lu′tion,** *n.*

ir·re·spec·tive (ir′i spek′tiv), *adj.* regardless: *All pupils, irrespective of age, may join the club.* —**ir′re·spec′tive·ly,** *adv.*

ir·re·spon·si·ble (ir′i spon′sə bəl), *adj.* **1** without a sense of responsibility; untrustworthy; unreliable. **2** not responsible; not able to be called to account: *A dictator is an irresponsible ruler.* —**ir′re·spon′si·bil′i·ty,** *n.* —**ir′re·spon′si·bly,** *adv.*

ir·re·triev·a·ble (ir′i trē′və bəl), *adj.* not able to be retrieved or recovered; impossible to recall or restore to its former condition. —**ir′re·triev′a·bly,** *adv.*

ir·rev·er·ence (i rev′ər əns), *n.* lack of reverence; disrespect.

ir·rev·er·ent (i rev′ər ənt), *adj.* not reverent; disrespectful. —**ir·rev′er·ent·ly,** *adv.*

ir·re·vers·i·ble (ir′i vèr′sə bəl), *adj.* not reversible; unable to be changed. —**ir′re·vers′i·bil′i·ty,** *n.* —**ir′re·vers′i·bly,** *adv.*

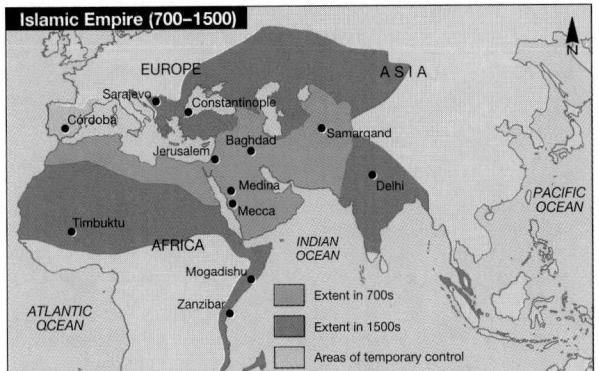

Islamic Empire (700–1500)

EUROPE
ASIA
Sarajevo
Córdoba
Constantinople
Jerusalem
Baghdad
Samarqand
Medina
Mecca
Delhi
Timbuktu
AFRICA
INDIAN OCEAN
PACIFIC OCEAN
Mogadishu
Zanzibar
ATLANTIC OCEAN

Extent in 700s
Extent in 1500s
Areas of temporary control

ir·rev·o·ca·ble (i rev′ə kə bəl), *adj.* not able to be revoked; final: *Nothing could change his irrevocable decision to leave.* —**ir·rev′o·ca·bil′i·ty,** *n.* —**ir·rev′o·ca·bly,** *adv.*

ir·ri·gate (ir′ə gāt), *v.* **1** to supply land with water by using ditches, by sprinkling, etc. **2** to supply some part of the body with a continuous flow of some liquid: *The doctor showed her how to irrigate her nose and throat with warm water.* ❑ *v.* **ir·ri·gat·ed, ir·ri·gat·ing.** —**ir′ri·ga′tion,** *n.* —**ir′ri·ga′tor,** *n.*

ir·ri·ta·bil·i·ty (ir′ə tə bil′ə tē), *n.* **1** condition of being irritable; impatience. **2** (in biology) the quality that living tissue has of responding to a stimulus.

ir·ri·ta·ble (ir′ə tə bəl), *adj.* **1** easily made angry; impatient: *When the rain spoiled her plans, she was irritable for the rest of the day.* **2** more sensitive than is natural or normal: *A baby's skin is often quite irritable.* **3** (in biology) able to respond to stimuli. —**ir′ri·ta·ble·ness,** *n.* —**ir′ri·ta·bly,** *adv.*

ir·ri·tant (ir′ə tənt), *n.* something that causes irritation: *Chlorine in swimming pools can be an irritant to the eyes.*

ir·ri·tate (ir′ə tāt), *v.* **1** to make impatient or angry; annoy; provoke; vex: *Their constant interruptions irritated me.* **2** to make unnaturally sensitive or sore: *Sunburn irritates the skin.* **3** (in biology) to stimulate an organ, muscle, tissue, etc., to a response: *A muscle contracts when it is irritated by an electric shock.* ❑ *v.* **ir·ri·tat·ed, ir·ri·tat·ing.** —**ir′ri·tat′ing·ly,** *adv.* —**ir′ri·ta′tor,** *n.*

ir·ri·ta·tion (ir′ə tā′shən), *n.* **1** act or process of irritating; annoyance; vexation. **2** irritated condition: *Irritation of your nose makes you sneeze.* **3** something that irritates: *The two irritations of sand and sunburn made his day at the beach uncomfortable.*

IRS or **I.R.S.,** Internal Revenue Service (the U. S. government agency that collects taxes).

Ir·ving (èr′ving), *n.* **Washington,** 1783-1859, American writer, author of *Rip Van Winkle.*

is (iz), *v.* form of the verb **be** used with *he, she, it,* and any singular noun to indicate the present tense: *He is at school. She is hall monitor this week. It is going to rain. Today is Tuesday. Soccer is a popular sport.*

is., **1** island or islands. **2** isle or isles.

I·saac (ī′zək), *n.* (in the Bible) the son of Abraham and Sarah, and father of Jacob and Esau.

Is·a·bel·la (iz′ə bel′ə), 1451-1504, queen of Castile and Aragon. She and her husband Ferdinand V paid for Columbus's voyages. [Isabella comes from Hebrew words meaning "oath of God."]

I·sai·ah (ī zā′ə), *n.* **1** a Hebrew prophet. **2** book of the Bible. [Isaiah comes from Hebrew words meaning "God's salvation."]

ISBN, International Standard Book Number.

Is·car·i·ot (i skar′ē ət), *n.* surname of Judas, the disciple who betrayed Jesus for money.

-ish, *suffix.* **1** somewhat ___: *sweetish = somewhat sweet.* **2** like a ___; like that of a ___: *childish = like a child.* **3** of or about ___: *English = of England.*

i·sin·glass (ī′zn glas′), *n.* **1** kind of gelatin obtained from certain fishes, used for making glue. **2** mica.

I·sis (ī′sis), *n.* the chief goddess of ancient Egypt, sister and wife of Osiris. She represented fertility.

Is·lam (is′ləm *or* i släm′), *n.* **1** religion based on the teachings of Muhammad as they appear in the Koran; religion of the Muslims. **2** Muslims as a group. **3** the countries under Muslim rule. —**Is·lam′ic,** *adj.*

Is·lam·a·bad (iz lä′mə bäd), *n.* capital of Pakistan, in the northeast part.

is·land (ī′lənd), *n.* **1** body of land smaller than a continent and completely surrounded by water: *Cuba is a large island.* **2** something that suggests a body of land surrounded by water. Platforms in the middle of busy streets are called **safety islands.**

is·land·er (ī′lən dər), *n.* person born or living on an island.

isle (īl), *n.* **1** a small island. **2** island. ■ Other words that sound like this are **aisle** and **I'll.**

Isle of Man. See **Man, Isle of.**

Isle Roy·ale National Park (roi′əl), a national park in N Michigan, containing a group of islands in Lake Superior.

is·let (ī′lit), *n.* a small island. ■ Another word that sounds like this is **eyelet.**

ism (iz′əm), *n.* doctrine, theory, system, or practice: *They dabbled in communism, socialism, and several other isms.*

-ism, *suffix.* **1** theory, system, or practice of ___: *Marxism = theories of Karl Marx.* **2** act of ___ing: *baptism = act of baptizing.* **3** condition of being a ___: *heroism = condition of being a hero.*

is·n't (iz′nt), is not.

i·so·bar (ī′sə bär), *n.* line on a weather map connecting places having the same average atmospheric pressure. Isobars show the distribution of atmospheric pressures at a particular time, and are used in making weather forecasts.

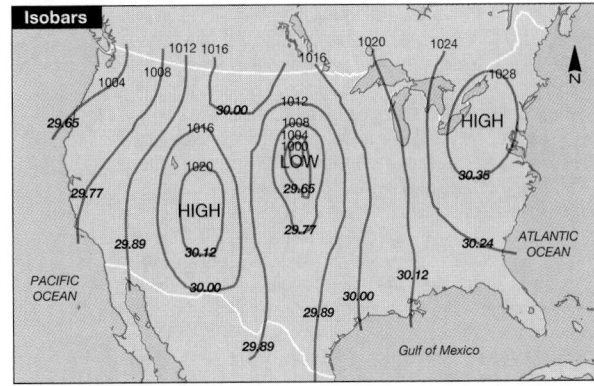

Isobars

1012 1016
1020 1024
1004 1008
1028
29.65
30.00
1012
HIGH
1016
1008
1004
1000
LOW
29.77
1020
29.65
30.35
HIGH
29.89
30.12
29.77
ATLANTIC OCEAN
30.24
PACIFIC OCEAN
30.00
30.12
29.89
30.00
29.89
Gulf of Mexico
N

i·so·late (ī′sə lāt), *v.* **1** to separate from others; keep alone: *A storm washed out the bridge, isolating the island from the mainland.* **2** to quarantine: *People with contagious diseases should be isolated.* ❑ *v.* **i·so·lat·ed, i·so·lat·ing.** [Isolate comes from a Latin word meaning "island." If you're isolated, you're cut off from others, like an island.] —**i′so·la′tion,** *n.* —**i′so·la′tor,** *n.*

i·so·la·tion·ism (ī′sə lā′shə niz′əm), *n.* principles or policy of avoiding political alliances and economic relationships with other nations.

i·so·la·tion·ist (ī′sə lā′shə nist), *n.* person who believes in the principles or policy of isolationism.

i·so·met·ric (ī′sə met′rik), *adj.* of or about isometrics: *isometric exercises.*

i·so·met·rics (ī′sə met′riks), *n.pl.* physical exercises done without athletic activity, by pressing one part of the body against another or against an object.

a	hat	ė	term	ȯ	order	ch	child		a in about
ā	age	i	it	oi	oil	ng	long		e in taken
ä	far	ī	ice	ou	out	sh	she	ə	i in pencil
â	care	o	hot	u	cup	th	thin		o in lemon
e	let	ō	open	ů	put	ŦH	then		u in circus
ē	equal	ȯ	saw	ü	rule	zh	measure		

i·sos·ce·les triangle (ī sos′ə lēz′), a triangle that has two equal sides. See picture at **triangle.**

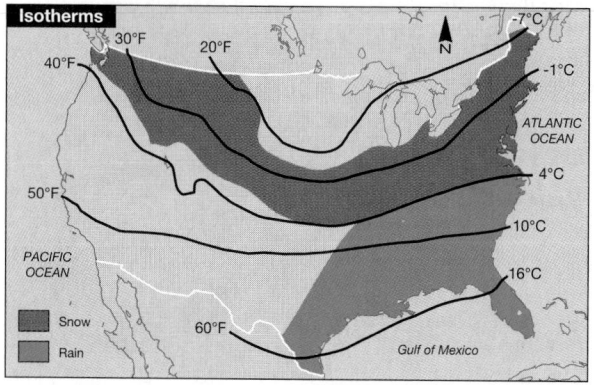

Isotherms
30°F 20°F -7°C
40°F N
ATLANTIC OCEAN
-1°C
50°F 4°C
PACIFIC OCEAN 10°C
16°C
Snow 60°F
Rain Gulf of Mexico

i·so·therm (ī′sə thėrm′), n. line on a weather map connecting places having the same average temperature.

i·so·tope (ī′sə tōp), n. any of two or more forms of a chemical element that have the same chemical properties and the same atomic number (number of protons), but different atomic weights (number of neutrons). Chlorine, whose atomic weight is 35.5, is a formation of two isotopes, one having an atomic weight of 37, the other, 35. Hydrogen and heavy hydrogen are isotopes. [**Isotope** comes from Greek words meaning "equal place." Isotopes of a chemical element all share one place in a chart of the elements.]

Is·ra·el (iz′rē əl), n. 1 country in SW Asia, on the Mediterranean, including the major part of Palestine. It was declared a Jewish state May 14, 1948. *Capital:* Jerusalem. 2 ancient Jewish kingdom in N Palestine. See **Judah** for map. 3 (in the Bible) a name given to Jacob after he had wrestled with the angel. 4 name given to his descendants; the Jews; the Hebrews.

Is·rae·li (iz rā′lē), 1 n. person born or living in Israel. 2 adj. of Israel. ❑ n., pl. **Is·rae·lis** or **Is·rae·li.**

Is·ra·el·ite (iz′rē ə līt), n. Jew; Hebrew; descendant of Israel.

Is·sei (ē′sā), n. a Japanese immigrant living in the United States or Canada. ❑ n., pl. **Is·sei.**

is·su·ance (ish′ü əns), n. act of issuing; issue.

is·sue (ish′ü), 1 v. to send out; put forth: *This magazine is issued every week. The government issues money and stamps.* 2 n. something sent out: *That newsstand sells the latest issues of all the popular magazines and newspapers.* 3 n. act of sending out; a putting forth: *The government controls the issue of stamps.* 4 v. to distribute officially to a person or persons: *Each soldier was issued a rifle.* 5 v. to come out; go out; proceed: *Smoke issues from the chimney.* 6 n. point to be debated; problem: *Peace is one of the main issues of this political campaign.* ❑ v. **is·sued, is·su·ing.** —**is′su·a·ble,** adj. —**is′su·er,** n.

at issue, in question; to be considered or decided: *Whether to go or not is what is at issue.*

take issue, to disagree: *I must take issue with you on that point.*

-ist, suffix. 1 an expert in a science: *botanist = an expert in botany.* 2 person in or working with ___: *journalist = a person working in journalism.* 3 person who believes in ___: *socialist = a person who believes in socialism.* 4 person who plays a musical instrument: *organist = a person who plays the organ.* 5 person who does or makes ___: *tourist = a person who makes a tour.*

Is·tan·bul (is′tän bül′), n. city in NW Turkey, on the Bosporus. Formerly called **Constantinople.**

isth·mus (is′məs), n. a narrow strip of land with water on both sides, connecting two larger bodies of land: *The Isthmus of Panama connects North America and South America.* ❑ n., pl. **isth·mus·es.**

it (it), 1 pron. the thing, object, person, or living thing spoken about: *Look at it carefully. What is it you want? It's my turn now.* 2 pron. the subject of an impersonal verb: *It snows in winter. It*

is cold. 3 pron. subject of a clause when the actual subject comes later: *It is hard to believe that she is dead.* 4 n. (in games) the player who must catch, find, guess, and so forth.

It., 1 Italian. 2 Italy.

ital., italic or italics.

Ital., 1 Italian. 2 Italy.

I·tal·ian (i tal′yən), 1 adj. of Italy, its people, or their language. 2 n. person born or living in Italy. 3 n. language of Italy.

Italian has given many words to the English language, including the words below.

alarm	confetti	macaroni	trampoline
artichoke	ditto	malaria	trombone
balcony	duet	ocarina	volcano
bandit	fiasco	piano[1]	zany
carnival	garb	pizza	zucchini
colonel	ghetto	spaghetti	

i·tal·ic (i tal′ik or ī tal′ik), 1 adj. of or in type whose letters slant to the right: *These words are in italic type.* 2 n.pl. **italics,** type whose letters slant to the right. ■ In writing and typing, italics are shown by single underline.

i·tal·i·cize (i tal′ə sīz), v. 1 to print in type in which the letters slant to the right: *This sentence is italicized.* 2 to underline with a single line to indicate italics. We italicize expressions which we wish to distinguish or emphasize. 3 to use italics. ❑ v. **i·tal·i·cized, i·tal·i·ciz·ing.**

It·a·ly (it′l ē), n. country in S Europe on the Mediterranean. *Capital:* Rome.

itch (ich), 1 n. a ticklish, prickling feeling in the skin that makes you want to scratch. 2 n. disease causing this feeling. 3 v. to cause this feeling: *Mosquito bites itch.* 4 v. to feel this way in the skin: *My nose itches.* 5 n. a restless, uneasy feeling, longing, or desire for anything: *an itch to get away.* 6 v. to have an uneasy desire: *I itched to find out their secret.* ❑ n., pl. **itch·es.**

itch·y (ich′ē), adj. 1 itching; like the itch: *My nose was itchy all morning.* 2 restless; nervous: *I get itchy if I have to stay indoors all day.* ❑ adj. **itch·i·er, itch·i·est.** —**itch′i·ness,** n.

-ite, suffix. inhabitant or native of ___: *Brooklynite = inhabitant or native of Brooklyn.*

i·tem (ī′təm), n. 1 a separate thing or article: *The list had twelve items on it.* 2 piece of news; bit of information: *There were several interesting items in today's paper.*

i·tem·ize (ī′tə mīz), v. to give each item of; list by items: *The grocery register itemized the bill to show each article purchased and its cost.* ❑ v. **i·tem·ized, i·tem·iz·ing.**

it·er·ate (it′ə rāt′), v. to say again or repeatedly; repeat. ❑ v. **it·er·at·ed, it·er·at·ing.** —**it·er·a′tion,** n.

Ith·a·ca (ith′ə kə), n. small island west of Greece, the legendary home of Ulysses. See **Troy** for map.

i·tin·er·ant (ī tin′ər ənt), 1 adj. traveling from place to place. 2 n. person who travels from place to place.

i·tin·er·ar·y (ī tin′ə rer′ē), n. 1 route of travel; plan of travel. 2 record of travel. 3 guidebook for travelers. ❑ n., pl. **i·tin·er·ar·ies.**

-itis, suffix. inflammation of; inflammatory disease: *appendicitis = inflammation of the appendix.*

it'll (it′l), 1 it will. 2 it shall.

its (its), adj. of it; belonging to it: *The dog wagged its tail.*

The possessive pronoun **its** is always written without an apostrophe: *The frog opened its eyes.* Only the contraction **it's,** meaning "it is," is written with an apostrophe: *It's almost dinnertime.*

it's (its), 1 it is: *It's my turn.* 2 it has: *It's been a beautiful day.* ■ See Usage Note at **its.**

it·self (it self′), pron. 1 form of it used to make a statement stronger: *The land itself is worth the money, without the house.* 2 form used instead of it in cases like: *The horse tripped and hurt itself.* 3 its normal or usual self: *After a few minor repairs my car was itself again.*

-ity, suffix. condition or fact of being ___: *sincerity = condition of being sincere.*

IU, international unit.

IUD, intrauterine device (a small plastic or metal device placed inside the uterus to prevent pregnancy).

IV or **i.v.,** intravenous.

I·van the Terrible (i′vən), 1530-1584, the first czar of Russia. ■ Ivan the Terrible expanded Russia's borders and power, but he also introduced secret police and even killed his oldest son with his own hands. [**Ivan** comes from Hebrew words meaning "God's gift."]

I've (īv), I have.

-ive, *suffix.* **1** of or about: *interrogative = of interrogation.* **2** likely to ___; inclined to ___: *active = inclined to act.*

Ives (īvz), *n.* **Charles Ed·ward** (ed′wərd), 1874-1954, American composer. His music emphasized American themes and used folk and popular music styles.

i·vied (ī′vēd), *adj.* covered or overgrown with ivy.

i·vor·y (ī′vər ē), **1** *n.* a hard, white substance making up the tusks of elephants, walruses, etc. Ivory is used for piano keys, billiard balls, combs, ornaments, etc. **2** *n.* substance like ivory. **3** *adj.* made of ivory. **4** *adj.* of or like ivory. **5** *n.* a creamy white. **6** *adj.* creamy white.

ivied mansion

WORD STORY **Ivory** comes from an Egyptian word meaning "elephant." **Elephant** comes from a Greek word meaning "ivory." It's like the chicken and the egg: whatever people named first, they named second, too.

Ivory Coast, former name of **Côte d'Ivoire.**

ivory tower, place or condition of withdrawing from the world of practical things into a world of ideas and dreams.

i·vy (ī′vē), *n.* **1** any of various climbing or trailing vines with smooth, shiny, evergreen leaves. **2** any of various other climbing plants, such as poison ivy. ❑ *n., pl.* **i·vies.**

Iwo Ji·ma (ē′wō jē′mə), a small island in the N Pacific, just south of Japan. U.S. forces defeated Japanese defenders here in 1945.

Iwo Jima—photograph from the 1945 battle

-ize, *suffix.* **1** to make or become ___: *legalize = make legal; crystallize = become crystal.* **2** to use ___: *criticize = to use criticism.*

USAGE NOTE The suffix is spelled **-ize** in words like *apologize, hospitalize,* and *realize.* In words such as *devise, exercise, improvise,* and *supervise,* **-ise** is not a suffix.

Iz·mir (iz′mir *or* iz mir′), *n.* port in W Turkey, on the Aegean Sea.

a	hat	ė	term	ô	order	ch	child	ə	a in about
ā	age	i	it	oi	oil	ng	long		e in taken
ä	far	ī	ice	ou	out	sh	she		i in pencil
â	care	o	hot	u	cup	th	thin		o in lemon
e	let	ō	open	ů	put	ŦH	then		u in circus
ē	equal	ò	saw	ü	rule	zh	measure		

J or **j** (jā), *n.* the tenth letter of the English alphabet. ❑ *n., pl.* **J's** or **j's.**

jab (jab), **1** *v.* to poke with something pointed; thrust forcefully: *He jabbed his fork into the potato.* **2** *n.* a poke with something pointed; a forceful thrust: *She gave him a jab with her elbow.* **3** in boxing: **a** *n.* a blow in which the arm is extended straight from the shoulder. **b** *v.* to hit with a jab. ❑ *v.* **jabbed, jab·bing.**

jab·ber (jab′ər), **1** *v.* to talk very fast in a confused, senseless way; chatter. **2** *n.* very fast, confused, or senseless talk; chatter. —**jab′ber·er,** *n.*

ja·bot (zha bō′ *or* zhab′ō), *n.* ruffle or frill of lace, worn at the throat or down the front of a shirt, dress, or blouse.

jac·a·ran·da (jak′ə ran′də), *n.* any of several American trees and bushes that grow in a warm climate. Jacarandas have showy blue flowers shaped like tubes and pretty, fragrant wood. ❑ *n., pl.* **jac·a·ran·das.**

jack (jak), **1** *n.* a portable tool or machine for lifting or pushing up heavy weights a short distance: *He raised the car off the ground with a jack to change the flat tire.* **2** *v.* to lift or push up with a jack: *jack up a car.* **3** *n.* a playing card with a picture of a servant or soldier on it; knave. **4** *n.* pebble or small six-pointed metal piece used in the game of jacks; jackstone. **5** *n.pl.* **jacks,** a children's game played with jacks and a small rubber ball; jackstones. Each player bounces the ball and picks up the jacks in between bounces. **6** *n.* a small flag used on a ship to show nationality or as a signal. **7** *n.* a male donkey. **8** *n.* man or fellow.

9 *n.* an electrical device which can receive a plug to make a connection in a circuit. [**Jack** comes from *Jack,* a nickname for the name *John.* First, people used it for any common person. Then it came to be used for any commonly found animal, machine, etc.]
jack up, INFORMAL. to raise prices, wages, etc.: *Supermarkets have jacked up prices in recent months.*

jack·al (jak′əl), *n.* any of several wild animals of Asia, Africa, and southeastern Europe. Jackals are related to dogs, but look like foxes. Jackals hunt in packs at night and feed on small animals or animals they find dead.

jack·a·napes (jak′ə nāps), *n.* an impertinent, forward person. ❑ *n., pl.* **jack·a·napes.**

jack·ass (jak′as′), *n.* **1** a male donkey. **2** a very stupid or foolish person. ❑ *n., pl.* **jack·ass·es.**

jack·boot (jak′büt′), *n.* a heavy military boot reaching above the knee.

jack·et (jak′it), *n.* **1** a short coat. **2** an outer covering. The paper cover for a book, the casing around a steam pipe, and the skin of a potato are jackets.

Jack Frost, frost or freezing weather thought of as a person.

jack·ham·mer (jak′ham′ər), *n.* a portable high-powered drill used to break up rock, pavement, etc.

jack·in·the·box (jak′in ᴛᴴə boks′), *n.* toy consisting of a figure that springs up from a box when the lid is opened. ❑ *n., pl.* **jack·in·the·box·es.**

jack-in-the-pul·pit (jak′in ᴛʜə pùl′pit), *n.* any of several North American plants with greenish, petallike sheaths arched over the flower stalks. ❑ *n., pl.* **jack-in-the-pul·pits.**

jack·knife (jak′nīf′), **1** *n.* a large, strong pocketknife. A jackknife may have several blades of different sizes that fold into the handle. **2** *n.* kind of dive in which a diver touches the feet with the hands in midair, and straightens out before entering the water. **3** *v.* to bend at a sharp angle: *When the tractor-trailer skidded, it jackknifed across the highway.* ❑ *n., pl.* **jack·knives** (jak′nivz′); *v.* **jack·knifed, jack·knif·ing.**

jack of all trades, person who can do many different kinds of work fairly well.

jack-o'-lan·tern (jak′ə lan′tərn), *n.* pumpkin hollowed out and cut to look like a face, used as a lantern at Halloween.

jack pine, a slender pine tree that grows in rocky soil in the northeastern and midwestern United States and Canada.

jack·pot (jak′pot′), *n.* **1** stakes that accumulate in a game until some player wins. **2** the big prize of a game.
hit the jackpot, 1 to get the big prize. **2** to have a stroke of very good luck.

jack·rab·bit (jak′rab′it), *n.* any of four kinds of large hares of western North America, with very long hind legs and long ears. A jackrabbit is not really a rabbit.

jack·screw (jak′skrü′), *n.* tool or machine that uses a screw to raise a heavy weight a short distance.

Jack·son (jak′sən), *n.* **1 Andrew,** 1767-1845, the seventh president of the United States, from 1829 to 1837. He was also a general in the War of 1812. **2 Hel·en Hunt** (hel′ən hunt), 1830-1885, American novelist who worked for American Indian rights. **3 Jes·se** (jes′ē), born 1941, American civil rights leader. **4 Thomas Jon·a·than** (jon′ə thən), 1824-1863, Confederate general. He was called "Stonewall" Jackson. **5** capital of Mississippi, in the central part.

Jack·son·ville (jak′sən vil), *n.* port in NE Florida, near the Atlantic.

jack·stone (jak′stōn′), *n.* **1** piece used in the game of jacks; jack. **2 jackstones,** *pl.* the game of jacks.

jack·straw (jak′strò′), *n.* **1** straw, strip of wood, bone, etc., used in the game of jackstraws. **2 jackstraws,** *pl.* a children's game played with these. A set of jackstraws is thrown down in a pile and each player tries to pick them up one at a time without moving any of the others.

Ja·cob (jā′kəb), *n.* (in the Bible) the son of Isaac and Rebecca, and younger twin brother of Esau. The 12 tribes of Israel traced their descent from Jacob's 12 sons. [See word history information at **James.**]

jade (jād), **1** *n.* a hard stone used for jewelry and ornaments. Most jade is green, but some is whitish. **2** *n.* a light green. **3** *adj.* light green. [**Jade** comes from a Spanish word meaning "stomachache." In old times, people thought jade could cure this pain, so they called it "stomachache stone."] —**jade′like′,** *adj.*

jad·ed (jā′did), *adj.* worn out; tired; weary. —**jad′ed·ly,** *adv.* —**jad′ed·ness,** *n.*

jag (jag), **1** *n.* a sharp point sticking out: *a jag of rock.* **2** *v.* to cut or tear unevenly. ❑ *v.* **jagged, jag·ging.**

jag·ged (jag′id), *adj.* with sharp points sticking out: *We cut our bare feet on the jagged rocks.* —**jag′ged·ly,** *adv.* —**jag′ged·ness,** *n.*

Jag·ger (jag′ər), *n.* **Mick** (mik), born 1943, British rock singer and songwriter. He is the leader of the band the Rolling Stones.

jag·uar (jag′wär), *n.* a large, fierce cat much like a leopard, but more heavily built. Jaguars live in forests in tropical America.

jai a·lai (hī′ ä lī′), game similar to handball, played on a walled court with a hard ball. The ball is caught and thrown with a kind of curved wicker basket fastened to the arm. [**Jai alai** comes from two words in Basque, a language in part of Spain and France. They mean "merry festival."]

jail (jāl), **1** *n.* prison, especially one for persons awaiting trial or being punished for some small offense. **2** *v.* to put or keep in jail.

WORD STORY **Jail** comes from a Latin word meaning "coop." **Cage** comes from the same word. A coop is a cage for birds, and prisoners are sometimes called "jailbirds."

jail·break (jāl′brāk′), *n.* an escape from jail or prison.

jail·er or **jail·or** (jā′lər), *n.* keeper of a jail.

Ja·kar·ta (jə kär′tə), *n.* port in NW Java, capital of Indonesia.

ja·la·pe·ño (hä′lə pā′nyō), *n.* a spicy, sharp-tasting Mexican pepper. ❑ *n., pl.* **ja·la·pe·ños.**

Ja·lis·co (hä lēs′kō *or* hə lis′kō), *n.* a state in W central Mexico.

ja·lop·y (jə lop′ē), *n.* INFORMAL. an old car in bad condition. ❑ *n., pl.* **ja·lop·ies.**

jal·ou·sie (jal′ə sē), *n.* a window shade or shutter made of horizontal slats that may be tilted to let in light and air but keep out sun and rain.

WORD STORY **Jalousie** comes from a French word meaning "jealousy." Jalousies keep passers-by from looking in the windows, but people inside can look out without being seen, as if jealously spying.

jam[1] (jam), **1** *v.* to press or squeeze tightly between two surfaces: *The ship was jammed between two rocks.* **2** *v.* to crush by squeezing; bruise: *I jammed my fingers in the door.* **3** *v.* to press or squeeze things or people tightly together: *They jammed us all into one bus.* **4** *n.* mass of people or things crowded together so that they cannot move freely: *She was delayed by the traffic jam.* **5** *v.* to fill or block up by crowding: *The river was jammed with logs.* **6** *v.* to stick or catch so that it cannot be worked: *The window has jammed; I can't open it.* **7** *v.* to cause to stick or catch so that it cannot be worked: *The key broke off and jammed the lock.* **8** *v.* to push hard or force; shove: *jam one more book into the bookcase.* **9** *n.* a difficulty or tight spot: *I was in a jam.* **10** *v.* to make radio signals, etc., unintelligible by sending out others of approximately the same frequency. ❑ *v.* **jammed, jam·ming.** ■ Another word that sounds like this is **jamb.**

jam[2] (jam), *n.* preserve made by boiling fruit with sugar until thick: *strawberry jam.* ■ Another word that sounds like this is **jamb.** —**jam′like′,** *adj.*

Ja·mai·ca (jə mā′kə), *n.* island country in the West Indies, south of Cuba. *Capital:* Kingston. —**Ja·mai·can,** *adj., n.*

jamb (jam), *n.* an upright piece forming the side of a doorway, window, or fireplace. [**Jamb** comes from a French word meaning "leg." Jambs are the legs that the top piece stands on.] ■ Another word that sounds like this is **jam.**

jam·ba·lay·a (jam′bə lī′ə), *n.* a Creole rice dish, usually made with ham or shrimp, tomatoes, and spices. ❑ *n., pl.* **jam·ba·lay·as.**

jam·bo·ree (jam′bə rē′), *n.* **1** a large rally or gathering of Boy Scouts or Girl Scouts. **2** a noisy party. ❑ *n., pl.* **jam·bor·ees.**

James (jāmz), *n.* **1** in the Bible: **a** one of the apostles of Jesus, sometimes called **James the Greater. b** another of the twelve apostles, sometimes called **James the Less. 2** book of the New Testament. **3** river in Virginia, flowing E to Chesapeake Bay. [**James** comes from a Hebrew word meaning "may God protect." **Jacob** comes from the same Hebrew word.]

jaguar—about 7 ft. (2 m) long with tail

a	hat	ė	term	ô	order	ch	child		a in about
ā	age	i	it	oi	oil	ng	long		e in taken
ä	far	ī	ice	ou	out	sh	she	ə ⟨	i in pencil
â	care	o	hot	u	cup	th	thin		o in lemon
e	let	ō	open	ù	put	ᴛʜ	then		u in circus
ē	equal	ò	saw	ü	rule	zh	measure		

J

James (jāmz), *n.* **1 Henry,** 1843-1916, American writer who lived in England. **2 Jes·se** (jes′ē), 1847-1882, American outlaw. ▪ **Jesse James** led about 25 robberies of banks, trains, and stagecoaches. He was killed by a fellow outlaw who wanted the reward that was offered for his arrest. **3 William,** 1842-1910, American psychologist and philosopher, brother of Henry James.

James I, 1566-1625, the first Stuart king of England, from 1603 to 1625. The King James version of the Bible was written during his reign.

James·town (jāmz′toun), *n.* restored village in SE Virginia. The first successful English settlement in North America was made there in 1607.

jam session, a gathering at which jazz musicians play compositions and improvise together.

Jan., January.

jan·gle (jang′gəl), **1** *v.* to sound harshly; make a loud, clashing noise: *The pots and pans jangled in the kitchen.* **2** *v.* to cause to make a harsh, clashing sound: *The boys jangled cowbells.* **3** *n.* a harsh sound; clashing noise or ring: *the jangle of the telephone.* **4** *v.* to have a harsh, unpleasant effect on: *All that racket jangles my nerves.* ❑ *v.* **jan·gled, jan·gling. —jan′gler,** *n.*

jan·i·tor (jan′ə tər), *n.* person hired to take care of a building or offices; caretaker. Janitors do cleaning and make some repairs. [Janitor comes from a Latin word meaning "door." In old times, a janitor was a doorman. Today these are two different jobs.]

Jan·u·ar·y (jan′yü er′ē), *n.* the first month of the year. It has 31 days.

WORD STORY   **January** comes from the name of the Roman god **Janus.** This month opens the door of a new year and closes the door of a year gone by.

Ja·nus (jā′nəs), *n.* Roman god of gates and doors, and of beginnings and endings, with two faces, one looking forward and the other looking backward. [See Word Story at **January.**]

ja·pan (jə pan′), **1** *n.* a hard, glossy varnish. **2** *v.* to put japan on. **3** *n.* articles varnished and ornamented in the Japanese manner. ❑ *v.* **ja·panned, ja·pan·ning.**

Ja·pan (jə pan′), *n.* **1** country made up of four large islands and many smaller ones, in the W Pacific east of the Asian mainland. *Capital:* Tokyo. The Japanese name for Japan is **Nippon. 2 Sea of,** sea between Japan and the Asian mainland.

Jap·a·nese (jap′ə nēz′), **1** *adj.* of Japan, its people, or their language. **2** *n.* person born or living in Japan. **3** *n.* language of Japan. ❑ *n., pl.* **Jap·a·nese** for 2.

Japan

RUSSIA

CHINA

Hokkaido

Sea of Japan

JAPAN

Honshu

Tokyo

Shikoku

Kyushu

PACIFIC OCEAN

N

WORD SOURCE   **Japanese** has given many words to the English language, including the words below.

bonsai	honcho	kimono	sushi
geisha	judo	ninja	tempura
ginkgo	jujitsu	origami	teriyaki
haiku	karate	soy	tycoon

Japanese beetle, a small, green and brown beetle that eats fruits, leaves, and grasses. It causes much damage to crops in the United States.

ja·pon·i·ca (jə pon′ə kə), *n.* an ornamental bush that comes from Asia. Japonicas have showy red, pink, or white flowers. ❑ *n., pl.* **ja·pon·i·cas.**

jar¹ (jär), *n.* **1** a deep container with a wide mouth, usually made of glass or plastic. **2** amount that it holds.

jar² (jär), **1** *v.* to cause to shake or rattle; vibrate: *Your heavy footsteps jar my table.* **2** *n.* a shake; rattle: *I felt the jar of a slight earthquake.* **3** *v.* to make a harsh, grating noise. **4** *n.* a harsh, grating noise. **5** *v.* to have a harsh, unpleasant effect on: *The chil-*

dren's screams jarred my nerves. **6** *n.* a slight shock to the ears, nerves, feelings, etc. **7** *v.* to clash; conflict: *We did not get on well together; our opinions always jarred.* ❑ *v.* **jarred, jar·ring. —jar′ring·ly,** *adv.*

jar·gon (jär′gən), *n.* **1** language of a special group, profession, etc. Doctors, actors, and sailors have jargons. **2** confused, meaningless talk or writing. **3** language that is a mixture of two or more languages.

jas·mine (jaz′mən *or* jas′mən), *n.* any of numerous bushes or vines of warm regions, with clusters of fragrant yellow, white, or reddish flowers.

jas·per (jas′pər), *n.* an opaque variety of quartz, usually red, brown, or yellow.

jaun·dice (jȯn′dis), **1** *n.* an unhealthy yellowness of the skin, eyes, and body fluids. It is caused by too much bile pigment in the blood. **2** *v.* to cause jaundice in. **3** *n.* a disturbed outlook due to envy, discontent, jealousy, etc. **4** *v.* to prejudice someone's mind and judgment by envy, discontent, jealousy, etc. ❑ *v.* **jaun·diced, jaun·dic·ing.**

WORD STORY   **Jaundice** comes from a Latin word meaning "yellow." Today, people are said to be "green with envy." In the past, envy was thought of as yellow.

jaunt (jȯnt), **1** *n.* a short journey, especially for pleasure: *a one-day jaunt to the seashore and back.* **2** *v.* to take such a trip.

jaun·ty (jȯn′tē), *adj.* **1** lively and self-confident: *The happy children walked with jaunty steps.* **2** smart; stylish: *a jaunty hat.* ❑ *adj.* **jaun·ti·er, jaun·ti·est.** [Jaunty comes from a Latin word meaning "noble." **Gentle** comes from the same word. Nobles used to have better manners and clothes than other people.] **—jaun′ti·ly,** *adv.* **—jaun′ti·ness,** *n.*

Ja·va (jä′və *or* jav′ə), *n.* **1** large island southeast of Sumatra. It is the most important island of Indonesia. **2** kind of coffee obtained from Java and nearby islands. **3** Usually, **java,** SLANG. coffee. ❑ *n., pl.* **ja·vas** for 3.

Java man, Homo erectus.

Jav·a·nese (jav′ə nēz′), **1** *adj.* of Java, its people, or their language. **2** *n.* person born or living in Java. **3** *n.* language of Java. ❑ *n., pl.* **Jav·a·nese** for 2.

jave·lin (jav′lən), *n.* **1** a light spear thrown by hand. **2** a wooden or metal spear, thrown for distance in track and field contests.

ja·ve·li·na (hä′və lē′nə), *n.* peccary. ❑ *n., pl.* **ja·ve·li·nas.**

jaw (jȯ), **1** *n.* the lower part of the face. **2** *n.* the upper or lower bone or set of bones, that together form the framework of the mouth. The lower jaw is movable. **3** *n.pl.* **jaws,** the parts in a tool or machine that grip and hold. A vise has jaws. **4** *v.* INFORMAL. to go on talking at great length, in a boring way. **—jaw′less,** *adj.*

jaw·bone (jȯ′bōn′), *n.* one of the bones in which the teeth are set, especially the lower jaw.

jaw·break·er (jȯ′brā′kər), *n.* **1** a large, hard piece of candy, usually in the shape of a ball. **2** word that is hard to pronounce.

jay (jā), *n.* any of various crested birds of Europe and North America, related to the crow. The **blue jay** is one kind of jay. [See word history information at **jaywalk.**]

Jay (jā), *n.* **John,** 1745-1829, first chief justice of the U.S. Supreme Court, from 1789 to 1795.

jay·walk (jā′wȯk′), *v.* to walk across a street without paying attention to traffic rules. [Jaywalk comes from an old meaning of jay, "stupid person," plus **walk.** It is like saying "birdbrain walk."] **—jay′walk′er,** *n.*

jazz (jaz), **1** *n.* a popular kind of music with a strong beat in which the accents fall at unusual places. Jazz is native to the United States, and developed from early African American spirituals and folk music. **2** *adj.* of or related to jazz: *a jazz band, jazz records.* **3** *n.* INFORMAL. similar things; stuff: *We had to give our age, height, color of hair, and all that jazz.*

jazz up, INFORMAL. to make lively; add flavor or interest to: *jazz up a speech with jokes and funny stories.*

jazz·y (jaz′ē), *adj.* **1** of or like jazz music. **2** INFORMAL. wildly active or lively: *jazzy action movies.* **3** INFORMAL. too fancy; flashy: *jazzy clothes.* ❑ *adj.* **jazz·i·er, jazz·i·est. —jazz′i·ly,** *adv.* **—jazz′i·ness,** *n.*

jeal·ous (jel′əs), *adj.* **1** fearful that someone you love may love or prefer someone else: *The child was jealous when anyone paid attention to the new baby.* **2** full of envy; envious: *She is jealous of her sister's good grades.* **3** watchful in keeping or guarding something; careful: *Our city is jealous of its rights within the state.* **4** close; watchful; suspicious: *The dog was such a jealous guardian of the little girl that he would not let her cross the street.* —**jeal′ous·ly,** *adv.* —**jeal′ous·ness,** *n.*

WORD STORY Jealous comes from a Greek word meaning "eager desire" or "enthusiasm." Zealous comes from the same word. A jealous person feels desire and fear or envy. A zealous person is strongly enthusiastic.

jeal·ous·y (jel′ə sē), *n.* condition of feeling jealous; envy.
jeans (jēnz), *n.pl.* pants made of heavy, coarse cotton cloth.

WORD STORY Today blue jeans are common, but once the cloth was so hard to get that people named it after the place where they could buy it. Jeans comes from Genoa, a city in Italy. Denim, another name for this cloth, comes from Nîmes (nēm), a city in France. Another name, serge, comes from a Greek word meaning "Chinese." The cloth was also made in India, where they called it by a name that turned into dungaree. So be glad you get yours close to home.

jeep (jēp), *n.* a small, powerful, general-purpose motor vehicle in which power is transmitted to all four wheels. It was originally designed for use by the U.S. Army. [**Jeep** comes from a fast way of pronouncing the abbreviation *G.P.,* which stands for *general purpose* car.]

jeer (jir), **1** *v.* to laugh at rudely or unkindly; mock; scoff: *Do not jeer at the mistakes or misfortunes of others.* **2** *n.* a mocking or insulting remark: *The mayor's speech asking for higher taxes was interrupted by jeers from the audience.* —**jeer′er,** *n.*

Jef·fer·son (jef′ər sən), *n.* **Thomas,** 1743-1826, the third president of the United States, from 1801 to 1809. He wrote most of the Declaration of Independence.

Jefferson City, capital of Missouri, in the central part, on the Missouri River.

Je·ho·vah (ji hō′və), *n.* one of the names of God in the Bible.

Jehovah's Witness, member of a Christian religious group that believes that governments and organized religions are evil, that the end of the world is near, and that a person's religious belief is more important than government authority.

jell (jel), *v.* **1** to become jelly; thicken. **2** to take definite form; become fixed: *His hunch soon jelled into a plan.* ■ Another word that sounds like this is **gel.**

jel·lied (jel′ēd), *adj.* turned into jelly.
Jell-O (jel′ō), *n.* trademark for a fruit-flavored gelatin dessert.
jel·ly (jel′ē), **1** *n.* fruit juice boiled with sugar and then cooked until firm. **2** *n.* a jellylike substance. **3** *v.* to become jelly or like jelly; thicken; congeal: *Some soup will jelly when it is chilled in the refrigerator.* □ *n., pl.* **jel·lies;** *v.* **jel·lied, jel·ly·ing.** —**jel′ly·like′,** *adj.*

jel·ly·bean (jel′ē bēn′), *n.* a small candy made of jellied sugar, often shaped like a bean.

jel·ly·fish (jel′ē fish′), *n.* any of numerous related sea animals without backbones, with bodies formed of a mass of almost transparent jellylike tissue; medusa. Most jellyfish have long, trailing tentacles that may bear stinging cells. □ *n., pl.* **jel·ly·fish** or **jel·ly·fish·es.**

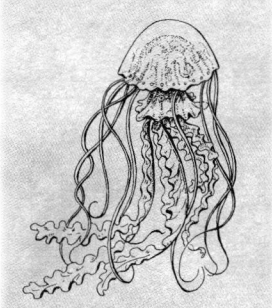
jellyfish

Jen·ner (jen′ər), *n.* **Ed·ward** (ed′wərd), 1749-1823, English physician who discovered vaccination.
jen·net (jen′it), *n.* **1** a small Spanish horse. **2** a female donkey.
jen·ny (jen′ē), *n.* **1** spinning jenny. **2** female of certain animals: *jenny wren.* □ *n., pl.* **jen·nies.**

jeop·ar·dize (jep′ər diz), *v.* to put in danger; risk; endanger; imperil: *The raging forest fire jeopardized many lives.* □ *v.* **jeop·ar·dized, jeop·ar·diz·ing.**

jeop·ar·dy (jep′ər dē), *n.* risk; danger; peril: *Many lives were in jeopardy during the forest fire.* [**Jeopardy** comes from French words meaning "an even game" or "a divided game," in which the chances of a win or a loss were about equal.]

jer·bo·a (jər bō′ə), *n.* any of several related, small, jumping, mouse-like mammals of Asia and northern Africa. □ *n., pl.* **jer·bo·as.**

Jer·e·mi·ah (jer′ə mī′ə), *n.* **1** a Hebrew prophet. **2** book of the Bible.

Jer·i·cho (jer′ə kō), *n.* city in ancient Palestine. According to the Bible, its walls fell down at the noise made by the trumpets of Joshua's attacking army. See **Canaan** for map.

jerk¹ (jėrk), **1** *v.* to pull or twist suddenly: *If the water is unexpectedly hot, you jerk your hand out.* ■ See Synonym Study at **pull. 2** *n.* a sudden, sharp pull, twist, or start: *The old car started with a jerk.* **3** *n.* a sudden movement of the muscles that you cannot control; twitch. **4** *v.* to move with a jerk: *The old wagon jerked along.* **5** *n.* INFORMAL. a stupid or foolish person. —**jerk′er,** *n.*

SYNONYM STUDY **Jerk**¹, **wrench,** and **twitch** all mean to pull suddenly. **Jerk** means to give a sudden sharp pull: *He jerked the handle and the door flew open.* **Wrench** means to twist something while pulling it: *My dog wrenched the shoe out of my hand.* **Twitch** means to pull with a short, quick tug: *She twitched the curtain aside.*

jerk² (jėrk), *v.* to preserve meat by cutting it into long, thin slices and drying it in the sun.

jer·kin (jėr′kən), *n.* a short, close-fitting coat or jacket without sleeves.

jerk·y¹ (jėr′kē), *adj.* with sudden starts and stops; with jerks. □ *adj.* **jerk·i·er, jerk·i·est.** —**jerk′i·ly,** *adv.* —**jerk′i·ness,** *n.*

jerk·y² (jėr′kē), *n.* strips of dried meat, usually beef.

jer·ry-built (jer′ē bilt), *adj.* built cheaply and not strongly: *We had to replace the jerry-built desk after a year.*

jer·sey (jėr′zē), *n.* **1** a soft, knitted cloth used for clothing. **2** shirt that is pulled over the head, made of this cloth: *Our hockey team wears red jerseys.* □ *n., pl.* **jer·seys.**

Jer·sey (jėr′zē), *n.* **1** one of the Channel Islands. **2** one of a breed of small, usually fawn-colored cattle that came from this island. **3** INFORMAL. New Jersey. □ *n., pl.* **Jer·seys** for 2.

Jersey City, city in NE New Jersey.

Je·ru·sa·lem (jə rü′sə ləm), *n.* capital of Israel, in the E part. It is a holy city to Jews, Christians, and Muslims.

jest (jest), **1** *n.* a joke: *His jests weren't very funny.* **2** *v.* to joke: *I was only jesting, but they took me seriously.* [**Jest** comes from a French word meaning "a story," any kind of story. Now a jest is only a funny story.] —**jest′ing·ly,** *adv.*
in jest, in fun; not seriously: *His words were spoken in jest.*

jest·er (jes′tər), *n.* person who jests. In the Middle Ages, royalty often had jesters to amuse them.

Jes·u·it (jezh′ü it *or* jez′yü it), *n.* member of the Society of Jesus, a Roman Catholic religious order of men founded by Saint Ignatius of Loyola in 1534.

Je·sus (jē′zəs), *n.* 4 B.C.?-A.D. 29?, founder of the Christian religion. [**Jesus** comes from Hebrew words meaning "God is salvation."]

Jesus Christ, Jesus.

jet¹ (jet), **1** *n.* aircraft driven by one or more jet engines. **2** *v.* to fly by jet plane: *to jet to Europe.* **3** *n.* stream of water, steam, gas, or any matter, sent with force, especially from a small opening: *A fountain sends up a jet of water.* **4** *n.* spout or nozzle for sending out a jet. **5** *v.* to shoot forth in a jet or forceful stream; gush out: *Water jetted from the broken pipe.* □ *v.* **jet·ted, jet·ting.**

WORD STORY Jet¹ comes from a Latin word meaning "to throw." A jet of water is thrown hard from the spout, and a jet plane throws itself fast through the air.

a	hat	ė	term	ô	order	ch	child		a in about
ā	age	i	it	oi	oil	ng	long		e in taken
ä	far	ī	ice	ou	out	sh	she	ə	i in pencil
â	care	o	hot	u	cup	th	thin		o in lemon
e	let	ō	open	ů	put	ŦH	then		u in circus
ē	equal	ò	saw	ü	rule	zh	measure		

J

jet² (jet), **1** *n.* a hard, black kind of coal, shiny when polished, used for making beads, buttons, and ornaments. **2** *n.* a deep, shiny black. **3** *adj.* deep, shiny black: *jet hair.*

jet-black (jet′blak′), *adj.* very black.

jet engine, engine which shoots out a jet of exhaust gases forcefully from the rear of the engine. The force of the jet drives the engine forward.

jet lag, the delayed effects, such as tiredness, that a person feels after a long flight through several time zones on a jet plane.

jet plane, jet.

jet-pro·pelled (jet′prə peld′), *adj.* driven by a jet engine: *Many aircraft are jet-propelled.*

jet propulsion, production of movement in one direction by a jet of air, gases, etc., forced in the opposite direction.

jet·sam (jet′səm), *n.* goods which are thrown overboard to lighten a ship in distress and afterwards are often washed ashore.

jet set, the social group of fashionable people who travel a lot by jet plane.

jet stream, a very large current of air traveling at very high speed, six to eight miles (10 to 13 kilometers) above the ground. The earth has five major jet streams, four circling the planet from west to east, one moving from east to west over southeast Asia and Africa.

jet·ti·son (jet′ə sən), *v.* **1** to throw goods overboard to lighten a ship in distress. **2** to throw away; discard.

jet·ty (jet′ē), *n.* **1** structure of stones or wooden piles built out from the shore to break the force of a current or waves; breakwater. **2** a landing place; pier. □ *n., pl.* **jet·ties.**

Jew (jü), *n.* **1** person descended from the Semitic people led by Moses, who settled in Palestine and now live in Israel and many other countries; Hebrew; Israelite. **2** person whose religion is Judaism.

jew·el (jü′əl), **1** *n.* a precious stone; gem. **2** *n.* a valuable ornament to be worn, often made of gold or silver and set with gems. **3** *n.* person or thing that is very precious. **4** *n.* gem or other hard material used as a bearing in some watches. **5** *v.* to set or decorate with jewels or with things like jewels: *a jeweled comb, a sky jeweled with stars.* □ *v.* **jew·eled, jew·el·ing** or **jew·elled, jew·el·ling.** —**jew′el·like′,** *adj.*

jew·el·er or **jew·el·ler** (jü′ə lər), *n.* person who makes, sells, or repairs jewelry and watches.

jew·el·ry (jü′əl rē), *n.* **1** jewels and ornaments set with gems: *She keeps her jewelry in a small, locked box.* **2** ring, bracelet, necklace, or other ornament to be worn, usually set with imitation gems or made of silver- or gold-colored metal, etc.

Jew·ish (jü′ish), *adj.* of the Jews or their religion: *the Jewish faith.* —**Jew′ish·ness,** *n.*

jew's-harp or **jews'-harp** (jüz′härp′), *n.* a simple musical instrument, held between the teeth and played by striking the free end of a flexible piece of metal with a finger.

jib (jib), *n.* a triangular sail in front of the most forward mast on a sailboat.

jibe¹ (jib), *v.* to be in harmony; agree: *Our opinions jibe; we like the same music.* □ *v.* **jibed, jib·ing.** ■ Another word that sounds like this is **gibe.**

jibe² (jib), *v.* **1** to shift a sail from one side of a ship to the other when sailing before the wind. **2** to shift itself in this way: *Be careful or your mainsail will jibe.* **3** to change the course of a ship so that the sails shift in this way. □ *v.* **jibed, jib·ing.** ■ Another word that sounds like this is **gibe.**

jibe³ (jib), *n., v.* gibe. □ *v.* **jibed, jib·ing.** —**jib′er,** *n.*

jif·fy (jif′ē), *n.* INFORMAL. a very short time; moment: *He was on his bike in a jiffy, pedaling down the drive.*

jig¹ (jig), **1** *n.* a lively dance, often in triple time. **2** *n.* music for it. **3** *v.* to dance a jig. □ *v.* **jigged, jig·ging.** [Jig¹ may come from a French word meaning "a fiddle." Jigs are usually danced to fiddle music.]

the jig is up, it's all over; there are no more chances.

jig² (jig), *n.* **1** a fishing lure consisting of a fishhook or a set of fishhooks. It is bobbed up and down or pulled through the water. **2** any of various devices used to hold a piece of work and guide a drill, file, saw, etc., toward it.

jig·ger (jig′ər), *n.* a small glass or metal cup, used to measure alcoholic liquor. It holds about 1½ ounces (44 milliliters).

jig·gle (jig′əl), **1** *v.* to shake or jerk slightly: *Don't jiggle the desk when I'm trying to write.* **2** *n.* a slight shake; light jerk. □ *v.* **jig·gled, jig·gling.**

jig·saw (jig′sô′), *n.* saw with a narrow blade mounted in a frame and worked with an up-and-down motion. It is used to cut curves or irregular lines.

jigsaw puzzle, picture glued onto cardboard or wood and sawed into differently shaped pieces that can be fitted together again.

ji·had (ji häd′), *n.* **1** a holy war carried on by Muslims as a religious duty. **2** any bitter fight or crusade.

jilt (jilt), *v.* to end a relationship with a lover, sweetheart, or someone you are engaged to, especially suddenly.

Jim Crow (jim′ krō), discrimination against African Americans, especially when widely and openly practiced.

jim·my (jim′ē), **1** *n.* a short crowbar used especially by burglars to force open windows, doors, or other things. **2** *v.* to force open with a jimmy. □ *n., pl.* **jim·mies;** *v.* **jim·mied, jim·my·ing.**

jim·son·weed (jim′sən wēd′), *n.* a tall, bushy, bad-smelling North American plant with long, white or purplish, funnel-shaped flowers and poisonous leaves.

jin·gle (jing′gəl), **1** *v.* to make or cause to make a sound like bells, coins, or keys striking together: *The sleigh bells jingle as we ride.* **2** *n.* a sound like that of little bells, or of coins or keys striking together. **3** *n.* verse or song that has repetition of similar sounds, or a catchy rhyme. "Higgledy, piggledy, my black hen" is a jingle. □ *v.* **jin·gled, jin·gling.**

jin·go (jing′gō), **1** *n.* person who supports a foreign policy so aggressive that it might lead to war. **2** *adj.* of or like jingoes or their attitude: *That car has a jingo bumper sticker.* □ *n., pl.* **jin·goes.**

by jingo! exclamation used to show strong feeling.

jin·go·ism (jing′gō iz əm), *n.* beliefs or actions of jingoes.

jin·rick·sha or **jin·rik·i·sha** (jin rik′shə *or* jin rik′shô), *n.* (earlier) a small, two-wheeled carriage with a folding top, pulled by a runner, used in Asia; rickshaw. □ *n., pl.* **jin·rick·shas** or **jin·rik·i·shas.**

jinx (jingks), **1** *n.* person or thing that brings bad luck. **2** *v.* to bring bad luck to. □ *n., pl.* **jinx·es.**

jit·ney (jit′nē), *n.* any car or small bus that carries passengers for a low fare, usually along a regular route. □ *n., pl.* **jit·neys.**

jit·ter·bug (jit′ər bug′), **1** *n.* a lively dance for couples, with rapid twirling movements and acrobatics. It was especially popular in the 1940s. **2** *v.* to dance the jitterbug. □ *v.* **jit·ter·bugged, jit·ter·bug·ging.**

jit·ters (jit′ərz), *n.pl.* extreme nervousness: *I had a case of jitters when I had to sing in public.* [Jitters may come from a word used in one part of England meaning "to shiver." People who are very nervous find it hard to hold still.]

jit·ter·y (jit′ər ē), *adj.* nervous: *He felt a little jittery before his first airplane ride.*

jiu·jit·su (jü jit′sü), *n.* jujitsu.

jive (jīv), **1** *n.* INFORMAL. swing (def. 10). **2** *n.* SLANG. the latest slang. **3** *n.* SLANG. misleading or tiresome talk. **4** *v.* SLANG. to mislead; deceive: *Are you trying to jive me?* □ *v.* **jived, jiv·ing.**

Joan of Arc (jōn′ əv ärk′), 1412-1431, French heroine who led armies against the invading English. She was captured by the English, condemned as a witch, and burned to death. In 1920 she was made a saint. [Joan comes from a Hebrew word meaning "God has been gracious."]

job (job), *n.* **1** work done for pay; employment: *My sister is hunting for a job.* **2** anything a person has to do: *I'm not going to wash the dishes; this week that's your job.* **3** a definite piece of work undertaken for a fixed price: *If you want your house painted, they will do the job for $2500.*

SYNONYM STUDY **Job, chore,** and **errand** all mean a certain amount of work. **Job** is the general word: *My job this Saturday is sweeping out the garage.* A **chore** is a job that is done regularly: *One of his chores is weeding the garden.* An **errand** is a job that requires making a trip: *She went on an errand to the drugstore.*

Job (jōb), *n.* **1** (in the Bible) a very patient man who kept his faith in God in spite of many troubles. **2** book of the Bible that tells about him.

job·ber (job′ər), *n.* person who buys goods from manufacturers in large quantities and sells them to retail dealers in small quantities.

job·less (job′lis), **1** *adj.* unable to find a job. **2** *n.pl.* **the jobless,** people who cannot find jobs: *The jobless are a forgotten problem.* —**job′less·ness,** *n.*

jock (jok), *n.* SLANG. athlete.

jock·ey (jok′ē), **1** *n.* person whose occupation is riding horses in races. **2** *v.* to ride a horse in a race. **3** *v.* to trick; cheat: *Swindlers jockeyed them into buying some worthless land.* **4** *v.* to maneuver so as to get advantage: *The crews were jockeying their boats to get into the best position.* ❑ *n., pl.* **jock·eys;** *v.* **jock·eyed, jock·ey·ing.**

jock·strap (jok′strap′), *n.* athletic supporter.

jo·cose (jō kōs′), *adj.* jesting; humorous; joking. —**jo·cose′ly,** *adv.* —**jo·cose′ness,** *n.*

joc·u·lar (jok′yə lər), *adj.* funny; joking. —**joc′u·lar·ly,** *adv.*

joc·u·lar·i·ty (jok′yə lar′ə tē), *n.* **1** jocular quality. **2** jocular talk or behavior. **3** a jocular remark or act. ❑ *n., pl.* **joc·u·lar·i·ties** for 3.

joc·und (jok′ənd), *adj.* cheerful; merry; happy. —**joc′und·ly,** *adv.*

jodh·purs (jod′pərz), *n.pl.* breeches for horseback riding, loose above the knees and close-fitting below the knees.

Jo·el (jō′əl), *n.* **1** a Hebrew prophet. **2** book of the Bible. [**Joel** comes from a Hebrew word meaning "The Lord is God."]

jog[1] (jog), **1** *v.* to trot or run slowly: *I jog daily for exercise.* ■ See Synonym Study at **run. 2** *v.* to shake with a push or jerk: *She jogged my elbow to get my attention.* **3** *n.* a shake, push, or nudge. **4** *v.* to stir up with a hint or reminder: *He tied a string around his finger to jog his memory.* **5** *n.* a hint or reminder: *give your memory a jog.* **6** *v.* to move up or down with a jerk or a shaking motion: *The rider jogged up and down on the horse's back.* **7** *n.* a trot or slow run. ❑ *v.* **jogged, jog·ging.**

jog[2] (jog), *n.* part that sticks out or in: *a jog in the wall.*

jog·ger (jog′ər), *n.* person who jogs for exercise.

jog·ging (jog′ing), *n.* slow running, done for exercise: *She does half an hour of jogging every morning.*

jog·gle (jog′əl), **1** *v.* to shake slightly. **2** *n.* a slight shake. ❑ *v.* **jog·gled, jog·gling.**

Jo·han·nes·burg (jō han′is bėrg′), *n.* city in NE South Africa.

John (jon), *n.* **1** (in the Bible) one of Jesus' twelve apostles. **2** the fourth book of the New Testament. **3 King John,** 1167?-1216, king of England from 1199 to 1216. He signed the Magna Carta in 1215. [**John** and **Jonathan** come from a Hebrew word meaning "God has been gracious."]

John XXIII, 1881-1963, pope from 1958 to 1963.

John Bull, 1 a typical Englishman. **2** the English nation.

John Doe, a made-up name used in legal forms or proceedings for the name of an unknown person. **Jane Doe** is often used for the name of an unknown woman.

John Hancock, a person's signature: *Put your John Hancock where it says "Signature."* [**John Hancock** comes from the bold and prominent signature of John Hancock, the first signer of the Declaration of Independence.]

john·ny·cake (jon′ē kāk′), *n.* cornbread in the form of a flat cake.

John Paul I, 1912-1978, pope in August and September 1978.

John Paul II, born 1920, pope since October 1978.

Johns (jonz), *n.* **Jas·per** (jas′pər), born 1930, American artist. His most famous works include realistic pictures of the U.S. flag.

John·son (jon′sən), *n.* **1 Andrew,** 1808-1875, the 17th president of the United States, from 1865 to 1869. ■ **Andrew Johnson** was impeached, but was found not guilty. He was the only former President to serve as a senator, which he did in 1875. **2 Jack** (jak), 1878-1946, American boxer. He was the first African American to win the world heavyweight championship. **3 James Wel·don** (wel′dən), 1871-1938, American poet. His most famous book is *God's Trombones.* His poems combine African American folklore with Biblical tales. **4 Lyn·don Baines** (lin′dən bānz′), 1908-1973, the 36th president of the United States from 1963 to 1969. **5 Mag·ic** (maj′ik), born 1959, American basketball player. In his first nine years as a professional, his team were champi-

ons five times. **6 Samuel,** 1709-1784, English author and dictionary maker.

John the Baptist, (in the Bible) a Hebrew prophet. John the Baptist foretold the coming of Jesus and baptized him.

join (join), *v.* **1** to come into the company of: *Go now, and I'll join you later.* **2** to become a member of: *She joined a tennis club. My uncle has joined the army.* **3** to bring or put together; connect, fasten, or clasp together: *join an island to the mainland by a bridge.* **4** to come together; meet: *The brook joins the river just below the mill.* **5** to make or become one; combine; unite: *join in marriage. The two clubs joined forces during the campaign.* **6** to take part with others: *join in a song.* **7** to be next to; adjoin: *Our farm joins theirs.*

> **USAGE NOTE** Do not use **together** after **join,** because "together" is already in the meaning of **join** ("to bring or put together"). SAY: *Our clubs should join to organize the fair.* NOT: *Our clubs should join together to organize the fair.*

join·er (joi′nər), *n.* **1** person or thing that joins. **2** carpenter who makes doors, windows, molding, and other inside woodwork.

joint (joint), **1** *adj.* shared or done by two or more persons: *By our joint efforts we managed to push the car back on the road.* **2** *adj.* joined together; sharing: *My sister and I are joint owners of this boat.* **3** *n.* one of the parts of which a jointed thing is made: *the middle joint of the finger.* **4** *n.* part in an animal where two bones join, allowing motion, and the way those bones are fitted together. **5** *n.* the way parts are joined: *The square ends of the wood made a perfect joint.* **6** *n.* the place at which two things or parts are joined together. A pocketknife has a joint to fold the blade inside the handle. **7** *n.* part of the stem of a plant from which a leaf or branch grows. **8** *n.* INFORMAL. a cheap, run-down restaurant, bar, hotel, etc.

out of joint, 1 out of place at the joint: *The fall put my shoulder out of joint.* **2** out of order; in bad condition.

joint·ed (join′tid), *adj.* having a joint or joints: *Lobsters have jointed legs.*

joint·ly (joint′lē), *adv.* together; as partners: *The two girls owned the boat jointly.*

joist (joist), *n.* one of the parallel beams of timber or steel which support the boards of a floor or ceiling.

jo·jo·ba (hō hō′bə), *n.* **1** a large evergreen bush that grows in dry places in Mexico and the southwestern United States. Jojobas have large, oily seeds. **2** oil from these seeds. Jojoba is used in lotions and medicine. ❑ *n., pl.* **jo·jo·bas** for 1.

joke (jōk), **1** *n.* something said or done to make somebody laugh; remark that is clever and funny; something funny; jest: *Looking for the hat that was on my head was a good joke on me.* **2** *v.* to make jokes; say or do something as a joke; jest: *As it got colder, we joked about the possibility of snow in July.* **3** *n.* person or thing laughed at: *Some of the new clothing styles are a joke.* ❑ *v.* **joked, jok·ing.** [See Word Story at **juggle.**] —**jok′ing·ly,** *adv.*

no joke, a serious matter: *The loss of my bicycle was no joke.*

> **SYNONYM STUDY** **Joke, wisecrack,** and **quip** are all things said or done to make someone laugh. **Joke** is the general word: *She thought the joke was funny, but her cousin didn't even smile.* A **wisecrack** is a clever remark, often one that makes fun of someone else: *His brother's wisecrack made him furious.* A **quip** is a short clever saying: *Our teacher keeps us interested with quips about the lesson.*

jok·er (jō′kər), *n.* **1** person who jokes. **2** an extra playing card used in some games.

Jo·li·et (jō′lē et), *n.* **Louis,** 1645-1700, French explorer, born in what is now Canada. He and Jacques Marquette were the first Europeans to reach the upper Mississippi.

Jo·li·ot-Cur·ie (zhô lyō′ kyùr′ē), *n.* **I·rène** (ē ren′), 1897-1956, French physicist. ■ **Irène Joliot-Curie** and her husband Frédéric

a	hat	ė	term	ô	order	ch	child		
ā	age	i	it	oi	oil	ng	long		a in about
ä	far	ī	ice	ou	out	sh	she		e in taken
â	care	o	hot	u	cup	th	thin	ə	i in pencil
e	let	ō	open	ù	put	ŦH	then		o in lemon
ē	equal	ò	saw	ü	rule	zh	measure		u in circus

shared the 1935 Nobel Prize for chemistry. She was the daughter of Nobel Prize-winning physicists Marie and Pierre Curie.

jol·li·ty (jol′ə tē), *n.* fun; merriment.

jol·ly (jol′ē), **1** *adj.* full of fun; very cheerful; merry. **2** *adj.* INFORMAL. pleasant or delightful. **3** *adv.* BRITISH. extremely; very: *a jolly good time.* ❑ *adj.* **jol·li·er, jol·li·est. —jol′li·ness,** *n.*

Jolly Rog·er (roj′ər), a pirates' black flag with a white skull and crossbones on it.

Jol·son (jōl′sən), *n.* **Al** (al), 1886-1950, American entertainer, born in Lithuania. He starred in the first important sound movie, *The Jazz Singer.*

jolt (jōlt), **1** *v.* to shake up; jar: *The wagon jolted us when the wheel went over a rock.* **2** *n.* a jerk, shock, or jar: *I put the brakes on suddenly and the car stopped with a jolt.* **3** *n.* a sudden surprise or shock: *News of the plane crash gave them a jolt.* **4** *v.* to move in a jerky or jarring way: *The car jolted across the rough ground.* **—jolt′er,** *n.*

Jo·nah (jō′nə), *n.* **1** a Hebrew prophet who was thrown overboard during a storm because he disobeyed God. He was swallowed by a large fish and later cast up on land. **2** book of the Bible that tells about him. [Jonah comes from a Hebrew word meaning "dove."]

Jon·a·than (jon′ə thən), *n.* (in the Bible) a son of Saul, and devoted friend of David. [See word history information at **John.**]

Jones (jōnz), *n.* **1 Cas·ey** (kā′sē), 1863-1900, American railroad engineer and folk hero. ■ **Casey Jones** gave his own life to save his passengers and crew when his train crashed into two freight trains that were blocking the tracks. He stayed in the engine to brake until the last minute. He was the only one killed. **2 John Paul,** 1747-1792, American naval commander in the Revolutionary War, born in Scotland. **3 Mary Har·ris** (har′əs), 1830-1930, American labor organizer, born in Ireland. She helped found the Industrial Workers of the World. She was known as "Mother Jones."

jon·quil (jong′kwəl), *n.* any of several plants with yellow or white flowers and long slender leaves, something like a daffodil. A jonquil is a narcissus.

Jop·lin (jop′lən), *n.* **Scott,** 1868-1917, American composer, known for his use of ragtime. ■ **Scott Joplin's** most famous song was "Maple Leaf Rag." He also wrote two operas.

Jor·dan (jôrd′n), *n.* **1** river flowing from SW Syria through Israel and Jordan into the Dead Sea. **2** country in SW Asia, east of Israel. Part of Palestine was added to it in 1950. *Capital:* Amman. **3 Michael,** born 1963, American sports star. ■ **Michael Jordan** is one of the most talented basketball players ever. He led the Chicago Bulls to three straight NBA championships. In 1993 he retired from basketball to play professional baseball, but in 1995 he returned to the game. **—Jor·da·ni·an** (jôr dā′nē ən), *adj., n.*

Jo·seph (jō′zəf), *n.* **1** (in the Bible) the favorite son of Jacob. His jealous brothers sold him into slavery in Egypt, where he finally became governor. **2** (in the Bible) the husband of Mary, mother of Jesus. **3 Chief,** 1840?-1904, American Indian leader of the Nez Perce tribe. [Joseph comes from a Hebrew word meaning "may God add."]

Jo·se·phine (jō′zə fēn′), *n.* 1763-1814, first wife of Napoleon Bonaparte.

josh (josh), *v.* INFORMAL. to make good-natured fun of; tease playfully. **—josh′er,** *n.*

Josh·u·a (josh′ü ə), *n.* **1** (in the Bible) the successor of Moses. Joshua led the Israelites into the Promised Land. **2** book of the Bible. [Joshua comes from a Hebrew word meaning "God is salvation."]

Joshua tree, a yucca tree that grows in dry places in the southwestern United States. It has long, bare branches tipped with bunches of narrow, pointed leaves.

Joshua tree—up to 30 ft. (9.1 m) tall

jos·tle (jos′əl), *v.* to shove, push, or crowd against; elbow roughly: *We were jostled by the big crowd at the entrance to the circus.* ❑ *v.* **jos·tled, jos·tling. —jos′tler,** *n.*

jot (jot), **1** *v.* to write briefly or in haste: *The waiter jotted down our order.* **2** *n.* a little bit; very small amount: *I do not care a jot.* ❑ *v.* **jot·ted, jot·ting.**

joule (jül *or* joul), *n.* unit of work equal to ten million ergs, or to the work done when a force of one newton moves an object one meter. Joules are used to measure all kinds of energy. ■ Another word that can sound like this is **jowl.**

jounce (jouns), **1** *v.* to shake up and down; bounce; bump; jolt: *The car jounced along on the rough road.* **2** *n.* a bump or jolt: *to sit down with a jounce.* ❑ *v.* **jounced, jounc·ing.**

jour·nal (jėr′nl), *n.* **1** newspaper, magazine, or other periodical: *My aunt subscribes to a monthly gardening journal.* **2** a daily record of events or occurrences. A diary is a journal of what a person does, thinks, feels, and notices. A ship's log is a journal of what happens on a ship. **3** (in bookkeeping) a book in which every item of business is written down, so that the item can be entered under the proper account. **4** the part of a shaft or axle that turns in a bearing.

jour·nal·ese (jėr′nl ēz′), *n.* style of writing often found in newspapers and magazines.

jour·nal·ism (jėr′nl iz′əm), *n.* work of gathering, writing, and presenting news in newspapers and magazines or on radio or TV.

jour·nal·ist (jėr′nl ist), *n.* person whose job is in journalism. Editors and reporters are journalists.

jour·nal·is·tic (jėr′nl is′tik), *adj.* of or like journalism or journalists. **—jour′nal·is′ti·cal·ly,** *adv.*

jour·ney (jėr′nē), **1** *n.* act or process of traveling from one place to another; trip: *a journey around the world.* ■ See Synonym Study at **trip. 2** *n.* distance traveled: *a week's journey.* **3** *v.* to take a trip; travel: *to journey through Europe.* ❑ *n., pl.* **jour·neys;** *v.* **jour·neyed, jour·ney·ing. —jour′ney·er,** *n.*

jour·ney·man (jėr′nē mən), *n.* **1** worker who has served an apprenticeship and is qualified to practice a trade. **2** an ordinary but not outstanding worker or employee. ❑ *n., pl.* **jour·ney·men.**

joust (joust), in the Middle Ages: **1** *v.* to fight with lances on horseback. Knights used to joust for fun. **2** *n.* combat between two armored knights on horseback, armed with lances. **—joust′er,** *n.*

Jove (jōv), *n.* Jupiter.

by Jove, exclamation of surprise, pleasure, etc.

jo·vi·al (jō′vē əl), *adj.* good-hearted and full of fun; merry: *Santa Claus is pictured as a jovial fellow.* **—jo′vi·al·ly,** *adv.*

jo·vi·al·i·ty (jō′vē al′ə tē), *n.* jollity; merriment.

jowl[1] (joul), *n.* **1** jaw, especially the lower jaw. **2** cheek. ■ Another word that can sound like this is **joule.**

jowl[2] (joul), *n.* fold of flesh hanging from or under the lower jaw. ■ Another word that can sound like this is **joule.**

joy (joi), *n.* **1** a strong feeling of pleasure; gladness; happiness: *They jumped for joy when they saw the clowns.* **2** something that causes gladness or happiness: *Her surprise visit was a joy.*

Joyce (jois), *n.* **James,** 1882-1941, Irish writer. His works include *Ulysses* and *The Dubliners.*

joy·ful (joi′fəl), *adj.* **1** glad; happy: *a joyful heart.* **2** causing joy: *joyful news.* **3** showing joy: *a joyful look.* **—joy′ful·ly,** *adv.* **—joy′ful·ness,** *n.*

joy·less (joi′lis), *adj.* without joy; sad; dismal. **—joy′less·ly,** *adv.* **—joy′less·ness,** *n.*

joy·ous (joi′əs), *adj.* joyful; glad; happy: *The birth of their first child was a joyous occasion.* **—joy′ous·ly,** *adv.* **—joy′ous·ness,** *n.*

joy·ride (joi′rīd′), INFORMAL. **1** *n.* a ride in a car for pleasure, especially when the car is driven recklessly or without the owner's permission. **2** *v.* to go for a joyride. ❏ *v.* **joy·rode, joy·rid·den, joy·rid·ing.** —**joy·rid·er,** *n.*

joy·stick (joi′stik′), *n.* an electronic device used to control video games and computer games. It is an upright rod that can be tilted forward and back, from side to side, or in other directions.

J.P., Justice of the Peace.

jr. or **Jr.,** Junior.

Juan Car·los I (hwän kär′lōs), born 1938, king of Spain since 1975.

Juà·rez (hwär′es), *n.* **Be·ni·to Pa·blo** (bä nē′tō pä′blō), 1806-1872, president of Mexico from 1861 to 1865 and from 1867 to 1872.

ju·bi·lant (jü′bə lənt), *adj.* expressing or showing joy: *She was jubilant when her team won the game.* —**ju′bi·lant·ly,** *adv.*

> **WORD STORY** Jubilant and jubilee have similar meanings, and they look as if they come from the same word, but they don't. **Jubilant** comes from a Latin word meaning "wild shout." **Jubilee** comes from a Hebrew word meaning "ram's horn," used as a trumpet. Because they have similar meanings, people have made the two words look and sound more alike over time.

ju·bi·la·tion (jü′bə lā′shən), *n.* great joy.

ju·bi·lee (jü′bə lē), *n.* **1** an anniversary thought of as a time of rejoicing: *a twenty-fifth or fiftieth wedding jubilee.* **2** time of rejoicing or great joy; celebration. ❏ *n., pl.* **ju·bil·ees.** [See Word Story at **jubilant**.]

Ju·dah (jü′də), *n.* ancient Hebrew kingdom in S Palestine. [Judah comes from a Hebrew word meaning "praised." **Judas** and **Jude** come from the same word.]

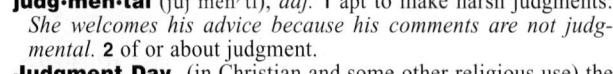

Judah (about 930 B.C.)

Ju·da·ic (jü dā′ik), *adj.* of the Jews or Judaism.

Ju·da·ism (jü′dē iz′əm), *n.* religion based on the teachings of Moses as found in the Hebrew Scriptures and in the laws of the Talmud.

Ju·das (jü′dəs), *n.* **1** (in the Bible) Judas Iscariot, the disciple who betrayed Jesus for money. **2** an utter traitor; person treacherous enough to betray a friend. [See word history information at **Judah**.]

Jude (jüd), *n.* **1** (in the Bible) one of Jesus' twelve apostles. **2** book of the Bible. [See word history information at **Judah**.]

Ju·de·a (jü dē′ə), *n.* the S part of Palestine when it was a province of the Roman Empire. See **Galilee** for map.

Ju·de·o-Chris·tian (jü dā′ō kris′chən), *adj.* of or about the beliefs, ideas, and religious books shared by Judaism and Christianity: *the Judeo-Christian tradition.*

judge (juj), **1** *n.* a public official appointed or elected to hear and decide cases in a court of law. **2** *v.* to hear and decide a case in a court of law; act as a judge. **3** *n.* person chosen to settle a dispute or decide who wins a race, contest, etc. **4** *v.* to settle a dispute; decide who wins a race, contest, etc. **5** *n.* person who can decide how good a thing is: *a good judge of character, a poor judge of poetry.* **6** *v.* to form an opinion of: *The librarian judged the merits of the new book.* **7** *v.* to consider and blame; criticize; condemn: *You had little cause to judge him so harshly.* ❏ *v.* **judged, judg·ing.** —**judg′er,** *n.*

judge·ment (juj′mənt), *n.* judgment.

Judg·es (juj′iz), *n.* book of the Bible dealing with the period in Jewish history between the death of Joshua and Saul's reign.

judge·ship (juj′ship), *n.* position, duties, or term of office of a judge.

judg·ment (juj′mənt), *n.* **1** result of judging; opinion or estimate: *In my judgment dogs make better pets than cats.* ■ See Synonym Study at **opinion.** **2** ability to form sound opinions; power to judge well; good sense: *Since she has judgment in such matters, we will ask her.* **3** act of judging, especially a decision, decree, or sentence given by a judge in a court of law: *After the trial was over, the prisoner awaited the judgment of the court.* **4** decision made by anybody who judges. **5** criticism; condemnation; *pass judgment on your neighbors.* Also, **judgement.**

judg·men·tal (juj men′tl), *adj.* **1** apt to make harsh judgments: *She welcomes his advice because his comments are not judgmental.* **2** of or about judgment.

Judgment Day, (in Christian and some other religious use) the day of God's final judgment of all people at the end of the world; doomsday.

ju·di·cial (jü dish′əl), *adj.* **1** of or by judges; of or about courts or the administration of justice: *The judicial branch of government enforces the laws.* **2** of or suitable for a judge; impartial; fair: *a judicial mind.* —**ju·di′cial·ly,** *adv.*

ju·di·ci·ar·y (jü dish′ē er′ē), **1** *n.* branch of government that administers justice; system of courts of law of a country. **2** *n.* judges of a country, state, or city. **3** *adj.* of courts, judges, or the administration of justice. ❏ *n., pl.* **ju·di·ci·ar·ies.**

ju·di·cious (jü dish′əs), *adj.* having, using, or showing good judgment; wise; sensible: *Judicious parents encourage their children to make their own decisions.* —**ju·di·cious·ly,** *adv.* —**ju·di·cious·ness,** *n.*

ju·do (jü′dō), *n.* a modern form of jujitsu practiced as a sport or a means of self-defense.

> **WORD STORY** Judo comes from Japanese words meaning "soft way." **Jujitsu** comes from Japanese words meaning "soft art." Instead of strength, these methods often use yielding movements to defeat an opponent.

jug (jug), *n.* container for holding liquids. A jug usually has a short, narrow neck and a handle.

jug band, a small band that uses simple instruments such as harmonicas, guitars, or kazoos, and homemade ones such as jugs and washboards. Jug bands usually play blues and folk music.

jug·ger·naut (jug′ər nôt), *n.* something to which someone blindly devotes himself or herself or is cruelly sacrificed.

jug·gle (jug′əl), *v.* **1** to keep several objects in the air at the same time by quickly tossing and catching them: *She can juggle four balls at once.* **2** to manage the conflicting demands of two or more duties, activities, etc.: *juggle schoolwork and sports.* **3** to change by trickery: *He juggled the store's accounts to hide his thefts.* ❏ *v.* **jug·gled, jug·gling.**

> **WORD STORY** Juggle comes from a Latin word meaning "a joke." **Joke** comes from the same word. In old times, jugglers made jokes, did tricks, told stories, sang songs—whatever entertained people.

jug·gler (jug′lər), *n.* **1** person who can do juggling tricks. **2** person who uses tricks, deception, or fraud.

jug·u·lar (jug′yə lər), **1** *adj.* of or relating to the neck or throat. **2** *adj.* of or relating to the jugular vein. **3** *n.* jugular vein.

jugular vein, one of the two large veins in each side of the neck and head that return blood from the head and neck to the heart.

juice (jüs), *n.* **1** the liquid part of fruits, vegetables, and meats: *the juice of a lemon, meat juice.* **2** fluid in the body. The juices of the stomach help to digest food. **3** SLANG. electricity. —**juice′less,** *adj.*

juic·er (jü′sər), *n.* mechanical device used to get juice from fruits and vegetables.

juic·y (jü′sē), *adj.* **1** full of juice; having much juice: *a juicy orange.* **2** full of interest; lively: *juicy gossip.* ❏ *adj.* **juic·i·er, juic·i·est.** —**juic′i·ly,** *adv.* —**juic′i·ness,** *n.*

ju·jit·su (jü jit′sü), *n.* a Japanese way of wrestling or of fighting without weapons that uses the strength and weight of an opponent to your own advantage. Also, **jiujitsu.** [See Word Story at **judo**.]

juke·box (jük′boks′), *n.* an automatic, coin-operated record or CD player. ❏ *n., pl.* **juke·box·es.** [Jukebox comes from an African American word meaning "rowdy" and the English word *box*. Jukeboxes were first used in bars, where people sometimes behave badly.]

Jul., July.

Jul·ian (jü′lyən), *adj.* of Julius Caesar.

a	hat	ė	term	ô	order	ch	child		
ā	age	i	it	oi	oil	ng	long	ə	a in about
ä	far	ī	ice	ou	out	sh	she		e in taken
â	care	o	hot	u	cup	th	thin		i in pencil
e	let	ō	open	ů	put	ŦH	then		o in lemon
ē	equal	ò	saw	ü	rule	zh	measure		u in circus

Julian calendar, calendar introduced by Julius Caesar in 46 B.C. and widely used until 1582. The average length of a year in this calendar was 365¼ days. It was replaced by the Gregorian calendar.

Ju·li·et (jü′lē et *or* jü′lyət), *n.* heroine of Shakespeare's play *Romeo and Juliet.*

Julius Caesar. See **Caesar.**

Ju·ly (jù lī′), *n.* the seventh month of the year. It has 31 days. ❑ *n., pl.* **Ju·lys.** [July comes from Julius Caesar. It was named in his honor after he introduced the Julian calendar.]

jum·ble (jum′bəl), **1** *n.* a mixed-up mess; state of confusion; muddle: *The broken radio was a jumble of wires and loose parts.* **2** *v.* to mix or confuse: *She jumbled up everything in the drawer while hunting for her other blue sock.* ❑ *v.* **jum·bled, jum·bling.**

jum·bo (jum′bō), **1** *n.* a big, clumsy person, animal, or thing; something unusually large of its kind. **2** *adj.* very big: *a jumbo soda.* ❑ *n., pl.* **jum·bos.**

WORD STORY Jumbo comes from the name of a very large elephant exhibited by P. T. Barnum. No one knows how the elephant got his name. The explanation that it comes from a Swahili word meaning "hello" is not supported by evidence.

jumbo jet, a large airplane holding about 500 passengers.

jump (jump), **1** *v.* to spring from the ground; leap; bound: *Jump across the puddle.* **2** *n.* a spring from the ground; leap; bound: *The horse made a fine jump.* **3** *v.* to leap over: *jump a stream. The speeding car jumped the curb and crashed.* **4** *v.* to cause to jump: *jump a horse over a fence.* **5** *n.* thing to be jumped over: *The horse cleared the jump.* **6** *n.* distance jumped: *a ten-foot jump.* **7** *n.* contest in jumping for height or distance. **8** *v.* to give a sudden movement or jerk: *He jumped when the loud noise startled him.* **9** *n.* a sudden nervous start or jerk: *She gave a jump at the crash of thunder.* **10** *v.* to rise

jump (def. 2)

suddenly: *Prices jumped.* **11** *n.* a sudden rise: *a jump in the cost of living.* **12** *v.* to attack; pounce on: *Who would dare to jump someone with a black belt in karate?*

get the jump on or **have the jump on,** INFORMAL. to get or have an advantage over.

jump at, to accept eagerly and quickly: *I jumped at the chance to spend the summer on a ranch.*

jump on or **jump all over,** to blame; scold; criticize: *My brother jumped on me when he found out I'd eaten all the ice cream.*

SYNONYM STUDY Jump, leap, and spring all mean to move suddenly through the air. **Jump** is the general word: *He jumped into the swimming pool.* **Leap** means to jump high: *Leaping suddenly, she shot the basketball at the hoop.* **Spring** means to jump quickly and gracefully: *The dancers spring onto the stage.*

jump ball, (in basketball) the upward toss of a ball by the referee between two opposing players. Each player jumps up for the ball and tries to tap it to a teammate, putting it into play.

jump·er¹ (jum′pər), *n.* someone or something that jumps.

jump·er² (jum′pər), *n.* **1** a sleeveless dress to wear over a blouse. **2** a loose jacket. Jumpers are often worn to protect clothes.

jumper cables, pair of electric wires to connect a live battery to a dead battery, for jump-starting a motor vehicle.

jumping bean, Mexican plant seed that has a tiny caterpillar inside it. When the caterpillar moves, the seed tumbles or jumps.

jumping jack, **1** a toy person or animal that can be made to jump by pulling a string. **2** a physical exercise performed by jumping from an erect position with feet together and arms at the sides to a position with legs spread wide and hands touching overhead, and then returning to the original position.

jump rope, **1** game or exercise in which someone jumps over a rope that is being turned around him or her, underfoot and overhead. **2** the rope used in this game or exercise. Jump ropes often have handles.

jump shot, (in basketball) a shot made while jumping, especially when the player is at the highest point of the jump.

jump-start (jump′stärt′), **1** *v.* to start the engine of a motor vehicle by using jumper cables: *My car wouldn't start this morning, so I had to jump-start it.* **2** *n.* the act of jump-starting a motor vehicle.

jump·suit (jump′süt′), *n.* **1** a one-piece suit worn by parachutists. **2** any similar one-piece suit, usually for informal wear.

jump·y (jum′pē), *adj.* **1** easily excited or frightened; nervous. **2** moving by jumps; making sudden, sharp jerks. ❑ *adj.* **jump·i·er, jump·i·est.** **—jump′i·ness,** *n.*

jun·co (jung′kō), *n.* any of several small North American birds with gray or brown bodies and white bellies. Juncos are related to sparrows. ❑ *n., pl.* **jun·cos** or **jun·coes.**

junc·tion (jungk′shən), *n.* **1** place of joining or meeting. A railroad junction is a place where railroad lines meet or cross. **2** act of joining or the condition of being joined: *The junction of the two rivers results in a large flow of water downstream.*

junc·ture (jungk′chər), *n.* **1** point of time, especially a critical time or state of affairs: *At this juncture we must decide what move to make next.* **2** point or line where two things join; joint.

June (jün), *n.* the sixth month of the year. It has 30 days.

WORD STORY June comes from **Juno,** the Roman goddess who was queen of the gods. She was also the goddess of marriage, and June is a favorite time for weddings.

Ju·neau (jü′nō), *n.* port and capital of Alaska, in the SE part.

June bug or **June beetle,** any of several large brown beetles of North America that appear in June.

Jung (yùng), *n.* **Carl Gus·tav** (kärl gùs′täf), 1875-1961, Swiss psychologist and psychiatrist.

jun·gle (jung′gəl), *n.* wild land thickly overgrown with bushes, vines, trees, etc. Jungles are hot and humid regions with many kinds of plants and wild animals.

WORD STORY Jungle comes from a word in Sanskrit, a language of ancient India, meaning "a desert." Later, the word came to mean "a rough, wild place." When the English came to India, the land that looked wildest to them had the most trees and vines and bushes, so they called that *jungle.*

jungle gym, framework of steel bars for children to climb or swing on as a pastime.

jun·ior (jü′nyər), **1** *adj.* the younger (used of a son having the same name as his father): *Juan Bolivar, Junior, is the son of Juan Bolivar, Senior.* **2** *adj.* a younger person: *She is her sister's junior by two years.* **3** *adj.* of or for younger people: *a junior choir.* **4** *adj.* of lower rank or shorter service; of less standing than some others: *a junior partner.* **5** *n.* person of lower rank or shorter service. **6** *n.* student in the third year of high school or college. **7** *adj.* of or referring to these students: *the junior class.*

junior college, school offering the first two years of a regular four-year college course.

junior high school, school consisting of grades seven and eight, and sometimes six or nine, attended after elementary school and followed by high school.

junior varsity, a high school or college sports team that participates in competitions on a level just below the varsity.

ju·ni·per (jü′nə pər), *n.* any of several evergreen bushes or trees related to cypresses, with tiny bluish cones that look like berries. The cones of one kind of juniper contain an oil used in flavoring gin and in medicines.

junk¹ (jungk), **1** *n.* old metal, paper, rags, etc.; rubbish; trash. **2** *n.* anything that is worthless. **3** *v.* to throw away or discard as junk.

WORD STORY Junk¹ comes from an old English word meaning "worn-out rope." On sailing ships this rope was cut up and used for stopping leaks. People who saw piles of junk on ships used the word to mean any old trash.

junk² (jungk), *n.* a Chinese sailing ship.

jun·ket (jung′kit), **1** *n.* a sweet, custardlike dessert made from milk, thickened with rennet. **2** *n.* a trip, supposedly for official or business reasons, but actually for pleasure: *The lobby sponsored the senators' fact-finding junket to Hawaii.* **—jun′ket·er,** *n.*

junk food, INFORMAL. food that contains calories but has little other nutritional value.

junk·ie (jung′kē), *n.* **1** SLANG. person who enjoys something a great deal and cannot do without it; enthusiast; fan: *My brother's a chocolate junkie.* **2** INFORMAL. person who is addicted to drugs.

junk mail, printed matter that consists mostly of circulars, catalogs, and advertising pieces, and is sent through the mail to a large number of addresses.

junk·man (jungk′man′), *n.* (earlier) person who bought and sold old metal, paper, rags, etc. ❏ *n., pl.* **junk·men.**

junk·yard (jungk′yärd′), *n.* yard where junk, such as car parts, old metal, or used paper, is kept and sold.

Ju·no (jü′nō), *n.* the Roman goddess of marriage. She was the wife of Jupiter. The Greeks called her Hera.

jun·ta (jun′tə *or* hün′tə), *n.* **1** a political or military group holding power after a revolution. **2** an assembly or council for deliberation or administration, especially in Spain and Latin America. ❏ *n., pl.* **jun·tas.**

Ju·pi·ter (jü′pə tər), *n.* **1** the largest planet in the solar system, fifth in distance from the sun. **2** a Roman god, king of the gods and husband of Juno; Jove. The Greeks called him Zeus.

Jupiter (def. 1)—with some of its moons

Ju·ras·sic (jù ras′ik), *n.* (in geology) time between about 180 million and 135 million years ago. During this time, dinosaurs dominated the earth, and birds first appeared.

jur·is·dic·tion (jùr′is dik′shən), *n.* **1** right or power to give out justice; the giving out of justice. **2** authority; power; control: *The principal has jurisdiction over the teachers in a school.* **3** the things over which authority extends: *A school is the principal's jurisdiction.* **4** territory over which authority extends.

jur·is·pru·dence (jùr′i sprüd′ns), *n.* **1** science or philosophy of law. **2** system of laws. **3** branch of law. Medical jurisprudence deals with the use of medical knowledge in certain questions of law.

jur·ist (jùr′ist), *n.* **1** an expert in law. **2** a learned writer on law.

jur·or (jùr′ər), *n.* member of a jury.

jur·y (jùr′ē), *n.* **1** group of citizens selected to hear evidence in a case brought before a court of law. A jury must make its decision based on the evidence presented to it. **2** group of persons chosen to give a judgment or to decide who is the winner in a contest: *The jury gave her poem the first prize.* ❏ *n., pl.* **jur·ies.**

jur·y·man (jùr′ē mən), *n.* member of a jury; juror. ❏ *n., pl.* **jur·y·men.**

jur·y·wom·an (jùr′ē wùm′ən), *n.* a woman member of a jury. ❏ *n., pl.* **jur·y·wom·en.**

just (just), **1** *adv.* a very little while ago: *She has just gone.* **2** *adv.* barely: *The shot just missed the mark.* **3** *adv.* quite; truly; positively: *The weather is just glorious.* **4** *adv.* no more than; only; merely: *He went just because his friend was going.* **5** *adv.* exactly: *That is just a pound.* **6** *adv.* almost exactly; nearly: *See the picture just above.* **7** *adj.* right; fair: *We felt that $100 was not a* just price for our old car. **8** *adj.* deserved; merited: *a just reward.* **9** *adj.* having good grounds; well-founded: *just anger.* **10** *adj.* true; correct; exact: *just weights, a just description.* **11** *adj.* good; righteous: *The old man had led a just life.* **—just′ness,** *n.*

just about, almost; nearly; practically: *I was just about ready to give up when my experiment finally worked.*

just now, only a very short time ago: *I saw her just now.*

WORD FAMILY	Just and the words below are related. They all come from a Latin word meaning "a right" or "a law."

adjust	judge	jury	maladjusted
conjure	judicious	justice	perjury
injury	jurisdiction	justify	prejudice

jus·tice (jus′tis), *n.* **1** just conduct; fair dealing: *Judges should have a sense of justice.* **2** quality of being just; fairness; rightness: *the justice of a claim, uphold the justice of our cause.* **3** well-founded reason; rightfulness; lawfulness: *They complained with justice of the bad treatment they had received.* **4** just treatment; deserved reward or punishment. **5** trial and judgment by process of law: *a court of justice.* **6** a judge. The Supreme Court has nine justices.

do justice to, 1 to treat fairly. **2** to see the good points of; show proper appreciation for.

do yourself justice, to do as well as you really can do: *He did not do himself justice on the test.*

justice of the peace, a local magistrate who tries minor cases, administers oaths, performs civil marriages, etc.

jus·ti·fi·a·ble (jus′tə fī′ə bəl), *adj.* able to be justified; proper: *Striking the person in self-defense was ruled a justifiable act.* **—jus′ti·fi·a·bil′i·ty,** *n.* **—jus′ti·fi′a·bly,** *adv.*

jus·ti·fi·ca·tion (jus′tə fə kā′shən), *n.* **1** fact or circumstance that justifies; good reason or excuse: *What is your justification for being so late?* **2** act of justifying or condition of being justified.

jus·ti·fy (jus′tə fī), *v.* **1** to give a good reason for: *The fine quality of the cloth justifies its high price.* **2** to show to be just or right: *Can you justify your act?* **3** to clear of blame or guilt: *The court ruled that he was justified in hitting the man in self-defense.* ❏ *v.* **jus·ti·fied, jus·ti·fy·ing.**

just·ly (just′lē), *adv.* **1** in a just manner: *deal justly with others.* **2** rightly: *You argue justly.*

jut (jut), *v.* to stick out; stand out; project: *The pier juts out from the shore into the water.* ❏ *v.* **jut·ted, jut·ting.**

jute (jüt), *n.* **1** a strong fiber used for making coarse fabrics, rope, etc. Jute is obtained from two tropical plants. **2** either of these plants.

Jute (jüt), *n.* member of a Germanic tribe that, with the Angles and Saxons, conquered England in the A.D. 400s and 500s.

Jut·land (jut′lənd), *n.* peninsula on which most of Denmark and part of Germany are located.

juv., juvenile.

ju·ve·nile (jü′və nəl *or* jü′və nīl), **1** *adj.* young; youthful: *a juvenile audience, to have a juvenile appearance.* ■ See Synonym Study at **young. 2** *adj.* childish; infantile: *That game is too juvenile for high school seniors.* **3** *n.* a young person, especially someone under 18 years old. **4** *adj.* of or for boys and girls: *juvenile books.* **5** *n.* book for boys and girls. **6** *n.* actor who plays youthful parts.

juvenile court, court of law where cases involving children are heard.

juvenile delinquency, unlawful behavior by a boy or girl usually under 18 years of age.

juvenile delinquent, boy or girl usually under 18 years of age who has committed a legal offense.

jux·ta·pose (juk′stə pōz′), *v.* to put close together; place side by side. ❏ *v.* **jux·ta·posed, jux·ta·pos·ing.**

jux·ta·po·si·tion (juk′stə pə zish′ən), *n.* **1** act of putting things close together or side by side; **2** position close together or side by side.

J

a	hat	ė	term	ô	order	ch	child		
ā	age	i	it	oi	oil	ng	long		a in about
ä	far	ī	ice	ou	out	sh	she		e in taken
â	care	o	hot	u	cup	th	thin	ə	i in pencil
e	let	ō	open	ù	put	ŦH	then		o in lemon
ē	equal	ò	saw	ü	rule	zh	measure		u in circus

K¹ or **k** (kā), *n.* the 11th letter of the English alphabet. ❑ *n., pl.* **K's** or **k's.**

K² (kā), *n.* **1** unit of computer memory size, equal to 1024 (2^{10}). 8K bytes = 8192 (8 × 1024) bytes. **2** 1000: *The advertised salary for the job is $38 K.* ❑ *n., pl.* **K.** [**K** is short for **kilo-.** 1024 is the power of 2 closest to 1000.]

K, symbol for potassium.

k., **1** karat. **2** kilogram or kilograms. **3** kopeck.

Kaa·ba (kä′bə), *n.* the most sacred shrine of Islam, at Mecca, that is the goal of pilgrims. Muslims face this shrine while praying.

ka·bob (kə bob′), *n.* shish kebab.

Ka·bu·ki (kä bü′kē), *n.* a form of Japanese drama with song and dance, elegant costumes, and exaggerated acting. It dates from the 1600s.

Ka·bul (kä′bùl), *n.* capital of Afghanistan, in the E part.

ka·chi·na (kə chē′nə), *n.* **1** one of several supernatural ancestral spirits, in Pueblo religion, who bring rain, crops, and healing. **2** a masked dancer who acts as one of these spirits in religious ceremonies. **3** doll carved to stand for one of these spirits. ❑ *n., pl.* **ka·chi·nas.**

Kaf·ka (käf′kə), *n.* **Franz** (fränts), 1883-1924, Austrian writer. His most famous works are the story "The Metamorphosis" and the novel *The Trial.*

kaf·tan (kaf′tən *or* käf tän′), *n.* caftan.

Kai·lu·a (kī lü′ə), *n.* city on Oahu, Hawaii.

kai·ser (kī′zər), *n.* **1** title of the rulers of Germany and Austria before 1918. **2** title of the emperors of the Holy Roman Empire.

WORD STORY **Kaiser** comes from the name of Julius Caesar, who ruled Rome. **Czar** comes from the same word. Roman emperors used *Caesar* as an official title. German and Russian emperors borrowed the title to suggest they were as great as Caesar.

Ka·laal·lit Nu·naat (kä′lä lit′ nü′nät), official name of **Greenland.**

Ka·la·ha·ri Desert (kä′lä här′ē), desert and plateau region in S Africa.

kale (kāl), *n.* a garden vegetable with loose, curled, dark green leaves. Kale is related to cabbage.

ka·lei·do·scope (kə lī′də skōp), *n.* **1** tube containing bits of colored glass and two mirrors. As it is turned, it reflects continually changing patterns. **2** a continually changing pattern. [**Kaleidoscope** comes from Greek words meaning "pretty," "form," and "look at." The word began as a trade name in 1817.]

ka·lei·do·scop·ic (kə lī′də skop′ik), *adj.* of or like a kaleidoscope; continually changing. **—ka·lei′do·scop′i·cal·ly,** *adv.*

Ka·me·ha·me·ha I (kä mā′hä mā′hä), 1758?-1819, king of Hawaii. He founded the kingdom of Hawaii.

ka·mi·ka·ze (kä′mi kä′zē), **1** *n.* a Japanese pilot in World War II, ordered to fly an airplane loaded with bombs into a target, usually a ship. The pilot would be blown up together with the target. **2** *n.* airplane flown by such a pilot. **3** *adj.* acting in a dangerous, seemingly self-destructive way: *a kamikaze cabdriver.*

Kam·pa·la (käm pä′lä), *n.* capital of Uganda, near Lake Victoria.

Kam·pu·che·a (kam′pü chē′ə), *n.* Cambodia. **—Kam′pu·che′an,** *adj., n.*

Kan·din·sky (kan din′skē), *n.* **Was·si·ly** (vä′sə lē), 1866-1944, Russian painter. He is called the founder of abstract painting.

Ka·ne·o·he (kä nē ō′ē), *n.* city on Oahu, Hawaii.

kan·ga·roo (kang′gə rü′), *n.* any of various plant-eating mammals of Australia and New Guinea with small front legs and very strong hind legs which give them great leaping power. Kangaroos use their tails to balance themselves. The female kangaroo has a pouch in front in which she carries her young. ❑ *n., pl.* **kan·ga·roos** or **kan·ga·roo.** **—kan′ga·roo′like′,** *adj.*

kangaroo court, an unofficial, self-appointed court, such as a mock court by prisoners in a jail.

kangaroo rat, any of several small, burrowing rodents of dry areas of North America. Kangaroo rats have cheek pouches and long hind legs and tails.

Kans., Kansas.

Kan·sas (kan′zəs), *n.* one of the midwestern states of the United States. *Abbreviation:* KS or Kans. *Capital:* Topeka. [Kansas comes from the name of an American Indian tribe. The name means "people of the south wind."] **—Kan·san** (kan′zən), *n.*

Kansas City, 1 city in W Missouri, on the Missouri River. **2** city in NE Kansas adjoining it.

Kant (kant), *n.* **Im·man·u·el** (i man′yü əl), 1724-1804, German philosopher. ■ **Immanuel Kant** believed that people should follow only principles that they believe everyone else should follow too.

ka·o·lin (kā′ə lən), *n.* a fine white clay, used in making porcelain.

ka·pok (kā′pok), *n.* the silky fibers around the seeds of a tropical tree, used for stuffing mattresses and life preservers.

Ka·po·si's sar·co·ma (kä′pə sēz sär kō′mə), a form of cancer with purplish blotches on the skin, common in people with AIDS.

ka·put (kə put′), *adj.* INFORMAL. finished; destroyed: *Their romance is kaput.*

  go kaput, be unsuccessful; fail: *His business went kaput.*

Ka·ra·chi (kə rä′chē), *n.* city in S Pakistan, formerly the capital.

kar·a·o·ke (kar′ē ō′kē), *n.* music system that plays a recorded accompaniment while a person or group sings into a microphone so that the singing is played with the music. The system can record singing and music together for later listening. [Karaoke comes from Japanese words meaning "vacant" and "band." The music is recorded without the vocal part.]

kar·at (kar′ət), *n.* 1/24 part of gold by weight in an alloy; carat. A gold ring of 18 karats is 18 parts pure gold and six parts other metals. ■ Other words that sound like this are **caret** and **carrot.**

ka·ra·te (kə rä′tē), *n.* a Japanese method of fighting without weapons by striking with the hands, elbows, knees, and feet at parts of the opponent's body which can easily be injured. [Karate comes from Japanese words meaning "empty hands." It got the name because it uses no weapons.]

Kar·loff (kär′lof), *n.* **Bor·is** (bôr′əs), 1887-1969, English horror movie actor. His most famous role was that of the monster in *Frankenstein.*

kar·ma (kär′mə), *n.* **1** (in Buddhism and Hinduism) all of a person's acts, words, and thoughts, believed to determine the form of reincarnation and the next life. **2** fate; destiny. ❑ *n., pl.* **kar·mas.**

Kar·pov (kar′pof), *n.* **An·a·to·ly** (an′ə tō′lē), born 1951, Russian chess player. He was the world chess champion from 1975 to 1985.

ka·sha (kä′shə *or* kash′ə), *n.* **1** a grain like buckwheat, wheat, or millet. **2** porridge or mush made with this hulled or crushed grain.

Kash·mir (kash mir′), *n.* area north of India, claimed by both India and Pakistan.

Kas·par·ov (kas′pər of), *n.* **Gar·y** (gâr′ē), born 1963, Russian chess player. He has been the world chess champion since 1985.

Kath·man·du or **Kat·man·du** (kät′män dü′), *n.* capital of Nepal.

Kat·mai National Park (kat′mī), national park in SW Alaska, containing a number of volcanoes, several of them active.

ka·ty·did (kā′tē did′), *n.* any of various large, green, long-horned grasshoppers. The male katydid makes a shrill noise by rubbing its front wings together.

Kau·ai (kou ī′ *or* kou′ī), *n.* the fourth largest island of Hawaii.

kay·ak (kī′ak), *n.* **1** an Eskimo canoe made of skins stretched over a light frame of wood or bone with an opening in the middle for a person. **2** a similar craft of other material.

Ka·zakh·stan (kə zäk′stän), *n.* country in SW Asia. *Capital:* Alma-Ata.

ka·zoo (kə zü′), *n.* a toy musical instrument that makes a buzzing sound when the player hums into it. ❑ *n., pl.* **ka·zoos.**

Keat·on (kēt′n), *n.* **Bus·ter** (bus′tər), 1895-1966, American silent movie actor.

Keats (kēts), *n.* **John,** 1795-1821, English poet. His poems include "On a Grecian Urn" and "To a Nightingale."

kayak (def. 2)

ke·bab (kə bob′), *n.* shish kebab.

keel (kēl), *n.* the main timber or steel piece that extends the whole length of the bottom of a ship or boat.

  keel over, 1 to turn upside down; upset: *The sailboat keeled over in the storm.* **2** to fall over suddenly: *keel over in a faint.*

  on an even keel, 1 horizontal. **2** calm; steady: *In spite of all the confusion, they managed to remain on an even keel.*

keen[1] (kēn), *adj.* **1** having a sharp edge for cutting: *a keen blade.* **2** piercing; sharp: *a keen wind, keen hunger, keen wit.* **3** strong; vivid: *keen competition.* **4** quickly and clearly aware; able to work quickly and carefully: *She has a keen mind.* ■ See Synonym Study at **sharp. 5** full of enthusiasm; eager: *He is keen about sailing.* ■ See Synonym Study at **eager. 6** SLANG. excellent; wonderful: *That's a keen bike.* **—keen′ly,** *adv.* **—keen′ness,** *n.*

keen[2] (kēn), **1** *n.* a wailing lament for the dead. **2** *v.* to wail; lament.

keep (kēp), **1** *v.* to have for a long time or forever: *You may keep this book.* **2** *v.* to have and not let go: *Can you keep a secret?* **3** *v.* to guard; take care of and protect: *The bank keeps money for people.* **4** *v.* to hold back; prevent: *Shutters keep rain away from the windows.* **5** *v.* to maintain in good condition; preserve: *A refrigerator keeps food fresh.* **6** *v.* to stay in good condition: *Milk does not keep long in hot weather.* **7** *v.* to stay or cause to stay the same; continue: *Keep the fire burning.* **8** *v.* to do the right thing with; celebrate; observe: *keep Thanksgiving as a holiday.* **9** *v.* to be faithful to: *keep a promise.* **10** *v.* to have and take care of; raise: *She keeps chickens.* **11** *n.* food and a place to sleep: *He works for his keep.* **12** *n.* the strongest part of a castle or fort. ❑ *v.* **kept, keep·ing.**

  for keeps, 1 for the winner to keep his or her winnings: *We were playing marbles for keeps.* **2** forever: *They have moved away for keeps.*

  keep on, to continue; go on: *We kept on swimming in spite of the rain.*

  keep to yourself, 1 to avoid associating with others: *That man always keeps to himself.* **2** to keep something secret.

  keep up, 1 to continue; prevent from ending: *We kept up a small fire.* **2** to maintain in good condition. **3** to not fall behind.

  keep up with, 1 to not fall behind; go or move as fast as: *You walk so fast that I cannot keep up with you.* **2** to stay informed about: *I couldn't keep up with sports news while I was studying for my test.*

keep·er (kē′pər), *n.* **1** someone who watches, guards, or takes care of people, animals, or things: *a lighthouse keeper, a zoo keeper.* **2** something large enough, good enough, etc., to be kept, not put back or discarded.

keep·ing (kē′ping), *n.* **1** care; charge: *The two older children were left in their grandparents' keeping.* **2** celebration; observance: *The keeping of Thanksgiving Day is an old American custom.* **3** agreement; harmony: *Don't trust him; his actions are not in keeping with his promises.*

a	hat	ė	term	ô	order	ch	child		
ā	age	i	it	oi	oil	ng	long	ə	a in about
ä	far	ī	ice	ou	out	sh	she		e in taken
â	care	o	hot	u	cup	th	thin		i in pencil
e	let	ō	open	u̇	put	ŦH	then		o in lemon
ē	equal	ȯ	saw	ü	rule	zh	measure		u in circus

keep·sake (kēp′sāk′), *n.* something kept in memory of the giver: *Before my friend moved, she gave me her photo as a keepsake.*

keg (keg), *n.* a small barrel, usually holding less than 10 gallons (38 liters).

Kel·ler (kel′ər), *n.* **Hel·en** (hel′ən), 1880-1968, American writer and lecturer. Though unable to see or hear because of a sickness in infancy, she nevertheless learned to speak and read.

Kel·ly (kel′ē), *n.* **Grace** (grās), 1929-1982, American movie actress. ■ **Grace Kelly** won an Academy Award in *The Country Girl* in 1954. In 1956 she married Prince Rainier III of Monaco, becoming Princess Grace of Monaco.

kelp (kelp), *n.* **1** any of various large, tough, brown seaweeds. **2** ashes of these seaweeds, used as a source of iodine.

Kel·vin (kel′vən), *adj.* of, based on, or according to a scale for measuring temperature on which 273 degrees marks the freezing point of water, 373 degrees marks the boiling point, and 0 degrees marks absolute zero.

ken (ken), **1** *n.* range of knowledge: *What happens on Mars is no longer beyond our ken.* **2** *v.* SCOTTISH. to know. ❑ *v.* **kenned** or **kent** (kent), **ken·ning.**

Ke·nai Fjords National Park (kē′nī), a national park in S Alaska, containing a rugged seacoast and a huge floating ice sheet.

Ken·ne·dy (ken′ə dē), *n.* **1 Ed·ward** (ed′wərd), born 1932, American political leader. He has been a senator from Massachusetts since 1962. He is the younger brother of John and Robert. **2 John Fitzgerald**, 1917-1963, the 35th president of the United States, 1961-1963. He was assassinated in Dallas, Texas on November 22, 1963. **3 Rob·ert** (rob′ərt), 1925-1968, American political leader. He was the attorney general of the United States from 1961 to 1964 and a senator from New York from 1965 to 1968. He was assassinated in Los Angeles in June 1968, while running for president. **4 Cape**, former name of **Cape Canaveral**, used from 1963 to 1973.

ken·nel (ken′l), **1** *n.* house for a dog or dogs. **2** *n.* Often, **kennels**, *pl.* place where dogs are bred or boarded. **3** *v.* to put into or keep in a kennel. ❑ *v.* **ken·neled, ken·nel·ing** or **ken·nelled, ken·nel·ling.** [Kennel comes from a Latin word meaning "dog." Canine comes from the same word.]

Ken·nel·ly-Heav·i·side layer (ken′ə lē hev′ē sīd), E region.

Ken·tuck·y (kən tuk′ē), *n.* one of the south central states of the United States. *Abbreviation:* KY or Ky. *Capital:* Frankfort. [Kentucky comes from a Cherokee word meaning "land of tomorrow" or "meadow land."] —**Ken·tuck′i·an,** *n.*

Ken·ya (ken′yə *or* kē′nyə), *n.* country in E Africa. *Capital:* Nairobi. —**Ken′yan,** *adj., n.*

Ken·yat·ta (ken yä′tə), *n.* **Jo·mo** (jō′mō), 1890?-1978, first president of Kenya from 1964 to 1978.

Kep·ler (kep′lər), *n.* **Jo·hann** (yō′han), 1571-1630, German astronomer. ■ **Johann Kepler** discovered three important laws of planetary motion. He was the first person to realize that planets moved around the sun in ellipses, instead of circles.

kept (kept), *v.* past tense and past participle of **keep**: *I gave him the book and he kept it. The milk was kept cool.*

ker·a·tin (ker′ə tin), *n.* protein substance that makes up hair, horns, feathers, toenails, and fingernails.

ker·chief (kėr′chif), *n.* **1** piece of cloth worn over the head or around the neck. **2** handkerchief. [Kerchief comes from French words meaning "to cover the head."]

Ke·ren·sky (kə ren′skē), *n.* **Alexander**, 1881-1970, Russian revolutionary leader and premier. He was active in the Russian Revolution of 1917.

ker·nel (kėr′nl), *n.* **1** the softer part inside the hard shell of a nut or inside the stone of a fruit. **2** a grain or seed of a cereal plant, such as wheat or corn. **3** the central or most important part of anything; core. ■ Another word that sounds like this is **colonel.**

ker·o·sene or **ker·o·sine** (ker′ə sēn′), *n.* a thin oil distilled from petroleum; coal oil. It is used as fuel in lamps, stoves, and some kinds of engines.

Ker·o·uac (ker′ə wak), *n.* **Jack** (jak), 1922-1969, American writer. His most famous novel is *On the Road.*

kes·trel (kes′trəl), *n.* any of various small falcons of North and South America that often hover facing the wind; sparrow hawk. Kestrels eat birds, insects, and other small animals.

ketch (kech), *n.* a small sailing ship with a large mainmast toward the bow and a smaller mast toward the stern. ❑ *n., pl.* **ketch·es.**

ketch·up (kech′əp), *n.* sauce to use with meat, fish, etc. Tomato ketchup is made of tomatoes, onions, salt, sugar, and spices. Also, **catchup** or **catsup.**

ket·tle (ket′l), *n.* **1** any metal container for boiling liquids, cooking fruit, etc. **2** teakettle.

a fine kettle of fish, an awkward state of affairs; mess; muddle.

ket·tle·drum (ket′l drum′), *n.* a large brass or copper drum with a round bottom and a skin called parchment stretched over the top.

key¹ (kē), **1** *n.* a small metal tool for locking and unlocking the lock of a door, a padlock, etc. **2** *n.* anything shaped like it: *a roller-skate key.* **3** *n.* one of a set of levers pressed down by the fingers in playing a piano or other instruments, and in operating a typewriter or computer. **4** *n.* the answer to a puzzle or a problem: *The key to this puzzle will be published next week.* **5** *n.* sheet or book of answers: *a key to a test.* **6** *n.* list or table that explains abbreviations, symbols, etc., used in a dictionary, map, etc. There is a pronunciation key in this dictionary. **7** *n.* place that commands or gives control of a sea, a district, etc., because of its position: *Gibraltar is the key to the Mediterranean.* **8** *adj.* controlling; very important: *the key industries of a nation.* **9** *n.* an important or essential person, thing, etc. **10** *n.* pin, bolt, wedge, or other piece put in a hole or space to hold parts together. **11** *v.* to fasten or adjust with a key. **12** *n.* scale or system of related tones in music which are based on a keynote: *a song written in the key of C.* **13** *n.* tone of voice; style of thought or expression: *The poet wrote in a melancholy key.* **14** *v.* to regulate the pitch of; tune: *key a musical instrument.* **15** *n.* samara. ❑ *n., pl.* **keys;** *v.* **keyed, key·ing.** ■ Other words that can sound like this are **cay** and **quay.** —**key′less,** *adj.*

key up, to excite; make nervous: *He was keyed up for the party.*

key² (kē), *n.* a low island; reef; cay. There are keys south of Florida. ❑ *n., pl.* **keys.** ■ Another word that can sound like this is **quay.**

WORD STORY Key² comes from an American Indian word of the Caribbean area. Spanish explorers in this area came to so many islands of this sort that they borrowed the local name, which became a Spanish word and then an English one.

Key (kē), *n.* **Fran·cis Scott** (fran′sis), 1779-1843, American writer who wrote the words to "The Star-Spangled Banner."

key·board (kē′bôrd′), **1** *n.* the set of keys in a piano, organ, typewriter, computer, etc. **2** *v.* to type data into a computer or calculator.

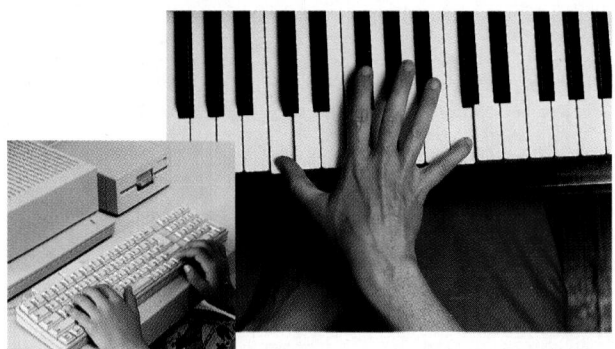

keyboards

key card, a magnetized plastic card used like a key for doors that have electronic lock systems.

key·hole (kē′hōl′), *n.* opening in a lock through which a key is inserted.

Keynes (kānz), *n.* **John May·nard** (mā′nərd), 1883-1946, British economist. He believed that governments should increase spending and lower interest rates to avoid economic depressions.

key·note (kē′nōt′), *n.* **1** tone on which a scale or system of tones in music is based; tonic. **2** main idea; guiding principle: *World peace was the keynote of the speech.*

key·pad (kē′pad′), *n.* group of keys like the keys of a typewriter or computer, but arranged like the keys of a calculator and having a special purpose, such as entering large sets of numbers into a computer.

key·punch (kē′punch′), *n.* machine having a keyboard similar to that of a typewriter, used to record and code information by punching patterns of holes in cards or tapes. ❏ *n., pl.* **key·punch·es.**

key signature, a group of sharp signs or flat signs written on a musical score after a clef to indicate the key of the music.

key·stone (kē′stōn′), *n.* **1** the middle stone at the top of an arch, holding the other stones or pieces in place. **2** part on which other related parts depend.

key·stroke (kē′strōk′), *n.* a stroke of a single key on a computer, calculator, typewriter, or similar machine.

kg or **kg.,** kilogram or kilograms.

Khadafy (kä dä′fē), *n.* See **Qaddafi.**

khak·i (kak′ē *or* kä′kē), **1** *n.* a dull yellowish brown. **2** *adj.* dull yellowish brown. **3** *n.* a heavy twilled cloth of this color, used especially for soldiers' uniforms. **4** *n.pl.* **khakis, a** uniform made of this cloth: *Khakis will be worn in the parade.* **b** pants made of khaki or of khaki-colored cloth. [**Khaki** comes from a Persian word meaning "dust." The cloth got its name in India because it didn't show the dust of travel.]

khan (kän), *n.* **1** (formerly) a title of a ruler among Tartar or Mongol tribes. **2** title of respect in Iran, Afghanistan, India, etc.

Khar·kov (kär′kóf), *n.* city in NE Ukraine.

Khar·toum (kär tüm′), *n.* capital of Sudan, on the Nile.

Khoi·khoi (koi′koi′), *n.* member of a people who live mainly in southwest Africa. ▪ See Usage Note at **Hottentot.** ❏ *n., pl.* **Khoi·khois** or **Khoi·khoi.**

Kho·mei·ni (kō mā′nē *or* hō mā′nē), *n.* Ayatollah **Ru·hol·lah** (rü-hōl′ə), 1900-1989, Iranian political and religious leader.

Khru·shchev (krüsh chóf′), *n.* **Ni·ki·ta** (ni kē′tə), 1894-1971, premier of the Soviet Union from 1958 to 1964.

Khy·ber Pass (ki′bər), important mountain pass between N Pakistan and E Afghanistan.

kib·ble (kib′əl), *n.* dry dog food.

kib·butz (ki büts′), *n.* an Israeli communal settlement, especially a farm cooperative. ❏ *n., pl.* **kib·butz·im** (ki bü tsēm′).

kib·itz (kib′its), *v.* INFORMAL. to look on and give unwanted advice: *She doesn't want him to kibitz while she is pitching.* **–kib′itz·er,** *n.*

kick (kik), **1** *v.* to strike or strike out at with the foot: *That horse kicks when anyone comes near it.* **2** *v.* to drive, force, or move by kicking: *kick a ball along the ground.* **3** *v.* to make a score by kicking: *kick a field goal in football.* **4** *n.* act of kicking: *lined up for the kick.* **5** *n.* ball that has been kicked, as in football or soccer. **6** *n.* distance that a kicked ball travels: *a long, high kick.* **7** *n.* motion of the legs in swimming to move the swimmer along. **8** *n.* a blow with the foot: *The horse's kick knocked me down.* **9** *n.* the recoil or backward motion of a gun when it is fired. **10** *v.* to spring back when fired; recoil: *This shotgun kicks.* **11** *v.* to get rid of; free yourself of: *He finally kicked the habit of smoking.* **12** *v.* INFORMAL. to find fault; complain; grumble: *My sister didn't kick when I ate her piece of cake.* **13** *n.* INFORMAL. complaint; objection. **14** *n.* excitement; thrill: *She got a kick out of winning the game.*

kick around, INFORMAL. **1** to treat roughly. **2** to go about aimlessly. **3** to consider or discuss a plan, topic, etc.

kick back, 1 to spring back suddenly and unexpectedly: *The gun kicked back with great force.* **2** INFORMAL. to return a portion of money received as a fee. **3** INFORMAL. to relax.

kick off, 1 to put a football in play with a kick at the beginning of each half and after a score has been made. **2** INFORMAL. to begin; start: *The sale will kick off the store's new hours.*

kick out, to expel or turn out in a humiliating or disgraceful way: *be kicked out of school.*

kick up, INFORMAL. to start; cause: *kick up a fuss.*

kick·back (kik′bak′), *n.* INFORMAL. portion or amount of a fee returned, especially as a bribe for having received a contract.

kick·ball (kik′bôl′), *n.* a game similar to baseball, in which the ball is rolled instead of thrown and kicked instead of hit.

kick·off (kik′ôf′), *n.* **1** kick that puts a football in play at the beginning of each half and after a score has been made. **2** an event that marks a beginning: *The sale is a kickoff for the new store.*

kick·stand (kik′stand′), *n.* a metal rod or other device attached to the frame or rear axle of a bicycle or motorcycle, holding the bike upright when it is not in use.

kid[1] (kid), **1** *n.* INFORMAL. child. **2** *adj.* INFORMAL. younger: *They're playing in the yard with my kid brother.* **3** *n.* a young goat. **4** *n.* leather made from the skin of young goats: *kid gloves.*

kid[2] (kid), *v.* **1** to tease playfully; talk in a joking way; banter. ▪ See Synonym Study at **ridicule.** **2** to deceive; fool. ❏ *v.* **kid·ded, kid·ding. –kid′der,** *n.*

Kidd (kid), *n.* **William,** 1645?-1701, Scottish privateer and pirate, known as "Captain Kidd."

kid·die or **kid·dy** (kid′ē), **1** *n.* child; kid. **2** *adj.* for or involving children. ❏ *n., pl.* **kid·dies.**

kid gloves, gloves made of soft kidskin.

handle with kid gloves, to treat with great care.

kid·nap (kid′nap), *v.* to carry off someone by force. ❏ *v.* **kid·napped, kid·nap·ping** or **kid·naped, kid·nap·ing. –kid′nap·per** or **kid′nap·er,** *n.*

kid·ney (kid′nē), *n.* **1** one of the pair of organs in the body that separates waste matter from the blood and passes it off through the bladder as urine. **2** kidney or kidneys of an animal, cooked for food. ❏ *n., pl.* **kid·neys.**

kidney bean, a large, red bean, shaped like a kidney and used as a vegetable.

kid·skin (kid′skin′), *n.* leather made from the skin of young goats.

Kiel (kēl), *n.* port in NW Germany, on the Baltic Sea.

kiel·ba·sa (kēl bä′sə), *n.* a garlic-flavored, smoked sausage. ❏ *n., pl.* **kiel·ba·sas, kiel·ba·sy** (kēl bä′sē).

Kiel Canal, a ship canal in NW Germany from the North Sea to the Baltic Sea.

Kier·ke·gaard (kir′kə gärd), *n.* **Sö·ren Aa·bye** (sėr′ən ô′bü), 1813-1855, Danish philosopher and theologian. ▪ **Kierkegaard** believed that people couldn't achieve religious belief by reason alone. He felt that people needed to make "a leap of faith" in order to believe wholeheartedly.

Ki·ev (kē′ef *or* kē ev′), *n.* capital of Ukraine, in the N part.

Ki·ga·li (ki gä′lē), *n.* capital of Rwanda, in the central part.

Ki·lau·e·a (kē′lou ā′ə), *n.* crater on the volcano Mauna Loa, in Hawaii, 4040 feet (1231 m) high.

Kil·i·man·ja·ro (kil′ə mən jär′ō), *n.* **Mount,** the highest mountain in Africa, in NE Tanzania, 19,340 feet (5895 meters) high.

Kilimanjaro

a	hat	ė	term	ô	order	ch	child		a in about
ā	age	i	it	oi	oil	ng	long		e in taken
ä	far	ī	ice	ou	out	sh	she	ə	i in pencil
â	care	o	hot	u	cup	th	thin		o in lemon
e	let	ō	open	u̇	put	ŦH	then		u in circus
ē	equal	ò	saw	ü	rule	zh	measure		

kill (kil), **1** *v.* to put to death; cause the death of: *A bolt of lightning killed the tree.* **2** *v.* to cause death: *"Thou shalt not kill."* **3** *n.* act of killing. **4** *n.* animal killed. **5** *v.* to get rid of; destroy: *kill odors.* **6** *v.* to cancel a word, item, etc.; delete. **7** *v.* to defeat or veto a legislative bill. **8** *v.* to use up time: *We killed an hour at the zoo.* **9** *v.* to cause pain to: *My sore foot is killing me.* **10** INFORMAL. *v.* to turn something off: *Please kill the lights.* ■ Another word that can sound like this is **kiln.**

> **SYNONYM STUDY** **Kill, murder,** and **massacre** all mean to cause death. **Kill** is the general word: *The cat killed the mouse.* **Murder** means to kill someone on purpose and against the law: *No one knows who murdered the lawyer.* **Massacre** means to kill cruelly and in large numbers: *Buffalo were massacred for their hides and horns.*

kill·deer (kil′dir′), *n.* an American shorebird that has two black bands across its breast. It has a loud, shrill cry that sounds like its name. A killdeer is a kind of plover. ◻ *n., pl.* **kill·deers** or **kill·deer.**
kill·er (kil′ər), *n.* person, animal, or thing that kills.
killer bee, a kind of bee that is a crossbreed of African and European honeybees, noted for its readiness to sting; Africanized honeybee. First bred in Brazil, these bees are now wild from Argentina to the southern United States.
killer whale, a large dolphin that travels in groups and kills and eats large fish, seals, and even whales; orca.

killer whale—up to 30 ft. (9 m) long

kill·ing (kil′ing), **1** *adj.* deadly; fatal: *A killing frost ruined the tomato plants.* **2** *n.* a sudden large profit: *She made a killing in the stock market.*
kill·joy (kil′joi′), *n.* someone who spoils other people's fun.
kiln (kil *or* kiln), *n.* furnace or oven for burning, baking, or drying something. Limestone is burned in a kiln to make lime. Bricks and pottery are baked in a kiln. [**Kiln** comes from a Latin word meaning "kitchen," another place to bake.] ■ Another word that can sound like this is **kill.**
ki·lo (kē′lō), *n.* **1** kilogram. **2** kilometer. ◻ *n., pl.* **ki·los.**
kilo-, *prefix.* **1** one thousand: *kilogram = one thousand grams.* **2** (in data processing) 1024: *kilobyte = 1024 bytes.*
kil·o·byte (kil′ə bīt′), *n.* unit of computer information, equal to 1024 bytes.
kil·o·cal·or·ie (kil′ə kal′ə rē), *n.* 1000 small calories; large calorie.
kil·o·cy·cle (kil′ə sī′kəl), *n.* kilohertz.
kil·o·gram (kil′ə gram), *n.* the basic unit of weight or mass in the metric system, equal to 1000 grams.
kil·o·hertz (kil′ə herts′), *n.* 1000 hertz, used to express the frequency of radio waves. ◻ *n., pl.* **kil·o·hertz.**
kil·o·li·ter (kil′ə lē′tər), *n.* unit of volume equal to 1000 liters, or one cubic meter.
ki·lom·e·ter (kə lom′ə tər), *n.* unit of length equal to 1000 meters.
kil·o·ton (kil′ə tun′), *n.* **1** unit of weight equal to 1000 tons. **2** unit of atomic power equal to the energy released by one thousand tons of exploding TNT.
kil·o·watt (kil′ə wot′), *n.* unit of electrical power, equal to 1000 watts.
kil·o·watt-hour (kil′ə wot′our′), *n.* unit of electrical power equal to the work done by one kilowatt in one hour.

kilt (kilt), *n.* a pleated skirt reaching to the knees, worn especially by men in the Scottish Highlands. [**Kilt** probably comes from Danish words meaning "to tuck up." Originally, a kilt was one large piece of cloth tucked at the waist with a belt.]
kil·ter (kil′tər), *n.* **out of kilter,** out of working order; not in good condition: *Our radio is so out of kilter that we cannot tune in most stations.*
Kim (kim), *n.* **1 Il Sung** (il′ sung′), 1912-1994, president of North Korea and head of the Communist party of North Korea from 1948 to 1994. **2 Jong Il** (jong′ il), born 1942, president of North Korea since 1994, son of Kim Il Sung.
kim·chi or **kim·chee** (kim′chē), *n.* pickled or fermented cabbage, eaten in Korea.
ki·mo·no (kə mō′nə), *n.* **1** a loose outer garment held in place by a sash, worn by Japanese men and women. **2** a woman's loose robe. ◻ *n., pl.* **ki·mo·nos.**
kin (kin), **1** *n.* a person's family or relatives; kinfolk: *All our kin came to the family reunion.* **2** *n.* family relationship; connection by birth or marriage: *What kin is she to you?* **3** *adj.* related: *Your cousin is also kin to me.*
next of kin, nearest living relative.
-kin, *suffix.* little: *lambkin = a little lamb.*
kind¹ (kīnd), *adj.* **1** doing good rather than harm; friendly: *Kind people try to help others. Sharing your lunch was a kind thing to do.* **2** gentle: *Be kind to animals.*

> **SYNONYM STUDY** **Kind¹, gentle,** and **good-natured** all mean friendly and thoughtful. **Kind** means friendly and good to others: *It was kind of them to offer us a ride home.* **Gentle** can mean kind and careful to avoid hurting others: *He is very gentle with his baby brother.* **Good-natured** means kind and cheerful: *Mom is very good-natured about all the frogs and snakes I bring home.*

kind² (kīnd), *n.* **1** group of individuals or objects having characteristics in common; class; sort: *He likes many kinds of candy. A kilt is a kind of skirt.* **2** natural group; race: *The wolf hunted with others of its kind.*
in kind, 1 in goods or produce, not in money: *They made payments in kind.* **2** in something of the same sort: *I returned their insults in kind by insulting them.* **3** in nature or quality: *There was a difference in kind, not merely in amount.*
kind of, INFORMAL. nearly; almost; somewhat; rather: *The room was kind of dark.*
of a kind, of the same sort; alike: *The cakes were all of a kind—chocolate.*
kin·der·gar·ten (kin′dər gärt′n), *n.* school or class for children from about four to six years old that educates them by games, toys, and pleasant occupations.

> **WORD STORY** **Kindergarten** comes from German words meaning "children" and "garden." People thought that children should grow in this class like flowers grow in a garden.

kin·der·gart·ner or **kin·der·gar·ten·er** (kin′dər gärt′nər), *n.* child who goes to kindergarten.
kind·heart·ed (kīnd′här′tid), *adj.* having or showing a kind heart; kindly; sympathetic. **—kind′heart′ed·ly,** *adv.* **—kind′heart′ed·ness,** *n.*
kin·dle (kin′dl), *v.* **1** to set on fire; light: *I used a match to kindle the wood.* **2** to catch fire; begin to burn: *This damp wood will never kindle.* **3** to stir up; arouse: *kindle anger, kindle enthusiasm.* **4** to light up; brighten: *The girl's face kindled as she told about the circus.* ◻ *v.* **kin·dled, kin·dling.**

> **SYNONYM STUDY** **Kindle** and **ignite** both mean to set on fire. **Kindle** means to get something like wood to burn, usually by working at it: *He tried to kindle the charcoal in the barbecue grill.* **Ignite** means to set fire to something that burns easily: *Sparks ignited the dry grass, and the fire spread quickly.*

kind·li·ness (kīnd′lē nis), *n.* **1** kindly feeling or quality. **2** a kindly act. ◻ *n., pl.* **kind·li·ness·es** for 2.
kin·dling (kind′ling), *n.* small pieces of wood for starting a fire.

kind·ly (kīnd′lē), **1** *adj.* kind; friendly: *kindly faces, kindly people.* **2** *adv.* in a kind or friendly way: *We thank you kindly for your help.* **3** *adj.* pleasant; agreeable: *a kindly shower.* **4** *adv.* pleasantly; agreeably: *He does not take kindly to criticism.* **5** *adv.* please: *Kindly help me lift this box of books.* ❑ *adj.* **kind·li·er, kind·li·est.**

kind·ness (kīnd′nis), *n.* **1** kind nature; being kind: *We admire her kindness.* **2** kind treatment: *Thank you for your kindness.* **3** a kind act. ❑ *n., pl.* **kind·ness·es** for 3.

kin·dred (kin′drid), **1** *adj.* like; similar; related: *We are studying about dew, frost, and kindred facts of nature.* **2** *n.* a person's family or relatives.

kin·es·thet·ic (kin′əs thet′ik), *adj.* of or related to sensations of motion from the muscles and joints.

ki·net·ic (ki net′ik), *adj.* **1** of motion. **2** caused by motion.

kinetic energy, energy of an object in motion.

kin·folk (kin′fōk′), *n.pl.* a person's family or relatives; kin. Also, **kinsfolk.**

kin·folks (kin′fōks), *n.pl.* kinsfolk.

king (king), *n.* **1** the male ruler of a nation; male sovereign, usually with a hereditary position and with either absolute or limited power. **2** man supreme in a certain sphere: *a baseball king, a software king.* **3** something most important, especially economically: *Before synthetic fibers were invented, cotton was king.* **4** an important piece in chess. A king can move one square in any direction. **5** piece that has moved entirely across the board in checkers. It can move in any direction. **6** a playing card bearing a picture of a king. —**king′like′,** *adj.*

King (king), *n.* **1 Bill·ie Jean** (bil′ē jēn′), born 1943, American tennis star. In 1971, she became the first woman tennis player to win $100,000 in a single year. **2 Cor·et·ta Scott** (kôr et′ə), born 1927, American civil rights leader. She is the widow of Martin Luther King, Jr. **3 Mar·tin Luther, Jr.** (mär′tən), 1929-1968, American minister who led a nonviolent movement to end racial discrimination in the United States. He was assassinated in Memphis, Tennessee on April 4, 1968. **4 William Ly·on Mac·Ken·zie** (lī′ən mə ken′zē), 1874-1950, Canadian political leader. He was the prime minister of Canada from 1921 to 1926, from 1926 to 1930, and from 1935 to 1948.

king·bird (king′bėrd′), *n.* any of several American flycatchers, especially a bold, black and white flycatcher of the eastern United States and Canada.

king crab, 1 a large crab found on the shores of the northern Pacific that is good to eat. **2** horseshoe crab.

king·dom (king′dəm), *n.* **1** nation that is governed by a king or a queen; land or territory ruled by one monarch. **2** a realm, domain, or province: *The mind is the kingdom of thought.* **3** the basic category used in classifying living things. Mice belong to the animal kingdom, maples to the plant kingdom, and mushrooms to the kingdom of fungi.

king·fish·er (king′fish′ər), *n.* any of numerous bright-colored birds with large heads, crests, and strong beaks. Kingfishers eat fish and insects.

King James Version, an English translation of the Bible written with the support of James I, published in 1611. The King James Version is still used by many Protestants.

king·ly (king′lē), **1** *adj.* of or like a king; royal; noble: *kingly pride.* **2** *adj.* fit for a king: *a kingly crown.* **3** *adv.* as a king does; royally. ❑ *adj.* **king·li·er, king·li·est.** —**king′li·ness,** *n.*

Kings (kingz), *n.* **1** (in the Protestant Bible) either of two books (I Kings or II Kings) containing the history of the reigns of the Hebrew kings after David. **2** (in the Roman Catholic Bible) any of the four books that correspond to I and II Samuel and I and II Kings in the Protestant Bible.

Kings Canyon National Park, a national park in central California, containing high peaks of the Sierra Nevada Mountains and many giant sequoias.

king·ship (king′ship), *n.* **1** position, rank, or dignity of a king. **2** rule of a king; government by a king.

king-size (king′sīz′), *adj.* large or long for its kind: *a king-size bed.*

king-sized (king′sīzd′), *adj.* king-size.

king snake, any of various large, harmless snakes found in North America and Central America. King snakes eat mice, rats, and other snakes.

Kings·ton (king′stən), *n.* port and capital of Jamaica, in the SE part.

Kings·town (kingz′toun), *n.* capital of St. Vincent and the Grenadines.

kink (kingk), **1** *n.* a twist or curl in thread, rope, hair, etc. **2** *v.* to form a kink or kinks; make kinks in: *The rope kinked as she rolled it up.* **3** *n.* pain or stiffness in the muscles of the neck, back, etc.; crick. **4** *n.* an odd idea; a mental quirk.

kin·ka·jou (king′kə jü), *n.* a yellowish brown mammal found in Central and South America. It is related to the raccoon. A kinkajou has a long tail, lives in trees, and feeds at night on insects and fruit.

kink·y (king′kē), *adj.* **1** full of kinks; twisted; curly. **2** INFORMAL. quite unusual; odd; extreme: *kinky styles in clothing.* ❑ *adj.* **kink·i·er, kink·i·est.** —**kink′i·ness,** *n.*

kins·folk (kinz′fōk′), *n.pl.* kinfolk.

Kin·sha·sa (kēn shä′sä), *n.* capital of Zaïre, in the W part, on the Congo River.

kin·ship (kin′ship), *n.* **1** family relationship. **2** relationship. **3** resemblance.

kins·man (kinz′mən), *n.* a male relative. ❑ *n., pl.* **kins·men.**

kins·wom·an (kinz′wùm′ən), *n.* a female relative. ❑ *n., pl.* **kins·wom·en.**

ki·osk (kē′osk *or* kē osk′), *n.* **1** a small building with one or more sides open, used as a newsstand, bandstand, or opening to a subway. **2** a cylindrical structure, placed on or near a sidewalk, on which advertisements, notices, etc., are displayed.

Ki·o·wa (kī′ə wə), *n.* member of an American Indian tribe living formerly in the southern Great Plains and now in Oklahoma. ❑ *n., pl.* **Ki·o·wa** or **Ki·o·was.**

Kip·ling (kip′ling), *n.* **Rud·yard** (rud′yərd), 1865-1936, English writer, born in India. His works include *The Jungle Book* and *Kim.*

kip·per (kip′ər), **1** *v.* to salt and dry or smoke herring, salmon, etc. **2** *n.* herring or salmon that has been kippered.

Ki·ri·bati (kir′ə bäs), *n.* island country in the central Pacific near the equator. *Capital:* Tarawa.

kirk (kėrk), *n.* SCOTTISH. church.

Kish·i·nev (kish′ə nef), *n.* capital of Moldova.

kiss (kis), **1** *v.* to touch with the lips as a sign of love, greeting, or respect: *The two sisters kissed. He kissed his mother good-by.* **2** *n.* a touch with the lips as a sign of love, greeting, or respect. **3** *v.* to touch gently: *A soft wind kissed the treetops.* **4** *n.* a gentle touch. **5** *v.* to put, bring, take, etc., by kissing: *kiss away tears.* **6** *n.* a small piece of candy, usually of chocolate. ❑ *n., pl.* **kiss·es.** —**kiss′a·ble,** *adj.*

kiss·er (kis′ər), *n.* **1** person who kisses. **2** SLANG. face or mouth.

Kis·sing·er (kis′in jər), *n.* **Henry,** born 1923, American diplomat and foreign policy adviser, born in Germany.

kit (kit), *n.* **1** the parts of anything to be put together by the buyer: *a radio kit, a model airplane kit.* **2** a person's equipment packed for traveling: *a soldier's kit.* **3** outfit of tools or supplies: *a plumber's kit, a first-aid kit.*

kitch·en (kich′ən), *n.* room or area where food is cooked.

WORD STORY **Kitchen** comes from a Latin word meaning "to cook." **Cook** comes from the same word. **Kitchen** went from Latin to German to English. **Cook** went straight from Latin to English. Because these two words went different ways, a cook cooks in a kitchen, but a baker bakes in a bakery.

kitch·en·ette (kich′ə net′), *n.* **1** a very small kitchen. **2** part of a room fitted up as a kitchen.

kitch·en·ware (kich′ən wâr′), *n.* kitchen utensils. Pots, kettles, and pans are kitchenware.

kite (kīt), *n.* **1** a light wooden frame covered with paper, cloth, or plastic. Kites are flown in the air on the end of long strings.

a	hat	ė	term	ô	order	ch	child		
ā	age	i	it	oi	oil	ng	long		a in about
ä	far	ī	ice	ou	out	sh	she		e in taken
â	care	o	hot	u	cup	th	thin	ə	i in pencil
e	let	ō	open	ù	put	ŦH	then		o in lemon
ē	equal	ò	saw	ü	rule	zh	measure		u in circus

2 any of various hawks with long, pointed wings and long, forked or notched tails.

kith (kith), *n.* **kith and kin,** friends and relatives.

kit·ten (kit′n), *n.* a young cat.

kit·ty (kit′ē), *n.* **1** kitten. **2** a pet name for a cat. ❑ *n., pl.* **kit·ties.**

kit·ty-cor·ner (kit′ē kôr′nər), *adj., adv.* cater-corner.

kit·ty-cor·nered (kit′ē kôr′nərd), *adj., adv.* cater-cornered.

Kitty Hawk, village in NE North Carolina. Wilbur and Orville Wright made the first successful airplane flight there in 1903.

Kitty Litter, trademark for small pieces of dry clay kept in a box or pan as a toilet for cats and other pets.

ki·va (kē′və), *n.* a one-room building used by Pueblos for religious and other purposes. It is often partly underground and is usually entered by an opening in its roof. ❑ *n., pl.* **ki·vas.**

ki·wi (kē′wē), *n.* any of three birds of New Zealand with shaggy feathers, tiny undeveloped wings, and long flexible bills. Kiwis cannot fly. ❑ *n., pl.* **ki·wis.**

kiwi fruit, a fuzzy, egg-shaped fruit that grows on a vine in New Zealand. Kiwi fruit is brownish on the outside and green on the inside. It is eaten raw.

KKK or **K.K.K.,** Ku Klux Klan.

Klee·nex (klē′neks), *n.* trademark for a disposable paper tissue used as a handkerchief, etc.

klep·to·ma·ni·a (klep′tə mā′nē ə), *n.* an abnormal, irresistible desire to steal, especially things which you do not need or cannot use.

klep·to·ma·ni·ac (klep′tə mā′nē ak), *n.* a person who has kleptomania.

klieg light (klēg), a bright, hot light used in making movies.

Klon·dike (klon′dīk), *n.* region in NW Canada, along the Yukon River, famous for its gold fields.

km or **km.,** kilometer or kilometers.

knack (nak), *n.* special skill; power to do something easily: *That clown has the knack of making very funny faces.*

WORD STORY   Why are some words spelled with **kn-** but pronounced with only *n*? In old days, the *k* was pronounced, too. **Knack** was pronounced (kə nak′). Because this is harder to say than just (nak), the pronunciation changed, but the spelling didn't.

knack·wurst (nok′wėrst), *n.* a short, thick, spicy sausage. Also **knockwurst.**

knap·sack (nap′sak′), *n.* a cloth bag with two shoulder straps, used for carrying clothes, equipment, etc., on the back; backpack; rucksack. [**Knapsack** comes from a Germanic word meaning "to eat" and **sack.** In old times, a traveler who wanted a meal needed to carry it.]

knave (nāv), *n.* **1** a tricky, dishonest person; rogue; rascal. **2** the jack, a playing card with a picture of a servant or soldier on it. **3** OLD USE. a male servant; man of humble birth or position. [See Word Story at **knight.**] ■ Another word that sounds like this is **nave.**

knav·ish (nā′vish), *adj.* tricky; dishonest. **−knav′ish·ly,** *adv.* **−knav′ish·ness,** *n.*

knead (nēd), *v.* **1** to press or mix together dough or clay into a soft mass: *A baker kneads dough.* **2** to make or shape by kneading. **3** to press and squeeze with the hands; massage: *Kneading the muscles in a stiff shoulder helps to take away the stiffness.* ■ Another word that sounds like this is **need. −knead′er,** *n.*

knee (nē), **1** *n.* the joint between the thigh and the lower leg. **2** *n.* any joint in a four-footed animal corresponding to the human knee or elbow. **3** *n.* anything like a bent knee in shape or position. **4** *n.* part of a piece of clothing covering the knee. **5** *v.* to hit or touch with the knee: *When both outfielders went for the fly ball, one kneed the other in the hip.* ❑ *n.* **knees;** *v.* **kneed, knee·ing.**
bring someone to his or her knees, to force someone to yield.

knee·cap (nē′kap′), *n.* the flat, movable bone at the front of the knee; patella.

knee-deep (nē′dēp′), *adj.* **1** up to the knees: *She was standing knee-deep in mud.* **2** so deep as to reach the knees: *The snow was knee-deep.* **3** very involved; deeply concerned: *knee-deep in work.*

knee-jerk (nē′jėrk′), *adj.* without thought; automatic: *He gave a knee-jerk answer to my question.*

kneel (nēl), *v.* **1** to go down on your knee or knees: *She knelt down to pull a weed from the flower bed.* **2** to remain in this position: *They knelt in prayer for half an hour.* ❑ *v.* **knelt** or **kneeled, kneel·ing. −kneel′er,** *n.*

knell (nel), **1** *n.* sound of a bell rung slowly after a death or at a funeral. **2** *v.* to ring slowly. **3** *n.* a warning sign of death, failure, etc.: *Their refusal rang the knell of our hopes.* **4** *v.* to give such a warning sign.

knelt (nelt), *v.* a past tense and a past participle of **kneel:** *She knelt and prayed.*

knew (nü), *v.* past tense of **know:** *She knew the right answer.* ■ Other words that sound like this are **gnu** and **new.**

knick·er·bock·ers (nik′ər bok′ərz), *n.pl.* knickers.

knick·ers (nik′ərz), *n.pl.* short, loose-fitting trousers gathered in at, or just below, the knee.

knick·knack (nik′nak′), *n.* ornament; trinket. Also, **nicknack.**

knife (nīf), **1** *n.* a thin, flat metal blade fastened in a handle so that it can be used to cut or spread. **2** *n.* a sharp blade forming part of a tool or cutting machine. **3** *v.* to cut or stab with a knife. ❑ *n., pl.* **knives;** *v.* **knifed, knif·ing. −knife′like′,** *adj.*

knight (nīt), **1** *n.* (in the Middle Ages) a man raised to an honorable military rank and pledged to do good deeds. After serving as a page and squire, a man was made a knight by the king or a lord. **2** *n.* (in modern times) a man raised to an honorable rank because of great achievement or service. A British knight ranks just below a baronet and uses the title *Sir* before his name. EXAMPLE: Sir John Smith or Sir John. **3** *v.* to raise to the rank of knight: *He was knighted by the queen.* **4** *n.* one of the pieces in the game of chess. ■ Another word that sounds like this is **night.**

knight (def. 1)

WORD STORY   **Knight** comes from an old English word meaning "servant." **Knave** comes from another old English word with the same meaning. People of the upper classes distrusted people of the lower classes and that distrust changed the meaning of **knave.** But since a knight was an upper-class servant of the king, the word still suggests honor instead of dishonesty.

knight-er·rant (nīt′er′ənt), *n.* (in the Middle Ages) knight traveling in search of adventure. ❑ *n., pl.* **knights-er·rant.**

knight·hood (nīt′hùd), *n.* **1** rank of a knight. **2** profession or occupation of a knight. **3** character or qualities of a knight. **4** knights as a group or class: *All the knighthood of France came to the aid of the king.*

knight·ly (nīt′lē), *adj.* having qualities admired in a knight; chivalrous. **−knight′li·ness,** *n.*

Knights Templars, (tem′plərs), a religious and military order of the Middle Ages.

knit (nit), *v.* **1** to make cloth or an article of clothing by looping yarn or thread together with long needles, or by machinery which forms loops instead of weaving: *knit a pair of socks.* **2** to join closely and firmly together: *The players were all knit into a team that played together smoothly.* **3** to grow together: *A broken bone knits.* **4** to draw the brows together in wrinkles: *She knits her brows when she frowns.* ❑ *v.* **knit** or **knit·ted, knit·ting.** ■ Another word that sounds like this is **nit. −knit′ter,** *n.*

knit·ting (nit′ing), *n.* knitted work.

knives (nīvz), *n.* plural of **knife.**

knob (nob), *n.* **1** a rounded lump: *The walking stick had a large knob at the top.* **2** a handle, object, or part often shaped like a rounded lump: *the knobs on a bureau drawer.* **3** a rounded hill or mountain. **−knob′like′,** *adj.*

knob·by (nob′ē), *adj.* **1** covered with knobs. **2** rounded like a knob. ❑ *adj.* **knob·bi·er, knob·bi·est. −knob′bi·ness,** *n.*

knock (nok), **1** *v.* to give a hard blow or blows to; hit: *She almost knocked the ball over the fence.* **2** *v.* to hit and cause to fall: *The speeding car knocked down several signs.* **3** *v.* to hit with a noise: *He knocked on the door.* **4** *n.* a hit with a noise: *I heard a knock at the door.* **5** *n.* trouble or problem; misfortune: *For someone who has suffered a lot of hard knocks, he seems very good-natured.* **6** *n.* a hit: *A foul ball gave a fan a nasty knock on the head.* **7** *v.* to make a noise, especially a rattling or pounding noise: *The engine is knocking.* **8** *n.* sound in an internal-combustion engine caused by loose parts or improper burning of fuel; ping: *a knock in the engine.* **9** *v.* INFORMAL. to find fault with; criticize: *The critics knocked the new book.*

knock about, **1** INFORMAL. to wander from place to place. **2** to be too rough with; mistreat: *Over the years, life has knocked him about.*

knock down, to take apart: *We knocked down the stage set.*

knock off, **1** to take off; deduct: *He will knock off a dollar from the price if you pay cash.* **2** INFORMAL. to stop work: *We knock off at noon for lunch.* **3** INFORMAL. to stop; quit doing something: *Knock off that noise!* **4** INFORMAL. to finish; complete: *They knocked off the whole job in two days.*

knock out, to hit so hard as to make helpless or unconscious.

knock together, to make or put together hastily: *The children knocked together a raft out of old boards.*

knock·a·bout (nok′ə bout′), *adj.* suitable for rough use.

knock·er (nok′ər), *n.* **1** a hinged knob, ring, or the like, usually of iron or brass, fastened on a door for use in knocking. **2** person or thing that knocks.

knock·kneed (nok′nēd′), *adj.* having legs bent inward at the knees.

knock-knock joke (nok′nok′), a joke in the form of a conversation, beginning with the imitation of someone at a door: *"knock, knock."*

knock·off (nok′ôf′), *n.* SLANG. imitation that costs less and is made worse than the original: *knockoffs of designer clothes.*

knock·out (nok′out′), *n.* a blow that makes an opponent helpless or unconscious: *The boxer won the fight by a knockout.*

knock·wurst (nok′wėrst), *n.* knackwurst.

knoll (nōl), *n.* a small, rounded hill; mound.

knot (not), **1** *n.* a fastening made by tying or twining together pieces of one or more ropes, cords, strings, etc.: *a square knot, a slip knot.* **2** *v.* to tie or twine together in a knot: *He knotted two ropes together.* **3** *v.* to tangle in knots: *My thread has knotted.* **4** *n.* group; cluster: *A knot of students stood talking outside the classroom.* **5** *v.* to unite closely in a way that is hard to undo. **6** *n.* the hard mass of wood formed in a tree where a branch grows out, which shows as a roundish, cross-grained piece in a board. **7** *n.* a hard lump. A knot sometimes forms in a tired muscle. **8** *v.* to form into a hard lump. **9** *n.* nautical mile. **10** *n.* unit of speed used on ships and aircraft, equal to one nautical mile per hour: *The ship averaged 12 knots.* **11** *n.* difficulty or problem. □ *v.* **knot·ted, knot·ting.** ■ Another word that sounds like this is **not.**

knot·hole (not′hōl′), *n.* hole in a board where a knot has fallen out.

knot·ty (not′ē), *adj.* **1** full of knots: *knotty wood.* **2** difficult; puzzling: *a knotty problem.* □ *adj.* **knot·ti·er, knot·ti·est. —knot′ti·ness,** *n*

know (nō), *v.* **1** to have the facts of; be skilled in: *She knows arithmetic. A carpenter must know his trade.* **2** to have the facts and be sure that they are true: *We know that 2 and 2 are 4. She was there at the time; she will know.* **3** to have knowledge: *I know from experience how to drive on icy roads.* ■ See Synonym Study at **understand. 4** to be acquainted with: *I know her very well, but I don't know her sister.* **5** to tell apart from others; distinguish: *You will know his house by the red roof.* □ *v.* **knew, known, know·ing.** ■ Another word that sounds like this is **no. —know′a·ble,** *adj.* **—know′er,** *n.*

in the know, having inside information.

know what's what, be well-informed.

know-how (nō′hou′), *n.* ability to do something.

know·ing (nō′ing), *adj.* **1** having knowledge; well-informed. **2** clever; shrewd. **3** suggesting shrewd or secret understanding of matters: *Her only answer was a knowing look.*

know·ing·ly (nō′ing lē), *adv.* **1** in a knowing way. **2** on purpose; intentionally: *I would not knowingly hurt anyone.*

know-it-all (nō′it ôl′), *n.* person who claims to know more than anybody else: *Don't be such a know-it-all! We're all aware of what's going on.*

knowl·edge (nol′ij), *n.* **1** what you know: *a gardener's knowledge of flowers.* **2** all that is known or can be learned: *Science is a part of knowledge.* **3** fact of knowing: *The knowledge of our victory caused great joy.*

to the best of your knowledge, as far as you know: *I have never met them, to the best of my knowledge.*

knowl·edge·a·ble (nol′i jə bəl), *adj.* well-informed, especially about a particular subject. **—knowl′edge·a·bil′i·ty,** *n.*

known (nōn), **1** *v.* past participle of **know: 1** *George Washington is known as the father of his country.* **2** *adj.* familiar to all; generally recognized; well-known: *a person of known ability.*

Knox·ville (noks′vil), *n.* city in E Tennessee.

knuck·le (nuk′əl), **1** *n.* a joint in a finger, especially one of the joints between a finger and the rest of the hand. **2** *v.* to hit or press with the knuckles. **3** *n.* knee or hock joint of an animal used as food: *boiled pigs' knuckles.* □ *v.* **knuck·led, knuck·ling.**

knuckle down, to work hard; study hard.

knuckle under, to submit; yield: *knuckle under to their demands.*

knuck·le·ball (nuk′əl bôl′), *n.* a slow, unpredictable baseball pitch thrown with the fingertips, having little speed or spin; knuckler.

knuck·ler (nuk′lər), *n.* knuckleball.

KO (kā′ō′), SLANG. **1** *v.* to knock out. **2** *n.* knockout. □ *v.* **KO'd, KO'ing;** *n., pl.* **KO's.**

K.O. or **k.o.,** knockout.

ko·a·la (kō ä′lə), *n.* a gray, furry mammal of Australia that looks like a small bear and lives in trees. The female koala carries her young in a pouch on her belly. Koalas eat mainly the leaves and green shoots of eucalyptus trees. □ *n., pl.* **ko·a·las.**

ko·ban (kō′bän), *n.* a small police substation located in a commercial area to deter crime. There are kobans in Baltimore, Philadelphia, and some other cities. [**Koban** comes from a Japanese word for a similar substation.]

Ko·be (kō′bē *or* kō′bā), *n.* port in W Japan.

koala— about 2 ft. (61 cm) long

Ko·buk Valley National Park (kō′buk), a national park in NW Alaska, containing wilderness forest and tundra and rare Arctic sand dunes.

Koch (kôk), *n.* **Ro·bert** (rob′ərt), 1843-1910, German physician. ■ Robert Koch won the Nobel Prize for physiology or medicine in 1905. He discovered the germ that causes tuberculosis.

Ko·dak (kō′dak), *n.* trademark for a small camera with rolls of film on which photographs are taken.

kohl·ra·bi (kōl′rä′bē), *n.* plant related to the cabbage that has a turnip-shaped stem that is eaten as a vegetable. □ *n., pl.* **kohl·ra·bies.**

Ko·ko·pel·i (kō′kō pel′ē), *n.* character in the mythology of southwestern American Indians, often shown in rock carvings as a flute player with a curved or humped back.

Ko·mo·do dragon (kə mō′dō), a very large lizard found on certain islands of Indonesia, thought to be the largest living lizard. Komodo dragons eat other animals.

kook (kük), *n.* SLANG. an odd or foolish person.

kook·a·bur·ra (kùk′ə bėr′ə), *n.* a large kingfisher of Australia and New Guinea that has a cackling call. □ *n., pl.* **kook·a·bur·ras.**

a	hat	ė	term	ô	order	ch	child		a in about
ā	age	i	it	oi	oil	ng	long		e in taken
ä	far	ī	ice	ou	out	sh	she	ə	i in pencil
â	care	o	hot	u	cup	th	thin		o in lemon
e	let	ō	open	ů	put	ŦH	then		u in circus
ē	equal	ò	saw	ü	rule	zh	measure		

Knights and Castles

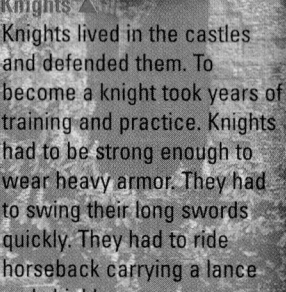

The castle was the center of people's lives in the Middle Ages. Most people lived outside its walls, but the castle was their safety in danger, the focus of law and order, the source of authority and command. The high castle towers and walls could be seen from far away. Even now, after hundreds of years, they still show their strength.

Knights ▲
Knights lived in the castles and defended them. To become a knight took years of training and practice. Knights had to be strong enough to wear heavy armor. They had to swing their long swords quickly. They had to ride horseback carrying a lance and shield.

Castle Construction ◄
Building a castle took hundreds of workers and could go on for months or years.

Castle Life ▲ ▶
For the lords and ladies, knights and maidens, life was often pleasant. In summer, they might stroll in the castle garden. In winter, there was feasting, music, and merriment. The battle behind the table is only a picture on a curtain.

Peasant Life ▲
Around the castle lived the peasants who farmed the land belonging to the lord of the castle. The peasants were not free; they had to stay and work. But they did share the crop, and they were protected from the threats of a dangerous time.

Armor
Armor had to be made by hand. Skilled armorers worked at the castles and traveled with armies. A suit of armor was actually many pieces worn together, strapped or hinged so that the knight inside could move.

Battle
In battle, knights on horses charge others standing with their lances in defensive formation.

485B

kook·y (kü′kē), *adj.* SLANG. odd; foolish. ◻ *adj.* **kook·i·er, kook·i·est. −kook′i·ness,** *n.*

ko·peck or **ko·pek** (kō′pek), *n.* a coin of Russia. 100 kopecks make one ruble.

Ko·ran (kô rän′ *or* kô ran′), *n.* the sacred book of the Muslims, believed by them to consist of revelations to the prophet Muhammad. It is the standard by which Muslims live.

Ko·re·a (kô rē′ə), *n.* former country on a peninsula in E Asia, divided into North Korea and South Korea after World War II.

Ko·re·an (kô rē′ən), **1** *adj.* of Korea, its people, or their language. **2** *n.* person born or living in Korea. **3** *n.* language of Korea.

Korean War, war between South Korea, aided by the United Nations, and North Korea, aided by the People's Republic of China. The war lasted from June 1950 to July 1953.

Ko·ror (kô′rôr), *n.* capital of Palau.

Kos·ci·us·ko (kos′ē us′kō), *n.* **Thad·de·us** (thad′ē əs), 1746-1817, Polish general who served in the American army during the Revolutionary War.

ko·sher (kō′shər), **1** *adj.* right or clean according to Jewish law: *kosher meat.* **2** *v.* to prepare food according to the Jewish law. **3** *adj.* INFORMAL. all right; fine: *It's not kosher to change the rules while you are playing the game.* [**Kosher** comes from a Hebrew word meaning "proper." Kosher food is food that has been prepared properly, that is, according to Jewish law.]

ko·to (kō′tō), *n.* a Japanese wooden musical instrument with seven to thirteen strings. ◻ *n., pl.* **ko·tos.**

Kou·fax (kō′faks), *n.* **San·dy** (san′dē), born 1935, American baseball player. He was the first person to pitch four no-hitters in the major leagues.

kow·tow (kou′tou′), *v.* to show slavish respect or obedience. [**Kowtow** comes from Chinese words meaning "to knock the head." In old times, kneeling and touching the forehead to the floor was a way of showing deep respect in China.]

K.P., a military duty of helping the cook prepare and serve food, wash dishes, and clean up the kitchen: *He's on K.P. for a week.* [**K.P.** stands for "kitchen police." In military language, **police** means "to keep clean and in order."]

Kr, symbol for krypton.

kraal (kräl), *n.* **1** village of South African blacks. **2** pen for cattle or sheep in South Africa.

Kra·ka·to·a (krak′ə tō′ə), *n.* a small volcanic island in Indonesia, between Java and Sumatra.

Krem·lin (krem′lən), *n.* citadel of Moscow. The chief offices of the Soviet government were in the Kremlin.

Kremlin

krill (kril), *n.pl.* various small, shrimplike shellfish that feed on plankton, and are eaten by whales and other sea animals.

Krish·na (krish′nə), *n.* a Hindu god and hero, worshiped as an incarnation of Vishnu.

Kriss Krin·gle (kris′ kring′gəl), Santa Claus.

kryp·ton (krip′ton), *n.* a colorless gas that forms a tiny part of the air. It is a chemical element. Krypton is used to fill some fluorescent lamps. *Symbol:* Kr

KS, Kansas (used with postal Zip Code).

kt., **1** karat. **2** kiloton.

K2 (kā′tü), *n.* mountain in the NW Himalayas, in N India. It is the second highest mountain in the world, 28,250 feet (8611 meters) high.

Kua·la Lum·pur (kwä′lə lüm′púr′), capital of Malaysia, in W Malaya.

Kub·lai Khan (kü′blī kän′), 1216-1294, Mongol emperor from 1259 to 1294. He was the first Mongol ruler of China.

ku·dos (kü′dos), *n.* praise; glory; fame.

> **USAGE NOTE** **Kudos** is a singular noun in formal English: *Kudos is the reward that matters most to her.* Because it looks like a plural noun, it is sometimes used that way: *His performance won many kudos from the audience.* Some people make a singular noun, "kudo," from that plural use. Careful writers use only the singular **kudos.** But time may change this rule, as time has changed many rules.

ku·du (kü′dü), *n.* either of two large African antelopes with spiral, curving horns. The **greater kudu** is reddish brown with white stripes. The **lesser kudu,** somewhat smaller, is yellowish gray with white stripes.

kud·zu (kúd′zü), *n.* vine originally found in Japan and China, now widespread in the southern United States. Kudzu grows quickly and can become a nuisance.

Ku Klux Klan (kü′ kluks′ klan′), **1** a secret society of white people formed in the southern United States after the Civil War to suppress certain minority groups and maintain white supremacy. **2** a secret society founded in 1915 in the United States, violently opposed to African Americans, Jews, Catholics, and foreigners.

Ku·kul·can or **Ku·kul·kan** (kü′kül kän′), *n.* Maya name for Quetzalcoatl.

kum·quat (kum′kwät), *n.* a yellow or orange fruit something like a small orange. It has a sour pulp and a sweet rind, and is used in preserves and candy. First grown in China, the kumquat is cultivated in warm parts of the United States.

kung fu (kúng′ fü′), any of various styles of Chinese boxing, most of which use punches, kicks, and blocking actions similar to those of karate.

Ku·shan Empire, (kə shän′), empire in the region now part of Afghanistan, Pakistan, and NW India, from about A.D. 50 to about A.D. 250. It was an important link between the cultures of ancient Rome, ancient China, and ancient India. Buddhism reached China from India through the Kushan territories.

Ku·wait (kü wāt′), *n.* **1** country in E Arabia, on the Persian Gulf. **2** its capital.

kvetch (kvech), **1** *n.* a complainer; whiner. **2** *v.* to complain; whine. ◻ *n., pl.* **kvetch·es.**

kw., kilowatt.

Kwa·ki·u·tl (kwä′kē ü′təl), *n.* member of a tribe of American Indians that live in British Columbia. ◻ *n., pl.* **Kwa·ki·u·tl.** [**Kwakiutl** may come from a word in the language of this tribe meaning "beach on the other side of the river." It is not known why.]

Kwang·chow (kwäng′jō′), *n.* a former spelling of **Guangzhou.**

Kwan·zaa or **Kwan·za** (kwän′zə), *n.* an African American celebration commemorating various African festivals, especially one for the new planting season. It lasts from December 26 to January 1. [**Kwanzaa** comes from a Swahili word meaning "first (fruits)," which comes from a Swahili word meaning "to begin."]

K.W.H., kilowatt-hour or kilowatt-hours.

KY, Kentucky (used with postal Zip Code).

Ky., Kentucky.

Kyo·to (kyō′tō), *n.* city in central Japan. It was formerly the capital.

Kyr·gyz·stan (kir gēz′stän), *n.* country in central Asia, north of Afghanistan. *Capital:* Bishkek.

Kyu·shu (kyü′shü), *n.* large island at the SW end of Japan.

Kushan Empire (about 100 A.D.)

Aral Sea · Caspian Sea · CHINA · KUSHAN EMPIRE · TIBET · Indus R. · Ganges R. · INDIA · Arabian Sea

L¹ or **l** (el), *n.* **1** the 12th letter of the English alphabet. **2** the Roman numeral for 50. ❑ *n., pl.* **L's** or **l's.**

L² (el), *n.* anything shaped like the letter L. ❑ *n., pl.* **L's.**

l or **l.,** liter or liters.

L, 1 large. **2** Latin. **3** length. **4** longitude.

L or **L.,** liter or liters.

l. or **l, 1** left. **2** length. **3** line. **4** lira or lire.

L., 1 lake. **2** Latin.

£, pound or pounds sterling.

la (lä), *n.* the sixth tone of the musical scale.

La, symbol for lanthanum.

LA, Louisiana (used with postal Zip Code).

La., Louisiana.

L.A., Los Angeles.

lab (lab), *n.* INFORMAL. laboratory.

Lab., Labrador.

la·bel (lā′bəl), **1** *n.* slip of paper, plastic, or other material attached to anything and marked to show what or whose it is, or where it is to go: *Can you read the label on the bottle?* **2** *v.* to put or write a label on: *The bottle is labeled "Poison."* **3** *n.* a word or phrase used to describe some person, thing, or idea: *In winter, Chicago deserves its label of "the Windy City."* **4** *v.* to describe as; call; name: *label someone a liar.* **5** *n.* brand; trademark. ❑ *v.* **la·beled, la·bel·ing** or **la·belled, la·bel·ling.** —**la′bel·er** or **la′bel·ler,** *n.*

la·bi·al (lā′bē əl), **1** *adj.* of the lips. **2** *adj.* pronounced with the lips closed, nearly closed, or rounded. **3** *n.* sound made in this way. *B, p,* and *m* are labials.

la·bor (lā′bər), **1** *n.* effort in doing or making something; work; toil: *Her understanding of the subject shows the amount of labor she puts into her homework.* **2** *n.* piece of work to be done; task: *The king gave Hercules 12 labors to perform.* **3** *n.* work, especially manual work, done by skilled and unskilled workers for wages: *Digging ditches is manual labor.* ■ See Synonym Study at **work. 4** *n.* workers as a group: *Labor favors safe working conditions.* **5** *v.* to do work; work hard; toil: *I labored all day at the factory.* **6** *v.* to move slowly and heavily: *The ship labored in the heavy seas.* **7** *n.* childbirth.

lab·o·ra·to·ry (lab′rə tôr′ē), *n.* **1** place with apparatus for conducting scientific experiments, investigations, tests, etc.: *a chemical laboratory.* **2** place for manufacturing drugs, medicines, chemicals, etc. ❑ *n., pl.* **lab·o·ra·to·ries.**

Labor Day, the first Monday in September, a legal holiday throughout the United States and Canada in honor of working people.

a	hat	ė	term	ô	order	ch	child		
ā	age	i	it	oi	oil	ng	long	(a	in about
ä	far	ī	ice	ou	out	sh	she		e	in taken
â	care	o	hot	u	cup	th	thin	ə ⟨ i	in pencil
e	let	ō	open	ù	put	ŦH	then		o	in lemon
ē	equal	ò	saw	ü	rule	zh	measure	(u	in circus

la·bored (lā′bərd), *adj.* done with much effort; forced: *labored breathing, a labored attempt at humor.*

la·bor·er (lā′bər ər), *n.* **1** person who does work that requires strength rather than skill or training. **2** worker.

la·bo·ri·ous (lə bôr′ē əs), *adj.* **1** needing or taking much effort; requiring hard work: *Climbing a mountain is laborious.* **2** showing signs of effort; labored: *The tardy student made up laborious excuses.* **3** willing to work hard; industrious: *a careful and laborious painter.* —**la·bo′ri·ous·ly,** *adv.* —**la·bo′ri·ous·ness,** *n.*

la·bor·sav·ing (lā′bər sā′ving), *adj.* able to reduce or replace human effort: *A washing machine is a laborsaving device.*

labor union, group of workers joined together to protect and promote their interests by dealing as a group with their employers; union.

Lab·ra·dor (lab′rə dôr), *n.* **1** peninsula in NE North America, between Hudson Bay and the Atlantic Ocean. **2** the E part of this peninsula, part of the Canadian province of Newfoundland.

Labrador retriever, a medium-sized, strongly built dog used to retrieve game. It has a thick, water-resistant coat of short black, brown, or yellow fur.

la·bur·num (lə bėr′nəm), *n.* any of three small trees or bushes related to peas, with bright yellow flowers hanging in clusters.

lab·y·rinth (lab′ə rinth′), *n.* **1** a set of connected passages arranged so that it is hard to find the way through them; maze. **2** Labyrinth, (in Greek myths) the maze built by Daedalus for Minos to imprison the Minotaur. **3** any confusing, complicated arrangement: *I cannot keep track of this novel's labyrinth of a story.*

labyrinth (def. 1)

lab·y·rin·thine (lab′ə rin′thən), *adj.* confusing and complicated; intricate.

lac (lak), *n.* a sticky substance deposited on various trees by scale insects. Lac is used in making sealing wax and shellac. ■ Another word that sounds like this is **lack.**

lace (lās), **1** *n.* a delicate netlike fabric woven from fine thread in an ornamental pattern. **2** *v.* to trim with lace: *a velvet cloak laced with gold.* **3** *n.* cord, string, or leather strip passed through holes to pull or hold together the opposite edges of a shoe, garment, etc.: *These shoes need new laces.* **4** *v.* to put laces through; pull or hold together with a lace or laces: *Lace up your shoes.* **5** *v.* to interlace; intertwine: *She sat with her fingers laced.* ❑ *v.* **laced, lac·ing.** —**lace′like′,** *adj.*

lace into, 1 to strike again and again; lash: *The two angry children laced into each other until the teacher separated them.* **2** to criticize severely: *The coach laced into the team for not trying hard enough to win.*

> **WORD STORY** **Lace** comes from a Latin word meaning "a noose." **Lasso** comes from the same word. The earliest meaning of **lace** in written English was "cord" or "string" (def. 3).

lac·e·rate (las′ə rāt′), *v.* **1** to tear roughly; mangle: *The bear's claws lacerated the hunter's arm.* **2** to cause pain or suffering to; distress: *The coach's sharp words lacerated my feelings.* ❑ *v.* **lac·e·rat·ed, lac·e·rat·ing.**

lac·e·ra·tion (las′ə rā′shən), *n.* **1** a torn, jagged wound. **2** act of lacerating.

lack (lak), **1** *n.* condition of being without: *Lack of a fire made us cold.* **2** *v.* to have no; be without: *Some guinea pigs lack tails.* **3** *v.* to not have enough; need: *This book lacks excitement.* **4** *n.* shortage; not having enough: *Lack of rest made her tired.* ■ Another word that sounds like this is **lac.**

lack·a·dai·si·cal (lak′ə dā′zə kəl), *adj.* lacking interest or enthusiasm; languid; listless. —**lack′a·dai′si·cal·ly,** *adv.*

lack·ey (lak′ē), *n.* **1** a male servant; footman. **2** follower who obeys orders like a servant; toady. ❑ *n., pl.* **lack·eys.**

lack·ing (lak′ing), *adj.* **1** not having enough; deficient: *A weak person is lacking in strength.* **2** absent; not here: *Water was lacking, so the crops began to dry up.*

lack·lus·ter (lak′lus′tər), *adj.* lacking brightness; dull and drab.

la·con·ic (lə kon′ik), *adj.* using few words; brief in speech or expression; concise. —**la·con′i·cal·ly,** *adv.*

lac·quer (lak′ər), **1** *n.* any varnish used to give a protective coating or a shiny appearance to metals, wood, paper, etc. Lacquers are made from various natural materials. **2** *v.* to coat with lacquer. —**lac′quer·er,** *n.*

la·crosse (lə krôs′), *n.* game played on a field with a ball and long-handled, loosely strung rackets, called sticks, by two teams, usually of 10 players each. The players carry the ball in the rackets, trying to hurl it into the other team's goal.

lac·tase (lak′tās), *n.* enzyme present in mammals that breaks down lactose in milk into simpler sugars that can be absorbed into the blood.

lac·tate (lak′tāt), *v.* to produce milk: *Mothers begin to lactate after they give birth.* ❑ *v.* **lac·tat·ed, lac·tat·ing.** —**lac·ta′tion,** *n.*

lac·te·al (lak′tē əl), *adj.* of milk; milky.

lac·tic (lak′tik), *adj.* of milk; found in milk; from milk.

lactic acid, a colorless, odorless acid formed when milk sours, vegetable juices ferment, etc. It also forms in tired muscle tissue and causes temporary soreness.

lac·tose (lak′tōs), *n.* a crystalline sugar present in milk; milk sugar.

lactose intolerant, lacking amounts of lactase necessary to digest lactose properly, and so made uncomfortable by food containing lactose. Many healthy people are lactose intolerant.

lac·y (lā′sē), *adj.* **1** made of lace: *a lacy collar.* **2** like lace: *the lacy leaves of a fern.* ❑ *adj.* **lac·i·er, lac·i·est.** —**la′ci·ness,** *n.*

lad (lad), *n.* boy; youth.

lad·der (lad′ər), *n.* **1** set of rungs or steps fastened to two side pieces for use in climbing up or down. **2** means of climbing higher: *Hard work is often a ladder to success.*

lad·die (lad′ē), *n.* SCOTTISH. lad.

lad·en (lād′n), *adj.* loaded; burdened: *We saw a ship laden with goods. The camels were laden with bundles of silk.*

lad·ing (lā′ding), *n.* **1** act of loading. **2** load; freight; cargo.

la·dle (lā′dl), **1** *n.* a large cup-shaped spoon with a long handle, for dipping out liquids. **2** *v.* to dip: *The cook ladled out the soup into large bowls.* ❑ *v.* **la·dled, la·dling.** [**Ladle** comes from an old English word meaning "to load." For loading cups with water or bowls with stew, a ladle is the tool you need.] —**la′dler,** *n.*

la·dy (lā′dē), *n.* **1** a polite term for any woman. "Ladies" is often used in speaking or writing to a group of women. **2** woman of good family and high social position: *a lady by birth.* **3** woman having good manners. **4** woman who has the rights and authority of a lord. **5** woman whom a man loves or who is a man's social companion: *He brought his lady over to meet us.* **6** Lady, title used in writing or speaking about women of certain high ranks in Great Britain: *Lord and Lady Grey attended the Queen's reception.* **7** Our Lady, a title of the Virgin Mary. ❑ *n., pl.* **la·dies** for 1–5, **La·dies** for 6.

> **WORD STORY** **Lady** comes from old English words meaning "loaf" and "to knead." In old times, bread was baked at home by the woman in charge of the house. The idea of "the woman in charge" probably caused the word to be used for women of high rank.

la·dy·bird (lā′dē bėrd′), *n.* ladybug.

la·dy·bug (lā′dē bug′), *n.* any of numerous small beetles with rounded backs, often red or yellow with black spots. Ladybugs eat harmful insects.

la·dy·fin·ger (lā′dē fing′gər), *n.* a small sponge cake shaped something like a finger.

la·dy-in-wait·ing (lā′dē in wā′ting), *n.* lady who accompanies or serves a queen or princess. ❑ *n., pl.* **la·dies-in-wait·ing.**

la·dy·like (lā′dē līk′), *adj.* like a lady; suitable for a lady; well-bred; polite.

la·dy·ship (lā′dē ship), *n.* **1** rank or position of a lady. **2 Ladyship,** title used in speaking to or of a woman having the rank of Lady: *your Ladyship, her Ladyship.*

la·dy's-slip·per (lā′dēz slip′ər), *n.* any of several wild orchids with slipper-shaped flowers. The pink lady's-slipper is the provincial flower of Prince Edward Island.

La·fa·yette (lä′fē et′ *or* laf′ē et′), *n.* **Marquis de,** 1757-1834, French general and political leader who served in the American army during the Revolutionary War. ■ **Lafayette** was not immediately accepted by the Americans, but after he offered to serve without pay, he was made a major general in the army.

La·fitte (lə fēt′), *n.* **Jean** (zhän), 1780?-1826?, New Orleans smuggler and pirate, born in France. ■ **Jean Lafitte** was also an American patriot. During the war of 1812, the British offered to make him a captain and give him money if he helped them attack New Orleans. He and his fellow smugglers fought for the United States instead and he received a pardon.

lag (lag), **1** *v.* to move too slowly; fall behind: *Our group lagged behind the others and missed the bus.* **2** *n.* act of falling behind; lagging: *There was a long lag in forwarding mail to us after we moved.* **3** *n.* amount by which someone or something falls behind: *There was a month's lag between the order for our car and its delivery.* **4** *v.* to become weaker; flag: *Our interest lagged as we watched the dull program.* ❑ *v.* **lagged, lag·ging.** —**lag′ger,** *n.*

lag·gard (lag′ərd), **1** *n.* person who moves too slowly or falls behind; loiterer. **2** *adj.* falling behind; slow; backward. —**lag′gard·ly,** *adv.* —**lag′gard·ness,** *n.*

la·goon (lə gün′), *n.* **1** pond or small lake, especially one connected with a larger body of water. **2** shallow water separated from the sea by low ridges of sand. **3** water within a ring-shaped coral island.

La·gos (lä′gōs *or* lā′gos), *n.* port in SW Nigeria, on the Atlantic.

La Guar·di·a (lə gwär′dē ə), **Fi·o·rel·lo Henry** (fē′ə rel′ō), 1882-1947, American political leader, mayor of New York City from 1934 to 1945.

laid (lād), *v.* past tense and past participle of **lay**[1]: *He laid down the heavy bundle. Those eggs were laid this morning.*

laid-back (lād′bak′), *adj.* relaxed; calm; not easily excited or upset; easygoing: *a laid-back attitude.*

lain (lān), *v.* past participle of **lie**[2]: *The snow has lain on the ground a week.* ■ Another word that sounds like this is **lane.**

lair (lâr), *n.* den or resting place of a wild animal. [**Lair** comes from an old English word meaning "a place to lie down." In the past, it had more definitions, including "a bed" and "a grave."]

laird (lârd), *n.* SCOTTISH. owner of land.

lais·sez faire *or* **lais·ser faire** (les′ā fâr′), the principle that trade, business, industry, etc., should operate with a minimum of regulation and interference by government.

la·i·ty (lā′ə tē), *n.* persons who are not members of the clergy or of a particular profession: *Doctors use many words that the laity do not know.*

lake (lāk), *n.* **1** body of water entirely or nearly surrounded by land. A lake usually consists of fresh water and is larger than a pond. **2** pool of liquid.

Lake Clark National Park, a national park in S Alaska near Anchorage, containing two active volcanoes and unexplored wilderness.

lake dweller, person who lived in a house built on piles over a lake in prehistoric times. —**lake dwelling.**

lake·shore (lāk′shôr′), *n.* lakeside.

lake·side (lāk′sīd′), *n.* the edge or shore of a lake.

lake trout, large, dark trout of the lakes of Canada and the northern United States. It is good to eat.

lake trout—up to 4 ft. 2 in. (1.3 m) long

Lake·wood (lāk′wùd), *n.* city in central Colorado.

La·ko·ta (lə kō′tə), *n.* Sioux, especially those living in the western section of their lands. ■ See Usage Note at **Sioux.** ❑ *n., pl.* **La·ko·ta.** [See word history information at **North Dakota.**]

la·ma (lä′mə), *n.* a Buddhist priest or monk in Tibet and Mongolia. ❑ *n., pl.* **la·mas.** ■ Another word that sounds like this is **llama.**

la·ma·ser·y (lä′mə ser′ē), *n.* a monastery of lamas in Tibet and Mongolia. ❑ *n., pl.* **la·ma·ser·ies.**

lamb (lam), **1** *n.* a young sheep. **2** *n.* meat from a lamb: *roast lamb.* **3** *n.* lambskin. **4** *v.* to give birth to a lamb or lambs. **5** *n.* a young, gentle, or dear person. [See Word Story at **meat.**] —**lamb′like′,** *adj.*

lam·baste (lam bāst′), *v.* **1** to strike again and again; beat severely; thrash. **2** to scold roughly. ❑ *v.* **lam·bast·ed, lam·bast·ing.**

lam·bent (lam′bənt), *adj.* **1** moving lightly over a surface: *a lambent flame.* **2** playing lightly and brilliantly over a subject: *lambent wit.* **3** shining with a soft, clear light: *Moonlight is lambent.* —**lam′bent·ly,** *adv.*

lamb·kin (lam′kən), *n.* a little lamb.

lamb·skin (lam′skin′), *n.* **1** leather made from the skin of a lamb. **2** skin of a lamb, especially with the wool on it. **3** parchment.

lame (lām), **1** *adj.* not able to walk properly; having an injured leg or foot; crippled: *He limps because he has been lame since birth.* **2** *adj.* stiff and sore: *My arm is lame from playing ball.* **3** *v.* to make lame; cripple: *The accident lamed me for life.* **4** *adj.* not very good; unsatisfactory; poor: *Oversleeping is a lame excuse for being late.* ❑ *adj.* **lam·er, lam·est;** *v.* **lamed, lam·ing.** —**lame′ly,** *adv.* —**lame′ness,** *n.*

a	hat	ė	term	ô	order	ch	child		a in about
ā	age	i	it	oi	oil	ng	long		e in taken
ä	far	ī	ice	ou	out	sh	she	ə	i in pencil
â	care	o	hot	u	cup	th	thin		o in lemon
e	let	ō	open	u̇	put	ŦH	then		u in circus
ē	equal	ȯ	saw	ü	rule	zh	measure		

la·mé (la mā′), *n.* a rich fabric made with gold or silver threads.

lame duck, a public official who has been defeated for reelection and is serving the last part of a term. **—lame′-duck,** *adj.*

la·ment (lə ment′), **1** *v.* to feel or show grief for; mourn aloud for: *We lament the dead.* **2** *n.* expression of grief or sorrow; wail. **3** *n.* poem, song, or tune that expresses grief. **4** *v.* to feel sorry about; regret: *We lamented her absence.* **—la·ment′er,** *n.*

lam·en·ta·ble (lam′ən tə bəl *or* lə men′tə bəl), *adj.* **1** to be regretted or pitied; giving cause for sorrow: *It was a lamentable day when our dog was run over.* **2** not so good; inferior; pitiful: *The singer gave a lamentable performance.* **—lam′en·ta·bly,** *adv.*

lam·en·ta·tion (lam′ən tā′shən), *n.* loud grief; cries of sorrow; mourning; wailing.

Lam·en·ta·tions (lam′ən tā′shənz), *n.* book of the Bible. According to tradition it was written by Jeremiah.

lam·i·na (lam′ə nə), *n.* a thin plate, scale, or layer. ◻ *n., pl.* **lam·i·nae** (lam′ə nē′), **lam·i·nas.**

lam·i·nate (lam′ə nāt), *v.* **1** to make plywood, plastics, glass, etc., by fastening together layer on layer of one or more materials. **2** to beat or roll into a thin plate. ◻ *v.* **lam·i·nat·ed, lam·i·nat·ing. —lam′i·na′tion,** *n.* **—lam′i·na′tor,** *n.*

lam·i·nat·ed (lam′ə nā′tid), *adj.* **1** made of layers of material. **2** coated with a thin layer, often plastic, for protection: *The photographs in the kitchen are laminated in case food gets on them.*

lamp (lamp), *n.* **1** device that gives artificial light. A gas or electric light is called a lamp. Oil lamps hold oil and a wick by which the oil is burned. **2** a similar device that gives heat or radiant energy: *an ultraviolet lamp.* [**Lamp** comes from an old Greek word meaning "to shine." **Lantern** comes from the same word.]

lamp·black (lamp′blak′), *n.* a fine black soot that is deposited when oil, gas, etc., burn incompletely. Lampblack is used as a coloring matter in paint and ink.

lamp·light (lamp′līt′), *n.* light from a lamp.

lamp·light·er (lamp′lī′tər), *n.* (long ago) someone employed to light gas-burning street lamps.

lam·poon (lam pün′), **1** *n.* piece of writing that attacks and makes fun of someone. **2** *v.* to attack and make fun of in a lampoon.

WORD STORY **Lampoon** comes from a French word meaning "let us drink," used as a refrain in insulting poems and songs. It is not known why the English borrowed a French word for this idea.

lamp·post (lamp′pōst′), *n.* post used to support a street lamp.

lam·prey (lam′prē), *n.* any of various related eellike, jawless fishes with large, round mouths. Lampreys attach themselves to fishes with their mouths, gnaw holes, and suck the body fluids as their food. ◻ *n., pl.* **lam·preys.**

La·nai (lä nī′), *n.* **1** island in the central part of the Hawaiian islands. **2 lanai,** porch.

Lan·ca·shire (lang′kə shər), *n.* county in NW England.

Lan·cas·ter (lang′kə stər), *n.* **1** the English royal house from 1399 to 1461. Its emblem was a red rose. **2** Lancashire.

lance (lans), **1** *n.* a long, wooden spear with a sharp iron or steel head: *The knights carried lances as they rode into battle.* **2** *n.* lancer. **3** *n.* any tool like a soldier's lance. A spear for harpooning a whale is called a lance. **4** *v.* to pierce with a lance: *lance a fish.* **5** *v.* to cut open with a lancet: *The doctor lanced the boil.* ◻ *v.* **lanced, lanc·ing.** [See Word Story at **launch**[1].]

lance corporal, a military rank. See chart on page 712.

Lan·ce·lot (lan′sə lot), *n.* (in legends of the Middle Ages) the bravest of King Arthur's knights of the Round Table.

lanc·er (lan′sər), *n.* a mounted soldier armed with a lance; lance.

lan·cet (lan′sit), *n.* a small, pointed knife with two sharp edges, used by doctors and surgeons in opening boils, abscesses, etc.

land (land), **1** *n.* the solid part of the earth's surface: *After weeks at sea, the voyagers sighted land.* **2** *v.* to come to land; bring to land: *The ship landed at the pier. The pilot landed the airplane in Seattle.* **3** *v.* to come down from the air; come to rest: *The airplane landed at the airport. The eagle landed on a rock.* **4** *v.* to put on land; set ashore: *The ship landed its passengers.* **5** *v.* to go on shore from a ship or boat: *The passengers landed.* **6** *n.* ground; soil: *This is good land for a garden.* **7** *n.* ground or soil

used as property: *People often buy land as an investment.* **8** *n.* country; region: *Switzerland is a mountainous land.* **9** *n.* people of a country; nation: *She collected folk songs from all the land.* **10** *v.* to come to a stop; arrive: *The burglar landed in jail. The car landed in the ditch.* **11** *v.* to cause to arrive: *This train will land you in London.* **12** *v.* to get; catch: *land a job, land a fish.* **13** *v.* to strike; hit: *I landed a blow on his chin.*

land breeze, breeze blowing from the land toward the sea.

land·ed (lan′did), *adj.* **1** owning land: *landed nobles.* **2** made up of land: *Landed property is real estate.*

landed immigrant, an immigrant admitted into Canada in order to become a permanent resident.

land element, CANADIAN. branch of the armed forces that fights on land, including infantry, armor, and artillery.

land·er (lan′dər), *n.* spacecraft or part of a spacecraft built to land on a planet, moon, etc.

Lan·ders (lan′dərz), *n.* **Ann** (an), born 1918, American advice columnist. ■ **Ann Landers'** twin sister also writes an advice column. She uses the name Abigail Van Buren.

land·fall (land′fôl′), *n.* **1** act of sighting land. **2** the land sighted or reached.

land·fill (land′fil′), *n.* place where garbage is buried, to dispose of it and often to build up low-lying or wet land.

landfill

land·form (land′fôrm′), *n.* a physical feature of the earth's surface. Plains, plateaus, hills, and mountains are landforms.

land·hold·er (land′hōl′dər), *n.* person who owns or occupies land.

land·ing (lan′ding), *n.* **1** act of coming to land or something solid like land: *the landing of the Pilgrims at Plymouth. There are many millions of takeoffs and landings at the nation's airports each year.* **2** place where persons or goods are landed from a ship, helicopter, etc. A wharf, dock, or pier is a landing for boats. **3** platform between flights of stairs.

landing field, field large enough and smooth enough for aircraft to land on and take off from safely.

landing gear, wheels, pontoons, etc., under an aircraft. When on land or water an aircraft rests on its landing gear.

landing strip, airstrip.

land·la·dy (land′lā′dē), *n.* **1** woman who owns buildings or land that is rented to others. **2** woman who runs an inn or rooming house. ◻ *n., pl.* **land·la·dies.**

land·less (land′lis), *adj.* without land; owning no land.

land·locked (land′lokt′), *adj.* **1** shut in, or nearly shut in, by land: *The landlocked harbor was protected from the full force of the wind and waves.* **2** living in waters shut off from the sea: *Landlocked salmon have to spend their lives in fresh water instead of migrating to salt water.*

land·lord (land′lôrd′), *n.* **1** person who owns buildings or land that is rented to others. **2** person who runs an inn or rooming house.

land·lub·ber (land′lub′ər), *n.* person not used to being on ships; person who is awkward on board ship because of lack of experience.

land·mark (land′märk′), *n.* **1** something familiar or easily seen, used as a guide: *The traveler did not lose her way in the forest because the rangers' high tower served as a landmark.* **2** any important fact or event; any happening that stands out above others: *The inventions of the printing press, telephone, telegraph, radio, television, and fiber optics are landmarks in the history of communication.* **3** a building, monument, or place designated as important or interesting: *That old building is a historical landmark.* **4** stone or other object that marks the boundary of a piece of land.

land·mass (land′mas′), *n.* a large area of land, especially a continent. □ *n., pl.* **land·mass·es.**

Land of the Midnight Sun, the regions north of the Arctic Circle; the Arctic.

land·own·er (land′ō′nər), *n.* person who owns land.

land reform, act or process of breaking up large properties of land into smaller properties with new owners, often the farmers who work on them.

land·scape (land′skāp), **1** *n.* view of scenery on land that can be taken in at a glance from one point of view: *From the church tower the valley formed a beautiful landscape.* **2** *n.* painting, etching, etc., showing such a view. **3** *v.* to make more pleasant to look at by arranging trees, bushes, flowers, etc.: *This park is landscaped.* □ *v.* **land·scaped, land·scap·ing.** —**land′scap′er,** *n.*

WORD STORY **Landscape** comes from two Dutch words meaning "land" and "-ship." In this word, *-ship* has the meaning "quality" or "condition." A painting that shows the quality or condition of some outdoor scene gives an idea of its "landship."

land·slide (land′slīd′), *n.* **1** mass of earth or rock that slides down a steep slope. **2** an overwhelming majority of votes for one candidate or political party in an election: *She won the election by a landslide.*

land·ward (land′wərd), *adv., adj.* toward the land or shore.

land·wards (land′wərdz), *adv.* landward.

lane (lān), *n.* **1** path between hedges, walls, or fences. **2** a narrow country road or city street. **3** any narrow way: *The bride and groom walked down a lane formed by two lines of wedding guests.* **4** course or route used by cars, ships, or aircraft going in the same direction. **5** bowling alley. ■ Another word that sounds like this is **lain.**

Lange (lang), *n.* **Dor·o·the·a** (dor′ō thē′ə), 1895-1965, American photographer. She is best known for her photographs of migrant workers and troubled farms during the Depression.

lan·guage (lang′gwij), *n.* **1** human speech, spoken or written: *Civilization would be impossible without language.* **2** the speech used by one nation, tribe, or other large group of people: *the French language, the Navajo language.* **3** communication among animals: *Our class did a project on dolphin language.* **4** a form, style, or kind of language; manner of expression: *poetic language.* **5** wording or words: *The lawyer explained the language of the contract.* **6** the special terms used by a science, art, or profession, or by a kind of people: *the language of chemistry.* **7** system of words, numbers, symbols, and abbreviations that stand for information and instructions in a computer. **8** expression of thoughts and feelings in a system other than speech or writing: *sign language.* **9** the study of language or languages; linguistics. [**Language** comes from a Latin word meaning "tongue."]

SYNONYM STUDY **Language, tongue,** and **speech** all mean the words shared by a particular group of people. **Language** is the general word: *The official languages of Canada are English and French.* **Tongue** is used mostly in writing: *The armies of Islam carried the Arabic tongue to many lands.* **Speech** means spoken language: *Words often become common in speech before they are accepted in writing.*

language arts, course of study in elementary schools and high schools that includes reading, spelling, speech, composition, and other subjects that develop skill in using language.

lan·guid (lang′gwid), *adj.* **1** feeling weak; without energy; drooping: *A hot, sticky day makes a person languid.* **2** without interest or enthusiasm; indifferent: *The lazy child felt too languid to do anything.* —**lan′guid·ly,** *adv.* —**lan′guid·ness,** *n.*

lan·guish (lang′gwish), *v.* **1** to grow weak; become weary; lose energy; droop: *The flowers languished from lack of water.* **2** to become weak or wasted through pain, hunger, etc.; suffer under any unfavorable conditions: *Wild animals often languish in captivity.* **3** to droop with longing; pine with love or grief: *The refugees languished for the homeland they had been forced to leave.* —**lan′guish·er,** *n.*

lan·guor (lang′gər), *n.* **1** lack of energy; weakness; weariness: *A long illness caused my languor.* **2** softness or tenderness of mood. **3** quietness; stillness: *the languor of a summer afternoon.*

lank (langk), *adj.* **1** long and thin; slender: *a lank child, lank grasses.* **2** straight and flat; not curly or wavy: *lank locks of hair.* —**lank′ly,** *adv.* —**lank′ness,** *n.*

lank·y (lang′kē), *adj.* awkwardly long and thin; tall and ungraceful: *a lanky teenager.* □ *adj.* **lank·i·er, lank·i·est.** —**lank′i·ly,** *adv.* —**lank′i·ness,** *n.*

lan·o·lin (lan′l ən), *n.* fatty substance obtained from the natural coating on wool fibers, used in cosmetics, ointments, shoe polish, etc.

Lan·sing (lan′sing), *n.* capital of Michigan, in the S part.

lan·tern (lan′tərn), *n.* a portable lamp with a transparent container around it to protect it from wind, rain, etc. [See word history information at **lamp.**]

lan·tha·num (lan′thə nəm), *n.* a metallic element which occurs in various minerals. It is easily shaped and is used in making alloys. *Symbol:* La

lan·yard (lan′yərd), *n.* **1** a short rope or cord used on ships to fasten rigging. **2** a loose cord around the neck on which to hang a knife, whistle, etc. **3** a short cord with a hook at one end, used in firing certain kinds of cannon.

La·os (lā′os *or* lä′ōs), *n.* country in SE Asia, west of Vietnam. *Capital:* Vientiane.

La·o·tian (lā ō′shən *or* lou′shən), **1** *adj.* of Laos, its people, or their language. **2** *n.* person born or living in Laos.

La·o Tzu (lou′ dzu′), 500s? B.C. Chinese philosopher. According to legend, he wrote the main book of Taoism.

Lange photograph

lap¹ (lap), *n.* **1** the front part from the waist to the knees of a person sitting down, with the clothing that covers it: *I held the baby on my lap.* **2** a loosely hanging edge of clothing; flap. [**Lap¹** comes from an old English word meaning "edge of a garment." The bottom of a shirt or jacket usually hangs about at the **lap.**]

in the lap of luxury, in luxurious circumstances.

lap² (lap), **1** *v.* to lay or lie together, one partly over or beside another; overlap: *We lapped shingles on the roof.* **2** *n.* the part that laps over. **3** *n.* amount that a part laps over. **4** *v.* to extend out beyond a limit: *The reign of Elizabeth I (queen of England from 1558 to 1603) lapped over into the 1600s.* **5** *v.* to wind or wrap; fold: *Lap this edge over that.* **6** *n.* the entire length of something, as a running course or swimming pool: *I swam three laps before breakfast.* **7** *n.* part of any course traveled: *The last lap of our all-day hike was the toughest.* □ *v.* **lapped, lap·ping.**

a	hat	ė	term	ô	order	ch	child		a in about
ā	age	i	it	oi	oil	ng	long		e in taken
ä	far	ī	ice	ou	out	sh	she	ə {	i in pencil
â	care	o	hot	u	cup	th	thin		o in lemon
e	let	ō	open	ù	put	ᴛʜ	then		u in circus
ē	equal	ò	saw	ü	rule	zh	measure		

lap³ (lap), **1** *v.* to drink by lifting up with the tongue: *Cats and dogs lap water.* **2** *v.* to move or beat gently with a lapping sound; splash gently: *Little waves lapped against the boat.* **3** *n.* act of lapping: *With one lap of the tongue the bear finished the honey.* **4** *n.* sound of lapping: *The lap of the waves against the shore always puts me to sleep.* ❑ *v.* **lapped, lap·ping.** —**lap′per,** *n.*

lap up, to take in eagerly or greedily; devour: *The scouts were so hungry after the long hike that they lapped up their dinners. The children lapped up the tales about frontier adventures.*

La Paz (lä päs′), one of the two capitals of Bolivia, in the W part. Sucre is the other capital.

lap dog, a small pet dog.

la·pel (lə pel′), *n.* either of the two front parts of a coat folded back just below the collar.

lap·i·dar·y (lap′ə der′ē), *n.* person who cuts, polishes, or engraves precious stones. ❑ *n., pl.* **lap·i·dar·ies.**

lap·is laz·u·li (lap′is laz′ə li), **1** a deep blue, semiprecious stone. **2** deep blue. ❑ *pl.* **lap′is laz′u·lis** for 1.

Lap·land (lap′land′), *n.* region in N Norway, N Sweden, N Finland, and NW Russia.

Lap·land·er (lap′lan′dər), *n.* person born or living in Lapland.

Lapp (lap), *n.* **1** one of a group of people that live in Lapland. **2** language of the Lapps.

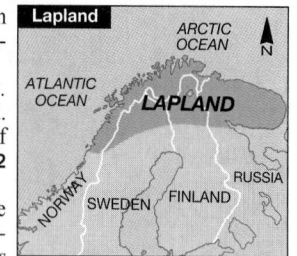

Lapland

ARCTIC OCEAN

ATLANTIC OCEAN

LAPLAND

NORWAY SWEDEN FINLAND RUSSIA

lapse (laps), **1** *n.* a slight mistake or error: *Due to a lapse of memory, I could not remember his name.* **2** *n.* act of slipping by or passing away: *A minute is a short lapse of time.* **3** *v.* to slip by; pass away: *His interest in the dull story soon lapsed.* **4** *n.* act of slipping into a lower condition: *War is a lapse into savage ways.* **5** *v.* to slip back; sink down: *I tried to be tidy, but soon lapsed into my old sloppy ways.* **6** *n.* act of falling or passing into any state: *a lapse into silence.* **7** *v.* to fall or pass into any state: *Our discussion lapsed into silence.* **8** *n.* the ending of a right or privilege because not renewed, not used, or otherwise neglected: *the lapse of a lease.* **9** *v.* to end in this way: *My driver's license lapsed when I failed to renew it.* ❑ *v.* **lapsed, laps·ing.**

WORD STORY **Lapse** comes from a Latin word meaning "to fall" or "to slip." A little mistake is like losing your balance or tripping on something. A little mistake in talking is called a slip of the tongue. **Lava** comes from the same Latin word because it slips down mountainsides.

lap·top (lap′top′), *n.* a small portable computer, easily balanced and used on your lap.

lar·board (lär′bərd), **1** *n.* the left or port side of a ship. **2** *adj.* on the left side of a ship.

lar·ce·nous (lär′sə nəs), *adj.* **1** involving larceny; guilty of larceny: *Burglary is a larcenous offense.* **2** thievish: *Blue jays are known for their larcenous habits.*

lar·ce·ny (lär′sə nē), *n.* crime of unlawfully taking and using the personal property of another person; theft. ❑ *n., pl.* **lar·ce·nies.** [**Larceny** comes from a Greek word meaning "pay." In old times, generals had to hire professional soldiers, who had no loyalty and stole whatever they could.]

larch (lärch), *n.* **1** any of several trees related to the pine, with small woody cones and needles that fall off in autumn. **2** the strong, tough wood of this tree. ❑ *n., pl.* **larch·es.**

lard (lärd), **1** *n.* the fat of hogs, melted down for use in cooking: *The cook uses lard in making pies.* **2** *v.* to put lard on or in; grease: *Lard the pan well.* **3** *v.* to give variety to; enrich: *The speaker larded his speech with jokes and stories.*

lar·der (lär′dər), *n.* **1** place where food is kept; pantry. **2** supply of food.

large (lärj), *adj.* of more than the usual size, amount, or number; big: *A hundred thousand dollars is a large sum of money. There was a large crowd at the game.* ❑ *adj.* **larg·er, larg·est.** —**large′ness,** *n.*

at large, 1 at liberty; free: *Is the escaped prisoner still at large?*

2 as a whole; altogether: *The people at large want peace.* **3** representing the whole of a state or district, not merely one division of it: *a congresswoman at large.*

large-heart·ed (lärj′här′tid), *adj.* generous; liberal.

large intestine, the wide, lower part of the intestines into which the small intestine discharges food that has not been digested. Water is absorbed in, and wastes are eliminated from, the large intestine.

large·ly (lärj′lē), *adv.* to a great extent; mainly: *This region consists largely of desert.*

large-scale (lärj′skāl′), *adj.* **1** involving many persons or things; great; extensive: *The great Chicago fire of 1871 was a large-scale disaster.* **2** made or drawn to a large scale: *This large-scale map shows many details.*

larg·ess or **larg·esse** (lär′jis), *n.* **1** generous giving. **2** a generous gift or gifts.

larg·ish (lär′jish), *adj.* rather large.

lar·go (lär′gō), in music: **1** *adj.* slow and dignified; stately. **2** *adv.* in a slow and dignified manner. **3** *n.* a slow, stately passage or piece of music. ❑ *n., pl.* **lar·gos.**

lar·i·at (lar′ē ət), *n.* a long rope with a loop at the end, used for catching horses and cattle; lasso. [**Lariat** comes from a Spanish word meaning "rope."]

lark¹ (lärk), *n.* **1** any of numerous small songbirds of Europe, Asia, America, and northern Africa with brown feathers and long hind claws. The skylark is one kind. Larks often sing while soaring in the air. **2** any of several similar unrelated American songbirds such as the meadowlarks.

lark² (lärk), **1** *n.* something that is good fun; a merry or happy time; frolic: *What a lark we had at the circus!* **2** *v.* to have fun; play; frolic.

lark·spur (lärk′spėr′), *n.* any of numerous plants with spurlike projections at the bottoms of their blue, pink, or white flowers; delphinium.

lar·ri·gan (lar′ə gən), *n.* CANADIAN. moccasin or boot made of oiled leather.

lar·va (lär′və), *n.* **1** the wormlike early form of an insect from the time it leaves the egg until it becomes a pupa or adult. A caterpillar is the larva of a butterfly or moth. The silkworm is a larva. **2** an immature form of some animals that is different in structure from the adult form and must undergo a change to become like the parent. A tadpole is the larva of a frog or toad. ❑ *n., pl.* **lar·vae** (lär′vē), **lar·vas.**

WORD STORY **Larva** comes from a Latin word meaning "a mask." This stage of an insect's life was called a mask because it does not look like its adult form. **Pupa** comes from a Latin word meaning "a doll." In this stage, an insect looks something like its adult form.

lar·val (lär′vəl), *adj.* **1** of or about larvae. **2** in the form of a larva.

lar·yn·gi·tis (lar′ən jī′tis), *n.* inflammation of the larynx, usually accompanied by hoarseness or loss of voice.

lar·ynx (lar′ingks), *n.* the upper end of the windpipe, where the vocal cords are; voice box. ❑ *n., pl.* **la·ryn·ges** (lə rin′jēz), **lar·ynx·es.**

la·sa·gna (lə zä′nyə), *n.* food made of chopped meat, cheese, and tomato sauce, baked with layers of wide noodles.

WORD STORY **Lasagna** comes from the Italian name of this food. The Italian word comes from a Greek word meaning "cooking pot." Originally the meaning was "a stand for a pot." The word for the stand was used for the pot; the word for the pot was used for the food. Similarly, in English today, **dish** can mean either a kind of food or the plate it's served on.

La Salle (lə sal′), **Ro·bert Ca·ve·lier** (rȯ ber′ kä və lyā′), Sieur de (syėr də), 1643-1687, French explorer. He led the first European expedition down the Mississippi River to the Gulf of Mexico.

las·civ·i·ous (lə siv′ē əs), *adj.* feeling, showing, or causing physical desire or lust. —**las·civ′i·ous·ly,** *adv.* —**las·civ′i·ous·ness,** *n.*

Las Cru·ces (läs krü′sis), city in SW New Mexico, on the Rio Grande.

la·ser (lā′zər), *n.* device that produces a very narrow and intense beam of light of only one wavelength going in only one direction. Laser beams are used to cut or melt hard materials, remove diseased body tissues, make holograms, play optical disks, etc.

WORD STORY **Laser** comes from the words **l**ight **a**mplification by **s**timulated **e**mission of **r**adiation. It was formed by using the first letter of most of these words. It is easier to understand how this word was formed than to understand how lasers are formed.

laser disk, a thin plastic-coated metal disk, about twice as wide as a compact disk. It is a form of optical disk. Movies, pictures, music, and computer information can be recorded on laser disks.

laser printer, a computer printer that uses a laser to print out documents at high speed and with high resolution.

lash[1] (lash), **1** *n.* the part of a whip that is not the handle: *The leather lash cut the side of the horse.* **2** *n.* a stroke or blow with a whip: *The driver gave his horse a lash.* **3** *v.* to strike with a whip; flog: *The driver of the team lashed her horses on.* **4** *v.* to beat back and forth: *The lion lashed its tail.* **5** *n.* a sudden, swift movement: *the lash of an animal's tail.* **6** *v.* to strike violently; hit: *The rain lashed against the windows.* **7** *v.* to attack severely in words; scold sharply: *In her speech she lashed out at corrupt politicians.* **8** *n.* eyelash. ❑ *n., pl.* **lash·es.** —**lash′er,** *n.*

lash[2] (lash), *v.* to tie or fasten with a rope or cord: *We lashed logs together to make a raft.* —**lash′er,** *n.*

lash·ing (lash′ing), *n.* rope or cord, used in tying or fastening.

lass (las), *n.* a girl or young woman. ❑ *n., pl.* **lass·es.**

Las·sen Volcanic National Park (las′ən), a national park in NE California, containing volcanic formations, hot springs, and glacial lakes.

las·sie (las′ē), *n.* girl; lass.

las·si·tude (las′ə tüd), *n.* lack of energy; a feeling of weakness; weariness: *a period of renewed excitement after an interval of lassitude.*

las·so (las′ō *or* la sü′), **1** *n.* a long rope with a loop at one end, used for catching horses and cattle; lariat. **2** *v.* to catch with a lasso. ❑ *n., pl.* **las·sos** *or* **las·soes;** *v.* **las·soed, las·so·ing.** [See Word Story at **lace.**]

last[1] (last), **1** *adj.* coming after all others; being at the end; final: *the last page of the book. Z is the last letter of the alphabet; A is the first.* **2** *adv.* after all others; at the end; finally: *He came last in the line.* **3** *adv.* latest: *When did you see her last?* **4** *adj.* most unlikely: *Fighting is the last thing I would do.* **5** *n.* someone or something that comes after all others: *He was the last in the line.* **6** *n.* end: *You have not heard the last of this.*

at last *or* **at long last,** at the end; after a long time; finally: *At last the baby fell asleep.*

breathe your last, to die.

SYNONYM STUDY **Last**[1] and **final** both mean at the end. **Last** means after all others: *He is last in line.* **Final** means that there will be no more: *Today is the final day of the contest.*

last[2] (last), *v.* **1** to go on; hold out; continue in time; endure: *The storm lasted three days. Can you last through the race? How long will our money last?* ■ See Synonym Study at **continue. 2** to continue in good condition, force, etc.: *I hope these shoes last a year.*

WORD STORY **Last**[2] comes from an old German word meaning "footprint." **Last**[3] comes from the same word. To track a person or animal by footprints requires endurance and lasting patience, and so **last**[2] got its present meanings.

last[3] (last), *n.* block shaped like a person's foot, on which shoes and boots are made or repaired. [See Word Story at **last**[2].]

last-ditch (last′dich′), *adj.* **1** final; very late and with all remaining strength; used in a final attempt when other attempts have failed: *a last-ditch effort to win the election by giving speeches all day.* **2** refusing to give in: *The last-ditch fans sat in the snow watching their team lose.*

last·ing (las′ting), *adj.* existing for a long time; permanent: *The thrilling voyage had a lasting effect on me.* —**last′ing·ly,** *adv.*

last·ly (last′lē), *adv.* in conclusion; finally: *Lastly, I want to thank all of you for your help.*

last-min·ute (last′min′it), *adj.* at the latest possible time; just before it is too late: *last-minute shoppers.*

last quarter, 1 period of time between the second half moon and the new moon. **2** phase of the moon represented by the half moon after the full moon.

last rites, religious rites performed for a dying person or at a funeral.

last straw, last of a series of troublesome things that finally causes a collapse, outburst, etc.

Last Supper, supper of Jesus and His disciples on the evening before He was crucified; Lord's Supper.

last word, 1 last thing said. **2** authority to make the final decision. **3** the latest thing. **4** something that cannot be improved.

Las Ve·gas (läs vā′gəs), city in SE Nevada.

lat., latitude.

Lat., Latin.

latch (lach), **1** *n.* a catch for fastening a door, gate, or window, often one not needing a key. A latch consists of a movable piece of metal or wood that fits into a notch or opening. **2** *v.* to fasten with a latch: *Latch and bar the door.* ❑ *n., pl.* **latch·es.** ■ See Synonym Study at **lock**[1].

latch onto, INFORMAL. to get as your own; get and hold: *He latched onto the basketball and wouldn't let anyone else play.*

latch·key (lach′kē′), *n.* key used to draw back or unfasten the latch on a door. ❑ *n., pl.* **latch·keys.**

latchkey child, a young child who comes home from school before any adult comes home, and who uses a key to get in.

late (lāt), **1** *adj., adv.* after the usual or proper time: *We had a late dinner last night. He worked late.* **2** *adj., adv.* near the end: *She reached success late in life.* **3** *adj.* not long past; recent: *My parents just bought a late model car.* **4** *adj.* recently dead: *The late Mary Lee was a good citizen.* **5** *adj.* gone out of or retired from office: *The late president is still working actively.* **6** *adv.* recently but no longer: *Jane Smith, late of Boston.* ❑ *adj.* **lat·er** *or* **lat·ter, lat·est** *or* **last;** *adv.* **lat·er, lat·est** *or* **last.** —**late′ness,** *n.*

of late, lately; recently: *I haven't seen them of late.*

late·com·er (lāt′kum′ər), *n.* person or group that has arrived late or recently: *The latecomers to the play missed the first act.*

la·teen sail (la tēn′), a triangular sail held up by a long beam on a short mast.

late·ly (lāt′lē), *adv.* a little while ago; not long ago; recently: *He has not been looking well lately.*

la·tent (lāt′nt), *adj.* present but not active; hidden: *The power of a seed to grow into a plant remains latent if it is not planted.* —**la′tent·ly,** *adv.*

lat·er·al (lat′ər əl), **1** *adj.* of the side; at the side; from the side; toward the side: *A lateral fin of a fish grows from its side.* **2** *n.* lateral pass. —**lat′er·al·ly,** *adv.*

lateral pass, (in football) a pass thrown sideways or slightly backward, not forward.

la·tex (lā′teks), *n.* **1** a milky liquid found in milkweed, poppies, and plants yielding rubber. It hardens in the air, and is used to make rubber, chewing gum, and other products. **2** rubber or plastic mixed into but not dissolved in water, used especially in paints. ❑ *n., pl.* **la·tex·es** *or* **lat·i·ces.**

lath (lath), *n.* **1** a thin, narrow strip of wood used with others like it to form a support for the plaster of a wall or ceiling. **2** a wire cloth or sheet metal with holes in it, used in place of laths. ❑ *n., pl.* **laths** (laᴛʜz *or* laths).

lathe (lāᴛʜ), *n.* machine for holding pieces of wood, metal, etc., and turning them rapidly against a cutting tool which shapes them.

lath·er (laᴛʜ′ər), **1** *n.* foam made from soap and water. **2** *v.* to put lather on: *He lathers his face before shaving.* **3** *v.* to form a lather: *This soap lathers well.* **4** *n.* foam formed in sweating: *the lather on a horse after a race.*

lat·i·ces (lat′ə sēz), *n.* a plural of **latex.**

a	hat	ė	term	ô	order	ch	child		
ā	age	i	it	oi	oil	ng	long		a in about
ä	far	ī	ice	ou	out	sh	she		e in taken
â	care	o	hot	u	cup	th	thin	ə	i in pencil
e	let	ō	open	u̇	put	ᴛʜ	then		o in lemon
ē	equal	ò	saw	ü	rule	zh	measure		u in circus

Lat·in (lat′n), **1** *n.* language of the ancient Romans, used in written form by scholars through the Middle Ages. It is still used in official documents of the Roman Catholic Church. **2** *adj.* of Latin; in Latin: *Latin poetry, Latin grammar, a Latin scholar.* **3** *n.* member of any of the peoples whose languages came from Latin. The Italians, French, Spanish, Portuguese, and Romanians are Latins. **4** *adj.* of these peoples or their languages.

WORD SOURCE **Latin** has given thousands of words to the English language, including the words below.

audio	grace	map	reptile
author	hospital	menu	republic
binoculars	human	model	salary
bus	index	motor	salmon
cereal	insect	muscle	salute
clock	insult	noble	student
companion	introduce	notice	stupid
demonstration	jelly	obey	tornado
education	join	order	tuba
erase	journey	peace	umbrella
face	kitchen	pigeon	video
fool	language	pupil	virus
fossil	library	question	volcano

La·ti·na (lə tē′nə *or* la tē′nə), *n.* a girl or woman of Hispanic descent. ❑ *n., pl.* **La·ti·nas.** ■ See Usage Note at **Hispanic.**

Latin America, South America, Central America, Mexico, and most of the West Indies. Many Latin American countries use Spanish, Portuguese, or French, all of which came from Latin, as official languages.

Latin American, 1 of or from Latin America. **2** person born or living in Latin America.

La·ti·no (lə tē′nō *or* la tē′nō), *n.* a boy or man of Hispanic descent. ❑ *n., pl.* **La·ti·nos.** ■ See Usage Note at **Hispanic.**

lat·ish (lā′tish), *adj., adv.* rather late.

lat·i·tude (lat′ə tüd), *n.* **1** distance north or south of the equator, measured in degrees. A degree of latitude is about 69 miles (111 kilometers). **2** place or region having a certain latitude: *Polar bears live in the cold latitudes.* **3** room to act or think; freedom from narrow rules; scope: *Artists enjoy much latitude in their work.* [*Latitude* comes from a Latin word meaning "wide." Roman maps were much wider than they were long, and lines of latitude went across the wide way.]

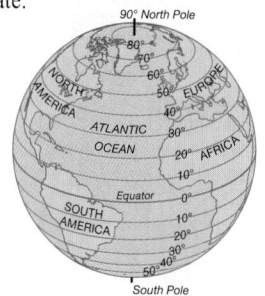

90° North Pole
NORTH AMERICA
EUROPE
ATLANTIC OCEAN
AFRICA
Equator
SOUTH AMERICA
South Pole

la·trine (lə trēn′), *n.* toilet, especially in a camp, factory, or army barracks.

lat·ter (lat′ər), *adj.* **1** the second of two: *Canada and the United States are in North America; the former lies north of the latter.* **2** more recent; nearer the end; later: *Friday comes in the latter part of the week.* ❑ *adj.* **late, latest** or **last.**

Lat·ter-day Saint (lat′ər dā′), Mormon.

lat·ter·ly (lat′ər lē), *adv.* at a recent time; lately.

lat·tice (lat′is), **1** *n.* structure of crossed wooden or metal strips with open spaces between them. **2** *v.* to furnish with a lattice: *The windows are latticed with iron bars.* **3** *n.* window, gate, etc., having a lattice. **4** *v.* to form into a lattice: *The cook latticed strips of dough across the pie.* ❑ *v.* **lat·ticed, lat·tic·ing.** —**lat′tice·like′,** *adj.*

lat·tice·work (lat′is wèrk′), *n.* **1** a lattice. **2** lattices: *Many old New Orleans houses are decorated with latticework of wrought iron.*

Lat·vi·a (lat′vē ə), *n.* a country in N Europe, on the Baltic Sea. *Capital:* Riga. —**Lat′vi·an,** *adj., n.*

laud (lôd), *v.* to praise highly; commend: *Our teacher lauded our efforts to raise money for the new library.*

laud·a·ble (lô′də bəl), *adj.* deserving praise; commendable: *Her desire to help her mother in the store is laudable.* —**laud′a·ble·ness,** *n.* —**laud′a·bly,** *adv.*

lau·da·num (lôd′n əm), *n.* solution of opium in alcohol, formerly used to lessen pain.

laud·a·to·ry (lô′də tôr′ē), *adj.* expressing praise; very complimentary: *a laudatory review.*

laugh (laf), **1** *v.* to make the sounds and movements of the face and body that show you are happy or amused: *We all laughed at the joke.* **2** *n.* act or sound of laughing: *a hearty laugh.* **3** *v.* to drive, put, bring, etc., by or with laughing: *The children laughed their tears away.* —**laugh′er,** *n.* —**laugh′ing·ly,** *adv.*

have the last laugh, to get the better of someone after appearing to lose: *In the race between the hare and the tortoise, the tortoise had the last laugh.*

laugh at, to make fun of; ridicule: *They laughed at me for believing in ghosts.*

laugh off, to get out of by laughing; treat as a joke: *My friend just laughs off any nasty comments the older kids make.*

SYNONYM STUDY **Laugh, chuckle,** and **giggle** all mean to make sounds and motions that show amusement. **Laugh** is the general word: *She laughed loudly at the joke.* **Chuckle** means to laugh softly: *I could barely hear him chuckling beside me.* **Giggle** means to laugh in a silly way: *He got embarrassed and began to giggle for no reason.*

laugh·a·ble (laf′ə bəl), *adj.* causing laughter; amusing; funny: *a laughable mistake.* —**laugh′a·bly,** *adv.*

laugh·ing (laf′ing), *adj.* **no laughing matter,** matter that is serious.

laughing gas, nitrous oxide.

laugh·ing·stock (laf′ing stok′), *n.* person or thing that is made fun of.

laugh·ter (laf′tər), *n.* **1** sound of laughing: *Laughter filled the room.* **2** action of laughing: *The clown's antics brought forth laughter from the children.*

laugh track, recording of laughter, played during a TV or radio show to make it seem funnier.

launch[1] (lônch), **1** *v.* to cause to slide into the water; set afloat: *The new ship was launched from the supports on which it was built.* **2** *v.* to send into the air or into outer space: *The satellite was launched in a rocket.* **3** *n.* act of launching a rocket, missile, aircraft, ship, etc.: *The launch of the first space shuttle was a historic event.* **4** *v.* to get going; set out; start: *Our friends launched us in business by lending us money.* ❑ *n., pl.* **launch·es.** —**launch′er,** *n.*

WORD STORY **Launch**[1] comes from a Latin word meaning "a spear." **Lance** comes from the same word. When horseback soldiers began wearing armor, the light throwing spear became the heavy hand-held lance.

launch[2] (lônch), *n.* **1** an open motorboat used for pleasure trips, for ferrying passengers, etc. **2** the largest boat carried by a warship. ❑ *n., pl.* **launch·es.**

launching pad, surface or platform on which a rocket or missile is prepared for launching and from which it is launched.

launch pad, launching pad.

laun·der (lôn′dər), *v.* **1** to wash and iron clothes, tablecloths, towels, etc. **2** to be able to be washed; stand washing: *Cotton materials usually launder well.* **3** to transfer money that someone gets illegally through a legitimate business, so that the money appears to have been legally earned. —**laun′der·a·ble,** *adj.* —**laun′der·er,** *n.*

laun·dress (lôn′dris), *n.* woman whose work is washing and ironing clothes, tablecloths, towels, etc. ❑ *n., pl.* **laun·dress·es.**

Laun·dro·mat (lôn′drə mat), *n.* trademark for a self-service laundry that has coin-operated washing machines and dryers.

laun·dry (lôn′drē), *n.* **1** clothes, tablecloths, towels, etc., washed or to be washed. **2** room or building where clothes, tablecloths, towels, etc., are washed and ironed. ❑ *n., pl.* **laun·dries** for 2.

laun·dry·man (lôn′drē mən), *n.* person who works in or for a laundry: *Our laundryman collects and delivers our laundry every Monday.* ❑ *n., pl.* **laun·dry·men.**

lau·re·ate (lôr′ē it), *n.* poet laureate.

lau·rel (lôr′əl), *n.* **1** a small evergreen tree of southern Europe, with smooth, shiny leaves; bay. **2** the leaves of this tree. The ancient Greeks and Romans made wreaths of laurel to put on the heads of persons they wished to honor. **3** any tree or bush related to the European laurel. **4** mountain laurel. **5 laurels**, *pl.* **a** high honor; fame. **b** victory.

rest on your laurels, be satisfied with the honors that you have already won or the achievements you have already attained: *Instead of resting on her laurels, she went on to further success.*

la·va (lä′və *or* lav′ə), *n.* **1** hot, melted rock flowing from a volcano. **2** rock formed by the cooling of this melted rock. Some lavas are hard and glassy; others are light and porous. □ *n., pl.* **lavas.** [See Word Story at **lapse.**]

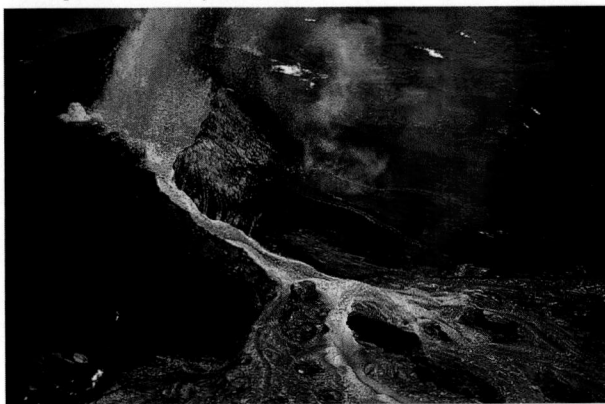

lava (def. 1)

lav·a·to·ry (lav′ə tôr′ē), *n.* **1** bathroom; toilet. **2** bowl or basin to wash in. □ *n., pl.* **lav·a·to·ries.** [See Word Story at **lavish.**]

lave (lāv), *v.* OLD USE. **1** to wash; bathe. **2** to wash or flow against. □ *v.* **laved, lav·ing.**

lav·en·der (lav′ən dər), **1** *adj.* pale purple. **2** *n.* a pale purple. **3** *n.* any of several small bushes with stalks of thickly growing fragrant, pale purple flowers. Oil from lavender is used in perfumes. **4** *n.* dried flowers, leaves, and stalks of these plants, used to perfume linens or clothes.

lav·ish (lav′ish), **1** *adj.* very free in giving or spending; extravagant: *A very rich person can be lavish with money.* **2** *adj.* very abundant; more than is needed: *a lavish helping of dessert.* **3** *v.* to give or spend very freely or too freely: *We lavished kindness on our sick friend.* —**lav′ish·er**, *n.* —**lav′ish·ly**, *adv.* —**lav′ish·ness**, *n.*

WORD STORY Lavish comes from a Latin word meaning "to wash." **Lavatory** comes from the same word. Because washing involves pouring out water, the Latin word became an old French word meaning "rainstorm." **Lavish** suggests a downpour of gifts or money.

La·voi·sier (lä vwä zyā′), *n.* **An·toine Lau·rent** (an′twon lô rän′), 1743-1794, French chemist. ■ **Lavoisier** was the first to explain fire scientifically. He also proved the law of conservation of matter and was the first person to write a chemical equation.

law (lô), *n.* **1** rule or regulation made by a country, state, etc., for all the people who live there: *a traffic law. Good citizens obey the laws.* **2** system of such rules formed to protect society: *English law is different from French law.* **3** the study of such a system of rules; the profession of a lawyer: *My cousin is planning a career in law.* **4** controlling influence of these rules: *The police maintain law and order.* **5** system of enforcement of the rules: *courts of law.* **6** police or similar organization that makes sure that government rules and regulations are obeyed: **7** all the rules concerned with a particular subject: *commercial law, criminal law.* **8** any rule that must be obeyed: *the laws of hospitality.* **9** statement of what always occurs under certain conditions: *the law of gravitation. Scientists study the laws of nature.* **10 the Law,** the first five books of the Bible, containing the Mosaic law.

lay down the law, 1 to give orders that must be obeyed: *There is no official to lay down the law on this question.* **2** to give a scolding: *The teacher laid down the law to the noisy class.*

take the law into your own hands, to protect your rights or punish a crime without appealing to courts of law: *In the early days of the American West, settlers often took the law into their own hands.*

law·a·bid·ing (lô′ə bī′ding), *adj.* obeying the law; peaceful and orderly: *As a law-abiding citizen, I don't litter.*

law·break·er (lô′brā′kər), *n.* someone who breaks the law.

law court, court of law.

law·ful (lô′fəl), *adj.* **1** according to law; done as the law directs: *lawful arrest.* **2** allowed by law; rightful: *lawful demands.* —**law′ful·ly**, *adv.* —**law′ful·ness**, *n.*

law·giv·er (lô′giv′ər), *n.* someone who prepares and puts into effect a system of laws for a people.

law·less (lô′lis), *adj.* **1** paying no attention to the law; breaking the law: *A thief leads a lawless life.* **2** having no laws: *In pioneer days much of the American West was lawless.* **3** hard to control; disorderly; unruly: *a wild and lawless sea.* —**law′less·ly**, *adv.* —**law′less·ness**, *n.*

law·mak·er (lô′mā′kər), *n.* someone who helps make the laws of a country; member of a legislature, congress, or parliament; legislator.

law·mak·ing (lô′mā′king), **1** *adj.* having the duty and power of making laws; legislative: *Congress is a lawmaking group.* **2** *n.* the making of laws; legislation.

law·man (lô′mən), *n.* a law enforcement officer. □ *n., pl.* **law·men.**

lawn¹ (lôn), *n.* piece of land covered with grass kept closely cut, especially near or around a house.

lawn² (lôn), *n.* a kind of thin, sheer linen or cotton cloth.

lawn bowling, game played on a lawn by rolling a ball as close as possible to a smaller ball at the other end of the lawn.

lawn mower *or* **lawn·mow·er** (lôn′mō′ər), *n.* machine with revolving blades for cutting the grass on a lawn.

lawn tennis, tennis, especially when played on a grass court.

law·ren·ci·um (lô ren′sē əm), *n.* a short-lived radioactive element produced artificially from californium. Symbol: Lr

law·suit (lô′süt′), *n.* case in a court of law started by one person to claim something from another; claim brought before a court of law to obtain justice.

Law·ton (lô′tən), *n.* city in SW Oklahoma.

law·yer (lô′yər *or* loi′yər), *n.* person whose profession is giving advice about the laws or acting for others in a court of law.

lax (laks), *adj.* **1** not tight or firm; slack: *The package was tied so loosely that the cord was lax.* **2** not strict; careless: *Don't become lax about the schedule for doing your homework.* **3** not exact; vague. [See Word Story at **lease.**] —**lax′ly**, *adv.* —**lax′ness**, *n.*

lax·a·tive (lak′sə tiv), **1** *n.* a medicine that causes the intestines to empty. **2** *adj.* causing the intestines to empty.

lax·i·ty (lak′sə tē), *n.* lax condition or quality.

lay¹ (lā), *v.* **1** to place in a certain position; put down: *Lay your hat on the table.* **2** to bring down; beat down: *A storm laid the crops low.* **3** to place in a lying-down position: *Lay the baby down gently.* **4** to place or set: *Lay your hand on your heart. The scene of this story is laid in New York.* **5** to put: *Lay aside that book for me. The horse laid its ears back.* **6** to put in place: *lay bricks. They laid the carpet on the floor.* **7** to put down as a bet; offer as a bet; wager: *I lay five dollars that she won't come.* **8** to blame; attribute: *I laid my failure on my lack of effort.* **9** to set forth; present: *The lawyers will lay their arguments before the jury.* **10** to give forth; produce an egg or eggs: *Birds, fish, and reptiles lay eggs. All the hens were laying well.* □ *v.* **laid, lay·ing.** ■ Another word that sounds like this is **lei.**

lay about, to hit out on all sides: *Attacked by thieves, the merchant laid about with his walking stick.*

lay aside, lay away, *or* **lay by,** to put away for future use; save: *I laid away a dollar a week to buy a new bicycle.*

lay down, 1 to declare; state: *lay down conditions.* **2** to give; sacrifice: *lay down your life for the cause of liberty.*

lay for, to stay hidden ready to attack.

lay in, to put aside for the future; provide: *The trapper laid in enough supplies for the winter.*

a	hat	ė	term	ô	order	ch	child		
ā	age	i	it	oi	oil	ng	long		a in about
ä	far	ī	ice	ou	out	sh	she		e in taken
â	care	o	hot	u	cup	th	thin	ə	i in pencil
e	let	ō	open	ů	put	ŦH	then		o in lemon
ē	equal	ò	saw	ü	rule	zh	measure		u in circus

lay into, 1 to beat; thrash: *She laid into the vicious dog with a stick.* **2** INFORMAL. to scold: *My parents laid into me for not doing my homework.*

lay off, 1 to put out of work for a time: *During the slack season many workers were laid off.* **2** to mark off: *The coach laid off the boundaries of the tennis court.* **3** INFORMAL. to stop teasing or interfering with: *Lay off me! I'm trying to study.*

lay open, 1 to make bare; expose: *The captured spy laid open to us the whole scheme of the attack.* **2** to make an opening in; wound.

lay out, 1 to spread out: *Supper was laid out on the table.* **2** to arrange; plan: *The road was laid out but not yet paved.* **3** to pay out; spend: *I had to lay out a lot of money for my new bicycle.* **4** to prepare a dead body for burial.

lay over, to stop for a time in a place: *It was raining so hard one day on our trip that we laid over until the rain stopped.*

lay to, to head into the wind and stand still: *The ship lay to until the fog lifted.*

lay up, 1 to put away for future use: *After the sailing season was over we laid our boat up for the winter.* **2** to cause to stay in bed or indoors because of illness: *I was laid up with a bad cold last week.*

lay yourself out, to make a big effort; take great pains: *He laid himself out to be agreeable.*

USAGE NOTE **Lay**¹ and **lie**² are sometimes confused, because the past tense of **lie**² is **lay**²: *He lay on the couch.* **Lay**¹ means "to put down": *Lay your hat there. She laid her book on the desk.* Don't use **lay** to mean "rest flat." Use **lie**: *The wallet was lying in the street. I want to lie down.*

lay² (lā), *v.* past tense of **lie**²: *I took a long walk and then lay down for a rest.* ■ Another word that sounds like this is **lei.**

lay³ (lā), *adj.* **1** of or relating to the people of a church who do not belong to the clergy. A lay sermon is one given by someone who is not a member of the clergy. **2** of or relating to the people who do not belong to a particular profession: *I am not a doctor, but my lay opinion is that you have the flu.* ■ Another word that sounds like this is **lei.**

lay⁴ (lā), *n.* **1** poem to be sung, especially one that tells a story or legend in simple verse form. **2** song; tune. ■ Another word that sounds like this is **lei.**

lay·a·way (lā′ə wā′), **1** *n.* a way of buying in which a buyer pays a bit at a time and the seller holds the item until the buyer has paid in full. **2** *adj.* of or relating to this method of buying: *I worked out a layaway plan to buy a color TV.*

lay·er (lā′ər), **1** *n.* a thickness of some material: *The runner wore a warm layer of clothing next to her skin.* **2** *n.* person or thing that lays: *That hen is a champion layer.* **3** *v.* to spread by layers.

layer cake, cake made in layers put together with frosting or filling.

lay·ette (lā et′), *n.* set of clothes and bedding for a newborn baby.

lay·man (lā′mən), *n.* **1** member of a church who is not a clergyman: *The priest and several laymen planned the church budget.* **2** someone who is not a member of a particular profession: *It is hard for most laymen to understand doctors' prescriptions.* ❑ *n., pl.* **lay·men.**

lay·off (lā′ôf′), *n.* **1** act of putting people out of work temporarily. **2** time during which the people are out of work.

lay of the land, 1 the nature of a place; the position of hills, water, woods, etc. **2** the situation as it exists; how things are: *Careful planning includes a good look at the lay of the land.*

lay·out (lā′out′), *n.* **1** arrangement; plan: *This map shows the layout of the camp.* **2** a plan or design for an advertisement, book, etc. **3** something laid or spread out; display.

lay·o·ver (lā′ō′vər), *n.* a short stay in a place: *After a twenty-minute layover in Chicago we flew on to Los Angeles.*

lay·per·son (lā′pėr′sən), *n.* someone who does not belong to a particular profession, or who does not have technical training: *a layperson's guide to computer programming.*

lay·up or **lay·up** (lā′up′), *n.* (in basketball) a shot made close to the basket, often a bank shot.

Laz·a·rus (laz′ər əs), *n.* (in the Bible) the brother of Mary and Martha. Jesus raised him from the dead. [**Lazarus** comes from a Hebrew word meaning "one whom God helped."]

Laz·a·rus (laz′ər əs), *n.* **Emma** (em′ə), 1849-1887, American poet. She wrote the poem that is on the pedestal of the Statue of Liberty.

laze (lāz), *v.* to be lazy or idle. ❑ *v.* **lazed, laz·ing.**

la·zy (lā′zē), *adj.* **1** not willing to work or be active: *He lost his job because he was lazy.* **2** moving slowly; not very active: *A lazy stream winds through the meadow.* ❑ *adj.* **la·zi·er, la·zi·est.** —**la′zi·ly,** *adv.* —**la′zi·ness,** *n.*

SYNONYM STUDY **Lazy, idle,** and **sluggish** all mean not active. **Lazy** means unwilling to work: *He acts lazy because this job bores him.* **Idle** means not doing anything: *She hates being idle, so she has many hobbies.* **Sluggish** means without energy: *The old dog is sluggish.*

la·zy·bones (lā′zē bōnz′), *n.* INFORMAL. a very lazy person.

lb., pound. ❑ *pl.* **lb.** or **lbs.**

WORD STORY Why is **lb.** the abbreviation for **pound**? You may know the Latin name **Libra,** meaning "a scale for weighing," as the name of a constellation. The word was also used to mean an amount of weight, one pound. In old England, most people who could write knew Latin. They were used to the abbreviation **lb.** from Latin, and they borrowed it for the English word with the same meaning.

lc or **l.c.,** lowercase.

LCD, liquid crystal display.

lea (lē), *n.* a grassy field; meadow. ■ Another word that sounds like this is **lee.**

leach (lēch), *v.* to dissolve soluble parts from ashes, ores, etc., by running water through slowly: *Potash is leached from wood ashes and used to make soap.* ■ Another word that sounds like this is **leech.** —**leach′a·ble,** *adj.* —**leach′er,** *n.*

lead¹ (lēd), **1** *v.* to show the way by going along with or in front of: *The guide dog led its owner safely across the street.* ■ See Synonym Study at **guide. 2** *v.* to be first among: *She leads the class in spelling.* **3** *n.* guidance or direction; leadership: *The scientists followed the lead of the director of the expedition.* **4** *v.* to guide or direct in action, policy, opinion, etc.; influence; persuade: *Such actions lead us to distrust them.* **5** *v.* to be a way or road: *Hard work leads to success.* **6** *v.* to pass or spend time in some special way: *He leads a*

lead¹ (def. 1)

quiet life in the country. **7** *v.* to go first; begin a game or other activity: *You may lead this time.* **8** *v.* to be chief of; command; direct: *She leads the community orchestra.* **9** *n.* place of a leader; place in front: *She always takes the lead when we plan to do anything.* **10** *n.* right to go or begin first: *It is your lead this time.* **11** *n.* the principal part in a play. **12** *n.* person who plays this part. **13** *n.* amount that you are ahead: *I had a narrow lead in the race.* **14** *n.* suggestion or clue: *He was not sure where to look for the information, but the librarian gave him several good leads.* **15** *n.* the opening paragraph in a newspaper or magazine article. A lead often summarizes the information in the body of the article. **16** *n.* (in baseball) position where a base runner stands, a short distance off one base in the direction of the next. ❑ *v.* **led, lead·ing.**

lead off, 1 to begin; start. **2** (in baseball) be the first player in the batting order or the first to come to bat in any inning.

lead on, to mislead, deceive, or persuade someone to do something unwise or illegal: *The suspect admitted the burglary, but claimed his friends had led him on.*

lead up to, 1 to come before something. **2** to approach a topic gradually.

lead² (led), **1** *n.* a soft, heavy, bluish gray metallic element which is used to make pipe, radiation shields, etc. *Symbol:* Pb **2** *adj.* made of lead: *a lead pipe.* **3** *n.* bullets; shot: *a hail of lead.* **4** *n.* a long, thin piece of graphite used in pencils. **5** *n.* weight on a line used to find out the depth of water; plumb. **6** *v.* to cover, frame, or weight with lead. ■ Another word that sounds like this is **led.**

lead·en (led′n), *adj.* **1** made of lead: *a leaden coffin.* **2** hard to lift or move; heavy: *leaden arms tired from working.* **3** dull; gloomy. **4** bluish gray: *Do you suppose those leaden clouds mean snow?* —**lead′en·ly,** *adv.* —**lead′en·ness,** *n.*

lead·er (lē′dər), *n.* someone who leads, or is well fitted to lead: *an orchestra leader. That girl is a born leader.* —**lead′er·less,** *adj.*

lead·er·ship (lē′dər ship), *n.* **1** condition of being a leader. **2** ability to lead: *Leadership is a great asset to an officer.* **3** guidance or direction: *Our group needs some leadership.* **4** people in charge of a group; leaders: *The leadership doesn't like to explain the exact process for making decisions.*

lead·ing (lē′ding), *adj.* **1** most important; chief; principal: *She has the leading role in the play.* **2** in the front position; foremost: *the leading float in the parade.* **3** showing the way; guiding; directing: *to ask someone a leading question.*

lead·off (lēd′ôf′), **1** *n.* act of beginning or starting something. **2** *n.* (in baseball) the first player of the batting order or the first to come to bat in any inning. **3** *adj.* beginning or leading off.

leaf (lēf), **1** *n.* one of the thin, usually flat, green parts of a tree or other plant that grow on the stem or grow up from the roots. **2** *v.* to put forth leaves: *The trees along the river leaf earlier than those on the hill.* **3** *n.* sheet of paper. Each side of a leaf is called a page. **4** *v.* to turn the pages: *to leaf through a book.* **5** *n.* a very thin sheet of metal, etc.: *gold leaf.* **6** *n.* a flat, movable piece in the top of a table: *We put two extra leaves in the table for the party.* ❏ *n., pl.* **leaves.** —**leaf′less,** *adj.* —**leaf′like′,** *adj.*

turn over a new leaf, to start all over again; try to do or be better in the future: *He promised to turn over a new leaf and behave.*

leaf·age (lē′fij), *n.* leaves; foliage.

leaf·let (lēf′lit), *n.* **1** a small, flat or folded sheet of printed matter: *advertising leaflets.* **2** a small or young leaf. **3** one of the separate blades or divisions of a compound leaf.

leaf·stalk (lēf′stók′), *n.* petiole.

leaf·y (lē′fē), *adj.* **1** having many leaves; covered with leaves. **2** resembling a leaf. ❏ *adj.* **leaf·i·er, leaf·i·est.** —**leaf′i·ness,** *n.*

league¹ (lēg), **1** *n.* a union of persons, parties, or nations formed to help one another. **2** *v.* to unite in a league; form a union. **3** *n.* association of sports clubs or teams: *a baseball league.* ❏ *v.* **leagued, lea·guing.**

in league, associated by agreement; allied.

league² (lēg), *n.* (long ago) unit for measuring distance, usually about 3 miles (5 kilometers).

League of Nations, organization intended to promote cooperation among nations and to maintain peace. It was established in 1920 and disbanded in 1946.

League of Women Voters, organization of women and men founded in 1920 to work for informed public activity in elections and other government affairs.

lea·guer (lē′gər), *n.* member of a league.

leak (lēk), **1** *n.* hole or crack not meant to be there that lets something in or out: *a leak in the roof.* **2** *v.* to go in or out through a hole or crack, or in ways suggesting a hole or crack: *Water leaked into the basement.* **3** *v.* to let something in or out which is meant to stay where it is: *My boat leaks and lets water in. That pipe leaks gas.* **4** *n.* leakage: *a leak of water, a leak of information.* **5** *v.* to become known gradually: *The secret leaked out.* ■ Another word that sounds like this is **leek.** —**leak′er,** *n.*

leak·age (lē′kij), *n.* **1** entrance or escape by a leak. **2** something that leaks in or out. **3** amount of leaking: *a leakage of a pailful an hour.*

Lea·key (lē′kē), *n.* **1 Louis,** 1903-1972, British anthropologist and paleontologist, born in Kenya. He found evidence of human beings living millions of years ago in Africa. **2 Mary Douglas Nic·ol** (nik′l), born 1913, British anthropologist, wife of Louis

Leakey. **3 Richard,** born 1944, Kenyan anthropologist, son of Mary and Louis Leakey.

leak·y (lē′kē), *adj.* having a leak or leaks; leaking: *a leaky faucet.* ❏ *adj.* **leak·i·er, leak·i·est.** —**leak′i·ness,** *n.*

lean¹ (lēn), **1** *v.* to stand slanting, not upright; bend: *The small tree leans over in the wind.* **2** *v.* to rest part of your weight against someone or something for support: *Lean against me.* **3** *v.* to set or put in a leaning position: *Lean the ladder against the wall.* **4** *n.* act of leaning; inclination. **5** *v.* to depend; rely: *lean on a friend's advice.* **6** *v.* to be inclined; bend: *My parents lean toward the candidate running for reelection.* ■ Another word that sounds like this is **lien.**

lean² (lēn), **1** *adj.* not fat; thin: *a lean and hungry stray dog.* **2** *n.* meat having little fat. **3** *adj.* producing little; not plentiful: *a lean harvest, a lean year for business.* ■ Another word that sounds like this is **lien.** —**lean′ness,** *n.*

lean·ing (lē′ning), *n.* tendency; inclination.

lean-to (lēn′tü′), **1** *n.* a small building attached to another, with a roof sloping downward from the side of the larger building. **2** *adj.* having supports or a roof so arranged: *a lean-to shed.* **3** *n.* a crude shelter built against a tree or post. It is usually open on one side. ❏ *n., pl.* **lean-tos.**

leap (lēp), **1** *n.* a jump or spring. **2** *n.* thing to be jumped. **3** *n.* distance covered by a jump. **4** *v.* to jump: *The basketball player leaped high to block the opponent's shot.* ■ See Synonym Study at **jump. 5** *v.* to jump over: *He leaped the wall.* **6** *v.* to cause to leap: *She leaped her horse over fences and ditches.* **7** *v.* to pass, come, rise, etc., as if with a leap or bound: *An idea leaped to her mind.* ❏ *v.* **leaped** or **leapt, leap·ing.** —**leap′er,** *n.*

leap (def. 1)

leap·frog (lēp′frog′), **1** *n.* game in which players take turns jumping over another player who is bending over. **2** *v.* to jump over someone or something as in this game. ❏ *v.* **leap·frogged, leap·frog·ging.** —**leap′frog′ger,** *n.*

leapt (lept *or* lēpt), *v.* a past tense and a past participle of **leap.**

leap year, year having 366 days. The extra day is February 29. A year is a leap year if its number can be divided exactly by four, except years at the end of a century, which must be exactly divisible by 400. The years 1980 and 2000 are leap years; 1981 and 1900 are not.

learn (lėrn), *v.* **1** to gain knowledge or skill: *Some children learn slowly.* **2** to memorize: *learn a poem by heart.* **3** to find out;

a	hat	ė	term	ô	order	ch	child		a in about
ā	age	i	it	oi	oil	ng	long		e in taken
ä	far	ī	ice	ou	out	sh	she	ə	i in pencil
â	care	o	hot	u	cup	th	thin		o in lemon
e	let	ō	open	ů	put	ŦH	then		u in circus
ē	equal	ô	saw	ü	rule	zh	measure		

come to know: *He learned that Brussels is the capital of Belgium.* **4** to find out about; gain knowledge of: *She is learning science and social studies.* **5** to become able by study or practice: *In school we learn to read.* **—learn′er,** *n.*

Some people use **learn** when they mean "teach." This is not correct standard usage. You should avoid it especially when you are writing.

learn·ed (lėr′nid), *adj.* having, showing, or requiring much knowledge; scholarly: *a learned professor.* **—learn′ed·ly,** *adv.* **—learn′ed·ness,** *n.*

learn·ing (lėr′ning), *n.* **1** the gaining of knowledge or skill. **2** possession of knowledge gained by study; scholarship: *men and women of great learning.* **3** knowledge.

learning disability, any of several conditions that make it difficult for someone to learn a specific skill, such as reading or writing. Learning disabilities can affect people of normal or above-normal intelligence. The disabilities are thought to be caused by various limited functions of the central nervous system.

lease (lēs), **1** *n.* the right to use property for a certain length of time by paying rent for it. **2** *n.* a written statement saying for how long a certain property is rented and how much money shall be paid for it. **3** *n.* the property held by a lease. **4** *n.* length of time for which a lease is made. **5** *v.* to give a lease on. **6** *v.* to rent: *We have leased an apartment for one year.* ❑ *v.* **leased, leas·ing.** **—leas′a·ble,** *adj.* **—leas′er,** *n.*

WORD STORY **Lease** comes from a Latin word meaning "loose." **Lax** comes from the same word. A person who gives a lease lets go of the property for another to hold.

leash (lēsh), **1** *n.* a strap or chain for holding an animal in check: *He led the dog on a leash.* **2** *v.* to fasten or hold in with a leash; control: *He leashed his anger and did not say a harsh word.* ❑ *n., pl.* **leash·es.**

least (lēst), **1** *adj.* less than any other; smallest; slightest: *Ten cents is a little money; five cents is less; one cent is least.* **2** *n.* smallest amount; smallest thing: *The least you can do is to thank them.* **3** *adv.* to the smallest extent, amount, or degree: *She liked that book least of all.* ❑ *adj.,* superlative of **little;** *adv.,* superlative of **less.**

at least, 1 at the lowest estimate: *The temperature was at least 95 degrees yesterday.* **2** at any rate; in any case: *He may have been late, but at least he came.*

not in the least, not at all.

least common denominator, the smallest number that is a multiple of all the denominators of a group of fractions. 30 is the least common denominator of ⅔, ⅘, and ⅙, because it is the smallest number divisible by 3, 5, and 6.

least common multiple, the smallest number that is divisible by all the numbers in a particular group. The least common multiple of 6 and 8 is 24.

least·wise (lēst′wiz′), *adv.* INFORMAL. at least; at any rate.

leath·er (leᴛʜ′ər), **1** *n.* material made from the skins of animals by removing the hair and then tanning them: *Shoes are usually made of leather.* **2** *adj.* made of leather: *leather gloves.*

Leath·er·ette (leᴛʜ′ə ret′), *n.* trademark for imitation leather, made of plastic, paper, or cloth.

leath·ern (leᴛʜ′ərn), *adj.* made of leather.

leath·er·y (leᴛʜ′ər ē), *adj.* like leather; tough: *leathery skin.*

leave¹ (lēv), *v.* **1** to go away: *We leave tonight.* **2** to go away from: *They left the room.* **3** to stop living in, belonging to, or working at or for: *leave the country, leave your job.* **4** to go without taking; let stay behind: *I left a book on the table.* **5** to let stay in a certain condition: *leave the dishes unwashed. I was left alone as before.* **6** to let alone: *The potatoes must be left to boil for half an hour.* **7** to give to family, friends or charity when you die: *She left a fortune to her children.* **8** to give or hand over to someone else to do: *I left the driving to my sister.* **9** to not attend to: *I shall leave my homework until tomorrow.* **10** to let remain uneaten, unused, unremoved, etc.: *Did the girls leave any lemonade for the rest of us?* **11** to have as a remainder after subtraction: *4 from 10*

leaves 6. ❑ *v.* **left, leav·ing.** ■ See Usage Note at **let¹.** **—leav′er,** *n.*

leave off, to stop: *Continue the story from where I left off.*

leave out, 1 to not do, say, or put in; omit: *She left out two words when she read the sentence.* **2** to neglect; forget: *Since everyone was busy, he felt that he was left out.*

leave² (lēv), *n.* **1** permission; consent: *They gave him leave to go.* **2** permission to be absent from duty. A **leave of absence** is an official permission to be absent from your work, school, or military duty. **3** length of time for which you have a leave of absence: *The soldier went home for a fifteen-day leave.*

on leave, absent with permission.

take leave of, to say good-by to.

leave³ (lēv), *v.* to put forth leaves; leaf: *Trees leave in the spring.* ❑ *v.* **leaved, leav·ing.**

leav·en (lev′ən), **1** *n.* any substance, such as yeast, that will cause fermentation and raise dough. **2** *v.* to raise with a substance that causes fermentation; make dough light or lighter. **3** *n.* an influence which, spreading silently and strongly, changes conditions or opinions. **4** *v.* to spread through and transform.

WORD FAMILY **Leaven** and the words below are related. They all come from a Latin word meaning "light in weight."

alleviate	legerdemain	lever	levy
elevate	levee	levity	relieve

leav·en·ing (lev′ə ning), *n.* thing that leavens.

leaves (lēvz), *n.* **1** plural of **leaf.** **2** a present tense of **leave:** *I cry every time she leaves us.*

leave-tak·ing (lēv′tā′king), *n.* act of taking leave; saying good-by.

leav·ings (lē′vingz), *n.pl.* things left; leftovers; remnants.

Leb·a·nese (leb′ə nēz′), **1** *adj.* of Lebanon or its people. **2** *n.* person born or living in Lebanon. ❑ *n., pl.* **Leb·a·nese.**

Leb·a·non (leb′ə nən), *n.* country in the Middle East, at the E end of the Mediterranean. *Capital:* Beirut.

lech·er·ous (lech′ər əs), *adj.* full of lust; lewd. **—lech′er·ous·ly,** *adv.* **—lech′er·ous·ness,** *n.*

lech·er·y (lech′ər ē), *n.* lustful behavior; lewdness.

lec·i·thin (les′ə thən), *n.* a fatty substance found in plant and animal tissues. Lecithin is extracted from egg yolk, soybeans, and corn. It is used in candy, drugs, paints, etc.

Le Cor·bus·ier (lə kôr bü zyā′), 1887-1965, French architect and city planner, born in Switzerland. ■ Le Corbusier was one of the most important architects of the twentieth century. His buildings often had long horizontal windows and featured columns that raised the building from the ground.

Le Corbusier building

lec·tern (lek′tərn), *n.* **1** a reading desk in a church, especially the desk from which the lessons are read at daily prayer. **2** a reading desk or stand.

lec·ture (lek′chər), **1** *n.* a planned talk on a chosen subject given before an audience; such a talk written down or printed; speech. ■ See Synonym Study at **speech.** **2** *v.* to give a lecture: *The explorer lectured on the Arctic.* **3** *n.* a scolding: *My parents give me a lecture when I come home late.* **4** *v.* to scold; reprove: *They lectured me about it.* ❑ *v.* **lec·tured, lec·tur·ing.** **—lec′tur·er,** *n.*

led (led), *v.* past tense and past participle of **lead**[1]: *She led her younger brother across the street. We were led through the cave by an experienced guide.* ■ Another word that sounds like this is **lead**[2].

LED, light-emitting diode (a tiny electronic device that produces light, usually red light, when electricity flows through it, used in clocks, calculators etc.).

ledge (lej), *n.* **1** a narrow shelf: *a window ledge.* **2** shelf or ridge of rock.

ledg·er (lej′ər), *n.* book of accounts in which a business keeps a record of all money transactions.

lee (lē), **1** *n.* a shelter. **2** *n.* side or part sheltered or away from the wind: *The wind was so fierce that we ran to the lee of the house.* **3** *adj.* sheltered from the wind: *the lee side of a ship.* ■ Another word that sounds like this is **lea.**

Lee (lē), *n.* **1** **Har·per** (här′pər), born 1926, American writer. Her only novel is *To Kill a Mockingbird.* It won the 1961 Pulitzer Prize for fiction. **2** **Rob·ert E.** (rob′ərt), 1807-1870, Confederate commanding general in the Civil War. Lee surrendered to Grant at Appomattox Courthouse on April 9, 1865. ■ A graduate of West Point, **Robert E. Lee** was offered the command of the U.S. Army. He declined, feeling his first loyalty was to Virginia, although he did not believe in slavery or secession. **3** **Spike** (spīk), born 1957, American movie director. His films include *Do The Right Thing* and *Malcolm X.*

leech (lēch), *n.* **1** any of numerous worms living in freshwater ponds and streams that suck the blood of animals. Doctors long ago used leeches to suck blood from sick people, thinking to remove diseased blood. **2** person who tries persistently to get money and favors from others, without doing anything to earn them. ❑ *n., pl.* **leech·es.** ■ Another word that sounds like this is **leach.**

Leeds (lēdz), *n.* city in N England.

leek (lēk), *n.* vegetable something like an onion, but with larger leaves, a smaller bulb shaped like a cylinder, and a milder flavor. ■ Another word that sounds like this is **leak.**

leer (lir), **1** *v.* to give a sly, evil glance: *The prisoner leered at the spectators in the courtroom during the trial.* **2** *n.* a sly, nasty look to the side; evil glance. —**leer′ing·ly,** *adv.*

leer·y (lir′ē), *adj.* suspicious; wary: *We are leery of his advice.* ❑ *adj.* **leer·i·er, leer·i·est.** —**leer′i·ly,** *adv.* —**leer′i·ness,** *n.*

Leeu·wen·hoek (lā′vən hůk), *n.* **An·ton van** (än′tôn vän), 1632-1723, Dutch scientist. He was the first to study blood cells and tiny living things through microscopes.

lee·ward (lē′wərd *or* lü′ərd), **1** *adj., adv.* on the side away from the wind. **2** *n.* the side away from the wind; lee. **3** *adj., adv.* in the direction toward which the wind is blowing.

Lee·ward Islands (lē′wərd), the N part of the Lesser Antilles in the West Indies.

lee·way (lē′wā′), *n.* **1** extra space at the side; more time, money, etc., than needed; margin of safety: *By leaving 20 minutes early, I allowed myself a good deal of leeway.* **2** the sideways movement of a ship to leeward, out of its course.

WORD STORY **Leeway** means extra space, time, money, etc., because ships need extra room on the lee side—the side away from the wind. Even when at anchor with no sails up, ships drift leeward in the direction that the wind is blowing.

left[1] (left), **1** *adj.* belonging to the side of this dictionary entry where the boldface word appears; of the side of a keyboard or calculator where the letter *A* or the numeral 1 appear. **2** *adj.* on this side when viewed from in front: *Take a left turn at the next light.* **3** *adv.* on or to the left side: *Turn left.* **4** *n.* the left side or hand: *I sat at her left.* **5** *n.* part of a lawmaking body consisting of the more liberal or radical groups. **6** *adj.* having liberal or radical ideas in politics.

WORD STORY **Left**[1] comes from an old English word meaning "weak." Most people's left hand is weaker than the right. The meaning in politics came from a custom in lawmaking groups of Europe, where the more liberal members sat on the left side.

left[2] (left), *v.* past tense and past participle of **leave**[1]: *I left my hat in the hall. A light was left burning in the window.*

left field, 1 in baseball: **a** the section of the outfield beyond third base. **b** position of the player in this area. **2** odd, unreasonable, or unrealistic state of mind: *an opinion out in left field.* —**left fielder.**

left-hand (left′hand′), *adj.* **1** on or to the left. **2** of, for, or with the left hand.

left-hand·ed (left′han′did), **1** *adj.* using the left hand more easily and readily than the right. **2** *adj.* done with the left hand. **3** *adj.* made to be used with the left hand. **4** *adj.* turning from right to left: *a left-handed screw.* **5** *adj.* doubtful or insincere: *a left-handed compliment.* ■ This meaning of **left-handed** is sometimes considered offensive. **6** *adv.* toward the left; with the left hand. —**left′-hand′ed·ly,** *adv.* —**left′hand′ed·ness,** *n.*

left-hand·er (left′han′dər), *n.* a left-handed person, especially a baseball pitcher; southpaw.

left·ist (lef′tist), **1** *n.* person who has liberal or radical ideas in politics. **2** *n.* member of a liberal or radical political organization. **3** *adj.* having liberal or radical ideas.

left·o·ver (left′ō′vər), **1** *n.* thing that is left. Scraps of food from a meal are leftovers. **2** *adj.* uneaten; unused; remaining: *I made some sandwiches with the leftover meat.*

left wing, the liberal or radical members, especially of a political party.

left-wing (left′wing′), *adj.* belonging to or like the left wing. —**left-wing·er** (left′wing′ər), *n.*

left·y (lef′tē), *n.* INFORMAL. a left-handed person. ❑ *n., pl.* **left·ies.**

leg (leg), **1** *n.* one of the body parts on which people and animals stand and walk. **2** *n.* part of clothing that covers a leg: *I fell and tore my pants' leg.* **3** *n.* anything shaped or used like a leg; any support that is much longer than it is wide: *a table leg.* **4** *n.* one of the parts of any process or activity: *the last leg of a trip.* **5** *v.* INFORMAL. to walk or run: *We could not get a ride, so we had to leg it.* **6** *n.* either of the two sides of a right triangle that is not the hypotenuse. ❑ *v.* **legged, leg·ging.** —**leg′less,** *adj.*

not have a leg to stand on, to have no defense or reason for doing something.

on your last legs, about to fail, collapse, or die.

pull someone's leg, to fool, trick, or make fun of someone.

shake a leg, INFORMAL. to hurry up: *Shake a leg; we have to go now.*

leg·a·cy (leg′ə sē), *n.* **1** money or other property left to a person by the will of someone who has died. **2** something handed down from an ancestor or predecessor; heritage. ❑ *n., pl.* **leg·a·cies.**

le·gal (lē′gəl), *adj.* **1** of or about law: *legal knowledge.* **2** of or from lawyers: *legal advice.* **3** according to law; lawful: *Hunting is legal only during certain seasons.* —**le′gal·ly,** *adv.*

SYNONYM STUDY **Legal** and **legitimate** both mean according to the law. **Legal** is a general word: *She has a legal claim to the money.* **Legitimate** suggests that something is sensible and real, as well as according to the law: *The inventor has a legitimate claim to be paid for any use of her invention.*

legal age, age at which the law grants someone full rights and responsibilities, including the right to vote and make contracts; majority.

le·gal·i·ty (li gal′ə tē), *n.* lawfulness.

le·gal·ize (lē′gə līz), *v.* to make legal; authorize by law; sanction. ❑ *v.* **le·gal·ized, le·gal·iz·ing.** —**le′gal·i·za′tion,** *n.*

legal tender, money that must, by law, be accepted in payment of debts.

leg·ate (leg′it), *n.* ambassador or representative, especially a representative of the pope.

leg·a·tee (leg′ə tē′), *n.* person to whom a legacy is left. ❑ *n., pl.* **leg·a·tees.**

le·ga·tion (li gā′shən), *n.* **1** the diplomatic representative of a country and a staff of assistants. A legation ranks next below an embassy. **2** the official residence, offices, etc., of such a representative in a foreign country.

a	hat	ė	term	ô	order	ch	child		a in about
ā	age	i	it	oi	oil	ng	long		e in taken
ä	far	ī	ice	ou	out	sh	she	ə	i in pencil
â	care	o	hot	u	cup	th	thin		o in lemon
e	let	ō	open	ů	put	ᴛʜ	then		u in circus
ē	equal	ô	saw	ü	rule	zh	measure		

le·ga·to (li gä′tō), in music: **1** *adj.* smooth and connected; without breaks between successive tones. **2** *adv.* in a smooth and connected manner.

leg·end (lej′ənd), *n.* **1** story coming down from the past, which may be based on actual people and events but is not regarded as historically true: *The stories about King Arthur and his knights of the Round Table are legends.* **2** such stories as a group: *Legend tells us that King Arthur was brave.* **3** a living person whose achievements and deeds are already part of history: *a basketball legend.* **4** what is written on a coin or medal: *Read the legend on a five-cent piece.* **5** words accompanying a picture or diagram: *The legend underneath the picture identified the woman as Queen Elizabeth I.*

SYNONYM STUDY **Legend** and **myth** both mean a story not supposed to be historically true. **Legend** means a story about great deeds done by people in the past. The story praises them and their nation or group: *I enjoy legends of Robin Hood.* **Myth** means a story about gods or superhuman beings. The story helps explain religious beliefs or something in nature: *This is a myth from Alaska about why there is night and day.*

leg·end·ar·y (lej′ən der′ē), *adj.* **1** of or described in a legend or legends; not historical: *Robin Hood is a legendary person.* **2** well-known; famous.

leg·er·de·main (lej′ər də mān′), *n.* **1** sleight of hand; magic tricks. **2** trickery; deceit.

-legged, *suffix.* having a certain kind or number of legs: *long-legged = having long legs.*

leg·gings (leg′ingz), *n.pl.* **1** extra outer coverings of cloth or leather for the legs, for use out of doors. **2** close-fitting pants usually made of knit cloth, sometimes worn under a skirt or dress.

leg·gy (leg′ē), *adj.* **1** having long legs. **2** having awkwardly long legs. ❑ *adj.* **leg·gi·er, leg·gi·est. —leg′gi·ness,** *n.*

Leg·horn (leg′hôrn *or* leg′ərn), *n.* a rather small chicken which produces large numbers of eggs.

leg·i·ble (lej′ə bəl), *adj.* easy to read; plain and clear: *legible handwriting.* **—leg′i·bil′i·ty,** *n.* **—leg′i·bly,** *adv.*

WORD FAMILY **Legible** and the words below are related. They all come from a Latin word meaning "to read, choose, or select."

coil	elite	legion	negligence
collect	intellect	legume	recollect
cull	intelligent	lesson	sacrilege
diligent	intelligible	lignite	select
elect	lecture	neglect	
eligible	legend		

le·gion (lē′jən), *n.* **1** a large group of soldiers; army. **2** Often, **Legion,** any of various military or honorary groups, especially a national organization of former members of a country's armed forces: *the Royal Canadian Legion.* **3** a great many; very large number: *Legions of grasshoppers destroyed the crops.* **4** a division in the ancient Roman army containing several thousand soldiers on foot and several hundred horsemen.

le·gion·ar·y (lē′jə ner′ē), **1** *adj.* of or belonging to a legion. **2** *n.* member of a legion. ❑ *n., pl.* **le·gion·ar·ies.**

le·gion·naire (lē′jə nâr′), *n.* **1** Often, **Legionnaire,** member of a group using the title of Legion. **2** soldier in a legion.

Le·gion·naires' disease (lē′jə nârz′), a serious contagious respiratory disease caused by a bacterium, with symptoms of high fever, coughing, headache, and often pneumonia.

leg·is·late (lej′ə slāt), *v.* **1** to make laws: *Congress legislates for the United States.* **2** to force or bring about by legislation: *The council legislated new standards for pollution control.* ❑ *v.* **leg·is·lat·ed, leg·is·lat·ing.**

leg·is·la·tion (lej′ə slā′shən), *n.* **1** laws that have been passed: *Important legislation is reported in today's newspaper.* **2** the making of laws: *Congress has the power of legislation.*

leg·is·la·tive (lej′ə slā′tiv), *adj.* **1** involving the making of laws: *legislative reforms.* **2** having the duty and power of making laws: *Congress is a legislative group.* **3** ordered by law; made to be as it is by law: *recent legislative decrees.* **—leg′is·la′tive·ly,** *adv.*

legislative assembly, (in Canada) the provincial legislature in all provinces except Quebec.

leg·is·la·tor (lej′ə slā′tər), *n.* member of a legislative group; lawmaker. Senators and Representatives are legislators.

leg·is·la·ture (lej′ə slā′chər), *n.* group of persons that has the duty and power of making laws for a state or country.

le·git (lə jit′), *adj.* SLANG. legitimate.

le·git·i·ma·cy (lə jit′ə mə sē), *n.* quality of being legitimate or lawful; being recognized as lawful or proper.

le·git·i·mate (lə jit′ə mit), *adj.* **1** allowed or admitted by law; rightful; lawful: *a legitimate ruler.* **2** valid; acceptable: *a legitimate reason for being absent.* ▪ See Synonym Study at **legal.** **3** born of parents who are married to each other. **—le·git′i·mate·ly,** *adv.*

le·git·i·mize (lə jit′ə mīz), *v.* to make or declare to be legitimate. ❑ *v.* **le·git·i·mized, le·git·i·miz·ing.**

leg·ume (leg′yüm *or* li gyüm′), *n.* **1** any of many plants that bear pods containing a number of seeds. Beans and peas are legumes. Unlike many other plants, legumes absorb nitrogen from the air and so fertilize the soil they grow in. **2** the pod of such a plant.

legume

le·gu·mi·nous (li gyü′mə nəs), *adj.* **1** of or belonging to the same group of plants as beans and peas. **2** of or bearing legumes.

leg·warm·ers (leg′wôr′merz), *n.pl.* coverings for the legs, from the ankles to above the knees, usually knitted and worn for exercise or dancing.

leg·work (leg′werk′), *n.* work that involves much moving about or traveling, usually in order to find information.

Le Ha·vre (lə hä′vrə), port in N France, on the English Channel.

lei (lā), *n.* wreath of flowers, leaves, etc., worn as an ornament around the neck or on the head. ❑ *n., pl.* **leis.** ▪ Another word that sounds like this is **lay.**

Leip·zig (līp′sig), *n.* city in E Germany.

lei·sure (lē′zhər *or* lezh′ər), **1** *n.* time free from required work in which you may rest, amuse yourself, and do the things you like to do: *She's been too busy to have much leisure.* **2** *adj.* free; not busy: *leisure hours.*

at your leisure, when you have leisure; at your convenience: *Let me hear from you at your leisure.*

lei·sure·ly (lē′zhər lē), *adj., adv.* without hurry; taking plenty of time: *a leisurely stroll in the park. He walked leisurely across the bridge.* ▪ See Synonym Study at **slow.** **—lei′sure·li·ness,** *n.*

lem·ming (lem′ing), *n.* any of several small, mouselike, arctic rodents, with short tails and furry feet. When food is scarce, lemmings sometimes migrate in large groups. A mistaken common belief is that such groups hurl themselves suicidally into the sea.

lem·on (lem′ən), **1** *n.* a sour, light yellow citrus fruit that grows on a thorny tree in warm climates. **2** *adj.* pale yellow. **3** *n.* a pale yellow. **4** *n.* INFORMAL. something that is worthless: *The car is cheap because it's a lemon.*

lem·on·ade (lem′ə nād′), *n.* a drink made of lemon juice, sugar, and water.

lemon law, a law requiring carmakers to repair, replace, or refund the purchase price of defective cars.

le·mur (lē′mər), *n.* any of several small mammals something like monkeys, but with foxlike faces and woolly fur. Lemurs are found mainly in Madagascar. They live in trees and are active mostly at night.

Le·na (lē′nə *or* lā′nə), *n.* river in E Russia, flowing from Siberia into the Arctic Ocean.

lend (lend), *v.* **1** to let someone else have or use for a time: *Will you lend me your bicycle for an hour?* **2** to give the use of money for a fixed or specified amount of payment: *Banks lend money and charge interest.* **3** to give for a time; add; contribute: *The Red Cross lends aid in time of disaster.* ❑ *v.* **lent, lend·ing. —lend′er,** *n.*

lend itself to or **lend yourself to,** to help or be suitable for.

length (lengkth *or* length), *n.* **1** how long a thing is; what a thing measures from end to end; the longest way a thing can be measured: *the length of a room, an animal eight inches in length.* **2** how long something lasts or goes on: *the length of a visit, the length of a book.* **3** distance: *The length of this race is one kilometer.* **4** a long stretch or extent: *It's been quite a length of time since our last meeting.* **5** piece of cloth, etc., of a given length: *a length of rope.*

at full length, with the body stretched out flat: *The snake lay at full length on the rock, sunning itself.*

at length, 1 at last; finally: *At length, after many delays, the conference started.* **2** with all the details; in full: *She told of her adventures at length.*

go to any length, to do everything possible: *I will go to any length to help you.*

keep at arm's length, to discourage from becoming friendly.

length·en (lengk′thən *or* leng′thən), *v.* to make or become longer: *Tailors lengthen trousers. Your legs lengthen as you grow.*

SYNONYM STUDY **Lengthen, extend,** and **prolong** all mean to make longer. **Lengthen** is the general word: *She lengthened the skirt. Days lengthen in spring.* **Extend** and **prolong** are mostly used about time: *We extended our visit two more days. Medicine prolonged his life.*

length·ways (lengkth′wāz′ *or* length′wāz′), *adv., adj.* lengthwise.

length·wise (lengkth′wīz′ *or* length′wīz′), *adv., adj.* in the direction of the length: *I cut the cloth lengthwise. The tailor made a lengthwise cut.*

length·y (lengk′thē *or* leng′thē), *adj.* long; too long: *His directions were so lengthy that everybody lost interest.* □ *adj.* **length·i·er, length·i·est.** —**length′i·ly,** *adv.* —**length′i·ness,** *n.*

len·ience (lē′nyəns), *n.* leniency.

len·ien·cy (lē′nyən sē), *n.* lenient quality; mildness; gentleness; mercy.

len·ient (lē′nyənt), *adj.* mild or gentle; not harsh or stern; merciful: *a lenient judge, a lenient punishment.* —**len′ient·ly,** *adv.*

Len·in (len′ən), *n.* **Vlad·i·mir Il·yich** (vlad′ə mir il′yich), 1870-1924, Russian revolutionary and political leader. He created the Soviet government and was its first premier, from 1918 to 1924.

Len·in·grad (len′ən grad), *n.* a former name of **St. Petersburg.**

Len·non (len′ən), *n.* **John,** 1940-1980, British rock musician. He was a member of the rock group the Beatles. He was shot by an insane admirer.

lens (lenz), *n.* **1** a curved piece of glass or other transparent material that brings rays of light passing through it closer together or sends them wider apart. The lens of a camera forms images on film. The lenses of a telescope make distant objects look larger and nearer. **2** the part of an eye that focuses light rays onto the retina. See picture at **eye.** □ *n., pl.* **lens·es.** [**Lens** comes from a Latin word meaning "lentil." Early lenses were small and shaped like seeds.]

lent (lent), *v.* past tense and past participle of **lend:** *I lent you my pencil. He had lent me his eraser.*

Lent (lent), *n.* the 40 weekdays between Ash Wednesday and Easter, observed in many Christian churches as a time for fasting and repenting of sins.

Lent·en (len′tən), *adj.* of or during Lent; suitable for Lent.

len·til (len′tl), *n.* a small, flat, beanlike seed that is eaten as a vegetable, often in soup. Lentils grow on plants like pea plants.

Le·o (lē′o), *n.* **1** a group of stars shaped something like a lion. **2** the fifth sign of the zodiac, associated with the period from mid-July to mid-August.

Le·o·nar·do da Vin·ci (lē′ə när′dō də vin′chē), 1452-1519, Italian painter, musician, sculptor, architect, engineer, and scientist. ∎ **Leonardo da Vinci's** most famous painting is the Mona Lisa. He kept notebooks of his drawings and ideas for machines, but he wrote all of his notes backward. They can be read only in a mirror. [**Leonardo** is the Italian form of *Leonard,* which comes from old German words meaning "lion" and "powerful."]

le·o·nine (lē′ə nīn), *adj.* of or like a lion.

leop·ard (lep′ərd), *n.* a large, fierce cat of Africa and southern Asia, having a dull yellowish fur spotted with black. Some leopards are black and are often called panthers.

leopard—about 8 ft. (2.4 m) long with the tail

le·o·tard (lē′ə tärd), *n.* **1** a tight-fitting one-piece garment, with or without sleeves. Dancers, gymnasts, etc., wear leotards. **2** Usually, **leotards,** *pl.* tights. [**Leotard** comes from the name of Jules Léotard, a famous French trapeze artist of the 1800s. So many people saw him perform in this garment that they named it after him.]

lep·er (lep′ər), *n.* person who has leprosy.

lep·re·chaun (lep′rə kän), *n.* (in Irish legends) a kind of elf resembling a little old man, believed to possess hidden gold.

lep·ro·sy (lep′rə sē), *n.* disease caused by certain rod-shaped bacteria that attack the skin and nerves, causing lumps or spots which may become ulcers; Hansen's disease. If not treated, the injury to the nerves results in numbness, paralysis, and eventual loss of tissue.

lep·rous (lep′rəs), *adj.* **1** having leprosy: *a leprous person.* **2** of or like leprosy: *white, leprous scabs.*

les·bi·an *or* **Les·bi·an** (lez′bē ən), **1** *n.* a woman who has sexual feelings for other women. **2** *adj.* of or relating to a lesbian or lesbians.

le·sion (lē′zhən), *n.* an abnormal change in the structure of an organ or body tissue, caused by disease or injury.

Le·so·tho (lə sō′tō), *n.* country in S Africa. It is entirely surrounded by the Republic of South Africa. *Capital:* Maseru.

less (les), **1** *adj.* smaller: *of less width, less importance.* **2** *adj.* not so much; not so much of: *to have less rain, to put on less butter, to eat less meat.* **3** *adj.* lower in age, rank, or importance: *no less a person than the President.* **4** *n.* a smaller amount or quantity: *could do no less, weigh less than before. I won't take less than $5.* **5** *adv.* to a smaller extent or degree; not so; not so well: *less known, less important.* **6** *prep.* with something taken away; without; minus: *five less two, a coat less one sleeve.* □ *adj., adv., comparative of* **little.** ∎ Another word that can sound like this is **loess.**

-less, *suffix.* **1** without a ___; having no ___: *homeless = without a home.* **2** that cannot be ___ed: *countless = that cannot be counted.*

les·see (le sē′), *n.* someone to whom a lease is granted. □ *n., pl.* **les·sees.**

less·en (les′n), *v.* **1** to grow less: *The fever lessened during the night.* **2** to make less; decrease. ∎ Another word that sounds like this is **lesson.**

less·er (les′ər), *adj.* **1** less; smaller: *Instead of the mile, she chose to run the lesser distance.* **2** the less important of two.

lesser panda, panda (def. 2).

a	hat	ė	term	ô	order	ch	child		
ā	age	i	it	oi	oil	ng	long		a in about
ä	far	ī	ice	ou	out	sh	she		e in taken
â	care	o	hot	u	cup	th	thin	ə	i in pencil
e	let	ō	open	u̇	put	ŦH	then		o in lemon
ē	equal	ò	saw	ü	rule	zh	measure		u in circus

501

les·son (les′n), *n.* **1** something to be learned or taught; something that has been learned or taught: *Children study many different lessons in school.* **2** unit of learning or teaching; what is to be studied or taught at one time: *Tomorrow we take the tenth lesson.* **3** an instructive experience, serving to encourage or warn: *The accident taught me a lesson: always look before you leap.* **4** a selection from the Bible, read as part of a church service. ■ Another word that sounds like this is **lessen.**

les·sor (les′ôr), *n.* someone who grants a lease.

lest (lest), *conj.* **1** for fear that: *Be careful lest you fall from that tree.* **2** that (after words meaning fear, danger, etc.): *I was afraid lest they should come too late to save us.*

let[1] (let), *v.* **1** to not stop from doing or having something; allow; permit: *Let the dog have a bone.* **2** to allow to pass, go, or come: *They let the visitor on board the ship.* **3** *Let* is used in giving suggestions and commands. "Let's go home" means "I suggest that we go home." **4** to suppose; assume: *Let the two lines be parallel.* **5** to hire out; rent: *to let rooms to students.* ❑ *v.* **let, let·ting.**

let down, 1 to lower: *We let the box down from the roof.* **2** to disappoint: *Don't let us down today; we're counting on you to win.*

let in, to permit to enter; admit: *Let in some fresh air.*

let off, to allow to go free; excuse from punishment, etc.: *I was let off with a warning to do better in the future.*

let on, 1 to allow to be known; reveal your knowledge of: *He didn't let on that he knew their secret.* **2** to make believe; pretend: *She let on that she didn't see me.*

let out, 1 to permit to go out. **2** to make larger: *Let out the hem on this skirt.* **3** to dismiss or be dismissed: *School lets out at three o'clock.* **4** to rent: *Has the room been let out yet?*

let up, to stop; pause: *They refused to let up in the fight.*

> **USAGE NOTE** People sometimes mix up **let**[1] and **leave**[1]. **Let** means not to stop something from happening. **Leave** means to go away. In writing and in most speech, you should use sentences such as *"Let her be"* or *"Let him go if he wants to."* Except in very relaxed conversation, you should not use **leave** in those sentences or others like them. In *"Leave me alone,"* of course, the meaning is "go away!"

let[2] (let), *n.* interference with the ball in tennis and similar games, especially a serve that hits the net and must be played over.

-let, *suffix.* little ___: *booklet = a little book.*

let·down (let′doun′), *n.* **1** disappointment: *Losing the contest was a letdown for me.* **2** a reduced effort.

le·thal (lē′thəl), *adj.* causing death; deadly: *lethal weapons, a lethal dose of a drug.* **—le′thal·ly,** *adv.*

le·thar·gic (lə thär′jik), *adj.* **1** unnaturally drowsy; sluggish; dull: *A hot, humid day makes most people feel lethargic.* **2** apathetic. **—le·thar′gi·cal·ly,** *adv.*

leth·ar·gy (leth′ər jē), *n.* **1** drowsy dullness; lack of energy; sluggish inactivity. **2** a state of unconsciousness resembling deep sleep.

let's (lets), let us.

let·ter (let′ər), **1** *n.* a written or printed message: *He told me about his vacation in a letter.* **2** *n.* a mark or sign that stands for any one of the sounds that make up words. There are 26 letters in our alphabet. **3** *v.* to mark with letters: *Please letter a new sign.* **4** *n.* exact wording; actual terms: *They kept the letter of the law but not the spirit.* **5** *n.* a block of type bearing a letter, used in printing. **6** *n.* the initial of a school, college, or other institution, given as an award or trophy to members of a sports team, etc. It is usually made of cloth and sewn to a garment. **7** *n.pl.* **letters,** literature: *English letters.*

to the letter, very exactly; just as you have been told: *I carried out your orders to the letter.*

> **WORD FAMILY** **Letter** and the words below are related. They all come from a Latin word meaning "letter (of the alphabet)."
>
> | alliteration | literacy | literary | literature |
> | illiterate | literal | literate | obliterate |

letter carrier, person who collects and delivers mail; mail carrier; postman.

let·ter·head (let′ər hed′), *n.* **1** words printed at the top of a sheet of paper, usually a name and address. **2** a sheet of paper so printed.

let·ter·ing (let′ər ing), *n.* **1** letters drawn, painted, or stamped. **2** act of making letters.

letter of credit, document issued by a bank, allowing the person named in it to draw money from other specified banks.

let·ter-per·fect (let′ər pèr′fikt), *adj.* **1** knowing your part or lesson perfectly: *My speech was letter-perfect.* **2** correct in every detail: *letter-perfect copies.*

let·tuce (let′is), *n.* the large, crisp, green leaves of a garden plant, used in salad. [**Lettuce** comes from a Latin word meaning "milk." Many lettuce plants have milky white juice.]

let·up (let′up′), *n.* a stop or pause: *There was no letup in the storm.*

leu·ke·mi·a (lü kē′mē ə), *n.* a form of cancer, in which there is a large excess of white blood cells in the blood.

leu·ko·cyte (lü′kə sīt), *n.* white blood cell.

Le·vant (lə vant′), *n.* the region about the E Mediterranean from Greece to Egypt, especially Syria, Lebanon, and Israel.

Le·van·tine (lə van′tən), **1** *adj.* of or relating to the Levant. **2** *n.* person or ship of the Levant.

lev·ee (lev′ē), *n.* **1** a high bank built to keep a river from overflowing: *There are levees in many places along the lower Mississippi River.* **2** a landing place for boats. ❑ *n., pl.* **lev·ees.** ■ Another word that sounds like this is **levy.**

levee (def. 1)

lev·el (lev′əl), **1** *adj.* having the same height everywhere; flat; even: *a level floor.* **2** *adj.* of equal height, importance, etc.: *The table is level with the sill of the window.* **3** *n.* something that is level; level or flat surface, tract of land, etc. **4** *n.* a tool for showing whether a surface is level. **5** *n.* a level position or condition. **6** *v.* to make level; put on the same level: *level the ground with a bulldozer.* **7** *v.* to lay low; bring to the level of the ground: *The tornado leveled every house in the valley.* **8** *v.* to raise and hold level for shooting; aim: *She leveled her rifle at the target.* **9** *n.* height: *The river rose to a level of 60 feet.* **10** *n.* stage of learning, achievement, etc.; position; rank: *She reads at a high level for her class.* **11** *adj.* well-balanced; sensible: *a level head.* **12** *v.* to be truthful or frank: *He wouldn't level with me.* ❑ *v.* **lev·eled, lev·el·ing** or **lev·elled, lev·el·ling. —lev′el·er** or **lev′el·ler,** *n.* **—lev′el·ly,** *adv.* **—lev′el·ness,** *n.*

level off, 1 to come to an equilibrium; even off; steady. **2** to return an aircraft to a horizontal position in landing, or after a climb or dive.

on the level, fair and straightforward; honest; legitimate.

> **SYNONYM STUDY** **Level, flat**[1], and **horizontal** all mean with the same height everywhere. **Level** is used about buildings or furniture: *Be sure the shelf is level before you nail it up.* **Flat** suggests a low height everywhere: *The flood spread quickly over the flat land.* **Horizontal** means parallel with the horizon: *The plane reached 30,000 feet and began horizontal flight.*

level best, the very best that you are able to do: *You don't have to be the world champion; just do your level best.*

level crossing, (in Canada) grade crossing.

lev·el·head·ed (lev′əl hed′id), *adj.* having good common sense or good judgment; sensible: *Levelheaded people stay calm in emergencies.* ■ See Synonym Study at **wise**[1]. **—lev′el·head′ed·ness,** *n.*

lev·er (lev′ər *or* lē′vər), **1** *n.* bar that turns on a fixed support called the fulcrum, used to transmit effort and motion. It is a simple machine. **2** *n.* any bar working on an axis or support: *the gearshift lever of a car.* **3** *v.* to move, lift, push, etc., with a lever: *The movers levered the sofa in through the window.* [**Lever** comes from a Latin word meaning "not heavy."]

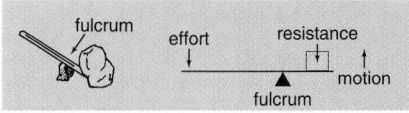

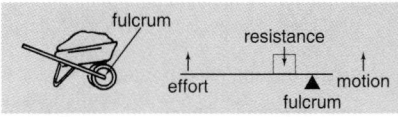

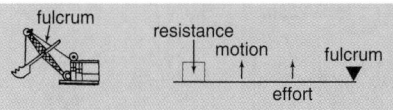

lever (def. 1)

lev·er·age (lev′ər ij *or* lē′vər ij), *n.* **1** action of a lever. **2** advantage or power gained by using a lever. **3** increased power of action.

Le·vi (lē′vī), *n.* (in the Bible) a son of Jacob. [**Levi** comes from a Hebrew word meaning "a join."]

le·vi·a·than (lə vī′ə thən), *n.* **1** (in the Bible) a huge sea animal. **2** any great and powerful person or thing.

Le·vi's (lē′vīz), *n.pl.* trademark for tight-fitting, heavy blue denim trousers reinforced at strain points with copper rivets or extra stitching.

lev·i·tate (lev′ə tāt), *v.* **1** to rise or float in the air. **2** to cause something to rise in the air, especially with nothing visible to hold it up: *The magician levitated her assistant.* ❑ *v.* **lev·i·tat·ed, lev·i·tat·ing.** —**lev′i·ta′tion,** *n.*

Le·vite (lē′vīt), *n.* member of the tribe descended from Levi, from which assistants to the Jewish priests were chosen.

Le·vit·i·cus (lə vit′ə kəs), *n.* book of the Bible, containing the laws for the priests and Levites and the rituals for Jewish ceremonies.

lev·i·ty (lev′ə tē), *n.* lack of proper seriousness or earnestness: *Giggling in class shows levity.*

lev·y (lev′ē), **1** *v.* to order to be paid: *The government levies taxes to pay its expenses.* **2** *n.* money collected by authority or force. **3** *v.* to draft citizens for an army: *When war threatened, the government levied a large number of soldiers from each state.* **4** *v.* to undertake or begin; wage: *to levy war against the enemy.* **5** *n.* citizens drafted for an army. ❑ *v.* **lev·ied, lev·y·ing;** *n., pl.* **lev·ies.**
■ Another word that sounds like this is **levee.**

lewd (lüd), *adj.* not decent; obscene: *lewd stories.* —**lewd′ly,** *adv.* —**lewd′ness,** *n.*

Lew·is (lü′is), *n.* **1** C. S., 1898-1963, British writer. His most famous books are a series of seven children's novels, *The Chronicles of Narnia.* C. S. stands for Clive Staples. **2** Meriwether (mer′i weтн′ər), 1774-1809, American explorer of the American northwest together with William Clark. **3** Sinclair (sin klâr′), 1885-1951, American novelist. He was the first American to win the Nobel Prize for literature, in 1930.

Lew·is·ton (lü′is tən), *n.* city in SW Maine.

lex·i·cog·ra·pher (lek′sə kog′rə fər), *n.* writer or editor of a dictionary.

lex·i·cog·ra·phy (lek′sə kog′rə fē), *n.* the writing or editing of dictionaries.

lex·i·con (lek′sə kən), *n.* dictionary, especially of Greek, Latin, or Hebrew.

Lex·ing·ton (lek′sing tən), *n.* **1** town in E Massachusetts where the first battle of the Revolutionary War was fought on April 19, 1775. **2** city in N Kentucky.

Ley·den jar (līd′n), an early device for storing an electric charge, made of a glass jar partly lined inside and outside with tin or aluminum foil and sealed with a stopper containing a metal rod connected to the foil inside. Electricity passed through the rod charges the inside foil, and this draws an opposite charge to the outside foil.

LF, L.F., or **l.f.,** low frequency.

l.h., (in music) left hand.

Lha·sa (lä′sə), *n.* capital of Tibet, in the S part.

Lha·sa ap·so (lä′sə ap′sō), any of a breed of small dogs originally from Tibet, with long heavy fur and the tail curled over the back.

Li, symbol for lithium.

L.I., Long Island.

li·a·bil·i·ty (lī′ə bil′ə tē), *n.* **1** condition of being liable: *liability for an accident.* **2** debt. **3** something that is to your disadvantage: *Her poor handwriting was a liability in school.* ❑ *n., pl.* **li·a·bil·i·ties** for 2,3.

li·a·ble (lī′ə bəl), *adj.* **1** likely; unpleasantly likely: *That glass is liable to break. You are liable to slip on ice.* **2** in danger of having, doing, etc.: *We are all liable to diseases.* **3** responsible; under obligation; bound by law to pay: *The Postal Service is not liable for damage to a parcel unless it is insured.*

li·ai·son (lē′ā zon′ *or* lē ā′zon), *n.* **1** person or group that makes or maintains connections between different organizations, companies, schools, departments, etc. **2** connection between military units to secure proper cooperation.

li·a·na (lē ä′nə *or* lē an′ə), *n.* any climbing plant or vine, especially one of those with woody stems that twine around the trunks of tropical trees. ❑ *n., pl.* **li·a·nas.**

li·ar (lī′ər), *n.* person who tells lies; person who says what is not true.

li·bel (lī′bəl), **1** *n.* a written or published statement that is likely to harm the reputation of the person about whom it is made; false or damaging statement. **2** *v.* to write or publish such a statement about. **3** *n.* act or crime of writing or publishing such a statement. ❑ *v.* **li·beled, li·bel·ing** or **li·belled, li·bel·ling.** —**li′bel·er,** *n.*

WORD STORY **Libel** comes from a Latin word meaning "the inner bark of a tree." **Library** comes from the same word. In ancient times, this bark was used to write on. **Libel** used to mean "a piece of writing," especially a legal statement of damage. Then it came to mean any damaging writing.

li·bel·ous (lī′bə ləs), *adj.* **1** containing a libel: *a libelous communication.* **2** spreading libels: *a libelous tongue.*

lib·er·al (lib′ər əl), **1** *adj.* giving or given freely; generous: *a liberal giver, a liberal donation.* **2** *adj.* plentiful; abundant: *There was a liberal supply of food at the party.* **3** *adj.* not narrow in your ideas; broad-minded; tolerant: *a liberal thinker.* **4** *adj.* not limited; broad. A liberal education develops the mind broadly by including courses in the liberal arts. **5** *adj.* favoring progress and reforms. **6** *n.* person favorable to progress and reforms. **7** *adj.* Often, **Liberal,** of or belonging to a political party that favors progress and reforms. **8** *n.* person who is too ready to try solving social problems by government regulation or government programs. ■ This meaning of **liberal** is sometimes considered offensive. —**lib′er·al·ly,** *adv.*

liberal arts, subjects studied for culture rather than for immediate practical use. Literature, languages, history, and philosophy are some of the liberal arts.

lib·er·al·ism (lib′ər ə liz′əm), *n.* liberal views or opinions; belief in progress and reforms.

lib·er·al·i·ty (lib′ə ral′ə tē), *n.* **1** generous acts or behavior; generosity. **2** tolerant and progressive nature; broad-mindedness.

lib·er·al·ize (lib′ər ə liz), *v.* to make or become liberal. ❑ *v.* **lib·er·al·ized, lib·er·al·iz·ing.** —**lib′er·al·i·za′tion,** *n.* —**lib′er·al·iz′er,** *n.*

liberal party, 1 a political party that favors progress and reforms. **2 Liberal Party,** a major political party of Canada.

lib·e·rate (lib′ə rāt′), *v.* to set free: *liberate political prisoners.* ❑ *v.* **lib·e·rat·ed, lib·e·rat·ing.** —**lib′e·ra′tion,** *n.* —**lib′e·ra′tor,** *n.*

a	hat	ė	term	ô	order	ch	child		
ā	age	i	it	oi	oil	ng	long		a in about
ä	far	ī	ice	ou	out	sh	she		e in taken
â	care	o	hot	u	cup	th	thin	ə	i in pencil
e	let	ō	open	ù	put	ŧн	then		o in lemon
ē	equal	ò	saw	ü	rule	zh	measure		u in circus

Li·ber·i·a (lī bir′ē ə), *n.* country in W Africa, settled in 1822 by African Americans who had been freed from slavery. *Capital:* Monrovia. —**Li·ber′i·an,** *adj., n.*

lib·er·tar·i·an (lib′ər ter′ē ən), *n.* person who advocates liberty, especially in thought or conduct.

lib·er·tine (lib′ər tēn′), *n.* person without moral restraints; immoral or licentious person.

lib·er·ty (lib′ər tē), *n.* **1** condition of being free; freedom; independence: *The American colonies won their liberty.* **2** right or power to do as you please; power or opportunity to do something. **3** right of being in, using, etc.: *We give our dog the liberty of the yard.* **4** too great freedom: *The author took liberties with the facts to make the story more interesting.* **5** permission granted to a sailor to go ashore. ❏ *n., pl.* **lib·er·ties** for 2,4.

at liberty, **1** free: *The escaped lion is still at liberty.* **2** allowed; permitted: *You are at liberty to make any choice you please.* **3** not busy: *The doctor will see us as soon as she is at liberty.*

SYNONYM STUDY **Liberty** and **independence** both mean freedom to act without control. **Liberty** suggests free choice: *I have liberty to spend my allowance however I like.* **Independence** suggests the end of outside control: *Haiti declared its independence in 1804.*

Liberty Bell, bell that was rung at Philadelphia on July 8, 1776, when the Continental Congress passed the Declaration of Independence. It is regarded as a symbol of liberty.

Li·bra (lē′brə), *n.* **1** a group of stars shaped something like a pair of scales. **2** the seventh sign of the zodiac, associated with the period from mid-September to mid-October.

li·brar·i·an (lī brer′ē ən), *n.* **1** person in charge of a library. **2** person trained for work in a library.

li·brar·y (lī′brer′ē), *n.* **1** collection of books, magazines, films, recordings, etc., either public or private. **2** room or building where such a collection is kept for public use and borrowing. **3** room in a home where books are kept. ❏ *n., pl.* **li·brar·ies.** [See Word Story at **libel.**]

Liberty Bell

library science, science of the organization, management, and maintenance of libraries.

li·bret·tist (lə bret′ist), *n.* writer of a libretto.

li·bret·to (lə bret′ō), *n.* **1** the words of an opera or other long musical composition. **2** book containing the words. ❏ *n., pl.* **li·bret·tos, li·bret·ti** (lə bret′ē).

Li·bre·ville (lē′brə vil), *n.* port and capital of Gabon, on the Atlantic.

Lib·y·a (lib′ē ə), *n.* country in N Africa, west of Egypt. *Capital:* Tripoli. —**Lib′y·an,** *adj., n.*

lice (līs), *n.* plural of **louse.**

li·cense (lī′sns), **1** *n.* permission given by law to do something: *A license to drive a car is issued by the state.* **2** *n.* paper, card, plate, etc., showing such permission: *The policeman asked the reckless driver for her license.* **3** *v.* to give a license to; permit by law: *A doctor is licensed to practice medicine.* **4** *n.* freedom of action, speech, thought, etc., that is permitted or conceded. **Poetic license** is the freedom from rules that is permitted in poetry and other arts. **5** *n.* too much liberty of action; lack of proper control; abuse of liberty. ❏ *v.* **li·censed, li·cens·ing.** —**li′cens·a·ble,** *adj.* —**li′cens·er** or **li′cen·sor,** *n.*

license plate, a metal plate with letters and numbers, attached to a motor vehicle as proof of registration with a government agency.

li·cen·tious (lī sen′shəs), *adj.* unrestrained in sexual activities; immoral. —**li·cen′tious·ly,** *adv.* —**li·cen′tious·ness,** *n.*

li·chen (lī′kən), *n.* any of very many living things that look something like moss but are actually combinations of a fungus and an alga growing together as one. Lichens grow in patches on rocks, trees, and other surfaces, often in places that are very cold or dry. They are gray, yellow, brown, black, or green. ■ Another word that sounds like this is **liken.**

Lich·ten·stein (lik′tən stīn), *n.* **Roy** (roi), born 1923, American painter. Many of his paintings are large single frames of comic strips.

lick (lik), **1** *v.* to pass the tongue over: *lick a stamp.* **2** *v.* to lap up with the tongue: *The cat licked the milk.* **3** *n.* a stroke of the tongue over something: *He gave the ice-cream cone a big lick.* **4** *v.* to pass about or play over like a tongue: *The flames were licking the roof of the burning house.* **5** *n.* INFORMAL. a blow: *Though I lost the fight, I got in a few good licks.* **6** *v.* INFORMAL. to beat or thrash. **7** *v.* INFORMAL. to defeat in a fight, etc.; conquer: *I licked him at chess.* **8** *n.* a small quantity: *She didn't do a lick of work.* **9** *n.* salt lick. —**lick′er,** *n.*

lick·e·ty-split (lik′ə tē split′), *adv.* INFORMAL. at full speed; headlong; rapidly: *The rabbit ran lickety-split into the bushes.*

lick·ing (lik′ing), *n.* a beating; a whipping.

lic·or·ice (lik′ər ish *or* lik′ər is), *n.* **1** candy flavored with a black substance from the sweet-tasting dried root of a plant growing in southern Europe and parts of Asia. **2** the black substance. **3** the root. **4** the plant.

lid (lid), *n.* **1** a movable cover; top: *a jar lid.* **2** eyelid. —**lid′less,** *adj.*

lie¹ (lī), **1** *n.* something said that is not true; something that is not true said to deceive: *I went to school today; saying I didn't is a lie.* **2** *v.* to speak falsely; tell a lie: *He says that he has never lied, but I think he is lying when he says it.* **3** *v.* to give a false impression; mislead: *That clock must be lying; it isn't noon yet.* ❏ *v.* **lied, ly·ing.** ■ Another word that sounds like this is **lye.**

give the lie to, to show to be false: *Her actions gave the lie to her statement.*

lie² (lī), *v.* **1** to have your body in a flat position along the ground or other surface: *lie on the grass, lie in bed.* **2** to rest on a surface: *The book was lying on the table.* **3** to be kept or stay in a given state: *lie idle, lie hidden, lie unused.* **4** to be; be placed: *a ship lying offshore at anchor. The lake lies to the south of us.* **5** to exist; be found to be: *The cure for ignorance lies in education.* **6** to be buried; be in a grave: *Here lie the fallen soldiers of many wars.* ❏ *v.* **lay, lain, ly·ing.** ■ See Usage Note at **lay¹.** ■ Another word that sounds like this is **lye.**

lie to, (of a ship, etc.) to come almost to a stop, facing the wind: *During the storm, the sailing ship lay to.*

take something lying down, to yield to something; not stand up to something: *He's not going to take that rejection lying down; he's made an appointment to talk to the dean of the school.*

Liech·ten·stein (lik′tən stīn), *n.* small country between W Austria and E Switzerland. *Capital:* Vaduz.

lied (līd), *v.* past tense and past participle of **lie¹**: *That girl lied about her work. She has lied before.*

lie detector, device that records the physical reaction of an emotion, used especially to determine whether someone is lying; polygraph.

liege (lēj), (in the Middle Ages: **1** *n.* lord having a right to the homage and loyal service of his vassals. **2** *adj.* having a right to the homage and loyal service of vassals. **3** *n.* vassal obliged to give homage and loyal service to his lord. **4** *adj.* obliged to give homage and loyal service to a lord.

liege·man (lēj′mən), *n.* **1** (in the Middle Ages) vassal. **2** a faithful follower. ❏ *n., pl.* **liege·men.**

lien (lēn), *n.* (in law) a claim on the property of another for payment of a debt: *The garage owner has a lien upon my car until I pay his bill.* ■ Another word that sounds like this is **lean.**

lieu (lü), *n.* **in lieu of,** in place of; instead of.

Lieut., Lieutenant.

lieu·ten·an·cy (lü ten′ən sē), *n.* rank, commission, or authority of a lieutenant.

lieu·ten·ant (lü ten′ənt), *n.* **1** a military rank. See chart on page 712. **2** a police or fire department officer, usually ranking next below a captain and next above a sergeant. **3** person who acts in the place of someone higher in authority: *The scoutmaster used the two boys as his lieutenants.*

lieutenant colonel, a military rank. See chart on page 712.

lieutenant commander, a military rank. See chart on page 712.

lieutenant general, a military rank. See chart on page 712.

lieutenant governor, 1 (in the United States) a public official next in rank to the governor of a state, who takes the governor's place when necessary. **2** (in Canada) the official head of a provincial government, appointed by the Governor General as the representative of Elizabeth II, Queen of Great Britain and Canada.

lieutenant junior grade, a military rank. See chart on page 712.

life (lif), *n.* **1** condition of living or being alive. People, animals, plants, bacteria, and all living things have life. Rocks and minerals do not. Life is shown by growing and reproducing. **2** time of being alive: *During her life she was an outstanding doctor.* **3** time of existence or action of inanimate things: *The life of the battery was about five years.* **4** a living being; person: *Five lives were lost.* **5** living things: *The desert island had almost no animal or vegetable life.* **6** way of living: *a dull life, a country life.* **7** account of someone's life: *Several lives of Lincoln have been written.* **8** spirit; vigor: *Put more life into your work.* ❑ *n., pl.* **lives** for 3,4,7.

bring to life, **1** to restore consciousness, breathing, or heartbeat to someone who has lost it; revive: *Artificial respiration can often bring to life a drowning victim.* **2** to cause to live; give life to: *The scientist's creature was brought to life by a lightning bolt.*

come to life, be restored to consciousness; be revived.

for dear life, to save your life: *She ran for dear life away from the burning house.*

not on your life, by no means; absolutely not: *Help you cheat? Not on your life!*

life-and-death (lif′ən deth′), *adj.* **1** involving life or death; critical: *a life-and-death medical emergency.* **2** extremely important; vital: *Good business at holiday season is a life-and-death matter for many stores.*

life belt, a life preserver made like a belt.

life·blood (lif′blud′), *n.* **1** source of strength and energy: *Employees are the lifeblood of the company.* **2** blood necessary to life.

life·boat (lif′bōt′), *n.* a strong open boat with oars, especially built for saving lives at sea. Lifeboats are usually carried aboard larger ships.

life buoy, a life preserver.

life cycle, the series of forms that one kind of living thing passes through, in development from a specific form in one generation to the same form in the next.

life expectancy, 1 the total number of years that someone can expect to live, based on year of birth, sex, ethnic group, country of residence, etc. **2** lifespan (def. 1).

life·guard (lif′gärd′), *n.* person employed at a beach or pool to help in case of accident or danger to bathers.

life insurance, insurance by which a specified sum of money is paid to the insured person's survivors at the death of that person.

life jacket, a sleeveless, canvas jacket filled with a light material such as kapok, or with air, worn as a life preserver.

life·less (lif′lis), *adj.* **1** without life: *a lifeless planet.* **2** dead: *a lifeless body.* **3** dull: *a lifeless party.* **—life′less·ly,** *adv.* **—life′less·ness,** *n.*

lifelike wax statue next to a real person

life·like (lif′līk′), *adj.* like life; looking as if alive: *a lifelike portrait.* **—life′like′ness,** *n.*

life·line (lif′līn′), *n.* **1** rope for saving life, such as one thrown to someone in the water. **2** a diver's signaling line. **3** anything that helps to maintain something that cannot exist by itself, such as a remote military position, etc.

life·long (lif′lông′), *adj.* lasting all your life: *a lifelong friendship.*

life net, a strong net or sheet of canvas, used to catch people jumping from burning buildings.

life preserver, a wide belt, jacket, circular tube, etc., usually made of plastic or cork, to keep a person afloat in the water.

lif·er (li′fər), *n.* SLANG. someone sentenced to prison for life.

life raft, raft for saving lives in a shipwreck or the wreck of an aircraft at sea.

life·sav·er (lif′sā′vər), *n.* **1** person who saves people from drowning. **2** any lifesaving person or thing.

life·sav·ing (lif′sā′ving), **1** *n.* skills and actions used in saving people's lives by keeping them from drowning. **2** *adj.* designed or used to save people's lives.

life sciences, the sciences that deal with living things: biology, biochemistry, medicine, etc.

life-size (lif′sīz′), *adj.* as big as the living person, animal, etc.: *a life-size statue.*

life-sized (lif′sīzd′), *adj.* life-size.

life-span (lif′span′), *n.* **1** the length of time something can be expected to live; life expectancy: *The lifespan of a wild elephant is 65 years.* **2** lifetime.

life-style (lif′stīl′), *n.* a person's or group's characteristic manner of living; your style of life.

life-support system (lif′sə pôrt′), **1** equipment that helps or replaces a bodily process, such as breathing, for a person who would not otherwise survive. **2** equipment that provides air and maintains conditions necessary for human life in an environment that cannot support human life, such as outer space.

life·time (lif′tīm′), *n.* time of being alive; period during which a life lasts: *My grandparents have seen many changes during their lifetime.*

life·work (lif′wėrk′), *n.* work that takes or lasts a whole lifetime; main work in life.

life zone, region that supports or is capable of supporting life.

lift (lift), **1** *v.* to raise into the air; raise up higher; take up; pick up: *Please help me lift this heavy box.* **2** *v.* to raise someone's thoughts, feelings, etc.: *The good news lifted our spirits.* **3** *n.* an elevating influence or effect: *The promotion gave her a lift.* **4** *v.* to rise and go; go away: *The fog lifted at dawn.* **5** *v.* to go up; be raised: *The box lid lifts up when you press the button.* **6** *n.* act of lifting: *With a lift of her eyebrow she showed surprise.* **7** *n.* distance through which something is lifted. **8** *n.* a helping hand: *Give me a lift with this heavy crate.* **9** *n.* a ride in a vehicle: *Can you give the children a lift to school?* **10** *v.* to pick or take up; steal: *lift things from a store.* **11** *n.* BRITISH. elevator. **12** *n.* one of the layers of leather in the heel of a shoe. **13** *n.* the quantity or weight that can be lifted at one time: *A lift of 50 pounds is my limit.* **14** *n.* ski lift. **15** *v.* to end or bring an end to a boycott, embargo, siege, etc. [Lift comes from an Icelandic word meaning "air." If you lift something, you put it up in the air.] **—lift′a·ble,** *adj.* **—lift′er,** *n.*

SYNONYM STUDY **Lift** and **raise** both mean to pull or push something up. **Lift** suggests hard work: *Can he lift that heavy bag?* **Raise** suggests less work: *If you know the answer, raise your hand.*

lift·off (lift′ôf′), *n.* the firing or launching of a rocket.

lig·a·ment (lig′ə mənt), *n.* band of strong tissue that connects bones or holds organs of the body in place.

WORD FAMILY **Ligament** and the words below are related. They all come from a Latin word meaning "to tie."

alliance	league	lien	rally[1]
alloy	legato	ligature	rely
ally	liable	obligate	self-reliant
furl	liaison	oblige	

lig·a·ture (lig′ə chür), *n.* **1** anything used to bind or tie up; band, bandage, cord, etc. **2** thread, wire, etc., used by surgeons to tie up a bleeding artery or vein. **3** two or three letters joined in printing. Æ and ffl are ligatures.

a	hat	ė	term	ô	order	ch	child		
ā	age	i	it	oi	oil	ng	long		a in about
ä	far	ī	ice	ou	out	sh	she	ə	e in taken
â	care	o	hot	u	cup	th	thin		i in pencil
e	let	ō	open	ů	put	ŦH	then		o in lemon
ē	equal	ȯ	saw	ü	rule	zh	measure		u in circus

light¹ (līt), **1** *n.* form of energy that the eye can see. Light is certain frequencies of electromagnetic waves. It travels at a speed of 186,282 miles (299,728 kilometers) per second in a vacuum. **2** *n.* any similar form of energy that the eye cannot see, such as ultraviolet rays or infrared rays, or other frequencies of electromagnetic waves. **3** *adj.* having light: *a light room.* **4** *n.* thing that gives light. A lamp is called a light. **5** *n.* supply of light: *A tall building cuts off our light.* **6** *v.* to cause to give light: *She lit the lamp.* **7** *v.* to give light to; provide with light: *The room is lit by six windows.* **8** *adj.* bright; clear: *The moonlit night seemed as light as day.* **9** *n.* brightness; clearness; illumination; particular amount of this: *a strong or dim light.* **10** *n.* a bright part: *light and shade in a painting.* **11** *v.* to make bright or clear: *Her face was lighted by a smile.* **12** *v.* to show the way by means of a light: *Here is a flashlight to light your way to the cellar.* **13** *v.* to become light: *The sky lights up at dawn.* **14** *n.* daytime; dawn: *The baker gets up before light.* **15** *adj.* pale in color: *light hair, light blue.* **16** *n.* thing with which to start something burning: *He wanted a light for the barbecue grill.* **17** *v.* to start burning: *She lit the candles.* **18** *v.* to take fire: *Matches light when you strike them.* **19** *n.* knowledge; information: *We need more light on this subject.* **20** *n.* public knowledge; open view: *The reporter brought to light graft in the city government.* **21** *n.* the way in which a thing is viewed: *The principal put the matter in the right light.* **22** *n.* shining model or example: *leading lights of social reform.* **23** *n.* a traffic light: *Turn left at the second light.* ❑ *v.* **lit** or **light·ed, light·ing.**

in light of, because of; considering: *In light of all these facts, what you did was completely right.*

see the light, 1 be born. **2** be made public. **3** to get the right idea.

see the light of day, 1 be born. **2** be made public.

shed light on or **throw light on,** to make clear; explain.

light² (līt), **1** *adj.* easy to carry; not heavy: *a light load.* **2** *adj.* having little weight for its size: *Feathers are light.* **3** *adj.* having less than usual weight: *light summer clothing.* **4** *adj.* less than usual in amount, force, etc.: *a light sleep, a light rain, a light meal.* **5** *adj.* easy to do or bear; not hard or severe: *light punishment, a light task.* **6** *adj.* not looking heavy; graceful; delicate: *a light bridge, light carving.* **7** *adj.* moving easily; nimble: *a light step.* **8** *adj.* cheerfully careless; happy: *a light laugh.* **9** *adj.* not serious enough; fickle: *a light mind, light of purpose.* **10** *adj.* aiming to entertain; not serious: *light reading.* **11** *adj.* not important: *light losses.* **12** *adj.* porous; sandy: *a light soil.* **13** *adj.* having risen properly; not soggy: *light dough.* **14** *adj.* lightly armed or equipped: *light infantry.* **15** *adv.* lightly. **16** *adj.* having fewer calories than similar food or drinks; lite: *a light soda, light yogurt.*

make light of, to treat as of little importance.

light³ (līt), *v.* **1** to come down to the ground; alight: *light from a horse.* **2** to come down from flight: *A bird lit on the branch.* **3** to come by chance: *Her eye lit upon a coin on the sidewalk.* ❑ *v.* **lit** or **light·ed, light·ing.**

light into, INFORMAL. **1** to attack. **2** to scold.

light out, INFORMAL. to leave suddenly; go away quickly.

light bulb, a ball or tube of glass containing a very fine wire that becomes white-hot and gives off light when electric current flows through it.

light·en¹ (līt'n), *v.* to make or become brighter; brighten: *Dawn lightens the sky.*

light·en² (līt'n), *v.* **1** to reduce the load of; make or become lighter: *Your help lightened our work.* **2** to make or become more cheerful: *The good news lightened our hearts.*

lighten up, to become less serious; be more relaxed and cheerful: *We told her to lighten up about the schedule.*

light¹ (def. 4)

light·er¹ (lī'tər), *n.* thing or person that starts something burning.

light·er² (lī'tər), **1** *n.* a flat-bottomed barge used for loading and unloading ships. **2** *v.* to carry goods in such a barge.

light·face (līt'fās'), *n.* printing type that has thin, light lines. This sentence is in lightface.

light·foot·ed (līt'fut'id), *adj.* stepping lightly. —**light'-foot'ed·ly,** *adv.* —**light'-foot'ed·ness,** *n.*

light·head·ed (līt'hed'id), *adj.* **1** dizzy; giddy; out of your head: *The sick man was light-headed from fever.* **2** empty-headed; silly; thoughtless: *That frivolous, light-headed crowd thinks of nothing but parties and games.* —**light'-head'ed·ly,** *adv.* —**light'-head'ed·ness,** *n.*

light·heart·ed (līt'här'tid), *adj.* without worry; carefree; cheerful. —**light'heart'ed·ly,** *adv.* —**light'heart'ed·ness,** *n.*

light heavyweight, boxer who weighs more than 160 pounds (73 kilograms) and less than 175 pounds (79 kilograms).

light·house (līt'hous'), *n.* tower or framework with a bright light that shines far out over the water. It is located on or near the shore to guide ships and warn of danger. ❑ *n., pl.* **light·hous·es** (līt'hou'ziz).

light industry, industry that makes consumer goods rather than products for businesses, using small machines and simple processes.

light·ing (lī'ting), *n.* **1** illumination; providing with light. **2** way in which lights are arranged: *overhead lighting.*

light·ly (līt'lē), *adv.* **1** with little weight or force: *Cares rested lightly on her.* **2** to a small degree or extent; not much: *lightly clad.* **3** quickly; easily: *She jumped lightly aside.* **4** cheerfully: *take bad news lightly.* **5** thoughtlessly; carelessly; frivolously: *take a warning lightly.*

light·mind·ed (līt'mīn'did), *adj.* empty-headed; thoughtless; frivolous. —**light'-mind'ed·ly,** *adv.* —**light'-mind'ed·ness,** *n.*

light·ness¹ (līt'nis), *n.* **1** brightness; clearness. **2** paleness.

light·ness² (līt'nis), *n.* **1** quality of being light in weight: *The lightness of this load is a relief after the heavy one I was carrying.* **2** cheerfulness: *lightness of spirit.* **3** lack of proper seriousness: *Such lightness of conduct is out of place in a courtroom.*

light·ning (līt'ning), *n.* flash of light in the sky caused by a discharge of electricity between clouds, or between a cloud and the earth's surface. The sound the discharge makes is thunder.

lightning bug, firefly.

lightning rod, a metal rod fastened to a building or ship to conduct lightning safely into the earth or water and prevent damage.

light pen, device like a pen which produces an electrical signal when it is pointed at light. It is used for directing a computer to add, change, or remove information shown on its display screen.

light rail, a system of lightweight streetcars used as urban transportation. —**light'-rail',** *adj.*

light·ship (līt'ship'), *n.* ship with a bright light, anchored at a dangerous place to warn ships away.

light·weight (līt'wāt'), **1** *n.* person or thing of less than average weight. **2** *adj.* light in weight. **3** *n.* boxer who weighs more than 126 pounds (57 kilograms) and less than 135 pounds (61 kilograms).

light·year (līt'yir'), *n.* unit of distance used in astronomy. It is equal to the distance that light travels in one year, about six trillion miles (ten trillion kilometers). The star closest to the Sun is about four light-years away.

lig·nite (lig'nīt), *n.* a dark brown coal, often having a woody texture.

lik·a·ble (lī'kə bəl), *adj.* having qualities that win goodwill or friendship; popular; pleasing: *the most likable boy in the whole school.* Also, **likeable.** —**lik'a·ble·ness,** *n.*

like¹ (līk), **1** *prep.* resembling something or each other; similar to: *Our house is like theirs.* **2** *prep.* in the same way as; as well as: *sing like a bird.* **3** *adj.* of the same form, kind, amount, etc.; the same or almost the same; similar: *Her aunt promised her $25 if she could earn a like sum.* **4** *prep.* such as you would expect of; characteristic of: *Isn't it just like him to be late?* **5** *prep.* in the right condition for: *I feel like working.* **6** *prep.* as if there will be: *It looks like rain.* **7** *n.* person or thing like another; counterpart or equal: *We shall not see her like again.* **8** *conj.* INFORMAL. as if: *He acted like he was afraid.* **9** *conj.* INFORMAL. in the same way as;

as: *Snakes attract him like puppies attract other people.*
and the like, 1 and so forth: *He studied music, painting, and the like.* **2** and other like things: *At the zoo we saw lions, tigers, bears, zebras, and the like.*

USAGE NOTE **Like¹** is used with nouns and pronouns: *She looks like her mother and talks like her too.* **As** is used with verbs: *He didn't behave as he should.* Many people feel that using **like** with a verb is wrong. Others feel that this use is only informal.

like² (līk), **1** *v.* to be pleased with; be satisfied with: *My cat likes milk.* **2** *v.* to have a kindly or friendly feeling for: *to like a person.* **3** *v.* to wish for; wish: *I'd like more time to finish this. Come whenever you like.* **4** *n.pl.* **likes,** liking; preference: *You know all my likes and dislikes.* ❑ *v.* **liked, lik·ing.**

-like, *suffix.* like a ___; like that of a ___: *childlike = like a child or child's.*

like·a·ble (lī′kə bəl), *adj.* likable. **—like′a·ble·ness,** *n.*

like·li·hood (līk′lē hùd), *n.* a strong chance; probability: *Is there any likelihood of rain today?*

like·ly (līk′lē), **1** *adj.* probable: *One likely result of this heavy rain is the rising of the river.* **2** *adv.* probably: *He will very likely be home all day.* **3** *adj.* to be expected: *It is likely to be hot in August.* **4** *adj.* suitable: *Is this a likely place to fish?* **5** *adj.* promising: *a likely student.* ❑ *adj.* **like·li·er, like·li·est.**

like-mind·ed (līk′mīn′did), *adj.* **1** in agreement or accord. **2** thinking along the same lines. **—like′-mind′ed·ness,** *n.*

lik·en (lī′kən), *v.* to compare: *Her voice was likened to that of a famous singer.* ■ Another word that sounds like this is **lichen.**

like·ness (līk′nis), *n.* **1** similarity; quality of being alike: *The girl's likeness to her aunt was striking.* **2** something that is like; copy; picture: *This photograph is a good likeness of him.* **3** appearance; shape: *I watched a large cloud assume the likeness of a sailing ship.* ❑ *n., pl.* **like·ness·es.**

like·wise (līk′wīz′), *adv.* **1** the same: *Watch what I do. Now you do likewise.* **2** also; moreover; too: *I must go now, and you likewise.*

lik·ing (lī′king), *n.* kindly feeling; preference; fondness: *a liking for apples, a liking for children.*

li·lac (lī′lək *or* lī′lak), **1** *n.* bush with clusters of tiny, fragrant, pale pinkish purple or white flowers. **2** *n.* a pale pinkish purple. **3** *adj.* pale pinkish purple. [**Lilac** comes from a Persian word meaning "blue." Often colors are named for plants, but this is a plant named for a color.]

Li·li·u·o·ka·la·ni (lē lē′ü ō kä lä′nē), *n.* **Ly·di·a Ka·me·ke·ha** (lid′ē-ə kä′me kä′hä), 1838-1917, queen of Hawaii from 1891 to 1893. ■ Liliuokalani wrote the song "Aloha Oe" which is now the traditional farewell song of Hawaii. Wealthy Americans living in Hawaii revolted against her in 1893 and established a republic in 1894.

Li·long·we (li lóng′wā), *n.* capital of Malawi.

lilt (lilt), **1** *v.* to sing or play a tune in a light, lively manner. **2** *n.* a lively song or tune with a swing. **3** *n.* a lively, springing movement: *She walks with a lilt.* **—lilt′ing·ly,** *adv.*

lil·y (lil′ē), **1** *n.* any of very many plants with flowers that are usually large, bell-shaped, and showy, and are often divided into six parts. Lilies grow from bulbs. The white lily is a symbol of purity. The white garden lily is the provincial flower of Quebec. **2** *adj.* like a white lily; pure and lovely. **3** *n.* any of various plants similar but unrelated to true lilies, such as the calla lily or water lily. ❑ *n., pl.* **lil·ies. —lil′y· like′,** *adj.*

lily (def. 1)

lily of the valley, plant with tiny, sweet-smelling, bell-shaped white flowers arranged along a single flower stem. ❑ *pl.* **lilies of the valley.**

Li·ma (lē′mə), *n.* capital of Peru, in the W part.

li·ma bean (lī′mə), a broad, flat, pale green bean, eaten as a vegetable.

limb (lim), *n.* **1** leg, arm, or wing. **2** a large branch: *They sawed the dead limb off the tree.* ■ Another word that sounds like this is **limn. —limb′less,** *adj.*

lim·ber (lim′bər), **1** *adj.* bending easily; flexible: *A piano player should have limber fingers.* **2** *v.* to make or become limber: *He is stiff when he begins to skate, but limbers up quickly.* **—lim′ber·ly,** *adv.* **—lim′ber·ness,** *n.*

lim·bo (lim′bō), *n.* **1** Often, **Limbo,** (in the belief of Roman Catholics) a region for souls of people who die unbaptized but who do not deserve the punishment of sinners. **2** place for persons and things forgotten, cast aside, or out of date: *The belief that the earth is flat belongs to the limbo of outworn ideas.* ❑ *n., pl.* **lim·bos** for 2.

Lim·burg·er (lim′bėr′gər), *n.* a soft cheese having a strong smell.

lime¹ (līm), **1** *n.* a solid, white compound of calcium and oxygen obtained by burning limestone, shells, bone, etc.; quicklime; calcium oxide. Lime is used in making mortar and on fields to improve acid soil. **2** *v.* to put lime on. ❑ *v.* **limed, lim·ing. —lime′less,** *adj.*

lime² (līm), *n.* a juicy, greenish yellow citrus fruit of two trees grown in warm climates. Limes are smaller and sourer than lemons.

lime³ (līm), *n.* the linden tree.

lime·ade (līm′ād′ *or* līm′ād′), *n.* drink made of lime juice, sweetener, and water.

lime·light (līm′līt′), *n.* **1** center of public attention and interest: *Some people are never happy unless they are in the limelight.* **2** a strong light produced by heating lime in a flame, formerly used in theaters to light up certain persons or objects and draw attention to them.

lim·er·ick (lim′ər ik), *n.* kind of humorous verse of five lines.

lime·stone (līm′stōn′), *n.* a sedimentary rock made mostly of calcium carbonate, used for building and for making lime.

lime·wa·ter (līm′wä′tər), *n.* solution of slaked lime in water. It is used to counteract excess acid in the digestive tract.

lim·it (lim′it), **1** *n.* farthest point or edge; where something ends or must end: *the limit of your vision, the limit of your patience.* **2** *n.* the largest amount allowed: *Every day last week my aunt managed to catch the legal limit of five fish a day.* **3** *n.pl.* **limits,** boundary; bounds: *Keep within the limits of the school grounds.* **4** *v.* to set a limit to; restrict: *We must limit the expense to $10.* [See Word Story at **term.**] **—lim′it·a·ble,** *adj.* **—lim′it·er,** *n.*

SYNONYM STUDY **Limit** and **restrict** both mean to control what is done. **Limit** means to say when or where something must stop: *Each speaker is limited to three minutes.* **Restrict** means to allow only certain choices: *When we bought a house, our budget became restricted.*

lim·i·ta·tion (lim′ə tā′shən), *n.* **1** act of limiting or condition of being limited. **2** a limiting rule or circumstance; restriction; boundary.

lim·it·ed (lim′ə tid), *adj.* kept within limits; restricted: *a limited space, a limited number.* **—lim′it·ed·ness,** *n.*

lim·it·less (lim′it lis), *adj.* without limits; boundless; infinite. **—lim′it·less·ly,** *adv.* **—lim′it·less·ness,** *n.*

limn (lim), *v.* OLD USE. **1** to paint or draw a picture. **2** to portray in words. ■ Another word that sounds like this is **limb.**

lim·o (lim′ō), *n.* INFORMAL. limousine. ❑ *n., pl.* **lim·os.**

lim·ou·sine (lim′ə zēn′ *or* lim′ə zēn′), *n.* **1** a large car with specially comfortable seating for a number of passengers, separated from the driver by a partition. Limousines are often hired for special trips or occasions. **2** a large car or small bus used to take passengers to or from an airport, railway, or bus station, etc.

limp¹ (limp), **1** *n.* a lame step or walk. **2** *v.* to walk with a limp: *After falling down the stairs, she limped for several days.* **—limp′er,** *n.* **—limp′ing·ly,** *adv.*

a	hat	ė	term	ô	order	ch	child		
ā	age	i	it	oi	oil	ng	long		a in about
ä	far	ī	ice	ou	out	sh	she	ə	e in taken
â	care	o	hot	u	cup	th	thin		i in pencil
e	let	ō	open	ù	put	ŦH	then		o in lemon
ē	equal	ò	saw	ü	rule	zh	measure		u in circus

limp² (limp), *adj.* not at all stiff or firm; ready to bend or droop: *Spaghetti gets limp when it is cooked. I am so tired I feel as limp as a rag.* ▪ See Synonym Study at **soft.** **–limp′ly,** *adv.* **–limp′-ness,** *n.*

lim·pet (lim′pit), *n.* any of several small shellfish that cling to rocks and other objects, used for bait and sometimes for food.

lim·pid (lim′pid), *adj.* clear or transparent: *a spring of limpid water, limpid eyes.* **–lim′pid·ness,** *n.*

lim·pid·i·ty (lim pid′ə tē), *n.* limpid quality or condition.

lim·y (lī′mē), *adj.* of, containing, or resembling lime. ❑ *adj.* **lim·i·er, lim·i·est.**

linch·pin (linch′pin′), *n.* pin inserted through a hole in the end of an axle to keep the wheel on.

Lin·coln (ling′kən), *n.* **1** Abraham, 1809-1865, the 16th president of the United States, from 1861 to 1865. He was assassinated by John Wilkes Booth. **2** capital of Nebraska, in the SE part.

Lind·bergh (lind′bėrg′), *n.* **1** Anne Mor·row (mor′ō), born 1906, American poet and writer. Her husband was Charles Lindbergh. **2 Charles Au·gus·tus** (ə gus′təs), 1902-1974, American aviator who made the first solo flight across the Atlantic, in 1927.

lin·den (lin′dən), *n.* any of several trees with heart-shaped leaves and clusters of small, sweet-smelling, yellowish flowers; basswood; lime³. Lindens are often used for shade and ornament.

line¹ (līn), **1** *n.* a long narrow mark: *Draw two lines along the margin.* **2** *n.* anything that is like a long narrow mark: *the lines in your face.* **3** *v.* to mark with lines: *Please line your paper with a pencil and ruler.* **4** *n.* a row of words across a page or in a column. **5** *n.* a single verse of poetry. **6** *n.* (in mathematics) the path traced by a moving point, extending at both ends; line segment. It has length, but no thickness. **7** *n.* piece of rope, cord, or wire: *a fishing line.* **8** *n.* a cord for measuring, making level, etc. A plumb line is used to see if a wall is vertical or to find the depth of water. **9** *n.* an edge or boundary: *the line between Texas and Mexico.* **10** *n.* row of persons or things: *a line of cars.* **11** *v.* to arrange in a line: *Line your shoes along the edge of the shelf.* **12** *v.* to form a line along: *Trees lined the road for a mile.* **13** *n.* a short letter; note: *Drop me a line.* **14** *n.* a connected series of persons or things following one another in time: *The latest in a long line of fine novels by this author. The Stuarts were a line of English rulers.* **15** *n.* family or ancestry: *of noble line.* **16** *n.* direction of something moving: *the line of flight of migrating birds.* **17** *n.* a certain way of doing: *Please proceed on these lines till further notice.* **18** *n.* (in warfare) a front row of trenches or other defenses. **19** *n.* formation of soldiers or ships placed side by side. **20** *n.* wire or system of wires connecting users of a telegraph or telephone system. **21** *n.* a telephone connection: *I'm sorry, the line is busy.* **22** *n.* any wire, pipe, hose, etc., from one point to another: *a steam line, a natural-gas line.* **23** *n.* a single track of railroad. **24** *n.* one branch of a system of transportation: *The main line of the railroad uses six tracks.* **25** *n.* a whole system of transportation: *a bus line.* **26** *n.* a related set of goods: *Her store carries the best line of shoes in town.* **27** *n.pl.* **lines,** words that an actor speaks in a play: *forget your lines.* **28** *n.* in football: **a** a line of scrimmage. **b** players along the line of scrimmage at the start of a play. Usually the offensive team has seven players in the line, and the defensive team has four. **29** *n.* INFORMAL. talk, usually intended to deceive or confuse: *The police didn't believe the driver's line about an emergency.* **30** *n.* one of the horizontal lines that make a staff in music. ❑ *v.* **lined, lin·ing.** **–line′less,** *adj.* **–line′like′,** *adj.*

all along the line, at every point; everywhere: *This car has given us trouble all along the line.*

bring into line, to cause to agree or conform.

line (def. 1)—line marking the start of a race

come into line, to agree; conform.

down the line, 1 the whole way; to the end. **2** later; in the future.

draw a line or **draw the line,** to set a limit.

get a line on or **have a line on,** INFORMAL. to get or have information about.

hold the line, 1 to stand firm; maintain a position: *The librarians sometimes let us stay a little late, but when it comes to eating in the library, they really hold the line.* **2** to wait in the middle of a telephone conversation for the other person to return: *Can you hold the line a moment? I have another call.*

in line, 1 in a row: *The children are all in line.* **2** in agreement: *This plan is in line with their thinking.*

in line for, expected or scheduled to receive: *in line for a promotion.*

line out, 1 (in baseball) to hit a line drive that is caught. **2** to draw a line or lines to indicate an outline.

line up, to form a line; form into a line: *They lined up by the door.*

on a line, even; level.

out of line, 1 uncalled-for; not suitable or proper. **2** in disagreement.

read between the lines, to get more from the words than they say; find a hidden meaning.

toe the line, to conform to a certain standard of duty, conduct, etc.

line² (līn), *v.* **1** to put a layer of paper, cloth, felt, etc., inside of a dress, hat, box, bag, etc. **2** to fill: *line your pockets with money.* **3** to serve as a lining for: *This piece of silk would line your coat very nicely.* ❑ *v.* **lined, lin·ing.**

lin·e·age (lin′ē ij), *n.* **1** descent in a direct line from an ancestor. **2** family or origin.

lin·e·al (lin′ē əl), *adj.* **1** in the direct line of descent: *She is a lineal descendant of her grandmother.* **2** of or like a line. **–lin′e·al·ly,** *adv.*

lin·e·a·ment (lin′ē ə mənt), *n.* part or feature, especially a part or feature of a face with attention to its outline.

lin·e·ar (lin′ē ər), *adj.* **1** of a line or lines: *linear succession to the throne.* **2** changing in a regular way or direction: *a story's linear development from beginning to end.* **3** made of lines; making use of lines: *linear designs.* **4** of length: *An inch is a linear measure.* **5** like a line; long and narrow: *A pine tree has linear leaves.* **–lin′e·ar·ly,** *adv.*

linear equation, an equation with solutions that lie on a straight line when they are placed on a graph.

linear measure, 1 system of units, such as foot and mile or meter and kilometer, used for measuring length. See table on page 975A. **2** a measured length: *The linear measure of the path is two miles.*

line·back·er (līn′bak′ər), *n.* (in football) a defensive player whose position is directly behind the line.

line drive, baseball hit so that it goes in almost a straight line, usually close to the ground; liner.

line graph, graph on which points that show amounts are connected by short straight lines.

line·man (līn′mən), *n.* **1** person who sets up or repairs telephone, telegraph, or electric power lines; linesman. **2** (in football) a player in the line; a center, guard, tackle, or end. **3** person who carries the line in surveying. ❑ *n., pl.* **line·men.**

lin·en (lin′ən), **1** *n.* cloth or thread made from flax. **2** *n.* articles made of linen or some substitute. Tablecloths, napkins, sheets, towels, and shirts are all called linen. **3** *adj.* made of linen.

line of scrimmage, an imaginary line running across a football field at any point where the ball is placed after a play has ended, and before the next play.

lin·er¹ (lī′nər), *n.* **1** ship or airplane belonging to a transportation system. **2** person or thing that makes lines. **3** line drive.

lin·er² (lī′nər), *n.* **1** person who lines or fits a lining to anything. **2** something that serves as a lining.

line segment, any section between two points on a line; segment.

lines·man (līnz′mən), *n.* **1** lineman (def. 1). **2** (in certain games) person who watches the lines which mark out the field, court, etc., and assists the umpire. ❑ *n., pl.* **lines·men.**

line·up or **line-up** (līn′up′), *n.* **1** list of the players who will take part or are taking part in a game. **2** formation of persons or things into a line. A police lineup is an arrangement of a group of persons for identification.

-ling, *suffix.* **1** little ___: *duckling* = *little duck.* **2** one belonging to ___: *earthling* = *one belonging to the earth.*

lin·ger (ling′gər), *v.* **1** to stay on; go slowly, as if unwilling to leave: *He lingered after the others had left.* ■ See Synonym Study at **lag.** **2** to remain in existence; persist: *Her fever went away, but the fatigue lingered.* **—lin′ger·er,** *n.* **—lin′ger·ing·ly,** *adv.*

lin·ge·rie (lan′zhə rē′ *or* län′zhə rā′), *n.* women's underwear, nightgowns, etc.

lin·go (ling′gō), *n.* INFORMAL. language or talk that sounds strange or is not understood: *baseball lingo.* ❏ *n., pl.* **lin·goes.**

lin·gua fran·ca (ling′gwə frang′kə), **1** a language made up of Italian mixed with French, Spanish, Greek, Arabic, and Turkish, used especially by traders in the eastern Mediterranean. **2** any language used as a trade or communications medium by people speaking different languages. ❏ *n., pl.* **lin·gua fran·cas.**

lin·gui·ne (ling gwē′nē), *n.* kind of pasta similar to spaghetti, cut into long, thin, flat pieces. Linguine is often served with clam sauce.

lin·guist (ling′gwist), *n.* **1** an expert in languages or linguistics. **2** person skilled in a number of languages.

lin·guis·tic (ling gwis′tik), *adj.* of or relating to language or the study of languages. **—lin·guis′ti·cal·ly,** *adv.*

lin·guis·tics (ling gwis′tiks), *n.* science of language; comparative study of languages.

lin·i·ment (lin′ə mənt), *n.* a soothing liquid which is rubbed on the skin to relieve the pain of sore muscles, sprains, bruises, etc.

lin·ing (lī′ning), *n.* layer of material covering the inner surface of something: *the lining of a coat.*

link (lingk), **1** *n.* any ring or loop of a chain. **2** *n.* anything that joins or connects as a link does: *a link in a chain of evidence.* **3** *v.* to join as a link does; unite or connect: *Don't try to link me with this scheme.* **4** *n.* cuff link.

link·age (ling′kij), *n.* **1** act of linking or condition of being linked. **2** arrangement or system of links.

linking verb, verb with little or no meaning of its own, used to connect a subject with a predicate adjective or a predicate noun. In *"The trees are maples," are* is a linking verb. *Am, are, is,* and *seem* are linking verbs.

links (lingks), *n.pl.* a golf course. ■ Another word that sounds like this is **lynx.**

link·up (lingk′up′), *n.* connection or tie between objects, people, groups, etc.: *a linkup between computers.*

Lin·nae·us (li nē′əs), *n.* **Car·o·lus** (kar′ə ləs), 1707-1778, Swedish botanist. ■ **Linnaeus** developed the modern scientific method of naming living things. In his system, each living thing has a two-part name. The first part of the name is for the genus and the second is for the species.

li·no·le·um (lə nō′lē əm), *n.* **1** a floor covering made by putting a hard surface of ground cork mixed with linseed oil on a canvas or burlap back. **2** any similar floor covering.

lin·seed (lin′sēd′), *n.* flaxseed.

linseed oil, a yellowish oil obtained by pressing linseed. It is used in making paints, printing inks, and linoleum.

lin·sey-wool·sey (lin′zē wùl′zē), *n.* (long ago) a strong, coarse fabric made of linen and wool or of cotton and wool.

lint (lint), *n.* **1** tiny bits of thread or fluff of any material. **2** the soft down or fleecy material obtained by scraping linen. Formerly, lint was put on wounds to keep out air and dirt. **—lint′less,** *adj.*

lin·tel (lin′tl), *n.* a horizontal beam or stone above a door or window to support the structure above it.

lint·y (lin′tē), *adj.* **1** full of or marked with lint. **2** like lint. ❏ *adj.* **lint·i·er, lint·i·est.**

li·on (lī′ən), *n.* **1** a large, fierce cat, with a dull yellowish coat, found in Africa and southern Asia. The male has a full, flowing mane of coarse hair. **2** mountain lion. **3** a very brave or strong person: *a lion on defense.* **4** a famous person: *a literary lion.*

li·on·ess (lī′ə nis), *n.* a female lion. ❏ *n., pl.* **li·on·ess·es.**

li·on·heart·ed (lī′ən här′tid), *adj.* brave; courageous.

li·on·ize (lī′ə nīz), *v.* to treat someone as very important. ❏ *v.* **li·on·ized, li·on·iz·ing. —li′on·i·za′tion,** *n.* **—li′on·iz′er,** *n.*

lion's share, the biggest or best part.

lip (lip), *n.* **1** either of the two fleshy, movable edges of the mouth.

2 the folding or bent-out edge of any opening: *the lip of a pitcher.* **—lip′less,** *adj.* **—lip′like′,** *adj.*

keep a stiff upper lip, be brave and firm; show no fear or discouragement

Li Peng (lē′ pung′), born 1928, Chinese political leader, prime minister of China since 1987.

lip·id (lip′id), *n.* any of various organic chemical compounds that feel oily and cannot be dissolved in water. Fats and waxes are lipids.

lip·py (lip′ē), *adj.* INFORMAL. impertinent. ❏ *adj.* **lip·pi·er, lip·pi·est.**

lip-read (lip′rēd′), *v.* to understand speech by watching the movements of the speaker's lips. ❏ *v.* **lip-read** (lip′red′), **lip-read·ing. —lip′read′er,** *n.*

lip reading, understanding of speech by watching the movements of the speaker's lips.

lip service, promises without action; an insincere claim of belief, goodwill, commitment, etc.: *The dictator may pay lip service to democracy but he is really interested only in power.*

lip·stick (lip′stik′), *n.* a small stick of a waxlike cosmetic, used for coloring the lips.

lip-sync or **lip-synch** (lip′singk′), *v.* **1** to move the lips at exactly the right times to match a recording, especially of a singer. **2** to speak or sing so as to make sounds matching lip movements in a film or video.

liq·ue·fac·tion (lik′wə fak′shən), *n.* **1** process of changing into a liquid. **2** liquefied condition.

liq·ue·fy (lik′wə fi), *v.* to change into a liquid; make or become liquid. ❏ *v.* **liq·ue·fied, liq·ue·fy·ing. —liq′ue·fi′er,** *n.*

li·queur (li kėr′), *n.* a strong, sweet, highly flavored alcoholic liquor.

liq·uid (lik′wid), **1** *n.* substance that is not a solid or a gas; substance that flows freely like water. Mercury is a liquid at room temperature. **2** *adj.* in the form of a liquid; melted: *liquid soap.* **3** *adj.* clear and bright like water. **4** *adj.* clear and smooth-flowing in sound: *the liquid notes of a bird.* **5** *adj.* easily turned into cash: *U.S. bonds are a liquid investment.* **—liq′uid·ly,** *adv.* **—liq′uid·ness,** *n.*

SYNONYM STUDY **Liquid** and **fluid** both mean a substance that flows. **Liquid** means a substance that is not a solid or a gas: *At room temperature, water is a liquid.* **Fluid** means a liquid or a gas: *At room temperature, water and air are both fluids.*

liquid air, an intensely cold liquid formed by putting air under very great pressure and then cooling it.

liq·ui·date (lik′wə dāt), *v.* **1** to pay off completely: *liquidate a debt.* **2** to close down a business firm by selling its assets. **3** to kill ruthlessly; exterminate: *The Russian Revolution liquidated the nobility.* ❏ *v.* **liq·ui·dat·ed, liq·ui·dat·ing. —liq′ui·da′tion,** *n.* **—liq′ui·da′tor,** *n.*

lion (def. 1)—about 3 ft. (91 cm) high at the shoulder

a	hat	ė	term	ô	order	ch	child		
ā	age	i	it	oi	oil	ng	long	ə	a in about
ä	far	ī	ice	ou	out	sh	she		e in taken
â	care	o	hot	u	cup	th	thin		i in pencil
e	let	ō	open	ù	put	ᴛʜ	then		o in lemon
ē	equal	ò	saw	ü	rule	zh	measure		u in circus

liquid crystal, any of several chemicals with structures between those of liquids and solids, and with appearance changeable by electricity or heat, used to show numbers on clocks, calculators, etc.

li·quid·i·ty (li kwid′ə tē), *n.* liquid condition or quality.

liquid measure, system for measuring the volume of liquids, using such units as quarts or liters. See table on page 975A.

liquid oxygen, an intensely cold liquid formed by putting oxygen under very great pressure and then cooling it; lox.

liq·uor (lik′ər), *n.* **1** an alcoholic drink, such as brandy, gin, rum, vodka, or whiskey. **2** any liquid, especially a liquid in which food is packaged, canned, or cooked.

lir·a (lir′ə), *n.* the unit of money in Italy, Malta, and Turkey. ❑ *n., pl.* **lir·e** (lir′ā), **lir·as.**

Lis·bon (liz′bən), *n.* port and capital of Portugal, near the Atlantic.

lisle (līl), **1** *n.* a fine, strong linen or cotton thread, used for making stockings, gloves, etc. **2** *adj.* made of lisle.

lisp (lisp), **1** *v.* to use the sound of *th* in *thin* and *then* instead of the sound of *s* or the sound of *z* in speaking: *A person who lisps might say, "Thing a thong" for "Sing a song."* **2** *n.* act, habit, or sound of saying a *th* sound for *s* and *z*: *He spoke with a lisp.* **3** *v.* to speak imperfectly: *Young children sometimes lisp.*

lis·some or **lis·som** (lis′əm), *adj.* bending easily; lithe; limber; supple. —**lis′some·ly,** *adv.* —**lis′some·ness,** *n.*

list[1] (list), **1** *n.* series of names, numbers, words, or phrases: *a shopping list.* **2** *v.* to make a list of; enter in a list: *A dictionary lists words in alphabetical order.*

list[2] (list), **1** *n.* act of tipping to one side; tilt: *the list of a ship.* **2** *v.* to tip to one side; tilt: *The sinking ship was listing so that water lapped its decks.*

list[3] (list), *v.* OLD USE. to listen; listen to.

lis·ten (lis′n), *v.* **1** to try to hear; attend with the ears so as to hear: *She listened for the sound of a car. I like to listen to music.* **2** to give heed to advice, temptation, etc.; pay attention. —**lis′ten·er,** *n.*

listen in, 1 to listen to others talking on a telephone: *I listened in on the extension to hear what they were saying.* **2** to listen to the radio: *Listen in next week for the exciting conclusion of our story.*

Lis·ter (lis′tər), *n.* **Joseph,** 1827-1912, English surgeon. He was the first to use antiseptic methods in performing operations.

list·ing (lis′ting), *n.* **1** a list. **2** act of making a list. **3** item in a list; something listed: *Did you check the job listings in today's paper?*

list·less (list′lis), *adj.* showing a lack of energy or enthusiasm; not interested in things: *a dull and listless mood.* —**list′less·ly,** *adv.* —**list′less·ness,** *n.*

list price, price of an item as it appears in a catalog, advertisement, or list. Discounts are figured on the list price.

lists (lists), *n.pl.* (in the Middle Ages) place where knights fought in tournaments.

enter the lists, to join in a contest; take part in a fight, argument, etc.

Liszt (list), *n.* **Franz** (fränz), 1811-1886, Hungarian composer and pianist, a leader in romanticism and the development of modern music.

lit[1] (lit), *v.* a past tense and a past participle of **light**[1]: *She lit the lamp. The stove was lit already.*

lit[2] (lit), *v.* a past tense and a past participle of **light**[3]: *He lit upon a pleasing thought. A butterfly had lit upon his head.*

lit., **1** liter. **2** literature.

lit·a·ny (lit′n ē), *n.* prayer consisting of a series of requests and responses said by a minister or priest and the congregation in turn. ❑ *n., pl.* **lit·a·nies.**

li·tchi (lē′chē), **1** *n.* the small nut-shaped fruit of a Chinese tree. It has a thin, brittle, rough red shell enclosing a sweet, white jellylike pulp with a single brown seed. **2** the tree it grows on. Also, **lichee.**

lite (līt), *adj.* INFORMAL. light[2] (def. 16).

li·ter (lē′tər), *n.* unit of volume in the metric system, equal to 1000 cubic centimeters.

-liter, suffix. **1** liters: *kiloliter = one thousand liters.* **2** part of a liter: *centiliter = one hundredth of a liter.*

lit·er·a·cy (lit′ər ə sē), *n.* **1** ability to read and write. **2** having understanding of the essentials of a particular area of knowledge: *computer literacy.*

lit·er·al (lit′ər əl), *adj.* **1** taking words in their usual meaning, without exaggeration or imagination; matter-of-fact: *the literal*

meaning of a phrase, a literal type of mind.* **2** following the exact words of the original: *a literal translation.* **3** true to fact: *a literal account.*

lit·er·al·ly (lit′ər ə lē), *adv.* **1** word for word; without exaggeration or imagination: *Write the story literally as it happened.* **2** actually: *The earthquake destroyed literally thousands of houses.*

lit·er·ar·y (lit′ə rer′ē), *adj.* **1** of or referring to literature. **2** knowing much about literature. **3** engaged in literature as a profession. —**lit′er·ar′i·ly,** *adv.*

lit·er·ate (lit′ər it), **1** *adj.* able to read and write. **2** *n.* someone who can read and write. **3** *adj.* knowledgeable about literature; educated. **4** *adj.* having understanding of the essentials of a particular subject: *courses designed to make students literate in science.*

lit·er·a·ture (lit′ər ə chùr *or* lit′ər ə chər), *n.* **1** writings of a period or of a country, especially those kept alive by their beauty of style or thought: *English literature.* **2** all the books and articles on a subject: *the literature of stamp collecting.* **3** writing books as a profession. **4** the study of literature: *I took literature this spring.* **5** printed matter of any kind: *election campaign literature.*

lithe (līᴛʜ), *adj.* bending easily; supple: *a lithe gymnast.* —**lithe′ly,** *adv.* —**lithe′ness,** *n.*

lith·i·um (lith′ē əm), *n.* a soft, silver white metallic element which occurs in various minerals. Lithium is the lightest of all metals. *Symbol:* Li

lith·o·graph (lith′ə graf), **1** *n.* print made from a flat stone or metal plate on which the picture, design, etc., is made with a greasy material that will hold printing ink. The rest of the surface is made ink-repellent with water. **2** *v.* to print from such a stone or plate. —**li·thog·ra·pher** (li thog′rə fər), *n.*

li·thog·ra·phy (li thog′rə fē), *n.* art or process of making lithographs.

lith·o·sphere (lith′ə sfir), *n.* the solid outer part of the earth, including the crust and upper mantle.

Lith·u·a·ni·a (lith′ü ā′nē ə), *n.* a country in N Europe, on the Baltic Sea. *Capital:* Vilnius. —**Lith′u·a′ni·an,** *adj., n.*

lit·i·gant (lit′ə gənt), *n.* person engaged in a lawsuit.

lit·i·ga·tion (lit′ə gā′shən), *n.* **1** act of carrying on a lawsuit or going to law. **2** a lawsuit or legal proceeding.

lit·mus (lit′məs), *n.* a blue dye obtained from lichens, used in litmus paper as a chemical indicator.

litmus paper, paper treated with litmus. Blue litmus paper turns red when put into acid; red litmus paper turns blue when put into alkali.

litter (def. 3)

lit·ter (lit′ər), **1** *n.* little bits of things left scattered around in disorder: *He picked up the litter.* **2** *v.* to leave stuff lying around; scatter things about; make untidy: *litter the room with papers.* **3** *n.* the young animals produced at one time: *a litter of kittens.* **4** *v.* to give birth to young animals. **5** *n.* straw, hay, etc., used as bedding for animals. **6** *n.* shredded clay used to absorb cat urine. **7** *n.* stretcher for carrying a sick or wounded person. **8** *n.* framework to be carried on the shoulders or by beasts of burden, with a couch usually enclosed by curtains. [**Litter** comes from a Latin word meaning "bed." Because farm animals sleep in loose straw or hay, their beds are very messy.] —**lit′ter·er,** *n.*

lit·ter·bug (lit'ər bug'), *n.* someone who throws trash along a highway or sidewalk, in a park, etc.

lit·tle (lit'l), **1** *adj.* not big or large; small. A grain of sand or the head of a pin is little. **2** *adj.* younger or youngest: *I take my little sister to day care every morning.* **3** *adj.* not long in time or in distance; short: *Wait a little while and I'll go a little way with you.* **4** *adj.* not much; small in number, amount, degree, or importance: *A very sick child has little strength and can eat only a little food.* **5** *adj.* mean; narrow-minded: *the pettiness of little minds.* **6** *n.* a small amount: *She had a big box of candy but gave her sister only a little.* **7** *n.* a short time or distance: *Move a little to the left.* **8** *n.* not much; not enough: *Little is being done to aid the victims of the hurricane.* **9** *adv.* to a small extent: *The teacher read from an interesting book that was little known to us.* **10** *adv.* not at all: *Little do they know what I plan to do.* ❏ *adj.* **less** or **less·er, least; lit·tler, lit·tlest;** *adv.* **less, least. —lit'tle·ness,** *n.*
little by little, by a small amount at a time; slowly; gradually.
make little of, to treat or represent as of little importance.
not a little, much; very: *We were not a little upset by the accident.*
think little of, to not value much; consider as unimportant.

A LITTLE POEM

Mary had a little lamb; she called it "lamb" plus "**-let,**"
Or sometimes other suffixes, like "**-ling**" or "**-kin**" or "**-ette.**"
Sometimes a prefix she would use, and "**mini-**" lamb she'd call.
Each one means "**little,**" takes less time, and is in use. Try all.

Little Bear, Ursa Minor.
Little Dipper, group of seven bright stars in the constellation Ursa Minor.
Little League, a group of baseball teams organized for children from eight to twelve years of age.
lit·tle·neck (lit'l nek'), *n.* a young quahog clam.
Little Rock, capital of Arkansas, in the central part.
little theater, a small theater that presents amateur or experimental plays.
li·tur·gi·cal (lə tèr'jə kəl), *adj.* of, about, or used in liturgies. **—li·tur'gi·cal·ly,** *adv.*
lit·ur·gy (lit'ər jē), *n.* a form of public worship. Different churches use different liturgies. ❏ *n., pl.* **lit·ur·gies.**
liv·a·ble (liv'ə bəl), *adj.* **1** fit to live in: *a livable house.* **2** worth living; endurable. **—liv'a·ble·ness,** *n.*
live[1] (liv), *v.* **1** to make one's home in; dwell: *live in the country. Who lives in this house?* **2** to have life; be alive; exist: *All creatures have an equal right to live.* **3** to remain alive: *She lived until the following year.* **4** to last; endure: *His good name will live forever.* **5** to keep up life: *Most of us live by working.* **6** to feed or subsist: *Lions live upon other animals.* **7** to pass life: *live a life of ease, live well.* **8** to carry out or show in life: *live your ideals.* **9** to have a rich and full life. ❏ *v.* **lived, liv·ing.**
live down, to live in such a way that people will overlook or forget something bad you did in the past.
live it up, to live in an exciting, pleasant, and often extravagant manner: *They are living it up, always at a dance or a show.*
live up to, to act according to; do what is expected or promised.
live with, 1 to live in the same house, apartment, etc., with; share a home with: *I live with two friends, and we share chores and expenses.* **2** to accept quietly; tolerate; put up with: *I like some of my classmates, but there are others that I just live with.*

SYNONYM STUDY **Live**[1] and **dwell** both mean to have a home somewhere. **Live** is the general word: *Who lives downstairs? Our dog lives in the garage.* **Dwell** is a formal word used about people: *The queen dwells in a palace.*

live[2] (liv), *adj.* **1** having life; alive: *a live dog.* **2** burning or glowing: *live coals.* **3** full of energy or activity: *a live person.* **4** of present interest; up-to-date: *a live question.* **5** still in use or to be used: *live stream.* **6** carrying an electric current: *a live wire.* **7** loaded: *a live cartridge.* **8** not previously recorded on tape or film; broadcast during the actual performance: *a live TV show.*

live·li·hood (līv'lē hůd), *n.* means of keeping alive; what is needed to support life; a living: *She earns her livelihood by working as an editor.*
live·long (liv'lông), *adj.* whole length of; whole; entire: *She is busy the livelong day.*
live·ly (līv'lē), **1** *adj.* full of life and spirit; active; vigorous: *A good night's sleep made us all lively again.* **2** *adj.* exciting: *We had a lively time during the blizzard.* **3** *adj.* bright; vivid: *lively colors.* **4** *adj.* cheerful: *a lively conversation.* **5** *adj.* bouncing well and quickly: *a lively tennis ball.* **6** *adv.* in a lively manner. ❏ *adj.* **live·li·er, live·li·est. —live'li·ly,** *adv.* **—live'li·ness,** *n.*

SYNONYM STUDY **Lively** and **active** both mean full of energy. **Lively** is the general word: *We had a lively chat. That's a lively tune.* **Active** means energetic in motion: *The puppy is so active that she never sits still for long.*

liv·en (lī'vən), *v.* **1** to put life into; cheer up. **2** to become more lively; brighten: *As he grew well, his spirits began to liven again.*
live oak (līv), an evergreen oak of the southeastern United States.
liv·er[1] (liv'ər), *n.* **1** the large, reddish brown organ that makes bile and helps the body absorb food. The liver frees the blood of its waste matter and changes sugar into glycogen. **2** the liver of an animal used as food.
liv·er[2] (liv'ər), *n.* person who lives in a certain way: *a carefree liver.*
liv·er·ied (liv'ər ēd), *adj.* clothed in livery.
Liv·er·pool (liv'ər pül), *n.* port in W England.
liv·er·wort (liv'ər wèrt'), *n.* **1** any of very many small plants that grow mostly on damp ground, rotten logs, and other moist places. Liverworts are something like mosses. **2** hepatica.
liv·er·wurst (liv'ər wèrst'), *n.* sausage, mostly liver.
liv·er·y (liv'ər ē), *n.* **1** business of keeping cars, boats, bicycles, etc., for hire. **2** business of keeping horses and carriages for hire. **3** business of stabling and caring for horses. **4** livery stable. **5** any uniform provided for servants, or adopted by any group: *a chauffeur in green livery.* ❏ *n., pl.* **liv·er·ies** for 4,5.
livery stable, stable where horses are taken care of for pay or where horses can be hired.
lives (līvz), *n.* plural of **life.**
live·stock (līv'stok'), *n.* farm animals. Cows, horses, sheep, and pigs are livestock.
live wire (līv), **1** INFORMAL. an energetic, wide-awake person. **2** wire in which an electric current is flowing.
liv·id (liv'id), *adj.* **1** very angry: *Their insults made me livid.* **2** having a dull bluish or grayish color, as from a bruise: *livid marks on an arm.* **3** very pale: *livid with shock.* **4** flushed; reddish: *livid with rage.* **—liv'id·ly,** *adv.*
liv·ing (liv'ing), **1** *adj.* having life; being alive: *a living plant.* **2** *n.* condition of being alive: *The young people were filled with the joy of living.* **3** *n.* means of keeping alive; livelihood: *work for a living.* **4** *n.* manner of life: *healthful living.* **5** *adj.* full of life; vigorous; strong; active: *a living faith.* **6** *adj.* in actual existence; still in use; alive: *a living language.* **7** *adj.* true to life; vivid; lifelike: *televised in living color.* **8** *adj.* of life; for living in: *the poor living conditions in the slums.* **9** *adj.* sufficient to live on: *a living wage.* **10** *adj.* of human beings: *within living memory.*
living room, room for general family use; sitting room.
living will, document in which someone lists medical procedures that may be used if that person is near death.
liz·ard (liz'ərd), *n.* any of many reptiles with long bodies and tails, movable eyelids, and usually four legs. Some lizards have no legs and look much like snakes. Iguanas, chameleons, and horned toads are lizards. **—liz'ard·like',** *adj.*
lizard-hipped (liz'ərd hipt'), *adj.* with a pelvic structure like a lizard's: *lizard-hipped dinosaurs.*
Lju·blja·na (lē ü'blē ä'nə), *n.* capital of Slovenia, in the central part.

a	hat	ė	term	ô	order	ch	child		
ā	age	i	it	oi	oil	ng	long		a in about
ä	far	ī	ice	ou	out	sh	she		e in taken
â	care	o	hot	u	cup	th	thin	ə	i in pencil
e	let	ō	open	ů	put	ŦH	then		o in lemon
ē	equal	ò	saw	ü	rule	zh	measure		u in circus

lla·ma (lä′mə), *n.* a domesticated South American mammal that chews the cud and has woolly hair. Llamas are related to camels, but do not have humps. Llamas are used as beasts of burden. ❑ *n., pl.* **lla·ma** or **lla·mas.** ▪ Another word that sounds like this is **lama.**

lla·no (lä′nō), *n.* a broad, treeless, grassy plain in Spanish America. ❑ *n., pl.* **lla·nos.**

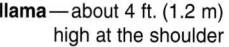
llama—about 4 ft. (1.2 m)
high at the shoulder

Lloyd Web·ber (loid′ web′ər), **Andrew,** born 1948, British composer of musicals. His musicals include *Cats, Evita,* and *Phantom of the Opera.*

lo (lō), *interj.* look! see! behold! ▪ Another word that sounds like this is **low.**

load (lōd), **1** *n.* what you are carrying; burden: *The cart has a load of hay. That's a load off my mind.* **2** *n.* amount that usually is carried: *Send us four loads of sand.* **3** *v.* to place on or in something so that it can be carried somewhere; heap up: *load grain into a ship.* **4** *v.* to put something in or onto a vehicle or support: *load a ship with grain.* **5** *v.* to take on what will be carried: *The ship loaded in five days.* **6** *v.* to burden; oppress: *load the mind with worries.* **7** *v.* to give in large amounts or in excess: *They loaded the singer with compliments.* **8** *n.pl.* **loads,** INFORMAL. a great quantity or number. **9** *v.* to put film into a camera. **10** *v.* **a** to move data or a program from a disk, tape, etc., into a computer's main memory: *As soon as the graphics software is loaded, we can start.* **b** to put a floppy disk or a tape into a computer drive: *I just finished creating my document, and now I'm loading a backup disk.* **11** *n.* the weight supported by a structure or part. **12** *n.* the total amount of power supplied by a dynamo, generator, or other source of electricity in a certain time. **13** *v.* (in baseball) to put runners on first, second, and third bases: *That walk has loaded the bases.* **14** *n.* one charge of ammunition for a gun. **15** *v.* to put a charge in a gun: *The frontiersman loaded his musket with powder and shot.* ▪ Another word that sounds like this is **lode.** —**load′er,** *n.*

get a load of, SLANG. to have a look at; notice; observe: *Get a load of the paint job on that truck!*

load·ed (lō′did), *adj.* **1** full of meaning and implications: *a loaded question.* **2** INFORMAL. having plenty of money; rich.

loaf[1] (lōf), *n.* **1** bread baked as one piece. **2** anything like a loaf. Meat loaf is meat chopped and mixed with other things and then baked. ❑ *n., pl.* **loaves.**

loaf[2] (lōf), *v.* to spend time idly; do nothing: *I can loaf all day Saturday.* —**loaf′er,** *n.*

Loaf·er (lō′fər), *n.* trademark for a shoe resembling a moccasin, but with sole and heel stitched to the upper.

loam (lōm), *n.* rich, fertile earth in which decaying leaves and other plant matter are mixed with clay and sand.

loam·y (lō′mē), *adj.* of or like loam.

loan (lōn), **1** *n.* act of lending: *She asked for the loan of his pen.* **2** *n.* anything that is lent, especially money: *He asked his brother for a small loan.* **3** *v.* to make a loan; lend: *Her friend loaned her the money.* ▪ Another word that sounds like this is **lone.**

on loan, borrowed for temporary use: *books on loan from the library.*

loan·er (lō′nər), *n.* car, TV, watch, etc., lent by the repairer while your own is being repaired. ▪ Another word that sounds like this is **loner.**

loath (lōth *or* lōᴛʜ), *adj.* unwilling or reluctant: *They were loath to admit that they were wrong.*

loathe (lōᴛʜ), *v.* to feel strong dislike and disgust for; abhor; hate: *We loathe rotten food.* ❑ *v.* **loathed, loath·ing.** ▪ See Usage Note at **loath.**

loath·ing (lō′ᴛʜing), *n.* strong dislike and disgust.

loath·some (lōᴛʜ′səm), *adj.* making you feel sick; disgusting: *Rotten lettuce has a loathsome odor.* —**loath′some·ly,** *adv.* —**loath′some·ness,** *n.*

loaves (lōvz), *n.* plural of **loaf**[1].

lob (lob), **1** *n.* a ball hit or thrown in a high arc. **2** *v.* to hit or throw a ball in a high arc. ❑ *v.* **lobbed, lob·bing.**

lob·by (lob′ē), **1** *n.* entrance hall; passageway: *A hotel lobby usually has chairs and couches to sit on.* **2** *n.* person or persons that try to influence members of a lawmaking group. **3** *v.* to try to influence the members of a lawmaking group: *The conservation group lobbied to outlaw the use of certain traps by hunters.* ❑ *n., pl.* **lob·bies;** *v.* **lob·bied, lob·by·ing.** —**lob′by·er,** *n.*

lob·by·ist (lob′ē ist), *n.* person who tries to influence members of a lawmaking group.

lobe (lōb), *n.* a rounded part that sticks out or down. The lobe of the ear is the lower rounded end.

lobed (lōbd), *adj.* having a lobe or lobes.

lo·bel·ia (lō bē′lyə), *n.* any of numerous plants with tube-shaped blue, red, yellow, purple, or white flowers. ❑ *n., pl.* **lo·bel·ias.**

lob·lol·ly pine (lob′lol′ē), **1** a pine tree of the southeastern United States that has thick bark, long needles, and cones with spiny tips. **2** its coarse wood, used for lumber.

lob·ster (lob′stər), *n.* **1** any of several large shellfish having five pairs of legs, with large claws on the front pair. Their shells turn a bright red when boiled. **2** flesh of a lobster, used as food.

lobster (def. 1)—up to 2 ft.
(61 cm) long with claws

lobster pot, trap used to catch lobsters.

lo·cal (lō′kəl), **1** *adj.* of or for a certain place or places: *local news.* **2** *adj.* of or referring to just one part of the body: *a local anesthetic.* **3** *adj.* making all, or almost all, stops: *a local commuter train.* **4** *n.* train, bus, subway, etc., that stops at all, or almost all, of the stations on its route. **5** *n.* branch or chapter of a labor union, fraternity, etc.

lo·cale (lō kal′), *n.* a place, especially with reference to events or circumstances connected with it: *The locale of the movie is California in 1849.*

lo·cal·ism (lō′kə liz′əm), *n.* a local expression, custom, etc.

lo·cal·i·ty (lō kal′ə tē), *n.* local region, district, or neighborhood: *I know few people in the locality of Boston.* ❑ *n., pl.* **lo·cal·i·ties.**

lo·cal·ize (lō′kə līz), *v.* to limit or be limited to a particular place or locality: *The infection seemed to be localized in the foot.* ❑ *v.* **lo·cal·ized, lo·cal·iz·ing.** —**lo′cal·i·za′tion,** *n.*

lo·cal·ly (lō′kə lē), *adv.* in a local manner; with regard to place; in one place; in a number of places, but not widely: *Outbreaks of the disease occurred locally.*

lo·cate (lō′kāt), *v.* **1** to find out the exact position of: *We followed the stream until we located its source.* **2** to set up or build something in a place: *They located their new store on Elm Street.* **3** to settle: *Pioneers located where there was water.* **4** to state or show the position of: *Can you locate Africa on the globe?* ❑ *v.* **lo·cat·ed, lo·cat·ing.** —**lo′cat·a·ble,** *adj.* —**lo′ca·ter** or **lo′ca·tor,** *n.*

be located, be situated; lie: *Buffalo is located on Lake Erie.*

lo·ca·tion (lō kā′shən), *n.* **1** position or place: *The camp was in a bad location as there was no water near it.* **2** act or process of locating: *The scouts argued about the location of the camp.*

on location, away from a movie studio: *Several of the movie scenes were shot on location in the desert.*

loch (lok), *n.* SCOTTISH. **1** lake: *Loch Ness.* **2** arm of the sea partly shut in by land. ❑ *n., pl.* **lochs.** ▪ Another word that sounds like this is **lock.**

Loch Ness (lok′ nes′), a long, narrow and very deep lake in N Scotland. The **Loch Ness Monster,** a large sea animal, is believed by some people to live in the lake.

lo·ci (lō′sī), *n.* plural of **locus.**

lock[1] (lok), **1** *n.* device for fastening doors, boxes, etc., with a bolt, usually needing a key to open it: *The front door of most houses has a lock.* **2** *n.* a similar device, often with a numbered dial to open it, for a locker, briefcase, etc. **3** *v.* to fasten with such a device: *Lock the door.* **4** *v.* to shut something in or out or up: *We lock up jewels in a safe.* **5** *v.* to hold fast: *The ship was locked in ice.* **6** *n.* an enclosed section of a canal or dock in which the level of the water can be changed by letting water in or out, to raise or lower ships. **7** *n.* (long ago) a part of a gun for exploding the charge. **8** *v.* to join, fit, jam, or link together: *The girls locked arms and walked away together.* **9** *n.* a kind of hold in wrestling. ■ Another word that sounds like this is **loch. –lock′a·ble,** *adj.*
lock out, to refuse to let employees work until they accept the employer's terms.

SYNONYM STUDY **Lock**[1] and **latch** both mean to fasten something shut. **Lock** means to use a device that can be opened only by a key or a set of numbers: *She locked her bike to the rack.* **Latch** means to use a catch that holds something shut but not locked: *We latch the backyard gate to keep our dog from getting out.*

lock[2] (lok), *n.* **1** curl of hair. **2** portion of hair, wool, flax, etc. **3 locks,** *pl.* the hair of the head: *The child has curly locks.* ■ Another word that sounds like this is **loch.**
lock·er (lok′ər), *n.* **1** a chest, small closet, cupboard, or other compartment that can be locked. **2** a refrigerated compartment for storing frozen foods.
locker room, room for changing clothes, with lockers for storing clothes and sports equipment. There are usually locker rooms in or near gymnasiums, swimming pools, health clubs, etc.
lock·et (lok′it), *n.* a small, ornamental case for holding a picture of someone or a lock of hair. A locket is usually worn around the neck on a chain.
lock·jaw (lok′jò′), *n.* a form of tetanus in which the jaws become firmly closed.
lock·out (lok′out′), *n.* the refusal of an employer to let employees work, used as a means of making them accept the employer's terms.
lock·smith (lok′smith′), *n.* person who makes or repairs locks.
lock·up (lok′up′), *n.* jail.
Lock·wood (lok′wŭd), *n.* **Bel·va Ann Ben·nett** (bel′və an ben′ət), 1830-1917, American political reformer and suffragist. ■ Belva Ann Lockwood was the first woman lawyer to argue before the Supreme Court. She was nominated for President in 1884 and 1888.
lo·co (lō′kō), **1** *adj.* SLANG. unreasonable; silly; foolish; very strange: *Exam week always makes my big sister loco.* **2** *n.* locoweed. **3** *n.* harmful effects caused by eating locoweed.
lo·co·mo·tion (lō′kə mō′shən), *n.* act or power of moving from place to place. Walking, swimming, and flying are common forms of locomotion.
lo·co·mo·tive (lō′kə mō′tiv), **1** *n.* engine that moves from place to place under its own power, used to pull railroad trains. **2** *adj.* moving from place to place: *locomotive bacteria.* **3** *adj.* of or referring to the power to move from place to place.
lo·co·weed (lō′kō wēd′), *n.* any of numerous plants found in western North America. If eaten by livestock, locoweed can poison the animals' brains.
lo·cus (lō′kəs), *n.* **1** place or locality. **2** (in mathematics) the set of all the points, and only those points, that satisfy a given condition. The locus of all the points which are equidistant from a given point is the surface of a sphere. ❑ *n., pl.* **lo·ci.**
lo·cust (lō′kəst), *n.* **1** any of various kinds of grasshoppers that migrate in great swarms, often destroying crops along the way. **2** cicada. **3** any of several North American trees and bushes, especially one shade and lumber tree with small rounded leaflets and clusters of sweet-smelling white or pink flowers. Its waxy seeds grow in long, shiny pods.
lo·cu·tion (lō kyü′shən), *n.* **1** style of speech. **2** form of expression.
lode (lōd), *n.* a vein of metal ore: *The miners struck a rich lode of copper.* ■ Another word that sounds like this is **load.**
lode·star (lōd′stär′), *n.* **1** star that shows the way. **2** the North Star. **3** a guide.

lode·stone (lōd′stōn′), *n.* **1** piece of iron ore that attracts iron and steel. It is a natural magnet. **2** something that attracts: *Gold was the lodestone that drew people to Alaska.*
lodge (loj), **1** *v.* to live in a place for a time: *We lodged in motels on our trip.* **2** *v.* to supply with a place to live in or sleep in for a time: *Can you lodge us for the weekend?* **3** *n.* a place to live in; a house, especially a small or temporary house: *My aunt rents a lodge in the mountains for the summer.* **4** *n.* inn or resort hotel: *Our cousins went skiing for a week and stayed at a lodge near the slopes.* **5** *v.* to live in a rented room in another's house: *We are merely lodging at present.* **6** *v.* to get caught or stuck somewhere: *My kite lodged in the branches of a big tree.* **7** *v.* to put or send into a particular place: *The archer lodged an arrow in the trunk of the tree.* **8** *v.* to put before some authority: *We lodged a complaint with the police.* **9** *n.* branch of a secret society. **10** *n.* the place where a secret society meets. **11** *n.* the den of an animal, such as a beaver or an otter. ❑ *v.* **lodged, lodg·ing.**
lodge·pole pine (loj′pōl′), either of two related pine trees of western North America. One is short and grows in coastal regions; the other is tall, grows inland, and is a source of timber.
lodg·er (loj′ər), *n.* someone who lives in a rented room in someone else's house.
lodg·ing (loj′ing), *n.* **1** place where you are living only for a time: *a lodging for the night.* **2 lodgings,** *pl.* a rented room or rooms in a house, not in a hotel.
lodg·ment (loj′mənt), *n.* **1** act of lodging. **2** condition of being lodged: *the lodgment of a claim against a company.*
lo·ess (lō′is *or* les), *n.* yellowish brown fertile soil, usually deposited by the wind, often quite thick. ■ Another word that can sound like this is **less.**
loft (lòft), **1** *n.* space just below the roof in a cabin; attic. **2** *n.* room under the roof of a barn: *This loft is full of hay.* **3** *n.* gallery in a church or hall: *a choir loft.* **4** *n.* an upper floor of a business building or warehouse. **5** *v.* to hit or throw a ball high in the air.
loft·y (lòf′tē), *adj.* **1** very high: *lofty mountains.* ■ See Synonym Study at **high. 2** exalted; dignified; grand: *lofty aims.* **3** proud; haughty: *a lofty contempt for others.* ❑ *adj.* **loft·i·er, loft·i·est. –loft′i·ly,** *adv.* **–loft′i·ness,** *n.*
log (lòg), **1** *n.* a length of wood just as it comes from the tree. **2** *adj.* made of logs: *a log house.* **3** *v.* to cut down trees, cut them into logs, and get them out of the forest. **4** *v.* to cut trees into logs. **5** *n.* the daily record of a ship's voyage. **6** *v.* to enter in a ship's log. **7** *v.* to travel a distance, especially as written down: *They logged six miles a day on their hiking trip.* **8** *n.* record of an airplane trip, performance of an engine, etc. **9** *n.* a float for measuring the speed of a ship. ❑ *v.* **logged, log·ging.**
log in or **log on,** to begin use of a computer or communication with a computer network: *She logs on to check her e-mail.*
log off or **log out,** to finish use of a computer or communication with a computer network: *He didn't log off until eleven o'clock.*
lo·gan·ber·ry (lō′gən ber′ē), *n.* a large, purplish red fruit of a plant which is a cross between a dewberry and a red raspberry. ❑ *n., pl.* **lo·gan·ber·ries.**
lo·ga·rithm (lò′gə riŦH′əm), *n.* the power to which a fixed number or base (usually 10) must be raised in order to produce a given number. If the fixed number or base is 10, the logarithm of 1000 is 3; the logarithm of 10,000 is 4; the logarithm of 100,000 is 5.
log·book (lòg′bŭk′), *n.* **1** book in which a daily record of a ship's voyage is kept. **2** a book for records of an airplane's trip. **3** journal of travel.

WORD STORY **Logbook** comes from an old way of telling how far a ship had gone in a certain time. Sailors threw a log of wood in the water behind them, tied to a long rope. After sailing a while, they hauled in the rope and knew by its length the distance traveled. A book recording the daily total was the logbook.

a	hat	ė	term	ô	order	ch	child		
ā	age	i	it	oi	oil	ng	long	ə	a in about
ä	far	ī	ice	ou	out	sh	she		e in taken
â	care	o	hot	u	cup	th	thin		i in pencil
e	let	ō	open	ů	put	ŦH	then		o in lemon
ē	equal	ò	saw	ü	rule	zh	measure		u in circus

loge (lōzh), *n.* **1** box in a theater or opera house. **2** seating area in a theater, made up of the first few rows on the ground floor or in the lowest balcony.

loge (def. 2)—shown in a painting

log·ger (lȯ′gər), *n.* **1** person whose work is logging. **2** machine for loading or hauling logs.

log·ger·head (lȯ′gər hed′), *n.* a large sea turtle of the western Atlantic.

log·ger·heads (lȯ′gər hedz′), *n.pl.* **at loggerheads,** in strong or total disagreement: *Committee members were at loggerheads over the budget.*

log·gia (loj′ə), *n.* gallery or arcade open to the air on at least one side. □ *n., pl.* **log·gias.**

log·ging (lȯ′ging), *n.* work of cutting down trees, sawing them into logs, and moving the logs out of the forest.

log·ic (loj′ik), *n.* **1** science of proof of and of reasoning. **2** use of argument; reasoning. **3** sound sense; reason: *There is much logic in what you say.* **4** the basic data processing operations performed by a computer, in which it compares and changes data according to set rules; computer logic. **5** electronic circuits, or arrangement of circuits, used by a computer for such basic data processing.

WORD FAMILY   **Logic** and the words below are related. They all come from old Greek words meaning "word, speech, or reason" or "to pick, gather, or speak."

analogous	dialect	ideology	prologue
analogy	dialogue	lexicographer	psychology
anthropology	doxology	lexicon	sociology
apologist	dyslexia	logarithm	syllogism
apology	ecology	logistic	tautology
archaeology	entomology	monologue	technology
astrology	epilogue	mythology	terminology
biology	etymology	ornithology	theology
catalog	eulogy	pathology	travelogue
chronological	genealogy	philology	trilogy
Decalogue	geology	phrenology	zoology

log·i·cal (loj′ə kəl), *adj.* **1** according to the principles of logic: *logical reasoning.* **2** reasonable; reasonably expected: *An upset stomach is a logical result of overeating.* **3** reasoning correctly: *a logical person.* **—log′i·cal·ly,** *adv.* **—log′i·cal·ness,** *n.*

lo·gi·cian (lō jish′ən), *n.* an expert in logic.

lo·gis·tic (lō jis′tik), *adj.* of or about logistics.

lo·gis·tics (lō jis′tiks), *n.* the planning and carrying out of any complex or large-scale operation, especially one of military movement, evacuation, and supply.

log·jam (lȯg′jam′), *n.* **1** point at which no further progress can be made; deadlock; standstill: *The negotiators tried to break the logjam by a lengthy meeting.* **2** act of blocking the movement of logs downstream so that they become jumbled together in the river.

lo·go (lō′gō *or* log′ō), *n.* symbol or trademark of a company, magazine, etc., that has been designed especially for advertising. □ *n., pl.* **lo·gos.**

LOGO (lō′gō), *n.* computer programming language designed to be usable by children.

log·roll·ing (lȯg′rō′ling), *n.* **1** act of giving political aid in return for a like favor. **2** act of rolling logs, especially by treading on them.

lo·gy (lō′gē), *adj.* heavy, sluggish, or dull. □ *adj.* **lo·gi·er, lo·gi·est.**

-logy, *suffix.* science or study of: *biology = the science of life.*

loin (loin), *n.* **1** Usually, **loins,** *pl.* the part of the body of an animal or human being between the ribs and the hipbones. The loins are on both sides of the backbone and nearer to it than the flanks are. **2** a piece of meat from this part of an animal: *a loin of pork.*

loin·cloth (loin′klȯth′), *n.* piece of cloth worn around the hips and between the thighs. □ *n., pl.* **loin·cloths** (loin′klȯᴛʜz′ *or* loin′klȯths′).

Loire (lwär), *n.* river flowing from S France into the Bay of Biscay.

loi·ter (loi′tər), *v.* **1** to linger idly; stop and play along the way: *She loitered along the street, looking into all the store windows.* **2** to spend time idly: *loiter the hours away.* **—loi′ter·er,** *n.*

WORD STORY   **Loiter** comes from a Dutch word meaning "to be loose," used about teeth or anything else that isn't firmly attached. Someone who loiters is not really staying or going, just sort of wobbling around.

Lo·ki (lō′kē), *n.* the Scandinavian god of destruction.

loll (lol), *v.* **1** to recline or lean in a lazy manner: *loll on a sofa.* **2** to hang loosely or droop: *A dog's tongue lolls out in hot weather.* **3** to allow to hang or droop: *The dog lolled out its tongue.* **—loll′er,** *n.*

lol·li·pop or **lol·ly·pop** (lol′ē pop), *n.* piece of hard candy, usually on the end of a small stick.

Lom·bar·di (lom bär′dē), *n.* **Vince** (vins), 1913-1970, American football coach. ■ **Vince Lombardi** was one of the most successful coaches in professional football history. He is remembered for the saying, "Winning isn't everything: it's the only thing."

Lom·bard·y (lom′bər dē), *n.* region in N Italy.

Lo·mé (lō mā′), *n.* port and capital of Togo, on the Atlantic.

Lo·mond (lō′mənd), *n.* **Loch,** lake in SW central Scotland.

Lon·don (lun′dən), *n.* **1** capital of the United Kingdom of Great Britain and Northern Ireland, in SE England, on the Thames. London is one of the largest cities in the world. **2** **Jack** (jak), 1876-1916, American writer. He wrote stories of the Alaskan frontier and of the sea.

lone (lōn), *adj.* **1** without others; alone; solitary; single: *The lone traveler was glad to reach home.* **2** standing apart; isolated: *a lone house.* ■ Another word that sounds like this is **loan.**

lone·ly (lōn′lē), *adj.* **1** feeling yourself alone and longing for company or friends: *He was lonely while his brother was away.* **2** without many people: *a lonely road.* **3** alone; isolated: *a lonely tree.* □ *adj.* **lone·li·er, lone·li·est. —lone′li·ly,** *adv.* **—lone′li·ness,** *n.*

lon·er (lō′nər), *n.* person who lives or works alone, especially by choice. ■ Another word that sounds like this is **loaner.**

lone·some (lōn′səm), *adj.* **1** feeling lonely: *I was lonesome while you were away.* **2** making you feel lonely: *a lonesome journey.* **3** unfrequented; desolate: *a lonesome road.* **4** solitary: *One lonesome pine stood in the yard.* □ *adj.* **lone·som·er, lone·som·est. —lone′some·ly,** *adv.* **—lone′some·ness,** *n.*

lone wolf, person who likes to be alone or work alone; loner.

long¹ (lȯng), **1** *adj.* measuring a great distance from end to end: *A year is a long time. I read a long story.* **2** *adj.* in length: *My table is three feet long.* **3** *adj.* having a long narrow shape: *a long board.* **4** *n.* a long time: *It won't be long until summer comes.* **5** *adv.* for a long time: *I can't stay long.* **6** *adv.* for its whole length: *all day long.* **7** *adv.* at a point of time far distant from the time indicated: *long before.* **8** *adj.* A vowel like *a* in *late, e* in *be, i* in *fine, o* in *note,* or *u* as in *rule* is a **long vowel.** □ *adj.* **long·er** (lȯng′gər), **long·est** (lȯng′gist). **—long′ly,** *adv.*

as long as or **so long as,** provided that.

before long, in a short time; soon: *Before long it will be summer and we'll be swimming outside.*

long² (lông), *v.* to wish very much; desire greatly: *long to see a good friend.*

Long (lông), *n.* **Hu·ey** (hyü′ē), 1893-1935, American political leader. He was the governor of Louisiana from 1928 until 1932, and a U.S. senator from 1930 to 1935, when he was assassinated.

long., longitude.

long·boat (lông′bōt′), *n.* the largest boat carried by a sailing ship.

long·bow (lông′bō′), *n.* a large bow for shooting a long, feathered arrow.

long distance, operator or exchange that takes care of long-distance calls.

long-dis·tance (lông′dis′təns), *adj.* **1** of telephone service between distant places. **2** from or covering a great distance: *long-distance trucking, a long-distance race.*

long division, method of division in which each step is written out. Long division is used to divide large numbers.

lon·gev·i·ty (lon jev′ə tē), *n.* long life: *A good diet promotes longevity.*

Long·fel·low (lông′fel′ō), *n.* **Henry Wads·worth** (wädz′wèrth), 1807-1882, American poet. His poems include *The Song of Hiawatha* and "Paul Revere's Ride."

long·hand (lông′hand′), *n.* ordinary writing, not shorthand or typewriting.

long·horn (lông′hôrn′), *n.* one of a breed of cattle with very long horns, formerly common in the southwestern United States.

long·house (lông′hous′), *n.* a large, rectangular dwelling of certain North American Indians, especially the Iroquois. Many families lived together in one longhouse. ❑ *n., pl.* **long·hous·es** (lông′houz′iz).

long·ing (lông′ing), **1** *n.* earnest desire: *a longing for home.* **2** *adj.* having or showing earnest desire: *a child's longing look at a window full of toys.* —**long′ing·ly,** *adv.*

long·ish (lông′ish), *adj.* somewhat long.

Long Island, large island south of Connecticut. It is part of New York State.

Long Island Sound, long, narrow strip of water between Connecticut and Long Island. It is an inlet of the Atlantic.

lon·gi·tude (lon′jə tüd), *n.* distance east or west on the earth's surface, measured in degrees from a certain meridian, usually the one through Greenwich, England. A degree of longitude is about 69 miles (111 kilometers) at the equator.

lon·gi·tu·di·nal (lon′jə tüd′n-əl), *adj.* **1** of or in length: *longitudinal measurements.* **2** running lengthwise: *The flag of the United States has longitudinal stripes.* **3** of or in longitude: *The longitudinal difference between New York and Seattle is about 50 degrees.* —**lon′gi·tu′di·nal·ly,** *adv.*

long johns (jonz), INFORMAL. long, warm underwear.

long jump, an athletic contest in which each contestant takes a running start and then jumps to cover as much ground as possible; broad jump.

long-last·ing (lông′las′ting), *adj.* **1** lasting a long time: *a long-lasting relationship.* **2** good or effective for a period of time: *long-lasting pain relief.*

long-lived (lông′līvd′ *or* lông′livd′), *adj.* living or lasting a long time. —**long′-lived′ness,** *n.*

long-range (lông′rānj′), *adj.* **1** looking ahead; future: *long-range plans.* **2** able to go a great distance: *a long-range ballistic missile.*

long·shore·man (lông′shôr′mən), *n.* someone whose work is loading and unloading ships. ❑ *n., pl.* **long·shore·men.**

long shot, 1 effort that has little chance of success: *Writing to the President for help is a long shot, but we'll try it.* **2** an attempt at something difficult. **3** in a horse race or similar contest, an entry that has little chance of winning.

not by a long shot, not at all.

long·stand·ing (lông′stan′ding), *adj.* having lasted for a long time: *a longstanding feud.*

long-suf·fer·ing (lông′suf′ər ing), *adj.* enduring trouble, pain, or injury long and patiently. —**long′suf′fer·ing·ly,** *adv.*

long-term (lông′tèrm′), *adj.* of or for a long period of time: *It's time to start thinking about long-term goals like college.*

long·time or **long-time** (lông′tīm′), *adj.* **1** of or for a long period of time: *a longtime friend.* **2** lasting or having lasted for a long time: *their longtime association. Thanks for your longtime support.*

long-wind·ed (lông′win′did), *adj.* talking or writing at great length; tiresome: *a long-winded speaker, a long-winded magazine article.* —**long′-wind′ed·ly,** *adv.* —**long′-wind′ed·ness,** *n.*

look (lùk), **1** *v.* to direct your eyes toward; see; try to see: *Look at the pictures.* **2** *v.* to gaze or stare in a certain way; look hard: *look questioningly at someone.* **3** *v.* to search: *I looked through the drawer to see if I could find my keys.* **4** *n.* a glance; seeing: *He took a quick look at the magazine.* **5** *v.* to have a view; face: *Our house looks out on the garden.* **6** *v.* to seem; appear: *She looks pale.* **7** *n.* appearance; aspect: *A deserted house has a desolate look.* **8** *v.* to show how you feel by your appearance: *He said nothing but looked his disappointment.* **9** *n.pl.* **looks,** personal appearance: *He has his mother's good looks.*

look after, to attend to; take care of: *He looked after the younger children.*

look alive, hurry up! be quick!

look at, to examine; pay attention to: *You must look at all the facts.*

look back, to think about the past; recollect.

look down on, to despise; scorn.

look for, to expect: *We'll look for you tonight.*

look forward to, to expect with pleasure; be eager for.

look in, to make a short visit.

look into, to examine; inspect.

look on, 1 to watch without taking part: *The teacher conducted the experiment while we looked on.* **2** to regard; consider: *I look on her as a very able person.*

look out, be careful; watch out: *Look out for cars as you cross the street.*

look over, to examine; inspect: *I looked over my report for spelling errors.*

look to, 1 to attend to; take care of. **2** to turn to for help. **3** to look forward to; expect.

look up, 1 to refer to; find: *She looked up the unfamiliar word in a dictionary.* **2** to call on; visit: *Look me up when you come to town.* **3** to get better; improve: *Things are looking up for me since I got the new job.*

look upon, to regard; consider.

look up to, to respect; admire.

look yourself, to seem like yourself; seem well.

look-a·like (lùk′ə līk′), **1** *n.* person or thing that looks very similar to another; double: *They couldn't get the actor they wanted for the part, so they found a look-alike.* **2** *adj.* looking just alike; very similar: *look-alike blouses.*

looking glass, mirror.

look·out (lùk′out′), *n.* **1** a sharp watch for someone to come or for something to happen: *Keep a lookout for Mother.* **2** place from which to watch. A crow's-nest is a lookout. **3** the person who has the duty of watching: *The lookout cried, "Land ho!"* **4** INFORMAL. something unpleasant or unfortunate that you have to look after or worry about yourself: *If you lost your keys, that's your lookout.*

loom¹ (lüm), *n.* frame or machine for weaving cloth.

loom² (lüm), *v.* **1** to appear dimly or vaguely as a large, threatening shape: *A large iceberg loomed through the thick fog.* **2** to appear likely to happen, especially in a threatening way: *Problems loomed ahead for the candidate.*

a	hat	ė	term	ô	order	ch	child		
ā	age	i	it	oi	oil	ng	long		a in about
ä	far	ī	ice	ou	out	sh	she	ə	e in taken
â	care	o	hot	u	cup	th	thin	{	i in pencil
e	let	ō	open	ù	put	ŦH	then		o in lemon
ē	equal	ȯ	saw	ü	rule	zh	measure		u in circus

loon¹ (lün), *n.* any of four large, web-footed diving birds of the Northern Hemisphere. Loons eat fish and have loud, wild cries.

loon¹—about 30 in. (76 cm) long

loon² (lün), *n.* INFORMAL. an unreasonable, foolish, or very strange person.

loon·y (lü′nē), *adj.* INFORMAL. foolish or silly. ❑ *adj.* **loon·i·er, loon·i·est. —loon′i·ness,** *n.*

loop (lüp), **1** *n.* the part of a curved string, ribbon, bent wire, etc., that crosses itself. **2** *n.* thing, bend, course, or motion shaped like this: *The road makes a wide loop around the lake.* **3** *n.* a fastening formed of cord or rope bent and crossed. **4** *v.* to make a loop of. **5** *v.* to make loops in. **6** *v.* to fasten with a loop: *She looped the gate shut with a rope.* **7** *v.* to encircle with a loop. **8** *v.* to form a loop or loops. **9** *v.* to cause an airplane to fly in a loop. **10** *n.* a loop-shaped turn, especially one made by an airplane. **11** *n.* a closed electric circuit. **12** *n.* a set of instructions that a computer carries out repeatedly.

loop·hole (lüp′hōl′), *n.* **1** a means of escape: *The clever lawyer found a loophole in the law to save his client.* **2** a small opening in a wall for looking through, for letting in air, or for firing through at an enemy outside.

loose (lüs), **1** *adj.* not fastened: *a loose thread.* **2** *adj.* not tight: *loose clothing.* **3** *adj.* not firmly set or fastened in: *a loose tooth.* **4** *adj.* not bound together: *loose papers.* **5** *adj.* not put up in a box, can, etc.: *loose coffee.* **6** *adj.* not shut in or up; free: *The dog has been loose all night.* **7** *adj.* not pressed close together: *loose earth, cloth with a loose weave.* **8** *adj.* not strict, close, or exact: *a loose account of the accident.* **9** *adj.* OLD USE. careless about morals or conduct: *a loose character.* **10** *v.* to set free; let go: *With an effort I loosed my arm from her grip.* **11** *v.* to loosen. **12** *v.* to shoot an arrow, bullet, etc. **13** *v.* to make loose; untie; unfasten: *loose a knot.* **14** *adv.* in a loose manner. ❑ *adj.* **loos·er, loos·est;** *v.* **loosed, loos·ing. —loose′ly,** *adv.* **—loose′ness,** *n.*

break loose, to run away; free yourself.

let loose, set loose, or **turn loose,** to set free; let go; release.

loose-joint·ed (lüs′join′tid), *adj.* able to move very freely; limber. **—loose′-joint′ed·ness,** *n.*

loose-leaf (lüs′lēf′), *adj.* having pages or sheets that can be taken out and replaced: *a loose-leaf notebook.*

loos·en (lü′sn), *v.* **1** to make loose or looser; untie; unfasten: *After our picnic we had to loosen our belts.* **2** to become loose or looser: *My clothes loosened as I lost weight.*

loot (lüt), **1** *v.* to steal things by force, especially during war, riot, or natural disaster: *Rioters looted supermarkets and liquor stores.* **2** *n.* things or money stolen; plunder; booty: *loot taken by soldiers from a captured town, burglar's loot.* **3** *n.* INFORMAL. expensive items, especially gifts. ■ Another word that sounds like this is **lute. —loot′er,** *n.*

lop¹ (lop), *v.* **1** to cut; cut off. **2** to cut branches or twigs from. ❑ *v.* **lopped, lop·ping. —lop′per,** *n.*

lop² (lop), **1** *v.* to hang loosely; droop. **2** *v.* to flop. **3** *adj.* hanging loosely; drooping: *lop ears.* ❑ *v.* **lopped, lop·ping.**

lope (lōp), **1** *v.* to run with a long, easy stride: *The horse loped along the trail.* **2** *n.* a long, easy stride. ❑ *v.* **loped, lop·ing. —lop′er,** *n.*

lop-eared (lop′ird′), *adj.* having ears that hang loosely or droop: *a lop-eared dog.*

lop·sid·ed (lop′sī′did), *adj.* larger or heavier on one side than the other; leaning to one side. **—lop′sid′ed·ly,** *adv.* **—lop′sid′ed·ness,** *n.*

lo·qua·cious (lō kwā′shəs), *adj.* talking much; fond of talking. **—lo·qua′cious·ly,** *adv.* **—lo·qua′cious·ness,** *n.*

lo·quac·i·ty (lō kwas′ə tē), *n.* inclination to talk a great deal; talkativeness.

lo·ran or **Lo·ran** (lôr′an), *n.* system of navigation in which an aircraft or ship can learn its position by measuring two or more radio signals from radio beacons at known locations.

lord (lôrd), **1** *n.* ruler, master, or chief; person who has power. **2** *v.* to rule proudly or absolutely. **3** *n.* a feudal superior. **4** *n.* **Lord, a** God. **b** Jesus: *the year of our Lord.* **5** *n.* **Lord, a** title used in writing or speaking about noblemen of certain high ranks in Great Britain: *Lord Tennyson.* **b** title given by courtesy to men of certain ranks in Great Britain: *the Lord Chief Justice, the Lord Mayor of London.* **6** *n.pl.* **the Lords, a** House of Lords. **b** members of the House of Lords.

lord it over, to domineer over: *The star lorded it over the extras.*

lord·ly (lôrd′lē), *adj.* **1** like a lord; suitable for a lord; grand; magnificent. **2** haughty; insolent; scornful.

lord·ship (lôrd′ship), *n.* **1** rank or position of a lord. **2 Lordship,** title used in speaking to or of a man having the rank of Lord: *your Lordship, his Lordship.*

Lord's Prayer, the prayer given by Jesus to his disciples, which begins with the words "Our Father who art in Heaven."

Lord's Supper, 1 Last Supper. **2** Holy Communion.

lore (lôr), *n.* **1** facts and stories about a certain subject: *fairy lore, bird lore, Irish lore.* **2** learning; knowledge.

lor·gnette (lôr nyet′), *n.* eyeglasses or opera glasses mounted on a handle.

Lor·raine (lə rān′), *n.* region in NE France, formerly part of Alsace-Lorraine.

lor·ry (lôr′ē), *n.* BRITISH. truck. ❑ *n., pl.* **lor·ries.**

Los Al·a·mos (lôs al′ə mōs), town in N New Mexico. It was a center of research leading to the creation of the atomic bomb.

Los An·ge·les (lòs an′jə ləs *or* lòs an′jə lēz′), port in S California. It is the second largest city in the United States.

lose (lüz), *v.* **1** to be defeated: *Our team lost.* **2** to be unable to find: *lose a book.* **3** to not have any longer; have taken away from you by accident, carelessness, parting, death, etc.: *lose a finger, lose a friend, lose your life.* **4** to fail to keep, preserve, or maintain; cease to have: *lose patience, lose your temper.* **5** to fail to follow with eye, hearing, mind, etc.: *lose a few words of what was said.* **6** to fail to have, get, catch, etc.: *lose a sale.* **7** to fail to win: *lose the prize.* **8** to bring to destruction; ruin: *The ship and its crew were lost.* **9** to spend or let go by without any result; waste: *lose an opportunity, lose time waiting.* **10** to be or become worse off in money, in numbers, etc.: *lose at poker, lose heavily in a battle.* **11** to cause the loss of: *Delay lost the battle.* **12** to cause to lose: *That one act of misconduct lost me my job.* ❑ *v.* **lost, los·ing.**

lose it, to fail to keep your emotions under control.

lose out, be unsuccessful; fail, especially in competition or a choice: *I applied for the job, but I lost out.*

lose yourself, 1 to become absorbed. **2** to let yourself go astray; become bewildered.

los·er (lü′zər), *n.* **1** someone or something that loses or suffers loss: *Our team was the loser.* **2** someone or something that loses consistently, or fails; failure: *a born loser.*

los·ing (lü′zing), **1** *adj.* not able to win or be won: *You are playing a losing game if you cheat on exams.* **2** *n.pl.* **losings,** losses.

loss (lòs), *n.* **1** fact of losing or having lost something: *Loss of your health is serious but the loss of a pencil is not.* **2** someone or something lost: *Her house was a complete loss to the fire.* **3** harm or disadvantage caused by losing something; value of the thing lost: *The loss from the fire was $10,000.* **4** a defeat: *Our hockey team only had two losses this season.* □ *n., pl.* **loss·es.**

at a loss, not sure; puzzled; uncertain; in difficulty: *The embarrassed child was at a loss as to how to act.*

lost (lòst), **1** *v.* past tense and past participle of **lose:** *I lost my new pen. I had already lost my ruler.* **2** *adj.* no longer possessed or kept: *lost friends.* **3** *adj.* no longer to be found; missing: *lost articles.* **4** *adj.* not in a known location; not sure where you are: *We were lost in the woods for an hour.* **5** *adj.* not won: *a lost battle.* **6** *adj.* hopeless: *a lost cause.* **7** *adj.* not used to good purpose; wasted: *lost time.* **8** *adj.* destroyed or ruined: *a lost soul.* **9** *adj.* bewildered: *a lost expression.* **–lost′ness,** *n.*

lost (def. 4)—Lost, the girls looked at their map.

be lost on, to have no effect on; fail to influence: *The hint was lost on him.*

lost in, completely absorbed or interested in: *He was lost in a book.*

lost to, insensible to: *They were having such a good time that they were lost to all sense of responsibility.*

lot (lot), *n.* **1** a number of persons or things considered as a group; collection: *This lot of oranges is better than the last.* **2** a plot of ground: *Her house is between two empty lots.* **3** a portion or part: *I divided the fruit into ten lots.* **4** one of a set of objects, such as bits of paper, wood, etc., used to decide something by chance. **5** such a method of deciding: *It was settled by lot.* **6** choice made in this way: *The lot fell to me.* **7** what you get by lot; your share or portion. **8** your fate or fortune: *It was his lot later to become president.* **9** a movie studio and its grounds.

a lot or **lots,** a great deal; much: *I feel a lot better.*

a lot of or **lots of,** a great many; much: *a lot of ties, lots of rope.*

cast lots or **draw lots,** to use lots to decide something: *We drew lots to see who should be captain.*

lo·tion (lō′shən), *n.* a liquid medicine or cosmetic which is applied to the skin. Lotions are used to relieve pain, to heal, to cleanse, or to benefit the skin.

lot·ter·y (lot′ər ē), *n.* a scheme for distributing prizes by lot or chance. In a lottery a large number of tickets are sold, some of which win prizes. □ *n., pl.* **lot·ter·ies.**

lo·tus (lō′təs), *n.* **1** any of several water lilies that grow in Egypt, Asia, and North America. **2** (in Greek legends) a plant with fruit supposed to cause a dreamy mental state and forgetfulness of real life. □ *n., pl.* **lo·tus·es.**

loud (loud), **1** *adj.* making a great sound; not quiet or soft: *a loud voice, a loud noise.* **2** *adj.* noisy: *a loud place to study.* **3** *adv.* in a loud manner: *The hunter called long and loud.* **4** *adj.* clamorous; insistent: *be loud in demands.* **5** *adj.* showy in dress or manner: *loud clothes.* **6** *adj.* vulgar; calling attention to yourself in a tasteless manner: *a loud show-off.* **–loud′ly,** *adv.* **–loud′ness,** *n.*

loud·mouth (loud′mouth′), *n.* **1** person who talks too loudly; someone who is offensively noisy. **2** person who talks too much, especially about matters that other people do not wish to have widely known: *John is such a loudmouth that when I flunked the*

test he told everybody right away. □ *n., pl.* **loud·mouths** (loud′-mouths′ *or* loud′mouᴛʜz′).

loud·speak·er (loud′spē′kər), *n.* device for making sounds louder, especially in a public address system.

Lou Gehrig's disease, amyotrophic lateral sclerosis.

Lou·i·si·an·a (lü ē′zē an′ə), *n.* one of the south central states of the United States. *Abbreviation:* LA or La. *Capital:* Baton Rouge. **–Lou·i′sian′i·an** or **Lou·i′si·an′an,** *n.*

Louisiana Purchase, large region that the United States bought from France in 1803. It extended from the Mississippi River to the Rocky Mountains and from Canada to the Gulf of Mexico.

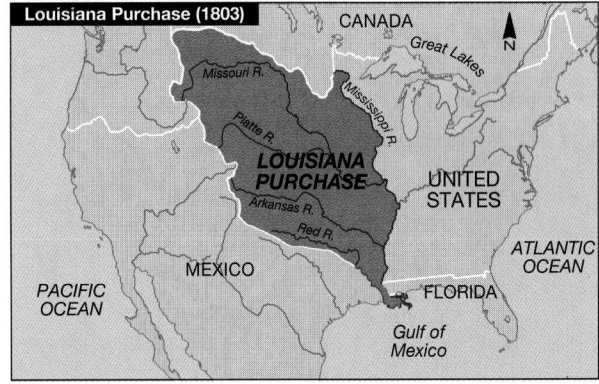

Lou·is·ville (lü′ē vil *or* lü′ə vil), *n.* city in N Kentucky, on the Ohio River.

Lou·is XIV (lü′ē), 1638-1715, king of France from 1643 to 1715. He ruled longer than any other modern European monarch, and he made France a great power in Europe and America. [Louis comes from an old French word meaning "loud fight."]

Louis XVI, 1754-1793, king of France from 1774 to 1792. He was beheaded during the French Revolution.

Lou·is (lü′is), *n.* **Joe** (jō), 1914-1981, American boxer. He was the world heavyweight boxing champion longer than any other champion, from 1937 to 1949. He defended his title 25 times.

lounge (lounj), **1** *v.* to stand, stroll, sit, or lie at ease in a lazy way: *He lounged in an old chair.* **2** *v.* to pass time lazily or at your ease. **3** *n.* a comfortable and informal room in which you can lounge and be at ease: *a theater lounge.* **4** *n.* a couch or sofa. □ *v.* **lounged, loung·ing. –loung′er,** *n.*

louse (lous), **1** *n.* any of many small, wingless insects that live on the hair or skin of people and animals and suck blood. **2** *n.* any of many other insects that live on and bite birds and a few other animals. **3** *n.* INFORMAL. a mean, contemptible person. **4** *v.* **louse up,** INFORMAL. to spoil; get something all confused or wrong: *louse up a deal.* □ *n., pl.* **lice;** *v.* **loused, lous·ing.**

lous·y (lou′zē), *adj.* **1** infested with lice. **2** INFORMAL. bad; poor; of low quality. □ *adj.* **lous·i·er, lous·i·est. –lous′i·ly,** *adv.* **–lous′i·ness,** *n.*

lout (lout), *n.* an awkward, stupid person; boor.

lou·ver (lü′vər), *n.* **1** any of several overlapping horizontal slats or strips of wood, aluminum, or glass set at a slant in a window or other opening, that keep out rain, but provide ventilation and light. **2** window or other opening covered with these strips.

Lou·vre (lü′vrə), *n.* a famous museum in Paris, formerly a palace of the kings of France.

lov·a·ble (luv′ə bəl), *adj.* worthy of being loved; endearing: *She was a most lovable person, always kind and thoughtful.* Also, **loveable. –lov′a·ble·ness,** *n.* **–lov′a·bly,** *adv.*

a	hat	ė	term	ô	order	ch	child		
ā	age	i	it	oi	oil	ng	long		a in about
ä	far	ī	ice	ou	out	sh	she		e in taken
â	care	o	hot	u	cup	th	thin	ə	i in pencil
e	let	ō	open	ù	put	ᴛʜ	then		o in lemon
ē	equal	ò	saw	ü	rule	zh	measure		u in circus

love (luv), **1** *n.* a warm and tender liking; deep feeling of fondness and friendship; great affection or devotion: *love of your family, love for a sweetheart.* **2** *v.* to have such a warm liking or deep feeling for: *We love our parents. I love my country.* **3** *n.* person who is loved; sweetheart. **4** *n.* a strong liking: *a love of books.* **5** *v.* to like very much; take great pleasure in: *She loves music.* **6** *n.* a score of zero in tennis. ❑ *v.* **loved, lov·ing.**

fall in love, to begin to love; come to feel love.

make love, to caress, kiss, etc., as lovers do; pay loving attention; woo.

SYNONYM STUDY Love and **affection** both mean a strong liking. **Love** means a liking of the strongest kind: *My parents fell in love while they were working together.* **Affection** is not as strong a word as love: *She has a special affection for the elderly couple upstairs.*

love·a·ble (luv′ə bəl), *adj.* lovable. **—love′a·ble·ness,** *n.* **—love′a·bly,** *adv.*

love affair, 1 a relationship or romantic episode between lovers; romance. **2** a strong interest in something or enthusiasm for something: *a love affair with Olympic sports.*

love·bird (luv′bėrd′), *n.* any of several small parrots that show great affection for their mates. They are often kept in cages as pets.

love·less (luv′lis), *adj.* without love; not loved. **—love′less·ly,** *adv.* **—love′less·ness,** *n.*

love·lorn (luv′lôrn′), *adj.* suffering because of love; forsaken by the person whom you love. **—love′lorn′ness,** *n.*

love·ly (luv′lē), *adj.* **1** beautiful or endearing in appearance or character; lovable: *They are the loveliest children we know.* **2** very pleasing; delightful: *We had a lovely holiday.* ❑ *adj.* **love·li·er, love·li·est. —love′li·ness,** *n.*

lov·er (luv′ər), *n.* **1** person who is in love with another. **2** person having a strong liking: *a lover of books.*

love seat, seat or small sofa for two persons.

love·sick (luv′sik′), *adj.* acting in an abnormal way because of love. **—love′sick′ness,** *n.*

lov·ing (luv′ing), *adj.* feeling or showing love; affectionate; fond. **—lov′ing·ly,** *adv.* **—lov′ing·ness,** *n.*

loving cup, a large cup with handles, awarded as a trophy.

lov·ing-kind·ness (luv′ing kind′nis), *n.* kindness coming from love: *the loving-kindness of your parents.*

low¹ (lō), **1** *adj.* not high or tall; short: *low walls. This footstool is very low.* **2** *adj.* near the ground or floor: *a low shelf, a low jump.* **3** *adj.* of humble rank; lowly: *to rise rapidly from a low position as an editorial assistant to president of the company.* **4** *adj.* less than usual in amount, degree, force, value, etc.; small: *a low price, low temperature, low speed.* **5** *adj.* nearly used up: *Our supply of oil is very low.* **6** *adj.* unfavorable; poor: *I have a low opinion of their work.* **7** *adj.* mean; contemptible: *low tricks.* **8** *adj.* feeble; weak: *a low state of health.* **9** *adj.* sad; depressed: *low in spirit.* **10** *adj.* deep in pitch: *a low note.* **11** *adj.* not loud; soft: *a low voice.* **12** *adv.* at or to a low point, place, rank, amount, degree, price, pitch, etc.: *The sun sank low. Supplies are running low.* **13** *n.* a low point, level, position, etc.: *Yesterday the temperature fell to a record low for that date.* **14** *n.* arrangement of gears to give the lowest speed and the greatest power. **15** *n.* area of low air pressure. ■ Another word that sounds like this is **lo. —low′ness,** *n.*

lay low, 1 to knock down: *The boxer laid his opponent low.* **2** to kill.

lie low, to stay hidden; keep still: *The robbers lay low for a time.*

low² (lō), **1** *v.* to make the sound of a cow; moo. **2** *n.* the sound a cow makes; mooing. ■ Another word that sounds like this is **lo.**

Low (lō), *n.* **Ju·li·ette Gor·don** (jü′ lē et gôr′dən), 1860-1927, founder of the Girl Scouts of America, in 1912.

low beam, beam from a motor vehicle's headlights that is focused low, for use when facing oncoming traffic.

low·born (lō′bôrn′), *adj.* of humble birth: *The knight, although lowborn, won the hand of the princess.*

low·boy (lō′boi′), *n.* a low chest of drawers, usually with legs.

low·brow (lō′brou′), INFORMAL. **1** *n.* person who is not cultured or intellectual. **2** *adj.* of or suitable for a lowbrow. ■ **Lowbrow** is often considered offensive.

low comedy, comedy that involves slapstick and lots of physical action and silly situations instead of witty dialogue.

Low Countries, the Netherlands, Belgium, and Luxembourg.

low·down (lō′doun′), *n.* INFORMAL. actual facts or truth: *She gave me the lowdown on several confusing rumors that I had heard.*

low-down (lō′doun′), *adj.* INFORMAL. mean; contemptible: *Selling me a broken radio was a low-down trick.*

Low·ell (lō′əl), *n.* city in NE Massachusetts.

low·er (lō′ər), **1** *v.* to let down or haul down: *We lower the flag at night.* **2** *v.* to make lower: *lower the volume of a radio.* **3** *v.* to sink; become lower: *Prices lowered during the summer.* **4** *v.* to bring down in rank, station, or estimation; dishonor. **5** *adj., adv.* more low: *Prices were lower last year than this.*

Lower California, a narrow peninsula in NW Mexico, south of California.

Lower Canada, Quebec, especially before 1841, when Upper Canada and Lower Canada formed the Province of Canada.

low·er·case (lō′ər kās′), in printing: **1** *n.* small letters, not capitals. **2** *adj.* in small letters, not capitals. **3** *v.* to print in small letters, not capitals. ❑ *v.* **low·er·cased, low·er·cas·ing.**

lower class, the social class considered below the middle class, usually thought to be made up of unskilled workers and the unemployed. People in the lower class generally have less money and education than people in the middle class. **—low′er-class′,** *adj.*

low·er·class·man (lō′ər klas′mən), *n.* freshman or sophomore. ❑ *n., pl.* **low·er·class·men.**

lower house or **Lower House,** the larger and more representative branch of a lawmaking group that has two branches, made up of members usually elected by popular vote. The House of Representatives is the lower house of Congress and the House of Commons is the lower house in the Canadian Parliament.

low·er·ing (lou′ər ing), *adj.* dark and threatening; gloomy: *lowering skies.* **—low′er·ing·ly,** *adv.*

Lower Lakes, Lakes Erie and Ontario.

low·er·most (lō′ər mōst), *adj.* lowest.

lower world, (in Greek myths) hell; Hades.

lowest common denominator, least common denominator.

low frequency, the band of radio frequencies between 30 and 300 kilohertz.

low-grade (lō′grād′), *adj.* **1** of poor quality; inferior: *The prospectors were disappointed to find only low-grade ore.* **2** unimportant; minor: *only a low-grade fever.*

low-key (lō′kē′), *adj.* without excitement or display; not noisy, flashy, or complicated; restrained: *To reduce expenses, the couple planned a low-key wedding.*

low·land (lō′lənd), *n.* **1** country or region that is lower and flatter than the neighboring country. **2 Lowlands,** *pl.* a low, flat region in S and E Scotland.

low·land·er (lō′lən dər), *n.* **1** person born or living in a lowland. **2 Lowlander,** person born or living in the Lowlands of Scotland.

low·ly (lō′lē), **1** *adj.* low in rank, position, or development: *a lowly clerk, a lowly job.* **2** *adj.* modest in feeling, behavior, or condition; humble; meek: *He held a lowly opinion of himself.* **3** *adv.* humbly; meekly. ❑ *adj.* **low·li·er, low·li·est. —low′li·ness,** *n.*

low-pitched (lō′picht′), *adj.* **1** having a low tone or sound; deep. **2** having little slope: *a low-pitched roof.*

low-pressure (lō′presh′ər), *adj.* **1** having or using less than the usual amount of pressure: *a low-pressure pump.* **2** having low air pressure: *a low-pressure region.* **3** easygoing; not applying much pressure: *a low-pressure teacher.*

low profile, a moderate attitude or position, deliberately chosen in order to avoid notice. **—low′-pro′file,** *adj.*

low-spir·it·ed (lō′spir′ə tid), *adj.* sad; depressed. **—low′-spir′it·ed·ly,** *adv.* **—low′-spir′it·ed·ness,** *n.*

low spirits, sadness; depression: *The loss of the homecoming game had the whole school in low spirits.*

low-tech (lō′tek′), *adj.* not made or working by advanced modern technology; not very sophisticated in methods or materials: *low-tech sun-heated cooking stoves.*

low tide, 1 the lowest level of the tide. Low tides occur twice daily. **2** time when the tide is lowest.

low tide

lox[1] (loks), *n.* salmon preserved in salt, then soaked in fresh water before being eaten.

lox[2] (loks), *n.* liquid oxygen.

loy·al (loi′əl), *adj.* **1** true and faithful to someone or something: *Loyal friends don't desert you.* **2** faithful to your king, government, or country. —**loy′al·ly,** *adv.*

SYNONYM STUDY **Loyal** and **faithful** both mean always on the same side. **Loyal** suggests support despite difficulty: *The fans stayed loyal when the team had a bad year.* **Faithful** suggests being trustworthy for a long time: *Faithful to the end, the knight died defending his king.*

loy·al·ist (loi′ə list), *n.* **1** person who supports the ruler or the existing government, especially in time of revolt. **2 Loyalist,** an American colonist who opposed independence for the American colonies at the time of the American Revolution; United Empire Loyalist. Many of these colonists moved to Canada during or after the American Revolution.

loy·al·ty (loi′əl tē), *n.* loyal feeling or behavior; faithfulness. ❑ *n., pl.* **loy·al·ties.**

Loy·o·la (loi ō′lə), *n.* **Ig·na·tius** (ig nā′shəs), 1491-1556, Spanish soldier, priest, and saint. ■ Ignatius Loyola lived in a cave for almost two years before he became a priest. He had mystical experiences there that he later wrote about. He founded the Jesuit order in 1534.

loz·enge (loz′inj), *n.* **1** design or figure shaped like this: ◇; diamond; rhombus. **2** a small tablet of any shape used as medicine or candy. Cough drops are sometimes called lozenges. [**Lozenge** may come from an old French word meaning "windowpane."]

LP, long-playing record.

Lr, symbol for lawrencium.

LSD, an extremely powerful drug which produces hallucinations and distorted perceptions.

Lt., Lieutenant.

Ltd. or **ltd.,** limited.

Lu, symbol for lutetium.

Lu·an·da (lü än′də), *n.* port and capital of Angola, on the Atlantic.

Lu·ang Pra·bang (lü äng′ prä bäng′), city in Laos, formerly the royal capital, in the N part.

lu·au (lü′ou), *n.* a Hawaiian feast, generally held outdoors, with roast pig as the main dish.

lub·ber (lub′ər), *n.* **1** a big, clumsy, stupid fellow. **2** a clumsy sailor.

lube (lüb), INFORMAL. **1** *n.* lubricant. **2** *n.* lubrication. **3** *v.* to lubricate. ❑ *v.* **lubed, lub·ing.**

lu·bri·cant (lü′brə kənt), *n.* a slippery substance, such as oil or grease, for putting on parts of machines that slide or move against one another. A lubricant reduces friction by making the parts smooth and slippery so that they will work easily.

lu·bri·cate (lü′brə kāt), *v.* **1** to make machinery smooth, slippery, and easy to work by putting on oil, grease, etc. **2** to make slippery or smooth. ❑ *v.* **lu·bri·cat·ed, lu·bri·cat·ing.** —**lu′bri·ca′tion,** *n.* —**lu′bri·ca′tive,** *adj.* —**lu′bri·ca′tor,** *n.*

Lu·cas (lü′kəs), *n.* **George,** born 1944, American movie director, producer, and writer. He wrote and directed *Star Wars* and produced *Raiders of the Lost Ark.*

Luce (lüs), *n.* **1 Clare Boothe** (klâr büth), 1903-1987, American political leader and playwright. She was a member of the House of Representatives from 1943 to 1947 and U.S. ambassador to Italy from 1953 to 1956. **2 Henry Rob·in·son** (rob′ən sən), 1898-1967, American publisher and editor, born in China. He started the magazines *Time, Life, Fortune,* and *Sports Illustrated.* He was married to Clare Boothe Luce.

lu·cent (lü′snt), *adj.* **1** bright or shining; luminous. **2** letting the light through; clear. —**lu′cent·ly,** *adv.*

lu·cid (lü′sid), *adj.* **1** easy to follow or understand: *A good explanation is lucid.* **2** rational: *After the crash, she wasn't quite lucid.* **3** clear; transparent: *a lucid stream.* **4** shining; bright. —**lu′cid·ly,** *adv.* —**lu·cid′i·ty,** *n.* —**lu′cid·ness,** *n.*

Lu·ci·fer (lü′sə fər), *n.* the chief rebel angel who was cast out of heaven; Satan; the Devil.

Lu·cite (lü′sīt), *n.* trademark for a clear plastic compound used instead of glass for airplane windows, lenses, etc.

luck (luk), *n.* **1** something which seems to happen or come to you by chance; fortune; chance: *I won the game by luck, not by skill.* **2** good luck: *She gave me a penny for luck.*

down on your luck, having bad luck; unlucky: *He's down on his luck right now, but he's hoping to get a job next month.*

in luck, having good luck; lucky: *I am in luck today; I found a five-dollar bill.*

luck out, INFORMAL. be successful in a difficult situation because of good luck.

out of luck, having bad luck; unlucky: *The tornado missed the city, but the trailer camp was out of luck.*

try your luck, to see what you can do: *After success as a model, she decided to try her luck at acting.*

SYNONYM STUDY **Luck, fortune,** and **chance** all mean a way things happen by accident. **Luck** can be good or bad: *I thought I could win, but I had tough luck.* **Fortune** suggests good luck: *Her fortune at finding the lost ring was amazing.* **Chance** suggests that things really happen for no reason: *By chance they chose the same restaurant for dinner.*

luck·i·ly (luk′ə lē), *adv.* by good luck; fortunately.

luck·less (luk′lis), *adj.* having or bringing bad luck; unlucky. —**luck′less·ly,** *adv.* —**luck′less·ness,** *n.*

luck·y (luk′ē), *adj.* **1** having good luck: *a lucky person.* **2** bringing good luck: *The coach thinks that his hat is lucky, so he wears it to every game.* ❑ *adj.* **luck·i·er, luck·i·est.** —**luck′i·ness,** *n.*

lu·cra·tive (lü′krə tiv), *adj.* bringing in money; profitable. —**lu′cra·tive·ly,** *adv.* —**lu′cra·tive·ness,** *n.*

lu·cre (lü′kər), *n.* money considered as bad or degrading.

lu·di·crous (lü′də krəs), *adj.* amusingly absurd; very silly; ridiculous: *the ludicrous acts of a clown.* —**lu′di·crous·ly,** *adv.* —**lu′di·crous·ness,** *n.*

luff (luf), **1** *v.* to turn the bow of a ship toward the wind. **2** *n.* act of turning the bow of a ship toward the wind. **3** *n.* the forward edge of a fore-and-aft sail.

lug[1] (lug), *v.* to pull along or carry with effort; drag: *We lugged the rug to the yard to clean it.* ❑ *v.* **lugged, lug·ging.**

lug[2] (lug), *n.* a part that sticks out, used to hold or grip something.

luge (lüzh), **1** *n.* a racing sled, used by one or two persons. **2** *v.* to race on a luge. ❑ *v.* **luged, lug·ing** or **luge·ing.** —**lug′er,** *n.*

lug·gage (lug′ij), *n.* suitcases or handbags that a traveler carries on a trip. [**Luggage** comes from **lug**[1]. It is what you have to lug around with you.] —**lug′gage·less,** *adj.*

lug·ger (lug′ər), *n.* boat with lugsails.

lug·sail (lug′sāl′ *or* lug′səl), *n.* a four-cornered sail held by a yard that slants across the mast.

a	hat	ė	term	ô	order	ch	child		
ā	age	i	it	oi	oil	ng	long		a in about
ä	far	ī	ice	ou	out	sh	she	ə	e in taken
â	care	o	hot	u	cup	th	thin		i in pencil
e	let	ō	open	u̇	put	ŦH	then		o in lemon
ē	equal	ȯ	saw	ü	rule	zh	measure		u in circus

lu·gu·bri·ous (lü gü′brē əs), *adj.* too sad; overly mournful: *the lugubrious howl of a dog.* —**lu·gu′bri·ous·ly,** *adv.* —**lu·gu′bri·ous·ness,** *n.*

lug·worm (lug′wėrm′), *n.* any of several worms that burrow in sand underwater along the seashore.

Luke (lük), *n.* **1** (in the Bible) a physician who was the companion of the apostle Paul. **2** the third book of the New Testament. It tells the story of the life of Jesus. [Luke comes from a Latin word meaning "light."]

luke·warm (lük′wôrm′), *adj.* **1** neither hot nor cold; moderately warm: *She likes her soup hot, not lukewarm.* **2** showing little enthusiasm; halfhearted: *a lukewarm greeting.* —**luke′warm′ly,** *adv.* —**luke′warm′ness,** *n.*

lull (lul), **1** *v.* to soothe with sounds or caresses; cause to sleep: *The soft music lulled me to sleep.* **2** *v.* to make or become calm or more nearly calm; quiet: *Their confidence lulled my fears. The wind lulled.* **3** *n.* period of less noise or violence; brief calm: *a lull in a storm.*

lul·la·by (lul′ə bī), *n.* song for singing to a child in a cradle; soft song to lull a baby to sleep. ❑ *n., pl.* **lul·la·bies.**

lu·lu (lü′lü), *n.* SLANG. an unusual person or thing: *The thunderstorm was a lulu.*

lum·ba·go (lum bā′gō), *n.* pain in the muscles of the lower part of the back.

lum·bar (lum′bər), *adj.* of or relating to the lower part of the back: *the lumbar region.* ■ Another word that sounds like this is **lumber.**

lum·ber¹ (lum′bər), **1** *n.* timber that has been roughly cut into boards, planks, etc., and prepared for use. **2** *v.* to cut and prepare lumber. ■ Another word that sounds like this is **lumbar.** —**lum′ber·er,** *n.*

lum·ber² (lum′bər), *v.* to move along heavily and noisily; roll along with difficulty: *The old truck lumbered down the road.* ■ Another word that sounds like this is **lumbar.**

lum·ber·ing¹ (lum′bər ing), *n.* business of cutting and preparing timber for use.

lumber¹ (def. 1)

lum·ber·ing² (lum′bər ing), *adj.* moving along heavily, noisily, or with difficulty. —**lum′ber·ing·ly,** *adv.*

lum·ber·jack (lum′bər jak′), *n.* person whose work is cutting down trees and sending the logs to the sawmill; woodsman; logger.

lum·ber·man (lum′bər mən), *n.* **1** lumberjack. **2** someone who prepares lumber or buys and sells lumber. ❑ *n., pl.* **lum·ber·men.**

lum·ber·yard (lum′bər yärd′), *n.* place where lumber is stored and sold.

lu·mi·nar·i·a (lü′mə ner′ ē ə), *n.* a lighted candle placed outdoors in a small paper bag filled with sand and sometimes decorated. Luminarias are traditional in Mexico and parts of the southern United States on Christmas and other holidays. ❑ *n., pl.* **lu·mi·nar·i·as.**

lu·mi·nar·y (lü′mə ner′ē), *n.* **1** a heavenly body that gives or reflects light. **2** a famous person. ❑ *n., pl.* **lu·mi·nar·ies.**

lu·mi·nes·cence (lü′mə nes′ns), *n.* production of light without much heat, at a temperature below that of incandescent objects. Luminescence includes phosphorescence and fluorescence.

lu·mi·nes·cent (lü′mə nes′nt), *adj.* giving off light without much heat. Fireflies and fluorescent lamps are luminescent.

lu·mi·nos·i·ty (lü′mə nos′ə tē), *n.* **1** luminous quality or condition. **2** something luminous. ❑ *n., pl.* **lu·mi·nos·i·ties** for 2.

lu·mi·nous (lü′mə nəs), *adj.* **1** shining by its own light: *The sun and stars are luminous bodies.* **2** full of light; bright: *She painted luminous pictures of sunlit scenes.* **3** easily understood; clear; enlightening. —**lu′mi·nous·ly,** *adv.* —**lu′mi·nous·ness,** *n.*

lump¹ (lump), **1** *n.* a small, solid mass of no particular shape: *a lump of coal.* **2** *n.* a swelling; bump: *a lump on the head.* **3** *adj.* in lumps; in a lump: *lump coal, lump sugar.* **4** *v.* to put together;

deal with in a mass or as a whole: *We will lump our expenses together.* **5** *adj.* not in parts; whole: *I was given a lump sum of money for all of my living expenses.* **6** *v.* to form into a lump or lumps: *The cornstarch lumped because we cooked it too fast.*
a lump in the throat, feeling of inability to swallow, caused by pity, sorrow, or other strong emotion.

lump² (lump), *v.* INFORMAL. to put up with; endure: *If you don't like it, you can lump it.*

lump·ec·to·my (lum pek′tə mē), *n.* the surgical removal of a breast tumor or cyst, instead of removing the entire breast.

lump·ish (lum′pish), *adj.* **1** like a lump; heavy and clumsy. **2** dull; stupid. —**lump′ish·ly,** *adv.* —**lump′ish·ness,** *n.*

lump·y (lum′pē), *adj.* **1** full of lumps: *lumpy gravy.* **2** covered with lumps: *lumpy ground.* ❑ *adj.* **lump·i·er, lump·i·est.** —**lump′i·ly,** *adv.* —**lump′i·ness,** *n.*

lu·na·cy (lü′nə sē), *n.* **1** insanity. **2** extreme folly.

luna moth or **Luna moth** (lü′nə), a large moth of North America that has light green wings with moon-shaped spots. Each of the luna moth's hind wings has a long tail.

lu·nar (lü′nər), *adj.* **1** of or like the moon: *a lunar landscape.* **2** measured by the moon's revolution around the earth: *a lunar month.*

lunar module, an independent part of a spacecraft for carrying astronauts from the moon-orbiting craft to the surface of the moon and back.

lunar month, the period of one complete revolution of the moon around the earth; the interval between one new moon and the next; about 29½ days.

lu·na·tic (lü′nə tik), **1** *n.* a mentally ill person. **2** *adj.* mentally ill. **3** *adj.* for mentally ill people: *a lunatic asylum.* **4** *adj.* extremely foolish; idiotic: *a lunatic search for buried treasure.* [Lunatic comes from a Latin word meaning "moon." It was once thought that mental illness was caused by changes of the moon.]

USAGE NOTE Lunatic is no longer used by doctors. They, and careful writers and speakers, use "mentally ill." Definitions 1, 2, and 3 of **lunatic** are considered offensive. People still use definition 4, especially in conversation, but there are many other words for the idea.

---

lunch (lunch), **1** *n.* a light meal between breakfast and dinner: *We usually have lunch at noon.* **2** *n.* food for a lunch. **3** *v.* to eat lunch. ❑ *n., pl.* **lunch·es.** —**lunch′er,** *n.*

lunch·eon (lun′chən), *n.* a lunch, especially one for a group of people, for a special occasion: *a women's club luncheon.*

lunch·eon·ette (lun′chə net′), *n.* restaurant in which light meals are served.

lunch·room (lunch′rüm′), *n.* **1** restaurant in which light meals are served. **2** room in a school, factory, office building, etc., where light meals are served.

lunch·time (lunch′tīm′), *n.* time at which lunch is eaten or served.

lung (lung), *n.* either one of a pair of saclike, spongy organs in the chest of mammals, reptiles, and birds, used in breathing. Lungs give the blood the oxygen it needs, and take away carbon dioxide. See picture at **heart.**

lunge (lunj), **1** *n.* any sudden forward movement, such as a thrust with a sword or other weapon. **2** *v.* to move suddenly forward; thrust: *The dog lunged at the stranger.* ❑ *v.* **lunged, lung·ing.** —**lung′er,** *n.*

lung·fish (lung′fish′), *n.* any of six kinds of fishes with lunglike sacs in addition to gills, enabling them to obtain oxygen both in and out of the water. Lungfishes are found in Australia, Africa, and South America. Most resemble eels. ❑ *n., pl.* **lung·fish** or **lung·fish·es.**

lu·pine (lü′pən), *n.* any of numerous plants with long spikes of flowers, clusters of hairy leaflets, and flat pods with bean-shaped seeds.

lurch¹ (lėrch), **1** *n.* a sudden leaning or roll to one side, like that of a ship, a car, or a staggering person: *The boat gave a lurch and tipped over.* **2** *v.* lean or roll suddenly; stagger: *The injured animal lurched forward.* ❑ *n., pl.* **lurch·es.**

lurch² (lėrch), *n.* **leave someone in the lurch,** to leave someone in a helpless condition or difficult situation.

lure (lŭr), **1** *n.* power of attracting or fascinating; charm; allure; attraction: *Many people feel the lure of the sea.* **2** *n.* something that attracts or tempts: *Gold was the lure that brought miners to California in 1849.* **3** *v.* to lead away or into something by arousing desire; attract; tempt: *Bees are lured by the scent of flowers.* **4** *n.* a bait, especially an artificial bait used in fishing. **5** *v.* to attract with a bait: *We lured the rat into a trap.* ❑ *v.* **lured, lur·ing.** **–lur′er,** *n.*

lur·id (lŭr′id), *adj.* **1** lighted up with a red or fiery glare: *The sky was lurid with the flames of the burning city.* **2** glaring in brightness or color: *a lurid red.* **3** terrible; sensational; startling: *The magazine had stories about murders and other lurid crimes.* **–lur′id·ly,** *adv.* **–lur′id·ness,** *n.*

lurk (lėrk), *v.* **1** to stay about without arousing attention; wait out of sight; be hidden: *A tiger was lurking in the jungle.* **2** to move about in a secret and sly manner: *Several people were seen lurking near the house before it was robbed.* **–lurk′ing·ly,** *adj.*

Lu·sa·ka (lü sä′kə), *n.* capital of Zambia, in the central part.

lus·cious (lush′əs), *adj.* **1** delicious; richly sweet: *a luscious peach.* ■ See Synonym Study at **delicious.** **2** very pleasing to taste, smell, hear, see, or feel: *a painting filled with luscious colors.* **–lus′cious·ly,** *adv.* **–lus′cious·ness,** *n.*

lush (lush), *adj.* **1** tender and juicy; growing thick and green: *Lush grass grows along the river banks.* **2** having thick growth; covered with growing things: *The hillside was lush with spring flowers.* **3** luxurious. **–lush′ly,** *adv.* **–lush′ness,** *n.*

lust (lust), **1** *n.* strong desire. **2** *n.* strong sexual desire. **3** *v.* to have a strong desire: *lust after money and power.*

lus·ter (lus′tər), *n.* **1** a bright shine on the surface: *the luster of pearls.* **2** brightness: *the luster in the eyes of a happy child.* **3** fame; glory; brilliance: *Many prizes added luster to the artist's reputation.* **4** a shiny, metallic, often iridescent surface on pottery or china. **–lus′ter·less,** *adj.*

lust·ful (lust′fəl), *adj.* full of lust or desire; lewd. **–lust′ful·ly,** *adv.* **–lust′ful·ness,** *n.*

lus·trous (lus′trəs), *adj.* having luster; shining; glossy: *lustrous satin.* **–lus′trous·ly,** *adv.* **–lus′trous·ness,** *n.*

lust·y (lus′tē), *adj.* strong and healthy; full of vigor: *a lusty athlete.* ❑ *adj.* **lust·i·er, lust·i·est. –lust′i·ly,** *adv.* **–lust′i·ness,** *n.*

lute (lüt), *n.* a musical instrument, much used in the 1500s and 1600s, having a pear-shaped body and usually six pairs of strings. It is played by plucking the strings. ■ Another word that sounds like this is **loot.**

lu·te·ti·um (lü tē′shē əm), *n.* a metallic element which usually occurs in nature with ytterbium. *Symbol:* Lu

Lu·ther (lü′thər), *n.* Martin (mar′-tən), 1483-1546, leader of the Protestant Reformation in Germany. ■ **Martin Luther** denied the authority of the pope. He believed that the Bible was the only source of religious truth. He translated the Latin Bible into German.

lute

Lu·ther·an (lü′thər ən), **1** *adj.* of or about Luther or the church that was named for him. **2** *n.* member of the Lutheran Church.

Lux·em·bourg or **Lux·em·burg** (luk′səm bėrg′), *n.* **1** small country in W Europe, bordered by Germany, France, and Belgium. **2** its capital.

lux·u·ri·ance (lug zhŭr′ē əns *or* luk shŭr′ē əns), *n.* luxuriant growth or productiveness; rich abundance.

lux·u·ri·ant (lug zhŭr′ē ənt *or* luk shŭr′ē ənt), *adj.* **1** growing thick and green. **2** producing abundantly. **3** rich in ornament. **–lux·u′ri·ant·ly,** *adv.*

lux·u·ri·ate (lug zhŭr′ē āt *or* luk shŭr′ē āt), *v.* **1** to indulge in luxury. **2** to take great delight: *The campers planned to luxuriate in hot baths when they returned home.* **3** to grow very abundantly. ❑ *v.* **lux·u·ri·at·ed, lux·u·ri·at·ing.**

lux·u·ri·ous (lug zhŭr′ē əs *or* luk shŭr′ē əs), *adj.* **1** giving luxury; very comfortable and beautiful: *a luxurious apartment.* **2** fond of luxury; tending toward luxury; self-indulgent: *a luxurious taste for fine food.* **–lux·u′ri·ous·ly,** *adv.* **–lux·u′ri·ous·ness,** *n.*

lux·u·ry (luk′shər ē *or* lug′zhər ē), **1** *n.* comforts and beauties of life beyond what is really necessary. **2** *n.* use of the best and most costly food, clothes, houses, furniture, and amusements: *The movie star was accustomed to luxury.* **3** *n.* something that you enjoy, usually something choice and costly: *luxuries such as fine paintings.* **4** *n.* something pleasant but not necessary: *Candy is a luxury.* **5** *adj.* providing lavish comfort and enjoyment; luxurious: *a luxury hotel.* ❑ *n., pl.* **lux·u·ries.**

Lu·zon (lü zon′), *n.* chief island of the Philippines.

-ly[1], *suffix.* **1** in a ___ way: *cheerfully = in a cheerful way.* **2** of or from ___: *financially = of finance; northerly = of or from the north.*

-ly[2], *suffix.* like a ___; like that of a ___: *ghostly = like a ghost.*

ly·ce·um (lī sē′əm), *n.* **1** lecture hall; place where lectures are given. **2** an association for instruction and entertainment through lectures, debates, and concerts.

Lyd·i·a (lid′ē ə), *n.* ancient country in W Asia Minor, famous for its wealth and luxury. See **Etruria** for map. **–Lyd′i·an,** *adj., n.*

lye (lī), *n.* any of several strong alkaline solutions used in making soap and in cleaning. ■ Another word that sounds like this is **lie.**

ly·ing[1] (lī′ing), **1** *n.* act of telling a lie; habit of telling lies. **2** *adj.* false; untruthful. **3** *v.* present participle of **lie**[1]: *I was not lying; I told the truth.* **–ly′ing·ly,** *adv.*

ly·ing[2] (lī′ing), *v.* present participle of **lie**[2]: *I was lying on the bed.*

Lyme disease (līm), a serious disease, caused by a bacterium and spread by ticks. Lyme disease usually begins with a rash, followed by fever, headache, joint pain, and exhaustion.

lymph (limf), *n.* a nearly colorless liquid in the tissues of the body, filtered from the blood. Lymph bathes and nourishes the tissues.

lym·phat·ic (lim fat′ik), *adj.* **1** of or related to lymph; carrying lymph. **2** sluggish; pale; lacking energy.

lymphatic vessel, tube or canal through which lymph is carried from different parts of the body.

lymph node or **lymph gland,** any of the small oval bodies occurring along the paths of the lymphatic vessels. Lymph nodes filter out harmful microorganisms from the lymph.

lymph·o·cyte (lim′fə sit), *n.* a type of white blood cell, produced by lymph tissues.

lynch (linch), *v.* to put an accused person to death, usually by hanging, without a lawful trial: *The angry mob lynched an innocent man.* **–lynch′er,** *n.*

lynx (lingks), *n.* a medium-sized fierce cat of the northern United States and Canada with a short tail, rather long legs, and tufts of hair at the ends of its ears. ■ Another word that sounds like this is **links.** ❑ *n., pl.* **lynx** or **lynx·es.**

lynx—about 3 ft. (91 cm) long

a	hat	ė	term	ô	order	ch	child		
ā	age	i	it	oi	oil	ng	long		a in about
ä	far	ī	ice	ou	out	sh	she		e in taken
â	care	o	hot	u	cup	th	thin	ə	i in pencil
e	let	ō	open	u̇	put	ᵺ	then		o in lemon
ē	equal	ô	saw	ü	rule	zh	measure		u in circus

lynx-eyed (lingks′id′), *adj.* having sharp eyes or keen sight.

ly·on·naise (lī′ə nāz′), *adj.* fried with pieces of onions: *lyonnaise potatoes.*

Ly·ons (lī′ənz *or* lē ȯn′), *n.* city in E central France, on the Rhone River.

Ly·ra (lī′rə), *n.* a small northern constellation shaped something like a lyre. It contains the bright star Vega. Also, **Lyre.**

lyre (līr), *n.* **1** an ancient stringed musical instrument somewhat like a small harp. **2 Lyre,** Lyra.

lyre·bird (līr′bėrd′), *n.* either of two Australian birds. The male has a long showy tail that is lyre-shaped when spread.

lyr·ic (lir′ik), **1** *n.* a short poem expressing personal emotion. A love poem, a patriotic song, a lament, and a hymn might all be lyrics. **2** *adj.* of or about such poems: *a lyric poet.* **3** *adj.* of or about a spontaneous expression of feeling. **4** *adj.* of or suitable for singing. **5** *n.* Usually, **lyrics,** *pl.* the words for a song.

lyr·i·cal (lir′ə kəl), *adj.* **1** expressing strong emotion in a beautiful manner, as in poetry; poetic: *She became almost lyrical when she described the scenery.* **2** lyric. **—lyr′i·cal·ly,** *adv.*

lyr·i·cism (lir′ə siz′əm), *n.* lyric character, form, or expression.

lyr·i·cist (lir′ə sist), *n.* **1** person who writes the words for a song; writer of lyrics. **2** a lyric poet.

lyre (def. 1)

lyrebird—about 3 ft. (91 cm) long with the tail

ly·sin (lī′sn), *n.* antibody that can dissolve bacteria, red blood cells, and other cellular elements.

M or m (em), *n.* **1** the 13th letter of the English alphabet. **2** the Roman numeral for 1000. □ *n., pl.* **M's** or **m's.**

m or **m.,** meter or meters.

M, megabyte.

m. or **m, 1** mile or miles. **2** minute or minutes.

M., 1 Monday. **2** Monsieur.

ma (mä), *n.* INFORMAL. mamma; mother. □ *n., pl.* **mas.**

MA, Massachusetts (used with postal Zip Code).

M.A., Master of Arts.

ma'am (mam), *n.* madam.

Ma'at (mät), *n.* the Egyptian goddess of truth and justice, shown as a crouching woman wearing an ostrich feather.

ma·ca·bre (mə kä′brə *or* mə käb′), *adj.* gruesome; horrible; ghastly.

ma·cad·am (mə kad′əm), *n.* **1** small, broken stones. Layers of macadam are rolled until solid and smooth to make roads. **2** road or pavement made of this.

mac·a·da·mi·a nut (mak′ə dā′mē ə), the large, smooth nut of the macadamia, a tree found in Australia and grown in Hawaii.

mac·cad·am·ize (mə kad′ə mīz), *v.* to make or cover a road with macadam. □ *v.* **ma·cad·am·ized, ma·cad·am·iz·ing.**

Ma·ca·o (mə kou′), *n.* **1** a seaport on a peninsula on the S coast of China. **2** a Portuguese colony that includes this peninsula and two small nearby islands.

ma·caque (mə käk′), *n.* any of several short-tailed monkeys of Asia, the East Indies, and North Africa. The rhesus is a macaque.

mac·a·ro·ni (mak′ə rō′nē), *n.* a mixture of flour and water that has been dried, usually in the form of hollow tubes, to be cooked for food. Macaroni is a form of pasta.

WORD STORY Macaroni and macaroon look alike because they both come from the same Italian word, meaning "flour paste." A French writer borrowed the Italian word to name the cookie, first made with a ground paste of almonds.

mac·a·roon (mak′ə rün′), *n.* a very rich cookie, made of egg whites, sugar, and ground almonds or coconut. [See Word Story at **macaroni.**]

Mac·Ar·thur (mək är′thər), *n.* Douglas, 1880-1964, American general in World War II and the Korean War. ■ Douglas MacArthur won the Medal of Honor for his defense of the Philippines. His father had won the same medal for heroism in the Civil War. The MacArthurs are the only father and son who have both won this medal.

ma·caw (mə kô′), *n.* any of about 20 large parrots of South and Central America, with long tails, brilliant feathers, and harsh voices. Macaws can be taught to imitate human speech.

a	hat	ė	term	ô	order	ch	child		
ā	age	i	it	oi	oil	ng	long	ə	a in about
ä	far	ī	ice	ou	out	sh	she		e in taken
â	care	o	hot	u	cup	th	thin		i in pencil
e	let	ō	open	ù	put	ŦH	then		o in lemon
ē	equal	ò	saw	ü	rule	zh	measure		u in circus

Mac·beth (mǝk beth′), *n.* **1** play by Shakespeare. **2** the principal character in this play, who murders his king and becomes king himself.

mace[1] (mās), *n.* **1** a club with a heavy metal head, often spiked, used as a weapon in the Middle Ages. **2** staff carried by or before an official as a symbol of authority.

mace[2] (mās), *n.* spice made from the dried outer covering of nutmegs.

Mace (mās), *n.* trademark for a powerful tear gas that is dispensed as a spray.

Mac·e·do·ni·a (mas′ǝ dō′nē ǝ), *n.* **1** ancient country in SE Europe, north of Greece. It now forms the modern country of Macedonia and parts of Bulgaria and Greece. See **Etruria** for map. **2** modern country in SE Europe, north of Greece. *Capital:* Skopje. —**Mac′e·do′ni·an,** *adj., n.*

Mach (mäk), *n.* Mach number.

ma·chet·e (mǝ shet′ē *or* mǝ chet′ē), *n.* a large, heavy knife, used in South America, Central America, and the West Indies as a tool to cut heavy vegetation, and as a weapon.

Mach·i·a·vel·li (mak′ē ǝ vel′ē), *n.* **Nic·co·lo** (nē′kō lō′), 1469-1527, Italian diplomat and writer. He advised leaders to use any method to preserve their political power, including cruelty and force if nothing else worked.

Mach·i·a·vel·li·an (mak′ē ǝ vel′ē ǝn), *adj.* **1** of Machiavelli or his political theory. **2** cunning in a subtle or unscrupulous way; crafty.

mach·i·na·tion (mak′ǝ nā′shǝn *or* mash′ǝ nā′shǝn), *n.* **1** evil or clever plotting; scheming against authority. **2** Usually, **machinations,** *pl.* an evil plot; secret or cunning scheme: *The election of our candidate was prevented by the machinations of the opponent.*

ma·chine (mǝ shēn′), **1** *n.* device containing an arrangement of fixed and moving parts for doing work, powered usually by electricity. **2** *adj.* of a machine or machines: *the machine age, machine action.* **3** *v.* to make or finish with a machine: *The steel was machined to exact specifications.* **4** *adj.* by or with a machine, not by hand: *machine printing.* **5** *n.* device for applying force or changing its direction. Levers and pulleys are simple machines. **6** *n.* person or group that acts without thinking. **7** *n.* group of people controlling an organization, especially a political party: *a political machine.* ❑ *v.* **ma·chined, ma·chin·ing.** —**ma·chin′a·ble** *or* **ma·chine′a·ble,** *adj.* —**ma·chine′like′,** *adj.*

machine gun, gun that fires bullets rapidly and automatically.

ma·chine-gun (mǝ shēn′gun′), *v.* to fire at with a machine gun. ❑ *v.* **ma·chine-gunned, ma·chine-gun·ning.**

machine language, a computer programming language written with only the binary digits 0 and 1. A computer can use a machine language directly, while other computer languages must be translated to machine language for computer use.

ma·chine-read·a·ble (mǝ shēn′rē′dǝ bǝl), *adj.* able to be entered into a computer directly from the printed form: *machine-readable numbers on checks.*

ma·chin·er·y (mǝ shē′nǝr ē), *n.* **1** machines: *A factory contains much machinery.* **2** the working parts of a machine: *The machinery of a computer should be kept clean.* **3** any combination of persons or things by which something is kept going or something is done: *Police officers are part of the machinery of the law.*

machine shop, workshop where machines are used to cut or shape metals and other hard substances.

machine tool, a power-driven tool or machine used to form metal into desired shapes by cutting, hammering, squeezing, etc.

ma·chin·ist (mǝ shē′nist), *n.* **1** a skilled worker who shapes metal by using machine tools. **2** person who makes and repairs machinery.

ma·chis·mo (mä chēz′mō), *n.* manliness, especially when strong or aggressive in nature; excessive concern over your manliness.

Mach number (mäk), number expressing the ratio of the speed of an object to the speed of sound in the same medium. An aircraft traveling at the speed of sound has a Mach number of 1; at twice the speed of sound, its Mach number is 2. Also, **Mach.**

ma·cho (mä′chō), **1** *n.* a strong, virile man. **2** *n.* machismo. **3** *adj.* showing machismo: *a macho attitude.* ❑ *n., pl.* **ma·chos** for 1.

Mac·ken·zie (mǝ ken′zē), *n.* river in NW Canada, flowing from Great Slave Lake northwest into the Arctic Ocean.

mack·er·el (mak′ǝr ǝl), *n.* any of numerous saltwater fishes, especially a common food fish of the northern Atlantic. ❑ *n., pl.* **mack·er·el** *or* **mack·er·els.**

mackerel sky, sky with scattered, small, white, fleecy clouds.

Mack·i·nac (mak′ǝ nȯ), *n.* **Straits of,** strait connecting Lake Michigan and Lake Huron.

mack·i·naw (mak′ǝ nȯ), *n.* **1** kind of short coat made of heavy woolen cloth. **2** kind of thick woolen blanket, often with bars of color, used in the northern and western United States and Canada.

mack·in·tosh (mak′ǝn tosh), *n.* **1** a waterproof coat; raincoat. **2** waterproof cloth. ❑ *n., pl.* **mack·in·tosh·es** for 1.

Ma·con (mā′kǝn), *n.* city in central Georgia.

mac·ra·mé *or* **mac·ra·me** (mak′rǝ mā), *n.* a coarse lace or fringe made by knotting thread or cord in patterns. ❑ *n., pl.* **mac·ra·més** *or* **mac·ra·mes.**

mac·ro (mak′krō), *n.* a set of instructions for a particular computer function, stored together for quick activation, in order to avoid entering each instruction separately: *He made a macro that pasted his address and the date in the letter.* ❑ *n., pl.* **mac·ros.**

macro-, *prefix.* large or long: *macromolecule = large molecule.*

mac·ro·bi·ot·ic (mak′rō bī ot′ik), *adj.* of a diet that is believed to prolong life, based on brown rice and other whole grains, fish, etc., but not including foods such as meat and eggs: *a macrobiotic lunch.*

ma·cron (mā′kron), *n.* a straight, horizontal line placed over a vowel to show that it is pronounced as a long vowel. EXAMPLES: came (kām), be (bē).

mac·ro·phage (mak′rǝ fāj), *n.* a kind of white blood cell that surrounds and destroys germs or harmful materials.

mad (mad), *adj.* **1** very annoyed; angry: *The insult made me mad.* **2** foolish; unwise: *a mad undertaking.* **3** unreasonably fond: *She is mad about skiing.* **4** mentally ill. ▪ See Usage Note at **crazy. 5** wildly joyful; merry: *Tomorrow will be the maddest, merriest day of the year.* **6** having rabies: *A mad dog often foams at the mouth and may bite people.* ❑ *adj.* **mad·der, mad·dest.** —**mad′ly,** *adv.*

like mad, very hard, fast, etc.: *I ran like mad to catch the train.*

SYNONYM STUDY **Mad** and **furious** both mean angry. **Mad** means that you have lost your temper: *It makes me mad when people call me "little boy."* **Furious** means wildly angry: *After the accident, the two drivers were furious with each other.*

Mad·a·gas·car (mad′ǝ gas′kǝr), *n.* island country in the Indian Ocean, east of S Africa. *Capital:* Antananarivo.

mad·am (mad′ǝm), *n.* a polite title used in writing or speaking to any woman: *May I help you, madam?* ❑ *n., pl.* **mad·ams** *or* **mes·dames.** ▪ Another word that can sound like this is **madame.**

mad·ame (mad′ǝm *or* mä däm′), *n.* FRENCH. Mrs.; madam. ❑ *n., pl.* **mes·dames.** ▪ Another word that can sound like this is **madam.**

mad·cap (mad′kap′), **1** *n.* person who carries out reckless ideas without stopping to think first. **2** *adj.* impulsive; hasty: *madcap schemes.*

mad·den (mad′n), *v.* to make or become mad: *The crowd was maddened by the umpire's decision.*

mad·den·ing (mad′n ing), *adj.* very annoying; irritating: *maddening delays.* —**mad′den·ing·ly,** *adv.*

made (mād), **1** *v.* past tense and past participle of **make:** *The cook made the cake. It was made of flour, milk, butter, eggs, and sugar.* **2** *adj.* built; formed: *a strongly made swing.* ▪ Another word that sounds like this is **maid.**

Ma·dei·ra (mǝ dir′ǝ), *n.* **1** group of Portuguese islands in the Atlantic, west of N Africa. **2** the most important island of this group. **3** Often, **madeira,** kind of wine made there.

mad·e·moi·selle (mad′ǝ mǝ zel′ *or* mad′mwä zel′), *n.* FRENCH. Miss. ❑ *n., pl.* **mes·de·moi·selles.**

made-up (mād′up′), *adj.* **1** not real; invented; imaginary: *a made-up story.* **2** wearing makeup: *made-up faces.*

mad·house (mad′hous′), *n.* **1** place of uproar and confusion: *The arena was a madhouse after the home team won the championship game.* **2** hospital for mentally ill people. ❑ *n., pl.* **mad·hous·es** (mad′hou′ziz).

Mad·i·son (mad′ə sən), *n.* **1 Dol·ley Payne** (dol′ē pān′), 1768-1849, American first lady, wife of James Madison. When the British invaded Washington during the War of 1812, she saved important state papers. **2 James,** 1751-1836, the fourth president of the United States, from 1809 to 1817. Earlier, he had an important part in creating the Constitution of the United States. **3** capital of Wisconsin, in the S part.

mad·man (mad′man′), *n.* **1** man who is mentally ill. **2** man who is foolish and unreasonable: *What madman built a house with no windows?* ❑ *n., pl.* **mad·men.**

mad·ness (mad′nis), *n.* **1** mental illness. **2** folly: *It would be madness to try to sail a boat in this storm.*

Ma·don·na (mə don′ə), *n.* **1** Mary, the mother of Jesus. **2** Also, **madonna,** picture or statue of her. ❑ *n., pl.* **Ma·don·nas** or **ma·don·nas** for 2.

mad·ras (mad′rəs *or* mə dras′), *n.* a closely woven cotton cloth, used for shirts, dresses, jackets, etc.

Ma·dras (mə dras′), *n.* seaport in SE India.

Ma·drid (mə drid′), *n.* capital of Spain, in the central part.

mad·ri·gal (mad′rə gəl), *n.* **1** song with parts for several voices, usually sung without instrumental accompaniment. **2** a short poem, often about love, that can be set to music.

mad·wo·man (mad′wŭm′ən), *n.* **1** woman who is mentally ill. **2** woman who is foolish and unreasonable: *When we got to the sale, she became a madwoman, buying wildly.*

mael·strom (māl′strəm), *n.* **1** a violent confusion of feelings, ideas, or activity. **2** any great whirlpool. **3 Maelstrom,** a dangerous whirlpool off the NW coast of Norway.

maes·tro (mī strō′), *n.* **1** a great composer, teacher, or conductor of music. **2** master of any art. ❑ *n., pl.* **maes·tros.**

Ma·fi·a or **ma·fi·a** (mä′fē ə), *n.* **1** a secret organization of criminals supposed to control underworld activities in various parts of the world. **2** a secret Sicilian terrorist society.

WORD STORY **Mafia** may come from an Arabic word meaning "boasting." That became an Italian word meaning "courage," and the members of the group in Sicily took it for the group's name.

mag·a·zine (mag′ə zēn′ *or* mag′ə zēn′), *n.* **1** a publication issued at regular intervals, especially weekly or monthly, which contains stories, articles, photographs, etc., by various contributors. **2** place in a repeating or automatic gun from which cartridges are fed into the firing chamber. **3** place for holding a roll or reel of film in a camera or projector. **4** room in a fort or warship for storing gunpowder and other explosives. **5** a building for storing gunpowder, guns, food, or other military supplies.

WORD STORY **Magazine** comes from an Arabic word meaning "warehouse." A printed magazine is like a warehouse of information, pictures, ideas, and notices of things to buy.

Ma·gel·lan (mə jel′ən), *n.* **1 Ferdinand,** 1480?-1521, Portuguese explorer. Although he was killed soon after he had explored the Philippine Islands, his ship was the first to sail around the world. **2 Strait of,** strait at the S tip of South America.

ma·gen·ta (mə jen′tə), **1** *n.* a purplish red dye. **2** *adj.* purplish red. **3** *n.* a purplish red. ❑ *n., pl.* **ma·gen·tas.**

WORD STORY **Magenta** comes from the name of a town in Italy. France won a battle there in 1859. A bloody battle was fought there just before the dye, which looks like blood, was discovered.

mag·got (mag′ət), *n.* the wormlike larva of various kinds of flies. Maggots usually live in decaying matter.

Ma·gi (mā′jī), *n.pl.* (in the Bible) the Three Wise Men, who followed the star to Bethlehem and brought gifts to the infant Jesus. ❑ *n., sing.* **Ma·gus.**

mag·ic (maj′ik), **1** *n.* the pretended art of using secret words, acts, or objects to make unnatural things happen: *The fairy's magic changed the brothers into swans.* **2** *n.* art or skill of creating illusions, especially by sleight of hand. **3** *adj.* done by magic or as if by magic: *A magic palace stood in place of their hut.* **4** *n.* something that produces results as if by magic; mysterious influence; unexplained power: *the magic of music.*

mag·i·cal (maj′ə kəl), *adj.* done by magic or as if by magic: *a magical effect.* —**mag′i·cal·ly,** *adv.*

ma·gi·cian (mə jish′ən), *n.* **1** (in stories) person skilled in the use of magic: *The wicked magician cast a spell over the princess.* **2** person who entertains by magic tricks: *The magician pulled not one, but three rabbits out of his hat!*

Magic Marker, trademark for a marking and drawing pen with a broad felt tip.

mag·is·te·ri·al (maj′ə stir′ē əl), *adj.* **1** of or suited to a magistrate: *A judge has magisterial rank.* **2** showing authority: *The principal spoke with a magisterial voice.* **3** domineering; overbearing: *He paced up and down with a magisterial stride.* —**mag′is·ter′i·al·ly,** *adv.*

mag·is·trate (maj′ə strāt), *n.* **1** a government official who has power to apply the law and put it in force. **2** judge in a minor court. A justice of the peace is a magistrate.

mag·lev (mag′lev), *n.* a high-speed railroad system in which magnetic force lifts a train a small distance above a rail and propels it forward.

maglev

mag·ma (mag′mə), *n.* the very hot, melted rock beneath the earth's crust from which igneous rock is formed.

WORD STORY **Magma** comes from a Greek word meaning "to squeeze in the hands." Magma oozes and spreads as dough or clay does if you squeeze it.

Mag·na Car·ta or **Mag·na Char·ta** (mag′nə kär′tə), the great charter which the English barons forcibly secured from King John in 1215. The Magna Charta provided a basis for guaranteeing the personal and political liberties of the people of England, and placed the king under the rule of the law.

mag·nan·i·mous (mag nan′ə məs), *adj.* noble in soul or mind; generous in forgiving; free from mean feelings or acts: *She has a magnanimous attitude toward her children when they misbehave.* —**mag·nan′i·mous·ly,** *adv.*

mag·nate (mag′nāt), *n.* an important, powerful, or prominent person: *The shipping magnate owned many freighters.*

mag·ne·sia (mag nē′zhə), *n.* a white, tasteless powder, used in medicine as an antacid and a laxative, and in industry in making fertilizers and heat-resistant building materials. It is a compound of magnesium and oxygen.

mag·ne·si·um (mag nē′zē əm), *n.* a light, silver-white metallic element that burns with a dazzling white light. Magnesium is used in magnesia, fireworks, and metal alloys that form strong, lightweight parts for cars and spacecraft. *Symbol:* Mg

mag·net (mag′nit), *n.* **1** piece of metal or ore that attracts iron or steel. A lodestone is a natural magnet. **2** anything that attracts: *On hot days the swimming pool was a magnet for neighborhood children.*

a	hat	ė	term	ô	order	ch	child		
ā	age	i	it	oi	oil	ng	long	⎧	a in about
ä	far	ī	ice	ou	out	sh	she	⎪	e in taken
â	care	o	hot	u	cup	th	thin	ə ⎨	i in pencil
e	let	ō	open	ù	put	₮H	then	⎪	o in lemon
ē	equal	ò	saw	ü	rule	zh	measure	⎩	u in circus

mag·net·ic (mag net′ik), *adj.* **1** of a magnet; that is a magnet: *the magnetic needle of a compass.* **2** of or producing magnetism: *a magnetic circuit.* **3** of or about the earth's magnetism: *a magnetic pole.* **4** able to be magnetized or attracted by a magnet: *magnetic nickel.* **5** very attractive: *He has a magnetic personality.* —**mag·net′i·cal·ly,** *adv.*

magnetic field, space around a magnet or electric current in which its magnetic force is felt.

magnetic needle, a slender bar of magnetized steel used as a compass. When it can turn easily, it points approximately north and south, toward the earth's magnetic poles.

magnetic north, the northerly direction shown by the needle of a compass.

magnetic pole, 1 one of the two poles of a magnet. **2** one of the two places on the earth's surface toward which a compass needle points. The **North Magnetic Pole** is in the Arctic; the **South Magnetic Pole** is in Antarctica.

magnetic resonance imaging, the use of a device that produces images by placing the subjects in controlled magnetic fields. In medicine, this method allows doctors to see tissues inside the body without the use of X rays.

magnetic south, the southerly direction shown by the needle of a compass.

magnetic tape, plastic tape, coated with magnetic iron oxide or a similar substance, on which sounds, images, or data can be recorded.

mag·net·ism (mag′nə tiz′əm), *n.* **1** the kind of force that magnets have: *the magnetism of iron and steel.* **2** branch of physics dealing with magnets and magnetic effects. **3** power to attract or charm: *A person with magnetism has many friends and admirers.*

mag·net·ite (mag′nə tit), *n.* an important iron ore that is strongly attracted by a magnet.

mag·net·ize (mag′nə tīz), *v.* **1** to give magnetic force to: *You can magnetize a needle by rubbing it with a magnet.* **2** to attract or influence someone: *Her stirring speech magnetized the audience.* ❑ *v.* **mag·net·ized, mag·net·iz·ing.** —**mag′net·i·za′tion,** *n.*

mag·net·o (mag nē′tō), *n.* a small electric generator that uses a magnetic field to produce an electric current. In some internal-combustion engines, a magneto supplies an electric spark to explode the gasoline vapor. ❑ *n., pl.* **mag·ne·tos.**

magnet school, school with special programs in certain subjects, that are designed to attract students from all parts of a city or district.

mag·nif·i·cence (mag nif′ə səns), *n.* richness of material, color, and ornament; grand beauty; splendor: *We were dazzled by the magnificence of the mountain scenery.*

mag·nif·i·cent (mag nif′ə sənt), *adj.* splendid; richly handsome; grand; stately: *a magnificent palace, a magnificent view of the mountains.* ■ See Synonym Study at **grand.** —**mag·nif′i·cent·ly,** *adv.*

mag·ni·fi·er (mag′nə fī′ər), *n.* **1** someone or something that magnifies. **2** magnifying glass.

mag·ni·fy (mag′nə fī), *v.* **1** to cause something to look larger than it actually is; increase the apparent size of an object: *A microscope magnifies bacteria so that they can be seen and studied.* **2** to make too much of; go beyond the truth in telling: *Was the fish really that big, or are you magnifying its size?* ❑ *v.* **mag·ni·fied, mag·ni·fy·ing.** —**mag′ni·fi·ca′tion,** *n.*

magnifying glass, lens or combination of lenses that causes things to look larger than they really are.

mag·ni·tude (mag′nə tüd), *n.* **1** greatness of size: *The magnitude of destruction caused by the hurricane had to be seen to be believed.* **2** great importance or effect: *The war brought problems of immense magnitude to many nations.* **3** measure of brightness of a star. Stars of the first magnitude are the brightest.

mag·nol·ia (mag nō′lyə), *n.* any of numerous trees or bushes of the Americas and Asia, with large white, yellow, pink, or purplish flowers. ❑ *n., pl.* **mag·nol·ias.**

mag·pie (mag′pī), *n.* **1** either of two related North American, European, and Asian black and white birds that chatter a great deal. Magpies have long tails and short wings and are related to the jays. **2** person who chatters.

Ma·gritte (mə grēt′), *n.* **Re·né** (rə nā′), 1898-1967, Belgian painter. His surreal paintings often contain everyday items painted very realistically.

mag·uey (mag′wā), *n.* **1** any of several desert plants with fleshy leaves, found especially in Mexico. **2** fiber obtained from any of these plants, used for making rope. ❑ *n., pl.* **mag·ueys.**

Ma·gus (mā′gəs), *n.* one of the Magi. ❑ *n., pl.* **Ma·gi.**

Mag·yar (mag′yär), **1** *n.* member of the chief group of people living in Hungary. **2** *n.* their language; Hungarian. **3** *adj.* of or about the Magyars or their language.

Ma·ha·bha·ra·ta (mə hä′bär′ə tə), *n.* a Hindu epic poem and religious text telling the story of a long civil war. The Bhagavad-Gita is part of it.

ma·ha·ra·ja (mä′hə rä′jə), *n.* formerly, a ruling prince in India, especially one who ruled a state. ❑ *n., pl.* **ma·ha·ra·jas.**

ma·ha·ra·jah (mä′hə rä′jə), *n.* maharaja.

ma·ha·ra·nee (mä′hə rä′nē), *n.* **1** wife of a maharaja. **2** formerly, a ruling princess in India, especially one who ruled a state. ❑ *n., pl.* **ma·ha·ra·nees.**

ma·ha·ra·ni (mä′hə rä′nē), *n.* maharanee. ❑ *n., pl.* **ma·ha·ra·nis.**

ma·hat·ma (mə hät′mə), *n.* a wise and holy person, especially in India. ❑ *n., pl.* **ma·hat·mas.**

Mah·fouz (mä füz′), *n.* **Na·guib** (nä′gēb), born 1911, Egyptian writer. He was the first writer in Arabic to receive the Nobel Prize for literature, in 1988. His works include *The Beggar* and *Miramar.*

Ma·hi·can (mə hē′kən), *n.* member of a tribe of American Indians formerly living in the Hudson River valley, now mostly living in Wisconsin. ❑ *n., pl.* **Ma·hi·can** or **Ma·hi·cans.** Also, **Mohican.** ■ See Usage Note at **Mohican.**

mah·jongg or **mah·jong** (mä′jong′), *n.* game of Chinese origin played by four people with many small tiles resembling dominoes. Each player tries to form winning combinations by drawing or discarding.

Mah·ler (mä′lər), *n.* **Gus·tav** (gùs′täv), 1860-1911, Austrian composer and conductor. He composed nine complete symphonies and many songs. His music is philosophical and often tragic.

ma·hog·a·ny (mə hog′ə nē), **1** *n.* any of several large tropical American and African trees that yield a hard, reddish brown wood. **2** *n.* their wood, used in making furniture. **3** *n.* any of several Philippine trees valued for a similar wood. **4** *adj.* dark reddish brown. **5** *n.* a dark reddish brown.

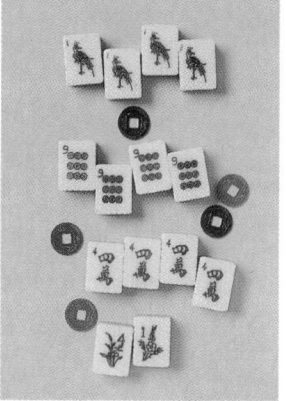

mah-jongg

ma·hout (mə hout′), *n.* (in the East Indies) the keeper and driver of an elephant.

maid (mād), *n.* **1** a girl or young woman who has not married. **2** a woman servant. ■ Another word that sounds like this is **made.**

maid·en (mād′n), **1** *n.* a girl or young woman who has not married; maid. **2** *adj.* of a maiden: *maiden grace.* **3** *adj.* never married: *a maiden aunt.* **4** *adj.* first: *a ship's maiden voyage, the senator's maiden speech in the Senate.*

maid·en·hair (mād′n hâr′), *n.* any of several ferns with very slender stalks and delicate, finely divided fronds.

maid·en·hood (mād′n hùd), *n.* condition or time of being a maiden.

maid·en·ly (mād′n lē), *adj.* of, like, or suited to a maiden. —**maid′en·li·ness,** *n.*

maiden name, a woman's last name before marriage.

maid of honor, 1 an unmarried woman who accompanies the bride and stands with her at a wedding. **2** an unmarried noble lady who attends a queen or princess. ❑ *n., pl.* **maids of honor.**

maid·serv·ant (mād′sėr′vənt), *n.* a woman servant.

mail[1] (māl), **1** *n.* letters, postcards, magazines, packages, etc., to be sent by a postal service. **2** *n.* system by which such mail is sent, managed by the postal service: *You can pay most bills by* *mail.* **3** *n.* all that comes by one post or delivery: *Has the mail come yet?* **4** *v.* to send by mail; put in a mailbox: *Should I mail that letter for you?* **5** *n.* e-mail. **6** *adj.* of or for mail. ∎ Another word that sounds like this is **male.** —**mail′a·ble,** *adj.*

mail² (māl), *n.* a flexible armor made of metal rings or small loops of chain linked together, or of overlapping plates, for protecting the body against arrows, spears, etc. ∎ Another word that sounds like this is **male.**

mail·box (māl′boks′), *n.* **1** a public box from which mail is collected. **2** a private box at your home or business to which mail is delivered. ❏ *n., pl.* **mail·box·es.**

mail carrier, person who carries or delivers mail; mailman; postman.

Mail·gram (māl′gram), *n.* **1** trademark for a speedy electronic message service which transmits a message to a local post office for regular mail delivery on the next business day. **2** a message sent by this service.

mail·ing list (mā′ling), a list of names and addresses used to send out advertising or other mail: *Somehow my name got on the mailing list for this catalog.*

mail·man (māl′man′), *n.* mail carrier. ❏ *n., pl.* **mail·men.**

mail order, order for goods sent by mail.

maim (mām), *v.* to cut off or make useless an arm, leg, ear, etc.; disable: *His foot was maimed in the accident.*

main (mān), **1** *adj.* most important; largest: *the main dish at dinner, the main street of town.* **2** *n.* a large pipe or conductor which carries water, gas, sewage, or electricity to or from smaller branches: *the water main, a gas main.* **3** *n.* OLD USE. the open sea; ocean. **4** *adj.* exerted to the utmost; full; sheer: *I moved the piano by main strength.* ∎ Another word that sounds like this is **mane.**
in the main, for the most part; chiefly; mostly: *Her grades are excellent in the main.*

main clause, independent clause.

Maine (mān), *n.* one of the northeastern states of the United States. *Abbreviation:* ME or Me. *Capital:* Augusta. —**Main′er,** *n.*

main·frame (mān′frām′), *n.* a large computer, not portable, needing a cabinet to hold it.

main·land (mān′land′ *or* mān′lənd), *n.* the main part of a continent or country, apart from islands or small peninsulas along the shores.

main·line (mān′līn′), *v.* SLANG. to inject a drug, especially heroin, into a vein. ❏ *v.* **main·lined, main·lin·ing.** —**main′lin′er,** *n.*

main·ly (mān′lē), *adv.* for the most part; chiefly; mostly: *Our garden is mainly vegetables.*

main·mast (mān′mast′ *or* mān′məst), *n.* the principal mast of a ship.

main·sail (mān′sāl′ *or* mān′səl), *n.* the largest sail of a ship on the mainmast.

main·spring (mān′spring′), *n.* **1** the principal spring in a clock or watch that is wound. **2** the main cause, motive, or influence.

main·stay (mān′stā′), *n.* **1** main support: *Loyal friends are a person's mainstay in time of trouble.* **2** rope or wire supporting the mainmast.

main·stream (mān′strēm′), **1** *n.* a main course or direction in the development of an idea, institution, etc. **2** *v.* to put disabled students in regular school classes.

main·tain (mān tān′), *v.* **1** to keep; keep up; carry on: *You must maintain your footing in a tug-of-war.* **2** to provide for; support: *They could not maintain their family in comfort on such a small*

income. **3** to uphold or defend: *The troops maintained their position under heavy fire.* **4** to keep supplied, equipped, or in repair: *The company employs people to maintain the machinery.* **5** to declare to be true: *He maintains that he is innocent.* **6** to affirm; assert against opposition: *He maintains his innocence.* [**Maintain** comes from Latin words meaning "to hold in the hand." Maintaining something carefully is like carrying it around with you.] —**main·tain′a·ble,** *adj.*

main·tain·er (mān tā′nər), *n.* a metal dental device used to maintain the position of teeth after straightening them with braces.

main·te·nance (mān′tə nəns), *n.* **1** act or process of keeping in good repair. **2** condition of being maintained; support: *A government collects taxes to pay for its maintenance.* **3** enough to support life; means of living: *Their small farm barely provides a maintenance.* **4** act or process of maintaining: *Maintenance of quiet is necessary in a hospital.*

main·top (mān′top′), *n.* platform on the mainmast.

maize (māz), *n.* **1** corn; Indian corn. **2** the color of ripe corn; yellow. ∎ Another word that sounds like this is **maze.**

Maj., Major.

ma·jes·tic (mə jes′tik), *adj.* of or having majesty; impressive; grand; noble; dignified; stately: *Majestic mountains towered above us.* ∎ See Synonym Study at **grand.** —**ma·jes′ti·cal·ly,** *adv.*

majestic

maj·es·ty (maj′ə stē), *n.* **1** royal dignity; stately appearance; nobility: *the majesty of the starry heavens, the great majesty of the Grand Canyon.* **2** supreme power or authority: *Judges uphold the majesty of the law.* **3** **Majesty,** title used in speaking to or of a king, queen, emperor, empress, etc.: *Your Majesty, His Majesty, Her Majesty.* ❏ *n., pl.* **Maj·es·ties** for 3.

ma·jor (mā′jər), **1** *adj.* more important; larger; greater: *Take the major share of the profits.* ∎ See Synonym Studies at **main** and **important.** **2** *n.* a military rank. See chart on page 712. **3** in music: **a** *adj.* greater by a half step than the corresponding minor interval: *a major chord.* **b** *adj.* noting a scale or key having half steps after the third and seventh tones: *the C major scale or key.* **c** *n.* a major scale, key, chord, interval, etc. **4** *n.* subject or course of study to which a student gives most time and attention: *Her major is mathematics.* **5** *v.* to have or take as a major subject of study: *to major in mathematics.* **6** *adj.* INFORMAL. real; important: *He's a major bore. This is a major opportunity for me.* [See word history information at **mayor.**]

Ma·jor (mā′jər), *n.* **John,** born 1943, British political leader, prime minister of Great Britain since 1990.

ma·jor-do·mo *or* **ma·jor·do·mo** (mā′jər dō′mō), *n.* **1** person in charge of a royal or noble household. **2** butler; steward. ❏ *n., pl.* **ma·jor-do·mos** *or* **ma·jor·do·mos.**

ma·jor·ette (mā′jə ret′), *n.* drum majorette.

major general, a military rank. See chart on page 712.

a	hat	ė	term	ô	order	ch	child		
ā	age	i	it	oi	oil	ng	long	∂	a in about
ä	far	ī	ice	ou	out	sh	she		e in taken
â	care	o	hot	u	cup	th	thin		i in pencil
e	let	ō	open	ü	put	ŦH	then		o in lemon
ē	equal	ô	saw	ü	rule	zh	measure		u in circus

ma·jor·i·ty (mə jôr′ə tē), *n.* **1** the larger number or part; more than half: *A majority of the children chose red covers for the books they had made.* **2** the number by which the votes on one side are more than those on the other: *He had 18 votes, and she had 12; so he had a majority of 6.* **3** the legal age of responsibility. Under the varying laws of the states of the United States, a person reaches his or her majority at the age of 18 in some states, at 21 in others. ❑ *n., pl.* **ma·jor·i·ties** for 2.

major league, either of the two chief leagues in American professional baseball (National League and American League), the National Basketball Association, and the National Hockey League.

ma·jor-league (mā′jər lēg′), *adj.* **1** of or about a major league or the major leagues. **2** first-class; of the highest quality: *a major-league law firm.*

major scale, a musical scale containing eight notes, with half steps instead of whole steps after the third and seventh notes.

Ma·ju·ro (mə jur′ō), *n.* capital of the Marshall Islands.

make (māk), **1** *v.* to bring into being; put together; build; form; shape: *make a new coat, make a fire, make jelly.* **2** *n.* way in which a thing is made; style; build; character: *Do you like the make of that coat?* **3** *n.* kind; brand: *What make of car is this?* **4** *v.* to have the qualities needed for: *Wood makes a good fire.* **5** *v.* to cause; bring about: *make trouble, make a noise, make peace.* **6** *v.* to cause to; force to: *We made them go home.* **7** *v.* to cause to be or become; cause yourself to be: *make a room warm, make a fool of yourself.* **8** *v.* to turn out to be; become: *He will make a good legislator.* **9** *v.* to get ready for use; arrange: *I make my own bed.* **10** *v.* to get; obtain; acquire; earn: *make a fortune, make your living.* **11** *v.* to do; perform: *make a speech, make an attempt, make a mistake.* **12** *v.* to amount to; add up to; count as: *Two and two make four.* **13** *v.* to think of as; figure to be: *I make the distance across the room 15 feet.* **14** *v.* to reach; arrive at: *The ship made port.* **15** *v.* to go; travel: *The caravan made 20 miles a day.* **16** *v.* to cause the success of: *One successful book made the young author.* **17** *v.* to get on; get a place on: *She made the tennis team.* ❑ *v.* **made, mak·ing.** —**mak′a·ble** or **make′a·ble,** *adj.*

make after, to follow; chase; pursue.

make away with, 1 to get rid of. **2** to kill. **3** to steal: *The treasurer made away with the club's funds.*

make believe, to pretend: *She liked to make believe she was a pilot.*

make fast, to attach firmly.

make for, 1 to go toward: *Make for the hills!* **2** to help bring about; favor: *New facts made for the prisoner's release.*

make it, to succeed.

make off, to leave suddenly.

make off with, to steal: *They made off with our car.*

make out, 1 to write out: *I made out a shopping list.* **2** to show to be; try to prove: *That makes me out most selfish.* **3** to understand: *The boy had a hard time making out the problem.* **4** to see with difficulty: *I can barely make out three ships near the horizon.* **5** to get along; manage: *We must try to make out with what we have.*

make over, 1 to alter; make different: *I had to make over my costume because it was too big.* **2** to hand over; transfer ownership of: *Grandfather made over the farm to my mother last year.*

make up, 1 to put together: *make up cloth into a shirt.* **2** to invent: *make up a story.* **3** to settle a dispute; reconcile: *make up your differences.* **4** to give or do in place of: *I took a shortcut to make up for lost time.* **5** to become friends again after a quarrel: *We were always fighting and then making up.* **6** to put rouge, lipstick, powder, etc., on the face. **7** to arrange type, pictures, etc., in the pages of a book, paper, or magazine: *make up a page of type.* **8** to compose; constitute: *Children made up the audience.* **9** to do work missed or take a test or an examination missed at a later time. **10** to take a failed test, course, etc., again.

make up to, to try to get the friendship of; flatter: *We all made up to the new boy the first day.*

make-be·lieve (māk′bi lēv′), **1** *n.* pretense: *Elves live in the land of make-believe.* **2** *adj.* pretended: *Some children have make-believe playmates.*

mak·er (mā′kər), *n.* **1** person or thing that makes; manufacturer. **2 Maker,** God.

make·shift (māk′shift′), **1** *n.* something used for a time instead of the right thing; temporary substitute: *When the lights went out, we used candles as a makeshift.* **2** *adj.* used for a time instead of the right thing: *makeshift awnings.*

make·up or **make-up** (māk′up′), *n.* **1** way of being put together: *The makeup of the class includes children from different parts of the town.* **2** nature; disposition: *a nervous makeup.* **3** way in which an actor is dressed and painted to look the part. **4** rouge, lipstick, powder, etc., put on the face; cosmetics. **5** special examination taken by a student who has missed or failed the original one. **6** arrangement of type, pictures, etc., in a book, paper, or magazine.

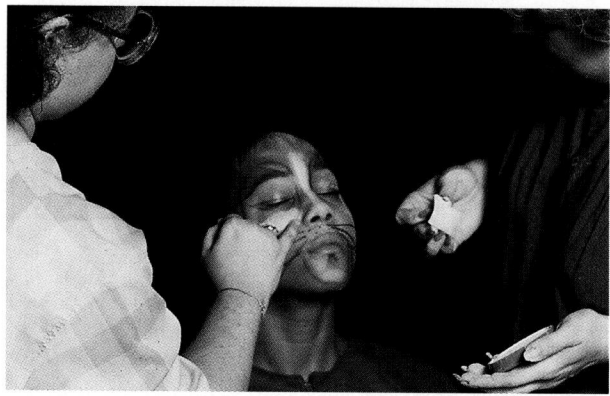

makeup (def. 4)

mak·ings (mā′kingz), *n.pl.* **the makings, a** qualities or potential for becoming something: *She has the makings of a fine basketball player.* **b** parts or ingredients necessary for making something: *Do we have the makings for tacos?*

mal-, *prefix.* bad or badly; poor or poorly: *maladjusted = badly adjusted.*

Mal·a·bo (mal′ə bō), *n.* capital of Equatorial Guinea.

Mal·a·chi (mal′ə kī), *n.* **1** Hebrew prophet. **2** book of the Bible. [**Malachi** comes from Hebrew words meaning "my messenger."]

mal·a·chite (mal′ə kīt), *n.* a green mineral that is an ore of copper and is used for ornamental items and carvings.

mal·ad·just·ed (mal′ə jus′tid), *adj.* badly adjusted; not in a healthy relation with your environment.

mal·ad·just·ment (mal′ə just′mənt), *n.* a bad adjustment.

mal·a·droit (mal′ə droit′), *adj.* unskillful; awkward; clumsy. —**mal′a·droit′ly,** *adv.* —**mal′a·droit′ness,** *n.*

mal·a·dy (mal′ə dē), *n.* **1** any bodily disorder or disease: *Cancer and malaria are serious maladies.* **2** any unwholesome or disordered condition: *Poverty and slums are social maladies.* ❑ *n., pl.* **mal·a·dies.**

Mál·a·ga (mal′ə gə), *n.* province in S Spain.

ma·laise (ma lāz′), *n.* **1** a vague feeling of sickness. **2** an uneasy, disturbed, or disordered condition: *a country gripped by political malaise.*

mal·a·mute (mal′ə myüt), *n.* Alaskan malamute. Also, **malemute.**

mal·a·prop·ism (mal′ə prop′iz′əm), *n.* **1** ridiculous misuse of words, especially a confusion of two words that are similar in sound but different in meaning. **2** an example of this kind of misuse of words. Malapropisms are often used to be funny: *Irrelevant never forgets.*

ma·lar·i·a (mə lâr′ē ə), *n.* disease with symptoms of periodic chills, fever, and sweating. Malaria is caused by tiny one-celled animals in the blood and is transmitted by the bite of certain mosquitoes which have bitten infected persons. [**Malaria** comes from two Italian words meaning "bad air." In old times, people thought that the disease was caused by polluted air.] —**ma·lar′i·al,** *adj.*

Ma·la·wi (mə lä′wē), *n.* country in SE Africa. *Capital:* Lilongwe. —**Ma·la′wi·an,** *adj., n.*

Ma·lay (mā′lā), **1** *n.* member of the people of the Malay Peninsula and nearby islands. **2** *n.* their language. **3** *adj.* of the Malays or their language.

Ma·lay·a (mə lā′ə), *n.* **1** Malay Peninsula. **2** former country on the Malay Peninsula, now part of Malaysia.

Ma·lay·an (mə lā′ən), *n., adj.* Malay.

Malay Archipelago, group of islands between SE Asia and Australia; East Indies; Indonesia.

Malay Peninsula, peninsula in SE Asia, north of Sumatra; Malaya.

Ma·lay·sia (mə lā′zhə), *n.* country consisting of Sabah, Sarawak, Malaya, and many small islands of the Malay Archipelago. *Capital:* Kuala Lumpur. —**Ma·lay′sian,** *adj., n.*

Mal·colm X (mal′kəm eks′), 1925-1965, African American Islamic leader. ■ **Malcolm X** worked to unite African Americans and people of African descent throughout the world. He was assassinated in New York City in 1965.

mal·con·tent (mal′kən tent′), **1** *adj.* discontented; rebellious. **2** *n.* a discontented person; rebellious person.

Mal·dive Islands (mal′dīv), group of islands in the Indian Ocean.

Mal·dives (mal′dīvz), *n.* **the,** country in the Indian Ocean southwest of Ceylon, consisting of the Maldive Islands. *Capital:* Malé.

male (māl), **1** *n.* man or boy. **2** *adj.* of men or boys. **3** *adj.* belonging to the sex that can fertilize eggs and father young. Bucks, bulls, and roosters are male animals. **4** *n.* animal belonging to this sex. **5** *adj.* (of a plant) having stamens but not pistils. **6** *n.* plant bearing flowers only with stamens. ■ Another word that sounds like this is **mail.** —**male′ness,** *n.*

Ma·lé or **Ma·le** (mä′lā), *n.* capital of the Maldives.

mal·e·dic·tion (mal′ə dik′shən), *n.* a curse.

mal·e·fac·tor (mal′ə fak′tər), *n.* a criminal; evildoer.

mal·e·mute (mal′ə myüt), *n.* Alaskan malamute. Also, **malamute.**

ma·lev·o·lence (mə lev′ə ləns), *n.* the wish that evil may happen to others; ill will; spite.

ma·lev·o·lent (mə lev′ə lənt), *adj.* wishing evil to happen to others; showing ill will; spiteful. —**ma·lev′o·lent·ly,** *adv.*

mal·fea·sance (mal fē′zns), *n.* official misconduct; violation of a public trust or duty: *A judge who accepts a bribe is guilty of malfeasance.*

mal·for·ma·tion (mal′fôr mā′shən), *n.* lack of proper shape or complete development in a body part: *The duck walks everywhere because it was born with a malformation in one wing.*

mal·formed (mal fôrmd′), *adj.* badly formed; having an abnormal form: *a malformed toe.*

mal·func·tion (mal′fungk′shən), **1** *n.* an improper functioning; failure to work or perform: *a malfunction in a machine.* **2** *v.* to function badly; work or perform improperly.

Ma·li (mä′lē), *n.* country in W Africa, site of the historic Mali Empire. *Capital:* Bamako. [**Mali** comes from a word in a language of its people meaning "hippopotamus," a symbol there of power.] —**Ma′li·an,** *adj., n.*

Mali Empire (1235–1468)

TUAREG
N
Senegal R.
MALI EMPIRE
Niger R.
SONGHAI
MOSSI
ATLANTIC OCEAN

mal·ice (mal′is), *n.* a wish to hurt or make suffer; spite: *His mistake was genuine, not caused by malice.*

ma·li·cious (mə lish′əs), *adj.* wishing to hurt or make suffer; spiteful: *That story is malicious gossip.* —**ma·li′cious·ly,** *adv.* —**ma·li′cious·ness,** *n.*

ma·lign (mə līn′), **1** *v.* to speak evil of; slander: *You malign an honest person when you call that person a liar.* **2** *adj.* evil; injur-

ious: *Gambling can have a malign influence.* **3** *adj.* hateful; malicious. —**ma·lign′er,** *n.* —**ma·lign′ly,** *adv.*

ma·lig·nan·cy (mə lig′nən sē), *n.* **1** malignant quality or tendency. **2** something malignant, as a tumor. ❑ *n., pl.* **ma·lig·nan·cies** for 2.

ma·lig·nant (mə lig′nənt), *adj.* **1** very evil, hateful, or malicious. **2** very harmful or dangerous; able to cause death: *A cancer is a malignant growth.* —**ma·lig′nant·ly,** *adv.*

ma·lig·ni·ty (mə lig′nə tē), *n.* **1** great malice; extreme hate or ill will. **2** great harmfulness; dangerous quality; deadliness.

ma·lin·ger (mə ling′gər), *v.* to pretend to be sick in order to escape work or duty; shirk. —**ma·lin′ger·er,** *n.*

mall (môl), *n.* **1** shopping center with stores, shops, restaurants, etc., that open onto a wide walking area or passageway. **2** a central walk in a shopping center. **3** a shaded walk; public walk or promenade. ■ Another word that sounds like this is **maul.**

mal·lard (mal′ərd), *n.* a wild duck of Europe, northern Asia, and North America. The male has a greenish black head and a white band around its neck. ❑ *n., pl.* **mal·lard** or **mal·lards.**

mal·le·a·ble (mal′ē ə bəl), *adj.* **1** able to be hammered, rolled, or extended into various shapes without being broken. Gold, silver, copper, and tin are malleable; they can be beaten into thin sheets. **2** adaptable; yielding: *A malleable person can adjust to changed plans.* —**mal′le·a·bil′i·ty, —mal′le·a·ble·ness,** *n.*

mal·let (mal′it), *n.* a hammer with a large head. Wooden mallets with long handles are used to play croquet and polo. Rubber mallets are used to pound out dents in metal.

mallet

mal·low (mal′ō), *n.* any of many plants with purple, pink, or white five-petaled flowers, hairy leaves and stems, and sticky sap.

mal·nour·ished (mal nėr′isht), *adj.* improperly nourished: *The stray cat looked malnourished.*

mal·nu·tri·tion (mal′nü trish′ən), *n.* a poorly nourished condition. People suffer from malnutrition because of eating wrong kinds of food as well as from lack of food.

mal·oc·clu·sion (mal′ə klü′zhən), *n.* failure of the upper and lower teeth to meet properly.

mal·o·dor·ous (mal ō′dər əs), *adj.* smelling bad. —**mal·o′dor·ous·ly,** *adv.* —**mal·o′dor·ous·ness,** *n.*

mal·prac·tice (mal prak′tis), *n.* **1** criminal neglect or unprofessional treatment of a patient by a doctor. **2** improper practice or conduct in any official or professional position; misconduct.

malt (môlt), *n.* **1** barley or other grain soaked in water until it sprouts, and then dried and aged. Malt has a sweet taste and is used in making beer and ale. **2** malted milk.

Mal·ta (môl′tə), *n.* **1** island in the Mediterranean, south of Sicily. **2** country including Malta and smaller islands nearby. *Capital:* Valletta. [**Malta** comes from a Phoenician word meaning "shelter." Phoenician sailors took shelter from storms at Malta about 3000 years ago.]

malt·ed (môl′tid), *n.* malted milk.

malted milk, drink prepared by mixing a powder made of dried milk, malted barley, and wheat flour with milk, flavoring, and often ice cream.

Mal·tese (môl tēz′), **1** *n.* person born or living in Malta. **2** *n.* language of Malta. **3** *adj.* of or about Malta, its people, or their language. **4** *n.* a small dog with a long, silky white coat. ❑ *n., pl.* **Mal·tese** for 1,4.

M

a	hat	ė	term	ô	order	ch	child		
ā	age	i	it	oi	oil	ng	long	ə	a in about
ä	far	ī	ice	ou	out	sh	she		e in taken
â	care	o	hot	u	cup	th	thin		i in pencil
e	let	ō	open	ù	put	ŦH	then		o in lemon
ē	equal	ò	saw	ü	rule	zh	measure		u in circus

Maltese cat, a short-haired, bluish gray pet cat.

Maltese cross, a cross with four equal arms resembling arrowheads pointed toward the center.

malt extract, a sugary substance obtained by soaking malt in water.

mal·tose (mȯl′tōs), *n.* a white, crystalline sugar made by the action of various enzymes on starch; malt sugar. It is formed in the body during digestion and is also used in making beer, ale, etc.

mal·treat (mal trēt′), *v.* to treat roughly or cruelly; abuse: *maltreat animals, maltreat a fine car.* **—mal·treat′ment,** *n.*

malt sugar, maltose.

ma·ma (mä′mə), *n.* mother. ❑ *n., pl.* **ma·mas.**

mam·ba (mam′bə), *n.* any of a group of poisonous snakes of Africa. Mambas are related to the cobra but do not have hoods. ❑ *n., pl.* **mam·bas.**

mam·bo (mäm′bō), **1** *n.* a ballroom dance of Caribbean origin, similar to the rumba. **2** *n.* music for this dance. **3** *v.* to dance the mambo. ❑ *n., pl.* **mam·bos;** *v.* **mam·boed, mam·bo·ing.**

mam·ma (mä′mə), *n.* mother. ❑ *n., pl.* **mam·mas.**

mam·mal (mam′əl), *n.* any of a great many warm-blooded animals with a backbone and usually with hair. Female mammals bear live young and secrete milk from mammary glands to nourish them. Human beings, horses, dogs, lions, bats, and whales are all mammals. **—mam·ma·li·an** (ma mā′lē ən), *adj.*

mam·mar·y gland (mam′ər ē), gland in the breast of mammals, enlarged in females and capable of producing milk.

mam·mo·gram (mam′ə gram), *n.* an X-ray picture of a woman's breast, taken to find tumors.

mam·mon or **Mam·mon** (mam′ən), *n.* riches thought of as an evil; greed for wealth.

mam·moth (mam′əth), **1** *n.* any of several very large, extinct elephants with hairy skins and long, curved tusks. **2** *adj.* huge; gigantic: *a mammoth undertaking.*

Mammoth Cave National Park, a national park in central Kentucky, containing part of the world's longest known group of caves.

man (man), **1** *n.* an adult male person. When a boy grows up, he becomes a man. **2** *n.* human being; person: *No man can be certain of the future.* **3** *n.* the human race: *man's search for peace.* **4** *n.* a male follower, servant, or employee: *Robin Hood and his merry men.* **5** *n.* husband: *man and wife.* **6** *n.* one of the pieces used in games such as chess and checkers. **7** *v.* to supply with a crew: *We can man ten ships.* **8** *v.* to serve or operate; get ready to operate: *Man the guns.* ❑ *n., pl.* **men;** *v.* **manned, man·ning.**

as one man, with complete agreement.

be your own man, 1 be free to do as you please. **2** to have complete control of yourself.

to a man, without an exception; all: *We accepted the idea to a man.*

Man (man), *n.* **Isle of,** small island in the Irish Sea, west of N England. See **British Isles** for map.

-man, *suffix.* **1** man from a certain place: *Irishman = man from Ireland; Frenchman = man from France.* **2** person who deals with ___ or is part of ___: *fireman = person who deals with fire; policeman = person who is part of the police.*

Man., Manitoba.

man·a·cle (man′ə kəl), **1** *n.* Usually, **manacles,** *pl.* handcuffs. **2** *v.* to put manacles on: *to manacle a prisoner.* **3** *v.* to restrain; hamper. ❑ *v.* **man·a·cled, man·a·cling.**

man·age (man′ij), *v.* **1** to guide or handle with skill or authority; control; direct: *manage a business, manage a horse.* **2** to succeed in accomplishing; contrive; arrange: *I shall manage to keep warm.* **3** to get along: *manage on your allowance.* ❑ *v.* **man·aged, man·ag·ing.** **—man′age·a·ble,** *adj.*

SYNONYM STUDY **Manage, conduct,** and **direct** all mean to plan and guide what other people do. **Manage** suggests being in charge: *He manages the younger children after school.* **Conduct** suggests keeping things going: *She conducts her business from an office at home.* **Direct** suggests controlling things to get results: *The mayor directed the townspeople's efforts to block the flood.*

man·age·ment (man′ij mənt), *n.* **1** act or process of managing or handling; control; direction: *Bad management caused the bank's failure.* **2** people that manage a business or an institution: *a dispute between labor and management.*

man·ag·er (man′ə jər), *n.* someone who manages, especially someone who manages a business: *She is the manager of the department store.*

man·a·ger·i·al (man′ə jir′ē əl), *adj.* necessary for a manager: *managerial skills.* **—man′a·ger′i·al·ly,** *adv.*

Ma·na·gua (mə nä′gwə), *n.* capital of Nicaragua, in the W part.

Ma·na·ma (mə nä′mə), *n.* capital of Bahrain.

ma·ña·na (mä nyä′nä), *n., adv.* sometime; later on; eventually.

Ma·nas·sas (mə nas′əs), *n.* town in NE Virginia. Two Civil War battles were fought near here, along Bull Run, both resulting in Confederate victories.

man-at-arms (man′ət ärmz′), *n.* **1** soldier. **2** a heavily armed soldier on horseback. ❑ *n., pl.* **men-at-arms.**

man·a·tee (man′ə tē′), *n.* any of three large plant-eating water mammals with flippers and flat, oval tails; sea cow. Manatees live in warm, shallow water in the Americas and West Africa. ❑ *n., pl.* **man·a·tees.**

WORD STORY **Manatee** comes from a Caribbean Indian word meaning "a breast." Manatees are mammals and nurse their young with milk. This is very unusual for water animals.

Man·ches·ter (man′ches′tər), *n.* **1** a city in W England, important in textile manufacturing. **2** city in S New Hampshire.

Man·chu (man′chü), **1** *n.* member of a people living in Manchuria, who conquered China in 1644 and ruled it until 1911. **2** *n.* their language. **3** *adj.* of the Manchus, their country, or their language.

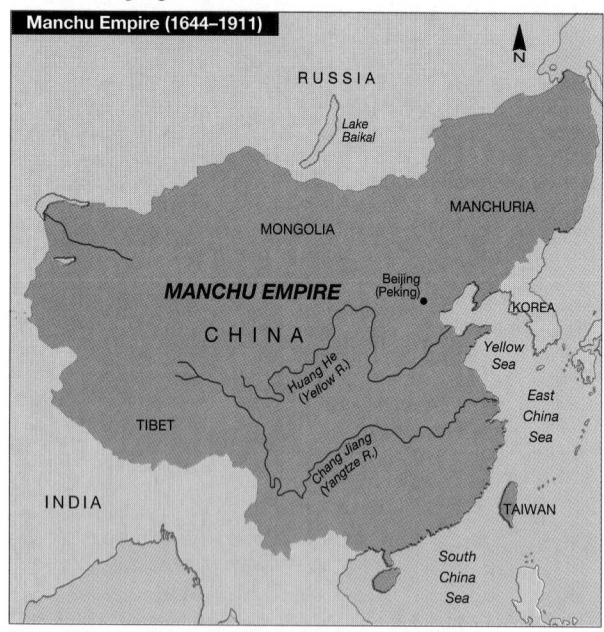

Manchu Empire (1644–1911)

Man·chur·i·a (man chúr′ē ə), *n.* region in NE China, including several provinces of China. **—Man·chur′i·an,** *adj., n.*

man·dar·in (man′dər ən), *n.* **1** an official of high rank in the Chinese empire. **2 Mandarin,** the dialect of Chinese spoken by officials and educated people. **3** a small, sweet, spicy citrus fruit with a very loose thin orange peel and segments that separate easily.

man·date (man′dāt), **1** *n.* the expressed will of voters to their representative. **2** *n.* an order or command, especially a legal order from a higher court or official to a lower one. **3** *n.* authority given to one nation by a group of nations to manage the government and affairs of a territory. **4** *v.* to put a territory under the management of another nation. **5** *n.* a mandated territory. ❏ *v.* **man·dat·ed, man·dat·ing.**

man·da·to·ry (man′də tôr′ē), *adj.* of or containing a command; commanded; required.

Man·del·a (man del′ə), *n.* **Nelson,** born 1918, South African reformer and political leader. He was imprisoned from 1962 to 1990. He became the president of South Africa in 1994.

man·di·ble (man′də bəl), *n.* **1** one of a pair of mouthparts in insects for seizing and biting: *The ant grasped the leaf with its mandibles.* **2** either part of a bird's beak. **3** a jaw, especially the lower jaw.

man·do·lin (man′də lin′ *or* man′dl ən), *n.* a musical instrument with a pear-shaped body and four to six pairs of metal strings. It is played with a pick.

man·drake (man′drāk), *n.* **1** either of two plants of southern Europe and Asia, related to the nightshade. A mandrake has a very short stem and a thick, often forked root thought to resemble the human form. Mandrake roots were formerly used in medicine. **2** May apple.

man·drill (man′drəl), *n.* a large monkey of western Africa, something like a baboon. The face of the male mandrill is marked with blue and scarlet.

mane (mān), *n.* the long, heavy hair growing on the back of the neck of a horse, or around the head of a male lion. ■ Another word that sounds like this is **main.**

man-eat·ing shark (man′ēt′ing), any shark that attacks or has been known to attack human beings, especially the great white shark.

Ma·net (mä nā′), *n.* **É·douard** (ā-dwär′), 1832-1883, French painter. He was one of the artists who helped create impressionism.

ma·neu·ver (mə nü′vər), **1** *n.* a planned movement of troops or warships: *Every year the army and navy hold maneuvers for practice.* **2** *v.* to perform or cause troops to perform maneuvers. **3** *n.* a skillful plan or movement; clever trick: *When we refused to use his idea, he tried to force it on us by a series of maneuvers.* **4** *v.* to plan skillfully; use clever tricks; scheme: *A scheming person is always maneuvering for some advantage.* **5** *v.* to force by skillful plans; get by clever tricks: *She maneuvered her lazy sister out of bed.* **6** *v.* to move or

Manet painting

handle skillfully: *I was able to maneuver the car through the heavy traffic with ease.* Also, **manoeuvre.** —**ma·neu′ver·a·bil′i·ty,** *n.* —**ma·neu′ver·a·ble,** *adj.* —**ma·neu′ver·er,** *n.*

man Friday, a faithful, efficient servant.

man·ful (man′fəl), *adj.* manly. —**man′ful·ly,** *adv.*

man·ga·nese (mang′gə nēz′), *n.* a hard, brittle, grayish white metallic element. Manganese is used in making alloys of steel, in paints, dyes, insecticides, and industrial chemicals. *Symbol:* Mn

mange (mānj), *n.* an itching skin disease of animals, causing scabs and loss of hair. It is caused by parasitic mites.

WORD STORY Mange and manger both come from a Latin word meaning "to chew." If an animal has mange, it bites itself to scratch the itch.

man·gel-wur·zel (mang′gəl wèr′zəl), *n.* a large, coarse variety of beet grown as food for cattle or other livestock.

man·ger (mān′jər), *n.* box or trough in which hay or other food can be placed for horses or cows to eat. [See Word Story at **mange.**]

man·gle[1] (mang′gəl), *v.* **1** to cut or tear roughly: *His hand was badly mangled when it was caught by some moving machinery.* **2** to spoil; ruin: *The song was too difficult for the children and they mangled it badly.* ❏ *v.* **man·gled, man·gling.** —**man′gler,** *n.*

man·gle[2] (mang′gəl), **1** *n.* machine with rollers for pressing and smoothing sheets, towels, and other flat things after washing. **2** *v.* to press or smooth in a mangle. ❏ *v.* **man·gled, man·gling.** —**man′gler,** *n.*

man·go (mang′gō), *n.* the slightly sour, juicy, oval fruit of a tropical tree. Mangoes have a thick, yellowish red rind and are eaten ripe or are pickled when green. ❏ *n., pl.* **man·goes** or **man·gos.**

man·grove (mang′grōv), *n.* any of several tropical trees or bushes with branches that send down many long roots that look like additional trunks. Mangroves grow in swamps and along riverbanks.

mang·y (mān′jē), *adj.* **1** having mange; caused by mange; with the hair falling out. **2** shabby and dirty: *a mangy dog, a mangy, smelly old blanket.* ❏ *adj.* **mang·i·er, mang·i·est.** —**mang′i·ly,** *adv.* —**mang′i·ness,** *n.*

man·han·dle (man′han′dl), *v.* to treat roughly; pull or push about. ❏ *v.* **man·han·dled, man·han·dling.**

Man·hat·tan (man hat′n), *n.* island on which the chief business section of New York City is located. It is a borough of New York City.

Manhattan Project, the scientific project organized by the U.S. government in 1942 to produce the first atomic bomb.

man·hole (man′hōl′), *n.* hole in a street with a removable metal cover. Through a manhole, a worker can enter a sewer, or a chamber that contains electrical wiring, water mains, or telephone lines, in order to repair them.

man·hood (man′hud), *n.* **1** condition or time of being a man: *The boy was about to enter manhood.* **2** character or qualities of a man. **3** men as a group: *the manhood of the United States.*

man·hour (man′our′), *n.* hour of work by one person, used as a unit of labor in industry to determine production time and cost: *Updating the index for that book will take 200 man-hours.*

man·hunt (man′hunt′), *n.* an organized hunt for a criminal, escaped prisoner, etc: *The manhunt for the escaped murderer lasted a week and covered three states.*

ma·ni·a (mā′nē ə), *n.* **1** kind of mental illness in which the symptoms are great excitement, excessive activity, and sometimes violence. **2** unusual or unreasonable fondness; craze: *a mania for dancing.* ❏ *n., pl.* **ma·ni·as** for 2.

ma·ni·ac (mā′nē ak), **1** *n.* a wildly excited person who may be violent. **2** *adj.* wildly excited and possibly violent.

ma·ni·a·cal (mə nī′ə kəl), *adj.* violently insane. —**ma·ni′a·cal·ly,** *adv.*

man·ic (man′ik), *adj.* **1** of or like mania. **2** suffering from mania.

man·ic-de·pres·sive (man′ik di pres′iv), **1** *adj.* having alternating periods of mania and depression. **2** *n.* someone who has such mental illness.

man·i·cure (man′ə kyur), **1** *n.* trimming, cleaning, and polishing of fingernails. **2** *v.* to trim, clean, and polish the fingernails. ❏ *v.* **man·i·cured, man·i·cur·ing.**

man·i·cur·ist (man′ə kyur′ist), *n.* person whose work is manicuring.

man·i·fest (man′ə fest), **1** *adj.* apparent to the eye or to the mind; plain; clear: *The error was manifest. The merits of his plan were manifest.* **2** *v.* to show plainly; display: *She manifests all the symptoms of a serious psychological disorder.* **3** *n.* a list of the cargo of a ship or aircraft. —**man′i·fest′ly,** *adv.*

manifest destiny, a belief in the 1840s in the inevitable territorial expansion of the United States to the Pacific coast.

man·i·fes·ta·tion (man′ə fə stā′shən), *n.* an act that shows or proves something: *Entering the burning building was a manifestation of courage.*

a	hat	ė	term	ô	order	ch	child		a in about
ā	age	i	it	oi	oil	ng	long		e in taken
ä	far	ī	ice	ou	out	sh	she	ə	i in pencil
â	care	o	hot	u	cup	th	thin		o in lemon
e	let	ō	open	ů	put	ŦH	then		u in circus
ē	equal	ò	saw	ü	rule	zh	measure		

M

man·i·fes·to (man′ə fes′tō), *n.* a public declaration of intentions, purposes, or motives by an important person or group; proclamation. ❏ *n., pl.* **man·i·fes·tos** or **man·i·fes·toes.**

man·i·fold (man′ə fōld), **1** *adj.* of many kinds; many and various: *manifold duties.* **2** *adj.* having many parts or forms: *a manifold way to control prices.* **3** *n.* pipe with several openings for connection with other pipes. The exhaust manifold on a car connects the cylinders in the engine with the exhaust pipe. —**man′i·fold′ly,** *adv.*

man·i·kin (man′ə kən), *n.* **1** a little man; dwarf. **2** mannequin (def. 1).

ma·nil·a (mə nil′ə), *n.* Manila paper.

Ma·nil·a (mə nil′ə), *n.* port and capital of the Philippines, on the island of Luzon.

Manila paper, a strong, brown or brownish yellow wrapping paper.

man·i·oc (man′ē ok), *n.* cassava.

ma·nip·u·late (mə nip′yə lāt), *v.* **1** to handle or treat, especially with skill: *She manipulated the controls of the airplane.* **2** to manage by clever use of personal influence, especially unfair influence: *He manipulated the class so that he was elected president instead of his more qualified opponent.* **3** to change for your own purpose or advantage; treat unfairly or dishonestly: *The bookkeeper manipulated the company's accounts to conceal her theft.* ❏ *v.* **ma·nip·u·lat·ed, ma·nip·u·lat·ing.** —**ma·nip′u·la·tive,** *adj.* —**ma·nip′u·la·tor,** *n.*

ma·nip·u·la·tion (mə nip′yə lā′shən), *n.* **1** skillful handling or treatment. **2** clever use of influence. **3** a change made for your own advantage.

man·i·to (man′ə tō), *n.* spirit worshiped by Algonquian Indians as a force of nature with supernatural powers. Also, **manitou.**

Man·i·to·ba (man′ə tō′bə), *n.* **1** province in S central Canada. *Capital:* Winnipeg. **2 Lake,** lake in S Manitoba. [Manitoba probably comes from **manito.** People living near Lake Manitoba believed that the lake was sacred to the spirit.] —**Man′i·to′ban,** *adj., n.*

man·i·tou (man′ə tü), *n.* manito.

man·kind (man′kīnd′ *for 1;* man′kīnd′ *for 2*), *n.* **1** the human race; all human beings: *Mankind has populated most areas of the earth.* **2** men as a group. ∎ See Usage Note at **man.**

man·like (man′līk′), *adj.* **1** like a man. **2** suitable for a man.

man·ly (man′lē), *adj.* **1** having qualities traditionally thought of as belonging to a man: *a manly show of strength.* **2** suitable for a man; masculine: *the manly sport of boxing.* ❏ *adj.* **man·li·er, man·li·est.** —**man′li·ness,** *n.*

man-made (man′mād′), *adj.* made by people; not natural; artificial: *a man-made satellite.* ∎ See Usage Note at **man.**

Mann (man *for 1,* män *for 2*), *n.* **1 Hor·ace** (hôr′əs), 1796-1859, American educator. He established the first school for training teachers in the United States. **2 Thomas,** 1875-1955, American novelist, born in Germany. He won the 1929 Nobel Prize for literature. He left Germany after the Nazis came to power.

man·na (man′ə), *n.* **1** (in the Bible) the food miraculously supplied to the Israelites in the wilderness. **2** a much needed thing that is unexpectedly supplied: *Amid the medical bills, her inheritance came as manna.*

manned (mand), *adj.* occupied or controlled by one or more people: *a manned space vehicle.* ∎ See Usage Note at **man.**

man·ne·quin (man′ə kən), *n.* **1** a model or figure of a person used by tailors, artists, stores, etc. Also, **manikin. 2** person whose work is wearing new clothes to show them to customers; model.

man·ner (man′ər), *n.* **1** way of doing, being done, or happening: *We went to school in the usual manner.* **2** way or style of acting or behaving: *She has a kind manner.* **3 manners,** *pl.* polite ways of behaving: *People with manners say "Please" and "Thank you."* **4** kind or kinds: *We saw all manner of birds in the forest.* ∎ Another word that sounds like this is **manor.**

in a manner of speaking, as you might say; so to speak.

man·nered (man′ərd), *adj.* affected; artificial; having many mannerisms: *a mannered style of writing.*

man·ner·ism (man′ə riz′əm), *n.* an odd trick or habit; peculiar way of acting, speaking, or writing.

man·ner·ly (man′ər lē), **1** *adj.* having or showing good manners; polite. **2** *adv.* politely. —**man′ner·li·ness,** *n.*

man·nish (man′ish), *adj.* (of a woman) having qualities or characteristics traditionally considered to be masculine. ∎ **Mannish** is often considered offensive. —**man′nish·ly,** *adv.* —**man′nish·ness,** *n.*

ma·noeu·vre (mə nü′vər), *n., v.* maneuver. ❏ *v.* **ma·noeu·vred, ma·noeu·vring.**

man-of-war (man′ə wôr′), *n.* warship of a type used in former times. ❏ *n., pl.* **men-of-war.**

ma·nom·e·ter (mə nom′ə tər), *n.* device for measuring the pressure of a gas or vapor.

man·or (man′ər), *n.* **1** (in the Middle Ages) a feudal estate, part of which was set aside for the lord and the rest divided among the peasants, who paid the owner rent in goods, services, or money. If the lord sold the manor, the peasants or serfs were sold with it. **2** a large estate. **3** the main house or mansion of an estate. ∎ Another word that sounds like this is **manner.** —**ma·no·ri·al** (mə nôr′ē əl), *adj.*

man·pow·er (man′pou′ər), *n.* **1** strength thought of in terms of the number of people needed or available: *a country's industrial manpower.* **2** power supplied by human physical labor.

man·sard (man′särd), *n.* **1** roof with two slopes on each side. **2** the story under such a roof.

manse (mans), *n.* a minister's house; parsonage.

man·serv·ant (man′sėr′vənt), *n.* a male servant. ❏ *n., pl.* **men·serv·ants.**

man·sion (man′shən), *n.* a large house; stately residence.

man·slaugh·ter (man′slò′tər), *n.* (in law) the accidental, unplanned killing of someone: *a charge of manslaughter.*

man·ta (man′tə), *n.* any of several large rays that move by a flapping motion of broad fins; devilfish. ❏ *n., pl.* **man·tas.**

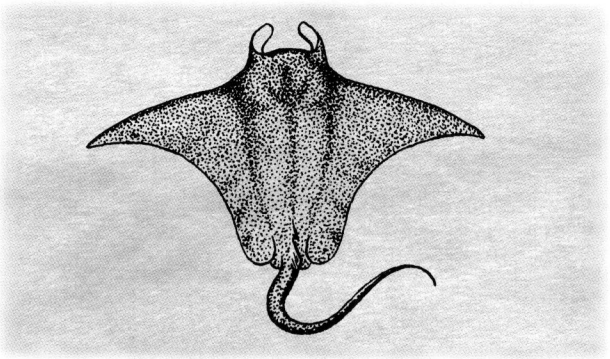

manta

man·tel (man′tl), *n.* **1** shelf above a fireplace; mantelpiece. **2** the decorative framework around a fireplace: *a mantel of tile.* ∎ Another word that sounds like this is **mantle.**

man·tel·piece (man′tl pēs′), *n.* mantel (def. 1).

man·til·la (man til′ə *or* man tē′yə), *n.* a veil or scarf, often of lace, covering the hair and falling over the shoulders. Spanish and Latin American women sometimes wear mantillas. ❏ *n., pl.* **man·til·las.**

man·tis (man′tis), *n.* any of several insects that hold their forelegs doubled up as if praying, especially the praying mantis. Mantises eat other insects. ❏ *n., pl.* **man·tis·es, man·tes** (man′-tēz). [Mantis comes from a Greek word meaning "prophet." The folded front legs of the insect suggested a religious posture.]

man·tle (man′tl), **1** *n.* a loose coat without sleeves. **2** *n.* anything that covers like a coat: *The ground had a mantle of snow.* **3** *v.* to cover with a coat or something like a coat. **4** *n.* a lacelike tube around a flame in a gas lantern. It gets so hot it glows and gives light. **5** *n.* fold of the body wall of a mollusk lining the shell and producing the material that forms the shell. **6** *n.* the layer of the earth beneath the crust and above the core. ❏ *v.* **man·tled, man·tling.** ∎ Another word that sounds like this is **mantel.**

Man·tle (man′tl), *n.* **Mick·ey** (mik′ē), 1931-1995, American baseball player. He hit 18 World Series home runs and led the American League in home runs four times.

man·u·al (man′yü əl), **1** *adj.* of the hands: *Performing surgery requires manual skill.* **2** *adj.* done with the hands: *Digging a trench with a shovel is manual labor.* **3** *n.* a small book that helps its readers to understand and use something; handbook: *A manual came with my pocket calculator.* —**man′u·al·ly,** *adv.*

manual training, training in work done with the hands; especially in making things out of wood or metal.

man·u·fac·ture (man′yə fak′chər), **1** *v.* to make by hand or by machine. A big factory manufactures goods in large quantities by using machines and dividing the work up among many people. **2** *n.* act or process of making articles by hand or by machine, especially in large quantities. **3** *v.* to make into something useful: *manufacture steel into rails.* **4** *v.* to make up; invent: *manufacture an excuse.* ❑ *v.* **man·u·fac·tured, man·u·fac·tur·ing.**

man·u·fac·tur·er (man′yə fak′chər ər), *n.* person or company whose business is manufacturing; owner of a factory.

ma·nure (mə nùr′), **1** *n.* animal waste, especially when put in or on the soil to make it rich. **2** *v.* to put manure in or on. ❑ *v.* **ma·nured, ma·nur·ing.**

man·u·script (man′yə skript), *n.* a handwritten or keyboarded book or article. Manuscripts are sent to publishers to be made into printed books, magazine articles, and the like.

Manx (mangks), **1** *adj.* of the Isle of Man, its people, or the language formerly spoken there. **2** *n.pl.* people of the Isle of Man. **3** *n.* the extinct Celtic language of the Isle of Man.

Manx cat, a short-haired, tailless pet cat.

man·y (men′ē), **1** *adj.* consisting of a great number; numerous: *many years ago. There are many children in the city.* **2** *n., pron.* a great number: *Do you know many of them?* **3** *n., pron.* a large number of people or things: *There were many at the dance.* ❑ *adj.* **more, most.**

a good many, a fairly large number.
a great many, a very large number.
how many, what number of: *How many days until vacation?*

WORD POWER **MANY ■** Many times, many people use many words in many ways for many reasons. With prefixes, people need many fewer words. It's not surprising that two well-known prefixes both mean "many." But why have two? **Multi-** comes from Latin, and **poly-** comes from Greek. In the same way, when you mean more than many, **omni-** comes from Latin, and **pan-** comes from Greek, and they both mean "all."

man·y-sid·ed (men′ē sī′did), *adj.* **1** having many sides. **2** having many interests or abilities. —**man′y-sid′ed·ness,** *n.*

Ma·o·ri (mou′rē), **1** *n.* member of the Polynesian people who were the original inhabitants of New Zealand. **2** *n.* their language. **3** *adj.* of the Maori or their language. ❑ *n., pl.* **Ma·o·ri** or **Ma·o·ris** for 1. [**Maori** means "native" or "usual" in Maori.]

Ma·o Tse-tung (mä′ō dzù′dùng′ *or* mou′ tse′tùng′), 1893–1976, Chinese revolutionary and Communist Party leader.

Mao Ze·dong (zù dùng′), Mao Tse-tung.

map (map), **1** *n.* a drawing representing the earth's surface or part of it, usually showing countries, cities, rivers, seas, lakes, and mountains. **2** *n.* a drawing of the sky or a part of it, showing the position of stars, galaxies, etc. **3** *v.* to make a map of; show on a map: *Explorers have mapped most of the earth.* **4** *v.* to plan; arrange in detail: *Each Monday we map out the week's work.* ❑ *v.* **mapped, mapping.** [**Map** comes from a Latin word meaning "napkin." Early maps were painted on cloth.] —**map′pa·ble,** *adj.* —**map′per,** *n.*

ma·ple (mā′pəl), *n.* **1** any of numerous related trees grown for shade, ornament, wood, or sugary sap. Maples have leaves with deep notches and winged seeds that grow in pairs. **2** the hard, light-colored wood of maple trees. **3** flavor of maple sugar or maple syrup.

maple leaf, **1** leaf of the maple tree. **2** this leaf as the national emblem of Canada.

maple sugar, sugar made by boiling maple syrup.

maple syrup, syrup made by boiling the sap maples.

Ma·pu·to (mä pü′tō), *n.* capital of Mozambique, in the S part.

mar (mär), *v.* to spoil the beauty of; damage; injure; ruin: *The nails in my shoes marred the floor.* ❑ *v.* **marred, mar·ring.**

mar., **1** marine. **2** maritime. **3** married.

Mar., March.

ma·ra·ca (mə rä′kə), *n.* a percussion instrument consisting of seeds, pebbles, etc., enclosed in a dry gourd and shaken like a rattle. Maracas are usually played in pairs. ❑ *n., pl.* **ma·ra·cas.**

Mar·a·cai·bo (mar′ə kī′bō), *n.* **1** port in NW Venezuela. **2** Lake, lake in NW Venezuela.

mar·a·schi·no cherry (mar′ə skē′nō *or* mar′ə shē′nō), cherry preserved in a sweet syrup. It is used to decorate and add flavor to drinks, desserts, etc.

mar·a·thon (mar′ə thon), *n.* **1** a foot race of 26 miles, 385 yards (42.2 kilometers), named for Marathon. **2** any long race or contest. **3 Marathon,** plain in Greece about 25 miles (40 kilometers) northeast of Athens. After the Athenians defeated the Persians there in 490 B.C., a runner ran all the way to Athens with the news of the victory. See **Sparta** for map.

WORD STORY **Marathon** was first used as the name of a race at the first modern Olympic Games in 1896. People began to use the word about any long physical activity, in phrases like *dance marathon.* Today people combine the last part of *marathon* with other words to make new words like *bikeathon* and *walkathon.*

ma·raud (mə rôd′), *v.* to roam about, looking for something to steal or for someone to rob or kill. —**ma·raud′er,** *n.*

mar·ble (mär′bəl), **1** *n.* a hard rock formed from limestone by heat and pressure. It may be white or colored, plain or patterned, and can be polished to be smooth and shiny. Marble is used for statues and in buildings. **2** *adj.* like marble; hard, cold, or unfeeling: *a marble heart.* **3** *v.* to color in imitation of the patterns in marble: *Some books have marbled paper lining the covers.* **4** *n.* a small, usually colored glass ball used in games. **5** *n.pl.* **marbles,** a children's game played with these glass balls. Each player uses a larger ball to knock the smaller ones out of a ring. ❑ *v.* **mar·bled, mar·bling.** —**mar′ble·like′,** *adj.*

Mar·ceau (mar sō′), *n.* **Mar·cel** (mar sel′), born 1923, French mime artist.

march (märch), **1** *v.* to walk as soldiers do, in time and with steps of the same length: *The members of the band marched in the parade to the beat of the drums.* ■ See Synonym Study at **walk. 2** *n.* act or fact of marching: *The band began their march.* **3** *n.* music meant for marching. **4** *n.* distance marched: *The camp is a day's march away.* **5** *n.* a long, hard walk. **6** *v.* to walk or go on steadily: *She marched to the front of the room and began her speech.* **7** *v.* to cause to march or go: *The teacher marched her class out to the playground.* **8** *v.* to move forward; advance: *History*

march (def. 1)

a	hat	ė	term	ô	order	ch	child		a in about
ā	age	i	it	oi	oil	ng	long		e in taken
ä	far	ī	ice	ou	out	sh	she	ə	i in pencil
â	care	o	hot	u	cup	th	thin		o in lemon
e	let	ō	open	ù	put	ŦH	then		u in circus
ē	equal	ò	saw	ü	rule	zh	measure		

533

marches on. **9** *n.* an advance; progress: *History records the march of events.* ❏ *n., pl.* **march·es. —march′er,** *n.*

steal a march, to gain an advantage without being noticed.

March (märch), *n.* the third month of the year. It has 31 days. [March comes from Mars, the Roman god of war. The name Mark and the word martial also come from this word.]

mar·chio·ness (mär′shə nis), *n.* **1** wife or widow of a marquis. **2** woman equal in rank to a marquis. ❏ *n., pl.* **mar·chio·ness·es.**

march·pane (märch′pān′), *n.* marzipan.

Mar·ci·a·no (mär sē a′nō), *n.* **Rock·y** (rok′ē), 1923-1969, American boxing champion. He was the world heavyweight champion from 1952 to 1956, the only one never to have lost a professional fight.

Mar·co·ni (mär kō′nē), *n.* **Gu·gliel·mo** (gü lyel′mō), 1874-1937, Italian inventor who perfected radio. He shared the 1909 Nobel Prize for physics.

Marco Polo. See Polo.

Mar·di gras (mär′dē grä′), the last day before Lent; Shrove Tuesday. It is celebrated in New Orleans and other cities with parades and festivities. [Mardi gras comes from French words meaning "fat Tuesday." On the Tuesday before Lent, people typically enjoy a feast as part of the celebrations.]

mare[1] (mâr), *n.* a female horse, donkey, or zebra.

ma·re[2] (mär′ē), *n.* **1** any of various dark regions on the surface of the moon. **2** a similar dark region on any planet or moon. ❏ *n., pl.* **ma·ri·a** (mär′ē ə).

mar·gar·ine (mär′jər ən *or* mär′jə rēn′), *n.* substitute for butter, made from cottonseed oil, soybean oil, or other vegetable oils; oleomargarine. [Margarine comes from a Greek word meaning "pearl." A chemical that shines like a pearl was discovered in the research that led to margarine.]

mar·gin (mär′jən), *n.* **1** the blank space around the writing or printing on a page: *Do not write in the margin.* **2** amount of difference: *In an election, the winning margin may be less than 1 percent.* **3** an extra amount; amount beyond what is necessary: *We try to allow a margin of 15 minutes in catching a train.* **4** an edge or border: *the margin of a lake.*

mar·gin·al (mär′jə nəl), *adj.* **1** written or printed in a margin. **2** of, in, or on a margin. **3** not really important: *marginal issues.* **4** barely able to produce goods, crops, etc., profitably: *marginal land.* **—mar′gin·al·ly,** *adv.*

mar·gue·rite (mär′gə rēt′), *n.* any of several plants with white petals around a yellow center.

Mar·i·an·a Islands (mar′ē an′ə), group of 15 small islands in the Pacific, east of the Philippines. The largest island, Guam, belongs to the United States. The other islands voted in 1975 to become a self-governing commonwealth under the protection of the United States.

Ma·rie An·toi·nette (mə rē′ an′twə net′), 1755-1793, wife of King Louis XVI of France. She was beheaded during the French Revolution.

mar·i·gold (mar′ə gōld), *n.* any of numerous American plants, several of which are grown in gardens for their yellow, orange, brownish, or red flowers.

mar·i·jua·na (mar′ə wä′nə), *n.* **1** the dried leaves and flowers of the hemp plant; cannabis. Marijuana is a drug, sometimes smoked for its effect. **2** hemp plant.

ma·rim·ba (mə rim′bə), *n.* a musical instrument something like a xylophone. ❏ *n., pl.* **ma·rim·bas.**

ma·ri·na (mə rē′nə), *n.* a small harbor with a dock where small boats may tie up, refuel, buy supplies, etc. ❏ *n., pl.* **ma·ri·nas.**

mar·i·nade (mar′ə nād′), **1** *n.* a spiced vinegar, wine, etc., used for soaking meat or fish before it is cooked. **2** *v.* to soak in a marinade. ❏ *v.* **mar·i·nad·ed, mar·i·nad·ing.**

ma·ri·na·ra (mar′ə när′ə), *n.* sauce flavored with tomatoes, onion, and garlic, used with Italian foods such as spaghetti and lasagna.

mar·i·nate (mar′ə nāt), *v.* to soak in a marinade. ❏ *v.* **mar·i·nat·ed, mar·i·nat·ing. —mar′i·na′tion,** *n.*

ma·rine (mə rēn′), **1** *adj.* of the sea; found in the sea; produced by the sea: *Seals and whales are marine animals.* **2** *adj.* of shipping; of the navy; for use at sea: *marine law, marine power, ma-*

rine supplies. **3** *n.* soldier formerly serving only at sea, now also serving on land and in the air. **4** *n.* Also, **Marine,** person serving in the Marine Corps. **5** *n.pl.* **marines,** Marine Corps.

marine biology, branch of biology that deals with things living in the sea.

Marine Corps, a branch of the armed forces of the United States. Its members are trained especially for landing operations. The Marine Corps has its own sea, air, and land units.

mar·i·ner (mar′ə nər), *n.* one who navigates a ship; sailor; seaman.

mar·i·o·nette (mar′ē ə net′), *n.* puppet moved by strings or wires, often on a little stage.

mar·i·tal (mar′ə təl), *adj.* of or about marriage: *marital vows.* **—mar′i·tal·ly,** *adv.*

mar·i·time (mar′ə tīm), *adj.* **1** of or about the sea; of shipping and sailing: *Ships and sailors are governed by maritime law.* **2** on or near the sea: *Boston is a maritime city.* **3** living near the sea: *Maritime peoples engage in fishing.*

Maritime Provinces, New Brunswick, Nova Scotia, and Prince Edward Island.

Mar·i·tim·er (mar′ə tī′mər), *n.* person born or living in Canada's Maritime Provinces.

mar·jor·am (mär′jər əm), *n.* any of various fragrant herbs related to mint, used as flavoring in cooking. Oregano is a kind of marjoram.

mark[1] (märk), **1** *n.* trace or impression made by some object on another. A line, dot, spot, stain, or scar is a mark. ■ See Synonym Study at **spot. 2** *n.* line or dot to show position: *This mark shows how far you jumped.* **3** *n.* the line where a race starts: *On the mark; get set; go.* **4** *n.* sign or indication of: *Saying "thank you" is a mark of good manners.* **5** *n.* a written or printed stroke or sign: *punctuation marks.* **6** *n.* grade or rating: *My mark in arithmetic was B.* **7** *v.* to give grades to; rate: *The teacher marked our examination papers.* **8** *n.* a cross or other sign made in place of a signature by someone who cannot write: *Make your mark here.* **9** *v.* to make a mark on or put your name on something to show ownership. **10** *v.* to make a mark on by stamping, cutting, writing, etc.: *Be careful not to mark the table.* **11** *v.* to put in a pin, make a line, etc., to show where a place is: *Mark all the large cities on this map.* **12** *v.* to show clearly; be a sign or indication of: *A tall pine marks the beginning of the trail. A frown marked her displeasure.* **13** *n.* something to be aimed at; target; goal: *The arrow failed to hit the mark.* **14** *n.* what is usual, proper, or expected; standard: *A tired person does not feel up to the mark.* **15** *n.* influence; impression: *The Industrial Revolution left its mark on society.* **16** *v.* to distinguish; set off: *Many important inventions mark the last 150 years.* **17** *v.* to give attention to; notice; observe; see: *Mark my words: their plan will fail.*

beside the mark, not to the point; not relevant.

hit the mark, 1 to succeed in doing what you tried to do. **2** be exactly right.

make your mark, to become well known; succeed.

mark down, 1 to write down; note down. **2** to mark for sale at a lower price.

mark off or **mark out,** to make lines, etc., to show the position of or to separate: *The hedge marks off one yard from another. We marked out a tennis court.*

mark out for, to set aside for; select for: *She seemed marked out for success.*

mark up, 1 to spoil the appearance of; damage: *Don't mark up the desks.* **2** to mark for sale at a higher price.

miss the mark, 1 to fail to do what you tried to do. **2** be not exactly right.

mark[2] (märk), *n.* **1** deutsche mark. **2** markka.

Mark (märk), *n.* **1** (in the Bible) one of Jesus' twelve apostles. He was one of the four Evangelists. **2** book of the Bible. It tells the story of the life of Jesus. [See word history information at **March.**]

Mark Antony. See Antony.

mark·down (märk′doun′), *n.* **1** a decrease in the price of an article. **2** the amount of this decrease.

marked (märkt; märkt *or* mär′kəd *for* 2), *adj.* **1** having a mark or marks. **2** very noticeable; very plain; easily recognized: *There* *are marked differences between apples and oranges.* **3** distinguished or singled out as if by a mark: *Even as a young person she was marked for success.* **—mark′ed·ly,** *adv.*

mark·er (mär′kər), *n.* **1** kind of pen used to write or draw with: *We used markers to make signs.* **2** person or thing that marks, especially someone who marks schoolwork. **3** bookmark.

mar·ket (mär′kit), **1** *n.* a meeting of people for buying and selling. **2** *n.* the people at such a meeting: *Excitement stirred the market.* **3** *n.* an open space or covered building where food, clothes, etc., are shown for sale. **4** *v.* to buy food and other things: *We go marketing on Saturday morning.* **5** *v.* to sell: *The farmers can't market all of their corn.* **6** *n.* a store for the sale of food: *a produce market.* **7** *n.* opportunity to sell or buy: *There is always a market for wheat.* **8** *n.* the demand for something; price offered: *The drought created a high market for corn.* **9** *n.* a particular area or group to which goods may be sold: *The United States is a large market for South American coffee.* **10** *n.* the stock market. [See Word Story at **mercy.**] **—mar′ket·er,** *n.*

be in the market for, be a possible buyer of.

on the market, for sale: *That house has been on the market for months.*

mar·ket·a·ble (mär′kə tə bəl), *adj.* able to be sold; salable. **—mar′ket·a·bil′i·ty,** *n.*

mar·ket·ing (mär′kə ting), **1** *n.* business or process of selling, pricing, and advertising goods to a particular market: *The marketing of toys is very competitive.* **2** *adj.* of or about such business: *marketing research.* **3** *n.* shopping for groceries.

mar·ket·place (mär′kət plās′), *n.* **1** place where a market is held. **2** the business world; world of commerce.

mark·ing (mär′king), *n.* **1** mark or marks. **2** arrangement of marks: *The bird had beautiful markings.*

mark·ka (mär′kä), *n.* unit of money in Finland. ❏ *n., pl.* **mark·kaa** (mär′kä).

marks·man (märks′mən), *n.* **1** someone who shoots well: *She is noted as a marksman.* **2** someone who shoots: *a poor marksman.* ❏ *n., pl.* **marks·men.**

marks·man·ship (märks′mən ship), *n.* skill in shooting.

Mark Twain. See **Twain.**

mark·up (märk′up′), *n.* percentage or amount added to the cost of an article to determine the selling price.

marl (märl), *n.* a loose, crumbly rock containing calcium carbonate, used as fertilizer and in making cement.

mar·lin (mär′lən), *n.* any of several large sea fishes related to the swordfish and the sailfish. ❏ *n., pl.* **mar·lin** or **mar·lins.**

mar·ma·lade (mär′mə lād), *n.* a preserve similar to jam, made of oranges or of other fruit. The peel is usually sliced up and boiled with the fruit.

WORD STORY **Marmalade** comes from Greek words meaning "honey apple." People in Portugal used that name for the quince, a kind of fruit from which the first marmalade was made. You may come across a story that **marmalade** comes from French words meaning "sick Mary." This was made up by people who knew French but not Greek.

Mar·ma·ra (mär′mər ə), *n.* **Sea of,** a small sea between Europe and Asia Minor. It is connected with the Aegean Sea by the Dardanelles and with the Black Sea by the Bosporus. See **Dardanelles** for map.

mar·mo·set (mär′mə set), *n.* any of ten kinds of very small monkeys with soft, thick fur that live in South and Central America.

mar·mot (mär′mət), *n.* any of several gnawing, burrowing animals of the Northern Hemisphere with thick bodies and bushy tails. Marmots are rodents, related to squirrels. Woodchucks are marmots.

Marne (märn), *n.* river flowing from NE France into the Seine.

ma·roon¹ (mə rün′), **1** *adj.* very dark brownish red. **2** *n.* a very dark brownish red.

ma·roon² (mə rün′), *v.* **1** to put someone ashore alone in a deserted place: *Pirates used to maroon people on desert islands.* **2** to leave someone in a lonely, helpless position.

mar·quee (mär kē′), *n.* a rooflike shelter over an entrance, especially of a theater or hotel. Theater marquees usually display the names of shows being featured. ❏ *n., pl.* **mar·quees.** ■ Another word that can sound like this is **marquis.**

market (def. 3)

mar·quess (mär′kwis), *n.* BRITISH. marquis. ❏ *n., pl.* **mar·quess·es.**

Mar·quette (mär ket′), *n.* Father **Jacques** (zhäk), 1637-1675, French Jesuit missionary. He and Louis Joliet were the first known Europeans to explore the upper part of the Mississippi River and its valley.

mar·quis (mär′kwis *or* mär kē′), *n.* **1** a British nobleman ranking below a duke and above an earl. **2** nobleman having a similar rank in certain other countries. ❏ *n., pl.* **mar·quis·es, mar·quis** (mär kē′). ■ Another word that can sound like this is **marquee.**

mar·quise (mär kēz′), *n.* marchioness.

mar·riage (mar′ij), *n.* **1** condition of living together as husband and wife; married life: *We wished the bride and groom a happy marriage.* **2** the ceremony of being married; act of marrying; wedding. **3** a close union: *The marriage of words and melody in that song was unusually effective.*

mar·riage·a·ble (mar′i jə bəl), *adj.* fit for marriage; old enough to marry: *of marriageable age.* **—mar′riage·a·bil′i·ty,** *n.*

mar·ried (mar′ēd), **1** *adj.* living together as husband and wife: *a married couple.* **2** *adj.* having a husband or wife: *a married man.* **3** *adj.* of or about marriage; of husbands and wives: *Married life has many rewards.* **4** *n.pl.* **marrieds,** a married couple.

mar·row (mar′ō), *n.* **1** bone marrow. **2** the inmost or important part: *The icy wind chilled me to the marrow.*

mar·ry (mar′ē), *v.* **1** to take as husband or wife: *She plans to marry him.* **2** to become married; take a husband or wife: *He married late in life.* **3** to join as husband and wife: *The minister married them.* **4** to give in marriage: *They have married off all of their children.* **5** to bring together in any close union. ❏ *v.* **mar·ried, mar·ry·ing.**

Mars (märz), *n.* **1** the planet next beyond Earth. It is the seventh largest planet in the solar system and the fourth in distance from the sun. **2** Roman god of war. The Greeks called him Ares.

Mars (def. 1)

Mar·seil·laise (mär′sā yez′ *or* mär′sə läz′), *n.* the French national anthem, written in 1792 during the French Revolution.

Mar·seilles (mär sā′), *n.* port in SE France, on the Mediterranean.

a	hat	ė	term	ô	order	ch	child		a in about
ā	age	i	it	oi	oil	ng	long		e in taken
ä	far	ī	ice	ou	out	sh	she	ə	i in pencil
â	care	o	hot	u	cup	th	thin		o in lemon
e	let	ō	open	ů	put	ŦH	then		u in circus
ē	equal	ò	saw	ü	rule	zh	measure		

M

Marine Life

The ocean covers more than 70% of the world. Near the continents, water is only a few hundred feet or meters deep, but farther out the average depth is about 14,000 feet (4300 meters). The greatest known distance to the bottom is 36,198 feet (11,033 meters), almost 7 miles below the Pacific Ocean surface.

Underwater Forests

Near the coast, where water is shallow and full of light, grow tangles of giant kelp plants. With hundreds of branches and thousands of long leaves, a giant kelp may grow to 150 feet (45 meters) long, and together they cover large areas. Like the birds and squirrels of forests on land, sea animals gather in these submarine forests.

High in the topmost branches of a kelp forest, at the surface of the water, a sea otter takes a nap.

Plankton

Plankton includes thousands of different kinds of plants and animals, most too small to be seen except with a microscope. These tiny plants are the foundation of the ocean ecosystem. Tiny animals eat these plants and are themselves eaten by larger animals, which nourish other animals, and so on. Animal life in the plankton includes huge numbers of eggs and larvae, as well as shellfish, jellyfish, worms, and more. The ocean's largest animals, great baleen whales such as blue and fin whales, feed mostly on plankton. That shows how rich a food source plankton is.

Top to Bottom

Water forms different environments at different depths. Sunlight shines through only a thin upper layer of water, so plants do not grow below about 300 feet (100 meters) from the surface. There is also much more oxygen in the upper layer. Life is plentiful there.

Surface Life

At the top of the ocean live animals that depend on the natural resources above them. Whales and dolphins breathe air; they must come to the surface regularly. Flying fish leap into the air and soar on extended fins like wings to escape predators.

A scuba diver using common equipment can safely descend to about 130 feet (40 meters) below the surface of the ocean.

1000m

A sperm whale hunting for squid to eat can easily dive to 1300 feet (400 meters). Some are reported to have gone five or six times as far down.

2000m

Glowing Monsters of the Deep

In the dark deep waters, prey is hard to find. Hunters have huge mouths and long, sharp teeth—but they need more weapons. The most common is light, which attracts other animals. Bioluminescence, light made by their bodies, acts as a lure. The anglerfish does even more. Its bioluminescent lure wiggles slowly like a fishing worm over its large mouth. A fish that tries to catch that worm will be lucky to get away.

Alvin, a submersible vehicle, carries three people. It has repeatedly descended to about 13,000 feet (4000 meters), deep enough to reach much of the ocean floor.

marsh (märsh), *n.* low, soft land covered at times by water, where grasses and reeds but not trees grow. ❑ *n., pl.* **marsh·es.** —**marsh′like′,** *adj.*

mar·shal (mär′shəl), **1** *n.* officer of various kinds, especially a police officer. A U.S. marshal is an officer of a federal court whose duties are like those of a sheriff. **2** *n.* chief of police or head of the fire department in some cities. **3** *n.* a high officer in an army. A Marshal of France is a general of the highest rank in the French Army. **4** *n.* person in charge of a parade or ceremony: *She is our parade marshal.* **5** *v.* to arrange in proper order: *marshal facts for a debate.* **6** *n.* person in charge of events or ceremonies. ❑ *v.* **mar·shaled, mar·shal·ing** or **mar·shalled, mar·shal·ling.** ■ Another word that sounds like this is **martial.**

Mar·shall (mär′shəl), *n.* **1 John,** 1755-1835, chief justice of the U.S. Supreme Court from 1801 to 1835. **2 Thur·good** (thėr′gud), 1908-1993, American lawyer and judge. He was the first African American justice of the U.S. Supreme Court, from 1967 to 1991.

Marshall Islands, country made up of a group of islands in the N Pacific, near the equator. *Capital:* Majuro

marsh gas, methane.

marsh·mal·low (märsh′mal′ō *or* märsh′mel′ō), *n.* a soft, white, spongy candy, covered with powdered sugar.

marsh mallow, herb related to mallows that grows in swampy places in Europe and North America and has pink flowers. Its root was formerly used in marshmallows.

marsh marigold, plant with bright yellow flowers that grows in moist meadows and swamps of Europe and North America; cowslip.

marsh·y (mär′shē), *adj.* soft and wet like a marsh: *a marshy field.* ❑ *adj.* **marsh·i·er, marsh·i·est.** —**marsh′i·ness,** *n.*

mar·su·pi·al (mär sü′pē əl), *n.* any of numerous mammals that carry their young in pouches. Kangaroos, koalas, and opossums are marsupials.

marsupial

mart (märt), *n.* center of trade; market: *New York and London are two great marts of the world.*

mar·ten (märt′n), *n.* **1** any of several slender, meat-eating mammals of the Northern Hemisphere similar to large weasels, valued for their fur. **2** their fur. ❑ *n., pl.* **mar·ten** or **mar·tens.** ■ Another word that sounds like this is **martin.**

Martha's Vineyard, island south of Cape Cod. It is part of Massachusetts. [*Martha's Vineyard* comes from the many wild grape vines on the island. But who was Martha? No one knows.]

Mar·tí (mar tē′), *n.* **Jo·sé** (hō sā′), 1853-1895, Cuban journalist, patriot, and poet. He worked to make Cuba independent of Spain, and was killed during a battle with Spanish troops.

mar·tial (mär′shəl), *adj.* **1** of war; suitable for war: *martial music.* **2** fond of fighting; warlike: *a martial nation.* [See word history information at **March.**] ■ Another word that sounds like this is **marshal.** —**mar′tial·ly,** *adv.*

martial art, any of the arts of fighting or self-defense, mainly Asian in origin. Aikido, judo, and tae kwon do are martial arts.

martial law, rule by the army in a time of trouble or of war instead of by the ordinary civil authorities.

Mar·tian (mär′shən), **1** *adj.* of or about the planet Mars. **2** *n.* a supposed inhabitant of the planet Mars.

mar·tin (märt′n), *n.* any of several swallows with long, pointed wings and a forked tail. The **purple martin** is a large martin of North America with dark purplish feathers on the males. ■ Another word that sounds like this is **marten.**

mar·ti·net (märt′n et′), *n.* someone who believes in and enforces very strict discipline.

mar·tin·gale (märt′n gāl′), *n.* strap of a horse's harness that prevents the horse from rising on its hind legs or throwing back its head.

mar·ti·ni (mär tē′nē), *n.* an alcoholic drink containing gin or vodka and vermouth. ❑ *n., pl.* **mar·ti·nis.**

Mar·ti·nique (märt′n ēk′), *n.* French island in the West Indies.

Martin Luther King Day, the third Monday in January, celebrated as a holiday in some states of the United States in honor of King's birth.

mar·tyr (mär′tər), **1** *n.* person who is put to death or made to suffer greatly because of his or her religion or other beliefs. **2** *v.* to put someone to death or torture because of religious or other beliefs. **3** *n.* person who suffers greatly. **4** *v.* to cause to suffer greatly; torture. [*Martyr* comes from a Greek word meaning "a witness." A person who suffers or dies for a belief shows evidence of complete faith.]

mar·tyr·dom (mär′tər dəm), *n.* **1** death or suffering of a martyr. **2** great suffering; torment.

mar·vel (mär′vəl), **1** *n.* something wonderful; astonishing thing: *The airplane is one of the marvels of science.* **2** *v.* to be filled with wonder; be astonished: *She marveled at the beautiful sunset.* ❑ *v.* **mar·veled, mar·vel·ing** or **mar·velled, mar·vel·ling.**

mar·vel·ous or **mar·vel·lous** (mär′və ləs), *adj.* **1** causing wonder; extraordinary: *The walk on the moon was a marvelous event.* **2** excellent; splendid; fine: *We had a marvelous time.* ■ See Synonym Study at **wonderful. 3** improbable: *Children like tales of marvelous things, like that of Dorothy in Oz.* —**mar′vel·ous·ly** or **mar′vel·lous·ly,** *adv.* —**mar′vel·ous·ness** or **mar′vel·lous·ness,** *n.*

Marx (märks), *n.* **1 Grouch·o** (grou′chō), 1890-1977, American comedian and movie star. ■ The **Marx** brothers, Groucho, Chico, Harpo, and Zeppo, starred in comedy movies, and Groucho hosted a popular TV show. Their real first names were Julius, Leonard, Arthur, and Herbert. **2 Karl** (kärl), 1818-1883, German writer on economics, coauthor of "The Communist Manifesto."

Marx·ism (märk′siz′əm), *n.* theories of Karl Marx.

Marx·ist (märk′sist), **1** *adj.* of or about Marx or his theories. **2** *n.* follower of Marx; believer in his theories.

Mar·y (mâr′ē), *n.* the mother of Jesus; Madonna. [*Mary* comes from a Hebrew word meaning "bitterness" or "desired child."]

Mar·y·land (mer′ə lənd), *n.* one of the southeastern states of the United States. *Abbreviation:* MD or Md. *Capital:* Annapolis. [*Maryland* comes from the name of Queen Henrietta Maria of England. Her husband, King Charles I, suggested the name.] —**Mar′y·land·er,** *n.*

Mary Mag·da·lene (mag′də lēn), (in the Bible) a woman from whom Jesus cast out seven devils. She is often shown in art as a repentant sinner.

Mary, Queen of Scots, 1542-1587, queen of Scotland from 1542 to 1567. She was beheaded by order of her cousin, Queen Elizabeth I.

mar·zi·pan (mär′zə pan), *n.* candy made of ground almonds and sugar, molded into various forms; marchpane.

masc., masculine.

mas·car·a (ma skar′ə), *n.* preparation used for coloring the eyelashes.

mas·con (mas′kon), *n.* one of several areas on the moon where gravity is increased as if by a concentration of dense matter under the surface.

mas·cot (mas′kot), *n.* animal, person, or thing supposed to bring good luck.

mas·cu·line (mas′kyə lin), *adj.* **1** of or about men or boys. **2** like a man; manly. **3** of or belonging to the male sex. **4** (in grammar) of the gender to which nouns and adjectives referring to males

belong. *He is a masculine pronoun; she is a feminine pronoun.*
—**mas·cu·line·ly,** *adv.* —**mas·cu·line·ness,** *n.*

mas·cu·lin·i·ty (mas′kyə lin′ə tē), *n.* masculine quality or condition.

ma·ser (mā′zər), *n.* device that amplifies or generates microwaves with precise control of wavelengths and with high energies. A maser works like a laser. Masers are used in long-distance radar and radio astronomy.

Mas·e·ru (maz′ə rü′), *n.* capital of Lesotho, in the NW part.

mash (mash), **1** *v.* to beat into a soft mass; crush to a uniform mass: *I'll mash the potatoes.* **2** *v.* to crush; smash: *mash a finger with a hammer.* **3** *n.* a soft mixture; soft mass. **4** *n.* a warm mixture of bran or meal and water for horses and other animals. **5** *n.* crushed malt or meal soaked in hot water for making beer. ❑ *n., pl.* **mash·es.**

mash·er (mash′ər), *n.* kitchen tool used for mashing vegetables, fruit, etc.

mask (mask), **1** *n.* a covering to hide the face. Masks may be artistic, religious, disguising, or just for fun. **2** *n.* a covering that protects the face: *a catcher's mask, a welder's mask.* **3** *v.* to cover the face with a mask. **4** *n.* a clay, wax, or plaster likeness of a person's face. **5** *n.* a disguise: *She hid her dislike under a mask of politeness.* **6** *v.* to disguise: *A smile masked his disappointment.* ■ Another word that sounds like this is **masque.** —**mask′like′,** *adj.*

part in a masquerade. **5** *n.* false pretense; disguise. ❑ *v.* **mas·que·rad·ed, mas·que·rad·ing.** —**mas′que·rad′er,** *n.*

mass[1] (mas), **1** *n.* a lump: *a mass of dough.* **2** *n.* a large quantity together: *a mass of flowers.* **3** *n.* majority; greater part: *The great mass of the population wants to live in peace.* **4** *n.pl.* **the mass·es,** the common people; the working classes; the lower classes of society. **5** *adj.* of or by many people: *a mass protest.* **6** *adj.* on a large scale: *mass migration.* **7** *n.* bulk or size: *They were awed by the sheer mass of the iceberg.* **8** *n.* the quantity of matter an object contains; the quality of a physical object that gives it inertia. The mass of an object is always the same on Earth, in outer space, etc.; its weight, which depends on the force of gravity, can vary. When the force of gravity does not vary, mass can be considered as weight, so units of mass are also used as units of weight. **9** *v.* to form or collect together; assemble: *She massed the peonies behind the roses. Many people massed in the square.* ❑ *n., pl.* **mass·es** for 1,2,8.

in the mass, as a whole.

Mass or **mass**[2] (mas), *n.* **1** the central service of worship in the Roman Catholic Church and in some other churches. The ritual of the Mass consists of Holy Communion and various prayers and ceremonies. **2** music written for certain parts of it. ❑ *n., pl.* **Mass·es** or **mass·es.**

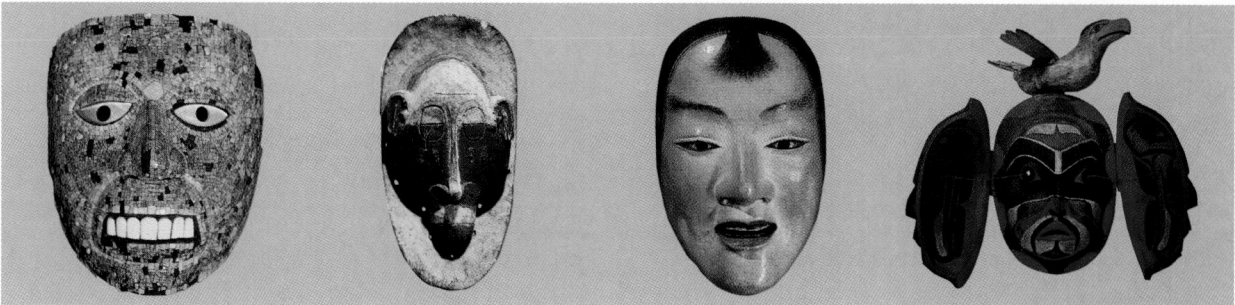

masks (def. 1)

masked (maskt), *adj.* **1** wearing or using a mask: *a masked outlaw.* **2** hidden; secret: *masked treachery.*

masked ball, dance at which masks are worn.

masking tape, a gummed tape used to hold things in place or protect surfaces when painting, spraying, etc.

mas·och·ist (mas′ə kist), *n.* someone who gets pleasure from being physically abused by other people; someone who enjoys suffering.

ma·son (mā′sn), *n.* **1** someone whose work is building with stone, brick, or similar materials. **2 Mason,** Freemason.

Ma·son-Dix·on line (mā′sn dik′sən), boundary between Pennsylvania and Maryland, formerly thought of as separating the North and the South of the United States.

WORD STORY **Mason-Dixon line** comes from the names of the two English surveyors who drew it. Maryland and Pennsylvania hired them to settle a quarrel about the boundary. The work took four years in the middle 1700s. Because people used to think of the line as where the South began, you might expect that **Dixie** comes from Dixon. People have said so, but there is no good evidence.

Ma·son·ic (mə son′ik), *adj.* of Masons, or the society of Freemasons.

Mason jar, a glass jar with a wide mouth and screw top, used in preserving food at home.

ma·son·ry (mā′sn rē), *n.* **1** wall, foundation, or part of a building made of brick or stone; stonework or brickwork. **2** the trade or skill of a mason.

masque (mask), *n.* **1** an amateur dramatic entertainment with fine costumes and scenery. Masques were popular in England in the 1500s and 1600s, at court and at the homes of nobles. **2** masked ball; masquerade. ■ Another word that sounds like this is **mask.**

mas·que·rade (mas′kə rād′), **1** *v.* to disguise yourself; go about under false pretenses: *The king masqueraded as a beggar.* **2** *n.* party or dance at which masks and fancy costumes are worn. **3** *n.* the costume and mask worn at such a party or dance. **4** *v.* to take

Mass., Massachusetts.

Mas·sa·chu·setts (mas′ə chü′sits), *n.* one of the northeastern states of the United States. *Abbreviation:* MA or Mass. *Capital:* Boston.

WORD STORY **Massachusetts** comes from the name of an American Indian tribe living near Boston. The name probably meant "at the big hills," which are south of where the city is now.

mas·sa·cre (mas′ə kər), **1** *n.* a pitiless killing of many people or animals. **2** *v.* to kill many people or animals needlessly or cruelly. ■ See Synonym Study at **kill.** **3** *n.* a severe defeat. **4** *v.* to defeat badly: *The football team massacred their rival 49 to 0.* ❑ *v.* **mas·sa·cred, mas·sa·cring.**

mas·sage (mə säzh′), **1** *n.* action of rubbing and kneading the muscles and joints to increase the circulation of blood: *A thorough massage feels good when you are tired.* **2** *v.* to give a massage to. ❑ *v.* **mas·saged, mas·sag·ing.** —**mas·sag′er,** *n.*

Mas·sa·soit (mas′ə soit), *n.* 1580?-1661, American Indian chief who was friendly to the Pilgrims. He and some of his tribe were part of the first Thanksgiving.

mas·seur (mə sėr′), *n.* person whose work is massaging people.

mas·seuse (mə süs′ *or* mə süz′), *n.* woman whose work is massaging people.

mas·sif (mas′if), *n.* the main part of a mountain range, surrounded by valleys.

mas·sive (mas′iv), *adj.* **1** big and heavy; bulky: *a massive boulder.* **2** great in amount, scale, or effect: *massive doses of medicine, a massive mural, a massive stroke.* —**mas′sive·ly,** *adv.* —**mas′sive·ness,** *n.*

a	hat	ė	term	ô	order	ch	child	
ā	age	i	it	oi	oil	ng	long	a in about
ä	far	ī	ice	ou	out	sh	she	e in taken
â	care	o	hot	u	cup	th	thin	ə { i in pencil
e	let	ō	open	u̇	put	ŦH	then	o in lemon
ē	equal	ȯ	saw	ü	rule	zh	measure	u in circus

mass media, all forms of communication, such as the press, TV, and radio, that reach large numbers of people from a central source.

mass meeting, a large assembly to hear or discuss some matter of common interest.

mass noun, noun that does not usually have a plural form, since it refers to something not normally counted. Mass nouns normally are preceded by *some,* not by *a* or *an. Butter* is a mass noun; *page* is not.

mass number, the sum of the number of protons and neutrons in the nucleus of an atom.

mass·pro·duce (mas′prə düs′), *v.* to make any product in large quantities, especially with the use of machinery. ❑ *v.* **mass·pro·duced, mass·pro·du·cing.**

mass-produce

mass production, the making of goods in large quantities, especially by machinery.

mass transit, public transportation in a city and its surrounding urban and suburban areas. Mass transit includes buses, subways, commuter railroads, etc.

mast (mast), *n.* **1** a long pole of wood or metal set upright on a ship to support the sails and rigging. **2** any tall, upright pole: *the mast of a TV antenna.* —**mast′less,** *adj.*

before the mast, serving as a common sailor. Such sailors used to sleep in the forward part of the ship.

mas·tec·to·my (ma stek′tə mē), *n.* the surgical removal of a breast, often to prevent the spread of cancer. ❑ *n., pl.* **mas·tec·to·mies.**

mas·ter (mas′tər), **1** *n.* person who has power or authority over others: *The dog ran away from its master. The salesperson asked to speak to the master of the house.* **2** *n.* a male teacher, especially in private schools: *The master taught his pupils how to read.* **3** *n.* title of respect for a boy: *First prize goes to Master Henry Adams.* **4** *n.* an expert, such as a great artist or skilled worker; person who knows all there is to know about a subject. **5** *n.* picture or painting by a great artist: *an old master.* **6** *adj.* being master of; of a master; by a master. **7** *adj.* very skilled: *She is a master painter.* **8** *adj.* main; controlling: *a master plan, a master switch.* **9** *v.* to become master of; conquer; control: *Learn to master your temper.* **10** *v.* to become expert in; become skillful at; learn: *She has mastered algebra.* **11** *n.* person who has taken a degree above bachelor and below doctor at a college or university. **12** *n.* an original version, especially of a recording or document, used as a source to make duplicate copies.

mas·ter·ful (mas′tər fəl), *adj.* **1** fond of power or authority; authoritative: *a masterful leader.* **2** expert or skillful: *a masterful performance.* —**mas′ter·ful·ly,** *adv.* —**mas′ter·ful·ness,** *n.*

mas·ter·ly (mas′tər lē), **1** *adj.* very skillful; expert: *a masterly argument, a masterly painter.* **2** *adv.* in an expert or skillful way. —**mas′ter·li·ness,** *n.*

mas·ter·mind (mas′tər mīnd′), **1** *n.* someone who plans and supervises a scheme or operation. **2** *v.* to devise and conduct a plan of action.

master of ceremonies, person in charge of a ceremony or entertainment who welcomes guests and introduces speakers, performers, etc.

mas·ter·piece (mas′tər pēs′), *n.* **1** anything done or made with wonderful skill; perfect piece of art or workmanship. **2** a person's greatest piece of work.

master sergeant, any of several military ranks. See chart on page 712.

mas·ter·work (mas′tər werk′), *n.* masterpiece.

mas·ter·y (mas′tər ē), *n.* **1** a very great skill or knowledge: *The teacher had a mastery of the subject.* **2** power such as a master has; rule; control. **3** the upper hand; victory: *The two teams vied for mastery.*

mast·head (mast′hed′), *n.* **1** top of a ship's mast. A crow's-nest near the masthead of the lower mast is used as a lookout. **2** the part of a newspaper or magazine that gives its name, owner, address, rates, etc.

mas·tic (mas′tik), *n.* **1** a yellowish resin obtained from the bark of a small Mediterranean evergreen tree. It is used in making varnish. **2** the tree it comes from.

mas·ti·cate (mas′tə kāt), *v.* to chew. ❑ *v.* **mas·ti·cat·ed, mas·ti·cat·ing.** —**mas′ti·ca′tion,** *n.*

mas·tiff (mas′tif), *n.* a large, strong dog with a short, thick coat and drooping ears.

mas·to·don (mas′tə don), *n.* any of several extinct animals much like mammoths and elephants, but somewhat smaller.

mas·toid (mas′toid), *n.* the small bone behind the ear.

mas·tur·bate (mas′tər bāt), *v.* to touch or rub the sexual organs for sexual pleasure. ❑ *v.* **mas·tur·bat·ed, mas·tur·bat·ing.** —**mas′·tur·ba′tion,** *n.*

mat[1] (mat), **1** *n.* a small rug of woven straw, rubber, or the like, used to protect a floor: *I stepped from the shower onto the bath mat.* **2** *n.* piece of material to put under a dish, vase, lamp, etc. A mat is put under a hot dish when it is brought to the table. **3** *n.* anything growing thickly packed or tangled together: *a mat of weeds.* **4** *v.* to pack or tangle like a mat: *The swimmer's wet hair was matted.* **5** *n.* a large, thick pad covered with canvas or plastic that is spread on the floor for use in exercising, tumbling, wrestling, or relaxing. ❑ *v.* **mat·ted, mat·ting.**

mat[2] (mat), **1** *n.* border or background for a picture, used as a frame or placed between the picture and its frame. **2** *v.* to put a mat around or under. ❑ *v.* **mat·ted, mat·ting.**

mat[3] (mat), *adj., n., v.* matte. ❑ *v.* **mat·ted, mat·ting.**

mat·a·dor (mat′ə dôr), *n.* the chief performer in a bullfight who kills the bull with a sword.

Ma·ta Ha·ri (mä′tə hä′rē), 1876-1917, Dutch dancer. She was executed by the French as a German spy.

match[1] (mach), *n.* a short, slender piece of wood or pasteboard tipped with a mixture that catches fire when you rub it on a rough or specially prepared surface. ❑ *n., pl.* **match·es.**

match[2] (mach), **1** *n.* person or thing equal to another or much like another; an equal: *A child is not a match for an adult.* **2** *v.* to be equal to in a contest: *No one could match the skill of the unknown archer.* **3** *n.* two persons or things that are alike or go well together: *Those two horses make a good match.* **4** *v.* to be alike; go well together: *The hat and scarf match.* **5** *v.* to find the equal of or one exactly like: *match a vase so as to have a pair.* **6** *v.* to make alike; fit together. **7** *n.* game; contest: *a tennis match.* **8** *v.* to try your skill or strength against; oppose: *He matched his throwing arm against his brother's.* **9** *n.* marriage. **10** *v.* to arrange a match for; marry. **11** *n.* person considered as a possible husband or wife. ❑ *n., pl.* **match·es.** [Match[2] comes from an old English word meaning "a companion." Things that are alike or that go together are like friends.] —**match′er,** *n.*

SYNONYM STUDY **Match**[2], **coincide,** and **correspond** all mean to be the same or nearly the same. **Match** suggests exact likeness: *His fingerprints matched the ones on the cash register.* **Coincide** suggests agreeing: *The two drivers' descriptions of the accident generally coincide.* **Correspond** suggests likeness with minor differences: *The plot of the movie corresponds with the book.*

match·book (mach′bùk′), *n.* a folder of safety matches, especially a folder of two rows of safety matches, with a surface for striking at the bottom.

match·box (mach′boks′), *n.* a small box for holding matches. ❏ *n., pl.* **match·box·es**

match·less (mach′lis), *adj.* so great or wonderful that it cannot be equaled: *matchless courage.* —**match′less·ly,** *adv.* —**match′-less·ness,** *n.*

match·mak·er (mach′mā′kər), *n.* **1** person who arranges, or tries to arrange, marriages for others. **2** person who arranges contests, prizefights, races, etc.

match point (in tennis, Ping-Pong, etc.) the final point needed to win a match.

mate[1] (māt), **1** *n.* one of a pair: *Where is the mate to this glove?* **2** *v.* (of animals) to have sexual intercourse in order to produce young: *Birds mate in the spring.* **3** *n.* husband or wife. **4** *n.* either the male or female of a pair of breeding animals. **5** *v.* to marry. **6** *n.* officer on a merchant ship ranking next below the captain. **7** *n.* assistant: *cook's mate.* ❏ *v.* **mat·ed, mat·ing.**

mate[2] (māt), *n., v.* checkmate. ❏ *v.* **mat·ed, mat·ing.**

ma·té (mä′tā), *n.* kind of tea made from the dried leaves and twigs of a South American holly; yerba maté. Maté is a popular drink in Argentina and Uruguay.

ma·te·ri·al (mə tir′ē əl), **1** *n.* what a thing is made from or used for: *Wood, steel, and plastic are building materials.* **2** *n.* ideas, information, etc., used to write an article, book, play, etc.: *I think her childhood experiences are fine material for a play.* **3** *n.* fabric; cloth: *I chose a colorful material for the curtains.* **4** *n.pl.* **materials,** tools or other things needed for making or doing something: *writing materials, teaching materials.* **5** *adj.* of matter or things; physical: *the material world.* **6** *adj.* of the body: *Food and shelter are material comforts.* **7** *adj.* leaving out or forgetting the spiritual side of things; worldly: *a material point of view.* **8** *adj.* important: *Hard work was a material factor in their success.*

ma·te·ri·al·ism (mə tir′ē ə liz′əm), *n.* **1** belief that reality is made up of material things only and not of ideas. **2** tendency to care too much for the things of this world and to neglect spiritual needs.

ma·te·ri·al·ist (mə tir′ē ə list), *n.* **1** believer in materialism. **2** person who cares too much for the things of this world and neglects spiritual needs.

ma·te·ri·al·is·tic (mə tir′ē ə lis′tik), *adj.* of or about materialism or materialists. —**ma·te·ri·al·is′ti·cal·ly,** *adv.*

ma·te·ri·al·ize (mə tir′ē ə līz), *v.* **1** to become an actual fact; be realized: *Our plans for the party did not materialize.* **2** to appear or cause to appear in material or bodily form: *A spirit materialized from the smoke of the magician's fire.* ❏ *v.* **ma·te·ri·al·ized, ma·te·ri·al·iz·ing.** —**ma·te·ri·al·i·za′tion,** *n.*

ma·te·ri·al·ly (mə tir′ē ə lē), *adv.* **1** with regard to material things; physically: *They improved both materially and morally.* **2** considerably; greatly: *Extra study helped the students to improve their understanding materially.*

ma·ter·nal (mə tėr′nl), *adj.* **1** of or like a mother; motherly: *maternal instincts.* **2** related on the mother's side of the family: *maternal grandparents.* **3** received or inherited from your mother: *His blue eyes were a maternal inheritance.* —**ma·ter′nal·ly,** *adv.*

ma·ter·ni·ty (mə tėr′nə tē), *n.* **1** motherhood; condition of being a mother. **2** motherliness; qualities of a mother. **3** *adj.* for a woman soon to have a baby: *maternity clothes.*

math (math), *n.* mathematics.

math·e·mat·i·cal (math′ə mat′ə kəl), *adj.* **1** of or about mathematics: *Mathematical problems are not always easy.* **2** exact; accurate: *mathematical measurements.* —**math′e·mat′i·cal·ly,** *adv.*

math·e·ma·ti·cian (math′ə mə tish′ən), *n.* an expert in mathematics.

math·e·mat·ics (math′ə mat′iks), *n.* science dealing with the measurement, properties, and relationships of quantities, as expressed in numbers or symbols. Mathematics includes arithmetic, algebra, geometry, calculus, etc. [Mathematics comes from a Greek word meaning "learn." Mathematics is a subject you have to learn in school.]

mat·i·nee or **mat·i·née** (mat′n ā′), *n.* an afternoon performance or showing of a play or movie. ❏ *n., pl.* **mat·i·nees** or **mat·i·nées.**

mat·ins (mat′nz), *n.pl.* a church service held at dawn or in the morning.

Ma·tisse (mä tēs′), *n.* **Hen·ri** (on rē′), 1869-1954, French painter and sculptor. His paintings often used brilliant colors, and he was influenced by African art.

Matisse painting

ma·tri·arch (mā′trē ärk), *n.* **1** mother who is the ruler of a family or tribe. **2** a highly respected elderly woman. ❏ *n., pl.* **ma·tri·archs.**

ma·tri·ar·chal (mā′trē är′kəl), *adj.* **1** under the rule of a matriarch: *a matriarchal society.* **2** of or suitable for a matriarch.

ma·tri·ar·chy (mā′trē är′kē), *n.* **1** a social system in which the mother is the ruler of a family or tribe. **2** government by women. ❏ *n., pl.* **ma·tri·ar·chies** for 1.

ma·tri·ces (mā′trə sēz′ *or* mat′rə sēz′), *n.* a plural of **matrix.**

ma·tri·cide (mat′rə sīd), *n.* **1** act of killing your mother. **2** someone who kills his or her mother. —**ma′tri·cid′al,** *adj.*

ma·tric·u·late (mə trik′yə lāt), *v.* to enroll as a student, especially in a college or university. ❏ *v.* **ma·tric·u·lat·ed, ma·tric·u·lat·ing.** —**ma·tric′u·la′tion,** *n.*

mat·ri·mo·ny (mat′rə mō′nē), *n.* the condition of being married. —**mat′ri·mo′ni·al,** *adj.* —**mat′ri·mo′ni·al·ly,** *adv.*

ma·trix (mā′triks *or* mat′riks), *n.* something that produces or gives form to something else it surrounds or encloses. A mold for a casting is called a matrix. ❏ *n., pl.* **ma·trix·es** *or* **ma·tri·ces.**

ma·tron (mā′trən), *n.* **1** wife or widow, especially an older married woman. **2** woman who manages the household affairs or supervises the inmates of a school, hospital, dormitory, or other institution. **3** woman who has charge of female prisoners in a jail.

ma·tron·ly (mā′trən lē), *adj.* like a matron; suitable for a matron; dignified. —**ma′tron·li·ness,** *n.*

matte (mat), **1** *adj.* not shiny; dull. **2** *n.* a dull surface or finish. **3** *v.* to give a dull surface or finish to. Also, **mat**[3]. ❏ *v.* **mat·ted, mat·ting.**

mat·ted (mat′id), *adj.* formed into a mat; roughly tangled.

mat·ter (mat′ər), **1** *n.* what things are made of; material; substance. Matter occupies space, has weight, and can exist as a solid, liquid, or gas. **2** *n.* event, idea, question, etc., that needs to be thought about and dealt with: *business matters.* **3** *n.* an instance or case; thing or things: *a matter of fact, a matter of accident.* **4** *n.* things written or printed: *Second-class matter requires less postage than first-class matter.* **5** *n.* amount; quantity: *a matter of two days.* **6** *n.* importance; significance: *Let it go since it is of no matter.* **7** *v.* to be important: *Nothing seems to matter when you are very sick.* **8** *n.* something given off from the body, such as pus. **9** *n.* problem; difficulty: *What's the matter with your bike?*
as a matter of course, as something that is to be expected.
as a matter of fact, in truth; in reality; actually.
for that matter, so far as that is concerned.
no matter, 1 it is not important; let it go. **2** regardless of.

a	hat	ė	term	ô	order	ch	child		
ā	age	i	it	oi	oil	ng	long		a in about
ä	far	ī	ice	ou	out	sh	she	ə	e in taken
â	care	o	hot	u	cup	th	thin		i in pencil
e	let	ō	open	ů	put	ŦH	then		o in lemon
ē	equal	ò	saw	ü	rule	zh	measure		u in circus

M

Mat·ter·horn (mat′ər hôrn), *n.* mountain peak in the Alps, between Switzerland and Italy, 14,685 feet (4480 meters) high.

mat·ter-of-fact (mat′ər əv fakt′), *adj.* sticking to facts; not imaginative or fanciful. —**mat′ter-of-fact′ly**, *adv.* —**mat′ter-of-fact′ness**, *n.*

Mat·thew (math′yü), *n.* **1** (in the Bible) one of Jesus' twelve apostles. He was a tax collector who became one of the four Evangelists. **2** the first book of the New Testament. It tells the story of the life of Jesus. [The name **Matthew** comes from a Hebrew word meaning "gift of God."]

mat·ting (mat′ing), *n.* **1** fabric of grass, straw, hemp, or other fiber, for mats, floor covering, wrapping material, etc. **2** mats.

mat·tock (mat′ək), *n.* a large tool with a steel head like a pickax, but having a flat blade on one side or flat blades on both sides, used for loosening soil and cutting roots.

mat·tress (mat′ris), *n.* a covering of strong cloth stuffed with cotton, foam rubber, or some other material, and sometimes containing springs. It is used on a bed or as a bed. ❏ *n., pl.* **mat·tress·es.**

WORD STORY **Mattress** comes from an Arabic word meaning "to throw." Before there were mattresses, people used to sleep on cushions thrown onto the floor.

mat·u·rate (mach′ù rāt′), *v.* to mature (def. 2). ❏ *v.* **mat·u·rat·ed, mat·u·rat·ing.** —**mat′u·ra′tion**, *n.*

ma·ture (mə chúr′ *or* mə tùr′), **1** *adj.* ripe or full-grown: *to reach a mature age. Grain is harvested when it is mature.* **2** *v.* to ripen; come to full growth: *These apples are maturing fast.* **3** *v.* to bring to full growth. **4** *adj.* mentally or physically like an adult: *He is very mature for one so young.* **5** *adj.* fully worked out; carefully thought out; fully developed: *mature plans.* **6** *adj.* due; payable. **7** *v.* to fall due: *This note to the bank matured yesterday.* ❏ *adj.* **ma·tur·er, ma·tur·est;** *v.* **ma·tured, ma·tur·ing.** —**ma·ture′ly**, *adv.* —**ma·ture′ness**, *n.*

ma·tur·i·ty (mə chúr′ə tē *or* mə tùr′ə tē), *n.* **1** full development; ripeness: *Frost struck before the peaches could reach maturity.* **2** condition of being mature: *He reached maturity at an early age.* **3** the time when a note or debt is payable.

mat·zo (mät′sə), *n.* a thin piece of unleavened bread, eaten especially during the Jewish holiday of Passover. ❏ *n., pl.* **mat·zos.**

maud·lin (môd′lən), *adj.* **1** sentimental in a weak, silly way: *We saw a maudlin movie about two children who lost their dog.* **2** tearfully silly because of drunkenness or excitement.

Mau·i (mou′ē), *n.* the second largest island of Hawaii.

maul (môl), **1** *n.* a very heavy hammer or mallet. **2** *v.* to beat and pull about; handle roughly: *The lion mauled its keeper badly.* ■ Another word that sounds like this is **mall.** —**maul′er**, *n.*

Mau·na Ke·a (mou′nə kē′ə), an extinct volcano on the island of Hawaii, the highest peak in the Pacific, 13,796 feet (4205 meters) high. [**Mauna Kea** comes from Hawaiian words meaning "white mountain."]

Mau·na Lo·a (lō′ə), an active volcano on the island of Hawaii, 13,675 feet (4170 meters) high. [**Mauna Loa** comes from Hawaiian words meaning "long mountain."]

maun·der (môn′dər), *v.* **1** to talk in a rambling, foolish way: *People who maunder talk much but say little.* **2** to move or act in an aimless, confused manner: *The injured man maundered about in a daze.*

Mau·ri·ta·ni·a (môr′ə tā′nē ə *or* môr′ə tā′nyə), *n.* country in W Africa, on the Atlantic. *Capital:* Nouakchott. —**Mau′ri·ta′ni·an**, *adj., n.*

Mau·ri·tius (mô rish′əs), *n.* island country in the Indian Ocean, east of Madagascar. *Capital:* Port Louis.

mau·so·le·um (mô′sə lē′əm), *n.* a large, magnificent tomb. ❏ *n., pl.* **mau·so·le·ums, mau·so·le·a** (mô′sə lē′ə).

mauve (mōv), **1** *adj.* delicate, pale purple. **2** *n.* a delicate, pale purple.

ma·ven (mā′vən), *n.* person who knows all about a subject, especially as a devoted amateur; expert: *a restaurant maven, a railroad maven.* Also, **mavin.**

mav·er·ick (mav′ər ik), *n.* **1** calf or other animal not marked with an owner's brand. **2** person who refuses to affiliate with a regular political party.

ma·vin (mā′vən), *n.* maven.

maw (mò), *n.* **1** mouth, throat, or gullet, especially of a meat-eating animal. **2** stomach.

mawk·ish (mò′kish), *adj.* **1** sickening. **2** sickly sentimental; weakly emotional. —**mawk′ish·ly**, *adv.* —**mawk′ish·ness**, *n.*

max (maks), *n.* SLANG. maximum.

max., maximum.

max·il·la (mak sil′ə), *n.* jaw or jawbone, especially the upper jawbone. ❏ *n., pl.* **max·il·lae** (mak sil′ē), **max·il·las.**

max·il·lar·y (mak′sə ler′ē), **1** *adj.* of or about the jaw or jawbone, especially the upper jawbone. **2** *n.* maxilla. ❏ *n., pl.* **max·il·lar·ies.**

max·im (mak′səm), *n.* a short rule of conduct; proverb: *"Look before you leap" is a maxim.*

Max·i·mil·ian (mak′sə mil′yən), *n.* 1832-1867, archduke of Austria, emperor of Mexico from 1864 to 1867. ■ During the American Civil War, the French attempted to gain control of Mexico and offered the country to Maximilian. When the United States forced French troops to leave, Maximilian was defeated by soldiers loyal to Juárez and then executed.

max·i·mize (mak′sə mīz), *v.* to increase or magnify to the highest possible amount or degree: *to maximize sales.* ❏ *v.* **max·i·mized, max·i·miz·ing.** —**max′i·mi·za′tion**, *n.* —**max′i·miz′er**, *n.*

max·i·mum (mak′sə məm), **1** *n.* the largest or highest amount; greatest possible amount: *Twenty kilometers in a day is the maximum that I can walk.* **2** *adj.* largest; highest; greatest possible: *The maximum score on this test is 100.* ❏ *n., pl.* **max·i·mums, max·i·ma** (mak′sə mə).

may (mā), *v.* **1** to be permitted or allowed to: *May I have an apple?* **2** to be possible that it will: *It may rain.* **3** it is hoped that: *May you prosper.* **4** *May* is used to express possibility, acknowledgment, purpose, result, etc.: *That may be true. I may be small but I'm strong.* ■ See Usage Note at **can.** ❏ *v., past tense* **might.**

May (mā), *n.* the fifth month of the year. It has 31 days. [**May** comes from the name of the Roman goddess of spring and growth.]

Ma·ya (mī′ə), *n.* member of an American Indian tribe that lived in central America and Mexico. The Maya had a highly developed culture from about A.D. 350 to about A.D. 800. ❏ *n., pl.* **Ma·ya** or **Ma·yas.** —**Ma′yan**, *adj., n.*

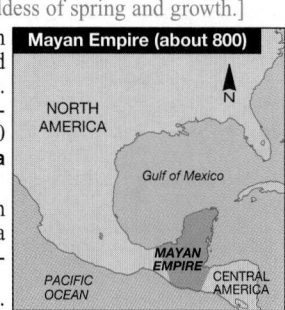

Mayan Empire (about 800)

NORTH AMERICA

Gulf of Mexico

MAYAN EMPIRE

PACIFIC OCEAN

CENTRAL AMERICA

N

May apple, a North American plant with a large, white flower, a single, yellowish fruit, and poisonous leaves and roots; mandrake.

may·be (mā′bē), *adv.* it may be; possibly; perhaps: *Maybe you'll have better luck next time.* ■ **Maybe** is an adverb. It goes with verbs: *Maybe it will be sunny tomorrow.* **May be** is a verb phrase: *It may be sunny tomorrow.*

may·day (mā′dā′), *n.* the international radio spoken call for help. [**Mayday** comes from the pronunciation of a French phrase meaning "help me!" It has no connection to **May Day.**]

May Day, the first day of May, often celebrated by crowning a queen of May, dancing around the maypole, etc. In some parts of the world, labor parades and meetings are held on May Day.

May Day, the first day of May, often celebrated by crowning a queen of May, dancing around the maypole, etc. In some parts of the world, labor parades and meetings are held on May Day.

may·flow·er (mā′flou′ər), *n.* any of several plants whose flowers blossom in May, especially the trailing arbutus.

May·flow·er (mā′flou′ər), *n.* ship on which the Pilgrims sailed in 1620.

may·fly (mā′flī), *n.* any of numerous slender insects, with lacy front wings that are much larger than the hind wings. Mayflies die soon after reaching the adult stage. ❏ *n., pl.* **may·flies.**

may·hem (mā′hem), *n.* **1** crime of intentionally maiming or injuring someone. **2** needless or intentional damage or disorder: *The stampeding cattle caused great mayhem on the ranch.*

may·n't (mā′ənt), may not.

may·o (mā′ō), *n.* INFORMAL. mayonnaise.

may·on·naise (mā/ə nāz/), *n.* a salad dressing made of egg yolks, vegetable oil, vinegar or lemon juice, and seasoning, beaten together until thick.

may·or (mā/ər), *n.* person at the head of a city or town government; chief official of a city or town. [**Mayor** comes from a Latin word meaning "greater." The mayor is of greater importance than any other city official. **Major** comes from the same Latin word.]
■ See Usage Note at **capital letter.**

may·or·al (mā/ər əl *or* mā ôr/əl), *adj.* of, about, or like a mayor: *a mayoral election.*

may·or·al·ty (mā/ər əl tē *or* mer/əl tē), *n.* **1** position of mayor. **2** mayor's term of office. ❑ *n., pl.* **may·or·al·ties.**

may·pole *or* **May·pole** (mā/pōl/), *n.* a high pole decorated with flowers or ribbons, used as part of May Day festivities.

maypole

maze (māz), *n.* **1** network of paths through which it is hard to find your way: *A guide led us through a maze of caves.* **2** confusion; muddle: *I couldn't find what I wanted in the maze of papers on the desk.* ■ Another word that sounds like this is **maize.** [**Maze** comes from **amaze.** If you go into a maze, you may be amazed at how hard it is to get out.]

ma·zur·ka (mə zèr/kə *or* mə zùr/kə), *n.* **1** a lively Polish dance. **2** music for it. ❑ *n., pl.* **ma·zur·kas.**

maz·y (mā/zē), *adj.* like a maze; intricate. ❑ *adj.* **maz·i·er, maz·i·est.**

M·ba·bane (əm bä bän/ *or* əm bä/nä), *n.* capital of Swaziland, in the NW part.

M.C., Master of Ceremonies.

Mc·Car·thy (mə kar/thē), *n.* **Joseph,** 1908-1957, American political leader. ■ **Joseph** McCarthy was a senator from Wisconsin. He accused other branches of the U.S. government and the military of protecting Communist agents in their organizations. His accusations received support from many Americans, which he later lost after his own staff was accused of improper conduct.

Mc·Cart·ney (mə kärt/nē), *n.* **Paul,** born 1942, English musician, a member of the Beatles.

Mc·Cor·mick (mə kôr/mik), *n.* **Cy·rus Hall** (sī/rəs hôl/), 1809-1884, American inventor of harvesting machinery.

Mc·Cul·lers (mə kul/ərz), *n.* **Carson,** 1917-1967, American writer. Her books include *The Heart is a Lonely Hunter* and *The Member of the Wedding.*

Mc·Kin·ley (mə kin/lē), *n.* **1 William,** 1843-1901, the 25th president of the United States, from 1897 to 1901, when he was assassinated. **2 Mount,** mountain in central Alaska, 20,320 feet (6194 meters) high. It is the highest peak in North America.

Md, symbol for mendelevium.

MD, Maryland (used with postal Zip Code).

Md., Maryland.

M.D., Doctor of Medicine.

me (mē), *pron.* I and *me* mean the person speaking. *She said, "Give the dog to me. I like it and it likes me."* ■ Another word that sounds like this is **mi.**

ME, Maine (used with postal Zip Code).

Me., Maine.

mead[1] (mēd), *n.* OLD USE. meadow.

mead[2] (mēd), *n.* an alcoholic drink made from fermented honey and water.

Mead (mēd), *n.* **Mar·ga·ret** (mär/gret), 1901-1978, American anthropologist. Her most famous work is *Coming of Age in Samoa,* in which she discussed the interaction of culture and personality.

mead·ow (med/ō), *n.* piece of grassy land, especially one used for growing hay or as a pasture.

mead·ow·lark (med/ō lärk/), *n.* either of two American songbirds with thick bodies, short tails, and yellow breasts marked with black. Meadowlarks are not larks, but are related to blackbirds.

mea·ger *or* **mea·gre** (mē/gər), *adj.* **1** poor or scanty: *a meager meal.* **2** thin; lean: *a meager face.* —**mea/ger·ly** *or* **mea/gre·ly,** *adv.* —**mea/ger·ness** *or* **mea/gre·ness,** *n.*

meal[1] (mēl), *n.* **1** breakfast, lunch, dinner, supper, or tea. **2** food served or eaten at any one time: *We enjoyed each meal at the hotel.*

meal[2] (mēl), *n.* **1** coarsely ground grain: *corn meal.* **2** anything ground to a powder.

meal·time (mēl/tīm/), *n.* the usual time for eating a meal.

meal·y (mē/lē), *adj.* **1** like meal; dry and powdery: *mealy potatoes.* **2** of meal. **3** covered with meal: *the miller's mealy hands.* **4** pale: *a mealy complexion.* ❑ *adj.* **meal·i·er, meal·i·est.** —**meal/i·ness,** *n.*

meal·y-mouthed (mē/lē mou̵т̵нd/ *or* mē/lē moutht/), *adj.* unwilling to tell the truth plainly; using soft words insincerely.

mean[1] (mēn), *v.* **1** to have as its thought; signify; import; denote: *What does this word mean?* **2** to be a sign of; indicate: *Red means stop and green means go.* **3** to intend to say or indicate: *"Keep out! That means you!"* **4** to have a certain degree of importance or value; matter: *Good friends mean a lot to a person.* **5** to plan; have in mind; intend: *Do you think they mean to visit us?* **6** to design or intend for a definite purpose; destine: *Fate meant us for each other.* ❑ *v.* **meant, mean·ing.** ■ Another word that sounds like this is **mien.**
mean well by, to have kindly feelings toward.

mean[2] (mēn), *adj.* **1** unkind: *It is mean to spread gossip about your friends.* ■ See Synonym Study at **unkind. 2** cruel: *Don't be mean to your pet.* **3** low in quality or grade; poor: *"He is no mean scholar" means "he is a good scholar."* **4** low in social position or rank; humble: *A peasant is of mean birth; a queen is of noble birth.* **5** of poor appearance; shabby: *The poor family lived in a mean hut.* **6** stingy or selfish: *A miser is mean about money.* **7** hard to manage; troublesome; bad-tempered: *a mean horse.* **8** INFORMAL. excellent; clever; skillful: *strums a mean banjo, plays a mean game of tennis.* ■ Another word that sounds like this is **mien.** —**mean/ly,** *adv.*

mean[3] (mēn), **1** *adj.* halfway between two extremes; average: *Six is the mean number between three and nine.* **2** *n.* condition, quality, or course of action halfway between two extremes: *Eight hours is a happy mean between too much sleep and too little.* **3** *n.* (in mathematics) quantity having a value intermediate between the values of other quantities, especially the average obtained by dividing the sum of all the quantities by the total number of quantities: *Six is the mean of three, seven, and eight.* **4** *n.pl.* **means, a** the method used to bring something about: *We won the game by fair means. Her quick thinking was the means of saving my life.* **b** wealth: *a person of means.* ■ Another word that sounds like this is **mien.** [**Mean**[3] comes from a Latin word meaning "middle."]
by all means, without fail; certainly: *By all means stop in to see us.*
by any means, at all; in any possible way; at any cost.
by means of, by the use of; through; with: *I found my dog by means of a notice in the paper.*
by no means, certainly not; not at all; in no way.

me·an·der (mē an/dər), **1** *v.* to follow a winding course: *A brook meanders through the meadow.* **2** *n.* a winding course. **3** *v.* to wan-

a	hat	ė	term	ô	order	ch	child		a in about
ā	age	i	it	oi	oil	ng	long		e in taken
ä	far	ī	ice	ou	out	sh	she	ə	i in pencil
â	care	o	hot	u	cup	th	thin		o in lemon
e	let	ō	open	ů	put	Ŧн	then		u in circus
ē	equal	ȯ	saw	ü	rule	zh	measure		

der aimlessly: *We meandered through the park.* [Meander comes from the Latin name for a river in Asia Minor that had many twists and turns.] **—me·an′der·er,** *n.* **—me·an′der·ing·ly,** *adv.*

mean·ing (mē′ning), **1** *n.* that which is meant or intended; significance: *The meaning of the sentence is clear.* **2** *adj.* meaningful; expressive: *a meaning look.*

SYNONYM STUDY **Meaning** and **sense** both mean the idea communicated by words or actions. **Meaning** is a general word: *What is the meaning of those cheers?* **Sense** often means a particular definition of a word: *Two common senses of "funny" are "comical" and "peculiar."*

---

mean·ing·ful (mē′ning fəl), *adj.* full of meaning; having much meaning; significant. **—mean′ing·ful·ly,** *adv.* **—mean′ing·ful·ness,** *n.*

mean·ing·less (mē′ning lis), *adj.* without meaning; not making sense; not significant. **—mean′ing·less·ly,** *adv.* **—mean′ing·less·ness,** *n.*

mean·ness (mēn′nis), *n.* **1** a mean act. **2** quality of being selfish in small things; stinginess. **3** quality of being mean in grade or quality; poorness. ❏ *n., pl.* **mean·ness·es** for 1.

meant (ment), *v.* past tense and past participle of **mean**[1]: *She explained what she meant. That sign was meant as a warning.*

mean·time (mēn′tīm′), **1** *n.* time between: *Dinner isn't ready yet; in the meantime, let's set the table.* **2** *adv.* in the time between. **3** *adv.* at the same time.

mean·while (mēn′hwīl′), *adv.* **1** in the time between: *I have to leave in an hour; meanwhile I'm going to rest.* **2** at the same time: *The children got lost in the woods; meanwhile, their parents were searching for them.*

mea·sles (mē′zəlz), *n.sing. or pl.* **1** a contagious disease caused by a virus, with symptoms of a bad cold, fever, and a breaking out of small, red spots on the skin. Measles is more common in children than in adults. **2** a less severe disease with a similar breaking out; German measles.

mea·sly (mē′zlē), *adj.* **1** ridiculously small. **2** of or like measles. **3** having measles. ❏ *adj.* **mea·sli·er, mea·sli·est.**

meas·ur·a·ble (mezh′ər ə bəl), *adj.* able to be measured. **—meas′ur·a·bil′i·ty,** *n.* **—meas′ur·a·bly,** *adv.*

meas·ure (mezh′ər), **1** *v.* to find the size or amount of; find out how long, wide, deep, large, much, etc., something is: *We measured the room and found it was 20 feet long and 15 feet wide.* **2** *v.* to mark off or out in inches, feet, meters, quarts, liters, etc.: *measure off two yards of silk, measure out a bushel of potatoes.* **3** *v.* to compare with a standard or with some other person or thing by estimating, judging, or acting: *I measured my swimming ability with hers by racing her across the pool.* **4** *v.* to be of a certain size or amount: *Buy some paper that measures 8 by 10 inches.* **5** *v.* to take measurements; find out size or amount: *Can he measure accurately?* **6** *v.* to serve as a measure of: *A clock measures time.* **7** *n.* size or amount: *His waist measure is 30 inches.* **Short measure** means less than it should be; **full measure** means all it should be. **8** *n.* something with which to measure. A yardstick, a meterstick, and a cup are common measures. **9** *n.* a unit or standard of measure, such as an inch, mile, kilometer, acre, peck, quart, gallon, pound, gram, or liter. **10** *n.* any standard of comparison, estimation, or judgment: *Academic achievement is not the only measure of success in school.* **11** *n.* system of measuring: *square measure.* **12** *n.* limit; bound: *Her joy knew no measure.* **13** *n.* quantity, degree, or proportion: *Carelessness is in large measure responsible for many accidents.* **14** *n.* rhythmical movement or arrangement in poetry or music: *the measure in which a poem is written.* **15** *n.* a bar of music. **16** *n.* action meant as means to an end: *What measures shall we take to solve the problem?* **17** *n.* a proposed law; a law: *This measure has passed the Senate.* ❏ *v.* **meas·ured, meas·ur·ing.** **—meas′ur·er,** *n.*

■ See **Table of Weights and Measures** on page 975A.

beyond measure, without limit; very greatly; exceedingly: *They were grateful beyond measure.*

for good measure, as something extra.

measure up to, to meet the standard of: *The movie did not measure up to my expectations.*

take measures, to do something; act.

take someone's measure, to judge someone's character.

meas·ured (mezh′ərd), *adj.* **1** regular; uniform: *measured portions of food.* **2** rhythmical; metrical: *measured lines of poetry.* **3** deliberate and restrained: *measured speech.*

meas·ure·less (mezh′ər lis), *adj.* without measure; unlimited; vast: *the measureless universe.*

meas·ure·ment (mezh′ər mənt), *n.* **1** size or amount found by measuring: *The measurements of the room are 10 by 15 feet.* **2** act or fact of measuring; finding the size or amount: *The measurement of length by a yardstick is easy.* **3** system of measuring or of measures: *Metric measurement is used in most countries.*

measuring worm, inchworm.

meat (mēt), *n.* **1** animal flesh used for food. Fish and poultry are not usually called meat. **2** food of any kind: *meat and drink.* **3** part of anything that can be eaten: *The meat of the walnut is tasty.* **4** the essential part or parts: *the meat of an argument, the meat of a book.*

■ Other words that sound like this are **meet** and **mete.**

WORD STORY Several kinds of **meat** have names in English that were the names of animals in Latin. **Beef** and **pork** come from Latin words meaning "ox" and "pig." **Mutton** and **veal** come from Latin words too, meaning "ram" and "calf." **Chicken** and **lamb** are also the names of animals, but they've been English words as long as they've been English food. It was the French who brought the first four words from Latin into England, when they conquered it in A.D. 1066. It's a good bet that French conquerors ate most of the beef and pork for a long time after that, while conquered English people got mostly chicken and lamb.

---

meat·ball (mēt′bôl′), *n.* ball of chopped or ground meat, cooked and usually served in gravy or sauce, especially with spaghetti.

meat·y (mē′tē), *adj.* **1** like meat. **2** full of meat. **3** full of substance; solid and nourishing: *It was a meaty lesson containing many valuable ideas.* ❏ *adj.* **meat·i·er, meat·i·est.** **—meat′i·ness,** *n.*

Mec·ca (mek′ə), *n.* **1** city in Saudi Arabia, in the W part. Because Muhammad was born there, Muslims turn toward Mecca when praying and go there on pilgrimages. **2** Also, **mecca,** place that many people visit or that a person longs to visit. ❏ *n., pl.* **mec·cas** for 2.

me·chan·ic (mə kan′ik), *n.* worker skilled with tools, especially one who repairs machines: *an airplane mechanic.*

me·chan·i·cal (mə kan′ə kəl), *adj.* **1** of or involving a machine, a mechanism, or machinery: *mechanical problems.* **2** made or worked by machinery: *a mechanical doll.* **3** like a machine; automatic; without expression: *The performance was very mechanical.* **4** of or according to the science of mechanics.

mechanical advantage, the increase of force gained by using a machine to do work, measured by comparing the force produced to the force put in. A longer lever has greater mechanical advantage than a short one.

mechanic

mechanical drawing, drawing of machines, tools, etc., done to exact scale with rulers, squares, compasses, etc.

me·chan·i·cal·ly (mə kan′ik lē), *adv.* **1** in a mechanical manner: *He greeted us mechanically.* **2** in mechanical respects: *mechanically perfect.* **3** toward mechanics: *She is mechanically inclined.*

me·chan·ics (mə kan′iks), *n.* **1** *sing.* branch of physics dealing with the effects of forces applied to solid objects, liquid substances, or gases that are in motion or at rest. Mechanics was developed by Galileo, Newton, and others. **2** *sing.* knowledge about machinery. **3** *pl.* physical skills; technique: *The mechanics of playing the piano are easy for some people to acquire.*

mech·a·nism (mek′ə niz′əm), *n.* **1** a machine or its working parts: *the mechanism of a watch.* **2** system of parts working together as the parts of a machine do: *The bones and muscles are parts of the mechanism of the body.* **3** means or way by which something is done: *a mechanism for increasing sales.*

mech·a·nis·tic (mek′ə nis′tik), *adj.* **1** of or about mechanics or mechanical theories. **2** of or about the belief that everything in the universe is produced by and can be explained by mechanical or material forces.

mech·a·nize (mek′ə nīz), *v.* **1** to make mechanical. **2** to do by machinery, rather than by hand: *Much housework can be mechanized.* **3** to replace people or animals by machinery in a business, farming, etc. ❑ *v.* **mech·a·nized, mech·a·niz·ing. —mech′a·ni·za′tion,** *n.* **—mech′a·niz′er,** *n.*

med·al (med′l), *n.* piece of metal like a coin, with a figure or inscription stamped on it: *She won the gold medal for figure skating at the Olympic games.* ■ Another word that sounds like this is **meddle.**

> ■ **WORD STORY** **Medal** may come from a Latin word meaning "metal." Or it may come from another Latin word, meaning "halfway, in the middle," used about coins worth half as much as others. Word stories are often uncertain, and they change. People used to think metal, but now they mostly think middle.

med·al·ist (med′l ist), *n.* someone who has won a medal: *an Olympic gold medalist in gymnastics.*

me·dal·lion (mə dal′yən), *n.* **1** a large medal. **2** design, ornament, etc., shaped like a medal. A design on a book or a pattern in lace may be called a medallion.

Medal of Freedom, the highest decoration awarded to a civilian in the United States.

Medal of Honor, the highest military decoration of the United States, given by Congress to members of the armed forces for extreme bravery in combat.

med·dle (med′l), *v.* to busy yourself with or in other people's things or affairs without being asked or needed: *Don't meddle with my things. That busybody meddles in everyone's business.* ❑ *v.* **med·dled, med·dling.** ■ Another word that sounds like this is **medal. —med′dler,** *n.*

> ■ **SYNONYM STUDY** **Meddle, interfere,** and **tamper** all mean to get involved in someone else's business in unwelcome, unhelpful ways. **Meddle** means to try to do more than one should: *The reporter felt that her editor had meddled with her story.* **Interfere** means to meddle in another person's quarrel: *If you interfered in their quarrel, it's not surprising they're both mad at you.* **Tamper** means to meddle with something and spoil the way it works: *Someone had tampered with the lock, and it wouldn't open.*

med·dle·some (med′l səm), *adj.* likely to meddle in other people's affairs; meddling; interfering. **—med′dle·some·ness,** *n.*

Mede (mēd), *n.* person who was born or lived in Media.

Me·de·a (mi dē′ə), *n.* (in Greek legends) an enchantress who helped Jason win the Golden Fleece.

me·di·a (mē′dē ə), *n.* **1** Often, **the media,** radio, TV, newspapers, magazines, and other such means of mass communication: *The media has a great responsibility in the modern world.* **2** a plural of **medium** (defs. 3-5,7,8).

> ■ **USAGE NOTE** **Media** was originally a plural of **medium. Mediums** is now the usual plural. Because people often think of all forms of mass communication together, **media** has become a common singular noun. Some people still use it as a plural, however.

Me·di·a (mē′dē ə), *n.* ancient country in SW Asia, south of the Caspian Sea. See **Persia** for additional map. **—Me′di·an,** *adj., n.*

me·di·al (mē′dē əl), *adj.* **1** in the middle. **2** average; ordinary. **—me′di·al·ly,** *adv.*

me·di·an (mē′dē ən), **1** *n.* the middle number of a series: *The median of 1, 3, 4, 8, 9 is 4. The median of 8, 12, 16, 20 is 14.* **2** *n.* median strip. **3** *n.* a line from any angle of a triangle to the midpoint of the opposite side. **4** *adj.* in the middle: *the median vein of a leaf.* **—me′di·an·ly,** *adv.*

median strip, strip of land, usually grass-covered, between the lanes for traffic going in opposite directions on some highways; median.

me·di·ate (mē′dē āt), *v.* **1** to come in to help settle a dispute; be a go-between; act in order to bring about an agreement between persons or sides: *The mayor tried to mediate between the bus company and its striking employees.* **2** to settle by intervening: *mediate an agreement, mediate a strike.* ❑ *v.* **me·di·at·ed, me·di·at·ing. —me′di·a′tion,** *n.* **—me′di·a·tor,** *n.*

med·ic (med′ik), *n.* **1** person who is trained to perform medical services, especially giving first aid in emergencies or in combat. **2** physician. **3** a medical student.

Med·i·caid or **med·i·caid** (med′ə kād′), *n.* program that provides medical benefits for needy or disabled persons not covered by social security. It is sponsored by the federal, state, and local governments.

med·i·cal (med′ə kəl), *adj.* of or about healing or the science and art of medicine: *medical advice, medical schools.* **—med′i·cal·ly,** *adv.*

me·dic·a·ment (mə dik′ə mənt), *n.* medicine.

Med·i·care or **med·i·care** (med′ə kâr′), *n.* a government-sponsored program of medical care and hospital services for elderly people covered by social security.

med·i·cate (med′ə kāt), *v.* **1** to treat with medicine: *medicate an infection.* **2** to put medicine on or in: *medicate a skin cream.* ❑ *v.* **med·i·cat·ed, med·i·cat·ing.**

med·i·cat·ed (med′ə kā′tid), *adj.* containing medicine: *medicated bandages.*

med·i·ca·tion (med′ə kā′shən), *n.* **1** medicine. **2** treatment with medicine. **3** act of putting medicine on or in.

Med·i·ci (med′ə chē′), *n.pl.* a rich, famous, and powerful family of Florence, Italy, during the 1400s and 1500s. The Medici were patrons of many painters, sculptors, and writers.

me·dic·i·nal (mə dis′n əl), *adj.* having value as medicine; healing; helping; relieving. **—me·dic′i·nal·ly,** *adv.*

med·i·cine (med′ə sən), *n.* **1** substance, such as a drug, used to treat, prevent, or cure disease: *The patient must take this medicine three times a day.* **2** science of treating, preventing, or curing disease; study of maintaining and improving health. **3** the work of doctors, especially those who treat all sorts of illnesses. **4** any object or ceremony that American Indian tribes believe has brought contact with the spirit world, or has aided in curing sickness. **5** power possessed by such an object or ceremony.

medicine ball, a large, heavy, stuffed leather ball tossed from one person to another for exercise.

medicine man, shaman.

me·di·e·val (mē dē′vəl *or* mē ē′vəl), *adj.* of or belonging to the Middle Ages (the years from about A.D. 500 to about 1450). **—me′di·e′val·ly,** *adv.*

Me·di·na (mə dē′nə), *n.* city in W Saudi Arabia. Muhammad's tomb is there.

M

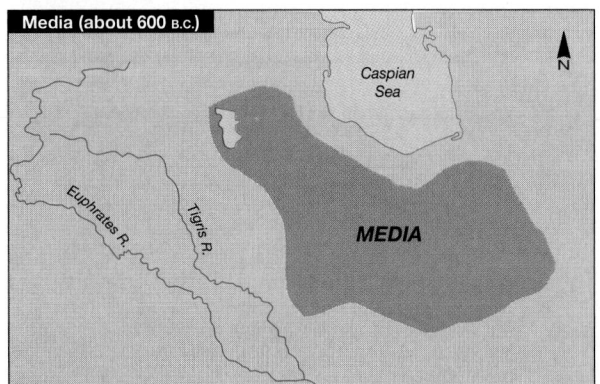

Media (about 600 B.C.)

a	hat	ė	term	ô	order	ch	child		a in about
ā	age	i	it	oi	oil	ng	long		e in taken
ä	far	ī	ice	ou	out	sh	she	ə {	i in pencil
â	care	o	hot	u	cup	th	thin		o in lemon
e	let	ō	open	ù	put	ᴛʜ	then		u in circus
ē	equal	ò	saw	ü	rule	zh	measure		

me·di·o·cre (mē′dē ō′kər *or* mē′dē ō′kər), *adj.* neither good nor bad; of average or lower than average quality; ordinary: *a mediocre book, a mediocre poet.* [**Mediocre** comes from Latin words meaning "halfway up the mountain," not high or low.]

me·di·oc·ri·ty (mē′dē ok′rə tē), *n.* **1** quality that is neither good nor bad; mediocre quality. **2** mediocre ability or accomplishment. **3** a mediocre person. ❏ *n., pl.* **me·di·oc·ri·ties** for 2,3.

med·i·tate (med′ə tāt), *v.* **1** to think quietly; reflect, especially about serious things. **2** to think about; consider; plan; intend: *She meditated a subject for her report.* ❏ *v.* **med·i·tat·ed, med·i·tat·ing.** —**med′i·ta′tor,** *n.*

med·i·ta·tion (med′ə tā′shən), *n.* quiet thought; reflection, especially about serious things.

med·i·ta·tive (med′ə tā′tiv), *adj.* fond of meditating; thoughtful. —**med′i·ta′tive·ly,** *adv.* —**med′i·ta′tive·ness,** *n.*

Med·i·ter·ra·ne·an (med′ə tə rā′nē ən), **1** *adj.* of or about the Mediterranean Sea or the countries and peoples around it. **2** *n.* Mediterranean Sea.

WORD STORY **Mediterranean** comes from a Latin word meaning "middle of the world." When this sea was named, people didn't know very much about geography.

Mediterranean Sea, large sea bordered by Europe, Asia, and Africa.

me·di·um (mē′dē əm), **1** *adj.* having a middle position, quality, or condition; moderate: *He is of medium height.* **2** *n.* that which is in the middle; neither one extreme nor the other: *a happy medium between city and country life.* **3** *n.* something or someone through which anything acts or through which an effect is produced; a means: *Money is a medium of exchange.* **4** *n.* Usually, **media,** *pl.* a means of communication, especially to large numbers of people: *TV, radio, and other media of advertising.* **5** *n.* substance in which something can live; environment: *Water is the medium in which fish live.* **6** *n.* someone who claims to send messages from the spirits of the dead to the living. **7** *n.* a material or technique with which an artist works: *the medium of photography, a quick-drying medium such as watercolor.* **8** *n.* a liquid or solid substance in or on which tiny living things are grown for study. ❏ *n., pl.* **me·di·ums** or **media** for 3-5,7,8; **mediums** for 6.

medium frequency, the band of radio frequencies between 300 kilohertz and 3 megahertz.

med·ley (med′lē), *n.* **1** mixture of things that ordinarily do not belong together. **2** piece of music made up of parts from other pieces. ❏ *n., pl.* **med·leys.**

me·dul·la (mi dul′ə), *n.* **1** medulla oblongata. **2** the inner part or tissue of a body organ or structure. ❏ *n., pl.* **me·dul·las, me·dul·lae** (mi dul′ē).

medulla ob·lon·ga·ta (ob′long gä′tə), the lowest part of the brain, at the top end of the spinal cord, containing nerve centers which control breathing and other involuntary functions. ❏ *pl.* **medulla ob·lon·ga·tas, medullae ob·lon·ga·tae** (ob′long gä′tē).

me·du·sa (mə dü′sə), *n.* jellyfish. ❏ *n., pl.* **me·du·sas, me·du·sae** (mə dü′sē).

Me·du·sa (mə dü′sə), *n.* (in Greek legends) a Gorgon that was killed by Perseus. ❏ *n., pl.* **Me·du·sas.**

meek (mēk), *adj.* **1** not easily angered; mild; patient. **2** submitting tamely when ordered about or injured by others; too shy or humbled; yielding: *Don't be meek about asking for a promotion.* ■ See Synonym Study at **modest.** —**meek′ly,** *adv.* —**meek′ness,** *n.*

meer·schaum (mir′shəm), *n.* **1** a soft, white mineral used to make tobacco pipes. **2** a tobacco pipe made of this material.

meet[1] (mēt), **1** *v.* to come face to face with someone at a certain time or place: *We met last week at the football game.* **2** *v.* to be introduced to; become acquainted: *Have you met my sister?* **3** *v.* to keep an appointment with: *Meet me at 4:15 by the front door.* **4** *v.* to receive and welcome on arrival: *I must go to the station to meet my mother.* **5** *v.* to come together; come into contact or connection with; join: *Two roads meet near the church.* **6** *v.* to be perceived by; be seen or heard by: *There is more to this matter than meets the eye.* **7** *v.* to fulfill; put an end to; satisfy: *The campers took along enough food to meet their needs for a week.*

8 *v.* to pay your debts when due: *I did not have enough money to meet my bills.* **9** *v.* to fight with; oppose; deal with: *meet an enemy in battle.* **10** *v.* to face directly: *He met her glance with a smile.* **11** *v.* to experience: *He met open scorn before he won fame.* **12** *v.* to come together; assemble: *Congress will meet next month.* **13** *n.* a gathering for athletic competition: *Everyone is going to the track meet.* ❏ *v.* **met, meet·ing.** ■ Other words that sound like this are **meat** and **mete.**

meet with, 1 to find by chance; encounter: *We met with bad weather.* **2** to have; get: *The plan met with approval.*

SYNONYM STUDY **Meet**[1], **encounter,** and **confront** all mean to come face to face. **Meet** is a general word: *Meet me at the library tomorrow.* **Encounter** is a formal word. It suggests unexpected meeting: *The two armies encountered each other at Gettysburg.* **Confront** suggests an unpleasant meeting, close together: *She confronted her neighbor about the garbage on the stairs.*

meet[2] (mēt), *adj.* OLD USE. suitable; proper; fitting: *It is meet that you should help your friends.* ■ Other words that sound like this are **meat** and **mete.** —**meet′ly,** *adv.*

meet·ing (mē′ting), *n.* **1** any gathering or assembly of people: *The club held a meeting.* **2** act of coming together: *The meeting of the two streams produces a large river.* **3** a gathering or assembly of people for worship: *a Quaker meeting, a prayer meeting.* **4** place where things meet; junction: *a meeting of roads.*

meet·ing·house (mē′ting hous′), *n.* a building used for worship; church. ❏ *n., pl.* **meet·ing·hous·es** (mē′ting hou′ziz).

mega-, *prefix.* **1** large: *megaphone = large horn.* **2** one million: *megacycle = one million cycles.*

meg·a·buck (meg′ə buk′), INFORMAL. **1** *n.* a million dollars. **2** *adj.* Also, **megabucks,** involving a million dollars or more: *a megabuck business deal.* **3** *n.* any very large amount of money: *a movie costing megabucks to make.*

meg·a·byte (meg′ə bīt′), *n.* unit of computer information, equal to one million bytes.

meg·a·cy·cle (meg′ə sī′kəl), *n.* one million cycles.

meg·a·hertz (meg′ə hėrts′), *n.* unit of frequency equal to one million hertz, used to express frequency of radio waves. ❏ *n., pl.* **meg·a·hertz.**

meg·a·lith (meg′ə lith), *n.* a stone of great size, especially in monuments built by people of prehistoric times.

megalith

meg·a·lo·ma·ni·a (meg′ə lō mā′nē ə), *n.* a mental disorder marked by delusions of great personal power, wealth, etc.

meg·a·lop·o·lis (meg′ə lop′ə lis), *n.* **1** a large metropolis. **2** a large metropolitan area, often including several cities.

meg·a·lo·saur (meg′ə lə sôr′), *n.* any of a group of large meat-eating dinosaurs that stood on two legs, found all over the world.

meg·a·phone (meg′ə fōn), *n.* device shaped like a funnel and used to increase the loudness of the voice.

meg·a·ton (meg′ə tun′), *n.* **1** unit of weight equal to one million tons. **2** unit of atomic power equal to the energy released by one million tons of exploding TNT.

meg·a·watt (meg′ə wät′), *n.* unit of electrical power, equal to one million watts.

mei·o·sis (mī ō′sis), *n.* the process by which living cells divide to form reproductive cells. Each new cell contains one-half the number of chromosomes of the original cell.

Me·ir (mā ir′), *n.* **Gol·da** (gōl′də), 1898-1978, Israeli political leader, born in Ukraine. She was prime minister of Israel from 1969 to 1974.

Me·kong (mā′kong), *n.* river flowing from E Tibet through S China and Indochina.

mel·an·chol·ic (mel′ən kol′ik), *adj.* melancholy; gloomy.

mel·an·chol·y (mel′ən kol′ē), **1** *n.* depression; sadness; tendency to be sad. **2** *adj.* sad; gloomy: *a melancholy person.* **3** *adj.* causing sadness; depressing: *a melancholy scene.*

Mel·a·ne·sia (mel′ə nē′zhə), *n.* group of islands in the Pacific, northeast of Australia. —**Mel′a·ne′sian,** *adj., n.*

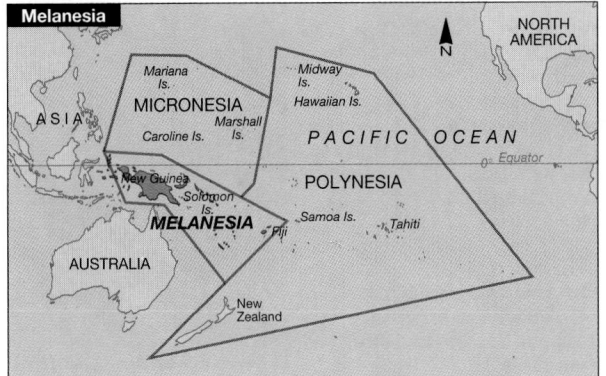

Melanesia

mé·lange (mā länzh′), *n.* mixture; medley. ❑ *n., pl.* **mé·langes.**

mel·a·nin (mel′ə nən), *n.* any of a group of dark brown or black substances that give color to skin, hair, and other body tissues.

mel·a·no·ma (mel′ə nō′mə), *n.* a dark-colored cancerous tumor of the cells that produce melanin in the skin or eye. ❑ *n., pl.* **mel·a·no·mas.**

Mel·bourne (mel′bərn), *n.* port and capital of Victoria, Australia.

meld[1] (meld), **1** *v.* to announce and show cards for a score in pinochle, etc. **2** *n.* act of melding. **3** *n.* cards which can be melded.

meld[2] (meld), *v.* to merge; blend; flow together: *If your eyes blur, images and colors seem to meld together.*

me·lee (mā′lā), *n.* a confused fight; hand-to-hand fight among a number of fighters. ❑ *n., pl.* **me·lees.**

mel·lif·lu·ous (mə lif′lü əs), *adj.* sweetly or smoothly flowing: *The actor spoke in a mellifluous voice.* —**mel·lif′lu·ous·ly,** *adv.* —**mel·lif′lu·ous·ness,** *n.*

mel·low (mel′ō), **1** *adj.* soft and full-flavored from ripeness; sweet and juicy: *a mellow apple.* **2** *adj.* fully matured: *mellow wine.* **3** *adj.* soft and rich: *a violin with a mellow tone, a mellow color.* **4** *adj.* made gentle and wise by age and experience: *He has grown mellow with the passing years.* **5** *v.* to make or become mellow: *The apples mellowed after we picked them. Time had mellowed her youthful temper.* —**mel′low·ly,** *adv.* —**mel′low·ness,** *n.*

me·lod·ic (mə lod′ik), *adj.* **1** of or about melody. **2** melodious. —**me·lod′i·cal·ly,** *adv.*

me·lo·di·ous (mə lō′dē əs), *adj.* **1** sweet-sounding; pleasing to the ear; musical: *a melodious voice.* **2** producing melody: *melodious birds.* —**me·lo′di·ous·ly,** *adv.* —**me·lo′di·ous·ness,** *n.*

mel·o·dra·ma (mel′ə drä′mə *or* mel′ə dram′ə), *n.* **1** a sensational drama with exaggerated appeal to the emotions and, usually, a happy ending: *Most mystery shows are melodramas.* **2** any sensational writing, speech, or action with exaggerated appeal to the emotions. ❑ *n., pl.* **mel·o·dra·mas.**

mel·o·dra·mat·ic (mel′ə drə mat′ik), *adj.* of, like, or suitable for melodrama; sensational and exaggerated. —**mel′o·dra·mat′i·cal·ly,** *adv.*

mel·o·dy (mel′ə dē), *n.* **1** sweet music; any sweet sound. **2** succession of single tones in music; tune. Most music has melody, harmony, and rhythm. **3** the main tune in a piece of music: *He sang the melody to a piano accompaniment.* ❑ *n., pl.* **mel·o·dies** for 1,3.

mel·on (mel′ən), *n.* any of several large, sweet, juicy fruits with hard rinds. Melons grow on vines. Watermelons, cantaloupes, and honeydew melons are different kinds. [**Melon** comes from Greek words meaning "apple" and "gourd." Melons grow on vines like gourds and taste sweet like apples.]

melt (melt), **1** *v.* to turn from a solid into a liquid by heating. Ice becomes water when it melts. **2** *v.* to dissolve: *Sugar melts in water.* **3** *v.* to disappear or cause to disappear gradually: *The clouds melted away, and the sun came out.* **4** *v.* to change very gradually; blend; merge: *In the rainbow, the green melts into blue, the blue into violet.* **5** *v.* to make or become gentle; soften: *Their kindness melted her heart.* **6** *n.* sandwich topped with melted cheese: *a tuna melt.* —**melt′er,** *n.*

melt·down (melt′doun′), *n.* a possible accident in a nuclear reactor, involving failure of cooling systems and buildup of heat in the nuclear fuel until it melts through and escapes from its container.

melting point, temperature at which a particular solid substance melts. Different substances have different melting points. The melting point of water is 32°F (0°C).

melting pot, 1 a place where immigrants from many regions and cultures live together and become more alike than different. The United States has been called a melting pot. **2** pot in which substances are melted.

Mel·ville (mel′vil), *n.* **Her·man** (hėr′mən), 1819-1891, American novelist. His most famous book, *Moby Dick,* is the story of a hunt for a great white whale.

mem·ber (mem′bər), *n.* **1** person, animal, or thing belonging to a group: *The lion is a member of the cat family.* **2** element or part of a whole: *a member of an equation, the members of a set.* **3** part or organ of an animal, person, or plant, especially a leg, arm, or wing.

mem·ber·ship (mem′bər ship), *n.* **1** fact or state of being a member: *Do you enjoy your membership in the Girl Scouts?* **2** members as a group: *The whole membership was present.* **3** number of members: *Our club has a large membership.*

mem·brane (mem′brān), *n.* a thin, soft layer of tissue that lines or covers a living thing or some part of a living thing.

mem·bra·nous (mem′brə nəs), *adj.* of or like membrane.

me·men·to (mə men′tō), *n.* something that is a reminder of something in the past; souvenir: *These postcards are mementos of our trip abroad.* ❑ *n., pl.* **me·men·tos** *or* **me·men·toes.**

mem·o (mem′ō), *n.* memorandum. ❑ *n., pl.* **mem·os.**

mem·oir (mem′wär), *n.* **1** biography. **2 memoirs,** *pl.* **a** record of facts and events written from personal knowledge or special information: *The retired general wrote his memoirs of army life.* **b** record of someone's own life and experiences; autobiography.

mem·o·ra·bil·i·a (mem′ər ə bil′ē ə), *n.pl.* things or events worth remembering.

mem·o·ra·ble (mem′ər ə bəl), *adj.* worth remembering; not to be forgotten; notable: *Graduation from school is a memorable occasion.* —**mem′or·a·ble·ness,** *n.* —**mem′or·a·bly,** *adv.*

mem·o·ran·da (mem′ə ran′də), *n.* a plural of **memorandum.**

mem·o·ran·dum (mem′ə ran′dəm), *n.* **1** a short written statement for future use; note to aid your memory: *Make a memorandum of the things we'll need for the trip.* **2** an informal letter, note, or report: *She sent him a memorandum suggesting a meeting tomorrow.* ❑ *n., pl.* **mem·o·ran·dums** *or* **mem·o·ran·da.**

me·mo·ri·al (mə môr′ē əl), **1** *n.* something that is a reminder of some event or person, such as a statue, an arch or column, a book, or a holiday. **2** *adj.* helping people to remember some person, thing, or event: *memorial services.* —**me·mo′ri·al·ly,** *adv.*

Memorial Day, holiday for remembering and honoring members of the U.S. armed services who have died for their country; Decoration Day. It is celebrated in most states on the last Monday in May.

me·mo·ri·al·ize (mə môr′ē ə līz), *v.* to preserve the memory of; commemorate. ❑ *v.* **me·mo·ri·al·ized, me·mo·ri·al·iz·ing.** —**me·mo′ri·al·i·za′tion,** *n.* —**me·mo′ri·al·iz′er,** *n.*

M

a	hat	ė	term	ô	order	ch	child		a in about
ā	age	i	it	oi	oil	ng	long		e in taken
ä	far	ī	ice	ou	out	sh	she	ə	i in pencil
â	care	o	hot	u	cup	th	thin		o in lemon
e	let	ō	open	ů	put	ᴛʜ	then		u in circus
ē	equal	ò	saw	ü	rule	zh	measure		

mem·o·rize (mem′ə rīz′), *v.* to commit to memory; learn by heart: *memorize the alphabet.* □ *v.* **mem·o·rized, mem·o·riz·ing.** —**mem′or·i·za′tion,** *n.* —**mem′o·riz′er,** *n.*

mem·or·y (mem′ər ē), *n.* **1** ability to remember or keep in the mind: *She will recall when that happened, for she has a good memory.* **2** act of remembering; remembrance: *My memory of the trip is still fresh.* **3** person, thing, or event that is remembered: *I was so young when we moved that our old house is only a vague memory.* **4** all that someone remembers. **5** length of past time that is remembered: *This is the hottest summer in anyone's memory.* **6** part of a computer or computer system in which information and instructions can be stored, temporarily or permanently; storage. **7** amount of information that a computer device or computer system can store. □ *n., pl.* **mem·or·ies** for 1-3,6.

in memory of, to help in remembering; as a reminder of: *I send you this gift in memory of our summer together.*

Mem·phis (mem′fis), *n.* city in SW Tennessee, on the Mississippi. —**Mem·phi·an** (mem′fē ən), *adj., n.*

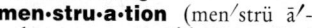

WORD STORY **Memphis** comes from the name of a city in Egypt, which comes from Egyptian words meaning "beauty endures." The ruler who built the city expected it to last a long time.

men (men), *n.pl.* **1** plural of **man. 2** human beings; people in general: *Men are mortal.* ■ See Usage Note at **man.**

men·ace (men′is), **1** *n.* threat: *In dry weather forest fires are a great menace.* **2** *v.* to threaten: *Floods menaced the valley towns with destruction.* □ *v.* **men·aced, men·ac·ing.** —**men′ac·ing·ly,** *adv.*

me·nag·er·ie (mə naj′ər ē), *n.* **1** a collection of wild animals kept in cages for exhibition. **2** place where such animals are kept.

mend (mend), **1** *v.* to put in good condition again; make whole; repair: *mend a road, mend a broken doll, mend stockings.* ■ See Synonym Study at **repair**[1]. **2** *v.* to correct faults in; set right; improve: *to mend your manners.* **3** *n.* place that has been mended: *The mend in your shirt scarcely shows.* **4** *v.* to get back your health; recover from illness or injury: *My sprained ankle has mended.* —**mend′a·ble,** *adj.* —**mend′er,** *n.*

on the mend, getting better; improving.

men·da·cious (men dā′shəs), *adj.* **1** lying; untruthful. **2** false; untrue. —**men·da′cious·ly,** *adv.*

men·dac·i·ty (men das′ə tē), *n.* **1** habit of telling lies; untruthfulness. **2** a lie. □ *n., pl.* **men·dac·i·ties** for 2.

Men·del (men′dl), *n.* **Greg·or** (greg′ər), 1822-1884, Austrian monk and biologist. His investigations of heredity began the science of genetics.

Men·de·le·ev (men′də lā′ev), *n.* **D·mit·ri I·va·no·vich** (də mē′trē i-va′nō vich), 1834-1907, Russian chemist. ■ **Mendeleev's** work led to the periodic table of elements. He predicted the nature of three unknown elements. These elements were later discovered, and his predictions were confirmed.

men·de·le·vi·um (men′dl ē′vē əm), *n.* a radioactive metallic element, produced artificially from einsteinium. *Symbol:* Md

Men·dels·sohn (men′dl sən), *n.* **Fe·lix** (fē′liks), 1809-1847, German composer. He helped revive interest in the music of J. S. Bach.

men·di·cant (men′də kənt), **1** *adj.* begging: *Mendicant friars ask alms for charity.* **2** *n.* a beggar: *We were surrounded by mendicants asking for money.*

Men·e·la·us (men′ə lā′əs), *n.* (in Greek legends) a king of Sparta, husband of Helen of Troy, and brother of Agamemnon.

men·folk (men′fōk′), *n.pl.* men.

men·ha·den (men hād′n), *n.* any of several sea fishes common along the eastern coast of the United States, used for making oil and fertilizer. □ *n., pl.* **men·ha·den.**

me·ni·al (mē′nē əl), **1** *adj.* of or suited to a servant; unskilled; tedious: *Cinderella had to do menial tasks.* **2** *n.* servant who does the humblest and most unpleasant tasks. —**me′ni·al·ly,** *adv.*

men·in·gi·tis (men′in jī′tis), *n.* a very serious bacterial disease in which the membranes surrounding the brain or spinal cord become inflamed.

me·nis·cus (mə nis′kəs), *n.* the curved upper surface of a column of liquid. □ *n., pl.* **me·nis·cus·es** or **me·nis·ci** (mə nis′ī).

Men·non·ite (men′ə nīt), *n.* member of any of several Christian churches opposed to infant baptism, taking oaths, holding public office, and military service. Mennonites often wear very plain clothes and live simply.

Me·nom·i·nee (mə nom′ə nē), *n.* member of a tribe of American Indians living in Wisconsin. □ *n., pl.* **Me·nom·i·nee** or **Me·nom·i·nees.**

WORD STORY **Menominee** comes from Algonquian words meaning "wild rice," a plant that grows widely in the region inhabited by the Menominee, and is important to their way of life.

men·o·pause (men′ə pòz), *n.* the time of life when a woman stops having menstrual periods, occurring usually between ages 45 and 50. —**men′o·paus′al,** *adj.*

me·no·rah (mə nôr′ə), *n.* candlestick with eight branches used during the Jewish festival of Hanukkah.

menorah

men·serv·ants (men′sėr′-vənts), *n.* plural of **manservant.**

men·ses (men′sēz′), *n.sing. or pl.* menstruation.

men·stru·al (men′strü əl *or* men′strəl), *adj.* of or about menstruation.

men·stru·ate (men′strü āt *or* men′strāt), *v.* to experience menstruation. □ *v.* **men·stru·at·ed, men·stru·at·ing.**

men·stru·a·tion (men′strü ā′-shən *or* men strā′shən), *n.* the flow of blood that occurs about every four weeks, from the uterus of a woman who is not pregnant. Menstruation normally begins at puberty and ends at menopause.

mens·wear (menz′wâr′), *n.* clothing designed for men.

-ment, *suffix.* **1** act of ___ing: *enjoyment = act of enjoying.* **2** condition of being ___ed: *amazement = condition of being amazed.* **3** product of ___ing: *pavement = product of paving.*

men·tal (men′tl), *adj.* **1** of or about the mind: *a mental test, mental illness.* **2** for the mind; done by the mind: *mental arithmetic.* **3** having a mental disease or disorder: *a mental patient.* **4** for people having a mental disease or disorder: *a mental hospital.*

mental deficiency, mental retardation.

mental health, the state of having a healthy mind, with good awareness of reality, emotional balance, and normal mental skills.

men·tal·i·ty (men tal′ə tē), *n.* **1** mental capacity; mind: *a student with a high mentality.* **2** attitude or outlook: *a mature mentality.* □ *n., pl.* **men·tal·i·ties** for 2.

men·tal·ly (men′tl ē), *adv.* in the mind; with the mind: *mentally alert.*

mental retardation, condition of having below-normal intelligence.

men·thol (men′thòl), *n.* a white, crystalline substance obtained from oil of peppermint, used in medicine.

men·tho·lat·ed (men′thə lā′tid), *adj.* **1** containing menthol. **2** treated with menthol.

men·tion (men′shən), **1** *v.* to speak about; refer to: *I mentioned your idea to the planning committee.* **2** *n.* a short statement; reference: *A mention of the game appeared in the newspaper.* **3** *n.* formal written praise for some high achievement: *The student did not win the essay contest but did receive honorable mention.* —**men′tion·a·ble,** *adj.* —**men′tion·er,** *n.*

make mention of, to speak of; refer to: *She made mention of a book she had read recently.*

not to mention, not even considering; besides.

men·tor (men′tər), *n.* a wise and trusted adviser.

men·u (men′yü), *n.* **1** list of the food served in a restaurant or other place where people go to eat; bill of fare. **2** the food served: *Everybody enjoyed the fine menu.* **3** a list of things to choose from, shown by a computer to the user: *Choose "print" from the menu.* □ *n., pl.* **men·us.**

WORD STORY **Menu** comes from a Latin word meaning "to make small." **Minute**[2] comes from the same word. The Latin word turned into a French word meaning "a detail." A menu lists the details of food served.

me·ow (mē ou′), **1** *n.* sound made by a cat or kitten. **2** *v.* to make this sound.

Meph·is·toph·e·les (mef′ə stof′ə lēz′), *n.* the devil of the Faust legend.

mer·can·tile (mėr′kən til), *adj.* of merchants or trade; commercial: *a mercantile firm, mercantile law.*

mer·can·til·ism (mėr′kən ti liz′əm), *n.* the economic system of Europe in the 1500s and 1600s. It favored acquiring colonies and keeping exports larger than imports. Its goal was to increase a country's wealth, especially gold and silver.

Mercator projection (mər kā′tər), method of drawing maps with parallel straight lines instead of curved lines for latitude and longitude.

mer·ce·nar·y (mėr′sə ner′ē), **1** *adj.* working for money only; acting with money as the motive. **2** *adj.* done for money or gain. **3** *n.* soldier serving for pay in a foreign army. ❑ *n., pl.* **mer·ce·nar·ies.** —**mer′ce·nar′i·ly,** *adv.*

mer·chan·dise (mėr′chən dīz *or* mėr′chən dīs *for noun;* mėr′chən·dīz *for verb*), **1** *n.* goods for sale; articles bought and sold: *Most drugstores sell games, books, pencils, and other sorts of merchandise besides medicines.* **2** *v.* to buy and sell; trade. **3** *v.* to further the sales of goods and services by advertising and other methods. ❑ *v.* **mer·chan·dised, mer·chan·dis·ing.** —**mer′chan·dis′er,** *n.*

mer·chant (mėr′chənt), **1** *n.* person who buys and sells for profit; trader: *Some merchants do most of their business with foreign countries.* **2** *n.* storekeeper. **3** *adj.* trading; of or about trade; commercial: *merchant ships.* [See Word Story at **mercy.**]

mer·chant·man (mėr′chənt mən), *n.* ship used in commerce. ❑ *n., pl.* **mer·chant·men.**

merchant marine, 1 the trading ships of a nation; ships used in commerce. **2** the group of officers and sailors who serve on such ships: *His brother is in the merchant marine.*

mer·ci·ful (mėr′si fəl), *adj.* having mercy; showing or feeling mercy; full of mercy. —**mer′ci·ful·ly,** *adv.* —**mer′ci·ful·ness,** *n.*

mer·ci·less (mėr′si lis), *adj.* without mercy; having no mercy; showing no mercy. —**mer′ci·less·ly,** *adv.* —**mer′ci·less·ness,** *n.*

mer·cu·ri·al (mər kyur′ē əl), *adj.* **1** sprightly and animated; quick. **2** changeable; fickle. —**mer·cur′i·al·ly,** *adv.*

mer·cu·ric (mər kyur′ik), *adj.* (of compounds) containing mercury.

Mer·cu·ro·chrome (mər kyur′ə krōm′), *n.* trademark for a red liquid containing mercury, used as an antiseptic.

mer·cu·ry (mėr′kyər ē), *n.* **1** a heavy, silver-white, metallic element that is liquid at ordinary temperatures; quicksilver. **2** the column of mercury in a thermometer or barometer. *Symbol:* Hg

Mer·cu·ry (mėr′kyər ē), *n.* **1** the eighth largest planet in the solar system and the one nearest to the sun. **2** Roman god of commerce, travel, and eloquence, the messenger of the gods. The Greeks called him Hermes.

mer·cy (mėr′sē), *n.* **1** more kindness than justice requires; kindness beyond what can be claimed or expected: *The judge showed mercy to the young offender.* **2** kindly treatment; pity. **3** something to be thankful for; blessing: *It's a mercy that she wasn't injured in the accident.* ❑ *n., pl.* **mer·cies** for 3.

at the mercy of, in the power of.

WORD STORY **Mercy** comes from a Latin word meaning "goods for sale." **Market** and **merchant** come from the same word, because they are words about selling goods. The Latin word was also used to mean "profit" or "reward," and so it became common in descriptions of the heavenly rewards promised by religion. Because that idea is so important to people, it became a separate word.

mercy killing, euthanasia.

mere (mir), *adj.* nothing else than; only; simple: *The cut was a mere scratch.* ❑ *adj., superlative* **mer·est.**

mere·ly (mir′lē), *adv.* simply; only; and nothing more; and that is all: *She is merely a member of the club, not one of the officers.*

mer·gan·ser (mər gan′sər), *n.* any of several large, fish-eating ducks with long, slender bills that are hooked at the tip. They often have crested heads. ❑ *n., pl.* **mer·gan·ser** *or* **mer·gan·sers.**

merge (mėrj), *v.* to combine or unite separate things into one: *The newspapers merged as the "Star-Sentinel."* ❑ *v.* **merged, merg·ing.**

merg·er (mėr′jər), *n.* act of merging; combination; consolidation: *One big company was formed by the merger of four small ones.*

me·rid·i·an (mə rid′ē ən), *n.* **1** an imaginary circle passing through any place on the earth's surface and through the North and South Poles. **2** the half of such a circle running from the North to the South Pole. All places on the same meridian have the same longitude. **3** the highest point: *The meridian of life is the prime of life.*

me·ringue (mə rang′), *n.* **1** a mixture of white of egg and sugar, beaten stiff. Meringue is often spread on pies, puddings, etc., and lightly browned in the oven. **2** a shell made of this mixture and filled with fruit, whipped cream, etc.

me·ri·no (mə rē′nō), *n.* **1** Often, **Merino,** kind of sheep with long, fine wool. **2** a soft, woolen yarn or cloth made from this wool or some substitute. ❑ *n., pl.* **me·ri·nos** or **Me·ri·nos** for 1.

mer·it (mer′it), **1** *n.* worth or value; goodness: *Students will be graded according to the merit of their work.* **2** *n.* something that deserves praise or reward. **3** *v.* to deserve: *Your excellent work merits praise.* **4** *n.* Usually, **merits,** *pl.* actual facts or qualities, whether good or bad: *I approve of your plan on its merits, not just because you are my friend.* —**mer′it·less,** *adj.*

mer·i·to·ri·ous (mer′ə tôr′ē əs), *adj.* deserving reward or praise; having merit; worthy: *The student's work at school was meritorious, but not brilliant.* —**mer′i·to′ri·ous·ly,** *adv.* —**mer′i·to′ri·ous·ness,** *n.*

merit system, system in which jobs and promotions in the civil service are made on the basis of merit or good performance rather than on allegiance to a political party.

Mer·lin (mėr′lən), *n.* magician who helped King Arthur.

mer·maid (mėr′mād′), *n.* an imaginary creature of the sea, with the head and body of a woman, and the tail of a fish.

mer·man (mėr′man′), *n.* an imaginary creature of the sea, with the head and body of a man, and the tail of a fish. ❑ *n., pl.* **mer·men.**

Mer·ri·mac (mer′ə mak), *n.* a U.S. frigate rebuilt with iron armor by the Confederates during the Civil War and renamed the *Virginia.* The Merrimac was the first armored warship.

Mer·ri·mack (mer′ə mak), *n.* river flowing from central New Hampshire through NE Massachusetts into the Atlantic.

mer·ri·ment (mer′ē mənt), *n.* laughter; fun; mirth; merry enjoyment.

mer·ry (mer′ē), *adj.* **1** laughing and cheerful; full of fun: *merry friends.* **2** joyful: *a merry holiday.* ❑ *adj.* **mer·ri·er, mer·ri·est.** —**mer′ri·ly,** *adv.* —**mer′ri·ness,** *n.*

make merry, to laugh and be joyful; have fun.

mer·ry-go-round (mer′ē gō round′), *n.* **1** set of animal figures and seats on a circular platform that is driven round and round by machinery; carousel. People ride on them for fun. **2** any whirl or rapid round: *The holidays were a merry-go-round of parties.*

merry-go-round (def. 1)

a	hat	ė	term	ô	order	ch	child		
ā	age	i	it	oi	oil	ng	long		a in about
ä	far	ī	ice	ou	out	sh	she		e in taken
â	care	o	hot	u	cup	th	thin	ə	i in pencil
e	let	ō	open	u̇	put	ŦH	then		o in lemon
ē	equal	ò	saw	ü	rule	zh	measure		u in circus

mer·ry·mak·er (mer′ē mā′kər), *n.* person who is being merry; person engaged in merrymaking.

mer·ry·mak·ing (mer′ē mā′king), **1** *n.* laughter and happiness; fun. **2** *n.* a happy festival; merry entertainment. **3** *adj.* happy and full of fun; having a merry time.

me·sa (mā′sə), *n.* a small, high plateau with a flat top and steep sides, common in dry regions of the western and southwestern United States. ❑ *n., pl.* **me·sas.** [Mesa comes from a Latin word meaning "table." The flat top of a mesa looks like a table.]

Me·sa (mā′sə), *n.* city in central Arizona.

Mesa Ver·de National Park (vėrd *or* ver′dē), a national park in SW Colorado, containing cliff dwellings 700 years old.

Mesa Verde National Park

mes·cal (mes kal′), *n.* a small cactus of northern Mexico and the southwestern United States, with buttonlike tops that are dried and chewed as a drug, especially in some Native American religious ceremonies; peyote.

mes·cal·ine (mes′kə lēn), *n.* a drug found in the small buttonlike tops of a mescal; peyote.

mes·dames (mā däm′), *n.* **1** a plural of **madam.** **2** FRENCH. plural of **madame.**

mes·de·moi·selles (mād mwä zel′), *n.* FRENCH. plural of **mademoiselle.**

mesh (mesh), **1** *n.* cord, wire, etc., used in a net or screen: *We found an old fly swatter made of wire mesh.* **2** *v.* to bring or come closely together; fit together; blend: *After a few meetings, the group meshed.* **3** *v.* to fit together; connect: *The teeth of a small gear mesh with the teeth of a larger one.* **4** *n.* an open space of a net, sieve, or screen: *This net has half-inch meshes.* **5** *n.* a woven or knitted material: *a shirt made of mesh.* **6** *n.pl.* **meshes,** a network: *Seaweed was caught in the meshes of the net.* **b** snares: *The spy was entangled in the meshes of his own plot to steal defense secrets.* ❑ *n., pl.* **mesh·es** for 4,5.

in mesh, in gear; fitted together.

mes·mer·ism (mez′mə riz′əm *or* mes′mə riz′əm), *n.* hypnotism.

mes·mer·ize (mez′mə riz′ *or* mes′mə riz′), *v.* to hypnotize. ❑ *v.* **mes·mer·ized, mes·mer·iz·ing.** —**mes′mer·i·za′tion,** *n.* —**mes′mer·iz′er,** *n.*

mes·o·derm (mes′ə dėrm′), *n.* the middle layer of cells formed during the early development of animal embryos. Muscles, bones, etc., grow from the mesoderm. —**mes′o·der′mal,** *adj.*

mes·on (mes′on *or* mē′zon), *n.* any of various extremely unstable subatomic particles, having masses greater than that of an electron and less than or more than that of a proton. A meson may have a positive, negative, or neutral charge.

Mes·o·po·ta·mi·a (mes′ə pə tā′mē ə), *n.* ancient country in SW Asia, between the Tigris and Euphrates rivers. —**Mes′o·po·ta′mi·an,** *adj., n.*

mes·o·sphere (mes′ə sfir), *n.* region of the atmosphere between the stratosphere and the ionosphere, extending from about 35 to 50 miles (56 to 80 kilometers) above the earth's surface. Most of the ozone in the atmosphere is created in the mesosphere, and there is almost no variation in the temperature there.

Mes·o·zo·ic (mes′ə zō′ik), *n.* (in geology) time between about 230 and 70 million years ago, including the Triassic, Jurassic, and Cretaceous.

me·squite (me skēt′), *n.* any of several trees or bushes common in the southwestern United States and Mexico, which often grow in dense clumps or thickets. Mesquite pods furnish a valuable food for cattle. The wood is used in grilling food.

mess (mes), **1** *n.* a dirty or untidy mass or group of things; dirty or untidy condition: *Please clean up the mess in your room.* **2** *v.* to make dirty or untidy: *She messed up her book by scribbling in it.* **3** *n.* confusion or difficulty: *His business affairs are in a mess.* **4** *v.* to make a failure of; spoil: *He messed up his chances of winning the race.* **5** *n.* an unpleasant, difficult, or unsuccessful situation: *She made a mess of her final examinations.* **6** *n.* group of people who take meals together regularly, especially such a group in the armed forces. **7** *n.* meal of such a group: *The officers ate early mess.* **8** *v.* to take your meals with. ❑ *n., pl.* **mess·es.**

mess about or **mess around,** be busy without really accomplishing anything.

mess around with or **mess with,** to fool with; get involved with: *Don't mess with the dog; it bites.*

> **WORD STORY** **Mess** comes from a Latin word meaning "to send." **Message** comes from the same word. In old times, a mess was a dish of food sent to the table from the kitchen. People began using the word mostly about messy foods like stew, and now a mess is not appetizing.

mes·sage (mes′ij), *n.* **1** words sent or delivered from one person or group to another: *a telephone message.* **2** an official speech or writing: *the President's message to Congress.* **3** lesson or moral contained in a story, play, speech, etc. [See Word Story at **mess.**]

mes·sen·ger (mes′n jər), *n.* **1** person who carries a message or goes on an errand. **2** a sign that something is coming; forerunner; herald: *Dawn is the messenger of day.*

messenger RNA, a form of RNA that carries instructions for making proteins from the cell nucleus to the rest of the cell.

Mes·si·ah (mə sī′ə), *n.* **1** the expected deliverer of the Jewish people. **2** (in Christian use) Jesus. **3** Often, **messiah,** any person hailed as or thought of as a savior. [See Word Story at **Christ.**]

Mes·si·an·ic (mes′ē an′ik), *adj.* **1** of or about the Messiah. **2** Often, **messianic,** of or like a messiah or savior.

mes·sieurs (mes′ərz; *French* mā syü′), *n.* plural of **monsieur.**

mess kit, a shallow, metal container that includes a fork, spoon, knife, and metal cup, for use by a soldier in the field, a camper, etc.

mess·mate (mes′māt′), *n.* one of a group of people who eat together regularly.

Messrs., messieurs, used before names as the plural of **Mr.:** *Messrs. Smith and Jones.*

mess·y (mes′ē), *adj.* **1** in a mess; like a mess; untidy; in disorder; dirty. **2** difficult: *Getting the two former friends to apologize to each other was a messy situation.* ❑ *adj.* **mess·i·er, mess·i·est.** —**mess′i·ly,** *adv.* —**mess′i·ness,** *n.*

mes·ti·za (me stē′zä), *n.* a woman of mixed ancestry, especially the child of a Spaniard and an American Indian in Latin America. ❑ *n., pl.* **mes·ti·zas.**

mes·ti·zo (me stē′zō), *n.* someone of mixed ancestry, especially the child of a Spaniard and an American Indian in Latin America. ❑ *n., pl.* **mes·ti·zos.**

met (met), *v.* past tense and past participle of **meet**[1]: *They met us this morning. We were met at the gate by our dog.*

met·a·bol·ic (met′ə bol′ik), *adj.* of or about metabolism. —**met′a·bol′i·cal·ly,** *adv.*

me·tab·o·lism (mə tab′ə liz′əm), *n.* all the processes by which living things use energy to form living tissue and to continue the functions of life. In metabolism some substances are broken down to produce energy, which is then used to build up new cells and tissues, provide heat, engage in physical activity, etc. Growth and action depend on metabolism.

me·tab·o·lize (mə tab′ə liz), *v.* **1** to change a substance by metabolism. **2** to undergo metabolism. ❑ *v.* **me·tab·o·lized, me·tab·o·liz·ing.**

met·a·car·pal (met/ə kär/pəl), **1** *adj.* of or about the metacarpus. **2** *n.* any bone of the metacarpus.

met·a·car·pus (met/ə kär/pəs), *n.* part of the hand, especially the bones, between the wrist and the fingers. ❑ *n., pl.* **met·a·car·pi** (met/ə kär/pī).

Met·air·ie (met/ər ē), *n.* city in SE Louisiana.

met·al (met/l), *n.* **1** any of a group of chemical elements that usually have a shiny surface, are good conductors of heat and electricity, and can be melted, hammered into thin sheets, or drawn out into wires. Metals form alloys with each other and react with nonmetals to form salts. Iron, gold, sodium, copper, lead, tin, and aluminum are metals. **2** any alloy of such elements, for example steel, bronze, and brass. ■ Another word that sounds like this is **mettle**.

me·tal·lic (mə tal/ik), *adj.* **1** of, containing, or consisting of metal: *a metallic substance.* **2** like metal; characteristic of metal; that suggests metal: *a metallic luster, a metallic voice.*

met·al·loid (met/l oid), *n.* an element with characteristics of both a metal and a nonmetal. Arsenic is a metalloid.

met·al·lur·gy (met/l ėr/jē), *n.* science of working with metals, including the study of their qualities and structure, the separation and refining of metals from their ores, and the production of alloys. —**met/al·lur/gi·cal,** *adj.* —**met/al·lur/gist,** *n.*

met·al·work (met/l wėrk/), *n.* **1** things made out of metal. **2** act or process of making things out of metal.

met·al·work·ing (met/l wėr/king), *n.* act or process of making things out of metal.

met·a·mor·phic (met/ə môr/fik), *adj.* **1** of or about metamorphosis; having to do with change of form. **2** changed in structure by heat, moisture, and pressure. Slate is a metamorphic rock that is formed from shale, a sedimentary rock.

met·a·mor·phose (met/ə môr/fōz), *v.* to change in form; transform: *A caterpillar metamorphoses into a butterfly.* ❑ *v.* **met·a·mor·phosed, met·a·mor·phos·ing.**

met·a·mor·pho·sis (met/ə môr/fə sis), *n.* **1** change of form of an animal as it develops from an embryo. Tadpoles become frogs by metamorphosis; they lose their tails and grow legs. **2** the changed form. **3** a noticeable or complete change of character or appearance. ❑ *n., pl.* **met·a·mor·pho·ses** (met/ə môr/fə sēz/).

met·a·phor (met/ə fôr), *n.* a figure of speech in which something is described by comparing it to something else, without using the words *like* or *as.* "A heart of stone" is a metaphor.

USAGE NOTE Metaphor compares things without using *like* or *as: I have a mountain of work to do.* **Simile** compares things using *like* or *as: He is as strong as an ox.* Some metaphors are so common that they are now standard phrases, including *head of government, career path,* and *window of opportunity.*

met·a·phor·i·cal (met/ə fôr/ə kəl), *adj.* using metaphors; figurative: *a metaphorical expression.* —**met/a·phor/i·cal·ly,** *adv.*

met·a·phys·i·cal (met/ə fiz/ə kəl), *adj.* **1** of or about metaphysics; about the real nature of things. **2** highly abstract; hard to understand. —**met/a·phys/i·cal·ly,** *adv.*

met·a·phys·ics (met/ə fiz/iks), *n.* branch of philosophy that tries to explain reality and knowledge; the study of the real nature of things.

me·tas·ta·sis (mə tas/tə sis), *n.* **1** the spread of cancerous cells from one body organ or part to another. **2** a cancerous growth that has spread from another part of the body. ❑ *n., pl.* **me·tas·ta·ses** (mə tas/tə sēz) for 2.

me·tas·ta·size (mə tas/tə sīz), *v.* to spread by metastasis. ❑ *v.* **me·tas·ta·sized, me·tas·ta·siz·ing.**

met·a·tar·sal (met/ə tär/səl), **1** *adj.* of or about the metatarsus. **2** *n.* any bone of the metatarsus.

met·a·tar·sus (met/ə tär/səs), *n.* part of the foot, especially the bones, between the ankle and the toes. ❑ *n., pl.* **met·a·tar·si** (met/ə tär/sī).

met·a·zo·an (met/ə zō/ən), *n.* any animal with more than one cell. Metazoans have cells organized into tissues and organs.

mete (mēt), *v.* to give to each person a proper or fair share; distribute; allot: *mete out punishment, mete out praise.* ❑ *v.* **met·ed, met·ing.** ■ Other words that sound like this are **meat** and **meet**.

me·te·or (mē/tē ər), *n.* mass of stone or metal that enters Earth's atmosphere from outer space with enormous speed; shooting star. Meteors become so hot from rushing through the air that they glow and often burn up. [Meteor comes from a Greek word meaning "a thing in the air." **Meteorite** adds an ending meaning "rock." **Meteorology** is the study of clouds, rain, snow, fog, wind, and other things in the air.]

meteor

me·te·or·ic (mē/tē ôr/ik), *adj.* **1** of or about meteors: *meteoric dust.* **2** flashing like a meteor; brilliant and soon ended; swift: *a meteoric rise to fame.* —**me/te·or/i·cal·ly,** *adv.*

me·te·or·ite (mē/tē ə rīt/), *n.* mass of stone or metal that has fallen from outer space to a planet or moon; a fallen meteor. [See word history information at **meteor**.]

me·te·or·oid (mē/tē ə roid/), *n.* mass of stone or metal that travels through space and will become a meteor if it enters a planet's atmosphere.

me·te·or·o·log·i·cal (mē/tē ər ə loj/ə kəl), *adj.* of or about meteorology. —**me/te·or·o·log/i·cal·ly,** *adv.*

me·te·or·ol·o·gy (mē/tē ə rol/ə jē), *n.* science dealing with the atmosphere and weather. Meteorology includes the study of atmospheric conditions, such as winds, moisture, temperature, etc., and weather forecasts. [See word history information at **meteor**.] —**me/te·or·ol/o·gist,** *n.*

me·ter[1] (mē/tər), *n.* **1** any kind of poetic rhythm; the arrangement of beats or accents in a line of poetry: *The meter of "Jack and Jill went up the hill" is not the meter of "One, two, buckle my shoe."* **2** musical rhythm; the arrangement of beats in music: *Three-fourths meter is waltz time.*

me·ter[2] (mē/tər), *n.* the basic unit of length in the metric system.

me·ter[3] (mē/tər), **1** *n.* device that measures, or measures and records, the amount of gas, water, electricity, etc., used: *an electric meter.* **2** *v.* to measure or record with a meter.

-meter, *suffix.* **1** device for measuring ___: *speedometer = device for measuring speed.* **2** meter: *millimeter = one thousandth of a meter; kilometer = one thousand meters.*

me·ter-kil·o·gram-sec·ond (mē/tər kil/ə gram sek/ənd), *adj.* of or about a system of measurement in which the meter is the basic unit of length, the kilogram is the basic unit of mass or weight, and the second is the basic unit of time.

me·ter·stick (mē/tər stik/), *n.* a stick one meter long, used for measuring.

meth·a·done (meth/ə dōn), *n.* a narcotic drug used to relieve pain and to aid in curing heroin addiction.

M

a	hat	ė	term	ô	order	ch	child		a in about
ā	age	i	it	oi	oil	ng	long		e in taken
ä	far	ī	ice	ou	out	sh	she	ə {	i in pencil
â	care	o	hot	u	cup	th	thin		o in lemon
e	let	ō	open	u̇	put	ᴛʜ	then		u in circus
ē	equal	ò	saw	ü	rule	zh	measure		

meth·ane (meth′ān), *n.* a colorless, odorless, flammable gas, the simplest of the hydrocarbons; marsh gas. Methane occurs in marshes, oil wells, volcanoes, and coal mines.

meth·a·nol (meth′ə nȯl), *n.* a poisonous, flammable liquid made from wood, coal, or other organic matter, or made synthetically; methyl alcohol; wood alcohol.

me·thinks (mi thingks′), *v.* OLD USE. it seems to me. ❑ *v., past tense* **me·thought.**

meth·od (meth′əd), *n.* **1** way of doing something: *Roasting is one method of cooking meat.* ■ See Synonym Study at **way.** **2** order or system in getting things done or in thinking: *If you used more method, you wouldn't waste so much time.*

me·thod·i·cal (mə thod′ə kəl), *adj.* **1** done according to a method; systematic; orderly: *a methodical check of your work.* **2** acting according to a method: *A scientist is usually a methodical person.* —**me·thod′i·cal·ly,** *adv.* —**me·thod′i·cal·ness,** *n.*

Meth·od·ist (meth′ə dist), **1** *n.* member of a church that had its origin in the teachings and work of John Wesley; Wesleyan. **2** *adj.* of the Methodists.

me·thought (mi thȯt′), *v.* OLD USE. past tense of **methinks.**

Me·thu·se·lah (mə thü′zə lə), *n.* **1** (in the Bible) a man who lived 969 years. **2** any very old man.

meth·yl alcohol (meth′əl), wood alcohol; methanol.

me·tic·u·lous (mə tik′yə ləs), *adj.* extremely careful about small details. —**me·tic′u·lous·ly,** *adv.* —**me·tic′u·lous·ness,** *n.*

Mé·tis or **Me·tis** (mā tē′, mā′tē, *or* mā tēs′), *n.* CANADIAN. someone of mixed descent, especially one of French and North American Indian descent. ❑ *n., pl.* **Mé·tis** or **Me·tis** (mā tēs′ *or* mā tēz′).

met·ric (met′rik), *adj.* **1** of or about the metric system. **2** metrical.

met·ri·cal (met′rə kəl), *adj.* **1** of or written in meter, not in prose; having a regular arrangement of accents: *metrical verse.* **2** of, about, or used in measurement. —**met′ri·cal·ly,** *adv.*

met·ri·ca·tion (met′rə kā′shən), *n.* act or process of adopting the metric system.

metric system, the system of measurement used by almost all countries except the United States. It is based on the meter as its unit of length, and the kilogram as its unit of mass or weight. A common unit of volume in the metric system is the liter. See chart on page 975A.

metric ton, unit of weight or mass equal to 1000 kilograms.

met·ro or **Met·ro** (met′rō), *n.* (in Montreal, Paris and certain other cities) the subway system; subway. ❑ *n., pl.* **met·ros** or **Met·ros.**

met·ro·nome (met′rə nōm), *n.* device that can be adjusted to make loud ticking sounds at different speeds. Metronomes are used especially to mark time for persons practicing on musical instruments.

me·trop·o·lis (mə trop′ə lis), *n.* **1** a large city; important center: *Chicago is a busy metropolis.* **2** the most important city of a country or region: *New York is the metropolis of the United States.* ❑ *n., pl.* **me·trop·o·lis·es.**

metronome

met·ro·pol·i·tan (met′rə pol′ə-tən), **1** *adj.* of, about, or belonging to large cities: *metropolitan newspapers.* **2** *n.* person who lives in a large city and knows its ways. **3** *n.* archbishop presiding over a church province.

metropolitan area, region including a large city and its suburbs.

met·tle (met′l), *n.* spirit; courage. ■ Another word that sounds like this is **metal.**

on your mettle, ready to do your best.

met·tle·some (met′l səm), *adj.* spirited; courageous.

MeV, mev, or **Mev** (mev), *n.* a million electron volts, used as a unit for measuring in nuclear physics. ❑ *n., pl.* **MeV, mev,** or **Mev.**

mew (myü), **1** *n.* sound made by a cat or kitten. **2** *v.* to make this sound: *Our kitten mews when it gets hungry.*

mewl (myül), *v.* to cry like a baby; whimper. ■ Another word that sounds like this is **mule.**

mews (myüz), *n.sing. or pl.* stables, usually converted into living quarters, built around a court or alley. ■ Another word that sounds like this is **muse.**

Mex., **1** Mexican. **2** Mexico.

Mex·i·can (mek′sə kən), **1** *adj.* of or about Mexico or its people. **2** *n.* person born or living in Mexico.

Mexican Spanish, the Spanish language as it is spoken in Mexico.

WORD SOURCE **Mexican Spanish** has given a number of words to the English language. The words below are some of them.

abalone	chaps	macho
burrito	cholla	stampede
canyon	jalapeño	tamale

Mexican War, war between the United States and Mexico from 1846 to 1848.

Mex·i·co (mek′sə kō), *n.* **1** country in North America, just south of the W United States. *Capital:* Mexico City. **2** **Gulf of,** gulf of the Atlantic, south of the United States and east of Mexico. [Mexico comes from an Aztec word meaning either "place of the war god" or "moon center place."]

Mé·xi·co (me′hē kō), *n.* a state in S central Mexico.

Mexico City, capital of Mexico, in the central part.

me·zuz·ah (me züz′ə), *n.* a small container holding a parchment scroll inscribed with certain biblical passages and God's name on the outside. It is attached by Jews to the right-hand doorposts of their homes as a symbol of their religion.

mez·za·nine (mez′n ēn′), *n.* a low story, usually extending above part of the main floor to form a balcony.

mez·zo·so·pran·o (met′sō sə pran′ō), *n.* **1** a voice between soprano and contralto. **2** singer with such a voice. ❑ *n., pl.* **mez·zo·so·pran·os.**

Mg, symbol for magnesium.

mg or **mg.,** milligram or milligrams.

mgr., manager.

mi (mē), *n.* the third note of the musical scale. ❑ *n., pl.* **mis.** ■ Another word that sounds like this is **me.**

MI, Michigan (used with postal Zip Code).

mi., mile or miles.

MIA, missing in action.

Mi·am·i (mī am′ē), *n.* port in SE Florida, near the Atlantic.

mi·as·ma (mī az′mə), *n.* a foul-smelling vapor rising from decaying organic matter in swamps or marshes. It was formerly supposed to cause disease. ❑ *n., pl.* **mi·as·mas.**

mi·ca (mī′kə), *n.* mineral containing silicon, aluminum, and oxygen, which splits easily into thin, partly transparent layers; isinglass. —**mi′ca·like′,** *adj.*

Mi·cah (mī′kə), *n.* **1** Hebrew prophet. **2** book of the Bible. [Micah comes from Hebrew words meaning "Who is like the Lord?"]

mice (mīs), *n.* **1** plural of **mouse** (defs. 1,4). **2** a plural of **mouse** (def. 5).

Mich., Michigan.

Mi·chael (mī′kəl), *n.* **Saint,** (in the Bible) archangel who led the loyal angels in defeating the revolt of Lucifer. [Michael comes from a Hebrew word meaning "Who is like God?"]

Mi·chel·an·ge·lo (mī′kə lan′jə lō), *n.* 1475-1564, Italian sculptor, painter, architect, and poet. ■ Two of **Michelangelo's** most famous works are the statue of David and the ceiling of the Sistine Chapel. He was the most important architect of St. Peter's Cathedral.

Michelangelo painting

Mich·i·gan (mish′ə gən), *n.* **1** one of the north central states of the United States. *Abbreviation:* MI or Mich. *Capital:* Lansing. **2 Lake,** one of the five Great Lakes. It is entirely in the United States. [Michigan comes from an Algonquian word meaning "big lake." The state was named for the lake.] —**Mich·i·gan·der** (mish′i gan′dər), **Mich·i·gan·ite,** *n.*

Mi·cho·a·cán (mē′chō ä kän′), *n.* a state in SW Mexico.

Mic·mac (mik′mak), *n.* member of a tribe of American Indians living in eastern Canada. □ *n., pl.* **Mic·mac** or **Mic·macs.**

micro-, *prefix.* **1** small; very small: *microscope = device for seeing very small things.* **2** one millionth part of: *microsecond = one millionth part of a second.*

mi·crobe (mī′krōb), *n.* microorganism.

mi·cro·bi·ol·o·gy (mī′krō bī ol′ə jē), *n.* science dealing with microorganisms. —**mi·cro·bi·ol′o·gist,** *n.*

mi·cro·chip (mī′krō chip′), *n.* chip (def. 7).

mi·cro·com·pu·ter (mī′krō kəm pyü′tər), *n.* personal computer.

mi·cro·cop·y (mī′krō kop′ē), **1** *n.* a copy of a book or other printed work made on microfilm. **2** *v.* to make a copy on microfilm. □ *n., pl.* **mi·cro·cop·ies;** *v.* **mi·cro·cop·ied, mi·cro·cop·y·ing.**

mi·cro·cosm (mī′krō koz′əm), *n.* **1** a little world; universe in miniature. **2** someone or something thought of as a miniature representation of the universe.

mi·cro·fiche (mī′krō fēsh′), *n.* a small sheet of microfilm showing many pages of a book or other printed work. □ *n., pl.* **mi·cro·fiche** or **mi·cro·fich·es** (mī′krō fēsh′).

mi·cro·film (mī′krō film′), **1** *n.* a kind of film for making very small photographs of pages of a book, newspapers, records, etc., to preserve them in a very small space. **2** *v.* to photograph on microfilm.

mi·crom·e·ter (mī krom′ə tər), *n.* **1** device for measuring very small distances, angles, objects, etc. Certain kinds are used with a microscope or telescope. **2** a micrometer caliper.

micrometer caliper, a caliper having a screw with a very fine thread, used for very accurate measurement.

mi·cron (mī′kron), *n.* unit of length equal to one millionth of a meter.

Mi·cro·ne·sia (mī′krō nē′zhə), *n.* **1** group of many small islands in the W Pacific. See **Melanesia** for map. **2 Federated States of,** country including many of these islands. *Capital:* Palikir. —**Mi′cro·ne′sian,** *adj., n.*

mi·cro·or·gan·ism (mī′krō ôr′gə niz′əm), *n.* any living thing too small to be seen except with a microscope. Bacteria are microorganisms.

mi·cro·phone (mī′krə fōn), *n.* device for magnifying or transmitting sounds by changing sound waves into electrical signals. Microphones are used for broadcasting and recording.

mi·cro·proc·es·sor (mī′krō pros′əs ər *or* mī′krō prō′səs ər), *n.* an integrated circuit that functions as a small computer. Microprocessors are used to control the operations of cars, video games, microwave ovens, and other machines as well as in computers.

mi·cro·scope (mī′krə skōp), *n.* **1** device with a lens or combination of lenses for making small things look larger. Bacteria, blood cells, and other objects not visible to the naked eye are clearly visible through a microscope. **2** any of several kinds of devices using advanced electronic methods to magnify small objects many more times than lenses can: *an electron microscope.*

mi·cro·scop·ic (mī′krə skop′ik), *adj.* **1** not able to be seen without using a microscope; tiny: *microscopic germs.* **2** like a microscope; suggesting a microscope: *a microscopic eye for mistakes.* **3** of or done with a microscope: *a microscopic examination of a fly's wing.* **4** in great detail: *microscopic criticism of the book.* —**mi′cro·scop′i·cal·ly,** *adv.*

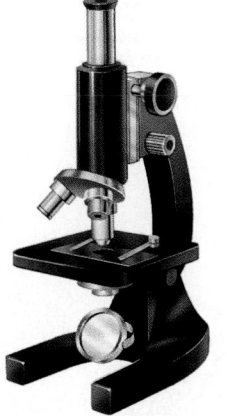

microscope

mi·cros·co·py (mī kros′kə pē), *n.* the use of a microscope; microscopic investigation.

mi·cro·sec·ond (mī′krō sek′ənd), *n.* unit of time equal to one millionth of a second.

mi·cro·sur·ger·y (mī′krō sėr′jər ē), *n.* surgery done on tiny structures of the body, using very small tools under high magnification.

mi·cro·wave (mī′krō wāv′), **1** *n.* an electromagnetic wave, with a wavelength between one millimeter and 30 centimeters. **2** *v.* to cook or heat food in a microwave oven. **3** *n.* microwave oven. □ *v.* **mi·cro·waved, mi·cro·wav·ing.**

microwave oven, oven in which food is cooked by the heat produced by microwaves. The microwaves penetrate the food and cook it quickly.

mid[1] (mid), *adj.* in the middle of; middle.

mid[2] or **'mid** (mid), *prep.* OLD USE. amid.

mid-, *prefix.* the middle part of; in the middle of: *midday = the middle part of the day; midsummer = in the middle of summer.*

mid·air (mid′âr′), *n.* the middle of the air; the air above the ground: *The acrobat made a somersault in midair.*

Mi·das (mī′dəs), *n.* (in Greek myths) a king of ancient times who had the power to turn everything he touched into gold. —**Mi′das·like′,** *adj.*

mid·day (mid′dā′), **1** *n.* the middle part of the day; noon. **2** *adj.* of midday: *a midday meal.*

mid·dle (mid′l), **1** *n.* the point or part that is the same distance from each end or side; the center: *the middle of the road.* **2** *adj.* halfway between; in the center; at the same distance from either end or side: *the middle house in the row.* **3** *adj.* in between; medium: *a man of middle size.* **4** *n.* the middle part of a person's body; waist.

middle age, time of life between youth and old age, from about 40 to 65 years of age.

mid·dle-aged (mid′l ājd′), *adj.* of middle age; between youth and old age.

Middle Ages, period in European history between ancient and modern times, from about A.D. 500 to about 1450.

Middle America, 1 the area between the United States and South America. It includes Mexico, Central America, and usually the islands of the West Indies. **2** ordinary middle-class Americans, especially those having moderately conservative or traditional attitudes and values. —**Middle American.**

middle C, the musical note on the first added line below the treble staff and the first above the bass staff. See picture at **clef.**

middle class, class of people who are socially and economically between the very wealthy class and the class of unskilled laborers and unemployed people. The middle class includes business and professional people, office workers, and many skilled workers. —**mid′dle-class′,** *adj.*

Middle Colonies, the four British colonies in North America south of New England and north of the Mason-Dixon line before the American Revolution: New York, New Jersey, Pennsylvania, and Delaware.

middle ear, a hollow space between the eardrum and the inner ear. In human beings it contains three small bones which pass on sound waves from the eardrum to the inner ear. See picture at **ear**[1].

Middle East, region extending from Sudan, Egypt, and Turkey in the west to Iran in the east, and including the countries of SW Asia. Iraq, Israel, Jordan, Syria, and Saudi Arabia are countries in the Middle East. Also, **Mideast.** —**Middle Eastern.**

Middle English, 1 period in the development of the English language between Old English and Modern English, lasting from about 1100 to about 1500. **2** language of this period. Chaucer wrote in Middle English.

mid·dle·man (mid′l man′), *n.* **1** seller or company that buys goods from the producer and sells them to a retailer or directly to the consumer. **2** person who acts as a go-between for two per-

a	hat	e	term	ô	order	ch	child		a in about
ā	age	i	it	oi	oil	ng	long		e in taken
ä	far	ī	ice	ou	out	sh	she	ə	i in pencil
â	care	o	hot	u	cup	th	thin		o in lemon
e	let	ō	open	u̇	put	ŦH	then		u in circus
ē	equal	ȯ	saw	ü	rule	zh	measure		

sons or groups concerned in some matter of business. ❑ *n., pl.* **mid·dle·men.**

mid·dle-of-the-road (mid'l əv ᴛнə rōd'), *adj.* moderate, not extreme, especially in politics: *a middle-of-the-road candidate.* —**mid'dle-of-the-road'er,** *n.*

middle school, school between elementary school and high school, usually including grades five through eight.

mid·dle·weight (mid'l wāt'), *n.* **1** person of average weight. **2** boxer who weighs more than 147 pounds (67 kilograms) and less than 160 pounds (73 kilograms).

Middle West, Midwest.

Middle Western, Midwestern. —**Middle Westerner.**

mid·dling (mid'ling), *adj.* medium in size, quality, grade, etc.; ordinary; average. —**mid'dling·ly,** *adv.*

mid·dy (mid'ē), *n.* **1** INFORMAL. midshipman. **2** middy blouse. ❑ *n., pl.* **mid·dies.**

middy blouse, a loose blouse having a collar with a broad flap at the back, worn by sailors and others.

Mid·east (mid'ēst'), *n.* Middle East.

Mid·east·ern (mid'ē'stərn), *adj.* Middle Eastern.

midge (mij), *n.* any of many small two-winged flies that resemble mosquitoes but do not bite.

midg·et (mij'it), **1** *n.* someone very much smaller than normal but shaped the same as other people; a tiny person. **2** *n.* anything much smaller than the usual size for its type or kind. **3** *adj.* very small; miniature; diminutive. ▪ See Usage Note at **dwarf.**

mid·land (mid'lənd), **1** *n.* the middle part of a country; the interior. **2** *n.pl.* **Midlands,** the central part of England. **3** *adj.* in, of, or from the midland.

mid·most (mid'mōst'), *adj.* in the exact middle; nearest the middle.

mid·night (mid'nīt'), **1** *n.* 12 o'clock at night; the middle of the night. **2** *adj.* of or at midnight. **3** *adj.* dark as midnight: *a midnight blue dress.*

midnight sun, sun seen all day and all night in the arctic and antarctic regions during their summers.

mid-o·cean ridge (mid'ō'shən), a mountain range rising from the middle of an ocean floor, but not reaching the surface. There are mountains of this sort under most of the world's oceans.

mid·point (mid'point'), *n.* **1** the middle part of anything; midway point: *the midpoint of a journey.* **2** (in mathematics) the point on a line segment that divides it into two equal segments.

mid·riff (mid'rif), *n.* the middle portion of the human body.

mid·sec·tion (mid'sek'shən), *n.* **1** section in the middle. **2** midriff.

mid·ship (mid'ship'), *adj.* in, of, or belonging to the middle part of a ship.

mid·ship·man (mid'ship'mən), *n.* student at the U.S. Naval Academy at Annapolis. ❑ *n., pl.* **mid·ship·men.**

mid·ships (mid'ships'), *adv.* amidships.

midst[1] (midst), *n.* position or condition of being surrounded, especially by a number of persons: *a stranger in their midst.*

in the midst of, 1 in the middle of; among; surrounded by: *in the midst of a forest.* **2** during: *in the midst of a storm.*

midst[2] or **'midst** (midst), *prep.* OLD USE. amidst; amid.

mid·stream (mid'strēm'), *n.* the middle of a stream.

mid·sum·mer (mid'sum'ər), **1** *n.* the middle of summer. **2** *n.* the time around June 21. **3** *adj.* in the middle of summer.

mid·term (mid'tėrm'), **1** *n.* the middle of a school term or of a term of political office. **2** *adj.* taking place in the middle of a school term: *midterm exams.* **3** *n.* examination given in the middle of a school term.

mid·town (mid'toun'), **1** *n.* middle section of a city or town, between downtown and uptown. **2** *adj.* of or located in midtown.

Midway (mid'wā'), *n.* a small group of islands in the central Pacific, NW of Honolulu, Hawaii. A naval battle, the **Battle of Midway,** was fought near here in June 1942, resulting in the loss of four Japanese aircraft carriers and a victory for the U.S. Navy.

mid·way (mid'wā'), **1** *adv., adj.* in the middle; halfway: *midway between the trees and the lake, a midway position.* **2** *n.* place for games, rides, and other amusements at a fair.

mid·week (mid'wēk'), **1** *n.* the middle of the week. **2** *adj.* in the middle of the week.

Mid·west (mid'west'), *n.* part of the United States west of the Appalachian Mountains, east of the Rocky Mountains, and north of the Ohio River and the S boundaries of Missouri and Kansas. Also, **Middle West.**

Mid·west·ern (mid'wes'tərn), *adj.* of the Midwest. Also, **Middle Western.** —**Mid'wes'ter·ner,** *n.*

mid·wife (mid'wīf'), *n.* nurse trained to help women in childbirth. ❑ *n., pl.* **mid·wives.**

mid·win·ter (mid'win'tər), **1** *n.* the middle of winter. **2** *n.* the time around December 21. **3** *adj.* in the middle of winter.

mid·year (mid'yir'), **1** *adj.* happening in the middle of the year: *a midyear examination.* **2** *n.pl.* **midyears,** INFORMAL. midyear examinations.

mien (mēn), *n.* manner of holding the head and body that shows personality, mood, or attitude: *have the mien of a judge.* ▪ Another word that sounds like this is **mean.**

Mies van der Rohe (mēz' van dər rō'ə), **Lud·wig** (lüt'vik), 1886-1969, American architect, born in Germany. His buildings have simple rectangular forms with much glass. His philosophy of design was often described by the phrase "less is more."

miffed (mift), *adj.* offended; irritated; annoyed: *My friend seemed a little miffed when I didn't accept the invitation.*

might[1] (mit), *v.* **1** past tense of **may:** *Mom told me I might go to the movies.* **2** possibly did: *We thought he might have missed the train.* **3** possibly would: *She might like basketball if she were taller.* ▪ Another word that sounds like this is **mite.**

might[2] (mit), *n.* great power; strength: *Work with all your might.* ▪ Another word that sounds like this is **mite.** —**might'less,** *adj.*

with might and main, with all your strength.

might·i·ly (mi'tə lē), *adv.* **1** in a mighty manner; powerfully; vigorously: *We pushed mightily and finally freed the car from the snowbank.* **2** very much; greatly: *We were mightily pleased at our win.*

might·n't (mit'nt), might not.

might·y (mi'tē), **1** *adj.* showing strength or power; powerful; strong: *a mighty ruler, mighty force.* **2** *adj.* very great: *a mighty famine.* **3** *adv.* INFORMAL. very: *a mighty long time.* ❑ *adj.* **might·i·er, might·i·est.** —**might'i·ness,** *n.*

mi·graine (mi'grān), *n.* a severe headache, usually on one side only, and often with nausea. [Migraine comes from two Greek words meaning "half skull."]

mi·grant (mi'grənt), **1** *n.* person or animal that migrates. **2** *n.* worker, especially a farm worker, who travels from one area to another in search of work. **3** *adj.* migrating; roving: *a migrant worker.*

mi·grate (mi'grāt), *v.* **1** to move from one place to settle in another: *Pioneers from New England migrated to all parts of the United States.* **2** to go from one region to another with the change in the seasons: *Most birds migrate to warmer countries in the winter.* ❑ *v.* **mi·grat·ed, mi·grat·ing.** —**mi'gra·tor,** *n.*

mi·gra·tion (mi grā'shən), *n.* **1** act of migrating: *Some kinds of birds travel thousands of miles on their migrations.* **2** number of people or animals migrating together.

migration

mi·gra·to·ry (mī′grə tôr′ē), *adj.* **1** moving from one place to another; migrating: *migratory laborers, migratory birds.* **2** of or relating to migration: *the migratory pattern of elephants.*

mi·ka·do (mə kä′dō), *n.* a former title of the emperor of Japan. It is seldom used now except in poetry. □ *n., pl.* **mi·ka·dos.**

mike (mīk), INFORMAL. **1** *n.* microphone. **2** *v.* to provide with a microphone or transmit by means of a microphone: *The actors are all miked.* □ *v.* **miked, mik·ing.**

mil., **1** military. **2** militia.

mi·la·dy (mi lā′dē), *n.* a polite title used in writing or speaking to an English noblewoman. □ *n., pl.* **mi·la·dies.**

Mi·lan (mi lan′), *n.* city in N Italy.

mild (mīld), *adj.* **1** gentle or kind: *a mild disposition.* **2** warm; calm; temperate; not harsh or severe: *a mild climate, a mild winter.* **3** soft or sweet to the senses; not sharp, sour, bitter, or strong in taste: *mild cheese.* —**mild′ly,** *adv.* —**mild′ness,** *n.*

mil·dew (mil′dü), **1** *n.* any of various kinds of fungi producing a whitish coating or discoloration on plants or on paper, clothes, leather, etc., during damp weather: *Mildew killed the rosebuds in our garden.* **2** *n.* the coating, discoloration, or damage produced by such a fungus: *Damp clothes left in a pile will show mildew in a few days.* **3** *v.* to cover or become covered with mildew: *A pile of damp clothes in the closet had mildewed.*

mile (mīl), *n.* **1** unit of distance equal to 5280 feet; statute mile. **2** nautical mile. [**Mile** comes from a Latin word meaning "one thousand." The Romans measured a mile by taking a thousand long steps.]

mile·age (mī′lij), *n.* **1** miles traveled: *Our car's mileage last year was 10,000 miles.* **2** miles traveled per gallon of gasoline: *Do you get good mileage with your car?* **3** length, extent, or distance in miles: *The mileage of a railroad is its total number of miles of roadbed.* **4** an allowance for traveling expenses at so much a mile: *When I use my car for company business, I am given a mileage of 25 cents per mile.* **5** long use or wear: *We got a lot of mileage out of that old TV.*

mile·post (mil′pōst′), *n.* post set up to show the distance in miles to a certain place or the distance covered.

mile·stone (mil′stōn′), *n.* **1** stone set up to show the distance in miles to a certain place. **2** an important event: *The invention of printing was a milestone in progress.*

mi·lieu (mē lyü′), *n.* surroundings; environment.

mil·i·tan·cy (mil′ə tən sē), *n.* warlike behavior or tendency; militant spirit or policy.

mil·i·tant (mil′ə tənt), **1** *adj.* aggressive; fighting; warlike: *a militant group.* **2** *adj.* active in serving a cause or in spreading a belief: *a militant isolationist.* **3** *n.* a warlike person. —**mil′i·tant·ly,** *adv.*

mil·i·ta·rism (mil′ə tə riz′əm), *n.* **1** policy of making military organization and power very strong. **2** military spirit and ideals.

mil·i·tar·ist (mil′ə tər ist), *n.* **1** someone who believes in a very powerful military organization. **2** an expert in warfare and military matters. —**mil′i·ta·ris′tic,** *adj.* —**mil′i·ta·ris′ti·cal·ly,** *adv.*

mil·i·ta·rize (mil′ə tə rīz′), *v.* **1** to make the military organization of a country very powerful. **2** to fill with military spirit and ideals. □ *v.* **mil·i·ta·rized, mil·i·ta·riz·ing.** —**mil′i·tar·i·za′tion,** *n.*

mil·i·tar·y (mil′ə ter′ē), **1** *adj.* of or about armed forces or war: *military training, military history.* **2** *adj.* done by armed forces: *military maneuvers.* **3** *adj.* fit for or typical of armed forces: *military discipline.* **4** *adj.* suitable for war; warlike: *military valor.* **5** *n.* **the military,** the armed forces: *an officer of the military.* —**mil′i·tar′i·ly,** *adv.*

military police, soldiers or marines who act as police for the Army or Marine Corps.

mil·i·tate (mil′ə tāt), *v.* to have or exert force; act; work; operate against or in favor of: *Bad reviews militated against the play's success.* □ *v.* **mil·i·tat·ed, mil·i·tat·ing.** ■ See Usage Note at **mitigate.**

mi·li·tia (mə lish′ə), *n.* army of citizens who are not regular soldiers but who undergo training for emergency duty or national defense. Every state of the United States has a militia called the National Guard. □ *n., pl.* **mi·li·tias.**

mi·li·tia·man (mə lish′ə mən), *n.* soldier in the militia. □ *n., pl.* **mi·li·tia·men.**

milk (milk), **1** *n.* the white liquid secreted by female mammals for the nourishment of their young, especially that from cows, which we drink and use in cooking. **2** *n.* any kind of liquid resembling this, such as the white juice of a plant, tree, or nut: *the milk of a coconut.* **3** *v.* to draw milk from a cow, goat, etc. **4** *v.* to drain contents, strength, information, wealth, etc., from; exploit: *The dishonest treasurer milked the club treasury.* —**milk′less,** *adj.*

cry over spilled milk, to waste sorrow or regret on what has happened and cannot be changed.

milk·er (mil′kər), *n.* **1** someone who milks. **2** machine that milks. **3** cow, goat, etc., that gives milk.

milk·maid (milk′mād′), *n.* woman who milks cows.

milk·man (milk′man′), *n.* person who sells milk or delivers it to customers. □ *n., pl.* **milk·men.**

milk of magnesia, a milk-white medicine, used as a laxative and to counteract acidity.

milk shake, a drink consisting of milk, flavoring, and often ice cream, shaken or beaten until frothy.

milk snake, a large harmless king snake of North America, often found in barns.

milk·sop (milk′sop′), *n.* someone who lacks courage; coward.

milk sugar, lactose.

milk tooth, one of the first set of teeth; temporary tooth of a young child or animal.

milk·weed (milk′wēd′), *n.* any of numerous plants with white juice that looks like milk.

milk·y (mil′kē), *adj.* **1** like milk; white as milk; whitish. **2** of or containing milk. □ *adj.* **milk·i·er, milk·i·est.** —**milk′i·ly,** *adv.* —**milk′i·ness,** *n.*

Milky Way, **1** a broad band of faint light that stretches across the sky at night. It is made up of countless stars too far away to be seen separately without a telescope. **2** the galaxy in which these countless stars are found; Galaxy. Earth, the sun, and all the other planets around the sun are part of the Milky Way.

Milky Way (def. 1)

mill (mil), **1** *n.* a building containing a machine for grinding grain into flour or meal. **2** *n.* a machine for grinding grain into flour or meal. **3** *v.* to grind grain into flour or meal. **4** *n.* any machine for crushing or grinding: *a coffee mill, a pepper mill.* **5** *v.* to grind into powder or pulp; grind very fine. **6** *n.* a building where manufacturing is done: *Cotton cloth is made in a cotton mill.* **7** *v.* to cut a series of fine notches or ridges on the edge of a coin: *A dime is milled.* **8** *v.* to move about in a confused way: *The frightened cattle began to mill around.*

Mill (mil), *n.* **John Stu·art** (stü′ərt), 1806-1873, English economist and philosopher. ■ **Mill** believed that workers should get more of the profits of the businesses they worked for and he believed in increased rights for women.

a	hat	ė	term	ô	order	ch	child		
ā	age	i	it	oi	oil	ng	long		a in about
ä	far	ī	ice	ou	out	sh	she		e in taken
â	care	o	hot	u	cup	th	thin	ə	i in pencil
e	let	ō	open	ủ	put	ŦH	then		o in lemon
ē	equal	ò	saw	ü	rule	zh	measure		u in circus

M

Mil·lay (mə lā′), *n.* **Ed·na St. Vin·cent** (ed′nə sänt′ vin′sənt), 1892-1950, American poet. She won the Pulitzer Prize for poetry in 1923.

mil·len·ni·al (mə len′ē əl), *adj.* of or about a millennium.

mil·len·ni·um (mə len′ē əm), *n.* **1** period of a thousand years: *The world is many milleniums old.* **2** period of a thousand years during which Jesus is expected by some churches to reign on earth. **3** period of righteousness and happiness. ❑ *n., pl.* **mil·len·ni·ums, mil·len·ni·a** (mə len′ē ə).

mill·er (mil′ər), *n.* **1** someone who owns or runs a mill, especially a flour mill. **2** any of several moths with wings that look as if they were powdered with flour.

Mil·ler (mil′ər), *n.* **1 Arthur**, born 1915, American playwright. His plays include *Death of A Salesman* and *The Crucible*. **2 Glenn** (glen), 1904-1944, American bandleader and trombone player. He was among the musicians who made the "big band" style widely popular.

mil·let (mil′it), *n.* any of several cereal grasses, grown for food or hay. The grain seeds are small and round.

milli-, *prefix.* one thousandth part of: *milligram = one thousandth part of a gram.*

mil·li·bar (mil′ə bär), *n.* unit for measuring atmospheric pressure. It is equal to 1000 dynes per square centimeter. Standard atmospheric pressure at sea level is about 1013 millibars, or 14.69 pounds per square inch.

mil·li·gram (mil′ə gram), *n.* unit of weight or mass equal to ¹⁄₁₀₀₀ of a gram.

Mil·li·kan (mil′ə kən), *n.* **Ro·bert** (rob′ərt), 1868-1953, American physicist. He won the Nobel Prize for physics in 1923.

mil·li·li·ter (mil′ə lē′tər), *n.* unit of volume equal to ¹⁄₁₀₀₀ of a liter.

mil·li·me·ter (mil′ə mē′tər), *n.* unit of length equal to ¹⁄₁₀₀₀ of a meter.

mil·li·ner (mil′ə nər), *n.* someone who makes, trims, or sells women's hats.

mil·li·ner·y (mil′ə ner′ē), *n.* **1** women's hats. **2** business of making, trimming, or selling women's hats.

mil·lion (mil′yən), **1** *n., adj.* one thousand thousand; 1,000,000. **2** *adj.* a very large number; very many: *millions of stars.*

mil·lion·aire (mil′yə nâr′), *n.* **1** someone whose wealth amounts to a million or more dollars, pounds, francs, etc. **2** a very wealthy person.

mil·lionth (mil′yənth), *adj., n.* **1** last in a series of a million. **2** one of a million equal parts.

mil·li·pede (mil′ə pēd′), *n.* any of very many small, wormlike animals that have two pairs of legs apiece for most of their many body segments.

mil·li·sec·ond (mil′ə sek′ənd), *n.* unit of time equal to ¹⁄₁₀₀₀ of a second.

mill·pond (mil′pond′), *n.* pond supplying water to drive a mill wheel.

mill·race (mil′rās′), *n.* **1** current of water that drives a mill wheel. **2** channel in which it flows to the mill.

mill·stone (mil′stōn′), *n.* **1** either of a pair of round, flat stones for grinding corn, wheat, etc. **2** a heavy burden. **3** anything that grinds or crushes.

mill·stream (mil′strēm′), *n.* the stream in a millrace.

mill wheel, wheel that is turned by water and supplies power for a mill.

Milne (miln), *n.* **A. A.**, 1882-1956, English writer. He created the characters of Christopher Robin and Winnie-the-Pooh.

mi·lord (mi lôrd′), *n.* a polite title used in speaking or writing to an English nobleman.

milt (milt), *n.* the sperm cells of male fishes with the milky fluid containing them.

Mil·ton (milt′n), *n.* **John**, 1608-1674, English poet. His most famous work is *Paradise Lost.*

Mil·wau·kee (mil wȯ′kē), *n.* port in SE Wisconsin, on Lake Michigan. [**Milwaukee** probably comes from an Algonquian word meaning "good land."]

mime (mīm), **1** *n.* actor, especially in a pantomime. **2** *v.* to imitate; mimic. **3** *n.* pantomime. **4** *v.* to act in a pantomime; act without using words. ❑ *v.* **mimed, mim·ing. —mim′er,** *n.*

mim·e·o·graph (mim′ē ə graf), **1** *n.* machine for making copies of written or typewritten materials by means of stencils. **2** *v.* to make copies with a mimeograph.

mim·ic (mim′ik), **1** *v.* to make fun of by imitating: *The children tried to annoy the baby-sitter by mimicking her accent.* ■ See Synonym Study at **imitate. 2** *n.* person or thing that imitates. **3** *v.* to copy closely; imitate: *A parrot can mimic a person's voice.* **4** *v.* to resemble closely in form, color, etc. **5** *adj.* not real, but imitated or pretended for some purpose: *We staged a mimic rescue of a drowning person in our first-aid class.* **6** *adj.* imitative: *mimic gestures.* ❑ *v.* **mim·icked, mim·ick·ing. —mim′ick·er,** *n.*

mim·ic·ry (mim′ik rē), *n.* **1** act of mimicking. **2** the close outward resemblance of an animal to its surroundings or to some different animal, especially for protection or concealment.

mi·mo·sa (mi mō′sə), *n.* any of several trees, bushes, or herbs growing in warm regions, usually having fernlike leaves and heads of small pink, purple, or white flowers. ❑ *n., pl.* **mi·mo·sas.**

min., 1 minimum. **2** minute or minutes.

min·a·ret (min′ə ret′), *n.* a slender, high tower attached to a Muslim mosque with one or more balconies, from which a muezzin, or crier, calls the people to prayer. [**Minaret** comes from an Arabic word meaning "lighthouse" or "candlestick." The tall, slender minaret is shaped like those other things.]

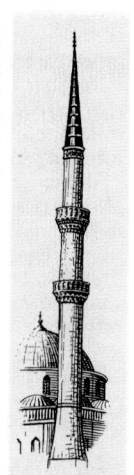

minaret

mince (mins), **1** *v.* to chop up into very small pieces. **2** *n.* mincemeat. **3** *v.* to put on fine airs in speaking or walking. **4** *v.* to walk with little short steps. ❑ *v.* **minced, minc·ing.** [**Mince** comes from a Latin word meaning "small."] **—minc′er,** *n.*

not to mince matters or **not to mince words,** to speak plainly and frankly.

mince·meat (mins′mēt′), *n.* mixture of chopped apples, suet, raisins, currants, spices, etc., and sometimes meat, used as a filling for pies.

mince pie, pie filled with mincemeat.

minc·ing (min′sing), *adj.* **1** putting on a dainty and refined manner: *a mincing voice.* **2** walking with little short steps. **—minc′ing·ly,** *adv.*

mind (mīnd), **1** *n.* the part of a person that knows, remembers, thinks, feels, wishes, wills, etc. **2** *n.* mental ability; intelligence; intellect: *have a good mind.* **3** *n.* person who has intelligence: *the greatest minds of the period.* **4** *n.* mental health: *in your right mind.* **5** *n.* what one thinks or feels; opinion; view: *change your mind.* **6** *n.* attention; mental effort: *Keep your mind on your work.* **7** *n.* remembrance or recollection; memory: *Keep the rules in mind.* **8** *v.* to give heed to: *Mind my words!* **9** *v.* to take notice; observe. **10** *v.* to be careful concerning: *Mind the step.* **11** *v.* to take care: *Mind that you come on time.* **12** *v.* to look after; take care of; tend: *Mind the baby.* **13** *v.* to obey: *Mind your father and mother.* **14** *v.* to feel bad about; object to: *Do you mind closing the door for me? Some people don't mind cold weather.* **15** *v.* DIALECT. to remember. **—mind′er,** *n.*

bear in mind or **keep in mind,** to remember.

be of one mind, to have the same opinion; agree: *We are of one mind in loving chocolate ice cream.*

cross your mind, to occur to you; come into your thoughts suddenly.

have a mind to, to intend to; think of doing.

have in mind, to be thinking of: *That's a good suggestion; what else do you have in mind?*

keep in mind, to give your attention to; remember: *I hope you will keep my suggestions in mind.*

make up your mind, to decide: *I made up my mind to study harder and get better grades.*

never mind, don't let it trouble you; it does not matter.

on your mind, in your mind; in your thoughts.

out of your mind, very foolish; senseless.

put in mind, to remind: *Your joke puts me in mind of a joke I heard yesterday.*

set your mind on, to want very much: *She set her mind on going to college.*

to your mind, in your opinion; to your way of thinking.

USAGE NOTE **Mind,** meaning "mental health," is not commonly used now. Careful writers and speakers avoid the phrase *out of your mind* except to mean foolish and senseless.

Min·da·na·o (min′də nä′ō), *n.* the second largest island in the Philippines.

mind-bog·gling (mind′bog′ling), *adj.* overwhelming to the mind; extremely exciting but difficult to believe or understand: *It's mind-boggling to think that dinosaurs once walked right where we live.*

mind·ed (min′did), *adj.* inclined; disposed: *Come a little early, if you are so minded.*

mind·ful (mīnd′fəl), *adj.* **1** having in mind; heedful: *Mindful of your advice, I went slowly.* **2** taking thought; careful: *We had to be mindful of every step we took on the slippery sidewalk.* —**mind′ful·ly,** *adv.* —**mind′ful·ness,** *n.*

mind·less (mīnd′lis), *adj.* **1** without mind or intelligence; stupid. **2** not taking thought; careless. —**mind′less·ly,** *adv.* —**mind′less·ness,** *n.*

mind·set or **mind-set** (mīnd′set′), *n.* frame of mind; attitude resulting from events and environment: *Because she has been in two accidents, she drives with a very defensive mindset.*

mind's eye, mental view or vision; imagination.

mine[1] (mīn), **1** *pron.* the one or ones belonging to me: *This book is mine.* **2** *adj.* OLD USE: my (used only before a vowel or *h*): *mine eyes.*

mine[2] (mīn), **1** *n.* a large hole dug in the earth to get out ores, precious stones, coal, salt, etc.: *a gold mine, a copper mine.* **2** *v.* to dig such a hole. **3** *v.* to dig in for coal, gold, etc.: *to mine the earth.* **4** *v.* to get by digging: *to mine coal, to mine gold.* **5** *v.* to work in a mine. **6** *n.* a rich or plentiful source: *The book proved to be a mine of information about radio.* **7** *n.* an underground passage in which an explosive is placed to blow up an enemy's trenches, fort, etc. **8** *v.* to make underground passages below. **9** *n.* bomb put under water or shallowly buried to blow up enemy troops or equipment. **10** *v.* to lay such bombs under: *to mine the mouth of a harbor.* ❑ *v.* **mined, min·ing.** —**min′a·ble** or **mine′a·ble,** *adj.*

mine[2] (def. 1)

min·er (mī′nər), *n.* person who works in a mine: *a coal miner.* ■ Another word that sounds like this is **minor.**

min·er·al (min′ər əl), **1** *n.* substance obtained by mining. Coal, gold, and mica are minerals. **2** *n.* any substance that is not alive or has not been alive. Sand is a mineral. **3** *adj.* containing minerals. **4** *n.* any chemical element the body needs to get in small amounts from food in order to function properly, such as calcium, potassium, etc.

min·er·al·o·gy (min′ə rol′ə jē), *n.* science of minerals. —**min′er·a·log′i·cal,** *adj.* —**min′er·al′o·gist,** *n.*

mineral oil, **1** any oil that comes from minerals. **2** a colorless, odorless, tasteless oil made from petroleum and often used as a laxative.

mineral water, water containing mineral salts or gases. People drink various mineral waters for their health.

Mi·ner·va (mə nėr′və), *n.* Roman goddess of wisdom, the arts, and war. The Greeks called her Athena.

min·e·stro·ne (min′ə strō′nē), *n.* a thick soup containing vegetables, vermicelli, etc.

mine·sweep·er (mīn′swē′pər), *n.* ship used to remove, disarm, or harmlessly explode underwater mines.

min·gle (ming′gəl), *v.* **1** to combine in a mixture; mix; blend: *Two rivers that join mingle their waters.* ■ See Synonym Study at **mix.** **2** to associate: *I tried to mingle with everyone at the party.* ❑ *v.* **min·gled, min·gling.** —**min′gler,** *n.*

min·i (min′ē), **1** *adj.* small or short for its kind: *Our weekend in New York was a mini vacation.* **2** *n.* anything very small in size: *They have a regular TV in the den and a mini in the bedroom.* ❑ *n., pl.* **min·is.**

mini-, *prefix.* small: *minibus = a small bus.*

min·i·a·ture (min′ē ə chùr *or* min′ə chər), **1** *n.* anything represented on a small scale: *In the museum there is a miniature of the ship "Mayflower."* **2** *adj.* done or made on a very small scale; tiny: *miniature cars, miniature furniture for a dollhouse.* ■ See Synonym Study at **tiny.** **3** *n.* a very small painting, usually a portrait. [**Miniature** comes from a Latin word meaning "to paint something red." Red paint was often used in painting illustrations in ancient books. Those illustrations were often very small.]

miniature pinscher, a breed of dog resembling a small Doberman pinscher.

min·i·a·tur·ize (min′ē ə chə rīz′ *or* min′ə chə rīz′), *v.* to reduce to a very small size: *to miniaturize electronic devices.* ❑ *v.* **min·i·a·tur·ized, min·i·a·tur·iz·ing.** —**min′i·a·tur·i·za′tion,** *n.*

min·i·bike (min′ē bīk′), *n.* a small motorcycle.

min·i·cam (min′ē kam), *n.* a miniature camera, especially a television or video camera.

min·i·mal (min′ə məl), *adj.* least possible; very small: *minimal damage, a minimal cost.* —**min′i·mal·ly,** *adv.*

min·i·mize (min′ə mīz), *v.* **1** to reduce to the least possible amount or extent: *The polar explorers took every precaution to minimize the dangers of their trip.* **2** to make something seem smaller, less important, etc., than it actually is: *She minimized the work involved in order to get me to do the job.* **3** to make a computer program take up less space on a computer screen, by changing its display from full information to an icon. ❑ *v.* **min·i·mized, min·i·miz·ing.** —**min′i·mi·za′tion,** *n.* —**min′i·miz′er,** *n.*

min·i·mum (min′ə məm), **1** *n.* the least possible amount; lowest amount: *Each of the children had to drink some milk at breakfast; half a glass was the minimum.* **2** *adj.* least possible; lowest: *Eighteen is the minimum age for voting in the United States.* ❑ *n., pl.* **min·i·mums, min·i·ma** (min′ə mə).

minimum wage, the pay set by law or agreement as the lowest given to certain workers.

min·ing (mī′ning), *n.* **1** the work or business of taking ores, coal, or other minerals from the earth. **2** the laying of bombs underground or underwater.

min·i·ser·ies (min′ē sir′ēz), *n.* a TV program telling a single story in a number of episodes shown on more than one day. ❑ *n., pl.* **min·i·ser·ies.**

min·i·skirt (min′ē skėrt′), *n.* a very short skirt, with a hemline several inches above the knee.

min·is·ter (min′ə stər), **1** *n.* member of the clergy; spiritual guide; pastor. **2** *v.* to act as a servant or nurse; be of service or aid; be helpful: *minister to a sick person's needs.* **3** *n.* person who is in charge of a department of a parliamentary government: *the Minister of Labor.* **4** *n.* person sent to a foreign country to represent his or her own government: *the U.S. Minister to Switzerland.*

min·is·ter·i·al (min′ə stir′ē əl), *adj.* **1** of or about a minister. **2** suited to a minister: *a ministerial manner.*

a	hat	ė	term	ô	order	ch	child		a in about
ā	age	i	it	oi	oil	ng	long		e in taken
ä	far	ī	ice	ou	out	sh	she	ə	i in pencil
â	care	o	hot	u	cup	th	thin		o in lemon
e	let	ō	open	ù	put	ᴛʜ	then		u in circus
ē	equal	ò	saw	ü	rule	zh	measure		

M

min·is·tra·tion (min′ə strā′shən), *n.* **1** service as a minister of a church. **2** help; aid: *give ministration to the poor.*

min·is·try (min′ə strē), *n.* **1** office, duties, or time of service of a minister. **2** ministers of a church; clergy. **3** ministers of a government in certain countries. Government ministers in these countries are often the same as cabinet members in the United States. **4** a government department under a minister. **5** act of ministering or serving. □ *n., pl.* **min·is·tries** for 1,4,5.

min·i·van (min′ē van′), *n.* a small van.

mink (mingk), *n.* **1** either of two small mammals that resemble weasels and live in water part of the time. One came originally from North America, the other from northern Europe and Asia. **2** the valuable fur of North American minks. —**mink′like′**, *adj.*

min·ke whale (ming′kə), a small, common whale of tropical and temperate waters.

Minn., Minnesota.

Min·ne·ap·o·lis (min′ē ap′ə lis), *n.* city in SE Minnesota, on the Mississippi.

Min·ne·so·ta (min′ə sō′tə), *n.* one of the midwestern states of the United States. *Abbreviation:* MN or Minn. *Capital:* St. Paul. [Minnesota comes from a Sioux word meaning "sky-colored water." The name was given first to the Minnesota River, then to the state.] —**Min′ne·so′tan**, *n.*

min·now (min′ō), *n.* **1** any of very many small freshwater fishes related to the carp. **2** any tiny fish. □ *n., pl.* **min·nows** or **min·now.**

mi·nor (mī′nər), **1** *adj.* less important; smaller; lesser: *a minor fault. Your paper is good; it contains only a few minor errors.* **2** *adj.* of a lower rank or order: *a minor poet, a minor political party.* **3** *n.* someone under 18 or 21 years, the legal age of responsibility. **4** in music: **a** *adj.* less by a half step than the corresponding major interval: *a minor chord.* **b** *adj.* noting a scale or key whose third tone is minor in relation to the main tone: *the C minor scale or key.* **c** *n.* a minor scale, key, chord, interval, etc. **5** *n.* subject or course of study to which a student gives less time than a major subject: *His minor is French.* **6** *v.* to have or take as a minor subject of study: *She will minor in French.* ▪ Another word that sounds like this is **miner.**

mi·nor·i·ty (mə nôr′ə tē *or* mī nôr′ə tē), *n.* **1** the smaller number or part; less than half: *A minority of the voters wanted a tax increase, but the majority defeated it.* **2** a group within a country, state, etc., that differs in race, religion, national origin, etc., from the larger part of the population. **3** condition or time of being under the legal age of responsibility. □ *n., pl.* **mi·nor·i·ties** for 1,2.

minor league, any professional sports league or association, especially in baseball, other than the major leagues.

mi·nor-league (mī′nər lēg′), *adj.* **1** of or about a minor league or the minor leagues. **2** inferior or cheap: *a minor-league writer.*

Mi·nos (mī′nəs), *n.* (in Greek legends) a king, who built the Labyrinth at Crete and kept the Minotaur in it.

Mi·not (mī′not), *n.* city in N central North Dakota.

Min·o·taur (min′ə tôr′), *n.* (in Greek legends) a monster with a bull's head and a man's body, kept in the Labyrinth at Crete and fed with human flesh. Theseus killed the Minotaur.

Minsk (minsk), *n.* capital of Belarus.

min·strel (min′strəl), *n.* **1** singer or musician in the Middle Ages who entertained in the household of a noble or went about singing or reciting poems. **2** member of a minstrel show.

minstrel show, show or entertainment in which the performers blackened their faces with burnt cork and played music, sang songs, and told jokes. Minstrel shows were very popular until the end of the 1800s.

mint¹ (mint), *n.* **1** any of a great many sweet-smelling plants used for flavoring. Peppermint and spearmint are kinds of mint. **2** piece of candy flavored with mint.

mint² (mint), **1** *n.* place where money is coined by government authority. **2** *v.* to coin money: *The government hasn't minted silver dollars lately.* **3** *n.* a large amount: *That furniture must have cost a mint.* **4** *adj.* without a blemish; as good as new: *a ten-year-old car in mint condition.* [See Word Story at **money.**] —**mint′er**, *n.*

min·u·end (min′yü end), *n.* number or quantity from which another is to be subtracted: *In 100 − 23 = 77, the minuend is 100.*

min·u·et (min′yü et′), *n.* **1** a slow, stately dance, fashionable in the 1600s and 1700s. **2** music for it.

Min·u·it (min′ü it), *n.* Peter, 1580-1638, Dutch colonial governor, born in Germany. In 1626 he bought Manhattan Island from the Indians for trinkets that cost about $24.

mi·nus (mī′nəs), **1** *prep.* decreased by; less: *5 minus 2 leaves 3.* **2** *prep.* without; lacking: *a book minus its cover.* **3** *adj.* less than: *A grade of B minus is not so high as a grade of B.* **4** *n.* minus sign. **5** *adj.* below zero: *Yesterday the temperature was −10 degrees.* □ *n., pl.* **mi·nus·es.**

mi·nus·cule (min′əs kyül′ *or* mi nus′kyül), *adj.* extremely small: *a minuscule insect.*

minus sign, the sign (−), indicating that the number or quantity following it is to be subtracted, or is a negative number or quantity.

min·ute¹ (min′it), *n.* **1** one of the 60 equal periods of time that make an hour; sixty seconds. **2** a short time; instant: *I'll be there in a minute.* **3** an exact point in time: *The minute you see her coming, please tell me.* **4** one sixtieth of a degree of arc. 10° 10′ means 10 degrees and 10 minutes. **5** minutes, *pl.* a written summary of what happened at a meeting, kept by the secretary. **up to the minute,** up to date.

mi·nute² (mī nüt′), *adj.* **1** very small; tiny: *Even a minute speck of dust makes him cough.* ▪ See Synonym Study at **tiny. 2** going into or concerned with small details: *minute instructions.* [See Word Story at **menu.**] —**mi·nute′ly**, *adv.* —**mi·nute′ness**, *n.*

min·ute hand (min′it), hand on a clock or watch that indicates minutes. It moves around the whole dial once in an hour.

min·ute·man (min′it man′), *n.* member of the American militia just before and during the Revolutionary War. The minutemen kept themselves ready for military service at a minute's notice. □ *n., pl.* **min·ute·men.**

minx (mingks), *n.* a bold or mischievous girl. □ *n., pl.* **minx·es.** ▪ **Minx** is sometimes considered offensive.

Mi·o·cene (mī′ə sēn′), *n.* (in geology) time between about 25 million and 12 million years ago. During this time, grasses developed and grazing mammals flourished.

mir·a·cle (mir′ə kəl), *n.* **1** a wonderful happening that is contrary

minuteman

to, or independent of, the known laws of nature: *It would be a miracle if the sun were to set in the east.* **2** something marvelous; a wonder: *It was a miracle you weren't hurt!* **3** a remarkable example: *She was a miracle of patience to put up with their noise.*

mi·rac·u·lous (mə rak′yə ləs), *adj.* **1** contrary to, or independent of, the known laws of nature: *The miraculous fountain of youth was supposed to make the old young again.* **2** marvelous; wonderful: *The famous actor gave a miraculous performance.* —**mi·rac′u·lous·ly**, *adv.* —**mi·rac′u·lous·ness**, *n.*

mi·rage (mə räzh′), *n.* an optical illusion, usually in the desert, at sea, or on a paved road, in which some distant scene appears to be much closer than it actually is. It is caused by the refraction of light rays by air layers of different temperatures. Often, an object in a mirage is seen upside down or as something other than it really is. Travelers on the desert may see a mirage of palm trees and water. [Mirage comes from a Latin word meaning "to gaze in wonder." Mirror comes from the same Latin word. People have different ideas of what is wonderful.]

Mi·ran·da (mə ran′də), *adj.* of, about, or carrying out a Supreme Court decision requiring that someone under arrest be informed of his or her constitutional rights to remain silent, and to have a lawyer present during questioning.

mire (mīr), **1** *n.* soft, deep mud; slush. **2** *n.* wet, swampy ground; bog. **3** *v.* to get stuck in mire: *He mired his car and had to go for help.* □ *v.* **mired, mir·ing.**

mir·ror (mir/ər), **1** *n.* a piece of glass that reflects images; looking glass. It is coated on one side with silver or aluminum. **2** *v.* to reflect as a mirror does: *The still water mirrored the trees along the bank.* **3** *n.* whatever reflects or gives a true description: *This book is a mirror of the life of the pioneers.* [See word history information at **mirage.**] —**mir/ror·like/,** *adj.*

mirror image, an image in reverse; reflection.

mirth (mėrth), *n.* merry fun; joy; glee; laughter.

mirth·ful (mėrth/fəl), *adj.* merry; joyous; laughing. —**mirth/ful·ly,** *adv.* —**mirth/ful·ness,** *n.*

mirth·less (mėrth/lis), *adj.* without mirth; joyless; gloomy. —**mirth/less·ly,** *adv.* —**mirth/less·ness,** *n.*

mis-, *prefix.* bad or badly; wrong or wrongly: *misbehave = behave badly; mispronunciation = wrong pronunciation.*

mis·ad·ven·ture (mis/əd ven/chər), *n.* an unfortunate accident; bad luck; mishap.

mis·ap·pli·ca·tion (mis/ap/lə kā/shən), *n.* act of misapplying or condition of being misapplied; wrong application.

mis·ap·ply (mis/ə pli/), *v.* to apply wrongly: *to misapply your knowledge.* ❑ *v.* **mis·ap·plied, mis·ap·ply·ing.**

mis·ap·pre·hend (mis/ap/ri hend/), *v.* to misunderstand.

mis·ap·pre·hen·sion (mis/ap/rī hen/shən), *n.* wrong idea; misunderstanding.

mis·ap·pro·pri·ate (mis/ə prō/prē āt), *v.* to use dishonestly as your own: *The treasurer misappropriated the club's funds.* ❑ *v.* **mis·ap·pro·pri·at·ed, mis·ap·pro·pri·at·ing.** —**mis/ap·pro/pri·a/tion,** *n.*

mis·be·got·ten (mis/bi got/n), *adj.* badly thought out or carried out: *misbegotten plans.*

mis·be·have (mis/bi hāv/), *v.* to behave badly. ❑ *v.* **mis·be·haved, mis·be·hav·ing.** —**mis/be·hav/er,** *n.*

mis·be·hav·ior (mis/bi hā/vyər), *n.* bad behavior.

misc., miscellaneous.

mis·cal·cu·late (mis kal/kyə lāt), *v.* to calculate wrongly or incorrectly. ❑ *v.* **mis·cal·cu·lat·ed, mis·cal·cu·lat·ing.** —**mis/cal/cu·la/tion,** *n.*

mis·call (mis kol/), *v.* to call by a wrong name.

mis·car·riage (mis kar/ij), *n.* **1** birth of a baby before it is able to live. **2** failure: *Because the judge was unfair, that trial resulted in a miscarriage of justice.*

mis·car·ry (mis kar/ē), *v.* **1** to give birth to a baby before it is able to live. **2** to go wrong; be unsuccessful: *Our plans miscarried, and we could not come.* ❑ *v.* **mis·car·ried, mis·car·ry·ing.**

mis·cast (mis kast/), *v.* to put in a role for which you are not suited. ❑ *v.* **mis·cast, mis·cast·ing.**

mis·ce·ge·na·tion (mis/ə jə nā/shən), *n.* intermarriage between a white person and someone of another race. Miscegenation was illegal in some states until the 1960s.

mis·cel·la·ne·ous (mis/ə lā/nē əs), *adj.* not all of one kind or nature: *He had a miscellaneous collection of stones, butterflies, stamps, and many other things.* —**mis/cel·la/ne·ous·ly,** *adv.* —**mis/cel·la/ne·ous·ness,** *n.*

mis·cel·la·ny (mis/ə lā/nē), *n.* **1** a miscellaneous collection; mixture. **2** Also, **miscellanies,** *pl.* a collection of miscellaneous articles in one book. ❑ *n., pl.* **mis·cel·la·nies.**

mis·chance (mis chans/), *n.* **1** bad luck; misfortune: *By some mischance she didn't receive my message.* **2** piece of bad luck; an unlucky accident.

mis·chief (mis/chif), *n.* **1** conduct that causes harm or trouble, often unintentionally: *The children were playing with matches, and their mischief resulted in a serious fire.* **2** harm or injury, usually done by some person: *Spreading gossip can do a lot of mischief.* **3** someone who does harm or causes annoyance, often just in fun: *You little mischief! You have hidden my glasses.* **4** merry teasing: *Her eyes were full of mischief.*

mis·chie·vous (mis/chə vəs), *adj.* **1** causing mischief; naughty: *mischievous behavior.* ■ See Synonym Study at **naughty.** **2** harmful: *mischievous gossip.* **3** full of pranks and teasing fun: *mischievous children.* —**mis/chie·vous·ly,** *adv.* —**mis/chie·vous·ness,** *n.*

USAGE NOTE **Mischievous** is sometimes pronounced as if it were spelled with an *i* after the *v.* This pronunciation and spelling are not accepted in standard English, and it is wise to avoid them.

mis·con·ceive (mis/kən sēv/), *v.* to have wrong ideas about; misunderstand. ❑ *v.* **mis·con·ceived, mis·con·ceiv·ing.** —**mis/con·ceiv/er,** *n.*

mis·con·cep·tion (mis/kən sep/shən), *n.* a mistaken idea or notion; wrong conception.

mis·con·duct (mis kon/dukt *for noun;* mis/kən dukt/ *for verb*), **1** *n.* bad behavior: *The children were punished for their misconduct.* **2** *v.* to behave badly. **3** *n.* bad management: *The misconduct of that business nearly ruined it.* **4** *v.* to manage badly.

mis·con·struc·tion (mis/kən struk/shən), *n.* wrong or mistaken meaning; misunderstanding: *What you said was open to misconstruction.*

mis·con·strue (mis/kən strü/), *v.* to take in a wrong or mistaken sense; misunderstand: *Shyness is sometimes misconstrued as unfriendliness.* ❑ *v.* **mis·con·strued, mis·con·stru·ing.**

mis·count (mis kount/ *for verb;* mis/kount/ *for noun*), **1** *v.* to count wrongly or incorrectly. **2** *n.* a wrong or incorrect count.

mis·cre·ant (mis/krē ənt), **1** *adj.* having little or no conscience; wicked. **2** *n.* a wicked person; villain.

mis·cue (mis kyü/), *n.* error; mistake.

mis·deal (mis dēl/ *for verb;* mis/dēl/ *for noun*), **1** *v.* to deal wrongly at cards. **2** *n.* a wrong deal at cards. ❑ *v.* **mis·dealt** (mis·delt/), **mis·deal·ing.**

mis·deed (mis dēd/), *n.* a bad act; wicked deed.

mis·de·mean·or (mis/di mē/nər), *n.* **1** act of breaking the law, not so serious as a felony. Disturbing the peace and breaking traffic laws are misdemeanors. **2** a wrong deed.

mis·di·rect (mis/də rekt/ *or* mis/di rekt/), *v.* to direct wrongly; give wrong directions to. —**mis/di·rec/tion,** *n.*

mis·di·vi·sion (mis/də vizh/ən), *n.* a wrong or mistaken division of a word or phrase at a place that is not correct. The word *apron* resulted from a misdivision of the Middle English phrase *a napron* as *an apron.*

WORD SOURCE **Misdivision** has caused several English words to change from one form to another. Usually this happens when the letter *n* leaves one word and joins another: *a nadder = an adder; ekename = a nickname.* Other words formed this way are: **apron, auger, newt, nonce,** and **umpire.**

The same process can happen before words get to English. For example, a Spanish word meaning "orange" began with an *n,* but the French word that came from it did not have that letter, and neither does the English word.

mi·ser (mi/zər), *n.* someone who loves money for its own sake; one who lives poorly in order to save money and keep it. [**Miser** comes from a Latin word meaning "wretched," which is how people think misers are.]

mis·er·a·ble (miz/ər bəl), *adj.* **1** very unhappy or unfortunate; wretched: *The sick child was miserable.* **2** causing trouble or unhappiness: *a miserable cold.* **3** poor; pitiful: *The run-down old house stood in miserable surroundings.* —**mis/er·a·ble·ness,** *n.* —**mis/er·a·bly,** *adv.*

mi·ser·ly (mi/zər lē), *adj.* of, like, or suited to a miser; stingy. —**mi/ser·li·ness,** *n.*

mis·er·y (miz/ər ē), *n.* **1** great distress or suffering caused by being unhappy, poor, or in pain: *Think of the misery of having no home or friends.* **2** poor, mean, miserable circumstances: *a life of misery.* **3** a cause or source of trouble and unhappiness: *That house has been a misery to her.* ❑ *n., pl.* **mis·er·ies** for 1,3.

SYNONYM STUDY **Misery** and **agony** both mean great sadness or pain. **Misery** suggests sadness that is painful to bear: *Misery at his wife's death has made him look much older.* **Agony** suggests intense pain of body or mind: *Until forest rangers found the lost child, her parents were in agony.*

mis·file (mis fil/), *v.* to file incorrectly. ❑ *v.* **mis·filed, mis·fil·ing.**

a	hat	ė	term	ô	order	ch	child	
ā	age	i	it	oi	oil	ng	long	a in about
ä	far	ī	ice	ou	out	sh	she	e in taken
â	care	o	hot	u	cup	th	thin	ə i in pencil
e	let	ō	open	ú	put	₮H	then	o in lemon
ē	equal	ò	saw	ü	rule	zh	measure	u in circus

mis·fire (mis fīr′), **1** *v.* to fail to fire or explode properly: *The pistol misfired.* **2** *n.* failure to discharge or start. **3** *v.* to go wrong; fail: *I tried to sneak into the movie without paying, but my plan misfired.* ❑ *v.* **mis·fired, mis·fir·ing.**

mis·fit (mis′fit′), *n.* **1** person who does not fit in a job, a group, etc.; maladjusted person. **2** a bad fit: *Do not buy shoes that are misfits.*

mis·for·tune (mis fôr′chən), *n.* **1** bad luck: *She had the misfortune to break her arm.* **2** piece of bad luck; unlucky accident: *The flood was a great misfortune for the people whose homes were damaged.*

mis·giv·ing (mis giv′ing), *n.* a feeling of doubt, suspicion, or anxiety: *We started off through the storm with some misgivings.*

mis·gov·ern (mis guv′ərn), *v.* to govern or manage badly. —**mis·gov′ern·ment,** *n.*

mis·guide (mis gīd′), *v.* to lead into mistakes or wrongdoing; mislead. ❑ *v.* **mis·guid·ed, mis·guid·ing.**

mis·guid·ed (mis gī′did), *adj.* led into mistakes or wrongdoing; misled: *a misguided person, misguided plans.* —**mis·guid′ed·ly,** *adv.* —**mis·guid′ed·ness,** *n.*

mis·han·dle (mis han′dl), *v.* to handle badly; maltreat. ❑ *v.* **mis·han·dled, mis·han·dling.**

mis·hap (mis′hap′), *n.* an unlucky accident: *By some mishap the letter went astray.*

mish·mash (mish′mash′), *n.* a confused mixture; hodgepodge; jumble. ❑ *n., pl.* **mish·mash·es.**

mis·in·form (mis′in fôrm′), *v.* to give wrong or misleading information to. —**mis·in·for·ma′tion,** *n.* —**mis·in·form′er,** *n.*

mis·in·ter·pret (mis′in tėr′prit), *v.* to interpret wrongly; explain wrongly; misunderstand. —**mis·in′ter·pre·ta′tion,** *n.*

mis·judge (mis juj′), *v.* to judge wrongly or unjustly: *misjudge distance, misjudge a person's character.* ❑ *v.* **mis·judged, mis·judg·ing.** —**mis·judg′ment,** *n.*

mis·laid (mis lād′), *v.* past tense and past participle of **mislay:** *The boy mislaid his books. I have mislaid my pen.*

mis·lay (mis lā′), *v.* **1** to put something in a place and then forget where it is; lose temporarily: *I am always mislaying my glasses.* **2** to put in an incorrect place. ❑ *v.* **mis·laid, mis·lay·ing.**

mis·lead (mis lēd′), *v.* **1** to cause to go in the wrong direction; lead astray: *Our guide misled us and we got lost.* **2** to cause to do wrong; lead into wrongdoing: *Bad companions can mislead a person.* **3** to lead to think what is not so; deceive: *Some advertisements are so exaggerated that they mislead people.* ❑ *v.* **mis·led, mis·lead·ing.**

mis·lead·ing (mis lē′ding), *adj.* causing mistakes or wrong conclusions; deceiving: *misleading statements in advertising.* —**mis·lead′ing·ly,** *adv.*

mis·led (mis led′), *v.* past tense and past participle of **mislead:** *We were misled by the false claims.*

mis·man·age (mis man′ij), *v.* to manage badly: *If you mismanage the business, you will lose money.* ❑ *v.* **mis·man·aged, mis·man·ag·ing.** —**mis·man′age·ment,** *n.*

mis·match (mis mach′ *for verb;* mis′mach *or* mis mach′ *for noun*), **1** *v.* to match badly or unsuitably. **2** *n.* a bad or unsuitable match. ❑ *n., pl.* **mis·match·es.**

mis·name (mis nām′), *v.* to call by a wrong or misleading name. ❑ *v.* **mis·named, mis·nam·ing.**

mis·place (mis plās′), *v.* **1** to put something in a place and then forget where it is; mislay: *I have misplaced my pencil.* **2** to put in the wrong place or position: *The street light is misplaced; it should be near the corner.* **3** to give your love or trust to the wrong person: *misplace one's confidence in an untrustworthy friend.* ❑ *v.* **mis·placed, mis·plac·ing.** —**mis·place′ment,** *n.*

mis·play (mis′plā *or* mis plā′ *for noun;* mis plā′ *for verb*), **1** *n.* a wrong play. **2** *v.* to play wrongly: *I misplayed my hand in the card game.*

mis·print (mis′print′ *for noun;* mis print′ *for verb*), **1** *n.* a mistake in printing. **2** *v.* to print wrongly.

mis·pro·nounce (mis′prə nouns′), *v.* to pronounce incorrectly. ❑ *v.* **mis·pro·nounced, mis·pro·nounc·ing.**

mis·pro·nun·ci·a·tion (mis′prə nun′sē ā′shən), *n.* an incorrect pronunciation.

mis·quo·ta·tion (mis′kwō tā′shən), *n.* an incorrect quotation.

mis·quote (mis kwōt′), *v.* to quote incorrectly. ❑ *v.* **mis·quot·ed, mis·quot·ing.**

mis·read (mis rēd′), *v.* **1** to read wrongly. **2** to interpret wrongly; misunderstand: *misread a person's intentions.* ❑ *v.* **mis·read** (mis-red′), **mis·read·ing.**

mis·rep·re·sent (mis′rep′ri zent′), *v.* to represent falsely; give a wrong idea of: *He misrepresented the barren property by claiming it was good farmland.*

mis·rep·re·sen·ta·tion (mis′rep ri zen tā′shən), *n.* **1** a false representation: *Tell the truth; do not resort to misrepresentation.* **2** an incorrect story or explanation: *The report is a misrepresentation of the facts in the case.*

mis·rule (mis rül′), **1** *n.* bad or unwise government: *After years of misrule, the country was ready for a new leader.* **2** *v.* to govern badly: *The cruel king misruled his people.* ❑ *v.* **mis·ruled, mis·rul·ing.**

miss (mis), **1** *v.* to fail to hit: *I swung at the ball and missed it.* **2** *n.* failure to hit or reach: *make more misses than hits.* **3** *v.* to fail to find, get, or meet: *I set out to meet my father, but in the dark I missed him.* **4** *v.* to let slip by; not seize: *I missed the chance of a ride to town.* **5** *v.* to fail to catch: *We were caught in traffic and missed the plane.* **6** *v.* to leave out: *miss a word in reading.* **7** *v.* to fail to do or answer correctly: *I missed two problems in today's math lesson.* **8** *v.* to fail to see, hear, or understand: *She missed the point of my remark.* **9** *v.* to fail to keep, do, or be present at: *I missed my music lesson today.* **10** *v.* to fail to see or notice: *I missed my favorite TV program last night.* **11** *v.* to escape or avoid: *I barely missed being hit by a car.* **12** *v.* to notice the absence of; feel keenly the absence of: *I missed you while you were away.* ❑ *n., pl.* **miss·es.**

Miss (mis), *n.* **1** title put before a girl's or unmarried woman's name: *Miss Brown, the Misses Brown, the Miss Browns.* **2 miss,** a young unmarried woman; girl. **3 miss,** a way to politely address a young woman whose name you do not know: *Oh, miss, may I see a menu, please?* ❑ *n., pl.* **Miss·es** for 1, **miss·es** for 2. ■ See Usage Note at **Ms.**

Who, him? That's 'Smiley'!

misname

Miss., Mississippi.

mis·sal (mis′əl), *n.* book containing the prayers, etc., for celebrating the Roman Catholic Mass throughout the year. ■ Another word that sounds like this is **missile.**

mis·shap·en (mis shā′pən), *adj.* badly shaped; deformed.

mis·sile (mis′əl), *n.* **1** object that is thrown or shot, such as a stone, an arrow, a bullet, or a lance. **2** rocket that delivers a bomb to a target. **3** a similar jet-propelled vehicle. ■ Another word that sounds like this is **missal.**

miss·ing (mis′ing), *adj.* not found when looked for; lacking; absent; gone: *One book is missing from the set.*

mis·sion (mish′ən), *n.* **1** errand or task that people are sent somewhere to do: *a diplomatic mission.* **2** a military or scientific operation or expedition. An expedition by a spacecraft to another planet is called a mission. **3** group sent on some special business: *She was one of a mission sent by our government to France.* **4** group of people sent by a religious organization into other parts of the world to spread its beliefs. **5 missions,** *pl.* an organized effort by a religious group to set up churches, schools, hospitals, etc.: *foreign missions.* **6** business on which a mission is sent: *carry out a mission.* **7** center or headquarters for religious or social work: *The church set up a mission with a soup kitchen to help local homeless people.* **8** business or purpose in life; calling: *It seemed to be her mission to help improve living conditions in the city.*

> **WORD FAMILY** Mission and the words below are related. They all come from a Latin word meaning "to send."
>
> | | | | |
> |---|---|---|---|
> | admit | emit | missile | premise |
> | commission | intermission | missionary | promise |
> | commit | Mass | omit | submit |
> | compromise | mess | permission | transmit |
> | dismiss | message | permit | |

mis·sion·ar·y (mish′ə ner′ē), **1** *n.* someone who carries on the work of a religious mission: *Missionaries helped start churches, schools, and hospitals in many places.* **2** *n.* person who works to advance some cause or idea. **3** *adj.* of or related to religious missions or missionaries. ❑ *n., pl.* **mis·sion·ar·ies.**

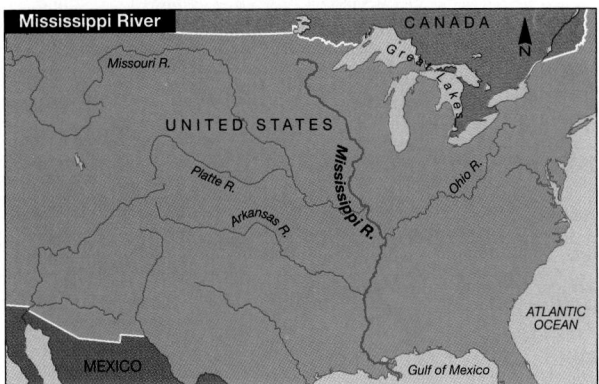

Mississippi River

Mis·sis·sip·pi (mis′ə sip′ē), *n.* **1** one of the south central states of the United States. *Abbreviation:* MS or Miss. *Capital:* Jackson. **2** largest river in the United States. It flows south from N Minnesota to the Gulf of Mexico.

> **WORD STORY** Mississippi comes from an American Indian word meaning "big river." The state got its name from the river. If this story sounds familiar, see the Word Story at **Yukon.**

Mis·sis·sip·pi·an (mis′ə sip′ē ən), *n.* **1** (in geology) time between about 350 million and 310 million years ago. During this time, winged insects first appeared. **2** someone born or living in Mississippi.

Mis·sou·la (mi zü′lə), *n.* city in W Montana.

> **WORD STORY** Missoula comes from a Flathead word meaning "by the cold water." The original word also suggests fear, but no one knows why the name was given.

Mis·sour·i (mə zùr′ē *or* mə zùr′ə), *n.* **1** one of the Midwestern states of the United States. *Abbreviation:* MO or Mo. *Capital:* Jefferson City. **2** large river in the N part of the United States, flowing from SW Montana into the Mississippi near St. Louis. —**Mis·sour′i·an,** *n.*

> **WORD STORY** Missouri comes from the name of an American Indian tribe who lived near the place where the Missouri and Mississippi Rivers meet. The name probably meant "people of the big canoes." The state got its name from the river.

Missouri Compromise, set of laws passed by the U.S. Congress in 1820 and 1821 to limit the expansion of slavery, according to which Missouri was admitted as a slave state, and Maine as a free state. Slavery was prohibited north of latitude 36°30′, except for Missouri.

mis·spell (mis spel′), *v.* to spell incorrectly. ❑ *v.* **mis·spelled** or **mis·spelt** (mis spelt′), **mis·spell·ing.**

mis·spell·ing (mis spel′ing), *n.* an incorrect spelling.

mis·spent (mis spent′), *adj.* spent foolishly or wrongly; wasted: *a misspent fortune, a misspent life.*

mis·state (mis stāt′), *v.* to state wrongly or incorrectly. ❑ *v.* **mis·stat·ed, mis·stat·ing.** —**mis·state′ment,** *n.*

mis·step (mis step′), *n.* **1** a wrong step. **2** error or slip in conduct.

miss·y (mis′ē), *n.* INFORMAL. little miss; miss. ❑ *n., pl.* **miss·ies.** ▪ Missy is often considered offensive.

mist (mist), **1** *n.* cloud of very fine drops of water suspended in the air; haze. **2** *n.* cloud of very fine drops of any liquid in the air: *A mist of perfume spread over the room.* **3** *v.* to come down in mist; rain in very fine drops. **4** *n.* anything that dims, blurs, or obscures: *She did not cry, but a mist came over her eyes. A mist of prejudice spoiled his judgment.* **5** *v.* to become covered with a mist; become dim: *The windows are misting.* **6** *v.* to cover with a mist; put a mist before; make dim: *Tears misted his eyes.*

mis·take (mə stāk′), **1** *n.* misunderstanding of something's use or meaning; error; blunder: *It was a mistake to leave before the snow stopped. I used your towel by mistake.* **2** *v.* to misunderstand what is seen or heard; take in a wrong sense: *We mistook her polite words for friendliness.* **3** *v.* to take wrongly; take to be some other person or thing: *I mistook him for his brother.* ❑ *v.* **mis·took, mis·tak·en, mis·tak·ing.** —**mis·tak′er,** *n.*

> **SYNONYM STUDY** Mistake and blunder both mean something you do wrong. Mistake is a general word: *I made a mistake in addressing the letter.* Blunder means a careless or foolish mistake: *Leaving for the airport without the tickets was a serious blunder.*

mis·tak·en (mə stā′kən), **1** *adj.* wrong in opinion; having made a mistake: *I saw I was mistaken and admitted my error.* **2** *adj.* wrongly judged; wrong; misplaced: *It was a mistaken kindness to give that boy more candy; it will make him sick.* **3** *v.* past participle of **mistake**: *I was mistaken for someone else.* —**mis·tak′en·ly,** *adv.*

Mis·ter (mis′tər), *n.* **1** Mr., a title put before a man's name or the name of his office: *Mr. Stein, Mr. President.* **2 mister,** a polite way to address a man whose name you do not know: *Do you need directions, mister?*

mis·tle·toe (mis′əl tō), *n.* any of several North American and European plants with small, waxy, white berries, growing as a parasite on trees. Mistletoe is used as a Christmas and New Year's decoration.

mis·took (mə stùk′), *v.* past tense of **mistake**: *I mistook you for your sister yesterday.*

Mis·tral (mēs träl′), *n.* **Gab·ri·el·a** (gä brē e′lä), 1889-1957, Chilean poet. In 1945 she became the first Latin American writer to win the Nobel Prize for literature.

mis·treat (mis trēt′), *v.* to treat badly: *It is cruel to mistreat animals.* —**mis·treat′ment,** *n.*

mis·tress (mis′tris), *n.* **1** woman who is at the head of a household. **2** woman who owns or controls something: *The kitten greeted its mistress with loud meows.* **3** woman who has a thorough knowledge or mastery: *She is a complete mistress of the art of cooking.* **4** woman teaching in a school, or at the head of a school, or giving lessons in a special subject: *the dancing mistress.* **5** woman who has a sexual relationship with a man without being married to him. **6 Mistress,** OLD USE. Mrs., Madam, or Miss. ❑ *n., pl.* **mis·tress·es** for 1-5, **Mis·tress·es** for 6.

a	hat	ė	term	ȯ	order	ch	child		⟨ a in about
ā	age	i	it	oi	oil	ng	long		e in taken
ä	far	ī	ice	ou	out	sh	she	ə	i in pencil
â	care	o	hot	u	cup	th	thin		o in lemon
e	let	ō	open	ù	put	ᴛʜ	then		⟨ u in circus
ē	equal	ȯ	saw	ü	rule	zh	measure		

mis·tri·al (mis trī′əl), *n.* **1** trial in which the jury fails to come to a decision. **2** trial of no effect in law because of some error in the proceedings.

mis·trust (mis trust′), **1** *v.* to feel no trust or confidence in; distrust; doubt: *I mistrusted my ability to swim.* **2** *n.* lack of trust or confidence; suspicion: *He looked with mistrust at the dog.*

mis·trust·ful (mis trust′fəl), *adj.* distrustful; doubting; suspicious. **—mis·trust′ful·ly,** *adv.* **—mis·trust′ful·ness,** *n.*

mist·y (mis′tē), *adj.* **1** full of or covered with mist: *misty hills.* **2** as if seen through a mist; vague; indistinct: *a misty form, a misty memory.* □ *adj.* **mist·i·er, mist·i·est.** **—mist′i·ly,** *adv.* **—mist′i·ness,** *n.*

mis·un·der·stand (mis′un′dər stand′), *v.* **1** to understand wrongly: *I completely misunderstood the poem's meaning.* **2** to take in a wrong sense; give the wrong meaning to: *We tried to help, but they misunderstood our intentions.* □ *v.* **mis·un·der·stood, mis·un·der·stand·ing.**

mis·un·der·stand·ing (mis′un′dər stan′ding), *n.* **1** wrong understanding; failure to understand; mistake as to meaning. **2** disagreement: *After their misunderstanding they scarcely spoke to each other for months.*

mis·un·der·stood (mis′un′dər stüd′), *v.* past tense and past participle of **misunderstand:** *She misunderstood what the teacher said and so did the wrong homework.*

mis·use (mis yüz′ *for verb;* mis yüs′ *for noun*), **1** *v.* to use for the wrong purpose: *He misuses his knife at the table by lifting food with it.* **2** *v.* to treat badly; mistreat; abuse: *The children misused their dog by trying to ride on its back.* **3** *n.* a wrong use: *I notice a misuse of the word "who" in your letter.* □ *v.* **mis·used, mis·us·ing.** **—mis·us′er,** *n.*

Mit·chell (mich′əl), *n.* **Mar·ga·ret** (mar′gret), 1900-1949, American writer. Her novel *Gone With the Wind* won the 1937 Pulitzer Prize for fiction.

mite[1] (mīt), *n.* any of many very tiny animals related to spiders and having eight legs. Mites live in foods, on plants, on other animals, in water, and elsewhere. ■ Another word that sounds like this is **might.**

mite[2] (mīt), *n.* **1** anything very small; little bit: *a mite of supper.* **2** coin of slight value. **3** a very small child: *What a mite your baby sister is!* ■ Another word that sounds like this is **might.**
a mite, a little; slightly: *After all that exercise, I'm a mite tired.*

mi·ter (mī′tər), **1** *n.* a tall, pointed, folded cap worn by bishops during sacred ceremonies. **2** *n.* kind of joint or corner where two pieces of wood are fitted together at right angles with the ends cut slanting. **3** *v.* to join in this way; prepare ends of wood for such joining. The corners of a picture frame are mitered.

mit·i·gate (mit′ə gāt), *v.* to make or become milder or less harsh; soften. Anger, grief, heat, cold, and other conditions may be mitigated. □ *v.* **mit·i·gat·ed, mit·i·gat·ing.** **—mit′i·ga′tion,** *n.*

mi·to·chon·dri·a (mī′tə kon′drē ə), *n.pl.* very tiny sausage-shaped structures found inside every cell with a nucleus. Mitochondria produce the energy needed for cell processes. □ *n., sing.* **mi·to·chon·dri·on** (mī′tə kon′drē ən).

mi·to·sis (mī tō′sis), *n.* process by which a living cell divides to form two new cells, each containing the same number of chromosomes as the original cell.

mitt (mit), *n.* **1** glove with a big pad over the palm and fingers, used by baseball players: *a catcher's mitt.* **2** mitten.

mit·ten (mit′n), *n.* kind of winter glove covering the four fingers together and the thumb separately.

Mit·ter·rand (mē tə rän′), *n.* **Fran·çois** (frän′swä), 1916–1996, president of France from 1981 to 1995.

mix (miks), **1** *v.* to put together; combine and stir well: *We mix butter, sugar, milk, flour, eggs, and flavoring for a cake.* **2** *v.* to

prepare by putting different things together: *She mixed pancakes for breakfast.* **3** *v.* to join: *mix business and pleasure.* **4** *v.* to be mixed; blend: *Oil and water do not mix.* **5** *v.* to associate together; get along together: *She likes people and mixes well in almost any group.* **6** *n.* a mixture: *A strange mix of people attended the opening of the play.* **7** *n.* preparation that is already mixed: *a cake mix.* □ *v.* **mixed, mix·ing;** *n., pl.* **mix·es.**
mix up, 1 to confuse: *I was so mixed up that I put sugar on my eggs.* **2** to involve; concern: *He was mixed up in a plot to take the mascot.*

mixed (mikst), *adj.* **1** formed of different kinds: *mixed candies.* **2** of or for both sexes: *We belong to a mixed chorus.*

mixed marriage, marriage in which the husband and wife are of different religions, races, or ethnic groups.

mixed number, number consisting of a positive or negative integer and a fraction. EXAMPLES: $1\frac{1}{2}$, $16\frac{2}{3}$, $-25\frac{9}{10}$.

mix·er (mik′sər), *n.* **1** machine that mixes: *a bread mixer, an electric mixer.* **2** someone who mixes. A person who gets along well with others is called a good mixer.

Mix·tec (mēs′tek), *n.* member of an American Indian tribe living in southern Mexico. □ *n., pl.* **Mix·tecs** or **Mix·tec.**

mix·ture (miks′chər), *n.* **1** something that has been mixed; a product of mixing: *Orange is a mixture of yellow and red.* **2** mixed condition: *The audience felt a mixture of relief and disappointment.* **3** act or process of mixing: *The mixture of the paints took almost 10 minutes.* **4** two or more substances mixed together but not chemically combined, so that they can be easily separated: *a mixture of salt and sand.*

mix-up (miks′up′), *n.* confusion; mess.

miz·zen (miz′n), *n.* **1** a fore-and-aft sail on a mizzenmast. **2** mizzenmast.

miz·zen·mast (miz′n mast′ *or* miz′n məst), *n.* mast nearest the stern in a two-masted or three-masted ship.

mks or **MKS,** meter-kilogram-second.

ml or **ml.,** milliliter or milliliters.

mL or **mL.,** milliliter or milliliters.

Mlle., Mademoiselle. □ *pl.* **Mlles.**

mm or **mm.,** millimeter or millimeters.

Mma·ba·tho (mä bä′tō), *n.* capital of Bophuthatswana.

Mme., Madame. □ *pl.* **Mmes.**

Mn, symbol for manganese.

MN, Minnesota (used with postal Zip Code).

mne·mon·ic (ni mon′ik), *adj.* **1** aiding the memory. **2** intended to aid the memory. **—mne·mon′i·cal·ly,** *adv.*

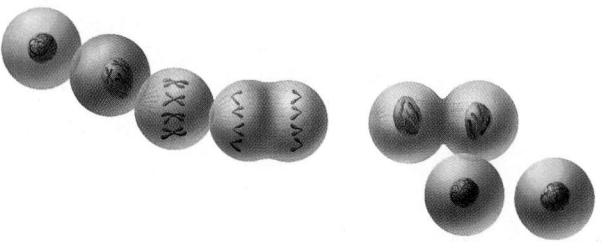

mitosis—Chromosomes in the cell nucleus duplicate themselves, then separate as the cell divides, producing two cells with identical chromosomes.

Mo, symbol for molybdenum.

MO, Missouri (used with postal Zip Code).

mo., month. ❑ *pl.* **mo.**

Mo., Missouri.

M.O., 1 money order. 2 mail order.

mo·a (mō′ə), *n.* any of several extinct flightless birds of New Zealand. Moas were something like ostriches. ❑ *n., pl.* **mo·as.**

Mo·ab (mō′ab), *n.* ancient kingdom in the region east of the Dead Sea and the lower Jordan River in what is now Jordan. See **Judah** for map.

moan (mōn), 1 *n.* a long, low sound of pain or grief. 2 *n.* any similar sound: *the moan of the winter wind.* 3 *v.* to make moans. 4 *v.* to utter with a moan: *"I'm so stiff I can't move," she moaned.* 5 *v.* to complain; grieve: *He was always moaning about his bad luck.* ■ Another word that sounds like this is **mown.**

moat

moat (mōt), *n.* 1 a deep, wide ditch, usually filled with water, dug around a castle or town. A moat was used as a protection against enemies in the Middle Ages. 2 a similar ditch used to separate animals in zoos. ■ Another word that sounds like this is **mote.**

WORD STORY Moat comes from a French word meaning "a mound." Early castles were built on hills made by digging dirt and piling it up. The ditch where the dirt came from often filled up with water. People saw that the ditches were a good defense, so they began to make them on purpose and borrowed the name.

mob (mob), 1 *n.* a lawless crowd, easily moved to act without thinking. 2 *n.* a large number of people; crowd. 3 *v.* to crowd around in curiosity, anger, etc.: *We eagerly mobbed the ice-cream truck the moment it appeared.* 4 *v.* to attack with violence, as a mob does. 5 *n.* the common mass of people. 6 *n.* group of criminals who work together; gang. 7 *n.* **the mob,** organized crime, especially the Mafia. ❑ *v.* **mobbed, mob·bing.** [Mob comes from mobile, because a mob is easily moved to act and may change its feelings quickly.]

mo·bile (mō′bəl *for adj;* mō′bēl′ *for noun*), 1 *adj.* easy to move; movable: *Several mobile classrooms were brought to the crowded school.* 2 *adj.* moving easily; changing easily: *a face with mobile features.* 3 *n.* pieces of metal, wood, paper, etc., suspended on wires or threads and so balanced as to move in a slight breeze, used for decoration. 4 *adj.* (of a society) known for freely allowing mixing of social classes and upward movement of individuals from lower to higher social classes.

Mo·bile (mō bēl′), *n.* port in SW Alabama, near the Gulf of Mexico.

mobile home, a house trailer, especially a large one set on a more or less permanent site.

mo·bil·i·ty (mō bil′ə tē), *n.* condition of being mobile; ability or readiness to move or be moved.

mo·bi·lize (mō′bə līz), *v.* 1 to call troops or ships into active military service; organize for war. 2 to assemble and prepare for war: *The troops mobilized quickly.* 3 to put into motion or active use: *mobilize the wealth of a country.* ❑ *v.* **mo·bi·lized, mo·bi·liz·ing. —mo′bi·li·za′tion,** *n.*

mob·ster (mob′stər), *n.* INFORMAL. a criminal; gangster.

moc·ca·sin (mok′ə sən), *n.* 1 a soft leather shoe or sandal without an attached heel. In former times, many American Indians wore moccasins, often of deerskin. 2 water moccasin.

moccasin flower, a pink or white North American lady's-slipper.

mo·cha (mō′kə), 1 *n.* a choice variety of coffee originally coming from Arabia. 2 *adj.* flavored with coffee, or with chocolate and coffee.

mock (mok), 1 *v.* to laugh at; make fun of: *Rude people in the audience mocked the new play.* 2 *v.* to make fun of by copying or imitating: *My friends mocked the way I hobbled around on my sore foot.* ■ See Synonym Study at **ridicule.** 3 *v.* to imitate; copy. 4 *adj.* not real; pretended; copying; imitation: *The troops took part in a mock battle.* 5 *n.* an action or speech that mocks; mockery. —**mock′er,** *n.* —**mock′ing·ly,** *adv.*

mock·er·y (mok′ər ē), *n.* 1 act of making fun; ridicule: *Their mockery of my new clothes hurt my feelings.* 2 someone or something to be made fun of. 3 a false, worthless, or useless imitation of something: *The unfair trial made a mockery of justice.* ❑ *n., pl.* **mock·er·ies** for 2,3.

mock·ing·bird (mok′ing bėrd′), *n.* a grayish American songbird that imitates the calls of other birds.

mock orange, syringa.

mock·up or **mock-up** (mok′up′), *n.* a full-sized model of a structure, used for teaching or for testing.

mod (mod), *adj.* very stylish or up-to-date; extremely modern: *mod fashions, mod music.*

mo·dal (mō′dəl), *adj.* 1 of or about mode, manner, or form. 2 (in grammar) having to do with the mood of a verb. —**mo′dal·ly,** *adv.*

mode[1] (mōd), *n.* 1 way or manner in which a thing is done: *Riding a donkey is a slow mode of travel.* 2 (in grammar) mood. 3 (in music) any of various arrangements of the tones of an octave. 4 (in statistics) number that occurs most often in a set of data.

mode[2] (mōd), *n.* style, fashion, or custom that is current; the way most people are behaving, talking, dressing, etc.: *Blue jeans have been the mode in student dress for years.*

mod·el (mod′l), 1 *n.* a small copy: *a model of a ship or an engine.* 2 *n.* figure in clay or wax that is to be copied in marble, bronze, etc.: *a model for a statue.* 3 *v.* to make, shape, or fashion; design; plan: *to model a horse in clay.* 4 *n.* way in which a thing is made; design; style: *Our TV set is a new model.* 5 *n.* formula, diagram, or theory used to explain or describe a thing, a process, or a relationship between things: *the germ model of infection.* 6 *n.* someone or something to be copied or imitated: *Your mother is a fine person; make her your model.* 7 *v.* to follow as a pattern or example: *Model yourself on your father.* 8 *adj.* just right or perfect, especially in conduct: *They tried very hard to be model parents.* 9 *adj.* serving as a pattern or example: *a model house.* 10 *n.* someone who poses for artists, photographers, etc. 11 *n.* someone employed to wear or be photographed in clothing so that customers can see how the clothing looks; mannequin. 12 *v.* to be a model: *I modeled for an illustrator.* ❑ *v.* **mod·eled, mod·el·ing** or **mod·elled, mod·el·ling.**

WORD FAMILY Model and the words below are related. They all come from a Latin word meaning "measure" or "manner."

accommodate	mode[1]	moderate	mold[1]
a la mode	mode[2]	modest	mood
commodity	modem	modify	outmoded

mo·dem (mō′dem), *n.* an electronic device that enables a computer to send or receive information or instructions by telephone lines.

mod·er·ate (mod′ər it *for adj., noun;* mod′ə rāt′ *for verb*), 1 *adj.* kept or keeping within proper bounds; not extreme: *The bus traveled at moderate speed.* 2 *adj.* not violent; calm: *moderate in opinion.* 3 *adj.* not very large or good; fair; medium: *make a moderate profit.* 4 *n.* person who holds opinions that are not extreme: *a political moderate.* 5 *v.* to make or become less extreme

a	hat	ė	term	ô	order	ch	child			a in about
ā	age	i	it	oi	oil	ng	long			e in taken
ä	far	ī	ice	ou	out	sh	she	ə		i in pencil
â	care	o	hot	u	cup	th	thin			o in lemon
e	let	ō	open	u̇	put	ŦH	then			u in circus
ē	equal	ò	saw	ü	rule	zh	measure			

M

or violent: *The wind is moderating.* **6** *v.* to act as moderator; preside over. □ *v.* **mod·er·at·ed, mod·er·at·ing.** —**mod′er·ate·ly,** *adv.*

mod·e·ra·tion (mod′ə rā′shən), *n.* freedom from excess; proper restraint; temperance: *The nutritionist recommended moderation in eating sweets.*

in moderation, without going to extremes: *It is all right to eat candy in moderation.*

mod·e·ra·to (mod′ə rä′tō), *adj., adv.* (in music) in moderate time.

mod·e·ra·tor (mod′ə rā′tər), *n.* a presiding officer; chairman: *the moderator of a panel discussion.*

mod·ern (mod′ərn), **1** *adj.* of or relating to the present time; of times not long past: *Color TV is a modern invention.* **2** *adj.* up-to-date; not old-fashioned: *They are young and have modern views.* **3** *n.* someone who has up-to-date ideas and tastes. **4** *adj.* **Modern,** of or about a language or group of languages used from about the year 1500 to the present: *Modern English, Modern Italian.* [Modern comes from a Latin word meaning "just now."]

modern dance, a form of artistic dancing using motions that are less formal and limited than the motions used in ballet dancing.

Modern English, 1 period in the development of the English language from about 1500 through the present. **2** the English language of this period.

mod·ern·ism (mod′ėr niz′əm), *n.* **1** modern attitudes or methods. **2** a modern word, phrase, or usage.

mod·ern·is·tic (mod′ər nis′tik), *adj.* **1** modern. **2** having modern attitudes, methods, or style.

mod·ern·ize (mod′ər nīz), *v.* **1** to make modern; bring up to present ways or standards. **2** to become modern. □ *v.* **mod·ern·ized, mod·ern·iz·ing.** —**mod′ern·i·za′tion,** *n.* —**mod′ern·iz′er,** *n.*

mod·est (mod′ist), *adj.* **1** not thinking too highly of yourself; not vain; humble: *In spite of many honors, the scientist remained a modest person.* **2** shy; not bold; held back by a sense of what is fit and proper: *The modest child sat quietly next to his mother during the party.* **3** not displaying or calling attention to your body. **4** not too great; not asking too much: *a modest request.* **5** not expensive or showy: *a modest little house.* —**mod′est·ly,** *adv.*

mod·est·y (mod′ə stē), *n.* **1** freedom from vanity; being modest or humble. **2** shyness; bashfulness. **3** act or habit of not displaying or calling attention to your body.

mod·i·fi·ca·tion (mod′ə fə kā′shən), *n.* **1** partial alteration or change: *With these modifications your composition will do for the school paper.* **2** act of making less severe or strong; a toning down: *A modification of the workers' demands helped settle the long strike.* **3** a changed form; variety. **4** limitation of meaning; qualification.

mod·i·fi·er (mod′ə fī′ər), *n.* **1** (in grammar) a word or group of words that limits the meaning of another word or group of words. In "a very tight coat," the adjective *tight* is a modifier of *coat,* and the adverb *very* is a modifier of *tight.* **2** someone or something that modifies.

mod·i·fy (mod′ə fī), *v.* **1** to change somewhat: *modify the design of a car, modify the terms of a lease.* **2** to make less; tone down; make less severe or strong: *He has modified his demands.* **3** to limit the meaning of; qualify. Adverbs modify verbs, adjectives, and other adverbs. □ *v.* **mod·i·fied, mod·i·fy·ing.** —**mod′i·fi′a·ble,** *adj.*

mod·ish (mō′dish), *adj.* fashionable; stylish. —**mod′ish·ly,** *adv.* —**mod′ish·ness,** *n.*

mod·u·lar (moj′ə lər), *adj.* **1** of or about a module. **2** built or designed with interchangeable units for easy assembly, arrangement, and repair: *modular furniture.*

mod·u·late (moj′ə lāt), *v.* **1** to regulate or adjust; soften; tone down. **2** to alter the voice in pitch, tone, or volume for expression. **3** to change from one musical key to another. **4** (in radio or television) to change the amplitude, frequency, or phase of a carrier wave to match the sound, picture, or information being sent. □ *v.* **mod·u·lat·ed, mod·u·lat·ing.** —**mod′u·la′tor,** *n.*

mod·u·la·tion (moj′ə lā′shən), *n.* **1** a change from one key to another during a piece of music. **2** (in electronics) a change of the amplitude, frequency, or phase of an electromagnetic wave, to carry signals.

mod·ule (moj′ül), *n.* **1** a self-contained unit or system within a larger system, often designed for a particular function. **2** a standard unit for measuring. **3** (in architecture) the size of some part taken as a unit of measure for other parts. **4** unit of instruction, usually covering a single topic.

Mog·a·di·shu (mog′ə dē′shü), *n.* port and capital of Somalia, on the Indian Ocean.

Mo·gul or **Mo·ghul** (mō′gəl), **1** *n.* one of the Mongol conquerors of India in the 1500s, or one of their descendants. **2** *adj.* of or about these conquerors. **The Mogul Empire** included large sections of India and Afghanistan and lasted about 200 years. **3** *n.* a very important or wealthy person: *a software mogul.* Also, **Mughal.**

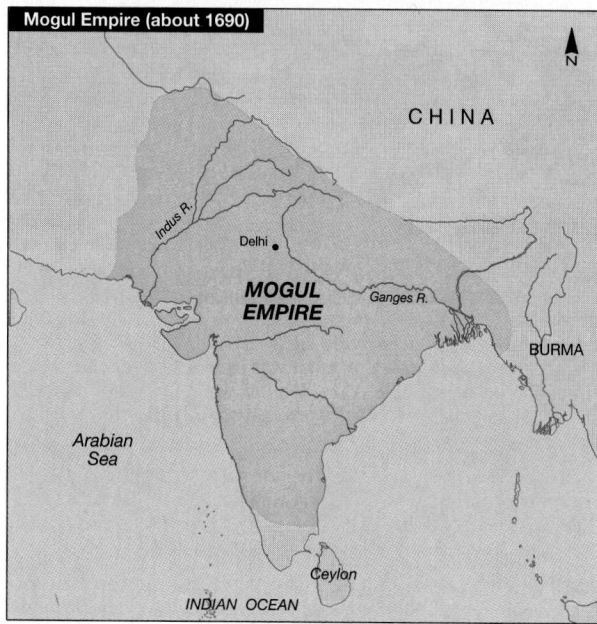

Mogul Empire (about 1690)

mo·hair (mō′hâr), *n.* **1** cloth made from the long, silky hair of the Angora goat; angora. **2** a similar cloth made of wool and cotton.

Mo·ham·med (mō ham′id), *n.* Muhammad.

Mo·ham·med·an (mō ham′ə dən), **1** *adj.* of or about Muhammad. **2** *adj.* Muslim. **3** *n.* a Muslim.

Mo·ham·med·an·ism (mō ham′ə də niz′əm), *n.* Islam, the religion of the Muslims.

Mo·hawk (mō′hôk), *n.* member of a tribe of American Indians living in New York, Ontario, and Quebec. □ *n., pl.* **Mo·hawk** or **Mo·hawks.** [Mohawk comes from a word in the language of a neighboring tribe, meaning "they eat people." The Mohawk were warlike, and their enemies may have believed that they did this.]

Mo·he·gan (mō hē′gən), *n.* member of a tribe of American Indians formerly living in eastern Connecticut. □ *n., pl.* **Mo·he·gan** or **Mo·he·gans.** Also, **Mohican.** ■ See Usage Note at **Mohican.**

Mo·hi·can (mō hē′kən), *n.* **1** Mahican. **2** Mohegan. □ *n., pl.* **Mo·hi·can** or **Mo·hi·cans.**

moist (moist), *adj.* slightly wet; damp. ■ See Synonym Study at damp. —**moist′ly,** *adv.* —**moist′ness,** *n.*

mois·ten (moi′sn), *v.* to make or become moist: *His eyes moistened with tears.* —**mois′ten·er,** *n.*

mois·ture (mois′chər), *n.* slight wetness; water or other liquid suspended in very small drops in the air or spread on a surface. Dew is moisture that collects at night on the grass.

mois·tur·ize (mois′chə rīz′), *v.* to add moisture to. ❑ *v.* **mois·tur·ized, mois·tur·iz·ing.** —**mois′tur·iz·er,** *n.*

Mo·ja·ve (mō hä′vē), *n.* large desert in S California.

mo·lar (mō′lər), *n.* tooth with a broad surface for grinding. A person's back teeth are molars.

mo·las·ses (mə las′iz), *n.* a sweet syrup produced during the process of making sugar from sugar cane.

WORD STORY   **Molasses** comes from a Latin word meaning "honey." Europeans did not grow sugar cane until the Middle Ages. Before then, they used honey for sweetening. When they got a new sweetener, they named it after the old one.

mold[1] (mōld), **1** *n.* a hollow shape in which anything is formed, cast, or solidified, such as the mold into which melted metal is poured to harden into shape, or the mold in which gelatin is left to stiffen. **2** *n.* the shape or form which is given by a mold: *The molds of ice cream were turkeys and pumpkins.* **3** *n.* the model according to which anything is shaped: *Those students are formed in their teacher's mold.* **4** *v.* to form; shape: *Children mold figures out of clay.* **5** *v.* to make or form something into shape: *We molded the dough into loaves to be baked.* **6** *v.* to determine or influence the quality or nature of something: *Her character was molded by her experiences.* **7** *n.* nature; character: *a person of ambitious mold.* —**mold′a·ble,** *adj.* —**mold′er,** *n.*

mold[2] (mōld), **1** *n.* a woolly or furry fungous growth, often greenish, that appears on food and other animal or vegetable substances when they are left too long in a warm, moist place. **2** *v.* to become covered with such a growth: *This food will mold unless you refrigerate it.*

mold[3] (mōld), *n.* loose earth; fine, soft, rich soil.

mold·er (mōl′dər), *v.* to turn into dust by natural decay; waste away; crumble.

mold·ing (mōl′ding), *n.* **1** act of shaping: *the molding of dishes from clay.* **2** something molded; a decorative outline used in architecture. **3** a strip, usually of wood, around the upper walls of a room, used to support pictures, to cover electric wires, for decoration, etc.

Mol·do·va (mòl dō′və), *n.* a country in E Europe, E of Romania. *Capital:* Kishinev.

mold·y (mōl′dē), *adj.* **1** covered with mold: *a moldy crust of bread, moldy cheese.* **2** musty; stale: *The closet had a moldy smell.* ❑ *adj.* **mold·i·er, mold·i·est.** —**mold′i·ness,** *n.*

mole[1] (mōl), *n.* a spot on the skin, usually brown, that was there at birth.

mole[2] (mōl), *n.* **1** any of several small mammals that live underground most of the time. Moles have dark, velvety fur and very small eyes that cannot see well. **2** person who begins to work as an enemy spy after a long period as a trusted citizen. —**mole′like′,** *adj.*

mole[3] (mōl), *n.* the number of grams of an element or compound that equals the number of its molecular weight; gram molecule.

mo·lec·u·lar (mə lek′yə lər), *adj.* of, between, caused by, or made of molecules.

molecular weight, the sum of the atomic weights of all the atoms in a molecule.

mol·e·cule (mol′ə kyül), *n.* **1** the smallest amount into which a chemical element or compound can be divided without changing its chemical properties. A molecule of an element consists of one or more like atoms. A molecule of a compound consists of two or more different atoms. **2** a very small particle; little bit: *not a molecule of evidence.*

mole·hill (mōl′hil′), *n.* a small mound or ridge of earth raised up by moles burrowing under the ground.

mo·lest (mə lest′), *v.* **1** to meddle with and injure; interfere with and trouble; disturb: *It is cruel to molest animals.* **2** to interfere with in an indecent manner, especially by making improper sexual advances to women and children. —**mo·les·ta′tion,** *n.* —**mo·lest′er,** *n.*

Mol·ière (mō lyer′), *n.* 1622-1673, French playwright. His comedies are known for their understanding of people's characters and follies.

mol·lie (mol′ē), *n.* any of several small, bright-colored or black fishes of North and South America, often kept in aquariums. Mollies give birth to live fish, rather than lay eggs. Also, **molly.**

mol·li·fy (mol′ə fī), *v.* to reduce someone else's anger: *I tried to mollify my parents by apologizing for losing my jacket.* ❑ *v.* **mol·li·fied, mol·li·fy·ing.** —**mol′li·fi·ca′tion,** *n.*

mol·lusk or **mol·lusc** (mol′əsk), *n.* any of about 100,000 kinds of animals with soft bodies not composed of segments, sometimes covered with a hard shell. Squids, octopuses, snails, slugs, oysters, and clams are mollusks.

mollusk

mol·ly (mol′ē), *n.* mollie. ❑ *n., pl.* **mol·lies.**

mol·ly·cod·dle (mol′ē kod′l), **1** *v.* to fuss over; pamper. **2** *n.* someone, especially a boy or man, accustomed to being fussed over. ❑ *v.* **mol·ly·cod·dled, mol·ly·cod·dling.** —**mol′ly·cod′dler,** *n.*

Mo·loch (mō′lok), *n.* (in the Bible) a fire god of the Phoenicians. Some parents sacrificed their children to Moloch.

Mo·lo·kai (mō′lō kī′), *n.* the fifth largest island of Hawaii.

molt (mōlt), **1** *v.* to shed the feathers, skin, etc., before a new growth: *We saw the snake molt its skin.* **2** *n.* act or process of such shedding. —**molt′er,** *n.*

mol·ten (mōlt′n), *adj.* **1** made liquid by heat; melted: *molten steel.* **2** made by melting and casting: *a molten image.*

mo·lyb·de·num (mə lib′də nəm), *n.* a heavy, hard, grayish metallic element. Molybdenum is much used to strengthen and harden steel. *Symbol:* Mo

mom (mom), *n.* INFORMAL. mother.

mom-and-pop (mom′ən pop′), *adj.* being owned and operated by a married couple: *The mom-and-pop grocery on our corner has better vegetables than the supermarket.*

mo·ment (mō′mənt), *n.* **1** a very short space of time; instant: *I'll be with you in a moment.* **2** a particular point of time: *I can't recall her name at the moment.* **3** importance: *Congress is busy on a matter of moment.*

mo·men·tar·i·ly (mō′mən ter′ə lē), *adv.* **1** for a moment: *She hesitated momentarily and then made her decision.* **2** at every moment; from moment to moment: *The danger was increasing momentarily.* **3** at any moment; very soon: *He was expecting visitors momentarily.*

mo·men·tar·y (mō′mən ter′ē), *adj.* lasting only a moment: *There was a momentary hesitation before she spoke.* —**mo′men·tar′i·ness,** *n.*

mo·men·tous (mō men′təs), *adj.* very important: *Choosing between peace and war is a momentous decision.* —**mo·men′tous·ly,** *adv.* —**mo·men′tous·ness,** *n.*

mo·men·tum (mō men′təm), *n.* **1** amount measuring the motion of an object, equal to the product of its mass and its velocity: *A falling object gains momentum as it falls.* **2** tendency to keep moving, resulting from movement: *The runner's momentum carried him far beyond the finish line.*

mom·ma (mom′ə), *n.* INFORMAL. mama; mother. ❑ *n., pl.* **mom·mas.**

mom·my (mom′ē), *n.* INFORMAL. mother. ❑ *n., pl.* **mom·mies.**

a	hat	ė	term	ô	order	ch	child	
ā	age	i	it	oi	oil	ng	long	a in about
ä	far	ī	ice	ou	out	sh	she	e in taken
â	care	o	hot	u	cup	th	thin	ə i in pencil
e	let	ō	open	u̇	put	ᴛʜ	then	o in lemon
ē	equal	ò	saw	ü	rule	zh	measure	u in circus

Mon., Monday.

Mon·a·co (mon′ə kō *or* mə nä′kō), *n.* **1** very small country on the SE coast of France, on the Mediterranean. **2** its capital. [See Word Story at **monarch**.] —**Mon′a·can**, *adj., n.*

mon·arch (mon′ərk), *n.* **1** king, queen, emperor, etc.; ruler. **2** someone or something like a monarch: *The tall, solitary pine was monarch of the forest.* **3** a large orange and black butterfly, known for autumn migrations in North America. ❑ *n., pl.* **mon·archs.**

WORD STORY Monarch comes from a Greek word meaning "alone." In old times, a monarch ruled alone, and a country has only one monarch at a time. **Monastery** and **monk** come from the same word. The earliest monks lived alone, and monasteries are places for monks to live by themselves. **Monaco** also comes from this word, because in ancient times one temple stood alone there.

mo·nar·chi·cal (mə när′kə kəl), *adj.* **1** of or about a monarch or monarchy. **2** favoring a monarchy.

mon·ar·chist (mon′ər kist), *n.* someone who supports or favors government by a monarch.

mon·ar·chy (mon′ər kē), *n.* **1** government by a monarch. **2** nation governed by a monarch. ❑ *n., pl.* **mon·ar·chies** for 2.

mon·as·ter·y (mon′ə ster′ē), *n.* building or buildings where monks live and work together. ❑ *n., pl.* **mon·as·ter·ies.** [See Word Story at **monarch**.]

mo·nas·tic (mə nas′tik), **1** *adj.* of or about monks or nuns: *the monastic vows of chastity, poverty, and obedience.* **2** *adj.* like that of monks or nuns. **3** *n.* monk. —**mo·nas′ti·cal·ly**, *adv.*

mo·nas·ti·cism (mə nas′tə siz′əm), *n.* system or condition of living a monastic life.

mon·au·ral (mon ôr′əl), *adj.* **1** of or about the recording or reproduction of sound by means of a single channel; monophonic: *monaural recordings.* **2** of, with, or for one ear: *a monaural hearing aid.* —**mon·au′ral·ly**, *adv.*

Mon·day (mun′dā′ *or* mun′dē), *n.* the second day of the week; day after Sunday. [**Monday** comes from an Old English word meaning "day of the moon." It got this name because it follows Sunday, the sun's day.]

mo·ner·an (mə nir′ən), *n.* any living thing that does not have a cellular nucleus. Bacteria and some algae are monerans.

Mo·net (mō nā′), *n.* **Claude** (klōd), 1840-1926, French painter. He was a leader of the impressionist movement. Many of his later paintings are of his garden and lily pond.

mon·e·tar·y (mon′ə ter′ē), *adj.* **1** of or about the money of a country: *The monetary unit in the United States is the dollar.* **2** of or about money: *a monetary reward.* —**mon′e·tar·i·ly**, *adv.*

mon·ey (mun′ē), *n.* **1** coins of gold, silver, copper, or other metal, or paper notes which represent these metals, issued by a government for use in buying and selling. **2** anything of value used for buying and selling, such as checks drawn on a bank, gold nuggets, or gold dust. **3** wealth: *He is a man of money.* **4 moneys** or **monies**, *pl.* sums of money. ❑ *n., pl.* **mon·eys** (or **mon·ies** for 4.)
make money, 1 to get money. **2** to become rich.

WORD STORY Money comes from a Latin word meaning "she who protects." This was a description of the goddess Juno, in whose temple the Romans made coins. **Mint**[2] comes from the same Latin word.

mon·ey·bag (mun′ē bag′), *n.* **1** bag for money. **2** INFORMAL. **moneybags**, a wealthy person.

mon·ey·chang·er (mun′ē chān′jər), *n.* **1** someone whose business is to exchange money, usually that of one country for that of another. **2** machine that takes in bills and gives out coins.

mon·eyed (mun′ēd), *adj.* **1** having money; wealthy. **2** consisting of or representing money: *moneyed resources.*

mon·ey·lend·er (mun′ē len′dər), *n.* someone whose business is lending money at interest.

money order, order for the payment of a certain sum of money. You can buy a money order at a post office, bank, etc., and send it to a person in another city, who can cash it there.

Mon·gol (mong′gəl), **1** *n.* member of an Asian people now living in Mongolia and nearby parts of China and Siberia. **2** *adj.* of or about this people.

Mongol Empire, former empire of the Mongols, which included most of Asia and part of E Europe during the late 1200s.

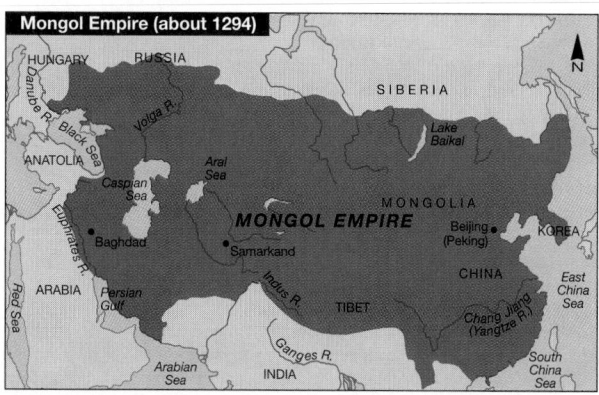

Mongol Empire (about 1294)

Mon·go·li·a (mong gō′lē ə), *n.* vast region in Asia, south of Siberia. Mongolia includes part of N China and the Mongolian People's Republic.

Mon·go·li·an (mong gō′lē ən), **1** *adj.* of or about Mongolia, the Mongols, or their languages. **2** *n.* language or languages of the Mongols or Mongolia. **3** *n.* someone born or living in Mongolia; Mongol.

Mongolian People's Republic, country in central Asia, north of China and south of Siberia. *Capital:* Ulan Bator.

mon·gol·ism or **Mon·gol·ism** (mong′gə liz′əm), *n.* Down syndrome. ■ **Mongolism** is now considered offensive.

Mon·gol·oid (mong′gə loid), **1** *adj.* of or resembling the Mongols. **2** *n.* someone whose ancestors belonged to the group of people living in central and eastern Asia. **3** *adj.* of or about people of this background. **4** *n.* someone having Down syndrome. **5** *adj.* having characteristics associated with Down syndrome. ■ Definitions 4 and 5 are considered offensive.

mon·goose (mong′güs), *n.* any of several slender, flesh-eating mammals of Asia and Africa that resemble ferrets. Some mongooses are noted for their ability to kill cobras and other poisonous snakes. ❑ *n., pl.* **mon·goos·es.**

mon·grel (mung′grəl *or* mong′grəl), **1** *n.* animal or plant of mixed breed, especially a dog. **2** *adj.* having a mixed breed, origin, nature, etc.: *mongrel puppies.*

mon·ies (mun′ēz), *n.* a plural of money.

mon·i·tor (mon′ə tər), **1** *n.* pupil in school with special duties, such as helping to keep order and taking attendance. **2** *n.* someone who gives advice or warning. **3** *n.* **Monitor,** a low, armored Union warship, that had a big gun in a revolving turret. It fought the Merrimac during the Civil War. **4** *n.* any of several large, flesh-eating lizards of Africa, southern Asia, Australia, and the East Indies. **5** *n.* receiver used for listening to and checking radio or television transmissions, telephone messages, etc. **6** *n.* screen on which a computer shows information and instructions. A TV set may be used as a monitor with some computers. **7** *v.* to listen to and check radio or television transmissions, telephone messages, etc., by using a receiver.

mon·i·to·ry (mon′ə tôr′ē), *adj.* admonishing; warning: *the monitory growl of a dog.*

monk (mungk), *n.* man who enters a monastery to live a life devoted to religion. [See Word Story at **monarch**.]

Monk (mungk), *n.* **The·lon·i·ous** (thə lō′nē əs), 1917-1982, American jazz composer and pianist. He was famous for his very unusual rhythm and harmony.

mon·key (mung′kē), **1** *n.* any of numerous mammals of the kind most closely resembling human beings. **2** *n.* one of the smaller mammals of this kind, not a chimpanzee, gorilla, or other large ape. Most monkeys have long tails. **3** *n.* someone, especially a child, who is full of mischief. **4** *v.* Also, **monkey around,** to play in a mischievous way; fool; trifle: *Don't monkey with the TV. She monkeyed around with the sprinkler, and now it's broken.* ❑ *n., pl.* **mon·keys;** *v.* **mon·keyed, mon·key·ing.** —**mon′key·like′**, *adj.*
make a monkey out of, to make a fool of.

monkey bars, jungle gym.

monkey business, 1 wrong or misleading action; fraud. **2** idiotic, foolish behavior; nonsense.

mon·key·shines (mung′kē shīnz′), *n.pl.* INFORMAL. mischievous tricks; clownish jokes.

monkey wrench, a wrench with a movable jaw that can be adjusted to fit different sizes of nuts.

monk·ish (mung′kish), *adj.* of or like a monk or monks. —**monk′ish·ly,** *adv.* —**monk′ish·ness,** *n.*

monks·hood (mungks′húd′), *n.* any of numerous plants with purple or white hooded flowers.

mon·o[1] (mon′ō), *n.* INFORMAL. mononucleosis.

mon·o[2] (mon′ō), **1** *adj.* monaural. **2** *n.* monaural recording or broadcast technique: *This song is in mono.*

mono-, *prefix.* one: *monosyllable = one syllable.*

mon·o·chrome (mon′ə krōm), *n.* a painting, drawing, etc., in a single color or shades of a single color.

mon·o·cle (mon′ə kəl), *n.* (earlier) eyeglass for one eye.

mon·o·cot (mon′ə kot), *n.* any of a great many flowering plants with seeds that have one seed leaf. Monocots have petals in groups of three. Daffodils, bananas, oats, and palm trees are monocots.

mon·o·cot·y·le·don (mon′ə kot′l ēd′n), *n.* monocot.

mo·nog·a·my (mə nog′ə mē), *n.* practice or condition of being married to only one person at a time. —**mo·nog′a·mous,** *adj.*

mon·o·gram (mon′ə gram), *n.* someone's initials combined in one design. Monograms are used on note paper, table linen, clothing, jewelry, etc.

mon·o·graph (mon′ə graf), *n.* book or article, especially a scholarly one, about a particular subject.

mon·o·lith (mon′l ith), *n.* **1** a single large block of stone. **2** monument, column, statue, etc., formed from a single large block of stone. —**mon′o·lith′ic,** *adj.*

mon·o·logue or **mon·o·log** (mon′l òg), *n.* **1** a long speech by one person in a group. **2** entertainment by a single speaker. **3** a play for a single actor. **4** part of a play in which a single actor speaks alone.

mon·o·mi·al (mon ō′mē əl), **1** *n.* expression in algebra containing a single term. The expression $2x^2$ is a monomial. **2** *n.* a one-word scientific name of a living thing. *Orca* (killer whale) is a monomial. **3** *adj.* made up of a single word or term.

Mo·non·ga·he·la (mə non′gə hē′lə), *n.* river flowing from N West Virginia which joins the Allegheny River to form the Ohio River at Pittsburgh. [**Monongahela** comes from an Algonquian word meaning "high falling banks."]

mon·o·nu·cle·o·sis (mon′ə nü′klē ō′sis), *n.* a very contagious disease with fever, sore throat, swelling of the lymph glands, exhaustion, and an abnormal increase in the number of certain kinds of cells in the blood.

mon·o·phon·ic (mon′ə fon′ik), *adj.* **1** monaural. **2** singing or playing one tune together.

mon·o·plane (mon′ə plān), *n.* airplane with only one pair of wings. Most modern airplanes are monoplanes.

mo·nop·o·list (mə nop′ə list), *n.* **1** someone who has a monopoly. **2** someone who favors monopoly.

mo·nop·o·lis·tic (mə nop′ə lis′tik), *adj.* **1** having a monopoly. **2** of or about monopolies or monopolists. —**mo·nop′o·lis′ti·cal·ly,** *adv.*

mo·nop·o·lize (mə nop′ə līz), *v.* **1** to have or get complete possession or control of a product or service: *One company monopolized the production of copper wire.* **2** to keep other people from sharing in: *monopolize a conversation.* ❑ *v.* **mo·nop·o·lized, mo·nop·o·liz·ing.** —**mo·nop′o·li·za′tion,** *n.* —**mo·nop′o·liz′er,** *n.*

mo·nop·o·ly (mə nop′ə lē), *n.* **1** the complete control of a product or service: *The electric company has a monopoly on providing electrical service in the area it serves.* **2** such control granted by a government: *Inventors have a monopoly on their inventions for a certain number of years.* **3** a commercial product or service that is exclusively controlled or nearly so. **4** person or company that has a monopoly on some commodity or service. **5** the exclusive possession or control of something: *a monopoly on another person's time.* ❑ *n., pl.* **mo·nop·o·lies** for 3,4.

mon·o·rail (mon′ə rāl), *n.* **1** a single rail serving as a track for the vehicles that run on it. **2** railway in which cars run on a single rail, either balanced on it or suspended from it.

monorail (def. 2)

mon·o·so·di·um glu·ta·mate (mon′ə sō′dē əm glü′tə māt), a white crystalline substance that helps bring out the natural flavors of foods.

mon·o·syl·lab·ic (mon′ə sə lab′ik), *adj.* **1** having only one syllable. **2** made up of a word or words of one syllable: *"No" is a monosyllabic reply.* —**mon′o·syl·lab′i·cal·ly,** *adv.*

mon·o·syl·la·ble (mon′ə sil′ə bəl), *n.* word of one syllable. *Yes, no,* and *grand* are monosyllables.

mon·o·tone (mon′ə tōn), *n.* sameness of tone, style of writing, color, etc.: *Don't read in a monotone; use expression.*

mo·not·o·nous (mə not′n əs), *adj.* **1** continuing in the same tone or few tones: *a monotonous voice, a monotonous tune.* **2** tiring or boring because of its sameness: *monotonous work, a monotonous diet.* —**mo·not′o·nous·ly,** *adv.* —**mo·not′o·nous·ness,** *n.*

mo·not·o·ny (mə not′n ē), *n.* **1** sameness of tone or pitch: *The monotony of the man's voice was irritating.* **2** tiring or boring sameness.

mon·ox·ide (mo nok′sīd), *n.* oxide containing one oxygen atom in each molecule.

Mon·roe (mən rō′), *n.* **1 James,** 1758-1831, the fifth president of the United States, from 1817 to 1825. **2 Mar·i·lyn** (mar′ə lin), 1926-1962, American movie star. Famous for her beauty, she played many comic parts as well.

Monroe Doctrine, doctrine that European nations should not interfere with American nations or try to acquire more territory in the Western Hemisphere. The Monroe Doctrine was derived from President Monroe's message to Congress on December 2, 1823.

Mon·ro·vi·a (mon rō′vē ə), *n.* port and capital of Liberia, on the Atlantic. [**Monrovia** is named for James Monroe, president of the United States when Liberia was founded with U.S. assistance.]

mon·sieur (mə syėr′), *n.* FRENCH. Mr.; sir. ❑ *n., pl.* **mes·sieurs.**

mon·si·gnor or **Mon·si·gnor** (mon sē′nyər), *n.* **1** title given to certain dignitaries in the Roman Catholic Church. **2** person having this title.

mon·soon (mon sün′), *n.* **1** a seasonal wind of the Indian Ocean and southern Asia. It blows from the southwest from April to October and from the northeast during the rest of the year. **2** the rainy season during which this wind blows from the southwest. [**Monsoon** comes from an Arabic word meaning "a season," because the direction of this wind depends on the season of the year.]

mon·ster (mon′stər), **1** *n.* an imaginary creature of strange and horrible appearance, such as a sea serpent. **2** *n.* any animal or plant that is very unlike those usually found in nature. A cow with two heads is a monster. **3** *n.* person too wicked to be considered human: *a ghastly crime committed by a monster of cruelty.* **4** *n.* a huge creature or thing. **5** *adj.* huge: *a monster success.*

a	hat	ė	term	ô	order	ch	child		
ā	age	i	it	oi	oil	ng	long	ə {	a in about
ä	far	ī	ice	ou	out	sh	she		e in taken
â	care	o	hot	u	cup	th	thin		i in pencil
e	let	ō	open	ù	put	ŦH	then		o in lemon
ē	equal	ò	saw	ü	rule	zh	measure		u in circus

mon·stros·i·ty (mon stros′ə tē), *n.* **1** monster. **2** condition or character of being monstrous. ❑ *n., pl.* **mon·stros·i·ties** for 1.

mon·strous (mon′strəs), *adj.* **1** huge; enormous: *A monstrous wave sank the tiny fishing boat.* **2** wrongly formed or shaped; like a monster. **3** so wrong or absurd as to be almost unheard of. **4** shocking; horrible; dreadful: *Murder is a monstrous crime.* **—mon′strous·ly,** *adv.* **—mon′strous·ness,** *n.*

Mont., Montana.

mon·tage (mon täzh′), *n.* **1** the combination of several photographs to make one picture. **2** a picture made in this way. **3** (in TV, movies, etc.) any combining or blending of pictures, at once or following one other quickly. **4** a similar effect in literature, music, etc., using a series of brief ideas following one another quickly.

Mon·tan·a (mon tan′ə), *n.* **1** one of the western states of the United States. *Abbreviation:* MT or Mont. *Capital:* Helena. **2 Joe** (jō), born 1956, American football player. He was the quarterback for the San Francisco 49ers from 1979 to 1993, during which time they won four Super Bowls. [Montana comes from a Spanish word meaning "mountainous." The Rocky Mountains cover the western part of the state.] **—Mon·tan′an,** *n.*

Mont Blanc (mȯn blän′), the highest mountain in the Alps, between France and Italy, 15,771 feet (4807 meters) high.

Mon·te Car·lo (mon′tə kär′lō), town in Monaco, noted as a gambling resort.

Mon·te·ne·gro (mon′tə neg′rō *or* mon′tə nē′grō), *n.* a former kingdom in SE Europe, later part of Yugoslavia. **—Mon·te·ne·grin** (mon′tə neg′rin *or* mon′tə nē′grin), *adj., n.*

Mon·tes·so·ri (mon′tə sôr′ē), *n.* **Ma·ri·a** (mə rē′ə), 1870-1952, Italian educator. She was the first Italian woman to receive a medical degree. Her educational methods are the basis of the schools named for her.

Montessori method, system of education intended to develop positive learning habits and attitudes in students. It is taught in special Montessori schools.

Mon·te·vi·de·o (mon′tə vi dā′ō), *n.* port and capital of Uruguay, in the S part, near the Atlantic.

WORD STORY Montevideo comes from Spanish words meaning "I see a mountain." A lookout on a ship of the explorer Ferdinand Magellan called out this phrase, and the place kept the name.

Mon·te·zu·ma II (mon′tə zü′mə), 1466?-1520, Aztec emperor of Mexico, from 1502 to 1520, defeated by Cortés.

Mont·gom·er·y (mont gum′ər ē), *n.* capital of Alabama, in the central part, on the Alabama River.

month (munth), *n.* **1** one of the 12 parts that make a year. September, April, June, and November have 30 days; February has 28 days except in leap years, when it has 29; all the other months have 31 days. **2** time from any day of one month to the day with the same number in the next month. **3** lunar month.

a month of Sundays, INFORMAL. a very long time: *I haven't seen them in a month of Sundays.*

WORD STORY Month comes from an old English word related to **moon.** The time from one full moon to the next is about a month long—which is probably why we have months at all.

month·ly (munth′lē), **1** *adj.* of or for a month; lasting a month: *a monthly supply.* **2** *adj.* done, happening, payable, etc., once a month: *a monthly meeting.* **3** *adv.* once a month; every month: *Some magazines come monthly.* **4** *n.* magazine published once a month. ❑ *n., pl.* **month·lies.**

Mon·ti·cel·lo (mon′tə sel′ō *or* mon′tə chel′ō), *n.* home of Thomas Jefferson, in central Virginia.

WORD STORY Monticello comes from an Italian word meaning "little mountain." The name was given by Thomas Jefferson because the house is on a hilltop.

Mont·pel·ier (mont pē′lyər), *n.* capital of Vermont, in the central part.

Mon·tre·al (mon′trē ȯl′), *n.* port and largest Canadian city, in S Quebec, on the St. Lawrence River. [Montreal comes from two Latin words meaning "royal mountain." The city is built around a mountain.]

mon·u·ment (mon′yə mənt), *n.* **1** something set up to honor a person or an event. A monument may be a building, pillar, arch, statue, tomb, or stone. **2** an enduring or prominent instance: *The Hoover Dam is a monument of engineering.*

mon·u·men·tal (mon′yə men′-tl), *adj.* **1** of or about a monument. **2** serving as a monument. **3** like a monument. **4** weighty and lasting; important: *The Constitution of the United States is a monumental document.* **5** very great: *monumental ignorance.* **—mon′u·men′tal·ly,** *adv.*

monument (def. 1)

moo (mü), **1** *n.* sound made by a cow. **2** *v.* to make this sound. ❑ *n., pl.* **moos;** *v.* **mooed, moo·ing.**

mooch (müch), *v.* INFORMAL. to get from someone else by begging or sponging. **—mooch′er,** *n.*

mood¹ (müd), *n.* state of mind or feeling: *I am in the mood to play now; I don't want to study.* ■ See Synonym Study at **feeling.**

mood² (müd), *n.* form of a verb which shows whether the act or state it expresses is thought of as a fact, condition, command, etc. In "I am hungry," *am* is in the indicative mood. In "I demand that she answer," *answer* is in the subjunctive mood. In "Open the window," *open* is in the imperative mood. Also, **mode.**

mood·y (mü′dē), *adj.* **1** likely to have changes of mood, often becoming sad or depressed: *She has been moody ever since she lost her job.* **2** sunk in sadness; gloomy; sullen: *They sat in moody silence.* ❑ *adj.* **mood·i·er, mood·i·est. —mood′i·ly,** *adv.* **—mood′i·ness,** *n.*

moon (mün), **1** *n.* the large shining object that revolves around the earth once in about 29½ days. It is a natural satellite of the earth and is held in orbit by the earth's gravity. The force of the moon's gravity on the earth causes ocean tides. **2** *n.* the moon as it looks at a certain point in its revolving: *a new moon, a full moon.* **3** *n.* the American Indian month of about 29½ days. **4** *n.* moonlight. **5** *n.* something shaped like the moon in any of its appearances. **6** *n.* satellite of any planet: *the moons of Jupiter.* **7** *v.* to wander around idly or gaze dreamily: *Don't sit there mooning when you have work to do.* [See Word Story at **month.**] **—moon′less,** *adj.* **—moon′like′,** *adj.*

moon·beam (mün′bēm′), *n.* ray of moonlight.

moon·light (mün′līt′), **1** *n.* light of the moon. **2** *adj.* having the light of the moon: *a moonlight night.* **3** *adj.* while the moon is shining; by night: *a moonlight swim.* **4** *v.* to work at a second job, often at night.

moon·lit (mün′lit′), *adj.* lighted by the moon.

moon·shine (mün′shīn′), *n.* **1** moonlight. **2** empty talk; foolish talk or ideas; nonsense. **3** INFORMAL. intoxicating liquor made unlawfully.

moon·stone (mün′stōn′), *n.* a whitish gem with a pearly luster. Moonstone is a variety of feldspar.

moon·struck (mün′struk′), *adj.* dazed or confused.

moon·walk (mün′wȯk′), **1** *n.* a walk on the moon's surface: *The astronauts gathered rocks on their moonwalk.* **2** *v.* to take such a walk. **3** *n.* a dance step with shifting of the feet in a backward motion. **4** *v.* to dance using this step. **—moon′walk′er,** *n.*

moor¹ (mur), *v.* **1** to put or keep a boat or ship in place by means of ropes or chains fastened to the shore or to anchors. **2** to fix firmly; secure. **3** to tie down or anchor a ship: *They moored in a bay.*

moor² (mur), *n.* an open wasteland, usually covered with heather.

Moor (mur), *n.* member of a Muslim people of mixed Arab and Berber ancestry, living in northwestern Africa. In the A.D. 700s the Moors invaded and conquered Spain. They were driven out in 1492.

Moore (mur *or* môr), *n.* **1 Henry,** 1898-1986, English sculptor. Many of his sculptures are very large humanlike forms, often with holes through them. **2 Mar·i·anne** (mar′ē an′), 1887-1972, American poet. She won the 1952 Pulitzer Prize for poetry.

moor·ings (mur′ingz), *n.* **1** *pl.* ropes, cables, or anchors by which a ship is fastened. **2** *sing.* place where a ship is moored.

Moor·ish (mur′ish), *adj.* of or relating to the Moors.

moose (müs), *n.* a large mammal of northern forests, in Europe called elk. The male has a large head and broad antlers. It is related to the deer. ❏ *n., pl.* **moose.** ■ Another word that sounds like this is **mousse.** [Moose comes from an Algonquian word meaning "he strips off the bark." The moose strips off and eats the bark of young trees.]

moot (müt), *adj.* **1** doubtful or debatable: *a moot point.* **2** having no practical importance; hypothetical; unreal, especially in contrast to actual circumstances: *The question of how to spend the prize money is moot, because we're not going to win.*

USAGE NOTE **Moot** is commonly used now to describe a question or topic that is unimportant because it has already been settled in practical terms. This is a fairly new meaning of the word, which formerly meant only "for discussion" or "debatable." A moot point was one that needed talking over. Now it is usually one that doesn't need talking over. Some people still object to the new meaning, but it is becoming more and more common.

mop (mop), **1** *n.* bundle of coarse yarn, cloth, etc., or a sponge fastened at the end of a stick or handle, for cleaning floors, dishes, etc. **2** *v.* to wash or wipe up; clean with a mop: *to mop up the floor.* **3** *v.* to wipe tears or sweat from: *to mop your forehead with your handkerchief.* **4** *n.* INFORMAL. a thick head of hair like a mop. ❏ *v.* **mopped, mop·ping.** —**mop′per,** *n.*

mop up, 1 to clean with a mop: *mop up a kitchen floor.* **2** to finish, especially remaining details: *Dad stayed late at work mopping up the installing of new computers.*

mope (mōp), **1** *v.* to be dull, silent, and sad. **2** *n.* someone who is dull, silent, and sad. ❏ *v.* **moped, mop·ing.** —**mop′er,** *n.*

mo·ped (mō′ped), *n.* motorbike that can be pedaled as a bicycle or operated with a motor at up to 30 miles (50 kilometers) an hour. [Moped is a blend of motor and pedal.]

mop·pet (mop′it), *n.* a little child.

mo·raine (mə rān′), *n.* heap or ridge of dirt and rocks that were scraped up and then dropped by a glacier.

mo·ral (môr′əl), **1** *adj.* good in character or conduct; virtuous according to traditional standards of right and wrong; right; just: *a moral act, a moral person.* **2** *n.pl.* **morals,** principles in regard to conduct; character or behavior in matters of right and wrong. **3** *adj.* capable of understanding right and wrong: *A little baby is not a moral being.* **4** *adj.* of or about character or the difference between right and wrong: *Whether to keep a large sum of money you have found or to turn it over to the police is a moral question.* **5** *n.* lesson, inner meaning, or teaching of a fable, a story, or an event: *The moral of the story was "Look before you leap."* **6** *adj.* teaching a good lesson; having a good influence: *moral instruction.* **7** *adj.* raising morale; inspiring confidence: *We gave moral support to the team by cheering them enthusiastically.*

USAGE NOTE **Moral** and **morale** look alike, and they both come from a Latin word meaning "customs." So it is easy to confuse them. One way to remember the difference is that **morale** ends in *e,* for energy, efficiency, and enthusiasm.

mo·rale (mə ral′), *n.* moral or mental condition as regards courage, confidence, enthusiasm, etc.: *The morale of the team was low after its defeat.* ■ See Usage Note at **moral.**

mo·ral·is·tic (môr′ə lis′tik), *adj.* **1** of or concerned with morals. **2** narrow-minded in moral judgment or beliefs. —**mo′ral·is′ti·cal·ly,** *adv.*

mo·ral·i·ty (mə ral′ə tē), *n.* **1** the right or wrong of an action: *They spent the evening arguing about the morality of war.* **2** doing right; virtue: *They have high standards of morality.* **3** system of morals; set of rules or principles of conduct. ❏ *n., pl.* **mo·ral·i·ties** for 3.

mo·ral·ize (môr′ə līz), *v.* **1** to think, talk, or write about questions of right and wrong. **2** to point out the lesson or inner meaning of. **3** to improve, or try to improve, someone's morals, especially by talking. ❏ *v.* **mo·ral·ized, mo·ral·iz·ing.** —**mo′ral·i·za′tion,** *n.* —**mo′ral·iz′er,** *n.*

mo·ral·ly (môr′ə lē), *adv.* **1** in a moral manner: *to behave morally.* **2** in morals; as to morals: *The king was a good man morally but too easily swayed by his crafty advisers.* **3** from a moral point of view; ethically: *What they did was morally wrong.*

moral victory, defeat that has the effect on the mind that a victory would have.

mo·rass (mə ras′), *n.* **1** piece of low, soft, very wet ground; swamp; marsh; bog. **2** a difficult situation. ❏ *n., pl.* **mo·rass·es.**

mor·a·to·ri·um (môr′ə tôr′ē əm), *n.* **1** a legal authorization to delay payments of money due. **2** period during which such authorization is in effect. **3** a temporary stopping of action on any issue. ❏ *n., pl.* **mo·ra·to·ri·ums, mo·ra·to·ri·a** (môr′ə tôr′ē ə).

Mo·ra·vi·a (mô rā′vē ə), *n.* region in E Czech Republic. —**Mo·ra′vi·an,** *adj., n.*

mo·ray (môr′ā), *n.* any of numerous, often brightly colored eels of tropical seas.

mor·bid (môr′bid), *adj.* **1** not wholesome; unhealthy; sickly: *morbid fancies, a morbid book.* **2** caused by disease; characteristic of disease; diseased: *Cancer is a morbid growth.* **3** horrible; gruesome; grisly: *the morbid details of a murder.* —**mor′bid·ly,** *adv.* —**mor′bid·ness,** *n.*

mor·bid·i·ty (môr bid′ə tē), *n.* **1** morbid condition or quality. **2** proportion of sickness or disease in a given population.

moray—up to 6 ft. (1.8 m) long

mor·dant (môrd′nt), *adj.* biting; cutting; sarcastic: *The mordant criticism hurt my feelings.* —**mor′dant·ly,** *adv.*

more (môr), **1** *adj.* greater in amount, degree, or number: *more people, more help. A foot is more than an inch.* **2** *n.* a greater or additional amount, degree, or number: *Tell me more about your camping trip.* **3** *adv.* in a higher degree; to a greater extent: *A burn hurts more than a scratch does.* **4** *adv.* in addition; farther: *Take one step more. Sing once more.* **5** *adj.* further; additional: *This plant needs more sun.* **6** *adv.* More helps to make the comparative form of most adverbs, and of most adjectives longer than one syllable: *more easily, more truly, more careful.* "More common" means "commoner." ❏ *adj., comparative of* **much;** *adv., comparative of* **much.**

more or less, 1 somewhat: *Most people are more or less generous.* **2** about; approximately: *The distance is 50 miles more or less.*

More (môr), *n.* Sir **Thomas,** 1478-1535, English judge and author. He was made a saint by the Roman Catholic church in 1935.

mo·rel (mə rel′), *n.* any of several small mushrooms that can be eaten, with pitted brown caps.

Mo·re·los (mō re′lōs or mə rā′lōs), *n.* a state in S central Mexico.

more·o·ver (môr ō′vər), *adv.* in addition to that; also; besides: *Our field trip was informative; moreover, it was fun.*

mo·res (môr′āz), *n.pl.* the traditional rules of a people or society.

Mor·gan le Fay (môr′gən lə fā′), King Arthur's half sister, a fairy.

morgue (môrg), *n.* **1** place in which the bodies of unknown persons found dead are kept until they can be identified and claimed. **2** the reference library in a newspaper office.

WORD STORY **Morgue** comes from a French word meaning "pride." The word was also the name of a room in French prisons where new prisoners were examined by the guards. Prisoners often tried to look proud, as if they were not embarrassed or nervous. The idea of examining new arrivals is still in the English meaning of definition 1.

mo·ri·bund (môr′ə bund), *adj.* dying.

a	hat	ė	term	ô	order	ch	child		
ā	age	i	it	oi	oil	ng	long		a in about
ä	far	ī	ice	ou	out	sh	she	ə	e in taken
â	care	o	hot	u	cup	th	thin		i in pencil
e	let	ō	open	ú	put	ŦH	then		o in lemon
ē	equal	ȯ	saw	ü	rule	zh	measure		u in circus

Mor·mon (môr′mən), **1** *n.* member of the Church of Jesus Christ of Latter-day Saints, founded in 1830 by Joseph Smith. **2** *adj.* of or about the Mormons or their religion.

Mormon Trail, trail from Nauvoo, Illinois, across Iowa, Nebraska, and Wyoming, to Salt Lake City, Utah, used by Mormons in the 1800s.

morn (môrn), *n.* OLD USE. morning. ■ Another word that sounds like this is **mourn.**

morn·ing (môr′ning), **1** *n.* the early part of the day, ending at noon. **2** *adj.* of or in the morning. ■ Another word that sounds like this is **mourning.**

morning glory, any of numerous climbing vines that have heart-shaped leaves and funnel-shaped blue, pink, or white flowers. A morning glory's flowers open early in the morning but close later in the sunlight. ❑ *pl.* **morn·ing glo·ries.**

morning star, a bright planet, especially Venus, seen in the eastern sky before sunrise.

mo·roc·co (mə rok′ō), *n.* a fine leather made from goatskin, used in binding books. ❑ *n., pl.* **mo·roc·cos.**

Mo·roc·co (mə rok′ō), *n.* country in NW Africa. *Capital:* Rabat. —**Mo·roc′can,** *adj., n.*

mo·ron (môr′on), *n.* a very stupid or foolish person. —**mo·ron′ic,** *adj.* —**mo·ron′i·cal·ly,** *adv.*

Mo·ro·ni (mō rō′nē), *n.* capital of the Comoros Islands.

mo·rose (mə rōs′), *adj.* gloomy; sullen; ill-humored. —**mo·rose′ly,** *adv.* —**mo·rose′ness,** *n.*

morph (môrf), *v.* **1** to change one picture into another, so that the process of change is either invisible or very smooth, especially by use of a computer: *He morphed the picture of a baby's face into a picture of a kitten's face.* **2** to change in this way from one appearance to another: *The alien morphed from lizard form to tiger form.*

mor·pheme (môr′fēm), *n.* any meaningful part of a word that cannot be divided into smaller meaningful parts. Morphemes may be words, prefixes, suffixes, or endings that show inflection. In the word *carelessness,* the morphemes are *care, -less,* and *-ness.*

Mor·pheus (môr′fē əs), *n.* Greek god of dreams.

mor·phine (môr′fēn′), *n.* drug made from opium, used to dull pain and to cause sleep.

mor·phol·o·gy (môr fol′ə jē), *n.* **1** branch of biology that deals with the form and structure of living things. **2** form and structure of a living thing or a part of a living thing. —**mor′pho·log′i·cal,** *adj.* —**mor′pho·log′i·cal·ly,** *adv.*

mor·row (môr′ō), *n.* **1** the following day or time. **2** OLD USE. morning.

Morse (môrs), *n.* **Samuel,** 1791-1872, American inventor and painter who made the first telegraph. The Morse code is named for him.

Morse code, system by which letters, numbers, and other signs are represented by dots, dashes, and spaces or by long and short sounds or flashes of light.

mor·sel (môr′səl), *n.* **1** a small portion of food: *I was so hungry I ate every morsel on my plate.* **2** piece; fragment.

mor·tal (môr′tl), **1** *adj.* sure to die sometime. **2** *n.* a being that is sure to die sometime. All living creatures are mortals. **3** *adj.* of or about human beings or mortals: *Mortal bodies feel pain.* **4** *n.* human being: *"Lord, what fools these mortals be!"* **5** *adj.* of or about death. **6** *adj.* causing death: *a mortal illness.* **7** *adj.* to the death: *a mortal enemy, a mortal battle.* **8** *adj.* very great; extreme: *mortal terror.* **9** *adj.* (in the Roman Catholic Church) causing damnation of the soul: *Murder is a mortal sin.*

mor·tal·i·ty (môr tal′ə tē), *n.* **1** mortal nature; being sure to die sometime. **2** loss of life on a large scale: *The mortality from car accidents is dreadful.* **3** death rate; number of deaths in proportion to population or to a specified part of a population: *The mortality from typhoid fever is decreasing.*

mor·tal·ly (môr′tl ē), *adv.* **1** fatally; so as to cause death: *The soldier fell mortally wounded.* **2** very greatly; bitterly; grievously: *She was mortally offended.*

mor·tar¹ (môr′tər), *n.* mixture of lime, cement, sand, and water, for holding bricks or stones together.

mor·tar² (môr′tər), *n.* **1** bowl of porcelain, glass, or other very hard material, in which substances may be pounded to a powder with a pestle. **2** a very short cannon for shooting shells or fireworks high into the air.

mor·tar·board (môr′tər bôrd′), *n.* **1** a flat, square board used by masons to hold mortar while working with it. **2** cap with a close-fitting crown topped by a stiff, flat, cloth-covered square piece from which a tassel usually hangs, worn at graduation exercises and other academic occasions.

mort·gage (môr′gij), **1** *n.* a loan made to the buyer of a building, or of land, used to pay for the property. The lender holds a claim to the property until the loan is repaid. **2** *n.* document that gives such a claim. **3** *v.* to give a lender a claim to your property in case a debt is not paid when due. **4** *v.* to put under some obligation; pledge: *Faust mortgaged his soul to the Devil.* ❑ *v.* **mort·gaged, mort·gag·ing.**

> **WORD STORY** **Mortgage** comes from French words meaning "dead" and "promise." When borrowed money is paid back as promised by a mortgage, the lender's claim on property ceases to exist, as if the claim were dead.

mort·gag·ee (môr′gi jē′), *n.* someone to whom property is mortgaged. ❑ *n., pl.* **mort·gag·ees.**

mort·ga·gor or **mort·gag·er** (môr′gi jər), *n.* someone who mortgages property.

mor·tice (môr′tis), *n., v.* mortise. ❑ *v.* **mor·ticed, mor·tic·ing.**

mor·ti·cian (môr tish′ən), *n.* funeral director.

mor·ti·fi·ca·tion (môr′tə fə kā′shən), *n.* **1** a feeling of shame; humiliation: *mortification at having spilled food on the table.* **2** a cause of shame or humiliation. **3** act of mortifying or condition of being mortified: *the mortification of the body by fasting.*

mor·ti·fy (môr′tə fī), *v.* **1** to wound the feelings of; make feel humbled and ashamed; humiliate: *Their bad behavior mortified their parents.* ■ See Synonym Study at **ashamed. 2** to overcome bodily desires and feelings by pain and going without things: *The saint mortified her body.* ❑ *v.* **mor·ti·fied, mor·ti·fy·ing.** [Mortify comes from Latin words meaning "to make dead." You may have heard someone say, "I was so ashamed, I wished I could die."] —**mor′ti·fi′er,** *n.*

mor·tise (môr′tis), **1** *n.* hole in one piece of wood cut to receive the tenon on another piece so as to form a joint. **2** *v.* to fasten by a mortise. ❑ *v.* **mor·tised, mor·tis·ing.** Also, **mortice.**

mor·tu·ar·y (môr′chü er′ē), **1** *n.* a building where the dead are kept until burial or cremation. **2** *adj.* of or about death or burial. ❑ *n., pl.* **mor·tu·ar·ies.**

mos., months.

mo·sa·ic (mō zā′ik), **1** *n.* decoration made of small pieces of stone, glass, wood, etc., of different colors inlaid to form a picture or design. **2** *n.* such a picture or design. Mosaics are used in the floors, walls, or ceilings of some fine buildings. **3** *adj.* formed by or resembling a mosaic. **4** *n.* anything like a mosaic: *Her music is a mosaic of folk tunes.* [See Word Story at **museum.**]

Mo·sa·ic (mō zā′ik), *adj.* of or from Moses: *the Mosaic law.*

Mos·cow (mos′kou or mos′kō), *n.* capital of Russia, and formerly of the Soviet Union, in the W part.

Mo·ses (mō′ziz), *n.* (in the Bible) the great leader and lawgiver of the Hebrews, who led them out of Egypt. [Moses may come from an Egyptian word meaning "son."]

Mo·ses (mō′ziz), *n.* **Grandma,** 1860-1961, American artist. ■ **Grandma Moses** began to paint in her 70s and painted 25 paintings the year after she turned 100.

mo·sey (mō′zē), *v.* INFORMAL. **1** to shuffle along. **2** to stroll; saunter. ❑ *v.* **mo·seyed, mo·sey·ing.**

Mos·lem (moz′ləm or mùz′ləm), *n., adj.* Muslim.

mosque (mosk), *n.* a Muslim place of worship.

Moscow

mos·qui·to (mə skē/tō), *n.* any of many small, slender insects with two wings, related to flies. The female of some kinds bites and sucks blood from people and animals, causing itching. One kind of mosquito transmits malaria; another transmits yellow fever. Many kinds of mosquitoes do not bite and eat only plant juices. ❑ *n., pl.* **mos·qui·toes** or **mos·qui·tos.**

moss (mȯs), *n.* any of the very many small, soft, green or brown rootless plants that grow close together like a carpet on the ground, on rocks, on trees, etc. ❑ *n., pl.* **moss·es.** —**moss′like′,** *adj.*

Mos·si (mos/ē), *n.* any of a group of people living mostly in Burkina Faso. ❑ *n., pl.* **Mos·sis** or **Mos·si.**

moss·y (mȯ/sē), *adj.* **1** covered with moss: *a mossy bank.* **2** like moss: *This sweater is mossy green.* ❑ *adj.* **moss·i·er, moss·i·est.** —**moss′i·ness,** *n.*

most (mōst), **1** *adj.* greatest in amount, degree, or number: *The winner gets the most money.* **2** *n.* the greatest amount, degree, or number: *He did most of the work. Who gave the most?* **3** *adv.* in the highest degree; to the greatest extent: *This tooth hurts most. She was most kind to me.* **4** *adj.* almost all: *Most people like ice cream.* **5** *adv. Most* helps to make the superlative form of almost all adverbs, and of almost all adjectives longer than one syllable: *most easily, most truly, most careful. "Most common" means "commonest."* ❑ *adj., superlative of* **many** or **much;** *adv., superlative of* **much.**

at most or **at the most,** not more than.

for the most part, mainly; usually.

make the most of, to make the best use of.

mos·tac·cio·li (mos/tə chō/lē), *n.* a kind of pasta similar to large macaroni, cut diagonally into short pieces and sometimes grooved, usually served with a cheese or meat sauce.

most·ly (mōst/lē), *adv.* almost all; for the most part; mainly; chiefly.

mote (mōt), *n.* speck of dust. ■ Another word that sounds like this is **moat.**

mo·tel (mō tel/), *n.* roadside hotel or group of furnished cottages or cabins providing overnight lodging for motorists. Most motels have parking next to or near the units. [Motel is a blend of **motor** and **hotel.**]

moth (mȯth), *n.* any of about 100,000 kinds of broad-winged insects very much like butterflies, but flying mostly at night. Some moths are destructive in the larval stage. One kind lays eggs in cloth, fur, etc., and its larvae eat holes in the material. Some larvae, such as the silkworm, are useful. ❑ *n., pl.* **moths** (mȯᴛʜz *or* mȯths).

moth—about 5 in. (13 cm) across

moth·ball (mȯth/bȯl/), *n.* a small ball of camphor or other strong-smelling substance, used to keep moths away from wool, silk, fur, etc.

in mothballs or **into mothballs,** in or into storage to protect against damage.

moth-eat·en (mȯth/ēt/n), *adj.* **1** eaten by moths; having holes made by moths. **2** worn-out.

moth·er[1] (muᴛʜ/ər), **1** *n.* a female parent. **2** *v.* to take care of; act as mother to: *She mothers her baby sister.* **3** *n.* the cause or source of anything. **4** *n.* mother superior. **5** *adj.* of or like a mother: *mother love, the mother church.* **6** *n.* someone who is like a mother. **7** *v.* to give birth to; bring forth. **8** *adj.* native: *our mother tongue, one's mother country.*

moth·er[2] (muᴛʜ/ər), *n.* a stringy, sticky substance formed in vinegar or on the surface of liquids that are turning to vinegar. Mother consists of bacteria and yeast cells.

moth·er·board (muᴛʜ/ər bôrd/), *n.* the main electrical system of a computer, containing the circuits for the CPU, monitor, and keyboard, and often with available connections for optional additional devices.

Mother Goose, the imaginary author of nursery rhymes.

moth·er·hood (muᴛʜ/ər hủd), *n.* condition of being a mother.

moth·er-in-law (muᴛʜ/ər in lô/), *n.* mother of your husband or wife. ❑ *n., pl.* **moth·ers-in-law.**

moth·er·land (muᴛʜ/ər land/), *n.* **1** your native country. **2** land of your ancestors.

moth·er·less (muᴛʜ/ər lis), *adj.* having no mother: *a motherless child.* —**moth′er·less·ness,** *n.*

moth·er·ly (muᴛʜ/ər lē), *adj.* like a mother; like a mother's; kindly: *a motherly person, motherly love.* —**moth′er·li·ness,** *n.*

moth·er-of-pearl (muᴛʜ/ər əv pėrl/), *n.* the hard, smooth, shiny lining of the shell of the pearl oyster, mussel, and abalone. It changes colors as the light changes. It is used to make buttons.

Mother's Day, the second Sunday of May, set apart in the United States and Canada in honor of mothers.

mother superior, woman who is the head of a convent of nuns; mother. ❑ *n., pl.* **mother superiors** or **mothers superior.**

mother tongue, 1 one's native language. **2** an original language to which other languages owe their origin.

mo·tif (mō tēf/), *n.* **1** a subject for development or treatment in art, literature, or music; a principal idea or feature: *This opera contains a love motif.* **2** a distinctive figure in a design.

mo·tion (mō/shən), **1** *n.* change of position or place; movement; moving. Anything is in motion which is not at rest. *Can you feel the motion of the ship?* **2** *v.* to make a movement, as of the hand or head, to show your meaning: *He motioned to show us the way.* **3** *v.* to show someone what to do by such a movement: *He motioned me out.* **4** *n.* a formal suggestion made in a meeting or court of law, to be voted on: *The motion to adjourn was carried.*

go through the motions, to do something required, without enthusiasm or effort: *I went through the motions of looking at his photos.*

mo·tion·less (mō/shən lis), *adj.* not moving. —**mo′tion·less·ly,** *adv.* —**mo′tion·less·ness,** *n.*

motion picture, movie. —**mo′tion-pic′ture,** *adj.*

motion sickness, nausea and dizziness, sometimes caused by the motion of a plane, car, ship, or other vehicle.

mo·ti·vate (mō/tə vāt), *v.* to provide with a motive; cause to act. ❑ *v.* **mo·ti·vat·ed, mo·ti·vat·ing.**

mo·ti·va·tion (mō/tə vā/shən), *n.* **1** something that motivates; reason for action: *The winner's scholarship is her motivation to practice.* **2** act of furnishing with a motive or cause for action.

mo·tive (mō/tiv), *n.* **1** thought or feeling that makes you act; reason for doing something: *My motive in taking the trip was a wish to travel.* **2** motif.

mot·ley (mot/lē), **1** *adj.* made up of parts or kinds that are different: *In the drawer I found a motley collection of butterflies, shells, and stamps.* **2** *adj.* of different colors like a clown's suit. **3** *n.* suit of more than one color worn by clowns: *At the costume party he wore motley.* ❑ *n., pl.* **mot·leys.**

mo·to·cross (mō/tō kròs/), *n.* a motorcycle race run over rugged trails with hills and curves, rather than on a flat paved track. ❑ *n., pl.* **mo·to·cross·es.**

mo·tor (mō/tər), **1** *n.* engine that makes a machine go: *an electric motor.* **2** *n.* an internal-combustion engine. **3** *adj.* run by a motor: *a motor vehicle.* **4** *adj.* of or by means of cars: *a motor tour.* **5** *v.* to travel by car. **6** *adj.* causing or having to do with motion. Motor nerves arouse muscles to action. —**mo′tor·less,** *adj.*

mo·tor·bike (mō/tər bik/), *n.* **1** bicycle with a small motor. **2** motorcycle, especially a small, light one.

mo·tor·boat (mō/tər bōt/), *n.* boat that is propelled by a motor.

mo·tor·cade (mō/tər kād), *n.* procession or long line of cars grouped for some reason: *the presidential motorcade.*

mo·tor·car (mō/tər kär/), *n.* car.

mo·tor·cy·cle (mō/tər si/kəl), **1** *n.* a two-wheeled motor vehicle with a large internal-combustion engine between the wheels and often two seats. **2** *v.* to travel by motorcycle. ❑ *v.* **mo·tor·cy·cled, mo·tor·cy·cling.**

a	hat	ė	term	ô	order	ch	child		
ā	age	i	it	oi	oil	ng	long		a in about
ä	far	ī	ice	ou	out	sh	she		e in taken
â	care	o	hot	u	cup	th	thin	ə	i in pencil
e	let	ō	open	ủ	put	ᴛʜ	then		o in lemon
ē	equal	ȯ	saw	ü	rule	zh	measure		u in circus

mo·tor·cy·clist (mō'tər sī'klist), *n.* someone who rides a motorcycle.

motor home, a motor vehicle having living space, used for traveling, camping, etc.

mo·tor·ist (mō'tər ist), *n.* someone who drives or travels in a car.

mo·tor·ize (mō'tə rīz'), *v.* **1** to furnish with a motor. **2** to supply with motor-driven vehicles in place of horses and horse-drawn vehicles. ❑ *v.* **mo·tor·ized, mo·tor·iz·ing. —mo'tor·i·za'tion,** *n.*

mo·tor·man (mō'tər mən), *n.* someone who drives a subway train, streetcar, etc. ❑ *n., pl.* **mo·tor·men.**

motor scooter, a short, lightweight two-wheeled motor vehicle with a seat for the driver, a small footboard, and the engine mounted over the rear wheel.

motor vehicle, any vehicle propelled by a motor and traveling on wheels on roads and highways. Cars, trucks, buses, vans, RVs, motorcycles, and motor scooters are motor vehicles.

Mott (mot), *n.* **Lu·cre·tia** (lü krē'shə), 1793-1880, American Abolitionist and suffragist. She and Elizabeth Cady Stanton organized the first women's rights meeting in the United States.

mot·tle (mot'l), **1** *v.* to mark with spots or streaks of different colors. **2** *n.* a spotted or streaked coloring or pattern. ❑ *v.* **mot·tled, mot·tling.**

mot·to (mot'ō), *n.* **1** a brief sentence adopted as a rule of conduct: *"Think before you speak" is a good motto.* **2** sentence, word, or phrase written or engraved on some object. ❑ *n., pl.* **mot·toes** or **mot·tos.**

mound (mound), **1** *n.* a bank or mass of earth or stones. **2** *v.* to heap up: *He mounded the sand.* **3** *n.* a small hill. **4** *n.* a pile or heap: *He poured gravy over a mound of mashed potatoes on his plate.* **5** *n.* the slightly elevated ground from which a baseball pitcher pitches.

> **WORD STORY**   **Mound** looks like **mount**[2], but the words are not related. No one knows where **mound** comes from. It used to mean "a fence" or "a hedge." People changed the meaning to "low hill" just because the word reminded them of **mount.**

Mound Builders, prehistoric Native Americans who lived in central and eastern North America, especially in the valleys of the Mississippi and Ohio rivers and the Great Lakes region. They built immense mounds of shaped earth, perhaps to bury their dead, to use as temples, or to defend themselves.

mount[1] (mount), **1** *v.* to go up; ascend: *mount stairs.* ■ See Synonym Study at **climb. 2** *v.* to get up on: *mount a horse, mount a platform.* **3** *v.* to get on a horse: *The riders mounted quickly.* **4** *v.* to put on a horse; furnish with a horse. **5** *n.* horse provided for riding: *The riding instructor had an excellent mount.* **6** *v.* to rise; increase; rise in amount: *The cost of living mounts steadily.* **7** *v.* to put in proper position or order for use: *mount specimens on slides.* **8** *v.* to have or carry guns as a fortress or ship does: *The ship mounts eight guns.* **9** *v.* to fix in a setting, backing, support, etc.: *mount a picture on cardboard.* **10** *n.* a setting; backing; support: *the mount for a picture.* **11** *v.* to organize; prepare: *mount an attack on the enemy.* **—mount'a·ble,** *adj.* **—mount'er,** *n.*

mount[2] (mount), *n.* mountain; high hill. *Mount* is often used before the names of mountains, as in *Mount Rainier.* [See Word Story at **mound.**]

moun·tain (moun'tən), *n.* **1** a very high hill, especially one that rises 2000 feet (600 meters) or more above surrounding land. **2** a very large heap or pile of anything: *a mountain of rubbish.* **3** a huge amount: *She overcame a mountain of difficulties.*

make a mountain out of a molehill, to give great importance to something that really doesn't matter.

> **WORD FAMILY**   **Mountain** and the words below are related. They all come from a Latin word meaning "mountain."
>
> | amount | mount[2] | promontory |
> | catamount | paramount | surmount |
> | insurmountable | Piedmont | tantamount |
> | mount[1] | | |

mountain ash, any of several trees and bushes with featherlike leaves, white flowers, and bright red berries.

mountain a·vens (av'ənz), a low evergreen plant with yellow and white flowers, related to roses. It is found in mountains and arctic regions of the Northern Hemisphere. The white mountain avens is the territorial plant of Canada's Northwest Territories.

moun·tain·eer (moun'tə nir'), **1** *n.* someone who lives in the mountains. **2** *n.* someone skilled in mountain climbing. **3** *v.* to climb mountains.

mountain goat, a white, goatlike antelope of the Rocky Mountains with slender, backward-curving black horns.

mountain goat—3 ft. (91 cm) high at the shoulder

mountain laurel, a North American evergreen bush with shiny leaves and pale pink or white flowers.

mountain lion, a large, fierce cat found in many parts of North and South America; cougar; puma.

moun·tain·ous (moun'tə nəs), *adj.* **1** covered with mountain ranges: *mountainous country.* **2** huge: *a mountainous wave.* **—moun'tain·ous·ly,** *adv.*

mountain range, row of connected mountains; large group of mountains.

mountain sheep, 1 bighorn. **2** any of various wild sheep living in mountains.

moun·tain·side (moun'tən sīd'), *n.* the slope of a mountain below the summit.

Mountain Standard Time, the standard time in the Rocky Mountain regions of the United States and Canada. It is seven hours behind Greenwich Time.

moun·tain·top (moun'tən top'), *n.* top or summit of a mountain.

mount·ed (moun'tid), *adj.* **1** on a horse, mule, bicycle, etc. **2** serving on horseback: *mounted police.*

Mount·ie (moun'tē), *n.* INFORMAL. member of the Royal Canadian Mounted Police.

mount·ing (moun'ting), *n.* support, setting, etc. The mounting of a photograph is the paper or cardboard on which it is pasted.

Mount Rainier National Park, a national park in W central Washington, containing the mountain, its glaciers, and its forests.

Mount Ver·non (ver'nən), home of George Washington in Virginia, on the Potomac River near Washington, D.C.

mourn (môrn), *v.* **1** to grieve: *People mourned the death of their neighbors in the tornado.* **2** to feel or show grief over: *mourn a lost dog.* ■ Another word that sounds like this is **morn.**

mourn·er (môr'nər), *n.* someone who mourns, especially at a funeral.

mourn·ful (môrn'fəl), *adj.* **1** full of grief; sad; sorrowful: *a mournful voice.* **2** causing sorrow or mourning.

mourn·ing (môr'ning), **1** *n.* the wearing of black clothing or a black armband to show sorrow for someone's death. **2** *n.* a draping of buildings, flying flags at half-mast, etc., as an outward sign of sorrow for death. **3** *n.* grief caused by death, especially of a loved one. ■ See Synonym Study at **sorrow. 4** *n.* clothes or decorations that show sorrow for death. **5** *adj.* of or about mourning; used in mourning. ■ Another word that sounds like this is **morning. —mourn'ing·ly,** *adv.*

mourning dove, a wild dove of North America that has a mournful call.

mouse (mous *for noun;* mous *or* mouz *for verb*), **1** *n.* any of many small, gnawing rodents with soft fur, pointed snouts, and long, thin tails. Some kinds of mice are commonly found in houses. Others live in fields and meadows. **2** *v.* to hunt for mice; catch mice for food: *Cats and owls go mousing at night.* **3** *v.* to search as a cat does; move about as if searching. **4** *n.* a shy, timid person. **5** *n.* box small enough to fit in one hand, connected to a computer by an electric cord, usually with a button or buttons for giving commands. Moving it across a flat surface controls the movement of a pointer on the computer screen. ❑ *n., pl.* **mice** for 1,4, **mous·es** (mou′siz) or **mice** for 5; *v.* **moused, mous·ing. . —mouse′like′,** *adj.*

mouse

mouse around, to explore a computer program or database by use of a mouse.

mous·er (mou′sər), *n.* animal that catches mice.

mouse·trap (mous′trap′), *n.* trap for catching mice.

mous·sa·ka (mü′sä kä′), *n.* a Greek baked food made of layers of ground meat with eggplant or zucchini between them, olive oil, and a topping of cheese and dough.

mousse (müs), *n.* **1** food made with whipped cream, either frozen or stiffened with gelatin: *chocolate mousse.* **2** a foam used to style the hair. ■ Another word that sounds like this is **moose.** [**Mousse** comes from a Latin word meaning "honey." People used to make wine with honey, and it was foamy. So is mousse.]

mous·tache (mus′tash *or* mə stash′), *n.* mustache.

mous·y (mou′sē), *adj.* **1** resembling or suggesting a mouse in color, odor, behavior, etc.: *mousy hair.* **2** quiet as a mouse. ❑ *adj.* **mous·i·er, mous·i·est.**

mouth (mouth *for noun;* mouᴛʜ *for verb*), **1** *n.* the opening through which a person or animal takes in food; space inside the jaws. **2** *n.* any opening suggesting a mouth: *the mouth of a cave, the mouth of a bottle.* **3** *n.* the part of a river or stream where its water flows into some other water: *the mouth of the Ohio River at the Mississippi River.* **4** *v.* to utter words in an overly formal, artificial way: *I dislike actors who mouth their speeches.* **5** *v.* to form silent words with your mouth: *mouth a warning.* **6** *v.* to chew or rub with the mouth: *The baby mouths her toys.* ❑ *n., pl.* **mouths** (mouᴛʜz). **—mouth′like′,** *adj.*

down in the mouth, INFORMAL. in low spirits; discouraged.

mouth·ful (mouth′fúl), *n.* **1** the amount the mouth can easily hold. **2** what is taken into the mouth at one time. **3** a small amount. **4** word or phrase that is very long or difficult to say. **5** important comment; true remark: *When she said we need help, she said a mouthful.* ❑ *n., pl.* **mouth·fuls.**

mouth organ, harmonica.

mouth·parts (mouth′pärts′), *n.pl.* the biting or feeding parts of the mouth of an insect or crustacean.

mouth·piece (mouth′pēs′), *n.* **1** the part of a pipe, horn, etc., that is placed in or against someone's mouth. **2** person, newspaper, etc., that speaks for others.

mouth·wash (mouth′wäsh′), *n.* a mildly antiseptic liquid to cleanse the mouth and teeth.

mov·a·ble (mü′və bəl), **1** *adj.* able to be moved: *Our fingers are movable.* **2** *adj.* able to be carried from place to place as personal belongings are. **3** *adj.* changing from one date to another in different years: *Thanksgiving is a movable holiday.* **4** *n.* piece of furniture that can be moved to another place. Also, **moveable.** **—mov′a·ble·ness,** *n.* **—mov′a·bly,** *adv.*

move (müv), **1** *v.* to change the place or position of: *Move your chair to the other side of the table.* **2** *v.* to change place or position: *The child moved in her sleep.* **3** *v.* to change your place of living: *We move to the country next week.* **4** *v.* to put or keep in motion; shake; stir: *The wind moves the leaves.* **5** *v.* to make progress; go: *The train moved slowly.* **6** *n.* act of moving; movement: *an impatient move of the head.* **7** *v.* to act: *The government*

must move in a decisive fashion. **8** *n.* action taken to bring about some result: *His next move was to earn some money.* **9** *v.* to cause to do something: *What moved you to get up so early?* **10** *v.* to affect with emotion; excite to tender feeling: *The sad story moved us to tears.* **11** *v.* (in games) to change to a different square according to rules: *move a pawn in chess.* **12** *n.* the moving of a piece in a game: *That was a good move.* **13** *n.* a player's turn to move in a game: *It's your move now.* **14** *v.* to make a formal request, application, or proposal; propose: *Madam Chairman, I move that we adjourn.* **15** *v.* to cause the intestines to empty. **16** *v.* to be active: *move in the best society.* ❑ *v.* **moved, mov·ing.**

get a move on, INFORMAL. to hurry; start moving: *If we want to leave at 9 A.M., we'll have to get a move on.*

move in, to move yourself, your family, your belongings, etc., into a new place to live.

move out, to move yourself, your family, your belongings, etc., out of the place where you have been living.

on the move, moving about: traveling: *Dolphins are always on the move.*

WORD FAMILY **Move** and the words below are related. They all come from a Latin word meaning "to move."

commotion	mobile	motor	remote
emotion	motion	movie	removal
immobilize	motive	promote	

move·a·ble (mü′və bəl), *adj., n.* movable. **—move′a·ble·ness,** *n.* **—move′a·bly,** *adv.*

move·ment (müv′mənt), *n.* **1** act or fact of moving: *We run by movements of the legs.* **2** a change in the placing of troops or ships. **3** the moving parts of a machine; special group of connected parts that move together. **4** one division of a symphony, sonata, or other long selection: *the second movement of Beethoven's Fifth Symphony.* **5** the efforts and results of a group of people working together to reach a common goal: *the civil rights movement.* **6** act of emptying the intestines. **7** the waste matter emptied from the intestines.

mov·er (mü′vər), *n.* **1** someone or something that moves. **2** person or company whose occupation is moving furniture, etc., from one house or place to another.

mov·ie (mü′vē), *n.* **1** series of pictures shown on a screen quickly enough that the persons and things pictured seem to be moving; motion picture. A movie is usually accompanied by a sound recording. **2** story told by means of such pictures. **3** **the movies,** a showing of such a story: *to go to the movies.* **4** **movies** or **the movies,** industry that makes such stories: *to work in movies as an actress or writer.*

mov·ing (mü′ving), *adj.* **1** in motion: *a moving car.* **2** causing action: *She was the moving spirit in planning for the party.* **3** stirring pity, tender feelings, or other emotions: *a moving story.* **4** in the business of moving furniture, etc.: *a moving van.* **—mov′ing·ly,** *adv.*

moving picture, movie.

mow[1] (mō), *v.* **1** to cut down with a machine or a scythe: *mow grass.* **2** to cut down the grass or grain from: *mow a field.* **3** to cut down grass, etc.: *We are mowing today.* ❑ *v.* **mowed, mowed** or **mown, mow·ing. —mow′er,** *n.*

mow down, to destroy in great numbers: *The enemy fire mowed down a platoon of soldiers.*

mow[2] (mou), *n.* **1** the place in a barn where hay, grain, or the like is piled or stored. **2** a pile or stack of hay, grain, etc., in a barn.

mown (mōn), *v.* a past participle of **mow**[1]. ■ Another word that sounds like this is **moan.**

mox·ie (mok′sē), *n.* SLANG. **1** courage; bravery. **2** daring; boldness. **3** know-how; skill; experience.

Mo·zam·bique (mō′zam bēk′), *n.* country in SE Africa. *Capital:* Maputo.

M

a	hat	ė	term	ô	order	ch	child		
ā	age	i	it	oi	oil	ng	long		a in about
ä	far	ī	ice	ou	out	sh	she		e in taken
â	care	o	hot	u	cup	th	thin	ə	i in pencil
e	let	ō	open	ů	put	ᴛʜ	then		o in lemon
ē	equal	ô	saw	ü	rule	zh	measure		u in circus

Mo·zart (mōt′särt), *n.* **Wolf·gang Am·a·de·us** (vȯlf′gäng ä mə dā′əs), 1756-1791, Austrian composer. ■ Mozart is one of the best loved composers of all time. He began performing in public as a very young child. Before his early death, he wrote 41 symphonies and more than 600 compositions in all.

moz·za·rel·la (mot′sə rel′ə), *n.* a soft, white, mild Italian cheese.

MP or **M.P.,** 1 Member of Parliament. 2 Military Police. 3 Mounted Police.

mph or **m.p.h.,** miles per hour.

Mr. or **Mr** (mis′tər), Mister, a title put in front of a man's name or the name of his position: *Mr. Stern, Mr. President.* ❑ *pl.* **Messrs.**

MRI, magnetic resonance imaging.

mRNA, messenger RNA.

Mrs. or **Mrs** (mis′iz), a title put in front of a married woman's name: *Mrs. Weiss.* ■ See Usage Note at **Ms.**

MS, 1 Mississippi (used with postal Zip Code). 2 multiple sclerosis.

ms., Ms., or **MS.,** manuscript. ❑ *pl.* **mss., Mss.,** or **MSS.**

Ms. (miz), a title put in front of a woman's name: *Ms. Karen Johnson.* ❑ *pl.* **Mses.**

USAGE NOTE **Ms.** is used by both married and unmarried women. **Mrs.** is used by married women. **Miss** is used by unmarried women, and sometimes in speaking to a woman whose name is not known. **Ms.** is often used when writing to a woman if you do not know whether she is married or not. In speaking or referring to someone in person, it is wise to ask which title she prefers.

M.S. or **M.Sc.,** Master of Science.

MSG, monosodium glutamate.

Msgr., Monsignor.

M-16 (em′siks ten′), *n.* a lightweight military rifle that operates as either an automatic or a semiautomatic weapon.

M.S.T. or **MST,** Mountain Standard Time.

MT, Montana (used with postal Zip Code).

mt., mountain. ❑ *pl.* **mts.**

Mt., Mount: *Mt. Everest.* ❑ *pl.* **Mts.**

Mu·ba·rak (mu̇ bär′äk), *n.* **Hos·ni** (hos′nē), born 1928, president of Egypt since October 1981.

much (much), 1 *adj.* in great amount or degree: *much money, not much time.* 2 *n.* a great amount: *I did not hear much of the talk. Don't eat too much.* 3 *adv.* to a high degree; greatly: *I was much pleased.* 4 *adv.* nearly; about: *This is much the same as the other.* ❑ *adj.* **more, most;** *adv.* **more, most.** —**much′ness,** *n.*

as much as, 1 all; everything possible: *Take as much as you want.* **2** practically; in effect: *They as much as told us we had to leave.*

how much, 1 what price: *How much is that shirt?* **2** what amount: *How much of this spaghetti can you eat?* **3** what amount of: *How much ice cream did you eat?*

make much of, to pay much attention to or do much for.

not much of a, not a very good: *Five dollars an hour is not much of a wage.*

too much for, more than a match for.

mu·ci·lage (myü′sə lij), *n.* a sticky, gummy substance used to make things stick together.

muck (muk), *n.* 1 dirt; filth. 2 moist farmyard manure, used as a fertilizer. 3 a heavy, moist, dark soil made up mostly of decayed plants.

muck·rake (muk′rāk′), *v.* to hunt for and expose corruption in government, big business, etc. ❑ *v.* **muck·raked, muck·rak·ing.**

muck·rak·er (muk′rā′kər), *n.* someone, especially a journalist, who muckrakes.

mu·cous (myü′kəs), *adj.* 1 of or like mucus. 2 containing or secreting mucus. ■ Another word that sounds like this is **mucus.**

mucous membrane, the mucus-producing lining of the nose, throat, and other cavities of the body that open to the air.

mu·cus (myü′kəs), *n.* a slimy substance produced in the nose, throat, and some other body cavities, to moisten and protect them. [Mucus is a Latin word that came directly into English. A related Latin word means "to blow your nose."] ■ Another word that sounds like this is **mucous.**

mud (mud), *n.* earth so wet that it is soft and sticky.

mud·dle (mud′l), 1 *v.* to mix up; get things into a mess: *to muddle a piece of work.* 2 *v.* to think or act in a confused, blundering way:

muddle through a difficulty. 3 *v.* to make confused or stupid: *The more you talk, the more you muddle me.* 4 *n.* mess; disordered state: *My notes are in a muddle.* ❑ *v.* **mud·dled, mud·dling.**

mud·dle·head·ed (mud′l hed′id), *adj.* stupid; confused.

mud·dy (mud′ē), 1 *adj.* of or like mud: *muddy footprints on the floor.* 2 *adj.* covered with mud: *a muddy road, muddy shoes.* 3 *adj.* clouded with mud; dull; not pure: *muddy water, a muddy color.* 4 *adj.* confused; not clear: *muddy thinking.* 5 *v.* to make or become muddy: *His boots muddied the kitchen floor when he came inside.* ❑ *adj.* **mud·di·er, mud·di·est;** *v.* **mud·died, mud·dy·ing.** —**mud′di·ly,** *adv.* —**mud′di·ness,** *n.*

mud·guard (mud′gärd′), *n.* fender (def. 1).

mud hen, coot.

mud puppy, any of several large freshwater salamanders that live in the eastern and central parts of the United States.

mu·ez·zin (myü ez′n), *n.* crier who, at certain hours, calls Muslims to prayer.

muff (muf), 1 *n.* (earlier) a covering of fur or other material for keeping both hands warm. One hand is put in at each end. 2 *v.* to fail to catch a ball when it comes into your hands. 3 *n.* a failure to catch a ball that comes into your hands: *The catcher's muff allowed the runner to score.* 4 *v.* to handle awkwardly; bungle: *He muffed his chance to get the job.* 5 *n.* an awkward handling; bungling.

muf·fin (muf′ən), *n.* a small, round cake made of wheat flour, corn meal, or the like. Muffins are often served hot.

muf·fle (muf′əl), *v.* 1 to wrap or cover up in order to keep warm and dry: *She muffled her throat in a warm scarf.* 2 to wrap in something in order to soften or stop the sound: *A bell can be muffled with cloth.* 3 to dull or deaden a sound: *The wind muffled our voices.* ❑ *v.* **muf·fled, muf·fling.**

muf·fler (muf′lər), *n.* 1 wrap or scarf worn around the neck for warmth. 2 anything used to deaden sound. A car muffler, attached to the exhaust pipe, deadens the sound of the engine's exhaust.

mug (mug), 1 *n.* a heavy china or metal drinking cup with a handle. 2 *n.* amount a mug holds: *to drink a mug of milk.* 3 *n.* SLANG. face or mouth. 4 *v.* to attack someone, usually to rob. 5 *v.* to exaggerate your facial expressions, as in acting; make funny faces. 6 *v.* INFORMAL. to make a photograph of someone's face for police records. ❑ *v.* **mugged, mug·ging.**

mug·ger (mug′ər), *n.* someone who attacks another, usually to rob.

mug·gy (mug′ē), *adj.* warm and humid; damp and close: *Yesterday the weather was very muggy.* ❑ *adj.* **mug·gi·er, mug·gi·est.** —**mug′gi·ness,** *n.*

Mu·ghal (mü′gəl), *n., adj.* Mogul.

mug shot, photograph of a suspected criminal's face taken by the police.

mug·wump (mug′wump′), *n.* person who is independent in politics.

Mu·ham·mad (mu̇ ham′əd), *n.* A.D. 570?-632, Arab prophet, founder of Islam, the religion of the Muslims. Also, **Mohammed.** [Muhammad comes from an Arabic word meaning "praised one."]

Mu·ham·mad (mu̇ ham′əd), *n.* **Elijah,** 1897-1975, American religious leader. He encouraged African Americans to live and work separately in the Nation of Islam.

muk·luk (muk′luk), *n.* 1 a high, waterproof boot, often made of sealskin, worn in arctic regions. 2 boot with a soft leather sole.

mu·lat·to (mə lat′ō *or* myü lat′ō), *n.* OLD USE. 1 person having one white parent and one African American parent. 2 any person of mixed white and African American descent. ❑ *n., pl.* **mu·lat·toes.** ■ Mulatto is considered offensive.

mul·ber·ry (mul′ber′ē), *n.* 1 any of several trees with small, berrylike fruit that can be eaten. The leaves of one kind are used for feeding silkworms. 2 its sweet, usually dark purple fruit. 3 a dark purplish red. ❑ *n., pl.* **mul·ber·ries.**

mulch (mulch), 1 *n.* a loose material, such as straw, leaves, sawdust, etc., spread on the ground around trees or plants. Mulch is used to protect the roots from cold or heat, to prevent weed growth and evaporation of moisture from the soil, and to enrich the soil. 2 *v.* to cover with straw, leaves, etc. ❑ *n., pl.* **mulch·es.**

mule¹ (myül), *n.* **1** offspring of a male donkey and a female horse. It has the form and size of a horse and the large ears, small hoofs, and tufted tail of a donkey. **2** INFORMAL. a stubborn person. ■ Another word that sounds like this is **mewl**.

mule² (myül), *n.* kind of slipper that leaves the heel uncovered. ■ Another word that sounds like this is **mewl**. [**Mule**² comes from a Latin word meaning "red." High red leather shoes were part of the uniform of certain Roman public officials. People later called fancy shoes of all kinds by the same name.]

mule¹ (def. 1)—4 to 5 ft. (1.2 to 1.5 m) high at the shoulder

mule skinner, INFORMAL. muleteer.

mu·le·teer (myü′lə tir′), *n.* driver of mules.

mul·ish (myü′lish), *adj.* like a mule; stubborn; obstinate. —**mul′ish·ly,** *adv.* —**mul′ish·ness,** *n.*

mull¹ (mul), *v.* to think about without making much progress; ponder.

mull² (mul), *v.* to make wine, beer, cider, etc., into a warm drink, adding sugar and spices.

mul·lah (mul′ə), *n.* a title of respect for someone who is learned in Islamic law; a religious scholar or leader.

mul·lein (mul′ən), *n.* any of numerous weeds, especially the North American **common mullein,** with coarse, woolly leaves and spikes of yellow flowers.

mul·let (mul′it), *n.* any of various fishes that live in warm and temperate waters. **Gray mullet** are larger, live close to shore, and are good to eat. **Red mullet** are small and brightly colored. □ *n.,* pl. **mul·let** or **mul·lets.**

multi-, *prefix.* many: *multicultural = of many cultures.*

mul·ti·cel·lu·lar (mul′ti sel′yə lər), *adj.* having or formed of many cells.

mul·ti·col·ored (mul′ti kul′ərd), *adj.* having many colors.

mul·ti·cul·tur·al (mul′ti kul′chər əl), *adj.* having or representing many different cultures: *a multicultural society.*

mul·ti·cul·tur·al·ism (mul′ti kul′chər ə liz′əm), *n.* **1** quality or condition of being multicultural. **2** policy that promotes multicultural conditions in a society.

mul·ti·eth·nic (mul′tē eth′nik), *adj.* designed for or involving different ethnic groups: *I learned about different cultures at the multiethnic festival.*

mul·ti·fac·et·ed (mul′ti fas′ə tid), *adj.* **1** having many sides: *a multifaceted gemstone.* **2** having many talents, interests, etc.: *a multifaceted personality.*

mul·ti·far·i·ous (mul′tə fâr′ē əs), *adj.* having many different parts, elements, forms, etc. —**mul′ti·far′i·ous·ly,** *adv.* —**mul′ti·far′i·ous·ness,** *n.*

mul·ti·lat·er·al (mul′ti lat′ər əl), *adj.* **1** having many sides. **2** involving three or more nations. —**mul′ti·lat′er·al·ly,** *adv.*

mul·ti·me·di·a (mul′ti mē′dē ə), *adj.* using a combination of different media, such as tapes, films, compact disk recordings, and photographs, to entertain, communicate, teach, etc.: *Our presentation was a multimedia event.*

mul·ti·mil·lion·aire (mul′ti mil′yə nâr′), *n.* someone who owns property worth several millions of dollars, pounds, francs, etc.; millionaire many times over.

mul·ti·na·tion·al (mul′ti nash′ə nəl), **1** *adj.* of or about many nations. **2** *n.* a corporation with branches in many nations.

mul·ti·ple (mul′tə pəl), **1** *adj.* of, having, or involving many parts, elements, relations, etc.: *a person of multiple interests.* **2** *n.* number that contains another number a certain number of times without a remainder: *12 is a multiple of 3.*

mul·ti·ple-choice (mul′tə pəl chois′), *adj.* containing two or more suggested answers from which the correct or best one must be chosen: *a multiple-choice test.*

multiple scle·ro·sis (sklə rō′sis), disease of the nervous system that attacks the brain and the spinal cord, with slow loss and scarring of tissue, followed by paralysis, muscle spasms, impaired speech, etc.

mul·ti·pli·cand (mul′tə plə kand′), *n.* number to be multiplied by another: *In 497 multiplied by 5, the multiplicand is 497.*

mul·ti·pli·ca·tion (mul′tə plə kā′shən), *n.* **1** operation of multiplying one number by another. **2** act or process of multiplying.

multiplication sign, the symbol × or a centered dot, used to show the operation of multiplying. EXAMPLES: $2 \times 2 = 4$; $2 \cdot 2 = 4$.

mul·ti·plic·i·ty (mul′tə plis′ə tē), *n.* a great many; a large variety: *a multiplicity of interests.*

mul·ti·pli·er (mul′tə pli′ər), *n.* number by which another number is to be multiplied: *In 83 multiplied by 5, the multiplier is 5.*

mul·ti·ply (mul′tə pli), *v.* **1** to add a number a given number of times: *To multiply 16 by 3 means to add 16 three times, making 48.* **2** to increase in number or amount: *My problems multiplied rapidly.* ■ See Synonym Study at **increase.** □ *v.* **mul·ti·plied, mul·ti·ply·ing.**

mul·ti·pur·pose (mul′ti pèr′pəs), *adj.* having many purposes or functions; versatile: *a multipurpose wrench.*

mul·ti·ra·cial (mul′ti rā′shəl), *adj.* having a number of races: *a multiracial community.*

mul·ti·tude (mul′tə tüd), *n.* a great many; crowd: *a multitude of difficulties, a multitude of enemies.*

mul·ti·vi·ta·min (mul′ti vi′tə min), *adj.* **1** containing many vitamins: *a multivitamin cereal.* **2** a tablet or capsule containing many vitamins.

mum¹ (mum), **1** *adj.* saying nothing; silent: *Keep mum about this; tell no one.* **2** *interj.* be silent! say nothing!

mum's the word, be silent; say nothing.

mum² (mum), *n.* INFORMAL. chrysanthemum.

mum·ble (mum′bəl), **1** *v.* to speak indistinctly, as a person does when the lips are partly closed. ■ See Synonym Study at **whisper.** **2** *n.* act of mumbling: *There was a mumble of protest from the team against the umpire's decision.* □ *v.* **mum·bled, mum·bling.** —**mum′bler,** *n.*

mum·ble·ty·peg (mum′bəl tē peg′), *n.* game in which the players in turn flip a knife from various positions, trying to make it stick in the ground.

mum·bo jum·bo (mum′bō jum′bō), foolish or meaningless words, used to confuse or to conceal a purpose: *When we asked why the car wasn't ready, they gave us a lot of mumbo jumbo.*

mum·mi·fy (mum′ə fi), *v.* **1** to make into a mummy; make like a mummy. **2** to shrivel; dry up. □ *v.* **mum·mi·fied, mum·mi·fy·ing.** —**mum′mi·fi·ca′tion,** *n.*

mum·my (mum′ē), *n.* a dead body preserved from decay. Egyptian mummies have lasted more than 3000 years. □ *n.,* pl. **mum·mies.** [**Mummy** comes from a Persian word meaning "wax." Wax was used in the preserving of dead bodies.]

mumps (mumps), *n.* a contagious viral disease marked by swelling of the glands in the neck and difficulty in swallowing.

munch (munch), *v.* to chew vigorously and steadily; chew noisily: *The horse munched its oats.* —**munch′er,** *n.*

munch·ies (mun′chēz), *n.pl.* INFORMAL. **1** food to munch on; snacks. **2** **the munchies,** a strong wish for food, especially snacks: *I never shop for groceries when I have the munchies.*

mun·dane (mun dān′ or mun′dān), *adj.* **1** ordinary; commonplace: *mundane conversation.* **2** of this world, not of heaven; earthly: *mundane goals.* —**mun·dane′ly,** *adv.* —**mun·dane′ness,** *n.*

Mu·nich (myü′nik), *n.* large city in S Germany.

mu·nic·i·pal (myü nis′ə pəl), *adj.* **1** of or about the affairs of a city or town: *The state police assisted the municipal police.* **2** run by a city, town, or other municipality. —**mu·nic′i·pal·ly,** *adv.*

mu·nic·i·pal·i·ty (myü nis′ə pal′ə tē), *n.* city or town having local self-government. □ *n.,* pl. **mu·nic·i·pal·i·ties.**

a	hat	ė	term	ô	order	ch	child		⟨ a in about
ā	age	i	it	oi	oil	ng	long		e in taken
ä	far	ī	ice	ou	out	sh	she	ə ⟨	i in pencil
â	care	o	hot	u	cup	th	thin		o in lemon
e	let	ō	open	ù	put	ŦH	then		u in circus
ē	equal	ò	saw	ü	rule	zh	measure		

M

mu·ni·tions (myü nish′ənz), *n.pl.* materials used in war. Munitions are military supplies, such as guns, ammunition, or bombs.

mur·al (myür′əl), **1** *n.* picture painted on a wall. **2** *adj.* on a wall.

mural (def. 1)

Mu·ra·sa·ki Shi·ki·bu (mü′rä sä′kē shē′kē bü′), 975?–1031?, Japanese writer. Her novel *The Tale of Genji* is considered a masterpiece of Japanese literature. She is also called Lady Murasaki.

mur·der (mėr′dər), **1** *n.* the unlawful killing of a human being when it is planned beforehand. ■ See Synonym Study at **kill.** **2** *n.* an instance of such a crime: *The detective solved the murder.* **3** *v.* to kill a human being intentionally: *Cain murdered his brother Abel.* **4** *v.* to do very badly; spoil or ruin: *I really murdered my recital piece.* **5** *n.* INFORMAL. anything extremely difficult or unpleasant: *That test was murder.*

mur·der·er (mėr′dər ər), *n.* person who murders somebody.

mur·der·ous (mėr′dər əs), *adj.* **1** able to kill: *a murderous blow.* **2** ready to murder: *a murderous villain.* **3** causing murder: *a murderous hate.* **4** INFORMAL. extremely difficult: overwhelming: *a murderous set of exercises.* **—mur′der·ous·ly,** *adv.*

Mur·doch (mėr′dok), *n.* **Ru·pert** (rü′pərt), born 1931, American businessman born in Australia, famous for buying newspapers, magazines, publishers, and movie and broadcasting companies.

murk (mėrk), *n.* darkness; gloom: *the murk of the night.*

murk·y (mėr′kē), *adj.* **1** dark; gloomy: *a murky prison.* **2** very thick and dark; misty; hazy: *murky smoke.* **3** discolored with sediment: *the murky waters of the pond.* ❑ *adj.* **murk·i·er, murk·i·est. —murk′i·ly,** *adv.* **—murk′i·ness,** *n.*

mur·mur (mėr′mər), **1** *n.* a soft, low, indistinct sound that rises and falls a little and goes on without breaks: *the murmur of a stream.* **2** *v.* to make a soft, low, indistinct sound. **3** *n.* a sound in the heart or lungs, especially an abnormal sound due to a leaky valve in the heart. **4** *v.* to say in a murmur: *The shy child murmured her thanks.* ■ See Synonym Study at **whisper.** **5** *n.* complaint made under the breath, not aloud. **6** *v.* to complain under the breath. **—mur′mur·er,** *n.* **—mur′mur·ing·ly,** *adv.*

mur·mur·ous (mėr′mər əs), *adj.* with murmurs; murmuring. **—mur′mur·ous·ly,** *adv.*

mus., 1 museum. **2** music.

Mus·cat (mus′kat), *n.* port and capital of Oman, in the N part, on the Gulf of Oman.

mus·cle (mus′əl), *n.* **1** a body tissue composed of fibers, each of which is a long cell. The fibers can tighten or loosen to move parts of the body. **2** a special bundle of such tissue which moves some particular bone or part. The biceps muscle bends the arm. **3** strength: *He didn't have enough muscle to budge the piano.* ■ Another word that sounds like this is **mussel.**

> **WORD STORY** **Muscle** comes from a Latin word meaning "little mouse." **Mussel** comes from the same word. Some muscles look like mice scampering under a covering. People called the shellfish "muscles" because that is what they saw when the shells were opened. After a while they started spelling the two meanings differently.

mus·cle-bound (mus′əl bound′), *adj.* having some of the muscles enlarged or tight, and lacking normal elasticity, usually as a result of too much exercise.

mus·cu·lar (mus′kyə lər), *adj.* **1** of or affecting the muscles: *a muscular strain.* **2** having well-developed muscles; strong: *a muscular arm.* **3** consisting of muscle. **—mus·cu·lar·i·ty** (mus′kyə lar′ə tē), *n.* **—mus′cu·lar·ly,** *adv.*

muscular dys·tro·phy (dis′trə fē), a disease in which the muscles gradually weaken and waste away.

mus·cu·la·ture (mus′kyə lə chùr), *n.* system or arrangement of muscles.

muse (myüz), *v.* to think in a dreamy way; think; meditate: *The boy spent the whole afternoon in musing.* ❑ *v.* **mused, mus·ing.** ■ Another word that sounds like this is **mews. —mus′ing·ly,** *adv.*

Muse (myüz), *n.* **1** one of the nine Greek goddesses of the fine arts and sciences. **2** Often, **muse,** spirit that inspires a poet or composer.

mu·se·um (myü zē′əm), *n.* a building or rooms where a collection of objects illustrating science, ancient life, art, history, or other subjects is kept and displayed.

mush[1] (mush), *n.* **1** corn meal boiled in water or milk. **2** a soft, thick mass: *After the heavy rain the dirt road turned to mush.* **3** INFORMAL. sentimental and silly words: *a Valentine's Day card full of mush.*

mush[2] (mush), **1** *n.* to travel through snow, driving a dog sled. **2** *interj.* a shout to a team of sled dogs to start or to speed up. ❑ *n., pl.* **mush·es. —mush′er,** *n.*

mush·room (mush′rüm), **1** *n.* any of many small fungi shaped like umbrellas, that grow very fast. Many mushrooms are good to eat; some are powerfully poisonous. **2** *adj.* of or like a mushroom: *a mushroom cloud.* **3** *v.* to grow rapidly: *Their business mushroomed when they opened the new store.*

> **WORD STORY** The French name for this fungus was *mousseron,* a difficult word for English speakers to pronounce. But *mush* meaning "soft stuff," already existed and seemed to make sense here. Some people then said *mushroon,* but others couldn't accept *roon* as an ending, so they used the familiar word *room.*

mush·y (mush′ē), *adj.* **1** like mush; pulpy. **2** INFORMAL. weakly sentimental. ❑ *adj.* **mush·i·er, mush·i·est. —mush′i·ly,** *adv.* **—mush′i·ness,** *n.*

Mus·i·al (myü′zē əl), *n.* **Stan** (stan), born 1920, American baseball player. He played for the St. Louis Cardinals from 1941 to 1963, and was known as "Stan the Man." His lifetime batting average is .331.

mu·sic (myü′zik), *n.* **1** art of putting sounds together in beautiful, pleasing, or interesting arrangements. **2** beautiful, pleasing, or interesting arrangements of sounds. **3** written or printed signs for tones: *Can you read music?* **4** any pleasant sound: *the music of a bubbling brook, the music of the wind.*

face the music, to meet trouble boldly or bravely.

set to music, to provide with music: *The piano teacher set the poem to music so that I could sing it at the school concert.*

> **WORD BANK** **Music** has a large vocabulary of its own, with many different words. If you want to learn more about music, you can begin by looking up these words in this dictionary and by seeing the Word Bank at **instrument.**

accompaniment	folk music	prelude
air	fugue	ragtime
anthem	gavotte	reggae
ballad	gospel music	requiem
bluegrass	heavy metal	rhapsody
blues	hymn	rock
calypso	interlude	roundelay
cantata	intermezzo	salsa
chamber music	jazz	scherzo
classical	lullaby	serenade
concerto	march	sonata
country music	nocturne	suite
dirge	opera	swing
disco	oratorio	symphony
Dixieland	overture	variation
étude	polonaise	zydeco

mu·si·cal (myü′zə kəl), **1** *adj.* of or producing music: *a musical composer.* **2** *adj.* sounding beautiful or pleasing; like music: *a musical voice.* **3** *adj.* set to music; accompanied by music: *a musical performance.* **4** *adj.* fond of music. **5** *adj.* skilled in music. **6** *n.* musical comedy.

musical comedy, play or movie with songs, choruses, and dances.

mu·si·cale (myü′zə kal′), *n.* a social gathering to enjoy music.

mu·si·cal·ly (myü′zik lē), *adv.* **1** in a musical manner: *The bells rang musically.* **2** in music: *She is well educated musically.*

music box, box or case containing apparatus for producing music mechanically.

music hall, 1 hall for musical performances. **2** theater for vaudeville.

mu·si·cian (myü zish′ən), *n.* **1** someone skilled in music. **2** someone who sings or who plays a musical instrument, especially as a profession or business: *An orchestra is composed of many musicians.* **3** composer of music. **—mu·si′cian·ship,** *n.*

mu·si·col·o·gy (myü′zə kol′ə jē), *n.* the systematic study of music, especially its history, forms, and principles. **—mu′si·col′o·gist,** *n.*

music video, a short musical film on videotape or videodisc, often a dramatized version of a rock'n'roll song.

musk (musk), *n.* **1** substance with a strong and lasting odor, used in making perfumes. Musk is found in a special gland in the male musk deer. **2** a similar substance found in the glands of other animals, such as the mink and muskrat. **3** odor of musk.

musk deer, a small, hornless deer of central Asia, the male of which has a gland containing musk.

mus·keg (mus′keg), *n.* **1** swamp or marsh. **2** swamp or marsh filled with moss and other decaying plant life, especially in northern forest regions.

mus·kel·lunge (mus′kə lunj), *n.* a very large North American fish, a kind of pike, valued as a food and game fish. ❑ *n., pl.* **mus·kel·lunge.**

mus·ket (mus′kit), *n.* kind of old gun used before rifles were invented.

mus·ket·eer (mus′kə tir′), *n.* (earlier) soldier armed with a musket.

mus·ket·ry (mus′kə trē), *n.* **1** muskets. **2** art of shooting with muskets or rifles.

mus·kie (mus′kē), *n.* INFORMAL. a muskellunge. Also, **musky**[2].

musk·mel·on (musk′mel′ən), *n.* a small, sweet melon with a hard rind. The cantaloupe, casaba, and honeydew melon are varieties of muskmelon.

musk ox, a large arctic mammal with a shaggy coat, downward curving horns, and a strong, musky smell.

musk ox—up to 5 ft. (1.5 m) high at the shoulder

musk·rat (musk′rat′), *n.* **1** a water rodent of North America something like a rat but larger; water rat. **2** its valuable, dark brown fur, used in making coats. ❑ *n., pl.* **musk·rat** or **musk·rats.**

musk·y[1] (mus′kē), *adj.* of or like musk; like that of musk: *a musky odor.* ❑ *adj.* **musk·i·er, musk·i·est. —musk′i·ness,** *n.*

mus·ky[2] (mus′kē), *n.* muskie. ❑ *n., pl.* **mus·kies.**

Mus·lim (muz′ləm or mûz′ləm), **1** *n.* someone who believes in and follows the teachings of Muhammad. **2** *adj.* of or about Muhammad, his followers, or the religion of Islam. [Muslim comes from an Arabic word meaning "a person who submits." Muslims submit their lives to God, whom they call Allah.]

mus·lin (muz′lən), **1** *n.* a thin, fine cotton cloth, used for dresses, curtains, etc. **2** a heavier cotton cloth, used for sheets, undergarments, etc.

muss (mus), **1** *v.* to put into disorder; rumple: *The child's new outfit was mussed.* **2** *n.* INFORMAL. untidy state; mess: *What a muss the room was!*

mus·sel (mus′əl), *n.* any of numerous shellfish that resemble clams. Sea mussels can be eaten. [See Word Story at **muscle.**] ■ Another word that sounds like this is **muscle.**

Mus·so·li·ni (mùs′ə lē′nē or mü′sə lē′nē), *n.* **Be·ni·to** (ben ē′tō), 1883-1945, leader of the Italian Fascists and prime minister of Italy from 1922 to 1943. He ruled as a dictator.

muss·y (mus′ē), *adj.* INFORMAL. untidy; messy; rumpled. ❑ *adj.* **muss·i·er, muss·i·est. —muss′i·ly,** *adv.* **—muss′i·ness,** *n.*

must (must), **1** *v.* to have to; be forced to: *You must eat to live.* **2** *v.* to feel a duty to; be obligated to: *When we learned that our grandmother was ill, we knew that we must return home.* **3** *v.* to be certain or likely to be, do, etc.: *You must be joking.* **4** *n.* something necessary; obligation: *This rule is a must.* **5** *adj.* demanding attention or doing; necessary: *a must item.* ❑ *v., past tense* **must.**

mus·tache (mus′tash or mə stash′), *n.* **1** the hair growing on a man's upper lip. **2** hairs or bristles growing near the mouth of an animal. Also, **moustache.**

mus·tang (mus′tang), *n.* a small wild or stray horse of the North American plains.

mus·tard (mus′tərd), *n.* **1** any of several plants with seeds that have a sharp, hot taste. **2** a yellow powder or paste made from the seeds, used as seasoning.

mustard plaster, mixture of mustard and water, or of mustard, flour, and water, spread on cloth and applied to the body to reduce pain or inflammation.

mus·ter (mus′tər), **1** *v.* to gather together; assemble; collect: *The guards were mustered for roll call.* **2** *n.* assembly; collection. **3** *v.* to summon: *muster up courage.* **4** *n.* act of bringing together troops or others for review or service: *There was a muster of all the guards.* **5** *n.* list of those assembled.

muster out, to discharge.

pass muster, be inspected and approved; meet the required standards.

must·n't (mus′nt), must not.

mus·ty (mus′tē), *adj.* **1** having a smell or taste suggesting mold or damp; moldy: *a musty room, musty crackers.* **2** stale; out-of-date: *musty laws about witches.* ❑ *adj.* **mus·ti·er, mus·ti·est. —mus′ti·ly,** *adv.* **—must′i·ness,** *n.*

mu·tant (myüt′nt), *n.* a new variety of living thing resulting from mutation.

mu·tate (myü′tāt), *v.* **1** to change. **2** to undergo or produce mutation. ❑ *v.* **mu·tat·ed, mu·tat·ing.**

mu·ta·tion (myü tā′shən), *n.* **1** a change within a gene or genes, resulting in a new feature or character that appears suddenly in a living thing and can be inherited. **2** such a new feature or character. **3** mutant. **4** a change; alteration.

mute (myüt), **1** *adj.* not making any sound; silent: *The little girl stood mute with astonishment.* **2** *adj.* unable to speak; dumb. **3** *n.* person who cannot speak. **4** *n.* clip, pad, or other device put on a musical instrument to muffle the sound. **5** *v.* to put such a device on; muffle the sound of with a mute: *He muted the strings of his violin.* **6** *adj.* not pronounced. The *e* in *mute* is mute. ❑ *v.* **mut·ed, mut·ing. —mute′ly,** *adv.* **—mute′ness,** *n.*

a	hat	ė	term	ô	order	ch	child		
ā	age	i	it	oi	oil	ng	long	ə	a in about
ä	far	ī	ice	ou	out	sh	she		e in taken
â	care	o	hot	u	cup	th	thin		i in pencil
e	let	ō	open	ù	put	ŦH	then		o in lemon
ē	equal	ò	saw	ü	rule	zh	measure		u in circus

mu·ti·la·te (myü′tl āt), *v.* **1** to cut off or tear off a limb or other important part of; injure seriously by cutting off or tearing off some part; maim: *Several passengers were mutilated in the train wreck.* **2** to destroy or ruin some part of: *The book was badly mutilated by someone who had torn out some pages.* ❑ *v.* **mu·ti·lat·ed, mu·ti·lat·ing.** —**mu′ti·la′tion,** *n.* —**mu′ti·la′tor,** *n.*

mu·ti·neer (myüt′n ir′), *n.* someone who takes part in a mutiny.

mu·ti·nous (myüt′n əs), *adj.* rebellious: *a mutinous crew.* —**mu′ti·nous·ly,** *adv.* —**mu′ti·nous·ness,** *n.*

mu·ti·ny (myüt′n ē), **1** *n.* open rebellion against lawful authority, especially by sailors or soldiers against their officers. **2** *v.* to take part in a mutiny; rebel. ❑ *n., pl.* **mu·ti·nies;** *v.* **mu·ti·nied, mu·ti·ny·ing.**

mutt (mut), *n.* INFORMAL. dog, especially a mongrel.

mut·ter (mut′ər), **1** *v.* to speak or utter words low and indistinctly, with lips partly closed. **2** *v.* to complain; grumble. **3** *n.* muttered words: *We heard a mutter of discontent.* —**mut′ter·er,** *n.*

mut·ton (mut′n), *n.* meat from a fully grown sheep: *We had roast mutton for dinner.* [See Word Story at **meat.**]

mut·ton·chops (mut′n chops′), *n.pl.* sideburns that are narrow at the temples and wide near the chin.

mu·tu·al (myü′chü əl), *adj.* **1** done, said, felt, etc., by each toward the other; given and received: *mutual promises, mutual dislike. They had mutual affection for each other.* **2** each to the other: *mutual enemies.* **3** belonging to each of several: *We are happy to have him as our mutual friend.* —**mu·tu·al·i·ty** (myü′chü al′ə tē), *n.* —**mu′tu·al·ly,** *adv.*

mutual fund, a financial organization that invests the money of its members into a variety of stocks and bonds.

mu·tu·al·ism (myü′chü ə liz′əm), *n.* relationship between two living things in which they both benefit. Birds that eat insects pulled from the skin of a large animal live in mutualism with that animal.

mutualism

muu·muu (mü′mü′), *n.* a long, loose-fitting cotton dress, originally worn by Polynesian women. ❑ *n., pl.* **muu·muus.**

muz·zle (muz′əl), **1** *n.* the nose, mouth, and jaws of an animal, especially a mammal. **2** *n.* a cover or cage of straps or wires to put over the head and mouth of an animal to keep it from biting or eating. **3** *v.* to put such a muzzle on: *muzzle a dog.* **4** *v.* to compel someone to keep silent about something: *Fear of losing their jobs muzzled the workers.* **5** *n.* the open front part of the barrel of a gun, pistol, etc. ❑ *v.* **muz·zled, muz·zling.** —**muz′zler,** *n.*

MVP, most valuable player.

MX, an intercontinental ballistic missile equipped with multiple nuclear warheads. ❑ *n., pl.* **MXes.**

my (mī), **1** *adj.* of or belonging to me: *My house is around the corner. I learned my lesson.* **2** *interj.* exclamation of surprise.

My·an·mar (mī än′mär), *n.* country in SE Asia, on the Indian Ocean. *Capital:* Yangon (Rangoon). Formerly called **Burma.**

my·ce·li·um (mī sē′lē əm), *n.* the growing part of a fungus, formed of interwoven fibers. ❑ *n., pl.* **my·ce·li·a** (mī sē′lē ə).

My·ce·nae (mī sē′nē), *n.* city in the southern part of ancient Greece. See **Troy** for map.

my·col·o·gy (mī kol′ə jē), *n.* branch of biology that deals with fungi. —**my·col′o·gist,** *n.*

my·e·lin (mī′ə lən), *n.* a soft, whitish, fatty substance that forms a covering around the core of certain nerve fibers.

My·lar (mī′lär), *n.* trademark for a tough polyester film used as a packaging material, a substitute for glass, a floor or wall covering, an electrical insulator, etc.

my·na (mī′nə), *n.* any of several Asian birds related to starlings, which can imitate human speech. ❑ *n., pl.* **my·nas.**

my·nah (mī′nə), *n.* myna.

my·o·pi·a (mī ō′pē ə), *n.* nearsightedness.

my·op·ic (mī op′ik), *adj.* nearsighted. —**my·op′i·cal·ly,** *adv.*

myr·i·ad (mir′ē əd), **1** *adj., n.* ten thousand. **2** *n.* a very great number: *myriads of stars.* **3** *adj.* countless.

myrrh (mėr), *n.* a fragrant, gummy substance with a bitter taste, used in medicines, perfumes, and incense. It is obtained from a bush that grows in Arabia and eastern Africa.

myr·tle (mėr′tl), *n.* **1** an evergreen bush of southern Europe and of Asia, with shiny leaves, fragrant white flowers, and black berries. **2** periwinkle.

my·self (mī self′), *pron.* **1** form of *me* or *I* used to make a statement stronger: *I myself will go.* **2** form used instead of *me* or *I* in cases like: *I can cook for myself. I hurt myself.* **3** my real or true self: *I am not myself today.*

mys·ter·i·ous (mi stir′ē əs), *adj.* **1** hard to explain or understand; full of mystery: *The mysterious, haunting call of a bird echoed across the lake.* **2** suggesting mystery: *a mysterious look.* —**mys·ter′i·ous·ly,** *adv.* —**mys·ter′i·ous·ness,** *n.*

mysterious (def. 2)

mys·ter·y (mis′tər ē), *n.* **1** something that is hidden or unknown; secret: *Astronomers seek out the mysteries of the universe.* **2** secrecy; obscurity. **3** something that is not explained or understood: *the mystery of the migration of birds.* **4** novel, story, etc., about a mysterious event or events which are not explained until the end, so as to keep the reader in suspense. **5** a religious rite, especially one to which only initiated persons are admitted. ❑ *n., pl.* **mys·ter·ies** for 1,3-5.

mystery play, (in the Middle Ages) a kind of religious play based on a Bible story.

mys·tic (mis′tik), **1** *adj.* mystical. **2** *n.* someone who believes that truth or God can be known directly through faith, spiritual insight, intuition, etc.

mys·ti·cal (mis′tə kəl), *adj.* **1** having some secret meaning; beyond human understanding; mysterious. **2** spiritually symbolic: *The lamb, the dove, and the wheel are mystical religious symbols.* **3** of or concerned with mystics or mysticism. —**mys′ti·cal·ly,** *adv.*

mys·ti·cism (mis′tə siz′əm), *n.* **1** beliefs or mode of thought of mystics. **2** vague or fuzzy thinking.

mys·ti·fi·ca·tion (mis′tə fə kā′shən), *n.* **1** condition of being mystified; bewilderment; perplexity. **2** something that mystifies.

mys·ti·fy (mis′tə fī), *v.* **1** to confuse completely; puzzle; perplex: *The magician's tricks mystified the audience.* **2** to make mysterious. ❑ *v.* **mys·ti·fied, mys·ti·fy·ing.**

mys·tique (mi stēk′), *n.* atmosphere of mystery about someone or something; mystic quality or air.

myth (mith), *n.* **1** legend or story, usually one that attempts to account for something in nature: *The myth of Proserpina is the ancient Roman explanation of summer and winter.* ■ See Synonym Study at **legend. 2** any invented story. **3** an imaginary person or thing: *Her trip to Europe was a myth invented to impress others.* **4** popular belief, opinion, or theory that is not based on fact.

myth·ic (mith′ik), *adj.* mythical.

myth·i·cal (mith′ə kəl), *adj.* **1** of or like a myth; in myths: *a mythical interpretation of nature, mythical monsters, mythical places.* **2** not real; made-up; imaginary: *His great wealth is merely mythical.* —**myth′i·cal·ly,** *adv.*

myth·o·log·i·cal (mith′ə loj′ə kəl), *adj.* of or about mythology: *The phoenix is a mythological bird.* —**myth′o·log′i·cal·ly,** *adv.*

my·thol·o·gy (mi thol′ə jē), *n.* a group of myths about a particular country or person: *Greek mythology.* ❑ *n., pl.* **my·thol·o·gies.**

mystify

a	hat	ė	term	ô	order	ch	child	
ā	age	i	it	oi	oil	ng	long	a in about
ä	far	ī	ice	ou	out	sh	she	e in taken
â	care	o	hot	u	cup	th	thin	ə i in pencil
e	let	ō	open	ů	put	ŦH	then	o in lemon
ē	equal	ȯ	saw	ü	rule	zh	measure	u in circus

M

N or **n** (en), *n.* the 14th letter of the English alphabet. ❏ *n., pl.* **N's** or **n's.**

n, (in algebra) an indefinite number.

N, symbol for nitrogen.

N or **N.,** **1** North. **2** Northern.

n., **1** north. **2** northern. **3** noun.

Na, symbol for sodium.

N.A., North America.

NAACP or **N.A.A.C.P.,** National Association for the Advancement of Colored People.

nab (nab), *v.* **1** to catch or seize suddenly; grab. **2** to arrest: *The police soon nabbed the thief.* ❏ *v.* **nabbed, nab·bing. —nab′ber,** *n.*

na·cho (nä′chō), *n.* a baked tortilla chip, often with a topping of cheese, beans, and hot peppers. ❏ *n., pl.* **na·chos.**

Na·der (nä′dər), *n.* **Ralph** (ralf), born 1934, American lawyer and consumer safety activist.

na·dir (nä′dər), *n.* **1** the lowest point: *This scandal is the nadir of her career.* **2** the point in the sky directly beneath the observer, on the other side of the earth; the point opposite the zenith. [**Nadir** comes from an Arabic word meaning "opposite."]

NAFTA (naf′tə), *n.* North American Free Trade Association (a comprehensive plan for free trade, without tariffs, among Canada, the United States, and Mexico; it also calls for labor and environmental regulations, and was approved by the U.S. Congress in 1993).

nag[1] (nag), **1** *v.* to find fault with someone all the time; irritate or annoy by peevish complaints; scold: *I will clean up in a minute; please don't nag me.* **2** *v.* to trouble; cause distress; disturb: *The unanswered questions nagged at her. My sore back is nagging me.* **3** *n.* someone who nags: *Don't be such a nag.* ❏ *v.* **nagged, nag·ging. —nag′ger,** *n.*

nag[2] (nag), *n.* **1** INFORMAL. a horse. **2** an old or inferior horse.

Na·ga·sa·ki (nä′gə sä′kē), *n.* port in SW Japan, target of the second atomic bomb to be used in war, on August 9, 1945. [**Nagasaki** comes from Japanese words meaning "long cape." The port is sheltered by a cape.]

Na·hua·tl (nä′wä təl), *n.* language of the Aztecs, Olmecs, Toltecs, and other American Indians of central Mexico and parts of Central America.

WORD SOURCE The **Nahuatl** language has given a number of words to the English language, including the words below.

avocado	chili	guacamole	quetzal
cacao	chocolate	mesquite	sapodilla
chicle	coyote	ocelot	tomato

Na·hum (nä′əm), *n.* **1** a Hebrew prophet. **2** book of the Bible. [**Nahum** comes from a Hebrew word meaning "compassionate."]

nai·ad (nä′ad), *n.* (in Greek and Roman myths) a nymph guarding a stream or spring.

nail (nāl), **1** *n.* a slender piece of metal with a point at one end and usually a flat or rounded head at the other end. Nails are hammered into pieces of wood to hold them together. **2** *v.* to fasten with a nail or nails: *She nailed plywood over the broken window.* **3** *v.* INFORMAL. to catch; seize: *The police were able to nail the thief.* **4** *n.* the thin, hard, horny layer on the upper side of the end of a finger or toe. **5** *n.* a claw; talon. **—nail′er,** *n.*

hit the nail on the head, to guess or understand correctly; say or do something just right.

nail down, to make certain of; agree to: *The buyer and seller nailed down the terms of the sale.*

Nai·ro·bi (nī rō′bē), *n.* capital of Kenya, in the SW part.

Nai·smith (nā′smith), *n.* James, 1861-1939, Canadian creator of basketball. He invented the game in Massachusetts in 1891.

na·ive or **na·ïve** (nä ēv′), *adj.* simple in nature; lacking in understanding of how things really are; unsophisticated. ❑ *adj.* **na·iv·er, na·iv·est** or **na·ïv·er, na·ïv·est.** [**Naive** comes from a Latin word meaning "born." We still say, if someone is being naive, "Were you born yesterday?"] **—na·ive′ly** or **na·ïve′ly,** *adv.*

na·i·ve·té, na·ï·ve·té (nä ē′və tā′), *n.* **1** quality of being naive. **2** a naive action, remark, etc. ❑ *n., pl.* **na·i·ve·tés, na·i·ve·tes** or **na·ï·ve·tés** for 2.

na·ked (nā′kid), *adj.* **1** with no clothes on; nude; bare. **2** not covered; stripped: *naked fields.* **3** not protected; exposed: *a naked light bulb.* **4** without the addition of anything else; plain: *The naked truth sometimes hurts.* **—na′ked·ly,** *adv.* **—na′ked·ness,** *n.*

naked eye, the eye unaided by a telescope, microscope, or other device.

Nam or **'Nam** (năm *or* nam), *n.* INFORMAL. Vietnam.

Na·math (nā′məth), *n.* Joe (jō), born 1943, American football player. He was the first quarterback to pass for more than 4000 yards in a season.

nam·by-pam·by (nam′bē pam′bē), **1** *adj.* weakly simple, silly, or sentimental; lacking strength or firmness. **2** *n.* a namby-pamby person. ❑ *n., pl.* **nam·by-pam·bies.** **—nam′by-pam′bi·ness,** *n.*

name (nām), **1** *n.* word or words by which a person, animal, place, or thing is spoken of or to: *Our dog's name is Shep. "The Corn State" is a name for Iowa.* **2** *n.* an insulting word or phrase: *to call a person names.* **3** *v.* to give a name to: *name a newborn baby.* **4** *v.* to call by name; mention by name: *Three persons were named in the report.* **5** *v.* to give the right name for: *Can you name these flowers?* **6** *n.* reputation; fame: *get a bad name. Make a name for yourself.* **7** *v.* to mention; speak of; state: *name several reasons.* **8** *v.* to specify or fix; settle on: *name a price. The class named the day for its party.* **9** *v.* to choose for some duty or office; nominate; appoint: *He was named captain of the team.* **10** *adj.* well-known: *a name author, name products.* ❑ *v.* **named, nam·ing. —nam′a·ble** or **name′a·ble,** *adj.* **—nam′er,** *n.*

call names, to call bad names; swear at; curse.

in name only, supposed to be, but not really so: *a ruler in name only.*

in the name of, **1** for the sake of. **2** acting for: *I ordered the supplies in the name of my supervisor.*

know only by name, to know only by hearing about.

to your name, belonging to you: *I haven't a penny to my name.*

name brand, brand name.

name·less (nām′lis), *adj.* **1** having no name: *We fed the nameless kitten.* **2** not marked with a name: *a nameless grave.* **3** that cannot be named or described: *a strange, nameless longing.* **4** not fit to be mentioned: *nameless crimes.* **5** not named; unknown; obscure: *a book by some nameless writer.* **—name′less·ly,** *adv.* **—name′less·ness,** *n.*

name·ly (nām′lē), *adv.* that is to say: *The railroad connects two cities—namely, New York and Chicago.*

name·sake (nām′sāk′), *n.* someone having the same name as another, especially someone named for another: *My sister Linda is the namesake of our aunt.*

Na·mib·i·a (nä mib′ē ə), *n.* country in SW Africa. *Capital:* Windhoek. It was formerly called **South-West Africa.**

Nam·pa (nam′pə), *n.* city in SW Idaho.

Nan·jing (nän′jing′), *n.* city in E China, on the Chang Jiang River. It was the capital of China from 1928 to 1937 and from 1946 to 1949. Formerly called **Nanking.**

Nan·king (nän′king′), *n.* former name of **Nanjing.**

nan·ny (nan′ē), *n.* a child's nurse. ❑ *n., pl.* **nan·nies.**

nan·ny goat (nan′ē), a female goat.

nano-, *prefix.* **1** one billionth of a ___: *nanosecond = one billionth of a second.* **2** extremely small; on the molecular level: *nanoengineering.*

na·no·en·gi·neer·ing (nan′ō en′jə nir′ing), *n.* science of planning or building extremely small structures or machines.

na·no·sec·ond (nan′ə sek′ənd *or* nā′nə sek′ənd), *n.* one billionth of a second. [**Nanosecond** comes from a Greek word meaning "dwarf" and **second**².]

nan·o·struc·ture (nan′ə struk′chər), *n.* a very small structure, microscopic or even molecular in scale.

Nan·tuck·et (nan tuk′it), *n.* island south of Cape Cod. It is part of Massachusetts.

Na·o·mi (nā ō′mē), *n.* (in the Bible) the mother-in-law of Ruth. [**Naomi** comes from a Hebrew word meaning "pleasantness."]

nap¹ (nap), **1** *n.* a short sleep: *The baby takes a nap after lunch.* **2** *v.* to take a short sleep: *Grandfather naps in his armchair.* **3** *v.* to be off guard; be unprepared: *The test caught me napping.* ❑ *v.* **napped, nap·ping.**

nap² (nap), *n.* the soft, short, woolly threads or hairs on the surface of cloth: *the nap on velvet.* **—nap′less,** *adj.*

na·palm (nā′päm′), **1** *n.* jellied gasoline, used for making fire bombs and in flamethrowers. **2** *v.* to attack with napalm.

nape (nāp *or* nap), *n.* the back of the neck.

naph·tha (naf′thə *or* nap′thə), *n.* a flammable liquid made from petroleum, coal tar, etc., used as fuel and to clean clothing.

nap·kin (nap′kin), *n.* **1** piece of cloth or paper used at meals for protecting the clothing or for wiping the lips or fingers. **2** sanitary napkin.

Na·ples (nā′pəlz), *n.* port in SW Italy, on the Tyrrhenian Sea.

Na·po·le·on I (nə pō′lē ən), 1769-1821, Napoleon Bonaparte, French general who made himself emperor of France in 1804. He conquered a large part of Europe, but was defeated at Waterloo in 1815 and exiled to the island of St. Helena.

Napoleon III, 1808-1873, president of France from 1848 to 1852 and emperor of France from 1852 to 1870. He was the nephew of Napoleon I.

Na·po·le·on·ic (nə pō′lē on′ik), *adj.* of or resembling Napoleon I.

narc (närk), *n.* SLANG. a law-enforcement agent who investigates the illegal sale and use of narcotics.

nar·cis·sism (när′sə siz′əm), *n.* too much love or admiration of yourself.

nar·cis·sus (när sis′əs), *n.* any of several spring plants with yellow or white flowers and long thin leaves. Jonquils and daffodils are narcissuses. ❑ *n., pl.* **nar·cis·sus·es, nar·cis·sus,** or **nar·cis·si** (när sis′ī).

narcissus

N

a	hat	ė	term	ô	order	ch	child		a in about
ā	age	i	it	oi	oil	ng	long		e in taken
ä	far	ī	ice	ou	out	sh	she	ə	i in pencil
â	care	o	hot	u	cup	th	thin		o in lemon
e	let	ō	open	ů	put	ŦH	then		u in circus
ē	equal	ȯ	saw	ü	rule	zh	measure		

Nar·cis·sus (när sis′əs), *n.* (in Greek myths) a beautiful youth who fell in love with his own reflection in a pool.

nar·co·lep·sy (när′kə lep′sē), *n.* disorder in which the symptoms are attacks of drowsiness or deep sleep during normal waking hours. **—nar′co·lep′tic,** *adj.*

nar·cot·ic (när kot′ik), **1** *n.* any drug that produces drowsiness, sleep, dullness, or an insensible condition, and lessens pain by dulling the nerves. Prescribed to relieve pain, narcotics tend to become addictive if abused. Opium, heroin, morphine, and codeine are narcotics. **2** *adj.* having the properties and effects of a narcotic. **3** *adj.* of or relating to narcotics or their use. **—nar·cot′i·cal·ly,** *adv.*

Nar·ra·gan·sett Bay (nar′ə gan′sit), bay of the Atlantic, in E Rhode Island.

nar·rate (nar′āt *or* na rāt′), *v.* **1** to tell; relate. **2** to add an explanation, comments, or a story to a TV show or movie: *narrate a nature series.* ❑ *v.* **nar·rat·ed, nar·rat·ing. —nar′rat·a·ble,** *adj.* **—nar′ra·tor,** *n.*

nar·ra·tion (na rā′shən), *n.* **1** act of telling. **2** the form of composition that relates an event or a story. Novels, short stories, histories, and biographies are forms of narration. **3** story or account.

nar·ra·tive (nar′ə tiv), **1** *n.* story; tale: *Her three-month trip through the Near East made an interesting narrative.* **2** *n.* narration; storytelling. **3** *adj.* narrating: *"Hiawatha" is a narrative poem.* **—nar′ra·tive·ly,** *adv.*

nar·row (nar′ō), **1** *adj.* not wide; having little width; less wide than usual for its kind: *a narrow path.* **2** *n.pl.* **narrows,** the narrow part of a river, strait, sound, valley, pass, etc. **3** *adj.* limited or small in extent, space, amount, range, scope, opportunity, etc.: *a narrow circle of friends.* **4** *v.* to make or become narrower; decrease in breadth, extent, etc.; limit: *The doctor narrowed his interest to diseases of the throat. The road narrows above the bend.* **5** *adj.* with little margin; close: *a narrow escape.*

narrow—a narrow street

6 *adj.* not ready to listen to new ideas and judge them fairly; prejudiced: *A person with a narrow mind is often afraid of new ideas.* **7** *adj.* with barely enough to live on: *live in narrow circumstances.* **—nar′row·ly,** *adv.* **—nar′row·ness,** *n.*

nar·row·cast·ing (nar′ō kas′ting), *n.* broadcasting to a limited, specific audience, as by cable TV.

nar·row-mind·ed (nar′ō mīn′did), *adj.* unwilling to consider new ideas or the opinions of other people. **—nar′row-mind′ed·ly,** *adj.* **—nar′row-mind′ed·ness,** *n.*

nar·whal (när′wəl), *n.* a large, spotted whale of arctic seas. The male has a single long, slender tusk extending forward from the upper jaw.

nar·y (nâr′ē), *adj.* DIALECT. not: *nary a one.*

NASA (nas′ə), *n.* National Aeronautics and Space Administration (an agency of the U.S. government set up to direct and aid civilian research and development in aeronautics and aerospace technology).

na·sal (nā′zəl), *adj.* **1** of, in, or from the nose: *nasal passages, nasal sprays.* **2** spoken through the nose. The letters *m, n,* and *ng* represent nasal sounds. **3** sounding as if speaking through the nose: *When you have a cold, you sound nasal.* **—na′sal·ly,** *adv.*

Nash (nash), *n.* **Og·den** (og′dən), 1902-1971, American poet. His humorous poems often used long lines with irregular rhythms.

Nash·u·a (nash′ü ə), *n.* city in S New Hampshire.

Nash·ville (nash′vil), *n.* capital of Tennessee, in the central part, on the Cumberland River.

Nas·sau (nas′ô), *n.* capital of the Bahamas. **—Nas·sau′vi·an** (na-sò′vē ən), *adj., n.*

Nas·ser (näs′ər), *n.* **Gam·al Ab·del** (gə mäl′ ab′dəl), 1918-1970, president of Egypt from 1956 to 1970. He led the revolt that overthrew the king of Egypt and made it a republic.

na·stur·tium (nə stėr′shəm), *n.* any of several garden plants with yellow, orange, or red flowers, and sharp-tasting leaves that are eaten in salads.

> **WORD STORY**   **Nasturtium** comes from Latin words meaning "nose" and "to twist." The leaves and seeds of nasturtiums have a strong smell, which may cause people to wrinkle their noses.

nas·ty (nas′tē), *adj.* **1** mean; cruel; hateful: *Several nasty people threw rocks at the birds on the lake. He made nasty remarks about my science project.* ■ See Synonym Study at **unkind. 2** very unpleasant: *The nasty weather ruined our plans for a picnic.* **3** dirty; filthy: *Dead fish and garbage littered the surface of the nasty creek.* **4** rather serious; bad: *a nasty cut on the hand.* ❑ *adj.* **nas·ti·er, nas·ti·est. —nas′ti·ly,** *adv.* **—nas′ti·ness,** *n.*

na·tal (nā′tl), *adj.* of your birth: *Her natal day is September 3.*

Na·tal (nə tal′), *n.* province of the Republic of South Africa, on the E coast.

> **WORD STORY**   **Natal** comes from the same Latin word that also became **natal.** The explorer Vasco da Gama reached this part of Africa on Christmas Day, 1497. Since Christmas is celebrated as Jesus' birthday, da Gama named the region, in Latin, "Birthday Land."

na·tion (nā′shən), *n.* **1** people occupying the same country, united under the same government, and usually speaking the same language: *The President appealed to the nation for support of his policies.* **2** a sovereign state; country: *the nations of the West.* **3** a people, race, or tribe; those having the same descent, language, and history: *the Armenian nation.* **4** a North American Indian tribe or federation: *the Five Nations of the Iroquois.*

> **WORD FAMILY**   **Nation** and the following words are related: **innate, international, natal, native, nature,** and **supernatural.** They all come from a Latin word meaning "born."

Na·tion (nā′shən), *n.* **Car·ry** (kar′ē), 1846-1911, American temperance activist. She often destroyed saloons with a hatchet.

na·tion·al (nash′ə nəl), **1** *adj.* of or relating to a nation; belonging to a whole nation: *national laws, a national disaster.* **2** *n.* citizen of a nation: *Many nationals of Canada visit our country.* **3** *adj.* owned by or operated by the federal government: *national forests.*

national anthem, the official patriotic song or hymn of a nation, sung and played on public occasions.

National Guard, the reserve militia of each state of the United States, supported in part by the federal government. The National Guard may be called upon to serve either the state or the federal government in time of emergency.

na·tion·al·ism (nash′ə nə liz′əm), *n.* **1** patriotic feelings or efforts. **2** desire and plans for national independence.

na·tion·al·ist (nash′ə nə list), **1** *n.* person who believes in or upholds nationalism. **2** *adj.* nationalistic.

Nationalist China, Taiwan; China.

na·tion·al·is·tic (nash′ə nə lis′tik), *adj.* of or relating to nationalism or nationalists. **—na′tion·al·is′ti·cal·ly,** *adv.*

na·tion·al·i·ty (nash′ə nal′ə tē), *n.* **1** fact or condition of belonging to a nation. Citizens of the same country have the same nationality. **2** political existence as an independent nation. ❑ *n., pl.* **na·tion·al·i·ties** for 1.

na·tion·al·ize (nash′ə nə līz), *v.* **1** to make national. **2** to bring land, industries, railroads, etc., under the control or ownership of a nation. ❑ *v.* **na·tion·al·ized, na·tion·al·iz·ing. —na′tion·al·i·za′tion,** *n.*

na·tion·al·ly (nash′ə nə lē), *adv.* **1** in a national manner; as a nation. **2** throughout the nation: *The program was broadcast nationally.*

national monument, an area of land set aside by a government because of special historical or natural importance.

national park, land kept by the national government for people to enjoy because of its beautiful scenery, historical interest, etc.

National Road, a highway built in the early 1800s, extending from Cumberland, Maryland, to St. Louis, Missouri. It served as a gateway to the West for pioneer migration.

National Socialist Party, a fascist political party which ruled Germany from 1933 to 1945, under the leadership of Adolf Hitler; the Nazi party.

Nation of Islam, an African American organization that follows many Muslim teachings and calls for complete segregation between blacks and whites.

na·tion-state (nā′shən stāt′), *n.* an independent country in which most of the people share a common language and cultural background.

na·tion·wide (nā′shən wīd′), *adj.* taking place throughout the nation: *a nationwide election.*

na·tive (nā′tiv), **1** *n.* someone born in a certain place or country. **2** *adj.* born in a certain place or country: *People born in New York are native sons and daughters of New York.* **3** *adj.* belonging to you because of your birth: *The United States is my native land.* **4** *adj.* belonging to you because of your nation or ancestors: *French is his native language.* **5** *adj.* born in a person; natural: *native ability.* **6** *n.* one of the people originally living in a place or country and found there by explorers or settlers. **7** *adj.* of these people: *native customs.* **8** *n.* a living thing that originated in a place: *The lion is a native of Africa.* **9** *adj.* originating, grown, or produced in a certain place: *Tobacco is native to America.* **10** *adj.* found pure in nature: *native copper.* —**na′tive·ly,** *adv.* —**na′tive·ness,** *n.*

WORD STORY **Native** looks like **naive,** and both words come from the same Latin word, meaning "born." As different meanings turned into separate words, one lost its middle *t* in pronunciation and spelling, and the other shifted its accent to the first syllable. Words like these are called doublets. **Costume** and **custom** are doublets, and there are hundreds more in English. See Word Source at **doublet.**

Native American, one of the people who have lived in the Americas from long before the time of the first European settlers; American Indian.

USAGE NOTE Many members of this group prefer to use the term **American Indian,** which has a long history and wide recognition. Many other members now prefer to use the term **Native American.** This term emphasizes the fact that these people were the first to settle America. It avoids the word *Indian,* which comes from Columbus's mistaken belief that he had sailed to Asia. It is wise to find out about people's preferences before using either term. Another possibility is to use a more precise name, such as Cherokee or Hopi.

na·tive-born (nā′tiv bôrn′), *adj.* born in the place or country indicated: *a native-born American.*

na·tiv·i·ty (nə tiv′ə tē), *n.* **1** birth. **2 the Nativity, a** birth of Jesus. **b** Christmas. ❑ *n., pl.* **na·tiv·i·ties** for 1.

natl., national.

NATO (nā′tō), *n.* North Atlantic Treaty Organization (an alliance of sixteen European and North American nations providing for joint military cooperation).

nat·u·ral (nach′ər əl), **1** *adj.* instinctively felt to be right and fair: *natural law, natural rights.* **2** *adj.* belonging to the nature you are born with; instinctive; inborn: *natural ability. It is natural for ducks to swim.* **3** *adj.* produced by nature; coming or occurring in the ordinary course of events: *natural feelings and actions, a natural death.* **4** *adj.* not artificial; not made by human beings: *Coal and oil are natural products.* **5** *adj.* in accordance with the nature of things or the circumstances of the case: *a natural conclusion.* **6** *adj.* like nature; true to nature: *The picture looked natural.* **7** *adj.* free from control; without planning: *a natural manner.* ■ See Synonym Study in music: **a** *adj.* neither sharp nor flat; not changed in pitch by a sharp or a flat: *C natural.* **b** *n.* a natural tone or note. **c** *n.* a sign (♮) used to cancel the effect of a preceding sharp or flat. **9** *n.* person who is especially suited for something because of inborn talent or ability: *He is a natural on the saxophone.* —**nat′ur·al·ness,** *n.*

natural food, food that is not processed, and to which no preservatives or artificial colorings or flavorings have been added.

natural gas, a fuel gas formed naturally in the earth. It is a mixture of methane and some other substances.

natural history, the study of living things, minerals, the atmosphere, and other things in nature.

nat·u·ral·ist (nach′ər ə list), *n.* person who makes a study of living things.

nat·u·ral·is·tic (nach′ər ə lis′tik), *adj.* of, like, or in accordance with nature. —**nat′ur·al·is′ti·cal·ly,** *adv.*

nat·u·ral·ize (nach′ər ə līz), *v.* **1** to admit to citizenship. After living in the United States for a certain number of years, an immigrant can be naturalized after passing a test. **2** to adopt a foreign word or custom: *"Chauffeur" is a French word that has been naturalized in English.* **3** (of living things) to introduce and make at home in another country: *The English oak has become naturalized in parts of Massachusetts.* ❑ *v.* **nat·u·ral·ized, nat·ur·al·iz·ing.** —**nat′ur·al·i·za′tion,** *n.* —**nat′ur·al·iz′er,** *n.*

nat·u·ral·ly (nach′ər ə lē), *adv.* **1** in a natural way: *Speak naturally; don't try to imitate someone else.* **2** by nature: *She was a naturally athletic child.* **3** as might be expected; of course: *She offered me some candy; naturally, I took it.*

natural number, a positive integer. 1,2,3,4, etc., are natural numbers.

natural resources, materials supplied by nature. Minerals, forests, and water power are natural resources.

natural science, any science dealing with the facts of nature or the physical world. Biology and physics are natural sciences.

natural selection, process in nature by which living things that are best adapted to their environment tend to survive and reproduce more often than those not so well adapted.

na·ture (nā′chər), *n.* **1** the world; all things except those made by human beings: *the wonders of nature.* **2** Also, **Nature,** all the forces at work throughout the world: *the laws of nature.* **3** the instincts or inborn tendencies that direct behavior: *It is the nature of birds to fly.* **4** life without artificial things: *to live in a state of nature.* **5** what a thing really is; quality; character: *It is against her nature to be petty.* **6** sort; kind: *books of a scientific nature.* **7** scenery of the natural world: *photographs of nature.*

Nau·ga·hyde (nò′gə hīd), *n.* a trademark for a fabric for covering furniture. It is made from vinyl, and resembles leather.

naught (nòt), *n.* **1** nothing: *All my studying came to naught; I failed the test.* **2** zero; 0. Also, **nought.** [Naught is from two old English words meaning "no" and "thing." Old English had two different words meaning "thing" so we have two words meaning "no thing," **naught** and **nothing.**]

naugh·ty (nò′tē), *adj.* **1** bad; not obedient: *The naughty child hit the baby.* **2** somewhat improper: *a naughty joke.* ❑ *adj.* **naugh·ti·er, naugh·ti·est.** —**naugh′ti·ly,** *adv.* —**naugh′ti·ness,** *n.*

SYNONYM STUDY **Naughty, mischievous,** and **rowdy** all mean not behaving well. **Naughty** is used mostly about children and animals: *The naughty puppy refuses to come inside.* **Mischievous** means taking pleasure in behaving badly: *Some mischievous person has put my bicycle in a tree.* **Rowdy** means noisy and making trouble: *The rowdy class quieted down fast when the principal walked in.*

natural food

a	hat	ė	term	ô	order	ch	child		
ā	age	i	it	oi	oil	ng	long	ə	a in about
ä	far	ī	ice	ou	out	sh	she		e in taken
â	care	o	hot	u	cup	th	thin		i in pencil
e	let	ō	open	ù	put	ŦH	then		o in lemon
ē	equal	ò	saw	ü	rule	zh	measure		u in circus

Na·u·ru (nä ü′rü), *n.* small island country in the central Pacific, northeast of the Solomon Islands. *Capital:* Yaren. **—Na·u′ru·an,** *adj., n.*

nau·se·a (nò′zē ə *or* nò′shə), *n.* **1** the feeling that you have when about to vomit. **2** extreme disgust; loathing.

nau·se·ate (nò′zē āt *or* nò′shē āt), *v.* **1** to feel nausea or cause nausea in; make or become sick. **2** to cause to feel loathing. ❑ *v.* **nau·se·at·ed, nau·se·at·ing. —nau′se·at/ing·ly,** *adv.*

nau·seous (nò′shəs *or* nò′zē əs), *adj.* **1** causing nausea; sickening. **2** feeling nausea; nauseated. **—nau′seous·ly,** *adv.* **—nau′seous·ness,** *n.*

nau·ti·cal (nò′tə kəl), *adj.* of or about ships, sailors, or navigation. **—nau′ti·cal·ly,** *adv.*

nautical mile, unit of distance equal to 6076.11549 feet (1.852 kilometers).

nau·ti·lus (nò′tl əs), *n.* either of two distantly related sea animals with shells. The **pearly nautilus** or **chambered nautilus** has a spiral shell divided into many compartments that have a pearly lining. The **paper nautilus** resembles an octopus, and the female has a very thin shell. ❑ *n., pl.* **nau·ti·lus·es, nau·ti·li** (nò′tl ī).

pearly nautilus

Nau·voo (nò vü′ *or* nò′vü), *n.* city in W Illinois. It was settled by Mormons under Joseph Smith's leadership in the late 1830s.

Nav·a·ho (nav′ə hō), *n.* Navajo. ❑ *n., pl.* **Nav·a·ho** or **Nav·a·hos.**

Nav·a·jo (nav′ə hō), *n.* member of a tribe of American Indians living in New Mexico, Arizona, and Utah. ❑ *n., pl.* **Nav·a·jo** or **Nav·a·jos.** [**Navajo** comes from a word in a Pueblo language meaning "a river valley with large fields." It was originally the name of a particular place.]

na·val (nā′vəl), *adj.* **1** of or for warships or the navy: *a naval officer, naval supplies, naval bases.* **2** having a navy: *Spain was once a great naval power.* ■ Another word that sounds like this is **navel.**

Na·varre (nə vär′), *n.* former kingdom including parts of SW France and N Spain.

nave (nāv), *n.* the main part of a church or cathedral, between the side aisles. ■ Another word that sounds like this is **knave.**

na·vel (nā′vəl), *n.* the mark or scar in the middle of the surface of the abdomen. It is what remains after cutting the cord that connects a newborn infant to its mother's body. ■ Another word that sounds like this is **naval.**

navel orange, a seedless orange with a small growth at one end shaped something like a navel.

nav·i·ga·ble (nav′ə gə bəl), *adj.* **1** able to be traveled by ships: *The river is deep enough to be navigable for hundreds of miles.* **2** able to be steered: *a navigable balloon.* **—nav/i·ga·bil/i·ty, nav′·i·ga·ble·ness,** *n.* **—nav/i·ga·bly,** *adv.*

nav·i·gate (nav′ə gāt), *v.* **1** to operate or steer a ship, aircraft, etc. **2** to sail on a sea or river. **3** to move, walk, or swim about: *I can barely navigate with this sprained ankle.* ❑ *v.* **nav·i·gat·ed, nav·i·gat·ing.**

nav·i·ga·tion (nav′ə gā′shən), *n.* **1** skill or process of finding a ship's or aircraft's position and course. **2** act or process of navigating. **—nav/i·ga′tion·al,** *adj.*

nav·i·ga·tor (nav′ə gā′tər), *n.* **1** person in charge of finding the position and course of a ship or aircraft. **2** (long ago) explorer of the seas.

Nav·ra·ti·lo·va (nav′rə ti lō′və), *n.* **Mar·ti·na** (mar tē′nə), born 1956, American tennis player, born in Czechoslovakia. In 1992 she won her 158th tournament, a career record.

na·vy (nā′vē), **1** *n.* Often, **Navy,** the branch of a nation's armed forces which includes its ships of war, the officers and personnel who run them, and the department that manages them. **2** *n.* OLD USE. fleet of ships. **3** *n.* a dark blue; navy blue. **4** *adj.* having this color: *She wore a navy sweater.* ❑ *n., pl.* **na·vies.**

navy bean, a small, common, white bean, dried for use. [Navy beans got their name during the 1880s, when they were served to sailors in the U.S. Navy every day.]

navy blue, a dark blue.

nay (nā), **1** *adv.* OLD USE. no. **2** *adv.* not only that, but also: *We are willing, nay, eager to go.* **3** *n.* no; a denial or refusal. **4** *n.* a negative vote or voter: *The yeas outnumber the nays, so the plan is approved.* ■ Other words that sound like this are **nee** and **neigh.**

Na·ya·rit (ni ə rēt′), *n.* a state in W Mexico.

Naz·a·rene (naz′ə rēn′ *or* naz′ə rēn′), *n.* **1** someone born or living in Nazareth. **2 the Nazarene,** Jesus.

Naz·ar·eth (naz′ər əth), *n.* town in N Israel. It was the childhood home of Jesus. See **Galilee** for map.

Na·zi (nä′tsē *or* nat′sē), **1** *n.* member or supporter of the National Socialist Party, a fascist political party in Germany, led by Adolf Hitler. **2** *adj.* of or about the Nazis. ❑ *n., pl.* **Na·zis.**

Na·zi·ism (nä′tsē iz/əm *or* nat′sē iz/əm), *n.* Nazism.

Na·zism (nä′tsiz/əm *or* nat′siz/əm), *n.* the doctrines and practices of the Nazis, including totalitarian government, state control of industry, anti-Semitism, and opposition to communism.

Nb, symbol for niobium.

N.B., New Brunswick.

N.B. or **n.b.,** note well; observe carefully.

NBA, National Basketball Association.

NBC, National Broadcasting Company.

NC, North Carolina (used with postal Zip Code).

N.C., North Carolina.

NCO, noncommissioned officer.

NC-17, no children under 17 (a rating between PG-13 and R for a movie that is recommended only for people over age 17).

Nd, symbol for neodymium.

ND, North Dakota (used with postal Zip Code).

N.Dak. or **N.D.,** North Dakota.

N'Dja·me·na (en/jə mä′nə), *n.* capital of Chad, in the S part.

Ne, symbol for neon.

NE, Nebraska (used with postal Zip Code).

NE or **N.E.,** **1** northeast. **2** northeastern.

Ne·an·der·thal (nē an′dər täl *or* nē an′dər thòl), **1** *adj.* of or belonging to a kind of prehistoric people who lived in caves in Europe, North Africa, and parts of Asia, in the early Stone Age. **2** *n.* one of these people. Neanderthals had large, heavy skulls, low foreheads, flat noses, heavy lower jaws, and large brains.

Ne·a·pol·i·tan (nē′ə pol′ə tən), **1** *adj.* of or about Naples. **2** *n.* someone born or living in Naples.

neap tide (nēp), tide that occurs when the difference in height between high and low tide is least; the lowest level of high tide. Neap tide comes twice a month, when the pulls of the moon and sun are most different in direction.

near (nir), **1** *adv.* to or at a short distance; not far; close: *They searched far and near. The holiday season is drawing near.* **2** *adj.* close by; not distant; less distant: *The post office is quite near.* **3** *prep.* close to in space, time, condition, etc.: *Our house is near the river.* **4** *v.* to come or draw near to; approach: *The ship neared the land.* **5** *adj.* close in feeling; intimate; familiar: *a near friend.* **6** *adj.* closely related: *a near relative.* **7** *adv.* all but; almost: *The war lasted near a year.* **8** *adj.* short; direct: *Go by the nearest route.* **9** *adj.* by a close margin: *We had a near escape.* **—near′·ness,** *n.*
come near doing, to almost do: *I came near forgetting my glasses.*
near at hand, 1 within easy reach. **2** not far in the future.

near·by (nir′bī′), *adj., adv.* near; close at hand: *a nearby house. They went nearby to visit.*

Near East, the countries of SW Asia, sometimes including the Balkan States and Egypt. **—Near Eastern.**

near·ly (nir′lē), *adv.* **1** almost: *I nearly missed the train.* **2** closely: *It will cost too much, as nearly as I can figure.*

near·sight·ed (nir′sī′tid), *adj.* not able to see far; seeing distinctly at a short distance only. Nearsighted people usually wear glasses. —**near′sight′ed·ly,** *adv.* —**near′sight′ed·ness,** *n.*

neat (nēt), *adj.* **1** clean and in order: *a neat desk, a neat room.* **2** able and willing to keep things in order: *a neat child.* **3** well-formed; in proportion: *a neat design.* **4** skillful; clever: *a neat trick.* **5** INFORMAL. wonderful; fine: *It was a neat party.* [Neat comes from a Latin word meaning "to shine." Things that are neat are usually clean and shining.] —**neat′ly,** *adv.* —**neat′ness,** *n.*

neath or **'neath** (nēth), *prep.* OLD USE. beneath.

Nebr., Nebraska.

Ne·bras·ka (nə bras′kə), *n.* one of the midwestern states of the United States. *Abbreviation:* NE or Nebr. *Capital:* Lincoln. —**Ne·bras′kan,** *n.*

Neb·u·chad·nez·zar II (neb ə kəd nez′ər), king of Babylonia from 605 to 562 B.C. He captured Jerusalem and destroyed the city in 587 or 586 B.C. He probably built the Hanging Gardens of Babylon, one of the wonders of the ancient world.

neb·u·la (neb′yə lə), *n.* **1** mass of dust particles and gases in outer space. A nebula may either be dark or appear as a glowing haze illuminated by stars. **2** galaxy outside our own or a cloud-like cluster of stars inside our galaxy. ❑ *n., pl.* **neb·u·las, neb·u·lae** (neb′yə lē′).

neb·u·lar (neb′yə lər), *adj.* of or about a nebula or nebulas.

neb·u·lous (neb′yə ləs), *adj.* **1** hazy; vague; indistinct; confused. **2** of or like a nebula or nebulas. —**neb′u·lous·ly,** *adv.* —**neb′u·lous·ness,** *n.*

nec·es·sar·i·ly (nes′ə ser′ə lē), *adv.* **1** always; of necessity: *Leaves are not necessarily green.* **2** as a logical result: *War necessarily causes misery and waste.*

nec·es·sar·y (nes′ə ser′ē), **1** *adj.* needed; needing to be done: *a necessary repair.* **2** *adj.* following as a logical result; inevitable: *Illness is often a necessary consequence of poor nutrition.* **3** *n.* something essential, or impossible to do without: *Food, clothing, and shelter are necessaries of life.* ❑ *n., pl.* **nec·es·sar·ies.**

ne·ces·si·tate (nə ses′ə tāt), *v.* to make necessary: *Her broken leg necessitated an operation.* ❑ *v.* **ne·ces·si·tat·ed, ne·ces·si·tat·ing.** —**ne·ces′si·ta′tion,** *n.*

ne·ces·si·ty (nə ses′ə tē), *n.* **1** fact of being necessary; extreme need: *We understand the necessity of eating the proper foods.* **2** something that is necessary: *Water is a necessity.* **3** something that forces you to act in a certain way: *Necessity often drives people to do disagreeable things.* **4** need; poverty: *a family in great necessity.* ❑ *n., pl.* **ne·ces·si·ties** for 2.

neck (nek), *n.* **1** the part of the body that connects the head with the shoulders. **2** the part of a piece of clothing that fits the neck: *the neck of a shirt.* **3** any narrow part like a neck: *She held the bottle by the neck.*

neck and neck, 1 abreast. **2** running even in a race or contest.

neck of the woods, neighborhood; region; area: *Do you live in my neck of the woods?*

risk your neck, to put yourself in a dangerous position.

stick your neck out, to put yourself in a dangerous position.

neck·er·chief (nek′ər chif), *n.* cloth worn around the neck.

neck·lace (nek′lis), *n.* string of jewels, gold, silver, beads, etc., worn around the neck as an ornament.

neck·line (nek′lin′), *n.* edge of a piece of clothing where it ends at the front of the neck.

neck·tie (nek′tī′), *n.* a narrow length of cloth worn around the neck, under the collar of a shirt, and tied in front.

neck·wear (nek′wâr′), *n.* ties, scarfs, and other articles that are worn around the neck.

nec·ro·man·cy (nek′rə man′sē), *n.* **1** act or practice of foretelling the future by communicating with the dead. **2** magic; sorcery. —**nec′ro·man′cer,** *n.*

nec·tar (nek′tər), *n.* **1** (in Greek myths) the drink of the gods. **2** any delicious drink. **3** a sweet liquid found in many flowers. Bees gather nectar and make it into honey. —**nec′tar·like′,** *adj.*

nec·ta·rine (nek′tə rēn′), *n.* kind of peach without any fuzz on its skin.

nee or **née** (nā), *adj.* born. ■ Nee is placed after the name of a married woman to show her maiden name: *Pamela Smith, nee Adams.* ■ Other words that sound like this are **nay** and **neigh.**

need (nēd), **1** *v.* to be unable to do without; lack: *I need a new hat. Plants need water.* **2** *n.* something that has to be; necessity: *There is no need to hurry.* **3** *n.* lack of something useful or desired: *Your handwriting shows a need of practice.* **4** *n.* situation or time of difficulty: *When I lacked money, my uncle was a friend in need.* **5** *n.* lack of money; extreme poverty: *This family's need was so great the children did not have shoes.* **6** *v.* must; should; have to; ought to: *You need not go. Need she go?* **7** *n.* something that you must have: *In the jungle their need was fresh water.* ■ Another word that sounds like this is **knead.**

if need be, if it has to be.

nebula (def. 2)

need·ful (nēd′fəl), *adj.* needed; necessary: *a needful change.* —**need′ful·ly,** *adv.* —**need′ful·ness,** *n.*

nee·dle (nē′dl), **1** *n.* a very thin tool, pointed at one end and with a hole to pass a thread through, used in sewing. **2** *n.* a thin rod used in knitting. **3** *n.* rod with a hook at one end used in crocheting. **4** *n.* a thin steel pointer in a compass, dial, gauge, etc., that shows amount, speed, pressure, etc. **5** *n.* a very thin steel tube with a sharp point at one end. It is used at the end of a hypodermic syringe, for injecting a liquid into the body or for withdrawing blood or other bodily fluid. **6** *n.* the small, pointed piece in a record player that touches the record and vibrates in the grooves. **7** *n.* the thin, pointed leaf of a pine tree, fir tree, yew tree, etc. **8** *n.* any of various small objects resembling a needle in sharpness: *needles of broken glass.* **9** *v.* to annoy or provoke someone with repeated teasing or mocking: *They kept needling me about my new glasses.* ❑ *v.* **nee·dled, nee·dling.** —**nee′dle·like′,** *adj.* —**nee′dler,** *n.*

nee·dle·leaf (nē′dl lēf′), *adj.* of or from trees that have thin, pointed leaves. Firs and pines are needleleaf trees.

a	hat	ė	term	ô	order	ch	child		
ā	age	i	it	oi	oil	ng	long	ə	a in about
ä	far	ī	ice	ou	out	sh	she		e in taken
â	care	o	hot	u	cup	th	thin		i in pencil
e	let	ō	open	ů	put	ṪH	then		o in lemon
ē	equal	ȯ	saw	ü	rule	zh	measure		u in circus

nee·dle·point (nē′dl point′), *n.* embroidery made on a canvas cloth, usually with woolen yarn.

need·less (nēd′lis), *adj.* not needed; unnecessary: *It is silly to take a needless risk.* —**need′less·ly,** *adv.* —**need′less·ness,** *n.*

nee·dle·work (nē′dl werk′), *n.* work done with a needle; sewing; embroidery.

need·n't (nēd′nt), need not.

need·y (nē′dē), *adj.* very poor; not having enough to live on: *a needy family.* ■ See Synonym Study at **poor.** ❑ *adj.* **need·i·er, need·i·est.** —**need′i·ness,** *n.*

ne'er (ner), *adv.* OLD USE. never.

ne'er-do-well (ner′dü wel′), *n.* an irresponsible or good-for-nothing person.

ne·far·i·ous (ni fâr′ē əs), *adj.* very wicked; villainous: *The nefarious deeds of the movie villain included stealing a freight train and robbing a bank.* —**ne·far′i·ous·ly,** *adv.* —**ne·far′i·ous·ness,** *n.*

Nef·er·ti·ti (nef′ər tē′tē), *n.* ancient Egyptian queen who ruled from 1367 to 1350 B.C. Several famous sculptured portraits of her have been found by archaeologists.

ne·gate (ni gāt′), *v.* **1** to destroy, nullify, or make ineffective. **2** to declare not to exist; deny. ❑ *v.* **ne·gat·ed, ne·gat·ing.** —**ne·ga′tor** or **ne·gat′er,** *n.*

ne·ga·tion (ni gā′shən), *n.* **1** act of denying; denial: *Shaking the head is a sign of negation.* **2** absence or opposite of some positive thing or quality: *Death is the negation of life.*

Nefertiti

neg·a·tive (neg′ə tiv), **1** *adj.* stating that something is not so; saying no: *His answer was negative.* **2** *n.* word or statement that says no or denies: *"I won't" is a negative.* ■ See Usage Note at **double negative. 3** *n.* the side that says no or argues against a question being debated; side opposing the affirmative. **4** *adj.* not positive; unfavorable; critical: *Her negative suggestions are not helpful.* **5** *adj.* less than zero; minus: *−5 is a negative number.* **6** *n.* a negative number or quantity: *Multiplying two negatives produces a positive.* **7** *adj.* of the kind of electricity that electrons have. Negative electricity travels along wires and is used for power. **8** *adj.* showing the lights, shadows, and colors reversed: *the negative image on photographic film.* **9** *n.* a photographic image in which the lights, shadows, and colors are reversed. Prints are made from it. **10** *adj.* showing the absence of a particular disease, condition, germ, etc.: *Tests were negative for cancer.* —**neg′a·tive·ly,** *adv.* —**neg′a·tive·ness, neg·a·tiv·i·ty** (neg′ə tiv′ə tē), *n.* **in the negative,** expressing disagreement by saying no; denying.

neg·a·tiv·ism (neg′ə tə viz′əm), *n.* tendency to say or do the opposite of what is suggested.

ne·glect (ni glekt′), **1** *v.* to give too little care or attention to: *neglect your health.* **2** *v.* to leave undone; not attend to: *neglect your work.* **3** *v.* to omit; fail: *Don't neglect to water the plants before you leave.* **4** *n.* act or fact of neglecting; disregard: *a persistent neglect of duty.* **5** *n.* lack of care or attention: *That car has been ruined by neglect.* **6** *n.* condition of being neglected: *The children suffered from neglect.* —**ne·glect′er,** *n.*

ne·glect·ful (ni glekt′fəl), *adj.* careless; negligent: *neglectful of your duty.* —**ne·glect′ful·ly,** *adv.* —**ne·glect′ful·ness,** *n.*

neg·li·gee (neg′lə zhā′), *n.* a woman's soft, loose dressing gown. ❑ *n., pl.* **neg·li·gees.**

neg·li·gence (neg′lə jəns), *n.* lack of proper care or attention; carelessness; neglect: *Negligence was the cause of the accident.*

neg·li·gent (neg′lə jənt), *adj.* **1** given to neglect; showing neglect; neglectful. **2** careless; indifferent. —**neg′li·gent·ly,** *adv.*

neg·li·gi·ble (neg′lə jə bəl), *adj.* not worth worrying about: *The loss of ten cents is negligible.* —**neg′li·gi·bil′i·ty,** *n.* —**neg′li·gi·bly,** *adv.*

ne·go·tia·ble (ni gō′shə bəl), *adj.* **1** able to be negotiated: *negotiable demands.* **2** transferrable: *negotiable securities.* —**ne·go′·tia·bil′i·ty,** *n.* —**ne·go′tia·bly,** *adv.*

ne·go·ti·ate (ni gō′shē āt), *v.* **1** to talk over and arrange terms; confer; consult: *Both countries negotiated for peace.* **2** to arrange for: *They finally negotiated a peace treaty.* **3** to get past or over: *The car negotiated the sharp curve easily.* ❑ *v.* **ne·go·ti·at·ed, ne·go·ti·at·ing.** —**ne·go′ti·a′tor,** *n.*

ne·go·ti·a·tion (ni gō′shē ā′shən), *n.* Often, **negotiations,** *pl.* act or process of negotiating; arrangement: *treaty negotiations.*

Ne·gro (nē′grō), **1** *n.* person whose ancestors belonged to the group of people living in Africa south of the Sahara; black; in the United States, African American. **2** *adj.* of or about people of this background. ■ Most people prefer to use **African American** or **black** instead of **Negro,** which is now often considered offensive. ❑ *n., pl.* **Ne·groes.**

Ne·he·mi·ah (nē′ə mī′ə), *n.* **1** a Hebrew leader. He rebuilt the walls of Jerusalem about 444 B.C. **2** book of the Bible describing his achievements. [**Nehemiah** comes from a Hebrew word meaning "comforted by Jehovah."]

Neh·ru (nā′rü), *n.* **Ja·wa·har·lal** (jə wä′hər läl′), 1889-1964, prime minister of India from 1947 to 1964.

neigh (nā), **1** *n.* sound that a horse makes. **2** *v.* to make this sound. ■ Other words that sound like this are **nay** and **nee.**

neigh·bor (nā′bər), **1** *n.* someone who lives in the next house or nearby. **2** *n.* something or someone that is near another: *The big tree brought down several of its smaller neighbors as it fell.* **3** *v.* to be near or next to; adjoin: *Canada neighbors the United States.* **4** *n.* a fellow human being.

neigh·bor·hood (nā′bər hùd), **1** *n.* region near some place or thing: *She lives in the neighborhood of the mill.* **2** *n.* place or district: *Is North Street a good neighborhood?* **3** *n.* people living near one another; people of a place: *The whole neighborhood came to the big party.* **4** *n.* neighborly feeling or conduct. **5** *adj.* of or for a neighborhood: *a neighborhood newspaper.* **in the neighborhood of,** somewhere near; about: *The car cost in the neighborhood of $12,500.*

neigh·bor·ing (nā′bər ing), *adj.* living or being near; bordering; near: *We heard the bird calls from the neighboring woods.*

neigh·bor·ly (nā′bər lē), *adj.* like or befitting a good neighbor; kindly, friendly, or sociable: *It was very neighborly of them to help us move in.* —**neigh′bor·li·ness,** *n.*

nei·ther (nē′Thər *or* nī′Thər), **1** *adj., conj., pron.* not either: *Neither statement is true. Neither you nor I will go. Neither of the statements is true.* **2** *conj.* nor yet; nor: *They didn't go; neither did we.*

nek·ton (nek′ton), *n.* living things such as fish, which are large enough to swim freely, unlike plankton, which float or drift.

Nel·son (nel′sən), *n.* Viscount **Hor·a·tio** (hə rā′shō), 1758-1805, British admiral, noted for victories over Napoleon I.

nem·a·tode (nem′ə tōd), *n.* roundworm.

Nem·e·sis (nem′ə sis), *n.* **1** the Greek goddess of vengeance. **2 nemesis,** someone who punishes another for evil deeds: *Sherlock Holmes was the nemesis of many criminals.* ❑ *n., pl.* **nem·e·ses** (nem′ə sēz′) for 2.

ne·o·clas·sic (nē′ō klas′ik), *adj.* of or about the revival of classical principles or practices in art, music, and literature.

ne·o·dym·i·um (nē′ō dim′ē əm), *n.* a yellowish metallic element found in various rare minerals. The pink salts of neodymium are used to color glass. *Symbol:* Nd

Ne·o·lith·ic (nē′ə lith′ik), *adj.* of or about the latest part of the Stone Age, when agriculture began and people used stone tools.

ne·ol·o·gism (nē ol′ə jiz′əm), *n.* a new word or expression, or a new meaning for an old word or phrase.

ne·on (nē′on), *n.* a colorless, odorless gas, forming a very small part of the air. It is a chemical element. Neon glows bright orange-red when electricity is passed through it, and it is used in neon signs. *Symbol:* Ne [**Neon** comes from a Greek word meaning "new." Neon was a newly discovered element in 1898.]

neon sign, advertising sign made with neon or other gases that glow in various colors when electricity is passed through them.

neon sign

ne·o·phyte (nē′ə fit), *n.* **1** beginner; novice. **2** a new convert; someone recently admitted to a religious group.

ne·o·prene (nē′ə prēn), *n.* a synthetic rubber which resists oil, heat, and harsh weather conditions. It is used in gaskets, shoe soles, gasoline hoses, etc.

Ne·pal (nə pôl′), *n.* country between India and Tibet. *Capital:* Kathmandu.

neph·ew (nef′yü), *n.* son of your brother or sister; son of your brother-in-law or sister-in-law.

ne·phri·tis (ni frī′tis), *n.* inflammation of the kidneys.

neph·ron (nef′ron), *n.* any of many tiny sections of the kidney that filter waste matter from the blood. A human kidney has more than one million nephrons.

nep·o·tism (nep′ə tiz′əm), *n.* the showing of favoritism to relatives by someone in power, especially by giving them desirable positions.

Nep·tune (nep′tün), *n.* **1** the fourth largest planet in the solar system and the eighth in distance from the sun. It is visible only through a telescope. **2** the Roman god of the sea. The Greeks called him Poseidon.

nep·tu·ni·um (nep tü′nē əm), *n.* a radioactive metallic element that occurs in tiny amounts in uranium ore. It is also obtained artificially from uranium that has absorbed neutrons. *Symbol:* Np

nerd (nėrd), *n.* SLANG. **1** a clumsy, unattractive person. **2** person who spends much time on an interest that allows little social contact: *a computer nerd.*

Ner·o (nir′ō), *n.* A.D. 37-68, Roman emperor from 54 to 68 A.D. He was noted for vice and tyranny.

Ner·u·da (nā rü′də), *n.* **Pab·lo** (pä′blō), 1904-1973, Chilean poet. He won the 1971 Nobel Prize for literature.

nerve (nėrv), **1** *n.* fiber or bundle of fibers that connects the brain or spinal cord with the other parts of the body. Nerves carry sensations and commands for action to and from the brain and spinal cord. **2** *n.* mental strength; courage: *Don't lose your nerve.* **3** *v.* to arouse strength or courage in: *The players nerved themselves for the big game.* **4** *n.* rude boldness; impudence. **5** *n.* pulp of a tooth. **6** *n.pl.* **nerves, a** nervousness. **b** attack of nervousness. ❑ *v.* **nerved, nerv·ing.**

get on someone's nerves, to annoy or irritate someone: *His whistling really gets on my nerves.*

strain every nerve, to use all your strength and energy in order to do something difficult.

nerve cell, 1 neuron. **2** the cell body of a neuron, without its fibers.

nerve fiber, any of the threadlike parts of a neuron; an axon or a dendrite.

nerve gas, any of several poisonous gases that attack the nervous system, causing weakness and death.

nerve impulse, series of chemical and electrical charges moving along and between nerve cells, carrying sensation or directing physical action.

nerve·less (nėrv′lis), *adj.* **1** without strength or vigor; feeble; weak. **2** not nervous; controlled; calm: *be nerveless before an examination.* —**nerve′less·ly,** *adv.* —**nerve′less·ness,** *n.*

nerve-rack·ing or **nerve-wrack·ing** (nėrv′rak′ing), *adj.* extremely irritating; causing great annoyance; very trying: *a nerve-racking commotion.*

nerv·ous (nėr′vəs), *adj.* **1** easily excited or upset; restless, uneasy, or timid: *Are you nervous about staying alone at night?* **2** having easily excited nerves; jumpy: *a nervous, impatient person.* **3** of or about the nerves: *a nervous disorder, nervous energy.* —**nerv′ous·ly,** *adv.* —**nerv′ous·ness,** *n.*

nervous system, system in a person or animal by which sensations are received and interpreted, and commands directing physical action are carried to muscles. The nervous system of animals with backbones includes the brain, spinal cord, and nerves, all formed of neurons.

nerv·y (nėr′vē), *adj.* **1** INFORMAL. rude and bold. **2** requiring courage or firmness. ❑ *adj.* **nerv·i·er, nerv·i·est.** —**nerv′i·ness,** *n.*

-ness, *suffix.* **1** quality of being ___: *preparedness = the quality of being prepared.* **2** ___ action; ___ behavior: *carefulness = careful action; careful behavior.*

nest (nest), **1** *n.* structure shaped something like a bowl, built by birds out of twigs, straw, mud, etc., as a place to lay their eggs and protect their young ones: *a robin's nest.* **2** *n.* structure or place used by insects, fishes, turtles, rabbits, etc., for a similar purpose. **3** *n.* the birds or animals living in a nest: *We found a nest of rabbits in our backyard.* **4** *n.* a snug resting place: *He cuddled down in the nest he'd made among the sofa cushions.* **5** *n.* a place that swarms, usually with something bad: *a nest of thieves.* **6** *v.* to make and use a nest: *The bluebirds are nesting here now.* **7** *v.* to settle or place in, or as if in, a nest. **8** *n.* a set or series of objects, from large to small, such that each fits within the next: *a nest of drinking cups.* —**nest′er,** *n.*

nest (def. 1)

feather your nest, to make yourself rich, especially at the expense of other people.

nest egg, something, usually a sum of money, saved up for future use.

nes·tle (nes′əl), *v.* **1** to settle yourself comfortably or cozily: *She nestled down into the big chair.* **2** to be settled comfortably or cozily; be sheltered: *The little house nestled among the trees.* **3** to press close in affection or for comfort: *nestle a baby in one's arms.* ❑ *v.* **nes·tled, nes·tling.** —**nes′tler,** *n.*

nest·ling (nest′ling), *n.* bird too young to leave the nest.

Nes·tor (nes′tər), *n.* (in Greek legends) the oldest and wisest of the Greeks at the siege of Troy.

a	hat	ė	term	ô	order	ch	child		
ā	age	i	it	oi	oil	ng	long		a in about
ä	far	ī	ice	ou	out	sh	she	ə	e in taken
â	care	o	hot	u	cup	th	thin		i in pencil
e	let	ō	open	ù	put	ŦH	then		o in lemon
ē	equal	ò	saw	ü	rule	zh	measure		u in circus

net¹ (net), **1** *n.* an open fabric made of string, cord, or thread, knotted together in such a way as to leave holes regularly arranged. **2** *n.* anything made of net. Nets are used to catch butterflies, birds, and fish, to keep your hair in place, and to separate opposing players in games such as tennis and volleyball. **3** *n.* a trap or snare: *caught in the net of their own lies.* **4** *n.* a ball that hits the net in tennis, volleyball, and other games played with a net. **5** *v.* to catch in a net: *net a fish.* **6** *v.* to cover, confine, or protect with a net. ❑ *v.* **net·ted, net·ting.** —**net′like′,** *adj.* —**net′ter,** *n.*

net² (net), **1** *adj.* remaining after deductions; free from deductions. A net gain or profit is the actual gain after all working expenses have been paid. The net weight of a glass jar of candy is the weight of the candy itself. The net price of a book is the real price, from which no discount can be made. **2** *n.* the net weight, profit, price, etc. **3** *v.* to gain: *The sale netted me a good profit.* ❑ *v.* **net·ted, net·ting.**

net³ (net), **the Net,** the Internet: *She spends hours surfing the Net.*

Neth., the Netherlands.

neth·er (neᴛʜ′ər), *adj.* lower.

Neth·er·lands (neᴛʜ′ər ləndz), *n.* **the,** country in NW Europe, west of Germany and north of Belgium; Holland. *Capitals:* Amsterdam and The Hague. —**Neth·er·land·er** (neᴛʜ′ər lan′dər *or* neᴛʜ′ər lən dər), *n.*

WORD STORY **Netherlands** is an English translation of a very similar Dutch word meaning "lowlands." The country is lower than the land around it—in fact, much of it is actually below sea level.

Netherlands Antilles, territory of the Netherlands consisting of five islands in the S Caribbean. *Capital:* Willemstad.

neth·er·most (neᴛʜ′ər mōst), *adj.* lowest.

net·ting (net′ing), *n.* **1** a netted or meshed material: *wire netting for window screens.* **2** process of making a net.

net·tle (net′l), **1** *n.* any of several plants with sharp hairs on the leaves and stems that sting the skin when touched. **2** *v.* to make angry; irritate; provoke; vex: *Their refusal to help nettled me.* ❑ *v.* **net·tled, net·tling.**

net·work (net′wėrk′), *n.* **1** any system of lines that cross: *a network of vines, a network of railroads.* **2** group of radio or TV stations that work together so that what is broadcast by one may be broadcast by all. **3** any group of people or things connected so that they can work together: *a network of computers.* **4** a netting; net.

net·work·ing (net′wėr′king), *n.* **1** process of developing and using personal contacts, recommendations, memberships, etc., to get a job, acceptance by a school, or other desirable goals. **2** process of linking computers in networks.

neur·al (nur′əl), *adj.* of or about a nerve, neuron, or nervous system. —**neu′ral·ly,** *adv.*

neu·ral·gia (nu̇ ral′jə), *n.* a sharp pain along the course of a nerve.

neu·ri·tis (nu̇ rī′tis), *n.* inflammation of a nerve or nerves.

neu·rol·o·gy (nu̇ rol′ə jē), *n.* study of the nervous system and its diseases. —**neu′ro·log′ical,** *adj.* —**neu·rol′o·gist,** *n.*

neur·on (nur′on), *n.* one of the cells forming the brain, spinal cord, and nerves; nerve cell. Neurons conduct nerve impulses. A neuron has a cell body, containing the nucleus, and usually several threadlike branching parts, including several shorter dendrites and a single longer axon.

neu·ro·sis (nu̇ rō′sis), *n.* any of various mental or emotional disorders, in which the symptoms are depression, anxiety, abnormal fears, compulsive behavior, etc. ❑ *n., pl.* **neu·ro·ses** (nu̇ rō′sēz′).

neu·ro·sur·geon (nur′ō sėr′jən), *n.* physician who specializes in neurosurgery.

neu·ro·sur·ger·y (nur′ō sėr′jər ē), *n.* surgery on the brain or other parts of the nervous system.

neu·rot·ic (nu̇ rot′ik), **1** *adj.* having or suffering from a neurosis. **2** *n.* someone having or suffering from a neurosis. —**neu·rot′·i·cal·ly,** *adv.*

neu·ter (nü′tər), **1** in grammar: **a** *adj.* neither masculine nor feminine. *It* is a neuter pronoun. **b** *n.* a neuter word or form. **c** *n.* the neuter gender. **2** *adj.* without sex organs or with sex organs that are not fully developed. Worker bees are neuter. **3** *n.* an animal or plant that is neuter. **4** *v.* to alter; sterilize.

neu·tral (nü′trəl), **1** *adj.* on neither side in a quarrel or war. **2** *n.* person or country not taking part in a quarrel or war. **3** *adj.* of or about such a country or area: *neutral territory.* **4** *adj.* neither one thing nor the other; indefinite. **5** *adj.* having little or no color: *White and gray are neutral colors.* **6** *adj.* (in chemistry) neither an acid nor a base. **7** *adj.* having neither a positive nor a negative electric charge. **8** *n.* position of gears when they do not transmit motion from the engine to the wheels or other working parts. —**neu′tral·ly,** *adv.*

neu·tral·i·ty (nü tral′ə tē), *n.* condition of being neutral; the attitude or policy of a nation that does not take part directly or indirectly in a war between other nations; neutral status.

neu·tral·ize (nü′trə līz), *v.* **1** to make neutral; keep war out of: *The city was neutralized so that peace talks could be held there.* **2** to make of no effect by some opposite force; counterbalance: *I neutralized the bright colors in my room by using a tan rug.* ❑ *v.* **neu·tral·ized, neu·tral·iz·ing.** —**neu′tral·i·za′tion,** *n.* —**neu′tral·iz′er,** *n.*

neutral vowel, schwa.

neu·tri·no (nü trē′nō), *n.* a subatomic particle having no electric charge and a mass equal or close to zero, produced in various radioactive decay events. ❑ *n., pl.* **neu·tri·nos.**

neu·tron (nü′tron), *n.* a subatomic particle that is neutral electrically and has about the same mass as a proton. Neutrons occur in the nucleus of every atom except hydrogen.

neutron star, a collapsed star with about the same mass as the sun, but measuring only a few miles across, in which extreme gravity has forced most of the electrons and protons together to form neutrons.

Nev., Nevada.

Ne·vad·a (nə vad′ə *or* nə vä′də), *n.* one of the western states of the United States. *Abbreviation:* NV or Nev. *Capital:* Carson City. [**Nevada** comes from a Spanish word meaning "snowy." The state has many snow-capped mountains.] —**Ne·vad′an,** *n.*

nev·er (nev′ər), *adv.* **1** not ever; at no time: *I have never been to New York.* **2** in no case; not at all: *He will be never the wiser.*

nev·er·more (nev′ər môr′), *adv.* never again.

nev·er·the·less (nev′ər ᴛʜə les′), *adv.* however; nonetheless; in spite of it: *She was very tired; nevertheless she kept on working.*

new (nü), **1** *adj.* never having existed before; just recently made, thought out, known or heard of, felt, or discovered: *a new invention, a new idea.* **2** *adj.* lately grown, come, or made; not old: *a new bud.* **3** *adj.* not used before; not worn or used up: *We bought some new furniture.* **4** *adj.* beginning again: *Sunrise marks a new day.* **5** *adj.* changed or renewed: *to go on with new courage.* **6** *adj.* not familiar: *She is new to the work.* **7** *adj.* later; modern; recent: *new dances.* **8** *adj.* having recently arrived in a new place or position: *a new arrival, a new president.* **9** *adj.* further; additional; more: *He sought new information on the subject.* **10** *adv.* newly; recently or lately; freshly: *new-fallen snow, a new-found friend.* ■ Other words that sound like this are **gnu** and **knew.** —**new′ness,** *n.*

WORD STORY **New words** and **new meanings** sometimes bother people, who criticize them and try to keep them from being used. If a word or meaning is useful enough, however, it becomes part of the language in spite of these efforts. Thirty years ago, many people disliked the use of *contact* as a verb. Now most people use the word that way. Other words that people objected to using, in certain ways or at all, include:

belittle	fix	lengthy	progress
clever	guess	locate	talkative
demoralize	intriguing		

New Age, 1 of or about a faith in a number of religious and spiritual traditions, often including reincarnation, the importance of the natural world, the powers of crystals, spiritualism, and beliefs taken from American Indian religions: *New Age healing.* **2** Also, **new age,** kind of music blending popular forms of jazz and quiet forms of rock in a mixture meant for easy listening, thought to encourage peace of mind.

New Amsterdam, name of New York City when it was a Dutch colonial town.

New·ark (nü′ərk *for 1;* nü′ärk *for 2*), *n.* **1** city in NE New Jersey, near New York City. **2** city in N Delaware.

new·born (nü′bôrn′), **1** *adj.* recently or only just born: *a newborn baby.* **2** *adj.* ready to start a new life; born again: *newborn hope.* **3** *n.* a newborn infant. ❑ *n., pl.* **new·born** or **new·borns.**

New Bruns·wick (brunz′wik), province in SE Canada. *Capital:* Fredericton. [New Brunswick comes from Brunswick, a region in Germany formerly ruled by the family that now rules the United Kingdom.] **—New Brunswicker.**

New Canadian, person who has recently arrived in Canada and plans to become, or has become, a citizen of Canada.

new·com·er (nü′kum′ər), *n.* person who has just come or who came not long ago.

New Deal, the policies and measures introduced by President Franklin D. Roosevelt in the 1930s as a means of improving the economic and social welfare of the United States.

New Del·hi (del′ē), capital of India, in the N part.

New Democratic Party, a political party in Canada.

New England, the NE part of the United States. Maine, New Hampshire, Vermont, Massachusetts, Rhode Island, and Connecticut are the New England states.

New Eng·land·er (ing′glən dər), someone born or living in New England.

new·fan·gled (nü′fang′gəld), *adj.* lately come into fashion; of a new kind: *a newfangled design.*

New·found·land (nü′fənd lənd *or* nü′found′land′), *n.* **1** large island in the Atlantic northeast of Nova Scotia. **2** province in E Canada that includes Newfoundland and Labrador. *Capital:* St. John's. **3** a very large, intelligent dog, shaggy and usually black, developed in Newfoundland. [Newfoundland comes from *new found land.* It was probably named by the explorer who first took news of it to England.]

New France, the territory in North America that belonged to France from 1609 to 1763.

New Frontier, the policies and measures introduced by President John F. Kennedy in the early 1960s.

New Guinea, large island north of Australia; Papua. The W part of New Guinea belongs to Indonesia. The E part is included in the country of Papua New Guinea. [New Guinea comes from Guinea, a country in Africa. To Spanish explorers, the two places and their inhabitants looked alike.]

New Hamp·shire (hamp′shər), one of the NE states of the United States. *Abbreviation:* NH or N.H. *Capital:* Concord. [New Hampshire comes from Hampshire, a county in England.] **—New Hampshirite.**

New Haven, port in S Connecticut, on Long Island Sound.

New Jersey, one of the NE states of the United States. *Abbreviation:* NJ or N.J. *Capital:* Trenton. [New Jersey comes from Jersey, an island near England.] **—New Jerseyite.**

new·ly (nü′lē), *adv.* **1** lately; recently: *newly discovered.* **2** once again; freshly: *a newly painted room.*

new·ly·wed (nü′lē wed′), *n.* someone who has recently married.

newlyweds

New·man (nü′mən), *n.* **Paul,** born 1925, American movie star. He won an Academy Award in 1986 for his role in the movie *The Color of Money.*

New Mexico, one of the SW states of the United States. *Abbreviation:* NM or N.Mex. *Capital:* Santa Fe. [New Mexico comes from Mexico. Spanish governors there sent explorers northward.] **—New Mexican.**

new moon, **1** moon when seen as a thin crescent with the hollow side on the left. **2** moon when its side toward the earth is dark, appearing almost invisible.

New Neth·er·land (neᴛн′ər lənd), former Dutch colony in America, from 1613 to 1664. England captured it in 1664 and divided it into the colonies of New York and New Jersey.

New Or·le·ans (ôr′lē ənz, ôr lēnz′, *or* ôr′lənz), port in SE Louisiana, near the mouth of the Mississippi River.

WORD STORY New Orleans comes from the title of the Duke of Orléans (ôr lā än′), brother of the king of France. The duke controlled France when the city was founded.

news (nüz), *n.* **1** information about something that has just happened or will soon happen: *The news that our teacher was leaving made us sad.* ■ See Synonym Study at **information.** **2** a report of a current happening or happenings in a newspaper, on TV, radio, etc. **3** newscast: *the 10 o'clock news.* **—news′less,** *adj.*

WORD BANK News has a large vocabulary of its own. If you want to know more about the news, you can start by looking up these words in this dictionary.

anchor	commentary	headline	Pulitzer Prize
announcer	correspondent	interview	reporter
banner	documentary	journalist	scoop
bulletin	edition	lead[1]	subhead
byline	editorial	media	syndicate
columnist	fourth estate	newscast	tabloid

news·boy (nüz′boi′), *n.* boy who delivers or sells newspapers; paperboy.

news·cast (nüz′kast′), *n.* a TV or radio broadcast devoted to current events and news bulletins.

news·cast·er (nüz′kas′tər), *n.* **1** someone who reports or reads the news on a newscast. **2** commentator on the news.

news·deal·er (nüz′dē′lər), *n.* seller of newspapers and magazines.

news·girl (nüz′gėrl′), *n.* girl who delivers or sells newspapers; papergirl.

news·let·ter (nüz′let′ər), *n.* letter or report giving informal or confidential news. Organizations often issue newsletters to members or subscribers.

New South Wales, state in SE Australia. *Capital:* Sydney.

New Spain, a former Spanish governmental division including all Spanish territory in North and Central America, the Caribbean, and the Philippines. Created in 1535, it ceased to exist in 1821.

news·pa·per (nüz′pā′pər), *n.* a daily or weekly publication printed on large sheets of paper folded together, telling the news, carrying advertisements, and having stories, pictures, articles, and useful information.

news·pa·per·man (nüz′pā′pər man′), *n.* a reporter, editor, or other person who works for a newspaper. ❑ *n., pl.* **news·pa·per·men.**

news·pa·per·wom·an (nüz′pā′pər wùm′ən), *n.* a woman working for a newspaper as a reporter, editor, etc. ❑ *n., pl.* **news·pa·per·wom·en.**

news·print (nüz′print′), *n.* a soft, cheap paper made from wood pulp, on which newspapers are usually printed.

news·room (nüz′rüm′), *n.* a newspaper, radio, or TV office in which news is prepared for publication or broadcast.

news·stand (nüz′stand′), *n.* place where newspapers and magazines are sold.

a	hat	ė	term	ô	order	ch	child		⟨ a in about
ā	age	i	it	oi	oil	ng	long		e in taken
ä	far	ī	ice	ou	out	sh	she	ə	i in pencil
â	care	o	hot	u	cup	th	thin		o in lemon
e	let	ō	open	ù	put	ᴛн	then		u in circus
ē	equal	ò	saw	ü	rule	zh	measure		

New Sweden, a Swedish colony in North America from 1638 to 1655, including parts of present-day Pennsylvania, New Jersey, and Delaware. It was taken over by the Dutch in 1655.

news·wor·thy (nüz′wėr′тнē), *adj.* having enough public interest to be printed in a newspaper. —**news′wor′thi·ness,** *n.*

news·y (nü′zē), *adj.* INFORMAL. full of news: *a newsy letter.* ❏ *adj.* **news·i·er, news·i·est.** —**news′i·ness,** *n.*

newt (nüt), *n.* any of several small, slimy, poisonous salamanders that breed in water.

newt—about 4 in. (10 cm) long

New Testament, the later part of the Bible, which contains the life and teachings of Jesus recorded by His followers, together with their own experiences and teachings.

new·ton (nüt′n), *n.* unit for measuring force, used in the metric system. It is the amount of force required to give a mass of one kilogram an acceleration of one meter per second per second.

New·ton (nüt′n), *n.* Sir **Isaac,** 1642-1727, English scientist and mathematician who discovered the law of gravitation. —**New·to·ni·an** (nü tō′nē ən), *adj.*

New World, the Western Hemisphere; North America and South America. Until 1492, the Western Hemisphere was unknown to Europeans. It was a "new world" to the explorers who reached its shores.

new-world or **New-World** (nü′wėrld′), *adj.* of the Western Hemisphere; not of the Old World: *new-world monkeys.*

New Year or **New Year's,** January 1; the first day or days of the year.

New Year's Day, January 1, usually observed as a legal holiday.

New Year's Eve, the eve of New Year's Day; December 31. New Year's Eve is often celebrated with parties and public festivities.

New York, 1 Often, **New York State,** one of the NE states of the United States. *Abbreviation:* NY or N.Y. *Capital:* Albany. 2 Often, **New York City,** port in SE New York State, at the mouth of the Hudson River. It is the largest city in the United States. [**New York** comes from the title of the Duke of York. His brother, King Charles II of England, granted him this region.]

New York·er (yôr′kər), person born or living in New York City or New York State.

New Zea·land (zē′lənd), country in the S Pacific, consisting of North Island, South Island, and other small islands. *Capital:* Wellington. —**New Zealander.**

WORD STORY **New Zealand** comes from the name of a region in the Netherlands. Its name means "sea land." Dutch explorers were the first Europeans here.

next (nekst), 1 *adj.* following at once; nearest: *The telephone is in the next room.* 2 *adv.* the first time after this: *When you next come, bring it.* 3 *adv.* in the place or time or position that is nearest: *Your name comes next on the list.* 4 *prep.* nearest to: *the house next the church.*

next to, 1 nearest to. 2 almost; nearly.

next door, 1 in or at the next house, apartment, etc.: *They live next door.* 2 very close: *Her requests are next door to commands.*

next-door (nekst′dôr′), *adj.* in or at the next house: *my next-door neighbor.*

next of kin, the nearest relative or relatives: *The form asked us to list our next of kin.*

Nez Perce or **Nez Percé** (nez′ pėrs′), member of a North American Indian tribe living in Idaho, Oregon, and Washington. ❏ *n., pl.* **Nez Perce, Nez Perc·es, Nez Percé,** or **Nez Perc·és.**

WORD STORY **Nez Perce** comes from French words meaning "pierced nose." In fact, few of the Nez Perce people wore ornaments in their noses. A French interpreter happened to meet some who did.

Nfld., Newfoundland.

N.G., National Guard.

NH, New Hampshire (used with postal Zip Code).

N.H., New Hampshire.

Ni, symbol for nickel.

ni·a·cin (nī′ə sən), *n.* nicotinic acid.

Ni·ag·a·ra (nī ag′rə), *n.* 1 short river flowing from Lake Erie into Lake Ontario over Niagara Falls. 2 Niagara Falls. [**Niagara** comes from an Iroquois word meaning "a neck." It was the name of the thin strip of land between Lakes Erie and Ontario.]

Niagara Falls, great waterfall of the Niagara River, on the boundary between the United States and Canada.

Niagara Falls

Nia·mey (nyä′mā), *n.* capital of Niger, in the SW part.

nib (nib), *n.* 1 point of a pen. 2 point or tip of anything. —**nib′like′,** *adj.*

nib·ble (nib′əl), 1 *v.* to eat away with quick, small bites, as a rabbit or mouse does. 2 *v.* to bite gently or lightly: *A small fish nibbled at the bait.* 3 *n.* act of nibbling; small bite. ❏ *v.* **nib·bled, nib·bling.** —**nib′bler,** *n.*

Nic·a·ra·gua (nik′ə rä′gwə), *n.* country in Central America, north of Costa Rica. *Capital:* Managua. [**Nicaragua** comes from the name of a ruler of people living there at the time the Spanish invaded. He assisted Spanish conquerors, who called it "Nicaragua's land."] —**Nic·a·ra′guan,** *adj., n.*

nice (nīs), *adj.* 1 good or pleasing; agreeable; satisfactory: *a nice ride, a nice day.* 2 thoughtful or kind: *He was nice to us.* 3 delicately skillful; requiring care, skill, or tact: *a nice try, a nice shot.* 4 refined; cultured: *nice manners.* 5 making very fine distinctions; exact; precise: *a nice ear for music.* 6 very fine; minute; subtle: *a nice distinction, a nice shade of meaning.* ❏ *adj.* **nic·er, nic·est.** ■ Another word that sounds like this is **gneiss.** —**nice′ly,** *adv.* —**nice′ness,** *n.*

nice and, pleasantly: *The cabin was nice and cozy.*

WORD STORY **Nice** comes from a Latin word meaning "ignorant." When it came into English, it meant "stupid." What happened? Caring about little things may show a lack of intelligence, but it can also show carefulness. Something that people have been careful about is often quite pleasant. So the idea of caring about very small differences (def. 6) connected the old meaning of **nice** to the one we use now.

Nice (nēs), *n.* resort city in SE France, on the Mediterranean.

ni·ce·ty (nī′sə tē), *n.* 1 exactness; accuracy; delicacy: *The dental surgery was performed with great nicety.* 2 a fine point; small distinction; detail: *I play tennis but have not mastered its niceties.* 3 something elegant or refined. ❏ *n., pl.* **ni·ce·ties** for 2,3.

niche (nich), *n.* 1 a hollow place made in a wall for a statue, vase, etc., to stand. 2 a suitable place or position; place for which a person is suited: *I found my niche in the drama club.* 3 of or about a market for specific product, or a specific kind of consumer: *This niche publishing company targets their magazine to disabled people making more than $50,000 a year.* 4 (in biology) a usual way of life of a particular species or living thing in an environment or community: *The cat's original niche was as a predator of small animals.*

Nicholas II (nik′ə ləs), 1868-1918, the last czar of Russia, from 1894 to 1917. He and his family were executed during the Russian Revolution.

nick (nik), **1** *n.* place where a small bit has been cut or broken out; notch; groove: *She cut nicks in a stick to keep score.* **2** *v.* to make a nick or nicks in.

in the nick of time, just in time.

nick·el (nik′əl), *n.* **1** a coin of the United States and Canada worth five cents. **2** a hard, silvery white metallic element found in igneous rocks. It is used in electroplating and is mixed with other metals to make alloys. Nickel and copper are used to make five-cent coins. *Symbol:* Ni

nickel-cadmium battery (nik′əl kad′mē əm), a kind of battery made of nickel and cadmium, able to be recharged with electricity, after its energy is gone, by running an electric current through it.

nick·el·o·de·on (nik′ə lō′dē ən), *n.* **1** former movie theater with an admission of only five cents. **2** a former jukebox that played records for only five cents.

nickel silver, a white alloy of copper, zinc, and nickel, used for ornaments, utensils, wire, etc.

nick·er (nik′ər), **1** *v.* to neigh: *The horse nickered when it saw my armful of hay.* **2** *n.* a neigh: *When I heard a nicker, I knew a horse must be nearby.*

Nick·laus (nik′ləs), *n.* **Jack** (jak), born 1940, American golfer. He was the first to win all of golf's major tournaments twice.

nick·nack (nik′nak′), *n.* knickknack.

nick·name (nik′nām′), **1** *n.* name added to someone's real name or used instead of it: *"Ed" is a nickname for "Edward." Roy's nickname was "Buzz."* **2** *v.* to give a nickname to: *They nicknamed the redheaded girl "Rusty."* □ *v.* **nick·named, nick·nam·ing.**

Nic·o·si·a (nik′ə sē′ə), *n.* capital of Cyprus, in the N central part.

nic·o·tine (nik′ə tēn′), *n.* poison contained in the leaves, roots, and seeds of tobacco. —**nic′o·tine′less,** *adj.*

nic·o·tin·ic acid (nik′ə tin′ik), a vitamin of the vitamin B complex, found especially in lean meat, yeast, liver, and wheat germ; niacin. It is used to treat and prevent pellagra.

niece (nēs), *n.* daughter of your brother or sister; daughter of your brother-in-law or sister-in-law.

Nietz·sche (nē′chə), *n.* **Fried·rich** (frē′drik), 1844-1900, Swiss philosopher, born in Germany. ■ **Nietzsche** believed that people's behavior is based on desire for power, both over others and over their own emotions.

nif·ty (nif′tē), *adj.* INFORMAL. attractive or stylish. □ *adj.* **nif·ti·er, nif·ti·est.** —**nif′ti·ly,** *adv.* —**nif′ti·ness,** *n.*

Ni·ger (nī′jər), *n.* **1** country in W Africa north of Nigeria. *Capital:* Niamey. **2** river in W Africa, flowing S through Nigeria into the Atlantic.

Ni·ger·i·a (nī jir′ē ə), *n.* country in W Africa. *Capital:* Abuja. —**Ni·ger′i·an,** *adj., n.*

nigh (nī), **1** *adj., adv., prep.* near. **2** *adv.* nearly.

night (nīt), **1** *n.* the time between evening and morning; the time from sunset to sunrise, especially when it is dark. **2** *n.* the darkness of night; the dark. **3** *n.* sadness of the mind, spirit, or emotions: *"the deep, dark night of the soul."* **4** *n.* evening; nightfall: *The fireworks will begin as soon as it is night.* **5** *adj.* of, for, or at night. ■ Another word that sounds like this is **knight.**

night blindness, condition in which a person cannot see or cannot see well at night or in a dim light.

night·cap (nīt′kap′), *n.* **1** (earlier) a cap to be worn in bed. **2** drink taken just before going to bed.

night·clothes (nīt′klōz′), *n.pl.* clothes worn for sleeping.

night·club (nīt′klub′), *n.* place for dancing, eating, and entertainment, open only at night.

night crawler, any of various large earthworms that come to the surface of the ground at night.

night·dress (nīt′dres′), *n.* nightgown. □ *n., pl.* **night·dress·es.**

night·fall (nīt′fôl′), *n.* the coming of night; dusk.

night·gown (nīt′goun′), *n.* a long, loose garment worn by a woman or child in bed.

night·hawk (nīt′hôk′), *n.* **1** any of several American birds related to the whippoorwill that hunt insects in the air after dark. They are not hawks. **2** person who often stays up late; night owl.

night·ie (nī′tē), *n.* INFORMAL. nightgown or nightshirt. Also, **nighty.**

night·in·gale (nīt′n gāl), *n.* a small, reddish brown European bird. The male sings sweetly at night as well as in the daytime.

WORD STORY **Nightingale** comes from old English words meaning "to sing" and "night." The male nightingale sings night and day, but because few birds sing at night, its beautiful song can be heard clearly then.

Night·in·gale (nīt′n gāl), *n.* **Flor·ence** (flor′əns), 1820-1910, English nurse who brought about great improvements in nursing, especially military nursing.

night-light (nīt′līt), *n.* a small light to be kept burning all night.

night-long (nīt′lông′), **1** *adj.* lasting all night. **2** *adv.* through the whole night.

night·ly (nīt′lē), **1** *adj.* done, happening, or appearing every night: *the nightly news on TV.* **2** *adv.* every night: *Performances are given nightly except on Sunday.* **3** *adj.* done, happening, or appearing at night: *nightly dew.* **4** *adv.* at night; by night: *Many animals come out only nightly.*

night·mare (nīt′mâr′), *n.* **1** a terrible dream: *I had a nightmare about falling off a high building.* **2** a terrible experience: *The hurricane was a nightmare.*

WORD STORY **Nightmare** does not come from a horse. It comes from an old English word meaning "night goblin." People gradually stopped believing in goblins, but they kept having nightmares. Sometimes they made up stories about "riding the nightmare" to explain the word to themselves.

night·mar·ish (nīt′mâr′ish), *adj.* like a nightmare; causing fear or anxiety; very distressing: *a nightmarish experience.* —**night′-mar′ish·ly,** *adv.* —**night′mar′ish·ness,** *n.*

night owl, person who often stays up late.

night school, school held in the evening for people who work during the day.

night·shade (nīt′shād′), *n.* any of many plants including potatoes, tomatoes, and other vegetables, but also including many poisonous plants. The **black nightshade** has white flowers and black berries. Belladonna, or the deadly nightshade, has red flowers and black berries.

night·shirt (nīt′shėrt′), *n.* a long, loose shirt worn by someone in bed.

night·stick (nīt′stik′), *n.* a police officer's club; billyclub.

night·time (nīt′tīm′), *n.* time between evening and morning.

night watch, 1 watch or guard kept during the night. **2** person or persons keeping such a watch. —**night watchman.**

night·y (nī′tē), *n.* nightie. □ *n., pl.* **night·ies.**

nil (nil), *n.* nothing; zero.

Nile (nīl), *n.* river in E Africa flowing north from Lake Victoria through Uganda, Sudan, and Egypt into the Mediterranean Sea. South of Khartoum, the Nile divides into the **White Nile** and the **Blue Nile.** The Nile is the longest river in the world.

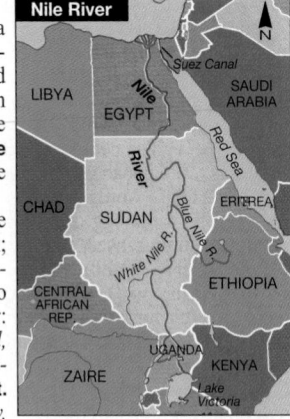

Nile River

nim·ble (nim′bəl), *adj.* **1** active and surefooted; light and quick; agile: *Goats are nimble in climbing among the rocks.* **2** quick to understand and to reply; clever: *The student had a nimble mind, and could quickly solve problems.* □ *adj.* **nim·bler, nim·blest.** —**nim′ble·ness,** *n.* —**nim′bly,** *adv.*

a	hat	ė	term	ô	order	ch	child		
ā	age	i	it	oi	oil	ng	long		a in about
ä	far	ī	ice	ou	out	sh	she		e in taken
â	care	o	hot	u	cup	th	thin	ə	i in pencil
e	let	ō	open	ù	put	ᵀH	then		o in lemon
ē	equal	ô	saw	ü	rule	zh	measure		u in circus

nim·bo·stra·tus (nim′bō strā′təs), *n.* a low, dark gray layer of cloud that usually produces long periods of rain or snow; nimbus. ❑ *n., pl.* **nim·bo·stra·ti** (nim′bō strā′tī).

nim·bus (nim′bəs), *n.* **1** nimbostratus. **2** a bright cloud surrounding a god or a representation of a god, person, or thing. **3** halo. ❑ *n., pl.* **nim·bus·es, nim·bi** (nim′bī).

Nim·rod (nim′rod), *n.* (in the Bible) a great hunter.

nin·com·poop (nin′kəm püp), *n.* a silly person.

nine (nīn), **1** *adj., n.* one more than eight; 9. **2** *n.* set of nine persons or things: *a baseball nine.*

nine·pins (nīn′pinz′), *n.* game in which nine large wooden pins are set up to be bowled over with a ball.

nine·teen (nīn′tēn′), *n., adj.* nine more than ten; 19.

nine·teenth (nīn′tēnth′), *adj., n.* **1** next after the 18th; last in a series of 19. **2** one of 19 equal parts.

nine·ti·eth (nīn′tē ith), **1** *adj., n.* next after the 89th; last in a series of 90. **2** *n.* one of 90 equal parts.

nine·ty (nīn′tē), *adj., n.* nine times ten; 90. ❑ *n., pl.* **nine·ties.**

Nin·e·veh (nin′ə və), *n.* capital of ancient Assyria. Its ruins are on the Tigris River. See **Assyria** for map.

nin·ja (nin′jə), *n.* **1** someone trained in martial arts developed by a group active in Japan hundreds of years ago. **2** member of that group, hired as a spy or assassin. ❑ *n., pl.* **nin·ja** or **nin·jas.**

nin·ny (nin′ē), *n.* a silly person. ❑ *n., pl.* **nin·nies.**

ninth (nīnth), **1** *adj., n.* next after the eighth; last in a series of nine. **2** *n.* one of nine equal parts.

ni·o·bi·um (nī ō′bē əm), *n.* a soft, steel-gray metallic element that is found in nature with tantalum. It is used in stainless steel and in other alloys. *Symbol:* Nb

nip[1] (nip), **1** *v.* to squeeze tight and suddenly; pinch; bite: *The crab nipped my toe.* **2** *n.* a tight squeeze; pinch; sudden bite. **3** *v.* to take off by biting, pinching, or snipping: *nip twigs from a bush.* **4** *v.* to hurt at the tips; spoil; injure: *Some of our tomato plants were nipped by frost.* **5** *v.* to have a sharp, biting effect on: *A cold wind nipped our ears.* **6** *n.* sharp cold; chill: *There is a nip in the air on a frosty morning.* ❑ *v.* **nipped, nip·ping.**

nip and tuck, so close in a race or contest that you can't tell who will win; neck and neck.

nip[2] (nip), *n.* a small drink.

nip·per (nip′ər), *n.* **1** someone or something that nips. **2** a big claw of a lobster or crab. **3** nippers, *pl.* pincers, forceps, pliers, or any tool that nips.

nip·ple (nip′əl), *n.* **1** a roundish tip on the front of the breast, slightly darker than the surrounding skin. Infants and baby animals suck milk from the female nipple. **2** the rubber cap or mouthpiece of a baby's bottle, through which the baby gets milk and other liquids. **3** anything shaped or used like a nipple.

Nip·pon (ni pon′), *n.* OLD USE. Japanese name for **Japan.**

nip·py (nip′ē), *adj.* **1** very chilly; biting; *a nippy wind.* **2** sharp; pungent: *nippy cheese.* ❑ *adj.* **nip·pi·er, nip·pi·est.**

nir·va·na or **Nir·va·na** (nir vä′nə), *n.* **1** the Buddhist idea of heavenly peace; condition in which the soul is free from all desire and pain. **2** any condition like this; blessed oblivion. ❑ *n., pl.* **nir·va·nas** or **Nir·va·nas** for 2.

Ni·sei (nē′sā′), *n.* person born in the United States or Canada whose parents were Japanese immigrants. ❑ *n., pl.* **Ni·sei.** [Nisei comes from Japanese words meaning "second" and "generation."]

nit (nit), *n.* **1** the egg of a louse or similar insect. **2** a very young louse or similar insect. ■ Another word that sounds like this is **knit.**

ni·ter (nī′tər), *n.* saltpeter.

nit-pick (nit′pik′), *v.* to correct something in a petty or trivial way; search for small, unimportant faults.

ni·trate (nī′trāt), *n.* **1** any salt of nitric acid. **2** potassium nitrate or sodium nitrate when used as fertilizers.

ni·tric (nī′trik), *adj.* of or containing nitrogen.

nitric acid, a clear, colorless liquid that eats into flesh, clothing, metal, and other substances. It is used in etching and metallurgy and in making dyes and explosives.

ni·tro·gen (nī′trə jən), *n.* a colorless, odorless, tasteless gas which forms about four fifths of the atmosphere. It is a necessary part of all animal and vegetable tissues. *Symbol:* N

nitrogen cycle, the process in which nitrogen and its compounds are transformed by living things in nature. Nitrogen in the air passes into the soil, where it is changed into nitrates by bacteria and used by green plants. Then the plants are eaten by animals. Decaying plants and animals, and animal waste products, are then broken down by bacteria, and the nitrogen in them passes into the air or soil again.

nitrogen cycle

nitrogen-fixing bacteria, bacteria in the soil or on the roots of some plants, able to change nitrogen from the air into ammonia and other compounds that can be used by plants to form proteins.

ni·trog·e·nous (nī troj′ə nəs), *adj.* containing nitrogen.

ni·tro·glyc·er·in or **ni·tro·glyc·er·ine** (nī′trə glis′ər ən), *n.* an oily, pale yellow, explosive liquid made by treating glycerin with nitric and sulfuric acids. Nitroglycerin is used in making dynamite and in medicine.

ni·trous (nī′trəs), *adj.* of or containing nitrogen.

nitrous acid, a weak acid that changes readily into other chemical compounds.

nitrous oxide, a colorless gas that causes laughing and dulls pain; laughing gas. It is sometimes used as an anesthetic.

nit·ty-grit·ty (nit′ē grit′ē), *n.* INFORMAL. the basic or fundamental facts: *Let's forget that and focus on the nitty-gritty of the problem.*

nit·wit (nit′wit′), *n.* a very stupid person.

nix (niks), *v.* to put a stop to; disapprove of; deny: *His parents nixed his plan to take skydiving lessons.*

Nix·on (nik′sən), *n.* Richard Mil·hous (mil′hous), 1913-1994, the 37th president of the United States, from 1969 to 1974, vice-president from 1953 to 1961. He was the first president to resign from office.

NJ, New Jersey (used with postal Zip Code).

N.J., New Jersey.

NM, New Mexico (used with postal Zip Code).

N.M. or **N.Mex.,** New Mexico.

no (nō), **1** *adv.* word used to indicate that you can't or won't, or that something is wrong; word used to deny, refuse, or disagree: *Will you come? No.* **2** *adv.* not in any degree; not at all: *He is no better.* **3** *adj.* not any; not a: *They have no friends.* **4** *n.* denial; refusal. **5** *n.* a vote against; person voting against: *The noes won.* ❑ *n., pl.* **noes.** ■ Another word that sounds like this is **know.**

No, symbol for nobelium.

no. or **No.,** number.

No·ah (nō′ə), *n.* (in the Bible) a man whom God told to make an ark to save himself, his family, and a pair of each kind of animal from the Flood. [Noah comes from a Hebrew word meaning "rest."]

No·bel (nō bel′), *n.* Alfred Bern·hard (bèrn′härd), 1833-1896, Swedish inventor of dynamite and manufacturer of explosives. He left his fortune to create the Nobel prizes.

no·be·li·um (nō bē′lē əm), *n.* a radioactive chemical element produced artificially in curium that absorbs carbon ions. *Symbol:* No

Nobel Prize, any of five money prizes established by Alfred B. Nobel to be given annually to those persons or organizations who have done outstanding work in physics, chemistry, medicine or physiology, literature, and the promotion of peace. A sixth category, economics, was added in 1969.

no·bil·i·ty (nō bil′ə tē), *n.* **1** people of noble rank, title, or birth. Earls, counts, countesses, and marquises belong to the nobility. **2** noble character: *the nobility of a great deed.*

no·ble (nō′bəl), **1** *adj.* high and great in character; showing greatness of mind; good: *a noble person, a noble deed.* **2** *adj.* excellent; fine; splendid; magnificent: *Niagara Falls is a noble sight.* **3** *adj.* high and great by birth, rank, or title: *a noble family.* **4** *n.* person high and great by birth, rank, or title. □ *adj.* **no·bler, no·blest.** —**no′ble·ness,** *n.* —**no′bly,** *adv.*

no·ble·man (nō′bəl mən), *n.* man of noble rank, title, or birth. □ *n., pl.* **no·ble·men.**

no·ble·wom·an (nō′bəl wum′ən), *n.* woman of noble rank, title, or birth. □ *n., pl.* **no·ble·wom·en.**

no·bod·y (nō′bod′ē), **1** *pron.* no one; no person: *Nobody would help me.* **2** *n.* someone of no importance: *I was ignored and made to feel like a nobody.* □ *n., pl.* **no·bod·ies** for 2.

no-brain·er (nō′brā′nər), *n.* SLANG. problem or question that requires little or no thought: *Deciding to help was a no-brainer.*

noc·tur·nal (nok tėr′nl), *adj.* **1** of or about the night: *Stars are a nocturnal sight.* **2** in the night: *a nocturnal visitor.* **3** active in the night: *The owl is a nocturnal bird.* **4** closed by day, open by night: *a nocturnal flower.* —**noc·tur′nal·ly,** *adv.*

noc·turne (nok′tėrn′), *n.* **1** a dreamy or pensive musical piece. **2** a painting of a night scene.

nod (nod), **1** *v.* to bow the head slightly and raise it again quickly. **2** *v.* to express by nodding: *I quietly nodded my approval.* **3** *n.* act of nodding the head: *She gave us a nod as she passed.* **4** *v.* to let the head fall forward when sleepy or falling asleep. **5** *v.* to be sleepy; become careless and dull. **6** *v.* to droop or sway back and forth: *Trees nod in the wind.* □ *v.* **nod·ded, nod·ding.** —**nod′der,** *n.*

node (nōd), *n.* **1** a knot, knob, or swelling. **2** a joint on a stem where a leaf or leaves grow out. —**nod′al,** *adj.*

nod·u·lar (noj′ə lər), *adj.* having nodules.

nod·ule (noj′ül), *n.* **1** a small knot, knob, or swelling. **2** a small rounded mass or lump: *nodules of pure gold.*

No·el or **No·ël** (nō el′), *n.* **1** Christmas. **2** noel or noël, a Christmas song; carol. □ *n., pl.* **no·els** or **no·ëls** for 2. [Noel comes from a Latin word meaning "to be born." It has often been used as a name for boys and girls born on Christmas Day.]

no-fault (nō′fôlt′), *adj.* **1** covering a policy-holder involved in a motor vehicle accident, no matter who is at fault: *no-fault auto insurance.* **2** with no accusations and no blame: *no-fault divorce.*

nog·gin (nog′ən), *n.* **1** a small cup or mug. **2** a small drink; ¼ pint. **3** INFORMAL. a person's head.

no-good (nō′gud′), **1** *n.* a worthless or evil person. **2** *adj.* not good for anything; worthless: *a no-good villain.*

no-hit·ter (nō′hit′ər), *n.* a baseball game in which a pitcher gives up no base hits to the opposing team.

noise (noiz), **1** *n.* a sound that is not musical or pleasant; loud or harsh sound: *The noise of traffic kept me awake.* **2** *n.* any sound: *the noise of rain on the roof.* **3** *n.* loud sounds of voices and movements; shouting; outcry; clamor: *They made so much noise that they were asked to leave the theater.* **4** *n.* any disturbance in a signal, such as interference in a radio or TV broadcast. **5** *v.* to spread the news of; tell: *It was noised abroad that the prime minister was ill.* □ *v.* **noised, nois·ing.** [See Word Story at **nausea.**]

SYNONYM STUDY **Noise, racket**[1], and **clatter** all mean an unpleasant sound. **Noise** is a general word: *The car alarm makes an awful noise.* **Racket** means a banging noise: *The workers tearing up the street made quite a racket.* **Clatter** means a noise of things hitting each other: *Can't you wash the pots without all that clatter?*

noise·less (noiz′lis), *adj.* making no noise; making little noise. —**noise′less·ly,** *adv.* —**noise′less·ness,** *n.*

noise·mak·er (noiz′mā′kər), *n.* **1** someone who makes too much noise. **2** something that makes noise, especially a horn, rattle, etc., used to make noise at a party.

nois·y (noi′zē), *adj.* **1** making much noise: *a noisy crowd, a noisy machine.* **2** full of noise: *a noisy street, the noisy city.* **3** having much noise with it: *a noisy quarrel.* ■ See Synonym Study at **loud.** □ *adj.* **nois·i·er, nois·i·est.** —**nois′i·ly,** *adv.* —**nois′i·ness,** *n.*

noisemakers (def. 2)

no·mad (nō′mad), *n.* **1** member of a tribe which moves from place to place to have food or pasture for its herds. **2** wanderer.

no·mad·ic (nō mad′ik), *adj.* of nomads or their life; wandering; roving: *Nomadic people often live in tents.* —**no·mad′i·cal·ly,** *adv.*

no man's land, 1 the land between opposing lines of trenches in warfare. **2** tract of land to which no one has a valid claim. **3** activity over which no jurisdiction or authority exists.

nom de plume (nom′ də plüm′), a pen name.

Nome (nōm), *n.* port and mining town in W Alaska, on the Bering Sea. [**Nome** comes from a mistake. On an early map of the region, someone wrote "Name?" near this port. Someone else copied the map and wrote "Nome." And so it stayed.]

no·men·cla·ture (nō′mən klā′chər), *n.* set or system of names or terms: *the nomenclature of music.*

nom·i·nal (nom′ə nəl), *adj.* **1** existing in name only; not real: *The president is the nominal head of our club, but the secretary really runs things.* **2** too small to be considered: *We paid our friend a nominal rent for the cottage—$25 a month.* —**nom′i·nal·ly,** *adv.*

nom·i·nate (nom′ə nāt), *v.* **1** to name as candidate for an office; designate: *William Jennings Bryan was nominated three times for President, but he was never elected.* **2** to appoint to an office or duty: *In 1933 Roosevelt nominated the first woman cabinet member in U.S. history.* □ *v.* **nom·i·nat·ed, nom·i·nat·ing.** —**nom′i·na·tor,** *n.*

nom·i·na·tion (nom′ə nā′shən), *n.* **1** act of naming a candidate for office: *a meeting for nomination of new club officers.* **2** a name of a person who has been nominated: *, The nominations for president of the club were written on the blackboard.* **2** selection for office or duty; appointment to office or duty: *Her nomination as Ambassador to France was approved by the Senate.* **3** condition of being nominated: *Her friends were pleased by her nomination.*

nom·i·na·tive (nom′ə na tiv), **1** *adj.* showing the subject of a verb or the words agreeing with the subject. *I, he, she, we,* and *they* are in the nominative case. **2** *n.* the nominative case. **3** *n.* a word in that case. *Who* and *I* are nominatives. —**nom′i·na·tive·ly,** *adv.*

nom·i·nee (nom′ə nē′), *n.* person nominated for an office or to be a candidate for election to an office. □ *n., pl.* **nom·i·nees.**

non-[1], *prefix.* not; not a; lack of: *nonessential = not essential; nonresident = not a resident; nonconformity = lack of conformity.* ■ **Non-** is such a useful prefix that it gets added to many words, with a hyphen or without one, whichever way seems easier to read. For more about **non-**, see the Word Power at **negative.**

non-[2], *prefix.* nine: *nonagon = nine-sided shape.*

non·ag·gres·sion (non′ə gresh′ən), *n.* the practice of refraining from aggression: *A pact of nonaggression was signed by the two nations.*

non·a·gon (non′ə gon), *n.* a plane figure having nine angles and nine sides.

non·al·co·hol·ic (non′al kə hò′lik), *adj.* containing no alcohol: *a nonalcoholic drink.*

non·a·ligned (non′ə lind′), *adj.* not taking sides politically; neutral: *nonaligned nations.* Also, **unaligned.**

non·break·a·ble (non brā′kə bəl), *adj.* not breakable.

nonce (nons), *n.* **for the nonce,** for the present time or occasion.

a	hat	ė	term	ô	order	ch	child		
ā	age	i	it	oi	oil	ng	long		a in about
ä	far	ī	ice	ou	out	sh	she		e in taken
â	care	o	hot	u	cup	th	thin	ə	i in pencil
e	let	ō	open	ù	put	ŦH	then		o in lemon
ē	equal	ò	saw	ü	rule	zh	measure		u in circus

nonce word, word formed or used for a single occasion. "Three-peat" is a nonce word used when a team may win a third championship in a row.

non·cha·lance (non′shə ləns *or* non′shə läns′), *n.* calmness; cool unconcern; indifference: *She received the prize with pretended nonchalance.*

non·cha·lant (non′shə lənt *or* non′shə länt′), *adj.* calm; without enthusiasm; coolly unconcerned; indifferent. [Nonchalant comes from Latin words meaning "not" and "warm." Or as we say in English, cool.] —**non′cha·lant·ly,** *adv.*

non·cir·cu·lat·ing (non′sėr′kyə lā ting), *adj.* not circulating.

non·com (non′kom′), *n.* INFORMAL. a noncommissioned officer.

non·com·bat·ant (non′kəm bat′nt *or* non kom′bə tənt), **1** *n.* someone in the armed forces who takes no part in combat. Surgeons, nurses, chaplains, etc., are noncombatants. **2** *adj.* not fighting; having civilian status in wartime.

non·com·mer·cial (non′kə mėr′shəl), *adj.* not commercial.

non·com·mis·sioned officer (non′kə mish′ənd), officer in the armed forces who does not hold a commission or a warrant, especially one with the rank of corporal, sergeant, or petty officer.

non·com·mit·tal (non′kə mit′l), *adj.* not committing yourself; not saying yes or no: *"I will think it over" is a noncommittal answer.* —**non′com·mit′tal·ly,** *adv.*

non·com·mu·ni·ca·ble disease (non′kə myü′nə kə bəl), disease that cannot be spread from one person to another; disease that is not contagious.

non·com·pli·ance (non′kəm pli′əns), *n.* fact of not complying; failure to comply: *noncompliance with a court order.*

non·con·duc·tor (non′kən duk′tər), *n.* any substance that does not readily conduct heat, electricity, or sound. Rubber is a nonconductor of electricity.

non·con·form·ist (non′kən fôr′mist), *n.* person who refuses to be bound by or accept the established customs or practices of a social group, business, or church.

non·con·form·i·ty (non′kən fôr′mə tē), *n.* lack of conformity; refusal to conform.

non·con·ta·gious (non′kən tā′jəs), *adj.* not contagious.

non·dair·y (non′dâr′ē), *adj.* containing no milk, cream, or other dairy products.

non·dem·o·crat·ic (non′dem ə krat′ik), *adj.* **1** not like a democracy. **2** not treating other people as equals.

non·de·nom·i·na·tion·al (non′di nom′ə nā′shə nəl), *adj.* not controlled by a particular religious group; open to all religious groups: *nondenominational services.*

non·de·script (non′də skript′), *adj.* not easily classified; not of any one particular kind: *We drove past a block of nondescript houses.*

none (nun), **1** *pron.* not any: *We have none of that paper left.* **2** *pron.* no one; not one: *None of these is a typical case.* **3** *pron.* no persons or things: *None have arrived.* **4** *adv.* to no extent; in no way; not at all: *Our supply is none too great.* ■ Another word that sounds like this is **nun.**

USAGE NOTE **None** is used as a plural pronoun and as a singular pronoun: *None of the cousins have met before. None of these umbrellas is the one I lost.* Some people believe that **none** should be used only as a singular pronoun. Scholars do not agree with that belief. In many sentences with **none,** either a singular or a plural verb is correct. See also the Usage Note at **neither.**

non·en·ti·ty (non en′tə tē), *n.* someone or something of little or no importance. ❑ *n., pl.* **non·en·ti·ties.**

non·es·sen·tial (non′ə sen′shəl), **1** *adj.* not essential; not necessary. **2** *n.* person or thing not essential.

none·the·less (nun′THə les′), *adv.* nevertheless.

non·ex·ist·ence (non′ig zis′təns), *n.* condition of not existing.

non·ex·ist·ent (non′ig zis′tənt), *adj.* having no existence.

non·fat (non′fat′), *adj.* without the fat content that is normally present: *nonfat milk.*

non·fat·ten·ing (non fat′ning), *adj.* not likely to make people gain weight: *to eat nonfattening foods.*

non·fic·tion (non fik′shən), *n.* writing that is not fiction. Biographies and histories are nonfiction. —**non·fic′tion·al,** *adj.*

non·flam·ma·ble (non flam′ə bəl), *adj.* not able to catch fire: *a nonflammable paint remover.*

non·in·ter·ven·tion (non′in tər ven′shən), *n.* **1** failure or refusal to intervene. **2** a government policy of staying out of the affairs of other governments.

non·liv·ing (non liv′ing), *adj.* not living.

non·met·al (non met′l), *n.* a chemical element lacking the physical and chemical properties of a metal.

non·me·tal·lic (non′mə tal′ik), *adj.* not like a metal. Carbon, oxygen, sulfur, and nitrogen are nonmetallic elements.

no-no (nō′nō′), *n.* INFORMAL. something that someone must not do, say, or use: *Telling fibs is a no-no.* ❑ *n., pl.* **no-nos, no-no's,** *or* **no-noes.**

no-non·sense (nō′non′sens), *adj.* permitting no foolishness or nonsense; serious: *My parents are no-nonsense when it comes to school.*

non·pa·reil (non′pə rel′), **1** *adj.* having no equal. **2** *n.* person or thing having no equal.

non·par·ti·san (non pär′tə zən), *adj.* not partisan; not supporting, or controlled by, any of the regular political parties: *a nonpartisan voter.*

non·pay·ment (non pā′mənt), *n.* failure to pay or condition of not being paid.

non·plus (non plus′ *or* non′plus), *v.* to puzzle completely; make unable to say or do anything: *We were nonplused to see two roads leading off to the left where we had expected only one.* ❑ *v.* **non·plused, non·plus·ing** *or* **non·plussed, non·plus·sing.**

non·poi·son·ous (non poi′zn əs), *adj.* containing no poison.

non·pro·duc·tive (non′prə duk′tiv), *adj.* **1** not productive. **2** not directly connected with production. —**non′pro·duc′tive·ly,** *adv.* —**non′pro·duc′tive·ness,** *n.*

non·prof·it (non prof′it), *adj.* not for profit; without profit: *The Salvation Army is a nonprofit organization.*

non·re·new·a·ble (non′ri nü′ə bəl), *adj.* not able to be renewed or replenished: *Oil is a nonrenewable natural resource.*

non·res·i·dent (non rez′ə dənt), **1** *adj.* living elsewhere; not living in a particular place. **2** *adj.* not living where official duties require you to live. **3** *n.* a nonresident person.

non·re·stric·tive (non′ri strik′tiv), *adj.* not restricting or limiting.

nonrestrictive clause, (in grammar) any clause which adds descriptive detail but is not an essential part of the sentence in which it appears. It is set off by commas. EXAMPLE: *My bicycle, which had a flat tire, was stolen today.*

non·sched·uled (non skej′üld), *adj.* not operating according to regular schedule: *a nonscheduled flight.*

non·sec·tar·i·an (non′sek ter′ē ən), *adj.* not connected with any religious denomination.

non·sense (non′sens), *n.* **1** words, ideas, or acts without meaning; foolish talk or doings; a plan or suggestion that is foolish: *That tale about the ghost that haunts the old mansion is nonsense.* **2** worthless stuff; junk: *a drawer full of useless gadgets and other nonsense.*

non·sen·si·cal (non sen′sə kəl), *adj.* foolish or absurd. —**non·sen′si·cal·ly,** *adv.* —**non·sen′si·cal·ness,** *n.*

non·smok·er (non′smō′kər), *n.* someone who does not smoke cigarettes.

non·stan·dard (non stan′dərd), *adj.* **1** not in agreement with particular standards. **2** (of pronunciation, grammar, vocabulary, etc.) not like the language of educated speakers and writers.

non·stick (non′stik′), *adj.* having a coating to prevent food from sticking during cooking.

non·stop (non′stop′), *adj., adv.* without stopping: *a nonstop flight to Paris, fly nonstop from New York to Denver.*

non·tax·a·ble (non tak′sə bəl), *adj.* not able to be taxed.

non·un·ion (non yü′nyən), *adj.* **1** not belonging to a trade union. **2** not following trade-union rules. **3** not recognizing or favoring trade unions.

non·vas·cu·lar (non vas′kyə lər), *adj.* without tubes that carry blood, sap, etc: *nonvascular plants.*

non·ver·bal (non vėr′bəl), *adj.* not verbal; without words: *Pantomime is a nonverbal form of expression.*

non·vi·o·lence (non vī′ə ləns), *n.* belief in the use of peaceful methods to achieve any goal; opposition to any form of violence.

non·vi·o·lent (non vī′ə lənt), *adj.* not violent; opposing violence: *I only watch nonviolent movies.* —**non·vi·o·lent·ly,** *adv.*

nonviolent—a nonviolent demonstration

noo·dle[1] (nü′dl), *n.* a mixture of flour, water, and eggs, dried into hard flat strips.

noo·dle[2] (nü′dl), *n.* SLANG. **1** a very stupid person; fool. **2** head.

nook (nůk), *n.* **1** a cozy little corner: *The cat likes to sleep in a nook by the furnace.* **2** a hidden spot; sheltered place: *There is a wonderful nook in the woods behind our house.*

noon (nün), **1** *n.* 12 o'clock in the daytime; middle of the day. **2** *adj.* of or at noon. [**Noon** comes from a Latin word meaning "ninth." In old English, noon meant nine hours after sunrise, about 3 P.M.]

noon·day (nün′dā′), *n., adj.* noon.

no one, no person; nobody.

noon·time (nün′tīm′), *n.* noon.

noose (nüs), **1** *n.* a loop at the end of a rope with a knot through which the rope can slip to tighten the loop. **2** *n.* a snare or bond. **3** *v.* to catch with a noose; snare. ❑ *v.* **noosed, noos·ing.**

Noot·ka (nůt′kə), *n.* member of a group of tribes of American Indians living on and near Vancouver Island, British Columbia. ❑ *n., pl.* **Noot·ka** or **Noot·kas.**

nope (nōp), *adv.* INFORMAL. no.

nor (nôr), *conj.* **1** and no: *We had neither food nor drink left.* **2** neither: *Nor silver nor gold can buy it.* **3** and not: *I have not gone there, nor will I ever go.*

Nor·dic (nôr′dik), **1** *adj.* belonging to or characteristic of the people of northern Europe. **2** *n.* a northern European. Scandinavians are Nordics.

Nor·folk (nôr′fək), *n.* port in SE Virginia, near the mouth of Chesapeake Bay.

norm (nôrm), *n.* standard for a certain group; type, model, or pattern: *In arithmetic this class is above the norm for the eighth grade.*

nor·mal (nôr′məl), **1** *adj.* usual; most commonly occurring: *The normal temperature of the human body is 98.6 degrees.* **2** *n.* the usual state or level: *After the rains, the river was 10 feet above normal.* **3** *adj.* being healthy in body or mind: *Your teeth look normal.*

WORD STORY **Normal** comes from a Latin word meaning "a carpenter's square," a tool to be sure that pieces of wood meet at right angles. **Regular** comes from a Latin word meaning "a carpenter's ruler," a tool to be sure that a piece of wood is straight and long enough. In old times, most buildings and pieces of furniture were made by carpenters, and anyone who had a good carpenter could live a normal, regular life.

nor·mal·cy (nôr′məl sē), *n.* normal condition.

nor·mal·i·ty (nôr mal′ə tē), *n.* normal condition.

nor·mal·ize (nôr′mə līz), *v.* to make normal: *normalize the relations between two countries.* ❑ *v.* **nor·mal·ized, nor·mal·iz·ing.** —**nor′mal·i·za′tion,** *n.* —**nor′mal·iz′er,** *n.*

nor·mal·ly (nôr′mə lē), *adv.* **1** in a normal way: *to act normally.* **2** if things are normal: *Children normally begin to lose their baby teeth when they are six years old.*

Nor·man (nôr′mən), **1** *n.* someone born or living in Normandy. **2** *n.* member of the people descended from the Scandinavians who settled in Normandy in the 900s A.D. and the French who lived there. **3** *adj.* of or about the Normans or Normandy. **4** *n.* city in central Oklahoma.

Norman Conquest, conquest of England by the Normans in 1066, under the leadership of William I.

Nor·man·dy (nôr′mən dē), *n.* region and former province in NW France. On June 6, 1944, Allied forces landed on the Normandy beaches of the English Channel to begin the invasion of Nazi-occupied Europe in World War II.

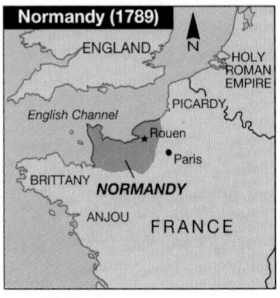

Normandy (1789)

Norse (nôrs), **1** *adj.* of or about ancient Scandinavia, its people, or their language. **2** *n.pl.* people of ancient Scandinavia; Norsemen; Northmen. **3** *n.* language of these people. **4** *adj.* of or about Norway or its people. **5** *n.pl.* Norwegians. **6** *n.* language of Norway.

Norse·man (nôrs′mən), *n.* one of the Nordic people of ancient Scandinavia. The Vikings were Norsemen. ❑ *n., pl.* **Norse·men.**

north (nôrth), **1** *n.* direction to which a compass needle points; direction to the right as you face the setting sun. **2** *adj., adv.* toward the north; farther toward the north: *We live on the north side of town. Drive north for the next mile.* **3** *adj.* from the north: *a north wind.* **4** *n.* Also, **North,** the part of any country toward the north. **5** *n.* **the North, a** the northern part of the United States; the states north of Maryland, the Ohio River, and Missouri, making up most of the states that formed the Union side in the Civil War. **b** (in Canada) the northern regions of provinces lying west of Quebec, together with the Northwest Territories and Yukon Territory. **c** the economically developed nations of the world, located mainly in the Northern Hemisphere.

north of, further north than: *Canada is north of the United States.*

North Africa, the northern section of Africa, especially countries containing parts of the Sahara. —**North African.**

North America, the northern continent of the Western Hemisphere. The United States, Mexico, and Canada are the three largest countries in North America.

North American, 1 of or about North America or its people. **2** someone born or living in North America.

North Atlantic Treaty Organization, NATO.

north·bound (nôrth′bound′), *adj.* going north.

North Carolina, one of the southeastern states of the United States. *Abbreviation:* NC or N.C. *Capital:* Raleigh. [**North Carolina** was named in honor of Charles I, king of England. His name in Latin is Carolus.] —**North Carolinian.**

North Cascades National Park, a national park in NW Washington, containing beautiful mountain ridges, valleys, waterfalls, and forests.

North Charleston, city in SE South Carolina.

North Dakota, one of the midwestern states of the United States. *Abbreviation:* ND, N.Dak., or N.D. *Capital:* Bismarck. [**North Dakota** was named for the Sioux Indians. The Sioux call themselves **Dakota** or **Lakota,** meaning "allies" or "friends."] —**North Dakotan.**

north·east (nôrth′ēst′), **1** *adj.* direction halfway between north and east. **2** *adj.* toward the northeast: *the northeast corner of the building.* **3** *n.* a place that is in the northeast part or direction. **4** *adv.* toward the northeast. **5** *adj.* from the northeast: *a northeast*

a	hat	ė	term	ô	order	ch	child		a in about
ā	age	i	it	oi	oil	ng	long		e in taken
ä	far	ī	ice	ou	out	sh	she	ə	i in pencil
â	care	o	hot	u	cup	th	thin		o in lemon
e	let	ō	open	ů	put	ŦH	then		u in circus
ē	equal	ò	saw	ü	rule	zh	measure		

wind. **6** *n.* **the Northeast,** the northeastern part of the United States, including New England, New York, Pennsylvania, and New Jersey.

north·east·er (nôrth/ē/stər), *n.* a wind or storm that blows from the northeast.

north·east·er·ly (nôrth/ē/stər lē), *adj., adv.* **1** toward the northeast. **2** from the northeast.

north·east·ern (nôrth/ē/stərn), *adj.* **1** toward the northeast. **2** from the northeast. **3** of or in the northeast. **4 Northeastern,** of or in the northeastern part of the United States.

north·east·ward (nôrth/ēst/wərd), *adv., adj.* toward the northeast.

north·er (nôr/ᴛʜər), *n.* a wind or storm that blows from the north.

north·er·ly (nôr/ᴛʜər lē), **1** *adj., adv.* toward the north: *a northerly exposure.* **2** *adj., adv.* from the north: *a northerly wind.* **3** *n.* wind that blows from the north. ❏ *n., pl.* **north·er·lies.**

north·ern (nôr/ᴛʜərn), *adj.* **1** toward the north: *a northern view.* **2** from the north: *a northern breeze.* **3** of or in the north: *northern countries.* **4 Northern,** of or in the northern part of the United States.

north·ern·er (nôr/ᴛʜər nər), *n.* **1** someone born or living in the north. **2 Northerner,** someone born or living in the northern part of the United States.

Northern Hemisphere, the half of the earth that is north of the equator.

Northern Ireland, self-governing district in NE Ireland that voted not to join the Republic of Ireland and is a part of the United Kingdom of Great Britain and Northern Ireland. *Capital:* Belfast. See **United Kingdom** for map.

northern lights, aurora borealis.

Northern Mar·i·an·as (mar/ē an/əz), a self-governing group of islands in the W Pacific, east of the Philippines. They are under the protection of the United States. *Capital:* Saipan.

north·ern·most (nôr/ᴛʜərn mōst), *adj.* farthest north.

Northern Territory, territory in N central Australia. *Capital:* Darwin.

North Island, the northernmost main island of New Zealand.

North Korea, country on the Korean peninsula, north of the 38th parallel. *Capital:* Pyongyang. **—North Korean.**

north·land (nôrth/lənd), *n.* **1** land in the north; the northern part of a country. **2 Northland,** the northern regions of the world.

North Little Rock, city lying on the north shore of the Arkansas River near Little Rock, Arkansas.

North·man (nôrth/mən), *n.* Norseman. ❏ *n., pl.* **North·men.**

North Pole, the northern end of the earth's axis. See **arctic** for map.

North Sea, sea that is part of the Atlantic Ocean, east of Great Britain, west of Denmark, and south of Norway.

North Star, the bright star seen almost directly above the North Pole, formerly used as a guide by sailors; Polaris; polestar; lodestar.

North·um·bri·a (nôr thum/brē ə), *n.* ancient kingdom in N England. **—North·um/bri·an,** *adj., n.*

North Vietnam, former country in SE Asia, now part of Vietnam.

north·ward (nôrth/wərd), **1** *adv., adj.* toward the north; north: *I walked northward. The orchard is on the northward slope of the hill.* **2** *n.* a northward part, direction, or point.

north·wards (nôrth/wərdz), *adv.* northward.

north·west (nôrth/west/), **1** *adj.* direction halfway between north and west. **2** *adj.* toward the northwest: *the northwest corner of the building.* **3** *n.* a place that is in the northwest part or direction. **4** *adv.* toward the northwest. **5** *adj.* from the northwest: *a northwest wind.* **6** *n.* **the Northwest,** the northwestern part of the United States, including Washington, Oregon, and Idaho.

north·west·er (nôrth/wes/tər), *n.* wind or storm that blows from the northwest.

north·west·er·ly (nôrth/wes/tər lē), *adj., adv.* **1** toward the northwest. **2** from the northwest.

north·west·ern (nôrth/wes/tərn), *adj.* **1** toward the northwest. **2** from the northwest. **3** of or in the northwest. **4 Northwestern,** of or in the northwestern part of the United States.

Northwest Passage, sea route for ships from the Atlantic to the Pacific along the N coast of North America.

Northwest Territories, a territory of N Canada, east of the Yukon Territory. *Capital:* Yellowknife.

Northwest Territory, former name for lands north of the Ohio River and east of the Mississippi River, now forming Ohio, Indiana, Illinois, Michigan, Wisconsin, and part of Minnesota.

Northwest Territory (1803-1848)

north·west·ward (nôrth/west/wərd), *adv., adj.* toward the northwest.

Nor·way (nôr/wā), *n.* country in N Europe, west and north of Sweden. *Capital:* Oslo.

Nor·we·gian (nôr wē/jən), **1** *adj.* of or relating to Norway, its people, or their language. **2** *n.* person born or living in Norway. **3** *n.* language of Norway.

nose (nōz), **1** *n.* the part of the face or head just above the mouth. The nose has openings for breathing and smelling. **2** *n.* sense of smell: *That dog has a good nose for hunting.* **3** *v.* to smell; investigate or discover by smell: *The hounds nosed the scent of the fox.* **4** *n.* ability to perceive or detect: *A reporter must have a nose for news.* **5** *v.* to touch, rub, or push with the nose: *The cat nosed its kittens.* **6** *n.* part that stands out, especially at the front of anything: *the nose of an airplane.* **7** *v.* to move forward carefully: *The boat nosed along the uneven shoreline.* **8** *v.* to search for; pry into: *nose into someone's business.* ❏ *v.* **nosed, nos·ing. —nose/like/,** *adj.*

count noses, to find out how many people are present.

follow your nose, to go straight ahead.

lead by the nose, to have complete control over.

look down your nose at or **turn up your nose at,** to treat with contempt or scorn.

nose out, 1 to find out by looking around quietly or secretly: *nose out the truth.* **2** to defeat by a small margin: *nosed out the champions, 10 to 9.*

on the nose, INFORMAL. **1** exactly. **2** solidly.

pay through the nose, to pay a great deal too much.

poke your nose into, to pry or meddle in a nosy way: *Our neighbors were always poking their noses into other people's business.*

under your nose, in plain sight.

win by a nose, 1 to win a horse race by no more than the length of a horse's nose. **2** to win by a small margin.

nose·bleed (nōz/blēd/), *n.* flow of blood from the nose.

nose cone, the cone-shaped front section of a missile or rocket, made to carry a bomb to a target or machines or passengers into space. The nose cone is made to resist high temperatures from friction with air molecules. It usually separates from the rest of the missile or rocket after the fuel runs out.

nose·dive (nōz/dīv/), *n.* **1** a swift plunge straight downward by an aircraft. **2** a sudden, sharp drop: *The thermometer took a nosedive the first day of winter.*

nose-dive (nōz/dīv/), *v.* to take a nosedive. ❏ *v.* **nose-dived, nose-div·ing.**

nos·ey (nō/zē), *adj.* nosy. ❏ *adj.* **nos·i·er, nos·i·est.**

nosh (nosh), SLANG. **1** *v.* to eat between meals; snack: *to nosh before dinner, noshing on potato chips.* **2** *n.* a snack. ❏ *n., pl.* **nosh·es. —nosh/er,** *n.*

nos·tal·gia (no stal/jə), *n.* an affectionate longing for your home, country, city, or for anything far removed in space or time.

nos·tal·gic (no stal/jik), *adj.* feeling or showing nostalgia. **—nos·tal/gi·cal·ly,** *adv.*

nos·tril (nos/trəl), *n.* either of the two openings in the nose. Air is breathed into the lungs, and smells come into the sensitive parts of the nose, through the nostrils.

nos·trum (nos/trəm), *n.* **1** medicine made by the person who is selling it; quack remedy; patent medicine. **2** a pet scheme for producing wonderful results; cure-all.

nos·y (nō/zē), *adj.* prying; inquisitive, or overly curious about other people's business: *Our nosy neighbors were always asking questions about our family.* ■ See Synonym Study at **curious.** ❏ *adj.* **nos·i·er, nos·i·est. —nos/i·ly,** *adv.* **—nos/i·ness,** *n.*

Nosy Par·ker (pär′kər), a nosy person; busybody.

not (not), *adv.* word that says no; a negative: *not in any way, not to any extent. Six and two are not ten.* ■ Another word that sounds like this is **knot.**

no·ta·ble (nō′tə bəl), **1** *adj.* worthy of notice; striking; remarkable; important: *Last week's volcano eruption was a notable event.* **2** *n.* someone who is notable: *Many notables came to the reception at the White House.* **—no′ta·bil′i·ty, no′ta·ble·ness,** *n.*

no·ta·bly (nō′tə blē), *adv.* **1** in a notable manner; to a notable degree: *Many countries are notably lacking in fertile soil and minerals.* **2** especially; particularly: *Some deserts, notably the Sahara and Death Valley, are extremely hot.*

no·ta·rize (nō′tə rīz′), *v.* to certify a contract, deed, will, etc. ❑ *v.* **no·ta·rized, no·ta·riz·ing. —no′tar·i·za′tion,** *n.*

no·tar·y (nō′tər ē), *n.* notary public. ❑ *n., pl.* **no·tar·ies.**

notary public, a public officer authorized to certify deeds and contracts, to record the fact that a certain person swears that something is true, and to attend to other legal matters. ❑ *pl.* **notaries public** or **notary publics.**

no·ta·tion (nō tā′shən), *n.* **1** a set of signs or symbols used to represent numbers, quantities, or other values: *In arithmetic we use the Arabic notation (1, 2, 3, 4, etc.) and sometimes the Roman notation (I, II, III, IV, etc.).* **2** the representing of numbers, quantities, or other values by symbols or signs: *Music has a special system of notation, and so has chemistry.* **3** a note to assist memory; record; jotting: *He made a notation on the margin of the paper.* **4** act of noting. **—no·ta′tion·al,** *adj.*

notch (noch), **1** *n.* a V-shaped nick or cut made in an edge or on a curving surface: *People used to cut notches on a stick to keep count of numbers.* **2** *v.* to make a notch or notches in. **3** *n.* a deep, narrow pass or gap between mountains. **4** *n.* grade; step; degree: *In hot weather we often set the air conditioner several notches higher.* ❑ *n., pl.* **notch·es.**

note (nōt), **1** *n.* a short sentence, phrase, or single word written down to remind you of what was in a book, a speech, an agreement, etc.: *Her notes helped her remember what the speaker said. I must make a note of that.* **2** *n.* a very short letter: *a note of thanks.* **3** *v.* to write down as a thing to be remembered: *Our class notes the weather daily on a chart.* **4** *n.* a comment, remark, or piece of information added concerning a word or a passage in a book, often to help pupils in studying the book: *There are many helpful notes at the back of our science textbook.* **5** *n.* promissory note. **6** *n.* certificate of a government or bank used as money. **7** *n.* piece of paper money. **8** *n.* greatness; fame: *a person of note.* **9** *v.* to notice; observe carefully; give attention to: *Now, please note what I do next.* **10** *v.* to mention specially. **11** *n.* in music: **a** a written sign to show the pitch and length of a sound. **b** a single sound of definite pitch made by an instrument or voice: *Sing this note for me.* **c** any one of the black or white keys of a piano: *to strike the wrong note.* **12** *n.* a song or call of a bird. **13** *n.* a special tone or way of expression: *There was a note of determination in her voice.* ❑ *v.* **not·ed, not·ing.**

compare notes, to exchange ideas or opinions.

strike the right note, to say or do something suitable.

take note of, to take notice of; give attention to; observe.

take notes, to write down things to be remembered.

note·book (nōt′bůk′), *n.* book in which to write notes of things to be learned or remembered.

not·ed (nō′tid), *adj.* especially noticed; conspicuous; well-known; celebrated; famous: *"Little Women" was written by the noted American author Louisa May Alcott.* ■ See Synonym Study at **famous. —not′ed·ly,** *adv.*

note·pad (nōt′pad′), *n.* a pad of paper for writing down notes: *Be sure to bring a notepad to the meeting.*

note·pa·per (nōt′pā pər), *n.* writing paper, especially paper for writing letters: *Use the blue notepaper for your thank-you notes.*

note·wor·thy (nōt′wėr′THē), *adj.* worthy of notice; remarkable: *The first flight across the Atlantic was a noteworthy achievement.* **—note′wor′thi·ly,** *adv.* **—note′wor′thi·ness,** *n.*

not-for-prof·it (not′fôr prof′it), *adj.* nonprofit: *a not-for-profit political organization.*

noth·ing (nuth′ing), **1** *n.* not anything; no thing: *Nothing arrived by mail.* **2** *n.* thing that does not exist: *create a world out of nothing.* **3** *n.* thing or person of no importance or value: *Don't worry, it's nothing.* **4** *n.* zero; naught. **5** *adv.* not at all: *She looks nothing like her sister.* [See word history information at **naught.**]

nothing doing, INFORMAL. certainly not; by no means: *You expect me to clean up all this mess? Nothing doing.*

nothing less than, just the same as.

noth·ing·ness (nuth′ing nis), *n.* **1** condition of being nothing or not existing. **2** worthlessness.

no·tice (nō′tis), **1** *n.* attention; observation; awareness: *escape your notice. A sudden movement caught his notice.* **2** *v.* to give attention to; observe; see: *I noticed a hole in my sock.* **3** *n.* announcement or warning: *The whistle blew to give notice that the boat was about to leave.* **4** *n.* a written or printed sign; paper posted in a public place; a large sheet of paper giving information or directions: *We saw a notice of today's city planning meeting.* **5** *n.* act of telling that you are leaving or must leave rented quarters or a job at a given time: *I gave two weeks' notice when I quit my job.* **6** *n.* a written or printed account in a newspaper: *There is a notice in the paper describing the wedding.* ❑ *v.* **no·ticed, no·tic·ing. —no′tic·er,** *n.*

serve notice, to give warning; announce: *The landlord served notice that the noisy tenants would have to move.*

take notice of, to give attention to; observe: *Take no notice of them.*

no·tice·a·ble (nō′ti sə bəl), *adj.* **1** easily seen or noticed; observable. **2** worth noticing: *The class has made a noticeable improvement in spelling.* **—no′tice·a·bly,** *adv.*

no·ti·fi·ca·tion (nō′tə fə kā′shən), *n.* **1** act of notifying. **2** notice: *We received a notification of the meeting.*

no·ti·fy (nō′tə fī), *v.* to give notice to; let know; announce to; inform: *Our teacher notified us that there would be a test on Monday.* ❑ *v.* **no·ti·fied, no·ti·fy·ing.**

no·tion (nō′shən), *n.* **1** idea or understanding: *I have no notion of what you mean.* **2** opinion, view, or belief: *People have different notions about how children should be raised.* **3** intention: *He has no notion of risking his money.* **4** a desire or thought that suddenly occurs to someone: *I had a notion to take a short vacation, but changed my mind.* **5** a foolish idea or opinion: *Grow oranges in Alaska? What a notion!* **6 notions,** *pl.* small, useful articles, such as pins, needles, thread, tape, etc.

no·tion·al (nō′shə nəl), *adj.* **1** in your imagination or thought only; not real. **2** full of notions; having strange notions.

no·to·chord (nō′tə kôrd), *n.* **1** a flexible, rodlike structure of cells running lengthwise in the back of some animals that have no backbones. It forms the main supporting structure of the body. Animals with notochords are thought to be the closest relatives of animals with backbones. **2** a similar structure in the embryos of animals with backbones. It turns into the backbone.

no·to·ri·e·ty (nō′tə rī′ə tē), *n.* well-known or famous for something bad: *A scandal brings notoriety to those involved in it.*

no·to·ri·ous (nō tôr′ē əs), *adj.* well-known or commonly known, especially because of something bad: *a notorious outlaw. Our neighbors are notorious for giving noisy parties.* **—no·to′ri·ous·ly,** *adv.* **—no·to′ri·ous·ness.** *n.*

Not·ting·ham (not′ing əm), *n.* city in central England. Many of Robin Hood's adventures took place there.

not·with·stand·ing (not′with stan′ding *or* not′with stan′-ding), **1** *prep.* in spite of: *I bought it notwithstanding the high price.* **2** *conj.* in spite of the fact that; although: *Notwithstanding there was need for haste, they still delayed.* **3** *adv.* in spite of it; nevertheless: *It is raining; but I shall go, notwithstanding.*

Nouak·chott (nə wäk shot′), *n.* capital of Mauritania, in the W part, near the Atlantic.

nou·gat (nü′gət), *n.* a kind of soft candy containing nuts.

nought (not), *n.* naught.

a	hat	ė	term	ô	order	ch	child		a in about
ā	age	i	it	oi	oil	ng	long		e in taken
ä	far	ī	ice	ou	out	sh	she	ə	i in pencil
â	care	o	hot	u	cup	th	thin		o in lemon
e	let	ō	open	ů	put	ᴛʜ	then		u in circus
ē	equal	ȯ	saw	ü	rule	zh	measure		

N

noun (noun), **1** *n.* word used as the name of a person, place, thing, quality, or event. Words like *Lisa, table, school, bookcase, kindness, skill,* and *party* are nouns. **2** *adj.* used as a noun.

WORD POWER **Nouns** ■ Words are always trying to turn into other words. Verbs and adjectives try to become nouns, at the same time that nouns are turning into adjectives and verbs. The fastest way to make these changes is with suffixes. For various reasons, there are especially many suffixes to form nouns. We have listed some separately; see the Word Powers at **inhabitant** and **person.**

One reason for these many suffixes is that they come from several languages, like **-hood** from old English and **-ity** from Latin and **-age** from French. Another reason is that some kinds of words seem to sound better with one suffix than with another. *Happiness* and *sadness,* for instance, would sound odd if they were *happihood* and *sadship.* Among the many suffixes forming nouns are:

-ability	-ation	-fication	-ment
-age	-cy	-graph	-ness
-al²	-ence	-hood	-ship
-ance	-ent	-ism	-ure
-athon	-ery	-ity	-y²

nour·ish (nėr′ish), *v.* **1** to make grow, or keep alive and well, with food; feed; nurture: *Milk nourishes a baby.* **2** to support; encourage: *Getting a letter published in the paper nourished her hopes of being a writer.* —**nour′ish·er,** *n.*

nour·ish·ing (nėr′ish ing), *adj.* keeping well-fed and healthy; producing health and growth: *a nourishing diet.*

nour·ish·ment (nėr′ish mənt), *n.* **1** food. **2** act of nourishing or condition of being nourished.

Nov., November.

no·va (nō′və), *n.* star that suddenly becomes brighter and then gradually fades back to its normal brightness. ❑ *n., pl.* **no·vas, no·vae** (nō′vē′).

nova

No·va Sco·tia (nō′və skō′shə), province in SE Canada consisting of a peninsula that extends into the Atlantic, and Cape Breton Island. *Capital:* Halifax. [**Nova Scotia** comes from Latin words meaning "New Scotland." It is north of New England, as Scotland is north of England.] —**Nova Scotian.**

nov·el (nov′əl), **1** *n.* a made-up story with characters and a plot, long enough to fill one or more volumes. Novels are usually about people, scenes, and happenings such as might be met in real life. **2** *adj.* of a new kind or nature; strange; new; unfamiliar: *a novel idea, a novel sensation.*

nov·el·ette (nov′ə let′), *n.* a short novel.

nov·el·ist (nov′ə list), *n.* writer of novels.

no·vel·la (nō vel′ə), *n.* **1** a short story with a simple plot. **2** a short novel. ❑ *n., pl.* **no·vel·las.**

nov·el·ty (nov′əl tē), *n.* **1** novel character; newness: *After the novelty of ice-skating wore off, we did not want to do it any more.* **2** a new or unusual thing: *Staying up late was a novelty to the children.* **3 novelties,** *pl.* small, unusual articles, such as toys or cheap jewelry. ❑ *n., pl.* **nov·el·ties** for 2,3.

No·vem·ber (nō vem′bər), *n.* the 11th month of the year. It has 30 days. [**November** comes from a Latin word meaning "nine." November was the ninth month of the earliest Roman calendar, which began with March.]

no·ve·na (nō vē′nə), *n.* (in the Roman Catholic Church) a devotion for some special purpose, made up of prayers or services on nine successive days. ❑ *n., pl.* **no·ve·nas.**

nov·ice (nov′is), *n.* **1** one who is new to something; beginner: *Novices are likely to make some mistakes.* **2** person in the period of trial and preparation before becoming a monk or a nun.

no·vi·ti·ate (nō vish′ē it), *n.* **1** the period of trial and preparation in a religious order. **2** the state or period of being a beginner.

No·vo·cain (nō′və kān), *n.* trademark for a drug used to numb feeling in dentistry and medicine.

now (nou), **1** *adv.* at this time: *He is here now. Most people do not believe in ghosts now.* **2** *adv.* by this time: *She must have reached the city now.* **3** *n.* the present; this time: *by now, until now, from now on.* **4** *adv.* at once: *Do it now!* **5** *conj.* inasmuch as; now that; since: *Now you mention it, I do remember.* **6** *adv.* as things are; as it is: *I would believe almost anything now.* **7** *adv.* then; next: *Now you see it; now you don't.* **8** *adv.* at the time referred to: *The clock now struck three.* **9** *adv.* Now is also used to introduce or emphasize, with little or no change of meaning. *Now what do you mean? Oh, come now!*
now and then or now and again, from time to time; once in a while.

NOW (nou), *n.* National Organization for Women.

now·a·days (nou′ə dāz′), *adv.* at the present day; in these times: *Nowadays people travel in cars rather than carriages.*

no·way (nō′wā), *adv.* in no way; not at all; by no means; nowise: *Noway could we believe the story.*

no way, INFORMAL. certainly not; it is impossible: *"I won't discuss the details. No way!" he insisted.*

no·where (nō′hwãr), **1** *adv.* in no place; at no place; to no place. **2** *n.* a place that is not well-known or is far from everything else: *Our car broke down in the middle of nowhere.*
nowhere near, not nearly; not by a long way.

no·wise (nō′wiz), *adv.* noway.

nox·ious (nok′shəs), *adj.* very harmful; poisonous: *Clouds of noxious fumes came from the back of the old bus.* —**nox′ious·ly,** *adv.* —**nox′ious·ness,** *n.*

noz·zle (noz′əl), *n.* a tip put on a hose, pipe, etc., forming an outlet: *A fine spray came from the nozzle.* [**Nozzle** comes from baby talk for **nose.**]

Np, symbol for neptunium.

N.S., Nova Scotia.

N.T. or **NT,** New Testament.

nth (enth), *n., adj.* last in the series 1, 2, 3, 4…*n;* being of the indefinitely large or small amount denoted by *n.*
to the nth degree, to the utmost: *silly to the nth degree.*

nt. wt., net weight.

nu·ance (nü′äns or nü äns′), *n.* **1** shade of expression, meaning, feeling, etc. **2** shade of color or tone.

nub (nub), *n.* **1** part sticking out; knob. **2** lump or small piece. **3** point or main idea of anything.

nub·bin (nub′ən), *n.* **1** a small or imperfect ear of corn. **2** an undeveloped fruit. **3** a small part that sticks out of something.

nub·bly (nub′lē), *adj.* nubby. ❑ *adj.* **nub·bli·er, nub·bli·est.**

nub·by (nub′ē), *adj.* having nubs: *nubby fabric.* ❑ *adj.* **nub·bi·er, nub·bi·est.**

Nu·bi·a (nü′bē ə), *n.* a region in NE Africa between the Red Sea and the Nile River, including parts of Egypt and Sudan. —**Nu′bi·an,** *adj., n.*

nu·bile (nü′bəl or nü′bīl), *adj.* **1** well developed physically; sexually attractive: *a nubile young woman.* **2** (of girls) old enough to be married; marriageable.

nu·cle·ar (nü′klē ər), *adj.* **1** of or about a nucleus, especially the nucleus of an atom: *nuclear mass.* **2** of or about atoms, atomic energy, or atomic weapons; atomic: *a nuclear reactor.*

USAGE NOTE **Nuclear** is pronounced as nü kyə lər by many people. Many other people feel that this pronunciation is wrong, but it is so common that it will probably be accepted into the language. This is how pronunciation and other parts of language change. It may even become the usual pronunciation. If it does, people in the future will wonder why the word is spelled the way it is.

nuclear energy, energy that exists inside the nucleus of an atom; atomic energy. Nuclear energy can be released by splitting or combining the nuclei of some kinds of atoms.

nuclear family, family consisting of father, mother, and child or children living together in one household.

nuclear fission, fission (def. 3).

nuclear fusion, fusion (def. 3).

nuclear physics, branch of physics dealing with the structure of atomic nuclei and the nature of nuclear particles, such as protons and neutrons.

nuclear reactor, reactor.

nuclear winter, period of intense cold weather thought to follow a nuclear war, when a blotting out of the sun's rays by dense smoke would result in the destruction of plant life, and hence mass starvation of animals and humans.

nu·cle·ic acid (nü klē′ik), any of several complex chemical compounds found in living cells and viruses and necessary for growth and reproduction. The two basic kinds of nucleic acid are DNA and RNA. Nucleic acids carry genetic information and control the production of proteins.

nu·cle·o·lus (nü klē′ə ləs), *n.* a small, usually round structure found within the nucleus of a cell, important to production of one kind of RNA. ❑ *n., pl.* **nu·cle·o·li** (nü klē′ə lī).

nu·cle·on (nü′klē on), *n.* a proton or a neutron.

nu·cle·us (nü′klē əs), *n.* **1** a central part or thing around which other parts or things are collected: *An encyclopedia and a dozen novels formed the nucleus of the classroom library.* **2** the central part of an atom. The nucleus carries a positive charge and most of an atom's mass. It is much smaller than the atom, and electrons move around it. **3** mass of specialized protoplasm found in many living cells, which controls their growth and their division to form new cells. **4** a beginning to which additions are made: *Her $50 bill became the nucleus of a flourishing bank account.* ❑ *n., pl.* **nu·cle·i** (nü′klē ī), **nu·cle·us·es.**

nude (nüd), **1** *adj.* with no clothes on; naked. **2** *n.* a naked figure in painting, sculpture, or photography.
in the nude, in a naked condition.

nudge (nuj), **1** *v.* to push slightly to attract attention: *She nudged me with her elbow when it was my turn to play.* **2** *n.* a slight push. ❑ *v.* **nudged, nudg·ing.** **–nudg′er,** *n.*

nud·ism (nü′diz′əm), *n.* practice of going naked, for health or as a fad.

nu·di·ty (nü′də tē), *n.* a naked condition; nakedness.

Nue·vo Le·on (nwā′vō lā ōn′), a state in N Mexico.

nug·get (nug′it), *n.* **1** valuable lump; lump: *nuggets of gold.* **2** anything valuable: *nuggets of wisdom.*

nui·sance (nü′sns), *n.* something or someone that annoys, troubles, offends, or is disagreeable; annoyance: *Flies are a nuisance.*

nuisance ground, CANADIAN. dump (def. 2).

nuke (nük), **1** *n.* INFORMAL. a nuclear weapon. **2** *v.* INFORMAL. to attack or destroy with or as if by nuclear weapons. **3** *v.* SLANG. to cook in a microwave oven. ❑ *v.* **nuked, nu·king.**

Nu·ku·a·lo·fa (nü′kü ä lō′fä), *n.* capital of Tonga.

null (nul), *adj.* **1** not binding; of no effect; as if not existing: *A promise obtained by force is legally null.* **2** unimportant; meaningless; empty; valueless. **3** not any; zero.
null and void, without legal force or effect; worthless.

nul·li·fy (nul′ə fī), *v.* **1** to make not binding; render void: *nullify a law.* **2** to make of no effect; wipe out; destroy; cancel: *The difficulties of the plan nullify its advantages.* ❑ *v.* **nul·li·fied, nul·li·fy·ing.** **–nul′li·fi·ca′tion,** *n.* **–nul′li·fi′er,** *n.*

null set, empty set.

numb (num), **1** *adj.* having lost the power of feeling or moving: *fingers numb with cold.* **2** *v.* to make numb: *The dentist gave me a shot to numb my jaw.* **3** *v.* to dull the feelings of: *The news numbed us with grief.* [Numb comes from an old English word meaning "taken away." If part of you is really numb, it feels gone.] **–numb′ly,** *adv.* **–numb′ness,** *n.*

num·ber (num′bər), **1** *n.* the count or sum of a group of things or persons; amount: *The number of students in our class is twenty.* **2** *n.* word that tells exactly how many. Two, fourteen, twenty-six, and one hundred are such numbers. **3** *n.* word that tells rank or place in a series. Second, fourteenth, and twenty-sixth are such numbers. **4** *v.* to find out the number of; count. **5** *n.* figure or mark that stands for a number; numeral. 2, 7, and 9 are numbers. **6** *v.* to mark with a number; give a number to; distinguish with a number: *The pages of this book are numbered.* **7** *v.* to be or amount to a given number: *The states in the Union number 50.* **8** *n.* quantity, especially a rather large quantity: *We saw a number of birds.* **9** *n.pl.* **numbers,** **a** arithmetic. **b** many: *There were numbers who stayed out of school that day.* **10** *v.* to reckon as one of a class or collection: *I number you among my best friends.* **11** *n.* a single issue of a magazine: *The May number has an unusually good story.* **12** *n.* one of a numbered series, often a particular numeral identifying someone or something: *a telephone number, a house number.* **13** *n.* a single part of a program: *The program consisted of four musical numbers.* **14** *v.* to fix the number of; limit: *Our old dog's days are numbered.* **15** *n.* (in grammar) a word form or ending which shows whether one or more is meant. *Girl, child,* and *this* are in the singular number; *girls, children,* and *these* are in the plural number. **–num′ber·er,** *n.*
beyond number, too many to count.
without number, too many to be counted: *stars without number.*

Number can be a singular or plural noun: *The number of tickets available is very small. A large number of people have bought tickets already.* Used with *the,* it is singular. Used with *a,* it is plural. See also Usage Note at **collective noun.**

num·ber·less (num′bər lis), *adj.* very numerous; too many to count: *There are numberless fish in the sea.*

number line, line divided into equal segments by points corresponding to integers. The points to the right of 0 are positive; those to the left are negative. The set of all the points on the line corresponds to the set of real numbers.

number one, 1 yourself: *to look out for number one.* **2** first in rank; leading: *The book was a number one best seller.*

Num·bers (num′bərz), *n.* book of the Bible. It tells about the counting of the Israelites after they left Egypt.

numb·skull (num′skul′), *n.* numskull.

nu·mer·a·ble (nü′mər ə bəl), *adj.* countable.

nu·mer·al (nü′mər əl), *n.* **1** a word, figure, or group of figures standing for a number. One, five, and ten are numerals. 7, 25, and 463 are Arabic numerals. III, VI, and XIX are Roman numerals for 3, 6, and 19. **2 numerals,** *pl.* big cloth numbers given by a school for excellence in some sport. They state the year in which the person who wins them will graduate.

nu·me·rate (nü′mə rāt′), *v.* to number, count, or enumerate. ❑ *v.* **nu·me·rat·ed, nu·me·rat·ing.**

nu·me·ra·tion (nü′mə rā′shən), *n.* **1** act of numbering, counting, or enumerating. **2** the reading of numbers expressed in figures.

nu·me·ra·tor (nü′mə rā′tər), *n.* number above or to the left of the line in a fraction, which shows how many equal parts of the whole make up the fraction: *In ⅜, 3 is the numerator and 8 is the denominator.*

nu·mer·ic (nü mer′ik), *adj.* numerical.

nu·mer·i·cal (nü mer′ə kəl), *adj.* **1** of or about a number or numbers; in numbers; by numbers. **2** shown by numbers, not by letters: *10 is a numerical quantity; bx is an algebraic quantity.* **–nu·mer′i·cal·ly,** *adv.*

nu·mer·ous (nü′mər əs), *adj.* very many: *The child asked numerous questions.* **–nu′mer·ous·ly,** *adv.*

Numerous, countless, and **innumerable** all mean a lot. **Numerous** suggests a large number: *There are numerous stories about President Lincoln.* **Countless** means too many to be worth counting: *The beach was covered with countless shells.* **Innumerable** means impossible to count: *Innumerable herds of bison once roamed the prairie.*

a	hat	ė	term	ô	order	ch	child		a in about
ā	age	i	it	oi	oil	ng	long		e in taken
ä	far	ī	ice	ou	out	sh	she	ə	i in pencil
â	care	o	hot	u	cup	th	thin		o in lemon
e	let	ō	open	ů	put	ŦH	then		u in circus
ē	equal	ò	saw	ü	rule	zh	measure		

N

nu·mis·mat·ics (nü′miz mat′iks), *n.* the study or collecting of coins and medals.

nu·mis·ma·tist (nü miz′mə tist), *n.* an expert in numismatics.

num·skull (num′skul′), *n.* a stupid person; blockhead.

nun (nun), *n.* woman who gives up many worldly things and lives a life devoted to religion. ▪ Another word that sounds like this is **none.**

nun·chucks (nun′chuks′), *n.pl.* an Oriental defensive weapon made of two hard wooden sticks joined by a rawhide cord or chain.

nun·ci·o (nun′shē ō), *n.* an official representative or ambassador from the pope to a government. ❑ *n., pl.* **nun·ci·os.**

nun·ner·y (nun′ər ē), *n.* building or buildings where nuns live; convent. ❑ *n., pl.* **nun·ner·ies.**

nup·tial (nup′shəl), **1** *adj.* of or about marriage or weddings. **2** *n.pl.* **nuptials,** a wedding or marriage.

Nur·em·berg (nür′əm bėrg′), *n.* city in SE Germany.

Nu·rey·ev (nər ā′ef), *n.* **Ru·dolf** (rü′dolf), 1938-1993, Austrian ballet dancer and choreographer, born in the former Soviet Union. He danced more than 100 roles.

nurse (nėrs), **1** *n.* someone who is trained to take care of the sick, the injured, or the old. Nurses often work with doctors in hospitals, assisting them and carrying out their instructions. **2** *v.* to be or act as a nurse for sick people; wait on or take care of the sick: *They nursed their children through the flu.* **3** *v.* to cure or try to cure by care: *She nursed a bad cold by going to bed.* **4** *n.* woman who cares for and brings up the young children or babies of another person. **5** *v.* to act as a nurse; have charge of or bring up another's baby or young child. **6** *v.* to make grow; nourish; protect: *nurse a plant, nurse a fire.*

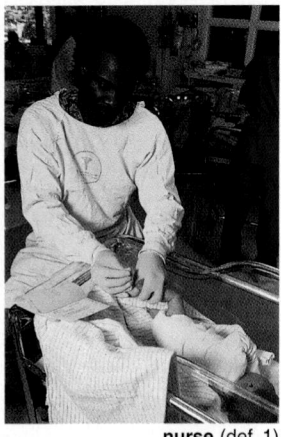

nurse (def. 1)

7 *v.* to use or treat with special care: *He nursed his sore arm by using it very little.* **8** *v.* to feed milk to a baby at the breast. **9** *v.* to suck milk from the breast of a mother. ❑ *v.* **nursed, nurs·ing.**

nurse·maid (nėrs′mād′), *n.* person employed to care for children.

nurs·er·y (nėr′sər ē), *n.* **1** room set apart for the care of babies. **2** a place where babies and small children are cared for during the day. **3** place where young trees and plants are raised for transplanting or sale. **4** nursery school. ❑ *n., pl.* **nurs·er·ies.**

nurs·er·y·man (nėr′sər ē mən), *n.* person who grows or sells young trees and plants. ❑ *n., pl.* **nurs·er·y·men.**

nursery rhyme, a short poem for children. "Sing a Song of Sixpence" is a famous nursery rhyme.

nursery school, school for children not old enough for kindergarten.

nursing home, place for the care of old people or anyone who needs nursing care over a long period of time.

nur·ture (nėr′chər), **1** *v.* to bring up; care for; foster; rear; train: *They nurtured the child as if she were their own.* **2** *n.* act or process of bringing up; rearing; training; education. **3** *v.* to nourish: *nurture resentment.* **4** *n.* nourishment. ❑ *v.* **nur·tured, nur·tur·ing.** —**nur′tur·er,** *n.*

nut (nut), *n.* **1** a dry fruit or seed with a hard, woody or leathery shell and a kernel inside which is often good to eat. **2** kernel of a nut: *chopped nuts.* **3** a small piece of metal or plastic with a hole in the center containing a screw thread. It screws on to a bolt to hold the bolt in place. **4** INFORMAL. **a** an odd or silly person. **b** a devoted fan: *a baseball nut.* —**nut′like′,** *adj.*

Nut (nŭt), *n.* Egyptian goddess of the sky, shown as a woman carrying a water jar on her head.

nut·crack·er (nut′krak′ər), *n.* **1** device for cracking the shells of nuts. **2** any of several birds related to crows and feeding especially on pine seeds.

nut·hatch (nut′hach′), *n.* any of several small, sharp-beaked birds that feed on small nuts, seeds, and insects while climbing along tree trunks and branches. ❑ *n., pl.* **nut·hatch·es.** [A nuthatch does not try to hatch nuts like eggs. It hacks nuts open. The old English form of **hack**[1] was pronounced like **hatch.** The pronunciation may have changed to avoid confusion.]

nut·meat (nut′mēt′), *n.* kernel of a nut.

nut·meg (nut′meg), *n.* a hard, spicy seed about as big as a marble, obtained from the fruit of a tree of the East Indies. The seed is grated and used for flavoring food.

nu·tri·a (nü′trē ə), *n.* **1** a large water rodent of South America, also found in parts of the southern United States, especially Louisiana; coypu. **2** its beaverlike fur. ❑ *n., pl.* **nu·tri·as.**

nu·tri·ent (nü′trē ənt), *n.* any substance that a living thing needs to eat for energy, growth, and repair of tissues: *vitamins, minerals, and other nutrients.*

nu·tri·ment (nü′trə mənt), *n.* nourishment; food.

nu·tri·tion (nü trish′ən), *n.* **1** act or process of providing with food; nourishment: *A balanced diet provides nutrition for your body.* **2** series of processes by which food is used in the bodies of living things for growth, energy, etc.

nu·tri·tion·al (nü trish′ə nəl), *adj.* of or about nutrition. —**nu·tri′tion·al·ly,** *adv.*

nu·tri·tion·ist (nü trish′ə nist), *n.* an expert in the study of nutrition.

nu·tri·tious (nü trish′əs), *adj.* valuable as food; nourishing. —**nu·tri′tious·ly,** *adv.* —**nu·tri′tious·ness,** *n.*

nu·tri·tive (nü′trə tiv), *adj.* **1** of or about foods and the use of foods. Digestion is part of the nutritive process. **2** nutritious. —**nu′tri·tive·ly,** *adv.*

nuts (nuts), *adj.* INFORMAL. totally unthinking; extremely foolish: *He's nuts to try a fool stunt like that.*
be nuts about, INFORMAL. be very fond of: *nuts about water-skiing.*

nuts and bolts, the most basic and important parts; practical details: *the nuts and bolts of a trade agreement.*

nut·shell (nut′shel′), *n.* shell of a nut.
in a nutshell, in very brief form; in a few words.

nut·ty (nut′ē), *adj.* **1** containing many nuts: *nutty cake.* **2** like nuts; tasting like nuts: *This cereal has a nutty flavor.* **3** INFORMAL. odd or silly: *We did nutty things like jumping in a pool with our clothes on.* **4** INFORMAL. very interested or enthusiastic. ❑ *adj.* **nut·ti·er, nut·ti·est.** —**nut′ti·ly,** *adv.* —**nut′ti·ness,** *n.*

nuz·zle (nuz′əl), *v.* **1** to poke or rub with the nose; press the nose against: *The horse nuzzled its owner's ear.* **2** to nestle; snuggle; cuddle. ❑ *v.* **nuz·zled, nuz·zling.** —**nuz′zler,** *n.*

NV, Nevada (used with postal Zip Code).

NW or **N.W.,** **1** northwest. **2** northwestern.

N.W.T., Northwest Territories.

NY, New York (used with postal Zip Code).

N.Y., New York State.

Ny·as·a·land (nī as′ə land′), *n.* former name of Malawi.

N.Y.C., New York City.

ny·lon (nī′lon), **1** *n.* a synthetic substance that is very strong, somewhat elastic, and wears well. Clothing, tents, stockings, and brushes are made of nylon. **2** *n.pl.* **nylons,** stockings made of nylon. **3** *adj.* made of nylon: *nylon carpeting, nylon casters.*

nymph (nimf), *n.* **1** (in Greek and Roman myths) a lesser goddess of nature. **2** a beautiful young woman. **3** form of various insects in the stage of development between the egg and the adult form. A nymph resembles the adult but has no wings. —**nymph′like′,** *adj.*

N.Z., New Zealand.

O¹ or **o** (ō), *n.* **1** the 15th letter of the English alphabet. **2** zero. ❑ *n., pl.* **O's** or **o's.**

O² (ō), *interj.* oh! ■ Another word that sounds like this is **owe.**

o' (ə *or* ō), *prep.* OLD USE. of: *will-o'-the-wisp.*

O, symbol for oxygen.

O., Ohio.

oaf (ōf), *n.* **1** a very stupid person. **2** a clumsy person. [Oaf comes from an Icelandic word meaning "elf." In old times, people believed that the elves took human children and left stupid elf children in their place.]

oaf·ish (ō′fish), *adj.* very stupid; clumsy. **—oaf′ish·ly,** *adv.* **—oaf′ish·ness,** *n.*

O·a·hu (ō ä′hü), *n.* the third largest island of Hawaii. Honolulu, the capital of Hawaii, is on Oahu.

oak (ōk), *n.* **1** any of numerous trees or bushes of the Northern Hemisphere, with strong, hard, durable wood and nuts called acorns. **2** their wood, used in building, especially for floors. **—oak′like′,** *adj.*

oak·en (ō′kən), *adj.* made of oak: *the old oaken bucket.*

Oak·land (ōk′lənd), *n.* city in W California, just east of San Francisco, on San Francisco Bay.

Oak·ley (ō′klē), *n.* **An·nie** (an′ē), 1860-1926, American sharpshooter. ■ Annie Oakley starred in Buffalo Bill's Wild West show for 17 years. The musical *Annie Get Your Gun* is based on her life.

Oak Ridge, city in E Tennessee. Oak Ridge is a research center for studying atomic energy.

oar (ôr), **1** *n.* a long pole with a flat blade at one end, used in rowing. Sometimes an oar is used to steer a boat. **2** *v.* to use an oar; row. **3** *n.* person who rows: *She is the best oar in our crew.* ■ Other words that sound like this are **o'er, or,** and **ore. —oar′less,** *adj.* **—oar′like′,** *adj.*

put your oar in, to meddle; interfere.

oar·lock (ôr′lok′), *n.* a notch or U-shaped support for holding the oar in place while rowing; rowlock.

oars·man (ôrz′mən), *n.* someone who rows, especially a member of a rowing crew. ❑ *n., pl.* **oars·men.**

oars·wom·an (ôrz′wům′ən), *n.* woman who rows, especially a member of a rowing crew. ❑ *n., pl.* **oars·wom·en.**

OAS, Organization of American States (association of 35 American countries formed to promote cooperation and to further the interests of peace and justice).

o·a·sis (ō ā′sis), *n.* **1** a place in a desert where there is water and where trees and plants can grow. **2** any pleasant place in a desolate region. ❑ *n., pl.* **o·a·ses** (ō ā′sēz′).

oat·en (ōt′n), *adj.* of or about oats or oatmeal.

a	hat	ė	term	ô	order	ch	child		
ā	age	i	it	oi	oil	ng	long		a in about
ä	far	ī	ice	ou	out	sh	she		e in taken
â	care	o	hot	u	cup	th	thin	ə	i in pencil
e	let	ō	open	ů	put	ŦH	then		o in lemon
ē	equal	ȯ	saw	ü	rule	zh	measure		u in circus

oath (ōth), *n.* **1** a solemn promise: *The oath bound him to secrecy.* **2** statement that something is true, which God or some holy person or thing is called on to witness. **3** name of God or some holy person or thing used as an exclamation to add force or to express anger. **4** a curse; word used in swearing. ❑ *n., pl.* **oaths** (ōтнz *or* ōths).

under oath, bound by an oath.

oat·meal (ōt′mēl′), *n.* **1** oats partially ground up and flattened into small flakes. **2** a cooked cereal made from this.

oats (ōts), *n.* grain from any of several cereal grasses, or the plants that it grows on. The grain is used to make oatmeal and as a food for horses and other farm animals.

feel your oats, INFORMAL. **1** be lively and frisky. **2** to feel pleased or important and show it.

Oa·xa·ca (wä hä′kə), *n.* a state in SE Mexico.

O·ba·di·ah (ō′bə dī′ə), *n.* **1** a Hebrew prophet. **2** book of the Bible. [**Obadiah** comes from a Hebrew word meaning "servant of God."]

o·be·di·ence (ō bē′dē əns), *n.* act of obeying; doing what you are told to do; submission to authority or law: *He must act in obedience to the judge's order.*

o·be·di·ent (ō bē′dē ənt), *adj.* doing what you are told; willing to obey: *The obedient dog came at its owner's whistle.* —**o·be′di·ent·ly,** *adv.*

o·bei·sance (ō bā′sns *or* ō bē′sns), *n.* **1** movement of the body expressing deep respect; deep bow: *The villagers made obeisance to the queen.* **2** deference; homage: *acts of obeisance.*

ob·e·lisk (ob′ə lisk), *n.* a tapering, four-sided stone pillar with a top shaped like a pyramid.

o·bese (ō bēs′), *adj.* extremely fat. —**o·bese′ly,** *adv.* —**o·bese′ness,** *n.*

o·bes·i·ty (ō bē′sə tē), *n.* extreme fatness.

o·bey (ō bā′), *v.* **1** to do what you are told to do; follow orders: *The dog obeyed its owner and went home.* **2** to act in agreement with; carry out: *A good citizen obeys the laws.* **3** to yield to the control of: *A trained horse obeys the rein.* ❑ *n., pl.* **o·beyed, o·bey·ing.** [**Obey** comes from Latin words meaning "to listen to."] —**o·bey′er,** *n.*

obelisk

o·bi (ō′bē), *n.* a long, broad sash worn by Japanese women around the waist of a kimono. ❑ *n., pl.* **o·bis.**

o·bit·u·ar·y (ō bich′ü er′ē), **1** *n.* a printed report of someone's death, often with a brief account of the person's life. **2** *adj.* of a death; recording a death: *the obituary notices in the newspaper.* ❑ *n., pl.* **o·bit·u·ar·ies.**

obj., **1** object. **2** objection. **3** objective.

ob·ject (ob′jikt *for noun;* əb jekt′ *for verb*), **1** *n.* something that can be seen or touched; thing: *What is that object by the fence?* **2** *n.* person or thing toward which feeling, thought, or action is directed: *an object of someone's affection.* **3** *n.* thing aimed at; end; purpose; goal: *My object in coming here was to help you.* **4** *n.* (in grammar) a word or group of words which receives the action of a verb, or which follows a preposition. In "He threw the ball to his sister," *ball* is the object of *threw,* and *sister* is the object of *to.* **5** *v.* to make objections; be opposed; feel dislike: *Many people object to loud noise.* **6** *v.* to give as a reason against something; bring forward in opposition; oppose: *I objected that it was too cold for camping.* —**ob·jec′tor,** *n.*

ob·jec·tion (əb jek′shən), *n.* **1** something said as a reason or argument against something: *One of his objections to the plan was that it would cost too much.* **2** feeling of disapproval or dislike: *an energetic person with no objection to hard work.*

ob·jec·tion·a·ble (əb jek′shə nə bəl), *adj.* very unpleasant; disagreeable: *objectionable odors.* —**ob·jec′tion·a·ble·ness,** *n.* —**ob·jec′tion·a·bly,** *adv.*

ob·jec·tive (əb jek′tiv), **1** *n.* something you are trying to do, get to, etc.; purpose; goal: *My objective this summer will be learning to play tennis better.* **2** *adj.* existing outside the mind as an actual object and not merely in the mind as an idea; real. Buildings are objective; ideas are subjective. **3** *adj.* true to the facts; not influenced by personal thoughts or feelings: *The witness gave an objective report of the accident.* **4** *adj.* showing the direct object of a verb or the object of a preposition. In "She saw me," *me* is in the objective case. **5** *n.* the objective case. **6** **objective pronoun,** word in that case. *Whom* and *me* are objective pronouns. **7** *n.* lens or lenses nearest to the thing seen through a telescope, microscope, etc. —**ob·jec′tive·ly,** *adv.* —**ob·jec′tive·ness,** *n.*

USAGE NOTE **Objective pronouns** should be used with prepositions. *I will go with her. She is angry at me.* Some people break this rule with the preposition **between,** but careful writers and speakers do not. "Between you and I" is wrong. Say or write "Between you and me."

ob·jec·tiv·i·ty (ob′jek tiv′ə tē), *n.* condition or quality of being objective.

object lesson, a practical illustration of a principle: *Many accidents are object lessons in the dangers of carelessness.*

ob·li·gate (ob′lə gāt), *v.* to make someone feel strongly that he or she must do something: *A promise obligates a person to carry out what is promised.* ❑ *v.* **ob·li·gat·ed, ob·li·gat·ing.**

ob·li·ga·tion (ob′lə gā′shən), *n.* **1** duty under the law or from personal feeling: *We have an obligation to help our friends when they need something.* **2** the binding power of a law, promise, sense of duty, etc.: *The person who did the damage is under obligation to pay for it.* **3** a binding legal agreement; bond; contract: *The firm was not able to meet its obligations.* **4** act of binding yourself or condition of being bound by oath, promise, etc., to do something: *It was his obligation to return my favor.*

o·blig·a·to·ry (ə blig′ə tôr′ē), *adj.* required by law, duty, or custom: *Jury service is obligatory.* —**o·blig′a·to′ri·ly,** *adv.*

o·blige (ə blīj′), *v.* **1** to force someone to do something because of a promise, contract, duty, etc.; require; compel: *The law obliges parents to send their children to school.* **2** to make someone grateful by doing a favor: *We are very much obliged for your kind offer.* **3** to do a favor for: *Kindly oblige me by closing the door.* ❑ *v.* **o·bliged, o·blig·ing.** —**o·blig′er,** *n.*

o·blig·ing (ə blī′jing), *adj.* willing to do favors; helpful: *Her obliging nature wins friends.* —**o·blig′ing·ly,** *adv.* —**o·blig′ing·ness,** *n.*

o·blique (ə blēk′), *adj.* **1** not straight up and down; not straight across; slanting. **2** not straightforward; indirect: *She made an oblique reference to her illness, but did not mention it directly.* —**o·blique′ly,** *adv.* —**o·blique′ness,** *n.*

oblique angle, any angle that is not a right angle. Acute angles and obtuse angles are oblique angles.

o·blit·er·ate (ə blit′ə rāt′), *v.* **1** to remove all traces of: *The heavy rain obliterated the footprints.* **2** to destroy completely: *An earthquake obliterated the village.* ❑ *v.* **o·blit·er·at·ed, o·blit·er·at·ing.** —**o·blit′er·a′tion,** *n.* —**o·blit′er·a′tor,** *n.*

o·bliv·i·on (ə bliv′ē ən), *n.* **1** condition of being entirely forgotten: *Many ancient cities have long since passed into oblivion.* **2** forgetfulness: *the oblivion of deep sleep.*

o·bliv·i·ous (ə bliv′ē əs), *adj.* forgetful; not conscious of: *The book was so interesting that I was oblivious of my surroundings.* ■ **Oblivious** is used with *of* or *to: oblivious to danger, oblivious of danger.* —**o·bliv′i·ous·ly,** *adv.* —**o·bliv′i·ous·ness,** *n.*

ob·long (ob′lông), **1** *adj.* longer than broad: *an oblong loaf of bread.* **2** *n.* rectangle that is not a square.

ob·nox·ious (əb nok′shəs), *adj.* very disagreeable; offensive: *Their rudeness and bad manners made them obnoxious to me.* —**ob·nox′ious·ly,** *adv.* —**ob·nox′ious·ness,** *n.*

o·boe (ō′bō), *n.* a woodwind instrument in which a thin, high-pitched tone is produced by a double reed mouthpiece. [**Oboe** comes from French words meaning "high" and "wood." The oboe is made of wood and makes high-pitched sounds.]

o·bo·ist (ō′bō ist), *n.* someone who plays the oboe.

ob·scene (əb sēn′), *adj.* offending modesty or decency; impure; filthy; vile. **—ob·scene′ly,** *adv.*

ob·scen·i·ty (əb sen′ə tē), *n.* **1** obscene quality. **2** obscene language or behavior; an obscene word or act. ❑ *n., pl.* **ob·scen·i·ties** for 2.

ob·scure (əb skyùr′), **1** *adj.* not clearly expressed; hard to understand; vague: *an obscure passage in a book, an obscure style of writing.* **2** *adj.* not well known; attracting no notice: *an obscure little village, an obscure poet.* **3** *adj.* not easily discovered; hidden: *an obscure path, an obscure meaning.* **4** *adj.* not distinct; not clear: *an obscure shape, obscure sounds.* **5** *adj.* dark; dim: *an obscure corner.* **6** *v.* to hide from view; dim; darken: *Clouds obscure the sun.* ❑ *adj.* **ob·scur·er, ob·scur·est;** *v.* **ob·scured, ob·scur·ing.** **—ob·scure′ly,** *adv.* **—ob·scure′ness,** *n.*

> **SYNONYM STUDY** **Obscure** and **vague** both mean hard to understand. **Obscure** means not clear: *"Too believable" was his obscure comment about the movie.* **Vague** means not precise or specific: *"Pretty much OK" was her vague comment about the movie.*

ob·scur·i·ty (əb skyùr′ə tē), *n.* **1** lack of clearness; difficulty in being understood: *The obscurity of the book caused an argument over its meaning.* **2** something obscure; thing hard to understand; point or passage not clearly expressed; doubtful or vague meaning. **3** condition of being unknown: *Lincoln rose from obscurity to fame.* **4** lack of light; dimness: *The dog hid in the obscurity of the thick bushes.* ❑ *n., pl.* **ob·scur·i·ties** for 2.

ob·se·qui·ous (əb sē′kwē əs), *adj.* overly attentive to someone thought to be important: *Obsequious courtiers greeted the royal couple.* **—ob·se′qui·ous·ly,** *adv.* **—ob·se′qui·ous·ness,** *n.*

ob·serv·a·ble (əb zėr′və bəl), *adj.* **1** able to be noticed; noticeable; easily seen: *That star is observable on a dark night.* **2** able to be followed or practiced: *This rule may not be observable.* **—ob·serv′a·bly,** *adv.*

ob·serv·ance (əb zėr′vəns), *n.* **1** act of observing or keeping laws or customs: *Observance of traffic laws is the sign of a good driver.* **2** act performed as a sign of worship or respect; religious ceremony.

ob·serv·ant (əb zėr′vənt), *adj.* **1** quick to notice; watchful: *If you are observant in the fields and woods, you will find many flowers that others fail to notice.* **2** careful in observing a law, custom, etc.: *A good driver is observant of the traffic rules.* **—ob·serv′ant·ly,** *adv.*

ob·ser·va·tion (ob′zər vā′shən), *n.* **1** act, habit, or power of seeing and noting: *By trained observation a doctor can tell much about the condition of a patient.* **2** something seen and noted: *During science experiments she kept careful records of her observations.* **3** fact or condition of being seen; notice: *The spy avoided observation.* **4** act of watching for some special purpose; study: *The observation of nature is important in science.* **5** a remark; comment: *"Haste makes waste" was Father's observation when I spilled the milk.* **—ob′ser·va′tion·al,** *adj.* **—ob′ser·va′tion·al·ly,** *adv.*

ob·serv·a·to·ry (əb zėr′və tôr′ē), *n.* **1** building equipped with telescopes and other devices for watching and studying astronomical objects. **2** a high place or building giving a wide view. ❑ *n., pl.* **ob·serv·a·to·ries.**

ob·serve (əb zėrv′), *v.* **1** to see and note; notice: *I observed nothing strange in her behavior.* ▪ See Synonym Study at **see**[1]. **2** to examine for some special purpose; study: *An astronomer observes the stars.* **3** to remark; comment: *"Bad weather ahead," she observed.* **4** to keep; follow in practice: *observe silence, serve a rule.* **5** to show regard for; celebrate: *observe a holiday.* ❑ *v.* **ob·served, ob·serv·ing.** **—ob·serv′er,** *n.*

ob·serv·ing (əb zėr′ving), *adj.* observant; quick to notice. **—ob·serv′ing·ly,** *adv.*

ob·sess (əb ses′), *v.* **1** to fill someone's mind; keep the attention of: *I was obsessed with the fear that I might fail.* **2** to think or worry about something all the time: *She obsesses about getting her computer to work properly.* **—ob·ses′sor,** *n.*

ob·ses·sion (əb sesh′ən), *n.* **1** influence of a feeling, idea, or impulse that a person cannot escape. **2** the feeling, idea, or impulse itself.

ob·ses·sive (əb ses′iv), *adj.* of or causing obsession: *an obsessive fear.* **—ob·ses′sive·ly,** *adv.* **—ob·ses′sive·ness,** *n.*

ob·sess·ive-com·pul·sive disorder (əb ses′iv kəm pul′siv), a mental illness in which the symptoms often include performing an action, such as washing the hands, over and over, or persistent unwanted or unpleasant thoughts.

ob·sid·i·an (ob sid′ē ən), *n.* a hard, dark, glassy rock that is formed when lava cools.

ob·so·les·cence (ob′sə les′ns), *n.* process of passing out of use; getting out of date; becoming obsolete.

ob·so·les·cent (ob′sə les′nt), *adj.* passing out of use; tending to become out of date: *an obsolescent machine.*

ob·so·lete (ob′sə lēt *or* ob′sə lēt′), *adj.* **1** no longer in use: *"Eft" (meaning again) is an obsolete word.* **2** out of date; old-fashioned: *We still use this machine though it is obsolete.*

ob·sta·cle (ob′stə kəl), *n.* something that prevents or stops progress; hindrance: *A fallen tree was an obstacle to traffic. He overcame the obstacle of blindness and became a computer programmer.*

> **SYNONYM STUDY** **Obstacle, hindrance,** and **barrier** all mean something that prevents or delays action. **Obstacle** is a general word: *The mountain climbers overcame all obstacles and reached the peak.* **Hindrance** suggests something that holds back or gets in the way: *Despite the hindrance of asthma, she is a champion athlete.* **Barrier** suggests something in the way like a wall: *The treaty removed barriers to trade between the two countries.*

ob·stet·ric (ob stet′rik), *adj.* of or about the care of women before, in, and after childbirth.

ob·stet·ri·cal (ob stet′rə kəl), *adj.* obstetric. **—ob·stet′ri·cal·ly,** *adv.*

ob·ste·tri·cian (ob′stə trish′ən), *n.* a doctor who specializes in obstetrics.

ob·stet·rics (ob stet′riks), *n.* branch of medicine concerned with treating women before, in, and after childbirth.

ob·sti·na·cy (ob′stə nə sē), *n.* stubbornness.

ob·sti·nate (ob′stə nit), *adj.* **1** very determined; stubborn: *They were obstinate and wanted to do everything their own way.* **2** hard to control or treat: *an obstinate cough.* **—ob′sti·nate·ly,** *adv.* **—ob′sti·nate·ness,** *n.*

ob·struct (əb strukt′), *v.* **1** to make hard to pass through; block up: *Fallen trees obstruct the road.* **2** to be in the way of; hinder: *Trees obstruct our view of the ocean.* **—ob·struc′tor,** *n.*

ob·struc·tion (əb struk′shən), *n.* **1** something that is in the way; obstacle: *The old path was blocked by such obstructions as boulders and fallen trees.* **2** act or process of blocking or hindering: *Obstruction of justice is a crime.*

ob·struc·tion·ism (əb struk′shə niz′əm), *n.* act or practice of hindering the progress or business of a meeting, legislature, etc.

ob·struc·tion·ist (əb struk′shə nist), *n.* person who hinders progress, legislation, reform, etc.

ob·struc·tive (əb struk′tiv), *adj.* tending or serving to block or hinder something: *obstructive tactics.* **—ob·struc′tive·ness,** *n.*

ob·tain (əb tān′), *v.* **1** to get something through effort; come to have: *obtain a job you applied for, obtain knowledge through study.* ▪ See Synonym Study at **get.** **2** to be in use; prevail: *Different rules obtain in different schools.* **—ob·tain′a·ble,** *adj.* **—ob·tain′er,** *n.*

ob·trude (əb trüd′), *v.* **1** to put forward unasked and unwanted; force: *Don't obtrude your opinions on others.* **2** to come unasked and unwanted; force yourself; intrude. ❑ *v.* **ob·trud·ed, ob·trud·ing.** **—ob·trud′er,** *n.*

ob·tru·sive (əb trü′siv), *adj.* putting yourself forward in an unpleasant way; intrusive. **—ob·tru′sive·ly,** *adv.* **—ob·tru′sive·ness,** *n.*

ob·tuse (əb tüs′), *adj.* **1** slow in understanding; stupid: *They were too obtuse to take the hint.* **2** not sharp or acute; blunt. **—ob·tuse′ly,** *adv.* **—ob·tuse′ness,** *n.*

a	hat	ė	term	ô	order	ch	child		
ā	age	i	it	oi	oil	ng	long		a in about
ä	far	ī	ice	ou	out	sh	she		e in taken
â	care	o	hot	u	cup	th	thin	ə	i in pencil
e	let	ō	open	u̇	put	₮H	then		o in lemon
ē	equal	ò	saw	ü	rule	zh	measure		u in circus

obtuse angle, angle larger than a right angle but less than 180 degrees. See picture at **angle**[1].

obtuse triangle, triangle having one obtuse angle. See picture at **triangle**.

ob·verse (ob′vèrs′), *n.* **1** side of a coin, medal, etc., that has the principal design on it. **2** the face of anything that is meant to be turned toward the observer; front. —**ob·verse′ly,** *adv.*

ob·vi·ate (ob′vē āt), *v.* to meet and dispose of a need, difficulty, etc.; clear out of the way; remove: *obviate possible objections.* ❑ *v.* **ob·vi·at·ed, ob·vi·at·ing.** —**ob′vi·a′tor,** *n.*

ob·vi·ous (ob′vē əs), *adj.* easily seen or understood; clear to the eye or mind; not to be doubted; plain: *It was obvious that she was angry.* ■ See Synonym Study at **clear.** [**Obvious** comes from a Latin word meaning "in the way." If something is obvious, you can't get past it without noticing.] —**ob′vi·ous·ly,** *adv.* —**ob′vi·ous·ness,** *n.*

oc·a·ri·na (ok′ə rē′nə), *n.* a small wind instrument with finger holes and a mouthpiece like a whistle. It produces a soft sound. ❑ *n., pl.* **oc·a·ri·nas.**

oc·ca·sion (ə kā′zhən), **1** *n.* a particular time: *We have met them on several occasions.* **2** *n.* a special event: *The jewels were worn only on great occasions.* **3** *n.* a good chance; opportunity: *The trip gave us an occasion to get better acquainted.* **4** *n.* a cause; reason: *The dog that was the occasion of the quarrel had run away.* ■ See Synonym Study at **cause.** **5** *v.* to cause; bring about: *His strange behavior occasioned talk.*
on occasion, now and then; once in a while.

oc·ca·sion·al (ə kā′zhə nəl), *adj.* **1** happening sometimes or once in a while: *We had fine weather all through July except for an occasional thunderstorm.* **2** caused by or used for some special time or event: *A piece of occasional music was played at the inauguration.* **3** for use once in a while: *occasional chairs.*

oc·ca·sion·al·ly (ə kā′zhə nə lē), *adv.* now and then; once in a while.

Oc·ci·dent (ok′sə dənt), *n.* countries in Europe and the Americas, considered separately from those in Asia; the West.

Oc·ci·den·tal (ok′sə den′tl), **1** *adj.* Western; of the Occident. **2** *n.* person born in the West. Europeans are Occidentals. **3** *adj.* **occidental,** western. ■ See Usage Note at **Oriental.**

oc·cip·i·tal (ok sip′ə təl), *adj.* of or about the back part of the head or skull. —**oc·cip′i·tal·ly,** *adv.*

oc·clude (o klüd′), *v.* **1** to stop up or block off something that is normally open; obstruct. **2** to meet closely in proper position. The teeth in the upper jaw and those in the lower jaw should occlude. ❑ *v.* **oc·clud·ed, oc·clud·ing.**

occluded front, a weather front formed when two cold air masses meet, forcing upward a warm air mass that had been between the cold ones, and often causing clouds, rain, or snow.

oc·clu·sion (ə klü′zhən), *n.* act of occluding or condition of being occluded.

oc·cult (ə kult′ *or* ok′ult), **1** *adj.* beyond the bounds of ordinary knowledge; mysterious. **2** *adj.* outside the laws of the natural world; magical: *Astrology and alchemy are occult sciences.* **3** *n.* **the occult,** knowledge of or study of magical, supernatural matters. —**oc·cult′ly,** *adv.* —**oc·cult′ness,** *n.*

oc·cult·ism (ə kul′tiz′əm *or* ok′ul tiz′əm), *n.* **1** belief in occult powers. **2** study or use of supposed occult knowledge.

oc·cu·pan·cy (ok′yə pən sē), *n.* act of occupying; holding land, houses, etc., by being in possession: *After five years of occupancy the homesteaders received a title to the land they lived on.*

oc·cu·pant (ok′yə pənt), *n.* **1** someone who occupies: *The occupants of the car stepped out as I approached.* **2** person in actual possession of a house, estate, office, etc.

oc·cu·pa·tion (ok′yə pā′shən), *n.* **1** work someone does regularly or to earn a living; business; employment; trade: *Caring for the sick is a nurse's occupation.* **2** invasion and physical possession: *the occupation of a town by the enemy.*

oc·cu·pa·tion·al (ok′yə pā′shə nəl), *adj.* of or about someone's occupation. An occupational hazard or disease is one that results from someone's work or occupation.

oc·cu·py (ok′yə pī), *v.* **1** to live in: *Two families occupy the house next door.* **2** to take possession of: *The enemy occupied our fort.*

3 to have; hold: *A judge occupies an important position.* **4** to take up; fill: *The building occupies an entire block.* **5** to keep busy; engage; employ: *Composing music occupied her attention.* ❑ *v.* **oc·cu·pied, oc·cu·py·ing.** —**oc′cu·pi′er,** *n.*

oc·cur (ə kėr′), *v.* **1** to take place; happen: *Storms often occur in winter.* ■ See Synonym Study at **happen.** **2** to be found; exist: *"E" occurs in print more than any other letter.* **3** to come to mind; suggest itself: *Did it occur to you to close the window?* ❑ *v.* **oc·curred, oc·cur·ring.**

oc·cur·rence (ə kėr′əns), *n.* **1** event; happening: *Her visit was an unexpected occurrence.* **2** act or fact of occurring: *The occurrence of storms delayed our trip.*

OCD, obsessive-compulsive disorder.

o·cean (ō′shən), *n.* **1** the salt water that covers almost three fourths of the earth's surface; sea. **2** any of its four main parts; the Atlantic, Pacific, Indian, and Arctic oceans. The waters around Antarctica are considered by some people to form a fifth ocean. —**o′cean·like′,** *adj.*

o·cean·go·ing (ō′shən gō′ing), *adj.* **1** designed and built to travel on the ocean: *an oceangoing ship.* **2** of or by travel on the ocean: *oceangoing trade.*

O·ce·an·i·a (ō′shē an′ē ə *or* ō′shē ā′nē ə), *n.* **1** islands of the central and south Pacific, north, northeast, and east of Australia. **2** these islands, together with Australasia and the Malay Archipelago. —**O·ce·an′i·an,** *adj., n.*

o·ce·an·ic (ō′shē an′ik), *adj.* **1** of or in the ocean: *oceanic islands, oceanic fish.* **2** like the ocean; wide; vast.

o·cean·og·ra·pher (ō′shə nog′rə fər), *n.* an expert in oceanography.

o·cean·og·ra·phy (ō′shə nog′rə fē), *n.* science that deals with oceans and seas and with the living things in them.

oc·e·lot (os′ə lot *or* ō′sə lot), *n.* a medium-sized fierce cat, something like a small leopard. Ocelots are found from Texas through Mexico and into parts of South America.

o·cher or **o·chre** (ō′kər), *n.* **1** a yellow, brown, or red earthy mixture containing clay and iron oxide, used as a pigment. **2** a pale brownish yellow.

o·clock (ə klok′), *adv.* **1** of or by the clock: *It is one o'clock.* **2** as if on the dial of a clock. 12 o'clock in an airplane is the horizontal direction straight ahead, or the vertical position straight overhead.

O·Con·nor (ō kon′ər), *n.* **1 Flan·ner·y** (flan′ər ē), 1925-1964, American writer. Her stories are violent and often have disturbed or deformed characters. **2 San·dra Day** (san′drə dā), born 1930, U.S. Supreme Court justice since 1981. She was the first woman appointed to the Supreme Court.

o·co·til·lo (ō kə tē′yō), *n.* a bush of Mexico and the southwestern United States with tall, thin, thorny stems and red flowers, often grown as a hedge. ❑ *n., pl.* **o·co·til·los.**

Oct., October.

oct-, *prefix.* eight: *octagon = a figure with eight angles and sides.*

oc·ta·gon (ok′tə gon), *n.* a plane figure having eight angles and eight sides. —**oc·tag·o·nal** (ok tag′ə nəl), *adj.* —**oc·tag′o·nal·ly,** *adv.*

oc·ta·he·dron (ok′tə hē′drən), *n.* a solid form with eight surfaces. ❑ *n., pl.* **oc·ta·he·drons, oc·ta·he·dra** (ok′tə hē′drə).

oc·tane (ok′tān), *n.* a colorless, liquid hydrocarbon that occurs in petroleum. High quality gasoline contains more octane than the lower grades.

oc·tave (ok′tiv *or* ok′tāv), *n.* **1** interval between a musical tone and another tone having twice or half as many vibrations per second. From one tone called C to the next tone called C is an octave. **2** the eighth tone above or below a given tone, having twice or half as many vibrations per second. **3** series of tones or of keys of an instrument, filling the interval between a tone and its octave. **4** the sounding together of a tone and its octave.

oc·ta·vo (ok tā′vō *or* ok tä′vō), *n.* **1** the size of a page that is one eighth of a whole sheet of printing paper. **2** book having pages of this size, usually about 6 by 9 inches (15 by 23 centimeters). ❑ *n., pl.* **oc·ta·vos.**

oc·tet (ok tet′), *n.* **1** piece of music for eight voices or instruments. **2** group of eight singers or players performing together. **3** any group of eight.

Oc·to·ber (ok tō′bər), *n.* the tenth month of the year. It has 31 days. [**October** comes from a Latin word meaning "eight." October was the eighth month of the earliest Roman calendar, which began with March.]

oc·to·ge·nar·i·an (ok′tə jə ner′ē ən), **1** *n.* person who is 80 years old or between 80 and 90 years old. **2** *adj.* 80 years old or between 80 and 90 years old.

oc·to·pus (ok′tə pəs), *n.* **1** any of numerous sea animals with soft bodies and eight arms with suckers on them; devilfish. **2** anything like an octopus. A powerful, grasping organization with far-reaching influence is often called an octopus. ❑ *n., pl.* **oc·to·pus·es, oc·to·pi** (ok′tə pī). [**Octopus** comes from Greek words meaning "eight" and "foot." We think of the octopus as having eight arms, but clearly the Greeks had another idea.]

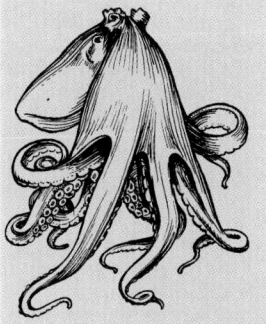

octopus (def. 1)—arms 6 in. (15 cm) to 20 ft. (6.1 m) across

oc·u·lar (ok′yə lər), *adj.* **1** of the eye: *an ocular muscle.* **2** received by actual sight; seen: *ocular proof.*

oc·u·list (ok′yə list), *n.* earlier: **1** ophthalmologist. **2** optometrist.

odd (od), *adj.* **1** strange; peculiar; unusual: *The odd house has no windows.* **2** leaving a remainder of 1 when divided by 2: *Three and seven are odd numbers.* **3** having an odd number. **4** being one of a pair or set of which the rest is missing: *an odd sock.* **5** left over; extra: *Pay him and keep the odd change.* **6** occasional: *odd jobs.* **7** with some extra: *thirty-odd dollars.* **—odd′ly,** *adv.* **—odd′ness,** *n.*

odd·ball (od′bȯl′), *n.* INFORMAL. a very eccentric person.

odd·i·ty (od′ə tē), *n.* **1** a strange, unusual, or peculiar person or thing. **2** strangeness; peculiarity. ❑ *n., pl.* **odd·i·ties** for 1.

oddity

odds (odz), *n.pl.* **1** the probability that something is true or that it will happen: *The odds are in our favor and we should win.* **2** this probability expressed as a number or ratio: *If you bet $10 on a horse at 3 to 1 odds, and it wins, you win $30.*

at odds, quarreling; disagreeing: *My sisters were often at odds.*

by all odds, in all ways; without doubt: *It is by all odds the best choice.*

odds and ends, things left over; extra bits; scraps; remnants.

odds-on (odz′ȯn′), *adj.* having the odds in your favor; having a good chance to win in a contest.

ode (ōd), *n.* a lyric poem full of noble feeling expressed with dignity. It is often addressed to some person or thing.

O·der (ō′dər), *n.* river flowing from the Czech Republic through W Poland into the Baltic Sea.

O·des·sa (ō des′ə), *n.* port in S Ukraine, on the Black Sea.

O·din (ōd′n), *n.* the chief Scandinavian god. Odin was the god of wisdom, war, and the dead. The Anglo-Saxons called him Woden.

o·di·ous (ō′dē əs), *adj.* very displeasing; hateful; offensive: *an odious smell, odious lies.* **—o′di·ous·ly,** *adv.* **—o′di·ous·ness,** *n.*

o·dom·e·ter (ō dom′ə tər), *n.* device for measuring the distance a vehicle has gone, by recording the number of revolutions of a wheel. Every car has an odometer showing its total distance traveled.

o·dor (ō′dər), *n.* smell or scent: *the odor of roses.*

o·dor·if·er·ous (ō′də rif′ər əs), *adj.* having an odor, especially an unpleasant odor: *an odoriferous flower.*

o·dor·less (ō′dər lis), *adj.* without any odor: *Water is odorless.* **—o′dor·less·ness,** *n.*

o·dor·ous (ō′dər əs), *adj.* giving forth an odor, especially a pleasant odor; fragrant: *Spices are odorous.* **—o′dor·ous·ly,** *adv.* **—o′dor·ous·ness,** *n.*

O·dys·se·us (ō dis′ē əs), *n.* Ulysses.

Od·ys·sey (od′ə sē), *n.* **1** a Greek epic poem describing the ten years of wandering of Ulysses after the Trojan War and his return home. Homer is supposed to be its author. **2 odyssey,** any long series of wanderings and adventures. ❑ *n., pl.* **od·ys·seys** for 2.

OECD, Organization for Economic Cooperation and Development.

Oed·i·pus (ed′ə pəs *or* ē′də pəs), *n.* (in Greek legends) a king who unknowingly killed his father and married his own mother.

o′er (ôr), *prep., adv.* OLD USE. over. ∎ Other words that sound like this are **oar, or,** and **ore.**

of (ov *or* uv), *prep.* **1** belonging to: *a friend of my childhood, the news of the day, the driver of the car.* **2** made from: *a house of bricks, castles of sand.* **3** having; containing; with: *a house of six rooms.* **4** having as a quality: *a look of pity, a word of encouragement.* **5** named: *the city of Chicago.* **6** away from; from: *north of Boston.* **7** about; in regard to; concerning: *think well of someone, be hard of heart, be fifteen years of age.* **8** as a result of having or using; out of; owing to: *expect much of a new medicine, die of a disease.* **9** among: *a friend of mine.* **10** before: *The time is twenty of seven.* **11** *Of* connects nouns and adjectives having the meaning of a verb with the noun which would be the object of the verb: *the eating of fruit, the love of truth, in search of a ball, a hall smelling of onions.* ∎ See Usage Note at **have.**

off (ȯf), **1** *adv.* from the usual or correct position, condition, etc.: *I took off my hat.* **2** *prep.* from; away from: *I jumped off the step. We are miles off the main road.* **3** *adv.* away; at or to a distance: *go off on a journey. Christmas is only five weeks off.* **4** *prep.* subtracted from: *25 dollars off the regular price.* **5** *prep.* near to; by: *They live right off the bus route.* **6** *adv.* so as to stop or lessen: *Turn the water off.* **7** *adj.* no longer planned; cancelled: *The game is off.* **8** *prep., adj.* not on; not connected: *The electricity is off.* **9** *adv., adj.* without work: *an afternoon off. He pursues his hobby during off hours.* **10** *adj.* in a specified condition in regard to money, property, etc.: *How well off are the Smiths?* **11** *adj.* not very good; not up to average: *Because I hadn't played in weeks, my tennis game was off.* **12** *adj.* possible but not likely: *I came on the off chance that I would find you.* **13** *adv.* on one's way: *Her friends saw her off at the airport.* **14** *adj.* in error; wrong: *Your figures are way off.* **15** *prep.* seaward from: *The ship anchored off Maine.* **16** *prep.* from the food provided by: *live off the land.* **17** *prep.* at the expense of; with the financial aid of: *He's been living off his family for years.* **18** *prep.* out of the possession of; from: *I bought it off her last week.*

be off, to go away; leave quickly: *I'm off to the party.*

off and on, at some times and not at others; now and then: *She has lived in Europe off and on for ten years.*

off with, 1 to take off. **2** away with!

| USAGE NOTE | **Off** is often used in everyday speech with **of** after it, but many people feel that careful writers and speakers should avoid **of. SAY:** *I stepped off the sidewalk. The cat jumped off the table.* NOT: *I stepped off of the sidewalk. The cat jumped off of the table.* The word **of** adds no meaning to such sentences. It's a mystery why so many people use it. |

a	hat	ė	term	ô	order	ch	child
ā	age	i	it	oi	oil	ng	long
ä	far	ī	ice	ou	out	sh	she
â	care	o	hot	u	cup	th	thin
e	let	ō	open	ů	put	₮ℎ	then
ē	equal	ò	saw	ü	rule	zh	measure

ə { a in about / e in taken / i in pencil / o in lemon / u in circus

off·beat (ôf′bēt′), **1** *adj.* out of the ordinary; unusual; unconventional: *an offbeat play.* **2** *n.* a musical beat with little or no accent.

off-cam·er·a (ôf′kam′ər ə), **1** *adj.* not planned to be recorded or filmed: *off-camera interviews.* **2** *adv.* beyond the range of the camera.

off-col·or (ôf′kul′ər), *adj.* **1** not of the right color. **2** somewhat improper: *an off-color joke.*

of·fence (ə fens′), *n.* BRITISH. offense.

of·fend (ə fend′), *v.* **1** to hurt the feelings of someone; make angry; displease; pain: *My friend was offended by my laughter.* **2** to affect in an unpleasant or disagreeable way. **3** to sin or do wrong: *In what way have I offended?*

of·fend·er (ə fen′dər), *n.* **1** person who offends. **2** person who does wrong or breaks a law: *No trespassing; offenders will be prosecuted.*

of·fense (ə fens′ *for 1-5;* ə fens′ *or* ô′fens *for 6*), *n.* **1** act of breaking the law; crime or sin. Offenses against the law are punished by fines or imprisonment. **2** condition of being offended; hurt feelings; anger: *He tried not to cause offense.* **3** act of offending; hurting someone's feelings: *No offense was meant.* **4** something that offends or causes displeasure. ■ See Synonym Study at **crime.** **5** act of attacking; attack: *A gun is a weapon of offense.* **6** an attacking team or force. —**of·fense′less,** *adj.*
give offense, to offend.
take offense, to be offended.

of·fen·sive (ə fen′siv), **1** *adj.* giving offense; irritating; annoying: *"That's a dumb idea" is an offensive remark.* ■ See Synonym Study at **rude. 2** *adj.* unpleasant; disagreeable; disgusting: *Bad eggs have an offensive odor.* **3** *adj.* used for attack; relating to attack: *offensive weapons, an offensive war for conquest.* **4** *n.* position or attitude of attack: *The army took the offensive.* **5** *n.* an attack: *an all-out offensive against polio.* —**of·fen′sive·ly,** *adv.* —**of·fen′sive·ness,** *n.*

of·fer (ô′fər), **1** *v.* to hold out to be taken or refused; present: *She offered us her help.* **2** *v.* to be willing if another approves: *They offered to help us.* **3** *v.* to propose; advance; suggest: *She offered a few ideas to improve the plan.* **4** *v.* to present in worship: *offer prayers.* **5** *v.* to give or show intention; attempt; try: *The thieves offered no resistance to the police.* **6** *v.* to suggest a price you are willing to pay for something: *She offered $90,000 for the house.* **7** *n.* thing that is offered: *She made an offer of $90,000 for a house.* —**of′fer·er** or **of′fe·ror,** *n.*

of·fer·ing (ô′fər ing), *n.* **1** something given as an act of worship. **2** contribution; gift. **3** act of one that offers.

of·fer·to·ry (ô′fər tôr′ē), *n.* **1** verses said or the music sung or played while the offering is received. **2** collection at a religious service. □ *n., pl.* **of·fer·to·ries.**

off·hand (ôf′hand′ *for adv.;* ôf′hand′ *for adj.*), **1** *adv.* without previous thought or preparation; at once: *The carpenter could not tell offhand how much the work would cost.* **2** *adj.* done or made offhand: *His offhand remarks were sometimes very wise.* **3** *adj.* casual; informal: *They played in an offhand way, without even keeping score.* **4** *adj.* without due courtesy; impolite: *The child's offhand ways angered her parents.*

off·hand·ed (ôf′han′did), *adj.* offhand. —**off′hand′ed·ly,** *adv.* —**off′hand′ed·ness,** *n.*

of·fice (ô′fis), *n.* **1** place in which the work of a business or profession is done; room or rooms in which to work: *The doctor's office is on the second floor.* **2** staff of persons carrying on work in an office: *Half the office is on vacation.* **3** position, especially in the public service: *The President holds the highest office in the United States.* **4** duty of your position; task; job; work: *A teacher's office is teaching.* **5** act of kindness or unkindness; attention; service; injury: *Through the good offices of a friend, I was able to get a job.* **6** a religious ceremony or prayer: *the daily office.*

of·fice·hold·er (ô′fis hōl′dər), *n.* person who holds a public office; government official.

of·fi·cer (ô′fə sər), *n.* **1** (in the armed forces) someone who commands others, especially someone who holds a commission, such as a major, a general, a captain, or an admiral. **2** someone who holds a public, government, or other office: *a police officer, an officer of a company.* **3** the president, vice-president, secretary, treasurer, etc., of a club, society, or similar organization.

of·fi·cial (ə fish′əl), **1** *n.* someone who holds a public position or who is in charge of some public work or duty: *The mayor is a government official.* **2** *n.* someone holding office; officer: *bank officials.* **3** *adj.* of an office or officers: *official duties, an official uniform.* **4** *adj.* having authority: *An official record is kept of the proceedings of Congress.* **5** *adj.* suitable for someone in office: *the official dignity of a judge.* —**of·fi′cial·ly,** *adv.*

of·fi·ci·ate (ə fish′ē āt), *v.* **1** to perform the duties of any office or position: *The president officiates at all club meetings.* **2** to perform the duties of a priest, minister, or rabbi: *The rabbi officiated at the bar mitzvah.* **3** to act as an official at a sports event. □ *v.* **of·fi·ci·at·ed, of·fi·ci·at·ing.**

of·fi·cious (ə fish′əs), *adj.* too ready to offer services or advice; minding other people's business; fond of meddling. —**of·fi′cious·ly,** *adv.* —**of·fi′cious·ness,** *n.*

off·ing (ô′fing), *n.* **in the offing,** in the near future: *trouble in the offing.*

off·ish (ô′fish), *adj.* INFORMAL. inclined to keep aloof; distant and reserved in manner. —**off′ish·ly,** *adv.* —**off′ish·ness,** *n.*

officiate (def. 3)

off-key (ôf′kē′), **1** *adv.* not in the right musical key: *to sing off-key.* **2** *adj.* somewhat inappropriate: *awkward, off-key remarks.*

off-lim·its (ôf′lim′its), *adj.* not to be used or entered; forbidden: *The street is off-limits for play.*

off-line or **off·line** (ôf′līn′), *adv., adj.* **1** not controlled by a computer. **2** not connected to a computer.

off-sea·son (ôf′sē′zn), **1** *n.* time of year during which business is least active: *The tourist shops close in the off-season.* **2** *adj., adv.* during that time of year: *Take advantage of off-season airline fares. You can get discounts if you travel off-season.*

off·set (ôf′set′ *for verb;* ôf′set′ *for noun*), **1** *v.* to make up for; compensate for: *A good offense helps offset a weak defense in sports.* **2** *n.* something which makes up for something else; compensation: *In tennis, her speed and control were an offset to her lack of strength.* **3** *n.* any offshoot. **4** *n.* process of printing in which the inked impression is first made on a rubber roller and transferred to the paper, instead of being printed directly on the paper. □ *v.* **off·set, off·set·ting.**

off·shoot (ôf′shüt′), *n.* **1** branch growing out from the main stem of a plant, tree, etc. **2** anything coming, or thought of as coming, as a branch from a main part: *an offshoot of a mountain range.*

off·shore (ôf′shôr′), *adj., adv.* off or away from the shore: *off-shore fisheries, a wind blowing offshore.*

off·side (ôf′sīd′), *adj.* (in sports) ahead of the ball or puck according to the rules.

off·spring (ôf′spring′), *n.* the young of a person, animal, plant, or other living thing; descendant: *Every one of their offspring had red hair.* □ *n., pl.* **off·spring.**

off·stage (ôf′stāj′), *adj., adv.* away from the part of the stage that the audience can see: *describe events that took place offstage.*

off-the-rec·ord (ôf′тнə rek′ərd), *adj.* not intended for publication; not to be repeated publicly or issued as news: *an off-the-record opinion.*

off-the-wall (ôf′тнə wôl′), *adj.* INFORMAL. odd; silly; highly unusual: *an off-the-wall suggestion.*

off-white (ôf′wīt′), **1** *n.* a very light shade of color, very close to white. **2** *adj.* almost white: *an off-white ceiling.*

oft (ôft), *adv.* OLD USE. often.

of·ten (ô′fən *or* ôf′tən), *adv.* in many cases; many times; frequently: *Blame is often misdirected. We come here often.*

of·ten·times (ô′fən tīmz′), *adv.* often.

o·gle (ō′gəl), *v.* to stare at someone in a way that shows sexual interest. □ *v.* **o·gled, o·gling.** —**o′gler,** *n.*

o·gre (ō′gər), *n.* **1** (in fairy tales) giant or monster that eats people. **2** person like such a monster in appearance or character.

oh or **Oh** (ō), *interj.* word used to express surprise, joy, grief, pain, and other feelings: *Oh, dear me!* Also, **O.** ■ Another word that sounds like this is **owe.**

OH, Ohio (used with postal Zip Code).

O·hi·o (ō hī′ō), *n.* **1** one of the north central states of the United States. *Abbreviation:* OH or O. *Capital:* Columbus. **2** river in the United States, flowing SW from Pittsburgh into the Mississippi River. [**Ohio** may come from an Iroquois word meaning "great," "fine," or "beautiful." The state was named for the river.] —**O·hi·o·an,** *n.*

ohm (ōm), *n.* unit for measuring electrical resistance. A wire in which one volt produces a current of one ampere has a resistance of one ohm.

ohm·me·ter (ōm′mē′tər), *n.* device for measuring electrical resistance in ohms.

Ohm's law, a scientific law that electrical current is directly proportional to electromotive force and inversely proportional to resistance.

-oid, *suffix.* **1** like ___: *humanoid = like a human.* **2** thing like a ___: *spheroid = thing like a sphere.*

oil (oil), **1** *n.* any thick, fatty or greasy liquid that is lighter than water, burns easily, and dissolves in alcohol but not in water. Mineral oils, such as kerosene, are used for fuel. Animal and vegetable oils, such as olive oil, are used in cooking, medicine, etc. **2** *n.* petroleum. **3** *v.* to put an oil on or in: *oil a door's squeaky hinges.* **4** *n.* oil paint. **5** *n.* oil painting. [**Oil** comes from a Greek word meaning "olive." **Olive** comes from the same word. Olive oil was the most important kind of oil in ancient Greece.]

burn the midnight oil, to study or work late at night.

strike oil, 1 to find petroleum by boring a hole in the earth. **2** to find something very profitable.

oil·cloth (oil′klôth′), *n.* **1** cloth made waterproof by coating it with paint or oil. It is used to cover shelves, tables, etc. **2** piece of this cloth; oilskin: *an oilcloth on a kitchen table.* □ *n., pl.* **oil·cloths** (oil′klô̇тнz′ or oil′klôths′) for 2.

oil color, 1 oil paint. **2** pigment mixed with oil to make oil paint. **3** oil painting.

oil·er (oi′lər), *n.* **1** person or thing that oils. **2** can with a long spout used in oiling machinery.

oil paint, paint made by mixing a pigment with oil.

oil painting, 1 picture painted with oil paint. **2** art of painting with oil paint.

oil shale, shale rock from which petroleum may be obtained.

oil·skin (oil′skin′), *n.* **1** cloth treated with oil to make it waterproof. **2** Usually, **oilskins,** *pl.* coat and trousers made of this cloth.

oil slick, a film of oil floating on the surface of water.

oil·stone (oil′stōn′), *n.* any stone which is oiled and used for sharpening tools.

oil well, well drilled in the earth to get oil.

oil·y (oi′lē), *adj.* **1** of oil: *an oily smell.* **2** containing oil: *oily salad dressing.* **3** covered or soaked with oil: *oily rags.* **4** like oil; smooth; slippery: *an oily liquid.* **5** too smooth or polite; suspiciously or disagreeably smooth or polite: *an oily manner.* □ *adj.* **oil·i·er, oil·i·est.** —**oil′i·ness,** *n.*

oint·ment (oint′mənt), *n.* substance made from oil or fat, often containing medicine, used on the skin to heal, soothe, or soften it. Cold cream and salve are ointments.

oil well with pump

O·jib·wa (ō jib′wä), *n.* member of an American Indian tribe formerly living around Lake Superior and now living in many places in the north central United States and south central Canada; Chippewa. □ *n., pl.* **O·jib·wa** or **O·jib·was.**

OK (ō′kā′), **1** *adj., adv., interj.* all right; correct; approved: *The new schedule was OK. She's doing OK at work.* "*OK, OK!*" he yelled. **2** *v.* to endorse; approve: *My teacher has to OK my class schedule.* **3** *n.* approval: *She gave the plan her OK.* Also, **O.K.** or **okay.** □ *v.* **OK'd, OK'ing;** *n., pl.* **OK's.**

OK, Oklahoma (used with postal Zip Code).

O.K. (ō′kā′), *adj., adv., interj., v., n.* OK. □ *v.* **O.K.'d, O.K.'ing;** *n., pl.* **O.K.'s.**

o·ka·pi (ō kä′pē), *n.* a mammal of central Africa, related to the giraffe, but smaller, without spots, and with a much shorter neck. It has stripes like a zebra's on parts of its legs. □ *n., pl.* **o·ka·pi** or **o·ka·pis.**

o·kay (ō′kā′), *adj., adv., interj., v., n.* OK.

O'Keeffe (ō kēf′), *n.* **Georgia,** 1887-1986, American painter. She often painted flowers and desert landscapes.

O·khotsk (ō kotsk′), *n.* **Sea of,** part of the Pacific Ocean, east of Siberia and north of Japan.

O·kie (ō′kē), *n.* INFORMAL. a migrant farm worker, especially one originally from Oklahoma. ■ The word *Okie* is often considered offensive.

O·ki·na·wa (ō′kə nä′wə), *n.* island in the W Pacific belonging to Japan. The last large battle of World War II took place here beginning in April 1945. U.S. forces finally defeated the Japanese defenders in late June. —**O′ki·na′wan,** *adj., n.*

Okla., Oklahoma.

O·kla·ho·ma (ō′klə hō′mə), *n.* one of the southwestern states of the United States. *Abbreviation:* OK or Okla. *Capital:* Oklahoma City. —**O′kla·ho′man,** *adj., n.*

Oklahoma City, capital of Oklahoma, in the central part.

o·kra (ō′krə), *n.* plant grown for its sticky pods, which are used in soups and as a vegetable; gumbo. □ *n., pl.* **o·kras.**

old (ōld), **1** *adj.* not young; having existed for a long time; aged: *old people, an old oak tree.* **2** *adj.* of age; in age: *The baby is ten months old.* **3** *adj.* not new; not recent; made long ago; ancient: *an old excuse, an old tomb, an old debt, an old family.* **4** *adj.* much worn by age or use: *old clothes.* **5** *adj.* looking or seeming old; like an old person in thought, behavior, etc.; mature: *That child is old for her years.* **6** *adj.* of long standing; over a long period of time: *We are old friends.* **7** *adj.* former: *An old student returned to visit her teacher.* **8** *adj.* familiar; dear: *good old fellow.* **9** *n.* time long ago; the past: *the heroes of old.* **10** *n.pl.* **the old,** old people: *a home for the old.* □ *adj.* **old·er, old·est** or **eld·er, eld·est.** ■ See Usage Note at **elder**[1]. —**old′ness,** *n.*

old age, years of life from about 65 on.

old-boy network, a group of men in the same profession or social class who help each other out in business, politics, etc.

old country, country an emigrant comes from.

old·en (ōl′dən), *adj.* of or from a time long ago; old; ancient: *King Arthur lived in olden times.*

a	hat	ė	term	ô	order	ch	child		a in about
ā	age	i	it	oi	oil	ng	long		e in taken
ä	far	ī	ice	ou	out	sh	she	ə {	i in pencil
â	care	o	hot	u	cup	th	thin		o in lemon
e	let	ō	open	u̇	put	тн	then		u in circus
ē	equal	ȯ	saw	ü	rule	zh	measure		

O

Old English, 1 period in the history of the English language before 1100. **2** language of this period; Anglo-Saxon.

WORD SOURCE Old English has given many words to the English language—perhaps one fourth of the vocabulary, including the words below.

answer	door	lady	send
back	eye	make	shoulder
bed	gate	milk	sparrow
bee	ghost	penny	stone
bird	iron	queen	tall
body	island	roof	walnut
day	ivy	salt	

old-fash·ioned (ōld′fash′ənd), *adj.* **1** out of date in style, construction, etc.; of or typical of an old style or time: *an old-fashioned dress.* **2** preferring old ways, ideas, etc.: *They are very old-fashioned in their ideas.*

old-fashioned (def. 1)
an old-fashioned sleigh

Old Glory, flag of the United States; the Stars and Stripes.

old hand, a very skilled or experienced person; expert: *an old hand at skiing.*

old·ie (ōl′dē), *n.* INFORMAL. something old, popular, or familiar, such as a song or a movie.

old-line (ōld′līn′), *adj.* **1** following old ideas and ways; conservative. **2** having a long history; established.

old maid, 1 woman who has not married and seems unlikely to. ■ This meaning of **old maid** is often considered offensive. **2** a prim, fussy person. ■ This meaning of **old maid** is often considered offensive. **3** a simple card game in which players draw cards from each other's hands to make pairs. The player holding the extra card at the end of the game loses.

Old Testament, the earlier part of the Bible, which contains the religious and social laws of the Jews and a record of their history, important literary works, and prophetic writings.

old-time (ōld′tīm′), *adj.* of former times; like old times: *old-time cars.*

old-tim·er (ōld′tī′mər), *n.* person who has lived a long time or been a member of a group for a long time: *The neighborhood old-timers remember when the streets were not paved.*

old wives' tale, a foolish story; silly or superstitious belief. ■ This phrase is sometimes considered offensive.

Old World, the Eastern Hemisphere; Europe, Asia, and Africa.

old-world (ōld′wėrld′), *adj.* **1** Also, **Old-World,** of or about the Eastern Hemisphere; not of the New World: *old-world monkeys.* **2** belonging to or characteristic of a former period: *old-world manners.*

o·le·an·der (ō′lē an′dər), *n.* a poisonous evergreen bush with fragrant red, pink, white, or purple flowers.

o·le·fin (ō′lə fin), *n.* a chemical compound containing carbon and hydrogen, used to make synthetic textiles.

o·le·o (ō′lē ō), *n.* oleomargarine.

o·le·o·mar·gar·ine (ō′lē ō mär′jər ən *or* ō′lē ō mär′jə rēn′), *n.* a substitute for butter made from vegetable oils; margarine.

ol·fac·to·ry (ol fak′tər ē), **1** *adj.* of or about the sense of smell. The nose is an olfactory organ. **2** *n.* an olfactory organ. ❑ *n., pl.* **ol·fac·to·ries.**

Ol·i·go·cene (ol′ə gō sēn′), *n.* (in geology) time between about 40 million and 25 million years ago. During this time, the first apes appeared and modern mammals became dominant.

ol·ive (ol′iv), **1** *n.* the small, oval, purplish black fruit of an evergreen tree that grows in warm regions. Olives have an oily pulp around a hard stone. They are eaten green or ripe as a relish and are used to make olive oil. **2** *n.* a yellowish green. **3** *adj.* yellowish green. **4** *n.* a yellowish brown. **5** *adj.* yellowish brown. [See word history information at **oil.**]

olive branch, 1 branch of the olive tree, especially used as an emblem or symbol of peace. **2** anything offered as a sign of peace.

olive drab, 1 a dark greenish yellow color. **2** a dark greenish yellow woolen cloth, formerly used by the U.S. Army for uniforms.

olive oil, oil pressed from olives, used in salad dressings, cooking, cosmetics, medicine, etc.

O·liv·i·er (ō liv′ē ā), *n.* **Laur·ence** (lôr′əns), 1907-1989, English actor. ■ **Laurence Olivier** won an Academy Award for his performance in *Hamlet,* another for producing, directing, and starring in *Richard III,* and a special Academy Award for lifetime achievement in movies.

Ol·mec (ōl′mek), *n.* member of a tribe of American Indians who ruled an empire in southeastern Mexico from about 1200 B.C. to 100 B.C. The Olmec influenced the culture of the Maya. ❑ *n., pl.* **Ol·mec** or **Ol·mecs.** [Olmec comes from a word in the Mayan language meaning "rubber." The Olmec lived in a region where rubber-producing plants grow.]

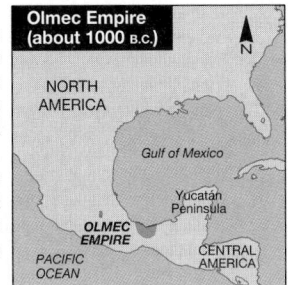
Olmec Empire
(about 1000 B.C.)
NORTH AMERICA
Gulf of Mexico
Yucatán Peninsula
OLMEC EMPIRE
PACIFIC OCEAN
CENTRAL AMERICA

O·lym·pi·a (ō lim′pē ə), *n.* **1** plain in ancient Greece where the Olympic games were held. **2** capital of Washington, in the W part.

O·lym·pi·ad (ō lim′pē ad), *n.* celebration of the modern Olympic games.

O·lym·pi·an (ō lim′pē ən), **1** *adj.* of or about Olympia in Greece or Mount Olympus. **2** *adj.* like a god; heavenly; magnificent; superior: *Olympian calm.* **3** *n.* one of the major Greek gods. **4** *n.* contender in the Olympic games.

O·lym·pic (ō lim′pik), **1** *adj.* of or about the Olympic games. **2** *n.pl.* **Olympics,** Olympic games.

Olympic games, 1 international athletic contests, held once every four years in a different country. Separate summer and winter games are held, alternating every two years. **2** contests in athletics, poetry, and music, held every four years by the ancient Greeks in honor of Zeus.

Olympic National Park, a national park in NW Washington near Seattle, containing mountains, rainforests, and seacoast.

O·lym·pus (ō lim′pəs), *n.* **Mount,** mountain in NE Greece, which the ancient Greeks believed to be the home of the major Greek gods, 9570 feet (2917 meters) high. See **Sparta** for map.

Olympic Games

O·ma·ha (ō′mə hò *or* ō′mə hä), *n.* city in E Nebraska, on the Missouri River. [Omaha comes from the name of an Indian tribe who lived in this area. The name may mean "going up the river."]

Omaha Beach, part of the Normandy beach assaulted by U.S. forces on June 6, 1944.

O·man (ō män′), *n.* **1** country in SE Arabia. *Capital:* Muscat. **2 Gulf of,** gulf of the Arabian Sea, between Oman and S Iran.

om·buds·man (om budz′mən), *n.* a government official appointed to receive and investigate grievances of citizens against the government. ❑ *n., pl.* **om·buds·men.**

o·meg·a (ō meg′ə *or* ō mē′gə), *n.* **1** the last letter of the Greek alphabet (Ω or ω). **2** the last of a series; end. ❑ *n., pl.* **o·meg·as.**

ome·let (om′lit), *n.* eggs beaten up with milk or water, fried or baked, and then folded over, often around a filling.

o·men (ō′mən), *n.* something supposed to be a sign of what is to happen; object or event that is believed to mean good or bad fortune: *Spilling salt is said to be an omen of bad luck.*

om·i·nous (om′ə nəs), *adj.* unfavorable; threatening: *Those black clouds look ominous.* —**om′i·nous·ly,** *adv.* —**om′i·nous·ness,** *n.*

o·mis·sion (ō mish′ən), *n.* **1** something omitted: *Her song was the only omission from the program.* **2** act of omitting or condition of being omitted: *the omission of a paragraph in copying a story.*

o·mit (ō mit′), *v.* **1** to leave out: *omit a letter in a word.* **2** to fail to do; neglect: *They omitted to make their beds.* ❑ *v.* **o·mit·ted, o·mit·ting.**

omni-, *prefix.* all; completely: *omnipotent = all powerful.* ■ See Word Power at **many.**

om·ni·bus (om′nə bus), **1** *n.* bus. **2** *n.* volume of works by a single author or of similar works by several authors: *an omnibus of sports stories.* **3** *adj.* covering many things at once: *an omnibus law.* ❑ *n.,* *pl.* **om·ni·bus·es.** [See word history information at **bus.**]

om·nip·o·tence (om nip′ə təns), *n.* complete power; unlimited power.

om·nip·o·tent (om nip′ə tənt), **1** *adj.* having all power; almighty. **2** *n.* the Omnipotent, God.

om·ni·pres·ence (om′nə prez′ns), *n.* presence everywhere at the same time.

om·ni·pres·ent (om′nə prez′nt), *adj.* present everywhere at the same time.

om·nis·cience (om nish′əns), *n.* knowledge of everything; complete or infinite knowledge.

om·nis·cient (om nish′ənt), *adj.* knowing everything; having complete or infinite knowledge. **—om·nis′cient·ly,** *adv.*

om·ni·vore (om′nə vôr′), *n.* person or animal that eats all kinds of food.

om·niv·or·ous (om niv′ər əs), *adj.* **1** eating every kind of food; eating both animal and vegetable food. Human beings and bears are omnivorous. **2** taking in everything; fond of all kinds: *An omnivorous reader reads all kinds of books.* **—om·niv′or·ous·ly,** *adv.* **—om·niv′or·ous·ness,** *n.*

on (on), **1** *prep.* above and supported by: *The book is on the table.* **2** *prep.* touching so as to cover, be around, etc.: *a ring on your finger.* **3** *prep.* close to: *a house on the shore.* **4** *prep.* in the direction of; toward: *The protesters marched on the Capitol.* **5** *prep.* against; upon: *The picture is on the wall.* **6** *adv.* atop something: *The walls are up, and the roof is on.* **7** *adv.* to something: *Hold on, or you may fall.* **8** *adv.* toward something: *Some played; the others looked on.* **9** *adv.* farther: *March on.* **10** *prep.* by means of; by the use of: *talk on the phone.* **11** *prep.* in the condition of; in the process of; in the way of: *on fire, on duty.* **12** *adv.* in or into a condition, process, manner, action, position, etc.: *Turn the gas on.* **13** *adj.* taking place: *The race is on.* **14** *adj.* in use; operating: *The radio is on.* **15** *prep.* being broadcast by: *The game is on Channel 5.* **16** *prep.* at the time of; during: *They greeted us on our arrival.* **17** *adv.* from a time; forward: *later on, from that day on.* **18** *prep.* about; in relation to; in connection with: *a book on animals.* **19** *prep.* for the purpose of: *I went on an errand.* **20** *prep.* in addition to: *Defeat on defeat discouraged them.* **21** *prep.* among: *I am not on the committee.* ■ See Usage Note at **onto.**

and so on, and more of the same.

on and off, at some times and not at others; now and then.

on and on, without stopping: *The music played on and on.*

once (wuns), **1** *adv.* one time: *Read it once more.* **2** *n.* a single occasion: *Once is enough.* **3** *adv.* at some one time in the past; formerly: *a once powerful nation.* **4** *adv.* even a single time; ever: *if the facts once become known.* **5** *conj.* when; if ever: *Most people like to swim, once they have learned how.*

all at once, suddenly: *All at once the lights went out.*

at once, 1 immediately: *Come at once.* **2** at the same time: *Everyone started shouting at once.*

for once, for one time at least.

once and for all or **once for all,** finally; decisively.

once in a while, not very often; now and then: *We see our cousins once in a while.*

once or twice, a few times.

once upon a time, long ago; once.

once-o·ver (wuns′ō′vər), *n.* a short, quick look.

on·com·ing (on′kum′ing), *adj.* approaching or advancing: *oncoming winter.*

one (wun), **1** *n.* the first and lowest whole number; the number 1. **2** *adj.* being a single unit or individual: *one apple, one dozen.* **3** *n.* a single person or thing: *I gave her the one she wanted.* **4** *adj.* some: *One day you'll be sorry.* **5** *pron.* some person or thing: *Two of you may go, but one must stay.* **6** *pron.* any person, standing for people in general: *One must work hard to achieve success.* **7** *adj.* a single; the same: *All the people in line faced one way.* **8** *pron.* the same person or thing: *In Robert Louis Stevenson's story, the kind Dr. Jekyll and the evil Mr. Hyde were one.* **9** *adj.* joined together; united: *The class was one in its approval.* **10** *adj.* a certain: *One Maria Serra was elected.* ■ Another word that sounds like this is **won.**

all one, 1 exactly the same. **2** making no difference; of no consequence.

at one, in agreement or harmony.

make one, 1 to form or be one of a number, assembly, or party. **2** to join together; unite in marriage.

one and all, everyone.

one by one, one after another.

one or two, a few.

one another, each other: *They looked at one another.* ■ See Usage Note at **each other.**

one-celled (wun′seld′), *adj.* having only one cell: *Bacteria are one-celled living things.*

O·nei·da (ō nī′də), *n.* member of a tribe of American Indians formerly living in New York, now living in New York, Ontario, and Wisconsin. ❑ *n., pl.* **O·nei·da** or **O·nei·das.** [**Oneida** comes from a word in their language meaning "standing rock." A large rock was a landmark near their main village.]

O'Neill (ō nēl′), *n.* **Eu·gene** (yü jēn′), 1888-1953, American playwright. He won the Nobel Prize for literature in 1936.

one·ness (wun′nis), *n.* **1** quality of being one in number or the only one of its kind; singleness. **2** quality of being the same in kind; sameness. **3** fact of forming one whole; unity. **4** agreement in mind, feeling, or purpose; harmony.

one-on-one (wun′on′wun′), **1** *adv.* directly against one opposing person: *guarding a pass receiver one-on-one.* **2** *adv.* directly between one person and another: *to bargain one-on-one.* **3** *adj.* directly between one person and another: *one-on-one basketball.*

one·self (wun self′), *pron.* your own self: *One should not praise oneself too much.*

be oneself, 1 to have control of your mind or body. **2** to act naturally.

one-sid·ed (wun′sī′did), *adj.* **1** seeing only one side of a question; partial; unfair; prejudiced: *The umpire seemed one-sided in his decisions, always favoring the home team.* **2** uneven; unequal: *If one team is much better than the other, a game is one-sided.* **—one′-sid′ed·ly,** *adv.* **—one′-sid′ed·ness,** *n.*

one-time (wun′tīm′), *adj.* of the past; former.

one-track (wun′trak′), *adj.* **1** having only one track. **2** understanding or doing only one thing at a time; narrow: *a one-track mind.*

one-way (wun′wā′), *adj.* moving or allowing movement in only one direction: *a one-way street.*

on·go·ing (on′gō′ing), *adj.* continuous; uninterrupted.

on·ion (un′yən), *n.* bulb of a garden vegetable plant eaten raw or cooked. Onions have a sharp, strong smell and taste. [See Word Story at **union.**] **—on′ion·like′,** *adj.*

onion

on·ion·skin (un′yən skin′), *n.* a thin, shiny, translucent paper.

on-line or **on·line** (on′līn′), *adj.* **1** available or communicating by computer, especially through e-mail or the Internet: *an on-*

a	hat	ė	term	ô	order	ch	child		a in about
ā	age	i	it	oi	oil	ng	long		e in taken
ä	far	ī	ice	ou	out	sh	she	ə {	i in pencil
â	care	o	hot	u	cup	th	thin		o in lemon
e	let	ō	open	ů	put	ŦH	then		u in circus
ē	equal	ò	saw	ü	rule	zh	measure		

line dictionary. *My aunt just went on-line and sent me three messages.* **2** controlled by a computer. **3** connected to a computer.

on·look·er (on′lük/ər), *n.* person who watches without taking part; spectator.

on·ly (ōn′lē), **1** *adj.* by itself or themselves; one and no more; sole or single: *an only child. This is the only road to the cabin.* **2** *adv.* merely; just: *She sold only two.* **3** *adv.* and no one else; and nothing more; and that is all: *Only he remained.* **4** *conj.* except that; but: *She would have started, only it rained.* **5** *adj.* in a class by itself; best; finest: *He is the only writer for my taste.* **6** *conj.* but then; it must be added that: *We had camped right beside a stream, only the water was not fit to drink.*

if only, I wish: *If only the sun would shine!*

only too, very: *She was only too glad to help us.*

> **USAGE NOTE** Only should go right in front of the word it describes: *I saw only six ducks.* You didn't see any more. *I only saw six ducks.* You didn't hear them, just saw them. In everyday speech, people often put **only** near the verb of a sentence, whatever it's supposed to describe. Careful writers and speakers do this only rarely.

on·o·mat·o·poe·ia (on′ə mat′ə pē′ə), *n.* formation of a name or word by imitating the sound associated with the thing designated, as in *buzz, hum, slap, splash.* ■ See Word Source at **imitative.**

On·on·da·ga (on′ən dô′gə), *n.* member of a tribe of American Indians living in New York and southern Ontario. □ *n., pl.* **On·on·da·ga** or **On·on·da·gas.** [**Onondaga** comes from a word in their language meaning "on top of the hill." Their main village had this name.]

on·rush (on′rush/), *n.* a very strong or forceful forward rush: *He was knocked down by the onrush of water.* □ *n., pl.* **on·rush·es.**

on·screen (on′skrēn), *adj.* **1** of or about a computer environment, especially for game-playing: *His onscreen nickname was "Dogboy."* **2** on a TV or computer monitor screen: *The onscreen image is better than the printout.*

on·set (on′set/), *n.* **1** the beginning or start: *The onset of this disease is gradual.* **2** attack: *The onset of the enemy took us by surprise.*

on·shore (on′shôr/), *adv., adj.* toward or on the shore.

on·side (on′sīd/), *adj.* (in sports) not ahead of the ball or puck according to the rules; not offside.

on·slaught (on′slôt/), *n.* a vigorous attack: *The pirates made an onslaught on the ship.*

on·stage (on′stāj/), *adj., adv.* on the part of a stage that the audience can see: *the actor's first onstage appearance, walk onstage.*

Ont., Ontario.

On·tar·i·o (on tãr′ē ō), *n.* **1** province in Canada, north of the Great Lakes. *Capital:* Toronto. **2 Lake,** the smallest of the five Great Lakes. [**Ontario** probably comes from an Iroquois word meaning "beautiful lake."] **—On·tar′i·an,** *adj., n.*

on-the-job (on′ᴛᴀᴀ job′), *adj.* learned, done, or happening as part of a job: *An intern receives on-the-job training.*

on·to (on′tü), *prep.* **1** on to; to a position on: *throw a ball onto the roof.* **2** familiar with; aware of: *I was soon onto their tricks.*

> **USAGE NOTE** Onto and on to are used in similar ways, and it can be hard to decide which one you want. If a sentence would sound complete without the part that begins with **to,** you probably want to use the two-word form: *She held on to the rope.* If the sentence would not sound complete, you probably want to use the one-word form: *The boy climbed onto the rock.*

o·nus (ō′nəs), *n.* burden; responsibility: *The onus of caring for the invalid fell upon his children.* □ *n., pl.* **o·nus·es.**

on·ward (on′wərd), *adv., adj.* toward the front; further on; on; forward: *The crowd around the store window began to move onward. An onward movement began.*

on·wards (on′wərdz), *adv.* onward.

on·yx (on′iks), *n.* a kind of quartz with layers of different colors. Onyx is often dyed and carved to make cameos.

oo·dles (ü′dlz), *n.pl.* ɪɴꜰᴏʀᴍᴀʟ. large or unlimited quantities; heaps; loads: *oodles of money.*

Ook·pik (ük′pik/), *n.* ᴄᴀɴᴀᴅɪᴀɴ. trademark for an owllike doll, designed in 1963 by an Inuit artist, honored as a symbol of Canadian handicrafts.

oomph (ümf), *n.* ɪɴꜰᴏʀᴍᴀʟ. force; strength; effect: *The ad is too cute to have any oomph.*

oops (üps), *interj.* exclamation of sudden error: *Oops! I dropped the eggs!*

Oort cloud (ôrt), a vast cloud of comets believed to orbit the sun far beyond the orbit of Pluto.

ooze[1] (üz), **1** *v.* to pass out slowly through small openings; leak out slowly and quietly: *Blood oozed from the cut.* **2** *n.* a slow flow. **3** *n.* something that oozes. □ *v.* **oozed, ooz·ing.**

ooze[2] (üz), *n.* a soft mud or slime, especially at the bottom of a pond or river or on the ocean bottom.

oo·zy[1] (ü′zē), *adj.* oozing. □ *adj.* **oo·zi·er, oo·zi·est. —oo′zi·ly,** *adv.*

oo·zy[2] (ü′zē), *adj.* muddy and soft; slimy: *an oozy meadow.* □ *adj.* **oo·zi·er, oo·zi·est. —oo′zi·ly,** *adv.* **—oo′zi·ness,** *n.*

op., opus.

o·pac·i·ty (ō pas′ə tē), *n.* a being opaque; darkness.

o·pal (ō′pəl), *n.* gem that shows beautiful changes of color. Opals are often milky white with streaks of different colors.

o·pal·es·cence (ō′pə les′ns), *n.* a play of colors like that of an opal.

o·pal·es·cent (ō′pə les′nt), *adj.* having a play of colors like that of an opal.

o·paque (ō pāk′), *adj.* **1** not letting light through; not transparent: *A brick wall is opaque.* **2** not shining; dark; dull: *The car's finish had become opaque.* **3** obscure; hard to understand. **—o·paque′ly,** *adv.* **—o·paque′ness,** *n.*

OPEC (ō′pek), *n.* Organization of Petroleum Exporting Countries.

o·pen (ō′pən), **1** *adj.* not shut; not closed; letting anyone or anything in or out: *She climbed in through the open window.* **2** *adj.* not closed up, fastened, or tied: *The drawer was open. Your dress is open in the back.* **3** *adj.* not closed in: *an open field, the open sea.* **4** *adj.* ready for customers to enter: *The bank is open from 9 to 3 on Tuesdays.* **5** *n.* **the open, a** clear or open space; open country, air, sea, etc.: *sleep out in the open.* **b** public view or knowledge: *Their secret is now out in the open.* **6** *adj.* having spaces or holes: *open ranks, cloth of open texture.* **7** *adj.* unfilled; not taken: *a position still open.* **8** *adj.* able to be entered, used, shared, competed for, etc., by all, or by a person or persons mentioned: *an open meeting, an open market.* **9** *adj.* not covered or protected; exposed: *an open fire, open to temptation.* **10** *adj.* exposed to general view, knowledge, etc.; not secret: *open disregard of rules.* **11** *adj.* ready to listen to new ideas and judge them fairly; not prejudiced: *She has an open mind.* **12** *adj.* frank and sincere: *an open heart.* **13** *adj.* generous; liberal: *give with an open hand.* **14** *v.* to make or become open: *Open the window. The door opened.* **15** *v.* to have an opening or passage: *This door opens into the dining room.* **16** *v.* to spread out or unfold: *open a letter.* **17** *v.* to come apart or burst open: *a crack where the earth had opened.* **18** *v.* to start or set up; establish: *They opened a new store.* **19** *v.* to begin: *School opens today.* **20** *adj.* free from hindrance, especially from ice: *open water on the lake.* **—o′pen·ly,** *adv.*

open to, ready to take; willing to consider.

open up, to make or become open; open a way to.

open air, outdoors: *Children like to play in the open air.*

open-air (ō′pən ãr′), *adj.* outdoor: *an open-air concert.*

open-air—an open-air market

o·pen-and-shut (ō′pən ən shut′), *adj.* simple and direct; obvious; straightforward: *It seemed to be an open-and-shut case of murder.*

open door, 1 opportunity for anyone to meet with an official: *The principal believes in an open door and will meet with any student.* **2** a free and equal chance for all countries to do business in another country. —**o′pen-door′**, *adj.*

o·pen-end·ed (ō′pən en′did), *adj.* **1** not settled permanently; open to later change. **2** not limited; having no restrictions: *open-ended opportunity.* **3** having no definite answer: *an open-ended question.*

o·pen·er (ō′pə nər), *n.* **1** person or thing that opens. **2** something that is used to open closed containers: *Where is the can opener?* **3** (in sports) the first game of a scheduled series.

o·pen-eyed (ō′pən īd′), *adj.* **1** having eyes wide open as in wonder. **2** watchful or vigilant; observant.

o·pen-faced (ō′pən fāst′), *adj.* **1** having a face that shows thoughts and feelings frankly and sincerely. **2** (of a sandwich) having the filling uncovered rather than between two slices of bread.

o·pen-hand·ed (ō′pən han′did), *adj.* generous; liberal. —**o′pen-hand′ed·ly**, *adv.* —**o′pen-hand′ed·ness**, *n.*

o·pen-heart (ō′pən härt′), *adj.* of or referring to a heart that has been stopped and opened by surgery to correct an injury or defect. During the operation, the heart's circulatory function is carried on by a machine which pumps and oxygenates the blood.

o·pen-heart·ed (ō′pən här′tid), *adj.* free in expressing your real thoughts, opinions, and feelings; candid; frank; unreserved. —**o′pen-heart′ed·ly**, *adv.* —**o′pen-heart′ed·ness**, *n.*

o·pen-hearth process (ō′pən härth′), process of making steel in a furnace that reflects the heat onto the raw material.

open house, 1 party or other social event that is open to all who wish to come. **2** an occasion on which an open house is held: *The High School open house is every other Friday evening.*

o·pen·ing (ō′pə ning), **1** *n.* an open or clear space; gap; hole: *an opening in a wall, an opening in the forest.* **2** *n.* the first part; the beginning: *the opening of a story.* **3** *adj.* first; beginning: *the opening words of his speech.* **4** *n.* a formal beginning: *The opening of the art exhibit will be at three o'clock.* **5** *n.* job that is open or vacant: *an opening for a teller in a bank.* **6** *n.* a favorable chance or opportunity: *I kept waiting for an opening to ask for a new bike.* **7** *n.* act of making open or fact of becoming open.

open letter, letter of protest, criticism, or appeal addressed to someone but published in a newspaper, magazine, etc.

o·pen-mind·ed (ō′pən mīn′did), *adj.* having or showing a mind open to new arguments or ideas. —**o′pen-mind′ed·ly**, *adv.* —**o′pen-mind′ed·ness**, *n.*

o·pen-mouthed (ō′pən mouṯнd′ *or* ō′pən moutht′), *adj.* **1** having the mouth open. **2** gaping with surprise or astonishment. **3** having a wide mouth: *an open-mouthed jar.* —**o′pen-mouth′ed·ness**, *n.*

o·pen·ness (ō′pən nis), *n.* **1** condition of being open. **2** lack of secrecy. **3** frankness. **4** willingness to consider new ideas or arguments.

open secret, a supposed secret that is actually generally known: *Their romance is an open secret.*

open ses·a·me (ses′ə mē), **1** the magic command that made the door of the robbers' cave fly open in the story of Ali Baba. **2** anything which removes the barriers to entering a restricted place or to reaching a certain goal.

open shop, factory or business that employs both members of labor unions and nonunion workers on equal terms.

o·pen·work (ō′pən wėrk′), **1** *n.* ornamental work with small gaps or openings. **2** *adj.* resembling such ornamental work.

op·er·a[1] (op′ər ə), *n.* a play in which music is an essential and prominent part, featuring arias, choruses, etc., with orchestral accompaniment. ❑ *n., pl.* **op·er·as.**

op·er·a[2] (ō′pər ə *or* op′ər ə), *n.* a plural of **opus.**

op·er·a·ble (op′ər ə bəl), *adj.* **1** able to be operated; in a condition to be used: *The old motorcycle is still operable.* **2** able to be treated by a surgical operation: *It was clear from the X ray that the cancerous growth was operable.*

opera glasses or **opera glass,** small binoculars for use at the opera and in theaters.

op·er·ate (op′ə rāt′), *v.* **1** to be at work; run: *The machinery operates night and day.* **2** to keep at work; control or manage: *operate an elevator. The company operates three factories.* **3** to produce an effect; work; act: *Several causes operated to bring on the war.* **4** to produce a desired effect: *The medicine operated quickly.* **5** to perform surgery: *The doctor operated on the damaged lung.* ❑ *v.* **op·er·at·ed, op·er·at·ing.**

op·er·at·ic (op′ə rat′ik), *adj.* of, in, or like an opera: *an operatic soprano.* —**op′er·at′i·cal·ly**, *adv.*

operating system, the basic set of programs that controls the working of a computer and enables other programs to be carried out. It controls both information and machinery.

op·er·a·tion (op′ə rā′shən), *n.* **1** act or process of working: *The operation of an airline requires many people.* **2** the way a thing works: *The operation of this machine is simple.* **3** action; activity: *the operation of organizing an expedition.* **4** a treatment of diseases and injuries involving surgery: *Removing an inflamed appendix is a common operation.* **5** movements of soldiers, ships, supplies, etc.: *military and naval operations.* **6** (in mathematics) something done to one or more numbers or quantities according to specific rules. Addition, subtraction, multiplication, and division are the four commonest operations in arithmetic.
in operation, in action or in use.

op·er·a·tion·al (op′ə rā′shə nəl), *adj.* **1** of or about operations of any kind. **2** in condition to operate effectively.

Operation Desert Storm, the Persian Gulf War.

op·er·a·tive (op′ər ə tiv), **1** *adj.* in operation; effective: *the laws operative in a community.* **2** *n.* worker; laborer: *The company hired a skilled machine operative.* **3** *adj.* of or about work or productiveness: *operative sections of a factory.* **4** *n.* detective. **5** *n.* secret agent; spy. —**op′er·a·tive·ly**, *adv.*

op·er·a·tor (op′ə rā′tər), *n.* **1** person who operates a machine or other device: *a telephone operator, a computer operator.* **2** person who runs a factory, mine, etc. **3** a shrewd person who manipulates people or events for his or her own purposes.

op·er·et·ta (op′ə ret′ə), *n.* a short, amusing opera with some spoken dialogue. ❑ *n., pl.* **op·er·et·tas.**

oph·thal·mol·o·gist (of′thəl mol′ə jist *or* op′thəl mol′ə jist), *n.* doctor who specializes in ophthalmology; oculist.

oph·thal·mol·o·gy (of′thəl mol′ə jē *or* op′thəl mol′ə jē), *n.* branch of medicine dealing with the structure, functions, and diseases of the eye.

o·pi·ate (ō′pē it *or* ō′pē āt), **1** *n.* any medical preparation containing opium that dulls pain or brings sleep. **2** *adj.* containing opium. **3** *n.* anything that quiets. **4** *adj.* bringing sleep or ease.

o·pine (ō pīn′), *v.* to hold or express an opinion; think: *She opined that the book was exciting.* ❑ *v.* **o·pined, o·pin·ing.**

o·pin·ion (ə pin′yən), *n.* **1** what you think; belief not based on actual knowledge or proof; judgment: *In my opinion, their plan will never succeed.* **2** judgment of worth; impression; estimate: *I have a good opinion of her.* **3** a formal judgment by an expert; professional advice: *He wanted the doctor's opinion about the cause of his headache.*

SYNONYM STUDY **Opinion, view,** and **judgment** all mean what someone thinks about something. **Opinion** means a belief based on facts but still personal: *Do you share his opinion that Chinese food is the best food?* **View** means a very personal belief: *It's my sister's view that she has a beautiful voice.* **Judgment** means a belief based on careful thought and decision: *In the officer's judgment, neither driver was at fault.*

o·pin·ion·at·ed (ə pin′yə nā′tid), *adj.* stubborn or conceited with regard to your opinions; dogmatic: *He is too opinionated to listen to anybody else.*

o·pi·um (ō′pē əm), *n.* a powerful narcotic drug that causes sleep and eases pain. It is made from a kind of poppy.

a	hat	ė	term	ô	order	ch	child		
ā	age	i	it	oi	oil	ng	long		a in about
ä	far	ī	ice	ou	out	sh	she		e in taken
â	care	o	hot	u	cup	th	thin	ə	i in pencil
e	let	ō	open	ů	put	ᴛʜ	then		o in lemon
ē	equal	ȯ	saw	ü	rule	zh	measure		u in circus

o·pos·sum (ə pos′əm), *n.* any of several small mammals of the Western Hemisphere that live in trees, are active mainly at night, and carry their young in a pouch; possum. One kind, common in the southern and eastern United States, often gives the appearance of being dead when it is frightened or caught. ◻ *n., pl.* **o·pos·sums** or **o·pos·sum.**

Op·pen·hei·mer (op′ən hī′-mər), *n.* **J. Rob·ert** (rob′ərt), 1904-1967, American physicist. He directed the laboratory where the first atomic bomb was designed and built.

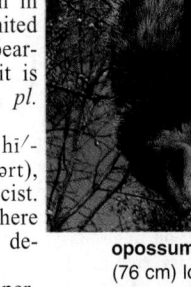

opossum—about 30 in. (76 cm) long with the tail

op·po·nent (ə pō′nənt), **1** *n.* person who is on the other side in a fight, game, or discussion; person fighting, struggling, or speaking against another: *She defeated her opponent in the election.* **2** *adj.* opposing.

op·por·tune (op′ər tün′), *adj.* fortunate or well-chosen; suitable; favorable. —**op′por·tune′ly,** *adv.* —**op′por·tune′ness,** *n.*

op·por·tun·ism (op′ər tü′niz′əm), *n.* policy or practice of using every opportunity to your advantage without considering whether the action is right or wrong: *an opportunistic person.*

op·por·tun·ist (op′ər tü′nist), *n.* person who uses every opportunity to gain advantage, regardless of right or wrong.

op·por·tun·is·tic (op′ər tü nis′tik), *adj.* **1** of or given to opportunism. **2** caused by a microorganism that can become dangerous to health when someone's immune system is weakened by a disease such as AIDS: *an opportunistic infection.*

op·por·tu·ni·ty (op′ər tü′nə tē), *n.* a good chance; favorable time; convenient occasion: *I had an opportunity to earn some money baby-sitting.* ◻ *n., pl.* **op·por·tu·ni·ties.**

op·pos·a·ble (ə pō′zə bəl), *adj.* able to be used by holding opposite something else. The human thumb is opposable to the fingers for grasping.

op·pose (ə pōz′), *v.* **1** to be against; be in the way of; act, fight, or struggle against; try to hinder; resist: *Many people opposed building a new highway because of the cost.* **2** to put in contrast: *Love is opposed to hate.* ◻ *v.* **op·posed, op·pos·ing.** —**op·pos′er,** *n.*

op·posed (ə pōzd′), *adj.* in opposition to: *opposed to a tax hike.* **as opposed to,** in contrast with: *She prefers butterscotch as opposed to chocolate flavoring.*

op·pos·ing (ə pō′zing), *adj.* in opposition to; on the other side; competing: *the opposing team.*

op·po·site (op′ə zit), **1** *adj.* placed directly across from something else; face to face; back to back: *The house straight across the street is opposite to ours.* **2** *adj.* as different as can be: *North and south are opposite directions. Sour is opposite to sweet.* **3** *n.* person or thing as different as can be: *Night is the opposite of day.* **4** *prep.* opposite to: *opposite the church.* —**op′po·site·ly,** *adv.* —**op′po·site·ness,** *n.*

op·po·si·tion (op′ə zish′ən), *n.* **1** action against; resistance: *There was some opposition to the workers' request for higher wages.* **2** contrast: *His views are in opposition to mine.* **3** Also, **Opposition, a** a political party opposed to the party which is in power. **b** any party or group of opponents. **4** an opposing team: *We beat the opposition 17-2.*

op·press (ə pres′), *v.* **1** to govern harshly; keep down unjustly or by cruelty: *The dictator oppressed the people.* **2** to weigh down; lie heavily on; burden: *A sense of trouble ahead oppressed her spirits.* —**op·pres′sor,** *n.*

op·pres·sion (ə presh′ən), *n.* **1** cruel or unjust treatment; tyranny; persecution: *The oppression of the people by the invaders caused much suffering.* **2** a heavy, weary feeling.

op·pres·sive (ə pres′iv), *adj.* **1** hard to bear; burdensome: *The great heat was oppressive.* **2** harsh; severe; unjust: *Oppressive measures were taken to crush the rebellion.* —**op·pres′sive·ly,** *adv.* —**op·pres′sive·ness,** *n.*

opt (opt), *v.* to choose: *The class opted to go on a field trip.*

op·tic (op′tik), *adj.* of or about the eye or the sense of sight.

op·ti·cal (op′tə kəl), *adj.* **1** of or about the eye or the sense of sight; visual: *Nearsightedness is an optical defect.* **2** made to assist sight: *Telescopes and microscopes are optical devices.* **3** of or about optics. —**op′ti·cal·ly,** *adv.*

optical disk, a thin, plastic-coated metal disk, on which information is recorded in the form of very tiny marks or dents that can be detected by a laser. The marks or dents stand for numbers, and the numbers can be used to produce music, pictures, or computer information. Unlike magnetic disks, optical disks are mostly used for only one recording, not erased and rerecorded. Compact disks and laser disks are optical disks.

optical fiber, a very thin, transparent thread of glass or plastic, able to carry light from end to end without loss or change. Optical fibers are used to send voices, images, and other information.

optical illusion, something that looks different from what it really is. A mirage is an optical illusion.

op·ti·cian (op tish′ən), *n.* maker or seller of eyeglasses and other devices that aid sight.

optic nerve, the nerve of sight, which goes from the retina of the eye to the brain. See picture at **eye.**

op·tics (op′tiks), *n.* branch of physics that deals with light and vision.

op·ti·mal (op′tə məl), *adj.* most favorable; best; optimum. —**op′-ti·mal·ly,** *adv.*

optical illusion—The parallel vertical lines appear slanted because of the diagonal lines.

op·ti·mism (op′tə miz′əm), *n.* **1** tendency to look on the bright side of things: *Her optimism always lifts my spirits.* **2** something that can be chosen; a choice: *Power windows are an option on many new cars.* **3** belief that everything will turn out for the best: *I questioned his optimism about our school's financial situation.* **4** doctrine that the existing world is the best of all possible worlds.

op·ti·mist (op′tə mist), *n.* **1** person who looks on the bright side of things. **2** person who believes that everything in life will turn out for the best.

op·ti·mis·tic (op′tə mis′tik), *adj.* **1** inclined to look on the bright side of things: *She is an optimistic person.* **2** hoping for the best: *I am optimistic about the chance of continued good weather.* **3** of or about optimism. —**op′ti·mis′ti·cal·ly,** *adv.*

op·ti·mize (op′tə mīz), *v.* to make the most of; make as good as possible: *optimize your chances of winning the contest.* ◻ *v.* **op·ti·mized, op·ti·miz·ing.** —**op·ti·mi·za·tion** (op′tə mə zā′shən), *n.* —**op′ti miz′er,** *n.*

op·ti·mum (op′tə məm), **1** *n.* the best or most favorable point, degree, amount, etc., for the purpose. **2** *adj.* most favorable; best: *A home alarm system provides optimum security.* ◻ *n., pl.* **op·ti·mums, op·ti·ma** (op′tə mə).

op·tion (op′shən), *n.* **1** right or freedom of choice: *Pupils in our school have the option of taking Spanish, French, or German.* **2** something that can be chosen; a choice: *Power windows are an* *option on many new cars.* **3** act of choosing: *Where to travel should be left to each person's option.* **4** right to buy or sell something at a certain price within a certain time: *She paid $5,000 for an option on the land.*

op·tion·al (op′shə nəl), *adj.* left to your choice; not required: *Attendance at the school picnic is optional.* **—op′tion·al·ly,** *adv.*

op·tom·e·trist (op tom′ə trist), *n.* person skilled in examining the eyes and prescribing eyeglasses. An optometrist is not an M.D. but is legally authorized to do such work.

op·tom·e·try (op tom′ə trē), *n.* measurement of the powers of sight; practice or occupation of testing eyes for glasses.

op·u·lence (op′yə ləns), *n.* **1** much money or property; wealth; riches. **2** abundance; plenty.

op·u·lent (op′yə lənt), *adj.* **1** having wealth; rich. **2** abundant; plentiful. **—op′u·lent·ly,** *adv.*

o·pus (ō′pəs), *n.* **1** a musical work or composition, especially numbered according to the order in which they were written: *The orchestra played Beethoven's Symphony No. 5 in C Minor, Opus 67.* **2** any work or composition. ❑ *n., pl.* **op·er·a** or **o·pus·es.**

WORD FAMILY   **Opus** and the following words are related: **co-operate, inoperative, opera, operable, operation,** and **operetta.** They all come from a Latin word meaning "work."

or (ôr), *conj.* **1** word used to express a choice or a difference, or to connect words or groups of words of equal importance in a sentence: *You can go or stay. Is it sweet or sour?* ■ See Usage Note at **either. 2** and if not; otherwise: *Either eat this or go hungry. Hurry, or you will be late.* **3** that is; being the same as: *an igloo or Eskimo snow house. This is the end or last part.* ■ Other words that sound like this are **oar, o'er,** and **ore.**

-or, *suffix.* person or thing that ___s: *actor = person who acts; accelerator = thing that accelerates.*

OR, Oregon (used with postal Zip Code).

o·ra·cle (ôr′ə kəl), *n.* **1** (in ancient times) an answer believed to be given by a god through a priest or priestess. It often had a hidden meaning that was hard to understand. **2** place where the god was believed to give such answers. A famous oracle was at Delphi. **3** the priest or priestess by whom the god's answer was believed to be given. **4** person or thing regarded as a reliable guide. ■ Another word that sounds like this is **auricle.**

o·rac·u·lar (ô rak′yə lər), *adj.* **1** of or like an oracle. **2** with a hidden meaning that is difficult to make out. **3** very wise. **—o·rac′u·lar·ly,** *adv.*

o·ral (ôr′əl), *adj.* **1** using speech; spoken: *An oral agreement is not enough; we must have a written promise.* **2** of or in the mouth: *oral hygiene.* ■ Another word that sounds like this is **aural. —o′ral·ly,** *adv.*

USAGE NOTE   **Oral** is sometimes confused with **verbal. Oral** means "spoken," not written. **Verbal** means "in words," not by pictures, actions, or anything else.

oral history, 1 a report of historical events in spoken form, usually tape-recorded conversations with people who experienced the events. **2** a written version of such a report.

-orama, *suffix.* INFORMAL. **1** store or business offering a large amount of one product or activity: *a 50-lane bowlorama.* **2** a large amount of a particular item or activity at one place or time: *That park is always a pigeonorama.*

o·range (ôr′inj), **1** *n.* the round, reddish yellow, juicy citrus fruit of an evergreen that grows in warm climates. **2** *adj.* reddish yellow. **3** *n.* a reddish yellow.

o·range·ade (ôr′inj ād′), *n.* a drink made of orange juice, sugar, and water.

orange pekoe, a black tea, made from the young leaves at the tips of the branches.

o·rang·ou·tang (ə rang′ə tang′), *n.* orangutan.

orange (def.1)

o·rang·u·tan (ə rang′ə tan′), *n.* a large ape of the forests of Borneo and Sumatra, with very long arms and long, reddish brown hair. [**Orangutan** comes from Malay words meaning "man of the woods."]

o·rate (ô rāt′), *v.* to make an oration; talk in a grand manner. ❑ *v.* **o·rat·ed, o·rat·ing.**

o·ra·tion (ô rā′shən), *n.* a formal public speech delivered on a special occasion: *a funeral oration.*

WORD FAMILY   **Oration** and the following words are related: **adore, oracle, orate, oratory, inexorable, oracular,** and **oratorio.** They all come from a Latin word meaning "to speak formally" or "to pray."

o·ra·tor (ôr′ə tər), *n.* **1** person who makes an oration. **2** person who can speak very well in public.

o·ra·tor·i·cal (ôr′ə tôr′ə kəl), *adj.* **1** of or relating to orators or oratory: *an oratorical contest.* **2** like orators or oratory: *She often talks in an oratorical manner.* **—o′ra·tor′i·cal·ly,** *adv.*

o·ra·to·ri·o (ôr′ə tôr′ē ō), *n.* a musical composition, usually based on a religious theme, for solo voices, chorus, and orchestra. It is dramatic in character but is performed without action, costumes, or scenery. ❑ *n., pl.* **o·ra·to·ri·os.**

o·ra·to·ry[1] (ôr′ə tôr′ē), *n.* **1** skill in public speaking; fine speaking. **2** the art of public speaking.

o·ra·to·ry[2] (ôr′ə tôr′ē), *n.* a small chapel; room set apart for prayer. ❑ *n., pl.* **o·ra·to·ries.**

orb (ôrb), *n.* anything round like a ball; sphere; globe.

or·bit (ôr′bit), **1** *n.* the curved path of any astronomical object about another object in space. **2** *v.* to travel in such a path: *The communications satellite orbits the earth once each day.* **3** *v.* to put or go into such a path. **4** *n.* orbital. **5** *n.* socket in which the eyeball is set. **—or′bit·al,** *adj.*

or·bit·al (ôr′bi tl), *n.* region around the nucleus of an atom in which a particular electron may be located. Formerly, electrons were thought of as orbiting the nucleus like planets around the sun.

or·ca (ôr′kə), *n.* killer whale. ❑ *n., pl.* **or·cas.**

or·chard (ôr′chərd), *n.* **1** piece of ground on which fruit trees are grown. **2** fruit trees grown together: *The orchard should bear a good crop this year.*

or·ches·tra (ôr′kə strə), *n.* **1** group of musicians playing together on various stringed, wind, and percussion instruments. Orchestras usually play at concerts, operas, or plays. **2** the violins, cellos, clarinets, and other instruments played together by such a group. **3** the part of a theater just in front of the stage, where the musicians sit to play. **4** the main floor of a theater, especially the part near the front: *Buy two seats in the orchestra.* ❑ *n., pl.* **or·ches·tras.**

WORD STORY   **Orchestra** comes from a Greek word meaning "to dance." Greek theaters had floors for dancers in front of the stages. Later this area was used either by musicians or for audience seats. So **orchestra** now means musicians or an area of theater seats.

or·ches·tral (ôr kes′trəl), *adj.* of or about an orchestra; composed for or performed by an orchestra. **—or·ches′tral·ly,** *adv.*

or·ches·trate (ôr′kə strāt), *v.* to compose or arrange music for performance by an orchestra. ❑ *v.* **or·ches·trat·ed, or·ches·trat·ing. —or′ches·tra′tion,** *n.* **—or′ches·tra′tor,** *n.*

or·chid (ôr′kid), **1** *n.* any of a great many plants with beautiful flowers with three petals that often have unusual shapes and colors. **2** *adj.* light purple. **3** *n.* a light purple.

or·dain (ôr dān′), *v.* **1** to appoint officially as a minister, priest, or rabbi in a formal ceremony. **2** to pass as a law; order; fix; decide; appoint: *The law ordains that all citizens shall have equal rights.* **—or·dain′er,** *n.* **—or·dain′ment,** *n.*

or·deal (ôr dēl′), *n.* **1** a severe test or experience: *I dreaded the ordeal of going to the dentist.* **2** (in the Middle Ages) an effort to

a	hat	ė	term	ô	order	ch	child		
ā	age	i	it	oi	oil	ng	long		a in about
ä	far	ī	ice	ou	out	sh	she	ə	e in taken
â	care	o	hot	u	cup	th	thin		i in pencil
e	let	ō	open	ů	put	ŦH	then		o in lemon
ē	equal	ȯ	saw	ü	rule	zh	measure		u in circus

decide the guilt or innocence of an accused person by making that person do something dangerous like holding fire or taking poison. The idea was that God would not let an innocent person be harmed by such danger.

or·der (ôr′dər), **1** *v.* to give an order to; tell what to do; command; bid: *The teacher ordered the noisy students to be quiet.* ■ See Synonym Study at **command. 2** *n.* a command; telling what to do: *Troops are expected to obey orders.* **3** *v.* to ask for; give someone a request for: *order a sandwich. Please order for me.* **4** *n.* a spoken or written request for goods: *We telephoned an order for two pizzas to be delivered to the house.* **5** *n.* goods so requested: *When will you be able to deliver my order?* **6** *n.* the way one thing follows another: *in order of size, in alphabetical order, to copy them in order.* **7** *n.* condition in which every part or piece is in its right place: *put a room in order.* **8** *v.* to put in proper condition; arrange: *order your affairs.* **9** *n.* condition; state: *My affairs are in good order.* **10** *n.* the way the world works; way things happen: *the order of nature.* **11** *n.* state or condition of things in which the law is obeyed and there is no trouble: *Order was established after the riot.* **12** *n.* principles and rules by which a meeting is run. **13** *n.* a paper saying that money is to be given or paid, or that something is to be handed over: *a postal money order.* **14** *n.* portion or serving of food in a restaurant, delicatessen, etc. **15** *v.* to decide; will: *The gods ordered it otherwise.* **16** *n.* kind or sort: *have ability of a high order.* **17** *n.* (in biology) a group of related living things ranking below a class and above a family. The rose family, the pea family, and several others belong to one order. **18** *n.* a social rank, grade, or class: *all orders of society.* **19** *n.* rank or position in a church: *the order of bishops.* **20** *n.* a society of monks, friars, or nuns: *the Franciscan order.* **21** *n.* society to which people may be admitted as an honor: *the Order of the Garter.* **22** *n.* a modern fraternal organization: *the Order of Masons.* **23** *n.* any of several styles of columns and architecture: *the Doric, Ionic, and Corinthian orders of Greek architecture.* —**or′der·er,** *n.*

by order, according to a command: *The bank was closed by order of the governor.*

call to order, to ask to be quiet and start work: *The chairperson called the meeting to order.*

in order, 1 in the right arrangement or condition. **2** working right. **3** allowed by the rules.

in order that, so that; with the purpose that.

in order to, for the purpose of; as a way of; as a means to: *She worked hard in order to win the prize.*

in short order, quickly: *The broken window was replaced in short order.*

on order, having been sent for but not yet received.

on the order of, 1 something like; similar to. **2** about: *on the order of 10 million dollars.*

order around or **order about,** to send here and there; tell to do this and that.

out of order, 1 in the wrong arrangement or condition. **2** not working right. **3** against the rules.

take holy orders, to become ordained as a Christian minister or priest.

to order, according to the buyer's wishes or needs.

WORD FAMILY Order and the words below are related. They all come from a Latin word meaning "row" or "series."

coordinate	ordain	ordinary
extraordinary	ordinal	ordnance
inordinate	ordinance	subordinate

ordered pair, (in mathematics) any two numbers written in a special order with one first and the other second. (2,5) is an ordered pair.

Order in Council, (in Canada) a rule ordered by the federal cabinet or a provincial cabinet, authorized by the Governor General or a lieutenant governor.

or·der·ly (ôr′dər lē), **1** *adj.* in order; with regular arrangement, method, or system: *an orderly arrangement of dishes on shelves, an orderly mind.* **2** *adj.* keeping order; well-behaved or regulated: *an orderly class.* **3** *n.* soldier who attends a superior officer to carry orders and perform other duties. **4** *n.* a hospital attendant who keep things clean and in order. ❑ *n., pl.* **or·der·lies.** —**or′der·li·ness,** *n.*

order of magnitude, (in mathematics) number of times that 10 is multiplied by itself in the expression of a particular value. 10^3 is two orders of magnitude less than 10^5.

or·di·nal (ôrd′n əl), **1** *adj.* showing something's position or order in a series. **2** *n.* an ordinal number. **3** *adj.* of or about an order of related living things. **4** *n.* Also **Ordinal,** book of church ceremonies, such as the daily office in the Roman Catholic Church.

or·di·nal number (ôrd′n əl), number that shows order or position in a series. First, second, third, etc., are ordinal numbers; one, two, three, etc., are cardinal numbers.

or·di·nance (ôrd′n əns), *n.* rule or law made by authority; decree: *a city ordinance that outlaws firecrackers.*

or·di·nar·i·ly (ôrd′n er′ə lē), *adv.* **1** usually; regularly; normally: *We ordinarily go to the movies on Saturday.* **2** to the usual extent.

or·di·nar·y (ôrd′n er′ē), *adj.* **1** according to habit or custom; usual; regular; normal: *an ordinary day's work. My ordinary lunch is a sandwich and an apple.* **2** not special; common; everyday; average: *an ordinary person, an ordinary situation.* ■ See Synonym Study at **common. 3** somewhat below the average: *The speaker was ordinary and tiresome.* [See Word Story at **ornery.**] —**or′di·nar·i·ness,** *n.*

out of the ordinary, not regular or customary; unusual; extraordinary.

or·di·na·tion (ôrd′n ā′shən), *n.* **1** act or ceremony of making someone a member of the clergy. **2** act of being made a member of the clergy.

ord·nance (ôrd′nəns), *n.* **1** military weapons of all kinds. **2** cannon or artillery.

Or·do·vi·cian (ôr′də vish′ən), *n.* (in geology) time between about 500 million and 425 million years ago. During this time, primitive fishes, the first animals with backbones, appeared.

ore (ôr), *n.* rock containing enough of a metal or metals to make mining profitable. After it is mined, ore must be treated to extract the metal. ■ Other words that sound like this are **oar, o′er,** and **or.**

Ore. or **Oreg.,** Oregon.

o·reg·a·no (ə reg′ə nō), *n.* a sweet-smelling herb related to mint, with leaves used for seasoning.

O·re·gon (ôr′ə gən *or* or′ə gən), *n.* one of the Pacific states of the United States. *Abbreviation:* OR or Ore. *Capital:* Salem. —**O·re·go·ni·an** (ôr′ə gō′nē ən), *n.*

WORD STORY **Oregon** is a mystery. It may come from a French word meaning "hurricane," once used as the name of the Columbia River. It may come from a Spanish word meaning "big ears," describing people who lived there. It may simply be a mistake in spelling on a map. But even that idea is puzzling—the word on the map was supposed to be **Wisconsin!** It was a French map, and in French the two words look more alike.

Oregon Trail, trail from Missouri northwest into Oregon, much used by early pioneers and settlers in the 1800s.

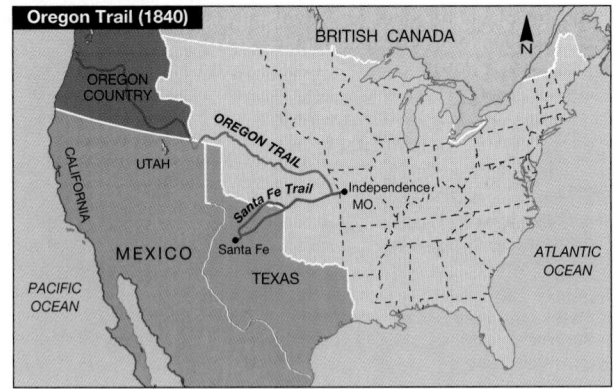

Oregon Trail (1840)

O·res·tes (ô res′tēz), *n.* (in Greek legends) the son of Agamemnon and Clytemnestra, who killed his mother because she had murdered his father.

or·gan (ôr′gən), *n.* **1** part of a living thing, performing some particular function. The eyes, stomach, heart, and lungs are organs of the body. Stamens and pistils are organs of flowers. **2** a musical instrument that has pipes of different sizes and often several sets of keys. The tones are produced by air blown through the pipes by a bellows. **3** a similar instrument with one or more sets of keys but without pipes. The tones are produced by electronic devices. **4** any of various other musical instruments, such as a hand organ or a reed organ. **5** newspaper or magazine that gives the views of a political party or some other organization: *a company's house organ newsletter.*

or·gan·dy or **or·gan·die** (ôr′gən dē′), *n.* a fine, thin, stiff muslin, used for dresses, curtains, etc. ❑ *n., pl.* **or·gan·dies.**

or·gan·elle (ôr′gə nel′), *n.* (in biology) a tiny part of a cell, doing some particular job. An organelle has a function for the cell similar to the function of an organ in a larger living thing.

organ grinder, person who plays a hand organ by turning a crank.

or·gan·ic (ôr gan′ik), *adj.* **1** of or from living things: *organic fertilizer.* **2** grown by using decaying things that were once alive instead of artificial fertilizers and pesticides: *organic foods.* **3** in chemistry: **a** containing carbon. Starch is an organic compound. **b** of or about compounds containing carbon. Organic chemistry deals with food, fuels, etc. **4** of or about the bodily organs: *an organic disease.* **5** made up of related parts, but being a whole: *The United States is an organic federation of 50 states.* **—or·gan′i·cal·ly,** *adv.*

or·gan·ism (ôr′gə niz′əm), *n.* **1** a living thing formed of separate parts, such as cells, tissues, and organs, which work together to carry on the various processes of life; an individual animal, plant, fungus, etc. **2** a whole made of related parts that work together. Human society is a social organism.

or·gan·ist (ôr′gə nist), *n.* person who plays an organ.

or·gan·i·za·tion (ôr′gə nə zā′shən), *n.* **1** group of persons united for some purpose. Churches, clubs, and political parties are organizations. **2** act of organizing; grouping and arranging parts to form a whole: *The organization of a big picnic takes time and thought.* **3** the way in which a thing's parts are arranged to work together: *The organization of the human body is very complicated.* **—or·gan·i·za′tion·al,** *adj.* **—or·gan·i·za′tion·al·ly,** *adv.*

or·gan·ize (ôr′gə nīz), *v.* **1** to put into working order; get together and arrange: *We helped our teacher organize a trip to the city zoo.* **2** to combine in a company, political party, labor union, etc.: *organize the miners.* ❑ *v.* **or·gan·ized, or·gan·iz·ing.** **—or·gan·iz′a·ble,** *adj.* **—or·gan·iz′er,** *n.*

organize (def. 1)—organized files

or·gan·za (ôr gan′zə), *n.* a thin cloth of rayon, silk, or nylon, similar to organdy, used especially for dresses.

or·gasm (ôr′gaz′əm), *n.* the highest point of sexual excitement, accompanied by strong pleasure and in males by ejaculation of semen. Following orgasm, sexual excitement weakens or lessens.

or·gy (ôr′jē), *n.* **1** a wild, drunken party. **2 orgies,** *pl.* secret rites or ceremonies in the worship of certain Greek and Roman gods, especially the god of wine, celebrated with drinking, wild dancing, and singing. ❑ *n., pl.* **or·gies.**

o·ri·ent (ôr′ē ənt *for noun;* ôr′ē ent *for verb*), **1** *n.* the east. **2** *n.* **the Orient,** the East; Eastern countries. China and Japan are important nations of the Orient. The Orient usually includes Asia and countries east and southeast of the Mediterranean. **3** *v.* to place so as to face any indicated direction: *The building is oriented north and south.* **4** *v.* to adjust to a new situation: *I had to orient myself on coming to a new city. The college has a program to orient freshman students.*

O·ri·en·tal (ôr′ē en′tl), **1** *adj.* Eastern; of the Orient: *Oriental customs.* **2** *n.* person born or living in the East, especially the Far East. **3** *n.* person whose ancestors came from the Far East.

USAGE NOTE **Oriental** is considered offensive by some people when used to mean "a person whose ancestors came from the Far East." **Occidental,** meaning "a person born in the West," is not considered offensive. Why not? Probably the reason is that people whose ancestors come from the Far East have experienced more discrimination against them as a group in the United States than have people born in Europe or America. Careful writers and speakers avoid using both words with these meanings.

O·ri·en·tal·ist (ôr′ē en′tl ist), *n.* person skilled in Oriental languages, literature, history, etc.

o·ri·en·tate (ôr′ē en tāt), *v.* to orient. ❑ *v.* **o·ri·en·tat·ed, o·ri·en·tat·ing.**

o·ri·en·ta·tion (ôr′ē en tā′shən), *n.* **1** act of bringing into the right relationship with surroundings; adjustment to a new situation: *the orientation of freshman students.* **2** someone's set of interests, ideas, or inclinations: *political orientation.*

o·ri·en·teer·ing (ôr′ē ən tir′ing), *n.* sport in which the contestants use a map and compass to get from one place to another over unfamiliar territory. The person who takes the shortest time to make the journey is the winner.

o·ri·fice (ôr′ə fis), *n.* an opening or hole; mouth: *the orifice of a tube or pipe.*

orig., **1** origin. **2** original.

o·ri·ga·mi (ôr′ə gä′mē), *n.* the Japanese art of folding paper to make decorative objects, such as birds, animals, and flowers.

o·ri·gin (ôr′ə jin), *n.* **1** thing from which anything comes; starting point; source; beginning: *the origin of a quarrel, the origin of a disease.* **2** parentage, ancestry, or birth: *He is of Mexican origin.* **3** (in mathematics) the point where the horizontal and vertical axes cross in a system of coordinates.

origami

SYNONYM STUDY **Origin** and **source** both mean the thing or place that something comes from. **Origin** is a general word. It often suggests the reasons for the new thing: *This huge traffic jam had its origin in one flat tire.* **Source** suggests a steady supply: *Her new cat is a constant source of amusement.*

o·rig·i·nal (ə rij′ə nəl), **1** *adj.* of or from the beginning; first; earliest: *They were the original owners of that house. The hat has been marked down from its original price.* **2** *adj.* new; fresh; novel: *It is hard to plan original games for a party.* **3** *adj.* able to do, make, or think something new; inventive: *a very original writer.* **4** *adj.* not copied, imitated, or translated from something else: *She wrote an original poem.* **5** *n.* thing from which another is copied, imitated, or translated: *The original of this picture is in Rome.*

o·rig·i·nal·i·ty (ə rij′ə nal′ə tē), *n.* **1** ability to do, make, or think up something new: *She is an artist with great originality.* **2** newness; freshness: *I was impressed by the play's originality.* **3** quality of being original.

a	hat	ė	term	ô	order	ch	child		
ā	age	i	it	oi	oil	ng	long		a in about
ä	far	ī	ice	ou	out	sh	she	ə	e in taken
â	care	o	hot	u	cup	th	thin		i in pencil
e	let	ō	open	u̇	put	ᴛʜ	then		o in lemon
ē	equal	ȯ	saw	ü	rule	zh	measure		u in circus

o·rig·i·nal·ly (ə rij′ə nə lē), *adv.* **1** by origin: *He is originally from Canada.* **2** at first; in the first place: *Though originally the house was small, rooms have been added.* **3** in a fresh or novel manner: *We want this room decorated originally.*

original sin, (in Christian belief) a tendency to do evil, believed to be natural in human beings and passed from Adam to the human race as a result of his sin in eating the forbidden fruit.

o·rig·i·nate (ə rij′ə nāt), *v.* **1** to cause to be; invent: *originate a new style of painting.* **2** to come into being; begin; arise: *Where did that story originate?* ❑ *v.* **o·rig·i·nat·ed, o·rig·i·nat·ing.** **—o·rig′i·na′tion,** *n.* **—o·rig′i·na·tor,** *n.*

o·rig·i·na·tive (ə rij′ə nā′tiv), *adj.* having originality; inventive; creative. **—o·rig′i·na′tive·ly,** *adv.*

O·ri·no·co (ôr′ə nō′kō), *n.* large river in South America, flowing through Venezuela into the Atlantic.

o·ri·ole (ôr′ē əl), *n.* any of several American songbirds with yellow and black or orange and black feathers.

O·ri·on (ə rī′ən), *n.* constellation near the celestial equator containing the extremely bright stars Betelgeuse and Rigel, and shaped something like a man wearing a belt and a sword and holding up a club.

Ork·ney Islands (ôrk′nē), group of islands northeast of, and belonging to, Scotland. See **British Isles** for map.

Or·lon (ôr′lon), *n.* trademark for a lightweight synthetic fiber that resists sun, rain, and acids. It is used for clothing, sails, awnings, etc.

or·na·ment (ôr′nə mənt *for noun;* ôr′nə ment *for verb*), **1** *n.* something pretty or decorative; something to add beauty; adornment; decoration: *Lace, jewels, vases, and statues are ornaments.* **2** *v.* to add beauty to; make more pleasing or attractive; adorn; decorate: *The dress was ornamented with beads.* ■ See Synonym Study at **decorate.**

or·na·men·tal (ôr′nə men′tl), *adj.* **1** of or for ornament; used as an ornament: *ornamental plants.* **2** decorative: *ornamental designs in wallpaper.* **—or′na·men′tal·ly,** *adv.*

or·na·men·ta·tion (ôr′nə men tā′shən), *n.* **1** decorations; ornaments. **2** act of ornamenting or condition of being ornamented.

or·nate (ôr nāt′), *adj.* having much decoration; much ornamented: *an ornate vase.* **—or·nate′ly,** *adv.* **—or·nate′ness,** *n.*

or·ner·y (ôr′nər ē), *adj.* INFORMAL. very mean; bad-tempered: *an ornery horse.* ❑ *adj.* **or·ner·i·er, or·ner·i·est. —or′ner·i·ness,** *n.*

WORD STORY Ornery comes from **ordinary.** Writers spelled the word a new way to show how people were pronouncing it. The new spelling developed a new meaning. Something just ordinary isn't very good. People used **ornery** to mean "not good, unpleasant, annoying," and then "mean."

or·nith·is·chi·an (ôr′nə this′kē ən), **1** *adj.* (of dinosaurs) having hip joints and pelvic bones that resemble those of birds. **2** *n.* a dinosaur with such hips and pelvis. The ornithischians were planteaters, such as triceratops and stegosaurus.

or·ni·tho·log·i·cal (ôr′nə thə loj′ə kəl), *adj.* of birds or ornithology. **—or′ni·tho·log′i·cal·ly,** *adv.*

or·ni·thol·o·gy (ôr′nə thol′ə jē), *n.* branch of zoology dealing with the study of birds. **—or′ni·thol′o·gist,** *n.*

or·phan (ôr′fən), **1** *n.* child whose parents are dead; child whose father or mother is dead. **2** *adj.* of or for such a child or children: *an orphan asylum.* **3** *adj.* without a father or mother or both. **4** *v.* to make an orphan of: *The war orphaned him at an early age.*

or·phan·age (ôr′fə nij), *n.* home for orphans.

Or·phe·us (ôr′fē əs), *n.* (in Greek myths) a musician who played so sweetly that animals, trees, and rocks followed him.

Orr (ôr), *n.* **Bob·by** (bob′ē), born 1948, American hockey player. He was the first defenseman to score more than 100 points in one season.

or·tho·don·tia (ôr′thə don′chə), *n.* orthodontics.

or·tho·don·tics (ôr′thə don′tiks), *n.* branch of dentistry that deals with straightening and adjusting teeth.

or·tho·don·tist (ôr′thə don′tist), *n.* dentist who specializes in orthodontics.

or·tho·dox (ôr′thə doks), *adj.* **1** generally accepted, especially in religion. **2** having generally accepted views or opinions, especially in religion; adhering to established customs and traditions: *an orthodox Methodist, an orthodox Jew.* **3** approved by custom; usual; customary: *orthodox ideas about bringing up children.*

Orthodox Church, Eastern Church.

or·tho·dox·y (ôr′thə dok′sē), *n.* the holding of generally accepted beliefs; orthodox practice, especially in religion.

or·tho·graph·ic (ôr′thə graf′ik), *adj.* **1** of or about orthography. **2** correct in spelling. **—or′tho·graph′i·cal·ly,** *adv.*

or·thog·ra·phy (ôr thog′rə fē), *n.* **1** correct spelling; spelling considered as right or wrong. **2** art of spelling; study of spelling.

or·tho·pe·dic (ôr′thə pē′dik), *adj.* of or for orthopedics. **—or′tho·pe′di·cal·ly,** *adv.*

or·tho·pe·dics (ôr′thə pē′diks), *n.* branch of medicine that deals with the deformities and diseases of bones and joints.

or·tho·pe·dist (ôr′thə pē′dist), *n.* physician who specializes in orthopedics.

Or·well (ôr′wel), *n.* **George,** 1903-1950, English writer. His novel *1984* is a description of a totalitarian world.

-ory, *suffix.* **1** ___ing: *contradictory = contradicting.* **2** of ___ion: *illusory = of illusion.* **3** place for ___ing: *depository = place for depositing.*

o·ryx (ôr′iks), *n.* any of several African and Middle Eastern antelopes with long, nearly straight horns. ❑ *n., pl.* **o·ryx** or **o·ryx·es.**

Os, symbol for osmium.

O·sage (ō′sāj), *n.* member of a tribe of American Indians formerly living in the region of the Arkansas and Missouri rivers, now living in Oklahoma. ❑ *n., pl.* **O·sage** or **O·sag·es.**

O·sa·ka (ō sä′kə), *n.* port in S Japan.

Os·car (os′kər), *n.* **1** Academy Award. **2** a small golden statue given to Academy Award winners.

WORD STORY Oscar comes from a comment made about the little statue given to winners of the Academy Awards. Soon after the awards started being given, a woman involved in giving them said that the statue reminded her of her uncle Oscar. The name stuck.

Os·ce·o·la (os′ē ō′lə), *n.* 1804?-1838, Seminole leader. ■ **Osceola** fought attempts by the U.S. Army to move the tribe west of the Mississippi River. Captured and imprisoned while meeting under a flag of truce, he died in prison.

os·cil·late (os′l āt), *v.* **1** to swing to and fro like a pendulum; move to and fro between two points. **2** to vary between moods, opinions, purposes, etc. ❑ *v.* **os·cil·lat·ed, os·cil·lat·ing.**

os·cil·la·tion (os′l ā′shən), *n.* **1** act or process of swinging to and fro like a pendulum. **2** a single swing in such motion: *Each oscillation of the pendulum takes one second.* **3** a change of a quantity from one extreme amount to another, such as the change in voltage of an alternating current.

os·cil·la·tor (os′l ā′tər), *n.* **1** device that converts direct current into alternating current of a particular frequency. Radios and TVs contain oscillators, as do broadcasting transmitters, to control the frequencies of electric signals. **2** person or thing that oscillates.

os·cil·lo·scope (ə sil′ə skōp), *n.* device for showing oscillations of a voltage or current on the screen of a CRT.

O·si·ris (ō sī′ris), *n.* one of the chief gods of ancient Egypt, ruler of the lower world and judge of the dead. He represented good and productivity and is identified with the Nile.

Os·lo (oz′lō), *n.* capital of Norway, in the SE part.

os·mi·um (oz′mē əm), *n.* a hard, heavy, bluish white metallic element that is found with platinum and iridium. Osmium is the heaviest, densest known element. It is used in alloys and for electric light filaments. *Symbol:* Os

os·mo·sis (oz mō′sis), *n.* **1** tendency of two different fluids separated by a membrane to go through it and become mixed. Osmosis is the main way that the body circulates nutrients and wastes. Fluid moves between the blood vessels and other tissues by osmosis. **2** a gradual, often unconscious, absorbing of facts, theories, ideas, etc.: *to learn by osmosis.*

os·mot·ic (oz mot′ik), *adj.* of or caused by osmosis. **—os·mot′i·cal·ly,** *adv.*

os·prey (os′prē), *n.* a large hawk that feeds on fish; fish hawk. ❑ *n., pl.* **os·preys.**

osprey—about 2 ft. (61 cm) long

os·ten·si·ble (o sten′sə bəl), *adj.* according to appearances but not necessarily true; apparent; pretended; professed: *My ostensible purpose for going to the library was to study, but I was really reading magazines.* **—os·ten′si·bly,** *adv.*

os·ten·ta·tion (os′ten tā′shən), *n.* showy display intended to impress others: *the ostentation of a newly rich family.*

os·ten·ta·tious (os′ten tā′shəs), *adj.* **1** done for display; intended to attract notice: *ostentatious jewels.* **2** showing off; liking to attract notice. **—os′ten·ta′tious·ly,** *adv.* **—os′ten·ta′tious·ness,** *n.*

os·te·o·path (os′tē ə path), *n.* person who specializes in osteopathy.

os·te·o·path·ic (os′tē ə path′ik), *adj.* of or about osteopathy. **—os′te·o·path′i·cal·ly,** *adv.*

os·te·op·a·thy (os′tē op′ə thē), *n.* treatment of diseases by manipulating the bones and muscles. Osteopathy also includes other types of medical and physical therapy.

os·te·o·po·ro·sis (os′tē ō pə rō′sis), *n.* disease in which the bones become weak and easily broken. The disease, caused by loss of calcium from the bones, occurs mainly in older women.

os·tra·cism (os′trə siz′əm), *n.* **1** condition of being shut out from society, from favor, from privileges, or from association with others. **2** banishment from your native country.

os·tra·cize (os′trə siz), *v.* **1** to shut out from society, from favor, from privileges, etc.: *The cheater was ostracized.* **2** to condemn to leave a country; banish. The ancient Greeks ostracized an unpopular citizen by public vote. ❑ *v.* **os·tra·cized, os·tra·ciz·ing. —os′tra·ciz′a·ble,** *adj.* **—os′tra·ci·za′tion,** *n.* **—os′tra·ciz′er,** *n.*

os·trich (os′trich), *n.* a large African and Arabian bird that can run swiftly but cannot fly. Ostriches have only two toes and are the largest birds alive. They have large plumes which were formerly much used as ornaments. ❑ *n., pl.* **os·trich·es.**

Os·wald (oz′wôld), *n.* **Lee Harvey,** 1939-1963, American assassin of President John F. Kennedy, on November 22, 1963. He himself was murdered two days later.

O.T. or **OT,** Old Testament.

OTC, over-the-counter.

O·thel·lo (ə thel′ō), *n.* **1** play by Shakespeare. **2** the principal character in this play, a brave but jealous Moor who kills his wife after being falsely persuaded that she is not true to him.

oth·er (uŦH′ər), **1** *adj.* remaining: *First she painted one wall, then the other walls.* **2** *adj.* additional or further: *I have no other place to go.* **3** *adj.* not the same as one or more already mentioned: *Come some other day.* **4** *adj.* different: *I would not have you other than you are.* **5** *pron.* the other one; not the same ones: *Each praises the other.* **6** *pron.* other person or thing: *There are others to be considered.* **7** *adv.* in any different way; otherwise: *I could not do other than I did.*

every other, every second; alternate: *We buy milk every other day.*

the other day (**night,** etc.), recently: *I saw her the other day.*

oth·er·wise (uŦH′ər wiz′), **1** *adv.* in a different way; differently: *I could not do otherwise.* **2** *adj.* different: *It might have been otherwise.* **3** *adv.* in other ways: *It is windy, but otherwise a very nice day.* **4** *adv.* under other circumstances: *She reminded me of what I would otherwise have forgotten.* **5** *conj.* or else; if not: *Come at once; otherwise you will be too late.*

Ot·ta·wa (ot′ə wə), *n.* **1** capital of Canada, in SE Ontario. **2** member of a tribe of American Indians who live in Michigan, Ontario, Kansas, and Oklahoma. ❑ *n., pl.* **Ot·ta·wa** or **Ot·ta·was** for 2.

> **WORD STORY** **Ottawa** comes from an Algonquian word meaning "to trade." The Ottawa traveled hundreds of miles to exchange goods with tribes to their east and west.

ot·ter (ot′ər), *n.* **1** any of several water mammals, related to the weasel, that have webbed toes with claws and thick, glossy, brown fur. Otters live near water and are good swimmers. **2** their fur. ❑ *n., pl.* **ot·ter** or **ot·ters.**

ot·to·man (ot′ə mən), *n.* **1** a low, cushioned seat without back or arms. **2** a cushioned footstool. ❑ *n., pl.* **ot·to·mans.**

Ot·to·man (ot′ə mən), **1** *n.* Turk. **2** *adj.* Turkish. ❑ *n., pl.* **Ot·to·mans.**

Ottoman Empire, a former Turkish empire which occupied Asia Minor and parts of N Africa, SE Europe, and SW Asia in the middle 1500s.

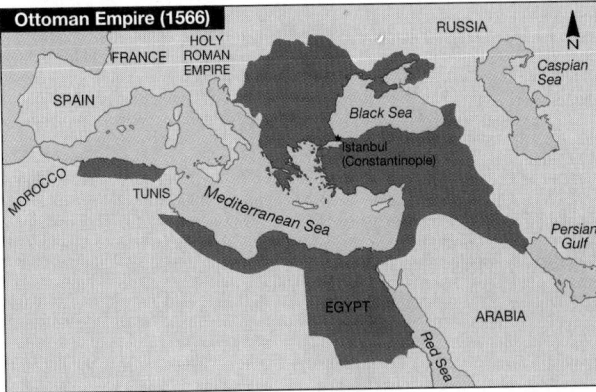

Ottoman Empire (1566)

Oua·ga·dou·gou (wä′gə dü′gü), *n.* capital of Burkina Faso, in the central part.

ouch (ouch), *interj.* exclamation of sudden pain.

ought (ôt), *v.* **1** to have a duty; be obliged: *You ought to obey your parents.* **2** to be right or suitable: *Cruelty and bullying ought not to be allowed.* **3** to be wise: *I ought to go before it rains.* **4** to be expected: *At your age you ought to know better.* **5** to be very likely: *It ought to be a fine day tomorrow.* ◼ Another word that sounds like this is **aught.**

> **USAGE NOTE** **Ought** is used in the negative with **not** or as the contraction **oughtn't.** Careful writers and speakers avoid such phrases as *shouldn't ought* or *hadn't ought.*

ought·n't (ôt′nt), ought not.

ounce¹ (ouns), *n.* **1** unit of weight equal to 1/16 of a pound in avoirdupois weight, and 1/12 of a pound in troy weight. **2** fluid ounce. **3** a little bit; small amount: *"An ounce of prevention is worth a pound of cure."*

> **WORD STORY** **Ounce¹** comes from a Latin word meaning "a twelfth." **Inch** comes from the same word. An inch is a twelfth of a foot, but what about an ounce? In troy weight and other old measuring systems, an ounce was a twelfth of a pound. The word still means a part of a pound, but today that part is usually a sixteenth of a pound.

ounce² (ouns), *n.* snow leopard.

a	hat	ė	term	ô	order	ch	child		a in about
ā	age	i	it	oi	oil	ng	long		e in taken
ä	far	ī	ice	ou	out	sh	she	ə	i in pencil
â	care	o	hot	u	cup	th	thin		o in lemon
e	let	ō	open	ů	put	ŦH	then		u in circus
ē	equal	ô	saw	ü	rule	zh	measure		

our (our), *adj.* of us; belonging to us: *We need our coats now.* ■ Another word that sounds like this is **hour.**

ours (ourz), *pron.* the one or ones belonging to us: *This garden is ours.*

our·selves (our selvz′), *pron. pl.* **1** form of *we* or *us* used to make a statement stronger: *We ourselves will do the work.* **2** form used instead of *we* or *us* in cases like: *We cook for ourselves.* **3** our real or true selves: *We weren't ourselves after the accident.* ■ See Usage Note at **myself.**

-ous, *suffix.* **1** having much; full of: *famous = having much fame; joyous = full of joy.* **2** like: *thunderous = like thunder.* **3** being a ___: *carnivorous = being a carnivore.*

oust (oust), *v.* to force out; drive out: *The sparrows have ousted the bluebirds from their nest.*

oust·er (ou′stər), *n.* act of ousting; expulsion.

out (out), **1** *adv.* away; forth: *The water will rush out.* **2** *adj.* not in use, action, control, or fashion: *The fire is out. Election results show the present mayor is out. That style is out this year.* **3** *adv.* outside: *It's raining out.* **4** *adv.* not at home; away from your office, work, etc.: *My mother is out just now.* **5** *adj.* (in baseball) not successful in reaching base or advancing from one base to another: *The outfielder caught the fly and the batter was out.* **6** *n.* condition of being out or act of putting out in baseball: *A team's turn at bat lasts until three outs are made.* **7** *adv.* from the usual place, condition, position, etc.: *Put the light out.* **8** *adv.* suffering the lack of: *be out ten dollars.* **9** *prep.* forth from; out of: *He went out the door.* **10** *adv.* into the open; made public; made known; into being; so as to be seen: *The secret is out now. Her new book is out.* **11** *adv.* to or at an end: *Let them play the game out.* **12** *prep.* out along: *Drive out Second Street.* **13** *v.* to go or come out; be disclosed: *The truth will out.* **14** *adv.* aloud; plainly: *Speak out so that all can hear.* **15** *adv.* so as to project or extend: *stand out.* **16** *adv.* to others: *let out rooms. Give out the books.* **17** *adv.* from among others: *Pick out an apple for me.* **18** *n.* a defense or excuse: *have an out for stealing.* **19** *adj.* external; exterior; outer; outlying: *an out island.* **20** *adj.* not possible; not to be considered: *I have no money, so going to the movies is out.*
on the outs, quarreling; disagreeing: *Tom and Debbie have been on the outs for weeks now.*
out for, looking for; trying to get: *He is out for the best deal he can get.*
out of, 1 from within: *He came out of the house.* **2** not within: *He is out of town.* **3** away from; beyond: *36 miles out of Atlanta. She was out of sight.* **4** not having; without: *She is out of work. We are out of coffee.* **5** so as to take away: *I was cheated out of my money.* **6** from: *made out of silk.* **7** from among: *We picked our puppy out of that litter.* **8** because of: *I went out of curiosity.*
out to, eagerly trying to.

out-, *prefix.* **1** outward: *outbound = outward bound.* **2** outside: *outlying = lying outside.* **3** more than or longer than: *outlive = live longer than.* **4** better than: *outdo = do better than.*

out·age (ou′tij), *n.* an unexpected interruption of service, especially of electricity.

out-and-out (out′n out′), *adj.* thorough; complete: *an out-and-out defeat.*

out·back (out′bak′), *n.* **1** the Australian back country far from any cities or towns. **2** the thinly settled parts of any country.

out·bal·ance (out bal′əns), *v.* to outweigh. ❑ *v.* **out·bal·anced, out·bal·anc·ing.**

out·bid (out bid′), *v.* to bid higher than someone else. ❑ *v.* **out·bid, out·bid·den** or **out·bid, out·bid·ding.**

out·board (out′bôrd′), *adj., adv.* outside the hull of a ship or boat.

outboard motor, a gasoline motor, often portable, attached to the outside of the stern of a boat or canoe.

out·bound (out′bound′), *adj.* outward bound: *an outbound ship, outbound flights.*

out·break (out′brāk′), *n.* **1** act of breaking out: *outbreaks of disease.* **2** a riot; public disturbance.

out·build·ing (out′bil′ding), *n.* a shed or building built against or near a main building: *Barns are outbuildings on a farm.*

out·burst (out′bėrst′), *n.* act of bursting forth: *There was an outburst of laughter when the clowns stumbled.*

out·cast (out′kast′), **1** *n.* person driven away from home and friends: *The criminal was an outcast.* **2** *adj.* being an outcast; homeless; friendless.

out·class (out klas′), *v.* to be of a higher class than; be much better than.

out·come (out′kum′), *n.* something that happens, especially as a result: *the outcome of a race.* ■ See Synonym Study at **effect.**

out·crop (out′krop′ *for noun;* out krop′ *for verb*), **1** *n.* area of rock that sticks out above the surrounding ground: *The outcrop that we found proved to be very rich in gold.* **2** *v.* to come to the surface; appear. ❑ *v.* **out·cropped, out·crop·ping.**

out·cry (out′krī′), *n.* **1** a crying out; sudden cry or scream. **2** a great noise or clamor. ❑ *n., pl.* **out·cries.**

out·dat·ed (out dā′tid), *adj.* out-of-date; old-fashioned: *a person with outdated ideas.*

out·did (out did′), *v.* past tense of **outdo:** *She outdid the others in diving.*

out·dis·tance (out dis′təns), *v.* to leave behind; outstrip: *The winner outdistanced all the other runners in the race.* ❑ *v.* **out·dis·tanced, out·dis·tanc·ing.**

out·do (out dü′), *v.* to do more or better than; surpass: *He can outdo the others in running.* ❑ *v.* **out·did, out·done, out·doing.**

out·done (out dun′), *v.* past participle of **outdo:** *She has outdone her previous track record.*

out·door (out′dôr′), *adj.* done, used, or living outdoors: *outdoor games, an outdoor meal.*

out·doors (out′dôrz′), **1** *adv.* outside; not indoors or in the house: *Let's go outdoors to play.* **2** *n.* the world outside of houses; the open air: *We must protect the wildlife of the great outdoors.*

outdoors

out·er (ou′tər), *adj.* on the outside; farther out: *Shingles are used as an outer covering for many roofs.*

outer ear, the outer part of the ear, including the passage leading to the middle ear. See picture at **ear¹.**

out·er·most (ou′tər mōst), *adj.* farthest out.

outer space, 1 space beyond the earth's atmosphere: *The moon is in outer space.* **2** space beyond the solar system.

out·er·wear (ou′tər wâr′), *n.* jackets, coats, and other clothing worn over regular clothing for warmth in cold weather.

out·field (out′fēld′), *n.* **1** the part of a baseball field beyond the diamond or infield. **2** the three players in the outfield.

out·field·er (out′fēl′dər), *n.* a baseball player in the outfield.

out·fight (out fīt′), *v.* to fight better than; surpass in a fight. ❑ *v.* **out·fought** (out fôt′), **out·fight·ing.**

out·fit (out′fit), **1** *n.* a set of clothes that match or go well together: *That jacket and dress make a lovely outfit.* **2** *n.* all the articles necessary for any activity: *a skiing outfit.* **3** *v.* to furnish with everything necessary for any purpose; equip: *She outfitted herself for camp.* **4** *n.* group working together, such as a military unit, business organization, etc. ❑ *v.* **out·fit·ted, out·fit·ting.**

out·fit·ter (out′fit′ər), *n.* person who outfits, especially a dealer in outfits for traveling, athletic sports, etc.

out·flank (out flangk′), *v.* **1** to go or extend beyond the flank of an opposing army; turn the flank of. **2** to get the better of; outmaneuver. —**out·flank′er,** *n.*

out·flow (out′flō′), *n.* **1** act of flowing out: *the outflow from a pipe, an outflow of sympathy.* **2** that which flows out.

out·fox (out foks′), *v.* to outsmart.

out·go (out′gō′), *n.* what goes out; amount spent. ❑ *n., pl.* **out·goes.**

out·go·ing (out′gō′ing), *adj.* **1** outward bound; departing: *outgoing steamships.* **2** friendly and helpful to others; sociable: *An outgoing person can usually make friends.*

out·grow (out grō′), *v.* **1** to grow too large for: *outgrow your clothes.* **2** to grow beyond or away from; get rid of by growing older: *outgrow a babyish habit.* **3** to grow faster or taller than: *This variety of tomato will outgrow most other kinds.* ❑ *v.* **out·grew** (out grü′), **out·grown** (out grōn′), **out·grow·ing.**

out·growth (out′grōth′), *n.* **1** a natural development, product, or result: *This big store is an outgrowth of a little shop.* **2** offshoot; something that has grown out: *A corn is an outgrowth on a toe.* **3** act or process of growing out or forth: *the outgrowth of new leaves in the spring.*

out·guess (out ges′), *v.* to be too clever for; get the better of.

out·gun (out′gun′), *v.* **1** to have more firepower than. **2** to overwhelm: *When they told me all their reasons for going, I felt outgunned.* ❑ *v.,* **out·gunned, out·gun·ning.**

out·house (out′hous′), *n.* **1** an outdoor toilet. **2** outbuilding. ❑ *n., pl.* **out·hous·es** (out′hou′ziz).

out·ing (ou′ting), *n.* a short pleasure trip; walk or airing; holiday spent outdoors away from home: *On Sunday the family went on an outing to the beach.*

out·land·ish (out lan′dish), *adj.* not familiar; odd; strange or ridiculous: *The singer wore an outlandish purple wig.* —**out·land′ish·ly,** *adv.* —**out·land′ish·ness,** *n.*

out·last (out last′), *v.* to last longer than.

out·law (out′lô′), **1** *n.* a lawless person; criminal. **2** *n.* person outside the protection of the law; exile; outcast. **3** *v.* to make or declare illegal: *outlaw gambling.*

out·lay (out′lā *for noun;* out lā′ *for verb*), **1** *n.* act of laying out money; spending; expense: *a large outlay for clothing.* **2** *n.* the amount spent: *an outlay of eleven dollars.* **3** *v.* to expend: *outlay money in improvements.* ❑ *v.* **out·laid, out·lay·ing.**

out·let (out′let), *n.* **1** means or place of letting out or getting out; way out; vent; opening; exit: *the outlet of a lake, an outlet for your energies.* **2** store that sells a particular product or products. **3** point in an electric circuit where an electric plug may be inserted to receive power. An outlet is usually set in a wall.

out·line (out′lin′), **1** *n.* line that shows the shape of an object: *The outline of Italy suggests a boot.* **2** *n.* a drawing or style of drawing that gives only outer lines: *Make an outline of the scene before you paint it.* **3** *v.* to draw the outer line of: *Outline a map of America.* **4** *n.* a general plan; rough draft: *Make an outline before trying to write a composition.* **5** *v.* to give a plan of; sketch: *She outlined their trip abroad.* ❑ *v.* **out·lined, out·lin·ing.**
in outline, 1 with only the outline shown. **2** with only the main features.

out·live (out liv′), *v.* to live or last longer than; survive; outlast: *She outlived her older sister.* ❑ *v.* **out·lived, out·liv·ing.**

out·look (out′lük′), *n.* **1** way of thinking about things; attitude of mind; point of view: *a cheerful outlook on life.* **2** what seems likely to happen; prospect: *The outlook for our picnic is not very good; it looks as if it will rain.* **3** what you see on looking out; view: *The room has a pleasant outlook.* **4** lookout; place to watch from.

out·ly·ing (out′lī′ing), *adj.* lying outside the boundary; far from the center; remote: *an outlying suburb of the city.*

out·ma·neu·ver (out′mə nü′vər), *v.* to outdo in maneuvering; get the better of by maneuvering.

out·mod·ed (out mō′did), *adj.* out-of-date: *outmoded ideas.*

out·most (out′mōst), *adj.* farthest out.

out·num·ber (out num′bər), *v.* to be more than; exceed in number: *They outnumbered us three to one.*

out-of-bounds (out′əv boundz′), *adj., adv.* outside the boundary line; out of play: *an out-of-bounds ball. He kicked the ball out-of-bounds.*

out-of-date (out′əv dāt′), *adj.* not in present use; old-fashioned: *A horse and buggy is an out-of-date vehicle.*

out-of-door (out′əv dôr′), *adj.* outdoor.

out-of-doors (out′əv dôrz′), **1** *adj.* outdoor. **2** *n., adv.* outdoors.

out-of-the-way (out′əv ᴛнə wā′), *adj.* **1** seldom visited; remote; unfrequented; secluded: *an out-of-the-way cottage.* **2** seldom met with; unusual: *out-of-the-way bits of information.*

out·pa·tient (out′pā′shənt), *n.* patient receiving treatment at a hospital or clinic but not staying there.

out·place·ment (out plās′mənt *or* out′plās′mənt), *n.* the act or service of helping a fired or unwanted employee find a new job, paid for by the company releasing the employee.

out·play (out plā′), *v.* to play better than.

out·port (out′pôrt′), *n.* CANADIAN. a small fishing village on the Newfoundland coast.

out·post (out′pōst′), *n.* **1** a guard, or small number of soldiers, placed at some distance from an army or camp to prevent surprise attacks. **2** place where they are stationed. **3** a settlement or village in an outlying place: *a frontier outpost.*

out·pour·ing (out′pôr′ing), *n.* **1** act of pouring out. **2** anything that is poured out. **3** an outburst: *an outpouring of grief.*

out·put (out′pùt′), **1** *n.* what is put out; amount produced; product; yield: *a factory's daily output of cars.* **2** *n.* act of putting forth: *With a sudden output of effort we moved the rock.* **3** *n.* information put out or produced by a computer. **4** *v.* to produce information: *Can you output these answers as a graph?* ❑ *v.* **out·put·ted** *or* **out·put, out·put·ting.**

out·rage (out′rāj), **1** *n.* an act showing no regard for the rights or feelings of others; overturning of the rights of others by force; act of violence; offense; insult: *The tyrant was guilty of many outrages.* **2** *n.* the anger caused by such an act. **3** *v.* to offend greatly; insult: *The British government outraged the colonists by taxing them unfairly.* **4** *v.* to break the law, a rule of morality, etc., openly; treat as nothing at all: *He outraged all rules of politeness by insulting his guests.* ❑ *v.* **out·raged, out·rag·ing.**

> **WORD STORY** **Outrage** does not come from **out** or from **rage.** It comes from a Latin word meaning "beyond," and its oldest meaning in English is "an act going beyond what is right or proper." Because an act of that sort makes people angry, and because of the word's spelling, people gave it the meaning "fury aroused by a misdeed."

out·ra·geous (out rā′jəs), *adj.* very bad or insulting; shocking: *outrageous language.* —**out·ra′geous·ly,** *adv.* —**out·ra′geous·ness,** *n.*

out·ran (out ran′), *v.* past tense of **outrun:** *She outran me easily.*

out·rank (out rangk′), *v.* to rank higher than: *A captain outranks a lieutenant.*

out·ré (ü trā′), *adj.* outside the bounds of what is usual and considered proper; eccentric; bizarre: *Green hair and blue goggles is an outré combination.*

out·rig·ger (out′rig′ər), *n.* **1** framework extending outward from the side of a light boat or canoe and ending in a float. It keeps the boat from turning over. **2** boat equipped with brackets extending outward from either side to hold oarlocks.

outrigger

a	hat	ė	term	ô	order	ch	child		
ā	age	i	it	oi	oil	ng	long		a in about
ä	far	ī	ice	ou	out	sh	she		e in taken
â	care	o	hot	u	cup	th	thin	ə	i in pencil
e	let	ō	open	ů	put	ᴛн	then		o in lemon
ē	equal	ò	saw	ü	rule	zh	measure		u in circus

out·right (out′rīt′), **1** *adj.* downright; straightforward; direct: *an outright refusal.* **2** *adj.* complete; total; absolute: *an outright criminal, an outright lie.* **3** *adv.* without restraint; openly: *I laughed outright.* **4** *adv.* not gradually; altogether; entirely: *We paid for our car outright.* **5** *adv.* at once; on the spot. —**out′right′ness**, *n.*

out·run (out run′), *v.* **1** to run faster than: *She can outrun her older sister.* **2** to leave behind; run beyond; pass the limits of: *This month's expenses have outrun our budget.* ❑ *v.* **out·ran, out·run, out·run·ning.**

out·sell (out sel′), *v.* **1** to outdo in selling; sell more than: *He outsold every other salesperson in the company last year.* **2** to be sold in greater quantity than: *This brand outsells the other brands on the market.* ❑ *v.* **out·sold** (out sōld′), **out·sell·ing.**

out·set (out′set′), *n.* act of setting out; start; beginning: *At the outset, it looked like a nice day.*

out·shine (out shin′), *v.* **1** to shine more brightly than. **2** to be more brilliant or excellent than; surpass. ❑ *v.* **out·shone** (out-shōn′), **out·shin·ing.**

out·side (out′sīd′; *for 5,6 also* out′sīd′), **1** *n.* the side or surface that is out; outer part: *polish the outside of a car, the outside of a house.* **2** *adj.* on the outside; of or nearer the outside; outer: *The outside covering of a nut is the hull.* **3** *adv.* on or to the outside; outdoors: *Run outside and play.* **4** *n.* space that is beyond or not inside. **5** *adv.* INFORMAL. with the exception of: *Outside of him, none of us liked the play.* **6** *prep.* out of; beyond the limits of: *Stay outside the house. That is outside my plans.* **7** *adj.* not belonging to a certain group, set, district, etc.: *We may need outside help on this project.* **8** *adj.* highest; largest; reaching the utmost limit: *an outside estimate of the cost.* **9** *adj.* barely possible; very slight: *The team has an outside chance to win.*

at the outside, at the utmost limit: *I can do it in a day, at the outside.*
outside of, with the exception of: *Outside of tennis, she has no interest in sports.*

out·sid·er (out′sī′dər), *n.* person not belonging to a particular group, set, company, party, district, etc.

out·size (out′sīz′), *adj.* larger than the usual size.

out·sized (out′sīzd′), *adj.* outsize.

out·skirts (out′skėrts′), *n.pl.* the outer parts or edges of a town, district, etc., or of a subject of discussion; outlying parts: *We have a farm on the outskirts of town.*

out·smart (out smärt′), *v.* to be more clever than; get the better of: *I outsmarted everyone and won the game.*

out·spo·ken (out′spō′kən), *adj.* not reserved; frank: *an outspoken person, outspoken criticism.* —**out′spo′ken·ly,** *adv.* —**out′spo′ken·ness,** *n.*

out·spread (out′spred′ *for adj.;* out spred′ *for verb*), **1** *adj.* spread out; extended: *an eagle with outspread wings.* **2** *v.* to spread out; extend. ❑ *v.* **out·spread, out·spread·ing.**

out·stand·ing (out stan′ding), *adj.* **1** standing out from others; well-known; important: *an outstanding student.* **2** unpaid: *outstanding debts.* —**out·stand′ing·ly,** *adv.*

out·stay (out stā′), *v.* to stay longer than.

out·stretched (out′strecht′), *adj.* stretched out; extended: *He welcomed his old friend with outstretched arms.*

out·strip (out strip′), *v.* **1** to do better than; excel: *She can outstrip most of her classmates in mathematics.* **2** to go faster than; leave behind in a race: *A horse can outstrip a human being.* ❑ *v.* **out·stripped, out·strip·ping.**

out·ward (out′wərd), **1** *adj.* going toward the outside; turned toward the outside: *She gave one outward glance.* **2** *adv.* toward the outside; away: *A porch extends outward from the house.* **3** *adj.* outer: *to all outward appearances.* **4** *adv.* on the outside: *I turned the coat with the lining outward.* **5** *adj.* that can be seen; plain to see: *Her outward behavior was calm and quiet.* —**out′ward·ness,** *n.*

out·ward·ly (out′wərd lē), *adv.* **1** on the outside or outer surface. **2** in appearance: *Though frightened, she remained outwardly calm.*

out·wards (out′wərdz), *adv.* outward.

out·wear (out wār′), *v.* **1** to wear longer than. **2** to wear out: *outwear someone's patience.* **3** to outgrow. ❑ *v.* **out·wore** (out wôr′), **out·worn, out·wear·ing.**

out·weigh (out wā′), *v.* **1** to exceed in value, importance, influence, etc.: *The advantages of the plan outweigh its disadvantages.* **2** to weigh more than.

out·wit (out wit′), *v.* to get the better of by being more intelligent; be too clever for: *She usually outwits me and wins at checkers.* ❑ *v.* **out·wit·ted, out·wit·ting.**

out·work (out wėrk′), *v.* to surpass in working; work harder or faster than.

out·worn (out′wôrn′ *for adj.;* out wôrn′ *for verb*), **1** *adj.* out-of-date; outgrown: *outworn habits.* **2** *adj.* worn out: *outworn clothes.* **3** *v.* past participle of **outwear:** *I have outworn the coat I bought last year.*

o·va (ō′və), *n.* plural of **ovum.**

o·val (ō′vəl), **1** *adj.* shaped like an egg. **2** *adj.* shaped like an ellipse. **3** *n.* something having an oval shape. —**o′val·ly,** *adv.* —**o′val·ness,** *n.*

o·var·i·an (ō vâr′ē ən), *adj.* of or on an ovary or ovaries.

o·var·y (ō′vər ē), *n.* **1** the organ of a female animal in which eggs are produced. **2** the enlarged lower part of the pistil of a flowering plant, enclosing the young seeds. ❑ *n., pl.* **o·var·ies.**

o·vate (ō′vāt), *adj.* egg-shaped: *an ovate leaf.* —**o′vate·ly,** *adv.*

o·va·tion (ō vā′shən), *n.* an enthusiastic public welcome; burst of loud clapping or cheering: *The soprano received a great ovation.* —**o·va′tion·al,** *adj.*

ovation

ov·en (uv′ən), *n.* **1** an enclosed space usually in a stove, for baking, roasting, and sometimes broiling food. **2** a small furnace for heating or drying pottery; kiln.

ov·en·bird (uv′ən bėrd′), *n.* a small American warbler that builds a nest with a dome-shaped roof.

o·ver (ō′vər), **1** *prep.* above in place or position: *the roof over your head.* **2** *prep.* above in authority, power, etc.: *We have a captain over us.* **3** *prep.* above and to the other side of; across: *leap over a wall. Can you climb over that hill?* **4** *adv.* across a space or distance: *Come over to my house.* **5** *adv.* down; out and down from an edge or from an upright position: *If you go too near the edge, you may fall over.* **6** *prep.* out and down from; down from the edge of: *The ball rolled over the side of the porch.* **7** *adv.* so as to cover the surface, or affect the whole surface: *Cover the tar over with sand until it has hardened.* **8** *prep.* about or upon, so as to cover: *Spread the canvas over the new cement.* **9** *prep.* at all or various places on; on; upon: *a blanket lying over a bed. A blush came over her face. Farms were scattered over the valley.* **10** *prep.* here and there on or in; round about; all through: *We shall travel over Europe.* **11** *prep.* from end to end of; along: *We drove over the new thruway.* **12** *adv.* from beginning to end: *read a newspaper over.* **13** *adv.* again: *I had to write my paper over.* **14** *prep.* during: *We were out of town over the weekend.* **15** *adj.* at an end: *The play is over.* **16** *prep.* about; concerning; in connection with: *He is worried over his health.* **17** *prep.* more than; beyond: *It costs over ten dollars.* **18** *prep.* by means of: *They spoke over the telephone.* **19** *adv.* in excess or addition; too; more; besides: *I ate two apples and had one left over.* **20** *adv.* more than: *Over fifty people came to the party.* **21** *adv.* so that the other side is up or showing; upside down: *turn over a page.* **22** *adj.* surplus; extra: *There was a copy for everyone and three copies over.* **23** *adv.* on the other side; at some distance: *over in Europe, over by the hill.* **24** *adv.* in a place for a period of time: *We stayed over in New York City until Monday.* **25** *adv.* at someone's home: *Can they sleep over?*

over again, once more: *Let's do that over again.*

over and above, besides; in addition to: *We had repairs to pay for over and above the cost of the car.*

over and over, again and again: *Practice the song over and over until you do it right.*

over with, done; finished.

over-, *prefix.* **1** above: *overhead = above the head.* **2** higher in rank; superior: *overlord = superior lord.* **3** across: *overseas = across the seas.* **4** too ___: *overcrowded = too crowded.* **5** above normal; extra: *oversize = above normal size; overtime = extra time.* **6** outer: *overcoat = outer coat.* **7 over-** also begins words meaning to take away power or effect, such as *overthrow* and *overturn.*

o·ver·a·chieve (ō′vər ə chēv′), *v.* to do more or better than seems likely considering abilities or resources: *an overachieving little school with two state championships.* ❑ *v.* **o·ver·a·chieved, o·ver·a·chiev·ing.** —**o′ver·a·chiev′er,** *n.*

o·ver·act (ō′vər akt′), *v.* to act a part in an exaggerated manner.

o·ver·ac·tive (ō′vər ak′tiv), *adj.* too active; active to too high a degree: *overactive youngsters.* —**o′ver·ac·tiv′i·ty,** *n.*

o·ver·all (ō′vər ȯl′), **1** *adj.* from one end to the other: *an overall measurement.* **2** *adj.* including everything: *an overall estimate.* **3** *adv.* generally; considering everything: *Overall, it was a very exciting movie.*

o·ver·alls (ō′vər ȯlz′), *n.pl.* loose trousers with a piece covering the chest. Overalls are usually worn over clothes to keep them clean.

o·ver·anx·ious (ō′vər angk′shəs), *adj.* too anxious. —**o′ver·anx′ious·ly,** *adv.* —**o′ver·anx′ious·ness,** *n.*

o·ver·arm (ō′vər ärm′), *adj.* with the arm raised above the shoulder; overhand.

o·ver·ate (ō′vər āt′), *v.* past tense of **overeat:** *I have a stomachache because I overate.*

o·ver·awe (ō′vər ȯ′), *v.* to overcome or restrain with awe: *The queen's courage overawed her rebellious subjects.* ❑ *v.* **o·ver·awed, o·ver·aw·ing.**

o·ver·bal·ance (ō′vər bal′əns), *v.* **1** to be greater than in weight, importance, value, etc.: *The gains overbalanced the losses.* **2** to cause to lose balance: *As I leaned over the side, my weight overbalanced the canoe and it upset.* ❑ *v.* **o·ver·bal·anced, o·ver·bal·anc·ing.**

o·ver·bear (ō′vər bâr′), *v.* **1** to overcome by weight or force; oppress; master: *My friends overbore all my objections.* **2** to bear down by weight or force; overthrow; upset. ❑ *v.* **o·ver·bore, o·ver·borne, o·ver·bear·ing.**

o·ver·bear·ing (ō′vər bâr′ing), *adj.* inclined to dictate; forcing others to your own will; domineering: *Promoted too quickly, the young executive became overbearing.* —**o′ver·bear′ing·ly,** *adv.*

o·ver·bid (ō′vər bid′), *v.* **1** to bid more than the value of a thing. **2** to outbid. **3** to bid too high. ❑ *v.* **o·ver·bid, o·ver·bid·ding.**

o·ver·bite (ō′vər bīt′), *n.* a condition in which someone's upper teeth are far in front of the lower teeth when the mouth is closed.

o·ver·board (ō′vər bôrd′), *adv.* from a ship or boat into the water: *to fall overboard.*

go overboard, to go too far in an effort because of extreme enthusiasm.

throw overboard, to throw into the water.

o·ver·bore (ō′vər bôr′), *v.* past tense of **overbear.**

o·ver·borne (ō′vər bôrn′), *v.* past participle of **overbear.**

overbite

o·ver·bur·den (ō′vər bėrd′n), *v.* to load with too great a burden: *I felt overburdened by so much homework.*

o·ver·came (ō′vər kām′), *v.* past tense of **overcome:** *I finally overcame my fear.*

o·ver·cast (ō′vər kast′), **1** *adj.* cloudy and dark; gloomy: *The sky was overcast before the storm.* **2** *n.* a cloud covering. **3** *v.* to sew over and through the edges of a seam with long stitches to prevent raveling. ❑ *v.* **o·ver·cast, o·ver·cast·ing.**

o·ver·cau·tious (ō′vər kȯ′shəs), *adj.* too careful; unwilling to take any chances. —**o′ver·cau′tious·ly,** *adv.* —**o′ver·cau′tious·ness,** *n.*

o·ver·charge (ō′vər chärj′ *for verb;* ō′vər chärj′ *for noun*), **1** *v.* to charge too high a price: *The grocer overcharged you for the eggs.* **2** *n.* a charge that is too great. **3** *v.* to load too heavily; fill too full: *The overcharged old musket burst.* ❑ *v.* **o·ver·charged, o·ver·charg·ing.**

o·ver·coat (ō′vər kōt′), *n.* an outer coat worn over the regular clothing for warmth in cold weather.

o·ver·come (ō′vər kum′), *v.* **1** to get the better of; win the victory over; conquer; defeat: *overcome an enemy, overcome difficulties.* **2** to make weak or helpless: *Weariness overcame her and she fell asleep.* ❑ *v.* **o·ver·came, o·ver·come, o·ver·com·ing.**

o·ver·con·fi·dent (ō′vər kon′fə dənt), *adj.* too confident. —**o′ver·con′fi·dent·ly,** *adv.*

o·ver·cooked (ō′vər kùkt′), *adj.* cooked too much or too long.

o·ver·crowd (ō′vər kroud′), *v.* to crowd too much; put in too much or too many: *Don't overcrowd the elevator.*

o·ver·de·vel·op (ō′vər di vel′əp), *v.* to develop too much or too long. If a photograph is overdeveloped, it is too dark. —**o′ver·de·vel′op·ment,** *n.*

o·ver·did (ō′vər did′), *v.* past tense of **overdo:** *She overdid her exercises and became very tired.*

o·ver·do (ō′vər dü′), *v.* **1** to do or attempt to do too much: *When getting over an illness, you mustn't overdo.* **2** to exaggerate: *The funny scenes in the play were overdone.* **3** to cook too much: *The vegetables were overdone.* **4** to exhaust; tire. ❑ *v.* **o·ver·did, o·ver·done, o·ver·do·ing.** —**o′ver·do′er,** *n.*

o·ver·done (ō′vər dun′), *v.* past participle of **overdo.**

o·ver·dose (ō′vər dōs′ *for noun;* ō′vər dōs′ *for verb*), **1** *n.* too big a dose. **2** *v.* to give too large a dose to. ❑ *v.* **o·ver·dosed, o·ver·dos·ing.**

o·ver·draft (ō′vər draft′), *n.* **1** act of overdrawing an account, especially a bank account. **2** amount overdrawn.

o·ver·draw (ō′vər drȯ′), *v.* **1** to write a check or checks against a bank account for more money than is in your account. **2** to exaggerate: *The characters in the book were greatly overdrawn.* ❑ *v.* **o·ver·drew** (ō′vər drü′), **o·ver·drawn** (ō′vər drȯn′), **o·ver·draw·ing.**

o·ver·dress (ō′vər dres′), *v.* to dress too elaborately: *My sister hopes that she didn't overdress for the party.*

o·ver·drive (ō′vər drīv′), *n.* an arrangement of gears in a car that produces greater speed while using less power than when the car is in high.

o·ver·dub (ō′vər dub′), *v.* to add sound or music to an existing recording: *He overdubbed the sound of a creaking door on the movie sound track.* ❑ *v.,* **o·ver·dubbed, o·ver·dub·bing.**

o·ver·due (ō′vər dü′), *adj.* more than due; due some time ago but not yet arrived, paid, etc.: *The plane is overdue. This bill is overdue.*

o·ver·eat (ō′vər ēt′), *v.* to eat too much. ❑ *v.* **o·ver·ate, o·ver·eat·en, o·ver·eat·ing.**

o·ver·eat·en (ō′vər ēt′n), *v.* past participle of **overeat:** *Nearly everyone has overeaten at the picnic.*

o·ver·em·pha·sis (ō′vər em′fə sis), *n.* too much emphasis.

o·ver·em·pha·size (ō′vər em′fə sīz), *v.* to give too much force or emphasis to; stress too much. ❑ *v.* **o·ver·em·pha·sized, o·ver·em·pha·siz·ing.**

a	hat	ė	term	ȯ	order	ch	child		a	in about
ā	age	i	it	oi	oil	ng	long		e	in taken
ä	far	ī	ice	ou	out	sh	she	ə	i	in pencil
â	care	o	hot	u	cup	th	thin		o	in lemon
e	let	ō	open	ù	put	ᴛʜ	then		u	in circus
ē	equal	ȯ	saw	ü	rule	zh	measure			

o·ver·es·ti·mate (ō′vər es′tə māt *for verb;* ō′vər es′tə mit *for noun*), **1** *v.* to estimate at too high a value, amount, rate, etc. **2** *n.* an estimate that is too high. ❑ *v.* **o·ver·es·ti·mat·ed, o·ver·es·ti·mat·ing. —o′ver·es′ti·ma′tion,** *n.*

o·ver·ex·pose (ō′vər ek spōz′), *v.* **1** to expose too much. **2** (in photography) to expose a film or negative too long to light. ❑ *v.* **o·ver·ex·posed, o·ver·ex·pos·ing.**

o·ver·ex·po·sure (ō′vər ek spō′zhər), *n.* too much or too long an exposure.

o·ver·feed (ō′vər fēd′), *v.* to feed too much. ❑ *v.* **o·ver·fed** (ō′vər fed′), **o·ver·feed·ing.**

o·ver·fish (ō′vər fish′), *v.* to fish too much in certain waters; to use up the supply of fish in an area: *The lake has been overfished and now there are no more trout.*

o·ver·flow (ō′vər flō′ *for verb;* ō′vər flō′ *for noun*), **1** *v.* to flow over or beyond the limits: *Rivers often overflow in the spring.* **2** *v.* to cover or flood: *The river overflowed my garden.* **3** *v.* to have the contents flowing over: *My cup is overflowing.* **4** *v.* to flow over the top of: *The milk overflowed the cup.* **5** *v.* to extend out beyond; be too many for: *The crowd overflowed the small room and filled the hall.* **6** *v.* to be very abundant: *an overflowing harvest, overflowing kindness.* **7** *n.* act of overflowing; excess. **8** *n.* outlet or container for overflowing liquid. ❑ *v.* **o·ver·flowed, o·ver·flown** (ō′vər flōn′), **o·ver·flow·ing.**

o·ver·graze (ō′vər grāz′), *v.* to destroy pasture land by allowing animals to graze too long or eat too much of the grass cover. ❑ *v.,* **o·ver·grazed, o·ver·graz·ing.**

o·ver·grew (ō′vər grü′), *v.* past tense of **overgrow:** *Vines overgrew the wall.*

o·ver·grow (ō′vər grō′), *v.* **1** to grow over: *The wall is overgrown with vines.* **2** to grow too fast; become too big. ❑ *v.* **o·ver·grew, o·ver·grown, o·ver·grow·ing.**

o·ver·grown (ō′vər grōn′), **1** *adj.* grown too big or too fast: *an overgrown hedge.* **2** *v.* past participle of **overgrow:** *The vines have overgrown the wall.*

o·ver·growth (ō′vər grōth′), *n.* **1** too much growth. **2** growth overspreading or covering something.

o·ver·hand (ō′vər hand′), *adj., adv.* **1** with the hand raised above the shoulder: *an overhand throw, to throw overhand.* **2** with the knuckles upward.

o·ver·hang (ō′vər hang′ *for verb;* ō′vər hang′ *for noun*), **1** *v.* to hang over; stick out over: *Trees overhang the street to form an arch of branches.* **2** *n.* something that sticks out: *The overhang of the roof shaded the bush.* ❑ *v.* **o·ver·hung, o·ver·hang·ing.**

o·ver·haul (ō′vər hól′ *for verb;* ō′vər hól′ *for noun*), **1** *v.* to examine thoroughly so as to make any repairs or changes that are needed: *Once a year we overhaul our boat.* **2** *n.* act of overhauling: *We give our boat an annual overhaul.* **3** *v.* to gain upon; overtake: *The pirate's ship was overhauling ours.*

o·ver·head (ō′vər hed′ *for adv.;* ō′vər hed′ *for adj., noun*), **1** *adv.* over the head; from above: *the stars overhead.* **2** *adj.* placed above; placed high up: *overhead wires.* **3** *n.* general expenses of running a business, such as rent, lighting, heating, taxes, and repairs.

o·ver·hear (ō′vər hir′), *v.* to hear when you are not meant to hear: *They spoke so loud that I could not help overhearing what they said.* ❑ *v.* **o·ver·heard, o·ver·hear·ing.**

overhead—picture taken from an overhead camera

o·ver·heard (ō′vər hėrd′), *v.* past tense and past participle of **overhear:** *I overheard what you told her.*

o·ver·heat (ō′vər hēt′), *v.* to make or become too hot, especially beyond the point of safety or comfort: *My car overheated when we drove through the mountains.*

o·ver·hung (ō′vər hung′ *for adj.;* ō′vər hung′ *for verb*), **1** *adj.* hung from above: *an overhung door.* **2** *v.* past tense and past participle of **overhang:** *A big awning overhung the sidewalk.*

o·ver·in·dulge (ō′vər in dulj′), *v.* to indulge too much. ❑ *v.* **o·ver·in·dulged, o·ver·in·dulg·ing.**

o·ver·joyed (ō′vər joid′), *adj.* very joyful; filled with joy; delighted.

o·ver·kill (ō′vər kil′ *for verb;* ō′vər kil′ *for noun*), **1** *v.* to destroy with greater force or damage than necessary. **2** *n.* act or process of overkilling. **3** *n.* capacity of a force or weapon to cause greater destruction than necessary.

o·ver·laid (ō′vər lād′), *v.* past tense and past participle of **overlay**[1]: *The workers overlaid the dome with gold.*

o·ver·lain (ō′vər lān′), *v.* past participle of **overlie.**

o·ver·land (ō′vər land′), *adj., adv.* on land; by land: *travel overland from New York to Florida, an overland route.*

Overland Park, city in NE Kansas.

WORD STORY   **Overland Park** was named for its location on the stagecoach route carrying overland mail in the early 1800s. Much mail then went to and from the Pacific coast by ship, but it was slow. The overland mail was faster, but driving stagecoaches could be difficult and dangerous work.

o·ver·lap (ō′vər lap′ *for verb;* ō′vər lap′ *for noun*), **1** *v.* to lap over; partly cover and extend beyond: *Shingles are laid to overlap each other.* **2** *n.* act of lapping over. **3** *n.* part that overlaps. ❑ *v.* **o·ver·lapped, o·ver·lap·ping.**

o·ver·lay[1] (ō′vər lā′ *for verb;* ō′vər lā′ *for noun*), **1** *v.* to lay or place one thing over or upon another. **2** *v.* to put a coating over the surface of; finish with a layer or applied decoration of something: *wood overlaid with gold.* **3** *n.* something laid over something else; layer or decoration; covering: *an overlay of gold on a statue.* ❑ *v.* **o·ver·laid, o·ver·lay·ing.**

o·ver·lay[2] (ō′vər lā′), *v.* past tense of **overlie.**

o·ver·lie (ō′vər lī′), *v.* to lie over; lie upon. ❑ *v.* **o·ver·lay, o·ver·lain, o·ver·ly·ing.**

o·ver·load (ō′vər lōd′ *for verb;* ō′vər lōd′ *for noun*), **1** *v.* to load too heavily: *overload a boat.* **2** *n.* too great a load: *The overload of electric current blew the fuse.*

o·ver·look (ō′vər lůk′ *for verb;* ō′vər lůk′ *for noun*), **1** *v.* to fail to see: *overlook a bill.* **2** *v.* to pay no attention to; excuse: *I will overlook your bad behavior this time.* **3** *v.* to have a view of from above; be higher than: *This high window overlooks half the city.* **4** *n.* a high place from which scenery or points of interest may be viewed.

o·ver·lord (ō′vər lôrd′), *n.* person who is lord over another lord or other lords: *The duke was the overlord of barons and knights who held land from him.*

o·ver·ly (ō′vər lē), *adv.* too; too much; excessively: *Our city is overly populated.*

o·ver·mas·ter (ō′vər mas′tər), *v.* to overcome; overpower.

o·ver·match (ō′vər mach′), *v.* to be more than a match for; surpass.

o·ver·night (ō′vər nīt′ *for adv.;* ō′vər nīt′ *for adj.*), **1** *adv.* during the night: *stay overnight.* **2** *adj.* done, occurring, etc., during the night: *an overnight stop.* **3** *adj.* for the night: *overnight guests.* **4** *adv.* at once; immediately; in a very short time: *Change will not come overnight.*

o·ver·pass (ō′vər pas′), *n.* bridge over a road, railroad, canal, etc. ❑ *n., pl.* **o·ver·pass·es.**

o·ver·pay (ō′vər pā′), **1** to pay too much. **2** to pay more than an amount due. ❑ *v.* **o·ver·paid** (ō′vər pād′), **o·ver·pay·ing. —o′ver·pay′ment,** *n.*

o·ver·play (ō′vər plā′), *v.* to play a part in an exaggerated manner.

o·ver·pop·u·late (ō′vər pop′yə lāt), *v.* to fill with too many people for available natural resources, food supply, etc. ❑ *v.* **o·ver·pop·u·lat·ed, o·ver·pop·u·lat·ing. —o′ver·pop′u·la′tion,** *n.*

o·ver·pow·er (ō′vər pou′ər), *v.* **1** to overcome or conquer; overwhelm: *overpower your enemies. Several people were overpowered by the heat.* ■ See Synonym Study at **conquer. 2** to be much greater or stronger than: *The wind brought a terrible smell that overpowered all others.* **—o′ver·pow′er·ing·ly,** *adv.*

o·ver·priced (ō′vər prīst′), *adj.* costing more than it is worth: *These poorly made shirts are overpriced.* ■ See Synonym Study at **expensive.**

o·ver·pro·duce (ō′vər prə düs′), *v.* to produce more than is needed or more than can be sold. ❑ *v.* **o·ver·pro·duced, o·ver·pro·**

duc·ing. **−o′ver·pro·duc′er,** *n.* **−o·ver·pro·duc·tion** (ō′vər prə‑duk′shən), *n.*

o·ver·pro·tect (ō′vər prə tekt′), *v.* to protect someone or something more thoroughly than is necessary. **−o′ver·pro·tec′tion,** *n.* **−o′ver·pro·tec′tive,** *adj.*

o·ver·ran (ō′vər ran′), *v.* past tense of **overrun.**

o·ver·rate (ō′vər rāt′), *v.* to rate or estimate too highly: *I overrated my strength and soon had to ask for help.* ❑ *v.* **o·ver·rat·ed, o·ver·rat·ing.**

o·ver·reach (ō′vər rēch′), *v.* **1** to reach over or beyond. **2** to reach too far. **−o′ver·reach′er,** *n.*

overreach yourself, **1** to fail or miss by trying for too much. **2** to fail by being too crafty or tricky.

o·ver·re·act (ō′vər rē akt′), *v.* to react with more force or emotion than is necessary. **−o′ver·re·ac′tion,** *n.*

o·ver·ride (ō′vər rīd′), *v.* **1** to act in spite of: *override advice or objections.* **2** to prevail over: *The new rule overrides all previous ones.* **3** to ride over; trample on. ❑ *v.* **o·ver·rode** (ō′vər rōd′), **o·ver·rid·den** (ō′vər rid′n), **o·ver·rid·ing.**

o·ver·ripe (ō′vər rīp′), *adj.* too ripe; more than ripe.

o·ver·rule (ō′vər rül′), *v.* **1** to rule or decide against a plea, argument, objection, etc.; set aside: *The president overruled my plan.* **2** to prevail over; be stronger than: *I was overruled by the majority.* ❑ *v.* **o·ver·ruled, o·ver·rul·ing.**

o·ver·run (ō′vər run′), *v.* **1** to spread over and spoil or harm in some way: *Weeds had overrun the old garden.* **2** to defeat and occupy: *Enemy troops overran the fort.* **3** to spread over: *Vines overran the wall.* **4** to run or go beyond; exceed: *The TV show overran its time limit.* ❑ *v.* **o·ver·ran, o·ver·run, o·ver·run·ning.**

o·ver·saw (ō′vər sò′), *v.* past tense of **oversee.**

o·ver·seas (ō′vər sēz′ *for adv.;* ō′vər sēz′ *for adj.*), **1** *adv.* across the sea; beyond the sea; abroad: *travel overseas.* **2** *adj.* done, used, or serving overseas: *overseas service.* **3** *adj.* of countries across the sea; foreign: *overseas trade.*

o·ver·see (ō′vər sē′), *v.* to look after and direct work or workers; supervise; manage: *oversee a factory.* ❑ *v.* **o·ver·saw, o·ver·seen** (ō′vər sēn′), **o·ver·see·ing.**

o·ver·se·er (ō′vər sir′ *or* ō′vər sē′ər), *n.* person who oversees others or their work.

o·ver·shad·ow (ō′vər shad′ō), *v.* **1** to be more important than: *Preparations for the school play soon overshadowed other activities.* **2** to cast a shadow over; make dark or gloomy.

o·ver·shoe (ō′vər shü′), *n.* a waterproof shoe or boot, often made of rubber, worn over another shoe to keep the foot dry and warm.

o·ver·shoot (ō′vər shüt′), *v.* **1** to shoot over, higher than, or beyond: *overshoot a target.* **2** to go beyond or past: *The airplane overshot the runway.* ❑ *v.* **o·ver·shot, o·ver·shoot·ing.**

o·ver·shot (ō′vər shot′ *for adj.;* ō′vər shot′ *for verb*), **1** *adj.* having the upper jaw sticking out beyond the lower. **2** *adj.* driven by water flowing from above. **3** *v.* past tense and past participle of **overshoot.**

o·ver·sight (ō′vər sīt′), *n.* **1** failure to notice or think of something: *Through an oversight, the kitten got fed twice last night.* **2** watchful care: *to work under a teacher's oversight and direction.*

o·ver·sim·pli·fy (ō′vər sim′plə fī), *v.* to make something too simple, causing misunderstanding or error. ❑ *v.* **o·ver·sim·pli·fied, o·ver·sim·pli·fying. −o′ver·sim′pli·fi·ca′tion,** *n.*

o·ver·size (ō′vər sīz′), *adj.* too big; larger than the proper or usual size.

o·ver·sized (ō′vər sīzd′), *adj.* oversize.

o·ver·sleep (ō′vər slēp′), *v.* to sleep beyond a certain hour; sleep too long. ❑ *v.* **o·ver·slept, o·ver·sleep·ing.**

o·ver·slept (ō′vər slept′), *v.* past tense and past participle of **oversleep:** *I overslept and missed the bus. I have overslept three days in a row.*

o·ver·spread (ō′vər spred′), *v.* to spread over: *Ivy overspread the old cabin.* ❑ *v.* **o·ver·spread, o·ver·spread·ing.**

o·ver·state (ō′vər stāt′), *v.* to state too strongly; exaggerate. ❑ *v.* **o·ver·stat·ed, o·ver·stat·ing. −o′ver·state′ment,** *n.*

o·ver·stay (ō′vər stā′), *v.* to stay beyond the time of: *overstay your planned visit.*

o·ver·step (ō′vər step′), *v.* to go beyond; exceed: *overstep your authority.* ❑ *v.* **o·ver·stepped, o·ver·step·ping.**

o·ver·stock (ō′vər stok′ *for verb;* ō′vər stok′ *for noun*), **1** *v.* to supply with more than is needed. **2** *n.* too great a supply.

o·ver·stuffed (ō′vər stuft′), *adj.* **1** stuffed too full. **2** made soft and comfortable by thick padding: *overstuffed furniture.*

o·ver·sup·ply (ō′vər sə plī′ *for verb;* ō′vər sə plī′ *for noun*), **1** *v.* to supply with more than is needed. **2** *n.* too great a supply. ❑ *v.* **o·ver·sup·plied, o·ver·sup·ply·ing;** *n., pl.* **o·ver·sup·plies.**

o·vert (ō vèrt′ *or* ō′vèrt′), *adj.* open or public; evident; not hidden: *Hitting someone is an overt act.* **−o·vert′ly,** *adv.* **−o·vert′ness,** *n.*

o·ver·take (ō′vər tāk′), *v.* **1** to catch up with: *I ran and overtook my friends.* **2** to come upon suddenly: *A storm overtook the children.* ❑ *v.* **o·ver·took, o·ver·tak·en, o·ver·tak·ing.**

o·ver·tak·en (ō′vər tā′kən), *v.* past participle of **overtake.**

o·ver·tax (ō′vər taks′), *v.* **1** to tax too heavily. **2** to put too heavy a burden on. **−o′ver·tax·a′tion,** *n.*

o·ver-the-count·er (ō′vər ᴛнə koun′tər), *adj.* for sale without a doctor's prescription.

o·ver·threw (ō′vər thrü′), *v.* past tense of **overthrow.**

o·ver·throw (ō′vər thrō′ *for verb;* ō′vər thrō′ *for noun*), **1** *v.* to take away the power of; defeat: *overthrow a government.* **2** *v.* to put an end to; destroy: *overthrow slavery.* **3** *v.* to overturn; upset; knock down. **4** *v.* to throw a ball past the place where it should go: *overthrow third base.* **5** *n.* a defeat; upset: *the overthrow of the government.* **6** *n.* act of throwing a ball past where it should go: *The runner at first was safe on the overthrow from the shortstop.* ❑ *v.* **o·ver·threw, o·ver·thrown, o·ver·throw·ing.**

o·ver·thrown (ō′vər thrōn′), *v.* past participle of **overthrow.**

o·ver·time (ō′vər tīm′), **1** *n.* extra time; time beyond the regular hours. **2** *n.* wages for this period. **3** *adv.* beyond the regular hours: *to work overtime.* **4** *adj.* of or for overtime: *overtime work.* **5** *n.* an extra period of time at the end of a tied sports event.

o·ver·tone (ō′vər tōn′), *n.* **1** a fainter and higher musical tone heard along with the main or fundamental tone; harmonic. **2** hint or suggestion of something felt, believed, etc.: *an overtone of anger.*

o·ver·took (ō′vər tùk′), *v.* past tense of **overtake.**

o·ver·top (ō′vər top′), *v.* **1** to rise above; be higher than: *The new building will overtop all the others.* **2** to surpass; excel. ❑ *v.* **o·ver·topped, o·ver·top·ping.**

o·ver·ture (ō′vər chər), *n.* **1** proposal or offer: *The enemy is making overtures for peace.* **2** a musical composition played by the orchestra as an introduction to an opera, oratorio, or other long musical composition.

WORD STORY **Overture** comes from a Latin word meaning "an opening." **Aperture,** the hole that lets light into a camera, comes from the same word. An overture opens negotiations or opens a concert.

o·ver·turn (ō′vər tèrn′), *v.* **1** to turn upside down. **2** to upset; fall down; fall over: *The boat overturned.* **3** to make fall down; overthrow; defeat; destroy the power of: *The rebels overturned the government.*

o·ver·use (ō′vər yüz′ *for verb;* ō′vər yüs′ *for noun*), **1** *v.* to use too much. **2** *v.* to use too hard or too often. **3** *n.* too much or too hard use. ❑ *v.* **o·ver·used, o·ver·us·ing.**

o·ver·view (ō′vər vyü′), *n.* a broad view; survey; summary: *an overview of railroad history.*

o·ver·weight (ō′vər wāt′), **1** *adj.* having more weight than is medically ideal or more weight than is wanted: *overweight for your height.* **2** *n.* more weight than is medically ideal or more weight than is wanted.

o·ver·whelm (ō′vər hwelm′), *v.* **1** to overcome completely; crush: *overwhelm with grief.* ▪ See Synonym Study at **conquer.** **2** to cover completely as a flood would: *A great wave overwhelmed the boat.*

o·ver·whelm·ing (ō′vər hwel′ming), *adj.* too many, too great,

a	hat	ė	term	ô	order	ch	child	
ā	age	i	it	oi	oil	ng	long	a in about
ä	far	ī	ice	ou	out	sh	she	e in taken
â	care	o	hot	u	cup	th	thin	ə i in pencil
e	let	ō	open	u̇	put	ᴛн	then	o in lemon
ē	equal	ȯ	saw	ü	rule	zh	measure	u in circus

or too much to be resisted; overpowering: *an overwhelming majority of votes.* **−o′ver·whelm′ing·ly,** *adv.*

o·ver·work (ō′vər wėrk′ *for noun;* ō′vər wėrk′ *for verb*), **1** *n.* too much or too hard work: *exhausted from overwork.* **2** *v.* to cause to work too hard or too long: *She overworks her staff.* **3** *n.* extra work.

o·ver·wrought (ō′vər rôt′), *adj.* **1** wearied or exhausted by too much work or excitement; greatly excited: *overwrought nerves.* **2** too elaborate.

o·vi·duct (ō′və dukt), *n.* tube through which an egg passes from an ovary.

o·vip·ar·ous (ō vip′ər əs), *adj.* producing eggs that hatch after leaving the body. Birds are oviparous.

o·vi·pos·i·tor (ō′və poz′ə tər), *n.* an organ of some female insects at the end of the abdomen, by which eggs are deposited. It often looks like a stinger.

o·void (ō′void), **1** *adj.* egg-shaped. **2** *n.* an egg-shaped object.

o·vo·vi·vip·ar·ous (ō′vō vī vip′ər əs), *adj.* producing eggs that hatch inside the mother's body, so that the young are born without covering. Many reptiles and some fishes are ovoviviparous. **−o′vo·vi·vip′ar·ous·ly,** *adv.*

o·vu·late (ō′vyə lāt *or* ov′yə lāt), *v.* to release a mature egg from the ovary. ❑ *v.* **o·vu·lat·ed, o·vu·lat·ing. −o′vu·la′tion,** *n.*

o·vule (ō′vyül), *n.* **1** a small ovum, especially when immature or unfertilized. **2** part of a plant that develops into a seed.

o·vum (ō′vəm), *n.* a female reproductive cell produced in the ovary; egg. After the ovum is fertilized, an embryo develops. ❑ *n., pl.* **o·va** (ō′və).

owe (ō), *v.* **1** to have to pay; be in debt for: *I owe her $2.* **2** to be in debt: *I am always owing for something.* **3** to have to give: *I really think you owe me an apology for what you just said.* **4** to be obliged or indebted for: *I owe a great deal to my parents.* ❑ *v.* **owed, ow·ing.** ■ Other words that sound like this are **O** and **oh.**

Ow·ens (ō′ənz), *n.* **Jes·se** (jes′ē), 1913-1980, American track-and-field star. ■ **Jesse Owens** won four gold medals at the 1936 Olympic Games in Berlin, Germany. Such a triumph by an African American embarrassed Hitler, who expected German athletes to prove themselves superior to athletes of other races.

Ow·ens·bor·o (ō′ənz bėr′ō), *n.* city in N Kentucky.

ow·ing (ō′ing), *adj.* due; owed: *pay what is owing.*

owing to, on account of; because of; as a result of: *Owing to the bad weather, we canceled our trip.*

owl (oul), *n.* any of numerous birds with big heads, big eyes, and short, hooked beaks. Owls hunt mice and small birds at night. Some kinds have tufts of feathers on their heads, called horns or ears. **−owl′like′,** *adj.*

owl·et (ou′lit), *n.* **1** a young owl. **2** a small owl.

owl·ish (ou′lish), *adj.* like an owl; like an owl's: *owlish eyes, an owlish look of wisdom.* **−owl′ish·ly,** *adv.* **−owl′ish·ness,** *n.*

own (ōn), **1** *v.* to have or possess: *They own much land.* **2** *adj.* of the person or thing mentioned: *We have our own troubles. The house is her own.* **3** *v.* to acknowledge; admit; confess: *She owns to her guilt. I own you are right.*

come into your own, 1 to get what belongs to you. **2** to get the success or credit that you deserve.

hold your own, to keep your position; not be forced back.

of your own, belonging to yourself: *a room of my own.*

on your own, not ruled or directed by someone else.

own up, to confess fully: *own up to a crime.*

own·er (ō′nər), *n.* one who owns: *Who is the owner of this dog?* **−own′er·less,** *adj.*

own·er·ship (ō′nər ship), *n.* condition of being an owner; the possessing of something; right of possession: *He claimed ownership of the abandoned car.*

ox (oks), *n.* **1** a full-grown castrated male of domestic cattle, used for farm work or for beef. **2** any of several kinds of mammals that chew their cud and have horns and cloven hoofs, including domestic cattle, buffaloes, bison, and yaks. ❑ *n., pl.* **ox·en. −ox′-like′,** *adj.*

ox·blood (oks′blud′), *n.* a deep red color.

ox·bow (oks′bō′), *n.* **1** a U-shaped piece of wood placed under

and around the neck of an ox, with the upper ends inserted in the bar of the yoke. **2** a U-shaped bend in a river.

ox·cart (oks′kärt′), *n.* cart drawn by oxen.

ox·en (ok′sən), *n.* plural of **ox.**

ox·eye daisy (oks′ī′), the common American daisy.

ox·ford (ok′sfərd), *n.* **1** kind of low shoe, laced over the instep. **2** kind of cotton or rayon cloth used for shirts, blouses, and other garments.

Ox·ford (ok′sfərd), *n.* **1** city in S England. **2** the very old and famous English university located there.

ox·i·da·tion (ok′sə dā′shən), *n.* **1** act or process of oxidizing; the combining of oxygen with another element to form one or more new substances. Burning is one kind of oxidation. **2** condition of being oxidized.

ox·ide (ok′sid), *n.* compound of oxygen with another element or radical.

ox·i·dize (ok′sə dīz), *v.* to combine or cause to combine with oxygen: *Water oxidizes some metals, producing rust.* ❑ *v.* **ox·i·dized, ox·i·diz·ing. −ox′i·diz′a·ble,** *adj.* **−ox′i·di·za′tion,** *n.*

ox·i·diz·er (ok′sə dī′zər), *n.* **1** something that oxidizes; an oxidizing substance or device. **2** substance that helps a fuel to burn.

ox·y·a·cet·y·lene (ok′sē ə set′l ēn′), *adj.* using a mixture of oxygen and acetylene. An oxyacetylene torch is used for welding or cutting metals.

ox·y·gen (ok′sə jən), *n.* a colorless, odorless gas that forms about one fifth of the air, and about one third of water. Oxygen is a chemical element present in combined form in water, carbon dioxide, iron ore, and many other substances. Animals and plants cannot live, and fire will not burn, without oxygen. *Symbol:* O

ox·y·gen·ate (ok′sə jə nāt), *v.* to treat or combine with oxygen. ❑ *v.* **ox·y·gen·at·ed, ox·y·gen·at·ing. −ox′y·gen·a′tion,** *n.* **−ox′y·gen·a′tor,** *n.*

oxygen mask, device worn over the nose and mouth through which oxygen is supplied from an attached container. Oxygen masks are used by aviators at high altitudes, by firefighters, by submarine crews, etc.

oxygen tent, a small, usually transparent tent which is supplied with a constant, regulated flow of oxygen. It is placed over the head and shoulders of a patient who has difficulty breathing.

ox·y·mo·ron (ok′si môr′on), *n.* a figure of speech in which words of opposite meaning or suggestion are used together. *Burning cold, bittersweet, sad laughter,* and *jumbo shrimp* are oxymorons. [**Oxymoron** comes from Greek words meaning "sharp" and "stupid." An oxymoron looks stupid at first but has a real point.]

o·yez (ō′yes), *interj., n.* hear! attend! a cry uttered, usually three times, by a public or court crier to command silence and attention before a proclamation is made.

oys·ter (oi′stər), *n.* any of several shellfish with rough, irregular shells in two hinged halves. Oysters are found in shallow water along seacoasts. Many kinds are good to eat and some kinds yield pearls.

oyster bed, a place where oysters breed or are cultivated.

oz., ounce. ❑ *pl.* **oz.**

O·zark Mountains (ō′zärk), a low mountain range in S Missouri, N Arkansas, and E Oklahoma.

WORD STORY **Ozark** comes from French words meaning "to Arkansas." The shortened form of **Arkansas** was used by the French. If you want to get to Arkansas from Missouri or Oklahoma, the Ozarks are on your way.

O·zarks (ō′zärks), *n.pl.* the Ozark Mountains.

o·zone (ō′zōn), *n.* a form of oxygen with a sharp, pungent odor, produced by electricity and especially present in the air after a thunderstorm. Ozone high in the atmosphere forms the protective ozone layer, but ozone near the ground pollutes the air, especially in smog.

ozone layer, a part of the atmosphere containing large amounts of ozone. It is about 10 to 30 miles (16 to 48 kilometers) above the earth's surface. It shields the earth from unhealthy amounts of ultraviolet radiation.

P or **p** (pē), *n.* the 16th letter of the English alphabet. ❑ *n., pl.* **P's** or **p's.**

mind your p's and q's, be careful about what you say and do.

> **WORD STORY** The phrase **p's and q's** may come from printing, in the days when each letter was a separate piece of metal type. Because **p** and **q** look like reflections of each other, it was easy to confuse them unless people were careful. Or the phrase may have come from businesses that sold liquids. The **p's** and **q's** may have stood for pints and quarts. A quart costs more than a pint, so it was important not to get them mixed up.

P, symbol for phosphorus.

p., **1** page. **2** participle.

pa (pä), *n.* INFORMAL. papa; father. ❑ *n., pl.* **pas.**

Pa, symbol for protactinium.

PA, **1** Pennsylvania (used with postal Zip Code). **2** public address system.

Pa., Pennsylvania.

PAC (pak), *n.* Political Action Committee (committee formed by a corporation, labor union, trade association, etc., that collects money from its members and gives it to political candidates that it wishes to see elected).

Pac., Pacific.

pace (pās), **1** *n.* a step. **2** *v.* to walk with regular steps: *The tiger paced up and down its cage.* **3** *v.* to walk over with regular steps: *pace the floor.* **4** *n.* the length of a step in walking; about 2½ feet

(76 centimeters): *There were perhaps ten paces between me and the bear.* **5** *v.* to measure by paces: *We paced off the distance and found it to be 72 paces.* **6** *n.* a particular way of stepping of some horses in which the feet on the same side are lifted and put down together. **7** *v.* to move at a pace: *Some horses are trained to pace.* **8** *n.* rate or speed: *walk at a fast pace.* **9** *v.* to set the pace for: *A motorboat will pace the rowing crew.* ❑ *v.* **paced, pac·ing.**

keep pace with, to keep up with; go as fast as.

put you through your paces, to try you out; find out what you can do.

set the pace, 1 to set an example of speed for others to keep up with. **2** be an example for others to follow.

> **WORD FAMILY** **Pace** and the words below are related. They all come from a Latin word meaning "to stretch."
>
> | compass | pass | passenger | pastime |
> | impasse | passage | passport | surpass |
> | pacemaker | passbook | past | trespass |

pace·mak·er (pās′mā′kər), *n.* **1** person, animal, or thing that sets the pace. **2** an electronic device implanted in the chest wall to maintain or restore the normal rhythm of the heartbeat.

a	hat	ė	term	ô	order	ch	child		a in about
ā	age	i	it	oi	oil	ng	long		e in taken
ä	far	ī	ice	ou	out	sh	she	ə {	i in pencil
â	care	o	hot	u	cup	th	thin		o in lemon
e	let	ō	open	ù	put	ŦH	then		u in circus
ē	equal	ò	saw	ü	rule	zh	measure		

pac·er (pā′sər), *n.* **1** person or thing that paces. **2** horse that lifts and puts down the feet on the same side together.

pa·chi·si (pə chē′zē), *n.* game something like backgammon, played on a cross-shaped board.

pach·y·derm (pak′ə dėrm′), *n.* any of several thick-skinned mammals with hoofs, formerly classed together, such as the elephant, hippopotamus, and rhinoceros. [Pachyderm comes from two Greek words meaning "thick" and "skin."]

pa·cif·ic (pə sif′ik), *adj.* **1** loving peace; not warlike: *The Quakers are a pacific people.* **2** peaceful; calm; quiet: *pacific weather.* —**pa·cif′i·cal·ly,** *adv.*

Pa·cif·ic (pə sif′ik), **1** *n.* ocean west of North and South America. It extends to Asia and Australia. **2** *adj.* of or about the Pacific Ocean. **3** *adj.* on, in, over, or near the Pacific Ocean: *Pacific air routes.* **4** *adj.* of or on the Pacific coast of the United States: *California is one of the Pacific states.*

WORD STORY Pacific comes from **pacific** (def. 2), meaning "peaceful." It was chosen as the ocean's name by Ferdinand Magellan, who commanded the first European ships to cross it. They had suffered from storms in the Atlantic Ocean, but they had calm weather the whole time in the Pacific.

Pacific Rim, countries bordering the Pacific Ocean, thought of or acting as a business and trade group.

Pacific Standard Time, the standard time in the westernmost parts of the continental United States and Canada, not including most of Alaska. It is eight hours behind Greenwich Time.

Pacific yew, kind of yew found on the Pacific coast of North America; western yew. Its bark is used in medicine.

pac·i·fi·er (pas′ə fī′ər), *n.* **1** a rubber or plastic nipple or ring given to a baby to suck. **2** person or thing that pacifies.

pac·i·fism (pas′ə fiz′əm), *n.* the principle or policy of universal peace; settlement of all differences between nations by peaceful means; opposition to war.

pac·i·fist (pas′ə fist), *n.* person who is opposed to war and favors settling all disputes between nations by peaceful means.

pac·i·fy (pas′ə fī), *v.* **1** to make peaceful; quiet down: *pacify angry demonstrators, pacify a crying baby.* ∎ See Synonym Study at **appease.** **2** to bring under control; control by force; subdue: *pacify a rebellious region.* ❑ *v.* **pac·i·fied, pac·i·fy·ing.** —**pac′i·fi′a·ble,** *adj.* —**pac′i·fi·ca′tion,** *n.*

pack[1] (pak), **1** *v.* to put things together in a bundle, box, bale, etc.: *Pack your clothes in this bag.* **2** *v.* to fill with things; put your things into: *Pack your trunk.* **3** *n.* a small package, usually containing a certain number of items: *a pack of gum.* **4** *n.* bundle of things wrapped up or tied together for carrying. **5** *n.* backpack. **6** *v.* to put into a container to be sold or stored: *Meat, fish, and vegetables are often packed in cans.* **7** *v.* to press or crowd closely together: *A hundred people were packed into one small room.* **8** *v.* to fill a space with all that it will hold: *A large audience packed the small theater.* **9** *n.* a set; lot; a number together: *a pack of thieves, a pack of nonsense, a pack of lies.* **10** *n.* a number of animals of the same kind hunting together: *Wolves hunt in packs; tigers hunt alone.* **11** *n.* a complete set of playing cards, usually 52. **12** *n.* ice pack. **13** *v.* to make tight with something that water, steam, air, etc., cannot leak through: *The plumber packed the pipe joint with tape.* **14** *v.* to carry: *pack a gun.* —**pack′a·ble,** *adj.*

pack off, to send away: *The child was packed off to bed.*

send packing, to send away in a hurry.

pack[2] (pak), *v.* to arrange unfairly. To pack a jury is to fill it with those who will favor one side.

pack·age (pak′ij), **1** *n.* bundle of things packed or wrapped together; box with things packed in it; parcel. **2** *v.* to put in a package. ❑ *v.* **pack·aged, pack·ag·ing.** —**pack′ag·er,** *n.*

pack animal, animal used for carrying loads or packs.

pack·er (pak′ər), *n.* person or company that packs meat, fruit, vegetables, etc., to be sold to wholesalers.

pack·et (pak′it), *n.* **1** a small package; parcel: *a packet of letters.* **2** packet boat.

packet boat, (earlier) boat that carried mail, passengers, and goods regularly on a fixed route.

pack·ing (pak′ing), *n.* **1** material used to keep water, steam, etc., from leaking through. **2** material placed around goods to protect them from damage in shipment, storage, etc. **3** business of preparing and packing meat, fish, fruit, vegetables, etc., to be sold.

pack·ing·house (pak′ing hous′), *n.* place where foods are prepared and packed to be sold. ❑ *n., pl.* **pack·ing·hous·es** (pak′ing hou′ziz).

pack rat, wood rat, especially one kind found in the Rocky Mountains that carries away bits of food, clothing, small tools, etc., and hides them in its nest.

pact (pakt), *n.* a formal agreement; compact: *a peace pact.*

pad[1] (pad), **1** *n.* piece of something soft, such as cotton, foam rubber, etc., used for comfort, protection, or stuffing; cushion: *The baby's carriage has a pad.* **2** *v.* to fill with something soft; stuff: *pad a chair.* **3** *n.* one of the cushionlike parts on the bottom side of the feet of dogs, cats, and some other animals. **4** *n.* foot of a dog, cat, etc. **5** *n.* a large floating leaf of a water lily. **6** *n.* a number of sheets of paper fastened along one edge; tablet. **7** *n.* cloth soaked with ink to use with a rubber stamp. **8** *v.* to make longer by the use of unnecessary words: *He padded his report so that it would fill the required 10 pages.* **9** *n.* launching pad: *The rocket rose from the pad.* **10** *n.* SLANG. room, house, or apartment: *Her pad is on the third floor.* ❑ *v.* **pad·ded, pad·ding.**

pad[2] (pad), **1** *v.* to go on foot; walk; tramp; trudge. **2** *v.* to walk or trot softly: *I padded barefoot across the rug.* **3** *n.* a dull sound, as of footsteps on the ground. ❑ *v.* **pad·ded, pad·ding.**

pad·ding (pad′ing), *n.* **1** material used to pad with, such as cotton or foam rubber. **2** words used in making a speech or a written paper longer.

pad·dle[1] (pad′l), **1** *n.* a short, lightweight oar with a broad blade at one end or both ends, usually held with both hands in rowing a boat or canoe. **2** *v.* to row a boat or canoe with a paddle or paddles. **3** *n.* one of the broad boards fastened to a water wheel or a paddle wheel to push, or be pushed by, the water. **4** *n.* a broad piece of wood with a handle at one end, used for stirring, for mixing, etc. **5** *n.* a paddle-shaped piece of wood with a short handle, used to hit the ball in table tennis; racket. **6** *v.* to beat with a paddle; spank. **7** *n.* an electronic device used to control video games and computer games. It is a flat handle containing a wheel and a button. ❑ *v.* **pad·dled, pad·dling.** —**pad′dle·like,** *adj.* —**pad′dler,** *n.*

pad·dle[2] (pad′l), *v.* to move the hands or feet about in water: *Children love to paddle at the beach.* ❑ *v.* **pad·dled, pad·dling.**

pad·dle·fish (pad′l fish′), *n.* either of two large scaleless fishes with long, flat paddlelike snouts, especially one kind found in the Mississippi and rivers that join it. ❑ *n., pl.* **pad·dle·fish** or **pad·dle·fish·es.**

paddle wheel, wheel with large flat boards fastened around it for moving a ship through the water.

pad·dock (pad′ək), *n.* **1** a small, enclosed field near a stable or house, used for exercising animals or as a pasture. **2** pen at a race track where horses are saddled before a race.

pad·dy (pad′ē), *n.* flooded area with raised banks around its sides, for growing rice. ❑ *n., pl.* **pad·dies.** [Paddy comes from a Malay word meaning "rice."]

pad·lock (pad′lok′), **1** *n.* a lock that can be put on and removed. It hangs by a curved bar, hinged at one end and snapped shut at the other. **2** *v.* to fasten with a padlock.

pa·dre (pä′drā), *n.* father. It is used as a name for a priest, especially in regions where Spanish, Portuguese, or Italian is spoken.

paddy

pae·an (pē′ən), *n.* song of praise, joy, or triumph.

pa·el·la (pä el′ə *or* pä ā′yə), *n.* a Spanish dish of rice and vegetables, cooked with meat, seafood, etc., and flavored with saffron. ❑ *n., pl.* **pa·el·las.**

pa·gan (pā′gən), **1** *n.* person who is not a Christian, Jew, or Muslim; one who worships many gods or no god; a heathen. *The ancient Greeks and Romans were pagans.* **2** *adj.* of or about pagans; heathen: *pagan customs.* **3** *n.* person who has no religion.

WORD STORY   **Pagan** comes from a Latin word meaning "village." People in country villages continued to worship many gods long after people in Rome and other cities had become Christians.

pa·gan·ism (pā′gə niz′əm), *n.* **1** a pagan attitude toward religion or morality. **2** the beliefs and practices of pagans. **3** condition of being a pagan.

page[1] (pāj), **1** *n.* one side of a leaf or sheet of paper: *a page in this book.* **2** *n.* the print or writing on one side of a leaf. **3** *n.* a record: *the pages of history.* **4** *n.* a happening or time considered as part of history: *The settling of the West is an exciting page in American history.* **5** *v.* to number the pages of. **6** *v.* to turn the pages of: *He paged through the first few chapters of the book.* ❑ *v.* **paged, pag·ing.**

page[2] (pāj), **1** *n.* someone who runs errands or delivers messages at a hotel, private club, office building, or government legislature. **2** *v.* to try to find someone in a public place by having his or her name called out. **3** *v.* to deliver a message to, or signal someone by electronic means, such as a pager or beeper. **4** *n.* a youth who attends a person of rank. **5** *n.* (in the Middle Ages) a youth who was preparing to be a knight. ❑ *v.* **paged, pag·ing.**

pag·eant (paj′ənt), *n.* **1** an elaborate spectacle; procession in costume; pomp; display; show: *The coronation of a new ruler is always a splendid pageant.* **2** a public entertainment that represents scenes from history, legend, or the like: *Our school gave a pageant about the Pilgrims.*

pag·eant·ry (paj′ən trē), *n.* **1** a splendid show; gorgeous display; pomp. **2** mere show; empty display.

pag·er (pā′jər), *n.* beeper.

pag·i·nate (paj′ə nāt), *v.* to mark the number of pages of. ❑ *v.* **pag·i·nat·ed, pag·i·nat·ing.** —**pag′i·na′tion,** *n.*

pa·go·da (pə gō′də), *n.* temple having many stories, with a roof curving upward from each story. There are pagodas in India, China, and Japan. ❑ *n., pl.* **pa·go·das.**

Pa·go Pa·go (päng′ō päng′ō *or* pä′gō pä′gō), capital of American Samoa.

paid (pād), **1** *adj.* receiving money; hired: *a paid worker, a paid informer.* **2** *v.* past tense and past participle of **pay:** *I paid my bills. These bills have been paid.*

Paige (pāj), *n.* **Satch·el** (sach′əl), 1906?-1982, American baseball player. ■ Satchel Paige was the

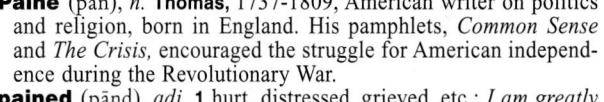
pagoda

first African American to pitch in the American League. He had previously played in leagues for African Americans for twenty years.

pail (pāl), *n.* **1** a round container for carrying liquids, etc.; bucket: *a milk pail.* **2** the amount a pail holds; pailful. ■ Another word that sounds like this is **pale.**

pail·ful (pāl′fūl), *n.* amount that fills a pail. ❑ *n., pl.* **pail·fuls.**

pain (pān), **1** *n.* a feeling of being hurt; suffering: *A cut gives pain. The death of someone we love causes pain.* **2** *v.* to cause to suffer; give pain: *Does your tooth pain you?* ■ Another word that sounds like this is **pane.**

on pain of or **under pain of,** subject to punishment or penalty of unless a certain thing is done: *The traitor was ordered to leave the country on pain of death.*

take pains, to work hard and carefully: *I took great pains with my book report.*

SYNONYM STUDY   **Pain** and **ache** both mean the bad feeling you have when you hurt yourself or when you are sick. **Pain** is a general word: *If I eat ice cream too fast, I get a pain behind my eyes.* **Ache** means a steady pain: *The ache in his back gets worse if he doesn't exercise.*

Paine (pān), *n.* **Thomas,** 1737-1809, American writer on politics and religion, born in England. His pamphlets, *Common Sense* and *The Crisis,* encouraged the struggle for American independence during the Revolutionary War.

pained (pānd), *adj.* **1** hurt, distressed, grieved, etc.: *I am greatly pained to learn of your refusal.* **2** expressing or showing pain: *a pained look.*

pain·ful (pān′fəl), *adj.* **1** causing pain; hurting: *a painful illness.* **2** unpleasant: *painful memories.* —**pain′ful·ly,** *adv.* —**pain′ful·ness,** *n.*

pain·kill·er (pān′kil′ər), *n.* any drug that relieves pain.

pain·less (pān′lis), *adj.* without pain; causing no pain. —**pain′less·ly,** *adv.* —**pain′less·ness,** *n.*

pains·tak·ing (pānz′tā′king), *adj.* very careful; particular; diligent: *a painstaking painter.* —**pains′tak′ing·ly,** *adv.* —**pains′tak′ing·ness,** *n.*

paint (pānt), **1** *n.* substance made of solid coloring matter or pigment mixed with a liquid, that can be spread on a surface to make a layer or film of white, black, or colored matter. **2** *v.* to cover or decorate with paint: *paint a house.* **3** *v.* to use paint. **4** *v.* to make a picture of, using paint: *The artist painted animals.* **5** *v.* to make pictures. **6** *v.* to picture vividly in words. **7** *n.* coloring matter put on the face or body. **8** *v.* to put on like paint: *paint iodine on a cut.* —**paint′less,** *adj.*

paint·brush (pānt′brush′), *n.* **1** brush for putting on paint. **2** any of several plants, related to the snapdragon, with showy crimson, yellow, or pink leaves on the flower stalk. ❑ *n., pl.* **paint·brush·es.**

paint·er[1] (pān′tər), *n.* **1** person who paints pictures; artist. **2** person who paints houses, woodwork, etc.

paint·er[2] (pān′tər), *n.* a rope, usually fastened to the bow of a boat, for tying it to a ship, pier, etc.

paint·er[3] (pān′tər), *n.* mountain lion.

paint·ing (pān′ting), *n.* **1** something painted; picture. **2** act of someone who paints.

WORD BANK   **Painting** has a large vocabulary, including many different styles and techniques. If you want to know more about them, you can begin by looking up these words in this dictionary.

abstract	easel	oil color	Renaissance
acrylic	foreshorten	oil painting	romanticism
airbrush	fresco	palette	self-portrait
baroque	impressionism	perspective	sketch
brush[1]	landscape	pigment	still life
canvas	miniature	portrait	surrealism
cartoon	mural	primitive	tempera
cubism	naturalistic	realism	watercolor

pair (pâr), **1** *n.* a set of two; two that go together: *a pair of shoes.* **2** *n.* a single thing consisting of two parts that cannot be used separately: *a pair of scissors, a pair of trousers.* **3** *v.* to arrange or be arranged in pairs: *The socks were neatly paired in a drawer.* **4** *n.* man and woman who are married or are engaged to be married: *They make a great pair.* **5** *v.* to join in love and marriage. **6** *n.* two animals that are mated. **7** *v.* to mate. **8** *n.* two cards of the same value in different suits, considered as a unit in your hand: *a pair of sixes.* ❑ *n., pl.* **pairs** or (sometimes after a numeral) **pair.** ■ Other words that sound like this are **pare** and **pear.**

pair off, to arrange in pairs; form into pairs: *The campers paired off and set out to start the first day of wilderness training.*

pais·ley (pāz′lē), *adj.* having a detailed and colorful pattern: *a paisley shirt.*

Pai·ute (pī yüt′ *or* pī′yüt), *n.* member of a tribe of American Indians living in Arizona, Nevada, Utah, California, and Oregon. ❑ *n., pl.* **Pai·ute** or **Pai·utes.**

pa·ja·ma (pə jä′mə *or* pə jam′ə), *adj.* of or in pajamas: *pajama tops, pajama party.*

P

a	hat	ė	term	ô	order	ch	child		
ā	age	i	it	oi	oil	ng	long		a in about
ä	far	ī	ice	ou	out	sh	she		e in taken
â	care	o	hot	u	cup	th	thin	ə	i in pencil
e	let	ō	open	ù	put	ŦH	then		o in lemon
ē	equal	ò	saw	ü	rule	zh	measure		u in circus

Painting

Painting is a very ancient activity. Tens of thousands of years ago, cave dwellers painted animals on the rock walls. People have painted ever since, all over the world, for many reasons and in many ways. Some ways of painting are familiar to you. Others look strange. It would take dozens of books to show all the kinds of paintings that people have admired. Here is a sample of paintings from many times and places. For more information on this subject, see the Word Bank at **painting**.

Village by a Stream
R. Mervilus
(late 1900s)

Mayan
Wall Painting
(700s)

Japanese
Screen Painting
(early 1800s)

Composition
Joan Miró
(middle 1900s)

Mona Lisa
Leonardo da Vinci
(about 1500)

Egyptian Wall
(about 1200 B.C.)

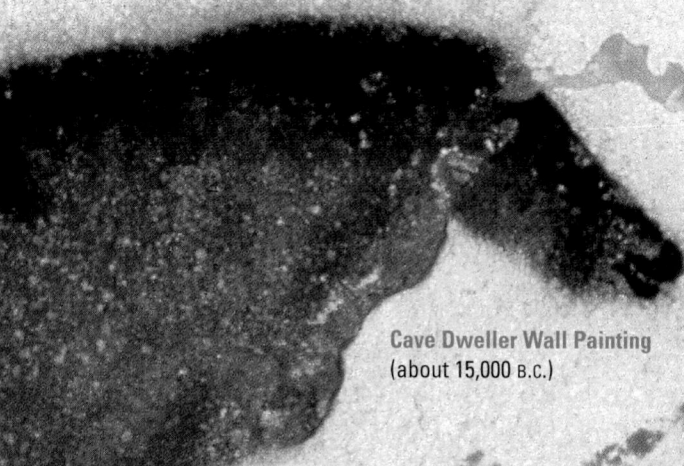

Cave Dweller Wall Painting
(about 15,000 B.C.)

Starry Night
Vincent Van Gogh
(late 1800s)

The Toy Seller
Jean B. Discart (middle 1800s)

pa·ja·mas (pə jä′məz *or* pə jam′əz), *n.pl.* clothing to sleep or lounge in, made up of a shirt and loose trousers. Also, **pyjamas.**

WORD STORY **Pajamas** comes from Persian words meaning "leg" and "clothing." People in Persia and India wore loose trousers as daytime clothes. Europeans began wearing them to sleep in, with a loose shirt, and called both parts **pajamas.**

Pak·i·stan (pak′ə stan), *n.* country in S Asia, west of India. *Capital:* Islamabad.

WORD STORY **Pakistan** comes from words in a language of the region meaning "land of the pure." The country was founded in hopes of creating a purely Islamic nation.

Pak·i·stan·i (pak′ə stan′ē), **1** *n.* person born or living in Pakistan. **2** *adj.* of Pakistan. ❑ *n., pl.* **Pak·i·stan·is** or **Pak·i·stan·i.**

pal (pal), **1** *n.* a close friend; playmate; comrade. **2** *v.* to associate as pals. ❑ *v.* **palled, pal·ling.** [**Pal** comes from a word in Romany, the language of Gypsies, meaning "brother." Sometimes a friend can feel as close as a brother.]

pal·ace (pal′is), *n.* **1** the official home of a king, queen, bishop, or some other ruler. **2** a very fine house or building. **—pal′ace·like′,** *adj.*

pal·at·a·ble (pal′ə tə bəl), *adj.* **1** agreeable to the taste; pleasing: *That was a most palatable lunch.* **2** agreeable to the mind or feelings; acceptable. **—pal′at·a·bil′i·ty, pal′at·a·ble·ness,** *n.* **—pal′at·a·bly,** *adv.*

pal·ate (pal′it), *n.* **1** the roof of the mouth. The bony part in front is the hard palate, and the fleshy part in back is the soft palate. **2** sense of taste: *The new flavor pleased my palate.* ■ Other words that sound like this are **palette** and **pallet.**

pa·la·tial (pə lā′shəl), *adj.* like a palace; fit for a palace; magnificent: *a palatial apartment.* **—pa·la′tial·ly,** *adv.*

Pa·lau (pä lou′), *n.* island country in the W Pacific. *Capital:* Koror. Also, **Belau.**

pa·lav·er (pə lav′ər), **1** *n.* any smooth, persuading talk; flattery. **2** *v.* to talk fluently and flatteringly. **—pa·lav′er·er,** *n.*

pale[1] (pāl), **1** *adj.* without much color; whitish: *When you have been ill, your face is sometimes pale.* **2** *adj.* not bright; dim: *pale blue. The bright stars are surrounded by hundreds of pale ones.* **3** *v.* to turn pale: *Her face paled at the bad news.* ❑ *adj.* **pal·er, pal·est;** *v.* **paled, pal·ing.** ■ Another word that sounds like this is **pail. —pale′ly,** *adv.* **—pale′ness,** *n.*

pale[2] (pāl), **1** *n.* a long, narrow board, pointed at the top, used for fences. **2** *n.* boundary: *Their behavior was beyond the pale of common decency.* **3** *v.* to build a fence around; enclose with pales. ❑ *v.* **paled, pal·ing.** ■ Another word that sounds like this is **pail.**

pale·face (pāl′fās′), *n.* a white person. The American Indians are said to have called European settlers palefaces.

Pa·le·o·cene (pā′lē ə sēn′), *n.* (in geology) time between about 70 million and 60 million years ago. During this time, modern birds developed and the primates first appeared.

Pa·le·o·lith·ic (pā′lē ə lith′ik), *adj.* of or about the earliest part of the Stone Age. Paleolithic tools were chipped out of stone.

pa·le·on·tol·o·gy (pā′lē on tol′ə jē), *n.* science of the forms of life existing in prehistoric time, as represented by fossil animals and plants. **—pa′le·on·tol′o·gist,** *n.*

Pa·le·o·zo·ic (pā′lē ə zō′ik), *n.* (in geology) time between about 600 million and 230 million years ago. During this time, fishes, insects, and reptiles developed.

Pal·es·tine (pal′ə stīn), *n.* region in SW Asia between the Mediterranean Sea and the Jordan River. The name has been applied since ancient times to the land of the Jews. Palestine is often called the Holy Land and in the Bible is called Canaan. It is now divided mostly between Israel and Jordan. [**Palestine** comes from **Philistine.** The Philistines lived along the coast here, and the Greeks called the whole region after them.]

Pal·es·tin·i·an (pal′ə stin′ē ən), **1** *adj.* of, in, or from Palestine. **2** *adj.* of or for Arabs living in Palestine. **3** *n.* an Arab born or living in Palestine.

pal·ette (pal′it), *n.* **1** a thin board, usually oval or oblong, with a thumb hole at one end, used by painters to lay and mix colors on. **2** set of colors used by a painter. ■ Other words that sound like

this are **palate** and **pallet.** [**Palette** comes from a Latin word meaning "a spade." A palette looks something like the blade of a shovel.] **—pal′ette·like′,** *adj.*

pal·frey (pôl′frē), *n.* OLD USE. a gentle riding horse, especially one used by women. ❑ *n., pl.* **pal·freys.**

Pa·li·kir (päl i kir′), *n.* capital of the Federated States of Micronesia.

pal·i·mo·ny (pal′ə mō′nē), *n.* money paid to a former lover because of a court order requiring it.

pal·in·drome (pal′in drōm), *n.* word, verse, sentence, or number which reads the same backward or forward. *Madam, radar,* "Madam, I'm Adam," and 247742 are palindromes.

pal·ing (pā′ling), *n.* **1** fence of pales. **2** pale in a fence.

pal·i·sade (pal′ə sād′), **1** *n.* a fence of stakes set firmly in the ground to enclose or defend. **2** *v.* to surround with a palisade. **3** *n.pl.* **palisades,** line of high, steep cliffs. **4** *n.* a long, strong, wooden stake pointed at the top end. ❑ *v.* **pal·i·sad·ed, pal·i·sad·ing.**

palisade (def. 1)

pall[1] (pôl), *n.* **1** a dark, gloomy covering: *A thick pall of smog shut out the sun.* **2** a heavy cloth of black, purple, or white velvet spread over a coffin, a hearse, or a tomb.

pall[2] (pôl), *v.* to become distasteful or very tiresome because there has been too much of something: *Even the most tasty food palls if it is served every day.*

pal·la·di·um (pə lā′dē əm), *n.* a soft, light, silver-white metallic element which occurs in nature with platinum. Palladium is used in making scientific devices, in alloys with precious metals such as gold and silver, and as a catalyst. *Symbol:* Pd

pall·bear·er (pôl′bâr′ər), *n.* one of the people who walk with or carry the coffin at a funeral.

pal·let[1] (pal′it), *n.* bed or mattress of straw. ■ Other words that sound like this are **palate** and **palette.**

pal·let[2] (pal′it), *n.* a small, low platform, usually made of wood, on which loads are stacked to keep them off the ground and to make them easy to pick up with a forklift. ■ Other words that sound like this are **palate** and **palette.**

pal·li·a·tive (pal′ē ā′tiv), **1** *adj.* useful to lessen, relieve, or soften; excusing. **2** *n.* something that lessens, relieves, softens, or excuses. **—pal′li·a′tive·ly,** *adv.*

pal·lid (pal′id), *adj.* lacking normal color; pale: *a pallid face.* **—pal′lid·ly,** *adv.*

pal·lor (pal′ər), *n.* lack of normal color from fear, illness, death, etc.; paleness.

palm[1] (päm), **1** *n.* the inside of the hand between the wrist and the fingers. **2** *n.* the width of a hand; 3 to 4 inches. **3** *n.* the part of a glove covering the palm. **4** *v.* to conceal in the hand: *The magician palmed the nickel.*

palm off, to pass off or get accepted by tricks, fraud, or false claims.

palm[2] (päm), *n.* **1** any of many trees or bushes that grow in warm climates. Most palms have tall trunks, no branches, and many large leaves at the top. **2** leaf or stalk of leaves of a palm tree, used as a symbol of victory or triumph. **—palm′like′,** *adj.*

pal·mate (pal′māt), *adj.* shaped like a hand with the fingers spread out: *a palmate leaf.* **—pal′mate·ly,** *adv.*

Pal·mer (pä′mər), *n.* **Arnold,** born 1929, American golfer. He was the first player to win the Masters Tournament, one of golf's main competitions, four times.

pal·met·to (pal met′ō), *n.* any of several rather small palm trees with fan-shaped leaves, common on the southeastern coast of the United States. ❏ *n., pl.* **pal·met·tos** or **pal·met·toes.**

palm·ist (pä′mist), *n.* person who claims to be able to tell fortunes by examining the palm of the hand.

palm·is·try (pä′mə strē), *n.* the supposed art of telling someone's fortune from lines and marks in the palm of the hand.

Palm Sunday, the Sunday before Easter Sunday.

palm·top (päm′top′), *n.* a personal computer small enough to be held in the palm of the hand.

palm·y (pä′mē), *adj.* **1** having many palms; shaded by palms. **2** flourishing; prosperous; glorious: *palmy days of peace.* ❏ *adj.* **palm·i·er, palm·i·est.**

pal·o·mi·no (pal′ə mē′nō), *n.* a cream colored or golden tan horse of Arabian stock. Its mane and tail are usually lighter colored. ❏ *n., pl.* **pal·o·mi·nos.** [Palomino comes from a Latin word meaning "dove." The color of the horse's coat resembles the color of some doves.]

pal·pa·ble (pal′pə bəl), *adj.* **1** easily seen or heard and recognized; obvious: *a palpable error.* **2** able to be felt by touching; tangible. **—pal′pa·bil′i·ty,** *n.* **—pal′pa·bly,** *adv.*

pal·pate (pal′pāt), *v.* to examine by touch, especially in medical diagnosis. ❏ *v.* **pal·pat·ed, pal·pat·ing. —pal·pa′tion,** *n.*

pal·pi·tate (pal′pə tāt), *v.* **1** to beat very rapidly; throb: *Your heart palpitates when you are excited.* **2** to quiver; tremble: *His entire body palpitated with terror.* ❏ *v.* **pal·pi·tat·ed, pal·pi·tat·ing. —pal′pi·tat′ing·ly,** *adv.*

pal·pi·ta·tion (pal′pə tā′shən), *n.* **1** a very rapid beating of the heart; throb. **2** act of quivering; trembling.

pal·sied (pȯl′zēd), *adj.* **1** having palsy; paralyzed. **2** shaking; trembling.

pal·sy (pȯl′zē), **1** *n.* paralysis, especially a form of paralysis occurring late in life, with symptoms of trembling and muscular weakness. **2** *v.* to afflict with palsy; paralyze. ❏ *v.* **pal·sied, pal·sy·ing.**

pal·try (pȯl′trē), *adj.* almost worthless; trifling; petty; mean: *paltry gossip, a paltry sum of money.* ❏ *adj.* **pal·tri·er, pal·tri·est. —pal′tri·ly,** *adv.* **—pal′tri·ness,** *n.*

pam·pas (pam′pəz), *n.pl.* the vast, grassy, treeless plains of South America, especially in Argentina.

pam·per (pam′pər), *v.* to give in to the wishes of; allow too many privileges: *pamper a child, pamper a sick person.* **—pam′per·er,** *n.*

pam·phlet (pam′flit), *n.* booklet in paper covers. It often deals with information of current interest.

pam·phlet·eer (pam′flə tir′), **1** *n.* writer of pamphlets. **2** *v.* to write and issue pamphlets.

pan¹ (pan), **1** *n.* dish for cooking and other household uses, usually broad, shallow, and with no cover: *pots and pans.* **2** *n.* anything like this. The dishes on a pair of scales are called pans. **3** *v.* to cook in a pan. **4** *v.* to wash gravel, sand, etc., in a pan to separate the gold. **5** *n.* (earlier) the hollow part of the lock that held a little gunpowder to set the gun off. **6** *v.* to criticize severely: *The drama critic panned the new play.* ❏ *v.* **panned, pan·ning.**

pan out, INFORMAL. to succeed; work out: *Her scheme panned out.*

pan² (pan), *v.* **1** to move a movie, TV, or video camera horizontally or vertically so as to take in all of a scene, or to follow a moving object: *The camera panned from the speaker to the audience.* **2** to move a camera in this way. ❏ *v.* **panned, pan·ning.**

Pan (pan), *n.* the Greek god of forests, pastures, flocks, and shepherds. Pan is described as a man with the legs, horns, and ears of a goat.

pan-, *prefix.* all; of all; entirely: *Pan-American = of all the Americas.* ■ See Word Power at **many.**

pan·a·ce·a (pan′ə sē′ə), *n.* a remedy for all diseases or ills; cure-all. ❏ *n., pl.* **pan·a·ce·as.**

Pan·a·ma (pan′ə mä), *n.* **1 Isthmus of,** a narrow neck of land which connects North America with South America. **2** country on the Isthmus of Panama. The Panama Canal runs through it. **3** its capital, a seaport on the Bay of Panama. **4 Bay of,** bay of the Pacific on the S coast of the Isthmus of Panama. **—Pan·a·ma·ni·an** (pan′ə mä′nē ən), *adj., n.*

Panama Canal, canal cut across the Isthmus of Panama to connect the Atlantic and Pacific oceans. It was built and formerly controlled by the United States.

Panama Canal Zone. See **Canal Zone.**

Panama hat, a lightweight hat made from braided leaves of a plant that grows in Ecuador.

Pan-A·mer·i·can (pan′ə mer′ə kən), *adj.* of or about all the people or countries of North, Central, and South America.

pan·cake (pan′kāk′), *n.* a thin, flat cake made of batter and fried in a pan or on a griddle.

pan·chro·mat·ic (pan′krō mat′ik), *adj.* sensitive to light of all colors: *a panchromatic photographic film.*

pan·cre·as (pan′krē əs), *n.* a large gland near the stomach that secretes insulin into the blood and pancreatic juice, a digestive juice containing various enzymes into the small intestine. The pancreas of animals when used for food is called sweetbread.

pan·cre·at·ic (pan′krē at′ik), *adj.* of or from the pancreas: *pancreatic secretions.*

pan·da (pan′də), *n.* **1** a bearlike mammal of Tibet and parts of southern and southwestern China, mostly white with black legs; giant panda. **2** a reddish brown mammal that looks something like a raccoon and lives in the Himalayas; lesser panda. ❏ *n., pl.* **pan·das.**

panda (def. 1)—about 5 ft. (1.5 m) long

pan·dem·ic (pan dem′ik), **1** *adj.* spreading over an entire country or continent, or over the whole world. **2** *n.* a pandemic disease.

pan·de·mo·ni·um (pan′də mō′nē əm), *n.* **1** wild uproar or confusion. **2** place of wild disorder or lawless confusion.

pan·der (pan′dər), **1** *n.* person who helps other people indulge desires, passions, or vices. **2** *v.* to act as a pander; supply material or opportunity for vices: *The newspaper pandered to people's liking for sensational stories.* **—pan′der·er,** *n.* **—pan′der·ing·ly,** *adv.*

Pan·do·ra (pan dôr′ə), *n.* (in Greek myths) the first woman, created by the gods. Curiosity led her to open a box (**Pandora's box**) and thus let out all evils and ills into the world.

pane (pān), *n.* a single sheet of glass or plastic in a division of a window, a door, or a sash: *Hailstones and gusts of wind broke several panes of glass.* ■ Another word that sounds like this is **pain. —pane′less,** *adj.*

pan·el (pan′l), **1** *n.* a strip or surface that is different in some way from what is around it. A panel is often sunk below or raised above the rest, and used for a decoration. Panels may be in a door or other woodwork, on large pieces of furniture, or made as parts

a	hat	ė	term	ô	order	ch	child		a in about
ā	age	i	it	oi	oil	ng	long		e in taken
ä	far	ī	ice	ou	out	sh	she	ə	i in pencil
â	care	o	hot	u	cup	th	thin		o in lemon
e	let	ō	open	u̇	put	ᴛʜ	then		u in circus
ē	equal	ȯ	saw	ü	rule	zh	measure		

P

of a dress. **2** *n.* a flat piece or section of material used in construction or as decoration: *oak panels.* **3** *v.* to arrange in panels; furnish or decorate with panels: *Her dining room was paneled with oak.* **4** *n.* picture, photograph, or design much longer than wide. **5** *n.* list of persons called as jurors; the members of a jury. **6** *n.* group formed for discussion: *A panel of experts gave its opinion on ways to solve the traffic problem.* **7** *n.* board containing the devices, controls, or indicators used in operating a car, aircraft, computer, or other mechanism. ❑ *v.* **pan·eled, pan·el·ing** or **pan·elled, pan·el·ling.** [See Word Story at **pane.**]

pan·el·ing (pan′l ing), *n.* **1** wood or other material for panels. **2** panels applied as decoration.

pan·el·ist (pan′l ist), *n.* person who takes part in a panel organized to discuss a specific topic.

pang (pang), *n.* **1** a sudden, short, sharp pain: *the pangs of a toothache.* **2** a sudden feeling: *He felt a pang of remorse.*

pan·go·lin (pang′gə lən), *n.* scaly anteater.

pan·han·dle (pan′han′dl), **1** *n.* handle of a pan. **2** *n.* a narrow strip of land projecting like a handle: *the Texas panhandle.* **3** *v.* to beg, especially in the streets. ❑ *v.* **pan·han·dled, pan·han·dling.** [**Panhandle,** meaning "to beg," is about 100 years old. What does begging have to do with pans or handles? No one knows.] —**pan′han′dler,** *n.*

pan·ic (pan′ik), **1** *n.* a fear spreading through a crowd of people so that they lose control of themselves; unreasoning fear: *When the theater caught fire, there was a panic.* **2** *n.* great fear of financial loss: *When several banks failed in one day, there was a panic among investors.* **3** *adj.* caused by panic; showing panic; unreasoning: *panic terror, panic haste.* **4** *v.* to affect or be affected with panic: *The audience panicked when the fire broke out.* ❑ *v.* **pan·icked, pan·ick·ing.**

pan·ick·y (pan′ə kē), *adj.* **1** caused by or showing panic: *panicky haste, panicky actions.* **2** feeling panic; liable to panic: *When fire broke out in the theater, the audience became panicky.*

pan·ic-strick·en (pan′ik strik′ən), *adj.* frightened out of your wits; demoralized by fear.

Pank·hurst (pangk′hərst), *n.* **Em·me·line** (em′ə lēn), 1858-1928, English suffragist. She and her daughters often used violent tactics, such as breaking windows, to get attention for their cause. Women became able to vote in England the year she died.

Pan·mun·jom (pän′mùn′jom′), *n.* town on the border between North Korea and South Korea. Truce talks were held here during the Korean War, from 1951 to 1953.

pan·ni·er (pan′ē ər), *n.* pack or basket, especially one of a pair to be slung across the shoulders, across the back of a pack animal, or hung over the rear wheel of a bicycle or motorcycle.

pan·o·ram·a (pan′ə ram′ə), *n.* **1** a wide, unbroken view of a surrounding region: *a panorama of beach and sea.* **2** a complete survey of some subject: *a panorama of history.* **3** picture of a landscape or other scene, often shown as if seen from a central point; picture unrolled a part at a time and made to pass continuously before the spectators. **4** a continuously passing or changing scene: *the panorama of city life.* ❑ *n., pl.* **pan·o·ram·as.**

pan·o·ram·ic (pan′ə ram′ik), *adj.* of or like a panorama: *a panoramic view.* —**pan′o·ram′i·cal·ly,** *adv.*

pan·pipe (pan′pīp′), *n.* an early musical instrument made of reeds or tubes of different lengths, fastened together side by side, in order of their length; syrinx. The reeds or tubes were closed at one end and the player blew across their open tops.

pan·sy (pan′zē), *n.* flower like a violet but much larger, with flat, velvety petals, usually of several colors. ❑ *n., pl.* **pan·sies.** [**Pansy** comes from a French word meaning "a thought." Pansies are still used to mean "remembrance."]

pant (pant), **1** *v.* to breathe hard and quickly: *She is panting from playing tennis.* **2** *n.* a short, quick breath. **3** *v.* to speak with short, quick breaths: *"Hurry, hurry," he panted.* **4** *v.* to wait for something eagerly: *I'm just panting for my turn.* —**pant′ing·ly,** *adv.*

pan·ta·loons (pan′tl ünz′), *n.pl.* tight-fitting trousers.

pan·the·ism (pan′thē iz′əm), *n.* belief that God and the universe are the same; doctrine that God is an expression of the physical forces of nature.

pan·the·ist (pan′thē ist), *n.* believer in pantheism.

pan·the·is·tic (pan′thē is′tik), *adj.* of or about pantheism or pantheists. —**pan′the·is′ti·cal·ly,** *adv.*

Pan·the·on (pan′thē on), *n.* **1** temple for all the gods, built at Rome about 27 B.C. and later used as a Christian church. **2** all the gods and goddesses, or heroes and heroines, of a group or country: *the pantheon of sports.*

pan·ther (pan′thər), *n.* **1** leopard, especially a black leopard. **2** mountain lion. **3** jaguar. ❑ *n., pl.* **pan·thers** or **pan·ther.**

pan·ties (pan′tēz), *n.pl.* kind of underpants worn by women or children.

pan·to·mime (pan′tə mīm), **1** *n.* a play without words, in which the actors express themselves by gestures. **2** *n.* gestures without words. **3** *v.* to express by gestures: *They pantomimed being hungry by pointing to their mouths and their stomachs.* ❑ *v.* **pan·to·mimed, pan·to·mim·ing.**

pan·try (pan′trē), *n.* a small room in which food, dishes, silverware, or table linen is kept. ❑ *n., pl.* **pan·tries.** [**Pantry** comes from a Latin word meaning "bread." Originally a pantry was a room where bread was kept.]

pants (pants), *n.pl.* **1** trousers. **2** underpants.

pantomime

pant·suit (pant′süt′), *n.* a woman's or girl's suit consisting of a jacket and trousers.

pan·ty·hose (pan′tē hōz′), *n.* underwear that combines panties and stockings.

pap (pap), *n.* **1** soft food for infants or invalids. **2** ideas or facts watered down in order to appear easier or more interesting. —**pap′like′,** *adj.*

pa·pa (pä′pə), *n.* father; daddy. ❑ *n., pl.* **pa·pas.**

pa·pa·cy (pā′pə sē), *n.* **1** position, rank, or authority of the pope. **2** time during which a pope rules. **3** all the popes. ❑ *n., pl.* **pa·pa·cies** for 2.

pa·pal (pā′pəl), *adj.* **1** of or from the pope: *a papal letter.* **2** of or about the papacy. —**pa·pal·ly,** *adv.*

pa·paw (pò′pò), *n.* **1** the oblong, yellowish fruit of a small North American tree. It is good to eat. **2** papaya. Also, **pawpaw.**

pa·pa·ya (pə pä′yə), *n.* the fruit of a palmlike tropical American tree. Papayas look something like melons, have yellowish pulp, and are good to eat. ❑ *n., pl.* **pa·pa·yas.**

pa·per (pā′pər), **1** *n.* a material used for writing, printing, drawing, wrapping packages, and covering walls. Paper is made in thin sheets from wood pulp, rags, etc. **2** *n.* piece or sheet of paper. **3** *n.* newspaper. **4** *n.* piece or sheet of paper with writing or printing on it; document: *Important papers were stolen.* **5** *n.pl.* **papers,** documents telling who or what you are. **6** *n.* wrapper, container, or sheet of paper containing something: *a paper of pins.* **7** *n.* article; essay: *The professor read a paper on the teaching of English.* **8** *n.* a written promise to pay money; note. **9** *adj.* made of paper: *paper dolls, paper money.* **10** *adj.* like paper; thin: *almonds with paper shells.* **11** *n.* wallpaper. **12** *v.* to cover with wallpaper: *paper a room.* —**pa′per·er,** *n.* —**pa′per·like′,** *adj.* **on paper, 1** in writing or print. **2** in theory.

pa·per·back (pā′pər bak′), *n.* book with a paper binding or cover.

pa·per·boy (pā′pər boi′), *n.* boy who delivers or sells newspapers; newsboy.

paper clip, a flat, bent piece of wire forming a clip to hold papers together.

pa·per·girl (pā′pər gėrl′), *n.* a girl who delivers or sells newspapers; newsgirl.

pa·per·hang·er (pā′pər hang′ər), *n.* person whose business is to cover walls with wallpaper.

paper money, money made of paper, not metal. A dollar bill is paper money.

pa·per·weight (pā′pər wāt′), *n.* a small, heavy object put on papers to keep them from being scattered.

pa·per·work (pā′pər wėrk′), **1** *n.* office work or clerical work, such as checking, sorting, and filing forms, letters, etc. **2** work done on paper, such as reports, letters, applications, etc.

pa·pier-mâ·ché (pā′per mə shā′), **1** *n.* a paper pulp mixed with some stiffener and molded into various shapes when moist. It becomes hard and strong when dry. **2** *adj.* made of papier-mâché.

pa·pil·la (pə pil′ə), *n.* any of the tiny bulges on the surface of the tongue that contain the taste buds. □ *n., pl.* **pa·pil·lae** (pə pil′ē).

pa·poose (pa püs′), *n.* an American Indian baby. ■ **Papoose** is often considered offensive.

pa·pri·ka (pə prē′kə *or* pap′rə kə), *n.* a red spice used to season food, made of finely ground sweet red peppers.

Papua New Guinea (pap′yü ə *or* pä′pü ä′), country consisting of the E part of the island of New Guinea and many nearby islands. *Capital:* Port Moresby.

pa·py·rus (pə pī′rəs), *n.* **1** a tall water plant from which the ancient Egyptians, Greeks, and Romans made a material to write on. **2** this writing material. **3** an ancient record written on this material. □ *n., pl.* **pa·py·rus·es, pa·py·ri** (pə pī′rī) for 3.

par (pär), **1** *n.* an equal level; equality: *The gains and losses are about on a par. He is quite on a par with his sister in intelligence.* **2** *n.* an average or normal amount, degree, or condition: *A sick person feels below par.* **3** *adj.* average; normal. **4** *n.* the value of a bond, a note, a share of stock, etc., that is printed on it; face value: *That stock is selling above par.* **5** *adj.* of or at par. **6** *n.* (in golf) a score which is used as a standard for a particular hole or course and which represents the number of strokes that will be taken if the hole or course is played well. Par is based on the length and difficulty of the hole or course.

par., **1** paragraph. **2** parallel.

par·a·ble (par′ə bəl), *n.* a brief story used to teach some truth or moral lesson: *The teacher explained the parable.*

pa·rab·o·la (pə rab′ə lə), *n.* a curve formed by all the points that are equally distant from a line and a point not on that line. A parabola is also produced by the intersection of a cone and a plane parallel to a side of the cone. The trajectory of a missile is a parabola. □ *n., pl.* **pa·rab·o·las.**

par·a·chute (par′ə shüt), **1** *n.* device shaped like an umbrella, made of nylon or silk, that allows people or objects to fall slowly after dropping out of an aircraft. **2** *v.* to come down by, or as if by, a parachute: *The pilot of the burning plane parachuted to the ground.* **3** *v.* to drop by parachute: *to parachute emergency supplies.* □ *v.* **par·a·chut·ed, par·a·chut·ing.** —**par′a·chut′er,** *n.*

par·a·chut·ist (par′ə shü′tist), *n.* person who uses a parachute or is skilled in making descents with a parachute.

parachute

pa·rade (pə rād′), **1** *n.* a march for display; procession: *The circus had a parade.* **2** *v.* to march in procession; walk proudly as if in a parade: *After the football victory, the students paraded through the neighborhood.* **3** *n.* group of people walking for display or pleasure. **4** *n.* a great show or display: *The modest man did not make a parade of his wealth.* **5** *v.* to make a great show of: *parade your wealth.* **6** *n.* a military display or review of troops. **7** *v.* to come together in military order for review or inspection. **8** *v.* to assemble troops for review. **9** *n.* the place used for the regular parade of troops. □ *v.* **pa·rad·ed, pa·rad·ing.** —**pa·rade′like′,** *adj.* —**pa·rad′er,** *n.*

par·a·digm (par′ə dīm), *n.* **1** pattern; example. **2** example of a noun, verb, pronoun, etc., in all its inflections.

par·a·dise (par′ə dīs), *n.* **1** heaven. **2** place or condition of great happiness: *The summer camp was a paradise for her.* **3** place of great beauty. **4** Also, **Paradise,** the garden of Eden.

Paradise, *n.* city in SE Nevada.

par·a·dox (par′ə doks), *n.* **1** statement that may be true but seems to say two opposite things: *"More haste, less speed"* and *"The child is father to the man"* are paradoxes. **2** statement that is false because it says two opposite things. **3** person or thing that seems to be full of contradictions. □ *n., pl.* **par·a·dox·es.**

par·a·dox·i·cal (par′ə dok′sə kəl), *adj.* **1** seeming to say opposite things; self-contradictory: *a paradoxical statement.* **2** of or being a paradox. —**par′a·dox′i·cal·ly,** *adv.* —**par′a·dox′i·cal·ness,** *n.*

par·af·fin (par′ə fin), **1** *n.* a white, tasteless, waxy substance, used for making candles and for sealing jars of jelly or jam. It is obtained chiefly from crude petroleum. **2** *v.* to treat with paraffin.

par·a·gon (par′ə gon), *n.* model of excellence or perfection.

par·a·graph (par′ə graf), **1** *n.* group of sentences relating to the same idea or topic and forming a distinct part of a chapter, letter, or other piece of writing. Paragraphs usually begin on a new line and are indented. **2** *v.* to divide into paragraphs. **3** *n.* a separate note or item of news in a newspaper. **4** *n.* sign (¶) used to show where a paragraph begins or should begin. It is used mostly in correcting written work.

Par·a·guay (par′ə gwā *or* par′ə gwī), *n.* **1** country in central South America, bordered by Bolivia, Brazil, and Argentina. *Capital:* Asunción. **2** river in central South America. —**Par′a·guay′an,** *adj., n.*

par·a·keet (par′ə kēt), *n.* any of several small parrots with slender bodies and long tails.

WORD STORY **Parakeet** comes from the old French form of the name *Peter.* **Parrot** comes from the same name. In the same way that *Polly* is a familiar name for parrots today, French people used to call a parrot *Peter,* and they called a parakeet *little Peter.*

par·a·le·gal (par′ə lē′gəl), *n.* person trained to assist a lawyer.

par·al·lax (par′ə laks), *n.* the apparent change in the position of an object when it is seen from two different points on different lines with the object. Parallax is used in surveying, astronomy, etc., to determine distances of objects.

par·al·lel (par′ə lel), **1** *adj.* at the same distance apart everywhere, like the two rails of a railroad track. **2** *v.* to stay at the same distance from something: *The street parallels the railroad.* **3** *n.* a line or surface at an unchanging distance from another. **4** *adj.* **a** of or about the performance of several different computer operations at the same time: *parallel processing.* **b** of or about the sending of computer information over separate wires at one time: *a parallel printer.* **5** *n.* any of the imaginary circles around the earth parallel to the equator, showing degrees of latitude. **6** *n.* comparison to show likeness: *He drew a parallel between this winter and last winter.* **7** *v.* to compare in order to show likeness. **8** *v.* to find a case that is similar to another: *Can you parallel that for friendliness?* **9** *adj.* similar; matching: *parallel customs in different countries.* **10** *n.* thing like another: *Her experience was an interesting parallel to ours.* **11** *v.* to be like; be similar to: *Your story closely parallels his.* **12** *n.* an arrangement of the wiring of batteries, lights, etc., in which all the positive terminals are connected to one conductor, and all the negative terminals to the other. □ *v.* **par·al·leled, par·al·lel·ing** or **par·al·lelled, par·al·lel·ling.**

parallel bars, a pair of raised bars horizontal to the ground, used in gymnastics to develop the muscles of the arms, chest, etc.

par·al·lel·e·pi·ped (par′ə lel′ə pī′pid), *n.* a solid with six surfaces, all parallelograms.

par·al·lel·ism (par′ə lel′iz′əm), *n.* **1** condition of being parallel. **2** likeness; similarity; correspondence; agreement.

par·al·lel·o·gram (par′ə lel′ə gram), *n.* a four-sided plane figure whose opposite sides are parallel and equal.

pa·ral·y·sis (pə ral′ə sis), *n.* **1** loss of part or all of the power of motion or sensation in any part of the body: *Polio can cause paralysis.* **2** condition of powerlessness or helpless inactivity;

a	hat	ė	term	ô	order	ch	child		a in about
ā	age	i	it	oi	oil	ng	long		e in taken
ä	far	ī	ice	ou	out	sh	she	ə	i in pencil
â	care	o	hot	u	cup	th	thin		o in lemon
e	let	ō	open	ů	put	ŦH	then		u in circus
ē	equal	ȯ	saw	ü	rule	zh	measure		

P

crippling: *The war caused a paralysis of trade.* ■ Some people feel that this meaning of **paralysis** should not be used because it focuses on the negative effects of a health problem. ❑ *n., pl.* **pa·ral·y·ses** (pə ral′ə sēz′).

par·a·lyt·ic (par′ə lit′ik), **1** *adj.* of or having paralysis. **2** *n.* person who has paralysis. ■ Some people feel that this meaning of **paralytic** should not be used because it labels a person in terms of a condition. —**par′a·lyt′i·cal·ly,** *adv.*

par·a·lyze (par′ə līz), *v.* **1** to affect with loss of part or all of the power of motion or feeling: *The patient's arm was paralyzed.* **2** to make powerless; stun: *Fear paralyzed my mind.* ❑ *v.* **par·a·lyzed, par·a·lyz·ing. —par′a·lyz′er,** *n.* **—par′a·lyz′ing·ly,** *adv.*

Par·a·mar·i·bo (par′ə mar′ə bō), *n.* port and capital of Suriname, on the Atlantic.

par·a·me·ci·um (par′ə mē′sē əm), *n.* any of several one-celled living things shaped like a slender slipper, with a groove along one side leading into an open mouth. Paramecia live in fresh water and move by means of hairlike cilia. They are protists. ❑ *n., pl.* **par·a·me·ci·a** (par′ə mē′sē ə).

par·a·med·ic (par′ə med′ik), *n.* someone who assists a doctor, especially someone who gives medical treatment at the scene of an emergency.

par·a·med·i·cal (par′ə med′ə kəl), *adj.* of or about paramedics or their work.

pa·ram·e·ter (pə ram′ə tər), *n.* **1** (in mathematics) a fixed or variable amount that controls a result such as the shape of a mathematical curve or the location of points in mathematical space. **2** a particular quality; characteristic feature: *The parameters of the pollution problem include population, technology, weather, and other factors.* **3** a limit or boundary: *as much information as the parameters of an encyclopedia allow.*

par·a·mil·i·tar·y (par′ə mil′ə ter′ē), *adj.* organized in a military way, but not part of the official armed forces of a country.

par·a·mount (par′ə mount), *adj.* chief in importance; above others; supreme: *Truth is of paramount importance.* —**par′a·mount′ly,** *adv.*

par·a·noi·a (par′ə noi′ə), *n.* **1** a mental illness in which the symptoms are feelings of persecution. **2** an irrational distrust of others.

par·a·noid (par′ə noid), **1** *adj.* like or tending toward paranoia. **2** *adj.* having the characteristics of paranoia. **3** *n.* a person suffering from paranoia.

par·a·pet (par′ə pet), *n.* **1** a low wall at the edge of a balcony, roof, bridge, etc. **2** a low wall or mound of stone, earth, etc., to protect soldiers.

par·a·pher·nal·ia (par′ə fər nā′lyə), *n.pl. or sing.* **1** personal belongings: *My paraphernalia are ready to be shipped.* **2** equipment; outfit: *A photographer's paraphernalia includes cameras, film, lenses, lights, tripods, etc.*

par·a·phrase (par′ə frāz′), **1** *v.* to state the meaning of a passage in other words. **2** *n.* an expression of the meaning of a passage in other words. ❑ *v.* **par·a·phrased, par·a·phras·ing. —par′a·phras′a·ble,** *adj.*

parapet

par·a·ple·gi·a (par′ə plē′jē ə), *n.* paralysis of the legs and the lower part of the body.

par·a·ple·gic (par′ə plē′jik), **1** *n.* person who has paraplegia. **2** *adj.* having paraplegia or about paraplegia.

par·a·pro·fes·sion·al (par′ə prə fesh′ə nəl), *n.* person who is trained to assist a doctor, lawyer, etc., but who does not have full professional training.

par·a·psy·chol·o·gy (par′ə sī kol′ə jē), *n.* branch of psychology dealing with psychic phenomena, such as extrasensory perception, telepathy, and clairvoyance. —**par′a·psy·chol′o·gist,** *n.*

par·a·site (par′ə sīt), *n.* **1** any living thing that lives on or in another, from which it gets its food, often harming the other in the process. Lice and tapeworms are parasites on animals. Mistletoe is a parasite on oak trees. **2** person who lives on others without making any useful return; hanger-on.

par·a·sit·ic (par′ə sit′ik), *adj.* of or like a parasite; living on others. —**par′a·sit′i·cal·ly,** *adv.*

par·a·sol (par′ə sȯl), *n.* a light umbrella used as a protection from the sun.

par·a·sym·pa·thet·ic nervous system (par′ə sim′pə thet′ik), part of the nervous system that widens blood vessels, increases the activity of the digestive system, contracts the pupils of the eyes, and slows the heartbeat.

par·a·thy·roid glands (par′ə thī′roid), small glands in or near the thyroid gland. Their secretion, which enables the body to use calcium, is necessary for life.

par·a·troop·er (par′ə trü′pər), *n.* soldier trained to use a parachute for dropping from an aircraft into a battle area.

par·a·troops (par′ə trüps′), *n.pl.* paratroopers.

par·a·ty·phoid fever (par′ə tī′foid), a disease like typhoid fever but usually milder, caused by salmonella bacteria.

par·boil (pär′boil′), *v.* to boil till partly cooked: *parboil beans before baking them.*

par·cel (pär′səl), **1** *n.* bundle of things wrapped or packed together; package: *She had her arms filled with parcels of gifts.* **2** *n.* piece: *a parcel of land.* **3** *n.* pack: *The peddler had a parcel of odds and ends in his sack.* **4** *v.* to make into a parcel; put up in parcels. ❑ *v.* **par·celed, par·cel·ing** or **par·celled, par·cel·ling.**
parcel out, to divide into, or distribute in, portions.

parcel post, branch of the postal service which carries parcels.

parch (pärch), *v.* **1** to make or become hot and dry or thirsty: *I am parched with the heat.* **2** to dry by heating; roast slightly: *Corn is sometimes parched.*

parch·ment (pärch′mənt), *n.* **1** the skin of sheep or goats, prepared for use as a writing material. **2** manuscript or document written on parchment. **3** paper that looks like parchment. —**parch′ment·like′,** *adj.*

par·don (pärd′n), **1** *n.* act of passing over an offense without punishment; forgiveness. **2** *v.* to forgive: *Grandmother pardoned the mischievous children.* **3** *n.* excuse or toleration: *I beg your pardon, but I missed your last remark.* **4** *v.* to set free from punishment: *The governor pardoned the prisoner.* **5** *n.* act of setting someone free from punishment. **6** *n.* a legal document setting someone free from punishment. —**par′don·er,** *n.*

SYNONYM STUDY **Pardon, forgive,** and **excuse** all mean not to punish. **Pardon** means to stop a punishment, especially officially: *The governor pardoned the prisoner.* **Forgive** means to choose not to punish someone: *I will forgive you for insulting me if you promise not to do it again.* **Excuse** means to forgive because of some reason: *The teacher excused his lateness when he explained about his mother's illness.*

par·don·a·ble (pärd′n ə bəl), *adj.* able to be pardoned; excusable. —**par′don·a·ble·ness,** *n.* —**par′don·a·bly,** *adv.*

pare (pâr), *v.* **1** to cut, trim, or shave off the outer part of; peel: *pare an apple.* **2** to cut away little by little: *We had to pare down expenses.* ❑ *v.* **pared, par·ing.** ■ Other words that sound like this are **pair** and **pear.**

par·e·gor·ic (par′ə gôr′ik), *n.* a soothing medicine containing camphor and a very little opium.

pa·ren·chy·ma (pə reng′kə mə), *n.* **1** the basic tissue of most plants, especially the soft parts of leaves and fruits, formed of thin-walled, unspecialized cells. Cells in the parenchyma are active in photosynthesis and in storage of resulting food. **2** tissue of any animal organ that is special to that organ. Many organs have the same kind of connecting tissue and supporting tissue, but each organ has its own special parenchyma.

par·ent (pâr′ənt), *n.* **1** father or mother. **2** any animal or plant that produces offspring. **3** source; cause; origin: *Fear is often the parent of anger.* —**par′ent·like′,** *adj.*

par·ent·age (pâr′ən tij), *n.* descent from parents; family line; ancestry.

pa·ren·tal (pə ren′tl), *adj.* of, for, or about a parent or parents; like a parent's: *parental advice.* **—pa·ren′tal·ly,** *adv.*

parental leave, a leave of absence from work to care for a new baby or a recently adopted child. Parental leave is usually without pay.

pa·ren·the·sis (pə ren′thə sis), *n.* **1** word, phrase, sentence, etc., inserted within a sentence to explain or qualify something. **2** either or both of two curved lines ( ) used to set off such an expression. ❑ *n., pl.* **pa·ren·the·ses** (pə ren′thə sēz′).

par·en·thet·ic (par′ən thet′ik), *adj.* **1** serving or helping to explain; qualifying. **2** enclosed in parentheses. **3** using parentheses. **—par′en·thet′i·cal·ly,** *adv.*

par·en·thet·i·cal (par′ən thet′ə kəl), *adj.* parenthetic.

par·ent·hood (pâr′ənt hud), *n.* condition of being a parent.

par·ent·ing (pâr′ən ting), *n.* the activity of being a father or mother; the raising of children.

pa·re·o (pär′ā ō), *n.* a lightweight and usually brightly colored length of cloth used as a skirt or dress, or as a covering over a bathing suit. ❑ *n., pl.* **pa·re·os.**

par·fait (pär fā′), *n.* **1** ice cream with syrup or crushed fruit and whipped cream, served in a tall glass. **2** a rich ice cream containing eggs and whipped cream.

pa·ri·ah (pə rī′ə), *n.* outcast.

par·i·mu·tu·el (par′i myü′chü əl), *n.* **1** system of betting on horse races in which those who have bet on the winning horses divide all the money bet, except for a part withheld by the management for costs, profits, taxes, etc. **2** machine for recording such bets.

par·ing (pâr′ing), *n.* the part pared off; skin; rind: *apple parings.*

Par·is (par′is), *n.* **1** capital and largest city of France, in the N part. Paris is on the Seine River. **2** (in Greek legends) a son of Priam, king of Troy. He kidnapped Helen and so started the Trojan War.

par·ish (par′ish), *n.* **1** district that has its own church and clergyman. **2** people of a parish. **3** members of the congregation of a particular church. **4** (in Louisiana) county. ❑ *n., pl.* **par·ish·es.**

pa·rish·ion·er (pə rish′ə nər), *n.* member of a parish.

Pa·ri·sian (pə rizh′ən), **1** *adj.* of or about Paris or its people. **2** *n.* person born or living in Paris.

par·i·ty (par′ə tē), *n.* similarity or close correspondence with regard to state, position, condition, value, quality, degree, etc.; equality.

Paris (def. 1)

park (pärk), **1** *n.* land set apart for the pleasure of the public: *Many cities have beautiful parks.* **2** *n.* field or stadium, especially for ball games and other sports events. **3** *v.* to leave a motor vehicle for a time in a certain place: *Park your car here.* **4** *n.* arrangement of gears, in an automatic transmission, in which the gears do not turn the wheels and the brake is on. **5** *n.* area set aside for a specific business use: *research park.* **—park′er,** *n.* **—park′like′,** *adj.*

par·ka (pär′kə), *n.* a heavy waterproof coat or jacket with a hood, originally worn in the Arctic and made of skins. ❑ *n., pl.* **par·kas.**

Par·ker (pär′kər), *n.* **1 Char·lie** (chär′lē), 1920-1955, American jazz saxophonist and composer. His nickname was "Bird." He often worked with Dizzy Gillespie and Thelonious Monk. **2 Dor·o·thy** (dor′ə thē), 1893-1967, American writer of poems and short stories. Her poems were often cynical and ironic, dealing with subjects such as unhappy relationships.

Par·kers·burg (pär′kərs bərg), *n.* city in W West Virginia.

parking lot, an open area used for parking motor vehicles, often for a fee.

parking meter, device containing a clock started by inserting coins. It allows a car to occupy a parking space for an amount of time that depends on the coin or coins inserted.

Par·kin·son's disease (pär′kin sənz), a disease of the nervous system that causes trembling muscles, weakness, and paralysis. It usually occurs after middle age and progresses slowly for years.

park·land (pärk′land′), *n.* in Canada: **1** area between the foothills of the Rockies and the prairies. **2** the wooded area between the Barren Ground and the prairies. **3** land protected from development, kept as a public park.

Parks (pärks), *n.* **Ro·sa** (rō′zə), born 1913, American activist. ■ In 1955, **Rosa Parks** refused to give up her seat on a bus to a white passenger in Montgomery, Alabama, as required by law. She was arrested, and other African Americans, led by Martin Luther King, Jr., boycotted the bus system.

park·way (pärk′wā′), *n.* a broad road with spaces planted with grass, trees, etc.

par·lance (pär′ləns), *n.* way of speaking; talk; language: *legal parlance.*

par·lay (pär′lā), *v.* **1** to increase money, skill, influence, etc.: *She parlayed her athletic ability into a career in professional tennis.* **2** to risk the winnings of one bet on another bet. ❑ *v.* **par·layed, par·lay·ing.**

par·ley (pär′lē), **1** *n.* conference or informal talk to discuss terms or matters in dispute: *The general held a parley with the enemy about exchanging prisoners.* **2** *v.* to discuss matters, especially with an enemy. ❑ *n., pl.* **par·leys;** *v.* **par·leyed, par·ley·ing.**

par·lia·ment (pär′lə mənt), *n.* council or congress that is the highest lawmaking group in some countries, including Canada, Great Britain, and other countries having the British system of government. [See Word Story at **parlor.**]

par·lia·men·tar·i·an (pär′lə men ter′ē ən), *n.* person skilled in parliamentary procedure or debate.

par·lia·men·tar·y (pär′lə men′tər ē), *adj.* **1** of or about a parliament: *parliamentary authority.* **2** done by a parliament: *parliamentary statutes.* **3** according to formal rules and customs for meetings: *The U.S. Congress functions in accordance with the rules of parliamentary procedure.* **4** having a parliament: *a parliamentary form of government.* **—par′lia·men·tar′i·ly,** *adv.*

par·lor (pär′lər), *n.* **1** formerly, a room for receiving or entertaining guests; sitting room. **2** room or set of rooms used for various business purposes; shop: *a funeral parlor, a beauty parlor.*

WORD STORY **Parlor** comes from a French word meaning "to talk." **Parliament** comes from the same word. A parlor is used mostly for conversation. Parliament is where politicians make speeches.

parlor car, a railroad passenger car for day travel, with more expensive reserved individual seats.

Par·me·san (pär′mə zän *or* pär′mə zən), *n.* a hard, dry Italian cheese made from skim milk.

Par·mi·gia·na (pär′mə jä′nə *or* pär′mə zhä′nə), *adj.* cooked or sprinkled with grated Parmesan cheese.

pa·ro·chi·al (pə rō′kē əl), *adj.* **1** of or in a parish: *parochial calls, a parochial church.* **2** narrow; limited: *a parochial viewpoint.* **—pa·ro′chi·al·ly,** *adv.*

parochial school, school maintained by a church or a religious organization.

par·o·dy (par′ə dē), **1** *n.* a humorous imitation of a serious writing. A parody follows the form of the original, but often changes its sense to nonsense, thus making fun of the writer's style. **2** *v.* to make fun of by imitating; make a parody of. ❑ *n., pl.* **par·o·dies;** *v.* **par·o·died, par·o·dy·ing.**

pa·role (pə rōl′), **1** *n.* release from prison or jail before the full term is served on the condition that future behavior be lawful, and that periodic reporting be made to an officer of the court. **2** *v.* to grant an early release from jail or prison before the full term

a	hat	ė	term	ô	order	ch	child		a in about
ā	age	i	it	oi	oil	ng	long		e in taken
ä	far	ī	ice	ou	out	sh	she	ə	i in pencil
â	care	o	hot	u	cup	th	thin		o in lemon
e	let	ō	open	ú	put	ᴛʜ	then		u in circus
ē	equal	ò	saw	ü	rule	zh	measure		

is served: *The prisoner was paroled after serving two years of a three-year sentence.* ❑ *v.* **pa·roled, pa·rol·ing.** **—pa·rol′a·ble,** *adj.*

pa·rol·ee (pə rō/lē′), *n.* person who is on parole from prison. ❑ *n., pl.* **pa·rol·ees.**

par·ox·ysm (par′ək siz′əm), *n.* **1** a sudden, severe attack of the symptoms of a disease, usually recurring periodically: *a paroxysm of coughing.* **2** a sudden outburst of emotion or activity: *a paroxysm of rage.*

par·quet (pär kā′), **1** *n.* an inlaid wooden flooring. **2** *adj.* made of parquet: *parquet floors.* **3** *n.* the main floor of a theater; orchestra.

par·quet·ry (pär′kə trē), *n.* mosaic of wood used for floors, wainscoting, etc.

Parr (pär), *n.* **Catherine,** 1512-1548, English queen, sixth and last wife of Henry VIII, whom she outlived.

par·ri·cide (par′ə sīd), *n.* **1** the crime of killing your parent or parents. **2** person who commits this crime.

par·rot (par′ət), **1** *n.* any of numerous birds with stout, hooked bills and often with bright-colored feathers. Some parrots can imitate sounds and repeat words and sentences. **2** *n.* person who repeats words or ideas without understanding them. **3** *v.* to repeat without understanding. [See Word Story at **parakeet.**] **—par′rot·like′,** *adj.*

par·ry (par′ē), **1** *v.* to ward off; turn aside; evade a thrust, stroke, weapon, question, etc.: *He parried the sword with his dagger. She parried our question by asking us one.* **2** *n.* act of parrying; avoiding. ❑ *v.* **par·ried, par·ry·ing;** *n., pl.* **par·ries.**

parse (pärs), *v.* **1** to analyze a sentence grammatically, telling its parts of speech and their uses in the sentence. **2** to describe a word grammatically, telling what part of speech it is, its form, and its use in a sentence. ❑ *v.* **parsed, pars·ing.** **—pars′a·ble,** *adj.* **—pars′er,** *n.*

par·sec (pär′sek), *n.* unit of distance used in astronomy, equal to 3.26 light-years (19.2 trillion miles or 30.9 trillion kilometers).

Par·see or **Par·si** (pär′sē), *n.* member of a Zoroastrian sect in India, descended from Persians who settled there in the A.D. 700s. ❑ *n., pl.* **Par·sees** or **Par·sis.**

par·si·mo·ni·ous (pär′sə mō′nē əs), *adj.* too economical; stingy. **—par′si·mo′ni·ous·ly,** *adv.* **—par′si·mo′ni·ous·ness,** *n.*

par·si·mo·ny (pär′sə mō′nē), *n.* extreme economy; stinginess.

par·sley (pär′slē), *n.* a garden plant with finely divided, fragrant leaves. Parsley is used to flavor food and to trim platters of meat, fish, etc.

par·snip (pär′snip), *n.* the long, narrow, whitish root of a garden plant, eaten as a vegetable. It looks very much like a carrot.

par·son (pär′sən), *n.* **1** minister in charge of an Episcopal parish. **2** any clergyman; minister.

par·son·age (pär′sə nij), *n.* house provided for a minister by a church.

part (pärt), **1** *n.* something less than the whole; not all: *He ate part of an apple.* **2** *n.* each of several equal quantities into which a whole may be divided; fraction: *A dime is a tenth part of a dollar.* **3** *n.* thing that helps to make up a whole: *An engine has many parts.* **4** *n.* share: *I had no part in the mischief.* **5** *n.* side in a dispute or contest: *He always takes her sister's part.* **6** *n.* character in a play, movie, etc.; role: *He played the part of Hamlet.* **7** *n.* the words spoken by a character: *She spoke the part of the heroine in our play.* **8** *v.* to divide into two or more pieces. **9** *v.* to force apart; divide: *Several mounted police parted the crowd.* ■ See Synonym Study at **separate.** **10** *v.* to go apart; separate: *The friends parted in anger.* **11** *n.* a dividing line left in combing your hair. **12** *v.* to comb the hair away from a dividing line. **13** *n.* one of the voices or instruments in a piece of music: *the tenor part, the violin part.* **14** *n.* the music for it. **15** *adj.* less than the whole: *part Irish.* **16** *adv.* in some measure or degree; partly. **17** *n.pl.* **parts, a** ability; talent: *a man of parts.* **b** regions; districts; places: *She has traveled much in foreign parts.*

for the most part, mostly: *The plan was for the most part successful.*

for your part, as far as you are concerned: *For his part, it just doesn't matter.*

in good part, in a friendly or gracious way.

in part, in some measure or degree; to some extent; partly.

on someone's part, by: *The decision has been delayed by the refusal on the part of the manager to consider the problem.*

part and parcel, a necessary part.

part from, to go away from; leave.

part with, to give up; let go.

take part, to take or have a share.

par·take (pär tāk′), *v.* **1** to eat or drink something: *We are eating lunch. Will you partake?* **2** to take or have a share. ❑ *v.* **par·took, par·tak·en, par·tak·ing.** **—par·tak′a·ble,** *adj.* **—par·tak′er,** *n.*

partake of, 1 to take some; have a share in: *Will you partake of this cake?* **2** to have to some extent the nature or character of: *Her modesty partakes of shyness.*

par·tak·en (pär tā′kən), *v.* past participle of **partake.**

par·the·no·gen·e·sis (pär′thə nō jen′ə sis), *n.* reproduction by means of eggs that have not been fertilized. Some insects reproduce by parthenogenesis.

Par·the·non (pär′thə non), *n.* temple of Athena on the Acropolis in Athens, regarded as the finest example of Doric architecture.

Parthenon

par·tial (pär′shəl), *adj.* **1** not complete; not total: *My parents made a partial payment on our new car.* **2** inclined to favor one side more than another; favoring unfairly: *Parents should not be partial to any one of their children.* **3** having a liking for; favorably inclined: *I am partial to sports.* **—par′tial·ness,** *n.*

par·ti·al·i·ty (pär′shē al′ə tē), *n.* **1** the favoring of one more than another or others; favorable prejudice; being partial. **2** a particular liking; fondness; preference; bent: *a partiality for word games.*

par·tial·ly (pär′shə lē), *adv.* **1** in part; not generally or totally; partly. **2** in a partial manner; with undue bias.

par·tic·i·pant (pär tis′ə pənt), *n.* person who shares or participates.

par·tic·i·pate (pär tis′ə pāt), *v.* to take part in something; have a share: *The teacher participated in the children's games.* ❑ *v.* **par·tic·i·pat·ed, par·tic·i·pat·ing.** **—par·tic′i·pa′tion,** *n.* **—par·tic′i·pa′tor,** *n.*

par·ti·cip·i·al (pär′tə sip′ē əl), *adj.* of or resembling a participle. We often use participial adjectives (a *masked* man, a *becoming* dress) and participial nouns (in *giving* a speech, the fatigue of *marching*). **—par′ti·cip′i·al·ly,** *adv.*

par·ti·ci·ple (pär′tə sip′əl), *n.* a verb form that keeps all the qualities of a verb, such as tense, voice, power to take an object, and modification by adverbs, but that may be used as an adjective. EXAMPLES: the students *writing* sentences at the blackboard, the people *waiting* for a train, the *polished* silver, the jewels *stolen* last night. In these phrases, *writing* and *waiting* are present participles; *polished* and *stolen* are past participles.

par·ti·cle (pär′tə kəl), *n.* **1** a very little bit: *I got a particle of dust in my eye.* **2** any of the extremely small units of matter that all atoms are made of, such as the electron, proton, and neutron: *subatomic particles.* **3** in grammar: **a** prefix or suffix. *Un-* and *-ment* are particles. **b** preposition, conjunction, article, or interjection. *In, if, an,* and *ah* are particles.

particle accelerator, any of several machines, such as the betatron and cyclotron, that produce streams of protons, electrons, and other subatomic particles moving with great energy at high speeds; accelerator. The accelerated particles may strike the nuclei of atoms in a target, causing the nuclei to release new particles, or they may be aimed so that the streams collide and produce new particles on impact.

par·ti·col·ored (pär′tē kul′ərd), *adj.* colored differently in different parts: *a parti-colored shirt.*

par·tic·u·lar (pər tik′yə lər), **1** *adj.* apart from others; considered separately; single: *That particular chair is already sold.* **2** *adj.* belonging to some one person, thing, group, occasion, etc.: *His particular task is to care for the dog.* **3** *adj.* different from others; unusual; special: *He is a particular friend of mine.* ■ See Synonym Study at **special. 4** *adj.* hard to please; wanting everything to be just right; very careful: *She is very particular; nothing but the best will do.* **5** *n.* an individual part; item; point: *All the particulars of the accident are now known.*

in particular, especially; specific: *We strolled around, going nowhere in particular.*

par·tic·u·lar·i·ty (pər tik′yə lar′ə tē), *n.* **1** detailed quality; minuteness. **2** special carefulness. **3** attentiveness to details. **4** a particular feature or trait. □ *n., pl.* **par·tic·u·lar·i·ties** for 4.

par·tic·u·lar·ize (pər tik′yə lə rīz′), *v.* **1** to mention particularly; treat in detail. **2** to mention individually; state or discuss in detail. □ *v.* **par·tic·u·lar·ized, par·tic·u·lar·iz·ing. —par·tic′u·lar·i·za′tion,** *n.* **—par·tic′u·lar·iz′er,** *n.*

par·tic·u·lar·ly (pər tik′yə lər lē), *adv.* **1** in a high degree; especially: *I am particularly fond of her.* **2** specifically: *He mentioned that point particularly.*

par·tic·u·late (pär tik′yə lit), **1** *adj.* of or containing particles. **2** *n.* a very small particle of dust, soot, etc.

part·ing (pär′ting), **1** *n.* act of going away; taking leave; departure: *The friends were sad at parting.* **2** *adj.* given, taken, done, etc., at parting: *a parting request.* **3** *adj.* departing. **4** *adj.* dividing; separating. **5** *n.* division; separation.

Par·ti Qué·béc·ois (pär tē′kä bek wä), (in Canada) a major political party of Quebec.

par·ti·san (pär′tə zən), **1** *n.* a strong supporter of a person, party, or cause; one whose support is based on feeling rather than on reasoning. **2** *n.* member of light, irregular troops; guerrilla. **3** *adj.* of or like a partisan: *There are often partisan favors in politics.* **—par′ti·san·ship,** *n.*

par·ti·tion (pär tish′ən), **1** *n.* wall, screen, etc., between rooms or spaces. **2** *v.* to divide into parts: *partition a territory into three states, partition a house into rooms.* **3** *v.* to separate by a partition. **4** *n.* division into parts: *the partition of a person's estate after death.* **—par·ti′tion·er,** *n.* **—par·ti′tion·ment,** *n.*

part·ly (pärt′lē), *adv.* in part; in some measure or degree: *You are partly to blame.*

part·ner (pärt′nər), *n.* **1** member of a company or firm who shares the risks and profits of the business. **2** wife or husband. **3** companion in a dance. **4** player on the same team or side in a game. **5** one who shares: *My sister was the partner of my walks.* **—part′ner·less,** *adj.*

part·ner·ship (pärt′nər ship), *n.* **1** condition of being a partner; joint interest; association: *a business partnership, the partnership of marriage.* **2** company or firm with two or more members who share in the risks and profits of the business: *a law partnership.* **3** the contract that creates such a relation.

part of speech, any of the classes into which words are divided according to their use or function in sentences. The traditional parts of speech are the noun, pronoun, adjective, verb, adverb, preposition, conjunction, and interjection.

par·took (pär tůk′), *v.* past tense of **partake:** *We partook of food and drink.*

par·tridge (pär′trij), *n.* any of several game birds of the United States, such as the ruffed grouse and the bobwhite. □ *n., pl.* **par·tridge** or **par·tridg·es.**

part song, song with parts in simple harmony for two or more voices, especially one meant to be sung without an accompaniment.

part-time (pärt′tim′), *adj.* for part of the usual time: *A part-time job helped her finish college.*

partridge—about 1 ft. (30 cm) long

part·way (pärt′wā), *adv.* not completely; only partly: *The bridge is only partway finished.*

par·ty (pär′tē), **1** *n.* a gathering of a group of people to have a good time together: *On her birthday she had a party and invited her friends.* **2** *n.* group of people doing something together: *a dinner party, a scouting party of three soldiers.* **3** *n.* group of people organized to gain political influence and control: *the Democratic Party.* **4** *adj.* of or about a party of people: *They have strong party loyalties.* **5** *n.* one who takes part in, aids, or knows about: *He was a party to our secret.* **6** *n.* each of the persons or sides in a contract, lawsuit, etc. **7** *n.* person: *The party you were calling is on the telephone now.* □ *n., pl.* **par·ties.**

Pas·a·de·na (pas′ə dē′nə), *n.* city in SW California, near Los Angeles.

WORD STORY Pasadena comes from Ojibwa words meaning "of the valley." The people of Pasadena wanted a Native American name for their town, but no Native Americans were living any longer in their area, so they sent to the Lake Superior region for help.

Pas·cal[1] (pa skal′), *n.* **Blaise** (blez), 1623-1662, French philosopher, mathematician, and physicist. ■ **Blaise Pascal** was educated by his father, who refused to teach him any sciences. When his father discovered he had taught himself geometry at age 12, and written a book on it by age 16, he was finally allowed to work in science and mathematics.

Pas·cal[2] or **PASCAL** (pa skal′ *or* pas′kəl), *n.* computer programming language designed to be used in teaching programming and to make programs easier to understand and check.

pa·sha (pə shä′), *n.* a former title used after the name of Turkish civil or military officials of high rank. □ *n., pl.* **pa·shas.**

pasque·flow·er (pask′flou′ər), *n.* any of several plants with slender stems and small cup-shaped purple or white flowers that bloom early in the spring. One kind is the provincial flower of Manitoba.

pass (pas), **1** *v.* to go by; move past: *The parade passed. We passed the big truck. Many people pass our house every day.* **2** *v.* to move on; go: *The days pass quickly. The salesman passed from house to house.* **3** *v.* to go from one to another: *The property passed from the father to the daughter.* **4** *v.* to hand from one to another; hand around: *Please pass the butter.* **5** *v.* to go across or over: *The truck passed the state line.* **6** *v.* to move: *Pass your hand over the velvet and feel how soft it is.* **7** *v.* to be successful in an examination, a course, etc.: *She passed French.* **8** *n.* success in an examination, etc.; passing an examination but without honors. **9** *n.* act of passing; passage. **10** *v.* to cause or allow to go through something; sanction or approve: *The inspector passed the item after examining it.* **11** *v.* to ratify or enact: *pass a bill or law.* **12** *v.* to be approved by a lawmaking group, etc.: *The new law passed the city council.* **13** *v.* to come to an end; die: *The king passed in peace.* **14** *v.* to go beyond; exceed; surpass: *That strange story passes belief.* **15** *v.* to use or spend: *We passed the days pleasantly.* **16** *v.* to change: *Water passes from a liquid to a*

a	hat	ė	term	ô	order	ch	child		
ā	age	i	it	oi	oil	ng	long		a in about
ä	far	ī	ice	ou	out	sh	she		e in taken
â	care	o	hot	u	cup	th	thin	ə	i in pencil
e	let	ō	open	ů	put	ŦH	then		o in lemon
ē	equal	ò	saw	ü	rule	zh	measure		u in circus

solid state when it freezes. **17** *v.* to take place; happen: *Tell me all that passed.* **18** *v.* to be accepted for or as: *She could pass for twenty.* **19** *v.* to express; pronounce: *A judge passes sentence on guilty persons.* **20** *v.* to give a judgment or opinion: *Please pass upon this question.* **21** *v.* to go without notice: *They were rude, but I let it pass.* **22** *n.* a note, license, etc., permitting one to do something: *They needed a pass to enter the fort.* **23** *n.* a free ticket: *She won a pass to the circus.* **24** *n.* state; condition: *Things have come to a strange pass when children give orders to their parents.* **25** *n.* motion of the hand or hands. **26** *n.* a narrow road, path, way, channel, etc.: *A pass crosses the mountains.* **27** in sports: **a** *v.* to throw or hit a ball or puck to another player. **b** *n.* act of throwing or hitting a ball or puck to another player. **28** *v.* to refrain from bidding or playing a hand of cards. **29** *n.* a thrust in fencing. ❑ *n., pl.* **pass·es.** ■ See Usage Note at **past.** —**pass′-er,** *n.* —**pass′less,** *adj.*

bring to pass, to cause to be; accomplish.

come to pass, to take place; happen.

pass away, to come to an end; die.

pass off, to use trickery or dishonesty to get something accepted as something else.

pass on, to die.

pass out, 1 to give out; distribute. **2** to faint; lose consciousness.

pass over, to fail to notice; overlook; disregard.

pass up, 1 to let go by; fail to take advantage of: *pass up a chance to go to college.* **2** to do without; give up; refuse: *I'll pass up the extra piece of pie.*

pass·a·ble (pas′ə bəl), *adj.* **1** fairly good; moderate: *She has a passable knowledge of geography.* **2** able to be traveled over or crossed: *The flooded road was barely passable.* —**pass′a·bly,** *adv.*

pas·sage (pas′ij), *n.* **1** hall or way through a building; passageway. **2** means of passing; way through: *open a passage through a crowd.* **3** right, liberty, or leave to pass: *The guard refused us passage.* **4** act of passing: *Our tastes can change with the passage of time.* **5** piece from a speech, writing, or musical composition: *The author read a passage from his latest book.* **6** journey by ship; voyage: *We had a stormy passage across the Atlantic.* **7** the right to have transportation, especially by boat: *obtain passage for Europe.* **8** act of making into law by a favoring vote of a legislature: *the passage of a bill.*

pas·sage·way (pas′ij wā′), *n.* way along which you can pass. Halls and alleys are passageways.

pass·book (pas′bùk′), *n.* bankbook.

pas·sé (pa sā′), *adj.* out-of-date.

passed ball, (in baseball) a pitched ball that the catcher should have caught but fails to catch, allowing a runner or runners to advance.

pas·sel (pas′əl), *n.* INFORMAL. a numerous group: *a passel of birds, a passel of troubles.*

pas·sen·ger (pas′n jər), *n.* traveler in an aircraft, bus, ship, train, etc., usually one that pays a fare.

passenger pigeon, a kind of wild pigeon of North America, now extinct, that flew in very large flocks.

pass·er·by (pas′ər bī), *n.* one that passes by. ❑ *n., pl.* **pass·ers·by.**

pass-fail (pas′fāl′), *adj.* of or with a grading system in which the usual letter grades are not used, and students either pass or fail.

pass·ing (pas′ing), **1** *adj.* going by; moving past: *a passing train.* **2** *n.* act of someone or something that passes; a going by; a departure: *the passing of spring.* **3** *adj.* done or given quickly; hurried; hasty: *She gave the book only a passing glance.* **4** *adj.* short; brief; not lasting long: *He made only a passing mention of his last visit here.* **5** *adj.* allowing one to pass an examination or test: *75 will be a passing grade.* **6** *n.* means or place of passing. **7** *n.* death: *the passing of a great leader.* —**pass′ing·ly,** *adv.*

in passing, by the way; incidentally.

pas·sion (pash′ən), *n.* **1** very strong feeling: *Hate and fear are passions.* **2** violent anger; rage: *He flew into a passion.* **3** romantic love. **4** very strong liking: *She has a passion for music.* **5** thing for which a strong liking is felt: *Music is her passion.* **6 the Passion, a** the sufferings of Jesus after the Last Supper until he died on the Cross. **b** story of these sufferings retold in music or art. —**pas′sion·less,** *adj.*

pas·sion·ate (pash′ə nit), *adj.* **1** having or showing strong feelings: *She has always been a passionate believer in human rights.* **2** easily moved to a fit or mood of some emotion, especially to anger. **3** resulting from strong feeling: *He made a passionate speech against death sentences.* —**pas′sion·ate·ly,** *adv.* —**pas′sion·ate·ness,** *n.*

pas·sion·flow·er (pash′ən flou′ər), *n.* **1** any of numerous climbing vines of warm regions, grown for their yellow or purple fruit and large, showy flowers. **2** flower of any of these plants.

passion play or **Passion play,** play representing the sufferings and death of Jesus.

pas·sive (pas′iv), **1** *adj.* being acted on without itself acting; not acting in return: *a passive mind, a passive disposition.* **2** *adj.* not resisting; yielding or submitting to the will of another: *The children gave passive obedience to their strict parents.* **3** *adj.* (in grammar) showing the subject as acted on. In "The race was won by her," *was won* is in the passive voice. **4** *n.* a verb form in the passive voice. —**pas′sive·ly,** *adv.* —**pas′sive·ness,** *n.*

passive resistance, peaceful refusal to follow a law, order, etc., especially in opposition to a government or other authority.

passive smoking, the breathing in of tobacco smoke by a nonsmoker, because someone nearby is smoking.

pas·siv·i·ty (pa siv′ə tē), *n.* condition of being passive; lack of action or resistance.

pass·key (pas′kē′), *n.* **1** key for opening several locks. **2** a private key. ❑ *n., pl.* **pass·keys.**

Pass·o·ver (pas′ō′vər), *n.* an annual Jewish holiday in memory of the escape of the Hebrews from Egypt, where they had been enslaved. It comes in March or April and lasts eight days.

pass·port (pas′pôrt), *n.* **1** paper or book giving official permission to travel abroad, under the protection of your own government. **2** anything that gives someone admission or acceptance: *A sense of curiosity can be a passport to knowledge.*

pass·word (pas′wėrd′), *n.* **1** a secret word that allows someone who says it to pass a guard. **2** a series of characters needed to be able to access a computer system.

past (past), **1** *adj.* gone by; ended: *Summer is past. Our troubles are past.* **2** *adj.* just gone by: *the past year, the past century.* **3** *n.* time gone by; time before; what has happened: *forget the past. History is a study of the past.* **4** *n.* a past life or history: *He cannot change his past.* **5** *prep.* beyond; farther on than: *The arrow went past the mark.* **6** *prep.* after; later than: *It is past noon.* **7** *adv.* so as to pass by or beyond: *The cars sped past.* **8** *prep.* beyond in number, amount, or degree. **9** *prep.* beyond the ability, range, scope, etc., of: *absurd fancies that are past belief.* **10** *adj.* having served a term in office: *a past president.* **11** *n.* the past tense or a verb form in the past tense.

USAGE NOTE **Past** began as another way of spelling **passed.** Then people used the different spellings for different meanings. Now **passed** is used only as a verb: *She passed him. Has the bus passed my stop?* **Past** is used as an adjective, adverb, noun, and preposition—but not as a verb.

pas·ta (pä′stə), *n.* dough made of wheat flour, water, salt, and sometimes milk or eggs and shaped into various forms. Macaroni, spaghetti, and ravioli are kinds of pasta. [See Word Story at **paste¹.**]

paste¹ (pāst), **1** *n.* mixture used to stick things together. It is often made of flour and water boiled together. **2** *n.* food prepared from tomatoes, ground nuts, meat, or fish cooked down to a soft, thick mass: *The cook used tomato paste in the sauce.* **3** *v.* to stick with paste. **4** *n.* dough for pastry. **5** *n.* a hard, glassy material used in making imitations of precious stones. ❑ *v.* **past·ed, past·ing.** —**past′er,** *n.*

WORD STORY **Paste¹** comes from a Greek word meaning "porridge." **Pasta** and **pastry** come from the same word. Flour and water make paste, and they also make pasta or pastry. The difference between the words is just a difference in recipe.

paste² (pāst), *v.* SLANG. to hit with a hard, sharp blow. ❑ *v.* **past·ed, past·ing.**

paste·board (pāst′bôrd′), *n.* a stiff material made of sheets of paper pasted together or of paper pulp pressed and dried.

pas·tel (pa stel′), **1** *n.* kind of chalklike crayon used in drawing. **2** *n.* a drawing made with such crayons. **3** *n.* a soft, pale shade of some color. **4** *adj.* soft and pale: *The room was painted pastel blue.*

pas·tern (pas′tərn), *n.* the part of a horse's foot between the fetlock and the hoof.

Pas·teur (pa stėr′), *n.* **Louis,** 1822-1895, French chemist. He invented a way of keeping milk and other foods from spoiling by heating them. He also discovered a vaccine for rabies.

pas·teur·ize (pas′chə riz′), *v.* to heat milk, beer, etc., to a high enough temperature and for a long enough time to destroy harmful bacteria. ❑ *v.* **pas·teur·ized, pas·teur·iz·ing. —pas′teur·i·za′tion,** *n.* **—pas′teur·iz′er,** *n.*

pas·time (pas′tim′), *n.* a pleasant way of passing time; amusement; recreation. Games and sports are pastimes.

past master, person who has much experience in some skill, art, study, etc.; expert.

pas·tor (pas′tər), *n.* minister in charge of a church; spiritual guide. **—pas′tor·ship,** *n.*

WORD STORY **Pastor** comes from a Latin word meaning "to feed." **Pasture** comes from the same word. **Pastor** was Latin for "shepherd," and people have long thought of spiritual leaders as shepherds providing food for the soul. This is why the Bible says that the Lord brings a worshiper "to lie down in green pastures."

pas·tor·al (pas′tər əl), *adj.* **1** of or about shepherds or country life: *The pastoral villagers graze their sheep on the hillsides.* **2** simple or naturally beautiful like the country: *a pastoral landscape.* **3** of or from a pastor: *a pastoral letter.* **—pas′tor·al·ly,** *adv.*

pas·tor·ate (pas′tər it), *n.* **1** position or duties of a pastor. **2** term of service of a pastor. **3** pastors as a group.

past participle, participle that indicates time gone by, or a former action or condition. *Played* in "She has played all day," and *thrown* in "The ball should have been thrown to me" are past participles.

past perfect, 1 a verb tense that describes an action completed before a certain time in the past. In "She had learned to read before she went to school," *had learned* is in the past perfect tense. **2** a verb form in this tense. In the same example, *had learned* is the past perfect of *learn.*

pas·tra·mi (pə strä′mē), *n.* a smoked and well-seasoned cut of beef, especially a shoulder cut.

pas·try (pā′strē), *n.* **1** pies, tarts, or other baked food made with dough rich in butter or other shortening. **2** one piece of such baked food. **3** the dough for such food. ❑ *n., pl.* **pas·tries** for 2. [See Word Story at **paste**[1].]

past tense, 1 tense expressing time gone by, or a former action or condition. **2** a verb form in the past tense.

pas·tur·age (pas′chər ij), *n.* **1** the growing grass and other plants for cattle, sheep, or horses to feed on. **2** pasture land.

pas·ture (pas′chər), **1** *n.* a grassy field or hillside; grasslands on which cattle, sheep, or horses can feed. **2** *n.* grass and other growing plants: *These lands afford good pasture.* **3** *v.* to put cattle, sheep, etc., out to graze: *The farmer pastured his cattle near the stream.* **4** *v.* to feed on growing grass, etc. ❑ *v.* **pas·tured, pas·tur·ing.** [See Word Story at **pastor**.]

past·y[1] (pā′stē), *adj.* **1** like paste. **2** pale. **3** flabby. ❑ *adj.* **past·i·er, past·i·est. —past′i·ness,** *n.*

pas·ty[2] (pas′tē), *n.* pie filled with meat, fish, etc.: *a venison pasty.* ❑ *n., pl.* **pas·ties.**

pat (pat), **1** *v.* to strike or tap lightly with something flat: *He patted the dough into a flat cake.* **2** *v.* to tap with the hand as a sign of sympathy, approval, or affection: *pat a dog.* **3** *n.* a light stroke or tap with the hand or with something flat. **4** *n.* sound made by patting. **5** *n.* a small mass, especially of butter. **6** *adj.* apt; suitable; to the point: *a pat reply.* **7** *adj.* prepared in advance; too ready to seem real: *pat words of sympathy.* ❑ *v.* **pat·ted, pat·ting;** *adj.* **pat·ter, pat·test. —pat′ly,** *adv.* **—pat′ness,** *n.*

have pat or **have down pat,** INFORMAL. to have perfectly; know thoroughly.

pat on the back, praise; compliment.

stand pat, to hold to things as they are and refuse to change.

Pat·a·go·ni·a (pat′ə gō′nē ə), *n.* region in the extreme south of South America. The larger part of Patagonia is in Argentina; the rest is in Chile. **—Pat′a·go′ni·an,** *adj., n.*

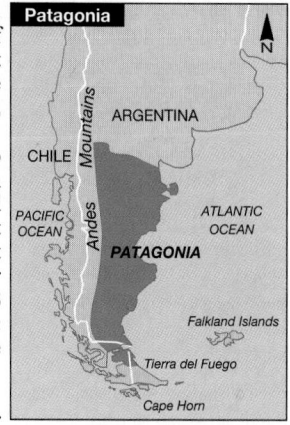
Patagonia

patch (pach), **1** *n.* piece put on to mend a hole or a tear. **2** *n.* a cloth bandage or pad put over a wound or a sore. **3** *n.* a pad over a hurt eye to protect it. **4** *v.* to put patches on; mend; protect or adorn with a patch or patches. **5** *n.* a small, uneven spot: *a patch of brown on the skin.* **6** *n.* piece of ground: *a garden patch.* **7** *n.* scrap or bit of cloth left over. **8** *v.* to make by joining patches or pieces together: *patch a quilt.* **9** *v.* to piece together; make hastily. ❑ *n., pl.* **patch·es. —patch′a·ble,** *adj.* **—patch′er,** *n.*

patch up, 1 to settle: *patch up a quarrel.* **2** to make right hastily or for a time: *patch up a leaking faucet.*

patch·work (pach′wėrk′), **1** *n.* pieces of cloth of various colors or shapes sewed together: *I made a cover of patchwork for the old cushion.* **2** *adj.* made of such pieces of cloth. **3** *n.* anything with a patchwork design: *From the airplane, we saw a patchwork of fields and woods.*

patch·y (pach′ē), *adj.* **1** having or marked by patches. **2** occurring in, forming, or resembling patches. ❑ *adj.* **patch·i·er, patch·i·est. —patch′i·ly,** *adv.* **—patch′i·ness,** *n.*

pate (pāt), *n.* top of the head; head: *a bald pate.*

pa·tel·la (pə tel′ə), *n.* kneecap. ❑ *n., pl.* **pa·tel·las, pa·tel·lae** (pə tel′ē).

pat·ent (pat′nt *for 1-4;* pāt′nt *or* pat′nt *for 5*), **1** *n.* a government grant which gives a person or company sole rights to make, use, or sell a new invention for a certain number of years. **2** *adj.* of or about patents: *patent law.* **3** *v.* to get a patent for: *She patented her new invention.* **4** *n.* invention that is patented. **5** *adj.* open to view or knowledge; evident; plain: *It is patent that cats dislike dogs.* **—pat′ent·a·ble,** *adj.*

pat·ent·ee (pat′n tē′), *n.* person to whom a patent is granted. ❑ *n., pl.* **pat·ent·ees.**

pat·ent leather (pat′nt), leather with a very glossy, smooth surface, usually black.

pa·tent·ly (pāt′nt lē *or* pat′nt lē), *adv.* plainly or openly; clearly; obviously.

pat·ent medicine (pat′nt), **1** any medicine that may be purchased without a doctor's prescription. **2** medicine sold by a company which has a patent on its manufacture and trade name.

pa·ter·nal (pə tėr′nl), *adj.* **1** of or like a father; fatherly: *Their uncle has taken a paternal interest in their welfare since their father died.* **2** related on the father's side of the family: *Everyone has two paternal grandparents and two maternal grandparents.* **3** derived or inherited from your father: *Her blue eyes were a paternal inheritance.* **—pa·ter′nal·ly,** *adv.*

pa·ter·nal·ism (pə tėr′nl iz′əm), *n.* principle or practice of taking responsibility for managing the affairs of a country or group of people as some fathers manage family affairs.

pa·ter·nal·is·tic (pə tėr′nl is′tik), *adj.* marked by paternalism. **—pa·ter′nal·is′ti·cal·ly,** *adv.*

pa·ter·ni·ty (pə tėr′nə tē), *n.* **1** quality of being a father; fatherhood. **2** paternal origin: *King Arthur's paternity was unknown.*

pat·er·nos·ter (pat′ər nos′tər *or* pā′tər nos′tər), *n.* the Lord's Prayer, especially in Latin.

Pat·er·son (pat′ər sən), *n.* city in NE New Jersey.

P

a	hat	ė	term	ô	order	ch	child		
ā	age	i	it	oi	oil	ng	long	ə	a in about
ä	far	ī	ice	ou	out	sh	she		e in taken
â	care	o	hot	u	cup	th	thin		i in pencil
e	let	ō	open	ů	put	ŦH	then		o in lemon
ē	equal	ò	saw	ü	rule	zh	measure		u in circus

path (path), *n.* **1** track made by people or animals walking. It is usually too narrow for cars or trucks. **2** track made to walk upon or to ride horses, bicycles, etc.: *a garden path.* **3** line along which someone or something moves; route: *The moon has a regular path through the sky.* **4** way of acting or behaving; way of life: *paths of glory, paths of ease.* ❑ *n., pl.* **paths** (paᴛʜz or paths). —**path′less,** *adj.*

path (def. 1)

pa·thet·ic (pə thet′ik), *adj.* causing pity; pitiful: *The stray dog was a pathetic sight.* —**pa·thet′i·cal·ly,** *adv.*

path·find·er (path′fīn′dər), *n.* one who finds a path or way, as through a wilderness.

path·o·gen (path′ə jən), *n.* anything capable of producing disease, especially a living microorganism or virus.

path·o·gen·ic (path′ə jen′ik), *adj.* producing disease.

path·o·log·ic (path′ə loj′ik), *adj.* pathological.

path·o·log·i·cal (path′ə loj′ə kəl), *adj.* **1** of or about pathology; dealing with diseases or concerned with diseases: *pathological studies.* **2** due to disease or accompanying a physical disease or mental disorder: *a pathological heart condition, a pathological liar.* —**path·o·log′i·cal·ly,** *adv.*

pa·thol·o·gy (pa thol′ə jē), *n.* **1** study of the causes and nature of diseases. **2** unhealthy conditions caused by a disease. ❑ *n., pl.* **pa·thol·o·gies** for 2. —**pa·thol′o·gist,** *n.*

pa·thos (pā′thos), *n.* quality in speech, writing, music, events, or a scene that causes pity or sadness.

WORD FAMILY Pathos and the words below are related. They all come from a Greek word meaning "feeling" or "suffering."

antipathy	osteopath	pathology	sympathy
apathy	pathetic	psychopath	telepathic
empathy	pathogen	sympathetic	telepathy

path·way (path′wā′), *n.* path.

pa·tience (pā′shəns), *n.* willingness to put up with waiting, pain, trouble, etc.; calm endurance of anything that annoys, troubles, or hurts: *He showed great patience with the quarreling children.*

pa·tient (pā′shənt), **1** *adj.* having or showing patience. **2** *n.* person who is being treated by a doctor. —**pa′tient·ly,** *adv.*

SYNONYM STUDY Patient and tolerant both mean able to bear something. **Patient** means able to bear trouble or suffering, without complaining: *The coach is always patient, even when we make mistakes.* **Tolerant** means able to bear ideas or behavior that you are not used to or do not agree with: *Freedom of speech requires the law to be tolerant of people's opinions and statements.*

pat·i·o (pat′ē ō), *n.* **1** terrace for outdoor eating, lounging, etc. **2** an inner court or yard open to the sky, found especially in houses of Spanish or Spanish American design. ❑ *n., pl.* **pat·i·os.**

pat·ois (pat′wä), *n.* a local or regional dialect: *the patois of the French Canadians.* ❑ *n., pl.* **pat·ois** (pat′wäz).

pa·tri·arch (pā′trē ärk), *n.* **1** father who is the ruler of a family or tribe. **2** a highly respected elderly man. **3** bishop of the highest rank in the Eastern Church and the Roman Catholic Church. ❑ *n., pl.* **pa·tri·archs.**

pa·tri·ar·chal (pā′trē är′kəl), *adj.* **1** of or suitable for a patriarch. **2** under the rule of a patriarch: *a patriarchal church.*

pa·tri·ar·chy (pā′trē är′kē), *n.* **1** a form of society in which the father is head of the family and children belong to the father's clan. **2** any group ruled by men. ❑ *n., pl.* **pa·tri·ar·chies.**

pa·tri·cian (pə trish′ən), **1** *n.* member of the nobility of ancient Rome. **2** *n.* a noble; aristocrat. **3** *adj.* of high social rank; aristocratic. **4** *adj.* suitable for an aristocrat.

pat·ri·cide (pat′rə sīd), *n.* **1** the act of killing your own father. **2** person who kills her or his father. —**pat′ri·cid′al,** *adj.*

Pat·rick (pat′rik), *n.* **Saint,** A.D. 389?-461?, British missionary and bishop. He is the patron saint of Ireland. [**Patrick** comes from a Latin word meaning "noble."]

pat·ri·mo·ny (pat′rə mō′nē), *n.* **1** property inherited from your father or ancestors. **2** property belonging to a church, monastery, or convent. **3** any heritage. ❑ *n., pl.* **pat·ri·mo·nies.** —**pat′ri·mo′ni·al,** *adj.*

pa·tri·ot (pā′trē ət), *n.* person who loves and loyally supports his or her country.

pa·tri·ot·ic (pā′trē ot′ik), *adj.* **1** loving your country. **2** showing love and loyal support of your own country. —**pa′tri·ot′i·cal·ly,** *adv.*

pa·tri·ot·ism (pā′trē ə tiz′əm), *n.* love and loyal support of your country.

pa·trol (pə trōl′), **1** *v.* to go around in an area watching and guarding in order to protect life and property: *The police patrolled once every hour.* **2** *v.* to go around a town, camp, etc., to watch or guard. **3** *n.* act of making the rounds to watch or guard. **4** *n.* persons who patrol: *The patrol was changed at midnight.* **5** *n.* group of soldiers, ships, or airplanes, sent to find out all they can about the enemy. **6** *n.* unit of eight boy or girl scouts. ❑ *v.* **pa·trolled, pa·trol·ling.** —**pa·trol′er,** *n.*

patrol car, car used by the police to patrol an area.

patrol wagon, a closed wagon or truck used by the police for carrying prisoners.

pa·tron (pā′trən), **1** *n.* a regular customer; someone who buys regularly at a certain store or goes regularly to a certain restaurant, hotel, etc. **2** *n.* person who gives approval and support to some person, art, cause, or undertaking: *A well-known patron of art, she has helped several young painters.* **3** *n.* a guardian saint or god; protector. **4** *adj.* guarding; protecting: *a patron saint.*

pa·tron·age (pā′trə nij or pat′rə nij), *n.* **1** regular business given to a store, hotel, etc., by customers. **2** favor, encouragement, or support given by a patron. **3** condescending favor: *an air of patronage.* **4** power to give jobs or favors: *the patronage of a governor, a mayor, or a member of Congress.* **5** political jobs or favors.

pa·tron·ize (pā′trə nīz or pat′rə nīz), *v.* **1** to be a regular customer of; give regular business to: *We patronize our neighborhood stores.* **2** to act as a patron toward; support or protect: *patronize the ballet.* **3** to treat in a condescending way: *We dislike to have anyone patronize us.* ❑ *v.* **pa·tron·ized, pa·tron·iz·ing.** —**pa′tron·iz′er,** *n.* —**pa′tron·iz′ing·ly,** *adv.*

patron saint, saint who is thought of as the special protector of a person, church, city, etc.

pa·troon (pə trün′), *n.* landowner who had certain privileges under the old Dutch governments of New York and New Jersey.

pat·sy (pat′sē), *n.* INFORMAL. an easy victim; the person who is blamed: *If the plan doesn't work out, don't let them make you the patsy.* ❑ *n., pl.* **pat·sies.**

pat·ter[1] (pat′ər), **1** *v.* to make rapid taps: *The rain patters on a windowpane.* **2** *v.* to move with a rapid tapping sound: *Bare feet pattered along the hard floor.* **3** *n.* series of quick taps or the sound they make: *the patter of rain.* —**pat′ter·er,** *n.*

pat·ter[2] (pat′ər), *n.* rapid and easy talk: *a magician's patter.*

pat·tern (pat′ərn), **1** *n.* arrangement of forms and colors; design: *Every rug seemed to have a different pattern.* **2** *n.* a model or guide for something to be made: *I used a paper pattern in cutting the cloth for my coat.* **3** *n.* a fine example; model to be followed: *He was a pattern of generosity.* **4** *n.* way of doing things that is repeated in the same order or manner: *The migration patterns of birds are studied by many scientists.* **5** *v.* to make according to a pattern: *Pattern yourself after your mother.* **6** *n.* any arrangement: *behavior pattern, a speech pattern.* —**pat′tern·less,** *adj.*

pattern (def. 1)

Pat·ton (pat′n), *n.* **George,** 1885-1945, American general in World War II. His nickname was "Old Blood and Guts."

pat·ty (pat′ē), *n.* **1** a small, round, flat piece of food or candy: *a hamburger patty.* **2** a hollow form of pastry filled with chicken, oysters, etc. ❑ *n., pl.* **pat·ties.**

pau·ci·ty (pô′sə tē), *n.* **1** a small number; fewness. **2** a small amount; scarcity; lack.

Paul (pôl), *n.* **Saint,** died A.D. 67?, apostle who started many Christian groups and wrote many books of the New Testament. [**Paul** comes from a Latin word meaning "small."]

Paul·ing (pô′ling), *n.* **Li·nus** (lī′nəs), 1901-1994, American scientist. He won the 1954 Nobel Prize in chemistry and the 1962 Nobel Peace Prize.

Paul VI, 1897-1978, pope from 1963 to 1978. In 1965 he became the first pope to visit the United States.

paunch (pônch), *n.* belly, especially a big belly. ❑ *n., pl.* **paunch·es.**

paunch·y (pôn′chē), *adj.* having a big belly. ❑ *adj.* **paunch·i·er, paunch·i·est. –paunch′i·ness,** *n.*

pau·per (pô′pər), *n.* a very poor person; person supported by charity.

pau·per·ize (pô′pə rīz′), *v.* to make a pauper of. ❑ *v.* **pau·per·ized, pau·per·iz·ing. –pau′per·i·za′tion,** *n.*

pause (pôz), **1** *v.* to stop for a time; wait: *I paused for a moment to look in a store window.* **2** *n.* a brief stop or rest: *After a pause for lunch the employees returned to work. After a short pause I went on reading.* **3** *v.* to dwell; linger: *pause upon a word.* **4** *n.* a sign (◡ or ⌒) above or below a musical note or rest, meaning that it is to be held for a longer time. ❑ *v.* **paused, paus·ing.** [See Word Story at **pose.**]

Pav·a·rot·ti (pä vä rot′ē), *n.* **Lu·ci·a·no** (lü chē än′ō), born 1935, Italian opera singer.

pave (pāv), *v.* **1** to cover a street, sidewalk, etc., with a pavement: *The driveway leading to the garage was paved with concrete.* **2** to make smooth or easy; prepare: *The invention paved the way for new discoveries.* ❑ *v.* **paved, pav·ing. –pav′er,** *n.*

pave·ment (pāv′mənt), *n.* **1** a covering or surface for streets, sidewalks, etc., made of asphalt, concrete, gravel, stones, etc. **2** a paved road.

pa·vil·ion (pə vil′yən), *n.* **1** a light building, usually somewhat open, used for shelter, pleasure, etc.: *The swimmers took shelter from the sudden storm in the beach pavilion.* **2** a large tent with a floor raised on posts. **3** part of a building higher and more decorated than the rest. **4** one of a group of buildings forming a hospital. **5** any building that houses an exhibition at a fair.

pav·ing (pā′ving), *n.* **1** material for pavement. **2** pavement.

Pav·lov (pav′lov), *n.* **Ivan,** 1849-1936, Russian physiologist. He won the 1904 Nobel Prize for physiology or medicine. ■ **Ivan Pavlov** did a series of experiments with dogs. He showed them food while a metronome was clicking and they salivated. Later he had the dogs hear the same clicking metronome, without showing them food, and they still salivated, because they associated the clicking sound with food.

paw (pô), **1** *n.* foot of a four-footed animal with claws. **2** *v.* to strike or scrape with the paws or feet: *The cat pawed the yarn. The horse pawed the ground, eager to be going.* **3** *v.* to handle awkwardly, roughly, or in too familiar a manner: *Stop pawing the tomatoes; you'll bruise them.* **–paw′er,** *n.*

pawl (pôl), *n.* a bar arranged to catch in the teeth of a ratchet so as to prevent backward movement or to allow forward movement.

pawn¹ (pôn), **1** *v.* to leave something with another person as security that borrowed money will be repaid; pledge: *I pawned my watch to buy food until I could get work.* **2** *n.* something left as security. **–pawn′a·ble,** *adj.*

pawn² (pôn), *n.* **1** (in chess) one of the 16 pieces of lowest value. **2** an unimportant person or thing used by someone to gain some advantage.

pawn·bro·ker (pôn′brō′kər), *n.* person who lends money at interest on articles that are left as a pledge that the money will be paid back.

Paw·nee (pô nē′), *n.* member of a tribe of American Indians formerly living in Nebraska and Kansas, now living in Oklahoma. ❑ *n., pl.* **Paw·nee** or **Paw·nees.**

WORD STORY **Pawnee** may come from a word in the language of neighboring Indians meaning "horn." Some Pawnee wore their hair in a stiff ridge like an animal's horn.

pawn·shop (pôn′shop′), *n.* pawnbroker's shop.

paw·paw (pô′pô), *n.* papaw.

Paw·tuck·et (pô tuk′it), *n.* city in NE Rhode Island. [**Pawtucket** comes from an Algonquian word meaning "at the falls in the river." You can imagine why.]

pay (pā), **1** *v.* to give money to for things, work, etc.: *He paid the doctor.* **2** *n.* money given for things or work: *She gets her pay every Friday.* **3** *v.* to give money for: *Pay your fare.* **4** *v.* to give what is due: *She owes it and must pay.* **5** *v.* to return for favors or hurts; reward or punish: *He paid them for their insults by causing them trouble.* **6** *n.* a return for favors or hurts: *Dislike is the pay for being mean.* **7** *v.* to give; offer; make: *pay attention, pay a visit.* **8** *v.* to be worthwhile: *It pays to be polite.* **9** *v.* to yield as a return: *pay a dividend.* **10** *adj.* containing a device for receiving money for use: *a pay telephone.* ❑ *v.* **paid, pay·ing.** [**Pay** comes from a Latin word meaning "peace." **Peace** comes from the same word. One way of living in peace is to pay debts.] **–pay′er,** *n.*

in the pay of, paid by and working for: *The spy was in the pay of a foreign state.*

pay back, 1 to return borrowed money. **2** to give the same treatment as received: *I hope to be able to pay back her help.*

pay off, 1 to give all the money that is owed; pay in full: *He used the money to pay off the loan.* **2** to have a good result: *Years of practice paid off, and she is now a successful violinist.* **3** to get even with; get revenge on.

pay out, to let out a rope. ■ The past tense of **pay out** is **payed out.**

pay up, to pay; pay in full.

SYNONYM STUDY **Pay** and **compensate** both mean to give money in return for something. **Pay** is a general word: *I paid the clerk for the things I bought.* **Compensate** suggests some loss or extra effort: *The oil company will compensate the state for the damages from the oil spill.*

pay·a·ble (pā′ə bəl), *adj.* **1** required to be paid; due: *I must spend $100 soon on bills payable.* **2** to be paid to a specific person.

pay·back (pā′bak′), *n.* INFORMAL. **1** act or process of returning a favor or other deed: *Watering her plants was payback for her picking up my mail.* **2** a revenge: *"It's payback time!" he shouted, and threw the water balloon.*

pay·check (pā′chek′), *n.* check given in payment of wages or salary.

pay·day (pā′dā′), *n.* day on which wages are paid.

pay dirt, earth, rock, etc., containing enough metal to be worth mining.

hit pay dirt, to do or find something that yields a large profit or extremely favorable results: *The company hit pay dirt with its new advertising slogan.*

pay·ee (pā ē′), *n.* person to whom money is paid or is to be paid. ❑ *n., pl.* **pay·ees.**

pay·load (pā′lōd′), *n.* load carried by a vehicle. Passengers are the payload of a bus, train, or airplane. The payload of a rocket is contained in the nose cone, and may be machines or astronauts. The payload of a missile is the warhead.

pay·mas·ter (pā′mas′tər), *n.* person whose job is to pay wages.

pay·ment (pā′mənt), *n.* **1** act of paying: *Payment of bills is very important.* **2** amount paid: *a monthly payment of $250 on our car.* **3** something paid; pay: *The pleasure of helping you is payment enough for me.* **4** reward or punishment.

a	hat	ė	term	ô	order	ch	child		
ā	age	i	it	oi	oil	ng	long		a in about
ä	far	ī	ice	ou	out	sh	she		e in taken
â	care	o	hot	u	cup	th	thin	ə	i in pencil
e	let	ō	open	u̇	put	ᴛʜ	then		o in lemon
ē	equal	ȯ	saw	ü	rule	zh	measure		u in circus

P

pay·off (pā′ôf′), *n.* **1** act of paying wages. **2** time of such payment. **3** returns from an enterprise, action, etc. **4** INFORMAL. climax of a story, situation, etc.

pay-per-view (pā′pər vyü′), *n.* system in which a cable TV company shows a movie or program only to people who have paid extra for it, usually over the telephone.

pay·roll (pā′rōl′), *n.* **1** list of persons to be paid and the amount that each one is to receive. **2** the total amount to be paid to them.

pay television, pay TV.

Pay·ton (pā′tən), *n.* **Wal·ter** (wôl′tər), born 1954, American football player. He rushed for a record 16,726 yards during his career with the Chicago Bears, from 1975 to 1987.

pay TV, system for sending TV programs only to subscribers who pay a monthly fee.

Pb, symbol for lead.

PBS, Public Broadcasting Service.

PC, 1 personal computer. **2** politically correct.

PCR, polymerase chain reaction (a process for making many copies of particular DNA from a small sample, using an enzyme).

PD, Police Department.

Pd, symbol for palladium.

pd., paid.

PE, physical education.

pea (pē), *n.* one of the round seeds inside the long green pod of a climbing garden plant. Peas are eaten as a vegetable. ❑ *n., pl.* **peas.**
as alike as two peas in a pod, exactly alike.

> **WORD STORY** **Pea** is a back-formation from **pease,** which used to mean "a pea." People thought that **pease** was plural, so they used **pea** as the singular. If someone thought **series** was plural and spoke of "a serie," that would be a mistake. But if a lot of people made that same mistake, a back-formation might start.

peace (pēs), *n.* **1** freedom from quarreling or disagreement of any kind; condition of quiet, order, and security: *It was nice to have peace in the house.* **2** freedom from war: *He works for world peace.* **3** agreement between enemies to end war: *The leaders of the warring countries signed the peace.* **4** a quiet condition; calm; stillness: *peace of mind.* [See word history information at **pay.**] ■ Another word that sounds like this is **piece.**
at peace, 1 not in a state of war. **2** not quarreling. **3** in a state of quietness; quiet; peaceful.
hold your peace or **keep your peace,** be silent.

peace·a·ble (pē′sə bəl), *adj.* **1** liking peace; keeping peace: *Peaceable people keep out of quarrels.* **2** peaceful. **—peace′a·bly,** *adv.*

Peace Corps, agency of the U.S. government, established in 1961, which sends trained volunteers to help developing countries.

peace·ful (pēs′fəl), *adj.* **1** full of peace; quiet; calm: *a peaceful vacation.* **2** liking peace; keeping peace: *peaceful neighbors.* **3** of or about peace: *peaceful means.* **—peace′ful·ly,** *adv.* **—peace′ful·ness,** *n.*

peace·keep·ing (pēs′kē′ping), *n.* process of keeping the peace between nations or communities, especially by means of an international military force.

peace·mak·er (pēs′mā′kər), *n.* person who makes peace.

peace officer, police officer, sheriff, or other civil officer responsible for keeping the public peace and enforcing the laws.

peace pipe, pipe smoked by American Indians as a token or pledge of peace; calumet.

peace·time (pēs′tīm′), **1** *n.* a time of peace. **2** *adj.* of a time of peace.

peach (pēch), **1** *n.* a juicy round fruit with fuzz-covered skin and a rough stone called a pit. Peaches grow on trees in temperate climates. **2** *n.* a yellowish pink. **3** *adj.* yellowish pink. **4** *n.* INFORMAL. an attractive or excellent person or thing. ❑ *n., pl.* **peach·es. —peach′like′,** *adj.*

peach (def. 1)

peach·y (pē′chē), *adj.* INFORMAL. fine; wonderful. ❑ *adj.* **peach·i·er, peach·i·est. —peach′i·ness,** *n.*

pea·cock (pē′kok′), *n.* either of two large birds with beautiful green, blue, and gold feathers. The males of one kind have long feathers on their backs with spots like eyes. These feathers may be spread out and held upright like a fan. ■ **Peacock** used to mean only males of these birds. Today most people call these birds peacocks regardless of sex. ❑ *n., pl.* **pea·cocks** or **pea·cock.**

pea green, light green.

pea·hen (pē′hen′), *n.* a female peacock.

pea jacket, a short coat of thick woolen cloth, worn by sailors.

peak (pēk), *n.* **1** the pointed top of a mountain or hill: *We saw the snowy peaks in the distance.* **2** mountain that stands alone: *Pikes Peak.* **3** any pointed end or top: *the peak of a roof.* **4** the highest point: *She has reached the peak of her profession.* **5** the front part or the brim of a cap, which stands out. ■ Other words that sound like this are **peek** and **pique.**

peaked¹ (pēkt), *adj.* having a peak; pointed: *a peaked hat.*

peak·ed² (pē′kid), *adj.* sickly in appearance; wan; thin. **—peak′-ed·ness,** *n.*

peal (pēl), **1** *n.* a loud, long sound: *a peal of thunder.* **2** *n.* the loud ringing of bells. **3** *n.* set of bells; chimes. **4** *v.* to sound out in a long loud sound or ring: *The bells pealed forth their message of joy.* ■ Another word that sounds like this is **peel.**

pea·nut (pē′nut′), *n.* **1** the large, nutlike seed of a plant related to the pea. Peanuts are contained in pods that ripen underground. They are roasted and used as food or pressed to get an oil for cooking. **2** **peanuts,** *pl.* INFORMAL. a relatively small amount of money.

peanut brittle, a hard, easily broken candy that contains peanuts.

peanut butter, food made of roasted peanuts ground until soft and smooth. It is spread on bread, crackers, etc.

peanut oil, oil pressed from peanuts, used especially in cooking and in margarine.

pear (pâr), *n.* a sweet, juicy, yellowish fruit rounded at one end and smaller toward the stem end. Pears grow on trees. ■ Other words that sound like this are **pair** and **pare.**

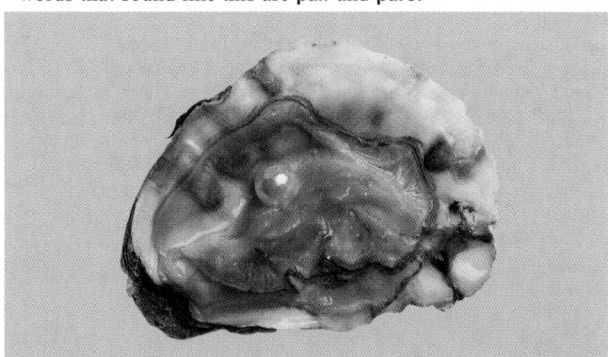

pearl (def. 1)

pearl (pėrl), **1** *n.* a white or nearly white gem that has a soft shine like satin cloth. Pearls are formed inside the shells of a kind of oyster, or of other similar shellfish. **2** *n.* thing that looks like a pearl, such as a dewdrop or a tear. **3** *n.* a very fine one of its kind: *His writings contain many pearls of wisdom.* **4** *n.* a very pale, clear, bluish gray. **5** *adj.* very pale, clear bluish gray. **6** *n.* mother-of-pearl. ■ Another word that sounds like this is **purl. —pearl′-like′,** *adj.*

> **WORD STORY** **Pearl** comes from a Latin word meaning "ham." Pearls were most often found in ancient times in a kind of shellfish shaped like a ham.

pearl gray, a soft, pale, bluish gray.

Pearl Harbor, U.S. naval base near Honolulu, Hawaii. A Japanese attack on it on December 7, 1941, was the immediate cause of American entry into World War II.

pearl·y (pėr′lē), *adj.* like a pearl in color or luster: *She has pearly white teeth.* ❑ *adj.* **pearl·i·er, pearl·i·est. —pearl′i·ness,** *n.*

Pear·y (pir′ē), *n.* **Rob·ert Ed·win** (rob′ərt ed′win), 1856-1920, American naval officer and arctic explorer. He led an expedition to the North Pole in 1909.

peas·ant (pez′nt), **1** *n.* farmer of the working class in Europe, Asia, and Latin America. **2** *adj.* of or about peasants: *peasant labor.*

peas·ant·ry (pez′n trē), *n.* peasants.

pease (pēz), *n.* OLD USE. pea: *pease porridge hot.*

pea·shoot·er (pē′shüt′ər), *n.* tube through which a small, round pellet or pea is blown.

peat (pēt), *n.* kind of turf made of partly rotted moss and plants that have partially turned into carbon, found in bogs. It is dried and used as fertilizer, or in Ireland and Great Britain as fuel. **—peat′like′,** *adj.*

peat moss, sphagnum.

peb·ble (peb′əl), **1** *n.* a small stone, usually worn smooth and round by being rolled about by water. **2** *v.* to pave with pebbles: *pebble a walk.* ❑ *v.* **peb·bled, peb·bling.**

peb·bly (peb′lē), *adj.* having many pebbles; covered with pebbles: *a pebbly beach.* ❑ *adj.* **peb·bli·er, peb·bli·est.**

pe·can (pi kän′ *or* pi kan′), *n.* an olive-shaped nut with a smooth, thin shell, that grows on a kind of hickory tree common in the southern United States. It is good to eat.

pec·ca·dil·lo (pek′ə dil′ō), *n.* a slight sin or fault. ❑ *n., pl.* **pec·ca·dil·loes** or **pec·ca·dil·los.**

pec·ca·ry (pek′ər ē), *n.* any of three hoofed mammals resembling pigs, found in South America and as far north as Texas. The most common kind is also called a javelina. ❑ *n., pl.* **pec·car·ies** or **pec·ca·ry.**

peck[1] (pek), **1** *v.* to strike at and pick up with the beak or a pointed tool: *The hen pecked corn.* **2** *n.* stroke made with the beak or a pointed tool: *The hen gave me a peck.* **3** *v.* to make by striking with the beak or a pointed tool: *Woodpeckers peck holes in trees.* **4** *n.* hole or mark made by pecking. **5** *v.* to make a pecking motion. **6** *n.* a light, quick kiss.

peck at, 1 to try to peck. **2** to eat only a little, bit by bit: *Because she is not feeling well, she just pecks at her food.* **3** to keep criticizing.

peck[2] (pek), *n.* **1** unit of volume for measuring grain, fruit, vegetables, and other dry things, equal to eight quarts or one fourth of a bushel: *a peck of beans, a peck of potatoes.* **2** container that holds a peck. **3** a great deal: *They have had a peck of trouble this year.*

pecking order, order of relative power or status among the members of a group: *As a rookie, she's low in the team's pecking order.*

pec·tin (pek′tən), *n.* any of several substances that occur in ripe fruits. When added to jams and jellies as they are cooking, pectin forms a gel that makes them stiff.

pec·tor·al (pek′tər əl), *adj.* of, in, or on the breast or chest.

pe·cul·iar (pi kyü′lyər), *adj.* **1** strange; odd; unusual: *It was peculiar that the fish market had no fish last Friday.* **2** belonging to one area, person, or thing and not to another; special: *a type of pottery peculiar to the ancient Egyptians.* **—pe·cul′iar·ly,** *adv.*

pe·cu·li·ar·i·ty (pi kyü′lē ar′ə tē), *n.* **1** condition of being peculiar; strangeness; oddness: *We noticed the peculiarity of her manner at once.* **2** some little thing that is strange or odd: *One of his peculiarities is that his eyes are not the same color.* **3** a peculiar or characteristic quality. ❑ *n., pl.* **pe·cu·li·ar·i·ties** for 2,3.

pe·cu·ni·ar·y (pi kyü′nē er′ē), *adj.* of or in the form of money.

ped·a·gog·ic (ped′ə goj′ik), *adj.* of or about teachers or teaching. **—ped′a·gog′i·cal·ly,** *adv.*

ped·a·gog·i·cal (ped′ə goj′ə kəl), *adj.* pedagogic.

ped·a·gogue (ped′ə gog), *n.* **1** teacher of children. **2** a dull, narrow-minded teacher; pedant. [**Pedagogue** comes from Greek words meaning "to lead" and "child."]

ped·a·go·gy (ped′ə gō′jē), *n.* science or art of teaching.

ped·al (ped′l), **1** *n.* lever worked by the foot; the part on which the foot is placed to move any kind of machinery. Organs and pianos have pedals for changing the tone. The two pedals of a bicycle, pushed down one after the other, make it go. **2** *v.* to work or use the pedals of; move by pedals: *He pedaled his bicycle slowly up the hill.* ❑ *v.* **ped·aled, ped·al·ing** or **ped·alled, ped·al·ling.** ■ Another word that sounds like this is **peddle.**

pedal

ped·ant (ped′nt), *n.* **1** person who makes an unnecessary or tiresome display of knowledge. **2** a dull, narrow-minded teacher.

pe·dan·tic (pi dan′tik), *adj.* **1** displaying your knowledge more than is necessary. **2** scholarly in a dull and narrow way. **—pe·dan′ti·cal·ly,** *adv.*

ped·ant·ry (ped′n trē), *n.* **1** an unnecessary or tiresome display of knowledge. **2** too much emphasis on rules, details, etc., especially in learning.

ped·dle (ped′l), *v.* **1** to carry from place to place and sell: *The salesman peddled brushes from house to house.* **2** to sell or deal out in small quantities: *peddle gossip.* **3** to travel about with things to sell. ❑ *v.* **ped·dled, ped·dling.** ■ Another word that sounds like this is **pedal.**

ped·dler (ped′lər), *n.* person who travels about selling things carried in a pack or in a truck, wagon, or cart.

ped·es·tal (ped′i stəl), *n.* **1** base on which a column or a statue stands. **2** base of a tall vase, lamp, etc. **3** any base; support; foundation.

place on a pedestal or **put on a pedestal,** to admire greatly; idolize.

pe·des·tri·an (pə des′trē ən), **1** *n.* person who goes on foot; walker: *Drivers should watch for pedestrians.* **2** *adj.* going on foot; walking. **3** *adj.* without imagination; dull; slow: *a pedestrian style of writing.*

pe·di·at·ric (pē′dē at′rik), *adj.* of or about pediatrics.

pe·di·a·tri·cian (pē′dē ə trish′ən), *n.* doctor who specializes in pediatrics.

pe·di·at·rics (pē′dē at′riks), *n.* branch of medicine dealing with children's diseases and the care of babies and children.

ped·i·cab (ped′ə kab′), *n.* a three-wheeled vehicle with a roofed cab for one or two passengers, pedaled by the driver. Pedicabs are used especially in Southeast Asia.

ped·i·cel (ped′ə səl), *n.* a small stalk or stalklike part.

ped·i·cure (ped′ə kyūr), *n.* care or beauty treatment of the feet and toenails.

ped·i·gree (ped′ə grē′), *n.* **1** list of ancestors of a person or animal; family tree. **2** ancestry; line of descent. ❑ *n., pl.* **ped·i·grees.**

a	hat	ė	term	ô	order	ch	child		
ā	age	i	it	oi	oil	ng	long		a in about
ä	far	ī	ice	ou	out	sh	she		e in taken
â	care	o	hot	u	cup	th	thin	ə	i in pencil
e	let	ō	open	ů	put	ŦH	then		o in lemon
ē	equal	ô	saw	ü	rule	zh	measure		u in circus

P

ped·i·greed (ped′ə grēd′), *adj.* having a known pedigree: *Her dog is pedigreed.* Horses, cows, dogs, and other animals of known and recorded ancestry are called pedigreed stock.

ped·i·ment (ped′ə mənt), *n.* **1** a low, wide, triangular section of some buildings, on the roof and facing forward. A pediment is something like a gable. **2** any similar decorative part on a building, door, bookcase, etc.

pe·dom·e·ter (pi dom′ə tər), *n.* device for recording the number of steps taken and thus measuring the distance traveled.

ped·o·phile (ped′ə fil), *n.* an adult who has sexual feelings for children.

pe·dun·cle (pi dung′kəl), *n.* stalk; stem; stalklike part.

peek (pēk), **1** *v.* to look quickly and slyly; peep: *You must not peek while you are counting in hide-and-seek.* **2** *n.* a quick, sly look: *I took a peek into the oven to see what we were having for dinner.* ■ Other words that sound like this are **peak** and **pique**.

peek·a·boo (pē′kə bü), *n.* a children's game in which someone hides his or her face and then suddenly shows it, calling "peekaboo!"

peel (pēl), **1** *n.* the rind or outer covering of fruit. **2** *v.* to strip the skin, rind, or bark from: *to peel an orange.* **3** *v.* to strip: *I peeled the tape off my hand.* **4** *v.* to come off: *When I was sunburned, my skin peeled.* [Peel comes from a Latin word meaning "hair." Peeling a fruit is like skinning an animal for its fur or hide.] ■ Another word that sounds like this is **peal.** —**peel′a·ble,** *adj.* —**peel′er,** *n.*
keep your eyes peeled, INFORMAL. be on the alert.

peel·ing (pē′ling), *n.* part peeled off or pared off.

peep[1] (pēp), **1** *v.* to look quickly or secretly, often from a hiding place: *My kid sister peeped through the curtains at our guests.* **2** *n.* a quick or secret look: *When no one was around, he took a peep at his birthday presents.* **3** *v.* to look out, as if peeping; come partly out: *Violets peeped among the leaves.* **4** *n.* the first appearance or coming out: *at the peep of day.*

peep[2] (pēp), **1** *n.* the cry of a young bird or chicken; a sound like a chirp or squeak. **2** *v.* to make such a sound; chirp.

peep·er[1] (pē′pər), *n.* INFORMAL. eye.

peep·er[2] (pē′pər), *n.* **1** person or thing that peeps. **2** any of certain frogs that make peeping noises.

peep·hole (pēp′hōl′), *n.* hole through which you may peep.

peer[1] (pir), *n.* **1** person of the same rank, ability, etc., as another; equal: *He is so fine a man that it would be hard to find his peer.* **2** man belonging to the nobility, especially a British nobleman having the rank of duke, marquis, earl, count, viscount, or baron. ■ Another word that sounds like this is **pier.**

peer[2] (pir), *v.* **1** to look closely to see clearly, as a nearsighted person does: *She peered at the tag to read the price.* **2** to come out slightly; peep out: *The sun was peering from behind a cloud.* ■ Another word that sounds like this is **pier.**

peer·age (pir′ij), *n.* **1** rank or dignity of a peer. **2** peers of a country. **3** book giving a list of peers of a country and their family histories.

peer·ess (pir′is), *n.* **1** wife or widow of a peer. **2** woman having the rank of peer in her own right. ❑ *n., pl.* **peer·ess·es.**

peer group, group of people of about the same age or the same social background.

peer·less (pir′lis), *adj.* without an equal; matchless: *His peerless performance won him a prize.*

peeve (pēv), **1** *v.* to make peevish. **2** *n.* an annoyance: *my pet peeve.* ❑ *v.* **peeved, peev·ing.**

pee·vish (pē′vish), *adj.* feeling cross; fretful; complaining: *A peevish child is unhappy and makes others unhappy.* —**pee′vish·ly,** *adv.* —**pee′vish·ness,** *n.*

pee·wee (pē′wē), *n.* a very small person or thing. ❑ *n., pl.* **pee·wees.**

peg (peg), **1** *n.* pin or small bolt of wood, metal, etc., used to fasten parts together, to hang things on, to stop a hole, to make fast a rope or string, to mark the score in a game, etc. **2** *v.* to fasten or hold with pegs: *peg down a tent.* **3** *v.* to mark with pegs. **4** *v.* to work hard: *I pegged away at my studies so that I would get good grades.* **5** *n.* step; degree: *Her work is several pegs above yours.* **6** *n.* a hard throw of a ball, especially in baseball. **7** *v.* to throw hard: *peg the ball to the shortstop.* ❑ *v.* **pegged, peg·ging.**
take down a peg, to lower the pride of; humble.

Peg·a·sus (peg′ə səs), *n.* (in Greek myths) a horse with wings.

peg·board (peg′bôrd′), *n.* board with evenly spaced holes in which pegs or hooks are inserted to hold tools, displays, etc.

Pei (pā), *n.* **I. M.,** born 1917, American architect, born in China. His buildings are often made up of large irregular shapes. He designed the East Building of the National Gallery of Art in Washington, D.C.

P.E.I., Prince Edward Island.

Pei·ping (pā′ping′ *or* bā′ping′), *n.* a former name of **Beijing.**

pe·jo·ra·tive (pe jôr′ə tiv), *adj.* tending to belittle; negative; not favorable: *pejorative language.* —**pe·jor′a·tive·ly,** *adv.*

Pe·kin·ese (pē′kə nēz′), *n.* Pekingese. ❑ *n., pl.* **Pe·kin·ese.**

Pe·king (pē′king′), *n.* a former name of **Beijing.**

Pe·king·ese (pē′kə nēz′), *n.* a small dog with long hair and a broad, flat face. ❑ *n., pl.* **Pe·king·ese.** Also, **Pekinese.**

pe·koe (pē′kō), *n.* kind of black tea form Sri Lanka or India, made from very young leaves.

Pe·lé (pā′lā), *n.* born 1940, Brazilian soccer player. He scored 1281 goals in his career, and is the only soccer player to have played on three world championship teams.

Pekingese—about 1 ft. (30 cm) high at the shoulder

pelf (pelf), *n.* money or riches, thought of as bad or degrading.

pel·i·can (pel′ə kən), *n.* any of several kinds of very large, fish-eating water birds with huge bills and pouches on the underside of the bills for scooping up fish.

pel·la·gra (pə lag′rə), *n.* disease marked by inflammation and scaling of the skin, nervousness, and sometimes mental disorders. It is caused by a lack of nicotinic acid in the diet.

pel·let (pel′it), *n.* **1** a little ball of mud, paper, food, medicine, etc.; pill. **2** bullet. —**pel′let·like′,** *adj.*

pell-mell or **pell·mell** (pel′mel′), **1** *adv.* in a rushing, tumbling mass or crowd: *The children dashed pell-mell down the beach and into the waves.* **2** *adv.* in headlong haste: *He ran pell-mell down the street.* **3** *adj.* headlong; tumultuous.

Pel·o·pon·ne·sus (pel′ə pə nē′səs), *n.* peninsula forming the S part of Greece. —**Pel·o·pon·ne·sian** (pel′ə pə nē′zhən), *adj., n.*

pe·lo·ta (pe lō′tə), *n.* **1** jai alai. **2** ball used in jai alai. ❑ *n., pl.* **pe·lo·tas** for 2.

pelt[1] (pelt), **1** *v.* to throw things at; attack: *Children were pelting each other with snowballs.* **2** *v.* to beat heavily: *The rain came pelting down.* **3** *v.* to throw: *The clouds pelted rain upon us.*

pelt[2] (pelt), *n.* skin of a sheep, goat, or other hairy or woolly animal, before it is tanned. —**pelt′less,** *adj.*

pel·vic (pel′vik), *adj.* of or about the pelvis.

pel·vis (pel′vis), *n.* **1** the basin-shaped cavity formed by the hipbones and the end of the backbone. **2** bones forming this cavity. ❑ *n., pl.* **pel·vis·es, pel·ves** (pel′vēz).

Pem·ba (pem′bə), *n.* island off E Africa. It is part of Tanzania.

pem·mi·can (pem′ə kən), *n.* dried meat pounded into a paste with melted fat. It is lightweight and stays good for a long time, so it is useful on journeys.

pen[1] (pen), **1** *n.* tool used for writing or drawing with ink. Most pens are either ballpoint pens or fountain pens. **2** *v.* to write: *I penned a brief note.* ❑ *v.* **penned, pen·ning.** —**pen′like′,** *adj.*

WORD STORY Pen[1] comes from a Latin word meaning "a feather." The first pens were made from feathers. **Penknife** comes from the use of small knives to sharpen the points of feather pens.

pen[2] (pen), **1** *n.* a small, closed yard for cows, sheep, pigs, chickens, etc. **2** *n.* enclosure for keeping a baby, a dog, etc., confined. **3** *v.* to shut in a pen. **4** *v.* to shut in; confine closely: *The fox was penned in a corner with no way of escape.* ❑ *v.* **penned, pen·ning.** —**pen′like′,** *adj.*

pen[3] (pen), *n.* SLANG. penitentiary.

pe·nal (pē′nl), *adj.* **1** of, about, or given as punishment: *penal laws, penal labor.* **2** liable to be punished: *Robbery is a penal offense.* —**pe′nal·ly,** *adv.*

pe·nal·ize (pē′nl īz *or* pēn′l īz), *v.* **1** to declare punishable by law or by rule; set a penalty for: *Fouls are penalized in many games.* **2** to inflict a penalty on; punish: *Our football team was penalized five yards for being offside.* ❑ *v.* **pe·nal·ized, pe·nal·iz·ing.** —**pe′nal·iz′a·ble,** *adj.* —**pe′nal·i·za′tion,** *n.*

pen·al·ty (pen′l tē), *n.* **1** punishment imposed by law: *The penalty for speeding is usually a fine.* **2** disadvantage imposed on a side or player for breaking the rules of some game or contest. **3** unfortunate or painful result of some act or condition: *the penalties of being poor.* ❑ *n., pl.* **pen·al·ties.**

penalty box, a seating area to the side of an hockey rink where players are sent after receiving a penalty.

pen·ance (pen′əns), *n.* **1** punishment that someone endures to show sorrow for sin, to make up for a wrong done, and to obtain pardon for sin. **2** any act done to show that you are sorry or repent.

pence (pens), *n.* a plural of **penny** (defs. 2 and 3).

pen·chant (pen′chənt), *n.* a strong taste or liking; inclination: *a penchant for taking long walks.*

pen·cil (pen′səl), **1** *n.* tool used for writing or drawing, made of a slender rod of graphite enclosed in wood or in a metal tube. **2** *v.* to mark or write with a pencil. **3** *n.* stick of coloring matter. ❑ *v.* **pen·ciled, pen·cil·ing.** —**pen′cil·like′,** *adj.*

WORD STORY **Pencil** comes from a Latin word meaning "a tail." A paintbrush looks something like a tail, and **pencil** used to mean "little brush." When people invented graphite pencils, the word changed meaning, about 400 years ago.

pend·ant (pen′dənt), **1** *n.* a hanging ornament, such as a locket. **2** *adj.* pendent.

pend·ent (pen′dənt), *adj.* **1** hanging: *the pendent branches of a willow.* **2** overhanging. **3** pending. —**pend′ent·ly,** *adv.*

pend·ing (pen′ding), **1** *adj.* waiting to be decided or settled: *while the agreement was pending.* **2** *prep.* while waiting for; until: *Pending your return, we'll get everything ready.* **3** *prep.* during: *pending the investigation.* **4** *adj.* likely to happen soon; threatening; about to occur.

pen·du·lous (pen′jə ləs), *adj.* **1** hanging loosely: *The oriole builds a pendulous nest.* **2** swinging. —**pen′du·lous·ly,** *adv.* —**pen′du·lous·ness,** *n.*

pen·du·lum (pen′jə ləm), *n.* a weight hung from a fixed point so that it is free to swing to and fro. The movement of the works of a tall clock is often timed by a pendulum.

Pe·nel·o·pe (pə nel′ə pē), *n.* (in Greek legends) the faithful wife of Ulysses. She waited twenty years for his return, meanwhile rejecting many suitors.

WORD STORY **Penelope** comes from a Greek word meaning "weaver." The Penelope of legend told her suitors that she would marry one of them when she finished the weaving she had on her loom. Each night she undid the part she had woven during the day.

pen·e·tra·ble (pen′ə trə bəl), *adj.* able to be penetrated. —**pen′e·tra·bil′i·ty,** *n.* —**pen′e·tra·bly,** *adv.*

pen·e·trate (pen′ə trāt), *v.* **1** to get into or through: *The bullet penetrated this wall, and two inches into the one beyond.* **2** to see through: *Our eyes could not penetrate the darkness.* **3** to soak through; spread through: *The rain penetrated our clothes. The odor penetrated the whole house.* **4** to see into; understand: *I could not penetrate the mystery.* ❑ *v.* **pen·e·trat·ed, pen·e·trat·ing.** —**pen′e·tra′tor,** *n.*

SYNONYM STUDY **Penetrate** and **pierce** both mean to go through something. **Penetrate** suggests force: *The drill penetrated the rock.* **Pierce** suggests a sharp point: *She had her ears pierced for earrings.*

pen·e·trat·ing (pen′ə trā′ting), *adj.* **1** sharp; piercing. **2** having an acute mind; understanding thoroughly. —**pen′e·trat′ing·ly,** *adv.*

pen·e·tra·tion (pen′ə trā′shən), *n.* **1** act or power of penetrating. **2** sharpness of intellect; insight.

pen·e·tra·tive (pen′ə trā′tiv), *adj.* penetrating; piercing; acute; keen. —**pen′e·tra′tive·ly,** *adv.* —**pen′e·tra′tive·ness,** *n.*

pen·guin (pen′gwin), *n.* any of several web-footed, short-legged seabirds that have black and white plumage and wings like flippers, which they use for diving and swimming, not for flying. Penguins live in Antarctica and other cold areas of the Southern Hemisphere.

pen·i·cil·lin (pen′ə sil′ən), *n.* any of a group of antibiotics made from penicillium molds and used to treat diseases caused by certain bacteria.

pen·i·cil·li·um (pen′ə sil′ē əm), *n.* any of several green or bluish green fungi that grow on citrus fruits, cheeses, etc. ❑ *n., pl.* **pen·i·cil·li·ums, pen·i·cil·li·a** (pen′ə sil′ē ə).

pe·nin·su·la (pə nin′sə lə), *n.* piece of land almost surrounded by water, or extending far out into the water. Florida is a peninsula. ❑ *n., pl.* **pe·nin·su·las.** —**pe·nin′su·lar,** *adj.*

pe·nis (pē′nis), *n.* the sex organ of a male animal. Urine leaves the body of male mammals through the penis. ❑ *n., pl.* **pe·nis·es, pe·nes** (pē′nēz).

pen·i·tence (pen′ə təns), *n.* a feeling of sorrow for sinning or doing wrong; repentance.

pen·i·tent (pen′ə tənt), **1** *adj.* sorry for sinning or doing wrong; repenting: *The penitent child promised never to cheat again.* **2** *n.* person who is sorry for sin, especially someone who confesses and does penance under the direction of a church. —**pen′i·tent·ly,** *adv.*

pen·i·ten·tial (pen′ə ten′chəl), *adj.* of or about penitence or penance. —**pen′i·ten′tial·ly,** *adv.*

pen·i·ten·tia·ry (pen′ə ten′chər ē), **1** *n.* prison for criminals, especially a state or federal prison. **2** *adj.* making you liable to punishment in a prison: *a penitentiary offense.* ❑ *n., pl.* **pen·i·ten·tiar·ies.**

pen·knife (pen′nīf′), *n.* a small pocketknife. ❑ *n., pl.* **pen·knives** (pen′nīvz′). [See Word Story at **pen**¹.]

pen·man·ship (pen′mən ship), *n.* writing with pen, pencil, etc.; handwriting.

Penn (pen), *n.* **William,** 1644-1718, English Quaker who founded the colony of Pennsylvania.

Penn. or **Penna.,** Pennsylvania.

pen name, name used by a writer instead of his or her real name; pseudonym.

pen·nant (pen′ənt), *n.* **1** flag, usually long and narrow, used on ships, in signaling, as a school banner, etc. **2** flag that indicates championship, especially of a professional baseball league season.

pen·ni·less (pen′ē lis), *adj.* without a cent of money; very poor: *I've lost all my money and now I'm penniless.* ■ See Synonym Study at **poor.** —**pen′ni·less·ly,** *adv.* —**pen′ni·less·ness,** *n.*

pen·non (pen′ən), *n.* **1** a long, usually triangular flag, originally carried on the lance of a knight. **2** any flag or banner.

Penn·syl·va·nia (pen′səl vā′nyə), *n.* one of the northeastern states of the United States. *Abbreviation:* PA or Pa. *Capital:* Harrisburg. [**Pennsylvania** is named for William Penn and a Latin word meaning "woods." The name was given by King Charles II of England, who gave Penn the land for the colony.] —**Penn′syl·van′ian,** *n.*

Pennsylvania Dutch, 1 the descendants of immigrants of the 1600s and 1700s to southeastern Pennsylvania from southern Germany and Switzerland. **2** dialect of German with English intermixed, spoken by them.

Penn·syl·va·ni·an (pen′sil vā′nyən), *n.* (in geology) time between about 310 million and 260 million years ago. During this time, reptiles appeared, amphibians were common, and huge, swampy forests grew that would later turn into coal.

pen·ny (pen′ē), *n.* **1** cent. 100 pennies make one dollar. **2** a British coin. 100 pennies make one pound. **3** a former British coin equal to one twelfth of a shilling. Until 1971, 240 pennies made one pound. ❑ *n., pl.* **pen·nies** (or **pence** for 2,3).

a pretty penny, INFORMAL. a large sum of money.

pen·ny·weight (pen′ē wāt′), *n.* 24 grains or ¹⁄₂₀ of an ounce in troy weight.

pen·ny-wise (pen′ē wīz′), *adj.* saving in regard to small sums.

penny-wise and pound-foolish, saving in small expenses and wasteful in big ones.

a	hat	ė	term	ô	order	ch	child		a in about
ā	age	i	it	oi	oil	ng	long		e in taken
ä	far	ī	ice	ou	out	sh	she	ə	i in pencil
â	care	o	hot	u	cup	th	thin		o in lemon
e	let	ō	open	u̇	put	ᴛʜ	then		u in circus
ē	equal	ȯ	saw	ü	rule	zh	measure		

pen·ny·worth (pen′ē wėrth′), *n.* **1** as much as can be bought for a penny. **2** a small amount: *Give me a pennyworth of advice.*

Pe·nob·scot (pə nob′skot), *n.* **1** river flowing from NW Maine into the Atlantic. **2** member of an American Indian tribe living near this river. □ *n., pl.* **Pe·nob·scot** or **Pe·nob·scots** for 2. [Penobscot comes from an Algonquian word meaning "tilted rocks," used to describe a part of the river with steep banks.]

pen pal, person with whom you exchange letters regularly, often in another country and without ever having met.

pen·sion (pen′shən), **1** *n.* a regular payment by an employer or government to someone who is retired or disabled. **2** *v.* to give a pension to: *The company pensioned several employees who were sixty-five years old.* —**pen′sion·a·ble,** *adj.*

pen·sion·er (pen′shə nər), *n.* person who receives a pension.

pen·sive (pen′siv), *adj.* thoughtful in a serious or sad way. —**pen′sive·ly,** *adv.* —**pen′sive·ness,** *n.*

pent (pent), *adj.* closely shut in; confined: *pent up inside all winter.*

pen·ta·gon (pen′tə gon), *n.* **1** a plane figure having five sides and five angles. **2 the Pentagon,** a five-sided building that is the headquarters of the Department of Defense of the United States. It is in Arlington, Virginia. —**pen·tag·o·nal** (pen tag′ə nəl), *adj.*

pentagons

pen·tam·e·ter (pen tam′ə tər), *n.* line of poetry having five feet or measures.
EXAMPLE: "If win|ter comes, | can spring | be far | behind?"

Pen·ta·teuch (pen′tə tük), *n.* the first five books of the Bible: Genesis, Exodus, Leviticus, Numbers, and Deuteronomy.

pen·tath·lon (pen tath′lən), *n.* an athletic contest consisting of five different events entered by each contestant.

Pen·te·cost (pen′tə kòst), *n.* **1** the seventh Sunday after Easter; Whitsunday. Pentecost is a Christian festival in memory of the descent of the Holy Spirit upon the apostles. **2** Shavuot. [Pentecost comes from a Greek word meaning "fiftieth," because it is nearly fifty days after Easter.]

Pen·te·cos·tal (pen′tə kòs′təl), **1** *adj.* of or belonging to certain churches that encourage members to be inspired by the Holy Spirit, as the Apostles were. **2** *n.* member of a Pentecostal church.

pent·house (pent′hous′), *n.* apartment or house built on the top of a building. □ *n., pl.* **pent·hous·es** (pent′hou′ziz).

pent-up (pent′up′), *adj.* shut up; closely confined: *Her pent-up anger could no longer be restrained, and she walked out, slamming the door.*

pe·num·bra (pi num′brə), *n.* the faint shadow beside the complete shadow cast by the sun, moon, or the earth during an eclipse. □ *n., pl.* **pe·num·bras, pe·num·brae** (pi num′brē).

pe·nur·i·ous (pi nùr′ē əs), *adj.* stingy about spending or giving money. —**pe·nur′i·ous·ly,** *adv.* —**pe·nur′i·ous·ness,** *n.*

pen·ur·y (pen′yər ē), *n.* very great poverty.

pe·on (pē′on), *n.* **1** (in Spanish America) someone doing work that requires little skill. **2** (earlier, in the southwestern United States and Mexico) a worker held for service to work off a debt. **3** someone who does humble, unpleasant tasks; drudge. ■ This meaning of **peon** is often considered offensive.

pe·on·age (pē′ə nij), *n.* **1** condition or service of a peon. **2** practice of holding persons to work off debts.

pe·o·ny (pē′ə nē), *n.* any of several garden plants with large red, pink, or white flowers. □ *n., pl.* **pe·o·nies.**

peo·ple (pē′pəl), **1** *n.pl.* men, women, and children; human beings; persons: *There were ten people present.* **2** *n.* race; nation: *the peoples of Asia, the American people.* **3** *n.pl.* group of citizens of a state; the public. **4** *n.pl.* persons of a place, class, or group: *City people live in a noisier environment than country people do.* **5** *n.pl.* the common people; lower classes: *The French nobles oppressed the people.* **6** *n.pl.* persons in relation to a superior: *a queen and her people.* **7** *n.pl.* family; relatives: *He spends his holidays with his people.* **8** *v.* to fill with people; populate: *Immigrants from many nations peopled the Americas.* □ *n., pl.* **peo·ples** for 2; *v.* **peo·pled, peo·pling.**

peony

USAGE NOTE **People** is a plural noun except when it means "one population group, considered among many groups." This is definition 2, and it is a singular noun. It has a plural form, **peoples,** meaning "several population groups, considered as groups." If the groups have their own names and clear identities, they are peoples. But most of the time, human beings are people.

Pe·o·ri·a (pē ôr′ē ə), *n.* city in central Illinois.

pep (pep), **1** *n.* spirit; energy; vim. **2** *v.* **pep up,** to fill or inspire with energy, etc.; put new life into. □ *v.* **pepped, pep·ping.** [Pep was shortened from **pepper.**]

pep·per (pep′ər), **1** *n.* a seasoning with a hot, spicy taste, made from the berries of a tropical plant and used for soups, meats, vegetables, etc. **Black pepper** is made from whole berries; **white pepper** is made from husked berries. **2** *n.* any of several hollow red or green vegetables with many seeds and mild or hot taste. They are eaten raw, cooked, pickled, or dried and ground for use as seasoning. **3** *v.* to season or sprinkle with pepper. **4** *v.* to sprinkle thickly: *His face is peppered with freckles.* **5** *v.* to hit with items sent thick and fast: *Reporters peppered the mayor with questions.*

pep·per·corn (pep′ər kôrn′), *n.* one of the dried berries that are ground up to make pepper.

pep·per·mint (pep′ər mint), *n.* **1** herb grown for its tasty oil, used in medicine and in candy. **2** this oil. **3** candy flavored with this oil.

pep·per·o·ni (pep′ə rō′nē), *n.* a very highly spiced Italian sausage. □ *n., pl.* **pep·per·o·nis** or **pep·per·o·ni.**

pep·per·y (pep′ər ē), *adj.* **1** full of pepper; like pepper. **2** hot; sharp. **3** having a hot temper; easily made angry. **4** angry and sharp: *peppery words.* —**pep′per·i·ness,** *n.*

pep·py (pep′ē), *adj.* full of pep; energetic; lively. □ *adj.* **pep·pi·er, pep·pi·est.** —**pep′pi·ly,** *adv.* —**pep′pi·ness,** *n.*

pep·sin (pep′sən), *n.* **1** enzyme in the juice of the stomach that helps to digest meat, eggs, cheese, and other proteins. **2** preparation containing this enzyme, used as medicine to help digestion.

pep talk, speech or short talk designed to fill or inspire with energy or enthusiasm.

pep·tic (pep′tik), *adj.* **1** made worse by the action of digestive juices: *peptic ulcer.* **2** of or for the digestion of food; digestive.

Pe·quot (pē′kwot), *n.* member of a tribe of American Indians living in Connecticut. □ *n., pl.* **Pe·quot** or **Pe·quots.** [Pequot comes from an Algonquian word meaning "destroyers," because of their success in battle.]

per (pər; *stressed* pėr), *prep.* **1** for each; for every: *two dollars per pound.* **2** by means of; by; through: *I send this per my son.* **3** according to: *Per your instructions, we are shipping your order express.* ■ Another word that can sound like this is **purr.**

per·am·bu·late (pə ram′byə lāt), v. 1 to walk through. 2 to walk or travel about; stroll. 3 to walk through and examine. ❑ v. **per·am·bu·lat·ed, per·am·bu·lat·ing. —per·am·bu·la′tion,** n.

per·am·bu·la·tor (pə ram′byə lā′tər), n. BRITISH. a baby's carriage.

per an·num (pər an′əm), per year; for each year; yearly: *Her salary was $40,000 per annum.*

per·cale (pər kāl′), n. a closely woven cotton cloth with a smooth finish.

per cap·i·ta (pər kap′ə tə), for each person: *a poor country with a low per capita income.*

per·ceive (pər sēv′), v. 1 to be aware of through the senses; see, hear, taste, smell, or feel: *Many animals do not perceive color as we do.* 2 to take in with the mind; understand; observe: *I soon perceived that I could not make them change their minds.* ❑ v. **per·ceived, per·ceiv·ing. —per·ceiv′a·ble,** adj. **—per·ceiv′a·bly,** adv. **—per·ceiv′er,** n.

per·cent (pər sent′), n.sing. or pl. 1 parts in each hundred; hundredths. 5 percent is 5 of each 100, or ⁵/₁₀₀ of the whole. 2 percentage: *A large percent of the state's apple crop was ruined.*

per cent, percent.

per·cent·age (pər sen′tij), n.sing. or pl. 1 rate or proportion of each hundred; part of each hundred; percent: *What percentage of children were absent?* 2 part or proportion: *Illness caused a large percentage of children to be absent.* 3 allowance, commission, discount, rate of interest, etc., figured by percent. ■ See Usage Note at **percent.**

per·cen·tile (pər sen′tīl), n. any one of a hundred sections into which a group is divided, each section of equal size but ranking differently in score, performance, weight, or other measure: *A student in the ninetieth percentile of a class on a test is in the top ten percent.*

per·cep·ti·ble (pər sep′tə bəl), adj. able to be perceived: *The other ship was barely perceptible in the fog.* **—per·cep′ti·bly,** adv.

per·cep·tion (pər sep′shən), n. 1 the understanding that is the result of perceiving: *She had a clear perception of the problem, and soon solved it.* 2 power of perceiving: *a keen perception.* 3 act of being aware of something: *My perception of time became confused when I flew from New York to Hawaii.*

per·cep·tive (pər sep′tiv), adj. able to perceive; intelligent: *a perceptive audience.* **—per·cep′tive·ly,** adv. **—per·cep′tive·ness,** n.

perch[1] (pėrch), 1 n. a bar, branch, or anything else on which a bird can come to rest. 2 v. to come to rest; settle: *A robin perched on our porch railing.* 3 n. a rather high seat or position. 4 v. to sit rather high: *I perched on a stool.* 5 v. to place high up: *a village perched high among the hills.* ❑ n., pl. **perch·es. —perch′er,** n.

perch[2] (pėrch), n. 1 any of numerous small freshwater fishes, used for food, especially the North American **yellow perch.** 2 any similar saltwater fish. ❑ n., pl. **perch** or **perch·es.**

per·chance (pər chans′), adv. perhaps.

per·co·late (pėr′kə lāt), v. 1 to drip or drain through small holes or spaces: *Let the coffee percolate for seven minutes.* 2 to filter through; permeate: *Water percolates sand.* ❑ v. **per·co·lat·ed, per·co·lat·ing. —per·co·la′tion,** n.

per·co·la·tor (pėr′kə lā′tər), n. kind of coffeepot in which boiling water drains over and over again through ground coffee.

per·cus·sion (pər kush′ən), n. 1 act of striking one object against another with force; stroke; blow. 2 shock made by the striking of one object against another with force; impact. 3 the striking of sound upon the ear.

percussion cap, a small cap containing powder. When struck, it explodes and sets off a larger charge.

percussion instrument, a musical instrument played by striking it, such as a drum, cymbal, or piano.

per·cus·sion·ist (pər kush′ə nist), n. person who plays a percussion instrument.

per di·em (pər dē′əm), per day; for each day: *Rental of the boat per diem was $50.*

per·di·tion (pər dish′ən), n. (in Christian use) loss of your soul and the joys of heaven.

per·e·grine (per′ə grən), n. a large, very fast, powerful falcon.

pe·remp·to·ry (pə remp′tər ē), adj. 1 leaving no choice; decisive; final; absolute: *a peremptory decree.* 2 allowing no denial or refusal: *a peremptory command.* 3 harsh in manner; dictatorial: *a peremptory professor.* **—pe·remp′tor·i·ly,** adv. **—pe·remp′tor·i·ness,** n.

pe·ren·ni·al (pə ren′ē əl), 1 adj. lasting for a very long time; enduring: *the perennial beauty of the hills.* 2 adj. living more than two years: *perennial plants.* 3 n. a plant that lives more than two years. Roses are perennials. 4 adj. lasting through the whole year: *a perennial stream.* **—per·en′ni·al·ly,** adv.

peregrine—18 in. (46 cm) long

per·fect (pėr′fikt *for adj.;* pər fekt′ *for verb*), 1 adj. without defect; not spoiled at any point; faultless: *a perfect spelling paper, a perfect apple, a perfect life.* 2 v. to remove all faults from; make perfect; add the finishing touches to: *perfect an invention. The artist was perfecting his picture.* 3 adj. completely skilled; expert: *a perfect golfer.* 4 adj. having all its parts; whole; complete: *The set was perfect; nothing was missing or broken.* 5 adj. exact: *a perfect copy, a perfect circle.* 6 v. to carry through; complete: *perfect a plan.* 7 adj. entire; complete; absolute: *a perfect stranger.* 8 adj. (in grammar) showing an action or event completed at the time of speaking or at the time spoken of. Three perfect tenses in English are: **present perfect,** *I have eaten;* **past perfect,** *I had eaten;* and **future perfect,** *I will have eaten.* **—per·fect′er,** n. **—per′fect·ly,** adv. **—per′fect·ness,** n.

per·fect·i·ble (pər fek′tə bəl), adj. capable of becoming, or being made, perfect. **—per·fect′i·bil′i·ty,** n.

per·fec·tion (pər fek′shən), n. 1 perfect condition; highest excellence; faultlessness: *Her goal was to achieve perfection in her work.* 2 a perfect person or thing. 3 act of making complete or perfect: *Perfection of our plans will take another week.*

to perfection, perfectly: *She played the difficult music to perfection.*

per·fec·tion·ist (pər fek′shə nist), n. person who is not content with anything that is not perfect or nearly perfect.

perfect number, a positive whole number that is equal to the sum of its factors, not including itself. Six, being the sum of its factors one, two, and three, is a perfect number.

perfect square, number having a whole number as its square root.

per·fid·i·ous (pər fid′ē əs), adj. deliberately faithless; treacherous. **—per·fid′i·ous·ly,** adv. **—per·fid′i·ous·ness,** n.

per·fo·rate (pėr′fə rāt′), v. 1 to make a hole or holes through: *Bullets perforated the target.* 2 to make a row or rows of holes through: *Sheets of postage stamps are perforated.* ❑ v. **per·fo·rat·ed, per·fo·rat·ing. —per′fo·ra′tor,** n.

a	hat	ė	term	ô	order	ch	child		
ā	age	i	it	oi	oil	ng	long		a in about
ä	far	ī	ice	ou	out	sh	she	ə	e in taken
â	care	o	hot	u	cup	th	thin		i in pencil
e	let	ō	open	ù	put	ᴛʜ	then		o in lemon
ē	equal	ò	saw	ü	rule	zh	measure		u in circus

per·fo·ra·tion (pėr′fə rā′shən), *n.* **1** hole bored or punched through something: *the perforations in the top of a salt shaker.* **2** act of perforating.

per·force (pər fôrs′), *adv.* by necessity; necessarily.

per·form (pər fôrm′), *v.* **1** to do; carry out: *Perform your duties well.* ■ See Synonym Study at **do**[1]. **2** to put into effect; carry out: *The surgeon performed an operation.* **3** to go through; render: *perform a piece of music.* **4** to act, play, sing, or do tricks in public: *The school band performed at yesterday's assembly.* —**per·form′a·ble**, *adj.*

per·form·ance (pər fôr′məns), *n.* **1** act of carrying out; doing; performing: *The firefighter was injured in the performance of his duties.* **2** thing performed; act; deed: *The child's kicks and screams made a disgraceful performance.* **3** the giving of a play, concert, circus, or other show: *The performance is at 8 o'clock.*

per·form·er (pər fôr′mər), *n.* person who performs, especially someone who performs to entertain others. Singers, dancers, and magicians are performers.

per·fume (pėr′fyüm *or* pər fyüm′ *for noun;* pər fyüm′ *for verb*), **1** *n.* liquid having a sweet smell. **2** *v.* to put a sweet-smelling liquid on. **3** *n.* a sweet smell; fragrance: *the perfume of flowers.* **4** *v.* to give a sweet smell to; fill with sweet odor: *Flowers perfumed the air.* ❑ *v.* **per·fumed, per·fum·ing.**

WORD STORY **Perfume** comes from Latin words meaning "through" and "smoke." In old times, people often gave rooms a sweet smell by burning incense. Other kinds of sweet-smelling substances were named for that smoke.

per·func·to·ry (pər fungk′tər ē), *adj.* **1** done merely out of duty; done from force of habit; mechanical; indifferent: *I gave my room a perfunctory cleaning.* **2** acting in a perfunctory way: *The new clerk was perfunctory; she did not really care about her work.* —**per·func′to·ri·ly**, *adv.* —**per·func′to·ri·ness**, *n.*

per·haps (pər haps′), *adv.* it may be; maybe; possibly: *Perhaps a letter will come to you today.*

per·i·car·di·um (per′ə kär′dē əm), *n.* the sac of thin, soft tissue that encloses the heart. ❑ *n., pl.* **per·i·car·di·a.**

Per·i·cles (per′ə klēz′), *n.* 490?-429 B.C., Athenian political leader. He reformed the government, improved the Athenian navy, and caused many famous temples to be built.

per·i·gee (per′ə jē), *n.* point closest to the earth in the orbit of the moon or any other earth satellite. ❑ *n., pl.* **per·i·gees.**

per·i·he·lion (per′ə hē′lyən), *n.* point closest to the sun in the orbit of a planet or comet. ❑ *n., pl.* **per·i·he·lia** (per′ə hē′lyə).

per·il (per′əl), **1** *n.* chance of harm; danger: *This bridge is not safe; cross it at your peril.* ■ See Synonym Study at **danger. 2** *v.* to put in danger. ❑ *v.* **per·iled, per·il·ing.**

per·il·ous (per′ə ləs), *adj.* full of peril; dangerous: *a perilous ocean voyage.* —**per′il·ous·ly**, *adv.* —**per′il·ous·ness**, *n.*

pe·rim·e·ter (pə rim′ə tər), *n.* **1** the outer boundary of a figure or area: *the perimeter of a circle, the perimeter of a garden.* **2** distance around such a boundary. The perimeter of a square equals four times the length of one side.

per·i·od (pir′ē əd), *n.* **1** portion of time: *He visited us for a short period.* **2** portion of time marked between events that happen again and again; time after which the same things begin to happen again: *the period from new moon to new moon.* **3** a particular time: *the period of World War II.* **4** one of several portions of a game during which there is actual play. **5** one of the portions of time into which a school day is divided. **6** dot (.) marking the end of a declarative sentence or showing an abbreviation. **7** one of the portions of time into which a geological era may be divided. **8** the time of menstruating; menstruation.

per·i·od·ic (pir′ē od′ik), *adj.* **1** occurring, appearing, or done again and again at regular times: *The coming of the new moon is a periodic event.* **2** happening every now and then: *Our school has periodic fire drills.* —**per′i·od′i·cal·ly**, *adv.*

per·i·od·i·cal (pir′ē od′ə kəl), **1** *n.* magazine that is published at regular times, less often than daily: *This periodical comes out monthly.* **2** *adj.* of or about periodicals. **3** *adj.* published at regular intervals, less often than daily. **4** *adj.* periodic.

periodic table, table in which the chemical elements, arranged in the order of their atomic numbers, are shown in related groups.

pe·riph·er·al (pə rif′ər əl), **1** *adj.* of, situated in, or forming an outside boundary: *the peripheral areas of the city.* **2** *n.* a separate device connected to and used with a computer. —**pe·riph′er·al·ly**, *adv.*

peripheral vision, ability to see outside the central focus area of the eye, at the edges of sight.

pe·riph·er·y (pə rif′ər ē), *n.* an outside boundary. The periphery of a circle is its circumference. ❑ *n., pl.* **pe·riph·er·ies.**

per·i·scope (per′ə skōp), *n.* device that allows those in a submarine to obtain a view of the surface. It is a tube with an arrangement of prisms or mirrors that reflect light rays down the tube to an eyepiece.

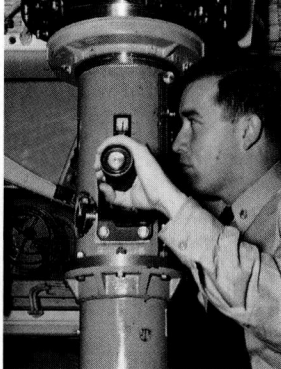

periscope

per·ish (per′ish), *v.* to be destroyed; die: *Three people perished in the fire. Flowers perish when frost comes.*

per·ish·a·ble (per′i shə bəl), **1** *adj.* liable to spoil or decay: *Bananas are perishable.* **2** *n.pl.* **perishables,** perishable things, especially food: *Milk and eggs are perishables.* —**per′ish·a·bil′i·ty,** **per′ish·a·ble·ness**, *n.* —**per′ish·a·bly**, *adv.*

per·i·stal·sis (per′ə stol′sis *or* per′ə stal′sis), *n.* the wavelike contractions of the alimentary canal or other tubular organ by which its contents are moved onward.

per·i·to·ne·um (per′ə tə nē′əm), *n.* membrane that lines the walls of the abdomen and covers the organs in it. ❑ *n., pl.* **per·i·to·ne·ums, per·i·to·ne·a** (per′ə tə nē′ə).

per·i·to·ni·tis (per′ə tə nī′tis), *n.* inflammation of the peritoneum.

per·i·win·kle[1] (per′ē wing′kəl), *n.* a low, trailing evergreen plant with blue flowers; myrtle.

per·i·win·kle[2] (per′ē wing′kəl), *n.* any of several sea snails with thick shells, used for food in Europe.

per·jure (pėr′jər), *v.* to make yourself guilty of perjury: *The witness perjured himself by lying about what he did on the night of the crime.* ❑ *v.* **per·jured, per·jur·ing.** —**per′jur·er**, *n.*

per·ju·ry (pėr′jər ē), *n.* act of swearing that something is true which you know to be false.

perk[1] (pėrk), *v.* **1** to raise smartly or briskly: *The dog perked its ears when it heard its owner's voice.* **2** to make trim or smart: *They are perked out in their best clothes.*

perk up, to brighten up; become more cheerful and lively: *The birds perked up as the sun rose over the hill.*

perk[2] (pėrk), *n.* INFORMAL. perquisite.

Per·kins (pėr′kinz), *n.* **Fran·ces** (fran′sis), 1882-1965, American political leader. She was the secretary of labor in Franklin D. Roosevelt's cabinet. She was the first woman to be a Cabinet member.

perk·y (pėr′kē), *adj.* smart; brisk; saucy; pert: *a perky squirrel.* ❑ *adj.* **perk·i·er, perk·i·est.** —**perk′i·ly**, *adv.* —**perk′i·ness**, *n.*

perm (pėrm), INFORMAL. **1** *n.* a permanent wave. **2** *v.* to give a permanent wave to.

per·ma·frost (pėr′mə frôst), *n.* layer of permanently frozen soil, under surface soil in most arctic regions.

per·ma·nence (pėr′mə nəns), *n.* condition of being permanent; lasting quality or condition.

per·ma·nen·cy (pėr′mə nən sē), *n.* permanence.

per·ma·nent (pėr′mə nənt), **1** *adj.* intended to last; not for a short time only; lasting: *a permanent filling in a tooth. After doing odd jobs for a week, I got a permanent position as salesclerk.* **2** *n.* permanent wave. —**per′ma·nent·ly**, *adv.*

per·ma·nent-press (pėr′mə nənt pres′), *adj.* treated by a chemical process so that creases and pleats are permanently set, resisting wrinkles: *permanent-press fabrics.*

permanent wave, wave put in the hair by a special process so as to last several months; permanent.

per·me·a·ble (pėr′mē ə bəl), *adj.* able to be permeated: *A sponge is permeable by water.* **−per′me·a·bil′i·ty,** *n.* **−per′me·a·bly,** *adv.*

per·me·ate (pėr′mē āt), *v.* **1** to spread through the whole of; pass through: *Smoke permeated the house.* **2** to penetrate: *Water permeates cotton.* ❑ *v.* **per·me·at·ed, per·me·at·ing. −per′me·a′tion,** *n.*

Per·mi·an (per′mē ən), *n.* (in geology) time between about 260 million and 230 million years ago. During this time, reptiles increased and amphibians decreased.

per·mis·si·ble (pər mis′ə bəl), *adj.* permitted; allowable. **−per·mis′si·ble·ness,** *n.* **−per·mis′si·bly,** *adv.*

per·mis·sion (pər mish′ən), *n.* consent; leave: *My sister gave me her permission to use her camera.*

per·mis·sive (pər mis′iv), *adj.* tending to permit; tolerant: *a permissive attitude.* **−per·mis′sive·ly,** *adv.* **−per·mis′sive·ness,** *n.*

per·mit (pər mit′ *for verb;* pėr′mit *or* pər mit′ *for noun*), **1** *v.* to let; allow: *My parents will not permit me to stay up late.* **2** *v.* to make possible; provide an opportunity for: *I will go on Monday, if the weather permits.* **3** *n.* license or written order giving permission to do something: *Have you a permit to fish in this lake?* ❑ *v.* **per·mit·ted, per·mit·ting. −per·mit′ter,** *n.*

per·mu·ta·tion (pėr′myü tā′shən), *n.* **1** a change from one condition, position, or form to another. **2** in mathematics: **a** the act of changing the order of a set of things. **b** one of several orders that a set of things may occur in or be put in. The permutations of *a, b,* and *c* are *abc, acb, bac, bca, cab,* and *cba.*

per·ni·cious (pər nish′əs), *adj.* very harmful; causing great harm or damage; injurious: *Taking drugs is a pernicious habit.* **−per·ni′cious·ly,** *adv.*

per·nick·e·ty (pər nik′ə tē), *adj.* INFORMAL. persnickety.

Per·ón (pə rōn′), *n.* **Juan** (wän), 1895-1974, president of Argentina from 1946 to 1955 and from 1973 to 1974. After a military revolt ended his first presidency, he left Argentina, returning in 1973. ■ **Juan Perón's** second wife, Eva, was very popular and helped him become president. She considered running for vice-president with him, but decided not to when military leaders objected. His third wife, Isabel, was his vice-president in 1973, and she became president when he died.

Pe·rot (pə rō′), *n.* **H. Ross,** born 1930, American business leader and presidential candidate in 1992.

pe·rox·ide (pə rok′sīd), *n.* **1** oxide that contains the greatest possible proportion of oxygen. **2** hydrogen peroxide.

perp (pėrp), *n.* INFORMAL. perpetrator, especially of a crime.

per·pen·dic·u·lar (pėr′pən dik′yə lər), **1** *adj.* standing straight up; vertical; upright: *a perpendicular cliff.* **2** *adj.* at right angles. One line is perpendicular to another when it makes a square corner with another. The floor of a room is perpendicular to the side walls and parallel to the ceiling. **3** *n.* a perpendicular line or plane. **−per·pen·dic′u·lar·ly,** *adv.*

per·pe·trate (pėr′pə trāt), *v.* to do or commit a crime, fraud, trick, or anything bad or foolish: *arrested for perpetrating a robbery.* ❑ *v.* **per·pe·trat·ed, per·pe·trat·ing. −per′pe·tra′tion,** *n.* **−per′pe·tra′tor,** *n.*

per·pet·u·al (pər pech′ü əl), *adj.* **1** never ceasing; continuous: *a perpetual stream of visitors.* **2** lasting throughout life: *a perpetual income.* **3** lasting forever; eternal: *the perpetual hills.* **−per·pet′u·al·ly,** *adv.*

per·pet·u·ate (pər pech′ü āt), *v.* to cause to continue; make perpetual; keep from being forgotten: *a monument built to perpetuate the memory of Abraham Lincoln.* ❑ *v.* **per·pet·u·at·ed, per·pet·u·at·ing. −per·pet′u·a′tion,** *n.* **−per·pet′u·a′tor,** *n.*

per·pe·tu·i·ty (pėr′pə tü′ə tē), *n.* condition of being perpetual. **in perpetuity,** forever.

per·plex (pər pleks′), *v.* to trouble with doubt; puzzle; confuse; bewilder: *This problem even perplexed the teacher.* **−per·plex′ed·ly,** *adv.* **−per·plex′ing·ly,** *adv.*

per·plex·i·ty (pər plek′sə tē), *n.* **1** perplexed condition; being puzzled; a not knowing what to do or how to act; confusion: *My perplexity was so great that I asked many persons for advice.* **2** something that perplexes: *There are many perplexities in such a complicated job.* ❑ *n., pl.* **per·plex·i·ties** for 2.

per·qui·site (pėr′kwə zit), *n.* anything received for work besides the regular pay: *The company pays medical benefits as a perquisite.*

Per·ry (per′ē), *n.* **1 Matthew C.,** 1794-1858, American naval officer. He arranged a treaty between the United States and Japan that opened Japan to American trade. **2** his brother, **Ol·i·ver Haz·ard** (ol′ə vər haz′ərd), 1785-1819, American naval commander in the War of 1812.

per se (pər sā), by itself; in itself.

per·se·cute (pėr′sə kyüt), *v.* **1** to treat badly; do harm to again and again; oppress: *Those bullies persecute the children by attacking them on their way home.* **2** to treat badly because of your principles or beliefs: *Christians were persecuted in ancient Rome.* **3** to annoy; harass: *persecuted by silly questions.* ❑ *v.* **per·se·cut·ed, per·se·cut·ing. −per′se·cu′tion,** *n.* **−per′se·cu′tor,** *n.*

Per·seph·o·ne (pər sef′ə nē), *n.* (in Greek myths) the daughter of Zeus and Demeter, made queen of the lower world by Pluto. The Romans called her Proserpina.

Per·se·us (pėr′sē əs), *n.* (in Greek legends) hero who killed the hideous Gorgon Medusa and used her head to turn his enemies to stone.

per·se·ver·ance (pėr′sə vir′əns), *n.* act or quality of sticking to a purpose or an aim; never giving up what you have set out to do: *By perseverance I finally learned to swim.*

per·se·vere (pėr′sə vir′), *v.* to keep on doing something hard; persist. ❑ *v.* **per·se·vered, per·se·ver·ing. −per′se·ver′ing·ly,** *adv.*

Per·shing (pėr′shing), *n.* **John Joseph,** 1860-1948, general in command of the U.S. Army in World War I. His nickname was "Black Jack."

Per·sia (pėr′zhə), *n.* **1** former name of **Iran. 2** ancient empire in W and SW Asia.

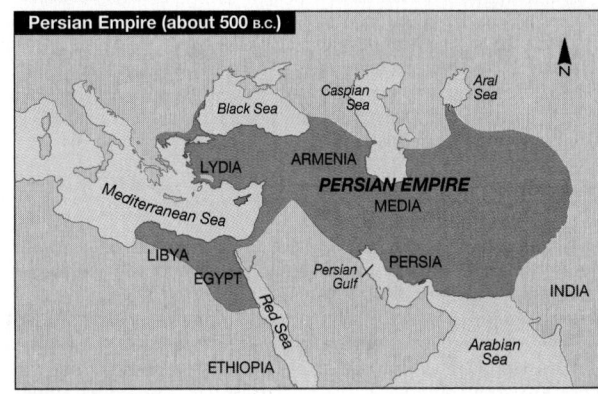

Persian Empire (about 500 B.C.)

Per·sian (pėr′zhən), **1** *adj.* of or about Persia, its people, or their language. **2** *n.* person born or living in Persia. **3** *n.* language of Persia; Farsi.

WORD SOURCE **Persian** is the official language of Iran, and one of the official languages of Afghanistan. The following words came into English from Persian.

bazaar	jasmine	mummy	shawl
candy	khaki	orange	spinach
caravan	lemon	pajamas	taffeta
divan	Magi	pistachio	tulip
jackal	magic	seersucker	turban

a	hat	ė	term	ô	order	ch	child	ə	a in about
ā	age	i	it	oi	oil	ng	long		e in taken
ä	far	ī	ice	ou	out	sh	she		i in pencil
â	care	o	hot	u	cup	th	thin		o in lemon
e	let	ō	open	u̇	put	ᵺ	then		u in circus
ē	equal	ȯ	saw	ü	rule	zh	measure		

P

Persian Gulf, gulf of the Arabian Sea, between Iran and Saudi Arabia.

Persian Gulf War, a multinational military operation authorized by the United Nations and led by U.S. forces against Iraq in 1991; Gulf War; Operation Desert Storm.

per·sim·mon (pər sim′ən), *n.* any of numerous related small trees, especially a North American tree with yellowish orange, plumlike fruit. Persimmons are bitter when green, but sweet and good when very ripe.

per·sist (pər sist′), *v.* **1** to keep on; refuse to stop or be changed: *Though we've asked her not to, she persists in reading at the table.* **2** to remain in existence; last; stay: *On the tops of very high mountains snow persists all year.* **3** to say again and again; maintain: *He persisted that he was innocent of the crime.* **—per·sist′er,** *n.*

per·sist·ence (pər sis′təns), *n.* **1** act of refusing to stop or be changed: *I was annoyed by the persistence of a fly buzzing around my head.* **2** continuing existence: *the persistence of a cough.*

per·sist·ent (pər sis′tənt), *adj.* **1** refusing to stop or give up: *She was persistent in her demands for more freedom to choose her own clothing.* **2** going on; continuing; lasting: *a persistent headache that lasted for days.* **—per·sist′ent·ly,** *adv.*

per·snick·e·ty (pər snik′ə tē), *adj.* INFORMAL. very hard to please, especially about minor details; picky. Also, **pernickety.**

per·son (pėr′sən), *n.* **1** man, woman, or child; human being: *Any person who wishes may come to the fair.* ■ See Usage Note at **individual. 2** the human body: *The person of the queen was well guarded.* **3** bodily appearance: *He kept his person neat and trim.* **4** (in grammar) a form of pronouns or verbs used to show the person speaking, the person spoken to, or the person or thing spoken of. *I* and *we* are used for the first person; *you,* for the second person; *he, she, it,* and *they,* for the third person. ❑ *n., pl.* **peo·ple** or **per·sons** for 1, **per·sons** for 2,3. [Person comes from a Latin word meaning "a mask." In old times, actors wore masks on stage. Each mask showed what sort of person the actor was pretending to be.]

in person, personally: *The author will appear in person.*

WORD POWER   **PERSON** ■ A person who fights fires is a firefighter. A person who studies the economy is an economist. A person who edits is an editor. A person who has dignity is a dignitary. A person who presides is a president. A person who assists is an assistant. A person who escapes is an escapee. Are you tired of reading "a person who"? Do you see why people use suffixes instead?

Some of those suffixes are:

-ant	-ent	-man
-ary	-er	-or
-ee	-ist	-woman

per·son·a·ble (pėr′sə nə bəl), *adj.* having a pleasing appearance; good-looking; attractive. **—per′son·a·ble·ness,** *n.* **—per′son·a·bly,** *adv.*

per·son·age (pėr′sə nij), *n.* **1** person of importance. **2** person. **3** character in a book or play.

per·son·al (pėr′sə nəl), **1** *adj.* of or about a person; individual; private: *a personal letter, a personal matter.* **2** *adj.* done in person; directly by yourself, not through others or by letter or telephone: *The author made personal appearances at several bookstores to autograph her books.* **3** *adj.* of or about the body or bodily appearance: *personal cleanliness.* **4** *adj.* about or against someone: *personal remarks, personal abuse.* **5** *adj.* (in grammar) showing person. *I, we, you, he, she, it,* and *they* are personal pronouns. **6** *adj.* (in law) of property that can be moved, such as furniture and clothing. **7** *n.* a short newspaper advertisement for a friend, companion, etc.

personal computer, a small, moderately priced computer, designed to fit on a table or desk top, used for various educational, business, and home functions; microcomputer.

per·son·al·i·ty (pėr′sə nal′ə tē), *n.* **1** the personal or individual quality that makes one person be different or act differently from another: *She has a warm, friendly personality that makes her popular with other students.* **2** pleasing or attractive qualities of a person: *The boy is developing a personality.* **3** a well-known person; personage: *I collect autographs of famous personalities*

in the entertainment world. **4 personalities,** *pl.* remarks made about or against some particular person: *Please refrain from personalities and stick to the issues.* ❑ *n., pl.* **per·son·al·i·ties.**

per·son·al·ly (pėr′sə nə lē), *adv.* **1** as far as you are concerned: *Personally, I like apples better than oranges.* **2** by yourself; not by the aid of others: *The owner of this store deals personally with customers.* **3** physically; present at the place mentioned; yourself: *You must apply for the job personally, not by mail or telephone.* **4** as a person: *I don't know her personally, but I've been told she is a talented writer.* **5** as being meant for yourself: *Don't take what I said personally; I didn't intend to insult you.*

personal pronoun, a pronoun that shows the person or persons speaking (*I, me, we, us*), the person or persons spoken to (*you*), or the person, or persons, thing, or things being talked about (*he, she, it, they, him, her, them*).

per·son·i·fi·ca·tion (pər son′ə fə kā′shən), *n.* **1** a clear example; embodiment; type: *A miser is the personification of greed.* **2** an imaginary person who stands for an idea. Uncle Sam, Cupid, Justice, and Father Time are personifications. **3** figure of speech in which a lifeless thing or quality is spoken of as if alive. EXAMPLES: The music sobbed. The company shrugged off its losses.

per·son·i·fy (pər son′ə fi), *v.* **1** to be a type of; embody: *Hitler and Stalin personified evil.* **2** to regard or represent as a person. We personify time and nature when we refer to *Father Time* and *Mother Nature.* ❑ *v.* **per·son·i·fied, per·son·i·fy·ing. —per·son′i·fi′er,** *n.*

per·son·nel (pėr′sə nel′), *n.* people employed in any work, business, or service.

per·spec·tive (pər spek′tiv), *n.* **1** art of picturing objects on a flat surface so as to give the appearance of distance. **2** effect of distance on the appearance of objects: *Faraway objects look small in perspective.* **3** effect of the distance of events upon the mind: *Perspective makes many happenings of last year seem less important.* **4** ability to think about or look at things or facts in their true relations to each other: *keep things in perspective.* **5** a view in front; distant view: *a perspective of lakes and hills.* **—per·spec′tive·ly,** *adv.*

perspective (def. 2)

per·spi·ca·cious (pėr′spə kā′shəs), *adj.* keen in observing and understanding; discerning.

per·spi·ra·tion (pėr′spə rā′shən), *n.* **1** sweat. **2** process of sweating.

per·spire (pər spir′), *v.* to sweat: *The room was so hot I began to perspire.* ❑ *v.* **per·spired, per·spir·ing.**

per·suade (pər swād′), *v.* to cause someone to do or believe something; make willing or sure by urging or arguing: *I knew I should study, but he persuaded me to go to the movies. We persuaded her that she was wrong.* ❑ *v.* **per·suad·ed, per·suad·ing. —per·suad′er,** *n.*

SYNONYM STUDY   **Persuade** and **convince** both mean to make someone do or believe something, usually by words. **Persuade** means to make someone agree with you: *She persuaded me to offer him an apology.* **Convince** means to make someone believe that something is true: *He tried to convince the teacher that the dog ate his homework.*

per·sua·sion (pər swā′zhən), *n.* **1** act or process of persuading: *All our attempts at persuasion were useless; she would not come with us.* **2** power of persuading. **3** firm belief; conviction: *different political persuasions.* **4** religious belief or denomination: *All Christians are not of the same persuasion.*

per·sua·sive (pər swā′siv), *adj.* able, intended, or likely to persuade: *The salesman had a very persuasive way of talking.* —**per·sua′sive·ly,** *adv.* —**per·sua′sive·ness,** *n.*

pert (pèrt), *adj.* **1** too forward or bold in speech or action; saucy: *a pert reply.* **2** stylish; jaunty: *a pert outfit.* —**pert′ly,** *adv.* —**pert′ness,** *n.*

per·tain (pər tān′), *v.* **1** to belong or be connected as a part or possession: *We own the house and the land pertaining to it.* **2** to refer; be related: *My question pertains to yesterday's homework.*

Perth (pèrth), *n.* capital of Western Australia, near the Indian Ocean.

per·ti·nence (pèrt′n əns), *n.* condition of being to the point; fitness; relevance: *The pertinence of the girl's replies showed that she was alert and intelligent.*

per·ti·nent (pèrt′n ənt), *adj.* relating to what is being considered; to the point; relevant: *If your question is pertinent, I will answer it.* —**per′ti·nent·ly,** *adv.*

per·turb (pər tèrb′), *v.* to disturb greatly; make uneasy or troubled: *My parents were perturbed by my grades.* —**per′tur·ba′tion,** *n.*

Pe·ru (pə rü′), *n.* mountainous country on the W coast of South America. *Capital:* Lima.

pe·ruke (pə rük′), *n.* wig, especially of the type worn in the 1600s and 1700s.

pe·rus·al (pə rü′zəl), *n.* act of reading: *the perusal of a letter.*

pe·ruse (pə rüz′), *v.* to read, especially thoroughly and carefully: *peruse the newspaper at breakfast.* ❑ *v.* **pe·rused, pe·rus·ing.** —**pe·rus′er,** *n.*

Pe·ru·vi·an (pə rü′vē ən), **1** *adj.* of or about Peru or its people. **2** *n.* person born or living in Peru.

per·vade (pər vād′), *v.* to go or spread throughout; be throughout: *The odor of pines pervades the air.* ❑ *v.* **per·vad·ed, per·vad·ing.** —**per·vad′er,** *n.*

per·va·sive (pər vā′siv), *adj.* **1** tending to pervade. **2** having power to pervade. —**per·va′sive·ly,** *adv.* —**per·va′sive·ness,** *n.*

per·verse (pər vèrs′), *adj.* **1** contrary and willful; stubborn: *The perverse child did just what we told him not to do.* **2** persistent in wrong. **3** morally wrong; wicked. **4** not correct; wrong: *perverse reasoning.* —**per·verse′ly,** *adv.* —**per·verse′ness,** *n.*

per·ver·sion (pər vèr′zhən), *n.* **1** abnormal sexual behavior. **2** a change to what is unnatural, abnormal, or wrong: *A tendency to eat sand is a perversion of appetite.*

per·ver·si·ty (pər vèr′sə tē), *n.* **1** quality of being perverse. **2** perverse character or conduct. **3** a perverse act. ❑ *n., pl.* **per·ver·si·ties** for 3.

per·vert (pər vèrt′ *for verb;* pèr′vèrt′ *for noun*), **1** *v.* to lead or turn from what is true, desirable, good, or morally right; corrupt: *pervert the cause of justice.* **2** *v.* to give a wrong meaning to: *pervert a friendly remark and make it into an insult.* **3** *v.* to use for wrong purposes or in a wrong way: *pervert your talents.* **4** *n.* a perverted person, especially one whose sexual behavior is abnormal. —**per·vert′ed·ly,** *adv.* —**per·vert′er,** *n.*

pe·se·ta (pə sā′tə), *n.* unit of money in Spain. ❑ *n., pl.* **pe·se·tas.**

pes·ky (pes′kē), *adj.* troublesome; annoying: *A pesky mosquito kept buzzing around my head.* ❑ *adj.* **pes·ki·er, pes·ki·est.** —**pes′ki·ly,** *adv.* —**pes′ki·ness,** *n.*

pe·so (pā′sō), *n.* unit of money in various countries of Latin America and in the Philippines. ❑ *n., pl.* **pe·sos.** [**Peso** comes from a Latin word meaning "to weigh." In old times, the value of a coin depended on the weight of precious metal in it.]

pes·si·mism (pes′ə miz′əm), *n.* **1** tendency to look on the dark side of things or to see all the difficulties and disadvantages. **2** belief that things naturally tend to evil, or that the evil in life outweighs the good.

pes·si·mist (pes′ə mist), *n.* **1** person inclined to look on the bad side of things or to see all the difficulties and disadvantages. **2** person who believes that things naturally tend to evil, or that the evil in life outweighs the good.

pes·si·mis·tic (pes′ə mis′tik), *adj.* inclined to look on the bad side of things or to see all the difficulties and disadvantages; expecting the worst: *I was pessimistic about passing the test because I hadn't studied.* —**pes′si·mis′ti·cal·ly,** *adv.*

pest (pest), *n.* **1** insect, animal, etc., that is harmful or destructive: *garden pests.* **2** something or someone that is annoying; nuisance: *Don't be such a pest.*

pes·ter (pes′tər), *v.* to annoy; trouble; vex: *Flies pester us. Don't pester me with foolish questions.*

pes·ti·cide (pes′tə sīd), *n.* substance used to kill pests. Farmers often use pesticides to kill insects that might destroy their crops.

pes·ti·lence (pes′tl əns), *n.* any disease that spreads rapidly, often causing many deaths. Smallpox, yellow fever, and plague are pestilences that killed many people in former times.

pes·ti·lent (pes′tl ənt), *adj.* **1** often causing death: *Smallpox is a pestilent disease.* **2** harmful to morals; destroying peace: *the pestilent effects of war.*

pes·ti·len·tial (pes′ti en′shəl), *adj.* **1** of or like a pestilence. **2** causing or likely to cause pestilence. **3** morally harmful. —**pes′ti·len′tial·ly,** *adv.*

pes·tle (pes′əl), *n.* tool for pounding or crushing substances into powder in a mortar.

pes·to (pes′tō), *n.* an Italian sauce made of fresh basil, ground pine nuts, olive oil, and grated Parmesan cheese.

pet[1] (pet), **1** *n.* animal kept as a companion and treated with affection. **2** *adj.* treated as a pet: *a pet rabbit.* **3** *v.* to treat as a pet; touch lovingly and gently; stroke or pat. **4** *n.* a darling or favorite: *teacher's pet.* **5** *adj.* favorite: *a pet theory.* **6** *adj.* showing affection: *a pet name.* ❑ *v.* **pet·ted, pet·ting.**

pet[2] (pet), *n.* fit of childish anger: *When he didn't get his way, he jumped on his bicycle and rode off in a pet.*

pet·al (pet′l), *n.* one of the parts of a flower that often stick out around the edge and are usually colored or white. —**pet′al·like′,** *adj.*

pet·aled or **pet·alled** (pet′ld), *adj.* having petals: *six-petaled.*

pet·cock (pet′kok′), *n.* a small faucet or valve in a pipe or cylinder, for reducing pressure or draining liquids.

pe·ter (pē′tər), *v.* INFORMAL. **peter out,** to come to an end gradually; fail; run out: *The path petered out among the trees.*

Pe·ter (pē′tər), *n.* **1** Saint, died A.D. 67?, one of Jesus' twelve apostles. He was also called Simon or Simon Peter. **2** either of two books in the New Testament that bear his name. [**Peter** comes from a Greek word meaning "a rock."]

Peter I, 1672-1725, czar of Russia from 1682 to 1725. He introduced many western customs to Russia and caused St. Petersburg to be built. He was called "Peter the Great."

pet·i·ole (pet′ē ōl), *n.* the slender stalk by which a leaf is attached to the stem; leafstalk.

pe·tite (pə tēt′), *adj.* of small size; little; tiny: *a petite young woman.* —**pe·tite′ness,** *n.*

pe·ti·tion (pə tish′ən), **1** *n.* a written request to someone in authority for some right or privilege, often signed by many people: *The residents on our street signed a petition asking the city council for a new sidewalk.* **2** *v.* to make such a request to: *We petitioned the principal to improve school lunches.* —**pe·ti′tion·er,** *n.*

pet·it jury (pet′ē), group of 12 persons chosen to decide a case in court.

pet·nap·ping (pet′nap′ing), *n.* the stealing of a pet or pets, especially for ransom. —**pet′nap′per,** *n.*

pet·rel (pet′rəl), *n.* any of various seabirds, especially the storm petrel. ■ Another word that sounds like this is **petrol.**

pe·tri dish (pē′trē), a shallow, circular glass or plastic dish with a loose cover, used in growing bacteria.

Petrified Forest National Park, a national park in N central Arizona, containing colorful giant fossilized trees.

pet·ri·fy (pet′rə fī), *v.* **1** to turn into stone; change plant or animal matter into a substance like stone: *Ancient tree trunks that have*

a	hat	ė	term	ô	oil	ch	child		a in about
ā	age	i	it	oi	oil	ng	long		e in taken
ä	far	ī	ice	ou	out	sh	she	ə	i in pencil
â	care	o	hot	u	cup	th	thin		o in lemon
e	let	ō	open	u̇	put	ᵺ	then		u in circus
ē	equal	ȯ	saw	ü	rule	zh	measure		

P

647

petrified can be seen in Arizona. **2** to paralyze with fear, horror, or surprise: *I was petrified when lightning struck our house.* ❏ *v.* **pet·ri·fied, pet·ri·fy·ing.**

pet·ro·chem·i·cal (pet′rō kem′ə kəl), **1** *n.* any chemical substance made from petroleum or natural gas. Plastics, paint, fertilizers, and the like are make with petrochemicals. **2** *adj.* of or with petrochemicals.

pet·ro·glyph (pet′rə glif′), *n.* a carving made on a rock, usually a picture or pattern, often in groups, such as were made by American Indians, especially in the Southwest.

petroglyphs

Pet·ro·grad (pet′rə grad), *n.* former capital of Russia, now called **St. Petersburg.**

pet·rol (pet′rəl), *n.* BRITISH. gasoline. ■ Another word that sounds like this is **petrel.**

pe·tro·le·um (pə trō′lē əm), *n.* an oily, dark, flammable liquid found in the earth, containing a mixture of various hydrocarbons. Gasoline, kerosene, and many other products such as plastics are made from petroleum. [**Petroleum** comes from Greek words meaning "rock" and "oil." It was first found seeping up through cracks in rocks.]

PET scan (pet), **1** process of making images of the brain, heart, or other internal body parts, using gamma rays. A PET scan shows the changing activity of living body parts. **2** image produced by this process.

pet·ti·coat (pet′ē kōt), *n.* a thin skirt or slip worn beneath a dress or outer skirt by women and girls.

pet·tish (pet′ish), *adj.* bad-tempered: *a pettish child.*

pet·ty (pet′ē), *adj.* **1** having little importance or value; small: *Don't let petty disturbances upset you.* ■ See Synonym Study at **unimportant. 2** mean; narrow-minded: *A gossip is a petty person.* **3** lower in rank or importance; subordinate: *a petty official.* ❏ *adj.* **pet·ti·er, pet·ti·est.** —**pet′ti·ly,** *adv.* —**pet′ti·ness,** *n.*

Pet·ty (pet′ē), *n.* **Richard,** born 1937, American race car driver. He has won more money and more races than any other stock car driver.

petty cash, 1 small sums of money spent or received. **2** sum of money kept on hand to pay small expenses.

petty officer, any of several military ranks. See chart on page 712.

pet·u·lance (pech′ə ləns), *n.* quality of being upset over unimportant things.

pet·u·lant (pech′ə lənt), *adj.* upset over unimportant things.

pe·tun·ia (pə tü′nyə), *n.* any of several common garden plants with white, pink, red, or purple flowers shaped like funnels. ❏ *n., pl.* **pe·tun·ias.** [**Petunia** comes from a native South American word meaning "tobacco." The plants are closely related.]

pew (pyü), *n.* bench in a church for people to sit on, fastened to the floor and with a back.

pe·wee (pē′wē), *n.* any of several small American birds with gray or olive backs. A pewee's call sounds something like its name. ❏ *n., pl.* **pe·wees.**

pew·ter (pyü′tər), **1** *n.* metal made by combining tin with lead, copper, or other metals. **2** *n.pl.* dishes or other utensils made of this. **3** *adj.* made of pewter: *a pewter mug.*

pe·yo·te (pā ō′tē), *n.* **1** mescal. **2** the buttonlike tops of the

mescal, which are used by some members of some tribes of Native Americans during religious ceremonies. **3** mescaline.

Pfc., Pfc, or **PFC,** private first class.

PG, Parental Guidance (a rating for a movie that is recommended for everyone, but with parental guidance for young people).

pg. or **pg,** page.

PG-13, Parental Guidance under 13 (a rating between PG and R for a movie that is recommended for everyone, but with parental guidance for young people under 13).

pH, symbol used with a number from 0 to 14 that tells how acid or basic a chemical substance is. pH 7 is neutral, pH 6 to pH 0 increasingly acid, and pH 8 to pH 14 increasingly basic.

phag·o·cyte (fag′ə sit), *n.* a kind of white blood cell that envelops and absorbs agents that cause diseases, destroying them.

WORD STORY Words that use *ph* for the sound of *f* are words coming from Greek. The ancient Greeks spelled this sound with a letter that is not in the English alphabet. They had a letter that looked like *f,* but it was pronounced like *w.* The Romans used *f* the way we do. When they took words from Greek that had an *f* sound, they used *ph* to avoid questions about whether to say *f* or *w.*

pha·lan·ges (fə lan′jēz), *n.pl.* the bones of the fingers and toes.

pha·lanx (fā′langks), *n.* **1** (in ancient Greece) a special battle formation of infantry fighting in close ranks with their shields joined and long spears overlapping each other. **2** a compact or closely massed group of people, animals, or things: *A phalanx of sheep blocked the road.* **3** number of persons united for a common purpose. ❏ *n., pl.* **pha·lanx·es.**

phan·tasm (fan′taz əm), *n.* **1** thing seen only in your imagination; unreal fancy: *the phantasms of a dream.* **2** a deceiving likeness of something.

phan·tom (fan′təm), **1** *n.* image in the mind which seems to be real: *phantoms of a dream.* **2** *n.* a vague, dim, or shadowy appearance; ghost. **3** *adj.* like a ghost; unreal: *a phantom ship.*

Phar·aoh (fâr′ō), *n.* any of the kings of ancient Egypt.

WORD STORY **Pharaoh** comes from an Egyptian word meaning "great house." **House** can mean "a noble family." In old times, only powerful leaders and their families lived in large houses.

Phar·i·see (far′ə sē), *n.* **1** member of a Jewish sect at the time of Jesus that was very strict in keeping to tradition and the laws of its religion. **2** pharisee, person who makes a show of religion rather than following its spirit; hypocrite. ❏ *n., pl.* **Phar·i·sees** for 1, **phar·i·sees** for 2.

WORD STORY **Pharisee** comes from an Aramaic word meaning "separated." According to the Bible, Pharisees ate only with other members of their own group.

phar·ma·ceu·ti·cal (fär′mə sü′tə kəl), **1** *adj.* of or about pharmacy. **2** *n.* a medicinal drug. —**phar′ma·ceu′ti·cal·ly,** *adv.*

phar·ma·cist (fär′mə sist), *n.* person trained and licensed to fill prescriptions.

phar·ma·col·o·gy (fär′mə kol′ə jē), *n.* science of drugs, their preparation, uses, and effects. —**phar′ma·col′o·gist,** *n.*

phar·ma·cy (fär′mə sē), *n.* **1** place where drugs and medicines are prepared or sold; drugstore. **2** preparation and dispensing of drugs and medicines; occupation of a druggist. ❏ *n., pl.* **phar·ma·cies** for 1.

phar·ynx (far′ingks), *n.* cavity at the back of the mouth where the passages to the nose, lungs, and stomach begin. ❏ *n., pl.* **phar·ynx·es, pha·ryn·ges** (fə rin′jēz).

phase (fāz), **1** *n.* one of the changing stages of development of someone or something: *At present his voice is changing; that is a phase all boys go through.* **2** *n.* one part, side, or view of something: *What phase of arithmetic are you studying now?* **3** *n.* the shape of the lighted part of the moon or a planet at a particular time. **4** *v.* to do something gradually, by steps: *phase an army's withdrawal over months.* ❏ *v.* **phased, phas·ing.** ■ Another word that sounds like this is **faze.**

phase in, to start something new one step at a time: *phase in new regulations, one a week.*

phase out, to stop something one step at a time.

Ph.D., Doctor of Philosophy.

pheas·ant (fez′nt), *n.* any of several large game birds with brightly colored feathers on the male, and long, pointed tail feathers. Pheasants are native to Asia but now live in many parts of Europe and North America. ❑ *n., pl.* **pheas·ant** or **pheas·ants.**

pheasant—about 42 in. (1 m) long with the tail

phe·nol (fē′nol *or* fē′nōl), *n.* carbolic acid.

phe·nom·e·na (fə nom′ə nə), *n.* a plural of **phenomenon.**

phe·nom·e·nal (fə nom′ə nəl), *adj.* **1** extraordinary: *a phenomenal memory.* **2** of or like a phenomenon or phenomena. —**phe·nom′e·nal·ly,** *adv.*

phe·nom·e·non (fə nom′ə non), *n.* **1** fact, event, or circumstance that can be observed. **2** any sign or symptom: *Fever and inflammation are phenomena of disease.* **3** something or someone that is extraordinary or remarkable: *The Grand Canyon is a phenomenon of nature.* ❑ *n., pl.* **phe·nom·e·na** (or **phe·nom·e·nons** for 3).

WORD FAMILY	

Phenomenon and the words below are related. They all come from a Greek word meaning "to show."

diaphanous	epiphany	fantasy	phantom
emphasis	fancy	pant	phase
emphatic	fantastic	phantasm	phenomenal

phe·no·type (fē′nə tīp), *n.* the physical appearance of a living thing, resulting from the interaction of its genes with its environment.

pher·o·mone (fer′ə mōn), *n.* any chemical substance that is given off by members of a species and causes other members of the same species to react. Some insect pheromones sexually attract other members of a species.

Phil·a·del·phi·a (fil′ə del′fē ə), *n.* city in SE Pennsylvania, on the Delaware River. —**Phil′a·del′phi·an,** *adj., n.*

WORD STORY	

Philadelphia comes from Greek words meaning "love" and "brother." William Penn, founder of Pennsylvania, named the city after a city mentioned in the Bible, in hopes that brotherly love would be common there.

phil·an·throp·ic (fil′ən throp′ik), *adj.* charitable; benevolent; kindly: *a philanthropic nature.* —**phil′an·throp′i·cal·ly,** *adv.*

phil·an·throp·i·cal (fil′ən throp′ə kəl), *adj.* philanthropic.

phi·lan·thro·pist (fə lan′thrə pist), *n.* person who practices philanthropy, especially by giving sizable donations of money to worthy causes.

phi·lan·thro·py (fə lan′thrə pē), *n.* **1** love of humanity shown by practical kindness and helpfulness: *The charity appealed to philanthropy.* **2** thing that benefits humanity; a philanthropic agency, enterprise, gift, act, etc.: *A hospital is a useful philanthropy.* ❑ *n., pl.* **phi·lan·thro·pies** for 2.

phi·lat·e·list (fə lat′l ist), *n.* collector of postage stamps, postmarks, etc.

phi·lat·e·ly (fə lat′l ē), *n.* the collecting, arranging, and study of postage stamps, stamped envelopes, post cards, etc.

phil·har·mon·ic (fil′här mon′ik), **1** *n.* symphony orchestra: *The New York Philharmonic gave a concert last night.* **2** *adj.* devoted to music; loving music: *A musical club is often called a philharmonic society.*

Phil·ip (fil′əp), *n.* (in the Bible) one of Jesus' twelve apostles. [**Philip** comes from a Greek word meaning "lover of horses."]

Phil·ip (fil′əp), *n.* ?-1676, American Indian leader. He was often called King Philip. ■ Unlike his father Massasoit, **King Philip** felt that the European settlers would soon become unfriendly to the Indians and eventually destroy them. He led attacks on settlements in 1675 and had almost destroyed the English settlements in New England before he was killed in 1676.

Phil·ip·pine (fil′ə pēn′), *adj.* of or about the Philippines or its inhabitants; Filipino.

Philippine Islands, Philippines.

Phil·ip·pines (fil′ə pēnz′), *n.sing. or pl.* country in the W Pacific, southeast of China and northeast of Borneo, consisting of over 7000 islands. The Philippines were governed by the United States from 1898 until 1946. *Capital:* Manila. [**Philippines** is named for Philip II, who was king of Spain when the first Spanish settlements were started in the islands.]

Phil·is·tine (fil′ə stēn′), **1** *n.* (in the Bible) one of the warlike people in southwestern Palestine who fought the Israelites many times. **2** Also, **philistine, a** *n.* person who is commonplace in ideas and tastes. **b** *adj.* lacking culture; commonplace.

phil·o·den·dron (fil′ə den′drən), *n.* any of numerous climbing evergreen plants with shiny leaves, often grown as houseplants.

phi·lol·o·gy (fə lol′ə jē), *n.* **1** the study of the historical development of language. **2** the study of literary and other records. —**phil′o·log′i·cal,** *adj.* —**phi·lol′o·gist,** *n.*

phi·los·o·pher (fə los′ə fər), *n.* **1** person who studies philosophy a great deal. **2** author or founder of a system of philosophy. **3** person who is calm and reasonable under hard conditions, accepting life and making the best of it.

phil·o·soph·ic (fil′ə sof′ik), *adj.* philosophical.

phil·o·soph·i·cal (fil′ə sof′ə kəl), *adj.* **1** of or about philosophy or philosophers: *a philosophical discussion.* **2** knowing much about philosophy. **3** devoted to philosophy. **4** wise; calm; reasonable: *I tried to be philosophical about my disappointments.* —**phil′o·soph′i·cal·ly,** *adv.*

phi·los·o·phize (fə los′ə fīz), *v.* to think or reason as a philosopher does; try to understand and explain things: *The old woman philosophized about life and death.* ❑ *v.* **phi·los·o·phized, phi·los·o·phiz·ing.** —**phi·los′o·phiz′er,** *n.*

phi·los·o·phy (fə los′ə fē), *n.* **1** the study that attempts to discover and understand the basic nature of knowledge and reality. **2** explanation or theory of the universe, especially the particular explanation or system of a philosopher: *the philosophy of Plato.* **3** system for guiding life. **4** the general principles of a particular subject or field of activity: *the philosophy of history, the army's military philosophy.* **5** a calm and reasonable attitude; accepting things as they are and making the best of them. ❑ *n., pl.* **phi·los·o·phies** for 2-4.

phil·ter (fil′tər), *n.* drug or magic potion which is supposed to make someone fall in love. ■ Another word that sounds like this is **filter.**

phlegm (flem), *n.* the thick mucus that forms in the mouth and throat during a cold or other respiratory disease.

phleg·mat·ic (fleg mat′ik), *adj.* not easily excited; indifferent; calm: *My parents are phlegmatic; they never seem to get upset about anything.* —**phleg·mat′i·cal·ly,** *adv.*

phlo·em (flō′em), *n.* tissue in a plant or tree through which the sap containing dissolved food materials passes from leaves downward to the stems and roots.

phlox (floks), *n.* any of several tall garden plants with round clusters of pink, purple, or red flowers. ❑ *n., pl.* **phlox** or **phlox·es.**

Phnom Penh (pə nòm′ pen′), capital of Cambodia, in the S part.

pho·bi·a (fō′bē ə), *n.* a deep, irrational fear of a certain thing or group of things: *a phobia about snakes.* ❑ *n., pl.* **pho·bi·as.** —**pho′bic,** *adj.*

a	hat	ė	term	ȯ	order	ch	child		a in about
ā	age	i	it	oi	oil	ng	long		e in taken
ä	far	ī	ice	ou	out	sh	she	ə	i in pencil
â	care	o	hot	u	cup	th	thin		o in lemon
e	let	ō	open	ù	put	ŦH	then		u in circus
ē	equal	ȯ	saw	ü	rule	zh	measure		

P

phoe·be (fē′bē), *n.* any of several small, dark North American flycatchers, some of which have a call like their name.

Phoe·be (fē′bē), *n.* the Greek goddess of the moon. Phoebe was also called Artemis by the Greeks and Diana by the Romans. [**Phoebe** comes from a Greek word meaning "bright."]

Phoe·bus (fē′bəs), *n.* **1** Apollo. **2** the sun.

Phoe·ni·cia (fə nish′ə), *n.* ancient country on the Mediterranean Sea, in the region of Lebanon, W Syria, and N Israel. It was famous for its traders. See **Canaan** for additional map.

Phoe·ni·cian (fə nish′ən), **1** *adj.* of or about Phoenicia, its people, or their language. **2** *n.* one of the people of Phoenicia. **3** *n.* language of Phoenicia.

phoe·nix (fē′niks), *n.* a mythical bird, the only one of its kind, said to live 500 or 600 years, to burn itself on a funeral pyre, and to rise again from the ashes, fresh and beautiful, for another long life. ❑ *n., pl.* **phoe·nix·es.**

Phoe·nix (fē′niks), *n.* capital of Arizona, in the central part.

WORD STORY   **Phoenix** was named for the bird. Traces of an ancient American Indian settlement were found at the site, and the new inhabitants hoped that it would rise again like the phoenix and become a great city.

phone (fōn), *n., v.* telephone. ❑ *v.* **phoned, phon·ing.**

-phone, *suffix.* **1** sound: *homophone = word with the same sound as another word.* **2** device for sound: *telephone = device for sending and receiving sound.*

pho·neme (fō′nēm), *n.* any one of a set of speech sounds by which the words of a language are distinguished one from another; the smallest meaningful unit of speech in a language. The words *pat* and *bat* are distinguished by their initial phonemes /p/ and /b/.

pho·ne·mic (fō nē′mik), *adj.* of or involving a phoneme or phonemes: *The difference between "p" and "b" is phonemic.* **−pho·ne′mi·cal·ly,** *adv.*

pho·net·ic (fə net′ik), *adj.* **1** of or about sounds made with the voice. Phonetic exercises are drills in pronunciation. **2** representing sounds made with the voice. Systems of phonetic spelling spell words as they are pronounced and represent the same sound by the same letter. Phonetic symbols are marks used to show pronunciation. We use ᴛʜ as the phonetic symbol for the sound of *th* in *the* or *then.* **3** of or about phonetics. **−pho·net′i·cal·ly,** *adv.*

pho·ne·ti·cian (fō′nə tish′ən), *n.* an expert in phonetics.

pho·net·ics (fə net′iks), *n.* science dealing with sounds made in speech and the art of pronunciation.

pho·ney (fō′nē), *adj., n.* INFORMAL. phony. ❑ *adj.* **pho·ni·er, pho·ni·est;** *n., pl.* **pho·nies.**

phon·ic (fon′ik), *adj.* **1** of or about sound. **2** of or about sounds made in speech; phonetic.

phon·ics (fon′iks), *n.* simplified phonetics for teaching reading.

pho·no·graph (fō′nə graf), *n.* device that reproduces sounds from phonograph records; record player. As a record turns, the grooves on its surface cause the phonograph needle to vibrate. These vibrations are changed into electricity which causes a loudspeaker to produce sound.

pho·no·graph·ic (fō′nə graf′ik), *adj.* of or about a phonograph. **−pho′no·graph′i·cal·ly,** *adv.*

phonograph record, record (def. 5).

pho·ny (fō′nē), **1** *adj.* not genuine; counterfeit; fake. **2** *n.* a fake; pretender: *The doctor turned out to be a phony who had no medical training.* Also, **phoney.** ❑ *adj.* **pho·ni·er, pho·ni·est;** *n., pl.* **pho·nies. −pho′ni·ly,** *adv.* **−pho′ni·ness,** *n.*

WORD STORY   **Phony** may come from an Irish word meaning "a ring." Criminals used to cheat people with rings that looked like gold, but were actually phony.

phoo·ey (fü′ē), *interj.* exclamation used to express disgust, frustration, or contempt.

phos·phate (fos′fāt), *n.* **1** any salt of phosphoric acid. Bread contains phosphates. **2** fertilizer containing such salts. **3** a drink of carbonated water flavored with fruit syrup, and containing a little phosphoric acid.

phos·phor (fos′fər), *n.* substance which gives off light when exposed to certain types of energy, such as ultraviolet rays or X rays. Phosphor is widely used in fluorescent lamps and television tubes.

phos·pho·res·cence (fos′fə res′ns), *n.* **1** act or process of giving out light without burning or by very slow burning that seems not to give out heat: *the phosphorescence of fireflies.* **2** light given out in this way.

phos·pho·res·cent (fos′fə res′nt), *adj.* showing phosphorescence.

phos·phor·ic (fo sfôr′ik), *adj.* of or containing phosphorus.

phosphoric acid, a colorless, odorless acid containing phosphorus, used in making fertilizers.

phos·phor·ous (fos′fər əs), *adj.* of or containing phosphorus.

phos·phor·us (fos′fər əs), *n.* a nonmetallic element whose most common form is a yellow or white, poisonous, waxy substance which burns slowly at ordinary temperatures and glows in the dark. *Symbol:* P

pho·to (fō′tō), *n.* a photograph. ❑ *n., pl.* **pho·tos.**

photo-, *prefix.* **1** of light; with light: *photoelectric = of electricity produced with light.* **2** of photography; by photography: *photocopy = copy made by photography.*

pho·to·chem·i·cal smog (fō′tō kem′ə kəl), air pollution caused when chemical compounds containing only hydrogen and carbon react with compounds of nitrogen and oxygen in sunlight. It is found especially in cities.

pho·to·cop·i·er (fō′tō kop′ē ər), *n.* a machine for reproducing documents photographically.

pho·to·cop·y (fō′tō kop′ē), **1** *n.* a photographic copy or reproduction of something written, typed, or drawn. **2** *v.* to produce a photocopy of. ❑ *n., pl.* **pho·to·cop·ies;** *v.* **pho·to·cop·ied, pho·to·cop·y·ing. −pho′to·cop′i·er,** *n.*

pho·to·e·lec·tric (fō′tō i lek′trik), *adj.* of or about electrical effects produced by the action of light.

photoelectric cell, electronic device that varies the flow of current according to the amount of light reaching its sensitive part; electric eye. Interruptions of the light can start machines that open doors, set off alarms, etc.

photo finish, **1** a finish in a race so close that a photograph is necessary to decide the winner. **2** any contest decided by a close difference.

pho·to·gen·ic (fō′tə jen′ik), *adj.* having characteristics that photograph very well: *a photogenic face.*

pho·to·gram·me·try (fō′tō gram′ə trē), *n.* art or science of making maps or surveys with the help of photographs, especially aerial photographs.

pho·to·graph (fō′tə graf), **1** *n.* picture made with a camera. A photograph is made by the action of light rays from the thing pictured passing through the lens of the camera onto the film. **2** *v.* to take a photograph of. **3** *v.* to look a certain way in a photograph: *I do not photograph well.*

pho·tog·ra·pher (fə tog′rə fər), *n.* **1** person who takes photographs. **2** person whose business is taking photographs.

pho·to·graph·ic (fō′tə graf′ik), *adj.* **1** of or like photography: *photographic accuracy.* **2** used in or produced by photography: *photographic supplies, a photographic record of a trip.* **−pho′to·graph′i·cal·ly,** *adv.*

pho·tog·ra·phy (fə tog′rə fē), *n.* the taking of photographs.

pho·to·jour·nal·ism (fō′tō jėr′nl iz′əm), *n.* journalism that uses dramatic photographs instead of written material as the basis of stories.

pho·tom·e·ter (fō tom′ə tər), *n.* any of various devices for measuring the intensity of light, light distribution, intensity, etc.

pho·tom·e·try (fō tom′ə trē), *n.* branch of physics dealing with measurements of the intensity of light, light distribution, illumination, etc.

pho·to·mon·tage (fō′tō mon-
täzh′), *n.* **1** process of combining
several photographs, or parts of
them, into a single picture. **2** picture made in this way.

pho·ton (fō′ton), *n.* an elementary particle that moves at the
speed of light. It is the basic unit
of electromagnetic energy, and
so the smallest possible amount
of light.

pho·to·re·al·ism (fō′tō rē′ə-
liz′əm), *n.* style of painting in
which the artist uses many precise details and careful coloring
in order to achieve an image that
is almost as realistic as a photograph of the scene.

photomontage

pho·to·stat (fō′tə stat), **1** *n.* photograph made with a special camera for making photocopies directly on specially prepared paper. **2**
n. **Photostat,** trademark for a camera of this kind. **3** *v.* to make a
photostat of something. ❑ *v.* **pho·to·stat·ted, pho·to·stat·ting.**

pho·to·syn·the·sis (fō′tō sin′thə sis), *n.* process in which plant
cells make carbohydrates from carbon dioxide and water in the presence of chlorophyll and light, and release oxygen as a by-product.

pho·tot·ro·pism (fō to′trə piz′əm), *n.* tendency of plants to turn
toward light.

phrasal verb, any verb combined with an adverb or preposition
in a phrase used repeatedly with a familiar meaning that cannot
be understood from the separate meanings of the verb and the
adverb or preposition. **Go along, go in for,** and **go off** are examples of phrasal verbs. Phrasal verbs are often considered as idioms, and they are the most common kind of idiom.

phrase (frāz), **1** *n.* two or more words that have a meaning but do
not contain a subject and verb, and do not form a complete sentence. *At school, in the house,* and *hoping to see you soon* are
phrases. **2** *n.* expression often used: *"Run out" is a common
phrase for "come to an end."* **3** *n.* a short, striking expression;
slogan. EXAMPLES: Liberty or death. All for one and one for all. No
pain, no gain. **4** *v.* to express in a particular way: *I tried to phrase
my excuse politely.* **5** *n.* division of a piece of music, usually several measures in length. ❑ *v.* **phrased, phras·ing.** —**phras′al,** *adj.*
—**phras′al·ly,** *adv.*

phrase book, book or pamphlet of familiar phrases and sentences from one language, with pronunciations and translations
into a second language, meant for use by speakers of the second
language who are not familiar with the first language.

phra·se·ol·o·gy (frā′zē ol′ə jē), *n.* selection and arrangement of
words; the particular way in which thoughts are expressed in language: *scientific phraseology.*

phre·nol·o·gist (fri nol′ə jist), *n.* someone who professes to tell
a person's character from the shape of the person's skull.

phre·nol·o·gy (fri nol′ə jē), *n.* **1** theory that the shape of the
skull shows what sort of mind and character someone has. **2**
practice of reading character from the shape of the skull.

Phryg·i·a (frij′ē ə), *n.* ancient country in the central and NW part
of Asia Minor. See **Troy** for map. —**Phryg′i·an,** *adj., n.*

phy·lum (fī′ləm), *n.* (in biology) the first kind of group into
which a living kingdom is divided, ranking above a class. ❑ *n.,
pl.* **phy·la** (fī′lə).

phys ed or **phys. ed.** (fiz′ ed′), physical education.

phys·i·cal (fiz′ə kəl), **1** *adj.* of or for the body: *physical exercise,
physical strength, a physical disability.* **2** *n.* a medical examination by a doctor: *I had to have a physical before I could go to
summer camp.* **3** *adj.* of or about matter; material: *The tide is a
physical force.* **4** *adj.* according to the laws of nature: *It is a physical impossibility to travel faster than the speed of light.* **5** *adj.* of
or about the science of physics. —**phys′i·cal·ly,** *adv.*

physical change, a change in which the shape or form of a substance becomes different but the nature of the substance stays the
same. A change from a liquid to a solid, as when water freezes
into ice, is a physical change.

physical education, instruction in how to exercise and take
care of the body, especially as a course at a school or college.

physical examination, physical (def. 2).

physical geography, branch of geography that deals with the
natural features of the earth's surface, such as landforms, climate, winds, and ocean currents.

physical science, physics, chemistry, geology, astronomy, and
other sciences that study nonliving matter.

physical therapy, treatment of diseases and defects by physical
remedies, such as exercise and massage, rather than by drugs;
physiotherapy.

phy·si·cian (fə zish′ən), *n.* doctor of medicine.

phys·i·cist (fiz′ə sist), *n.* an expert in physics.

phys·ics (fiz′iks), *n.* science that deals with matter and energy
and the relationships between them. Physics includes the study of
mechanics, heat, light, sound, electricity, magnetism, and atomic
energy.

phys·i·og·no·my (fiz′ē og′nə mē), *n.* **1** kind of features or type
of face you have; your face: *a ruddy physiognomy.* **2** art of estimating character from the features of the face or the form of the
body. **3** the general aspect or looks of a countryside, a situation,
etc.: *the rugged physiognomy of northern Scotland.* ❑ *n., pl.*
phys·i·og·no·mies for 1,3.

phys·i·ol·o·gy (fiz′ē ol′ə jē), *n.* **1** branch of biology dealing with
the normal functions of living things and their parts: *animal
physiology, plant physiology.* **2** all the functions and activities of
a living thing or of any of its parts: *the physiology of the liver.*
—**phys′i·o·log′i·cal,** —**phys′i·ol′o·gist,** *n.*

phys·i·o·ther·a·py (fiz′ē ō ther′ə pē), *n.* physical therapy.
—**phys′i·o·ther′a·pist,** *n.*

phy·sique (fə zēk′), *n.* bodily structure or development; body.

pi (pī), *n.* the Greek letter π, used as the symbol for the ratio of the
circumference of any circle to its diameter. π is equal to about
3.14159. ❑ *n., pl.* **pis.** ■ Another word that sounds like this is **pie.**

P.I., Philippine Islands.

pi·a·nis·si·mo (pē′ə nis′ə mō), in music: **1** *adj.* very soft. **2** *adv.*
very softly.

pi·an·ist (pē an′ist *or* pē′ə nist), *n.* person who plays the piano.

pi·an·o[1] (pē an′ō), *n.* a large musical instrument whose tones
come from many wires. Pressing the keys on a keyboard causes
small hammers to strike the wires, which vibrate, producing
sound. ❑ *n., pl.* **pi·an·os.**

pi·an·o[2] (pē an′ō), in music: **1** *adj.* soft. **2** *adv.* softly.

pi·an·o·for·te (pē an′ə fôr′tē), *n.* piano[1].

pi·az·za (pē az′ə *for 1;* pē ät′sə
for 2), *n.* **1** a large porch along
one or more sides of a house. **2**
an open public square in Italian
towns. ❑ *n., pl.* **pi·az·zas.**

pi·ca (pī′kə), *n.* **1** size of type, 12
point. **2** this size used as a measure; about ⅙ inch. ❑ *n., pl.* **pi·
cas** for 2. ■ Another word that
sounds like this is **pika.**

Pic·ar·dy (pik′ər dē), *n.* region in
N France. See **Normandy** for map.

Pi·cas·so (pi kä′sō), *n.* **Pa·blo**
(pä′blō), 1881-1973, French
painter and sculptor, born in
Spain. He painted in many different styles. His early paintings
were often done in many shades of
blue or pink. He created cubism.

Picasso painting

a	hat	ė	term	ô	order	ch	child		a in about
ā	age	i	it	oi	oil	ng	long		e in taken
ä	far	ī	ice	ou	out	sh	she	ə {	i in pencil
â	care	o	hot	u	cup	th	thin		o in lemon
e	let	ō	open	u̇	put	₮H	then		u in circus
ē	equal	ò	saw	ü	rule	zh	measure		

P

pic·a·yune (pik′ə yün′), *adj.* small; petty; mean: *picayune criticism.*

pic·ca·lil·li (pik′ə lil′ē), *n.* relish made of chopped pickles, onions, tomatoes, hot spices, etc.

pic·co·lo (pik′ə lō), *n.* a small, shrill flute, sounding an octave higher than an ordinary flute. ❑ *n., pl.* **pic·co·los.**

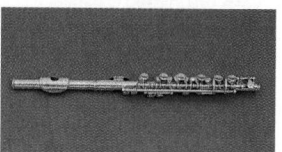

piccolo

pick[1] (pik), **1** *v.* to choose out of a number or quantity; select: *I picked a winning horse at the races.* ■ See Synonym Study at **choose. 2** *n.* choice; selection: *This red rose is my pick. Who is your pick to win the championship?* **3** *n.* the best or most desirable part: *We got a high price for the pick of our peaches.* **4** *v.* to pull away with the fingers; gather: *We pick fruit and flowers.* **5** *v.* to use something pointed to remove things from: *pick your teeth, pick a bone.* **6** *v.* to open with a pointed tool, wire, etc.: *The burglar picked the lock on the garage.* **7** *v.* to steal the contents of: *In the crowded waiting room I didn't feel the hand that picked my pocket.* **8** *v.* to prepare for use by removing feathers, waste parts, etc.: *pick a chicken.* **9** *v.* to pluck the strings of a musical instrument: *I picked the banjo.* **10** *n.* thing held in the fingers and used to pull on the strings of a musical instrument; plectrum. **11** *v.* to seek and find occasion for; seek and find: *pick a quarrel, pick flaws.* **—pick′er**, *n.*

pick at, 1 to pull on with the fingers, etc.: *She picked at the scab on her finger.* **2** to eat only a little at a time: *The bird picks at the bread.*

pick off, 1 to hit something after taking careful aim. **2** (in baseball) to catch a runner off base and throw him or her out. **3** to shoot one at a time.

pick on, to annoy; tease: *My older brother and sister always pick on me.*

pick out, 1 to choose with care; select: *Pick out a coat you will like to wear.* **2** to tell someone or something apart from its surroundings; recognize: *Can you pick me out in this group picture?*

pick up, 1 to take up: *She picked up the hammer.* **2** to get by chance: *pick up a bargain.* **3** to learn without being taught: *He picks up games easily.* **4** to take into a vehicle or ship; give a ride to: *The bus picked up passengers at every other corner.* **5** to get and take along with you: *I picked up a pizza on my way home.* **6** to recover; improve: *He seemed to pick up quickly after his fever went down.* **7** to go faster: *The bus picked up speed on its way down the mountain.* **8** to succeed in seeing, hearing, etc.: *She picked up a radio broadcast from Paris.* **9** INFORMAL. to become acquainted with someone without being introduced. **10** to tidy up; put in order: *pick up a room.*

pick up on, to understand; see; get: *I didn't pick up on what he was trying to tell me.*

pick[2] (pik), *n.* **1** pickax. **2** a sharp-pointed tool. Ice is broken into pieces with a pick.

pick·ax or **pick·axe** (pik′aks′), *n.* tool with a heavy metal bar, pointed at one or both ends, attached through the center to a wooden handle; pick. It is used for breaking up dirt, rocks, etc. ❑ *n., pl.* **pick·ax·es.** [**Pickax** probably comes from a Latin word meaning "woodpecker." A pickax looks like a woodpecker's beak.]

pick·er·el (pik′ər əl), *n.* any of three freshwater fishes with long, narrow pointed heads, used for food. Pickerels are pike. ❑ *n., pl.* **pick·er·el** or **pick·er·els.**

pick·et (pik′it), **1** *n.* person stationed by a labor union near a factory, store, etc., where there is a strike. Pickets try to prevent employees from working or customers from buying. **2** *n.* person who takes part in a public demonstration or boycott to support a cause or to protest something. **3** *v.* to station pickets at or near: *picket a factory.* **4** *n.* a small group of troops, or a single soldier, posted at some place to watch for the enemy and guard against surprise attacks. **5** *v.* to station as pickets. **6** *v.* to walk about or stand near as a picket. **7** *n.* a pointed stake or peg placed upright to make a fence, to tie a horse to, etc. **8** *v.* to tie to a picket: *picket a horse.* **9** *v.* to enclose with pickets; fence. **—pick′et·er**, *n.*

picket fence, fence made of pickets.

picket line, a line of people picketing a factory, place of business, school, or the like.

pick·ings (pik′ingz), *n.pl.* **1** amount picked. **2** things left over; scraps.

pick·le (pik′əl), **1** *n.* cucumber or other vegetable preserved in a spicy liquid containing salt water, vinegar, etc. **2** *n.* salt water, vinegar, or other liquid in which meat and vegetables can be preserved. **3** *v.* to preserve in pickle: *We pickled several quarts of beets yesterday.* **4** *n.* INFORMAL. trouble; difficulty: *I got in a bad pickle today.* ❑ *v.* **pick·led, pick·ling.**

pick·pock·et (pik′pok′it), *n.* person who steals from people's pockets.

WORD STORY   **Pickpocket** is one of a small number of English words that are formed from a verb followed by its object noun. **Scarecrow** and **scofflaw** are others. You can probably think of more. These words let you imagine people naming things for the first time, putting old words together to do it.

pick·up (pik′up′), *n.* **1** act of picking up: *the daily pickup of mail.* **2** process of getting better; improvement: *a pickup in business, a pickup in your health.* **3** increase in speed; acceleration; going faster: *Although our car is ten years old, it still has good pickup.* **4** cartridge (def. 4). **5** reception of sounds or images in radio or television and their conversion into electric waves for broadcasting. **6** equipment for such reception or the place where it occurs. **7** pickup truck.

pickup truck, a small truck with an open back, used for light hauling; pickup.

pick·y (pik′ē), *adj.* **1** choosy; particular: *Some customers are very picky when it comes to selecting shoes.* **2** finding fault about trifles; nagging: *The driving instructor was picky about details, but he taught me a lot about driving in highway traffic.* ❑ *adj.* **pick·i·er, pick·i·est. —pick′i·ness**, *n.*

pic·nic (pik′nik), **1** *n.* a pleasure trip with a meal in the open air. **2** *v.* to go on such a trip: *Our family often picnics at the beach.* **3** *v.* to eat in picnic style. ❑ *v.* **pic·nicked, pic·nick·ing. —pic′nick·er**, *n.*

pi·co·sec·ond (pē′kō sek′ənd), *n.* one trillionth of a second.

pics (piks), *n.pl.* INFORMAL. pictures, especially photographs: *Have you seen our vacation pics?*

Pict (pikt), *n.* member of an ancient people formerly living in Scotland, especially northern Scotland, between A.D. 200s and 900s.

pic·to·gram (pik′tə gram), *n.* diagram that uses pictures to show numerical information or relationships.

pic·to·graph (pik′tə graf), *n.* **1** picture used as a sign or symbol: *Chinese characters developed from pictographs.* **2** chart or diagram showing facts or information by using pictures of different colors, sizes, or numbers. **—pic′to·graph′ic**, *adj.*

pic·to·ri·al (pik tôr′ē əl), *adj.* **1** of or about pictures; expressed in pictures. **2** illustrated by pictures: *a pictorial history, a pictorial magazine.* **3** of or about painters or painting: *pictorial skill.* **—pic·to′ri·al·ly**, *adv.*

pic·ture (pik′chər), **1** *n.* a drawing, painting, portrait, or photograph; a print of any of these: *The book contains a good picture of a tiger.* **2** *n.* scene: *The trees and brook make a lovely picture.* **3** *n.* something beautiful: *The old stone castle was a picture in the bright sunlight.* **4** *v.* to draw, paint, etc.; make into a picture: *The artist pictured life in the old West.* **5** *n.* image; likeness: *He is the picture of his father. She was the picture of happiness.* **6** *v.* to form a picture of in the mind; imagine: *It is hard to picture life a hundred years ago.* **7** *n.* a mental picture; idea: *have a clear picture of the problem.* **8** *n.* a vivid description: *The speaker gave us a good picture of life in the old West.* **9** *v.* to show by words; describe vividly: *The speaker pictured the suffering of the poor.* **10** *n.* a movie. **11** *n.* image on a TV set. **12** *n.* state of affairs; condition: *the employment picture.* ❑ *v.* **pic·tured, pic·tur·ing.**

pic·tur·esque (pik′chə resk′), *adj.* **1** quaint or interesting enough to be used as the subject of a picture. **2** making a picture for the mind; vivid: *picturesque language.* **—pic′tur·esque′ly**, *adv.* **—pic′tur·esque′ness**, *n.*

picture tube, a cathode-ray tube, narrow at one end and widening at the other to form a screen on which television pictures or computer information appear.

pidg·in (pij′ən), *n.* **1** a language with a limited grammar and vocabulary, spoken by people with different native languages, in order to communicate or engage in trade. **2** pidgin English.

pidgin English, one of several forms of English, with simplified grammatical structure and often a mixed vocabulary, used as a language of trade in western Africa, Australia, Melanesia, and China.

pie (pī), *n.* fruit, meat, etc., baked in a crust: *apple pie, chicken pie.* ■ Another word that sounds like this is **pi.**

pie·bald (pī′bôld′), **1** *adj.* spotted in two colors, especially black and white. **2** *n.* a piebald horse.

piece (pēs), **1** *n.* one of the parts into which a thing is divided or broken; bit: *The cup broke in pieces.* **2** *n.* portion; limited part; small quantity: *a piece of land containing two acres, a piece of bread.* **3** *n.* a single thing of a set or class: *This set of china has 144 pieces.* **4** *n.* a single composition in an art: *a piece of music.* **5** *n.* coin: *a five-cent piece.* **6** *n.* example; instance: *That silly story is a piece of nonsense.* **7** *n.* an amount of work done: *paid by the piece.* **8** *n.* gun; cannon. **9** *v.* to make or repair by adding or joining pieces: *piece a quilt.* ❑ *v.* **pieced, piec·ing.** ■ Another word that sounds like this is **peace.**

give someone a piece of your mind, to scold: *I gave him a piece of my mind for coming late again.*

go to pieces, 1 to fall apart; break up: *Another ship had gone to pieces on the rocks.* **2** to break down; collapse: *When her business failed, she went completely to pieces.*

of a piece, of the same kind; similar to: *That plan is of a piece with the rest of their silly suggestions.*

piece together, to join the pieces or parts of: *After listening to all four witnesses, we were able to piece together the story of what happened.*

piece·meal (pēs′mēl′), **1** *adv.* piece by piece; a little at a time: *work done piecemeal.* **2** *adv.* piece from piece; to pieces; into fragments. **3** *adj.* done piece by piece.

piece of cake, INFORMAL. something easy to do: *After lots of practice, the performance was a piece of cake.*

piece of eight, an old Spanish peso, used during the Spanish colonization of America.

piece·work (pēs′wėrk′), *n.* work paid for by the amount done, not by the time it takes.

pie chart, a circular chart divided into sections like slices of a pie. The size of a section shows the size of the amount it stands for.

pied (pīd), *adj.* having patches of two or more colors; many-colored.

Pied·mont (pēd′mont), *n.* **1** plateau in the United States between the Appalachian Mountains and the lowland along the Atlantic coast. The Piedmont extends over parts of New Jersey, Pennsylvania, Delaware, New York, Maryland, Virginia, North Carolina, South Carolina, Georgia, and Alabama. **2** region in NW Italy. [Piedmont comes from French words meaning "foot" and "mountain," because this region is at the foot of the Appalachians.]

State Business Income

service 24%
trade 21%
other 6%
agriculture 14%
finance 11%
transport 7%
manufacturing 17%

pie chart

pier (pir), *n.* **1** structure supported on columns extending into the water, used as a walk or a landing place for ships. **2** breakwater. **3** one of the solid supports on which the arches of a bridge rest; pillar. **4** the solid part of a wall between windows, doors, etc. ■ Another word that sounds like this is **peer.**

pierce (pirs), *v.* **1** to make a hole in; bore into or through: *A nail pierced the tire of our car.* ■ See Synonym Study at **penetrate. 2** to go into; go through: *A tunnel pierces the mountain.* **3** to force a way; force a way through or into: *A sharp cry pierced the air.* **4** to make a way through with the eye or mind: *pierce a disguise, pierce a mystery.* **5** to affect sharply with some feeling: *a heart pierced with grief.* ❑ *v.* **pierced, pierc·ing. —pierce′a·ble,** *adj.* **—pierc′er,** *n.*

Pierce (pirs), *n.* **Franklin,** 1804-1869, the 14th president of the United States, from 1853 to 1857. ■ **Franklin Pierce** was his party's fifth choice for the presidential nomination. He was considered only after 34 nominating votes had been taken without a winner. He won on the 49th vote.

pierc·ing (pir′sing), *adj.* able to pierce; penetrating; sharp; keen: *piercing cold, a piercing look.* **—pierc′ing·ly,** *adv.*

Pierre (pir), *n.* capital of South Dakota, in the central part. [Pierre was named for Pierre Chouteau, an early fur trader.]

pi·e·ty (pī′ə tē), *n.* **1** reverence for God; devotion to religion; holiness; goodness. **2** dutiful regard for your parents. **3** a pious act, remark, belief, etc. ❑ *n., pl.* **pi·e·ties** for 3.

pig (pig), *n.* **1** a four-footed mammal with a stout, heavy body, cloven hoofs, and a broad snout; hog; swine. Pigs are raised for their meat. **2** a young animal of this kind. **3** pork. **4** INFORMAL. person who acts as a pig is thought to act; someone who is greedy, dirty, dull, sullen, or stubborn. **—pig′like′,** *adj.*

pig out, INFORMAL. to stuff yourself with food; gorge: *pig out on junk food.*

pig (def. 1)—28 in. (71 cm) high at the shoulder

pig·eon (pij′ən), *n.* any of numerous birds with thick bodies, short tails and legs, and often cooing calls, including doves. There are many domesticated varieties of the common pigeon.

pig·eon·hole (pij′ən hōl′), **1** *n.* one of a set of boxlike compartments for holding papers and other articles in a desk, a cabinet, etc. **2** *v.* to put in a pigeonhole; put away. **3** *v.* to classify and lay aside in memory where one can refer to it. **4** *v.* to put aside with the idea of dismissing, forgetting, or neglecting: *The city council pigeonholed the people's request for a new park.* **5** *n.* a small place built, usually as one of a series, for a pigeon to nest in. ❑ *v.* **pig·eon·holed, pig·eon·hol·ing.**

pig·eon·toed (pij′ən tōd′), *adj.* having the toes or feet turned inward.

pig·gish (pig′ish), *adj.* **1** very selfish; greedy. **2** dirty; filthy. **—pig′gish·ly,** *adv.* **—pig′gish·ness,** *n.*

WORD STORY Piggish and other words about pigs make clear that people don't have a high opinion of these animals. In fact, most words from domestic animal names suggest criticism. It isn't good to be catty, chicken, or sheepish. It's respectable to be dogged, but not to be a cur. People seem to think better of wild animals: if you're foxy enough, you could end up being lionized.

pig·gy (pig′ē), **1** *n.* a little pig. **2** *adj.* piggish. ❑ *n., pl.* **pig·gies.**

pig·gy·back (pig′ē bak′), **1** *adj.* on the back: *a piggyback ride.* **2** *adv.* on railroad flatcars: *Loaded truck trailers are first transported piggyback and then by road.* **3** *v.* to use one thing as a means to do or have something else: *She piggybacked on her success as a model to start an acting career.*

piggy bank, 1 a small container in the shape of a pig, with a slot in the top for coins. **2** any coin bank.

a	hat	ė	term	ô	order	ch	child		a in about
ā	age	i	it	oi	oil	ng	long		e in taken
ä	far	ī	ice	ou	out	sh	she	ə	i in pencil
â	care	o	hot	u	cup	th	thin		o in lemon
e	let	ō	open	u̇	put	ŦH	then		u in circus
ē	equal	ȯ	saw	ü	rule	zh	measure		

P

pig·head·ed (pig′hed′id), *adj.* stupidly obstinate or stubborn; refusing to change your opinion or action: *Some people can be very pigheaded.* —**pig′head′ed·ly,** *adv.* —**pig′head′ed·ness,** *n.*

pig iron, crude iron as it first comes from the blast furnace or smelter. It is used to make steel, cast iron, and wrought iron.

pig Latin, a form of English, popular with children, in which each word is pronounced with the first consonant sound placed at the end and the sound ā added. *Ellohay, ischray = Hello, Chris.*

pig·let (pig′lit), *n.* a young pig.

pig·ment (pig′mənt), *n.* **1** a coloring material, especially a powdered dry substance. Paint and dyes are made by mixing pigments with liquid. **2** substance that occurs in and colors the tissues of a living thing. The color of a person's hair, skin, and eyes is produced by pigments.

pig·men·ta·tion (pig′mən tā′shən), *n.* process of coloring the tissues of a living thing by deposits of pigment. Freckles are caused by pigmentation.

pig·my (pig′mē), *adj., n.* pygmy. ❏ *n., pl.* **pig·mies.**

pig·pen (pig′pen′), *n.* **1** pen where pigs are kept; sty. **2** a filthy place.

pig·skin (pig′skin′), *n.* **1** the skin of a pig. **2** leather made from it. **3** INFORMAL. a football.

pig·sty (pig′stī′), *n.* pigpen. ❏ *n., pl.* **pig·sties.**

pig·tail (pig′tāl′), *n.* braid of hair hanging from the back of the head.

pi·ka (pī′kə), *n.* a small, tailless mammal related to and resembling a rabbit, but with short ears. Several kinds of pikas live in mountains of Asia and western North America. ❏ *n., pl.* **pi·kas.**
■ Another word that sounds like this is **pica.**

pike[1] (pīk), *n.* a long, wooden shaft with a sharp-pointed metal head; spear. Foot soldiers used to carry pikes.

pike[2] (pīk), *n.* a sharp point; spike.

pike[3] (pīk), *n.* any of several large, fierce, slender, freshwater fish of the Northern Hemisphere, with long, pointed heads, especially the **northern pike,** a common game and food fish. The muskellunge and pickerels are pikes. ❏ *n., pl.* **pike** or **pikes.**

pike[4] (pīk), *n.* turnpike.

pik·er (pī′kər), *n.* INFORMAL. **1** person who does things in a small or cheap way. **2** a stingy person.

Pikes Peak (pīks), mountain of the Rocky Mountains in central Colorado, 14,110 feet (4301 meters) high.

pi·laf (pi läf′ or pē′läf), *n.* an Asian food made of rice or cracked wheat, flavored with spices, raisins, etc.

pi·las·ter (pə las′tər), *n.* a rectangular pillar, especially when not standing alone, but supporting a part of a wall from which it sticks out a little.

Pi·late (pī′lət), *n.* **Pon·tius** (pon′shəs), Roman governor who ruled over Judea in Palestine from A.D. 26 to 36?. During his rule Jesus was crucified.

pile[1] (pīl), **1** *n.* many things lying on each other in a more or less orderly way: *a pile of wood.* **2** *n.* a heap like a hill or mound: *a pile of dirt.* **3** *v.* to heap up; stack: *The campers piled the extra wood near the fire.* **4** *v.* to gather or rise in heaps: *Snow piled against the fences.* **5** *n.* a large amount: *I have a pile of work to do.* **6** *v.* to cover with large amounts: *pile a plate with food.* **7** *v.* to go in a confused, rushing crowd or group: *pile out of a bus, pile into a car.* **8** *n.* reactor. ❏ *v.* **piled, pil·ing.**

pile[2] (pīl), *n.* a heavy beam driven upright into the earth, often under water, to help support a bridge, wharf, building, etc.

pile[3] (pīl), *n.* **1** a soft, thick nap on velvet, plush, and many carpets: *The pile of that rug is almost half an inch long.* **2** a soft, fine hair or down.

pile driver, machine for driving down piles or stakes, usually a tall framework in which a heavy weight is raised and then allowed to fall upon the pile.

pil·fer (pil′fər), *v.* to steal in small quantities; steal: *The hungry hikers pilfered apples from an orchard.* —**pil′fer·er,** *n.*

pil·grim (pil′grəm), *n.* **1** person who goes on a journey to a sacred or holy place as an act of religious devotion. In the Middle Ages, many people went as pilgrims to Jerusalem and to holy places in Europe. **2** traveler; wanderer. **3 Pilgrim,** one of the Puritan settlers of Plymouth Colony in 1620.

pil·grim·age (pil′grə mij), *n.* **1** a pilgrim's journey; a journey to some sacred place as an act of religious devotion. **2** a long journey.

pil·ing (pī′ling), *n.* **1** piles or heavy beams driven into the ground. **2** structure made of piles.

pill (pil), *n.* **1** medicine made up into a small pellet, tablet, or capsule to be swallowed whole. **2 the pill,** pill taken by women to prevent pregnancy.

pil·lage (pil′ij), **1** *v.* to rob with violence; plunder: *Pirates pillaged the towns along the coast.* **2** *n.* plunder; robbery. ❏ *v.* **pillaged, pil·lag·ing.** —**pil′lag·er,** *n.*

pil·lar (pil′ər), *n.* **1** a slender, upright structure; column. Pillars are usually made of stone, wood, or metal and used as supports or ornaments for a building. Sometimes a pillar stands alone as a monument. **2** anything slender and upright like a pillar: *Pillars of smoke arose from the burning building.* **3** an important support or supporter: *a pillar of society, a pillar of the church.*
from pillar to post, from one thing or place to another without any definite purpose.

pill·box (pil′boks′), *n.* **1** a small box, usually shallow and often round, for holding pills. **2** a small, low fortress with thick, concrete walls and roof, equipped with machine guns and other weapons. ❏ *n., pl.* **pill·box·es.**

pil·lion (pil′yən), *n.* seat attached behind a motorcycle saddle, for a passenger to ride on.

pil·lo·ry (pil′ər ē), **1** *n.* frame of wood with holes through which someone's head and hands were put. The pillory was formerly used as a punishment, being set up in a public place where the crowd could make fun of the offender. **2** *v.* to put in the pillory. **3** *v.* to expose to public ridicule, contempt, or abuse: *The newspapers pilloried the unpopular mayor.* ❏ *n., pl.* **pil·lo·ries;** *v.* **pil·lo·ried, pil·lo·ry·ing.**

pil·low (pil′ō), **1** *n.* bag or case filled with feathers, down, foam rubber, or other soft material, usually used to support the head when resting or sleeping. **2** *v.* to rest on a pillow. **3** *v.* to be a pillow for: *He lay with his arm pillowing his head.*

pil·low·case (pil′ō kās′), *n.* a cloth cover pulled over a pillow.

pil·low·slip (pil′ō slip′), *n.* pillowcase.

pi·lot (pī′lət), **1** *n.* person trained to operate the controls of an aircraft or spacecraft in flight. **2** *n.* person trained to steer ships in or out of a harbor or through dangerous waters. A ship takes on a pilot before coming into a strange harbor. **3** *n.* person who steers a ship or boat. **4** *v.* to steer or operate controls: *to pilot an airplane.* **5** *n.* a guide; leader. **6** *v.* to guide; lead: *The manager piloted us through the big factory.* **7** *n.* a sample show of a planned TV series. [**Pilot** comes from a Greek word meaning "an oar." In old times, ships were steered by a special oar instead of a rudder.] —**pi′lot·less,** *adj.*

pi·lot·house (pī′lət hous′), *n.* an enclosed place on the deck of a ship, sheltering the steering wheel and pilot; wheelhouse. ❏ *n., pl.* **pi·lot·hous·es** (pī′lət hou′ziz).

pilot light, a small flame used to light a main burner. Gas stoves and gas water heaters have pilot lights.

Pi·ma (pē′mə), *n.* member of a tribe of American Indians living in Arizona. ❏ *n., pl.* **Pi·mas** or **Pi·ma.**

pi·men·to (pə men′tō), *n.* pimiento. ❏ *n., pl.* **pi·men·tos.**

pi·mien·to (pə men′tō), *n.* kind of fleshy sweet pepper, used as a vegetable, relish, and stuffing for green olives. ❏ *n., pl.* **pi·mien·tos.**

pim·per·nel (pim′pər nel), *n.* a European and Asian plant with small scarlet, purple, blue, or white flowers that close in bad weather.

pim·ple (pim′pəl), *n.* a small, inflamed swelling of the skin. —**pim′ple·like′,** *adj.*

pim·pled (pim′pəld), *adj.* pimply.

pim·ply (pim′plē), *adj.* having pimples. ❏ *adj.* **pim·pli·er, pim·pli·est.**

pin (pin), **1** *n.* a short, slender piece of wire with a point at one end and a head at the other, for fastening things together. **2** *n.* badge with a pin or clasp to fasten it to the clothing: *She wore her class pin.* **3** *n.* brooch. **4** *n.* peg made of wood, metal, or plastic, used to fasten things together, hold something, hang things on, etc. **5** *n.* any of various fastenings, such as a clothespin or safety pin. **6** *v.* to fasten with a pin or pins; put a pin through: *He pinned a notice on the bulletin board.* **7** *v.* to hold fast in one position: *When the tree fell, it pinned the lumberjack's leg to the ground.* **8** *n.* (in bowling) one of the bottle-shaped pieces of wood that you aim the ball at. ❑ *v.* **pinned, pin·ning. —pin′like′,** *adj.*

on pins and needles, very worried or uneasy.

pin down, to force someone to state or do something.

pin on, to fix blame, responsibility, etc., on: *You're not going to pin the blame on me!*

pin·a·fore (pin′ə fôr′), *n.* **1** a child's apron that covers most of the dress. **2** a light dress without sleeves.

pi·ña·ta (pē nyä′tə), *n.* a decorated pottery jar filled with candy, fruit, or other treats. It is a Hispanic custom to hang a piñata at birthday parties and Christmastime above the heads of blindfolded children. They swing sticks at the jar to break it and get what is inside. ❑ *n., pl.* **pi·ña·tas.** [**Piñata** probably comes from an Italian word meaning "pine cone." One kind of Italian clay pot was shaped like a large pine cone, and the pot's name was borrowed into Spanish.]

piñata

pin·ball (pin′bôl′), *n.* game in which a ball is propelled by a spring so that it rolls down a slanting board. Points are scored when the ball strikes or passes through various bumpers and alleys.

pince-nez (pans′nā′ *or* pins′nā′), *n.* eyeglasses kept in place by a spring that clips onto the bridge of the nose. ❑ *n., pl.* **pince-nez** (pans′nāz′ *or* pins′nāz′). [**Pince-nez** comes from French words meaning "to pinch" and "nose."]

pin·cers (pin′sərz), *n.pl. or sing.* **1** tool for gripping and holding tight, made like scissors but with jaws instead of blades. **2** the large claw or pair of claws of crabs, lobsters, etc., which are used to grip and hold the prey. Also, **pinchers.**

pinch (pinch), **1** *v.* to squeeze between two hard edges; squeeze with thumb and forefinger: *pinch a baby's cheek playfully.* **2** *n.* act of pinching; a squeeze between two hard edges. **3** *v.* to press so as to hurt; squeeze: *These new shoes pinch my feet.* **4** *n.* sharp pressure that hurts; squeeze: *the pinch of tight shoes.* **5** *n.* sharp discomfort or distress: *the pinch of cold.* **6** *v.* to cause to shrink or become thin: *a face pinched by hunger.* **7** *n.* time of special need; emergency: *I will help you in a pinch.* **8** *n.* as much as can be taken up with the tips of finger and thumb; a very small amount: *a pinch of salt.* **9** *v.* to be stingy; be stingy with: *The miser even pinched pennies.* **10** *v.* SLANG. to arrest. **11** *n.* SLANG. an arrest. **12** *v.* SLANG. to steal: *The grocer caught them pinching apples.* **13** *n.* SLANG. act of stealing. ❑ *n., pl.* **pinch·es. —pinch′er,** *n.*

pinch·ers (pin′chərz), *n.pl. or sing.* pincers.

pinch-hit (pinch′hit′), *v.* **1** (in baseball) to bat for another player, especially when a hit is badly needed. **2** to take another's place in an emergency: *I had to pinch-hit for my brother when he was sick and couldn't drive.* ❑ *v.* **pinch-hit, pinch-hit·ting. —pinch hitter.**

pin·cush·ion (pin′kush′ən), *n.* a small cushion to stick pins in until they are needed.

pine[1] (pīn), *n.* **1** any of numerous evergreen trees of the Northern Hemisphere that have cones and clusters of needle-shaped leaves. Pines are valuable for timber, turpentine, resin, etc. **2** the wood of any of these trees.

pine[2] (pīn), *v.* **1** to long eagerly; yearn: *The homesick children pined to see their parents.* **2** to waste away with pain, hunger, grief, or desire. ❑ *v.* **pined, pin·ing. —pin′er,** *n.*

pin·e·al (pin′ē əl), *adj.* of or about the pineal body.

pineal body or **pineal gland,** a small, cone-shaped part of the brain, which produces and releases hormones. It is thought to sense light and to act as a biological clock.

pine·ap·ple (pī′nap′əl), *n.* the large, juicy fruit of a tropical plant with slender, stiff leaves. Pineapples look something like big pine cones.

Pine Bluff, city in S central Arkansas.

pine nut, seed found in the cones of several kinds of pine trees, such as the piñon. It is good to eat.

pin·ey (pī′nē), *adj.* piny. ❑ *adj.* **pin·i·er, pin·i·est.**

pin·feath·er (pin′feᴛʜ′ər), *n.* an undeveloped feather, especially one just growing through the skin.

pineapple

ping (ping), **1** *n.* a high-pitched sound like that of a rifle bullet whistling through the air or striking something metal. **2** *v.* to make this sound. **3** *n.* knock (def. 8).

Ping-Pong (ping′pong′), *n.* trademark for table tennis.

pin·head (pin′hed′), *n.* **1** the head of a pin. **2** something very small or worthless. **3** SLANG. very stupid person; jerk.

pin·hole (pin′hōl′), *n.* **1** hole made by or as if by a pin. **2** hole for a pin or peg to go in.

pin·ion[1] (pin′yən), **1** *n.* the last joint of a bird's wing. **2** *n.* a wing. **3** *n.* any one of the stiff flying feathers of the wing. **4** *v.* to cut off or tie the pinions of a bird to prevent flying. **5** *v.* to bind the arms of; bind: *The bank robbers pinioned the guard to a chair.*

pin·ion[2] (pin′yən), *n.* a small gear with teeth that fit into those of a rack or those of a larger gear.

pink[1] (pingk), **1** *n.* the color obtained by mixing red with white; light or pale red. **2** *adj.* having this color. **3** *n.* any of numerous garden plants with spicy-smelling flowers of various colors, mostly white, pink, and red. A carnation is a kind of pink. **—pink′ness,** *n.*

in the pink, in excellent health and physical condition.

pink[2] (pingk), *v.* **1** to prick or pierce with a sword, spear, or dagger. **2** to cut the edge of cloth in small notches to prevent raveling. **3** to decorate with small, round holes.

pink·eye (pingk′ī′), *n.* a contagious disease that causes inflammation of the membrane that forms the inner surface of the eyelids and the front part of the eyeball.

pink·ie (ping′kē), *n.* the smallest finger. Also, **pinky.**

pinking shears, shears for cutting the edges of cloth in small notches to prevent raveling.

pink·ish (ping′kish), *adj.* somewhat pink.

pink·y (ping′kē), *n.* pinkie. ❑ *n., pl.* **pink·ies.**

pin money, a small amount of money used to buy extra things for your own use.

pin·na (pin′ə), *n.* a skin-covered flap of cartilage that forms the external ear; auricle. ❑ *n., pl.* **pin·nae** (pin′ē), **pin·nas.**

pin·na·cle (pin′ə kəl), *n.* **1** a high peak or point of rock, ice, etc.: *a snow-covered pinnacle of the Alps.* **2** the highest point: *at the pinnacle of your fame.* **3** a slender turret or spire.

pin·nate (pin′āt), *adj.* **1** like a feather. **2** (of a leaf) having leaflets on each side of a stalk. **—pin′nate·ly,** *adv.*

pi·noch·le (pē′nuk′əl), *n.* game played with a double deck of all cards from the nine to the ace. There are 48 cards in the deck.

piñ·on (pin′yən *or* pē′nyōn), *n.* any of four small pine trees of the southwestern United States, producing large, nutlike seeds that are good to eat. ❑ *n., pl.* **piñ·ons.**

pin·point (pin′point′), **1** *v.* to aim at accurately; determine precisely: *The pilot pinpointed a field for landing.* **2** *adj.* extremely accurate or precise: *pinpoint bombing.* **3** *n.* something very small or sharp: *pinpoints of light.* **4** *n.* the point of a pin.

pint (pīnt), *n.* **1** unit of volume for measuring liquids, equal to ½

a	hat	e̤	term	ô	order	ch	child		a in about
ā	age	i	it	oi	oil	ng	long		e in taken
ä	far	ī	ice	ou	out	sh	she	ə	i in pencil
â	care	o	hot	u	cup	th	thin		o in lemon
e	let	ō	open	ù	put	ᴛʜ	then		u in circus
ē	equal	ò	saw	ü	rule	zh	measure		

P

quart; 2 cups; 16 fluid ounces. **2** unit of volume for measuring dry things, equal to ¹⁄₆₄ bushel.

pin·to (pin′tō), **1** *adj.* spotted in two or more colors; pied: *a pinto pony.* **2** *n.* a spotted, white and black or white and brown horse. ❑ *n., pl.* **pin·tos.** [Pinto comes from a Latin word meaning "to paint." This kind of horse is sometimes called "a paint" in English.]

pinto bean, kind of kidney bean that is pink with dark spots.

pin·wheel (pin′wēl′), *n.* **1** toy made of a wheel fastened to a stick by a pin so that it revolves in the wind. **2** kind of firework that revolves when lighted.

pin·worm (pin′wėrm′), *n.* any of several small, threadlike worms, especially one that sometimes inhabits the large intestine and rectum of children, causing intense itching.

pin·y (pī′nē), *adj.* **1** abounding in or covered with pine trees: *piny mountains.* **2** of or suggesting pine trees: *a piny odor.* ❑ *adj.* **pin·i·er, pin·i·est.** Also, **piney.**

Pin·yin or **pin·yin** (pin′yin), *n.* system for spelling the sounds of Mandarin Chinese in the English alphabet. Pinyin was created in 1958 and officially adopted by the Chinese government in 1978.

pi·o·neer (pī′ə nir′), **1** *n.* person who settles in a part of a country, preparing it for others: *The pioneers of the American West included trappers, explorers, and farming families.* **2** *n.* person who goes first, or does something first, and so prepares a way for others: *a pioneer in medical science.* **3** *v.* to prepare or open up for others; take the lead in doing: *Astronauts are pioneering in exploring outer space.*

> **WORD STORY** **Pioneer** comes from a Latin word meaning "foot." Groups of foot soldiers used to go ahead of an army to make roads and build bridges, preparing the way for others, as later pioneers prepared for settlements.

pi·ous (pī′əs), *adj.* **1** having or showing deep respect for God; religious. **2** done under pretense of religion or of serving a good cause: *a pious fraud.* **−pi′ous·ly,** *adv.* **−pi′ous·ness,** *n.*

pip¹ (pip), *n.* seed of an apple, orange, etc.

pip² (pip), *n.* an infectious disease of birds that causes the production of thick mucus in the mouth and throat.

pip³ (pip), *n.* one of the spots on playing cards, dominoes, or dice.

pipe (pip), **1** *n.* tube through which a liquid or gas flows. **2** *v.* to carry by means of a pipe or pipes: *Water is piped from the lake into the reservoir.* **3** *v.* to supply with pipes: *Our street is being piped for gas.* **4** *n.* tube with a bowl of clay, wood, or other material at one end, for smoking. **5** *n.* a musical instrument with a single tube into which the player blows. **6** *n.pl.* **pipes,** a set of musical tubes: *the pipes of Pan.* **b** bagpipe. **7** *v.* to play on a pipe. **8** *n.* any one of the tubes in an organ. **9** *v.* to make a shrill noise; speak or sing in a shrill voice: *"I'm hungry!" piped the child.* **10** *n.* a shrill sound, voice, or song: *the pipe of the lark.* ❑ *v.* **piped, pip·ing.** [See Word Story at **fife.**] **−pipe′like′,** *adj.*

pipe down, INFORMAL. be quiet! shut up!

pipe dream, INFORMAL. an impractical idea or plan that is impossible to make real: *His singing career is just a pipe dream.*

pipe·line (pīp′līn′), *n.* **1** line of pipes for carrying oil or other liquids, usually over a considerable distance. **2** source of information, usually secret. **3** the group of projects or products in development or planned; things to come: *A new class on computer graphics is in the pipeline for next year.*

pipe organ, organ with pipes of different lengths that produce various musical notes when air is blown through them.

pip·er (pī′pər), *n.* person who plays on a pipe or bagpipe.

pay the piper, to pay for your pleasure; bear the consequences.

pi·pette (pī pet′), *n.* a slender tube for transferring or measuring small quantities of liquids. Liquid is held in the tube by closing the top end; when the top end is uncovered, the liquid flows from the bottom end.

pip·ing (pī′ping), **1** *n.* a shrill sound: *the piping of frogs in the spring.* **2** *adj.* shrill: *a high, piping voice.* **3** *n.* pipes: *copper piping.* **4** *n.* music of pipes. **5** *n.* a narrow band of material, sometimes containing a cord, used for trimming along edges and seams of clothing, slipcovers, etc.

piping hot, so hot as to hiss; very hot; boiling: *The tea is piping hot.*

pip·it (pip′it), *n.* either of two small, brownish North American birds, something like larks, that sing while flying. Pipits build nests on the ground.

pip·pin (pip′ən), *n.* any of several kinds of apple: *a yellow pippin.*

pi·quan·cy (pē′kən sē), *n.* **1** quality of exciting the mind pleasantly. **2** quality of exciting the appetite, being odd to the taste, or pleasantly sharp.

pi·quant (pē′kənt), *adj.* **1** stimulating to the mind, interest, etc.: *a piquant bit of news, a piquant face.* **2** pleasantly sharp; stimulating to the taste: *a piquant sauce.* **−pi′quant·ly,** *adv.* **−pi′quant·ness,** *n.*

pique (pēk), **1** *n.* a feeling of anger at being slighted; wounded pride: *In a pique, the couple left the party.* **2** *v.* to cause a feeling of anger in; wound the pride of: *It piqued her that we had a secret she did not share.* **3** *v.* to arouse; stir up: *Our curiosity was piqued by the locked trunk.* ❑ *v.* **piqued, pi·quing.** ■ Other words that sound like this are **peak** and **peek.**

pi·qué (pi kā′), *n.* fabric of cotton, rayon, or silk, with narrow ribs or raised stripes.

pi·ra·cy (pī′rə sē), *n.* **1** robbery on the sea. **2** act of publishing or using a book, play, invention, etc., without permission.

pi·ra·nha (pi rä′nyə), *n.* any of several small South American freshwater fishes with very sharp teeth. Piranhas in groups will attack even large animals. ❑ *n., pl.* **pi·ra·nha** or **pi·ra·nhas.**

pi·rate (pī′rit), **1** *n.* person who attacks and robs ships; robber on the sea; buccaneer. **2** *v.* to be a pirate; plunder; rob. **3** *v.* to publish or use without the author's, inventor's, or owner's permission. ❑ *v.* **pi·rat·ed, pi·rat·ing.** **−pi′rate·like′,** *adj.*

pi·rat·i·cal (pī rat′ə kəl), *adj.* of or like pirates; like piracy. **−pi·rat′i·cal·ly,** *adv.*

pi·ro·gi (pi rō′gē), *n.* an eastern European dish, made of large pieces of dough stuffed with various mixtures of meat, fish, eggs, or cabbage. Pirogi are first boiled, then fried. ❑ *n., pl.* **pi·ro·gi** or **pi·ro·gies.**

pi·rogue (pə rōg′), *n.* dugout (def. 3).

pir·ou·ette (pir′ü et′), **1** *n.* act of whirling about on one foot or on the toes, as in dancing. **2** *v.* to whirl in this way. ❑ *v.* **pir·ou·et·ted, pir·ou·et·ting.** [Pirouette comes from the French word for a toy top. A person who makes a pirouette spins like a top.]

Pi·sa (pē′zə), *n.* city in NW Italy, famous for its leaning tower.

Pis·ces (pī′sēz), *n.* **1** group of stars shaped something like a fish. **2** the twelfth sign of the zodiac, associated with the period from mid-February to mid-March.

pis·ta·chi·o (pi stash′ē ō *or* pi stä′shē ō), **1** *n.* the greenish, almond-flavored seed of a small evergreen tree that grows in warm regions. The seeds are good to eat and are used to make flavoring. **2** *n.* a light green. **3** *adj.* light green. ❑ *n., pl.* **pis·ta·chi·os.**

pis·til (pis′tl), *n.* the part of a flower that produces seeds, containing an ovary, a style, and a stigma. ■ Another word that sounds like this is **pistol.**

pis·til·late (pis′tl āt), *adj.* having a pistil or pistils, especially when not having stamens.

pis·tol (pis′tl), *n.* a small, short gun held and fired with one hand. [Pistol comes from a Czech word meaning "a pipe." The barrel of a pistol is like a small metal pipe.] ■ Another word that sounds like this is **pistil.**

pis·ton (pis′tən), *n.* a short cylinder, or a flat, round piece of wood or metal, fitting closely inside a tube or cylinder in which it is moved back and forth by the force of exploding gasoline vapor, steam, etc. Pistons are used in pumps, engines, compressors, etc.

piston ring, a metal ring fitted in a groove around a piston to form a tight seal against the cylinder wall.

piston rod, a rod by which a piston transmits or receives motion.

pit¹ (pit), **1** *n.* a natural hole in the ground. **2** *n.* hole dug deep into the earth. A mine or the shaft of a mine is a pit. **3** *n.* a hollow place on the surface of anything: *the pit of the stomach.* **4** *n.* a little hollow place or scar, such as is left by smallpox. **5** *v.* to mark with small pits or scars: *The smallpox victim's face was deeply pitted.* **6** *n.* a covered hole used as a trap for wild animals. **7** *n.* place where dogs or cocks are made to fight. **8** *v.* to set to fight or compete; match: *She was pitted against her friend in the last* round of the tennis match. **9** *n.* **the pit,** hell. **10** *n.* **the pits,** SLANG. some thing, place, or situation thought to be utterly bad: *The movie was the pits.* ❑ *v.* **pit·ted, pit·ting.**

pit² (pit), **1** *n.* the hard seed of a cherry, peach, plum, date, etc.; stone. **2** *v.* to remove pits from fruit: *We pitted cherries to make a cherry pie.* ❑ *v.* **pit·ted, pit·ting.**

pi·ta (pē′tä *or* pē′tə), *n.* a flat, round bread commonly eaten in the Middle East. ❑ *n., pl.* **pi·tas.**

pit·a·pat (pit′ə pat′), *n.* pitter-patter.

pit bull, any of several kinds of dogs known for their ability and readiness to fight. Several breeds of terrier and some crossbreeds of terrier with a coat of short, stiff hair, are called pit bulls.

pitch¹ (pich), **1** *v.* to throw or fling; hurl; toss: *They were pitching horseshoes.* **2** *v.* (in baseball) to throw the ball to the batter. **3** *n.* act of pitching; a throw or toss: *The first pitch was a strike.* **4** *v.* to fix firmly in the ground; set up: *pitch a tent.* **5** *v.* to fall or plunge forward: *I lost my balance and pitched down the stairs.* **6** *v.* to plunge with the bow rising and then falling: *The ship pitched about in the storm.* **7** *v.* to set at a certain point, degree, or level. **8** *v.* to determine the key of a tune. **9** *n.* point; position; degree: *She reached the lowest pitch of bad fortune.* **10** *n.* degree of highness or lowness of a sound. Notes in music with a low pitch have a slower rate of vibration than those with a high pitch. **11** *v.* to slope downward; incline; dip. **12** *n.* a talk, argument, offer, plan, etc., used to persuade, as in selling: *The clerk had developed a strong sales pitch.* **13** *n.* amount of slope: *a road with a steep pitch.* ❑ *n., pl.* **pitch·es.**

pitch in, INFORMAL. to work vigorously: *All of us pitched in, and the job was soon finished.*

pitch² (pich), **1** *n.* thick, black, sticky substance made from tar or turpentine, used to fill the seams of wooden ships, to cover roofs, to make pavements, etc. **2** *v.* to cover with pitch. **3** *n.* resin from certain evergreen trees. ❑ *n., pl.* **pitch·es.** **−pitch′like′,** *adj.*

pitch-black (pich′blak′), *adj.* very black or dark.

pitch·blende (pich′blend′), *n.* mineral consisting largely of an oxide of uranium, occurring in black, pitchlike masses. It is a source of radium, uranium, and actinium.

pitch-dark (pich′därk′), *adj.* pitch-black. **−pitch′dark′ness,** *n.*

pitched battle, battle with the opposing troops arranged in definite positions.

pitch·er¹ (pich′ər), *n.* **1** container for holding and pouring liquids, with a lip on one side and a handle on the other. **2** amount that a pitcher holds. **−pitch′er·like′,** *adj.*

pitch·er² (pich′ər), *n.* a baseball player who pitches the ball to the batter.

pitcher plant, any of several plants with leaves shaped something like a pitcher. These leaves often contain a liquid in which insects are captured and digested by the plant. The flower of one of these plants is the provincial flower of Newfoundland.

pitch·fork (pich′fôrk′), *n.* a large fork with a long handle, for lifting and throwing hay, etc.; hayfork.

pitch·out (pich′out′), *n.* **1** (in baseball) an intentionally wide

pitcher²

pitch that the batter cannot reach, thrown in order to give the catcher a chance to catch a runner off base. **2** (in football) a lateral pass thrown behind the line of scrimmage to a running back.

pitch pipe, a small musical pipe having one or more notes, used to give the pitch for singing or for tuning an instrument.

pitch·y (pich′ē), *adj.* **1** full of pitch. **2** like pitch; sticky. **3** black. ❑ *adj.* **pitch·i·er, pitch·i·est.** **−pitch′i·ness,** *n.*

pit·e·ous (pit′ē əs), *adj.* very sad; causing pity; deserving pity: *A starving person is a piteous sight.* **−pit′e·ous·ly,** *adv.* **−pit′e·ous·ness,** *n.*

pit·fall (pit′fól′), *n.* **1** a hidden pit to catch animals in. **2** any trap or hidden danger.

pith (pith), *n.* **1** the important or essential part: *the pith of a speech.* **2** the central, spongy tissue in the stems of plants. **3** a similar tissue found in other parts of plants, like that lining the skin of an orange. **4** the soft inner substance of a bone, feather, etc.

Pith·e·can·thro·pus (pith′ə kan′thrə pəs), *n.* Homo erectus.

pith·y (pith′ē), *adj.* **1** full of substance, meaning, force, or vigor: *pithy phrases, a pithy speaker.* **2** of or like pith. **3** having much pith: *a pithy orange.* ❑ *adj.* **pith·i·er, pith·i·est.** **−pith′i·ly,** *adv.* **−pith′i·ness,** *n.*

pit·i·a·ble (pit′ē ə bəl), *adj.* **1** deserving pity. **2** deserving contempt; to be scorned: *Their halfhearted attempts to help with the work were pitiable.* **−pit′i·a·ble·ness,** *n.* **−pit′i·a·bly,** *adv.*

pit·i·ful (pit′i fəl), *adj.* **1** to be pitied; deserving pity: *The rabbit caught in the trap was a pitiful sight.* **2** feeling or showing pity; feeling sorrow for the trouble of others. **3** deserving contempt; mean; to be scorned: *a pitiful excuse.* **−pit′i·ful·ly,** *adv.*

pit·i·less (pit′ē lis), *adj.* without pity or mercy. **−pit′i·less·ly,** *adv.* **−pit′i·less·ness,** *n.*

pit·tance (pit′ns), *n.* **1** a small allowance of money. **2** a small amount or share.

pit·ter-pat·ter (pit′ər pat′ər), *n.* a quick succession of light beats or taps; pitapat: *the pitter-patter of rain, the pitter-patter of a child's steps.*

Pitts·burgh (pits′bėrg′), *n.* city in SW Pennsylvania, a center of the iron and steel industry.

pi·tu·i·tar·y gland (pə tü′ə ter′ē), a small, oval gland at the base of the brain. It releases hormones that increase growth, stimulate other glands, and control many bodily functions.

pit viper, any of several poisonous snakes with hollow fangs and a heat-sensing pit between the eye and nostril, including rattlesnakes, water moccasins, copperheads, and bushmasters.

pit·y (pit′ē), **1** *n.* sorrow for another's suffering or distress; feeling for the sorrows of others; sympathy. **2** *v.* to feel pity for: *I pitied the sobbing child.* **3** *n.* cause for pity or regret; thing to be sorry for: *It is a pity to be kept in the house in good weather.* ❑ *v.* **pit·ied, pit·y·ing.**

have pity on or **take pity on,** to show pity for.

piv·ot (piv′ət), **1** *n.* shaft, pin, or point on which something turns. The pin of a hinge is a pivot. **2** *v.* to turn on a pivot or as if on a pivot: *pivot on your heel.* **3** *n.* a turn on a pivot or as if on a pivot: *With a quick pivot he threw the ball to his teammate.* **4** *v.* to mount on, attach by, or provide with a pivot. **5** *n.* something or someone on which something turns, hinges, or depends; central point: *the pivot of your hopes.*

piv·ot·al (piv′ə təl), *adj.* **1** of, about, or serving as a pivot. **2** being that on which something turns, hinges, or depends; very important. **−piv′ot·al·ly,** *adv.*

pix·el (pik′səl), *n.* any one of the many tiny points, each able to be bright or dark and of various colors, that make up an electronic image.

pix·y or **pix·ie** (pik′sē), *n.* fairy or elf. ❑ *n., pl.* **pix·ies.**

a	hat	ė	term	ô	order	ch	child		a in about
ā	age	i	it	oi	oil	ng	long		e in taken
ä	far	ī	ice	ou	out	sh	she	ə	i in pencil
â	care	o	hot	u	cup	th	thin		o in lemon
e	let	ō	open	ů	put	ᴛʜ	then		u in circus
ē	equal	ó	saw	ü	rule	zh	measure		

P

Pi·zar·ro (pi zär′ō), *n.* **Fran·cis·co** (fran sis′kō), 1478?-1541, Spanish conqueror of Peru. ■ Pizarro and his men killed thousands of Incas and captured their ruler, Atahualpa. Pizarro held Atahualpa for ransom but killed him after receiving the payment. He founded the city of Lima in Peru.

pi·zazz (pə zaz′), *n.* INFORMAL. **1** liveliness; pep. **2** flashy style.

piz·za (pēt′sə), *n.* a spicy Italian dish made by baking a large flat layer of bread dough covered with cheese, tomato sauce, herbs, etc. ❑ *n., pl.* **piz·zas.**

piz·zazz (pə zaz′), *n.* INFORMAL. pizazz.

piz·ze·ri·a (pēt′sə rē′ə), *n.* restaurant or bakery where pizzas are baked and sold. ❑ *n., pl.* **piz·ze·ri·as.**

piz·zi·ca·to (pit′sə kä′ tō), in music: **1** *adj.* played by plucking the strings of a violin, viola, etc., with the finger instead of using the bow. **2** *n.* note or series of notes played in this way. ❑ *n., pl.* **piz·zi·ca·ti** (pit′sə kä′tē).

pj's or **p.j.'s** (pē′jāz′), *n.pl.* INFORMAL. pajamas.

pkg., package.

pl., **1** place. **2** plural.

plac·ard (plak′ärd *or* plak′ərd), **1** *n.* notice to be posted in a public place; poster. **2** *v.* to put placards on or in: *The circus placarded the city with advertisements.*

pla·cate (plā′kāt *or* plak′āt), *v.* to soothe or satisfy the anger of; make peaceful; appease: *placate a person you have offended.* ❑ *v.* **pla·cat·ed, pla·cat·ing.** —**pla′cat·er,** *n.*

place (plās), **1** *n.* the part of space occupied by someone or something: *a place to rest.* **2** *n.* city, town, village, district, etc.: *What place do you come from?* **3** *n.* building or spot used for a certain purpose: *A store or office is a place of business.* **4** *n.* house; house and grounds; dwelling: *Her parents have a beautiful place in the country.* **5** *n.* part or spot in a body or surface: *a sore place on your foot, to mark your place in a book.* **6** *n.* the proper or natural position: *There is a time and place for everything.* **7** *n.* rank; position; way of life: *She won first place in the essay contest. They have a high place in society.* **8** *n.* position in time; part of time occupied by an event: *The performance went too slowly in several places.* **9** *n.* (in arithmetic) position of a figure in a number or series: *In the number 365, the figure 3 is in the hundreds place.* **10** *n.* space or seat for a person: *We took our places at the table.* **11** *v.* to put in a spot, position, condition, or relation: *The orphan was placed in a good home. The people placed confidence in their leader.* **12** *v.* to identify by remembering the place, time, or situation in which someone or something was known before: *I know that person's face, but I can't place her.* **13** *v.* to finish among the leaders in a race or competition: *I failed to place in the first race and was eliminated.* **14** *n.* situation; post or office; official employment or position: *get a place in a store.* **15** *v.* to appoint a person to a post or office; find a situation, etc., for. **16** *n.* duty; business: *It is not her place to find fault.* **17** *n.* a step or point in order of proceeding: *In the first place, the room is too small; in the second place, it is too dirty.* **18** *n.* a short street or court: *Waverley Place.* ❑ *v.* **placed, plac·ing.** ■ Another word that sounds like this is **plaice.**

give place, 1 to make room. **2** to be followed by: *My anger gave place to remorse.*

in place, in the proper or usual place; in the original place: *Everything was in place before we began the experiment.*

in place of, instead of: *Use water in place of milk in that recipe.*

know your place, to act according to your position in life.

out of place, 1 not in the proper or usual place. **2** unsuitable.

take place, to happen; occur.

WORD STORY **Place** comes from a Greek word meaning "broad," which was often used in a Greek phrase meaning "broad street." **Place** is sometimes used as part of a street name today. In old cities, streets were mostly narrow, and a broad street would be an important place. **Plaza** comes from the same Greek word, because a plaza is a specially broad place in a city.

pla·ce·bo (plə sē′bō), *n.* medicine that has no effect, given to satisfy a patient or used in research as a comparison to test the effectiveness of a new medicine. ❑ *n., pl.* **pla·ce·bos.**

place kick, the kicking of a ball placed or held on the ground in football, soccer, etc. —**place′-kick′,** *v.* —**place′-kick′er,** *n.*

place mat, a mat of linen, plastic, paper, etc., put under someone's plate or table setting.

place·ment (plās′mənt), *n.* **1** act of placing or condition of being placed; location; arrangement. **2** the finding of work or a job for someone. **3** act of placing a football on the ground for a place kick.

pla·cen·ta (plə sen′tə), *n.* organ in most mammals by which the fetus is attached to the wall of the uterus and nourished. ❑ *n., pl.* **pla·cen·tas, pla·cen·tae** (plə sen′tē).

pla·cen·tal (plə sen′tl), *adj.* of, about, or having a placenta.

plac·er (plas′ər), *n.* deposit of sand, gravel, or earth in the bed of a stream, containing particles of gold or other valuable minerals.

place value, the value which a figure has because of its place in a number. In 438, the place values of the figures are 4×100, 3×10, and 8×1.

plac·id (plas′id), *adj.* pleasantly calm or peaceful; quiet: *a placid lake, a placid temper.* —**pla·cid·i·ty** (plə sid′ə tē), **plac′id·ness,** *n.* —**plac′id·ly,** *adv.*

placid

plack·et (plak′it), *n.* an opening or slit in a garment, especially at the top of a skirt, to make it easy to put on.

pla·gia·rism (plā′jə riz′əm), *n.* act of plagiarizing.

pla·giar·ist (plā′jər ist), *n.* person who plagiarizes.

pla·gia·rize (plā′jə rīz′), *v.* to take and use as your own the thoughts, writings, etc., of another, especially to take and use a passage, plot, etc., from the work of another writer. ❑ *v.* **pla·gia·rized, pla·gia·riz·ing.** —**pla′gia·riz′er,** *n.*

plague (plāg), **1** *n.* a very dangerous disease that spreads rapidly and often causes death. It occurs in several forms, one of which is bubonic plague. **2** *n.* any epidemic disease; pestilence. **3** *n.* punishment thought to be sent from God. **4** *v.* to cause to suffer from a plague. **5** *n.* thing or person that torments, vexes, annoys, troubles, offends, or is disagreeable: *Weeds are a plague to a gardener.* **6** *v.* to annoy; bother; trouble: *The people of the colony were plagued with high taxes.* ❑ *v.* **plagued, pla·guing.** —**pla′guer,** *n.*

plaice (plās), *n.* any of various North Atlantic flatfish caught for food. ❑ *n., pl.* **plaice** or **plaic·es.** ■ Another word that sounds like this is **place.**

plaid (plad), **1** *n.* a long piece of woolen cloth, usually having a pattern of checks or stripes in many colors, worn over one shoulder by the Scottish Highlanders. **2** *n.* any cloth with a pattern of checks or crisscross stripes. **3** *n.* a pattern of this kind. **4** *adj.* having a pattern of checks or crisscross stripes: *a plaid dress.*

plain (plān), **1** *adj.* easy to understand; easily seen or heard; clear: *The meaning is plain.* ■ See Synonym Study at **clear. 2** *adv.* in a plain manner; clearly. **3** *adj.* without ornament or decoration; simple: *a plain dress.* **4** *adj.* without figured pattern, varied weave, or variegated color: *a plain blue fabric.* **5** *adj.* not rich or highly seasoned: *plain food.* **6** *adj.* common; ordinary; simple in manner: *They were plain, hard-working people.* **7** *adj.* not pretty or handsome. **8** *adj.* frank; honest; sincere: *plain speech.* **9** *n.* Often, **plains,** a flat stretch of land; prairie: *Cattle and horses wandered over the plains.* [See Word Story at **plane**[1].] ■ Another word that sounds like this is **plane.** —**plain′ly,** *adv.* —**plain′ness,** *n.*

plain·clothes·man (plān′klōz′mən), *n.* police officer or detective who wears ordinary clothes, not a uniform, when on duty. ❑ *n., pl.* **plain·clothes·men.**

plain·clothes·wo·man (plān′klōz′wüm′ən), *n.* woman police officer or detective who wears ordinary clothes, not a uniform, when on duty. ❑ *n., pl.* **plain·clothes·wo·men.**

Plains Indian, member of any of the American Indian tribes that lived in the Great Plains.

plains·man (plānz′mən), *n.* person who lives on the plains. ❑ *n., pl.* **plains·men.**

Plains of Abraham, plain just west of Quebec City, site of a major British victory over the French in 1759, which resulted in British control of North America.

plain-spo·ken (plān′spō′kən), *adj.* plain or frank in speech. —**plain′-spo·ken·ness,** *n.*

plaint (plānt), *n.* **1** complaint. **2** OLD USE. lament.

plain·tiff (plān′tif), *n.* person who begins a lawsuit: *The plaintiff accused the defendant of fraud.*

plain·tive (plān′tiv), *adj.* mournful; sad: *a plaintive song.* —**plain′tive·ly,** *adv.* —**plain′tive·ness,** *n.*

plait (plāt *or* plat), **1** *n.* a braid of hair, ribbon, etc.: *She wore her hair in a plait.* **2** *v.* to braid: *She plaits her hair.* **3** *n.* a pleat. **4** *v.* to pleat. ■ Another word that can sound like this is **plate.**

plan (plan), **1** *n.* way of making or doing something that has been worked out beforehand; scheme of action: *Our summer plans were upset by Dad's illness.* **2** *v.* to think out beforehand how something is to be made or done; design, scheme, or devise: *plan a trip.* **3** *v.* to have in mind as a purpose; intend: *I plan to go to New York next week.* **4** *n.* a drawing or diagram to show how a garden, a floor of a house, etc., is arranged. **5** *v.* to make a drawing or diagram of: *The architect is planning a new garage for us.* ❑ *v.* **planned, plan·ning.** [See Word Story at **plane**[1].] —**plan′ner,** *n.*

> **SYNONYM STUDY** **Plan, design,** and **project** all mean an idea of how to do or make something. **Plan** is a general word: *She has a plan to make the boss notice how hard she works.* **Design** means a plan, especially a drawing: *The design for our treehouse shows how many boards we'll need.* **Project** means a plan, especially for doing something in a big way: *The city announced a five-million-dollar project to cut air pollution.*

pla·nar·i·an (plə nâr′ē ən), *n.* any of numerous flatworms that live in water, move by using hairlike cilia along their symmetrical bodies, and have an intestine divided into three main sections. Many planarians have simple eyes.

plane[1] (plān), **1** *n.* any flat or level surface. **2** *adj.* flat; level. **3** *n.* level; grade: *Try to keep your work on a high plane.* **4** *n.* airplane. **5** *n.* surface such that if any two points on it are joined by a straight line, the line will be contained wholly in the surface. **6** *adj.* of or about figures wholly in a plane: *plane geometry.* ■ Another word that sounds like this is **plain.**

> **WORD STORY** **Plane**[1] comes from a Latin word meaning "flat." **Plan** and **plain** come from the same Latin word. A plan was called a plane, in old times, because a plan was often a drawing on a flat surface. And a map of a plain would be a flat drawing of flat land.

plane[2] (plān), **1** *n.* tool with a blade for smoothing or shaping wood. **2** *v.* to smooth wood with a plane. **3** *v.* to remove with a plane. ❑ *v.* **planed, plan·ing.** ■ Another word that sounds like this is **plain.**

plane geometry, branch of geometry that deals with forms, such as squares, triangles, and circles, that have only two dimensions and lie in a plane.

plan·er (plā′nər), *n.* person or thing that planes, especially a machine for planing wood or for finishing flat surfaces on metal.

plan·et (plan′it), *n.* **1** one of the nine large astronomical objects that move around the sun in elliptical orbits. Mercury, Venus, Earth, Mars, Jupiter, Saturn, Uranus, Neptune, and Pluto are planets. **2** any similar body revolving around a star other than the sun. [**Planet** comes from a Greek word meaning "to wander." In old times, people thought the planets were stars. Most stars do not move, but the planets do, so they were called wandering stars.] —**plan′et·like′,** *adj.*

plan·e·tar·i·um (plan′ə târ′ē əm), *n.* **1** machine that shows the changing appearances and locations of the sun, moon, planets, and stars by projecting lights on the inside of a dome. **2** room or building with such an apparatus. ❑ *n., pl.* **plan·e·tar·i·ums, plan·e·tar·i·a** (plan′ə târ′ē ə).

planetarium

plan·e·tar·y (plan′ə târ′ē), *adj.* of a planet.

plan·et·oid (plan′ə toid), *n.* asteroid.

plank (plangk), **1** *n.* a long, flat piece of sawed timber thicker than a board. **2** *v.* to cover or furnish with planks. **3** *v.* to cook on a board: *Steak is sometimes planked.* **4** *n.* article or feature of the platform of a political party or other organization.

plank down, INFORMAL. to put down or pay then and there: *He planked down the package. She planked down her money.*

walk the plank, be put to death by being forced to walk off a plank extending from a ship's side over the water. Pirates used to make their prisoners do this.

plank·ton (plangk′tən), *n.* the small living things that float or drift in water, especially at or near the surface.

plant (plant), **1** *n.* any living thing that lacks a nervous system and sense organs, is unable to move about, and is able to use chlorophyll in chloroplasts to manufacture its own food; any member of the vegetable kingdom. **2** *n.* any living thing that has leaves, roots, and a soft stem, and is small in contrast with a tree or bush: *a tomato plant, a potted plant.* **3** *v.* to put in the ground to grow: *She planted sunflower seeds in the backyard.* **4** *v.* to put seed or seedlings in: *He planted his garden with beans.* **5** *v.* to set firmly; put; place: *The boy planted his feet far apart.* **6** *v.* to establish or set up a colony, city, etc.; settle. **7** *v.* to put in or teach principles, doctrines, ideas, etc.: *Parents try to plant ideals of honesty and kindness in their children.* **8** *n.* the buildings, machinery, etc., used in manufacturing any product. —**plant′like′,** *adj.*

Plan·tag·e·net (plan taj′ə nit), *n.* member of the royal family that ruled England from 1154 to 1485.

plan·tain[1] (plan′tən), *n.* a kind of large banana with hard starchy flesh, eaten cooked.

plan·tain[2] (plan′tən), *n.* any of several common weeds with large, spreading leaves close to the ground and long, slender spikes carrying flowers and seeds.

plan·ta·tion (plan tā′shən), *n.* **1** a large farm or estate, especially in a tropical or semitropical region, on which cotton, tobacco, sugar cane, rubber trees, etc., are grown. The work on a plantation is done by laborers who live there. **2** a large group of trees or other plants that have been planted: *a rubber plantation.*

plant·er (plan′tər), *n.* **1** person who owns or runs a plantation. **2** machine for planting seeds: *a corn planter.* **3** person who plants. **4** a box, stand, or other holder, usually decorative, for plants.

plant louse, aphid.

a	hat	è	term	ô	order	ch	child		
ā	age	i	it	oi	oil	ng	long		a in about
ä	far	ī	ice	ou	out	sh	she	ə	e in taken
â	care	o	hot	u	cup	th	thin		i in pencil
e	let	ō	open	ù	put	ᵀʜ	then		o in lemon
ē	equal	ò	saw	ü	rule	zh	measure		u in circus

659

plaque (plak), *n.* **1** an ornamental tablet of metal, porcelain, etc., often with writing carved on it. **2** a platelike ornament or badge. **3** a thin film of saliva and food particles, containing germs, that forms on the surface of the teeth.

plash (plash), *v., n.* splash. ❑ *n., pl.* **plash·es.**

plas·ma (plaz′mə), *n.* the clear, very pale, yellowish liquid part of blood or lymph. Blood cells float in this liquid.

plas·mid (plaz′mid), *n.* a small amount of DNA not in the chromosomes, found in some bacteria. Plasmids are genetically active, reproduce themselves, and can pass from cell to cell.

plas·mo·di·um (plaz mō′dē əm), *n.* any of several tiny parasitic protists, including those that cause malaria. ❑ *n., pl.* **plas·mo·di·a** (plaz mō′dē ə).

plas·ter (plas′tər), **1** *n.* a soft mixture of lime, sand, and water that hardens as it dries, used for covering walls or ceilings. **2** *v.* to cover walls, ceilings, etc., with plaster. **3** *v.* to spread with anything thickly: *Her shoes were plastered with mud.* **4** *v.* to make smooth and flat: *He plastered his hair down.* **5** *n.* a medical preparation consisting of some substance spread on cloth, that will stick to the body and protect cuts, relieve pain, etc. [See Word Story at **plastic.**] **—plas′ter·er,** *n.* **—plas′ter·like′,** *adj.*

plas·ter·board (plas′tər bôrd′), *n.* a large, flat board made of a layer of plaster between two layers of heavy paper and used to cover walls and partitions.

plaster of Paris, mixture of gypsum powder and water. This mixture hardens quickly. It is used for making molds, cheap statues, casts, etc.

plas·tic (plas′tik), **1** *n.* any of a large group of substances made chemically from materials such as coal, water, and limestone, and molded by heat, pressure, etc., into various forms, such as sheets, fibers, and bottles. Nylon, vinyl, and many cellulose products are plastics. **2** *adj.* made of plastic: *a plastic bottle.* **3** *adj.* easily molded or shaped: *Clay, wax, and plaster are plastic substances.* **4** *adj.* molding or giving shape to material: *Sculpture is a plastic art.*

> **WORD STORY** **Plastic** and **plaster** both come from a Greek word meaning "to form" or "to mold." Plastic and plaster both start soft and can be molded into shapes that harden for use. Plaster was discovered thousands of years ago, plastic a little more than 100 years ago. Definitions 3 and 4 of **plastic** are about 300 years old— so plastic things existed long before things were made out of plastic.

plastic explosive, an explosive charge, often containing TNT, that can be shaped like clay.

plas·tic·i·ty (pla stis′ə tē), *n.* plastic quality.

plastic surgery, surgery that restores or improves the outer appearance of the body. **—plastic surgeon.**

plastic wrap, a very thin sheet of plastic used for wrapping food and sold in rolls.

plas·tid (plas′tid), *n.* any of various small, identifiable parts of a plant cell that are found outside the nucleus. The chloroplasts, which contain chlorophyll, are plastids.

plate (plāt), **1** *n.* dish, usually round and almost flat. Food is served on plates. **2** *n.* contents of such a dish: *a small plate of stew.* **3** *n.* food served to one person at a meal: *The fundraising dinner cost $50 a plate.* **4** *n.* something having the shape of a flat dish: *A plate is passed in church to receive the collection.* **5** *n.* dishes and utensils covered with a thin layer of silver or gold, or made of those metals. **6** *v.* to cover with a thin layer of silver, gold, or other metal: *The spoon was plated with silver.* **7** *n.* a thin, flat piece of metal: *The warship was covered with steel plates.* **8** *v.* to cover with metal pieces for protection. **9** *n.* a thin, flat piece of metal on which something is stamped or engraved: *a license plate.* **10** *n.* something printed from an engraved piece of metal, especially a full-page illustration printed on special paper. **11** *n.* a piece of metal used to print pages of words. **12** *n.* a thin sheet of glass or metal coated with chemicals that are sensitive to light. Plates are sometimes used in taking photographs. **13** *n.* piece of metal, plastic, or other firm material with false teeth set into it. **14** *n.* one of the large, slowly drifting, often continent-size sections of the earth's crust. **15** *n.* **the plate,** (in baseball) home plate.

16 *n.* a thin cut of beef from the lower end of the ribs. **17** *n.* the positive electrode in a vacuum tube. ❑ *v.* **plat·ed, plat·ing.** ■ Another word that can sound like this is **plait. —plate′like′,** *adj.*

> **WORD FAMILY** **Plate** and the words below are related. They all come from a Greek word meaning "broad" or "flat."
>
> | displace | place | platform | platter |
> |---|---|---|---|
> | misplace | plaice | platinum | platypus |
> | piazza | plateau | platitude | plaza |

pla·teau (pla tō′), *n.* **1** a plain in the mountains or considerably above sea level; large, high plain; tableland. **2** a level or stage, especially one that someone reaches and then stays at for some time: *I hit a plateau juggling four balls, and it took weeks to get to five.* ❑ *n., pl.* **pla·teaus** or **pla·teaux** (pla tōz′).

plate·ful (plāt′fúl), *n.* as much as a plate will hold. ❑ *n., pl.* **plate·fuls.**

plate glass, thick and very clear glass made in smooth, polished sheets, used for large windowpanes, mirrors, etc.

plate·let (plāt′lit), *n.* one of many small disks that float in the blood plasma and are important to blood clotting.

plate tectonics, 1 theory that the changes in the earth's crust are caused by the movements of huge sections called plates. **2** movements of plates in the earth's crust. **3** forces causing such movements.

plat·form (plat′fôrm), *n.* **1** a raised level surface. There usually is a platform beside the track at a railroad station. A hall usually has a platform for speakers. **2** plan of action or statement of principles of a group. A political party has a platform made up of planks. **3** the operating system or hardware used by a software application: *Does that program run on this platform?*

platform tennis, kind of tennis played on a wooden platform enclosed with chicken wire. Players use wooden paddles to hit a small rubber ball.

Plath (plath), *n.* **Syl·vi·a** (sil′vē ə), 1932-1963, American poet. Her collected poems, published after her death, won the Pulitzer Prize for poetry in 1982.

plat·ing (plā′ting), *n.* a thin layer of silver, gold, or other metal.

plat·i·num (plat′n əm), *n.* a heavy, silver-white, metallic element with a very high melting point. Platinum is a precious metal which is resistant to acid and does not tarnish easily. It is used in chemical and industrial equipment and in jewelry. *Symbol:* Pt

plat·i·tude (plat′ə tüd), *n.* **1** a dull or commonplace remark, especially one given out solemnly as if it were fresh and important: *"Better late than never" is a platitude.* **2** flatness; triteness; dullness.

Pla·to (plā′tō), *n.* 427?-347? B.C., Greek philosopher who was the pupil of Socrates and the teacher of Aristotle. He was the first philosopher to explain his ideas at length in writing, and most of what is known about Socrates appears in Plato's books.

Pla·ton·ic (pla ton′ik), *adj.* **1** of or about Plato or his philosophy. **2** Also, **platonic,** friendly but not like a lover. **—pla·ton′i·cal·ly,** *adv.*

pla·toon (plə tün′), *n.* **1** a military unit made up of two or more squads, usually commanded by a lieutenant. Several platoons make up a company. **2** (in football) either of two groups of players, one specializing in offensive play, the other in defensive play.

Platte (plat), *n.* river flowing from central Nebraska into the Missouri River. [See Word Story at **Nebraska.**]

plat·ter (plat′ər), *n.* a large shallow dish for holding or serving food, especially meat and fish.

plat·y (plat′ē), *n.* any of several small freshwater fishes found in southern North America. Some of these brilliantly colored fish are popular as aquarium fish. ❑ *n., pl.* **plat·y, plat·ys,** or **plat·ies.**

plat·y·pus (plat′ə pəs), *n.* a small, egg-laying water mammal of Australia and Tasmania with webbed feet and a bill something like a duck's; duckbilled platypus. ❑ *n., pl.* **plat·y·pus·es.** [Platypus comes from Greek words meaning "wide" and "foot." Because the animal's feet are webbed, they are very broad.]

platypus—about 18 in. (46 cm) long

plau·dit (plô′dit), *n.* Usually, **plaudits,** *pl.* round of applause; enthusiastic expression of approval or praise: *The actress bowed in response to the plaudits of the audience.*

plau·si·ble (plô′zə bəl), *adj.* **1** appearing true, reasonable, or fair. **2** apparently worthy of confidence but often not really so: *a plausible liar.* —**plau′si·bil′i·ty, plau′si·ble·ness,** *n.* —**plau′si·bly,** *adv.*

play (plā), **1** *n.* something done to amuse oneself; fun; sport; recreation: *The children are happy at play.* **2** *v.* to have fun; do something in sport: *The kitten plays with its tail. He played a joke on his sister.* **3** *v.* to take part in a game: *Children play tag and ball.* **4** *v.* to take part in a game against: *Our team played the sixth-grade team.* **5** *n.* a turn, move, or act in a game: *It is your play next.* **6** *v.* to put into action in a game: *Play your ten of hearts.* **7** *n.* act of carrying on a game: *Play was slow in the first half of the game.* **8** *n.* a story written for or presented as a dramatic performance; drama: *"Peter Pan" is a charming play.* **9** *n.* the performance of such a story on TV, radio, or the stage, or in a movie. **10** *v.* to act a part; act the part of a character in a play, etc. **11** *v.* to act in a specified way: *play sick, play fair, play the fool.* **12** *n.* action; operation; working: *foul play, fair play. They brought all their strength into play to move the rock.* **13** *v.* to make believe; pretend in fun: *Let's play the hammock is a boat.* **14** *v.* to make music; produce music on an instrument. **15** *v.* to perform on a musical instrument: *play a piano.* **16** *v.* to cause to produce recorded or broadcast sound or pictures: *play a record, play the radio, play the VCR.* **17** *v.* to move lightly or quickly: *A breeze played on the water.* **18** *n.* a light, quick movement: *the play of sunlight on leaves, the play of color in an opal.* **19** *n.* freedom for action, movement, etc.: *The children gave their imaginations full play in telling what they could do with a million dollars.* **20** *v.* to cause to act, move, or work; direct on, over, or along: *play a hose on a burning building.* **21** *v.* to act carelessly; do foolish things: *Don't play with matches.* **22** *n.* gambling. **23** *v.* to gamble or bet on: *He plays the horses.*

play down, to make light of; understate.

played out, 1 exhausted. **2** finished; done with.

play off, 1 to play an additional game or match in order to decide a draw or tie. **2** to pit one person or thing against another, especially for your own advantage.

play on or **play upon,** to take advantage of; make use of: *We played on our friend's good nature, too often making her the victim of our jokes.*

play out, to play to the end; bring to an end.

play up, to make the most of; exploit.

play up to, to try to get the favor of; flatter: *play up to a celebrity.*

play·a·ble (plā′ə bəl), *adj.* **1** able to be played. **2** fit to be played on.

play·back (plā′bak′), *n.* the playing of a tape recording, videotape, etc., especially after it has just been made.

play·bill (plā′bil′), *n.* **1** a handbill or placard announcing a play. **2** program of a play.

play·boy (plā′boi′), *n.* man whose chief interest is in having a good time.

play·er (plā′ər), *n.* **1** person who plays: *a baseball player, a card player.* **2** actor in a theater. **3** musician: *a flute player.* **4** thing or device that plays: *a record player.*

player piano, piano played by machinery, rather than by a person.

play·fel·low (plā′fel′ō), *n.* playmate.

play·ful (plā′fəl), *adj.* **1** full of fun; fond of playing: *a playful puppy.* **2** joking; not serious: *a playful remark.* —**play′ful·ly,** *adv.* —**play′ful·ness,** *n.*

play·ground (plā′ground′), *n.* place for outdoor play.

play·house (plā′hous′), *n.* **1** a small house for a child to play in. **2** dollhouse. **3** theater. ❑ *n., pl.* **play·hous·es** (plā′hou′ziz).

playing card, card used in playing games like bridge, poker, and pinochle, usually being one of a set of 52 cards including 4 suits (spades, hearts, diamonds, and clubs) of 13 cards each.

play·mate (plā′māt′), *n.* person who plays with another.

play-off or **play·off** (plā′ôf′), *n.* **1** game or series of games played after the regular season to decide a championship. **2** an extra game or round played to settle a tie.

play on words, pun.

play·pen (plā′pen′), *n.* a small folding pen for a baby or young child to play in.

play·room (plā′rüm′), *n.* room for children to play in.

play·thing (plā′thing′), *n.* thing to play with; toy.

play·wright (plā′rīt′), *n.* writer of plays; dramatist.

plaz·a (plaz′ə or plä′zə), *n.* a public square in a city or town. ❑ *n., pl.* **plaz·as.** [See Word Story at **place.**]

plea (plē), *n.* **1** request or appeal; an asking: *a plea for help.* **2** an excuse or defense: *The man's plea was that he did not see the signal.* **3** answer made by a defendant to a charge in a court of law.

plead (plēd), *v.* **1** to offer reasons for or against; argue. **2** to ask earnestly; make an earnest appeal: *When the rent was due, the poor family pleaded for more time.* ■ See Synonym Study at **beg.** **3** to offer as an excuse: *The woman who stole pleaded poverty.* **4** to speak for or against in a court of law: *He had a good lawyer to plead his case.* **5** to answer to a charge in a court of law: *The defendant pleaded innocent.* ❑ *v.* **plead·ed** or **pled, plead·ing.** —**plead′a·ble,** *adj.* —**plead′er,** *n.* —**plead′ing·ly,** *adv.*

pleas·ant (plez′nt), *adj.* **1** giving pleasure; enjoyable: *a pleasant swim on a hot day.* **2** easy to get along with; friendly. **3** fair; not stormy. —**pleas′ant·ly,** *adv.* —**pleas′ant·ness,** *n.*

pleas·ant·ry (plez′n trē), *n.* **1** a good-natured joke; witty remark. **2** a casual, polite remark. ❑ *n., pl.* **pleas·ant·ries.**

please (plēz), *v.* **1** to give pleasure to: *Toys please children.* **2** to be satisfactory: *Such a fine meal cannot fail to please.* **3** to wish; think fit: *Do what you please.* **4** to be the will of: *May it please the court to show mercy.* **5** to be so kind as to (now used merely as a polite addition to requests or commands): *Please come here.* ❑ *v.* **pleased, pleas·ing.**

be pleased, 1 to feel pleasure. **2** to wish; choose; like.

if you please, if you like; with your permission.

pleas·ing (plē′zing), *adj.* giving pleasure; pleasant: *a pleasing smile, a well-mannered and pleasing young man.* —**pleas′ing·ly,** *adv.* —**pleas′ing·ness,** *n.*

pleas·ur·a·ble (plezh′ər ə bəl), *adj.* pleasant; agreeable. —**pleas′ur·a·ble·ness,** *n.* —**pleas′ur·a·bly,** *adv.*

pleas·ure (plezh′ər), *n.* **1** a feeling of being pleased; enjoyment; delight; joy: *The child's pleasure in the gift was good to see.* **2** something that pleases; cause of joy or delight: *It would be a pleasure to see you again.* **3** anything that amuses; sport; play: *She takes her pleasure in riding and hunting.* **4** one's will, desire, or choice: *What is your pleasure in this matter?*

pleat (plēt), **1** *n.* a flat, usually narrow, fold made in cloth by doubling it on itself. **2** *v.* to fold or arrange in pleats: *a pleated skirt.* —**pleat′er,** *n.*

ple·be·ian (pli bē′ən), **1** *adj.* of or about the common people; common; vulgar. ■ This meaning of **plebeian** is sometimes considered offensive. **2** *n.* one of the common people. **3** *adj.* of or about the lower class of citizens in ancient Rome. **4** *n.* member of this class.

pleb·i·scite (pleb′ə sīt), *n.* a direct vote by the qualified voters of a country, state, etc., on some important question.

plec·trum (plek′trəm), *n.* a small piece of plastic, metal, etc., used for plucking the strings of a guitar, mandolin, etc.; pick. ❑ *n., pl.* **plec·trums, plec·tra** (plek′trə).

pled (pled), *v.* pleaded; a past tense and past participle of **plead.**

pledge (plej), **1** *n.* a solemn promise: *They made a pledge to give money to charity.* **2** *v.* to promise solemnly: *We pledge allegiance to the flag.* ■ See Synonym Study at **promise.** **3** *v.* to cause to promise solemnly; bind by a promise: *pledge hearers to secrecy.* **4** *n.* something given to another as a guarantee of good faith or of a future action; security: *She left the jewelry as a pledge for the loan.* **5** *v.* to give as security. **6** *v.* to drink a health to; drink in honor of someone and wish that person well: *They rose from the table to pledge the queen.* **7** *n.* the drinking of a health or toast.

a	hat	ė	term	ô	order	ch	child	
ā	age	i	it	oi	oil	ng	long	a in about
ä	far	ī	ice	ou	out	sh	she	e in taken
â	care	o	hot	u	cup	th	thin	ə = i in pencil
e	let	ō	open	ů	put	ŧ͟h	then	o in lemon
ē	equal	ȯ	saw	ü	rule	zh	measure	u in circus

8 *n.* something given to show favor or love, or as a promise of something to come; sign; token. ❑ *v.* **pledged, pledg·ing.** **–pledg′er** or **pledg′or,** *n.*

Ple·ia·des (plē′ə dēz′), *n.pl.* cluster of several hundred stars in the constellation Taurus. Six of these stars can normally be seen with the naked eye.

Pleis·to·cene (plī′stə sēn), *n.* (in geology) time between about 2 million and 11 thousand years ago; Ice Age. During this time, glaciers came and went several times, and human beings first appeared.

ple·nar·y (plē′nər ē *or* plen′ər ē), *adj.* **1** attended by all of its qualified members: *a plenary session of a committee.* **2** not lacking in any way; full; complete; absolute: *an ambassador with plenary power.*

plen·i·po·ten·ti·ar·y (plen′ə pə ten′shē er′ē), **1** *n.* a diplomatic agent having full power or authority. **2** *adj.* having or giving full power and authority. The United States has either an ambassador or a minister plenipotentiary in every important foreign country. ❑ *n., pl.* **plen·i·po·ten·ti·ar·ies.**

plen·te·ous (plen′tē əs), *adj.* plentiful. **–plen′te·ous·ly,** *adv.* **–plen′te·ous·ness,** *n.*

plen·ti·ful (plen′ti fəl), *adj.* more than enough; ample; abundant: *a plentiful supply of food.* **–plen′ti·ful·ly,** *adv.* **–plen′ti·ful·ness,** *n.*

SYNONYM STUDY **Plentiful, ample,** and **abundant** all mean more than enough, but not too much. **Plentiful** is a general word: *Flowers are plentiful in summer.* **Ample** suggests a particular purpose: *The restaurant has ample parking.* **Abundant** means very plentiful: *The puppy's abundant energy makes it fun to play with.*

plen·ty (plen′tē), **1** *n.* a full supply; all that you need; a large enough number or quantity: *You have plenty of time to catch the train.* **2** *n.* quality or condition of being plentiful; abundance: *years of peace and plenty.* **3** *adj.* enough: *Six potatoes will be plenty.* **4** *adv.* INFORMAL. very; quite: *It was plenty hot.*

ple·si·o·saur (plē′sē ə sôr′), *n.* any of several large sea reptiles that lived about 200 million years ago. They had long necks and flippers instead of legs.

plesiosaur—about 50 ft. (15.3 m) long

pleth·or·a (pleth′ər ə), *n.* excessive fullness; too much; superabundance: *a plethora of words, a plethora of food.*

pleur·a (plùr′ə), *n.* a thin membrane covering each lung and lining the chest cavity. ❑ *n., pl.* **pleur·ae** (plùr′ē), **pleur·as. –pleur′-al,** *adj.*

pleur·i·sy (plùr′ə sē), *n.* inflammation of the pleura, often marked by fever, chest pains, and difficulty in breathing.

Plex·i·glas (plek′sə glas′), *n.* trademark for a light, transparent plastic that can be molded when heated. Plexiglas is often used instead of glass.

plex·us (plek′səs), *n.* network of nerve fibers or blood vessels. The solar plexus is a collection of nerves behind the stomach. ❑ *n., pl.* **plex·us·es** or **plex·us.**

pli·a·ble (plī′ə bəl), *adj.* **1** easily bent; flexible; supple: *Willow twigs are pliable.* **2** easily influenced; yielding: *He is too pliable to be a good leader.* **–pli′a·bil′i·ty, pli′a·ble·ness,** *n.* **–pli′a·bly,** *adv.*

pli·an·cy (plī′ən sē), *n.* pliant condition or quality.

pli·ant (plī′ənt), *adj.* **1** bending easily; flexible; supple: *pliant leather.* **2** easily influenced; yielding: *a pliant nature.* **3** changing easily to fit different conditions; adaptable. **–pli′ant·ly,** *adv.*

plied (plīd), *v.* past tense and past participle of **ply¹**: *He plied his trade in the big city.*

pli·ers (plī′ərz), *n.pl.* tool with pincers for holding small objects firmly, or for bending or cutting wire.

plies (plīz), **1** *n.* plural of **ply²**. **2** *v.* a present tense of **ply¹**.

plight¹ (plīt), *n.* condition or situation, usually bad: *He was in a sad plight when he became ill and had no money.*

plight² (plīt), *v.* OLD USE. to promise solemnly; pledge: *plight your loyalty.*

plinth (plinth), *n.* **1** the lower, square part of the base of a column. **2** a square base of a pedestal.

Pli·o·cene (plī′ə sēn′), *n.* (in geology) time between about 12 million and 2 million years ago. During this time, primates with some specifically human features first appeared.

PLO, Palestine Liberation Organization (an Arab political and military group formed in 1964 to bring about the creation of a Palestinian state as a homeland for the Arab people who formerly lived in Palestine and for their descendants).

plod (plod), *v.* **1** to walk heavily; trudge: *The hikers plodded wearily along the road.* **2** to proceed in a slow or dull way; work patiently with effort: *I plodded away at the lessons until I learned them.* ❑ *v.* **plod·ded, plod·ding. –plod′der,** *n.*

plop (plop), **1** *n.* sound like that of a flat object striking water without a splash. **2** *v.* to make such a sound. **3** *v.* to fall or cause to fall: *She plopped her bag down.* ❑ *v.* **plopped, plop·ping.**

plot (plot), **1** *n.* a secret plan, especially to do something wrong: *They formed a plot to rob the bank.* **2** *v.* to plan secretly with others; plan: *The rebels plotted against the government.* **3** *n.* plan or main story of a play, novel, poem, etc.: *I like plots filled with action and adventure.* **4** *n.* a small piece of ground: *a garden plot.* **5** *n.* map; diagram. **6** *v.* to make a map or diagram of: *The pilot plotted the plane's course.* **7** *v.* to mark the position of something on a map or diagram: *The nurse plotted the patient's temperature on a chart over several days.* ❑ *v.* **plot·ted, plot·ting.**

SYNONYM STUDY **Plot** and **conspiracy** both mean secret planning, especially to do wrong. **Plot** is a general word: *The spy's plot to steal the plans involved bribing a guard.* **Conspiracy** means secret planning with other people: *Police have uncovered a conspiracy of three clerks to defraud the business.*

plot·ter (plot′ər), *n.* **1** person who plots. **2** an electronic device that draws pictures or diagrams on paper, controlled by a computer.

plough (plou), *n., v.* plow.

plov·er (pluv′ər), *n.* any of several small shore birds with short tails and bills, long, pointed wings, and usually no rear toe. The killdeer is a plover. ❑ *n., pl.* **plov·er** or **plov·ers.** [**Plover** comes from a Latin word meaning "to rain." People believed that the bird's call was a sign of rain coming.]

plow (plou), **1** *n.* a large piece of farm equipment pulled by a tractor or farm animals, used for turning the soil over and cutting furrows. **2** *v.* to turn up the soil of with a plow: *plow a field.* **3** *n.* snowplow. **4** *v.* to use a plow. **5** *v.* to move through anything as a plow does; advance slowly and with effort: *The ship plowed through the waves.* Also, **plough. –plow′a·ble,** *adj.* **–plow′er,** *n.* **plow back,** to reinvest the profits from a business into the same business.

plow·boy (plou′boi′), *n.* boy who guides a plow or the horses drawing a plow.

plow·man (plou′mən), *n.* **1** person who guides a plow. **2** a farm worker. ❑ *n., pl.* **plow·men.**

plow·share (plou′shâr′), *n.* blade of a plow; the part of a plow that cuts the soil.

ploy (ploi), *n.* a clever move or trick used to gain an advantage over another person: *Her pretense of nervousness was just a ploy.*

pluck (pluk), **1** *v.* to pull off; pick: *He plucked flowers in the garden.* **2** *v.* to pull at; pull; tug; jerk: *She plucked at the loose threads of her coat.* **3** *n.* act of picking or pulling. **4** *v.* to pull on the strings of a musical instrument; play by picking at the strings: *She was plucking the banjo softly.* **5** *v.* to pull off the feathers or hair from: *pluck a chicken before cooking it.* **6** *n.* courage: *The cat showed pluck in fighting the dog.*

pluck·y (pluk′ē), *adj.* having or showing courage: *a plucky dog.* ❑ *adj.* **pluck·i·er, pluck·i·est.** —**pluck′i·ly,** *adv.* —**pluck′i·ness,** *n.*

plug (plug), **1** *n.* device at the end of a wire to make an electrical connection by fitting into a socket. **2** *n.* piece of wood or other substance used to fill a hole. **3** *v.* to fill with a plug: *They plugged the hole with cement.* **4** *n.* spark plug. **5** *n.* hydrant; fireplug. **6** *v.* to recommend or advertise, especially on a radio or TV show: *plug a new movie.* **7** *n.* advertisement or recommendation, especially on a radio or TV show. **8** *v.* SLANG. to hit; shoot. **9** *v.* INFORMAL. to work steadily; plod: *We plugged away at our keyboards.* **10** *n.* cake of pressed tobacco; piece of this cut off for chewing. **11** *n.* SLANG. a worn-out or inferior horse. ❑ *v.* **plugged, plug·ging.** —**plug′ger,** *n.*

plug in, to make an electrical connection by inserting a plug.

plum (plum), **1** *n.* a roundish, juicy fruit with a smooth skin and a stone inside. Plums grow on several kinds of related trees. There are purple, blue, red, green, and yellow plums. **2** *n.* something very good or desirable: *Her new job is a real plum.* **3** *n.* a dark, bluish purple. **4** *adj.* dark bluish purple. [See Word Story at **prune**[1].] ■ Another word that sounds like this is **plumb.** —**plum′like′,** *adj.*

plum·age (plü′mij), *n.* feathers of a bird: *Some ducks have bright plumage.*

plumb (plum), **1** *n.* a small weight hung on the end of a line, used to find the depth of water or to see if a wall is vertical; plumb bob; lead. **2** *v.* to test or measure by a plumb line; sound: *Our line was not long enough to plumb the depths of the lake.* **3** *adj.* vertical. **4** *v.* to get to the bottom of: *No one could plumb the deep mystery.* **5** *adv.* INFORMAL. completely; thoroughly: *That horse is plumb worn out.* ■ Another word that sounds like this is **plum.**

plumage

out of plumb or **off plumb,** not vertical.

plumb bob, plumb (def. 1).

plumb·er (plum′ər), *n.* person whose work is installing and repairing water pipes, sinks, bathtubs, etc., in buildings: *When the water pipe froze, we sent for a plumber.*

plumb·ing (plum′ing), *n.* **1** the water pipes, sinks, bathtubs, etc., in a building: *bathroom plumbing.* **2** work or trade of a plumber.

plumb line, line with a plumb bob at the end, used to find the depth of water or to see if a wall is vertical.

plume (plüm), **1** *n.* a large, long feather; feather. **2** *n.* a feather, bunch of feathers, or tuft of hair worn as an ornament on a hat, helmet, etc. **3** *v.* to furnish with plumes. **4** *v.* to smooth or arrange the feathers of: *The eagle plumed its wing.* ❑ *v.* **plumed, plum·ing.**

plum·met (plum′it), *v.* to plunge; drop: *The book plummeted from the window to the ground.*

WORD STORY **Plummet** comes from a Latin word meaning "the metal lead." **Plunge** comes from the same Latin word. Lead is very heavy, and so people used it to describe falling or sinking.

plump[1] (plump), **1** *adj.* pleasantly round and full: *plump cheeks.* **2** *v.* to make or become plump: *Plump the pillows on your bed.* —**plump′ness,** *n.*

plump[2] (plump), **1** *v.* to fall or drop heavily or suddenly: *All out of breath, she plumped down on a chair.* **2** *n.* a sudden plunge; heavy fall. **3** *n.* sound made by a plunge or fall. **4** *adv.* heavily or suddenly: *She dropped the bowling ball plump on the alley.* **5** *adv.* straight; directly: *He ran plump into me.*

plump for, to give your complete support to; champion vigorously: *plump for lower taxes.*

plum pudding, a rich, boiled or steamed pudding containing raisins, currants, spices, etc.

plum·y (plü′mē), *adj.* **1** having plumes or feathers. **2** adorned with a plume or plumes. **3** like a plume; feathery.

plun·der (plun′dər), **1** *v.* to rob by force; rob: *Pirates entered the harbor and plundered the town.* **2** *n.* things taken in plundering; booty; loot: *They carried off the plunder in their ships.* —**plun′der·er,** *n.*

plunge (plunj), **1** *v.* to throw or thrust with force into a liquid, place, or condition: *plunge your hand into water, plunge the world into war.* ■ See Synonym Study at **dip. 2** *v.* to throw yourself into water, danger, a fight, etc.: *She plunged into the lake to save the drowning swimmer.* **3** *v.* to fall or move suddenly downward or forward: *The plane plunged toward earth.* **4** *n.* a jump or thrust; a dive: *a sudden plunge into the lake.* **5** *v.* to pitch suddenly and violently: *The ship plunged about in the storm.* ❑ *v.* **plunged, plung·ing.** [See Word Story at **plummet.**]

plunge

plung·er (plun′jər), *n.* **1** a rubber suction cup on a long stick, used for unplugging drains and toilets that are stopped up. **2** part of a machine, such as a piston in a pump, that acts with a plunging motion. **3** person or thing that plunges.

plunk (plungk), **1** *v.* to put, drop, etc., heavily or suddenly: *I plunked a quarter down on the counter.* **2** *v.* to pluck a banjo, guitar, etc. **3** *v.* to make a sudden twanging sound like the plucking of a stringed musical instrument; twang: *Raindrops plunked into the puddles near the back door.* **4** *n.* act or sound of plunking.

plu·ral (plur′əl), **1** *adj.* more than one in number: *"Girl" is singular; "girls" is plural.* **2** *adj.* showing more than one in number: *the plural ending "-s," the plural noun "mice."* **3** *n.* the plural number in grammar. *Books* is the plural of *book; men,* of *man; are,* of *is; we,* of *I; these,* of *this.* **4** *n.* a word in the plural number. —**plur′al·ly,** *adv.*

plu·ral·i·ty (plu ral′ə tē), *n.* **1** difference between the number of votes received by the winner of an election and the number received by the next highest candidate. **2** the greater number; the majority. **3** condition of being plural. ❑ *n., pl.* **plu·ral·i·ties** for 1,2.

plu·ral·ize (plur′ə līz), *v.* to make plural; express in the plural form. ❑ *v.* **plur·al·ized, plur·al·iz·ing.** —**plur′al·i·za′tion,** *n.*

plus (plus), **1** *prep.* added to: *3 plus 2 equals 5.* **2** *prep.* and also: *The work of an engineer requires intelligence plus experience.* **3** *adj.* and more: *a grade average of B plus.* **4** *n.* plus sign. **5** *adj.* favorable; with good results; beneficial: *On the plus side, the rain will help the flowers.* **6** *n.* a positive quality or item; something favorable, welcome, or helpful: *Her sense of humor is a real plus.* **7** *adj.* greater than zero: *a temperature of plus 10 degrees.* ❑ *n., pl.* **plus·es** or **plus·ses.**

a	hat	ė	term	ô	order	ch	child		a in about
ā	age	i	it	oi	oil	ng	long		e in taken
ä	far	ī	ice	ou	out	sh	she	ə	i in pencil
â	care	o	hot	u	cup	th	thin		o in lemon
e	let	ō	open	ů	put	ŦH	then		u in circus
ē	equal	ò	saw	ü	rule	zh	measure		

plush (plush), **1** *n.* fabric like velvet but thicker and softer. **2** *adj.* luxurious; expensive; stylish: *a plush office.* ◻ *n., pl.* **plush·es.**

plush·y (plush′ē), *adj.* of or like plush. ◻ *adj.* **plush·i·er, plush·i·est. —plush′i·ness,** *n.*

plus sign, the sign (+), indicating that the number or quantity following is to be added, or is a positive number or quantity.

Plu·to (plü′tō), *n.* **1** the smallest planet in the solar system and the farthest from the sun. **2** the Greek god of the dead.

plu·toc·ra·cy (plü tok′rə sē), *n.* **1** government in which the rich rule. **2** a ruling class of wealthy people. ◻ *n., pl.* **plu·toc·ra·cies.**

plu·to·crat (plü′tə krat), *n.* **1** person who has power or influence because of wealth. **2** a wealthy person.

plu·to·ni·um (plü tō′nē əm), *n.* a radioactive metallic element produced artificially from uranium and found in minute quantities in pitchblende and other uranium ores. It is used as a source of energy in nuclear reactors and bombs. *Symbol:* Pu

ply[1] (plī), *v.* **1** to work with; use: *The dressmaker plies her needle.* **2** to keep up work on; work away at or on: *to ply your trade. We plied the water with our oars.* **3** to urge again and again: *She plied me with questions to make me tell her what was in the package.* **4** to keep on supplying: *ply a person with food or drink.* **5** to travel back and forth over or along a river or lake: *Hovercraft ply the English Channel.* ◻ *v.* **plied, ply·ing.**

ply[2] (plī), *n.* thickness, fold, or twist. ◻ *n., pl.* **plies.**

Plym·outh (plim′əth), *n.* **1** town in SE Massachusetts, founded by the Pilgrims. **2** port in SW England, on the English Channel.

Plymouth Colony, the settlement established by the Pilgrims in 1620, on the site of Plymouth, Massachusetts.

Plymouth Rock, 1 the rock at Plymouth, Massachusetts, on which the Pilgrims are said to have landed in 1620. **2** an American breed of chicken kept for the production of both meat and eggs.

ply·wood (plī′wůd′), *n.* board or boards made of several thin layers of wood glued together, usually with the grain of one layer lying at right angles to the grain of the next layer.

Pm, symbol for promethium.

p.m. or **P.M.,** the time from noon to midnight: *Our school day ends at 3 p.m.* [The abbreviation **p.m.** stands for the Latin phrase *post meridiem,* meaning "after noon."]

PMS, premenstrual syndrome (physical and emotional discomfort, sometimes severe, experienced before menstruation).

pneu·mat·ic (nü mat′ik), *adj.* **1** filled with air; containing air: *a pneumatic tire.* **2** worked by air: *a pneumatic drill.* **3** of or about air and other gases.

WORD STORY Words that start with **pn-** come from a Greek word meaning "to breathe." In Greek, both letters were pronounced. The sound is like breathing out. But it's easier to make just the *n* sound. So English kept the spelling, but people saved their breath.

pneu·mo·nia (nü mō′nyə), *n.* an infectious bacterial or viral disease that causes inflammation of the lungs and often a high fever and a hard, dry cough. It often follows a bad cold or other disease. Pneumonia in both lungs is called **double pneumonia.**

Po (pō), *n.* river flowing from NW Italy into the Adriatic Sea.

Po, symbol for polonium.

P.O. or **p.o.,** post office.

poach[1] (pōch), *v.* **1** to trespass on someone else's land, especially to hunt or fish. **2** to take game or fish without any right. **—poach′er,** *n.*

poach[2] (pōch), *v.* **1** to cook an egg by breaking it into gently boiling water. **2** to cook fish, chicken, etc., by simmering in gently boiling water.

WORD STORY Poach[2] comes from an old French word meaning "bag." **Pouch** comes from the same French word. When an egg is poached, the white hardens around the yolk, enclosing it in a kind of bag.

Po·ca·hon·tas (pō′kə hon′təs), *n.* 1595?-1617, American Indian who in her childhood is said to have saved the life of Captain John Smith. Later she was converted to Christianity, took the name Rebecca, and married an Englishman. She visited England and died there of smallpox. [Pocahontas comes from a word in the language of her people meaning "playful one."]

Po·ca·tel·lo (pō′kə tel′ō), *n.* city in SE Idaho.

pock (pok), *n.* pimple, mark, or pit on the skin, caused by smallpox and certain other diseases.

pock·et (pok′it), **1** *n.* a small bag sewed into clothing for carrying money or other small items. **2** *v.* to put into a pocket. **3** *adj.* meant to be carried in a pocket: *a pocket handkerchief.* **4** *adj.* small enough to go in a pocket: *a pocket camera.* **5** *n.* a small area or isolated group: *The candidate met pockets of resistance in his own party.* **6** *n.* bag at the corner or side of a pool table. **7** *n.* hole in the earth containing gold or other ore: *The miner struck a pocket of silver.* **8** *v.* to hold back; suppress; hide: *I pocketed my pride and said nothing.* **9** *v.* to take secretly or dishonestly: *Our partner pocketed the profits.* **10** *n.* air pocket. **—pock′et·like′,** *adj.*

be out of pocket, to spend or lose a sum of money: *He was out of pocket $50 for travel expenses.*

in someone's pocket, completely under someone's control or influence.

pock·et·book (pok′it bůk′), *n.* **1** a woman's purse. **2** wallet; billfold. **3** a person's supply of money; income: *This coat is too expensive for my pocketbook.*

WORD STORY Pocketbook today has no connection to pockets or books. Hundreds of years ago, it meant a notebook to carry in a pocket, which was a convenient place to keep money. So the notebook became a wallet, still called a pocketbook. Women often keep wallets in purses, so the word changed meaning again.

pock·et·ful (pok′it fůl′), *n.* as much as a pocket will hold. ◻ *n., pl.* **pock·et·fuls.**

pock·et·knife (pok′it nīf′), *n.* a small knife with one or more blades that fold into the handle. ◻ *n., pl.* **pock·et·knives** (pok′it-nīvz′).

pocket money, money for unexpected or minor expenses.

pock·et·size (pok′it sīz′), *adj.* small enough to go in a pocket: *a pocket-size camera.*

pocket veto, method of vetoing a bill that can be used by the President of the United States on a bill presented for signing within ten days of the end of a session of Congress. If the President does not sign the bill before Congress adjourns, it does not become a law.

pock·mark (pok′märk′), *n.* mark or pit on the skin; pock.

pock·marked (pok′märkt′), *adj.* marked with pocks.

pod (pod), **1** *n.* the case in which plants like beans and peas grow their seeds. Pods split open when they are ripe. **2** *v.* to produce pods. **3** *v.* to open pods and remove seeds: *podding peas.* ◻ *v.* **pod·ded, pod·ding.**

po·di·a·try (pə dī′ə trē), *n.* the branch of medicine that studies and treats diseases and problems of the human foot; chiropody. **—po·di′a·trist,** *n.*

po·di·um (pō′dē əm), *n.* a raised platform. The conductor of an orchestra or a speaker before an audience often stands on a podium. ◻ *n., pl.* **po·di·ums, po·di·a** (pō′dē ə). [Podium comes from a Greek word meaning "foot." A podium is a place to stand.]

Poe (pō), *n.* **Ed·gar Al·lan** (ed′gər al′ən), 1809-1849, American poet, short-story writer, and critic. His stories and poems often have a mysterious atmosphere and describe horrible events.

po·em (pō′əm), *n.* **1** a piece of writing that expresses the writer's imagination, usually about some inner feeling. A poem is often arranged in patterns of lines, rhyme, rhythm, or accent. **2** any composition showing great beauty or nobility of language or thought.

po·e·sy (pō′ə sē), *n.* OLD USE. poetry.

po·et (pō′it), *n.* person who writes poetry. Emily Dickinson and Walt Whitman were poets.

po·et·ic (pō et′ik), *adj.* **1** of or about poems or poets. **2** suitable for poems or poets. *Alas, o'er,* and *blithe* are poetic words. **3** showing beautiful or noble language, imagery, or thought: *poetic fancies.* **—po·et′i·cal·ly,** *adv.*

po·et·i·cal (pō et′ə kəl), *adj.* poetic.

poetic justice, ideal justice, with virtue being suitably rewarded and wickedness properly punished, as shown often in poems, plays, and stories.

poetic license, variations from facts and common usage, allowed in poetry for imaginative effect.

poet laureate, 1 (in Great Britain) a poet appointed by the king or queen to write poems in celebration of court and national events. 2 any poet regarded as the best or most typical of a country or region. ❏ *pl.* **poets laureate** or **poet laureates.**

po·et·ry (pō′i trē), *n.* 1 poems: *a collection of poetry.* 2 art of writing poems: *Our class is studying examples of English poetry.* 3 poetic quality; poetic spirit or feeling.

po·go stick (pō′gō), toy consisting of a stick that contains a spring, and has footrests near the bottom and a handle at the top. One can hop from place to place by jumping up and down on the footrests, while holding the handle.

po·grom (pō grom′), *n.* an organized massacre of a particular ethnic group, especially of Jews.

poi (poi), *n.* a Hawaiian food made of taro root that is baked, pounded, moistened, and fermented.

poign·an·cy (poi′nyən sē), *n.* condition of being poignant; sharpness; piercing quality: *poignancy of suffering.*

poign·ant (poi′nyənt), *adj.* 1 very painful; piercing: *poignant suffering.* 2 keen; intense: *a subject of poignant interest, a poignant delight.* —**poign′ant·ly,** *adv.*

poin·set·ti·a (poin set′ē ə *or* poin set′ə), *n.* a plant of Mexico and Central America, with a small, greenish yellow flower surrounded by large scarlet or white leaves that look like petals. Poinsettias are commonly used as a Christmas decoration. ❏ *n., pl.* **poin·set·ti·as.** [Poinsettia was named for Joel R. Poinsett, an American diplomat in Mexico, who introduced the plant in the United States in the middle 1800s.]

pogo stick

point (point), 1 *n.* a sharp end; something with a sharp end: *the point of a needle.* 2 *n.* period in writing; a decimal point in numbers. 3 *n.* (in mathematics) something that has position without length or width. Two lines meet or cross at a point. 4 *n.* a place; spot: *Stop at this point.* 5 *n.* any particular position, condition, or time; degree; stage: *boiling point, freezing point.* 6 *n.* item; detail: *He answered my questions point by point.* 7 *n.* a characteristic quality: *Courage and endurance were her good points.* 8 *n.* the main idea or purpose; important or essential thing: *I missed the point of the joke.* 9 *n.* a particular purpose, goal, or reason: *What's the point of rushing?* 10 *v.* to direct a finger, weapon, etc.; aim: *Point the arrow at the target.* 11 *v.* to show position or direction or to call attention with a finger: *He pointed the way to the village.* 12 *v.* (of a dog) to show the presence of game by standing rigid and looking toward it. 13 *v.* to show a particular direction: *The road sign points north.* 14 *n.* any of the 32 positions indicating direction marked around the edge of the card of a compass. North, south, east, and west are the four main, or cardinal, points of the compass. 15 *n.* piece of land with a sharp end sticking out into the water; cape. 16 *n.* unit of scoring or measuring: *We won by three points. The price of that stock has gone up a point.*

at the point of, in the act of; very near to: *at the point of leaving.*

beside the point, having nothing to do with the subject; not appropriate.

in point, relevant; connected: *a case in point.*

make a point of, to insist upon: *He made a point of arriving on time.*

on the point of, just about to do; at the moment of: *She was on the point of going out when a neighbor came in.*

point out, to show or call attention to: *Please point out my mistakes.*

stretch a point, 1 to exceed the reasonable limit. 2 to make an exception.

to the point, on the subject; relevant: *His speech was brief and to the point.*

point-blank (point′blangk′ *for adj.;* point′blangk′ *for adv.*), 1 *adj.* aimed straight at the mark. 2 *adj.* close enough for aim to be taken in this way: *I fired the gun from point-blank range.* 3 *adv.* straight at the mark: *to fire point-blank.* 4 *adj.* plain and blunt; direct: *a point-blank question.* 5 *adv.* plainly and bluntly; directly: *She gave excuses, but her friend refused point-blank.*

point·ed (poin′tid), *adj.* 1 having a point or points: *a pointed roof.* 2 sharp; piercing: *a pointed wit.* 3 directed; aimed: *a pointed remark.* 4 emphatic: *She showed me pointed attention.* —**point′ed·ly,** *adv.* —**point′ed·ness,** *n.*

point·er (poin′tər), *n.* 1 a long, tapering stick used in pointing things out on a map, blackboard, etc. 2 a hint; suggestion: *She gave him some pointers on improving his tennis.* 3 hand of a clock, gauge, or dial. 4 a short-haired hunting dog trained to show game by standing still with its head and body pointing toward the game. The **German shorthaired pointer** is a breed of pointer. 5 person or thing that points. 6 **Pointers,** *pl.* the two stars at the front of the Big Dipper that point to the North Star in the Little Dipper.

point·less (point′lis), *adj.* 1 without meaning or purpose: *a pointless question.* 2 without a point: *a pointless sword.* —**point′less·ly,** *adv.* —**point′less·ness,** *n.*

point of order, a question raised about whether official proceedings are being conducted according to the rules.

point of view, 1 attitude of mind: *Happy people and sad people have different points of view toward life.* 2 position from which you look at something.

poise (poiz), 1 *n.* calm; self-confidence: *He has perfect poise and never seems embarrassed.* 2 *n.* the way in which the body, head, etc., are held; carriage. 3 *v.* to balance: *Poise yourself on your toes.* 4 *v.* to hold or carry evenly or steadily: *The waiter poised the tray on his hand.* ❏ *v.* **poised, pois·ing.**

poi·son (poi′zn), 1 *n.* substance very dangerous to life or health. Arsenic and lead are both poisons. 2 *v.* to kill or harm by poison. 3 *v.* to put poison in or on. 4 *adj.* poisonous. 5 *n.* anything dangerous or deadly: *the poison of hate.* 6 *v.* to have a dangerous or harmful effect on: *Jealousy poisoned their friendship.* —**poi′son·er,** *n.*

WORD STORY **Poison** comes from a Latin word meaning "to drink." **Potion** comes from the same Latin word. In old times, people believed in the power of special drinks to heal illness, to work magic, to attract love, or to kill. Many of these drinks probably had no actual effect.

poison ivy, a climbing plant that looks like ivy, with shiny green leaves having three leaflets each. It causes a painful rash on the skin of most people who touch it.

poison oak, a plant closely related to poison ivy that grows as a bush. It causes a painful rash of the skin of most people who touch it.

poi·son·ous (poi′zn əs), *adj.* 1 containing poison; very harmful to life and health: *The rattlesnake's bite is poisonous.* 2 having a dangerous or harmful effect: *a poisonous lie.* —**poi′son·ous·ly,** *adv.* —**poi′son·ous·ness,** *n.*

poison sumac, plant closely related to poison ivy that grows as a bush, with leaves having seven to thirteen leaflets and white berrylike fruit. It causes a severe rash on the skin of most people who touch it.

poke¹ (pōk), 1 *v.* to push against with something pointed; prod: *She poked me in the ribs with her elbow.* 2 *v.* to thrust; push: *The dog poked its head out of the car window.* 3 *n.* act of poking; thrust; push. 4 *v.* to search; grope; pry. 5 *v.* to make by poking: *She poked a hole in the paper.* 6 *v.* to go lazily; loiter. 7 *n.* a slow, lazy person. 8 *v.* INFORMAL. to hit with the fist; punch: *poke someone in the nose.* 9 *n.* INFORMAL. a blow with the fist; a punch. ❏ *v.* **poked, pok·ing.**

poke² (pōk), *n.* DIALECT. bag; sack.

a	hat	è	term	ô	order	ch	child		
ā	age	i	it	oi	oil	ng	long		a in about
ä	far	ī	ice	ou	out	sh	she	ə	e in taken
â	care	o	hot	u	cup	th	thin		i in pencil
e	let	ō	open	ù	put	ᵺ	then		o in lemon
ē	equal	ò	saw	ü	rule	zh	measure		u in circus

P

poke³ (pōk), *n.* bonnet or hat with a large brim in front.

poke⁴ (pōk), *n.* pokeweed.

poke·ber·ry (pōk′ber′ē), *n.* **1** berry of the pokeweed. **2** pokeweed. □ *n., pl.* **poke·ber·ries.**

pok·er¹ (pō′kər), *n.* a metal rod for stirring a fire.

po·ker² (pō′kər), *n.* a card game in which the players bet on the value of the cards that they hold in their hands.

poke·weed (pōk′wēd′), *n.* a tall, branching plant of North America with greenish white flowers, deep purple, juicy berries, and poisonous roots; poke; pokeberry.

pok·ey¹ (pō′kē), *n.* SLANG. a jail. □ *n., pl.* **pok·eys.**

pok·y or **pok·ey²** (pō′kē), *adj.* **1** moving or acting slowly; puttering; slow; dull. **2** small and cramped; confined. □ *adj.* **pok·i·er, pok·i·est.** —**pok′i·ly,** *adv.* —**pok′i·ness,** *n.*

Po·land (pō′lənd), *n.* country in central Europe between Germany and Belarus. *Capital:* Warsaw.

WORD STORY **Poland** comes from a Slavic word meaning "field" or "plain." People living in this region 1000 years ago called themselves "plains people."

po·lar (pō′lər), *adj.* **1** of or near the North or South Pole: *It is very cold in the polar regions.* **2** of or about the poles of a magnet. **3** opposite in character, like the poles of a magnet: *Love and hatred are polar feelings.*

polar bear, a large, white bear of arctic regions.

polar bears—about 8 ft. (2.5 m) long

Po·lar·is (pō lar′is), *n.* the North Star.

po·lar·i·ty (pō lar′ə tē), *n.* **1** condition of having two opposite poles. A magnet has polarity. **2** condition of having two opposite principles or tendencies. □ *n., pl.* **po·lar·i·ties** for 2.

po·lar·ize (pō′lə rīz′), *v.* **1** to cause people to separate into two opposing sides: *School issues polarized the voters.* **2** to separate by the direction of vibration: *polarized light.* **3** to give polarity to. □ *v.* **po·lar·ized, po·lar·iz·ing.** —**po′lar·iz′a·ble,** *adj.* —**po′lar·i·za′tion,** *n.*

polarizing lens, lens that allows only electromagnetic waves vibrating in one particular direction to pass through. Polarizing lenses in sunglasses reduce glare by removing light reflected from horizontal surfaces.

Po·la·roid (pō′lə roid′), *n.* trademark for a thin, transparent, polarizing material that absorbs part of the light passing through it and reduces glare.

pole¹ (pōl), **1** *n.* a long, slender piece of wood, etc.: *a telephone pole.* **2** *v.* to make a boat go with a pole. □ *v.* **poled, pol·ing.** ■ Another word that sounds like this is **poll.**

pole² (pōl), *n.* **1** an end of the earth's axis. The North Pole and the South Pole are opposite each other. **2** an end of the axis of any planet or other sphere. **3** an end of a magnet. The magnetic force at one pole is opposite to the force at the other pole. ■ Another word that sounds like this is **poll.**

Pole (pōl), *n.* person born or living in Poland.

pole bean, any kind of bean that grows as a vine up a pole or other support.

pole·cat (pōl′kat′), *n.* **1** skunk. **2** any of three small, dark brown, meat-eating European and Asian mammals related to the weasel, that can emit a very disagreeable odor.

po·lem·ic (pə lem′ik), **1** *n.* strong argument against some position, belief, etc. **2** *adj.* of or about a strong argument. —**po·lem′i·cal·ly,** *adv.*

pole·star (pōl′stär′), *n.* **1** North Star. **2** a guiding principle; guide: *Friendship was her polestar.*

pole vault, a jump or leap over a high crossbar by using a long pole. —**pole′-vault′,** *v.* —**pole′-vault′er,** *n.*

po·lice (pə lēs′), **1** *n.* persons whose duty is keeping order and arresting people who break the law. **2** *n.* department of government that keeps order and arrests people who break the law. **3** *v.* to keep order in: *police the streets.* **4** *n.* the cleaning and keeping in order of a military camp, area, etc., or those who do it. **5** *v.* to keep a military camp, area, etc., clean and in order. □ *v.* **po·liced, po·lic·ing.** [See Word Story at politics.]

police (def. 1)

police dog, 1 German shepherd. **2** any dog trained to work with police officers.

po·lice·man (pə lēs′mən), *n.* member of the police. □ *n., pl.* **po·lice·men.**

police officer, member of a police force.

police state, a country strictly policed by its government and allowing only limited social, economic, and political liberties to its people.

po·lice·wom·an (pə lēs′wu̇m′ən), *n.* woman who is a member of the police. □ *n., pl.* **po·lice·wom·en.**

pol·i·cy¹ (pol′ə sē), *n.* **1** plan of action; way of management: *The candidates explained their policies.* **2** practical wisdom; prudence. □ *n., pl.* **pol·i·cies** for 1. [See Word Story at politics.]

pol·i·cy² (pol′ə sē), *n.* a written agreement about insurance. An insurance policy makes clear when money will be paid, and how much. □ *n., pl.* **pol·i·cies.**

po·li·o (pō′lē ō), *n.* a severe, infectious, viral disease that destroys nervous tissue in the spinal cord, causing fever, paralysis and wasting away of various muscles, and sometimes death; infantile paralysis; poliomyelitis. Before a vaccine was developed to control it, it attacked children especially, often causing permanent paralysis, partial or total.

po·li·o·my·e·li·tis (pō′lē ō mī′ə lī′tis), *n.* polio.

pol·ish (pol′ish), **1** *v.* to make smooth and shiny: *polish shoes.* **2** *v.* to become smooth and shiny; take on a polish. **3** *n.* substance used to give smoothness or shine: *silver polish.* **4** *v.* to put into a better condition; improve; refine: *polish your French.* **5** *n.* polished condition; smoothness; refinement: *Travel with polite people gave polish to his manners.* □ *n., pl.* **pol·ish·es** for 3. —**pol′ish·er,** *n.* polish off, **1** to get done with; finish. **2** to defeat; overcome. **3** to eat or drink up greedily.

Pol·ish (pō′lish), **1** *adj.* of or about Poland, its people, or their language. **2** *n.* language of Poland.

po·lite (pə līt′), *adj.* **1** having or showing good manners; behaving properly: *The polite girl gave the old woman her seat on the bus.* **2** refined; elegant: *He tried to learn all the customs of polite society.* □ *adj.* **po·lit·er, po·lit·est.** —**po·lite′ly,** *adv.* —**po·lite′ness,** *n.*

SYNONYM STUDY **Polite** and **courteous** both mean having good manners. **Polite** suggests doing what is proper: *It is polite to say "Excuse me" if you bump into someone.* **Courteous** suggests thoughtful kindness: *When our car broke down, a courteous young woman stopped and asked if she could help.*

pol·i·tic (pol′ə tik), *adj.* wise in looking out for your own interests; prudent: *A politic person tries not to offend people.* **—pol′-i·tic·ly,** *adv.*

po·lit·i·cal (pə lit′ə kəl), *adj.* **1** of or concerned with politics. **2** of or about citizens or government: *Treason is a political offense.* **3** of or about politicians or their methods: *a political party.* **—po·lit′i·cal·ly,** *adv.*

politically correct, completely following certain political principles, especially a belief that people should avoid language, images, or behavior possibly offensive to an ethnic group, age group, sexual group, etc.

political science, science of the principles and conduct of government. **—political scientist.**

pol·i·ti·cian (pol′ə tish′ən), *n.* **1** someone whose occupation or chief activity is government. **2** someone active in politics chiefly for personal or party profit. **3** someone holding a political office.

po·lit·i·co (pə lit′ə kō), *n.* a politician. ❏ *n., pl.* **po·lit·i·cos.**

pol·i·tics (pol′ə tiks), *n.sing. or pl.* **1** the work of government; management of public business: *Our senior senator has been engaged in politics for many years.* **2** political principles or opinions: *My parents' politics are strongly against rule by any one person.* **3** political methods or maneuvers.

WORD STORY **Politics** comes from a Greek word meaning "city." **Police** and **policy**[1] come from the same Greek word. In old times, large Greek cities were independent. Politics went on between cities and inside them. The city government kept order and made policy. The ancient Greeks even defined human beings as "the animal that lives in cities."

pol·i·ty (pol′ə tē), *n.* **1** government. **2** a particular form or system of government. **3** community with a government; state. ❏ *n., pl.* **pol·i·ties** for 2,3.

Polk (pōk), *n.* **James Knox** (noks), 1795-1849, the 11th president of the United States, from 1845 to 1849. He was the first president who didn't run for a second term.

pol·ka (pōl′kə *or* pō′kə), **1** *n.* a kind of lively dance. **2** *n.* music for it. **3** *v.* to do this dance. ❏ *n., pl.* **pol·kas.** *v.* **pol·kaed, pol·ka·ing.**

pol·ka dot (pō′kə), dot or round spot repeated to form a pattern on cloth.

poll (pōl), **1** *n.* act of voting; collection of votes: *The class had a poll to decide where it would have its picnic.* **2** *n.* number of votes cast. **3** *n.pl.* **polls,** place where votes are cast and counted: *The polls will be open all day.* **4** *n.* list of persons, especially a list of voters. **5** *v.* to receive at an election: *The mayor polled a record vote.* **6** *v.* to vote; cast a vote. **7** *v.* to take or register the votes of: *to poll a village.* **8** *n.* a survey of public opinion concerning a particular subject. **9** *v.* to ask for opinions from; question: *She polled the students to learn how many liked the cafeteria food.* **10** *n.* the head, especially the part of it on which the hair grows. ▪ Another word that sounds like this is **pole. —poll′er,** *n.*

pol·len (pol′ən), *n.* a fine, yellowish powder released from the anthers of flowers. Grains of pollen carried by insects, wind, etc., to the pistils of flowers fertilize them.

pollen count, a count of the number of grains of pollen to be found at a specified time and place in a cubic yard of air.

pol·li·nate (pol′ə nāt), *v.* to carry pollen from anthers to pistils; bring pollen to. Flowers are pollinated by bees, bats, birds, wind, etc. ❏ *v.* **pol·li·nat·ed, pol·li·nat·ing. —pol′li·na′tion,** *n.*

pol·li·wog (pol′ē wog), *n.* tadpole. Also, **pollywog.** [*Polliwog* comes from old English words meaning "head" and "wiggle." That's about all there is to a polliwog.]

Pol·lock (pol′ək), *n.* **Jackson,** 1912-1956, American artist. He dripped and poured paint on his canvases instead of using brushes.

pol·lock (pol′ək), *n.* (in Canada) a saltwater food fish, something like cod, but darker. ❏ *n., pl.* **pol·lock** or **pol·locks.**

poll·ster (pōl′stər), *n.* person who takes a poll of public opinion.

poll tax, a tax on every adult citizen, especially as a requirement to vote in public elections.

pol·lu·tant (pə lüt′nt), *n.* something that pollutes: *Water from a factory may be a pollutant of the stream it flows into.*

pol·lute (pə lüt′), *v.* to make dirty or impure: *The water at the beach was polluted by refuse.* ❏ *v.* **pol·lut·ed, pol·lut·ing.**

SYNONYM STUDY **Pollute** and **contaminate** both mean to make something filthy and unfit for use. **Pollute** suggests spreading harmful substances: *Automobile engines pollute the air.* **Contaminate** suggests touching with something unclean: *Trash from the hospital is contaminated by contact with infection.*

pol·lu·tion (pə lü′shən), *n.* **1** act or process of dirtying any part of the environment, especially with waste material. **2** anything that dirties the environment, especially waste material: *pollution of the air, pollution at the beach.* **—pol·lu·tion′-free′** *adj.*

pol·ly·wog (pol′ē wog), *n.* polliwog.

po·lo (pō′lō), *n.* game like hockey, played on horseback with long-handled mallets and a wooden ball. [*Polo* may come from a Tibetan word meaning "a ball."]

pollution (def. 2)

Po·lo (pō′lō), *n.* **Mar·co** (mär′kō), 1254-1324?, Italian merchant who wrote about his travels in Asia.

po·lo·naise (pol′ə nāz′ *or* pō′lə nāz′), *n.* **1** a slow, stately dance in three-quarter time. **2** music for it.

po·lo·ni·um (pə lō′nē əm), *n.* a radioactive metallic element found in pitchblende. *Symbol:* Po

polo shirt, a close-fitting shirt of knitted cotton or jersey with short sleeves and a collar.

pol·ter·geist (pōl′tər gīst), *n.* a supposed spirit or ghost that makes its presence known by making doors slam, small objects move, and other disturbances that cannot be explained.

poly-, *prefix.* many: *polygon = shape with many angles.* ▪ See Word Power at **many.**

pol·y·es·ter (pol′ē es′tər), *n.* any of a large group of synthetic resins used in making paints, synthetic fibers, films, and plastics.

pol·y·eth·yl·ene (pol′ē eth′ə lēn′), *n.* a lightweight plastic used to make containers, insulation, tubing, and packaging.

po·lyg·a·mist (pə lig′ə mist), *n.* person who practices polygamy.

po·lyg·a·my (pə lig′ə mē), *n.* practice or condition of being married to more than one person at the same time. **—po·lyg′a·mous,** *adj.*

pol·y·glot (pol′ē glot), **1** *adj.* knowing many languages. **2** *n.* person who knows many languages.

pol·y·gon (pol′ē gon), *n.* a closed plane figure with three or more straight sides and angles.

po·lyg·o·nal (pə lig′ə nəl), *adj.* of or about a polygon.

pol·y·graph (pol′ē graf), *n.* lie detector. **—pol′y·graph′ic,** *adj.*

pol·y·he·dron (pol′ē hē′drən), *n.* a solid figure having four or more faces. ❏ *n., pl.* **pol·y·he·drons, pol·y·he·dra** (pol′ē hē′drə).

pol·y·mer (pol′ē mər), *n.* a chemical compound in which each molecule is made up of many small molecules strung together. Nylon and cellulose are polymers.

pol·y·mer·ase chain reaction (pol′ə mə rās′), PCR.

pol·y·mer·i·za·tion (pol′ə mər ə zā′shən), *n.* a chemical reaction in which many small molecules join in a large, complex molecule. Many plastics are formed by polymerization.

pol·y·mer·ize (pol′i mə rīz′), *v.* to undergo or cause to undergo polymerization. ❏ *v.* **pol·y·mer·ized, pol·y·mer·iz·ing.**

Pol·y·ne·sia (pol′ə nē′zhə), *n.* group of many small islands in the Pacific, east of Micronesia and Melanesia. See **Melanesia** for map.

Pol·y·ne·sian (pol′ə nē′zhən), **1** *n.* member of the division of the human race that includes the original inhabitants of islands in the Pacific from Hawaii south to New Zealand, and their de-

a	hat	ė	term	ô	order	ch	child		a in about
ā	age	i	it	oi	oil	ng	long		e in taken
ä	far	ī	ice	ou	out	sh	she	ə	i in pencil
â	care	o	hot	u	cup	th	thin		o in lemon
e	let	ō	open	ủ	put	ᴛʜ	then		u in circus
ē	equal	ò	saw	ü	rule	zh	measure		

scendants throughout the world. **2** *n.* the languages of Polynesia, including Maori, Hawaiian, etc. **3** *adj.* of or about Polynesia, its people, or their languages.

pol·y·no·mi·al (pol/ē nō/mē əl), **1** *n.* an algebraic expression containing two or more terms connected by plus signs or minus signs. **2** *adj.* containing two or more algebraic terms.

pol·yp (pol/ip), *n.* any of very many small water animals with tube-shaped bodies having a mouth at one end surrounded by fingerlike tentacles to gather food. Polyps often grow in colonies, with their bases connected. Corals, hydras, and sea anemones are polyps.

pol·y·sty·rene (pol/ē stī/rēn), *n.* a clear plastic, sometimes in the form of a stiff foam, used for insulation and packaging, and in making household appliances.

pol·y·syl·lab·ic (pol/ē sə lab/ik), *adj.* having more than three syllables. —**pol/y·syl·lab/i·cal·ly,** *adv.*

pol·y·syl·la·ble (pol/ē sil/ə bəl), *n.* word of more than three syllables. *Politician* is a polysyllable, and so is *possibility.*

pol·y·tech·nic (pol/ē tek/nik), *adj.* of or dealing with many crafts or sciences: *a polytechnic school.*

pol·y·the·ism (pol/ē thē iz/əm), *n.* belief in more than one god. The religion of the ancient Greeks was polytheism.

pol·y·the·ist (pol/ē thē/ist), *n.* person who believes in more than one god. —**pol/y·the·is/tic,** *adj.*

pol·y·u·re·thane (pol/ē yùr/ə thān), *n.* any of several synthetic substances that are made in the form of foam, fibers, resins, etc. It is used to make cushions, insulating material, and various kinds of molded products.

po·made (pō mād/ *or* pom ād/), *n.* a perfumed ointment for the scalp and hair.

pom·e·gran·ate (pom/ə gran/it), *n.* the reddish gold fruit of a small tropical tree. It has a thick skin and many seeds in a red pulp with a pleasant, slightly sour taste.

Pom·e·ra·ni·an (pom/ə rā/nē ən), *n.* a small dog with a sharp nose, pointed ears, and long, thick, silky hair.

pom·mel (pum/əl *or* pom/əl), **1** *n.* part of a saddle that sticks up at the front. **2** *n.* a rounded knob on the hilt of a sword, dagger, etc. ❑ *v.* **pom·meled, pom·mel·ing** *or* **pom·melled, pom·mel·ling.** ■ Another word that can sound like this is **pummel.**

pomp (pomp), *n.* stately or showy display; splendor; magnificence: *The new ruler was crowned with great pomp.* [Pomp comes from a Greek word meaning "a parade."]

pom·pa·dour (pom/pə dôr), *n.* arrangement of hair in which it is puffed high over the forehead or brushed straight up and back from the forehead.

pom·pa·no (pom/pə nō), *n.* **1** any of several food fishes of the West Indies and the coasts of southern North America. **2** a similar fish of the California coast. ❑ *n., pl.* **pom·pa·no** *or* **pom·pa·nos.**

Pom·pei·an (pom pā/ən), *adj.* of or about Pompeii or its people.

Pom·peii (pom pā/), *n.* city in ancient Italy, which was buried by an eruption of Mount Vesuvius in A.D. 79. Its ruins have been partly laid bare by excavation.

pom·pom *or* **pom·pon** (pom/pom *or* pom/pon), *n.* **1** a colored, fluffy ball of paper strips or other material, waved by a cheerleader. **2** any chrysanthemum or dahlia with very small, rounded flowers. **3** an ornamental tuft or ball of feathers, silk, etc., worn on a hat, dress, or shoe.

pom·pos·i·ty (pom pos/ə tē), *n.* pompous show of self-importance. ❑ *n., pl.* **pom·pos·i·ties.**

pomp·ous (pom/pəs), *adj.* **1** trying to seem magnificent; fond of display; acting proudly; self-important: *The leader of the band bowed in a pompous manner.* **2** marked by pomp; splendid; magnificent; stately. —**pomp/ous·ly,** *adv.* —**pomp/ous·ness,** *n.*

Ponce de Le·ón (pons/ də lē/ən), **Juan** (wän), 1460?-1521, Spanish explorer and soldier. ■ **Ponce de León** led the first European expedition to Florida because he was looking for the Fountain of Youth, an imaginary spring said to make old people young again.

pon·cho (pon/chō), *n.* **1** a large piece of cloth, often waterproof, with a slit in the middle for the head to go through. Ponchos are worn in South America as cloaks. **2** a waterproof piece of cloth-

ing like this, worn by hikers, cyclists, etc., as a raincoat. ❑ *n., pl.* **pon·chos.**

pond (pond), *n.* body of still water, smaller than a lake.

pon·der (pon/dər), *v.* to consider carefully; think over: *ponder a problem.* —**pon/der·er,** *n.*

pon·der·o·sa pine (pon/də rō/sə), a tall pine tree of western North America, valuable for its lumber.

pon·der·ous (pon/dər əs), *adj.* **1** very heavy. **2** heavy and clumsy: *A hippopotamus is ponderous.* **3** dull; tiresome: *The speaker talked in a ponderous way.* —**pon/der·ous·ly,** *adv.* —**pon/der·ous·ness,** *n.*

pone (pōn), *n.* DIALECT. corn bread, popular in the southern United States.

pon·gee (pon jē/), *n.* fabric made of soft silk, usually left in natural brownish yellow color.

pon·iard (pon/yərd), *n.* OLD USE. dagger.

pons (ponz/), *n.* a wide band of nerve fibers in the base of the brain, just above the medulla oblongata, connecting various parts of the brain.

pon·tiff (pon/tif), *n.* **1** the pope. **2** bishop. **3** a high priest; chief priest.

pon·tif·i·cal (pon tif/ə kəl), *adj.* of or about a pope or bishop. —**pon·tif/i·cal·ly,** *adv.*

pon·tif·i·cate (pon tif/ə kāt), *v.* to behave or speak pompously. ❑ *v.* **pon·tif/i·cat·ed, pon·tif/i·cat·ing.** —**pon·tif/i·ca/tion,** *n.*

pon·toon (pon tün/), *n.* **1** a low, flat-bottomed boat. **2** such a boat, or some other floating structure, used as one of the supports of a temporary bridge. **3** either of two boat-shaped parts of an airplane, used for landing on or taking off from water.

pontoon bridge, a temporary bridge supported by low, flat-bottomed boats or other floating structures.

po·ny (pō/nē), *n.* kind of small horse. Ponies are usually less than 5 feet (1.5 meters) tall at the shoulder. ❑ *n., pl.* **po·nies.**

pony express, system of carrying letters and small packages in the western United States in 1860 and 1861 by relays of men riding fast ponies or horses.

po·ny·tail (pō/nē tāl/), *n.* a hair style in which the hair is pulled back and tied, with the ends falling free from where the hair is gathered.

pooch (püch), *n.* INFORMAL. dog. ❑ *n., pl.* **pooch·es.**

poo·dle (pü/dl), *n.* dog with thick, curly hair that is often clipped and shaved in an elaborate manner.

WORD STORY **Poodle** comes from a German word meaning "puddle." Poodles were bred as hunting dogs, and they used to run into water to retrieve game that had fallen there.

poof (púf *or* püf), *interj.* **1** an expression of contempt or impatience. **2** an expression to indicate a sudden appearance or disappearance of something.

pooh (pü), *interj.* exclamation of disrespect or disapproval: *Pooh! You don't dare jump.*

pooh-pooh (pü/pü/ *or* pü/pü/), *v.* to express contempt for; make light of.

Juan Ponce de León

pool¹ (pül), *n.* **1** tank of water to swim or bathe in: *a swimming pool.* **2** a small body of still water; small pond: *a forest pool.* **3** a still, deep place in a stream. **4** puddle: *a pool of grease under a car.*

pool² (pül), **1** *n.* game played with 16 hard, numbered balls on a special table with six pockets. The players try to drive the balls into the pockets with long sticks called cues. **2** *v.* to put things or money together for common advantage: *We plan to pool our savings for a year so that we can buy a boat.* **3** *n.* system or arrangement in which money, vehicles, or other things are put together by different people, so that they all may benefit: *a car pool. The hikers put all their food and money in a pool.* **4** *n.* group of people, usually having the same skills, who are drawn upon as needed: *the labor pool.* **5** *n.* persons who form a pool. **6** *n.* stake played for in some games.

WORD STORY   **Pool²** comes from a French word meaning "hen." **Poultry** comes from the same French word. French soldiers used this word as slang for whatever they could steal during a war. People then used the French word to mean "winnings," and it came into English with the idea of money put together by all players of a game and taken by the winner. The game pool was often played this way.

pool·room (pül′rüm′), *n.* room or place in which the game of pool is played.

poop (püp), *n.* **1** deck at the stern above the ordinary deck, often forming the roof of a cabin. **2** stern of a ship.

pooped (püpt), *adj.* INFORMAL. exhausted; tired; worn out: *After all that exercise I'm really pooped.*

poor (pùr), **1** *adj.* having few things or nothing; lacking money or property; needy: *He was so poor that he could not afford to buy a warm coat.* **2** *n.pl.* **the poor,** persons who are needy. **3** *adj.* not good in quality; lacking something needed: *poor soil, a poor crop, poor health.* **4** *adj.* needing pity; unfortunate: *This poor child is hurt.* **—poor′ness,** *n.*

SYNONYM STUDY   **Poor, penniless,** and **needy** all mean with little money. **Poor** is a general word: *Many poor people cannot afford to see a doctor.* **Penniless** means with no money at all: *I lost my wallet, and I am penniless.* **Needy** means without enough to live on: *The food bank provides groceries for needy families.*

poor box, box in a church in which money can be donated to help the poor: *This year the poor box donations were used to feed, clothe, and shelter thirty families in our parish.*

poor boy, hero sandwich.

poor·house (pùr′hous′), *n.* in old times, a house in which people with no money lived at public expense. ❑ *n., pl.* **poor·hous·es** (pùr′hou′ziz).

poor·ly (pùr′lē), *adv.* in a poor manner; not enough; badly; meanly: *A desert is poorly supplied with water. The student did poorly on the test.*

poor-mouth (pùr′mouth′ *or* pùr′mouTH′), *v.* INFORMAL. **1** to plead or claim poverty. **2** to criticize; make fun of: *The boxer poor-mouthed his opponent and promised to win easily.*

pop¹ (pop), **1** *v.* to make a short, quick, explosive sound: *The firecrackers popped in bunches.* **2** *n.* a short, quick, explosive sound: *the pop of a cork.* **3** *v.* to burst open or cause to burst open with such a sound: *The chestnuts were popping in the fire. He popped the balloon.* **4** *v.* to move, go, or come suddenly or unexpectedly: *Our neighbor popped in for a short visit. I popped over to the store for some milk.* **5** *v.* to thrust or put suddenly: *She popped her head out through the window.* **6** *v.* to fire a gun or pistol; shoot. **7** *n.* a shot from a gun, etc. **8** *v.* to bulge: *The surprise made her eyes pop out.* **9** *v.* (in baseball) to hit a short, high ball over the infield. **10** *n.* a nonalcoholic carbonated drink: *strawberry pop.* ❑ *v.* **popped, pop·ping.**

a pop, apiece; each time; each: *I bought my own ice skates because renting them cost three dollars a pop.*

pop the question, to ask someone to marry you; propose: *He's waiting to pop the question to Mary on her birthday.*

pop² (pop), *n.* INFORMAL. papa; father.

pop³ (pop), *adj.* INFORMAL. popular: *pop songs.*

pop., **1** popular. **2** population.

pop art, painting and sculpture based on the style of comic strips, advertising posters, etc.

pop art

pop·corn (pop′kôrn′), *n.* **1** kind of corn, the kernels of which burst open and puff out when heated. **2** the white, puffed-out kernels.

pope or **Pope** (pōp), *n.* the supreme head of the Roman Catholic Church: *the last three popes, the Pope.* [**Pope** comes from a Greek word meaning "father." The pope is thought of as a spiritual father by members of his church.] ■ See Usage Note at **capital letter.**

pop fly, (in baseball) a short, high fly ball.

pop·gun (pop′gun′), *n.* a toy gun that shoots with a popping sound.

pop·in·jay (pop′in jā), *n.* a vain, overly talkative, conceited person.

pop·lar (pop′lər), *n.* **1** any of several trees that grow very rapidly and produce light, soft wood. The cottonwood and the aspen are two kinds of poplars. **2** wood of such a tree.

pop·lin (pop′lən), *n.* a ribbed fabric, made of silk, wool, cotton, or rayon, and used for making dresses, curtains, etc.

pop·o·ver (pop′ō′vər), *n.* a very light and hollow muffin.

pop·pa (pop′ə), *n.* INFORMAL. father. ❑ *n., pl.* **pop·pas.**

pop·py (pop′ē), *n.* any of numerous plants with delicate, showy red, yellow, or white flowers. Opium is made from one kind of poppy. ❑ *n., pl.* **pop·pies.**

pop·py·cock (pop′ē kok′), *n., interj.* INFORMAL. nonsense; bosh.

Pop·si·cle (pop′sə kəl), *n.* a trademark for flavored, sweetened ice that is molded onto a stick.

pop-top (pop′top′), *adj.* having a metal tab that can be pulled loose to make an opening in the top of a container: *pop-top cans.*

pop·u·lace (pop′yə lis), *n.* the common people: *The king was well-liked by the populace.*

pop·u·lar (pop′yə lər), *adj.* **1** liked by most people: *a popular song.* **2** liked by acquaintances or associates: *Her good nature makes her the most popular girl in the class.* **3** of or for the people; by the people; representing the people: *a popular election.* **4** widespread among many people; common: *It is a popular belief that black cats bring bad luck.* **5** suited to or intended for ordinary people: *books on popular science.* **—pop′u·lar·ly,** *adv.*

pop·u·lar·i·ty (pop′yə lar′ə tē), *n.* fact or condition of being liked by most people.

pop·u·lar·ize (pop′yə lə rīz′), *v.* to make popular: *The Olympic medalist helped popularize gymnastics.* ❑ *v.* **pop·u·lar·ized, pop·u·lar·iz·ing. —pop′u·lar·i·za′tion,** *n.* **—pop′u·lar·iz′er,** *n.*

pop·u·late (pop′yə lāt), *v.* **1** to live in; inhabit: *This city is densely populated.* **2** to furnish with inhabitants: *Europe helped populate America.* ❑ *v.* **pop·u·lat·ed, pop·u·lat·ing.**

pop·u·la·tion (pop′yə lā′shən), *n.* **1** people of a city, country, or district. **2** the number of people living in a place. **3** part of the inhabitants distinguished in any way from the rest: *the urban population.* **4** all the living things of one kind in a single place: *Pollution has harmed the river's trout population.*

pop·u·lous (pop′yə ləs), *adj.* full of people; having many people per square mile. **—pop′u·lous·ly,** *adv.* **—pop′u·lous·ness,** *n.*

por·ce·lain (pôr′sə lin), *n.* **1** a hard, fine, lightweight ceramic material made from special clay. Teacups are often made of porcelain. **2** items made from this material; china: *On Sundays we use our porcelain at dinner.* [See Word Story at **porcupine.**]

porch (pôrch), *n.* **1** a covered entrance to a building. **2** a long, often open, structure along one or more sides of a house; veranda. ❑ *n., pl.* **porch·es.**

a	hat	ė	term	ô	order	ch	child		a in about
ā	age	i	it	oi	oil	ng	long		e in taken
ä	far	ī	ice	ou	out	sh	she	ə	i in pencil
â	care	o	hot	u	cup	th	thin		o in lemon
e	let	ō	open	ù	put	ŦH	then		u in circus
ē	equal	ȯ	saw	ü	rule	zh	measure		

P

por·cu·pine (pôr′kyə pīn), *n.* any of several heavy, short-legged rodents covered with coarse hair and spines called quills. One kind lives in North American forests.

WORD STORY Porcupine comes from Latin words meaning "pig" and "thorn." **Porpoise** comes from Latin words meaning "pig" and "fish." **Porcelain** comes from a Latin word meaning "pig." Obviously, many things reminded Romans of pigs. With the porcupine, it was probably shape and size. With the porpoise, it was the snout. Porcelain is named for a shiny white seashell that looks like china. To the Romans, the shell looked like a pig's back.

pore[1] (pôr), *v.* to study or think over carefully or earnestly: *pore over a book, pore over a problem.* ❑ *v.* **pored, por·ing.** ■ Another word that sounds like this is **pour.**

pore[2] (pôr), *n.* a very small opening. Sweat comes through the pores in the skin. ■ Another word that sounds like this is **pour.**

por·gy (pôr′gē), *n.* any of numerous saltwater food fishes of Mediterranean and Atlantic waters. ❑ *n., pl.* **por·gy** or **por·gies.**

pork (pôrk), *n.* meat of a pig or hog used for food. [See Word Story at **meat.**]

pork·er (pôr′kər), *n.* pig, especially one fattened to eat.

porn (pôrn), *n.* pornography.

por·nog·ra·phy (pôr nog′rə fē), *n.* writings or pictures about sexual activities, meant to arouse sexual desires. **—por·no·graph·ic** (pôr′nə graf′ik), *adj.*

po·ros·i·ty (pô ros′ə tē), *n.* porous quality or condition.

po·rous (pôr′əs), *adj.* full of pores or tiny holes through which liquids or gases can pass: *Cloth is porous but rubber is not.* **—po′rous·ness,** *n.*

por·phyr·y (pôr′fər ē), *n.* any igneous rock in which large crystals are scattered through a mass of smaller minerals.

por·poise (pôr′pəs), *n.* **1** any of several sea mammals with blunt, rounded snouts. Porpoises are small toothed whales, and they live in groups in the northern Atlantic and Pacific. **2** any of several other small sea mammals, especially a dolphin. ❑ *n., pl.* **por·poise** or **por·pois·es.** [See Word Story at **porcupine.**]

por·ridge (pôr′ij), *n.* food made of oatmeal or other grain boiled in water or milk until it thickens.

por·rin·ger (pôr′ən jər), *n.* (earlier) a small dish from which soup, porridge, bread and milk, etc., could be eaten.

port[1] (pôrt), *n.* **1** place where ships and boats can be sheltered from storms; harbor. **2** place where ships and boats can load and unload; city or town by a harbor: *New York, Baltimore, and San Francisco are important American ports.*

port[2] (pôrt), *n.* **1** porthole. **2** opening in a cylinder or pipe for steam, air, water, etc., to pass through. **3** socket on a computer for attaching cables from peripherals.

port[3] (pôrt), **1** *n.* the side of a ship, boat, or aircraft to the left of someone facing forward. **2** *adj.* on the left side of a ship, boat, or aircraft.

port[4] (pôrt), *n.* a strong, sweet, dark red wine.

Port., **1** Portugal. **2** Portuguese.

por·ta·ble (pôr′tə bəl), *adj.* capable of being carried; easily carried: *a portable typewriter, a portable radio.*

por·tage (pôr′tij), *n.* **1** act or process of carrying boats, provisions, etc., overland from one river or lake to another. **2** place where this is done. **3** cost of carrying anything.

por·tal (pôr′tl), *n.* door, gate, or entrance, usually an imposing one.

Port-au-Prince (pôrt′ō prins′), *n.* port and capital of Haiti, in the S part.

port·cul·lis (pôrt kul′is), *n.* a strong gate or grating of iron sliding up and down in grooves, used to close the gateway of an ancient castle or fortress. ❑ *n., pl.* **port·cul·lis·es.**

por·tend (pôr tend′), *v.* to indicate beforehand; give warning of: *Black clouds portend a storm.*

por·tent (pôr′tent), *n.* a warning, usually of coming evil; sign; omen: *The black clouds were a portent of bad weather.*

por·ten·tous (pôr ten′təs), *adj.* **1** indicating evil to come; ominous; threatening. **2** amazing; extraordinary. **—por·ten′tous·ly,** *adv.* **—por·ten′tous·ness,** *n.*

por·ter (pôr′tər), *n.* **1** person employed to carry loads or baggage: *Give your bags to the porter.* **2** attendant in a parlor car or sleeping car of a passenger train.

Por·ter (pôr′tər), *n.* **1 Cole** (kōl), 1891-1964, American songwriter. His first song was published when he was eleven years old. His later witty and sophisticated songs included "Night and Day" and "You're the Top." **2 Katherine Anne** (kath′ər in), 1890-1980, American short-story writer and novelist. A collection of her stories won the Pulitzer Prize for fiction in 1966. **3 William Sydney.** See **Henry, O.**

por·ter·house (pôr′tər hous′), *n.* a choice beefsteak containing the tenderloin.

porterhouse steak, porterhouse.

port·fo·li·o (pôrt fō′lē ō), *n.* **1** a portable case for loose papers, drawings, etc. **2** a set of drawings, photographs, etc., that show an artist's or model's work, usually carried in a large folder. **3** position and duties of a cabinet member or a minister of state: *The Secretary of Defense resigned his portfolio.* **4** holdings in the form of stocks, bonds, etc. ❑ *n., pl.* **port·fo·li·os.**

port·hole (pôrt′hōl′), *n.* **1** opening in a ship's side to let in light and air. **2** opening in a ship, wall, etc., through which to shoot.

por·ti·co (pôr′tə kō), *n.* roof supported by columns, forming a porch or a covered walk. ❑ *n., pl.* **por·ti·coes** or **por·ti·cos.**

por·tion (pôr′shən), **1** *n.* a part or share: *A portion of each school day is devoted to arithmetic.* ■ See Synonym Study at **part. 2** *n.* quantity of food served to someone at one time: *I can't eat such a large portion.* **3** *v.* to divide into parts or shares: *The money was portioned out among the children.* **4** *n.* dowry.

Port·land (pôrt′lənd), *n.* **1** port in SW Maine, near the Atlantic. **2** port in NW Oregon, on the Columbia River.

Port Lou·is (lü′is *or* lü′ē), port and capital of Mauritius, in the NW part.

port·ly (pôrt′lē), *adj.* **1** having a large body; stout. ■ See Synonym Study at **fat. 2** stately; dignified. ❑ *adj.* **port·li·er, port·li·est.** **—port′li·ness,** *n.*

port·man·teau (pôrt man′tō), *n.* a stiff traveling bag with two compartments opening like a book. ❑ *n., pl.* **port·man·teaus** or **port·man·teaux** (pôrt man′tōz).

Port Mores·by (môrz′bē), port and capital of Papua New Guinea, in SE New Guinea.

Port of Spain, Port-of-Spain.

Port-of-Spain (pôrt′əv spān′), *n.* port and capital of Trinidad and Tobago, in NW Trinidad.

Por·to-No·vo (pōr′tō nō′vō), *n.* port and capital of Benin, in the S part, on the Atlantic.

Por·to Ri·co (pôr′tō rē′kō), former name of **Puerto Rico.**

por·trait (pôr′trit *or* pôr′trāt), *n.* **1** picture of a person, especially of the face. **2** picture in words; description.

por·trait·ist (pôr′trā tist), *n.* person who makes portraits.

por·trai·ture (pôr′trə chùr), *n.* **1** act of portraying. **2** portrait.

por·tray (pôr trā′), *v.* **1** to make a likeness of in a drawing or painting; make a picture of: *portray a historical scene.* **2** to picture in words; describe: *The book "Black Beauty" portrays the life of a horse.* ■ See Synonym Study at **describe. 3** to act the part of in a play or movie: *He portrayed a clerk.* **—por·tray′a·ble,** *adj.* **—por·tray′er,** *n.*

por·tray·al (pôr trā′əl), *n.* **1** act of portraying by drawing or in words. **2** a picture or description.

Por·tu·gal (pôr′chə gəl), *n.* country in SW Europe, west of Spain. *Capital:* Lisbon.

Por·tu·guese (pôr′chə gēz′), **1** *adj.* of or about Portugal, its people, or their language. **2** *n.* person born or living in Portugal. **3** *n.* language of Portugal. ❑ *n., pl.* **Por·tu·guese.**

WORD SOURCE Portuguese has given many words to the English language, including the words below.

albino	coco	macaque	palaver
anchovy	dodo	macaw	zebra
cobra	emu		

Port-Vi·la (pôrt′vē′lə), *n.* capital of Vanuatu.

pose (def. 2)

pose (pōz), **1** *n.* position of the body; way of holding the body: *a natural pose, a pose taken in exercising.* **2** *v.* to hold a position of the body: *He posed an hour for his portrait.* **3** *v.* to put in a certain position: *The photographer posed her before taking her picture.* **4** *n.* attitude assumed for effect; pretense; affectation: *Her interest in other people is quite real; it is not just a pose.* **5** *v.* to pretend something; put on an attitude for effect: *They posed as a rich couple although they had little money.* ■ See Synonym Study at **pretend**. **6** *v.* to put forward for discussion; state: *pose a question.* ❏ *v.* **posed, pos·ing.** —**pos′er,** *n.*

WORD STORY **Pose** comes from a Latin word meaning "a pause." **Pause** comes from the same Latin word. A pose is the position you are in when you pause.

Po·sei·don (pə sīd′n), *n.* the Greek god of the sea. The Romans called him Neptune.

posh (posh), *adj.* elegant or fine in appearance; stylish.

po·si·tion (pə zish′ən), **1** *n.* place where a thing or person is: *The flowers grew in a sheltered position behind the house.* **2** *n.* way of being placed: *Sit in a more comfortable position.* **3** *n.* proper place: *The band got into position to march in the parade.* **4** *n.* condition with reference to place or circumstances: *I maneuvered for position before shooting the basketball. Your careless remark put me in an awkward position.* **5** *n.* job: *He has a position in a bank.* **6** *n.* rank or standing, especially high standing: *She was raised to the position of manager.* **7** *n.* way of thinking; set of opinions: *What is your position on this question?* **8** *v.* to place in a certain position: *The photographer positioned the tall students behind the shorter ones.*

pos·i·tive (poz′ə tiv), **1** *adj.* permitting no question; without doubt; sure: *We have positive evidence that the earth moves around the sun.* **2** *adj.* too sure; too confident: *A positive manner annoys some people.* **3** *adj.* definite; emphatic: *"No. I will not," was his positive refusal.* **4** *adj.* showing agreement or approval: *a positive answer to a question.* **5** *n.* the simple form of an adjective or adverb, different from the comparative and superlative. *Fast* is the positive; *faster* is the comparative; *fastest* is the superlative. **6** *adj.* of the simple form of an adjective or adverb. **7** *adj.* showing that a particular disease, condition, germ, etc., is present: *The test was positive.* **8** *adj.* adding something; helpful; practical: *Don't just make criticisms; give us some positive suggestions.* **9** *adj.* of the kind of electricity that protons have. Positive electricity does not travel along wires, but it pulls negative electricity toward it. **10** *adj.* greater than zero; plus: *Five above zero is a positive quantity.* **11** *n.* a positive number or quantity. **12** *adj.* (in photography) having the lines, shadows, and colors as in the original subject: *a positive image.* **13** *n.* print made from a photographic film or plate. **14** *adj.* (in biology) moving toward the source of a stimulus, such as light: *positive tropism.* —**pos′i·tive·ness,** *n.*

pos·i·tive·ly (poz′ə tiv lē), *adv.* **1** in a positive way: *The audience reacted positively to the play.* **2** to a great extreme; absolutely: *I was positively furious at them for being so rude.*

pos·i·tron (poz′ə tron), *n.* an elementary particle having the same mass as an electron, but with a positive charge.

pos·se (pos′ē), *n.* group of citizens called together by a sheriff to help maintain law and order.

posse

pos·sess (pə zes′), *v.* **1** to have as belonging to you; own: *My aunt possessed great intelligence and determination.* **2** to hold as property; hold; occupy. **3** to control; influence strongly: *She was possessed by the desire to be rich.* **4** to control by an evil spirit: *He fought like one possessed.* [**Possess** comes from Latin words meaning "to be able" and "to sit." If you own it, people can't tell you to get off it.]

pos·ses·sion (pə zesh′ən), *n.* **1** act or fact of possessing or having: *The troops fought hard for possession of a valuable airfield.* **2** ownership: *On her 21st birthday she came into possession of $50,000.* **3** **possessions,** *pl.* things possessed; property: *Please move your possessions from my room.* **4** territory under the rule of a country: *Guam is a possession of the United States.* **5** domination by a particular feeling, idea, evil spirit, etc. —**pos·ses′sor,** *n.*

pos·ses·sive (pə zes′iv), **1** *adj.* showing possession. *My, your, his,* and *our* are in the possessive case because they indicate who possesses or owns. **2** *n.* the possessive case. **3** *n.* word in this case. In "your book," *your* is a possessive. **4** *adj.* desirous of ownership: *She is very possessive of her books and will not lend them.* —**pos·ses′sive·ly,** *adv.* —**pos·ses′sive·ness,** *n.*

pos·si·bil·i·ty (pos′ə bil′ə tē), *n.* **1** condition of being possible: *There is a possibility that the train may be late.* **2** a possible thing, person, or event: *A whole week of rain is a possibility.* ❏ *n., pl.* **pos·si·bil·i·ties** for 2.

pos·si·ble (pos′ə bəl), *adj.* **1** capable of being, being done, or happening: *It is possible to cure tuberculosis. Space travel is now possible.* **2** not known to be true, but perhaps true: *It is possible that they left without us.* **3** capable of being done or chosen properly: *the only possible action, the only possible candidate.*

pos·si·bly (pos′ə blē), *adv.* **1** by any possibility; no matter what happens: *I cannot possibly go.* **2** perhaps: *Possibly you are right.*

pos·sum (pos′əm), *n.* opossum. ❏ *n., pl.* **pos·sums** or **pos·sum.** **play possum,** to pretend to be weak, inactive, or dead.

WORD STORY **Play possum** comes from an unusual behavior of the opossum. When threatened, the opossum appears to play dead by lying motionless on its side. Some scientists have wondered if the opossum is really fainting from fear. However, careful tests do not show the bodily changes that normally go with fainting. So it seems likely that an opossum does pretend, in order to save its life.

post¹ (pōst), **1** *n.* piece of timber, metal, etc., firmly set up, usually to support something else: *the posts of a door, a hitching post.* **2** *v.* to fasten a notice in a place where it can easily be seen: *Advertise-*

a	hat	ė	term	ô	order	ch	child		a in about
ā	age	i	it	oi	oil	ng	long		e in taken
ä	far	ī	ice	ou	out	sh	she	ə	i in pencil
â	care	o	hot	u	cup	th	thin		o in lemon
e	let	ō	open	ů	put	ŦH	then		u in circus
ē	equal	ò	saw	ü	rule	zh	measure		

ments for the new play were posted all over town. **3** *v.* to make known by, or as if by, a posted notice; make public: *post a reward.* **4** *v.* to put a name in a list that is published or posted up: *The names of the winners will be posted soon.* **5** *v.* to put up notices warning people to keep out of: *That farmer posts his land.*

post² (pōst), **1** *n.* the place where a soldier, police officer, guard, etc., is stationed; place where you are supposed to be when on duty: *When the fire alarm sounded, they all rushed to their posts.* **2** *n.* a military base where soldiers are stationed; fort. **3** *v.* to station at a post: *They posted guards at the door.* **4** *v.* to make a deposit of: *post bail.* **5** *n.* job or position: *the post of secretary, a diplomatic post.* **6** *n.* trading post.

post³ (pōst), **1** *n.* an established system for carrying letters, papers, packages, etc.; the mail: *I sent the package by post.* **2** *n.* a single delivery of mail: *this morning's post.* **3** *v.* to send by mail: *post a letter.* **4** *v.* to supply with up-to-date information; inform: *Keep me posted about your new job.*

post-, *prefix.* after; later: *postwar = after the war.*

post·age (pō′stij), *n.* amount paid on anything sent by mail.

postage meter, machine that stamps postage on a package or letter and postmarks it.

postage stamp, stamp (def. 1).

post·al (pō′stəl), *adj.* of or about mail and post offices: *postal rules.*

postal card, **1** an officially produced card sold by a post office, that has a government postage stamp printed on it and is used to send a message by mail. **2** postcard.

postal code, CANADIAN. a combination of six letters and numbers that identifies one of Canada's postal delivery areas.

Postal Service, an independent agency of the U.S. government that provides mail services, sells postage stamps, etc. It replaced the U.S. Post Office Department in 1971.

post·card (pōst′kärd′), *n.* **1** a privately produced card, usually about 3½ inches by 5½ inches (9 by 14 centimeters), for sending a message by mail, requiring a postage stamp and often having a picture on one side. **2** postal card.

post·date (pōst′dāt′), *v.* **1** to give a later date than the true date to a letter, check, etc. **2** to follow in time. ❏ *v.* **post·dat·ed, post·dat·ing.**

post·er (pō′stər), *n.* a large printed sheet or notice put up on a wall.

pos·te·ri·or (po stir′ē ər), **1** *adj.* situated behind; back; rear; hind. **2** *adj.* coming after; later. **3** *n.* the buttocks.

pos·ter·i·ty (po ster′ə tē), *n.* **1** generations of the future: *Posterity may travel to distant planets.* **2** anyone's children, and their children, and their children, and so on and on; all of a person's descendants.

pos·tern (pō′stərn *or* pos′tərn), *n.* a small back door or gate, especially one in a castle or fort.

poster paint, a kind of watercolor paint that contains egg yolk, gum, or glue to make it more opaque.

post exchange, PX.

post·grad·u·ate (pōst graj′ü it), **1** *n.* student who continues studying in college or at school after graduation. **2** *adj.* taking a course of study after graduation. **3** *adj.* of or for postgraduates: *postgraduate courses.*

post·haste (pōst′hāst′), *adv.* very speedily; in great haste.

post·hu·mous (pos′chə məs), *adj.* **1** happening after death: *posthumous fame.* **2** published after the death of the author: *a posthumous book.* **3** born after the death of the father: *a posthumous child.* —**post′hu·mous·ly,** *adv.*

post·man (pōst′mən), *n.* mail carrier. ❏ *n., pl.* **post·men.**

post·mark (pōst′märk′), **1** *n.* an official mark stamped on mail to cancel the postage stamp and record the place and date of mailing. **2** *v.* to stamp with a postmark.

post·mas·ter (pōst′mas′tər), *n.* person in charge of a post office.

postmaster general, **1** person at the head of the postal system of a country. **2** Postmaster General, the chief executive officer of the Postal Service. ❏ *n., pl.* **postmasters general** for 1, **Postmasters General** for 2.

post me·rid·i·em (pōst mə rid′ē əm), LATIN. after noon; P.M.

post·mis·tress (pōst′mis′tris), *n.* woman in charge of a post office. ❏ *n., pl.* **post·mis·tress·es.**

post·mor·tem (pōst′môr′təm), **1** *adj.* after death: *A postmortem examination showed that he had died of natural causes.* **2** *n.* autopsy.

post·na·tal (pōst nā′tl), *adj.* after birth: *postnatal care, postnatal diseases.* —**post·na′tal·ly,** *adv.*

post office, **1** place where mail is handled and postage stamps are sold. **2** Often, **Post Office,** the former government department in charge of mail, replaced by the Postal Service in 1971.

post·op·er·a·tive (pōst op′ər ə tiv), *adj.* occurring after a surgical operation: *postoperative pain.* —**post·op′er·a·tive·ly,** *adv.*

post·paid (pōst′pād′), *adj.* with the postage paid for.

post·pone (pōst pōn′), *v.* to put something off till later; put off to a later time; delay: *The softball game was postponed because of rain.* ❏ *v.* **post·poned, post·pon·ing.** —**post·pone′ment,** *n.* —**post·pon′er,** *n.*

post·script (pōst′skript), *n.* **1** addition to a letter, written after the writer's name has been signed. **2** a supplementary part added to any composition or literary work.

pos·tu·late (pos′chə lit *for noun;* pos′chə lāt *for verb*), **1** *n.* something taken for granted or assumed as a basis for reasoning; fundamental principle; necessary condition: *One postulate of plane geometry is that a straight line is the shortest distance between any two points.* **2** *v.* to assume without proof; take for granted: *Geometry postulates certain things as a basis for its reasoning.* ❏ *v.* **pos·tu·lat·ed, pos·tu·lat·ing.** —**pos·tu·la′tion,** *n.*

pos·ture (pos′chər), **1** *n.* position of the body; way of holding the body: *Good posture is important to health.* ▪ See Synonym Study at **bearing. 2** *v.* to take a certain position: *The dancer postured before the mirror, bending gracefully.* **3** *n.* attitude or policy toward a situation: *an aggressive posture in nuclear defense.* ❏ *v.* **pos·tured, pos·tur·ing.** —**pos′tur·al,** *adj.* —**pos′tur·er,** *n.*

post·war (pōst′wôr′), *adj.* after the war.

po·sy (pō′zē), *n.* **1** flower. **2** bunch of flowers; bouquet. ❏ *n., pl.* **po·sies.**

pot (pot), **1** *n.* kind of vessel or dish. There are many different kinds and shapes of pots. They are made of iron, aluminum, earthenware, and other substances. A pot may hold food or drink or contain earth for flowers to grow in. **2** *n.* amount a pot can hold: *He ate a small pot of beans.* **3** *n.* INFORMAL. a large sum of money. **4** *n.* INFORMAL. all the money bet at one time in a card game, lottery, etc. **5** *n.* SLANG. marijuana. **6** *v.* to put into a pot: *pot young tomato plants.* **7** *v.* to cook and preserve in a pot. **8** *v.* to take a potshot at; shoot. ❏ *v.* **pot·ted, pot·ting.** —**pot′like′,** *adj.*
go to pot, to go to ruin.

po·ta·ble (pō′tə bəl), *adj.* fit or suitable for drinking. —**po′ta·bil′i·ty,** *n.*

pot·ash (pot′ash′), *n.* any of several substances containing potassium made from various minerals, wood ashes, etc., used in making soap, fertilizers, and glass. ❏ *n., pl.* **pot·ash·es.**

po·tas·si·um (pə tas′ē əm), *n.* a soft, silver-white, metallic element, occurring in nature only in compounds. Potassium is one of the most abundant elements in the earth's crust, and is essential for the growth of plants. *Symbol:* K

po·tas·si·um-ar·gon dating, method of determining the age of rock by measuring the amount of radioactive potassium that has turned into argon.

potassium hydroxide, a white, solid substance which releases great heat when it dissolves in water; caustic potash. It is used in bleaching, in making liquid soaps, and in medicine.

potassium nitrate, a white or colorless crystalline compound, occurring naturally or produced from chloride of potassium; saltpeter; niter. It is used in explosives, fertilizers, medicine, and meat preservatives.

po·ta·to (pə tā′tō), *n.* **1** a round, hard, starchy vegetable with a thin skin; Irish potato; white potato. It is one of the most widely used vegetables. Potatoes grow underground. **2** sweet potato. ❏ *n., pl.* **po·ta·toes.**

WORD STORY **Potato** comes from a word in a Native American language of the Caribbean, meaning "sweet potato." Europeans learned the word but applied it to the unsweet potato.

potato chip, a thin slice of potato fried in deep fat.
pot·bel·lied (pot′bel′ēd), *adj.* **1** having a potbelly. **2** shaped like a potbelly: *a potbellied stove.*
pot·bel·ly (pot′bel′ē), *n.* a bulging belly. □ *n., pl.* **pot·bel·lies.**
po·ten·cy (pōt′n sē), *n.* power; strength: *the potency of an argument, the potency of a drug.*
po·tent (pōt′nt), *adj.* having great power; powerful; strong: *a potent remedy for a disease, potent reasons.* **–po′tent·ly,** *adv.*
po·ten·tate (pōt′n tāt), *n.* **1** person having great power; ruler.
po·ten·tial (pə ten′shəl), **1** *adj.* possible, not yet actual; able to come into being or action: *There is a potential danger of being bitten when playing with a strange dog.* **2** *n.* something possible: *a potential of danger.* **3** *n.* voltage. **–po·ten′tial·ly,** *adv.*
potential energy, energy that an object contains because of its position or structure. A coiled spring or a raised weight has potential energy.
po·ten·ti·al·i·ty (pə ten′shē al′ə tē), *n.* **1** potential condition or quality; possible power. **2** something potential; possibility. □ *n., pl.* **po·ten·ti·al·i·ties** for 2.
pot·ful (pot′ful), *n.* as much as a pot can hold. □ *n., pl.* **pot·fuls.**
pot·herb (pot′ėrb′ or pot′hėrb′), *n.* **1** any plant with leaves and stems that are boiled for use as a vegetable, such as spinach. **2** plant used as seasoning in cooking, such as sage.
pot·hold·er (pot′hōl′dər), *n.* a thick pad of cloth or other material for handling hot pots, lids, etc.
pot·hole (pot′hōl′), *n.* **1** a deep hole in the surface of a street or road. **2** a deep, round hole, especially one made in the rocky bed of a river by stones and gravel that are spun around in the current. **3** a shallow, poorly drained area on a prairie, where water accumulates at certain times of the year and forms a marsh or pond: *birds nesting in prairie potholes.*

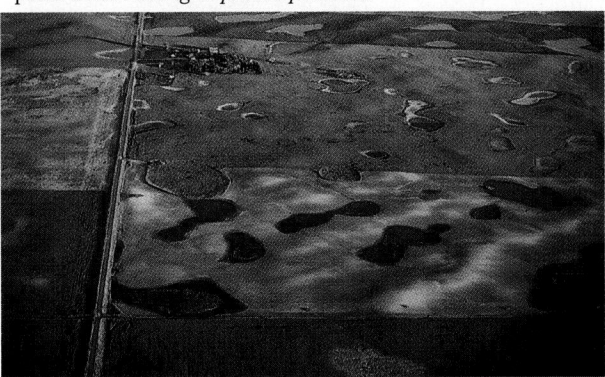

potholes (def. 3)

pot·hook (pot′hůk′), *n.* **1** hook for hanging a pot over an open fire. **2** rod with a hook for lifting hot pots.
po·tion (pō′shən), *n.* a drink, especially one that is used as a medicine or poison, or in magic. [See Word Story at **poison.**]
pot·latch (pot′lach′), *n.* a ceremonial festival among certain American Indians of the northern Pacific coast at which they gave away or destroyed valuable objects to show their wealth. □ *n., pl.* **pot·latch·es.**
pot·luck (pot′luk′), *n.* whatever food happens to be ready or on hand for a meal: *Come and take potluck with me.*
potluck supper, meal at which each guest brings a dish for everyone to share.
Po·to·mac (pə tō′mək), *n.* river flowing from E West Virginia between Maryland and Virginia, into Chesapeake Bay. Washington, D.C., is on the Potomac River.
pot·pie (pot′pī′), *n.* **1** meat, or poultry, and vegetables baked in a pie. **2** a stew with dumplings.
pot·pour·ri (pō′pu̇ rē′), *n.* **1** a fragrant mixture of dried flower petals and spices. **2** medley or mixture: *a potpourri of Italian, French, and Austrian folk songs.*
pot roast, beef browned in a pot and cooked slowly with only a little water.

pot·shot (pot′shot′), *n.* **1** a quick shot fired at something from close range without careful aim. **2** Often, **potshots,** *pl.* criticism, usually made in a careless manner.
pot·tage (pot′ij), *n.* OLD USE. a thick soup.
pot·ter (pot′ər), *n.* person who makes pottery.
Pot·ter (pot′ər), *n.* **Be·a·trix** (bē′ə triks), 1866-1943, English writer and illustrator. She wrote many children's stories about animals who wear clothes and use tools and furniture, including *The Tale of Peter Rabbit.*
potter's field, piece of public ground set aside for the burial of people who die without friends or money.

WORD STORY **Potter's field** comes from the Bible. After Judas killed himself, the money he had taken to betray Jesus was used to buy a field from a potter, to bury strangers in. Public cemeteries of this sort borrowed the name.

potter's wheel, a rotating horizontal disk upon which clay is molded into dishes, etc.
pot·ter·y (pot′ər ē), *n.* **1** pots, dishes, vases, etc., made from clay and hardened by heat. **2** art or business of making them. **3** place where such pots, dishes, vases, etc., are made. □ *n., pl.* **pot·ter·ies** for 3.

pouch (pouch), *n.* **1** bag or sack: *a mail pouch.* **2** a baglike fold of skin. A kangaroo carries its young in a pouch. **3** a small plastic sack or envelope for storing food in a freezer. □ *n., pl.* **pouch·es.** [See Word Story at **poach**².] **–pouch′like′,** *adj.*
poul·tice (pōl′tis), **1** *n.* a soft, moist mass of mustard, herbs, etc., applied to the body to reduce pain or swelling. **2** *v.* to put a poultice on. □ *v.* **poul·ticed, poul·tic·ing.**
poul·try (pōl′trē), *n.* birds such as chickens, turkeys, geese, and ducks, raised for their meat or eggs. [See Word Story at **pool**².]

pouch (def. 2)

pounce (pouns), **1** *v.* to come down with a rush and seize something: *The cat pounced upon the mouse.* **2** *v.* to seize something and turn it to your advantage, such as an opportunity, someone else's mistake, etc. **3** *n.* a sudden swoop or pouncing. □ *v.* **pounced, pounc·ing.** [**Pounce** comes from an old English word meaning "claw." When a hunting animal pounces it uses its claws.]
pound¹ (pound), *n.* **1** unit of weight equal to 16 ounces in avoirdupois weight and 12 ounces in troy weight. **2** pound sterling. **3** unit of money of Israel, Egypt, and certain other countries. □ *n., pl.* **pounds** or **pound.**

WORD STORY **Pound**¹, in Latin, is *libra,* also meaning "scales" as in the sign of the zodiac. It is from the Latin word that English gets the abbreviation **lb.** and the pound sterling symbol **£,** which looks like a fancy **L** and stands for *libra.*

pound² (pound), **1** *v.* to hit hard again and again; hit heavily: *She pounded the door with her fist.* ■ See Synonym Study at **beat. 2** *v.* to beat hard; throb: *After running fast you can feel your heart pound.* **3** *v.* to make into a powder or pulp by pounding: *They pounded the grains of corn into meal.* **4** *v.* to move with a pounding sound: *We pounded down the hill to catch the bus.* **5** *n.* a heavy blow, or its sound.
pound³ (pound), *n.* **1** an enclosed place in which to keep stray animals: *a dog or cat pound.* **2** enclosure for keeping, confining, or trapping animals or fish.

a	hat	ė	term	ô	order	ch	child		a in about
ā	age	i	it	oi	oil	ng	long		e in taken
ä	far	ī	ice	ou	out	sh	she	ə {	i in pencil
â	care	o	hot	u	cup	th	thin		o in lemon
e	let	ō	open	u̇	put	℔	then		u in circus
ē	equal	ȯ	saw	ü	rule	zh	measure		

P

pound cake, a rich, sweet cake, formerly made with one pound each of flour, sugar, and butter, and with many eggs.

pound-fool·ish (pound/fü/lish), *adj.* foolish or careless in regard to large sums of money.

pound sterling, unit of money of Great Britain. Since February, 1971, 1 pound = 100 pence; before that, 1 pound = 240 pence. £1 means one pound.

pour (pôr), **1** *v.* to flow or cause to flow in a steady stream: *I poured the milk from the bottle. The crowd poured out of the theater.* **2** *v.* to make known freely or without reserve: *pour out your grief.* **3** *v.* to rain heavily. **4** *n.* a heavy rain; downpour. ■ Another word that sounds like this is **pore. –pour/er,** *n.*

pout (pout), **1** *v.* to show unhappiness by pushing out the lips, sulking, or looking angry: *The child was pouting because he couldn't have the new toy.* **2** *n.* act of pushing out the lips when displeased or sulky.

pout·er (pou/tər), *n.* a kind of domestic pigeon that puffs out its crop.

pov·er·ty (pov/ər tē), *n.* **1** condition of being poor: *Their tattered clothing and broken furniture indicated their poverty.* **2** lack of what is needed; poor quality: *The poverty of the soil makes the crops small.* **3** a small amount; fewness: *A boring person's talk shows poverty of ideas.*

pov·er·ty-strick·en (pov/ər tē strik/ən), *adj.* extremely poor.

POW, prisoner of war.

pow·der (pou/dər), **1** *n.* a solid reduced to dust by pounding, crushing, or grinding. **2** *v.* to make into or become powder: *The soil powdered in the heat.* **3** *n.* some special kind of powder: *face powder, bath powder.* **4** *v.* to sprinkle or cover with powder. **5** *v.* to sprinkle: *The ground was powdered with snow.* **6** *v.* to put powder on the face, body, etc.: *She powdered her face.* **7** *n.* gunpowder. [**Powder** comes from a Latin word meaning "dust."] **–pow/der·er,** *n.*

powder blue, a light blue.

powder horn, case made of an animal's horn for carrying gunpowder.

powder puff, a soft puff or pad for applying powder to the skin.

powder room, lavatory for women, especially one with a dressing table.

pow·der·y (pou/dər ē), *adj.* **1** of or like powder; in the form of powder. **2** easily made into powder. **3** sprinkled or covered with powder.

pow·er (pou/ər), **1** *n.* strength or force; effectiveness; might: *a medicine of great power, military power.* **2** *n.* ability to do or act: *I will give you all the help in my power.* **3** *n.* particular ability: *He has great powers of concentration.* **4** *n.* authority; influence; control; right: *Congress has power to declare war.* **5** *n.* person, thing, group, or nation having authority or influence: *Five powers held a peace conference.* **6** *n.* energy that can do work: *water power for generating electricity, heating by solar power.* **7** *v.* to provide with energy: *a boat powered by an outboard motor.* **8** *adj.* operated by a motor; equipped with its own motor: *a power drill.* **9** *n.* product of a number multiplied by itself one or more times. 16 is the 4th power of 2 ($2 \times 2 \times 2 \times 2 = 16$). **10** *n.* ability of a device to magnify. An object seen through a microscope with a power of ten looks ten times its actual size. **11** *n.* the rate at which work is done, equal to the work divided by the time. Power is measured in watts and horsepower.

in power, having control or authority.

the powers that be, those who have control or authority.

pow·er·boat (pou/ər bōt/), *n.* boat propelled by an engine on board; motorboat.

pow·er·ful (pou/ər fəl), *adj.* having great power or force; mighty; strong: *a powerful person, a powerful medicine, a powerful argument, a powerful nation.* **–pow/er·ful·ly,** *adv.*

pow·er·house (pou/ər hous/), *n.* **1** a building containing boilers, engines, generators, etc., for producing electric power. **2** a powerful, energetic, or highly effective person or group. ❑ *n., pl.* **pow·er·hous·es** (pou/ər hou/ziz).

pow·er·less (pou/ər lis), *adj.* without power; helpless: *The mouse was powerless in the cat's claws.* **–pow/er·less·ly,** *adv.* **–pow/er·less·ness,** *n.*

power mower, a lawn mower powered by a gasoline engine or by electricity.

power of attorney, a written statement giving one person legal power to act for another.

power pack, device used to change the voltage of an electric line or battery to the lower voltage used in a radio, a toy, etc.

power plant, **1** building with machinery for generating power. **2** motor; engine.

power play, (in hockey) form of attack used when the opponents are without one or more players on defense because of penalty.

power surge, a large, sudden, brief increase in the amount of current in an electric circuit. A power surge can damage electrical equipment.

power tool, tool powered by electricity or a gasoline engine, such as a circular saw, a drill, or the like.

Pow·ha·tan (pou/ə tan/), *n.* 1550?-1618, American Indian chief in Virginia. He was the father of Pocahontas.

pow·wow (pou/wou/), **1** *n.* an American Indian spiritual ceremony, usually accompanied by feasting and dancing, performed for the cure of disease, success in hunting, etc. **2** *n.* council or conference of or with American Indians. **3** *n.* INFORMAL. any conference or meeting. **4** *v.* to hold a powwow; confer.

WORD STORY **Powwow** comes from an Algonquian word meaning "to tell the future by dreams." American Indian spiritual leaders often used their dreams this way, especially during ceremonies and conferences.

pox (poks), *n.* any disease that covers the body or parts of the body with sores, such as chicken pox or smallpox. ❑ *n., pl.* **pox** or **pox·es.**

pp., **1** pages. **2** past participle.

p.p., **1** parcel post. **2** past participle. **3** postpaid.

Pr, symbol for praseodymium.

pr., **1** pair. **2** price.

PR, 1 proportional representation. **2** public relations. **3** Puerto Rico (used with postal Zip Code).

P.R., Puerto Rico.

prac·ti·ca·ble (prak/tə kə bəl), *adj.* able to be done; capable of being put into practice: *a practicable idea.* **–prac/ti·ca·bil/i·ty,** *n.* **–prac/ti·ca·bly,** *adv.*

prac·ti·cal (prak/tə kəl), *adj.* **1** of or about action or practice rather than thought or theory: *Earning a living is a practical matter.* **2** suitable for an actual situation: *a practical plan.* **3** useful: *An outdoor swimming pool is more practical in Florida than in Minnesota.* **4** having good sense: *A practical person does not spend time foolishly.* **5** engaged in actual work: *She is a practical musician who knows how to please an audience.* **6** being such in effect; virtual: *So many of our players were injured that our victory was a practical defeat.* **–prac/ti·cal·ness,** *n.*

prac·ti·cal·i·ty (prak/tə kal/ə tē), *n.* **1** quality of being practical; practical usefulness; practical habit of mind. **2** a practical matter. ❑ *n., pl.* **prac·ti·cal·i·ties** for 2.

practical joke, trick or prank played on a person. **–practical joker.**

prac·ti·cal·ly (prak/tik lē), *adv.* **1** almost; nearly: *Our house is around the corner, so we are practically home.* **2** so far as the results will be; in effect; really. **3** in a practical way; in a useful way.

practical nurse, person whose occupation is to care for the sick, but who does not have the hospital training or diploma of a registered nurse.

prac·tice (prak/tis), **1** *n.* action done many times over to gain skill: *Practice makes perfect.* **2** *n.* skill gained by experience or exercise: *They were out of practice at batting.* **3** *v.* to do some act again and again to learn to do it well: *She practiced pitching the ball. I practice on the piano every day.* **4** *n.* a training session:

Coach says to play in the game, you must have attended practice.
5 *n.* action or process of doing or being something: *Your plan is good in theory, but not in actual practice.* **6** *v.* to follow, observe, or use day after day; make a custom of; do usually: *We should practice kindness to others.* **7** *n.* the usual way; custom: *It is the practice at the factory to blow a whistle at noon.* **8** *v.* to work at or follow as a profession, art, or occupation: *practice medicine.* **9** *n.* act of working at or following a profession or occupation: *She is engaged in the practice of law.* **10** *n.* business of a doctor or lawyer: *The old doctor sold his practice.* ❑ *v.* **prac·ticed, prac·tic·ing. —prac′tic·er,** *n.*

prac·ticed (prak′tist), *adj.* experienced; skilled; expert: *Years of study have made him a practiced musician.*

prac·ti·tion·er (prak tish′ə nər), *n.* person engaged in the practice of a profession.

prae·to·ri·an or **Prae·to·ri·an** (prē tôr′ē ən), **1** *adj.* of or about the bodyguard of a Roman commander or emperor. **2** *n.* soldier of the bodyguard of a Roman commander or emperor.

prag·mat·ic (prag mat′ik), *adj.* concerned with practical results or values; viewing things in a matter-of-fact way. **—prag·mat′i·cal·ly,** *adv.*

Prague (präg), *n.* capital and largest city of the Czech Republic, in the W part.

Pra·ia (prä′yə), *n.* capital of Cape Verde Islands.

prair·ie (prâr′ē), *n.* **1** a large area of level or rolling land with grass but few or no trees, especially such an area making up much of central North America. **2 the Prairies,** *pl.* plain that covers southern and central Manitoba, Saskatchewan, and Alberta.

prairie chicken, either of two brown, black, and white grouse that live on the prairies of North America.

prairie dog, any of several burrowing rodents about the size of a squirrel, living as groups in burrows on the Great Plains and in the Rocky Mountain region. Prairie dogs bark.

prairie lily, a wild lily of North America, found from Quebec west to British Columbia, and south to New Mexico. It is the provincial flower of Saskatchewan.

Prairie Provinces, Manitoba, Saskatchewan, and Alberta.

prairie schooner, a large covered wagon used in crossing the plains of North America before the railroads were built.

prairie schooner

praise (prāz), **1** *n.* act of saying that a thing or person is good; words that tell the worth or value of a thing or person. **2** *v.* to express approval or admiration of: *She praised the winning team.* **3** *v.* to worship in words or song: *praise God.* **4** *n.* words or song worshiping God. ❑ *v.* **praised, prais·ing. —prais′er,** *n.*

sing the praises of, to praise with enthusiasm.

praise·wor·thy (prāz′wėr′ŦHē), *adj.* worthy of praise; deserving approval. **—praise′wor′thi·ly,** *adv.* **—praise′wor′thi·ness,** *n.*

pra·line (prä′lēn′ *or* prā′lēn′), *n.* a small cake of brown candy made of brown or maple sugar and nuts, usually pecans or almonds.

prance (prans), **1** *v.* to spring about on the hind legs: *Horses prance when they feel lively.* **2** *v.* to ride on a horse doing this.

3 *v.* to move gaily or proudly: *The children pranced about in their new Halloween costumes.* **4** *n.* act of prancing. ❑ *v.* **pranced, pranc·ing. —pranc′er,** *n.* **—pranc′ing·ly,** *adv.*

prank (prangk), *n.* piece of mischief; playful trick: *On April Fools' Day people often play pranks on each other.*

prank·ish (prang′kish), *adj.* **1** full of pranks; fond of pranks. **2** like a prank. **—prank′ish·ly,** *adv.* **—prank′ish·ness,** *n.*

prank·ster (prangk′stər), *n.* person who plays pranks.

pra·se·o·dym·i·um (prā′zē ō dim′ē əm), *n.* a yellowish white metallic element which occurs with neodymium. Its green salts are used to tint glass. *Symbol:* Pr

prate (prāt), *v.* to talk a great deal in a foolish way. ❑ *v.* **prat·ed, prat·ing. —prat′er,** *n.* **—prat′ing·ly,** *adv.*

prat·tle (prat′l), **1** *v.* to tell freely and carelessly. **2** *v.* to talk in a foolish way; babble. **3** *n.* foolish talk. **4** *n.* sounds like baby talk; babble: *the cheerful prattle of a brook.* ❑ *v.* **prat·tled, prat·tling. —prat′tler,** *n.*

prawn (prȯn), *n.* any of several shellfish used for food. Prawns are much like shrimp but larger. ❑ *n., pl.* **prawns** or **prawn.**

pray (prā), *v.* **1** to ask for from God; speak to God in worship: *They prayed for God's help.* **2** to ask earnestly for: *pray your forgiveness.* **3** to be pleased to; choose; wish: *Pray come with me.* ■ Another word that sounds like this is **prey.** **—pray′er,** *n.*

prayer (prâr), *n.* **1** act of praying: *We knelt in prayer.* **2** thing prayed for: *Our prayers were granted.* **3** form of words to be used in praying: *the Lord's Prayer.* **4** form of worship. **5** an earnest or humble request.

prayer book, book of prayers.

prayer·ful (prâr′fəl), *adj.* having the habit of praying often; devout. **—prayer′ful·ly,** *adv.* **—prayer′ful·ness,** *n.*

praying mantis, **1** a European mantis introduced into the United States to eat harmful garden pests, now widespread in eastern states. **2** any mantis.

praying mantis (def. 1)—about 2 in. (5 cm) long

pre-, *prefix.* before; in advance: *prewar = before the war; prepay = to pay in advance.*

preach (prēch), *v.* **1** to speak on a religious subject; deliver a sermon. **2** to make known by preaching; proclaim: *preach the gospel.* **3** to recommend strongly; urge; advise: *The coach was always preaching exercise and fresh air. Practice what you preach.* **4** to give earnest advice: *preach about good manners.*

preach·er (prē′chər), *n.* person who preaches; member of the clergy; minister.

preach·y (prē′chē), *adj.* inclined to preach, especially in a judgmental way. ❑ *adj.* **preach·i·er, preach·i·est. —preach′i·ness,** *n.*

pre·am·ble (prē′am′bəl), *n.* introduction to a speech or a writing. The reasons for a law and its general purpose are often stated in a preamble.

a	hat	ė	term	ô	order	ch	child		a in about
ā	age	i	it	oi	oil	ng	long		e in taken
ä	far	ī	ice	ou	out	sh	she	ə	i in pencil
â	care	o	hot	u	cup	th	thin		o in lemon
e	let	ō	open	ủ	put	ŦH	then		u in circus
ē	equal	ȯ	saw	ü	rule	zh	measure		

P

pre·ar·range (prē′ə rānj′), v. to arrange beforehand. ❑ v. pre·ar·ranged, pre·ar·rang·ing. —pre′ar·range′ment, n.

Pre·cam·bri·an (prē′kam′brē ən), n. (in geology) time between about 3½ billion and 600 million years ago, including the Archeozoic and Proterozoic.

pre·car·i·ous (pri kâr′ē əs), adj. not safe or secure; uncertain; dangerous; risky: *A racecar driver leads a precarious life. His hold on the branch was precarious.* —pre·car′i·ous·ly, adv. —pre·car′i·ous·ness, n.

pre·cau·tion (pri kò′shən), n. 1 care taken beforehand; thing done beforehand to ward off evil or secure good results: *Locking doors is a precaution against thieves.* 2 act of taking care beforehand: *Proper precaution is wise.*

pre·cau·tion·ar·y (pri kò′shə ner′ē), adj. of or using precaution: *She took precautionary measures to avoid the flu.*

pre·cede (prē sēd′), v. 1 to go or come before something: *The letter A precedes B in the alphabet. The band preceded the floats in the parade.* 2 to be higher than in rank or importance: *A major precedes a captain.* ❑ v. pre·ced·ed, pre·ced·ing.

prec·e·dence (pres′ə dəns or pri sēd′ns), n. 1 act or fact of preceding; a going or coming before in time or order. 2 higher position or rank; greater importance: *This work takes precedence over all other work.* 3 right to precede others in ceremonies or social affairs; social superiority: *A Senator takes precedence over a Representative.*

prec·e·dent (pres′ə dənt *for noun;* pri sēd′nt or pres′ə dənt *for adj.*), 1 n. action that may serve as an example or reason for a later action: *A decision of a court often serves as a precedent in other courts. Last year's school picnic set a precedent for having one this year.* 2 adj. preceding.

pre·ced·ing (prē sē′ding), adj. going or coming before; previous: *Turn back and look for the answer on the preceding page.*

pre·cept (prē′sept), n. rule of action or behavior; guiding principle: *"If at first you don't succeed, try, try again" is a familiar precept.*

pre·cep·tor (pri sep′tər), n. instructor; teacher.

pre·cinct (prē′singkt), n. 1 a part or district of a city: *an election precinct, a police precinct.* 2 space within a boundary: *Do not leave the school precincts during school hours.*

pre·cious (presh′əs), 1 adj. having great value; worth much; valuable. Gold, platinum, and silver are often called the precious metals. Diamonds, rubies, and sapphires are precious stones. 2 adj. much loved; dear: *a precious child.* 3 adv. very: *precious little money.* —pre′cious·ly, adv. —pre′cious·ness, n.

prec·i·pice (pres′ə pis), n. a nearly vertical cliff or mountainside.

pre·cip·i·tate (pri sip′ə tāt *for verb;* pri sip′ə tit *for adj.;* pri sip′ə tit or pri sip′ə tāt *for noun*), 1 v. to hasten the beginning of; bring about suddenly: *Insults precipitated an argument.* 2 adj. sudden and forceful; plunging or rushing; hasty; rash: *a precipitate action.* 3 v. to throw headlong; hurl: *precipitated herself into the struggle.* 4 v. to fall from the air in the form of rain, snow, etc. 5 v. to separate a substance from a solution as a solid. 6 n. substance separated from a solution as a solid. ❑ v. pre·cip·i·tat·ed, pre·cip·i·tat·ing. [See Word Story at precipice.] —pre·cip′i·tate·ly, adv. —pre·cip′i·tate·ness, n.

pre·cip·i·ta·tion (pri sip′ə tā′shən), n. 1 the act or process of falling from the air in the form of rain, snow, etc. 2 the amount of water that falls from the air in a certain time. 3 the process of

separating a substance from a solution as a solid. 4 act or process of bringing on suddenly: *the precipitation of a quarrel.*

pre·cip·i·tous (pri sip′ə təs), adj. 1 like a precipice; very steep: *precipitous cliffs.* 2 hasty; rash. —pre·cip′i·tous·ly, adv. —pre·cip′i·tous·ness, n.

pre·cise (pri sīs′), adj. 1 very definite or correct; exact; accurate: *The directions they gave were so precise that we found our way easily. The precise sum was 34 cents.* 2 very careful: *precise handwriting. She is precise in her work.* 3 strict: *We had precise orders to leave at two o'clock.* —pre·cise′ly, adv. —pre·cise′ness, n.

pre·ci·sion (pri sizh′ən), n. condition of being exact; accuracy: *to speak with precision.*

pre·clude (pri klüd′), v. to shut out; make impossible; prevent: *The heavy thunderstorm precluded our going to the beach.* ❑ v. pre·clud·ed, pre·clud·ing.

pre·co·cious (pri kō′shəs), adj. developed earlier than usual in knowledge, skill, etc.: *This very precocious child could read well at the age of four.* [Precocious comes from a Latin word meaning "to ripen early."] —pre·co′cious·ly, adv. —pre·co′cious·ness, n.

pre·coc·i·ty (pri kos′ə tē), n. precocious development; early maturity: *Mozart's precocity was extraordinary, for when he was only five years old, he began to compose music.*

pre·Co·lum·bi·an (prē′kə lum′bē ən), adj. of or from the time before the arrival of Columbus in the Americas: *pre-Columbian art.*

pre·con·ceived (prē′kən sēvd′), adj. formed beforehand: *The beauty of the scenery surpassed all our preconceived notions.*

pre·con·cep·tion (prē′kən sep′shən), n. idea or opinion formed beforehand.

pre·con·cert·ed (prē′kən sèr′tid), adj. arranged beforehand: *At a preconcerted signal we sang "Happy Birthday."*

pre·cook (prē′kùk′), v. to cook something completely or partially in advance, for quick heating or final cooking later.

pre·cur·sor (pri kèr′sər or prē′kèr′sər), n. forerunner: *A severe cold may be the precursor of pneumonia.*

pred., predicate.

pre·date (prē dāt′), v. 1 to be or happen before; precede; antedate: *Radio predated TV.* 2 to give an earlier date to: *predate a check.* ❑ v. pre·dat·ed, pre·dat·ing.

pre·da·tion (pri dā′shən), n. 1 act of preying on another animal or animals; predatory behavior. 2 robbery.

pred·a·tor (pred′ə tər), n. animal or person that lives by killing and eating other animals.

pred·a·to·ry (pred′ə tôr′ē), adj. 1 living by hunting and eating other animals. Lions and tigers are predatory animals. Hawks and owls are predatory birds. 2 living by robbery or other violent crime: *Predatory pirates roamed the seas.*

pred·e·ces·sor (pred′ə ses′ər), n. any person or thing that came before another, performing the same functions or having the same title or office.

predecessor of modern cars

pre·des·ti·na·tion (prē des′tə nā′shən), n. 1 act of ordaining beforehand; destiny; fate. 2 action of God in deciding beforehand what shall happen; doctrine that by God's decree certain souls will be saved and others lost.

pre·des·tine (prē des′tən), v. to determine or settle beforehand; foreordain. ❑ v. pre·des·tined, pre·des·tin·ing.

pre·de·ter·mine (prē′di tèr′mən), v. to determine or decide beforehand: *We met at the predetermined time.* ❑ v. pre·de·ter·mined, pre·de·ter·min·ing. —pre·de·ter′mi·na′tion, n.

pre·dic·a·ment (pri dik′ə mənt), n. an unpleasant, difficult, or bad situation: *She was in a predicament when she missed the last train home.*

pred·i·cate (pred′ə kit *for noun, adj.;* pred′ə kāt *for verb*), **1** *n.* (in grammar) the word or words expressing what is said about the subject. EXAMPLES: Dogs *bark.* The dogs *dug holes.* The dogs *are beagles.* **2** *adj.* (in grammar) belonging to the predicate. In "Horses are strong," *strong* is a **predicate adjective.** In "The dogs are beagles," *beagles* is a **predicate noun. 3** *v.* to found or base a statement, action, etc., on something: *Democracy is predicated on the belief that people should choose their government.* **4** *v.* to declare, assert, or affirm to be real or true: *Many religions predicate life after death.* ❑ *v.* **pred·i·cat·ed, pred·i·cat·ing.**

pre·dict (pri dikt′), *v.* to tell beforehand; prophesy; forecast: *The Weather Service predicts rain for tomorrow.* **—pre·dict′a·ble,** *adj.* **—pre·dict′a·bly,** *adv.*

pre·dic·tion (pri dik′shən), *n.* **1** thing predicted; prophecy; forecast: *predictions about the weather.* **2** act of predicting.

pre·di·lec·tion (pred′ə lek′shən *or* prē′də lek′shən), *n.* a strong liking for something; preference.

pre·dis·pose (prē′dis pōz′), *v.* to give an inclination or tendency to; make liable or susceptible: *A cold predisposes a person to other diseases.* ❑ *v.* **pre·dis·posed, pre·dis·pos·ing.**

pre·dis·po·si·tion (prē′dis′pə zish′ən), *n.* inclination or tendency: *a predisposition to look on the dark side of things.*

pre·dom·i·nance (pri dom′ə nəns), *n.* quality of being predominant: *the predominance of weeds in a deserted garden.*

pre·dom·i·nant (pri dom′ə nənt), *adj.* **1** having more power, authority, or influence than others; superior: *The United States has become the predominant nation in the Western Hemisphere.* **2** most noticeable; prevailing: *Red was the predominant color in the fabric.* **—pre·dom′i·nant·ly,** *adv.*

pre·dom·i·nate (pri dom′ə nāt), *v.* to be greater in power, strength, influence, or numbers: *Sunny days predominate over rainy days in desert regions.* ❑ *v.* **pre·dom·i·nat·ed, pre·dom·i·nat·ing. —pre·dom′i·na′tion,** *n.*

pree·mie (prē′mē), *n.* INFORMAL. a premature baby.

pre·em·i·nence *or* **pre-em·i·nence** (prē em′ə nəns), *n.* condition of being outstanding or preeminent; superiority: *the preeminence of an Olympic skier.*

pre·em·i·nent *or* **pre-em·i·nent** (prē em′ə nənt), *adj.* standing out above all others; superior to others: *She is the preeminent researcher, teacher, and author in her field.* **—pre·em′i·nent·ly** *or* **pre-em′i·nent·ly,** *adv.*

pre·empt *or* **pre-empt** (prē empt′), *v.* **1** to take for yourself before someone else does; acquire beforehand: *preempt the most comfortable chair.* **2** to take over; replace: *A special feature preempted the regular TV program.* **3** to settle on land with the right to buy it before others.

preen (prēn), *v.* **1** to smooth or arrange feathers with the beak. **2** to dress or groom carefully.

pre·ex·ist *or* **pre-ex·ist** (prē′ig zist′), *v.* to exist beforehand, or before something else.

pre·ex·ist·ence (prē′ig zis′təns), *n.* previous existence.

pre·ex·ist·ent (prē′ig zis′tənt), *adj.* existing previously.

pre·fab (prē′fab′), *n.* INFORMAL. something prefabricated, especially a house.

pre·fab·ri·cate (prē fab′rə kāt), *v.* to make all standardized parts of a building, house, etc., at a factory. The erection of a prefabricated house requires merely the assembling of the various sections. ❑ *v.* **pre·fab·ri·cat·ed, pre·fab·ri·cat·ing. —pre·fab′ri·ca′tion,** *n.* **—pre·fab′ri·ca′tor,** *n.*

pref·ace (pref′is), **1** *n.* introduction to a book, writing, or speech: *My history book has a preface written by the author.* **2** *v.* to introduce by written or spoken remarks; give a preface to: *He prefaced his speech with a joke about the weather.* **3** *v.* to be a preface to; begin. ❑ *v.* **pref·aced, pref·ac·ing.**

pref·a·to·ry (pref′ə tôr′ē), *adj.* of or like a preface; made as a preface; introductory; preliminary. **—pref′a·to′ri·ly,** *adv.*

pre·fect (prē′fekt), *n.* **1** (in ancient Rome) the title of various military and civil officers. **2** the chief administrative official of a department of France.

pre·fer (pri fèr′), *v.* **1** to like better; choose; wish: *I will come later, if you prefer. She prefers swimming to fishing.* **2** to present a

charge against someone for consideration in a court of law: *The policeman preferred charges of speeding against the driver.* ❑ *v.* **pre·ferred, pre·fer·ring. —pre·fer′rer,** *n.*

pref·er·a·ble (pref′ər ə bəl), *adj.* to be preferred; more desirable. **—pref′er·a·ble·ness,** *n.* **—pref′er·a·bly,** *adv.*

pref·er·ence (pref′ər əns), *n.* **1** act or attitude or preferring; liking better: *My preference is for beef rather than lamb.* **2** thing preferred; first choice: *My preference in reading is a mystery story.* **3** act of favoring one above another: *A teacher should not show preference for any student.*

pref·er·en·tial (pref′ə ren′shəl), *adj.* of, giving, or receiving preference: *preferential treatment.* **—pref′e·ren′tial·ly,** *adv.*

pre·fer·ment (pri fèr′mənt), *n.* advancement; promotion: *seek preferment in your job.*

pre·fig·ure (prē fig′yər), *v.* **1** to reveal or suggest beforehand by a figure or type: *Christianity believes that many events in the history of Israel prefigured events in the life of Jesus.* **2** to imagine to yourself beforehand. ❑ *v.* **pre·fig·ured, pre·fig·ur·ing. —pre·fig′ur·a′tion,** *n.* **—pre·fig′ure·ment,** *n.*

pre·fix (prē′fiks), *n.* syllable, syllables, or word put at the beginning of a word to change its meaning or to make another word, as *pre-* in *prepaid, under-* in *underline, dis-* in *disappear, un-* in *unlike,* and *re-* in *redo.* ❑ *n., pl.* **pre·fix·es.**

preg·nan·cy (preg′nən sē), *n.* pregnant quality or condition. ❑ *n., pl.* **preg·nan·cies.**

preg·nant (preg′nənt), *adj.* **1** having one or more offspring developing in the womb; soon to have a baby. **2** filled; full: *words pregnant with meaning.* **3** meaningful; significant: *a pregnant pause.* **—preg′nant·ly,** *adv.*

pre·heat (prē hēt′), *v.* to heat before using: *Preheat the oven before putting the frozen pie in.*

pre·hen·sile (pri hen′səl), *adj.* able to seize, grasp, and hold something. Many monkeys have prehensile tails.

pre·his·to·ric (prē′hi stôr′ik), *adj.* of or belonging to times before histories were written: *Prehistoric peoples used stone tools.* **—pre′his·to′ri·cal·ly,** *adv.*

pre·his·to·ri·cal (prē′hi stôr′ə kəl), *adj.* prehistoric.

pre·his·tor·y (prē his′tər ē), *n.* time before recorded history; prehistoric life or times.

pre·judge (prē juj′), *v.* to judge beforehand; judge without knowing all the facts. ❑ *v.* **pre·judged, pre·judg·ing. —pre·judg′ment** *or* **pre·judge′ment,** *n.*

prehensile

prej·u·dice (prej′ə dis), **1** *n.* unreasonable dislike of an idea, group of people, etc. **2** *n.* opinion formed without sufficient knowledge or taking time and care to judge the facts fairly: *a prejudice against unfamiliar foods.* **3** *v.* to cause a prejudice in; fill with prejudice: *One bad experience prejudiced him against all lawyers.* **4** *n.* harm or injury: *I will do nothing to the prejudice of my cousin in this matter.* **5** *v.* to harm or injure. ❑ *v.* **prej·u·diced, prej·u·dic·ing.**

SYNONYM STUDY **Prejudice, intolerance,** and **discrimination** all mean unfairness. **Prejudice** means an unfair, usually bad opinion: *She has rid herself of prejudice against people from other countries.* **Intolerance** means unwillingness to let other people be different from you: *His intolerance of other opinions keeps him from making friends.* **Discrimination** means unfair treatment: *Discrimination in hiring by race is illegal.*

a	hat	ė	term	ô	order	ch	child		
ā	age	i	it	oi	oil	ng	long		a in about
ä	far	ī	ice	ou	out	sh	she		e in taken
â	care	o	hot	u	cup	th	thin	ə	i in pencil
e	let	ō	open	u̇	put	ŦH	then		o in lemon
ē	equal	ȯ	saw	ü	rule	zh	measure		u in circus

prej·u·di·cial (prej/ə dish/əl), *adj.* causing prejudice or disadvantage; hurtful: *acting in a manner prejudicial to others.* —**prej/u·di/cial·ly,** *adv.*

prel·ate (prel/it), *n.* a member of the clergy of high rank, such as a bishop.

pre·lim·i·nar·y (pri lim/ə ner/ē), **1** *adj.* coming before the main business; leading to something more important: *The speaker of the day gave an address after the preliminary song.* **2** *n.* a preliminary step; something preparatory: *An examination is a preliminary to entering that school.* ❑ *n., pl.* **pre·lim·i·nar·ies.** —**pre·lim/i·nar/i·ly,** *adv.*

prel·ude (prel/yüd *or* prā/lüd), *n.* **1** anything serving as an introduction: *Low barometric pressure was a prelude to a severe windstorm.* **2** in music: **a** a composition, or part of it, that introduces another composition or part. **b** an independent instrumental composition, usually short.

pre·mar·i·tal (prē mar/ə təl), *adj.* before marriage: *a premarital blood test.* —**pre·mar/i·tal·ly,** *adv.*

pre·ma·ture (prē/mə chúr/ *or* prē/mə túr/), *adj.* before the proper time; too soon: *Their arrival an hour before the party began was premature.* —**pre/ma·ture/ly,** *adv.*

pre·med (prē/med/), INFORMAL. **1** *n.* a premedical student. **2** *adj.* premedical.

pre·med·i·cal (prē med/ə kəl), *adj.* preparing for the study of medicine: *a premedical student, a premedical course.*

pre·med·i·tate (prē med/ə tāt), *v.* to consider or plan beforehand: *The murder was premeditated.* ❑ *v.* **pre·med·i·tat·ed, pre·med·i·tat·ing.** —**pre·med/i·ta/tion,** *n.*

pre·men·stru·al (prē men/strü əl), *adj.* before menstruation.

pre·mier (pri mir/), **1** *n.* prime minister. **2** *n.* (in Canada) the highest executive officer of a provincial government. **3** *adj.* first in rank; chief. **4** *adj.* first in time; earliest.

pre·miere (prə myer/ *or* pri mir/), **1** *n.* a first public performance: *the premiere of a new play.* **2** *adj.* premier; first.

prem·ise (prem/is), *n.* **1** (in logic) a statement assumed to be true and used to draw a conclusion. MAJOR PREMISE: CHILDREN SHOULD GO TO SCHOOL. MINOR PREMISE: THEY ARE CHILDREN. CONCLUSION: THEY SHOULD GO TO SCHOOL. **2** **premises,** *pl.* house or building with its grounds.

pre·mi·um (prē/mē əm), *n.* **1** a reward, especially one given as an incentive to buy; prize: *Some magazines give premiums for obtaining new subscriptions.* **2** something more than the ordinary price or wages. **3** money paid for insurance: *I pay premiums on my life insurance four times a year.* **4** unusual or unfair value: *put too high a premium on neatness.*

at a premium, at more than the usual value or price: *Tickets for the concert were scarce and selling at a premium.*

pre·mo·lar (prē mō/lər), *n.* bicuspid.

pre·mo·ni·tion (prē/mə nish/ən *or* prem/ə nish/ən), *n.* a forewarning: *a vague premonition of disaster.*

pre·mon·i·to·ry (pri mon/ə tôr/ē), *adj.* giving warning beforehand.

pre·na·tal (prē nā/tl), *adj.* occurring before birth: *A woman who is going to have a baby requires prenatal care.*

pre·oc·cu·pa·tion (prē ok/yə pā/shən), *n.* **1** something that preoccupies a person. **2** condition of being preoccupied.

pre·oc·cu·pied (prē ok/yə pīd), *adj.* having your attention focused on something; lost in thought: *She was too preoccupied to hear the doorbell.*

pre·oc·cu·py (prē ok/yə pī), *v.* to take up all the attention of; absorb: *The problem of how to pay her debts preoccupied her mind.* ❑ *v.* **pre·oc·cu·pied, pre·oc·cu·py·ing.**

pre·or·dain (prē/ôr dān/), *v.* to decide or settle beforehand; foreordain. —**pre·or·dain/ment,** *n.*

prep (prep), *v.* **1** to study. **2** to prepare: *to prep a patient for surgery.* **3** to go to preparatory school. ❑ *v.* **prepped, prep·ping.**

prep., preposition.

pre·paid (prē pād/), **1** *adj.* paid for in advance: *prepaid season tickets.* **2** *v.* past tense and past participle of **prepay:** *Has he prepaid the shipping fees?*

prep·a·ra·tion (prep/ə rā/shən), *n.* **1** act of preparing; making ready: *I sharpened the knife in preparation for carving the meat.* **2** thing done to get ready: *He made thorough preparations for his trip*

by carefully planning which routes to take. **3** condition of being ready; readiness. **4** a specially made medicine, food, or mixture of any kind: *There is a new preparation for removing rust.*

pre·par·a·to·ry (pri par/ə tôr/ē), *adj.* **1** of or for preparation; making ready; preparing. A **preparatory school** prepares pupils for college. **2** as an introduction; preliminary: *preparatory remarks.* —**pre·par/a·to/ri·ly,** *adv.*

pre·pare (pri pâr/), *v.* **1** to make ready; get ready: *prepare dinner.* **2** to make by a special process: *prepare aluminum from bauxite.* ❑ *v.* **pre·pared, pre·par·ing.** —**pre·par/er,** *n.*

pre·par·ed·ness (pri pâr/id nis), *n.* **1** condition of being prepared; readiness. **2** having adequate military forces and defenses to meet threats or outbreaks of war.

pre·pay (prē pā/), *v.* to pay or pay for in advance. ❑ *v.* **pre·paid, pre·pay·ing.** —**pre·pay/ment,** *n.*

pre·pon·der·ance (pri pon/dər-əns), *n.* **1** greater number or greater weight; greater power or influence. **2** condition of being the chief or most important element: *the preponderance of oaks in these woods.*

prepare (def. 1)

pre·pon·der·ant (pri pon/dər ənt), *adj.* **1** weighing more; being stronger or more numerous; having more power or influence. **2** most important; chief: *Lush vegetation is the preponderant characteristic of the jungle.*

prep·o·si·tion (prep/ə zish/ən), *n.* word that expresses some relation to a noun, pronoun, phrase, or clause which follows it. *With, for, by,* and *in* are prepositions in the sentence "A man *with* vegetables *for* sale drove *by* our house *in* the morning."

prep·o·si·tion·al (prep/ə zish/ə nəl), *adj.* **1** of or formed with a preposition: *a prepositional phrase.* **2** having the nature or function of a preposition.

pre·pos·sess·ing (prē/pə zes/ing), *adj.* making a favorable impression; attractive; pleasing: *In my old, ragged work clothes, my appearance was not very prepossessing.*

pre·pos·ter·ous (pri pos/tər əs), *adj.* contrary to nature, reason, or common sense; absurd; senseless; foolish: *That the moon is made of green cheese is a preposterous notion.* —**pre·pos/ter·ous·ly,** *adv.* —**pre·pos/ter·ous·ness,** *n.*

prep·py or **prep·pie** (prep/ē), SLANG. **1** *n.* student or graduate of a preparatory school. **2** *adj.* of or like that of preppies, especially in regard to clothes or behavior: *preppy fashions.* ❑ *n., pl.* **prep·pies;** *adj.* **prep·pi·er, prep·pi·est.**

prep school, preparatory school.

pre·quel (prē/kwəl), *n.* book, movie, TV show, or the like, in which the story or events take place before those of an earlier work. [Prequel comes from the prefix **pre-** and the last four letters of **sequel.**]

pre·re·cord (prē/ri kôrd/), *v.* to record ahead of time for later use: *a prerecorded TV show.*

pre·req·ui·site (prē rek/wə zit), **1** *n.* something required beforehand: *The completion of a high school course is the usual prerequisite to college work.* **2** *adj.* required beforehand.

pre·rog·a·tive (pri rog/ə tiv), *n.* right or privilege that nobody else has: *The government has the prerogative of coining money.*

pres., present.

Pres., President.

pres·age (pres/ij *for noun;* pres/ij *or* pri sāj/ *for verb*), **1** *n.* a sign felt as a warning; omen. **2** *v.* to give warning of; predict: *Some people think that a halo around the moon presages a storm.* ❑ *v.* **pre·saged, pre·sag·ing.** —**pre·sag/er,** *n.*

pres·by·ter (prez′bə tər), *n.* **1** a minister or a lay elder in the Presbyterian Church. **2** a minister or a priest in the Episcopal Church. [See Word Story at **priest.**]

Pres·by·ter·i·an (prez′bə tir′ē ən), **1** *adj.* of or belonging to a Protestant denomination or church governed by elected presbyters or elders, all of equal rank. **2** *n.* member of a Presbyterian church.

Pres·by·ter·i·an·ism (prez′bə tir′ē ə niz′əm), *n.* **1** system of church government by elders, all (including ministers) of equal rank. **2** beliefs of Presbyterian churches.

pre·school (prē′skül′), **1** *adj.* before the age of going to regular school: *preschool training, preschool children.* **2** *n.* school for children below the age of five: *My three-year-old sister is in preschool.*

pre·school·er (prē′skü′lər), *n.* child who attends a preschool: *This playground is suitable for the preschoolers.*

pre·sci·ence (prē′shē əns), *n.* knowledge of things before they exist or happen; foreknowledge; foresight: *Some people believe that animals have an instinctive prescience of the approach of danger.*

pre·sci·ent (prē′shē ənt), *adj.* knowing beforehand; foreseeing. **–pre′sci·ent·ly,** *adv.*

pre·scribe (pri skrib′), *v.* **1** to order as a medicine or treatment: *The doctor prescribed penicillin.* **2** to lay down as a rule to be followed; order; direct: *Good citizens do what the laws prescribe.* ❑ *v.* **pre·scribed, pre·scrib·ing. –pre·scrib′er,** *n.*

pre·scrip·tion (pri skrip′shən), *n.* **1** a written direction or order for preparing and using a medicine: *a prescription for cough medicine.* **2** the medicine ordered. **3** an eye doctor's written instructions for corrective lenses in glasses. **4** any order; direction.

pre·scrip·tive (pri skrip′tiv), *adj.* **1** prescribing. **2** established by law or custom. **–pre·scrip′tive·ly,** *adv.* **–pre·scrip′tive·ness,** *n.*

pres·ence (prez′ns), *n.* **1** condition of being present in a place: *I just learned of her presence in the city.* **2** a place where someone is: *The messenger was admitted to the king's presence.* **3** appearance; bearing: *The queen is a person of noble presence.* **4** something present, especially a ghost, spirit, or the like.
in the presence of, in the sight or company of: *I signed my name in the presence of two witnesses.*

presence of mind, ability to think calmly and quickly under stress.

pres·ent¹ (prez′nt), **1** *adj.* being in the place or thing in question; not absent: *Every member of the class was present. Oxygen is present in the air.* **2** *adj.* at this time; being or occurring now: *the present government, present prices.* **3** *n.* **the present,** the time being; this time; now: *That is enough for the present.* **4** *n.* the present tense or a verb form in that tense.
at present, at the present time; now.

pres·ent² (pri zent′ *for verb;* prez′nt *for noun*), **1** *v.* to give: *They presented flowers to their teacher.* **2** *n.* thing given; gift: *a birthday present.* **3** *v.* to offer formally; offer: *The host presented the sandwiches to each guest.* **4** *v.* to make acquainted; bring someone before somebody; introduce: *Miss Smith, may I present Mr. Brown?* **5** *v.* to offer to view or notice: *The new library presents a fine appearance.* **6** *v.* to bring before the public: *Our class presented a play.* **7** *v.* to set forth in words; offer: *The speaker presented arguments for his side.* **–pre·sent′er,** *n.*
present with, to give to: *Our class presented the school with a picture.*

pre·sent·a·ble (pri zen′tə bəl), *adj.* **1** fit to be seen; suitable in appearance: *to make a house presentable for company.* **2** suitable in appearance, dress, manners, etc., for being introduced into society or company. **–pre·sent′a·bil′i·ty, pre·sent′a·ble·ness,** *n.* **–pre·sent′a·bly,** *adv.*

pres·en·ta·tion (prez′n tā′shən *or* prē′zen tā′shən), *n.* **1** act of giving; delivering: *the presentation of a gift.* **2** the gift that is presented. **3** act of bringing forward; offering to be considered: *the presentation of a plan.* **4** an offering to be seen; exhibition: *a presentation of student art.* **–pres′en·ta′tion·al,** *adj.*

pres·ent-day (prez′nt dā′), *adj.* of the present time: *Present-day clothing is less formal than the clothing of the 1800s.*

pre·sen·ti·ment (pri zen′tə mənt), *n.* a feeling or impression that something bad is about to happen; vague sense of approaching misfortune; foreboding.

pres·ent·ly (prez′nt lē), *adv.* **1** before long; soon: *I will do the dishes presently.* **2** at the present time; at this time; now: *He is presently in sixth grade.*

pre·sent·ment (pri zent′mənt), *n.* **1** act of bringing forward; offering to be considered. **2** something brought forward or shown.

present participle, participle that indicates time that is now. In "Singing merrily, we turn our steps toward home," *singing* is a present participle.

present tense, 1 tense that expresses time that is now. **2** a verb form in the present tense.

pres·er·va·tion (prez′ər vā′shən), *n.* **1** act of preserving; keeping safe: *Doctors work for the preservation of our health.* **2** condition of being preserved; being kept safe: *Egyptian mummies have been in a state of preservation for thousands of years.*

pre·serv·a·tive (pri zėr′və tiv), **1** *n.* any substance that will prevent decay or injury: *Paint is a preservative for wood surfaces.* **2** *adj.* capable of preserving.

pre·serve (pri zėrv′), **1** *v.* to keep from harm or change; keep safe; protect: *Good nutrition helps to preserve your health.* **2** *v.* to keep; maintain: *You must preserve your calm.* **3** *v.* to keep from spoiling: *Ice helps to preserve food.* **4** *v.* to prepare food to keep it from spoiling. Boiling with sugar, salting, smoking, and pickling are different ways of preserving food. **5** *n.pl.* **pre·serves,** fruit cooked with sugar and sealed from the air: *plum preserves.* **6** *n.* a place where wild animals, fish, or trees and plants are protected: *People are not allowed to hunt in that preserve.* ❑ *v.* **pre·served, pre·serv·ing. –pre·serv′a·ble,** *adj.* **–pre·serv′er,** *n.*

preserve (def. 1)—fly preserved in amber

pre·set (prē set′), *v.* to set in advance: *The missile's course was preset before it was launched.* ❑ *v.* **pre·set, pre·set·ting.**

pre·shrunk (prē shrungk′), *adj.* shrunk while being made in order to prevent shrinking later: *preshrunk jeans.*

pre·side (pri zid′), *v.* **1** to hold the place of authority; have charge of a meeting: *preside at an election.* **2** to have authority; have control: *The manager presides over the business of this store.* ❑ *v.* **pre·sid·ed, pre·sid·ing. –pre·sid′er,** *n.*

pres·i·den·cy (prez′ə dən sē), *n.* **1** office of president: *She was elected to the presidency of the Junior Club.* **2** Often, **President·cy,** office of the highest executive officer of a republic. **3** time in which a president is in office: *The United States entered World War II during the presidency of Franklin D. Roosevelt.* ❑ *n., pl.* **pres·i·den·cies** for 1,3, **Presidencies** for 2.

pres·i·dent (prez′ə dənt), *n.* **1** the chief officer of a company, college, society, club, etc. **2** Often, **President,** the highest executive officer of a republic. ■ See Usage Note at **capital letter.**

WORD STORY **President** comes from a Latin word meaning "to sit in front." If a group is seated together at a public event, the leaders will be sitting at the front.

pres·i·dent-e·lect (prez′ə dənt i lekt′), *n.* president who has been elected but not yet inaugurated.

pres·i·den·tial (prez′ə den′shəl), *adj.* of or about a president or presidency: *a presidential election, a presidential candidate.* **–pres′i·den′tial·ly,** *adv.*

Presidents' Day, the third Monday in February, celebrated as a holiday in some states to commemorate the birthdays of Abraham Lincoln and George Washington.

a	hat	ė	term	ô	order	ch	child		a in about
ā	age	i	it	oi	oil	ng	long		e in taken
ä	far	ī	ice	ou	out	sh	she	ə	i in pencil
â	care	o	hot	u	cup	th	thin		o in lemon
e	let	ō	open	u̇	put	ŦH	then		u in circus
ē	equal	ȯ	saw	ü	rule	zh	measure		

pre·sid·i·o (pri sid′ē ō), *n.* military post in the southwestern United States and California, formerly under Spanish or Mexican control. ❑ *n., pl.* **pre·sid·i·os.**

Pres·ley (pres′lē), *n.* **El·vis** (el′vis), 1935-1977, American singer. He made 45 records that sold more than a million copies each. He also appeared in 33 movies, and his home, Graceland, in Memphis, Tennessee, is a tourist attraction.

press¹ (pres), **1** *v.* to use force or weight steadily against; push with steady force: *Press the button to ring the bell.* **2** *v.* to squeeze out; squeeze: *press apples for cider, press all the juice from the oranges.* **3** *v.* to make smooth; flatten: *press clothes with an iron.* **4** *v.* to clasp; hug: *I pressed the puppy to me.* **5** *n.* pressure; push: *The press of many duties keeps her very busy.* **6** *n.* machine for pressing, squeezing, etc.: *a cider press.* **7** *n.* a printing press. **8** *n.* business for printing books, etc. **9** *n.* the business of printing newspapers and magazines: *Many advertising dollars have gone from the press to broadcasting.* **10** *n.* newspapers, magazines, radio, and TV, and the people who report for them: *The fire was reported by the press.* **11** *v.* to push forward; keep pushing: *I pressed on in spite of the strong wind.* **12** *v.* to urge onward; cause to hurry. **13** *n.* a crowd; throng: *The little boy was lost in the press.* **14** *v.* to crowd; throng: *The people pressed about the famous actor.* **15** *v.* to keep asking someone earnestly; urge: *We pressed our guest to stay until the snow stopped.* **16** *v.* to compel; force. **17** *v.* to harass; oppress; trouble. **18** *n.* cupboard or closet for clothes, books, etc. **19** *n.* (in basketball) a defensive play in which players guard their opponents very closely. ❑ *n., pl.* **press·es** for 6-8,18,19. **—press′a·ble,** *adj.*

go to press, to begin to be printed: *The newspaper goes to press at midnight.*

press² (pres), *v.* to force into service, usually naval or military; impress: *Naval officers used to visit towns and merchant ships to press men for the fleet.*

press agent, agent in charge of publicity for a person, organization, etc.; publicist.

press conference, meeting arranged by a person or group with members of the press to release some news or give an interview.

press·ing (pres′ing), *adj.* requiring immediate action or attention; urgent: *A person with a broken leg is in pressing need of a doctor's help. She left town quickly on some pressing business.* **—press′ing·ly,** *adv.*

pres·sure (presh′ər), **1** *n.* the continued action of a weight or other force: *The small box was flattened by the pressure of the heavy book on it.* **2** *n.* force per unit of area: *There is a pressure of 27 pounds to the square inch in this tire.* **3** *n.* a condition of trouble or strain: *I don't work well under pressure.* **4** *n.* effort to control choice or action: *I was under pressure from the others to change my mind.* **5** *v.* to force by urging or threatening: *The car dealer tried to pressure my parents into buying a car.* **6** *n.* a need for prompt or decisive action; urgency: *the pressure of a deadline.* ❑ *v.* **pres·sured, pres·sur·ing.**

pressure cooker, an airtight container for cooking with steam under pressure.

pressure group, any business, professional, or labor group that attempts to influence legislation affecting its special concerns.

pres·sur·ize (presh′ə rīz′), *v.* **1** to keep the atmospheric pressure inside the cabin of an aircraft at a normal level in spite of the altitude. **2** to place under high pressure. ❑ *v.* **pres·sur·ized, pres·sur·iz·ing. —pres′sur·i·za′tion,** *n.* **—pres′sur·iz′er,** *n.*

pres·tige (pre stēzh′), *n.* reputation, influence, or distinction based on what is known about your abilities, achievements, opportunities, associations, etc.: *Her prestige rose when her classmates learned that she could ski.*

WORD STORY **Prestige** comes from a Latin word meaning "a magician's tricks." That Latin word comes from another Latin word meaning "to dazzle the eyes," as magicians' tricks and illusions do. Someone who can pull rabbits out of a hat or make coins vanish is likely to be admired and to seem special. That specialness turned into the word **prestige.**

pres·ti·gious (pre stij′əs), *adj.* having prestige. **—pres·ti′gious·ly,** *adv.* **—pres·ti′gious·ness,** *n.*

pres·to (pres′tō), **1** in music: **a** *adv.* very quickly. **b** *adj.* very quick. **c** *n.* a very quick part in a piece of music. **2** *interj.* exclamation used to express quick or sudden action: *Then—presto—the rabbit disappeared.* ❑ *n., pl.* **pres·tos.**

pre·sum·a·ble (pri zü′mə bəl), *adj.* able to be presumed or taken for granted; probable; likely: *the presumable cause of the accident.* **—pre·sum′a·bly,** *adv.*

pre·sume (pri züm′), *v.* **1** to take for granted without proving; suppose: *You'll play out of doors, I presume, if there is sunshine. The law presumes innocence until guilt is proved.* **2** to take upon yourself; venture; dare: *May I presume to tell you you are wrong?* **3** to take an unfair advantage: *Don't presume on his good nature by borrowing from him every week.* **4** to act with improper boldness; take liberties: *It would be presuming to camp in a farmer's field without permission.* ❑ *v.* **pre·sumed, pre·sum·ing. —pre·sum′ed·ly,** *adv.* **—pre·sum′er,** *n.*

pre·sump·tion (pri zump′shən), *n.* **1** thing taken for granted: *Since she took the coat, the presumption was that it was hers.* **2** unpleasant boldness: *It is presumption to go to a party when you have not been invited.* **3** cause or reason for presuming; probability. **4** act of presuming.

pre·sump·tive (pri zump′tiv), *adj.* **1** based on probability or likelihood: *a presumptive title to an estate.* **2** giving grounds for presumption or belief: *Their running away was regarded as presumptive evidence of their guilt.* **—pre·sump′tive·ly,** *adv.*

pre·sump·tu·ous (pri zump′chü əs), *adj.* acting without permission; too bold; forward. **—pre·sump′tu·ous·ly,** *adv.* **—pre·sump′tu·ous·ness,** *n.*

pre·sup·pose (prē′sə pōz′), *v.* **1** to take for granted in advance; assume beforehand: *Let's presuppose that we will be going and make some plans for the trip.* **2** to require as a condition; imply: *A debate presupposes debaters.* ❑ *v.* **pre·sup·posed, pre·sup·pos·ing.**

pre·sup·po·si·tion (prē′sup ə zish′ən), *n.* **1** act of presupposing. **2** thing presupposed: *The detective acted upon the presupposition that the thief knew the value of the jewels.*

pre·teen (prē′tēn′), **1** *n.* person younger than 13, especially one about 10 to 12 years of age. **2** *adj.* of, for, or characteristic of a preteen or preteens: *preteen styles.* **3** *adj.* being a preteen or preteens: *preteen children.*

pre·tend (pri tend′), **1** *v.* to make believe: *Let's pretend that we are grown-ups.* **2** *v.* to claim falsely: *I pretended to like the meal so that my host would be pleased.* **3** *v.* to claim falsely to have: *She pretended illness.* **4** *v.* I don't pretend to be a musician. **5** *v.* to lay claim: *The English king pretended to the French throne.* **6** *adj.* imaginary; make-believe: *The child had a pretend horse.*

SYNONYM STUDY **Pretend, pose,** and **bluff**² all mean to act in a way that is not real. **Pretend** is a general word: *He pretends to be friendly, but he's not.* **Pose** suggests trying to fool people: *The reporter posed as a homeless woman to find out about the shelter.* **Bluff** means trying to fool someone by acting confident: *She claims she got a perfect score, but she's bluffing.*

pre·tend·ed (pri ten′did), *adj.* claimed falsely; asserted falsely. **—pre·tend′ed·ly,** *adv.*

pre·tend·er (pri ten′dər), *n.* **1** person who pretends. **2** person who lays claim, especially falsely, to a title or throne.

pre·tense (prē′tens *or* pri tens′), *n.* **1** make-believe; act of pretending: *My anger was all pretense.* **2** a false appearance: *Under pretense of dropping a pencil, she looked at a classmate's test.* **3** a false claim: *She made a pretense of knowing our secret.* **4** a claim: *I make no pretense to a talent for art.* **5** act of showing off; display: *a manner free from pretense.*

pre·ten·sion (pri ten′shən), *n.* **1** a claim: *The young prince has pretensions to the throne.* **2** act of putting forward a claim; laying claim to. **3** act of doing things for show or to make a fine appearance; showy display: *We were annoyed by the pretensions of our wealthy neighbor.*

pre·ten·tious (pri ten′shəs), *adj.* **1** making claims to excellence or importance: *a pretentious book, pretentious art.* **2** doing things for show or to make a fine appearance: *a pretentious style of entertaining.* —**pre·ten′tious·ly,** *adv.* —**pre·ten′tious·ness,** *n.*

pre·ter·nat·u·ral (prē′tər nach′ər əl), *adj.* **1** out of the ordinary course of nature; abnormal. **2** due to something above or beyond nature; supernatural. —**pre′ter·nat′ur·al·ly,** *adv.*

pre·test (prē′test′), **1** *n.* test given to students to see if they are prepared enough to begin further study. **2** *v.* to give students a test like this. **3** *v.* to test something, such as a new product, in advance of its future use.

pre·text (prē′tekst), *n.* a false reason hiding the real reason; misleading excuse; pretense: *He did not go, on the pretext of being too tired.*

Pre·to·ri·a (pri tôr′ē ə), *n.* administrative capital of the Republic of South Africa, in the NE part.

pret·ti·fy (prit′ə fī), *v.* to make artificially pretty. ❑ *v.* **pret·ti·fied, pret·ti·fy·ing.** —**pret′ti·fi·ca′tion,** *n.*

pret·ty (prit′ē), **1** *adj.* pleasing to the eye, ear, etc.: *a pretty face, a pretty dress, a pretty tune.* **2** *adj.* not at all pleasing: *This is a pretty mess, indeed.* **3** *adv.* fairly; rather: *It is pretty late.* ❑ *adj.* **pret·ti·er, pret·ti·est.** —**pret′ti·ly,** *adv.* —**pret′ti·ness,** *n.*

sitting pretty, in an advantageous position: *They certainly are sitting pretty since they made all that money.*

WORD STORY **Pretty** comes from an old English word meaning "a trick." That turned into an adjective meaning "tricky" or "cunning." **Cunning** is used today about something pretty and cute. The oldest meaning of **cute** is "clever" or "cunning." See the Word Story at **cute.**

pret·zel (pret′səl), *n.* a crisp cracker, usually in the form of a knot or stick, salted on the outside.

WORD STORY **Pretzel** comes from a Latin word meaning "an arm." The knot-shaped pretzel looks like a pair of crossed arms. The English word came from a German form of the Latin, so it looks German.

pre·vail (pri vāl′), *v.* **1** to exist in many places; be in general use: *Making resolutions on New Year's Day is a custom that still prevails.* **2** to be the most usual or strongest: *Sadness prevailed in our minds.* **3** to be the stronger; gain the victory; succeed: *Reason prevailed over emotion.* —**pre·vail′er,** *n.*

prevail on or **prevail upon,** to persuade: *Can I prevail on you to stay?*

pre·vail·ing (pri vā′ling), *adj.* **1** in general use; common: *a prevailing style. The prevailing summer winds here are from the west.* **2** that prevails; having superior force or influence; victorious. —**pre·vail′ing·ly,** *adv.*

prevailing westerlies, the strong, steady west-to-east winds that blow between about 30° and 60° latitude, north and south.

prev·a·lence (prev′ə ləns), *n.* widespread occurrence; general use: *the prevalence of cars.*

prev·a·lent (prev′ə lənt), *adj.* in general use; widespread; common: *Colds are prevalent in the winter.* —**prev′a·lent·ly,** *adv.*

pre·vent (pri vent′), *v.* **1** to keep from: *Illness prevented him from working.* **2** to keep from happening: *Vaccination prevents smallpox.* **3** to hinder: *Doctors try to prevent diseases from spreading by treating them.* —**pre·vent′a·ble** or **pre·vent′i·ble,** *adj.* —**pre·vent′er,** *n.*

pre·vent·a·tive (pri ven′tə tiv), *adj., n.* preventive.

pre·ven·tion (pri ven′shən), *n.* act of preventing: *the prevention of fire.*

pre·ven·tive (pri ven′tiv), **1** *adj.* able to prevent or hinder: *Preventive measures were taken to stop the spread of the disease.* **2** *n.* something that prevents: *Vaccination is a preventive against smallpox.* —**pre·ven′tive·ly,** *adv.* —**pre·ven′tive·ness,** *n.*

pre·view (prē′vyü′), **1** *n.* an advance showing of scenes from a movie, play, TV show, etc. **2** *v.* to view beforehand. **3** *n.* a previous view, inspection, survey, etc.: *a preview of things to come.*

pre·vi·ous (prē′vē əs), *adj.* coming or being before; earlier: *She did better in the previous lesson.* —**pre′vi·ous·ly,** *adv.* —**pre′vi·ous·ness,** *n.*

WORD STORY **Previous** comes from Latin words meaning "road" and "ahead." These combined in a Latin word meaning "leading the way." A previous person or thing comes before the next one.

pre·war (prē′wôr′), *adj.* before the war.

pre·writ·ing (prē′rī′ting), *n.* creation and organization of ideas before writing them down.

prey (prā), *n.* **1** *sing.* or *pl.* animal or animals hunted and killed for food by another animal: *Mice and birds are the prey of cats.* **2** act or habit of hunting and killing other animals for food: *Hawks are birds of prey.* ❑ *n., pl.* **preyed, prey·ing.** ■ Another word that sounds like this is **pray.** —**prey′er,** *n.*

prey on or **prey upon,** **1** to hunt and kill for food: *Cats prey on mice.* **2** to be a strain upon; injure; irritate: *Worry about debts preys on her mind.* **3** to rob; plunder.

Pri·am (prī′əm), *n.* (in Greek legends) the king of Troy at the time of the Trojan War.

price (pris), **1** *n.* the amount for which a thing is sold or can be bought; the cost to the buyer: *The price of this coat is $90.* **2** *v.* to put a price on; set the price of: *The hat was priced at $10.* **3** *v.* to ask the price of; find out the price of: *Mother is pricing cars.* **4** *n.* reward offered for the capture of someone alive or dead: *Every member of the gang has a price on his head.* **5** *n.* what must be given, done, undergone, etc., to obtain a thing; amount paid for any result: *The Pilgrims paid a heavy price for staying in America, for half of them died during the first winter.* **6** *n.* value; worth: *a diamond of great price.* ❑ *v.* **priced, pric·ing.** —**price′a·ble,** *adj.* —**pric′er,** *n.*

at any price, at any cost, no matter how great: *We wanted to win at any price.*

beyond price or **without price,** so valuable that it cannot be bought, or be given a value in money.

Price (pris), *n.* **Le·on·tyne** (lē′ən tēn), born 1927, American opera singer. She is best known for singing *Aida.*

price cutting, act of reducing prices, especially reducing prices below cost in order to eliminate competition.

price fix·ing (prīs′ fiks′ing), **1** an illegal agreement by several manufacturers to set a noncompetitive price on a product which they all make. **2** control of prices by a government agency.

price·less (prīs′lis), *adj.* **1** extremely valuable: *Many museums have collections of priceless works of art.* ■ See Synonym Study at **precious. 2** INFORMAL. very amusing or absurd; delightful: *The look on her face when she found the frog was priceless.* —**price′less·ness,** *n.*

pri·cey (prī′sē), *adj.* INFORMAL. expensive: *pricey designer shoes.* Also, **pricy.** ❑ *adj.* **pric·i·er, pric·i·est.** —**pric′ey·ness,** *n.* —**pric′i·ly,** *adv.*

prick (prik), **1** *n.* a sharp point. **2** *n.* a little hole or mark made by a sharp point. **3** *v.* to make a little hole or mark on with a sharp point: *I pricked my finger on a thorn.* **4** *n.* a sharp pain from something pricking you. **5** *v.* to point upwards; raise or erect: *The dog pricked up its ears at the noise.* **6** *v.* OLD USE. to ride fast; spur. —**prick′er,** *n.*

prick·le (prik′əl), **1** *n.* a small, sharp point; thorn; spine. **2** *v.* to feel a prickly or smarting sensation: *My skin prickled as I listened to the scary story.* **3** *n.* such a sensation. **4** *v.* to cause such a sensation in. ❑ *v.* **prick·led, prick·ling.**

prick·ly (prik′lē), *adj.* **1** having many sharp points or thorns: *a prickly rosebush, the prickly porcupine.* **2** sharp and stinging; itching; smarting: *Heat sometimes causes a prickly rash on the skin.* ❑ *adj.* **prick·li·er, prick·li·est.** —**prick′li·ness,** *n.*

prickly heat, a red, itching rash on the skin caused by inflammation of the sweat glands.

prickly pear, **1** a pear-shaped fruit of any of several kinds of cactus. Some kinds are good to eat. **2** cactus that it grows on.

prickly rose, a wild rose of North American, with large pink flowers, found from Quebec to Alaska and south to Colorado. It is the provincial flower of Alberta.

pri·cy (prī′sē), *adj.* pricey. ❑ *adj.* **pric·i·er, pric·i·est.** —**pric′i·ness,** *n.* —**pric′i·ly,** *adv.*

P

a	hat	ė	term	ô	order	ch	child		a in about
ā	age	i	it	oi	oil	ng	long		e in taken
ä	far	ī	ice	ou	out	sh	she	ə	i in pencil
â	care	o	hot	u	cup	th	thin		o in lemon
e	let	ō	open	u̇	put	₮H	then		u in circus
ē	equal	ò	saw	ü	rule	zh	measure		

pride (prīd), **1** *n.* a sense of your own worth; self-respect. **2** *n.* pleasure or satisfaction in something concerned with oneself: *to take pride in an important victory.* **3** *n.* something that you are proud of: *Their children are their great pride.* **4** *n.* too high an opinion of oneself; scorn of others; haughtiness: *Pride goes before a fall.* **5** *n.* group of lions, usually including many that are related. **6** *v.* **pride oneself on,** to be proud of: *I pride myself on being punctual.* ❑ *v.* **prid·ed, prid·ing.** ■ Another word that sounds like this is **pried.**

pride (def. 2)

pried (prīd), *v.* past tense and past participle of **pry**[1] and **pry**[2]: *She pried the top off the jar. They have often pried into our business.* ■ Another word that sounds like this is **pride.**

pries (prīz), *v.* **1** a present tense of **pry**[1] and **pry**[2]. **2** plural of **pry**[2]. ■ Another word that sounds like this is **prize.**

priest (prēst), *n.* **1** a member of the clergy or minister of a Christian church. **2** a special servant of a god who performs certain public religious acts: *priests of Apollo.*

WORD STORY   **Priest** comes from a Greek word meaning "old man." **Presbyter** comes from the same Greek word. People with various religious opinions nevertheless agreed that old men were especially wise, and the leaders of most religious groups today are old men.

priest·ess (prē′stis), *n.* woman who serves at an altar or in sacred rites: *a priestess of Diana.* ❑ *n., pl.* **priest·ess·es.**

priest·hood (prēst′hud), *n.* **1** position or rank of priest: *He was admitted to the priesthood.* **2** priests as a group: *the priesthood of Spain.*

priest·ly (prēst′lē), *adj.* **1** of or about a priest. **2** like a priest; suitable for a priest. ❑ *adj.* **priest·li·er, priest·li·est.** —**priest′li·ness,** *n.*

prig (prig), *n.* person who is too particular about speech and manners, and prides himself or herself on being better than others.

prig·gish (prig′ish), *adj.* too particular about doing right in things that show outwardly; priding yourself on being better than others. —**prig′gish·ly,** *adv.* —**prig′gish·ness,** *n.*

prim (prim), *adj.* very proper and correct in speaking and dressing. ❑ *adj.* **prim·mer, prim·mest.** —**prim′ly,** *adv.* —**prim′ness,** *n.*

pri·ma·cy (prī′mə sē), *n.* **1** condition of being first in order, rank, importance, etc. **2** the position of a bishop of highest rank. ❑ *n., pl.* **pri·ma·cies** for 2. [See Word Story at **primitive.**]

pri·ma don·na (prē′mə don′ə), **1** the principal woman singer in an opera. **2** a temperamental person. ❑ *pl.* **pri·ma don·nas.**

pri·mal (prī′məl), *adj.* **1** of or about early times; first; primeval. **2** chief; fundamental. —**pri′mal·ly,** *adv.*

pri·mar·i·ly (prī mer′ə lē), *adv.* **1** above all; mostly; principally: *The scientist was primarily interested in physics.* **2** at first; originally.

pri·mar·y (prī′mer′ē), **1** *adj.* first in time or order; original; fundamental: *the primary causes of unemployment.* ■ See Synonym Study at **elementary. 2** *adj.* first in importance; chief: *A balanced diet is primary to good health.* **3** *n.* anything that is first in order,

rank, or importance. **4** *n.* an election in which members of a political party choose candidates for office. Primaries are held before the regular election. ❑ *n., pl.* **pri·mar·ies.** [See Word Story at primitive.] —**pri′mar·i·ness,** *n.*

primary accent, 1 the strongest accent in the pronunciation of a word. **2** mark (′) used to show this.

primary color, any of a group of pigments or colors which, when mixed together, yield all other colors. Red, yellow, and blue are the primary colors in pigments. In light they are red, green, and blue.

primary election, primary (def. 4).

primary school, the first three or four grades of elementary school.

primary source, any document that is direct evidence of historical events. Letters, photographs, and diaries are some primary sources.

pri·mate (prī′māt *for 1;* prī′mit *or* prī′māt *for 2*), *n.* **1** one of a group of mammals that have very advanced brains and hands with thumbs that can grasp things. Primates are the most highly developed mammals. Apes, monkeys, lemurs, and human beings are primates. **2** archbishop or bishop ranking above all other bishops in a country or church province. [See Word Story at primitive.]

prime[1] (prīm), **1** *adj.* first in rank; chief: *The town's prime need is a new school.* **2** *adj.* first in time or order; primary: *the prime causes of pollution.* **3** *adj.* first in quality; first-rate; excellent: *prime ribs of beef.* **4** *n.* prime number. [See Word Story at primitive.] —**prime′ly,** *adv.* —**prime′ness,** *n.*

prime[2] (prīm), *n.* **1** the best part; best time; best condition: *be in the prime of life.* **2** the first part; beginning. [See Word Story at primitive.]

prime[3] (prīm), *v.* **1** to prepare by putting something in or on. **2** to cover a surface with a first coat of paint or oil so that the finishing coat of paint will not soak in. **3** to equip someone with information, words, etc.: *prime a person with a speech.* **4** to supply a gun with powder. **5** to pour water into a pump to start action. ❑ *v.* **primed, prim·ing.**

prime meridian, meridian from which the longitude east and west is measured. It passes through Greenwich, England, and its longitude is 0 degrees.

prime minister, the chief minister or official in certain governments; premier. Canada and Great Britain have prime ministers.

prime number, number that can be divided without a remainder only by itself and 1; prime. 2, 3, 5, 7, and 11 are prime numbers; 4, 6, and 9 are composite numbers.

prim·er[1] (prim′ər), *n.* **1** a first book in reading. **2** a first book; beginner's book: *a primer of statistics.*

prim·er[2] (prī′mər), *n.* **1** person or thing that primes. **2** cap or cylinder containing a little gunpowder, used for firing a charge.

prime time, the hours during the evening, usually considered to be from 7 to 11 P.M., when the greatest number of people are watching TV.

pri·me·val (prī mē′vəl), *adj.* **1** of or about the first age or ages, especially of the world: *In its primeval state the earth was without any forms of life.* **2** ancient: *primeval forests untouched by the ax.* —**pri·me′val·ly,** *adv.*

prim·ing (prī′ming), *n.* **1** powder or other material used to set fire to an explosive. **2** a first coat of paint, oil, etc.

prim·i·tive (prim′ə tiv), **1** *adj.* of or about early times; of long ago: *Primitive people often lived in caves.* **2** *adj.* very simple; such as people had early in human history: *A primitive way of making fire is by rubbing two sticks together.* **3** *n.* artist belonging to an early period or whose art is like that of early periods. **4** *n.* work of art by such an artist. **5** *n.* person living in a primitive society or in primitive times. —**prim′i·tive·ly,** *adv.* —**prim′i·tive·ness,** *n.*

WORD STORY   **Primitive** comes from a Latin word meaning "first." So do **primacy, primary, primate, prime**[1], and **prime**[2]. In general, coming first suggests good things; when it happened long ago, however, it can suggest the absence of later advantages.

pri·mo·gen·i·ture (prī′mə jen′ə chùr *or* prī′mə jen′ə chər), *n.* **1** fact of being the first-born among the children of the same parents. **2** the right or rule by which the eldest son inherits his father's land and buildings; inheritance by the first-born son, formerly common.

pri·mor·di·al (prī môr′dē əl), *adj.* **1** existing at the very beginning; primitive. **2** original; elementary. —**pri·mor′di·al·ly,** *adv.*

primp (primp), *v.* to dress yourself with excessive care; dress carefully.

prim·rose (prim′rōz′), *n.* any of numerous plants with showy, bell-shaped or funnel-shaped flowers of various colors.

primrose path, a pleasant path; way of pleasure.

prin., principal.

prince (prins), *n.* **1** son of a king or queen; son of a king's or queen's son. **2** sovereign. **3** ruler of a small state or country. **4** the English equivalent of certain titles of nobility of varying importance or rank in other countries. **5** the greatest or best of a group; chief: *a merchant prince.*

WORD STORY **Prince** comes from Latin words meaning "first" and "take." In a group, a prince usually gets first choice. **Prince** was used to mean any ruler or leader until the title **Prince of Wales** was given to the English heir to the throne. From that use, the word got its main modern meaning, "son of a king or queen."

Prince Charming, **1** the fairy-tale prince who marries Cinderella. **2** an ideal type of man; the perfect suitor: *She says she'll keep dating until she finds Prince Charming.*

prince consort, prince who is the husband of a queen or empress.

prince·dom (prins′dəm), *n.* **1** lands ruled by a prince. **2** title or rank of a prince.

Prince Edward Island, province in E Canada consisting of an island in the Gulf of St. Lawrence, just north of Nova Scotia. *Capital:* Charlottetown. [Prince Edward Island was named in honor of a son of King George III.] —**Prince Edward Islander.**

prince·ling (prins′ling), *n.* a young, little, or petty prince.

prince·ly (prins′lē), *adj.* **1** of or about a prince or his rank; royal. **2** like a prince; noble: *a princely manner.* **3** fit for a prince; magnificent: *a princely salary.* ❑ *adj.* **prince·li·er, prince·li·est.** —**prince′li·ness,** *n.*

Prince of Wales, title given to the eldest son, or heir apparent, of the British sovereign. [See Word Story at **prince.**]

prince royal, the oldest son of a king or queen.

prin·cess (prin′ses *or* prin′sis), *n.* **1** daughter of a king or queen; daughter of a king's or queen's son. **2** wife or widow of a prince. **3** woman having the rank of a prince. ❑ *n., pl.* **prin·cess·es.** —**prin′cess·like′,** *adj.*

princess royal, the oldest daughter of a king or queen.

prin·ci·pal (prin′sə pəl), **1** *adj.* most important; main; chief: *Chicago is the principal city of Illinois.* ■ See Synonym Study at **main.** **2** *n.* a chief person; someone who gives orders. **3** *n.* the head of an elementary or secondary school. **4** *n.* sum of money on which interest is paid. **5** *n.* money, property, or investments from which income interest is received. ■ See Usage Note at **principle.**

prin·ci·pal·i·ty (prin′sə pal′ə tē), *n.* **1** a small state or country ruled by a prince. **2** the country from which a prince gets his title. ❑ *n., pl.* **prin·ci·pal·i·ties.**

prin·ci·pal·ly (prin′sə pə lē), *adv.* for the most part; above all; mostly; mainly.

principal parts, the main parts of a verb, from which the other forms can be derived. In English the principal parts are the present infinitive, past tense, and past participle. These parts, plus the present participle, are shown for many verbs in this dictionary. EXAMPLES: go, went, gone; do, did, done; drive, drove, driven; push, pushed, pushed.

prin·ci·ple (prin′sə pəl), *n.* **1** a truth that is a foundation for other truths: *the principles of mathematics.* **2** a fundamental belief: *religious principles.* **3** a rule of action or conduct: *I make it a principle to save some money each week.* **4** honor; integrity; uprightness: *a person of principle.* **5** a rule of science explaining how things act; law: *the uncertainty principle, a machine work-*

ing on principles of friction and leverage.

on principle, 1 for reasons of right conduct. **2** according to a particular belief or rule.

USAGE NOTE **Principle** and **principal** are often confused because they sound alike. They are spelled similarly because they both come from the same Latin word that **prince** does. A way to remember how to spell them is from their meanings. **Principle** means a basic truth or rule, and it ends in *-le* like *rule.* All other possible meanings—important, chief person, head of a school, money—are spelled the other way, to end in *-al.*

print (print), **1** *v.* to use plates, type, or other inked surfaces to transfer words, pictures, etc., onto paper. Books, magazines, newspapers, and pamphlets are printed. **2** *v.* to stamp words, designs, etc., onto paper or another surface with ink or dye. **3** *v.* to cause to be printed; publish: *The company prints 200 novels a year. The magazine will print her story.* **4** *v.* to transfer words or pictures onto paper or another surface by a method other than pressing or stamping: *letters printed by the computer's laser output, a photocopier that prints too light.* **5** *n.* words transferred onto paper with ink: *The book had very large print.* **6** *v.* to make words or letters the way they look in books instead of in writing: *Print your name clearly. Most children learn to print before learning to write.* **7** *n.* any cloth with a pattern on it: *This print will make a nice shirt.* **8** *n.* a picture or design transferred from an engraved plate, block, etc. **9** *n.* picture that is copied by photography from a painting. **10** *v.* to produce marks by pressure; stamp; impress. **11** *n.* a mark made by pressing or stamping: *the print of a foot.* **12** *n.* fingerprint. **13** *n.* photograph produced from a negative. **14** *v.* to produce a photograph by passing light through a negative onto treated paper.

in print, 1 in printed form. **2** (of books) still available for purchase from the publisher.

out of print, no longer sold by the publisher.

print out, (of a computer) to produce or display information in printed or readable form.

print·a·ble (prin′tə bəl), *adj.* **1** capable of being printed. **2** fit to be printed.

printed circuit, (in electronics) circuit in which the parts or connections are printed, painted, or sprayed onto an insulating surface usually at very small sizes and by automated machines.

print·er (prin′tər), *n.* **1** person whose business or work is printing or setting type. **2** machine that prints, controlled by a computer.

print·ing (prin′ting), *n.* **1** the producing of books, newspapers, or pamphlets by transferring words, pictures, or the like from type or other inked surface. **2** printed words, letters, etc. **3** all the copies printed at one time. **4** letters made like those in print.

printing press, machine for printing from movable type, plates, etc.

print·out (print′out′), *n.* the printed output of a computer.

pri·or[1] (prī′ər), *adj.* coming before; earlier: *I can't go with you because I have a prior engagement.*

prior to, coming before in time, order, or importance; earlier than; before.

pri·or[2] (prī′ər), *n.* head of a priory or monastery for men. Priors usually rank below abbots.

pri·or·ess (prī′ər is), *n.* head of a priory or convent for women. Prioresses usually rank below abbesses. ❑ *n., pl.* **pri·or·ess·es.**

pri·or·i·tize (prī ôr′ə tīz), *v.* **1** to arrange or do in order of priority: *Prioritize your errands, because there isn't time for all of them.* **2** to give something priority. ❑ *v.* **pri·or·i·tized, pri·or·i·tiz·ing.** —**pri·or′i·ti·za′tion,** *n.*

pri·or·i·ty (prī ôr′ə tē), *n.* **1** something given attention before anything else: *The young couple's first priority was to find a decent place to live.* **2** quality of coming before in order or importance: *Fire engines, police cars, and ambulances have priority over other traffic.* **3** condition of being earlier in time: *Their*

a	hat	ė	term	ô	order	ch	child		
ā	age	i	it	oi	oil	ng	long		a in about
ä	far	ī	ice	ou	out	sh	she		e in taken
â	care	o	hot	u	cup	th	thin	ə	i in pencil
e	let	ō	open	ů	put	ʈH	then		o in lemon
ē	equal	ȯ	saw	ü	rule	zh	measure		u in circus

claim to the land has priority because they were the first to live on it. ❑ *n., pl.* **pri·or·i·ties** for 1.

pri·or·y (prī′ər ē), *n.* a religious house governed by a prior or prioress. A priory is often, but not necessarily, dependent on an abbey. ❑ *n., pl.* **pri·or·ies.**

prism (priz′əm), *n.* **1** a solid form with parallel ends that have the same size and shape, and with sides that have two pairs of parallel edges each. A six-sided pencil before it is sharpened has the form of one kind of prism. **2** a transparent solid object, often made of glass, having the shape of a mathematical prism, usually with three-sided ends. Such objects can reflect or refract light, and some can separate white light into the colors of the spectrum by refraction.

prism (def. 2)

pris·mat·ic (priz mat′ik), *adj.* **1** of or like a prism. **2** formed by a transparent prism. **3** varied in color; brilliant. —**pris·mat′i·cal·ly,** *adv.*

prismatic colors, the seven colors formed when white light is separated by a prism: red, orange, yellow, green, blue, indigo, and violet. These are the colors of the spectrum.

pris·on (priz′n), *n.* **1** a public building in which criminals are confined: *The burglar was put in prison.* **2** any place where a person or animal is shut up unwillingly: *The small apartment was a prison to the big dog.* —**pris′on·like′,** *adj.*

pris·on·er (priz′n ər), *n.* **1** person who is under arrest or held in a jail or prison. **2** person who is confined unwillingly, or who is not free to move. **3** person taken by the enemy in war.

pris·sy (pris′ē), *adj.* **1** too careful; too fussy: *Don't be prissy; it's only a little dirt.* **2** too easily shocked. ❑ *adj.* **pris·si·er, pris·si·est.** —**pris′si·ly,** *adv.* —**pris′si·ness,** *n.*

pris·tine (pris′tēn′), *adj.* as it was in its earliest time or state; original; primitive: *The ancient paintings had kept their pristine freshness.* —**pris′tine′ly,** *adv.*

prith·ee (priᴛн′ē), *interj.* OLD USE. I pray thee; I ask you.

pri·va·cy (prī′və sē), *n.* **1** condition of being private; being away from others: *in the privacy of your home.* **2** absence of publicity; secrecy: *He told me his reasons in strict privacy. The negotiations were conducted in privacy.*

pri·vate (prī′vit), **1** *adj.* not for the public; for just a few special people or for one: *a private road, a private house, a private letter.* **2** *adj.* not public; individual; personal: *the private life of a famous person, my private opinion.* **3** *adj.* confidential; secret: *News reached her through private channels.* **4** *adj.* secluded: *some private corner.* **5** *adj.* having no public office: *He no longer seeks the presidency and is content to be a private citizen.* **6** *n.* a military rank. See chart on page 712. —**pri′vate·ly,** *adv.* —**pri′vate·ness,** *n.*

in private, 1 not publicly: *My parents spoke to the principal in private.* **2** secretly: *We met in private to plan his surprise party.*

private enterprise, free enterprise.

pri·va·teer (prī′və tir′), **1** *n.* an armed ship owned by civilians. Formerly, the U.S. government commissioned privateers to attack and capture enemy ships. **2** *n.* commander or one of the crew of a privateer. **3** *v.* to cruise as a privateer.

private eye, INFORMAL. person who has his or her own business doing detective work: *We hired a private eye to locate my missing aunt.*

private first class, a military rank. See chart on page 712.

private school, school owned and operated by a private group rather than by the government: *Both of their children go to a private school run by their church.*

pri·va·tion (prī vā′shən), *n.* **1** lack of the comforts or of the necessities of life: *Many people were hungry and homeless because of privation during the war.* **2** condition of being deprived; loss; absence: *suffer from the privation of love.*

priv·et (priv′it), *n.* any of several bushes often used for hedges.

priv·i·lege (priv′ə lij), *n.* a special right, advantage, or favor: *My sister has the privilege of driving the family car.*

priv·i·leged (priv′ə lijd), *adj.* having some privilege or privileges: *The nobility of Europe was a privileged class.*

priv·i·ly (priv′ə lē), *adv.* in a private manner; secretly.

priv·y (priv′ē), **1** *adj.* private. **2** *adj.* OLD USE. secret; hidden. **3** *n.* a small outhouse used as a toilet. ❑ *n., pl.* **priv·ies.**

privy to, having secret or private knowledge of.

privy council, group of personal advisers to a ruler. —**privy councilor.**

Privy Council, (in Canada) the group of personal advisers to the Governor General, including current ministers of the federal cabinet and all former cabinet ministers.

prize¹ (prīz), **1** *n.* a reward won after competing against other people: *Prizes will be given for the three best stories.* **2** *adj.* given as a prize. **3** *adj.* having won a prize: *prize livestock.* **4** *adj.* worthy of a prize: *prize vegetables.* **5** *n.* a reward worth working for. ■ Another word that sounds like this is **pries.**

prize² (prīz), *n.* thing or person captured in war, especially an enemy's ship and its cargo taken at sea. ■ Another word that sounds like this is **pries.**

prize³ (prīz), *v.* to value highly: *She prizes her new bicycle.* ❑ *v.* **prized, priz·ing.** ■ Another word that sounds like this is **pries.**

prize·fight (prīz′fīt′), *n.* a boxing match between professional boxers for money. —**prize′fight′er,** *n.*

pro¹ (prō), **1** *adv.* in favor of; for. **2** *n.* a reason in favor of. The pros and cons of a question are the arguments for and against it. ❑ *n., pl.* **pros.**

pro² (prō), *adj., n.* professional: *He plays tennis like a pro.* ❑ *n., pl.* **pros.**

pro-, *prefix.* in favor of; supporting: *prodemocracy = supporting democracy.*

prob·a·bil·i·ty (prob′ə bil′ə tē), *n.* **1** quality or fact of being likely or probable; good chance: *There is a probability of rain today.* **2** something likely to happen: *A storm is a probability for tomorrow.* **3** a number that tells how likely it is that a certain event will occur. This number is the number of occurrences divided by the number of all possible occurrences. The probability that a coin will come up heads is ½. ❑ *n., pl.* **prob·a·bil·i·ties** for 2.

in all probability, probably.

prob·a·ble (prob′ə bəl), *adj.* **1** likely to happen: *Cooler weather is probable after this shower.* **2** likely to be true: *Something I ate is the probable cause of my upset stomach.*

prob·a·bly (prob′ə blē), *adv.* more likely than not: *I think it will probably snow today.*

pro·bate (prō′bāt), **1** *n.* act or process of officially proving a will as genuine. **2** *adj.* of or concerned with the probating of wills: *a probate court.* **3** *v.* to prove by legal process the genuineness of a will. ❑ *v.* **pro·bat·ed, pro·bat·ing.**

pro·ba·tion (prō bā′shən), *n.* **1** the system of letting convicted lawbreakers go free under supervision without receiving the punishment which they are sentenced to unless there is a further offense: *He can't leave the state while he is on probation.* **2** time for trial or testing of character, qualifications, work habits, etc., especially of a new employee.

pro·ba·tion·er (prō bā′shə nər), *n.* person who is on probation.

probation officer, officer appointed by a court to supervise offenders who have been placed on probation.

probe (prōb), **1** *v.* to examine thoroughly; investigate; search into: *probe the causes of pollution.* **2** *n.* a thorough examination; investigation: *a probe into medical costs.* **3** *n.* an investigation, usually by a lawmaking group, in an effort to discover evidence of law violation: *the Senate probe of Watergate.* **4** *n.* a slender tool for exploring something. A doctor or dentist uses a probe to explore the depth or direction of a wound or cavity. **5** *v.* to examine with a probe. **6** *n.* spacecraft carrying scientific devices to record and report information: *a lunar probe.* ❑ *v.* **probed, probing.** —**prob′er,** *n.* —**prob′ing·ly,** *adv.*

pro·bi·ty (prō′bə tē), *n.* high principle; uprightness; honesty.

prob·lem (prob′ləm), **1** *n.* a question or situation, especially a difficult one: *Poverty is a national problem.* **2** *n.* something to be worked out: *a math problem.* **3** *adj.* causing difficulty: *a problem child.*

prob·lem·at·ic (prob′lə mat′ik), *adj.* having the nature of a problem; doubtful; uncertain; questionable: *What the weather will be is often problematic.* —**prob′lem·at′i·cal·ly,** *adv.*

prob·lem·at·i·cal (prob′lə mat′ə kəl), *adj.* problematic.

pro·bos·cis (prō bos′is), *n.* **1** an elephant's trunk. **2** a long, flexible snout, like that of the tapir. **3** the tubelike mouth parts of some insects, such as butterflies or mosquitoes, developed for piercing or sucking. ❑ *n., pl.* **pro·bos·cis·es, pro·bos·cid·es** (prōbos′i dēz).

proboscises (def. 1)

pro·car·y·ote (prō kar′ē ōt), *n.* prokaryote.

pro·ce·dure (prə sē′jər), *n.* **1** way of proceeding; method of doing things: *What is your procedure in making bread?* **2** the customary manners or ways of conducting business: *parliamentary procedure, legal procedure.* —**pro·ce′dur·al,** *adj.*

pro·ceed (prə sēd′), *v.* **1** to go on after having stopped; move forward: *Please proceed with your story. The train proceeded down the track.* ■ See Synonym Study at **advance. 2** to carry on any activity: *I proceeded to light the fire.* **3** to come forth; issue; go out; emanate: *Heat proceeds from fire.* —**pro·ceed′er,** *n.*

pro·ceed·ing (prə sē′ding), *n.* **1** course of action; conduct. **2 proceedings,** *pl.* **a** action in a case in a court of law. **b** record of what was done at the meetings of a society, club, etc.

pro·ceeds (prō′sēdz′), *n.pl.* money obtained from a sale, etc.: *The proceeds from the school play will be used to buy new books.*

proc·ess (pros′es *or* prō′ses), **1** *n.* set of actions taken to achieve a desired result: *By what process is cloth made from wool?* **2** *n.* series of changes that occurs naturally: *the digestive process.* **3** *v.* to treat or prepare by some special method: *This cloth has been processed to make it waterproof.* **4** *n.* part that grows out or sticks out: *the process of a bone.* **5** *n.* a written command or summons to appear in a court of law. ❑ *n., pl.* **proc·ess·es.**

in process, in the course or condition of being done: *The author has just finished one book and has another in process.*

pro·ces·sion (prə sesh′ən), *n.* **1** something that moves forward; persons marching or riding: *The opening procession started at noon.* **2** act of moving forward; progression: *march in procession.*

pro·ces·sion·al (prə sesh′ə nəl), **1** *adj.* of or for a procession. **2** *adj.* used or sung in a procession: *a processional hymn.* **3** *n.* processional music: *The choir marched in singing the processional.* **4** *n.* book containing hymns, etc., for use in religious processions.

proc·es·sor (pros′es ər *or* prō′ses ər), *n.* **1** the central processing unit of a computer, especially the part of this unit in which data are examined, compared, changed, and the like. **2** person or thing that processes: *She works as an order processor for a large mail-order company.*

process server, person who serves summonses, subpoenas, etc.

pro·claim (prə klām′), *v.* to make known publicly and officially; declare publicly: *proclaim a holiday. The congresswoman proclaimed that she would run for reelection.*

proc·la·ma·tion (prok′lə mā′shən), *n.* an official, public announcement: *a proclamation ending the war.*

pro·cliv·i·ty (prō kliv′ə tē), *n.* tendency; inclination. ❑ *n., pl.* **pro·cliv·i·ties.**

pro·cras·ti·nate (prō kras′tə nāt), *v.* to put things off until later; delay. ❑ *v.* **pro·cras·ti·nat·ed, pro·cras·ti·nat·ing.** —**pro·cras′ti·na′tion,** *n.* —**pro·cras′ti·na′tor,** *n.*

pro·cre·a·tion (prō′krē ā′shən), *n.* act or process of producing offspring; reproduction.

proc·tol·o·gy (prok tol′ə jē), *n.* branch of medicine which deals with the functions and diseases of the rectum and anus. —**proc·tol′o·gist,** *n.*

proc·tor (prok′tər), **1** *n.* officer in a university or school who keeps good order. **2** *v.* to serve as a proctor at an examination.

pro·cure (prə kyūr′), *v.* **1** to get by care or effort; obtain; secure: *procure a job in a bank. It is hard to procure water in a desert.* **2** to bring about; cause: *The lawyer procured the prisoner's release.* ❑ *v.* **pro·cured, pro·cur·ing.** —**pro·cur′a·ble,** *adj.* —**pro·cure′ment,** *n.*

prod (prod), **1** *v.* to poke or jab with something pointed: *prod an animal with a stick.* **2** *v.* to stir up; urge on: *My parents prodded me to clean my room.* **3** *n.* a poke; thrust: *That prod in the ribs hurt.* **4** *n.* a sharp-pointed stick; goad. **5** *n.* words, actions, or feelings that urge someone to act. ❑ *v.* **prod·ded, prod·ding.** —**prod′der,** *n.*

prod·i·gal (prod′ə gəl), **1** *adj.* spending too much; wasting money or other resources; wasteful: *prodigal of natural resources.* **2** *adj.* abundant; lavish. **3** *n.* person who is wasteful or extravagant; spendthrift: *The repentant prodigal was welcomed back home.* —**prod′i·gal′i·ty** (prod′ə gal′ə tē), *n.* —**prod′i·gal·ly,** *adv.*

pro·di·gious (prə dij′əs), *adj.* **1** very great; huge; vast: *The ocean contains a prodigious amount of water.* **2** wonderful; marvelous. —**pro·di′gious·ly,** *adv.* —**pro·di′gious·ness,** *n.*

prod·i·gy (prod′ə jē), *n.* **1** someone gifted with amazing brilliance, talent, etc. A child prodigy is remarkably brilliant in some respect. **2** a wonderful sign or omen: *The brilliant comet seemed a prodigy to all who saw it.* ❑ *n., pl.* **prod·i·gies.**

procession (def. 1)

pro·duce (prə düs′ *for verb;* prod′üs *or* prō′düs *for noun*), **1** *v.* to bring into existence; make: *This factory produces stoves.* **2** *v.*

a	hat	ė	term	ô	order	ch	child		ə {	a in about
ā	age	i	it	oi	oil	ng	long			e in taken
ä	far	ī	ice	ou	out	sh	she			i in pencil
â	care	o	hot	u	cup	th	thin			o in lemon
e	let	ō	open	ù	put	ᵺ	then			u in circus
ē	equal	ô	saw	ü	rule	zh	measure			

P

to bring about; cause: *Hard work produces success.* **3** *v.* to bring forth or yield offspring, crops, products, dividends, interest, etc. **4** *v.* to bring forth; supply; create; yield: *Hens produce eggs.* **5** *v.* to bring forward; show: *Produce your proof.* **6** *v.* to bring a play, movie, etc., before the public: *Our class produced a play.* **7** *n.* farm products, especially fruits and vegetables. ❑ *v.* **pro·duced, pro·duc·ing.** **–pro·duc′i·ble** or **pro·duce′a·ble,** *adj.*

pro·duc·er (prə dü′sər), *n.* **1** person in charge of presenting a play, a movie, or a TV or radio show. **2** one that produces, especially someone who grows or manufactures things that are used by others. **3** a living thing that can make its own food from minerals, water, and sunlight. All green plants and some bacteria are producers.

prod·uct (prod′əkt), *n.* **1** something that is produced; result of work or of growth: *factory products, farm products.* **2** number or quantity resulting from multiplying two or more numbers together: *40 is the product of 8 and 5.*

pro·duc·tion (prə duk′shən), *n.* **1** act or process of producing; creation; manufacture: *the production of cars.* **2** something produced: *the yearly production of a farm.* **3** amount produced: *a decline in production.*

pro·duc·tive (prə duk′tiv), *adj.* **1** producing much; fertile: *a productive farm, a productive writer.* **2** producing food or other articles of commerce: *Farming is productive labor.* **3** having good results: *Efforts to resolve the dispute were very productive.* **–pro·duc′tive·ly,** *adv.* **–pro·duc′tive·ness,** *n.*

pro·duc·tiv·i·ty (prō′duk tiv′ə tē), *n.* power to produce; productiveness.

Prof., professor.

prof·a·na·tion (prof′ə nā′shən), *n.* act of showing contempt or disregard toward something holy; treatment of something sacred as it should not be treated.

pro·fane (prə fān′), **1** *adj.* showing contempt or disregard for God or holy things: *a profane person, profane language.* **2** *v.* to treat holy things with contempt or disregard: *Soldiers profaned the church when they stabled their horses in it.* **3** *v.* to put to wrong or unworthy use. **4** *adj.* not sacred; worldly: *profane literature.* ❑ *v.* **pro·faned, pro·fan·ing.** **–pro·fane′ly,** *adv.* **–pro·fane′ness,** *n.* **–pro·fan′er,** *n.*

pro·fan·i·ty (prə fan′ə tē), *n.* **1** use of profane language; swearing. **2** act of being profane; lack of reverence. **3** a profane word or phrase. ❑ *n., pl.* **pro·fan·i·ties** for 2,3.

pro·fess (prə fes′), *v.* **1** to lay claim to; claim: *I don't profess to be an expert in chemistry.* **2** to declare your belief in: *Christians profess the Christian religion.* **3** to declare openly: *He professed his loyalty to the United States.* **4** to have as one's business or profession: *profess law.*

pro·fessed (prə fest′), *adj.* **1** stated or acknowledged; openly declared: *a professed Christian, a professed candidate for office.* **2** alleged or pretended: *accused by your professed friends.*

pro·fes·sion (prə fesh′ən), *n.* **1** an occupation requiring special education, such as law, medicine, teaching, or the ministry. **2** the people engaged in such an occupation: *the medical profession.* **3** act of professing; open declaration: *a profession of friendship.* **4** declaration of belief in a religion.

pro·fes·sion·al (prə fesh′ə nəl), **1** *adj.* of or about a profession; appropriate to a profession: *The surgeon showed great professional skill during the operation.* **2** *adj.* engaged in a profession: *A lawyer or a teacher is a professional person.* **3** *adj.* making a business or trade of something which others do for pleasure: *a professional athlete, professional musicians.* **4** *n.* person who works at a profession; a professional man or woman. **5** *adj.* engaged in by professionals rather than amateurs: *a professional ball game.* **–pro·fes′sion·al·ly,** *adv.*

pro·fes·sion·al·ize (prə fesh′ə nə līz), *v.* to make or become professional. ❑ *v.* **pro·fes·sion·al·ized, pro·fes·sion·al·iz·ing.** **–pro·fes′sion·al·i·za′tion,** *n.*

pro·fes·sor (prə fes′ər), *n.* **1** teacher of the highest rank in a college or university. **2** teacher. **–pro·fes′sor·ship,** *n.*

pro·fes·so·ri·al (prō′fə sôr′ē əl or prof′ə sôr′ē əl), *adj.* of or characteristic of a professor. **–pro′fes·so′ri·al·ly,** *adv.*

prof·fer (prof′ər), **1** *v.* to offer for acceptance; present; tender: *We proffered our regrets at having to leave so early.* **2** *n.* an offer made: *Her proffer of advice was accepted.* **–prof′fer·er,** *n.*

pro·fi·cien·cy (prə fish′ən sē), *n.* knowledge; skill; advanced state of expertness.

pro·fi·cient (prə fish′ənt), *adj.* very skilled or knowledgeable in any art, science, or subject; expert: *to be proficient in mathematics.* **–pro·fi′cient·ly,** *adv.* **–pro·fi′cient·ness,** *n.*

pro·file (prō′fīl), **1** *n.* a side view, especially of the human face. **2** *n.* outline. **3** *n.* a concise description of someone's abilities, personality, or career. **4** *v.* to draw or write a profile of. ❑ *v.* **pro·filed, pro·fil·ing.** [Profile comes from Latin words meaning "out" and "thread." A simple profile can be drawn with a single continuous line, like a curving thread stretched out.]

profile (def. 1)

prof·it (prof′it), **1** *n.* the money made from a business; what is left when the cost of goods and of carrying on the business is subtracted from the amount of money taken in: *The profits in this business are not large.* **2** *v.* to make a gain from business; make a profit. **3** *n.* advantage; benefit: *What profit is there in worrying?* **4** *v.* to get advantage; gain; benefit: *profit from your mistakes.* **5** *v.* to be an advantage or benefit to. ■ Another word that sounds like this is **prophet.** **–prof′it·less,** *adj.*

prof·it·a·ble (prof′ə tə bəl), *adj.* **1** yielding a financial profit: *The sale held by the Girl Scouts was very profitable.* **2** giving a gain or benefit; useful: *We spent a profitable afternoon in the library.* **–prof′it·a·bil′i·ty, prof′it·a·ble·ness,** *n.* **–prof′it·a·bly,** *adv.*

prof·it·eer (prof′ə tir′), **1** *n.* person who makes an unfair profit by charging excessive prices for scarce goods. **2** *v.* to seek or make such unfair profits.

profit sharing, the sharing of profits between employer and employees.

prof·li·ga·cy (prof′lə gə sē), *n.* **1** reckless extravagance. **2** great wickedness; vice.

prof·li·gate (prof′lə git), **1** *adj.* recklessly extravagant. **2** *adj.* very wicked; shamelessly bad. **3** *n.* person who is very wicked or extravagant. **–prof′li·gate·ly,** *adv.*

pro·found (prə found′), *adj.* **1** deeply felt; very great: *profound sympathy.* **2** going far deeper than what is easily understood; having or showing great knowledge or understanding: *a profound book, a profound thinker.* **3** far-reaching; thorough: *profound cultural changes.* **4** very deep: *a profound sigh, a profound sleep.* **–pro·found′ly,** *adv.* **–pro·found′ness,** *n.*

pro·fun·di·ty (prə fun′də tē), *n.* **1** condition of being profound; great depth. **2** a very deep thing or place. ❑ *n., pl.* **pro·fun·di·ties** for 2.

pro·fuse (prə fyüs′), *adj.* **1** very abundant: *profuse thanks.* **2** spending or giving freely; lavish; extravagant: *He was profuse in his praise of the book.* **–pro·fuse′ly,** *adv.* **–pro·fuse′ness,** *n.*

pro·fu·sion (prə fyü′zhən), *n.* **1** great abundance: *a profusion of books, a profusion of roses.* **2** extravagance; lavishness.

pro·gen·i·tor (prō jen′ə tər), *n.* ancestor in the direct line; forefather.

prog·e·ny (proj′ə nē), *n.pl.* children or offspring; descendants.

pro·ges·te·rone (prō jes′tə rōn′), *n.* hormone produced by the ovaries that makes the uterus ready to receive a fertilized ovum.

prog·no·sis (prog nō′sis), *n.* **1** forecast of the probable course of a disease. **2** estimate of what will probably happen. ❑ *n., pl.* **prog·no·ses** (prog nō′sēz).

prog·nos·ti·cate (prog nos′tə kāt), *v.* to tell what is going to happen; forecast. ❑ *v.* **prog·nos·ti·cat·ed, prog·nos·ti·cat·ing.** **–prog·nos′ti·ca′tion,** *n.* **–prog·nos′ti·ca′tor,** *n.*

pro·gram (prō′gram), **1** *n.* a broadcast on radio or TV: *a news program.* **2** *n.* the items making up an entertainment: *a program of modern dances.* **3** *n.* list or booklet showing items or events set down in order with a list of the performers: *Ask the usher for a program.* **4** *v.* to arrange or enter in a list. **5** *n.* a plan of what is to be done: *government economic programs.* **6** *v.* to draw up a plan for. **7** *n.* a set of instructions for a computer outlining the steps to be performed in a specific operation. **8** *v.* to prepare a set of instructions for a computer. **9** *v.* to give instructions to an automatic machine: *program a VCR to record a show.* **10** *v.* to train to think in a specific way: *programmed to expect rewards for good work.* ❑ *v.* **pro·grammed, pro·gram·ming** or **pro·gramed, pro·gram·ing.**

pro·gram·mer or **pro·gram·er** (prō′gram′ər), *n.* person who prepares a computer program or programs.

prog·ress (prog′res *for noun;* prə gres′ *for verb*), **1** *n.* an advance or growth; development; improvement: *the progress of science, showing rapid progress in your studies.* **2** *v.* to get better; advance; develop: *We progress in learning step by step.* **3** *n.* act of moving forward; going ahead: *We made rapid progress on our journey.* **4** *v.* to move forward; go ahead: *The building of the new school progressed quickly during the summer.*

WORD FAMILY
Progress and the words below are related. They all come from Latin words meaning "to walk" or "a step."

aggression	congress	digress	ingredient
biodegradable	degrade	grade	regress
centigrade	degree	gradual	transgression

pro·gres·sion (prə gresh′ən), *n.* **1** act or process of progressing; a moving forward; going ahead: *Creeping is a slow method of progression.* **2** a continuous series of acts or events; sequence: *A rapid progression of interesting scenes in the story led up to a surprising climax.* **3** (in mathematics) series of numbers in which there is always the same relation between a number and the one after it. 2, 4, 6, 8, 10 are in arithmetical progression. 2, 4, 8, 16, 32 are in geometric progression.

pro·gres·sive (prə gres′iv), **1** *adj.* making progress; advancing toward something better; improving: *a progressive nation.* **2** *adj.* favoring progress; wanting improvement or reform in government, business, etc. **3** *n.* person who favors improvement and reform in government, religion, or business. **4** *adj.* moving forward; developing: *a progressive disease.* **5** *adj.* (in grammar) showing an action that is in progress. *Is reading, was reading,* and *has been reading* are progressive forms of read. —**pro·gres′-sive·ly,** *adv.* —**pro·gres′sive·ness,** *n.*

Progressive Conservative Party, a political party in Canada.

pro·hib·it (prō hib′it), *v.* **1** to forbid by law or authority: *Swimming was prohibited when the water was contaminated.* ■ See Synonym Study at **forbid. 2** to prevent: *Rainy weather and fog prohibited flying.* —**pro·hib′it·er** or **pro·hib′i·tor,** *n.*

pro·hi·bi·tion (prō′ə bish′ən), *n.* **1** law or order that prohibits. **2** Often, **Prohibition,** law or laws against making or selling alcoholic liquors. National Prohibition existed in the United States between 1920 and 1933. **3** act of prohibiting: *The prohibition of swimming in the reservoir is sensible.*

prohibit (def. 1)

pro·hib·i·tive (prō hib′ə tiv), *adj.* enough to prohibit or prevent something: *prohibitive costs.* —**pro·hib′i·tive·ly,** *adv.* —**pro·hib′i·tive·ness,** *n.*

proj·ect (proj′ekt *for noun;* prə jekt′ *for verb*), **1** *n.* a plan; scheme; effort; undertaking: *a project for better sewage disposal.* ■ See Synonym Study at **plan. 2** *v.* to plan; scheme: *to project a tax decrease.* **3** *v.* to throw or cast forward: *A cannon projects shells.* **4** *v.* to cause to fall on a surface: *Motion pictures are projected on the screen. The tree projects a shadow on the grass.* **5** *v.* to stick out: *The rocky point projects far into the water.* **6** *n.* a special assignment planned and carried out by a student, a group

of students, or an entire class. **7** *n.* group of apartment buildings built and run as a unit, especially with government support. **8** *v.* to use your voice loudly and clearly enough to be heard and understood at a distance, as actors do. **9** *v.* to make a prediction that something will happen, based on performance up to that point: *project an election winner from poll results.*

pro·jec·tile (prə jek′təl), *n.* any object that is thrown, hurled, or shot, such as a stone or bullet.

pro·jec·tion (prə jek′shən), *n.* **1** part that projects or sticks out: *rocky projections on the face of a cliff.* **2** prediction based on past performance. **3** act of throwing or casting forward: *the projection of a photographic image on a screen.* **4** representation on a flat surface of all or part of the surface of the earth.

pro·jec·tion·ist (prə jek′shə nist), *n.* person who operates a movie projector.

pro·jec·tor (prə jek′tər), *n.* apparatus for projecting an image on a screen.

pro·kar·y·ote (prō kar′ē ōt), *n.* any one-celled living thing that has no nucleus or organelles. Bacteria are prokaryotes. Also, **pro·caryote.** —**pro·kar′y·ot′ic,** *adj.*

Pro·ko·fiev (prō kô′fyef), *n.* **Ser·gei Ser·ge·ye·vich** (ser′gā ser-gā′ə vich), 1891-1953, Russian composer. He wrote symphonies, music for movies, and *Peter and the Wolf.*

pro·le·tar·i·an (prō′lə târ′ē ən), **1** *adj.* of or belonging to the proletariat. **2** *n.* person belonging to the proletariat.

pro·le·tar·i·at (prō′lə târ′ē ət), *n.* the working class, especially industrial workers working for wages. [**Proletariat** comes from a Latin word meaning "good only for having children."]

pro·lif·e·rate (prō lif′ə rāt′), *v.* **1** to grow or produce by multiplication of parts: *The bacteria proliferated in a favorable environment.* **2** to multiply; spread: *Suburbs around many major cities have proliferated.* ❑ *v.* **pro·lif·e·rat·ed, pro·lif·e·rat·ing.** —**pro·lif′e·ra′tion,** *n.* —**pro·lif′er·a·tive,** *adj.*

pro·lif·ic (prə lif′ik), *adj.* **1** producing many offspring: *Rabbits are prolific.* **2** producing much: *a prolific garden, a prolific imagination, a prolific writer.* —**pro·lif′i·cal·ly,** *adv.* —**pro·lif′ic·ness,** *n.*

pro·logue (prō′lôg), *n.* **1** introduction to a novel, poem, or other literary work. **2** speech or poem addressed to the audience by one of the actors at the beginning of a play. **3** any introductory act or event.

pro·long (prə lông′), *v.* to make longer; extend; stretch; protract: *prolong a visit. Good care may prolong a sick person's life.* ■ See Synonym Study at **lengthen.** —**pro·long′er,** *n.*

pro·lon·ga·tion (prō′lông gā′shən), *n.* an extension in time or space: *the prolongation of a discussion.*

prom (prom), *n.* a formal dance given by a high school or college class: *the senior prom.*

prom·e·nade (prom′ə nād′ *or* prom′ə näd′), **1** *n.* a walk for pleasure or for show: *They took a promenade in their fine clothes.* **2** *v.* to walk about or up and down for pleasure or for show: *We promenaded back and forth on the ship's deck.* **3** *n.* a public place for such a walk: *Atlantic City has a famous promenade along the beach.* **4** *n.* a formal dance. **5** *n.* a march of all the guests at the opening of a formal dance. ❑ *v.* **prom·e·nad·ed, prom·e·nad·ing.** —**prom′e·nad′er,** *n.*

Pro·me·the·us (prə mē′thē əs), *n.* (in Greek myths) one of the Titans. He stole fire from heaven and taught people its use. Zeus punished him by chaining him to a rock.

pro·me·thi·um (prə mē′thē əm), *n.* a radioactive metallic element which is a product of the fission of uranium, thorium, and plutonium. *Symbol:* Pm

prom·i·nence (prom′ə nəns), *n.* **1** a prominent condition: *the prominence of Jefferson as a statesman, the prominence of football as a sport.* **2** something that sticks out, especially upward. A hill is a prominence. **3** cloud of gas that erupts from the sun and is seen as a glowing projection from the sun's surface during a solar eclipse.

a	hat	ė	term	ô	order	ch	child		a in about
ā	age	i	it	oi	oil	ng	long		e in taken
ä	far	ī	ice	ou	out	sh	she	ə {	i in pencil
â	care	o	hot	u	cup	th	thin		o in lemon
e	let	ō	open	u̇	put	ᴛʜ	then		u in circus
ē	equal	ȯ	saw	ü	rule	zh	measure		

prom·i·nent (prom′ə nənt), *adj.* **1** well-known or important; distinguished: *a prominent citizen.* **2** easy to see: *I hung the picture in a prominent place in the living room.* **3** standing out; projecting: *Some insects have prominent eyes.* —**prom′i·nent·ly,** *adv.*

prom·is·cu·i·ty (prom′i skyü′ə tē), *n.* fact or condition of being promiscuous.

pro·mis·cu·ous (prə mis′kyü əs), *adj.* **1** having sexual relations with many persons. **2** making no distinctions; not discriminating; careless: *Doctors warn about the promiscuous use of drugs.* **3** mixed and in disorder: *a promiscuous collection of notes.* —**pro·mis′cu·ous·ly,** *adv.* —**pro·mis′cu·ous·ness,** *n.*

prom·ise (prom′is), **1** *n.* words said or written that you will do or not do something: *You can count on her to keep her promise.* **2** *v.* to give your word; make a promise: *They promised to stay till we came.* **3** *v.* to make a promise of: *to promise help.* **4** *v.* to state positively that something is true; assure: *I've finished my homework, I promise.* **5** *n.* indication of what may be expected: *The clouds give promise of rain.* **6** *n.* that which gives hope of success: *a young scholar who shows promise.* **7** *v.* to give hope; give hope of: *The rainbow promises fair weather tomorrow.* ❑ *v.* **prom·ised, prom·is·ing.** —**prom′is·er,** *n.*

SYNONYM STUDY **Promise, pledge,** and **guarantee** all mean to give your word that you will do something. **Promise** is a general word: *If I tell you what I'm feeling, do you promise to keep it a secret?* **Pledge** means to promise in a very serious way: *Each morning we pledge allegiance to the flag.* **Guarantee** means to promise to fix or take back something sold: *The store guarantees that the microwave will work for a year with no problems.*

Promised Land, 1 country promised by God to Abraham and his descendants; Canaan. **2 promised land,** a place or condition of expected happiness: *The United States has been a promised land for many immigrants.*

prom·is·ing (prom′ə sing), *adj.* likely to turn out well: *a promising beginning, a promising future.* —**prom′is·ing·ly,** *adv.*

prom·is·so·ry (prom′ə sôr′ē), *adj.* containing a promise.

prom·is·so·ry note, a written promise to pay a stated sum of money to someone at a specific time.

prom·on·to·ry (prom′ən tôr′ē), *n.* a high peak of land that sticks out from the coast into the water; headland. ❑ *n., pl.* **prom·on·to·ries.**

Promontory, town in NW Utah, near which the final spike was driven on May 10, 1869, to complete the building of the first U.S. transcontinental railroad.

pro·mote (prə mōt′), *v.* **1** to raise in rank, condition, or importance: *Pupils who pass the test will be promoted to the next higher grade.* **2** to help to grow or develop; help to success: *A kindly feeling toward other countries will promote peace.* **3** to further the sale of something by advertising. **4** to help to organize; start: *Several bankers promoted the new company.* ❑ *v.* **pro·mot·ed, pro·mot·ing.** [See Word Story at demote.] —**pro·mot′a·ble,** *adj.*

SYNONYM STUDY **Promote, foster,** and **boost** all mean to help someone or something succeed. **Promote** is a general word: *UNICEF promotes the welfare of children everywhere.* **Foster** means to help growth or development: *That piano teacher has fostered many young talents.* **Boost** means to promote by praise: *Town leaders are boosting plans for a new highway.*

pro·mot·er (prə mō′tər), *n.* **1** person who organizes and secures money for sporting events, new companies, etc. **2** person or thing that encourages or furthers something: *a promoter of energy conservation.*

pro·mo·tion (prə mō′shən), *n.* **1** an advance in rank or importance: *The clerk was given a promotion and an increase in salary.* **2** act of helping to grow, develop, or succeed: *They are active in the promotion of better health care.* **3** act of helping to organize; starting: *It took much time and money for the promotion of the new company.* —**pro·mo′tion·al,** *adj.*

prompt (prompt), **1** *adj.* ready and willing; on time; quick: *Be prompt to obey.* **2** *adj.* done at once; made without delay: *I expect a prompt answer.* **3** *v.* to cause someone to do something: *Her curiosity prompted her to ask questions.* **4** *v.* to give rise to; suggest; inspire: *A kind thought prompted the gift.* **5** *v.* to remind a learn-

er, speaker, actor, etc., of the words or actions needed: *Please prompt me if I forget my lines.* **6** *n.* a word or symbol that appears on a computer screen when the system is read for new instructions or when it is asking for more information. —**prompt′ly,** *adv.* —**prompt′ness,** *n.*

prompt·er (promp′tər), *n.* person or device that tells actors, speakers, etc., what to say when they forget.

pron., 1 pronoun. **2** pronunciation.

prone (prōn), *adj.* **1** inclined or disposed; liable: *He is prone to forget to do his chores.* **2** lying down, usually with the face down: *He lay prone on the bed, sound asleep.* **3** lying flat: *fall prone on the ground.* —**prone′ly,** *adv.* —**prone′ness,** *n.*

prong (prông), *n.* one of the pointed ends of a fork, antler, etc.

pronged (prôngd), *adj.* having prongs.

prong·horn (prông′hôrn′), *n.* a very fast mammal that looks like an antelope, found on the plains of western North America. ❑ *n., pl.* **prong·horn** or **prong·horns.**

pronghorn—3 ft. (91 cm) high at the shoulder

pro·noun (prō′noun), *n.* word used instead of a noun. In "John did not want to go because he was sick," *he* is a pronoun used in the second part of the sentence to avoid repeating *John.*

pro·nounce (prə nouns′), *v.* **1** to make the sounds of; speak: *Pronounce your words clearly.* **2** to declare someone or something to be: *The doctor pronounced her cured.* **3** to declare solemnly or positively: *The judge pronounced sentence on the prisoner.* ❑ *v.* **pro·nounced, pro·nounc·ing.** —**pro·nounce′a·ble,** *adj.* —**pro·nounc′er,** *n.*

pro·nounced (prə nounst′), *adj.* strongly marked; emphatic; decided: *She has pronounced opinions on politics.*

pro·nounce·ment (prə nouns′mənt), *n.* **1** a formal statement; declaration. **2** opinion; decision.

pron·to (pron′tō), *adv.* INFORMAL. promptly; immediately; quickly: *They got the job done pronto.*

pro·nun·ci·a·tion (prə nun′sē ā′shən), *n.* **1** way of pronouncing. This book gives the pronunciation of each main word. **2** act of making the sounds of; speaking.

proof (prüf), *n.* **1** way showing the truth of something: *Do you have any proof of your story?* **2** act or process of showing the truth of anything. **3** act of testing; trial: *That box looks okay, but let us put it to the proof.* **4** a test copy of something printed. A book is first printed in proof so that errors can be corrected. **5** a test print of an etching, photograph, etc. **6** the alcohol content of a liquor, shown by a number that is the percentage of alcohol multiplied by two. An alcohol content of 50 percent = 100 proof.

-proof, *suffix.* safe from; able to resist effects of: *fireproof = safe from fire; weatherproof = able to resist bad weather.*

proof·read (prüf′rēd′), *v.* to read and mark errors to be corrected. ❑ *v.* **proof·read** (prüf′red′), **proof·read·ing.** —**proof′read′er,** *n.*

prop¹ (prop), **1** *v.* to hold up by placing a support under or against: *Prop the clothesline with a stick. He was propped up in bed with pillows.* **2** *v.* to support; sustain: *prop a failing cause.* **3** *n.* thing or person used to support another: *I used the book as a prop behind my painting.* ❑ *v.* **propped, prop·ping.**

prop² (prop), *n.* any piece of furniture or small item used in performing or making a making a movie or a TV show; property.

prop³ (prop), *n.* INFORMAL. an airplane propeller.

prop·a·gan·da (prop/ə gan/də), *n.* **1** organized efforts to spread information that is often biased or inaccurate, in order to influence public opinion: *Government propaganda is most effective when there is no freedom of the press.* **2** information spread in this way: *During the war, the enemies spread propaganda.*

prop·a·gan·dist (prop/ə gan/dist), **1** *n.* person who gives time or effort to the spreading of propaganda. **2** *adj.* of or about propaganda or propagandists.

prop·a·gan·dize (prop/ə gan/dīz), *v.* **1** to propagate or spread information by propaganda. **2** to carry on propaganda. □ *v.* **prop·a·gan·dized, prop·a·gan·diz·ing.**

prop·a·gate (prop/ə gāt), *v.* **1** to produce offspring; reproduce: *Trees propagate themselves by seeds.* **2** to cause to increase in number by the production of young: *Cows and sheep are propagated on farms.* **3** to spread news or knowledge: *The scientist propagated her new theory about life in outer space.* **4** to spread; pass on; send further: *Sound is propagated by vibrations.* □ *v.* **prop·a·gat·ed, prop·a·gat·ing.** —**prop/a·ga/tion,** *n.*

pro·pane (prō/pān), *n.* a heavy, colorless, flammable gas, a hydrocarbon. Propane occurs in crude petroleum and is used as a fuel, refrigerant, or solvent.

pro·pel (prə pel/), *v.* to drive forward; force ahead: *propel a boat by oars, a person propelled by ambition.* □ *v.* **pro·pelled, pro·pel·ling.**

pro·pel·lant (prə pel/ənt), *n.* **1** substance that propels, especially the fuel of a rocket. **2** a compressed gas that makes the contents of a spray can squirt out when the pressure is set free by pushing a button.

pro·pel·lent (prə pel/ənt), **1** *adj.* propelling; driving forward. **2** *n.* thing or person that propels.

pro·pel·ler (prə pel/ər), *n.* wheel with curved blades, powered by an engine, for propelling boats and aircraft.

pro·pen·si·ty (prə pen/sə tē), *n.* a natural tendency or inclination; leaning: *a propensity for athletics.* □ *n.*, *pl.* **pro·pen·si·ties.**

prop·er (prop/ər), *adj.* **1** right for the occasion; fitting: *Night is the proper time to sleep.* **2** decent; respectable: *proper conduct.* **3** belonging to one person or a few; not common to all. *Mary Jones* and *John Jones* are proper names. **4** strictly so called; in the strict sense of the word: *Puerto Rico is not part of the United States proper.* —**prop/er·ness,** *n.*

proper fraction, fraction less than 1. For example, ⅔, ⅛, and ⁹⁹/₁₀₀ are all proper fractions.

prop·er·ly (prop/ər lē), *adv.* **1** in a proper, correct, or fitting manner: *Eat properly.* ∎ See Synonym Study at **well¹.** **2** rightly; justly: *An honest person is properly indignant at the offer of a bribe.* **3** strictly: *Properly speaking, a whale is not a fish.*

proper noun, noun naming a particular person, place, or thing. *Maria, George, Chicago,* and *Monday* are proper nouns. A proper noun always begins with a capital letter.

prop·er·ty (prop/ər tē), *n.* **1** thing or things owned; possession or possessions: *This house is that man's property. That book is my property; please return it to me.* **2** piece of land or real estate: *She owns property in Florida.* **3** ownership. **4** quality or power belonging specially to something: *Copper has several important properties.* **5** prop². □ *n.*, *pl.* **prop·er·ties** for 2,4,5.

proph·e·cy (prof/ə sē), *n.* **1** act of telling what will happen; foretelling future events. **2** thing told about the future. **3** a divinely inspired revelation, writing, etc. □ *n.*, *pl.* **proph·e·cies** for 2,3.

proph·e·sy (prof/ə sī), *v.* **1** to tell what will happen; foretell; predict: *The fortuneteller prophesied that I would have good luck in the future.* **2** to speak when or as if inspired by God. □ *v.* **proph·e·sied, proph·e·sy·ing.** —**proph/e·si/er,** *n.*

proph·et (prof/it), *n.* **1** person who tells what will happen: *Don't be a bad-luck prophet.* **2** a religious leader who speaks as the voice of God: *Jeremiah was a Hebrew prophet.* [**Prophet** comes from Greek words meaning "before" and "to speak." A prophet speaks of something before it happens.] ∎ Another word that sounds like this is **profit.**

pro·phet·ic (prə fet/ik), *adj.* **1** belonging to a prophet; such as a prophet has: *prophetic power.* **2** giving warning of what is to happen; foretelling: *Thunder is prophetic of rain.* —**pro·phet/i·cal·ly,** *adv.*

pro·phy·lac·tic (prō/fə lak/tik), **1** *adj.* protecting from disease. **2** *n.* medicine or measure that protects against disease. **3** *n.* condom.

pro·pi·tious (prə pish/əs), *adj.* **1** suitable; favorable: *propitious weather for our trip.* **2** favorably inclined; gracious. —**pro·pi/tious·ly,** *adv.* —**pro·pi/tious·ness,** *n.*

pro·po·nent (prə pō/nənt), *n.* person who supports something; advocate: *Both candidates are proponents of more funds for schools.*

pro·por·tion (prə pôr/shən), **1** *n.* relation of two things in magnitude; size, number, amount, or degree compared to another: *climbers small in proportion to a boulder, water and orange juice in the proportion of three to one.* **2** *n.* a proper relation between parts: *The dog's short legs were not in proportion to its long body.* **3** *v.* to fit one thing to another so that they go together: *The designs in that rug are well proportioned.* **4** *v.* to adjust in proper proportion or relation: *to proportion correctly the various ingredients of a recipe.* **5** *n.* part; share: *A large proportion of Nevada is desert.* **6** *n.* statement of equality between two ratios. EXAMPLE: 4 is to 2 as 10 is to 5. **7** *n.pl.* **proportions, a** size; extent: *She left an art collection of considerable proportions.* **b** dimensions: *The dining room of the castle had the proportions of our entire apartment.*

proportion (def. 1)

pro·por·tion·al (prə pôr/shə nəl), *adj.* **1** in the proper proportion; corresponding: *The pay will be proportional to the amount of time put in.* **2** (in mathematics) having the same relationship in size. —**pro·por/tion·al·ly,** *adv.*

pro·por·tion·ate (prə pôr/shə nit), *adj.* in the proper proportion: *The money earned by the fair was really not proportionate to the effort we put into it.* —**pro·por/tion·ate·ly,** *adv.* —**pro·por/tion·ate·ness,** *n.*

pro·pos·al (prə pō/zəl), *n.* **1** what is proposed; plan, scheme, or suggestion: *The club will now hear this member's proposal.* **2** an offer of marriage. **3** act of proposing: *Proposal is easier than performance.*

pro·pose (prə pōz/), *v.* **1** to suggest; put forward: *I propose that we take turns using the computer.* **2** to present the name of someone for an office: *I am proposing Jack for president.* **3** to intend; plan: *She proposes to save half of all she earns.* **4** to make an offer of marriage. □ *v.* **pro·posed, pro·pos·ing.**

prop·o·si·tion (prop/ə zish/ən), *n.* **1** what is offered to be considered; proposal: *The corporation presented a proposition to buy several smaller businesses.* **2** statement. EXAMPLE: "All men are created equal." **3** statement that is to be proved true. EXAMPLE: Resolved: that our city should have a bird sanctuary. **4** problem to be solved: *a proposition in geometry.* **5** INFORMAL. something to be taken care of; task: *Getting a good grade in art will not be an easy proposition.*

pro·pound (prə pound/), *v.* to suggest; propose: *propound a theory, propound a riddle.* —**pro·pound/er,** *n.*

pro·pri·e·tar·y (prə prī/ə ter/ē), *adj.* **1** manufactured and sold by the holder of a patent, trademark, or copyright: *proprietary medicines.* **2** owned by a private person or company: *a proprietary business.* **3** of or about a proprietor or owner: *a proprietary interest in a business.*

pro·pri·e·tor (prə prī/ə tər), *n.* owner. —**pro·pri/e·tor·ship,** *n.*

a	hat	ė	term	ô	order	ch	child		
ā	age	i	it	oi	oil	ng	long		a in about
ä	far	ī	ice	ou	out	sh	she		e in taken
â	care	o	hot	u	cup	th	thin	ə	i in pencil
e	let	ō	open	ù	put	ŦH	then		o in lemon
ē	equal	ò	saw	ü	rule	zh	measure		u in circus

pro·pri·e·ty (prə prī′ə tē), *n.* **1** quality of being proper; fitness. **2** proper behavior: *She acted with propriety.* **3 proprieties,** *pl.* the customs and rules of proper behavior: *The proprieties require that we use good table manners.*

pro·pul·sion (prə pul′shən), *n.* **1** a propelling force: *the propulsion of jet engines.* **2** act of driving forward or onward.

pro·rate (prō rāt′ *or* prō′rāt′), *v.* to divide proportionally: *I prorated the money according to the number of days each person had worked.* ❑ *v.* **pro·rat·ed, pro·rat·ing. —pro·rat′a·ble,** *adj.* **—pro·ra′tion,** *n.*

pro·sa·ic (prō zā′ik), *adj.* like prose; matter-of-fact; ordinary; not exciting: *a prosaic style.* **—pro·sa′i·cal·ly,** *adv.*

pro·sce·ni·um (prō sē′nē əm), *n.* **1** the part of the stage in front of the curtain. **2** a stage curtain and the wall around it.

pro·scribe (prō skrīb′), *v.* **1** to prohibit as wrong or dangerous; talk against; condemn: *Some religions proscribe dancing, drinking, and card playing.* **2** to banish; outlaw. ❑ *v.* **pro·scribed, pro·scrib·ing. —pro·scrib′er,** *n.*

pro·scrip·tion (prō skrip′shən), *n.* act of proscribing or condition of being proscribed; banishment.

prose (prōz), **1** *n.* the ordinary form of spoken or written language; plain language not arranged in verses. **2** *adj.* of or in prose.

WORD STORY **Prose** comes from a Latin word meaning "straight." Latin poetry and English poetry often use words in fancy or complicated ways. Prose is more direct, like a straight road compared to a winding one.

pros·e·cute (pros′ə kyüt), *v.* **1** to bring before a court of law: *Reckless drivers will be prosecuted.* **2** to bring a case before a court of law. **3** to carry out; follow up: *The fire department started an inquiry into the cause of the fire, and prosecuted it for several weeks.* **4** to carry on a business or occupation. ❑ *v.* **pros·e·cut·ed, pros·e·cut·ing.**

pros·e·cu·tion (pros′ə kyü′shən), *n.* **1** act or process of carrying on a lawsuit: *The prosecution will be abandoned if the stolen money is returned.* **2** side that starts action against another in a court of law. The prosecution makes certain charges against the defense. **3** act of carrying out; following up: *the prosecution of a plan.*

pros·e·cu·tor (pros′ə kyü′tər), *n.* **1** the lawyer who takes charge of the government's side of a case against an accused person. **2** person who starts legal proceedings against another person: *Who is the prosecutor in this case?*

pros·e·lyte (pros′ə līt), **1** *n.* person who has changed from one opinion, religious belief, etc., to another. **2** *v.* to proselytize. ❑ *v.* **pros·e·lyt·ed, pros·e·lyt·ing.**

pros·e·lyt·ize (pros′ə lə tīz), *v.* to make converts; proselyte. ❑ *v.* **pros·e·lyt·ized, pros·e·lyt·iz·ing.**

Pro·ser·pi·na (prō sėr′pə nə), *n.* (in Roman myths) Persephone.

pros·o·dy (pros′ə dē), *n.* the science of poetic meters and versification.

pros·pect (pros′pekt), **1** *n.* thing expected or looked forward to: *The prospects from our gardens are good this year.* **2** *n.* act of looking forward; expectation: *The prospect of a vacation is pleasant.* **3** *n.* outlook for the future. **4** *n.* view; scene: *The prospect from the mountain was breathtaking.* **5** *v.* to search or look: *prospect for gold.* **6** *n.* person who may become a customer, buyer, candidate, etc.: *The salesman called on several prospects.*

pro·spec·tive (prə spek′tiv), *adj.* **1** likely to happen; probable; expected: *a prospective customer, a prospective raise in pay.* **2** looking forward in time; future. **—pro·spec′tive·ly,** *adv.*

pros·pec·tor (pros′pek tər), *n.* person who explores or examines a region, searching for gold, oil, uranium, or other valuable resources.

pro·spec·tus (prə spek′təs), *n.* a printed statement describing and advertising something. ❑ *n., pl.* **pro·spec·tus·es.**

pros·per (pros′pər), *v.* to be successful; have good fortune; flourish: *Our business prospered.*

pros·per·i·ty (pro sper′ə tē), *n.* prosperous condition; good fortune; success: *a time of peace and prosperity.* [**Prosperity** comes from Latin words meaning "hope" and "for." The way of life that people hope for is prosperity.]

pros·per·ous (pros′pər əs), *adj.* **1** wealthy; successful; thriving; fortunate: *a prosperous merchant.* **2** favorable; helpful: *prosperous weather for growing wheat.* **—pros′per·ous·ly,** *adv.* **—pros′per·ous·ness,** *n.*

pros·ta·glan·din (pros′tə glan′dən), *n.* any of a group of hormones made in the body, believed to control many bodily functions.

pros·tate (pros′tāt), *n.* a large gland surrounding the male urethra in front of the bladder. **—pros·tat·ic** (pro stat′ik), *adj.*

pros·the·sis (pros thē′sis), *n.* an artificial part that replaces a missing tooth, leg, arm, eye, etc. ❑ *n., pl.* **pros·the·ses** (pros thē′sēz). **—pros·thet·ic** (pros thet′ik), *adj.*

pros·ti·tute (pros′tə tüt), **1** *n.* person who has sexual relations with others for money. **2** *n.* person who does base things for money. **3** *v.* to put to an unworthy or base use: *to prostitute artistic skills.* ❑ *v.* **pros·ti·tut·ed, pros·ti·tut·ing.**

pros·ti·tu·tion (pros′tə tü′shən), *n.* **1** the act or business of having sexual relations with other people for money. **2** the use of your body, honor, talents, etc., in a dishonorable way.

pros·trate (pros′trāt), **1** *v.* to throw down flat; cast down: *The captives prostrated themselves before the conqueror.* **2** *adj.* lying flat with face downward: *They were humbly prostrate in prayer.* **3** *adj.* lying flat: *He stumbled and fell prostrate on the floor.* **4** *v.* to make very weak or helpless; exhaust: *Sickness often prostrates people.* **5** *adj.* helpless; overcome: *They were prostrate with grief.* ❑ *v.* **pros·trat·ed, pros·trat·ing.**

pros·tra·tion (pro strā′shən), *n.* **1** act of prostrating; bowing down low or lying face down before a ruler, before idols, or before God. Prostration is an act of submission, of respect, or of worship. **2** condition of being very much worn out or used up in body or mind; exhaustion.

pros·y (prō′zē), *adj.* like prose; commonplace; dull; tiresome. ❑ *adj.* **pros·i·er, pros·i·est. —pros′i·ly,** *adv.* **—pros′i·ness,** *n.*

pro·tac·tin·i·um (prō′tak tin′ē əm), *n.* a very rare, heavy, radioactive metallic element which occurs in pitchblende. It disintegrates to form actinium. *Symbol:* Pa

pro·tag·o·nist (prō tag′ə nist), *n.* the main character in a play, story, or novel.

pro·tect (prə tekt′), *v.* to shield from harm or danger; shelter; defend; guard: *Proper food protects a person's health.* ■ See Synonym Study at **guard. —pro·tect′ing·ly,** *adv.*

pro·tec·tion (prə tek′shən), *n.* **1** act of protecting; condition of being kept from harm; defense: *We have a dog for protection.* **2** thing or person that prevents damage: *A hat is protection from the sun.*

pro·tec·tion·ism (prə tek′shə niz′əm), *n.* an economic policy of taxing foreign goods, so that people are more likely to buy goods made in their own country.

pro·tec·tive (prə tek′tiv), *adj.* **1** defensive; protecting: *the hard protective covering of a turtle.* **2** preventing injury to those around: *a protective device on a machine.* **—pro·tec′tive·ly,** *adv.* **—pro·tec′tive·ness,** *n.*

protective coloration, appearance of some animals that makes it hard to tell them apart from the things they live among, or that makes them resemble a harmful or bad-tasting animal, and so protects them from their enemies.

protective coloration

pro·tec·tor (prə tek′tər), *n.* person or thing that protects; defender.

pro·tec·tor·ate (prə tek′tər it), *n.* **1** a weak country under the protection and partial control of a strong country. **2** such protection and control.

pro·té·gé (prō′tə zhā), *n.* person who has been taken under the protection or kindly care of a friend or patron. ❑ *n., pl.* **pro·té·gés.**

pro·tein (prō′tēn), *n.* any of the many complex substances containing nitrogen that are necessary parts of the cells of animals and plants. Proteins are a necessary part of human and animal diets. Meat, milk, cheese, eggs, and beans contain protein. A protein is made of several or many amino acids.

Prot·er·o·zo·ic (prot′ər ə zō′ik), *n.* (in geology) time between about 2 billion and 600 million years ago. During this time, sponges, algae, fungi, bacteria, and other forms of sea life developed.

pro·test (prō′test *for noun, adj.;* prə test′ *for verb*), **1** *n.* statement that denies or objects strongly: *They yielded only after protest.* **2** *v.* to make objections; object: *I protested against having to wash the dishes.* **3** *v.* to object to: *The coach protested the umpire's decision.* **4** *adj.* expressing objection against some condition: *a protest movement.* **5** *v.* to declare solemnly; assert: *The accused speeder protested her innocence.* —**pro·test′er** or **pro·tes′tor,** *n.*

under protest, unwillingly; objecting.

Prot·es·tant (prot′ə stənt), **1** *n.* member of any of certain Christian churches which split off from the Roman Catholic Church during the Reformation of the 1500s or developed thereafter. Lutherans, Baptists, Methodists, Quakers, and many others are Protestants. **2** *adj.* of or about Protestants or their religion.

Protestant Episcopal Church, a church in the United States that has about the same principles and beliefs as the Church of England.

Prot·es·tant·ism (prot′ə stən tiz′əm), *n.* **1** the religion of Protestants. **2** their principles and beliefs. **3** Protestants or Protestant churches as a group.

prot·es·ta·tion (prot′ə stā′shən), *n.* **1** a solemn declaration; act of protesting. **2** a protest.

pro·tist (prō′tist), *n.* any living thing that has characteristics of both animals and plants, or of neither; protoctist. Protists have definite nuclei and are usually one-celled. Amebas, slime molds, and many algae are protists. ❑ *n., pl.* **pro·tists, pro·tis·ta** (prō tis′tə).

pro·to·col (prō′tə kol), *n.* rules of etiquette of the diplomatic corps.

pro·toc·tist (prə tok′tist), *n.* protist.

pro·ton (prō′ton), *n.* a tiny particle in the nucleus of the atom, carrying one unit of positive electricity. A proton has a mass about 1,836 times that of an electron.

pro·to·plasm (prō′tə plaz′əm), *n.* the chemically active mixture of proteins, fats, and many other complex substances suspended in water that forms the living matter of all cells; the substance that is the basis of life. —**pro′to·plas′mic,** *adj.*

pro·to·type (prō′tə tip), *n.* the first or original type or model of anything that is designed or constructed.

pro·to·zo·an (prō′tə zō′ən), **1** *n.* any of a great many living things that are like animals, but that have only one cell and are microscopic in size. Most protozoans live in water. They are neither animals nor plants, but another kind of life called protists. Amebas and paramecia are protozoans. **2** *adj.* of or belonging to protozoans. ❑ *n., pl.* **pro·to·zo·ans, pro·to·zo·a** (prō′tə zō′ə).

pro·tract (prō trakt′), *v.* to prolong; lengthen in time: *a protracted visit.* —**pro·tract′i·ble,** *adj.* —**pro·trac′tion,** *n.*

pro·trac·tor (prō trak′tər), *n.* tool for drawing or measuring angles.

pro·trude (prō trüd′), *v.* **1** to push forth; stick out: *The turtle protruded its head.* **2** to be pushed forth; stick out: *teeth that protrude too far.* ❑ *v.* **pro·trud·ed, pro·trud·ing.**

pro·tru·sion (prō trü′zhən), *n.* **1** condition of sticking out: *Bending your arm causes a protrusion of the elbow.* **2** something that sticks out; projection: *A protrusion of rock gave us shelter from the storm.*

pro·tu·ber·ance (prō tü′bər əns), *n.* part that sticks out; bulge; swelling: *The protuberance in the coat pocket turned out to be a crumpled scarf.*

pro·tu·ber·ant (prō tü′bər ənt), *adj.* bulging out; sticking out; prominent.

proud (proud), *adj.* **1** having pride in yourself or your achievements. **2** feeling or showing pleasure or satisfaction in something connected with yourself or others: *I am proud to have been chosen to be class president.* **3** having respect for yourself, your position, or your character: *The family was too proud to ask for charity.* **4** thinking too well of yourself; haughty; arrogant. **5** very pleasing to your feelings or your pride: *It was a proud moment for her when she was awarded the scholarship.* **6** grand; magnificent: *The big ship was a proud sight.* [See Word Story at **prude.**] —**proud′ly,** *adv.* —**proud′ness,** *n.*

proud of, thinking well of; being well satisfied with.

> **SYNONYM STUDY** **Proud, conceited,** and **boastful** all mean pleased with yourself. **Proud** is a general word, and it often suggests having good reason to be pleased: *She is proud of her good grades.* **Conceited** means having too high an opinion of yourself: *He is conceited about his family's wealth, although he has never earned a dollar.* **Boastful** means fond of saying how good you are: *She sent a boastful letter from camp about all the prizes she had won there.*

Proust (prüst), *n.* **Mar·cel** (mär sel′), 1871-1922, French novelist. He continually revised his huge seven-volume novel *Remembrance of Things Past,* and the last three parts were published after his death.

prove (prüv), *v.* **1** to show that a thing is true and right: *Prove your statement.* **2** to turn out; be found to be: *This book proved interesting.* **3** to try out; test: *prove a new product.* ❑ *v.* **proved, proved** or **prov·en, prov·ing.** —**prov′a·ble,** *adj.* —**prov′a·bly,** *adv.* —**prov′er,** *n.*

> **WORD STORY** **Prove** comes from a Latin word meaning "to test," and **prove** still has "to test" as one definition. This is the meaning involved in the saying "The exception proves the rule." If you find an exception to a rule, you test how good the rule is. Often, a test shows that something is true and right, so that meaning of **prove** became more common. Many people now understand the saying to mean that an exception shows that a rule is a good one, because it applies to all *other* cases.

prov·en (prü′vən), *v.* **1** known to be true, accurate, good enough, etc.: *proven results, a proven manager.* **2** a past participle of **prove.**

Pro·ven·çal (prō′vən säl′), **1** *adj.* of or about Provence, its people, or their language. **2** *n.* person born or living in Provence. **3** *n.* language of Provence. In its medieval form, it was widely known in Europe as one of the chief languages of the troubadours.

Pro·vence (prò väns′), *n.* part of SE France, famous during the Middle Ages for chivalry and poetry. [See Word Story at **province.**]

Provence (1225)

Provence in 1225
Addditional territory occupied in 50 B.C.
GERMANY
FRANCE
ITALY
SPAIN
ATLANTIC OCEAN
Mediterranean Sea

prov·en·der (prov′ən dər), *n.* **1** dry food for animals, such as hay or corn. **2** food.

prov·erb (prov′ėrb′), *n.* a short, wise saying used for a long time by many people. "Haste makes waste" is a proverb.

pro·ver·bi·al (prə vėr′bē əl), *adj.* **1** of or about proverbs; expressed in a proverb; like a proverb: *a proverbial saying.* **2** having become a proverb: *the proverbial stitch in time.* **3** well-known: *the proverbial loyalty of dogs.* —**pro·ver′bi·al·ly,** *adv.*

Prov·erbs (prov′ėrbz′), *n.* book of the Bible made up of sayings of the wise men of Israel.

pro·vide (prə vid′), *v.* **1** to give what is needed or wanted; supply; furnish: *The school provided lunches for students.* **2** to take care for the future: *They saved and invested money to provide for*

a	hat	ė	term	ô	order	ch	child		
ā	age	i	it	oi	oil	ng	long		a in about
ä	far	ī	ice	ou	out	sh	she		e in taken
â	care	o	hot	u	cup	th	thin	ə	i in pencil
e	let	ō	open	ů	put	ᴛʜ	then		o in lemon
ē	equal	ò	saw	ü	rule	zh	measure		u in circus

their old age. **3** to arrange in advance; state as a condition beforehand: *Club rules provide that dues must be paid monthly.* ❑ *v.* **pro·vid·ed, pro·vid·ing. –pro·vid′a·ble,** *adj.* **–pro·vid′er,** *n.*

pro·vid·ed (prə vī′did), *conj.* on the condition that; if: *I will go provided my friends can go also.*

prov·i·dence (prov′ə dəns), *n.* **1** God's care and help: *Trusting in providence, the Pilgrims sailed for the unknown world.* **2 Prov·idence,** God. **3** care for the future; good management: *Greater providence on my part would have kept me out of debt.*

Prov·i·dence (prov′ə dəns), *n.* port and capital of Rhode Island, in the NE part.

prov·i·dent (prov′ə dənt), *adj.* having or showing foresight; careful in providing for the future: *Provident people save money.* [See Word Story at **prude.**] **–prov′i·dent·ly,** *adv.*

prov·i·den·tial (prov′ə den′shəl), *adj.* **1** fortunate: *Our delay seemed providential, for the train we had planned to take was wrecked.* **2** of or proceeding from God's care: *providential help.* **–prov′i·den′tial·ly,** *adv.*

pro·vid·ing (prə vī′ding), *conj.* on the condition that; if: *I shall go providing it doesn't rain.*

prov·ince (prov′əns), *n.* **1** one of the main divisions of a country. Canada is made up of provinces. **2 the provinces,** *pl.* part of a country outside the capital or the largest cities: *I was accustomed to city life and did not like living in the provinces.* ■ This meaning of **provinces** is often considered offensive. **3** proper work or activity: *Physics is not within the province of Grade 5.* **4** division; department: *the province of science.*

pro·vin·cial (prə vin′shəl), **1** *adj.* of or about a province: *provincial government.* **2** *n.* person born or living in a province. **3** *adj.* belonging or peculiar to some particular province or provinces rather than to the whole country; local: *provincial English, provincial customs.* **4** *adj.* lacking refinement or polish: *a provincial point of view.* ■ This meaning of **provincial** is often considered offensive. **5** *n.* a provincial person. **–pro·vin′cial·ly,** *adv.*

pro·vin·cial·ism (prə vin′shə liz′əm), *n.* **1** provincial manners, habit of thought, etc. **2** word, expression, or way of pronunciation peculiar to a district of a country; regionalism. *Reckon* for *think* is a provincialism.

provincial park, CANADIAN. land set aside by a province as a wildlife refuge and for public enjoyment.

pro·vi·sion (prə vizh′ən), **1** *n.* statement making a condition: *A provision of the lease is that the rent must be paid promptly.* **2** *n.* act of providing; preparation: *They made provision for their children's education.* **3** *n.* care taken for the future; arrangement made beforehand: *There is a provision for making the building larger if necessary.* **4** *n.pl.* **provisions,** a supply of food and drinks: *After a long winter the settlers were low on provisions.* **5** *v.* to supply with provisions: *The cabin was well provisioned with canned goods.* **–pro·vi′sion·er,** *n.*

pro·vi·sion·al (prə vizh′ə nəl), *adj.* for the time being; temporary: *a provisional agreement, a provisional governor.* **–pro·vi′sion·al·ly,** *adv.*

pro·vi·so (prə vī′zō), *n.* a condition that is part of an agreement; requirement; provision. ❑ *n., pl.* **pro·vi·sos** or **pro·vi·soes.**

prov·o·ca·tion (prov′ə kā′shən), *n.* **1** something that stirs you up; cause of anger: *Their insults were a provocation.* **2** act of provoking.

pro·voc·a·tive (prə vok′ə tiv), *adj.* tending or serving to call forth action, thought, laughter, anger, etc.: *a provocative remark.* **–pro·voc′a·tive·ly,** *adv.* **–pro·voc′a·tive·ness,** *n.*

pro·voke (prə vōk′), *v.* **1** to make angry; vex: *She provoked him by her teasing.* **2** to stir up; excite: *An insult provokes a person to anger.* **3** to call forth; bring about; start into action; cause: *The President's speech provoked much discussion.* ❑ *v.* **pro·voked, pro·vok·ing.**

prov·ost (prō′vōst), *n.* **1** a high administrative officer in some colleges and universities. **2** head or dean of the clergymen assigned to a cathedral.

pro·vost marshal (prō′vō), an officer who is the head of military police in a district or command.

prow (prou), *n.* **1** the front part of a ship or boat; bow. **2** the pointed front part of anything that sticks forward: *the prow of an aircraft.*

prow·ess (prou′is), *n.* **1** bravery, courage, or daring acts, especially in battle. **2** unusual skill or ability: *athletic prowess.*

prowl (proul), **1** *v.* to go about slowly and secretly like an animal hunting to eat or a thief looking for something to steal: *Many wild animals prowl at night.* ■ See Synonym Study at **sneak. 2** *v.* to wander: *He got up and prowled about his room.* **3** *n.* act of prowling: *It was only a wild animal on its nightly prowl.* **–prowl′er,** *n.*

prowl car, squad car.

prox·i·mate (prok′sə mit), *adj.* **1** next; nearest. **2** near the exact amount; approximate. **–prox′i·mate·ly,** *adv.*

prox·im·i·ty (prok sim′ə tē), *n.* nearness; closeness.

prox·y (prok′sē), *n.* **1** the authority to do something for another person. In marriage by proxy, someone takes the place of the absent bride or bridegroom during the ceremony. **2** someone having this kind of authority; agent; substitute: *The mayor sent a proxy to the meeting to act in her place.* **3** an official document that gives someone this authority. ❑ *n., pl.* **prox·ies** for 2,3.

prude (prüd), *n.* person who is too proper or too modest; person who puts on extremely proper or modest airs.

pru·dence (prüd′ns), *n.* **1** wise thought before acting; good judgment. **2** good management; economy.

pru·dent (prüd′nt), *adj.* planning carefully ahead of time; sensible; discreet: *My prudent friend saves part of her wages.* [See Word Story at **prude.**] **–pru′dent·ly,** *adv.*

pru·den·tial (prü den′shəl), *adj.* of, marked by, or showing prudence. **–pru·den′tial·ly,** *adv.*

prud·er·y (prü′dər ē), *n.* **1** extreme modesty or propriety, especially when not genuine. **2** a prudish act or remark. ❑ *n., pl.* **prud·er·ies** for 2.

Prud·hoe Bay (prü′dō), town in N Alaska, on the Arctic Ocean. The Alaska Pipeline begins there.

prud·ish (prü′dish), *adj.* like a prude; extremely proper or modest; too modest. **–prud′ish·ly,** *adv.* **–prud′ish·ness,** *n.*

prune[1] (prün), *n.* **1** kind of sweet plum that is dried. **2** plum suitable for drying.

prune[2] (prün), *v.* **1** to cut unnecessary or undesirable twigs or branches from a bush, tree, etc.: *prune fruit trees or grape vines.* **2** to cut off or out: *We pruned branches from the apple tree to improve next year's fruit.* **3** to cut out useless or undesirable parts from: *The editor pruned the writer's manuscript.* ❑ *v.* **pruned, prun·ing. –prun′a·ble,** *adj.* **–prun′er,** *n.*

Prus·sia (prush′ə), *n.* former duchy and kingdom in N Europe which became the most important state in the confederation of German states united in 1871. **–Prus′sian,** *adj., n.*

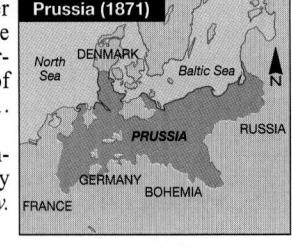

Prussia (1871)

pry[1] (prī), *v.* to look, peer, or inquire into something, especially someone's private business. ❑ *v.* **pried, pry·ing.**

pry² (prī), **1** *v.* to raise or move by force: *I used a large screwdriver to pry open the window.* **2** *n.* lever for prying. **3** *v.* to get with much effort: *We finally pried the secret out of him.* ❑ *v.* **pried, pry·ing;** *n., pl.* **pries.**

pry·ing (prī′ing), *adj.* looking or searching too curiously; unpleasantly inquisitive. —**pry′ing·ly,** *adv.*

P.S., 1 postscript. **2** Public School.

psalm (säm), *n.* **1** a sacred song or poem. **2** **Psalm,** any of the 150 sacred songs or hymns that together form a book of the Bible.

> **WORD STORY** Words that begin with **ps-** mostly come from Greek. In Greek, both letters are pronounced. It is easier to pronounce only the *s*, and so in English the *p* has become silent. As usual, however, English has kept the older spelling.

psalm·ist (sä′mist), *n.* **1** author of a psalm or psalms. **2** **the Psalmist,** King David, who according to tradition wrote many of the Psalms.

Psalms (sämz), *n.* book of the Bible made up of 150 psalms.

Psal·ter (sȯl′tər), *n.* **1** the book of Psalms. **2** version of the Psalms for use in religious services. **3** a prayer book containing such a version.

psal·ter·y (sȯl′tər ē), *n.* an ancient musical instrument played by plucking the strings. ❑ *n., pl.* **psal·ter·ies.**

pseu·do (sü′dō), *adj.* not genuine; false; pretended: *a pseudo science, pseudo anger.*

pseu·do·nym (süd′n im), *n.* name used by an author instead of his or her real name; pen name. Mark Twain is a pseudonym for Samuel Langhorne Clemens.

pseu·do·pod (sü′də pod), *n.* a temporary bulge or extension at the edge of a one-celled living thing, by which it moves and can envelop and absorb food.

pseu·do·sci·ence (sü′dō sī′əns), *n.* false science based on nonscientific method.

pshaw (shȯ), *interj., n.* exclamation expressing impatience, contempt, or dislike.

psi (sī), *n.* psychic abilities and phenomena, including telepathy, clairvoyance, and extrasensory perception: *a sci-fi story of psi in the sky.*

pso·ri·a·sis (sə rī′ə sis), *n.* an inflammatory skin disease in which the skin is dry, scaly, and reddened.

PST, Pacific Standard Time.

psych (sīk), *n.* INFORMAL. psychology.

psych out, to outsmart by understanding and foreseeing the thinking of: *psych out an opponent, psych out a test.*

psych up, to develop an enthusiastic or determined state of mind: *I psyched myself up for the big race.*

psy·che (sī′kē), *n.* **1** the human soul or spirit. **2** the mind. **3** **Psyche,** (in Greek and Roman myths) the human soul or spirit pictured as a beautiful young woman, usually with butterfly wings. Psyche was loved by Cupid and was made immortal.

psy·che·del·ic (sī′kə del′ik), *adj.* revealing new areas of consciousness, often accompanied by hallucinations or mental disorders: *psychedelic drugs.*

psy·chi·at·ric (sī′kē at′rik), *adj.* of or about the treatment of mental and emotional disorders. —**psy′chi·at′ri·cal·ly,** *adv.*

psy·chi·a·trist (sī kī′ə trist), *n.* doctor who treats mental and emotional disorders.

psy·chi·a·try (sī kī′ə trē), *n.* study and treatment of mental and emotional disorders.

psy·chic (sī′kik), **1** *adj.* especially sensitive to supernatural influences. **2** *n.* person supposed to be specially sensitive to supernatural influences. **3** *adj.* of the soul or mind; mental: *illness due to psychic causes.* **4** *adj.* outside the known laws of physics; supernatural. —**psy′chi·cal·ly,** *adv.*

psy·chi·cal (sī′kə kəl), *adj.* psychic.

psy·cho (sī′kō), *n.* SLANG. **1** psychopath. **2** psychotic. ❑ *n., pl.* **psy·chos.**

psycho-, *prefix.* of the mind; mental: *psychoanalysis = analysis of the mind.*

psy·cho·a·nal·y·sis (sī′kō ə nal′ə sis), *n.* method of psychotherapy that examines someone's mind to discover the unconscious desires, fears, anxieties, etc., which produce mental and emotional disorders.

psy·cho·an·a·lyst (sī′kō an′l ist), *n.* person who practices psychoanalysis.

psy·cho·an·a·lyze (sī′kō an′l īz), *v.* to treat by psychoanalysis. ❑ *v.* **psy·cho·an·a·lyzed, psy·cho·an·a·lyz·ing.**

psy·cho·log·i·cal (sī′kə loj′ə kəl), *adj.* **1** of or about the mind. Memories and dreams are psychological processes. **2** of or about psychology: *psychological research.* —**psy′cho·log′i·cal·ly,** *adv.*

psy·chol·o·gist (sī kol′ə jist), *n.* an expert in psychology.

psy·chol·o·gy (sī kol′ə jē), *n.* **1** science of the mind. Psychology tries to explain why people act, think, and feel as they do. **2** the mental states and processes of a person or persons; mental nature and behavior: *The long illness had a bad effect on his psychology.*

psy·cho·path (sī′kə path), *n.* person having a mental or personality disorder, especially someone who behaves in an immoral or criminal way because of the disorder. —**psy′cho·path′ic,** *adj.*

psy·cho·sis (sī kō′sis), *n.* any very severe form of mental illness which seriously disrupts normal behavior and social functioning. ❑ *n., pl.* **psy·cho·ses** (sī kō′sēz).

psy·cho·so·mat·ic (sī′kō sə mat′ik), *adj.* of or about physical symptoms or diseases caused by psychological problems: *psychosomatic disorders.*

psy·cho·ther·a·py (sī′kō ther′ə pē), *n.* treatment of mental or emotional disorders by psychological means.

psy·chot·ic (sī kot′ik), **1** *adj.* of, having, or caused by a psychosis. **2** *n.* a psychotic person. ■ This meaning of **psychotic** is sometimes considered offensive, because it identifies the person with the illness. —**psy·chot′i·cal·ly,** *adv.*

Pt, symbol for platinum.

pt., 1 past tense. **2** pint or pints.

P.T.A., Parent-Teacher Association.

Ptah (tä), *n.* Egyptian god of creation and fertility, shown as a mummy holding a scepter.

ptar·mi·gan (tär′mə gən), *n.* any of several kinds of grouse that have feathered feet and live in mountainous and cold regions. ❑ *n., pl.* **ptar·mi·gan** or **ptar·mi·gans.**

ptarmigan—about 13 in. (33 cm) long

> **WORD STORY** Unlike other English words that begin with **pt-**, **ptarmigan** comes from a Celtic word that begins with a *t*. It sounds like some Greek words, however, so English people gave it a Greek spelling. See the Word Story at **pteranodon.**

PT boat, a fast motorboat which carries torpedoes, depth bombs, etc., used to attack enemy ships.

pter·an·o·don (ter an′ə don′), *n.* any of several large pterodactyls with rods of bone extending from the back of the skull.

> **WORD STORY** Words that begin with **pt-** mostly come from Greek. In Greek, both letters are pronounced. In English, it is easier to pronounce only the *t*, and so the *p* has become silent. As usual, however, English has kept the older spelling.

pter·o·dac·tyl (ter′ə dak′təl), *n.* any of several extinct flying reptiles of various sizes that had wings something like a bat's.

> **WORD STORY** **Pterodactyl** comes from two Greek words meaning "wing" and "finger." The pterodactyl's wings were flaps of skin stretched from their bodies to the tips of very long fingers.

pter·o·saur (ter′ə sôr′), *n.* any of numerous extinct flying reptiles that had wings something like a bat's. Some were small and had long tails, while others were much larger and tailless. Pterodactyls were pterosaurs.

a	hat	ė	term	ô	order	ch	child			
ā	age	i	it	oi	oil	ng	long		a	in about
ä	far	ī	ice	ou	out	sh	she	ə {	e	in taken
â	care	o	hot	u	cup	th	thin		i	in pencil
e	let	ō	open	ů	put	ŦH	then		o	in lemon
ē	equal	ȯ	saw	ü	rule	zh	measure		u	in circus

P

Ptol·e·ma·ic (tol′ə mā′ik), *adj.* of or about the astronomer Ptolemy. The **Ptolemaic system** of astronomy taught that Earth was the fixed center of the universe and that the sun, moon, planets, and stars moved around it.

Ptol·e·my (tol′ə mē), *n.* **Claud·i·us** (klò′dē əs), Greek mathematician, astronomer, and geographer at Alexandria, Egypt. He believed that Earth stayed still while the sun, moon, planets, and stars revolved around it. He lived in the A.D. 100s.

pto·maine (tō′mān), *n.* any of several chemical compounds produced by bacteria in decaying matter. Some ptomaines are poisonous.

Pu, symbol for plutonium.

pub (pub), *n.* saloon; tavern.

pu·ber·ty (pyü′bər tē), *n.* **1** age at which a person is first able to produce children; the physical beginning of manhood and womanhood. Puberty is about 14 in boys and about 12 in girls. **2** the series of physical changes that begin at this age.

pu·bic (pyü′bik), *adj.* of or in the region of the front part of the pelvis.

pub·lic (pub′lik), **1** *n.* the people in general; all the people: *inform the public.* **2** *adj.* of the people as a whole: *public affairs, public buildings.* **3** *adj.* done, made, acting, etc., for the people as a whole: *public relief.* **4** *adj.* open to all the people; serving all the people: *a public park, public meetings.* **5** *adj.* of or engaged in the affairs or service of the people: *a public official.* **6** *adj.* known to many or all; not private: *The fact became public.* **7** *n.* a particular section of the people: *A popular actor has a large public.* **—pub′lic·ness,** *n.*

in public, not in private or secretly; publicly; openly: *to stand up in public for what you believe.*

public-address system, apparatus made up of one or more microphones, amplifiers, and loudspeakers for making sounds audible to a large audience, as on a street or in an auditorium.

pub·li·can (pub′lə kən), *n.* **1** BRITISH. keeper of a pub. **2** a tax collector of ancient Rome.

pub·li·ca·tion (pub′lə kā′shən), *n.* **1** book, newspaper, or magazine; anything that is published. **2** the printing and selling of books, newspapers, magazines, etc. **3** act of making known; condition of being made known; public announcement: *There is prompt publication of any important news over the radio.*

public defender, lawyer who defends people who cannot afford to hire a lawyer. Public defenders are assigned by the court and are paid from public funds.

public domain. in the public domain, available for anyone to use because not protected by copyright or patent.

public enemy, person, especially a criminal, who is a menace to the public: *The FBI declared the escaped murderer public enemy number one.*

public house, BRITISH. saloon; tavern.

pub·li·cist (pub′lə sist), *n.* **1** person skilled or trained in law or in public affairs. **2** writer on law, politics, or public affairs. **3** press agent.

pueblo (def. 1)

pub·lic·i·ty (pub lis′ə tē), *n.* **1** public notice, especially attention gained by giving out information: *The new movie received favorable publicity in newspapers and on TV.* **2** measures used for getting, or the process of getting, public notice: *I worked on the publicity for the concert.* **3** articles, announcements, etc., used to get public notice: *write publicity.*

pub·li·cize (pub′lə sīz), *v.* to give publicity to. ❑ *v.* **pub·li·cized, pub·li·ciz·ing.**

pub·lic·ly (pub′lik lē), *adv.* **1** in a public manner; openly: *She admitted her error publicly.* **2** by the public: *a publicly owned business.*

public opinion, opinion of the people in a country, community, etc.: *make a survey of public opinion.*

public relations, 1 activities of an organization, institution, or individual done to create or keep a favorable public image. **2** the business of such activities: *to work in public relations.*

public school, 1 (in the United States) a free school supported by taxes. **2** (in Great Britain) a private boarding school.

public servant, person who works for the government.

public service, 1 government service. **2** service performed by a public utility. **3** something done for the public good.

public speaking, act or art of speaking effectively before an audience: *Many people are frightened of public speaking.*

pub·lic-spir·it·ed (pub′lik spir′ə tid), *adj.* having or showing an unselfish desire for the public good.

public television, television that provides cultural and educational programs to the public. Public television is supported by donations and public funds rather than by advertising fees.

public utility, company formed or chartered to render essential services to the public, such as a company furnishing electricity, gas, water, communications, etc.

public works, things built by the government at public expense and for public use, such as roads, docks, dams, and waterworks.

pub·lish (pub′lish), *v.* **1** to prepare and offer a book, newspaper, magazine, sheet music, or other printed material for sale or distribution. **2** to make publicly or generally known: *Don't publish the faults of your friends.* **—pub′lish·a·ble,** *adj.*

pub·lish·er (pub′li shər), *n.* person or company whose business is to publish books, newspapers, magazines, etc.: *Look at the bottom of the title page of this book for the publisher's name.*

Puc·ci·ni (pü chē′nē), *n.* **Gia·co·mo** (jä′kō mō), 1858-1924, Italian composer of romantic operas. His operas include *La Bohème* and *Madama Butterfly.*

puck (puk), *n.* a rubber disk used in the game of hockey.

Puck (puk), *n.* a mischievous fairy in English folklore.

puck·er (puk′ər), **1** *v.* to draw into wrinkles or irregular folds: *pucker your brow, pucker cloth in sewing. My lips puckered as I tasted the sour persimmon.* **2** *n.* an irregular fold; wrinkle: *There are puckers at the shoulders of this ill-fitting coat.*

puck·ish (puk′ish), *adj.* mischievous; impish: *a puckish twinkling of the eyes.* **—puck′ish·ly,** *adv.* **—puck′ish·ness,** *n.*

pud·ding (pùd′ing), *n.* a soft cooked food, usually sweet: *rice pudding.*

pud·dle (pud′l), *n.* **1** a small pool of water, especially dirty water: *a puddle of rain water.* **2** a small pool of any liquid: *a puddle of ink.*

pudg·y (puj′ē), *adj.* short and fat or thick: *The plump baby had pudgy hands.* ❑ *adj.* **pudg·i·er, pudg·i·est.** ■ **Pudgy** is sometimes considered offensive. **—pudg′i·ly,** *adv.* **—pudg′i·ness,** *n.*

Pue·bla (pwe′blä), *n.* a state in SE Mexico.

pueb·lo (pweb′lō), *n.* **1** an American Indian village of homes grouped together to form a large building which is several stories high. Pueblos are built of adobe and stone and usually have flat roofs. **2** **Pueblo,** member of any American Indian tribe living in such villages. Pueblos, including Hopi and Zuñi, live in the southwestern United States and northern Mexico. ❑ *n., pl.* **pueb·los** for 1, **Pueb·lo** or **Pueb·los** for 2.

WORD STORY **Pueblo** comes from a Spanish word meaning "village" and "people." When Spanish explorers found American Indians living in villages of impressive buildings, the explorers called these people after the villages.

pu·er·ile (pyü′ər əl), *adj.* foolish or silly for a grown person to say or do; childish. **—pu′er·ile·ly,** *adv.*

Puer·to Ri·co (pwer′tō rē′kō), island in the E part of the West Indies. Puerto Rico is a self-governing commonwealth under the protection of the United States. *Abbreviation:* PR or P.R. *Capital:* San Juan. Formerly, **Porto Rico.** —**Puer′to Ri′can.**

WORD STORY **Puerto Rico** comes from Spanish words meaning "port" and "rich." Columbus named this island San Juan Bautista, meaning "St. John the Baptist." **Puerto Rico** was used at first for the island's main city and its harbor, because Spanish settlers hoped to become wealthy there. When people started calling the island Puerto Rico, the city got the name San Juan, so the names have just about reversed.

puff (puf), **1** *v.* to give out short quick blasts of air, smoke, etc.: *I puffed on the fire to make it burn better. Please don't puff smoke in my direction.* **2** *n.* a short, quick blast: *A puff of wind blew away the letter.* **3** *v.* to breathe quick and hard: *She puffed as she climbed the stairs.* **4** *v.* to give out puffs; move with puffs: *The old steam engine stood puffing in the station. The steamboat puffed around the bend in the river.* **5** *v.* to smoke: *puff a cigar.* **6** *v.* to swell: *My broken toe puffed up to twice its usual size.* **7** *n.* act or process of swelling. **8** *n.* a soft, round mass: *a puff of hair, a puff of cotton.* **9** *n.* a small pad for putting powder on the skin. **10** *n.* a light pastry filled with whipped cream, jam, etc.: *a cream puff.* **11** *v.* to praise in exaggerated language: *puff someone to the skies.* **12** *n.* exaggerated praise.

puff adder, a large and very poisonous African snake that puffs up its body when excited.

puff·ball (puf′bôl′), *n.* any of several ball-shaped fungi something like mushrooms. A ripe puffball gives off a cloud of tiny spores when it is suddenly broken.

puff·er (puf′ər), *n.* any of various fishes capable of inflating their bodies suddenly to defend against attack.

puf·fin (puf′ən), *n.* any of several seabirds of northern waters with thick bodies, large heads, and bills of several colors.

puff·y (puf′ē), *adj.* puffed out; swollen: *My eyes were puffy from crying.* ❑ *adj.* **puff·i·er, puff·i·est.** —**puff′i·ness,** *n.*

pug (pug), *n.* **1** a small, heavy-bodied dog with a curly tail and a short nose on a wide, wrinkled face. **2** pug nose.

Pu·get Sound (pyü′jit), a long narrow bay of the Pacific in NW Washington.

pu·gi·lism (pyü′jə liz′əm), *n.* art or sport of boxing.

pu·gi·list (pyü′jə list), *n.* boxer.

pu·gi·lis·tic (pyü′jə lis′tik), *adj.* of or about boxing.

pug·na·cious (pug nā′shəs), *adj.* having the habit of fighting; fond of fighting; quarrelsome. —**pug·na′cious·ly,** *adv.* —**pug·na′cious·ness,** *n.*

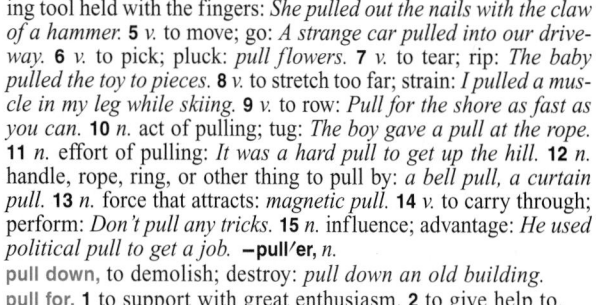

pug (def. 1)—10 in. (25 cm) high at the shoulder

pug·nac·i·ty (pug nas′ə tē), *n.* fondness for fighting; quarrelsomeness.

pug nose, a short, turned-up nose.

puke (pyük), *n., v.* SLANG. vomit. ❑ *v.* **puked, puk·ing.**

Pu·las·ki (pù las′kē), *n.* Count **Cas·i·mir** (kaz′ə mir), 1748-1779, Polish nobleman who was a general in the American army during the Revolutionary War.

pule (pyül), *v.* to cry in a thin voice, as a sick child does; whimper; whine. ❑ *v.* **puled, pul·ing.**

Pul·it·zer (pùl′it sər), *n.* **Joseph,** 1847-1911, American newspaper publisher, born in Hungary. ■ **Pulitzer's** newspapers were the first to print color comics. His will left money and instructions for establishing what were later called the Pulitzer prizes, which are given every year in journalism, literature, drama, and music.

Pulitzer Prize, any of various annual awards for high achievement in American journalism, literature, music, and the arts.

pull (pùl), **1** *v.* to move something by grasping it and moving it toward oneself: *Pull the door open; don't push it.* **2** *v.* to move, usually with effort or force: *pull a sled uphill.* **3** *v.* to take hold of and tug: *pull a person's hair. She pulled at my sleeve to get my atten-*

tion. **4** *v.* to take hold of and draw out with the fingers or a clutching tool held with the fingers: *She pulled out the nails with the claw of a hammer.* **5** *v.* to move; go: *A strange car pulled into our driveway.* **6** *v.* to pick; pluck: *pull flowers.* **7** *v.* to tear; rip: *The baby pulled the toy to pieces.* **8** *v.* to stretch too far; strain: *I pulled a muscle in my leg while skiing.* **9** *v.* to row: *Pull for the shore as fast as you can.* **10** *n.* act of pulling; tug: *The boy gave a pull at the rope.* **11** *n.* effort of pulling: *It was a hard pull to get up the hill.* **12** *n.* handle, rope, ring, or other thing to pull by: *a bell pull, a curtain pull.* **13** *n.* force that attracts: *magnetic pull.* **14** *v.* to carry through; perform: *Don't pull any tricks.* **15** *n.* influence; advantage: *He used political pull to get a job.* —**pull′er,** *n.*

pull down, to demolish; destroy: *pull down an old building.*

pull for, 1 to support with great enthusiasm. **2** to give help to.

pull in, to arrive: *They pulled in this morning.*

pull off, to do something successfully; succeed in.

pull out, to leave: *What time does the train pull out? It pulled out of the station an hour ago.*

pull over, to bring a vehicle to the side of the road or street and stop: *When our tire started going flat, we had to pull over and change it.*

pull through, to get through a difficult or dangerous situation.

pull up, to bring or come to a halt; stop.

pull yourself together, to gather your faculties, energy, etc.

SYNONYM STUDY **Pull, tug,** and **jerk**[1] all mean to make something move toward you. **Pull** is a general word: *He pulled his wagon up the hill.* **Tug** means to pull hard, sometimes stopping to rest between pulls: *She tugged at the rope until she got the anchor up.* **Jerk** means to pull quickly and suddenly: *The cook jerked his hand away from the hot stove.*

pul·let (pùl′it), *n.* a young hen, usually less than a year old.

pul·ley (pùl′ē), *n.* **1** wheel with a grooved rim in which a rope can run and so change the direction of a pull. It is a simple machine and is used to raise weights. **2** set of such wheels used to increase the power applied. ❑ *n., pl.* **pul·leys.**

Pull·man (pùl′mən), *n.* **1** sleeping car. **2** parlor car.

pull·out (pùl′out′), **1** *n.* withdrawal, especially of troops. **2** *n.* (of aircraft) the action of recovering from a dive and returning to level flight. **3** *n.* something that can be removed by pulling out, like a section of a newspaper. **4** *adj.* that pulls out: *a pullout shelf.* **5** *adj.* able to be removed by pulling out: *a pullout sports section.*

pull·o·ver (pùl′ō′vər), *n.* sweater or shirt put on by pulling it over the head.

pul·mo·nar·y (pul′mə ner′ē), *adj.* of or about the lungs. Pneumonia is a pulmonary disease.

pulp (pulp), **1** *n.* any soft, wet mass. Paper is made from wood that is ground to a pulp. **2** *n.* the soft, fleshy part of some fruits and vegetables. **3** *n.* the soft inner part of a tooth, containing blood vessels and nerves. **4** *v.* to make into pulp. **5** *n.* magazine printed on cheap paper, containing sensational stories of little literary value. —**pulp′like′,** *adj.*

pul·pit (pùl′pit), *n.* **1** platform or raised structure in a church from which the minister preaches. **2** preachers or preachings: *the influence of the pulpit.*

pulp·wood (pulp′wùd′), *n.* any soft wood suitable for reducing to pulp to make paper.

pulp·y (pul′pē), *adj.* like pulp; fleshy; soft. ❑ *adj.* **pulp·i·er, pulp·i·est.** —**pulp′i·ness,** *n.*

pul·sar (pul′sär), *n.* star that gives out a strong beam of radio waves. The beam reaches Earth very briefly at very short regular intervals. Pulsars are thought to be rapidly rotating neutron stars.

pul·sate (pul′sāt), *v.* **1** to beat; throb: *The patient's heart was pulsating rapidly.* **2** to vibrate; quiver. ❑ *v.* **pul·sat·ed, pul·sat·ing.**

a	hat	ė	term	ô	order	ch	child		
ā	age	i	it	oi	oil	ng	long		a in about
ä	far	ī	ice	ou	out	sh	she	ə	e in taken
â	care	o	hot	u	cup	th	thin		i in pencil
e	let	ō	open	ù	put	₮H	then		o in lemon
ē	equal	ò	saw	ü	rule	zh	measure		u in circus

pul·sa·tion (pul sā′shən), *n.* **1** act of beating; throbbing. **2** a beat; throb. **3** vibration; quiver.

pulse¹ (puls), **1** *n.* the regular beating of the arteries caused by the rush of blood into them after each contraction of the heart. By feeling a person's pulse in the artery of the wrist, you can count the number of times the heart beats each minute. **2** *n.* any regular, measured beat: *the pulse in music, the pulse of an engine.* **3** *v.* to beat; throb; vibrate: *My heart pulsed with excitement.* **4** *n.* feeling; sentiment: *the pulse of the nation.* ❑ *v.* **pulsed, puls·ing.**

pulse² (puls), *n.* **1** the seeds of plants such as peas, beans, and lentils, used as food. **2** any plant that has such seeds.

pul·ve·rize (pul′və rīz′), *v.* **1** to grind to powder or dust. **2** to become dust. **3** to break to pieces; demolish: *pulverize an enemy force, pulverize the hopes of the people.* ❑ *v.* **pul·ve·rized, pul·ve·riz·ing.** —**pul′ve·ri·za′tion,** *n.* —**pul′ve·riz′er,** *n.*

pu·ma (pyü′mə), *n.* mountain lion. ❑ *n., pl.* **pu·mas.**

pum·ice (pum′is), *n.* a light, porous lava used for cleaning, smoothing, and polishing.

pum·mel (pum′əl), *v.* to strike or beat; beat with the fists. ❑ *v.* **pum·meled, pum·mel·ing** or **pum·melled, pum·mel·ling.** ■ Another word that can sound like this is **pommel.**

pump¹ (pump), **1** *n.* machine for forcing liquids or gases into, through, or out of things: *a water pump, an oil pump.* **2** *v.* to move liquids, air, etc., by a pump. **3** *v.* to blow air into: *Pump up the car's tires.* **4** *v.* to remove water, etc., from by a pump: *Pump the well dry.* **5** *v.* to draw or force as if from a pump: *pump air into your lungs.* **6** *v.* to move by, or as if by, a pump handle: *to pump a person's hand.* **7** *v.* to get information out of; try to get information out of: *Don't let them pump you.* —**pump′er,** *n.*

pump² (pump), *n.* a low shoe with a thin sole and no fasteners.

pum·per·nick·el (pum′pər nik′əl), *n.* a heavy, dark, slightly sour bread made from whole, coarse rye.

pump·kin (pump′kin), *n.* the large, round, yellowish orange fruit of several trailing vines, used for making pies, as a vegetable, and for jack-o'-lanterns.

pun (pun), **1** *n.* a humorous use of a word where it can have different meanings, or of one word that sounds like another; play on words. **2** *v.* to make puns. ❑ *v.* **punned, pun·ning.**

> **WORD STORY** **Pun** is a short word with a clear meaning, and you might expect it to have a simple word story. In fact, it appeared in English suddenly, about 300 years ago. Where did it come from? No one knows.

punch¹ (def. 2)

punch¹ (punch), **1** *v.* to hit with the fist: *to punch someone on the arm.* **2** *n.* a quick thrust or blow with the fist. **3** *n.* tool for making holes. **4** *n.* tool or apparatus for piercing or stamping materials, impressing a design, etc. **5** *v.* to pierce, cut, stamp, or make with a punch: *punch tickets.* **6** *v.* to press a key, lever, etc., in order to make something happen: *punch data into a computer.* **7** *v.* to herd or drive cattle. ❑ *n., pl.* **punch·es.** —**punch′er,** *n.*

punch in, to get to a place of work: *Mom likes to punch in early on Fridays so she can have a longer weekend.*

punch out, to leave a place of work: *He punches out at 4:30.*

telegraph a punch, to make something obvious that should be kept secret, as a surprise.

punch² (punch), *n.* drink made of different liquids, often fruit juices or carbonated beverages, mixed together. ❑ *n., pl.* **punch·es.** [**Punch**² probably comes from a Sanskrit word meaning "five," because it was originally a drink made with five ingredients.]

Punch (punch), *n.* a hook-nosed, hunchbacked doll who quarrels violently with his wife Judy in the puppet show *Punch and Judy.*

pleased as Punch, very much pleased.

punch card, card on which information could be recorded by means of holes punched according to a code, formerly used in processing data by computers.

punch-drunk (punch′drungk′), *adj.* **1** (of a boxer) uncoordinated in movement, speech, etc., as the result of a brain concussion. **2** INFORMAL. dazed.

punching bag, a leather bag, filled with air or stuffed, and hung from the ceiling. Punching bags are hit with the fists for exercise or to develop boxing skills.

punch line, the line or sentence in a joke, story, play, or drama which makes or enforces the point.

punch·y (pun′chē), *adj.* INFORMAL. (of a boxer) uncoordinated in movement or speech because of brain concussion. ❑ *adj.* **punch·i·er, punch·i·est.**

punc·til·i·ous (pungk til′ē əs), *adj.* **1** very careful and exact: *punctilious in details.* **2** paying strict attention to details of conduct and ceremony. —**punc·til′i·ous·ly,** *adv.* —**punc·til′i·ous·ness,** *n.*

punc·tu·al (pungk′chü əl), *adj.* on time; prompt: *She is punctual to the minute.* [See Word Story at **punctuation.**] —**punc·tu·al·i·ty** (pungk′chü al′ə tē), **punc′tu·al·ness,** *n.* —**punc′tu·al·ly,** *adv.*

punc·tu·ate (pungk′chü āt), *v.* **1** to use periods, commas, and other marks in writing or printing to help make the meaning clear. **2** to put punctuation marks in. **3** to interrupt now and then: *a speech punctuated with cheers.* **4** to give point or emphasis to: *She punctuated her remarks with gestures.* ❑ *v.* **punc·tu·at·ed, punc·tu·at·ing.** —**punc′tu·a′tor,** *n.*

punc·tu·a·tion (pungk′chü ā′shən), *n.* **1** use of periods, commas, and other marks to help make the meaning of a sentence clear. Punctuation does for writing and printing what pauses and changes of voice do for speech. **2** punctuation marks.

> **WORD STORY** **Punctuation** and **punctual** both come from a Latin word meaning "a point." Punctuation marks are points (and short lines) that show meaning. A punctual person does things at the point in time they should be done.

punctuation mark, mark used in writing or printing to help make the meaning clear. Periods, commas, question marks, colons, etc., are punctuation marks.

punc·ture (pungk′chər), **1** *n.* hole made by something pointed. **2** *v.* to make such a hole in. **3** *v.* to have or get a puncture. **4** *n.* act or process of puncturing. **5** *v.* to reduce, spoil, or destroy as if by a puncture: *His pride was punctured by repeated criticisms.* ❑ *v.* **punc·tured, punc·tur·ing.** —**punc′tur·er,** *n.*

pun·dit (pun′dit), *n.* a very learned person; expert; authority.

pun·gen·cy (pun′jən sē), *n.* sharpness of taste, smell, feeling, etc.: *the pungency of pepper, the pungency of wit.*

pun·gent (pun′jənt), *adj.* **1** sharply affecting the organs of taste and smell: *a pungent pickle.* **2** sharp; biting: *pungent criticism.* **3** stimulating to the mind; keen; lively: *a pungent wit.* —**pun′gent·ly,** *adv.*

pun·ish (pun′ish), *v.* **1** to cause pain, loss, or discomfort to for some fault or offense: *punish criminals for wrongdoing.* **2** to cause pain, loss, or discomfort for: *The law punishes crimes.* **3** to deal with severely, roughly, or greedily: *punish a car by very fast driving.* —**pun′ish·er,** *n.*

pun·ish·a·ble (pun′i shə bəl), *adj.* **1** liable to punishment. **2** deserving punishment.

pun·ish·ment (pun′ish mənt), *n.* **1** act of punishing or condition of being punished. **2** penalty given for a fault or offense: *Her punishment for speeding was a fine.* **3** severe or rough treatment.

pu·ni·tive (pyü′nə tiv), *adj.* **1** of or about punishment: *punitive laws.* **2** inflicting punishment: *a punitive job review.* —**pu′ni·tive·ly,** *adv.* —**pu′ni·tive·ness,** *n.*

punk[1] (pungk), *n.* **1** a preparation that burns very slowly. A stick of punk is used to light fireworks. **2** decayed wood used as tinder.

punk[2] (pungk), INFORMAL. **1** *n.* a young hoodlum. **2** *n.* a young, inexperienced person. **3** *adj.* having to do with punk rock or punk rockers. **4** *n.* a young person who enjoys unusual, rough hairstyles, makeup, and clothing. **5** *adj.* poor or bad in quality.

punk rock, a kind of rock music that is performed in a very loud, furious, and energetic style. Punk rock songs often express violence and rudeness. —**punk′-rock′,** *adj.* —**punk rocker.**

pun·ster (pun′stər), *n.* person fond of making puns.

punt (punt), **1** *v.* to kick a ball before it touches the ground after dropping it. **2** *n.* a kick made this way. —**punt′er,** *n.*

pu·ny (pyü′nē), *adj.* **1** of less than usual size and strength; small and weak. **2** petty; not important. ❑ *adj.* **pu·ni·er, pu·ni·est.** [**Puny** comes from French words meaning "afterwards" and "born." A younger animal is smaller and weaker than an older one.] —**pu′ni·ness,** *n.*

punt

pup (pup), *n.* **1** a young dog; puppy. **2** a young fox, wolf, seal, etc.

pu·pa (pyü′pə), *n.* **1** stage between the larva and the adult in the development of many insects. **2** insect in this stage. Most pupae are inactive and some are enclosed in a tough case or cocoon. ❑ *n., pl.* **pu·pae** (pyü′pē), **pu·pas.** [See Word Story at **puppet.**] —**pu′pal,** *adj.*

pu·pate (pyü′pāt), *v.* to become a pupa. ❑ *v.* **pu·pat·ed, pu·pat·ing.** —**pu·pa′tion,** *n.*

pu·pil[1] (pyü′pəl), *n.* person who is learning in school or being taught by someone. [See Word Story at **puppet.**]

pu·pil[2] (pyü′pəl), *n.* the opening in the center of the iris of the eye that looks like a black spot. The size of the pupil is controlled by the expansion and contraction of the iris. See picture at **eye.** [See Word Story at **puppet.**]

puppet show, play performed with puppets on a small stage.

pup·py (pup′ē), *n.* a young dog. ❑ *n., pl.* **pup·pies.** [See Word Story at **puppet.**]

pup tent, a small, low tent, usually for one or two persons.

pur·blind (pėr′blīnd′), *adj.* **1** nearly blind. **2** slow to understand. —**pur′blind′ly,** *adv.* —**pur′blind′ness,** *n.*

pur·chase (pėr′chəs), **1** *v.* to get by paying a price; buy: *We purchased a new car.* ■ See Synonym Study at **buy.** **2** *n.* act of buying: *the purchase of a new car.* **3** *n.* thing bought: *That hat was a good purchase.* **4** *v.* to get in return for something: *purchase safety at the cost of happiness.* **5** *n.* a firm hold to help move something or to keep from slipping: *Wind the rope twice around the tree to get a better purchase.* ❑ *v.* **pur·chased, pur·chas·ing.** —**pur′chas·a·ble,** *adj.* —**pur′chas·er,** *n.*

pure (pyùr), *adj.* **1** not mixed with anything else; unadulterated; genuine: *pure gold.* **2** perfectly clean; spotless: *pure hands.* **3** perfect; correct; without defects: *speak pure French.* **4** nothing else than; mere; sheer: *pure accident.* **5** with no evil; without sin; chaste: *a pure mind.* **6** concerned with theory rather than practical use; not applied; abstract: *pure mathematics.* ❑ *adj.* **pur·er, pur·est.** —**pure′ness,** *n.*

pure·bred (pyùr′bred′), *adj.* of pure breed or stock; having ancestors all of one breed: *purebred Holstein cows.*

pu·rée (pyù rā′ *or* pyù rē′), **1** *n.* food boiled to a pulp and pushed through a sieve. **2** *n.* a thick soup. **3** *v.* to make into a purée. ❑ *n., pl.* **pu·rées;** *v.* **pu·réed, pu·rée·ing.**

pure·ly (pyùr′lē), *adv.* **1** in a pure manner. **2** exclusively; entirely. **3** merely. **4** innocently; chastely.

pur·ga·tive (pėr′gə tiv), **1** *n.* medicine that causes emptying of the intestines. Castor oil is a purgative. **2** *adj.* purging; cleansing.

pur·ga·to·ry (pėr′gə tôr′ē), *n.* **1** (in Roman Catholic belief) a temporary condition or place in which the souls of those who have died repenting are purified from sin by punishment. **2** any condition or place of temporary suffering or punishment. ❑ *n., pl.* **pur·ga·to·ries** for 2. —**pur′ga·to′ri·al,** *adj.*

purge (pėrj), **1** *v.* to wash away all that is not clean; make clean. **2** *n.* act of purging. **3** *v.* to clear of any undesired thing or person: *purge a city of dishonest officials.* **4** *n.* elimination of undesired persons from a nation or party. **5** *v.* to empty the intestines. **6** *n.* medicine that purges. ❑ *v.* **purged, purg·ing.** —**purge′a·ble,** *adj.* —**purg′er,** *n.*

pu·ri·fy (pyùr′ə fī), *v.* **1** to make pure: *Filters are used to purify water.* **2** to become pure. ❑ *v.* **pu·ri·fied, pu·ri·fy·ing.** —**pur′i·fi·ca′tion,** *n.* —**pur′i·fi′er,** *n.*

P

puppets (def. 1)

pup·pet (pup′it), *n.* **1** figure made to look like a person or animal and moved by wires, strings, or the hands. **2** anybody who is not independent, waits to be told how to act, and does what somebody else says. —**pup′pet·like′,** *adj.*

Pur·im (pùr′im), *n.* a Jewish holiday, celebrated each year in February or March. It celebrates Esther's saving of the Jews from a massacre.

> **WORD STORY** **Puppet** comes from a Latin word meaning "doll" or "child." **Pupa, pupil**[1], **pupil**[2], and **puppy** come from the same Latin word. A pupa is sometimes like a doll or puppet of the adult insect. A pupil in school is usually a child. A pupil in the eye shows a little reflection of the person looking in, like a doll. And a puppy is like a doll of a dog.

> **WORD STORY** **Purim** comes from a Hebrew word for a marker that was used to decide something by chance. The man who planned the massacre of the Hebrews drew lots to decide what day to do it on.

pup·pet·eer (pup′ə tir′), *n.* person who works with puppets.

a	hat	ė	term	ô	order	ch	child		
ā	age	i	it	oi	oil	ng	long		a in about
ä	far	ī	ice	ou	out	sh	she		e in taken
â	care	o	hot	u	cup	th	thin	ə	i in pencil
e	let	ō	open	ù	put	ᴛʜ	then		o in lemon
ē	equal	ò	saw	ü	rule	zh	measure		u in circus

pur·ist (pyur′ist), *n.* person who is very careful or too careful about purity of language, behavior, rules, etc. A purist of language dislikes slang and all expressions that are not formally correct.

Pur·i·tan (pyur′ə tən), **1** *n.* member of a group in the Church of England during the 1500s and 1600s who wanted simpler forms of worship and stricter morals. Many Puritans settled in New England. **2** *adj.* of or about the Puritans. **3** *n.* **puritan,** person who is very strict in morals and religion.

pur·i·tan·ic (pyur′ə tan′ik), *adj.* puritanical.

Pur·i·tan·i·cal (pyur′ə tan′ə kəl), *adj.* **1** of, about, or like the Puritans. **2** **puritanical,** of or like a puritan; very strict or too strict in morals or religion.

Pur·i·tan·ism (pyur′ə tə niz′əm), *n.* **1** the principles and practices of the Puritans. **2** **puritanism,** puritanical behavior or principles.

pur·i·ty (pyur′ə tē), *n.* **1** freedom from dirt or other substances; clearness; cleanness: *They tested the purity of the town's drinking water.* **2** freedom from evil; innocence: *a person of goodness and purity.* **3** careful correctness: *purity of style.*

purl[1] (pėrl), **1** *v.* to flow with rippling motions and a murmuring sound: *A shallow brook purls.* **2** *n.* a purling motion or sound. ■ Another word that sounds like this is **pearl.**

purl[2] (pėrl), *v.* to knit with inverted stitches. ■ Another word that sounds like this is **pearl.**

pur·loin (pər loin′), *v.* to steal. —**pur·loin′er,** *n.*

pur·ple (pėr′pəl), **1** *n.* a dark color made by mixing red and blue. **2** *adj.* of this color. **3** *adj., n.* crimson. This was the ancient meaning of purple. **4** *n.* purple cloth or clothing, especially as worn by emperors, kings, etc., to indicate high rank. **5** *n.* imperial, royal, or high rank. A prince is born to the purple. **6** *adj.* imperial; royal. **7** *v.* to make or become purple. ❑ *v.* **pur·pled, pur·pling.**

Purple Heart, medal awarded to members of the armed forces of the United States for wounds received in action against an enemy or as a result of enemy action.

WORD STORY The **Purple Heart** was originally a heart-shaped badge made of purple cloth, given for military bravery. George Washington created the award in 1782. In 1932, the Purple Heart was recreated as a medal for being wounded or killed by enemy forces.

purple martin, a large American swallow. The male has glossy blue-black feathers.

pur·plish (pėr′plish), *adj.* somewhat purple.

pur·port (pər pôrt′ *for verb;* pėr′pôrt *for noun*), **1** *v.* to claim or profess: *The document purported to be official.* **2** *v.* to have as its main idea; mean: *a paper purporting certain facts.* **3** *n.* meaning; main idea: *What was the purport of the letter?* —**pur·port′ed·ly,** *adv.*

pur·pose (pėr′pəs), **1** *n.* something you have in mind to get or do; plan; aim; intention. ■ See Synonym Study at **intention.** **2** *n.* object or end for which a thing is made, done, used, etc. **3** *v.* to plan; aim; intend. ❑ *v.* **pur·posed, pur·pos·ing.**

on purpose, with a purpose; not by accident.

to good purpose, with good results.

to little purpose or **to no purpose,** with few or no results.

pur·pose·ful (pėr′pəs fəl), *adj.* having a purpose: *She hurried about in a purposeful way, getting her work done quickly.* —**pur′pose·ful·ly,** *adv.* —**pur′pose·ful·ness,** *n.*

pur·pose·less (pėr′pəs lis), *adj.* lacking a purpose. —**pur′pose·less·ly,** *adv.* —**pur′pose·less·ness,** *n.*

pur·pose·ly (pėr′pəs lē), *adv.* on purpose; intentionally: *Did you leave the door open purposely?*

purr (pėr), **1** *n.* a low, murmuring sound, such as a cat makes when pleased. **2** *v.* to make this sound. ■ Another word that can sound like this is **per.**

purse (pėrs), **1** *n.* a small bag or container to hold small change, usually carried in a handbag or pocket. **2** *n.* handbag. **3** *n.* money; resources; treasury. **4** *n.* sum of money: *A purse was made up for the victims of the fire.* **5** *v.* to draw together; press into folds or wrinkles: *She pursed her lips and frowned.* ❑ *v.* **pursed, purs·ing.** [**Purse** comes from a Greek word meaning "a skin." Leather is made from animal skins, and the earliest purses were leather money bags.]

purs·er (pėr′sər), *n.* a ship's officer who keeps accounts, pays wages, and attends to the welfare and comfort of passengers.

pur·su·ance (pər sü′əns), *n.* act of carrying out; pursuit: *In pursuance of her duty, the lifeguard risked her life.*

pur·su·ant (pər sü′ənt), *prep.* **pursuant to,** acting according to; in accordance with.

pur·sue (pər sü′), *v.* **1** to follow to catch or kill; chase: *The dogs pursued the rabbit.* **2** to proceed along; follow: *He pursued a wise course by taking no chances.* **3** to strive for; try to get; seek: *pursue pleasure.* **4** to carry on; keep on with: *She pursued the study of botany.* **5** to continue to annoy or trouble: *pursue a teacher with questions.* ❑ *v.* **pur·sued, pur·su·ing.** —**pur·su′er,** *n.*

pur·suit (pər süt′), *n.* **1** act of pursuing; chase: *The dog is in pursuit of the cat.* **2** what one does, as a profession, business, recreation, etc.; occupation: *Fishing is her favorite pursuit; reading is mine.*

pur·vey (pər vā′), *v.* to supply food or provisions; provide; furnish: *purvey meat for an army.* ❑ *v.* **pur·vey, pur·vey·ing.**

pur·vey·or (pər vā′ər), *n.* **1** person who supplies provisions: *a purveyor of fine foods and meats.* **2** person who supplies anything: *a purveyor of gossip.*

pus (pus), *n.* a thick, yellowish white fluid formed in sores, abscesses, and other infected tissues in the body. It consists of dead white blood cells, bacteria, etc.

push (pùsh), **1** *v.* to move something away by pressing against it: *Push the door; don't pull it.* **2** *v.* to press hard: *We pushed with all our might.* **3** *v.* to thrust: *Trees push their roots down into the ground.* **4** *v.* to go forward by force: *We pushed through the crowd.* **5** *v.* to make go forward; urge: *Please push this job and get it done this week.* **6** *v.* to extend: *The railroad pushed its tracks across the prairie.* **7** *v.* to urge the use or purchase of: *That manufacturer is pushing its small cars this year.* **8** *n.* INFORMAL. force; energy; power to succeed: *She has plenty of push.* **9** *n.* act of pushing: *Give the door a push.* **10** *n.* hard effort; determined advance. ❑ *n., pl.* **push·es.**

push around, to treat roughly or with contempt; bully.

push off, to move from shore: *We pushed off in the boat.*

push on, to keep going; proceed.

SYNONYM STUDY **Push, shove,** and **thrust** all mean to move something away from you. **Push** is a general word: *She pushed the door open and stepped outside.* **Shove** means to push hard: *Please help me shove this desk into the next room.* **Thrust** means to push hard and quickly: *After thrusting his papers quickly into his briefcase, he ran for the bus.*

push button, a small button or knob pushed to turn an electric current on or off.

push·cart (pùsh′kärt′), *n.* a light cart pushed by hand.

push·er (pùsh′ər), *n.* **1** person who sells drugs illegally. **2** person or thing that pushes.

push·o·ver (pùsh′ō′vər), *n.* INFORMAL. **1** person very easy to beat in a contest. **2** something very easy to do.

push·up (pùsh′up′), *n.* exercise done by lying face down and raising the body with the arms while keeping the back straight and the toes on the ground.

push·y (pùsh′ē), *adj.* forward; aggressive. ❑ *adj.* **push·i·er, push·i·est.** —**push′i·ly,** *adv.* —**push′i·ness,** *n.*

puss (pùs), *n.* cat. ❑ *n., pl.* **puss·es.**

puss·y (pùs′ē), *n.* **1** cat. **2** catkin. ❑ *n., pl.* **puss·ies.**

puss·y·foot (pùs′ē fùt′), *v.* **1** to move softly and cautiously to avoid being seen. **2** to be cautious and timid about revealing your opinions or committing yourself.

pussy willow, a small American willow with silky catkins that bloom early in spring.

pus·tule (pus′chùl), *n.* a small, pus-filled bump on the skin.

put (pùt), *v.* **1** to cause to be in some place or position; place; lay: *Put away your toys.* **2** to cause to be in some state, condition, position, relation, etc.: *Put your room in order. We put our house on the market.* **3** to express: *The teacher puts things clearly.* **4** to set at a particular place, point, amount, etc., in a scale of estimation; appraise: *He puts the distance at five miles.* **5** to apply: *I put my writing skill to good use.* **6** to impose: *put a tax on gasoline.* **7** to throw or cast a heavy metal ball from the hand placed close to the shoulder: *to put the shot.* ❏ *v.* **put, put·ting.**

put about, (of a ship) to change direction.

put across, 1 to carry out successfully. **2** to get accepted or understood: *He could not put across his point of view to the audience.*

put away or **put by,** to save for future use.

put down, 1 to put an end to; suppress: *The rebellion was quickly put down.* **2** to write down. **3** to slight or belittle; snub.

put forth, 1 to grow; sprout; issue: *put forth buds.* **2** to use fully; exert: *put forth effort.*

put forward, to propose or submit for consideration, deliberation, etc.

put in, 1 to spend time as specified: *put in a full day of work.* **2** to enter a place for safety, supplies, etc.: *The ship put in at Singapore.* **3** to make a claim, plea, or offer: *put in for a loan.*

put off, 1 to lay aside; postpone: *We put off our meeting for a week.* **2** to cause to wait: *She refused to be put off any longer.* **3** to offend: *His sarcastic comments put people off.*

put on, 1 to present on a stage; produce: *The class put on a play.* **2** to take on or add to yourself: *put on weight.* **3** to assume or take on, especially as a pretense: *I put on an expression of innocence.* **4** to apply or exert: *They put on pressure to try to make me change my mind.* **5** to mislead deliberately: *I can't believe you won the lottery—you're putting me on.*

put out, 1 to extinguish; make an end to; destroy: *put out a fire, put out your eye.* **2** to go; turn; proceed: *The ship put out to sea.* **3** to offend; provoke: *I was quite put out by her lateness.* **4** to cause to be out in a game. **5** to publish. **6** to inconvenience someone: *I'm not going to put myself out for her anymore.*

put over, 1 to carry out successfully. **2** to do or carry out by trickery.

put through, to carry out successfully.

put to it, to force to a course; put in difficulty.

put up, 1 to offer: *put up a house for sale.* **2** to give or show: *put up a brave front.* **3** to build: *Several new houses were put up across the street from ours.* **4** to lay aside work. **5** to propose for election or adoption: *His name was put up for president of the club.* **6** to preserve food by canning or other means: *We put up six jars of blackberry jam.* **7** to give lodging or food to.

put upon, to take advantage of; impose upon; victimize.

put up to, to stir up; incite: *put someone up to mischief.*

put up with, to bear with patience; tolerate.

put-down (pút′doun′), *n.* **1** act of humiliating or belittling someone or something. **2** comment intended to humiliate or belittle.

put-on (pút′on′), **1** *adj.* assumed; affected; pretended: *a put-on air of innocence.* **2** *n.* a pretense or affectation: *Those tears were a put-on.* **3** INFORMAL. joke or trick played for fun on someone; practical joke.

put-out (pút′out′), *n.* (in baseball) act of putting out a batter or base runner.

pu·tre·fac·tion (pyü′trə fak′shən), *n.* decay; rotting.

pu·tre·fy (pyü′trə fī), *v.* to decay by the action of bacteria and fungi, producing bad-smelling gases; rot. ❏ *v.* **pu·tre·fied, pu·tre·fy·ing.**

pu·trid (pyü′trid), *adj.* **1** decaying; rotten: *putrid meat.* **2** caused by rot; foul: *a putrid odor.* **—pu′trid·ly,** *adv.* **—pu′trid·ness,** *n.*

putt (put), **1** *v.* to strike a golf ball gently and carefully in an effort to make it roll into the hole. **2** *n.* the stroke itself.

put·ter[1] (put′ər), *v.* to keep busy in an aimless or useless way: *I like to putter in the garden.* **—put′ter·er,** *n.*

putt·er[2] (put′ər), *n.* **1** a golf club used in putting. **2** person who putts.

put·ter[3] (put′ər), *n.* person or thing that puts.

putt·ing green (put′ing), the very smooth turf around the hole into which a player putts a golf ball.

put·ty (put′ē), **1** *n.* a soft, doughlike mixture of powdered chalk and linseed oil, used for fastening panes of glass in window frames and to fill holes and cracks in walls and woodwork. **2** *v.* to stop up or cover with putty: *We puttied the holes in the woodwork.* ❏ *v.* **put·tied, put·ty·ing. —put′ti·er,** *n.*

put-up·on (pút′ə pon′), *adj.* taken advantage of: *She feels put-upon by his expectation that she will listen to all his problems.*

puz·zle (puz′əl), **1** *n.* a hard problem: *How to get all my things into one suitcase is a puzzle.* ▪ See Synonym Study at **mystery. 2** *n.* problem or task to be done for fun: *This puzzle has seven*

pieces of wood you fit together. **3** *v.* to make unable to answer, solve, or understand something; perplex: *How the cat got out puzzled us.* **4** *v.* to be perplexed. **5** *v.* to exercise your mind on something hard: *She likes a mystery story that can keep her puzzling.* ❏ *v.* **puz·zled, puz·zling. —puz′zled·ly,** *adv.* **—puz′zler,** *n.* **—puz′zling·ly,** *adv.*

puzzle out, to find out by thinking or trying hard.

puzzle over, to think hard about; try hard to do or work out: *I puzzled over a hard math problem for a long time.*

puz·zle·ment (puz′əl mənt), *n.* puzzled condition.

Pvt., Private.

PWA or **P.W.A.,** Public Works Administration.

PX, post exchange (store on a military post where only military personnel and their dependents may buy goods and services).

pyg·my (pig′mē), **1** *n.* Pygmy, one of a group of people of equatorial Africa who are less than five feet (1.5 meters) tall. **2** *adj.* Pygmy, of or about the Pygmies. **3** *n.* a very small person; dwarf. **4** *adj.* very small: *a pygmy marmoset.* ❏ *n., pl.* **Pyg·mies** for 1, **pyg·mies** for 3. Also, **pigmy.**

> **USAGE NOTE** **Pygmy** is not the name used by these African people for themselves. It comes from a Greek word meaning "very short." Many of them, and the people who study or work with them, dislike the name and prefer specific local names which they use for themselves. If you are discussing these people, it is wise to consider your source and your audience. Used about a small person of other background, **pygmy** is often considered offensive.

pygmy chimpanzee, bonobo.

py·ja·mas (pə jä′məz *or* pə jam′əz), *n.pl.* BRITISH. pajamas.

py·lon (pī′lon), *n.* **1** a tall steel framework used to carry high-tension wires across country. **2** post or tower for guiding aviators. **3** one of a pair of high supporting structures that marks an entrance at either end of a bridge. **4** gateway, particularly to an ancient Egyptian temple, usually consisting of two huge towers.

py·lo·rus (pī lôr′əs), *n.* the opening that leads from the stomach into the intestine. ❏ *n., pl.* **py·lo·ri** (pī lôr′ī′).

Pyong·yang (pyung′yäng′), *n.* capital of North Korea, in the SW part.

py·or·rhe·a (pī′ə rē′ə), *n.* disease of the gums in which pockets of pus form about the teeth, the gums shrink, and the teeth become loose. **—py′or·rhe′al,** *adj.*

pyr·a·mid (pir′ə mid), **1** *n.* a solid figure having a polygon for a base and triangular sides which meet in a point. **2** *n.* anything having the form of a pyramid: *a pyramid of stones.* **3** *v.* to put in the form of a pyramid. **4** *v.* to raise or increase costs, wages, etc., gradually. **5** *n.pl.* **Pyramids,** the huge, massive stone pyramids, serving as royal tombs, built by the ancient Egyptians.

pyramid (def. 2) **Pyramids** (def. 5)

a	hat	ė	term	ô	order	ch	child		
ā	age	i	it	oi	oil	ng	long		a in about
ä	far	ī	ice	ou	out	sh	she	ə {	e in taken
â	care	o	hot	u	cup	th	thin		i in pencil
e	let	ō	open	u̇	put	⊥H	then		o in lemon
ē	equal	ȯ	saw	ü	rule	zh	measure		u in circus

P

py·ram·i·dal (pə ram′ə dəl), *adj.* shaped like a pyramid. **—py·ram′i·dal·ly,** *adv.*

pyre (pīr), *n.* pile of wood for burning a dead body.

Pyr·e·ne·an (pir′ə nē′ən), *adj.* of or about the Pyrenees.

Pyr·e·nees (pir′ə nēz′), *n.pl.* mountain range between France and Spain.

py·re·thrum (pī rē′thrəm), *n.* **1** any of several chrysanthemums with beautiful white, light purple, or red flowers. **2** an insect poison made from the powdered flower heads of two of these plants.

Py·rex (pī′reks), *n.* trademark for a kind of glassware that will not break when heated.

pyr·i·dox·ine (pir′ə dok′sēn′), *n.* vitamin necessary to human nutrition, found in wheat germ, fish, liver, etc.; vitamin B_6. Pyridoxine is an enzyme important in metabolism.

py·rite (pī′rit), *n.* a yellow mineral, a compound of iron and sulfur, which is often mistaken for gold; fool's gold. It is used to make sulfuric acid.

py·ri·tes (pī rī′tēz *or* pī′rīts), *n.* any of various chemical compounds of sulfur and a metal, such as tin pyrites, an ore of tin. ❏ *n., pl.* **py·ri·tes.**

py·ro·ma·ni·a (pī′rə mā′nē ə), *n.* an uncontrollable desire to set things on fire.

py·ro·ma·ni·ac (pī′rə mā′nē ak), *n.* person with an uncontrollable desire to set things on fire.

py·ro·tech·nic (pī′rə tek′nik), *adj.* **1** of or about fireworks: *a pyrotechnic display.* **2** resembling fireworks; brilliant; sensational: *pyrotechnic eloquence.* **—py′ro·tech′ni·cal·ly,** *adv.*

py·ro·tech·ni·cal (pī′rə tek′nə kəl), *adj.* pyrotechnic.

py·ro·tech·nics (pī′rə tek′niks), *n.* **1** the making of fireworks. **2** use of fireworks. **3** display of fireworks. **4** a brilliant or sensational display.

Pyr·rhic victory (pir′ik), victory won at too great a cost. [**Pyrrhic victory** comes from King Pyrrhus (pir′əs), who defeated the ancient Romans in a battle that wounded or killed almost all his soldiers.]

Py·thag·or·as (pə thag′ər əs), *n.* 582?-500? B.C., Greek philosopher, religious teacher, and mathematician. The Pythagorean theorem is named for him. He believed that people's souls were immortal and that after death souls move to another human or animal body.

Py·thag·o·re·an (pə thag′ə rē′ən), **1** *adj.* of or about Pythagoras, his teachings, or his followers. **2** *n.* a follower of Pythagoras.

Pythagorean theorem, theorem that the square of the hypotenuse of a right triangle equals the sum of the squares of the other two sides.

python—up to 30 ft. (9 m) long

py·thon (pī′thon), *n.* any of several very large snakes of Asia, Africa, and Australia that kill prey by squeezing and stopping breath.

Q or **q** (kyü), *n.* the 17th letter of the English alphabet. *Q* is followed by *u* in most English words. ❑ *n., pl.* **Q's** or **q's.**

Qad·da·fi (kä dä′fē), *n.* **Mu·am·mar al-** (mü ä mär′ äl), born 1942, Libyan political leader since 1969. He became the leader of Libya after he led a military overthrow of the king. Also, **Khadafy, Gadhafi.**

Qa·tar (kä′tär), *n.* country in E Arabia. *Capital:* Doha.

Q.E.D., which was to be proved.

qt., quart. ❑ *pl.* **qt.** or **qts.**

quack[1] (kwak), **1** *n.* the sound a duck makes. **2** *v.* to make such a sound.

WORD STORY   Most words that are spelled with **q** come from Latin. Latin had no letter *w*, so Romans used the letter *v* for that sound. However, they also used the letter *v* for the sound of *u*. To keep from getting confused, they added *q* to their alphabet and used *qu* for the sound spelled *kw* here. This is why *q* is still followed by *u* in English. Old English spelled this sound as *cw*, but after the Norman Conquest the spelling was changed to look like French and Latin, so that a *cwen* became a *queen.*

quack[2] (kwak), **1** *n.* a dishonest person who pretends to be a doctor. **2** *n.* an ignorant pretender to knowledge or skill of any sort. **3** *adj.* used by quacks: *quack medicine.*

WORD STORY   **Quack**[2] comes from an old Dutch word meaning "to brag." That word probably came from the sound a duck makes, because ducks are often noisy for no good reason.

quack·er·y (kwak′ər ē), *n.* methods or behavior of a quack.

quad (kwäd), *n.* **1** quadrangle. **2** INFORMAL. quadruplet. **3** INFORMAL. quadriceps.

quadr-, *prefix.* four: *quadrangle = shape with four angles.*

quad·ran·gle (kwäd′rang′gəl), *n.* **1** a four-sided space or court wholly or nearly surrounded by buildings: *the quadrangle of a palace, a college quadrangle.* **2** buildings around a quadrangle. **3** a plane figure with four angles and four sides; quadrilateral.

quad·rant (kwäd′rənt), *n.* **1** quarter of the circumference of a circle; arc of 90 degrees. **2** the area contained by such an arc and two radii drawn perpendicular to each other. **3** one of the four parts into which a plane is divided by two perpendicular lines. **4** device with a scale of 90 degrees, used in astronomy, navigation, and surveying for measuring altitudes.

quad·ra·phon·ic (kwäd′rə fon′ik), *adj.* of or referring to the recording or the reproduction of sound, using four separate channels instead of two as in ordinary stereo transmission.

qua·drat·ic (kwä drat′ik), *adj.* **1** of or like a square. **2** of or about an equation in which one or more of the terms is squared. $x^2 + 3x + 2 = 12$ is a quadratic equation.

a	hat	ė	term	ô	order	ch	child		
ā	age	i	it	oi	oil	ng	long		a in about
ä	far	ī	ice	ou	out	sh	she		e in taken
â	care	o	hot	u	cup	th	thin	ə	i in pencil
e	let	ō	open	ů	put	ŦH	then		o in lemon
ē	equal	ò	saw	ü	rule	zh	measure		u in circus

701

qua·dren·ni·al (kwä dren′ē əl), *adj.* **1** occurring every four years: *The United States has a quadrennial presidential election.* **2** lasting for four years. **—qua·dren′ni·al·ly,** *adv.*

quad·ri·ceps (kwäd′rə seps), *n.* the large muscle of the front of the thigh. It straightens the leg. □ *n., pl.* **quad·ri·ceps.**

quad·ri·lat·er·al (kwäd′rə lat′ər əl), **1** *adj.* having four sides and four angles. **2** *n.* a plane figure having four sides and four angles. Squares and rectangles are quadrilaterals.

qua·drille (kwä dril′), *n.* **1** a square dance for four couples that usually has five parts or movements. **2** music for such a dance.

qua·dril·lion (kwä dril′yən), *n.* **1** (in the United States and France) 1 followed by 15 zeros; one thousand trillions. **2** (in Great Britain) 1 followed by 24 zeros; one million trillions.

quad·ri·ple·gic (kwäd′rə plē′jik), *n.* someone with paralysis of both arms and both legs.

quad·ru·ped (kwäd′rə ped), *n.* animal that has four feet.

qua·dru·ple (kwä drü′pəl), **1** *adj.* consisting of four parts; including four parts or parties; fourfold: *a quadruple agreement.* **2** *adj., adv.* four times; four times as great. **3** *n.* number, amount, etc., four times as great as another: *80 is the quadruple of 20.* **4** *v.* to make or become four times as great. □ *v.* **qua·dru·pled, qua·dru·pling.**

qua·dru·plet (kwä drü′plit), *n.* **1** one of four children born at the same time to the same mother. **2** any group or combination of four.

quaff (kwäf *or* kwaf), *v.* to drink in large swallows; drink freely. **—quaff′er,** *n.*

quag·mire (kwag′mīr′), *n.* **1** soft, muddy ground; boggy or miry place. **2** a difficult situation.

qua·hog *or* **qua·haug** (kwô′-hòg′ *or* kwō′hòg′), *n.* a roundish clam of the Atlantic coast of North America. It is good to eat.

quail¹ (kwāl), *n.* any of various plump game birds belonging to the same family as the pheasant, especially the bobwhite. □ *n., pl.* **quail** *or* **quails.** **—quail′like′,** *adj.*

quail² (kwāl), *v.* to be afraid; lose courage; shrink back in fear: *The hikers quailed at the sight of a rattlesnake.*

quaint (kwānt), *adj.* strange or odd in an interesting, pleasing, or amusing way: *Many old photographs seem quaint to us today.* **—quaint′ly,** *adv.* **—quaint′ness,** *n.*

quail¹

WORD STORY Quaint comes from a Latin word meaning "known" or "learned." In old times, **quaint** meant "skilled" or "cunning" or "stylish." Styles change, and things that looked smart once look strange now.

quake (kwāk), **1** *v.* to shake; tremble: *I quaked with fear.* **2** *n.* act of shaking; trembling. **3** *n.* earthquake. □ *v.* **quaked, quak·ing.**

Quak·er (kwā′kər), *n.* member of a Christian group called the Society of Friends. Quakers favor simple religious services and are opposed to war and to taking oaths.

qual·i·fi·ca·tion (kwäl′ə fə kā′shən), *n.* **1** quality, skill, or ability that makes someone fit for a job, task, office, etc.: *A knowledge of trails is one qualification for a guide.* **2** modification; limitation; restriction: *She made the statement without qualification.*

qual·i·fied (kwäl′ə fīd), *adj.* **1** having the desirable or required qualifications; competent: *A qualified airplane pilot must have good eyesight and hold a license to fly.* **2** modified; limited: *His qualified answer was, "I will go, but only if you will come with me."*

qual·i·fi·er (kwäl′ə fī′ər), *n.* **1** person or thing that qualifies. **2** word that limits or modifies the meaning of another word. Adjectives and adverbs are qualifiers.

qual·i·fy (kwäl′ə fī), *v.* **1** to make competent: *qualify yourself for a job.* **2** to earn the right to have something: *qualify for a driver's license.* **3** to make less strong; change somewhat; limit; modify: *Qualify your statement that dogs are loyal by adding "usually."*

4 to limit or modify the meaning of: *Adverbs qualify verbs.* □ *v.* **qual·i·fied, qual·i·fy·ing.**

qual·i·ta·tive (kwäl′ə tā′tiv), *adj.* concerned with quality or qualities: *The qualitative facts about food have to do with vitamin content and nutritional value.* **—qual′i·ta′tive·ly,** *adv.*

qualitative analysis, a testing of a substance or mixture to find out what its chemical components are.

qual·i·ty (kwäl′ə tē), *n.* **1** something special about someone or something that makes it what it is; characteristic; attribute: *One quality of iron is hardness; one quality of sugar is sweetness. She has many fine qualities.* **2** nature, kind, or character of something: *the quality of a sound, the refreshing quality of a drink.* **3** grade of excellence; degree of worth: *food of poor quality.* **4** fineness; merit; excellence: *Look for quality rather than quantity.* **5** high rank; good or high social position: *people of quality.* □ *n., pl.* **qual·i·ties** for 1,2.

qualm (kwäm *or* kwòm), *n.* **1** a sudden disturbing feeling in the mind; uneasiness; misgiving; doubt: *I tried the test with some qualms.* **2** disturbance or scruple of conscience: *I had no qualms about neglecting my work on such a sunny day.* **3** a momentary feeling of faintness or nausea.

Qua·nah (kwä′nə), *n.* 1845-1911, Comanche Indian chief. ■ Quanah led warriors against the U.S. Army in 1875 to try to stop the killing of buffalo in Texas. He was the first chief to get U.S. citizenship for his people.

quan·dar·y (kwän′dər ē), *n.* state of doubtfulness or uncertainty; dilemma. □ *n., pl.* **quan·dar·ies.**

Quant (kwänt), *n.* **Mary,** born 1934, English fashion designer. She introduced the miniskirt in 1966.

quan·ti·fy (kwän′tə fī), *v.* to measure or express the quantity of something: *quantify public opinion by a poll.* □ *v.* **quan·ti·fied, quan·ti·fy·ing.**

quan·ti·ta·tive (kwän′tə tā′tiv), *adj.* **1** concerned with quantity or quantities. **2** measurable. **—quan′ti·ta′tive·ly,** *adv.*

quantitative analysis, a testing of a substance or mixture to find out the amounts and proportions of its chemical components.

quan·ti·ty (kwän′tə tē), *n.* **1** number; amount: *Use equal quantities of nuts and raisins in the cake.* **2** a large amount; large number: *The baker buys flour in quantity. She owns quantities of books.* **3** (in mathematics) figure or symbol which represents something having size, amount, extent, etc. □ *n., pl.* **quan·ti·ties.**

quan·tum (kwän′təm), **1** *n.* (in physics) the basic unit of radiant energy; the smallest amount in which energy can exist. Light and heat are given off and absorbed in quanta. **2** *adj.* (in physics) of or about quanta: *quantum theory.* **3** *adj.* involving totally different conditions; sudden; abrupt: *Automobiles brought a quantum change to society.* □ *n., pl.* **quan·ta** (kwän′tə).

quantum theory, theory that whenever radiant energy is transferred, the transfer occurs in pulsations rather than continuously, and that the amount transferred during each pulsation is a definite amount or quantum.

quar·an·tine (kwôr′ən tēn′ *or* kwär′ən tēn′), **1** *v.* to keep a person, animal, plant, ship, etc., away from others for a time to prevent the spread of an infectious disease: *People with smallpox were quarantined.* **2** *n.* condition of being quarantined: *The ship was in quarantine because several of the crew had smallpox.* **3** *n.* detention, isolation, and other measures taken to prevent the spread of an infectious disease. **4** *n.* place or time in which people, animals, plants, ships, etc., are held until it is sure that they have no infectious diseases, insect pests, etc. □ *v.* **quar·an·tined, quar·an·tin·ing.**

WORD STORY Quarantine comes from a Latin word meaning "forty." In old times, ships were forbidden to unload for forty days after reaching port, to prevent disease.

quark (kwôrk *or* kwärk), *n.* an elementary particle having an electric charge less than that of an electron. The several kinds of quarks are thought to form protons and neutrons.

quar·rel (kwôr′əl), **1** *n.* an angry dispute; a fight with words: *The children had a quarrel over the division of the candy.* **2** *v.* to fight with words; dispute or disagree angrily: *The two friends quar-*

reled and now they don't speak to each other. **3** *n.* cause for a dispute or disagreement; reason for breaking off friendly relations: *A bully likes to pick quarrels.* **4** *v.* to disagree: *Most people did not quarrel with the jury's decision.* ❑ *v.* **quar·reled, quar·rel·ing** or **quar·relled, quar·rel·ling. —quar′rel·er,** *n.*

quar·rel·some (kwôr′əl səm), *adj.* too ready to quarrel; fond of fighting and disputing: *a quarrelsome nature, a quarrelsome child.* **—quar′rel·some·ness,** *n.*

quar·ry[1] (kwôr′ē *or* kwär′ē), **1** *n.* place where stone is dug, cut, or blasted out for use in building. **2** *v.* to obtain from a quarry: *She watched the workers quarry out a huge block of stone.* ❑ *n., pl.* **quar·ries;** *v.* **quar·ried, quar·ry·ing. —quar′ri·er,** *n.*

> **WORD STORY** **Quarry**[1] comes from a Latin word meaning "a square." Blocks of stone cut from a quarry have straight edges and smooth surfaces. The hole has the same shape.

quar·ry[2] (kwôr′ē *or* kwär′ē), *n.* animal chased in a hunt; game; prey. ❑ *n., pl.* **quar·ries.**

quart (kwôrt), *n.* **1** unit of volume for liquids, equal to one fourth of a gallon: *a quart of milk.* **2** unit of capacity for dry things, equal to one eighth of a peck: *a quart of berries.* **3** container that holds a quart. [See Word Story at **quarter**.]

quar·ter (kwôr′tər), **1** *n.* one fourth; half of a half; one of four equal parts: *a quarter of an apple, a quarter of an hour.* **2** *v.* to divide into fourths: *She quartered the apple.* **3** *n.* coin of the United States and Canada equal to 25 cents. Four quarters make one dollar. **4** *n.* one of four equal periods of play in football, basketball, soccer, etc. **5** *n.* one fourth of a year; three months: *My bank pays interest every quarter.* **6** *n.* one fourth of a school year. **7** *n.* one of the four periods of the moon, lasting about seven days each. **8** *adj.* being one of four equal parts; being equal to one fourth of a whole. **9** *n.* a point of the compass; direction: *From what quarter did the wind blow?* **10** *n.* region; place; section: *the French quarter, visit a distant quarter of the globe.* **11** *n.* person or place not exactly identified: *Help came from many quarters.* **12** *n.pl.* **quarters,** place to live: *The circus has its winter quarters in the South.* **13** *v.* to give a place to live in: *Soldiers were quartered in all the houses of the town.* **14** *n.* mercy shown in sparing the life of a defeated enemy: *The pirates gave no quarter to their victims.* **15** *n.* one of the four legs of an animal, with its parts. **16** *n.* an assigned post or place to be, as on a ship: *sailors called to quarters.*

at close quarters, very close together; almost touching: *The cars had to pass at close quarters on the narrow road.*

> **WORD STORY** **Quarter** comes from a Latin word meaning "fourth." **Quart** comes from the same word. The meaning "a place to live," comes from the four main directions on a map: North, South, etc. People used **quarter** to mean "direction," "region," and then "neighborhood."

quar·ter·back (kwôr′tər bak′), *n.* an offensive back in football who stands directly behind the center. The quarterback begins each play by handing the ball to a running back, passing it to a teammate, or running with it.

quar·ter·deck (kwôr′tər dek′), *n.* part of the upper deck between the mainmast and the stern, used mostly by the officers of a ship.

quar·ter·fi·nal (kwôr′tər fī′nəl), **1** *adj.* of or about the four games, matches, or rounds that come before the semifinals and finals in a tournament. **2** *n.* Often, **quarterfinals,** *pl.* these four games.

quarter horse, a strong horse originally bred for racing on quarter-mile tracks, now used for herding cattle, playing polo, and riding.

quar·ter·ly (kwôr′tər lē), **1** *adj.* happening, done, etc., four times a year: *make quarterly payments on your insurance.* **2** *adv.* once each quarter of a year: *to pay your insurance premiums quarterly.* **3** *n.* magazine published every three months. ❑ *n., pl.* **quar·ter·lies.**

quar·ter·mas·ter (kwôr′tər mas′tər), *n.* **1** (in the army) an officer who has charge of providing quarters, clothing, fuel, transportation, etc., for troops. **2** (in the navy) a petty officer who has charge of the steering, the compasses, signals, etc., on a ship.

quarter note, (in music) a note played for one fourth as long a time as a whole note.

quar·ter·staff (kwôr′tər staf′), *n.* an old English weapon consisting of a stout pole 6 to 8 feet long, tipped with iron. ❑ *n., pl.* **quar·ter·staves** (kwôr′tər stāvz′).

quar·tet or **quar·tette** (kwôr tet′), *n.* **1** group of four singers or players performing together. **2** piece of music for four voices or instruments. **3** any group of four.

quar·to (kwôr′tō), **1** *n.* the page size of a book in which each leaf is one fourth of a whole sheet of paper. **2** *adj.* having this size. **3** *n.* book having this size. ❑ *n., pl.* **quar·tos.**

quartz (kwôrts), *n.* a very hard mineral made of silicon and oxygen and found in many different types of rocks, such as sandstone and granite. Crystals of pure quartz are colorless and transparent. Colored varieties of quartz include flint, jasper, agate, opal, and amethyst.

quartz

quartz·ite (kwôrts′sīt), *n.* a strong rock made of quartz, often formed from heavily compressed sandstone.

qua·sar (kwā′zär *or* kwā′sär), *n.* any of many astronomical objects, larger than stars but smaller than galaxies, thought to be the centers of extremely distant galaxies. Quasars produce extraordinarily powerful light and radio waves. [**Quasar** comes from the words **quasi-stellar.** *Quasi-stellar* means "like a star."]

quash[1] (kwosh), *v.* to put down; crush: *quash a revolt.*

quash[2] (kwosh), *v.* to make void; annul: *The judge quashed the charges against the defendant.*

qua·si (kwā′zī, kwā′sī, *or* kwä′sē), *adj.* seeming; not real; halfway: *quasi humor.*

quasi-, *prefix.* seemingly; somewhat; partly; sort of: *quasi-official = somewhat official.*

Qua·ter·nar·y (kwä′tər när′ē), *n.* (in geology) time between about two million years ago and now.

quat·rain (kwot′rān), *n.* stanza or poem of four lines.

qua·ver (kwā′vər), **1** *v.* to shake; tremble: *The old man's voice quavered.* **2** *v.* to sing or say in trembling tones. **3** *n.* act of shaking or trembling, especially of the voice. **4** *v.* to trill in singing or in playing on a musical instrument.

quay (kē *or* kā), *n.* a solid landing place for ships. ■ Other words that can sound like this are **cay** and **key.**

Que., Quebec.

quea·sy (kwē′zē), *adj.* **1** inclined to nausea; easily upset: *a queasy stomach.* **2** uneasy; uncomfortable. ❑ *adj.* **quea·si·er, quea·si·est. —quea′si·ly,** *adv.* **—quea′si·ness,** *n.*

Que·bec (kwi bek′ *or* kā′bek′), *n.* **1** province in E Canada. **2** its capital, on the St. Lawrence River. [**Quebec** comes from an Algonquian word meaning "where the river narrows."] **—Que·beck′er,** *n.*

Qué·béc·ois (kā′bek wä′), FRENCH. **1** *n.* Quebecker. **2** *adj.* of or for French-speaking Quebec or Quebeckers. ❑ *n., pl.* **Qué·béc·ois.**

que·bra·cho (kā brä′chō), *n.* a South American tree with very hard wood. The wood and sometimes the bark are used in tanning and dyeing. ❑ *n., pl.* **que·bra·chos.**

Quech·ua (kech′wä), *n.* member of an American Indian tribe that ruled the Inca empire. Forms of the Quechua language are spoken in the Andes Mountains region of South America. ❑ *n., pl.* **Quech·ua** or **Quech·uas. —Quech′uan,** *adj., n.*

> **WORD SOURCE** The **Quechua** language has given many words to the English language. The words below are some of them.

alpaca	guano	llama	puma
condor	jerk[2]	maté	quinine
guanaco	jerky[2]	pampas	vicuña

a	hat	ė	term	ô	order	ch	child
ā	age	i	it	oi	oil	ng	long
ä	far	ī	ice	ou	out	sh	she
â	care	o	hot	u	cup	th	thin
e	let	ō	open	ù	put	ᴛʜ	then
ē	equal	ò	saw	ü	rule	zh	measure

ə { a in about / e in taken / i in pencil / o in lemon / u in circus }

queen (kwēn), *n.* **1** wife of a king. **2** woman who rules a country and its people; female sovereign, usually with a hereditary position and with either limited or absolute power. **3** woman who is very important, stately, or beautiful: *the queen of society.* **4** a fully developed female in a colony of bees, ants, etc., that lays eggs. There is usually only one queen in a hive of bees. **5** a playing card bearing a picture of a queen. **6** the most powerful piece in chess. It can move in any straight or diagonal row across any number of empty squares.

Queen Anne's lace, a wild variety of the carrot, with lacy clusters of small, white flowers.

queen·ly (kwēn′lē), **1** *adj.* of or fit for a queen: *queenly rank or majesty.* **2** *adj.* like a queen; like a queen's: *queenly dignity.* **3** *adv.* in a queenly manner; as a queen does. ❑ *adj.* **queen·li·er, queen·li·est. —queen′li·ness,** *n.*

queen mother, widow of a former king and mother of a reigning king or queen.

Queens (kwēnz), *n.* borough of New York City, on Long Island, east of Brooklyn.

Queen's Birthday, Victoria Day.

Queen's Highway, (in Canada) a main road that the provincial government is responsible for maintaining.

queen-size (kwēn′sīz′), *adj.* larger than others of its kind, but smaller than king-size: *a queen-size mattress.*

Queens·land (kwēnz′lənd), *n.* state in E Australia. *Capital:* Brisbane.

queer (kwir), **1** *adj.* not usual or normal; strange; odd; peculiar: *That was a queer remark for him to make.* **2** *adj.* not well; faint; giddy: *The motion of the ship made him feel queer.* **3** *v.* INFORMAL. to spoil; ruin. **—queer′ly,** *adv.*

quell (kwel), *v.* to put down; subdue: *quell a riot.*

quench (kwench), *v.* **1** to put an end to; stop: *quench your thirst.* **2** to drown out; put out: *Water quenched the fire.*

Que·ré·ta·ro (ke re′tä rō′), *n.* a state in central Mexico.

quer·u·lous (kwer′ə ləs), *adj.* complaining; fretful: *Some people are very querulous when they are sick.* **—quer′u·lous·ly,** *adv.* **—quer′u·lous·ness,** *n.*

quer·y (kwir′ē), **1** *n.* a question; inquiry. **2** *v.* to ask; ask about; inquire into: *The teacher queried my reason for being late.* **3** *v.* to express doubt about: *Some of us queried the accuracy of the vote.* **4** *n.* the sign (?) put after a question or used to express doubt about something written or printed. ❑ *n., pl.* **quer·ies;** *v.* **quer·ied, quer·y·ing. —quer′i·er,** *n.*

quest (kwest), **1** *n.* a search or hunt: *She went to the library on a quest for something to read.* **2** *v.* to search or seek for; hunt. **3** *n.* expedition by knights in search of something: *There are many stories about the quests of King Arthur's knights.* **—quest′er,** *n.*

in quest of, trying to find; looking for: *In 1849 people rushed to California in quest of gold.*

ques·tion (kwes′chən), **1** *n.* thing asked in order to get information; inquiry: *The teacher answered the children's questions about the story.* **2** *v.* to ask in order to find out; seek information from: *Then the teacher questioned the children about what happened on the playground.* **3** *n.* matter of doubt or dispute; controversy: *A question arose about who owned the football.* **4** *v.* to doubt; dispute: *question the truth of a story.* **5** *n.* matter to be talked over, investigated, considered, etc.; problem: *Several family members raised the question of whether we need a new car.* **6** *n.* proposal to be voted on: *The president asked if the club members were ready for the question.* **7** *n.* act of asking: *to examine by question and answer.* **—ques′tion·er,** *n.* **—ques′tion·ing·ly,** *adv.*

beg the question, 1 to assume the idea that you should prove. **2** to avoid discussing what you can't prove.

beside the question, off the subject.

beyond question, without a doubt; not to be disputed: *The statements in that book are true beyond question.*

call in question, to dispute; challenge: *My honesty was called in question when they suggested I had cheated on the test.*

in question, 1 under consideration or discussion. **2** in dispute.

out of the question, not to be considered; impossible: *Our teacher said that postponing the test was out of the question.*

without question, without a doubt; not to be disputed: *That is without question a beautiful sunset.*

ques·tion·a·ble (kwes′chə nə bəl), *adj.* **1** open to question or dispute; doubtful; uncertain: *a questionable statement.* **2** of doubtful honesty, morality, etc.: *questionable behavior.* **—ques′tion·a·ble·ness,** *n.* **—ques′tion·a·bly,** *adv.*

question mark, mark (?) put after a question in writing or printing; interrogation mark.

ques·tion·naire (kwes′chə nâr′), *n.* a written or printed list of questions used to gather information, to obtain a sampling of opinion, etc.

quet·zal (ket säl′), *n.* any of four kinds of Central American birds, especially one kind with brilliant golden green and scarlet plumage. The male of this quetzal has long, flowing tail feathers. ❑ *n., pl.* **quet·zals.**

Quet·zal·co·a·tl (ket säl′kō-ät′l), *n.* Aztec god of learning and civilization, shown in the form of a feathered serpent. The Maya called him Kukulcan.

quetzal—tail feathers about 3 ft. (91 cm) long

queue (kyü), **1** *n.* a line of people, cars, etc.; cue: *There was a long queue in front of the theater.* **2** *v.* to form or stand in a long line; cue. **3** *n.* braid of hair hanging down from the back of the head. ❑ *v.* **queued, queu·ing** or **queue·ing.**

quib·ble (kwib′əl), **1** *n.* an unfair and petty evasion of the point or truth by using words with a double meaning: *a legal quibble.* **2** *v.* to evade the point or the truth by twisting the meaning of words. ❑ *v.* **quib·bled, quib·bling. —quib′bler,** *n.*

quiche (kēsh), *n.* a pastry shell filled with beaten eggs and cream, cheese, onion, bacon, or other ingredients, then baked.

quick (kwik), **1** *adj.* fast and sudden; swift: *The cat made a quick jump.* **2** *adj.* coming soon; prompt: *a quick reply.* **3** *adj.* not patient; hasty: *a quick temper.* **4** *adj.* acting quickly; ready; lively: *a quick wit.* **5** *adj.* understanding or learning fast: *a child who is quick in school.* **6** *adv.* quickly: *Find a bandage quick!* **7** *n.* tender, sensitive flesh under a fingernail or toenail: *bite your nails down to the quick.* **8** *n.* the tender, sensitive part of your feelings: *Their insults cut me to the quick.* [**Quick** comes from an old English word meaning "alive." Someone who is dead is certainly not quick.] **—quick′ly,** *adv.* **—quick′ness,** *n.*

the quick and the dead, living people and those not alive.

quick·en (kwik′ən), *v.* **1** to move more quickly; hasten: *Quicken your pace.* **2** to stir up; make alive: *Reading adventure stories quickens my imagination.* **3** to become more active or alive: *Her pulse quickened.*

quick-freeze (kwik′frēz′), *v.* to subject food to rapid freezing to prepare it for storing at freezing temperatures. ❑ *v.* **quick-froze** (kwik′frōz′), **quick-fro·zen** (kwik′frō′zn), **quick-freez·ing.**

quick·ie (kwik′ē), *n.* INFORMAL. something done very quickly or hastily.

quick·lime (kwik′līm′), *n.* lime[1].

quick·sand (kwik′sand′), *n.* a very deep, soft, wet sand that will not hold up a person's weight. Quicksand may swallow up people and animals.

quick·sil·ver (kwik′sil′vər), *n.* mercury.

quick·step (kwik′step′), *n.* **1** step used in marching in quick time. **2** a lively dance step. **3** music in a brisk march rhythm.

quick-tem·pered (kwik′tem′pərd), *adj.* easily angered.

quick-wit·ted (kwik′wit′id), *adj.* having a quick mind; clever. —**quick′-wit·ted·ly**, *adv.*

quid¹ (kwid), *n.* **1** piece to be chewed. **2** bite of chewing tobacco.

quid² (kwid), *n.* BRITISH SLANG. one pound, or 100 pence. □ *n., pl.* **quid** or **quids.**

qui·es·cence (kwī es′ns), *n.* absence of activity; quietness; stillness.

qui·es·cent (kwī es′nt), *adj.* inactive; quiet; still. —**qui·es′cent·ly**, *adv.*

qui·et (kwī′ət), **1** *adj.* making no sound; with little or no noise: *quiet footsteps, a quiet room.* **2** *adj.* moving very little; still: *a quiet river.* **3** *adj.* at rest; not busy: *a quiet evening at home.* **4** *adj.* peaceful; gentle: *quiet manners, a quiet person.* **5** *n.* state of rest; stillness; absence of motion or noise. **6** *n.* freedom from disturbance; peace: *to read in quiet.* **7** *v.* to make or become quiet: *Soft words quieted the frightened child. The wind quieted down.* **8** *adj.* not showy or bright: *Gray is a quiet color.* [See word history information at **quit.**] —**qui′et·ly**, *adv.* —**qui′et·ness**, *n.*

qui·e·tude (kwī′ə tüd), *n.* quietness; stillness; calmness.

qui·e·tus (kwī ē′təs), *n.* something that ends, finishes, or settles something: *Lack of money put the quietus on our vacation plans.* □ *n., pl.* **qui·e·tus·es.**

quill (kwil), *n.* **1** a large, stiff feather. **2** the hollow stem of a feather. **3** anything made from the hollow stem of a feather, especially a pen. **4** a stiff, sharp hair or spine like the pointed end of a feather. A porcupine has quills on its back. —**quill′-like′**, *adj.*

quilt (kwilt), **1** *n.* cover for a bed, usually made of two pieces of cloth with a soft pad between, held in place by stitching. **2** *v.* to make quilts. **3** *v.* to stitch together with a soft lining: *She was busy quilting a warm bathrobe for her granddaughter.* [**Quilt** comes from a Latin word meaning "a cushion."] —**quilt′er**, *n.*

quilt·ing (kwil′ting), *n.* **1** quilted work. **2** material for making quilts.

quince (kwins), *n.* the hard, yellowish, acid, pear-shaped fruit of a small tree, used for preserves and jelly.

quilt

qui·nine (kwī′nīn), *n.* a bitter drug made from the bark of a cinchona tree, used in treating malaria and fevers.

quin·sy (kwin′zē), *n.* tonsillitis with pus; a very sore throat with an abscess in the tonsils. [**Quinsy** comes from a Greek word meaning "dog collar." The pain of quinsy feels like a tight strap around the throat.]

quint (kwint), *n.* INFORMAL. quintuplet.

quint-, *prefix.* five: *quintuple = having five parts.*

Quin·ta·na Roo (kēn tä′nä rō′), a state in SE Mexico, on the Yucatán peninsula.

quin·tes·sence (kwin tes′ns), *n.* **1** the purest form of some quality; pure essence. **2** the most perfect example of something: *The ballerina was the quintessence of grace.*

quin·tet or **quin·tette** (kwin tet′), *n.* **1** group of five singers or players performing together. **2** piece of music for five voices or instruments. **3** any group of five.

quin·tu·ple (kwin tü′pəl), **1** *adj.* having five parts; fivefold. **2** *adj., adv.* five times; five times as great. **3** *n.* number, amount,

etc., five times as large as another: *100 is the quintuple of 20.* **4** *v.* to make or become five times as great. □ *v.* **quin·tu·pled, quin·tu·pling.**

quin·tu·plet (kwin tup′lit *or* kwin tü′plit), *n.* **1** one of five children born at the same time to the same mother. **2** any group or combination of five.

quintuplets

quip (kwip), **1** *n.* a clever or witty saying. ■ See Synonym Study at **joke. 2** *v.* to make quips. □ *v.* **quipped, quip·ping.**

quirk (kwėrk), *n.* **1** a peculiar way of acting: *We all have our own quirks.* **2** a sudden twist or turn: *a quirk of fate, a mental quirk.*

quirt (kwėrt), *n.* a riding whip with a short, stout handle and a lash of braided leather.

quis·ling (kwiz′ling), *n.* person who treacherously helps to prepare the way for enemy occupation of his or her own country.

Quis·ling (kwiz′ling), *n.* **Vid·kun** (vid′kun), 1887-1945, Norwegian traitor. Although he was a Norwegian army officer, he favored Nazi invaders and served as head of their puppet government of Norway.

quit (kwit), **1** *v.* to stop: *They quit work at five.* **2** *v.* to give up; leave: *quit your job. He quit college after one year.* **3** *v.* to stop working: *Our car engine overheated and quit.* **4** *adj.* free; clear; rid: *I gave them money to be quit of them.* □ *v.* **quit** or **quit·ted, quit·ting.** [**Quit** comes from a Latin word meaning "at rest." **Quite** and **quiet** come from the same word. If you quit, things get quite quiet.]

quit·claim (kwit′klām′), **1** *n.* act of formally giving up a claim. **2** *n.* document stating that somebody gives up a claim. **3** *v.* to give up claim to a possession, etc.

quite (kwīt), *adv.* **1** completely; entirely: *I am quite alone.* **2** actually; really; positively: *quite the thing.* **3** very; rather; somewhat: *quite pretty. It is quite hot.* [See word history information at **quit.**]

Qui·to (kē′tō), *n.* capital of Ecuador, in the N part.

quits (kwits), *adj.* even or on equal terms by having given or paid back something: *We each won a game, so we are quits.*

call it quits, to abandon an attempt to do something: *The roads were so icy we called it quits and drove home.*

quit·ter (kwit′ər), *n.* person who gives up a game, a project, or a challenge whenever it becomes difficult; person unwilling to try hard. ■ **Quitter** is often considered offensive.

quiv·er¹ (kwiv′ər), **1** *v.* to shake; shiver; tremble: *The dog quivered with excitement.* **2** *n.* act of quivering; shaking or trembling: *A quiver of his mouth showed that he was about to cry.* —**quiv′er·er**, *n.* —**quiv′er·ing·ly**, *adv.*

quiv·er² (kwiv′ər), *n.* case to hold arrows.

Quixote, Don. See **Don Quixote.**

quix·ot·ic (kwik sot′ik), *adj.* **1** resembling Don Quixote; extravagantly chivalrous or romantic. **2** visionary; not practical. —**quix·ot′i·cal·ly**, *adv.*

a	hat	ė	term	ô	order	ch	child		
ā	age	i	it	oi	oil	ng	long		a in about
ä	far	ī	ice	ou	out	sh	she	ə	e in taken
â	care	o	hot	u	cup	th	thin		i in pencil
e	let	ō	open	u̇	put	ŦH	then		o in lemon
ē	equal	ȯ	saw	ü	rule	zh	measure		u in circus

quiz (kwiz), **1** *n.* a short or informal test: *Each week the teacher gives us a quiz in social studies.* **2** *v.* to give such a test to: *quiz a class in spelling.* **3** *v.* to question; interrogate: *The lawyer quizzed the witness.* **4** *n.* act of questioning. ❑ *n., pl.* **quiz·zes;** *v.* **quizzed, quiz·zing.** —**quiz′zer,** *n.*

quiz program or **quiz show,** a radio or TV show in which contestants are asked questions and win prizes if they answer correctly.

quiz program

quiz·zi·cal (kwiz′ə kəl), *adj.* **1** teasing; mocking: *a quizzical smile.* **2** questioning; baffled: *She had a quizzical expression on her face.* **3** odd; comical. —**quiz′zi·cal·ly,** *adv.*

quoit (kwoit), *n.* **1 quoits,** *pl.* game similar to horseshoes, played by tossing a heavy, flat iron or rope ring onto a peg stuck in the ground. **2** one of the rings used in this game.

Quon·set hut (kwon′sit), a prefabricated metal building shaped like a half cylinder.

quo·rum (kwôr′əm), *n.* number of members of any society or assembly that must be present if the business done is to be legal or binding.

quo·ta (kwō′tə), *n.* **1** the share of a total due from or to a particular district, state, person, etc.: *Each member of the club was given a quota of tickets to sell.* **2** a set number or amount: *a quota of two sodas per day, a sales quota of $2000 a week.* ❑ *n., pl.* **quo·tas.**

quot·a·ble (kwō′tə bəl), *adj.* **1** able to be quoted. **2** suitable for quoting.

quo·ta·tion (kwō tā′shən), *n.* **1** somebody's words repeated exactly by another person; passage quoted from a book, speech, etc.: *From what author does this quotation come?* **2** act of quoting: *Quotation is a habit of some teachers.* **3** the current price of a stock, commodity, etc.: *today's market quotation on wheat.*

quotation mark, one of a pair of marks used to indicate the beginning and end of a quotation. For an ordinary quotation use these marks (" "). For a quotation within another quotation use these (' ').

USAGE NOTE A period or comma goes before a closing quotation mark. *"Yes," he said, "I can."* A colon or semicolon goes after a closing quotation mark. A question mark or exclamation point may go before or after a closing quotation mark. They go before a closing quotation mark if they are part of what is being quoted. If not, they go after: *Who shouted "Help!"?*

quote (kwōt), **1** *v.* to repeat the exact words of; give words or passages from: *Our teacher often quotes Shakespeare.* **2** *v.* to repeat exactly the words of another or a passage from a book: *She quoted from the senator's speech.* **3** *v.* to bring forward as an example or authority: *Judges quote various cases in support of their opinions.* **4** *v.* to give a price: *quote a price on a house up for sale.* **5** *n.* quotation. **6** *n.* a quotation mark. **7** *v.* (in speaking or reading aloud) to mark the beginning of a quotation. ❑ *v.* **quot·ed, quot·ing.** —**quot′er,** *n.*

quoth (kwōth), *v.* OLD USE. said.

quo·tient (kwō′shənt), *n.* number arrived at by dividing one number by another. In $26 ÷ 2 = 13$, 13 is the quotient.

q.v., which see.

R or **r** (är), *n.* the 18th letter of the English alphabet. ❑ *n., pl.* **R's** or **r's.**

the three R's, reading, writing, and arithmetic.

R, Restricted (a rating for a movie that is not recommended for people under the age of 17, except when accompanied by a parent or guardian).

r., 1 radius. 2 right. 3 roentgen.

R., 1 Rabbi. 2 Republican. 3 River. 4 Royal.

Ra[1] (rä), *n.* Egyptian god of the sun, one of the chief gods, shown as a man with a hawk's head and the sun on his head.

Ra[2], symbol for radium.

R.A., 1 Rear Admiral. 2 Royal Academy.

Ra·bat (rə bät′), *n.* capital of Morocco, on the Atlantic.

rab·bi (rab′ī), *n.* teacher of the Jewish law and religion; leader of a Jewish congregation. ❑ *n., pl.* **rab·bis.** [**Rabbi** comes from a Hebrew word meaning "my master."]

rab·bin·i·cal (rə bin′ə kəl), *adj.* of or about rabbis, their learning, teachings, etc. —**rab·bin′i·cal·ly,** *adv.*

rab·bit (rab′it), *n.* 1 any of several small burrowing mammals with soft fur, long ears, long hind legs, and short, fluffy tails. Rabbits are similar to hares, but smaller. 2 the fur of a rabbit. —**rab′bit·like′,** *adj.*

rabbit ears, INFORMAL. a small, indoor TV antenna with two adjustable, lightweight rods that may be set in an upright V shape resembling a rabbit's ears.

rabbit fever, tularemia.

rab·ble (rab′əl), *n.* 1 a disorderly crowd; mob. 2 **the rabble,** the lower classes: *The nobles scorned the rabble.* ■ This meaning of **rabble** shows contempt and is considered offensive.

rab·id (rab′id), *adj.* 1 unreasonably extreme; fanatical; violent: *The rebels are rabid idealists.* 2 furious; raging: *rabid with anger.* 3 having rabies; mad: *a rabid dog.* —**rab′id·ly,** *adv.* —**rab′id·ness,** *n.*

ra·bies (rā′bēz), *n.* a virus disease of warm-blooded animals that causes damage to brain cells and paralyzes muscles; hydrophobia. Human beings can get rabies from the bite or saliva of an infected animal. Unless it is prevented with a serum, rabies causes death.

WORD STORY **Rabies** comes from a Latin word meaning "to be mad." A dog that obviously has rabies is often called "a mad dog." **Rage** comes from the same Latin word.

rac·coon (ra kün′), *n.* 1 either of two medium-sized, grayish brown, meat-eating American mammals with bushy, ringed tails, and dark fur around the eyes. Raccoons live mostly in wooded areas near water and are active at night. 2 the fur of a raccoon. Also, **racoon.** ❑ *n., pl.* **rac·coons** or **rac·coon.**

a	hat	ė	term	ô	order	ch	child		a in about
ā	age	i	it	oi	oil	ng	long		e in taken
ä	far	ī	ice	ou	out	sh	she	ə	i in pencil
â	care	o	hot	u	cup	th	thin		o in lemon
e	let	ō	open	ů	put	ŦH	then		u in circus
ē	equal	ò	saw	ü	rule	zh	measure		

race¹ (rās), **1** *n.* contest of speed, as in running, driving, riding, sailing, etc.: *a dog race, a car race.* **2** *n.pl.* **races,** series of races run in one day. **3** *v.* to engage in a contest of speed. **4** *v.* to run or cause to run in a race with: *I'll race you to the corner.* **5** *n.* any contest that suggests a race: *a political race.* **6** *v.* to go swiftly: *race to catch a bus.* **7** *v.* to cause to run, move, or go swiftly. **8** *v.* to run an engine at high speed when the gears are in neutral position. **9** *n.* a strong or fast current of water. ❑ *v.* **raced, rac·ing.**

race² (rās), *n.* **1** a major group of human beings that passes on certain physical characteristics from one generation to another. **2** any group with similar characteristics or ancestry: *the human race, the canine race.* **3** (in biology) subspecies. **4** group of people of the same kind: *the brave race of pioneers.*

race·car (rās′kär), *n.* a car used for racing.

race·course (rās′kôrs′), *n.* racetrack.

race·horse (rās′hôrs′), *n.* horse bred, trained, or kept for racing.

ra·ceme (rā sēm′ *or* rə sēm′), *n.* a simple flower cluster with flowers on nearly equal stalks along a stem. The lily of the valley has a raceme.

rac·er (rā′sər), *n.* **1** person, animal, boat, car, etc., that takes part in races. **2** any of various North American snakes that can move very rapidly. The blacksnake is a racer.

race·track (rās′trak′), *n.* track laid out for racing, usually circular or oval.

race walking, sport of walking very quickly, always having one foot on the ground.

race·way (rās′wā′), *n.* **1** narrow channel or passage for a current of water. **2** racetrack for harness racing.

Ra·chel (rā′chəl), *n.* (in the Bible) the wife of Jacob, and the mother of Joseph and Benjamin. [Rachel comes from a Hebrew word meaning "ewe."]

Rach·ma·ni·noff (räk mä′ni nôf), *n.* **Ser·gei** (ser gā′), 1873-1943, Russian composer, conductor, and pianist. He wrote many works for piano, especially solo piano. He left Russia in 1917 and never returned.

ra·cial (rā′shəl), *adj.* **1** of or about a race: *racial traits.* **2** of or involving races: *racial discrimination.* **—ra′cial·ly,** *adv.*

Ra·cine (rə sen′ *or* rā sēn′), *n.* city in SE Wisconsin, on Lake Michigan. [Racine comes from a French word meaning "a root." It stands on the Root River. People must have grubbed for grub there sometime.]

rac·ism (rā′siz′əm), *n.* **1** belief that a particular race, especially your own, is superior to other races. **2** discrimination or prejudice against a race or races based on this belief.

rac·ist (rā′sist), **1** *n.* someone who believes in, supports, or practices racism. **2** *adj.* marked by racism: *racist opinions.*

rack¹ (rak), **1** *n.* a frame with bars, shelves, hooks, or pegs to hold, arrange, or keep things on: *a bike rack, a clothes rack, a tool rack.* **2** *n.* a triangular plastic frame used to arrange pool balls on the table at the start of a game. **3** *n.* device once used for torturing people by stretching them. **4** *v.* to hurt very much: *The accident victim was racked with pain.* **5** *v.* to stretch; strain. **6** *n.* a bar with notches on one edge. The pegs on the rim of a turning pinion wheel fit into the notches and shift the rack from side to side. ■ Another word that sounds like this is **wrack. —rack′er,** *n.*
on the rack, in great pain; suffering very much.
rack up, INFORMAL. to score: *We racked up three runs in the ninth inning.*

rack² (rak), *n.* **rack and ruin,** ruin; destruction: *Over the years, the vacant house went to rack and ruin.* ■ Another word that sounds like this is **wrack.**

rack·et¹ (rak′it), *n.* **1** loud noise; loud talk; din. ■ See Synonym Study at **noise. 2** scheme for getting money from people through bribery, threats of violence, and other illegal means.

rack·et² (rak′it), *n.* **1** an oval wooden or metal frame strung with netting and with a handle of various lengths, used to hit the ball in tennis, squash, badminton, racquetball, etc. **2** paddle. Also, **racquet. —rack′et·like′,** *adj.*

WORD STORY Racket² comes from an Arabic word meaning "palm of the hand." In English, *racket* originally meant "a kind of handball." Then someone, probably someone with a sore hand, invented the tool we call **racket** today.

rack·et·eer (rak′ə tir′), **1** *n.* person who gets money from people through bribery, threats of violence, and other illegal means. **2** *v.* to get money in this way.

ra·coon (ra kün′), *n.* raccoon. ❑ *n., pl.* **ra·coons** or **ra·coon.**

rac·quet (rak′it), *n.* racket². **—rac′quet·like′,** *adj.*

rac·quet·ball (rak′it bȯl′), *n.* game played in a four-walled court with a hollow rubber ball and a short-handled racket.

racquetball

rad¹ (rad), *n.* unit for measuring radiation absorbed.

rad² (rad), *interj., adj.* SLANG. terrific; great; wonderful.

ra·dar (rā′där), *n.* machine or system for measuring the distance, direction, speed, etc., of unseen objects by the reflection of microwave radio waves. [Radar comes from the beginning letters of the words radio detection and ranging.]

ra·di·al (rā′dē əl), *adj.* **1** of or like radii or rays. **2** arranged like or in radii or rays. **—ra′di·al·ly,** *adv.*

radial symmetry, a shape in which similar parts are arranged around a center, from which they spread out in all directions. Starfish have radial symmetry.

radial tire, a tire that has its inner fabric cords at right angles to the line of the tread, for greater tire strength.

ra·di·ance (rā′dē əns), *n.* vivid brightness: *the radiance of the sun, the radiance of a smile.*

ra·di·ant (rā′dē ənt), *adj.* **1** shining; bright; beaming: *a radiant smile.* ■ See Synonym Study at **bright. 2** sending out rays of light or heat: *The sun is a radiant body.* **3** sent off in rays from some source; radiated: *radiant heat.* **—ra′di·ant·ly,** *adv.*

radiant energy, energy in the form of waves, especially electromagnetic waves. Light, X rays, and radio waves are forms of radiant energy.

ra·di·ate (rā′dē āt), *v.* **1** to spread out from a center: *Roads radiate from the city in every direction.* **2** to give out rays of: *The sun radiates light and heat.* **3** to issue in rays: *Heat radiates from those hot steam pipes.* **4** to give out; send forth: *Her face radiates joy.* ❑ *v.* **ra·di·at·ed, ra·di·at·ing.**

ra·di·a·tion (rā′dē ā′shən), *n.* **1** particles or electromagnetic waves produced by the atoms of a radioactive substance as a result of nuclear decay; radioactivity. Radiation includes alpha particles, beta particles, gamma rays, and neutrons, and can be harmful to living tissue. **2** energy radiated, especially electromagnetic waves. **3** act or process of producing light or other radiant energy. **4** act or process of spreading out from a center.

ra·di·a·tor (rā′dē ā′tər), *n.* **1** a heating device made of a set of pipes through which steam or hot water circulates. **2** device for cooling water. The radiator of a car gives off heat very fast and so cools the water passing through it.

rad·i·cal (rad′ə kəl), **1** *adj.* basic; fundamental: *To lose weight, I had to make radical changes in my eating habits.* **2** *adj.* favoring fundamental changes or reforms; extreme. **3** *n.* person who favors fundamental changes or reforms, especially in politics; person with extreme opinions. **4** *n.* atom or molecule acting as a unit in chemical reactions. A carbonate molecule (CO_3) is a radical in sodium carbonate (Na_2CO_3), becoming part of that compound without changing, as if it were a single element instead of two. **5** *n.* radical sign. **—rad′i·cal·ly,** *adv.* **—rad′i·cal·ness,** *n.*

rad·i·cal·ism (rad′ə kə liz′əm), *n.* principles or practices of radicals; support or advocacy of extreme changes or reforms, especially in politics.

radical sign, a mathematical sign ($\sqrt{}$) put before a number or expression to show that a root of it is to be found by calculation.
EXAMPLES: $\sqrt{16}$ = the square root of 16 = 4.
$\sqrt[3]{27}$ = the cube root of 27 = 3.

rad·i·cand (rad′ə kand′), *n.* the number placed under a radical sign. 16 and 27 are radicands in the previous entry.

ra·dic·chi·o (rə dik′ē ō), *n.* a kind of chicory with a head of reddish and white striped leaves, used in salads.

rad·i·ces (rā′də sēz), *n.* a plural of **radix.**

ra·di·i (rā′dē ī), *n.* a plural of **radius.**

ra·di·o (rā′dē ō), **1** *n.* act or process of sending and receiving signals by means of electromagnetic waves without connecting wires between sender and receiver. The signals may carry information, sound, or pictures. **2** *n.* device for sending or receiving the signals sent in this way. **3** *n.* device that converts such signals into sound. **4** *adj.* of, used in, or sent by radio: *I enjoy listening to radio programs.* **5** *v.* to send by radio: *The ship radioed a call for help.* **6** *n.* business of broadcasting sound: *He left publishing and got a job in radio.* ❏ *n., pl.* **ra·di·os** for 2,3; *v.* **ra·di·oed, ra·di·o·ing.**

radio-, *prefix.* **1** radiation; radiant energy: *radioactivity = condition of giving off radiation.* **2** radioactive: *radiocarbon = radioactive carbon.* **3** radio; by radio: *radiotelephone = radio working by voice.*

ra·di·o·ac·tive (rā′dē ō ak′tiv), *adj.* of, having, or caused by radioactivity. Radium and uranium are radioactive. —**ra′di·o·ac′tive·ly,** *adv.*

radioactive dating, way of measuring the age of some object or material by measuring its radioactive elements and the other elements into which they have changed at a known rate.

ra·di·o·ac·tiv·i·ty (rā′dē ō ak tiv′ə tē), *n.* **1** the quality of producing radiation in the form of alpha particles, beta particles, or gamma rays as the result of nuclear decay in particular chemical elements. **2** the radiation given off.

radio astronomy, branch of astronomy studying astronomical objects by means of radio waves that these objects give off. It enables astronomers to study objects not visible through ordinary telescopes. —**radio astronomer.**

ra·di·o·car·bon (rā′dē ō kär′bən), *n.* a radioactive isotope of carbon, especially carbon 14.

radio frequency, any electromagnetic wave frequency suitable for radio or television broadcasting, usually above 10,000 hertz.

ra·di·o·gram (rā′dē ō gram′), *n.* message transmitted by radio.

ra·di·o·i·so·tope (rā′dē ō ī′sə tōp), *n.* a radioactive isotope. Artificially produced radioisotopes are widely used in medical research and treatment.

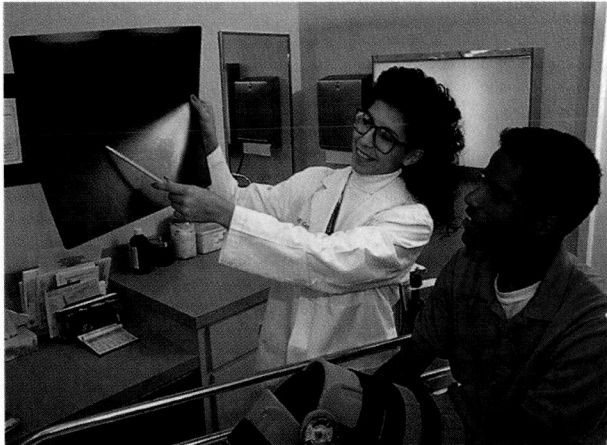

radiology

ra·di·ol·o·gy (rā′dē ol′ə jē), *n.* branch of medicine that uses X rays and other radiation or radioactive materials for diagnosis or treatment. —**ra′di·ol′o·gist,** *n.*

ra·di·om·e·ter (rā′dē om′ə tər), *n.* device for detecting and measuring radiant energy.

ra·di·o·sonde (rā′dē ō sond′), *n.* device carried into the atmosphere by a balloon from which it descends by parachute, automatically reporting data on atmospheric conditions to observers on the ground by means of a small radio transmitter.

ra·di·o·tel·e·phone (rā′dē ō tel′ə fōn), *n.* a radio transmitter that uses voice communication. —**ra·di·o·tel·e·phon·ic** (rā′dē ō·tel′ə fon′ik), *adj.*

radio telescope, a very large, bowl-shaped antenna with a radio receiver for detecting radio waves produced by objects in outer space.

radio wave, an electromagnetic wave within the radio frequencies. Radio waves are produced for use in radio and television broadcasting, radar, and microwave ovens.

rad·ish (rad′ish), *n.* the small, crisp, red or white root of a garden plant. Radishes are eaten raw as a relish and in salads. ❏ *n., pl.* **rad·ish·es.** —**rad′ish·like′,** *adj.*

ra·di·um (rā′dē əm), *n.* a radioactive metallic element found in very small amounts in uranium ores. Radium is very unstable and gives off alpha particles and gamma rays while breaking down into radon, polonium, and finally lead. *Symbol:* Ra

ra·di·us (rā′dē əs), *n.* **1** a line segment going straight from the center to the outside of a circle or a sphere. Any spoke in a wheel is a radius. **2** the length of such a line segment: *The radius of the circle is 6 centimeters.* **3** a circular area measured by the length of its radius: *The explosion could be heard within a radius of ten miles.* **4** the bone of the forearm on the same side as the thumb, across from the ulna. ❏ *n., pl.* **ra·di·i** or **ra·di·us·es.**

ra·dix (rā′diks), *n.* (in mathematics) a number taken as the base of a system of numbers, logarithms, or the like. The radix of the decimal system is 10. ❏ *n., pl.* **rad·i·ces** or **ra·dix·es.**

ra·don (rā′don), *n.* a heavy, radioactive, gaseous element formed by the decay of radium. *Symbol:* Rn

rad·waste (rad′wāst′), *n.* radioactive waste material, such as used nuclear fuel.

raf·fi·a (raf′ē ə), *n.* fiber from the leaf stalks of some palm trees, used in making baskets, mats, etc. ❏ *n., pl.* **raf·fi·as.**

raf·fle (raf′əl), **1** *n.* kind of lottery in which many people each pay a small sum for a chance to win a prize. **2** *v.* to give an article as a prize in a raffle. ❏ *v.* **raf·fled, raf·fling.** —**raf′fler,** *n.*

WORD STORY **Raffle** comes from a French word meaning "taking everything." This was the name of a game in which the winner took all. Today, raffles usually have many prizes.

raft[1] (raft), *n.* logs or boards fastened together to make a floating platform: *We crossed the stream on a raft.*

raft[2] (raft), *n.* INFORMAL. a large number; abundance: *a raft of troubles.*

raft·er (raf′tər), *n.* a slanting beam of a roof.

rag[1] (rag), **1** *n.* piece of cloth, often made from a scrap of old or torn material: *Use a clean rag to rub this mirror bright.* **2** *n.pl.* **rags,** clothing that is torn and in tatters. **3** *n.* a small piece of cloth. **4** *adj.* made from rags: *a rag doll, a rag rug.* —**rag′like′,** *adj.*

rag[2] (rag), *v.* INFORMAL. **1** to scold. **2** to tease; play jokes on. ❏ *v.* **ragged, rag·ging.**

rag[3] (rag), *n.* a ragtime musical composition.

rag·a·muf·fin (rag′ə muf′ən), *n.* a dirty, ragged person, especially a child. [**Ragamuffin** comes from two words, one in old English, one in old Dutch. Together they meant "ragged mittens."]

rage (rāj), **1** *n.* violent anger: *His voice quivered with rage.* **2** *v.* to be furious with anger. **3** *v.* to talk or act violently; move, proceed, or continue with great violence: *Keep your temper; don't rage. A storm is raging.* ❏ *v.* **raged, rag·ing.** [See Word Story at **rabies.**]
all the rage or **the rage,** what everybody wants for a short time; the fashion: *Red ties were all the rage last season.*

a	hat	ė	term	ô	order	ch	child		
ā	age	i	it	oi	oil	ng	long		a in about
ä	far	ī	ice	ou	out	sh	she		e in taken
â	care	o	hot	u	cup	th	thin	ə	i in pencil
e	let	ō	open	ù	put	ᴛʜ	then		o in lemon
ē	equal	ò	saw	ü	rule	zh	measure		u in circus

R

rag·ged (rag′id), *adj.* **1** worn or torn into rags: *ragged clothes.* **2** wearing torn or badly worn-out clothing: *ragged children in a war-torn city.* **3** having loose shreds or bits: *a ragged wound.* **4** having rough or sharp points; uneven; jagged: *ragged rocks.* **5** not done well: *a ragged performance.* **–rag′ged·ly,** *adv.* **–rag′ged·ness,** *n.*

rag·ged·y (rag′ə dē), *adj.* ragged: *a raggedy coat.* ❑ *adj.* **rag·ged·i·er, rag·ged·i·est.**

rag·lan (rag′lən), *adj.* having sleeves cut so as to continue up to the collar: *a raglan topcoat.*

ra·gout (ra gü′), *n.* a highly seasoned stew of meat and vegetables.

rag·time (rag′tīm′), *n.* **1** musical rhythm with accents falling at unusual places. **2** form of jazz using this rhythm. [**Ragtime** is short for *ragged time.* People gave it this name because the rhythm sounded uneven to them.]

rag·weed (rag′wēd′), *n.* any of several large weeds with pollen that often causes hay fever.

rah (rä), *interj., n.* hurrah.

raid (rād), **1** *n.* a sudden attack: *The pirates planned a raid on the harbor.* **2** *v.* to attack suddenly: *The enemy raided our camp.* **3** *n.* act of entering and seizing what is inside: *The hungry girls made a raid on the refrigerator.* **4** *v.* to force a way into; enter and seize what is inside: *The police raided the gambling house.* **–raid′er,** *n.*

rail¹ (rāl), **1** *n.* bar of wood or metal used to support, protect, or separate. There are stair rails, fence rails, and altar rails. **2** *n.* one of a pair of steel bars laid parallel on ties as a track for a railroad, subway, etc. **3** *n.* railroad: *ship freight by rail.* **4** *v.* to enclose with bars or a fence: *to rail off a space for horses.*

rail² (rāl), *v.* to complain bitterly; use violent and reproachful language: *rail at your hard luck.* **–rail′er,** *n.*

rail³ (rāl), *n.* any of several small birds with short wings and tails, narrow bodies, long toes, and harsh voices. They live in marshes and swamps. ❑ *n., pl.* **rail** or **rails.**

rail·ing (rā′ling), *n.* rail used as a guard or support on a stairway or platform; handrail.

rail·ler·y (rā′lər ē), *n.* good-humored ridicule; joking; teasing.

rail·road (rāl′rōd′), **1** *n.* track with parallel steel rails on which the wheels of the cars go. **2** *n.* trains, stations, and other property of a transportation business that uses tracks with rails, together with the people who manage them. **3** *v.* to work for such a business. **4** *v.* to carry out or put into effect quickly, in an unfair way: *to railroad a bill through without full debate.* **5** *v.* INFORMAL. to send someone to prison on false evidence, without a fair trial, etc.: *The convict claimed she was railroaded.* **–rail′road′er,** *n.*

WORD BANK			
Railroads and *trains* have a large vocabulary with many interesting words. If you want to learn more about railroads, you can start by looking up these words in this dictionary.			
boxcar	diner	freight train	sleeper
brakeman	el	gondola	station
caboose	elevated	local	subway
conductor	engine	locomotive	tank car
coupler	engineer	Pullman	tie
cowcatcher	excursion	rail¹	timetable
depot	express	redcap	track
derail	first class	roundhouse	trainman
diesel	flatcar	siding	transfer

rail·way (rāl′wā′), *n.* railroad.

rai·ment (rā′mənt), *n.* OLD USE. clothing; garments.

rain (rān), **1** *n.* water falling in drops from clouds. Rain is formed from moisture condensed from water vapor in the atmosphere. *The rain spattered the windows.* **2** *n.* the fall of such drops: *The rain lasted an hour.* **3** *v.* to fall in drops of water: *It rained all day.* **4** *n.* a thick, fast fall of anything: *A rain of petals fell from the blossoming apple tree.* **5** *v.* to fall like rain: *Sparks rained down from the burning roof.* **6** *v.* to send like rain: *The crowd rained confetti on the parade.* ■ Other words that sound like this are **reign** and **rein.** **–rain′less,** *adj.*

rain out, to postpone or cancel because of rain: *Today's game was rained out and will be played tomorrow in a doubleheader.*

rain·bow (rān′bō′), **1** *n.* a curve of colored light seen sometimes after rain in the sky opposite the sun, or in mist or spray. A rainbow shows all the colors of the spectrum: red, orange, yellow, green, blue, indigo, and violet. **2** *adj.* having many colors like a rainbow.

rainbow (def. 1)

rain check, **1** ticket for future use, given to the spectators at a baseball game or other outdoor performance stopped by rain. **2** a written offer giving a customer the right to purchase a sale item at a later time for the same sale price, because the item is out of stock.

rain·coat (rān′kōt′), *n.* a waterproof coat worn for protection from rain.

rain date, date chosen as an alternative date for an outdoor event or activity in case of bad weather on the original date.

rain·drop (rān′drop′), *n.* drop of rain.

rain·fall (rān′fôl′), *n.* **1** amount of water in the form of rain, sleet, or snow that falls in a particular time and area; precipitation: *The yearly rainfall in New York is much greater than that in Arizona.* **2** a shower of rain.

rain·for·est or **rain forest** (rān′fôr′ist), *n.* a very dense forest in a region where rain is heavy throughout the year. Rainforests are usually in tropical areas.

Rai·nier (rə nir′), **Mount,** mountain in W Washington, 14,410 feet (4392 meters) high.

rain·proof (rān′prüf′), *adj.* not letting rain through; waterproof.

rain shadow, the dry area on the side of a mountain range away from the usual winds.

rain·storm (rān′stôrm′), *n.* storm with much rain.

rain·wa·ter (rān′wò′tər), *n.* water that has fallen as rain.

rain·wear (rān′wâr′), *n.* rainproof clothes.

rain·y (rā′nē), *adj.* **1** having rain; having much rain: *The weather was gloomy, dark, and rainy.* **2** bringing rain: *The sky is filled with dark, rainy clouds.* **3** wet with rain: *rainy streets.* ❑ *adj.* **rain·i·er, rain·i·est.**

rainy day, possible time of greater need in the future: *to save money for a rainy day.*

raise (rāz), **1** *v.* to lift up; put up: *raise the flag. Children in school raise their hands to answer a question.* ■ See Synonym Study at **lift.** **2** *v.* to cause to rise: *The car raised a cloud of dust. Dough for bread is raised by yeast.* **3** *v.* to put into a higher position; make higher or nobler: *The store clerk was raised to manager.* **4** *v.* to increase in degree, amount, price, pay, etc.: *That store has raised its prices again. Raise your voice.* **5** *n.* an increase in amount, price, pay, etc.: *a raise in pay.* **6** *v.* to gather together; collect; manage to get: *Our parents helped to raise money for a hospital.* **7** *v.* to breed; grow: *The farmer raises crops and cattle.* **8** *v.* to bring about; cause: *A funny remark raises a laugh.* **9** *v.* to build; create; produce; start; set up: *They raised a monument to the famous poet.* **10** *v.* to bring up; rear: *Parents raise their children.* **11** *v.* to bring back to life: *raise the dead.* **12** *v.* to put an end to: *The soldiers raised the siege of the fort by driving away the enemy.* ❑ *v.* **raised, rais·ing.** ■ Another word that sounds like this is **raze.** **–rais′er,** *n.*

rai·sin (rā′zn), *n.* a sweet, dried grape.

ra·ja (rä′jə), *n.* rajah. ❑ *n., pl.* **ra·jas.**

ra·jah (rä′jə), *n.* ruler or chief in India, Java, Borneo, etc.

rake¹ (rāk), **1** *n.* a long-handled tool having a bar at one end with teeth in it. A rake is used for smoothing the soil or gathering together loose leaves, hay, straw, etc. **2** *v.* to move with a rake: *Rake the leaves off the grass.* **3** *v.* to make clear, clean, smooth, etc., with a rake, or as if with a rake: *Rake the yard.* **4** *v.* to search carefully: *I raked the want ads, hoping to find a bicycle for sale.* **5** *v.* to fire guns along the length of a ship, line of soldiers, etc. ❑ *v.* **raked, rak·ing.**

rake in, INFORMAL. to get a lot of something easily: *Their new business is raking in money.*

rake² (rāk), *n.* person who shamelessly indulges in vice; immoral or dissolute person.

rake-off (rāk′ôf′), *n.* INFORMAL. a share, especially taken illegally or without permission.

rak·ish¹ (rā′kish), *adj.* **1** smart; jaunty; dashing: *a hat set at a rakish angle.* **2** suggesting dash and speed: *They own a rakish boat.* —**rak′ish·ly,** *adv.* —**rak′ish·ness,** *n.*

rak·ish² (rā′kish), *adj.* like a rake; immoral; dissolute.

Ra·leigh (rô′lē), *n.* **1** Sir **Walter** (wôl′tər), 1552?-1618, English soldier, explorer, and author. He founded two colonies in North Carolina. The first colonists gave up and went back to England, and the second group of colonists mysteriously disappeared. ■ Sir Walter **Raleigh** was a favorite of Elizabeth I but not of her successor, James I, who imprisoned him for twelve years for treason. He was released to search for gold in South America, but he disobeyed James's orders and was executed when he returned to England. **2** capital of North Carolina, in the central part.

ral·ly¹ (ral′ē), **1** *v.* to bring together, especially to get in order again: *The commander was able to rally the fleeing troops.* **2** *v.* to come or bring together in a group for a common purpose or action: *The people rallied to rebuild the dike before the river flooded their homes.* **3** *v.* to come to help a person, party, or cause: *She rallied to the side of her injured friend.* **4** *v.* to recover health and strength: *My sick friend has begun to rally.* **5** *v.* (in sports) to come from behind in scoring. **6** *n.* act of rallying; recovery. **7** *n.* a mass meeting or assembly for a common purpose or action: *We all attended the rally in support of the presidential candidate.* ❑ *v.* **ral·lied, ral·ly·ing;** *n., pl.* **ral·lies.**

ral·ly² (ral′ē), *v.* to make fun of good-naturedly; tease: *We rallied our friend on her forgetfulness.* ❑ *v.* **ral·lied, ral·ly·ing.**

ram (ram), **1** *n.* a male sheep. **2** *v.* to crash hard against; strike violently; strike head-on: *One ship rammed the other ship.* **3** *v.* to push hard; drive down or in by heavy blows: *He rammed the fence post into the ground.* **4** *n.* machine or part of a machine that strikes heavy blows. The ram on a pile driver is the weight that drives the piles into the ground. **5** *n.* battering ram. ❑ *v.* **rammed, ram·ming.**

RAM (ram), *n.* random access memory (a form of temporary computer memory in which all data are equally available and can be put in or taken out at any time).

ram (def. 1)

Ram·a·dan (räm′ə dän′), *n.* the ninth month of the Muslim year, during which Muslims fast every day from dawn until sunset.

Ra·ma·ya·na (rä mä′yə nə), *n.* a Hindu epic poem and religious text describing the adventures of an exiled prince and his beloved wife.

ram·ble (ram′bəl), **1** *v.* to wander about: *We rambled here and there through the woods.* **2** *n.* a walk for pleasure, not to go to any special place. **3** *v.* to talk or write about first one thing and then another with no useful connections. **4** *v.* to spread irregularly in various directions: *Vines rambled over the wall.* ❑ *v.* **ram·bled, ram·bling.**

ram·bler (ram′blər), *n.* **1** person or thing that rambles. **2** a climbing rose with clusters of small red, yellow, or white flowers.

ram·bling (ram′bling), *adj.* **1** wandering about. **2** going from one thing to another with no useful connections: *The rambling speech bored us.* **3** growing or extending in irregular ways and various directions: *They live in a rambling old farmhouse.* —**ram′bling·ly,** *adv.*

ram·bunc·tious (ram bungk′shəs), *adj.* wild and noisy; boisterous. —**ram·bunc′tious·ly,** *adv.* —**ram·bunc′tious·ness,** *n.*

ram·i·fi·ca·tion (ram′ə fə kā′shən), *n.* any of several results of something done or decided; consequence: *What are the ramifications of the company's decision to relocate?*

ram·i·fy (ram′ə fī), *v.* to divide or spread out into branches or parts resembling branches. ❑ *v.* **ram·i·fied, ram·i·fy·ing.**

ramp (ramp), *n.* a sloping way connecting two different levels of a building, road, etc.; slope.

ram·page (ram′pāj′; *also* ram pāj′ *for verb*), **1** *n.* fit of rushing wildly about; spell of violent behavior; wild outbreak. **2** *v.* to rush wildly about; behave violently; rage. ❑ *v.* **ram·paged, ram·pag·ing.** —**ram·pag′er,** *n.*

ram·pant (ram′pənt), *adj.* **1** passing beyond restraint or usual limits; unchecked: *Looting was rampant during the riot.* **2** (in heraldry) standing up on the hind legs. —**ram′pant·ly,** *adv.*

ram·part (ram′pärt), *n.* **1** a wide bank of earth, often with a wall on top, built around a fort to help defend it. **2** anything that defends; defense; protection.

ram·pike (ram′pīk′), *n.* CANADIAN. a tall, dead tree, with its branches burned off by a forest fire.

ram·rod (ram′rod′), *n.* **1** rod for ramming down the charge in a gun that is loaded from the muzzle. **2** rod for cleaning the barrel of a gun.

Ram·ses (ram′sēz), *n.* the name of several kings of ancient Egypt. One, **Ramses II,** is believed to be the pharaoh described in the book of Exodus in the Bible. He ruled from about 1290 to 1224 B.C.

ram·shack·le (ram′shak′əl), *adj.* loose and shaky; likely to come apart.

ran (ran), *v.* past tense of **run:** *The dog ran after the cat.*

ranch (ranch), **1** *n.* a large farm with grazing land, used for raising cattle, sheep, or horses. **2** *n.* any farm, especially one used to raise one kind of animal or crop: *a chicken ranch, a fruit ranch.* **3** *v.* to work on a ranch; manage a ranch. ❑ *n., pl.* **ranch·es.**

ranch·er (ran′chər), *n.* person who owns, manages, or works on a ranch.

ran·cher·o (ran châr′ō), *n.* rancher in the southwestern United States. ❑ *n., pl.* **ran·cher·os.**

ran·cid (ran′sid), *adj.* **1** stale; spoiled: *rancid butter.* **2** tasting or smelling like stale fat or butter: *a rancid odor.* —**ran′cid·ly,** *adv.* —**ran′cid·ness,** *n.*

ran·cor (rang′kər), *n.* bitter resentment or ill will; extreme hatred or spite.

ran·cor·ous (rang′kər əs), *adj.* spiteful; bitterly malicious. —**ran′cor·ous·ly,** *adv.* —**ran′cor·ous·ness,** *n.*

r & b or **R & B,** rhythm and blues.

R & D, research and development.

ran·dom (ran′dəm), *adj.* by chance; with no plan; haphazard: *a random guess, random questions, pick a random number.* —**ran′dom·ly,** *adv.* —**ran′dom·ness,** *n.*

at random, by chance; with no plan or purpose: *She took a book at random from the shelf.*

SYNONYM STUDY **Random** and **chance** both mean without plan or choice. **Random** suggests lack of reason or purpose: *Her letter was full of random remarks without connection.* **Chance** suggests happening by accident: *The story begins with a chance meeting of old friends.*

random access memory. See **RAM.**

a	hat	ė	term	ô	order	ch	child		a in about
ā	age	i	it	oi	oil	ng	long		e in taken
ä	far	ī	ice	ou	out	sh	she	ə {	i in pencil
â	care	o	hot	u	cup	th	thin		o in lemon
e	let	ō	open	ù	put	ᴛʜ	then		u in circus
ē	equal	ò	saw	ü	rule	zh	measure		

R

rang (rang), *v.* past tense of **ring²**: *The telephone rang.*

range (rānj), **1** *n.* distance between certain limits; extent: *A dog has a greater range of hearing than a person.* **2** *n.* variety; number: *a range of colors to choose from.* **3** *v.* to vary within certain limits: *The prices ranged from $5 to $20.* **4** *n.* the greatest distance that something can go or at which it can operate: *This missile has a range of 1500 miles.* **5** *n.* a place to practice shooting: *a rifle range.* **6** *n.* land used for grazing. **7** *v.* to wander; rove; roam: *Our talk ranged over many subjects.* **8** *n.* line of mountains: *Mount Rainier is in the Cascade Range.* **9** *n.* a row; line: *ranges of books in perfect order.* **10** *v.* to put in a row or rows: *Range the books by size.* **11** *v.* to put in groups or classes. **12** *v.* to put in line: *The nobles ranged themselves behind the king.* **13** *v.* to extend in a line; run: *a boundary ranging east and west.* **14** *n.* region where a particular living thing is found: *The range of the fungus includes only three countries.* **15** *v.* to be found; occur: *a butterfly ranging from Canada to Mexico.* **16** *n.* a stove for cooking: *a gas range.* ❑ *v.* **ranged, rang·ing.**

range finder, device for estimating the distance to an object.

rang·er (rān′jər), *n.* **1** person employed to guard a tract of forest. **2** one of a group of armed troops employed in ranging over a region to police it. **3** person or thing that ranges; rover. **4** CANADIAN. **a. Ranger,** a member of the Girl Guides over 16 years old. **b** an Indian or Inuit military scout in the Far North.

Ran·goon (rang gün′), *n.* former name of **Yangon.**

rang·y (rān′jē), *adj.* slender and having long legs: *a rangy soccer player, a rangy horse.* ❑ *adj.* **rang·i·er, rang·i·est. —rang′i·ness,** *n.*

rank¹ (rangk), **1** *n.* row or line, especially of soldiers, placed side by side. **2** *n.pl.* **ranks, a** army; soldiers. **b** rank and file. **c** formation: *open ranks, close ranks.* **3** *v.* to arrange in a row or line. **4** *n.* position; grade; class: *the rank of colonel.* **5** *n.* high position: *A duchess is a woman of rank.* **6** *v.* to have a certain rank: *rank high in a spelling test.* **7** *v.* to put in some special order in a list: *Rank the states in the order of size.* **—rank′er,** *n.*

pull rank, to use your position to get something: *She pulled rank as president of the student council to get free tickets to the school talent show.*

rank² (rangk), *adj.* **1** growing in a thick, coarse way: *a rank growth of weeds.* **2** producing a dense and coarse growth: *rank swampland.* **3** having a strong, bad smell or taste: *rank meat, rank tobacco.* **4** strongly marked; extreme: *rank ingratitude, rank nonsense.* **—rank′ly,** *adv.* **—rank′ness,** *n.*

rank and file, 1 common soldiers, especially those with the rank of corporal or below; ranks. **2** common people. **—rank′-and-file′,** *adj.*

Ran·kin (rang′kin), *n.* **Jean·nette** (jə net′), 1880-1973, American political leader. ■ **Jeannette Rankin** was the first woman to be elected to the U.S. Congress. She was the only member of the House of Representatives to vote against entering World War II.

rank·ing (rang′king), **1** *adj.* of highest standing; leading; foremost: *the ranking U.S. Senator.* **2** *n.* position; standing: *a high ranking in tennis.*

ran·kle (rang′kəl), *v.* to cause anger; continue to irritate: *The memory of the insult rankled in my mind.* ❑ *v.* **ran·kled, ran·kling.**

WORD STORY **Rankle** comes from a Latin word meaning "little dragon." People also used that word to mean a sore place, as if a little dragon were biting them.

ran·sack (ran′sak), *v.* **1** to search thoroughly through: *A thief ransacked the house for jewelry.* **2** to rob; plunder: *The invading army ransacked the city and carried off its treasure.* **—ran′sack·er,** *n.*

ran·som (ran′səm), **1** *n.* price paid or demanded before a captive is set free: *The robbers held the travelers for ransom.* **2** *v.* to obtain the release of a captive by paying a price: *They ransomed the kidnaped child.* **3** *n.* act of ransoming. **—ran′som·er,** *n.*

rant (rant), **1** *v.* to speak wildly, extravagantly, violently, or noisily. **2** *n.* extravagant, violent, or noisy speech. **—rant′er,** *n.*

rap¹ (rap), **1** *n.* a light, sharp knock; a quick, light blow: *We heard a rap at the window.* **2** *v.* to knock sharply; tap: *The chairman rapped on the table for order.* **3** *v.* to say sharply: *rap out an answer.* **4** *n.* INFORMAL. punishment; blame: *Although his friends were also involved, he took the rap for the broken window.* ❑ *v.* **rapped, rap·ping.** ■ Another word that sounds like this is **wrap.**

rap² (rap), *n.* INFORMAL. the least bit: *I don't care a rap.* ■ Another word that sounds like this is **wrap.**

rap³ (rap), **1** *n.* SLANG. conversation; talk. **2** *v.* SLANG. to talk together in an informal way. **3** *n.* a kind of popular music with a strong beat and strongly rhymed words chanted rhythmically. ❑ *v.* **rapped, rap·ping.** ■ Another word that sounds like this is **wrap.**

ra·pa·cious (rə pā′shəs), *adj.* **1** seizing by force; plundering: *rapacious pirates.* **2** greedy; grasping: *a rapacious miser.* **3** living by the capture of prey; predatory: *rapacious birds.* **—ra·pa′cious·ly,** *adv.* **—ra·pa′cious·ness,** *n.*

ra·pac·i·ty (rə pas′ə tē), *n.* rapacious spirit, action, or practice; greed.

rape¹ (rāp), **1** *n.* crime of having sexual intercourse with someone against her or his will, often by using force. **2** *v.* to commit rape on. **3** *n.* act of seizing and carrying off by force. ❑ *v.* **raped, rap·ing.**

rape² (rāp), *n.* plant whose leaves are used as food for sheep and hogs. Rape seeds yield an oil that is used as a lubricant.

★★★★ **Ranks in the United States Armed Services**

ARMY	NAVY	AIR FORCE	MARINE CORPS
General	Admiral	General	General
Lieutenant General	Vice Admiral	Lieutenant General	Lieutenant General
Major General	Rear Admiral (upper)	Major General	Major General
Brigadier General	Rear Admiral (lower)	Brigadier General	Brigadier General
Colonel	Captain	Colonel	Colonel
Lieutenant Colonel	Commander	Lieutenant Colonel	Lieutenant Colonel
Major	Lieutenant Commander	Major	Major
Captain	Lieutenant	Captain	Captain
First Lieutenant	Lieutenant Junior Grade	First Lieutenant	First Lieutenant
Second Lieutenant	Ensign	Second Lieutenant	Second Lieutenant
Chief Warrant Officer	Chief Warrant Officer		Chief Warrant Officer
Warrant Officer	Warrant Officer		Warrant Officer
Sergeant Major	Master Chief Petty Officer	Chief Master Sergeant	Sergeant Major; Master Gunnery Sergeant
First Sergeant; Master Sergeant	Senior Chief Petty Officer	Senior Master Sergeant	First Sergeant; Master Sergeant
Sergeant First Class; Specialist 7	Chief Petty Officer	Master Sergeant	Gunnery Sergeant
Staff Sergeant; Specialist 6	Petty Officer First Class	Technical Sergeant	Staff Sergeant
Sergeant; Specialist 5	Petty Officer Second Class	Staff Sergeant	Sergeant
Corporal; Specialist 4	Petty Officer Third Class	Sergeant	Corporal
Private First Class	Seaman	Airman First Class	Lance Corporal
Private Second Class	Seaman Apprentice	Airman	Private First Class
Private	Seaman Recruit	Airman Basic	Private

Raph·a·el (raf′ē əl), *n.* 1483-1520, Italian painter. ■ **Raphael** painted many frescoes in the pope's quarters in the Vatican. His famous painting, *The School of Athens,* is there. This painting shows important Greek philosophers and scientists, including Plato and Aristotle.

Raphael painting

rap·id (rap′id), **1** *adj.* moving or doing with speed; very quick; swift: *a rapid worker.* ■ See Synonym Study at **quick. 2** *n.pl.* **rapids,** a part of a river's course where the water rushes quickly, often over rocks near the surface: *Their canoe overturned in the rapids.* —**rap′id·ly,** *adv.* —**rap′id·ness,** *n.*

WORD FAMILY **Rapid** and the words below are related. They all come from a Latin word meaning "to seize."

rapacious	raptor	ravenous	surreptitious
rape[1]	rapture	ravine	usurp
rapt	ravage	ravish	

Rapid City, city in SW South Dakota.

rap·id-fire (rap′id fir′), *adj.* **1** firing shots in quick succession. **2** ready and quick; occurring in quick succession: *rapid-fire commands.*

ra·pid·i·ty (rə pid′ə tē), *n.* swiftness; speed.

rapid transit, a fast system of public transportation in and around cities, using electric cars that run on tracks.

ra·pi·er (rā′pē ər), *n.* a long, very thin sword used for thrusting. —**ra′pi·er·like′,** *adj.*

rap·pel (ra pel′), **1** *v.* to lower yourself down the face of a cliff by means of a rope fastened at the top of the cliff and placed around your body so that the rope can gradually be lengthened. **2** *n.* act of lowering in this way. ❑ *v.* **rap·pelled, rap·pel·ling.**

rap·per (rap′ər), *n.* **1** a rap musician. **2** someone who raps.

rap·port (ra pôr′), *n.* relationship marked by understanding, communication, and harmony: *There is a special rapport between the twins.*

rap·scal·lion (rap skal′yən), *n.* rascal; rogue; scamp.

rapt (rapt), *adj.* **1** lost in delight. **2** so busy thinking of or enjoying one thing that you do not notice what else is happening: *Rapt in my work, I did not hear them.* **3** showing a rapt condition; caused by a rapt condition: *rapt attention.* —**rapt′ly,** *adv.* —**rapt′ness,** *n.*

rap·tor (rap′tər), *n.* **1** any bird that lives by hunting, such as an eagle, hawk, or owl; bird of prey. **2** velociraptor.

rap·ture (rap′chər), *n.* a strong feeling that absorbs the mind; very great joy: *In rapture the child gazed at the toys in the shop window.*

rap·tur·ous (rap′chər əs), *adj.* full of great joy; expressing or feeling great joy. —**rap′tur·ous·ly,** *adv.* —**rap′tur·ous·ness,** *n.*

rare[1] (râr), *adj.* **1** seldom seen or found: *Storks and peacocks are rare birds in the United States.* **2** not happening often; unusual: *Snow is rare in Florida.* **3** unusually good or great: *Edison had rare powers as an inventor.* **4** thin; not dense: *The higher we go above the earth, the rarer the air is.* ❑ *adj.* **rar·er, rar·est.** —**rare′ness,** *n.*

SYNONYM STUDY **Rare**[1] and **scarce** both mean not often or easily found. **Rare** means something that is always difficult to find: *Gold is a rare element.* **Scarce** means something once common but now not easily found: *During the drought, water became scarce.*

rare[2] (râr), *adj.* not cooked much: *a rare steak.* ❑ *adj.* **rar·er, rar·est.** —**rare′ness,** *n.*

rare·bit (râr′bit), *n.* Welsh rabbit.

rare-earth element (râr′ėrth′), any of a group of silver-colored metallic elements that are similar to each other and are usually listed together by chemists. They are used in lights, magnets, making glass, and refining petroleum.

rar·e·fy (râr′ə fi), *v.* **1** to make or become less dense: *The air on high mountains is rarefied.* **2** to refine; purify. ❑ *v.* **rar·e·fied, rar·e·fy·ing.**

rare·ly (râr′lē), *adv.* seldom; not often.

rar·ing (râr′ing), *adj.* INFORMAL. very eager: *raring to go.*

rar·i·ty (râr′ə tē), *n.* **1** something rare: *A person over a hundred years old is a rarity.* **2** scarcity: *The rarity of diamonds makes them valuable.* **3** lack of density; thinness: *The rarity of the air in the mountains is bad for some people.* ❑ *n., pl.* **rar·i·ties** for 1.

ras·cal (ras′kəl), *n.* **1** a bad, dishonest person. **2** a mischievous person.

ras·cal·i·ty (ra skal′ə tē), *n.* rascally character, conduct, or act. ❑ *n., pl.* **ras·cal·i·ties.**

ras·cal·ly (ras′kə lē), *adj.* mean; dishonest; bad: *a rascally trick.*

rash[1] (rash), *adj.* too hasty; careless; reckless; taking too much risk: *It is rash to cross the street without looking both ways.* —**rash′ly,** *adv.* —**rash′ness,** *n.*

rash[2] (rash), *n.* **1** a sudden appearance of many small red spots on the skin. Scarlet fever causes a rash. **2** a sudden increase: *a rash of bank robberies.* ❑ *n., pl.* **rash·es.**

rash·er (rash′ər), *n.* a thin slice of bacon or ham for frying or broiling.

rasp (rasp), **1** *v.* to utter with a grating sound: *rasp out a command.* **2** *v.* to make a harsh, grating sound: *The file rasped as she worked.* **3** *n.* a harsh, grating sound: *The rasp in his voice was due to a sore throat.* **4** *v.* to affect harshly; irritate; grate on: *Their constant squabbling began to rasp my nerves.* **5** *v.* to scrape with a rough surface or tool. **6** *n.* a coarse file with pointed teeth.

rasp·ber·ry (raz′ber′ē), *n.* **1** any of several small, soft fruits that grow on bushes. They are usually red or black, but some kinds are white or yellow. **2** INFORMAL. sound of disapproval made with the tongue and lips. ❑ *n., pl.* **rasp·ber·ries.**

Ras·pu·tin (ra spyüt′n), *n.* **Gri·go·ri** (gri gô′rē), 1871-1916, Russian monk and adviser to Nicholas II. The czar believed Rasputin could treat the crown prince's hemophilia. Rasputin was assassinated in 1916. The first attempt to poison him failed, so the killers shot and stabbed him and threw him in a nearby river.

rasp·y (ras′pē), *adj.* **1** grating; harsh; rough: *When I have a cold, my voice gets raspy.* **2** irritable: *a raspy disposition.* ❑ *adj.* **rasp·i·er, rasp·i·est.**

rat (rat), **1** *n.* any of numerous long-tailed rodents like mice but larger. Rats are gray, black, brown, or white. **2** *v.* to hunt for rats; catch rats. **3** *n.* SLANG. a hateful, disloyal person. **4** *v.* SLANG. to turn informer against friends or partners; squeal. ❑ *v.* **rat·ted, rat·ting.** —**rat′like′,** *adj.*

smell a rat, to suspect a trick or scheme.

ratch·et (rach′it), *n.* **1** wheel or bar with teeth that come against a catch or pawl so that motion is permitted in one direction but not in the other. **2** the catch or pawl. **3** the entire device, wheel or bar, and pawl.

rate (rāt), **1** *n.* quantity, amount, or degree measured in proportion to something else: *The yearly rate of interest is 6 cents on the dollar.* **2** *n.* speed; velocity: *The car was going at the rate of 40 miles an hour.* **3** *n.* number of times something happens in a period of time; frequency: *selling burgers at a rate of 150 an hour.* **4** *v.* to put a value on: *We rated the house as worth $90,000.* **5** *n.* price: *We pay the regular rate.* **6** *v.* to consider; regard: *He was rated as one of the richest men in town.* **7** *n.* class; grade; rating: *first rate, second rate.* **8** *n.* (in Canada) tax on property. **9** *v.* to put in a certain class or

R

a	hat	ė	term	ô	order	ch	child		a in about
ā	age	i	it	oi	oil	ng	long		e in taken
ä	far	ī	ice	ou	out	sh	she	ə	i in pencil
â	care	o	hot	u	cup	th	thin		o in lemon
e	let	ō	open	ů	put	ŦH	then		u in circus
ē	equal	ò	saw	ü	rule	zh	measure		

grade: *rate a baseball player.* **10** *v.* to be worthy of: *She rates the best seat in the house.* ❑ *v.* **rat·ed, rat·ing.**

at any rate, in any case; under any circumstances; anyway.

rate·pay·er (rāt′pā′ər), *n.* CANADIAN. taxpayer.

rath·er (raтн′ər), *adv.* **1** more readily; more willingly: *I would rather go today than tomorrow.* **2** more properly or justly; with better reason: *This is rather for your parents to decide than for you.* **3** more truly or correctly: *It was late Monday night or, rather, early Tuesday morning.* **4** to some extent; somewhat; more than a little: *After working so long she was rather tired.* **5** on the contrary: *The lesson wasn't difficult to do; rather, it was easy.*

rat·i·fy (rat′ə fī), *v.* to confirm; approve; sanction; authorize: *The Senate ratified the treaty.* ■ See Synonym Study at **approve.** ❑ *v.* **rat·i·fied, rat·i·fy·ing. —rat′i·fi·ca′tion,** *n.*

rat·ing (rā′ting), *n.* **1** position in a class or grade: *The judges gave the gymnast a high rating.* **2** class; grade. **3** level of popularity as determined by a survey: *television ratings.*

ra·ti·o (rā′shē ō), *n.* **1** relation between two quantities expressed as a quotient. "They have sheep and cows in the ratio of 10 to 3" means that they have ten sheep for every three cows. **2** quotient expressing this relation. The ratio between two quantities is the number of times one contains the other. The ratio of 10 to 3 is written as 10:3, 10/3, 10 ÷ 3, or ¹⁰⁄₃. The ratios of 3 to 5 and 6 to 10 are the same. ❑ *n., pl.* **ra·ti·os.**

> **WORD STORY** **Ratio** comes from a Latin word meaning "calculation" or "arithmetic." **Reason** and **rational** come from the same word. Arithmetic is a purely reasonable activity that achieves rational results.

ra·tion (rash′ən *or* rā′shən), **1** *n.* a fixed allowance of food; the daily allowance of food for a person or animal. **2** *n.* portion of anything dealt out; share; allotment: *After the flood, volunteers gave out food rations to homeless people.* **3** *v.* to allow only certain amounts to: *ration citizens when supplies are scarce.* **4** *v.* to distribute in limited amounts: *Food was rationed to the public during the war.*

ra·tion·al (rash′ə nəl), *adj.* **1** reasoned out; sensible; reasonable: *When very angry, people seldom act in a rational way.* **2** able to think and reason clearly: *Human beings are rational animals.* **3** of or based on reasoning: *There is a rational explanation for thunder and lightning.* [See Word Story at **ratio.**] **—ra′tion·al·ly,** *adv.*

ra·tion·ale (rash′ə nal′), *n.* the fundamental reason.

ra·tion·al·ism (rash′ə nə liz′əm), *n.* principle or habit of accepting reason as the supreme authority in matters of opinion, belief, or conduct.

ra·tion·al·ist (rash′ə nə list), *n.* person who accepts reason as the supreme authority in matters of opinion, belief, or conduct.

ra·tion·al·is·tic (rash′ə nə lis′tik), *adj.* of or about rationalism or rationalists.

ra·tion·al·i·ty (rash′ə nal′ə tē), *n.* the possession of reason; reasonableness: *That man is odd in some ways, but no one doubts his rationality.*

ra·tion·al·ize (rash′ə nə līz), *v.* **1** to find (often unconsciously) an explanation or excuse for: *I rationalized eating two portions of mashed potatoes by thinking "I must eat enough to keep up my strength."* **2** to make something reasonable: *rationalize a filing system.* **3** to treat or explain in a rational manner. ❑ *v.* **ra·tion·al·ized, ra·tion·al·iz·ing. —ra′tion·al·i·za′tion,** *n.* **—ra′tion·al·iz′er,** *n.*

rational number, any number that can be expressed as an integer or as a ratio between two integers, excluding zero as a denominator. The numbers 2, 5, and ½ are rational numbers.

rat·line (rat′lən), *n.* one of the small ropes that cross the shrouds of a ship, used as steps for going aloft.

rat race, INFORMAL. any activity or situation with too much confusion and competition: *the corporate rat race.*

rat·tan (ra tan′), *n.* the very long, thin stems of various palm trees, used for wickerwork, canes, etc.

rat·ter (rat′ər), *n.* one that catches rats: *Our terrier is a good ratter.*

rat·tle (rat′l), **1** *v.* to make or cause to make a number of short, sharp sounds: *The window rattled in the wind. He rattled the dishes.* **2** *n.* a number of short, sharp sounds: *the rattle of empty*

bottles. **3** *v.* to move with short, sharp sounds: *The old car rattled down the street.* **4** *n.* toy or musical instrument that makes such a noise when it is shaken: *a baby's rattle.* **5** *n.* a row of horny pieces at the end of a rattlesnake's tail. **6** *v.* to talk or say quickly, on and on. **7** *v.* to confuse; upset: *I was so rattled that I forgot my speech.* ■ See Synonym Study at **upset.** ❑ *v.* **rat·tled, rat·tling.**

rat·tler (rat′lər), *n.* rattlesnake.

rat·tle·snake (rat′l snāk′), *n.* any of several poisonous American snakes with thick bodies, broad, triangular heads, and horny rattles on their tails.

rat·tle·trap (rat′l trap′), *n.* **1** a rattling, rickety car or other vehicle. **2** any shaky, rattling object.

rat·ty (rat′ē), *adj.* **1** of or like rats: *a ratty odor.* **2** full of rats: *a ratty cellar.* **3** SLANG. poor; shabby: *a ratty apartment.* **4** SLANG. mean: *That was a ratty thing to do.* ❑ *adj.* **rat·ti·er, rat·ti·est.**

rau·cous (rô′kəs), *adj.* hoarse; harsh-sounding: *the raucous caw of a crow.* **—rau′cous·ly,** *adv.* **—rau′cous·ness,** *n.*

raunch·y (rôn′chē), *adj.* SLANG. **1** vulgar; crude; coarse: *some noisy, raunchy song.* **2** messy; filthy; squalid: *raunchy slum streets.* ❑ *adj.* **raunch·i·er, raunch·i·est. —raunch′i·ly,** *adv.* **—raunch′i·ness,** *n.*

rav·age (rav′ij), **1** *v.* to damage greatly; lay waste; destroy: *The forest was ravaged by fire.* **2** *n.* violence; destruction; great damage: *the ravages of war.* ❑ *v.* **rav·aged, rav·ag·ing. —rav′ag·er,** *n.*

rave (rāv), **1** *v.* to talk wildly. An excited, angry person may rave. **2** *v.* to talk with great enthusiasm: *They raved about the food.* **3** *v.* to howl; roar: *The wind raved about the lighthouse.* **4** *n.* great praise: *The new play drew raves from the critics.* ❑ *v.* **raved, rav·ing.**

rav·el (rav′əl), *v.* to separate into threads; fray: *The sweater has raveled at the elbow.* ❑ *v.* **rav·eled, rav·el·ing** *or* **rav·elled, rav·el·ling.**

Ra·vel (rə vel′), *n.* **Mau·rice** (mô rēs′), 1875-1937, French composer. ■ **Ravel** composed in a sophisticated form of impressionism, but he is most famous for his *Bolero,* which repeats one tune many times.

rav·el·ing (rav′ə ling), *n.* a thread drawn from a woven or knitted fabric.

ra·ven (rā′vən), **1** *n.* any of several birds like crows, but larger. **2** *n.* **Raven,** (in American Indian myths) a supernatural being, often described as a trickster, linked in stories with the creation of the world, light, and people, and with providing such human necessities as fire. **3** *adj.* deep, shiny black: *raven hair.*

raven (def. 1)—about 2 ft. (61 cm) long

rav·en·ing (rav′ə ning), *adj.* ravenous.

rav·en·ous (rav′ə nəs), *adj.* **1** very hungry. **2** greedy. **—rav′en·ous·ly,** *adv.* **—rav′en·ous·ness,** *n.*

ra·vine (rə vēn′), *n.* a long, deep, narrow valley eroded by running water.

rav·ing (rā′ving), *adj.* **1** talking wildly; delirious; frenzied; raging. ■ See Synonym Study at **hysterical.** **2** INFORMAL. remarkable; extraordinary: *a raving beauty.* **—rav′ing·ly,** *adv.*

rav·i·o·li (rav′ē ō′lē), *n.sing. or pl.* small, square pieces of dough filled with chopped meat, cheese, etc., and cooked by boiling in water. It is usually served with a tomato sauce. ❑ *n., pl.* **rav·i·o·li** *or* **rav·i·o·lis.**

rav·ish (rav′ish), *v.* **1** to fill with great delight; enrapture. **2** to carry off by force. **3** to rape. **—rav′ish·er,** *n.*

rav·ish·ing (rav′i shing), *adj.* very delightful; enchanting: *jewels of ravishing beauty.* **—rav′ish·ing·ly,** *adv.*

raw (rô), *adj.* **1** not cooked: *raw oysters, raw meat.* **2** in the natural state; not manufactured, treated, or prepared: *raw materials. Raw milk has not been pasteurized.* **3** not experienced; not trained: *Six months ago these well-trained soldiers were raw recruits.* **4** with the skin off; sore: *There was a raw spot on a horse where the harness rubbed.* **5** damp and cold: *A raw wind blew off the ocean.* **6** harsh; unfair: *a raw deal.* **—raw′ly,** *adv.* **—raw′ness,** *n.*

raw·boned (rȯ′bōnd′), *adj.* having little flesh on the bones; gaunt.

raw·hide (rȯ′hīd′), *n.* **1** the untanned skin of cattle. **2** rope or whip made of this.

raw material, substance in its natural state; anything that can be manufactured, treated, or prepared to make it more useful or increase its value. Coal, iron ore, petroleum, cotton, and soybeans are raw materials.

ray¹ (rā), *n.* **1** a beam of light: *rays of the sun.* ■ See Synonym Study at **beam.** **2** a beam of radiant energy: *X rays and other invisible rays of the electromagnetic spectrum.* **3** a slight trace; faint gleam: *Not a ray of hope pierced our gloom.* **4** a thin line or part coming out from a center. The petals of a daisy and the arms of a starfish are rays. **5** the part of a line on one side of any particular point on the line; half-line.

ray¹ (def. 1)

ray² (rā), *n.* any of numerous fishes with broad, flat bodies, very broad fins, and thin whiplike tails. They are related to sharks.

ray·on (rā′on), **1** *n.* fiber or fabric made from cellulose treated with chemicals. Rayon is often used to make lightweight clothing. **2** *adj.* made of rayon: *a rayon sweater.*

raze (rāz), *v.* to tear down; destroy completely. ❑ *v.* **razed, raz·ing.** ■ Another word that sounds like this is **raise.**

ra·zor (rā′zər), *n.* tool with one or more sharp blades for shaving.

ra·zor·back (rā′zər bak′), *n.* **1** a kind of thin, half-wild hog with a ridged back, common in the southeastern United States. **2** a sharp ridge on a hill, mountain, etc.

razz (raz), INFORMAL. **1** *v.* to laugh at; make fun of. **2** *n.* strong disapproval; derision. **3** *v.* to express disapproval of; boo: *The angry crowd razzed the umpire.*

Rb, symbol for rubidium.

RBI or **rbi,** (in baseball) run or runs batted in.

R.C., **1** Red Cross. **2** Roman Catholic.

rd., **1** road. **2** rod or rods.

Rd., Road.

R.D., Rural Delivery.

re¹ (rā), *n.* the second tone of the musical scale.

re² (rē), *prep.* with reference to; in the matter or case of; about; concerning: *re your letter of the 7th.*

Re, symbol for rhenium.

re-, *prefix.* **1** again; once more: *reappear = appear again.* **2** back: *repay = pay back.* **3** to ___ in new ways: *reclassify = classify in a new or different way.*

reach (rēch), **1** *v.* to get to; come to; arrive at: *reach the top of a hill, reach the end of a book, reach an agreement.* **2** *v.* to stretch out or hold out an arm or a hand: *I reached out in the dark and turned on the lights.* **3** *v.* to extend in space, time, influence, etc.: *Television reaches hundreds of millions of people.* **4** *v.* to touch: *I can reach to the top of the wall.* **5** *v.* to move to touch or seize something; try to get: *I reached for the rope.* **6** *v.* to get at; influence: *The speaker reached the hearts of the audience.* **7** *v.* to take or pass with the hand: *Please reach me the newspaper.* **8** *v.* to get in touch with someone: *I could not reach him today.* **9** *n.* act of stretching out; reaching: *With a long reach, the drowning man grasped the rope.* **10** *n.* extent or distance of reaching: *Food and water were left within reach of the dog.* **11** *n.* range; power; capacity: *The difficult lesson was beyond my reach.* **12** *n.* a continuous stretch or extent: *There are vast reaches of snow in the Antarctic.* ❑ *n., pl.* **reach·es** for 11,12. **—reach′a·ble,** *adj.*

re·act (rē akt′), *v.* **1** to act in response: *Dogs react to kindness by showing affection.* **2** to experience unpleasant effects because of something: *to react to a medicine with hives.* **3** to act chemically. Hydrogen reacts with oxygen to form water.
   react against, to act unfavorably toward or take an unfavorable attitude toward: *Some critics react against fads.*

re·act·ant (rē ak′tənt), *n.* a chemical that is involved in a reaction.

re·ac·tion (rē ak′shən), *n.* **1** action in response to some influence or force: *Our reaction to a joke is to laugh. The doctor observed carefully the patient's reactions to certain tests.* **2** action in the opposite direction: *The thrust of burned gases from a rocket engine produces a reaction that propels the rocket in flight.* **3** a political tendency toward a previous, usually more conservative, state of affairs. **4** the chemical change of one or more substances resulting in the formation of one or more additional substances. The reaction between nitrogen and hydrogen produces ammonia.

re·ac·tion·ar·y (rē ak′shə ner′ē), **1** *adj.* of or favoring a return to previous conditions, especially in politics: *The bad results of the revolution brought about a reactionary feeling.* **2** *n.* person who favors a return to previous conditions, especially in politics. ❑ *n., pl.* **re·ac·tion·ar·ies.** ■ **Reactionary** may be considered offensive.

re·ac·ti·vate (rē ak′tə vāt), *v.* to make active again; restore to active service. ❑ *v.* **re·ac·ti·vat·ed, re·ac·ti·vat·ing. —re·ac′ti·va′tion,** *n.*

re·ac·tive (rē ak′tiv), *adj.* **1** likely to react. **2** of or in reaction. **—re·ac′tive·ly,** *adv.*

re·ac·tor (rē ak′tər), *n.* machine for the release of atomic energy by a controlled chain reaction; pile; nuclear reactor. Reactors contain fissionable material such as uranium, controlling material such as graphite or heavy water, and coolant.

read¹ (rēd), *v.* **1** to get the meaning of writing or print: *read a book. The blind read by touching special raised print with their fingertips.* **2** to learn from writing or print: *I read of the event in the paper.* **3** to speak printed or written words; say aloud the words you see or touch: *Read to me.* **4** to show by letters, figures, signs, etc.: *The thermometer reads 70 degrees.* **5** to be worded in a certain way: *This line reads differently in the first edition.* **6** to get the meaning of; understand: *She seemed to read my thoughts.* **7** to give the meaning of; interpret: *A prophet reads the future.* **8** to understand or interpret something in a particular way, sometimes not the intended way: *read a hostile intent in a friendly letter.* **9** (in data processing) to copy data from a disk, tape, storage location, etc., often in order to enter the copy elsewhere. ❑ *v.* **read** (red), **read·ing.** ■ Another word that sounds like this is **reed.**
   read into, to interpret in a certain way, often attributing more than intended: *He read into the remark an insult.*
   read up on, to study or learn about by reading.

read² (red), **1** *adj.* having knowledge gained by reading; informed: *She is widely read in history.* **2** *v.* past tense and past participle of **read¹:** *I read that book last year. They have read it too.* ■ Another word that sounds like this is **red.**

a	hat	ė	term	ô	order	ch	child		a in about
ā	age	i	it	oi	oil	ng	long		e in taken
ä	far	ī	ice	ou	out	sh	she	ə	i in pencil
â	care	o	hot	u	cup	th	thin		o in lemon
e	let	ō	open	ů	put	ŦH	then		u in circus
ē	equal	ȯ	saw	ü	rule	zh	measure		

read·a·ble (rē′də bəl), *adj.* **1** easy to read; interesting: *a readable story with an interesting plot.* **2** capable of being read: *readable type.* —**read′a·bil′i·ty, read′a·ble·ness,** *n.*

read·er (rē′dər), *n.* **1** person who reads. **2** book for learning and practicing reading. **3** device that projects a readable image from microfilm.

read·i·ly (red′l ē), *adv.* **1** quickly; promptly; without delay: *The eager student answered readily.* **2** easily; without difficulty: *This information can be readily located in your science book.* **3** willingly.

read·i·ness (red′ē nis), *n.* **1** condition of being ready; preparedness. **2** quickness; promptness. **3** ease; facility. **4** willingness.

read·ing (rē′ding), **1** *n.* act or process of getting the meaning of writing or printing. **2** *n.* act of speaking written or printed words out loud; public recital. **3** *n.* written or printed matter read or to be read: *She has a lot of reading to do this weekend.* **4** *n.* amount shown by letters, figures, or signs on the scale of an device: *The reading of the thermometer was 96 degrees.* **5** *n.* interpretation: *Each actor gave the lines a different reading.* **6** *adj.* used in or for reading: *reading glasses.*

re·ad·just (rē′ə just′), *v.* to adjust again; arrange again. —**re′ad·just′ment,** *n.*

read-only memory. See ROM.

read·y (red′ē), **1** *adj.* prepared for action or use at once; prepared: *Dinner is ready. We are ready for the test.* **2** *adj.* willing: *I am ready to forget our disagreement.* **3** *adj.* quick; prompt: *a ready welcome, a ready wit.* **4** *adj.* apt; likely; liable: *She is too ready to find fault.* **5** *adj.* easy to get at; immediately available: *We always keep some ready money in the house.* **6** *v.* to make ready; prepare: *The expedition readied itself during the summer.* ❏ *adj.* **read·i·er, read·i·est;** *v.* **read·ied, read·y·ing.**

at the ready, prepared for action: *The soldiers walked down the road with their guns at the ready.*

read·y-made (red′ē mād′), *adj.* ready for immediate use; made for anybody who will buy; not made to order: *ready-made clothes.*

re·af·firm (rē′ə fėrm′), *v.* to affirm again or anew. —**re·af·fir·ma·tion** (rē′af ər mā′shən), *n.*

Rea·gan (rā′gən), *n.* **Ron·ald Wilson** (ron′əld), born 1911, the fortieth president of the United States, from 1981 to 1989.

re·a·gent (rē ā′jənt), *n.* substance used to detect, measure, or produce other substances by the chemical reactions it causes.

re·al[1] (rē′əl), **1** *adj.* existing as a fact; not imagined or made up; actual; true: *a real experience, the real reason.* **2** *adj.* genuine: *The bracelet is made of real gold.* **3** *adj.* (in law) of or about immovable property. Lands and houses are called real property. **4** *adv.* INFORMAL. very; extremely: *It was real kind of you to come.*

WORD FAMILY **Real**[1] and the words below are related. They all come from a Latin word meaning "a thing."

realistic	realize	realty	republic
reality	Realtor	rebus	surrealism

re·al[2] (rē′əl *or* rā äl′), *n.* a former small silver coin of Spain and Spanish America. ❏ *n., pl.* **re·als, re·a·les** (rā ä′lās).

real estate, land together with the buildings, fences, trees, water, minerals, etc., that belong with it. —**real′-es·tate′,** *adj.*

re·al·ism (rē′ə liz′əm), *n.* **1** thought and action based on realities: *Her realism caused her to dislike fanciful schemes.* **2** (in art and literature) the picturing of life as it actually is.

re·al·ist (rē′ə list), *n.* **1** person interested in what is real and practical rather than what is imaginary or theoretical. **2** artist or writer who represents things as they are in real life.

re·al·is·tic (rē′ə lis′tik), *adj.* **1** like the real thing; lifelike: *The speaker gave a very realistic picture of life a hundred years ago.* **2** seeing things as they are; prac-

realistic (def. 3)

tical: *She wanted to buy a car, but decided to be realistic and save her money for college.* **3** (in art and literature) representing life as it actually is. —**re′al·is′ti·cal·ly,** *adv.*

re·al·i·ty (rē al′ə tē), *n.* **1** actual existence; true state of affairs: *Ghosts have no place in reality.* **2** a real thing; actual fact: *Slaughter and destruction are terrible realities of war.* ❏ *n., pl.* **re·al·i·ties** for 2.

in reality, really; actually; in fact; truly: *They thought I was serious, but in reality I was joking.*

re·al·i·za·tion (rē′ə lə zā′shən), *n.* **1** clear understanding; full awareness; perception: *The explorers had a realization of the dangers that they were to face.* **2** act of making or becoming real: *Becoming a chemist was the realization of all his hopes.*

re·al·ize (rē′ə līz), *v.* **1** to understand clearly; be fully aware of: *I realize how hard you worked.* **2** to make real; bring into actual existence: *Her uncle's present made it possible for her to realize her dream of going to college.* **3** to obtain as a return or profit: *I realized $50 from mowing lawns.* ❏ *v.* **re·al·ized, re·al·iz·ing.**

re·al·ly (rē′ə lē), *adv.* **1** actually; truly; in fact: *Try to see things as they really are.* **2** indeed: *Oh, really?*

realm (relm), *n.* **1** kingdom. **2** region; range; extent: *This is beyond the realm of my understanding.* **3** a particular field of something: *the realm of biology, the realm of poetry.*

real number, any rational or irrational number.

real-time (rēl′tīm′), *adj.* of or about a computer process that updates information or user input as soon as it receives it, and responds immediately, without perceptible delay: *real-time animation, real-time communications.*

Re·al·tor (rē′əl tər), *n.* a real-estate agent who is a member of the National Association of Realtors.

re·al·ty (rē′əl tē), *n.* real estate.

ream[1] (rēm), *n.* **1** quantity of paper of the same sort and size, usually 500 sheets. A ream may include 480 or 516 sheets. **2** a very large quantity: *reams of nonsense.*

ream[2] (rēm), *v.* **1** to enlarge or shape a hole. **2** to remove with a reamer.

ream·er (rē′mər), *n.* **1** tool for enlarging or shaping a hole. **2** utensil for squeezing the juice out of oranges, lemons, etc.

reap (rēp), *v.* **1** to cut grain. **2** to gather a crop. **3** to cut grain or gather a crop from: *reap fields.* **4** to get as a return or reward: *Kind acts often reap happy smiles.*

reap·er (rē′pər), *n.* person or machine that cuts grain or gathers a crop.

re·ap·pear (rē′ə pir′), *v.* to appear again. —**re′ap·pear′ance,** *n.*

rear[1] (rir), **1** *n.* the back part; back: *the rear of the house.* **2** *adj.* at the back; in the back: *Leave by the rear door of the bus.* **3** *n.* the last part of an army, fleet, etc.

bring up the rear, to move onward as the rear part; come last in order.

rear[2] (rir), *v.* **1** to make grow; help to grow; bring up: *They reared their children to respect other people.* **2** to breed livestock. **3** to set up; build: *The Romans reared temples to their gods.* **4** to raise; lift up: *The snake reared its head.* **5** (of an animal) to rise on the hind legs; rise: *The horse reared and threw its rider.*

rear admiral, a military rank. See chart on page 712.

rear-end (rir′end′), *v.* to run into a motor vehicle from behind, damaging it: *The truck rear-ended my convertible.*

rear guard, troops assigned to protect the rear of an army.

re·arm (rē ärm′), *v.* **1** to arm again; arm yourself again. **2** to supply with new or better weapons. —**re·ar′ma·ment,** *n.*

re·ar·range (rē′ə rānj′), *v.* **1** to arrange in a new or different way: *They rearranged the living room furniture for the party.* **2** to arrange again: *I had to rearrange my papers after the wind blew them on the floor.* ❏ *v.* **re·ar·ranged, re·ar·rang·ing.** —**re′ar·range′ment,** *n.*

rear·view mirror (rir′vyü′), mirror mounted above the windshield or outside the door of a motor vehicle, enabling the driver to see traffic on the road behind.

rear·ward (rir′wərd), *adv., adj.* toward or in the rear.

rear·wards (rir′wərdz), *adv.* rearward.

rea·son (rē′zn), **1** *n.* cause or motive for an action, feeling, etc.: *I have my own reasons for doing this.* ■ See Synonym Study at **cause. 2** *n.* justification; explanation: *What is your reason for be-*

ing so late? **3** *n.* ability or power to think: *He was so angry he temporarily lost his reason.* **4** *v.* to think logically; think things out: *Most animals can't reason.* ■ See Synonym Study at **think. 5** *v.* to draw conclusions or inferences from facts or premises: *I reasoned that their alibi couldn't be true.* **6** *n.* right thinking; common sense. **7** *v.* to consider; discuss; argue: *If you reason with them they may change their minds.* [See Word Story at **ra-tio.**] —**rea′son·er,** *n.*

bring to reason, to cause to be reasonable: *The stubborn child was at last brought to reason.*

by reason of, on account of; because of: *School was dismissed by reason of the teachers' conference.*

in reason or **within reason,** within reasonable and sensible limits: *I will do anything in reason.*

stand to reason, be reasonable and sensible: *It stands to reason that you can't do your best if you're tired.*

rea·son·a·ble (rē′zn ə bəl), *adj.* **1** according to reason; sensible; not foolish. **2** not asking too much; fair; just. **3** not high in price; inexpensive: *a reasonable price.* **4** able to reason. —**rea′son·a·ble·ness,** *n.* —**rea′son·a·bly,** *adv.*

rea·son·ing (rē′zn ing), *n.* **1** process of drawing conclusions from facts or premises. **2** reasons; arguments.

re·as·sem·ble (rē′ə sem′bəl), *v.* to come or bring together again. □ *v.* **re·as·sem·bled, re·as·sem·bling.**

re·as·sur·ance (rē′ə shùr′əns), *n.* **1** new or fresh assurance. **2** restoration of courage or confidence.

re·as·sure (rē′ə shùr′), *v.* **1** to restore to confidence: *The crew's calmness during the storm reassured the passengers.* **2** to assure again or anew. □ *v.* **re·as·sured, re·as·sur·ing.** —**re′as·sur′ing·ly,** *adv.*

re·bate (rē′bāt), **1** *n.* a return of part of the money paid for something; partial refund; discount. **2** *v.* to return part of the money paid for something. □ *v.* **re·bat·ed, re·bat·ing.**

Re·bec·ca (ri bek′ə), *n.* (in the Bible) the wife of Isaac, and the mother of Esau and Jacob. [**Rebecca** comes from a Hebrew word meaning "cow."]

reb·el (reb′əl for noun, adj.; ri bel′ for verb), **1** *n.* person who resists or fights against authority instead of obeying: *The rebels armed themselves against the government.* **2** *adj.* defying law or authority: *a rebel army.* **3** *v.* to resist or fight against law or authority: *Unfair taxes made the colonists rebel.* **4** *v.* to feel a great dislike or opposition: *We rebelled at having to stay in on so fine a day.* □ *v.* **re·belled, re·bel·ling.**

WORD STORY **Rebel** comes from Latin words meaning "a war again." Sometimes, after the Romans conquered a country and added it to their empire, the conquered people would go to war again, trying to drive out the Roman rulers.

re·bel·lion (ri bel′yən), *n.* **1** armed resistance or fight against your government; revolt. ■ See Synonym Study at **revolt. 2** resistance or fight against any power or restriction.

re·bel·lious (ri bel′yəs), *adj.* **1** defying authority; acting like a rebel; mutinous: *The rebellious troops marched on the capital.* **2** hard to manage; hard to treat; disobedient: *a rebellious child.* —**re·bel′lious·ly,** *adv.* —**re·bel′lious·ness,** *n.*

re·bind (rē bīnd′), *v.* to bind again or anew: *This book with the broken back needs rebinding.* □ *v.* **re·bound, re·bind·ing.**

re·birth (rē′bėrth′ or rē bėrth′), *n.* a new birth; being born again: *a rebirth of national pride.*

re·born (rē bôrn′), *adj.* born again emotionally or spiritually.

re·bound[1] (ri bound′ for verb; rē′bound′ for noun), **1** *v.* to spring back. **2** *n.* act of springing back: *In handball, you hit the ball on the rebound.* **3** in basketball: **a** *n.* a ball that bounds back off the backboard or the rim of the basket after a shot has been made. **b** *v.* to catch a ball that bounds back in this way. —**re′bound·er,** *n.*

on the rebound, reacting to an unhappy situation, especially the sudden ending of a relationship: *He started dating her on the rebound, and now he's even more unhappy.*

re·bound[2] (rē bound′), *v.* past tense and past participle of **rebind:** *Send this book to be rebound.*

re·buff (ri buf′), **1** *n.* a blunt or sudden refusal to someone who makes advances, offers help, makes a request, etc.: *Her offer to*

help him met with the rebuff, "Leave me alone." **2** *v.* to give a rebuff to: *The friendly dog was rebuffed by a kick.*

re·build (rē bild′), *v.* to build again or anew. □ *v.* **re·built** (rē bilt′), **re·build·ing.**

re·buke (ri byük′), **1** *v.* to express disapproval of; reprove. **2** *n.* expression of disapproval; scolding: *The child feared the teacher's rebuke.* □ *v.* **re·buked, re·buk·ing.** —**re·buk′er,** *n.* —**re·buk′ing·ly,** *adv.*

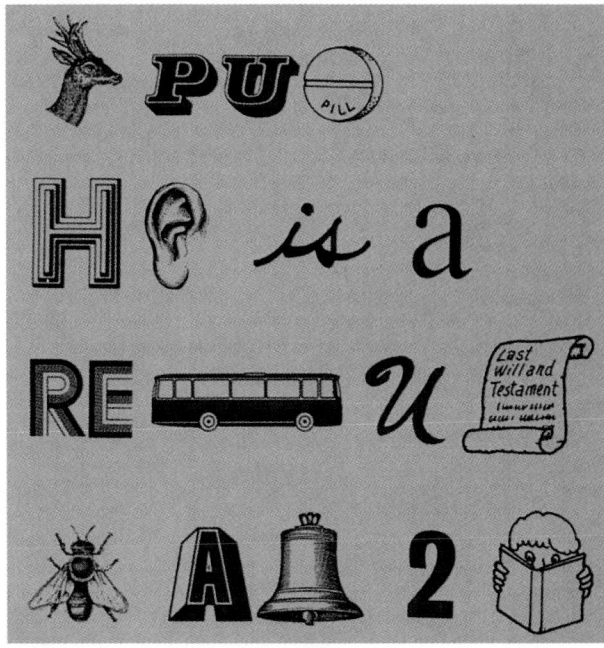

Dear pupil, Here is a rebus you will be able to read. **rebus**

re·bus (rē′bəs), *n.* a puzzle in which words are suggested by pictures, numbers, etc., that stand for syllables or words. A picture of a cat on a log is a rebus for catalog. □ *n., pl.* **re·bus·es.**

WORD STORY **Rebus** comes from Latin words meaning "by means of objects." In order to read a rebus, you need to know the names of the objects pictured.

re·but (ri but′), *v.* to offer arguments or reasons why something is untrue; try to disprove: *rebut an argument in a debate.* □ *v.* **re·but·ted, re·but·ting.** —**re·but′ta·ble,** *adj.* —**re·but′ter,** *n.*

re·but·tal (ri but′l), *n.* act of rebutting.

rec., **1** receipt. **2** recipe. **3** record. **4** recreation.

re·cal·ci·trance (ri kal′sə trəns), *n.* refusal to submit or comply.

re·cal·ci·trant (ri kal′sə trənt), *adj.* resisting authority or control; disobedient: *The recalcitrant patient would not take the pill.*

re·call (ri kól′ for verb; ri kól′ or rē′kól′ for noun), **1** *v.* to call back to mind; remember: *I can recall stories told to me when I was a small child.* ■ See Synonym Study at **remember. 2** *n.* act of recalling to mind. **3** *v.* to call back; order back: *The ambassador was recalled.* **4** *n.* act of calling back; ordering back. **5** *v.* to take back; withdraw: *The order has been given and cannot be recalled.* **6** *n.* act of taking back; revocation; annulment. **7** *v.* to call back something in order to replace or repair a defective part. **8** *n.* act of calling back a product in order to replace or repair a defective part. **9** *n.* procedure by which the people can vote to remove a public official before his or her term has expired.

re·cant (ri kant′), *v.* **1** to take back formally or publicly; withdraw or renounce a statement, opinion, purpose, etc.: *The re-*

a	hat	ė	term	ô	order	ch	child	
ā	age	i	it	oi	oil	ng	long	a in about
ä	far	ī	ice	ou	out	sh	she	e in taken
â	care	o	hot	u	cup	th	thin	ə i in pencil
e	let	ō	open	ù	put	ᴛʜ	then	o in lemon
ē	equal	ȯ	saw	ü	rule	zh	measure	u in circus

R

porter recanted the story when evidence proved it was false. **2** to renounce an opinion or allegiance: *The rebels knew there would be war, yet they would not recant.* **—re·can·ta′tion,** *n.*

re·cap¹ (rē kap′ *for verb;* rē′kap *for noun*), **1** *v.* to join a strip of rubber or similar material to a worn surface of a tire, by using heat and pressure. **2** *n.* a tire with such a strip on it. ❑ *v.* **re·capped, re·cap·ping. —re·cap′pa·ble,** *adj.*

re·cap² (rē kap′ *for verb;* rē′kap *for noun*), INFORMAL. **1** *v.* to recapitulate. **2** *n.* a recapitulation: *We heard a late news recap on the 10:30 news.* ❑ *v.* **re·capped, re·cap·ping.**

re·ca·pit·u·late (rē′kə pich′ə lāt), *v.* to repeat or recite the main points of; tell briefly; sum up. ❑ *v.* **re·ca·pit·u·lat·ed, re·ca·pit·u·lat·ing. —re′ca·pit′u·la′tion,** *n.*

re·cap·ture (rē kap′chər), **1** *v.* to capture again; have again. **2** *v.* to recall: *The picture album recaptured the past.* **3** *n.* act of capturing again. ❑ *v.* **re·cap·tured, re·cap·tur·ing.**

re·cast (rē kast′), *v.* **1** to cast again or anew: *recast a bell.* **2** to make over; remodel: *recast a sentence.* ❑ *v.* **re·cast, re·cast·ing.**

recd. or **rec'd.,** received.

re·cede (ri sēd′), *v.* **1** to go backward; move backward; withdraw: *When the tide receded we dug for clams.* **2** to slope backward: *a chin that recedes.* ❑ *v.* **re·ced·ed, re·ced·ing.**

re·ceipt (ri sēt′), **1** *n.* a written statement that money, a package, a letter, etc., has been received. **2** *v.* to write on a bill, etc., that something has been received or paid for: *Pay the bill and ask the grocer to receipt it.* **3** *n.pl.* **receipts,** money received; amount or quantity received: *Our expenses were less than our receipts.* **4** *n.* act of receiving or condition of being received: *On receipt of the news he went home.* **5** *n.* recipe.

re·ceiv·a·ble (ri sē′və bəl), *adj.* **1** fit for acceptance: *Gold is receivable all over the world.* **2** on which payment is to be received. Bills receivable are the opposite of bills payable.

re·ceive (ri sēv′), *v.* **1** to take something offered or sent; take into your hands or possession: *receive gifts.* **2** to be given or sent; get: *receive a letter from home.* **3** to take; support; bear; hold: *The foundation of a house receives its whole weight.* **4** to take or let into the mind; accept: *receive new ideas.* **5** to experience; suffer; endure: *He received swift punishment for cheating.* **6** to let into your house, society, etc.: *The people of the neighborhood were glad to receive the new couple.* **7** to change electromagnetic waves into sound or picture signals: *At night we can receive radio broadcasts from hundreds of miles away.* ❑ *v.* **re·ceived, re·ceiv·ing.**

re·ceiv·er (ri sē′vər), *n.* **1** person who receives. **2** thing that receives: *Public telephones have coin receivers.* **3** the part of a telephone held to the ear. **4** device that changes electromagnetic waves into sound or picture signals: *a radio or television receiver.* **5** someone appointed by law to take charge of the property of others: *He will act as receiver for the bankrupt firm.* **6** (in football) an offensive player eligible to receive a forward pass.

re·ceiv·er·ship (ri sē′vər ship), *n.* **1** position of a receiver in charge of the property of others. **2** condition of being in the control of a receiver.

re·cent (rē′snt), *adj.* **1** done or made not long ago: *This chair is a recent purchase.* **2** not long past; modern: *The recent period in history includes several wars.* [See word history information at **rinse.**] **—re′cent·ly,** *adv.* **—re′cent·ness,** *n.*

re·cep·ta·cle (ri sep′tə kəl), *n.* any container or place used to put things in to keep them conveniently. Bags, baskets, and vaults are all receptacles.

re·cep·tion (ri sep′shən), *n.* **1** manner of receiving: *She got a warm reception from her friend.* **2** a gathering to receive and welcome people: *Our school gave a*

reception for our new principal. **3** quality of the sound reproduced in a radio or of the sound and picture in a television receiver: *Reception was poor because we were so far from the transmitter.* **4** act of receiving or condition of being received: *calm reception of bad news. Her reception as a club member pleased her.* **5** (in football) a catch of a forward pass.

reception (def. 5)

re·cep·tion·ist (ri sep′shə nist), *n.* person employed to talk to customers or clients in a place of business, take telephone calls, etc.: *My sister is employed as a receptionist in a doctor's office.*

re·cep·tive (ri sep′tiv), *adj.* able, quick, or willing to receive ideas, suggestions, impressions, etc. **—re·cep′tive·ly,** *adv.* **—re·cep′tive·ness, re·cep·tiv′i·ty,** *n.*

re·cep·tor (ri sep′tər), *n.* a nerve cell or group of nerve cells sensitive to light, heat, taste, etc.

re·cess (rē′ses *or* ri ses′), **1** *n.* time during which work stops: *There will be a short recess before the next meeting.* ■ See Synonym Study at **intermission. 2** *v.* to take a recess: *The convention recessed until afternoon.* **3** *n.* part in a wall set back from the rest; alcove; niche. **4** *v.* to put in a recess; set back. **5** *n.* an inner place or part; quiet, secluded place: *the recesses of a cave, the recesses of your secret thoughts.* ❑ *n., pl.* **re·cess·es.**

re·ces·sion (ri sesh′ən), *n.* **1** time when business activity is somewhat slow and some people are out of work. It is shorter and less extreme than a depression. **2** act of going backward; moving or sloping backward; withdrawal.

re·ces·sion·al (ri sesh′ə nəl), *n.* hymn or piece of music sung or played while the clergy and the choir leave the church at the end of a service.

re·ces·sive (ri ses′iv), **1** *adj.* likely to go back; receding. **2** *n.* recessive gene. **3** *adj.* of or controlled by a recessive gene. **4** *n.* characteristic controlled by a recessive gene. **—re·ces′sive·ly,** *adv.* **—re·ces′sive·ness,** *n.*

recessive gene, gene that is overcome by the effect of another gene. The gene for blue eyes is a recessive gene. If it is paired with a gene for brown eyes, the gene for blue eyes will be overcome, and the eyes will be brown.

re·charge (rē chärj′), *v.* to charge again or anew: *recharge a battery.* ❑ *v.* **re·charged, re·charg·ing. —re·charge′a·ble,** *adj.*

rec·i·pe (res′ə pē), *n.* **1** set of directions for preparing something to eat: *Give me your recipe for cookies.* **2** set of directions for doing or preparing anything: *a recipe for happiness.*

re·cip·i·ent (ri sip′ē ənt), *n.* person or thing that receives something: *The recipients of the prizes had their names printed in the paper.*

re·cip·ro·cal (ri sip′rə kəl), **1** *adj.* in return: *Although she gave me a present, she expected no reciprocal gift from me.* **2** *adj.* existing on both sides; mutual: *reciprocal liking, reciprocal distrust.* **3** *adj.* (in grammar) expressing mutual action or relation. In "The two children like each other," *each other* is a reciprocal pronoun. **4** *n.* number so related to another that when multiplied together they give 1. 3 is the reciprocal of ⅓, and ⅓ is the reciprocal of 3. **—re·cip′ro·cal·ly,** *adv.*

re·cip·ro·cate (ri sip′rə kāt), *v.* **1** to give, do, feel, or show in return: *She likes me, and I reciprocate her liking.* **2** to interchange: *to reciprocate favors.* **3** to move or cause to move with an alternating backward and forward motion. ❑ *v.* **re·cip·ro·cat·ed, re·cip·ro·cat·ing. —re·cip′ro·ca′tion,** *n.*

rec·i·proc·i·ty (res′ə pros′ə tē), *n.* **1** reciprocal state; mutual action. **2** a mutual exchange, especially an exchange of special privileges in regard to trade between two countries.

re·cit·al (ri sī′tl), *n.* **1** a musical entertainment, given usually by a single performer: *My music teacher will give a piano recital Tuesday afternoon.* **2** act of reciting; telling facts in detail: *I hope that my lengthy recital of my problems hasn't bored you.* **3** story; account.

rec·i·ta·tion (res′ə tā′shən), *n.* **1** act of reciting a prepared lesson by pupils before a teacher. **2** act of telling facts in detail. **3** act of repeating something from memory. **4** piece repeated from memory.

rec·i·ta·tive (res′ə tə tēv′), *n.* **1** passage, part, or piece of music which is sung with the rhythm and phrasing of ordinary speech. Operas often contain long recitatives. **2** this style of singing.

re·cite (ri sīt′), v. **1** to say over; repeat: *He can recite that poem from memory.* **2** to say part of a lesson; answer a teacher's questions. **3** to give an account of in detail: *She recited the day's adventures.* ❏ v. **re·cit·ed, re·cit·ing.** —**re·cit′er,** n.

reck·less (rek′lis), adj. behaving or acting in a careless way, regardless of possible dangerous effects or results: *Reckless driving causes many accidents.* —**reck′less·ly,** adv. —**reck′less·ness,** n.

reck·on (rek′ən), v. **1** to find the number or value of; count: *Reckon the cost before you decide.* **2** to consider; judge; account: *He is reckoned the best speller in the class.* **3** DIALECT. to think; suppose. **4** to depend; rely: *You can reckon on our help.*
reckon with, to take into consideration.

reck·on·ing (rek′ə ning), n. **1** calculation; count; judgment of numbers or distances: *By my reckoning we are miles from home.* **2** settlement of an account: *a day of reckoning.* **3** bill, especially at an inn or tavern. **4** calculation of the position of a ship or aircraft.

re·claim (ri klām′), v. **1** to bring back to or put into a useful, good condition: *The farmer reclaimed the eroded land by terracing it and applying topsoil.* **2** to get from discarded things: *to reclaim rubber from old tires.* **3** to demand or ask for the return of: *We reclaimed our luggage at the end of the trip.* —**re·claim′a·ble,** adj. —**re·claim′er,** n.

rec·la·ma·tion (rek′lə mā′shən), n. restoration to a useful, good condition: *the reclamation of deserts by irrigation.*

re·cline (ri klīn′), v. to lean back; lie or lay down: *recline on a couch.* ❏ v. **re·clined, re·clin·ing.**

re·clin·er (ri klī′nər), n. a comfortable armchair with a seat and back that change position so that you can lean back comfortably.

rec·luse (rek′lüs or ri klüs′), n. someone who lives alone, away from society.

rec·og·ni·tion (rek′əg nish′ən), n. **1** act of recognizing. **2** condition of being recognized: *With a good disguise he escaped recognition.* **3** act of admitting or accepting that something is true: *We insisted on complete recognition of our rights.* **4** favorable notice; acceptance: *The author soon won recognition from the public.*

re·cog·ni·zance (ri kog′nə zəns), n. in law: **1** an agreement made in court by which someone promises to do something, such as to come to court again. **2** sum of money to be given up if the thing is not done.

rec·og·nize (rek′əg nīz), v. **1** to realize that someone or something has been seen or known before: *You have grown so much that I scarcely recognized you.* **2** to identify: *recognize a person from a description.* **3** to acknowledge acquaintance with; greet: *recognize a person on the street.* **4** to accept as true; admit; acknowledge: *They recognized and did their duty.* **5** to take notice of: *The delegate waited till the chairman recognized her.* **6** to show appreciation of. **7** to acknowledge and agree to deal with: *For some years other nations did not recognize the new government.* ❏ v. **rec·og·nized, rec·og·niz·ing.** —**rec′og·niz′a·ble,** adj. —**rec′og·niz′a·bly,** adv.

re·coil (ri koil′ *for verb;* ri koil′ *or* rē′koil *for noun*), **1** v. to pull yourself back; shrink back: *Most people would recoil at seeing a snake.* **2** v. to spring back: *The gun recoiled after I fired it.* **3** n. act of springing back: *The recoil of the shotgun hurt my shoulder.*

WORD STORY Recoil comes from two Latin words meaning "back" and "rump," used to suggest falling down into a sitting position. In the past, **recoil** meant a much larger backward movement than it does now.

rec·ol·lect (rek′ə lekt′), v. to call back to mind; remember. ■ See Synonym Study at **remember.**

re·col·lect (rē′kə lekt′), v. **1** to collect again. **2** to recover control of yourself.

rec·ol·lec·tion (rek′ə lek′shən), n. **1** thing remembered. **2** memory; remembrance: *This has been the hottest summer within my recollection.* **3** act or power of calling back to mind.

re·com·bi·nant DNA (ri com′bə nənt), DNA from different types of living cells that has been divided and recombined to produce new forms of life.

re·com·bine (rē′kəm bīn′), v. to combine again or anew. ❏ v. **re·com·bined, re·com·bin·ing.**

rec·om·mend (rek′ə mend′), v. **1** to speak in favor of; suggest favorably: *The teacher recommended him for the job. Can you recommend a good adventure story?* **2** to advise: *The doctor recommended that the patient stay in bed.* **3** to make pleasing or attractive: *The location of the camp recommends it as a summer home.* —**rec′om·mend′a·ble,** adj.

rec·om·men·da·tion (rek′ə men dā′shən), n. **1** thing recommended: *My recommendation is that you get plenty of sleep.* **2** words of advice or praise. **3** anything that recommends someone or something. **4** act of recommending.

rec·om·pense (rek′əm pens), **1** v. to pay someone; pay back; reward: *The travelers recompensed the man who so carefully directed them.* **2** v. to make a fair return for an action, anything lost, damage done, or hurt received: *The insurance company recompensed her for the loss of her car.* **3** n. payment; reward. **4** n. return; amends: *She received $8000 in recompense for the loss of her car.* ❏ v. **rec·om·pensed, rec·om·pens·ing.**

rec·on·cile (rek′ən sīl), v. **1** to make friends again: *The children had quarreled but were soon reconciled.* **2** to settle a quarrel or difference: *The teacher reconciled the dispute between the two pupils.* **3** to make agree; bring into harmony: *It is impossible to reconcile that story with the facts.* **4** to make satisfied; make no longer opposed: *reconcile yourself to the change in plans.* ❏ v. **rec·on·ciled, rec·on·cil·ing.** —**rec′on·cile′ment,** n. —**rec′on·cil′er,** n.

rec·on·cil·i·a·tion (rek′ən sil′ē ā′shən), n. **1** act of bringing together again in friendship. **2** settlement or adjustment of disagreements or differences: *a reconciliation of opposite points of view.*

re·con·di·tion (rē′kən dish′ən), v. to restore to a good or satisfactory condition by repairing, replacing used parts, etc.: *recondition an old car.*

re·con·nais·sance (ri kon′ə səns), n. examination or inspection of an area, especially for military purposes.

rec·on·noi·ter (rek′ə noi′tər or rē′kə noi′tər), v. **1** to approach and examine or observe in order to learn something: *Our scouts will reconnoiter the enemy's position before we attack.* **2** to approach a place and make a first survey of it: *It seemed wise to reconnoiter before entering the town.* —**rec′on·noi′ter·er,** n.

re·con·sid·er (rē′kən sid′ər), v. to consider again: *The assembly voted to reconsider a bill.* —**re′con·sid′er·a′tion,** n.

re·con·sti·tute (rē kon′stə tüt), v. to bring back to its original form or consistency: *to reconstitute frozen juice by adding water.* ❏ v. **re·con·sti·tut·ed, re·con·sti·tut·ing.** —**re·con′sti·tu′tion,** n.

re·con·struct (rē′kən strukt′), v. to construct again; rebuild; make over. ❏ v. **re·con·struct′i·ble,** adj.

re·con·struc·tion (rē′kən struk′shən), n. **1** act of reconstructing. **2** Reconstruction, **a** process by which the southern states after the Civil War were reorganized and their relations with the national government were reestablished. **b** period when this was done, from 1865 to 1877. **3** thing reconstructed.

re·cord (ri kôrd′ *for verb;* rek′ərd *for noun, adj.*), **1** v. to write down for future use: *Listen to the speaker and record what she says.* **2** v. to put in some permanent form; keep for remembrance: *We record history in books and pictures.* **3** n. the thing written or kept: *She made a record of her trip expenses.* **4** n. an official written account: *The secretary kept a record of what was done at the meeting.* **5** n. a thin, flat disk, usually of vinyl or other plastic, with narrow grooves on its surface, used on a phonograph. Variations in the grooves of the record are picked up by the needle of a phonograph and transformed into sound. **6** v. to copy music, words, or sounds, usually on magnetic tape, for future use. **7** n. the known facts about a person, group, organization, subject, etc.: *a fine record at school, a matter of record.* **8** n. a group of related pieces of information in a computer database. A person's name, address, and Zip Code form one record in a mailing list database. **9** n. the best yet done; best amount, rate, or speed yet reached: *Who holds*

a	hat	ė	term	ô	order	ch	child	
ā	age	i	it	oi	oil	ng	long	⎰ a in about
ä	far	ī	ice	ou	out	sh	she	ə ⎱ e in taken
â	care	o	hot	u	cup	th	thin	⎰ i in pencil
e	let	ō	open	ů	put	ŦH	then	o in lemon
ē	equal	ò	saw	ü	rule	zh	measure	u in circus

R

the record for the high jump? **10** *adj.* making or affording a record: *a record wheat crop.* **—re·cord′a·ble,** *adj.*

off the record, not to be recorded or quoted.

on record, recorded, especially publicly.

re·cord·er (ri kôr′dər), *n.* **1** person whose business is to make and keep records. **2** machine or part of a machine that records. The recorder of a cash register adds up and prints the amount of sales made. **3** tape recorder. **4** a wooden musical instrument with a tone something like a flute.

re·cord·ing (ri kôr′ding), *n.* magnetic tape, phonograph record, CD, laser disk, etc., on which sound or pictures and sound have been recorded.

record player (rek′ərd), device that reproduces sound from records; phonograph.

re·count¹ (ri kount′), *v.* to tell in detail; give an account of: *He recounted all the happenings of the day.*

re·count² or **re-count** (rē kount′ *for verb;* rē′kount′ *for noun*), **1** *v.* to count again: *I recounted the money to make certain it was the right amount.* **2** *n.* a second count: *The defeated candidate demanded a recount of the votes.*

re·coup (ri küp′), *v.* **1** to make up for: *recoup your losses.* **2** to repay: *I will recoup you for any money you spend.* **—re·coup′a·ble,** *adj.* **—re·coup′ment,** *n.*

re·course (rē′kôrs *or* ri kôrs′), *n.* **1** act of turning to someone for help or protection: *Our recourse in illness is to a doctor.* **2** person or thing appealed to or turned to for help or protection: *His only recourse in trouble was his family.*

have recourse to, to appeal to; turn to for help: *When we do not know what a word means, we have recourse to a dictionary.*

re·cov·er (ri kuv′ər), *v.* **1** to get well; get back to a normal condition: *She is recovering from a cold.* **2** to get back something lost, taken away, stolen, or sent out: *After the argument, I needed time to recover my temper. The police recovered the stolen car.* **3** to make up for something lost or damaged: *I hurried, trying to recover lost time.* **4** to regain in usable form; reclaim. Many useful substances are now recovered from materials that used to be thrown away. **—re·cov′er·a·ble,** *adj.* **—re·cov′er·er,** *n.*

SYNONYM STUDY **Recover** and **retrieve** both mean to get something back. **Recover** suggests something has been lost or given up: *The team recovered first place by winning this game.* **Retrieve** suggests much effort or search: *I had to go downtown to retrieve the book I left on the bus.*

re-cov·er (rē kuv′ər), *v.* to put a new cover on: *re-cover a couch.*

re·cov·er·y (ri kuv′ər ē), *n.* **1** act or process of coming back to health or normal condition: *She had a rapid recovery from surgery.* **2** act of getting back something that was lost, taken away, stolen, or sent out: *the recovery of a space capsule.* **3** act or process of getting back to a better situation: *an economic recovery.* □ *n., pl.* **re·cov·er·ies** for 1,3.

recovery room, room used in a hospital to treat patients recovering immediately after an operation or childbirth.

rec·re·ate (rek′rē āt), *v.* to take recreation. □ *v.* **rec·re·at·ed, rec·re·at·ing.**

re-cre·ate (rē′krē āt′), *v.* to create anew. □ *v.* **re-cre·at·ed, re-cre·at·ing. —re-′cre·a′tion,** *n.*

rec·re·a·tion (rek′rē ā′shən), *n.* play or amusement. Gardening, sports, games, and reading are all forms of recreation.

rec·re·a·tion·al (rek′rē ā′shə nəl), *adj.* of or used for recreation: *recreational opportunities, recreational areas.*

recreational vehicle, a motor vehicle designed for living and traveling in; motor home; RV.

recreation room, a room for informal entertaining or activities such as watching TV, listening to music, or playing games; rec room.

re·crim·i·na·tion (ri krim′ə nā′shən), *n.* Usually, **recriminations,** *pl.* accusations against someone who has accused you: *The quarreling children indulged in many recriminations, blaming each other for the argument.*

rec room (rek), INFORMAL. recreation room.

re·cruit (ri krüt′), **1** *n.* a newly enlisted member of one of the armed forces. **2** *v.* to get men and women to join one of the armed forces. **3** *n.* a new member of any group or class: *The Nature Club needs recruits.* **4** *v.* to get new members; get people to join: *recruit volunteers.* **—re·cruit′a·ble,** *adj.* **—re·cruit′er,** *n.* **—re·cruit′ment,** *n.*

rec·tal (rek′təl), *adj.* of or near the rectum. **—rec′tal·ly,** *adv.*

rec·tan·gle (rek′tang′gəl), *n.* a four-sided plane figure with four right angles. [See Word Story at **rector.**]

rec·tan·gu·lar (rek tang′gyə lər), *adj.* shaped like a rectangle. **—rec·tan′gu·lar·ly,** *adv.*

rec·ti·fi·er (rek′tə fī′ər), *n.* **1** device for changing alternating current into direct current. **2** person or thing that makes something right or corrects it.

rec·ti·fy (rek′tə fī), *v.* **1** to make right; put right; adjust; remedy: *The storekeeper admitted his mistake and was willing to rectify it.* **2** to purify or refine: *rectify a liquor by distilling it several times.* □ *v.* **rec·ti·fied, rec·ti·fy·ing. —rec′ti·fi′a·ble,** *adj.* **—rec′ti·fi·ca′tion,** *n.*

rec·ti·lin·e·ar (rek′tə lin′ē ər), *adj.* **1** formed by straight lines. **2** forming or moving in a straight line. **—rec′ti·lin′e·ar·ly,** *adv.*

rec·ti·tude (rek′tə tüd), *n.* upright conduct or character; honesty; righteousness.

rec·tor (rek′tər), *n.* **1** clergyman in the Protestant Episcopal Church or the Church of England who has charge of a parish. **2** priest in the Roman Catholic Church who has charge of a congregation or religious house. **3** the head of some schools, colleges, and universities.

WORD STORY **Rector** comes from a Latin word meaning "to keep straight." **Rectangle** comes from the same word plus **angle¹.** The Latin word was also used to mean "to steer," "to guide," and "to rule." **Ruler,** not surprisingly, comes from this same Latin word. In Latin as in English, a country's ruler guides people the way a straight-edged ruler guides a line.

rec·to·ry (rek′tər ē), *n.* a rector's house. □ *n., pl.* **rec·to·ries.**

rec·tum (rek′təm), *n.* the lowest part of the large intestine.

re·cum·bent (ri kum′bənt), *adj.* lying down; reclining; leaning. **—re·cum′bent·ly,** *adv.*

re·cu·pe·rate (ri kü′pə rāt′), *v.* **1** to recover from sickness, exhaustion, loss, etc.: *It took us a few days to recuperate after the long trip.* **2** to get back; regain: *She recuperated gradually everything she had lost.* □ *v.* **re·cu·pe·rat·ed, re·cu·pe·rat·ing. —re·cu·pe·ra′tion,** *n.* **—re·cu′pe·ra′tive,** *adj.*

re·cur (ri kėr′), *v.* **1** to come up again; occur again; be repeated: *Leap year recurs every four years.* **2** to return in thought or speech: *Seeing old friends made childhood memories recur to them. He recurred to the matter of cost.* □ *v.* **re·curred, re·cur·ring.**

re·cur·rence (ri kėr′əns), *n.* occurrence again; repetition; return: *prevent the recurrence of a mistake.*

re·cur·rent (ri kėr′ənt), *adj.* occurring again; repeated; recurring: *recurrent attacks of hay fever.*

re·cy·cle (rē sī′kəl), *v.* to process or treat something so that it can be used again. Paper, aluminum, and glass products are commonly recycled. □ *v.* **re·cy·cled, re·cy·cling. —re·cy′cla·ble,** *adj.* **—re·cy′cler,** *n.*

recycle—recycled bottle

red (red), **1** *n.* the color of blood or of a ruby. **2** *adj.* having the color of blood or of a ruby: *red paint, a red light, red ink.* **3** *adj.* being like or suggesting the color of blood: *red hair, a red fox.* **4** *n.* a red pigment or dye. **5** *n.* a red or reddish person, animal, or thing. **6 Red, a** *n.* a Communist or, sometimes, any extreme radical. Revolutionaries, socialists, and anarchists are often called Reds. **b** *adj.* Communist or extremely radical. ■ Another word that sounds like this is **read².** **—red′ly,** *adv.* **—red′ness,** *n.*

in the red, in debt; losing money.

see red, to become very angry.

red·bird (red′bėrd′), *n.* any of several birds with red feathers, such as the cardinal or the scarlet tanager.

red blood cell, cell in the blood that carries oxygen from the lungs to various parts of the body; red corpuscle; erythrocyte. Hemoglobin in these cells gives blood its red color.

red-blood·ed (red′blud′id), *adj.* full of life and spirit; vigorous.

red·breast (red′brest′), *n.* robin.

red·cap (red′kap′), *n.* porter at a railroad station whose uniform usually includes a red cap.

red-carpet (red′kär′pit), *adj.* extremely favorable and dignified; showing great respect: *When we won the contest, we received the red-carpet treatment.*

red cell, red blood cell.

Red Cloud, 1822-1909, a leader of the Lakota Sioux. ■ Red Cloud fought to keep white settlers on their way to Montana's gold fields out of Sioux territory. In 1868 the U.S. government agreed not to build roads and to give up their forts in Sioux territory. Because of this, Red Cloud has been called the only American Indian leader to defeat the U.S. government.

red·coat (red′kōt′), *n.* (long ago) a British soldier.

red corpuscle, red blood cell.

Red Cross, an international organization to care for the sick and wounded in war, and to relieve suffering caused by floods, fires, earthquakes, and other disasters. Its badge is a red cross on a white background.

red deer, deer native to the forests of Europe and Asia, formerly very common in England.

red·den (red′n), *v.* 1 to make or become red. 2 to blush: *She reddened with embarrassment at her mistake.*

red·dish (red′ish), *adj.* somewhat red. —**red′dish·ness,** *n.*

re·dec·o·rate (rē dek′ə rāt′), *v.* to decorate again, especially by painting or papering a room, etc.: *After we moved in, we decided to redecorate the dining room and the living room.* ❑ *v.* **re·dec·o·rat·ed, re·dec·o·rat·ing.**

re·ded·i·cate (rē ded′ə kāt), *v.* to dedicate again. ❑ *v.* **re·ded·i·cat·ed, re·ded·i·cat·ing.** —**re′ded·i·ca′tion,** *n.*

re·deem (ri dēm′), *v.* 1 to buy back: *The property on which money was lent was redeemed when the loan was paid back.* 2 to pay off: *We redeemed the mortgage.* 3 to make up for; balance: *A very good feature will sometimes redeem several bad ones.* 4 to turn in coupons or trading stamps for something valuable. 5 to set free; rescue; save; liberate; deliver; release: *redeemed from sin.*

re·deem·a·ble (ri dē′mə bəl), *adj.* 1 able to be redeemed. 2 to be redeemed or paid: *bonds redeemable in 2018.* —**re·deem′a·bly,** *adv.*

re·deem·er (ri dē′mər), *n.* 1 person who redeems. 2 **Redeemer,** Jesus.

re·demp·tion (ri demp′shən), *n.* 1 deliverance; rescue. 2 deliverance from sin; salvation. 3 act of buying back; paying off: *the redemption of a loan.* 4 a ransom.

Red·ford (red′fərd), *n.* **Rob·ert** (rob′ərt), born 1937, American movie actor and director. He won the 1980 Academy Award for best director for the movie *Ordinary People.*

red giant, a huge reddish star with a low surface temperature because it has used up much of its internal fuel.

red-hand·ed (red′han′did), *adj.* in the very act of crime, mischief, etc.: *be caught red-handed in a robbery.*

red·head (red′hed′), *n.* person having red hair: *Our class has ten blonds, fifteen brunettes, and three redheads.*

red·head·ed (red′hed′id), *adj.* having red hair.

redheaded woodpecker, a North American woodpecker with a red head. Its body and wings are black and white.

red herring, something used to draw attention away from the real issue.

red-hot (red′hot′), *adj.* 1 red with heat; very hot: *a red-hot iron.* 2 very enthusiastic; excited; violent: *a red-hot fanatic.* 3 fresh from the source: *red-hot rumors.*

re·did (rē did′), past tense of **redo.**

re·dis·cov·er (rē′dis kuv′ər), *v.* to discover again.

red-let·ter (red′let′ər), *adj.* memorable; especially happy: *Graduation is a red-letter day in your life.*

red light, 1 a red traffic light used to signal vehicles and pedestrians to stop. 2 an order denying permission to go ahead with something: *We thought we were going to be able to start a school recycling center, but the principal gave us the red light.*

red·line (red′līn′), *v.* to discriminate against by refusing to offer, or by charging unreasonably high rates for, mortgage loans or insurance: *to redline a neighborhood.* ❑ *v.* **red·lined, red·lin·ing.**

red line, in ice hockey, the line across the center of the rink that divides the rink in half. It is used as a boundary in ruling that a player is offside.

red line

re·do (rē dü′), *v.* to do again; do over: *My computer lost my term paper and I had to redo it last night.* ❑ *v.* **re·did, re·done** (rē-dun′), **re·do·ing.**

re·dou·ble (rē dub′əl), *v.* 1 to double again. 2 to increase greatly; double: *The swimmer redoubled her speed as she neared the finish line. We redoubled our efforts to finish our science project before the deadline.* 3 to double back: *The fox redoubled on its trail to escape the hunters.* ❑ *v.* **re·dou·bled, re·dou·bling.**

re·doubt (ri dout′), *n.* a small fort standing alone.

re·doubt·a·ble (ri dou′tə bəl), *adj.* causing fear or dread: *a redoubtable warrior, a redoubtable debater.* —**re·doubt′a·bly,** *adv.*

re·dound (ri dound′), *v.* to come back as a result; contribute: *The courage of the pioneers redounds to the glory of the nation.*

red pepper, 1 cayenne pepper. 2 any of several pepper plants that have hollow, mild or hot fruits, which are red when ripe.

re·dress (ri dres′ *for verb;* rē′dres *or* ri dres′ *for noun*), 1 *v.* to set right; repair; remedy: *King Arthur tried to redress wrongs in his kingdom.* 2 *n.* act or process of setting right; reparation; relief: *Anyone who has been injured deserves redress.* ❑ *n., pl.* **re·dress·es.**

Red River, 1 river flowing from NW Texas into the Mississippi. 2 **Red River of the North,** river flowing north from W Minnesota, between Minnesota and North Dakota into Lake Winnipeg in Manitoba.

Red River Rebellion, a Métis uprising in 1869-1870 to protest the takeover of their territory by the Canadian government from the Hudson's Bay Company.

Red Sea, narrow sea between the Arabian peninsula and Africa. It is part of the Indian Ocean and is connected with the Mediterranean Sea by the Suez Canal.

red shift, change toward red wavelengths in light from a star, galaxy, or other astronomical object moving away from Earth, caused by the Doppler effect. The discovery that many galaxies show a red shift led to the theory that the universe is expanding.

red·skin (red′skin′), *n.* a North American Indian. ■ **Redskin** is often considered offensive.

red·start (red′stärt′), *n.* a fly-catching American warbler. The male is black with bright orange patches on wings and tail.

red tape, too much attention to details and forms: *We had to deal with a lot of red tape from the city when we wanted to start our own recycling center at school.*

red tide, a reddish coloring on the surface of seawater, produced when some kinds of algae reproduce in large numbers. These algae also release poisons that can kill fish and make shellfish unsafe to eat.

re·duce (ri düs′), *v.* 1 to make less; make smaller; decrease: *We have reduced expenses this year. She is trying to reduce her weight.* 2 to become less in weight: *His doctor advised him to reduce.* 3 to bring down; lower: *The family's misfortunes reduced them to poverty. The major was reduced to the rank of captain.* 4

a	hat	ė	term	ô	order	ch	child		
ā	age	i	it	oi	oil	ng	long		a in about
ä	far	ī	ice	ou	out	sh	she		e in taken
â	care	o	hot	u	cup	th	thin	ə	i in pencil
e	let	ō	open	u̇	put	ᴛʜ	then		o in lemon
ē	equal	ò	saw	ü	rule	zh	measure		u in circus

R

to change to another form: *The chalk was reduced to powder. Reduce that statement to writing. If you reduce 3 lbs. 7 oz. to ounces, you have 55 ounces.* **5** to bring to a certain state, form, or condition: *The teacher soon reduced the noisy class to order. I was reduced to tears by the cruel words.* **6** to conquer; subdue: *The army reduced the fort by a sudden attack.* **7** to remove oxygen from. ❑ *v.* **re·duced, re·duc·ing. —re·duc′er,** *n.* **—re·duc′i·ble,** *adj.* **—re·duc′i·bly,** *adv.*

re·duc·tion (ri duk′shən), *n.* **1** act of reducing or condition of being reduced: *a reduction of ten pounds in weight. Failure to obey orders caused the corporal's reduction to the rank of private.* **2** amount by which a thing is reduced: *The reduction in cost was $5.* **3** form of something produced by reducing; copy of something on a smaller scale.

re·dun·dan·cy (ri dun′dən sē), *n.* **1** more than is needed. **2** a redundant thing, part, or amount. **3** the use of too many words for the same idea. ❑ *n., pl.* **re·dun·dan·cies** for 2.

re·dun·dant (ri dun′dənt), *adj.* **1** not needed; extra: *a redundant word.* **2** using too many words for the same idea; wordy: *"Two" in the phrase "the two twins" is redundant.* **—re·dun′dant·ly,** *adv.*

re·du·pli·cate (ri dü′plə kāt), *v.* to double; repeat. ❑ *v.* **re·du·pli·cat·ed, re·du·pli·cat·ing. —re·du′pli·ca′tion,** *n.*

red·wing (red′wing′), *n.* red-winged blackbird.

red-winged blackbird (red′wingd′), a North American blackbird. The male has a scarlet patch on each wing.

red wolf, a kind of wolf of the southeastern United States, now very rare, thought by some scientists to be a different species from the gray wolf. It has reddish fur and is smaller than a gray wolf.

red·wood (red′wud′), *n.* **1** a very large evergreen sequoia tree of California and Oregon coastal regions. Redwoods are the tallest living trees, many reaching a height of over 300 feet (90 meters). **2** its brownish red wood.

Redwood National Park, a national park in N California. The park contains the tallest known tree in the world.

re·ech·o or **re-ech·o** (rē ek′ō), *v.* to echo back; reverberate: *The house reechoes children's laughter. The thunder reechoed far behind.* ❑ *v.* **re·ech·oed, re·ech·o·ing** or **re-ech·oed, re-ech·o·ing.**

reed (rēd), *n.* **1** any of various kinds of tall grass with hollow, jointed stalks, growing in wet places. **2** a stalk of this grass. **3** anything made from the stalk of a reed, such as a musical pipe or an arrow. **4** a thin piece of wood, metal, or plastic in a musical instrument that produces sound when air is blown over it. ■ Another word that sounds like this is **read**[1].

reed instrument, a musical instrument that produces sound by means of a vibrating reed or reeds. Oboes, clarinets, and saxophones are reed instruments.

reed organ, a musical instrument producing tones by means of small metal reeds and played by keys; harmonium.

re·ed·u·cate (rē ej′ə kāt), *v.* **1** to educate or train someone for a new job or activity. **2** to educate or train someone to resume normal activities, for instance after a disabling injury or illness. ❑ *v.* **re·ed·u·cat·ed, re·ed·u·cat·ing. —re·ed′u·ca′tion,** *n.*

reed·y (rē′dē), *adj.* **1** full of reeds: *a reedy pond.* **2** like a reed or reeds: *reedy grass.* **3** sounding like a reed instrument: *a thin, reedy voice.* ❑ *adj.* **reed·i·er, reed·i·est. —reed′i·ness,** *n.*

reef[1] (rēf), *n.* ridge of rocks or coral at or near the surface of the water: *The ship was wrecked on a hidden reef.*

reef[2] (rēf), **1** *n.* the part of a sail that can be rolled or folded up to reduce the area exposed to the wind. **2** *v.* to reduce the area of a sail by rolling or folding up a part of it.

reef·er[1] (rē′fər), *n.* **1** SLANG. marijuana, especially rolled as a cigarette. **2** a short coat of thick cloth, worn especially at sea. **3** person who reefs a sail.

reef·er[2] (rē′fər), *n.* SLANG. a refrigerated trailer or railroad car.

reek (rēk), **1** *v.* to send out a strong, unpleasant smell: *The beach reeks of dead fish.* **2** *n.* a strong, unpleasant smell: *We noticed the reek of cooking cabbage as we entered the hall.* ■ Another word that sounds like this is **wreak. —reek′ing·ly,** *adv.*

reel[1] (rēl), **1** *n.* roller or spool for winding fishline, wire, hose, film, or anything that can be wound. **2** *n.* something wound on a reel: *two reels of movie film.* **3** *v.* to wind on a reel. **4** *v.* to draw with a reel or by winding: *She reeled in a fish.* **—reel′er,** *n.*
reel off, to say, write, or make in a quick, easy way: *She can reel off stories by the hour.*

reel[2] (rēl), **1** *v.* to suddenly sway or stagger from shock: *She reeled when the ball struck her.* **2** *v.* to sway in standing or walking: *The dazed boy reeled down the street.* **3** *v.* to be in a whirl; be dizzy: *My head was reeling after the fast dance.* **4** *n.* a reeling or staggering movement. **5** *v.* to become unsteady; waver: *The platoon reeled when the enemy attacked.*

reel[3] (rēl), *n.* **1** a lively dance. One kind is the Virginia reel. **2** music for it.

re·e·lect (rē′i lekt′), *v.* to elect again. **—re′e·lec′tion,** *n.*

re·en·list (rē′en list′), *v.* to enlist again or for an additional term. **—re′en·list′ment,** *n.*

re·en·ter (rē en′tər), *v.* to enter again; go in again: *The spacecraft reentered the atmosphere.*

re·en·try (rē en′trē), *n.* act or process of entering again or returning, especially of a rocket or spacecraft into the atmosphere after flight into outer space. ❑ *n., pl.* **re·en·tries.**

re·es·tab·lish or **re-es·tab·lish** (rē′ə stab′lish), *v.* to establish again; restore. **—re′es·tab′lish·ment** or **re′-es·tab′lish·ment,** *n.*

re·e·val·u·ate (rē′i val′yü āt), *v.* to evaluate again. ❑ *v.* **re·e·val·u·at·ed, re·e·val·u·at·ing. —re′e·val′u·a′tion,** *n.*

reeve (rēv), *n.* CANADIAN. **1** a local official of a village or township council in Ontario. **2** the elected head of a rural municipal council in Ontario and the western provinces.

re·ex·am·ine or **re-ex·am·ine** (rē′eg zam′ən), *v.* to examine again. ❑ *v.* **re·ex·am·ined, re·ex·am·in·ing** or **re-ex·am·ined, re-ex·am·in·ing. —re′ex·am′i·na′tion** or **re′-ex·am′i·na′tion,** *n.*

ref (ref), *n.* INFORMAL. referee.

re·fec·to·ry (ri fek′tər ē), *n.* a room for meals, especially in a monastery, convent, or school. ❑ *n., pl.* **re·fec·to·ries.**

re·fer (ri fér′), *v.* **1** to send or direct for information, help, or action: *Our teacher referred us to the librarian for some help with our questions.* **2** to hand over; submit: *Let's refer the dispute over who should be team captain to the teacher.* **3** to turn for information or help: *A person refers to a dictionary to find the meaning of words.* **4** to direct attention to or speak about: *The speaker referred to the Bible.* **5** to relate; apply: *The rule refers only to special cases.* ❑ *v.* **re·ferred, re·fer·ring. —re·fer′rer,** *n.*

ref·e·ree (ref′ə rē′), **1** *n.* person who rules on the plays in some games and sports: *a football referee.* **2** *n.* person to whom something is referred for decision or settlement. **3** *v.* to act as referee; act as referee in. ❑ *n., pl.* **ref·e·rees;** *v.* **ref·e·reed, ref·e·ree·ing.**

ref·er·ence (ref′ər əns), **1** *n.* act of calling someone's attention to something: *references to newspaper articles.* **2** *n.* statement referred to: *You will find that reference on page 16.* **3** *adj.* used for information or help: *The reference librarian can find the article you're looking for.* **4** *n.* person who can give information about another person's character or ability: *He gave his principal as a reference.* **5** *n.* statement about someone's character or ability: *When she left the company, she received an excellent reference from her boss.* **6** *n.* relation; respect; regard: *Everyone, without reference to age, was asked to volunteer during the emergency.*
in reference to or **with reference to,** about; concerning.
make reference to, to mention: *Don't make any reference to it.*

reference book, book containing helpful facts or information: *A dictionary is a reference book.*

ref·er·en·dum (ref/ə ren/dəm), *n.* **1** process of submitting a bill already passed by the lawmaking group to the direct vote of the citizens for approval or rejection. **2** act of submitting any matter to a direct vote. ❑ *n., pl.* **ref·er·en·dums, ref·er·en·da** (ref/ə ren/də).

re·fer·ral (ri fėr/əl), *n.* **1** act of referring. **2** person who is referred.

re·fill (rē fil/ *for verb;* rē/fil/ *for noun*), **1** *v.* to fill again: *refill a glass.* **2** *n.* something to refill with: *a refill for a pen.* **3** *n.* act of filling again: *I got a refill for my prescription.*

re·fi·nance (rē fi/nans), *v.* **1** to finance again, especially by arranging a loan at a new interest rate or over a different length of time. **2** to pay off debts or loans by arranging a loan with new terms. ❑ *v.* **re·fi·nanced, re·fi·nanc·ing.**

re·fine (ri fīn/), *v.* **1** to make or become pure: *Sugar, oil, and metals are refined before being used.* **2** to make or become fine, polished, or cultivated: *refine your way of speaking.* **3** to make very fine, subtle, or exact. ❑ *v.* **re·fined, re·fin·ing. —re·fin/er,** *n.*

    refine on or **refine upon,** 1 to improve. 2 to excel.

re·fined (ri fīnd/), *adj.* **1** freed from impurities; made pure: *refined sugar.* **2** showing education and good taste; well-bred: *refined tastes, a refined voice, refined manners.*

re·fine·ment (ri fīn/mənt), *n.* **1** fineness of feeling, taste, manners, or language: *Good manners and correct speech are marks of refinement.* **2** act or result of refining: *Gasoline is produced by the refinement of petroleum.* **3** improvement.

re·fin·er·y (ri fī/nər ē), *n.* a building and machinery for purifying petroleum, sugar, or other things. ❑ *n., pl.* **re·fin·er·ies.**

re·fin·ish (rē fin/ish), *v.* to give wood, metal, etc., a new finish. **—re·fin/ish·er,** *n.*

re·fit (rē fit/), *v.* to prepare or equip for use again: *The old ship was refitted for the voyage.* ❑ *v.* **re·fit·ted, re·fit·ting.**

re·flect (ri flekt/), *v.* **1** to turn back or throw back light, heat, sound, etc.: *A white roof reflects the heat of the sun.* **2** to give back a likeness or image of: *The sky was reflected in the still pond.* **3** to reproduce or show like a mirror: *The newspaper reflected the owner's opinions.* **4** to think carefully: *Take time to reflect before making a decision.* **5** to cast blame, reproach, or discredit: *The children's spoiled behavior reflected on their parents.* **6** to bring or give back: *A kind act reflects credit on the person who does it.*

reflecting telescope, telescope in which light is gathered and focused by a concave mirror.

re·flec·tion (ri flek/shən), *n.* **1** likeness; image: *the reflection of sailboats in the water.* **2** something reflected. **3** act of reflecting or condition of being reflected: *The reflection of the sun's rays by sand and water can cause sunburn.* **4** careful thinking: *On reflection, the plan seemed too dangerous.* **5** idea or remark resulting from careful thinking. **6** remark or action that casts blame or discredit. **7** blame; discredit.

reflection (def. 1)

re·flec·tive (ri flek/tiv), *adj.* **1** able to reflect; reflecting: *the reflective surface of polished metal.* **2** thoughtful: *The judge had a reflective look.* **—re·flec/tive·ly, adv. —re·flec/tive·ness, re·flec·tiv/i·ty,** *n.*

re·flec·tor (ri flek/tər), *n.* **1** any thing, surface, or device that reflects light, heat, sound, etc., especially a piece of glass or metal, usually concave, for reflecting light in a required direction. **2** reflecting telescope.

re·flex (rē/fleks), **1** *n.* an involuntary action in direct response to stimulation of particular nerve cells. Sneezing, vomiting, and shivering are reflexes. **2** *adj.* not voluntary; coming as a direct response to a stimulation of particular nerve cells. Yawning is a reflex action. ❑ *n., pl.* **re·flex·es. —re/flex·ly,** *adv.*

re·flex·ive (ri flek/siv), **1** *adj.* (in grammar) expressing an action that refers back to the subject. **2** *n.* a reflexive verb or pronoun. In "I hurt myself," *hurt* and *myself* are reflexives. **—re·flex/ive·ly, adv. —re·flex/ive·ness,** *n.*

re·flux (rē/fluks), *n.* act of flowing back; ebb of a tide. ❑ *n., pl.* **re·flux·es.**

re·fo·rest (rē fôr/ist), *v.* to replant an area with trees. **—re/fo·rest·a/tion,** *n.*

re·form (ri fôrm/), **1** *v.* to make better; improve by removing faults: *Some prisons try to reform criminals instead of just punishing them.* ■ See Synonym Study at **improve.** **2** *n.* a change intended to improve conditions; improvement: *The new government made many reforms.* **3** *v.* to become better: *They promised to reform if given another chance.* **—re·form/a·ble,** *adj.*

re-form (rē fôrm/), *v.* **1** to form again. **2** to take a new shape.

ref·or·ma·tion (ref/ər mā/shən), *n.* **1** act or process of reforming or condition of being reformed; change for the better; improvement. **2 Reformation,** the religious movement in Europe in the 1500s that aimed at reform within the Roman Catholic Church but led to the establishment of Protestant churches.

re·form·a·to·ry (ri fôr/mə tôr/ē), **1** *n.* an institution that is both a school and a prison for young people who have broken the law. **2** *adj.* serving or meant to reform. ❑ *n., pl.* **re·form·a·to·ries.**

re·form·er (ri fôr/mər), *n.* person who reforms, or tries to reform, some state of affairs, custom, etc.; supporter of reforms.

reform school, reformatory.

re·fract (ri frakt/), *v.* to bend a ray or waves from a straight course. Water refracts light. **—re·fract/ive,** *adj.*

refracting telescope, telescope in which light is gathered and focused by a lens.

re·frac·tion (ri frak/shən), *n.* act or process of bending a ray of light, sound waves, etc., when passing from one medium into another of different density.

re·frac·tor (ri frak/tər), *n.* **1** anything that bends waves, light rays, etc. **2** refracting telescope.

re·frac·to·ry (ri frak/tər ē), *adj.* **1** hard to manage; stubborn; obstinate: *Mules are refractory.* **2** not yielding readily to treatment: *She had a refractory cough.* **3** hard to melt, reduce, or work: *refractory ores.* **—re·frac/to·ri·ly, adv. —re·frac/to·ri·ness,** *n.*

re·frain¹ (ri frān/), *v.* to keep yourself from doing something: *Refrain from wrongdoing.* **—re·frain/er,** *n.* **—re·frain/ment,** *n.*

re·frain² (ri frān/), *n.* phrase or verse repeated regularly in a song or poem. In "The Star-Spangled Banner" the refrain is "O'er the land of the free and the home of the brave."

re·fresh (ri fresh/), *v.* to make fresh again; freshen up; renew: *His bath refreshed him. She refreshed her memory by a glance at the book.*

re·fresh·er (ri fresh/ər), *adj.* helping to renew knowledge or abilities, or to bring a person new needed knowledge: *take a refresher course in French.*

re·fresh·ing (ri fresh/ing), *adj.* **1** able to refresh: *Cool drinks are refreshing on a warm day.* **2** welcome as a pleasing change. **—re·fresh/ing·ly, adv.**

re·fresh·ment (ri fresh/mənt), *n.* **1** thing that refreshes: *Fruit juice was the only refreshment served.* **2 refreshments,** *pl.* food or drink: *Cake and lemonade were the refreshments at our party.* **3** act of refreshing.

re·fried beans (rē/frīd/), frijoles that have been cooked until soft, fried, then fried again after being mashed.

re·frig·er·ant (ri frij/ər ənt), *n.* something that cools. Ice is a refrigerant.

re·frig·er·ate (ri frij/ə rāt/), *v.* to make or keep food, etc., cold or cool: *Milk, meat, and ice cream must be refrigerated to prevent spoiling.* ❑ *v.* **re·frig·er·at·ed, re·frig·er·at·ing. —re·frig/er·a/tion,** *n.*

re·frig·er·a·tor (ri frij/ə rā/tər), *n.* appliance or room that keeps foods and other items cool, usually by mechanical means.

R

a	hat	ė	term	ô	order	ch	child		a in about
ā	age	i	it	oi	oil	ng	long		e in taken
ä	far	ī	ice	ou	out	sh	she	ə	i in pencil
â	care	o	hot	u	cup	th	thin		o in lemon
e	let	ō	open	ů	put	ŦH	then		u in circus
ē	equal	ò	saw	ü	rule	zh	measure		

re·fu·el (rē fyü′əl), *v.* **1** to supply with fuel again. **2** to take on a fresh supply of fuel. ❑ *v.* **re·fu·eled, re·fu·el·ing** or **re·fu·elled, re·fu·el·ling.**

ref·uge (ref′yüj), *n.* shelter or protection from danger or trouble; safety; security: *The cat took refuge in a tree.* ■ See Synonym Study at **shelter.**

ref·u·gee (ref′yə jē′ *or* ref′yə jē′), *n.* person who flees for refuge or safety, especially to a foreign country, in time of persecution, war, or disaster: *Refugees from the war were cared for in neighboring countries.* ❑ *n., pl.* **ref·u·gees.**

re·fund (ri fund′ *or* rē′fund *for verb;* rē′fund *for noun*), **1** *v.* to pay back: *If the refrigerator doesn't work, the store will refund your money.* **2** *n.* a return of money paid: *When the show was cancelled, refunds were given to ticket holders.* **3** *n.* the money paid back: *I put my tax refund in a savings account.* [See Word Story at **refuse**[1].] **—re·fund′er,** *n.*

re·fund·a·ble (ri fund′ə bəl), *adj.* able to be refunded or returned: *a refundable bottle deposit.*

re·fur·bish (rē fėr′bish), *v.* to polish up again; brighten; renovate: *refurbish an old house.* **—re·fur′bish·ment,** *n.*

re·fus·al (ri fyü′zəl), *n.* **1** act of refusing: *a refusal to lend money.* **2** the right to refuse or take a thing before it is offered to others: *Please give me first refusal if you decide to sell your car.*

re·fuse[1] (ri fyüz′), *v.* **1** to say no to; decline to accept; reject: *He refuses the offer. They refused to go with me, so I went by myself.* **2** to say no: *She is free to refuse.* **3** to say you will not do it, give it, etc.: *refuse to obey.* ❑ *v.* **re·fused, re·fus·ing. —re·fus′er,** *n.*

WORD STORY **Refuse**[1] comes from a Latin word meaning "to pour back." If someone said no to a drink, it was poured back into the jar. Something that everyone said no to became known as **refuse**[2]. **Refund** comes from the same Latin word.

---

ref·use[2] (ref′yüs), *n.* useless stuff; waste; rubbish: *The street-cleaning department took away all refuse from the streets.* [See Word Story at **refuse**[1].]

re·fuse·nik (ri fyüz′nik), *n.* **1** someone who refuses to do something that is expected of him or her: *The refusenik didn't perform her hit song at the concert, and a lot of fans were disappointed.* **2** (earlier) a citizen of the Soviet Union, usually Jewish, who was refused permission to emigrate.

re·fute (ri fyüt′), *v.* to show that a claim, opinion, or argument is false or incorrect; prove wrong; disprove: *He refuted the rumors with facts.* ❑ *v.* **re·fut·ed, re·fut·ing. —ref·u·ta·tion** (ref′yə tā′shən), *n.* **—re·fut′er,** *n.*

reg (reg), *n.* INFORMAL. regulation.

re·gain (ri gān′), *v.* **1** to get again; recover: *After the illness, she regained her health quickly.* **2** to get back to; reach again: *You can regain the main road by turning left two miles ahead.*

re·gal (rē′gəl), *adj.* **1** belonging to a king or queen; royal: *regal power.* **2** fit for a king or queen; stately; splendid; magnificent: *a regal banquet.* **—re′gal·ly,** *adv.*

re·gale (ri gāl′), *v.* **1** to entertain agreeably; delight with something pleasing: *Grandmother regaled us with exciting stories about her travels in Africa.* **2** to entertain with a choice meal; feast. ❑ *v.* **re·galed, re·gal·ing.**

re·ga·li·a (ri gā′lē ə), *n.pl.* **1** the emblems of royalty. Crowns and scepters are regalia. **2** the emblems or decorations of any society or order. **3** clothes, especially fine clothes: *in party regalia.*

re·gard (ri gärd′), **1** *v.* to think of; consider: *Our school band is regarded as the best in the state.* **2** *v.* to show thought or consideration for; care for; respect: *regard the rights of others.* **3** *v.* to take notice of; heed: *regard all traffic laws.* **4** *n.* consideration; thought; care: *Have regard for the feelings of others.* **5** *v.* to look at; look closely at; watch: *The cat regarded me anxiously when I picked up her kittens.* **6** *n.* esteem; favor; good opinion: *He has high regard for your ability.* **7** *n.pl.* **regards,** good wishes; greetings: *She sends her regards.* **8** *n.* point; particular matter: *You are wrong in this regard.* **—re·gard′a·ble,** *adj.*

as regards, with respect to; concerning: *As regards money, I have enough to go out to a fancy dinner once a week.*

in regard to or **with regard to,** relating to; concerning; about; regarding: *The teacher spoke to me in regard to being late.*

without regard to, not considering: *They decided where we would go for vacation without regard to my wishes.*

re·gard·ful (ri gärd′fəl), *adj.* heedful or observant; mindful. **—re·gard′ful·ly,** *adv.* **—re·gard′ful·ness,** *n.*

re·gard·ing (ri gär′ding), *prep.* with regard to; concerning; about: *A letter regarding the field trip was sent to parents.*

re·gard·less (ri gärd′lis), **1** *adj.* with no concern for; careless: *Regardless of the danger, they crossed the thin ice.* **2** *adv.* in spite of what happens: *We plan to leave on Monday, and we will leave then, regardless.* **—re·gard′less·ly,** *adv.* **—re·gard′less·ness,** *n.*

re·gat·ta (ri gat′ə), *n.* a boat race or a series of boat races. ❑ *n., pl.* **re·gat·tas.**

regatta

re·gen·cy (rē′jən sē), *n.* **1** the position, office, or function of a regent or group of regents: *The Queen Mother held the regency till the young king became of age.* **2** a group of regents. **3** a government consisting of regents. **4** the time during which there is a regency. ❑ *n., pl.* **re·gen·cies.**

re·gen·er·ate (ri jen′ə rāt′ *for verb;* ri jen′ər it *for adj.*), **1** *v.* to give a new and better spiritual life to; improve the moral condition of. **2** *v.* to put new life and spirit into. **3** *adj.* born again spiritually; formed anew morally. **4** *v.* to grow again; form new tissue, a new part, etc., to replace what is lost: *If a young crab loses a claw, it will often regenerate a new one.* ❑ *v.* **re·gen·er·at·ed, re·gen·er·at·ing. —re·gen′er·a′tion,** *n.* **—re·gen′er·a′tive,** *adj.*

re·gent (rē′jənt), *n.* **1** person who rules when the regular ruler is absent, disabled, or too young: *The Queen will be the regent till her son grows up.* **2** member of a governing board. Many universities have boards of regents.

WORD FAMILY **Regent** and the words below are related. They all come from a Latin word meaning "to rule," "to guide," or "to keep straight."

correct	directory	rector	regular
direct	erect	regime	regulate
directive	irregular	regiment	rule
director	rectify	region	ruler

---

reg·gae (reg′ā *or* rā′gā), *n.* kind of popular music that began in the West Indies, with a lively rhythm that combines blues and rock'n'roll.

re·gime or **ré·gime** (ri zhēm′ *or* rā zhēm′), *n.* **1** system of government or rule: *the Communist regime in China.* **2** regimen.

reg·i·men (rej′ə men), *n.* a set of rules or habits of diet, exercise, or manner of living, intended to improve health, reduce weight, etc.: *The baby's regimen includes two naps a day.*

reg·i·ment (rej′ə mənt *for noun;* rej′ə ment′ *for verb*), **1** *n.* a military unit made up of several battalions, usually commanded by a colonel. It is smaller than a brigade. **2** *v.* to treat in a strict or uniform manner: *A dictatorship regiments its citizens.*

reg·i·men·tal (rej′ə men′tl), **1** *adj.* of or about a regiment. **2** *n.pl.* **regimentals,** a military uniform. **—reg′i·men′tal·ly,** *adv.*

reg·i·men·ta·tion (rej′ə men tā′shən), *n.* **1** subjection to control. **2** formation into organized or uniform groups. **3** act of making uniform.

Re·gi·na (ri jī′nə), *n.* capital of Saskatchewan, Canada.

re·gion (rē′jən), *n.* **1** any place, space, or area: *a mountainous region.* ■ See Synonym Study at **zone. 2** a large part of the earth's surface: *the region near the equator.* **3** a part of the body: *the region of the heart.* **4** a field of thought or action; sphere: *the region of the imagination.* **5** (in Canada) a governmental unit in Ontario larger than a county, first set up in 1973.

re·gion·al (rē′jə nəl), *adj.* of or in a particular region: *a regional weather forecast.* —**re′gion·al·ly**, *adv.*

Regional word choices can be quite different, and the habits of word use formed in a particular region are usually very strong and long-lasting. If you live in a part of the country where a soft drink is called a *soda*, someone who asks for a can of *pop* will sound odd to you. Do you call a big sandwich on a roll a *submarine*, or *hero*, or something else? Do you call a soft paper container a *bag* or a *sack* or a *poke*? From these and other regional word choices, an expert in language can figure out where you're from, without even meeting you.

re·gion·al·ism (rē′jə nə liz′əm), *n.* **1** full knowledge of or strong loyalty to a certain region. **2** the use of regional customs, ways of life, etc., in literature and art. **3** expression, dialect, custom, etc., common in a region.

re·gion·al·ist (rē′jə nə list), **1** *n.* person who practices regionalism. **2** *adj.* of or inclined to regionalism.

reg·is·ter (rej′ə stər), **1** *v.* to write in a list or record: *Register the names of the new members.* **2** *v.* to have your name written in a list or record: *Citizens must register before they can vote.* **3** *n.* a list or record: *a register of class attendance.* **4** *n.* book in which a list or record is kept: *After signing the hotel register, we were shown to our rooms.* **5** *v.* to have a letter, parcel, etc., recorded in a post office, paying extra postage for special care in delivery: *She registered the letter containing the check.* **6** *n.* thing that records. A cash register shows the amount of money taken in. **7** *v.* to indicate; record: *The thermometer registers 90 degrees.* **8** *v.* to show surprise, joy, anger, etc., by the expression on your face or by actions. **9** *n.* the range of a voice or an instrument. **10** *n.* an opening in a wall or floor that has a device to regulate the amount of air coming from a furnace or central air conditioner.

registered nurse, a graduate nurse licensed by state authority to practice nursing.

reg·is·trant (rej′ə strənt), *n.* person who registers.

reg·is·trar (rej′ə strär), *n.* official who keeps a register; official recorder.

reg·is·tra·tion (rej′ə strā′shən), *n.* **1** act of registering: *Registration of new students is next Monday.* **2** an entry in a register. **3** a legal document showing proof that someone or something has been registered: *The police officer asked to see our car registration.* **4** number of people registered: *Registration for camp is higher than last year.*

reg·is·try (rej′ə strē), *n.* **1** act of registering; registration. **2** place where a register is kept; office of registration. **3** book in which a list or record is kept; register. ❏ *n., pl.* **reg·is·tries** for 2,3.

re·gress (ri gres′), *v.* to return to an earlier condition or stage of development. —**re·gres′sion**, *n.* —**re·gres′sor**, *n.*

re·gres·sive (ri gres′iv), *adj.* showing regression. —**re·gres′sive·ly**, *adv.* —**re·gres′sive·ness**, *n.*

re·gret (ri gret′), **1** *v.* to feel sorry for or about: *We regretted his absence.* **2** *v.* to feel sorry; mourn: *He wrote regretting that he could not visit us.* **3** *n.* the feeling of being sorry; sense of loss; sorrow: *With regret she remembered her forgotten promise.* **4** *n.pl.* **regrets,** a polite reply declining an invitation: *She could not come to the party, but she sent her regrets.* ❏ *v.* **re·gret·ted, re·gret·ting.** —**re·gret′ter**, *n.*

re·gret·ful (ri gret′fəl), *adj.* feeling or expressing regret; sorrowful; sorry. —**re·gret′ful·ly**, *adv.* —**re·gret′ful·ness**, *n.*

re·gret·ta·ble (ri gret′ə bəl), *adj.* deserving or giving cause for regret: *It is regrettable that our neighborhood school is being closed.* —**re·gret′ta·bly**, *adv.*

re·group (rē grüp′), *v.* **1** to form into a new group; reorganize: *The colonel regrouped the platoons after the battle.* **2** (in subtraction) to take one from the next digit on the left and add its place value to the digit being subtracted from; borrow: *To subtract 28 from 51, regroup 51 into 4 tens and 11 ones.*

reg·u·lar (reg′yə lər), **1** *adj.* fixed by custom or rule; usual; normal: *Six o'clock was her regular hour of rising.* ▪ See Synonym Study at **usual.** **2** *adj.* following some rule or principle; accord-

ing to rule: *A period is the regular ending for a sentence.* **3** *adj.* coming, acting, or done again and again at the same time: *I make regular visits to the dentist.* **4** *adj.* steady; habitual: *A regular customer shops often at the same store.* **5** *adj.* even in size, spacing, or speed; well-balanced: *regular features, regular breathing.* **6** *adj.* symmetrical. **7** *adj.* orderly; methodical: *He leads a regular life.* **8** *adj.* properly trained: *The regular cook in our school cafeteria is sick.* **9** *adj.* (of a word) having the usual endings; inflected in the usual way. "Ask" is a regular verb. **10** *adj.* INFORMAL. thorough; complete: *a regular bore.* **11** *adj.* INFORMAL. fine; agreeable: *He's a regular fellow.* **12** *n.* member of a regularly paid group of any kind: *The fire department was made up of regulars and volunteers.* **13** *adj.* of or belonging to the permanent army of a country. [See Word Story at **normal.**] —**reg′u·lar·ly**, *adv.*

reg·u·lar·i·ty (reg′yə lar′ə tē), *n.* condition of being regular; order; system; steadiness: *The seasons come and go with regularity.*

reg·u·lar·ize (reg′yə lə riz′), *v.* to make regular: *We hired a consultant to come in and regularize our bookkeeping.* ❏ *v.* **reg·u·lar·ized, reg·u·lar·iz·ing.** —**reg′u·lar·i·za′tion**, *n.*

reg·u·late (reg′yə lāt), *v.* **1** to control by rule, principle, or system: *The government regulates the coining of money.* **2** to put in condition to work properly: *My watch is losing time; I will have to have it regulated.* **3** to keep at a stated level, amount, or rate; control; adjust: *A thermostat regulates the temperature of the room.* ❏ *v.* **reg·u·lat·ed, reg·u·lat·ing.** —**reg′u·la·tive**, *adj.*

reg·u·la·tion (reg′yə lā′shən), **1** *n.* rule; law: *traffic regulations.* **2** *n.* act of controlling or condition of being controlled by rule, principle, or system: *Regulation of interstate truck travel is carried out by the federal government.* **3** *adj.* required by some rule; standard: *Soldiers wear a regulation uniform.*

reg·u·la·tor (reg′yə lā′tər), *n.* **1** person or thing that regulates. **2** device in a clock or watch for causing it to go faster or slower.

regulator gene, any gene that controls or influences the expression of another gene or genes.

reg·u·la·to·ry (reg′yə lə tôr′ē), *adj.* regulating.

re·gur·gi·tate (rē gėr′jə tāt), *v.* **1** to throw up; vomit: *regurgitate food from the stomach.* **2** to repeat something that you have written down or heard, but have not fully understood: *He just regurgitated the lecture from class; he hasn't read the chapter yet.* ❏ *v.* **re·gur·gi·tat·ed, re·gur·gi·tat·ing.** —**re·gur′gi·ta′tion**, *n.*

re·ha·bil·i·tate (rē′hə bil′ə tāt), *v.* **1** to restore to a good condition; make over in a new form: *The school is to be rehabilitated.* **2** to restore to a condition of good health or to a level of useful activity, by means of medical treatment and therapy. **3** to restore to former standing, rank, rights, privileges, reputation, etc.: *The former criminal was rehabilitated and became a respected citizen.* ❏ *v.* **re·ha·bil·i·tat·ed, re·ha·bil·i·tat·ing.** —**re′ha·bil′i·ta′tion**, *n.*

re·hash (rē hash′ *for verb;* rē′hash *for noun*), **1** *v.* to deal with again; work up old material in a

rehabilitate (def. 2)

new or different form: *The question has been rehashed again and again.* **2** *n.* act of rehashing; act of putting something old into a new or different form: *That play is simply a rehash of an old movie.* ❏ *n., pl.* **re·hash·es.**

re·hears·al (ri hėr′səl), *n.* act of rehearsing; process of preparing for a public performance: *The rehearsal for the show was a disaster, but the actual performance was great.*

a	hat	ė	term	ô	order	ch	child		
ā	age	i	it	oi	oil	ng	long	ə	a in about
ä	far	ī	ice	ou	out	sh	she		e in taken
â	care	o	hot	u	cup	th	thin		i in pencil
e	let	ō	open	u̇	put	ŦH	then		o in lemon
ē	equal	ȯ	saw	ü	rule	zh	measure		u in circus

R

re·hearse (ri hėrs′), *v.* **1** to practice a play, part, etc., for a public performance: *We rehearsed our parts for the school play.* **2** to drill or train a person or animal by repetition. ❑ *v.* **re·hearsed, re·hears·ing.** —**re·hears′er,** *n.*

WORD STORY Rehearse comes from an old French word meaning "harrow." A harrow is a farm tool for cutting and turning soil. Rehearsing is like digging through something over and over. **Hearse** comes from the same word, because an early piece of funeral equipment was shaped like the farm tool.

Rehn·quist (ren′kwist), *n.* **William,** born 1924, chief justice of the U.S. Supreme Court since 1986.

Reich (rīk), *n.* (formerly) Germany as a state; the German nation.

reign (rān), **1** *n.* period of power of a ruler: *Queen Victoria's reign lasted sixty-four years.* **2** *v.* to rule: *A king reigns over his kingdom.* **3** *n.* act of ruling; royal power; rule: *The reign of a wise ruler benefits a country.* **4** *v.* to exist everywhere; prevail: *On a still night silence reigns.* **5** *n.* existence everywhere; prevalence: *the reign of technology in this century.* ■ Other words that sound like this are **rain** and **rein.**

re·im·burse (rē′im bėrs′), *v.* to pay back; repay. You reimburse a person for expenses made for you. ❑ *v.* **re·im·bursed, re·im·burs·ing.** —**re′im·burs′a·ble,** *adj.* —**re′im·burse′ment,** *n.*

Reims (rēmz), *n.* city in NE France. Nearly all the French kings were crowned in its cathedral.

rein (rān), **1** *n.* Usually, **reins,** *pl.* a long, narrow strap or line fastened to the bit of a bridle, by which to guide and control an animal. **2** *v.* to check or pull with reins: *She reined the galloping horse hard to the left, trying to miss a low branch.* **3** *n.* Usually, **reins,** *pl.* a means of control and direction: *seize the reins of government.* **4** *v.* to guide and control: *Rein your tongue.* ■ Other words that sound like this are **rain** and **reign.**

draw rein, **1** to tighten the reins. **2** to slow down; stop.

give rein to, to let move or act freely, without guidance or control: *give rein to your feelings.*

take the reins, to assume control: *When the President was ill, the Vice-President took the reins of government.*

re·in·car·nate (rē′in kär′nāt), *v.* to give a new body to a soul. ❑ *v.* **re·in·car·nat·ed, re·in·car·nat·ing.**

re·in·car·na·tion (rē′in kär nā′shən), *n.* rebirth of the soul in a new body.

rein·deer (rān′dir′), *n.* a large deer with branching antlers that lives in northern regions. It is used to pull sleighs and also for meat, milk, and hides. North American reindeer are called caribou. ❑ *n., pl.* **rein·deer.**

reindeer—4 ft. 6 in. (1.4 m) high at the shoulder

re·in·force (rē′in fôrs′), *v.* **1** to strengthen with new force, materials, arguments, etc.: *More supports were added to reinforce the bridge. Scientists reinforce theories with new discoveries and new evidence.* **2** to strengthen by adding troops, warships, planes, or armor: *The general reinforced the small unit guarding the village.* ❑ *v.* **re·in·forced, re·in·forc·ing.** —**re′in·forc′er,** *n.*

re·in·force·ment (rē′in fôrs′mənt), *n.* **1** reinforcements, *pl.* extra soldiers, warships, planes, etc.: *Reinforcements were sent to the battlefront.* **2** act of reinforcing or condition of being reinforced: *Reinforcement of the rafters was necessary before repairing the roof.* **3** something that reinforces.

re·in·state (rē′in stāt′), *v.* to put someone or something back in a former position or condition; establish again. ❑ *v.* **re·in·stat·ed, re·in·stat·ing.** —**re′in·state′ment,** *n.*

re·in·ter·pret (rē′in tėr′prit), *v.* to interpret again. —**re′in·ter′pre·ta′tion,** *n.*

re·in·vest (rē′in vest′), *v.* to invest again or in a new way. —**re′in·vest′ment,** *n.*

re·it·e·rate (rē it′ə rāt′), *v.* to say or do something several times; repeat again and again: *The teacher reiterated his request for order.* ❑ *v.* **re·it·e·rat·ed, re·it·e·rat·ing.** —**re·it′e·ra′tion,** *n.*

re·ject (ri jekt′ *for verb;* rē′jekt *for noun*), **1** *v.* to refuse to take; turn down: *She rejected our help. He tried to join the army but was rejected because of poor health.* **2** *v.* to throw away as useless or unsatisfactory: *Reject all apples with soft spots.* **3** *n.* a rejected person or thing. —**re·ject′er** or **re·jec′tor,** *n.*

re·jec·tion (ri jek′shən), *n.* act of rejecting or condition of being rejected: *The inspector ordered the rejection of the faulty parts. Medicine is used to prevent rejection by the body of transplanted organs.*

re·joice (ri jois′), *v.* to be glad; be filled with joy: *She rejoiced at our success.* ❑ *v.* **re·joiced, re·joic·ing.** —**re·joic′er,** *n.*

re·joic·ing (ri joi′sing), *n.* the feeling or expression of joy.

re·join[1] (rē join′), *v.* **1** to join the company of again: *I will rejoin my family in April.* **2** to join again; unite again: *rejoin a broken plate.*

re·join[2] (ri join′), *v.* to answer; reply: *"Come with me!" "Not on your life," he rejoined.*

re·join·der (ri join′dər), *n.* an answer to a reply; response: *a debater's rejoinder.*

re·ju·ve·nate (ri jü′və nāt′), *v.* to make young or vigorous again; give youthful qualities to: *The long vacation rejuvenated her.* ❑ *v.* **re·ju·ve·nat·ed, re·ju·ve·nat·ing.** —**re·ju′ve·na′tion,** *n.*

re·laid (rē lād′), *v.* past tense and past participle of **re·lay:** *The pavement on our street has just been re-laid.*

re·lapse (ri laps′ *for verb;* ri laps′ *or* rē′laps *for noun*), **1** *v.* to fall or slip back into a former state or way of acting: *After one cry of surprise she relapsed into silence.* **2** *n.* act of falling or slipping back into a former state or way of acting: *He seemed to be getting over his illness but had a relapse.* ❑ *v.* **re·lapsed, re·laps·ing.** —**re·laps′er,** *n.*

re·late (ri lāt′), *v.* **1** to give an account of; tell: *The traveler related her adventures.* **2** to connect in thought or meaning: *"Better" and "best" are related to "good."* **3** to be connected in any way: *We are interested in what relates to ourselves.* **4** to respond favorably or sympathetically to: *I can relate to problems like that.* ❑ *v.* **re·lat·ed, re·lat·ing.** —**re·lat′er** or **re·la′tor,** *n.*

re·lat·ed (ri lā′tid), *adj.* **1** connected in any way. **2** belonging to the same family; connected by a common origin: *Cousins are related.* —**re·lat′ed·ness,** *n.*

re·la·tion (ri lā′shən), *n.* **1** connection in thought or meaning: *Your answer has no relation to the question.* **2** connection by family ties of blood or marriage; relationship: *What relation are you to her?* **3** person who belongs to the same family as another; relative. **4** relations, *pl.* dealings between persons, groups, countries, etc.: *international relations. Our firm has business relations with their firm.* **5** act of telling; account: *We enjoyed the relation of the traveler's adventures.*

in relation to or with relation to, in reference to; in regard to; about; concerning: *We must plan in relation to the future.*

re·la·tion·ship (ri lā′shən ship), *n.* **1** connection: *What is the relationship of clouds to rain?* **2** condition of belonging to the same family. **3** condition that exists between people or groups that deal with each other: *I have good relationships with all of my teachers this year.*

rel·a·tive (rel′ə tiv), **1** *n.* person who belongs to the same family as another, such as father, brother, aunt, nephew, or cousin. **2** *adj.* related or compared to each other: *We discussed the relative advantages of city and country life.* **3** *adj.* depending for meaning on a relation to something else: *East is a relative term; for example, Chicago is east of California but west of New York.* **4** *adj.* referring to someone or something mentioned. *Who, whose, whom, which, what,* and *that* are relative pronouns. **5** *n.* a relative pronoun. *Who, which, what,* *whom, whose,* and *that* are relatives. **—rel′a·tive·ness,** *n.*

relative to, 1 about; concerning: *They asked me some questions relative to my plans for the summer.* **2** in proportion to; in comparison with; for: *She is strong relative to her size.*

relative humidity, the ratio between the amount of water vapor present in the air and the greatest amount the air could contain at the same temperature.

rel·a·tive·ly (rel′ə tiv lē), *adv.* in relation to something else; comparatively: *You are relatively tall for your age.*

rel·a·tiv·i·ty (rel′ə tiv′ə tē), *n.* **1** theories known as **special relativity** and **general relativity,** created by Albert Einstein, and stating laws that describe motion, matter, space, and time. By these laws, all measurements of matter and time depend on relative motion, and the nature of space is relative to the matter it contains. **2** condition of being relative.

re·lax (ri laks′), *v.* **1** to loosen up; make or become less stiff or firm: *Relax when you dance.* **2** to make or become less strict or severe; lessen in force: *Discipline is relaxed on the last day of school.* **3** to relieve or be relieved from work or effort; give or take recreation or amusement: *Take a vacation and relax.* **4** to relieve or be relieved from work, effort, or worry: *We relaxed during the holidays. Relax! Everything will be all right.*

re·lax·a·tion (rē′lak sā′shən), *n.* **1** relief from work or effort; recreation; amusement: *Walking and reading are relaxations.* **2** act of loosening: *the relaxation of the muscles.* **3** act of lessening strictness, severity, force, etc.: *the relaxation of discipline over the holidays.* **4** condition of being relaxed.

re·lay (rē′lā *for noun;* rē′lā *or* ri lā′ *for verb*), **1** *v.* to take and carry farther: *Please relay this message to my parents.* **2** *n.* a relay race. **3** *n.* one part of a relay race. **4** *n.* a fresh supply: *A new relay of firefighters was rushed to fight the huge blaze.* **5** *n.* an electric switch that opens and closes a circuit in response to changing voltage or current. **6** *n.* device that receives a signal and transmits it again to send it farther: *a radio relay tower.* ❏ *v.* **re·layed, re·lay·ing.**

WORD STORY **Relay** comes from an old French word meaning "a reserve pack of hounds." During big hunts, an extra pack of hunting dogs was kept, in case the first pack got tired or hurt. In English, the word was also used about horses kept at certain places so that travelers could change tired animals for fresh ones. The first relay race may have been between riders.

re-lay (rē lā′), *v.* to lay again: *That floor must be re-laid.* ❏ *v.* **re-laid, re-lay·ing.**

re·lay race (rē′lā), race in which each member of a team runs, swims, etc., only a certain part of the distance.

re·lease (ri lēs′), **1** *v.* to let go; set free: *Prisoners were released after the war. She released him from his promise.* **2** *n.* act of letting go; setting free: *The end of the war brought the release of the prisoners.* **3** *v.* to relieve; free from obligation: *I will not be released from duty until seven o'clock.* **4** *n.* freedom; relief: *This medicine will give you release from pain.* **5** *n.* part of a machine that sets other parts free to move. **6** *n.* the legal surrender of a right, estate, etc., to another. **7** *v.* to give up legal right, claim, etc. **8** *n.* document that does this. **9** *v.* to permit to be published, shown, sold, etc. **10** *n.* permission for publication, exhibition, sale, etc. **11** *n.* article, statement, etc., distributed for publication. ❏ *v.* **re·leased, re·leas·ing.** [See Word Story at **relish.**]

rel·e·gate (rel′ə gāt), *v.* **1** to put away, usually to a lower position or condition: *She relegated the broken chair to the basement.* **2** to hand over a matter, task, etc., to someone else. ❏ *v.* **rel·e·gat·ed, rel·e·gat·ing. —rel′e·ga′tion,** *n.*

re·lent (ri lent′), *v.* to become less harsh; be more tender and merciful: *The trapper relented and set the panda free again.*

WORD STORY **Relent** comes from Latin words meaning "soft" and "again." They became an old English word meaning "to melt" or "to dissolve." When someone relents, a firm decision melts away.

re·lent·less (ri lent′lis), *adj.* without pity; not relenting; unyielding; harsh: *The storm raged with relentless fury.* **—re·lent′less·ly,** *adv.* **—re·lent′less·ness,** *n.*

rel·e·vance (rel′ə vəns), *n.* quality of being relevant.

rel·e·van·cy (rel′ə vən sē), *n.* relevance.

rel·e·vant (rel′ə vənt), *adj.* connected with the matter in hand; to the point: *relevant questions.* **—rel′e·vant·ly,** *adv.*

re·li·a·ble (ri lī′ə bəl), *adj.* worthy of trust; able to be depended on: *Send her to the bank for the money; she is reliable.* **—re·li′a·bil′i·ty, re·li′a·ble·ness,** *n.* **—re·li′a·bly,** *adv.*

re·li·ance (ri lī′əns), *n.* **1** trust or dependence: *an unhealthy reliance on other people's opinions.* **2** confidence.

re·li·ant (ri lī′ənt), *adj.* **1** trusting or depending; relying. **2** confident. **3** relying on yourself. **—re·li′ant·ly,** *adv.*

rel·ic (rel′ik), *n.* **1** something left over from the past: *This ruined bridge is a relic of the Civil War.* **2** something belonging to a holy person, kept as a sacred memorial. **3** object having interest because of its age or its associations with the past; keepsake; souvenir.

re·lief (ri lēf′), *n.* **1** act or process of reducing, or freeing from, a pain, burden, difficulty, etc.: *His relief from pain came as the medicine began to work.* **2** something that reduces, lessens, or frees from pain, burden, difficulty, etc.; aid; help: *Relief was sent to the people made homeless by the tornado.* **3** welfare (def. 2). **4** something that makes a pleasing change or lessens strain. **5** freedom from a post of duty: *The nurse was on duty all day, with only two hours' relief.* **6** change of persons on duty. **7** persons who relieve others from duty; person who does this: *The watchman's relief arrives at seven.* **8** projection of figures or designs from a surface in sculpture, drawing, or painting. **9** figure or design standing out from the surface from which it is cut, shaped, or stamped. **10** the appearance of standing out from a surface, given to a drawing or painting by the use of shading, color, etc. **11** differences in height between the summits and lowlands of a region.

relief (def. 9)

in relief, standing out from a surface.

on relief, receiving money to live on from public funds.

relief map, map that shows the different heights of a land surface by using shading, colors, or solid materials.

re·lieve (ri lēv′), *v.* **1** to reduce the pain or trouble of: *Aspirin will relieve a headache. We telephoned to relieve our parents' uneasiness.* **2** to set free: *Your coming relieves me of the job of writing a long letter.* **3** to free someone on duty by taking his or her place: *The cashier waited for someone to relieve him so that he could eat lunch.* **4** to bring aid to; help: *Food and medicine were sent to relieve the flood victims.* **5** to give variety or a pleasing change to: *The new red couch will relieve the drabness of the room.* ❏ *v.* **re·lieved, re·liev·ing. —re·liev′a·ble,** *adj.* **—re·liev′er,** *n.*

re·li·gion (ri lij′ən), *n.* **1** belief in and worship of God or gods. **2** a particular system of faith and worship: *the religion of Islam.*

re·li·gious (ri lij′əs), **1** *adj.* of or about religion: *religious meetings, religious books, religious differences.* **2** *adj.* much interested in religion; devoted to religion: *He is very religious and often goes to church to pray.* **3** *n.* monk, nun, friar, etc.; member of a religious order: *There are sixty religious teaching in this school.* **4** *adj.* very careful; strict; scrupulous: *I gave religious attention to the doctor's orders.* ❏ *n., pl.* **re·li·gious. —re·li′gious·ly,** *adv.* **—re·li′gious·ness,** *n.*

SYNONYM STUDY **Religious** and **devout** both mean caring much for religion. **Religious** means devoted to God: *Monks lead a religious life.* **Devout** means active in worship and prayer: *Devout Muslims pray five times every day.*

R

a	hat	ė	term	ô	order	ch	child		
ā	age	i	it	oi	oil	ng	long	⟨	a in about
ä	far	ī	ice	ou	out	sh	she	ə	e in taken
â	care	o	hot	u	cup	th	thin		i in pencil
e	let	ō	open	u̇	put	ŦH	then		o in lemon
ē	equal	ȯ	saw	ü	rule	zh	measure	⟨	u in circus

re·lin·quish (ri ling′kwish), *v.* to give up; let go: *The small dog relinquished his bone to the big dog.* —**re·lin′quish·er,** *n.* —**re·lin′quish·ment,** *n.*

rel·ish (rel′ish), **1** *n.* a pleasant taste; good flavor: *Hunger gives relish to simple food.* **2** *n.* something to add flavor to food. Olives and pickles are relishes. **3** *n.* liking; appetite; enjoyment: *We watched the old movie with great relish.* **4** *v.* to like the taste of; like; enjoy: *The cat relishes cream. We did not relish the prospect of a long winter.* ❑ *n., pl.* **rel·ish·es** for 2. [See Word Story at **zest.**]

> **WORD STORY** **Relish** comes from an old French word meaning "to release" or "to leave behind." **Release** comes from the same word. Cooking food releases its flavor, and eating food leaves the taste behind.

re·live (rē liv′), *v.* to live over or through again. ❑ *v.* **re·lived, re·liv·ing.**

re·lo·cate (rē lō′kāt), *v.* to move to a new place. ❑ *v.* **re·lo·cat·ed, re·lo·cat·ing.** —**re′lo·ca′tion,** *n.*

re·luc·tance (ri luk′təns), *n.* **1** a reluctant feeling or action; unwillingness: *She took part in the game with reluctance.* **2** slowness in action because of unwillingness.

re·luc·tant (ri luk′tənt), *adj.* **1** unwilling; showing unwillingness: *The teacher led the reluctant student to the principal.* **2** slow to act because unwilling: *I am reluctant to go out in very cold weather.* —**re·luc′tant·ly,** *adv.*

> **SYNONYM STUDY** **Reluctant** and **hesitant** both mean not wanting to do something. **Reluctant** suggests trying to avoid or resist: *She is reluctant to criticize other people.* **Hesitant** suggests holding back from doubt or fear: *Looking down from the diving board, he was hesitant about jumping.*

re·ly (ri li′), *v.* to depend or trust: *Rely on your own efforts. I relied upon your promise.* ■ See Synonym Study at **trust.** ❑ *v.* **re·lied, re·ly·ing.** —**re·li′er,** *n.*

REM (rem), rapid eye movement (movement of the eyes that occurs while asleep and dreaming).

re·main (ri mān′), **1** *v.* to continue in a place; stay: *We shall remain at the seashore till October.* ■ See Synonym Study at **stay¹. 2** *v.* to continue; last; keep on: *The town remains the same year after year.* **3** *v.* to be left: *A few apples remain on the trees. If you take 2 from 5, 3 remains.* **4** *n.pl.* **remains, a** what is left: *The remains of the fire at the campsite were stirred and soaked with water.* **b** a dead body: *Washington's remains are buried at Mount Vernon.*

re·main·der (ri mān′dər), *n.* **1** the part left over; the rest: *After studying an hour, she spent the remainder of the afternoon playing.* **2** in arithmetic: **a** a number left over after subtracting one number from another. In 9 − 2, the remainder is 7. **b** number left over after dividing one number by another. In 14 ÷ 3, the quotient is 4 with a remainder of 2.

re·make (rē māk′ *for verb;* rē′māk *for noun*), **1** *v.* to make again; make over. **2** *n.* something made again, especially a movie made in a new version. ❑ *v.* **re·made** (rē mād′), **re·mak·ing.**

re·mand (ri mand′), **1** *v.* to send a prisoner or an accused person back into custody. **2** *v.* to send back. **3** *n.* act of remanding.

re·mark (ri märk′), **1** *v.* to say in a few words; state; comment: *She remarked that it was a beautiful day.* **2** *n.* something said in a few words; short statement: *The president made a few remarks.* **3** *v.* to notice; observe: *Did you remark that strange cloud?* **4** *n.* act of noticing; observation. —**re·mark′er,** *n.*

re·mark·a·ble (ri mär′kə bəl), *adj.* worthy of notice; unusual: *He has a remarkable memory.* —**re·mark′a·ble·ness,** *n.* —**re·mark′a·bly,** *adv.*

re·mar·riage (rē mar′ij), *n.* any marriage after your first marriage.

re·mar·ry (rē mar′ē), *v.* to marry again. ❑ *v.* **re·mar·ried, re·mar·ry·ing.**

re·match (rē′mach′), *n.* a second or subsequent match between two opponents, teams, etc. ❑ *n., pl.* **re·match·es.**

Rem·brandt (rem′brant), *n.* 1606-1669, Dutch artist. He made many paintings, etchings, and drawings, including about 100 self-portraits.

re·me·di·a·ble (ri mē′dē ə bəl), *adj.* able to be remedied or cured. —**re·me′di·a·ble·ness,** *n.* —**re·me′di·a·bly,** *adv.*

re·me·di·al (ri mē′dē əl), *adj.* remedying; curing; helping; relieving. —**re·me′di·al·ly,** *adv.*

rem·e·dy (rem′ə dē), **1** *n.* a means of removing or relieving diseases or any bad condition; cure: *Aspirin is used as a remedy for headaches.* **2** *v.* to put right; make right; cure: *A nap remedied my weariness.* ❑ *n., pl.* **rem·e·dies;** *v.* **rem·e·died, rem·e·dy·ing.**

re·mem·ber (ri mem′bər), *v.* **1** to call back to mind: *I can't remember that man's name.* **2** to have something return to the mind: *Then I remembered where I was.* **3** to keep in mind; take care not to forget: *Remember me when I am gone.* **4** to keep in mind as deserving a reward, gift, etc.: *Uncle remembered us in his will.* **5** to mention someone as sending friendly greetings: *She asked to be remembered to you.* —**re·mem′ber·a·ble,** *adj.* —**re·mem′ber·er,** *n.*

> **SYNONYM STUDY** **Remember, recall,** and **recollect** all mean to call something back to mind. **Remember** is the general word: *I can remember my seventh birthday.* **Recall** suggests making an effort: *Try to recall where you left your keys.* **Recollect** suggests recalling something from a long time ago: *Grandpa likes to recollect his youth in Cuba.*

re·mem·brance (ri mem′brəns), *n.* **1** power to remember; act of remembering; memory: *I hold my old friend in fond remembrance.* **2** any thing or action that makes you remember someone; souvenir; keepsake. **3** **remembrances,** *pl.* greetings: *Give my remembrances to your sister.*

Remembrance Day, November 11, celebrated as a holiday in Canada and Great Britain to remember those who where killed in the World Wars.

remembrance (def. 1)—flowers placed in remembrance of a loved one

re·mind (ri mind′), *v.* to make you think of something; cause to remember: *This picture reminds me of a story I heard.*

re·mind·er (ri min′dər), *n.* something to help you remember: *The notes taped to the refrigerator door are reminders of things to do.*

Rem·ing·ton (rem′ing tən), *n.* **Fred·er·ic** (fred′ər ik), 1861-1909, American painter and sculptor. His art often showed cowboys, American Indians, and life in the West.

rem·i·nisce (rem′ə nis′), *v.* to talk or think about past experiences or events. ❑ *v.* **rem·i·nisced, rem·i·nisc·ing.**

rem·i·nis·cence (rem′ə nis′ns), *n.* **1** act of remembering; recalling past persons, events, etc. **2** Often, **reminiscences,** *pl.* account of something remembered; recollection: *childhood reminiscences.*

rem·i·nis·cent (rem′ə nis′nt), *adj.* **1** recalling past persons, events, etc.: *reminiscent talk.* **2** awakening memories of something else; suggestive: *a manner reminiscent of a past age.* —**rem′i·nis′cent·ly,** *adv.*

re·miss (ri mis′), *adj.* careless or slack in doing what you have to do; negligent: *to be remiss in your duties.* —**re·miss′ly,** *adv.* —**re·miss′ness,** *n.*

re·mis·sion (ri mish′ən), *n.* **1** decrease or disappearance of pain, symptoms, force, labor, etc.: *The storm continued without remission. His disease was in remission.* **2** act of releasing from debt, punishment, etc.: *The bankrupt sought remission of his debts.* **3** pardon; forgiveness: *remission of sins.*

re·mit (ri mit′), *v.* **1** to send money to a person or place: *Enclosed is our bill; please remit.* **2** to send money due: *Please remit $50.* **3** to refrain from carrying out; cancel: *The governor is remitting the prisoner's sentence.* **4** to pardon; forgive: *the power to remit sins.* **5** to make less; decrease: *After we had rowed the boat into calm water, we remitted our efforts.* ❑ *v.* **re·mit·ted, re·mit·ting.** —**re·mit′ter,** *n.*

re·mit·tance (ri mit′ns), *n.* **1** money that is sent to someone. **2** act of sending money to someone.

rem·nant (rem′nənt), *n.* **1** a small part left: *This town has only a remnant of its former population.* **2** piece of cloth, ribbon, lace, etc., left after the rest has been used or sold.

re·mod·el (rē mod′l), *v.* to make over; change or alter: *The old barn was remodeled into a house.* ❑ *v.* **re·mod·eled, re·mod·el·ing** or **re·mod·elled, re·mod·el·ling.**

re·mon·strance (ri mon′strəns), *n.* act of remonstrating; protest; complaint.

re·mon·strate (ri mon′strāt), *v.* to speak, reason, or plead in complaint or protest: *The teacher remonstrated with the class about their unruly behavior.* ❑ *v.* **re·mon·strat·ed, re·mon·strat·ing.** —**re′mon·stra·tion,** *n.* —**re·mon′stra·tor,** *n.*

rem·o·ra (rem′ər ə *or* rə môr′ə), *n.* any of several tropical fishes with a sucker disk on the top of the head. A remora attaches itself to ships or other fishes, especially sharks, for transportation, protection, and food. ❑ *n., pl.* **rem·o·ras.**

re·morse (ri môrs′), *n.* deep, painful regret for having done wrong: *I felt remorse for hurting her feelings, so I apologized.* [Remorse comes from a Latin word meaning "to bite back" or "to gnaw." Deep regret may feel like something chewing away at you.]

re·morse·ful (ri môrs′fəl), *adj.* feeling or expressing deep regret or remorse. —**re·morse′ful·ly,** *adv.* —**re·morse′ful·ness,** *n.*

re·morse·less (ri môrs′lis), *adj.* **1** without remorse. **2** pitiless; cruel: *a remorseless killer.* —**re·morse′less·ly,** *adv.* —**re·morse′less·ness,** *n.*

re·mote (ri mōt′), *adj.* **1** far away; far off: *The North Pole is a remote part of the world.* ∎ See Synonym Study at **distant. 2** out of the way; secluded: *Mail comes to this remote village only once a week.* **3** distant: *He is a remote relative.* **4** slight; faint: *I haven't the remotest idea what you mean.* ❑ *adj.* **re·mot·er, re·mot·est.** —**re·mote′ly,** *adv.* —**re·mote′ness,** *n.*

remote control, 1 control of a machine, operation, etc., from a distance by electric current, radio signals, or infrared light: *Some model airplanes can be flown by remote control.* **2** device used to control a TV set, garage door opener, toy car, etc., from a distance.

re·mov·a·ble (ri mü′və bəl), *adj.* able to be removed. —**re·mov′a·ble·ness,** *n.* —**re·mov′a·bly,** *adv.*

re·mov·al (ri mü′vəl), *n.* **1** act of removing; taking away: *We made arrangements for the removal of the dead tree.* **2** a change of place: *The store announced its removal to larger quarters.* **3** dismissal from an office or position.

re·move (ri müv′), **1** *v.* to move from a place or position; take off; take away: *They removed the furniture before refinishing the floor. Remove your hat.* **2** *v.* to get rid of; put an end to: *An experiment removed all our doubt about the fact that water is made up of two gases.* **3** *v.* to dismiss from an office or position: *The mayor removed the chief of police for failing to do his duty.* **4** *n.* step or degree of distance: *At every remove the mountain seemed smaller.* ❑ *v.* **re·moved, re·mov·ing.**

re·mov·er (ri mü′vər), *n.* something that removes: *a bottle of ink remover.*

re·mu·ne·rate (ri myü′nə rāt′), *v.* to pay for work, services, trouble, etc.; reward: *The club remunerated the speaker.* ❑ *v.* **re·mu·ne·rat·ed, re·mu·ne·rat·ing.** —**re·mu′ne·ra·tor,** *n.*

re·mu·ne·ra·tion (ri myü′nə rā′shən), *n.* a reward; pay; payment.

re·mu·ne·ra·tive (ri myü′nə rə tiv), *adj.* paying; profitable. —**re·mu′ne·ra·tive·ly,** *adv.* —**re·mu′ne·ra·tive·ness,** *n.*

Re·mus (rē′məs), *n.* (in Roman legends) the twin brother of Romulus, the founder of Rome.

ren·ais·sance (ren′ə säns′ *or* ren′ə säns), **1** *n.* a new birth; revival. **2** *n.* **the Renaissance, a** the great revival of art and learning in Europe during the 1300s, 1400s, and 1500s. **b** the period of time when this revival occurred. **3** *adj.* **Renaissance,** of the Renaissance or its style of art, architecture, etc.

re·nal (rē′nl), *adj.* of or about the kidneys.

re·name (rē nām′), *v.* to give a new name to; name again: *They bought a used boat and renamed it "Seagull."* ❑ *v.* **re·named, re·nam·ing.**

re·nas·cent (ri nā′snt), *adj.* being born again; reviving.

rend (rend), *v.* **1** to pull apart violently; tear: *Lions will rend a zebra to pieces.* **2** to split: *Lightning rent the tree.* **3** to disturb violently: *She was rent by a wish to keep the money she found and the knowledge that she ought to return it.* **4** to remove with force or violence. ❑ *v.* **rent, rend·ing.**

ren·der (ren′dər), *v.* **1** to cause to become; make: *Fright rendered me speechless.* **2** to give; provide: *She rendered us a great service by her help.* **3** to hand in; report: *The treasurer rendered an account of all the money spent.* **4** to give in return: *Render thanks for your blessings.* **5** to pay as due: *The conquered people rendered tribute to the conqueror.* **6** to bring out the meaning of; represent: *The actor rendered the part of the villain well.* **7** to play or sing music. **8** to change from one language to another; translate: *She rendered a French poem into English.* **9** to melt fat; clarify or extract by melting. Fat from hogs is rendered for lard.

ren·dez·vous (rän′də vü), **1** *n.* an appointment or engagement to meet at a fixed place or time; meeting by agreement. **2** *n.* a meeting place; gathering place: *The family's favorite rendezvous was the garden.* **3** *n.* place agreed on for a meeting at a certain time, especially of troops or ships. **4** *n.* a meeting at a fixed place or time: *the rendezvous of a lunar module and the command ship.* **5** *v.* to meet at a rendezvous. ❑ *n., pl.* **ren·dez·vous** (rän′də vüz); *v.* **ren·dez·voused** (rän′də vüd), **ren·dez·vous·ing** (rän′də vü′ing).

ren·di·tion (ren dish′ən), *n.* **1** act of rendering a dramatic part, music, etc., so as to bring out the meaning. **2** translation. **3** act of rendering.

ren·e·gade (ren′ə gād), **1** *n.* deserter from a religious faith, a political party, etc.; traitor. **2** *adj.* like a traitor; deserting; disloyal.

re·nege (ri nig′ *or* ri neg′), *v.* **1** to fail to play a card of the same suit as that first played, although you are able to do so. It is against the rules of card games to renege. **2** to back out; fail to carry out: *renege on a promise.* ❑ *v.* **re·neged, re·neg·ing.** —**re·neg′er,** *n.*

re·new (ri nü′), *v.* **1** to make new again; make like new; restore: *Rain renews the greenness of the fields.* **2** to begin again; get again; say, do, or give again: *He renewed his efforts to open the window.* **3** to replace by new material or a new thing of the same sort; fill again: *The well renews itself no matter how much water is taken away.* **4** to give or get for a new period: *We renewed our lease for another year.* —**re·new′er,** *n.*

re·new·a·ble (ri nü′ə bəl), *adj.* able to be renewed: *a renewable contract.* —**re·new′a·bly,** *adv.*

re·new·al (ri nü′əl), *n.* act of renewing or condition of being renewed: *When hot weather comes there will be a renewal of interest in swimming.*

ren·net (ren′it), *n.* substance containing rennin, prepared from the stomach lining of a calf or other cud-chewing mammal, used for making cheese and junket.

ren·nin (ren′ən), *n.* enzyme in the gastric juice that coagulates or curdles milk.

Re·no (rē′nō), *n.* city in W Nevada.

Ren·oir (ren′wär), *n.* **Pierre Au·guste** (pyer′ ō güst′), 1841-1919, French painter. He liked to paint happy groups, often his friends. Late in his life he suffered from arthritis and painted with brushes tied to his hands.

re·nounce (ri nouns′), *v.* **1** to declare that you give up; give up entirely; give up: *He renounces his claim to the money.* **2** to refuse to accept or recognize: *The colonists renounced royal authority.* ❑ *v.* **re·nounced, re·nounc·ing.** —**re·nounce′ment,** *n.*

ren·o·vate (ren′ə vāt), *v.* to make new again; make like new; restore to good condition: *renovate a house.* ❑ *v.* **ren·o·vat·ed, ren·o·vat·ing.** —**ren′o·va′tion,** *n.* —**ren′o·va′tor,** *n.*

re·nown (ri noun′), *n.* fame: *A doctor who finds a cure for a disease wins renown.*

re·nowned (ri nound′), *adj.* famous: *a renowned scientist.*

rent¹ (rent), **1** *n.* the money paid for the use of property. **2** *v.* to pay for the use of property: *Her parents rented a movie for the party.* **3** *v.* to receive money for the use of property: *The hardware store rents tools.* **4** *v.* to be rented: *This car rents for $50 a day.* —**rent′a·ble,** *adj.* —**rent′er,** *n.*

a	hat	ė	term	ȯ	order	ch	child		a in about
ā	age	i	it	oi	oil	ng	long		e in taken
ä	far	ī	ice	ou	out	sh	she	ə	i in pencil
â	care	o	hot	u	cup	th	thin		o in lemon
e	let	ō	open	ů	put	ᴛʜ	then		u in circus
ē	equal	ȯ	saw	ü	rule	zh	measure		

for rent, available in return for rent paid: *That large two-bedroom apartment we were admiring is for rent.*

rent² (rent), **1** *n.* a torn place; tear; split. **2** *adj.* torn; split. **3** *v.* past tense and past participle of **rend:** *The tree was rent by the wind.*

rent·al (ren′tl), **1** *n.* amount received or paid as rent: *The yearly rental of her house is $7200.* **2** *n.* something rented. **3** *adj.* of or about rent: *a rental agent.*

re·nun·ci·a·tion (ri nun′sē ā′shən), *n.* act of giving up a right, title, possession, etc.; act of renouncing.

re·o·pen (rē ō′pən), *v.* **1** to open again: *School will reopen in September.* **2** to discuss again or further: *The matter is settled and cannot be reopened.*

re·or·gan·ize (rē ôr′gə nīz), *v.* to organize again; form again; arrange in a new way: *Classes will be reorganized after the first four weeks.* ❏ *v.* **re·or·gan·ized, re·or·gan·iz·ing.** —**re·or′gan·i·za′- tion,** *n.* —**re·or′gan·iz′er,** *n.*

rep (rep), *n.* reputation: *He had a good rep at his old school.*

Rep., **1** Republic. **2** Republican.

re·paid (ri pād′), *v.* past tense and past participle of **repay:** *She repaid the money she had borrowed. All debts should be repaid.*

re·pair¹ (ri pâr′), **1** *v.* to put in good condition again; mend: *He repairs shoes.* **2** *n.* act or work of repairing: *After the storm, repair of the roof was necessary.* **3** *n.* Often, **repairs,** *pl.* instance or piece of repairing: *Repairs on the school building are made during the summer.* **4** *n.* condition fit to be used: *The state keeps the roads in repair.* **5** *n.* condition for use: *The house was in bad repair.* **6** *v.* to make up for: *How can I repair the harm done?* —**re·pair′a·ble,** *adj.* —**re·pair′er,** *n.*

> **SYNONYM STUDY** **Repair¹, fix,** and **mend** all mean to make something usable again. **Repair** suggests skill and experience: *The mechanic repaired the engine.* **Fix** suggests a smaller, easier job: *Dad fixed my coat zipper.* **Mend** suggests closing a hole: *That badly torn sleeve will not be easy to mend.*

re·pair² (ri pâr′), *v.* to go to a place: *After dinner we repaired to the porch.*

re·pair·man (ri pâr′man′), *n.* person whose work is repairing something. ❏ *n., pl.* **re·pair·men.**

rep·ar·a·ble (rep′ər ə bəl), *adj.* able to be repaired or remedied. —**rep′ar·a·bly,** *adv.*

rep·a·ra·tion (rep′ə rā′shən), *n.* **1 reparations,** *pl.* compensation for wrong or injury, especially payments made by a defeated country for the devastation of territory during war: *England and France demanded reparations from Germany after World War I.* **2** act of giving satisfaction or compensation for wrong or injury done.

rep·ar·tee (rep′ər tē′), *n.* **1** witty reply or replies. **2** cleverness and wit in making replies. ❏ *n., pl.* **rep·ar·tees.**

re·past (ri past′), *n.* meal; food: *A light repast was served at the party.*

re·pa·tri·ate (rē pā′trē āt), *v.* to send back or restore to your own country: *After peace was declared, refugees and prisoners of war were repatriated.* ❏ *v.* **re·pa·tri·at·ed, re·pa·tri·at·ing.** —**re·pa′tri·a′tion,** *n.*

re·pay (ri pā′), *v.* **1** to pay back; give back: *When can you repay me?* **2** to do something in return for something received: *No thanks can repay such kindness.* **3** to do in return for someone: *The student's success repaid the teacher for her efforts.* ❏ *v.* **re·paid, re·pay·ing.** —**re·pay′a·ble,** *adj.* —**re·pay′ment,** *n.*

re·peal (ri pēl′), **1** *v.* to take back; withdraw; do away with: *The law was finally repealed.* **2** *n.* act of repealing; withdrawal; abolition: *She voted for the repeal of that law.* —**re·peal′a·ble,** *adj.* —**re·peal′er,** *n.*

re·peat (ri pēt′ *for verb;* rē′pēt′ *or* ri pēt′ *for noun*), **1** *v.* to do or make again: *repeat an error.* **2** *v.* to say again: *repeat a word for emphasis.* **3** *v.* to say over; recite: *He can repeat many poems from memory.* **4** *v.* to say after another says: *Repeat the oath after me.* **5** *v.* to tell to another or others: *I promised not to repeat the secret.* **6** *n.* act of repeating; repetition. **7** *n.* thing repeated. **8** *n.* passage in music to be repeated. **9** *n.* radio or TV show that is broadcast again. —**re·peat′a·ble,** *adj.* —**re·peat′er,** *n.*

repeat yourself, to say what you have already said.

re·peat·ed (ri pē′tid), *adj.* said, done, or made more than once: *Her repeated efforts at last won success. His repeated complaints were ignored.* —**re·peat′ed·ly,** *adv.*

re·peat·er (ri pē′tər), *n.* **1** gun that can be fired several times without reloading. **2** a watch or clock that, if a spring is pressed, strikes the hour is struck last.

repeating decimal, decimal in which the same number or series of numbers is repeated indefinitely. For example, .3333+ and .7272+ are repeating decimals.

re·pel (ri pel′), *v.* **1** to force back; drive back; drive away: *They repelled the enemy attack.* **2** to keep off or out; fail to mix with: *Oil and water repel each other. This tent repels moisture.* **3** to force apart or away by some inherent force: *The like poles of two magnets repel each other.* **4** to be displeasing to; cause disgust in: *Spiders and worms repel me.* **5** to reject: *They repelled his offer of a loan.* ❏ *v.* **re·pelled, re·pel·ling.**

re·pel·lent (ri pel′ənt), **1** *adj.* disagreeable or distasteful; unattractive: *a person with a cold, repellent manner. Cheating is repellent to most people.* **2** *adj.* repelling; driving back. **3** *n.* anything that repels: *We sprayed ourselves with insect repellent before the picnic.* —**re·pel′lent·ly,** *adv.*

re·pent (ri pent′), *v.* **1** to feel sorry for having done wrong and seek forgiveness: *The criminal repented.* **2** to feel sorry for; regret: *They bought a white rug and repented their choice.* —**re·pent′er,** *n.*

re·pent·ance (ri pen′təns), *n.* sorrow for having done wrong; regret.

re·pent·ant (ri pen′tənt), *adj.* repenting; feeling regret; sorry for wrongdoing: *a repentant criminal.* —**re·pent′ant·ly,** *adv.*

re·per·cus·sion (rē′pər kush′ən), *n.* **1** an indirect influence or reaction from an event: *repercussions of war.* **2** sound flung back; echo. **3** act of springing back; rebound; recoil: *the repercussion of a cannon.*

rep·er·toire (rep′ər twär′), *n.* the list of plays, operas, parts, pieces, etc., that a company, an actor, a musician, or a singer is prepared to perform.

rep·er·to·ry (rep′ər tôr′ē), *n.* **1** repertoire. **2** store or stock of things ready for use. ❏ *n., pl.* **rep·er·to·ries.**

repertory theater, a company of actors which performs a series of plays in a season.

rep·e·ti·tion (rep′ə tish′ən), *n.* **1** something repeated; repeated occurrence. **2** act of repeating; doing again; saying again: *Repetition helps learning.*

rep·e·ti·tious (rep′ə tish′əs), *adj.* full of repetitions; repeating in a tiresome way: *repetitious excuses.* —**rep′e·ti′tious·ly,** *adv.* —**rep′e·ti′tious·ness,** *n.*

re·pet·i·tive (ri pet′ə tiv), *adj.* of or using repetition. —**re·pet′i·tive·ly,** *adv.* —**re·pet′i·tive·ness,** *n.*

re·phrase (rē frāz′), *v.* to phrase again; say or write in a different way. ❏ *v.* **re·phrased, re·phras·ing.**

re·place (ri plās′), *v.* **1** to fill or take the place of: *A substitute replaced our teacher.* **2** to get another in place of: *I will replace the cup I broke.* **3** to put back; put in place again: *Replace the books on the shelf.* ❏ *v.* **re·placed, re·plac·ing.** —**re·place′a·ble,** *adj.*

re·place·ment (ri plās′mənt), *n.* **1** something or someone that replaces: *She is a replacement for our usual shortstop.* **2** act of replacing or condition of being replaced: *the replacement of steam locomotives by diesel engines.*

re·plant (rē plant′), *v.* to place new plants or trees in an area, replacing previous ones: *After the city finished repairing the sidewalk, all the neighbors brought flowers to replant along the path.*

re·play (rē plā′ *for verb;* rē′plā′ *for noun*), **1** *v.* to play a match, game, etc., again. **2** *n.* a match or game played again. **3** *n.* a rerun of the videotape of a play, or portion of a game that is being televised: *We saw the touchdown again on the replay.*

re·plen·ish (ri plen′ish), *v.* to fill again; provide a new supply for: *Once our natural resources are used up we cannot replenish them.* —**re·plen′ish·er,** *n.* —**re·plen′ish·ment,** *n.*

re·plete (ri plēt′), *adj.* abundantly supplied; filled: *The tour of London was replete with unexpected thrills.* —**re·plete′ness,** *n.*

re·ple·tion (ri plē′shən), *n.* fullness.

rep·li·ca (rep′lə kə), *n.* copy; reproduction: *There is a replica of the Mayflower in Plymouth, Massachusetts.* □ *n., pl.* **rep·li·cas.**

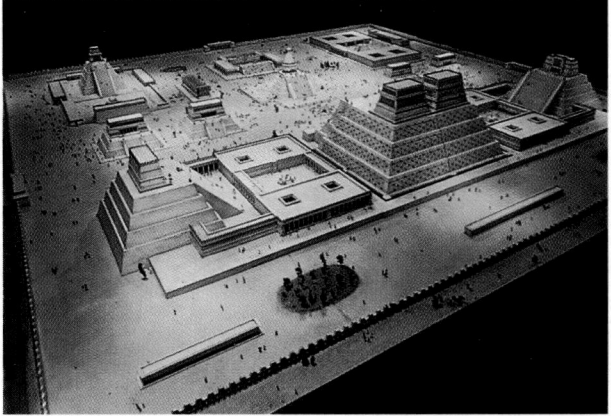

replica of an Aztec village

rep·li·cate (rep′lə kāt), *v.* **1** to copy exactly; reproduce; duplicate: *to replicate a lab experiment.* **2** to duplicate or reproduce itself: *molecules of DNA replicate themselves.* □ *v.* **rep·li·cat·ed, rep·li·cat·ing.** **—rep′li·ca′tion,** *n.*

re·ply (ri plī′), **1** *v.* to answer by words or action; respond: *She replied with a shout. The enemy replied to the attack with heavy gunfire.* **2** *n.* something said or done in answer; response: *They didn't hear your reply to the question.* □ *v.* **re·plied, re·ply·ing;** *n., pl.* **re·plies.**

re·port (ri pôrt′), **1** *n.* an account of something seen, heard, read, done, or considered. **2** *n.* an account officially or formally expressed, generally in writing: *a committee report.* **3** *v.* to make a report; give an account of something; announce or state: *Our treasurer reports that all dues are paid up.* **4** *v.* to repeat what you have heard, seen, etc.; bring back an account of; describe; tell: *The radio reports the news and weather.* **5** *v.* to present yourself; appear: *Report for work at 9 a.m.* **6** *v.* to announce as a wrongdoer; denounce: *report someone to the police.* **7** *n.* the sound of a shot or an explosion: *the report of a gun.* **8** *n.* rumor: *Report has it that our neighbors are leaving town.* **9** *n.* OLD USE. reputation: *a just man of good report.* **—re·port′a·ble,** *adj.*

SYNONYM STUDY **Report** and **describe** both mean to tell about something. **Report** means to tell in an organized way: *She will report to the class on her family's trip to Mexico City.* **Describe** means to tell what something is like: *The ad describes the missing cat in detail.*

report card, a written report sent regularly by a school to parents or guardians, indicating the quality of a student's work.

re·port·ed·ly (ri pôr′tid lē), *adv.* according to reports: *A new school is reportedly going to be built next year.*

re·port·er (ri pôr′tər), *n.* **1** person who gathers and reports news for a newspaper, radio or TV station, etc. **2** person who reports.

re·pose[1] (ri pōz′), **1** *n.* rest or sleep: *Do not disturb her repose.* **2** *v.* to lie at rest: *The cat reposed upon the cushion.* **3** *v.* to lay to rest: *Repose yourself in the hammock.* **4** *n.* quietness; ease: *repose of manner.* **5** *n.* peace; calmness: *the repose of the country.* □ *v.* **re·posed, re·pos·ing.**

re·pose[2] (ri pōz′), *v.* to put; place: *We repose complete confidence in his honesty.* □ *v.* **re·posed, re·pos·ing.**

re·pos·i·to·ry (ri poz′ə tôr′ē), *n.* place or container where things are stored or kept: *The box was a repository for old magazines.* □ *n., pl.* **re·pos·i·to·ries.**

re·pos·sess (rē′pə zes′), *v.* to possess again; get possession of again, especially from a buyer who has failed to pay.

rep·re·hend (rep′ri hend′), *v.* to blame; criticize.

rep·re·hen·si·ble (rep′ri hen′sə bəl), *adj.* deserving blame: *Cheating is a reprehensible act.* **—rep′re·hen′si·bly,** *adv.*

rep·re·sent (rep′ri zent′), *v.* **1** to stand for; be a sign or symbol of: *The 50 stars in our flag represent the 50 states.* **2** to act in place of; speak and act for: *Elected officials represent the voters.*

3 to act the part of: *Each child will represent an animal at the party.* **4** to show in a picture, statue, carving, etc.; give a likeness of; portray: *This painting represents the seasons.* **5** to be a type of; be an example of: *A raft represents a very simple kind of boat.* **6** to describe; set forth: *He represented the plan as safe, but it was not.* **—rep′re·sent′a·ble,** *adj.*

rep·re·sen·ta·tion (rep′ri zen tā′shən), *n.* **1** condition or fact of being represented: *"Taxation without representation is tyranny."* **2** act of representing. **3** representatives considered as a group. **4** likeness; picture; model. **5** performance of a play; presentation: *A representation of the story "Little Women" will be given today.* **6** account; statement: *They deceived us by false representations.* **—rep′re·sen·ta′tion·al,** *adj.*

rep·re·sent·a·tive (rep′ri zen′tə tiv), **1** *n.* person appointed or elected to act or speak for others: *She is the club's representative at the convention.* **2** *n.* **Representative,** member of the House of Representatives. ■ See Usage Note at **capital letter.** **3** *adj.* having its citizens represented by chosen persons: *a representative government.* **4** *adj.* representing: *Images representative of animals were made by the children.* **5** *n.* a typical example; type: *The tiger is a representative of the cat family.* **6** *adj.* serving as an example of; typical: *Oak and maple are representative American hardwoods.* **—rep′re·sent′a·tive·ly,** *adv.* **—rep′re·sent′a·tive·ness,** *n.*

re·press (ri pres′), *v.* **1** to prevent from acting; check: *She repressed an impulse to cough.* **2** to keep down; put down; suppress: *repress a revolt.* **—re·press′er** or **re·pres′sor,** *n.*

re·pres·sion (ri presh′ən), *n.* **1** act of repressing: *The repression of a laugh made him choke.* **2** condition of being repressed: *Repression made the people revolt against the government.*

re·pres·sive (ri pres′iv), *adj.* tending to repress; having power to repress.

re·prieve (ri prēv′), **1** *v.* to postpone the punishment of someone, especially the execution of someone condemned to death. **2** *n.* a delay in carrying out a punishment, especially of the death penalty. **3** *n.* the order giving authority for such delay. **4** *n.* temporary relief from any evil or trouble. **5** *v.* to give such relief to. □ *v.* **re·prieved, re·priev·ing.** **—re·priev′a·ble,** *adj.*

rep·ri·mand (rep′rə mand), **1** *n.* a severe or formal scolding, especially by a superior or official. **2** *v.* to scold severely or formally: *The captain was reprimanded and demoted.*

re·print (rē print′ *for verb;* rē′print′ *for noun*), **1** *v.* to print again; print a new impression of. **2** *n.* a new impression of a printed work. **—re·print′er,** *n.*

re·pris·al (ri prī′zəl), *n.* injury done in return for injury, especially by one nation to another.

re·prise (ri prēz′), **1** *n.* (in music) a repetition of a theme. **2** *v.* (in music) to repeat a theme. **3** *v.* to repeat something as before, with little or no variation: *The actor will reprise his role as the villain in the sequel.* □ *v.* **re·prised, re·pris·ing.**

re·proach (ri prōch′), **1** *n.* blame or censure: *Their conduct is above reproach.* **2** *v.* to blame; censure: *They reproached me for being late.* **3** *n.* a cause of blame or disgrace: *That run-down building is a reproach to the owners.* **4** *n.* expression of blame, censure, or disapproval. □ *n., pl.* **re·proach·es.** **—re·proach′a·ble,** *adj.* **—re·proach′a·bly,** *adv.* **—re·proach′er,** *n.*

re·proach·ful (ri prōch′fəl), *adj.* full of reproach; expressing disapproval: *a reproachful look.* **—re·proach′ful·ly,** *adv.* **—re·proach′ful·ness,** *n.*

rep·ro·bate (rep′rə bāt), **1** *n.* a very wicked or unprincipled person; scoundrel. **2** *adj.* very wicked; unprincipled.

re·pro·duce (rē′prə düs′), *v.* **1** to make a copy of: *to reproduce a photograph.* **2** to produce offspring: *Most plants reproduce by seeds.* **3** to produce again; make or create over: *to reproduce music from a recording.* □ *v.* **re·pro·duced, re·pro·duc·ing.** **—re′pro·duc′er,** *n.* **—re′pro·duc′i·ble,** *adj.*

R

a	hat	ė	term	ô	order	ch	child		a in about
ā	age	i	it	oi	oil	ng	long		e in taken
ä	far	ī	ice	ou	out	sh	she	ə	i in pencil
â	care	o	hot	u	cup	th	thin		o in lemon
e	let	ō	open	ù	put	ŦH	then		u in circus
ē	equal	ò	saw	ü	rule	zh	measure		

re·pro·duc·tion (rē′prə duk′shən), *n.* **1** a copy: *a reproduction of a painting.* **2** process by which living things produce offspring. **3** act or process of reproducing: *the reproduction of sounds by a cassette player.*

re·pro·duc·tive (rē′prə duk′tiv), *adj.* **1** capable of reproducing. **2** of or about reproduction. —**re′pro·duc′tive·ly,** *adv.* —**re′pro·duc′tive·ness,** *n.*

re·proof (ri prüf′), *n.* words of blame or disapproval; rebuke.

re·prove (ri prüv′), *v.* to show disapproval of; find fault with; scold: *I reproved the children for teasing the cat.* ❑ *v.* **re·proved, re·prov·ing.** —**re·prov′er,** *n.* —**re·prov′ing·ly,** *adv.*

rep·tile (rep′til), *n.* **1** any of many cold-blooded animals with backbones and lungs, usually covered with horny plates or scales. Snakes, lizards, turtles, alligators, and crocodiles are reptiles. Dinosaurs were reptiles. **2** a selfish and unfeeling person.

WORD STORY Reptile comes from a Latin word meaning "to crawl." Many reptiles have short legs and move with their belly close to the ground; snakes move with their bellies right on the ground.

rep·til·i·an (rep til′ē ən), **1** *adj.* of or about reptiles. **2** *adj.* like a reptile; base; mean. **3** *n.* a reptile.

re·pub·lic (ri pub′lik), *n.* **1** government in which the citizens elect representatives to manage the government, which is usually headed by a president. **2** nation or state that has such a government. The United States and Mexico are republics.

re·pub·li·can (ri pub′lə kən), **1** *adj.* of or like that of a republic: *Many countries have a republican form of government.* **2** *n.* person who favors a republic. **3 Republican, a** *adj.* of the Republican Party. **b** *n.* member of the Republican Party.

Republican Party, one of the two main political parties in the United States. The other is the Democratic Party.

re·pu·di·ate (ri pyü′dē āt), *v.* **1** to refuse to accept; reject: *repudiate a rumor.* **2** to refuse to acknowledge or pay: *repudiate a debt.* ❑ *v.* **re·pu·di·at·ed, re·pu·di·at·ing.** —**re·pu′di·a′tion,** *n.* —**re·pu′di·a′tor,** *n.*

re·pug·nance (ri pug′nəns), *n.* strong dislike, distaste, or aversion: *Some people feel a repugnance for snakes.*

re·pug·nant (ri pug′nənt), *adj.* disagreeable or offensive; distasteful: *a repugnant smell, a repugnant duty.* —**re·pug′nant·ly,** *adv.*

re·pulse (ri puls′), **1** *v.* to drive back; repel: *Our soldiers repulsed the enemy.* **2** *n.* act of driving or condition of being driven back: *After the second repulse, the enemy surrendered.* **3** *v.* to refuse to accept; reject: *She repulsed my invitation.* **4** *n.* refusal; rejection: *Her repulse was quite unexpected.* ❑ *v.* **re·pulsed, re·puls·ing.**

re·pul·sion (ri pul′shən), *n.* **1** strong dislike or aversion. **2** repulse.

re·pul·sive (ri pul′siv), *adj.* **1** causing strong dislike or aversion: *the repulsive smell of a skunk.* **2** tending to drive back or repel. —**re·pul′sive·ly,** *adv.* —**re·pul′sive·ness,** *n.*

rep·u·ta·ble (rep′yə tə bəl), *adj.* having a good reputation; well thought of; respectable: *a reputable citizen.* —**rep′u·ta·bly,** *adv.*

rep·u·ta·tion (rep′yə tā′shən), *n.* **1** what other people think and say the character of someone or something is; character in the opinion of others; name; repute: *This store has an excellent reputation for fair dealing.* **2** good name; good reputation: *Cheating ruined his reputation.* **3** fame: *an international reputation.*

re·pute (ri pyüt′), **1** *n.* reputation: *This is a district of bad repute because of the crime here.* **2** *v.* to suppose to be; consider; suppose: *They are reputed to be quite rich.* ❑ *v.* **re·put·ed, re·put·ing.**

re·put·ed (ri pyü′tid), *adj.* accounted or supposed to be such: *the reputed author of a book.* —**re·put′ed·ly,** *adv.*

re·quest (ri kwest′), **1** *v.* to ask for; ask as a favor: *She requested a loan from her friend.* ■ See Synonym Study at **ask. 2** *v.* to ask: *He requested her to go with him.* **3** *n.* act of asking: *a request for help.* **4** *n.* what is asked for: *He granted my request.*
by request, in response to a request.

req·ui·em or **Req·ui·em** (rek′wē əm), *n.* **1** Mass for the dead; musical church service for the dead. **2** music for it.

re·quire (ri kwīr′), *v.* **1** to have need for; need; want: *We shall require more help.* **2** to command; order; demand: *The rules require us all to be present.* ❑ *v.* **re·quired, re·quir·ing.**

re·quire·ment (ri kwīr′mənt), *n.* **1** a need; thing needed: *Patience is a requirement in teaching.* **2** a demand; thing demanded: *That school has a requirement that students wear uniforms.*

req·ui·site (rek′wə zit), **1** *adj.* required by circumstances; needed; necessary; essential; indispensable: *the qualities requisite for a leader, the number of votes requisite for election.* **2** *n.* thing needed; requirement: *Food and air are requisites for life.*

req·ui·si·tion (rek′wə zish′ən), **1** *v.* to demand or take by authority: *requisition supplies.* **2** *n.* a demand made, especially a formal, written demand: *The principal signed a requisition for new books.* **3** *v.* to make demands upon: *The hospital requisitioned the city for more funds.* **4** *n.* condition of being required for use or called into service: *The car was in constant requisition for errands.*

re·quite (ri kwīt′), *v.* to pay back; make return for: *requite kindness with love.* ❑ *v.* **re·quit·ed, re·quit·ing.** —**re·quit′er,** *n.*

re·read (rē rēd′), *v.* to read again: *reread a good book.* ❑ *v.* **re·read** (rē red′), **re·read·ing.**

re·route (rē rüt′ *or* rē rout′), *v.* to send by a new or different route. ❑ *v.* **re·rout·ed, re·rout·ing.**

re·run (rē run′ *for verb;* rē′run′ *for noun*), **1** *v.* to run again. **2** *n.* a TV show or movie that is shown again. **3** *n.* act of running again. ❑ *v.* **re·ran** (rē ran′), **re·run, re·run·ning.**

re·sale (rē′sāl′), *n.* act of selling again: *the resale of a house.*

re·scind (ri sind′), *v.* to annul; repeal; cancel: *rescind a law.* —**re·scind′a·ble,** *adj.* —**re·scind′er,** *n.*

res·cue (res′kyü), **1** *v.* to save from danger, capture, harm, etc.; free; deliver: *rescue someone from drowning.* ■ See Synonym Study at **save¹. 2** *n.* act of saving or freeing from danger, capture, harm, etc.: *The fireman was praised for his brave rescue of the children.* ❑ *v.* **res·cued, res·cu·ing.** —**res′cu·er,** *n.*

re·search (ri sėrch′ *or* rē′sėrch′), **1** *n.* act of hunting carefully for facts or truth; inquiry; investigation: *library research, cancer research.* **2** *v.* to hunt for facts or truth; inquire; investigate: *My father is researching the history of our family.* ❑ *n., pl.* **re·search·es.** —**re·search′er,** *n.*

research

re·sem·blance (ri zem′bləns), *n.* similar appearance; likeness: *Twins often show great resemblance.*

re·sem·ble (ri zem′bəl), *v.* to be like; be similar to; have likeness to in form, figure, or qualities: *An orange resembles a grapefruit.* ❑ *v.* **re·sem·bled, re·sem·bling.**

re·sent (ri zent′), *v.* to feel injured and angry at; feel indignation at: *I resented being called lazy.*

re·sent·ful (ri zent′fəl), *adj.* feeling resentment; injured and angry; showing resentment. —**re·sent′ful·ly,** *adv.*

re·sent·ment (ri zent′mənt), *n.* the feeling that you have at being injured or insulted; anger; bitterness: *Everyone feels resentment at being treated unfairly.*

res·er·va·tion (rez′ər vā′shən), *n.* **1** arrangement to have a room, a seat, etc., held in advance for your use later on: *make a reservation for a room in a hotel.* **2** land set aside by the government for a special purpose: *an Indian reservation.* **3** a doubt, especially one that is not expressed: *She didn't mention it, but she had reservations about their plan.* **4** a limiting condition: *We accepted the plan completely, without reservations.*

re·serve (ri zėrv′), **1** *v.* to keep back; keep to yourself: *Mother reserved judgment until she had heard both sides of the argument.* **2** *v.* to set apart: *He reserves his evenings to spend them with his family.* **3** *v.* to save for use later: *Reserve enough money for your fare home.* **4** *n.* the actual cash in a bank or assets that can be turned into cash quickly. Banks must keep a reserve of money. **5** *n.pl.* **reserves,** members of the armed forces not assigned to duty but ready to serve when needed. **6** *n.* public land set apart for a special purpose: *a forest reserve.* **7** *n.* (in Canada) reservation (def. 3). **8** *n.* anything kept back for future use; store: *a reserve of food or energy.* **9** *n.* act of keeping back or holding back; reservation: *You may speak before her without reserve.* **10** *n.* fact, state, or condition of being kept, set apart, or saved for use later: *keep money in reserve.* **11** *v.* to arrange to have set aside for the use of a particular person or persons: *reserve a table at a restaurant.* **12** *adj.* kept in reserve; forming a reserve: *a reserve stock, a reserve force.* **13** *n.* act or quality of keeping your thoughts, feelings, and affairs to yourself; self-restraint in action or speech; lack of friendliness. **14** *n.* a silent manner that keeps people from making friends easily. ❑ *v.* **re·served, re·serv·ing.** —**re·serv′er,** *n.*

re·served (ri zėrvd′), *adj.* **1** kept in reserve; kept by special arrangement: *a reserved seat.* **2** set apart. **3** self-restrained in action or speech. **4** disposed to keep to yourself: *A reserved person does not make friends easily.* —**re·serv·ed·ly** (ri zėr′vid lē), *adv.*

re·serv·ist (ri zėr′vist), *n.* member of the reserves; soldier or sailor not in active service but available if needed.

res·er·voir (rez′ər vwär), *n.* **1** place where water is collected and stored for use: *This reservoir supplies the entire city.* **2** anything to hold a liquid: *A fountain pen has an ink reservoir.* **3** place where anything is collected and stored: *Her mind was a reservoir of facts.* **4** a great supply: *a reservoir of weapons.*

re·set (rē set′), *v.* to set again: *The diamonds were reset in platinum. My broken arm had to be reset.* ❑ *v.* **re·set, re·set·ting.**

re·side (ri zīd′), *v.* **1** to live in or at a place for a long time; dwell: *This family has resided in our town for 100 years.* **2** to be; exist: *The power to declare war resides in Congress.* ❑ *v.* **re·sid·ed, re·sid·ing.** —**re·sid′er,** *n.*

res·i·dence (rez′ə dəns), *n.* **1** the place where a person lives; house; home; abode: *The President's residence is the White House in Washington, D.C.* **2** act of residing; living; dwelling: *Long residence in France made them very fond of the French.* **3** period of residing in a place: *They spent a residence of a year in France.*

res·i·den·cy (rez′ə dən sē), *n.* the period of time that a doctor spends practicing in a hospital after completing training as an intern.

res·i·dent (rez′ə dənt), **1** *n.* person living in a place permanently; dweller: *The residents of the town are proud of their new library.* **2** *adj.* staying; dwelling in a place: *Resident owners live on their property.* **3** *adj.* living in a place while on duty or doing active work: *She is a resident physician at the hospital.* **4** *n.* doctor practicing in a hospital after completing training as an intern.

WORD STORY **Resident** comes from a Latin word meaning "to sit back." A person who sits back in a chair intends to remain there, and a resident is someone who lives in a place permanently.

res·i·den·tial (rez′ə den′shəl), *adj.* **1** of or suitable for homes or residences: *They live in a large residential district outside the city.* **2** of or about residence: *The city is considering the adoption of a residential requirement for all city employees to live within the city limits.* —**res′i·den′tial·ly,** *adv.*

re·sid·u·al (ri zij′ü əl), *adj.* of or forming a residue; remaining; left over. —**re·sid′u·al·ly,** *adv.*

res·i·due (rez′ə dü), *n.* what remains after a part is taken; remainder: *His will directed that after the payment of all debts the residue of his property should go to his children. The syrup dried up, leaving a sticky residue.*

re·sign (ri zīn′), *v.* to give up a job, position, etc.; renounce: *I resigned my position on the school paper.*
resign yourself, to submit quietly; adapt yourself without complaint; yield: *He had to resign himself to a week in bed when he hurt his back.*

res·ig·na·tion (rez′ig nā′shən), *n.* **1** a written statement giving notice that you resign. **2** act of resigning: *There have been two resignations from the committee.* **3** patient acceptance; quiet submission: *bear pain with resignation.*

re·signed (ri zīnd′), *adj.* accepting what comes without complaint. —**re·sign·ed·ly** (ri zī′nid lē), *adv.*

re·sil·ience (ri zil′yəns), *n.* **1** power of springing back; elasticity; resilient quality or nature: *Rubber has resilience.* **2** power of recovering quickly; buoyancy; cheerfulness.

re·sil·ien·cy (ri zil′yən sē), *n.* resilience.

re·sil·ient (ri zil′yənt), *adj.* **1** springing back; returning to the original form or position after being bent, compressed, or stretched: *resilient steel.* **2** recovering quickly; buoyant; cheerful: *a resilient nature that throws off trouble.* —**re·sil′i·ent·ly,** *adv.*

res·in (rez′n), *n.* a sticky, yellow or brown substance that flows from some plants and trees, especially pines and firs. It is also made chemically and is used in medicine, varnish, plastics, etc. —**res′in·like′,** *adj.*

res·in·ous (rez′n əs), *adj.* of, like, or containing resin.

re·sist (ri zist′), *v.* **1** to act against; try to prevent; oppose: *She resisted the plan to close our neighborhood library.* ■ See Synonym Study at **oppose.** **2** to keep from doing something; struggle successfully against: *I could not resist laughing.* **3** to withstand the action or effect of an acid, storm, etc.: *A healthy body resists disease.* —**re·sist′er,** *n.*

re·sist·ance (ri zis′təns), *n.* **1** act of resisting: *The bank clerk made no resistance to the robbers.* **2** power to resist: *Some people have very little resistance to colds.* **3** thing or act that resists; opposing force; opposition: *Air resistance makes a feather fall more slowly than a pin.* **4 Resistance,** people who secretly organize and fight for their freedom in a country occupied and controlled by a foreign power: *the French Resistance in World War II.* **5** quality of an electric conductor that opposes the passage of current and changes electric energy into heat. Copper has a low resistance.

re·sist·ant (ri zis′tənt), *adj.* resisting.

re·sist·less (ri zist′lis), *adj.* **1** that cannot be resisted; irresistible. **2** offering no resistance. —**re·sist′less·ly,** *adv.* —**re·sist′·less·ness,** *n.*

re·sis·tor (ri zis′tər), *n.* an electric conductor used to control voltage by its resistance.

res·o·lute (rez′ə lüt), *adj.* determined; firm: *be resolute against all opposition. She was resolute in her attempt to climb to the top of the mountain.* —**res′o·lute′ly,** *adv.* —**res′o·lute′ness,** *n.*

res·o·lu·tion (rez′ə lü′shən), *n.* **1** decision; making up your mind to do or not do something: *We made a resolution to get up early.* **2** a formal expression of opinion: *The club passed a resolution thanking the teacher for his help.* **3** act of resolving or determining. **4** power of holding firmly to a purpose; determination: *The pioneers' resolution overcame many hardships.* **5** act or process of separating. **6** answer or solution: *the resolution of a problem, the resolution of a plot in a novel.* **7** ability of a device to form clear visual images. A telescope with high resolution shows separate pictures of stars that are close together. A high-resolution computer screen shows pictures or text in great detail.

re·solve (ri zolv′), **1** *v.* to make up your mind; determine; decide: *I resolved to do better work in the future.* ■ See Synonym Study at **decide.** **2** *n.* thing determined on; thing decided: *He kept his resolve to do better.* **3** *n.* firmness in carrying out a purpose; determination: *Helen Keller was a woman of resolve.* **4** *v.* to decide by vote: *It was resolved that our class should have a picnic.* **5** *v.* to answer and explain; solve: *The letter resolved our doubts.* **6** *v.* to separate into parts; break up: *Some chemical compounds resolve when heated.* **7** *v.* to change: *The assembly resolved itself into a committee.* ❑ *v.* **re·solved, re·solv·ing.** —**re·solv′a·ble,** *adj.* —**re·solv′er,** *n.*

R

a	hat	ė	term	ô	order	ch	child		a in about
ā	age	i	it	oi	oil	ng	long		e in taken
ä	far	ī	ice	ou	out	sh	she	ə	i in pencil
â	care	o	hot	u	cup	th	thin		o in lemon
e	let	ō	open	ù	put	ŦH	then		u in circus
ē	equal	ò	saw	ü	rule	zh	measure		

re·solved (ri zolvd′), *adj.* determined; firm; resolute.

res·o·nance (rez′n əns), *n.* **1** resounding quality; quality of being resonant: *the resonance of an organ.* **2** act of reinforcing and prolonging sound by reflection or by vibration of other objects. The hollow body of a guitar provides resonance.

res·o·nant (rez′n ənt), *adj.* **1** full; rich; vibrating: *The singer's resonant voice filled the auditorium.* **2** tending to increase or prolong sounds. —**res′o·nant·ly,** *adv.*

res·o·nate (rez′n āt), *v.* to produce full, vibrant sound; resound. ❑ *v.* **res·o·nat·ed, res·o·nat·ing.**

res·o·na·tor (rez′n ā′tər), *n.* something that produces resonance; device for making musical sounds louder by resonance.

re·sort (ri zôrt′), **1** *n.* a place people go to, usually for recreation: *There are many summer resorts in the mountains.* **2** *v.* to use as a method when others have failed: *When discussion doesn't solve a problem, some people resort to arguing and even fighting.* **3** *n.* act of using as a method: *By resort to legal action, they recovered the money.* **4** *n.* person or thing turned to for help: *Friends are the best resort in trouble.* —**re·sort′er,** *n.*

re·sound (ri zound′), *v.* **1** be filled with sound: *The room resounded with the children's shouts.* **2** to echo: *The hills resounded when we shouted.* **3** to sound loudly: *TV's resound from every apartment.* **4** be much talked about: *The fame of the first flight across the Atlantic resounded all over the world.*

re·sound·ing (ri zoun′ding), *adj.* **1** sounding very loud: *a resounding cheer.* **2** impressive; unmistakable: *a resounding victory.* —**re·sound′ing·ly,** *adv.*

re·source (ri sôrs′ *or* rē′sôrs), *n.* **1** any supply that will meet a need. We have resources of money, of knowledge, of strength, etc. **2 resources,** *pl.* the actual and potential wealth of a country: *natural resources, human resources.* **3** any means of getting success or getting out of trouble: *Climbing a tree is a cat's resource when chased by a dog.* **4** skill in meeting difficulties, getting out of trouble, etc.

re·source·ful (ri sôrs′fəl), *adj.* good at thinking of ways to do things; quick-witted: *The resourceful children mowed lawns to earn enough money to buy new bicycles.* —**re·source′ful·ly,** *adv.* —**re·source′ful·ness,** *n.*

re·spect (ri spekt′), **1** *n.* high regard; honor; esteem: *The children always showed great respect for their grandparents.* **2** *v.* to feel or show honor or esteem for: *We respect an honest person.* **3** *n.* consideration; care; regard: *Show respect for other people's property.* **4** *v.* to show consideration for; care for: *Respect the ideas and feelings of others.* **5** *n.pl.* **respects,** expressions of respect; regards: *We must pay our respects to the guest of honor.* **6** *n.* feature; point; matter; detail: *The plan is unwise in many respects.* **7** *n.* relation; reference: *We must plan with respect to the future.* —**re·spect′er,** *n.*

re·spect·a·ble (ri spek′tə bəl), *adj.* **1** worthy of respect; having a good reputation; honest and decent: *They are very respectable people.* **2** fairly good; moderate in size or quality: *His record in school was respectable but not brilliant.* **3** good enough to use; fit to be seen: *respectable clothes.* —**re·spect′a·bil′i·ty,** *n.* —**re·spect′a·bly,** *adv.*

re·spect·ful (ri spekt′fəl), *adj.* showing respect; considerate and polite. —**re·spect′ful·ly,** *adv.* —**re·spect′ful·ness,** *n.*

re·spect·ing (ri spek′ting), *prep.* regarding; about; concerning: *A discussion arose respecting the merits of different cars.*

re·spec·tive (ri spek′tiv), *adj.* belonging to each; particular; individual: *The classes went to their respective rooms.*

re·spec·tive·ly (ri spek′tiv lē), *adv.* as regards each of several persons or things in turn or in the order mentioned: *Pat, José, and Kathy are 16, 18, and 20 years old, respectively.*

re·spell (rē spel′), *v.* to spell over again, especially in a different alphabet.

res·pi·ra·tion (res′pə rā′shən), *n.* **1** act of inhaling and exhaling; breathing: *A bad cold can make respiration difficult.* **2** the process by which a living thing takes in oxygen from the air or water, distributes it, uses it for oxidation of food materials, and gives off carbon dioxide. **3** cellular respiration.

res·pi·ra·tor (res′pə rā′tər), *n.* **1** device worn over the nose and mouth to keep from breathing in harmful substances. **2** device used to help a person to breathe; ventilator. Respirators are used in giving artificial respiration.

res·pir·a·to·ry (res′pər ə tôr′ē), *adj.* of or used for respiration. The lungs are respiratory organs.

respiratory system, the organs in the body which take in oxygen from the air or water and remove carbon dioxide from the body. The nasal passages, bronchial tubes, and lungs are parts of the human respiratory system.

re·spire (ri spir′), *v.* to inhale and exhale; breathe. ❑ *v.* **re·spired, re·spir·ing.**

res·pite (res′pit), *n.* **1** time of relief and rest; lull: *A thick cloud brought a respite from the glare of the sun.* **2** delay, especially in carrying out a sentence of death; reprieve.

re·splend·ence (ri splen′dəns), *n.* great brightness; gorgeous appearance; splendor.

re·splend·ent (ri splen′dənt), *adj.* very bright; shining; splendid: *a gown resplendent with jewels, a face resplendent with joy.* —**re·splend′ent·ly,** *adv.*

re·spond (ri spond′), *v.* **1** to answer; reply: *He responded to the question.* **2** to act in answer; react: *A dog responds to kind treatment by loving its owner.*

WORD FAMILY **Respond** and the following words are related: **correspond, correspondence, response, responsibility, responsible,** and **responsive.** They all come from a Latin word meaning "to promise in return."

re·sponse (ri spons′), *n.* **1** an answer by word or act: *Her response to my letter was prompt. She laughed in response to his joke.* **2** words said or sung by the congregation or choir in answer to the minister. **3** the reaction by a living thing to some change in its surroundings: *When you look into bright light, the pupils of your eyes grow smaller in response.*

re·spon·si·bil·i·ty (ri spon′sə bil′ə tē), *n.* **1** act or fact of being responsible; obligation: *We agreed to share responsibility for planning the party.* **2** thing for which you are responsible: *Keeping my room clean and feeding the cat are my responsibilities.* ❑ *n., pl.* **re·spon·si·bil·i·ties** for 2.

re·spon·si·ble (ri spon′sə bəl), *adj.* **1** having the duty or obligation of taking care of someone or something: *You are responsible for keeping your room cleaned up.* **2** being the cause or reason: *Heavy rain was responsible for the small attendance.* **3** trustworthy; reliable: *Choose a responsible person to take care of the money.* **4** involving obligations or duties: *The presidency is a very responsible position.* —**re·spon′si·ble·ness,** *n.* —**re·spon′si·bly,** *adv.*

re·spon·sive (ri spon′siv), *adj.* **1** easily moved; responding readily: *a responsive nature.* **2** responding: *a responsive glance.* **3** using or containing responses: *responsive reading in church in which minister and congregation read in turn.* —**re·spon′sive·ly,** *adv.* —**re·spon′sive·ness,** *n.*

rest¹ (rest), **1** *n.* state of quiet and ease; sleep: *a good night's rest.* **2** *v.* to be still or quiet; sleep: *Lie down and rest.* **3** *n.* ease after work or effort: *After mowing the lawn, I needed rest.* **4** *n.* time of ease and freedom from activity or trouble: *I left the swimming pool for a short rest.* **5** *v.* to be free from work, effort, care, trouble, etc.: *Some people like to rest on weekends.* **6** *n.* absence of motion; stillness: *The ball came to rest at her feet.* **7** *v.* to give rest to; refresh by rest: *Stop and rest your feet.* **8** *v.* to place or be placed for support; lie; lay; lean: *He rested his rake against the fence. The roof of the porch rests on columns.* **9** *n.* a support; something to lean on: *a rest for a billiard cue.* **10** *v.* look directly at: *Our eyes rested on the open book.* **11** *v.* to be at ease: *Don't let her rest until she promises to visit us.* **12** *v.* to be or become inactive; let remain inactive: *Let the matter rest.* **13** *v.* to rely; trust; depend: *Our hope rests on you.* **14** *v.* to be found; be present; lie: *In a democracy, government rests with the people.* **15** *n.* place for resting: *a travelers' rest.* **16** *n.* in music: **a** a silence of definite length between notes. **b** a mark to show such a silence. **17** *n.* a pause in reading. **18** *n.* death; the grave. **19** *v.* to be dead;

lie in the grave: *The old man rests with his ancestors.* ■ Another word that sounds like this is **wrest**.

lay to rest, to bury: *lay a body to rest.*

rest² (rest), **1** *n.* what is left; those that are left: *The sun was out in the morning but it rained for the rest of the day. One horse was running ahead of the rest.* **2** *v.* to continue to be; remain: *You may rest assured that I will keep my promise. The final decision rests with you.* ■ Another word that sounds like this is **wrest**.

re·state (rē stāt′), *v.* **1** to state again. **2** to state in a new way. ❑ *v.* **re·stat·ed, re·stat·ing.**

re·state·ment (rē stāt′mənt), *n.* **1** a new statement. **2** statement made again. **3** act of stating again.

res·tau·rant (res′tər ənt *or* res′tə ränt′), *n.* place to buy and eat a meal.

res·tau·ra·teur (res′tər ə tėr′), *n.* person who owns or manages a restaurant.

rest·ful (rest′fəl), *adj.* **1** full of rest; giving rest: *He had a restful nap.* **2** quiet; peaceful. **—rest′ful·ly,** *adv.* **—rest′ful·ness,** *n.*

rest home, place where old people or people recovering from an illness can live and be cared for.

res·ti·tu·tion (res′tə tü′shən), *n.* **1** act of giving back what has been lost or taken away. **2** act of making good any loss, damage, or injury: *It is only fair that those who do the damage should make restitution.*

res·tive (res′tiv), *adj.* **1** restless; uneasy: *a restive audience.* **2** hard to manage: *a restive child.* **3** refusing to go ahead; balky: *a restive mule.* **—res′tive·ly,** *adv.* **—res′tive·ness,** *n.*

rest·less (rest′lis), *adj.* **1** unable to rest; uneasy: *The dog seemed restless, as if it sensed some danger.* **2** without rest or sleep; not restful: *The sick child passed a restless night.* **3** rarely or never still or quiet; always moving: *Some nervous people are very restless.* **—rest′less·ly,** *adv.* **—rest′less·ness,** *n.*

res·to·ra·tion (res′tə rā′shən), *n.* **1** act of restoring or condition of being restored; bringing back to a former condition: *the restoration of order after a period of rioting.* **2** something restored: *The house was a restoration of a colonial mansion.*

re·stor·a·tive (ri stôr′ə tiv), *adj.* capable of restoring; tending to restore health or strength: *a restorative medicine.* **—re·stor′a·tive·ly,** *adv.*

re·store (ri stôr′), *v.* **1** to bring back; establish again: *The police restored order.* **2** to bring back to a former condition or to a normal condition: *The old house has been restored.* **3** to give back; put back: *The boy restored the money he had found to its owner.* ❑ *v.* **re·stored, re·stor·ing.** **—re·stor′a·ble,** *adj.* **—re·stor′er,** *n.*

restoration (def. 1)

re·strain (ri strān′), *v.* to hold back; keep down; keep in check; keep within limits: *I could not restrain my curiosity to see what was in the box. We restrained the excited dog when guests came.* **—re·strain′a·ble,** *adj.* **—re·strain′ed·ly,** *adv.* **—re·strain′er,** *n.*

re·strain·ing order (ri strān′ing), an order by a judge that forbids an action until a legal decision is made: *They obtained a restraining order forbidding the county to tear down their house.*

re·straint (ri strānt′), *n.* **1** act of restraining or condition of being restrained: *Violent people sometimes need restraint.* **2** means of restraining. **3** device that restricts motion, such as a safety belt. **4** tendency to restrain natural feeling; reserve: *She was very angry, but she spoke with restraint.*

re·strict (ri strikt′), *v.* to keep within limits; confine: *Our club membership is restricted to twelve.* ■ See Synonym Study at **limit**.

re·strict·ed (ri strik′tid), *adj.* **1** limited; kept within limits: *She is on a very restricted diet, and can have no sweets.* **2** having restrictions or limiting rules: *Factories may not be built in this restricted residential section.* **—re·strict′ed·ly,** *adv.*

re·stric·tion (ri strik′shən), *n.* **1** something that restricts; limiting condition or rule: *The restrictions on the use of the playground are: No fighting; no damaging property.* **2** act of restricting or condition of being restricted: *This park is open to the public without restriction.*

re·stric·tive (ri strik′tiv), *adj.* restricting; limiting: *Restrictive laws limit the amount of pollution the factory can produce.* **—re·stric′tive·ly,** *adv.* **—re·stric′tive·ness,** *n.*

restrictive clause, (in grammar) any clause that qualifies a noun so definitely that it cannot be left out without changing the meaning of the sentence. EXAMPLE: All employees *who have been with this firm for five years* will receive bonuses.

rest·room (rest′rüm′), *n.* lavatory in a public building.

rest room, restroom.

re·sult (ri zult′), **1** *n.* what happens because of something else; what is caused; effect: *The result of the fall was a broken leg.* ■ See Synonym Study at **effect**. **2** *n.* good or useful effect: *The new medicine got results.* **3** *v.* to happen because of something: *Sickness often results from eating spoiled food.* **4** *v.* to have as a result; end: *Eating spoiled food often results in sickness.* **5** *n.* quantity, value, etc., obtained by calculation.

re·sult·ant (ri zult′nt), *adj.* resulting.

re·sume (ri züm′), *v.* **1** to begin again; go on: *Resume reading where we left off.* **2** to get or take again: *Those standing may resume their seats.* ❑ *v.* **re·sumed, re·sum·ing.** **—re·sum′a·ble,** *adj.*

rés·u·mé, re·su·mé, *or* **res·u·me** (rez′ə mā′), *n.* summary: *a résumé of your education and job experience.* ❑ *n., pl.* **ré·su·més, re·su·més,** *or* **re·su·mes.**

re·sump·tion (ri zump′shən), *n.* act of resuming: *the resumption of duties after absence.*

re·sur·face (rē sėr′fis), *v.* **1** to put a new surface on: *resurface a driveway.* **2** to rise to the surface again: *The submarine resurfaced.* **3** to reappear: *Many old suggestions resurfaced at the meeting last night.* ❑ *v.* **re·sur·faced, re·sur·fac·ing.**

re·sur·gence (re sėr′jəns), *n.* act of rising again: *resurgence of interest.*

re·sur·gent (ri sėr′jənt), *adj.* rising or tending to rise again: *Spring is a time of resurgent life.*

res·ur·rect (rez′ə rekt′), *v.* **1** to raise from the dead; bring back to life. **2** to bring back to sight, use, etc.: *resurrect an old custom.*

res·ur·rec·tion (rez′ə rek′shən), *n.* **1** act of coming to life again; rising from the dead. **2** **Resurrection,** (in Christian use) the rising again of Jesus after his death and burial. **3** restoration from decay or disuse; revival.

re·sus·ci·tate (ri sus′ə tāt), *v.* to bring or come back to life or consciousness; revive: *The paramedic resuscitated the man who was overcome by smoke.* ❑ *v.* **re·sus·ci·tat·ed, re·sus·ci·tat·ing.** **—re·sus′ci·ta′tion,** *n.*

re·sus·ci·ta·tor (ri sus′ə tā′tər), *n.* device used to revive persons overcome by gas, water in the lungs, etc. It produces artificial respiration by forcing air or oxygen into the lungs through a tight-fitting mask or cup attached to the victim's face.

re·tail (rē′tāl), **1** *n.* sale of goods in small quantities directly to the consumer: *Our grocer buys at wholesale and sells at retail.* **2** *adj.* of or about the sale of goods in small quantities: *The wholesale price of this coat is $40; the retail price is $60.* **3** *adj.* selling in small quantities: *the retail trade, a retail merchant.* **4** *v.* to sell or be sold in small quantities: *They retail these jackets at $50 each.* **—re′tail·er,** *n.*

WORD STORY **Retail** comes from an old French word meaning "to cut up." A retail store sells things already cut up (like meat or lumber), ready for people to buy and use.

re·tain (ri tān′), *v.* **1** to continue to have or hold; keep: *A china teapot retains heat for quite a long time. Our baseball team retained a lead throughout the game.* **2** to keep in mind; remember:

a	hat	ė	term	ô	order	ch	child	a in about
ā	age	i	it	oi	oil	ng	long	e in taken
ä	far	ī	ice	ou	out	sh	she	ə i in pencil
â	care	o	hot	u	cup	th	thin	o in lemon
e	let	ō	open	ù	put	ᴛʜ	then	u in circus
ē	equal	ò	saw	ü	rule	zh	measure	

R

She retained the tune but not the words of the song. **3** to hire by payment of a fee: *I retained a very good lawyer.*

re·tain·er¹ (ri tā′nər), *n.* **1** someone who serves a person of rank; vassal; attendant; follower: *The queen had many retainers.* **2** a metal wire used to hold teeth in place after they have been straightened by the wearing of braces.

re·tain·er² (ri tā′nər), *n.* fee paid to secure services: *This lawyer receives a retainer before he begins work on a case.*

re·tain·ing wall (ri tān′ing wôl), a wall used to hold back earth, especially at the edge of a terrace or excavation.

re·take (rē tāk′ *for verb;* rē′tāk′ *for noun*), **1** *v.* to take again. **2** *v.* to take back. **3** *n.* act of retaking: *a retake of a scene in a movie.* ❑ *v.* **re·took, re·tak·en** (rē tā′kən), **re·tak·ing.**

re·tal·i·ate (ri tal′ē āt), *v.* to pay back wrong, injury, etc.; return like for like, usually to return evil for evil: *If we insult them, they will retaliate.* —*v.* **re·tal·i·at·ed, re·tal·i·at·ing.** —**re·tal′i·a′tion,** *n.*

re·tal·i·a·to·ry (ri tal′ē ə tôr′ē), *adj.* returning like for like, especially evil for evil.

re·tard (ri tärd′), *v.* to slow up; delay the progress of; keep back; hinder: *Lack of education retards progress.*

re·tard·ant (ri tärd′nt), **1** *n.* something, especially a chemical, that delays a process: *treat cloth with a fire retardant.* **2** *adj.* tending to slow down or hinder something: *fire-retardant cloth.*

re·tar·da·tion (rē′tär dā′shən), *n.* **1** slowness in mental development. **2** act of retarding. **3** something that retards; hindrance.

re·tard·ed (ri tär′did), *adj.* slow in mental development.

USAGE NOTE **Retarded** is often considered offensive. Alternative terms include *developmentally disabled, challenged, special,* and *person with developmental disability* or *person with mental retardation.*

retch (rech), *v.* to make efforts to vomit. ■ Another word that sounds like this is **wretch.**

re·tell (rē tel′), *v.* to tell again. ❑ *v.* **re·told, re·tell·ing.**

re·ten·tion (ri ten′shən), *n.* **1** act of retaining or condition of being retained. **2** power to retain. **3** ability to remember.

re·ten·tive (ri ten′tiv), *adj.* **1** able to hold or keep: *a material retentive of moisture.* **2** able to remember easily: *a retentive memory.* —**re·ten′tive·ly,** *adv.* —**re·ten′tive·ness,** *n.*

re·test (rē test′), *v.* to test again.

ret·i·cence (ret′ə səns), *n.* tendency to be silent or say little; reserve in speech.

ret·i·cent (ret′ə sənt), *adj.* tending to keep silent or say little; reserved in speech: *We were all surprised when a reticent classmate became the star of the debate team.* —**ret′i·cent·ly,** *adv.*

re·tic·u·late (ri tik′yə lit *or* ri-tik′yə lāt), *adj.* covered with or resembling a network. Reticulate leaves have the veins arranged like the threads of a net. —**re·tic′u·late·ly,** *adv.*

Retin-A (ret′n ā′), *n.* a trademark for a substance related to vitamin A, used to treat wrinkles and acne.

ret·i·na (ret′n ə), *n.* inner membrane at the back of the eyeball that is sensitive to light and receives the images of things looked at. The retina transmits these images to the brain through the optic nerve. See picture at **eye.** ❑ *n., pl.* **ret·i·nas.**

ret·i·nal (ret′n əl), *adj.* of or on the retina.

reticulate skin pattern

ret·i·ni·tis pig·men·to·sa (ret′n ī′tis pig′men tō′sə), a disease of the eye involving degeneration of the retina, leading to night blindness and loss of peripheral vision. Retinitis pigmentosa eventually leads to tunnel vision or total blindness.

ret·i·nue (ret′n ü), *n.* group of attendants or retainers; a following: *The king's retinue accompanied him.*

re·tire (ri tīr′), *v.* **1** to give up an office, occupation, profession, etc., especially because of age: *Our teachers retire at 65.* **2** to remove from an office, occupation, etc. **3** to go away, especially to a place which is more quiet or private: *They retired to the country.* **4** to withdraw; draw back; send back: *The government retires worn or torn dollar bills from use.* **5** to go back; retreat: *The enemy retired before the advance of our troops.* **6** to go to bed: *We retire early.* **7** to withdraw from circulation and pay off bonds, loans, etc. **8** to put out a batter, side, etc., in baseball and cricket. ❑ *v.* **re·tired, re·tir·ing.**

re·tired (ri tīrd′), *adj.* **1** withdrawn from your occupation or office: *a retired accountant.* **2** secluded; shut off; hidden: *a retired spot.*

re·tir·ee (ri tī′rē), *n.* someone who has retired. ❑ *n., pl.* **re·tir·ees.**

re·tire·ment (ri tīr′mənt), *n.* **1** act of retiring; withdrawal: *The teacher's retirement was regretted by the school.* **2** a quiet way or place of living: *She lives in retirement in the country.*

re·tir·ing (ri tī′ring), *adj.* shrinking from society or publicity; reserved; shy: *a retiring nature.* —**re·tir′ing·ly,** *adv.*

re·told (rē tōld′), *v.* past tense and past participle of **retell:** *I then retold the story for the newcomers.*

re·took (rē tùk′), *v.* past tense of **retake:** *The photographer retook my picture.*

re·tool (rē tül′), *v.* to change the tools, machinery, designs, etc., of a factory in order to make new models or products.

re·tort¹ (ri tôrt′), **1** *v.* to reply quickly or sharply: *"It's none of your business," I retorted.* **2** *n.* a sharp or witty reply: *"Why are your teeth so sharp?" asked Red Ridinghood. "The better to eat you with," was the wolf's retort.* **3** *v.* to return in kind: *I told her what I thought of her, and she retorted insult for insult.*

re·tort² (ri tôrt′), *n.* container used for distilling or separating substances by heat.

re·touch (rē tuch′), *v.* to change or improve a photographic negative, painting, etc., by making slight changes with a brush, pencil, etc. —**re·touch′er,** *n.*

re·trace (ri trās′), *v.* to go back over: *We retraced our steps to where we started.* ❑ *v.* **re·traced, re·trac·ing.** —**re·trace′a·ble,** *adj.*

re·tract (ri trakt′), *v.* **1** to withdraw; take back: *retract an offer.* **2** to draw back or in: *The kitten retracted its claws and purred when I petted it.* —**re·tract′a·ble,** *adj.*

re·trac·tion (ri trak′shən), *n.* **1** act of taking back; withdrawal of a promise, statement, etc.: *The newspaper published a retraction of the inaccurate report about the actress.* **2** act of drawing or condition of being drawn back or in.

re·tread (rē tred′ *for verb;* rē′tred′ *for noun*), **1** *v.* to put a new tread on. **2** *n.* a tire that has been retreaded.

re·treat (ri trēt′), **1** *v.* to move back; withdraw: *The enemy retreated before the advance of our soldiers.* **2** *n.* act of moving back or withdrawing: *The army's retreat was orderly.* **3** *n.* a signal for retreat: *The drums beat a retreat.* **4** *n.* a signal on a bugle or drum, given at sunset during the lowering of the flag. **5** *n.* a safe, quiet place; place of rest or refuge. **6** *n.* a retirement, or period of retirement, by a group of people for religious exercises, meditation, etc.: *The monks conducted a retreat.*

beat a retreat, to run away; retreat: *We dropped the apples and beat a hasty retreat when the farmer chased us.*

re·trench (ri trench′), *v.* to cut down or reduce expenses, etc.: *In hard times, we must retrench to keep out of debt.* —**re·trench′-ment,** *n.*

re·tri·al (rē trī′əl), *n.* a second trial; new trial.

ret·ri·bu·tion (ret′rə byü′shən), *n.* a deserved punishment; return for wrongdoing.

re·trib·u·tive (ri trib′yə tiv), *adj.* bringing or inflicting punishment in return for wrongdoing: *retributive justice.*

re·triev·al (ri trē′vəl), *n.* act of retrieving; recovery.

re·trieve (ri trēv′), *v.* **1** to get back again; recover: *retrieve a lost pocketbook.* ■ See Synonym Study at **recover.** **2** to bring back to a former or better condition; restore: *retrieve your fortunes.* **3** to find and carry back to someone: *A dog can be trained to retrieve a ball.* **4** to copy computer data from storage, for display or for use by a program. ❑ *v.* **re·trieved, re·triev·ing.** —**re·triev′a·ble,** *adj.* —**re·triev′a·bly,** *adv.*

re·triev·er (ri trē′vər), *n.* dog that can be trained to find killed or wounded game and bring it to a hunter. Breeds of retriever include **Chesapeake Bay retrievers, golden retrievers,** and **Labrador retrievers.**

golden retriever

ret·ro (ret′rō), *adj.* of or in the style of an earlier time, especially if deliberately so: *That new restaurant has a retro 30s look.*

retro-, *prefix.* backward; back: *retrospective = looking back.*

ret·ro·ac·tive (ret′rō ak′tiv), *adj.* having an effect on what is past. A retroactive law applies to events that occurred before the law was passed. —**ret′ro·ac′tive·ly,** *adv.* —**ret′ro·ac·tiv′i·ty,** *n.*

ret·ro·grade (ret′rə grād), **1** *adj.* moving backward; retreating. **2** *v.* to move or go backward. **3** *adj.* becoming worse. **4** *v.* to fall back toward a worse condition; grow worse; decline. ❑ *v.* **ret·ro·grad·ed, ret·ro·grad·ing.** —**ret′ro·grade′ly,** *adv.*

ret·ro·gress (ret′rə gres *or* ret′rə gres′), *v.* **1** to move backward; go back. **2** to become worse. —**ret′ro·gres′sion,** *n.*

ret·ro·rock·et (ret′rō rok′it), *n.* a small rocket at the front of a spacecraft. It produces thrust opposite to the motion of the spacecraft in order to reduce speed for landing or for reentry.

ret·ro·spect (ret′rə spekt), *n.* survey of past time, events, etc.; thinking about the past.

in retrospect, when looking back: *She saw, in retrospect, that the problem could have been avoided.*

ret·ro·spec·tion (ret′rə spek′shən), *n.* act or process of looking back on things past; survey of past events or experiences.

ret·ro·spec·tive (ret′rə spek′tiv), *adj.* **1** looking back on things past; surveying past events or experiences. **2** applying to the past; retroactive. —**ret′ro·spec′tive·ly,** *adv.*

ret·ro·vi·rus (ret′rō vī′rəs), *n.* virus that contains RNA instead of DNA. Retroviruses cause AIDS and some kinds of cancer. ❑ *n., pl.* **ret·ro·vi·rus·es.**

re·turn (ri tėrn′), **1** *v.* to go back; come back: *Return home at once. My cousin will return this summer.* **2** *n.* act of going or coming back; happening again: *We look forward all winter to our return to the country. We wish you many happy returns of your birthday.* **3** *v.* to bring, give, send, put, or pay back: *Return that book to the library. I left a message for her to return my telephone call.* **4** *n.* act of bringing, giving, sending, putting, or paying back: *Such bad behavior was a poor return for kindness.* **5** *n.* something returned. **6** *n.* Often, **returns,** *pl.* profit; amount received: *The returns from the sale were more than a hundred dollars.* **7** *v.* to yield: *The concert returned about $5,000 over expenses.* **8** *n.* a report; an account: *election returns. I must make out my income-tax return.* **9** *v.* to report or announce officially: *The jury returned a verdict of guilty.* **10** *adj.* of or for a return: *a return ticket.* **11** *adj.* sent, given, done, etc., in return: *a return game.* **12** in football: **a** *v.* to run back a kick, fumble, or intercepted pass. **b** *n.* runback of a kick, fumble, or intercepted pass.

in return, as a return; in exchange: *If you let me use your skates, I'll lend you my skis in return.*

re·turn·a·ble (ri tėr′nə bəl), *adj.* **1** able to be returned. **2** meant or required to be returned.

re·turn·ee (ri tėr′nē′), *n.* person who has returned, especially from military service abroad. ❑ *n., pl.* **re·turn·ees.**

returning officer, (in Canada) an election official responsible for preparing voter lists and reporting the results of elections to the proper authorities.

Reu·ben sandwich (rü′bin), a grilled sandwich made of slices of corned beef and Swiss cheese on rye bread with sauerkraut.

re·un·ion (rē yü′nyən), *n.* **1** a social gathering of persons who have been separated or who have interests in common: *We have a family reunion every summer.* **2** act of coming together again: *the reunion of parted friends.*

re·u·nite (rē′yü nīt′), *v.* to bring together again; come together again: *The two friends were reunited after a long separation.* ❑ *v.* **re·u·nit·ed, re·u·nit·ing.**

re·use (rē yüz′ *for verb;* rē′yüs′ *for noun*), **1** *v.* to use again. **2** *n.* act of using again. ❑ *v.* **re·used, re·us·ing.** —**re·us′a·ble,** *adj.*

rev (rev), INFORMAL. **1** *v.* to increase the speed of an engine. **2** *n.* a revolution of an engine. ❑ *v.* **revved, rev·ving.**

Rev., Reverend.

re·vamp (rē vamp′), *v.* **1** to patch up; repair: *revamp an old car.* **2** to take apart and put together in a new form: *revamp plans.*

re·veal (ri vēl′), *v.* **1** to make known: *Never reveal my secret.* **2** to display; show: *Her smile revealed her even teeth.* —**re·veal′a·ble,** *adj.* —**re·veal′er,** *n.*

rev·eil·le (rev′ə lē), *n.* a signal on a bugle to waken members of the armed forces in the morning.

rev·el (rev′əl), **1** *v.* to take great pleasure: *The children revel in country life.* **2** *n.* a noisy good time; merrymaking: *Christmas revels with feasting and dancing were common in England.* **3** *v.* to make merry. ❑ *v.* **rev·eled, rev·el·ing** *or* **rev·elled, rev·el·ling.** —**rev′el·er,** *n.*

rev·e·la·tion (rev′ə lā′shən), *n.* **1** something made known: *Her true nature was a revelation to me.* **2** act of making known: *We all waited for the revelation of the winner's name.* **3** **Revelation,** the last book of the New Testament, supposed to have been written by the apostle John.

rev·el·ry (rev′əl rē), *n.* boisterous reveling or festivity; noisy merrymaking. ❑ *n., pl.* **rev·el·ries.**

re·venge (ri venj′), **1** *n.* harm done in return for a wrong; vengeance; returning evil for evil: *a blow struck in revenge.* **2** *n.* desire for vengeance. **3** *v.* to do harm in return for. ❑ *v.* **re·venged, re·veng·ing.**

be revenged or revenge yourself, to get revenge: *He swore to be revenged for the wrongs done to him.*

re·venge·ful (ri venj′fəl), *adj.* feeling or showing a strong desire for revenge. —**re·venge′ful·ly,** *adv.* —**re·venge′ful·ness,** *n.*

rev·e·nue (rev′ə nü′), *n.* money coming in; income: *The government gets revenue from taxes.*

re·ver·be·rate (ri vėr′bə rāt′), *v.* to echo; resound: *The deep, rumbling sound of the organ reverberated in the church.* ❑ *v.* **re·ver·be·rat·ed, re·ver·be·rat·ing.** —**re·ver′be·ra′tion,** *n.*

re·vere (ri vir′), *v.* to love and respect deeply; honor greatly; show reverence for: *People revered the saint.* ❑ *v.* **re·vered, re·ver·ing.**

Re·vere (ri vir′), *n.* **Paul,** 1735-1818, American patriot. He is famous for his night ride through eastern Massachusetts to warn colonists of the approach of British troops in 1775.

Paul Revere

a	hat	ė	term	ô	order	ch	child		
ā	age	i	it	oi	oil	ng	long		a in about
ä	far	ī	ice	ou	out	sh	she		e in taken
â	care	o	hot	u	cup	th	thin	ə	i in pencil
e	let	ō	open	ù	put	ᴛʜ	then		o in lemon
ē	equal	ò	saw	ü	rule	zh	measure		u in circus

rev·er·ence (rev′ər əns), **1** *n.* a feeling of deep respect, mixed with wonder, awe, and love. **2** *v.* to regard with reverence; revere. ❑ *v.* **rev·er·enced, rev·er·enc·ing.**

rev·er·end (rev′ər ənd), *adj.* **1** worthy of great respect. **2** Reverend, title for members of the clergy: *the Reverend Earl Johnson.*

rev·er·ent (rev′ər ənt), *adj.* feeling reverence; showing reverence: *a reverent prayer.* —**rev′er·ent·ly,** *adv.*

rev·e·ren·tial (rev′ə ren′shəl), *adj.* reverent. —**rev′e·ren′tial·ly,** *adv.*

rev·er·ie (rev′ər ē), *n.* dreamy thoughts; dreamy thinking of pleasant things: *He loved to indulge in reveries about the future.*

re·ver·sal (ri vėr′səl), *n.* **1** change to the opposite; act or process of reversing. **2** a change for the worse: *financial reversals.*

re·verse (ri vėrs′), **1** *n.* the opposite or contrary: *She did the reverse of what I suggested.* **2** *adj.* turned backward; opposite or contrary in position or direction: *the reverse side of a phonograph record.* **3** *n.* the back: *His name is on the reverse of the medal.* **4** *adj.* acting in a manner opposite or contrary to that which is usual. **5** *adj.* causing an opposite or backward movement. **6** *v.* to turn the other way; turn inside out; turn upside down: *Reverse that hose; don't point it at me.* **7** *n.* an opposite or contrary motion or direction: *a reverse in dancing.* **8** *n.* arrangement of gears that reverses the movement of machinery: *Put the car in reverse and back up.* **9** *v.* to change to the opposite; repeal: *The Supreme Court reversed the lower court's decision.* **10** *n.* a change to bad fortune; defeat; setback: *The business used to be profitable but has recently met with reverses.* ❑ *v.* **re·versed, re·vers·ing.** —**re·verse′ly,** *adv.*

re·vers·i·ble (ri vėr′sə bəl), *adj.* **1** able to be reversed; able to reverse. **2** (of a garment, fabric, etc.) finished on both sides so that it can be worn with either side showing.

re·ver·sion (ri vėr′zhən), *n.* return to a former condition, practice, belief, etc.; return.

re·vert (ri vėrt′), *v.* to go back; return: *My thoughts reverted to the last time that I had seen her.*

re·view (ri vyü′), **1** *v.* to look at again; study again: *Review today's lesson for tomorrow.* **2** *n.* act of looking at again; act of studying again: *Before the examinations we have a review of the term's work.* ■ See Synonym Study at **practice.** **3** *v.* to look back on: *Before falling asleep, she reviewed the day's happenings.* **4** *n.* act of looking back on; survey: *a review of recent events.* **5** *v.* to examine again; look at with care; examine: *A superior court may review decisions of a lower court.* **6** *n.* examination; inspection: *A review of the troops will be held during the general's visit.* **7** *v.* to inspect formally: *The admiral reviewed the fleet.* **8** *n.* opinion or judgment of a book, play, etc., giving its good and bad points: *Did that movie get good reviews?* **9** *v.* to examine and give an opinion or judgment of: *She reviews books for a living.*

re·view·er (ri vyü′ər), *n.* **1** person who reviews. **2** person who writes articles discussing books, plays, etc.

re·vile (ri vil′), *v.* to call bad names; abuse with words: *The pedestrian reviled the reckless driver.* ❑ *v.* **re·viled, re·vil·ing.** —**re·vil′er,** *n.* —**re·vile′ment,** *n.*

re·vise (ri viz′), *v.* **1** to read carefully in order to correct; look over and change; examine and improve: *She has revised her essay to make it read better.* **2** to change; alter: *revise your opinion.* ❑ *v.* **re·vised, re·vis·ing.** —**re·vis′er** or **re·vi′sor,** *n.*

re·vi·sion (ri vizh′ən), *n.* **1** act or work of revising. **2** a revised form: *a revision of a book.*

re·vi·tal·ize (rē vi′tə liz), *v.* to give new energy or vigor to; put new life into: *revitalize a neighborhood with new jobs.* ❑ *v.* **re·vi·tal·ized, re·vi·tal·iz·ing.** —**re·vi′tal·i·za′tion,** *n.*

re·viv·al (ri vi′vəl), *n.* **1** act or process of bringing or coming back to style, use, activity, etc.: *There has been a revival of interest in folk music.* **2** act of bringing or coming back to life or consciousness. **3** an awakening or increase of interest in religion. **4** a new production of an old play, movie, etc. **5** restoration to vigor or health. **6** special services or efforts made to awaken or increase interest in religion.

re·vive (ri viv′), *v.* **1** to bring back or come back to life or consciousness: *revive a half-drowned person. The half-drowned swimmer revived.* **2** to bring or come back to a fresh, lively condition: *Flowers revive in water.* **3** to make or become fresh; restore: *Hot cocoa revived the cold, tired hikers.* **4** to bring back or come back to notice, use, fashion, memory, activity, etc.: *An old play is sometimes revived on the stage.* ❑ *v.* **re·vived, re·viv·ing.** —**re·viv′er,** *n.*

rev·o·ca·tion (rev′ə kā′shən), *n.* a repeal; act of canceling; withdrawal: *the revocation of a law.*

re·voke (ri vōk′), *v.* to cancel; repeal; withdraw: *revoke a driver's license.* ❑ *v.* **re·voked, re·vok·ing.**

re·volt (ri vōlt′), **1** *n.* act or state of rebelling: *One cause of the revolt was unfair taxes.* **2** *v.* to turn away from and fight against a leader; rise against the government's authority: *The people revolted against the dictator.* **3** *v.* to cause to feel disgust: *Senseless cruelty revolts me.* [See Word Story at **revolution.**] —**re·volt′er,** *n.*

re·volt·ing (ri vōl′ting), *adj.* disgusting; repulsive: *a revolting odor.* —**re·volt′ing·ly,** *adv.*

rev·o·lu·tion (rev′ə lü′shən), *n.* **1** a complete overthrow of an established government or political system: *The American Revolution gave independence to the colonies.* ■ See Synonym Study at **revolt. 2** a complete change: *The car caused a revolution in ways of traveling.* **3** movement in a circle or curve around some point: *One revolution of the earth around the sun takes a year.* **4** act or fact of turning around a center or axis; rotation: *The motor makes more than one thousand revolutions per minute.* **5** time or distance of one such turn.

rev·o·lu·tion·ar·y (rev′ə lü′shə ner′ē), **1** *adj.* of or connected with political revolution: *revolutionary speeches, revolutionary leaders.* **2** *adj.* bringing or causing great changes: *Radio and TV were two revolutionary inventions of this century.* **3** *n.* person who advocates, or takes part in, a revolution. ❑ *n., pl.* **rev·o·lu·tion·ar·ies.**

Revolutionary War, the war from 1775 to 1783 by which the thirteen American colonies won independence from England; American Revolution.

Revolutionary War

rev·o·lu·tion·ize (rev′ə lü′shə nīz), v. to change completely; produce a very great change in: *The car, radio, TV, and the computer have revolutionized people's lives.* ❑ v. **rev·o·lu·tion·ized, rev·o·lu·tion·iz·ing.**

re·volve (ri volv′), v. **1** to move in a circle; move in a curve round a point: *The moon revolves around the earth.* **2** to turn round a center or axis; rotate: *The wheels of a moving car revolve.* **3** to cause to move round. ❑ v. **re·volved, re·volv·ing.** [See Word Story at **revolution**.] —**re·volv′a·ble,** adj.

> **WORD FAMILY** Revolve and the following words are related: **evolution, involve, revolution, vault**[1], **vault**[2], and **volume.** They all come from a Latin word meaning "to roll."

re·volv·er (ri vol′vər), n. pistol in which the part that holds the bullets turns each time a shot is fired. A revolver can be fired several times without being loaded again.

re·vue (ri vyü′), n. a theatrical entertainment with singing, dancing, parodies of recent plays, humorous treatments of happenings and fads of the year, etc.

re·vul·sion (ri vul′shən), n. a sudden, violent feeling of disgust: *Friendship turned to revulsion when I realized their dishonesty.*

re·ward (ri wôrd′), **1** n. something received in return for something done: *A summer at camp was her reward for getting high grades this year.* **2** n. a money payment given or offered for capture of criminals, the return of lost property, etc. **3** v. to give a reward to: *They rewarded me for finding their lost dog.* **4** v. to give a reward for: *Her display at the science fair was rewarded with a trip to New York.*

re·ward·ing (ri wôr′ding), adj. giving or likely to give a feeling of reward; satisfying: *a rewarding activity.*

re·word (rē werd′), v. to put into other words.

re·work (rē werk′), v. to work over again; revise.

re·write (rē rīt′), v. to write again; write in a different form; revise. ❑ v. **re·wrote** (rē rōt′), **re·writ·ten** (rē rit′n), **re·writ·ing.**

Reye's syndrome (rīz or rāz), a rare and often fatal disease that primarily occurs in children, usually after a viral infection. It can damage the liver, brain, and kidneys.

Rey·kja·vik (rā′kyə vēk′), n. port and capital of Iceland, in the SW part. [Reykjavik comes from Icelandic words meaning "smoky bay," probably because of nearby volcanoes.]

Reyn·ard (ren′ərd or rā′närd), n. fox who is the main character in a group of medieval fables about animals.

Rf, symbol for rutherfordium.

R.F.D., Rural Free Delivery.

Rh, symbol for rhodium.

rhap·sod·ic (rap sod′ik), adj. of or like rhapsody; extravagantly enthusiastic; ecstatic. —**rhap·sod′i·cal·ly,** adv.

rhap·so·dy (rap′sə dē), n. **1** (in music) an instrumental composition irregular in form: *Liszt's Hungarian Rhapsodies.* **2** extravagant enthusiasm in speech or writing: *go into rhapsodies over a present.* ❑ n., pl. **rhap·so·dies.**

rhe·a (rē′ə), n. either of two large South American birds that are much like the ostrich, but smaller and with three toes instead of two. ❑ n., pl. **rhe·as.**

Rhe·a (rē′ə), n. (in Greek myths) the mother of Zeus, Hera, Poseidon, and other important Greek gods.

Rhen·ish (ren′ish), adj. of the Rhine River or the regions near it.

rhe·ni·um (rē′nē əm), n. a rare, hard, grayish metallic element with a very high melting point, used in making alloys. *Symbol:* Re

rhe·o·stat (rē′ə stat), n. device for controlling the strength of an electric current by adding different amounts of resistance to the circuit.

rhe·sus monkey (rē′səs), n. a small, yellowish brown monkey with a short tail, found in India. It is used in medical research.

rhet·or·ic (ret′ər ik), n. **1** art of using words effectively in speaking or writing. **2** book about this art. **3** speech that sounds important, but is actually meaningless or insincere.

rhe·tor·i·cal (ri tôr′ə kəl), adj. **1** of or using rhetoric. **2** intended especially for display; artificial. **3** oratorical. —**rhe·tor′i·cal·ly,** adv.

rhetorical question, question asked only for effect, not for information. EXAMPLE: "Who can tell whether or not life exists in other galaxies?"

rhet·o·ri·cian (ret′ə rish′ən), n. **1** person skilled in rhetoric. **2** person given to display in language.

rheum (rüm), n. a watery discharge, such as mucus, tears, or saliva. ■ Another word that sounds like this is **room.**

rheu·mat·ic (rü mat′ik), **1** adj. of, having, or caused by rheumatism. **2** n. person who has rheumatism. —**rheu·mat′i·cal·ly,** adv.

rheumatic fever, disease more common among children than among adults, in which the symptoms are fever, pains in the joints, and often damage to the heart.

rheu·ma·tism (rü′mə tiz′əm), n. **1** disease with inflammation, swelling, and stiffness of the joints, such as arthritis, bursitis, or gout. **2** rheumatic fever.

rheum·y (rü′mē), adj. **1** full of rheum. **2** causing rheum; damp and cold. ❑ adj. **rheum·i·er, rheum·i·est.** ■ Another word that sounds like this is **roomy.**

Rh factor, a substance found in the red blood cells of most people. Blood containing this substance (**Rh positive**) may cause serious problems if donated to a person with blood lacking it (**Rh negative**).

Rhine (rīn), n. river flowing from central Switzerland through Germany and the Netherlands into the North Sea.

Rhine·land (rīn′land′), n. **1** the region along the Rhine. **2** the part of Germany west of the Rhine.

rhine·stone (rīn′stōn′), n. an imitation diamond, made of glass or paste.

rhi·no (rī′nō), n. INFORMAL. rhinoceros. ❑ n., pl. **rhi·no** or **rhi·nos.**

rhi·noc·er·os (rī nos′ər əs), n. any of five kinds of large, thick-skinned mammals of Africa and Asia with one or two upright horns on the snout. Rhinoceroses eat grass and other plants.
❑ n., pl. **rhi·noc·er·os·es** or **rhi·noc·er·os.** [Rhinoceros comes from Greek words meaning "nose" and "horn."]

rhi·no·vi·rus (rī′nō vī′rəs), n. any of a group of viruses that cause the common cold and similar diseases. ❑ n., pl. **rhi·no·vi·rus·es.**

rhi·zoid (rī′zoid), n. one of the rootlike filaments that attaches a moss, fern, or fungus to what it grows on.

rhi·zome (rī′zōm), n. an underground stem, usually horizontal, that sends out roots and leafy shoots; rootstock.

Rhode Island (rōd), one of the northeastern states of the United States. Rhode Island is the smallest state. *Abbreviation:* RI or R.I. *Capital:* Providence. [Rhode Island is named for the Greek island of Rhodes. An early explorer compared the state's largest island to Rhodes.]

Rhodes (rōdz), n. **1** Greek island in the Aegean Sea. See **Troy** for map. **2 Ce·cil John** (ses′əl), 1853-1902, British colonial political leader. He founded the Rhodes scholarships for study at Oxford University.

Rho·de·sia (rō dē′zhə), n. former name of **Zimbabwe.** —**Rho·de′sian,** adj., n.

rho·di·um (rō′dē əm), n. a silver-white metallic element found mostly in platinum ores. It is resistant to acids, and is used for plating silverware, jewelry, etc. *Symbol:* Rh

rho·do·den·dron (rō′də den′drən), n. any of several bushes, some of which are grown for their evergreen leathery leaves and clusters of showy pink, purple, or white flowers.

Rhine River [map]

R

a	hat	ė	term	ô	order	ch	child		a in about
ā	age	i	it	oi	oil	ng	long		e in taken
ä	far	ī	ice	ou	out	sh	she	ə {	i in pencil
â	care	o	hot	u	cup	th	thin		o in lemon
e	let	ō	open	ù	put	ℾH	then		u in circus
ē	equal	ò	saw	ü	rule	zh	measure		

rhom·boid (rom′boid), *n.* a four-sided shape with opposite sides that are parallel and unequal touching sides.

rhom·bus (rom′bəs), *n.* parallelogram with equal sides, usually having two obtuse angles and two acute angles. ❑ *n., pl.* **rhom·bus·es, rhom·bi** (rom′bī).

Rhone or **Rhône** (rōn), *n.* river flowing from S Switzerland through SE France into the Mediterranean Sea. See **Rhine** for map.

rhu·barb (rü′bärb), *n.* **1** the sour stalks of a garden plant with very large poisonous leaves. The stalks are used for making sauce, pies, etc. **2** INFORMAL. a violent argument or protest.

rhyme (rim), **1** *v.* to sound alike in the last part: *"Long" and "song" rhyme. "Go to bed" rhymes with "sleepyhead."* **2** *n.* word or line having the same last sound as another: *"Cat" is a rhyme for "mat."* **3** *n.* verses or poetry with some of the lines ending in similar sounds. **4** *n.* agreement in the final sounds of words or lines. **5** *v.* to put or make into rhyme: *rhyme a translation.* **6** *v.* to make rhymes. **7** *v.* to use a word with another that rhymes with it: *rhyme "love" and "dove."* ❑ *v.* **rhymed, rhym·ing.** [See Word Story at **rhythm**.] ▪ Another word that sounds like this is **rime²**. —**rhym′er,** *n.*

without rhyme or reason, having no system or sense.

rhythm (riᴛʜ′əm), *n.* **1** any movement with a regular repetition of a beat, accent, rise and fall, or the like: *the rhythm of dancing, the rhythm of the tides.* **2** repetition of an accent; arrangement of beats in a line of poetry or in a piece of music.

WORD STORY   **Rhythm** and **rhyme** have different meanings now, but once they were the same word, meaning "the kind of poetry that has a regular beat and lines ending in similar sounds." That word came from an old Greek word meaning "to flow." As people separated the two ideas, they used different spellings and pronunciations to make clear which one they had in mind.

rhythm and blues, popular music that began in the United States, influenced by blues and having a strong rhythm; R & B.

rhyth·mic (riᴛʜ′mik), *adj.* rhythmical.

rhyth·mi·cal (riᴛʜ′mə kəl), *adj.* having rhythm; of or about rhythm: *the rhythmical sound of the music.* —**rhyth′mi·cal·ly,** *adv.*

RI, Rhode Island (used with postal Zip Code).

R.I., Rhode Island.

rib (rib), **1** *n.* one of the curved bones extending from the backbone around the heart and lungs to the front of the body. **2** *n.* something like a rib. The curved timbers in a ship's frame are called ribs. The thick vein of a leaf is also called a rib. An umbrella has ribs. **3** *v.* to provide or strengthen with ribs. **4** *n.* ridge in cloth, knitting, etc. **5** *n.* a cut of meat containing a rib: *a rib of beef.* **6** *v.* to form riblike ridges on knitted or woven fabric. **7** *v.* to tease. ❑ *v.* **ribbed, rib·bing.** —**rib′ber,** *n.* —**rib′like′,** *adj.*

rib·ald (rib′əld), *adj.* offensive in speech; coarsely mocking; irreverent; indecent; obscene: *a ribald story.*

rib·ald·ry (rib′əl drē), *n.* ribald language.

ribbed (ribd), *adj.* having ribs or ridges: *ribbed cloth.*

rib·bon (rib′ən), *n.* **1** a strip or band of silk, satin, velvet, paper, or other material, used for decorating and tying things: *The gift was tied with a big, red ribbon.* **2** an inked strip of cloth or plastic used in a typewriter or electronic printer. **3** a colored strip of cloth given to a winner of a competition. **4** **ribbons,** *pl.* torn strips; tatters: *Strong winds tore the sails to ribbons.* —**rib′bon·like′,** *adj.*

rib·cage (rib′kāj′), *n.* the enclosure formed by the ribs of the chest.

ri·bo·fla·vin (ri′bō flā′vən), *n.* a B vitamin that helps growth and is present in liver, eggs, milk, and spinach. It is sometimes called vitamin G or B₂.

ri·bo·nu·cle·ic acid (ri′bō nü klē′ik), RNA.

ri·bose (ri′bōs), *n.* a sugar present in all living cells, part of riboflavin, RNA, and other molecules.

ri·bo·some (ri′bə sōm), *n.* a small structure that carries on protein formation in living cells.

rice (ris), **1** *n.* the starchy grain of a kind of cereal grass grown in warm regions. Rice is an important food in India, China, and Japan. **2** *v.* to press food through a sieve so that it looks like rice: *to rice potatoes.* ❑ *v.* **riced, ric·ing.**

rice·bird (ris′bėrd′), *n.* (in the southern United States) a bobolink.

rich (rich), **1** *adj.* having much money, land, goods, etc.: *a rich person.* **2** *n.pl.* **the rich,** rich people. **3** *adj.* well supplied; abounding: *a country rich in oil.* **4** *adj.* producing much; fertile: *rich soil, a rich mine.* **5** *adj.* having great worth; valuable: *a rich harvest, rich advice.* **6** *adj.* costly; elegant: *rich clothing, rich jewels, rich carpets.* **7** *adj.* containing plenty of butter, eggs, flavoring, etc.: *a rich fruit cake.* **8** *adj.* (of colors, sounds, smells, etc.) deep; full; vivid: *a rich red, a rich tone.* **9** *adj.* INFORMAL. very amusing; ridiculous. —**rich′ly,** *adv.* —**rich′ness,** *n.*

SYNONYM STUDY   **Rich** and **wealthy** both mean having a lot of money. **Rich** suggests having more money than you need: *He is rich and doesn't have to work.* **Wealthy** suggests being very rich, with great status or influence: *Three wealthy families gave most of the money for the art museum.*

Rich·ard I (rich′ərd), 1157-1199, king of England from 1189 to 1199. He was called "Richard the Lion-Hearted." [*Richard* comes form a German word meaning "rule" or "government."]

Rich·e·lieu (rish′ə lü), *n.* 1585-1642, French cardinal and political leader who controlled France from 1624 to 1642.

rich·es (rich′iz), *n.pl.* much money, land, goods, etc.; abundance of property; wealth.

Rich·mond (rich′mənd), *n.* capital of Virginia, in the E part, on the James River.

Rich·ter scale (rik′tər), a set of numbers for measuring the force of earthquakes. On this scale, light tremors register 1.5, while highly destructive earthquakes measure 8.3.

rick (rik), *n.* an outdoor stack of hay, straw, etc., especially one which is covered to protect it from rain.

rick·ets (rik′its), *n.* disease of childhood, caused by lack of vitamin D and calcium. It results in softening, and sometimes bending, of the bones.

rick·ett·si·a (ri ket′sē ə), *n.* a kind of bacteria that lives in the bodies of ticks and lice and is sometimes transmitted to humans, causing such diseases as Rocky Mountain spotted fever and typhus. ❑ *n., pl.* **rick·ett·si·as.**

rick·et·y (rik′ə tē), *adj.* **1** liable to fall or break down; shaky; weak: *a rickety old chair.* **2** having rickets; suffering from rickets. **3** feeble in the joints. —**rick′et·i·ness,** *n.*

rick·rack (rik′rak′), *n.* a narrow, zigzag braid used as trimming.

rick·shaw (rik′shò), *n.* jinricksha.

ric·o·chet (rik′ə shā′), **1** *v.* to skip or glance off a surface in a different direction: *The bullets struck the ground and ricocheted through the grass.* **2** *n.* the skipping or glancing motion of an object from a flat surface: *the ricochet of a stone thrown along the surface of water.* ❑ *v.* **ric·o·cheted** (rik′ə shād′), **ric·o·chet·ing** (rik′ə shā′ing).

ri·cot·ta (ri kot′ə), *n.* a soft, white Italian cheese similar to cottage cheese, made from the watery part of milk.

rid (rid), *v.* to make free: *What will rid a house of mice?* ❑ *v.* **rid** or **rid·ded, rid·ding.**

be rid of, be freed from: *After he pays off his student loans he will be rid of debt.*

get rid of, 1 to get free from: *I can't get rid of this cold.* **2** to do away with: *Poison will get rid of ants in the kitchen.*

rid·dance (rid′ns), *n.* act of clearing something away or out; removal.

good riddance, exclamation expressing relief that something or somebody has been removed.

rid·den (rid′n), *v.* past participle of **ride:** *I had ridden my horse all day.*

rid·dle¹ (rid′l), **1** *n.* a puzzling question, statement, problem, etc. EXAMPLE: When is a door not a door? ANSWER: When it is ajar. **2** *n.* person or thing that is hard to understand, explain, etc. **3** *v.* to speak in riddles. **4** *v.* to solve a riddle or question. ❑ *v.* **rid·dled, rid·dling.** —**rid′dler,** *n.*

rid·dle² (rid′l), *v.* **1** to pierce with holes: *Insects had riddled the old tree stump.* **2** to damage or weaken as if by making many holes in: *The witness's testimony was riddled with lies.* ❑ *v.* **rid·dled, rid·dling.**

ride (rīd), **1** *v.* to sit on something and make it go: *ride a camel, ride a bicycle.* **2** *v.* to be carried along by anything: *ride on a train, ride in a car.* **3** *v.* to ride over, along, or through: *ride the plains.* **4** *v.* to be carried on: *The eagle rides the winds.* **5** *n.* a trip on horseback, in a car, on a train, etc.: *We took a ride into the country.* **6** *v.* to move or float on the water: *The ship rode into port.* **7** *v.* to lie at anchor. **8** *v.* INFORMAL. to make fun of; tease. **9** *v.* to cause to ride; carry: *He rode his little sister on his shoulders.* **10** *n.* machine that carries people a short distance for their amusement or excitement: *The carnival had a roller coaster, a Ferris wheel, and other rides.* **11** *v.* to dominate or oppress: *be ridden by foolish fears.* ❑ *v.* **rode, rid·den, rid·ing.** —**rid′a·ble** or **ride′a·ble,** *adj.*

let ride, to leave undisturbed or undecided: *Let it ride until later.*
ride down, 1 to knock down while riding. **2** to overcome: *The club president rode down the opposition to his plan.* **3** to overtake by riding.
ride out, to endure successfully: *The small boat rode out the storm without damage.*

Ride (rīd), *n.* **Sal·ly** (sal′ē), born 1951, American astronaut. She was the first American woman to travel in space.

rid·er (rī′dər), *n.* **1** person who rides: *a horseback rider.* **2** anything added to a record, document, legislative bill, or statement after it was supposed to be complete: *They added a rider to the bill making small businesses exempt from the new regulations.* —**rid′er·less,** *adj.*

ridge (rij), **1** *n.* the long and narrow upper part of something: *the ridge of an animal's back.* **2** *n.* the line where two sloping surfaces meet: *the ridge of a roof.* **3** *n.* a long, narrow chain of hills or mountains: *the Blue Ridge of the Appalachian Mountains.* **4** *n.* any raised narrow strip: *the ridges on corduroy cloth, the ridges in plowed ground.* **5** *v.* to form or make into ridges. **6** *v.* to cover with ridges; mark with ridges. ❑ *v.* **ridged, ridg·ing.**

ridge·pole (rij′pōl′), *n.* the horizontal timber along the top of a roof or tent; rooftree.

rid·i·cule (rid′ə kyül), **1** *v.* to laugh at; make fun of: *People once ridiculed the idea of an airplane.* **2** *n.* laughter in mockery; words or actions that make fun of somebody or something: *I was very hurt by the ridicule of my classmates.* ❑ *v.* **rid·i·culed, rid·i·cul·ing.** —**rid′i·cul′er,** *n.*

SYNONYM STUDY **Ridicule, mock,** and **kid²** all mean to make fun of someone or something. **Ridicule** suggests making fun to belittle: *She ridiculed my plan, but hers was no better.* **Mock** suggests making fun by imitation: *The comedian mocks several famous actors in his performance.* **Kid** means playful teasing: *When people kid him about his height, he says he can't hear them down there.*

ri·dic·u·lous (ri dik′yə ləs), *adj.* deserving ridicule; absurd; laughable: *It would be ridiculous to walk backward all the time.* —**ri·dic′u·lous·ly,** *adv.* —**ri·dic′u·lous·ness,** *n.*

rid·ing (rī′ding), *n.* CANADIAN. a political subdivision of a province, represented by a member of Parliament, or of the legislative assembly; constituency.

rif or **riff** (rif), *v.* to dismiss employees in order to reduce payroll costs: *His father got riffed last year and is still looking for work.* ❑ *v.* **riffed, rif·fing.**

RIF (rif), *n.* reduction in force (act of dismissing a number of employees, in order to reduce payroll costs).

rife (rīf), *adj.* **1** happening often; common; numerous; widespread: *Noise is rife in the big city.* **2** well supplied; full; abounding: *Our town was rife with rumors that the bank had no funds.*

riff·raff (rif′raf′), *n.* **1** disreputable people. **2** trash; rubbish.

ri·fle¹ (rī′fəl), **1** *n.* gun with spiral grooves in its long barrel which spin or rotate the bullet as it is fired, giving the gun greater accuracy. A rifle is usually fired from the shoulder. **2** *v.* to cut such grooves in a gun. ❑ *v.* **ri·fled, ri·fling.**

ri·fle² (rī′fəl), *v.* to search thoroughly and rob; ransack and rob: *The burglars rifled through all the drawers and cabinets looking for valuables.* ❑ *v.* **ri·fled, ri·fling.** —**ri′fler,** *n.*

ri·fle·man (rī′fəl mən), *n.* **1** soldier armed with a rifle. **2** person skilled in the use of a rifle. ❑ *n., pl.* **ri·fle·men.**

rift (rift), **1** *n.* a split; break; crack: *The sun shone through a rift in the clouds.* **2** *v.* to split; break open.

rift valley, a long, narrow valley formed when a part of the earth's crust dropped, leaving steep walls on each side.

rig (rig), **1** *n.* outfit; equipment: *a camper's rig, an oil-drilling rig.* **2** *v.* to equip; fit out: *rig out a football team with uniforms.* **3** *v.* to get ready for use. **4** *n.* heavy equipment used for drilling into the earth: *an oil rig.* **5** *v.* to put together in a hurry or by using odds and ends: *The girls rigged up a tent with a rope and a blanket.* **6** *v.* INFORMAL. to dress: *On Halloween the children rig themselves up in funny clothes.* **7** *n.* INFORMAL. set of clothes; costume: *His rig consisted of a silk hat and overalls.* **8** *v.* to arrange in an unfair way: *The race was rigged.* **9** *n.* truck or other large motor vehicle: *His mother drives a big rig.* **10** *v.* to equip a ship with masts, sails, and ropes: *It took us 20 minutes to rig our sailboat.* **11** *n.* the arrangement of masts, sails, ropes, etc., on a ship. A schooner has a fore-and-aft rig; that is, the sails are set lengthwise on the ship. **12** *n.* (earlier) a carriage, with its horse or horses. ❑ *v.* **rigged, rig·ging.** —**rig′ger,** *n.*

Ri·ga (rē′gə), *n.* **1** port and capital of Latvia, on the Baltic Sea. **2 Gulf of,** gulf on the Baltic Sea.

rig·a·to·ni (rig′ə tō′nē), *n.sing. or pl.* short, ribbed tubes of pasta, bigger than macaroni.

Ri·gel (rī′jəl), *n.* a very bright star in the left foot of Orion.

rig·ging (rig′ing), *n.* **1** ropes, chains, and cables, used to support and control the masts, yards, sails, etc., on a ship: *The midshipmen climbed the rigging.* **2** equipment used for a specific purpose; gear; apparatus: *The stage crew handled the rigging for the school play.*

rigging (def. 1)

right (rīt), **1** *adj.* agreeing with what is good, just, or lawful: *She did the right thing when she told the truth.* **2** *adv.* in a way that is good, just, or lawful: *He acted right when he told the truth.* **3** *n.* that which is right, just, good, or true: *Do right, not wrong.* **4** *n.* a just claim; something that is due to someone: *Each member of the club has a right to vote. I demand my rights.* **5** *adj.* correct; true: *the right answer.* **6** *adv.* correctly; truly: *She guessed right.* **7** *adj.* proper; suitable; fitting: *Learn to say the right thing at the right time. Is this the right color for me?* **8** *adv.* properly; well: *It's faster to do a job right the first time.* **9** *adj.* in good condition; well; healthy: *I don't feel right; I think I'm getting the flu.* **10** *adj.* meant to be seen; most important: *the right side of cloth.* **11** *v.* to make correct; set right: *right a wrong.* **12** *v.* to do justice to: *right the oppressed.* **13** *n.* fair treatment; justice. **14** *v.* to get or put into proper position: *The ship righted as the wave passed. We righted the sailboat.* **15** *adj.* belonging to the side that is turned east when the main side is turned north; opposite of left. **16** *adj.* on this side when viewed from the front: *Make a right turn at the corner.* **17** *adv.* on or to the right side: *Turn right.* **18** *n.* the right side or hand: *Please sit on my right.* **19** *adv.* exactly; just; precisely: *Your cap is right where you left it.* **20** *adv.* at once; immediately: *Stop playing right away.* **21** *adv.* very: *the Right Honorable Lord Mayor.* **22** *adv.* DIALECT. extremely: *I'm right glad to see you.* **23** *adv.* in a straight line; directly: *Look me right in the eye.* **24** *adj.* straight: *a right line.* **25** *adv.* completely: *My hat was knocked right off.* **26** *n.* part of a lawmaking group consisting of the conservative or reactionary political groups. **27** *adj.* having conservative or reactionary ideas in politics. **28** *adj.* OLD

R

a	hat	ė	term	ô	order	ch	child		a in about
ā	age	i	it	oi	oil	ng	long		e in taken
ä	far	ī	ice	ou	out	sh	she	ə	i in pencil
â	care	o	hot	u	cup	th	thin		o in lemon
e	let	ō	open	u̇	put	ŧ͟h	then		u in circus
ē	equal	ȯ	saw	ü	rule	zh	measure		

USE. rightful; real: *Who is the right king of that country?* ■ Other words that sound like this are **rite** and **write**. **—right′er,** *n.* **—right′ness,** *n.*

by right or **by rights,** properly; rightly; correctly.

in the right, right.

right away, at once; immediately: *I'll do it right away.*

right on, SLANG. exactly right, correct, or true.

to rights, in or into proper condition, order, etc.

right angle, an angle that is formed by a line perpendicular to another line; angle of 90 degrees. The angles in a square are right angles. See picture at **angle**[1].

right-an·gled (rīt′ang′gəld), *adj.* containing a right angle or right angles; rectangular.

right·eous (rī′chəs), *adj.* **1** doing right; virtuous; morally good: *A righteous person treats others with kindness.* **2** proper; just; right: *righteous indignation.* **—right′eous·ly,** *adv.* **—right′eous·ness,** *n.*

right field, in baseball: **a** the section of the outfield beyond first base. **b** position of the player in this area. **—right fielder.**

right·ful (rīt′fəl), *adj.* **1** according to law; by rights: *the rightful owner of this dog.* **2** just and right; proper. **—right′ful·ly,** *adv.* **—right′ful·ness,** *n.*

right-hand (rīt′hand′), *adj.* **1** on or to the right. **2** of, for, or with the right hand. **3** most helpful or useful: *He is the scoutmaster's right-hand man.*

right-hand·ed (rīt′han′did), **1** *adj.* using the right hand more easily and readily than the left. **2** *adj.* done with the right hand. **3** *adj.* made to be used with the right hand: *a right-handed can opener, right-handed scissors.* **4** *adj.* turning from left to right: *a right-handed screw.* **5** *adv.* with the right hand. **—right′-hand′ed·ly,** *adv.* **—right′-hand′ed·ness,** *n.*

right·ist (rī′tist), **1** *n.* person who has conservative or reactionary ideas in politics. **2** *adj.* having conservative or reactionary ideas.

right·ly (rīt′lē), *adv.* **1** in a just manner; fairly: *She was rightly upset by their behavior.* **2** correctly: *She guessed rightly that it would rain.* **3** properly; suitably: *He rightly apologized after having missed his appointment.*

right of way, **1** the right to go first, especially the right of a vehicle to cross in front of another. **2** the right to pass over someone else's property.

right triangle, triangle with one right angle. See picture at **triangle**.

right·ward (rīt′wərd), *adj., adv.* on or toward the right.

right·wards (rīt′wərdz), *adv.* rightward.

right whale, any of several large whales with huge heads, no fin on their backs, and no throat grooves. A right whale has about 350 long whalebone plates on each side of its mouth. It feeds by swimming through plankton with its mouth open and catching some on the whalebone.

right wing, the conservative or reactionary members, especially of a political party.

rig·id (rij′id), *adj.* **1** not bending; stiff; firm: *Hold your arm rigid.* ■ See Synonym Study at **stiff.** **2** not changing; strict: *a rigid belief, a rigid rule.* **—rig′id·ly,** *adv.* **—rig′id·ness,** *n.*

ri·gid·i·ty (ri jid′ə tē), *n.* **1** stiffness; firmness. **2** strictness; severity.

rig·ma·role (rig′mə rōl′), *n.* foolish talk or activity; words or action without meaning; nonsense.

rig·or (rig′ər), *n.* **1** strictness; severity: *The new recruits were trained with great rigor.* **2** harshness: *endure the rigors of a long, cold winter.* **3** logical exactness: *the rigor of scientific method.*

rig·or mor·tis (rig′ər môr′tis), the stiffening of the muscles after death.

rig·or·ous (rig′ər əs), *adj.* **1** severe; strict: *the rigorous discipline in the army.* **2** harsh: *a rigorous climate.* **3** thoroughly logical and scientific; exact: *the rigorous methods of science.* **—rig′or·ous·ly,** *adv.* **—rig′or·ous·ness,** *n.*

rile (rīl), *v.* to anger; irritate; annoy greatly: *If you criticize them, it will just rile them up, and we'll never get the job done.* ❑ *v.* **riled, ril·ing.**

rill (ril), *n.* a tiny stream; little brook.

rim (rim), **1** *n.* an edge, border, or margin on or around anything: *the rim of a wheel, the rim of a glass.* ■ See Synonym Study at

edge. **2** *v.* to form a rim around; put a rim around: *Wildflowers and grasses rimmed the little pool.* ❑ *v.* **rimmed, rim·ming. —rim′less,** *adj.*

rime[1] (rīm), *n., v.* OLD USE. rhyme. ❑ *v.* **rimed, rim·ing.**

rime[2] (rīm), **1** *n.* white frost; hoarfrost. **2** *v.* to cover with rime. ❑ *v.* **rimed, rim·ing.** ■ Another word that sounds like this is **rhyme.**

Rim·sky-Kor·sa·kov (rim′skē kôr′sə kôf), *n.* **Nik·o·lay** (nik′ə-lī), 1844-1908, Russian composer. He taught Sergei Prokofiev and Igor Stravinsky. His works often have subjects from Russian history or folktales.

rind (rīnd), *n.* a firm outer covering, on melons, cheeses, etc.

ring[1] (ring), **1** *n.* a circle: *You can tell the age of a tree by counting the number of rings in its wood; one ring grows every year. We danced in a ring.* **2** *n.* a thin circle of metal or other material: *a napkin ring, a wedding ring, a key ring.* **3** *n.* persons or things arranged in a circle. **4** *n.* the outer edge or border of a coin, plate, wheel, or anything round. **5** *v.* to put a ring around; form a circle around: *Rosebushes ringed the backyard.* **6** *v.* to toss a horseshoe, ring, etc., over: *He ringed the post.* **7** *v.* to form a ring or rings. **8** *n.* an enclosed space for races or games: *a circus ring, a boxing ring.* **9** *n.* prizefighting. **10** *n.* group of people working together for a selfish or bad purpose: *The police arrested a ring of smugglers.* ❑ *v.* **ringed, ring·ing.** ■ Another word that sounds like this is **wring. —ring′like′,** *adj.*

run rings around, to surpass with ease; beat easily.

ring[2] (ring), **1** *v.* to give forth a clear sound, as a bell does: *Did the telephone ring?* **2** *v.* to cause to give forth a clear ringing sound: *Ring the bell.* **3** *v.* to cause a bell to sound: *She rang for the maid.* **4** *v.* to make a sound by ringing: *The bells rang a joyous peal.* **5** *n.* a sound of a bell: *Did you hear a ring?* **6** *n.* a sound like that of a bell: *On a cold night we can hear the ring of skates on ice.* **7** *v.* to announce or proclaim by bells; usher; conduct: *Ring out the old year; ring in the new.* **8** *v.* to proclaim or repeat loudly everywhere: *ring a person's praises.* **9** *v.* to resound; sound loudly: *The room rang with shouts of laughter.* **10** *v.* to echo; give back sound: *The mountains rang with the roll of thunder.* **11** *v.* to be filled with report or talk: *His words rang true.* **12** *v.* to sound: *His words rang true.* **13** *v.* to have a sensation as of sounds of bells; hear inner sounds: *My ears ring.* **14** *n.* a characteristic sound or quality: *a ring of sincerity.* **15** *v.* to call up on a telephone: *I'll ring you tomorrow.* **16** *n.* a call on the telephone: *I'll give you a ring later on.* ❑ *v.* **rang, rung, ring·ing.** ■ Another word that sounds like this is **wring.**

ring for, to summon by a bell.

ring up, to record a specific amount on a cash register.

ringed (ringd), *adj.* **1** having or wearing a ring or rings. **2** marked or decorated with a ring or rings. **3** surrounded by a ring or rings. **4** formed of or with rings; ringlike.

ring·er (ring′ər), *n.* **1** person or thing that rings; device for ringing a bell. **2** INFORMAL. person or thing very much like another. **3** contestant illegally entered in a competition. ■ Another word that sounds like this is **wringer.**

ring finger, the finger next to the little finger, especially the one on the left hand.

ring·lead·er (ring′lē′dər), *n.* person who leads others in opposition to authority or law: *the ringleaders of the mutiny.*

ring·let (ring′lit), *n.* **1** curl: *The baby's hair was in ringlets.* **2** a little ring: *Drops of rain made ringlets in the pond.*

ring·mas·ter (ring′mas′tər), *n.* person in charge of the performances in a circus. A ringmaster usually announces each performance.

ring·side (ring′sīd′), *n.* **1** a place just outside the ring at a circus, prizefight, etc. **2** a place affording a close view.

ringmaster

ring·worm (ring′wėrm′), *n.* any of several contagious skin diseases caused by fungi. One kind appears in the form of ring-shaped patches. Athlete's foot is a common type of ringworm.

rink (ringk), *n.* **1** sheet of ice for skating. **2** a smooth floor for roller-skating.

rinse (rins), **1** *v.* to wash with clean water: *Rinse all the soap out of your hair after you wash it.* **2** *v.* to wash lightly: *Rinse your mouth with warm water.* **3** *n.* act of rinsing: *Give the clothes a final rinse in cold water.* **4** *n.* a liquid preparation used after shampooing to add color or luster to the hair. ❑ *v.* **rinsed, rins·ing.** [**Rinse** and **recent** come from a Latin word meaning "new" or "fresh." Something that is recently rinsed has a fresh look.]

Ri·o de Ja·nei·ro (rē′ō dā zhə ner′ō), port in Brazil, in the SE part, near the Atlantic.

WORD STORY   **Rio de Janeiro** comes from Portuguese words meaning "river of January." The explorer who named the river that the port is on came to this spot on New Year's Day.

Ri·o Grande (rē′ō grand′ *or* rē′ō gran′dē), river forming part of the boundary between Texas and Mexico as it flows SE to the Gulf of Mexico.

ri·ot (rī′ət), **1** *n.* a wild, violent public disturbance; disorder caused by an unruly crowd or mob: *a riot in a prison.* **2** *v.* to behave in a wild, disorderly way. **3** *v.* to have a noisy good time. **4** *n.* a bright display: *The garden was a riot of color.* **5** *n.* INFORMAL. a very amusing person or performance: *She was a riot at the party.* **–ri′ot·er,** *n.*

read the riot act, to give orders for disturbance to cease.

run riot, 1 to act without restraint; run wild. **2** to grow wildly or luxuriantly.

ri·ot·ous (rī′ə təs), *adj.* **1** taking part in a riot. **2** boisterous; disorderly: *Sounds of riotous glee came from the playhouse.* **–ri′ot·ous·ly,** *adv.* **–ri′ot·ous·ness,** *n.*

rip[1] (rip), **1** *v.* to cut roughly; tear apart; tear off: *Rip the cover off this box.* ■ See Synonym Study at **tear**[2]. **2** *v.* to become torn apart. **3** *v.* to tear along the seam of a piece of clothing: *I ripped my jacket pocket on the door handle.* **4** *n.* a torn place, especially a seam in a piece of clothing: *Please sew up this rip in my sleeve.* **5** *v.* to cut or pull out the threads in the seams of a piece of clothing. **6** *v.* to saw wood along the grain, not across the grain. **7** *v.* to move fast or violently: *Fire ripped through the empty building.* ❑ *v.* **ripped, rip·ping. –rip′per,** *n.*

rip off, INFORMAL. to steal: *rip off an expensive camera.*

rip[2] (rip), *n.* **1** a stretch of rough water made by opposite currents meeting. **2** riptide.

rip·cord (rip′kôrd′), *n.* cord which is pulled to open a parachute.

ripe (rīp), *adj.* **1** full-grown and ready to be gathered and eaten: *ripe fruit.* **2** fully developed; mature: *a ripe cheese.* **3** ready: *That country is ripe for revolt.* **4** advanced in years: *the ripe age of 85.* ❑ *adj.* **rip·er, rip·est. –ripe′ly,** *adv.* **–ripe′ness,** *n.*

rip·en (rī′pən), *v.* to become or make ripe. **–rip′en·er,** *n.*

rip-off (rip′ôf′), *n.* INFORMAL. **1** theft. **2** something that cheats.

rip·ple (rip′əl), **1** *n.* a very little wave: *Throw a stone into still water and watch the ripples spread in rings.* **2** *n.* anything that seems like a tiny wave: *ripples in the sand.* **3** *n.* a sound that reminds you of little waves: *a ripple of laughter in the crowd.* **4** *v.* to make a sound like rippling water. **5** *v.* to form or have ripples. **6** *v.* to make ripples on: *A breeze rippled the quiet waters.* ❑ *v.* **rip·pled, rip·pling. –rip′pler,** *n.*

rip·rap (rip′rap′), **1** *n.* wall or foundation of broken stone put together irregularly. **2** *n.* broken stones used in this way. **3** *v.* to build with broken stones. ❑ *v.* **rip·rapped, rip·rap·ping.**

rip·saw (rip′sô′), *n.* saw for cutting wood along the grain, not across the grain.

rip·tide (rip′tīd′), *n.* a strong, narrow surface current that flows rapidly away from the shore; rip.

Rip Van Win·kle (rip′ van wing′kəl), hero of a story by Washington Irving, who wakes after twenty years of magical sleep to find everything changed.

rise (rīz), **1** *v.* to get up from a lying, sitting, or kneeling position; stand up: *Please rise from your seat when you recite.* **2** *v.* to get up from sleep or rest: *I rise at 7 every morning.* **3** *v.* to go up; come up; move up; ascend: *The curtain rose on the first act of the play. Mercury rises in a thermometer on a hot day.* **4** *v.* to go higher; increase: *Prices are rising. My anger rose at that remark.* **5** *n.* act or process of going up; act or process of going higher: *a rise in prices. We watched the rise of the balloon.* **6** *n.* an advance in rank, power, etc. **7** *v.* to advance in importance, rank, etc.: *He rose from clerk to president of the company.* **8** *v.* to slope upward: *Hills rise in the distance.* **9** *n.* an upward slope: *The rise of that hill is gradual.* **10** *n.* piece of rising or high ground; hill: *The house is situated on a rise.* **11** *n.* the vertical height of a step, slope, arch, etc. **12** *v.* to appear over the horizon: *The sun rises in the morning.* **13** *v.* to start; begin: *The river rises from a spring. Quarrels often rise from trifles.* **14** *v.* to come into being or action: *The wind rose rapidly.* **15** *n.* origin; beginning; start: *the rise of a river, the rise of a storm, the rise of a new problem.* **16** *v.* to become more cheerful; improve: *Our spirits rose at the good news.* **17** *v.* to revolt; rebel: *The people rose against the government.* **18** *v.* to grow larger and lighter; swell: *Yeast makes dough rise.* **19** *v.* to come to life again: *Jesus is risen.* ❑ *v.* **rose, ris·en, ris·ing.**

get a rise out of, to get an emotional reaction from: *My teasing got a rise out of them.*

give rise to, to bring about; start; begin; cause: *Their sudden wealth gave rise to rumors about where the money came from.*

rise to, be equal to; be able to deal with: *rising to the occasion.*

SYNONYM STUDY   **Rise, ascend,** and **soar** all mean to go up. **Rise** is the general word: *Smoke rises from the fire.* **Ascend** means to go upward steadily: *The airplane will ascend to an altitude of over 30,000 feet.* **Soar** means to fly upward quickly and smoothly: *The kite soared toward the clouds.*

ris·en (riz′n), *v.* past participle of **rise**: *They had risen before dawn.*

ris·er (rī′zər), *n.* **1** person or thing that rises: *an early riser.* **2** the vertical part of a step in a stairway.

risk (risk), **1** *n.* chance of harm or loss; danger: *If you drive carefully, there is no risk of being fined.* **2** *v.* to expose to the chance of harm or loss: *You risk your neck trying to climb that tree.* **3** *v.* to take the risk of: *She risked defeat in running against the popular candidate.*

run a risk or **take a risk,** to expose yourself to the chance of harm or loss.

risk·y (ris′kē), *adj.* full of risk; dangerous. ❑ *adj.* **risk·i·er, risk·i·est. –risk′i·ly,** *adv.* **–risk′i·ness,** *n.*

ri·tar·dan·do (rē′tär dän′dō), in music: **1** *adj.* becoming gradually slower. **2** *adv.* gradually more slowly. **3** *n.* movement or passage in which the tempo gradually becomes slower.

rite (rīt), *n.* a solemn ceremony. Most churches have rites for baptism, marriage, and burial. Secret societies have their special rites. ■ Other words that sound like this are **right** and **write.**

rit·u·al (rich′ü əl), **1** *n.* a form or system of rites. The rites of baptism, marriage, and burial are parts of the ritual of most churches. Secret societies have a ritual for initiating new members. **2** *adj.* of or about rites; done as a rite: *a ritual dance, ritual laws.* **3** *n.* any regularly followed routine. **–rit′u·al·ly,** *adv.*

rit·u·al·ism (rich′ü ə liz′əm), *n.* fondness for ritual; insistence upon ritual.

ritz·y (rit′sē), *adj.* INFORMAL. stylish; smart. ❑ *adj.* **ritz·i·er, ritz·i·est.**

WORD STORY   **Ritzy** comes from the name of César (sā zar′) Ritz, who opened his Ritz Hotel in Paris near the end of the 1800s. The hotel became so famous for its luxury that people used the name Ritz for everything stylish and smart.

ri·val (rī′vəl), **1** *n.* person who wants and tries to get the same thing as another or who tries to equal or do better than another; competitor: *The two girls were rivals for the same class office.*

a	hat	ė	term	ô	order	ch	child		
ā	age	i	it	oi	oil	ng	long	⟨	a in about
ä	far	ī	ice	ou	out	sh	she		e in taken
â	care	o	hot	u	cup	th	thin	ə	i in pencil
e	let	ō	open	u̇	put	ŦH	then		o in lemon
ē	equal	ô	saw	ü	rule	zh	measure		u in circus

R

They were also rivals in sports. **2** *adj.* wanting the same thing as another; trying to equal or outdo another; competing: *The rival supermarkets both cut their prices.* **3** *v.* to try to equal or outdo; compete with: *The sisters rivaled each other in the tennis tournament.* **4** *v.* to equal; match: *The sunset rivaled the sunrise in beauty.* **5** *n.* thing that will bear comparison with something else; equal; match. ❏ *v.* **ri·valed, ri·val·ing** or **ri·valled, ri·val·ling.**

ri·val·ry (rī′vəl rē), *n.* effort to obtain something another person wants; competition: *There is rivalry among business firms for trade.* ❏ *n., pl.* **ri·val·ries.**

riv·er (riv′ər), *n.* **1** a large, natural stream of water that flows into a lake, ocean, etc. **2** any large stream or flow: *rivers of lava.* [See Word Story at **rival.**]

Ri·ver·a (ri ver′ə), *n.* **Di·e·go** (dē ā′gō), 1886-1957, Mexican artist. He painted many murals about Mexican history and culture.

Rivera painting

riv·er·bank (riv′ər bangk′), *n.* the ground bordering a river.

river basin, land that is drained by a river and its tributaries.

riv·er·bed (riv′ər bed′), *n.* channel in which a river flows or used to flow.

riv·er·boat (riv′ər bōt′), *n.* boat for use on a river, usually made with a flat bottom.

riv·er·side (riv′ər sīd′), *n.* the bank of a river: *We walked along the riverside.*

riv·et (riv′it), **1** *n.* a metal bolt with a head at one end, the other end being hammered into a head after insertion. Rivets fasten heavy steel plates together. **2** *v.* to fasten with a rivet or rivets. **3** *v.* to fasten firmly; fix firmly: *Their eyes were riveted on the speaker.* **—riv′et·er,** *n.*

Riv·i·er·a (riv′ē er′ə), *n.* section of SE France and NW Italy along the Mediterranean Sea, famous as a resort.

riv·u·let (riv′yə lit), *n.* a very small stream.

Ri·yadh (ri yäd′), *n.* capital of Saudi Arabia, in the central part.

rm., **1** ream. **2** room. ❏ *pl.* **rms.**

Rn, symbol for radon.

R.N., **1** registered nurse. **2** Royal Navy.

RNA, a large, complex molecule found in all living cells; ribonucleic acid. It has important functions in the process of making proteins from the information contained in genes.

roach[1] (rōch), *n.* cockroach. ❏ *n., pl.* **roach·es.**

roach[2] (rōch), *n.* a silvery European freshwater fish related to the carp. ❏ *n., pl.* **roach** or **roach·es.**

road (rōd), *n.* **1** a smooth surface made for cars, trucks, etc., to travel on: *the road from New York to Boston.* **2** a way or course: *the road to ruin, a road to peace.* **3** railroad. **4** Also, **roads,** *pl.* roadstead. ■ Another word that sounds like this is **rode.**
on the road, traveling, especially in order to sell something.

road·bed (rōd′bed′), *n.* foundation for a road or for railroad tracks.

road·block (rōd′blok′), *n.* obstacle; hindrance; impediment.

road hog, INFORMAL. person who uses more of the road than is necessary, especially by driving in the center of the road.

road·ie (rō′dē), *n.* someone who travels with touring musicians in order to set up and take down equipment.

road·kill (rōd′kil′), *n.* an animal or animals killed on a road by a motor vehicle.

road map, map for car travel, showing the roads in a region and the distances between cities and towns.

road·run·ner (rōd′run′ər), *n.* a medium-sized bird of the deserts of the southwestern United States, with a long tail and a thick crest. The roadrunner is related to the cuckoo. It can run very fast.

road·side (rōd′sīd′), **1** *n.* the side of a road: *Flowers grew along the roadside.* **2** *adj.* beside a road: *a roadside inn.*

road·stead (rōd′sted), *n.* a place near the shore where ships may anchor; road.

road·ster (rōd′stər), *n.* (earlier) an open car with a single wide seat and sometimes a rumble seat in the back.

road test, **1** a test of a vehicle to determine if it is safe for use. **2** a test given to a driver before a driving license is issued.

road·way (rōd′wā′), *n.* **1** road. **2** the part of a road used by wheeled vehicles: *Do not walk in the roadway.*

road·work (rōd′wėrk′), *n.* physical training by running long distances, especially done by boxers.

roam (rōm), *v.* **1** to go about with no special plan or aim; wander: *roam through the fields.* **2** to wander over.

roan (rōn), **1** *adj.* yellowish brown or reddish brown sprinkled with gray or white. **2** *n.* horse or other animal of a roan color. **3** *n.* a roan color.

roar (rôr), **1** *v.* to make a loud, deep sound; make a loud noise: *The lion roared. The wind roared at the windows.* **2** *n.* a loud, deep sound; loud noise: *the roar of the cannon, a roar of laughter.* **3** *v.* to utter loudly: *roar out an order.* **4** *v.* to laugh loudly: *The audience roared at the clown.*

roast (rōst), **1** *v.* to cook by dry heat; bake: *We roasted meat and potatoes.* **2** *n.* piece of baked meat; piece of meat to be roasted. **3** *n.* an informal outdoor meal, at which some food is cooked over an open fire: *a wiener roast.* **4** *adj.* roasted: *roast beef, roast pork.* **5** *v.* to prepare by heating: *roast coffee, roast a metal ore.* **6** *v.* to make or become very hot: *He roasted in a heavy coat.* **7** *v.* INFORMAL. to make fun of; ridicule.

roast·er (rō′stər), *n.* **1** pan used in roasting. **2** something fit to be roasted.

rob (rob), *v.* **1** (in law) to take property unlawfully from someone by force or threat of force: *Bandits robbed the bank of thousands of dollars.* **2** to steal: *Some girls robbed fruit from the orchard.* ■ See Usage Note at **steal. 3** to take away some characteristic; keep from having or doing: *The disease has robbed him of his strength.* ❏ *v.* **robbed, rob·bing. —rob′ber,** *n.*

rob·ber·y (rob′ər ē), *n.* **1** (in law) the unlawful taking of property from someone by force or threat of force. **2** act of robbing; theft: *a bank robbery.* ❏ *n., pl.* **rob·ber·ies** for 2.

robe (rōb), **1** *n.* a long, loose outer garment: *I wore a robe over my pajamas.* **2** *n.* garment that shows rank, office, etc.: *a judge's robe, the queen's robes of state.* **3** *n.* a covering or wrap: *a beach robe.* **4** *v.* to put a robe on; dress: *They robed themselves all in white.* **5** *n.* bathrobe or dressing gown. ❏ *v.* **robed, rob·ing.**

Robe·son (rōb′sən), *n.* **Paul,** 1898-1976, American actor, singer, and activist. ■ **Paul Robeson** is especially famous for his concerts of spirituals and folk songs, and for his performance as Othello. The U.S. government canceled his passport in 1950 because of his association with Communists.

Robes·pierre (rōbz′pyer), *n.* **Max·i·mi·lien** (mäk′sē mē lyan′), 1758-1794, French political leader during the French Revolution. He brought about the execution of thousands of people during a period known as the Reign of Terror. He was eventually executed himself.

rob·in (rob′ən), *n.* **1** a large American thrush with a reddish breast. **2** a small European thrush with an orange breast.

Robin Hood, a legendary English outlaw who robbed the rich but gave money to the poor. [**Robin** is a nickname for *Robert.*]

Rob·in·son (rob′ən sən), *n.* **1 Jack·ie** (jak′ē), 1919-1972, American baseball player. ■ **Jackie Robinson** was the first African American to play major league baseball. He played for ten years with the Brooklyn Dodgers, and was elected to the National Baseball Hall of Fame in 1962. **2 Ray** (rā), 1921-1989, American boxer. He held the welterweight title for five years and won the middleweight championship five times. His nickname was "Sugar Ray."

Rob·in·son Cru·soe (rob′ən sən krü′sō), hero of Daniel Defoe's novel of the same name, a sailor shipwrecked on a desert island.

ro·bot (rō′bot *or* rō′bət), *n.* **1** machine with moving parts and sensing devices controlled by a computer. Computer programs enable a robot to carry out complex series of tasks repeatedly, without human supervision, and to change tasks with a change of programs. Robots are sometimes built to resemble human beings, though they can be of any shape and size. **2** person who acts or works in a dull, mechanical way.

robot (def. 1)

ro·bot·ic (rō bot′ik), *adj.* **1** of or for robots: *robotic design.* **2** like a robot: *tireless, robotic effort.* **—ro·bot′i·cal·ly,** *adv.*

ro·bot·ics (rō bot′iks), *n.* the study, design, manufacture, and use of robots: *a professor of robotics.*

ro·bust (rō bust′ *or* rō′bust), *adj.* **1** strong and healthy; sturdy: *a robust person.* ■ See Synonym Study at **strong. 2** able to deal with unexpected situations or problems: *a robust program, a robust set of guidelines.* [**Robust** comes from a Latin word meaning "like an oak." Oak trees are big and strong.] **—ro·bust′ly,** *adv.* **—ro·bust′ness,** *n.*

roc (rok), *n.* (in Arabian legends) a bird so large and strong that it could carry off an elephant. ■ Another word that sounds like this is **rock.**

Roch·es·ter (roch′es′tər), *n.* **1** city in W New York State. **2** city in SE New Hampshire.

rock¹ (rok), *n.* **1** any piece of stone; a stone: *I threw a rock in the lake.* **2** a large mass of stone: *The ship was wrecked on the rocks.* **3** the mass of mineral matter of which the earth's crust is made. **4** a particular layer or kind of such matter. **5** something firm like a rock; support; defense: *She was a rock when I needed strong support.* ■ Another word that sounds like this is **roc. —rock′like′,** *adj.*

on the rocks, 1 wrecked; ruined. **2** INFORMAL. bankrupt.

rock² (rok), **1** *v.* to move backward or forward, or from side to side; sway: *The waves rocked the ship.* ■ See Synonym Study at **swing. 2** *v.* to put to sleep, rest, etc., with swaying movements: *I rocked the baby to sleep.* **3** *n.* a rocking movement. **4** *n.* a kind of popular music, originally called rock'n'roll, with a strong beat and a simple, often repeated, melody. ■ Another word that sounds like this is **roc.**

rock and roll, rock² (def. 4).

rock bottom, the very bottom; lowest level.

rock candy, sugar in the form of large, hard crystals.

Rock·e·fel·ler (rok′ə fel′ər), *n.* **John D.,** 1839-1937, American capitalist and philanthropist. ■ **Rockefeller** created the Standard Oil company and the modern oil industry. During his lifetime, he gave away more than 500 million dollars, mostly to charitable foundations and organizations.

rock·er (rok′ər), *n.* **1** one of the curved pieces on which a cradle, rocking chair, etc., rocks. **2** rocking chair. **3** someone who plays rock music.

rock·et (rok′it), **1** *n.* device consisting of a tube open at one end in which an explosive or fuel is rapidly burned. The burning creates gases that escape from the open end and force the tube upward or forward. Some rockets, used for fireworks and signaling, shoot up high in the air and explode into showers of sparks or stars. Larger rockets are used as weapons or to propel spacecraft. **2** *n.* spacecraft, missile, etc., propelled by such a device. **3** *v.* to go like a rocket; rise very fast; skyrocket: *The author rocketed to fame when her book was published.*

rocket launcher, device consisting of a tube or cluster of tubes from which rockets are launched.

rock·et·ry (rok′ə trē), *n.* the science of building, using, and firing rockets.

Rock·ford (rok′fərd), *n.* city in N Illinois.

rock garden, garden of flowers and ornamental plants, planted on rocky ground or among rocks.

Rock·ies (rok′ēz), *n.pl.* Rocky Mountains.

rocking chair, chair mounted on rockers, or on springs, so that it can rock back and forth; rocker.

rocking horse, a toy horse on rockers for children to ride.

rock lobster, spiny lobster.

Rock·ne (rok′nē), *n.* **Knute** (nüt), 1888-1931, American college football coach, born in Norway. He studied, played, and coached at the University of Notre Dame. He won a higher percentage of games than any other college football coach.

rock'n'roll (rok′ən rōl′), *n.* rock² (def. 4).

rock-ribbed (rok′ribd′), *adj.* **1** having ridges of rock. **2** unyielding; rigid.

rock salt, common salt as it occurs in the earth in large crystals; halite. Rock salt is often used to melt ice on roads and sidewalks.

Rock Springs, city in SW Wyoming.

Rock·well (rok′wel), *n.* **Nor·man** (nor′mən), 1894-1978, American artist. His paintings of everyday small-town life were often published as magazine covers.

rock wool, woollike fibers made from rock or slag and used for insulation and soundproofing.

rock·y¹ (rok′ē), *adj.* **1** full of rocks: *a rocky shore.* **2** made of rock. **3** like rock; hard; firm: *rocky determination.* ❑ *adj.* **rock·i·er, rock·i·est. —rock′i·ness,** *n.*

rock·y² (rok′ē), *adj.* **1** likely to rock; shaky: *That table is a bit rocky; put a piece of wood under the short leg.* **2** sickish; weak; dizzy. **3** marked by difficulties: *She was having a rocky time with her new job.* ❑ *adj.* **rock·i·er, rock·i·est. —rock′i·ly,** *adv.* **—rock′i·ness,** *n.*

Rocky Mountains, chief group of mountain ranges in W North America; the Rockies. They extend from Alaska to New Mexico.

Rocky Mountain spotted fever, an infectious disease in which the symptoms are fever, pain, and a rash, formerly believed to occur mostly in the Rocky Mountain area. It is caused by a rickettsia bacterium and is transmitted by the bite of infected ticks.

ro·co·co (rō kō′kō), **1** *n.* style of architecture and decoration with elaborate ornamentation, combining scrolls, foliage, etc., much used in the 1700s. **2** *adj.* of this style.

rod (rod), *n.* **1** a thin, straight bar of metal, wood, or plastic. **2** a stick used to beat. **3** fishing rod. **4** unit of length equal to 5½ yards; 16½ feet. A square rod is 30¼ square yards, 272¼ square feet. **5** staff or wand carried as a symbol of rank or authority. **6** one of the many cells in the retina of the eye that are sensitive to dim light. **—rod′like′,** *adj.*

spare the rod, to fail to punish.

a	hat	ė	term	ô	order	ch	child		
ā	age	i	it	oi	oil	ng	long		a in about
ä	far	ī	ice	ou	out	sh	she	ə	e in taken
â	care	o	hot	u	cup	th	thin		i in pencil
e	let	ō	open	ů	put	ŦH	then		o in lemon
ē	equal	ò	saw	ü	rule	zh	measure		u in circus

R

rode (rōd), *v.* past tense of **ride:** *We rode ten miles yesterday.* ▪ Another word that sounds like this is **road.**

ro·dent (rōd′nt), *n.* any of many mammals with large front teeth that are used for gnawing. Rats, mice, squirrels, and beavers are rodents. [See Word Story at **erode.**]

ro·den·ti·cide (rō den′tə sid), *n.* substance used to kill rodents.

ro·de·o (rō′dē ō *or* rō dā′ō), *n.* **1** a contest or exhibition of skill in roping cattle, riding horses and bulls, etc. **2** (in the western United States) the driving of cattle together. ❏ *n., pl.* **ro·de·os.**

Rod·gers (roj′ərz), *n.* **Richard,** 1902-1979, American composer of musicals, including *Oklahoma!* and *The Sound of Music.*

Ro·din (rō dan′), *n.* **Au·guste** (ō-güst′), 1840-1917, French sculptor. He almost always sculpted human figures, of which the most famous is *The Thinker,* a seated man with his chin on his fist.

roe¹ (rō), *n.* a small deer of Europe and Asia, with forked antlers. ❏ *n., pl.* **roes** or **roe.** ▪ Other words that sound like this are **row¹** and **row².**

roe² (rō), *n.* fish eggs. ▪ Other words that sound like this are **row¹** and **row².**

roent·gen (rent′gən), *n.* unit for measuring the strength of X rays or gamma rays.

Roent·gen (rent′gən), *n.* **Wilhelm Kon·rad** (vil′helm kon′-rad), 1845-1923, German physicist who discovered X rays. He won the first Nobel Prize for physics for this discovery, in 1901.

rog·er (roj′ər), *interj.* INFORMAL. O.K.; message received and understood.

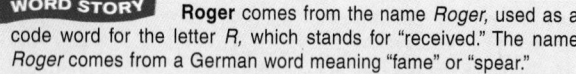
Rodin sculpture

WORD STORY **Roger** comes from the name *Roger,* used as a code word for the letter *R,* which stands for "received." The name *Roger* comes from a German word meaning "fame" or "spear."

Rog·ers (roj′ərs), *n.* **1 Gin·ger** (jin′jər), 1911-1995, American dancer and actress. She starred in many musical comedies with Fred Astaire. She won an Academy Award in 1940 for *Kitty Foyle.* **2 Will** (wil), 1879-1935, American humorist. He did rope tricks with a lasso while making jokes about current events in his stage show, and wrote a newspaper column. His most famous saying is "I never met a man I didn't like."

rogue (rōg), *n.* **1** a dishonest person; rascal; scoundrel. **2** a mischievous person: *The little rogue has his grandpa's glasses on.* **3** animal with a savage nature that lives apart from the herd.

rogues' gallery, collection kept by the police of photographs of known criminals.

ro·guish (rō′gish), *adj.* **1** of or like rogues; dishonest; rascally. **2** playfully mischievous: *She had a roguish twinkle in her eyes.* —**ro′guish·ly,** *adv.* —**ro′guish·ness,** *n.*

roil (roil), *v.* **1** to make water muddy by stirring up sediment. **2** to disturb; irritate; vex.

rois·ter (roi′stər), *v.* to be boisterous; swagger.

rois·ter·ous (rois′tər əs), *adj.* noisy; boisterous.

Ro·land (rō′lənd), *n.* (in legends of the Middle Ages) the leader of Charlemagne's knights. His story is told in a famous poem written about A.D. 1100 called *The Song of Roland.* [*Roland* comes from a German word meaning "fame" or "land."]

role or **rôle** (rōl), *n.* **1** an actor's part in a play, movie, etc.: *She played the leading role in the school play.* **2** a part played in real life: *He had the role of mediator in the recent strike.* ▪ Another word that sounds like this is **roll.**

WORD STORY **Role** comes from the French word for "roll of paper," on which an actor's part was written. That French word came from a Latin word meaning "wheel," because the rolled paper looked like a wheel. **Roll** comes from the same Latin word.

role model, person whose patterns of behavior influence someone else's actions and beliefs: *Parents are important role models for children.*

role-play (rōl′plā′), *v.* to act out a situation from real life and then discuss it. People role-play to help them recognize and deal with their problems.

roll (rōl), **1** *v.* to move along by turning over and over: *The ball rolled away.* **2** *v.* to turn round and round on itself or on something else; wrap; be wrapped round: *She rolled herself up in a blanket. Roll the string into a ball.* **3** *n.* something rolled up: *rolls of paper, a roll of carpet.* **4** *n.* a rounded or rolled-up mass: *a roll of cookie dough.* **5** *v.* to move or be moved on wheels or rollers: *The car rolled along.* **6** *v.* to move smoothly; sweep along: *Waves roll in on the beach. The years roll on.* **7** *v.* to move with a side-to-side motion: *roll your eyes. The freighter rolled in the waves.* **8** *n.* act of rolling; motion from side to side: *The ship's roll made some of the crew sick.* **9** *v.* to turn over, or over and over: *The horse rolled in the dust.* **10** *v.* to rise and fall again and again: *rolling country, rolling waves.* **11** *v.* to make flat or smooth with a roller; spread out with a rolling pin, etc.: *Roll the dough thin for these cookies.* **12** *v.* to make deep, loud sounds: *Thunder rolls.* **13** *n.* a deep, loud sound: *the roll of thunder.* **14** *v.* to beat a drum with rapid, continuous strokes. **15** *n.* a rapid, continuous beating on a drum. **16** *v.* to trill: *roll your r's.* **17** *n.* a list of names; record; list: *I will call the roll to find out who is absent.* **18** *n.* a kind of bread or cake: *a sweet roll.* [See Word Story at **role.**] ▪ Another word that sounds like this is **role.**

on a roll, having great success which seems likely to continue.

roll up, to pile up; increase: *Bills roll up fast.*

roll call, the calling of a list of names, as of soldiers, pupils, etc., to find out who is present.

roll·er (rō′lər), *n.* **1** a cylinder on which something is rolled along or rolled up. Window shades go up and down on rollers. Hair is curled on rollers. **2** a cylinder of metal, stone, or wood used for smoothing, spreading, pressing, or crushing: *A heavy roller was used to smooth the tennis court. The paint was applied with a small roller.* **3** thing that rolls, especially a small wheel: *Some articles of furniture have rollers under the legs.* **4** a long, swelling wave: *Huge rollers broke on the sandy beach.*

roller bearing, a bearing in which the shaft turns on rollers to lessen friction.

Roll·er·blades (rō′lər blādz′), *n.pl.* trademark for in-line skates.

roller coaster, a ride at an amusement park, consisting of inclined tracks along which trains of small cars roll and make steep drops and sudden turns.

roller skate, a shoe or metal base with four small wheels, used for skating on a floor, sidewalk, or other surface; skate.

roll·er-skate (rō′lər skāt′), *v.* to move on roller skates. ❏ *v.* **roll·er-skat·ed, roller-skat·ing.**

rol·lick·ing (rol′ə king), *adj.* frolicking; jolly; lively: *I had a rollicking good time at the picnic.*

rolling mill, 1 machine for rolling metal into sheets and bars. **2** factory where this is done.

rolling pin, cylinder of wood, plastic, or glass with a handle at each end, for rolling out dough.

rolling stock, the locomotives and cars of a railroad.

ro·ly-po·ly (rō′lē pō′lē), **1** *adj.* short and plump: *a roly-poly child.* **2** *n.* a short, plump person or animal. ❏ *n., pl.* **ro·ly-po·lies.**

ROM (rom), *n.* read-only memory (computer memory containing data that can be copied but not changed or erased).

Rom., 1 Roman. **2** Romance. **3** Romania. **4** Romans (book of the Bible).

ro·maine (rō mān′), *n.* a kind of lettuce with long, green, crinkly leaves joined loosely at the base.

Ro·man (rō′mən), **1** *adj.* of or about ancient or modern Rome or its people. **2** *n.* person born or living in Rome. **3** *n.* citizen of ancient Rome. **4** *adj.* of or about the Roman Catholic Church. **5 roman, a** *n.* the upright style of type most used in printing and typewriting. This sentence is in roman. **b** *adj.* of or in roman type.

Roman candle, a kind of firework that is a tube that shoots out balls of fire and sparks.

Roman Catholic, 1 of or belonging to the Christian church that recognizes the pope as the supreme head. **2** member of this church.

Roman Catholic Church, the Christian church that honors the pope as its head.

ro·mance (rō mans′ or rō′mans *for noun;* rō mans′ *for verb*), **1** *n.* a love affair: *"Cinderella" is the story of the romance between a beautiful girl and a prince.* **2** *n.* a love story. **3** *n.* story of adventure: *"The Arabian Nights" and "Treasure Island" are romances.* **4** *n.* story or poem telling of heroes: *Have you read the romances about King Arthur and his knights?* **5** *n.* real happenings that are like stories of heroes and are full of love, excitement, or noble deeds: *The children dreamed of traveling in search of romance. The explorer's life was filled with romance.* **6** *n.* a made-up story: *Nobody believes the romances she tells about her adventures.* **7** *v.* to make up stories: *Some children romance because of their lively imaginations.* **8** *v.* to treat or talk to someone in a romantic way. ❑ *v.* **ro·manced, ro·manc·ing. —ro·manc′er,** *n.*

> **WORD STORY** **Romance** and **romantic** come from **Rome.** Languages based on Latin are called **Romance languages.** Poems written in those languages long ago were called romances. The poems were full of adventure and love, so love and adventure were called romances too. What could be more romantic than a romance in Rome?

Romance languages, French, Italian, Spanish, Portuguese, Romanian, and other languages that came from Latin, the language of the Romans. [See Word Story at **romance.**]

Roman Empire, empire of ancient Rome lasting from 27 B.C. to A.D. 395. It was divided into the **Eastern Roman Empire** (A.D. 395-1453) and the **Western Roman Empire** (A.D. 395-476).

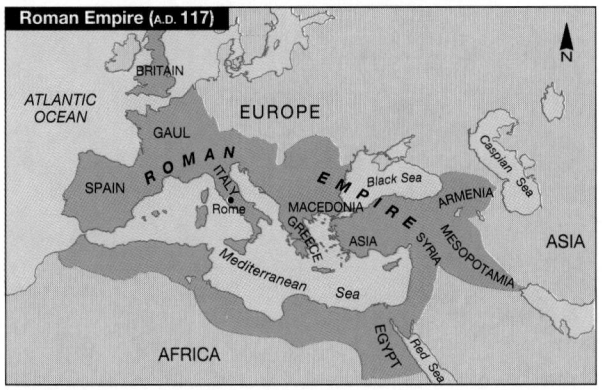

Roman Empire (A.D. 117)

Ro·man·esque (rō′mə nesk′), **1** *n.* style of architecture developed in Europe during the early Middle Ages before the Gothic period. Romanesque used round arches and vaults. **2** *adj.* of or in this style of architecture.

Ro·ma·ni·a (rō mā′nē ə), *n.* country in SE Europe. *Capital:* Bucharest. Also, **Rumania.**

> **WORD STORY** **Romania** comes from a Latin word meaning "Roman." This area was the last conquest added to the Roman Empire. Ever since, the people living there have identified themselves as coming from the Roman settlers almost 2000 years ago.

Ro·ma·ni·an (rō mā′nē ən), **1** *adj.* of or about Romania, its people, or their language. **2** *n.* person born or living in Romania. **3** *n.* language of Romania.

Roman nose, nose that has a prominent bridge.

Roman numerals, numerals like XXIII, LVI, and MDCCLX, used by the ancient Romans in numbering. In this system I = 1, V = 5, X = 10, L = 50, C = 100, D = 500, and M = 1000. Thus, MDCCCLXIII = 1963.

Ro·mans (rō′mənz), *n.* book of the New Testament, an epistle by Saint Paul to the Christians of Rome.

ro·man·tic (rō man′tik), **1** *adj.* suited to or bringing to mind thoughts of love: *The orchestra played soft, romantic music.* **2** *adj.* interested in adventure and love; having ideas or feelings suited to romance: *The old couple reminisced about the days of their courtship, when they were young and romantic.* **3** *adj.* full of love, adventure, mystery, or daring; characteristic of romances or romance: *romantic tales of love and adventure, a romantic life in exotic lands.* **4** *adj.* of or about romanticism in literature, art, and music. **5** *adj.* not based on fact; fanciful; imaginary; unreal. **6** *adj.* not customary or practical; fantastic; extravagant; quixotic: *romantic illusion.* **7** *n.* a romantic person. [See Word Story at **romance.**] **—ro·man′ti·cal·ly,** *adv.*

ro·man·ti·cism (rō man′tə siz′əm), *n.* a style of literature, art, and music especially widespread in the 1800s. Romanticism allows freedom of form and stresses strong feeling, imagination, and love of nature.

ro·man·ti·cize (rō man′tə sīz), *v.* to make romantic; give a romantic character to. ❑ *v.* **ro·man·ti·cized, ro·man·ti·ciz·ing. —ro·man′ti·ci·za′tion,** *n.*

Rom·a·ny (rom′ə nē), **1** *n.* language of the Gypsies. **2** *adj.* of or about the Gypsies, their customs, or their language. **3** *n.* Gypsy. ❑ *n., pl.* **Rom·a·nies** for 3.

> **WORD STORY** **Romany** does not come from **Rome.** It comes from a word in a language of India meaning "a man." The Romany language developed from the Indian language.

Rome (rōm), *n.* **1** capital of Italy, on the Tiber River. The headquarters of the pope and the Roman Catholic Church are in Vatican City, an independent state within Rome. **2** an ancient city in the same place, the capital of the Roman Empire. It was captured by the barbarians in A.D. 410. **3** the ancient Roman republic or the ancient Roman Empire.

Ro·me·o (rō′mē ō), *n.* hero of Shakespeare's play *Romeo and Juliet.*

romp (romp), **1** *v.* to play in a rough, boisterous way; rush, tumble, and punch in play. **2** *n.* a rough, lively play or frolic: *The kids had a romp on the beach.* **—romp′er,** *n.*

romp·ers (rom′pərz), *n.pl.* a loose outer garment, worn by young children at play.

Rom·u·lus (rom′yə ləs), *n.* (in Roman legends) the founder and first king of Rome. He and his twin brother, Remus, were abandoned as infants and nourished by a wolf.

rood (rüd), *n.* OLD USE. **1** 40 square rods; one fourth of an acre. **2** cross or crucifix. ▪ Another word that sounds like this is **rude.**

roof (rüf *or* rủf), **1** *n.* the top covering of a building. **2** *n.* something like it: *the roof of a cave, the roof of the mouth.* **3** *v.* to cover with a roof; form a roof over: *Tall trees roofed the road through the woods.* **—roof′less,** *adj.* **—roof′like′,** *adj.*

raise the roof, INFORMAL. to make a disturbance; create an uproar or confusion.

roof·er (rü′fər), *n.* person who makes or repairs roofs.

roof·ing (rü′fing), *n.* material used for roofs. Shingles are a common roofing for houses.

roof·top (rüf′top′), *n.* the outer surface of a roof.

roof·tree (rüf′trē′), *n.* ridgepole. ❑ *n., pl.* **roof·trees.**

rook[1] (rủk), **1** *n.* a European bird resembling a crow, that often nests in trees near buildings. **2** *v.* to cheat.

rook[2] (rủk), *n.* piece in the game of chess; castle. A rook can move in a straight line across any number of unoccupied squares.

rook·er·y (rủk′ər ē), *n.* **1** a breeding place of rooks; colony of rooks. **2** a breeding place or colony where other birds or animals are crowded together: *a rookery of seals.* ❑ *n., pl.* **rook·er·ies.**

rook·ie (rủk′ē), *n.* **1** player in his or her first year of professional athletics. **2** beginner; novice. **3** an inexperienced recruit.

room (rüm), **1** *n.* a part of a house, or other building, with walls of its own. **2** *n.* people in a room: *The whole room laughed.* **3** *n.* space occupied by, or available for, something: *The street was so crowded that the cars did not have room to move. There is room for one more in the car.* **4** *n.* opportunity: *There is room for im-*

R

a	hat	ė	term	ô	order	ch	child		a in about
ā	age	i	it	oi	oil	ng	long		e in taken
ä	far	ī	ice	ou	out	sh	she	ə {	i in pencil
â	care	o	hot	u	cup	th	thin		o in lemon
e	let	ō	open	ủ	put	ŦH	then		u in circus
ē	equal	ò	saw	ü	rule	zh	measure		

Rome: Life in Ancient Times

In ancient Rome, only a wealthy family could afford to live in a large town house like this one. Life in a house of this sort was as comfortable 2000 years ago as life anywhere until modern times. The family shown here probably ate well, owned good clothes and furniture, and had time for education and conversation. Good water supplies and sanitation helped to keep them healthy. We might not choose to live as they did, but it was a highly civilized way of life.

Kitchen
Food for the family was prepared by servants in a kitchen separated from the dining area and other parts of the house. The distance lessened the smell and the risk of a fire.

Dining
The meals of a wealthy Roman family might include such delicacies of the time as ostrich, flamingo with dates, and roast parrot. Family members lay on couches while they ate.

Courtyard
Ancient Roman town houses were usually built around a courtyard, which admitted light and air to the inside of the house. Courtyards often contained small gardens, fishponds, and fountains.

Getting Around
Small two-wheeled carts pulled by a donkey or a mule were commonly used to haul loads. A wealthy homeowner might own a riding horse or passenger chariot.

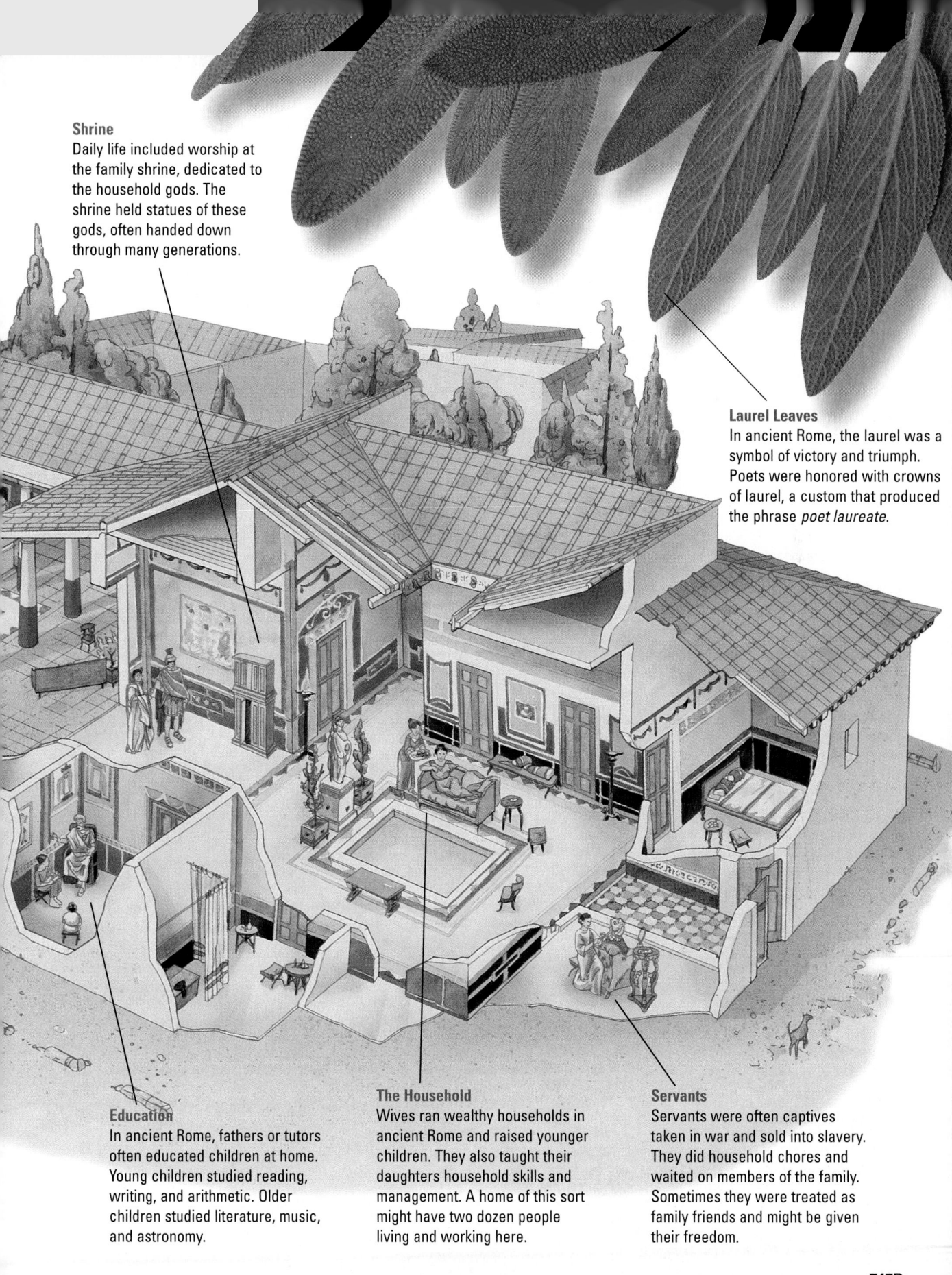

Shrine
Daily life included worship at the family shrine, dedicated to the household gods. The shrine held statues of these gods, often handed down through many generations.

Laurel Leaves
In ancient Rome, the laurel was a symbol of victory and triumph. Poets were honored with crowns of laurel, a custom that produced the phrase *poet laureate*.

Education
In ancient Rome, fathers or tutors often educated children at home. Young children studied reading, writing, and arithmetic. Older children studied literature, music, and astronomy.

The Household
Wives ran wealthy households in ancient Rome and raised younger children. They also taught their daughters household skills and management. A home of this sort might have two dozen people living and working here.

Servants
Servants were often captives taken in war and sold into slavery. They did household chores and waited on members of the family. Sometimes they were treated as family friends and might be given their freedom.

provement in his work. **5** *v.* to occupy a room; live in a room: *Three girls from our town roomed together at college.* **6** *n.pl.* **rooms,** lodgings. ■ Another word that sounds like this is **rheum.**

room·er (rü′mər), *n.* person who lives in a rented room or rooms in another's house; lodger.

room·ette (rü met′), *n.* **1** a small private bedroom in a railroad sleeping car. **2** a private room with box seats at a stadium, used for entertaining guests at a sporting event.

room·ful (rüm′fül), *n.* **1** enough to fill a room. **2** people or things in a room. ❑ *n., pl.* **room·fuls.**

rooming house, house with rooms to rent.

room·mate (rüm′māt′), *n.* person who shares a room with another or others.

room·y (rü′mē), *adj.* having plenty of room; large; spacious. ❑ *adj.* **room·i·er, room·i·est.** ■ Another word that sounds like this is **rheumy.** —**room′i·ly,** *adv.* —**room′i·ness,** *n.*

Roo·se·velt (rō′zə velt), *n.* **1 Eleanor,** 1884-1962, American author and political leader, wife of Franklin Delano Roosevelt. **2 Franklin Del·a·no** (del′ə nō), 1882-1945, the 32nd president of the United States, from 1933 to 1945. ■ Franklin Delano Roosevelt was the only U.S. president to be elected four times. **3 The·o·dore** (thē′ə dôr), 1858-1919, the 26th president of the United States, from 1901 to 1909. ■ Theodore Roosevelt was the youngest man to become President of the United States. He was only 42 when he took office.

roost (rüst), **1** *n.* bar, pole, or perch on which birds rest or sleep. **2** *v.* to sit as birds do on a roost; settle for the night. **3** *n.* place for birds to rest or sleep.

come home to roost, to come back so as to harm the doer or user; backfire; boomerang.

rule the roost, INFORMAL. be master.

roost·er (rü′stər), *n.* a full-grown male chicken.

root[1] (rüt *or* rüt), **1** *n.* a part of a plant that grows downward, usually into the ground, to hold the plant in place, absorb water and minerals from the soil, and often to store food material. **2** *n.* any underground part of a plant. **3** *n.* something like a plant's root in shape, position, use, etc.: *the root of a tooth, the roots of the hair.* **4** *n.* a part from which other things grow and develop; cause; source: *"The love of money is the root of all evil."* **5** *v.* to send out roots and begin to grow; become set in the ground: *Some plants root more quickly than others.* **6** *v.* to pull, tear, or dig up by the roots; get completely rid of: *We spent hours rooting up weeds.* **7** *n.* the essential part; base. **8** *n.pl.* **roots,** feeling of having ties to a particular place, people, or culture; awareness of your origins and background. **9** *n.* number that produces another number when multiplied by itself a certain number of times. 2 is the square root of 4 and the cube root of 8 (2 × 2 = 4, 2 × 2 × 2 = 8). **10** *n.* word or word part from which other words are made. *Room* is the root of *roominess, roomer, roommate,* and *roomy.* The Latin root of the words *portable, porter, import,* and *transport* is *port-,* meaning "to carry." ■ Another word that can sound like this is **route.** —**root′like,** *adj.*

take root, 1 to send out roots and begin to grow. **2** to become firmly fixed.

root[2] (rüt), *v.* **1** to dig with the snout: *The pigs rooted up the garden.* **2** to rummage: *She rooted through the closet looking for her hat.* ■ Another word that can sound like this is **route.** —**root′er,** *n.*

root[3] (rüt), *v.* to cheer or support a team, candidate, etc., enthusiastically. ■ Another word that can sound like this is **route.** —**root′er,** *n.*

root beer, a soft drink flavored with the juice of the roots of certain plants, such as sarsaparilla, sassafras, etc.

root canal, 1 passage in the root of a tooth through which nerves and blood pass to the soft inner part of the tooth. **2** a dental procedure to remove the inner part from the tooth and from this passage, and then to fill the space with a plug. The procedure treats or prevents infection.

root·ed (rü′tid), *adj.* **1** having roots. **2** having taken root; firmly fixed: *a deeply rooted belief.*

root hair, a hairlike growth from the root of a plant. Root hairs absorb water and minerals from the soil.

root·less (rüt′lis), *adj.* without a root or roots; not rooted.

root·let (rüt′lit), *n.* a little root; small branch of a root.

root·stock (rüt′stok′), *n.* rhizome.

rope (rōp), **1** *n.* a strong, thick line or cord made by twisting smaller cords together. A rope of twisted wires is a cable. **2** *v.* to tie, bind, or fasten with a rope. **3** *v.* to enclose or mark off with a rope: *In winter, they rope off the entrance to the beach.* **4** *n.* a lasso. **5** *v.* to catch a horse, calf, etc., with a lasso. **6** *n.* a number of things twisted or strung together: *a rope of pearls, a rope of onions.* **7** *n.* cord or noose for hanging someone. **8** *n.* a sticky, stringy mass: *Molasses candy forms a rope.* ❑ *v.* **roped, rop·ing.** —**rop′er,** *n.*

know the ropes, INFORMAL. to know about a business or activity.

rope in, INFORMAL. to get or lead in by tricking.

the end of your rope, the end of your resources, activities, etc.

rop·y (rō′pē), *adj.* **1** forming sticky threads; stringy: *a ropy syrup.* **2** like a rope or ropes. ❑ *adj.* **rop·i·er, rop·i·est.** —**rop′i·ness,** *n.*

Roque·fort (rōk′fərt), *n.* trademark for a strongly flavored French blue cheese made from sheep's milk.

ro·sar·y (rō′zər ē), *n.* **1** string of beads for keeping count in saying a series of prayers. **2** a series of prayers. ❑ *n., pl.* **ro·sar·ies.** [**Rosary** comes from a Latin word meaning "a rose." People sometimes put crowns of roses on statues of the Virgin Mary.]

rose[1] (rōz), **1** *n.* any of numerous bushes with thorny stems and pretty red, pink, white, or yellow flowers that usually smell very sweet. **2** *n.* any of various related or similar plants or flowers. **3** *adj.* pinkish red. **4** *n.* a pinkish red. **5** *n.* something shaped like a rose or suggesting a rose, such as a rosette. —**rose′like′,** *adj.*

rose[2] (rōz), *v.* past tense of **rise:** *The cat rose slowly.*

ro·se·ate (rō′zē it *or* rō′zē āt), *adj.* **1** rose-colored; rosy. **2** cheerful; optimistic. —**ro′se·ate·ly,** *adv.*

Ro·seau (rō zō′), *n.* port and capital of Dominica, in the S part.

rose·bud (rōz′bud′), *n.* the bud of a rose.

rose·bush (rōz′büsh′), *n.* bush or vine bearing roses. ❑ *n., pl.* **rose·bush·es.**

rose-col·ored (rōz′kul′ərd), *adj.* **1** pinkish red. **2** bright; cheerful.

rose·mar·y (rōz′mâr′ē), *n.* a fragrant evergreen bush with leaves used in making perfume and in seasoning food.

ro·sette (rō zet′), *n.* an ornament shaped like a rose. Rosettes are often made of ribbon. Carved or molded rosettes are used in architecture.

rose water, water made fragrant with oil of roses.

rose window, a round stained glass window, especially one with a pattern of sections like flower petals around its center.

rose·wood (rōz′wüd′), *n.* any of several tropical trees with beautiful reddish wood used in fine furniture.

Rosh Ha·sha·nah (rosh′ hə shä′nə), the Jewish New Year. It usually occurs in September.

rose window

ros·in (roz′n), **1** *n.* a hard, yellow substance that remains when turpentine is evaporated from pine resin. Rosin is rubbed on violin bows and on the shoes of acrobats and ballet dancers to keep them from slipping. **2** *v.* to cover or rub with rosin.

Ross (rôs), *n.* **Bet·sy** (bet′sē), 1752-1836, American woman who is said to have made the first U.S. flag.

ros·ter (ros′tər), *n.* **1** list giving each person's name and duties. **2** any list.

ros·trum (ros′trəm), *n.* platform for public speaking. ❑ *n., pl.* **ros·trums, ros·tra** (ros′trə).

Ros·well (roz′wel), *n.* city in SE New Mexico.

ros·y (rō′zē), *adj.* **1** like a rose; rose-red; pinkish red. **2** bright; cheerful: *a rosy future.* ❑ *adj.* **ros·i·er, ros·i·est.** —**ros′i·ly,** *adv.* —**ros′i·ness,** *n.*

rot (rot), **1** *v.* to become rotten; decay; spoil: *So much rain will make the fruit rot.* ■ See Synonym Study at **decay. 2** *v.* to cause to decay. **3** *n.* process of rotting; decay. **4** *n.* any of various diseases of plants and animals, especially sheep. **5** *v.* to lose vigor; degenerate. **6** *n.* INFORMAL. nonsense; rubbish. ◻ *v.* **rot·ted, rot·ting.**

ro·tar·y (rō′tər ē), **1** *adj.* turning like a top or a wheel; rotating. **2** *adj.* having parts that rotate. **3** *n.* traffic circle. ◻ *n., pl.* **ro·tar·ies.**

ro·tate (rō′tāt), *v.* **1** to move around a center or axis; turn in a circle; revolve. Wheels, tops, and the earth rotate. **2** to change in a regular order; take turns or cause to take turns: *The officials will rotate as chairman. Farmers rotate their crops in order to keep the soil productive.* ◻ *v.* **ro·tat·ed, ro·tat·ing.** —**ro′tat′a·ble,** *adj.* —**ro′ta·tor,** *n.*

> **WORD FAMILY** Rotate and the words below are related. They all come from a Latin word meaning "wheel."
>
> | enroll | roll | rotor |
> |---|---|---|
> | rodeo | roly-poly | roulette |
> | role | rotary | rowel |

ro·ta·tion (rō tā′shən), *n.* **1** act of turning around a center or axis; turning in a circle; revolving: *the rotation of a top. The earth's rotation causes night and day.* **2** a change in a regular order.
in rotation, in turn; in regular succession.

rotation of crops, the varying from year to year of crops grown in the same field to keep the soil from losing its fertility.

ro·ta·tor cuff (rō′tā tər), the structure of muscles and tendons that supports and strengthens the shoulder joint. Rotator cuff injuries are common among baseball pitchers.

ro·ta·to·ry (rō′tə tôr′ē), *adj.* **1** turning like a top or wheel; rotating. **2** causing rotation: *a rotatory muscle.*

R.O.T.C., Reserve Officers' Training Corps.

rote (rōt), *n.* a set, mechanical way of doing things. ▪ Another word that sounds like this is **wrote.**
by rote, by memory without thought of the meaning: *to learn a lesson by rote.*

rot·hole (rot′hōl′), *n.* CANADIAN. a soft place in the ice on a frozen lake or river.

ro·ti·fer (rō′tə fər), *n.* any of many very small water animals with hairlike parts that wave in circular patterns like turning wheels. Rotifers use these parts to move and to draw in food.

ro·tis·ser·ie (rō tis′ər ē), *n.* an electric appliance with a spit for roasting food, rotated by an electric motor.

ro·tor (rō′tər), *n.* **1** a rotating part of a machine. **2** set of rotating blades by which a helicopter is able to fly.

rot·ten (rot′n), *adj.* **1** decayed or spoiled: *a rotten egg.* **2** foul; disgusting: *a rotten smell.* **3** unsound; weak: *rotten ice, rotten beams.* **4** corrupt; dishonest: *rotten government.* **5** bad; nasty: *The weather was rotten yesterday. He had a rotten cold all last week.* —**rot′ten·ly,** *adv.* —**rot′ten·ness,** *n.*

Rot·ter·dam (rot′ər dam′), *n.* port in SW Netherlands.

rott·wei·ler or **Rott·wei·ler** (rot′wī′lər), *n.* a medium-sized, stocky dog with short black hair, brown markings on the face and legs, and a short tail.

ro·tund (rō tund′), *adj.* **1** round or plump: *a rotund face.* **2** sounding rich and full; full-toned: *a rotund voice.* —**ro·tund′ly,** *adv.* —**ro·tund′ness,** *n.*

ro·tun·da (rō tun′də), *n.* a round building or room, especially one with a dome: *The Capitol in Washington has a large rotunda.* ◻ *n., pl.* **ro·tun·das.**

ro·tun·di·ty (rō tun′də tē), *n.* **1** roundness or plumpness. **2** rounded fullness of tone.

Rou·en (rü än′), *n.* city in N France, on the Seine River, famous for its cathedral. Joan of Arc was burned at the stake in Rouen in 1431.

rouge (rüzh), **1** *n.* a red or pink powder, paste, or liquid for coloring the cheeks or lips. **2** *v.* to color with rouge. **3** *n.* a red powder, chiefly an oxide of iron, used for polishing metal, jewels, etc. **4** *n.* (in Canadian football) a single point scored by the kicking team when the receiving team chooses not to run a kick back from its own end zone. ◻ *v.* **rouged, roug·ing.**

rough (ruf), **1** *adj.* not smooth; not level; not even: *rough boards, the rough bark of an oak tree, a rough, rocky hill.* **2** *adj.* without luxury and ease: *She led a rough life at her summer camp.* **3** *adj.* unpleasant; hard; severe: *She had a rough time recovering from the accident.* **4** *adj.* stormy: *rough weather, a rough sea.* **5** *adj.*

likely to hurt others; not gentle; harsh; rude: *rough manners.* **6** *adv.* in a rough manner; roughly: *Those older children play too rough for me.* **7** *adj.* without polish or fine finish: *rough diamonds.* **8** *adj.* not completed or perfected; done as a first try; without details: *a rough drawing, a rough idea.* **9** *adj.* coarse and tangled: *rough fur.* **10** *n.* a coarse, violent person. **11** *v.* to shape or sketch roughly: *rough out a plan.* **12** *n.* ground where there is long grass, etc., on a golf course. ▪ Another word that sounds like this is **ruff.** —**rough′ness,** *n.*
in the rough, not polished or refined; coarse; crude.
rough it, to live without comforts and conveniences.
rough up, 1 to make rough: *A strong wind roughed up the waves.* **2** to treat roughly; beat: *The angry mob roughed up the suspected traitor.*

> **SYNONYM STUDY** Rough and uneven both mean not smooth. **Rough** suggests a surface with many sharp edges: *He caught his sweater on the rough wall.* **Uneven** suggests a surface that is not level or has holes in it: *The car bounced along the uneven road.*

rough·age (ruf′ij), *n.* the coarser parts or kinds of food which stimulate the movement of food and waste products through the intestines. Bran, fruit skins, and certain fruits are roughage.

rough·en (ruf′ən), *v.* to make or become rough.

rough·hew (ruf′hyü′), *v.* to shape timber, stone, etc., roughly, without smoothing or finishing. ◻ *v.* **rough-hewed, rough-hewed** or **rough-hewn, rough-hew·ing.**

rough·house (ruf′hous′), INFORMAL. **1** *n.* rough play; rowdy conduct; disorderly behavior. **2** *v.* to act in a rough, disorderly way. ◻ *v.* **rough-housed, rough-hous·ing.**

rough·ly (ruf′lē), *adv.* **1** in a rough manner: *They pushed him roughly out the door.* **2** approximately: *From her house to mine is roughly two miles.*

rough·neck (ruf′nek′), *n.* INFORMAL. a rough, coarse person.

rough·shod (ruf′shod′), *adj.* having horseshoes with sharp nails that stick out.
ride roughshod over, to domineer over; show no consideration for; treat roughly.

rou·lette (rü let′), *n.* **1** a gambling game in which the players bet on which numbered section of a revolving wheel a small ball will come to rest in. **2** a small wheel with sharp teeth for making lines of marks, dots, or perforations: *a roulette for perforating sheets of postage stamps.*

round (round), **1** *adj.* shaped like a ball, a circle, or a tree trunk; having a circular or curved outline: *Oranges are round. A ring is round. Most candles are round.* **2** *n.* anything shaped like a ball, a circle, or a tree trunk; thing that is circular, curved, cylindrical, etc. The rungs of a ladder are sometimes called rounds. **3** *adj.* plump: *The baby had round cheeks.* **4** *v.* to make or become round: *The carpenter rounded the corners of the table.* **5** *adv., prep.* around: *Wheels go round. They built a fence round the yard.* **6** *v.* to go around; make a turn to the other side of: *The car rounded the corner at high speed.* **7** *n.* Often, **rounds,** *pl.* a fixed course ending where it begins: *The watchman makes his rounds of the building every hour.* **8** *n.* movement in a circle or about an axis: *the earth's yearly round.* **9** *n.* series of duties, events, etc.; routine: *a round of pleasures.* **10** *n.* section of a game or sport: *a round in a boxing match.* **11** *n.* a complete game or unit: *a round of golf.* **12** *n.* discharge of guns by a group of soldiers at the same time. **13** *n.* bullets, powder, etc., for one such discharge, or for a single shot: *Three rounds of ammunition were left in the rifle.* **14** *n.* an act that a number of people do together: *a round of applause, a round of cheers.* **15** *n.* round dance. **16** *n.* a short song sung by several persons or groups beginning one after the other. "Row, Row, Row Your Boat" is a round. **17** *adj.* full; complete; large: *a round dozen, a good round sum of money.* **18** *v.* to change a number to the nearest hundredth, tenth, ten, hundred, etc. 7578

a	hat	ė	term	ô	order	ch	child		a in about
ā	age	i	it	oi	oil	ng	long		e in taken
ä	far	ī	ice	ou	out	sh	she	ə {	i in pencil
â	care	o	hot	u	cup	th	thin		o in lemon
e	let	ō	open	u̇	put	ŦH	then		u in circus
ē	equal	ò	saw	ü	rule	zh	measure		

rounded to the nearest hundred would be 7600. **19** *adj.* plainly expressed; frank; blunt: *I was scolded in good round terms for being so late.* **20** *adj.* with a full tone: *a mellow, round voice.* **21** *adj.* spoken with the lips rounded: *O is a round vowel.* **22** *v.* to utter a vowel with a small circular opening of the lips. **23** *n.* a cut of beef just above the hind leg and below the rump. **—round′ness,** *n.*

in the round, 1 in a form of sculpture in which the figures are apart from any background. **2** having seats all around a central stage: *theater in the round.*

make the rounds or **go the rounds, 1** to go from one place to another: *He made the rounds of the town looking for work.* **2** to spread from one person to another: *The story about his accident went the rounds in a day.*

round off or **round out, 1** to make or become round. **2** to finish; complete.

round up, to drive or bring together: *The cowboys rounded up the cattle.*

round·a·bout (round′ə bout′), *adj.* not straight; indirect: *a roundabout route, to speak in a roundabout way.*

round dance, 1 a dance in which the dancers stand in or move around a circle or ring. **2** a dance based on circular movement. The waltz is a round dance.

roun·de·lay (roun′dl ā), *n.* song in which a phrase or a line is repeated again and again.

round·house (round′hous′), *n.* **1** a circular building for storing or repairing locomotives. It is built around a rotating turntable. **2** cabin on the rear part of a ship's quarterdeck. ❏ *n., pl.* **round·hous·es** (round′hou′ziz).

roundhouse (def. 1)

round·ish (roun′dish), *adj.* somewhat round.

round·ly (round′lē), *adv.* **1** in a round manner; in a circle, curve, globe, etc. **2** plainly; bluntly; severely: *scold roundly.* **3** fully; completely.

round number, a number in even tens, hundreds, thousands, etc. 3874 in round numbers would be 3900 or 4000.

round robin, 1 system of scheduling a tournament, in which every player or team plays every other player or team. **2** petition or protest with the signatures written in a circle, so that it is impossible to tell who signed first. **3** letter passed from person to person in a group, with each person adding something.

round-shoul·dered (round′shōl′dərd), *adj.* having the shoulders bent forward.

round table, 1 group of people gathered for a discussion. **2 Round Table,** in legends of the Middle Ages: **a** table around which King Arthur and his knights sat. **b** King Arthur and his knights.

round trip, trip to a place and back again. **—round′-trip′,** *adj.*

round·up (round′up′), *n.* **1** act of driving or bringing cattle together from long distances. **2** the people and horses that do this. **3** any similar gathering: *a roundup of old friends.*

round·worm (round′wėrm′), *n.* any of very many worms that have long, thin, round bodies without segments and that live in soil or water, or as parasites in animals and plants; nematode. The hookworm and the pinworm are roundworms.

rouse (rouz), *v.* **1** to wake up; awake: *I was roused by the ring of the telephone.* **2** to excite; stir up: *She was roused to anger by the insult.* ❏ *v.* **roused, rous·ing.** **—rous′er,** *n.*

rous·ing (rou′zing), *adj.* stirring; vigorous; brisk: *a rousing speech.* **—rous′ing·ly,** *adv.*

Rous·seau (rü sō′), *n.* **Jean Jacques** (zhän zhäk), 1712-1778, French philosopher. He wrote about government and education. He believed that people are naturally kind and generous but that society makes people evil and selfish.

roust·a·bout (roust′ə bout′), *n.* an unskilled laborer on a wharf, a ship, a ranch, in a circus, etc.

rout[1] (rout), **1** *n.* flight of a defeated army in disorder: *The enemy's retreat soon became a rout.* **2** *v.* to put to flight in disorder: *rout an enemy.* **3** *n.* a complete defeat: *The game ended in a rout for our team.* **4** *v.* to defeat completely: *The baseball team routed its opponents by a score of ten to one.* ■ Another word that can sound like this is **route.**

rout[2] (rout), *v.* **1** to put out; force out: *be routed out of bed at five o'clock.* **2** to hollow out; scoop out; gouge. **3** root[2]. ■ Another word that can sound like this is **route.**

route (rüt *or* rout), **1** *n.* way to go; road: *Will you go to the coast by the northern route?* **2** *v.* to arrange a way for: *The travel club routed us through Montana on our vacation to Canada.* **3** *v.* to send by a particular way: *Traffic was routed around the construction work.* **4** *n.* a regular way or area assigned to someone making deliveries, sales, etc.: *a newspaper route.* ❏ *v.* **rout·ed, rout·ing.** ■ Other words that can sound like this are **root** and **rout.**

> **WORD STORY** **Route** comes from a Latin word meaning "to break." **Rupture** comes from the same word. Italy is mountainous, and the Romans often had to break through great amounts of rock to build roads.

rou·tine (rü tēn′), **1** *n.* a regular method of doing things; habit of doing the same things in the same way: *Getting up and going to bed are parts of your daily routine.* **2** *adj.* using regular methods: *a routine operation.* **3** *adj.* average; ordinary; run-of-the-mill: *a routine show with routine performances.* **4** *n.* a set of instructions that directs a computer to perform a certain task or group of tasks. **—rou·tine′ly,** *adv.*

rou·tin·ize (rü tē′nīz), *v.* to make habitual. ❏ *v.* **rou·tin·ized, rou·tin·iz·ing.** **—rou·tin′i·za′tion,** *n.*

roux (rü), *n.* a mixture of flour and butter, oil, etc., cooked and used to thicken soups, sauces, gumbos, etc. ❏ *n., pl.* **roux** (rüz).

rove (rōv), *v.* to wander about; wander; roam; ramble; range: *She loved to rove through the fields and woods.* ❏ *v.* **roved, rov·ing.**

rov·er[1] (rō′vər), *n.* **1** person who roves; wanderer. **2** (in lacrosse) a player without a specific position who roves over the whole field. **3 Rover,** (in Canada) member of the Boy Scouts who is more than 17 years old.

ro·ver[2] (rō′vər), *n.* **1** pirate. **2** a pirate ship.

row[1] (rō), *n.* **1** line of people or things: *Corn is planted in rows.* **2** street with a line of buildings on either side. ■ Another word that sounds like this is **roe.**

hard row to hoe, a difficult thing to do.

in a row, one after another; in succession: *They won the state championship three years in a row.*

row[2] (rō), **1** *v.* to use oars to move a boat: *We rowed across the lake.* **2** *v.* to cause a boat to move by the use of oars. **3** *v.* to carry in a rowboat: *I rowed them to shore.* **4** *n.* trip in a rowboat: *It's only a short row to the island.* ■ Another word that sounds like this is **roe.** **—row′er,** *n.*

row[3] (rou), *n.* a noisy quarrel or disturbance; squabble; ruckus: *The three children had a row over the bicycle.*

row·boat (rō′bōt′), *n.* boat moved by oars.

row·dy (rou′dē), **1** *adj.* rough; disorderly; quarrelsome: *The gym was full of rowdy kids.* ■ See Synonym Study at **naughty. 2** *n.* a rough, disorderly, quarrelsome person: *The rowdies were asked to leave the game.* ❏ *n., pl.* **row·dies;** *adj.* **row·di·er, row·di·est.** **—row′di·ly,** *adv.* **—row′di·ness,** *n.*

row·el (rou′əl), *n.* a small wheel with sharp points, attached to the end of a spur.

row house, one of a row of houses, each very like the others, each sharing its outer walls with the houses next to it; town house.

row houses

row·lock (rō′lok′), *n.* oarlock.

roy·al (roi′əl), *adj.* **1** of or about kings and queens: *the royal family.* **2** belonging to a king or queen: *royal power, a royal palace.* **3** from or by a king or queen: *a royal command.* **4** of or for a kingdom: *a royal army or navy.* **5** appropriate for a king or queen; splendid: *a royal welcome, a royal feast.* **6** like a king or queen; noble; majestic: *The lion is a royal beast.* **—roy′al·ly,** *adv.*

Royal Canadian Mounted Police, the federal Canadian police force.

roy·al·ist (roi′ə list), **1** *n.* supporter of a king or queen or of a royal government. The royalists supported the British king during the Revolutionary War. **2** *adj.* of or about royalists: *royalist principles, a royalist party.*

roy·al·ty (roi′əl tē), *n.* **1** a royal person or royal persons. Kings, queens, princes, and princesses are royalty. **2** rank or dignity of a king or queen; royal power: *The crown is the symbol of royalty.* **3** kingly or queenly nature; royal quality; nobility. **4** a share of the receipts or profits paid to an owner of a patent or copyright. Authors receive royalties from the publishers of their books. ❏ *n., pl.* **roy·al·ties** for 4.

rpm or **r.p.m.,** revolutions per minute.

rps or **r.p.s.,** revolutions per second.

R.R., railroad.

R.S.V.P. or **r.s.v.p.,** please answer.

rt., right.

rte., route.

Ru, symbol for ruthenium.

rub (rub), **1** *v.* to move one thing back and forth against another: *Rub your hands to warm them. He rubbed soap on his hands.* **2** *v.* to push and press along the surface of: *Please rub my sore back. That door rubs on the floor.* **3** *v.* to make or bring by rubbing: *rub silver bright.* **4** *v.* to clean, smooth, or polish by moving one thing firmly against another: *Rub the silver with a soft cloth.* **5** *n.* act of rubbing: *Give the silver a rub with the polish.* **6** *n.* thing that hurts the feelings: *He didn't like her mean rub at his slowness.* **7** *v.* to irritate or make sore by rubbing: *The new shoe rubbed his heel, causing a blister.* **8** *n.* difficulty: *The rub is that we all want the last piece of pie.* ❏ *v.* **rubbed, rub·bing.**

rub down, to rub the body; massage.

rub it in, to keep on mentioning something unpleasant.

rub off, to remove or be removed by rubbing: *Rub off the dust on your sleeve. Ink rubs off easily with this eraser.*

rub the wrong way, to annoy; irritate.

rub·ber[1] (rub′ər), **1** *n.* an elastic substance obtained from the milky juice of certain tropical plants, or produced artificially by a chemical process. Rubber will not let air or water through. **2** *n.* something made from this substance, such as a rubber band or eraser. **3** *n.pl.* **rubbers,** low-cut overshoes made of rubber. **4** *adj.* made of rubber: *a rubber tire.* [See Word Story at **erase.**] **—rub′-ber·like′,** *adj.*

rub·ber[2] (rub′ər), *n.* **1** series of two games out of three or three games out of five won by the same side. **2** the deciding game in such a series: *If each side has won two games, the fifth game will be the rubber.*

rubber band, a circular strip of rubber, used to hold things together; elastic.

rub·ber·ize (rub′ə rīz′), *v.* to cover or treat with rubber: *rubberized cloth.* ❏ *v.* **rub·ber·ized, rub·ber·iz·ing.**

rub·ber·neck (rub′ər nek′), *v.* INFORMAL. to stare curiously: *Crowds rubbernecked at the construction site.* **—rub′ber·neck′er,** *n.*

rubber plant, 1 a houseplant, originally found in tropical Asia, with round, shiny, leathery leaves. It is a kind of fig. **2** any plant yielding rubber.

rubber stamp, 1 stamp made of rubber, used with ink for printing dates, signatures, etc. **2** person or group that approves or endorses something without thought or without power to refuse.

rub·ber·y (rub′ər ē), *adj.* like rubber; elastic; tough.

rub·bing (rub′ing), *n.* a copy of a an engraved or raised design made by pressing paper on the surface and rubbing it with crayon, charcoal, chalk, etc.

rub·bish (rub′ish), *n.* **1** worthless or useless stuff; waste; trash: *Pick up the rubbish and burn it.* **2** silly words and thoughts; nonsense: *Gossip is often a lot of rubbish.*

rub·bish·y (rub′i shē), *adj.* **1** full of or covered with rubbish. **2** of or like rubbish; having no value.

rub·ble (rub′əl), *n.* **1** rough broken stones, bricks, etc.: *the rubble left by an explosion or an earthquake.* **2** masonry made of this: *The house was built of rubble and plaster.*

rub·down (rub′doun′), *n.* a massage.

ru·bel·la (rü bel′ə), *n.* German measles.

Ru·bens (rü′bənz), *n.* Peter Paul, 1577-1640, Flemish painter. He was a popular court painter and received so many commissions he had to train assistants to help him finish them.

ru·bid·i·um (rü bid′ē əm), *n.* a soft, silver-white, metallic element which reacts violently in water and burns spontaneously in air. *Symbol:* Rb

ru·ble (rü′bəl), *n.* unit of money in Russia.

ru·bric (rü′brik), *n.* **1** title or heading of a chapter, a law, etc., written or printed in red or in special lettering. **2** rule for the conducting of religious services inserted in a prayer book, ritual, etc. **3** category.

ru·by (rü′bē), **1** *n.* a clear, hard, deep red precious stone. Rubies are a variety of corundum. **2** *adj.* deep, glowing red: *ruby wine.* **3** *n.* a deep, glowing red. ❏ *n., pl.* **ru·bies** for 1. **—ru′by·like′,** *adj.*

ruck·sack (ruk′sak′), *n.* knapsack.

ruck·us (ruk′əs), *n.* INFORMAL. a noisy disturbance or uproar; row[3]. ❏ *n., pl.* **ruck·us·es.**

rud·der (rud′ər), *n.* **1** a flat piece of wood or metal hinged vertically to the rear end of a boat or ship and used to steer it. **2** a similar device on an aircraft.

rud·dy (rud′ē), *adj.* **1** red or reddish: *the ruddy glow of a fire.* **2** having a fresh, healthy, red look: *ruddy cheeks.* ❏ *adj.* **rud·di·er, rud·di·est. —rud′di·ly,** *adv.* **—rud′di·ness,** *n.*

rude (rüd), *adj.* **1** not courteous; impolite: *It is rude to stare at people.* **2** roughly made or done; without finish or polish; coarse: *We made a rude bed from the branches of evergreen trees.* **3** rough in manner or behavior; violent; harsh: *I had a rude shock when I discovered that my bicycle was gone.* **4** not having learned much; rather wild; barbarous: *a rude, primitive culture.* ❏ *adj.* **rud·er, rud·est.** ■ Another word that sounds like this is **rood.** **—rude′ly,** *adv.* **—rude′ness,** *n.*

SYNONYM STUDY **Rude, offensive,** and **blunt** all mean acting in an unpleasant way. **Rude** means showing bad manners: *The cab driver shouted something rude.* **Offensive** means rude and annoying: *I found his language offensive.* **Blunt** can mean to the point, without concern for other people's feelings: *She was blunt in her analysis of my handwriting.*

R

a	hat	ė	term	ô	order	ch	child		
ā	age	i	it	oi	oil	ng	long	ə	a in about
ä	far	ī	ice	ou	out	sh	she		e in taken
â	care	o	hot	u	cup	th	thin		i in pencil
e	let	ō	open	ù	put	ᴛʜ	then		o in lemon
ē	equal	ò	saw	ü	rule	zh	measure		u in circus

ru·di·ment (rü′də mənt), *n.* **1** part to be learned first; beginning: *the rudiments of grammar.* **2** something in an early stage: *the rudiments of wings on a baby chick.*

ru·di·men·tar·y (rü′də men′tər ē), *adj.* **1** to be learned or studied first; elementary: *It is almost impossible to learn multiplication without knowing the rudimentary steps of addition.* **2** in an early stage of development; undeveloped: *rudimentary wings.* —**ru·di·men·tar·i·ly** (rü′də mən ter′ə lē), *adv.*

rue[1] (rü), **1** *v.* to be sorry for; regret: *She will rue the day she left school.* **2** *n.* sorrow; regret. ◻ *v.* **rued, ru·ing.**

rue[2] (rü), *n.* any of several strong-smelling, woody European and Asian plants with bitter leaves.

rue·ful (rü′fəl), *adj.* **1** sorrowful; unhappy; mournful: *a rueful expression.* **2** causing sorrow or pity: *a rueful sight.* —**rue′ful·ly,** *adv.* —**rue′ful·ness,** *n.*

ruff (ruf), *n.* **1** a deep frill, stiff enough to stand out, worn around the neck by men and women in the 1500s and 1600s. **2** a collar-like growth of long or specially marked feathers or hairs on the neck of a bird or other animal. ■ Another word that sounds like this is **rough.**

ruffed (ruft), *adj.* having a ruff.

ruffed grouse, a North American game bird with a thick ruff of feathers and a fan-shaped tail.

ruf·fi·an (ruf′ē ən), *n.* a rough, brutal, or cruel person; bully; hoodlum.

ruf·fle (ruf′əl), **1** *v.* to destroy the smoothness of; make rough or uneven: *A breeze ruffled the lake. The chicken ruffled its feathers when the dog barked.* **2** *n.* a strip of cloth, ribbon, or lace gathered along one edge and used for trimming. **3** *v.* to gather into a ruffle. **4** *v.* to become ruffled: *The flag ruffled in the breeze.* **5** *v.* to disturb; annoy: *Nothing can ruffle her calm temper.* ◻ *v.* **ruf·fled, ruf·fling.**

rug (rug), *n.* **1** a piece of thick, heavy fabric, used as a floor covering: *a rag rug, a fur rug.* Rugs usually cover only part of a room's floor. **2** (earlier) a thick, warm cloth used as covering: *The coachman wrapped a rug around his legs.*

Rug·by (rug′bē), *n.* **1** a famous English school for boys. **2 rugby, a** an English game played with an oval ball and teams of 13 or 15 players who advance the ball in continuous play by kicking, dribbling, lateral passing, and tackling. No forward passing or blocking interference is permitted. **b** a Canadian version of this game, played by teams of 12.

rug·ged (rug′id), *adj.* **1** covered with rough edges; rough and uneven: *rugged ground, rugged rocks.* **2** able to do and endure much; sturdy; hardy: *Pioneers were rugged people.* **3** strong and irregular: *rugged features.* **4** harsh; stern; severe: *rugged times.* **5** rude; unpolished; unrefined: *rugged manners.* **6** stormy: *rugged weather.* —**rug′ged·ly,** *adv.* —**rug′ged·ness,** *n.*

Ruhr (rùr), *n.* **1** river in W Germany flowing into the Rhine. **2** a rich mining and industrial region along this river.

ru·in (rü′ən), **1** *n.* Often, **ruins,** *pl.* what is left after a building, wall, etc., has fallen to pieces: *the ruins of an ancient city.* **2** *n.* very great damage; destruction; overthrow; decay: *The ruin of property caused by the earthquake was enormous. Her enemies planned the queen's ruin.* **3** *n.* condition of destruction, decay, or downfall: *The house had gone to ruin from neglect.* **4** *n.* cause of destruction, decay, or downfall: *Reckless spending will be your ruin.* **5** *v.* to bring to ruin; destroy; spoil: *Rain ruined our picnic.* **6** *v.* to make bankrupt. —**ru′in·er,** *n.*

SYNONYM STUDY **Ruin** and **wreck** both mean the remains of something destroyed. **Ruin** is used mostly about buildings, often in the plural: *They went to see the ruins of the old castle.* **Wreck** is used about machines or vehicles: *After the collision the car was a wreck.*

ru·in·a·tion (rü′ə nā′shən), *n.* ruin; destruction; downfall.

ru·in·ous (rü′ə nəs), *adj.* **1** bringing ruin; causing destruction: *ruinous expense, a ruinous war.* **2** fallen into ruins; ruined: *a building in a ruinous condition.* —**ru′in·ous·ly,** *adv.* —**ru′in·ous·ness,** *n.*

rule (rül), **1** *n.* statement of what to do and not to do; a principle governing conduct, action, arrangement, etc.; law: *the rules of a club, to obey the rules of the game, the rules of the road.* **2** *v.* to make a rule; decide. **3** *v.* to make a formal decision: *The judge ruled against them.* **4** *v.* to control, govern, or manage: *The majority rules in a democracy.* **5** *n.* control; government: *In a democracy the people have the rule.* **6** *n.* period of power of a ruler; reign: *The Revolutionary War took place during the rule of George III.* **7** *n.* a regular method; thing that usually happens or is done; what is usually true: *Fair weather is the rule in Arizona.* **8** *v.* to prevail in; dominate: *Wit rules all her poems.* **9** *n.* ruler (def. 2). **10** *v.* to mark with lines: *I used a ruler to rule the paper.* ◻ *v.* **ruled, rul·ing.**

as a rule, normally; generally.

rule out, to decide against; exclude.

SYNONYM STUDY **Rule** and **govern** both mean to have political power over others. **Rule** can suggest absolute power: *Hitler ruled Germany for 12 years.* **Govern** suggests the wise use of limited power: *The county is governed by six commissioners.*

rule of thumb, 1 rule based on experience or practice rather than on scientific knowledge. **2** a rough, practical method of procedure: *As a rule of thumb, I get one quart of ice cream for every six guests.*

rul·er (rü′lər), *n.* **1** person who rules or governs. Kings and queens are rulers. **2** a straight strip of wood, metal, or plastic, often marked in inches or centimeters, used in drawing lines or in measuring; rule. [See Word Story at **rector.**]

rul·ing (rü′ling), **1** *n.* decision of a judge or court: *a ruling on a point of law.* **2** *adj.* governing; controlling: *the ruling class.* **3** *adj.* predominating; prevalent; chief: *Her tape collection is her ruling passion.*

rum (rum), *n.* **1** an alcoholic liquor distilled from sugar cane, molasses, etc. **2** any alcoholic liquor.

Ru·ma·ni·a (rü mā′nē ə), *n.* Romania. —**Ru·ma′ni·an,** *adj., n.*

rum·ba (rum′bə), *n.* **1** a lively ballroom dance that originated in Cuba. **2** music for this dance. ◻ *n., pl.* **rum·bas.**

rum·ble (rum′bəl), **1** *v.* to make a deep, heavy, continuous sound: *Thunder rumbled in the distance.* **2** *n.* a deep, heavy, continuous sound: *We heard the far-off rumble of thunder.* **3** *v.* to move with such a sound: *The train rumbled through the station.* ◻ *v.* **rum·bled, rum·bling.**

rumble seat, an extra, outside seat for two in the back of some early coupes and roadsters.

rumble seat

ru·mi·nant (rü′mə nənt), **1** *n.* any animal that chews the cud. Cows, sheep, and camels are ruminants. **2** *adj.* belonging to the group of such animals. **3** *adj.* thoughtful; meditative; reflective. —**ru′mi·nant·ly,** *adv.*

ruin (def. 1)

ru·mi·nate (rü′mə nāt), *v.* **1** to think or ponder; meditate; reflect: *She ruminated on the strange events of the past week.* **2** to chew the cud. ❑ *v.* **ru·mi·nat·ed, ru·mi·nat·ing.** **–ru′mi·na′tion,** *n.* **–ru′·mi·na′tor,** *n.*

ru·mi·na·tive (rü′mə nā′tiv), *adj.* meditative. **–ru′mi·na·tive·ly,** *adv.*

rum·mage (rum′ij), **1** *v.* to search thoroughly by moving things about: *I rummaged through three drawers before I found my gloves.* ■ See Synonym Study at **search.** **2** *v.* to search in a disorderly way: *He rummaged in the drawer for a sheet of paper.* **3** *v.* to pull from among other things; bring to light: *She rummaged change from the bottom of her purse.* **4** *n.* a thorough search in which things are moved about. ❑ *v.* **rum·maged, rum·mag·ing.** **–rum′mag·er,** *n.*

WORD STORY **Rummage** comes from a French word meaning "to put cargo into the hold of a ship." In the process of stowing the cargo, many things had to be moved around before it could all be neatly put away. Once it was put away, many things had to be moved to get anything out again. So **rummage** now means to search in a way that moves things around a lot.

rummage sale, sale of odds and ends, old clothing, etc., usually held to raise money for charity.

rum·my (rum′ē), *n.* a kind of card game in which points are scored by forming sets of three or four cards of the same rank or sequences of three or more cards of the same suit.

ru·mor (rü′mər), **1** *n.* story or statement talked of as news without any proof that it is true: *The rumor spread that a new school would be built here.* **2** *n.* vague, general talk: *Rumor has it that the new girl went to school in France.* **3** *v.* to tell or spread by rumor: *It was rumored that the government was going to increase taxes.*

rump (rump), *n.* **1** the hind part of the body of an animal, where the legs join the back. **2** a cut of beef from this part.

rum·ple (rum′pəl), **1** *v.* to wrinkle; crush; crumple: *a rumpled sheet of paper.* **2** *v.* to muss up; disorder: *The wind rumpled my hair.* **3** *n.* a wrinkle; crease. ❑ *v.* **rum·pled, rum·pling.**

rum·pus (rum′pəs), *n.* INFORMAL. a noisy disturbance or uproar.

run (run), **1** *v.* to go by moving the legs quickly; go faster than walking: *A horse can run faster than a person.* **2** *v.* to go in a hurry; hasten: *Run for help.* **3** *v.* to make a quick trip: *Let's run over to the lake for the weekend.* **4** *v.* to escape; flee: *Run for your life.* **5** *v.* to cause to run; cause to move: *run a horse up and down a track.* **6** *v.* to do by running: *run a race, run errands.* **7** *v.* to keep going; go; move: *This train runs from Kansas City to St. Louis. Does your watch run well?* **8** *v.* to amount; add up: *Prices of hats run as high as $50.* **9** *v.* to creep; trail; climb: *Vines run up the sides of the chimney.* **10** *v.* to pass or cause to pass quickly: *The thought ran through my mind that I might forget my speech. She ran her eyes over the old notes before discarding them.* **11** *v.* to stretch; extend: *Shelves run along the walls. A fence runs around the yard. The road runs from New York to Atlanta.* **12** *v.* to drive; force; thrust: *He ran a splinter into his hand.* **13** *v.* to flow with; flow: *Blood runs from a cut. The streets ran oil after an oil truck overturned.* **14** *v.* to discharge fluid, mucus, or pus: *My nose runs whenever I have a cold.* **15** *v.* to get; become; pass into a certain condition: *Never run into debt. The well ran dry.* **16** *v.* to have a specified character, quality, form, size, etc.: *That suit runs large.* **17** *v.* to spread: *The color ran when the shirt was washed.* **18** *v.* to continue; last: *a lease to run two years. The play ran for a whole season.* **19** *v.* to take part in a race or contest: *She's looking forward to running in the race tomorrow.* **20** *v.* to be a candidate for election: *run for class president.* **21** *v.* to expose yourself to: *run the risk of catching cold.* **22** *v.* to move easily, freely, or smoothly; keep operating: *A rope runs in a pulley. The engine ran all day without overheating.* **23** *v.* to cause to move easily, freely, or smoothly; cause to keep operating: *run a machine.* **24** *v.* to be worded or expressed: *How does the first verse run?* **25** *n.* act of running: *When the bell rang we set out at a run.* **26** *n.* spell or period of causing a machine, etc., to operate: *During a run of eight hours the factory produced 100 cars.* **27** *n.* amount of anything produced during such a period: *a run of 100 cars.* **28** *n.* a trip, especially a regular trip over a certain route: *She makes a*

daily run to town for the mail.* **29** *n.* a quick trip: *Let's take a run over to the lake.* **30** *v.* to conduct; manage: *run a business.* **31** *n.* unit of score in baseball or cricket. **32** *n.* time; period; spell: *a run of wet weather, a run of bad luck.* **33** *n.* succession of performances: *This play has had a run of two years.* **34** *n.* onward movement; progress; course; trend: *the run of events.* **35** *n.* a sudden demand or series of demands: *a run on the bank to draw out money.* **36** *n.* (in music) a rapid succession of tones. **37** *n.* kind or class: *the usual run of children's books.* **38** *n.* free use: *The guests were given the run of the house.* **39** *v.* to go without restraint: *The children were allowed to run about the garden.* **40** *n.* flow or rush of water; small stream. **41** *n.* number of fish moving together: *a run of salmon.* **42** *n.* stretch of ground or enclosed space for animals: *a dog run, a chicken run.* **43** *v.* to drop stitches; ravel: *Nylon stockings often run.* **44** *n.* a place where stitches have slipped out or become undone: *a run in a stocking.* **45** *v.* to sew by pushing a needle in and out with even stitches in a line. **46** *v.* to get past or through: *Enemy ships tried to run the blockade.* **47** *v.* to publish an advertisement, story, etc., in a newspaper, magazine, etc.: *run an ad in the paper.* **48** *v.* to be suffering from: *run a fever, run a temperature.* ❑ *v.* **ran, run, run·ning.**

a run for your money, 1 strong competition. **2** satisfaction for your expenditures, efforts, etc.: *The travel agent promised to give the tourists a run for their money.*

in the long run, on the whole; in the end.

on the run, 1 hurrying. **2** in retreat or rout; fleeing.

run across, to meet or find by chance: *I ran across several old photographs in the attic.*

run away with, to win easily over others: *He ran away with every prize in the tournament.*

run down, 1 to stop working or going: *The clock has run down.* **2** to chase till caught: *The fox ran down the hare.* **3** to knock down by running against. **4** to speak evil against.

run for it, to run for safety.

run in, 1 INFORMAL. to arrest and put in jail. **2** to pay a short visit.

run into, 1 to meet by chance. **2** to crash into; collide with.

run off, to print: *to run off 1000 copies for a first edition.*

run out, to come to an end: *After three minutes his time ran out on the telephone call.*

run out of, to use up; have no more.

run out on, 1 to leave suddenly; desert: *My friends didn't run out on me when I was having a difficult time.* **2** to back out of; not be faithful to: *They ran out on their promise to help me.*

run over, 1 to ride or drive over: *The car ran over some glass.* **2** to overflow. **3** to go through quickly.

run through, 1 to use up, spend, or consume rapidly or recklessly. **2** to make a hole through; pierce. **3** to review or rehearse: *The teacher ran through the homework assignment a second time.*

run up, 1 to make quickly: *The team ran up a big lead in the first quarter.* **2** to collect; accumulate: *Don't run up a big bill.*

SYNONYM STUDY **Run, jog**[1], and **sprint** all mean to move the legs quickly. **Run** is the general word: *An ostrich can run more than twice as fast as a human being.* **Jog** means to trot or run slowly, especially for exercise: *He jogs two miles every day.* **Sprint** means to run at full speed for a short distance: *Once around the track is as far as I can sprint.*

run·a·bout (run′ə bout′), *n.* **1** (earlier) a light, open car or carriage. **2** a small motorboat.

run·a·round (run′ə round′), *n.* avoidance or postponement of action, especially in regard to a request.

run·a·way (run′ə wā′), **1** *n.* person, horse, etc., that runs away. **2** *n.* a running away. **3** *adj.* running with nobody to guide or stop it; out of control: *a runaway horse.* **4** *adj.* done by runaways: *a runaway marriage.* **5** *adj.* easily won: *a runaway victory.*

R

a	hat	ė	term	ô	order	ch	child		
ā	age	i	it	oi	oil	ng	long	ə	a in about
ä	far	ī	ice	ou	out	sh	she		e in taken
â	care	o	hot	u	cup	th	thin		i in pencil
e	let	ō	open	ů	put	ᴛʜ	then		o in lemon
ē	equal	ȯ	saw	ü	rule	zh	measure		u in circus

run·back (run′bak′), *n.* (in football) a run made by a player after catching a kick, intercepting a pass, or recovering an opponent's fumble.

run·down (run′doun′), *n.* an account; summary: *a rundown of events.*

run·down (run′doun′), *adj.* **1** tired; sick: *People who don't eat properly may become run-down.* **2** falling to pieces; partly ruined: *a run-down shack in the mountains.* **3** no longer wound up.

run-down (def. 2)

rune (rün), *n.* **1** any letter of an ancient Germanic alphabet. **2** a mark, verse, or saying that is believed to have some mysterious, magic meaning.

rung[1] (rung), *v.* past participle of **ring**[2]: *The bell has rung.* ■ Another word that sounds like this is **wrung.**

rung[2] (rung), *n.* **1** a round rod or bar used as a step of a ladder. **2** crosspiece set between the legs of a chair or as part of the back or arm of a chair. ■ Another word that sounds like this is **wrung.**

ru·nic (rü′nik), *adj.* written in runes; marked with runes.

run-in (run′in′), *n.* INFORMAL. a sharp disagreement; argument; quarrel.

run·ner (run′ər), *n.* **1** person, animal, or thing that runs. **2** (in baseball) a player on the team at bat who either is on base or is running to the next base. **3** messenger: *a runner for a bank.* **4** one of the narrow pieces on which a sleigh, sled, or ice skate slides. **5** a long, narrow strip: *a runner of carpet in the hall.* **6** person or ship that tries to evade somebody; smuggler: *a blockade runner.* **7** a low, slender, horizontal stem that takes root along the ground, producing new plants. Strawberry plants spread by runners.

run·ner-up (run′ər up′), *n.* player or team that takes second place in a contest.

run·ning (run′ing), **1** *n.* act of a person, animal, or thing that runs: *Running is good exercise.* **2** *adj.* flowing: *running water.* **3** *adj.* going or carried on continuously: *a running commentary.* **4** *adv.* following in succession: *for three nights running.* **5** *adj.* performed with or during a run: *a running leap.* **6** *adj.* discharging fluid, mucus, or pus: *a running sore, a running nose.*

be in the running, to have a chance to win.

be out of the running, to have no chance to win.

running board, a step attached below the door on some cars and trucks.

running knot, slipknot.

running mate, candidate in an election who is paired with another candidate from the same political party running for a more important office.

run·ny (run′ē), *adj.* that runs: *a runny nose.* ❏ *adj.* **run·ni·er, run·ni·est.**

Run·ny·mede (run′ē mēd′), *n.* meadow near London where King John granted the Magna Charta in 1215.

run·off (run′ôf′), *n.* **1** a final, deciding race or contest: *There will be a runoff election next month if no candidate receives a majority of the votes cast.* **2** something that runs off, such as rain that flows from the land in streams.

run-of-the-mill (run′əv ᴛʜə mil′), *adj.* average or commonplace; ordinary.

run-on entry (run′ôn′ *or* run′on′), a dictionary entry which is not defined. It is formed by adding a common suffix to a defined entry and appears in heavy type at the end of that entry. The run-on entry **ruthlessly** appears at the end of the entry **ruthless.**

run-on sentence, sentence in which a comma is put between two main clauses where a period, semicolon, or conjunction belongs. EXAMPLE: We were early, the school was still closed.

runt (runt), *n.* animal, person, or plant which is smaller than the usual size. ■ If used about a person, **runt** is sometimes considered offensive.

runt·y (run′tē), *adj.* unusually small. ❏ *adj.* **runt·i·er, runt·i·est.** –**runt′i·ness,** *n.*

run·way (run′wā′), *n.* **1** a paved strip at an airport on which aircraft land and take off. **2** way, track, groove, trough, etc., along which something moves, slides, etc.

ru·pee (rü pē′), *n.* unit of money in India, Pakistan, and certain other countries. ❏ *n., pl.* **ru·pees.**

rup·ture (rup′chər), **1** *n.* act of breaking or the condition of being broken: *The rupture of a blood vessel usually causes the mark of a bruise.* **2** *n.* act of breaking off of friendly relations. **3** *v.* to break off; burst: *There was a bluish mark on his thigh where a blood vessel ruptured.* **4** *n.* hernia. **5** *v.* to affect with or suffer hernia. ❏ *v.* **rup·tured, rup·tur·ing.**

ru·ral (rùr′əl), *adj.* in the country; belonging to the country; like that of the country: *a rural school, rural roads.* –**rur′al·ly,** *adv.*

rural delivery or **rural free delivery,** free delivery of mail in country districts by regular carriers.

rural route, a mail route for country areas.

ruse (rüz *or* rüs), *n.* scheme to mislead others; trick.

rush[1] (rush), **1** *v.* to move with speed or force: *The river rushed past. We rushed to the station.* **2** *v.* to send, push, or force with speed or haste: *Rush this order, please.* **3** *v.* to go or act with speed or haste: *They rush into things without knowing anything about them.* **4** *v.* to attack with much speed and force: *The soldiers rushed the enemy.* **5** *n.* act of rushing; dash: *The rush of the flood swept everything before it.* **6** *n.* busy haste; hurry: *the rush of city life.* **7** *n.* a great or sudden effort of many people to go somewhere or get something: *a gold rush, the Christmas rush.* **8** *n.* eager demand; pressure: *a rush for tickets to a play. A sudden rush of business kept her working hard.* **9** *adj.* requiring haste: *A rush order must be filled at once.* ❏ *n., pl.* **rush·es.** –**rush′er,** *n.*

rush[2] (rush), *n.* **1** a grasslike plant with a hollow stem, that grows in wet soil or marshy places. **2** stem of such a plant, used for making chair seats, baskets, floor mats, etc. ❏ *n., pl.* **rush·es.** –**rush′like′,** *adj.*

rush hour, time of day when traffic is heaviest and trains, buses, etc., are most crowded.

Mount Rushmore

Rush·more (rush′môr′), *n.* **Mount,** mountain in the Black Hills of South Dakota. Huge heads of Washington, Jefferson, Theodore Roosevelt, and Lincoln are carved on its side.

WORD STORY The name of this mountain, **Mount Rushmore,** comes from a joke. A visitor named Rushmore asked the mountain's name, and someone said, "Oh, that's Mount Rushmore." People played along, and the name became permanent.

rusk (rusk), *n.* **1** piece of bread or cake toasted in the oven. **2** kind of light, soft, sweet biscuit.

Russ., **1** Russia. **2** Russian.

Rus·sell (rus′əl), *n.* **1** Ber·trand (bėr′trənd), 1872-1970, British philosopher, mathematician, and writer. He attempted to prove that all of mathematics is derived from logic and uses only concepts that can be logically defined. **2 Bill** (bil), born 1934, American basketball player and coach. He was the first African American head coach in major league professional sports when he was a player and the coach of the Boston Celtics from 1966 to 1969.

rus·set (rus′it), **1** *adj.* yellowish brown or reddish brown: *the scarlet, yellow, and russet leaves of autumn.* **2** *n.* a yellowish brown or a reddish brown. **3** *n.* kind of winter apple with a rough, brownish skin.

Rus·sia (rush′ə), *n.* **1** a country in E Europe and N Asia. From 1917 to 1991 it formed a large part of the Soviet Union. Before 1917 it was part of an empire ruled by a czar. *Capital:* Moscow. **2** the Soviet Union.

Rus·sian (rush′ən), **1** *adj.* of or about Russia, its people, or their language. **2** *n.* person born or living in Russia. **3** *n.* the chief language of Russia.

WORD SOURCE **Russian** has given many words to the English language. The words below are some of them.

babushka	Cossack	pogrom	steppe
Bolshevik	czar	samovar	tundra
borscht	gulag	shaman	vodka
borzoi	mammoth	soviet	yurt
commissar	parka	sputnik	

Russian dressing, a salad dressing made of mayonnaise, chili sauce, chopped pickles, onions, etc.

Russian Orthodox Church, the self-governing Russian branch of the Eastern Church. It was the national church of Russia before 1917.

Russian Revolution, revolution which overthrew the government of Nicholas II in 1917, and later that year established the Bolshevik government under Lenin.

Russian Soviet Federated Socialist Republic, formerly, the largest republic in the Soviet Union, occupying three fourths of the country's area; now called Russia.

Russian wolfhound, borzoi.

rust (rust), **1** *n.* the reddish brown or orange coating that forms on iron or steel exposed to air or moisture. **2** *v.* to cover or become covered with this coating: *Don't let the tools rust by leaving them out in the rain. The rain rusted the tools.* **3** *v.* to become spoiled by not being used: *Don't let your mind rust during vacation.* **4** *v.* to spoil by not using. **5** *n.* any plant disease that spots leaves and stems. **6** *n.* any of numerous fungi that produce such diseases. **7** *adj.* reddish brown or orange. **8** *n.* a reddish brown or orange. —**rust′less,** *adj.*

rus·tic (rus′tik), **1** *adj.* belonging to the country; suitable for the country; rural: *The play had a rustic setting.* **2** *adj.* simple; plain: *Their rustic speech and ways made them feel uncomfortable in the royal palace.* **3** *n.* a country person. **4** *adj.* made of branches with the bark still on them: *rustic furniture, a rustic fence.* —**rus′ti·cal·ly,** *adv.*

rus·tic·i·ty (rus′tis′ə tē), *n.* **1** rustic quality, characteristic, or peculiarity. **2** rural life.

rus·tle (rus′əl), **1** *v.* to make or cause to make a light, soft sound of things gently rubbing together: *The leaves rustled in the breeze. The wind rustled the papers.* **2** *n.* this sound. **3** *v.* to steal cattle, horses, etc. ❑ *v.* **rus·tled, rus·tling.**

rustle up, **1** to gather; find. **2** to get ready; prepare: *The cook rustled up some food.*

rus·tler (rus′lər), *n.* a cattle thief.

rust·proof (rust′prüf′), *adj.* resisting rust.

rust·y (rus′tē), *adj.* **1** covered with rust; rusted: *a rusty knife.* **2** made by rust: *a rusty stain, a rusty spot.* **3** colored like rust. **4** no longer good or effective from lack of use or practice: *She hadn't played tennis for months, so her game was rusty.* ❑ *adj.* **rust·i·er, rust·i·est.** —**rust′i·ly,** *adv.* —**rust′i·ness,** *n.*

rut (rut), **1** *n.* a track made in the ground by wheels. **2** *v.* to make ruts in. **3** *n.* a fixed or established way of acting; a boring routine: *He was so set in his ways that everyone said he was in a rut.* ❑ *v.* **rut·ted, rut·ting.**

ru·ta·ba·ga (rü′tə bā′gə), *n.* a kind of large, yellow or white root like a turnip, eaten as a vegetable and fed to animals. ❑ *n., pl.* **ru·ta·ba·gas.**

Ruth (rüth), *n.* **1** (in the Bible) a widow who was very devoted to her mother-in-law, Naomi. Ruth left her native land of Moab to go with Naomi to Bethlehem. **2** book of the Bible about her. [**Ruth** comes from a Hebrew word meaning "friend."]

Ruth (rüth), *n.* **George Her·man** (hėr′mən), 1895-1948, American baseball player. He was better known as Babe Ruth.

ru·the·ni·um (rü thē′nē əm), *n.* a brittle, white, metallic element which is found in platinum ores. *Symbol:* Ru

Ruth·er·ford (ruth′ər fərd), *n.* **Er·nest** (ėr′nəst), 1871-1937, British physicist, born in New Zealand, who developed the basic theories of nuclear physics.

ruth·er·ford·i·um (ruth′ər fôr′dē əm), *n.* proposed name for a radioactive metallic element, produced artificially from californium.

ruth·less (rüth′lis), *adj.* having no pity; showing no mercy; cruel. —**ruth′less·ly,** *adv.* —**ruth′less·ness,** *n.*

Rut·land (rut′lənd), *n.* city in S central Vermont.

RV, recreational vehicle.

Rwan·da (rü än′də), *n.* country in central Africa, north of Burundi. *Capital:* Kigali.

Ry., railway.

rye (rī), *n.* **1** a hardy annual cereal grass widely grown in cold regions. **2** its seeds, used for making flour, as food for livestock, and in making whiskey. **3** bread made from rye flour: *She ordered a ham on rye.* **4** whiskey made from rye. ■ Another word that sounds like this is **wry.**

a	hat	ė	term	ô	order	ch	child	
ā	age	i	it	oi	oil	ng	long	a in about
ä	far	ī	ice	ou	out	sh	she	e in taken
â	care	o	hot	u	cup	th	thin	ə i in pencil
e	let	ō	open	u̇	put	ŦH	then	o in lemon
ē	equal	ȯ	saw	ü	rule	zh	measure	u in circus

S or **s** (es), *n.* **1** the 19th letter of the English alphabet. **2** anything shaped like an S: *The road curved in a big S.* ❑ *n., pl.* **S's** or **s's.**

S, symbol for sulfur.

S or **S., 1** Saint. **2** Saturday. **3** September. **4** south. **5** southern. **6** Sunday.

s., 1 second. **2** shilling or shillings. **3** singular. **4** son. **5** south. **6** southern.

S.A., 1 South Africa. **2** South America.

Saar (sär *or* zär), *n.* **1** river flowing from NE France into W Germany. **2** state in W Germany, along the Saar River.

Saar·i·nen (sär′ə nen), *n.* **Ee·ro** (e′rō), 1910-1961, American architect, born in Finland. He designed many public and corporate buildings, including airport terminals in Washington, D.C., and New York.

Sa·bah (sä′bə), *n.* state in N Borneo, a part of Malaysia.

Sab·bath (sab′əth), *n.* day of the week used for rest and worship by some religious groups. Sunday is the Sabbath for most Christians; Saturday is the Jewish Sabbath.

sab·bat·i·cal (sə bat′ə kəl), *adj.* **1** of or suitable for the Sabbath. **2** of or for a rest from work. Once in seven years some teachers have a sabbatical leave for rest, study, or travel.

sa·ber (sā′bər), *n.* a heavy sword, usually slightly curved, having a single cutting edge. Also, **sabre.**

sa·ber-toothed tiger (sā′bər tütht′), any of several large, fierce cats something like tigers, extinct since about 10,000 years ago. They had very long, curved upper canine teeth.

Sa·bin (sā′bən), *n.* **Al·bert** (al′bərt), 1906-1993, American physician who developed a polio vaccine that can be taken by mouth.

sa·ble (sā′bəl), *n.* **1** a small, flesh-eating, Asian mammal similar to and related to weasels. **2** its dark brown, shiny, costly fur.

sab·o·tage (sab′ə täzh), **1** *n.* damage done by enemy agents or sympathizers, by civilians of a conquered nation, etc. **2** *n.* damage done to work, tools, machinery, etc., by workers as an attack or threat against an employer. **3** *v.* to damage or destroy deliberately: *to sabotage an ammunition plant.* ❑ *v.* **sab·o·taged, sab·o·tag·ing.**

WORD STORY **Sabotage** comes from a French word meaning "shoe damage." Angry French weavers sometimes threw their heavy, wooden shoes into the weaving machinery, breaking it.

sab·o·teur (sab′ə tėr′), *n.* person who sabotages.

sa·bra (sä′brə), *n.* a Jewish person born in Israel. ❑ *n., pl.* **sa·bras.**

sa·bre (sā′bər), *n.* saber.

sac (sak), *n.* a part like a bag in an animal or plant, often one containing liquids. ∎ Another word that sounds like this is **sack.** —**sac′like′,** *adj.*

Sac·a·ja·we·a (sak′ə jə wē′ə), *n.* 1787?-1812?, Shoshoni guide and interpreter. She accompanied the Lewis and Clark expedition to the Northwest. [**Sacajawea** comes from Shoshoni words meaning "bird woman."]

sac·char·in (sak′ər ən), *n.* a very sweet substance produced from coal tar, used as a substitute for sugar. It has no food value.

sac·char·ine (sak′ər ən), *adj.* **1** overly sweet; sugary: *a saccharine smile.* **2** of or like sugar. **—sac′char·ine·ly,** *adv.*

sac·er·do·tal (sas′ər dō′tl), *adj.* of or about priests or the priesthood; priestly. **—sac′er·do′tal·ly,** *adv.*

sa·chem (sā′chəm), *n.* (among some North American Indians) the chief of a tribe or confederation.

sa·chet (sa shā′), *n.* a small bag or pad containing perfumed powder, placed among articles of clothing. ■ Another word that sounds like this is **sashay.**

sack¹ (sak), **1** *n.* a large bag made of coarse cloth. Sacks are used for holding grain, flour, potatoes, and coal. **2** *n.* a paper or plastic bag. **3** *n.* amount that a sack will hold: *a sack of candy. We bought two sacks of corn.* **4** *v.* to put into a sack or sacks: *to sack grain or salt.* **5** *v.* (in football) to tackle the quarterback behind the line of scrimmage. **6** *n.* a loose coat: *a knitted sack for a baby.* **7** *v.* to dismiss from a job; fire. **8** *n.* INFORMAL. bed. ■ Another word that sounds like this is **sac. —sack′like′,** *adj.*

sack out, INFORMAL. to go to bed.

sack² (sak), **1** *v.* to plunder a captured city. **2** *n.* act or process of plundering a captured city: *the sack of Rome by the barbarians.* ■ Another word that sounds like this is **sac. —sack′er,** *n.*

sack·cloth (sak′klôth′), *n.* **1** coarse cloth for making sacks. **2** coarse cloth worn as a sign of mourning or penance.

sack·ful (sak′fůl), *n.* enough to fill a sack. ❑ *n., pl.* **sack·fuls.**

sack·ing (sak′ing), *n.* coarse cloth for making sacks.

sa·cra (sā′krə), *n.* a plural of **sacrum.**

sac·ra·ment (sak′rə mənt), *n.* **1** (in Christian churches) any of certain religious ceremonies. Baptism and the Eucharists are sacraments. **2** Often, **Sacrament,** the Eucharist; Holy Communion.

sac·ra·men·tal (sak′rə men′tl), *adj.* of or about a sacrament; used in a sacrament: *sacramental wine.*

Sac·ra·men·to (sak′rə men′tō), **1** capital of California, in the central part. **2** river flowing from N California to San Francisco Bay.

sa·cred (sā′krid), *adj.* **1** belonging to or dedicated to God; holy: *the sacred altar, a sacred building.* **2** connected with religion; religious: *sacred writings, sacred music.* **3** worthy of reverence: *the sacred memory of a dead hero.* **4** not to be violated or disregarded: *a sacred promise.* **—sa′cred·ness,** *n.*

WORD FAMILY Sacred and the words below are related. They all come from a Latin word meaning "holy."

consecrate	sacristan	sanction
desecrate	sacrosanct	sanctuary
sacrament	saint	sanctum
sacrifice	sanctify	Santa
sacrilege	sanctimonious	sexton

sacred cow, person or thing that is thought to be above criticism or opposition.

sac·ri·fice (sak′rə fis), **1** *n.* act of offering to a god. **2** *n.* the thing offered: *The ancient Hebrews killed animals on altars as sacrifices to God.* **3** *v.* to give or offer to a god: *They sacrificed oxen, sheep, and doves.* **4** *n.* act of giving up of one thing for another: *Our teacher does not approve of any sacrifice of studies to sports.* **5** *v.* to give up: *sacrifice your life for another, sacrifice business for pleasure.* **6** *n.* loss from selling something below its value: *They sold their house at a sacrifice because they needed the money.* **7** *v.* to sell at a loss. **8** *n.* (in baseball) a bunt that helps a base runner to advance, or a fly that allows a base runner to score, although the batter is put out. ❑ *v.* **sac·ri·ficed, sac·ri·fic·ing. —sac′ri·fic′er,** *n.*

sac·ri·fi·cial (sak′rə fish′əl), *adj.* of or used in a sacrifice: *sacrificial rites.* **—sac′ri·fi′cial·ly,** *adv.*

sac·ri·lege (sak′rə lij), *n.* an intentional injury to anything sacred; disrespectful treatment of anyone or anything sacred: *Robbing the church was a sacrilege.*

sac·ri·le·gious (sak′rə lij′əs), *adj.* injurious or insulting to sacred persons or things. **—sac′ri·le′gious·ly,** *adv.*

sac·ris·tan (sak′ri stən), *n.* person in charge of the sacred vessels, robes, etc., of a church.

sac·ris·ty (sak′ri stē), *n.* place where the sacred vessels, robes, etc., of a church are kept. ❑ *n., pl.* **sac·ris·ties.**

sac·ro·sanct (sak′rō sangkt), *adj.* very holy; very sacred.

sa·crum (sā′krəm), *n.* bone at the lower end of the spine, made by the joining of several vertebrae, forming the back of the pelvis. ❑ *n., pl.* **sa·cra** or **sa·crums.**

sad (sad), *adj.* **1** unhappy; full of sorrow: *You feel sad if your best friend goes away.* **2** causing sorrow: *a sad accident.* **3** extremely bad: *a sad state of affairs.* ❑ *adj.* **sad·der, sad·dest. —sad′ly,** *adv.* **—sad′ness,** *n.*

WORD STORY Sad comes from an old English word meaning "satisfied," used to describe people who had eaten or drunk all they wanted. Having no appetite and feeling full often makes people less than cheerful, as our modern phrase "fed up" suggests.

Sa·dat (sä dät′), *n.* **An·war** (an′wär), 1918-1981, president of Egypt from 1970 to 1981. He shared the 1978 Nobel Peace Prize with Menachem Begin.

sad·den (sad′n), *v.* to make or become sad: *Her face saddened at the news.*

sad·dle (sad′l), **1** *n.* seat for a rider on a horse's back, or on a bicycle or motorcycle. **2** *n.* thing shaped like a saddle. A ridge between two mountain peaks is called a saddle. **3** *v.* to put a saddle on. **4** *v.* to burden: *He is saddled with too many jobs.* **5** *n.* a cut of mutton, venison, lamb, etc., consisting of both loins and the back portion between them. ❑ *v.* **sad·dled, sad·dling.**

in the saddle, in a position of control.

sad·dle·bag (sad′l bag′), *n.* one of a pair of bags laid over an animal's back behind the saddle, or over the rear fender of a bicycle or motorcycle.

saddle horse, horse for riding.

sad·dler (sad′lər), *n.* person who makes or sells saddles and harnesses.

saddle shoe, a low shoe, usually white, with the instep crossed by a band of leather of a different color.

sa·dism (sā′diz′əm *or* sad′iz′əm), *n.* **1** practice of someone who gets pleasure from hurting someone else. **2** an unnatural love of cruelty.

sa·dist (sā′dist *or* sad′ist), *n.* **1** person who gets pleasure from hurting someone else. **2** person having an unnatural love of cruelty.

sa·dis·tic (sə dis′tik), *adj.* cruel; showing cruelty: *a sadistic villain.* **—sa·dis′ti·cal·ly,** *adv.*

sa·fa·ri (sə fär′ē), *n.* **1** journey or hunting expedition in eastern Africa. **2** any long trip or expedition. ❑ *n., pl.* **sa·fa·ris.**

safe (sāf), **1** *adj.* free from harm or danger: *Keep money in a safe place.* **2** *adj.* not harmed: *He returned from war safe and sound.* **3** *adj.* out of danger; secure: *We feel safe with the dog in the house.* **4** *adj.* not able to harm or injure: *Several wild dogs were locked up safe in the truck.* **5** *adj.* careful: *a safe guess, a safe move.* **6** *adj.* dependable: *a safe guide.* **7** *n.* a steel or iron box for money, jewels, papers, etc. **8** *adj.* (in baseball) reaching a base without being out. ❑ *adj.* **saf·er, saf·est. —safe′ly,** *adv.* **—safe′ness,** *n.*

safe (def. 8)

a	hat	ė	term	ô	order	ch	child		a in about
ā	age	i	it	oi	oil	ng	long		e in taken
ä	far	ī	ice	ou	out	sh	she	ə	i in pencil
â	care	o	hot	u	cup	th	thin		o in lemon
e	let	ō	open	ù	put	ŦH	then		u in circus
ē	equal	ò	saw	ü	rule	zh	measure		

S

safe·con·duct (sāf/kon/dukt), *n.* **1** privilege of passing safely through a region, especially in time of war: *At the start of the war, neutrals were given safe-conduct out of the country.* **2** paper granting this privilege.

safe-de·pos·it box (sāf/di poz/it), box for storing valuable things, especially in a bank vault.

safe·guard (sāf/gärd/), **1** *v.* to keep safe; guard against hurt or danger; protect: *Pure food laws safeguard our health.* **2** *n.* protection; defense: *Keeping clean is a safeguard against disease.*

safe·keep·ing (sāf/kē/ping), *n.* protection; keeping safe; care.

safe sex, sexual activity that does not include the exchange of bodily fluids, such as sperm or saliva.

safe·ty (sāf/tē), *n.* **1** the condition of being safe; freedom from harm or danger: *A bank assures safety for your money. You can cross the street in safety when the green light is on.* **2** device to prevent injury or accident. A gun cannot be fired if the safety is on. **3** in football: **a** a play in which an offensive player downs the ball, or is downed, behind the offensive goal line. A safety counts two points for the defensive team. **b** a defensive player who plays closest to the defensive goal line. □ *n., pl.* **safe·ties** for 2,3.

safety belt, seat belt.

safe·ty-de·pos·it box (sāf/tē di poz/it), CANADIAN. safe-deposit box.

safety glass, glass that resists shattering, made of two or more layers of glass joined together by a layer of transparent plastic.

safety match, match that will light only when you rub it against a specially prepared surface.

safety net, 1 a large net placed below a tightrope or trapeze so that it will catch anyone who falls or jumps. **2** something that provides security in case of failure or loss.

safety pin, pin bent back on itself to form a spring and having a guard that covers the point and prevents accidental unfastening.

safety razor, razor with the blade shielded to prevent it from cutting the skin deeply.

safety touch, (in Canadian football) safety (def. 3a).

safety valve, 1 valve in a steam boiler, etc., that opens and lets steam or fluid escape when the pressure becomes too great. Pressure cookers have a safety valve. **2** something that helps someone get rid of anger, nervousness, etc., in a harmless way.

saf·flow·er (saf/lou/ər), *n.* plant like a thistle, with large flower heads. Its seeds yield an oil used for cooking.

saf·fron (saf/rən), **1** *n.* a purple autumn crocus with yellowish orange stigmas. **2** *n.* a yellowish orange coloring obtained from the dried stigmas of this crocus. Saffron is used to color and flavor candy, drinks, etc. **3** *n.* a yellowish orange. **4** *adj.* yellowish orange.

sag (sag), **1** *v.* to sink under weight or pressure; bend down in the middle, as a rope, beam, cable, plank, etc. **2** *v.* to hang down unevenly: *Your dress sags in the back.* **3** *v.* to become weaker: *Our courage sagged.* **4** *n.* act, state, or degree of sagging. **5** *n.* place where anything sags. □ *v.* **sagged, sag·ging.**

sa·ga (sä/gə), *n.* **1** a Norse or Icelandic story of heroic deeds, written between the 1100s and the 1300s. **2** any story of heroic deeds. □ *n., pl.* **sa·gas.**

sa·ga·cious (sə gā/shəs), *adj.* wise in a keen, practical way; shrewd. **—sa·ga/cious·ly,** *adv.* **—sa·ga/cious·ness,** *n.*

sa·gac·i·ty (sə gas/ə tē), *n.* keen, sound judgment; mental acuteness; shrewdness: *The lawyer displayed sagacity in questioning the witnesses.*

sag·a·more (sag/ə môr/), *n.* (among some North American Indians) a chief or great man, sometimes loyal to a sachem.

Sa·gan (sā/gən), *n.* **Carl** (kärl), born 1934, American astronomer. He has helped popularize astronomy with his books and articles and his TV show.

sage[1] (sāj), **1** *adj.* showing wisdom or good judgment: *a sage reply.* **2** *adj.* wise: *The queen surrounded herself with sage advisers.* **3** *n.* a very wise man: *The sage gave advice to his king.* □ *adj.* **sag·er, sag·est.**

sage[2] (sāj), *n.* **1** any of numerous herbs related to mint, especially a small bush with gray-green leaves used to season food. **2** sagebrush.

sage·brush (sāj/brush/), *n.* any of several grayish bushes that smell like sage, especially one that is common on the dry plains of western North America.

Sag·it·tar·i·us (saj/ə tãr/ē əs), *n.* **1** group of stars that looks something like an archer. **2** the ninth sign of the zodiac, associated with the period from mid-November to mid-December.

sa·go (sā/gō), *n.* **1** a starchy food used in making puddings and soups. **2** sago palm. □ *n., pl.* **sa·gos** for 2.

sago palm, any of several palm trees that grow in the East Indies. Sago is obtained from their stems.

sa·gua·ro (sə gwär/ō), *n.* a very tall, branching cactus of southern Arizona and neighboring regions. □ *n., pl.* **sa·gua·ros.**

Sa·har·a (sə hãr/ə or sə här/ə), *n.* the world's largest desert, in N Africa. **—Sa·har/an,** *adj., n.*

sa·hib (sä/ib), *n.* sir; master (in colonial India, a term of respect used to or about Europeans).

said (sed), **1** *v.* past tense and past participle of **say:** *He said he would come. They had said "No" every time.* **2** *adj.* named or mentioned before: *the said witness, the said sum of money.*

Sai·gon (sī gon/), *n.* former name of **Ho Chi Minh City.**

sail (sāl), **1** *n.* piece of cloth attached to the rigging of a ship to catch the wind and make the ship move through the water. **2** *n.* something like a sail, such as the part of an arm of a windmill that catches the wind. **3** *n.* trip on a boat with sails or on any other vessel: *Let's go for a sail.* **4** *v.* to travel on water by the action of wind on sails. **5** *v.* to travel on a steamboat, etc. **6** *v.* to move smoothly like a ship with sails: *The eagle sailed by. The duchess sailed into the room.* **7** *v.* to sail upon, over, or through: *sail the seas.* **8** *v.* to manage a ship or boat: *The girls are learning to sail.* **9** *v.* to begin a trip by water: *We sail at 2 P.M.* ■ Another word that sounds like this is **sale. —sail/like/,** *adj.*

sail into, INFORMAL. **1** to attack; beat. **2** to criticize; scold: *She sailed into us for being late.*

set sail, to begin a trip by water.

under sail, with the sails spread out.

saguaro

sail·board (sāl/bôrd/), *n.* surfboard to which a mast and a hand-held sail are attached by a universal joint. Speed and direction are controlled by moving the sail.

sail·boat (sāl/bōt/), *n.* boat that is moved by a sail or sails. Schooners and sloops are kinds of sailboats.

sail·cloth (sāl/klôth/), *n.* canvas used for making sails.

sail·fish (sāl/fish/), *n.* any of several large saltwater fishes that have a long, high fin on the back. Sailfish are related to the swordfish. □ *n., pl.* **sail·fish** or **sail·fish·es.**

sail·ing (sā/ling), *n.* **1** act of someone or something that sails. **2** art of operating a ship; navigation.

sail·or (sā/lər), *n.* **1** person whose work is handling a boat or other vessel. **2** member of a ship's crew who is not an officer. **3** a flat-brimmed straw hat modeled after the kind of hat sailors used to wear long ago.

sail·plane (sāl/plān/), *n.* a lightweight glider. Its very long wings enable it to fly by taking advantage of rising air currents.

saint (sānt), *n.* **1** a very holy person. **2** person who has gone to heaven. **3** person declared a saint by the Roman Catholic Church. **4** person who is very humble, patient, etc., like a saint. **—saint/like/,** *adj.*

Saint. For names of saints look under the Christian name, and for other entries beginning with "Saint" look under the **St.** words.

Saint Ber·nard (bər närd′), a big, brown and white dog with a large head. This dog was first bred by monks to rescue travelers lost in the Swiss Alps.

saint·ed (sān′tid), *adj.* **1** declared to be a saint. **2** thought of as a saint; gone to heaven. **3** sacred; saintly.

saint·hood (sānt′hůd), *n.* character or status of a saint.

saint·ly (sānt′lē), *adj.* like a saint; very holy; very good. ❑ *adj.* **saint·li·er, saint·li·est. —saint′li·ness,** *n.*

Saint Bernard

Saint Nicholas, Santa Claus.

Saint Nick, Santa Claus.

Saint Patrick's Day, March 17. It is an Irish national holiday.

Saint Valentine's Day, February 14, day on which valentines are exchanged.

Sai·pan (sī pan′), *n.* **1** island in the W Pacific, one of the Mariana Islands. **2** capital of Northern Marianas.

saith (seth), *v.* OLD USE. says.

sake[1] (sāk), *n.* **1** cause; account; interest: *Put yourself to no trouble for our sakes.* **2** purpose; end: *We moved to the country for the sake of peace and quiet.*

sa·ke[2] (sä′kē), *n.* an alcoholic drink made from fermented rice, popular in Japan.

Sak·har·ov (sak′ə rôf), *n.* **An·drei** (än′drā), 1921-1989, Russian physicist and human rights leader. He won the 1975 Nobel Peace Prize.

sa·laam (sə läm′), **1** *n.* a greeting used especially in Muslim countries. **2** *n.* a very low bow, with the palm of the right hand placed on the forehead. **3** *v.* to greet with a salaam. [Salaam comes from an Arabic word meaning "peace."]

sal·a·ble (sā′lə bəl), *adj.* fit to be sold; easily sold. **—sal′a·bil′i·ty,** *n.*

sa·la·cious (sə lā′shəs), *adj.* **1** obscene; indecent. **2** lustful; lewd. **—sa·la′cious·ly,** *adv.* **—sa·la′cious·ness,** *n.*

sal·ad (sal′əd), *n.* raw green vegetables, such as lettuce, cabbage, and celery, served with a dressing. Often cold meat, fish, eggs, cooked vegetables, or fruits are used along with, or instead of, the raw green vegetables.

salad bar, a table with various salad ingredients, for customers to take whatever they want.

salad days, days of youthful inexperience.

salad dressing, sauce used in or on a salad.

sal·a·man·der (sal′ə man′dər), *n.* any of numerous animals shaped like lizards, but related to frogs and toads. Salamanders have moist, smooth skin and live in water or in damp places.

sa·la·mi (sə lä′mē), *n.* kind of thick sausage, often flavored with garlic. It is usually sliced and eaten cold. ❑ *n., pl.* **sa·la·mis.** [Salami comes from a Latin word meaning "salt." Salami contains much salt, which helps to preserve it.]

sal·a·ried (sal′ər ēd), *adj.* receiving or bringing in a salary: *a salaried employee, a salaried position.*

sal·ar·y (sal′ər ē), *n.* a fixed sum of money paid for work done: *Her yearly salary was $38,000.* ❑ *n., pl.* **sal·ar·ies.**

WORD STORY
Salary comes from a Latin word meaning "salt." Roman soldiers were given money for salt to preserve their food with. Even now, people who are good at their jobs are said to be "worth their salt."

sale (sāl), *n.* **1** act of selling; exchange of goods or property for money: *the sale of a house.* **2 sales,** *pl.* **a** amount sold: *Today's sales were larger than yesterday's.* **b** business of selling: *His first job was in sales.* **3** act of selling at lower prices than usual: *This store is having a sale on suits.* **4** an auction. ■ Another word that sounds like this is **sail.**

for sale, to be sold: *There are several houses in the neighborhood for sale, but none for rent.*

on sale, for sale at lower prices than usual: *The grocer has coffee on sale.*

Sa·lem (sā′ləm), *n.* **1** port in NE Massachusetts, settled in 1626. **2** capital of Oregon, in the NW part. [Salem comes from a Hebrew word meaning "peace."]

sales·clerk (sālz′klėrk′), *n.* person whose work is selling in a store.

sales·man (sālz′mən), *n.* person whose work is selling. ❑ *n., pl.* **sales·men.**

sales·man·ship (sālz′mən ship), *n.* **1** work of a salesman. **2** ability at selling.

sales·peo·ple (sālz′pē′pəl), *n.pl.* salespersons.

sales·per·son (sālz′pėr′sən), *n.* person whose work is selling, especially in a store.

sales talk, 1 a talk by a salesperson to sell something. **2** any talk intended to persuade: *She asked me to lunch, but it was just a sales talk for joining the neighborhood club.*

sales tax, tax based on the amount received for articles sold.

sales·wom·an (sālz′wům′ən), *n.* woman whose work is selling, especially in a store. ❑ *n., pl.* **sales·wom·en.**

sal·i·cyl·ic acid (sal′ə sil′ik), a white, crystalline powder used as a mild antiseptic and preservative, and in making aspirin.

sa·li·ent (sā′lē ənt), **1** *adj.* easily seen or noticed; most important; prominent: *The audience applauded the salient points in her speech.* **2** *n.* part of a fortification or line of trenches that sticks out toward an enemy.

Sa·li·nas de Gor·ta·ri (sä lē′näs dā gôr tär′ē), **Car·los** (kär′lōs), born 1948, president of Mexico from 1988 to 1994.

sa·line (sā′lēn′), **1** *adj.* of or like salt; salty. **2** *adj.* containing common salt or any other salts: *a saline solution.* **3** *n.* solution with a high concentration of salt, used in medical examinations and treatment. **—sa·lin·i·ty** (sə lin′ə tē), *n.*

WORD FAMILY	**Saline** and the words below are related. They all come from a Latin word meaning "salt."

salad	salt	sassy	sausage
salami	saltine	sauce	silt
salary	saltpeter	saucer	

Sa·lin·ger (sal′in jər), *n.* **J. D.,** born 1919, American writer. He wrote fiction about sensitive young people, especially in his novel *The Catcher in the Rye.* J. D. stands for Jerome David.

Sal·is·bur·y (sôlz′ber′ē), *n.* **1** city in S England. A famous cathedral is located there. **2** former name of **Harare.**

Salisbury steak, chopped beef shaped before cooking into a patty about twice the size of a hamburger, usually served with gravy.

Sa·lish (sā′lish), *n.* a member of a group of American Indian tribes living in the Pacific Northwest. ❑ *n., pl.* **Sa·lish** or **Sa·lish·es.**

sa·li·va (sə lī′və), *n.* liquid produced by glands in the mouth to keep it moist, help in chewing, and start digestion.

sal·i·var·y (sal′ə vâr′ē), *adj.* of or producing saliva: *the salivary glands.*

sal·i·vate (sal′ə vāt), *v.* to produce saliva, especially an increased amount. ❑ *v.* **sal·i·vat·ed, sal·i·vat·ing. —sal′i·va′tion,** *n.*

Salk (sôlk), *n.* **Jo·nas** (jō′nəs), 1914-1995, American physician who developed the first effective polio vaccine.

Salk vaccine, vaccine containing dead polio viruses which causes the body to produce antibodies. It protects against infection from live polio viruses.

sal·low (sal′ō), *adj.* having a sickly, yellowish color: *a sallow complexion.* **—sal′low·ness,** *n.*

sal·ly (sal′ē), **1** *v.* to set out briskly: *We sallied forth at dawn.* **2** *n.* act of rushing out suddenly: *The men in the fort made a brave sally and returned with many prisoners.* **3** *n.* excursion; jaunt. **4** *n.* a witty remark: *She continued her story undisturbed by the merry sallies of her hearers.* ❑ *v.* **sal·lied, sal·ly·ing;** *n., pl.* **sal·lies.**

sal·ma·gun·di (sal′mə gun′dē), *n.* **1** dish of chopped meat, anchovies, eggs, onions, oil, seasonings, etc. **2** any mixture of unlike things. ❑ *n., pl.* **sal·ma·gun·dis** or **sal·ma·gun·dies.**

S

a	hat	ė	term	ô	order	ch	child		a in about
ā	age	i	it	oi	oil	ng	long		e in taken
ä	far	ī	ice	ou	out	sh	she	ə	i in pencil
â	care	o	hot	u	cup	th	thin		o in lemon
e	let	ō	open	ů	put	ŦH	then		u in circus
ē	equal	ȯ	saw	ü	rule	zh	measure		

salm·on (sam′ən), **1** *n.* any of several large saltwater and fresh-water food fishes with silvery scales and yellowish pink flesh. They are common in the northern Atlantic and northern Pacific near the mouths of large rivers, which they swim up in order to spawn. **2** *n.* a yellowish pink. **3** *adj.* yellowish pink. ❑ *n., pl.* **salm·on** or **salm·ons.**

salmon (def. 1)—up to 19 in. (48 cm) long

salm·on·ber·ry (sam′ən ber′ē), *n.* the tasty, salmon-colored fruit of a plant related to the raspberry, found along the Pacific coast of North America.

sal·mo·nel·la (sal′mə nel′ə), *n.* one of a group of bacteria that cause food poisoning, typhoid fever, and other dangerous dis-eases. ❑ *n., pl.* **sal·mo·nel·lae** (sal′mə nel′ē), **sal·mo·nel·as.**

sa·lon (sə lon′), *n.* **1** a fashionable or stylish shop. **2** a gathering of distinguished persons, especially the regular gathering of fa-mous artists, writers, politicians, etc., as guests of a well-known host or hostess. **3** place used to exhibit works of art. **4** a large room for receiving or entertaining guests.

sa·loon (sə lün′), *n.* **1** place where alcoholic drinks are sold and drunk; tavern. **2** a large room for general or public use: *The ship's passengers ate in the dining saloon.*

sal·sa (säl′sə), *n.* **1** a spicy sauce made with onions, tomatoes, and hot peppers. **2** a popular style of music from Latin America, with influences from jazz and rock. **3** a lively dance performed to this music. ❑ *n., pl.* **sal·sas.**

sal soda (sal), sodium carbonate.

salt (sôlt), **1** *n.* a white mineral found in the earth and in seawa-ter; common table salt; sodium chloride. Salt is used to season and preserve food. **2** *adj.* of or containing salt: *a salt solution.* **3** *v.* to season with salt; sprinkle salt on: *to salt popcorn.* **4** *v.* to preserve with salt: *to salt cod.* **5** *v.* to scatter salt on; apply salt to: *salt roads to melt ice and snow.* **6** *adj.* cured or preserved with salt: *salt pork.* **7** *adj.* flooded with or growing in salt water: *salt marshes, salt grass.* **8** *v.* to make lively and interesting: *conver-sation salted with wit.* **9** *n.* something that gives liveliness or in-terest. **10** *n.* any chemical compound made from an acid by re-placing the hydrogen in the acid with a metal or a molecule acting like a metal. Sodium bicarbonate is a salt. **11** *n.pl.* **salts, a** a medicine that causes emptying of the intestines. **b** smelling salts. **12** *n.* INFORMAL. sailor. —**salt′er,** *n.* —**salt′like′,** *adj.*

salt away, to store for later: *She salted away money for her old age.*

salt down, to pack with salt to preserve: *salt down fish.*

salt of the earth, the best people.

worth your salt, worth what you receive in wages, meals, etc.

WORD STORY   Salt of the earth comes from Jesus' Sermon on the Mount in the Bible. He used this phrase to describe his disciples, because salt is used in preserving food, and a small amount of salt can save a lot of food from being lost. A few disciples can save many souls from being lost.

salt·box (sôlt′boks′), *n.* a wooden house with two stories in front, one in back, and a long sloping roof section usually over the kitchen. Saltboxes are common in New England. ❑ *n., pl.* **salt·box·es.**

salt·cel·lar (sôlt′sel′ər), *n.* shaker or dish for holding salt, used on the table.

salt flat, a large, level area of land coated with salt left by water that has evaporated from a lake or sea formerly there.

salt·ine (sôl tēn′), *n.* a thin, crisp, salted cracker.

Salt Lake City, capital of Utah, in the N part.

salt lick, a place where natural salt is found on the ground and where animals go to lick it up.

salt·pe·ter (sôlt′pē′tər), *n.* **1** potassium nitrate; niter. **2** sodium nitrate; niter. **Chile saltpeter** is a naturally occurring form of sodium nitrate used as a fertilizer.

salt·shak·er (sôlt′shā′kər), *n.* holder for salt, with holes in the top through which the salt is sprinkled.

salt·wa·ter (sôlt′wô′tər), *adj.* **1** made up of salt and water: *a saltwater solution.* **2** living in the sea or in water like seawater: *saltwater fish.* **3** working on the sea: *a saltwater fisherman.*

salt·y (sôl′tē), *adj.* **1** containing salt; tasting of salt. Sweat and tears are salty. **2** to the point; witty and a bit improper: *a salty re-mark.* ❑ *adj.* **salt·i·er, salt·i·est.** —**salt′i·ly,** *adv.* —**salt′i·ness,** *n.*

sa·lu·bri·ous (sə lü′brē əs), *adj.* healthful: *a salubrious diet.* —**sa·lu′bri·ous·ly,** *adv.* —**sa·lu′bri·ous·ness,** *n.*

sal·u·tar·y (sal′yə ter′ē), *adj.* **1** beneficial: *The teacher gave the boy salutary advice.* **2** good for the health; wholesome: *Walking is a salutary exercise.* —**sal′u·tar′i·ly,** *adv.* —**sal′u·tar′i·ness,** *n.*

sal·u·ta·tion (sal′yə tā′shən), *n.* **1** act of greeting or saluting: *The man raised his hand in salutation.* **2** something said, written, or done to salute: *Begin your letter with the salutation "Dear Sir." A curtsy was her parting salutation.*

sa·lu·ta·to·ri·an (sə lü′tə tôr′ē ən), *n.* student who gives the ad-dress of welcome at the graduation of a class. The salutatorian is often the student who ranks second in his or her class.

sa·lu·ta·to·ry (sə lü′tə tôr′ē), **1** *adj.* expressing greeting; wel-coming. **2** *n.* an opening address welcoming guests at the gradu-ation of a class. ❑ *n., pl.* **sa·lu·ta·to·ries.**

sa·lute (sə lüt′), **1** *v.* to honor in a formal manner by raising the hand to the head, by firing guns, by dipping flags, etc.: *The sol-dier saluted the officer.* **2** *v.* to meet with kind words, a bow, a kiss, etc.; greet: *The old gentleman walked along the avenue saluting his friends.* **3** *n.* act of saluting; sign of welcome, farewell, or honor: *The queen gracefully acknowledged the salutes of the crowd.* **4** *v.* to make a salute. **5** *n.* position of the hand, gun, etc., in saluting. ❑ *v.* **sa·lut·ed, sa·lut·ing.** —**sa·lut′er,** *n.*

Salvador, *n.* See El Salvador.

sal·vage (sal′vij), **1** *n.* act of saving a ship or its cargo from wreck, capture, etc. **2** *n.* payment for saving it. **3** *n.* rescue of property from fire, flood, shipwreck, etc. **4** *v.* to save from fire, flood, shipwreck, etc. **5** *n.* property salvaged: *the salvage from a shipwreck, the salvage from a fire.* ❑ *v.* **sal·vaged, sal·vag·ing.** —**sal′vage·a·ble,** *adj.* —**sal′vag·er,** *n.*

sal·va·tion (sal vā′shən), *n.* **1** act of saving or condition of being saved. **2** person or thing that saves. **3** (in Christian use) a saving of the soul; deliverance from sin and from punishment for sin.

Salvation Army, organization to preach to and help the poor, founded in England in 1865 by William Booth.

salve (sav), **1** *n.* a soft, greasy ointment put on wounds and sores to soothe or heal them. **2** *v.* to put salve on. **3** *n.* something sooth-ing; balm: *The kind words were a salve to his hurt feelings.* **4** *v.* to soothe; smooth over: *She salved her conscience by the thought that her lie harmed no one.* ❑ *v.* **salved, salv·ing.**

sal·vo (sal′vō), *n.* **1** act of firing several guns at the same time as a broadside or as a salute. **2** round of cheers or applause. ❑ *n., pl.* **sal·vos** or **sal·voes.**

Salz·burg (sôlz′bėrg′), *n.* city in W Austria. Annual music festi-vals are held there.

S. Am., South America.

sam·a·ra (sam′ər ə), *n.* any dry seedcase that has a winglike ex-tended part and does not split open when it is ripe; key. The seeds of maple trees grow in double samaras. ❑ *n., pl.* **sam·a·ras.**

Sa·mar·i·a (sə mâr′ē ə), *n.* **1** district in the N part of ancient Palestine, now in Jordan. **2** chief city of this district. See **Galilee** for map.

Sa·mar·i·tan (sə mâr′ə tən), *n.* **1** person born or living in Samaria. **2** person who helps another in trouble or distress; Good Samaritan.

sa·mar·i·um (sə mâr′ē əm), *n.* a metallic element that is hard, brittle, and grayish white. It is used in magnets. *Symbol:* Sm

Sam·ar·qand (sam′ər kand′), *n.* city in Uzbekistan, north of Afghanistan.

sam·ba (säm′bə), *n.* **1** a dance that began in Africa and changed into a ballroom dance in Brazil. **2** music for this dance. ❑ *n., pl.* **sam·bas.**

same (sām), **1** *adj.* not another; identical: *We came back the same way we went.* **2** *adj.* just alike; not different: *His name and mine are the same.* **3** *adj.* unchanged: *It is the same beautiful place.* **4** *adj.* just spoken of: *We were talking about my aunt. This same aunt will be visiting us next week.* **5** *pron.* the same person or thing. **6** *adv.* **the same,** in the same manner: *"Sea" and "see" are pronounced the same.*

all the same, notwithstanding; nevertheless.

just the same, 1 in the same manner. **2** nevertheless.

SYNONYM STUDY **Same** and **equal** both mean exactly alike. **Same** is a general word: *He and I are wearing the same shirt today.* **Equal** means alike in number, size, or amount: *Divide the pie so that everyone gets an equal piece.*

same·ness (sām′nis), *n.* **1** condition of being the same; exact likeness. **2** lack of variety; tiresomeness.

sam·i·sen (sam′ə sen), *n.* a Japanese instrument like a banjo, having three strings and played by plucking the strings.

Sa·mo·a (sə mō′ə), *n.* group of islands in the S Pacific. Several of these islands (**American Samoa**) belong to the United States and the rest make up the independent country of **Western Samoa.** —**Sa·mo′an,** *adj., n.*

sam·o·var (sam′ə vär), *n.* a metal urn used especially by Russians to heat water for tea.

Sam·o·yed (sam′ə yed′ *or* sam·oi′ed), *n.* a large, long-haired dog with a thick white coat, first bred in Siberia.

sam·pan (sam′pan), *n.* a type of small boat used in China, Japan, etc. A sampan is propelled by one or more oars at the stern; it usually has a single sail.

sam·ple (sam′pəl), **1** *n.* part to show what the rest is like; one thing to show what the others are like: *Here are some samples of drapery material for you to choose from.* **2** *adj.* serving as an example: *a sample copy.* **3** *v.* to take a part of; test a part of: *We sampled the cake and found it very good.* ❑ *v.* **sam·pled, sam·pling.**

samovar

sam·pler[1] (sam′plər), *n.* person who samples.

sam·pler[2] (sam′plər), *n.* piece of cloth embroidered to show skill in needlework.

sam·pling (sam′pling), *n.* **1** act or process of taking samples. **2** something taken or serving as a sample.

Samp·son (samp′sən), *n.* **Deborah,** 1760-1827, American soldier. ■ **Deborah Sampson** enlisted in the Revolutionary Army disguised as a man. When she was finally discovered, General Washington ordered that she be honorably discharged.

Sam·son (sam′sən), *n.* **1** (in the Bible) a man who had very great strength. He lost his strength when Delilah cut his hair. **2** any very strong man. [**Samson** comes from Hebrew words meaning "man of the sun."]

Sam·u·el (sam′yü əl), *n.* **1** a Hebrew leader, judge, and prophet of the 1000s B.C. **2** either one of two books of the Bible. [**Samuel** comes from Hebrew words meaning "name of God."]

sam·u·rai (sam′ú rī′), *n.* **1** the military class in feudal Japan, consisting of the retainers of the great nobles. **2** member of this class. ❑ *n., pl.* **sam·u·rai.**

San (sän), *n.* member of a roving hunting people of southern Africa. ❑ *n., pl.* **Sans** or **San.** ■ See Usage Note at **Bushman.**

Sa·naa (sä nä′), *n.* capital of Yemen.

San An·dre·as Fault (san än drā′əs), a large break in the earth's crust, located in California. It is a center of earthquake activity.

San An·to·ni·o (san an tō′nē ō), city in S Texas. The Alamo is there.

san·a·to·ri·um (san′ə tôr′ē əm), *n.* place for treatment of the sick or those recovering from illness. People who are suffering from a sickness that takes a long time to cure, like tuberculosis, often go to sanatoriums. ❑ *n., pl.* **san·a·to·ri·ums, san·a·to·ri·a** (san′ə tôr′ē ə). Also, **sanitarium.**

sanc·ti·fy (sangk′tə fī), *v.* **1** to make holy; make free from sin. **2** to set apart as sacred; observe as holy: *"Lord, sanctify this our offering to Thy use."* **3** to make right; justify or sanction: *a custom sanctified by law.* ❑ *v.* **sanc·ti·fied, sanc·ti·fy·ing.** —**sanc′ti·fi′a·ble,** *adj.* —**sanc′ti·fi·ca′tion,** *n.* —**sanc′ti·fi′er,** *n.*

sanc·ti·mo·ni·ous (sangk′tə mō′nē əs), *adj.* making a show of holiness; putting on airs of sanctity. —**sanc′ti·mo·ni·ous·ly,** *adv.* —**sanc′ti·mo·ni·ous·ness,** *n.*

sanc·tion (sangk′shən), **1** *n.* permission with authority; support; approval: *You need the owner's sanction to cross this property.* **2** *v.* to authorize; approve; allow: *Her conscience does not sanction stealing.* **3** *n.* a mild form of punishment, such as a blockade, trade limitations, or the like, carried out by one or more countries against some country, and intended to force it to obey international law: *economic sanctions.*

sanc·ti·ty (sangk′tə tē), *n.* **1** holiness; saintliness; godliness. **2** sacredness; holy character: *the sanctity of a church, the sanctity of the home.*

sanc·tu·ar·y (sangk′chü er′ē), *n.* **1** a sacred place. A church is a sanctuary. **2** part of a church around the altar. **3** place of refuge or protection: *a wildlife sanctuary.* **4** refuge or protection: *The cabin provided sanctuary from the rain.* ❑ *n., pl.* **sanc·tu·ar·ies** for 1-3.

WORD STORY **Sanctuary** comes from a Latin word meaning "a holy place." In the Middle Ages, people could avoid being arrested by staying in a church. The laws of that time said that a person could be protected there.

sanc·tum (sangk′təm), *n.* **1** a sacred place. **2** a private room or office where someone can be undisturbed. ❑ *n., pl.* **sanc·tums, sanc·ta** (sangk′tə).

sand (sand), **1** *n.* tiny grains of worn-down or disintegrated rock: *the sands of the desert, the sands of the seashore.* **2** *v.* to spread sand over: *The highway department sanded the icy road to prevent skidding.* **3** *v.* to smooth or polish with sandpaper: *to sand the edges of a board.*

san·dal (san′dl), *n.* **1** kind of shoe made of a sole fastened to the foot by straps. **2** any of various kinds of open shoes, slippers, etc. [See Word Story at **sandalwood**.]

san·dal·wood (san′dl wūd′), *n.* **1** the fragrant wood of various trees of Asia and Australia, used for making boxes, fans, etc., and burned as incense. **2** any of the trees it comes from.

WORD STORY **Sandalwood** is not used for sandals. The two words are not related. **Sandalwood** comes from the Sanskrit name of these trees, and **sandal** comes from the Greek word for this kind of shoe. People often spell and pronounce unrelated words in similar ways if the words are somewhat alike to start with. This is how we get homographs, homonyms, and homophones.

sand·bag (sand′bag′), **1** *n.* bag filled with sand. Sandbags are used to hold back floods and as ballast on balloons. **2** *v.* to furnish with sandbags: *Homeowners sandbagged their driveways to keep floodwater out of their houses.* **3** *n.* a small bag of sand used as a club. **4** *v.* to hit or stun with or as if with a sandbag. ❑ *v.* **sand·bagged, sand·bag·ging.** —**sand′bag′ger,** *n.*

S

a	hat	ė	term	ô	order	ch	child		a in about
ā	age	i	it	oi	oil	ng	long		e in taken
ä	far	ī	ice	ou	out	sh	she	ə	i in pencil
â	care	o	hot	u	cup	th	thin		o in lemon
e	let	ō	open	ů	put	ŦH	then		u in circus
ē	equal	ò	saw	ü	rule	zh	measure		

sand·bank (sand′bangk′), *n.* ridge of sand.

sand·bar (sand′bär′), *n.* ridge of sand in a river or along a shore, formed by the action of tides or currents.

sand·blast (sand′blast′), **1** *n.* blast of air or steam containing sand, used to clean, grind, cut, or decorate hard surfaces, such as glass, stone, or metal. **2** *v.* to use a sandblast on; clean, grind, cut, or decorate by a sandblast. **—sand′blast′er,** *n.*

sand·box (sand′boks′), *n.* box for holding sand, especially for children to play in. ❏ *n., pl.* **sand·box·es.**

Sand·burg (sand′bėrg′), *n.* **Carl** (kärl), 1878-1967, American poet and biographer of Abraham Lincoln.

sand dollar, a small, flat, round sea animal that lives on sandy bottoms of the ocean. It is a kind of sea urchin.

sand·er (san′dər), *n.* person or machine that sands or sandpapers.

San Di·e·go (san dē ā′gō), port in SW California.

S & L, savings and loan association.

sand·lot (sand′lot′), *adj.* of or about games or sports, especially baseball, played in vacant lots.

sand·man (sand′man′), *n.* (in stories) a man who makes children sleepy by sprinkling sand on their eyes.

sand·pa·per (sand′pā′pər), **1** *n.* a strong paper with a layer of sand or similar substance glued on it, used for smoothing, cleaning, or polishing. **2** *v.* to smooth, clean, or polish with sandpaper.

sand·pip·er (sand′pī′pər), *n.* any of numerous small birds with long bills, living on sandy shores and mud flats.

sand·stone (sand′stōn′), *n.* a sedimentary rock made mostly of sand, used in building.

sand·storm (sand′stôrm′), *n.* windstorm that carries along clouds of sand.

sand·wich (sand′wich), **1** *n.* two or more slices of bread with meat, jelly, cheese, or some other filling between them. **2** *v.* to put or squeeze in: *He was sandwiched between two large boxes.* ❏ *n., pl.* **sand·wich·es.**

WORD STORY **Sandwich** comes from the name of the Earl of Sandwich, a British nobleman of the 1700s, who supposedly invented it so that he would not have to leave a card game to eat.

sand·y (san′dē), *adj.* **1** containing sand; made up of sand: *sandy soil.* **2** covered with sand: *Most of the shore is rocky, but there is a sandy beach.* **3** yellowish red: *She has sandy hair.* ❏ *adj.* **sand·i·er, sand·i·est. —sand′i·ness,** *n.*

sane (sān), *adj.* **1** having a healthy mind; normal; sound; rational. **2** having or showing good sense; sensible: *A driver with a sane attitude doesn't take chances.* ❏ *adj.* **san·er, san·est.** ■ Another word that sounds like this is **seine. —sane′ly,** *adv.* **—sane′ness,** *n.*

San·for·ized (san′fə rīzd′), *adj.* trademark for fabrics that are preshrunk by a special process before they are made into articles of clothing.

San Fran·cis·co (san frən sis′kō), port in W California.

San Francisco

San Francisco Bay, bay of the Pacific on which San Francisco and Oakland, California, are located.

sang (sang), *v.* a past tense of **sing:** *The bird sang sweetly.*

san·gui·nar·y (sang′gwə ner′ē), *adj.* **1** bloody. **2** bloodthirsty. **—san′gui·nar′i·ly,** *adv.* **—san′gui·nar′i·ness,** *n.*

san·guine (sang′gwən), *adj.* **1** naturally cheerful and hopeful: *a sanguine disposition.* **2** confident; hopeful: *sanguine of success.* **3** having a healthy red color; ruddy: *a sanguine complexion.* **—san′guine·ly,** *adv.* **—san·guin·i·ty** (sang gwin′ə tē), *n.*

san·i·tar·i·um (san′ə ter′ē əm), *n.* sanatorium. ❏ *n., pl.* **san·i·tar·i·ums, san·i·tar·i·a** (san′ə ter′ē ə).

san·i·tar·y (san′ə ter′ē), *adj.* **1** of or about health; favorable to health; preventing disease: *sanitary regulations in a hospital.* **2** free from dirt and filth: *Food should be kept in a sanitary place.* **—san′i·tar′i·ly,** *adv.*

sanitary napkin, a soft, disposable pad of material used to absorb blood during menstruation.

san·i·ta·tion (san′ə tā′shən), *n.* the study, development, and practical application of sanitary measures. Disposal of sewage and government inspection of milk, meat, and other foods are important parts of sanitation.

san·i·tize (san′ə tīz), *v.* to make clean; remove germs from: *Dentists sanitize their tools after using them.* ❏ *v.* **san·i·tized, san·i·tiz·ing.**

san·i·ty (san′ə tē), *n.* **1** soundness of mind; mental health. **2** soundness of judgment; sensibleness.

San Ja·cin·to (san′ jə sin′tō), river in SE Texas, flowing into the Gulf of Mexico near Galveston. On April 21, 1836, American forces under General Sam Houston defeated the Mexican army under General Santa Anna here.

San Joa·quin (san′ wä kēn′), river in California, flowing NW into the Sacramento River.

San Jo·se (san hō zā′), city in W central California.

San Jo·sé (san hō zā′), capital of Costa Rica, in the central part.

San Juan (san wän′), port and capital of Puerto Rico, in the NE part.

sank (sangk), *v.* a past tense of **sink:** *The ship sank.*

San Lu·is Po·to·sí (sän′lwēs′pō tō sē′), a state in central Mexico.

San Ma·ri·no (san mə rē′nō), **1** tiny country in N Italy. **2** its capital.

sans (sanz), *prep.* without.

San Sal·va·dor (san sal′və dôr), **1** island of the central Bahamas. **2** capital of El Salvador, in the central part.

San·sei (sän′sā′), *n.* person born in the United States or Canada whose grandparents were Japanese immigrants. ❏ *n., pl.* **San·sei.**

San·skrit (san′skrit), *n.* the ancient literary language of India.

WORD SOURCE **Sanskrit** has given many words to the English language. The words below are some of them.

Buddha	karma	punch[2]	sugar
cheetah	loot	pundit	swami
chintz	maharaja	rajah	swastika
guru	mandarin	rupee	thug
juggernaut	musk	saccharin	yoga
jungle	pagoda	sapphire	yogi

San·ta (san′tə *for noun;* san′tə *or* sän′tä *for adj.*), **1** *n.* Santa Claus. **2** *adj.* a Spanish or an Italian word meaning *holy* or *saint,* used in combinations, as in *Santa Maria.*

San·ta An·na (san′tə *or* sän′tä ä′nä), **An·to·ni·o Ló·pez de** (an tō′nē ō lō′pez dā), 1795-1876, Mexican general and president. His army defeated the Texans at the Alamo, but soon afterward he was defeated and captured.

Santa Claus (klôz′), the spirit of Christmas giving; Saint Nicholas; Saint Nick. He is pictured as a fat, jolly old man with a white beard, dressed in a fur-trimmed red suit.

San·ta Fe (san′tə fā′), capital of New Mexico, in the N part.

Santa Fe Trail, an early trade route between Independence, Missouri, and Santa Fe, New Mexico. See **Oregon Trail** for map.

San·ti·a·go (san′tē ä′gō), *n.* capital of Chile, in the central part.

San·to Do·min·go (san′tō də ming′gō), capital of the Dominican Republic, in the S part. It was established in 1496 and was the first town founded by Europeans in the Western Hemisphere.

São Pau·lo (soun pou′lu̇), city in Brazil, in the SE part, near the Atlantic.

São To·mé (soun tü mā′), capital of São Tomé and Principe.

São To·mé and Prin·ci·pe (soun tü mā′ ənd prin′sə pə), country made up of two islands off W Africa. *Capital:* São Tomé.

sap[1] (sap), *n.* **1** liquid that circulates through a plant, carrying water, food, etc., as blood does in animals. Rising sap carries water and minerals from the roots; sap traveling downward carries sugar, gums, resins, etc. **2** INFORMAL. a fool.

sap[2] (sap), *v.* **1** to dig under or wear away the foundation of: *The walls of the boathouse had been sapped by the waves.* **2** to weaken; use up: *The heat sapped our strength.* ❑ *v.* **sapped, sap·ping**.

sa·pi·ence (sā′pē əns), *n.* wisdom.

sa·pi·ent (sā′pē ənt), *adj.* wise; sage. −**sa′pi·ent·ly,** *adv.*

Sa·pir (sə pir′), *n.* **Edward,** 1884-1939, American anthropologist and linguist, born in Germany. He studied many American Indian languages and investigated how culture and language affect personality.

sap·less (sap′lis), *adj.* **1** without sap; withered. **2** without energy or vigor. −**sap′less·ness,** *n.*

sap·ling (sap′ling), *n.* a young tree.

sap·o·dil·la (sap′ə dil′ə), *n.* a large evergreen tree of tropical America that yields chicle and bears large fruits tasting like pears. ❑ *n., pl.* **sap·o·dil·las.**

sa·pon·i·fy (sə pon′ə fī), *v.* **1** to make a fat or oil into soap by treating with an alkali. **2** to become soap. ❑ *v.* **sa·pon·i·fied, sa·pon·i·fy·ing.** −**sa·pon′i·fi′a·ble,** *adj.* −**sa·pon′i·fi′er,** *n.*

sap·phire (saf′īr), **1** *n.* a clear, hard, usually blue, precious stone. Sapphires are a variety of corundum. **2** *adj.* bright blue. **3** *n.* a bright blue.

sap·py (sap′ē), *adj.* **1** full of sap; juicy. **2** INFORMAL. silly; foolish. ❑ *adj.* **sap·pi·er, sap·pi·est.** −**sap′pi·ness,** *n.*

sap·ro·phyte (sap′rō fīt), *n.* any living thing that lives on decaying organic matter. Many fungi and bacteria are saprophytes.

sapphire

sap·suck·er (sap′suk′ər), *n.* any of several small North American woodpeckers that feed on the sap of trees.

sap·wood (sap′wùd′), *n.* the soft, new, living wood between the bark and the hard inner wood of most trees.

Sar·a·cen (sar′ə sən), **1** *n.* an Arab. **2** *n.* a Muslim at the time of the Crusades. **3** *adj.* of or about the Saracens.

Sar·ah (sâr′ə), *n.* (in the Bible) the wife of Abraham and the mother of Isaac. [**Sarah** comes from a Hebrew word meaning "princess."]

Sa·ra·je·vo (sar′ə yā′vō), *n.* capital of Bosnia and Herzegovina.

sa·ran (sə ran′), *n.* a plastic produced as a fiber, film, or molded form and highly resistant to damage and soiling, used to package food.

Sa·ra·to·ga (sar′ə tō′gə), *n.* village in E New York. It was the site of a major American victory in the Revolutionary War in 1777.

Sa·ra·wak (sə rä′wäk), *n.* state in N Borneo, a member of the Federation of Malaysia.

sar·casm (sär′kaz′əm), *n.* **1** a sneering or cutting remark, often ironical. **2** act of making fun of someone to hurt his or her feelings; harsh or bitter irony: *"How unselfish you are!" said the girl in sarcasm as her sister took the biggest piece of cake.*

WORD STORY **Sarcasm** comes from a Greek word meaning "to strip off flesh." Today we speak of cutting remarks that can wound feelings. Words used as weapons can cause serious pain.

sar·cas·tic (sär kas′tik), *adj.* using sarcasm; sneering; cutting: *"Don't hurry!" was my brother's sarcastic comment as I slowly dressed.* −**sar·cas′ti·cal·ly,** *adv.*

Sar·cee (sär′sē), *n.* member of a tribe of American Indians of the Great Plains, now living in Alberta, Canada. ❑ *n., pl.* **Sar·cee** or **Sar·cees.**

sar·coph·a·gus (sär kof′ə gəs), *n.* a stone coffin, especially an ornamental one. ❑ *n., pl.* **sar·coph·a·gi** (sär kof′ə jī), **sar·coph·a·gus·es.**

WORD STORY **Sarcophagus** comes from a Greek word meaning "to eat the flesh." The ancient Greeks buried their dead in coffins made of blocks of limestone. The stone's high lime content caused the bodies to decompose quickly.

sar·dine (sär dēn′), *n.* a young or small herring or related fish, often preserved in oil for food. ❑ *n., pl.* **sar·dine** or **sar·dines.**

packed like sardines, very crowded.

Sar·din·i·a (sär din′ē ə), *n.* large Italian island in the Mediterranean Sea, west of Italy. See **Castile** for map.

sar·don·ic (sär don′ik), *adj.* bitterly sarcastic, scornful, or mocking: *a sardonic laugh.* −**sar·don′i·cal·ly,** *adv.*

sar·gas·so (sär gas′ō), *n.* sargassum. ❑ *n., pl.* **sar·gas·sos.**

sar·gas·sum (sär gas′əm), *n.* any of several kinds of brown algae with air bladders like berries, floating in large, branching masses.

Sar·gent (sär′jənt), *n.* **John Sin·ger** (sing′ər), 1856-1925, American painter. He painted mainly portraits and spent most of his life in England.

sa·ri (sär′ē), *n.* a long piece of cotton or silk worn wound around the body with one end thrown over the head or shoulder. It is the outer garment of Hindu women. ❑ *n., pl.* **sa·ris.**

sa·rong (sə rông′), *n.* a rectangular piece of cloth, usually a brightly colored, printed material, worn as a skirt by men and women in the East Indies.

sar·sa·pa·ril·la (sas′pə ril′ə *or* sär′sə pə ril′ə), *n.* **1** any of various tropical American climbing or trailing plants. **2** the dried root of a sarsaparilla, used for flavoring. **3** a soft drink flavored with this root. ❑ *n., pl.* **sar·sa·pa·ril·las.**

sari

sar·to·ri·al (sär tôr′ē əl), *adj.* of or about tailors or their work: *His clothes were a sartorial triumph.* −**sar·to′ri·al·ly,** *adv.*

Sar·tre (sär′trə), *n.* **Jean-Paul** (zhän′pôl′), 1905-1980, French philosopher and writer. ■ Sartre believed that people are free to choose their own characters but that they avoid this knowledge. He was awarded the Nobel Prize for literature in 1964 but refused to accept it.

SASE, self-addressed stamped envelope.

sash[1] (sash), *n.* a long, broad strip of cloth, worn round the waist or over one shoulder. ❑ *n., pl.* **sash·es.**

sash[2] (sash), *n.* frame which holds the glass in a window or door. ❑ *n., pl.* **sash·es.**

sa·shay (sa shā′), *v.* INFORMAL. to glide, move, or go about. ■ Another word that sounds like this is **sachet.**

sa·shi·mi (sä shē′mē), *n.* a Japanese dish consisting of thin slices of raw fish, usually dipped in a sauce and eaten as an appetizer.

Sask., Saskatchewan.

Sas·katch·e·wan (sa skach′ə won), *n.* province in S Canada. *Capital:* Regina. [**Saskatchewan** comes from Cree words meaning "rapid" and "current." The province took its name from the Saskatchewan River, which flows through it.]

sas·ka·toon (sas kə tün′), *n.* CANADIAN. any of a group of North American bushes related to roses, with white flowers; shadbush; serviceberry.

sass (sas), INFORMAL. **1** *n.* rudeness; back talk; impudence. **2** *v.* to be rude or disrespectful to: *The little girl sassed her mother.*

sas·sa·fras (sas′ə fras), *n.* **1** a slender American tree that has fragrant yellow flowers and bluish black fruit. **2** the flavorful dried bark of its root, used in medicine, tea, soft drinks, etc.

sas·sy (sas′ē), *adj.* **1** rude. **2** lively; spirited: *a sassy attitude.* **3** stylish: *sassy designs.* ❑ *adj.* **sas·si·er, sas·si·est.**

sat (sat), *v.* past tense and past participle of **sit**: *Yesterday I sat in a train all day. The cat has sat at that mouse hole for hours.*

S

a	hat	ė	term	ô	order	ch	child	ə	a in about
ā	age	i	it	oi	oil	ng	long		e in taken
ä	far	ī	ice	ou	out	sh	she		i in pencil
â	care	o	hot	u	cup	th	thin		o in lemon
e	let	ō	open	ù	put	ŦH	then		u in circus
ē	equal	ò	saw	ü	rule	zh	measure		

Sat., Saturday.

Sa·tan (sāt′n), *n.* (in the Jewish and Christian religions) the supreme evil spirit; the Devil.

sa·tan·ic (sā tan′ik *or* sə tan′ik), *adj.* of or like Satan; like that of Satan; very wicked.

satch·el (sach′əl), *n.* a small bag for carrying clothes, books, etc.; handbag.

sate (sāt), *v.* **1** to satisfy fully any appetite or desire: *A long drink sated his thirst.* **2** to supply with more than enough, so as to weary or disgust. □ *v.* **sat·ed, sat·ing.**

sa·teen (sa tēn′), *n.* a cotton cloth made to imitate satin.

sat·el·lite (sat′l it), *n.* **1** an astronomical object that revolves around a planet; a moon. The moon is a satellite of Earth. **2** an artificial object launched by rocket into an orbit around Earth or some other astronomical object. **3** country that is supposedly independent but is actually controlled by a more powerful country.

satellite (def. 2)

sa·ti·ate (sā′shē āt), *v.* **1** to feed fully; satisfy fully. **2** to supply with too much; weary or disgust with too much: *She was so satiated with bananas that she would not even look at one.* □ *v.* **sa·ti·at·ed, sa·ti·at·ing. —sa′ti·a′tion,** *n.*

sat·in (sat′n), **1** *n.* a silk, rayon, nylon, or cotton cloth with one very smooth, glossy side. **2** *adj.* of or like satin; smooth and glossy.

sat·in·y (sat′n ē), *adj.* like satin in smoothness and gloss.

sat·ire (sat′īr), *n.* **1** the use of sarcasm, irony, or wit to attack or ridicule a habit, idea, custom, etc. **2** poem, essay, story, etc., that attacks or ridicules in this way.

sa·tir·ic (sə tir′ik), *adj.* satirical.

sa·tir·i·cal (sə tir′ə kəl), *adj.* of or containing satire; fond of using satire. **—sa·tir′i·cal·ly,** *adv.*

sat·i·rist (sat′ə rist), *n.* writer of satires; person who uses satire.

sat·i·rize (sat′ə rīz′), *v.* to attack with satire; criticize with mockery; seek to improve by ridicule. □ *v.* **sat·i·rized, sat·i·riz·ing. —sat′i·riz′a·ble,** *adj.* **—sat′i·ri·za′tion. —sat′i·riz′er,** *n.*

sat·is·fac·tion (sat′i sfak′shən), *n.* **1** condition of being satisfied, or pleased and contented: *She felt satisfaction at winning a prize.* **2** anything that makes us feel pleased or contented: *It is a great satisfaction to have things turn out just the way you want.* **3** act of satisfying; fulfillment: *The satisfaction of hunger requires food.* **4** payment of a debt; discharge of an obligation; making up for wrong or injury done.

give satisfaction, **1** to satisfy. **2** to fight a duel because of an insult.

sat·is·fac·to·ri·ly (sat′i sfak′tər ə lē), *adv.* in a satisfactory way.
■ See Synonym Study at **well**[1].

sat·is·fac·to·ry (sat′i sfak′tər ē), *adj.* satisfying; good enough to satisfy; pleasing or adequate. **—sat′is·fac′to·ri·ness,** *n.*

sat·is·fy (sat′i sfī), *v.* **1** to give enough to; fulfill desires, hopes, demands, etc.; put an end to needs, wants, etc.: *He satisfied his hunger with a sandwich and milk.* **2** to make contented; please: *Are you satisfied now?* **3** to pay; make right: *After the accident*

he satisfied all claims for the damage he had caused. **4** to set free from doubt; convince: *I am satisfied that it was an accident.* □ *v.* **sat·is·fied, sat·is·fy·ing. —sat′is·fi·a·ble,** *adj.* **—sat′is·fi′er,** *n.* **—sat′is·fy′ing·ly,** *adv.*

sat·u·rate (sach′ə rāt′), *v.* **1** to soak thoroughly; fill full: *Rain has saturated the ground, so any more will cause flooding.* **2** to cause a substance to combine with the greatest possible amount of another substance. A saturated salt solution cannot dissolve more salt. □ *v.* **sat·u·rat·ed, sat·u·rat·ing. —sat′u·ra′tor,** *n.*

sat·u·rat·ed fat, solid or semisolid animal fat, such as butter or lard. It contains fatty acids with carbon atoms that have combined with the greatest possible number of other atoms.

sat·u·ra·tion (sach′ə rā′shən), *n.* **1** act or process of saturating. **2** saturated condition. Saturation of a salt solution occurs when no more salt will dissolve in the water.

Sat·ur·day (sat′ər dā′ *or* sat′ər dē), *n.* the seventh day of the week, following Friday.

WORD STORY Saturday comes from **Saturn** and the old English word meaning "day." It is the only day with a name that comes from a Latin word. No one knows why.

Sat·urn (sat′ərn), *n.* **1** the second largest planet in the solar system and the sixth in distance from the sun. Saturn is encircled by a system of rings made of tiny particles of ice and rock. **2** the Roman god of agriculture, thought to have ruled during a golden age.

Sat·ur·na·li·a (sat′ər nā′lē ə), *n.pl. or sing.* the ancient Roman festival of Saturn, celebrated in December with much feasting and merrymaking.

sat·ur·nine (sat′ər nīn), *adj.* gloomy; unfriendly.

sa·tyr (sā′tər), *n.* a Greek deity of the woods, like a man with the tail of a goat or horse.

sauce (sôs), **1** *n.* something, usually a liquid, served with or on food to make it taste better. We eat mint sauce with lamb, egg sauce with fish, and many different sauces with puddings. **2** *n.* stewed fruit: *cranberry sauce.* **3** *v.* to prepare with sauce; season. **4** *n.* rudeness: *Don't give me any sauce!* □ *v.* **sauced, sauc·ing.**

sauce·pan (sôs′pan′), *n.* a small pan with a handle, used for stewing, boiling, etc.

sau·cer (sô′sər), *n.* **1** a shallow dish to set a cup on. **2** something round and shallow like a saucer. **—sau′cer·like′,** *adj.*

sau·cy (sô′sē), *adj.* showing lack of respect; rude: *saucy language or conduct.* □ *adj.* **sau·ci·er, sau·ci·est. —sau′ci·ly,** *adv.* **—sau′ci·ness,** *n.*

Sau·di (sou′dē *or* sô′dē), **1** *adj.* of or about Saudi Arabia. **2** *n.* person born or living in Saudi Arabia. □ *n., pl.* **Sau·dis.**

Saudi Arabia, country in central Arabia. *Capital:* Riyadh. **—Saudi Arabian.**

sauer·kraut (sour′krout′), *n.* cabbage cut up fine, salted, and allowed to sour.

Sauk (sôk), *n.* member of a tribe of American Indians formerly living in Michigan, Wisconsin, and Illinois, now living in Iowa, Kansas, and Oklahoma. □ *n., pl.* **Sauk** or **Sauks.** [Sauk comes from an Algonquian word meaning "yellow earth."]

Saul (sôl), *n.* in the Bible: **1** the first king of Israel. **2** the original name of the apostle Paul. [Saul comes from a Hebrew word meaning "desire."]

Sault Sainte Ma·rie or **Sault Ste. Ma·rie** (sü′ sānt mə rē′), rapids in the river connecting Lake Superior and Lake Huron. Canals around the rapids enable ships to pass between the two lakes.

sau·na (sou′nə *or* sô′nə), *n.* **1** a steam bath in which the steam is produced by water thrown on hot stones. **2** building or room used for such a steam bath. □ *n., pl.* **sau·nas.**

saun·ter (sôn′tər), **1** *v.* to walk along slowly and happily; stroll: *People sauntered through the park on summer evenings.* **2** *n.* a stroll. **—saun′ter·er,** *n.*

sau·ri·an (sôr′ē ən), *n.* **1** lizard. **2** any similar reptile, such as a crocodile.

saur·is·chi·an (sô ris′kē ən), **1** *adj.* (of dinosaurs) having hip joints and pelvic bones that resemble those of lizards. **2** *n.* dinosaur with such hips and pelvis. The tyrannosaur and the apatosaurus were both saurischians.

sau·sage (sȯ′sij), *n.* chopped pork, beef, or other meats, seasoned and usually stuffed into a very thin casing. **–sau′sage·like′,** *adj.*

sau·té (sō tā′ *or* sȯ tā′), **1** *adj.* cooked or browned in a little fat. **2** *n.* dish of food cooked or browned in a little fat. **3** *v.* to fry quickly in a little fat. ❑ *n., pl.* **sau·tés;** *v.* **sau·téed, sau·té·ing.**

sav·age (sav′ij), **1** *n.* member of a primitive, uncivilized people. ■ This meaning of **savage** is often considered offensive. **2** *adj.* not civilized; barbarian: *savage customs.* ■ See Synonym Study at **fierce. 3** *adj.* fierce; cruel; ready to fight; brutal: *a savage dog.* **4** *n.* a fierce, brutal, or cruel person. **5** *adj.* wild or rugged: *savage mountain scenery.* [**Savage** comes from a Latin word meaning "forest." Because many forest animals are fierce and ready to fight, **savage** got that meaning.] **–sav′age·ly,** *adv.* **–sav′age·ness,** *n.*

sav·age·ry (sav′ij rē), *n.* **1** cruelty; brutality. **2** wildness. **3** an uncivilized condition. ■ This meaning of **savagery** is often considered offensive. ❑ *n., pl.* **sav·age·ries** for 1.

sa·van·na (sə van′ə), *n.* a grassy plain with few or no trees, especially one in the southern United States or in tropical regions. ❑ *n., pl.* **sa·van·nas.**

sa·van·nah (sə van′ə), *n.* savanna.

Sa·van·nah (sə van′ə), *n.* port in SE Georgia, near the Atlantic.

save¹ (sāv), **1** *v.* to make or keep safe; rescue or protect from harm, danger, loss, etc.; rescue: *The dog saved the child's life. We covered the plants with straw to save them from the frost.* **2** *v.* to store up for use in the future: *save money. I save pieces of string.* **3** *v.* to keep from spending or wasting: *We took the shortcut to save time.* **4** *v.* to avoid expense or waste: *She saves in every way she can.* **5** *v.* to make less; prevent: *save work, save trouble.* **6** *v.* to treat carefully to keep in good condition: *Use a reading light and save your eyes.* **7** *v.* to prevent the loss of: *Another goal will save the game.* **8** *v.* to copy computer data to a protected form, either in another file or on another device. **9** *n.* (in baseball) action of a relief pitcher who keeps the opposing team from tying the score. **10** *v.* (in religious use) to set free from sin and its results. ❑ *v.* **saved, sav·ing. –sav′a·ble** *or* **save′a·ble,** *adj.* **–sav′er,** *n.*

SYNONYM STUDY Save¹ and **rescue** both mean to free someone or something from danger. **Save** is a general word: *Smoke alarms save many lives.* **Rescue** means to save with quick or strong actions: *The Coast Guard rescued the crew from the burning freighter.*

save² (sāv), *prep.* except; but: *He works every day save Sunday.*

sav·ing (sā′ving), **1** *adj.* tending to save up money; avoiding waste; economical. **2** *n.* way of saving money, time, etc.: *It will be a saving to take this shortcut.* **3** *n.* act of preserving, rescuing, etc. **4** *n.pl.* **savings,** money saved. **5** *prep.* with the exception of; save; except: *Saving a few crackers, we had eaten nothing all day.* **6** *prep.* with all due respect to or for. **7** *adj.* compensating; redeeming. **8** *conj.* except: *The pens are the same saving one has red ink and the other blue.*

savings account, account in a savings bank.

savings and loan association, association that uses depositors' savings to make loans, usually for mortgages.

savings bank, bank which accepts money only for savings and investment and which pays interest on all deposits.

savings bond, bond issued by the U.S. government to help pay its expenses. Savings bonds can be cashed with interest after a certain time.

sav·ior *or* **sav·iour** (sā′vyər), *n.* person who saves or rescues.

Sav·ior *or* **Sav·iour** (sā′vyər), *n.* Jesus.

sa·vor (sā′vər), **1** *v.* to enjoy very much: *She savored her win in the race.* **2** *v.* to enjoy the taste of: *We savored the apple turnovers.* **3** *n.* a taste or smell; flavor: *The soup has a savor of onion.* **4** *n.* a distinctive quality; noticeable trace: *There was a savor of humor in her conversation.* **–sa′vor·er,** *n.* **–sa′vor·ing·ly,** *adv.* **–sa′vor·less,** *adj.*

sa·vor·y¹ (sā′vər ē), *adj.* **1** pleasing in taste or smell: *the savory smell of roasting turkey.* **2** morally pleasing; agreeable.

sa·vor·y² (sā′vər ē), *n.* a fragrant herb related to mint, used for seasoning food.

Sa·voy (sə voi′), *n.* region in SE France.

sav·vy (sav′ē), INFORMAL. **1** *adj.* smart; clever: *a savvy person.* **2** *n.* understanding; intelligence; sense: *a person with savvy.* **3** *v.* to know; understand. ❑ *v.* **sav·vied, sav·vy·ing;** *adj.* **sav·vi·er, sav·vi·est.**

saw¹ (sȯ), **1** *n.* tool for cutting, made of a thin blade with sharp teeth on the edge. **2** *n.* a machine with such a tool for cutting. **3** *v.* to cut with a saw: *to saw wood.* **4** *v.* to make with a saw: *Boards are sawed from logs.* **5** *v.* to use a saw: *Can you saw straight?* **6** *v.* to be sawed: *Pine saws more easily than oak.* ❑ *v.* **sawed, sawed** *or* **sawn, saw·ing. –saw′er,** *n.* **–saw′like′,** *adj.*

saw² (sȯ), *v.* past tense of **see**¹: *I saw a robin yesterday.*

saw³ (sȯ), *n.* an old, familiar saying; proverb: *"A stitch in time saves nine" is a familiar saw.*

saw·buck (sȯ′buk′), *n.* **1** sawhorse. **2** SLANG. a ten-dollar bill.

saw·dust (sȯ′dust′), *n.* particles of wood made by sawing.

sawed-off (sȯd′ȯf′), *adj.* **1** having one end sawed or cut off: *a sawed-off shotgun.* **2** SLANG. small in size; short. ■ This meaning of **sawed-off** is often considered offensive.

saw·fish (sȯ′fish′), *n.* any of a group of sharklike fishes with long, flat snouts that have a row of sharp teeth along each edge. ❑ *n., pl.* **saw·fish** *or* **saw·fish·es.**

saw·horse (sȯ′hôrs′), *n.* frame for holding wood that is being sawed.

saw·mill (sȯ′mil′), *n.* **1** a building where machines saw timber into planks, boards, etc. **2** a machine for such sawing.

sawn (sȯn), *v.* a past participle of **saw**¹.

sax (saks), *n.* saxophone. ❑ *n., pl.* **sax·es.**

sax·i·frage (sak′sə frij), *n.* any of numerous plants with white, pink, purple, or yellow flowers, often grown in rock gardens.

Sax·on (sak′sən), **1** *n.* member of a Germanic tribe that, with the Angles and Jutes, conquered England in the A.D. 400s and 500s. **2** *n.* language of the Saxons. **3** *adj.* of or about the Saxons or their language: *Saxon laws.* **4** *adj., n.* Anglo-Saxon.

sax·o·phone (sak′sə fōn), *n.* a woodwind instrument having a curved metal body with keys for the fingers and a mouthpiece with a single reed.

saxophone

sax·o·phon·ist (sak′sə fō′nist), *n.* a saxophone player.

say (sā), **1** *v.* to speak; utter: *What did you say? "Thank you," she said.* **2** *v.* to put into words; express; declare: *Say what you think.* **3** *v.* to recite; repeat: *Say your prayers.* **4** *adv.* about; approximately: *You can learn to dance in, say, ten lessons.* **5** *v.* to express an opinion: *It is hard to say which shirt is nicer.* **6** *n.* chance to say something: *If you have all had your say, we will vote on the matter.* **7** *n.* power; authority: *Who has the final say in this matter?* ❑ *v.* **said, say·ing. –say′er,** *n.*

that is to say, that is; in other words.

SYNONYM STUDY Say, state, and **declare** all mean to put into words. **Say** is a general word: *She always says exactly what she means.* **State** means to say clearly and openly: *The judge asked the witness to state her name and occupation.* **Declare** means to state strongly and firmly: *He declares that he is innocent of any wrongdoing.*

say·ing (sā′ing), *n.* **1** something said; statement. **2** proverb: *"Haste makes waste" is a saying.*

go without saying, be too obvious to need mention.

sa·yo·na·ra (sä′yō nä′rä), *interj., n.* JAPANESE. good-by.

says (sez), *v.* a present tense of **say**: *He says he'll be late.*

say-so (sā′sō′), *n.* **1** one's mere word: *Do you believe that, just on his say-so?* **2** authority or power to decide. ❑ *n., pl.* **say-sos.**

Sb, symbol for antimony.

Sc, symbol for scandium.

SC, South Carolina (used with postal Zip Code).

a	hat	ė	term	ô	order	ch	child		
ā	age	i	it	oi	oil	ng	long	ə	a in about
ä	far	ī	ice	ou	out	sh	she		e in taken
â	care	o	hot	u	cup	th	thin		i in pencil
e	let	ō	open	u̇	put	ŦH	then		o in lemon
ē	equal	ȯ	saw	ü	rule	zh	measure		u in circus

S.C., South Carolina.

scab (skab), **1** *n.* the crust that forms over a sore or wound as it heals: *A scab started to form on my scraped knee.* **2** *v.* to become covered with a scab. **3** *n.* worker who will not join a labor union or who takes a striker's job. ❑ *v.* **scabbed, scab·bing. –scab′like′,** *adj.*

scab·bard (skab′ərd), *n.* a sheath or case for the blade of a sword, dagger, etc.

scab·by (skab′ē), *adj.* covered with scabs. ❑ *adj.* **scab·bi·er, scab·bi·est. –scab′bi·ness,** *n.*

sca·bies (skā′bēz), *n.* disease of the skin caused by mites that live under the skin and cause itching.

scads (skadz), *n.pl.* INFORMAL. a large quantity.

scaf·fold (skaf′əld), *n.* **1** a temporary structure for holding workers and materials. **2** a raised platform on which criminals are put to death. **3** any raised framework.

scaf·fold·ing (skaf′əl ding), *n.* **1** scaffold. **2** materials for scaffolds.

scal·a·ble (skā′lə bəl), *adj.* able to be changed by users so as to work on various data, tasks, or problems: *a scalable program for homework and home offices.*

scal·a·wag (skal′ə wag), *n.* a mischievous person; rascal.

scald (skôld), **1** *v.* to burn with hot liquid or steam: *I scalded myself with hot grease.* **2** *n.* a burn caused by hot liquid or steam: *The scald on his hand came from lifting a pot cover carelessly.* **3** *v.* to pour boiling liquid over; use boiling liquid on: *Scald the dishes before drying them.* **4** *v.* to heat almost to boiling, but not quite: *Scald the milk.* **5** *v.* to burn as if with boiling water.

scale¹ (skāl), **1** *n.* device for weighing: *a bathroom scale.* **2** *n.* Usually, **scales,** *pl.* a balance for weighing: *The statue of Justice carries a sword and scales.* **3** *n.* a dish or pan of a balance: *The heavier scale drops lower.* **4** *v.* to weigh: *I scale 95 pounds.* **5** *v.* to weigh, measure, or compare as if by weighing: *scaling two job offers.* ❑ *v.* **scaled, scal·ing.**

tip the scales, to weigh: *to tip the scales at 100 pounds.* **2** to give one side an advantage over another; decide: *The help of France tipped the scales in favor of the Colonies' independence.*
turn the scales, to give an advantage; decide.

scale² (skāl), **1** *n.* one of the thin, flat, hard plates forming the outer covering of some fishes, snakes, and lizards. **2** *n.* a thin layer like a scale: *My sunburn caused my skin to peel off in scales.* **3** *v.* to remove scales from: *She scaled the fish with a knife.* **4** *v.* to come off in scales: *The paint is scaling off the house.* **5** *n.* one of the parts that cover a bud or other plant part. **6** *n.* scale insect. ❑ *v.* **scaled, scal·ing. –scal′a·ble,** *adj.* **–scale′less,** *adj.* **–scale′like′,** *adj.*

scale³ (skāl), **1** *n.* series of steps or degrees; plan of graded amounts: *The salary scale for this job ranges from $20,000 now to $40,000 after ten years.* **2** *n.* series of marks made along a line at regular distances to use in measuring: *A thermometer has a scale.* **3** *n.* a tool marked in this way, used for measuring. **4** *n.* size of a plan, map, drawing, or model compared with what it shows: *This map is drawn to the scale of one inch for each 100 miles.* **5** *n.* size; extent; basis: *That rich family entertains on a large scale.* **6** *n.* system of numbering: *The decimal scale counts by tens, as in dimes, dollars.* **7** *v.* to reduce by a certain amount in relation to other amounts: *To draw this map, mileage was scaled down to one inch for each 100 miles.* **8** *n.* (in music) a series of tones ascending or descending in pitch according to fixed amounts: *She practices scales on the piano.* **9** *v.* to climb: *They scaled the wall by ladders.* **10** *v.* to make according to a scale. ❑ *v.* **scaled, scal·ing.**

scale insect, any of various small insects that feed on and often destroy plants by piercing them and sucking the sap. The females have the body and eggs covered by a scale or shield formed by a secretion from the body.

sca·lene (skā lēn′ or skā′lēn), *adj.* (of a triangle) having three sides unequal. See picture at **triangle.**

Sca·li·a (skə lē′ə), *n.* **Anthony,** born 1936, U.S. Supreme Court justice, appointed 1986.

scal·lion (skal′yən), *n.* **1** a young onion that has no large, distinct bulb. **2** leek.

scal·lop (skal′əp *or* skol′əp), **1** *n.* any of numerous shellfish

something like a clam, with a rounded, fan-shaped shell. In some kinds the large muscle that opens and closes the shell is good to eat. **2** *v.* to bake with sauce and bread crumbs in a dish; escallop: *scalloped oysters.* **3** *n.* one of a series of curves on the edge of anything: *This plate has scallops.* **4** *v.* to make such curves on: *scallop a quilt.*

scal·op·pi·ni (skal′ə pē′nē), *n.sing. or pl.* very thin slices of veal, quickly fried, or sometimes breaded, fried, and covered with cheese and tomato sauce.

scalp (skalp), **1** *n.* the skin on the top and back of the head, usually covered with hair. **2** *n.* part of this skin, kept in old days as a token of victory by some peoples. **3** *v.* to cut or tear the scalp from. [See Word Story at **scalpel**.]

scal·pel (skal′pəl), *n.* a small, straight knife used by surgeons.

WORD STORY **Scalpel** looks as it it should be related to **scalp. Scalp** comes from a Latin word meaning "knife." **Scalp** comes from an Icelandic word meaning "sheath," the cover a knife fits into. The scalp is a covering for the head. In spite of these similar meanings, the two words come from different sources and have no connection at all.

scal·y (skā′lē), *adj.* **1** covered with scales; having scales like a fish: *This iron pipe is scaly with rust.* **2** like scales. ❑ *adj.* **scal·i·er, scal·i·est. –scal′i·ness,** *n.*

scaly anteater, any of several scaly, toothless mammals of tropical Asia and Africa; pangolin. Scaly anteaters have long snouts and sticky tongues used to catch and eat ants. When in danger, a scaly anteater rolls itself into a ball.

scaly anteater—up to 5 ft. (1.5 m) long

scam (skam), INFORMAL. **1** *n.* a clever but dishonest trick; fraud. **2** *v.* to trick someone or to get something in a clever but dishonest way: *He scammed two tickets by claiming to be related to the band's drummer.* **–scam′mer,** *n.*

scamp (skamp), *n.* a mischievous person; rascal; rogue.

scam·per (skam′pər), **1** *v.* to run quickly: *The mice scampered away when the cat came.* **2** *n.* a quick run: *Let the dog out for a scamper.*

scan (skan), **1** *v.* to look at closely; examine with care: *You should scan every word in the contract before you sign it.* **2** *v.* to glance at; look over hastily. ■ See Usage Note at **first-degree. 3** *v.* (of poetry) to have the number of syllables and accents required by a meter: *This line doesn't scan.* **4** *v.* to mark off lines of poetry into feet. EXAMPLE: "Once up|on a | midnight | dreary|" **5** *v.* (in television) to expose a surface to beams of electrons in order to transmit or receive a picture. **6** *v.* to examine automatically by using a device such as a scanner. **7** *n.* the picture or other information provided by a scanner: *a brain scan.* ❑ *v.* **scanned, scan·ning. –scan′na·ble,** *adj.*

scan·dal (skan′dl), *n.* **1** a shameful action, condition, or event that brings disgrace or shocks public opinion: *It was a scandal for the city treasurer to take tax money for personal use.* **2** damage to reputation; disgrace. **3** public talk about someone which will hurt his or her reputation; evil gossip; slander.

scan·dal·ize (skan′dl īz), *v.* to offend by doing something thought to be wrong or improper; shock: *Our great-grandparents would be scandalized by the things we do today.* ❑ *v.* **scan·dal·ized, scan·dal·iz·ing. –scan′dal·i·za′tion,** *n.* **–scan′dal·iz′er,** *n.*

scan·dal·ous (skan′dl əs), *adj.* **1** bringing disgrace; shameful; shocking: *scandalous behavior.* **2** spreading scandal or slander: *a scandalous piece of gossip.* **–scan′dal·ous·ly,** *adv.* **–scan′dal·ous·ness,** *n.*

Scan·di·na·vi·a (skan′də nā′vē ə), *n.* **1** region of NW Europe that includes Norway, Sweden, Denmark, and sometimes Finland and Iceland. **2** peninsula on which Norway and Sweden are located.

Scan·di·na·vi·an (skan′də nā′vē ən), **1** *adj.* of or about Scandinavia, its people, or their languages. **2** *n.* person born or living in Scandinavia. **3** *n.* languages of Scandinavia, both modern and historical. Scandinavian includes Danish, Icelandic, Norwegian, and Swedish.

> **WORD SOURCE** **Scandinavian** languages have given many words to the English language. The words below are some of them. (See also Word Sources at **Danish** and **Icelandic**.)
>
> | | | | |
> |---|---|---|---|
> | fiord | guest | ombudsman | smorgasbord |
> | flaw | lemming | rump | tungsten |
> | floe | nag¹ | ski | vole |
> | gauntlet¹ | narwhal | slalom | |

scan·di·um (skan′dē əm), *n.* a silvery metallic element found in many minerals in Scandinavia. *Symbol:* Sc

scan·ner (skan′ər), *n.* device that examines something automatically, especially one that passes a beam of electrons or radiation over a surface.

scanning electron microscope, an electron microscope that forms images by passing a beam of electrons across the surface of the object being viewed.

scan·sion (skan′shən), *n.* the marking off of lines of poetry into feet; scanning. In the oral scansion of poetry, a reader stresses the accented syllables heavily.

scant (skant), **1** *adj.* not enough in size or quantity: *Her coat was short and scant.* **2** *adj.* barely enough; barely full; bare: *You have a scant hour in which to pack.* **3** *v.* to neglect; pay too little attention to: *He tends to scant important matters.* **–scant′ly,** *adv.* **–scant′ness,** *n.*

scant·y (skan′tē), *adj.* **1** not enough: *His scanty clothing did not keep out the cold.* **2** barely enough; meager: *The drought caused a very scanty harvest.* ❑ *adj.* **scant·i·er, scant·i·est. –scant′i·ly,** *adv.* **–scant′i·ness,** *n.*

scape·goat (skāp′gōt′), *n.* person or thing made to bear the blame for the mistakes or sins of others.

> **WORD STORY** **Scapegoat** comes from **escape** and **goat**. In the Bible, God commands the Hebrews to choose two goats as offerings to make up for their sins. One goat is for sacrifice. The other goat escapes sacrifice, for God commands that it be let go in the desert. People have understood this story to mean that the goat carried the weight of others' sins away with it.

scap·u·la (skap′yə lə), *n.* shoulder blade. ❑ *n., pl.* **scap·u·las, scap·u·lae** (skap′yə lē).

scar (skär), **1** *n.* the mark left by a healed cut, wound, burn, or sore: *My vaccination scar is small.* **2** *n.* any mark like this: *A fallen leaf leaves a scar where it joined the stem.* **3** *v.* to mark with a scar: *He scarred the wood with the hammer when he missed the nail.* **4** *v.* to form a scar; heal: *The wound is scarring quite well.* ❑ *v.* **scarred, scar·ring.**

> **WORD STORY** **Scar** comes from a Greek word meaning "fireplace." A fireplace always shows traces of old fires. The Greeks also used the word to mean the marks that fire left on burned skin.

scar·ab (skar′əb), *n.* **1** any of numerous beetles, especially the sacred beetle of the ancient Egyptians. **2** an image of this beetle. Scarabs were much used in ancient Egypt as charms or ornaments.

scarce (skârs), **1** *adj.* hard to get; rare: *Water is becoming scarce in some parts of the country.* ■ See Synonym Study at **rare**¹. **2** *adv.* scarcely. ❑ *adj.* **scarc·er, scarc·est. –scarce′ness,** *n.*

make yourself scarce, **1** to go away. **2** to stay away.

scarce·ly (skârs′lē), *adv.* **1** not quite; barely: *We could scarcely see the ship through the fog.* **2** decidedly not: *She can scarcely have said that.*

scar·ci·ty (skâr′sə tē), *n.* too small a supply; lack: *There is a scarcity of nurses.* ❑ *n., pl.* **scar·ci·ties.**

scare (skâr), **1** *v.* to make or become afraid; frighten: *We were scared and ran away. Courageous people don't scare easily.* **2** *n.* a fright. **3** *n.* a widespread state of fright or panic: *a bomb scare at the airport.* **4** *v.* to frighten away; drive off: *The watchdog scared away the robber with its loud barking.* ❑ *v.* **scared, scar·ing. –scar′er,** *n.*

scare up, INFORMAL. to get; raise: *scare up a few extra blankets by searching in the attic.*

> **SYNONYM STUDY** **Scare, frighten,** and **alarm** all mean to make someone afraid. **Scare** is a general word: *Her loud laughter scares the baby.* **Frighten** suggests sudden fear: *The dog's rush frightened me.* **Alarm** means to cause someone to worry about possible danger: *The sound of fire trucks alarmed the neighbors.*

scare·crow (skâr′krō′), *n.* **1** figure of a person dressed in old clothes, set in a field to frighten birds away from crops. **2** person, usually skinny, dressed in ragged clothes. [See Word Story at **pickpocket**.]

scarf¹ (skärf), *n.* **1** a long, broad strip of silk, lace, etc., worn around the neck, shoulders, head, or waist. **2** a long strip of linen, etc., used as a cover for a bureau, table, piano, etc. ❑ *n., pl.* **scarfs** or **scarves.**

scarf² (skärf), *v.* SLANG. Also, **scarf down,** to eat, especially hurriedly: *He scarfed down three hamburgers after practice.*

scar·i·fy (skar′ə fī), *v.* **1** to make scratches or cuts on skin, furniture, or other surfaces. **2** to criticize severely; hurt the feelings of. ❑ *v.* **scar·i·fied, scar·i·fy·ing. –scar′i·fi·ca′tion,** *n.* **–scar′i·fi′er,** *n.*

scar·la·ti·na (skär′lə tē′nə), *n.* scarlet fever, especially a mild form of the disease.

scar·let (skär′lit), **1** *n.* a very bright red. **2** *adj.* very bright red.

scarlet fever, a very contagious, bacterial disease that affects mostly children, causing a scarlet rash, sore throat, and fever.

scarlet tanager, a colorful songbird of eastern North America; redbird. The male has black wings and tail and a scarlet body.

scarves (skärvz), *n.* a plural of **scarf**¹.

scar·y (skâr′ē), *adj.* **1** causing fright or alarm: *scary sounds, a scary movie.* **2** easily frightened. ❑ *adj.* **scar·i·er, scar·i·est. –scar′i·ly,** *adv.* **–scar′i·ness,** *n.*

scat (skat), **1** *interj.* exclamation used to drive away an animal. **2** *v.* to go away, especially in a hurry. ❑ *v.* **scat·ted, scat·ting.**

scath·ing (skā′ᴛʜing), *adj.* very critical; bitterly severe: *scathing criticism.* **–scath′ing·ly,** *adv.*

scarlet tanager—up to 8 in. (20 cm) long

scat·ter (skat′ər), *v.* **1** to throw here and there; sprinkle: *I scattered salt on the sidewalk to melt the ice.* **2** to separate and drive off in different directions: *The police scattered the disorderly crowd.* **3** to separate and go in different directions: *The pigeons scattered when the dog ran toward them.* **–scat′ter·er,** *n.*

> **SYNONYM STUDY** **Scatter** and **strew** both mean to spread things out. **Scatter** means to throw without aiming, so that things land far apart: *She scatters bread for the pigeons to eat.* **Strew** means to throw or drop in no order: *His clothes are strewn all over his room.*

scat·ter·brain (skat′ər brān′), *n.* a thoughtless, flighty person.

a	hat	ė	term	ô	order	ch	child		
ā	age	i	it	oi	oil	ng	long		a in about
ä	far	ī	ice	ou	out	sh	she	ə {	e in taken
â	care	o	hot	u	cup	th	thin		i in pencil
e	let	ō	open	ů	put	ᴛʜ	then		o in lemon
ē	equal	ò	saw	ü	rule	zh	measure		u in circus

scat·ter·brained (skat′ər brānd′), *adj.* not able to think steadily; flighty; thoughtless.

scat·ter·ing (skat′ər ing), *n.* a small amount or number occurring here and there.

scatter rug, a small rug.

scat·ter·shot (skat′ər shot′), *adj.* **1** spreading widely like the burst of shot from a shotgun. **2** too general; vague; confused: *Her scattershot approach to the problem led to more difficulties.*

scav·enge (skav′ənj), *v.* to pick over discarded objects for things to use or sell. ❑ *v.* **scav·enged, scav·eng·ing.**

scav·en·ger (skav′ən jər), *n.* **1** living thing that feeds on decaying matter. Vultures and jackals are scavengers. **2** person who searches through discarded objects for something of value.

> **WORD STORY** **Scavenger** comes from a Flemish word meaning "to inspect." In old times, Flemish tax inspectors were also required to clean the streets. They liked to be called inspectors, but people thought of them as garbage pickers.

scavenger hunt, game in which each person or team is given a list of various objects to collect without buying them. The winner is whoever first returns to the starting point with all the objects on the list.

sce·nar·i·o (si nâr′ē ō *or* si när′ē ō), *n.* **1** the outline of a movie, giving the main facts about the scenes, persons, and acting. **2** the outline of any play, opera, etc. **3** an imagined or suggested series of events: *a scenario for settling the long strike.* ❑ *n., pl.* **sce·nar·i·os.**

sce·nar·ist (si nâr′ist *or* si när′ist), *n.* person who writes scenarios.

scene (sēn), *n.* **1** the time, place, circumstances, etc., of a play or story: *The scene of the novel is laid in Virginia during the Civil War.* **2** the place where something happens or takes place: *the scene of an accident.* **3** view; picture: *The white sailboats in the blue water made a pretty scene.* ■ See Synonym Study at **view.** **4** part of an act of a play: *The queen comes to the castle in Act I, Scene 2.* **5** the painted screens, hangings, etc., used in a theater to represent places: *The scene represents a city street.* **6** a particular incident of a play: *The scene in which the detective reveals the name of the murderer is the highlight of the play.* **7** action, incident, situation, etc., occurring in reality or represented in literature or art: *He has painted a series of pictures called "Scenes of My Boyhood."* **8** show of strong feeling in front of others; exhibition; display: *The child kicked, screamed, and made a dreadful scene.* **9** area of interest or activity: *the college scene, the rock scene.* **10** INFORMAL. a specific event or situation: *When the air conditioning failed on a very hot day, it was a bad scene.* ■ Another word that sounds like this is **seen.**

behind the scenes, 1 out of sight of the audience. **2** not publicly; privately; secretly.

> **WORD STORY** **Scene** and **scenery** both come from a Greek word meaning "tent." In ancient Greece, plays were given in outdoor theaters, and actors went into a tent to change costumes between parts of the plays. Later theaters had buildings behind the stage in place of tents, and the walls of those buildings were decorated with painted scenery.

scen·er·y (sē′nər ē), *n.* **1** the general appearance of a place; the natural features of a landscape: *She enjoys mountain scenery very much.* **2** the painted hangings, screens, etc., used in a theater to represent places: *The scenery pictures a garden in the moonlight.* [See Word Story at **scene.**]

scen·ic (sē′nik), *adj.* **1** of or about natural scenery: *The scenic splendors of Yellowstone Park are famous.* **2** having much fine scenery: *a scenic highway.* **3** of or about stage scenery or stage effects: *The production of the musical comedy was a scenic triumph.* **—scen′i·cal·ly,** *adv.*

scent (sent), **1** *n.* a smell: *The scent of roses filled the air.* **2** *v.* to smell: *The dog scented a rabbit and ran off after it.* **3** *n.* sense of smell: *Bloodhounds have a keen scent.* **4** *n.* smell left in passing: *The dogs followed the fox by its scent.* **5** *n.* means by which something or someone can be traced: *The police are on the scent of the thieves.* **6** *v.* to have a suspicion of; be aware of: *I scent a trick in their offer.* **7** *n.* a perfume: *She uses too much scent; it makes me sneeze.* **8** *v.* to fill with odor; perfume: *The bouquet of lilacs scented the entire room.* ■ Other words that sound like this are **cent** and **sent.** **—scent′less,** *adj.*

scep·ter (sep′tər), *n.* the rod or staff carried by a ruler as a symbol of royal power or authority.

scep·tic (skep′tik), *n.* skeptic.

scep·ti·cal (skep′tə kəl), *adj.* skeptical.

scep·ti·cism (skep′tə siz′əm), *n.* skepticism.

sched·ule (skej′ül *or* skej′əl), **1** *n.* a written or printed statement of when things will take place: *a TV schedule, an airline schedule. The teacher posted the schedule of classes.* **2** *v.* to make a schedule of; enter in a schedule: *He scheduled his work for all next week.* **3** *v.* to plan or

scepter

arrange something for a definite time or date: *We scheduled our vacation for July.* **4** *n.* the time fixed for doing something, arrival at a place, etc.: *The bus was an hour behind schedule.* ❑ *v.* **sched·uled, sched·ul·ing.**

sche·mat·ic (ski mat′ik), *adj.* of or like a diagram, plan, or scheme. **—sche·mat′i·cal·ly,** *adv.*

sche·ma·tize (skē′mə tīz), *v.* to arrange according to a scheme or formula. ❑ *v.* **sche·ma·tized, sche·ma·tiz·ing. —sche′ma·ti·za′-tion,** *n.* **—sche′ma·tiz′er,** *n.*

scheme (skēm), **1** *n.* program of action; plan: *He has a scheme for extracting salt from seawater.* **2** *n.* a plot: *a scheme to cheat the government.* **3** *v.* to devise plans, especially underhanded or evil ones; plot: *They schemed to bring the jewels into the country without paying duty.* **4** *n.* system of connected things, parts, thoughts, etc.: *The color scheme of the room is blue and gold.* ❑ *v.* **schemed, schem·ing. —schem′er,** *n.*

schem·ing (skē′ming), *adj.* making tricky schemes; crafty. **—schem′ing·ly,** *adv.*

scher·zo (sker′tsō), *n.* a light or playful movement of a sonata or symphony. ❑ *n., pl.* **scher·zos, scher·zi** (sker′tsē).

Schick test (shik), a test to determine if someone is immune to diphtheria, made by injecting a very small amount of diphtheria toxin under the skin.

schism (siz′əm *or* skiz′əm), *n.* division or separation into hostile groups, especially because of some difference of opinion about religion.

schist (shist), *n.* a kind of metamorphic rock, made mostly of mica, that splits easily into layers.

schiz·o·phre·ni·a (skit′sə frē′nē ə), *n.* a severe mental illness, with symptoms of withdrawal from reality and a gradual loss of personality. **—schiz·o·phren·ic** (skit′sə fren′ik), *adj., n.*

schnau·zer (shnou′zər), *n.* any of three kinds of terrier with wiry hair, a long head, and small ears, first bred in Germany.

Schoen·berg (shōn′bėrg), *n.* **Arnold,** 1874-1951, Austrian composer. He invented a system replacing traditional musical keys with sequences chosen from the 12 tones of an octave with sharps and flats.

schol·ar (skol′ər), *n.* **1** a learned person; person having much knowledge: *The professor was a famous scholar.* **2** pupil at school; learner. **3** student who is given a scholarship.

schol·ar·ly (skol′ər lē), *adj.* **1** having much knowledge; learned: *a scholarly person.* **2** of or fit for a scholar; like that of a scholar: *scholarly debates.* **3** fond of learning; studious. **4** thorough and orderly in methods of study: *a scholarly book.* **—schol′ar·li·ness,** *n.*

schol·ar·ship (skol′ər ship), *n.* **1** possession of knowledge gained by study; quality of learning and knowledge. **2** money or other aid given to help a student continue his or her studies: *The college offered her a scholarship of one thousand dollars.*

scho·las·tic (skə las′tik), *adj.* of or about schools, scholars, or education; academic: *scholastic methods.* **—scho·las′ti·cal·ly,** *adv.*

school¹ (skül), **1** *n.* place for teaching and learning: *Children go to school to study.* **2** *n.* learning in school; instruction: *Most children start school when they are about five years old.* **3** *n.* regular meetings of teachers and pupils for teaching and learning: *We attend school every day.* **4** *n.* the time or period of such meetings: *to stay after school.* **5** *n.* pupils who are taught and their teachers: *The entire school was present.* **6** *n.* group of people holding the same beliefs or opinions: *the Dutch school of painting.* **7** *n.* a particular department or group in a university: *a medical school, a law school.* **8** *v.* to teach; train; discipline: *School yourself to control your temper.* **9** *adj.* of or about a school or schools.

WORD STORY School¹ comes from a Greek word meaning "leisure." In ancient Greece, most children were put to work early. Only people with enough money for leisure could contine their educations.

school² (skül), **1** *n.* a large number of the same kind of fish or water animals swimming together: *a school of mackerel.* **2** *v.* to swim together in a school. [School² comes from a Dutch word meaning "large group."]

school age, 1 age at which a child begins to go to school. **2** years during which going to school is compulsory or customary.

school board, a group of people or committee managing the public schools of a community.

school·book (skül′bůk′), *n.* book for study in schools; textbook.

school·boy (skül′boi′), *n.* boy attending school.

school bus, bus that carries children to and from school.

school·child (skül′child′), *n.* schoolboy or schoolgirl. ❑ *n., pl.* **school·chil·dren** (skül′chil′drən).

school·fel·low (skül′fel′ō), *n.* schoolmate.

school·girl (skül′gėrl′), *n.* girl attending school.

school·house (skül′hous′), *n.* building used as a school. ❑ *n., pl.* **school·hous·es** (skül′hou′ziz).

schoolhouse—the oldest schoolhouse in the United States

school·ing (skü′ling), *n.* instruction in school; education received at school.

school·marm (skül′märm′), *n.* INFORMAL. schoolmistress.

school·mas·ter (skül′mas′tər), *n.* man who teaches in a school, or is its principal.

school·mate (skül′māt′), *n.* companion at school.

school·mis·tress (skül′mis′tris), *n.* woman who teaches in a school, or is its principal. ❑ *n., pl.* **school·mis·tress·es.**

school·room (skül′rüm′), *n.* room in which pupils are taught.

school·teach·er (skül′tē′chər), *n.* person who teaches in a school.

school·work (skül′wėrk′), *n.* a student's lessons and assignments.

school·yard (skül′yärd′), *n.* piece of ground around or near a school, used for play, games, etc.

school year, part of the year during which a school is in session.

schoon·er (skü′nər), *n.* **1** ship with two or more masts and fore-and-aft sails. **2** prairie schooner.

schot·tische (shot′ish), *n.* **1** a dance something like the polka but slower, popular in the 1800s. **2** music for this dance.

Schu·bert (shü′bərt), *n.* **Franz** (fränts), 1797-1828, Austrian composer. He wrote many different kinds of music, including more than 600 songs.

Schulz (shůlts), *n.* **Charles,** born 1922, American cartoonist. He created the comic strip "Peanuts."

Schu·mann (shü′män), *n.* **1 Clar·a** (klar′ə), 1819-1896, German pianist and composer, wife of Robert Schumann. She was the first pianist to memorize entire concerts. Her husband often used passages of her compositions in his works. **2 Rob·ert** (rob′ərt), 1810-1856, German composer and critic. He composed many works for piano and four symphonies. He suffered from mental illness and died in an asylum.

schwa (shwä), *n.* an unstressed vowel sound such as *a* in *about* or *u* in *circus,* represented by the symbol ə. ❑ *n., pl.* **schwas.**

Schweit·zer (shwī′tsər), *n.* **Al·bert** (al′bərt), 1875-1965, Alsatian physician, philosopher, musician, and missionary in Africa. He won the 1952 Nobel Peace Prize.

sci., 1 science. **2** scientific.

sci·at·i·ca (sī at′ə kə), *n.* pain in a sciatic nerve and its branches.

sci·at·ic nerve (sī at′ik), a large nerve which extends from the lower back down the back part of the thigh and leg.

sci·ence (sī′əns), *n.* **1** knowledge based on observed facts and tested truths arranged in an orderly system: *the laws of science.* **2** branch of such knowledge. Chemistry, physics, and astronomy are physical sciences. Zoology and botany are biological sciences. Economics and sociology are social sciences. **3** skill based on training and practice; technique: *the science of judo, the science of sailing.*

WORD BANK Science has a vocabulary of its own. Part of learning about science is learning many new words. The vocabulary of science includes a large number of prefixes and suffixes. When scientists make new discoveries and need new words, they often form them by combining words, prefixes, and suffixes that were being used before. For instance, if someone invented a method for recording the sounds of living things from far away, it might be called "biotelephonography." Among the many prefixes and suffixes of science are these:

aero-	geo-	-ist	photo-
astro-	-gon	-logy	psycho-
bio-	-graph	macro-	-scope
cyber-	-graphy	micro-	thermo-
electro-	hydro-	-phone	zoo-

science fair, group of school exhibits prepared by students, each demonstrating a scientific principle, process, development, etc.

science fiction, story or novel that combines science and fantasy. Science fiction deals with life in the future, in other galaxies, etc., but makes much use of the latest discoveries of science and technology.

sci·en·tif·ic (sī′ən tif′ik), *adj.* **1** using the facts and laws of science: *a scientific method, scientific farming.* **2** of or used in science: *scientific books.* —**sci′en·tif′i·cal·ly,** *adv.*

scientific method, a system used in scientific research, generally including identifying a question, gathering information, forming a theory about the information, performing experiments to test the theory, interpreting the results of the experiments, and stating a conclusion.

scientific notation, a short way to write a number by multiplying a power of 10 and a number between 1 and 10. EXAMPLE: 6.57×10^5 instead of 657,000.

sci·en·tist (sī′ən tist), *n.* **1** person who has expert knowledge of some branch of science. Persons specially trained in and familiar with the facts and laws of such fields of knowledge as biology, chemistry, mathematics, physics, geology, and astronomy are scientists. **2 Scientist,** Christian Scientist.

sci-fi (sī′fī′), INFORMAL. **1** *n.* science fiction. **2** *adj.* of or about science fiction.

scim·i·tar (sim′ə tər), *n.* a short, curved sword used by Turks, Persians, and other Asian peoples.

a	hat	ė	term	ô	order	ch	child		
ā	age	i	it	oi	oil	ng	long		a in about
ä	far	ī	ice	ou	out	sh	she		e in taken
â	care	o	hot	u	cup	th	thin	ə	i in pencil
e	let	ō	open	ů	put	ᵗʜ	then		o in lemon
ē	equal	ò	saw	ü	rule	zh	measure		u in circus

scin·til·la (sin til′ə), *n.* a tiny particle; trace: *not a scintilla of truth.* ❑ *n., pl.* **scin·til·las.**

scin·til·late (sin′tl āt), *v.* to sparkle; flash: *The snow scintillates in the sun like diamonds. Her brilliant wit scintillates.* ❑ *v.* **scin·til·lat·ed, scin·til·lat·ing.** —**scin′til·lat′ing·ly,** *adv.* —**scin′til·la′tion,** *n.*

sci·on (sī′ən), *n.* **1** descendant; heir: *the scion of a wealthy family.* **2** bud or branch cut for grafting or planting.

scis·sors (siz′ərz), *n.pl. or sing.* tool or device for cutting that has two sharp blades so fastened that their edges slide against each other.

scissors hold, a wrestling hold where the legs of one wrestler are locked around the opponent's head or body.

scissors kick, movement of the legs in swimming like the movement of scissors blades.

scler·a (sklir′ə), *n.* the tough, white outer membrane of the eyeball. ❑ *n., pl.* **scler·as.**

scle·ro·sis (sklə rō′sis), *n.* hardening of a part of the body, such as an artery or part of the nervous system, usually caused by disease. ❑ *n., pl.* **scle·ro·ses** (sklə rō′sēz). —**scle·rot·ic** (sklə rot′ik), *adj.*

scoff (skôf), *v.* to make fun of something to show you do not believe or respect it; mock: *We scoffed at the idea of swimming in three inches of water.* —**scoff′er,** *n.* —**scoff′ing·ly,** *adv.*

scoff·law (skôf′lô′), *n.* person who has little respect for the law; person who regularly fails to obey the law: *The scofflaw had not paid more than 150 parking tickets.* [See Word Story at **pickpocket.**]

scold (skōld), **1** *v.* to find fault with; blame with angry words: *She scolded the painters for doing such a poor job.* **2** *v.* to find fault; talk angrily: *Don't scold so much.* **3** *n.* person who scolds. —**scold′a·ble,** *adj.* —**scold′er,** *n.*

sco·li·o·sis (skō′lē ō′sis), *n.* an abnormal sideways curvature of the spine. It occurs most often during adolescence.

sconce (skons), *n.* a bracket sticking out from a wall, used to hold a candle or other light.

scone (skōn), *n.* a thick, flat, round cake cooked on a griddle or in an oven. Some scones taste much like bread; some are like buns.

scoop (sküp), **1** *n.* tool like a small shovel, with a short handle and a hollow part for dipping out or shoveling up things. A cuplike scoop is used to dish up ice cream. **2** *n.* the part of a dredge, power shovel, etc., that picks up or holds dirt, sand, etc. **3** *n.* amount picked up at one time by a scoop: *Use two scoops of flour and one of sugar.* **4** *n.* act of taking up with a scoop. **5** *v.* to pick up with a scoop, or as a scoop does: *The children scooped up snow with their hands to make snowballs.* **6** *v.* to hollow out; dig out: *The children scooped holes in the sand.* **7** *n.* act of publishing or broadcasting a piece of news before a rival newspaper, magazine, or TV station does. **8** *n.* such a piece of news. **9** *v.* to publish or broadcast a piece of news before a rival newspaper, magazine, or TV station does. —**scoop′er,** *n.*

scoop·ful (sküp′fúl), *n.* enough to fill a scoop. ❑ *n., pl.* **scoop·fuls.**

scoot (sküt), **1** *v.* to go quickly; dart: *He scooted out the door.* **2** *n.* (in Canada) a flat-bottomed boat, powered by an airplane propeller set at the back, for travel over water, ice, or snow.

scoot·er (skü′tər), *n.* **1** a child's vehicle consisting of a footboard between two wheels, one in front of the other, steered by a long, upright handlebar. It is moved by pushing one foot against the ground. **2** motor scooter. **3** sailboat with runners, for use on either water or ice.

scope (skōp), *n.* **1** extent or range of understanding or mental activity: *The scope of the child's interests was enlarged from reading many books.* **2** the area over which any activity extends: *This is not within the scope of our investigation.*

scope out, INFORMAL. to observe in order to evaluate or investigate; survey: *He scoped out the other dancers in the contest.*

-scope, *suffix.* device for viewing or examining: *telescope = device for viewing distant objects; stethoscope = device for examining the lungs and heart.*

sco·pol·a·mine (skō pol′ə mēn′), *n.* drug used to dilate the pupils of the eye. Scopolamine is also used to produce a drowsy state called **twilight sleep.** In this state pain is lessened and memories of what happens may be dulled or incomplete.

scorch (skôrch), **1** *v.* to burn slightly; burn on the outside: *He scorched his shirt while he was ironing it.* ▪ See Synonym Study at **burn**[1]. **2** *n.* a slight burn. **3** *v.* to dry up; wither: *The grass is scorched by the intense heat.* ❑ *n., pl.* **scorch·es.** —**scorch′ing·ly,** *adv.*

scorched-earth policy (skôrcht′ėrth′), policy of destroying anything that can be used by an invading army: *The defenders' scorched-earth policy required that they burn crops as they retreated.*

scorch·er (skôr′chər), *n.* a very hot day.

score (skôr), **1** *n.* the record of points made in a game, contest, or test: *He had nearly a perfect score on the history exam.* **2** *v.* to make points in a game, contest, or test: *She scored 85 per cent on the final exam.* **3** *v.* to succeed: *His poem scored with the contest judges.* **4** *v.* to keep a record of the number of points made in a game, contest, or test: *The teacher will score for both sides.* **5** *v.* to achieve; gain: *He scored a great success in the school play.* **6** *n.* group or set of twenty; twenty: *four score and seven years ago.* **7** *n.pl.* **scores,** a large number: *Scores died in the earthquake.* **8** *n.* a written or printed piece of music: *She studied the score of the symphony.* **9** *v.* to write or arrange a piece of music for particular instruments or voices: *score a sonata for piano and strings.* **10** *n.* a cut; scratch; mark; line: *The carpenter used a nail to make a score on the board.* **11** *v.* to cut; scratch; mark; line: *Moving the furniture across the floor scored the polish.* **12** *n.* an account; reason; ground: *Don't worry on that score.* **13** *n.* **the score,** the truth about anything or things in general; the facts: *Our new classmate doesn't know the score yet.* ❑ *n., pl.* **scores** for 1,8,10,12; **score** for 6; *v.* **scored, scor·ing.** —**score′less,** *adj.* —**scor′er,** *n.*

pay off a score or **settle a score,** to get even for an injury or wrong: *She had an old score to settle with them.*

score·board (skôr′bôrd′), *n.* a large board on which the scores of a sporting event are recorded and displayed.

scoreboard

score·card (skôr′kärd′), *n.* card on which to record the score of a game, especially while it is being played.

score·keep·er (skôr′kē′pər), *n.* person who keeps score.

score·less (skôr′lis), *adj.* having no score: *a scoreless tie.*

scorn (skôrn), **1** *v.* to look down upon; think of with contempt; despise: *Most people scorn tattletales.* **2** *v.* to reject or refuse as low or wrong: *The judge scorned to take a bribe.* **3** *n.* a feeling that a person, animal, or act is mean or low; contempt: *Most pupils feel scorn for those who cheat.* **4** *n.* person, animal, or thing that is scorned or despised. —**scorn′er,** *n.*

SYNONYM STUDY **Scorn** and **contempt** both mean a feeling that someone or something deserves no respect. **Scorn** suggests judging as worthless: *She listened to his lies with scorn.* **Contempt** suggests scorn, anger, and deep dislike: *His face showed his contempt for the vandals.*

scorn·ful (skôrn′fəl), *adj.* showing contempt; mocking; full of scorn: *a scornful glance.* —**scorn′ful·ly,** *adv.* —**scorn′ful·ness,** *n.*

Scor·pi·o (skôr′pē ō), *n.* **1** group of stars shaped something like a scorpion. **2** the eighth sign of the zodiac, associated with the period from mid-October to mid-November.

scor·pi·on (skôr′pē ən), *n.* any of several small animals related to spiders and having a poisonous sting at the end of the tail.

Scot (skot), *n.* person born or living in Scotland.

scotch (skoch), *v.* to stamp out or crush: *scotch a rumor.*

Scotch (skoch), **1** *n.sing.* whiskey made in Scotland. **2** *adj., n.pl.* Scottish. ■ The word *Scottish* should be used when referring to the people of Scotland or their customs. The word *Scotch* is often considered offensive.

Scotch·man (skoch′mən), *n.* Scotsman. ■ The use of **Scotchman** is often considered offensive. ❑ *n., pl.* **Scotch·men.**

scorpion—up to 8 in. (20 cm) long

Scotch pine, a pine tree originally found in northern Europe and Asia, now grown in eastern North America for its lumber and as a Christmas tree.

Scotch tape, trademark for a very thin, transparent or opaque adhesive tape used for mending, sealing, etc.

Scotch·wom·an (skoch′wùm′ən), *n.* Scotswoman. ■ The use of **Scotchwoman** is often considered offensive. ❑ *n., pl.* **Scotch·wom·en.**

scot-free (skot′frē′), *adj.* free from punishment, loss, or injury: *One of the speeding drivers was fined, but the other got off scot-free.*

Scot·land (skot′lənd), *n.* division of Great Britain north of England; the land of the Scottish people. *Capital:* Edinburgh. See **United Kingdom** for map.

Scotland Yard, 1 headquarters of the London police. **2** the London police, especially the department that does detective work.

Scots (skots), **1** *adj.* of or about Scotland; Scottish. **2** *n.pl.* the people of Scotland.

Scots·man (skots′mən), *n.* man born or living in Scotland. ❑ *n., pl.* **Scots·men.**

Scots·wom·an (skots′wùm′ən), *n.* woman born or living in Scotland. ❑ *n., pl.* **Scots·wom·en.**

Scott (skot), *n.* Sir **Wal·ter** (wôl′tər), 1771-1832, Scottish novelist and poet. He wrote many historical novels, including *Ivanhoe* and *Rob Roy.*

Scot·tie (skot′ē), *n.* INFORMAL. **1** Scottish terrier. **2** nickname for someone from Scotland.

Scot·tish (skot′ish), **1** *adj.* of or about Scotland, its people, or their language: *Scottish industry.* **2** *n.pl.* the people of Scotland. **3** *n.* form of English spoken by the people of Scotland.

Scottish terrier, a short-legged terrier with rough, wiry hair and pointed, standing ears.

scoun·drel (skoun′drəl), *n.* an evil, dishonorable person; villain; rascal: *The scoundrels who set fire to the barn have been caught.*

scour[1] (skour), **1** *v.* to clean or polish by hard rubbing: *I scoured the sink with cleanser.* **2** *v.* to remove dirt and grease by rubbing. **3** *v.* to make clear by flowing through or over: *The stream had scoured a channel.* **4** *n.* act of scouring. —**scour′er,** *n.*

scour[2] (skour), *v.* to move quickly over: *They scoured the countryside for the lost dog.*

scourge (skèrj), **1** *n.* a whip. **2** *n.* any means of punishment. **3** *v.* to whip; punish. **4** *n.* someone or something that causes great trouble or misfortune. Formerly, an outbreak of disease was called a scourge. **5** *v.* to cause great pain or destruction: *Tornadoes scourged the flatlands.* ❑ *v.* **scourged, scourg·ing.** —**scourg′er,** *n.* —**scourg′ing·ly,** *adv.*

scout[1] (skout), **1** *n.* person sent to find out what the enemy is doing. A scout usually wears a uniform; a spy does not. **2** *n.* something that acts as a scout. Some ships and airplanes are scouts. **3** *v.* to act as a scout; hunt around to find something: *Go and scout for firewood for the campfire.* **4** *n.* person who is sent out to get information. **5** *v.* to observe or examine to get information:

Campers scouted the valley to see if there was any drinking water. **6** *n.* act of scouting. **7** *n.* person belonging to the Boy Scouts or Girl Scouts. **8** *n.* INFORMAL. fellow; person: *He's a good scout.* —**scout′er,** *n.*

scout[2] (skout), *v.* to refuse to believe in; reject with scorn: *She scouted the idea of a dog with two tails.*

scout·ing (skou′ting), *n.* activities of scouts.

Scouting USA, Boy Scouts of America.

scout·mas·ter (skout′mas′tər), *n.* adult in charge of a troop or band of Boy Scouts.

scow (skou), *n.* a large, flat-bottomed boat used to carry ore, sand, garbage, etc.

scowl (skoul), **1** *v.* to look angry or sullen by lowering the eyebrows; frown: *She scowled at the man who stepped on her toes.* **2** *n.* an angry, sullen look; frown. —**scowl′er,** *n.* —**scowl′ing·ly,** *adv.*

scrab·ble (skrab′əl), **1** *v.* to scratch or scrape about with hands, claws, etc.; scramble. **2** *v.* to scrawl; scribble. **3** *n.* act of scraping; scramble. ❑ *v.* **scrab·bled, scrab·bling.** —**scrab′bler,** *n.*

scrag (skrag), **1** *n.* a skinny person or animal. An old bony horse is a scrag. ■ This meaning of **scrag** is often considered offensive. **2** *n.* the lean, bony end of a neck of veal or mutton.

scrag·gly (skrag′lē), *adj.* rough or irregular; ragged. ❑ *adj.* **scrag·gli·er, scrag·gli·est.**

scrag·gy (skrag′ē), *adj.* **1** having little flesh; lean; thin. ■ This meaning of **scraggy** is often considered offensive. **2** scraggly. ❑ *adj.* **scrag·gi·er, scrag·gi·est.** —**scrag′gi·ly,** *adv.* —**scrag′gi·ness,** *n.*

scram (skram), *v.* INFORMAL. to go at once. ❑ *v.* **scrammed, scram·ming.**

scram·ble (skram′bəl), **1** *v.* to make your way by climbing, crawling, etc.: *The girls scrambled up the steep, rocky hill.* **2** *n.* a climb or walk over rough ground: *It was a long scramble through bushes and over rocks to the top of the hill.* **3** *v.* to struggle with others for something: *The players scrambled to get the ball.* **4** *n.* a struggle to possess: *the scramble for wealth and power.* **5** *n.* any disorderly struggle or activity; scrambling: *They ran from the wasps in a wild scramble of arms and legs.* **6** *v.* to mix together out of order: *a coded message of letters scrambled together.* **7** *v.* to change an electronic signal so that a special receiver is needed to understand transmitted messages. Government agencies sometimes scramble signals that carry secret information. **8** *v.* to cook eggs with the whites and yolks mixed together. **9** *v.* to put aircraft into the air quickly to intercept enemy aircraft. ❑ *v.* **scram·bled, scram·bling.** —**scram′bler,** *n.*

scrap[1] (skrap), **1** *n.* a small piece; little bit; small part left over: *The cook gave some scraps of meat to the dog. Put the scraps of paper in the wastebasket.* **2** *n.* old metal fit only to be melted and used again. **3** *v.* to make into scraps; break up: *The army scrapped the old tanks.* **4** *v.* to throw aside as useless or worn out. **5** *adj.* in the form of scraps: *scrap metal.* ❑ *v.* **scrapped, scrap·ping.**

scrap[2] (skrap), INFORMAL. **1** *n.* a fight, quarrel, or struggle: *The dogs got into a scrap over a bone.* **2** *v.* to fight, quarrel, or struggle. ❑ *v.* **scrapped, scrap·ping.** —**scrap′per,** *n.*

scrap·book (skrap′bùk′), *n.* book in which pictures or clippings are pasted and kept.

scrape (skrāp), **1** *v.* to rub with something sharp or rough; make smooth or clean by doing this: *Scrape your muddy shoes with this old knife.* **2** *v.* to remove by rubbing with something sharp or rough: *We need to scrape the peeling paint off the house before we repaint it.* **3** *v.* to scratch or graze by rubbing against something rough: *She fell and scraped her knee on the sidewalk.* **4** *n.* act of scraping. **5** *n.* a scraped place. **6** *v.* to rub with a harsh sound; rub harshly: *The branch of the tree scraped against the window.* **7** *v.* to give a harsh sound; grate. **8** *n.* a harsh, grating sound: *the scrape of the bow of a violin.* **9** *v.* to collect by scraping or with difficulty: *I was so hungry I scraped every crumb*

a	hat	ė	term	ô	order	ch	child		a in about
ā	age	i	it	oi	oil	ng	long		e in taken
ä	far	ī	ice	ou	out	sh	she	ə	i in pencil
â	care	o	hot	u	cup	th	thin		o in lemon
e	let	ō	open	ù	put	₮ₕ	then		u in circus
ē	equal	ò	saw	ü	rule	zh	measure		

S

from my plate. I've finally scraped together enough money to buy a bicycle. **10** *v.* position hard to get out of; difficulty: *Children often get into scrapes.* **11** *v.* to bow with a drawing back of the foot. ❏ *v.* **scraped, scrap·ing.**

scrape through, to get through with difficulty: *I barely scraped through the examination.*

scrap·er (skrā′pər), *n.* device or tool for scraping: *We removed the loose paint with a scraper.*

scrap·py[1] (skrap′ē), *adj.* made of or containing disconnected parts; not complete or thoroughly prepared; fragmentary: *scrappy data.* ❏ *adj.* **scrap·pi·er, scrap·pi·est.**

scrap·py[2] (skrap′ē), *adj.* fond of fighting; ready to quarrel. ❏ *adj.* **scrap·pi·er, scrap·pi·est.**

scratch (skrach), **1** *v.* to break, mark, or cut slightly with something sharp or rough: *Your feet have scratched the chair.* **2** *n.* mark made by scratching: *There are deep scratches on this desk.* **3** *v.* to tear or dig with the nails or claws: *The cat scratched me.* **4** *n.* a very slight cut: *That scratch on your hand will soon be well.* **5** *v.* to rub or scrape to relieve itching: *Don't scratch your mosquito bites.* **6** *v.* to rub with a harsh noise; rub: *I scratched the match on the rock.* **7** *n.* sound of scratching: *the scratch of a pen.* **8** *v.* to write in a hurry or carelessly. **9** *n.* any act of scratching. **10** *v.* to draw a line through. **11** *v.* to withdraw a horse, candidate, etc., from a race or contest. **12** *v.* to have an effort in a game or contest not count because of a violation of a rule: *His foot went over the line on his first throw so he scratched.* **13** *adj.* for quick notes, a first draft, etc.: *scratch paper.* **14** *adj.* collected by chance: *a scratch football team.* ❏ *n., pl.* **scratch·es. —scratch′er,** *n.*

from scratch, with no advantages; without help.

up to scratch, up to standard; in good condition.

scratch test, test for allergy to a particular substance, such as pollen or mold, done by scratching the skin and applying a small dose of the substance.

scratch·y (skrach′ē), *adj.* **1** likely or apt to scratch, scrape, or grate: *a scratchy pen.* **2** made up of mere scratches: *It was only a quick, scratchy drawing.* ❏ *adj.* **scratch·i·er, scratch·i·est. —scratch′i·ly,** *adv.* **—scratch′i·ness,** *n.*

scrawl (skrôl), **1** *v.* to write or draw poorly or carelessly. **2** *n.* poor, careless handwriting. **3** *n.* something scrawled, such as a hastily or badly written letter or note. **—scrawl′er,** *n.*

scrawl·y (skrô′lē), *adj.* awkwardly written or drawn. ❏ *adj.* **scrawl·i·er, scrawl·i·est.**

scraw·ny (skrô′nē), *adj.* having little flesh; lean; thin; skinny: *Turkeys have scrawny necks.* ■ **Scrawny** is often considered offensive. ❏ *adj.* **scraw·ni·er, scraw·ni·est. —scraw′ni·ness,** *n.*

scream (skrēm), **1** *v.* to make a loud, sharp, piercing cry. People scream in fright, in anger, and in excitement. **2** *n.* a loud, sharp, piercing cry. **3** *v.* to utter loudly. **4** *n.* something or someone extremely funny. **—scream′er,** *n.*

scream·ing (skrē′ming), *adj.* **1** crying out; screeching. **2** evoking screams of laughter: *a screaming comedy.* **3** startling: *screaming headlines, screaming colors.* **—scream′ing·ly,** *adv.*

screech (skrēch), **1** *v.* to cry out sharply in a high voice; shriek. **2** *n.* a shrill, harsh scream. ❏ *n., pl.* **screech·es.**

screech owl, any of several small owls with hornlike tufts of feathers and shrill, wavering cries.

screen (skrēn), **1** *n.* a flat, white surface on which movies or slides are shown. **2** *v.* to show a movie on a screen. **3** *n.* movies; the movie industry: *a star of the screen, stage, and TV.* **4** *n.* a glass surface on which television pictures, computer information, or video game diagrams appear. **5** *n.* the information shown by a computer at any particular moment, or any particular diagram shown by a video game machine: *If you score enough points now, you get*

screech owl—up to 10 in. (25 cm) long

another turn on a different screen. **6** *n.* a covered frame that hides, protects, or separates: *hospital beds with a screen between them.* **7** *v.* to shelter, protect, or hide: *The lawyer tried to screen her client from the reporters.* **8** *n.* wires woven together with small openings: *We have screens at our windows to keep out flies.* **9** *n.* an ornamental divider: *painted Japanese screens.* **10** *n.* any surface or line that hides or protects: *A screen of trees shelters our house from the road.* **11** *n.* sieve for sifting sand, gravel, coal, seed, etc. **12** *v.* to sift: *The children screened dirt from the creek, looking for sapphires.* **13** *v.* to investigate someone's background: *Some government agencies screen their employees for loyalty.*

screen·play (skrēn′plā′), *n.* a movie story in manuscript form, including the dialogue, descriptions of scenes, action, camera directions, etc.

screen test, a brief scene filmed to test how an actor might perform and look in a movie. **—screen′-test′,** *v.*

screen·writ·er (skrēn′rī′tər), *n.* person who writes screenplays.

screw (skrü), **1** *n.* a slender piece of metal like a nail with a ridge twisted evenly around its length. It has a slot in its flat or rounded head for a screwdriver to fit into, and a sharp point at the other end. **2** *n.* cylinder with an inclined plane wound around it and fitting into a threaded, cylindrical hole. It is a simple machine. Screws are used in some jacks to lift heavy loads. **3** *v.* to turn as you turn a screw; twist: *Screw the lid on the jar.* **4** *n.* a turn of a screw; screwing motion. **5** *v.* to fasten or tighten with a screw or screws: *The carpenter screwed the hinges to the door.* **6** *v.* to force, press, or stretch tight by using screws. **7** *n.* anything that turns like a screw or looks like one. **8** *v.* to twist out of shape: *His face was screwed up with fear.* **9** *v.* to get by force or pressure: *screw money out of someone.* **10** *v.* to gather for an effort: *Screw up your courage and dive.* **11** *n.* propeller that moves a ship.

have a screw loose, INFORMAL. to be unreasonable or silly.

put the screws on, to use pressure or force to get something.

screw up, SLANG. to do something very badly: *I screwed up my exams.*

screw·ball (skrü′bôl′), **1** *n.* SLANG. an eccentric person. ■ This meaning of **screwball** is sometimes considered offensive. **2** *adj.* SLANG. eccentric; erratic: *a screwball idea.* ■ This meaning of **screwball** is sometimes considered offensive. **3** *n.* (in baseball) a pitch thrown with a spin opposite to that of a curve.

screw·driv·er (skrü′drī′vər), *n.* tool for putting in or taking out screws by turning them.

screw·y (skrü′ē), *adj.* INFORMAL. very odd or strange. ❏ *adj.* **screw·i·er, screw·i·est. —screw′i·ness,** *n.*

scrib·ble (skrib′əl), **1** *v.* to write or draw carelessly or hastily. **2** *v.* to make marks that do not mean anything. **3** *n.* something scribbled. ❏ *v.* **scrib·bled, scrib·bling.**

scrib·bler (skrib′lər), *n.* **1** person who scribbles. **2** author who has little or no importance.

scribe (skrīb), *n.* **1** person who copies manuscripts. Before printing was invented, there were many scribes. **2** (in ancient times) a teacher of the Jewish law. **3** writer; author. **4** a public clerk or secretary.

WORD FAMILY **Scribe** and the words below are related. They all come from a Latin word meaning "to write."

ascribe	inscription	proscribe	subscribe
circumscribe	manuscript	proscription	subscription
conscript	nondescript	scribble	superscript
describe	postscript	scrip	transcribe
description	prescribe	script	transcript
inscribe	prescription	Scripture	typescript

scrim·mage (skrim′ij), **1** *n.* a rough fight or struggle. **2** *v.* to take part in a rough fight or struggle. **3** *n.* (in football) the play that takes place when the ball is snapped back by the center and which continues until the ball is whistled dead. **4** *v.* to take part in such a play. **5** *n.* football playing for practice: *an hour of scrimmage between the first and second teams.* ❏ *v.* **scrim·maged, scrim·mag·ing. —scrim′mag·er,** *n.*

scrimp (skrimp), *v.* **1** to be very economical; stint; skimp: *Many parents have to scrimp to keep their children in school.* **2** to treat stingily or very economically.

scrimp·y (skrim′pē), *adj.* too small; too little; scanty. ❑ *adj.* **scrimp·i·er, scrimp·i·est.** —**scrimp′i·ly,** *adv.* —**scrimp′i·ness,** *n.*

scrim·shaw (skrim′shȯ′), *n.* **1** small carvings of whalebone, whale teeth, and the like, first made by American sailors. **2** the art or technique of producing these carvings.

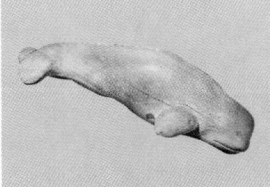

scrimshaw (def. 1)

scrip (skrip), *n.* **1** receipt showing a right to something. **2** paper money issued for temporary use in a time of emergency.

script (skript), *n.* **1** manuscript of a play, movie, or radio or TV show. **2** written letters, figures, characters, etc.; handwriting: *German script.* **3** a style of printing that looks like handwriting.

scrip·tur·al or **Scrip·tur·al** (skrip′chər əl), *adj.* of or about the Scriptures; according to the Scriptures; based on the Scriptures. —**scrip′tur·al·ly,** *adv.*

Scrip·ture (skrip′chər), *n.* **1** the Bible. **2** *n.pl.* **the Scriptures** or **the Holy Scriptures,** the Bible. **3 scripture,** any sacred writing.

script·writ·er (skript′rī′tər), *n.* person who writes scripts, especially for movies or TV.

scriv·en·er (skriv′nər), *n.* OLD USE. a public writer of letters or documents for others; clerk; notary.

scrod (skrod), *n.* a young cod, especially one split for cooking.

scroll (skrōl), **1** *n.* roll of parchment, papyrus, or paper, especially one with writing on it. **2** *n.* ornament resembling a partly open roll of paper, with a spiral or coiled form. **3** *v.* to move across a computer screen in a horizontal or vertical direction. To show a new line of text when the screen is full, the text scrolls upward to make room for the line.

scroll saw, a very narrow saw for cutting thin wood in curved ornamental patterns.

scroll·work (skrōl′wèrk′), *n.* **1** decorative work in which scroll shapes are used: *plaster scrollwork around the ceiling.* **2** ornamental work cut out with a scroll saw.

Scrooge (skrüj), *n.* the old miser in Dickens's story *A Christmas Carol.*

scro·tum (skrō′təm), *n.* pouch that contains the testicles. ❑ *n., pl.* **scro·tums, scro·ta** (skrō′tə).

scrounge (skrounj), **1** *v.* to search about for what you can find that is useful: *We scrounged enough material to build our stage set just by looking in our garages.* **2** *v.* to beg; get by begging: *scrounge a meal.* **3** *n.* person who scrounges. ❑ *v.* **scrounged, scroung·ing.** —**scroung′er,** *n.*

scroung·y (skroun′jē), *adj.* **1** dirty; shabby. **2** scrounging: *His scroungy friend came around again looking for a free meal.*

scrub[1] (skrub), **1** *v.* to rub hard; wash or clean by rubbing: *I scrubbed the floor with a brush and soap.* **2** *n.* act of scrubbing: *Give your hands a good scrub.* **3** *v.* to cancel; reject: *scrub a rocket launch.* ❑ *v.* **scrubbed, scrub·bing.**

scrub[2] (skrub), **1** *n.* low trees or bushes. **2** *n.* anything small, or below the usual size: *a little scrub of a dog.* **3** *adj.* small; poor; inferior. A scrub team is made up of inferior, substitute, or untrained players. **4** *n.* player not on the regular or varsity team.

scrub·ber (skrub′ər), *n.* someone or something that scrubs, especially a device attached to a factory smokestack to remove pollution from smoke, gas, etc., before it goes out into the air.

scrub·by (skrub′ē), *adj.* **1** below the usual size; low; stunted; small: *scrubby trees.* **2** covered with low, stunted trees or bushes. **3** shabby: *scrubby old clothes.* ❑ *adj.* **scrub·bi·er, scrub·bi·est.** —**scrub′bi·ness,** *n.*

scruff (skruf), *n.* the skin at the back of the neck; back of the neck.

scruf·fy (skruf′ē), *adj.* untidy; shabby: *scruffy clothes.* ❑ *adj.* **scruf·fi·er, scruf·fi·est.** —**scruf′fi·ly,** *adv.* —**scruf′fi·ness,** *n.*

scrump·tious (skrump′shəs), *adj.* very pleasing or satisfying, especially to the taste or smell; delightful: *a scrumptious meal.* —**scrump′tious·ly,** *adv.*

scrunch (skrunch), *v.* **1** to crunch; crush; crumple; squeeze: *He scrunched the wad of paper in his fist.* **2** to crouch: *He scrunched way down in his seat.*

scru·ple (skrü′pəl), **1** *n.* a feeling of uneasiness or doubt that keeps someone from doing something, especially for moral reasons: *He has scruples about playing cards for money.* **2** *v.* to hesitate or be unwilling to do something: *A dishonest person does not scruple to deceive others.* **3** *n.* measure of apothecaries' weight equal to 20 grains. Three scruples make one dram. ❑ *v.* **scru·pled, scru·pling.**

WORD STORY **Scruple** comes from a Latin word meaning "a small sharp stone." The ancient Romans compared doubt that holds you back to a painful stone in your shoe: it may be little, but it keeps you from going ahead.

scru·pu·lous (skrü′pyə ləs), *adj.* **1** very careful to do what is right. **2** attending thoroughly to details; very careful: *We tried to pay scrupulous attention to our orders.* —**scru′pu·lous·ly,** *adv.* —**scru′pu·lous·ness,** *n.*

scru·ti·nize (skrüt′n īz), *v.* to examine closely; inspect carefully: *The jeweler scrutinized the diamond for flaws.* ❑ *v.* **scru·ti·nized, scru·ti·niz·ing.** —**scru′ti·niz′er,** *n.*

scru·ti·ny (skrüt′n ē), *n.* close examination; careful inspection: *His work looks all right, but it will not bear scrutiny.* [See Word Story at **inscrutable.**]

scu·ba (skü′bə), **1** *n.* portable equipment for breathing underwater, used in skin diving. It consists of one or more tanks of compressed air strapped to the diver's back, a hose and mouthpiece with valves to regulate the air, and a glass face mask. **2** *adj.* using or consisting of such equipment: *scuba diving, scuba gear.*

WORD STORY **Scuba** comes from the words **s**elf-**c**ontained **u**nderwater **b**reathing **a**pparatus. It was formed by using the first letter of each of those words. Words formed in this manner are called acronyms. See Word Source at **acronym.**

scud (skud), **1** *v.* to run or move swiftly: *Clouds scud across the sky when there is a high wind.* **2** *n.* clouds or spray driven by the wind. ❑ *v.* **scud·ded, scud·ding.**

scuff (skuf), **1** *v.* to walk without lifting the feet; shuffle. **2** *v.* to wear or injure the surface of by hard use: *scuff your shoes.* **3** *n.* act of scuffing.

scuf·fle (skuf′əl), **1** *v.* to struggle or fight in a rough, confused manner: *The angry workers scuffled in the yard and several were injured.* **2** *n.* a confused, rough struggle or fight: *I lost my hat in the scuffle.* **3** *v.* to shuffle. **4** *n.* act of shuffling. ❑ *v.* **scuf·fled, scuf·fling.** —**scuf′fler,** *n.*

scull (skul), **1** *n.* oar worked with a side twist over the end of a boat to make it go. **2** *n.* one of a pair of oars used, one on each side, by a single rower. **3** *v.* to propel a boat by a scull or by sculls. **4** *n.* a light racing boat for one or more rowers. ■ Another word that sounds like this is **skull.** —**scull′er,** *n.*

scul·ler·y (skul′ər ē), *n.* a small room next to a kitchen where cleaning of dishes, pots, pans, etc., is done. ❑ *n., pl.* **scul·ler·ies.**

scul·lion (skul′yən), *n.* OLD USE. servant who cleans dishes, pots, pans, etc., in a kitchen.

sculpt (skulpt), *v.* to sculpture or make sculptures: *The class is learning to sculpt in clay.*

sculp·tor (skulp′tər), *n.* person who makes figures by carving, modeling, casting, etc.; artist in sculpture. Sculptors work in marble, wood, bronze, etc.

sculp·tur·al (skulp′chər əl), *adj.* of or like sculpture. —**sculp′-tur·al·ly,** *adv.*

sculp·ture (skulp′chər), **1** *n.* the art of making figures by carving, modeling, casting, etc. Sculpture includes the cutting of statues from blocks of marble, stone, or wood, casting in bronze, and modeling in clay or wax. **2** *v.* to make figures this way. **3** *n.* sculptured work; piece of such work. **4** *v.* to cover or ornament with sculpture. ❑ *v.* **sculp·tured, sculp·tur·ing.**

S

a	hat	ė	term	ȯ	order	ch	child		a in about
ā	age	i	it	oi	oil	ng	long		e in taken
ä	far	ī	ice	ou	out	sh	she	ə	i in pencil
â	care	o	hot	u	cup	th	thin		o in lemon
e	let	ō	open	ù	put	ŦH	then		u in circus
ē	equal	ȯ	saw	ü	rule	zh	measure		

Sculpture

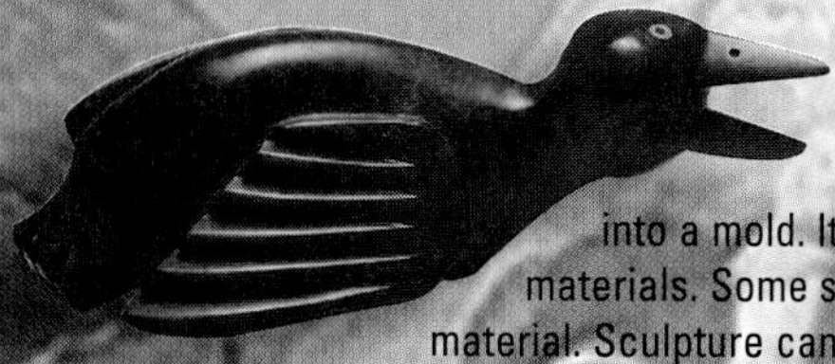

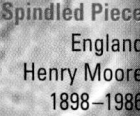

Loon
Canada
1900s

Sculpture can be huge, or it can be tiny. Sculpture can be carved or hammered, stuck together, or poured into a mold. It is made of stone, metal, clay, ivory, or many other materials. Some sculpture is brightly colored. Most is the color of its material. Sculpture can be solid as a rock, or open as space, or both. Some sculpture moves. Most stands still. Some sculpture shows what people, animals, or things look like. Some sculpture is shaped only like itself. Throughout history, people everywhere have made sculpture, too much for any book to show it all. Here is a sample of kinds of sculpture, from many countries and many times.

Mount Rushmore
United States
Gutzon Borglum
1867–1941

Spindled Piece
England
Henry Moore
1898–1986

**Mayan
Clay Figurine**
Mexico
700–1000

The Thinker
France
Auguste Rodin
1840–1917

Mobile
United States
Alexander Calder
1898–1976

Horn-Blower
Nigeria
1550–1680

Buddha
Japan
Ono Goroemon
1252

sculp·tured (skulp′chərd), *adj.* **1** covered or ornamented with sculpture. **2** molded or shaped by sculpture, or as if by sculpture: *finely sculptured facial features.*

scum (skum), *n.* **1** a thin layer that rises to the top of a liquid: *green scum floating on the pond.* **2** undesirable person or persons. ∎ This meaning of **scum** is often considered offensive.

scum·my (skum′ē), *adj.* **1** consisting of or containing scum. **2** disreputable. ∎ This meaning of **scummy** is often considered offensive. □ *adj.* **scum·mi·er, scum·mi·est. –scum′mi·ness,** *n.*

scup·per (skup′ər), *n.* an opening in the side of a ship to let water run off the deck.

scurf (skėrf), *n.* **1** small scales of dead skin. Dandruff is a kind of scurf. **2** any scaly matter on a surface. **–scurf′like′,** *adj.*

scur·ri·lous (skėr′ə ləs), *adj.* filled with foul and abusive language: *scurrilous accusations.* **–scur′ri·lous·ly,** *adv.* **–scur′ri·lous·ness,** *n.*

scur·ry (skėr′ē), **1** *v.* to run quickly; scamper; hurry: *Mice scurry in the walls.* **2** *n.* act of scurrying: *With much fuss and scurry, they at last got started.* □ *v.* **scur·ried, scur·ry·ing.**

scur·vy (skėr′vē), **1** *n.* disease caused by a lack of vitamin C in the diet. It results in swollen and bleeding gums, extreme weakness, and bruises on the skin. Scurvy used to be common among sailors who had no citrus fruits or leafy green vegetables to eat. **2** *adj.* mean; contemptible; base: *a scurvy trick.* □ *adj.* **scur·vi·er, scur·vi·est. –scur′vi·ly,** *adv.* **–scur′vi·ness,** *n.*

scutch·eon (skuch′ən), *n.* escutcheon.

scut·tle¹ (skut′l), *n.* kind of bucket for holding or carrying coal.

scut·tle² (skut′l), *v.* to scamper; scurry: *The crabs scuttled across the sand.* □ *v.* **scut·tled, scut·tling. –scut′tler,** *n.*

scut·tle³ (skut′l), **1** *n.* an opening in the deck or side of a ship, with a lid or cover. **2** *n.* the lid or cover for any such opening. **3** *v.* to cut a hole or holes through the bottom or sides of a ship to sink it: *The crew scuttled the old ship after its last voyage.* **4** *v.* to abandon; give up on: *Both sides scuttled the truce plans.* □ *v.* **scut·tled, scut·tling.**

scut·tle·butt (skut′l but′), *n.* INFORMAL. rumor; gossip: *The scuttlebutt is that they're quarreling.*

Scyl·la (sil′ə), *n.* **1** (in Greek legends) a monster with six heads and twelve arms that lived on a rock in the ocean and snatched sailors from ships. **2** the monster's rock, supposedly located off the southwestern tip of Italy, opposite the whirlpool Charybdis. **between Scylla and Charybdis,** between two equally serious dangers.

scythe (sīᴛʜ), **1** *n.* a long, slightly curved blade on a long handle, for cutting grass, grain, etc. **2** *v.* to cut or mow with a scythe. □ *v.* **scythed, scyth·ing.**

SD, South Dakota (used with postal Zip Code).

S. Dak. or **S.D.,** South Dakota.

SDI, Strategic Defense Initiative.

Se, symbol for selenium.

SE or **S.E.,** **1** southeast. **2** southeastern.

sea (sē), **1** *n.* the salt water that covers almost three fourths of the earth's surface; ocean. **2** *n.* any large body of salt water, smaller than an ocean, partly or wholly enclosed by land: *the Mediterranean Sea.* **3** *n.* a large lake of fresh or salt water: *the Caspian Sea.* **4** *n.* the swell of the ocean: *a heavy sea.* **5** *n.* an overwhelming amount or number: *a sea of worries.* **6** *n.* a broad, filled space: *a sea of faces.* **7** *adj.* of or about the sea; marine: *a sea animal, a sea route, a sea breeze.* **8** *n.* Often, **Sea,** one of the dark, flat plains of the moon, once thought to be seas; mare: *the Sea of Tranquility.* □ *n., pl.* **seas.** ∎ Other words that sound like this are **see** and **si.**

at sea, 1 out on the sea: *We were at sea out of sight of land for ten days.* **2** puzzled; confused: *This problem has me all at sea.*

follow the sea, to be a sailor.

go to sea, 1 to become a sailor. **2** to begin a voyage.

put to sea, to begin a voyage.

sea anemone, any of numerous small, flowerlike sea animals with fleshy, cylindrical bodies and with mouths surrounded by many brightly colored tentacles. A sea anemone is a kind of polyp.

sea·bed (sē′bed′), *n.* seafloor.

Sea·bee (sē′bē′), *n.* member of the construction battalion of the U.S. Navy. □ *n., pl.* **Sea·bees.**

sea·bird (sē′bėrd′), *n.* any bird that lives at sea or near the sea. The albatross is a seabird.

sea·board (sē′bôrd′), *n.* seacoast.

sea breeze, breeze blowing from the sea toward the land.

sea·coast (sē′kōst′), *n.* land along the sea; seaboard: *the seacoast of Maine.*

sea cow, any of several large plant-eating sea mammals with two flippers and a flat tail. The manatee is one kind of sea cow.

sea cucumber, any of numerous small, spiny sea animals with flexible bodies that resemble cucumbers.

sea dog, sailor, especially one with long experience.

sea element, CANADIAN. branch of the armed forces that uses combat ships.

sea·far·er (sē′fâr′ər), *n.* **1** sailor. **2** traveler on the sea.

sea·far·ing (sē′fâr′ing), **1** *adj.* going, traveling, or working on the sea: *a hardy seafaring people.* **2** *n.* business or calling of a sailor.

sea·floor (sē′flôr′), *n.* bottom of a sea or an ocean.

sea·food (sē′füd′), *n.* any saltwater fish or shellfish that is good to eat.

sea·front (sē′frunt′), *n.* seashore.

sea·go·ing (sē′gō′ing), *adj.* **1** going by sea; seafaring. **2** fit for going to sea: *a seagoing merchant ship.*

sea green, light bluish green.

sea gull, any gull, especially one living on or near the sea.

sea horse, 1 any of several small fishes with heads suggesting that of a horse and with tails that can grasp things. **2** an imaginary sea animal supposed to be half horse and half fish.

seal¹ (sēl), **1** *n.* design or pattern, used to show ownership or authority. The seal of the United States is attached to important government papers. **2** *n.* stamp for marking things with such a design: *a seal with your initials on it.* **3** *n.* piece of wax, paper, metal, etc., on which the design is stamped. **4** *v.* to mark a document with a seal to certify it or

sea horse (def. 1)—up to 12 in. (30 cm) long

make it binding: *The treaty was signed and sealed by both governments.* **5** *v.* to close tightly; shut; fasten: *Seal the letter before mailing it. Her promise sealed her lips.* **6** *n.* thing that fastens or closes something tightly. **7** *n.* something that secures; pledge: *under seal of secrecy.* **8** *n.* something that settles or determines: *the seal of authority.* **9** *v.* to settle; determine: *The judge's decision sealed the prisoner's fate.* **10** *v.* to give a sign that something is true: *They sealed their bargain by shaking hands.* **11** *n.* a special kind of stamp: *Easter seals.* **–seal′a·ble,** *adj.* **–seal′er,** *n.*

set your seal to, to approve.

seal² (sēl), **1** *n.* any of numerous flesh-eating sea mammals with large flippers, living usually in cold regions. **2** *n.* sealskin. **3** *v.* to hunt seals. □ *n., pl.* **seals** or **seal. –seal′like′,** *adj.*

seal·ant (sē′lənt), *n.* substance used for sealing.

sea legs, legs accustomed to walking steadily on a rolling or pitching ship.

seal·er (sē′lər), *n.* **1** person who hunts seals. **2** ship used for hunting seals.

sea level, level of the surface of the sea. Mountains, plains, seafloors, etc., are measured above or below sea level.

sea lily, any of several small sea animals that resemble flowers and are related to starfish.

sealing wax, a hard, brittle substance made of resin and shellac. It becomes soft when heated and is used for sealing letters, packages, etc.

sea lion, any of several large seals of the Pacific coast.

seal·skin (sēl'skin'), *n.* **1** skin or fur of the seal, prepared for use. **2** jacket, boots, etc., made of this fur.

seam (sēm), **1** *n.* line formed by sewing two pieces of cloth, canvas, leather, etc., together: *the seams of a coat, the seams of a sail.* **2** *n.* any line where edges join: *The seams of the boat must be filled in if they leak.* **3** *v.* to sew the seam of; join with a seam. **4** *n.* any mark like a seam: *The old cut had left a seam in his hand.* **5** *v.* to mark with seams, wrinkles, etc.: *Her face was seamed with age.* **6** *n.* layer; stratum: *a seam of coal.* ■ Another word that sounds like this is **seem.** —**seam'er,** *n.* —**seam'less,** *adj.*

sea·man (sē'mən), *n.* **1** sailor. **2** any of several military ranks. See chart on page 712. ❑ *n., pl.* **sea·men.** ■ Another word that sounds like this is **semen.**

sea·man·ship (sē'mən ship), *n.* skill in managing a ship.

sea mile, nautical mile.

sea·mount (sē'mount'), *n.* mountain that rises from the seafloor but does not reach sea level.

seam·stress (sēm'stris), *n.* woman whose work is sewing. ❑ *n., pl.* **seam·stress·es.**

seam·y (sē'mē), *adj.* worst; least pleasant: *Police officers often see the seamy side of life.* ❑ *adj.* **seam·i·er, seam·i·est.** —**seam'i·ness,** *n.*

sé·ance (sā'äns), *n.* a meeting of people trying to communicate with spirits of the dead by the help of a medium. ❑ *n., pl.* **sé·anc·es.**

sea otter, a large otter found in small numbers along the coasts of the northern Pacific, once hunted for its valuable fur.

sea·plane (sē'plān'), *n.* airplane that takes off from and lands on water, especially one which has floats instead of wheels.

sea·port (sē'pôrt'), *n.* port or harbor on the seacoast; city or town with a harbor that ships can reach from the sea: *San Francisco and New Orleans are seaports.*

sea·quake (sē'kwāk'), *n.* earthquake below the sea.

sear (sir), *v.* **1** to burn or char the surface of: *The cook seared the roast to seal in its juice. The hot iron seared my hand.* **2** to dry up; wither: *The hot sun seared the grain.* ■ Another word that sounds like this is **seer.**

search (sèrch), **1** *v.* to look through; go over carefully; examine, especially for something concealed: *The police searched the prisoners to see if they had weapons.* **2** *v.* to try to find by looking; seek; look for something: *We searched all day for the lost cat.* **3** *n.* act of searching; examination: *She found her book after a long search.* ❑ *n., pl.* **search·es.** [See Word Story at **circus.**] —**search'a·ble,** *adj.* —**search'er,** *n.*

in search of, trying to find; looking for: *The children went in search of their lost dog.*

search out, to find by searching: *She searched out the facts in the case.*

search·ing (sèr'ching), *adj.* **1** examining carefully; thorough: *a searching look, a searching examination.* **2** piercing; sharp: *a searching wind.* —**search'ing·ly,** *adv.* —**search'ing·ness,** *n.*

search·light (sèrch'līt'), *n.* **1** device that can throw a very bright beam of light in any direction desired. **2** the beam of light thrown by this device.

search warrant, a written court order authorizing the search of a house or building for stolen goods, criminals, illegal narcotics, etc.

sea·scape (sē'skāp'), *n.* **1** view of the sea. **2** picture of a scene on the sea.

Sea Scout, member of the Boy Scouts receiving training in seamanship.

sea serpent, **1** a huge, imaginary, snakelike animal supposed to live in the ocean. **2** sea snake.

sea·shell (sē'shel'), *n.* shell of any sea animal, especially a mollusk such as an oyster, a conch, etc.

sea·shore (sē'shôr'), *n.* land at the edge of a sea; seafront; seaside.

sea·sick (sē'sik'), *adj.* sick because of a ship's motion. —**sea'sick'ness,** *n.*

sea·side (sē'sīd'), *n.* seashore.

sea snake, any of many poisonous snakes with finlike tails that live in tropical seas; sea serpent.

sea·son (sē'zn), **1** *n.* one of the four periods of the year; spring, summer, autumn, or winter. **2** *n.* any special period of time: *the holiday season, the harvest season.* **3** *n.* period of time when something goes on, or occurs: *basketball season, tornado season.* **4** *v.* to improve the flavor of: *season soup with salt.* **5** *v.* to give interest or character to: *season conversation with wit.* **6** *v.* to make something fit for use by a period of keeping or treatment: *Wood is seasoned for building by drying it.* **7** *v.* to accustom; make used to: *Soldiers are seasoned to battle by experience in war.*

for a season, for a time.

in good season, early enough.

in season, **1** at the right or proper time. **2** in the time or condition for eating, hunting, etc.: *Cherries are in season in June.*

out of season, not in season.

sea·son·a·ble (sē'zn ə bəl), *adj.* **1** suitable to the season: *Hot weather is seasonable in July.* **2** coming at the right or proper time; timely: *Our business would have failed without your seasonable advice.* —**sea'son·a·ble·ness,** *n.* —**sea'son·a·bly,** *adv.*

sea·son·al (sē'zn əl), *adj.* of or about the seasons; depending on a season; happening at regular intervals: *seasonal variations in the weather, a seasonal business.* —**sea'son·al·ly,** *adv.*

sea·son·ing (sē'zn ing), *n.* **1** something that gives a better flavor. Salt, pepper, and herbs are seasonings. **2** something that gives interest or character: *We like conversation with a seasoning of humor.*

season ticket, ticket or pass entitling the holder to certain privileges for the season or for a specified period.

seat (sēt), **1** *n.* thing to sit on. Chairs, benches, and stools are seats. **2** *n.* place to sit: *Is there a seat on the bus?* **3** *n.* place in which you have the right to sit. If a person has a seat in Congress or a seat in the stock exchange, it means that person is a member. **4** *n.* that part of a chair, bench, stool, etc., on which you sit: *This bench has a broken seat.* **5** *n.* that part of the body on which you sit, or the clothing covering it: *The seat of her jeans was patched.* **6** *n.* manner of sitting on horseback: *That rider has a good seat.* **7** *v.* to set or place on a seat: *seat a person on a chair, seat yourself at the piano.*

seasonings

8 *v.* to have or provide seats for a specified number: *Our school assembly seats one thousand pupils.* **9** *n.* an established place or center: *A university is a seat of learning. The seat of our government is in Washington, D.C.* **10** *n.* residence; home: *The family seat of the Howards is in southern England.* —**seat'less,** *adj.*

by the seat of your pants, by guesses based on experience: *You can run a small store by the seat of your pants, but a large company needs plans and schedules.*

seat belt, belt or set of belts fastened to the seat or frame of a car or airplane. It helps hold a person in the seat in case of a crash, jolt, bump, etc.

seat·ed (sē'tid), *adj.* **1** sitting: *Seated at the piano, she played a little tune.* **2** located: *They retired to a village seated in a pleasant valley.*

be seated, to sit down: *If everyone will be seated, the meeting can begin.*

a	hat	ė	term	ô	order	ch	child		
ā	age	i	it	oi	oil	ng	long		a in about
ä	far	ī	ice	ou	out	sh	she	ə ⟨	e in taken
â	care	o	hot	u	cup	th	thin		i in pencil
e	let	ō	open	u̇	put	ᴛʜ	then		o in lemon
ē	equal	ò	saw	ü	rule	zh	measure		u in circus

S

seat·mate (sēt′māt′), *n.* person who sits next to you on a train, bus, plane, etc.

Seattle

Se·at·tle (sē at′l), *n.* port in W Washington, on Puget Sound.

WORD STORY **Seattle** is named for an American Indian leader who helped early settlers on this site. So everyone remembers his name, but no one knows what it meant.

sea urchin, any of numerous small, round sea animals with spiny shells.

sea·wall (sē′wôl′), *n.* a strong wall or embankment made to prevent the waves from wearing away the shore, to act as a breakwater, etc.

sea·ward (sē′wərd), **1** *adj., adv.* toward the sea: *a seaward breeze. Our house faces seaward.* **2** *n.* direction toward the sea: *The island lies a mile to seaward.*

sea·wards (sē′wərdz), *adv.* seaward.

sea·wa·ter (sē′wô′tər), *n.* the salt water of the sea.

sea·way (sē′wā′), *n.* **1** an inland waterway that is deep enough to permit ocean shipping: *Oceangoing freighters reach Detroit by passing through the St. Lawrence Seaway.* **2** a route over the sea.

sea·weed (sē′wēd′), *n.* any plant or any living thing like a plant growing in the sea.

sea·wor·thy (sē′wèr′ᴛʜē), *adj.* fit for sailing on the sea; able to stand storms at sea: *a seaworthy ship.* —**sea′wor′thi·ness,** *n.*

se·ba·ceous gland (si bā′shəs), gland in an inner layer of the skin that supplies oil to the skin and hair.

se·bum (sē′bəm), *n.* the oily substance produced by the sebaceous glands.

sec., **1** second or seconds. **2** secretary. **3** section or sections.

se·cant (sē′kənt), in geometry: **1** *n.* a straight line that intersects a curve at two or more points. **2** *adj.* intersecting: *a secant plane.*

se·cede (si sēd′), *v.* to withdraw formally from an organization. ❏ *v.* **se·ced·ed, se·ced·ing.** —**se·ced′er,** *n.*

se·ces·sion (si sesh′ən), *n.* **1** act of formally withdrawing from an organization. **2** Also, **Secession,** the seceding of the eleven Southern states from the Union in 1860-1861, which resulted in the Civil War.

se·ces·sion·ist (si sesh′ə nist), *n.* **1** person who favors secession. **2** person who secedes.

se·clude (si klüd′), *v.* to keep apart from company; shut off from others: *He secludes himself and sees only his close friends.* ❏ *v.* **se·clud·ed, se·clud·ing.**

se·clud·ed (si klü′did), *adj.* shut off from others; undisturbed: *He wrote that famous novel at a secluded cottage in the woods.* —**se·clud′ed·ly,** *adv.* —**se·clud′ed·ness,** *n.*

se·clu·sion (si klü′zhən), *n.* **1** condition of being secluded; retirement: *She lives in seclusion apart from her friends.* **2** a secluded place.

sec·ond[1] (sek′ənd), **1** *adj.* next after the first: *the second seat from the front, a second child.* **2** *adj.* below the first; inferior: *the second officer on a ship, cloth of second quality.* **3** *adj.* another; other: *Please give me a second chance.* **4** *adv.* in the second group, division, rank, etc.; secondly: *I finished second in the ten-*

nis finals. **5** *n.* person or thing that is second. **6** *n.pl.* **seconds, a** goods below first quality: *These stockings are seconds and have some slight defects.* **b** a second portion of food: *After I finished eating what was on my plate, I went back for seconds.* **7** *n.* person who supports or aids another; backer: *The prizefighter had a second.* **8** *v.* to express approval of; back up; support: *One member made a motion to adjourn the meeting, and another seconded it.* **9** *adj.* singing or playing a part lower in pitch: *second soprano.* —**sec′ond·er,** *n.*

sec·ond[2] (sek′ənd), *n.* **1** one of the 60 very short equal periods of time that make up a minute; 1/60 of a minute; 1/3600 of an hour. **2** any very short time; instant; moment. **3** 1/3600 of a degree of an angle. 12°10′30″ means 12 degrees, 10 minutes, 30 seconds.

sec·ond·ar·y (sek′ən der′ē), *adj.* **1** next after the first in order, place, time, or importance: *A secondary industry uses products of other industries as its raw materials.* **2** not main or chief; having less importance: *Reading fast is secondary to reading well.* **3** not original; derived: *a secondary source of the report.* —**sec′ond·ar′i·ly,** *adv.* —**sec′ond·ar′i·ness,** *n.*

secondary accent, **1** an accent that is weaker than the strongest accent in the pronunciation of a word but stronger than no accent. The second syllable of *ab·bre′vi·a′tion* has a secondary accent. **2** mark (′) used to show this.

secondary school, school attended after elementary school or junior high school; high school.

sec·ond-class (sek′ənd klas′), **1** *adj.* of or about the class next after the first: *second-class mail.* **2** *adv.* by the passenger service that is next to best and less expensive: *They could afford only to travel second-class.* **3** *adj.* of inferior grade, quality, position, etc.: *second-class goods.*

second class, **1** passenger service that is next to best and less expensive. **2** class of mail that includes newspapers, magazines, and the like.

Second Coming, (in Christian use) the coming of Jesus at the Last Judgment.

sec·ond-guess (sek′ənd ges′), *v.* to judge something or someone after the results are known: *The fans all second-guessed the manager's decision when the pinch hitter struck out.* —**sec′ond-guess′er,** *n.*

second hand, hand on a clock or watch, pointing to the seconds. It moves around the whole dial once in a minute.

sec·ond·hand (sek′ənd hand′), **1** *adj.* not new; used already by someone else: *secondhand clothes.* **2** *adj.* dealing in used goods: *a secondhand clothing store.* **3** *adj.* not original; obtained from another: *secondhand information.* **4** *adv.* from other than the original source; not firsthand: *The information came to us secondhand.*

second-hand smoke, smoke from a cigarette, cigar, or pipe that is inhaled by people other than the person smoking.

second lieutenant, a military rank. See chart on page 712.

sec·ond·ly (sek′ənd lē), *adv.* in the second place.

second nature, habit, quality, knowledge, etc., acquired so long ago that it seems to be almost a part of someone's nature: *Checking to make sure that everyone is in his or her seat before the bus moves is second nature to our regular bus driver.*

second person, form of a pronoun or verb used to refer to the person spoken to. *You* and *yours* are pronouns of the second person.

sec·ond-rate (sek′ənd rāt′), *adj.* poor in quality; inferior: *a second-rate performance.*

second wind, **1** the easier breathing that comes after a period of tiring physical activity. **2** renewed energy or strength: *By chatting for a few minutes, I got my second wind and continued studying.*

se·cre·cy (sē′krə sē), *n.* **1** condition of being secret or of being kept secret: *Plans for the birthday party were made in the greatest secrecy.* **2** ability to keep things secret: *Secrecy was necessary to keep them from finding out our plans for the party.*

se·cret (sē′krit), **1** *adj.* kept from the knowledge of others: *a secret errand, a secret formula, a secret weapon.* **2** *adj.* known only to a few: *a secret society, a secret sign.* **3** *adj.* kept from sight; hidden: *a secret drawer.* **4** *adj.* working or acting in secret: *secret police, a secret agent.* **5** *n.* something secret or hidden: *Can you* *keep a secret?* **6** *n.* a hidden cause or reason: *the secret of her success, the secret of his charm.* **—se′cret·ly,** *adv.*

in secret, in private; not openly; secretly.

secret agent, agent of a government secret service.

sec·re·tar·i·al (sek′rə ter′ē əl), *adj.* of a secretary; having to do with a secretary: *secretarial skills.*

sec·re·tar·i·at (sek′rə ter′ē it), *n.* **1** office or position of secretary or secretary-general. **2** the department or administrative unit controlled by a secretary or secretary-general: *the secretariat of the United Nations.*

sec·re·tar·y (sek′rə ter′ē), *n.* **1** person who writes letters, keeps records, etc., for a person, company, club, etc.: *Our club has a secretary who keeps the minutes of the meeting.* **2** Often, **Secretary,** person who has charge of a department of the government or similar organization. The Secretary of the Treasury is the head of the Treasury Department. **3** a writing desk with a set of drawers and often with shelves for books. ❏ *n., pl.* **sec·re·tar·ies** (or **Sec·re·tar·ies** for 2).

sec·re·tar·y-gen·er·al (sek′rə ter′ē jen′ər əl), *n.* the chief secretary; the administrative head of a secretariat: *the secretary-general of the United Nations.* ❏ *n., pl.* **sec·re·tar·ies-gen·er·al.**

se·crete[1] (si krēt′), *v.* to keep secret; hide: *She secreted money in a cupboard.* ❏ *v.* **se·cret·ed, se·cret·ing.**

se·crete[2] (si krēt′), *v.* to produce and let flow: *Glands in the mouth secrete saliva.* ❏ *v.* **se·cret·ed, se·cret·ing.**

se·cre·tion (si krē′shən), *n.* **1** substance that is secreted by some part of a living thing: *Bile is the secretion of the liver.* **2** process of secreting. **3** act of concealing or keeping secret.

se·cre·tive (sē′krə tiv *or si* krē′tiv *for 1*; si krē′tiv *for 2*), *adj.* **1** having the habit of secrecy; not frank and open. **2** causing or aiding secretion. **—se′cre·tive·ly,** *adv.* **—se′cre·tive·ness,** *n.*

secret police, police force that operates largely without the knowledge of citizens, using threats and often violence to suppress opposition to the government.

secret service, **1** branch of a government that makes secret investigations. **2 Secret Service,** branch of the U.S. Treasury Department concerned with discovering and preventing counterfeiting, with protecting the President, etc.

sect (sekt), *n.* group of people having the same principles, beliefs, or opinions: *a religious sect.*

sec·tar·i·an (sek ter′ē ən), *adj.* **1** of or about a sect; denominational. **2** characteristic of one sect only; strongly prejudiced in favor of a certain sect.

sec·tar·i·an·ism (sek ter′ē ə niz′əm), *n.* quality of being sectarian.

sec·tion (sek′shən), **1** *n.* a part separated or cut off; division; slice: *Divide the pizza into sections.* **2** *n.* division of a book, newspaper, law, etc.: *She always turns to the sports section first.* **3** *n.* part of a country, city, etc.; region or district: *The town has a business section and a residential section.* **4** *n.* act of cutting. **5** *v.* to cut or divide into parts: *section a pizza, section an orange.* **6** *n.* cross section (def. 3). **7** *n.* area of land one mile square; 640 acres. A township often contains 36 sections.

sec·tion·al (sek′shə nəl), *adj.* **1** of or for a particular section; regional or local: *sectional interests, sectional prejudices.* **2** made of sections: *a sectional bookcase.* **—sec′tion·al·ly,** *adv.*

sec·tion·al·ism (sek′shə nə liz′əm), *n.* too great regard for sectional interests; sectional prejudice or hatred.

sec·tor (sek′tər), **1** *n.* section; zone; quarter: *Our new house is in the northern sector of the city.* **2** *n.* area that a military unit is re-

sponsible for defending. **3** *n.* the part of a circle between two radii and the included arc. **4** *v.* to divide into sectors.

sec·u·lar (sek′yə lər), *adj.* **1** not religious or sacred; worldly: *secular music, a secular education.* **2** living in the world; not belonging to a religious order: *the secular clergy.* **—sec′u·lar·ly,** *adv.*

sec·u·lar·ism (sek′yə lə riz′əm), *n.* **1** a nonreligious system of politics, philosophy, or morals. **2** the view that religious instruction or worship should not occur in the public schools, or be publicly funded.

sec·u·lar·ize (sek′yə lə riz′), *v.* to make secular or worldly; separate from religious connection or influence. ❏ *v.* **sec·u·lar·ized, sec·u·lar·iz·ing. —sec′u·lar·i·za′tion,** *n.* **—sec′u·lar·iz′er,** *n.*

se·cure (si kyur′), **1** *adj.* safe against loss, attack, escape, etc.: *a secure hiding place, a secure investment.* **2** *v.* to make safe; protect: *Every loan was secured by bonds or mortgages.* **3** *adj.* sure; certain; that can be counted on: *We know in advance that our victory is secure.* **4** *v.* to make something sure or certain; ensure. **5** *adj.* free from care or fear: *They hoped for a secure old age.* **6** *adj.* firmly fastened; not liable to give way: *a secure lock.* **7** *v.* to make firm or fast: *Secure the locks on the windows.* **8** *v.* to get; obtain: *Secure your tickets early.* ❏ *v.* **se·cured, se·cur·ing. —se·cur′a·ble,** *adj.* **—se·cure′ly,** *adv.* **—se·cure′ment,** *n.* **—se·cure′ness,** *n.* **—se·cur′er,** *n.*

se·cu·ri·ty (si kyur′ə tē), *n.* **1** freedom from danger, care, or fear; feeling or condition of being safe: *We swam with a sense of security because we knew the lifeguard was nearby.* **2** something that secures or makes safe: *Her watchdog is a security against burglars.* **3** actions taken to prevent crime, sabotage, escape of prisoners, etc.: *Airport security is always strict.* **4** something given to another person as a guarantee of good faith or that something will be done in the future: *She used her car title as security for the loan.* **5** Usually, **securities,** *pl.* bond or stock certificates: *These securities can be sold for $5000.*

security blanket, **1** blanket, pillow, towel, etc., that a small child clings to for comfort and reassurance. **2** any person or thing that gives you comfort, protection, or reassurance.

secy., secretary.

se·dan (si dan′), *n.* **1** a car with a front and back seat, seating four or more persons. **2** sedan chair.

sedan chair, a covered chair carried on poles by two bearers. Sedan chairs were used as vehicles in the 1600s and 1700s.

se·date[1] (si dāt′), *adj.* quiet; calm; serious: *I was very sedate as a child and often preferred reading to playing.* **—se·date′ly,** *adv.* **—se·date′ness,** *n.*

se·date[2] (si dāt′), *v.* to give a sedative to. ❏ *v.* **se·dat·ed, se·dat·ing. —se·da′tion,** *n.*

section (def. 5)—pizza sectioned into six slices

sed·a·tive (sed′ə tiv), **1** *n.* medicine that lessens pain or excitement. **2** *adj.* lessening pain or excitement. **3** *adj.* soothing; calming.

a	hat	ė	term	ô	order	ch	child		ə	a in about
ā	age	i	it	oi	oil	ng	long			e in taken
ä	far	ī	ice	ou	out	sh	she			i in pencil
â	care	o	hot	u	cup	th	thin			o in lemon
e	let	ō	open	ů	put	ŦH	then			u in circus
ē	equal	ò	saw	ü	rule	zh	measure			

sed·en·tar·y (sed′n ter′ē), *adj.* **1** used to sitting still much of the time: *Sedentary people get little physical exercise.* **2** keeping you sitting still much of the time: *Bookkeeping is a sedentary occupation.* —**sed′en·tar′i·ly,** *adv.* —**sed′en·tar′i·ness,** *n.*

Se·der (sā′dər), *n.* the religious feast and service held in Jewish homes on the first night or first two nights of Passover.

sedge (sej), *n.* any of numerous grasslike plants that grow mostly in wet places.

sed·i·ment (sed′ə mənt), *n.* **1** material that settles to the bottom of a liquid: *Sediment often collects at the bottom of hot-water tanks.* **2** (in geology) sand, mud, etc., deposited by water, wind, or ice: *When glaciers melt, they leave behind much sediment.*

sed·i·men·tar·y (sed′ə men′tər ē), *adj.* **1** of or about sediment. **2** (in geology) formed by the depositing of sediment. Sandstone is a sedimentary rock.

sed·i·men·ta·tion (sed′ə men tā′shən), *n.* act or process of depositing sediment.

se·di·tion (si dish′ən), *n.* speech or action causing discontent or rebellion against the government.

se·di·tious (si dish′əs), *adj.* **1** stirring up discontent or rebellion. **2** taking part in sedition; guilty of sedition. **3** of or about sedition. —**se·di′tious·ly,** *adv.* —**se·di′tious·ness,** *n.*

se·duce (si düs′), *v.* **1** to tempt to wrongdoing; persuade to do wrong: *Benedict Arnold, seduced by offers of money, betrayed his country to the enemy.* **2** to persuade someone to have sexual intercourse. **3** to lead away from virtue; lead astray; beguile. ❑ *v.* **se·duced, se·duc·ing.** —**se·duc′i·ble** or **se·duce′a·ble,** *adj.* —**se·duc′er,** *n.* —**se·duc′ing·ly,** *adv.*

se·duc·tion (si duk′shən), *n.* **1** act of seducing or condition of being seduced. **2** something that seduces; temptation; attraction.

se·duc·tive (si duk′tiv), *adj.* **1** tempting or enticing; alluring: *a very seductive offer.* **2** captivating; charming: *a seductive smile.* —**se·duc′tive·ly,** *adv.* —**se·duc′tive·ness,** *n.*

sed·u·lous (sej′ə ləs), *adj.* hard-working; diligent; painstaking. —**sed′u·lous·ly,** *adv.* —**sed′u·lous·ness,** *n.*

see[1] (sē), *v.* **1** to be aware of by using the eyes; look at: *See that black cloud?* **2** to have the power of sight: *The blind do not see.* **3** to be aware of with the mind; understand: *I see what you mean.* **4** to find out; learn: *I will see what needs to be done.* **5** to take care; make sure: *See that you lock the back door.* **6** to have knowledge or experience of: *That coat has seen hard wear.* **7** to attend; escort; go with: *My parents will see you home.* **8** to have a talk with; call on; meet: *I went to see a friend.* **9** to receive a visit from: *He is too ill to see anyone.* **10** to socialize with someone often or regularly; date: *I hear you're seeing someone new.* **11** to visit; attend: *We saw the World's Fair.* ❑ *v.* **saw, seen, see·ing.** ■ Other words that sound like this are **sea** and **si.** —**see′a·ble,** *adj.*

see about, 1 to attend to. **2** to learn about. **3** to consider and decide later.

see fit, to think something is worth doing or worthwhile: *The city has given the school $10,000 to spend as it sees fit.*

see into, to understand the real character or hidden purpose of.

see off, to go with someone to the starting place of a journey.

see out, to go through with; finish: *Many people volunteered for the beach cleanup, but only a few saw out the whole day's job.*

see through, 1 to understand the real character or hidden purpose of. **2** to go through with; finish. **3** to watch over or help through: *Friends saw her through her time of illness.*

see to, to look after; take care of.

see[2] (sē), *n.* **1** position or authority of a bishop. **2** district under a bishop's authority; diocese; bishopric. ■ Other words that sound like this are **sea** and **si.**

seed (sēd), **1** *n.* the part of most plants from which another plant can grow. A seed has a protective outer coat enclosing an embryo that will become the new plant and a supply of food for the plant's growth. **2** *adj.* of or containing seeds; used for seeds: *seed corn for planting.* **3** *v.* to sow with seeds; scatter seeds over: *They seeded the field with corn.* **4** *v.* to produce seeds; shed seeds. **5** *v.* to remove the seeds from: *seed tomatoes.* **6** *n.* source or beginning of anything: *seeds of trouble.* **7** *n.* children; descendants: *The Jews are called the seed of Abraham.* ❑ *n., pl.* **seeds** or **seed.** ■ Another word that sounds like this is **cede.** —**seed′like′,** *adj.*

go to seed, 1 to come to the time of yielding seeds: *Dandelions go to seed when their heads turn white.* **2** to come to the end of vigor, usefulness, prosperity, etc.: *After the mines closed, the miners left and the town went to seed.*

seed·case (sēd′kās′), *n.* any pod, capsule, or other dry, hollow fruit that contains seeds.

seed coat, the outer covering of a seed.

seed·er (sē′dər), *n.* **1** person who seeds. **2** machine or device for planting seeds. **3** machine or device for removing seeds.

seed·less (sēd′lis), *adj.* without seeds: *seedless grapes.*

seed·ling (sēd′ling), *n.* **1** a young plant grown from a seed. **2** a young tree less than three feet (0.9 meter) high.

seed money, money needed or collected to begin a new project.

seed pearl, a very small pearl.

seed plant, any plant that bears seeds. Most seed plants have flowers and produce seeds in fruits; some form seeds on cones.

seed·y (sē′dē), *adj.* **1** shabby; no longer fresh or new: *seedy clothes.* **2** full of seed. **3** gone to seed. ❑ *adj.* **seed·i·er, seed·i·est.** —**seed′i·ly,** *adv.* —**seed′i·ness,** *n.*

see·ing (sē′ing), **1** *conj.* in view of the fact; considering: *Seeing that it is 10 o'clock, we will wait no longer.* **2** *n.* ability to see; sight.

Seeing Eye, organization that breeds and trains dogs as guides for people who cannot see.

Seeing Eye dog, trademark for a dog trained to work as a guide for someone who cannot see.

seek (sēk), *v.* **1** to try to find; look for; hunt; search: *We are seeking a new home.* ■ See Synonym Study at **search. 2** to try to get: *Friends sought her advice. Some people seek wealth.* **3** to try; attempt: *We seek to make peace with our enemies.* ❑ *v.* **sought, seek·ing.** —**seek′er,** *n.*

seem (sēm), *v.* **1** to look like; appear to be: *This apple seemed good but was rotten inside.* **2** to appear to yourself: *I still seem to hear the music.* **3** to appear to exist: *There seems no need to wait longer.* **4** to appear to be true or to be the case: *It seems likely to rain. This, it seems, is your idea of cleaning a room.* ■ Another word that sounds like this is **seam.**

Seeing Eye dog

seem·ing (sē′ming), **1** *adj.* apparent; appearing to be: *a seeming advantage.* **2** *n.* appearance: *It was worse in its seeming than in reality.* —**seem′ing·ly,** *adv.* —**seem′ing·ness,** *n.*

seem·ly (sēm′lē), OLD USE. **1** *adj.* suitable; proper: *That dance is not seemly.* **2** *adv.* properly; becomingly; fittingly: *Try to behave seemly.* ❑ *adj.* **seem·li·er, seem·li·est.** —**seem′li·ness,** *n.*

seen (sēn), *v.* past participle of **see**[1]: *Have you seen my parents?* ■ Another word that sounds like this is **scene.**

seep (sēp), *v.* to leak slowly; trickle; ooze: *Water seeps through sand.*

seep·age (sē′pij), *n.* **1** slow leakage. **2** moisture or liquid that seeps: *two feet of seepage in the cellar.*

seer (sir), *n.* person who foresees or foretells future events; prophet. ■ Another word that sounds like this is **sear.**

seer·suck·er (sir′suk′ər), *n.* cloth with alternate stripes of plain and crinkled material.

see·saw (sē′sò′), **1** *n.* plank resting on a support near its middle so the ends can move up and down; teeter-totter. **2** *n.* a children's game in which the children sit at opposite ends of such a plank and move alternately up and down. **3** *v.* to move up and down on such a plank: *The two children seesawed in the playground for some time.* **4** *v.* to move up and down or back and forth. **5** *adj.* moving up and down or back and forth. **6** *n.* movement up and down or back and forth: *the seesaw of a storm-tossed ship.*

seethe (sēᴛн), *v.* **1** to be excited; be disturbed: *She seethed with anger at being unjustly fired.* **2** to bubble and foam: *Water seethed under the falls.* ❑ *v.* **seethed, seeth·ing.** —**seeth′ing·ly,** *adv.*

seg·ment (seg′mənt), **1** *n.* piece or part that is cut, marked, or broken off; division; section: *A tangerine is easily pulled apart into its segments.* **2** *n.* (in geometry) part of a circle cut off by a straight line. **3** *n.* line segment. **4** *v.* to divide into segments.

se·go (sē′gō), *n.* sego lily. ❑ *n., pl.* **se·gos.**

sego lily, a plant related to lilies, with showy, white, trumpet-shaped flowers. It is found in the western United States, and its bulb was eaten by settlers.

seg·re·gate (seg′rə gāt), *v.* **1** to separate people of different races by having separate schools, restaurants, etc. **2** to separate from others; set apart; isolate: *The doctor segregated the sick child to protect the other patients.* ❑ *v.* **seg·re·gat·ed, seg·re·gat·ing.**

sego lily

seg·re·ga·tion (seg′rə gā′shən), *n.* **1** separation of people of different races, especially in schools, housing, etc. **2** separation from others; isolation.

seg·re·ga·tion·ist (seg′rə gā′shə nist), *n.* person who believes in or practices racial segregation.

se·gue (seg′wā *or* sā′gwā), **1** *v.* to go on without pause, especially from one musical item to another: *Each song in the medley segues into the next.* **2** *n.* act of going on without pause: *The text provided a good segue from the 70s into the 80s.* ❑ *v.* **se·gued, se·gue·ing.**

seiche (sāsh), *n.* a sudden rise in the water level along the shore of a lake or bay, which can produce waves up to 10 feet (3 meters) high. Seiches are caused by wind, earthquakes, etc.

seine (sān), **1** *n.* a fishing net that hangs straight down in the water. It has floats at the upper edge and sinkers at the lower. **2** *v.* to fish or catch fish with a seine. ❑ *v.* **seined, sein·ing.** ■ Another word that sounds like this is **sane.** —**sein′er,** *n.*

Seine (sān *or* sen), *n.* river flowing from E France into the English Channel. Paris is on the Seine. See **Rhine** for map.

seis·mic (sīz′mik), *adj.* of or caused by an earthquake: *seismic waves.*

seis·mo·graph (sīz′mə graf), *n.* device for recording the direction, strength, and time of earthquakes.

seis·mol·o·gy (sīz mol′ə jē), *n.* the scientific study of earthquakes. —**seis·mol′o·gist,** *n.*

seize (sēz), *v.* **1** to take hold of suddenly; clutch; grasp: *In fright I seized her arm.* **2** to take possession of by force: *The rebels seized the palace.* **3** to take prisoner; arrest; catch: *seize someone wanted for murder.* **4** to take possession of or come upon suddenly: *A fever seized him.* **5** to take possession of by legal authority: *seize smuggled goods.* **6** to grasp with the mind: *seize an idea.* ❑ *v.* **seized, seiz·ing.** —**seiz′a·ble,** *adj.* —**seiz′er,** *n.*

seize on or **seize upon, 1** to take hold of suddenly. **2** to take possession of.

sei·zure (sē′zhər), *n.* **1** a sudden attack of disease: *an epileptic seizure.* **2** act of seizing: *Seizure of smuggled jewels by government agents was reported yesterday.* **3** condition of being seized.

sel·dom (sel′dəm), *adv.* not often; rarely: *I am seldom ill.*

se·lect (si lekt′), **1** *v.* to pick out; choose: *Select the book you want.* ■ See Synonym Study at **choose. 2** *adj.* picked as best; chosen specially: *She was one of a select group of skiers going to the Olympics.* **3** *adj.* choice; superior: *That store carries a very select line of merchandise.* **4** *adj.* careful in choosing; particular as to friends, company, etc.: *She belongs to a very select club.* —**se·lect′ly,** *adv.* —**se·lect′ness,** *n.*

se·lec·tion (si lek′shən), *n.* **1** act of selecting; choice: *His selection of a hat took a long time.* **2** person, thing, or group chosen: *The plain blue hat was her selection.* **3** quantity or variety to choose from: *The shop offered a good selection of hats.* **4** condition of being chosen: *Her selection as a candidate was certain.*

se·lec·tive (si lek′tiv), *adj.* **1** having the power to select; selecting. **2** of or about selection. —**se·lec′tive·ly,** *adv.* —**se·lec′tiveness,** *n.* —**se·lec·tiv′i·ty,** *n.*

selective service, compulsory military service of persons selected from the general population according to age, physical fitness, etc.

se·lect·man (si lekt′mən), *n.* member of a board of town officers in New England, chosen each year to manage the town's public affairs. ❑ *n., pl.* **se·lect·men.**

se·lec·tor (si lek′tər), *n.* **1** person who selects. **2** a mechanical or electrical device that selects.

Se·le·ne (sə lē′nē), *n.* the Greek goddess of the moon. The Romans called her Luna.

se·le·ni·um (sə lē′nē əm), *n.* a grayish element found in various metallic ores. It is used in photoelectric cells. *Symbol:* Se

self (self), **1** *n.* one's own person: *his very self.* **2** *n.* one's own welfare or interests: *A selfish person puts self first.* **3** *n.* nature or character of someone or something: *She is not her old self.* **4** *pron.* myself; himself; herself; yourself: *a check made payable to self.* ❑ *n. and pron., pl.* **selves.**

self-, *prefix.* **1** of or over yourself: *self-conscious = conscious of yourself; self-control = control over yourself.* **2** by or in yourself or itself: *self-inflicted = inflicted by yourself; self-absorbed = absorbed in yourself.* **3** to or for yourself: *self-addressed = addressed to yourself.* **4** yourself or itself: *self-defeating = defeating yourself or itself.* **5** automatic; automatically: *self-winding = winding automatically.*

self-act·ing (self′ak′ting), *adj.* working by itself: *a self-acting machine.*

self-ad·dressed (self′ə drest′), *adj.* addressed to yourself: *a self-addressed envelope.*

self-ap·point·ed (self′ə poin′tid), *adj.* appointed by yourself, not by anyone else: *a self-appointed leader.*

self-as·ser·tion (self′ə sėr′shən), *n.* insistence on your own wishes, opinions, claims, etc.

self-as·ser·tive (self′ə sėr′tiv), *adj.* putting yourself forward; insisting on one's own wishes, opinions, etc. —**self′-as·ser′tively,** *adv.* —**self′-as·ser′tive·ness,** *n.*

self-as·sur·ance (self′ə shür′əns), *n.* self-confidence.

self-as·sured (self′ə shürd′), *adj.* self-confident; sure of yourself. —**self′-as·sured′ness,** *n.*

self-a·ware·ness (self′ə wâr′nes), *n.* awareness or perception of yourself as an individual personality.

self-cen·tered (self′sen′tərd), *adj.* **1** occupied with your own interests and affairs. **2** selfish. —**self′-cen′tered·ly,** *adv.* —**self′-cen′tered·ness,** *n.*

self-con·cept (self′kon′sept), *n.* a person's idea or view of herself or himself as an individual.

self-con·fi·dence (self′kon′fə dəns), *n.* belief in your own ability, power, judgment, etc.; confidence in yourself.

self-con·fi·dent (self′kon′fə dənt), *adj.* believing in your own ability, power, judgment, etc. —**self′-con′fi·dent·ly,** *adv.*

self-con·scious (self′kon′shəs), *adj.* embarrassed, especially by the presence of other people or by the opinions you believe other people have of you; shy: *I always feel self-conscious when I'm among people I don't know.* —**self′-con′scious·ly,** *adv.* —**self′-con′scious·ness,** *n.*

self-con·tained (self′kən tānd′), *adj.* **1** saying little; reserved. **2** containing in yourself or itself all that is necessary.

self-con·trol (self′kən trōl′), *n.* control of your actions, feelings, etc. —**self′-con·trolled′,** *adj.*

a	hat	ė	term	ô	order	ch	child	
ā	age	i	it	oi	oil	ng	long	a in about
ä	far	ī	ice	ou	out	sh	she	e in taken
â	care	o	hot	u	cup	th	thin	ə i in pencil
e	let	ō	open	ů	put	ᴛн	then	o in lemon
ē	equal	ȯ	saw	ü	rule	zh	measure	u in circus

S

self-de·feat·ing (self/di fē/ting), *adj.* defeating yourself or itself; contrary to your own purpose or interests.

self-de·fense (self/di fens/), *n.* defense of your own person, property, reputation, etc.: *After being hit, he fought back in self-defense.*

self-de·ni·al (self/di nī/əl), *n.* sacrifice of your own desires and interests; going without things you want.

self-de·ny·ing (self/di nī/ing), *adj.* unselfish; sacrificing your own wishes and interests.

self-de·struct (self/di strukt/), *v.* to destroy itself: *When it swerved from its intended course, the rocket self-destructed.* —**self/-de·struc/tion**, *n.*

self-de·struc·tive (self/di struk/tiv), *adj.* wanting or acting to destroy yourself; suicidal: *a self-destructive way of life.* —**self/-de·struc/tive·ness**, *n.*

self-de·ter·mi·na·tion (self/di tėr/mə nā/shən), *n.* **1** determination by a nation's people of the form of government they shall have, without reference to the wishes of any other nation. **2** act or process of choosing for yourself, without the help or interference of others.

self-dis·ci·pline (self/dis/ə plin), *n.* careful control and training of yourself.

self-doubt (self/dout/), *n.* lack of confidence in your own abilities or judgment.

self-ed·u·cat·ed (self/ej/ə kā/tid), *adj.* self-taught; educated by your own efforts.

self-em·ployed (self/em ploid/), *adj.* not employed by others; working for yourself. Doctors and farmers are usually self-employed.

self-es·teem (self/e stēm/), *n.* confidence in yourself; self-respect.

self-ev·i·dent (self/ev/ə dənt), *adj.* evident in itself; needing no proof. —**self/-ev/i·dent·ly**, *adv.*

self-ex·plan·a·to·ry (self/ek splan/ə tôr/ē), *adj.* explaining itself; needing no explanation; obvious.

self-ex·pres·sion (self/ek spresh/ən), *n.* expression of your personality.

self-ful·fill·ment (self/fül fil/mənt), *n.* achievement of ambitions, hopes, or the like, by your own efforts or actions.

self-gov·ern·ing (self/guv/ər ning), *adj.* ruling itself: *a self-governing territory.*

self-gov·ern·ment (self/guv/ərn mənt), *n.* **1** government of a group by its own members: *self-government through elected representatives.* **2** self-control.

self-help (self/help/), *n.* act of helping yourself; getting along without assistance from others.

self-im·age (self/im/ij), *n.* the conception you have of yourself, of your abilities and ambitions, etc.; your idea of your true self.

self-im·por·tance (self/im pôrt/ns), *n.* too high an opinion of your own importance; conceit; behavior showing conceit.

self-im·por·tant (self/im pôrt/nt), *adj.* having or showing too high an opinion of your own importance.

self-im·posed (self/im pōzd/), *adj.* imposed on yourself by yourself: *a self-imposed task.*

self-im·prove·ment (self/im prüv/mənt), *n.* improvement of your character, mind, etc., by your own efforts.

self-in·dul·gence (self/in dul/jəns), *n.* satisfaction of your own desires, passions, etc., with too little regard for the welfare of others.

self-in·dul·gent (self/in dul/jənt), *adj.* showing self-indulgence. —**self/-in·dul/gent·ly**, *adv.*

self-in·flict·ed (self/in flik/tid), *adj.* inflicted on yourself by yourself: *a self-inflicted wound.*

self-in·ter·est (self/in/tər ist), *n.* **1** interest in your own welfare with too little care for the welfare of others; selfishness. **2** personal advantage.

self·ish (sel/fish), *adj.* **1** caring too much for yourself; caring too little for others. Selfish people put their own interests first. **2** showing care solely or mostly for yourself: *selfish motives.* —**self/ish·ly**, *adv.* —**self/ish·ness**, *n.*

SYNONYM STUDY **Selfish** and **greedy** both mean wanting more than your share. **Selfish** means caring too much about yourself and what you want: *She is so selfish that she constantly borrows clothes but never lends any.* **Greedy** means with a strong desire to have a whole lot: *The greedy child cried for every toy in the store.*

self·less (self/lis), *adj.* having no regard or thought for self; unselfish. —**self/less·ly**, *adv.* —**self/less·ness**, *n.*

self-made (self/mād/), *adj.* **1** made by yourself. **2** successful through your own efforts.

self-pit·y (self/pit/ē), *n.* pity for yourself.

self-pol·li·na·tion (self/pol/ə nā/shən), *n.* the transfer of pollen from the anther to the stigma of the same flower, so that it produces seeds by itself.

self-por·trait (self/pôr/trit *or* self/pôr/trāt), *n.* portrait of yourself made by yourself.

self-pos·sessed (self/pə zest/), *adj.* having or showing control of your feelings and actions; not excited, embarrassed, or confused; calm.

self-pos·ses·sion (self/pə zesh/ən), *n.* control of your feelings and actions; composure; calmness.

self-pres·er·va·tion (self/prez/ər vā/shən), *n.* preservation of yourself from harm or destruction.

self-pro·pelled (self/prə peld/), *adj.* propelled by an engine, motor, etc., within itself: *a self-propelled missile.*

self-re·li·ance (self/ri lī/əns), *n.* reliance on your own acts, abilities, etc.

self-re·li·ant (self/ri lī/ənt), *adj.* having or showing self-reliance. —**self/-re·li/ant·ly**, *adv.*

self-re·proach (self/ri prōch/), *n.* blame by your own conscience.

self-re·spect (self/ri spekt/), *n.* respect for yourself; proper pride.

self-re·spect·ing (self/ri spek/ting), *adj.* having self-respect; properly proud.

self-re·straint (self/ri strānt/), *n.* self-control.

self-right·eous (self/rī/chəs), *adj.* thinking that you are more moral and virtuous than other people: *self-righteous disapproval of other people's habits.* —**self/-right/eous·ly**, *adv.* —**self/-right/eous·ness**, *n.*

self-rule (self/rül/), *n.* self-government.

self-sac·ri·fice (self/sak/rə fis), *n.* sacrifice of your own interests and desires, for your duty, another's welfare, etc.

self-sac·ri·fic·ing (self/sak/rə fī/sing), *adj.* unselfish; giving up things for someone else.

self·same (self/sām/), *adj.* very same: *We study the selfsame books that you do.* —**self/same/ness**, *n.*

self-sat·is·fac·tion (self/sat/is fak/shən), *n.* satisfaction with yourself or your achievements.

self-sat·is·fied (self/sat/i sfid), *adj.* pleased with yourself or your achievements.

self-seek·er (self/sē/kər), *n.* person who seeks his or her own interests too much.

self-seek·ing (self/sē/king), **1** *adj.* seeking to advance your own interests too much; selfish. **2** *n.* selfishness.

self-serve (self/sėrv/), *adj.* **1** able to be used without help: *self-serve gas pumps.* **2** offering self-service to customers: *a self-serve filling station.*

self-serv·ice (self/sėr/vis), *n.* act or process of serving yourself in a restaurant, store, etc.

self-serv·ing (self/sėr/ving), *adj.* serving someone's own wishes, without caring about the truth or about the feelings of others; selfish: *The committee prepared a self-serving report saying the problem was not their fault.*

self-styled (self/stild/), *adj.* called by yourself: *a self-styled leader whom no one follows.*

self-suf·fi·cien·cy (self/sə fish/ən sē), *n.* **1** ability to supply your own needs. **2** conceit; self-assurance.

self-suf·fi·cient (self/sə fish/ənt), *adj.* **1** asking no help; independent. **2** having too much confidence in your own resources, power, etc.; conceited.

self-sup·port·ing (self/sə pôr/ting), *adj.* earning your expenses; getting along without help.

self-taught (self/tot/), *adj.* taught by yourself without aid from others.

self-will (self/wil/), *n.* insistence on having your own way.

self-willed (self/wild/), *adj.* insisting on having your own way; objecting to doing what others ask or command.

self·wind·ing (self′wīn′ding), *adj.* winding itself. A self-winding watch winds itself by the movements of the person wearing it.

sell (sel), *v.* **1** to exchange for money or other payment: *sell a house.* **2** to deal in; keep for sale: *That store sells furniture.* **3** to be given in exchange; be on sale; be sold: *Strawberries sell at a high price in January.* **4** to give up; betray: *The traitor sold his country for money.* **5** to cause to be accepted, approved, or adopted by methods characteristic of salesmanship: *sell an idea to the public.* **6** to win acceptance, approval, or adoption: *I believe that her idea will sell.* ❑ *v.* **sold, sell·ing.** ■ Another word that sounds like this is **cell. —sell′a·ble,** *adj.*

sell out, 1 to sell all that you have of; get rid of by selling. **2** to betray by a secret bargain. **3** to give up your principles, pride, or identity in order to make money: *The rock band sold out by letting their song be used in a deodorant commercial.*

sell·er (sel′ər), *n.* **1** person who sells: *The stock exchange was filled with sellers of stocks.* **2** thing considered with reference to its sale: *This book is a good seller.* ■ Another word that sounds like this is **cellar.**

Sel·ma (sel′mə), *n.* city in SW Alabama. It was the site of a 1965 drive to register African American voters, led by Reverend Martin Luther King, Jr.

selt·zer (selt′sər), *n.* soda water.

sel·vage or **sel·vedge** (sel′vij), *n.* the edge of a woven fabric finished off to prevent raveling.

selves (selvz), *n., pron.* plural of **self:** *She had two selves—one that liked to save money and one that liked to spend it.*

se·man·tic (sə man′tik), *adj.* **1** having to do with the meanings of words. **2** having to do with semantics. **—se·man′ti·cal·ly,** *adv.*

se·man·tics (sə man′tiks), *n.* the scientific study of the meanings, and the development of meanings, of words.

sem·a·phore (sem′ə fôr), **1** *n.* device for signaling. **2** *n.* system of hand signals, using a flag in each hand. **3** *n.* a set of colored lights, or formerly, a post with a movable arm, for controlling railroad traffic. **4** *v.* to signal in any of these ways. ❑ *v.* **sem·a·phored, sem·a·phor·ing.**

sem·blance (sem′bləns), *n.* **1** outward appearance: *Their story had the semblance of truth but was really false.* **2** likeness: *These clouds have the semblance of a huge head.*

semaphore (def. 2)

se·men (sē′mən), *n.* a whitish fluid containing the male reproductive cells. ■ Another word that sounds like this is **seaman.**

se·mes·ter (sə mes′tər), *n.* a part, often one half, of a school year.

sem·i (sem′ī), *n.* INFORMAL. semitrailer. ❑ *n., pl.* **sem·is.**

semi-, *prefix.* **1** a half; half of: *semicircle = half of a circle.* **2** partly; incompletely: *semiskilled = partly skilled.* **3** twice; in or for each half; two times: *semimonthly = every half month, or twice a month.*

sem·i·an·nu·al (sem′ē an′yü əl), *adj.* **1** occurring every half year. **2** lasting a half year. **—sem′i·an′nu·al·ly,** *adv.*

sem·i·ar·id (sem′ē ar′id), *adj.* having little rainfall.

sem·i·au·to·mat·ic (sem′ē ò′tə mat′ik), **1** *adj.* partly automatic; self-acting in some part of its operation. **2** *n.* gun like an automatic but requiring a press of the trigger to fire each shot. **—sem′i·au′to·mat′i·cal·ly,** *adv.*

sem·i·cir·cle (sem′i sėr′kəl), *n.* half of a circle: *We sat in a semicircle around the fire.*

sem·i·cir·cu·lar (sem′i sėr′kyə lər), *adj.* having the form of half a circle. **—sem′i·cir′cu·lar·ly,** *adv.*

semicircular canal, any of three curved, tubelike canals in the inner ear that help to maintain balance.

sem·i·co·lon (sem′i kō′lən), *n.* mark of punctuation (;) that shows a separation not so complete as that shown by a period but more so than that shown by a comma. EXAMPLE: We arrived later than we had intended; consequently there was little time left for swimming before the volleyball game.

sem·i·con·duc·tor (sem′i kən duk′tər), *n.* a mineral substance, such as silicon, that conducts electricity better than an insulator but not so well as a metal. Semiconductors can convert alternating current into direct current and amplify weak electric signals. Transistors are made primarily of semiconductors.

sem·i·con·scious (sem′i kon′shəs), *adj.* half conscious; not fully conscious. **—sem′i·con′scious·ly,** *adv.* **—sem′i·con′scious·ness,** *n.*

sem·i·fi·nal (sem′i fī′nl *for adj.;* sem′i fī′nl *for noun*), **1** *adj.* of or about the two games, matches, or rounds that come before the final one in a tournament. **2** *n.* Often, **semifinals,** *pl.* one of these two games.

sem·i·fi·nal·ist (sem′i fī′nl ist), *n.* contestant in the semifinal game, match, or round.

sem·i·month·ly (sem′i munth′lē), **1** *adj.* occurring or appearing twice a month. **2** *adv.* twice a month. **3** *n.* magazine or newspaper published twice a month. ❑ *n., pl.* **sem·i·month·lies.**

sem·i·nal (sem′ə nəl), *adj.* **1** like seed; having the possibility of future development: *a seminal idea.* **2** of or about semen or seed. **—sem′i·nal·ly,** *adv.*

sem·i·nar (sem′ə när′), *n.* **1** group of students engaged in discussion and original research under the guidance of a professor. **2** meeting in class of such a group.

sem·i·nar·y (sem′ə ner′ē), *n.* **1** school or college for training students to be priests, ministers, rabbis, etc. **2** academy or boarding school, especially for young women. ❑ *n., pl.* **sem·i·nar·ies.**

sem·i·nif·er·ous (sem′ə nif′ər əs), *adj.* **1** (in botany) bearing or producing seed. **2** (in zoology) carrying, containing, or producing semen.

seminiferous tubule, any of the very small tubes that produce sperm in the testicles.

Sem·i·nole (sem′ə nōl), *n.* member of a tribe of American Indians that settled in Florida in the 1700s, now living in the Florida Everglades and in Oklahoma. ❑ *n., pl.* **Sem·i·nole** or **Sem·i·noles.**

WORD STORY Seminole comes from a Creek adaptation of an American Spanish word meaning "wild" or "escaped." Their lands in Florida were outside Spanish control and a refuge for people who had escaped from slavery.

sem·i·of·fi·cial (sem′ē ə fish′əl), *adj.* partly official; having some degree of authority. **—sem′i·of·fi′cial·ly,** *adv.*

sem·i·pre·cious (sem′i presh′əs), *adj.* having some value; somewhat precious. Garnets are semiprecious stones. They are less valuable than diamonds, which are precious stones.

sem·i·pri·vate (sem′i prī′vit), *adj.* not completely private: *a semiprivate hospital room with two beds.*

sem·i·pro (sem′i prō′), *n., adj.* semiprofessional. ❑ *n., pl.* **sem·i·pros.**

sem·i·pro·fes·sion·al (sem′i prə fesh′ə nəl), **1** *n.* a part-time professional athlete. **2** *adj.* about or for such athletes. **—sem′i·pro·fes′sion·al·ly,** *adv.*

sem·i·skilled (sem′i skild′), *adj.* partly skilled.

sem·i·sol·id (sem′i sol′id), **1** *adj.* partly solid. **2** *n.* a partly solid substance.

Sem·ite (sem′īt), *n.* member of a group of ancient and modern peoples speaking any of the Semitic languages. The ancient Hebrews, Phoenicians, and Assyrians were Semites. Arabs and Jews are sometimes called Semites. [Semite comes from Shem, the oldest son of Noah, thought of as the ancestor of these peoples.]

Se·mit·ic (sə mit′ik), **1** *adj.* of or about the Semites or their languages. **2** *n.* group of languages including Hebrew, Arabic, Aramaic, Phoenician, and Assyrian.

sem·i·tone (sem′i tōn′), *n.* (in music) half step; half tone.

sem·i·trail·er (sem′i trā′lər), *n.* type of truck trailer with wheels only at the back, the front end being supported by the tractor.

a	hat	ė	term	ô	order	ch	child		a in about
ā	age	i	it	oi	oil	ng	long		e in taken
ä	far	ī	ice	ou	out	sh	she	ə	i in pencil
â	care	o	hot	u	cup	th	thin		o in lemon
e	let	ō	open	ù	put	ŦH	then		u in circus
ē	equal	ò	saw	ü	rule	zh	measure		

S

sem·i·trop·i·cal (sem′i trop′ə kəl), *adj.* halfway between tropical and temperate: *The climate of Florida is semitropical.*

sem·i·week·ly (sem′i wēk′lē), **1** *adj.* occurring or appearing twice a week. **2** *adv.* twice a week. **3** *n.* newspaper or magazine published twice a week. ❑ *n., pl.* **sem·i·week·lies.**

sem·o·li·na (sem′ə lē′nə), *n.* the larger hard parts of ground wheat remaining after the fine flour has been sifted through. Semolina is used to make pasta, puddings, and the like.

Sen. or **sen., 1** Senate. **2** Senator.

sen·ate (sen′it), *n.* **1** a governing or lawmaking assembly. The highest council of state in ancient Rome was called the senate. **2** the upper and smaller branch of an assembly that makes laws. **3 Senate, a** the upper house of Congress or of a state legislature. **b** the upper house of the legislature of certain other countries, such as Canada and Australia.

WORD STORY Senate comes from a Latin word meaning "old." Senior, señor, señora, and señorita come from the same Latin word. The ancient Roman senate included only older men. Senior citizens are older than other citizens. The Spanish words began with a way of speaking to people of noble families. Because powerful people were often older, the word meaning "older" came to mean "lord" and "lady." Gradually it became good manners to use such words for everyone—even young ladies.

sen·a·tor (sen′ə tər), *n.* **1** member of a senate. **2 Senator,** member of the U.S. Senate.

sen·a·to·ri·al (sen′ə tôr′ē əl), *adj.* **1** of or suitable for a senator or senators. **2** made up of senators: *a senatorial fact-finding committee.* **3** entitled to elect a senator: *a senatorial district.* **–sen′a·to′ri·al·ly,** *adv.*

send (send), *v.* **1** to cause to go from one place to another: *send a child on an errand, send someone for a doctor.* **2** to cause to be carried: *send a letter, send news.* **3** to cause to come, occur, or be: *Send help at once.* **4** to drive; impel; throw: *The volcano sent clouds of smoke into the air.* ❑ *v.* **sent, send·ing. –send′a·ble,** *adj.* **–send′er,** *n.*

send for, 1 to tell or order to come; summon: *to send for help.* **2** to order to be delivered, usually by mail: *to send for a catalog.* **3** to send out for.

send out for, to order by telephone the delivery of something: *We got so hungry we sent out for a pizza.*

send-off (send′ôf′), *n.* **1** a friendly demonstration in honor of someone setting out on a journey, course, career, etc. **2** a public start for a person or project.

send-off (def. 1)

Sen·e·ca (sen′ə kə), *n.* member of a tribe of American Indians living in New York and Ontario. ❑ *n., pl.* **Sen·e·ca** or **Sen·e·cas.** [Seneca comes from an Algonquian word meaning "stone."]

Sen·e·gal (sen′ə gòl′ or sen′ə gäl), *n.* country in W Africa, on the Atlantic. *Capital:* Dakar.

sen·es·chal (sen′ə shəl), *n.* steward in charge of a royal palace or nobleman's estate in the Middle Ages. Seneschals often had the powers of judges or generals.

se·nile (sē′nil), *adj.* **1** showing the loss of mental and physical abilities caused by various diseases that can occur in old age. **2** caused by old age. ■ **Senile** is sometimes considered offensive. **–se′nile·ly,** *adv.*

se·nil·i·ty (sə nil′ə tē), *n.* loss of mental and physical abilities caused by various diseases that can occur in old age. ■ **Senility** is sometimes considered offensive.

sen·ior (sē′nyər), **1** *adj.* the older. The word senior is used of a father whose son has the same given name: *John Parker, Senior, is the father of John Parker, Junior.* **2** *adj.* older or elder: *a senior citizen.* **3** *n.* an older person: *She is her sister's senior by two years.* **4** *adj.* of higher position or standing; higher in rank or longer in service: *a senior officer.* **5** *n.* person of higher position or standing; person of higher rank or longer service. **6** *n.* student who is a member of the graduating class of a high school or college. **7** *adj.* of or for the last year of high school or college: *the senior class, the senior prom.* [See Word Story at **senate.**]

senior citizen, an older person, especially one who is old enough to retire.

senior high school, school attended after junior high school. It usually has grades 10, 11, and 12.

sen·ior·i·ty (sē nyôr′ə tē), *n.* **1** right to come before others because of length of service: *She has seniority because she has worked here longer than anyone else.* **2** condition of being greater in age or standing; a being older: *He felt that two years' seniority gave him the right to advise his sister.*

sen·na (sen′ə), *n.* the dried leaves of cassia plants, used as a laxative. ❑ *n., pl.* **sen·nas.**

se·ñor (sen yôr′), *n.* SPANISH. **1** Mr. or sir. **2** a gentleman. ❑ *n., pl.* **se·ño·res** (sen yô′res). [See Word Story at **senate.**]

se·ño·ra (sen yôr′ä), *n.* SPANISH. **1** Mrs. or Madam. **2** a lady. ❑ *n., pl.* **se·ño·ras.** [See Word Story at **senate.**]

se·ño·ri·ta (sen′yô rē′tä), *n.* SPANISH. **1** Miss. **2** a young lady. ❑ *n., pl.* **se·ño·ri·tas.** [See Word Story at **senate.**]

sen·sa·tion (sen sā′shən), *n.* **1** feeling: *a sensation of being watched.* **2** action of the senses; power to see, hear, feel, taste, smell, etc.: *An unconscious person is without sensation.* **3** strong or excited feeling: *The announcement of peace caused a sensation throughout the nation.* **4** anything causing excitement: *The new movie is a sensation.*

sen·sa·tion·al (sen sā′shə nəl), *adj.* **1** very good or exciting; outstanding; spectacular: *The outfielder's sensational catch made the crowd cheer wildly.* **2** arousing or trying to arouse strong or excited feeling: *a sensational newspaper.* **3** of or about the senses or sensation. **–sen·sa′tion·al·ly,** *adv.*

sen·sa·tion·al·ism (sen sā′shə nə liz′əm), *n.* sensational methods, writing, language, etc., aimed at arousing strong or excited feeling.

sense (sens), **1** *n.* power of a living thing to know what happens outside itself. Sight, hearing, touch, taste, and smell are some of the senses. **2** *n.* feeling: *The extra lock on the door gives us a sense of security.* **3** *v.* to be aware; feel; understand: *I sensed that he was tired.* **4** *n.* understanding; awareness: *He has a delightful sense of humor.* **5** *n.* Usually, **senses,** *pl.* normal, reasonable condition of mind: *They must be out of their senses to climb that steep cliff.* **6** *n.* good judgment; intelligence: *She had the sense to stay out of the argument.* **7** *n.* a reason; use: *What's the sense of going out in the rain?* **8** *n.* meaning: *Which sense of "funny" are you using?* ■ See Synonym Study at **meaning.** ❑ *v.* **sensed, sens·ing.**

in a sense, in some ways; to some amount.

make sense, to have a meaning; be understandable; be reasonable: *The statement "Cow cat bless lawn" doesn't make sense.*

WORD FAMILY Sense and the words below are related. They all come from a Latin word meaning "to feel" or "to perceive."

extrasensory	sensitive	sensual	sententious
sensation	sensitize	sensuous	sentient
sensible	sensory	sentence	sentiment

sense·less (sens′lis), *adj.* **1** unconscious: *A hard blow on the head knocked him senseless.* **2** foolish; stupid: *a senseless idea.* **3** meaningless: *senseless words.* **–sense′less·ly,** *adv.* **–sense′less·ness,** *n.*

sense organ, a part of the body by which a person or an animal receives sensations of heat, colors, sounds, smells, etc.; receptor.

sen·si·bil·i·ty (sen′sə bil′ə tē), *n.* **1** sensitiveness: *a sensibility to the beauties of nature.* **2** Usually, **sensibilities,** *pl.* sensitive or refined emotions, tastes, etc. **3** tendency to feel offended or hurt too easily. **4** ability to perceive: *Some drugs lessen a person's sensibilities.* ❑ *n., pl.* **sen·si·bil·i·ties** for 1,3,4.

sen·si·ble (sen′sə bəl), *adj.* **1** having or showing good sense or judgment; wise: *She is far too sensible to do anything foolish.* ■ See Synonym Study at **wise**[1]. **2** aware; conscious: *I am sensible of your kindness.* **3** noticeable: *There is a sensible difference between red and orange.* **4** able to be perceived by the senses. **5** sensitive. —**sen′si·ble·ness,** *n.* —**sen′si·bly,** *adv.*

sen·si·tive (sen′sə tiv), *adj.* **1** receiving impressions readily: *The eye is sensitive to light.* **2** easily affected or influenced: *This device is sensitive to changes in temperature. Sensitive people are quickly touched by something beautiful or sad.* **3** easily hurt or offended: *to be sensitive about your weight.* **4** aware of the feelings and needs of other people. —**sen′si·tive·ly,** *adv.* —**sen′si·tive·ness,** *n.*

sensitive plant, 1 a tropical American plant with fernlike leaves that fold together when touched. **2** any other plant that reacts to touch.

sen·si·tiv·i·ty (sen′sə tiv′ə tē), *n.* condition, quality, or degree of being sensitive.

sen·si·tize (sen′sə tīz), *v.* to make sensitive. Camera films have been sensitized to light. ❑ *v.* **sen·si·tized, sen·si·tiz·ing.** —**sen′si·ti·za′tion,** *n.* —**sen′si·tiz′er,** *n.*

sen·sor (sen′sər), *n.* any device that reacts to heat, light, pressure, etc., and transmits a signal. ■ Other words that sound like this are **censer** and **censor.**

sen·so·ry (sen′sər ē), *adj.* of or about sensation or the senses. The eyes and ears are sensory organs.

sen·su·al (sen′shü əl), *adj.* **1** of or about the bodily senses rather than with the mind or soul: *the sensual pleasures of eating.* **2** caring too much for the pleasures of the senses. —**sen·su·al·i·ty** (sen′shü al′ə tē), *n.* —**sen′su·al·ly,** *adv.*

sen·su·ous (sen′shü əs), *adj.* **1** of or derived from the senses; having an effect on the senses; perceived by the senses: *the sensuous thrill of a warm bath, a sensuous love of color.* **2** enjoying the pleasures of the senses. —**sen′su·ous·ly,** *adv.* —**sen′su·ous·ness,** *n.*

sent (sent), *v.* past tense and past participle of **send:** *They sent the trunks last week. She was sent on an errand.* ■ Other words that sound like this are **cent** and **scent.**

sen·tence (sen′təns), **1** *n.* a word or group of words that makes a statement, a request, a question, a command, or an exclamation. **2** *n.* group of mathematical symbols that expresses a complete idea or a requirement. $4 + 2 = 6$ is a closed sentence expressing a complete idea. $6 \div x = 2$ is an open sentence expressing a requirement. **3** *n.* decision by a judge on the punishment of a criminal: *By the sentence of the court, the thief was put in prison for five years.* **4** *n.* the punishment itself: *a sentence of five years.* **5** *v.* to pronounce punishment on: *The judge sentenced her to prison.* ❑ *v.* **sen·tenced, sen·tenc·ing.** —**sen′tenc·er,** *n.*

sentence fragment, a phrase that lacks a subject, a verb, or both. "Girls and women." "Fell down." and "Somewhere along the way." are sentence fragments.

sen·ten·tious (sen ten′shəs), *adj.* **1** full of meaning; saying much in few words. **2** inclined to give advice in a self-righteous way. **3** inclined to make wise sayings; speaking in proverbs. —**sen·ten′tious·ly,** *adv.* —**sen·ten′tious·ness,** *n.*

sen·tient (sen′shənt), *adj.* able to feel; having feeling: *sentient beings.* —**sen′tient·ly,** *adv.*

sen·ti·ment (sen′tə mənt), *n.* **1** mixture of thought and feeling. Admiration, patriotism, and loyalty are sentiments. **2** feeling, especially tender feeling: *Her letter expressed sentiments of friendship and sympathy.* **3** thought or saying that expresses feeling. **4** a mental attitude. **5** a personal opinion.

sen·ti·men·tal (sen′tə men′tl), *adj.* **1** having or showing much tender feeling: *sentimental poetry.* **2** likely to act from feelings rather than from logical thinking; having too much sentiment: *a sentimental person.* **3** of or dependent on sentiment: *These old family photographs have sentimental value.* —**sen′ti·men′tal·ly,** *adv.*

sen·ti·men·tal·ism (sen′tə men′tl iz′əm), *n.* sentimentality.

sen·ti·men·tal·ist (sen′tə men′tl ist), *n.* a sentimental person; someone who indulges in sentimentality.

sen·ti·men·tal·i·ty (sen′tə men tal′ə tē), *n.* **1** tendency to be influenced by sentiment rather than reason. **2** too much indulgence in sentiment. **3** feeling expressed too openly or emotionally. ❑ *n., pl.* **sen·ti·men·tal·i·ties** for 3.

sen·ti·men·tal·ize (sen′tə men′tl īz), *v.* **1** to indulge in sentiment. **2** to make sentimental. **3** to be sentimental about. ❑ *v.* **sen·ti·men·tal·ized, sen·ti·men·tal·iz·ing.** —**sen′ti·men′tal·i·za′tion,** *n.*

sen·ti·nel (sen′tə nəl), *n.* person stationed to keep watch and guard against surprise attacks.
stand sentinel, to act as a sentinel; keep watch.

sen·try (sen′trē), *n.* soldier stationed at a post to keep watch and guard against surprise attacks; sentinel. ❑ *n., pl.* **sen·tries.**
stand sentry, to keep watch; guard: *The sheepdog stood sentry over the sleeping flock.*

sentry box, a small building for sheltering a sentry.

Seoul (sōl), *n.* capital of South Korea, in the NW part.

se·pal (sē′pəl), *n.* one of the leaflike parts that form the calyx of a flower. The sepals are usually green and cover the unopened bud.

sep·a·ra·ble (sep′ər ə bəl), *adj.* able to be separated. —**sep′ar·a·bil′i·ty,** *n.* —**sep′ar·a·bly,** *adv.*

sentry

sep·a·rate (sep′ə rāt′ *for verb;* sep′ər it *for adj.*), **1** *v.* to keep apart; be between; divide: *The Atlantic Ocean separates the Americas from Europe and Africa.* **2** *v.* to divide into parts or groups: *separate a tangle of yarn.* **3** *v.* to draw, come, or go apart: *The rope separated under the strain.* **4** *v.* to live apart. A husband and wife may separate by agreement or by order of a court. **5** *v.* to put or set apart; keep away: *Separate your books from his.* **6** *adj.* apart from others: *in a separate room.* **7** *adj.* divided; not joined: *separate seats.* **8** *adj.* individual; single: *the separate parts of a machine.* ❑ *v.* **sep·a·rat·ed, sep·a·rat·ing.** —**sep′ar·ate·ly,** *adv.* —**sep′ar·ate·ness,** *n.*

SYNONYM STUDY **Separate, divide,** and **part** all mean to take things apart. **Separate** suggests taking one kind or part from another: *Separate the dark and light clothes before washing them.* **Divide** suggests cutting or breaking into parts equally or for sharing: *We divided the candy among the four of us.* **Part** suggests separating closely connected things: *The Civil War parted many families.*

separate school, in Canada: **1** a school for children of a religious minority. **2** a Roman Catholic parochial school. **3** a private school.

sep·a·ra·tion (sep′ə rā′shən), *n.* **1** act or fact of separating; dividing; taking apart. **2** condition of being apart; being separated: *The friends were glad to meet after so long a separation.* **3** line or point of separating: *We now come to the separation of the two branches of the river.* **4** the practice of living apart of husband and wife by agreement or by order of a court.

sep·a·ra·tism (sep′ər ə tiz′əm), *n.* **1** principle or policy of separation. **2 Separatism,** support for withdrawal of Quebec from the Confederation of Canada.

sep·a·ra·tist (sep′ər ə tist), *n.* member of a group that separates or withdraws from a larger group.

sep·a·ra·tor (sep′ə rā′tər), *n.* person or thing that separates, especially a machine for separating the cream from milk, wheat from chaff or dirt, etc.

a	hat	ė	term	ô	order	ch	child		a in about
ā	age	i	it	oi	oil	ng	long		e in taken
ä	far	ī	ice	ou	out	sh	she	ə	i in pencil
â	care	o	hot	u	cup	th	thin		o in lemon
e	let	ō	open	u̇	put	ŦH	then		u in circus
ē	equal	ȯ	saw	ü	rule	zh	measure		

S

se·pi·a (sē′pē ə), **1** *n.* a dark brown pigment prepared from the inky liquid produced by cuttlefish. **2** *n.* a dark brown. **3** *adj.* dark brown. **4** *adj.* done in tones of brown: *a sepia print.* □ *n., pl.* **se·pi·as.** —**se′pi·a·like′,** *adj.*

sept-, *prefix.* seven: *septet = group of seven.*

Sept., September.

sep·ta (sep′tə), *n.* plural of **septum.**

Sep·tem·ber (sep tem′bər), *n.* the ninth month of the year. It has 30 days. [**September** comes from a Latin word meaning "seven." It was the seventh month in the ancient Roman calendar.]

sep·tet (sep tet′), *n.* **1** piece of music for seven voices or instruments. **2** group of seven singers or musicians performing together. **3** any group of seven.

sep·tic (sep′tik), *adj.* **1** causing infection. **2** caused by infection.

sep·ti·ce·mi·a (sep′tə sē′mē ə), *n.* blood poisoning.

septic tank, an underground concrete or steel container for household sewage. Bacteria in the sewage break it down, while the liquid flows out through pipes into the soil.

sep·tum (sep′təm), *n.* a dividing wall; partition. There is a septum of bone and cartilage between the nostrils. □ *n., pl.* **sep·ta.**

sep·ul·cher (sep′əl kər), *n.* place of burial; tomb; grave.

se·pul·chral (sə pul′krəl), *adj.* **1** deep and gloomy; dismal; suggesting a tomb: *sepulchral darkness.* **2** of or about sepulchers or burial: *sepulchral ceremonies.* —**se·pul′chral·ly,** *adv.*

se·quel (sē′kwəl), *n.* **1** a complete story continuing an earlier one about the same people: *Louisa May Alcott's book "Little Men" is a sequel to her "Little Women."* **2** something that follows as a result of some earlier happening; result of something; outcome: *Among the sequels of the party were many stomachaches.*

se·quence (sē′kwəns), *n.* **1** the coming of one thing after another; succession; order of succession: *alphabetical sequence.* ∎ See Synonym Study at **succession. 2** a connected series: *a sequence of lessons.*

se·quen·tial (si kwen′shəl), *adj.* forming a sequence or connected series. —**se·quen′tial·ly,** *adv.*

se·ques·ter (si kwes′tər), *v.* **1** to remove or withdraw from public use or from public view: *The author sequestered herself in a seaside cottage while she worked on her new book.* **2** to take away property for a time from an owner until a debt is paid or some claim is satisfied. **3** to seize by authority; take and keep: *The soldiers sequestered food from the people they conquered.*

se·ques·tra·tion (sē′kwə strā′shən), *n.* **1** the seizing and holding of property until legal claims are satisfied. **2** forcible or authorized seizure; confiscation. **3** seclusion.

se·quin (sē′kwən), *n.* spangle used to decorate dresses, scarfs, etc.

se·quined or **se·quinned** (sē′kwənd), *adj.* decorated with sequins.

se·quoi·a (si kwoi′ə), *n.* **1** giant sequoia. **2** redwood. □ *n., pl.* **se·quoi·as.**

Sequoia National Park, a national park in central California. It contains thousands of giant sequoia trees.

Se·quoy·ah or **Se·quoy·a** (si-kwoi′ə), *n.* 1770?-1843, American Indian leader who invented a system of writing for the Cherokee language. The giant sequoia was named for him.

ser·a (sir′ə), *n.* a plural of **serum.**

se·ragl·io (sə ral′yō), *n.* harem. □ *n., pl.* **se·ragl·ios.**

se·ra·pe (sə rä′pē), *n.* shawl or blanket, often having bright colors, worn in Mexico and other Latin American countries.

ser·aph (ser′əf), *n.* one of the highest order of angels. □ *n., pl.* **ser·aphs** or **ser·a·phim.**

se·raph·ic (sə raf′ik), *adj.* **1** of or about seraphs. **2** like a seraph; angelic. —**se·raph′i·cal·ly,** *adv.*

ser·a·phim (ser′ə fim), *n.* a plural of **seraph.**

serape

Serb (sėrb), *n.* person born or living in Serbia.

Ser·bi·a (sėr′bē ə), *n.* country in SE Europe. *Capital:* Belgrade. —**Ser′bi·an,** *adj., n.*

Ser·bo-Cro·a·tian (sėr′bō krō ā′shən), **1** *n.* the Slavic language of Serbia and Croatia. **2** *adj.* of or about this language.

ser·e·nade (ser′ə nād′), **1** *n.* music played or sung outdoors at night, especially by a lover under someone's window. **2** *n.* piece of music suitable for such a performance. **3** *v.* to sing or play a serenade to. □ *v.* **ser·e·nad·ed, ser·e·nad·ing.** —**ser′e·nad′er,** *n.*

ser·en·dip·i·ty (ser′ən dip′ə tē), *n.* the ability to make fortunate discoveries by accident. [**Serendipity** comes from a story called "The Three Princes of Serendip," whose heroes made fortunate discoveries. Serendip is an old name for Sri Lanka.]

se·rene (sə rēn′), *adj.* **1** peaceful; calm: *a serene smile.* **2** not cloudy; clear; bright: *a serene sky.* —**se·rene′ly,** *adv.* —**se·rene′ness,** *n.*

se·ren·i·ty (sə ren′ə tē), *n.* **1** peace and quiet; calmness: *I enjoyed the serenity of the quiet woods.* **2** clearness; brightness.

serf (sėrf), *n.* **1** (in the feudal system of the Middle Ages) a peasant who could not be sold off the land, but passed from one owner to another with the land. **2** person treated almost like a possession; person who is mistreated, underpaid, etc. ∎ Another word that sounds like this is **surf.** —**serf′like′,** *adj.*

serf·dom (sėrf′dəm), *n.* **1** condition of a serf. **2** custom of having serfs. Serfdom existed all over Europe in the Middle Ages and lasted in Russia till the middle of the 1800s.

serge (sėrj), *n.* kind of cloth woven with slanting ridges in it. [See Word Story at **jeans.**] ∎ Another word that sounds like this is **surge.**

ser·geant (sär′jənt), *n.* **1** a military rank. See chart on page 712. **2** a police officer ranking next above an ordinary policeman and next below a captain or lieutenant.

sergeant at arms, officer who keeps order in a legislature, court of law, etc. □ *pl.* **sergeants at arms.**

sergeant first class, a military rank. See chart on page 712.

sergeant major, a military rank. See chart on page 712.

ser·i·al (sir′ē əl), **1** *n.* story published in installments in a magazine or newspaper, or televised as a series of individual programs. Formerly, radio and movie serials were popular. **2** *adj.* of or arranged in a series; making a series. ∎ Another word that sounds like this is **cereal.** —**ser′i·al·ly,** *adv.*

ser·i·al·ize (sir′ē ə līz), *v.* to publish or broadcast in a series of installments. □ *v.* **ser·i·al·ized, ser·i·al·iz·ing.** —**ser′i·al·i·za′tion,** *n.*

serial number, number given to one of a series of persons, articles, etc., as a means of easy identification.

series (def. 1)

ser·ies (sir′ēz), *n.* **1** number of similar things in a row: *A series of rooms opened off the hall.* **2** number of things or events coming one after the other: *We had a series of rainy days.* ∎ See Synonym Study at **succession. 3** a TV program shown at a regular time: *I watched the new mystery series last night.* **4** an electrical arrangement in which a number of batteries, condensers, etc., are connected so that a current flows in turn through each one. □ *n., pl.* **ser·ies.**

ser·i·ous (sir′ē əs), *adj.* **1** showing deep thought or purpose; thoughtful; grave: *a serious manner, a serious face.* **2** not fooling; in earnest; sincere: *Are you joking or are you serious?* **3** needing thought; important: *Choice of your life's work is a serious matter.* **4** important because it may do much harm; dangerous: *The patient was in serious condition.* **—ser′i·ous·ly,** *adv.* **—ser′i·ous·ness,** *n.*

SYNONYM STUDY **Serious, solemn,** and **earnest**¹ all mean not playful. **Serious** means showing deep thought: *He made a serious speech at graduation.* **Solemn** means serious and formal: *The President takes a solemn oath to uphold the Constitution.* **Earnest** means serious and full of strong feeling: *Our teacher made a earnest appeal for donations to the food drive.*

ser·i·ous-mind·ed (sir′ē əs mīn′dəd), *adj.* having a serious or earnest disposition. **—ser′i·ous-mind′ed·ness,** *n.*

ser·mon (ser′mən), *n.* **1** a public talk on religion or something connected with religion, usually given by a member of the clergy as part of a church service. **2** a serious talk about conduct or duty; moral lecture: *After the guests left, the children got a sermon on their bad table manners.*

ser·mon·ize (ser′mə nīz), *v.* to give a sermon; preach. ❑ *v.* **ser·mon·ized, ser·mon·iz·ing. —ser′mon·iz′er,** *n.*

Sermon on the Mount, (in the Bible) a sermon by Jesus to his disciples, which presents his basic teachings.

ser·o·pos·i·tive (sir′ō pos′i tiv), *adj.* having a high level of antibodies in the serum, showing previous contact with a particular infectious disease.

ser·ous (sir′əs), *adj.* **1** of or producing serum. **2** like serum; watery. Tears are drops of a serous fluid. ■ Another word that sounds like this is **cirrus.**

ser·pent (ser′pənt), *n.* **1** snake, especially a big snake. **2** a sly, treacherous person.

ser·pen·tine (ser′pən tēn′ or ser′pən tīn), *adj.* **1** of or like a serpent. **2** winding; twisting: *a serpentine creek.*

ser·rate (ser′āt), *adj.* notched like the edge of a saw; toothed.

ser·rat·ed (ser′ā tid), *adj.* serrate.

ser·ried (ser′ēd), *adj.* crowded closely together.

ser·um (sir′əm), *n.* **1** the clear, pale yellow, watery part that separates from blood when it clots. **2** liquid used to prevent or cure a disease, usually obtained from the blood of an animal that has been made immune to the disease. ❑ *n., pl.* **ser·ums, ser·a.**

serv·ant (ser′vənt), *n.* **1** person employed in a household, such as a cook or maid. **2** public servant. **3** person devoted to any service: *a servant of God.*

serve (serv), **1** *v.* to work for; give service to: *serve a worthwhile cause, serve customers in a store.* **2** *v.* to give service; perform duties: *She served as a counselor. My cousin served three years in the navy.* **3** *v.* to honor and obey; worship: *serve God.* **4** *v.* to wait on at table; bring food or drink to: *The waiter served us.* **5** *v.* to put food or drink on the table: *Serve crackers with the soup. Dinner is served.* **6** *v.* to supply with something needed; supply; furnish: *The dairy serves us with milk.* **7** *v.* to supply enough for: *One pie will serve six persons.* **8** *v.* to be useful; be what is needed; be used: *Boxes served as seats.* **9** *v.* to be useful to; fulfill: *This will serve my purpose.* **10** *v.* to pass; spend: *The thief served a term in prison.* **11** *v.* to deliver; present: *She was served with a notice to appear in court.* **12** *v.* to put the ball in play by hitting it in volleyball, and games played with a racket, such as tennis. **13** *n.* act of serving the ball in volleyball, and games played with a racket, such as tennis. **14** *n.* a player's turn to serve. ❑ *v.* **served, serv·ing.**

serve someone right, be just what a person deserves: *If you cheat and get punished, it serves you right.*

serv·er (ser′vər), *n.* **1** person who serves. **2** tray for dishes.

serv·ice (ser′vis), **1** *n.* helpful act or acts; aid; a being useful to others: *They performed many services for their community.* **2** *n.* business or system that supplies something useful or necessary: *a secretarial service. Bus service was good.* **3** *n.* occupation or employment as a servant: *go into domestic service.* **4** *n.* Usually, **services,** *pl.* **a** performance of duties: *She no longer needs the*

services of a doctor. **b** work in the service of others; useful labor: *We pay for services such as repairs, maintenance, and utilities.* **5** *n.* advantage; benefit; use: *This down coat has given me great service. Every available vehicle was pressed into service.* **6** *n.* department of government or public employment, or the persons engaged in it: *the diplomatic service.* **7** *n.* the armed forces: *We entered the service together.* **8** *n.* duty in the armed forces: *He was on active service during the war.* **9** *n.* Often, **services,** *pl.* a religious meeting, ritual, or ceremony: *a marriage service. They attend services on Friday evening.* **10** *n.* manner of serving food or the food served: *The service in this restaurant is excellent.* **11** *n.* set of dishes, etc.: *a solid silver tea service.* **12** *n.* (in law) the serving of a process or writ upon a person. **13** *v.* to make fit for service; keep fit for service: *The mechanic serviced our car.* **14** *n.* act of serving the ball in volleyball, and games played with a racket, such as tennis. **15** *v.* to provide with a service of any kind: *Only two trains a day service the town.* **16** *adj.* for use by people making deliveries, household servants, etc.: *a service entrance.* ❑ *v.* **serv·iced, serv·ic·ing.**

at your service, ready to do what you want.

of service, helpful; useful.

serv·ice·a·ble (ser′vi sə bəl), *adj.* **1** useful for a long time; able to stand much use: *We want to buy a serviceable secondhand car.* **2** capable of giving good service; useful. **—serv′ice·a·bil′i·ty,** *n.* **—serv′ice·a·bly,** *adv.*

serv·ice·ber·ry (ser′vis ber′ē), *n.* saskatoon. ❑ *n., pl.* **serv·ice·ber·ries.**

serv·ice·man (ser′vis man′), *n.* **1** member of the armed forces. **2** person who maintains or repairs machinery or some kind of equipment: *We called a serviceman to fix our dryer.* ❑ *n., pl.* **serv·ice·men.**

service station, filling station.

serv·ice·wom·an (ser′vis wùm′ən), *n.* woman who is a member of the armed forces. ❑ *n., pl.* **serv·ice·wom·en.**

ser·vi·ette (ser′vē et′), *n.* CANADIAN. napkin (def. 1).

ser·vile (ser′vil), *adj.* **1** showing too much respect because of fear; mean; base: *servile flattery.* **2** of or for enslaved persons: *servile work.* **—ser′vile·ly,** *adv.* **—ser·vil′i·ty** (ser vil′ə tē), *n.*

serv·ing (ser′ving), *n.* portion of food served to someone at one time; helping.

ser·vi·tor (ser′və tər), *n.* OLD USE. a male servant or attendant.

ser·vi·tude (ser′və tüd), *n.* **1** bondage; enslaved condition. **2** forced labor as punishment: *The criminal was sentenced to five years' servitude.*

ser·vo·mech·a·nism (ser′vō mek′ə niz′əm), *n.* any automatic device powered by its own motor, and regulated by feedback, that carries out instructions transmitted to it by another device. A power-steering system is a servomechanism that turns the wheels of a car in response to movements of the steering wheel.

ses·a·me (ses′ə mē), *n.* **1** the small seeds of a tropical plant, used in bread, candy, and other foods, and in making an oil used in cooking. **2** plant producing these seeds.

ses·sile (ses′əl), *adj.* **1** (in zoology) attached to one spot; not movable. Some barnacles are sessile. **2** (in botany) attached by the base instead of by a stem, like certain leaves.

ses·sion (sesh′ən), *n.* **1** a meeting of a court, council, legislature, etc.: *a session of Congress.* **2** a series of such meetings. **3** term or period of such meetings: *This year's session of Congress was unusually long.* **4** a meeting of a group for some special purpose: *The singer was late for the recording session.* **5** a single, continuous course or a period of lessons: *Our school has two sessions, one in the morning and one in the afternoon.* ■ Another word that sounds like this is **cession.**

in session, meeting: *The teachers were in session all Saturday morning. Congress is now in session.*

a	hat	ė	term	ô	order	ch	child		
ā	age	i	it	oi	oil	ng	long		a in about
ä	far	ī	ice	ou	out	sh	she		e in taken
â	care	o	hot	u	cup	th	thin	ə	i in pencil
e	let	ō	open	ù	put	ŦH	then		o in lemon
ē	equal	ò	saw	ü	rule	zh	measure		u in circus

set (set), **1** *v.* to put in some place; put; place: *Set the box on its end.* **2** *v.* to put in the right place, position, or condition; put in proper order; arrange: *The doctor set my broken leg. Set the clock. Set the table for dinner.* **3** *v.* to cause to be; put in some condition or relation: *Their friendliness set me at ease. The prisoner was set free.* **4** *v.* to arrange; specify; define: *set the rules of a contest, set a time limit for the quiz.* **5** *adj.* arranged beforehand; established: *a set time for meals. There are set rules in the game of chess.* **6** *adj.* prepared; ready: *They are all set to try again.* **7** *v.* to provide for others to follow: *set a good example.* **8** *v.* to put in a rigid or settled state: *She set her jaw in determination.* **9** *adj.* rigid; unmoving: *a set smile.* **10** *v.* to make or become firm or hard: *Jelly sets as it cools.* **11** *v.* to put in a frame or other thing that holds: *set a diamond in gold.* **12** *v.* to go down; sink: *The sun sets in the west.* **13** *n.* number of things or persons belonging together; group; outfit: *a set of dishes.* ■ See Synonym Study at **group**. **14** *n.* scenery of a play or for a movie. **15** *n.* device for receiving radio or TV signals and turning them into sounds and pictures: *a TV set.* **16** *n.* way a thing is put or placed; form; shape: *His jaw had a stubborn set.* **17** *n.* direction; tendency; course: *The set of opinion was toward building a new bridge.* **18** *v.* to turn in a particular direction; direct: *to set your feet homeward.* **19** *v.* to begin to move; start: *She set to work.* **20** *v.* to put a hen on eggs to hatch them; place eggs under a hen to be hatched. **21** *v.* (of a hen) to sit on eggs. **22** *n.* act or manner of setting. **23** *adj.* stubbornly firm and unchanging; obstinate: *They are set in their ways.* **24** *n.* group of games in tennis. One side must win six games and at least two more than the other side. **25** *n.* a young plant: *onion sets.* **26** *n.* (in mathematics) a collection of numbers, points, objects, or other items which are distinguished from all other items by specific common characteristics. The whole numbers form a set, and any number in this set is a member of the set. ❑ *v.* **set, set·ting.**

set about, to start work on; begin: *set about your business.*

set against, 1 to make unfriendly toward. **2** to balance; compare.

set aside, 1 to put to one side. **2** to keep for later use. **3** to discard, dismiss, or leave out; reject; annul: *Sometimes a higher court sets aside the decision in a lawsuit.*

set back, 1 to delay; hinder; check: *Road repairs were set back by bad weather.* **2** to cost; to cause someone to pay: *That car set them back about $17,000.*

set down, 1 to put down: *The bus set us down near town.* **2** to record in writing or printing. **3** to consider; regard: *set a person down as a gossip.* **4** to assign; attribute: *Your failure in the test can be set down to too much haste.*

set forth, 1 to make known; express; declare: *set forth your opinions on a subject.* **2** to start to go: *set forth on a trip.*

set in, to begin: *Winter set in early.*

set off, 1 to explode: *set off a string of firecrackers.* **2** to start to go: *set off for home.* **3** to increase or improve by contrast: *The green dress set off her red hair.* **4** to mark off; separate from the others: *One word was set off from the others by quotation marks.*

set on or **set upon, 1** to attack: *They were set on by a pack of dogs.* **2** to urge to attack.

set out, 1 to start to go: *They set out on the hike with plenty of water.* **2** to spread out to show, sell, or use: *set out a flag, set out goods for sale.* **3** to plant: *set out tomato plants in the spring.*

set to, 1 to begin to work enthusiastically: *We set to painting the scenery for the play.* **2** to begin to fight.

set up, 1 to build: *set up a monument.* **2** to begin; start: *set up a business.* **3** to put up; raise in place, position, power, pride, etc.: *They set him up as king.* **4** to claim; pretend: *The swindler set up as a millionaire.* **5** to plan, prepare, or establish: *set up a meeting.*

set your face against, to oppose; to refuse to consider: *He set his face against their marriage.*

set·back (set′bak′), *n.* something that delays or reverses progress: *The team had a setback when its best player became sick.*

Se·ton (sēt′n), *n.* Saint **Elizabeth Ann** (an), 1774-1821, American educator and religious worker. ■ **Elizabeth Ann Seton** was the first person born in the United States to be canonized by the Roman Catholic Church. She founded the first Catholic elementary school and the first Catholic orphanage in the United States.

set·tee (se tē′), *n.* sofa or long bench with a back and, usually, arms. ❑ *n., pl.* **set·tees.**

set·ter (set′ər), *n.* **1** a long-haired hunting dog, trained to stand motionless and point its nose toward the game that it scents. **2** someone or something that sets: *a setter of type, a setter of jewels.*

settee

set theory, branch of mathematics that deals with sets, their qualities, and their relationships.

set·ting (set′ing), *n.* **1** frame or other thing in which something is set. The mounting of a jewel is its setting. **2** scenery of a play. **3** place and time of a story, play, or movie: *The setting was a garden in England in the 1860s.* **4** surroundings; background: *a scenic mountain setting.* **5** music composed to go with a story, poem, etc. **6** the eggs that a hen sets on for hatching. **7** act of someone or something that sets. **8** dishes or cutlery required to set one place at a table: *a wedding present of six settings of china.*

set·tle[1] (set′l), *v.* **1** to determine; decide; agree upon: *settle an argument. They settled on a time for leaving.* **2** to put or be put in order; arrange: *I must settle all my affairs before going away for the winter.* **3** to pay; arrange payment of: *She settled a bill before leaving town. Let us settle up our expenses for the trip.* **4** to take up residence in a new country or place: *settle in New York.* **5** to establish colonies in; colonize: *The English settled New England.* **6** to set or be set in a fairly permanent position, place, or way of life: *We are settled in our new home.* **7** to come to rest in a particular place; become set or fixed: *A heavy fog settled over the airport. My cold settled in my chest.* **8** to place in or come to a desired or comfortable position: *The cat settled itself in the chair.* **9** to make or become quiet: *A vacation will settle your nerves.* **10** to go down; sink: *Our house has settled four inches since it was built.* ❑ *v.* **set·tled, set·tling.** —**set′tle·a·ble,** *adj.*

settle down, 1 to live a more regular life. **2** to direct steady effort or attention. **3** to calm down; become quiet: *settle down for a nap.*

settle for, to accept something less than what was expected: *The runner had to settle for second place.*

settle upon or **settle on,** to give money or property to someone by law: *She settled one thousand dollars a year upon her housekeeper.*

set·tle[2] (set′l), *n.* a long bench, usually with arms and a high back.

set·tle·ment (set′l mənt), *n.* **1** agreement or arrangement to settle a dispute: *No settlement of the dispute is possible unless each side yields some point.* **2** payment: *Settlement of all claims against the company will be made shortly.* **3** the settling of persons in a new country: *The settlement of the English along the Atlantic coast gave England claim to that section.* **4** colony: *England had many settlements along the Atlantic coast.* **5** group of buildings and the people living in them: *Ships brought supplies to the scattered settlements of the colonists.* **6** place in a poor, neglected neighborhood where work for its improvement is carried on; settlement house. **7** act of settling property upon someone.

settlement house, settlement (def. 6).

set·tler (set′lər), *n.* person who settles in a new country.

set-to (set′tü′), *n.* **1** a fight; dispute: *We had a set-to about whose turn it was to take out the garbage.* **2** a contest; match. ❑ *n., pl.* **set-tos.**

set-up (set′up′), *n.* **1** arrangement of apparatus, machinery, etc. **2** arrangement of an organization. **3** situation arranged in advance to obtain a specified result.

Seur·at (sə rä′), *n.* **Georges** (zhôrzh), 1859-1891, French painter. He painted using dots of different colors side by side. From a distance, the dots merge and look like other colors.

Seuss (süs), *n.* **Dr.,** 1904-1991, American writer and illustrator of children's books. His real name was Theodor Geisel.

sev·en (sev′ən), *n., adj.* one more than six; 7.

sev·en·fold (sev′ən fōld′), **1** *adj., adv.* seven times as much or as many. **2** *adj.* having seven parts. **3** *adv.* seven times as much or as often.

seven seas, all the seas and oceans of the world, traditionally believed to be the Arctic, Antarctic, N Atlantic, S Atlantic, N Pacific, S Pacific, and Indian oceans: *to sail the seven seas.*

Seuss character

sev·en·teen (sev′ən tēn′), *n., adj.* seven more than ten; 17.

sev·en·teenth (sev′ən tēnth′), *adj., n.* **1** next after the 16th; last in a series of 17. **2** one of 17 equal parts.

sev·enth (sev′ənth), *adj., n.* **1** next after the sixth; last in a series of seven. **2** one of seven equal parts.

Sev·enth-Day Ad·ven·tist (sev′ənth dā′ əd ven′tist), member of a Protestant church that observes Saturday as the Sabbath and emphasizes the doctrine of the Second Coming.

sev·en·ti·eth (sev′ən tē ith), *adj., n.* **1** next after the 69th; last in a series of 70. **2** one of 70 equal parts.

sev·en·ty (sev′ən tē), *adj., n.* seven times ten; 70. ❑ *n., pl.* **sev·en·ties.**

Seven Wonders of the World, the seven most remarkable structures of ancient times. These were the Pyramids of Egypt, the hanging gardens of Babylon, the statue of Zeus by Phidias at Olympia, the temple of Artemis at Ephesus, the Colossus of Rhodes, the mausoleum at a city in southwestern Asia Minor, and the lighthouse at Alexandria.

sev·er (sev′ər), *v.* **1** to cut apart; cut off: *I severed the rope with a knife.* **2** to part; divide; separate: *The rope severed and the swing fell down.* **3** to break off: *The two countries severed diplomatic relations.*

sev·er·al (sev′ər əl), **1** *adj., pron. pl.* more than two or three but not many; some; a few: *gain several pounds. Several have given their consent.* **2** *adj.* individual; different: *The children went their several ways after school.*

sev·er·al·ly (sev′ər ə lē), *adv.* separately; singly; individually: *Consider these points, first severally and then collectively.*

sev·er·ance (sev′ər əns), *n.* **1** act of severing or condition of being severed; separation; division. **2** act of breaking off: *the severance of diplomatic relations between two countries.*

se·vere (sə vir′), *adj.* **1** very strict; stern; harsh: *The judge gave the criminal a severe sentence.* **2** sharp or violent: *a severe headache, a severe storm.* **3** serious; grave: *a severe illness.* **4** very plain or simple; without ornament: *severe black clothes.* **5** difficult: *a series of severe tests.* ❑ *adj.* **se·ver·er, se·ver·est.** —**se·vere′ly,** *adv.* —**se·vere′ness,** *n.*

SYNONYM STUDY **Severe, strict,** and **stern**[1] all mean following the rules without making exceptions. **Severe** means without gentleness or sympathy: *Because it was the woman's third crime, the judge gave her a severe sentence.* **Strict** means very careful of the rules: *The space shuttle is launched with strict attention to proper procedure.* **Stern** means firm in control or judgment: *One stern word from the trainer makes the dogs quiet right away.*

se·ver·i·ty (sə ver′ə tē), *n.* **1** strictness; sternness; harshness: *The severity of the punishment seemed unfair to many people.* **2** sharpness or violence: *the severity of storms, the severity of pain, the severity of grief.* **3** simplicity of style or taste; plainness: *the severity of a modern steel and glass building.* **4** seriousness: *We did not realize the severity of her illness.* ❑ *n., pl.* **se·ver·i·ties** for 2.

Se·ville (sə vil′), *n.* city in SW Spain.

sew (sō), *v.* **1** to work with needle and thread. **2** to fasten with stitches: *sew on a button, sew a hem on a dress.* **3** to close with stitches: *The doctor sewed up the wound.* ❑ *v.* **sewed, sewed** or **sewn, sew·ing.** ▪ Other words that sound like this are **so** and **sow**[1]. —**sew′a·ble,** *adj.*

sew·age (sü′ij), *n.* the waste matter that passes through sewers.

Sew·ard (sü′ərd), *n.* **William Henry,** 1801-1872, American political leader. He was secretary of state from 1861 to 1869. During this time he arranged the purchase of Alaska from Russia.

sew·er[1] (sü′ər), *n.* an underground pipe or channel for carrying off waste water and refuse.

sew·er[2] (sō′ər), *n.* person or thing that sews.

sew·er·age (sü′ər ij), *n.* **1** removal of waste matter by sewers. **2** system of sewers. **3** the waste matter that passes through sewers; sewage.

sew·ing (sō′ing), **1** *n.* work done with a needle and thread. **2** *n.* something to be sewed. **3** *adj.* for sewing; used in sewing: *a sewing room.*

sewing machine, machine for sewing or stitching cloth, etc.

sewn (sōn), *v.* a past participle of **sew:** *I've sewn on the buttons.* ▪ Another word that sounds like this is **sown.**

sex (seks), *n.* **1** either of the two basic kinds of human beings and many other living things. The two sexes are males and females. **2** the character of being male or female: *The list of members of the club was arranged by age and by sex.* **3** sexual intercourse. ❑ *n., pl.* **sex·es** for 1.

sex chromosome, either of a pair of chromosomes, the X chromosome or the Y chromosome, which determine sex.

sex gland, gonad.

sex·ism (sek′siz əm), *n.* discrimination or prejudice against a sex or member of a sex, especially the female sex.

sex·ist (sek′sist), *adj.* of or about sexism: *sexist attitudes.*

sex·less (seks′lis), *adj.* without sex or the characteristics of sex. —**sex′less·ly,** *adv.* —**sex′less·ness,** *n.*

sex-linked (seks′lingkt′), *adj.* carried by genes located in the sex chromosomes. One kind of color blindness is sex-linked.

sext-, *prefix.* six: *sextet = group of six.*

sex·tant (sek′stənt), *n.* device used by navigators, surveyors, etc., for measuring the angular distance between two objects. Sextants are used at sea to measure the altitude of the sun or a star in order to determine latitude and longitude.

sex·tet (sek stet′), *n.* **1** piece of music for six voices or instruments. **2** group of six singers or players performing together. **3** any group of six.

sex·ton (sek′stən), *n.* person who takes care of a church building, rings the church bell, arranges burials, etc.

Sex·ton (sek′stən), *n.* **Anne,** 1928-1974, American poet. Her poems are often about events in her own life, especially her struggle with mental illness.

sex·u·al (sek′shü əl), *adj.* of or about sex or the sexes: *sexual development.* —**sex′u·al·ly,** *adv.*

sexual intercourse, insertion of the penis into the vagina.

sexually transmitted disease, disease spread by sexual activity; venereal disease.

sex·y (sek′sē), *adj.* INFORMAL. **1** sexually attractive. **2** exciting; desirable: *a sexy racing car.* ❑ *adj.* **sex·i·er, sex·i·est.**

Sey·chelles (sā shelz′), *n.pl. or sing.* country consisting of a group of islands in the Indian Ocean, off E Africa. *Capital:* Victoria.

Sey·mour (sē′môr), *n.* **Jane** (jān), 1509?-1537, English queen, third wife of Henry VIII, mother of Edward VI.

Sgt., Sergeant.

shab·by (shab′ē), *adj.* **1** much worn: *This old suit looks shabby.* **2** wearing old or much worn clothes: *a shabby beggar.* **3** poor or neglected; run-down: *a shabby old house.* ▪ See Synonym Study at **worn.** **4** not generous; mean; unfair: *a shabby way to treat a friend.* ❑ *adj.* **shab·bi·er, shab·bi·est.** —**shab′bi·ly,** *adv.* —**shab′bi·ness,** *n.*

a	hat	ė	term	ȯ	order	ch	child		
ā	age	i	it	oi	oil	ng	long		a in about
ä	far	ī	ice	ou	out	sh	she	ə {	e in taken
â	care	o	hot	u	cup	th	thin		i in pencil
e	let	ō	open	u̇	put	ŦH	then		o in lemon
ē	equal	ȯ	saw	ü	rule	zh	measure		u in circus

S

shack (shak), *n.* **1** a roughly built hut or cabin: *We built a shack of old boards in the backyard.* **2** house in bad condition: *Those run-down shacks are being torn down to make way for new housing.*

shack·le (shak′əl), **1** *n.* a metal band fastened around the ankle or wrist of a prisoner, enslaved person, etc. Shackles are usually fastened to each other, the wall, the floor, etc., by chains. **2** *n.pl.* **shackles,** chains; fetters. **3** *n.* link fastening together the two rings for the ankles and wrists of a prisoner. **4** *v.* to put shackles on. **5** *n.* Also, **shackles,** *pl.* anything that prevents freedom of action, thought, etc.: *to remove the shackles of poverty. Ignorance and fear are shackles of the mind.* **6** *v.* to restrain; hamper. ❑ *v.* **shack·led, shack·ling. —shack′ler,** *n.*

shad (shad), *n.* any of several saltwater food fishes related to the herring. Shad are common along the northern Atlantic coast and go up rivers in the spring to spawn. ❑ *n., pl.* **shad** or **shads.**

shad·bush (shad′bŭsh′), *n.* (in the Maritime Provinces) saskatoon. ❑ *n., pl.* **shad·bush·es.**

shade (shād), **1** *n.* a partly dark place, not in the sunshine: *We sat in the shade of a big tree.* **2** *n.* a slight darkness or coolness given by something that cuts off light: *Leafy trees cast shade.* **3** *n.* something that shuts out light: *Pull down the shades of the windows.* **4** *v.* to keep light from: *A big hat shades the eyes.* **5** *n.* lightness or darkness of color: *silks in all shades of blue.* ■ See Synonym Study at **color. 6** *n.* the dark part of a picture. **7** *v.* to make darker than the rest; use black or color to give the effect of shade in a picture. **8** *n.* a very small difference; little bit: *a shade too long, many shades of opinion.* **9** *v.* to show very small differences; change little by little: *This scarf shades from deep rose to pale pink.* **10** *n.* ghost; spirit: *the shades of departed heroes.* **11** *n.pl.* **the shades,** darkness of evening or night. **12** *n.pl.* **shades,** INFORMAL. sunglasses. ❑ *v.* **shad·ed, shad·ing. —shade′less,** *adj.* **—shad′er,** *n.*

in the shade, in or into a condition of being unknown or unnoticed.

shad·ing (shā′ding), *n.* **1** something that covers light, providing shade. **2** use of variation in black or color to give the effect of shade or depth in a picture. **3** a slight variation or difference of color, character, etc.

shad·ow (shad′ō), **1** *n.* shade made by some person, animal, or thing. Sometimes your shadow is much longer than your actual height, and sometimes much shorter. **2** *n.* Often, **shadows,** *pl.* darkness; partial shade: *There was someone lurking in the shadows.* **3** *n.* the dark part of a place or picture. **4** *v.* to cast a shadow on. **5** *n.* a little bit; small degree; slight suggestion: *They were innocent beyond the shadow of a doubt.* **6** *n.* ghost. **7** *n.* a faint image: *You look worn to a shadow.* **8** *n.* anything that is unreal or imaginary even though it seems to be real. **9** *v.* to follow closely and secretly: *The detective shadowed the suspect.* **10** *n.* person who follows another closely and secretly, as a detective. **11** *n.* constant companion; follower. **12** *n.* sadness; gloom. **—shad′ow·er,** *n.* **—shad′ow·less,** *adj.* **—shad′ow·like′,** *adj.*

shadow (def. 1)

shad·ow·box (shad′ō boks′), *v.* to box with an imaginary opponent for exercise or training. **—shad′ow·box′ing,** *n.*

shad·ow·y (shad′ə wē), *adj.* **1** having much shadow or shade;

shady: *We were glad to leave the hot sun and come into the cool, shadowy room.* **2** like a shadow; dim, faint, or slight: *We saw a shadowy outline on the window curtain.* **—shad′ow·i·ness,** *n.*

shad·y (shā′dē), *adj.* **1** in the shade; shaded: *We sat in a shady spot.* **2** giving shade: *We sat under a shady tree.* **3** of doubtful honesty, character, etc.: *a shady business deal.* ❑ *adj.* **shad·i·er, shad·i·est. —shad′i·ly,** *adv.* **—shad′i·ness,** *n.*

shaft (shaft), **1** *n.* a cylinder-shaped bar that supports turning parts in a machine or that transmits motion from one part of the machine to another. **2** *n.* a deep passage sunk in the earth. The entrance to a mine is called a shaft. **3** *n.* a passage that is like a well; high, narrow space: *an elevator shaft.* **4** *n.* the long, slender stem of an arrow, spear, etc. **5** *n.* arrow; spear. **6** *n.* something aimed at someone like an arrow or spear: *shafts of ridicule.* **7** *n.* ray or beam of light. **8** *n.* (earlier) one of the two wooden poles between which a horse is harnessed to a carriage, cart, etc. **9** *n.* the main part of a building column. **10** *n.* the long, straight handle of a hammer, ax, golf club, etc. **11** *v.* SLANG. to treat someone in a mean and harmful way, especially by cheating on an agreement.

get the shaft, be very badly treated, especially in an unfair way.

give someone the shaft, to treat very badly, especially in an unfair way.

shag (shag), *n.* **1** rough, matted hair, wool, etc. **2** the long, rough nap of some kinds of cloth or rugs. **3** cloth having such a nap. **—shag′like′,** *adj.*

shag·bark (shag′bärk′), *n.* a hickory tree with rough bark that peels off in long strips.

shag·gy (shag′ē), *adj.* **1** covered with a thick, rough mass of hair, wool, etc.: *a shaggy dog.* **2** long, thick, and rough: *shaggy eyebrows.* **3** untidy in appearance, especially needing a haircut or shave. **4** having a long, rough nap; of coarse texture: *a shaggy felt hat.* ❑ *adj.* **shag·gi·er, shag·gi·est. —shag′gi·ly,** *adv.* **—shag′gi·ness,** *n.*

shaggy (def. 1)—a shaggy alpaca

shah (shä), *n.* title of the former rulers of Iran.

shake (shāk), **1** *v.* to move quickly backward and forward, up and down, or from side to side: *shake a rug. The baby shook the rattle. The branches of the old tree shook in the wind.* **2** *v.* to bring, throw, force, rouse, scatter, etc., by or as if by movement: *shake snow off your clothes.* **3** *v.* to clasp hands in greeting, congratulating, etc., another: *shake hands.* **4** *v.* to tremble: *The kitten was shaking with cold.* **5** *v.* to make tremble: *The explosion shook the town.* **6** *v.* to disturb; make less firm: *His lie shook my faith in his honesty.* **7** *n.* act or fact of shaking: *A shake of the head was her answer.* **8** *n.pl.* **the shakes,** a trembling caused by chills or fear. **9** *v.* to get rid of: *Can't you shake your little cousin?* **10** *n.* milk shake. ❑ *v.* **shook, shak·en, shak·ing.** ■ Another word that can sound like this is **sheik. —shak′a·ble** or **shake′a·ble,** *adj.*

no great shakes, INFORMAL. not unusual, extraordinary, or important.

shake down, 1 to bring or throw down by shaking. **2** to become accustomed to something new. **3** to bring into working order. **4** INFORMAL. to get money from dishonestly. **5** to search a place thoroughly.

shake off, to get rid of: *shake off a cold.*

shake up, 1 to shake hard: *Shake up a mixture of oil and vinegar for the salad.* **2** to make a sudden and complete change in; reorganize completely: *The new manager shook up her office staff.* **3** to jar in body or nerves: *I was much shaken up by the experience.*

shake·down (shāk′doun′), **1** *n.* SLANG. way of getting money from someone by force or threats of force. **2** *adj.* INFORMAL. for testing and adjustment of a new product or equipment: *a shakedown cruise.*

shak·en (shā′kən), **1** *v.* past participle of **shake. 2** *adj.* upset; disturbed: *The shaken survivors of the tornado were examined for injuries.* ■ See Synonym Study at **upset.**

shak·er (shā′kər), *n.* **1** person who shakes something. **2** machine or utensil used in shaking. **3** container for pepper, salt, etc., having a top with holes in it. **4** Shaker, member of an American religious sect, called this from movements of the body forming part of their worship.

Shake·speare (shāk′spir), *n.* **William,** 1564-1616, English poet and playwright. His plays include *Hamlet, Julius Caesar, Othello, Romeo and Juliet, King Lear,* and *Macbeth.* He also wrote many sonnets. ■ **William Shakespeare** was an actor himself as well as a playwright. He performed before Elizabeth I and James I.

Shake·spear·e·an or **Shake·spear·i·an** (shāk spir′ē ən), *adj.* of or about Shakespeare, his time, or his works.

shake-up (shāk′up′), *n.* a sudden and complete change: *The mayor fired all her assistants in a shake-up.*

shak·o (shak′ō *or* shā′kō), *n.* a high, stiff military hat with a visor and a plume or other ornament. ❑ *n., pl.* **shak·os** or **shak·oes.**

shak·y (shā′kē), *adj.* **1** shaking: *a shaky voice.* **2** liable to break down; weak: *a shaky porch.* **3** not to be depended on; not reliable: *a shaky knowledge of history.* ❑ *adj.* **shak·i·er, shak·i·est.** **—shak′i·ly,** *adv.* **—shak′i·ness,** *n.*

shale (shāl), *n.* rock formed from hardened clay or mud in thin layers which split easily. **—shale′like′,** *adj.*

shall (shal), *v. Shall* is used to express future time, command, obligation, and necessity. *We shall come soon. You shall go to the party. I shall miss you.* ■ See Usage Note at **will**[1]. ❑ *v.,* past tense **should.**

shal·lop (shal′əp), *n.* a small, light, open boat with sails or oars.

shal·lot (shə lot′), *n.* a small bulb much like an onion, often used for seasoning cooked foods.

shal·low (shal′ō), **1** *adj.* not deep: *shallow water, a shallow dish.* **2** *adj.* lacking depth of thought, knowledge, feeling, etc.: *a shallow mind.* **3** *n.* Usually, **shallows,** *pl.* a shallow place: *splashing in the shallows of the pond.* **—shal′low·ly,** *adv.* **—shal′low·ness,** *n.*

sha·lom (shä lōm′), **1** *n., interj.* hello or good-by. **2** *interj.* peace. [Shalom comes from a Hebrew word meaning "peace."]

shalt (shalt), *v.* OLD USE. shall. "Thou shalt" means "You shall."

sham (sham), **1** *n.* pretense; fraud: *Their claim to be descended from royalty is a sham.* **2** *adj.* false; pretended; imitation: *a sham battle fought for practice, sham antiques.* **3** *v.* to pretend: *He shammed sickness so he wouldn't have to work.* **4** *n.* person who is not what he or she pretends to be; fraud. ❑ *v.* **shammed, sham·ming.**

sha·man (shä′mən, shā′mən, *or* sham′ən), *n.* **1** man in American Indian tribes believed to have close contact with the spirit world, and to be skilled in curing diseases; medicine man. **2** a similar man in certain other societies.

sham·ble (sham′bəl), **1** *v.* to walk awkwardly or unsteadily: *The exhausted hikers shambled into camp.* **2** *n.* an awkward or unsteady walk. ❑ *v.* **sham·bled, sham·bling.**

sham·bles (sham′bəlz), *n.pl. or sing.* **1** confusion; mess; general disorder: *They made a shambles of the clean room.* **2** place of butchery or of great bloodshed.

shame (shām), **1** *n.* fact to be sorry about; a pity: *It is a shame to be so wasteful.* **2** *n.* a painful feeling of having done something wrong, improper, or silly: *to blush with shame.* **3** *v.* to cause to feel shame: *My silly mistake shamed me.* **4** *v.* to drive or force by shame: *She was shamed into cleaning her room after guests saw it.* **5** *n.* a disgrace; dishonor: *brought shame to his family.* **6** *v.* to bring disgrace upon: *to shame your family.* **7** *n.* someone or something to be ashamed of; cause of disgrace. ❑ *v.* **shamed, sham·ing.**

for shame, shame on you!

put to shame, 1 to disgrace; make ashamed. **2** be better than; surpass: *Your careful work has put ours to shame.*

shame·faced (shām′fāst′), *adj.* **1** showing shame and embarrassment. **2** bashful; shy. **—shame·fac·ed·ly** (shām′fā′sid lē), *adv.* **—shame′fac′ed·ness,** *n.*

shame·ful (shām′fəl), *adj.* causing shame; bringing disgrace. **—shame′ful·ly,** *adv.* **—shame′ful·ness,** *n.*

shame·less (shām′lis), *adj.* **1** without shame. **2** not modest. **—shame′less·ly,** *adv.* **—shame′less·ness,** *n.*

sham·poo (sham pü′), **1** *n.* a liquid soap or detergent, often scented, used to wash the hair. **2** *v.* to wash the hair with shampoo. **3** *n.* act of washing the hair with shampoo. ❑ *v.* **sham·pooed, sham·poo·ing;** *n., pl.* **sham·poos.**

sham·rock (sham′rok), *n.* **1** a bright green leaf composed of three parts. The shamrock is the national emblem of Ireland. **2** plant, such as white clover, that has leaves like this.

shang·hai (shang′hī), *v.* **1** to make unconscious by drugs, liquor, etc., and put on a ship to serve as a sailor. **2** to force to do something by trickery or force. ❑ *v.* **shang·haied, shang·hai·ing.**

Shang·hai (shang′hī′), *n.* port in E China. [Shanghai comes from Chinese words meaning "at the sea."]

shank (shangk), *n.* **1** the part of the leg between the knee and the ankle. **2** the corresponding part in animals. **3** cut of meat from the upper part of the leg of an animal. **4** the whole leg. **5** any part like a leg, stem, or shaft. The shank of a fishhook is the straight part between the hook and the loop.

Shan·non (shan′ən), *n.* river flowing from N Republic of Ireland southwest into the Atlantic. It is the most important river in Ireland.

shan't (shant), shall not.

shan·tung (shan tung′), *n.* a silk, rayon, or cotton fabric having a rough, uneven surface.

Shan·tung (shan′tung′), *n.* **1** province in NE China. **2** peninsula in the E part of this province.

shan·ty (shan′tē), *n.* a roughly built hut or cabin. ❑ *n., pl.* **shan·ties. —shan′ty·like′,** *adj.*

shape (shāp), **1** *n.* the outward contour or outline; form; figure; appearance: *the shape of a triangle. A white shape stood at his bedside. A witch was supposed to take the shape of a cat or a bat.* **2** *v.* to form into a shape; mold: *The child shapes clay into balls. She shaped a clever reply.* ■ See Synonym Study at **make. 3** *v.* to adapt in form: *That hat is shaped to your head.* **4** *n.* condition: *Athletes exercise to keep themselves in good shape.* **5** *n.* definite form; proper arrangement; order: *Take time to get your thoughts into shape.* **6** *v.* to plan; devise; direct: *to shape your course in life.* ❑ *v.* **shaped, shap·ing.** **—shap′a·ble** or **shape′a·ble,** *adj.* **—shap′er,** *n.*

shape up, 1 to take on a certain form or appearance; develop: *Our school project is shaping up well.* **2** to show a certain tendency. **3** to behave properly; do what is expected: *He will have to shape up if he expects to get a good grade in this subject.*

take shape, to have or take on a definite form.

a	hat	ė	term	ô	order	ch	child	ə	a in about
ā	age	i	it	oi	oil	ng	long		e in taken
ä	far	ī	ice	ou	out	sh	she		i in pencil
â	care	o	hot	u	cup	th	thin		o in lemon
e	let	ō	open	ù	put	ŦH	then		u in circus
ē	equal	ò	saw	ü	rule	zh	measure		

shape·less (shāp′lis), *adj.* **1** without definite shape: *He wore a shapeless old hat.* **2** having an unattractive shape: *a shapeless figure.* —**shape′less·ly,** *adv.* —**shape′less·ness,** *n.*

shape·ly (shāp′lē), *adj.* having a pleasing shape. ❑ *adj.* **shape·li·er, shape·li·est.** —**shape′li·ness,** *n.*

shard (shärd), *n.* piece of broken earthenware or pottery.

share[1] (shâr), **1** *n.* part belonging to one individual; portion; part: *Do your share of the work. Each of the heirs was left an equal share of the property.* **2** *v.* to use together; enjoy together; have in common: *The sisters share the same room.* **3** *v.* to divide into parts, each taking a part: *The child shared his candy with his sister.* **4** *v.* to have a share; take part: *Everyone shared in making the picnic a success.* **5** *n.* each of the equal parts into which the ownership of a company or corporation is divided: *The ownership of this railroad is divided into several million shares.* ❑ *v.* **shared, shar·ing.** —**share′a·ble** or **shar′a·ble,** *adj.* —**shar′er,** *n.*

go shares, to share in something.

share[2] (shâr), *n.* plowshare.

share·crop (shâr′krop′), *v.* to farm as a sharecropper. ❑ *v.* **share·cropped, share·crop·ping.**

share·crop·per (shâr′krop′ər), *n.* person who farms land for the owner in return for part of the crops.

share·hold·er (shâr′hōl′dər), *n.* person owning shares of stock.

shark[1] (shärk), *n.* any of numerous, mainly flesh-eating fishes that generally are large and ferocious and live in warm seas. Sharks are valued for their hides, flesh, and liver oil, and are sometimes dangerous to human beings. —**shark′like′,** *adj.*

shark[1]—great white shark, up to 21 ft. (6.4 m) long

shark[2] (shärk), *n.* a dishonest person who preys on others.

sharp (shärp), **1** *adj.* having a thin cutting edge or a fine point: *a sharp knife, a sharp pencil.* **2** *adj.* having a point; not rounded: *a sharp nose, a sharp corner on a box.* **3** *adj.* with a sudden change of direction: *a sharp turn.* **4** *adj.* intelligent; shrewd; clever: *a sharp boy, a sharp lawyer, sharp at a bargain.* **5** *adj.* very cold: *a sharp wind.* **6** *adj.* severe; biting: *sharp words.* **7** *adj.* affecting the senses keenly: *a sharp taste, a sharp noise, a sharp pain.* **8** *adj.* clear; distinct: *the sharp contrast between black and white.* **9** *adj.* quick; brisk: *a sharp walk, a sharp run.* **10** *adj.* fierce; violent: *a sharp struggle.* **11** *adj.* keen; eager: *a sharp desire, a sharp appetite.* **12** *adj.* being aware of things quickly: *a sharp eye, sharp ears.* **13** *adj.* watchful; alert; wide-awake: *keep a sharp watch.* **14** *adv.* promptly; exactly: *Come at one o'clock sharp.* **15** *adj.* shrill; high in pitch: *a sharp voice.* **16** in music: **a** *adv.* above the true pitch: *sing sharp.* **b** *adj.* one half step or half tone above natural pitch: *Play a C sharp.* **c** *n.* such a tone or note. **d** *n.* sign (♯) that shows such a tone. **e** *adj.* (of a key) having sharps in the signature. **f** *v.* to raise in pitch. **17** *adv.* in a sharp manner; in an alert manner; keenly: *Look sharp!* **18** *adv.* suddenly: *pull a horse up sharp.* **19** *adj.* INFORMAL. attractive; stylish: *a sharp outfit.* —**sharp′ly,** *adv.* —**sharp′ness,** *n.*

Shar-Pei (shär′pā′), *n.* a medium-sized dog with wrinkly skin on the head and body, originally from China.

sharp·en (shär′pən), *v.* **1** to make sharp: *sharpen a pencil. Sharpen your wits.* **2** to become sharp. —**sharp′en·er,** *n.*

Sharps·burg (shärps′bərg), *n.* town in N Maryland, near the site of the battle fought on Antietam creek in 1862.

sharp·shoot·er (shärp′shü′tər), *n.* person who shoots very well, especially with a rifle.

sharp-sight·ed (shärp′sī′tid), *adj.* **1** having sharp sight. **2** sharp-witted: *a sharp-sighted move.*

sharp-wit·ted (shärp′wit′id), *adj.* having or showing a quick, keen mind. —**sharp′-wit′ted·ness,** *n.*

shat·ter (shat′ər), *v.* **1** to break into pieces suddenly: *A stone shattered the window. The glass shattered.* ■ See Synonym Study at **break. 2** to disturb greatly; destroy: *Her hopes were shattered. The great mental strain shattered his mind.* —**shat′ter·ing·ly,** *adv.*

shat·ter·proof (shat′ər prüf′), *adj.* made so that it will not shatter; almost impossible to shatter: *shatterproof glass.*

shave (shāv), **1** *v.* to remove hair with a razor; cut hair from the face, chin, etc., with a razor: *Father shaves every day. The actor shaved his head in order to portray a bald man.* **2** *n.* act or process of cutting off hair with a razor. **3** *v.* to cut off with a razor. **4** *v.* to cut off in thin slices: *She shaved the chocolate.* **5** *v.* to come very close to; graze: *The car shaved the corner.* **6** *v.* to reduce by a small amount: *She shaved two seconds off the old record.* ❑ *v.* **shaved, shaved** or **shav·en, shav·ing.** —**shav′a·ble** or **shave′a·ble,** *adj.*

shav·en (shā′vən), **1** *adj.* shaved. **2** *adj.* closely cut. **3** *v.* a past participle of **shave.**

shav·er (shā′vər), *n.* **1** person who shaves. **2** tool for shaving. **3** INFORMAL. youngster; small boy.

shav·ing (shā′ving), *n.* **1** a very thin piece or slice. Shavings of wood are cut off by a plane. **2** act or process of cutting hair from the face, chin, etc., with a razor.

Sha·vu·ot (shä vü′ōt *or* shə vü′ōs), *n.* a Jewish festival observed about seven weeks after Passover, celebrating the harvest and the giving of the law to Moses; Pentecost.

WORD STORY **Shavuot** comes from a Hebrew word meaning "a week." This holiday comes 49 days after the first day of Passover, a time thought of as seven times seven, a week of weeks.

Shaw (shò), *n.* **George Ber·nard** (bər närd′), 1856-1950, British playwright, critic, novelist, and social reformer, born in Ireland. He won the 1925 Nobel Prize for literature. He was a socialist and a vegetarian and supported women's rights and spelling reform.

shawl (shòl), *n.* a square or oblong piece of cloth to be worn about the shoulders or head. —**shawl′less,** *adj.* —**shawl′like′,** *adj.*

Shaw·nee (shò nē′), *n.* member of a tribe of American Indians formerly living in eastern North America, especially Ohio, Tennessee, and South Carolina, and now living in Oklahoma. ❑ *n., pl.* **Shaw·nee** or **Shaw·nees.** [**Shawnee** comes from a word in this people's language meaning "southern people."]

shay (shā), *n.* (earlier) a light carriage; chaise.

she (shē), **1** *pron.* girl, woman, or female animal spoken about or mentioned before: *My sister says she likes to read and her reading helps her in school.* **2** *pron.* anything thought of as female and spoken about or mentioned before: *She was a fine old ship.* **3** *n.* a female: *Is the baby a he or a she?*

sheaf (shēf), *n.* bundle of things of the same sort: *a sheaf of wheat, a sheaf of papers.* ❑ *n., pl.* **sheaves.**

shear (shir), *v.* **1** to cut the wool or fleece from. **2** to cut with shears or scissors. **3** to cut close; cut off; cut: *The airplane's wing was sheared off in the crash.* **4** to strip or deprive as if by cutting: *The assembly had been shorn of its legislative powers.* ❑ *v.* **sheared, sheared** or **shorn, shear·ing.** ■ Another word that sounds like this is **sheer.** —**shear′er,** *n.*

shears (shirz), *n.pl.* **1** large scissors: *barber's shears.* **2** any cutting device resembling shears: *grass shears, tin shears.*

shear·wa·ter (shir′wò′tər), *n.* any of several seabirds, related to petrels, that fly so low over water that their wings nearly skim the surface.

sheath (shēth), *n.* **1** case or covering for the blade of a sword, knife, etc. **2** any similar covering, especially on an animal or plant. ❑ *n., pl.* **sheaths** (shēᴛнz *or* shēths). **—sheath′like′,** *adj.*

sheathe (shēᴛн), *v.* **1** to put into a sheath. **2** to enclose in a case or covering: *a mummy sheathed in linen. The doors were sheathed in metal.* ❑ *v.* **sheathed, sheath·ing. —sheath′er,** *n.*

sheath·ing (shē′ᴛнing), *n.* casing; covering. The first covering of boards on a house is sheathing.

sheave (shēv), *v.* to gather and tie into a sheaf or sheaves. ❑ *v.* **sheaved, sheav·ing.**

sheaves (shēvz), *n.* plural of **sheaf.**

She·ba (shē′bə), *n.* **1** an ancient country in S Arabia. **2 Queen of,** (in the Bible) a queen who visited Solomon to learn of his great wisdom.

she·bang (shə bang′), *n.* SLANG. affair; event; matter; business: *An anonymous donor sponsored the opera and paid for the whole shebang.*

shed[1] (shed), *n.* a building used for shelter, storage, etc., usually having only one story: *The rake is in the tool shed.* ■ See Synonym Study at **hut. —shed′like′,** *adj.*

shed[2] (shed), *v.* **1** to pour out; let flow: *shed tears.* **2** to cast off; let drop or fall: *The snake sheds its skin. The umbrella sheds water.* **3** to get rid of: *shed your worries, shed your fears.* **4** to send out; give forth: *The sun sheds light. Flowers shed perfume.* ❑ *v.* **shed, shed·ding. —shed′a·ble** *or* **shed′da·ble,** *adj.* **—shed′der,** *n.*
shed blood, to destroy life; kill.

she'd (shēd), **1** she had. **2** she would.

sheen (shēn), *n.* brightness; luster. Satin and polished silver have a sheen.

sheep (shēp), *n.* **1** a cud-chewing mammal with a thick wooly coat and hoofs that chews its cud. Sheep are related to goats and are raised for wool, meat, and skin. **2** person who is timid, weak, or stupid. ❑ *n., pl.* **sheep. —sheep′like′,** *adj.*
make sheep's eyes, to give a longing, loving look.

sheep·dog (shēp′dȯg′), *n.* collie or other dog trained to help a shepherd herd and watch sheep.

sheep·fold (shēp′fōld′), *n.* pen or covered shelter for sheep.

sheep·herd·er (shēp′hėr′dər), *n.* person who watches and tends large numbers of sheep while they are grazing on unfenced land.

sheep·ish (shē′pish), *adj.* **1** awkwardly bashful or embarrassed: *a sheepish smile.* **2** like a sheep; timid; weak; stupid. **—sheep′ish·ly,** *adv.* **—sheep′ish·ness,** *n.*

sheepdog

sheep·skin (shēp′skin′), *n.* **1** skin of a sheep, especially with the wool on it. **2** leather or parchment made from the skin of a sheep. **3** INFORMAL. diploma.

sheer[1] (shir), *adj.* **1** complete; absolute: *sheer nonsense, sheer weariness.* **2** straight up and down; very steep: *From the top of the wall it was a sheer drop of 100 feet to the water below.* **3** very thin; almost transparent: *Those sheer curtains will let the light through.* ■ Another word that sounds like this is **shear. —sheer′ly,** *adv.* **—sheer′ness,** *n.*

sheer[2] (shir), *v.* to turn from a course; turn aside; swerve: *At the last minute, the boat sheered away from the rocks.* ■ Another word that sounds like this is **shear.**

sheet[1] (shēt), *n.* **1** a large piece of cotton, linen, or other cloth used to sleep on or under. **2** *n.* a single piece of paper. **3** *n.* a broad, thin piece of anything: *a sheet of glass.* **4** *n.* a broad, flat surface: *A sheet of ice covered the highway.* **5** *v.* to shroud.

sheet[2] (shēt), *n.* rope that controls the angle at which a sail is set.

sheet·ing (shē′ting), *n.* cotton, linen, or other cloth for bed sheets.

sheet lightning, heat lightning.

sheet metal, metal in thin, flat pieces.

sheet music, music printed on unbound sheets of paper.

Shef·field (shef′ēld), *n.* city in central England, famous for the manufacture of cutlery.

sheik *or* **sheikh** (shēk *or* shāk), *n.* an Arab chief or head of a family, village, or tribe. ■ Other words that can sound like this are **chic** and **shake.**

shek·el (shek′əl), *n.* **1** an ancient silver coin of the Hebrews that weighed about half an ounce. **2** an ancient unit of weight originating in Babylonia, equal to about half an ounce.

shel·drake (shel′drāk′), *n.* **1** shelduck. **2** merganser. ❑ *n., pl.* **shel·drakes** *or* **shel·drake.**

shel·duck (shel′duk′), *n.* any of various large ducks of Europe and Asia.

shelf (shelf), *n.* **1** a thin, flat piece of wood, metal, stone, etc., fastened to a wall or frame to hold things, such as books, dishes, etc. **2** anything like a shelf: *The ship hit a shelf of coral.* ❑ *n., pl.* **shelves. —shelf′like′,** *adj.*
on the shelf, no longer useful or desirable.

shelf life, length of time that a product can be stored without spoiling or becoming useless: *the shelf life of milk.*

shell (shel), **1** *n.* the hard outside covering of certain animals. Oysters, turtles, and snails all have shells. **2** *n.* the hard outside covering of a nut, seed, fruit, etc. **3** *n.* the hard outside covering of an egg. **4** *n.* tortoiseshell used in combs or ornaments. **5** *v.* to take out of a shell: *shell peas.* **6** *v.* to separate grains of corn from the cob. **7** *n.* something like a shell. The framework of a house and a hollow baked dough for pastry are called shells. **8** *n.* cartridge used in a rifle or shotgun. **9** *n.* a metal case filled with explosives that is fired by artillery and explodes either in the air or when it strikes something. **10** *v.* to fire cannon at; bombard with shells: *The enemy shelled the town.* **11** *n.* a long, narrow racing boat of light wood, rowed by a crew using long oars. **—shell′like′,** *adj.*
come out of your shell, to stop being shy or reserved; join in conversation, etc., with others.
shell out, INFORMAL. to hand over money; pay out: *We had to shell out five dollars for the movie.*

she'll (shēl), **1** she shall. **2** she will.

shel·lac (shə lak′), **1** *n.* a kind of varnish made from resin dissolved in alcohol. Shellac dries rapidly to give wood, metal, and other materials a smooth, shiny appearance, and protection from air and moisture. **2** *v.* to put this liquid on; cover with this liquid. **3** *v.* INFORMAL. to defeat completely. ❑ *v.* **shel·lacked, shel·lack·ing.**

Shel·ley (shel′ē), *n.* **1 Mary Woll·stone·craft** (wŭl′stən kraft′), 1797-1851, English writer. She wrote *Frankenstein.* **2 Per·cy Bysshe** (pėr′sē bish), 1792-1822, English poet, husband of Mary Shelley.

shell·fire (shel′fir′), *n.* the firing of explosive shells or projectiles.

shell·fish (shel′fish′), *n.* a water animal with a shell. Oysters, clams, crabs, and lobsters are shellfish. ❑ *n., pl.* **shell·fish** *or* **shell·fish·es.**

shell game, game used by swindlers in which someone tries to guess which of three shells or cups a small object is hidden under.

shell shock, a nervous or mental disorder resulting from the strain of war. **—shell′-shocked,** *adj.*

shel·ter (shel′tər), **1** *n.* something that covers or protects from weather, danger, or attack: *Trees are a shelter from the sun.* **2** *v.* to protect; shield; hide: *shelter a fugitive.* **3** *n.* protection; refuge: *We took shelter from the storm in a barn.* **4** *n.* a temporary place of shelter for poor or homeless people, or for animals without owners. **—shel′ter·er,** *n.* **—shel′ter·less,** *adj.*

SYNONYM STUDY **Shelter, haven,** and **refuge** all mean a place that protects you. **Shelter** means something that protects from weather or danger: *The shade of the tree gives the cows shelter from the sun.* **Haven** means a place of shelter and safety: *The church has opened its basement as a haven for the homeless.* **Refuge** suggests a place that is free of danger: *The whooping cranes spend winter at a wildlife refuge.*

a	hat	ė	term	ô	order	ch	child		a in about
ā	age	i	it	oi	oil	ng	long		e in taken
ä	far	ī	ice	ou	out	sh	she	ə	i in pencil
â	care	o	hot	u	cup	th	thin		o in lemon
e	let	ō	open	ů	put	ᴛн	then		u in circus
ē	equal	ȯ	saw	ü	rule	zh	measure		

shelve (shelv), *v.* **1** to put on a shelf: *shelve books.* **2** to lay aside: *Let us shelve that argument.* ❑ *v.* **shelved, shelv·ing. —shelv′er,** *n.*

shelves (shelvz), *n.* plural of **shelf.**

shelv·ing (shel′ving), *n.* **1** wood, metal, etc., for shelves: *I ordered 40 feet of pine shelving.* **2** shelves.

Shen·an·do·ah (shen′ən dō′ə), *n.* river flowing through N Virginia into the Potomac River.

Shenandoah National Park, a national park in N Virginia, containing a large section of the Blue Ridge Mountains and a famous mountain road.

Shenandoah National Park

she·nan·i·gans (shə nan′ə gənz), *n.pl.* INFORMAL. mischief or trickery.

She·ol (shē′ōl), *n.* a Hebrew name for the abode of the dead.

shep·herd (shep′ərd), **1** *n.* person who takes care of sheep. **2** *v.* to take care of: *to shepherd a flock.* **3** *v.* to guide; direct: *The teacher shepherded the children safely out of the burning building.* **4** *n.* a spiritual guide; pastor.

shep·herd·ess (shep′ər dis), *n.* woman who takes care of sheep. ❑ *n., pl.* **shep·herd·ess·es.**

sher·bet (shėr′bət), *n.* a frozen dessert made of fruit juice, sugar, and water or milk.

sher·iff (sher′if), *n.* **1** the most important law enforcement officer of a county. **2** (in Canada) an official who carries out such court orders as evicting people for nonpayment of rent, and escorting sentenced convicts to prison.

Sherlock Holmes. See **Holmes.**

Sher·man (sher′mən), *n.* **William Tecumseh,** 1820-1891, Union general in the Civil War. He led an army across Georgia, destroying much property.

Sher·pa (sher′pə), *n.* member of a people living in Nepal who have served as guides for many of the expeditions to climb Mount Everest. ❑ *n., pl.* **Sher·pas.**

sher·ry (sher′ē), *n.* a strong wine. It varies in color from pale yellow to brown.

Sher·wood Forest (sher′wud), a royal forest near Nottingham, where Robin Hood and his men are said to have lived.

she's (shēz), **1** she is. **2** she has.

Shet·land Islands (shet′lənd), group of British islands northeast of Scotland. See **British Isles** for map.

Shetland pony, a small, sturdy pony with a rough coat.

Shetland sheep dog, a long-haired working dog like a small collie, originally from the Shetland Islands.

Shi·a (shē′ä), *n.* **1** sect of Islam believing that Muslim leadership passed from Muhammad to his son-in-law Ali. **2** member of this sect; Shiite. ❑ *n., pl.* **Shi·a** or **Shi·as.**

shib·bo·leth (shib′ə lith), *n.* any test word, watchword, or pet phrase of a political party, a class, sect, etc.

WORD STORY Shibboleth comes from a Bible story in which soldiers asked everyone crossing a river to say "shibboleth," a Hebrew word meaning "river." Their enemies could not say **sh,** because that sound did not exist in the enemy language. During World War II, American passwords often included sounds difficult for Germans or Japanese to pronounce.

shied (shīd), *v.* **1** past tense and past participle of **shy**[1]: *The horse shied and threw the rider. It had never shied like that before.* **2** past tense and past participle of **shy**[2]: *The boy shied a stone at the tree. He has shied stones at birds.*

shield (shēld), **1** *n.* piece of armor carried on the arm to protect the body in battle. **2** *n.* anything used to protect: *I turned up my collar as a shield against the cold wind.* **3** *n.* something shaped like a shield. A police officer's badge and a coat of arms are called shields. **4** *v.* to be a shield to; protect; defend: *They shielded me from unjust punishment.* **—shield′like′,** *adj.*

shi·er (shī′ər), *adj.* a comparative of **shy**[1].

shi·est (shī′ist), *adj.* a superlative of **shy**[1].

shift (shift), **1** *v.* to move or change from one place, position, person, sound, etc., to another: *The wind has shifted to the southeast. I shifted the heavy bag from one hand to the other.* **2** *n.* a change of direction, position, attitude, etc.: *a shift of the wind, a shift in policy.* **3** *n.* group of workers who work during the same period of time: *The night shift begins work at 12:30 a.m.* **4** *n.* time during which such a group works: *She is on the night shift this week.* **5** *n.* scheme; trick: *The child tried every shift to avoid going to bed.* **6** *v.* to manage to get along; provide: *I left home at an early age and had to shift for myself.* **7** *v.* to change the position of gears, as in a car. **—shift′a·ble,** *adj.* **—shift′er,** *n.* **—shift′ing·ly,** *adv.*

make shift, 1 to manage to get along; do as well as you can. **2** to manage something with effort or difficulty.

shift·less (shift′lis), *adj.* lazy; inefficient: *The shiftless fellow refused to work.* **—shift′less·ly,** *adv.* **—shift′less·ness,** *n.*

shift·y (shif′tē), *adj.* not straightforward; tricky: *The suspect gave shifty answers to the police.* ❑ *adj.* **shift·i·er, shift·i·est. —shift′i·ly,** *adv.* **—shift′i·ness,** *n.*

Shih Tzu (shē′ dzü′), a small, lively dog, originally from China, with long, thick hair, short legs, a broad head and muzzle, and drooping ears.

Shi·ism (shē′iz′əm), *n.* beliefs of Shia Muslims.

Shi·ite (shē′īt), *n.* Shia (def. 2).

Shi·ko·ku (shi kō′kü), *n.* island of Japan, in the S part.

shil·le·lagh (shə lā′lē *or* shə lā′lə), *n.* IRISH. a stick to hit with; cudgel.

Shih Tzu—about 10 in. (25 cm) high at the shoulder

shil·ling (shil′ing), *n.* a former unit of money in Great Britain, equal to 12 pence or ¹⁄₂₀ of a pound.

shil·ly·shal·ly (shil′ē shal′ē), *v.* to be undecided; hesitate. ❑ *v.* **shil·ly·shal·lied, shil·ly·shal·ly·ing.**

Shi·loh (shī′lō), *n.* **Battle of,** battle of the Civil War in NW Tennessee on April 6-7, 1862. A Union retreat was halted by reinforcements, and Union troops then drove back the Confederate advance.

shim·mer (shim′ər), **1** *v.* to gleam faintly: *Both the sea and the sand shimmered in the moonlight.* **2** *n.* a faint gleam or shine: *The pearls have a beautiful shimmer.* **—shim′mer·ing·ly,** *adv.*

shim·mer·y (shim′ər ē), *adj.* shimmering; gleaming softly.

shim·my (shim′ē), **1** *n.* an unusual shaking or vibration: *a dangerous shimmy of a ladder.* **2** *v.* to shake; vibrate. ❑ *n., pl.* **shim·mies;** *v.* **shim·mied, shim·my·ing.**

shin (shin), **1** *n.* the front part of the leg from the knee to the ankle. **2** *v.* to climb by clasping or holding tight with the hands or arms and legs and pulling yourself up: *I shinned up the tree.* ❑ *v.* **shinned, shin·ning.** [See Word Story at **shinny**[2].]

shin·bone (shin′bōn′), *n.* the inner and thicker of the two bones of the leg between the knee and the ankle; tibia.

shin·dig (shin′dig), *n.* INFORMAL. a merry or noisy dance, party, etc.

shine (shīn), **1** *v.* to send out light; be bright with light; reflect light; glow: *The sun shines. His face is shining with soap and water.* **2** *n.* light; brightness: *the shine of a lamp.* **3** *n.* luster; polish: *the shine of a new penny.* **4** *n.* fair weather; sunshine: *He goes to school rain or shine.* **5** *v.* to do very well; be brilliant; excel: *She shines at sports.* **6** *v.* to make bright; polish: *shine shoes.* **7** *n.* polish put on shoes. **8** *v.* to cause to shine: *shine a light.* ❑ *v.* **shone** (or **shined**, especially for 6), **shin·ing.**

shine up to, INFORMAL. to try to please and get the friendship of.
take a shine to, INFORMAL. to become fond of; like.

shin·er (shī′nər), *n.* **1** someone or something that shines. **2** any of several small American freshwater fishes with glistening scales, related to carp. **3** INFORMAL. black eye.

shin·gle¹ (shing′gəl), **1** *n.* a thin piece of asbestos, wood, etc., used to cover roofs, walls, etc. Shingles are laid in overlapping rows with the thicker ends showing. **2** *v.* to cover with shingles: *shingle a roof.* **3** *n.* a small signboard, especially one outside a doctor's or lawyer's office. ❑ *v.* **shin·gled, shin·gling. –shin′gler,** *n.*

shin·gle² (shing′gəl), *n.* loose stones or pebbles that lie on the seashore; coarse gravel.

shin·gles (shing′gəlz), *n.sing. or pl.* a virus disease that causes pain in certain nerves and an outbreak of spots and blisters on the skin in the area of the affected nerves.

shin·guard (shin′gärd′), *n.* a protective leather or plastic covering for the shins and knees, worn by baseball catchers and hockey goalkeepers.

shin·ing (shī′ning), *adj.* glowing; brilliant; outstanding: *a shining star, a shining career.* **–shin′ing·ly,** *adv.*

shin·ny¹ (shin′ē), **1** *n.* a simple kind of field hockey, played with a ball or the like and clubs curved at one end. **2** *v.* to play shinny. ❑ *v.* **shin·nied, shin·ny·ing.**

shin·ny² (shin′ē), *v.* to climb by holding tight with the arms and legs and pulling yourself up; shin: *shinny up a tree.* ❑ *v.* **shin·nied, shin·ny·ing.**

shin·splints (shin′splints′), *n.sing. or pl.* pain and inflammation of muscles in the lower legs, caused by too much exercise, as in running or rapid walking on a hard surface.

Shin·to (shin′tō), *n.* the native religion of Japan, primarily a system of nature worship and ancestor worship.

Shin·to·ism (shin′tō iz′əm), *n.* the Shinto religion.

shin·y (shī′nē), *adj.* **1** shining; bright: *a shiny new penny.* **2** worn to a glossy smoothness: *a coat shiny from hard wear.* ❑ *adj.* **shin·i·er, shin·i·est. –shin′i·ly,** *adv.* **–shin′i·ness,** *n.*

ship (ship), **1** *n.* any large boat which can travel on oceans and deep waterways. Freighters, passenger liners, and oil tankers are common kinds of ships. **2** *n.* a large sailing boat, especially one with three masts and a bowsprit. **3** *v.* to send or carry from one place to another by a ship, train, truck, etc.: *Did you ship it by express or by freight?* **4** *n.* an airship, airplane, spacecraft, etc. **5** *n.* officers and crew of a ship. **6** *v.* to travel on a ship, especially as a member of the crew; sail: *He shipped as a cook.* **7** *v.* to send off: *They shipped him off to camp for the summer.* **8** *v.* to take in water over the side, as a boat does when the waves break over it. ❑ *v.* **shipped, ship·ping.**

when your ship comes in or **when your ship comes home,** when your fortune is made; when you have money.

-ship, *suffix.* **1** office, position, or occupation of ___: *governorship = office of a governor; authorship = occupation of an author.* **2** situation or condition of being ___: *partnership = condition of being a partner.* **3** skill, ability, or power of ___: *craftsmanship = skill of a craftsman.*

ship biscuit, hardtack.

ship·board (ship′bôrd′), *n.* **on shipboard,** on or inside a ship.

ship·build·ing (ship′bil′ding), *n.* the designing or building of ships. **–ship′build′er,** *n.*

ship·load (ship′lōd′), *n.* a full load for a ship.

ship·mas·ter (ship′mas′tər), *n.* master, commander, or captain of a ship.

ship·mate (ship′māt′), *n.* a fellow sailor on a ship.

ship·ment (ship′mənt), *n.* **1** act of shipping goods: *A thousand boxes of oranges were ready for shipment.* **2** goods sent at one time to a person or company: *We received two shipments today.*

ship·own·er (ship′ō′nər), *n.* person who owns a ship or ships.

ship·per (ship′ər), *n.* person who ships goods.

ship·ping (ship′ing), *n.* **1** the act or business of sending goods by ship, train, truck, or airplane. **2** ships, especially ships of a nation, city, or business: *Much of the world's shipping passes through the Panama Canal each year.*

ship·shape (ship′shāp′), *adj.* tidy; in good order: *We made the house shipshape before our visitors arrived.*

ship's papers, the documents giving information about a ship's nationality, owner, etc., which every ship must carry.

ship·worm (ship′wėrm′), *n.* any of various long, wormlike sea animals, covered with a shell, that burrow into the timbers of ships and wharves.

ship·wreck (ship′rek′), **1** *n.* destruction or loss of a ship: *Only two people were saved from the shipwreck.* **2** *n.* a wrecked ship. **3** *n.* destruction; ruin: *The shipwreck of her plans discouraged her.* **4** *v.* to wreck, ruin, or destroy.

ship·yard (ship′yärd′), *n.* place near the water where ships are built or repaired.

shire (shīr), *n.* one of the counties into which Great Britain is divided, especially one whose name ends in *-shire: Yorkshire.*

shirk (shėrk), *v.* to avoid or get out of doing work, a duty, etc.: *You will lose your job if you continue to shirk your responsibilities.* **–shirk′er,** *n.*

shirr (shėr), **1** *v.* to draw up or gather cloth on parallel threads. **2** *n.* a shirred arrangement of cloth, etc. **3** *v.* to bake eggs in a shallow dish with butter, etc.

shirt (shėrt), *n.* **1** piece of clothing for the upper part of the body. A shirt usually has a collar, long or short sleeves, and an opening in the front that is closed by buttons. **2** undershirt. **–shirt′like′,** *adj.*

keep your shirt on, INFORMAL. to stay calm; keep your temper.

shirt·ing (shėr′ting), *n.* cloth used for making shirts.

shirt·tail (shėrt′tāl′), *n.* the lower part of a shirt, especially the back part.

shirt·waist (shėrt′wāst′), *n.* **1** a woman's or girl's shirtlike blouse, worn with a separate skirt. **2** a one-piece dress with a shirtlike top.

shish ke·bab (shish′kə bob′), small pieces of seasoned meat, and sometimes tomatoes and onions, roasted and served on a skewer.

Shi·va (shē′və), *n.* Hindu god of destruction and renewal.

shiv·er¹ (shiv′ər), **1** *v.* to shake with cold, fear, or excitement: *I shivered in the cold wind.* ▪ See Synonym Study at **shake. 2** *n.* a shaking from cold, fear, or excitement: *A shiver ran down my back as I waited for the roller coaster ride to begin.* **–shiv′er·er,** *n.* **–shiv′er·ing·ly,** *adv.*

shiv·er² (shiv′ər), **1** *v.* to break into small pieces: *I shivered the mirror with a hammer.* **2** *n.* a small piece; splinter: *There were shivers of glass on the floor.*

shiver¹

S

a	hat	ė	term	ô	order	ch	child		a in about
ā	age	i	it	oi	oil	ng	long		e in taken
ä	far	ī	ice	ou	out	sh	she	ə	i in pencil
â	care	o	hot	u	cup	th	thin		o in lemon
e	let	ō	open	ů	put	ᴛʜ	then		u in circus
ē	equal	ò	saw	ü	rule	zh	measure		

shiv·er·y (shiv′ər ē), *adj.* **1** quivering from cold, fear, etc.; shivering. **2** chilly. **3** causing shivers: *a shivery experience.*

shoal[1] (shōl), **1** *n.* place in a sea, lake, or stream where the water is shallow. **2** *n.* sandbar that makes the water shallow, especially one that can be seen at low tide: *The ship was wrecked on the shoals.* **3** *adj.* shallow. **4** *v.* to become shallow.

shoal[2] (shōl), **1** *n.* a large number; crowd: *We saw a shoal of fish in the water.* **2** *v.* to form into a shoal; crowd together.

shoat (shōt), *n.* a young pig that no longer suckles.

shock[1] (shok), **1** *n.* a sudden, violent, or upsetting disturbance: *Her death was a great shock to her family.* **2** *n.* a sudden, violent shake, blow, or crash: *Earthquake shocks are often felt in Japan.* **3** *v.* to cause to feel surprise, horror, or disgust: *That child's bad language shocks everyone.* **4** *n.* condition of physical collapse or depression, together with a sudden drop in blood pressure, often resulting in unconsciousness. Shock may set in after a severe injury, great loss of blood, or a sudden emotional disturbance. **5** *n.* the feeling or physical effects produced by an electric current passing through the body. **6** *v.* to give an electric shock to: *That lamp shocked me when I touched it with my wet hands.* —**shock′·a·ble,** *adj.* —**shock′er,** *n.*

shock[2] (shok), **1** *n.* group of cornstalks or bundles of grain set up on end together in order to dry. **2** *v.* to make into shocks.

shock[3] (shok), *n.* a thick, bushy mass: *an untidy shock of red hair.*

shock ab·sorb·er (ab sôr′bər), device consisting of springs, hydraulic pistons, etc., used on cars, airplanes, etc., to absorb the force of sudden impacts.

shock·ing (shok′ing), *adj.* **1** causing very painful feelings or surprise: *We heard the shocking news of the airplane crash.* **2** causing disgust or horror: *The crimes of the convicted murderers were shocking.* —**shock′ing·ly,** *adv.*

shock·proof (shok′prüf′), *adj.* able to withstand a sudden, violent shake or blow without breaking: *a shockproof watch.*

shock troops, troops chosen and specially trained for making attacks.

shock wave, disturbance spreading as a wave through air, water, etc., and caused by motion of some object at a speed greater than the speed of sound in the disturbed substance. Pressure, density, and motion change suddenly as a shock wave passes.

shod (shod), *v.* a past tense and past participle of **shoe:** *The blacksmith shod the horses. They had never been shod before.*

shod·dy (shod′ē), *adj.* **1** of inferior quality: *shoddy furniture.* **2** mean; shabby: *a shoddy trick.* ❑ *adj.* **shod·di·er, shod·di·est.** —**shod′di·ly,** *adv.* —**shod′di·ness,** *n.*

shoe (shü), **1** *n.* an outer covering for a person's foot. Shoes are made of leather, vinyl, etc., and usually have a stiff sole and a heel. **2** *n.* thing like a shoe in shape or use. **3** *n.* a horseshoe. **4** *n.* the part of a brake that presses on a wheel to slow it down or stop it. **5** *v.* to furnish with a shoe or shoes: *A blacksmith shoes horses. Her feet were shod with silver slippers.* **6** *v.* to protect or arm at the point; edge or face with metal: *a stick shod with steel.* ❑ *v.* **shod** or **shoed, shoe·ing.** ■ Another word that sounds like this is **shoo.** —**shoe′less,** *adj.*

in someone else's shoes, in the place, situation, or circumstances of someone else.

shoe·horn (shü′hôrn′), *n.* a curved piece of metal, horn, etc., used to help slip a shoe more easily over the heel.

shoe·lace (shü′lās′), *n.* cord or a strip of leather or other material for fastening a shoe.

shoe·mak·er (shü′mā′kər), *n.* person who makes or mends shoes.

Shoe·mak·er (shü′mā′kər), *n.* **Wil·lie** (wil′ē), born 1931, American jockey. He has won more money and more races than any other jockey.

shoe·shine (shü′shīn′), *n.* **1** act of shining a pair of shoes. **2** the shiny surface on shoes produced by polishing.

shoe·string (shü′string′), *n.* **1** shoelace. **2** a very small amount of money used to start or carry on a business, investment, etc.: *The company was formed on a shoestring.*

shoe·tree (shü′trē′), *n.* a device shaped like a foot, placed in a shoe to keep its shape or to stretch it. ❑ *n., pl.* **shoe·trees.**

sho·far (shō′fär *or* shō′fər), *n.* a ram's horn sounded during certain Jewish religious services, especially on Rosh Hashanah and Yom Kippur. ■ Another word that can sound like this is **chauffeur.**

sho·gun (shō′gun), *n.* title given to the commander in chief of the Japanese army. Shoguns were the real rulers of Japan for hundreds of years until 1867.

shone (shōn), *v.* a past tense and a past participle of **shine:** *The sun shone all last week. It has not shone since.* ■ Another word that sounds like this is **shown.**

shoo (shü), **1** *interj.* an exclamation used to scare or drive away animals or small children: *"Shoo! You children get away from that cake!"* **2** *v.* to scare or drive away by calling "Shoo!": *Shoo those flies away from the sugar.* ❑ *v.* **shooed, shoo·ing.** ■ Another word that sounds like this is **shoe.**

shoo-in (shü′in′), *n.* INFORMAL. **1** an easy or sure winner: *He's a shoo-in to win the science fair this year.* **2** an easy race, contest, etc., to win: *The pie-throwing contest is a shoo-in for our star pitcher.*

shook (shuk), *v.* past tense of **shake:** *They shook hands.*

shoot (shüt), **1** *v.* to hit, wound, or kill with a bullet, arrow, etc.: *He shot a rabbit.* **2** *v.* to fire a gun: *She shot her rifle at the target.* **3** *v.* to send a bullet: *This gun shoots straight.* **4** *v.* to send swiftly: *A bow shoots an arrow. She shot question after question at us.* **5** *n.* a trip, gathering, or contest for shooting. **6** *v.* to move suddenly and swiftly: *Flames shot up from the burning house.* **7** *v.* to pass quickly along, through, over, or under: *Only a shallow boat can shoot this stretch of rapids.* **8** *v.* to go sharply through part of the body: *Pain shot up her arm.* **9** *v.* to send a ball, puck, marble, etc., toward the goal, pocket, etc., while scoring or trying to score: *We put up a basketball hoop and shot baskets for practice.* **10** *v.* to take a picture with a camera; photograph: *I shot several views of the mountains.* **11** *v.* to come forth; grow; grow rapidly: *Buds shoot forth in the spring.* **12** *n.* a session of taking photographs, videos, or TV images. **13** *v.* to stick out sharply: *a cape that shoots out into the sea.* **14** *n.* a new part growing out; young branch: *The rosebush is putting out new shoots.* **15** *n.* chute (def. 1). **16** *v.* to vary with some different color, etc.: *The fabric was shot with threads of gold.* ❑ *v.* **shot, shoot·ing.** —**shoot′er,** *n.*

shoot at or **shoot for,** INFORMAL. to aim at; work to achieve.

shoot down, 1 to bring down an aircraft by firing shells or missiles at it. **2** to defeat someone's ideas: *to shoot down a budget proposal.*

shooting star, meteor seen falling through the sky at night.

shop (shop), **1** *v.* to visit stores to look at or to buy things: *We shopped all morning for a coat.* **2** *n.* place where things are made or repaired: *He works in a carpenter's shop.* **3** *n.* place where a certain kind of work is done: *We got our hair cut at a barber shop.* **4** *n.* place where things are sold; store: *a small dress shop.* **5** *n.* schoolroom equipped for woodworking, auto repair, metalworking, printing, and other skills. **6** *n.* course offering instruction in these skills. ❑ *v.* **shopped, shop·ping.**

set up shop, to start work or business.

talk shop, to talk about your work or occupation.

shop·keep·er (shop′kē′pər), *n.* person who owns or manages a shop or store.

shop·lift (shop′lift′), *v.* to steal things from a store while pretending to be a customer. —**shop′lift′er,** *n.*

shop·lift·ing (shop′lif′ting), *n.* act of stealing things from a store while pretending to be a customer.

shop·per (shop′ər), *n.* person who visits stores to look at or to buy things.

shop·ping (shop′ing), *n.* act of visiting stores to look at or to buy things: *We usually do our shopping on Saturday morning.*

shopping center, group of stores built as a unit on or near a main road, especially in a suburban or new community. Most shopping centers have large parking lots.

shopping mall, mall (def. 1).

shopping plaza, CANADIAN. shopping center.

shop·talk (shop′tôk′), *n.* talk about your work or occupation, especially outside of working hours.

shop·worn (shop′wôrn′), *adj.* soiled or damaged by being displayed or handled in a store.

shore[1] (shôr), *n.* **1** the land at the edge of a sea, lake, etc. **2** any land: *After so many months at sea, it was good to be on shore again.*
off shore, in or on the water, not far from the shore.

shore[2] (shôr), **1** *n.* a prop placed against or beneath something to support it. **2** *v.* to prop up or support with shores. ❑ *v.* **shored**, **shor·ing.**

shore·bird (shôr′bėrd′), *n.* any bird that is often on the shores of seas, lakes, etc.

shore leave, leave for a member of a ship's crew to go ashore.

shore·line (shôr′līn′), *n.* line where shore and water meet: *The shoreline shifts during each big storm.*

shore[1] (def. 1)

shore patrol, enlisted persons who act as police for the Navy and Coast Guard.

shore·ward (shôr′wərd), *adv., adj.* toward the shore: *The winds blew shoreward. We felt the shoreward breeze.*

shorn (shôrn), **1** *v.* a past participle of **shear**: *The sheep was shorn of its wool.* **2** *adj.* sheared.

short (shôrt), **1** *adj.* not long; of little distance or amount from end to end: *a short distance, a short time.* **2** *adj.* not tall: *a short man, short grass.* **3** *adj.* lacking the right amount, measure, standard, etc.: *I would like to buy this, but I'm short a dime.* **4** *adj.* not having or being enough: *After two weeks of camping, we were short of food.* **5** *adj.* so brief as to be rude: *She was so short with me that I felt hurt.* **6** *adv.* failing to reach the point aimed at: *The arrows landed just short of the target.* **7** *adv.* in a very quick way; abruptly; suddenly: *The horse stopped short.* **8** *adj.* breaking or crumbling easily; crisp; flaky. Pastry is made short with butter or other shortening. **9** *adj.* (of vowels or syllables) taking little time to speak. A vowel like *a* in *fat, e* in *net, i* in *pin, o* in *not,* or *u* in *up* is a **short vowel. 10** *n.pl.* **shorts, a** short pants that do not reach the knees. **b** a similar kind of men's or boy's underwear. **11** *n.* a short circuit. **12** *v.* to short-circuit. **—short′ness,** *n.*
cut short, to end suddenly; interrupt: *Sickness cut short my vacation.*
fall short, 1 to fail to reach. **2** be insufficient.
for short, in order to make shorter: *Robert was called Rob for short.*
in short, briefly.
run short, 1 to not have enough. **2** not be enough.
short for, a shortened form of: *The word "phone" is short for "telephone."*
short of, 1 not up to; less than: *Nothing short of your best work will satisfy me.* **2** on the near side of.

short·age (shôr′tij), *n.* too small an amount; lack; deficiency: *The nation had a serious shortage of grain due to poor crops.*

short·bread (shôrt′bred′), *n.* a rich cake or cookie that crumbles easily.

short·cake (shôrt′kāk′), *n.* **1** cake made of rich biscuit dough and shortening, covered or filled with berries or other fruit. **2** a sweet cake filled with fruit.

short·change (shôrt′chānj′), *v.* **1** to give less than the right change to. **2** to cheat: *be shortchanged in getting an education.* ❑ *v.* **short·changed, short·chang·ing. —short′chang′er,** *n.*

short circuit, an unwanted, malfunctioning electric circuit like that formed when insulation wears off wires that touch each other or another conductor. A short circuit prevents electric devices from working. It may cause a fire unless it blows a fuse or activates a circuit breaker.

short-cir·cuit (shôrt′sėr′kit), *v.* **1** to make a short circuit in. **2** to make a short circuit.

short·com·ing (shôrt′kum′ing), *n.* flaw in your character or conduct; fault; defect: *Rudeness is one of her shortcomings.*

short·cut (shôrt′kut′), *n.* **1** a less distant or quicker way: *To save time we took a shortcut through a vacant lot.* **2** a way to save time.

short division, way of dividing numbers in which each step is worked out in the mind, not written out.

short·en (shôrt′n), *v.* **1** to make shorter; cut off: *The new highway shortens the trip. I've had my coat shortened.* **2** to become shorter: *The days shortened and soon snow began to fall.* **3** to make rich with butter, lard, etc.: *shorten a cake.* **—short′en·er,** *n.*

SYNONYM STUDY **Shorten, abbreviate,** and **abridge** all mean to make shorter. **Shorten** is a general word: *I shortened this skirt.* **Abbreviate** means to shorten a word: *Maryland is abbreviated as Md.* **Abridge** means to shorten a piece of writing by leaving words or sections out: *This abridged dictionary still contains all commonly used words.*

short·en·ing (shôrt′n ing), *n.* **1** butter, lard, vegetable oil, or other fat, used to make pastry, cake, etc., crisp or crumbly. **2** act of someone or something that shortens.

short·fall (shôrt′fôl′), *n.* amount by which something is less than expected; shortage: *a shortfall in the wheat harvest, a shortfall of two million dollars in the state's tax revenues.*

short·hand (shôrt′hand′), *n.* **1** method of rapid writing which uses symbols for abbreviations in place of letters, words, phrases, etc.; stenography. **2** writing in such symbols.

short·hand·ed (shôrt′han′did), *adj.* not having enough workers, helpers, etc.

short-haul (shôrt′hôl′), *adj.* of or about travel or transportation over short distances: *short-haul airlines.*

short·horn (shôrt′hôrn′), *n.* one of a breed of cattle with short horns, raised for beef.

short·ish (shôr′tish), *adj.* rather short.

short-lived (shôrt′livd′ or shôrt′līvd′), *adj.* living only a short time; lasting a short time. **—short′-lived′ness,** *n.*

short·ly (shôrt′lē), *adv.* **1** in a short time; before long; soon: *I will be with you shortly.* **2** in a few words; briefly. **3** briefly and rudely; curtly.

short order, any kind of food that is cooked or served quickly, such as food in a fast-food restaurant or at a lunch counter. **—short′-or′der,** *adj.*

short-range (shôrt′rānj′), *adj.* not reaching far in time or distance; not long-range: *a short-range forecast.*

short shrift, little or no consideration, mercy, or delay in dealing with a person or problem: *Violators of these new regulations will get short shrift.*

short·sight·ed (shôrt′sī′tid), *adj.* **1** nearsighted; not able to see far. **2** not taking careful thought for the future: *It was shortsighted of us not to bring umbrellas or raincoats on our trip.* **—short′sight′ed·ly,** *adv.* **—short′sight′ed·ness,** *n.*

short·stop (shôrt′stop′), *n.* a baseball player stationed between second and third base.

short story, a prose story which usually describes a single event, has a limited number of characters, and is much shorter than a novel.

short-tem·pered (shôrt′tem′pərd), *adj.* easily made angry; quick-tempered.

short-term (shôrt′tėrm′), *adj.* for a short period of time: *short-term plans.*

short·wave (shôrt′wāv′), **1** *n.* a radio wave with a wavelength between 10 meters and 200 meters (33 feet and 656 feet), and a frequency greater than 1600 kilohertz. **2** *adj.* using such waves: *a shortwave radio.* **3** *v.* to transmit by short waves. ❑ *v.* **short·waved, short·wav·ing.**

short-wind·ed (shôrt′win′did), *adj.* getting out of breath very easily; having difficulty in breathing.

Sho·sho·ne (shō shō′nē), *n.* Shoshoni. ❑ *n., pl.* **Sho·sho·ne** or **Sho·sho·nes.**

a	hat	ė	term	ô	order	ch	child	⎧ a in about
ā	age	i	it	oi	oil	ng	long	⎪ e in taken
ä	far	ī	ice	ou	out	sh	she	ə ⎨ i in pencil
â	care	o	hot	u	cup	th	thin	⎪ o in lemon
e	let	ō	open	ů	put	ŦH	then	⎩ u in circus
ē	equal	ò	saw	ü	rule	zh	measure	

Sho·sho·ni (shō shō′nē), *n.* member of a tribe of American Indians living in Wyoming, Idaho, Utah, California, and Nevada. ❑ *n., pl.* **Sho·sho·ni** or **Sho·sho·nis.**

Shos·ta·ko·vich (shos′tə kō′vich), *n.* **D·mi·tri** (də mē′trē), 1906-1975, Russian composer. He wrote 15 symphonies and was repeatedly criticized by the Soviet government for his modern style.

shot[1] (shot), *n.* **1** the firing of a gun: *We heard two shots.* **2** act of shooting. **3** tiny balls of steel, lead, etc., fired from a shotgun. **4** a single ball of lead, steel, etc., for a gun or cannon. **5** an attempt to hit by shooting: *take a shot at the target.* **6** the distance a weapon can shoot; range: *We were within rifle shot of the fort.* **7** person who shoots: *She is a good shot.* **8** something like a shot, especially an aimed throw or stroke in a game: *a shot at the basket, a difficult golf shot.* **9** injection of a vaccine or drug: *a flu shot.* **10** an unkind remark aimed at someone or something. **11** an attempt; try: *have a shot at the job.* **12** a heavy metal ball used in the shot-put. **13** picture taken with a camera or a movie film of a scene. **14** a drink, usually a jigger, of liquor. ❑ *n., pl.* **shots** (or **shot** for 3,4).

call the shots, INFORMAL. be in control; be in charge: *Since it's his project, he calls the shots.*

shot[2] (shot), **1** *v.* past tense and past participle of **shoot:** *I shot the gun.* **2** *adj.* woven so as to show a play of colors: *blue silk shot with gold.* **3** *adj.* used up, worn out, or ruined: *The car's brakes were shot.*

shot through with, full of: *a composition shot through with errors.*

shot·gun (shot′gun′), *n.* gun with no grooves in its barrel, for firing cartridges filled with small shot.

shot put, contest in which someone sends a heavy metal ball through the air as far as possible with one push.

should (shu̇d), *v.* **1** past tense of **shall. 2** ought to: *You should try to make fewer mistakes.* **3** *Should* is used to express uncertainty: *If it should rain, I won't go.* **4** *Should* is used in speaking of something which might have happened but did not. *I should have gone if you had asked me.* **5** *Should* is used to express a condition or reason for something. *He was pardoned on the condition that he should leave the country.*

shot put

shoul·der (shōl′dər), **1** *n.* a part of the body to which an arm, foreleg, or wing is attached. **2** *n.* a part of a piece of clothing covering a shoulder: *I ripped the shoulder of my jacket.* **3** *n.pl.* **shoulders,** the two shoulders and the part of the back between them: *The man carried a trunk on his shoulders.* **4** *n.* edge of a road, often unpaved: *We pulled onto the shoulder to fix a flat tire.* **5** *v.* to take onto or support with the shoulder or shoulders: *shoulder a pack.* **6** *v.* to push with the shoulders: *shoulder your way through a crowd.* **7** *v.* to bear responsibility, blame, expense, etc.: *She shouldered the costs of sending her niece to college.* **8** *n.* something that sticks out like a shoulder: *the shoulder of a hill.* **9** *n.* a cut of meat including an upper foreleg and the parts joined to it.

cry on someone's shoulder, tell someone your troubles or worries.
put your shoulder to the wheel, to make a serious effort.
shoulder to shoulder, 1 side by side; together. **2** with united effort.
straight from the shoulder, frankly; directly.
turn a cold shoulder to, to show dislike for; shun; avoid.

shoulder bag, purse with a strap for hanging it over the shoulder.

shoulder blade, the flat, triangular bone of either shoulder, in the upper back; scapula.

shoulder strap, 1 strap worn over the shoulder to hold up an article of clothing. **2** an ornamental strip fastened on the shoulder of an officer's uniform to show rank.

should·n't (shu̇d′nt), should not.

shout (shout), **1** *v.* to call or yell loudly: *I shouted for help when the boat sank. Somebody shouted, "Fire!" The crowd shouted with laughter.* **2** *n.* a loud call or yell: *Shouts of joy rang through the halls.* **3** *v.* to express by a shout or shouts. —**shout′er,** *n.*
shout down, to silence by very loud talk.

SYNONYM STUDY **Shout, yell,** and **shriek** all mean to call out in a loud voice. **Shout** suggests trying to get someone's attention: *The guard shouted at the boys who had climbed the fence.* **Yell** means to call out very loudly and excitedly: *The crowd yells when each race begins.* **Shriek** means to call out in a loud, shrill voice, with fear, anger, or excitement: *Shrieking happily, the children rode the roller coaster over and over.*

shove (shuv), **1** *v.* to move forward or along by applying force from behind; push: *She shoved the bookcase into place.* **2** *v.* to push roughly or rudely; jostle: *Someone shoved me out of the line. The people shoved to get on the crowded bus.* ■ See Synonym Study at **push. 3** *n.* a push: *We gave the boat a shove which sent it far out into the water.* ❑ *v.* **shoved, shov·ing.** —**shov′er,** *n.*
shove off, 1 to push away from the shore; row away. **2** to leave a place; start on your way.

shov·el (shuv′əl), **1** *n.* tool with a broad blade or scoop attached to a long handle, used to lift and throw loose material: *a snow shovel.* **2** *v.* to lift and throw with a shovel: *They shoveled the sand into the truck.* **3** *v.* to make with a shovel: *They shoveled a path through the snow.* **4** *n.* a shovelful. **5** *v.* to throw or lift as if with a shovel: *The hungry child greedily shoveled the food into her mouth.* ❑ *v.* **shov·eled, shov·el·ing** or **shov·elled, shov·el·ling.**

shov·el·er (shuv′ə lər), *n.* **1** any of several freshwater ducks with long, broad, flat bills. **2** someone or something that shovels.

shov·el·ful (shuv′əl fu̇l), *n.* as much as a shovel can hold. ❑ *n., pl.* **shov·el·fuls.**

show (shō), **1** *v.* to let be seen; put in sight; display: *She showed me her rock collection.* **2** *v.* to reveal; indicate: *show great energy, show signs of fear.* **3** *v.* to be in sight; appear; be seen: *Anger showed in his face.* **4** *v.* to point out: *They showed us the way to town.* **5** *v.* to direct; guide: *Show them out.* **6** *v.* to make clear; explain. **7** *v.* to make clear to; explain to: *Show us how to do the problem.* **8** *v.* to prove: *She showed that it was true.* **9** *v.* to grant; give: *The governor was asked to show mercy and pardon the criminal.* **10** *n.* a play, movie, etc., or a performance of one of these: *The late show is at 11:00.* **11** *n.* a display: *The jewels made a fine show.* **12** *n.* a display for effect: *He put on a show of learning to impress us.* **13** *n.* any kind of public exhibition or display: *We are going to the flower show and to the automobile show.* **14** *n.* act of showing: *The club voted by a show of hands.* **15** *n.* appearance: *There is some show of truth in his excuse.* **16** *n.* false appearance; pretense: *hide your dislike by a show of friendship.* **17** *n.* object of scorn; something odd; queer sight: *Don't make a show of yourself.* **18** *n.* operation or undertaking: *They are running the whole show.* ❑ *v.* **showed, shown** or **showed, show·ing.** —**show′a·ble,** *adj.* —**show′er,** *n.*
for show, for effect; to attract attention.
show off, to make a show of; display your good points or abilities: *to show off new clothes. My little sister likes to show off by doing handstands when we have company.*
show up, 1 to stand out. **2** to put in an appearance. **3** to do better than someone; make plain someone's shortcomings: *show up her older brother with faster work.* **4** to expose; reveal: *show up the business as a fraud.*

show bill, poster, placard, or the like, advertising a show.

show·biz (shō′biz′), *n.* INFORMAL. show business.

show·boat (shō′bōt′), *n.* a river steamboat with a theater for plays. Showboats carry their own actors and make frequent stops to give performances.

show business, the industry or world of entertainment.

show·case (shō′kās′), **1** *n.* a glass case to display and protect articles in a store, museum, etc. **2** *n.* any display or exhibit. **3** *v.* to make a display or exhibit of: *The TV network showcased her talents in a special program.* ❑ *v.* **show·cased, show·cas·ing.**

show·down (shō′doun′), *n.* a meeting face to face in order to settle an issue or dispute: *The showdown between the mayor and the council over the new budget resulted in a welcome compromise.*

show·er (shou′ər), **1** *n.* bath in which water pours down on the body from an overhead nozzle. **2** *v.* to take such a bath. **3** *n.* a short fall of rain. **4** *v.* to rain for a short time. **5** *v.* to wet with spray; sprinkle: *Water from the broken hose showered those standing nearby.* **6** *n.* anything like a fall of rain: *a shower of hail, a shower of tears, a shower of sparks from an engine.* **7** *v.* to give generously or in large amounts: *Her rich aunt showered gifts upon her.* **8** *n.* party for giving presents to a woman about to be married or to give birth. —**show′er·less,** *adj.* —**show′er·like′,** *adj.*

shower bath, shower (def. 1).

show·er·y (shou′ər ē), *adj.* **1** raining in showers. **2** having many showers. **3** like a shower. —**show′er·i·ness,** *n.*

show·ing (shō′ing), *n.* **1** show; display; exhibition: *a current showing of paintings.* **2** manner of appearance or performance: *make a good showing.*

show·man (shō′mən), *n.* **1** person skilled in presenting things in a dramatic and exciting way. **2** person who manages a show. ❑ *n., pl.* **show·men.** —**show′man·ship,** *n.*

shown (shōn), *v.* a past participle of **show:** *We were shown many apartments.* ■ Another word that sounds like this is **shone.**

show-off (shō′ôf′), *n.* person who shows off in an effort to attract attention: *Some athletes are terrible show-offs.*

show·piece (shō′pēs′), *n.* anything shown as an outstanding example of its kind.

show·room (shō′rüm′), *n.* room used for the display of goods or merchandise for sale.

show window, window in the front of a store, where things are shown for sale.

show window

show·y (shō′ē), *adj.* **1** making a display; likely to attract attention; striking: *Peacocks are showy birds.* **2** too bright and flashy to be in good taste. **3** making a display to impress others; doing things to attract attention. ❑ *adj.* **show·i·er, show·i·est.** —**show′i·ly,** *adv.* —**show′i·ness,** *n.*

SYNONYM STUDY **Showy, flashy,** and **gaudy** all mean likely to attract attention. **Showy** suggests something bright and easy to see: *Orchids are showy flowers.* **Flashy** suggests that something gets more attention than it deserves: *Cheap, flashy clothes are often badly made.* **Gaudy** means bright and colorful and not in good taste: *The car was painted with gaudy purple flames.*

shrank (shrangk), *v.* a past tense of **shrink:** *My shirt shrank in the wash.*

shrap·nel (shrap′nəl), *n.* **1** shell filled with metal balls and powder, set to explode in midair and scatter the fragments over a wide area. **2** metal fragments of an exploding shell.

shred (shred), **1** *n.* a very small piece torn off or cut off; very narrow strip; scrap: *The wind tore the sail to shreds.* **2** *n.* bit; fragment; particle: *There's not a shred of evidence that he took the money.* **3** *v.* to tear or cut into small pieces: *He shredded the lettuce for the salad.* ■ See Synonym Study at **tear**[2]. ❑ *v.* **shred·ded, shred·ding.** —**shred′der,** *n.*

Shreve·port (shrēv′pôrt), *n.* city in NW Louisiana.

shrew (shrü), *n.* **1** any of numerous mouselike mammals with long snouts and brownish fur. Shrews eat insects and worms. **2** a bad-tempered, quarrelsome woman. ■ This meaning of **shrew** is considered offensive. —**shrew′like′,** *adj.*

shrewd (shrüd), *adj.* having a sharp mind; showing a keen wit; clever; keen; sharp: *She is a shrewd store manager with a talent for knowing what people want to buy.* —**shrewd′ly,** *adv.* —**shrewd′ness,** *n.*

shrew·ish (shrü′ish), *adj.* scolding or bad-tempered. ■ **Shrewish** is considered offensive. —**shrew′ish·ly,** *adv.* —**shrew′ish·ness,** *n.*

shriek (shrēk), **1** *v.* to make a loud, sharp, shrill sound. People sometimes shriek because of terror, anger, pain, or amusement. ■ See Synonym Study at **shout.** **2** *n.* a loud, sharp, shrill sound: *Shrieks of laughter greeted the clown's tricks.* **3** *v.* to utter loudly and shrilly. —**shriek′er,** *n.* —**shriek′ing·ly,** *adv.*

shrift (shrift), *n.* OLD USE. confession of your sins to a priest, followed by the granting of forgiveness by the priest.

shrike (shrik), *n.* any of several songbirds with strong, hooked beaks. They feed on large insects, frogs, mice, and sometimes on other birds.

shrill (shril), **1** *adj.* having a high pitch; high and sharp in sound; piercing: *Crickets, locusts, and katydids make shrill noises.* **2** *v.* to make a piercing sound; sound sharply. —**shrill′ness,** *n.*

shril·ly (shril′lē), *adv.* in shrill tones: *A bird called shrilly to its mate.*

shrimp (shrimp), *n.* **1** any of numerous small, long-tailed shellfish with long feelers and five pairs of legs. Some shrimp are used for food. **2** a small, short, or insignificant person. ■ This meaning of **shrimp** is often considered offensive. ❑ *n., pl.* **shrimp** or **shrimps** for 1, **shrimps** for 2. —**shrimp′like′,** *adj.*

shrimp·er (shrim′pər), *n.* **1** person who catches shrimp. **2** boat used to catch shrimp.

shrine (shrin), *n.* **1** a sacred place; place where sacred things are kept. A shrine may be the tomb of a saint, an altar in a church, or a box holding a holy object. **2** any place or object sacred because of its history; something sacred because of memories connected with it: *Shakespeare's birthplace is visited by thousands as a literary shrine.* —**shrine′like′,** *adj.*

shrine (def. 1)

shrink (shringk), **1** *v.* to pull back: *I shrank from the large, hissing snake. They were shy people who shrank from strangers.* **2** *v.* to become smaller: *My wool sweater shrank when it was washed.* **3** *v.* to make smaller; cause to contract: *The heat of the dryer shrank my wool socks.* **4** *n.* INFORMAL. psychiatrist. ❑ *v.* **shrank** or **shrunk, shrunk** or **shrunk·en, shrink·ing.** —**shrink′a·ble,** *adj.* —**shrink′er,** *n.* —**shrink′ing·ly,** *adv.*

shrink·age (shring′kij), *n.* **1** act or process of shrinking. **2** the amount or degree of shrinking: *a shrinkage of two inches in the length of a sleeve.*

shrink-wrap (shringk′rap′), **1** *n.* kind of plastic wrapping used to package products. When heated, it becomes tight-fitting, protecting products from dust, water, and other damage. **2** *v.* to enclose in this kind of wrapping. ❑ *v.* **shrink-wrapped, shrink-wrap·ping.**

shrive (shriv), *v.* **1** to hear the confession of and grant absolution to. **2** OLD USE. to make confession. ❑ *v.* **shrove** or **shrived, shriv·en** or **shrived, shriv·ing.**

S

a	hat	ė	term	ô	order	ch	child		a in about
ā	age	i	it	oi	oil	ng	long		e in taken
ä	far	ī	ice	ou	out	sh	she	ə	i in pencil
â	care	o	hot	u	cup	th	thin		o in lemon
e	let	ō	open	ů	put	ŦH	then		u in circus
ē	equal	ò	saw	ü	rule	zh	measure		

shriv·el (shriv′əl), *v.* to dry up; wither; shrink and wrinkle: *The hot sunshine shriveled the grass.* ❑ *v.* **shriv·eled, shriv·el·ing** or **shriv·elled, shriv·el·ling.**

shriv·en (shriv′ən), *v.* a past participle of **shrive.**

shroud (shroud), **1** *n.* cloth or garment in which a dead person is wrapped or dressed for burial. **2** *v.* to wrap or dress for burial. **3** *n.* something that covers, conceals, or veils: *The thick fog was a shroud over the city.* **4** *v.* to cover; conceal; veil: *plans shrouded in secrecy.* **5** *n.* a rope from a mast to the side of a ship. Shrouds help support the mast. —**shroud′less,** *adj.* —**shroud′like′,** *adj.*

shrove (shrōv), *v.* a past tense of **shrive.**

Shrove Tuesday, the day before Ash Wednesday; last day before Lent.

shrub (shrub), *n.* bush. —**shrub′like′,** *adj.*

shrub·ber·y (shrub′ər ē), *n.* group of shrubs: *Shrubbery hid the house from the street.*

shrub·by (shrub′ē), *adj.* **1** like shrubs. **2** covered with shrubs. **3** consisting of shrubs. ❑ *adj.* **shrub·bi·er, shrub·bi·est.** —**shrub′bi·ness,** *n.*

shrug (shrug), **1** *v.* to raise the shoulders as an expression of doubt or lack of interest: *He shrugged his shoulders when I asked him who would win.* **2** *n.* act of raising the shoulders in this way: *A shrug was her only reply.* ❑ *v.* **shrugged, shrug·ging.**

shrunk (shrungk), *v.* a past tense and past participle of **shrink:** *These socks have shrunk and I can't get them on.*

shrunk·en (shrung′kən), **1** *adj.* grown smaller; shriveled: *I threw away the shrunken orange.* **2** *v.* a past participle of **shrink.**

shtick (shtik), *n.* SLANG. **1** a comedy act or skit. **2** a special activity or special quality: *Tap-dancing is her shtick.*

shuck (shuk), **1** *n.* a husk; pod. **2** *v.* to remove the husks from: *shuck corn.* **3** *v.* to take off; remove: *She likes to shuck her shoes when she's indoors.* —**shuck′er,** *n.*

shucks (shuks), *interj.* an exclamation of disappointment or disgust: *Shucks! My shoelace just broke.*

shud·der (shud′ər), **1** *v.* to tremble with horror, fear, cold, etc.: *shudder at a ghastly sight.* **2** *n.* act of trembling or quivering. —**shud′der·ing·ly,** *adv.*

shuf·fle (shuf′əl), **1** *v.* to scrape or drag the feet while walking: *We shuffled slowly along the slippery sidewalk.* **2** *n.* act of scraping or dragging the feet. **3** *v.* to mix cards so as to change the order. **4** *n.* act of mixing cards. **5** *n.* the right or turn to mix cards. **6** *v.* to push about; thrust or throw with clumsy haste: *Instead of cleaning his room, he shuffled everything into a drawer.* **7** *v.* to move this way and that: *shuffle a stack of papers.* **8** *n.* movement this way and that: *After a hasty shuffle through his papers, the speaker began to talk.* **9** *n.* unfair act; trick: *Through some legal shuffle she secured a new trial.* ❑ *v.* **shuf·fled, shuf·fling.** —**shuf′fler,** *n.*

shuffle off, to get rid of.

shuf·fle·board (shuf′əl bôrd′), *n.* game in which players use long sticks to push large disks along a smooth, flat surface to various numbered spaces.

shul (shül), *n.* YIDDISH. synagogue.

shun (shun), *v.* to keep away from; avoid: *She shuns housework.* ■ See Synonym Study at **avoid.** ❑ *v.* **shunned, shun·ning.** —**shun′ner,** *n.*

shunt (shunt), **1** *v.* to move out of the way; turn aside. **2** *n.* act of turning aside; shift. **3** *v.* to sidetrack; put aside; get rid of. **4** *v.* to switch a train from one track to another. **5** *n.* a railroad switch. **6** *n.* wire joining two points in an electric circuit and forming a path through which a part of the current may pass. Shunts are used to control the amount of current passing through the main circuit. **7** *v.* to carry a part of a current by means of such a wire. —**shunt′er,** *n.*

shush (shush), **1** *v.* to hush; stop making noise: *The librarian asked the noisy kids to shush.* **2** *interj.* hush! stop the noise!

shut (shut), *v.* **1** to close a container or opening by pushing or pulling a lid, door, or some part into place: *shut a box, shut a door, shut a window.* **2** to close your eyes, a book, etc., by bringing parts together: *Shut your mouth.* **3** to close tight; close securely; close doors or other openings of: *shut a house for the summer.* **4** to be-

come closed; be closed: *The baby's mouth shut and she refused to eat any more.* **5** to keep from going out; enclose; confine: *The canary was shut in its cage.* ❑ *v.* **shut, shut·ting.**

shut down, **1** to close a factory or the like for a time; stop work. **2** to put a stop to some illegal activity: *Police shut down the bookie.*

shut in, to keep from going out.

shut off, to turn off; close; obstruct; bar: *Shut off the radio.*

shut out, **1** to keep from coming in: *The curtains shut out the light. Shut the dog out of this room.* **2** to defeat a team without allowing it to score.

shut up, **1** to shut the doors and windows of. **2** to stop talking. **3** to keep from going out.

> **USAGE NOTE** Many people feel that **shut up** is impolite and should not be used. This feeling involves the command "Shut up!" more than other uses of the phrase. Fewer people object to a sentence such as *The boys shut up when they saw us listening.* In most writing and in formal speech, it is still wise to use some other way of saying that people stopped talking.

shut·down (shut′doun′), *n.* act of closing of a factory, or the like, for a time: *The factory had a partial shutdown last week to fix some faulty equipment.*

shut-in (shut′in′ *for adj.;* shut′in′ *for noun*), **1** *adj.* kept in; held in; confined. **2** *n.* person who does not go out because of sickness, weakness, etc.

shut·out (shut′out′), *n.* the defeat of a team without allowing it to score: *The final game was a shutout, with our soccer team winning 5-0.*

shut·ter (shut′ər), **1** *n.* device in a camera that opens and closes to allow light to reach the film and produce a picture. **2** *n.* a movable cover for a window. **3** *v.* to put a shutter or shutters on or over: *As the storm approached, we hurried to shutter the windows.* —**shut′ter·less,** *adj.*

shut·tle (shut′l), **1** *n.* device used in weaving that carries the thread back and forth across the piece being woven. **2** *n.* the sliding holder for the lower thread in a sewing machine, which moves back and forth once for each stitch. **3** *v.* to move quickly back and forth: *We shuttled between our old house and our new house many times on moving day.* **4** *n.* bus, train, airplane, etc., that runs back and forth regularly over a short distance. **5** *n.* space shuttle. ❑ *v.* **shut·tled, shut·tling.**

shut·tle·cock (shut′l kok′), *n.* the rounded object hit back and forth in the game of badminton; bird. A shuttlecock was originally a cork with feathers stuck in one end, but now is often made of plastic.

shuttle diplomacy, diplomatic negotiations carried on by a person who travels back and forth between the negotiating countries, sides, etc.

shy[1] (shī), **1** *adj.* uncomfortable in company; bashful: *He is shy and dislikes parties.* **2** *adj.* easily frightened away; timid: *A deer is a shy animal.* **3** *v.* to jump back or to the side suddenly, as when startled: *The horse shied at the newspaper blowing along the ground.* **4** *adj.* not having enough; short; lacking: *The store is shy on children's clothing. I am shy of cash this week.* ❑ *adj.* **shy·er, shy·est** or **shi·er, shi·est;** *v.* **shied, shy·ing.** —**shy′er,** *n.* —**shy′ly,** *adv.* —**shy′ness,** *n.*

fight shy of, to keep away from; avoid.

> **SYNONYM STUDY** **Shy**[1], **bashful,** and **timid** all mean uneasy in the presence of others. **Shy** is a general word: *He was too shy to try out for the chorus.* **Bashful** means shy and easily embarrassed: *He was so bashful in front of the new teacher that he couldn't say his own name.* **Timid** means shy and frightened: *The timid puppy ran under the sofa.*

shy[2] (shī), **1** *v.* to throw; fling: *The boy shied a stone at the tree.* **2** *n.* a throw; fling. ❑ *v.* **shied, shy·ing;** *n., pl.* **shies.**

Shy·lock (shī′lok), *n.* the harsh and pitiless moneylender in Shakespeare's play *The Merchant of Venice.*

shy·ster (shī′stər), *n.* INFORMAL. lawyer or other person who uses morally questionable or legally improper methods in business dealings or professional activities.

si (sē), *n.* ti. ◼ Other words that sound like this are **sea** and **see**.

Si, symbol for silicon.

Si·am (sī am′), *n.* former name of Thailand.

Si·a·mese (sī′ə mēz′), *adj., n.* Thai. ❑ *n., pl.* **Si·a·mese.**

Siamese cat, a short-haired, blue-eyed cat, usually with a light tan body and dark face, ears, feet, and tail.

Siamese twins, twins who are born joined together.

Siamese cat—2 ft. 6 in. (76 cm) long with the tail

WORD STORY **Siamese twins** comes from the most famous twins of this sort. Born in Siam (now called Thailand) in the early 1800s, they made public appearances all over the world. Because twins like these are rare, most people had never seen any before.

Si·ber·i·a (sī bir′ē ə), *n.* region in N Asia, extending from the Ural Mountains to the Pacific. It is part of Russia. **—Si·ber′i·an,** *adj., n.*

Siberian husky, a strong, medium-sized, arctic sled dog that has a thick coat and a bushy tail which curves over the back; husky.

sib·i·lant (sib′ə lənt), **1** *adj.* hissing. **2** *n.* a hissing sound, letter, or symbol. *S* and *sh* are sibilants. **—sib′i·lant·ly,** *adv.*

sib·ling (sib′ling), *n.* brother or sister. An only child has no siblings.

sib·yl (sib′əl), *n.* **1** (in Greek and Roman legends) a woman who could foretell the future. **2** any woman who is believed to be able to foretell the future.

sic (sik), *v.* **1** to set upon or attack (mostly used as a command to a dog). **2** to incite to set upon or attack: *sic a dog on a stranger.* ❑ *v.* **sicked, sick·ing.** Also, **sick²**.

Si·cil·ian (sə sil′yən), **1** *adj.* of or about Sicily or its people. **2** *n.* person born or living in Sicily.

Sic·i·ly (sis′ə lē), *n.* island near the SW tip of Italy, belonging to Italy since 1860. It is the largest island in the Mediterranean. See **Adriatic Sea** for map.

sick¹ (sik), **1** *adj.* in poor health; having some disease; ill. **2** *adj.* vomiting or feeling as though about to vomit: *The motion of the boat made me sick.* **3** *adj.* of or for a sick person; connected with sickness: *sick pay.* **4** *n.pl.* **the sick,** sick people: *The sick need special care.* **5** *adj.* weary; tired: *I'm sick of school.* **6** *adj.* disgusted: *Your constant fighting makes me sick.* **7** *adj.* affected by sorrow, longing, disgust, or other strong emotions: *It makes me sick to think I almost caused a serious accident.* ◼ Another word that sounds like this is **sic.**

SYNONYM STUDY **Sick¹** and **ill** both mean in poor health. **Sick** suggests a temporary condition and expected recovery: *He stayed home sick today.* **Ill** suggests a serious condition and a slow recovery: *Dad was ill for months.*

sick² (sik), *v.* to sic.

sick bay, a place on a ship used as a hospital.

sick·bed (sik′bed′), *n.* bed of a sick person.

sick·en (sik′ən), *v.* to make or become sick: *The sight of blood sickened him. The bird sickened when kept in the cage.* **—sick′en·er,** *n.*

sick·en·ing (sik′ə ning), *adj.* causing nausea, faintness, disgust, or loathing. **—sick′en·ing·ly,** *adv.*

sick·ish (sik′ish), *adj.* **1** somewhat sick. **2** somewhat sickening. **—sick′ish·ly,** *adv.* **—sick′ish·ness,** *n.*

sick·le (sik′əl), *n.* tool with a short, curved blade on a short handle, used to cut grass, grain, etc.

sickle cell, an abnormal, sickle-shaped red blood cell.

sickle cell anemia, an inherited blood disease in which the normally round red blood cells become sickle-shaped. These cells may block small blood vessels, blocking blood flow and causing painful damage to body organs.

sick·ly (sik′lē), *adj.* **1** often sick; not strong; not healthy: *The sickly baby needed medical care.* **2** of or caused by sickness: *Her face was damp with a sickly sweat.* **3** causing sickness: *a sickly climate.* **4** faint; weak; pale: *a sickly glow.* ❑ *adj.* **sick·li·er, sick·li·est.** **—sick′li·ness,** *n.*

sick·ness (sik′nis), *n.* **1** an abnormal, unhealthy condition; disease; illness. **2** nausea; vomiting. ❑ *n., pl.* **sick·ness·es** for 1.

sick pay, salary paid while someone is sick and unable to work.

sick·room (sik′rüm′), *n.* room in which a sick person is cared for.

side (sīd), **1** *n.* a surface or line that forms the boundary of something: *A cube has six square sides.* **2** *n.* a surface that is not the front, back, top, or bottom of an object: *There is a door at the side of the house.* **3** *n.* either of the two surfaces of paper, cloth, etc.: *Write on only one side of the paper.* **4** *n.* a particular surface: *the side of the moon turned toward the earth.* **5** *n.* the slope of a hill or mountain: *The side of the hill was very steep.* **6** *n.* either the right or the left part of a thing; either of two parts or regions divided by a central line: *the east side of a city, our side of the street.* **7** *n.* either the right or the left part of the body, between hip and shoulder: *I felt a sharp pain in my side.* **8** *n.* one of two or more ways of behaving or being considered: *the better side of his nature, the bright side of a difficulty.* **9** *n.* group of persons who oppose another group: *The children chose sides for a game of softball.* **10** *n.* position or point of view that is opposed to others: *Let's hear your side of the argument.* **11** *n.* part of a family: *He is English on his mother's side and Polish on his father's side.* **12** *adj.* at one side; on one side: *the side aisles of a theater, a side door.* **13** *adj.* from one side: *a side view.* **14** *adj.* toward one side: *a side glance.* **15** *adj.* less important: *Let's deal with the main problem and forget the side issues for now.* ❑ *v.* **sid·ed, sid·ing.** **—side′less,** *adj.*

by your side, near you.

on the side, in addition to your ordinary duties.

side by side, beside one another.

side with, to agree with; support: *His sisters always side with him.*

split your sides, to laugh very hard.

take sides, to join with one person or group against another.

side·arm (sīd′ärm′), *adj.* throwing or thrown from the side with the arm at waist height; not overhand or underhand: *a sidearm pitch.*

side arms, sword, revolver, bayonet, etc., carried at the side or in the belt.

side·board (sīd′bôrd′), *n.* a low cabinet with drawers and shelves for holding silver and linen, and space on top for dishes; buffet.

side·burns (sīd′bernz′), *n.pl.* whiskers in front of the ears, especially when the chin is shaved.

WORD STORY **Sideburns** comes from the name of a Civil War general, Ambrose E. Burnside, who had thick side whiskers that soldiers admired and named for him. Such whiskers were sometimes called **sideboards,** and **burnsides** soon turned into **sideburns.**

side effect, a secondary effect or reaction, usually undesirable or unpleasant: *Many drugs produce side effects on some people.*

side·kick (sīd′kik′), *n.* INFORMAL. partner or close friend.

side·light (sīd′līt′), *n.* **1** light coming from the side. **2** incidental information about a subject: *amusing sidelights in a biography.*

side·line (sīd′līn′), **1** *n.* a line at the side of something. **2** *n.* line that marks the limit of play on the side of the field in football, etc. **3** *n.pl.* **sidelines,** space just outside these lines: *watch a game from the sidelines.* **4** *n.* an additional line of goods, business, or activity. **5** *v.* to put on the sidelines; make inactive. ❑ *v.* **side·lined, side·lining.**

side·long (sīd′lông′), *adj., adv.* to one side; toward the side: *a sidelong glance. He glanced sidelong at me.*

S

a	hat	ė	term	ô	order	ch	child		a in about
ā	age	i	it	oi	oil	ng	long		e in taken
ä	far	ī	ice	ou	out	sh	she	ə	i in pencil
â	care	o	hot	u	cup	th	thin		o in lemon
e	let	ō	open	u̇	put	ŦH	then		u in circus
ē	equal	ȯ	saw	ü	rule	zh	measure		

si·der·e·al (sī dir′ē əl), *adj.* **1** of or about the stars. **2** measured by the apparent motion of the stars: *sidereal time.*

sidereal year, time it takes for the earth to make one complete revolution around the sun and return to the position among the stars that it had at the year's beginning. A sidereal year is 365 days, 6 hours, 9 minutes, and 9.54 seconds long.

side·sad·dle (sid′sad′l), **1** *n.* a woman's saddle made so that both of the rider's legs are on the same side of the horse. **2** *adv.* with both legs on the same side of the horse: *ride sidesaddle.*

sidesaddle (def. 2)

side·show (sid′shō′), *n.* a small show in connection with a principal one: *the sideshows of a circus.*

side·step (sid′step′), *v.* **1** to step aside: *I sidestepped the deep puddle on the sidewalk.* **2** to get away from; avoid: *She would never sidestep a responsibility.* ❑ *v.* **side·stepped, side·step·ping.** —**side′step′per,** *n.*

side·stream smoke (sid′strēm′), smoke given off by a burning cigarette, cigar, etc., between puffs.

side·stroke (sid′strōk′), *n.* a swimming stroke done lying on one side and pulling with one arm and then the other while performing a scissors kick.

side·swipe (sid′swip′), **1** *v.* to hit with a glancing blow along the side: *A truck sideswiped our bus.* **2** *n.* a glancing blow along the side. ❑ *v.* **side·swiped, side·swip·ing.** —**side′swip′er,** *n.*

side·track (sid′trak′), **1** *v.* to draw someone's attention away from something: *Don't sidetrack me with pointless questions.* **2** *n.* a railroad siding. **3** *v.* to switch a train to a siding.

side·walk (sid′wôk′), *n.* place to walk along the side of a street, usually paved.

side·way (sid′wā′), *adv., adj.* sideways.

side·ways (sid′wāz′), *adv., adj.* **1** to one side; toward one side: *walk sideways, a sideways tilt.* **2** from one side: *to hit sideways, a sideways glimpse.* **3** with one side toward the front: *stand sideways.*

side·wind·er (sid′win′dər), *n.* a small rattlesnake of the southwestern United States that travels sideways by looping its body.

side·wise (sid′wiz′), *adv., adj.* sideways.

sid·ing (si′ding), *n.* **1** boards, shingles, etc., forming the outside walls of a wooden building. **2** a short railroad track to which cars can be switched from a main track for loading, storage, etc.

si·dle (si′dl), *v.* to move sideways slowly so as not to attract attention: *The child shyly sidled up to the visitor.* ❑ *v.* **si·dled, si·dling.** —**si′dling·ly,** *adv.*

SIDS (sidz), sudden infant death syndrome.

siege (sēj), *n.* **1** the surrounding of a fortified place by an army trying to capture it: *The castle was under siege for several months before its defenders gave up.* **2** any long or persistent effort to overcome resistance; any long-continued attack: *I had a siege of bronchitis that lasted nearly a month.*

lay siege to, 1 to besiege: *The Greeks laid siege to Troy.* **2** to attempt to win or get by long and persistent effort.

Sieg·fried (sig′frēd *or* sēg′frēd), *n.* (in German legends) a hero who killed a dragon and won a treasure. [**Siegfried** comes from German words meaning "victory" and "peace."]

si·en·na (sē en′ə), *n.* **1** mixture of clay and iron oxide, used as a pigment. In its natural state, it is yellowish brown and is called raw sienna. After heating, it becomes reddish brown and is called **burnt sienna. 2** a yellowish brown or a reddish brown.

si·er·ra (sē er′ə), *n.* chain or ridge of jagged mountains or hills. ❑ *n., pl.* **si·er·ras.**

Si·er·ra Le·o·ne (sē er′ə lē ō′nē), country on the W coast of Africa. *Capital:* Freetown. —**Si·er′ra Le·o′ne·an.**

WORD STORY **Sierra Leone** comes from Portuguese words meaning "mountain" and "lion." Portuguese explorers anchored near the coast here thought that the sound of thunder in the coastal mountains was like the roaring of lions.

Si·er·ra Ma·dre (sē er′ə mä′drä), mountain ranges in E and W Mexico. The central plateau of Mexico lies between the ranges.

Si·er·ra Ne·vad·a (sē er′ə nə vad′ə *or* sē er′ə nə vä′də), a mountain range in E California.

si·es·ta (sē es′tə), *n.* a nap or rest taken at noon or in the afternoon. ❑ *n., pl.* **si·es·tas.**

sieve (siv), **1** *n.* utensil having holes that let liquids and smaller pieces pass through, but not the larger pieces: *Shaking flour through a sieve removes lumps.* **2** *v.* to put through a sieve. ❑ *v.* **sieved, siev·ing.** —**sieve′like′,** *adj.*

sift (sift), *v.* **1** to separate large pieces from small by shaking in a sieve: *Sift the gravel and put the larger stones in another pile.* **2** to put through a sieve: *Sift powdered sugar on the top of the cake.* **3** to fall through, or as if through, a sieve: *The snow sifted softly down.* **4** to examine very carefully: *sift all available evidence.* —**sift′er,** *n.*

sigh (si), **1** *v.* to let out a very long, deep breath because you are sad, tired, relieved, etc.: *We heard her sigh.* **2** *n.* act or sound of sighing: *a sigh of regret, a sigh of relief.* **3** *v.* to say or express with a sigh. **4** *v.* to make a sound like a sigh: *The wind sighed in the treetops.* **5** *v.* to wish very much; long: *He sighed for home.* **6** *v.* to show grief by sighing: *sigh over your unhappy fate.* —**sigh′er,** *n.*

sight (sit), **1** *n.* power of seeing; vision: *Birds have better sight than dogs.* **2** *n.* act or fact of seeing; look: *love at first sight.* **3** *n.* range of seeing: *Land was in sight.* **4** *n.* thing seen; view; glimpse: *I can't stand the sight of blood.* **5** *n.* something worth seeing: *see the sights of the city. Niagara Falls is one of the sights of the world.* ■ See Synonym Study at **view. 6** *n.* something that looks bad or odd: *Your room is a sight.* **7** *v.* to see: *The lifeboat drifted for several days before the survivors sighted land.* **8** *n.* device to guide the eye in taking aim or observing: *the sights on a rifle.* **9** *n.* the aim or observation taken by such devices. **10** *v.* to take aim or look at by means of a sight: *I sighted carefully, then I fired at the target.* **11** *n.* way of looking or thinking; regard; opinion: *This is very important in his sight.* [See Word Story at **batch.**] ■ Other words that sound like this are **cite** and **site.** —**sight′a·ble,** *adj.* —**sight′er,** *n.*

at sight or **on sight,** as soon as seen: *She reads music at sight.*

catch sight of, to see: *I caught sight of him.*

know by sight, to know sufficiently to recognize when seen.

out of sight of, 1 where you cannot see: *Our ship was out of sight of land for several weeks.* **2** where you cannot be seen: *out of sight of the neighbors.*

sight unseen, without seeing or examining in advance: *She bought that bicycle sight unseen.*

sight·ed (si′tid), **1** *adj.* able to see: *a sighted person.* **2** *n.pl.* **the sighted,** people who are able to see.

sight·ing (si′ting), *n.* act of seeing; condition of being seen: *The newspaper reported the sighting of a new comet.*

sight·less (sit′lis), *adj.* not able to see. —**sight′less·ly,** *adv.* —**sight′less·ness,** *n.*

sight·ly (sit′lē), *adj.* **1** pleasing to the sight. **2** affording a fine view. ❑ *adj.* **sight·li·er, sight·li·est.** —**sight′li·ness,** *n.*

sight-read (sit′rēd′), *v.* to play a piece of music or read text in a foreign language without having seen or practiced it before. ❑ *v.* **sight-read** (sit′red′), **sight-read·ing.**

sight·see·ing (sit′sē′ing), **1** *n.* act of going around to see objects or places of interest: *a weekend of sightseeing in London.* **2** *adj.* engaged in or used in seeing objects or places of interest: *a sightseeing tour.*

sight·se·er (sīt'sē'ər), *n.* person who goes around to see objects or places of interest.

sign (sīn), **1** *n.* any mark or thing used to mean, stand for, or point out something: *The signs for addition, subtraction, multiplication, and division are +, –, ×, and ÷.* **2** *v.* to put your name on; write your name. A person signs a letter, a note promising to pay a debt, a check, etc. We sign for delivered packages, registered letters, etc. **3** *v.* to write: *Sign your initials here.* **4** *v.* to hire by a written agreement: *sign a new player.* **5** *n.* an inscribed board, space, etc., serving for advertisement, information, etc.: *See the sign over the door? The sign reads, "Private."* **6** *v.* to accept employment: *They signed for three years.* **7** *n.* motion or gesture used to mean, stand for, or point out something: *A nod is a sign of agreement. She made the sign of the cross.* **8** *v.* to use sign language: *She signed her part of the conversation.* **9** *v.* to make gestures or motions that mean, stand for, or point out something: *She signed that he should be silent.* **10** *n.* indication: *There are no signs of life about the house.* **11** *n.* indication of a coming event; omen: *The robin is a sign of spring. Ancient people viewed comets as signs of evil.* **12** *n.* a trace: *The hunter found signs of deer.* **13** *n.* any of the twelve divisions of the zodiac, each named for a constellation and each denoted by a special symbol. ■ Another word that sounds like this is **sine.** —**sign'er,** *n.*

sign away, to give away by signing your name: *He signed away all rights to any inheritance.*

sign off, to stop broadcasting: *That radio station signs off at midnight.*

sign over, to hand over by signing your name: *He signed over his rights to the oil to his ex-wife.*

sign up, to enlist, join, etc., by written agreement: *sign up as a new member.*

sig·nal (sīg'nəl), **1** *n.* anything giving notice, warning, or pointing out something: *The raising of the flag was a signal to advance.* **2** *v.* to make a signal or signals to: *She signaled the bus to stop by raising her hand.* **3** *v.* to make known by a signal or signals: *A bell signals the end of a school period.* **4** *adj.* used as a signal or in signaling: *a signal flag.* **5** *adj.* remarkable; striking; notable: *The airplane was a signal invention.* **6** *n.* an electromagnetic wave controlled so as to carry sounds and pictures to be received by radios or TV sets. □ *v.* **sig·naled, sig·nal·ing** or **sig·nalled, sig·nal·ling.** —**sig'nal·er** or **sig'nal·ler,** *n.*

sig·nal·ize (sīg'nə līz), *v.* to make stand out; make notable: *Many great inventions signalize the last 150 years.* □ *v.* **sig·nal·ized, sig·nal·iz·ing.** —**sig'nal·i·za'tion,** *n.*

sig·nal·ly (sīg'nə lē), *adv.* in a remarkable manner; strikingly; notably.

sig·nal·man (sīg'nəl man'), *n.* person in charge of signals on a railroad, in the army or navy, etc. □ *n., pl.* **sig·nal·men.**

sig·na·ture (sīg'nə chər), *n.* **1** a person's name written by that person. **2** act of writing your name: *a document ready for signature.* **3** signs printed at the beginning of a staff to show the key and time of a piece of music. **4** music, sound effects, etc., used to identify a performer or a radio or TV show.

sign·board (sīn'bôrd'), *n.* board having a sign, notice, advertisement, inscription, etc., on it.

sig·net (sīg'nit), *n.* a small seal used to stamp documents: *The order was sealed with the king's signet.* ■ Another word that sounds like this is **cygnet.**

signet ring, a ring with a signet.

sig·nif·i·cance (sīg nif'ə kəns), *n.* **1** importance; consequence: *The President wanted to see him on a matter of significance.* **2** meaning: *She did not understand the significance of my nod.*

sig·nif·i·cant (sīg nif'ə kənt), *adj.* **1** full of meaning; important; of consequence: *July 4, 1776, is a significant date for Americans.* ■ See Synonym Study at **important. 2** having or expressing a hidden meaning: *A significant nod from his friend warned him to stop talking.* —**sig·nif'i·cant·ly,** *adv.*

sig·ni·fi·ca·tion (sīg'nə fə kā'shən), *n.* a meaning; sense.

sig·ni·fy (sīg'nə fī), *v.* **1** to be a sign of; mean: *"Oh!" signifies surprise.* **2** to make known by signs, words, or actions: *He signified his consent with a nod.* **3** to have importance; be of consequence; matter: *What a fool says does not signify.* □ *v.* **sig·ni·fied, sig·ni·fy·ing.** —**sig'ni·fi'er,** *n.*

sign language, language in which motions, especially of the hands, stand for words, ideas, etc.

sign language

si·gnor (sē'nyôr), *n.* ITALIAN. **1** Mr. or sir. **2** a gentleman. □ *n., pl.* **si·gno·ri** (sē nyôr'ē).

si·gno·ra (sē nyôr'ə), *n.* ITALIAN. **1** Mrs. or madam. **2** a lady. □ *n., pl.* **si·gno·re** (sē nyôr'ā).

si·gno·ri·na (sē'nyə rē'nə), *n.* ITALIAN. **1** Miss. **2** a young lady. □ *n., pl.* **si·gno·ri·ne** (sē'nyə rē'nā).

sign·post (sīn'pōst'), *n.* post having signs, notices, or directions on it; guidepost.

Sikh (sēk), *n.* member of a religious sect of northwestern India. Sikhs are famous as warriors.

Sik·kim (sik'əm), *n.* state of India in the Himalayas, between Tibet and India. It was formerly an independent country.

si·lage (sī'lij), *n.* green fodder for winter feeding of farm animals, preserved and stored in a silo or other airtight place; ensilage.

si·lence (sī'ləns), **1** *n.* absence of sound or noise; stillness: *The teacher asked for silence.* **2** *n.* act of keeping still; not talking: *His silence made us believe he agreed.* **3** *n.* act of not mentioning: *Mother passed over our foolish remarks in silence.* **4** *v.* to stop the speech or noise of; make silent; quiet: *Please silence that barking dog.* **5** *v.* to make silent by restraint; repress: *to silence the press.* **6** *interj.* keep still! be still! □ *v.* **si·lenced, si·lenc·ing.**

si·len·cer (sī'lən sər), *n.* device which muffles the sound of a gun.

si·lent (sī'lənt), *adj.* **1** quiet; still; noiseless: *a silent house, the silent hills.* **2** not speaking; saying little or nothing: *The stranger was silent about her early life.* **3** not spoken; not said out loud: *a silent prayer. The "e" in "time" is a silent letter.* **4** not active; taking no open or active part. A silent partner in a business has no share in managing the business. —**si'lent·ly,** *adv.* —**si'lent·ness,** *n.*

Si·le·sia (sə lē'shə *or* sī lē'shə), *n.* region in central Europe, most of which is now in SW Poland and the Czech Republic. —**Si·le'sian,** *adj., n.*

sil·hou·ette (sil'ü et'), **1** *n.* a dark image outlined against a lighter background: *Silhouettes of skyscrapers could be seen against the moonlit sky.* **2** *n.* picture that is cut out of black paper or filled in with some single color or to form an outline. **3** *v.* to show in outline: *The mountain was silhouetted against the sky.* □ *v.* **sil·hou·et·ted, sil·hou·et·ting.**

silhouette (def. 1)

S

a	hat	ė	term	ô	order	ch	child		a in about
ā	age	i	it	oi	oil	ng	long		e in taken
ä	far	ī	ice	ou	out	sh	she	ə	i in pencil
â	care	o	hot	u	cup	th	thin		o in lemon
e	let	ō	open	ů	put	₮H	then		u in circus
ē	equal	ò	saw	ü	rule	zh	measure		

sil·i·ca (sil′ə kə), *n.* a hard, white or colorless substance; silicon dioxide. Flint, quartz, and opal are forms of silica.

sil·i·cate (sil′ə kit *or* sil′ə kāt), *n.* compound containing silicon with oxygen and a metal. Mica, soapstone, asbestos, and feldspar are silicates.

sil·i·con (sil′ə kən), *n.* element found only combined with other elements, mostly with oxygen in silica. Silicon has the properties of both a metal and a nonmetal. Next to oxygen, it is the most abundant element in the earth's crust. It is used in making computer chips, transistors, and many other products. *Symbol:* Si

sil·i·cone (sil′ə kōn), *n.* any of many compounds of silicon, oxygen, and organic chemicals. Silicones can resist extreme heat and cold. They are used for lubricants, varnishes, and insulators.

silk (silk), **1** *n.* a fine, soft fiber spun by silkworms to form their cocoons. **2** *n.* thread or cloth made from this fiber. **3** *n.* an article of clothing made of silk. **4** *n.* fiber like silk, produced by spiders to make their webs. **5** *n.* anything like silk. The glossy threads at the end of an ear of corn are called **corn silk.** **6** *adj.* of or like silk: *silk embroidery.* ❑ *n., pl.* **silks** for 2,3. **—silk′like′,** *adj.*

> **WORD STORY** **Silk** comes from a Greek word meaning "Chinese." Chinese people were the first to discover methods of making silk. They made so much money selling silk that they threatened to execute anyone who revealed the secret of these methods. They kept the secret for 3000 years.

silk·en (sil′kən), *adj.* **1** made of silk: *The king wore silken robes.* **2** like silk; smooth, soft, and glossy: *silken hair.*

silk-stocking (silk′stok′ing), *adj.* **1** elegant; aristocratic: *a silk-stocking party.* **2** inhabited by people of wealth and high social standing: *a silk-stocking district.*

silk·worm (silk′wėrm′), *n.* any caterpillar that spins silk to form a cocoon, especially the larva of a moth that feeds on mulberry leaves.

silk·y (sil′kē), *adj.* of or like silk; smooth, soft, and glossy; silken: *A kitten has silky fur.* ❑ *adj.* **silk·i·er, silk·i·est. —silk′i·ly,** *adv.* **—silk′i·ness,** *n.*

sill (sil), *n.* **1** piece of wood or stone across the bottom of a door or window frame. **2** a large, wooden beam on which the wall of a house, etc., rests. **—sill′-like′,** *adj.*

sil·li·ness (sil′ē nis), *n.* quality of being silly; foolishness.

sil·ly (sil′ē), **1** *adj.* without sense or reason; foolish: *It's silly to be afraid of harmless insects like moths.* ■ See Synonym Study at **foolish.** **2** *adj.* stunned by a blow; dazed. **3** *n.* a foolish person. ❑ *adj.* **sil·li·er, sil·li·est;** *n., pl.* **sil·lies. —sil′li·ly,** *adv.*

silly season, a time of year when silly or exaggerated news stories are often published, usually in July or August.

si·lo (sī′lō), *n.* **1** a tall, cylinder-shaped, airtight building in which green food for farm animals can be stored without spoiling. **2** a vertical underground shaft for housing and launching missiles, rockets, etc. ❑ *n., pl.* **si·los.**

silt (silt), **1** *n.* very fine particles of dirt carried by moving water and deposited as sediment: *The harbor is being choked with silt.* **2** *v.* to fill or close up with silt. **—sil·ta′tion,** *n.*

silt·y (sil′tē), *adj.* of or like silt; full of silt. ❑ *adj.* **silt·i·er, silt·i·est.**

Si·lur·i·an (si lùr′ē ən), *n.* (in geology) time between about 425 million and 400 million years ago. During this time, life first left the seas, as land plants and air-breathing animals appeared.

sil·ver (sil′vər), **1** *n.* a shining white, precious metallic element that can be hammered into very thin sheets or drawn out into very fine wire. Silver conducts heat and electricity better than any other substance. It is used to make coins, jewelry, spoons, dishes, etc. *Symbol:* Ag **2** *n.* coins made from this or a similar metal: *a pocketful of silver.* **3** *n.* utensils or dishes made of or plated with silver; silverware: *table silver.* **4** *adj.* made of or plated with silver: *a silver spoon.* **5** *v.* to cover or coat with silver or something like silver: *glass silvered to make a mirror.* **6** *n.* the color of silver. **7** *adj.* having the color of silver: *a silver slipper.* **8** *v.* to make or become the color of silver: *Moonlight silvered the lake.* **—sil′ver·er,** *n.* **—sil′ver·like′,** *adj.*

sil·ver·back (sil′vər bak′), *n.* an older male gorilla with gray hair on its back. It is usually the leader of a group.

sil·ver·fish (sil′vər fish′), *n.* **1** any of several small, wingless insects with silvery scales, especially a kind that is harmful to books, wallpaper, fabrics, etc. **2** any of various silvery fishes, such as the tarpon. ❑ *n., pl.* **sil·ver·fish** or **sil·ver·fish·es.**

silver lining, the brighter side of a sad or unfortunate situation.

silver plate, 1 items covered with a thin layer of silver or similar material. **2** a plating of silver or an alloy of silver and another metal.

sil·ver-plate (sil′vər plāt′), *v.* to cover with silver plate. ❑ *v.* **sil·ver·plat·ed, sil·ver·plat·ing.**

sil·ver·smith (sil′vər smith′), *n.* person who makes articles of silver.

Silver Spring, city in S Maryland.

silver thaw, CANADIAN. **1** an ice storm. **2** ice on all exposed surfaces, following an ice storm.

sil·ver-tongued (sil′vər-tungd′), *adj.* eloquent.

sil·ver·ware (sil′vər wâr′), *n.* knives, forks, or spoons made of silver or a less precious metal: *We set the table with our everyday silverware unless we are having company.*

silverware

sil·ver·y (sil′vər ē), *adj.* like silver; like that of silver: *Grandmother has beautiful, silvery hair. We polished the metal to a silvery gleam.* **—sil′ver·i·ness,** *n.*

sim·i·an (sim′ē ən), **1** *adj.* apelike or monkeylike. **2** *n.* an ape; monkey.

sim·i·lar (sim′ə lər), *adj.* **1** much the same; alike; like: *The children in that family are very similar in appearance.* **2** (in geometry) having the same shape: *similar triangles.* **—sim′i·lar·ly,** *adv.*

> **SYNONYM STUDY** **Similar, comparable,** and **corresponding** all mean alike. **Similar** is a general word: *Synonyms have similar meanings.* **Comparable** means alike enough to be compared: *Only players using the same equipment and rules have comparable performance records.* **Corresponding** means with similar functions or positions: *As predators, wolves and killer whales have corresponding places in their food chains.*

sim·i·lar·i·ty (sim′ə lar′ə tē), *n.* **1** condition of being similar; likeness; resemblance. **2** similarities, *pl.* points of resemblance.

sim·i·le (sim′ə lē′), *n.* a statement that one thing is like another. EXAMPLES: a face like marble, as brave as a lion. ■ See Usage Note at **metaphor.**

si·mil·i·tude (sə mil′ə tüd), *n.* likeness; resemblance.

sim·mer (sim′ər), **1** *v.* to keep at or just below the boiling point; boil gently: *Simmer the milk, do not boil it. The soup should simmer for a few hours to improve its taste.* **2** *n.* process of cooking at or just below the boiling point: *Do not let the soup cook faster than at a simmer.* **3** *v.* to be nearly at the point of breaking out: *He simmered with anger, but said nothing.* **—sim′mer·ing·ly,** *adv.* **simmer down, 1** to cool off; calm down. **2** (of a liquid) to reduce in quantity through continued simmering.

Si·mon Peter (sī′mən). See **Peter, Saint.** [**Simon** comes from Hebrew words meaning "God has heard."]

si·mo·ny (sī′mə nē *or* sim′ə nē), *n.* act of buying and selling sacred things, especially positions or promotion in the church.

si·moom (sə müm′), *n.* a hot, suffocating, sand-carrying wind of the deserts of Arabia, Syria, and northern Africa.

sim·per (sim′pər), **1** *v.* to smile in a silly, affected way. **2** *n.* a silly, affected smile. **—sim′per·er,** *n.* **—sim′per·ing·ly,** *adv.*

sim·ple (sim′pəl), *adj.* **1** easy to do or understand: *a simple problem. This book is in simple language.* **2** not divided into parts; single; not compound. An oak leaf is a simple leaf. "John called his dog" is a simple sentence. **3** having few parts; not complex; elementary: *a simple one-celled animal.* **4** with nothing added; bare; mere: *My answer is the simple truth.* **5** without ornament; not rich or showy; plain: *simple food, simple clothing.* **6** natural; not showing off: *She has a pleasant, simple manner.* **7** honest; sincere: *a simple heart.* **8** not subtle; not sophisticated; innocent;

artless: *a simple child.* **9** common; ordinary: *a simple citizen.* **10** humble: *His parents were simple people.* **11** weak in mind; stupid. ■ This definition of **simple** is often considered offensive. ❑ *adj.* **sim·pler, sim·plest. –sim′ple·ness,** *n.*

simple fraction, fraction having a whole number in both the numerator and the denominator. EXAMPLES: $\frac{1}{3}$, $\frac{3}{4}$, $\frac{119}{125}$.

sim·ple-heart·ed (sim′pəl här′tid), *adj.* **1** having or showing a simple, unaffected nature. **2** guileless; sincere.

simple interest, interest paid only on the original sum of money borrowed or invested, not on the interest that has grown since.

simple machine, one of six basic mechanical devices that increase force or change its direction. The lever, wedge, pulley, wheel and axle, inclined plane, and screw are simple machines. Many parts of more complicated machines are based on these.

sim·ple-mind·ed (sim′pəl min′did), *adj.* **1** without awareness of conventions; artless; inexperienced. **2** ignorant; foolish. **3** slow in mental development. ■ This definition of **simple-minded** is often considered offensive. **–sim′ple-mind′ed·ly,** *adv.* **–sim′ple-mind′ed·ness,** *n.*

simple sentence, sentence consisting of one main clause. EXAMPLE: This book is a dictionary.

sim·ple·ton (sim′pəl tən), *n.* a stupid or silly person; fool.

sim·plic·i·ty (sim plis′ə tē), *n.* **1** condition of being simple: *Simplicity of design can keep building costs low.* **2** freedom from difficulty; clearness: *The simplicity of that book makes it suitable for children.* **3** plainness: *A room in a hospital should be furnished with simplicity.* **4** absence of show or pretense; sincerity. **5** lack of shrewdness; dullness: *Their simplicity made them easily fooled.*

sim·pli·ca·tion (sim′plə fə kā′shən), *n.* **1** act of making simpler or condition of being made simpler. **2** a change to a simpler form.

sim·pli·fy (sim′plə fī), *v.* to make simple or simpler; make plainer or easier: *The rules of the game were simplified for younger children.* ❑ *v.* **sim·pli·fied, sim·pli·fy·ing. –sim′pli·fi′er,** *n.*

sim·plis·tic (sim plis′tik), *adj.* trying to explain too much by a single idea: *a simplistic notion that all government is bad.* **–sim·plis′ti·cal·ly,** *adv.*

sim·ply (sim′plē), *adv.* **1** in a simple manner. **2** without much ornament; plainly: *She was simply dressed in blue jeans and a sweater.* **3** merely; only: *The baby did not simply cry; he yelled.* **4** absolutely: *The cool, sunny weather was simply perfect for hiking.*

sim·u·late (sim′yə lāt), *v.* **1** to put on a false appearance of; pretend; feign: *She simulated interest to please her friend.* **2** to act like; look like; imitate: *Certain insects simulate flowers or leaves.* ❑ *v.* **sim·u·lat·ed, sim·u·lat·ing. –sim′u·la′tor,** *n.*

sim·u·la·tion (sim′yə lā′shən), *n.* **1** imitation; false appearance: *a harmless insect's simulation of a poisonous one.* **2** act of putting on a false appearance; pretense; feigning.

si·mul·cast (sī′məl kast′), **1** *v.* to transmit a program over radio and television simultaneously. **2** *n.* a program that is simulcast. ❑ *v.* **si·mul·cast** or **si·mul·cast·ed, si·mul·cast·ing.**

si·mul·ta·ne·ous (sī′məl tā′nē əs), *adj.* existing, done, or happening at the same time: *The two simultaneous shots sounded like one.* **–si′mul·ta′ne·ous·ly,** *adv.* **–si′mul·ta′ne·ous·ness,** *n.*

sin (sin), **1** *n.* act of breaking the law of God on purpose. **2** *v.* to break the law of God; be a sinner. **3** *n.* wrongdoing of any kind; immoral act. Lying, stealing, dishonesty, and cruelty are sins. ■ See Synonym Study at **crime. 4** *v.* to do wrong. ❑ *v.* **sinned, sin·ning.**

sin, sine.

Si·nai (sī′nī), *n.* **1** Mount, (in the Bible) the mountain where God gave the Ten Commandments to Moses. It is thought to be located in the S part of the Sinai peninsula. **2** triangular peninsula in NE Egypt, between the Mediterranean Sea and the N end of the Red Sea.

Si·na·lo·a (sē′nä lō′ä), *n.* a state in W Mexico.

Si·na·tra (sə nä′trə), *n.* **Frank** (frangk), born 1915, American singer and movie actor. He won an Academy Award in 1953 for the movie *From Here to Eternity.*

Sin·bad (sin′bad), *n.* sea captain in *The Arabian Nights* who went on seven extraordinary voyages.

since (sins), **1** *prep.* from a past time till now: *The sun has been up since five.* **2** *conj.* after the time that; from the time when: *He has been home only once since he went to New York.* **3** *adv.* before now; ago: *I heard that old joke long since.* **4** *conj.* because: *Since you feel tired, you should rest.*

sin·cere (sin sir′), *adj.* honest; genuine; real: *I made a sincere effort to pass my exams. Her friendly greeting and invitation were certainly sincere.* ❑ *adj.* **sin·cer·er, sin·cer·est. –sin·cere′ly,** *adv.* **–sin·cere′ness,** *n.*

sin·cer·i·ty (sin ser′ə tē), *n.* honesty; truthfulness: *We doubted the sincerity of his apology.*

sine (sīn), *n.* the ratio of the length of the side opposite an acute angle of a right triangle to the length of the hypotenuse. ■ Another word that sounds like this is **sign.**

si·ne·cure (sī′nə kyúr *or* sin′ə kyúr), *n.* an extremely easy job requiring little or no work and usually paying well.

sin·ew (sin′yü), *n.* **1** tendon. **2** strength; energy. **3** Often, **sinews,** *pl.* means of strength; source of power: *Factories and money are the sinews of war.* **–sin′ew·less,** *adj.*

sin·ew·y (sin′yü ē), *adj.* **1** having strong sinews; strong; powerful: *A wrestler has sinewy arms.* **2** vigorous; forcible. **3** like sinews; having sinews; tough; stringy. **–sin′ew·i·ness,** *n.*

sin·ful (sin′fəl), *adj.* full of sin; wicked; wrong; immoral; evil: *a sinful person, a sinful act.* ■ See Synonym Study at **wicked. –sin′ful·ly,** *adv.* **–sin′ful·ness,** *n.*

sing (sing), **1** *v.* to make music with the voice: *She sings folk songs.* **2** *v.* to make pleasant musical sounds: *Birds sing.* **3** *v.* to speak musically: *He almost seemed to sing his lines from the play.* **4** *v.* to bring, send, put, etc., with or by singing: *Sing the baby to sleep.* **5** *v.* to tell in song or poetry: *Poets sang of Camelot.* **6** *v.* to proclaim: *sing a person's praises.* **7** *v.* to make a ringing, whistling, humming, or buzzing sound: *The teakettle sang on the stove. The taut cord sang with tension.* **8** *n.* an occasion of singing, especially in a group: *We went to a community sing.* ❑ *v.* **sang** or **sung, sung, sing·ing. –sing′a·ble,** *adj.* **–sing′ing·ly,** *adv.*

sing out, to call loudly; shout.

sing., singular.

Sing·a·pore (sing′ə pôr), *n.* **1** island country off the S tip of the Malay Peninsula. **2** its capital, on the S coast.

singe (sinj), **1** *v.* to burn a little; scorch: *A spark from the fireplace singed the rug.* ■ See Synonym Study at **burn**[1]. **2** *n.* a slight burn. **3** *v.* to burn the ends or edges of: *The candle singed my hair.* **4** *v.* to remove by a slight burning: *The cook singed the feathers from the chicken.* ❑ *v.* **singed, singe·ing. –sing′er,** *n.*

sing·er (sing′ər), *n.* person or bird that sings: *Our canary is a fine singer.*

sin·gle (sing′gəl), **1** *adj.* one and no more; only one: *Please give me a single piece of paper.* **2** *adj.* for only one; individual: *The sisters share one room with two single beds in it.* **3** *adj.* not married: *a single man.* **4** *adj.* with only one on each side: *The knights engaged in single combat.* **5** *n.pl.* **singles,** game played with only one person on each side: *In tennis, she likes to play singles rather than doubles.* **6** *v.* to pick from among others: *The teacher singled us out for praise.* **7** *n.* a single thing or person. **8** in baseball: **a** *n.* a hit that allows the batter to reach first base only. **b** *v.* to make such a hit. **9** *adj.* with only one set of petals. Most garden roses have double flowers with many petals; wild roses have single flowers with five petals. ❑ *v.* **sin·gled, sin·gling. –sin′gle·ness,** *n.*

sin·gle-dig·it (sing′gəl dij′ət), *adj.* of or about a percentage smaller than ten: *single-digit growth.*

sin·gle-breast·ed (sing′gəl bres′tid), *adj.* overlapping across the breast just enough to fasten with one row of buttons: *a suit with a single-breasted jacket.*

a	hat	ė	term	ô	order	ch	child			a in about
ā	age	i	it	oi	oil	ng	long			e in taken
ä	far	ī	ice	ou	out	sh	she	ə	{	i in pencil
â	care	o	hot	u	cup	th	thin			o in lemon
e	let	ō	open	ú	put	₮H	then			u in circus
ē	equal	ò	saw	ü	rule	zh	measure			

S

single file, line of persons or things arranged one behind another: *We walked along the narrow trail in single file.*

single file

sin·gle-hand·ed (sing′gəl han′did), **1** *adj., adv.* without help from others. **2** *adj.* using, requiring, or managed by only one hand or only one person: *a single-handed catch, a single-handed saw.* —**sin′gle-hand′ed·ly,** *adv.* —**sin′gle-hand′ed·ness,** *n.*

sin·gle-heart·ed (sing′gəl här′tid), *adj.* **1** sincere. **2** having only one purpose. —**sin′gle-heart′ed·ly,** *adv.* —**sin′gle-heart′ed·ness,** *n.*

sin·gle-mind·ed (sing′gəl min′did), *adj.* **1** having only one purpose in mind. **2** sincere; straightforward. —**sin′gle-mind′ed·ly,** *adv.* —**sin′gle-mind′ed·ness,** *n.*

single parent, parent who is raising a child or children without the other parent.

sin·gle·tree (sing′gəl trē′), *n.* whiffletree. ❑ *n., pl.* **sin·gle·trees.**

sin·gly (sing′glē), *adv.* **1** by itself; individually; separately: *Let us consider each point singly.* **2** one by one; one at a time: *Misfortunes never come singly.* **3** by your own efforts; without help.

sing·song (sing′sông′), **1** *n.* a monotonous, up-and-down rhythm and pitch. **2** *n.* a monotonous tone or sound in speaking. **3** *adj.* monotonous in rhythm and pitch: *a singsong recitation of the multiplication table.*

sin·gu·lar (sing′gyə lər), **1** *adj.* extraordinary; unusual: *a person of singular ability.* **2** *adj.* strange; odd; peculiar: *The detectives were greatly puzzled by the singular nature of the crime.* **3** *adj.* being the only one of its kind: *an event singular in history.* **4** *adj.* one in number. *Boy* is singular; *boys* is plural. **5** *n.* form of a word to show that it means only one. *Ox* is the singular of *oxen.* **6** *n.* a word in the singular number. —**sin′gu·lar·ly,** *adv.*

sin·gu·lar·i·ty (sing′gyə lar′ə tē), *n.* **1** oddness; strangeness; unusualness: *The singularity of their speech and clothing attracted much attention.* **2** something singular; peculiarity; oddity: *One of the giraffe's singularities is the length of its neck.* ❑ *n., pl.* **sin·gu·lar·i·ties** for 2.

sin·is·ter (sin′ə stər), *adj.* **1** bad; evil; dishonest: *a sinister plan.* **2** showing ill will; threatening: *a sinister rumor, a sinister look.* —**sin′is·ter·ly,** *adv.* —**sin′is·ter·ness,** *n.*

WORD STORY **Sinister** comes from a Latin word meaning "on the left side." The ancient Romans tried to to predict the future by omens—events that people thought were signs of what would happen. Their omens included birds in flight or a bolt of lightning. Omens on the left side were thought to mean bad luck, so the Latin word also meant "unlucky." In English the meaning is even more negative.

sink (singk), **1** *v.* to go down; fall slowly; go lower and lower: *sink to the floor in a faint.* ∎ See Synonym Study at **descend. 2** *v.* to make go under: *The submarine sank two ships.* **3** *v.* to go under: *The ship sank.* **4** *v.* to make go down; make fall: *Lack of rain sank the water level in the well.* **5** *v.* to make or become lower, weaker, or less in amount or volume: *Her voice sank to a whisper.* **6** *v.* to pass gradually into a state of sleep, silence, etc.: *The injured woman sank into unconsciousness.* **7** *v.* to go deeply: *Let the lesson sink into your mind.* **8** *v.* to make go deep; dig: *The men are sinking a well.* **9** *v.* to become worse: *My spirits sank.* **10** *v.* to invest money, especially unprofitably: *We sank $20 in a wrench we*

never used. **11** *n.* a shallow basin or tub with a drainpipe: *The dishes are in the kitchen sink.* **12** *n.* a low-lying inland area where water collects. ❑ *v.* **sank** or **sunk, sunk, sink·ing.** —**sink′a·ble,** *adj.*

sink·er (sing′kər), *n.* a lead weight for sinking a fish line or net.

sink·hole (singk′hōl′), *n.* **1** hole eroded in rock by running water and acting as a drain for surface water. **2** hole where water collects. **3** a large opening in the ground, often formed by the collapse of a cave roof.

sinkhole (def. 3)

sin·less (sin′lis), *adj.* without sin. —**sin′less·ly,** *adv.* —**sin′less·ness,** *n.*

sin·ner (sin′ər), *n.* person who sins or does wrong.

sin·u·os·i·ty (sin′yü os′ə tē), *n.* **1** sinuous form or character. **2** curve; bend; turn. ❑ *n., pl.* **sin·u·os·i·ties.**

sin·u·ous (sin′yü əs), *adj.* **1** having many curves or turns; winding: *The motion of a snake is sinuous.* **2** indirect; devious; untrustworthy. —**sin′u·ous·ly,** *adv.* —**sin′u·ous·ness,** *n.*

si·nus (sī′nəs), *n.* one of the spaces inside the bones in the front of the skull. The sinuses connect with the nose and may become infected by cold viruses. ❑ *n., pl.* **si·nus·es.**

si·nus·i·tis (sī′nə sī′tis), *n.* inflammation of one of the sinuses.

Si·on (sī′ən), *n.* Zion.

Sioux (sü), *n.* a group of American Indian tribes living on the plains of the northern United States and southern Canada; Dakota; Lakota. ❑ *n., pl.* **Sioux** (sü *or* süz).

USAGE NOTE **Sioux** probably comes from an Algonquian or Ojibwa word meaning "foreigner" or "enemy." Many Sioux prefer the name **Dakota** or **Lakota** instead. This name means "allies" in their own language.

Sioux City, city in W Iowa.

Sioux Falls, city in SE South Dakota.

sip (sip), **1** *v.* to drink a little bit at a time: *We sipped our tea.* ∎ See Synonym Study at **drink. 2** *n.* a very small drink: *She took a sip.* **3** *n.* act of sipping. ❑ *v.* **sipped, sip·ping.** —**sip′per,** *n.*

si·phon (sī′fən), **1** *n.* a bent tube through which liquid can be drawn from one container into another at a lower level by atmospheric pressure. **2** *v.* to draw or pass through a siphon: *They siphoned a gallon of gasoline from their car to ours.* **3** *n.* bottle for soda water with a tube through which the liquid is forced out by the pressure of the gas in the bottle. **4** *n.* a tube-shaped organ of some animals, such as certain shellfish, for drawing in and expelling water. —**si′phon·like′,** *adj.*

sir (sėr), *n.* **1** a polite title used in writing or speaking to any man. **2 Sir,** the title of a knight or baronet: *Sir Walter Scott.*

sire (sīr), **1** *n.* a male ancestor; forefather. **2** *n.* male parent; father: *Lightning was the sire of the racehorse Danger.* **3** *v.* to be the father of: *Lightning sired Danger.* **4** *n.* title of respect used formerly to a great noble and now to a king: *"Good morning, Sire,"* said the page to the king. ❑ *v.* **sired, sir·ing.**

si·ren (sī′rən), **1** *n.* device that makes a loud, wailing sound: *We heard the sirens of the fire engines.* **2** *n.* (in Greek legends) any of a group of nymphs who lured sailors by their sweet singing to shipwreck upon some rocks. **3** *n.* woman who lures or tempts. —**si′ren·like′,** *adj.*

Sir·i·us (sir′ē əs), *n.* the brightest star in the sky; Dog Star.

sir·loin (sėr′loin), *n.* cut of beef from the part of the loin in front of the rump.

si·roc·co (sə rok′ō), *n.* **1** a hot, dry, dust-carrying wind blowing from northern Africa across the Mediterranean Sea and southern Europe. **2** any hot, unpleasant wind. ❑ *n., pl.* **si·roc·cos.**

sir·rah (sir′ə), *n.* OLD USE. fellow, used to address men and boys when speaking contemptuously, angrily, impatiently, etc.

sir·up (sir′əp *or* sėr′əp), *n.* syrup.

sir·up·y (sir′ə pē *or* sėr′ə pē), *adj.* syrupy.

sis (sis), *n.* INFORMAL. sister.

sis·al (sī′səl *or* sis′əl), *n.* **1** a strong white fiber, used for making rope, twine, etc. **2** a Mexican plant that it comes from.

sisal hemp, sisal.

sis·sy (sis′ē), *n.* **1** a weak or cowardly person. **2** boy or man who behaves in an unmanly way. ■ **Sissy** is considered offensive. ❑ *n., pl.* **sis·sies.**

sissy bar, INFORMAL. a thin, U-shaped bar, fastened behind the seat of a motorcycle or bicycle. It prevents a rider or passenger from sliding backward off the seat.

sis·ter (sis′tər), *n.* **1** daughter of the same parents. A girl is a sister to the other children of her parents. **2** a close friend or companion. **3** a female member of the same group, club, union, or religious organization. **4** member of a religious order of women; nun: *Sisters of Charity.* –**sis′ter·less,** *adj.* –**sis′ter·like′,** *adj.*

sis·ter·hood (sis′tər hùd), *n.* **1** affectionate relationship between sisters; feeling of sister for sister. **2** association of women with some common aim, interest, or profession.

sis·ter-in-law (sis′tər in lô′), *n.* **1** sister of your husband or wife. **2** wife of your brother. ❑ *n., pl.* **sis·ters-in-law.**

sis·ter·ly (sis′tər lē), *adj.* **1** of or like a sister: *sisterly traits.* **2** very friendly; kindly: *sisterly interest.* –**sis′ter·li·ness,** *n.*

Sis·tine Chapel (sis′tēn′), chapel in the Vatican. It is decorated with frescoes by Michelangelo and other great artists.

sit (sit), *v.* **1** to rest on the lower part of the body with the weight off the feet: *She sat in a chair.* **2** to cause to sit; seat: *The woman sat the little boy in his stroller.* **3** to sit on: *He sat his horse well.* **4** to have place or position: *The clock has sat on that shelf for years.* **5** to have a seat in an assembly; be a member of a council: *sit in Congress.* **6** to hold a session: *The court sits next month.* **7** to place yourself in a position for having your picture made; pose: *sit for a portrait.* **8** to be in a state of rest; remain inactive: *He doesn't use the car, so it just sits there.* **9** to press or weigh: *His responsibilities sit heavy on his mind.* **10** to perch: *The birds were sitting on the fence rail.* **11** to cover eggs so that they will hatch; brood: *The hen will sit until the eggs are ready to hatch.* **12** to baby-sit: *I sit for the family next door.* **13** to fit: *The coat sits well.* ❑ *v.* **sat, sit·ting.** ■ See Usage Note at **set.**

sit down, to take a seat; put yourself in a sitting position.

sit in, 1 to take part in a game, talk, etc. **2** to take part in a sit-in.

sit in on, to take part in a meeting, conference, etc.

sit on or **sit upon, 1** to sit in judgment or council on. **2** to have a seat on a jury, committee, etc.

sit out, 1 to remain seated during a dance. **2** to stay until something has finished.

sit up, 1 to raise the body to a sitting position. **2** to keep such a position: *The sick child was able to sit up while eating.* **3** to stay up instead of going to bed.

si·tar (si tär′), *n.* a musical instrument of India, with a long neck and strings. It is played with a pick.

sit·com (sit′kom), *n.* INFORMAL. a situation comedy.

sit-down strike (sit′doun′), strike in which the workers stay in the factory, store, etc., without working until their demands are met or an agreement is reached.

site (sīt), *n.* position or place of something; location: *The site for the new school has not yet been chosen.* ■ Other words that sound like this are **cite** and **sight.**

sit-in (sit′in′), *n.* form of protest in which a group of people enter and remain seated for a long period of time in a public place. Sit-ins are organized to protest racial discrimination, government policies, etc.

Sit·ka (sit′kə), *n.* town in SE Alaska.

sit·ter (sit′ər), *n.* baby-sitter.

sit·ting (sit′ing), *n.* **1** meeting or session of a court of law, legislature, commission, etc. **2** time of remaining seated: *She read five chapters at one sitting.*

Sitting Bull, 1834?-1890, a leader of the Lakota Sioux. He led his people to their victory over Custer in 1876.

sitting duck, an easy target or mark.

sitting room, living room.

sit·u·ate (sich′ü āt), *v.* to place or locate. ❑ *v.* **sit·u·at·ed, sit·u·at·ing.**

sit·u·at·ed (sich′ü ā′tid), *adj.* **1** placed; located: *New York is a favorably situated city.* **2** in a certain financial or social position: *The doctor was quite well situated.*

sit·u·a·tion (sich′ü ā′shən), *n.* **1** circumstances; case; condition: *act calmly in a difficult situation.* **2** site; location; place: *Our house has a beautiful situation on a hill.* **3** place to work; job; position: *She is trying to find a good situation.*

situation comedy, comedy, especially a weekly TV series, about the same character or group of characters in various funny situations; sitcom.

sit-up (sit′up′), *n.* exercise done by lying on the back and then sitting up without raising the feet.

si·wash (sī′wäsh), CANADIAN. **1** *n.* a heavy sweater made of raw wool, with a knitted pattern on the back and sides. **2** *v.* to camp out, using no artificial shelter. ❑ *n., pl.* **si·wash·es** or **si·wash.**

six (siks), *adj., n.* one more than five; 6. ❑ *n., pl.* **six·es.**

at sixes and sevens, 1 in confusion. **2** in disagreement.

Six Nations, group of American Indians tribes formed when the Tuscarora joined the Five Nations, in the early 1700s. This group is also called the Iroquois.

six-pack (siks′pak′), *n.* a cardboard or plastic container holding six bottles, cans, or other items sold as a unit.

six·pence (siks′pəns), *n.* a former coin of Great Britain, equal to six pennies.

six-shoot·er (siks′shü′tər), *n.* revolver that can fire six shots without being reloaded.

six·teen (sik′stēn′), *n., adj.* six more than ten; 16.

six·teenth (sik′stēnth′), *adj., n.* **1** next after the 15th; last in a series of 16. **2** one of 16 equal parts.

sixteenth note, (in music) a note played for one sixteenth as long a time as a whole note.

sixth (siksth), *adj., n.* **1** next after the fifth; last in a series of six. **2** one of six equal parts.

sixth sense, an unusual power of perception; intuition.

six·ti·eth (sik′stē ith), *adj., n.* **1** next after the 59th; last in a series of 60. **2** one of 60 equal parts.

six·ty (sik′stē), *adj., n.* six times ten; 60. ❑ *n., pl.* **six·ties.**

siz·a·ble (sī′zə bəl), *adj.* fairly large. Also, **sizeable.** –**siz′a·ble·ness,** *n.* –**siz′a·bly,** *adv.*

size[1] (sīz), **1** *n.* amount of surface or space a thing takes up: *The two boys are of the same size.* **2** *n.* number, quantity, or amount: *The city's population has grown in size.* **3** *n.* one of a series of measures: *His shoes are size 10.* **4** *v.* to arrange according to size or in sizes: *He sized the shoe display.* ❑ *v.* **sized, siz·ing.** –**siz′er,** *n.*

of a size, of the same size.

size up, to form an opinion of; estimate.

WORD POWER **SIZE** ■ Your shoe size is just a number that everyone agrees to use, and many other sizes are the same. To be useful, a system of sizes has to be shared. To be convenient, it should be short. Scientists and many other people share a system of prefixes and suffixes to tell size—and weight, too. Some of these are:

centi-	-gram	-liter	micro-
deca-	hecto-	mega-	milli-
deci-	kilo-	-meter	nano-
giga-			

a	hat	ė	term	ô	order	ch	child	ə { a in about
ā	age	i	it	oi	oil	ng	long	e in taken
ä	far	ī	ice	ou	out	sh	she	i in pencil
â	care	o	hot	u	cup	th	thin	o in lemon
e	let	ō	open	ù	put	ᵺ	then	u in circus
ē	equal	ò	saw	ü	rule	zh	measure	

S

size² (sīz), **1** *n.* preparation made from glue, starch, or other sticky material. It is used to glaze paper, cover plastered walls, stiffen cloth, etc. **2** *v.* to coat or treat with size. □ *v.* **sized, siz·ing.**

size·a·ble (sī′zə bəl), *adj.* sizable. **−size′a·ble·ness,** *n.* **−size′a·bly,** *adv.*

siz·zle (siz′əl), **1** *v.* to make a hissing sound, as fat does when it is frying or burning. **2** *n.* a hissing sound. □ *v.* **siz·zled, siz·zling.**

siz·zler (siz′lər), *n.* INFORMAL. a very hot day.

S.J. or **SJ,** Society of Jesus.

skate¹ (skāt), **1** *n.* ice skate. **2** *n.* roller skate. **3** *n.* in-line skate. **4** *v.* to glide or roll along on skates. □ *v.* **skat·ed, skat·ing. −skat′er,** *n.*

skate² (skāt), *n.* any of several broad, flat fishes with fins growing along the sides of their heads and bodies. They swim by rippling movements of these fins. Skates are one group of rays. □ *n., pl.* **skates** or **skate.**

skate·board (skāt′bôrd′), **1** *n.* a narrow board resembling a surfboard, with roller-skate wheels attached to each end, used for gliding or moving on any hard surface. **2** *v.* to ride on a skateboard. **−skate′board′er,** *n.*

skeet (skēt), *n.* sport of shooting at targets, called clay pigeons, which are flung in the air at angles similar to those taken by a bird in flight.

skein (skān), *n.* a small, coiled bundle of yarn or thread. There are 120 yards in a skein of cotton yarn.

skel·e·tal (skel′ə təl), *adj.* of or like a skeleton; attached to a skeleton. **−skel′e·tal·ly,** *adv.*

skel·e·ton (skel′ə tən), *n.* **1** the bones supporting the muscles and internal organs of any animal with a backbone. **2** frame: *the steel skeleton of a building.* **3** the basic features or contents; outline: *the skeleton of a story.* **−skel′e·ton·like′,** *adj.*

skeleton in the closet, a secret source of embarrassment, grief, or shame, especially to a family.

skeleton key, key made to open many locks.

skep·tic (skep′tik), *n.* **1** person who questions the truth of theories or apparent facts; doubter.

■ See Synonym Study at **cynic. 2** person who doubts the truth of religious doctrines. Also, **sceptic.**

skep·ti·cal (skep′tə kəl), *adj.* of or like a skeptic; inclined to doubt; not believing easily. Also, **sceptical. −skep′ti·cal·ly,** *adv.*

skep·ti·cism (skep′tə siz′əm), *n.* skeptical attitude; doubt; unbelief. Also, **scepticism.**

sketch (skech), **1** *n.* a rough, quickly done drawing, painting, or design. **2** *v.* to make a sketch of; draw roughly. **3** *v.* to make sketches: *He sketches in his free time.* **4** *n.* outline; plan. **5** *n.* a short description, story, play, etc. □ *n., pl.* **sketch·es. −sketch′er,** *n.*

sketch·book (skech′bůk′), *n.* book to draw or paint sketches in.

sketch·y (skech′ē), *adj.* **1** incomplete; slight; imperfect: *The first news bulletins gave only a sketchy account of the disaster.* **2** like a sketch; having or giving only outlines or main features. □ *adj.* **sketch·i·er, sketch·i·est. −sketch′i·ly,** *adv.* **−sketch′i·ness,** *n.*

skew (skyü), **1** *adj.* twisted to one side; slanting. **2** *n.* a slant. **3** *v.* to give a slanting form, position, direction, etc., to; slant. **4** *v.* to represent unfairly; distort: *The data were skewed to support one side of the question.* **−skew′ness,** *n.*

skew·er (skyü′ər), **1** *n.* a long pin of wood or metal stuck through meat to hold it together while it is cooking. **2** *v.* to fasten with a skewer or skewers. **3** *v.* to pierce with or as if with a skewer. **−skew′er·er,** *n.*

ski (skē), **1** *n.* one of a pair of long, flat, slender pieces of hard wood, plastic, or metal, that can be fastened to shoes or boots to enable someone to glide over snow. **2** *n.* a similar object used to glide over water; water ski. **3** *v.* to glide over snow or water on skis. □ *n., pl.* **skis** or **ski;** *v.* **skied, ski·ing. −ski′a·ble,** *adj.* **−ski′er,** *n.*

skid (skid), **1** *v.* to slip or slide sideways while moving: *The car skidded on the slippery road.* **2** *n.* a slip or slide while moving: *The car went into a skid on the icy road.* **3** *n.* piece of wood or metal to prevent a wheel from turning. **4** *v.* to slide along without turning, as a wheel does when held by a skid. **5** *n.* timber, frame, etc., on which something rests, or on which something heavy may slide. **6** *v.* to slide along on a skid or skids. □ *v.* **skid·ded, skid·ding. −skid′der,** *n.* **−skid′ding·ly,** *adv.*

on the skids, INFORMAL. headed for dismissal, failure, or other disaster.

Ski·doo (ski dü′ *or* skē′dü), *n.* CANADIAN. trademark for a snowmobile.

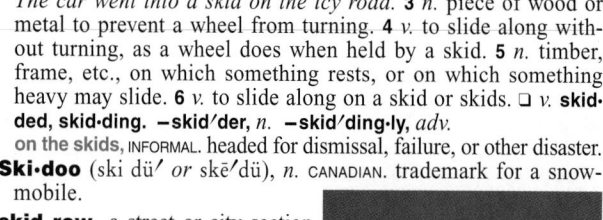

skid row, a street or city section full of run-down buildings and houses, cheap bars, etc., with many homeless or jobless people.

skies (skīz), *n.* plural of **sky.**

skiff (skif), *n.* **1** a light rowboat. **2** a small, light boat with a mast for a single triangular sail.

ski·ing (skē′ing), *n.* act or sport of gliding over snow or water on skis.

ski jump, 1 a jump made by someone on skis. **2** a raised track for making such jumps.

skil·ful (skil′fəl), *adj.* skillful. **−skil′ful·ly,** *adv.* **−skil′ful·ness,** *n.*

ski lift, machinery for carrying skiers to the top of a slope, such as chains moving on a cable; lift.

ski jump (def. 1)

skill (skil), *n.* **1** ability gained by practice, knowledge, etc.; expertness: *The trained teacher managed the children with skill.* **2** ability to do things well with your body or with tools: *It takes skill to tune a piano.* **3** an art or craft: *master the carpenter's skill.* **−skill′-less** or **skil′less,** *adj.*

skilled (skild), *adj.* **1** having skill; trained; experienced: *A carpenter is a skilled worker.* ■ See Synonym Study at **expert. 2** showing skill; requiring skill: *Bricklaying is skilled labor.*

skil·let (skil′it), *n.* a shallow pan with a long handle, used for frying; frying pan.

skill·ful (skil′fəl), *adj.* **1** having skill; expert: *a skillful surgeon.* **2** showing skill: *a skillful piece of bricklaying.* Also, **skilful. −skill′ful·ly,** *adv.* **−skill′ful·ness,** *n.*

skim (skim), *v.* **1** to remove from the top: *I skimmed the fat from the soup.* **2** to take something from the top of: *Skim milk by taking off the cream.* **3** to move lightly over: *The pebble I threw skimmed the surface of the water.* **4** to glide along: *The swallows were skimming by.* **5** to send skimming: *skim a flat stone over the water.* **6** to read hastily or carelessly; read with omissions: *It took me an hour to skim the book.* □ *v.* **skimmed, skim·ming.**

skim·mer (skim′ər), *n.* **1** a shallow ladle full of holes, with a long handle. It is used in skimming liquids. **2** any of three kinds of seabirds that fly along the surface of water with their lower bills in the water to catch food.

skim milk or **skimmed milk,** milk from which the cream has been removed.

skimp (skimp), *v.* **1** to supply in too small an amount: *Don't skimp the butter in making a cake.* **2** to be very saving or economical: *She had to skimp to send her children to camp.* **3** to do imperfectly: *She skimps on her chores.*

skimp·y (skim′pē), *adj.* scanty; not enough: *I was hungry all afternoon after my skimpy lunch.* □ *adj.* **skimp·i·er, skimp·i·est. −skimp′i·ly,** *adv.* **−skimp′i·ness,** *n.*

skin (skin), **1** *n.* the outer layer of tissue of the bodies of people and animals, especially when soft and flexible: *Sunburn reddens the skin.* **2** *n.* a hide; pelt: *The skin of a calf makes soft leather.* **3** *n.* any outer surface layer, such as the rind of a fruit, a sausage casing, etc. **4** *v.* to take the skin off: *He skinned his knees when he fell. The hunter skinned the deer.* **5** *n.* container made of skin for holding liquids. **6** *v.* SLANG. to swindle; cheat. □ *v.* **skinned, skin·ning. −skin′like′,** *adj.*

by the skin of your teeth, very narrowly; barely.

save your skin, to escape without harm.

skin-deep (skin′dēp′), *adj.* no deeper than the skin; shallow; slight.

skin-dive (skin′dīv′), *v.* to engage in skin diving. ❏ *v.* **skin·dived, skin·div·ing.**

skin diving, sport of swimming under water, equipped with a face mask, rubber flippers, and often a portable breathing device. **–skin diver.**

skin-flint (skin′flint′), *n.* a mean, stingy person.

skin graft, a piece of skin surgically moved from one part of the body to another, or from one person to another person. A skin graft replaces damaged skin.

skin·less (skin′lis), *adj.* having no skin: *skinless frankfurters.*

skin·ner (skin′ər), *n.* **1** person who skins. **2** person who prepares or deals in skins, furs, etc. **3** someone who drives draft animals.

Skin·ner (skin′ər), *n.* **B. F.,** 1904-1990, American psychologist. He believed that psychology should study outward behavior, not states of mind.

skin·ny (skin′ē), *adj.* very thin; very lean. ■ See Synonym Study at **thin.** ❏ *adj.* **skin·ni·er, skin·ni·est. –skin′ni·ness,** *n.*

skin·ny-dip (skin′ē dip′), INFORMAL. **1** *v.* to swim in the nude. **2** *n.* a swim in the nude. ❏ *v.* **skin·ny-dipped, skin·ny-dip·ping.**

skin-tight (skin′tīt′), *adj.* fitting closely to the skin: *skintight jeans.*

skip (skip), **1** *v.* to leap lightly; spring; jump: *The children skipped down the street.* **2** *v.* to leap lightly over: *children skipping rope.* **3** *v.* to pass over; omit: *I skipped the questions I couldn't answer.* **4** *n.* a light spring, jump, or leap: *The child gave a skip of joy.* **5** *v.* to go or send bounding along a surface; skim: *We liked to skip stones on the lake.* **6** *n.* act of passing over; omission. **7** *v.* to move ahead in school by being promoted one or more grades ahead of the next regular grade. **8** *v.* to leave in a hurry: *They skipped town to avoid paying their bills.* ❏ *v.* **skipped, skip·ping. –skip′pa·ble,** *adj.*

ski pants, close-fitting, often waterproof, pants with tapered legs, worn by skiers.

skip·jack (skip′jak′), *n.* any of various fishes that sometimes leap out of the water, such as a variety of tuna. ❏ *n., pl.* **skip·jack** or **skip·jacks.**

skip·per (skip′ər), *n.* **1** captain of a ship, especially of a small trading or fishing boat. **2** any captain or leader.

skir·mish (skėr′mish), **1** *n.* a small-scale fight between groups: *Army scouts had a skirmish with a small group of enemy troops.* **2** *n.* a slight conflict, argument, or contest: *The children had a skirmish over whose turn it was.* **3** *v.* to take part in a skirmish. ❏ *n., pl.* **skir·mish·es. –skir′mish·er,** *n.*

skirt (skėrt), **1** *n.* a woman's or girl's garment that hangs from the waist. **2** *n.* the part of a dress that hangs from the waist. **3** *n.* something like a skirt: *A skirt covered the legs of the chair.* **4** *n.* border; edge: *The rabbits fed at the skirts of the field.* **5** *n.* outskirts. **6** *v.* to pass along the border or edge; pass along the border or edge of: *We skirted the swamp.*

ski run, a snow-covered slope or steep track used by skiers.

skit (skit), *n.* a short sketch that contains humor or satire: *a TV skit.*

skit·ter (skit′ər), *v.* to move lightly or quickly; skim or skip along a surface: *A rabbit skittered across the road.*

skit·tish (skit′ish), *adj.* **1** apt to start, jump, or run; easily frightened: *a skittish horse.* **2** fickle; changeable: *a skittish wind.* **3** shy and timid; coy: *a skittish child.* **–skit′tish·ly,** *adv.* **–skit′tish·ness,** *n.*

skit·tles (skit′lz), *n.* game in which the players try to knock down nine wooden pins by rolling balls or throwing wooden disks at them.

skiv·vies (skiv′ēz), *n.pl.* men's underwear; shorts and an undershirt.

skoal (skōl), *n., interj.* a Scandinavian word used in making a toast. It means "Hail" or "May you prosper."

Skop·je (skôp′yä), *n.* capital of Macedonia.

skul·dug·ger·y (skul dug′ər ē), *n.* trickery; dishonesty.

skulk (skulk), *v.* **1** to keep out of sight to avoid danger, work, duty, etc.; hide or lurk in a cowardly way. **2** to move in a stealthy, sneaking way: *The wolf was skulking nearby.*

skull (skul), *n.* the bones of the head and face in human beings and other animals with backbones. The skull encloses and protects the brain. ■ Another word that sounds like this is **scull.**

skull and crossbones, picture of a human skull above two crossed bones. It was often used on pirates' flags as a symbol of death, and it is now sometimes used on labels of poisonous drugs, etc.

skull·cap (skul′kap′), *n.* a close-fitting cap without a brim.

skunk (skungk), **1** *n.* any of several black, bushy-tailed mammals of North America, especially one with white stripes along its back. A skunk is about the size of a cat. When frightened or attacked, skunks squirt a spray of liquid with a very strong, unpleasant smell from a pair of glands near the tail. **2** *n.* fur of the skunk. **3** *n.* INFORMAL. a mean, unpleasant person. **4** *v.* SLANG. to defeat utterly, as in an unequal contest where one side is held scoreless.

skunk cabbage, either of two low, broad-leaved, bad-smelling North American plants related to the jack-in-the-pulpit.

sky (skī), *n.* **1** the space above the earth, appearing as a great dome covering the world; the region of the clouds; the heavens. **2** heaven. **3** Often, **skies,** *pl.* climate; weather: *sunny skies.* ❏ *n., pl.* **skies.**

out of a clear blue sky, suddenly; unexpectedly.

to the skies, very highly: *to praise someone to the skies.*

sky blue, a clear, soft blue. **–sky′-blue′,** *adj.*

sky·cap (skī′kap′), *n.* person employed to handle baggage at an airport.

sky·dive (skī′dīv′), *v.* to take part in skydiving. ❏ *v.* **sky·dived, sky·div·ing.**

sky·div·ing (skī′dī′ving), *n.* act or sport of diving from an airplane and dropping for a great distance before opening a parachute. **–sky′div′er,** *n.*

sky-high (skī′hī′), *adv., adj.* very high.

Sky·lab (skī′lab′), *n.* the first U.S. space station. It was launched May 14, 1973, and fell to earth July 11, 1979.

sky·lark (skī′lärk′), **1** *n.* a common European lark that sings very sweetly as it flies upward. **2** *v.* to play; frolic.

sky·light (skī′līt′), *n.* window in a roof or ceiling.

sky·line (skī′līn′), *n.* **1** outline of buildings, mountains, trees, etc., as seen against the sky: *New York City has a remarkable skyline.* **2** horizon.

sky·rock·et (skī′rok′it), **1** *n.* firework that goes up high in the air and bursts into a shower of stars, sparks, etc. **2** *v.* to act like a skyrocket; rise suddenly and make a brilliant show: *The movie star skyrocketed to fame.* **3** *v.* to rise much and quickly: *The price of beef skyrocketed during the shortage.*

sky·scrap·er (skī′skrā′pər), *n.* a very tall building.

sky·ward (skī′wərd), *adv., adj.* toward the sky.

sky·wards (skī′wərdz), *adv.* skyward.

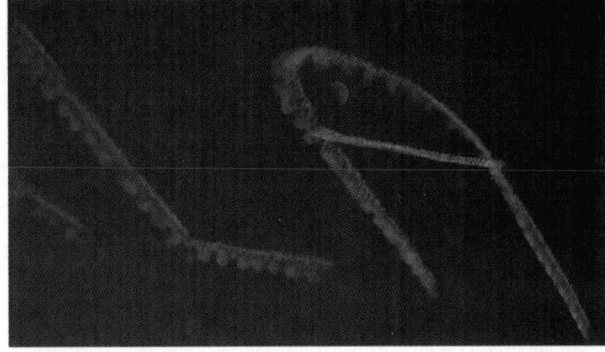

skywriting

sky·writ·ing (skī′rī′ting), *n.* the tracing of words, etc., against the sky from an airplane. Smoke, vapor, or some similar substance is used.

a	hat	ė	term	ô	order	ch	child			a in about
ā	age	i	it	oi	oil	ng	long			e in taken
ä	far	ī	ice	ou	out	sh	she	ə	{	i in pencil
â	care	o	hot	u	cup	th	thin			o in lemon
e	let	ō	open	ů	put	ŦH	then			u in circus
ē	equal	ò	saw	ü	rule	zh	measure			

S

slab (slab), *n.* a broad, flat, thick piece of stone, wood, meat, etc.: *a slab of cheese as big as my hand. This sidewalk is made of slabs of concrete.*

slack (slak), **1** *adj.* not tight or firm; loose: *a slack rope.* ■ See Synonym Study at **loose. 2** *n.* part that hangs loose: *Pull in the slack of the rope.* **3** *adj.* careless: *a slack worker.* **4** *adj.* slow: *The horse was moving at a slack pace.* **5** *adj.* not active; not brisk; dull: *Business is slack at this season.* **6** *v.* to make or become slack; let up: *He slacked his pace so we could catch up. The breeze slacked.* **—slack'ly,** *adv.* **—slack'ness,** *n.*

slack off, 1 to loosen. **2** to lessen your efforts.

slack up, to slow down; go more slowly.

slack·en (slak'ən), *v.* **1** to make or become slower: *We didn't slacken our efforts till the work was done. Their business always slackens in the winter.* **2** to make or become looser: *Slacken the rope. The rope slackened as the wave sent the boat toward the pier.*

slack·er (slak'ər), *n.* person who shirks work or evades duty.

slacks (slaks), *n.pl.* trousers for casual wear.

slag (slag), *n.* **1** the rough, hard waste left after metal is separated from ore by melting. **2** a light, spongy lava.

slain (slān), *v.* past participle of **slay:** *The lamb was slain by wolves.*

slake (slāk), *v.* **1** to satisfy thirst: *We slaked our thirst at the spring.* **2** to change lime to slaked lime by leaving it in the moist air or putting water on it. ❑ *v.* **slaked, slak·ing.**

slaked lime, a white powder obtained by exposing lime to moist air or by putting water on lime; calcium hydroxide. Slaked lime is used to refine metals and to purify water.

sla·lom (slä'ləm), *n.* (in skiing) a zigzag race downhill.

slam (slam), **1** *v.* to shut with force and noise; close with a bang: *She slammed the window down. The door slammed.* **2** *v.* to throw, push, hit, or move hard with force: *That car slammed into a truck.* **3** *n.* act of violent and noisy closing, striking, etc.; bang: *I threw my books down with a slam.* **4** *v.* to criticize harshly. **5** *n.* the winning of 12 (**little slam** or **small slam**) or all 13 (**grand slam**) tricks in the game of bridge. ❑ *v.* **slammed, slam·ming.**

slam-dunk (slam'dungk'), **1** *n.* a dunk shot. **2** *v.* to make a dunk shot.

slan·der (slan'dər), **1** *n.* a false spoken statement meant to harm someone's reputation: *The candidate for mayor accused his opponent of slander.* **2** *v.* to talk falsely about. **3** *n.* act or crime of spreading false reports: *Malicious slander had caused some people to doubt the mayor's honesty.* **—slan'der·er,** *n.*

slan·der·ous (slan'dər əs), *adj.* **1** containing a slander. **2** speaking or spreading slanders. **—slan'der·ous·ly,** *adv.* **—slan'der·ous·ness,** *n.*

slang (slang), *n.* **1** words, phrases, meanings, etc., not used when speaking or writing formal English. Slang is often very lively and expressive and is used in talk between friends but it is not usually proper in school themes. Slang is mostly made up of new words or meanings that are popular for only a short time. *Nerd* and *on the skids* are slang. **2** special talk of a particular class of people: *criminal slang.* [**Slang** came into English about 250 years ago. At that time the word **slang** was a slang word.]

slang·y (slang'ē), *adj.* **1** containing slang; full of slang. **2** using much slang. ❑ *adj.* **slang·i·er, slang·i·est. —slang'i·ly,** *adv.* **—slang'i·ness,** *n.*

slant (slant), **1** *v.* to slope: *Most handwriting slants to the right.* **2** *n.* a sloping direction, position, or movement: *The roof has a sharp slant.* **3** *adj.* sloping: *A lean-to has a slant roof.* **4** *n.* way of looking at or thinking about something; mental attitude.

slant·ing (slan'ting), *adj.* sloping: *slanting roofs.* **—slant'ing·ly,** *adv.*

slant·ways (slant'wāz'), *adv.* slantwise.

slant·wise (slant'wīz'), **1** *adv.* in a slanting manner; obliquely. **2** *adj.* slanting; oblique.

slap (slap), **1** *n.* a blow with the open hand or with something flat. **2** *v.* to strike with the open hand or with something flat: *I slapped the table with my hand.* **3** *n.* sound made by slapping. **4** *v.* to put, dash, or cast with force: *She slapped the book down angrily.* ❑ *v.* **slapped, slap·ping. —slap'per,** *n.*

slap·dash (slap'dash'), **1** *adv.* hastily and carelessly. **2** *adj.* hasty and careless.

slap shot, (in hockey) a fast shot made with a swinging stroke of the stick at the puck.

slap·stick (slap'stik'), **1** *n.* comedy full of rough play. **2** *adj.* full of rough play. In slapstick comedy, the actors knock each other around, throw pies at each other, etc., to make people laugh.

WORD STORY **Slapstick** comes from the name of a paddle used by clowns as long ago as the 1500s. Made of two thin boards joined at one end, a slapstick produced a loud slapping noise when it hit someone, but it did not hurt. Slapsticks were common in comedy full of rough play, and "slapstick comedy" became known simply as **slapstick.**

slash (slash), **1** *v.* to cut something with a sweeping blow of a sword, knife, or whip; gash: *I slashed the bark off the tree with my knife.* **2** *v.* to make a slashing stroke: *She slashed at the vines growing across the path with her knife.* **3** *n.* a sweeping, slashing stroke: *the slash of a sword, the slash of the rain.* **4** *n.* a cut or wound made by such a stroke; a gash: *When the screwdriver slipped, it made a deep slash on his thumb.* **5** *v.* to cut or slit to let a different cloth or color show through. **6** *v.* to whip severely; lash. **7** *v.* to criticize sharply, severely, or unkindly: *The critics slashed the new play.* **8** *v.* to cut down sharply; reduce a great deal: *My salary was slashed when business became bad.* **9** *n.* a sharp cutting down; great reduction: *a slash in prices.* ❑ *n., pl.* **slash·es. —slash'er,** *n.*

slash-and-burn (slash'ən bėrn'), *adj.* **1** of or about a way of farming in which wild plants are cut and then burned before crops are planted. This is a very destructive method and can be used for only a few years. **2** extremely destructive: *slash-and-burn criticism.*

slat (slat), *n.* a long, thin, narrow piece of wood, metal, or plastic: *the slats of a Venetian blind.*

slate (slāt), **1** *n.* a bluish gray rock that splits easily into thin, smooth layers. Slate is used to cover roofs and for blackboards. **2** *n.* a thin piece of this rock. Schoolchildren used to write on slates. **3** *v.* to cover a roof with slate. **4** *n.* a dark, bluish gray. **5** *adj.* dark bluish gray. **6** *n.* list of candidates, officers, etc., to be considered for appointment, nomination, election, etc. **7** *v.* to put on such a list: *She is slated as the Republican candidate for county clerk.* **8** *v.* to schedule: *slate the next speaker.* ❑ *v.* **slat·ed, slat·ing. —slate'like',** *adj.*

a clean slate, a record not marred by mistakes or faults.

slat·tern (slat'ərn), *n.* woman who is dirty, careless, or untidy in her dress, her ways, etc. ■ **Slattern** is considered offensive.

slat·tern·ly (slat'ərn lē), *adj.* like a slattern; slovenly; untidy. ■ **Slatternly** is considered offensive. **—slat'tern·li·ness,** *n.*

slat·y (slā'tē), *adj.* **1** of or like slate. **2** slate-colored. ❑ *adj.* **slat·i·er, slat·i·est.**

slaugh·ter (slô'tər), **1** *n.* the killing of an animal or animals for food; butchering: *the slaughter of a steer, to fatten hogs for slaughter.* **2** *n.* brutal killing; much or needless killing: *The battle resulted in a frightful slaughter.* **3** *v.* to kill an animal or animals for food; butcher: *Cattle are slaughtered in the stockyards.* **4** *v.* to kill brutally or in large numbers; massacre. **—slaugh'ter·er,** *n.*

slaugh·ter·house (slô'tər hous'), *n.* place where animals are killed for food. ❑ *n., pl.* **slaugh·ter·hous·es** (slô'tər hou'ziz).

Slav (släv), **1** *n.* member of a group of peoples in eastern, southeastern, and central Europe whose languages are related. Russians, Ukrainians, Poles, Czechs, Slovaks, Slovenes, Bulgarians, Serbs, and Croats are Slavs. **2** *adj.* of or about Slavs; Slavic.

slave (slāv), **1** *n.* person who is owned by another. **2** *n.* person who is controlled or ruled by some desire, habit, or influence: *a slave to drugs, a slave to your emotions.* **3** *n.* person who works like a slave. **4** *v.* to work like a slave: *We slaved all day long cleaning our house.* **5** *adj.* of or done by slaves: *slave labor.* ❑ *v.* **slaved, slav·ing. —slave'like',** *adj.*

USAGE NOTE **Slave** is considered by some people to be a misleading and undesirable word, because they feel it identifies a person with a condition that has been forcibly imposed by others, whose responsibility should be indicated. Other ways of expressing this idea include *enslaved person* and *person living in slavery.* It is wise to consider the preferences of your subject, your sources, and your audience. If in doubt, ask!

Slave (slāv), *n.* member of a tribe of American Indians living near Great Slave Lake in Canada. ❑ *n., pl.* **Slaves** or **Slave**. [Slave is an English translation of the Cree name for this tribe, whom the Cree defeated in battle and drove from their lands.]

slave driver, 1 overseer of enslaved people. **2** a harsh supervisor.

slave·hold·er (slāv′hōl′dər), *n.* person holding other people in slavery.

slave·hold·ing (slāv′hōl′ding), **1** *adj.* holding people in slavery. **2** *n.* act of holding people in slavery.

slav·er[1] (slā′vər), *n.* **1** person who buys and sells enslaved persons. **2** ship used in the slave trade.

slav·er[2] (slav′ər), **1** *v.* to let saliva run from the mouth. **2** *n.* saliva running from the mouth.

slav·er·y (slā′vər ē), *n.* **1** condition of being a enslaved person. **2** custom of holding people in slavery. **3** condition like that of an enslaved person. **4** hard work like that of an enslaved person.

Slave State, any of the 15 states of the United States in which slavery was legal before the Civil War.

slave trade, the business of obtaining and selling enslaved persons.

Slav·ic (slä′vik), **1** *adj.* of or about the Slavs or their languages. **2** *n.* language or group of languages spoken by the Slavs.

WORD SOURCE **Slavic** languages have given many words to the English language. The words below are some of them. (See also the Word Source at **Russian.**)

blintz	mazurka	robot
horde	pistol	sable
howitzer	polka	yarmulke

slav·ish (slā′vish), *adj.* **1** weak; helpless; obeying as enslaved people were forced to. **2** lacking originality and independence: *a slavish reproduction.* —**slav′ish·ly,** *adv.* —**slav′ish·ness,** *n.*

slaw (slò), *n.* coleslaw.

slay (slā), *v.* to kill with violence: *Jack slew the giant.* ❑ *v.* **slew, slain, slay·ing. ■** Another word that sounds like this is **sleigh.** —**slay′er,** *n.*

slea·zy (slē′zē), *adj.* **1** in poor condition; disreputable: *a sleazy hotel.* **2** flimsy and poor: *sleazy cloth.* ❑ *adj.* **slea·zi·er, slea·zi·est.** —**slea′zi·ly,** *adv.* —**slea′zi·ness,** *n.*

sled (sled), **1** *n.* framework mounted on runners and used for sliding on snow or ice. **2** *n.* a similar device of any form. **3** *v.* to ride or carry on a sled. ❑ *v.* **sled·ded, sled·ding.** —**sled′der,** *n.*

sled·ding (sled′ing), *n.* act or activity of riding or coasting on a sled: *two months of good sledding.*

hard sledding, unfavorable conditions; difficult going: *The bill will have hard sledding before the legislature passes it.*

sled dog, dog trained to pull a sled in arctic regions.

sledge[1] (slej), **1** *n.* a heavy sled or sleigh, usually pulled by horses. **2** *v.* to carry on or ride in a sledge. ❑ *v.* **sledged, sledg·ing.**

sledge[2] (slej), *n.* sledgehammer.

sledge·ham·mer (slej′ham′ər), *n.* a large, heavy hammer, usually swung with both hands.

sleek (slēk), **1** *adj.* soft and glossy; smooth: *sleek hair.* **2** *adj.* having smooth, soft skin, hair, fur, etc.: *a sleek cat.* **3** *adj.* smooth of manners and speech: *a sleek salesclerk.* **4** *adj.* having clean lines; trim: *a sleek jet plane.* **5** *v.* to smooth or make smooth: *He sleeked down his hair.* —**sleek′ly,** *adv.* —**sleek′ness,** *n.*

sled dogs

sleep (slēp), **1** *v.* to rest body and mind; be without ordinary thought or movement: *We sleep at night.* **2** *n.* a rest of body and mind occurring naturally and regularly: *Many people need eight hours of sleep a day.* **3** *v.* to be in a condition like sleep: *The seeds sleep in the ground all winter.* **4** *n.* condition like sleep. **The last sleep** means death. ❑ *v.* **slept, sleep·ing.** —**sleep′like′,** *adj.*

sleep away, to pass or spend in sleeping: *I slept away the whole day.*

sleep in, 1 to sleep later than usual, on purpose. **2** to sleep at your place of work.

sleep off, to get rid of by sleeping: *sleeping off a headache.*

sleep over, INFORMAL. to stay the night at someone else's home.

SYNONYM STUDY **Sleep, slumber,** and **doze** all mean not to be awake. **Sleep** is a general word: *The dog likes to sleep on the chair.* **Slumber,** a formal word, means to sleep lightly and peacefully: *He pulled a blanket over the slumbering child.* **Doze** means to be barely asleep, usually without meaning to: *She dozed on the bus and missed her stop.*

sleep·er (slē′pər), *n.* **1** someone or something that sleeps: *a sound sleeper.* **2** a railroad sleeping car. **3** a heavy horizontal beam used as a support.

sleep·ing (slē′ping), **1** *n.* sleep. **2** *adj.* asleep. **3** *adj.* used for sleeping on or in: *sleeping quarters.*

sleeping bag, a long, warmly lined or padded cloth bag made of nylon, Dacron, down, etc., used for sleeping in a tent or outdoors.

sleeping car, a railroad car with berths or small rooms for passengers to sleep in.

sleeping pill, pill or capsule containing a drug that helps people fall asleep.

sleeping sickness, 1 disease common in Africa and carried by the tsetse fly, causing fever, inflammation of the brain, weakness, sleepiness, and usually death. **2** a viral disease marked by inflammation of the brain, weakness, and extreme drowsiness.

sleep·less (slēp′lis), *adj.* **1** without sleep; restless: *a hot, sleepless night.* **2** watchful; wide-awake. **3** always moving or acting. —**sleep′less·ly,** *adv.* —**sleep′less·ness,** *n.*

sleep·ov·er (slēp′ō vər), *n.* a party that involves staying the night at the host's home with several other people: *Her birthday party was a big sleepover.*

sleep·walk·er (slēp′wò′kər), *n.* person who walks about while asleep.

sleep·walk·ing (slēp′wò′king), *n.* act of walking while asleep.

sleep·y (slē′pē), *adj.* **1** ready to go to sleep; inclined to sleep: *He never gets enough rest and is always sleepy.* **2** not active; quiet: *a sleepy little mountain town.* ❑ *adj.* **sleep·i·er, sleep·i·est.** —**sleep′i·ly,** *adv.* —**sleep′i·ness,** *n.*

sleep·y·head (slē′pē hed′), *n.* a sleepy, drowsy, or lazy person.

sleet (slēt), **1** *n.* partly frozen rain. Sleet forms when rain falls through a layer of cold air. **2** *v.* to come down as sleet: *It sleeted; then it snowed; then it rained.*

sleepy (def. 1)

sleet·y (slē′tē), *adj.* of or like sleet; accompanied by sleet: *a dismal and sleety morning.* ❑ *adj.* **sleet·i·er, sleet·i·est.** —**sleet′i·ness,** *n.*

sleeve (slēv), *n.* **1** the part of an article of clothing that covers the arm: *The sleeves of her coat were too long and hung down over her hands.* **2** tube into which a rod or another tube fits. —**sleeve′less,** *adj.*

laugh up your sleeve, be amused but not show it.

up your sleeve, in reserve; ready for use when needed.

sleeved (slēvd), *adj.* having sleeves.

sleigh (slā), **1** *n.* carriage or cart mounted on runners for use on ice or snow. **2** *v.* to travel or ride in a sleigh. **■** Another word that sounds like this is **slay.**

sleight (slīt), *n.* **1** skill, dexterity. **2** a clever trick. **■** Another word that sounds like this is **slight.**

sleight of hand, 1 skill and quickness in moving the hands. **2** tricks or skill of a modern magician.

a	hat	ė	term	ô	order	ch	child		
ā	age	i	it	oi	oil	ng	long	ə	a in about
ä	far	ī	ice	ou	out	sh	she		e in taken
â	care	o	hot	u	cup	th	thin		i in pencil
e	let	ō	open	ù	put	ᵺ	then		o in lemon
ē	equal	ò	saw	ü	rule	zh	measure		u in circus

S

slen·der (slen′dər), *adj.* **1** long and thin; not big around; slim: *a slender child. A pencil is a slender piece of wood.* ■ See Synonym Study at **thin. 2** slight; small; scanty: *a slender meal, a slender income, a slender hope.* —**slen′der·ly**, *adv.* —**slen′der·ness**, *n.*

slen·der·ize (slen′də rīz′), *v.* to make or become slender. ❑ *v.* **slen·der·ized, slen·der·iz·ing.**

slept (slept), *v.* past tense and past participle of **sleep:** *The child slept soundly. I haven't slept well for weeks.*

sleuth (slüth), *n.* detective.

slew¹ (slü), *v.* past tense of **slay:** *Jack slew the giant.*

slew² (slü), **1** *v.* to turn; swing; twist: *She slewed the front wheels sharply to avoid hitting the dog. The car suddenly slewed to the left.* **2** *n.* a turn; swing; twist. Also, **slue.**

slew³ (slü), *n.* slough¹ (def. 2).

slew⁴ (slü), *n.* INFORMAL. a lot; large number or amount: *The new girl quickly gained a slew of friends.* Also, **slue.**

slice (slīs), **1** *n.* a thin, flat, broad piece cut from something: *a slice of bread, meat, or cake.* **2** *v.* to cut into slices: *slice the bread.* **3** *v.* to cut off as a slice: *Slice her a piece of cake.* **4** *v.* to cut through or across: *The boat sliced the waves.* **5** *v.* (in sports) to hit a ball so that it curves to your right if hit right-handed. ❑ *v.* **sliced, slic·ing.**

slic·er (slī′sər), *n.* **1** tool or machine that slices: *a meat slicer.* **2** person who slices.

slick (slik), **1** *adj.* soft and glossy; smooth: *slick hair.* ■ See Synonym Study at **smooth. 2** *v.* to make sleek or smooth: *He slicked down his hair.* **3** *adj.* slippery; greasy: *a road slick with ice.* **4** *n.* a smooth place or spot. Oil makes a slick on the surface of water. **5** *adj.* clever; ingenious. **6** *adj.* sly; tricky. **7** *adj.* smooth of speech, manners, etc. —**slick′ly**, *adv.* —**slick′ness**, *n.*

slick·er (slik′ər), *n.* **1** a long, loose, waterproof coat, made of oilskin or the like. **2** INFORMAL. an unpleasantly smooth, tricky person: *a city slicker.*

slid (slid), *v.* past tense and past participle of **slide:** *The minutes slid by. She has slid past us.*

slide (slīd), **1** *v.* to move smoothly along a surface: *The bureau drawers slide in and out.* **2** *v.* to move easily, quietly, or secretly: *I hid by sliding behind the door.* **3** *v.* to slip, as when losing your foothold: *The car slid into the ditch.* **4** *v.* to pass little by little; slip: *They slid into bad habits.* **5** *v.* to pass or put quietly or secretly: *I slid the letter into my pocket.* **6** *n.* act of sliding: *The children each take a slide in turn.* **7** *n.* a smooth surface for sliding on: *a playground slide, a toboggan slide.* **8** *n.* a track, rail, etc., on which something slides. **9** *n.* something that slides or that works by sliding. **10** *n.* mass of earth, snow, etc., sliding down: *The slide cut off the valley from the rest of the world.* **11** *n.* a small, thin sheet of glass on which objects are placed in order to look at them under a microscope. **12** *n.* a small transparent photograph. Slides are put in a projector and shown on a screen. ❑ *v.* **slid, slid·ing.**

let slide, to neglect; not bother about: *He let his work slide, and now he has huge amounts to do.*

slide fastener, zipper.

slide projector, device for projecting onto a screen the images on photographic slides.

slide rule, ruler with a sliding section in the center, both parts marked with scales, formerly used for making rapid mathematical calculations.

sliding scale, system of wages, prices, taxes, etc., that can be adjusted according to economic conditions, or to someone's ability to pay.

sli·er (slī′ər), *adj.* comparative of **sly.**

sli·est (slī′ist), *adj.* superlative of **sly.**

slight (slīt), **1** *adj.* not much; not important; small: *I have a slight headache.* **2** *adj.* not big around; slender: *a slight figure.* **3** *v.* to treat as of little value; pay too little attention to; neglect: *They often slight their work. I felt slighted because I was not asked to the party.* **4** *n.* slighting treatment; act of neglect: *The unpopular student suffered many slights in school.* ■ Another word that sounds like this is **sleight.** —**slight′ness**, *n.*

slight·ing (slī′ting), *adj.* disrespectful; insulting: *a slighting remark.* —**slight′ing·ly**, *adv.*

slight·ly (slīt′lē), *adv.* **1** to a slight degree; somewhat; a little: *I knew him slightly.* **2** slenderly: *a slightly built person.*

slim (slim), **1** *adj.* slender; thin: *He was very slim, being 6 feet tall and weighing only 130 pounds.* **2** *adj.* small; slight; weak: *We had a slim attendance at the football game because of the rain. The invalid's chances for getting well were very slim.* **3** *v.* to make or become slim or slender: *slim down your weight by exercising more.* ❑ *adj.* **slim·mer, slim·mest;** *v.* **slimmed, slim·ming.** —**slim′ly**, *adv.* —**slim′ness**, *n.*

slime (slīm), *n.* **1** soft, sticky mud or something like it: *Thick slime surrounded the edge of the stagnant pool.* **2** a sticky substance given off by snails, slugs, fish, etc. **3** disgusting filth.

slime (def. 2)

slime mold, any of several kinds of fungi that gather into shapeless, slimy masses that move around slowly. Some are parasites of plants, while others surround and digest bacteria.

slim·y (slī′mē), *adj.* **1** covered with slime: *The pond is too slimy to swim in.* **2** of or like slime. **3** disgusting; filthy. ❑ *adj.* **slim·i·er, slim·i·est.** —**slim′i·ly**, *adv.* —**slim′i·ness**, *n.*

sling (sling), **1** *n.* strip of leather with a string fastened to each end, for throwing stones. **2** *n.* a slingshot. **3** *v.* to throw with a sling. **4** *v.* to throw; cast; hurl; fling: *I slung the bag of oats into the truck.* **5** *n.* a hanging loop of cloth fastened around the neck to support an injured arm. **6** *n.* loop of rope, band, chain, etc., by which heavy objects are lifted, carried, or held: *We lowered the heavy boxes over the railing with a sling.* **7** *v.* to raise, lower, etc., with a sling. **8** *v.* to hang in a sling; hang so as to swing loosely: *I slung the bag over my shoulder.* ❑ *v.* **slung, sling·ing.** —**sling′er**, *n.*

sling·shot (sling′shot′), *n.* a Y-shaped stick with a band of rubber between its prongs, used to shoot pebbles, etc.

slink (slingk), *v.* to move in a sneaking, guilty manner; sneak: *After stealing the meat, the dog slunk away.* ❑ *v.* **slunk, slink·ing.**

slink·y (sling′kē), *adj.* **1** fitting closely; clinging to the body: *a slinky dress.* **2** sneaky; furtive; stealthy. ❑ *adj.* **slink·i·er, slink·i·est.**

slip¹ (slip), **1** *v.* to go or move smoothly, quietly, easily, or quickly: *She slipped out of the room. Time slips by.* ■ See Synonym Study at **slide. 2** *v.* to slide; move out of place: *The knife slipped and cut his finger.* **3** *v.* to slide suddenly and lose your balance: *He slipped on the icy sidewalk.* **4** *n.* act or fact of slipping: *Her broken leg resulted from a slip on a banana peel.* **5** *v.* to cause to slip; put, pass, or draw smoothly, quietly, or secretly: *I slipped back the bolt on the door. I slipped the ring from my finger. Slip the note into her hand.* **6** *v.* to put or take something easily or quickly: *Slip on your coat and come with us. Slip off your shoes.* **7** *n.* pillowcase. **8** *n.* a sleeveless garment worn under a dress. **9** *v.* to pass without notice; lose through neglect; escape: *Don't let this opportunity slip.* **10** *v.* to get loose from; get away from; escape from: *The dog has slipped its collar. Your name has slipped my mind.* **11** *v.* to fall off; decline: *Sales are slipping.* **12** *v.* to make a mistake or error: *I slipped when I used the wrong Zip Code on the letter.* **13** *n.* mistake; error: *He makes slips in pronouncing words. That remark was a slip of the tongue.* **14** *n.* space for ships between wharves or in a dock. ❑ *v.* **slipped, slip·ping.**

give someone the slip, INFORMAL. to get away from someone completely; slip away.

let slip, to tell without meaning to: *They talked too much and let the secret slip.*

slip one over on, INFORMAL. to get the advantage of, especially by trickery: *The fox slipped one over on the hounds and got away.*

slip out, to become known.

slip up, to make a mistake or error: *I slipped up on that problem and got the answer all wrong.*

slip² (slip), **1** *n.* a small, narrow strip of paper, wood, etc.: *The teacher passed out slips of paper for us to write our names on.* **2** *n.* a young, slender person: *He is just a slip of a boy.* **3** *n.* a small branch or twig cut from a plant, used to grow a new plant: *She has promised us slips from her rosebush.* **4** *v.* to cut branches from a plant to grow new plants; take a part from a plant. ❑ *v.* **slipped, slip·ping.**

slip·case (slip′kās′), *n.* box or covering to protect one or more books, phonograph records, etc., so that only their edges are exposed.

slip·cov·er (slip′kuv′ər), *n.* a removable cloth or plastic cover for a chair, sofa, etc.

slip·knot (slip′not′), *n.* knot made to slip along the rope or cord around which it is made; running knot.

slip·on (slip′on′), **1** *adj.* able to be put on and taken off easily. **2** *n.* an item of clothing, such as a sweater or shirt, that is easy to put on and take off.

slip·o·ver (slip′ō′vər), *n.* pullover.

slipped disk (slipt), a painful condition caused by the slipping out of place of a disk of cartilage between the bones of the spine, causing pressure on the spinal nerves.

slip·per (slip′ər), *n.* a light, low shoe that is slipped on easily: *dancing slippers, bedroom slippers.*

slip·pered (slip′ərd), *adj.* wearing slippers.

slip·per·y (slip′ər ē), *adj.* **1** causing or likely to cause slipping: *The steps are slippery with ice.* ■ See Synonym Study at **smooth. 2** slipping away easily: *Wet soap is slippery.* **3** not to be depended on; tricky. **—slip′per·i·ness,** *n.*

slip·shod (slip′shod′), *adj.* careless in dress, habits, speech, etc.; untidy; slovenly.

slip·stream (slip′strēm′), *n.* current of air produced by the propeller of an aircraft.

slip·up (slip′up′), *n.* mistake; error: *Do this job right, with no slip-ups.*

slit (slit), **1** *v.* to cut or tear in a straight line; make a long, straight cut or tear in: *slit cloth into strips, slit a skirt to make a pocket.* **2** *n.* a straight, narrow cut, tear, or opening: *a slit in a bag, the slit in a mailbox.* ❑ *v.* **slit, slit·ting. —slit′ter,** *n.*

slith·er (slith′ər), **1** *v.* to go with a sliding motion: *The snake slithered into the weeds.* **2** *v.* to slide down or along a surface, especially unsteadily: *He tripped and slithered down the side of the hill.* **3** *n.* a slithering movement; a slide.

sliv·er (sliv′ər), **1** *n.* a long, thin piece that has been split off, broken off, or cut off; splinter. **2** *v.* to split or break into slivers.

slob (slob), *n.* a dirty, untidy, or clumsy person. [**Slob** comes from an Irish word meaning "mud." You can see why.]

slob·ber (slob′ər), **1** *v.* to let liquid run out of the mouth; drool. **2** *n.* saliva or other liquid running out of the mouth. **3** *v.* to speak in a silly, sentimental way. **—slob′ber·er,** *n.*

slob·ber·y (slob′ər ē), *adj.* **1** slobbering. **2** disagreeably wet; sloppy.

sloe (slō), *n.* **1** a dark purple, plumlike fruit. **2** the thorny bush that it grows on. ■ Another word that sounds like this is **slow.**

slog (slog), *v.* **1** to plod heavily. **2** to work hard at something. ❑ *v.* **slogged, slog·ging. —slog′ger,** *n.*

slo·gan (slō′gən), *n.* word or phrase used by a business, club, political party, etc., to advertise its purpose; motto: *"Service with a smile" was the store's slogan.*

WORD STORY **Slogan** comes from Gaelic words meaning "army" and "shout." Together they meant "battle cry." Some famous slogans have been intended to make people fight, as was "Give me liberty or give me death!" Modern slogans encourage people to choose a candidate, a food, or some other item competing for loyalty.

sloop (slüp), *n.* sailboat having one mast and at least two sails, one in front of the mast and the other behind it.

slop (slop), **1** *v.* to spill liquid upon; spill; splash: *She slopped water on me.* **2** *n.* liquid carelessly spilled or splashed about. **3** *n.* Often, **slops,** *pl.* dirty water; liquid garbage: *kitchen slops.* **4** *n.* a thin, liquid mud or slush. **5** *v.* to splash through mud, slush, or water. **6** *n.* weak, liquid food, such as gruel. ❑ *v.* **slopped, slop·ping.**

slope (slōp), **1** *v.* to go up or down at an angle; slant: *Our roof slopes very steeply.* **2** *n.* any line, surface, land, etc., that goes up or down at an angle: *If you roll a ball up a slope, it will roll down again.* **3** *n.* amount of slant: *The floor of the theater has a slope of four feet from back to front.* ❑ *v.* **sloped, slop·ing. —slop′er,** *n.*

slop·py (slop′ē), *adj.* **1** very wet; slushy: *sloppy ground, sloppy weather.* **2** careless: *do sloppy work.* **3** untidy; not neat: *She has a very sloppy desk.* ❑ *adj.* **slop·pi·er, slop·pi·est. —slop′pi·ly,** *adv.* **—slop′pi·ness,** *n.*

sloppy joe (jō), half of a hamburger bun covered with a mixture of ground beef and tomato sauce or chili sauce.

slosh (slosh), *v.* to splash in slush, mud, or water: *She sloshed around in the bathtub and got the floor all wet.*

slot (slot), **1** *n.* a small, narrow opening or depression: *Put a quarter in the slot to get candy from this machine.* **2** *n.* place or position in a schedule, list, organization, etc: *Her slot at the Youth Center is from six to eight on Monday evenings.* **3** *v.* to make a slot or slots in. ❑ *v.* **slot·ted, slot·ting.**

slot car, a plastic, toy racing car built to exact scale, electrically driven over a slotted track, and operated by a hand-held, remote control.

sloth (def. 2)—about 2 ft. (60 cm) long

sloth (slòth *or* slōth), *n.* **1** unwillingness to work or exert yourself; laziness; idleness. **2** either of two kinds of very slow-moving mammals of South and Central America that live in trees. Sloths hang upside down from tree branches.

WORD STORY **Sloth** comes from **slow,** like **warmth** from **warm.** In old English, **sloth** had the meaning "slowness." It stopped being used that way, probably because it also had the meaning "laziness," and it was easy to confuse the two ideas.

sloth·ful (slòth′fəl *or* slōth′fəl), *adj.* unwilling to work or exert yourself; lazy; idle. **—sloth′ful·ly,** *adv.* **—sloth′ful·ness,** *n.*

a	hat	ė	term	ô	order	ch	child		
ā	age	i	it	oi	oil	ng	long	ə	a in about
ä	far	ī	ice	ou	out	sh	she		e in taken
â	care	o	hot	u	cup	th	thin		i in pencil
e	let	ō	open	u̇	put	₮H	then		o in lemon
ē	equal	ò	saw	ü	rule	zh	measure		u in circus

S

slot machine, machine that is worked by dropping a coin or coins into a slot. Some slot machines are vending machines that sell peanuts, candy, etc.; others are used for gambling.

slouch (slouch), **1** *v.* to stand, sit, walk, or move in an awkward, drooping manner: *The weary traveler slouched along.* **2** *n.* act of bending forward the head and shoulders; awkward, drooping way of standing, sitting, or walking. **3** *v.* to droop or bend downward: *I slouched my shoulders.* **4** *n.* an awkward, careless, or inefficient person: *He's no slouch when it comes to hard work.* □ *n., pl.* **slouch·es.** **–slouch′er,** *n.*

slouch hat, a soft hat with a soft brim that bends easily.

slouch·y (slou′chē), *adj.* slouching awkwardly; carelessly untidy. □ *adj.* **slouch·i·er, slouch·i·est.** **–slouch′i·ly,** *adv.* **–slouch′i·ness,** *n.*

slough¹ (slou *for 1;* slü *for 2*), *n.* **1** a soft, deep, muddy place. **2** a swampy place; marshy inlet; slew; slue.

slough² (sluf) **1** *v.* to be shed or cast; drop or fall: *A scab sloughs off when new skin takes its place.* **2** *v.* to shed; drop off; throw off; cast: *I finally sloughed off my bad habits.* **3** *n.* the old skin shed by a reptile. **4** *n.* anything that has been or can be shed or cast off: *As people become adults, they cast off the slough of their childish ways.*

Slo·vak (slō′vak), **1** *n.* member of a Slavic people living in Slovakia. The Slovaks are related to the Bohemians and the Moravians. **2** *n.* their language. **3** *adj.* of or about Slovakia, its people, or their language: *Slovak writers.*

Slo·va·ki·a (slō vä′kē ə), *n.* country in E Europe, S of Poland. *Capital:* Bratislava. **–Slo·va′ki·an,** *adj., n.*

slov·en (sluv′ən), *n.* person who is untidy, dirty, or careless in dress, appearance, habits, work, etc.

Slo·vene (slō′vēn′), *n.* **1** member of a Slavic people living in Slovenia. The Slovenes are related to the Croats and Serbians. **2** their language.

Slo·ve·ni·a (slō vē′nē ə), *n.* country in SE Europe. *Capital:* Ljubljana. **–Slo·ve′ni·an,** *adj., n.*

slov·en·ly (sluv′ən lē) **1** *adj.* untidy, dirty, or careless in appearance, dress, habits, work, etc. **2** *adv.* in a slovenly manner. □ *adj.* **slov·en·li·er, slov·en·li·est.** **–slov′en·li·ness,** *n.*

slow (slō), **1** *adj.* taking a long time; taking longer than usual; not fast or quick: *a slow journey. She is slow to anger.* **2** *adj.* moving with little speed, or with less speed than others: *The slow runners couldn't keep up.* **3** *adj.* indicating time earlier than the correct time: *That clock is slow.* **4** *adj.* causing a low or lower rate of speed: *a slow track.* **5** *v.* to make slow or slower; reduce the speed of: *slow down a car.* **6** *v.* to become slow; go slower: *Cars should slow up when they pass a school.* **7** *adv.* in a slow manner: *Drive slow past a school.* **8** *adj.* not quick to understand: *a slow learner.* ■ This meaning of **slow** is sometimes considered offensive. **9** *adj.* sluggish; inactive: *Business is slow.* **10** *adj.* dull; not interesting: *a slow party.* ■ Another word that sounds like this is **sloe.** **–slow′ly,** *adv.* **–slow′ness,** *n.*

slow cooker, a cooking pot with a tight-fitting lid, used to cook soups, stews, etc., for several hours at a steady, low temperature.

slow·ish (slō′ish), *adj.* rather slow.

slow match, (earlier) a fuse that burns very slowly, used to fire gunpowder, dynamite, etc.

slow motion, (in movies and television) action shown at much less than its real speed. The effect is produced by taking pictures at a high speed and then showing them at usual speed.

slow-mo·tion (slō′mō′shən), *adj.* showing action at much less than its actual speed: *slow-motion photography.*

slow·poke (slō′pōk′), *n.* INFORMAL. a very slow person or thing.

sludge (sluj), *n.* **1** soft mud; mire; slush. **2** a soft, thick, muddy or oily mixture, deposit, sediment, etc.

sludg·y (sluj′ē), *adj.* made of sludge; slushy. □ *adj.* **sludg·i·er, sludg·i·est.**

slue¹ (slü), *n., v.* slew². □ *v.* **slued, slu·ing.**

slue² (slü), *n.* slough¹ (def. 2).

slue³ (slü), *n.* slew⁴.

slug¹ (slug), *n.* **1** any of numerous slow-moving animals like snails, without shells or with only partially developed shells. Slugs live mostly in forests, gardens, and damp places feeding on plants. **2** caterpillar or other larva that looks like a slug. **3** any slow-moving person. **4** a shaped piece of lead or other metal for firing from a gun. **5** a round metal disk or counterfeit coin illegally inserted in a coin-operated machine instead of a genuine coin.

slug² (slug), **1** *v.* to hit hard with the fist or with a baseball bat; hit hard. **2** *n.* a hard blow with the fist. □ *v.* **slugged, slug·ging.**

slug·gard (slug′ərd), *n.* a lazy, idle person.

slug·gish (slug′ish), *adj.* **1** slow-moving; not active; lacking energy or vigor: *When I stay up late, I am often sluggish the next day.* ■ See Synonym Study at **lazy.** **2** moving slowly; having little motion: *The stream was so sluggish that I could hardly tell which way it flowed.* **–slug′gish·ly,** *adv.* **–slug′gish·ness,** *n.*

sluice (slüs), **1** *n.* structure with a gate for holding back or controlling the water of a canal, river, or lake. **2** *n.* gate that holds back or controls the flow of water through a channel. When the water behind a dam gets too high, the sluices are opened. **3** *v.* to let out or draw off water by opening a sluice. **4** *v.* to flush or cleanse with a rush of water; pour or throw water over. **5** *n.* a long, sloping trough through which water flows, used to wash gold from sand, dirt, or gravel. **6** *n.* channel for carrying off overflow or surplus water. □ *v.* **sluiced, sluic·ing.**

sluice (def. 5)

slum (slum), **1** *n.* Often, **slums,** *pl.* a run-down, overcrowded part of a city or town. Poverty, dirt, and unhealthy living conditions are common in the slums. **2** *v.* to visit, go to, or work in any place thought of as much worse than your usual place: *We enjoyed having a professional play with our band until we learned that she thought of it as slumming.* □ *v.* **slummed, slum·ming.**

slum·ber (slum′bər), **1** *v.* to sleep lightly; doze: *The baby slumbered in the crib.* ■ See Synonym Study at **sleep.** **2** *n.* a light sleep: *He awoke from his slumber.* **3** *v.* to pass in sleep: *He slumbered all day.* **4** *v.* to be inactive: *The volcano had slumbered for years.* **5** *n.* an inactive state or condition. **–slum′ber·er,** *n.*

slum·ber·ous (slum′bər əs), *adj.* **1** sleepy; heavy with drowsiness: *slumberous eyelids.* **2** causing or inducing sleep. **–slum′ber·ous·ly,** *adv.*

slum·brous (slum′brəs), *adj.* slumberous.

slum·lord (slum′lôrd′), *n.* owner of a slum dwelling, especially one who charges high rents.

slump (slump), **1** *v.* to drop heavily; fall suddenly: *The thin air made me so faint that I slumped to the ground.* **2** *v.* to move, walk, sit, etc., in a drooping manner; slouch: *The bored students slumped in their seats.* **3** *n.* a heavy or sudden fall; collapse. **4** *n.* a great or sudden decline: *a slump in prices.*

slung (slung), *v.* past tense and past participle of **sling:** *They slung some stones and ran away. The girl had slung her laundry bag over her shoulder.*

slunk (slungk), *v.* past tense and past participle of **slink:** *The dog slunk away ashamed.*

slur (slėr), **1** *n.* a blot or stain upon someone's reputation; insulting or slighting remark: *a slur on his good name.* **2** *v.* to pass lightly over; go through hurriedly or in a careless way: *They slurred over their team's poor performance last year, thinking only of today's game.* **3** *v.* to pronounce indistinctly: *Many persons slur "how do you do."* **4** *n.* a slurred pronunciation, sound, etc. **5** in music: **a** *v.* to sing or play two or more tones of different pitch without a break; run together in a smooth, connected manner. **b** *n.* a slurring of tones. **c** *n.* a curved mark, ⌢ or ⌣, indicating this. **6** *v.* to harm the reputation of; insult; slight. ❑ *v.* **slurred, slur·ring.**

slurp (slėrp), **1** *v.* to eat or drink with a noisy, gurgling sound. **2** *n.* a noisy, gurgling sound.

slush (slush), *n.* **1** partly melted snow; snow and water mixed. **2** soft mud. **3** silly, sentimental talk, writing, etc.

slush fund, money collected or set aside for dishonest purposes, such as bribery.

slush·y (slush′ē), *adj.* **1** having much slush. **2** of or like slush. ❑ *adj.* **slush·i·er, slush·i·est. —slush′i·ness,** *n.*

slut (slut), *n.* **1** a dirty, untidy woman. **2** a sexually immoral woman. ■ **Slut** is considered offensive.

sly (slī), *adj.* **1** skillful in deceiving others; cunning; crafty; tricky; wily: *He was very sly in pretending to be unable to help get the job done.* **2** playfully mischievous or knowing: *a sly wink. Waiting for the surprise party to begin, the children exchanged many sly looks and smiles.* **3** acting secretly or stealthily. ❑ *adj.* **sly·er, sly·est** or **sli·er, sli·est. —sly′ly,** *adv.* **—sly′ness,** *n.*

on the sly, secretly.

Sly, cunning, and **crafty** all mean able to trick people. **Sly** suggests trickery to get something you want: *The sly dog eats dinner and then acts as if he never got it.* **Cunning** suggests cleverness: *Sherlock Holmes was too smart for even the most cunning criminals.* **Crafty** suggests skill and practice: *She is so crafty with her curve ball that batters never touch it.*

Sm, symbol for samarium.

smack[1] (smak), **1** *v.* to open the lips quickly so as to make a sharp sound: *She smacked her lips at the thought of cake.* **2** *n.* a smacking movement of the lips. **3** *n.* the sharp sound made in this way. **4** *v.* to kiss loudly. **5** *v.* to slap: *She smacked the horse on its rump.* **6** *n.* a loud kiss or slap. **7** *adv.* directly; squarely: *She rode the bicycle smack into the hedge.*

smack[2] (smak), **1** *n.* a slight taste or flavor: *The sauce had a smack of nutmeg.* **2** *n.* trace; suggestion: *The old sailor still had a smack of the sea about him.* **3** *v.* to have a taste or trace of: *The immigrant talked in a way that smacked of the old country.*

smack[3] (smak), *n.* **1** a small sailboat with one mast. **2** a fishing boat with a well for keeping fish alive.

small (smôl), **1** *adj.* not large; little; not large as compared with other things of the same kind: *A cottage is a small house.* **2** *adj.* not great in amount, time, value, strength, etc.: *a small dose, small hope of success. The cent is our smallest coin.* **3** *adj.* not important: *This is only a small matter.* **4** *adj.* having little land, capital, etc.; doing business on a limited scale: *a small farmer. They own a small business.* **5** *adj.* having little strength; gentle; soft; low: *a small voice.* **6** *adj.* mean; petty: *A person with a small nature is not generous.* **7** *adj.* (of letters) not capital. **8** *n.* a small, slender, or narrow part: *the small of the back.* **—small′ness,** *n.*

feel small, to be ashamed or humiliated.

small arms, weapons easily carried by a person, such as rifles or revolvers.

small change, 1 coins of small value, such as nickels, dimes, etc. **2** anything small and unimportant.

small fry, 1 young children. **2** people or things having little importance.

small hours, the early hours in the morning.

small intestine, the long winding tube between the stomach and the large intestine. The small intestine receives partly digested food from the stomach, completes the digestion of food, and passes the useful parts of it into the blood.

small·ish (smô′lish), *adj.* rather small.

small letter, an ordinary letter, not a capital.

small-mind·ed (smôl′mīn′did), *adj.* narrow-minded; petty; mean. **—small′-mind′ed·ly,** *adv.* **—small′-mind′ed·ness,** *n.*

small·pox (smôl′poks′), *n.* a very contagious viral disease that causes fever and red spots on the skin. These spots often leave permanent scars called pocks. Vaccination prevents smallpox.

small talk, conversation about unimportant matters; chitchat.

smart (smärt), **1** *v.* to feel sharp pain: *Her eyes smarted.* **2** *v.* to cause sharp pain: *The cut smarts.* **3** *n.* a sharp pain: *The smart of the wound kept me awake.* **4** *adj.* clever; bright: *a smart student.* **5** *adv.* in a smart manner; cleverly. **6** *v.* to feel distress or irritation: *I smarted from the scolding.* **7** *adj.* sharp; severe: *He gave the horse a smart blow.* **8** *adj.* keen; active; lively: *They walked home at a smart pace.* **9** *adj.* fresh and neat; in good order: *the smart new band uniforms.* **10** *adj.* stylish; fashionable: *some smart new clothes.* **11** *adj.* guided, controlled, or regulated by a computer: *smart bombs.* **—smart′ly,** *adv.* **—smart′ness,** *n.*

Smart, intelligent, and **clever** all mean having a good mind. **Smart** means learning easily and solving problems quickly: *One reason he is so smart is that he studies hard.* **Intelligent** means thinking clearly and making good decisions: *Scientists are still not sure how intelligent dolphins really are.* **Clever** means quick to think of good ideas: *Her mom is clever and has a job writing commercials.*

smart al·eck (al′ik), INFORMAL. person who is too pleased with herself or himself and very unpleasant to other people.

smart·en (smärt′n), *v.* **1** to improve in appearance; brighten. **2** to make or become brisker.

smash (smash), **1** *v.* to break into pieces with violence and noise: *smash a dish, smash a window with a stone.* ■ See Synonym Study at **break. 2** *v.* to destroy; shatter; ruin: *smash a person's hopes.* **3** *v.* to be broken to pieces: *The dishes smashed on the floor.* **4** *v.* to become ruined. **5** *v.* to rush violently; crash: *The car smashed into a tree.* **6** *n.* a violent crash or collision: *Two cars were involved in the smash.* **7** *n.* act or sound of smashing: *the smash of broken glass.* **8** *n.* a crushing defeat; disaster. **9** *n.* INFORMAL. a highly successful performance or production; great hit: *a theatrical smash.* **10** *adj.* INFORMAL. highly successful: *a smash Broadway musical.* ❑ *n., pl.* **smash·es. —smash′er,** *n.*

smash·ing (smash′ing), *adj.* INFORMAL. wonderful; fine. **—smash′ing·ly,** *adv.*

smash-up (smash′up′), *n.* **1** a bad collision; wreck. **2** a great misfortune; disaster.

smat·ter·ing (smat′ər ing), *n.* very slight knowledge: *a smattering of French.*

smear (smir), **1** *v.* to cover or stain with anything sticky, greasy, or dirty: *I smeared my fingers with jam.* **2** *v.* to rub or spread oil, grease, paint, etc. **3** *n.* a mark or stain left by smearing: *There are smears of paint on the wallpaper.* ■ See Synonym Study at **stain. 4** *v.* to receive a mark or stain; be smeared: *Wet paint smears easily.* **5** *v.* to harm; soil; spoil: *Enemies tried to smear his good reputation.* **6** *n.* a small sample of blood, cells, bacteria, etc., taken by rubbing or rubbed onto something for examination.

smell (smel), **1** *v.* to perceive by breathing in through the nose: *Can you smell the smoke?* **2** *n.* quality in a thing that is perceived by breathing in through the nose; odor: *The smell of burning rubber is not pleasant.* **3** *v.* to use the nose to smell; sniff: *Smell this rose.* **4** *v.* to sniff at: *pick up a rose and smell it.* **5** *v.* to give out a smell: *The garden smelled of roses.* **6** *v.* to give out a bad smell; have a bad smell: *That dirty, wet dog smells.* **7** *n.* sense of smelling: *Smell is keener in dogs than in people.* **8** *v.* to find a

a	hat	ė	term	ô	order	ch	child		
ā	age	i	it	oi	oil	ng	long	ə	a in about
ä	far	ī	ice	ou	out	sh	she		e in taken
â	care	o	hot	u	cup	th	thin		i in pencil
e	let	ō	open	ù	put	ŦH	then		o in lemon
ē	equal	ò	saw	ü	rule	zh	measure		u in circus

S

trace or suggestion of: *We smelled trouble.* **9** *v.* to have the smell of; have the trace of: *The plan smells of trickery.* **10** *n.* act of smelling: *Have a smell of this rose.* ❑ *v.* **smelled** or **smelt, smell·ing.** —**smell′er,** *n.*

SYNONYM STUDY **Smell, aroma,** and **fragrance** all mean an odor. **Smell** is a general word: *There is a smell of paint in the hall.* **Aroma** means a pleasant, spicy smell: *Wonderful aromas came from the bakery.* **Fragrance** means a sweet smell: *The flowers are tiny, but their fragrance fills the yard.*

smelling salts, a form of ammonia breathed in to relieve faintness, headaches, etc.

smell·y (smel′ē), *adj.* having or giving out a strong or unpleasant smell: *Rotten fish are smelly.* ❑ *adj.* **smell·i·er, smell·i·est.** —**smell′i·ness,** *n.*

smelt[1] (smelt), *v.* **1** to melt ore in order to get the metal out of it. **2** to refine impure metal by melting.

smelt[2] (smelt), *n.* any of several small saltwater or freshwater food fishes with silvery scales. ❑ *n., pl.* **smelts** or **smelt.**

smelt[3] (smelt), *v.* a past tense and a past participle of **smell.**

smelt·er (smel′tər), *n.* **1** furnace for smelting ores. **2** place where ores or metals are smelted. **3** person whose work or business is smelting ores or metals.

smidg·en, smidg·eon, or **smidg·in** (smij′ən), *n.* a tiny bit: *There isn't a smidgen of truth in this rumor.*

smile (smīl), **1** *v.* to look pleased or amused; show pleasure, favor, kindness, amusement, etc., by an upward curve of the mouth. **2** *v.* to show scorn, disapproval, etc., by a curve of the mouth: *She smiled bitterly.* **3** *v.* to bring, put, drive, etc., by smiling: *Smile your tears away.* **4** *v.* to give a smile: *She smiled a sunny smile.* **5** *v.* to express by a smile: *He smiled consent.* **6** *n.* act of smiling: *a friendly smile, a smile of pity.* **7** *v.* to look upon or regard with favor: *Good fortune always smiled on her.* ❑ *v.* **smiled, smil·ing.** —**smil′er,** *n.* —**smil′ing·ly,** *adv.*

smirch (smėrch), **1** *v.* to make dirty; soil with soot, dirt, dust, dishonor, disgrace, etc. **2** *n.* a dirty mark; blot; stain. ❑ *n., pl.* **smirch·es.**

smirk (smėrk), **1** *v.* to smile in a silly or self-satisfied way. **2** *n.* a silly or self-satisfied smile.

smite (smīt), *v.* **1** to strike hard; hit hard; strike: *The hero smote the giant with his sword.* **2** to affect with a strong feeling: *We were smitten with curiosity about the forbidden room.* ❑ *v.* **smote, smit·ten** or **smote, smit·ing.** —**smit′er,** *n.*

smith (smith), *n.* **1** worker in metal: *silversmith.* **2** blacksmith.

Smith (smith), *n.* **1 Adam,** 1723-1790, Scottish economist. He is considered the first modern economist. **2 Bes·sie** (bes′ē), 1894-1937, American blues singer. Although African Americans bought millions of her records, white audiences were unaware of her beautiful strong voice until shortly before her death. **3** Captain **John,** 1580-1631, English explorer and early settler in Virginia. Pocahontas was believed to have saved his life. **4 Joseph,** 1805-1844, American who founded the Church of Jesus Christ of Latter-day Saints, known as Mormons. **5 Mar·ga·ret Chase** (mär′gə ret chās), 1897-1995, American political leader. She was the first woman elected to both houses of the U.S. Congress and to campaign for the presidential nomination of a major political party.

smith·e·reens (smiтн′ə rēnz′), *n.pl.* small pieces; bits: *smash a chair into smithereens.*

smith·y (smith′ē), *n.* workshop of a blacksmith. ❑ *n., pl.* **smith·ies.**

smit·ten (smit′n), *v.* a past participle of **smite.**

smock (smok), **1** *n.* a loose outer article of clothing worn to protect other clothing. **2** *v.* to ornament a smock, dress, etc., with smocking.

smock·ing (smok′ing), *n.* a honeycomb pattern formed by lines of stitches crossing each other diagonally and gathering the material, used to ornament smocks, dresses, etc.

smog (smog), *n.* **1** a brownish haze of pollution, produced by sunlight acting on the exhaust gases from burning gasoline or petroleum products. It contains ozone and other irritating chemicals. **2** mixture of smoke and fog in the air, produced especially by smoke from burning coal. [**Smog** is a blend of **smoke** and **fog.**]

smog·gy (smog′ē), *adj.* full of smog: *Breathing in the smoggy air, she began to cough.* ❑ *adj.* **smog·gi·er, smog·gi·est.**

smoke (smōk), **1** *n.* the mixture of gases and particles of carbon that can be seen rising in a cloud from anything burning. **2** *n.* mist or vapor that looks something like this. **3** *v.* to give off smoke or steam: *The fireplace smokes. The ruins of the house were still smoking when the fire department left.* **4** *v.* to breathe in the smoke from a cigarette, cigar, pipe, etc., and breathe it out again. **5** *n.* something that is smoked; cigarette, cigar, pipe, etc. **6** *n.* act or period of smoking tobacco: *He went outside for a smoke.* **7** *v.* to preserve and flavor meat or fish by treating it with smoke. ❑ *v.* **smoked, smok·ing.** —**smoke′like′,** *adj.*

go up in smoke, to end without result; be unsuccessful: *Despite all our work, plans for the dance went up in smoke.*

smoke out, 1 to drive out by smoke: *We smoked the woodchuck out of its hole.* **2** to find out and make known: *smoke out a plot.*

smoke and mirrors, anything that distracts attention from facts, figures, etc.; clever deception: *The candidate answered reports of her failures with smoke and mirrors about the media conspiracy against her.*

smoke detector, an electronic device that detects the presence of smoke and sounds an alarm.

smoke·house (smōk′hous′), *n.* building or place in which meat, fish, etc., are treated with smoke to keep them from spoiling. ❑ *n., pl.* **smoke·hous·es** (smōk′hou′ziz).

smoke·jump·er (smōk′jum′pər), *n.* a forester trained to parachute into areas difficult to reach in order to fight fires.

smoke·less (smōk′lis), *adj.* making no smoke; having little smoke: *smokeless powder.*

smokeless tobacco, tobacco products that can be used without smoking, such as snuff and chewing tobacco.

smok·er (smō′kər), *n.* **1** person who smokes tobacco. **2** a railroad car or a part of it where smoking is allowed. **3** (earlier) an informal gathering of men.

smoke·screen (smōk′skrēn′), *n.* mass of thick smoke used to hide troops, ships, airplanes, etc., from the enemy.

smokejumper

smoke·stack (smōk′stak′), *n.* **1** a tall chimney. **2** pipe that discharges smoke: *the smokestack of a steamship.*

smoking gun, clear proof or evidence of something, especially of a crime: *The chocolate stain on his shirt was the smoking gun that identified him as the cake thief.*

smok·y (smō′kē), *adj.* **1** giving off much smoke: *a smoky fire.* **2** full of smoke: *a smoky kitchen.* **3** darkened or stained with smoke. **4** like smoke or suggesting smoke: *a smoky gray, a smoky taste.* ❑ *adj.* **smok·i·er, smok·i·est.** —**smok′i·ly,** *adv.* —**smok′i·ness,** *n.*

smog

smol·der (smōl′dər), **1** *v.* to burn and smoke without flame: *The campfire smoldered for hours after the blaze died down.* **2** *n.* a slow, smoky burning without flame; smoldering fire. **3** *v.* to exist or continue without being let out or expressed: *The people's discontent smoldered for years before it broke out into open rebellion.* **4** *v.* to show barely hidden feeling: *I smoldered with anger and nearly shouted out that the charges against me were all lies.* Also, **smoulder.**

smooch (smüch), SLANG. **1** *v.* to kiss. **2** *n.* a kiss. ❑ *n., pl.* **smooch·es.**

smooth (smüᴛʜ), **1** *adj.* having an even surface, like glass, silk, or still water; flat; level: *smooth stones.* **2** *adj.* free from unevenness or roughness: *smooth sailing, a smooth voyage.* **3** *adj.* without lumps: *smooth gravy.* **4** *v.* to make smooth or smoother; make flat, even, or level: *Smooth this dress with a hot iron. He smoothed out the ball of crushed paper and read it.* **5** *adj.* without trouble or difficulty; easy: *a smooth course of affairs.* **6** *v.* to make easy: *Her tact smoothed the way to an agreement.* **7** *adj.* calm; serene: *a smooth temper.* **8** *adj.* polished; pleasant; polite: *That salesclerk is a smooth talker.* **9** *adj.* not harsh in sound or taste: *smooth verses, smooth wine.* **10** *v.* to make less harsh or crude; polish or refine writing, manners, etc. **11** *adv.* in a smooth manner. —**smooth′ly,** *adv.* —**smooth′ness,** *n.*

smooth away, to get rid of troubles, difficulties, etc.: *He smoothed away all objections to the plan.*

smooth down, to calm; soothe: *She smoothed down her friend's anger.*

smooth over, to make something seem less wrong, unpleasant, or noticeable: *The teacher tried to smooth over the differences between the two students who always quarreled with each other.*

> **SYNONYM STUDY** Smooth, slippery, and slick all mean having no rough or uneven places. Smooth can mean soft or hard: *The baby's skin is so smooth! The stone is smooth from water running over it.* Slippery and slick both mean so smooth that things slide over them: *The road is slippery because of slick ice.*

smooth·bore (smüᴛʜ′bôr′), *n.* gun without grooves in its barrel. A shotgun is a smoothbore.

smooth-faced (smüᴛʜ′fāst′), *adj.* **1** having a smooth face or surface. **2** agreeable in speech and manner: *a smooth-faced hypocrite.*

smooth muscle, a kind of muscle with fibers in smooth layers; involuntary muscle. It contracts without a person's thinking about it. Muscles of the stomach and intestines are smooth muscles.

smor·gas·bord (smôr′gəs bôrd), *n.* a buffet meal with a large variety of meats, salads, appetizers, relishes, etc.

smote (smōt), *v.* a past tense and past participle of **smite:** *The blacksmith smote the horseshoe with a hammer.*

smoth·er (smuᴛʜ′ər), **1** *v.* to make unable to get air; kill by keeping air from: *The gas almost smothered the coal miners but they got out in time.* **2** *v.* to be unable to breathe freely; suffocate: *We are smothering in this stuffy room.* **3** *v.* to cover thickly: *In the fall the grass is smothered with leaves.* **4** *v.* to deaden or put out by covering thickly: *The fire is smothered by ashes.* **5** *v.* to keep back; check; suppress: *He smothered a sharp reply.* **6** *n.* cloud of dust, smoke, spray, etc. —**smoth′er·er,** *n.*

smoul·der (smōl′dər), *v., n.* smolder.

smudge (smuj), **1** *n.* a dirty mark; smear. **2** *v.* to mark with dirty streaks; smear: *The child's drawing was smudged.* **3** *n.* a smoky fire made to drive away insects or to protect fruit and plants from frost. ❑ *v.* **smudged, smudg·ing.**

smudge pot, pot or stove in which oil or other fuel is burned to produce a smoky fire.

smudg·y (smuj′ē), *adj.* smudged; marked with smudges. ❑ *adj.* **smudg·i·er, smudg·i·est.** —**smudg′i·ly,** *adv.* —**smudg′i·ness,** *n.*

smug (smug), *adj.* too pleased with your own goodness, cleverness, respectability, etc.; self-satisfied; complacent: *Nothing disturbs the smug beliefs of some prim, narrow-minded people.* ❑ *adj.* **smug·ger, smug·gest.** —**smug′ly,** *adv.* —**smug′ness,** *n.*

smug·gle (smug′əl), *v.* **1** to bring something into or take something out of a country secretly and against the law, especially without payment of legal duties. **2** to bring, take, put, etc., secretly: *I tried to smuggle my puppy into the house.* ❑ *v.* **smug·gled, smug·gling.** —**smug′gler,** *n.*

smut (smut), **1** *n.* a bit or bits of soot, dirt, etc. **2** *v.* to soil or be soiled with smut: *smut your hands with coal.* **3** *n.* indecent, obscene talk or writing. **4** *n.* any of several plant diseases in which the grain is replaced by black, dustlike spores. **5** *n.* any of several fungi that produce such a disease. ❑ *v.* **smut·ted, smut·ting.**

smut·ty (smut′ē), *adj.* **1** soiled with smut; dirty or sooty. **2** indecent; nasty; obscene. **3** (of plants) having the disease smut. ❑ *adj.* **smut·ti·er, smut·ti·est.** —**smut′ti·ly,** *adv.* —**smut′ti·ness,** *n.*

Smyr·na (smėr′nə), *n.* former name of **Izmir.**

Sn, symbol for tin.

snack (snak), **1** *n.* small amount of food eaten between meals. **2** *v.* to eat a small amount between meals.

snack bar, an eating place, usually with a counter, where quick, small meals are served.

snaf·fle (snaf′əl), **1** *n.* a slender, jointed bit used on a bridle. **2** *v.* to control or manage by such a bit. ❑ *v.* **snaf·fled, snaf·fling.**

snag (snag), **1** *n.* any sharp or rough point that sticks out, such as a bramble or thorn. **2** *v.* to catch on a snag: *She snagged her sweater on a nail.* **3** *n.* a tear made by a snag. **4** *n.* a hidden or unexpected obstacle: *Our plans hit a snag.* **5** *n.* tree or branch held fast in a river or lake. ❑ *v.* **snagged, snag·ging.**

snag·gle·tooth (snag′əl tüth′), *n.* an uneven, broken, or crooked tooth. ❑ *n., pl.* **snag·gle·teeth.**

snag·gy (snag′ē), *adj.* **1** having snags. **2** sticking out sharply or roughly. ❑ *adj.* **snag·gi·er, snag·gi·est.**

snail (snāl), *n.* **1** any of a great many small, soft-bodied animals that crawl very slowly. Most snails have spiral shells on their backs into which they can move for protection. Snails live in water and on land. **2** a lazy, slow-moving person. —**snail′like′,** *adj.*

snake (snāk), **1** *n.* any of many long, slender, crawling or swimming reptiles without limbs. A few snakes are poisonous. **2** *n.* a sly, treacherous person. **3** *n.* a long, flexible metal tool used by plumbers to clean out a drain. **4** *v.* to move, wind, or curve like a snake: *The narrow road snaked through the mountains.* ❑ *v.* **snaked, snak·ing.** —**snake′like′,** *adj.*

Snake, *n.* river flowing from NW Wyoming through Idaho into the Columbia River in Washington.

snake·skin (snāk′skin′), *n.* **1** skin of a snake. **2** leather made from it.

snak·y (snā′kē), *adj.* **1** like a snake; twisting; winding. **2** having many snakes. **3** sly; venomous; treacherous. ❑ *adj.* **snak·i·er, snak·i·est.** —**snak′i·ly,** *adv.* —**snak′i·ness,** *n.*

snap (snap), **1** *v.* to break suddenly or sharply: *The violin string snapped because it was fastened too tight.* **2** *v.* to make or cause to make a sudden, sharp sound: *The teacher snapped her fingers to get our attention.* **3** *n.* a quick, sharp sound: *The box shut with a snap.* **4** *v.* to move, shut, catch, etc., with a snap: *The latch snapped.* **5** *n.* act of breaking suddenly or the sound of breaking: *One snap made the knife useless.* **6** *v.* to make a sudden, quick bite or snatch: *The dog snapped up the meat.* **7** *v.* to seize suddenly; grab: *We snapped up several bargains at the sale.* **8** *n.* a quick, sudden bite or snatch: *The dog made a snap at a fly.* **9** *v.* to speak quickly and sharply: *Don't snap at him; he doesn't understand what you want.* **10** *v.* to move quickly and sharply: *The soldiers snapped to attention.* **11** *n.* a quick, sharp movement: *She moves with snap and energy.* **12** *adj.* made or done suddenly: *A snap judgment is likely to be wrong.* **13** *n.* fastener; clasp: *Several of the snaps of your dress are unfastened.* **14** *n.* a thin, crisp cookie: *We ate a few lemon snaps after school.* **15** *n.* snapshot. **16** *v.* to take a snapshot of. **17** *n.* INFORMAL. an easy job, piece of work, etc.: *Building the model was a snap.* **18** *adj.* INFORMAL. easy: *a snap task.* **19** in football: **a** *v.* to pass back the ball to begin a play. The center snaps the ball to an offensive back, usually the quarterback. **b** *n.* a pass from the center to an offensive back, usually the quarterback. ❑ *v.* **snapped, snap·ping.**

a	hat	ė	term	ô	order	ch	child		
ā	age	i	it	oi	oil	ng	long		a in about
ä	far	ī	ice	ou	out	sh	she		e in taken
â	care	o	hot	u	cup	th	thin	ə	i in pencil
e	let	ō	open	ù	put	ᴛʜ	then		o in lemon
ē	equal	ò	saw	ü	rule	zh	measure		u in circus

S

snap out of it, to change your attitude or habit suddenly: *He was in a bad mood, but then he snapped out of it and started to laugh.*

snap·drag·on (snap′drag′ən), *n.* any of several garden plants with spikes of showy flowers of crimson, purple, white, yellow, etc.

snap·per (snap′ər), *n.* **1** any of numerous large fishes of tropical seas used for food, especially the **red snapper** of the Gulf of Mexico. **2** snapping turtle. **3** someone or something that snaps. ❑ *n., pl.* **snapper** or **snappers** for 1; **snappers** for 2,3.

snapping turtle, either of two large American freshwater turtles that have powerful jaws with which they snap at and seize their prey.

snapdragons

snap·pish (snap′ish), *adj.* **1** quick and sharp in speech or manner; impatient. **2** apt to snap. —**snap′pish·ly,** *adv.* —**snap′pish·ness,** *n.*

snap·py (snap′ē), *adj.* **1** INFORMAL. having smartness, pungency, etc.; crisp; lively; stylish: *snappy cheese, a snappy sports jacket.* **2** snappish; sharp. **3** snapping or crackling in sound: *a snappy fire.* ❑ *adj.* **snap·pi·er, snap·pi·est. —snap′pi·ly,** *adv.* —**snap′pi·ness,** *n.*
make it snappy, INFORMAL. hurry up!

snap·shot (snap′shot′), *n.* photograph taken quickly with a small camera.

snare¹ (snâr), **1** *n.* noose for catching small animals and birds: *They made snares to catch rabbits.* **2** *v.* to catch with a snare: *One day they snared a skunk.* **3** *n.* a trap: *Flattery is a snare in which fools are caught.* **4** *v.* to trap. ❑ *v.* **snared, snar·ing.**

snare² (snâr), *n.* one of the strings of wire or gut stretched across the bottom of a snare drum.

snare drum, a small drum with strings of wire or gut stretched across the bottom to make a rattling sound.

snarl¹ (snärl), **1** *v.* to growl sharply and show your teeth: *The dog snarled at the stranger.* **2** *n.* a sharp, angry growl. **3** *v.* to say or express with a snarl; speak harshly in a sharp, angry tone: *snarl a nasty threat.* **4** *n.* a sharp, angry tone or remark: *She replied with a nasty snarl.* —**snarl′er,** *n.* —**snarl′ing·ly,** *adv.*

snarl² (snärl), **1** *n.* a tangle: *I combed the snarls out of my hair.* **2** *n.* confused situation; confusion: *An accident caused a snarl in traffic.* **3** *v.* to tangle or become tangled: *The kitten snarled the yarn by playing with it. Her hair snarls easily.* **4** *v.* to confuse: *Snow snarled traffic for hours.*

snatch (snach), **1** *v.* to seize suddenly; grasp hastily: *The hawk snatched the rabbit and flew away.* **2** *n.* act of snatching: *The girl made a snatch at the ball.* **3** *v.* to take suddenly: *He snatched off his hat and bowed.* **4** *n.* a short time: *She had a snatch of sleep sitting in her chair.* **5** *n.* a small amount; bit; scrap: *We heard snatches of their conversation as they raised their voices from time to time.* ❑ *n., pl.* **snatch·es.** —**snatch′er,** *n.*
snatch at, 1 to try to seize or grasp: *He snatched at the rail.* **2** to take advantage of eagerly: *She snatched at the chance to travel.*

snaz·zy (snaz′ē), *adj.* SLANG. fancy; flashy: *a snazzy suit.* ❑ *adj.* **snaz·zi·er, snaz·zi·est. —snaz′zi·ness,** *n.*

sneak (snēk), **1** *v.* to move in a stealthy, sly way: *The man sneaked about the barn watching for a chance to steal the horse.* **2** *v.* to get, put, pass, etc., in a stealthy, sly way: *They sneaked the puppy into the house.* **3** *v.* to act like a thief or someone who is ashamed to be seen: *He sneaked in by the back way.* **4** *n.* person who sneaks; a sneaking, cowardly person. **5** *adj.* sly and secret; sneaking: *a sneak attack.* ❑ *v.* **sneaked** or **snuck, sneak·ing.**

SYNONYM STUDY Sneak, prowl, and creep all mean to move in a way that tries to avoid being noticed. Sneak suggests trying to hide: *They got caught sneaking into the movie.* Prowl suggests waiting for a chance to get something: *Police caught the man prowling around the building with burglar's tools.* Creep suggests slow, secret motion: *Creeping toward the bird's nest, the photographer held her camera ready.*

sneak·er (snē′kər), *n.* **1 sneakers,** *pl.* light canvas shoes with rubber soles, used for games, sports, etc. **2** person who sneaks; sneak.

sneak·ing (snē′king), *adj.* **1** cowardly; underhand; concealed. **2** slight but likely: *She had a sneaking suspicion that they knew she had broken the vase.* —**sneak′ing·ly,** *adv.*

sneak·y (snē′kē), *adj.* like someone ashamed to be seen. ❑ *adj.* **sneak·i·er, sneak·i·est. —sneak′i·ly,** *adv.* —**sneak′i·ness,** *n.*

sneer (snir), **1** *v.* to show scorn or contempt by looks or words: *The students sneered at the sentimentality of the poem.* **2** *n.* a look or words expressing scorn or contempt: *She feared sneers more than blows.* **3** *v.* to say or express

sneakers

with scorn or contempt: *"Bah!" he sneered with a curl of his lip.* —**sneer′er,** *n.* —**sneer′ing·ly,** *adv.*

sneeze (snēz), **1** *v.* to force air suddenly and violently through the nose and mouth by an involuntary spasm. A person with a cold often sneezes. *The pepper made her sneeze.* **2** *n.* a sudden, violent forcing of air through the nose and mouth. ❑ *v.* **sneezed, sneez·ing. —sneez′er,** *n.*
sneeze at, INFORMAL. to treat with contempt; despise; scorn: *Ten dollars is not a sum to be sneezed at.*

snick·er (snik′ər), **1** *n.* a half-suppressed and often disrespectful laugh; sly or silly laugh; giggle. **2** *v.* to laugh in this way. Also, **snigger.**

snide (snīd), *adj.* mean or spiteful in a sly way: *a snide remark.* ❑ *adj.* **snid·er, snid·est. —snide′ly,** *adv.* —**snide′ness,** *n.*

sniff (snif), **1** *v.* to draw air through the nose in short, quick breaths that can be heard: *The man who had a cold was sniffing.* **2** *v.* to smell with sniffs: *The dog sniffed suspiciously at the stranger.* **3** *v.* to try the smell of: *I sniffed the medicine before taking a spoonful of it.* **4** *v.* to draw in through the nose with the breath: *He sniffed steam to clear his head.* **5** *n.* act or sound of sniffing: *He cleared his nose with a loud sniff.* **6** *v.* to show your contempt by sniffing: *sniff at an inexpensive gift.* **7** *n.* a single breathing in of something; breath. —**sniff′er,** *n.*

snif·fle (snif′əl), **1** *v.* to sniff again and again as you do from a cold in the head or in trying to stop crying. **2** *n.* act or sound of sniffling. **3** *n.pl.* **the sniffles,** a slight cold in the head. ❑ *v.* **snif·fled, snif·fling. —snif′fler,** *n.*

snig·ger (snig′ər), *n., v.* snicker.

snip (snip), **1** *v.* to cut with a small, quick stroke or series of strokes with scissors: *I snipped the thread.* **2** *n.* act of snipping: *With a few snips I cut out the picture.* **3** *n.* a small piece cut off: *Pick up the snips of cloth and thread from the floor.* **4** *n.pl.* **snips,** hand shears for cutting sheet metal. **5** *n.* INFORMAL. a small or unimportant person. ❑ *v.* **snipped, snip·ping. —snip′per,** *n.*

snipe (snīp), **1** *v.* to shoot at an enemy one at a time from a hidden place. **2** *n.* a marsh bird with a long bill. **3** *v.* to hunt for snipe. ❑ *n., pl.* **snipe** or **snipes;** *v.* **sniped, snip·ing.**

snip·er (snī′pər), *n.* person who shoots at someone from a hidden place; a hidden sharpshooter.

snip·pet (snip′it), *n.* a small piece snipped off; bit; scrap; fragment.

snip·py (snip′ē), *adj.* INFORMAL. **1** sharp; curt: *a snippy reply.* **2** haughty; disdainful. ❑ *adj.* **snip·pi·er, snip·pi·est. —snip′pi·ly,** *adv.* —**snip′pi·ness,** *n.*

snitch¹ (snich), *v.* INFORMAL. to snatch; steal. —**snitch′er,** *n.*

snitch² (snich), INFORMAL. **1** *v.* to be an informer; tell tales. **2** *n.* informer. ❑ *n., pl.* **snitch·es. —snitch′er,** *n.*

sniv·el (sniv′əl), *v.* **1** to cry with sniffling. **2** to put on a show of grief; whine. **3** to run at the nose; sniffle. ❑ *v.* **sniv·eled, sniv·el·ing** or **sniv·elled, sniv·el·ling. —sniv′el·er,** *n.*

snob (snob), *n.* person who cares too much for rank, wealth, position, etc., and too little for real merit; person who tries too hard to please superiors and ignores inferiors.

snob·ber·y (snob′ər ē), *n.* snobbishness.

snob·bish (snob′ish), *adj.* of or like a snob; looking down on those in a lower position: *a snobbish pride in being wealthy.* —**snob′bish·ly,** *adv.* —**snob′bish·ness,** *n.*

snood (snüd), *n.* net or bag worn over a woman's hair.

snoop (snüp), INFORMAL. **1** *v.* to go about in a sneaking, prying way; prowl; pry: *Our neighbor snoops into everybody's business.* **2** *n.* person who snoops. —**snoop′er,** *n.*

snoop·y (snü′pē), *adj.* INFORMAL. eager to pry into the lives of other people; nosy. ❑ *adj.* **snoop·i·er, snoop·i·est.**

snoot·y (snü′tē), *adj.* INFORMAL. having too high an opinion of yourself; apt to look down on others. ❑ *adj.* **snoot·i·er, snoot·i·est.** —**snoot′i·ly,** *adv.* —**snoot′i·ness,** *n.*

> **WORD STORY** **Snooty** comes from **snout.** As you can see from the idioms **look down your nose at** and **turn up your nose at,** stuck-up snooty people often hold their heads high. Their noses are lifted and pointed forward, like an animal's snout.

snooze (snüz), **1** *v.* to take a nap; sleep; doze: *The dog snoozed in the sun.* **2** *n.* a nap; doze. ❑ *v.* **snoozed, snooz·ing.** —**snooz′er,** *n.*

snore (snôr), **1** *v.* to breathe during sleep with a harsh rough sound: *The child had a stuffy nose and snored all night.* **2** *n.* sound made in snoring. ❑ *v.* **snored, snor·ing.** —**snor′er,** *n.*

snor·kel (snôr′kəl), **1** *n.* a curved tube that enables swimmers to breathe underwater while swimming near the surface. **2** *v.* to swim using a snorkel. **3** *n.* pair of metal tubes for taking air in and letting gases out. This device allows submarines to remain under water for a long time. It is like a periscope in shape.

snort (snôrt), **1** *v.* to force the breath violently through the nose with a loud, harsh sound: *The horse snorted.* **2** *v.* to make a sound like this: *The engine snorted.* **3** *n.* act or sound of snorting: *The horse leaped to the side with a loud snort.* **4** *v.* to show contempt, defiance, anger, etc., by snorting. **5** *v.* to say or express with a snort: *"Indeed!" snorted my aunt.* —**snort′er,** *n.*

snout (snout), *n.* **1** the part of an animal's head that sticks forward and contains the nose, mouth, and jaws. Pigs, dogs, and crocodiles have snouts. **2** anything like an animal's snout, such as a nozzle. —**snout′like′,** *adj.*

snow (snō), **1** *n.* water frozen into crystals that fall to earth in soft, white flakes and often spread upon it as a white layer. Rain falls in summer; snow falls in winter. **2** *n.* a fall of snow: *We had a heavy snow yesterday.* **3** *v.* to fall as snow: *to snow all day.* **4** *v.* to let fall or scatter like snow. —**snow′less,** *adj.* —**snow′like′,** *adj.*

snow in, to shut in by snow: *The mountain village was snowed in for almost a week after the blizzard.*

snow under, 1 to cover with snow: *The houses were snowed under by the blizzard.* **2** to overwhelm: *He is snowed under with work.*

snow apple, CANADIAN. a variety of eating apple with firm, white flesh and dark red skin.

snow·ball (snō′bôl′), **1** *n.* ball made of snow pressed together. **2** *v.* to throw balls of snow at: *The children snowballed each other.* **3** *n.* any of several bushes with white flowers in large clusters like balls. **4** *v.* to grow quickly in size, like a rolling snowball: *The number of signers of the petition for a new school snowballed.*

snow·bank (snō′bangk′), *n.* a large mass or drift of snow, especially at the side of a road.

snow·belt (snō′belt′), *n.* **1** any area in which snow falls every year, often heavily. **2 Snowbelt,** the northern area of the United States, especially the Midwest and northeastern states, where there are often heavy snowfalls every winter; frostbelt.

snow·bird (snō′bėrd′), *n.* **1** junco. **2** snow bunting. **3** INFORMAL. person who vacations in a warm climate to escape snow and cold weather.

snow·blind (snō′blīnd′), *adj.* affected with snow blindness.

snow blindness, temporary blindness caused by the reflection of sunlight from snow or ice.

snow·blow·er (snō′blō′ər), *n.* machine that clears snow from sidewalks and driveways by blowing the snow up into the air and off to one side.

snow·bound (snō′bound′), *adj.* shut in by snow; snowed in.

snow bunting, a small, white bird with black and brownish markings that lives in cold regions.

snow·cap (snō′kap′), *n.* covering of snow that piles up on a mountaintop.

snow·capped (snō′kapt′), *adj.* having its top covered with snow: *a snowcapped mountain.*

snow·drift (snō′drift′), *n.* mass or bank of snow piled up by the wind.

snow·drop (snō′drop′), *n.* any of several small plants with white flowers that bloom early in the spring.

snow·fall (snō′fôl′), *n.* **1** a fall of snow. **2** amount of snow falling within a certain time and area: *The snowfall today was 16 inches.*

snow·flake (snō′flāk′), *n.* a small, feathery piece of snow.

snow goose, a wild goose that breeds in the Arctic and migrates to the southern United States in the winter.

snow leopard, a large, fierce cat, something like a leopard, found in the mountains of central Asia; ounce. Snow leopards have thick light-colored fur with dark spots.

snow leopard—about 6 ft. 6 in. (2 m) long with the tail

snow line, line on mountains above which there is always snow.

snow·man (snō′man′), *n.* snow made into a figure something like that of a person. ❑ *n., pl.* **snow·men.**

snow·mo·bile (snō′mō bēl′), **1** *n.* motor vehicle used for traveling on snow. Runners like skis in front are steered by handlebars. Rear tracks or treads are powered by an engine. **2** *v.* to travel by snowmobile. ❑ *v.* **snow·mo·biled, snow·mo·bil·ing.** —**snow′mo·bil′er,** *n.*

snow·plow (snō′plou′), **1** *n.* motor vehicle or attachment for clearing away snow from streets, railroad tracks, etc. **2** *v.* to clear away snow with a snowplow. **3** in skiing: **a** *n.* movement in which the toes of the skis are brought toward one another and the inside edges are pressed into the snow, in order to slow down. **b** *v.* to do such a movement.

snow·shoe (snō′shü′), **1** *n.* a light, wooden frame with strips of leather stretched across it, worn on the feet to keep from sinking into deep, soft snow. **2** *v.* to walk on snowshoes. ❑ *v.* **snow·shoed, snow·shoe·ing.**

snowshoe rabbit or **snowshoe hare,** hare of northern North American with fur that is white in winter and brown in other seasons. Its large, furry hind feet enable it to run on snow.

snow·slide (snō′slīd′), *n.* an avalanche of snow down a steep slope.

snow snake, 1 game played by North American Indians, in which a wooden stick with a weighted head is slid over ice or snow. **2** the stick used to play this game.

snow·storm (snō′stôrm′), *n.* storm with much snow.

snow·suit (snō′süt′), *n.* a warm, lined winter coat and leggings, sometimes made as one piece, worn by children in the winter.

snow-white (snō′wīt′), *adj.* white as snow.

snow·y (snō′ē), *adj.* **1** having snow: *a snowy day.* **2** covered with snow: *a snowy roof.* **3** like snow; white as snow: *My gym teacher has snowy hair.* ❑ *adj.* **snow·i·er, snow·i·est.** —**snow′i·ly,** *adv.* —**snow′i·ness,** *n.*

a	hat	ė	term	ô	order	ch	child		
ā	age	i	it	oi	oil	ng	long		a in about
ä	far	ī	ice	ou	out	sh	she	ə	e in taken
â	care	o	hot	u	cup	th	thin		i in pencil
e	let	ō	open	ů	put	ŦH	then		o in lemon
ē	equal	ò	saw	ü	rule	zh	measure		u in circus

snowy owl, owl with white feathers and brown markings that lives in arctic and other northern regions.

snub (snub), **1** *v.* to treat coldly, scornfully, or with contempt: *snub your neighbors by ignoring them.* **2** *n.* cold, scornful, or disdainful treatment. **3** *v.* to check or stop a rope or cable running out suddenly. **4** *n.* a sudden check or stop. **5** *adj.* short and turned up at the tip: *a snub nose.* ❏ *v.* **snubbed, snub·bing.** **—snub′ber,** *n.*

snub-nosed (snub′nōzd′), *adj.* having a snub nose.

snuck (snuk), *v.* a past tense and past participle of **sneak.**

snuff[1] (snuf), **1** *n.* powdered tobacco taken into the nose. **2** *v.* to draw in through the nose; draw up into the nose. **3** *v.* to sniff; smell: *The dog snuffed at the track of the fox.*

up to snuff, INFORMAL. in perfect order or condition; as good as expected.

snuff[2] (snuf), *v.* **1** to cut or pinch off the burned wick of. **2** to put out a candle; extinguish. **—snuff′er,** *n.*

snuff out, to put an end to suddenly and completely; wipe out: *The new dictator snuffed out the people's hopes for freedom.*

snuff·box (snuf′boks′), *n.* a very small box for holding snuff. ❏ *n., pl.* **snuff·box·es.**

snuff·ers (snuf′ərz), *n.pl.* small tongs for taking off burned wick or putting out the light of a candle.

snuf·fle (snuf′əl), **1** *v.* to breathe noisily through the nose like someone with a cold in the head. **2** *n.* act or sound of breathing noisily through the nose. **3** *v.* to smell; sniff. ❏ *v.* **snuf·fled, snuf·fling. —snuf′fler,** *n.*

snug (snug), **1** *adj.* comfortable and warm; sheltered; cozy: *The cat has found a snug corner behind the stove.* **2** *adj.* fitting closely: *That coat is a little too snug.* **3** *adj.* neat; trim; compact: *The cabins on the boat are snug.* **4** *adv.* in a snug manner. ❏ *adj.* **snug·ger, snug·gest. —snug′ly,** *adv.* **—snug′ness,** *n.*

snug·gle (snug′əl), *v.* to lie or press closely for warmth or comfort or from affection; nestle; cuddle: *The newborn kittens snuggled together in the basket.* ❏ *v.* **snug·gled, snug·gling.**

so[1] (sō), **1** *adv.* in that way; in the same way or degree; as shown: *Do not walk so fast.* **2** *adj.* as stated; true: *Is that really so?* **3** *adv.* in such a way; to such a degree: *He is not so tall as his brother.* **4** *adv.* likewise; also: *She likes dogs; so do I.* **5** *conj.* with the result that; in order that: *Go away so I can rest.* **6** *adv.* very: *You are so kind.* **7** *adv.* very much: *My head aches so.* **8** *adv.* for that reason; accordingly; therefore: *The dog seemed hungry, so we fed it.* **9** *conj.* with the purpose or intention that: *I did the work so you would not need to.* **10** *interj.* So is sometimes used alone to exclaim or to ask a question. *So! late again! The train is late. So?* **11** *pron.* more or less: *It weighs a pound or so.* ■ Other words that sound like this are **sew** and **sow**[1].

and so, 1 likewise; also: *He is here and so is she.* **2** accordingly: *I said I would go, and so I shall.*

so as, with the result or purpose: *I go to bed early so as to get enough sleep.*

so that, with the result or purpose that: *Study so that you will do well.*

so[2] (sō), *n.* sol. ■ Other words that sound like this are **sew** and **sow**[1].

so., **1** south. **2** southern.

So., **1** South. **2** Southern.

soak (sōk), **1** *v.* to make or become very wet; wet through: *The rain soaked my clothes.* **2** *v.* to let remain in water or other liquid until wet clear through: *Soak the clothes all night before you wash them.* **3** *v.* to make its way; enter; go: *Water will soak through the earth.* **4** *n.* act or process of soaking: *Give the clothes a long soak.* **5** INFORMAL. to make pay too much; charge or tax heavily: *I was soaked in the deal.* **—soak′er,** *n.*

soak up, 1 to absorb: *The sponge soaked up the water.* **2** to take into the mind: *soak up knowledge.*

so-and-so (sō′ən sō′), *n.* some person or thing not named. ❏ *n., pl.* **so-and-sos.**

soap (sōp), **1** *n.* substance used for washing, usually made of a fat and lye. **2** *v.* to rub with soap: *Soap your hands well.* **3** *n.* INFORMAL. soap opera.

soap·box (sōp′boks′), *n.* an empty box used as a temporary platform by speakers addressing street meetings. ❏ *n., pl.* **soap·box·es.**

Soap Box Derby, a yearly series of races for young people in small motorless cars, which they must build themselves.

soap opera, a series of dramatic shows on radio or TV, usually broadcast on weekday mornings or afternoons, with many melodramatic emotional crises.

WORD STORY **Soap opera** comes from the fact that many early programs of this sort on radio were sponsored by soap manufacturers. They were called "operas" because of the melodrama.

soap·stone (sōp′stōn′), *n.* a soft rock that feels something like soap, used for carving, and for making heat- and acid-resistant surfaces.

soap·suds (sōp′sudz′), *n.pl.* bubbles and foam on soapy water.

soap·y (sō′pē), *adj.* **1** covered with soap or soapsuds. **2** containing soap: *soapy water.* **3** of or like soap: *a soapy taste.* ❏ *adj.* **soap·i·er, soap·i·est. —soap′i·ly,** *adv.* **—soap′i·ness,** *n.*

soar (sôr), *v.* **1** to fly at a great height; fly upward: *The eagle soared without flapping its wings.* ■ See Synonym Study at **rise.** **2** to rise beyond what is common and ordinary: *Prices are soaring. Her hope soared when she heard that she was a finalist in the contest.* ■ Another word that sounds like this is **sore. —soar′er,** *n.* **—soar′ing·ly,** *adv.*

sob (sob), **1** *v.* to cry or sigh with short, quick breaths: *She sobbed herself to sleep.* ■ See Synonym Study at **cry.** **2** *n.* act of catching short, quick breaths because of grief, anger, etc. **3** *v.* to make a sound like this: *The wind sobbed.* **4** *n.* a sound like this. **5** *v.* to say or express with short, quick breaths: *sob out a sad story.* ❏ *v.* **sobbed, sob·bing.**

so·ber (sō′bər), **1** *adj.* not drunk. **2** *adj.* temperate; moderate: *The Puritans led sober, hard-working lives.* **3** *adj.* quiet; serious; solemn: *He looked sober at the thought of missing the picnic.* **4** *adj.* calm; sensible; free from exaggeration: *sober facts. The judge's sober opinion was not influenced by prejudice or strong feeling.* **5** *v.* to make or become sober: *Seeing the car accident sobered us all.* **6** *adj.* quiet in color: *He was dressed in sober gray.* **—so′ber·ly,** *adv.* **—so′ber·ness,** *n.*

so·ber-mind·ed (sō′bər mīn′did), *adj.* having or showing a sober mind or self-control; sensible.

so·bri·e·ty (sə brī′ə tē), *n.* **1** soberness. **2** temperance in the use of strong drink. **3** moderation. **4** quietness; seriousness.

so·bri·quet (sō′brə kā), *n.* nickname.

soc., **1** social. **2** society.

Soc., **1** Socialist. **2** Society.

so-called (sō′kôld′), *adj.* called so, but really not so; called so improperly or incorrectly: *Her so-called friend hasn't even written to her.*

soc·cer (sok′ər), *n.* game played with a round ball between two teams of eleven players each. The players may strike the ball with any part of the body except the hands and arms. Only the goalkeeper may touch the ball with the hands and arms. Players score by hitting the ball into a net cage at either end of the field.

soccer

so·cia·ble (sō′shə bəl), **1** *adj.* liking company; friendly: *They are a sociable family and entertain a great deal.* **2** *adj.* marked by conversation and companionship: *We had a sociable afternoon together.* **3** *n.* an informal social gathering. **—so′cia·bil′i·ty,** *n.* **—so′cia·bly,** *adv.*

so·cial (sō′shəl), **1** *adj.* of or for human beings in their relations to each other; about the life of human beings in a community or society: *Schools and hospitals are social institutions.* **2** *adj.* liking company: *She has a social nature.* **3** *adj.* living, or liking to live, with others: *People are social beings.* **4** *adj.* connected with fashionable society: *They are the social leaders in our town.* **5** *n.* a friendly gathering or party. **6** *adj.* (of animals) living together in organized communities. Ants and bees are social insects. Lions and wolves are social animals. **7** *adj.* for companionship or friendliness: *They belong to several social clubs.*

WORD FAMILY Social and the words below are related. They all come from a Latin word meaning "companion" or "ally."

antisocial	sociable	socialize	sociology
associate	socialism	society	unsociable
dissociate	socialite		

Social Credit Party, a political party in Canada.

social insurance, (in Canada) monetary benefits paid from governmental or employer funds to people in need, including old-age pensions, social security, Family Allowance, disability insurance, etc.

so·cial·ism (sō′shə liz′əm), *n.* **1** theory or system of social organization by which the major means of production and distribution are owned, managed, or controlled by the government, by associations of workers, or by the community as a whole. **2** a political movement supporting or associated with this system.

so·cial·ist (sō′shə list), **1** *n.* person who favors or supports socialism. **2** *adj.* socialistic. **3** *n.* **Socialist,** member of a Socialist Party. **4** *adj.* **Socialist,** of or about a Socialist Party.

so·cial·is·tic (sō′shə lis′tik), *adj.* **1** of or about socialism or socialists. **2** favoring or supporting socialism. **—so′cial·is′ti·cal·ly,** *adv.*

so·cial·ite (sō′shə līt), *n.* member of the fashionable society of a community.

so·cial·ize (sō′shə līz), *v.* **1** to be social or sociable: *He has never learned to socialize with his fellow workers.* **2** to establish or regulate in accordance with socialism. **3** to make social; make fit for living with others. ❑ *v.* **so·cial·ized, so·cial·iz·ing. —so′cial·i·za′tion,** *n.* **—so′cial·iz′er,** *n.*

socialized medicine, system of providing medical care and hospital services for all citizens of a nation, either free or for a small cost, usually funded by government money.

so·cial·ly (sō′shə lē), *adv.* **1** in a social way or manner; in relation to other people. **2** as a member of society or of a social group: *He is an able man, but socially he is a failure.*

social science, study of people, their activities, their customs, and their institutions in relationship to other people. History, sociology, economics, geography, and civics are social sciences. **—social scientist.**

social security, system of federal old-age pensions and medical care for retired persons and their dependents. The program is financed by the government, the employee, and the employer.

social studies, course of study in elementary schools and high schools that includes history, civics, economics, geography, and other subjects in the social sciences.

social work, work directed toward the betterment of social conditions in a community. Social work includes such services as free medical clinics, counseling for families, and recreational activities for underprivileged children. **—social worker.**

so·ci·e·ty (sə sī′ə tē), *n.* **1** all the people; human beings living together as a group: *Society must work hard for world peace.* **2** the people of any particular time or place: *twentieth-century society, American society.* **3** group of persons joined together for a common purpose or by a common interest. A club, a fraternity, a lodge, or an association may be called a society. **4** the activities and customs of society or of a particular society: *Magic plays an important part in some societies.* **5** company; companionship: *I enjoy their society.* **6** fashionable people or their doings: *Her parents are leaders of society.* ❑ *n., pl.* **so·ci·e·ties** for 2-4.

Society Islands, group of French islands in the S Pacific that includes Tahiti.

Society of Friends, the Quakers.

Society of Jesus, the religious order of the Jesuits.

so·ci·o·log·i·cal (sō′sē ə loj′ə kəl), *adj.* **1** of or about human society or problems relating to it: *Unemployment is a sociological problem.* **2** of or about sociology. **—so′ci·o·log′i·cal·ly,** *adv.*

so·ci·ol·o·gy (sō′sē ol′ə jē), *n.* study of the nature, origin, and development of human society and community life; science of society. Sociology deals with social conditions, such as crime and poverty, and social institutions, such as marriage, the family, and the school. **—so′ci·ol′o·gist,** *n.*

sock¹ (sok), *n.* a short, close-fitting, knitted covering for the foot and ankle, sometimes one that reaches about halfway to the knee. **—sock′less,** *adj.* **—sock′like′,** *adj.*

sock² (sok), **1** *v.* to strike or hit hard. **2** *n.* a hard blow.

sock·et (sok′it), *n.* a hollow part or piece for receiving and holding something. A candlestick has a socket in which to set a candle. A person's eyes are set in sockets. An electric lamp has a socket into which a bulb is screwed.

sock·eye (sok′ī), *n.* a small greenish blue salmon of the coasts of Alaska and British Columbia, known for its flavorful, red, oily flesh.

Soc·ra·tes (sok′rə tēz′), *n.* 469?-399 B.C., Athenian philosopher whose teachings were written down by his disciple Plato. ■ Socrates was accused of corrupting the beliefs of the young people of Athens and of disrespecting religion. He was sentenced to death and drank hemlock poison.

So·crat·ic (sō krat′ik), *adj.* of or about Socrates, his philosophy, followers, etc.

sod (sod), **1** *n.* ground covered with grass. **2** *n.* piece or layer of this containing the grass and its roots. **3** *v.* to cover with sod: *We sodded the bare spots in our lawn.* ❑ *v.* **sod·ded, sod·ding.**

sod—house built of pieces of sod in horizontal layers

so·da (sō′də), *n.* **1** soda pop. **2** soda water flavored with fruit juice or syrup and with ice cream in it. **3** soda water. **4** any of several chemical substances containing sodium, such as sodium bicarbonate or baking soda, sodium carbonate or sal soda, and sodium hydroxide or caustic soda. ❑ *n., pl.* **so·das** for 1,2.

soda cracker, a light, thin cracker made with little or no sugar or fat.

soda fountain, counter with places for holding soda water, flavored syrups, ice cream, etc.

so·dal·i·ty (sō dal′ə tē), *n.* **1** fellowship; friendship. **2** (in the Roman Catholic Church) a lay society with religious or charitable purposes. ❑ *n., pl.* **so·dal·i·ties** for 2.

soda pop, soft drink.

soda water, water charged with carbon dioxide to make it bubble and fizz, often served with the addition of syrup, ice cream, etc.; club soda.

a	hat	ė	term	ô	order	ch	child		
ā	age	i	it	oi	oil	ng	long		a in about
ä	far	ī	ice	ou	out	sh	she	ə	e in taken
â	care	o	hot	u	cup	th	thin		i in pencil
e	let	ō	open	ù	put	ŦH	then		o in lemon
ē	equal	ò	saw	ü	rule	zh	measure		u in circus

S

sod·den (sod'n), *adj.* soaked through: *The girl's clothes were sodden with rain.* —**sod'den·ly**, *adv.* —**sod'den·ness**, *n.*

so·di·um (sō'dē əm), *n.* a soft, silver-white, metallic element that reacts violently with water. It occurs in nature only in combination with other elements. Salt and soda contain sodium. *Symbol:* Na

sodium bicarbonate, a white crystalline powder used in baking, medicine, manufacturing, etc.; baking soda; bicarbonate of soda.

sodium carbonate, a white crystalline powder used for softening water, making soap and glass, and in medicine and photography; sal soda.

sodium chloride, salt (def. 1).

sodium fluoride, a crystalline substance used in the fluoridation of water and to prevent tooth decay.

sodium hydroxide, a white solid substance that is a strong, corrosive alkali; caustic soda. It is used in making soap and as a bleaching agent.

sodium nitrate, a colorless, crystalline compound used in making fertilizer, rocket fuel, and explosives; saltpeter; niter.

Sod·om (sod'əm), *n.* (in the Bible) a wicked city destroyed, together with Gomorrah, by fire from heaven.

so·fa (sō'fə), *n.* a long, upholstered seat or couch having a back and arms. ❑ *n., pl.* **so·fas.**

So·fi·a (sō fē'ə), *n.* capital of Bulgaria, in the W part. [*Sofia* comes from a Greek word meaning "wisdom." It was named for a church honoring divine wisdom.]

soft (sôft), **1** *adj.* not hard; not stiff; yielding easily to touch: *a soft pillow. Feathers, cotton, and wool are soft.* **2** *adj.* not hard compared with other things of the same sort: *Pine is softer than oak. Copper and lead are softer than steel.* **3** *adj.* pleasant to the touch; not rough or coarse; smooth: *soft fur, soft silk.* **4** *adj.* not loud: *a soft voice.* **5** *adj.* quietly pleasant; mild; not harsh: *a soft spring morning, soft words, soft candlelight.* **6** *adj.* gentle; kind; tender: *a soft heart, soft eyes.* **7** *adj.* weak; out of condition; not fit: *become soft from lack of exercise.* **8** *adv.* softly; quietly; gently. **9** *adj.* free from minerals that keep soap from forming suds: *Soft water is easy to wash clothes with.* **10** *adj.* having a more or less hissing sound. The *c* is soft in *city* and hard in *corn; g* is soft in *gentle* and hard in *get.* **11** *adj.* easy; easygoing: *a soft job, a soft person.* —**soft'ly,** *adv.* —**soft'ness,** *n.*

SYNONYM STUDY Soft, limp², and **yielding** all mean not hard. **Soft** is a general word: *After a week in a sleeping bag, it is good to sleep in a soft bed.* **Limp** means so easy to bend that it will not stay straight: *Boil the noodles until they are limp.* **Yielding** means easy to push into: *The pigeons left footprints in the yielding cement.*

---

soft·ball (sôft'bôl'), *n.* **1** a kind of baseball that is played on a smaller field, with a larger and softer ball. A softball must be pitched underhand. **2** the ball used in this game.

soft-boiled (sôft'boild'), *adj.* (of an egg) boiled only a little so that the yolk is still soft.

soft coal, bituminous coal.

soft drink, a sweetened, flavored drink, made with soda water and containing no alcohol.

soft·en (sôf'ən), *v.* to make or become soft: *Hand lotion softens the skin.* —**soft'en·er,** *n.*

soft·en·er (sôf'ən ər), *n.* **1** any mixture added to a substance to make it softer or smoother. **2** water softener.

soft-heart·ed (sôft'här'tid), *adj.* gentle; kind; tender. —**soft'heart'ed·ly,** *adv.* —**soft'heart'ed·ness,** *n.*

soft landing, a landing of a spacecraft, module, scientific equipment, etc., at a speed slow enough to avoid serious damage.

soft palate, the fleshy back part of the roof of the mouth.

soft shoe, tap dance using shoes that have no metal taps.

soft-shoe (sôft'shü'), *v.* to dance a soft shoe. ❑ *v.* **soft-shoed, soft-shoe·ing.**

soft shoulder, soft earth along the edge of a paved road or highway.

soft-spo·ken (sôft'spō'kən), *adj.* **1** speaking with a soft voice. **2** spoken softly: *a soft-spoken reply.*

soft spot, **1** a tender or sentimental feeling: *I have a soft spot in my heart for Cape Cod.* **2** a weak or exposed part or area; a place easily attacked.

soft·ware (sôft'wâr'), *n.* instructions for a computer or computer system; programs.

soft·wood (sôft'wúd'), **1** *n.* the soft, easily cut wood of such trees as pine, fir, hemlock, and redwood. **2** *n.* any of such trees, having needles or lacking broad leaves. **3** *adj.* of such trees or wood: *softwood forests.*

soft·y (sôf'tē), *n.* INFORMAL. **1** a foolish or weak person. **2** someone easily moved to show emotion. ❑ *n., pl.* **soft·ies.**

sog·gy (sog'ē), *adj.* **1** thoroughly wet; soaked: *The wash on the line was soggy from the rain.* **2** damp and heavy: *We couldn't eat the heavy, soggy bread.* ■ See Synonym Study at **wet.** ❑ *adj.* **sog·gi·er, sog·gi·est.** [**Soggy** comes from a word used in some parts of England, meaning "a swamp." Things are likely to get soggy in a swamp.] —**sog'gi·ly,** *adv.* —**sog'gi·ness,** *n.*

soil¹ (soil), *n.* **1** ground; earth; dirt. **2** land; country: *This is my native soil.* —**soil'less,** *adj.*

soil² (soil), *v.* **1** to make or become dirty: *I soiled my clean clothes. White shirts soil easily.* **2** to disgrace; dishonor: *False rumors can soil your good name.*

soi·ree (swä rā'), *n.* an evening party or social gathering. ❑ *n., pl.* **soi·rees.**

soi·rée (swä rā'), *n.* soiree. ❑ *n., pl.* **soi·rées.**

so·journ (sō'jėrn ⌐ or sō jėrn' for verb; sō'jėrn' for noun), **1** *v.* to stay for a time: *The Israelites sojourned in the land of Egypt.* **2** *n.* a brief stay; a stay that is not permanent: *During his sojourn in Africa he learned much about tribal customs.* —**so'journ'er,** *n.*

sol (sōl), *n.* the fifth tone of the musical scale. Also, **so.** ■ Other words that sound like this are **sole** and **soul.**

Sol (sol), *n.* **1** the Roman god of the sun. **2** the sun.

sol·ace (sol'is), **1** *n.* comfort or relief: *She found solace from her troubles in music.* **2** *v.* to comfort or relieve; cheer: *He solaced himself with a book.* ❑ *v.* **sol·aced, sol·ac·ing.** —**sol'ac·er,** *n.*

so·lar (sō'lər), *adj.* **1** of or from the sun: *a solar eclipse, solar rays.* **2** measured by Earth's motion in relation to the sun: *solar time.* **3** working by means of sunlight: *solar heating.*

solar battery, battery containing a large number of solar cells.

solar cell, device that changes sunlight directly into electricity.

solar collector, device for collecting heat from sunlight. It usually has glass panels over a black surface with a space between for liquid or air to flow and collect heat.

solar flare, a sudden eruption on the surface of the sun, usually associated with sunspots.

so·lar·i·um (sə lâr'ē əm), *n.* room, porch, etc., where people can lie or sit in the sun. ❑ *n., pl.* **so·lar·i·ums, so·lar·i·a** (sə lâr'ē ə).

solar panel, panel of connected solar cells.

solar panel

solar plexus, network of nerves situated at the upper part of the abdomen, behind the stomach and in front and on the sides of the aorta.

solar system, the sun and all the planets, satellites, comets, etc., that revolve around it.

solar wind, a continuous flow of electrically charged particles from the sun, extending to the edge of the solar system.

solar year, time for the earth to make one revolution around the sun. It is about 365¼ days.

sold (sōld), *v.* past tense and past participle of **sell**: *She sold her car a week ago. She has sold it to a friend.*

sol·der (sod′ər), **1** *n.* metal or alloy that can be melted and used for joining or mending metal surfaces, parts, etc. **2** *v.* to fasten, mend, or join with such a metal or alloy: *She soldered the broken wires together.* —**sol′der·a·ble,** *adj.* —**sol′der·er,** *n.*

sol·dier (sōl′jər), **1** *n.* person who serves in an army. **2** *n.* an enlisted man or woman in the army who is not a commissioned officer. **3** *n.* person who serves in any cause: *Christian soldiers.* **4** *v.* to act or serve as a soldier.

WORD STORY Soldier comes from a Latin word meaning "solid." Solid comes from the same Latin word. One kind of gold coin in ancient Rome was called a solid coin (the phrase *solid gold* is still used in English). Soldier first meant someone who was paid to fight, unlike many people in old-time armies who were simply forced to serve. Paid armies tended to win wars, so after a while most troops were soldiers.

sol·dier·ly (sōl′jər lē), *adj.* like a soldier; like that of a soldier. —**sol′dier·li·ness,** *n.*

soldier of fortune, person serving or ready to serve as a soldier under any government for money, adventure, or pleasure.

sole¹ (sōl), *adj.* **1** one and only; single: *He was the sole heir to the fortune when his aunt died.* **2** only: *We three were the sole survivors from the wreck.* **3** not shared with others; of or for only one person or group and not others; exclusive: *That company has the sole right to manufacture this drug.* ■ Other words that sound like this are **sol** and **soul.** —**sole′ness,** *n.*

sole² (sōl), **1** *n.* the bottom or underside of the foot. **2** *n.* bottom of a shoe, slipper, boot, etc. **3** *v.* to put a sole on: *I must have my shoes soled.* ❑ *v.* **soled, sol·ing.** ■ Other words that sound like this are **sol** and **soul.**

sole³ (sōl), *n.* any of various flatfishes. European sole is valued highly as food. ❑ *n., pl.* **sole** or **soles.** ■ Other words that sound like this are **sol** and **soul.**

sol·e·cism (sol′ə siz′əm), *n.* **1** mistake in using words: *"I done it" is a solecism.* **2** mistake in social behavior; breach of good manners or etiquette.

sole·ly (sōl′lē), *adv.* **1** as the only one or ones; alone: *You will be solely responsible for providing the lunch.* **2** only: *Bananas grow outdoors solely in warm climates.*

sol·emn (sol′əm), *adj.* **1** serious; dignified; earnest: *to speak in a solemn voice. I gave my solemn promise to try harder.* ■ See Synonym Study at **serious.** **2** impressive; causing serious thoughts: *solemn music.* **3** done with form and ceremony: *a solemn procession.* **4** connected with religion; sacred. **5** gloomy; dark; somber in color. —**sol′emn·ly,** *adv.* —**sol′emn·ness,** *n.*

so·lem·ni·ty (sə lem′nə tē), *n.* **1** solemn feeling; seriousness; impressiveness: *The solemnity of the occasion was felt even by the children.* **2** a solemn, formal ceremony: *Passover is observed with solemnities.* ❑ *n., pl.* **so·lem·ni·ties** for 2.

sol·em·nize (sol′əm nīz), *v.* **1** to observe with ceremonies: *Christian churches solemnize the resurrection of Jesus at Easter.* **2** to hold or perform a ceremony or service: *The marriage was solemnized in the temple.* **3** to make serious; dignify. ❑ *v.* **sol·em·nized, sol·em·niz·ing.** —**sol′em·ni·za′tion,** *n.* —**sol′em·niz′er,** *n.*

sol·e·noid (sō′lə noid), *n.* a cylindrical coil of wire that becomes a magnet when an electric current passes through it. Solenoids are used in starters and other electromagnetic switches.

so·lic·it (sə lis′it), *v.* **1** to ask earnestly; try to get: *The new store is soliciting customers through newspaper advertising.* **2** to make appeals or requests: *solicit for contributions to the Red Cross.* —**so·lic′i·ta′tion,** *n.*

so·lic·i·tor (sə lis′ə tər), *n.* **1** person who solicits, especially for charity. **2** lawyer. In England a solicitor prepares a case and gives advice, but can plead a case only in a lower court. **3** lawyer for a town, city, state, etc.

so·lic·i·tous (sə lis′ə təs), *adj.* **1** showing care or concern; anxious; concerned: *Parents are solicitous for their children's progress in school.* **2** desirous; eager: *solicitous to please.* —**so·lic′i·tous·ly,** *adv.* —**so·lic′i·tous·ness,** *n.*

so·lic·i·tude (sə lis′ə tüd), *n.* anxious care; anxiety; concern.

sol·id (sol′id), **1** *n.* substance that is not a liquid or a gas. Iron, wood, and ice are solids. **2** *adj.* not liquid or gaseous: *Water becomes solid when it freezes.* **3** *adj.* in the form of a solid; not liquid: *After I had my tooth pulled I couldn't eat solid food.* **4** *adj.* not hollow: *A bar of iron is solid; a pipe is hollow.* **5** *n.* object or shape that has height, width, and thickness. A cube is a solid. **6** *adj.* strongly put together; hard; firm: *They were glad to leave the boat and put their feet on solid ground.* **7** *adj.* the same throughout: *The cloth is a solid blue.* **8** *adj.* firmly united: *The country was solid for peace.* **9** *adj.* real; serious: *Latin and physics are solid subjects.* **10** *adj.* able to be depended on: *a solid citizen.* **11** *adj.* having good judgment; sound; sensible; intelligent: *a serious book by a solid thinker.* **12** *adj.* unbroken; without interruption: *I spent a solid hour on my geometry.* **13** *adj.* undivided; continuous: *a solid row of houses.* **14** *adj.* having height, width, and thickness; three-dimensional. **15** *adv.* completely: *The subway was packed solid with commuters.* [See Word Story at **soldier.**] —**sol′id·ly,** *adv.* —**sol′id·ness,** *n.*

sol·i·dar·i·ty (sol′ə dar′ə tē), *n.* unity or fellowship arising from common responsibilities and interests.

solid geometry, branch of mathematics that deals with objects having the three dimensions of length, breadth, and thickness.

so·lid·i·fy (sə lid′ə fī), *v.* **1** to make or become solid; harden: *The melted butter solidified as it cooled.* **2** to unite firmly. ❑ *v.* **so·lid·i·fied, so·lid·i·fy·ing.** —**so·lid′i·fi′a·ble,** *adj.* —**so·lid′i·fi·ca′tion,** *n.* —**so·lid′i·fi′er,** *n.*

so·lid·i·ty (sə lid′ə tē), *n.* condition or quality of being solid; firmness or hardness; substantial quality: *the solidity of marble or steel, the solidity of a person's character.*

sol·id-state (sol′id stāt′), *adj.* **1** of or about solid-state physics. **2** made with transistors, printed circuits, etc. Tiny solid-state devices have replaced larger parts, such as vacuum tubes, in many radios, TVs, and other appliances.

solid-state physics, branch of physics that deals with the qualities of solid materials, such as mechanical strength, the movement of electrons, and the nature of crystals. Research in solid-state physics has produced the transistor and a number of other semiconductor devices.

so·lil·o·quize (sə lil′ə kwīz), *v.* to speak a soliloquy. ❑ *v.* **so·lil·o·quized, so·lil·o·quiz·ing.** —**so·lil′o·quiz′er,** *n.*

so·lil·o·quy (sə lil′ə kwē), *n.* **1** speech made by an actor to himself or herself. It reveals the actor's thoughts and feelings to the audience, but not to the other characters in the play. **2** act of talking to yourself. ❑ *n., pl.* **so·lil·o·quies.**

sol·i·taire (sol′ə târ), *n.* **1** any card game played by one person. **2** diamond or other gem set by itself.

sol·i·tar·y (sol′ə ter′ē), *adj.* **1** without companions; away from people; lonely. **2** alone; single; only: *A solitary rider was seen in the distance.* —**sol′i·tar′i·ly,** *adv.* —**sol′i·tar′i·ness,** *n.*

sol·i·tude (sol′ə tüd), *n.* **1** condition of being alone: *He likes company and hates solitude.* **2** a lonely place: *This forest is a solitude.* **3** loneliness.

so·lo (sō′lō), **1** *n.* piece of music for one voice or instrument: *She sang three solos.* **2** *adj.* arranged for and performed by one voice or instrument: *He played the solo part.* **3** *adj.* without a partner, teacher, etc.; alone: *The flying student made her first solo flight.* **4** *n.* anything done without a partner, teacher, etc. **5** *v.* to make a flight alone in an airplane. ❑ *n., pl.* **so·los;** *v.* **so·loed, so·lo·ing.**

WORD FAMILY Solo and the words below are related. They all come from a Latin word meaning "alone."

desolate	solely	solitaire	solitude
sole¹	soliloquy	solitary	sullen

so·lo·ist (sō′lō ist), *n.* person who sings or plays a solo or solos.

a	hat	ė	term	ô	order	ch	child	
ā	age	i	it	oi	oil	ng	long	a in about
ä	far	ī	ice	ou	out	sh	she	e in taken
â	care	o	hot	u	cup	th	thin	ə i in pencil
e	let	ō	open	u̇	put	ᴛʜ	then	o in lemon
ē	equal	ȯ	saw	ü	rule	zh	measure	u in circus

Sol·o·mon (sol′ə mən), *n.* (in the Bible) king of Israel who lived in the 900s B.C. Solomon was a son of David. He was famous for his wisdom and for the great temple which he had built in Jerusalem. [**Solomon** comes from a Hebrew word meaning "peaceful."]

Solomon Islands, island country consisting of many small islands in the S Pacific, northeast of Australia. *Capital:* Honiara. See **Australasia** for map.

so long, INFORMAL. good-by; farewell.

sol·stice (sol′stis), *n.* either of the two times in the year when the sun appears to be farthest north or south in the sky. In the Northern Hemisphere, June 21 or 22, the **summer solstice**, is the longest day of the year and December 21 or 22, the **winter solstice**, is the shortest.

sol·u·bil·i·ty (sol′yə bil′ə tē), *n.* quality of dissolving easily: *the solubility of sugar in water.*

sol·u·ble (sol′yə bəl), *adj.* 1 able to dissolve: *Salt is soluble in water.* 2 able to be solved: *This problem is soluble.* —**sol′u·ble·ness,** *n.*

sol·ute (sol′yüt *or* sō′lüt), *n.* substance that has dissolved in a solution: *Salt is a solute in seawater.*

so·lu·tion (sə lü′shən), *n.* 1 act or process of solving a problem: *That problem was hard; its solution required many hours.* 2 explanation: *The police are seeking a solution of the crime.* 3 mixture formed by combining one substance with another so that the molecules of each are evenly distributed throughout, but not chemically changed: *Salt and water form a solution.* 4 act or process of forming such a mixture: *the solution of carbon dioxide in water.* 5 (in mathematics) any number that makes an open sentence into a true statement.

solution set, the set which contains all the solutions of an equation or inequality.

solv·a·ble (sol′və bəl), *adj.* capable of being solved. —**solv′a·bil′i·ty,** *n.*

solve (solv), *v.* to find the answer to; clear up; explain: *The detective solved the mystery. He has solved all the problems in the lesson.* ❑ *v.* **solved, solv·ing.** —**solv′er,** *n.*

sol·ven·cy (sol′vən sē), *n.* ability to pay all you owe.

sol·vent (sol′vənt), 1 *adj.* able to pay all you owe: *A bankrupt company is not solvent.* 2 *n.* substance, usually a liquid, that can dissolve other substances: *Water is a solvent of sugar and salt.* 3 *adj.* able to dissolve: *Dry cleaning fluid is a solvent liquid that removes dirt.*

Sol·zhe·ni·tsyn (sol′zhə nē′tsən), *n.* **Alexander,** born 1918, Russian writer. ■ Alexander Solzhenitsyn wrote about his experiences in Soviet prison and labor camps. He won the 1970 Nobel Prize for literature. His citizenship was revoked in 1974, and he was deported from the Soviet Union.

So·ma·lia (sə mä′lyə), *n.* country in E Africa, on the Indian Ocean. *Capital:* Mogadishu.

so·mat·ic (sō mat′ik), *adj.* of or about the body.

somatic cell, any cell of a living thing, except a germ cell.

som·ber (som′bər), *adj.* 1 having deep shadows; dark; gloomy: *A cloudy winter day is somber. It was a somber room with dark furniture and heavy black hangings.* 2 sad; gloomy; dismal: *His losses made him very somber.* —**som′ber·ly,** *adv.* —**som′ber·ness,** *n.*

som·brer·o (som brer′ō), *n.* a hat with a broad brim worn in the southwestern United States, Mexico, and Spain. ❑ *n., pl.* **som·brer·os.**

WORD STORY Sombrero comes from a Spanish word that comes from Latin words meaning "under" and "shade." If you are wearing a sombrero, your face is in the shade under the brim.

some (sum), 1 *adj.* certain or particular, but not known or named: *Some dogs are larger than others.* 2 *adj.* a number of: *Ask some friends to help you. I left the city some years ago.* 3 *adj.* a quantity of: *Drink some milk.* 4 *pron.* a certain number or quantity: *She ate some and gave the rest away.* 5 *adj.* a; any: *Can't you find some kind person who will help you?* 6 *adv.* about: *Some twenty people asked for work.* 7 *adj.* INFORMAL. very big, bad, etc.; remarkable: *That was some storm!* ■ Another word that sounds like this is **sum.**

-some[1], *suffix.* 1 tending to ___: *meddlesome = tending to meddle.* 2 causing ___: *troublesome = causing trouble.*

-some[2], *suffix.* group of ___: *foursome = group of four.*

some·bod·y (sum′bod′ē), 1 *pron.* person not known or named; some person; someone: *Somebody has taken my pen.* 2 *n.* person of importance: *She acts as if she were somebody since she won the prize.* ❑ *n., pl.* **some·bod·ies.**

some·day (sum′dā), *adv.* at some future time.

some·how (sum′hou), *adv.* in a way not known or not stated; in one way or another: *I'll finish this work somehow.*

some·one (sum′wun), *pron.* some person; somebody: *Someone is coming.*

some·place (sum′plās), *adv.* in or to some place; somewhere: *I'm sure they live around here someplace.*

som·er·sault (sum′ər sôlt), 1 *n.* a run or jump, turning the heels over the head. 2 *v.* to run or jump, turning the heels over the head.

some·thing (sum′thing), 1 *n.* some thing; a particular thing not named or known: *I'm sure I've forgotten something.* 2 *n.* a certain amount or quantity; a part; a little: *There is something of his father in his smile.* 3 *adv.* somewhat; to some extent or degree: *She is something like her father.* 4 *n.* thing or person of some value or importance: *He thinks he's something.*

some·time (sum′tīm), 1 *adv.* at one time or another: *Come to see me sometime.* 2 *adv.* at an indefinite point of time: *It happened sometime last May.* 3 *adj.* former: *a sometime pupil of our school.*

some·times (sum′tīmz), *adv.* now and then; at times: *She comes to visit sometimes.*

some·way (sum′wā), *adv.* in some way.

some·what (sum′wät), 1 *adv.* to some extent or degree; slightly: *My hat is somewhat like yours.* 2 *n.* some part; some amount: *The large gift came as somewhat of a surprise.*

some·where (sum′wâr), *adv.* 1 in or to some place; in or to one place or another: *She lives somewhere in the neighborhood.* 2 at some time: *It happened somewhere in the last century.*

som·me·lier (sum′əl yā′), *n.* person who chooses wines for a restaurant and recommends them to customers.

som·nam·bu·lism (som nam′byə liz′əm), *n.* sleepwalking.

som·nam·bu·list (som nam′byə list), *n.* sleepwalker.

som·no·lence (som′nə ləns), *n.* sleepiness; drowsiness.

som·no·lent (som′nə lənt), *adj.* 1 sleepy; drowsy. 2 tending to produce sleep: *The music had a somnolent effect.* —**som′no·lent·ly,** *adv.*

son (sun), *n.* 1 a male child. A boy or man is the son of his father and mother. 2 a male descendant. 3 **the Son,** Jesus. ■ Another word that sounds like this is **sun.**

so·nar (sō′när), *n.* device for finding the depth of water or for detecting and locating underwater objects. Sonar sends sound waves into water, and they are reflected back when they strike the bottom or any object. [**Sonar** comes from sound navigation ranging.]

so·na·ta (sə nä′tə), *n.* piece of music for one or two instruments, having three or four movements in contrasted rhythms but related keys. ❑ *n., pl.* **so·na·tas.**

son·a·ti·na (son′ə tē′nə), *n.* a short or simple sonata. ❑ *n., pl.* **son·a·ti·nas.**

Sond·heim (sond′hīm), *n.* **Steph·en** (stē′vən), born 1930, American composer and lyricist. He wrote the lyrics for *West Side Story* and won a Pulitzer Prize in 1985 for *Sunday in the Park with George.*

song (sông), *n.* 1 something to sing; a short poem set to music. 2 music to fit a poem; singing: *The canary burst into song.* 3 poetry that has a musical sound. 4 any sound like singing: *the cricket's song, the song of the teakettle.*

for a song, very cheap: *He bought several sleeping bags for a song.*

song and dance, a long explanation or excuse, usually untrue: *When I asked him why he was late, he gave me some song and dance about the street signs being hidden by trees.*

song·bird (sông′bėrd′), *n.* bird that sings.

Son·ghai (song gī′), *n.* member of a group of people living mostly along the Niger river, where they ruled an empire in the 1400s and 1500s. □ *n., pl.* **Songhais** or **Son·ghai.**

Songhai Empire (1591)

SONGHAI EMPIRE

Walata

Senegal R.

Kumbi Saleh ● Timbuktu ● Gao

● Jenne

● Kangaba

Niger R.

ATLANTIC OCEAN

song·less (sòng′lis), *adj.* not able to sing. —**song′less·ly,** *adv.* —**song′less·ness,** *n.*

Song of Solomon, The, book of the Bible.

Song of Songs, Song of Solomon.

song sparrow, a small North American sparrow with a streaked chest and a central chest spot. It is known for its frequent, tuneful song.

song·writ·er (sòng′rī′tər), *n.* composer of popular songs or tunes.

song·writ·ing (sòng′rī′ting), *n.* the composition of popular songs or tunes.

son·ic (son′ik), *adj.* **1** of or about sound waves. **2** of or about the rate at which sound travels through air. At sea level the rate is 1087 feet (331 meters) per second. —**son′i·cal·ly,** *adv.*

sonic barrier, a sudden increase in air resistance against an aircraft or projectile as it nears the speed of sound; sound barrier.

sonic boom, a very loud noise caused by shock waves that are produced by an aircraft moving faster than the speed of sound. As the shock waves move down and touch the earth's surface, they produce explosive sounds.

son-in-law (sun′in lò′), *n.* husband of your daughter. □ *n., pl.* **sons-in-law.**

son·net (son′it), *n.* poem having 14 lines with a fixed measure and a formal arrangement of rhymes.

son·net·eer (son′ə tir′), *n.* writer of sonnets.

son·ny (sun′ē), *n.* little son. *Sonny* is used as a pet name, or as a way of speaking to a little boy. ■ Another word that sounds like this is **sunny.**

son·o·gram (son′ə gram′), *n.* image of an internal organ of the body or of a fetus, produced by ultrasound.

So·no·ra (sə nôr′ə), *n.* a state in NW Mexico.

so·no·ri·ty (sə nôr′ə tē), *n.* sonorous quality or condition.

so·no·rous (sə nôr′əs), *adj.* **1** giving out or having a deep loud sound: *a big, sonorous church bell.* **2** full and rich in sound: *a sonorous voice.* **3** having an impressive sound; high-sounding: *sonorous phrases, a sonorous style.* —**so·no′rous·ly,** *adv.*

Sons of Freedom, a sect of the Doukhobors that live mainly in British Columbia.

soon (sün), *adv.* **1** in a short time; before long: *I will see you again soon.* **2** before the usual or expected time; early: *Why have you come so soon?* **3** promptly; quickly: *As soon as I hear, I will let you know.* **4** readily; willingly: *I would as soon die as have to go through such a terrible experience again.*

soot (sùt), *n.* a black substance in the smoke from burning coal, wood, oil, etc. Soot collects on the inside of chimneys.

soothe (süŦH), *v.* **1** to quiet; calm; comfort: *The mother soothed the crying child.* **2** to make less painful; relieve; ease: *Heat soothes some aches; cold soothes others.* □ *v.* **soothed, sooth·ing.** —**sooth′er,** *n.*

sooth·ing (sü′ŦHing), *adj.* tending to soothe: *soothing cough syrup.* —**sooth′ing·ly,** *adv.* —**sooth′ing·ness,** *n.*

sooth·say·er (süth′sā′ər), *n.* person who claims to foretell the future; person who makes prophecies or predictions.

soothsayer

sooth·say·ing (süth′sā′ing), *n.* the foretelling of future events; prediction or prophecy.

soot·y (sùt′ē), *adj.* **1** covered or blackened with soot. **2** dark brown or black; dark-colored. □ *adj.* **soot·i·er, soot·i·est.** —**soot′i·ly,** *adv.* —**soot′i·ness,** *n.*

sop (sop), **1** *v.* to take up water, etc.; wipe; mop: *Please sop up that water with a cloth.* **2** *n.* piece of food dipped or soaked in milk, broth, etc. **3** *v.* to dip or soak: *to sop bread in milk.* **4** *n.* something given to soothe or quiet; bribe. **5** *v.* to soak thoroughly; drench. □ *v.* **sopped, sop·ping.**

sopping wet, soaked; drenched.

soph·ist (sof′ist), *n.* a clever but misleading reasoner.

so·phis·ti·cate (sə fis′tə kāt *for verb;* sə fis′tə kāt *or* sə fis′tə kit *for noun*), **1** *v.* to make less simple in your tastes or ideas; make more worldly. **2** *n.* a sophisticated person. □ *v.* **so·phis·ti·cat·ed, so·phis·ti·cat·ing.**

so·phis·ti·cat·ed (sə fis′tə kā′tid), *adj.* **1** knowing how to get along in the world; not simple in your tastes or ideas: *My cousin's sophisticated tastes are the result of having lived in several countries.* **2** very complex and advanced in design: *sophisticated laboratory equipment.* —**so·phis′ti·cat·ed·ly,** *adv.*

soph·ist·ry (sof′ə strē), *n.* **1** unsound reasoning. **2** a clever but misleading argument. —**soph·ist·ries** for 2.

soph·o·more (sof′ə môr), *n.* student in the second year of high school or college. —**soph′o·mor′ic,** *adj.*

so·po·rif·ic (sō′pə rif′ik *or* sop′ə rif′ik), **1** *adj.* causing or tending to cause sleep. **2** *adj.* sleepy; drowsy. **3** *n.* drug that causes sleep.

sop·ping (sop′ing), *adj.* soaked; drenched.

sop·py (sop′ē), *adj.* soaked; very wet; rainy: *soppy ground, soppy weather.* □ *adj.* **sop·pi·er, sop·pi·est.** —**sop′pi·ness,** *n.*

so·pran·o (sə pran′ō), **1** *n.* the highest singing voice in women and boys. **2** *n.* singer with such a voice. **3** *n.* part for such a voice or for a corresponding instrument. **4** *n.* instrument playing such a part. **5** *adj.* of or for a soprano. □ *n., pl.* **so·pran·os.**

sor·cer·er (sôr′sər ər), *n.* person believed to practice magic, especially with the supposed aid of evil spirits; wizard; magician.

sor·cer·ess (sôr′sər is), *n.* woman believed to practice magic, especially with the supposed aid of evil spirits; witch. □ *n., pl.* **sor·cer·ess·es.**

sor·cer·y (sôr′sər ē), *n.* magic believed to be performed with the supposed aid of evil spirits; witchcraft: *The prince had been changed into a lion by sorcery.*

sor·did (sôr′did), *adj.* **1** dirty; filthy: *a sordid back street, a sordid shack.* **2** immoral; foul; vile: *sordid crimes.* —**sor′did·ly,** *adv.* —**sor′did·ness,** *n.*

sore (sôr), **1** *adj.* causing sharp or continuous pain; painful; aching; tender; smarting: *a sore throat, a sore finger.* **2** *n.* a painful place on the body where the skin or flesh is broken or bruised. **3** *adj.* angry; vexed: *He is sore at missing the game.* **4** *adj.* causing misery, anger, or offense; vexing: *Their defeat is a sore subject with the members of the team.* **5** *n.* cause of pain, sorrow, sadness, anger, offense, etc. **6** *adj.* severe; distressing: *Your going away is a sore grief to us.* □ *adj.* **sor·er, sor·est.** ■ Another word that sounds like this is **soar.** —**sore′ness,** *n.*

sore·head (sôr′hed′), *n.* INFORMAL. person who is easily angered or offended.

sore·ly (sôr′lē), *adv.* **1** very much; urgently: *sorely needed political changes.* **2** in a sore way; painfully.

sor·ghum (sôr′gəm), *n.* **1** any of several tall grasses that resemble corn. One kind of sorghum has a sweet juice used for making molasses or syrup. Some kinds provide food for livestock either by their grain or as hay, and others furnish material for brushes or brooms. **2** molasses or syrup made from a sorghum plant.

so·ro·ri·ty (sə rôr′ə tē), *n.* club or society of women or girls, especially at a college. □ *n., pl.* **so·ro·ri·ties.**

a	hat	ė	term	ô	order	ch	child		
ā	age	i	it	oi	oil	ng	long		a in about
ä	far	ī	ice	ou	out	sh	she		e in taken
â	care	o	hot	u	cup	th	thin	ə	i in pencil
e	let	ō	open	ù	put	ŦH	then		o in lemon
ē	equal	ò	saw	ü	rule	zh	measure		u in circus

S

sor·rel¹ (sôr′əl), **1** *adj.* reddish brown. **2** *n.* a reddish brown. **3** *n.* a horse of this color.

sor·rel² (sôr′əl), *n.* any of several plants with sour leaves.

sor·row (sor′ō), **1** *n.* grief, sadness, or regret: *He felt sorrow at the loss of his kitten. He expressed sorrow at his mistake.* **2** *n.* cause of grief, sadness, or regret; trouble; suffering; misfortune: *Her sorrows have aged her.* **3** *v.* to feel or show grief, sadness, or regret; be sad; feel sorry; grieve: *She sorrowed over the end of their friendship.* —**sor′row·er,** *n.* —**sor′row·less,** *adj.*

SYNONYM STUDY **Sorrow, grief,** and **mourning** all mean strong unhappiness about some particular thing. **Sorrow** suggests a loss of something precious: *The idea of moving to another state filled the children with a mixture of excitement and sorrow.* **Grief** suggests deep sorrow and mental suffering: *His grief over the loss of the farm lasted for years.* **Mourning** suggests a period of grief caused by the death of a loved one: *She wore black as a sign of mourning.*

sor·row·ful (sor′ə fəl), *adj.* **1** full of sorrow; feeling sorrow; sad: *Our family has been sorrowful since our best friends moved away.* **2** showing sorrow: *a sorrowful expression.* **3** causing sorrow: *The funeral was a sorrowful occasion.* —**sor′row·ful·ly,** *adv.* —**sor′row·ful·ness,** *n.*

sor·ry (sor′ē), *adj.* **1** feeling pity, regret, sympathy; sad: *We are sorry that we cannot come to the party.* **2** wretched; poor; pitiful: *The ragged, hungry child was a sorry sight.* ❑ *adj.* **sor·ri·er, sor·ri·est.** —**sor′ri·ly,** *adv.* —**sor′ri·ness,** *n.*

sort (sôrt), **1** *n.* kind or class; type: *What sort of work does he do? I like this sort of candy best.* **2** *n.* character; quality; nature: *materials of an inferior sort.* **3** *n.* person or thing of a certain kind or quality: *He is a good sort.* **4** *v.* to arrange by kinds or classes; arrange in order: *Sort these cards according to their colors.* **5** *v.* to separate from others; put: *sort out the best apples for eating.* —**sort′a·ble,** *adj.* —**sort′er,** *n.*

of sorts, of a poor or mediocre quality: *a writer of sorts.*

out of sorts, ill, cross, or uncomfortable.

sort of, somewhat; rather: *In spite of her faults I sort of like her.*

sor·tie (sôr′tē), *n.* **1** (of troops) act of making an attack from a besieged fort, town, castle, etc., against the besiegers. **2** a single flight of an aircraft attacking an enemy.

so·rus (sôr′əs), *n.* any of the dotlike clusters of spore cases on the underside of a frond of a fern. ❑ *n., pl.* **so·ri** (sôr′ī).

SOS (es′ō′es′), *n.* **1** signal of distress consisting of the letters *S O S* of the international Morse code (•••−−−•••), used by ships, aircraft, etc. **2** any urgent call for help.

so-so (sō′sō′), **1** *adj.* neither very good nor very bad; fairly good: *The speech was only so-so, but we enjoyed the singing that followed.* **2** *adv.* in a passable or indifferent manner; tolerably: *"How is he doing his work?" "So-so."*

sot (sot), *n.* person made stupid and foolish by drinking too much alcoholic liquor; drunkard.

sou (sü), *n.* a former French coin, worth five centimes or 1/20 of a franc.

souf·flé (sü flā′), *n.* a frothy baked dish, usually made light by beaten eggs: *cheese soufflé.* ❑ *n., pl.* **souf·flés.**

sough (suf *or* sou), **1** *v.* to make a rustling or murmuring sound: *The pines soughed when the wind blew.* **2** *n.* a rustling or murmuring sound. ■ Another word that can sound like this is **sow².**

sought (sôt), *v.* past tense and past participle of **seek:** *For days she sought a job. They had sought the kitten for hours before they found it asleep in the back closet.*

soul (sōl), *n.* **1** the spiritual part of a human being, believed to be the source of thought, feeling, and action. Many religions teach that the soul is separate from the body and never dies. **2** energy of mind or feelings; spirit: *She puts her whole soul into her work.* **3** cause of inspiration and energy: *Florence Nightingale was the soul of the movement to reform nursing.* **4** the essential part: *"Brevity is the soul of wit."* **5** a distinctive emotional or spiritual quality associated with the culture of African Americans, especially as expressed through music. **6** person: *Don't tell a soul.* **7** embodiment: *the soul of grace.* ■ Other words that sound like this are **sol** and **sole.**

soul·ful (sōl′fəl), *adj.* **1** full of feeling; deeply emotional: *soulful music.* **2** expressing or suggesting deep feeling: *a soulful sigh.* —**soul′ful·ly,** *adv.* —**soul′ful·ness,** *n.*

soul·less (sōl′lis), *adj.* having no soul; without spirit or noble feelings. —**soul′less·ly,** *adv.*

sound¹ (sound), **1** *n.* what is or can be heard; sensation produced in the organs of hearing by vibrations of the air or some other substance: *the sound of music, the sound of thunder.* **2** *n.* energy in the form of waves passing through a vibrating substance such as air. This energy is heard as sound. Sound travels through air at a speed of 1087 feet (331 meters) per second at sea level. **3** *n.* volume; loudness: *Turn up the sound.* **4** *n.* one of the simple noises that make up speech: *a vowel sound.* **5** *v.* to make a noise: *The wind sounds like an animal howling.* **6** *v.* to pronounce: *Sound each syllable.* **7** *v.* to be pronounced: *"Rough" and "ruff" sound just alike.* **8** *v.* to cause to sound: *The ambulance sounded its siren.* **9** *v.* to order or direct by a sound: *Sound the retreat.* **10** *v.* to make known; announce; utter: *The police sounded a tornado warning.* **11** *v.* to seem: *That answer sounds wrong to me.* **12** *n.* style of music: *the New Age sound.* **13** *n.* effect produced on the mind by what is heard: *the sound of victory.*

within sound, near enough to hear: *within sound of her voice.*

sound² (sound), **1** *adj.* free from disease; healthy: *a sound body and mind.* **2** *adj.* free from injury, decay, or defect: *sound walls, a sound ship, sound fruit.* **3** *adj.* strong; safe; secure: *a sound business firm.* **4** *adj.* solid: *sound roof supports.* **5** *adj.* correct; right; reasonable; reliable: *sound advice, sound arguments.* **6** *adj.* morally good; honest; upright: *sound values.* **7** *adj.* deep; heavy; profound: *a sound sleep.* **8** *adj.* thorough; complete: *a sound whipping.* **9** *adv.* deeply; thoroughly: *sleep long and sound.*

sound³ (sound), *v.* **1** to measure the depth of water by letting down a weight fastened on the end of a line. **2** to try to find out the views of; test; examine: *We sounded them on the subject of a picnic.* **3** to go quickly toward the bottom; dive: *The whale sounded.*

sound⁴ (sound), *n.* **1** a long, narrow strip of water, larger than a strait, joining two larger bodies of water or separating an island from the mainland: *Long Island Sound.* **2** inlet of the sea: *Puget Sound.*

sound barrier, sonic barrier.

sound bite, a very brief recorded statement by a politician, intended to be used in a radio or TV news report.

sound·board (sound′bôrd′), *n.* sounding board (defs. 1 and 2).

sound box, the hollow part of a stringed instrument, such as a cello or violin, that makes the sound louder.

sound effects, sounds, such as thunder, footsteps, traffic, and the like, imitated by various devices or reproduced by recordings as part of a play, a movie, or a radio or TV show.

sound·er (soun′dər), *n.* someone or something that measures the depth of water.

sound·ing (soun′ding), *n.* **1** act of measuring the depth of water with a sounding line. **2** depth of water found this way. **3** **soundings,** *pl.* **a** depths of water found this way. **b** water not more than 600 feet (183 meters) deep, which can be measured by an ordinary sounding line.

sounding board, 1 a thin piece of wood on a violin, piano, etc., that vibrates and increases the fullness of the instrument's tone. **2** structure used to direct sound outward toward an audience. **3** person or group with whom you discuss your opinions, ideas, etc., to get their reactions.

sounding line, line having a weight fastened to the end, used to measure the depth of water.

sound·less¹ (sound′lis), *adj.* without sound; making no sound: *soundless footsteps.* —**sound′less·ly,** *adv.*

sound·less² (sound′lis), *adj.* so deep that the bottom cannot be reached: *the soundless depths of the ocean.*

sound·ly (sound′lē), *adv.* **1** deeply; heavily: *The tired child slept soundly.* **2** vigorously; thoroughly: *He scolded us soundly.* **3** with good judgment: *a soundly based decision.*

sound·ness (sound′nis), *n.* **1** good health: *soundness of body and mind.* **2** freedom from weakness or defect. **3** good judgment; correctness and reliability.

sound•proof (sound′prüf′), **1** *adj.* not letting sound pass through: *a soundproof room or ceiling.* **2** *v.* to make soundproof: *Carpenters soundproofed the music room.*

sound track, 1 a recording of the sounds of words, music, etc., made along one edge of movie film. **2** a recording featuring the songs or music used in a movie, TV show, etc.: *He liked the movie so much that he bought the sound track.*

soup (süp), *n.* a liquid food made by boiling meat, vegetables, etc.
in the soup, INFORMAL. in difficulty.
soup up, SLANG. to increase the horsepower of an engine, car, etc.

soup•y (sü′pē), *adj.* like soup. ❑ *adj.* **soup•i•er, soup•i•est.**

sour (sour), **1** *adj.* having a taste like vinegar or lemon juice; sharp and biting; acid: *This green fruit is sour.* **2** *adj.* spoiled: *sour milk.* **3** *adj.* having a sour or rank smell. **4** *adj.* disagreeable; bad-tempered: *a sour face, a sour remark.* **5** *adj.* unusually acid: *sour soil.* **6** *v.* to make or become sour; turn sour: *The milk soured while it stood in the hot sun.* **7** *v.* to make or become cross, bad-tempered, or disagreeable. **–sour′ly,** *adv.* **–sour′ness,** *n.*

SYNONYM STUDY **Sour** and **tart**[1] both mean tasting like lemons, without sweetness. **Sour** is a general word: *This salad dressing is too sour.* **Tart** suggests something that is pleasantly sour: *Tart cherries make good pies.*

sour•ball (sour′bôl′), *n.* a round piece of hard candy with a sour taste.

source (sôrs), *n.* **1** person or place from which anything comes or is obtained: *The newspaper gets news from many sources. Mines are the chief source of diamonds.* ■ See Synonym Study at **origin. 2** beginning of a brook or river; fountain; spring.

sour cream, a thick cream that has been soured, but has a pleasant taste. It is used on baked potatoes, on salads, and in cooking.

sour•dough (sour′dō′), *n.* **1** fermented dough saved from one baking to start fermentation in the next. **2** prospector or pioneer in Alaska or northwestern Canada.

sour grapes, act or fact of pretending that you dislike something because you cannot have it.

WORD STORY **Sour grapes** comes from a fable by Aesop. A fox sees some grapes but can't reach them. After many tries, the fox gives up, saying that the grapes were probably sour anyway.

Sou•sa (sü′zə), *n.* **John Philip,** 1854-1932, American conductor and composer of band music. He wrote more than a hundred marches, including *Stars and Stripes Forever.*

sou•sa•phone (sü′zə fōn′), *n.* a brass instrument similar to the tuba, but with a wider opening that faces forward. It is designed for use in marching bands.

sousaphone

souse (sous), **1** *v.* to plunge into liquid; throw liquid over; soak in a liquid. **2** *n.* act of plunging into a liquid; drenching. **3** *v.* to soak in vinegar, brine, etc.; pickle. **4** *n.* liquid used for pickling. **5** *n.* something soaked or pickled in brine, especially the head, ears, and feet of a pig. ❑ *v.* **soused, sous•ing.**

Sou•ter (sü′tər), *n.* **David,** born 1939, U.S. Supreme Court justice, appointed in 1990.

south (south), **1** *n.* direction to the left as you face the setting sun; direction just opposite north. **2** *adj., adv.* toward the south; farther toward the south: *the south side of town, drive south.* **3** *adj.* from the south: *a south wind.* **4** *n.* Also, **South,** the part of any country toward the south. **5** *n.* **a the South,** the southern part of the United States; the states south of Pennsylvania, the Ohio River, and Missouri, making up most of the states that formed the Confederate side in the Civil War. **b** the economically less developed nations of the world, located mainly in the Southern Hemisphere.
south of, further south than: *New York is south of Boston.*

South Africa, Republic of, country in S Africa. *Capitals:* Bloemfontein (judicial); Cape Town (legislative); Pretoria (administrative). **–South African.**

South African Dutch, Afrikaans.

South America, continent in the Western Hemisphere southeast of North America. **–South American.**

South•amp•ton (sou thamp′tən), *n.* port in S England.

South Australia, state in S Australia. *Capital:* Adelaide.

South Bend, city in N Indiana.

south•bound (south′bound′), *adj.* going south.

South Burlington, city in NW Vermont.

South Carolina, one of the southeastern states of the United States. *Abbreviation:* SC or S.C. *Capital:* Columbia. **–South Carolinian.**

WORD STORY **South Carolina** comes from the name of King Charles I of England. In Latin, **Charles** is *Carolus,* and **Carolina** means "of or about Charles." The colony of Carolina was divided into northern and southern parts in 1730.

South China Sea, part of the Pacific Ocean, southeast of Asia. It is connected to the East China Sea by the Taiwan Strait.

South Dakota, one of the midwestern states of the United States. *Abbreviation:* SD, S.D., or S. Dak. *Capital:* Pierre. **–South Dakotan.**

WORD STORY **South Dakota** comes from the name of the people who were living there when Europeans first came (See Usage Note at **Sioux.**) In 1889, the Dakota Territory was divided into northern and southern states.

south•east (south′ēst′), **1** *n.* direction halfway between south and east. **2** *adj., adv.* toward the southeast: *the southeast corner, driving southeast.* **3** *n.* a place that is in the southeast part or direction. **4 the Southeast,** the southeastern part of the United States, including Alabama, Georgia, Florida, South Carolina, North Carolina, and Virginia. **5** *adj.* from the southeast: *a southeast wind.*

Southeast Asia, region in Asia including Malaysia, the countries of Indochina, the islands of Indonesia, and sometimes, the Philippines.

south•east•er (south′ē′stər), *n.* wind or storm from the southeast.

south•east•er•ly (south′ē′stər lē), *adj., adv.* **1** toward the southeast. **2** from the southeast.

south•east•ern (south′ē′stərn), *adj.* **1** toward the southeast. **2** from the southeast. **3** of or in the southeast.

south•east•ward (south′ēst′wərd), *adv., adj.* toward the southeast.

south•er•ly (suᴛʜ′ər lē), **1** *adj., adv.* toward the south: *We hiked in a southerly direction.* **2** *adj., adv.* from the south: *a southerly wind.* **3** *n.* wind that blows from the south. ❑ *n., pl.* **south•er•lies.**

south•ern (suᴛʜ′ərn), *adj.* **1** toward the south: *a southern view.* **2** from the south: *a southern breeze.* **3** of or in the south: *southern countries.* **4 Southern,** of or in the southern part of the United States.

Southern Colonies, the five British colonies in North America south of the Mason-Dixon Line before the American Revolution: Maryland, Virginia, North Carolina, South Carolina, and Georgia.

Southern Cross, constellation in the form of a cross, visible in the Southern Hemisphere.

south•ern•er (suᴛʜ′ər nər), *n.* **1** person born or living in the south. **2 Southerner,** person born or living in the southern part of the United States.

Southern Hemisphere, the half of the earth that is south of the equator.

southern lights, the aurora australis.

south•ern•most (suᴛʜ′ərn mōst), *adj.* farthest south.

Southern Yemen, a former country in SW Arabia, now part of Yemen.

a	hat	ė	term	ô	order	ch	child	ə	a	in about
ā	age	i	it	oi	oil	ng	long		e	in taken
ä	far	ī	ice	ou	out	sh	she		i	in pencil
â	care	o	hot	u	cup	th	thin		o	in lemon
e	let	ō	open	ů	put	ᴛʜ	then		u	in circus
ē	equal	ȯ	saw	ü	rule	zh	measure			

S

South Island, the southern and larger of New Zealand's two main islands.

South Korea, country in the S part of the Korean peninsula. It is the area south of the 38th parallel. *Capital:* Seoul. **–South Korean.**

south·land (south′lənd *or* south′land′), *n.* land in the south; southern part of a country.

south·paw (south′pȯ′), INFORMAL. **1** *n.* a left-hander. **2** *adj.* left-handed.

South Pole, the southern end of the earth's axis.

South Sea Islands, islands in the S Pacific.

South Vietnam, former country in SE Asia, now part of Vietnam.

south·ward (south′wərd), **1** *adv., adj.* toward the south; south: *She walked southward. The orchard is on the southward slope of the hill.* **2** *n.* a southward part, direction, or point.

south·wards (south′wərds), *adv.* southward.

south·west (south′west′), **1** *n.* direction halfway between south and west. **2** *adj., adv.* toward the southwest: *the southwest corner, driving southwest.* **3** *n.* a place that is in the southwest part or direction. **4** *n.* **the Southwest,** the southwestern part of the United States, especially Texas, New Mexico, Oklahoma, Arizona, and sometimes, southern California. **5** *adj.* from the southwest: *a southwest wind.*

South-West Africa (south′west′), former name of **Namibia.**

south·west·er (south′wes′tər *for 1;* sou′wes′tər *for 2*), *n.* **1** wind or storm from the southwest. **2** a waterproof hat with a broad brim at the back to protect the neck, worn especially by sailors. Also, **sou'wester.**

south·west·er·ly (south′wes′tər lē), *adj., adv.* **1** toward the southwest. **2** from the southwest.

south·west·ern (south′wes′tərn), *adj.* **1** toward the southwest. **2** from the southwest. **3** of or in the southwest. **4 Southwestern,** of or in the southwestern part of the United States.

south·west·ward (south′west′wərd), *adv., adj.* toward the southwest.

sou·ve·nir (sü′və nir′ *or* sü′və nir), *n.* something given or kept for remembrance; memento; keepsake: *She bought a pair of moccasins as a souvenir of her trip out West.*

WORD STORY Souvenir comes from Latin words meaning "to come from under." When you buy a souvenir on a trip, you get something that you may find someday put away under other things, and that will bring memories of the trip up from under more recent memories.

sou'west·er (sou′wes′tər), *n.* southwester.

sove·reign (sov′rən), **1** *n.* supreme ruler; king or queen; monarch. Queen Victoria was the sovereign of Great Britain from 1837 to 1901. **2** *adj.* having supreme rank, power, or authority: *a sovereign prince, a sovereign court.* **3** *adj.* independent of the control of other governments: *The United States became a sovereign nation in 1776.* **4** *adj.* above all others; supreme; greatest: *Good character is of sovereign importance.* **5** *n.* a former British gold coin, equal to 20 shillings or one pound. **–sove′-reign·ly,** *adv.*

sove·reign·ty (sov′rən tē), *n.* **1** supreme power or authority: *The French Revolution rejected the sovereignty of the king.* **2** freedom from outside control; independence in exercising power or authority: *Countries that are satellites lack full sovereignty.* **3** state, territory, community, etc., that is independent or sovereign. **4** the rank, power, or jurisdiction of a sovereign. ❑ *n., pl.* **sove·reign·ties** for 3.

so·vi·et (sō′vē et), **1** *n.* any of the governing councils or assemblies of the former Soviet Union, including town soviets and village soviets as well as the **Supreme Soviet,** the national legislative group. **2** *adj.* of or about soviets. **3** *adj.* **Soviet,** of or about the former Soviet Union.

Soviet Russia, 1 the Russian Soviet Federated Socialist Republic, the largest republic in the former Soviet Union. **2** the former Soviet Union.

Soviet Union, a former union of fifteen republics in E Europe and W and N Asia; Union of Soviet Socialist Republics. In 1991, it broke up into several countries, including Russia, Ukraine, Georgia, etc. *Capital:* Moscow.

sow[1] (sō), *v.* **1** to scatter seed on the ground; plant seed: *He sows more wheat than oats.* **2** to plant seed in: *They sowed the field with oats.* **3** to scatter anything; spread abroad: *The rebels sowed discontent among the people.* ❑ *v.* **sowed, sown** or **sowed, sow·ing.** ■ Other words that sound like this are **sew** and **so. –sow′er,** *n.* **sow your wild oats,** to behave in a reckless, lawless, or indiscreet way, especially when you are young.

sow[2] (sou), *n.* a fully grown female pig. ■ Another word that can sound like this is **sough.**

sow bug (sou), wood louse.

sown (sōn), *v.* a past participle of **sow**[1]: *The field had been sown with oats for three years in a row.* ■ Another word that sounds like this is **sewn.**

sox (soks), *n.pl.* socks.

soy (soi), *n.* **1** soy sauce. **2** soybean.

soy·bean (soi′bēn′), *n.* **1** a small, light-colored bean grown as a major farm crop. Soybeans are an important protein-rich food, and are used to make tofu. The oil is removed and used in margarine, paints, etc. The remaining meal is fed to livestock or made into flour. **2** the plant this bean grows on, used to feed cattle.

So·yin·ka (shȯ ying′kə), *n.* **Wo·le** (wȯ′lā), born 1934, Nigerian writer. In 1986 he became the first African writer to win the Nobel Prize for literature.

soy sauce, a Chinese and Japanese sauce for fish, meat, etc., made from fermented soybeans. Also, **soy.**

sp., 1 special. **2** species. **3** spelling.

Sp., 1 Spain. **2** Spaniard. **3** Spanish.

spa (spä), *n.* **1** a mineral spring. **2** town, area, or resort where there is a mineral spring or springs. **3** a place with exercise equipment, saunas, etc. ❑ *n., pl.* **spas.**

space (spās), **1** *n.* the unlimited amount of room that extends in all directions and in which all things exist: *Motion is change of position in space.* **2** *n.* a limited place or room: *Is there enough space in the car for another person?* **3** *n.* area of ground, surface, etc.: *The trees covered acres of space.* **4** *n.* outer space: *a rocket launched into space.* **5** *adj.* of or about outer space: *space travel.* **6** *n.* distance: *The road is bad for a space of ten miles.* **7** *n.* length of time: *The flowers died in the space of a day.* **8** *n.* (in music) one of the gaps between the lines of a staff. **9** *v.* to separate; keep apart: *Space your words evenly when you write.* **10** *v.* to divide into areas; set limits on; place: *to space land into sections for sale.* ❑ *v.* **spaced, spac·ing.**

space age, the current period in history, since the exploration of outer space began. **–space′-age′,** *adj.*

space bar, the bar on a typewriter or computer keyboard that is used to insert a space.

space·borne (spās′bôrn′), *adj.* traveling through outer space: *spaceborne equipment, a spaceborne experiment.*

space cadet, SLANG. a person who seems to be silly, not paying attention, or out of touch with reality.

space capsule, capsule (def. 2).

space·craft (spās′kraft′), *n.* vehicle used for flight in outer space. ❑ *n., pl.* **space·craft.**

spaced-out (spāst′out′), *adj.* SLANG. distanced from experience or feeling; in a daze; out of touch with reality: *The strong painkillers the doctor gave him after his surgery made him feel spaced-out.*

space·flight (spās′flīt′), *n.* flight into or through outer space.

space heater, a small gas or electric heater, often portable, for warming a room or a portion of a room.

space·man (spās′man′), *n.* **1** astronaut. **2** alien; visitor to earth from space: *The movie was about an invasion of spacemen.* ❑ *n., pl.* **space·men.**

space medicine, branch of medicine that deals with the effects on the body of space travel.

space probe, spacecraft equipped with scientific devices to study the physical features of outer space or astronomical objects.

space·ship (spās′ship′), *n.* spacecraft.

space shot, act of launching a space vehicle, such as a rocket or shuttle, beyond the earth's atmosphere.

space shuttle, spacecraft with wings, which can orbit the earth, land like an airplane, and be used again. A space shuttle has two rockets and a large fuel tank which come off after use in launching the spacecraft.

space shuttle landing

space station, an earth satellite large enough for crew members to live there for weeks and months, used for experiments and observations, possibly for manufacturing or for construction of spacecraft.

space·suit (spās′süt′), *n.* an airtight, pressurized suit designed to protect astronauts from vacuum, radiation, and other hazards.

space·walk (spās′wok′), *n.* act of moving or floating outside a spacecraft in outer space.

spac·ing (spā′sing), *n.* **1** act or process of supplying or arranging spaces. **2** manner in which spaces are arranged: *open spacing in printed matter.* **3** a space or spaces in printing or other work.

spa·cious (spā′shəs), *adj.* containing much space; with plenty of room; vast: *The rooms were bright and spacious.* **–spa′cious·ly,** *adv.* **–spa′cious·ness,** *n.*

spade¹ (spād), **1** *n.* tool for digging, having an iron blade which can be pressed into the ground with the foot, and a long handle with a grip or crosspiece at the top. **2** *v.* to dig with a spade: *Spade up the garden.* ❑ *v.* **spad·ed, spad·ing.**

call a spade a spade, to call a thing by its real name; speak plainly and frankly.

spade² (spād), *n.* **1** figure shaped like this: ♠. **2** a playing card marked with one or more black figures like this. **3 spades,** *pl.* suit of such playing cards.

spade·work (spād′werk′), *n.* any work done in preparation for later use such as research, organization, training, or the like, especially if the work is long and detailed.

spa·dix (spā′diks), *n.* spike of tiny flowers on a fleshy stem. A spadix is usually enclosed in a spathe, as in the jack-in-the-pulpit and the calla lily. ❑ *n., pl.* **spa·dix·es, spa·di·ces** (spā′di sēz).

spa·ghet·ti (spə get′ē), *n.* a mixture of flour and water that has been dried in the form of long, thin rods, to be cooked for food. Spaghetti is a form of pasta.

Spahn (spän), *n.* **Warren,** born 1921, American baseball player. He won 363 games, more than any other left-handed pitcher.

Spain (spān), *n.* country in SW Europe. *Capital:* Madrid. [Spain may come from a Phoenician word meaning "mines," which the Phoenicians had there.]

spake (spāk), *v.* OLD USE. a past tense of **speak.**

span¹ (span), **1** *n.* period of time, often short or limited: *the span of human life.* **2** *n.* a part between two supports: *The bridge crossed the river in a single span.* **3** *n.* distance between two supports: *The arch had a fifty-foot span.* **4** *v.* to extend over: *A bridge spanned the river.* **5** *n.* distance between the tip of the thumb and the tip of the little finger when the fingers are spread out, about 9 inches. **6** *v.* to measure by the fingers spread out: *This pole can be spanned by two hands.* ❑ *v.* **spanned, span·ning.**

span² (span), *n.* pair of horses or other animals harnessed and driven together.

span·dex (span′deks), *n.* an elastic synthetic fabric used to make clothing. [Spandex comes from rearranging the letters of **expands,** because it is elastic. It is an anagram.]

span·gle (spang′gəl), **1** *n.* a small piece of glittering metal used for decoration: *The costume was covered with spangles.* **2** *n.* any small, bright bit: *This rock shows spangles of gold.* **3** *v.* to decorate with spangles: *The costume was spangled with gold.* **4** *v.* to sprinkle with small, bright bits: *The sky is spangled with stars.* ❑ *v.* **span·gled, span·gling.**

Span·iard (span′yərd), *n.* person born or living in Spain.

span·iel (span′yəl), *n.* a small or medium-sized dog with long, silky hair and drooping ears. Breeds of spaniel include **cocker spaniels, English Springer spaniels, Irish water spaniels,** and **Tibetan spaniels.** [Spaniel comes from a French word meaning "Spanish." Spaniels first came from Spain.] **–span′iel·like′,** *adj.*

Span·ish (span′ish), **1** *adj.* of or about Spain, its people, or their language: *Spanish literature.* **2** *n.pl.* the people of Spain. **3** *n.* the language of Spain. It is also the language of most Latin American countries.

WORD SOURCE Spanish has given many words to the English language. The words below are some of them. See also the Word Source at **Mexican Spanish.**

alligator	flotilla	patio	silo
armada	guerrilla	pimiento	stevedore
bonanza	hammock	plantain¹	tango
bongo	lariat	ranch	tornado
brocade	lasso	renegade	tuna
cigar	loco	rodeo	vamoose
cinch	machete	rumba	vanilla
corral	mosquito	savanna	vigilante
filibuster	palomino	sierra	yucca

Spanish America, countries and islands south and southeast of the United States, in which the principal language is Spanish.

Spanish American, person born or living in a Spanish-American country.

Span·ish-A·mer·i·can (span′ish ə mer′ə kən), *adj.* **1** of or about Spain and the Americas, or Spain and the United States. **2** of or about the parts of the Americas where Spanish is the principal language.

Spanish-American War, war between Spain and the United States in 1898, fought mostly in Cuba and the Philippines.

Spanish Main, 1 (formerly) the NW coast of South America, from which Spanish ships used to sail with gold for Spain. **2** (in later use) the Caribbean Sea.

Spanish moss, an American air plant of warm regions that grows on the branches of trees, from which it hangs in gray streamers like hair.

Spanish rice, rice cooked with onions, tomatoes, and green peppers.

spank (spangk), **1** *v.* to slap on the buttocks with the open hand. **2** *n.* a slap on the buttocks with the open hand.

spank·ing (spang′king), **1** *n.* act of slapping someone on the buttocks with the open hand. **2** *adj.* blowing briskly: *a spanking breeze.* **3** *adj.* unusually fine, great, large, etc.: *a spanking team of horses.*

Spanish moss

a	hat	ė	term	ô	order	ch	child		a in about
ā	age	i	it	oi	oil	ng	long		e in taken
ä	far	ī	ice	ou	out	sh	she	ə	i in pencil
â	care	o	hot	u	cup	th	thin		o in lemon
e	let	ō	open	ů	put	ᴛʜ	then		u in circus
ē	equal	ò	saw	ü	rule	zh	measure		

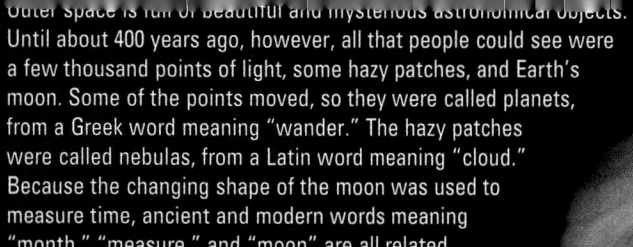

Outer space is full of beautiful and mysterious astronomical objects. Until about 400 years ago, however, all that people could see were a few thousand points of light, some hazy patches, and Earth's moon. Some of the points moved, so they were called planets, from a Greek word meaning "wander." The hazy patches were called nebulas, from a Latin word meaning "cloud." Because the changing shape of the moon was used to measure time, ancient and modern words meaning "month," "measure," and "moon" are all related.

Then, in 1609, the Italian scientist Galileo pointed a telescope at the sky, and the wonders of outer space came into view for the first time.

Saturn's Rings
Galileo looked at Saturn in 1610, and he saw what he described as "handles" on the planet. A few years later, another scientist with a stronger telescope recognized the handles as rings. Billions of ice fragments orbit the planet, here in a photograph through color filters to show cloud bands more clearly.

Surface of Earth's Moon
Galileo first discovered that Earth's moon is not smooth, as everyone had thought. Hammered by meteorites, it is scarred by millions of craters. Lava flows and mountains also roughen the surface.

Earthrise from the Moon
Half sunlit, half dark with night, Earth hangs above the moon's horizon. Someday, travelers in outer space may send back postcards with pictures like these.

Jupiter's Moons and Great Red Spot
In 1610, Galileo astonished the world of science with the news that the planet Jupiter has moons. He found and named four of the 16 we now know. Two can be seen here. Other scientists, later in the 1600s, discovered Jupiter's Great Red Spot, seen here behind one moon. The Great Red Spot is thought to be an enormous storm (more than wide enough to swallow Earth whole) that has raged for more than 300 years.

Nebula
Nebulas really are clouds, but not of water vapor like clouds on Earth. Hydrogen and helium gas, mixed with tiny particles of dust, float between the stars. Starlight makes them glow. Millions of miles across, trillions of miles away, they are often the birthplace of new stars. About 75 years ago, some hazy patches once called nebulas were discovered to be galaxies like the Milky Way. They look cloudy because they contain billions or trillions of stars.

spar¹ (spär), **1** *n.* a stout pole used to support or extend the sails of a ship; mast, yard, gaff, boom, etc., of a ship. **2** *v.* to provide a ship with spars. ❑ *v.* **sparred, spar·ring.**

spar² (spär), *v.* **1** to make motions of attack and defense with the arms and fists; box. **2** to argue: *Two people were sparring about who would win the election.* ❑ *v.* **sparred, spar·ring.**

spar³ (spär), *n.* any of various shiny minerals, such as feldspar, that split easily into flakes.

spare (spâr), **1** *v.* to show mercy to; decide not to harm or destroy: *spare a conquered enemy.* **2** *v.* to make free from labor, pain, etc.: *I did the work to spare you the trouble.* **3** *v.* to get along without; do without: *I can't spare the car, so you'll have to take the bus.* **4** *v.* to use in small quantities or not at all; be saving of: *to spare no expense.* **5** *adj.* free for other use: *spare time.* **6** *adj.* extra; in reserve: *a spare tire.* ■ See Synonym Study at **extra.** **7** *n.* an extra thing or part: *We keep spare car fuses in the glove compartment.* **8** *adj.* thin; lean: *Lincoln was a tall, spare man.* **9** *adj.* small in quantity; meager; scanty: *I'm still hungry after that spare meal.* **10** *n.* act of knocking down all the pins with two rolls of a bowling ball. ❑ *v.* **spared, spar·ing;** *adj.* **spar·er, spar·est.** **—spare′a·ble,** *adj.* **—spare′ly,** *adv.* **—spare′ness,** *n.* **—spar′er,** *n.*

spare·ribs (spâr′ribs′), *n.pl.* ribs of pork having less meat than the ribs near the loins.

spar·ing (spâr′ing), *adj.* avoiding waste; economical; frugal: *a sparing use of sugar.* **—spar′ing·ly,** *adj.* **—spar′ing·ness,** *n.*

spark (spärk), **1** *n.* a small bit of fire: *The burning wood threw off sparks.* **2** *v.* to send out small bits of fire; produce sparks. **3** *n.* flash made when electricity jumps across an open space. An electric spark ignites the gasoline vapor in the engine of a motor vehicle. **4** *n.* a bright flash; gleam: *We saw a spark of light through the trees.* **5** *v.* to flash; gleam; sparkle. **6** *n.* a small amount: *I haven't a spark of interest in the plan.* **7** *n.* a glittering bit: *The moving sparks we saw were fireflies.* **8** *v.* to stir to activity; stimulate: *Cruelty may spark a revolt.* **—spark′less,** *adj.*

spar·kle (spär′kəl), **1** *v.* to send out little sparks: *The fireworks sparkled.* **2** *n.* a little spark. **3** *v.* to shine; glitter; flash; gleam: *The diamonds sparkled.* ■ See Synonym Study at **flash.** **4** *n.* a shine; glitter; flash: *the sparkle of someone's eyes.* **5** *v.* to be brilliant; be lively: *Wit sparkles.* **6** *n.* brilliance; liveliness. **7** *v.* to bubble. Ginger ale and champagne sparkle. ❑ *v.* **spar·kled, spar·kling.**

spar·kler (spär′klər), *n.* **1** firework that shoots out little sparks when it is lit. **2** a sparkling gem, especially a diamond.

spar·kling (spär′kling), *adj.* **1** shining; glittering: *sparkling stars.* **2** brilliant: *She has a sparkling wit.* **3** bubbling: *sparkling drinks.*

spar·kly (spär′klē), *adj.* full of sparkles; glittering; shining. ❑ *adj.* **spar·kli·er, spar·kli·est.**

spark plug, device in the cylinder of a gasoline engine that produces an electric spark to ignite a mixture of fuel and air in the combustion chamber.

spar·row (spar′ō), *n.* any of various small, usually brownish songbirds common in North and South America and also in Europe, Asia, and Africa. **—spar′row·like′,** *adj.*

sparrow hawk, kestrel.

sparse (spärs), *adj.* **1** thinly scattered; occurring here and there: *a sparse population, sparse hair.* **2** scanty; meager: *a sparse diet.* ❑ *adj.* **spars·er, spars·est. —sparse′ly,** *adv.* **—sparse′ness, spar′si·ty,** *n.*

Spar·ta (spär′tə), *n.* one of the most important cities in ancient Greece, famous for its soldiers.

Spar·ta·cus (spär′tə kəs), *n.* ?-71 B.C., Roman gladiator and leader. ■ **Spartacus** led an army of 70,000 slaves that defeated the Romans in several battles before final defeat.

Spar·tan (spärt′n), **1** *adj.* of or about Sparta or its people. **2** *n.* person who was born or lived in Sparta. The Spartans were noted for living simply, saying little, being brave, and enduring pain without complaining. **3** *adj.* Often, **spartan,** like the Spartans; simple, frugal, and severe. **4** *n.* person who is like the Spartans. **—Spar′tan·ly** or **spar′tan·ly,** *adv.*

spasm (spaz′əm), *n.* **1** a sudden, abnormal, involuntary contraction of a muscle or muscles. **2** any sudden, brief fit or spell of unusual energy or activity: *a spasm of laughter.*

spas·mod·ic (spaz mod′ik), *adj.* **1** of or like spasms; resembling a spasm: *a spasmodic cough.* **2** occurring very irregularly: *a spasmodic interest in reading.* **3** having or showing bursts of excitement. **—spas·mod′i·cal·ly,** *adv.*

spas·tic (spas′tik), **1** *adj.* of or marked by spasms. **2** *n.* person with a form of motion disability that includes muscle spasms. ■ This meaning of **spastic** is often considered offensive. **—spas′-ti·cal·ly,** *adv.*

spat¹ (spat), **1** *n.* a slight quarrel. **2** *v.* to quarrel slightly. ❑ *v.* **spat·ted, spat·ting.**

spat² (spat), *v.* a past tense and a past participle of **spit¹**: *The cat spat at the dog.*

spat³ (spat), *n.* Usually, **spats,** *pl.* a short outer covering worn over the top part of the shoe and reaching just above the ankle.

spate (spāt), *n.* a large number or amount, especially in a short time: *This year saw a spate of new books on dinosaurs.*

spathe (spāᴛʜ), *n.* a large leaf, often resembling a petal, that encloses a flower cluster. The calla lily has a white spathe around a yellow spadix.

spa·tial (spā′shəl), *adj.* **1** of or about space. **2** existing in space. **—spa·tial·ly,** *adv.*

spat·ter (spat′ər), **1** *v.* to scatter or dash in drops or particles: *spatter mud.* **2** *v.* to fall in drops or particles: *Rain spattered on the sidewalk.* **3** *v.* to strike in a shower; strike in a number of places: *Bullets spattered the wall.* **4** *n.* act or sound of spattering: *We listened to the spatter of rain on the roof.* **5** *n.* a splash or spot.

spat·u·la (spach′ə lə), *n.* tool with a broad, flat, flexible blade, used for spreading, scraping, or stirring soft substances such as putty, cake frosting, etc. A wider kind of spatula is used to lift cooked food from a pan. ❑ *n., pl.* **spat·u·las.**

spav·ined (spav′ənd), *adj.* (of horses) having a disease in which a bony swelling forms in the lower leg, causing lameness.

spawn (spôn), **1** *n.* eggs of fish, frogs, shellfish, etc. **2** *n.* the young newly hatched from such eggs. **3** *v.* to bring forth; give birth to. **4** *n.* offspring, especially a large number of offspring. **—spawn′er,** *n.*

spay (spā), *v.* to remove the ovaries of a female animal.

S.P.C.A., Society for the Prevention of Cruelty to Animals.

speak (spēk), *v.* **1** to say words; talk: *speak clearly.* **2** to make a speech: *Who is going to speak at the meeting?* **3** to make known; tell; express; say: *Speak the truth.* **4** to use a language: *Do you speak French?* **5** to express an idea, feeling, etc.; communicate: *Actions speak louder than words.* ❑ *v.* **spoke, spo·ken, speak·ing. —speak′a·ble,** *adj.*

so to speak, to speak in such a manner; use that expression: *He has a chance to win; he is, so to speak, still in the running.*

speak for, to speak in the interest of; represent: *Why don't you speak for yourself instead of having others speak for you?*

speak of, to refer to; mention: *Speaking of school, how do you like the new gym? I have no complaints to speak of.*

speak out or **speak up,** to speak loudly, clearly, or freely: *No one dared to speak out against the big bully. The children all spoke up in favor of the teacher's suggestion to have a party.*

speak well for, to give a favorable idea of; be evidence in favor of: *Her behavior speaks well for her.*

> **SYNONYM STUDY** **Speak, talk,** and **chat** all mean to make words with the voice. **Speak** is a general word: *He speaks in a clear voice.* **Talk** suggests that this goes on for a while: *We talked about her problem.* **Chat** suggests talking with others in an easy, relaxed way: *They chatted during lunch.*

speak·eas·y (spēk′ē′zē), *n.* SLANG. place where alcoholic drinks were sold illegally. Speakeasies were popular during the 1920s in the United States because of Prohibition. ❑ *n., pl.* **speak·eas·ies.**

speak·er (spē′kər), *n.* **1** person who speaks. **2** Also, **Speaker,** person who presides over a legislative assembly. The Speaker of the

Sparta (about 450 B.C.)

★ Battlefield · N

Mount Olympus · Aegean Sea · Thermopylae · Delphi · Thebes · Marathon · Corinth · Athens · Sparta

House of Representatives is its presiding officer. **3** device for producing sound from electrical signals, as in a radio, stereo, or the like.

speak·ing (spē′king), **1** *n.* act, utterance, or discourse of someone who speaks. **2** *adj.* used in, suited to, or involving speech: *the speaking voice, within speaking distance, a speaking part in a play.* **3** *adj.* permitting conversation: *a speaking acquaintance with a person.* **4** *adj.* lifelike: *a speaking likeness.*

spear¹ (spir), **1** *n.* weapon with a long shaft and a sharp-pointed head. **2** *v.* to pierce with a spear: *I speared a fish.* **3** *v.* to pierce or stab with anything sharp: *spear string beans with a fork.* —**spear′er,** *n.*

spear² (spir), *n.* sprout or shoot of a plant: *a spear of grass.*

spear·head (spir′hed′), **1** *n.* the sharp-pointed striking end of a spear. **2** *n.* part that is first in an attack, endeavor, etc. **3** *v.* to lead or clear the way for; head: *Our group spearheaded the efforts to clean the lake.*

spear·man (spir′mən), *n.* soldier armed with a spear. ❑ *n., pl.* **spear·men.**

spear·mint (spir′mint′), *n.* a fragrant herb grown for its oil, which is used for flavoring.

spe·cial (spesh′əl), **1** *adj.* extraordinary; unusual; exceptional: *Today's topic is of special interest.* **2** *adj.* of a particular kind; distinct from others; not general: *This desk has a special lock. Have you any special color in mind for your new coat?* **3** *adj.* for a particular person, thing, purpose, etc.: *Send the letter by a special messenger.* **4** *n.* something special in importance, price, interest, etc.: *The store advertised a special on raincoats.* **5** *n.* a TV show produced especially for a single broadcast: *We watched a TV special on whales.* **6** *adj.* held in high regard; great; chief: *a special friend.* —**spe′cial·ly,** *adv.* —**spe′cial·ness,** *n.*

SYNONYM STUDY **Special, particular,** and **specific** all mean for one and not others. **Special** means of a kind different from others: *My birthday is a special day for me.* **Particular** means belonging to one person or thing only: *Each of the three authors will autograph copies of her particular book.* **Specific** means characteristic of one person or thing: *Every mineral has a specific hardness.*

special delivery, delivery of a letter or package by a special messenger instead of the regular mail carrier, for an additional fee: *This package must be sent special delivery.*

special education, **1** teaching methods designed for students with special needs. **2** classes using these methods.

special effects, pictures and sound effects added to a movie or TV show after being made separately and in special ways. Special effects often show things that cannot be photographed or tape-recorded, such as monsters, spaceflight, or ghosts.

special effects

Special Forces, part of the U.S. Army whose members train non-U.S. forces in guerrilla warfare tactics. They are often called **Green Berets** because of the special hats they wear.

spe·cial·ist (spesh′ə list), *n.* **1** person who pursues one particular branch of study, business, etc. A heart specialist is a doctor who treats diseases of the heart. **2** (in the U.S. Army) a soldier with administrative or technical duties only. See chart on page 712.

special interest, any group of people, especially a corporation or industry, that tries to get privileges or special treatment from the government, especially through legislation. Special interests often try to influence legislation through campaign contributions.

spe·cial·ize (spesh′ə līz), *v.* **1** to pursue some special branch of study, work, etc.: *Some doctors specialize in treating heart disease. She specializes in medieval literature.* **2** to adapt to a spe-

cial function or condition: *Lungs and gills are specialized for breathing.* **3** to develop in a special way: *Animals and plants are specialized to fit their surroundings.* ❑ *v.* **spe·cial·ized, spe·cial·iz·ing.** —**spe′cial·i·za′tion,** *n.*

spe·cial·ty (spesh′əl tē), *n.* **1** a special study, line of work, profession, trade, etc.: *American history is the specialty of my social studies teacher.* **2** product, article, etc., to which special attention is given: *This store makes a specialty of children's clothes.* **3** special character or quality. **4** a special or particular characteristic; peculiarity. ❑ *n., pl.* **spe·cial·ties.**

spe·cie (spē′shē), *n.* money in the form of coins; metal money. Silver dollars are specie.

spe·cies (spē′shēz), *n.* **1** a set of related living things that all have certain characteristics and that are able to interbreed. A species ranks next below a genus and may be divided into several varieties, races, or breeds. Spearmint is a species of mint. The lion is one species of cat. **2** a kind; sort; variety: *There are many species of advertisements.* **3** **the species,** the human race. ❑ *n., pl.* **spe·cies** for 1,2.

WORD FAMILY **Species** and the words below are related. They all come from a Latin word meaning "sort" or "appearance."

allspice	specialist	specie	specify
especially	specialize	specific	specious
special	specialty	specification	spice

spe·cif·ic (spi sif′ik), **1** *adj.* definite; precise; particular: *There was no specific reason for the quarrel.* **2** *adj.* distinctive; limited to: *Feathers are a feature specific to birds.* ■ See Synonym Study at **special. 3** *adj.* curing some particular disease. **4** *n.* a cure for some particular disease: *Vitamin C is a specific for scurvy.* **5** *adj.* produced by some special cause: *a specific disease.* **6** *adj.* of or about a species: *the specific name of spearmint.* **7** *n.pl.* **specifics,** details: *specifics of the new laws.*

spe·cif·i·cal·ly (spi sif′ik lē), *adv.* in a specific manner; definitely; particularly: *The doctor told her specifically not to eat eggs.* ■ See Synonym Study at **especially.**

spec·i·fi·ca·tion (spes′ə fə kā′shən), *n.* **1** act of specifying; definite mention; detailed statement of particulars: *She made careful specification as to the kinds of cake and candy for her party.* **2** Usually, **specifications,** *pl.* a detailed description of the dimensions, materials, etc., for a building, road, dam, boat, etc. **3** something specified; particular item, article, etc.

specific gravity, ratio of the weight of a volume of a substance to the weight of the same volume of water, hydrogen, or air. The specific gravity of gold is 19, because any volume of gold weighs 19 times as much as the same volume of water.

specific heat, number of calories needed to raise the temperature of one gram of some substance by one degree Celsius.

spec·i·fic·i·ty (spes′ə fis′ə tē), *n.* specific quality.

spec·i·fy (spes′ə fī), *v.* **1** to mention or name definitely: *Did you specify any particular time for us to call?* **2** to include in the specifications: *He delivered the paper as specified.* ❑ *v.* **spec·i·fied, spec·i·fy·ing.** —**spec′i·fi′er,** *n.*

spec·i·men (spes′ə mən), *n.* **1** one of a group or class taken to show what the others are like; sample: *He collects specimens of all kinds of rocks and minerals. The statue was a fine specimen of Greek sculpture.* **2** sample of blood, urine, etc., for analysis or examination.

spe·cious (spē′shəs), *adj.* seeming desirable, reasonable, or probable, but not really so; apparently good, but without real merit: *a specious excuse.* —**spe′cious·ly,** *adv.* —**spe′cious·ness,** *n.*

speck (spek), **1** *n.* a small spot; stain: *Can you clean the specks off this wallpaper?* ■ See Synonym Study at **spot. 2** *n.* a tiny bit; particle: *I have a speck in my eye.* **3** *v.* to mark with specks: *His shirt was specked with ink.*

a	hat	ė	term	ô	order	ch	child			
ā	age	i	it	oi	oil	ng	long		a	in about
ä	far	ī	ice	ou	out	sh	she		e	in taken
â	care	o	hot	u	cup	th	thin	ə	i	in pencil
e	let	ō	open	ů	put	₮ʜ	then		o	in lemon
ē	equal	ȯ	saw	ü	rule	zh	measure		u	in circus

speck·le (spek′əl), **1** *n.* a small spot or mark: *This hen is gray with white speckles.* **2** *v.* to mark with many small spots: *The shirt was speckled with paint.* ❑ *v.* **speck·led, speck·ling.**

speck·led (spek′əld), *adj.* marked with many small spots: *A speckled bird flew out of the bush.*

specs (speks), *n.pl.* INFORMAL. **1** specifications. **2** spectacles; eyeglasses.

spec·ta·cle (spek′tə kəl), *n.* **1** something to look at; sight: *The children at play among the flowers made a charming spectacle. A quarrel is an unpleasant spectacle.* **2** a public show or display: *The parade was a fine spectacle.* **3** **spectacles,** *pl.* eyeglasses.

spec·tac·u·lar (spek tak′yə lər), **1** *adj.* making a great display: *the spectacular eruption of a volcano.* **2** *adj.* of or about a spectacle or show. **3** *n.* a lengthy movie or TV show, usually produced on a lavish scale. —**spec·tac′u·lar·ly,** *adv.*

spec·ta·tor (spek′tā tər), *n.* person who looks on without taking part: *There were many spectators at the game.*

spec·ter (spek′tər), *n.* **1** ghost. **2** thing causing terror or dread: *the grim specter of war.*

spec·tral (spek′trəl), *adj.* **1** of or like a specter; ghostly: *the spectral form of a ship on a foggy sea.* **2** of or about the spectrum: *spectral colors.* —**spec′tral·ly,** *adv.* —**spec′tral·ness,** *n.*

spec·tro·gram (spek′trə gram), *n.* photograph of a spectrum.

spec·tro·graph (spek′trə graf), *n.* device used to photograph a spectrum. —**spec′tro·graph′ic,** *adj.* —**spec′tro·graph′i·cal·ly,** *adv.*

spec·tro·scope (spek′trə skōp), *n.* device for producing and examining the spectrum of a ray from any source. The spectrum of a light ray can be examined to determine the nature of the source of the ray.

spec·trum (spek′trəm), *n.* **1** the band of colors formed when a beam of light is passed through a prism or is broken up by some other means. A rainbow has all the colors of the spectrum: red, orange, yellow, green, blue, indigo, and violet. **2** a similar band produced from a beam of any electromagnetic radiation. **3** any range or spread: *the spectrum of grades on the test, the spectrum of political opinion.* ❑ *n., pl.* **spec·tra** (spek′trə), **spec·trums.**

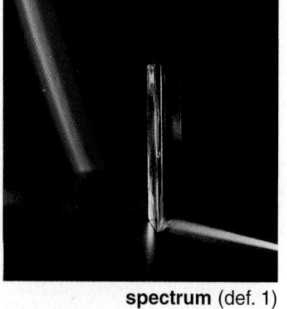
spectrum (def. 1)

spec·u·late (spek′yə lāt), *v.* **1** to think carefully; reflect; meditate; consider: *The philosopher speculated about time and space.* **2** to guess; conjecture: *She tried to speculate about the possible winner.* **3** to buy or sell when there is a large risk, with the hope of making a profit from future price changes: *He became poor after speculating in what turned out to be worthless oil wells.* ❑ *v.* **spec·u·lat·ed, spec·u·lat·ing.**

spec·u·la·tion (spek′yə lā′shən), *n.* **1** act of guessing; notion: *Our estimates of the cost were based on speculation.* **2** careful thought; reflection: *speculations about the nature of the universe.* **3** act of buying or selling when there is a large risk, with the hope of making a profit from future price changes: *Her speculations in the stock market made her a thousand dollars.*

spec·u·la·tive (spek′yə lā′tiv), *adj.* **1** carefully thoughtful; reflective. **2** theoretical rather than practical. **3** of or involving buying or selling at a large risk. —**spec′u·la′tive·ly,** *adv.* —**spec′u·la′-tive·ness,** *n.*

spec·u·la·tor (spek′yə lā′tər), *n.* person who speculates, usually in business. A ticket speculator buys tickets for shows, games, etc., in advance, hoping to sell them later at a higher price.

sped (sped), *v.* a past tense and a past participle of **speed:** *The police car sped down the road.*

speech (spēch), *n.* **1** act of speaking; talk: *Human beings express their thoughts by speech.* **2** power of speaking: *Animals lack speech.* **3** manner of speaking; dialect: *I could tell by their speech that they were from the South.* **4** language: *The native speech of most Americans is English.* ■ See Synonym Study at **language. 5** what is said; the words spoken: *We made the usual*

farewell speeches. **6** a public talk: *Our Congresswoman gave a fine speech at the fundraiser.* ❑ *n., pl.* **speech·es** for 5,6.

SYNONYM STUDY **Speech, lecture,** and **address** all mean a set of words spoken in public. **Speech** suggests minutes or hours in front of a large audience: *The candidate gave a speech outlining her plans for cutting taxes.* **Lecture** means speaking in order to teach: *The museum will present a lecture on why dinosaurs became extinct.* **Address** means a formal speech at a serious public event: *Lincoln's Gettysburg Address took only a few minutes.*

speech·i·fy (spē′chə fi), *v.* to make a speech or speeches. ❑ *v.* **speech·i·fied, speech·i·fy·ing.** —**speech′i·fi′er,** *n.*

speech·less (spēch′lis), *adj.* **1** not able to speak: *He was speechless with anger.* **2** silent: *Her frown gave a speechless message.* —**speech′less·ly,** *adv.* —**speech′less·ness,** *n.*

speech recognition, voice recognition.

speed (spēd), **1** *n.* rate of movement: *The children ran at top speed.* **2** *n.* rapid movement: *This game requires speed and strength.* **3** *v.* to go fast: *The boat sped over the water.* ■ See Synonym Study at **hurry. 4** *v.* to make go fast: *If we all help, that will speed the work.* **5** *v.* to go faster than is lawful: *Several drivers were caught speeding.* **6** *n.* arrangement of gears to give a certain rate of movement. A motor vehicle usually has several speeds forward and one backward. **7** *v.* to help succeed; promote: *speed an undertaking.* **8** *n.* OLD USE. good luck; success. ❑ *v.* **sped** or **speed·ed, speed·ing.**

speed up, to go or cause to go faster; increase speed.

speed·boat (spēd′bōt′), *n.* motorboat built to go fast.

speed bump, a raised ridge, often made of asphalt, placed crosswise on the surface of a street, driveway, or parking lot. A speed bump forces drivers to slow down.

speed·er (spē′dər), *n.* person who drives a motor vehicle at a higher speed than is safe or lawful.

speed limit, a maximum or minimum motor vehicle speed that is set by law in a specific area.

speed·om·e·ter (spē dom′ə tər), *n.* **1** device to show the speed of a motor vehicle. **2** odometer.

speed-read·ing (spēd′rē′ding), *n.* method of reading quickly by understanding several words or phrases at a time, or by scanning the middle of each page from top to bottom.

speed trap, a place where police cars often hide by the side of a road in order to catch speeders.

speed·up (spēd′up′), *n.* an increase in speed.

speed·way (spēd′wā′), *n.* a road or track for car or motorcycle racing.

speed·well (spēd′wel), *n.* any of several low plants with small blue, purple, pink, or white flowers.

speed·y (spē′dē), *adj.* moving, going, or acting with speed; fast; rapid; quick; swift: *speedy workers, a speedy decision.* ❑ *adj.* **speed·i·er, speed·i·est.** —**speed′i·ly,** *adv.* —**speed′i·ness,** *n.*

speed zone, a part of a road where drivers are limited to a speed much lower than the limit on other parts of the road.

spe·le·ol·o·gy (spē′lē ol′ə jē), *n.* the scientific study of caves. —**spe′le·ol′o·gist,** *n.*

spell¹ (spel), *v.* **1** to write or say the letters of a word in order: *Some words are easy to spell.* **2** to spell words: *We learn to spell in school.* **3** to make up or form a word: *C-a-t spells cat.* **4** to mean: *These clouds spell a storm. Delay spells danger.* ❑ *v.* **spelled, spell·ing.** —**spell′a·ble,** *adj.*

spell out, 1 to read with difficulty: *If you have to spell out each sentence in the story, you'll never understand what it is about.* **2** to explain carefully, step by step, and in detail: *We asked him to spell out his plan for raising more money.*

spell² (spel), *n.* **1** word or set of words supposed to have magic power. **2** magic influence; fascination; charm: *A spell of mystery seemed to hang over the old castle.* —**spell′-like′,** *adj.*

cast a spell on, to put under the influence of a spell; fascinate.

under a spell, controlled by a spell; fascinated; spellbound: *The adventure story held the children under a spell.*

spell³ (spel), **1** *n.* period or time of anything: *There was a long spell of rainy weather in August.* **2** *n.* a brief period: *rest for a* *spell.* **3** *v.* to work in place of someone else for a while: *I'll spell you at cutting the grass.* **4** *n.* period of illness: *The child has spells of coughing.* **5** *v.* to give a time of rest to. **6** *n.* relief of one person by another in doing something. **7** *n.* period of work or duty: *The rower's spell at the oars was half an hour.* ❑ *v.* **spelled, spell·ing.**

spell·bind (spel′bīnd′), *v.* to make spellbound; fascinate; enchant. ❑ *v.* **spell·bound, spell·bind·ing.**

spell·bind·er (spel′bīn′dər), *n.* speaker who can hold listeners spellbound.

spell·bound (spel′bound′), *adj.* too interested to move; fascinated; enchanted: *The children were spellbound by the circus performance.*

spell-check·er (spel′chek ər), *n.* a computer program for checking spelling in a file: *His spell-checker automatically changes "teh" to "the."*

spell·er (spel′ər), *n.* **1** person who spells words. **2** book for teaching spelling.

spell·ing (spel′ing), *n.* **1** act of writing or saying the letters of a word in order: *He is good at spelling.* **2** the way a word is spelled: *"Ax" has two spellings, "ax" and "axe."*

spelling bee, a spelling contest.

spe·lunk·er (spi lung′kər), *n.* person who explores and maps caves.

spend (spend), *v.* **1** to pay out: *She spent ten dollars shopping for food today.* **2** to pay out money: *Earn before you spend.* **3** to use; use up: *Don't spend any more time on that lesson.* **4** to pass: *She spent last summer at the lake.* **5** to wear out: *The storm has spent its force.* **6** to waste; squander: *He spent his fortune on horse racing.* ❑ *v.* **spent, spend·ing.** **—spend′a·ble,** *adj.* **—spend′er,** *n.*

WORD STORY **Spend** comes from a Latin word meaning "to weigh." **Expend** comes from the same Latin word. In old times, money was made of precious metals, such as gold and silver, and it was worth what it weighed. This is why some countries still use the pound as an unit of money.

spend·thrift (spend′thrift′), **1** *n.* person who wastes money. **2** *adj.* extravagant with money; wasteful.

spent (spent), **1** *v.* past tense and past participle of **spend**: *Saturday was spent in playing. How have you spent your time today?* **2** *adj.* used up. **3** *adj.* worn out; tired: *a spent swimmer, a spent horse.*

sperm (spėrm), *n.* **1** sperm cell. **2** semen. ❑ *n., pl.* **sperm** or **sperms** for 1.

sper·ma·cet·i (spėr′mə set′ē *or* spėr′mə sē′tē), *n.* a whitish, waxy substance obtained from the oil in the head of the sperm whale and formerly used in making fine candles, ointments, cosmetics, etc.

sper·mat·o·phyte (spėr mat′ə fīt), *n.* a seed-bearing plant.

sper·ma·to·zo·on (spėr′mə tə zō′ən), *n.* sperm cell. ❑ *n., pl.* **sper·ma·to·zo·a** (spėr′mə tə zō′ə).

sperm cell, a male reproductive cell; sperm. A sperm cell from the father unites with a mother's ovum to fertilize it.

sperm whale, a very large, gray, square-headed toothed whale that eats squid.

spew (spyü), *v.* to throw out; cast forth; vomit. **—spew′er,** *n.*

sp. gr., specific gravity.

sphag·num (sfag′nəm), *n.* any of a group of soft mosses, living mostly in swampy places; peat moss. When sphagnum decays and becomes compressed, it forms peat. Sphagnum is also used for potting or packing plants.

sphere (sfir), *n.* **1** a round solid object. Every point on the surface of a sphere is the same distance from the center. ■ See Synonym Study at **ball**¹. **2** ball or globe. The sun, moon, earth, and stars are spheres. **3** a place or surroundings in which someone or something exists, acts, works, etc.: *The woman's sphere today includes both business and home.* **4** a range; extent; region: *England's sphere of influence.* **5** a place, position, or rank in society: *the sphere of the aristocracy.*

spher·i·cal (sfir′ə kəl *or* sfer′ə kəl), *adj.* **1** shaped like a sphere. **2** of or about a sphere or spheres. **—spher′i·cal·ly,** *adv.*

spher·oid (sfir′oid), *n.* object or geometric figure shaped something like a sphere, but not perfectly round.

sphinc·ter (sfingk′tər), *n.* a ringlike muscle that surrounds an opening or passage of the body, and can contract to close it.

sphinx (sfingks), *n.* **1** statue of a lion's body with the head of a man, ram, or hawk. There are many sphinxes in Egypt. The **Great Sphinx** is a huge statue with a man's head and a lion's body, near Cairo. **2** **Sphinx,** (in Greek myths) a winged monster with the head of a woman and the body of a lion. The Sphinx asked every passerby a riddle and killed those unable to guess it. **3** any puzzling or mysterious person. ❑ *n., pl.* **sphinx·es** for 1,3.

sphyg·mo·ma·nom·e·ter (sfig′mō mə nom′ə tər), *n.* device for measuring blood pressure.

spice (spīs), **1** *n.* any of various seasonings obtained from plants and used to flavor food. Pepper, cinnamon, cloves, ginger, and nutmeg are common spices. **2** *v.* to put spice in; season: *spiced peaches.* **3** *n.* something that adds flavor or interest: *"Variety is the spice of life."* **4** *v.* to add flavor or interest to: *The principal spiced her speech with stories and jokes.* ❑ *v.* **spiced, spic·ing.**

spices (def. 1)

spice·bush (spīs′bush′), *n.* a North American bush with small yellow flowers and spicy-smelling bark and leaves. ❑ *n., pl.* **spice·bush·es.**

spick-and-span (spik′ən span′), *adj.* neat and clean; fresh; new: *a spick-and-span room.*

spic·ule (spik′yül), *n.* a small, slender, sharp-pointed piece, usually bony or crystalline, especially such a piece in a sponge.

spic·y (spī′sē), *adj.* **1** flavored with spice: *The cookies were rich and spicy.* **2** like spice: *Those apples have a spicy smell and taste.* **3** lively; spirited: *spicy conversation full of gossip.* **4** somewhat improper or indecent. ❑ *adj.* **spic·i·er, spic·i·est. —spic′i·ly,** *adv.* **—spic′i·ness,** *n.*

spi·der (spī′dər), *n.* **1** any of a great many small animals with eight legs, no wings, and bodies divided into two parts. Spiders are arachnids, not insects. **2** frying pan, especially one with legs to raise it above coals. **—spi′der·like′,** *adj.*

spider monkey, any of several monkeys living in Central and South America, with long, slim bodies, arms, and legs, a long grasping tail, and either undeveloped thumbs or no thumbs.

spider plant, a popular houseplant with long, thin leaves, often striped, and clusters of blue, purple, or white flowers. Spider plants grow by extending a thin stalk with a bunch of leaves at the end that looks something like a spider.

spi·der·web (spī′dər web′), *n.* web spun by a spider.

spi·der·y (spī′dər ē), *adj.* **1** long and thin like a spider's legs. **2** suggesting a spider web.

spied (spīd), *v.* past tense and past participle of **spy**: *He spied his friend in the crowd. Who had spied on us?*

spiel¹ (spēl), INFORMAL. **1** *n.* a speech, especially a long one. **2** *v.* to speak at length.

spiel² (spēl), *n.* CANADIAN. bonspiel.

a	hat	ė	term	ô	order	ch	child		
ā	age	i	it	oi	oil	ng	long		a in about
ä	far	ī	ice	ou	out	sh	she		e in taken
â	care	o	hot	u	cup	th	thin	ə	i in pencil
e	let	ō	open	ù	put	ŦH	then		o in lemon
ē	equal	ò	saw	ü	rule	zh	measure		u in circus

Spiel·berg (spēl′bərg), *n.* **Ste·ven** (stē′vən), born 1947, American movie director. ■ **Steven Spielberg's** movies include *Jaws, Raiders of the Lost Ark,* and *E.T.: The Extra-Terrestrial.* He won an Academy Award as best director for the movie *Schindler's List.*

spi·er (spī′ər), *n.* a spy.

spies (spīz), **1** *n.* plural of **spy. 2** *v.* a present tense of **spy.**

spiff·y (spif′ē), *adj.* INFORMAL. stylish; neat; trim: *a spiffy new suit.* ❑ *adj.* **spiff·i·er, spiff·i·est. —spiff′i·ly,** *adv.* **—spiff′i·ness,** *n.*

spig·ot (spig′ət), *n.* **1** faucet. **2** peg or plug used to stop up the small hole of a cask, barrel, or keg; bung.

spike[1] (spīk), **1** *n.* a large, strong nail. **2** *v.* to fasten with spikes: *The work crew laid the track by spiking the rails to the ties.* **3** *n.* a sharp-pointed piece of wood, metal, plastic, etc.: *fence spikes. Ballplayers wear shoes with spikes.* **4** *v.* to provide with spikes: *Runners wear spiked shoes to keep from slipping.* **5** *v.* to pierce or injure with a spike. **6** *v.* (earlier) to make a cannon useless by driving a spike into the opening where the powder is set off. **7** *v.* to put an end to or stop to; make useless; block: *The mayor spiked the talk of an increase in taxes.* **8** *v.* to drive a volleyball down into the opponent's court by a powerful hit above the net. **9** *n.* a volleyball hit in this way. **10** *v.* INFORMAL. to add alcoholic liquor to a nonalcoholic drink. ❑ *v.* **spiked, spik·ing. —spik′er,** *adj.*

spike[2] (spīk), *n.* **1** ear of grain. **2** a long, pointed flower cluster.

spike·nard (spīk′nərd *or* spik′närd), *n.* **1** (long ago) a sweet-smelling ointment. **2** the fragrant Asian plant from which it was obtained.

spik·y (spī′kē), *adj.* **1** having spikes; set with sharp, projecting points. **2** having the shape of a spike. ❑ *adj.* **spik·i·er, spik·i·est. —spik′i·ly,** *adv.* **—spik′i·ness,** *n.*

spill[1] (spil), **1** *v.* to let liquid or any loose matter run or fall: *spill milk or salt.* **2** *v.* to fall or flow out: *Water spilled from the pail.* **3** *v.* to shed blood. **4** *v.* to cause to fall from a horse, car, boat, etc.: *The boat upset and spilled all of us into the water.* **5** *n.* act of spilling. **6** *n.* quantity spilled. **7** *n.* a fall: *She took a bad spill while roller-skating.* **8** *v.* to make known; tell: *spill a secret.* ❑ *v.* **spilled** *or* **spilt, spill·ing. —spill′er,** *n.*

spill[2] (spil), *n.* a thin piece of wood, or a folded or twisted piece of paper, used to light a candle, pipe, etc.

spill·way (spil′wā′), *n.* channel or passage for the release of surplus water from a dam, river, etc.

spilt (spilt), *v.* a past tense and a past participle of **spill**[1].

spin (spin), **1** *v.* to turn around rapidly: *The wheel spins.* **2** *v.* to make something turn around rapidly: *The child spun the top.* **3** *v.* to feel as if you were turning around; feel dizzy: *My head is spinning.* **4** *v.* to draw out and twist cotton, flax, wool, etc., into thread. **5** *v.* to make thread or yarn by drawing out and twisting cotton, wool, flax, etc. **6** *v.* to make a thread, web, cocoon, etc., by giving out sticky material that hardens in air. A spider spins a web. **7** *v.* to tell in a long way: *My grandparents often spin yarns about life on the farm.* **8** *n.* act of spinning. **9** *n.* a rapid run, ride, drive, etc.: *Get your bicycle and come for a spin with me.* **10** *n.* a rapid turning around of an airplane as it falls. ❑ *v.* **spun, spin·ning. —spin′ner,** *n.*

spin out, to make long and slow; draw out: *spin out a story.*

> **SYNONYM STUDY** **Spin, twirl,** and **whirl** all mean to turn rapidly, many times. **Spin** is a general word: *As a CD spins, a laser converts its markings into music or information.* **Twirl** suggests speed and grace: *The figure skater twirled on the ice.* **Whirl** suggests great speed and force: *The whirling propeller lifted the helicopter.*

spin·ach (spin′ich), *n.* the green leaves of a garden plant, cooked and eaten as a vegetable, or used uncooked in a salad.

spi·nal (spī′nl), *adj.* of or about the backbone. **—spi′nal·ly,** *adv.*

spinal column, backbone.

spinal cord, the thick, whitish cord of nerve tissue that extends from the brain down through most of the backbone. Nerves branch off from the spinal cord to various parts of the body.

spin·dle (spin′dl), **1** *n.* the rod or pin used in spinning to twist, wind, and hold thread. **2** *n.* any rod or pin that turns around, or on which something turns. **3** *n.* something shaped like a spindle. **4** *v.* to grow very long and thin. ❑ *v.* **spin·dled, spin·dling.**

spin·dle-leg·ged (spin′dl leg′id *or* spin′dl legd′), *adj.* having long, thin legs.

spin·dling (spind′ling), *adj.* spindly.

spin·dly (spind′lē), *adj.* very long and slender; too tall and thin: *a spindly plant.* ❑ *adj.* **spin·dli·er, spin·dli·est.**

spin·drift (spin′drift′), *n.* spray blown or splashed up from the waves.

spine (spīn), *n.* **1** backbone. **2** anything like a backbone; long, narrow ridge or support. **3** a stiff, sharp-pointed growth; thorn or something like it. A cactus has spines; so has a porcupine. **4** the back portion of a book cover, often with the title on it.

spine·less (spīn′lis), *adj.* **1** without courage; weak: *a spineless coward.* **2** invertebrate. **3** having no spines: *a spineless cactus.* **—spine′less·ly,** *adv.* **—spine′less·ness,** *n.*

spin·et (spin′it), *n.* **1** a compact upright piano. **2** an old-fashioned musical instrument like a small harpsichord.

Spin·garn (spin′gärn), *n.* **Joel El·i·as** (ə lī′əs), 1875-1939, American literary critic and social reformer. ■ **Joel Spingarn** was one of the first white leaders of the NAACP. In 1914, he established the **Spingarn Medal,** which is given each year to an outstanding African American.

spin·na·ker (spin′ə kər), *n.* a large, triangular sail which is used as an extra sail when sailing downwind, to increase the speed of a boat.

spin·ner·et (spin′ə ret′), *n.* organ with which spiders and certain insect larvae, such as silkworms, spin their threads.

spinning jenny, an early type of spinning machine having more than one spindle, whereby one person could spin a number of threads at the same time; jenny.

spinning wheel, a large wheel with a spindle, arranged for spinning cotton, flax, wool, etc., into thread or yarn.

spin-off *or* **spin·off** (spin′ôf′), *n.* **1** product or products of research done for some other reason: *civilian spin-offs of military devices.* **2** something that comes from an earlier work: *The film is a spin-off of the original book.*

spin·ster (spin′stər), *n.* an unmarried woman, especially an older woman. ■ **Spinster** is often considered offensive.

spin·y (spī′nē), *adj.* **1** covered with spines; having spines; thorny: *a spiny cactus.* **2** stiff and sharp-pointed; spinelike: *the spiny quills of a porcupine.* ❑ *adj.* **spin·i·er, spin·i·est. —spin′i·ness,** *n.*

spiny anteater, echidna.

spiny lobster, a kind of lobster without large claws; rock lobster.

spi·ra·cle (spī′rə kəl *or* spir′ə kəl), *n.* an opening for breathing. Insects take in air through tiny spiracles. The blowhole of a whale is a large spiracle.

spi·rae·a (spī rē′ə), *n.* spirea. ❑ *n., pl.* **spi·rae·as.**

spi·ral (spī′rəl), **1** *n.* a winding and gradually widening coil. The thread of a screw is a spiral. **2** *adj.* winding; coiled: *a spiral staircase.* **3** *v.* to move in a spiral: *The flaming airplane spiraled to earth.* **4** *v.* to form into a spiral. ❑ *v.* **spi·raled, spi·ral·ing,** *or* **spi·ralled, spi·ral·ling. —spi′ral·ly,** *adv.*

spire[1] (spīr), *n.* **1** the top part of a tower or steeple that narrows to a point. **2** anything tapering and pointed: *The sunset shone on the rocky spires of the mountains.*

spire[2] (spīr), *n.* a coil; spiral.

spi·re·a (spī rē′ə), *n.* any of several bushes with clusters of small white, pink, or red flowers with five petals. ❑ *n., pl.* **spi·re·as.**

spi·ril·lum (spī ril′əm), *n.* any of numerous bacteria with spirally twisted forms. ❑ *n., pl.* **spi·ril·la** (spī ril′ə).

spir·it (spir′it), **1** *n.* the part of a human being that is not bodily; soul: *Some religions teach that at death the spirit leaves the body.* **2** *n.* a person's moral, religious, or emotional nature: *a proud spirit.* **3** *n.* a supernatural being. Angels are spirits. Ghosts and fairies are spirits. **4** *n.* **the Spirit, a** God. **b** the Holy Spirit. **5** *n.* Often, **spirits,** *pl.* state of mind; mood; temper: *She is in good spirits.* **6** *n.* person; person-

spire[1] (def. 1)

ality: *He is one of the more active spirits in our town.* **7** *n.* feeling that inspires and excites: *people with a spirit of progress.* **8** *n.* courage; vigor; liveliness: *A show horse must have spirit.* **9** *n.* enthusiasm and loyalty: *team spirit.* **10** *n.* what is really meant, separated from what is said or written: *The spirit of a law, she argued, is more important than its words.* **11** *n.* a general character, quality, or tendency: *the true Irish spirit.* **12** *n.* Often, **spirits,** *pl.* **a** a strong alcoholic liquor. **b** solution of a substance in alcohol: *spirits of camphor.* **13** *v.* to carry something away or off secretly: *The child has been spirited away.* **14** *adj.* of or about spirits or spiritualism: *the spirit world.*

out of spirits, sad or gloomy.

spir·it·ed (spir′ə tid), *adj.* full of energy and spirit; lively; dashing; brave: *a spirited race horse.* —**spir′it·ed·ly,** *adv.* —**spir′it·ed·ness,** *n.*

spir·it·less (spir′it lis), *adj.* without spirit or courage; depressed; tame. —**spir′it·less·ly,** *adv.* —**spir′it·less·ness,** *n.*

spir·i·tu·al (spir′ə chü əl), **1** *adj.* of or about the spirit or spirits. **2** *adj.* caring much for things of the spirit or soul. **3** *adj.* of the church; sacred; religious: *spiritual teachings.* **4** *adj.* supernatural. **5** *n.* a religious song which originated among African Americans of the southern United States. —**spir′i·tu·al·ly,** *adv.* —**spir′i·tu·al·ness,** *n.*

spir·i·tu·al·ism (spir′ə chü ə liz′əm), *n.* **1** the belief that spirits of the dead communicate with the living, especially through persons called mediums. **2** spiritual quality.

spir·i·tu·al·ist (spir′ə chü ə list), *n.* person who believes that the dead communicate with the living.

spir·i·tu·al·i·ty (spir′ə chü al′ə tē), *n.* devotion to spiritual things; spiritual quality.

spir·i·tu·al·ize (spir′ə chü ə līz), *v.* to make spiritual. ❏ *v.* **spir·i·tu·al·ized, spir·i·tu·al·iz·ing.** —**spir′i·tu·al·i·za′tion,** *n.*

spi·ro·chete (spī′rə kēt′), *n.* any of several bacteria that are spiral, slender, and very flexible.

spi·ro·gy·ra (spī′rə jī′rə), *n.* any of numerous green algae that grow in masses like scum in freshwater ponds. ❏ *n., pl.* **spi·ro·gy·ras.**

spit[1] (spit), **1** *v.* to throw out saliva, bits of food, etc., from the mouth. **2** *v.* to hurl: *A gun spits fire. The crew spit curses.* **3** *n.* saliva. **4** *n.* sound or act of spitting. **5** *v.* to make a spitting sound: *The cat spits when angry.* ❏ *v.* **spit** or **spat, spit·ting.** —**spit′ter,** *n.*

spit and image, spitting image.

spit up, to throw up or vomit.

spit[2] (spit), **1** *n.* a sharp-pointed, slender rod or bar on which meat is roasted. **2** *v.* to run a spit through; pierce; stab: *The cook spitted two rabbits.* **3** *n.* a narrow point of land that sticks out into the water. ❏ *v.* **spit·ted, spit·ting.**

spit·ball (spit′bôl′), *n.* **1** a small ball of chewed-up paper, used as a missile. **2** (in baseball) an illegal curve thrown by the pitcher after moistening one side of the ball with saliva, grease, etc.

spite (spīt), **1** *n.* ill will; grudge: *He broke my new radio out of spite.* **2** *v.* to show ill will toward; annoy: *They let the weeds grow in their yard to spite their neighbors.* ❏ *v.* **spit·ed, spit·ing.**

in spite of, regardless of: *I went out in spite of the snowstorm.*

spite·ful (spīt′fəl), *adj.* full of spite; eager to annoy; behaving with ill will: *My spiteful little cousin tore up all my drawings.* —**spite′ful·ly,** *adv.* —**spite′ful·ness,** *n.*

spit·fire (spit′fīr′), *n.* person, especially a woman or girl, who has a quick and fiery temper.

spitting image, the exact likeness; spit and image: *She is the spitting image of her mother.*

spit·tle (spit′l), *n.* saliva; spit.

spit·toon (spi tün′), *n.* container to spit into; cuspidor.

spitz (spits), *n.* any of various sturdy, small dogs with long hair, pointed noses, and tails curled up over their backs. ❏ *n., pl.* **spitz·es.**

splash (splash), **1** *v.* to cause water, mud, etc., to fly about. **2** *v.* to dash liquid about: *The baby likes to splash in the tub.* **3** *v.* to dash in scattered masses or drops: *The waves splashed on the beach.* **4** *v.* to wet, spatter, or soil: *Our car is all splashed with mud.* **5** *n.* act or sound of splashing; splashing: *The splash of the wave knocked him over. The boat upset with a loud splash.* **6** *v.* to fall, move, or go with a splash or splashes: *He splashed across the*

brook. **7** *n.* spot of liquid splashed upon a thing: *She had splashes of grease on her clothes.* **8** *n.* spot; patch: *The dog is white with brown splashes.* ❏ *n., pl.* **splash·es.**

make a splash, to attract attention; cause excitement.

splash

splash·down (splash′doun′), *n.* the landing of a capsule or other spacecraft in the ocean after reentry.

splash·y (splash′ē), *adj.* **1** making a splash. **2** full of spots or streaks. **3** attracting attention; causing excitement. ❏ *adj.* **splash·i·er, splash·i·est.** —**splash′i·ly,** *adv.* —**splash′i·ness,** *n.*

splat·ter (splat′ər), **1** *v.* to splash or spatter: *splattered with paint.* **2** *n.* a splash or spatter.

splay (splā), **1** *v.* to spread out. **2** *adj.* wide and flat: *splay feet.*

spleen (splēn), *n.* **1** a ductless, glandlike organ located near the stomach. It filters germs and nonfunctioning blood cells from the blood. **2** bad temper; spite; anger: *criticism full of spleen.*

splen·did (splen′did), *adj.* **1** brilliant or glorious; magnificent; grand: *a splendid sunset, a splendid palace, splendid jewels, a splendid victory.* **2** very good; fine; excellent: *a splendid opportunity.* —**splen′did·ly,** *adv.* —**splen′did·ness,** *n.*

splen·dif·er·ous (splen dif′ər əs), *adj.* INFORMAL. splendid. —**splen·dif′er·ous·ly,** *adv.* —**splen·dif′er·ous·ness,** *n.*

splen·dor (splen′dər), *n.* **1** great brightness; brilliant light: *The sun set in a golden splendor.* **2** magnificent show; pomp; glory.

splice (splīs), **1** *v.* to join ropes by weaving together ends which have been untwisted. **2** *v.* to join two pieces of timber by overlapping. **3** *v.* to join film, tape, wire, etc., by gluing or cementing the ends. **4** *n.* act of joining ropes, timbers, film, etc., by splicing: *How neat a splice can you make?* ❏ *v.* **spliced, splic·ing.** —**splic′er,** *n.*

splint (splint), *n.* **1** arrangement of wood or metal to hold a broken or dislocated bone in place. **2** a thin strip of wood, such as is used in making baskets.

splin·ter (splin′tər), **1** *n.* a thin, sharp piece of wood, bone, glass, etc.: *I have a splinter in my hand.* **2** *v.* to split or break into thin, sharp pieces: *to splinter wood with an ax.*

splin·ter·y (splin′tər ē), *adj.* **1** apt to splinter: *splintery wood.* **2** rough and jagged, as if from splintering. **3** full of splinters.

split (split), **1** *v.* to break or cut from end to end, or in layers: *We split the logs into firewood.* **2** *v.* to separate into parts; divide: *We split the cost of the dinner between us.* **3** *n.* a break; crack; fracture: *Frost caused the split in the rock.* **4** *adj.* broken or cut from end to end; divided. **5** *v.* to divide into different groups. **6** *n.* division in a group: *There was a split in the club for a time, but agreement was restored at last.* **7** *v.* to divide a molecule or atomic nucleus into two or more smaller parts. **8** *n.* Often, **splits,** *pl.* an acrobatic trick of sinking to the floor with one leg straight forward and the other leg straight back. **9** *v.* SLANG. to go away; leave. ❏ *v.* **split, split·ting.** —**split′ter,** *n.*

a	hat	ė	term	ô	order	ch	child		a in about
ā	age	i	it	oi	oil	ng	long		e in taken
ä	far	ī	ice	ou	out	sh	she	ə {	i in pencil
â	care	o	hot	u	cup	th	thin		o in lemon
e	let	ō	open	ů	put	ŦH	then		u in circus
ē	equal	ò	saw	ü	rule	zh	measure		

split infinitive, infinitive having one or more words between *to* and the verb. EXAMPLE: Last summer I learned *to really enjoy* swimming.

> **USAGE NOTE** **Split infinitives** are regarded as incorrect usage by many people. Others say that there is no strong reason for a rule against this usage. It is wise to avoid split infinitives in formal speech or in writing.

split-lev·el (split′lev′əl), *n.* house with two or more floor levels, each level about half a story above or below the adjacent level.

split personality, 1 personality that shows patterns of behavior so different at various times that it is difficult to understand how they can be one person's. **2** INFORMAL. schizophrenia or person with schizophrenia.

split second, a very brief moment of time; instant.

split·ting (split′ing), *adj.* very severe; extreme; violent: *a splitting headache.*

splotch (sploch), **1** *n.* a large, irregular spot; splash. **2** *v.* to make such spots or splashes on. ❑ *n., pl.* **splotch·es.**

splotch·y (sploch′ē), *adj.* marked with splotches. ❑ *adj.* **splotch·i·er, splotch·i·est. —splotch′i·ness,** *n.*

splurge (splėrj), **1** *v.* to spend more money than you should: *We splurged and ate at a fancy restaurant.* **2** *n.* act of showing off. **3** *v.* to show off. ❑ *v.* **splurged, splurg·ing.**

splut·ter (splut′ər), **1** *v.* to talk in a hasty, confused way. People sometimes splutter when they are excited. **2** *v.* to make spitting or popping noises; sputter: *The baked apples are spluttering in the oven.* **3** *n.* a spluttering noise.

Spock (spok), *n.* **Ben·ja·min** (ben′jə mən), born 1903, American doctor and author. He has written many books about how to care for children and infants.

spoil (spoil), **1** *v.* to damage or injure something so as to make it unfit or useless; ruin; destroy: *The rain spoiled the picnic.* **2** *v.* to be damaged; become bad or unfit for use: *The fruit spoiled because I kept it too long.* **3** *v.* to injure the character or disposition of: *They spoiled him by always giving him what he wanted.* ■ See Synonym Studies at **gratify** and **pamper.** **4** *n.* Often, **spoils,** *pl.* **a** things taken by force; things won: *The victors returned with the spoils of war.* **b** offices and positions filled by the political party that has won an election. ❑ *v.* **spoiled** or **spoilt, spoil·ing.**

be spoiling for, be longing for a fight, etc.: *spoiling for a quarrel.*

spoil·age (spoi′lij), *n.* **1** act of spoiling. **2** fact of being spoiled. **3** something spoiled.

spoil·er (spoi′lər), *n.* **1** person or thing that spoils. **2** person who takes spoils. **3** anything that reveals the end of a book, movie, etc., to those who have not yet read or seen it: *That movie review was a real spoiler and told who was the murderer.*

spoil·sport (spoil′spôrt′), *n.* person who keeps others from having fun.

spoils system, system or practice in which public offices with their salaries and advantages are awarded to supporters of the winning political party.

spoilt (spoilt), *v.* a past tense and a past participle of **spoil.**

Spo·kane (spō kan′), *n.* city in E Washington.

spoke[1] (spōk), *v.* past tense of **speak:** *She spoke about that yesterday.*

spoke[2] (spōk), *n.* **1** one of the rods that connect the center of a wheel to the rim. **2** rung of a ladder.

spo·ken (spō′kən), **1** *v.* past participle of **speak:** *They have spoken about coming to visit.* **2** *adj.* expressed with the mouth; uttered; told: *I usually understand a spoken direction better than a written one.* **3** *adj.* speaking in a certain way: *a soft-spoken person, plain-spoken advice.*

be spoken for, be saved or reserved for someone: *I'm sorry, seats on the aisle are all spoken for.*

spokes·man (spōks′mən), *n.* person who speaks for another or others: *I am the spokesman for my class in the student council.* ❑ *n., pl.* **spokes·men.**

spokes·per·son (spōks′pėr′sən), *n.* person who speaks for another or others.

spokes·wom·an (spōks′wùm′ən), *n.* woman who speaks for another or others. ❑ *n., pl.* **spokes·wom·en.**

sponge (spunj), **1** *n.* any of very many motionless water animals resembling plants, but feeding on living matter in water that they suck in through tiny pores in their bodies. Most sponges live in large colonies on the bottom of the ocean, attached to stones, plants, etc. **2** *n.* the soft, light skeleton of any of these animals, used for soaking up water in bathing, cleaning, etc. **3** *n.* a similar item made of rubber, plastic, etc. **4** *v.* to wipe or rub with a wet sponge; make clean or damp in this way: *Sponge the mud spots off the car.* **5** *v.* to absorb: *sponge up knowledge.* **6** *n.* something used like a sponge, such as a pad of gauze used by doctors to absorb blood in surgery. **7** *v.* to live or profit at the expense of someone else in a mean or selfish way: *They are sponging on their relatives instead of working.* ❑ *v.* **sponged, spong·ing.** **—sponge′like′,** *adj.*

throw in the sponge, to give up; admit defeat: *After the opposing team scored their sixth touchdown, our guys threw in the sponge.*

sponge (def. 1)

sponge cake, a light, spongy cake made with eggs, sugar, flour, etc., but no shortening.

spong·er (spun′jər), *n.* **1** person who lives at the expense of others. **2** person or boat engaged in gathering sponges.

spon·gy (spun′jē), *adj.* **1** like a sponge; soft, light, and full of holes: *spongy moss, spongy dough.* **2** full of holes: *a spongy rock.* ❑ *adj.* **spon·gi·er, spon·gi·est. —spon′gi·ness,** *n.*

spon·sor (spon′sər), **1** *n.* person or group that endorses, supports, or is responsible for a person or thing: *the sponsor of a law, the sponsor of a student applying for a scholarship.* **2** *n.* person who stands with the parents at an infant's baptism, agreeing to assist in the child's religious upbringing if necessary; godparent. **3** *n.* business firm or other organization that pays the costs of a radio or TV show advertising its products or services. **4** *v.* to act as sponsor for. **—spon′sor·ship,** *n.*

spon·ta·ne·i·ty (spon′tə nē′ə tē), *n.* spontaneous action, movement, etc.

spon·ta·ne·ous (spon tā′nē əs), *adj.* **1** caused by natural impulse or desire; not forced or compelled; not planned beforehand: *both sides burst into spontaneous cheers at the skillful play.* **2** taking place without external cause or help; caused entirely by inner forces: *the eruption of a volcano is spontaneous.* **—spon·ta′ne·ous·ly,** *adv.* **—spon·ta′ne·ous·ness,** *n.*

spontaneous combustion, the act or process of something's bursting into flame without anyone's having set it on fire. In spontaneous combustion, the heat produced by internal chemical action causes the fire.

spontaneous generation, the supposed production of living things from nonliving matter. People long ago believed that flies were born from rotting food or that worms were born from dirt.

spoof (spüf), **1** *n.* parody; takeoff. **2** *n.* a trick, hoax, or joke. **3** *v.* to play tricks. **4** *v.* to parody something.

spook (spük), **1** *n.* ghost. **2** *n.* SLANG. a spy. **3** *v.* to scare; frighten: *The storm spooked the horses.*

spook·y (spü′kē), *adj.* **1** strange and frightening; suited to or suggesting spooks: *We were afraid to enter the spooky old house.*

2 easily frightened: *a spooky horse.* ❏ *adj.* **spook·i·er, spook·i·est.** **—spook′i·ly,** *adv.* **—spook′i·ness,** *n.*

spool (spül), **1** *n.* cylinder of wood or metal on which thread, wire, recording tape, film, etc., is wound. **2** *v.* to wind on a spool.

spoon (spün), **1** *n.* tool consisting of a small, shallow bowl at the end of a handle. Spoons are used to pick up or stir food or drink. **2** *v.* to pick up in a spoon: *to spoon heaps of mashed potatoes onto a plate.* **3** *n.* something shaped like a spoon. **—spoon′like′,** *adj.*

born with a silver spoon in your mouth, born lucky or rich.

spoon·bill (spün′bil′), *n.* any of several long-legged, pink wading birds that have long, flat bills with spoon-shaped tips.

spoon bread, mixture of corn meal with milk, eggs, shortening, etc., cooked by baking but always soft enough to be served with a spoon.

spoon·er·ism (spü′nə riz′əm), *n.* a usually accidental reversal of the first sounds of two or more words. EXAMPLE: "well-boiled icicle" for "well-oiled bicycle."

spoon-feed (spün′fēd′), *v.* **1** to feed with a spoon. **2** to provide information, aid, etc., to someone who passively receives it. ❏ *v.* **spoon-fed** (spün′fed′), **spoon-feed·ing.**

spoon·ful (spün′fül), *n.* as much as a spoon can hold. ❏ *n., pl.* **spoon·fuls.**

spoor (spür), *n.* trail of a wild animal; track.

spo·rad·ic (spə rad′ik), *adj.* occurring in scattered cases; appearing here and there or now and then: *sporadic outbreaks of scarlet fever.* **—spo·rad′i·cal·ly,** *adv.*

spo·ran·gi·um (spə ran′jē əm), *n.* spore case. ❏ *n., pl.* **spo·ran·gi·a** (spə ran′jē ə).

spore (spôr), *n.* cell produced by some living things that can develop into a new living thing. Ferns, mosses, and many fungi and bacteria produce spores.

spore case, case containing spores; sporangium. The little brown spots on the underside of ferns are collections of spore cases.

spo·ro·phyte (spôr′ə fit), *n.* a plant or a generation of plants producing asexual spores, when the generations before and after produce sexual seeds.

spo·ro·zo·an (spôr′ə zō′ən), *n.* any of numerous one-celled parasitic protists that reproduce sexually and asexually in alternate generations. Certain sporozoans cause diseases, such as malaria, in humans and other animals.

spor·ran (spôr′ən), *n.* a large purse, commonly of fur, hanging from the belt in front of a Scottish Highlands costume.

sport (spôrt), **1** *n.* game, contest, or other pastime requiring some skill and usually involving a certain amount of physical exercise. Baseball and fishing are outdoor sports; bowling and basketball are indoor sports. **2** *n.* any pastime or amusement: *They fly kites for sport.* **3** *adj.* of or suitable for sports. **4** *n.* ridicule: *The fool's actions were a source of sport to the villagers.* **5** *n.* object of jokes and ridicule: *The awkward beginner was the sport of the experienced golfers.* **6** *n.* sportsman. **7** *n.* person who behaves in a fair and honorable manner and knows how to be a good loser: *to be a sport.* **8** *v.* to display: *to sport a new hat.* [**Sport** comes from **disport,** which comes from Latin words meaning "to carry away." Sport carries our attention away from work or study.]

for sport or **in sport,** in fun; as a joke: *She teased them in sport.*

make sport of, to make fun of; laugh at; ridicule: *Don't make sport of me.*

WORD BANK There are many different kinds of **sports,** and many names for them. If you want to learn more about sports, you can begin by looking up these words in this dictionary.

aikido	figure skating	polo	swimming
archery	football	racquetball	table tennis
baseball	golf	rugby	tennis
basketball	gymnastics	running	touch football
bowling	handball	skiing	track and field
boxing	hockey	soccer	volleyball
cricket[2]	jai alai	softball	water-skiing
curling	judo	squash[1]	wrestling
fencing	karate	surfing	
field hockey	lacrosse		

sport·ing (spôr′ting), *adj.* **1** of, interested in, or engaging in sports: *a sporting event.* **2** playing fair; sportsmanlike: *The loser made a sporting gesture in shaking the winner's hand.* **—sport′-ing·ly,** *adv.*

sporting chance, offering the kind of risk that is fair and even: *The inexperienced team hardly had a sporting chance of winning.*

spor·tive (spôr′tiv), *adj.* playful; merry: *The old dog seemed as sportive as the puppy.* **—spor′tive·ly,** *adv.* **—spor′tive·ness,** *n.*

sports (spôrts), *adj.* of sports; suitable for sports: *sports clothes.*

sports car, a small, low, fast car, usually with two seats and an open top.

sports·cast (spôrts′kast′), *n.* broadcast of a sports event.

sports·cast·er (spôrts′kas′tər), *n.* person who does the spoken part of a broadcast or telecast sports event.

sport shirt, shirt meant to be worn informally, without a tie.

sports·man (spôrts′mən), *n.* **1** person who takes part in or is interested in sports, especially hunting and fishing. **2** person who plays fair and is a good loser. ❏ *n., pl.* **sports·men.** **—sports′man·ly,** *adj.*

sports·man·like (spôrts′mən līk′), *adj.* like or suitable for a sportsman; fair and honorable.

sports·man·ship (spôrts′mən ship), *n.* **1** qualities or conduct of a sportsman; fair play. **2** ability in sports.

sports medicine, branch of medicine dealing with the proper working of the human body during physical activity and with the prevention and treatment of sports injuries.

sports·wear (spôrts′wâr′), *n.* clothes designed for informal, outdoor, or athletic wear.

sports·wom·an (spôrts′wúm′ən), *n.* woman who engages in or is interested in sports. ❏ *n., pl.* **sports·wom·en.**

sports·writ·er (spôrts′rī′tər), *n.* journalist who writes about sports.

sport·y (spôr′tē), *adj.* INFORMAL. **1** showy; flashy: *a sporty convertible.* **2** smart in dress, appearance, manners, etc. **3** sportsmanlike; sporting. ❏ *adj.* **sport·i·er, sport·i·est.** **—sport′i·ly,** *adv.* **—sport′i·ness,** *n.*

spot (spot), **1** *n.* a small mark or stain that discolors or disfigures: *You have grease spots on your suit. That spot on her arm is a bruise.* **2** *n.* a small part unlike the rest: *a blue tie with red spots.* **3** *n.* a place: *From this spot you can see the ocean.* **4** *v.* to place in a certain spot; scatter in various spots: *Lookouts were spotted all along the coast.* **5** *v.* to pick out; find out; recognize: *I spotted my sister in the crowd. The teacher spotted every mistake.* **6** *n.* a blemish or flaw in character or reputation: *His record is without spot.* **7** *v.* to make or become spotted: *The tablecloth was spotted with gravy.* **8** *adj.* ready; on hand: *a spot answer, spot cash.* **9** *n.* figure or dot on playing cards, dominoes, or dice to show their kind and value. ❏ *v.* **spot·ted, spot·ting.**

hit the spot, INFORMAL. be just right; be satisfactory.

in a spot, in trouble or difficulty.

on the spot, 1 at the very place where needed: *A doctor on the spot gave the injured player first aid.* **2** at once: *Your orders will be carried out on the spot.* **3** in an awkward or difficult position: *He put me on the spot by asking a question I could not answer.*

SYNONYM STUDY **Spot, mark**[1], and **speck** all mean a point different from the surface around it. **Spot** suggests a spill: *He got ink spots on his jacket.* **Mark** suggests a touch: *There's a mark on the wall where the chair rubbed it.* **Speck** suggests something tiny and only lying on a surface: *She cleans every speck of dust off her computer each morning.*

spot check, 1 a brief, rough sampling. **2** a checkup made without warning. **—spot′-check′,** *v.*

spot·less (spot′lis), *adj.* without a spot: *a spotless white shirt.* **—spot′less·ly,** *adv.* **—spot′less·ness,** *n.*

S

a	hat	ė	term	ô	order	ch	child		a	in about
ā	age	i	it	oi	oil	ng	long		e	in taken
ä	far	ī	ice	ou	out	sh	she	ə	i	in pencil
â	care	o	hot	u	cup	th	thin		o	in lemon
e	let	ō	open	ù	put	ŦH	then		u	in circus
ē	equal	ò	saw	ü	rule	zh	measure			

spot·light (spot′līt′), **1** *n.* a spot or circle of bright light thrown upon a particular place or person. **2** *n.* lamp that gives such light: *a spotlight in a theater.* **3** *v.* to light up with a spotlight or spotlights: *spotlight the conductor.* **4** *n.* public notice; anything that directs attention on a person or thing: *Movie stars are often in the spotlight.* **5** *v.* to call attention to; give public notice to: *The newspaper article spotlights the growth of the soybean industry.* ❑ *v.* **spot·light·ed** or **spot·lit** (spot′līt′), **spot·light·ing.**

spotlight (def. 3)

spot·ted (spot′id), *adj.* **1** marked with spots: *a spotted dog.* **2** stained with spots: *a spotted reputation.*

spot·ty (spot′ē), *adj.* **1** having spots; spotted. **2** not of uniform quality; irregular: *Your work is spotty.* ❑ *adj.* **spot·ti·er, spot·ti·est.** —**spot′ti·ly,** *adv.* —**spot′ti·ness,** *n.*

spous·al (spou′zəl), *adj.* of or about marriage or a spouse: *spousal abuse.*

spouse (spous), *n.* husband or wife: *Mr. Smith is Mrs. Smith's spouse, and she is his spouse.* —**spouse′less,** *adj.*

spout (spout), **1** *v.* to throw out a liquid in a stream or spray: *A whale spouts water when it breathes.* **2** *v.* to flow out with force: *Water spouted from a break in the pipe.* **3** *n.* stream; jet: *A spout of water shot up from the hole in the pipe.* **4** *n.* pipe for carrying off water: *Rain runs down a spout from our roof to the ground.* **5** *n.* tube or lip from which liquid is poured. A teakettle and a coffeepot have spouts. **6** *v.* INFORMAL. to speak in loud and very emotional tones: *The hammy actor spouted his lines.* —**spout′er,** *n.*

sprain (sprān), **1** *v.* to stretch or tear ligaments in a joint by a sudden twist or wrench: *I sprained my ankle.* **2** *n.* injury caused by a sudden twist or wrench: *The sprain took a long time to heal.*

sprang (sprang), *v.* a past tense of **spring:** *The hungry tiger sprang at the antelope.*

sprat (sprat), *n.* a small herring of the Atlantic coast of Europe. ❑ *n., pl.* **sprat** or **sprats.**

sprawl (spról), **1** *v.* to lie or sit with the arms and legs spread out, especially in an awkward manner: *The children were sprawled in front of the TV.* **2** *v.* to spread out in an irregular or awkward manner: *His large handwriting sprawled across the page.* **3** *n.* act or position of sprawling.

spray[1] (sprā), **1** *n.* liquid going through the air in small drops: *We were wet with the sea spray.* **2** *n.* liquid stored under pressure in a container, that can be released as a spray or mist. **3** *n.* device that sends a liquid out as spray. **4** *v.* to scatter spray on; sprinkle: *Spray the apple tree.* **5** *v.* to fire bullets or small missiles at: *A squad of riflemen sprayed the enemy position.* —**spray′er,** *n.*

spray[2] (sprā), *n.* a small branch or piece of some plant with its leaves, flowers, or fruit: *a spray of lilacs.*

spray can, container from which an insecticide, paint, cosmetic, etc., can be released as a spray or mist.

spray gun, device used to spray paint, pesticide, and the like.

spread (spred), **1** *v.* to cover or cause to cover a large or larger area; stretch out; unfold; open out: *to spread rugs on the floor. The bird spread its wings.* **2** *v.* to move farther out apart: *Spread out your fingers.* **3** *v.* to put on as a thin layer: *He spread jam on his bread.* **4** *v.* to cover with a thin layer: *She spread each slice with*

butter. **5** *v.* to extend; lie: *Fields of corn spread out before us.* **6** *v.* to scatter; distribute: *She spread the news. She spread grain for the chickens.* **7** *n.* act of spreading: *to fight the spread of infection, encourage the spread of knowledge.* **8** *n.* width; extent; amount of or capacity for spreading: *the spread of a bird's wings.* **9** *n.* a covering for a bed or table. **10** *v.* to set or put food on a table. **11** *n.* food put on the table; feast. **12** *n.* a soft food to spread on bread, crackers, etc. Butter and jam are spreads. **13** *n.* advertisement, article, etc., occupying a number of adjoining columns or pages in a magazine or newspaper: *The ad was given a three-column spread.* ❑ *v.* **spread, spread·ing.** —**spread′er,** *n.*

spread·sheet (spred′shēt′), *n.* type of computer program designed to process numerical information, especially for financial purposes. Such a program can calculate rapidly the changes produced in whole sets of data by a change in a single category, such as the effect on an entire budget of one increased expense.

spree (sprē), *n.* a short period of activity, fun, or pleasure, especially when done to excess: *I went on a buying spree.*

spri·er (sprī′ər), *adj.* comparative of **spry.**

spri·est (sprī′ist), *adj.* superlative of **spry.**

sprig (sprig), *n.* twig or small branch: *a sprig of mint.*

spright·ly (sprīt′lē), *adj.* lively; vigorous. ❑ *adj.* **spright·li·er, spright·li·est.** —**spright′li·ness,** *n.*

spring (spring), **1** *n.* season when plants begin to grow; season of the year between winter and summer. **2** *adj.* of or in this season. Spring wheat is sown in the spring. **3** *v.* to rise suddenly and lightly; leap; jump: *I sprang to my feet.* ■ See Synonym Study at **jump. 4** *n.* an elastic device that returns to its original shape after being pulled or held out of shape. Springs are usually made of metal formed into coils or curves. **5** *n.* a leap; jump: *a spring over the fence.* **6** *v.* to move back or away as if by an elastic device: *The door sprang shut.* **7** *v.* to cause to move in this way: *The slightest pressure will spring the trap.* **8** *n.* elastic quality: *The old man's knees have lost their spring.* **9** *n.* a small stream of water flowing naturally from the earth. **10** *v.* to come from some source; arise; grow: *The argument sprang from a misunderstanding.* **11** *n.* source; beginning; origin. **12** *v.* to begin to move, act, grow, etc., suddenly; burst forth: *Towns spring up where oil is discovered.* **13** *v.* to bring out, produce, or make suddenly: *to spring a surprise on someone.* **14** *v.* to bend or break: *Frost has sprung the rock wall. The door has sprung and won't close properly.* ❑ *v.* **sprang** or **sprung, sprung, spring·ing.** —**spring′er,** *n.*

spring·board (spring′bôrd′), *n.* **1** a flexible board used to give added spring in diving, jumping, and vaulting. **2** anything that serves as a way to get to something else: *Hard work is often a springboard to success.*

spring·bok (spring′bok′), *n.* a small antelope of southern Africa. It leaps almost directly upward when excited or disturbed. ❑ *n., pl.* **spring·bok** or **spring·boks.**

springbok—2 ft. 6 in. (76 cm) high

spring fever, a lazy feeling that some people get during the first warm weather of spring.

Spring·field (spring′fēld′), *n.* **1** capital of Illinois, in the central part. **2** city in S Massachusetts. **3** city in SW Missouri.

spring salmon, CANADIAN. chinook salmon.

Spring·steen (spring′stēn), *n.* Bruce (brüs), born 1949, American rock musician and composer. His nickname is "The Boss."

spring·tide (spring′tīd′), *n.* springtime.

spring tide, the especially high and low tides that come at the time of the new moon or the full moon.

spring·time (spring′tīm′), *n.* the season of spring.

spring·y (spring′ē), *adj.* full of bounce; elastic: *a springy step.* ❑ *adj.* **spring·i·er, spring·i·est.** —**spring′i·ly,** *adv.* —**spring′i·ness,** *n.*

sprin·kle (spring′kəl), **1** *v.* to scatter in drops or tiny bits: *I sprinkled salt on the icy sidewalk.* **2** *v.* to spray or cover with small drops: *sprinkle flowers with water.* **3** *n.* small quantity: *The cook put a sprinkle of nuts on the cake.* **4** *v.* to rain a little. **5** *n.* a light rain. ❑ *v.* **sprin·kled, sprin·kling.**

sprin·kler (spring′klər), *n.* device for sprinkling water on gardens and lawns.

sprinkler system, system for putting fires out in a building, using overhead sprinklers that come on automatically when the temperature rises too high.

sprin·kling (spring′kling), *n.* a small quantity or number scattered here and there: *He has a sprinkling of gray hair.*

sprint (sprint), **1** *v.* to run at full speed, especially for a short distance. ■ See Synonym Study at **run. 2** *n.* a race or any short spell of running, rowing, etc., at top speed. **—sprint′er,** *n.*

sprit (sprit), *n.* a small pole running diagonally from the foot of the mast to the top corner of a fore-and-aft sail, to support and stretch it.

sprite (sprit), *n.* elf; fairy; goblin.

sprit·sail (sprit′sāl′ *or* sprit′səl), *n.* sail supported and stretched by a sprit.

sprock·et (sprok′it), *n.* **1** one of a set of teeth on the rim of a wheel, arranged so as to fit into the links of a chain. The sprockets keep the chain from slipping. **2** Also, **sprocket wheel,** wheel made with sprockets.

sprout (sprout), **1** *v.* to produce new leaves, shoots, or buds: *The wheat sprouted early this year.* **2** *v.* to begin to grow; come forth: *Buds sprout in the spring.* **3** *n.* a young growth of a plant: *The gardener had gently set out sprouts.* **4** *n.pl.* **sprouts, a** the first stalks of germinating beans, alfalfa seeds, etc., eaten as a vegetable. **b** Brussels sprouts. **5** *v.* to appear or develop quickly: *Malls seem to have sprouted overnight.*

spruce¹ (sprüs), *n.* **1** any of several evergreen trees related to the pine. Spruces have cones and needle-shaped leaves. They are sometimes used as Christmas trees in North America. **2** the wood of these trees, used for making paper, boxes, lumber, etc.

WORD STORY **Spruce¹** and **spruce²** both probably come from **Prussia.** The tree was common there, and a kind of leather made there was considered so good-looking that its name may have been borrowed for anything neat and stylish. An old English form of **Prussia** began with an *S.*

spruce² (sprüs), **1** *adj.* neat; trim: *You look very spruce in your new suit.* **2** *v.* to make or become spruce: *Spruce up before you go back to school.* ❑ *adj.* **spruc·er, spruc·est;** *v.* **spruced, spruc·ing.** [See Word Story at **spruce¹.**] **—spruce′ly,** *adv.* **—spruce′ness,** *n.*

sprung (sprung), *v.* a past tense and the past participle of **spring:** *The mouse sprung the trap. The mousetrap was sprung.*

spry (sprī), *adj.* active; lively; nimble: *The spry old woman traveled all over the country.* ❑ *adj.* **spri·er, spri·est** *or* **spry·er, spry·est. —spry′ly,** *adv.* **—spry′ness,** *n.*

spud (spud), *n.* **1** INFORMAL. potato. **2** tool with a narrow blade for digging up or cutting the roots of weeds.

spume (spyüm), **1** *n.* frothy matter; foam; froth. ❑ *v.* **spumed, spum·ing.**

spu·mo·ni *or* **spu·mo·ne** (spə mō′nē), *n.* an Italian ice cream made with layers of different colors and flavors, usually containing fruit and nuts.

spum·y (spyü′mē), *adj.* foamy; frothy. ❑ *adj.* **spum·i·er, spum·i·est.**

spun (spun), *v.* past tense and past participle of **spin:** *The car skidded and spun on the ice. The thread was spun from silk.*

spun glass, fiberglass.

spunk (spungk), *n.* INFORMAL. courage; spirit: *a little puppy full of spunk.*

spunk·y (spung′kē), *adj.* INFORMAL. courageous; brave; spirited: *a spunky person.* ❑ *adj.* **spunk·i·er, spunk·i·est. —spunk′i·ly,** *adv.* **—spunk′i·ness,** *n.*

spur (spėr), **1** *n.* a metal point or pointed wheel, worn on a rider's boot heel for urging a horse on. **2** *v.* to urge with spurs: *The riders spurred their horses to a gallop.* **3** *v.* to urge on: *Anger spurred her to speak bluntly.* **4** *n.* anything that urges on: *Ambition was the spur that made him work.* **5** *n.* something like a spur; point sticking out. A rooster has spurs on its legs. **6** *n.* ridge

sticking out from or smaller than the main part of a mountain or mountain range. **7** *n.* any short branch or section: *a spur of a railroad.* ❑ *v.* **spurred, spur·ring. —spur′like′,** *adj.*

on the spur of the moment, on a sudden impulse, without previous thought or preparation.

win your spurs, to make a reputation for yourself or to gain a desired rank or position.

spur·i·ous (spyůr′ē əs), *adj.* resembling something genuine, but false; counterfeit: *a spurious document, spurious anger.* **—spur′i·ous·ly,** *adv.* **—spur′i·ous·ness,** *n.*

spurn (spėrn), *v.* to refuse with scorn; scorn: *The judge spurned the bribe.* **—spurn′er,** *n.*

spurred (spėrd), *adj.* having spurs or a spur: *a spurred boot, spurred feet.*

spurt (spėrt), **1** *v.* to flow suddenly in a stream or jet; gush out; squirt: *Water spurted from the drinking fountain.* **2** *n.* a sudden rushing forth; jet: *a spurt of blood from a cut.* **3** *n.* a great increase of effort or activity for a short time: *To win the race he put on a spurt of speed at the end.* **4** *v.* to put forth great energy for a short time; show great activity for a short time: *The runners spurted near the end of the race.*

sput·nik (sput′nik *or* spůt′nik), *n.* any of the earth satellites put into orbit by the Soviet Union.

sput·ter (sput′ər), **1** *v.* to make spitting or popping noises: *fat sputtering in the frying pan. The firecrackers sputtered.* **2** *v.* to throw out drops of saliva, bits of food, etc., in excitement or in talking too fast. **3** *v.* to talk in a hasty confused way: *Embarrassed, he began to sputter and make silly excuses.* **4** *n.* confused talk. **5** *n.* a sputtering noise. **—sput′ter·er,** *n.*

spu·tum (spyü′təm), *n.* **1** saliva; spit. **2** mixture of saliva and mucus coughed up and spat out.

spy (spī), **1** *n.* person paid by a government to get secret information about another government or country, especially in time of war. **2** *n.* person who keeps secret watch on the action of others. **3** *v.* to keep secret watch: *He saw two men spying on him from behind a tree.* **4** *v.* to act as a spy; be a spy. The punishment for spying in wartime is death. **5** *v.* to catch sight of; see: *She was the first to spy the rescue party in the distance.* ❑ *n., pl.* **spies;** *v.* **spied, spy·ing.**

spy·glass (spī′glas′), *n.* a small telescope. ❑ *n., pl.* **spy·glass·es.**

sq., square.

squab (skwäb), *n.* a very young bird, especially a young pigeon. ❑ *n., pl.* **squabs** *or* **squab.**

squab·ble (skwäb′əl), **1** *n.* a petty, noisy quarrel: *Children's squabbles annoy their parents.* **2** *v.* to take part in a petty, noisy quarrel: *I won't squabble over a nickel.* ❑ *v.* **squab·bled, squab·bling. —squab′bler,** *n.*

squad (skwäd), *n.* **1** any small group of persons working together: *a police squad, a rescue squad.* **2** an athletic team: *He made the football squad last fall.* **3** a military unit usually made up of ten to twelve men. It is the basic unit for drill, inspection, or work. It is usually commanded by a sergeant or a corporal.

squad car, police patrol car which has a special radio to keep in communication with headquarters.

squad·ron (skwäd′rən), *n.* **1** part of a naval fleet used for special service: *a destroyer squadron.* **2** formation of eight or more airplanes that fly or fight together. **3** any group or formation.

squal·id (skwäl′id), *adj.* **1** very dirty; filthy; wretched: *a squalid tenement.* **2** repulsive; sordid; morally degraded: *a squalid existence.* **—squal′id·ly,** *adv.* **—squal′id·ness,** *n.*

squall¹ (skwôl), **1** *n.* a sudden, violent gust of wind, often with rain, snow, or sleet. **2** *v.* to blow as a squall.

squall² (skwôl), **1** *v.* to cry out loudly; scream violently: *The hungry baby squalled.* **2** *n.* a loud, harsh cry: *The parrot's squall was heard all over the house.* **—squall′er,** *n.*

a	hat	ė	term	ô	order	ch	child		a in about
ā	age	i	it	oi	oil	ng	long		e in taken
ä	far	ī	ice	ou	out	sh	she	ə	i in pencil
â	care	o	hot	u	cup	th	thin		o in lemon
e	let	ō	open	ů	put	ŦH	then		u in circus
ē	equal	ò	saw	ü	rule	zh	measure		

S

squall·y (skwȯ′lē), *adj.* having many sudden and violent gusts of wind: *squally weather.* ❑ *adj.* **squall·i·er, squall·i·est.**

squal·or (skwäl′ər), *n.* **1** misery and dirt; filth. **2** condition of being morally sordid.

squan·der (skwän′dər), *v.* to spend foolishly; waste: *squander your time and money in playing video games.* —**squan′der·er,** *n.*

square (skwâr), **1** *n.* a plane figure with four equal sides and four right angles (□). **2** *adj.* having this shape: *a square box. A block of stone is usually square.* **3** *n.* anything having this shape or nearly this shape: *I gave the child a square of chocolate.* **4** *adj.* of or for square measure. A square foot is the area of a square with edges that are each one foot long. Any other square unit is the area of a square with each side of the length named. **5** *adj.* having length and width. The square content of a field is its entire space in two dimensions. **6** *n.* an open space in a city or town bounded by streets on four sides, often planted with grass, trees, etc.: *The library is in the square directly opposite the city hall.* **7** *n.* any similar open space, such as at the meeting of streets. **8** *adj.* of a specified length on each side of a square: *a room ten feet square.* **9** *adj.* forming a right angle: *a square corner.* **10** *v.* to bring to the form of a right angle. **11** *v.* to make square; make rectangular; make cubical: *square a block of granite.* **12** *n.* tool shaped like a T or an L, used for drawing right angles and testing the squareness of anything. **13** *adj.* straight; level; even. **14** *v.* to make straight, level, or even: *square a picture on a wall.* **15** *adj.* leaving no balance; even: *make accounts square.* **16** *v.* to adjust; settle: *Let us square our accounts.* **17** *v.* to agree; conform: *Her acts do not square with her promises.* **18** *adj.* just; fair; honest: *You will get a square deal at this shop.* **19** *adj.* satisfying: *a square meal.* **20** *n.* sum that results when a number is multiplied by itself: *16 is the square of 4.* **21** *v.* to multiply a number by itself: *25 squared makes 625.* **22** *n.* SLANG. person who is too conventional or old-fashioned. **23** *adj.* SLANG. too conventional or old-fashioned. ❑ *adj.* **squar·er, squar·est;** *v.* **squared, squar·ing.** —**square′ly,** *adv.* —**square′ness,** *n.*

on the square, 1 at right angles. **2** justly; fairly; honestly.

square away, 1 to set the sails so that the ship will stay before the wind. **2** to get things ready or in order: *We squared away our business affairs before leaving on vacation.*

square off, to put yourself in a position of defense or attack.

square one, the original position; the starting point: *After all our planning for the cruise, we found ourselves back at square one when the ship couldn't sail.*

square yourself, INFORMAL. **1** to make up for something you have said or done: *I needed to square myself with my friend after our quarrel.* **2** to get even: *After being tricked, she stormed off, determined to square herself eventually.*

square dance, dance done by groups of four couples in a square formation. The dancers form different patterns according to the directions of a caller. —**square′-dance′,** *v.*

square dance

square knot, knot firmly joining two loose ends of rope or cord. Each end is formed into a loop which both encloses and passes through the other.

square measure, system of units, such as square feet or square meters, used for measuring area. See table on page 975A.

square-rigged (skwâr′rigd′), *adj.* having the principal sails set at right angles across the masts.

square-rig·ger (skwâr′rig′ər), *n.* a square-rigged ship.

square root, number that produces a given number when multiplied by itself: *The square root of 16 is 4.*

square shooter, INFORMAL. a fair and honest person.

squash[1] (skwäsh), **1** *v.* to press or be pressed until soft or flat; crush: *She squashed the bug. Carry the cream puffs carefully, for they squash easily.* **2** *n.* act, fact, or sound of squashing. **3** *v.* to put an end to; stop by force: *The police quickly squashed the riot.* **4** *v.* to crowd; squeeze. **5** *n.* either of two games something like handball and tennis, played in a walled court with rackets and a rubber ball. ❑ *n., pl.* **squash·es** for 2. —**squash′er,** *n.*

squash[2] (skwäsh), *n.* the fruit of any of several trailing garden vines related to the pumpkin and cucumber. Squashes have different shapes and colors, usually yellow, green, or white. Many are good to eat. ❑ *n., pl.* **squash** or **squash·es.**

square (def. 7)

squash·y (skwäsh′ē), *adj.* **1** easily squashed: *The baby liked soft, squashy toys.* **2** soft and wet: *squashy ground.* ❑ *adj.* **squash·i·er, squash·i·est.** —**squash′i·ly,** *adv.* —**squash′i·ness,** *n.*

squat (skwät), **1** *v.* to crouch on the heels: *Squatting on the grass, she was watching a caterpillar.* **2** *v.* to sit on the ground or floor with the legs drawn up closely beneath or in front of the body: *The campers squatted around the fire.* **3** *adj.* crouching: *A squat figure sat in front of the fire.* **4** *n.* act of squatting; squatting posture. **5** *v.* to settle on another's land without title or right. **6** *v.* to settle on public land to acquire ownership of it. **7** *adj.* short and thick; low and broad: *a squat man, a squat teapot.* ❑ *v.* **squat·ted, squat·ting;** *adj.* **squat·ter, squat·test.** —**squat′ly,** *adv.* —**squat′ness,** *n.*

squat·ter (skwät′ər), *n.* **1** person who settles on another's land without any right to do so. **2** person who settles on public land to gain ownership of it.

squat·ty (skwät′ē), *adj.* short and thick; squat. ❑ *adj.* **squat·ti·er, squat·ti·est.**

squaw (skwȯ), *n.* a North American Indian woman. ■ **Squaw** is often considered offensive.

squawk (skwȯk), **1** *v.* to make a loud, harsh sound: *Hens and ducks squawk when frightened.* **2** *n.* such a sound. **3** *v.* INFORMAL. to complain loudly: *They squawked about the large repair bill.* **4** *n.* INFORMAL. a loud complaint. —**squawk′er,** *n.*

squeak (skwēk), **1** *v.* to make a short, sharp, shrill sound: *A mouse squeaks.* **2** *n.* such a sound: *We heard the squeak of the rocking chair.* **3** *v.* to get or pass by or through with difficulty: *The Senate will block the bill even if it squeaks through the House of Representatives.* **4** *n.* a chance to get by or through; chance of escape: *a narrow squeak.*

squeak·y (skwē′kē), *adj.* squeaking. ❑ *adj.* **squeak·i·er, squeak·i·est.** —**squeak′i·ly,** *adv.* —**squeak′i·ness,** *n.*

squeal (skwēl), **1** *v.* to make a long, sharp, shrill cry or noise like a cry: *A pig squeals when it is hurt. The rear tires squealed as the truck turned left in the intersection.* **2** *n.* such a cry or noise. **3** *v.* SLANG. to inform on someone: *One thief squealed on the others.* —**squeal′er,** *n.*

squeam·ish (skwē′mish), *adj.* **1** easily affected with nausea; queasy. **2** slightly sick to your stomach; nauseated. **3** too proper, modest, etc.; easily shocked. —**squeam′ish·ly,** *adv.* —**squeam′ish·ness,** *n.*

squee·gee (skwē′jē′), **1** *n.* tool consisting of a blade of rubber and a handle, used for removing water from windows after washing, sweeping water from wet decks, etc. **2** *v.* to clean or smooth with a squeegee. ❑ *n., pl.* **squee·gees;** *v.* **squee·geed, squee·gee·ing.**

squeeze (skwēz), **1** *v.* to press hard; compress: *Don't squeeze the kitten; you'll hurt it.* **2** *n.* act of squeezing; tight pressure: *a squeeze of the hand. She gave her sister's arm a squeeze.* **3** *v.* to hug: *She squeezed her child.* **4** *v.* to force by pressing: *I can't squeeze another thing into my trunk.* **5** *v.* to force out by pressure: *squeeze juice from a lemon.* **6** *v.* to get by pressure, force, or effort: *The dictator squeezed money from the people.* **7** *v.* to yield to pressure: *Sponges squeeze easily.* **8** *v.* to force a way: *squeeze through a crowd.* **9** *v.* to crush; crowd: *Six people squeezed into the little car.* ❑ *v.* **squeezed, squeez·ing.** —**squeez′a·ble,** *adj.*

squeez·er (skwē′zər), *n.* device for squeezing juice from fruits or vegetables.

squelch (skwelch), *v.* to cause to be silent; crush: *She squelched him with a look of contempt.* —**squelch′er,** *n.*

squib (skwib), *n.* a short, witty attack in speech or writing.

squid (skwid), *n.* any of numerous sea animals having ten arms with suckers, and a pair of tail fins. Squid are mollusks and are related to octopuses. ❑ *n., pl.* **squid** or **squids.**

squig·gle (skwig′əl), **1** *n.* a wriggly twist or curve. **2** *v.* to make with twisting or curving lines. **3** *v.* to twist and turn about; writhe; squirm; wriggle. ❑ *v.* **squig·gled, squig·gling.**

squinch (skwinch), *v.* to squeeze together; squint: *I squinched my eyes and tried to read the distant sign.*

squint (skwint), **1** *v.* to look with the eyes partly closed. **2** *n.* act of looking with partly closed eyes. **3** *n.* a sidelong look; hasty look: *The squint she gave me indicated she doubted my story.* **4** *v.* to look sideways; look askance. **5** *n.* tendency to look sideways or askance. **6** *v.* to be cross-eyed. **7** *n.* cross-eyed condition. —**squint′er,** *n.*

squire (skwīr), **1** *n.* (in Great Britain) a country gentleman, especially the chief landowner in a district. **2** *n.* (in the United States) a justice of the peace or a local judge. **3** *n.* (in the Middle Ages) a young man of noble family who attended a knight till he himself was made a knight. **4** *n.* attendant. **5** *v.* to attend as squire. **6** *n.* a woman's escort. **7** *v.* to escort a woman. ❑ *v.* **squired, squir·ing.**

squirm (skwėrm), **1** *v.* to turn and twist; writhe: *The restless boy squirmed in his chair.* **2** *n.* a wriggle; twist. **3** *v.* to show great embarrassment, annoyance, confusion, etc.

squirm·y (skwėr′mē), *adj.* squirming; wriggling. ❑ *adj.* **squirm·i·er, squirm·i·est.**

squir·rel (skwir′əl *or* skwėrl), *n.* **1** any of numerous small furry rodents, some of which have long tails and live in trees. Others, called ground squirrels, have short tails and do not climb trees. **2** the gray, reddish, or dark brown fur of these animals. —**squir′rel·like′,** *adj.*

squirrels—about 18 in. (45 cm) long with tail

WORD STORY **Squirrel** comes from Greek words meaning "shadow" and "tail." The long, bushy tails of many squirrels curl over their backs and seem to keep them in a shadow.

squirt (skwėrt), **1** *v.* to force liquid out through a narrow opening: *squirt water through a tube.* **2** *v.* to come out in a jet or stream: *Water squirted from the hose.* **3** *v.* to wet or soak by shooting liquid in a jet or stream: *The elephant squirted me with its trunk.* **4** *n.* act of squirting. **5** *n.* jet of liquid, etc.: *I soaked her with squirts of water from the hose.* **6** *n.* something that squirts. **7** *n.* INFORMAL. an insignificant person who is impudent or conceited: *a little squirt of a man.* —**squirt′er,** *n.*

squirt gun, water pistol.

squish (skwish), **1** *v.* to press something soft and wet, or to move in a soft, wet, oozing way: *The mud squished between my toes.* **2** *n.* sound of something soft and wet being pressed: *the squish of wet shoes.* **3** *v.* to make a sound like this: *My wet shoes squished as I walked.* ❑ *n., pl.* **squish·es.**

squish·y (skwish′ē), *adj.* **1** easily squished; oozy. **2** making soft, splashing sounds: *squishy mud between her toes.* ❑ *adj.* **squish·i·er, squish·i·est.** —**squish′i·ness,** *n.*

Sr, symbol for strontium.

Sr., Senior.

Sri Lan·ka (srē′ läng′kə), island country in the Indian Ocean, just off S India. *Capital:* Colombo. [**Sri Lanka** means "splendid land" in the language spoken by most of the country's people.]

SS or **S.S.,** steamship.

SS, a select military unit of highly trained, fanatical Nazis who served as Hitler's bodyguard and in special security units.

SST, supersonic transport (a large passenger or cargo airplane that flies faster than the speed of sound).

St., **1** Saint. **2** Street.

stab (stab), **1** *v.* to pierce or wound with something pointed: *He was stabbed with a knife.* **2** *v.* to thrust with something pointed; jab: *I stabbed at the onion with my fork.* **3** *n.* a thrust or blow made with something pointed. **4** *n.* any thrust or sudden, sharp blow. **5** *n.* wound made by stabbing. **6** *v.* to wound sharply or deeply in the feelings: *The parents were stabbed to the heart by their son's ingratitude.* **7** *n.* an attempt: *I've never skied, but I'd like to take a stab at it.* ❑ *v.* **stabbed, stab·bing.** —**stab′ber,** *n.*

sta·bil·i·ty (stə bil′ə tē), *n.* **1** condition of being stable; firmness: *A concrete wall has more stability than a light wooden fence.* **2** permanence. **3** steadfastness of character, purpose, etc.: *the stability of someone who helps a friend in need.*

sta·bi·lize (stā′bə līz), *v.* **1** to make stable or firm: *stabilize a government.* **2** to prevent changes in; hold steady: *stabilize prices.* **3** to keep well balanced. ❑ *v.* **sta·bi·lized, sta·bi·liz·ing.** —**sta′bi·li·za′tion,** *n.*

sta·bi·liz·er (stā′bə lī′zər), *n.* **1** device for keeping an airplane, ship, etc., steady. **2** any person or thing that stabilizes.

sta·ble[1] (stā′bəl), **1** *n.* building where horses or cattle are kept and fed: *I went with her to the stable where she took riding lessons.* **2** *n.* group of animals housed in such a building. **3** *v.* to put or keep in a stable. **4** *n.* group of race horses belonging to one owner. ❑ *v.* **sta·bled, sta·bling.**

sta·ble[2] (stā′bəl), *adj.* **1** not likely to move or change position; steadfast; firm; steady: *We held the ladder to make it stable for the painter.* **2** not likely to fall or be overturned: *a stable government.* —**sta′ble·ness,** *n.* —**sta′bly,** *adv.*

stac·ca·to (stə kä′tō), in music: **1** *adj.* with breaks between the successive tones; disconnected; abrupt. **2** *adv.* in a staccato manner.

stack (stak), **1** *n.* pile of anything: *a stack of books.* **2** *v.* to pile or arrange in a stack: *stack hay, stack firewood.* **3** *n.* a large pile of hay, straw, etc. **4** *n.* a large number or quantity: *a stack of compliments.* **5** *v.* to arrange playing cards unfairly: *stack the deck.* **6** *n.* chimney. **7** *n.* rack with shelves for books. **8** *n.pl.* **stacks,** part of a library in which the main collection of books is shelved. —**stack′a·ble,** *adj.* —**stack′er,** *n.*

sta·di·um (stā′dē əm), *n.* an oval, U-shaped, or round building, usually without a roof. Tiers of seats for spectators surround the playing field.

WORD STORY **Stadium** comes from a Greek word meaning "a unit of length." About 600 feet long, this was the usual length of a running track in ancient Greece, and so the word was also used to mean "a running track." English borrowed the word to mean "any place that people get exercise," and then to mean "a big building for athletic games."

S

a	hat	ė	term	ô	order	ch	child		a in about
ā	age	i	it	oi	oil	ng	long		e in taken
ä	far	ī	ice	ou	out	sh	she	ə	i in pencil
â	care	o	hot	u	cup	th	thin		o in lemon
e	let	ō	open	ù	put	ᵀH	then		u in circus
ē	equal	ò	saw	ü	rule	zh	measure		

staff (staf), **1** *n.* group of employees: *Our school has a staff of twenty teachers.* **2** *n.* (in the armed forces) group of officers assisting a commanding officer with administration, planning, etc., but without command or combat duties. **3** *v.* to provide with officers or employees. **4** *n.* a stick, pole, or rod used as a support, as an emblem of office, as a weapon, etc.: *The woman leaned on her staff.* **5** *n.* something that supports or sustains. Bread is called the staff of life because it will support life. **6** *n.* set of five lines and the four spaces between them on which music is written; stave. ❑ *n., pl.* **staffs** for 1,2,5; **staves** or **staffs** for 4,6.

staff·er (staf′ər), *n.* member of a staff.

staff sergeant, a military rank. See chart on page 712.

stag (stag), **1** *n.* a full-grown male deer. **2** *adj.* for men only: *a stag dinner.*

stage (stāj), **1** *n.* one step or time in a process. Childhood, adolescence, and adulthood are stages in a person's life. **2** *n.* the raised platform in a theater on which the actors perform. **3** *v.* to present in a theater: *The play was very well staged.* **4** *n.* **the stage,** theater; drama; actor's profession: *Shakespeare was a man of the stage.* **5** *n.* scene of action: *the stage of a famous battle.* **6** *v.* to organize and carry out: *The city stages an art exhibit every summer.* **7** *n.* section of a rocket or missile with its own engine and fuel. **8** *n.* (earlier) stagecoach. **9** *n.* a place of rest on a journey; regular stopping place. **10** *n.* distance between two stopping places on a journey. **11** *n.* platform; flooring. ❑ *v.* **staged, stag·ing.**

by easy stages, a little at a time; slowly; often stopping.

on the stage, being an actor or actress.

stage·coach (stāj′kōch′), *n.* (earlier) coach pulled by horses and carrying passengers, parcels, and mail over a regular route. ❑ *n., pl.* **stage·coach·es.**

stage fright, nervous fear of appearing before an audience.

stage·hand (stāj′hand′), *n.* person whose work is moving scenery, arranging lights, etc., in a theater.

stage-struck (stāj′struk′), *adj.* extremely interested in acting; wanting very much to become an actor.

stage whisper, a loud whisper on a stage meant for the audience to hear but not the other characters in the play.

stag·ger (stag′ər), **1** *v.* to move or walk unsteadily: *I staggered and fell while trying to carry too many books.* **2** *v.* to cause someone to almost fall down: *The blow staggered me for a moment.* **3** *n.* act of swaying or reeling. **4** *v.* to become unsteady; waver: *The troops staggered under the severe gunfire.* **5** *v.* to confuse or astonish greatly: *He was staggered by the news of his friend's death.* **6** *v.* to arrange in a zigzag order or way. **7** *v.* to arrange to begin at different times: *Vacations were staggered so that only one person was away at a time.* **8** *n.* **staggers,** a nervous disease of horses, cattle, etc., that makes them sway or fall suddenly. —**stag′ger·er,** *n.* —**stag′ger·ing·ly,** *adv.*

stag·nant (stag′nənt), *adj.* **1** not running or flowing: *stagnant air, stagnant water.* **2** foul from standing still: *a stagnant pool of water.* **3** not active; sluggish; dull: *During the summer, business is often stagnant.* —**stag′nant·ly,** *adv.*

stag·nate (stag′nāt), *v.* **1** to be stagnant; become stagnant. **2** to make stagnant. ❑ *v.* **stag·nat·ed, stag·nat·ing.** —**stag·na′tion,** *n.*

staid (stād), *adj.* having a settled, quiet character; sober; sedate: *We think of the Puritans as staid people.* —**staid′ly,** *adv.* —**staid′ness,** *n.*

stain (stān), **1** *v.* to discolor with streaks of dirt, blood, etc.; soil; spot: *Spilled food stained the tablecloth.* **2** *n.* a discoloration made by soiling; a spot: *He has ink stains on his shirt.* **3** *v.* to spot by wrongdoing or disgrace; dishonor: *His crimes stained the family honor.* **4** *n.* mark of disgrace; dishonor: *Her character is without stain.* **5** *v.* to color or dye: *He stained the chair green.* **6** *n.* a coloring or dye: *She applied a brown stain to the table.* —**stain′a·ble,** *adj.* —**stain′er,** *n.*

stained glass (stānd), colored glass used in sheets or fitted pieces to form a picture or design.

stain·less (stān′lis), *adj.* without stain; spotless. —**stain′less·ly,** *adv.* —**stain′less·ness,** *n.*

stainless steel, steel containing a high percentage of chromium, making it very resistant to rust and corrosion.

stair (stâr), *n.* **1** one of a series of steps for going from one level or floor to another. **2** Also, **stairs,** *pl.* set of such steps; stairway: *the top of the stairs.* ∎ Another word that sounds like this is **stare.**

stair·case (stâr′kās′), *n.* flight of stairs with its framework; stairs.

stair·way (stâr′wā′), *n.* way up and down by stairs; a flight or flights of stairs: *the back stairway.*

stair·well (stâr′wel′), *n.* the vertical passage or open space containing the stairs of a building.

stake¹ (stāk), **1** *n.* a stick or post pointed at one end for driving into the ground. **2** *n.* **the stake,** a (long ago) post to which someone was tied and then burned to death: *Joan of Arc was burned at the stake.* **b** (long ago) death by being burned in this way. **3** *v.* to fasten to a stake or with a stake: *stake down a tent.* **4** *v.* to mark with stakes; mark the boundaries of: *stake out a mining claim.* ❑ *v.* **staked, stak·ing.** ∎ Another word that sounds like this is **steak.**

pull up stakes, to move away: *Constant flooding of their land led the farmers to pull up stakes and leave the valley for the highland.*

stake² (stāk), **1** *v.* to risk money or something valuable on the result of a game or on any chance: *She staked all her money on the black horse.* **2** *n.* money risked; what is staked: *They played for high stakes.* **3** *n.* Often, **stakes,** *pl.* prize in a race or contest: *The stakes were divided up among the winners.* **4** *n.* something to gain or lose; interest; share in a property: *Each of us has a stake in the future of our country.* **5** *v.* to assist or back someone with money, etc.: *I'll stake you to a dinner if you'll come.* ❑ *v.* **staked, stak·ing.** ∎ Another word that sounds like this is **steak.** —**stak′er,** *n.*

at stake, to be won or lost; risked: *Your health is at stake if you smoke.*

sta·lac·tite (stə lak′tīt), *n.* a mineral formation shaped like an icicle hanging from the roof of a cave. It is formed by dripping water that contains calcium carbonate or another mineral.

sta·lag·mite (stə lag′mīt), *n.* a mineral formation shaped like a cone on the floor of a cave. It is formed by dripping water that contains calcium carbonate or another mineral.

stalactites and stalagmites

stale (stāl), **1** *adj.* not fresh: *stale bread.* **2** *adj.* no longer new or interesting: *a stale joke.* **3** *adj.* out of condition: *The tennis player practiced every day to avoid becoming stale.* **4** *v.* to make or become stale. ❑ *adj.* **stal·er, stal·est;** *v.* **staled, stal·ing.** —**stale′ly,** *adv.* —**stale′ness,** *n.*

stale·mate (stāl′māt′), **1** *n.* any position in which no action can be taken; complete standstill. **2** *v.* to put in such a position; bring to a complete standstill. **3** *n.* (in chess) a draw which results when you cannot move any of your pieces without putting your own king in check. ❑ *v.* **stale·mat·ed, stale·mat·ing.**

Sta·lin (stä′lin), *n.* **Joseph,** 1879-1953, Soviet political leader, dictator of the Soviet Union from 1929 to 1953. ∎ Stalin was responsible for the deaths of millions of people, whom he had executed or sent to prison camps.

Sta·lin·grad (stä′lin grad′), *n.* former name of **Volgograd.**

stalk¹ (stôk), *n.* **1** the main stem of a plant. **2** stem¹ (def. 2). **3** any similar part. The eyes of a crayfish are on stalks.

stalk² (stôk), **1** *v.* to hunt by following silently and carefully: *The hungry lion stalked a zebra.* **2** *v.* to spread silently and steadily: *Disease stalked through the land.* **3** *v.* to walk with slow, stiff, or haughty strides: *She became angry and stalked out of the room.* **4** *n.* a haughty gait. **5** *n.* act of stalking. —**stalk′a·ble,** *adj.* —**stalk′er,** *n.*

stall[1] (stôl), **1** *n.* place for one animal in a barn or stable. **2** *n.* a small place for selling things: *At the public market different things were sold in different stalls under one big roof.* **3** *n.* seat in the choir of a church. **4** *n.* a small enclosed space: *a shower stall.* **5** *v.* to put or keep in a stall: *The horses were safely stalled.* **6** *v.* to stop or bring to a standstill, usually against your wish: *The engine stalled.* **7** *n.* a parking space. **—stall′-like′,** *adj.*

stall[2] (stôl), **1** *n.* a delay to prevent action, the accomplishment of a purpose, etc. **2** *v.* to act or speak evasively or uncertainly in order to avoid doing something: *When I ask for a raise my boss stalls.*

stal·lion (stal′yən), *n.* a male horse that can be used for breeding.

stal·wart (stôl′wərt), **1** *adj.* strong and brave: *a stalwart knight.* **2** *adj.* firm; steadfast: *a stalwart refusal.* **3** *n.* a stalwart person. **—stal′wart·ly,** *adv.* **—stal′wart·ness,** *n.*

sta·men (stā′mən), *n.* the part of a flower that contains the pollen. A stamen has a slender stem that supports the anther. [See Word Story at **stamina.**]

stam·i·na (stam′ə nə), *n.* strength; endurance: *He didn't have enough stamina to finish the race.*

WORD STORY **Stamina** comes from a Latin word meaning "thread." In Roman mythology, the three Fates determined the length of everyone's life: the first Fate spun the thread of life; the second measured it; and the third cut it. Today, **stamina** doesn't mean how long you will live, but the word still means how long you can go on or endure. **Stamen** comes from the same Latin word, because this part of a flower looks like a thread.

stam·mer (stam′ər), **1** *v.* to repeat the same sound in an effort to speak; hesitate in speaking. People may stammer when nervous, embarrassed, or afraid. **2** *v.* to say in this manner: *stammer an excuse.* **3** *n.* act of stammering; stuttering: *He has a nervous stammer.* **—stam′mer·er,** *n.* **—stam′mer·ing·ly,** *adv.*

stamp (stamp), **1** *n.* a small piece of paper with a sticky back, put on letters, papers, packages, etc., to show that a charge for mailing has been paid; postage stamp. **2** *n.* trading stamp. **3** *n.* any official mark or label required by law to be affixed to a paper or item to show that a fee, duty, tax, etc., has been paid. **4** *v.* to put a stamp on: *stamp a letter.* **5** *v.* to bring down your foot with force: *He stamped on the spider. He stamped his foot in anger.* **6** *n.* act of stamping. **7** *v.* to pound, crush, trample, or tread: *She stamped out the fire.* **8** *v.* to fix firmly or deeply: *an event stamped on your memory.* **9** *n.* tool that cuts, shapes, or impresses a design on paper, wax, metal, etc.; thing that puts a mark on: *The rubber stamp had her name on it.* **10** *v.* to mark with such a tool: *She stamped the papers with the date.* **11** *n.* the mark made by such a tool. **12** *v.* to show to be of a certain quality or character; indicate: *Her speech stamps her as an educated woman.* **13** *n.* impression; marks: *a face bearing the stamp of suffering.* **14** *n.* kind; type: *People of his stamp are rare.* **—stamp′a·ble,** *adj.* **—stamp′er,** *n.* **—stamp′less,** *adj.* **—stamp′like′,** *adj.*

stam·pede (stam pēd′), **1** *n.* a sudden headlong rush by a frightened herd of cattle, horses, etc. **2** *n.* any headlong rush of a large group: *the stampede of people from a burning building.* **3** *v.* to rush or scatter in a stampede. **4** *v.* to cause to rush: *The thunder stampeded the herd.* □ *v.* **stam·ped·ed, stam·ped·ing.** **—stam·ped′er,** *n.*

stampede (def. 1)

stance (stans), *n.* **1** manner of standing; posture: *an erect stance.* **2** position of the feet of a player when making a stroke in golf or other games. **3** attitude; point of view: *a political stance toward full employment.*

stanch[1] (stônch), *v.* **1** to stop or check the flow of blood. **2** to stop the flow of blood from a wound. Also, **staunch.** **—stanch′a·ble,** *adj.* **—stanch′er,** *n.*

stanch[2] (stônch), *adj.* staunch[1]. **—stanch′ly,** *adv.* **—stanch′ness,** *n.*

stan·chion (stan′shən), *n.* an upright bar, post, or support in a window, in a stall for cattle, on a ship, etc.

stand (stand), **1** *v.* to be upright on your feet: *Don't stand if you are tired; sit down.* **2** *v.* to have a certain height when upright: *He stands six feet in his socks.* **3** *v.* to rise to your feet: *We stood when the guest entered the room.* **4** *v.* to be set upright; be placed; be located: *The box stands over there.* **5** *v.* to set upright or in an indicated position, condition, etc.: *Stand the box here.* **6** *v.* to be in a certain place, rank, or position: *He stood first in his class.* **7** *v.* to take or keep a certain position: *"Stand back!" called the policeman to the crowd.* **8** *v.* to hold to a way of thinking or acting: *stand on your rights.* **9** *v.* to be in a special condition: *The poor child stands in need of food and clothing. The door stood ajar.* **10** *v.* to think or act: *How does your congresswoman stand on tax reform?* **11** *v.* to be unchanged; remain the same: *The rule against being late will stand.* **12** *v.* to stay in place; last: *The old house has stood for a hundred years.* **13** *v.* to put up with; tolerate: *I can't stand that singer.* **14** *v.* to bear; endure; withstand: *Because those plants cannot stand cold, we bring them inside in October.* ■ See Synonym Study at **bear**[1]. **15** *v.* to bear the expense of: *I'll stand you a dinner.* **16** *v.* to stop moving; halt; stop: *The cars stood and waited for the light to change.* **17** *n.* act of standing. **18** *n.* a halt; stop. **19** *n.* a stop for defense, resistance, etc.: *We made a last stand against the enemy.* **20** *n.* place where someone stands; position: *The usher took her stand near the door.* **21** *n.* a moral position: *We took a strong stand against pumping sewage into the lake.* **22** *n.* Also, **stands,** *pl.* a raised place where people can watch or listen: *The mayor sat on the reviewing stand at the parade.* **23** *n.* something to put things on or in: *Leave your wet umbrella in the stand in the hall.* **24** *n.* stall, booth, table, etc., for a small business: *a newspaper stand.* **25** *n.* group of growing trees or plants: *a stand of timber.* □ *v.* **stood, stand·ing.**

stand by, 1 be near. **2** to help; support: *stand by a friend.* **3** be or get ready for use, action, etc.

stand for, 1 to mean; signify: *What does the abbreviation IRS stand for?* **2** be on the side of; take the part of; uphold: *Our team stands for fair play.* **3** to put up with: *The teacher said she would not stand for talking during class.*

stand in for, to take the place of; substitute for.

stand off, to keep off; keep away: *stand off an angry dog.*

stand out, 1 to stick out: *His ears stood out.* **2** be noticeable or prominent: *Certain facts stand out.*

stand up, 1 to get to your feet: *She stood up and began to speak.* **2** to endure; last: *That old car has stood up for years.* **3** to fail to keep a date with someone.

stand up for, to take the part of; defend; support: *I always stand up for my friends.*

stand up to, to meet or face boldly.

stan·dard (stan′dərd), **1** *n.* anything taken as a basis of comparison; model: *Your work is not up to the class standard.* **2** *adj.* used as a standard; according to rule: *standard spelling, standard pronunciation.* **3** *adj.* having recognized excellence or authority: *Use a standard encyclopedia to look up these subjects.* **4** *adj.* of the accepted or normal size, amount, power, quality, etc.: *the standard rate of pay, a standard gauge.* **5** *n.* flag, emblem, or symbol: *The dragon was the standard of China.* **6** *n.* an upright support: *The floor lamp has a long standard.*

S

a	hat	ė	term	ô	order	ch	child		
ā	age	i	it	oi	oil	ng	long		a in about
ä	far	ī	ice	ou	out	sh	she		e in taken
â	care	o	hot	u	cup	th	thin	ə	i in pencil
e	let	ō	open	ù	put	ŦH	then		o in lemon
ē	equal	ò	saw	ü	rule	zh	measure		u in circus

stan·dard·ize (stan′dər dīz), v. to make standard in size, shape, weight, quality, strength, etc.: *Bicycle tires are standardized.* ❑ v. **stan·dard·ized, stan·dard·iz·ing.** —**stan′dard·i·za′tion,** n.

standard of living, way of living that is usual for a person, a community, or an area, considering food, clothes, housing, and possessions such as cars, TV sets, and the like. A high standard of living is a very comfortable and secure one.

standard time, time officially used in a region or country.

stand·by (stand′bī′), n. 1 person or thing that can be relied upon; chief support; ready resource. 2 person or thing held in reserve, especially as a possible replacement or substitute. ❑ n., pl. **stand·bys.**

stand·ee (stan dē′), n. person who has to stand on a subway, bus, etc. ❑ n., pl. **stand·dees.**

stand·in (stand′in′), n. 1 person whose work is standing in the place of a movie actor or actress while the lights and camera are being arranged, or during scenes in which dangerous action occurs. 2 person or thing that takes the place of another; substitute.

stand·ing (stan′ding), n. 1 n. position; reputation: *a person of good standing.* 2 n. duration: *a family feud of long standing.* 3 adj. established; permanent: *a standing invitation, a standing army.* 4 adj. straight up; erect: *standing timber.* 5 adj. done from an erect position: *a standing jump.* 6 adj. not flowing; stagnant: *standing water.*

Stan·dish (stan′dish), n. **Miles** (mīlz), 1584?-1656, the military leader of the English colony at Plymouth, Massachusetts.

stand·off (stand′ôf′), n. 1 situation in which neither opposing force will move, bargain, etc., until the other force does something. 2 a tie in a game.

stand·off·ish (stand′ô′fish), adj. reserved; aloof: *A cool, stand-offish attitude does not help you make friends.* —**stand′off′ish·ly,** adv. —**stand′off′ish·ness,** n.

stand·out (stand′out′), n. person or thing that is especially excellent: *She is a standout as a basketball player.*

stand·pipe (stand′pīp′), n. a large, upright pipe or tower to hold water at a height great enough to provide pressure for a water system.

stand·point (stand′point′), n. point of view; mental attitude.

stand·still (stand′stil′), n. a complete stop; halt.

stank (stangk), v. a past tense of **stink:** *The dead fish stank.*

Stan·ley (stan′lē), n. Sir **Henry Mor·ton** (môrt′n), 1841-1904, British explorer in Africa. ■ **Henry Stanley** found the Scottish missionary and explorer, David Livingstone, who had disappeared in Africa. When Stanley finally met Livingstone near Lake Tanganyika, he said "Dr. Livingstone, I presume?"

Stanley Cup, a trophy given to the champion of the National Hockey League each year.

Stan·ton (stan′tən), n. **Elizabeth Ca·dy** (kā′dē), 1815-1902, American leader in the movement for women's rights. She and Lucretia Mott organized the first women's rights convention in Seneca Falls, New York, in 1848.

stan·za (stan′zə), n. group of lines of poetry, usually four or more, arranged according to a fixed plan; verse of a poem: *They sang the first and last stanzas of "America."* ❑ n., pl. **stan·zas.**

staph (staf), n. staphylococcus or staphylococci.

staph·y·lo·coc·cus (staf′ə lə kok′əs), n. any of numerous spherical bacteria that bunch together in irregular masses. ❑ n., pl. **staph·y·lo·coc·ci** (staf′ə lə kok′sī).

sta·ple[1] (stā′pəl), 1 n. a U-shaped piece of metal with pointed ends. Staples are driven into wood or other material to hold hooks, wiring, insulation, etc. 2 n. a bent piece of wire used to hold together papers, parts of a book, etc. 3 v. to fasten with a staple or staples. ❑ v. **sta·pled, sta·pling.**

sta·ple[2] (stā′pəl), 1 n. product, especially a food sold and used all the time. Bread, milk, sugar, and salt are common staples in this country. 2 n. the most important or principal product grown or manufactured in a place: *Cotton is the staple in many Southern states.* 3 n. chief element or material. 4 adj. most important; principal: *Bread is a staple food.* 5 n. a raw material. 6 n. fiber of cotton or wool. 7 adj. regularly produced in large quantities for the market.

sta·pler (stā′plər), n. device for fastening together papers, parts of a book, etc., with wire staples.

star (stär), 1 n. any astronomical object that shines by its own light. Stars are made of extremely hot gas. They vary in size from smaller than Earth to several million times as large as the sun. 2 n. any of the astronomical objects appearing as bright points in the sky at night. A planet may be called a star. 3 n. a shape having five or more points, like these: ★ ✻. 4 n. thing having or suggesting this shape. 5 n. a very talented or famous person in some art, sport, etc., especially someone who plays the lead in a performance: *a movie star, a basketball star.* 6 adj. best; leading; excellent: *the star player on the team.* 7 v. to be a leading performer; be prominent; excel: *She has starred in many movies.* 8 v. to present as a leading performer: *a movie starring a dog.* 9 n. asterisk (*). 10 v. to mark with an asterisk. 11 n. fate; fortune. ❑ v. **starred, star·ring.**

star·board (stär′bərd), 1 n. the right side of a boat or aircraft when facing forward. 2 adj. on the right side of a boat or aircraft.

starch (stärch), 1 n. a white, tasteless food substance. Potatoes, wheat, rice, and corn contain much starch. 2 n.pl. **starches,** foods containing a lot of starch. 3 n. a preparation of this substance used to stiffen clothes, curtains, etc. 4 v. to stiffen clothes, curtains, etc., with starch: *to starch curtains.* 5 n. a stiff, formal manner; stiffness. —**starch′less,** adj.

starch·y (stär′chē), adj. 1 like or containing starch: *starchy food.* 2 stiffened with starch: *a starchy collar.* 3 stiff in manner; formal. ❑ adj. **starch·i·er, starch·i·est.** —**starch′i·ly,** adv. —**starch′i·ness,** n.

star·dom (stär′dəm), n. 1 condition of being a star actor or performer. 2 star actors or performers as a group.

stare (stâr), 1 v. to look long and directly with the eyes wide open: *The children stared at the toys in the window.* ■ See Synonym Study at **watch.** 2 n. a long and direct look with the eyes wide open: *an unwinking stare.* ❑ v. **stared, star·ing.** ■ Another word that sounds like this is **stair.** —**star′er,** n. —**star′ing·ly,** adv. **stare down,** to confuse or embarrass by staring.

star·fish (stär′fish′), n. any of several star-shaped sea animals with flattened bodies and usually five or more arms. Starfish are echinoderms, not fish. ❑ n., pl. **star·fish** or **star·fish·es.**

star·gaze (stär′gāz′), v. 1 to gaze at the stars. 2 to be absent-minded; daydream. ❑ v. **star·gazed, star·gaz·ing.**

stark (stärk), 1 adj. downright; complete: *That fool is talking stark nonsense.* 2 adv. entirely; completely: *The boys went swimming stark naked.* 3 adj. bare; barren; desolate: *a stark landscape.* —**stark′ly,** adv. —**stark′ness,** n.

star·less (stär′lis), adj. without stars; without starlight: *a dark, starless night.* —**star′less·ly,** adv. —**star′less·ness,** n.

star·let (stär′lit), n. a young actress who is being trained for leading roles in movies. ■ **Starlet** is sometimes considered offensive.

star·light (stär′līt′), n. light from the stars.

star·like (stär′līk′), adj. 1 shaped like a star: *pattern of starlike snowflakes.* 2 shining like a star.

star·ling (stär′ling), n. any of several birds with sharp bills and pointed wings, especially one kind with glossy, greenish black or brownish black feathers, common in Europe and North America.

starling—about 8 in. (20 cm) long

star·lit (stär′lit′), adj. lighted by the stars: *a starlit night.*

Star of David, a Jewish emblem (✡), in the form of a six-pointed star made of two triangles, one placed upon the other.

Starr (stär), n. 1 **Belle** (bel), 1848-1889, American outlaw. ■ **Belle Starr** was a cattle and horse thief and a robber. She was called the "bandit queen." 2 **Ring·o** (ring′gō), born 1940, English musician, a member of the Beatles.

starred (stärd), adj. 1 full of or decorated with stars. 2 marked with a star or asterisk.

star·ry (stär′ē), adj. 1 lighted by stars; containing many stars: *a starry sky.* 2 shining like stars: *starry eyes.* ❑ adj. **star·ri·er, star·ri·est.** —**star′ri·ness,** n.

star·ry–eyed (stär′ē īd′), *adj.* too optimistic or hopeful; unrealistic; dreamy.

Stars and Stripes, the flag of the United States.

star·ship (stär′ship′), *n.* an imaginary vehicle that can travel through outer space from one star to another; spaceship.

star–span·gled (stär′spang′gəld), *adj.* sprinkled with stars.

Star–Spangled Banner, 1 the national anthem of the United States. The words were composed by Francis Scott Key during the War of 1812. **2** flag of the United States; Stars and Stripes.

start (stärt), **1** *v.* to begin to move, go, or act: *The movie started on time.* **2** *v.* to begin: *start reading a book. School starts next week.* **3** *v.* to set going; put into action: *start a car, start a fire.* **4** *n.* act of setting in motion: *We pushed the car to give the motor a start.* **5** *n.* a beginning to move, go, or act: *see a race from start to finish.* **6** *v.* to move suddenly: *He started in surprise.* **7** *n.* a sudden movement; jerk: *I awoke with a start.* **8** *v.* to come, rise, or spring out suddenly: *Tears started from the baby's eyes.* **9** *n.* advantage over others; lead: *The fox had a mile start over the hounds.* **10** *n.* place, line, etc., where a race begins. **11** *v.* to rouse: *start a rabbit.* **12** *v.* to put in the original lineup in a contest: *The manager started a left-handed pitcher.*

start in, start out, or **start up,** to begin to do something.

start·er (stär′tər), *n.* **1** an electric motor for starting an internal-combustion engine. **2** the first in a series of things: *How about salad as a starter?* **3** person who gives the signal for starting: *the starter of a race.* **4** any person or thing that starts.

for starters, as a beginning; for the first thing, with more to follow: *For starters, we have to read 100 pages a week.*

star·tle (stär′tl), *v.* **1** to frighten suddenly; surprise: *The dog jumped at the girl and startled her.* **2** to move suddenly in fear or surprise. □ *v.* **star·tled, star·tling. —star′tle·ment,** *n.*

star·tling (stärt′ling), *adj.* surprising; frightening: *startling tales.* **—star′tling·ly,** *adv.*

star·va·tion (stär vā′shən), *n.* **1** suffering from extreme hunger; being starved: *Starvation caused his death.* **2** act of starving: *Starvation of prisoners is barbarous.*

starve (stärv), *v.* **1** to die because of hunger. **2** to suffer severely because of hunger. **3** to weaken or kill with hunger: *They starved the enemy into surrendering.* **4** to feel very hungry: *I'm starving! Let's eat.* □ *v.* **starved, starv·ing.**

starve for, to suffer or cause to suffer from lack of: *That lonely child is starving for affection.*

starve·ling (stärv′ling), *n.* OLD USE. person or animal that is suffering from lack of food.

Star Wars, Strategic Defense Initiative.

stash (stash), **1** *v.* to hide or put away for safekeeping or future use: *The thieves stashed the stolen money in a drainpipe.* **2** *n.* something hidden: *a stash of candy bars.* □ *n., pl.* **stash·es.**

state (stāt), **1** *n.* condition; situation: *The house is in a bad state of repair.* **2** *n.* a particular condition: *a state of excitement.* **3** *n.* the physical condition of a material. A substance may exist in a solid, liquid, or gaseous state. Ice is water in a solid state. **4** *n.* group of people occupying an area and organized under a government; commonwealth; nation. **5** *n.* Often, **State,** one of several organized political groups of people that together form a nation: *The state of Alaska is one of the United States.* **6** *n.* territory of a state. **7** *n.* the civil government; highest civil authority: *affairs of state.* **8** *n.* position in life; rank: *a person of respectable state.* **9** *v.* to tell in speech or writing; express; say: *State your opinion of the new school rules.* ■ See Synonym Study at **say. 10** *v.* to specify; declare: *to state a price.* **11** *n.* high style; dignity; pomp: *The royal family lived in great state.* □ *v.* **stat·ed, stat·ing. —stat′a·ble** or **state′a·ble,** *adj.*

lie in state, to lie in a coffin in a public place where formal respects may be paid before burial: *The dead hero lay in state.*

stat·ed (stā′tid), *adj.* **1** put into words; said: *the stated facts of a case.* **2** specified; declared: *School begins daily at a stated time.*

state·hood (stāt′hud), *n.* condition of being a state, especially a state of the United States.

state·house or **State·house** (stāt′hous′), *n.* building in which the legislature of a state meets; capitol of a state.

state·less (stāt′lis), *adj.* not belonging to any country; having no citizenship or nationality: *a stateless refugee.*

state·ly (stāt′lē), *adj.* having dignity; imposing; grand; majestic: *The Capitol at Washington is a stately building.* □ *adj.* **state·li·er, state·li·est. —state′li·ness,** *n.*

state·ment (stāt′mənt), *n.* **1** something stated; report; account: *Her statement was correct.* **2** act of stating; manner of stating something: *The statement of an idea helps me to remember it.* **3** summary of an account, showing the amount owed or due: *a bank statement.* **4** a single instruction given to a computer; command.

Stat·en Island (stat′n), island at the mouth of the Hudson River, south of Manhattan. It is a borough of New York City.

state of the art, the present-day level of development of a technology or area of scientific study. **—state′–of–the–art′,** *adj.*

state·room (stāt′rüm′), *n.* a private room on a ship or, formerly, on a railroad train.

state·side (stāt′sīd′), *adj.* from or in the United States.

states·man (stāts′mən), *n.* person skilled in the management of public or national affairs. □ *n., pl.* **states·men. —states′man·like′,** *adj.* **—states′man·ship,** *n.*

states' rights, powers belonging to the individual states of the United States, under the Constitution. The doctrine of states' rights holds that all powers which the Constitution does not specifically delegate to the federal government and does not specifically deny to the individual states belong to the states.

states·wom·an (stāts′wum′ən), *n.* a woman skilled in the management of public or national affairs. □ *n., pl.* **states·wom·en.**

state·wide (stāt′wīd′), *adj.* covering an entire state; over all of a state.

stat·ic (stat′ik), **1** *adj.* at rest; standing still: *Technology does not remain static; it changes constantly.* **2** *adj.* of or about electric charges produced by friction. **Static electricity** can be produced by rubbing a glass rod with a silk cloth. **3** *n.* noises and other interference with radio and TV reception caused by electric disturbances. **4** *adj.* of or about objects at rest or forces that balance each other. **5** *adj.* acting by weight without producing motion: *static pressure.*

stat·ics (stat′iks), *n.* branch of mechanics that deals with objects at rest or with forces that balance each other.

sta·tion (stā′shən), **1** *n.* a regular stopping place along a route: *a train station.* **2** *n.* place or equipment for sending out or receiving programs, messages, etc., by radio or TV. **3** *n.* place to stand in; place which a person is appointed to occupy in the performance of some duty; assigned post: *The policeman took his station at the corner.* **4** *n.* building or place used for a definite purpose: *a police station.* **5** *v.* to assign a station to; place: *She stationed herself just outside the main doorway to collect tickets.* **6** *n.* social position; rank: *A serf was a person of humble station in life.*

station (def. 1)

a	hat	ė	term	ô	order	ch	child	⟨ a in about
ā	age	i	it	oi	oil	ng	long	i in taken
ä	far	ī	ice	ou	out	sh	she	ə ⟨ i in pencil
â	care	o	hot	u	cup	th	thin	o in lemon
e	let	ō	open	ů	put	ŦH	then	⟨ u in circus
ē	equal	ò	saw	ü	rule	zh	measure	

sta·tion·ar·y (stā'shə ner'ē), *adj.* **1** not movable: *A furnace is stationary.* **2** standing still; not moving: *A parked car is stationary.* **3** not changing in size, number, activity, etc.: *The population of this town has been stationary for the last ten years at about 5000 people.* ■ Another word that sounds like this is **stationery**.

stationary front, boundary between warm and cold air masses, neither of which is moving.

station break, pause during a radio or TV program, or between programs, to identify the broadcasting station or network.

sta·tion·er (stā'shə nər), *n.* person who sells paper, pens, pencils, ink, etc.

sta·tion·er·y (stā'shə ner'ē), *n.* writing materials such as paper, cards, and envelopes. ■ Another word that sounds like this is **stationary**.

sta·tion·mas·ter (stā'shən mas'tər), *n.* person in charge of a railroad station.

station wagon, car with a rear door for loading and unloading and seats in the rear that can be folded down, for use as a light truck.

sta·tis·tic (stə tis'tik), **1** *adj.* statistical. **2** *n.* any value, item, etc., used in statistics: *an important statistic.*

sta·tis·ti·cal (stə tis'tə kəl), *adj.* of or about statistics; consisting of or based on statistics. **—sta·tis'ti·cal·ly,** *adv.*

sta·tis·ti·cian (stat'ə stish'ən), *n.* an expert in statistics; person who prepares statistics.

sta·tis·tics (stə tis'tiks), *n.* **1** *pl.* numerical facts about people, the weather, business conditions, etc. Statistics are collected and classified systematically. **2** *sing.* science of collecting and using such facts.

stat·u·ar·y (stach'ü er'ē), *n.* **1** statues. **2** art of making statues.

stat·ue (stach'ü), *n.* image of a person or animal carved in stone or wood, cast in bronze, or modeled in clay or wax: *Nearly every city has a statue of some famous person.* **—stat'ue·like',** *adj.*

WORD FAMILY Statue and the words below are related. They all come from a Latin word meaning "to stand."

estate	stanza	stationery	status
stage	state	statistic	statute
stance	station	stature	stay[1]
stanchion	stationary		

Statue of Liberty, a huge statue of a woman holding aloft a lighted torch, given to the United States by France. It stands on an island in New York Bay.

stat·u·esque (stach'ü esk'), *adj.* like a statue in dignity, formal grace, or classic beauty. **—stat'u·esque'ly,** *adv.* **—stat'u·esque'ness,** *n.*

stat·u·ette (stach'ü et'), *n.* a small statue.

stat·ure (stach'ər), *n.* **1** height: *a young woman of average stature.* **2** physical, mental, or moral growth; accomplishment: *Thomas Jefferson was a man of great stature among his countrymen.*

Statue of Liberty

sta·tus (stā'təs *or* stat'əs), *n.* **1** social or professional standing; position; rank: *to lose status, to seek status. What is her status in the government?* **2** state; condition: *Diplomats are interested in the status of world affairs.* **3** high rank or position. ◻ *n., pl.* **stat·us·es.**

status quo (kwō), the way things are; existing state of affairs.

stat·ute (stach'üt), *n.* law enacted by a legislative group: *The statutes for the United States are made by Congress.*

statute mile, mile (def. 1).

stat·u·to·ry (stach'ù tôr'ē), *adj.* **1** of or about a statute. **2** fixed by statute. **3** punishable by statute.

St. Au·gus·tine (sänt ô'gə stēn'), city in NE Florida, on the Atlantic. It is the oldest city in the United States, founded by the Spanish in 1565.

staunch[1] (stônch), *adj.* **1** loyal; steadfast: *staunch friends, staunch supporters of the law.* **2** strong or firm: *staunch walls, a staunch defense.* **3** watertight: *a staunch boat.* Also, **stanch.** **—staunch'ly,** *adv.* **—staunch'ness,** *n.*

staunch[2] (stônch), *v.* to stanch.

stave (stāv), **1** *n.* one of the curved pieces of wood that form the sides of a barrel, tub, etc. **2** *n.* stick or staff. **3** *v.* to break a hole in a barrel, boat, etc. **4** *n.* verse or stanza of a poem or song. **5** *n.* the musical staff. **6** *v.* to furnish with staves. ◻ *v.* **staved** *or* **stove, stav·ing.**

stave off, to put off; delay or prevent: *The lost campers ate birds' eggs to stave off starvation.*

staves (stāvz), *n.* **1** a plural of **staff** (defs. 4 and 6). **2** plural of **stave.**

stay[1] (stā), **1** *v.* to continue to be as indicated; remain: *Stay still. The cat stayed out all night. Shall I go or stay?* **2** *v.* to live for a while; dwell: *She is staying with her aunt for a few weeks.* **3** *n.* period of time spent: *a pleasant stay in the country.* **4** *v.* to stop; halt: *We have no time to stay.* **5** *v.* to put an end to for a while; satisfy: *He ate some cheese to stay his hunger.* **6** *v.* to put off; hold back; delay; restrain: *The teacher stayed judgment till he could hear both sides.* **7** *n.* restraint: *a stay on your activity.* **8** *n.* a delay in carrying out the order of a court: *The judge granted a stay of execution.* **9** *v.* to last; endure: *The runner was unable to stay to the end of the race.*

stay put, to remain where or as placed; remain fixed: *We stayed put in the tent until the rain stopped.*

SYNONYM STUDY **Stay**[1] and **remain** both mean to continue to be in a place for a while. **Stay** suggests not leaving: *They stayed for dinner.* **Remain** suggests staying after others have gone: *Remain in your seat until your name is called.*

stay[2] (stā), **1** *n.* a support; prop; brace: *The oldest child was the family's stay.* **2** *v.* to strengthen mentally or spiritually; fix or rest in dependence or reliance; hold up; support; prop. **3** *n.pl.* **stays,** corset, especially a stiffened one.

stay[3] (stā), **1** *n.* a strong rope, often of wire, which supports the mast of a ship. **2** *n.* any rope or chain attached to something to steady it. **3** *v.* to support or secure with stays.

staying power, power to hold out and not give in even though weakened or tired; power or will to endure.

STD, sexually transmitted disease.

stead (sted), *n.* place: *Our regular baby-sitter could not come, but sent her brother in her stead.*

stand in good stead, be of advantage or service to: *Her ability to swim stood her in good stead when the boat upset.*

stead·fast (sted'fast'), *adj.* constant; not moving or changing: *a steadfast friend.* **—stead'fast'ly,** *adv.* **—stead'fast'ness,** *n.*

stead·y (sted'ē), **1** *adj.* changing very little; regular: *He is making steady progress at school.* **2** *adj.* firm; not swaying or shaking: *This post is steady as a rock. Hold the ladder steady.* **3** *adj.* not easily excited; calm: *Airplane pilots must have steady nerves.* **4** *adj.* steadfast; firm: *steady friendship.* **5** *adj.* having good habits; reliable: *He is a steady young man.* **6** *v.* to make steady; keep steady: *Steady the ladder while I climb to the roof.* **7** *v.* to become steady: *Our sails filled as the wind steadied from the east.* **8** *n.* one's regular sweetheart. ◻ *adj.* **stead·i·er, stead·i·est;** *v.* **stead·ied, stead·y·ing;** *n., pl.* **stead·ies.** **—stead'i·ly,** *adv.* **—stead'i·ness,** *n.*

go steady, to have an agreement with a person to date only that person.

steady state theory, theory that the universe is much the same as it has always been and that matter is always being created to take the place of matter constantly vanishing or scattered.

steak (stāk), *n.* **1** slice of meat or fish for broiling or frying. *Steak* often means *beefsteak.* **2** finely ground meat shaped and cooked like a steak: *hamburger steak.* ■ Another word that sounds like this is **stake.**

steal (stēl), **1** *v.* to take something that does not belong to you; take dishonestly: *Robbers stole the money.* **2** *v.* to take, get, or do secretly: *She stole time from her lessons to read a story.* **3** *v.* to take, get, or win by art, charm, etc.: *The baby stole our hearts.*

4 *v.* to move secretly or quietly: *She stole softly out of the house.* **5** *n.* act of stealing; theft. **6** *n.* INFORMAL. something obtained at a very low cost or with very little effort: *This table is such a bargain it's a steal.* **7** *v.* (in baseball) to run to second base, third base, or home plate as the pitcher throws the ball to the catcher. ❑ *v.* **stole, sto·len, steal·ing.** ■ Another word that sounds like this is **steel.** —**steal′er,** *n.*

SYNONYM STUDY **Steal** and **rob** both mean to take something from someone. However, they are not really synonyms because of the way they are used. The object of **steal** is the thing that is taken. The object of **rob** is the person or place that something is taken from: *They stole over $50,000 when they robbed the bank.*

stealth (stelth), *n.* secret or sly action: *He obtained the letter by stealth, taking it while nobody was in the room.*

stealth·y (stel′thē), *adj.* done in a secret manner; secret; sly: *The cat crept in a stealthy way toward the bird.* ❑ *adj.* **stealth·i·er, stealth·i·est.** —**stealth′i·ly,** *adv.* —**stealth′i·ness,** *n.*

steam (stēm), **1** *n.* the invisible vapor or gas into which water is changed when heated to the boiling point. Steam may be used to heat homes or drive turbines to generate electricity. **2** *n.* the white cloud or mist formed by the condensation of this invisible vapor or gas. **3** *v.* to give off steam. **4** *v.* to become covered with steam: *The windshield had completely steamed up inside the heated car.* **5** *v.* to move by steam: *The ship steamed off.* **6** *v.* to cook, soften, or freshen by steam: *steamed vegetables. Steam those curtains to get the wrinkles out.* **7** *n.* power; energy; force: *She has worked hard all day and is running out of steam.* **8** *adj.* of or using steam; produced or worked by steam: *Many large office buildings and apartments have steam heat.* —**steam′less,** *adj.*

let off steam, to relieve your feelings.

steam·boat (stēm′bōt′), *n.* boat moved by a steam engine. In former times, steamboats carried passengers and cargo on large rivers.

steam engine, engine that works by the action of steam under pressure. The steam, produced in a boiler, expands and pushes a piston in a cylinder. Steam engines were formerly used to drive locomotives, ships, and large machines.

steam·er (stē′mər), *n.* **1** boat, ship, car, etc., moved by a steam engine. **2** container in which something is steamed.

steam·fit·ter (stēm′fit′ər), *n.* person who installs or repairs steam pipes, radiators, boilers, etc.

steam iron, an electric iron which releases steam through holes in its undersurface to dampen cloth while pressing it.

steam·roll·er (stēm′rō′lər), **1** *n.* vehicle with a heavy roller, formerly moved by steam but now usually by an internal-combustion engine, used to crush and level materials in making roads. **2** *n.* method of crushing opposition. **3** *v.* to crush: *to steamroller all political opposition.*

steam·ship (stēm′ship′), *n.* ship moved by steam.

steam shovel, machine for digging, formerly run by steam but now usually by an internal-combustion engine.

steam·y (stē′mē), *adj.* **1** of or like steam: *a steamy vapor.* **2** full of steam; giving off steam: *a steamy room.* ❑ *adj.* **steam·i·er, steam·i·est.** —**steam′i·ly,** *adv.* —**steam′i·ness,** *n.*

steed (stēd), *n.* **1** horse, especially a riding horse. **2** a high-spirited horse.

steel (stēl), **1** *n.* an alloy of iron and carbon. Steel has greater hardness and flexibility than cast iron and is used for tools and machinery. **2** *n.* something made from steel, such as a sword, a rod of steel for sharpening knives, etc. **3** *adj.* like or made of steel: *Steel beams are used in building skyscrapers and bridges.* **4** *v.* to make hard or strong like steel: *steel yourself against a possible failure.* **5** *n.* steellike hardness or strength: *nerves of steel.* ■ Another word that sounds like this is **steal.** —**steel′like′,** *adj.*

steel band, a kind of West Indian musical band that performs on percussion instruments usually made from oil drums.

steel wool, pad of long, fine steel threads used in cleaning or polishing surfaces.

steel·work·er (stēl′wėr′kər), *n.* person who works in a place where steel is made.

steel·works (stēl′wėrks′), *n.pl. or sing.* place where steel is made.

steel·y (stē′lē), *adj.* **1** made of steel. **2** like steel in color, strength, or hardness. ❑ *adj.* **steel·i·er, steel·i·est.** —**steel′i·ness,** *n.*

steel·yard (stēl′yärd *or* stil′yərd), *n.* balance for weighing, with arms of unequal length. The longer arm has a movable weight and is marked in units of weight; the shorter arm has a hook for holding the object to be weighed.

steep¹ (stēp), *adj.* **1** having a sharp slope; almost straight up and down: *The hill is steep.* **2** too high; unreasonable: *a steep price.* —**steep′ly,** *adv.* —**steep′ness,** *n.*

steep² (stēp), *v.* **1** to soak: *Let the tea steep in boiling water for five minutes.* **2** to involve deeply in something: *to steep yourself in history.* —**steep′er,** *n.*

steeped in, filled with; absorbed in: *ruins steeped in gloom.*

steep·en (stē′pən), *v.* to make or become steep or steeper.

stee·ple (stē′pəl), *n.* **1** a high tower on a church. Steeples usually have spires. **2** spire on top of the tower or roof of a church or similar building.

stee·ple·chase (stē′pəl chās′), *n.* a horse race over a course having ditches, hedges, and other obstacles.

stee·ple·jack (stē′pəl jak′), *n.* person who climbs steeples, tall chimneys, or the like, to make repairs, etc.

steer¹ (stir), *v.* **1** to guide the course of: *steer a ship, steer a car.* **2** to be guided: *This car steers easily.* **3** to direct your way or course: *Steer for the harbor.* **4** to set and follow: *She steered a middle course during the debate, agreeing with speakers on both sides.* —**steer′a·ble,** *adj.* —**steer′er,** *n.*

steer clear of, to keep away from; avoid.

steer² (stir), *n.* a young male of cattle raised for beef, usually two to four years old.

steer·age (stir′ij), *n.* **1** (earlier) the part of a ship occupied by passengers traveling at the cheapest rate. **2** act of steering.

steering wheel, wheel that is turned to steer a car, bus, etc.

steers·man (stirz′mən), *n.* person who steers a boat or ship. ❑ *n., pl.* **steers·men.**

steg·o·saur (steg′ə sôr′), *n.* stegosaurus.

steg·o·sau·rus (steg′ə sôr′əs), *n.* a plant-eating dinosaur of great size, with bony armor in the form of plates and spikes along the back and tail. ❑ *n., pl.* **steg·o·sau·rus·es** or **steg·o·sau·ri** (steg′ō sôr′ī). [**Stegosaurus** comes from Greek words meaning "roof" and "lizard." The plates on its back reminded people of the edge of a roof.]

stein (stīn), *n.* a mug for beer.

Stein (stīn), *n.* **Ger·trude** (gėr′trüd), 1874-1946, American writer. ■ **Gertrude Stein** lived in Paris for much of her life, where she encouraged and influenced other writers and artists, including Pablo Picasso and Ernest Hemingway.

steel band

a	hat	ė	term	ô	order	ch	child		a in about
ā	age	i	it	oi	oil	ng	long		e in taken
ä	far	ī	ice	ou	out	sh	she	ə	i in pencil
â	care	o	hot	u	cup	th	thin		o in lemon
e	let	ō	open	u̇	put	ŦH	then		u in circus
ē	equal	ȯ	saw	ü	rule	zh	measure		

Stein·beck (stĭn′bek), *n.* **John,** 1902-1968, American writer. ■ **John Steinbeck** won the 1962 Nobel Prize for literature. His novels are often about the struggles of poor or disadvantaged people.

Stein·em (stī′nəm), *n.* **Gloria,** born 1934, American political activist and writer. She founded the magazine *Ms.*

stel·lar (stel′ər), *adj.* **1** of or like the stars or a star. **2** leading; main; chief: *a stellar role.*

St. El·mo's fire (sānt el′mōz), ball of light caused by a discharge of atmospheric electricity, often seen on towers, masts of ships, etc.

stem¹ (stem), **1** *n.* the main part of a plant, usually above the ground. The stem supports the branches, leaves, flowers, etc. **2** *n.* the part of a flower, a fruit, or a leaf that joins it to the plant or tree; stalk¹. **3** *n.* anything like the stem of a plant: *the stem of a goblet, the stem of a pipe.* **4** *n.* the part of a word to which endings are added and in which changes are made. *Run* is the stem of *running, runner, ran,* etc. **5** *v.* to remove the stem from a leaf, fruit, etc. **6** *n.* the bow or front end of a boat. ❑ *v.* **stemmed, stem·ming.** —**stem′like**, *adj.*

from stem to stern, 1 from one end of a ship to the other. **2** completely; thoroughly.

stem from, to come from; have as a source or cause: *The difficulty stems from their failure to plan properly.*

stem² (stem), *v.* **1** to stop; check; dam up: *I put a tight bandage over the cut to stem the flow of blood.* **2** to make headway or progress against: *When you swim upstream you have to stem the current.* ❑ *v.* **stemmed, stem·ming.**

stem·less (stem′lis), *adj.* having no stem or no visible stem.

stemmed (stemd), *adj.* **1** having a stem. **2** having the stem removed.

stench (stench), *n.* a very bad smell; stink: *the stench of a garbage dump.* ❑ *n., pl.* **stench·es.**

sten·cil (sten′səl), **1** *n.* a thin sheet of metal, paper, plastic, cardboard, etc., having letters or designs cut through it. When it is laid on a surface and ink or color is spread over it, these letters or designs are made on the surface underneath. **2** *n.* the letters or designs made in this way. **3** *v.* to mark, paint, or make with a stencil: *to stencil your name on a box.* ❑ *v.* **sten·ciled, sten·cil·ing** or **sten·cilled, sten·cil·ling.**

stencil

Steng·el (steng′gəl), *n.* **Ca·sey** (kā′sē), 1890-1975, American baseball manager. ■ **Casey Stengel** managed the New York Yankees from 1949 to 1960, during which time they won the World Series seven times. He was also the first manager of the New York Mets.

ste·nog·ra·pher (stə nog′rə fər), *n.* person whose work is taking dictation in shorthand and transcribing it, usually with a typewriter.

sten·o·graph·ic (sten′ə graf′ik), *adj.* **1** made by stenography. **2** using stenography. —**sten′o·graph′i·cal·ly,** *adv.*

ste·nog·ra·phy (stə nog′rə fē), *n.* **1** method of rapid writing that uses symbols, abbreviations, etc.; shorthand. **2** act of writing in such symbols.

sten·to·ri·an (sten tôr′ē ən), *adj.* very loud or powerful in sound: *a stentorian voice.* —**sten·to′ri·an·ly,** *adv.*

step (step), **1** *n.* movement made by lifting a foot and putting it down again in a new position; one motion of the leg in walking, running, dancing, etc. **2** *n.* distance covered by one such movement: *We were three steps away when she called us back.* **3** *v.* to put a foot down: *He stepped on a bug.* **4** *n.* the sound made by putting a foot down: *I hear steps upstairs.* **5** *n.* a place for a foot in going up or coming down. A stair or a rung of a ladder is a step. **6** *v.* to move the legs as in walking, running, dancing, etc.: *Step lively!* **7** *n.* a short distance; little way: *The school is only a step from our house.* **8** *v.* to walk a short distance: *Step this way.* **9** *n.* way of dancing: *The dance instructor taught me several new steps.* **10** *v.* to measure by taking steps: *She stepped off the distance from the door to the window.* **11** *n.* footprint: *I see steps in the mud.* **12** *n.* action; deed; movement: *Agreeing to a conference was the first step toward peace.* **13** *n.* a level or degree in a scale; a grade in rank: *A colonel is three steps above a captain.* **14** *n.* stage or action in a gradual process, operation, etc.: *a step in a chemical experiment.* **15** *n.* (in music) a level or degree of the staff or the scale. C is two steps above A. ❑ *v.* **stepped, step·ping.** ■ Another word that sounds like this is **steppe.** —**step′per,** *n.*

in step, 1 moving the same leg at the same time as another person does: *Band members must learn to march in step.* **2** making your actions or ideas agree with those of another person or persons; in harmony or agreement.

keep step, to move the same leg at the same time that another person does while walking or marching.

out of step, not in step; not at a uniform pace or in harmony with another or others.

step by step, little by little; slowly.

step down, 1 to surrender or resign from an office or position. **2** to lower by steps or degrees; decrease.

step in, to intervene; take part.

step into, to come into, acquire, or receive, especially without particular effort or by chance: *step into a fortune.*

step on it, INFORMAL. to go faster; hurry up: *Step on it or we'll be late.*

step out, to go out for entertainment.

step up, to increase bit by bit; go faster, higher, etc.: *step up the production of cars, step up the pressure in a boiler.*

take steps, to do things considered likely to achieve a goal: *The principal took steps to stop needless absence from school.*

watch your step, be careful: *Watch your step when you ride down that steep hill on the bicycle.*

step-, *prefix.* related by the remarriage of a parent: *stepfather = husband in the mother's remarriage.*

step·broth·er (step′bruᴛн′ər), *n.* a stepfather's or stepmother's son by a former marriage.

step-by-step (step′bī step′), *adj.* progressing by stages; gradual.

step·child (step′chīld′), *n.* child of your husband or wife by a former marriage. ❑ *n., pl.* **step·chil·dren** (step′chil′drən).

step·dad (step′dad′), *n.* INFORMAL. stepfather.

step·daugh·ter (step′dȯ′tər), *n.* daughter of your husband or wife by a former marriage.

step·fam·i·ly (step′fam′ə lē), *n.* **1** the people who are part of your family because they are related to your stepparent. **2** a family with stepchildren.

step·fa·ther (step′fä′ᴛнər), *n.* man who has married your mother after the death or divorce of your father.

step·lad·der (step′lad′ər), *n.* ladder with flat steps instead of rungs, and a folding support attached to the back by hinges.

step·moth·er (step′muᴛн′ər), *n.* woman who has married your father after the death or divorce of your mother.

step·par·ent (step′pâr′ənt), *n.* stepfather or stepmother.

steppe (step), *n.* **1** one of the vast, treeless plains in southeastern Europe and in Asia, especially in Russia. **2** any vast, treeless plain. ■ Another word that sounds like this is **step.**

step·ping·stone (step′ing stōn′), *n.* **1** stone or one of a line of stones in shallow water, a marshy place, or the like, used in crossing. **2** stone for use in mounting or ascending. **3** anything serving as a means of advancing yourself or getting ahead.

step·sis·ter (step′sis′tər), *n.* a stepfather's or stepmother's daughter by a former marriage.

step·son (step'sun'), *n.* son of your husband or wife by a former marriage.

-ster, *suffix.* **1** person who ___s: *trickster = a person who tricks or cheats.* **2** person who makes ___: *punster = a person who makes puns.*

ster·e·o (ster'ē ō *or* stir'ē ō), **1** *adj.* stereophonic. **2** *n.* a set of connected devices used to produce stereophonic sound, including speakers, an amplifier, a radio tuner, and often a CD player, tape deck, and phonograph. ❑ *n., pl.* **ster·e·os.**

ster·e·o·phon·ic (ster'ē ə fon'ik *or* stir'ē ə fon'ik), *adj.* giving the effect of lifelike sound by using two or more sets of equipment for recording or broadcasting. Stereophonic sound also needs two or more speakers, which produce different sounds at the same time. Together, these different sounds have the same effects of depth and direction as the original source of sound. —**ster'e·o·phon'i·cal·ly,** *adv.*

ster·e·op·ti·con (ster'ē op'tə kən *or* stir'ē op'tə kən), *n.* projector arranged to combine two images on a screen so that they gradually become one image, with three-dimensional effect.

ster·e·o·scope (ster'ē ə skōp' *or* stir'ē ə skōp'), *n.* viewing device through which two pictures of the same object or scene, taken from slightly different angles, are seen, one by each eye. The object or scene thus viewed appears to have three dimensions.

ster·e·o·scop·ic (ster'ē ə skop'ik *or* stir'ē ə skop'ik), *adj.* of or about stereoscopes.

ster·e·o·type (ster'ē ə tīp' *or* stir'ē ə tīp'), **1** *n.* an oversimplified conventional notion or idea about a person, group, thought, etc., held in common by members of a group, and which allows for no individual judgments. Long John Silver, in Stevenson's *Treasure Island,* is the stereotype of a pirate. **2** *v.* to give a fixed or settled form to. **3** *n.* a printing plate cast from a mold. ❑ *v.* **ster·e·o·typed, ster·e·o·typ·ing.** —**ster'e·o·typ'er,** *n.* —**ster·e·o·typ·ic** (ster'ē ə tip'ik *or* stir'ē ə tip'ik), **ster·e·o·typ'i·cal,** *adj.* —**ster'e·o·typ'i·cal·ly,** *adv.*

ster·e·o·typed (ster'ē ə tīpt' *or* stir'ē ə tīpt'), *adj.* **1** conventional: *"It gives me great pleasure to be with you tonight" is a stereotyped opening for a speech.* **2** cast in the form of, or printed from, a stereotype.

ster·ile (ster'əl), *adj.* **1** free from germs: *Bandages should always be kept sterile.* **2** not producing seed, offspring, crops, etc.; not fertile; barren: *sterile land, a sterile cow.* —**ster'ile·ly,** *adv.* —**ster'ile·ness, ste·ril·i·ty** (stə ril'ə tē), *n.*

ster·i·lize (ster'ə līz), *v.* **1** to make free from germs: *The water had to be sterilized by boiling to make it fit to drink.* **2** to make incapable of bearing offspring. ❑ *v.* **ster·i·lized, ster·i·liz·ing.** —**ster'i·li·za'tion,** *n.*

ster·i·liz·er (ster'ə lī'zər), *n.* any device for killing germs.

ster·ling (ster'ling), **1** *adj.* made of silver that is 92.5 percent pure. *Sterling* is stamped on solid silver knives, forks, spoons, and jewelry. **2** *n.* sterling silver or things made of it. **3** *adj.* genuine; excellent; dependable; reliable: *a person of sterling character.* **4** *n.* British money, especially the pound as a monetary unit in international trade: *to pay in sterling.* **5** *adj.* of British money; payable in British money.

sterling silver, silver that is 92.5 percent pure.

stern[1] (stern), *adj.* **1** harshly firm; hard; strict: *a stern parent. Our teacher's stern frown silenced us.* ■ See Synonym Study at **severe. 2** very severe; rigorous; harsh: *stern necessity.* —**stern'ly,** *adv.* —**stern'ness,** *n.*

stern[2] (stern), *n.* the rear part of a ship or boat.

ster·num (ster'nəm), *n.* breastbone. ❑ *n., pl.* **ster·nums** *or* **ster·na** (ster'nə).

stern-wheel·er (stern'wē'lər), *n.* (earlier) steamboat driven by a paddle wheel at the stern.

ster·oid (stâr'oid), *n.* any of a group of organic chemical compounds including bile acids, cholesterol, and the sex hormones. Some steroids are sometimes used illegally to build muscle tissue, although they have dangerous side effects.

steth·o·scope (steth'ə skōp'), *n.* device used to hear the sounds produced in the lungs, heart, or other parts of the body.

ste·ve·dore (stē'və dôr'), *n.* person who loads and unloads ships.

Ste·vens (stē'vənz), *n.* **1 John Paul,** born 1920, U.S. Supreme Court justice, appointed in 1975. **2 Wallace,** 1879-1955, American poet. His *Collected Poems* won the 1955 Pulitzer Prize.

Ste·ven·son (stē'vən sən), *n.* **Rob·ert Lou·is** (rob'ərt lü'əs), 1850-1894, Scottish writer. ■ **Robert Louis Stevenson** is best known for his novels of adventure and suspense, including *Treasure Island* and *The Strange Case of Dr. Jekyll and Mr. Hyde.*

stew (stü), **1** *v.* to cook by slow boiling: *The cook stewed the chicken for a long time.* **2** *n.* food cooked by slow boiling: *beef stew.* **3** *v.* to worry; fret. **4** *n.* condition of being worried: *They were in a stew over their lost luggage.* —**stew'a·ble,** *adj.*

stew·ard (stü'ərd), *n.* **1** man employed on an airplane, a ship, etc., to look after passengers. **2** person who manages another's property or finances. **3** person who has charge of the food and table service for a club, restaurant, etc.

stew·ard·ess (stü'ər dis), *n.* woman employed on an airplane, a ship, etc., to look after passengers. ❑ *n., pl.* **stew·ard·ess·es.**

stew·ard·ship (stü'ərd ship), *n.* position or work of a steward.

Stew·art (stü'ərt), *n.* **James,** born 1908, American movie actor. He won an Academy Award for best actor for *The Philadelphia Story* in 1940.

St. George's, capital of Grenada.

St. He·le·na (sānt hə lē'nə), British island in the S Atlantic. Napoleon I was exiled there from 1815 until his death in 1821.

St. Hel·ens (sānt hel'ənz), **Mount,** volcano in the Cascade Range in W Washington. It erupted in 1980, causing great damage. 8364 feet (2549 meters) high.

stick[1] (stik), *n.* **1** a long, thin piece of wood: *Put some sticks on the fire.* **2** such a piece of wood shaped for a special use: *a walking stick.* **3** a slender branch or twig of a tree or bush, especially when cut or broken off. **4** something like a stick in shape: *a stick of candy.* **5** INFORMAL. a stiff, awkward, or stupid person. **6** device used in some small airplanes to control the ailerons and elevators. **7 the sticks,** *pl.* INFORMAL. the outlying or undeveloped districts; backwoods. —**stick'like',** *adj.*

stick[2] (stik), *v.* **1** to pierce with a pointed tool; thrust a point into; stab: *She stuck a fork into the potato.* **2** to fasten by pushing the point or end into or through something: *He stuck a flower in his buttonhole.* **3** to put into a position: *Don't stick your head out of the window.* **4** to come out from; extend: *My arms stick out of my coat sleeves.* **5** to fasten; attach: *Stick a stamp on the letter.* **6** to keep close: *The puppy stuck to my heels.* **7** to be or become fastened; be at a standstill: *Two pages of the book stuck together.* **8** to bring to a stop: *Our car was stuck in the mud.* **9** to hold your position; hold fast; cling: *She stuck on the horse's back. Let's stick to the task until we've finished it.* **10** to puzzle; baffle: *I got really stuck on that arithmetic problem.* **11** SLANG. to cheat; swindle. **12** to take advantage of; burden: *I got stuck washing dishes when everyone else went out.* ❑ *v.* **stuck, stick·ing.** —**stick'a·ble,** *adj.*

stick around, INFORMAL. to stay or wait nearby.

stick at, to hesitate or stop for: *He'll stick at nothing to win.*

stick by *or* **stick to,** to remain faithful to; refuse to desert: *She sticks by her friends when they need her help.*

stick up, INFORMAL. to hold up; rob.

stick up for, to stand up for; support; defend: *Stick up for your friends when they are in trouble.*

SYNONYM STUDY **Stick**[2], **cling,** and **adhere** all mean to touch something and stay touching. **Stick** often suggests things that are gummy or that have dried together: *The mud stuck to his shoes.* **Cling** suggests something that hangs on in spite of efforts to get rid of it: *My cat's hairs cling to my dress.* **Adhere** suggests flat things: *Electricity makes the paper adhere to the glass.*

stick·ball (stik'bôl'), *n.* form of baseball played with a rubber ball and a stick or broom handle for a bat.

stick·er (stik'ər), *n.* **1** a gummed label. **2** thorn or bur.

a	hat	ė	term	ô	order	ch	child		
ā	age	i	it	oi	oil	ng	long		a in about
ä	far	ī	ice	ou	out	sh	she		e in taken
â	care	o	hot	u	cup	th	thin	ə	i in pencil
e	let	ō	open	u̇	put	ŦH	then		o in lemon
ē	equal	ȯ	saw	ü	rule	zh	measure		u in circus

S

847

stick·le·back (stik′əl bak′), *n.* any of several small, scaleless fishes with a row of sharp spines on the back. The male builds an elaborate nest for the eggs and guards them carefully. ❑ *n., pl.* **stick·le·back** or **stick·le·backs.**

stick·ler (stik′lər), *n.* **1** person who contends or insists stubbornly, sometimes over trifles: *a stickler for accuracy.* **2** something that puzzles: *That's a real stickler; I don't know the answer.*

stick·pin (stik′pin′), *n.* pin worn in a necktie for ornament.

stick·shift (stik′shift′), *n.* a lever, especially one mounted on the floor, used to change gears in a motor vehicle.

stick·up (stik′up′), *n.* INFORMAL. robbery; holdup.

stick·y (stik′ē), *adj.* **1** apt to stick: *sticky candy.* **2** covered with a layer of material that will stick: *Adhesive tape is sticky.* **3** hot and damp: *sticky weather.* **4** difficult: *a sticky problem.* ❑ *adj.* **stick·i·er, stick·i·est.** —**stick′i·ly,** *adv.* —**stick′i·ness,** *n.*

Stieg·litz (stē′glits), *n.* **Alfred,** 1864-1946, American photographer. He helped popularize the idea of photography as art. He was the husband of Georgia O'Keeffe.

sties (stīz), *n.* **1** plural of **sty**[1]. **2** plural of **sty**[2].

stiff (stif), **1** *adj.* not easily bent; fixed; rigid: *stiff work gloves.* **2** *adj.* not able to move easily: *My neck is stiff today.* **3** *adj.* not fluid; firm: *Beat the egg whites until they are stiff.* **4** *adj.* not easy or natural in manner; formal: *The magician made a a stiff bow to the audience.* **5** *adj.* strong: *a stiff breeze.* **6** *adj.* hard to move: *The old hinges on the barn door are stiff.* **7** *adj.* hard to deal with; hard: *There was stiff competition at the track meet.* **8** *adj.* more than seems suitable: *a stiff price for a house.* **9** *adv.* very much; extremely: *I was scared stiff.* —**stiff′ly,** *adv.* —**stiff′ness,** *n.*

Stieglitz photograph

Stiff and **rigid** both mean not easy to bend. **Stiff** suggests that bending something takes effort: *Grandma's joints are stiff when she gets up in the morning.* **Rigid** suggests that something is very hard or impossible to bend: *He uses a rigid case for his eyeglasses because he thinks it's safer.*

stiff·en (stif′ən), *v.* to make or become stiff: *The jelly will stiffen as it cools. Her muscles stiffened in the cold wind.* —**stiff′en·er,** *n.*

stiff-necked (stif′nekt′), *adj.* **1** having a stiff neck. **2** stubborn; obstinate. —**stiff′-neck′ed·ness,** *n.*

sti·fle (stī′fəl), *v.* **1** to be unable to breathe freely: *I am stifling in this close room.* **2** to keep back; stop: *The conversation was so boring I had to stifle a few yawns.* **3** to stop someone's breath; smother: *The smoke stifled the firefighters.* ❑ *v.* **sti·fled, sti·fling.** —**sti′fler,** *n.*

stig·ma (stig′mə), *n.* **1** a mark of disgrace or shame; stain on your reputation. **2** a spot in the skin that bleeds or turns red. **3** the part of a pistil of a plant that receives pollen. ❑ *n., pl.* **stig·mas, stig·ma·ta** (stig mä′tə).

Stigma comes from a Greek word meaning "to mark" or "to tattoo." In old times, criminals were marked for life by branding or tattooing. A stigma remains a mark of disgrace, but one less visible than a tattoo.

stig·ma·tize (stig′mə tīz), *v.* to set some mark of disgrace upon; reproach; brand: *He always felt that his father's prison record stigmatized both of them.* ❑ *v.* **stig·ma·tized, stig·ma·tiz·ing.** —**stig′ma·ti·za′tion,** *n.* —**stig′ma·tiz′er,** *n.*

stile (stīl), *n.* **1** step or steps for getting over a fence or wall. **2** turnstile. ■ Another word that sounds like this is **style.**

sti·let·to (stə let′ō), *n.* dagger with a narrow blade. ❑ *n., pl.* **sti·let·tos** or **sti·let·toes.**

still[1] (stil), **1** *adj.* staying in the same position or at rest; without motion; motionless: *to stand or lie still. Sit still. The lake is still today.* **2** *adj.* without noise; quiet: *a still night. The room was so still that you could have heard a pin drop.* ■ See Synonym Study at **quiet.** **3** *v.* to make or become calm or quiet: *The father stilled the crying baby.* **4** *n.* quiet; silence: *in the still of the night.* **5** *adv.* in spite of; yet; nevertheless: *Proof was given, but they still doubted. Though she liked her other jobs, she still favors this one.* **6** *adv.* at or until the present, or some other stated time: *Was the store still open? Were they still up when you got home last night?* **7** *adv.* without moving; quietly. **8** *adv.* even; yet: *You can read better still if you try.*

still[2] (stil), *n.* apparatus for distilling liquids, especially alcoholic liquors.

still·birth (stil′bėrth′), *n.* birth of a dead baby.

still·born (stil′bôrn′), *adj.* dead when born.

still life, a picture of inanimate objects, such as fruit, flowers, pottery, and the like, artistically arranged to be the subject of a picture. —**still′-life′,** *adj.*

still·ness (stil′nis), *n.* **1** absence of noise; quiet; silence. **2** absence of motion; calm. ❑ *n., pl.* **still·ness·es.**

stilt (stilt), *n.* **1** one of a pair of poles, each with a support for a foot at some distance above the ground. Stilts are used by circus performers, or by children for amusement. **2** a long post or pole used to support a house, shed, etc., above water, swampland, etc. **3** any of several wading birds with long, slender legs and long bills, living in marshes. ❑ *n., pl.* **stilts** (or **stilt** for 3). —**stilt′like′,** *adj.*

stilt·ed (stil′tid), *adj.* stiffly dignified or formal: *a stilted manner of speaking.* —**stilt′ed·ly,** *adv.* —**stilt′ed·ness,** *n.*

stim·u·lant (stim′yə lənt), **1** *n.* food, drug, medicine, etc., that temporarily increases the activity of the body or some part of the body. Tea and coffee are stimulants. **2** *n.* something that excites, stirs, or stimulates: *Advertising is a stimulant to business.* **3** *adj.* stimulating.

stim·u·late (stim′yə lāt), *v.* **1** to make more active; encourage; rouse to action: *The new factory helped to stimulate the growth of the town.* **2** to act as a stimulant or a stimulus. ❑ *v.* **stim·u·lat·ed, stim·u·lat·ing.** —**stim′u·la′tion,** *n.* —**stim′u·lat′or** or **stim′u·la′ter,** *n.*

stim·u·li (stim′yə lī), *n.* plural of **stimulus.**

stim·u·lus (stim′yə ləs), *n.* **1** something that encourages action or effort: *The lecture on self-improvement was the stimulus that led me to go back to school.* **2** something that causes a reaction in a living thing: *The stimulus of a bright light makes the pupils of the eyes become smaller.* ❑ *n., pl.* **stimuli.**

sting (sting), **1** *v.* to wound with a sharp-pointed part: *A bee stung her.* **2** *n.* act of stinging. **3** *n.* a wound caused by stinging: *The sting on his knee began to swell.* **4** *n.* stinger (def. 1). **5** *v.* to cause to suffer: *The actor was stung by the insults of the critics.* **6** *n.* sharp pain: *The ball team felt the sting of defeat.* **7** *v.* to cause a feeling like that of a sting: *Hot peppers can sting your mouth.* **8** *v.* SLANG. to cheat by charging too high a price. **9** *n.* INFORMAL. any complicated trap, especially one carried out by police out of uniform, or other law enforcement agents, to catch criminals. ❑ *v.* **stung, sting·ing.** —**sting′less,** *adj.*

sting·er (sting′ər), *n.* **1** the sharp-pointed part of an insect that wounds and often poisons; sting. **2** anything that stings: *a leaf with stingers on it.*

sting·ray (sting′rā′), *n.* any of numerous large rays that can cause severe wounds with sharp spines on their tails.

stin·gy (stin′jē), *adj.* **1** unwilling to spend or give money; not generous: *He tried to save money without being stingy.* **2** scanty; meager. ❑ *adj.* **stin·gi·er, stin·gi·est.** —**stin′gi·ly,** *adv.* —**stin′gi·ness,** *n.*

stink (stingk), **1** *n.* a very bad smell. **2** *v.* to have a bad smell: *Decaying fish stink.* **3** *v.* to cause to have a very bad smell: *Damp garbage stunk up the basement.* **4** *v.* to have a very bad reputation; be in great disfavor. ❑ *v.* **stank** or **stunk, stunk, stink·ing.**

stink·er (sting′kər), *n.* **1** person or thing that stinks. **2** INFORMAL. a mean or naughty person. **3** SLANG. something very hard or difficult: *a stinker of a test.*

stink·y (sting′kē), *adj.* stinking. ❑ *adj.* **stink·i·er, stink·i·est.**

stint (stint), **1** *n.* period of time spent on an assigned task: *She did a three month stint as a reporter for the local newspaper.* **2** *v.* to keep on short allowance; be saving or careful in using or spending; limit: *The parents stinted themselves of food to give it to their children.* **3** *n.* a limit; limitation: *a generous person who gives without stint.* **4** *v.* to be saving; get along on very little. **5** *n.* amount or share set aside. —**stint′er,** *n.* —**stint′ing·ly,** *adv.*

sti·pend (stī′pend), *n.* regular pay; salary: *The scholarship winner received a monthly stipend to cover her college expenses.*

stip·u·late (stip′yə lāt), *v.* to arrange definitely; demand as a condition of agreement: *He stipulated that he should receive a month's vacation every year if he took the job.* ❑ *v.* **stip·u·lat·ed, stip·u·lat·ing.** —**stip·u·la′tor,** *n.*

stip·u·la·tion (stip′yə lā′shən), *n.* a definite arrangement; agreement; condition in an agreement or bargain: *We rented the apartment with the stipulation that it should be decorated.*

stip·ule (stip′yül), *n.* one of the pair of little leaflike parts at the base of a leaf stem.

stir (stėr), **1** *v.* to mix by moving around with a spoon, fork, stick, etc.: *stir sugar into your tea.* **2** *v.* to set in motion; move: *The wind stirred the leaves.* **3** *v.* to move about: *No one was stirring in the house.* **4** *v.* to set going; affect strongly; excite: *Don't stir up trouble.* **5** *n.* movement: *There was a stir in the bushes where the children were hiding.* **6** *n.* excitement: *The news caused a great stir.* **7** *n.* act of stirring: *She gave the mixture a hard stir.* ❑ *v.* **stirred, stir·ring.** —**stir′rer,** *n.*

stir-fry (stėr′frī′), **1** *v.* to cook food in a small amount of hot fat, stirring constantly to prevent sticking and to be sure all sides of the food are fried. **2** *n.* meal cooked this way: *a beef and broccoli stir-fry.* ❑ *v.* **stir-fried, stir-fry·ing;** *n., pl.* **stir-fries.**

stir·ring (stėr′ing), *adj.* **1** moving, active, or lively: *stirring times.* **2** rousing; exciting: *a stirring speech.* —**stir′ring·ly,** *adv.*

stir·rup (stėr′əp *or* stir′əp), *n.* **1** a loop or ring of metal or wood that hangs from a saddle to support a rider's foot. **2** the innermost of the three tiny bones in the middle ear. It looks like a stirrup. See picture at **ear**[1].

stitch (stich), **1** *n.* one complete movement of a threaded needle through cloth in sewing, or through skin or tissue in surgery. **2** *n.* one complete movement in knitting, crocheting, embroidering, etc. **3** *n.* a particular method of taking stitches: *buttonhole stitch.* **4** *n.* loop of thread, etc., made by a stitch: *The doctor will take the stitches out of the wound tomorrow.* **5** *v.* to make stitches in; fasten with stitches: *The doctor stitched the cut.* **6** *v.* to sew. **7** *n.* piece of cloth or clothing: *He hadn't a dry stitch on.* **8** *n.* a small bit: *She wouldn't do a stitch of work.* **9** *n.* a sudden, sharp pain: *I had a stitch in my side.* ❑ *n., pl.* **stitch·es.** —**stitch′er,** *n.*

St. John's (sānt jonz′), **1** capital of Newfoundland, Canada, on the Atlantic. **2** capital of Antigua and Barbuda.

St. Jo·seph (sānt jō′zəf), city in NW Missouri. In 1860 it was the eastern end of the pony express route.

St. Kitts and Nevis (sānt kits′ənd nē′vis), an island country in the West Indies. *Capital:* Basseterre.

St. Law·rence (sānt lôr′əns), **1** river in SE Canada flowing northeast from Lake Ontario to the Gulf of St. Lawrence. **2 Gulf of,** arm of the Atlantic Ocean in E Canada.

St. Lawrence Seaway, waterway that links the Great Lakes to the Atlantic Ocean by means of canals and the St. Lawrence River.

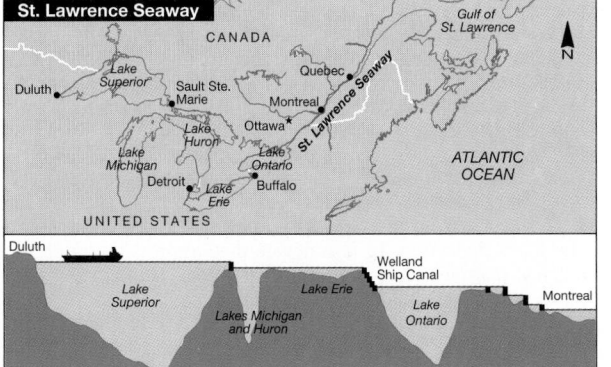

St. Lou·is (sānt lü′is), port in E Missouri, on the Mississippi River.

St. Lu·cia (sānt lü′shə), island country in the West Indies. *Capital:* Castries.

stoat (stōt), *n.* ermine in its summer coat of brown fur. ❑ *n., pl.* **stoats** or **stoat.**

stock (stok), **1** *n.* things for use or for sale: *This store keeps a large stock of toys.* **2** *v.* to get or keep regularly for use or for sale: *A toy store stocks toys.* **3** *adj.* kept regularly: *stock sizes of dresses.* **4** *adj.* in common use; commonplace; everyday: *The weather is a stock subject of conversation.* **5** *v.* to provide with a supply; equip: *Our camp is stocked with everything we need for a week.* **6** *v.* to get a supply: *stock up salt for the winter.* **7** *n.* livestock. **8** *v.* to furnish with livestock: *stock a farm.* **9** *n.* shares owned in a company. **10** *n.* family or ancestors: *a person of aristocratic stock.* **11** *n.* group of closely related living things. **12** *n.* a part used as a support or handle: *a rifle stock.* **13** *n.* raw material: *Rags are used as a stock for making fine paper.* **14** *n.* water in which meat or fish has been cooked, used as a base for soups, sauces, etc. **15** *n.* trunk or stump of a tree. **16** *n.* main stem of a plant. **17** *n.* stem in which a graft is inserted. **18** *n.pl.* **the stocks,** an old punishment device consisting of a heavy wooden frame with holes to put someone's feet and sometimes hands through. —**stock′a·ble,** *adj.* —**stock′er,** *n.* —**stock′like′,** *adj.*

in stock, ready for use or sale; available: *The store has many brands of CD players in stock.*

out of stock, not available; lacking: *That item is out of stock just now, but we should have some in very soon.*

take stock, 1 to find out how much stock you have. **2** to make an estimate or examination: *take stock of a problem.*

take stock in, to take an interest in; consider important; trust: *He took little stock in the story.*

stock·ade (sto kād′), **1** *n.* a defensive pen or barrier made of large, strong posts fixed upright in the ground: *A heavy stockade protected the pioneers from attack.* **2** *v.* to protect, fortify, or surround with a stockade. ❑ *v.* **stock·ad·ed, stock·ad·ing.**

stock·boy (stok′boi′), *n.* person who puts merchandise on the shelves in stores, supermarkets, etc.

stock·bro·ker (stok′brō′kər), *n.* person who buys and sells stocks and bonds for others for a commission.

stock car, 1 a standard passenger automobile, modified for racing. **2** a railroad freight car for livestock.

stock company, 1 company whose capital is divided into shares. **2** a theatrical company employed usually at one theater to perform many different plays.

stock exchange, 1 place where stocks and bonds are bought and sold. **2** association of brokers and dealers in stocks and bonds.

stock·hold·er (stok′hōl′dər), *n.* owner of stocks or shares in a company.

Stock·holm (stok′hōm *or* stok′hōlm), *n.* port and capital of Sweden, in the SE part. [Stockholm comes from Swedish words meaning "stockade" and "island." The city began as an island settlement defended by a fort of wooden posts.]

Stockholm

stock·ing (stok′ing), *n.* a close-fitting, knitted covering of wool, cotton, silk, nylon, etc., for the foot and leg.

stocking cap, a close-fitting, knitted cap with a long, pointed end that falls over the back or shoulder, worn for skiing, sledding, etc.

a	hat	ė	term	ô	order	ch	child		
ā	age	i	it	oi	oil	ng	long		a in about
ä	far	ī	ice	ou	out	sh	she		e in taken
â	care	o	hot	u	cup	th	thin	ə	i in pencil
e	let	ō	open	u̇	put	ŦH	then		o in lemon
ē	equal	ò	saw	ü	rule	zh	measure		u in circus

stock·man (stok′mən), *n.* person who raises livestock. □ *n., pl.* **stock·men.**

stock market, 1 place where stocks and bonds are bought and sold; stock exchange. **2** activity of buying and selling in such a place. **3** prices of stocks and bonds.

stock·pile (stok′pīl′), **1** *n.* a supply of raw materials, essential items, etc., built up and held in reserve for use during a time of emergency or shortage. **2** *n.* such a reserve of weapons for warfare. **3** *v.* to collect or bring together a stockpile. □ *v.* **stock·piled, stock·pil·ing. —stock′pil′er, n.**

stock·room (stok′rüm′), *n.* room where a stock is kept.

stock-still (stok′stil′), *adj.* motionless.

stock·y (stok′ē), *adj.* having a solid or sturdy form or build; thick for its height: *a stocky little child, a stocky building.* □ *adj.* **stock·i·er, stock·i·est. —stock′i·ly, adv. —stock′i·ness, n.**

stock·yard (stok′yärd′), *n.* place with pens and sheds to keep cattle, sheep, hogs, and horses in before shipping or slaughtering them.

stodg·y (stoj′ē), *adj.* **1** dull or uninteresting; boring: *a stodgy book.* **2** old-fashioned: *a stodgy attitude.* □ *adj.* **stodg·i·er, stodg·i·est. —stodg′i·ly, adv. —stodg′i·ness, n.**

sto·gie or **sto·gy** (stō′gē), *n.* a long, slender, cheap cigar. □ *n., pl.* **sto·gies.**

WORD STORY **Stogie** is short for **Conestoga wagon.** Men who drove early Conestoga wagons westward over the Allegheny Mountains were said to be fond of smoking such cigars.

sto·ic (stō′ik), **1** *n.* person who remains calm and self-controlled, and appears to be indifferent to pleasure and pain. **2** *adj.* stoical.

sto·i·cal (stō′ə kəl), *adj.* like a stoic; self-controlled; indifferent to pleasure and pain. **—sto′i·cal·ly, adv. —sto′i·cal·ness, n.**

sto·i·cism (stō′ə siz′əm), *n.* patient endurance; indifference to pleasure and pain.

stoke (stōk), *v.* **1** to stir up and feed fuel to a fire; tend the fire of a furnace. **2** to tend a fire. □ *v.* **stoked, stok·ing.**

stok·er (stō′kər), *n.* **1** worker who tends the fires of a furnace or boiler. **2** a mechanical device for putting coal in a furnace.

stole¹ (stōl), *v.* past tense of **steal:** *They stole my car.*

stole² (stōl), *n.* **1** a woman's collar or scarf of fur or cloth with ends hanging down in front. **2** a narrow strip of silk or other material worn over the shoulders by a member of the clergy during certain church functions.

sto·len (stō′lən), *v.* past participle of **steal:** *The money was not stolen; it was lost.*

stol·id (stol′id), *adj.* not easily excited; showing no emotion. **—stol′id·ly, adv. —sto·lid·i·ty** (stə lid′ə tē), **stol′id·ness, n.**

sto·lon (stō′lon), *n.* a slender plant stem along or beneath the ground, that takes root at the tip and grows into a new plant.

sto·ma (stō′mə), *n.* a small opening or pore in a plant or animal. A leaf contains many stomata, which let water and gases in and out of the plant. □ *n., pl.* **sto·ma·ta** or **sto·mas.**

stom·ach (stum′ək), **1** *n.* the large muscular bag in the body that receives swallowed food, and that partly digests it before passing it on to the intestines. **2** *n.* the part of the body containing this organ; abdomen; belly: *I was hit in the stomach.* **3** *n.* appetite. **4** *n.* desire; liking: *I have no stomach for prizefights.* **5** *v.* to put up with; bear; endure: *She could not stomach such insults.* □ *n., pl.* **stom·achs.**

stom·ach·ache (stum′ək āk′), *n.* pain in the stomach.

sto·ma·ta (stō′mə tə or stom′ə tə), *n.* a plural of **stoma.**

stomp (stomp), **1** *v.* to stamp or trample on with the foot. **2** *v.* INFORMAL. to defeat decisively: *Our team really stomped Central High in last week's soccer game.* **3** *n.* act of stomping. **—stomp′er, n. —stomp′ing·ly, adv.**

stone (stōn), **1** *n.* the hard, mineral material of which rocks are made. Stone such as granite and marble is used in building. **2** *n.* a small piece of rock: *They threw stones into the pond.* **3** *n.* piece of rock of definite size or shape, used for a particular purpose: *The grave is marked by a fine stone.* **4** *adj.* of or about stone: *stone carving.* **5** *n.* gem; jewel: *The diamonds were very fine stones.* **6** *n.* a hard, solid object that sometimes forms in the kidneys or gall bladder, causing sickness and pain. **7** *v.* to throw

stones at: *The martyr was stoned as a heretic.* **8** *n.* a hard seed: *peach stones.* **9** *v.* to take such seeds out of: *to stone cherries or plums.* **10** *n.* a British unit of weight equal to 14 pounds. □ *n., pl.* **stones** for 2,3,6,7,8; **stone** for 10; *v.* **stoned, ston·ing. —ston′er, n. —stone′like′, adj.**

Stone (stōn), *n.* **Lu·cy** (lü′sē), 1818-1893, American leader in the women's rights and antislavery movements.

Stone Age, the earliest known period of human culture, in which people used tools and weapons made from stone. It was followed by the Bronze Age.

stone-blind (stōn′blīnd′), *adj.* totally blind. ▪ See Usage Note at **blind.**

stone-broke (stōn′brōk′), *adj.* INFORMAL. totally without money.

stone-cut·ter (stōn′kut′ər), *n.* **1** person who cuts or carves stones. **2** machine for cutting or dressing stone.

stoned (stōnd), *adj.* **1** SLANG. drunk from alcohol. **2** under the influence of a drug.

stone-deaf (stōn′def′), *adj.* totally deaf. ▪ See Usage Note at **deaf.**

Stone·henge (stōn′henj), *n.* a prehistoric ruin in southern England, consisting of huge slabs of roughly shaped stone in a circular arrangement. It may have been a kind of observatory used by astronomers.

WORD STORY **Stonehenge** comes from old English words meaning "stone" and "to hang." It was probably named for the huge stones that rest on top of other stones, high in the air.

stone·ma·son (stōn′mā′sn), *n.* person who cuts stone or builds walls, etc., of stone.

stone's throw, a short distance: *We live only a stone's throw from the school.*

stone·wall (stōn′wôl′), *v.* to refuse to give information to a person or investigating agency; refuse to cooperate with.

stone·ware (stōn′wâr′), *n.* a coarse, hard, glazed pottery.

stone·work (stōn′wèrk′), *n.* **1** wall, foundation, or other structure made of stone. **2** the part of a building made of stone.

ston·y (stō′nē), *adj.* **1** having many stones: *The beach is stony.* **2** without expression or feeling: *After our argument, whenever we met she would always give me a stony stare.* □ *adj.* **ston·i·er, ston·i·est. —ston′i·ly, adv. —ston′i·ness, n.**

stood (stüd), *v.* past tense and past participle of **stand:** *She stood in the corner for five minutes. I had stood in line all morning to buy tickets to the game.*

stooge (stüj), *n.* INFORMAL. **1** a fool. **2** person on the stage who asks questions of a comedian and is the butt of the comedian's jokes. **3** person who follows and flatters another; hanger-on.

stool (stül), *n.* **1** seat without back or arms. **2** a low bench used to rest the feet on, or to kneel on. **—stool′like′, adj.**

stool pigeon, SLANG. a spy for the police; informer.

stoop¹ (stüp), **1** *v.* to bend forward: *He stooped to pick up the money. She stooped over her work.* **2** *v.* to carry head and shoulders bent forward: *The old man stoops.* **3** *n.* a forward bend of the head and shoulders: *My uncle walks with a stoop.* **4** *v.* to lower yourself; descend: *He stooped to cheating.* **—stoop′er, n.**

stoop² (stüp), *n.* a porch or platform at the entrance of a house.

stop (stop), **1** *v.* to not be happening any longer; come to an end; cease: *The baby stopped crying. The rain is stopping.* **2** *v.* to stay for a short time: *She stopped at the bank for a few minutes.* **3** *v.* to keep from moving, acting, doing, being, working, etc.: *I stopped the children from teasing the cat. I stopped the car.* **4** *v.* to close a hole or opening by filling it: *I will stop up the rats' holes.* **5** *v.* to close a container with a cork, plug, or other stopper: *stop up a bottle.* **6** *v.* to close up or block; plug: *Scraps of food stopped up the sink.* **7** *n.* act of coming to a stop: *Her sudden stop startled us. The singing came to a stop.* **8** *n.* place where a stop is made: *a bus stop.* **9** *n.* thing that blocks, hinders, or checks: *a door stop.* **10** *n.* a device that controls the pitch of a musical instrument. **11** *n.* (in musical organs) a graduated set of pipes of the same kind, or the knob or handle that controls them. **12** *n.* aperture of a camera lens. □ *v.* **stopped, stop·ping. —stop′less, adj. —stop′pa·ble, adj.**

pull out all the stops, to make every possible effort while doing something: *The town pulled out all the stops for its 100th anniversary celebration.*

put a stop to, to stop; end.

stop by or **stop in,** to visit briefly.

stop off, to stop for a short stay.

stop over, 1 to make a short stay. **2** to stop in the course of a trip.

WORD STORY **Stop** comes from a Greek word meaning "fiber." In old times, sailors pulled apart ropes and used the fibers as stuffing to fill leaks in their boats. The fibers stopped water from coming in.

stop-and-go (stop/ən gō/), *adj.* with frequent stops, caused by heavy traffic or traffic signals.

stop·cock (stop/kok/), *n.* device, such as a valve, for turning the flow of a liquid or gas on or off.

stop·gap (stop/gap/), *n.* something that fills the place of something lacking; a temporary substitute.

stop·light (stop/līt/), *n.* **1** traffic light. **2** a red light, on the rear end of a vehicle, that turns on automatically when the brakes are applied.

stop order, order given to a stockbroker to buy or sell a stock whenever a stated price is reached.

stop·o·ver (stop/ō/vər), *n.* a layover during a trip, especially with the privilege of proceeding later using the ticket originally issued for the trip.

stop·page (stop/ij), *n.* **1** act of stopping: *The foreman called for a stoppage of operations to oil the machinery.* **2** condition of being stopped: *During the work stoppage many workers looked for other jobs.* **3** a block; obstruction.

Stop·pard (stop/ərd), *n.* **Tom** (tom), born 1937, English playwright, born in what is now the Czech Republic. His plays are noted for their philosophical themes and witty dialogue.

stop·per (stop/ər), *n.* plug or cork for closing a bottle, tube, etc.

stop·watch (stop/wäch/), *n.* watch that can be stopped or started at any instant. A stopwatch indicates fractions of a second and is used for timing races and contests. ❏ *n., pl.* **stop·watch·es.**

stor·age (stôr/ij), *n.* **1** act or fact of storing goods: *the storage of storm windows in summertime.* **2** condition of being stored. Cold storage is used to keep eggs and meat from spoiling. **3** place for storing: *She has put her furniture in storage.* **4** price for storing: *She paid $30 storage on her furniture.* **5** the part of a computer in which information and instructions are stored; memory.

storage battery, any kind of battery that can be recharged with electricity, after its energy is used up, by running an electric current through it. The battery of a car is a storage battery.

store (stôr), **1** *n.* place where goods are kept for sale: *a clothing store.* **2** *n.* something put away for use later; supply; stock: *We have a large store of frozen food in the freezer.* **3** *v.* to supply or stock. **4** *v.* to put away for use later: *The squirrel stores away nuts.* **5** *n.* place where supplies are kept for future use; storehouse. **6** *v.* to put in a warehouse or place used for preserving. ❏ *v.* **stored, stor·ing.** —**stor/a·ble,** *adj.* —**stor/er,** *n.*

in store, be expected; waiting to happen: *Lots of new experiences were in store for us.*

mind the store, to take care of what you are responsible for.

set store by, to value; esteem: *She sets great store by her friend's opinions.*

store-bought (stôr/bòt/), *adj.* purchased in a store rather than homemade: *We had a store-bought cake at his birthday party.*

store·front (stôr/frunt/), *n.* the front part of a store.

store·house (stôr/hous/), *n.* **1** place where things are stored; warehouse: *After the harvest the storehouses were full.* **2** person or thing resembling such a place: *She was a storehouse of ideas.* ❏ *n., pl.* **store·hous·es** (stôr/hou/ziz).

store·keep·er (stôr/kē/pər), *n.* person who owns or manages a store or stores.

store·room (stôr/rüm/), *n.* room where things are stored.

sto·ried (stôr/ēd), *adj.* celebrated in story or history: *the storied Wild West.*

-storied, *suffix.* having ___ stories or floors: *a two-storied house = a house having two stories.*

stork (stôrk), *n.* any of several large, long-legged wading birds with long necks and long bills. —**stork/like/,** *adj.*

---

storm (stôrm), **1** *n.* a strong wind, usually with heavy rain, snow, or hail, and sometimes thunder and lightning. A storm blows at 64 to 72 miles (103 to 116 kilometers) per hour. **2** *n.* a heavy fall of rain, snow, or hail. **3** *v.* to blow hard; rain; snow; hail: *It stormed all night.* **4** *n.* anything like a windstorm: *a storm of arrows.* **5** *n.* a violent outburst or disturbance: *a storm of tears, a storm of angry words.* **6** *v.* to be violent; rage. **7** *v.* to rush violently: *He stormed out of the room.* **8** *v.* to attack violently: *The troops stormed the city.* **9** *n.* a violent attack: *The castle was taken by storm.*

storm (def. 1)

WORD BANK There are many different words for **storms.** If you want to learn more about them, you can start by looking these words up in this dictionary.

blizzard	electrical storm	simoom	torrent
cloudburst	hailstorm	snowstorm	sirocco
cyclone	monsoon	squall	twister
deluge	northeaster	tempest	typhoon
downpour	rainstorm	thunderstorm	waterspout
dust storm	sandstorm	tornado	whirlwind

storm cellar, cellar for shelter during cyclones, tornadoes, etc.

storm center, 1 center of a cyclone, where there is very low air pressure and comparative calm. **2** any center of trouble, uproar, etc.

storm door, an extra door outside of an ordinary door, to keep out snow, rain, cold air, etc.

storm petrel, any of several small black and white seabirds with long, pointed wings, whose presence is supposed to give warning of a storm. Also, **stormy petrel.**

storm window, an extra window outside of an ordinary window, to keep out snow, rain, cold air, etc.

storm·y (stôr/mē), *adj.* **1** having storms; likely to have storms; affected by storms: *stormy weather, a stormy sea, a stormy night.* **2** marked by violence or harsh criticism: *They had stormy quarrels.* ❏ *adj.* **storm·i·er, storm·i·est.** —**storm/i·ly,** *adv.* —**storm/i·ness,** *n.*

stormy petrel, storm petrel.

sto·ry[1] (stôr/ē), *n.* **1** an account of some happening or group of happenings: *Tell us the story of your life.* **2** such an account, either true or made up, intended to interest the reader or hearer; tale: *fairy stories, stories of adventure.* **3** a newspaper article. **4** falsehood: *That's not true; you're telling stories.* ❏ *n., pl.* **sto·ries.**

SYNONYM STUDY **Story**[1], **anecdote,** and **tale** all mean a set of events told in words. **Story** is a general word: *He wrote a story about boys lost in a cave.* **Anecdote** means a brief story, usually spoken, often of a personal or funny event: *She told us an anecdote about her time in the army.* **Tale** usually means an imaginary story: *Fairy tales have been told for thousands of years.*

sto·ry[2] (stôr/ē), *n.* all the rooms or space on one level of a building; floor: *That building has nine stories.* ❏ *n., pl.* **sto·ries.**

sto·ry·book (stôr/ē buk/), **1** *n.* book containing one or more stories or tales, especially for children. **2** *adj.* of or similar to that of a storybook; romantic; fictional: *a storybook hero, a storybook ending.*

sto·ry·tell·er (stôr/ē tel/ər), *n.* person who tells stories.

sto·ry·tell·ing (stôr/ē tel/ing), *n.* act or art of telling stories.

stout (stout), **1** *adj.* fat and large: *That boy could run much faster if he weren't so stout.* ■ See Synonym Study at **fat.** **2** *adj.* strongly built; firm; strong: *The fort has stout walls.* **3** *adj.* brave; bold: *Robin Hood was a stout fellow.* **4** *adj.* not yielding; stubborn: *stout resistance.* **5** *n.* a strong, dark brown ale. —**stout/ly,** *adv.* —**stout/ness,** *n.*

S

a	hat	ė	term	ô	order	ch	child
ā	age	i	it	oi	oil	ng	long
ä	far	ī	ice	ou	out	sh	she
â	care	o	hot	u	cup	th	thin
e	let	ō	open	ů	put	ŦH	then
ē	equal	ò	saw	ü	rule	zh	measure

ə { a in about / e in taken / i in pencil / o in lemon / u in circus }

stout·heart·ed (stout/här/tid), *adj.* having courage; brave; bold: *The stouthearted boy plunged into the icy river to save his friend.* **—stout/heart/ed·ly,** *adv.* **—stout/heart/ed·ness,** *n.*

stove[1] (stōv), *n.* appliance for cooking or heating. There are gas, electric, oil, wood, and coal stoves.

stove[2] (stōv), *v.* a past tense and a past participle of **stave.**

stove·pipe (stōv/pīp/), *n.* **1** a metal pipe that carries smoke and gases from a stove to a chimney. **2** a tall silk hat.

stow (stō), *v.* **1** to pack: *stow books in a trunk. The cargo was stowed in the ship's hold.* **2** to pack things closely in; fill by packing: *stow a pantry with cans of food.* **—stow/a·ble,** *adj.* **—stow/er,** *n.*

stow away, to hide on a ship, airplane, etc., to get a free ride or to escape secretly.

stow·a·way (stō/ə wā/), *n.* person who hides on a ship, airplane, etc., to get a free ride or to make an escape.

Stowe (stō), *n.* **Har·ri·et Beech·er** (har/ē ət bē/chər), 1811-1896, American writer, author of *Uncle Tom's Cabin.*

St. Paul, capital of Minnesota, in the SE part, on the Mississippi River.

St. Pe·ters·burg (sānt pē/tərz bėrg/), **1** seaport and former capital of Russia, on the Gulf of Finland. Formerly called **Petrograd** and **Leningrad. 2** city in W Florida, on Tampa Bay.

St. Pierre and Mi·que·lon (san pyer/ənd me/kə lōn/), two small groups of French islands in the N Atlantic off Newfoundland.

strad·dle (strad/l), *v.* **1** to have a leg on each side of a horse, bicycle, chair, ditch, etc. **2** to stand or lie across; be on both sides of: *the town straddles the state line.* **3** to walk, stand, or sit with the legs wide apart. **4** to spread the legs wide apart. **5** to avoid taking sides; attempt to favor both sides of a question: *All three political candidates straddled the issue of higher taxes.* ❑ *v.* **strad·dled, strad·dling. —strad/dler,** *n.*

Strad·i·var·i·us (strad/ə vâr/ē əs), *n.* violin, viola, or cello made by Antonio Stradivari, a famous Italian violin maker who lived from about 1644 to 1737.

strafe (strāf), *v.* (of aircraft) to fly low over enemy troops or positions and attack with machine-gun fire. ❑ *v.* **strafed, straf·ing. —straf/er,** *n.*

WORD STORY **Strafe** comes from a German word meaning "to punish." During World War I, Germany used a slogan, "God Punish England." Warplanes were first used in World War I, and British troops receiving fire from the air commented that they were being punished. They used a form of the German word, and it became an English word.

strag·gle (strag/əl), *v.* **1** to wander from or lag behind your group, a leader, etc.: *Several hikers straggled into camp a half hour after the others. Cows straggled along the lane.* **2** to stray from the rest. **3** to spread out in an irregular way: *Vines straggled over the yard.* ❑ *v.* **strag·gled, strag·gling. —strag/gler,** *n.*

strag·gly (strag/lē), *adj.* spread out in an irregular, rambling way; straggling. ❑ *adj.* **strag·gli·er, strag·gli·est.**

straight (strāt), **1** *adj.* without a bend or curve; not crooked or irregular: *a straight line, a straight path, straight hair.* **2** *adv.* in a line; directly: *He went straight home.* **3** *adj.* going in a line; direct: *a straight course, a straight throw.* **4** *adj.* frank; honest; upright: *a straight answer.* **5** *adj.* right; correct: *straight thinking, a straight thinker.* **6** *adj.* in proper order or condition: *Keep your accounts straight.* **7** *adj.* having nothing added; pure; undiluted: *straight whiskey.* **8** *adj.* showing no emotion, humor, etc.: *I kept a straight face, though I wanted to laugh.* **9** *adj.* supporting the candidates of one party only: *to vote a straight Republican ticket.* ■ Another word that sounds like this is **strait. —straight/ly,** *adv.* **—straight/ness,** *n.*

straight away or **straight off,** at once.

straight angle, angle of 180 degrees.

straight·a·way (strāt/ə wā/ *for noun, adj.;* strāt/ə wā/ *for adv.*), **1** *n.* a straight course. **2** *adj.* in a straight course. **3** *adv.* straightway.

straight·edge (strāt/ej/), *n.* strip of wood, metal, or plastic having one edge accurately straight, used to make or test straight lines and level surfaces.

straight·en (strāt/n), *v.* **1** to make straight: *He straightened the bent pin.* **2** to become straight: *She straightened up and walked out of the room.* **3** to put in the proper order or condition: *Straighten up your room. We must straighten out our bank account.* **—straight/en·er,** *n.*

straight·for·ward (strāt/fôr/wərd), **1** *adj.* honest; frank: *a straightforward answer.* **2** *adj.* going straight ahead; direct. **3** *adv.* directly. **—straight/for/ward·ly,** *adv.* **—straight/for/ward·ness,** *n.*

straight man, one of a pair of comedians who makes statements or asks questions to which the other makes funny responses.

straight·way (strāt/wā/), *adv.* at once; immediately: *I will leave straightway.*

strain[1] (strān), **1** *n.* any severe, trying, or wearing pressure: *the strain of worry. The strain of overwork can make you ill.* **2** *n.* effect of such pressure on the body or mind. **3** *v.* to injure by too much effort or by stretching: *I strained a muscle.* **4** *n.* injury caused by too much effort or by stretching: *The injury to his back was only a slight strain.* **5** *v.* to draw tight; stretch: *The weight strained the rope.* **6** *v.* to pull hard: *The dog strained at its leash.* **7** *n.* force or weight that stretches: *The strain on the rope made it break.* **8** *v.* to stretch as much as possible: *She strained the truth in telling the story.* **9** *v.* to use to the utmost: *I strained every muscle to lift the rock. She strained her eyes to see.* **10** *v.* to make a very great effort. **11** *v.* to press or pour through a strainer: *Straining orange juice removes the pulp.* **12** *n.* manner or style of action, speaking, or writing: *a cynical strain.*

strain[2] (strān), *n.* **1** line of descent; ancestors: *He is proud of his Spanish strain.* **2** group that forms part of a subspecies or variety. **3** an inherited quality: *There is a strain of musical talent in that family.* **4** trace or streak: *That horse has a mean strain.* **5** *n.* part of a piece of music; melody; song.

strained (strānd), *adj.* forced; not natural: *a strained greeting.* **—strained/ly,** *adv.*

strain·er (strā/nər), *n.* utensil having holes that let liquids and smaller pieces pass through, but not the larger pieces.

strait (strāt), **1** *n.* a narrow channel connecting two larger bodies of water: *The Strait of Gibraltar connects the Mediterranean Sea and the Atlantic Ocean.* **2** *adj.* OLD USE. narrow; limited; confining. **3** *n.pl.* **straits,** difficulty; need; distress: *be in desperate straits for money.* ■ Another word that sounds like this is **straight.**

strait·ened (strāt/nd), *adj.* limited by lack of money: *in straitened circumstances.*

strait·jack·et (strāt/jak/it), *n.* a strong, tight jacket or coat that binds the arms close to the sides. It keeps a violent person from doing harm.

strait-laced (strāt/lāst/), *adj.* very strict in matters of conduct; prudish. **—strait/-lac/ed·ly,** *adv.* **—strait/-lac/ed·ness,** *n.*

strand[1] (strand), **1** *v.* to leave in a helpless position: *She was stranded a thousand miles from home with no money.* **2** *v.* to run aground; drive on the shore: *The ship was stranded on the rocks.* **3** *n.* shore; land bordering a sea, lake, or river.

strand[2] (strand), *n.* **1** one of the threads, strings, or wires that are twisted together to make a rope or cable. **2** thread or string: *a strand of pearls, a strand of hair.*

strange (strānj), *adj.* **1** unusual; odd; peculiar: *a strange accident, a strange experience. There was a strange quiet throughout the city.* **2** not known, seen, or heard of before; not familiar: *She is moving to a strange place. A strange cat is on our steps.* **3** not used to: *He is strange to the work but will soon learn.* **4** out of place; not at home: *The poor child felt strange in the palace.* ❑ *adj.* **strang·er, strang·est. —strange/ly,** *adv.* **—strange/ness,** *n.*

stran·ger (strān/jər), *n.* **1** person not known, seen, or heard of before: *She is a stranger to us.* **2** person or thing new to a place: *I am a stranger in New York.* **3** person who is out of place or not at home in something: *He is no stranger to hard work.* **4** person from another country: *The king received the strangers with kindness.*

stran·gle (strang/gəl), *v.* **1** to kill by squeezing the throat to prevent breathing. **2** to choke: *She almost strangled on a piece of meat that caught in her throat.* **3** to choke down; suppress; hold back: *I strangled an impulse to cough.* ❑ *v.* **stran·gled, stran·gling. —stran/gler,** *n.*

stran·gu·la·tion (strang′gyə lā′shən), *n.* act of strangling or condition of being strangled.

strap (strap), **1** *n.* a narrow strip of leather, cloth, or other material used for fastening things or holding them together: *The strap on my sandal broke. She placed a strap around the box.* **2** *v.* to fasten with a strap: *He strapped on a helmet.* **3** *v.* to beat with a strap. **4** *n.* a strop. ❑ *v.* **strapped, strap·ping.** —**strap′pa·ble,** *adj.* —**strap′per,** *n.*

strap·less (strap′lis), *adj.* having no strap or straps: *a strapless gown.*

strapped (strapt), *adj.* INFORMAL. having very little or no money.

strap·ping (strap′ing), *adj.* tall, strong, and healthy: *a fine, strapping youngster.*

Stras·bourg (stras′bėrg′), *n.* city in NE France, on the Rhine River.

stra·ta (strā′tə), *n.* a plural of **stratum.**

strat·a·gem (strat′ə jəm), *n.* scheme or plan for deceiving the enemy; trick; trickery: *The spy got into the country by the stratagem of pretending to be a student.*

stra·te·gic (strə tē′jik), *adj.* **1** of or based on strategy; useful in strategy: *a strategic retreat.* **2** important in strategy: *The Air Force is a strategic link in our national defense.* —**stra·te′gi·cal·ly,** *adv.*

Strategic Defense Initiative, program of the U.S. government to develop a missile-defense system, based mainly in space, made up of sophisticated rockets, lasers, and other weapons, capable of destroying incoming offensive rockets before they reach their targets.

strat·e·gist (strat′ə jist), *n.* person trained or skilled in strategy: *a military strategist, a chess strategist, a football strategist.*

strat·e·gy (strat′ə jē), *n.* **1** science or art of war; planning and directing of large-scale military movements and operations. **2** the skillful planning and management of anything. **3** plan based on strategy: *We need some strategy to win this game.* ❑ *n., pl.* **strat·e·gies** for 3.

Strat·ford-on-A·von (strat′fərd on ā′vən), *n.* town in central England on the Avon River. It is Shakespeare's birthplace and burial place.

strat·i·fy (strat′ə fī), *v.* to arrange in layers or strata; form into layers or strata. ❑ *v.* **strat·i·fied, strat·i·fy·ing.** —**strat′i·fi·ca′tion,** *n.*

stra·to·cu·mu·lus (strā′tō kyü′myə ləs), *n.* cloud formation of large, round dark clouds above a flat base, usually seen in winter and occurring at heights under 6000 feet (1800 meters). ❑ *n., pl.* **stra·to·cu·mu·li** (strā′tō kyü′myə lī).

strat·o·sphere (strat′ə sfir *or* strā′tə sfir), *n.* region of the atmosphere between the troposphere and the mesosphere, extending from about 10 to 35 miles (16 to 56 kilometers) above the earth's surface. In the stratosphere, temperature varies little with changes in altitude, and the winds are mostly horizontal. —**strat′o·spher′ic,** *adj.*

stra·tum (strā′təm *or* strat′əm), *n.* **1** layer of material, especially one of several parallel layers placed one upon another: *Several strata of rock are visible on the side of the hill where erosion has exposed them.* **2** social level: *rise from a low stratum to a high stratum of society.* ❑ *n., pl.* **stra·ta** *or* **stra·tums.**

stra·tus (strā′təs *or* strat′əs), *n.* a low, horizontal layer of gray cloud that spreads over a large area. ❑ *n., pl.* **stra·ti** (strā′tī).

Strauss (strous), *n.* **1 Jo·hann** (yō′hän), 1804-1849, Austrian composer of dance music. **2** his son, **Jo·hann** (yō′hän), 1825-1899, Austrian composer of dance music and light operas. He wrote the waltz "On the Beautiful Blue Danube." **3 Levi,** 1829-1902, American clothing manufacturer, born in Germany. He was the first maker of denim jeans. **4 Richard,** 1864-1949, German composer and conductor.

Stra·vin·sky (strə vin′skē), *n.* **I·gor** (ē′gôr), 1882-1971, American composer, born in Russia. ■ During the first performance of **Igor Stravinsky's** unconventional ballet, *The Rite of Spring,* the audience rioted.

straw (strô), **1** *n.* the stems of grain after drying and threshing. **2** *n.* one such stem. **3** *n.* tube made of waxed paper, plastic, or glass, used for sucking up drinks. **4** *n.* bit; trifle: *He doesn't care a straw.* —**straw′like′,** *adj.*

straw·ber·ry (strô′ber′ē), *n.* the small, bumpy, juicy, red fruit of any of several plants that grow close to the ground. Strawberries are good to eat. ❑ *n., pl.* **straw·ber·ries.**

straw man, a weak or imaginary opponent or opposing argument, set up in order to be easily defeated or refuted.

straw vote, an unofficial vote taken to find out general opinion.

stray (strā), **1** *v.* to lose your way; wander; roam: *Our dog has strayed off somewhere.* **2** *adj.* wandering; lost: *A stray cat is crying at the door.* **3** *n.* wanderer; lost animal: *The cat is a stray that we took in.* **4** *v.* to lose your concentration on something: *He strayed from his topic.* **5** *adj.* scattered; here and there: *The beach was empty except for a few stray swimmers.* —**stray′er,** *n.*

streak (strēk), **1** *n.* a long, thin mark or line: *a streak of dirt on your face.* **2** *n.* a long flash: *We saw a streak of lightning.* **3** *n.* layer: *Bacon has streaks of fat and streaks of lean.* **4** *n.* a part of someone's character: *He has a streak of humor, though he looks very serious.* **5** *n.* a line of powder produced when a mineral specimen is rubbed on a hard surface or scratched. The color of a streak is an important way of identifying a mineral. **6** *v.* to put long, thin marks or lines on: *The children streaked their faces with water colors.* **7** *n.* a brief period; spell: *a streak of luck, a winning streak.* **8** *v.* to move very fast; go at full speed: *She streaked past the others and over the finish line.* —**streak′er,** *n.*

like a streak, very fast; at full speed: *When her dog saw her, it ran like a streak to greet her.*

streak·y (strē′kē), *adj.* **1** marked with streaks: *These jeans have faded so much that the color is streaky.* **2** occurring in streaks. **3** varying; uneven; unreliable: *streaky quality.* ❑ *adj.* **streak·i·er, streak·i·est.** —**streak′i·ly,** *adv.* —**streak′i·ness,** *n.*

stream (strēm), **1** *n.* a flow of water in a channel. Small rivers and large brooks are both called streams. *Because of the lack of rain many streams dried up.* **2** *n.* any steady flow: *a stream of words, a stream of cars.* **3** *v.* to flow: *Tears streamed from her eyes.* ■ See Synonym Study at **flow.** **4** *v.* to move steadily and swiftly: *People streamed out of the theater.* **5** *v.* to pour out: *The gash in his arm streamed blood.* **6** *adj.* be so wet as to drip in a stream: *a streaming umbrella.* **7** *v.* to float or wave: *Flags streamed in the wind.* —**stream′less,** *adj.* —**stream′like′,** *adj.*

stratum (def. 1)

stream·er (strē′mər), *n.* **1** any long, narrow, flowing thing: *Streamers of ribbon hung from the new boat.* **2** a long, narrow flag.

stream·let (strēm′lit), *n.* a small stream.

stream·line (strēm′līn′), **1** *v.* to give a streamlined shape to. **2** *v.* to bring up to date; make more efficient: *streamline rail service.* **3** *adj.* streamlined. ❑ *v.* **stream·lined, stream·lin·ing.**

a	hat	ė	term	ô	order	ch	child		⟨ a	in about
ā	age	i	it	oi	oil	ng	long		e	in taken
ä	far	ī	ice	ou	out	sh	she	ə	i	in pencil
â	care	o	hot	u	cup	th	thin		o	in lemon
e	let	ō	open	ù	put	₮н	then		⟨ u	in circus
ē	equal	ò	saw	ü	rule	zh	measure			

stream·lined (strēm′lind′), *adj.* **1** shaped so as to cause the least possible resistance to motion through air or water. The fastest cars, airplanes, and boats have streamlined bodies. **2** brought up to date; made more efficient: *streamlined methods of production.*

street (strēt), **1** *n.* road in a city or town, usually with buildings on both sides. **2** *n.* roadway for motor vehicles: *Be careful crossing the street.* **3** *adj.* of or about a street or streets: *a street map.* **4** *adj.* for the street or streets: *street clothes.* **5** *n.* people who live in the buildings on a street: *The whole street planted new trees.*

street·car (strēt′kär′), *n.* an electrically powered light-rail vehicle for public transportation; trolley car.

streetcar

street·light (strēt′līt′), *n.* an overhead light for a street.

street-smart (strēt′smärt′), *adj.* streetwise.

street smarts, practical knowledge that enables someone to deal with life on inner-city streets.

street·wise (strēt′wīz′), *adj.* having the knowledge necessary to deal with life on the streets of inner cities.

Strei·sand (strī′sənd), *n.* **Bar·bra** (bär′brə), born 1942, American singer, stage and movie actress and director. ■ **Barbra Streisand** won Academy awards for her performance in the movie *Funny Girl* in 1968 and for her song "Evergreen" in 1976.

strength (strengkth), *n.* **1** quality of being strong; power; force; vigor: *I do not have the strength to lift that heavy box.* ■ See Synonym Study at **power. 2** power to resist force or to endure: *the strength of a rope.* **3** military force measured in numbers of soldiers, warships, fighter planes, etc.: *an army at full strength.* **4** degree of strength; intensity: *Some flavorings lose their strength in cooking.* **5** something a person does very well: *Mathematics and music are two of her strengths.*

on the strength of, relying or depending on; with the support or help of: *They bought the dog on the strength of the children's promise to take care of it.*

strength·en (strengk′thən), *v.* to make or grow stronger: *Exercise strengthens muscles.* —**strength′en·er,** *n.*

stren·u·ous (stren′yü əs), *adj.* **1** requiring much energy: *Running is strenuous exercise.* **2** full of energy: *Beavers are strenuous workers.* **3** very active: *We had a strenuous day moving into our new house.* —**stren′u·ous·ly,** *adv.* —**stren′u·ous·ness,** *n.*

strep (strep), *n.* INFORMAL. streptococcus.

strep throat, a serious throat inflammation caused by a streptococcus, and marked by fever, aching muscles, headache, etc.

strep·to·coc·cus (strep′tə kok′əs), *n.* any of a group of spherical bacteria that multiply by dividing in only one direction, usually forming chains. Many serious infections and diseases, such as scarlet fever and rheumatic fever, are caused by streptococci. ❑ *n., pl.* **strep·to·coc·ci** (strep′tə kok′sī).

strep·to·my·cin (strep′tō mī′sn), *n.* a powerful antibiotic effective against tuberculosis, typhoid fever, and certain other bacterial infections.

stress (stres), **1** *n.* great pressure or force, especially a force that can cause damage to a structure: *The roof collapsed under the stress of the heavy snow.* **2** *n.* emphasis; importance: *Our teacher lays stress upon punctuation and spelling.* **3** *n.* tension, pressure, or strain that affects the mind and body: *A person's blood pressure may increase under stress.* **4** *v.* to cause mental or physical strain in: *Worry can stress a person.* **5** *v.* to treat as important; emphasize: *He stressed the value of teamwork.* **6** *n.* loudness in the pronunciation of syllables, words in a sentence, etc.; accent: *In "zero," the stress is on the first syllable.* **7** *v.* to pronounce with stress: *"Accept" is stressed on the second syllable.* **8** *v.* (in physics) to apply a distorting force to. ❑ *n., pl.* **stress·es.** —**stress′less,** *adj.*

> **WORD FAMILY** Stress and the words below are related. They all come from a Latin word meaning "to pull straight or tight."
>
> | | | | |
> |---|---|---|---|
> | constraint | district | strain[1] | strait-laced |
> | constriction | restrain | strait | strict |
> | distress | restrictive | straitjacket | stringent |

stress·ful (stres′fəl), *adj.* full of stress; producing stress: *stressful conditions.* —**stress′ful·ly,** *adv.*

stress mark, accent (def. 2).

stress test, a medical test in which someone exercises on a treadmill or stationary bicycle while the electrical activity of the heart, and the blood pressure, pulse, etc., are recorded.

stretch (strech), **1** *v.* to extend your body, arms, legs, wings, etc., to full length: *The bird stretched its wings. She stretched herself out on the grass to rest.* **2** *v.* to extend your body or limbs: *I stretched out on the couch.* **3** *v.* to continue over a distance; extend from one place to another; fill space; spread: *The forest stretches for miles. She stretched the hammock from a tree to a pole.* **4** *v.* to reach out; hold out: *I stretched out my hand for the money.* **5** *v.* to pull out to greater size: *Stretch the damp sweater so it won't shrink as it dries.* **6** *v.* to become longer or wider without breaking: *Rubber stretches.* **7** *v.* to pull tight; strain: *stretch a guitar string until it breaks.* **8** *v.* to extend beyond proper limits: *They stretched the law to suit their own purpose.* **9** *v.* to exaggerate: *stretch the truth.* **10** *n.* an unbroken length; extent: *A stretch of sand hills lay between the road and the ocean.* **11** *n.* a continuous length of time: *He worked for a stretch of five hours.* **12** *n.* act of stretching or condition of being stretched: *We began our calisthenics with a good stretch.* **13** *n.* extent to which something can be stretched: *The stretch of that bird's wings is two feet.* **14** *n.* homestretch. ❑ *n., pl.* **stretch·es.** —**stretch′a·ble,** *adj.*

stretch·er (strech′ər), *n.* **1** canvas stretched on a frame for carrying the sick, wounded, or dead. **2** person or thing that stretches.

stretcher (def. 1)

strew (strü), *v.* **1** to scatter or sprinkle: *She strewed seeds in her garden.* ■ See Synonym Study at **scatter. 2** to cover with something scattered or sprinkled: *The ground was strewn with leaves.* ❑ *v.* **strewed, strewed** or **strewn, strew·ing.**

strewn (strün), *v.* a past participle of **strew.**

stri·at·ed muscle (strī′ā′tid), type of muscle with fibers in cross bands; voluntary muscle. It is contracted by choice. Muscles that move the arms and legs are striated muscles.

strick·en (strik′ən), **1** *adj.* hit, wounded, or affected by a weapon, disease, trouble, sorrow, etc.: *a stricken deer. They fled from the stricken city. The stricken man was taken immediately to a hospital.* **2** *v.* a past participle of **strike.**

strict (strikt), *adj.* **1** very careful in following a rule or in making others follow it: *The teacher was strict but fair.* ■ See Synonym Study at **severe. 2** harsh; severe: *strict discipline.* **3** exact; precise; accurate: *She told the strict truth.* **4** perfect; complete; absolute: *strict secrecy.* —**strict′ly,** *adv.* —**strict′ness,** *n.*

stric·ture (strik′chər), *n.* **1** an unfavorable criticism; critical remark. **2** an unhealthy narrowing of some duct or tube of the body.

stride (strīd), **1** *v.* to walk with long steps: *She strides rapidly, as though always late.* **2** *v.* to pass with one long step: *They strode over the brook.* **3** *n.* a long step: *The child could not keep up with* his father's stride. **4** *n.* distance covered by a stride. ❑ *v.* **strode, strid·den** (strid′n), **strid·ing. —strid′er,** *n.* **—strid′ing·ly,** *adv.*

hit your stride, to reach your regular speed or normal activity.

make great strides or **make rapid strides,** to make great progress; advance quickly: *Under a new teacher the class is making great strides in math.*

take in stride, to deal with easily; do or take without difficulty, hesitation, or special effort.

stri·den·cy (strīd′n sē), *n.* quality of being strident.

stri·dent (strīd′nt), *adj.* making or having a harsh sound; grating; shrill: *a strident voice.* **—stri′dent·ly,** *adv.*

strife (strīf), *n.* **1** a quarreling; fighting: *bitter strife between rivals.* **2** a quarrel; fight: *to find out the cause of a strife.*

strike (strīk), **1** *v.* to hit: *Lightning struck the barn. The car struck a fence.* **2** *v.* to give forth or out; deal: *strike a blow in self-defense.* **3** *v.* to make by stamping, printing, etc.: *They will strike a medal in memory of the great victory.* **4** *v.* to set or be set on fire by hitting or rubbing: *strike a match.* **5** *v.* to impress in a certain way: *The plan strikes me as silly.* **6** *v.* to sound: *The clock strikes twelve times at noon. This clock strikes the hour and the half hour.* **7** *v.* to affect deeply; influence; overcome by death, disease, suffering, fear, etc.: *They were struck with terror. The town was struck with a flu epidemic.* **8** *v.* to attack: *The enemy will strike at dawn.* **9** *n.* an attack: *a strike by bombers on a target.* **10** *v.* to come into your mind; occur to: *An amusing thought struck her.* **11** *v.* to find or come upon suddenly: *After drilling several holes, they finally struck oil.* **12** *n.* act or fact of finding rich ore in mining, oil in boring, etc.; sudden success: *He made a rich strike in the Yukon.* **13** *v.* to stop work to get better pay, shorter hours, etc.: *The coal miners struck when the company refused to improve safety conditions in the mines.* **14** *n.* an act of stopping work: *The workers were home for six weeks during the strike last year.* **15** *v.* to assume: *strike an amusing pose.* **16** *v.* to make; decide; enter upon: *The employer and the workers have struck an agreement.* **17** *v.* to lower or take down a sail, flag, tent, etc.: *The ship struck its flag as a sign of surrender.* **18** *n.* act of striking. **19** *n.* baseball pitched through the strike zone and not swung at, any pitch that is swung at and missed, or any pitch that is hit foul under the rules of the game. **20** *n.* (in bowling) act of knocking down all the pins with the first ball bowled. ❑ *v.* **struck, struck** or **strick·en, strik·ing.**

on strike, stopping work to get more pay, shorter hours, etc.: *Most of the workers voted to go on strike.*

strike it rich, 1 to find rich ore, oil, etc. **2** to have a sudden or unexpected great success.

strike off, to take off or remove, especially from a list: *After she moved away, her name was struck off the class attendance roll.*

strike out, 1 to remove; cross out: *Strike out the incorrect answers.* **2** (in baseball) to put out or be put out by three strikes: *The pitcher struck out six batters. The batter struck out.* **3** to go; advance: *We walked along the road a mile, then struck out across the fields.*

strike up, to begin: *The two children struck up a friendship.*

strike·break·er (strīk′brā′kər), *n.* person who helps to break up a strike of workers by taking a striker's job or by furnishing people who will do so.

strike·break·ing (strīk′brā′king), *n.* forceful measures taken to halt a strike.

strike·out (strīk′out′), *n.* in baseball: **1** an out caused by three strikes. **2** act of striking out.

strik·er (strī′kər), *n.* **1** worker who is on strike: *The union won't accept any settlement that does not greatly improve the working conditions of the strikers.* **2** person or thing that strikes.

strike zone, (in baseball) zone or area above home plate, between the batter's knees and armpits, through which a pitch must be thrown to be called a strike.

strik·ing (strī′king), *adj.* **1** attracting attention; very noticeable: *a striking performance by an actor.* **2** on strike: *The striking miners hope to return to work.* **—strik′ing·ly,** *adv.* **—strik′ing·ness,** *n.*

string (string), **1** *n.* a thick thread; small cord; very thin rope: *The package is tied with red string.* **2** *n.* such a thread with things on it:

She wore a string of beads around her neck. **3** *v.* to put on a string: *The child is stringing beads.* **4** *n.* one of the wires that make sound on a stringed instrument: *the strings of a violin.* **5** *n.pl.* **strings,** a violins, cellos, and other stringed instruments, especially as a group. **b** secret or hidden condition: *an offer with strings attached to it.* **6** *v.* to provide with strings: *She had her tennis racket strung.* **7** *n.* anything used for tying: *apron strings.* **8** *v.* to tie with string or rope; hang up with a string or rope: *We dry herbs by stringing them from the rafters in the barn.* **9** *v.* to extend or stretch from one point to another: *Telephone lines are strung on poles or placed underground.* **10** *n.* a cordlike part of a plant. String beans have little strings connecting the two halves of a pod. **11** *v.* to remove strings from: *String the beans before cooking them.* **12** *v.* to form into a string or strings. **13** *n.* number of things in a line or row: *A string of cars came down the street.* ❑ *v.* **strung, string·ing. —string′less,** *adj.* **—string′like′,** *adj.*

on a string, under someone's control.

pull strings, 1 to control the actions of others secretly. **2** to use secret influence.

string along, 1 to fool; hoax. **2** to go along: agree. **3** to believe or trust completely.

string out, to stretch; extend: *He strung out his report with pictures.*

string up, INFORMAL. to kill by hanging.

string bean, the long, green or yellow seed pod of a garden plant, cooked and eaten as a vegetable.

stringed instrument, a musical instrument having strings, played either with a bow or by plucking. A harp, a violin, and a guitar are stringed instruments.

strin·gen·cy (strin′jən sē), *n.* strictness; severity.

strin·gent (strin′jənt), *adj.* strict; severe: *stringent laws against speeding.* **—strin′gent·ly,** *adv.*

string·er (string′ər), *n.* **1** a long, horizontal timber in a building, bridge, railroad bridge, etc. **2** person or thing that strings.

string·y (string′ē), *adj.* **1** like a string or strings: *a person with stringy hair.* **2** having tough fibers: *stringy meat.* **3** lean and sinewy: *He is a boy of about sixteen, tall and stringy.* ❑ *adj.* **string·i·er, string·i·est. —string′i·ness,** *n.*

strip¹ (strip), *v.* **1** to make bare or naked; undress. **2** to remove; pull off: *The birds stripped the fruit from the trees.* **3** to rob: *Thieves stripped the house of everything valuable.* **4** to take off the covering of: *to strip a log by removing the bark.* **5** to take away the titles, rights, etc., of someone or something. **6** to tear off the teeth of a gear, etc. **7** to break the thread of a bolt, nut, etc. ❑ *v.* **stripped, strip·ping. —strip′per,** *n.*

strip² (strip), *n.* **1** a long, narrow, flat piece of cloth, paper, bark, etc. **2** airstrip.

stripe (strīp), **1** *n.* line or long narrow part of different color, material, etc.: *A tiger has stripes. The American flag has thirteen stripes.* **2** *v.* to mark with stripes. **3** *n.* sort; type: *a man of quite a different stripe.* ❑ *v.* **striped, strip·ing. —stripe′less,** *adj.*

striped (strīpt), *adj.* having stripes; marked with stripes: *He wore a striped shirt.*

strip·ling (strip′ling), *n.* boy just coming into manhood; youth; lad.

strip mine, a mine worked from the surface by digging away layers of earth that cover the ore.

strip mining, process of removing ore from a strip mine.

strip search, 1 to require someone to remove clothing as part of a search for weapons, drugs, etc. Strip searching may also involve inspecting body cavities. **2** act of searching someone in this way.

striped—a striped fish

S

a	hat	ė	term	ô	order	ch	child		a in about
ā	age	i	it	oi	oil	ng	long		e in taken
ä	far	ī	ice	ou	out	sh	she	ə	i in pencil
â	care	o	hot	u	cup	th	thin		o in lemon
e	let	ō	open	ù	put	ŦH	then		u in circus
ē	equal	ò	saw	ü	rule	zh	measure		

strive (strīv), *v.* **1** to try hard; work hard: *strive for self-control. Strive to succeed.* **2** to struggle; fight: *The swimmer strove against the tide.* □ *v.* **strove** or **strived, striv·en** or **strived, striv·ing.** —**striv′er,** *n.*

striv·en (striv′ən), *v.* a past participle of **strive:** *She has striven hard to make the business a success.*

strode (strōd), *v.* past tense of **stride:** *He strode into the room.*

stroke[1] (strōk), **1** *n.* act of striking; blow: *drive in a nail with several strokes of a hammer.* ■ See Synonym Study at **blow**[1]. **2** *n.* a sudden event that has a powerful impact or effect: *The house was hit by a stroke of lightning.* **3** *n.* sound made by striking: *the stroke of a bell. We arrived at the stroke of three o'clock.* **4** *n.* a sudden attack of illness, especially one caused by a blood clot or bleeding in the brain; apoplexy. **5** *n.* piece of good or bad luck, fortune, etc.: *a stroke of bad luck.* **6** *n.* a single complete movement to be made again and again: *He rowed with a strong stroke of the oars. She swims a fast stroke.* **7** *n.* movement or mark made by a pen, pencil, brush, etc.: *I write with a heavy down stroke.* **8** *n.* a very successful effort; act: *a stroke of genius.* **9** *n.* a single effort; act: *I felt lazy and didn't do a stroke of work all day.* **10** *n.* rower who sets the time for the other oarsmen. **11** *v.* to be the stroke of: *Who stroked their crew?* □ *v.* **stroked, strok·ing.**

stroke[2] (strōk), **1** *v.* to move the hand gently over: *She stroked the kitten.* **2** *n.* a stroking movement: *to brush away the crumbs with one stroke.* □ *v.* **stroked, strok·ing.** —**strok′er,** *n.*

stroll (strōl), **1** *v.* to take a quiet walk for pleasure; walk: *We strolled through the park after dinner.* ■ See Synonym Study at **walk. 2** *n.* a leisurely walk. **3** *v.* to go from place to place: *strolling musicians.*

stroll·er (strō′lər), *n.* **1** a kind of light baby carriage in which a small child can ride sitting up; go-cart. **2** person who strolls: *There were many strollers in the park.*

strong (strông), **1** *adj.* having much force or power: *A strong person can lift heavy things. A strong wind blew down the trees. A strong nation has many able citizens and great resources.* **2** *adj.* having good bodily strength or health: *Several months after the operation she was well and strong again.* **3** *adj.* able to last, endure, or resist; not easy to break: *a strong rope.* **4** *adj.* having great mental force; not easily influenced or changed; firm: *a strong will.* **5** *adj.* having great force or effectiveness: *strong arguments.* **6** *adj.* having a certain number: *A group that is 100 strong has 100 members.* **7** *adj.* having a lot of a particular quality: *strong perfume. Strong tea has more flavor than weak tea.* **8** *adv.* with force; powerfully; vigorously; in a strong manner: *A gale blew strong from the northeast.* □ *adj.* **strong·er** (strông′-gər), **strong·est** (strông′gəst). —**strong′ly,** *adv.*

SYNONYM STUDY **Strong, sturdy,** and **robust** all mean having great power and strength. **Strong** is a general word: *A strong wind damaged the tree.* **Sturdy** means strong and solidly built: *The old oak table is extremely sturdy.* **Robust** means strong and healthy: *Her weightlifting program has made her robust and trim.*

strong·box (strông′boks′), *n.* a strongly made box to hold valuable things: *The diamonds were kept in a strongbox.* □ *n.,* pl. **strong·box·es.**

strong·hold (strông′hōld′), *n.* a strong place; safe place; fortress: *The robbers have a stronghold in the mountains.*

stron·ti·um (stron′shē əm *or* stron′tē əm), *n.* a metallic element that occurs only in combination with other elements. It is used in making alloys and in fireworks and signal flares. *Symbol:* Sr

strontium 90, a radioactive isotope of strontium that occurs in the fallout from a nuclear explosion. It is extremely dangerous because it is easily absorbed by the bones and tissues.

strop (strop), **1** *n.* a leather strap used for sharpening razors. **2** *v.* to sharpen on a strop. □ *v.* **stropped, strop·ping.**

stro·phe (strō′fē), *n.* group of lines of poetry; stanza.

strove (strōv), *v.* a past tense of **strive:** *They strove hard, but did not win the game.*

struck (struk), *v.* past tense and a past participle of **strike:** *The clock struck four. The barn was struck by lightning.*

struc·tur·al (struk′chər əl), *adj.* **1** used in building. Structural

steel is steel made into beams, girders, etc. **2** of, about, or affecting a structure or structures: *The geologist showed the structural difference in rocks of different ages.* —**struc′tur·al·ly,** *adv.*

struc·ture (struk′chər), **1** *n.* something built; a building or construction. Dams, bridges, tunnels, and skyscrapers are very large structures; apartment houses are smaller structures. **2** *n.* anything composed of parts arranged together: *The human body is a wonderful structure.* **3** *n.* manner of building; way parts are put together; construction: *The structure of the school was excellent.* **4** *n.* arrangement of parts, elements, etc.: *the structure of a molecule, the structure of a flower, sentence structure.* **5** *v.* to make into a structure; build; construct: *to structure a sentence.* □ *v.* **struc·tured, struc·tur·ing.** —**struc′ture·less,** *adj.*

stru·del (strü′dl), *n.* light, flaky pastry wrapped around fruit.

strug·gle (strug′əl), **1** *v.* to try hard; work hard against difficulties: *The poor have to struggle for a living. The swimmer struggled against the tide.* **2** *v.* to get, move, or make your way with great effort: *The old horse struggled to its feet.* **3** *n.* great effort; hard work: *It was a struggle for the couple to send all three children to college.* **4** *v.* to fight: *The brave dog struggled fiercely with the large wildcat.* **5** *n.* act of fighting; conflict: *The struggle between the two countries went on for years.* □ *v.* **strug·gled, strug·gling.** —**strug′gler,** *n.*

strum (strum), **1** *v.* to play by running the fingers lightly across the strings or keys: *strum a guitar.* **2** *n.* act or sound of strumming. □ *v.* **strummed, strum·ming.** —**strum′mer,** *n.*

strung (strung), *v.* past tense and past participle of **string:** *The children strung the beads according to size. The vines had been strung on poles.*

strut[1] (strut), **1** *v.* to walk in a vain, important manner: *The rooster struts about the barnyard.* **2** *n.* a strutting walk. □ *v.* **strut·ted, strut·ting.** —**strut′ter,** *n.*

strut[2] (strut), *n.* a supporting piece; brace.

strych·nine (strik′nin), *n.* a poisonous drug used as a pesticide, formerly used in medicine in tiny doses as a tonic or stimulant.

Stu·art (stü′ərt), *n.* **1** the royal family that ruled Scotland from 1371 to 1603, and England and Scotland for most of the time from 1603 to 1714. James I and II and Charles I and II belonged to the house of Stuart. **2 Mary.** See **Mary, Queen of Scots.**

stub (stub), **1** *n.* a short piece that is left: *the stub of a pencil.* **2** *n.* the short piece of a ticket or each check in a checkbook kept as a record. **3** *n.* pen having a short, blunt point. **4** *n.* stump of a tree, a broken tooth, etc. **5** *v.* to strike your toe against something: *I stubbed my toe on a sharp rock.* □ *v.* **stubbed, stub·bing.**

stub·ble (stub′əl), *n.* **1** the lower ends of stalks of grain left in the ground after the grain is cut: *The corn stubble hurt the child's bare feet.* **2** any short, rough growth: *Since he had not shaved for three days, there was stubble on his face.*

stub·bly (stub′lē), *adj.* **1** covered with stubble. **2** resembling stubble; bristly: *a stubbly mustache.* □ *adj.* **stub·bli·er, stub·bli·est.** —**stub′bli·ness,** *n.*

stub·born (stub′ərn), *adj.* **1** determined in purpose or opinion; not giving in to argument or requests: *The stubborn child refused to listen to reasons for not going out in the rain.* **2** hard to deal with or manage: *a stubborn cough.* —**stub′born·ly,** *adv.* —**stub′born·ness,** *n.*

WORD STORY **Stubborn** may come from **stub** (def. 4). Because tree stumps are held in place by long roots, getting them out of the ground is very hard work. People who refuse to change their minds are like stumps that can't be moved.

stub·by (stub′ē), *adj.* **1** short and thick: *stubby fingers.* **2** short, thick, and stiff: *a stubby beard.* **3** having many stubs or stumps. □ *adj.* **stub·bi·er, stub·bi·est.** —**stub′bi·ness,** *n.*

stuc·co (stuk′ō), **1** *n.* plaster used for covering walls. One kind is used for covering the outer walls of buildings; another kind is used for cornices, moldings, and other interior decoration. **2** *v.* to cover with stucco: *We had our house stuccoed last year.* □ *n.,* pl. **stuc·cos** or **stuc·coes;** *v.* **stuc·coed, stuc·co·ing.**

stuck (stuk), *v.* past tense and past participle of **stick**[2]: *She stuck her arm out of the car window. We were stuck in the mud.*

stuck-up (stuk′up′), *adj.* INFORMAL. having too high an opinion of yourself; conceited; haughty: *We didn't join that group at the Valentine's Day party because they seemed stuck-up.*

stud¹ (stud), **1** *n.* an upright piece of lumber to which boards or laths are nailed in making walls in houses. **2** *n.* head of a nail, knob, etc., sticking out from a surface, used especially for ornament. **3** *v.* to set with studs or something like studs: *The dagger handle was studded with jewels.* **4** *n.* a kind of small, removable button used in men's dress shirts. **5** *v.* to be set or scattered over: *Little islands stud the harbor. In late summer, shocks of corn studded the fields.* ❑ *v.* **stud·ded, stud·ding.**

stud² (stud), *n.* **1** a male horse or other male animal kept for breeding. **2** collection of horses kept for breeding.

stu·dent (stüd′nt), *n.* **1** person who is studying in a school, college, or university: *That high school has 3000 students.* **2** person who studies: *She is a student of birds.*

stud·ied (stud′ēd), *adj.* carefully planned; done on purpose; deliberate: *What she said to me was a studied insult.* —**stud′ied·ly**, *adv.* —**stud′ied·ness**, *n.*

stu·di·o (stü′dē ō), *n.* **1** workroom of a painter, sculptor, photographer, etc. **2** place where movies are made. **3** place from which a radio or TV show is broadcast. ❑ *n., pl.* **stu·di·os.**

studio couch, an upholstered couch, without a back or arms, that can be used as a bed by sliding a single cot from underneath it.

stu·di·ous (stü′dē əs), *adj.* **1** fond of study: *a studious pupil.* **2** showing careful consideration; careful; thoughtful: *The clerk made a studious effort to please customers.* —**stu′di·ous·ly**, *adv.* —**stu′di·ous·ness**, *n.*

stud·y (stud′ē), **1** *n.* effort to learn by reading or thinking: *After an hour's hard study, he knew his lesson.* **2** *v.* to try to learn: *She studied her spelling lesson for half an hour.* **3** *n.* a careful examination; investigation: *make a study of the life of Mark Twain.* **4** *v.* to examine carefully: *We studied the map to find the shortest way home.* **5** *n.* subject that is studied; branch of learning; thing investigated or to be investigated. History, music, and law are studies. **6** *n.* a room for study, reading, writing, etc.: *The author was at work in her study.* **7** *n.* piece of writing or work of art that deals in careful detail with one particular subject: *a study of art in Germany.* **8** *n.* sketch for a picture, story, etc. **9** *v.* to consider with care; think out; plan: *The mayor studied ways to cut expenses.* ■ See Synonym Study at **consider.** **10** *n.* deep thought; reverie: *The judge was absorbed in study about the case.* **11** *n.* piece of music intended to develop skill; étude. ❑ *n., pl.* **stud·ies;** *v.* **stud·ied, stud·y·ing.** [**Study** comes from a Latin word meaning "eagerness." If you're eager to learn, you're likely to study.] —**stud′i·a·ble**, *adj.* —**stud′i·er**, *n.*

study hall, 1 classroom in a school where students study during the school day. **2** period of the school day during which students study.

stuff (stuf), **1** *n.* thing or things; substance: *Some kind of stuff was floating on the pond.* **2** *n.* possessions; belongings: *He was told to move his stuff out of the room.* **3** *n.* worthless material; trash: *Their attic is full of old stuff.* **4** *n.* what a thing is made of; material: *He bought some white stuff for curtains.* **5** *n.* silly words and thoughts: *a lot of stuff and nonsense.* **6** *n.* inward qualities; character: *That girl has good stuff in her.* **7** *n.* capability; knowledge: *They really showed their stuff at the dance competition.* **8** *v.* to pack full; fill: *They stuffed the pillows with feathers.* **9** *v.* to put dishonest votes in a ballot box. **10** *v.* to stop up; block; choke up: *My head is stuffed up by a cold.* **11** *v.* to fill the skin of a dead animal to make it look as it did when alive: *We saw many stuffed animals at the museum.* **12** *v.* to prepare meat, fowl, or vegetables by filling with stuffing: *stuff a turkey.* **13** *v.* to force; push; thrust: *She stuffed her clothes into the drawer.* **14** *v.* to fill too much with food: *After I stuffed myself with candy, I felt sick.* —**stuff′er**, *n.*

WORD STORY **Stuff** comes from a French word meaning "to fill a space by packing it with something." From that word came another French word, meaning "something to pack a space with." So whatever stuff you might stuff a turkey with, it's stuffing you're using, and stuffing you're doing.

stuffed shirt, INFORMAL. person who tries to seem very important.

stuff·ing (stuf′ing), *n.* **1** material used to fill or pack something: *The stuffing is coming out of the pillow.* **2** seasoned bread crumbs, ground nuts, etc., used to stuff a chicken, turkey, fish, etc., before cooking.

stuff·y (stuf′ē), *adj.* **1** lacking fresh air: *a stuffy room.* **2** lacking freshness or interest; dull: *a stuffy conversation, a stuffy person.* **3** stopped up: *A cold makes your head feel stuffy.* ❑ *adj.* **stuff·i·er, stuff·i·est.** —**stuff′i·ly**, *adv.* —**stuff′i·ness**, *n.*

stum·ble (stum′bəl), **1** *v.* to trip by striking the foot against something: *He stumbled over the stool in the dark kitchen.* **2** *v.* to walk unsteadily: *The tired hikers stumbled along.* **3** *v.* to speak, act, etc., in a clumsy or hesitating way: *The actors made many blunders as they stumbled through the play.* **4** *v.* to make a mistake; do wrong. **5** *n.* a wrong act; mistake. **6** *v.* to come upon by accident or chance: *While in the country, we stumbled upon some fine antiques.* **7** *n.* act of stumbling. ❑ *v.* **stum·bled, stum·bling.** —**stum′bler**, *n.* —**stum′bling·ly**, *adv.*

stumbling block, obstacle; hindrance.

stump (stump), **1** *n.* the lower end of a tree or plant, left after the main part is cut off: *She sat on top of a stump.* **2** *n.* anything left after the main or important part is removed: *The dog wagged its stump of a tail.* **3** *n.* place where a political speech is made. **4** *v.* to make political speeches in: *The candidates for governor will stump the state.* **5** *v.* to walk in a stiff, clumsy way. **6** *v.* to puzzle: *The riddle stumped me.*

stump·y (stum′pē), *adj.* **1** short and thick: *a stumpy person.* ■ **Stumpy** may be considered offensive. **2** having many stumps: *stumpy ground.* ❑ *adj.* **stump·i·er, stump·i·est.** —**stump′i·ness**, *n.*

stun (stun), *v.* **1** to daze; bewilder; shock; overwhelm: *She was stunned by the news of her friend's death.* **2** to make senseless; knock unconscious: *He was stunned by the fall.* ❑ *v.* **stunned, stun·ning.**

stung (stung), *v.* past tense and past participle of **sting**: *A wasp stung me. He had been stung on the neck by a hornet.*

stunk (stungk), *v.* a past tense and past participle of **stink**: *The garbage stunk. Rotten eggs had stunk up the kitchen.*

stun·ning (stun′ing), *adj.* **1** having striking excellence, beauty, etc.; very attractive: *a stunning outfit.* **2** shocking; bewildering: *a stunning defeat.* —**stun′ning·ly**, *adv.*

stunt¹ (stunt), *v.* to hinder or slow down normal growth or development: *Lack of proper food stunts a child.*

stunt²

stunt² (stunt), *n.* an act that attracts attention, especially one that shows boldness or skill: *Circus riders perform stunts on horseback.*

a	hat	ė	term	ô	order	ch	child		
ā	age	i	it	oi	oil	ng	long	ə	a in about
ä	far	ī	ice	ou	out	sh	she		e in taken
â	care	o	hot	u	cup	th	thin		i in pencil
e	let	ō	open	u̇	put	ᵺ	then		o in lemon
ē	equal	ò	saw	ü	rule	zh	measure		u in circus

stu·pe·fac·tion (stü′pə fak′shən), *n.* overwhelming amazement; total shock.

stu·pe·fy (stü′pə fī), *v.* **1** to overwhelm with shock or amazement; astound: *They were stupefied by the news of the disaster.* **2** to make stupid, dull, or senseless: *be stupefied by a drug.* ◻ *v.* **stu·pe·fied, stu·pe·fy·ing.** —**stu′pe·fy′ing·ly,** *adv.*

stu·pen·dous (stü pen′dəs), *adj.* amazing; marvelous; immense: *Niagara Falls is a stupendous sight.* —**stu·pen′dous·ly,** *adv.* —**stu·pen′dous·ness,** *n.*

stu·pid (stü′pid), *adj.* **1** not intelligent; dull: *a stupid remark.* **2** not interesting: *a stupid book.* **3** dazed; senseless. —**stu′pid·ly,** *adv.*

stu·pid·i·ty (stü pid′ə tē), *n.* **1** lack of intelligence; dullness. **2** a foolish act, idea, etc. ◻ *n., pl.* **stu·pid·i·ties** for 2.

stu·por (stü′pər), *n.* a dazed condition; loss or decrease of the power to feel: *The injured mountain climber lay in a stupor, unable to tell what had happened.*

stur·dy (ster′dē), *adj.* **1** strong; stout: *a sturdy chair.* ■ See Synonym Study at **strong.** **2** not yielding; firm: *The enemy put up a sturdy defense.* ◻ *adj.* **stur·di·er, stur·di·est.** —**stur′di·ly,** *adv.* —**stur′di·ness,** *n.*

stur·geon (ster′jən), *n.* any of several large food fishes with long bodies that have tough skin and rows of bony plates. Caviar is made from sturgeon eggs. ◻ *n., pl.* **stur·geon** or **stur·geons.**

sturgeon

stut·ter (stut′ər), **1** *v.* to repeat the same sound in an effort to speak. People may stutter when nervous, embarrassed, or afraid. **2** *n.* act or habit of stuttering: *to speak with a stutter.* —**stut′ter·er,** *n.* —**stut′ter·ing·ly,** *adv.*

St. Vin·cent and the Gren·a·dines (sānt vin′sənt ənd тнə gren′ə dēnz′), island country in the West Indies. *Capital:* Kingstown.

sty[1] (stī), *n.* **1** pen for pigs. **2** any filthy place. ◻ *n., pl.* **sties.**

sty[2] (stī), *n.* a painful swelling on the edge of the eyelid. A sty is a small boil. ◻ *n., pl.* **sties.**

style (stīl), **1** *n.* manner; method; way: *She learned several styles of swimming.* **2** *n.* way of writing or speaking: *I like this author's clear, easy style.* **3** *n.* fashion: *My clothes are out of style.* **4** *n.* good taste; flair: *She dresses with style.* **5** *v.* to make in a particular way or form: *Her hair is styled with care.* **6** *v.* to name; call: *She styles herself an actress.* **7** *n.* the stemlike part of the pistil of a flower. ◻ *v.* **styled, styl·ing.** ■ Another word that sounds like this is **stile.** —**style′less,** *adj.* —**style′less·ness,** *n.* —**styl′er,** *n.*

WORD STORY   **Style** comes from **stylus.** In Latin, *stylus* meant both "a tool for writing on wax" and "a way of writing." Because people stopped writing on wax, they stopped talking about the tool, and the form *stylus* with that meaning did not change. Because people always care about style—in writing, dressing, and design—they kept on using *stylus* with that meaning, and its form gradually changed with use.

styl·ish (stī′lish), *adj.* having style; fashionable: *He wears stylish clothes.* —**styl′ish·ly,** *adv.* —**styl′ish·ness,** *n.*

styl·ist (stī′list), *n.* **1** person who designs, arranges, or advises concerning interior decorations, clothes, hair styles, etc. **2** writer, speaker, artist, etc., who is considered to be an expert or a master of style.

sty·lis·tic (stī lis′tik), *adj.* of or about style: *stylistic details.* —**sty·lis′ti·cal·ly,** *adv.*

styl·ize (stī′līz), *v.* to make or design something according to a particular or conventional style. ◻ *v.* **styl·ized, styl·iz·ing.** —**styl′i·za′tion,** *n.* —**styl′iz·er,** *n.*

sty·lus (stī′ləs), *n.* **1** a needlelike point used in making or playing phonograph records. **2** a pointed tool for writing on wax. ◻ *n., pl.* **sty·lus·es, sty·li** (stī′lī). [See Word Story at **style.**]

sty·mie (stī′mē), *v.* to block completely; hinder; thwart: *His plans were stymied by lack of money.* ◻ *v.* **sty·mied, sty·mie·ing.**

sty·rene (stī′rēn′), *n.* a mixture of hydrogen and carbon, used to make plastics and synthetic rubber.

Sty·ro·foam (stī′rə fōm′), *n.* trademark for a lightweight, waterproof plastic foam, used to insulate buildings and to make small boats, buoys, etc.

suave (swäv), *adj.* smoothly agreeable or polite. —**suave′ly,** *adv.* —**suave′ness, sua′vi·ty,** *n.*

sub[1] (sub), **1** *n.* substitute. **2** *v.* to act as a substitute: *My mother subbed for our regular teacher in school today.* ◻ *v.* **subbed, sub·bing.**

sub[2] (sub), *n.* submarine.

sub[3] (sub), *n.* hero sandwich.

sub-, *prefix.* **1** below; beneath: *subsoil = earth below surface soil.* **2** near; nearly: *subtropical = nearly tropical.* **3** smaller; less important; part of another: *subcommittee = a smaller committee.*

sub., **1** subscription. **2** substitute. **3** suburban.

sub·arc·tic (sub ärk′tik *or* sub är′tik), *adj.* near or just below the arctic region; having to do with or occurring in regions just south of the arctic circle.

sub·a·tom·ic (sub′ə tom′ik), *adj.* of or about the parts that form an atom or atoms.

sub·com·mit·tee (sub′kə mit′ē), *n.* a small committee chosen from a larger general committee for some special duty. ◻ *n., pl.* **sub·com·mit·tees.**

sub·com·pact (sub′kom′pakt), *n.* car smaller than a compact, usually having a four-cylinder engine.

sub·con·scious (sub kon′shəs), **1** *adj.* not wholly conscious; existing in the mind but not fully perceived or recognized: *Some students drop out of school not really because they have to go to work, but because of a subconscious fear of failure in school.* **2** *n.* thoughts, feelings, etc., that are present in the mind but not fully perceived or recognized. —**sub·con′scious·ly,** *adv.*

sub·con·ti·nent (sub kon′tə nənt), *n.* a landmass or region that is very large, but smaller than a continent. India is a subcontinent.

sub·con·tract (sub kon′trakt), **1** *n.* contract for carrying out a previous contract or part of it: *The contractor for the new building gave out subcontracts to a plumber and an electrician.* **2** *v.* to make a subcontract.

sub·cu·ta·ne·ous (sub′kyü tā′nē əs), *adj.* **1** under the skin: *subcutaneous tissue.* **2** placed under the skin: *a subcutaneous injection.* —**sub′cu·ta·ne·ous·ly,** *adv.*

sub·di·vide (sub′də vīd′ *or* sub′də vīd′), *v.* to divide again; divide into smaller parts: *A real estate developer bought the farm and subdivided it into building lots.* ◻ *v.* **sub·di·vid·ed, sub·di·vid·ing.**

sub·di·vi·sion (sub′də vizh′ən *or* sub′də vizh′ən), *n.* **1** division into smaller parts. **2** part of a larger part. **3** tract of land divided into building lots.

sub·dom·i·nant (sub dom′ə nənt), *n.* the fourth note in a musical scale. F is the subdominant in the key of C.

sub·duc·tion (səb duk′shən), *n.* a geological process in which one plate of the earth's crust descends underneath another plate where their edges meet.

sub·due (səb dü′), *v.* **1** to overcome by superior force; conquer: *The Romans subdued all the peoples of the Mediterranean.* **2** to keep down; hold back; suppress: *We subdued a desire to laugh.* **3** to tone down; soften: *Pulling down the shades subdued the light in the room.* ◻ *v.* **sub·dued, sub·du·ing.** —**sub·du′a·ble,** *adj.* —**sub·du′er,** *n.*

sub·fam·i·ly (sub fam′ə lē), *n.* group of related living things ranking below a family. ◻ *n., pl.* **sub·fam·i·lies.**

sub·freez·ing (sub frē′zing), *adj.* below freezing: *subfreezing temperatures.*

sub·group (sub′grüp′), *n.* a subordinate group; division of a group.

sub·head (sub′hed′), *n.* **1** a subordinate heading or title: *Many magazine articles have subheads.* **2** a subordinate division of a heading or title. Lesson subheads are often indicated by numbers or letters in parentheses, such as (1) and (a).

sub·hu·man (sub hyü′mən), *adj.* less than human. ■ **Subhuman** is often considered offensive.

subj., **1** subject. **2** subjective. **3** subjectively. **4** subjunctive.

sub·ject (sub′jikt *for noun, adj.;* səb jekt′ *for verb*), **1** *n.* something that is thought about, discussed, investigated, etc.; topic: *The subject for our composition was "An Exciting Moment."* **2** *n.* something learned or taught; course of study in some branch of knowledge: *English, science, and arithmetic are some of the subjects we take up in school.* **3** *n.* person under the power, control, or influence of another: *subjects of the king.* **4** *adj.* bound by loyalty or allegiance to; obedient to some power or influence: *We are subject to our country's laws.* **5** *adj.* under some power or influence: *the subject nations of an empire.* **6** *v.* to bring under some power or influence: *Rome subjected all Italy to its rule.* **7** *v.* to cause to undergo or experience something: *The school subjected new students to many tests.* **8** *adj.* liable to suffer from; prone to: *I am subject to colds.* **9** *v.* lay open to; expose: *The location of the island in the middle of the ocean subjected it to frequent hurricanes.* **10** *n.* person or thing that undergoes or experiences something: *Rabbits and mice are often subjects for medical experiments.* **11** *adj.* depending on; on the condition of: *I bought the car subject to your approval.* **12** *n.* (in grammar) a word or group of words about which something is said in a sentence. The subject is usually the performer of the action of an active verb or the receiver of the action of a passive verb. *I* is the subject of the following sentences: *I saw the deer. I was seen by the deer. I could see.*

WORD STORY Subject comes from a Latin word meaning "to throw under." A school subject is under study; a king's subject is under the king's rule; and the subject of an experiment is under scientific investigation.

sub·jec·tion (səb jek′shən), *n.* **1** act or process of bringing under some power or influence; conquering: *The subjection of the rebels took years.* **2** condition of being under some power or influence: *The peasants lived in subjection to the nobility.*

sub·jec·tive (səb jek′tiv), *adj.* **1** existing in the mind; belonging to the person thinking rather than to the object thought of: *Base your subjective opinions on objective facts.* **2** about the thoughts and feelings of the speaker, writer, painter, etc.; personal: *a subjective poem.* —**sub·jec′tive·ly,** *adv.* —**sub·jec′tive·ness,** *n.*

sub·jec·tiv·i·ty (sub′jek tiv′ə tē), *n.* tendency to understand things according to how they affect you personally; use of personal reactions and perceptions as a basis for judgment or description: *The author's subjectivity makes the guidebook interesting but incomplete.*

subject matter, **1** something thought about, discussed, studied, written about, etc. **2** what a talk, book, play, movie, etc., is about, as distinguished from its form or style: *The speaker's subject matter was better than her presentation.*

sub·ju·gate (sub′jə gāt), *v.* to subdue; conquer. ❏ *v.* **sub·ju·gat·ed, sub·ju·gat·ing.** —**sub′ju·ga′tion,** *n.* —**sub′ju·ga′tor,** *n.*

sub·junc·tive (səb jungk′tiv), **1** *adj.* (in grammar) referring to a verb form which expresses a condition, act, or event as possible or dependent, rather than actual. **2** *n.* form of a verb which expresses this. In "I insist that he go" and "If I were you," *go* and *were* are subjunctives. **3** *n.* mood of such a verb.

sub·king·dom (sub king′dəm), *n.* a group of related living things ranking below a kingdom.

sub·lease (sub′lēs′ *for noun;* sub lēs′ *or* sub′lēs′ *for verb*), **1** *n.* a lease granted by someone on property which he or she has leased. **2** *v.* to give a sublease of. **3** *v.* to take a sublease of. ❏ *v.* **sub·leased, sub·leas·ing.**

sub·let (sub let′ *or* sub′let′), *v.* **1** to rent to another person something which has been rented to you; give a sublease of: *She sublet her house for the summer.* **2** to take a sublease of: *I have sublet an apartment whose tenants went away for the summer.* **3** to give part of a contract to another: *The contractor for the whole building sublet the contract for the plumbing.* ❏ *v.* **sub·let, sub·let·ting.**

sub·li·mate (sub′lə māt), *v.* to change an undesirable impulse or trait into a desirable activity: *He sublimated his shyness in art.* ❏ *v.* **sub·li·mat·ed, sub·li·mat·ing.** —**sub′li·ma′tion,** *n.*

sub·lime (sə blīm′), **1** *adj.* lofty or elevated in thought, feeling, language, etc.; noble; grand; exalted: *sublime devotion, sublime poetry. Mountain scenery is often sublime.* **2** *n.* whatever is lofty, noble, exalted, etc.: *the sublime in literature and art.* —**sub·lime′ly,** *adv.* —**sub·lime′ness, sub·lim′i·ty,** *n.*

sub·ma·chine gun (sub′mə shēn′), a lightweight automatic or semiautomatic gun, designed to be fired from the shoulder or hip.

sub·ma·rine (sub′mə rēn′ *or* sub′mə rēn′), **1** *n.* boat that can go under water. Submarines are used in warfare for attacking enemy ships with torpedoes and for launching missiles. **2** *adj.* under the surface of the sea; underwater: *submarine plants, submarine warfare.* **3** *n.* hero sandwich.

submarine (def. 1)

sub·merge (səb mėrj′), *v.* **1** to put under water; cover with water: *A big wave submerged us.* **2** to cover; bury: *His talent was submerged by his shyness.* **3** to sink under water; go below the surface: *The submarine submerged to escape attack.* ❏ *v.* **sub·merged, sub·merg·ing.**

sub·mer·gence (səb mėr′jəns), *n.* act of submerging or condition of being submerged.

sub·merse (səb mėrs′), *v.* to submerge. ❏ *v.* **sub·mersed, sub·mers·ing.** —**sub·mer·sion** (səb mėr′zhən), *n.*

sub·mers·i·ble (səb mėr′sə bəl), **1** *adj.* able to be submerged. **2** *n.* a submarine.

sub·mis·sion (səb mish′ən), *n.* **1** act of yielding to the power, control, or authority of another; submitting: *The defeated general showed his submission by giving up his sword.* **2** obedience; humbleness: *They all bowed in submission to the queen's order.* **3** act of referring or condition of being referred to the consideration or judgment of some person or group. **4** something that is referred in this manner.

sub·mis·sive (səb mis′iv), *adj.* yielding to the power, control, or authority of another; obedient; humble. —**sub·mis′sive·ly,** *adv.* —**sub·mis′sive·ness,** *n.*

sub·mit (səb mit′), *v.* **1** to yield to the power, control, or authority of some person or group; surrender; yield: *They submitted to the wishes of the majority.* **2** to refer to the consideration or judgment of some person or group: *The secretary submitted a report of the last meeting.* **3** to suggest or urge respectfully: *I submit that more evidence is needed to support the case.* ❏ *v.* **sub·mit·ted, sub·mit·ting.** —**sub·mit′ter,** *n.*

sub·nor·mal (sub nôr′məl), *adj.* below normal: *a subnormal temperature.* —**sub·nor·mal·i·ty** (sub′nor mal′ə tē), *n.* —**sub·nor′mal·ly,** *adv.*

sub·or·bit·al (sub ôr′bə təl), *adj.* involving less than a full orbit: *a suborbital space flight.*

sub·or·der (sub′ôr dər), *n.* a group of related living things ranking below an order.

sub·or·di·nate (sə bôrd′n it *for adj., noun;* sə bôrd′n āt *for verb*), **1** *adj.* lower in rank: *In the military, lieutenants are sub-*

a	hat	ė	term	ô	order	ch	child		a in about
ā	age	i	it	oi	oil	ng	long		e in taken
ä	far	ī	ice	ou	out	sh	she	ə	i in pencil
â	care	o	hot	u	cup	th	thin		o in lemon
e	let	ō	open	ů	put	ŦH	then		u in circus
ē	equal	ò	saw	ü	rule	zh	measure		

S

ordinate to captains. **2** *adj.* having less importance; secondary; dependent: *An assistant has a subordinate position.* **3** *n.* a subordinate person or thing: *Our supervisor seldom takes advice from her subordinates.* **4** *v.* to make subordinate: *He was an agreeable person, who often subordinated his wishes to those of other people.* ❏ *v.* **sub·or·di·nat·ed, sub·or·di·nat·ing. –sub·or′di·nate·ly,** *adv.* **–sub·or′di·nate·ness,** *n.*

subordinate clause, dependent clause.

subordinating conjuction, a conjunction, such as *that, which, who,* or *where,* that introduces a dependent clause. In *The house where I grew up is gone now,* the subordinating conjunction *where* introduces the dependent clause *where I grew up.*

sub·or·di·na·tion (sə bôrd′n ā′shən), *n.* **1** submission to authority; willingness to obey; obedience. **2** act of subordinating. **3** subordinate position or importance.

sub·orn (sə bôrn′), *v.* **1** to persuade, bribe, or cause someone to do an illegal or evil deed. **2** to persuade or cause a witness to give false testimony in court. **–sub′or·na′tion,** *n.* **–sub·orn′er,** *n.*

sub·poe·na (sə pē′nə), **1** *n.* an official written order commanding someone to appear in a court of law to give testimony or offer certain records, documents, etc. **2** *v.* to order that certain records, documents, etc., be brought to a court of law. ❏ *n., pl.* **sub·poe·nas;** *v.* **sub·poe·naed, sub·poe·na·ing.**

sub·rou·tine (sub′rü tēn′), *n.* a set of computer instructions that carries out a specific part of the main routine.

sub·scribe (səb skrīb′), *v.* **1** to promise to take and pay for: *We subscribe to a few magazines.* **2** to promise to give or pay a sum of money: *She subscribed $50 to the hospital fund.* **3** to write your name at the end of a document, etc.; show your consent or approval by signing: *The men who subscribed to the Declaration of Independence are now famous.* **4** to give your consent or approval; agree: *She does not subscribe to my opinion.* ❏ *v.* **sub·scribed, sub·scrib·ing. –sub·scrib′er,** *n.*

sub·script (sub′skript), *n.* number, letter, etc., written underneath and to one side of a symbol. In H_2SO_4 the 2 and 4 are subscripts.

sub·scrip·tion (səb skrip′shən), *n.* **1** the right to receive something, obtained by paying a certain sum: *Our subscription to the newspaper expires next week.* **2** act of subscribing.

sub·sec·tion (sub′sek′shən), *n.* part of a section.

sub·se·quent (sub′sə kwənt), *adj.* coming after; later: *Subsequent events proved that she was right.* **–sub′se·quent·ly,** *adv.*

sub·ser·vi·ence (səb sėr′vē əns), *n.* willingness to do what other people want you to do; excessive obedience.

sub·ser·vi·ent (səb sėr′vē ənt), *adj.* very willing to do what other people want you to do; submissively polite. **–sub·ser′vi·ent·ly,** *adv.*

sub·set (sub′set′), *n.* (in mathematics) a set, each of whose members is a member of a second set: *Sixth graders are a subset of the set which includes all students attending elementary school.*

sub·side (səb sīd′), *v.* **1** to become less; die down: *The storm finally subsided. Her fever subsided after she took the medicine.* **2** to sink to a lower level: *Several days after the rain stopped, the floodwaters subsided.* ❏ *v.* **sub·sid·ed, sub·sid·ing.**

sub·sid·ence (səb sīd′ns *or* sub′sə dəns), *n.* act or process of subsiding: *the subsidence of a flood.*

sub·sid·i·ar·y (səb sid′ē er′ē), **1** *adj.* useful to assist or supplement; auxiliary; supplementary: *The teacher sold books as a subsidiary occupation.* **2** *n.* thing or person that assists or supplements. **3** company having over half of its stock owned or controlled by another company: *The publisher was a subsidiary of the media conglomerate.* **4** *adj.* maintained by a subsidy. ❏ *n., pl.* **sub·sid·i·ar·ies.**

sub·si·dize (sub′sə dīz), *v.* to aid or assist with a grant of money: *The government subsidizes airlines that carry mail.* ❏ *v.* **sub·si·dized, sub·si·diz·ing. –sub′si·di·za′tion,** *n.* **–sub′si·diz′er,** *n.*

sub·si·dy (sub′sə dē), *n.* grant or contribution of money, especially one made by a government: *a subsidy for education.* ❏ *n., pl.* **sub·si·dies.**

sub·sist (səb sist′), *v.* **1** to stay alive without much food, cloth-

ing, or shelter: *The lost hiker subsisted on wild berries for two days.* **2** to continue to be; persist: *Many superstitions still subsist.*

sub·sist·ence (səb sis′təns), *n.* **1** condition of subsisting: *Selling papers was his only means of subsistence.* **2** means of keeping alive; livelihood: *The sea provides a subsistence for fishermen.* **3** existence; continuance.

sub·soil (sub′soil′), *n.* layer of earth that lies just under the surface soil.

sub·son·ic (sub son′ik), *adj.* **1** of or about a speed less than the speed of sound, about 1087 feet (331 meters) per second at sea level. **2** moving slower than the speed of sound: *a subsonic airplane.* **–sub·son′i·cal·ly,** *adv.*

sub·spe·cies (sub′spē′shēz), *n.* group of related living things ranking below a species. ❏ *n., pl.* **sub·spe·cies.**

sub·stance (sub′stəns), *n.* **1** material that something is made of; matter: *Ice and water are the same substance in different forms.* **2** the real, main, or important part of anything: *The substance of an education is its effect on your life, not just learning lessons.* **3** real meaning: *Give the substance of the speech in your own words.* **4** solid quality; body: *Pea soup has more substance than water.* **5** wealth; property: *a person of substance.*

substance abuse, abuse of a substance, such as alcohol, heroin, etc., that causes dangerous and destructive addiction.

sub·stand·ard (sub stan′dərd), *adj.* below standard: *substandard housing.*

sub·stan·tial (səb stan′shəl), *adj.* **1** real; actual: *People and things are substantial; dreams and ghosts are not.* **2** strong; firm; solid: *The house is substantial enough to last a hundred years.* **3** large; important; ample: *Your work shows substantial improvement.* **4** providing ample or abundant nourishment: *Eat a substantial breakfast.* **5** in the main; in essentials: *The stories told by the two children were in substantial agreement.* **6** well-to-do; wealthy.

sub·stan·tial·ly (səb stan′shə lē), *adv.* **1** essentially; mainly: *This report is substantially correct.* **2** really; actually. **3** strongly; solidly: *a substantially built house.*

sub·stan·ti·ate (səb stan′shē āt), *v.* to establish by evidence; prove: *substantiate a rumor, substantiate a claim.* ❏ *v.* **sub·stan·ti·at·ed, sub·stan·ti·at·ing. –sub·stan′ti·a′tion,** *n.*

sub·stan·tive (sub′stən tiv), **1** *n.* noun or pronoun; the name of a person or thing. **2** *adj.* used as a noun. **3** *adj.* showing or expressing existence. The verb *to be* is the substantive verb. **4** *adj.* substantial: *substantive discussions.*

sub·sta·tion (sub′stā′shən), *n.* a branch station; subordinate station: *Besides the main post office in our city, there are six substations.*

sub·sti·tute (sub′stə tüt), **1** *n.* thing used instead of another; person taking the place of another: *A substitute taught us at school today.* **2** *v.* to put in the place of another: *We substituted brown sugar for molasses in these cookies.* **3** *v.* to take the place of another: *She substituted for our teacher, who is ill.* **4** *adj.* put in or taking the place of another: *a substitute teacher.* ❏ *v.* **sub·sti·tut·ed, sub·sti·tut·ing.**

sub·sti·tu·tion (sub′stə tü′shən), *n.* the use of one thing for another; a putting one person or thing in the place of another; a taking the place of another.

sub·stra·tum (sub strā′təm), *n.* layer lying under another layer: *Beneath the sandy soil there was a substratum of clay.* ❏ *n., pl.* **sub·stra·ta** (sub strā′tə), **sub·stra·tums.**

sub·struc·ture (sub′struk′chər), *n.* structure that forms the foundation of another structure, such as the columns holding up a bridge.

sub·sys·tem (sub′sis′təm), *n.* a separate, self-contained part of a larger system.

sub·teen (sub′tēn′), *n.* boy or girl nearly thirteen years old.

sub·ter·fuge (sub′tər fyüj), *n.* trick or excuse used to escape something unpleasant: *The child's headache was only a subterfuge to avoid doing chores.*

sub·ter·ra·ne·an (sub′tə rā′nē ən), *adj.* **1** underground: *A subterranean passage led from the castle to a cave.* **2** carried on secretly; hidden: *subterranean plotting.*

sub·ti·tle (sub′tī′tl), **1** *n.* an additional title of a book, article, etc. **2** *n.* word or words shown on a movie screen, especially as the translation of the words spoken in a foreign-language film; caption. **3** *v.* to give a subtitle to. ❑ *v.* **sub·ti·tled, sub·ti·tling.**

sub·tle (sut′l), *adj.* **1** slight; delicate: *a subtle odor of perfume.* **2** not obvious; difficult to perceive: *Subtle humor is often hard to understand.* **3** working secretly: *a subtle poison.* **4** mysterious: *a subtle smile.* **5** marked by a quick ability to understand: *a subtle mind.* ❑ *adj.* **sub·tler, sub·tlest.** —**sub′tle·ness,** *n.*

sub·tle·ty (sut′l tē), *n.* **1** subtle quality. **2** something subtle. ❑ *n., pl.* **sub·tle·ties** for 2.

sub·tly (sut′lē *or* sut′l ē), *adv.* in a subtle manner.

sub·top·ic (sub′top′ik), *n.* a secondary or subordinate topic.

sub·to·tal (sub tō′tl), **1** *n.* something less than the total. **2** *adj.* not quite total; less than complete.

sub·tract (səb trakt′), *v.* to take away: *Subtract 2 from 10 and you have 8.* —**sub·tract′er,** *n.*

sub·trac·tion (səb trak′shən), *n.* operation of subtracting one number or quantity from another; finding the difference between two numbers or quantities: *10−2 = 8 is a simple subtraction.*

sub·tra·hend (sub′trə hend), *n.* number or quantity to be subtracted from another: *In 10−2 = 8, the subtrahend is 2.*

sub·trop·i·cal (sub trop′ə kəl), *adj.* **1** bordering on the tropics. **2** nearly tropical.

sub·trop·ics (sub′trop′iks), *n.pl.* region bordering on the tropics.

sub·urb (sub′ėrb′), *n.* district, town, or village just outside or near a city: *Many people who work in the city live in the suburbs.*

sub·ur·ban (sə bėr′bən), *adj.* **1** of or in a suburb: *We have excellent suburban train service.* **2** like a suburb or its inhabitants.

sub·ur·ban·ite (sə bėr′bə nīt), *n.* person who lives in a suburb.

sub·ur·bi·a (sə bėr′bē ə), *n.* **1** suburbs. **2** suburbanites or their way of life, attitudes, and the like.

sub·ver·sion (səb vėr′zhən), *n.* act or process of overthrowing a government, political system, etc.

sub·ver·sive (səb vėr′siv), **1** *adj.* tending to overthrow a government, political system, etc. **2** *n.* person who seeks to overthrow or weaken a government, political system, etc. —**sub·ver′sive·ly,** *adv.* —**sub·ver′sive·ness,** *n.*

sub·vert (səb vėrt′), *v.* **1** to overthrow something established or existing, especially a government, political system, etc.: *Dictators subvert democracy.* **2** to weaken the principles of; corrupt: *subvert a peaceful society.* —**sub·vert′er,** *n.*

sub·way (sub′wā′), *n.* **1** an electric railroad running beneath the surface of the streets in a city. **2** an underground passage.

subway

suc·ceed (sək sēd′), *v.* **1** to turn out well; do well; have success: *Her plans succeeded.* **2** to accomplish what you intended to do: *She succeeded in completing the project.* **3** to come next after; follow; take the place of: *John Adams succeeded Washington as President.* **4** to come next after another; follow another; take the place of another: *When George VI died, Elizabeth II succeeded to the throne.* —**suc·ceed′er,** *n.*

suc·cess (sək ses′), *n.* **1** accomplishment of what you intended to do: *Success in school comes from intelligence and work.* **2** the gaining of wealth, a high position, etc.: *He has had little success*

in life. **3** person or thing that succeeds: *The circus was a great success.* **4** result; outcome; fortune: *What success did you have in finding a new apartment?* ❑ *n., pl.* **suc·cess·es.**

suc·cess·ful (sək ses′fəl), *adj.* having success; ending in success; prosperous; fortunate: *a successful writer, a successful campaign.* —**suc·cess′ful·ly,** *adv.* —**suc·cess′ful·ness,** *n.*

suc·ces·sion (sək sesh′ən), *n.* **1** group of things happening one after another; series: *A succession of accidents spoiled our trip.* **2** act or process in which one person or thing comes after another. **3** a right of succeeding to an office, property, or rank: *The vice-president has succession to the presidency.* **4** order or arrangement of persons having such a right of succeeding: *The king's oldest daughter is next in succession to the throne.* **5** the order in which one species of living thing replaces another as an ecosystem gradually develops.

in succession, one after another: *We visited our sick friend several days in succession.*

SYNONYM STUDY **Succession, series,** and **sequence** all mean several things in order, one after another. **Succession** means things that are all part of one process: *A carefully planned succession of space flights led up to the first moon voyage.* **Series** suggests that the things are similar: *Have you heard about the series of robberies?* **Sequence** suggests a clear pattern in which one thing leads to the next: *The camping merit badges must be earned in sequence.*

suc·ces·sive (sək ses′iv), *adj.* coming one after another; following in order: *It rained for three successive days.* —**suc·ces′-sive·ly,** *adv.* —**suc·ces′sive·ness,** *n.*

suc·ces·sor (sək ses′ər), *n.* one that follows or succeeds another in office, position, or ownership of property; thing that comes next after another in a series: *John Adams was Washington's successor as President.*

suc·cinct (sək singkt′), *adj.* expressed briefly and clearly; concise: *a succinct one-page memo.* —**suc·cinct′ly,** *adv.* —**suc·cinct′ness,** *n.*

suc·cor (suk′ər), *n., v.* help; aid. ■ Another word that sounds like this is **sucker.** —**suc′cor·er,** *n.*

suc·co·tash (suk′ə tash), *n.* kernels of sweet corn and beans, usually lima beans, cooked together.

Suc·coth (sùk′əs), *n.* Sukkoth.

suc·cu·lence (suk′yə ləns), *n.* juiciness.

suc·cu·lent (suk′yə lənt), *adj.* juicy: *a succulent peach.* —**suc′-cu·lent·ly,** *adv.*

suc·cumb (sə kum′), *v.* **1** to give in to; yield: *I succumbed to temptation and ate the last piece of candy.* **2** to die: *She succumbed of old age.*

such (such), **1** *adj.* of that kind; of the same kind or degree: *We had never seen such a sight.* **2** *adj.* of a particular kind; of the kind that: *The child had such a fever that she nearly died.* **3** *adj.* of the kind already spoken of or suggested: *They did not like tea and coffee and such drinks.* **4** *adj.* so great, so bad, so good, etc.: *He is such a liar. Such weather!* **5** *pron.* person or thing of that kind; persons or things of that kind: *There were rowboats, canoes, surfboards, and such on sale at the store last week.* **6** *adv.* so very: *We had such good times last summer.*

as such, as being what is indicated or implied: *A friend, as such, deserves understanding.*

such as, 1 similar to; like: *A good friend such as you is rare.* **2** for example: *members of the dog family, such as the wolf and fox.*

suck (suk), **1** *v.* to draw into the mouth by using the lips and tongue: *Lemonade can be sucked through a straw.* **2** *v.* to draw liquid from with the mouth: *suck oranges.* **3** *v.* to draw milk from the breast or a bottle. **4** *v.* to draw or be drawn by sucking: *He sucked at his pipe.* **5** *v.* to draw; take in; absorb: *The fan sucked the smoke from the room. A sponge sucks in water.* **6** *v.* to hold in the mouth and lick: *The child sucked a lollipop.* **7** *n.* act of sucking: *The baby took one suck at the empty bottle and pushed it away.*

a	hat	ė	term	ô	order	ch	child		
ā	age	i	it	oi	oil	ng	long	ə	a in about
ä	far	ī	ice	ou	out	sh	she		e in taken
â	care	o	hot	u	cup	th	thin		i in pencil
e	let	ō	open	ù	put	ᴛʜ	then		o in lemon
ē	equal	ò	saw	ü	rule	zh	measure		u in circus

S

suck·er (suk′ər), *n.* **1** animal or thing that sucks. **2** any of several freshwater fishes with large, fleshy lips that suck in food. **3** organ of some animals for sucking or holding by sucking. **4** a growth from an underground stem or root. **5** lollipop. **6** INFORMAL. person easily deceived. ■ Another word that sounds like this is **succor.**

suck·le (suk′əl), *v.* **1** to feed with milk from the breast or udder: *The cat suckles her kittens.* **2** to suck at the breast or udder. ❑ *v.* **suck·led, suck·ling.**

suck·ling (suk′ling), *n.* a very young animal or child, especially one not yet weaned.

Su·cre (sü′krā), *n.* one of the two capitals of Bolivia, in the S part. La Paz is the other capital.

su·crose (sü′krōs), *n.* ordinary sugar obtained from sugar cane, sugar beets, etc.

suc·tion (suk′shən), **1** *n.* process of drawing liquids or gases into a space by sucking out or removing part of the air from that space to produce a vacuum. We draw lemonade through a straw by suction. Vacuum cleaners and some pumps work by suction. **2** *n.* the force caused by suction. **3** *n.* act or process of sucking. **4** *adj.* causing a suction; working by suction: *a suction valve.*

Su·dan (sü dan′), *n.* **1** country in NE Africa. *Capital:* Khartoum. **2 the Sudan,** vast region in Africa, south of the Sahara Desert and extending from the Atlantic to the Red Sea. [**Sudan** comes from Arabic words meaning "land of the blacks." People living in Sudan usually have darker skin than people living in Egypt or Arabia.]

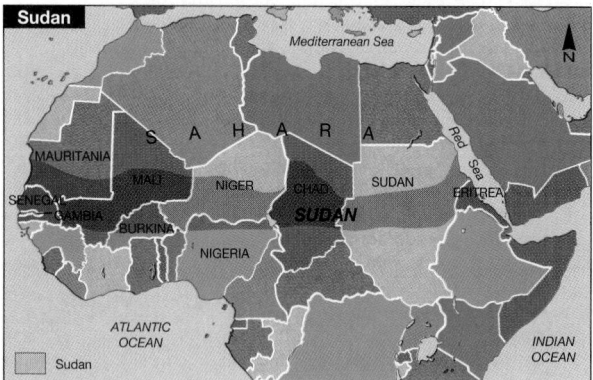

Su·da·nese (süd′n ēz′), **1** *adj.* of or about Sudan or the Sudan or their inhabitants. **2** *n.* person born or living in Sudan or the Sudan. ❑ *n., pl.* **Su·da·nese.**

sud·den (sud′n), *adj.* **1** happening without warning or notice; not expected: *a sudden stop, a sudden rainstorm, a sudden rise to power.* **2** found or hit upon unexpectedly; abrupt: *There was a sudden turn in the road.* **3** quick; rapid: *The cat made a sudden jump at the mouse.* **−sud′den·ly,** *adv.* **−sud′den·ness,** *n.*
all of a sudden, in a sudden manner; unexpectedly or quickly.

sudden death, (in sports) an overtime period played to decide the winner of a game that has ended in a tie. The first team to score wins the game.

sudden infant death syndrome, death from an unknown cause of a sleeping infant that has shown no signs of serious illness; crib death.

suds (sudz), *n.pl.* **1** soapy water. **2** bubbles and foam on soapy water; soapsuds.

suds·y (sud′zē), *adj.* full of soapsuds. ❑ *adj.* **suds·i·er, suds·i·est.**

sue (sü), *v.* **1** to start a lawsuit against: *She sued the driver of the car that hit her.* **2** to take action in law: *sue for damages.* **3** to beg or ask for; plead: *Messengers came suing for peace.* ❑ *v.* **sued, su·ing. −su′a·ble,** *adj.* **−su′er,** *n.*

suede (swād), **1** *n.* a soft leather that has a velvety surface on one or both sides. **2** *n.* kind of cloth that has a similar appearance. **3** *adj.* made of suede: *suede shoes, a suede jacket.*

su·et (sü′it), *n.* the hard fat around the kidneys and loins of cattle and sheep. Suet is used as shortening and for making tallow.

Su·ez Canal (sü ez′), canal in the NE part of Egypt, connecting the Mediterranean and Red seas.

suf·fer (suf′ər), *v.* **1** to have pain, grief, injury, etc.: *Sick people suffer.* **2** to have or feel pain, grief, etc.: *I suffered sunburn from being at the beach all day.* **3** to experience harm, loss, etc.: *His business suffered greatly last year.* **4** to bear with patiently; endure: *I will not suffer such insults.* **−suf′fer·a·ble,** *adj.* **−suf′fer·er,** *n.*

suf·fer·ance (suf′ər əns), *n.* permission or consent given only by a failure to object or prevent.

suf·fer·ing (suf′ər ing), *n.* **1** condition of being in pain: *Hunger causes suffering.* **2** the enduring of pain, trouble, or distress: *the suffering of a poor family.*

suf·fice (sə fīs′), *v.* **1** to be enough; be sufficient: *Fifty dollars will suffice to buy that coat.* **2** to satisfy; make content: *A small amount of cake sufficed the baby.* ❑ *v.* **suf·ficed, suf·fic·ing.**

suf·fi·cien·cy (sə fish′ən sē), *n.* **1** a sufficient amount; large enough supply: *The ship had a sufficiency of provisions for a voyage of two months.* **2** condition or fact of being sufficient; adequacy; ability. ❑ *n., pl.* **suf·fi·cien·cies** for 1.

suf·fi·cient (sə fish′ənt), *adj.* as much as is needed; enough: *sufficient proof.* **−suf·fi′cient·ly,** *adv.*

suf·fix (suf′iks *for noun;* sə fiks′ *or* suf′iks *for verb),* **1** *n.* syllable or syllables put at the end of a word to change its meaning or to make another word, as *-ly* in *badly, -ness* in *goodness,* and *-ful* in *spoonful.* **2** *v.* to add at the end; put after. ❑ *n., pl.* **suf·fix·es.**

suf·fo·cate (suf′ə kāt), *v.* **1** to kill by stopping the breath: *Thick smoke suffocated them.* **2** to keep someone from breathing; choke: *I was suffocating under too many blankets.* **3** to gasp for breath; choke. **4** to die for lack of oxygen; be suffocated: *The diver suffocated when his air hose became twisted.* ❑ *v.* **suf·fo·cat·ed, suf·fo·cat·ing. −suf′fo·cat′ing·ly,** *adv.* **−suf′fo·ca′tion,** *n.*

suf·frage (suf′rij), *n.* **1** the right to vote; franchise: *The United States granted suffrage to women in 1920.* **2** a vote, usually in support of a proposal, candidate, etc. **3** act of casting votes.

suffragettes

suf·fra·gette (suf′rə jet′), *n.* woman advocating suffrage for women.

suf·fra·gist (suf′rə jist), *n.* person who favors giving suffrage to more people, especially to women.

suf·fuse (sə fyüz′), *v.* to spread over with a liquid, dye, etc.: *eyes suffused with tears. At twilight the sky was suffused with glorious color.* ❑ *v.* **suf·fused, suf·fus·ing. −suf·fu′sion,** *n.*

sug·ar (shug′ər), **1** *n.* a sweet substance obtained mostly from sugarcane or sugar beets and widely used in food products; sucrose. **2** *n.* any of the class of carbohydrates to which this substance belongs. Glucose, lactose, and maltose are other sugars. **3** *v.* to put sugar in or on; sweeten with sugar: *She sugared her tea.* **4** *v.* to cover with sugar; sprinkle with sugar: *to sugar doughnuts.* **5** *v.* to form sugar crystals: *Honey sugars if kept too long.* **6** *v.* to cause to seem pleasant or agreeable: *He sugared his criticism of the play with some praise for the performers.* **−sug′ar·free′,** *adj.*

sugar beet, a large beet with a white root that yields sugar.

sug·ar·cane (shug′ər kān′), *n.* a very tall grass growing in warm regions, with long, flat leaves and a strong, jointed stem that yields sugar.

sug·ar·coat (shŭg′ər kōt′), v. 1 to cover with sugar. 2 to cause to seem more pleasant or agreeable: *to sugarcoat the news about the cancellation of the party with plans for a vacation.*

sug·ar·less (shŭg′ər lis), adj. without sugar: *sugarless candy.*

sugar loaf, 1 a solid cone-shaped mass of molded sugar. 2 something shaped like a sugar loaf, especially a cone-shaped hill.

sugar maple, a maple tree of eastern North America, valued for its hard, tough wood and for its sweet sap, from which maple sugar and maple syrup are made.

sug·ar·plum (shŭg′ər plum′), n. piece of candy; bonbon.

sug·ar·y (shŭg′ər ē), adj. 1 containing sugar; like sugar; sweet: *sugary drinks.* 2 outwardly, but not sincerely, pleasant or agreeable: *a sugary greeting.* —**sug′ar·i·ness,** n.

sug·gest (səg jest′ *or* sə jest′), v. 1 to put forward; propose: *She suggested a swim, and we all agreed.* 2 to bring to mind; call up the thought of: *The thought of summer suggests swimming, tennis, and hot weather.* 3 to show in an indirect way; hint: *His yawns suggest that he would like to go to bed.* —**sug·gest′er,** n. —**sug·gest′i·ble,** adj. —**sug·gest′i·bil′i·ty,** n.

sug·ges·tion (səg jes′chən *or* sə jes′chən), n. 1 thing suggested; proposal: *The picnic was an excellent suggestion.* 2 act of suggesting: *The suggestion of a swim made the children jump with joy.* 3 a very small amount; slight trace: *She spoke with just a suggestion of a French accent.*

sug·ges·tive (səg jes′tiv *or* sə jes′tiv), adj. 1 tending to suggest ideas, acts, or feelings: *The teacher gave an interesting and suggestive list of composition subjects.* 2 communicating a suggestion or hint of something: *a story suggestive of mystery.* 3 tending to suggest something that is improper or indecent. —**sug·ges′tive·ly,** adv. —**sug·ges′tive·ness,** n.

su·i·cid·al (sü′ə sī′dl), adj. 1 of or about suicide; leading to or causing suicide: *suicidal thoughts.* 2 inclined toward suicide: *Sick and depressed, he soon became suicidal.* 3 ruinous to your own interests; disastrous to yourself: *It would be suicidal for a store to sell many things below cost.* —**su′i·cid′al·ly,** adv.

su·i·cide (sü′ə sīd), n. 1 act of killing yourself on purpose. 2 person who commits suicide. 3 destruction of your own interests.

suit (süt), 1 n. set of clothes to be worn together. A man's suit consists of a coat, pants, and sometimes a vest. A woman's suit consists of a coat and either a skirt or pants. 2 v. to be agreeable, convenient, or acceptable to; please; satisfy: *Which date suits you best?* 3 v. to be suitable for; agree with: *A cold climate suits apples and wheat, but not oranges and tea.* 4 v. to make suitable; make fit: *to suit the punishment to the crime.* 5 v. to be becoming to: *That blue sweater suits you.* 6 n. case in a court of law; application to a court for justice: *He started a suit to collect damages for his injuries.* 7 n. one of the four sets of cards (spades, hearts, diamonds, and clubs) making up a deck. [See Word Story at **suite.**]

follow suit, 1 to play a card of the same suit as that first played. 2 to follow the example of another.

suit yourself, to do as you please.

suit·a·ble (sü′tə bəl), adj. right for the occasion; fitting; proper: *The park gives the children a suitable playground.* —**suit′a·bil′i·ty, suit′a·ble·ness,** n. —**suit′a·bly,** adv.

suit·case (süt′kās′), n. a flat, rectangular case for carrying clothing and other things while traveling.

suite (swēt), n. 1 set of connected rooms to be used by one person or family: *They have a suite of rooms at the hotel—a living room, bedroom, and bath.* 2 set of furniture that matches. 3 in music: **a** a series of connected instrumental movements: *a suite for strings.* **b** a set of dance tunes. 4 group of attendants: *The queen traveled with a suite of twelve.* ∎ Another word that sounds like this is **sweet.**

sui·tor (sü′tər), n. 1 man who is courting a woman. 2 person bringing suit in a court of law. 3 anyone who sues or petitions.

su·ki·ya·ki (sü′kē yä′kē *or* skē yä′kē), n. a Japanese dish consisting mainly of fried meat, onions, and other vegetables.

Suk·koth *or* **Suk·kot** (sŭk′əs), n. a Jewish harvest festival lasting eight or nine days, celebrated in September or October. Also, **Succoth.**

Su·la·we·si (sü′lä wä′sē), n. Celebes.

sul·fa (sul′fə), adj. of or belonging to a group of drugs derived from sulfanilamide, used in treating various bacterial infections.

sul·fa·nil·a·mide (sul′fə nil′ə mīd), n. an organic chemical compound containing sulfur. Sulfanilamide is the basis for most sulfa drugs.

sul·fate (sul′fāt), n. any salt of sulfuric acid.

sul·fide (sul′fīd), n. any compound of sulfur with another element or with a radical.

sul·fur (sul′fər), n. a light yellow nonmetallic element that burns easily, producing a suffocating odor. Sulfur is common in volcanic regions, occurring in nature in both free and combined forms, and is also in proteins. It is used in making matches, gunpowder, paper pulp, fertilizers, insecticides, etc., and in medicine. Also, **sulphur.** *Symbol:* S

sulfur dioxide, a heavy, colorless gas with a sharp odor, used as bleach, disinfectant, or preservative. Sulfur dioxide produced as a by-product of industry is a major environmental pollutant.

sul·fur·ic (sul fyür′ik), adj. of or containing sulfur.

sulfuric acid, a heavy, oily, colorless, and very corrosive acid containing sulfur. Sulfuric acid is used in making explosives and fertilizers, in refining petroleum, and in many other industrial processes.

sul·fur·ous (sul′fər əs *or* sul′fyər əs), adj. 1 of or containing sulfur. 2 like sulfur; like burning sulfur. 3 of or like the fires of hell; infernal.

sulk (sŭlk), 1 v. to be silent and bad-tempered; be sulky. 2 n. act of sulking; a fit of sulking: *When he didn't get the lead in the play, he went into a sulk that lasted a week.* 3 n.pl. **the sulks,** bad humor shown by sulking: *He seems to have a fit of the sulks.*

sulk·y (sul′kē), 1 adj. silent and bad-tempered because of resentment; sullen: *Some people become sulky when they cannot have their own way.* 2 n. a light one-horse carriage with two wheels, for one person, now commonly used in trotting races. ❑ adj. **sulk·i·er, sulk·i·est;** n., pl. **sulk·ies.** —**sulk′i·ly,** adv. —**sulk′i·ness,** n.

sul·len (sul′ən), adj. 1 silent because of bad temper or anger: *The sullen child refused to answer my question.* 2 gloomy; dismal: *The sullen skies threatened rain.* —**sul′len·ly,** adv. —**sul′len·ness,** n.

Sul·li·van (sul′ə vən), n. 1 Sir Arthur, 1842-1900, English composer and conductor. He wrote the music for many comic operettas created with Sir William Gilbert. 2 John L., 1858-1918, American boxer. ∎ John L. Sullivan won the heavyweight title in 1882 and defended it in 1888 and 1889. He was the last boxer to win a championship bout fighting with bare knuckles. 3 Louis, 1856-1924, American architect. He believed that "form follows function" and that buildings should express their structure in their appearance.

sul·ly (sul′ē), v. to soil, stain, or tarnish: *Smog sullied the usually attractive skyline of the city.* ❑ v. **sul·lied, sul·ly·ing.**

Sullivan building

S

a	hat	ė	term	ô	order	ch	child		a in about
ā	age	i	it	oi	oil	ng	long		e in taken
ä	far	ī	ice	ou	out	sh	she	ə ⟨	i in pencil
â	care	o	hot	u	cup	th	thin		o in lemon
e	let	ō	open	ù	put	ŦH	then		u in circus
ē	equal	ò	saw	ü	rule	zh	measure		

sul·phur (sul′fər), *n.* sulfur.

sul·tan (sult′n), *n.* ruler of a Muslim country.

sul·tan·a (sul tan′ə), *n.* **1** wife of a sultan. **2** mother, sister, or daughter of a sultan. ❑ *n., pl.* **sul·tan·as.**

sul·tan·ate (sult′n āt), *n.* **1** position, authority, or period of rule of a sultan. **2** territory ruled over by a sultan.

sul·try (sul′trē), *adj.* **1** hot, close, and moist: *We expect sultry weather during July.* ■ See Synonym Study at **hot. 2** hot or fiery: *a sultry sun, a sultry glance.* ❑ *adj.* **sul·tri·er, sul·tri·est. –sul′tri·ly,** *adv.* **–sul′tri·ness,** *n.*

sum (sum), **1** *n.* amount of money: *We paid a large sum for the house.* **2** *n.* number or quantity obtained by adding two or more numbers or quantities together: *The sum of 2 and 3 and 4 is 9.* **3** *n.* problem in arithmetic: *He can do easy sums in his head, but he has to use pencil and paper for hard ones.* **4** *n.* the whole amount; total amount: *The sum of scientific knowledge has increased greatly in this century.* **5** *v.* to find the total of. ❑ *v.* **summed, sum·ming.** ■ Another word that sounds like this is **some.**

sum up, to express or tell briefly: *Sum up the main points of the lesson in three sentences.*

> **WORD STORY**   **Sum** comes from a Latin word meaning "highest." **Summary** and **summit** come from the same Latin word. When Romans added numbers, they put the sum at the top. A summary sums up the main points. And a summit is the highest point.

su·mac (sü′mak *or* shü′mak), *n.* **1** any of numerous bushes or small trees with divided leaves that turn scarlet in the autumn and clusters of red or white fruit. Some sumacs are poisonous to the touch. **2** the dried leaves of certain sumacs, used in tanning and dyeing.

Su·ma·tra (sü mä′trə), *n.* large island in Indonesia, off the SE coast of Asia. **–Su·ma′tran,** *adj., n.*

Su·mer (sü′mər), *n.* ancient region in the valley of the Euphrates River, north of its mouth. See **Babylonia** for map.

Su·mer·i·an (sü mir′ē ən), **1** *adj.* of or about the people of Sumer or their language. **2** *n.* person who was born or lived in Sumer. **3** *n.* their language. Sumerian is recorded in cuneiform inscriptions.

sum·ma·rize (sum′ə rīz′), *v.* to make a summary of; give only the main points of; express briefly: *summarize the story of a book.* ❑ *v.* **sum·ma·rized, sum·ma·riz·ing. –sum′ma·ri·za′tion,** *n.* **–sum′ma·riz′er,** *n.*

sum·ma·ry (sum′ər ē), **1** *n.* a brief statement giving the main points: *The history book had a summary at the end of each chapter.* **2** *adj.* giving only the main points; brief; short. **3** *adj.* direct and prompt; without delay or formality: *summary vengeance. The governor took summary action to aid the flood victims.* ❑ *n., pl.* **sum·mar·ies.** [See Word Story at **sum.**] ■ Another word that sounds like this is **summery. –sum·mar′i·ly,** *adv.*

sum·ma·tion (sə mā′shən), *n.* **1** (in law) the final presentation of facts and arguments by the counsel for each side. **2** process of finding the sum or total; addition. **3** the total.

sum·mer (sum′ər), **1** *n.* the warmest season of the year; season of the year between spring and autumn. **2** *adj.* of or for summer; coming in summer: *summer heat, summer clothes.* **3** *v.* to pass the summer: *to summer at the seashore.*

sum·mer·house (sum′ər hous′), *n.* building in a park or garden in which to sit in warm weather. Summerhouses often have no walls. ❑ *n., pl.* **sum·mer·hous·es** (sum′ər hou′ziz).

summer school, classes taught during the summer so that students can make up failures or graduate earlier.

sum·mer·time (sum′ər tīm′), *n.* the summer season.

sum·mer·y (sum′ər ē), *adj.* of or for summer; like summer: *summery heat, a summery day in spring.* ■ Another word that sounds like this is **summary.**

sum·mit (sum′it), *n.* the highest point; top: *the summit of a mountain. The summit of her ambition was to be a doctor.* [See Word Story at **sum.**]

summit meeting, a meeting between heads of governments, especially for the purpose of settling disagreements.

sum·mon (sum′ən), *v.* **1** to call with authority; order to come; send for: *I was summoned to the principal's office. An urgent phone call summoned me home.* ■ See Synonym Study at **call. 2** to call together: *summon an assembly.* **3** to order or notify formally to appear before a court of law or judge, especially to answer a charge. **4** to stir to action; rouse: *We summoned our courage and entered the deserted house.* **–sum′mon·er,** *n.*

sum·mons (sum′ənz), *n.* **1** a formal order or notice to appear before a court of law or judge, especially to answer a charge: *I received a summons for speeding.* **2** an urgent call; a summoning command, message, or signal: *I hurried in response to my friend's summons for help.* ❑ *n., pl.* **sum·mons·es.**

sump (sump), *n.* pit or reservoir for collecting water or other liquid waste in a basement, factory, mine, etc.

sump pump, pump which removes liquid from a sump when the liquid reaches a certain level.

sump·tu·ous (sump′chü əs), *adj.* involving great expense; lavish and costly; magnificent; rich: *sumptuous jewels, a sumptuous banquet.* **–sump′tu·ous·ly,** *adv.* **–sump′tu·ous·ness,** *n.*

Sum·ter (sum′tər), *n.* Fort, fort in the harbor of Charleston, South Carolina. The Civil War began with a Confederate attack on this fort on April 12, 1861.

sun (sun), **1** *n.* the brightest object in the sky; the star around which Earth and the other planets revolve and which supplies them with light and heat. It is a glowing ball of hot gases about 93 million miles (150 million kilometers) from Earth. **2** *n.* the light and warmth of the sun: *to sit in the sun.* **3** *v.* to expose to the sun's rays: *The swimmers sunned themselves on the beach.* **4** *n.* any star. ❑ *v.* **sunned, sun·ning.** ■ Another word that sounds like this is **son.**

Sun., Sunday.

sun·bathe (sun′bāтн′), *v.* to expose yourself to the sun's rays or to a sunlamp. ❑ *v.* **sun·bathed, sun·bath·ing. –sun′bath′er,** *n.*

sun·beam (sun′bēm′), *n.* ray of sunlight: *A sunbeam brightened the child's hair to gold.*

Sun·belt or **sun·belt** (sun′belt′), *n.* those areas that form the southern boundaries of the United States, from Virginia to southern California.

sun·block (sun′blok′), *n.* a very effective sunscreen that protects the skin against sunburn and blocks ultraviolet rays.

sun·bon·net (sun′bon′it), *n.* a large bonnet that shades the face and neck.

sun·burn (sun′bėrn′), **1** *n.* redness or blistering of the skin, caused by the sun's rays or by a sunlamp. A sunburn is often red and painful. **2** *v.* to burn the skin by the sun's rays or by a sunlamp. **3** *v.* to become sunburned: *My skin sunburns very quickly.* ❑ *v.* **sun·burned** or **sun·burnt, sun·burn·ing.**

sun·burnt (sun′bėrnt′), *v.* a past tense and a past participle of **sunburn.**

sun·dae (sun′dā′ *or* sun′dē), *n.* dish of ice cream served with syrup, crushed fruits, nuts, etc., over it.

sunbonnet

Sun·da Islands (sun′də), a chain of islands mostly in Indonesia, including Sumatra, Borneo, Bali, and Timor.

Sun·day (sun′dā′ *or* sun′dē), **1** *n.* the first day of the week. **2** *adj.* of or on Sundays; not everyday or regular; occasional: *a Sunday driver, Sunday painters.* [See word history information at **Monday.**]

Sunday school, 1 school held on Sunday for teaching religion. **2** its members.

sun·der (sun′dər), *v.* to break apart; separate; part; sever; split: *Distance often sunders friends.*

sun·dew (sun′dü′), *n.* any of several small plants, related to the Venus's-flytrap, that grow in bogs and have hairy, sticky leaves with which they capture and digest insects.

sun·di·al (sun′dī/əl), *n.* device for telling the time of day by the position of a shadow; dial. The sun strikes an upright pointer, casting a shadow onto a dial indicating the hours.

sun·down (sun′doun/), *n.* sunset: *We'll be home by sundown.*

sun·dried (sun′drīd/), *adj.* dried in the sun: *sun-dried tomatoes.*

sun·dries (sun′drēz), *n.pl.* various things; items not named; odds and ends: *I spent $15 for sundries at the drugstore.*

sun·dry (sun′drē), *adj.* several; various: *From sundry hints, I guessed I was to be given a bicycle for my birthday.*

sun·fish (sun′fish/), *n.* **1** any of several very large fishes with very small fins and no scales, living in warm seas. **2** any of numerous small freshwater fishes of North America, used for food. Sunfish are related to perch. □ *n., pl.* **sun·fish** or **sun·fish·es.**

sun·flow·er (sun′flou/ər), *n.* any of several tall plants that have large yellow flowers with brown centers. Sunflower seeds are used as food and to produce oil for cooking.

sunflower

sung (sung), *v.* a past tense and past participle of **sing:** *Many songs were sung at the concert.*

sun·glass·es (sun′glas/iz), *n.pl.* eyeglasses with colored lenses, worn to protect the eyes from the glare of the sun.

sun god, god of the sun. Many different peoples have worshiped sun gods. Apollo and Ra were sun gods.

sunk (sungk), *v.* a past tense and past participle of **sink:** *The ship had sunk to the bottom.*

sunk·en (sung′kən), *adj.* **1** sunk: *They discovered a sunken ship.* **2** submerged; underwater: *The boat struck a sunken rock.* **3** lower than the surrounding level: *We walked down three steps to the sunken garden.* **4** fallen in; hollow: *After the long illness, his cheeks were pale and sunken.*

sun·lamp (sun′lamp/), *n.* lamp for producing ultraviolet rays similar to those in sunlight.

sun·less (sun′lis), *adj.* without sun; without sunlight: *a sunless day.*

sun·light (sun′līt/), *n.* the light of the sun: *We hung the wash out to dry in the sunlight.*

sun·lit (sun′lit/), *adj.* lit by the sun: *They held the reception in a sunlit room overlooking the garden.*

Sun·ni (sun′ē), *n.* **1** sect of Islam believing that Muslim leadership passed from Muhammad to elected members of his tribe. **2** member of this sect; Sunnite. □ *n., pl.* **Sun·ni** or **Sun·nis** for 2.

Sun·nism (sun′iz əm), *n.* beliefs of Sunni Muslims.

Sun·nite (sun′it), *n.* Sunni (def. 2).

sun·ny (sun′ē), *adj.* **1** having much sunshine or sunlight: *a sunny day.* **2** exposed to, lighted by, or warmed by the direct rays of the sun: *a sunny room.* **3** bright; cheerful; happy: *The baby gave a sunny smile.* □ *adj.* **sun·ni·er, sun·ni·est.** ■ Another word that sounds like this is **sonny.**

sun parlor, room with many windows to let in sunlight.

sun porch, porch enclosed largely by glass.

sun·rise (sun′rīz/), *n.* **1** the first appearance of the sun above the horizon in the morning. **2** the time when the sun first appears; the beginning of day. **3** the display of light or color in the sky at this time.

sun·room (sun′rüm/), *n.* room with many windows to let in sunlight.

sun·screen (sun′skrēn/), *n.* a chemical compound that screens out the ultraviolet rays of the sun, used in skin lotions to prevent sunburn.

sun·set (sun′set/), *n.* **1** the last appearance of the sun above the horizon in the evening. **2** the time when the sun last appears; the close of day. **3** the display of light or color in the sky at this time.

sun·shade (sun′shād/), *n.* an umbrella, parasol, awning, etc., used to provide protection against the sun.

sun·shine (sun′shīn/), *n.* **1** light or rays of the sun. **2** brightness; cheerfulness; happiness: *Her weekly visits bring sunshine to her grandparents.*

sun·shin·y (sun′shī/nē), *adj.* **1** having much sunshine. **2** bright; cheerful; happy: *He had a sunshiny smile.* □ *adj.* **sun·shin·i·er, sun·shin·i·est.**

sun·spot (sun′spot/), *n.* one of the dark spots that appear from time to time on the surface of the sun, not visible to the naked eye. Disturbances of Earth's magnetic field often occur when sunspots appear.

sun·stroke (sun′strōk/), *n.* a sudden illness caused by too much or too long an exposure to the sun's rays. Sunstroke results in fever, dry skin, extreme exhaustion, and often loss of consciousness.

sun·tan (sun′tan/), *n.* the reddish brown color of someone's skin tanned by the sun or by a sunlamp.

sun·up (sun′up/), *n.* sunrise.

sun·ward (sun′wərd), *adv., adj.* toward the sun: *to glance sunward, the sunward side of the tree.*

Sun Yat-sen (sun′ yät′sen′), 1866-1925, Chinese revolutionary and political leader, president of China from 1921 to 1922. He played a central part in the overthrow of the Chinese empire.

sup (sup), *v.* to eat the evening meal; take supper: *We supped on pasta.* □ *v.* **supped, sup·ping.**

sup., **1** above. **2** superior. **3** superlative. **4** supplement. **5** supplementary.

su·per (sü′pər), **1** *n.* superintendent. **2** *n.* a supernumerary. **3** *adj.* INFORMAL. excellent: *We thought the movie was super and stayed to see it again.* **4** *adj.* special; more than normal: *super heroes, super powers.*

super-, *prefix.* **1** very large, powerful, or remarkable: *supercomputer = a very powerful computer.* **2** in large amounts; in a major way; very: *superabundant = very abundant.* **3** more than: *supernatural = more than natural; superhuman = more than human.* **4** above; on top of: *superscript = something written above.*

su·per·a·bun·dance (sü′pər ə bun′dəns), *n.* **1** very great abundance: *This year we have had a superabundance of rain.* **2** a greater amount than is needed.

su·per·a·bun·dant (sü′pər ə bun′dənt), *adj.* **1** very abundant. **2** more than enough.

su·perb (sù pėrb′), *adj.* **1** very fine; first-rate; excellent: *The singer gave a superb performance.* **2** rich; elegant: *a superb dinner.* **3** grand and stately; majestic; magnificent; splendid: *Mountain scenery is superb.* —**su·perb′ly,** *adv.* —**su·perb′ness,** *n.*

su·per·charge (sü′pər chärj′), *v.* to increase the power of an internal-combustion engine by fitting it with a supercharger. □ *v.* **su·per·charged, su·per·charg·ing.**

su·per·charg·er (sü′pər chär′jər), *n.* a pump, compressor, or similar device that increases the amount of fuel vapor forced into the cylinders of an internal-combustion engine. Superchargers are used to increase the power of racecar and aircraft engines.

su·per·cil·i·ous (sü′pər sil′ē əs), *adj.* proud, haughty, and contemptuous; disdainful; showing scorn or indifference because of a feeling of superiority: *a supercilious smile, a supercilious stare.* —**su′per·cil′i·ous·ly,** *adv.* —**su′per·cil′i·ous·ness,** *n.*

su·per·com·put·er (sü′pər kəm pyü′tər), *n.* a very powerful, high-speed computer that can perform several hundred million operations a second and work on many parts of a problem simultaneously.

su·per·con·duc·tiv·i·ty (sü′pər kon′duk tiv′ə tē), *n.* ability to conduct electric current with no resistance at very low temperatures.

su·per·con·duc·tor (sü′pər kən duk′tər), *n.* any chemical compound or metal that can conduct electric current with no resistance at extremely low temperatures.

su·per·con·ti·nent (sü′pər kon′tə nənt), *n.* a very large landmass, believed by earth scientists to have formed long ago when several continents drifted together, and to have separated again into continental landmasses.

su·per·cool (sü′pər kül′), *v.* to cool a liquid below its usual freezing point without causing it to solidify.

a	hat	ė	term	ô	order	ch	child		
ā	age	i	it	oi	oil	ng	long	ə	a in about
ä	far	ī	ice	ou	out	sh	she		e in taken
â	care	o	hot	u	cup	th	thin		i in pencil
e	let	ō	open	ů	put	ŦH	then		o in lemon
ē	equal	ò	saw	ü	rule	zh	measure		u in circus

S

su·per·fi·cial (sü′pər fish′əl), *adj.* **1** of, on, or at the surface: *superficial measurement. His burns were superficial and soon healed.* **2** concerned with or understanding only what is on the surface; not thorough; shallow: *superficial knowledge.* **3** not real or genuine: *a superficial friendship.* **—su′per·fi′cial·ly,** *adv.* **—su′per·fi′cial·ness,** *n.*

su·per·fi·ci·al·i·ty (sü′pər fish′ē al′ə tē), *n.* **1** superficial quality or condition; shallowness. **2** something superficial. ❑ *n., pl.* **su·per·fi·ci·al·i·ties** for 2.

su·per·fine (sü′pər fīn′), *adj.* **1** very fine; extra fine: *superfine sugar.* **2** too refined; too nice.

su·per·flu·i·ty (sü′pər flü′ə tē), *n.* **1** a greater amount than is needed; excess: *Our orchard gives us a superfluity of apples.* **2** something not needed: *Luxuries are superfluities.* ❑ *n., pl.* **su·per·flu·i·ties** for 2.

su·per·flu·ous (sü pèr′flü əs), *adj.* **1** more than is needed; excessive; surplus: *Superfluous words made the message seem confusing.* **2** needless; unnecessary: *A raincoat is superfluous on a clear day.* **—su·per′flu·ous·ly,** *adv.* **—su·per′flu·ous·ness,** *n.*

su·per·gi·ant (sü′pər jī′ənt), *n.* any of many huge, extremely bright stars. Some are 10,000 times as bright as the sun.

su·per·high·way (sü′pər hī′wā), *n.* highway for fast traveling. Superhighways are often very long and have two or more lanes for traffic in each direction, divided by a median strip.

su·per·hu·man (sü′pər hyü′mən), *adj.* **1** above or beyond what is human: *superhuman beings.* **2** above or beyond ordinary human power, experience, etc.: *With a superhuman burst of speed, the runner set a new Olympic record.* **—su′per·hu′man·ly,** *adv.*

su·per·im·pose (sü′pər im pōz′), *v.* to put on top of something else: *The technician superimposed one photographic image over another.* ❑ *v.* **su·per·im·posed, su·per·im·pos·ing.**

su·per·in·tend (sü′pər in tend′), *v.* to oversee and direct work or workers; manage a place, institution, etc.

su·per·in·tend·ence (sü′pər in ten′dəns), *n.* guidance and direction; management.

su·per·in·tend·ent (sü′pər in ten′dənt), *n.* person who oversees, directs, or manages; supervisor: *a superintendent of schools, a factory superintendent.*

su·per·i·or (sə pir′ē ər), **1** *adj.* above the average; very good; excellent: *superior work in school.* ■ See Synonym Study at **excellent.** **2** *adj.* higher in quality; better; greater: *a superior blend of coffee. We lost the baseball game to a superior team.* **3** *adj.* higher in position, rank, importance, etc.: *a superior officer.* **4** *n.* person who is superior in rank, position, or ability: *As a violin player, he has no superior. A captain is a lieutenant's superior.* **5** *adj.* showing a feeling of being above others; proud: *superior airs, superior manners.* **6** *n.* head of a monastery or convent. **—su·per′i·or·ly,** *adv.*

superior to, 1 higher than; above: *Apes are considered superior to most other animals in intelligence.* **2** better than; greater than: *This restaurant's food is superior to any other.* **3** not giving in to; above yielding to: *A wise person is superior to flattery.*

Superior, *n.* **Lake,** the largest of the five Great Lakes. It is the largest body of fresh water in the world.

WORD STORY Lake Superior got its name from definition 3 of superior, "higher in position." It is 600 feet (183 meters) above sea level, 21 feet (6 meters) higher than Lake Huron, into which its waters flow.

su·per·i·or·i·ty (sə pir′ē ôr′ə tē), *n.* superior state or quality: *Our team showed its superiority by winning all its matches this year.*

su·per·la·tive (sə pèr′lə tiv), **1** *adj.* very good; above all others; supreme: *superlative skills, superlative wisdom.* **2** *n.* person or thing above all others; supreme example. **3** *n.* a form of a word or combination of words to show the extreme degree or greatest amount. *Fastest* is the superlative of *fast. Best* is the superlative of *good. Most quickly* is the superlative of *quickly.* **4** *adj.* showing the highest degree of comparison of an adjective or adverb. *Best* is the superlative form of *good.* **—su·per′la·tive·ly,** *adv.* **—su·per′la·tive·ness,** *n.*

talk in superlatives, to exaggerate.

su·per·man (sü′pər man′), *n.* person having more than human powers. ❑ *n., pl.* **su·per·men.**

su·per·mar·ket (sü′pər mär′kit), *n.* a large store for groceries and household articles in which customers select their purchases from open shelves and pay for them just before leaving.

su·per·nat·u·ral (sü′pər nach′ər əl), **1** *adj.* beyond the forces or laws of nature; of or about God, angels, ghosts, or other spirits: *The movie was a supernatural horror film.* **2** *n.* **the supernatural,** events, beings, or powers beyond the forces or laws of nature. **—su′per·nat′ur·al·ly,** *adv.* **—su′per·nat′ur·al·ness,** *n.*

su·per·nat·u·ral·ism (sü′pər nach′ər ə liz′əm), *n.* **1** supernatural character or agency. **2** belief in the supernatural.

su·per·no·va (sü′pər nō′və), *n.* a kind of star that explodes and becomes far brighter than an ordinary nova, as much as 10 billion times as bright as the sun. ❑ *n., pl.* **su·per·no·vas, su·per·no·vae** (sü′pər nō′vē).

su·per·nu·me·rar·y (sü′pər nü′mə rer′ē), **1** *adj.* more than the usual or necessary number; extra. **2** *n.* an extra person or thing. ❑ *n., pl.* **su·per·nu·me·rar·ies.**

su·per·pow·er (sü′pər pou′ər), *n.* **1** nation so great or strong as a power that its actions and policies greatly affect those of smaller, less powerful nations. **2** power on an extraordinary or extensive scale.

su·per·script (sü′pər skript), **1** *n.* number, letter, etc., written above and to one side of a symbol. In $a^3 = b^n$ the *3* and the *n* are superscripts. **2** *adj.* written above.

su·per·sede (sü′pər sēd′), *v.* **1** to take the place of; cause to be set aside; displace: *Refrigerators have superseded iceboxes.* **2** to fill the place of; replace: *A new governor superseded the old one.* ❑ *v.* **su·per·sed·ed, su·per·sed·ing.**

su·per·sen·si·tive (sü′pər sen′sə tiv), *adj.* extremely sensitive. **—su′per·sen′si·tive·ly,** *adv.* **—su′per·sen′si·tive·ness,** *n.*

su·per·set (sü′pər set′), *n.* (in mathematics) a set that includes all members of another set.

su·per·son·ic (sü′pər son′ik), *adj.* **1** faster than the speed of sound in air, about 1087 feet (331 meters) per second at sea level. **2** able to move faster than the speed of sound: *supersonic aircraft.* **3** of or about sound waves beyond the limit of human ability to hear (above frequencies of 20,000 hertz). **—su′per·son′i·cal·ly,** *adv.*

su·per·star (sü′pər stär′), *n.* person, often an entertainer or athlete, who is exceptionally successful in his or her field.

su·per·sta·tion (sü′pər stā′shən), *n.* a TV or radio broadcasting company that uses cable or satellite systems to reach a national audience.

su·per·sti·tion (sü′pər stish′ən), *n.* **1** belief or practice founded on ignorant fear or mistaken reverence: *A common superstition considers 13 an unlucky number.* **2** an unreasoning fear of what is unknown or mysterious; unreasoning expectation.

su·per·sti·tious (sü′pər stish′əs), *adj.* full of superstition; likely to believe superstitions; of or caused by superstition: *a superstitious habit, a superstitious belief.* **—su′per·sti′tious·ly,** *adv.* **—su′per·sti′tious·ness,** *n.*

su·per·struc·ture (sü′pər struk′chər), *n.* **1** all of a building above the foundation. **2** parts of a ship above the main deck. **3** structure built on something else.

su·per·tank·er (sü′pər tang′kər), *n.* a very large tanker ship, able to carry more than 100,000 tons (90,000 metric tons) of cargo.

su·per·vene (sü′pər vēn′), *v.* to happen as a consequence of, or in reaction to. ❑ *v.* **su·per·vened, su·per·ven·ing.**

su·per·vise (sü′pər vīz), *v.* to look after and direct work or workers, a process, etc.; oversee; superintend; manage: *Study halls are supervised by teachers.* ❑ *v.* **su·per·vised, su·per·vis·ing.**

su·per·vi·sion (sü′pər vizh′ən), *n.* management; direction: *The house was built under the careful supervision of an architect.*

su·per·vi·sor (sü′pər vī′zər), *n.* person who supervises.

su·per·vi·so·ry (sü′pər vī′zər ē), *adj.* **1** of or about a supervisor; having to do with supervision: *supervisory responsibilities.* **2** supervising.

su·pine (sü pīn′), *adj.* **1** lying flat on the back: *a supine person.* **2** lazily inactive; listless. **—su·pine′ly,** *adv.* **—su·pine′ness,** *n.*

sup·per (sup′ər), *n.* the evening meal; meal eaten early in the evening if dinner is near noon, or late in the evening if dinner is at six or later. **—sup′per·less,** *n.*

sup·per·time (sup′ər tīm′), *n.* the time at which supper is served.

sup·plant (sə plant′), *v.* **1** to take the place of; displace or set aside: *Machinery has supplanted hand labor.* **2** to take the place of by unfair methods or by treacherous means: *The prince plotted to supplant the king.* **—sup′plan·ta′tion,** *n.* **—sup·plant′er,** *n.*

sup·ple (sup′əl), *adj.* **1** bending or folding easily: *supple leather.* **2** capable of bending easily; moving easily or nimbly: *a supple dancer.* **3** readily adaptable to different ideas, circumstances, people, etc.; yielding: *a supple mind.* ❑ *adj.* **sup·pler, sup·plest.** **—sup′ple·ly,** *adv.* **—sup′ple·ness,** *n.*

sup·ple·ment (sup′lə mənt *for noun;* sup′lə ment *for verb*), **1** *n.* something added to complete a thing, or to make it larger or better. Many newspapers and periodicals have supplements that are usually of a special character and issued as an additional feature. **2** *v.* to supply what is lacking in; add to; complete: *He supplements his diet with vitamin pills.* **3** *n.* something added to supply a deficiency: *a diet supplement.* **—sup′ple·men·ta′tion,** *n.*

sup·ple·men·tal (sup′lə men′tl), *adj.* supplementary.

sup·ple·men·tar·y (sup′lə men′tər ē), *adj.* added to supply what is lacking; additional: *supplementary instruction.*

supplementary angle, either of two angles which together form an angle of 180 degrees: *A 60-degree angle is the supplementary angle of a 120-degree angle.* See picture at **angle**[1].

sup·pli·ant (sup′lē ənt), **1** *adj.* asking humbly and earnestly: *He sent a suppliant message for help.* **2** *n.* person who asks humbly and earnestly: *I knelt as a suppliant before her.* **—sup′pli·ant·ly,** *adv.*

sup·pli·cant (sup′lə kənt), *n., adj.* suppliant.

sup·pli·cate (sup′lə kāt), *v.* **1** to beg humbly and earnestly: *They supplicated the judge to pardon the prisoner.* **2** to pray humbly. ❑ *v.* **sup·pli·cat·ed, sup·pli·cat·ing.** **—sup′pli·cat′ing·ly,** *adv.* **—sup′pli·ca′tor,** *n.*

sup·pli·ca·tion (sup′lə kā′shən), *n.* **1** a humble and earnest request or prayer: *Supplications to God arose from many of the people in the besieged town.* **2** act of supplicating.

sup·ply (sə plī′), **1** *v.* to provide what someone or something needs; furnish: *Many cities supply books for children in school.* **2** *n.* quantity ready for use; stock: *The school gets its supplies of books, paper, pencils, chalk, etc., from the city.* **3** *n.* quantity of an article in the market ready for purchase, especially at a given price: *a supply of coffee.* **4** *n.pl.* **supplies,** the food, equipment, etc., necessary for an army, expedition, or the like. **5** *v.* to satisfy a want, need, etc.: *There was just enough to supply the demand.* **6** *n.* act of supplying. ❑ *v.* **sup·plied, sup·ply·ing;** *n., pl.* **sup·plies.** **—sup·pli′er,** *n.*

sup·port (sə pôrt′), **1** *v.* to give strength or courage to; keep up; help: *Hope supported us during our troubles.* **2** *v.* to provide for: *support a large family.* **3** *v.* to maintain, keep up, or keep going: *This city supports two orchestras.* **4** *v.* to be in favor of; back; second: *She supports the amendment.* **5** *v.* to help prove; bear out: *The facts support her claim.* **6** *n.* act of supporting: *He spoke in support of the new proposal.* **7** *v.* to keep from falling; hold up: *Walls support the roof.* **8** *n.* condition of being supported: *This argument lacks support.*

support (def. 10)

9 *n.* help or assistance: *They need our financial support.* **10** *n.* person or thing that holds something up; prop: *The neck is the support of the head.* **—sup·port′er,** *n.*

sup·port·a·ble (sə pôr′tə bəl), *adj.* capable of being supported; bearable or endurable. **—sup·port′a·bil′i·ty,** *n.* **—sup·port′a·bly,** *adv.*

sup·por·tive (sə pôr′tiv), *adj.* providing support; supporting: *supportive evidence.* **—sup·por′tive·ly,** *adv.* **—sup·por′tive·ness,** *n.*

sup·pose (sə pōz′), *v.* **1** to consider as possible; take for granted; assume: *Suppose you are late, what excuse will you make?* **2** to believe, think, or imagine: *I suppose he will stay.* **3** to expect; require: *I'm supposed to be there early.* ❑ *v.* **sup·posed, sup·pos·ing.**

WORD STORY **Suppose** comes from Latin words meaning "to put" and "under." **Hypothesis** comes from Greek words meaning "to put" and "under." Today we may ask whether thoughts have any basis, or foundation. The notion of ideas resting on top of each other, like stones in a wall, occurs in many different languages.

sup·posed (sə pōzd′), *adj.* accepted as true; considered as possible or probable; accepted as true: *The supposed beggar was really a prince.* **—sup·pos·ed·ly** (sə pō′zid lē), *adv.*

sup·pos·ing (sə pō′zing), *conj.* in the event that; if: *Supposing it rains, shall we go?*

sup·po·si·tion (sup′ə zish′ən), *n.* **1** thing supposed; belief; opinion: *the supposition that he was already there.* **2** act of supposing.

sup·pos·i·to·ry (sə poz′ə tôr′ē), *n.* medicine in the form of a cone or cylinder to be put into the rectum or vagina, where it dissolves. ❑ *n., pl.* **sup·pos·i·to·ries.**

sup·press (sə pres′), *v.* **1** to put an end to; stop by force; put down: *suppress a rebellion.* **2** to keep in; hold back; keep from appearing: *She suppressed a yawn.* **3** to hold in a feeling, etc.: *suppress a desire.* **4** to keep secret; prevent from being published: *suppress the news.* **—sup·press′or** or **sup·pres′ser,** *n.*

sup·pres·sant (sə pres′ənt), *n.* substance that prevents some unwanted action or condition: *an allergy suppressant.*

sup·pres·sion (sə presh′ən), *n.* **1** act of putting down by force or authority; putting an end to: *the suppression of the revolt.* **2** act of keeping secret: *the suppression of the facts about the case.*

sup·pres·sive (sə pres′iv), *adj.* tending to suppress; causing suppression.

su·pra·re·nal gland (sü′prə rē′nl), adrenal gland.

su·prem·a·cist (sə prem′ə sist), *n.* person who believes that one group of people is superior to another: *a white supremacist.*

su·prem·a·cy (sə prem′ə sē), *n.* **1** condition of being supreme. **2** supreme authority or power.

su·preme (sə prēm′), *adj.* **1** highest in rank or authority: *a supreme ruler.* **2** highest in degree or quality; greatest; utmost: *supreme courage.* **—su·preme′ly,** *adv.* **—su·preme′ness,** *n.*

Supreme Being, God.

United States Supreme Court building

Supreme Court, **1** the highest court in the United States, which meets at Washington, D.C. It is made up of a chief justice and eight associate justices. **2** the highest court in some states of the United States. **3** a similar court in other countries.

a	hat	ė	term	ô	order	ch	child		
ā	age	i	it	oi	oil	ng	long	⎧	a in about
ä	far	ī	ice	ou	out	sh	she	ə ⎨	e in taken
â	care	o	hot	u	cup	th	thin		i in pencil
e	let	ō	open	ů	put	ŦH	then		o in lemon
ē	equal	ò	saw	ü	rule	zh	measure	⎩	u in circus

S

Supt. or **supt.,** superintendent.

sur·charge (sèr′chärj′), **1** *n.* an additional or extra charge: *We had to pay a surcharge for the extra weight of our luggage.* **2** *v.* to charge extra. **3** *v.* to overload; overburden: *The mourner's heart was surcharged with grief.* **4** *n.* an additional mark printed on a postage stamp to change its value, date, etc. **5** *v.* to print a surcharge on a postage stamp. ❑ *v.* **sur·charged, sur·charg·ing.**

sur·coat (sèr′kōt′), *n.* an outer coat, especially such a coat worn by knights over their armor.

surd (sèrd), *n.* irrational number.

sure (shùr), **1** *adj.* free from doubt; certain; having ample reason for belief; confident; positive: *She is sure of success.* **2** *adj.* to be trusted; safe; reliable: *The only sure way of sending a message was by radio.* **3** *adj.* never missing, slipping, etc.; unfailing; unerring: *sure aim, a sure touch.* **4** *adj.* without any doubt or question: *sure proof.* **5** *adj.* firm; stable: *sure ground.* **6** *adj.* certain to come, to be, or to happen: *It is sure to snow this winter.* **7** *adv.* INFORMAL. surely; certainly. ❑ *adj.* **sur·er, sur·est.** —**sure′ness,** *n.*

for sure, certainly; undoubtedly.

make sure, 1 to do something that makes an event certain to happen: *Make sure your brother does his homework.* **2** to get precise knowledge of: *Did you make sure of the weekend bus schedule?*
to be sure, of course; certainly: *The weather, to be sure, was unfavorable.*

sure·fire (shùr′fīr′), *adj.* INFORMAL. sure to be successful: *a sure-fire solution to the problem.*

sure·foot·ed (shùr′fùt′id), *adj.* unlikely to stumble, slip, or fall. —**sure′foot′ed·ly,** *adv.* —**sure′foot′ed·ness,** *n.*

sure·ly (shùr′lē), *adv.* **1** undoubtedly; certainly; of course: *Half a loaf is surely better than none.* **2** without mistake; without missing, slipping, etc.; firmly: *The goat leaped surely from rock to rock.*

sur·e·ty (shùr′ə tē), *n.* **1** security against loss, damage, or failure to do something: *An insurance company gives surety against loss by fire.* **2** person who agrees to be responsible for another: *She was surety for her sister's appearance in court on the day set.* **3** OLD USE. a sure thing; certainty. ❑ *n., pl.* **sur·e·ties.**

surf (sèrf), **1** *n.* waves of the sea breaking in a foaming mass on the shore or upon shoals, reefs, etc. **2** *n.* the deep pounding or thundering sound of waves. **3** *v.* to ride on the crest of a wave, especially with a surfboard. **4** *v.* to search or investigate in a rapid, random way: *surfing the Internet, to surf on cable TV for an hour.* ■ Another word that sounds like this is **serf.** —**surf′er,** *n.*

sur·face (sèr′fis), **1** *n.* the outside of anything: *the surface of a golf ball. An egg has a smooth surface.* **2** *n.* the top of the ground or soil, or of a body of water or other liquid: *The stone sank beneath the surface of the water.* **3** *n.* any face or side of a thing: *A cube has six surfaces.* **4** *n.* the outward appearance: *He seems rough, but you will find him very kind below the surface.* **5** *adj.* of or on the surface; about the surface: *a surface view.* **6** *adj.* superficial; external: *surface emotions.* **7** *v.* to put a surface on; make smooth: *surface a road.* **8** *v.* to rise to the surface: *The submarine surfaced.* **9** *v.* to come into public notice: *News of the new drug surfaced last week.* ❑ *v.* **sur·faced, sur·fac·ing.**

surf·board (sèrf′bôrd′), *n.* a long, narrow board for riding the surf.

surf·cast·ing (sèrf′kast′ing), *n.* sport of fishing in the sea by casting a line from the shore.

sur·feit (sèr′fit), **1** *n.* too much; excess: *A surfeit of food makes you sick.* **2** *n.* disgust or nausea caused by too much of anything. **3** *v.* to feed or supply too much.

surf·ing (sèr′fing), *n.* **1** act or sport of riding the surf on a surfboard. **2** act or process of looking for something, such as information on the Internet or an interesting TV show, in a random, rapid way: *I've been surfing on-line for an hour but I still can't find anyone to discuss Jane Austen with.*

surge (sèrj), **1** *v.* to rise and fall; move like waves: *A great wave surged over us. The crowd surged through the streets.* **2** *n.* a swelling motion; sweep or rush, especially of waves: *Our boat was upset by a surge.* **3** *n.* something like a wave: *A surge of anger swept over him.* **4** *n.* power surge. ❑ *v.* **surged, surg·ing.** ■ Another word that sounds like this is **serge.**

sur·geon (sèr′jən), *n.* doctor who performs operations: *A surgeon removed the patient's ruptured appendix.*

Surgeon General, 1 chief medical officer of the U.S. Public Health Service. **2** chief medical officer of one of the armed forces of the United States.

surge protector, an electronic device that prevents a power surge from reaching and damaging electrical equipment such as a computer or TV set.

sur·ger·y (sèr′jər ē), *n.* **1** art and science of treating diseases, injuries, etc., by operations and instruments: *The discovery of anesthesia transformed surgery.* **2** operating room or other area where surgical operations are performed. **3** the work performed by a surgeon; operation. ❑ *n., pl.* **sur·ger·ies** for 2,3.

sur·gi·cal (sèr′jə kəl), *adj.* **1** of or about surgery: *a surgical patient.* **2** used in surgery: *surgical instruments:* **3** performed by a surgeon: *a surgical operation.* —**sur′gi·cal·ly,** *adv.*

sur·gi·cen·ter (sùr′jə sen′tər), *n.* a medical center where minor surgery is performed on outpatients.

Sur·i·name (sùr′ə nä′mə), *n.* country in N South America, on the Atlantic. *Capital:* Paramaribo.

sur·ly (sèr′lē), *adj.* unfriendly; rude; bad-tempered: *They got a surly answer from their grouchy neighbor.* ❑ *adj.* **sur·li·er, sur·li·est.** —**sur′li·ness,** *n.*

sur·mise (sər mīz′ *for verb;* sər mīz′ *or* sèr′mīz *for noun*), **1** *v.* to guess: *We surmised that the delay was caused by some accident.* **2** *n.* formation of an idea with little or no evidence; act of guessing: *Their guilt was a matter of surmise; there was no proof.* ❑ *v.* **sur·mised, sur·mis·ing.**

sur·mount (sər mount′), *v.* **1** to overcome: *She surmounted many difficulties.* **2** to rise above: *That mountain surmounts all the peaks near it.* **3** to be above or on top of: *A statue surmounts the monument.* —**sur·mount′a·ble,** *adj.*

sur·name (sèr′nām′), **1** *n.* a last name; family name: *Stein is the surname of Jane Stein.* **2** *n.* name added to someone's real name: *William I of England had the surname "the Conqueror."* **3** *v.* to give an added name to; call by a surname. ❑ *v.* **sur·named, sur·nam·ing.**

sur·pass (sər pas′), *v.* **1** to do better than; be greater than; excel: *She surpasses her sister in arithmetic.* **2** to be too much or too great for; go beyond; exceed: *The beauty of the sunset surpassed description.* —**sur·pass′a·ble,** *adj.* —**sur·pass′ing·ly,** *adv.*

sur·plice (sèr′plis), *n.* a white gown with broad sleeves worn by members of the clergy and choir singers over their other clothes.

sur·plus (sèr′pləs *or* sèr′plus), **1** *n.* amount over and above what is needed; extra quantity left over; excess: *The bank keeps a large surplus of money in reserve.* **2** *adj.* more than is needed; extra; excess: *Surplus wheat and cotton are shipped abroad.* ■ See Synonym Study at **extra.** ❑ *n., pl.* **sur·plus·es.**

sur·prise (sər prīz′), **1** *n.* something unexpected: *Our grandparents always have a surprise for us on holidays.* **2** *n.* the feeling caused by something that happens suddenly or unexpectedly; astonishment; wonder: *His face showed surprise at the news.* **3** *v.* to cause to feel surprised; astonish: *The victory surprised us.* **4** *adj.* not expected; surprising; coming suddenly and without warning: *a surprise visit.* **5** *v.* to catch unprepared; come upon suddenly; attack suddenly: *The enemy surprised the fort.* **6** *n.* the act of coming upon suddenly; act of catching unprepared: *The fort was captured by surprise.* ❑ *v.* **sur·prised, sur·pris·ing.**

take by surprise, 1 to catch unprepared; come on unexpectedly: *Her call took him by surprise.* **2** to astonish: *News of the award took him by surprise.*

sur·pris·ing (sər prī′zing), *adj.* causing surprise or wonder; amazing: *a surprising recovery.* —**sur·pris′ing·ly,** *adv.*

sur·re·al (sə rē′əl), *adj.* **1** surrealistic. **2** eerie; bizarre.

sur·re·al·ism (sə rē′ə liz′əm), *n.* a modern movement in painting, sculpture, literature, movies, etc., that tries to show what takes place in dreams and in the subconscious mind. Surrealism is characterized by unusual and unexpected arrangements and distortions of images.

sur·re·al·ist (sə rē′ə list), *n.* artist or writer who uses surrealism.

sur·re·al·is·tic (sə rē′ə lis′tik), *adj.* of or about surrealism or surrealists. —**sur·re·al·is′ti·cal·ly,** *adv.*

sur·ren·der (sə ren′dər), **1** *v.* to stop fighting and give up; yield: *The town surrendered to the ene-*

surrealism

my. They surrendered themselves to bitter grief. **2** *n.* act of surrendering: *The surrender of the town saved it from bombardment.*

sur·rep·ti·tious (sèr′əp tish′əs), *adj.* **1** stealthy: *a surreptitious look.* **2** secret and unauthorized: *surreptitious meetings.* —**sur′-rep·ti′tious·ly,** *adv.* —**sur′rep·ti′tious·ness,** *n.*

sur·rey (sèr′ē), *n.* a light, four-wheeled carriage with two seats. ❑ *n., pl.* **sur·reys.**

sur·ro·gate (sèr′ə git *or* sèr′ə gāt), **1** *n.* person or thing that takes the place of another; substitute. **2** *adj.* serving as a substitute: *The baby-sitter became a surrogate parent to the children.* **3** *n.* (in certain states of the United States) a judge having charge of the probate of wills, the administration of estates, etc.

sur·round (sə round′), *v.* **1** to shut in on all sides; be around: *A high fence surrounds the field.* ■ See Synonym Study at **enclose.** **2** to form an enclosure around; encircle: *They surrounded the sick person with every comfort.*

sur·round·ings (sə roun′dingz), *n.pl.* surrounding things, conditions, etc.: *We enjoyed the peaceful surroundings at the cabin.*

sur·tax (sèr′taks′), *n.* an additional or extra tax on something already taxed. ❑ *n., pl.* **sur·tax·es.**

sur·veil (sər vāl′), *v.* to put someone under surveillance. ❑ *v.* **sur·veilled, sur·veil·ling.**

sur·veil·lance (sər vā′ləns), *n.* **1** a close watch kept over someone: *The police kept the suspected criminal under surveillance.* **2** supervision.

sur·vey (sər vā′ *for verb;* sèr′vā *or* sər vā′ *for noun*), **1** *v.* to look over; view; examine: *The buyers surveyed the goods offered for sale.* **2** *n.* a general look; view; examination; inspection: *We were pleased with our first survey of the house.* **3** *n.* a formal or official inspection, study, poll, etc.: *The institute conducted a survey of public opinion.* **4** *v.* to measure for size, shape, position, boundaries, etc.: *They are surveying the land before it is divided into house lots.* **5** *n.* a careful measurement: *A survey showed that the northern boundary was not correct.* **6** *n.* plan or description of such a measurement: *She pointed out the route of the railroad on the government survey.* ❑ *n., pl.* **sur·veys;** *v.* **sur·veyed, sur·vey·ing.**

sur·vey·ing (sər vā′ing), *n.* business or act of making surveys of land.

sur·vey·or (sər vā′ər), *n.* person who surveys land.

sur·viv·al (sər vī′vəl), *n.* **1** act or fact of surviving; continuance of life; living or lasting longer than others. **2** person, thing, custom, belief, etc., that has lasted from an earlier time: *Belief in the evil eye is a survival of ancient magic.*

sur·vive (sər vīv′), *v.* **1** to live longer than: *He survived his wife by three years.* **2** to remain alive after: *The crops survived the dry weather. Only ten of the crew survived the shipwreck.* **3** to continue to exist; remain: *These cave paintings have survived for over 15,000 years.* ❑ *v.* **sur·vived, sur·viv·ing.**

sur·vi·vor (sər vī′vər), *n.* person or other living thing that remains alive; thing that continues to exist: *There were two survivors from the plane crash.*

sus·cep·ti·bil·i·ty (sə sep′tə bil′ə tē), *n.* **1** quality of being susceptible; sensitiveness. **2 susceptibilities,** *pl.* sensitive feelings.

sus·cep·ti·ble (sə sep′tə bəl), *adj.* easily influenced by feelings or emotions; very sensitive: *Poetry appealed to his susceptible nature.* —**sus·cep′ti·ble·ness,** *n.* —**sus·cep′ti·bly,** *adv.*

susceptible of, capable of receiving, undergoing, or being affected by: *The preliminary plans were susceptible of a great deal of improvement.*

susceptible to, easily affected by; liable to; open to: *Young children are susceptible to many diseases.*

su·shi (sü′shē), *n.* a Japanese meal of cooked rice mixed with vinegar, cooled, and served with slices of raw fish and sometimes vegetables or seaweed.

sus·pect (sə spekt′ *for verb;* sus′pekt *for noun;* sus′pekt *or* sə-spekt′ *for adj.*), **1** *v.* to imagine to be so; think likely; suppose: *I suspect that some accident has delayed her.* **2** *v.* to believe to be guilty, false, bad, etc., without proof: *The police suspected them of being shoplifters.* **3** *v.* to feel no confidence in; doubt: *I suspected the truth of my guest's excuse.* **4** *n.* person believed to be guilty: *The police have arrested two suspects in connection with the bank robbery.* **5** *adj.* open to or seen with suspicion.

sus·pend (sə spend′), *v.* **1** to stop for a while: *We suspended building operations during the winter.* **2** to cause a law, regulation, etc., to be for a time no longer in force. **3** to keep or prevent someone from attending school, being on a team, doing a job, etc., for a short time: *They were all suspended from school for a week for bad conduct.* **4** to defer; postpone; delay; put off: *The court suspended judgment till next Monday.* **5** to cancel temporarily: *The judge suspended her driver's license.* **6** to hang by fastening to something above: *The lamp was suspended from the ceiling.* **7** to hold in place as if by hanging: *We saw the smoke suspended in the still air.*

suspended animation, an unconscious state that appears like death, in which breathing and pulse appear to stop.

sus·pend·ers (sə spen′dərz), *n.pl.* straps worn over the shoulders to hold up the trousers.

sus·pense (sə spens′), *n.* **1** condition of being uncertain: *The detective story kept me in suspense until the last chapter.* **2** anxious uncertainty; anxiety: *There was an air of suspense in the room as the teacher graded our tests.*

sus·pen·sion (sə spen′shən), *n.* **1** act of suspending or condition of being suspended: *suspension from school, the suspension of a driver's license for speeding.* **2** arrangement of springs for supporting the body of a wheeled vehicle on its axles. **3** mixture in which very small particles of one substance remain floating throughout another substance. **4** any support on which something is suspended.

suspension bridge, bridge with its roadway anchored at each end and suspended from cables or chains hung between towers.

suspension bridge

a	hat	ė	term	ô	order	ch	child		a in about
ā	age	i	it	oi	oil	ng	long		e in taken
ä	far	ī	ice	ou	out	sh	she	ə	i in pencil
â	care	o	hot	u	cup	th	thin		o in lemon
e	let	ō	open	ů	put	ŦH	then		u in circus
ē	equal	ȯ	saw	ü	rule	zh	measure		

S

sus·pi·cion (sə spish′ən), *n.* **1** belief; feeling; thought: *I have a suspicion that the weather will be very hot today.* **2** state of mind of someone who suspects; act of suspecting: *The real thief tried to turn suspicion toward others.* **3** condition of being suspected.
above suspicion, not to be suspected: *Don't blame my friend; he is above suspicion.*
on suspicion of, because of being suspected of: *They were arrested on suspicion of robbery.*
under suspicion, suspected.

sus·pi·cious (sə spish′əs), *adj.* **1** feeling suspicion; suspecting: *Our dog is suspicious of strangers.* **2** causing someone to suspect: *a suspicious manner.* **3** showing suspicion: *The dog gave a suspicious sniff at my leg.* —**sus·pi′cious·ly,** *adv.* —**sus·pi′cious·ness,** *n.*

Sus·que·han·na (sus′kwə han′ə), *n.* river flowing from central New York State through Pennsylvania and Maryland into Chesapeake Bay.

sus·tain (sə stān′), *v.* **1** to keep up; keep going: *Hope sustains him in his misery.* **2** to supply with food, provisions, etc.: *sustain a family.* **3** to hold up; support: *Several arches sustain the weight of the roof.* **4** to bear; endure: *The sea wall sustains the shock of the waves.* **5** to suffer; experience: *She sustained a great loss in the death of her parents.* **6** to allow; admit; favor: *The court sustained his suit.* **7** to agree with; confirm: *The facts sustain her theory.* —**sus·tain′a·ble,** *adj.* —**sus·tain′er,** *n.*

sus·te·nance (sus′tə nəns), *n.* **1** means of sustaining life; food or provisions: *The lost campers went for two days without sustenance.* **2** means of living; support: *She gave money for the sustenance of the poor.*

Sutt·ner (zùt′nər), *n.* **Ber·tha von** (bėr′tä fən), 1843-1914, Austrian writer and pacifist. In 1905 she became the first woman to win the Nobel Peace Prize.

su·ture (sü′chər), **1** *n.* process of sewing together or joining of two surfaces, especially the edges of a cut or wound. **2** *n.* seam formed in sewing up a wound. **3** *n.* one of the stitches or fastenings used. **4** *v.* to unite by suture or in a similar manner. **5** *n.* line where two bones, especially of the skull, join. ❑ *v.* **su·tured, su·tur·ing.**

Su·va (sü′və), *n.* capital of Fiji.

svelte (svelt), *adj.* slender; stylish: *The countess was tall, svelte, and very pale.* —**svelte′ness,** *n.*

SW, S.W., or **s.w., 1** southwest. **2** southwestern.

swab (swäb), **1** *n.* a bit of sponge, cloth, or cotton for cleansing some part of the body or for applying medicine to it. **2** *v.* to clean with a swab; apply a swab to: *swab a person's throat.* **3** *n.* a mop for cleaning decks, floors, etc. **4** *n.* a cleaner for the bore of a firearm. ❑ *v.* **swabbed, swab·bing.** —**swab′ber,** *n.*

swad·dle (swäd′l), *v.* to bind a baby with long, narrow strips of cloth; wrap tightly with clothes, bandages, etc. ❑ *v.* **swad·dled, swad·dling.**

swaddling clothes, 1 long, narrow strips of cloth, formerly used for wrapping a newborn infant. **2** long clothes for an infant.

swag (swag), *n.* SLANG. things stolen or gotten in a dishonest way.

swag·ger (swag′ər), **1** *v.* to walk with a bold, rude, or superior air; strut about or show off in a conceited or bragging way: *The actor swaggered onto the stage.* **2** *v.* to boast or brag noisily. **3** *n.* a swaggering way of walking, acting, or speaking. —**swag′ger·er,** *n.* —**swag′ger·ing·ly,** *adv.*

Swa·hi·li (swä hē′lē), *n.* a Bantu language containing many Arabic and other foreign words, spoken in much of eastern Africa and parts of Zaïre. *Safari* came into English from Swahili.

swain (swān), *n.* OLD USE. **1** lover. **2** a young man who lives in the country.

swal·low¹ (swäl′ō), **1** *v.* to take into the stomach through the throat: *We swallow all our food and drink.* **2** *v.* to perform the act of swallowing: *I cannot swallow.* **3** *v.* to take in; absorb: *The waves swallowed up the swimmer.* **4** *v.* to believe too easily; accept without question or suspicion: *He will swallow any story.* **5** *v.* to put up with; take meekly; accept without opposing or resisting: *He had to swallow the insult.* **6** *v.* to take back: *swallow words said in anger.* **7** *v.* to keep back; keep from expressing: *She*

swallowed her displeasure and smiled. **8** *n.* act of swallowing: *She took the medicine at one swallow.* **9** *n.* amount swallowed at one time: *There are only about four swallows of water left in the bottle.* —**swal′low·er,** *n.*

swal·low² (swäl′ō), *n.* any of numerous small, swift-flying birds with long, pointed wings. Swallows are known for their regular migrations, in large numbers and over very long distances. Some kinds have deeply forked tails.

swal·low·tail (swäl′ō tāl′), *n.* **1** any of numerous large butterflies with taillike extensions of the hind wings. **2** swallow-tailed coat.

swal·low-tailed coat (swäl′ō tāld′), a man's coat with tails, worn at certain formal events.

swam (swam), *v.* past tense of **swim:** *We swam all afternoon.*

swa·mi (swä′mē), *n.* title of a Hindu religious teacher. ❑ *n., pl.* **swa·mis.**

swamp (swämp), **1** *n.* wet, soft land; marsh: *the swamp along the river's edge.* **2** *v.* to plunge or sink into a swamp: *The truck is swamped in the muddy field.* **3** *v.* to fill with water and sink: *Their boat swamped. The wave swamped the boat.* **4** *v.* to overwhelm or be overwhelmed as if by a flood; make or become helpless: *He was swamped with work.*

swamp·land (swämp′land′), *n.* area of land covered by swamps.

swamp·y (swäm′pē), *adj.* **1** like a swamp; soft and wet: *The front yard is swampy from the heavy rain.* **2** containing swamps: *a swampy region.* **3** of or about swamps. ❑ *adj.* **swamp·i·er, swamp·i·est.** —**swamp′i·ness,** *n.*

swan (swän), *n.* any of several large, graceful water birds with long, slender, curving necks. The adults of some species are pure white. —**swan′like′,** *adj.*

swan dive, a graceful dive in which the legs are held straight, the back is curved, and the arms are extended out and back.

swank (swangk), *adj.* INFORMAL. stylish; smart; dashing: *a swank new restaurant.*

swank·y (swang′kē), *adj.* INFORMAL. swank. ❑ *adj.* **swank·i·er, swank·i·est.** —**swank′i·ly,** *adv.* —**swank′i·ness,** *n.*

swan song, 1 someone's last appearance or last piece of work. **2** song which, according to fable, a swan sings as it is about to die.

swap (swäp), **1** *v.* to exchange, barter, or trade: *The children swapped books.* **2** *n.* an exchange, barter, or trade. ❑ *v.* **swapped, swap·ping.** Also, **swop.** —**swap′per,** *n.*

swan dive

WORD STORY **Swap** comes from an old English word meaning "to hit." That word may have imitated the sound of a hand hitting something. In the Middle Ages, people who had agreed on a trade would slap each other's hand as a sign that they had made a deal. This may be why we still speak of striking a bargain. Today, people show the same thing by shaking hands, and perhaps someday **shake** will mean "to trade."

sward (swôrd), *n.* a grassy surface; turf.

swarm (swôrm), **1** *n.* group of bees led by a queen that leaves a hive and flies off together to start a new colony. **2** *v.* to fly off together in this way to start a new colony. **3** *n.* group of bees settled together in a hive. **4** *n.* a large group of insects, animals, people, etc., moving about together: *Swarms of children were playing in the park.* ■ See Synonym Study at **crowd. 5** *v.* to fly or move about in great numbers; be in very great numbers: *The mosquitoes swarmed about us.* **6** *v.* to be crowded; crowd: *The mall swarms with shoppers.* —**swarm′er,** *n.*

swarth·y (swôr′ᴛʜē *or* swôr′ᴛʜē), *adj.* having a dark skin: *The ship's crew was swarthy from the sun of the tropics.* ❑ *adj.* **swarth·i·er, swarth·i·est.** —**swarth′i·ly,** *adv.* —**swarth′i·ness,** *n.*

swash (swäsh), **1** *v.* to dash water, etc., about; splash. **2** *n.* a swashing action or sound: *the swash of waves against a boat.* □ *n., pl.* **swash·es.**

swash·buck·ler (swäsh′buk′lər), *n.* a swaggering swordsman, bully, or boaster.

swash·buck·ling (swäsh′buk′ling), *n., adj.* swaggering; bullying; boasting: *military swashbuckling, a swashbuckling adventurer.*

swas·ti·ka (swäs′tə kə), *n.* an ancient symbol or ornament like a cross with the arms bent. Swastikas were thought in early times to bring good luck. The swastika with arms turning clockwise was the symbol of the Nazis in Germany. □ *n., pl.* **swas·ti·kas.**

swat (swät), **1** *v.* to hit sharply or violently: *swat a fly.* **2** *n.* a sharp or violent blow. □ *v.* **swat·ted, swat·ting.** **—swat′ter,** *n.*

SWAT (swät), *n.* Special Weapons and Tactics (a group of police specially trained to deal with criminals who have barricaded themselves in a building).

swatch (swäch), *n.* sample of cloth or other material. □ *n., pl.* **swatch·es.**

swath (swäth), *n.* **1** the space covered by a single cut of a scythe or by one cut of a mowing machine. **2** row of grass, grain, etc., cut by a scythe or mowing machine. **3** a strip.

swathe (swäᴛʜ *or* swāᴛʜ), **1** *v.* to wrap up closely or fully: *swathed in a blanket.* **2** *v.* to bind, wrap, or bandage. **3** *n.* a wrapping or bandage. **4** *v.* to envelop or surround like a wrapping: *White clouds swathed the mountain.* □ *v.* **swathed, swath·ing.**

sway (swā), **1** *v.* to swing back and forth; rock from side to side, or to one side: *The pail swayed in her hands as she ran.* ■ See Synonym Study at **swing. 2** *v.* to make move; cause to sway: *The wind swayed the branches.* **3** *n.* act of swinging back and forth or from side to side: *The sway of the pail caused some water to spill out.* **4** *v.* to move to one side; turn aside: *The horse swayed left at the crossroads.* **5** *v.* to change in opinion or feeling: *Nothing could sway her after she had made up her mind.* **6** *v.* to influence, control, or rule: *The speaker's words swayed the audience.* **7** *n.* an influence, control, or rule: *The country was under the sway of a dictator.* **—sway′er,** *n.*

sway·backed (swā′bakt′), *adj.* having a back that sags to an unusual degree.

Swa·zi·land (swä′zē land′), *n.* country in SE Africa. *Capital:* Mbabane.

swear (swâr), *v.* **1** to use profane language; curse: *They raged and swore when they were captured.* **2** to make a solemn statement, appealing to God or some other sacred being or object; take an oath: *A witness at a trial is asked, "Do you swear to tell the truth, the whole truth, and nothing but the truth, so help you God?"* **3** to promise on oath or solemnly to observe or do something; vow; pledge: *The governor swore to uphold the constitution.* **4** to bind by an oath; require to promise or pledge: *sworn to secrecy.* □ *v.* **swore, sworn, swear·ing. —swear′er,** *n.*

swear by, 1 to name as your witness in taking an oath. **2** to have great confidence in.

swear in, to admit to office or service by giving an oath: *to swear in a jury.*

swear off, to promise to give up: *to swear off smoking.*

swear out, to get by swearing that a certain charge is true: *He swore out a warrant for the arrest of the man who had hit him.*

swear·word (swâr′wėrd′), *n.* word used in cursing; oath.

sweat (swet), **1** *n.* moisture that comes through the pores of the skin: *After mowing the lawn I wiped the sweat from my face.* **2** *v.* to give out moisture through the pores of the skin: *We sweated because it was very hot.* **3** *v.* to cause to sweat: *She sweated her horse by riding it too hard.* **4** *v.* to get rid of by sweating or as if by sweating: *to sweat off excess weight.* **5** *n.* a fit or condition of sweating: *He was in a cold sweat from fear.* **6** *v.* SLANG. to worry about: *He's really sweating his exams.* **7** *n.* INFORMAL. condition of anxiety, impatience, or anything that might make someone sweat: *We were all in a sweat over the big test.* **8** *n.* moisture given out by something or that condenses on its surface. **9** *v.* to give out moisture; collect moisture from the air: *A pitcher of ice water sweats on a hot day.* **10** *v.* to cause to work hard and under bad conditions: *a company that sweats its workers.* **11** *v.* INFORMAL. to work very hard. **12** *n.pl.* **sweats,** sweatpants, sweatshirts, sweatsuits, and the like. □ *v.* **sweat** or **sweat·ed, sweat·ing.**

sweat out, INFORMAL. **1** to wait for something anxiously: *sweat out the results of a test.* **2** to work hard for something: *sweat out a college degree.*

sweat·band (swet′band′), *n.* **1** a band of cloth worn around the head or wrists to absorb sweat during exercise. **2** a band of leather or cloth on the inside of a hat or cap to protect it from sweat.

sweat·er (swet′ər), *n.* a knitted article of clothing made of wool, cotton, nylon, etc., worn on the upper part of the body.

sweat gland, gland of the skin that secretes sweat. A sweat gland is connected with the surface of the skin by a tube or duct that ends in a pore.

sweat·pants (swet′pants′), *n.pl.* pair of baggy pants gathered with elastic at the waist and ankles, worn to keep warm before and after exercise.

sweat·shirt (swet′shėrt′), *n.* a heavy pullover with long sleeves, sometimes with a fleece lining, worn especially by athletes to keep warm before and after exercise.

sweat·shop (swet′shop′), *n.* place where workers are employed at low pay for long hours under bad conditions.

sweat·suit (swet′süt′), *n.* an exercise suit made of a sweatshirt and sweatpants.

sweat·y (swet′ē), *adj.* **1** covered or wet with sweat; sweating. **2** causing sweat. **3** laborious. □ *adj.* **sweat·i·er, sweat·i·est. —sweat′i·ly,** *adv.* **—sweat′i·ness,** *n.*

sweaty (def. 1)

Swede (swēd), *n.* person born or living in Sweden.

Swe·den (swēd′n), *n.* country in N Europe, east and south of Norway. *Capital:* Stockholm.

Swed·ish (swē′dish), **1** *adj.* of or about Sweden, its people, or their language: *a Swedish movie.* **2** *n.pl.* the people of Sweden. **3** *n.* language of Sweden.

sweep (swēp), **1** *v.* to clean with a broom, brush, etc.; use a broom or something like one to remove dirt; brush: *He sweeps the floor every morning.* **2** *v.* to move with or as if with a broom, brush, etc.: *Please sweep the dust into a pan.* **3** *n.* act of sweeping: *I need to give the room a good sweep.* **4** *v.* to remove; carry along: *A flood swept away the bridge.* **5** *v.* to pass over with a steady movement: *His eyes swept the crowd, looking for his friend.* **6** *v.* to move swiftly; come or go swiftly: *The hawk swept down on the mouse.* **7** *n.* a steady, driving motion or swift onward rush: *the sweep of the wind across the prairie.* **8** *v.* to move with dignity: *She swept out of the room.* **9** *v.* to move or stretch in a long line or curve: *The shore sweeps to the south for miles.* **10** *n.* a swinging or curving motion: *With a sweep of the bat, she hit the ball over the fence.* **11** *n.* a continuous area; stretch: *The house looks upon a wide sweep of farming country.* **12** *n.* distance of effectiveness or perception: *The mountain is beyond the sweep of your eye.* **13** *n.* act of winning all the games in a series, match, contest, etc.; complete victory. **14** *n.* (earlier) person who sweeps chimneys, streets, etc. **15** *n.* a long oar used to row or steer a boat. **16** *n.* a long pole that pivots on a high post, used to raise or lower a bucket in a well. □ *v.* **swept, sweep·ing.**

sweep·er (swē′pər), *n.* someone or something that sweeps: *a carpet sweeper.*

sweep·ing (swē′ping), **1** *adj.* passing over a wide space: *Her sweeping glance took in the whole room.* **2** *adj.* having wide range: *a sweeping victory, a sweeping statement.* **3** *n.pl.* **sweepings,** dust, rubbish, scraps, etc., swept out or up. **—sweep′ing·ly,** *adv.*

sweep·stake (swēp′stāk′), *n.* sweepstakes.

a	hat	ė	term	ô	order	ch	child		
ā	age	i	it	oi	oil	ng	long		a in about
ä	far	ī	ice	ou	out	sh	she		e in taken
â	care	o	hot	u	cup	th	thin	ə	i in pencil
e	let	ō	open	u̇	put	ᴛʜ	then		o in lemon
ē	equal	ò	saw	ü	rule	zh	measure		u in circus

S

sweep·stakes (swēp′stāks′), *n.* **1** system of gambling on horse races, etc. People buy tickets, and the money they pay goes to the holder or holders of winning tickets. **2** the race or contest. **3** prize in such a race or contest. ❑ *n., pl.* **sweep·stakes.**

sweet (swēt), **1** *adj.* having a taste like that of sugar or honey: *Pears are much sweeter than lemons.* **2** *adj.* having a pleasant taste or smell: *Perfume is sweet.* **3** *adj.* pleasant; agreeable: *a sweet child, a sweet smile, sweet music.* **4** *adj.* fresh; not sour, salty, bitter, or spoiled: *sweet cream.* **5** *n.* a dear; darling. **6** *n.* something sweet. **7** *n.pl.* **sweets,** candy or other sweet things. **8** *adv.* in a sweet manner. ■ Another word that sounds like this is **suite. —sweet′ly,** *adv.* **—sweet′ness,** *n.*

sweet·bread (swēt′bred′), *n.* the pancreas or thymus of a calf, lamb, etc., used as meat.

sweet cider, unfermented cider.

sweet corn, kind of corn which is eaten by people, usually when it is young and tender. It may be preserved by canning or freezing.

sweet·en (swēt′n), *v.* **1** to make sweet: *He sweetened his coffee with sugar.* **2** to become sweet: *Those pears will sweeten as they ripen.*

sweet·en·er (swēt′n ər), *n.* substance that sweetens something: *Do you prefer sugar or an artificial sweetener?*

sweet·en·ing (swēt′n ing), *n.* something that sweetens. Sugar is the most common sweetening.

sweet·heart (swēt′härt′), *n.* a loved one; lover.

sweet·ish (swē′tish), *adj.* somewhat sweet.

sweet·meats (swēt′mēts′), *n.pl.* candied fruits, sugar-covered nuts, etc.; candy.

sweet pea, any of several garden plants related to vegetable pea plants, with delicate, fragrant flowers of various colors.

sweet pepper, plant bearing a mild-flavored kind of pepper.

sweet potato, the sweet, thick, yellow or orange root of a creeping vine grown in warm regions. Sweet potatoes are eaten as a vegetable or in pies.

sweet-tem·pered (swēt′tem′pərd), *adj.* having a gentle or pleasant nature.

sweet tooth, fondness for sweets.

sweet william or **sweet William,** plant with dense, rounded clusters of small flowers in various shades of white and red.

swell (swel), **1** *v.* to grow or make bigger: *Bread dough swells as it rises. The bee sting swelled his finger up.* ■ See Synonym Study at **expand. 2** *v.* to be larger or thicker in a particular place; stick out: *A barrel swells in the middle.* **3** *n.* act of swelling; an increase in size, amount, etc. **4** *n.* condition of being swollen. **5** *v.* to rise or cause to rise above the level: *Rounded hills swell gradually from the plain.* **6** *n.* piece of higher ground; rounded hill. **7** *n.* a long, unbroken wave or waves: *The boat rocked in the swell.* **8** *v.* to grow or make louder: *The sound swelled from a murmur to a roar.* **9** *v.* to become filled with emotion: *to swell with pride.* **10** *n.* a tone or sound that becomes louder. **11** *n.* in music: **a** a gradual increase in sound followed by a decrease. **b** sign for this (< >). **12** *n.* INFORMAL. a fashionable person. **13** *adj.* INFORMAL. stylish; grand. **14** *adj.* INFORMAL. excellent; first-rate. ❑ *v.* **swelled, swelled** or **swol·len, swell·ing.**

swell·ing (swel′ing), *n.* an increase in size; swollen part: *There is a swelling on her head where she bumped it.*

swel·ter (swel′tər), **1** *v.* to suffer from heat. **2** *v.* to perspire freely; sweat. **3** *n.* a sweltering condition.

swel·ter·ing (swel′tər ing), *adj.* extremely and uncomfortably hot: *sweltering summer nights.* ■ See Synonym Study at **hot. —swel′ter·ing·ly,** *adv.*

swept (swept), *v.* past tense and past participle of **sweep:** *I swept the room. It was swept clean.*

swept·back (swept′bak′), *adj.* (of the wings of an aircraft) extending outward and sharply backward from the fuselage.

swerve (swėrv), **1** *v.* to turn aside: *The car swerved sharply to avoid hitting the truck. Nothing could swerve her from reaching her goal.* **2** *n.* act of turning aside: *The car made a quick swerve to avoid a pothole.* ❑ *v.* **swerved, swerv·ing.**

swift (swift), **1** *adj.* moving very fast: *a swift car.* **2** *adj.* coming or happening quickly: *a swift response.* **3** *adj.* quick or prompt to act: *He is swift to repay a kindness.* **4** *adv.* in a quick manner. **5**

n. any of several small birds with long wings, looking something like swallows. Swifts spend much of their lives in flight. **—swift′ly,** *adv.* **—swift′ness,** *n.*

Swift (swift), *n.* **Jonathan,** 1667-1745, English writer of satires, born in Ireland. He wrote *Gulliver's Travels.*

swift-foot·ed (swift′fut′id), *adj.* able to run swiftly.

swig (swig), INFORMAL. **1** *n.* a big or hearty drink. **2** *v.* to drink heartily or greedily. ❑ *v.* **swigged, swig·ging. —swig′ger,** *n.*

swill (swil), **1** *n.* kitchen refuse, especially when partly liquid; garbage; slops. Swill is sometimes fed to pigs. **2** *v.* to drink greedily; drink too much.

swim (swim), **1** *v.* to move along on or in the water by using arms, legs, fins, etc.: *Fish swim. Most boys and girls like to swim.* **2** *v.* to swim across: *She swam the river.* **3** *v.* to make swim: *He swam his horse across the stream.* **4** *v.* to float: *The roast lamb was swimming in gravy.* **5** *v.* to overflow or be flooded with: *Her eyes were swimming with tears.* **6** *n.* act, time, motion, or distance of swimming: *Her swim had tired her. They had had an hour's swim.* **7** *n.* **the swim,** the current of affairs, activities, etc.: *An active and sociable person likes to be in the swim.* **8** *v.* to go smoothly; glide: *White clouds swam across the sky.* **9** *v.* to be dizzy; whirl: *The heat and noise made my head swim.* ❑ *v.* **swam, swum, swim·ming. —swim′mer,** *n.*

swim·mer·et (swim′ə ret′), *n.* an abdominal limb or appendage in many crustaceans, such as lobsters and shrimp. It may be used for respiration, for carrying eggs, or for swimming.

swim·ming (swim′ing), **1** *n.* practice or sport of swimming: *My friend is an expert at both swimming and diving. She is our teacher in swimming.* **2** *n.* act of swimming: *Can you reach the island by swimming?* **3** *adj.* of or for swimming or swimmers: *a swimming teacher, a swimming pool.* **4** *adj.* dizzy: *a swimming sensation.*

swim·ming·ly (swim′ing lē), *adv.* with great ease or success: *Everything went swimmingly at our party.*

swim·suit (swim′süt′), *n.* bathing suit.

swin·dle (swin′dl), **1** *v.* to cheat; defraud: *Honest storekeepers do not swindle their customers.* **2** *v.* to get by fraud. **3** *n.* act of cheating; fraud. ❑ *v.* **swin·dled, swin·dling. —swin′dler,** *n.*

swine (swīn), *n.* **1** a hog or pig. **2** a coarse person. ❑ *n., pl.* **swine.**

swine·herd (swīn′hėrd′), *n.* person who tends hogs or pigs.

swing (swing), **1** *v.* to move back and forth, especially with a regular motion: *The hammock swings. He swings his arms as he walks.* **2** *v.* to move in a curve: *to swing a bat, to swing a golf club.* **3** *n.* act or manner of swinging. **4** *n.* a swinging blow: *With a powerful swing, the batter hit a home run.* **5** *n.* seat hung from ropes or chains in which you can sit and swing. **6** *v.* to hang: *We swung the hammock between two trees.* **7** *v.* to move with a free, swaying motion: *The children came swinging down the street.* **8** *n.* a swinging gait or movement; steady, marked rhythm: *The song "Dixie" has a swing.* **9** *n.* movement; activity: *It's hard to get into the swing of school after summer vacation.* **10** *n.* jazz music with a lively, steady rhythm, in which the players improvise freely on the original melody; jive. **11** *v.* INFORMAL. to manage successfully; complete satisfactorily: *swing a business deal.* ❑ *v.* **swung, swing·ing. —swing′er,** *n.*

in full swing, going on actively and completely; without restraint: *By five o'clock the party was in full swing.*

SYNONYM STUDY **Swing, rock²,** and **sway** all mean to move back and forth. **Swing** suggests regular, even movement: *The trapeze swings back and forth.* **Rock** suggests movement back and forth on a steady base: *She rocked from one foot to the other, over and over, as she waited in line.* **Sway** suggests unsteady movement back and forth: *The train swayed on the rough track.*

swin·ish (swī′nish), *adj.* **1** very selfish; greedy. **2** dirty; filthy; beastly. **—swin′ish·ly,** *adv.* **—swin′ish·ness,** *n.*

swipe (swīp), **1** *v.* SLANG. to steal: *Someone swiped her bike.* **2** *v.* INFORMAL. to strike with a sweeping blow: *He swiped at the mosquito, but missed it.* **3** *n.* INFORMAL. a sweeping stroke; hard blow: *He made two swipes at the golf ball without hitting it.* ❑ *v.* **swiped, swip·ing.**

swirl (swėrl), **1** *v.* to move or drive along with a twisting motion; whirl: *dust swirling in the air, a stream swirling over rocks. The heat and noise made my head swirl.* **2** *n.* a swirling movement; whirl; eddy. **3** *v.* to twist or curl: *a lock of hair swirled against his neck.* **4** *n.* a twist or curl: *a swirl of whipped cream on top of a sundae.*

WORD STORY Swirl, twirl, and **whirl** all look and sound alike, so you might think they come from the same word. They don't, though. **Swirl** comes from an old English word meaning "little whirlpool." **Whirl** comes from an old Scandinavian word meaning "to turn." **Twirl** doesn't come from either of those words, but no one knows where it does come from.

swish (swish), **1** *v.* to move or cause to move with a thin, light, hissing or brushing sound: *The whip swished through the air. The child swished the stick.* **2** *v.* to make such a sound: *The long gown swished as she danced across the floor.* **3** *n.* a swishing movement or sound: *the swish of little waves on the shore.* □ *n., pl.* **swish·es.**

Swiss (swis), **1** *adj.* of or about Switzerland or its people: *the Swiss lakes.* **2** *n.sing.* person born or living in Switzerland. **3** *n.pl.* the people of Switzerland.

Swiss chard, chard.

Swiss cheese, a firm, pale yellow or whitish cheese with many large holes.

switch (swich), **1** *v.* to change; shift: *They switched hats.* **2** *n.* a change; shift: *a last-minute switch of plans.* **3** *n.* device for making or breaking a connection in an electric circuit. **4** *v.* to turn on or turn off by using such a device: *Switch off the light.* **5** *n.* pair of movable rails by which a train is shifted from one track to another. **6** *v.* to shift by using such rails: *to switch railroad cars from one track to another.* **7** *n.* a slender stick used in whipping. **8** *v.* to whip or strike: *She switched the horse to make it gallop.* **9** *n.* a stroke or sweep: *The dog knocked a vase off the table with a switch of its tail.* **10** *v.* to move or swing like a whip or fan: *The horse switched its tail to drive off the flies.* □ *n., pl.* **switch·es.** —**switch'a·ble,** *adj.* —**switch'er,** *n.*

switch·back (swich'bak'), *n.* section of a railroad track or highway built in a zigzag course up a steep hill.

switch·blade (swich'blād'), *n.* pocketknife with a blade that springs out at the push of a button or knob on the handle.

switch·board (swich'bôrd'), *n.* panel containing switches, plugs, and other devices for opening, closing, combining, or controlling electric circuits.

switch-hit·ter (swich'hit'ər), *n.* a baseball player who bats either right- or left-handed.

switch·man (swich'mən), *n.* person in charge of a railroad switch. □ *n., pl.* **switch·men.**

Switz., Switzerland.

Swit·zer·land (swit'sər lənd), *n.* small country in central Europe, north of Italy. *Capital:* Bern.

swiv·el (swiv'əl), **1** *n.* a fastening that allows the thing fastened to turn round freely upon it. **2** *n.* a chain link having two parts, one of which turns freely in the other. **3** *n.* support on which a chair, gun, etc., can turn round. **4** *v.* to turn on a swivel. □ *v.* **swiv·eled, swiv·el·ing** or **swiv·elled, swiv·el·ling.**

switchboard for telephones in earlier times

swivel chair, chair having a seat that turns on a swivel.

swol·len (swō'lən), **1** *adj.* swelled: *a swollen ankle.* **2** *v.* a past participle of **swell.**

swoon (swün), **1** *v.* to faint: *swoon at the sight of blood.* **2** *n.* a faint: *Cold water may help to bring someone out of a swoon.* —**swoon'ing·ly,** *adv.*

swoop (swüp), **1** *v.* to come down with a rush, as a hawk does; sweep rapidly down upon in a sudden attack: *Bats swooped down from the roof of the cave.* **2** *n.* a rapid downward sweep; sudden, swift descent or attack: *With one swoop the hawk seized the*

chicken and flew away. **3** *v.* to snatch: *The nurse rushed after the running child and swooped him up in her arms.* —**swoop'er,** *n.*

at one fell swoop or **in one fell swoop,** in a single action; all at once: *The careless investor lost all his money at one fell swoop.*

swop (swop), *n., v.* swap. □ *v.* **swopped, swop·ping.**

sword (sôrd), *n.* **1** weapon, usually metal, with a long, sharp blade fastened to a handle or hilt. **2 the sword,** fighting, war, or military power: *Those who live by the sword will die by the sword.* —**sword'like',** *adj.*

at swords' points, very unfriendly.

cross swords, 1 to fight. **2** to quarrel; dispute.

sword·fish (sôrd'fish'), *n.* a very large saltwater food fish with a long, swordlike projection from its upper jaw. □ *n., pl.* **sword·fish** or **sword·fish·es.**

sword·play (sôrd'plā'), *n.* action, practice, or art of wielding a sword; fencing.

swords·man (sôrdz'mən), *n.* **1** person skilled in using a sword. **2** person using a sword. □ *n., pl.* **swords·men.** —**swords'man·ship,** *n.*

sword·tail (sôrd'tāl'), *n.* a small, freshwater fish found in Central America, popular in home aquariums because of its bright colors. Male swordtails have long, tapering tails.

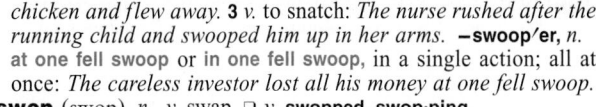
swordtail—5 in. (13 cm) long

swore (swôr), *v.* past tense of **swear:** *I swore to keep her secret.*

sworn (swôrn), **1** *v.* past participle of **swear:** *A solemn oath of loyalty was sworn by all the knights.* **2** *adj.* having taken an oath; bound by an oath: *There were ten sworn witnesses.* **3** *adj.* declared, promised, etc., with an oath: *We have her sworn statement.*

swum (swum), *v.* past participle of **swim:** *He had never swum before.*

swung (swung), *v.* past tense and past participle of **swing:** *She swung her arms as she walked. The door had swung open.*

syc·a·more (sik'ə môr'), *n.* **1** a tall North American shade tree with broad leaves, small, round fruit, and bark that breaks or peels off; buttonwood. **2** a large maple tree of Europe and Asia. **3** a fig tree of Egypt and Syria.

Syd·ney (sid'nē), *n.* port and capital of New South Wales. It is the largest city in Australia.

syl·lab·ic (sə lab'ik), *adj.* **1** of or consisting of syllables. **2** forming a separate syllable by itself. The second *l* sound in *little* (lit'l) is syllabic. —**syl·lab'i·cal·ly,** *adv.*

syl·lab·i·cate (sə lab'ə kāt), *v.* to divide into syllables. □ *v.* **syl·lab·i·cat·ed, syl·lab·i·cat·ing.** —**syl·lab'i·ca'tion,** *n.*

syl·lab·i·fy (sə lab'ə fi), *v.* to divide into syllables. □ *v.* **syl·lab·i·fied, syl·lab·i·fy·ing.** —**syl·lab'i·fi·ca'tion,** *n.*

syl·la·ble (sil'ə bəl), *n.* **1** word or part of a word pronounced as a unit. A syllable usually consists of a vowel alone or a vowel with one or more consonants. The word *syllable* (sil'ə bəl), has three syllables. Certain consonant sounds may be used as a vowel sound in syllables, such as the (l) in *bottle* (bot'l) or the (n) in *hidden* (hid'n). **2** letter or group of letters representing a syllable in writing and printing. A syllable may be separated from other syllables of a word by a dot, space, hyphen, or other mark to show where the word may be divided at the end of a line. *Strength* has only one syllable; *ap·prox·i·mate* has four.

a	hat	ė	term	ô	order	ch	child		
ā	age	i	it	oi	oil	ng	long		a in about
ä	far	ī	ice	ou	out	sh	she		e in taken
â	care	o	hot	u	cup	th	thin	ə	i in pencil
e	let	ō	open	ů	put	ŦH	then		o in lemon
ē	equal	ȯ	saw	ü	rule	zh	measure		u in circus

syl·la·bus (sil′ə bəs), *n.* a brief statement of the main points of a speech, a book, a course of study, etc. ❑ *n., pl.* **syl·la·bus·es, syl·la·bi** (sil′ə bī).

syl·lo·gism (sil′ə jiz′əm), *n.* a form of argument or reasoning, consisting of two statements and a conclusion drawn from them. EXAMPLE: All trees have roots; an oak is a tree; therefore, an oak has roots.

sylph (silf), *n.* **1** a slender, graceful girl or woman. **2** an imaginary spirit of the air. —**sylph′like′,** *adj.*

syl·van (sil′vən), *adj.* of or in the woods; wooded: *They lived in a sylvan retreat.*

sym·bi·o·sis (sim′bē ō′sis), *n.* condition or process in which two unlike living things live together for the benefit of each. Most lichens, which are composed of an alga and a fungus, are examples of symbiosis; the alga provides the food, and the fungus provides water and protection.

sym·bi·ot·ic (sim′bē ot′ik), *adj.* of or living in symbiosis. —**sym′bi·ot′i·cal·ly,** *adv.*

sym·bol (sim′bəl), *n.* something that stands for or represents something else. ∎ Another word that sounds like this is **cymbal.**

sym·bol·ic (sim bol′ik), *adj.* **1** used as a symbol: *A lily is symbolic of purity.* **2** of or expressed by a symbol or symbols; using symbols or symbolism: *a symbolic poem. Writing is a symbolic form of expression.* —**sym·bol′i·cal·ly,** *adv.*

sym·bol·i·cal (sim bol′ə kəl), *adj.* symbolic.

sym·bol·ism (sim′bə liz′əm), *n.* **1** use of symbols; representation by symbols: *The cross, the crown, the lamb, and the lily are parts of Christian symbolism.*

sym·bol·ize (sim′bə līz), *v.* **1** to be a symbol of; stand for; represent: *A dove symbolizes peace.* **2** to represent by a symbol or symbols: *The ancient Egyptians symbolized the sun as a boat.* **3** to use symbols. ❑ *v.* **sym·bol·ized, sym·bol·iz·ing.** —**sym′bol·i·za′tion,** *n.* —**sym′bol·iz′er,** *n.*

sym·met·ric (si met′rik), *adj.* symmetrical: *symmetric patterns.*

sym·met·ri·cal (si met′rə kəl), *adj.* having symmetry; well-proportioned: *symmetrical figures.* —**sym·met′ri·cal·ly,** *adv.*

sym·me·try (sim′ə trē), *n.* **1** exact agreement in size, shape, and arrangement of parts on opposite sides of a line or plane, or around a center or axis. **2** pleasing proportions between the parts of a whole; well-balanced arrangement of parts; harmony.

sym·pa·thet·ic (sim′pə thet′ik), *adj.* **1** having or showing kind feelings toward others; sympathizing: *a sympathetic friend.* ∎ See Synonym Study at **thoughtful. 2** approving; agreeing: *The teacher was sympathetic to the class's plan for a trip to the museum.* **3** enjoying the same things and getting along well together. **4** harmonious; agreeable: *a sympathetic environment for creativity.* **5** of or about the part of the nervous system that reacts to fear or stress by speeding up heart rate, raising blood pressure, and narrowing blood vessels. —**sym′pa·thet′i·cal·ly,** *adv.*

sym·pa·thize (sim′pə thīz), *v.* **1** to feel or show sympathy: *I sympathized with the injured child.* **2** to share in or agree with a feeling or opinion: *My parents sympathize with my plan to be a painter.* ❑ *v.* **sym·pa·thized, sym·pa·thiz·ing.** —**sym′pa·thiz′er,** *n.* —**sym′pa·thiz′ing·ly,** *adv.*

sym·pa·thy (sim′pə thē), *n.* **1** act of sharing another's sorrow or trouble: *We feel sympathy for a person who is ill.* ∎ See Synonym Study at **pity. 2** agreement in feeling; condition or fact of having the same feeling: *The sympathy between the twins was so great that they always smiled or cried at the same things.* **3** agreement; approval; favor: *I am in sympathy with your plan.* ❑ *n., pl.* **sym·pa·thies** for 1,3. [Sympathy comes from Greek words meaning "to feel together." That is what sympathetic people do.]

sym·phon·ic (sim fon′ik), *adj.* of or like a symphony: *symphonic music.* —**sym·phon′i·cal·ly,** *adv.*

sym·pho·ny (sim′fə nē), *n.* **1** an elaborate musical composition for an orchestra. A symphony usually has three or more movements in different rhythms but related keys. **2** symphony orchestra: *the Chicago Symphony.* **3** harmony of sounds. **4** harmony of colors: *In autumn the woods are a symphony in red, brown, and yellow.* ❑ *n., pl.* **sym·pho·nies** for 1,2.

symphony orchestra

symphony orchestra, a large orchestra that plays symphonies, made up of brass, woodwind, percussion, and stringed instruments.

sym·po·si·um (sim pō′zē əm), *n.* **1** a meeting or conference for the discussion of some subject: *hold a symposium on science.* **2** a collection of the opinions of several persons on some subject: *This magazine contains a sports symposium.* ❑ *n., pl.* **sym·po·si·ums, sym·po·si·a** (sim pō′zē ə).

symp·tom (simp′təm), *n.* **1** a sign or indication: *Shaking knees and paleness are symptoms of fear or shock.* **2** a noticeable change in the normal working of the body that indicates or accompanies disease, sickness, etc.: *The doctor made her diagnosis after studying the patient's symptoms.*

symp·to·mat·ic (simp′tə mat′ik), *adj.* being a sign or symptom: *Headaches are sometimes symptomatic of eyestrain. Riots are symptomatic of political or social unrest.*

syn., 1 synonym. **2** synonymous.

syn·a·gogue (sin′ə gog), *n.* **1** building used by Jews for worship and religious instruction. **2** a Jewish congregation.

syn·apse (sin′aps *or* si naps′), *n.* place where a nerve impulse passes from one nerve cell to another.

syn·ap·tic (si nap′tik), *adj.* of or at a synapse. —**syn·ap′ti·cal·ly,** *adv.*

syn·chro·nize (sing′krə nīz), *v.* **1** to make agree in time: *synchronize all the clocks in a building.* **2** to occur at the same time; agree in time. **3** to move or take place at the same rate and exactly together. ❑ *v.* **syn·chro·nized, syn·chro·niz·ing.** —**syn′chro·ni·za′tion,** *n.*

syn·chro·nous (sing′krə nəs), *adj.* **1** occurring at the same time; simultaneous. **2** going on at the same rate and exactly together: *the synchronous movements of the two dancers.* —**syn′chro·nous·ly,** *adv.*

syn·chro·tron (sing′krə tron), *n.* machine that causes atomic particles to move in circular paths at very high speeds by varying magnetic and electric fields in time with particle motion.

syn·cline (sing′klin), *n.* (in geology) a fold of rock layers that bends down from the sides to the center. —**syn·cli′nal,** *adj.*

syn·co·pate (sing′kə pāt), *v.* (in music) to begin a tone on an unaccented beat and hold it into an accented one. ❑ *v.* **syn·co·pat·ed, syn·co·pat·ing.** —**syn′co·pa′tion,** *n.* —**syn′co·pa′tor,** *n.*

syn·di·cate (sin′də kit *for noun;* sin′də kāt *for verb*), **1** *n.* a combination of persons or companies formed to carry out some undertaking, especially one requiring a large capital investment. **2** *n.* agency that sells special articles, photographs, etc., to a large number of newspapers or magazines for publication at the same time. **3** *v.* to combine into a syndicate. **4** *v.* to manage by a syndicate. **5** *v.* to publish through a syndicate. ❑ *v.* **syn·di·cat·ed, syn·di·cat·ing.** —**syn′di·ca′tion,** *n.* —**syn′di·ca′tor,** *n.*

syn·drome (sin′drōm), *n.* group of symptoms considered together that indicate the presence of a particular disease.

syn·er·gism (sin′ər jiz′əm), *n.* synergy.

syn·er·gis·tic (sin′ər jis′tik), *adj.* of or showing synergy. —**syn′er·gis′ti·cal·ly,** *adv.*

syn·er·gy (sin′ər jē), *n.* a combination of various actions that produces a greater effect than all the individual actions separately; synergism.

syn·fu·el (sin′fyü′əl), *n.* synthetic fuel.

syn·od (sin′əd), *n.* a council of churches or church officials.

syn·o·nym (sin′ə nim), *n.* word that means the same or nearly the same as another word. "Keen" is a synonym of "sharp."

WORD FAMILY Synonym and the following words are related: **acronym, anonymous, antonym, homonym,** and **pseudonym.** They all come from a Greek word meaning "name."

syn·on·y·mous (si non′ə məs), *adj.* having the same or nearly the same meaning. "Little" and "small" are synonymous. **—syn·on′y·mous·ly,** *adv.*

syn·on·y·my (si non′ə mē), *n.* 1 condition of being synonymous; sameness in meaning. 2 the study of synonyms. 3 a set, list, or system of synonyms.

syn·op·sis (si nop′sis), *n.* a brief statement giving a general view of some subject, book, play, etc.; summary. ❑ *n., pl.* **syn·op·ses** (si nop′sēz).

sy·no·vi·al fluid (si nō′vē əl), a thick, clear fluid produced by membranes in joints of the body. It lubricates the joints.

syn·tac·tic (sin tak′tik), *adj.* syntactical.

syn·tac·ti·cal (sin tak′tə kəl), *adj.* of or about syntax; in accordance with the rules of syntax. **—syn·tac′ti·cal·ly,** *adv.*

syn·tax (sin′taks), *n.* 1 way in which the words and phrases of a sentence are arranged to show how they relate to each other. 2 part of grammar dealing with this.

syn·the·sis (sin′thə sis), *n.* 1 combination of parts into a whole: *a synthesis of various cultures in a nation.* 2 formation of a chemical compound from elements or simpler compounds, by one or more chemical reactions. ❑ *n., pl.* **syn·the·ses** (sin′thə sēz).

syn·the·size (sin′thə sīz), *v.* 1 to combine into a complex whole. 2 manufacture synthetically: *to synthesize an antibiotic.* ❑ *v.* **syn·the·sized, syn·the·siz·ing.**

syn·the·siz·er (sin′thə sī′zər), *n.* 1 an electronic instrument that can imitate and mix together many types of sounds, including those of traditional musical instruments. 2 someone or something that synthesizes.

syn·thet·ic (sin thet′ik), 1 *adj.* made artificially by chemical synthesis. Nylon is a synthetic fiber. ■ See Synonym Study at **artificial.** 2 *n.pl.* **synthetics,** artificially made substances formed by chemical synthesis. Plastics are synthetics. 3 *adj.* of or about synthesis: *synthetic chemistry.* 4 *adj.* not real or genuine; artificial: *synthetic laughter.* **—syn·thet′i·cal·ly,** *adv.*

synthetic fuel, any liquid fuel or fuel gas that is made from coal, from certain kinds of rock or sand, or from plant material such as grain; synfuel.

syph·i·lis (sif′ə lis), *n.* a sexually transmitted disease that attacks the skin, internal organs, and finally the brain and spinal cord.

Syr·i·a (sir′ē ə), *n.* country in W Asia, south of Turkey. *Capital:* Damascus. [Syria may come from a Phoenician word meaning "stone." It has a rocky coast.] **—Syr′i·an,** *adj., n.*

sy·rin·ga (sə ring′gə), *n.* bush with fragrant white flowers blooming in early summer; mock orange. ❑ *n., pl.* **sy·rin·gas.**

sy·ringe (sə rinj′), 1 *n.* a narrow tube fitted with a plunger or rubber bulb for drawing in a quantity of fluid and then forcing it out in a stream. Syringes are used for cleaning wounds, injecting fluids into the body, etc. 2 *n.* hypodermic syringe. 3 *v.* to clean, wash, inject, etc., by means of a syringe. ❑ *v.* **sy·ringed, sy·ring·ing.**

syr·inx (sir′ingks), *n.* 1 panpipe. 2 the vocal organ of birds, located close to the bottom of the windpipe. ❑ *n., pl.* **syr·inx·es.**

syr·up (sir′əp *or* sėr′əp), *n.* a sweet, thick liquid. Sugar boiled with water or fruit juice makes a syrup. A cough syrup contains medicine to relieve coughing. Maple syrup is made from the sap of maple trees. Also, **sirup. —syr′up·like′,** *adj.*

syr·up·y (sir′ə pē *or* sėr′ə pē), *adj.* like syrup in consistency or sweetness. Also, **sirupy.**

sys·tem (sis′təm), *n.* 1 set of things or parts forming a whole: *a mountain system, a railroad system, the digestive system.* 2 an ordered group of facts, principles, beliefs, etc.: *a system of government, a system of education.* 3 plan, scheme, or method: *a system of classification.* 4 an orderly way of getting things done: *the current system of education. They work by a system, not by chance.* ■ See Synonym Study at **way.** 5 the body as a whole: *Exercise is good for your system.*

sys·tem·at·ic (sis′tə mat′ik), *adj.* 1 according to a system; having a system, method, or plan: *systematic work.* 2 orderly in arranging things or in getting things done: *a systematic person.* **—sys′tem·at′i·cal·ly,** *adv.*

sys·tem·a·tize (sis′tə mə tīz), *v.* to arrange according to a system; make into a system; make more systematic. ❑ *v.* **sys·tem·a·tized, sys·tem·a·tiz·ing. —sys′te·ma·ti·za′tion,** *n.* **—sys′tem·a·tiz′er,** *n.*

sys·tem·ic (si stem′ik), *adj.* of or affecting the body as a whole: *a systemic disease.*

sys·to·le (sis′tl ē), *n.* the normal rhythmic contraction of the heart as its chambers pump blood into the arteries.

sys·tol·ic pressure (si stol′ik), the blood pressure measured when the heart is contracting to pump blood. Systolic pressure is higher than diastolic pressure.

a	hat	ė	term	ô	order	ch	child	
ā	age	i	it	oi	oil	ng	long	⎧ a in about
ä	far	ī	ice	ou	out	sh	she	⎪ e in taken
â	care	o	hot	u	cup	th	thin	ə ⎨ i in pencil
e	let	ō	open	u̇	put	ŦH	then	⎪ o in lemon
ē	equal	ȯ	saw	ü	rule	zh	measure	⎩ u in circus

875

T¹ or **t** (tē), *n.* the 20th letter of the English alphabet. ❏ *n., pl.* **T's** or **t's.**

to a T, exactly; perfectly: *That suits me to a T.*

T² (tē), *n.* anything shaped like the letter T. ❏ *n., pl.* **T's.**

t., 1 teaspoon or teaspoons. 2 temperature. 3 tenor. 4 tense. 5 territory. 6 time. 7 ton or tons. 8 transitive. 9 true.

T. or **T,** 1 tablespoon or tablespoons. 2 Territory. 3 Testament. 4 ton or tons. 5 Tuesday.

Ta, symbol for tantalum.

TA or **T.A.,** Transit Authority.

tab (tab), *n.* 1 a small extension of or attachment to a card, used for labeling, numbering, coding, etc., in filing. 2 a small metal flap attached to the top of a can so that the top may be easily pulled off. 3 a small flap, strap, loop, or piece: *a fur cap with tabs over the ears.* 4 INFORMAL. a bill or check: *pick up the tab.*

keep tab on or **keep tabs on,** to keep track of; keep watch on; check: *Please keep tabs on the children while I'm out.*

tab·ard (tab′ərd), *n.* 1 a short, loose coat worn by heralds in the Middle Ages. 2 mantle worn over armor by knights.

Ta·bas·co (tä bäs′kō *or* tə bas′kō *for 1;* tə bas′kō *for 2*), *n.* 1 a state in SE Mexico. 2 trademark for a spicy sauce used on meat or fish. It is made from hot peppers.

tab·bou·leh (tə bü′lə *or* tə bü′lē), *n.* a Middle Eastern salad made of cracked wheat, onions, parsley, tomatoes, mint, olive oil, and lemon juice.

tab·by (tab′ē), *n.* 1 a yellowish brown cat with dark stripes. 2 a female cat. ❏ *n., pl.* **tab·bies.**

tab·er·nac·le (tab′ər nak′əl), *n.* 1 place of worship for a large congregation. 2 a Jewish temple. 3 **Tabernacle,** the covered, wooden framework carried by the Jews for use as a place of worship during their journey from Egypt to Palestine. 4 recess covered with a canopy and used as a shrine. 5 container for something holy or precious; container for the consecrated bread used in the Mass.

ta·ble (tā′bəl), 1 *n.* piece of furniture having a smooth, flat top on legs. 2 *n.* information arranged in rows or columns; list: *a table of contents in the front of a book, the multiplication table.* 3 *n.* food put on a table to be eaten: *Our hosts set a good table.* 4 *n.* the persons seated at a table, especially at a dinner or for informal discussion: *The whole table joined in the conversation.* 5 *v.* to make a list or statement in tabulated form. 6 *n.* a thin, flat piece of wood, stone, metal, etc.; tablet: *The Ten Commandments were written on tables of stone.* 7 *n.* tableland. 8 *v.* to put off discussing a bill, motion, etc., until a future time. ❏ *v.* **ta·bled, ta·bling.**

at table, having a meal; eating: *We were at table when my brother unexpectedly arrived.*

turn the tables, to reverse conditions or circumstances totally.

under the table, in a secret way: *Illegal arrangements were made under the table.*

tab·leau (tab′lō), *n.* **1** a striking scene; picture. **2** representation of a picture, statue, scene, etc., by a person or group posing in appropriate costume: *Our school is going to present several tableaux from American history.* ❑ *n., pl.* **tab·leaux** (tab′lōz), **tab·leaus.**

ta·ble·cloth (tā′bəl klôth′), *n.* cloth for covering a table. ❑ *n., pl.* **ta·ble·cloths** (tā′bəl klôᴛʜz′ *or* tā′bəl klôths′).

ta·ble·land (tā′bəl land′), *n.* a high plain; plateau; table.

ta·ble·spoon (tā′bəl spün′), *n.* **1** a large spoon used to serve food. **2** unit of measure in cooking equal to three teaspoons or ½ fluid ounce.

ta·ble·spoon·ful (tā′bəl spün′fůl), *n.* as much as a tablespoon holds. ❑ *n., pl.* **ta·ble·spoon·fuls.**

tab·let (tab′lit), *n.* **1** a small, flat piece of medicine, candy, etc.: *aspirin tablets.* **2** a thin, flat sheet of stone, wood, ivory, etc., used to write or draw on. The ancient Romans used tablets as we use pads of paper. **3** number of sheets of writing paper fastened together at the edge. **4** a small, flat surface with an inscription: *The Hall of Fame is a building that has many tablets in memory of famous people.*

table talk, conversation at meals.

table tennis, game played on a large table marked somewhat like a tennis court, using small wooden rackets and a light, hollow ball.

ta·ble·ware (tā′bəl wâr′), *n.* dishes, knives, forks, spoons, etc., used at meals.

tab·loid (tab′loid), *n.* a newspaper, usually having half the ordinary size newspaper page, that has many pictures and gives the news in short articles.

WORD STORY **Tabloid** comes from a trademark for a compressed form of drugs, sold in tablets about 100 years ago. People used the word about anything made smaller or shorter, including short newspaper stories and smaller-sized newspapers.

ta·boo (tə bü′), **1** *adj.* forbidden by custom or tradition; prohibited; banned. **2** *v.* to forbid; prohibit; ban. **3** *n.* system or act of setting things apart as forbidden; prohibition; ban. ❑ *v.* **ta·booed, ta·boo·ing;** *n., pl.* **ta·boos.** Also, **tabu.**

ta·bu (tə bü′), *adj., v., n.* taboo. ❑ *v.* **ta·bued, ta·bu·ing.**

tab·u·lar (tab′yə lər), *adj.* **1** of or arranged in tables or lists; written or printed in columns. **2** flat like a table: *a tabular rock.*

tab·u·late (tab′yə lāt), *v.* to arrange facts, figures, etc., in tables or lists. ❑ *v.* **tab·u·lat·ed, tab·u·lat·ing.** —**tab′u·la′tion,** *n.* —**tab′u·la′tor,** *n.*

ta·chom·e·ter (tak·om′ə tər *or* tə kom′ə tər), *n.* device for measuring the speed of rotation of a shaft, wheel, etc. Some cars have a tachometer dial in the instrument panel.

tach·y·car·di·a (tak′i kär′dē ə), *n.* an extremely rapid heartbeat.

tac·it (tas′it), *adj.* **1** implied or understood without being openly expressed: *His eating the food was a tacit admission that he liked it.* **2** unspoken; silent: *a tacit prayer.* —**tac′it·ly,** *adv.* —**tac′it·ness,** *n.*

tac·i·turn (tas′ə tėrn′), *adj.* not fond of talking; saying very little. —**tac·i·tur·ni·ty** (tas′ə tėr′nə tē), *n.* —**tac′i·turn′ly,** *adv.*

tack (tak), **1** *n.* a short, sharp-pointed nail or pin having a broad, flat head: *carpet tacks.* **2** *v.* to fasten with tacks: *She tacked mosquito netting over the windows.* **3** *v.* to attach; add: *He tacked a postscript to the end of the letter.* **4** *v.* to sail in a zigzag course against the wind: *The ship was tacking, trying to make the harbor.* **5** *n.* a zigzag course against the wind. **6** *n.* a zigzag movement; one of the movements in a zigzag course. **7** *n.* direction in which a ship moves in regard to the position of its sails. When on port tack, a ship has the wind on its left. **8** *n.* act of zigzagging; a turn from one direction to the next. **9** *n.* course of action or conduct: *Ordering rather than asking her to help was the wrong tack to take.* **10** *n.* stitch used as a temporary fastening. **11** *v.* to sew with temporary stitches. —**tack′er,** *n.*

tack·le (tak′əl), **1** *v.* to try to deal with: *We have a difficult problem to tackle.* **2** *v.* to grab; seize: *He tackled the boy who was running away and pulled him to the ground.* **3** *v.* (in football) to seize and stop, or throw to the ground, an opponent who has the ball. **4** *v.* (in soccer and field hockey) to strike or kick the ball

away from an opponent. **5** *n.* act of tackling. **6** *n.* an offensive or defensive player next to the end on either side of the line in football. **7** *n.* equipment; apparatus; gear. Fishing tackle means the rod, line, hooks, etc., used in catching fish. **8** *n.* set of ropes and pulleys for lifting, lowering, or moving heavy things. The sails of a ship are raised and moved by tackle. ❑ *v.* **tack·led, tack·ling.**

tack·y¹ (tak′ē), *adj.* sticky. ❑ *adj.* **tack·i·er, tack·i·est.**

tack·y² (tak′ē), *adj.* **1** in poor taste: *It was tacky of her to ask how much money I make.* **2** shabby; dowdy. ❑ *adj.* **tack·i·er, tack·i·est.** —**tack′i·ly,** *adv.* —**tack′i·ness,** *n.*

ta·co (tä′kō), *n.* tortilla filled with chopped meat, chicken, cheese, etc., and served hot. ❑ *n., pl.* **ta·cos.**

Ta·co·ma (tə kō′mə), *n.* port in W Washington, on Puget Sound.

WORD STORY **Tacoma** comes from an American Indian word that may mean "mountain spirit." Originally, it was the name of Mount Rainier. The mountain gave its name to the city nearby, but then people changed the name of the mountain.

tact (takt), *n.* ability to say and do the right things; skill in dealing with people or handling difficult situations: *Mother's tact kept her from talking about things likely to be unpleasant to her guests.*

tact·ful (takt′fəl), *adj.* **1** having tact: *a tactful person.* **2** showing tact: *a tactful reply.* —**tact′ful·ly,** *adv.* —**tact′ful·ness,** *n.*

tac·tic (tak′tik), *n.* **1** any skillful move; gambit. **2** detail of military tactics; maneuver.

tac·ti·cal (tak′tə kəl), *adj.* **1** marked by skillful procedure or methods. **2** relating to the disposal of military or naval forces in action against an enemy. **3** of or concerning tactics. —**tac′ti·cal·ly,** *adv.*

tac·ti·cian (tak tish′ən), *n.* an expert in tactics.

tac·tics (tak′tiks), *n.* **1** *pl.* ways to gain advantage or success; methods: *When coaxing failed, they changed their tactics and began to threaten.* **2** *sing.* art or science of disposing military or naval forces in action. **3** *pl.* the operations themselves: *The tactics of pretending to retreat fooled the enemy.*

tac·tile (tak′təl), *adj.* **1** of or about touch. **2** having the sense of touch. **3** able to be felt by touch; tangible.

tact·less (takt′lis), *adj.* **1** without tact; blunt: *a tactless person.* **2** showing no tact: *a tactless reply.* —**tact′less·ly,** *adv.* —**tact′less·ness,** *n.*

tad (tad), *n.* INFORMAL. **a tad,** a little bit; slightly: *This job pays a tad more than my last one.*

tad·pole (tad′pōl′), *n.* a very young frog or toad in the larval stage when it lives in water and has gills, a long tail, and no limbs.

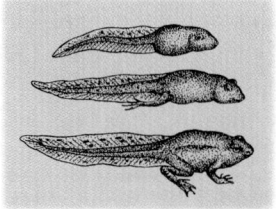

stages of a **tadpole**

WORD STORY **Tadpole** comes from old English words meaning "toad" and "head." A tadpole is mostly head at first; eventually, the head grows a toad or a frog behind it.

tae kwon do (tī′kwon′dō′), a Korean method of self-defense, similar to karate.

taf·fe·ta (taf′ə tə), *n.* a light, stiff silk, linen, or rayon cloth with a smooth, glossy surface. ❑ *n., pl.* **taf·fe·tas.**

taf·fy (taf′ē), *n.* kind of candy made of brown sugar or molasses boiled and pulled repeatedly until it is chewy: *saltwater taffy.*

Taft (taft), *n.* **William Howard,** 1857-1930, the 27th president of the United States, from 1909 to 1913, and Chief Justice of the Supreme Court, from 1921 to 1930.

tag¹ (tag), **1** *n.* piece of card, paper, leather, etc., to be tied or fastened to something: *a price tag.* **2** *n.* a metal or plastic cover at the end of a string. A shoelace has a tag on each end. **3** *n.* quotation, moral, etc., added for ornament or effect. **4** *n.* the last line or lines of a song, play, actor's speech, etc. **5** *v.* to furnish with a

a	hat	ė	term	ô	order	ch	child	
ā	age	i	it	oi	oil	ng	long	a in about
ä	far	ī	ice	ou	out	sh	she	e in taken
â	care	o	hot	u	cup	th	thin	ə i in pencil
e	let	ō	open	ů	put	ᴛʜ	then	o in lemon
ē	equal	ò	saw	ü	rule	zh	measure	u in circus

tag or tags: *All his bags are tagged with his name and address.* **6** *v.* to follow closely: *The baby tagged after his sister.* **7** *v.* to fasten a tag or label onto, especially in order to identify a biological specimen. ❑ *v.* **tagged, tag·ging.** **–tag′ger,** *n.* **–tag′like′,** *adj.*

tag² (tag), **1** *n.* a children's game in which one player who is "it" chases the others and tries to touch them. The first person touched is then "it" and must chase the others. **2** *v.* to touch or tap with the hand. **3** in baseball: **a** *v.* to touch a base runner with the ball to make an out. **b** *n.* the act of touching a base runner with the ball to make an out. ❑ *v.* **tagged, tag·ging.** **–tag′ger,** *n.*

Ta·ga·log (tä gä′log), *n.* **1** member of the chief Malay people in the Philippines. **2** their language. ❑ *n., pl.* **Ta·ga·log** or **Ta·ga·logs** for 1.

tag·a·long (tag′ə lòng′), *n.* person who always follows the lead of another, often in an annoying way.

Ta·gore (tə gôr′), *n.* **Ra·bin·dra·nath** (rə bin′drə nät′), 1861-1941, Indian poet and philosopher. He won the 1913 Nobel Prize for literature.

Taj Mahal

ta·hi·ni (tä hē′nē), *n.* a thick food paste or sauce made of ground sesame seeds.

Ta·hi·ti (tə hē′tē), *n.* French island in the S Pacific.

Ta·hi·tian (tə hē′shən), **1** *adj.* of or about Tahiti, its people, or their language. **2** *n.* person born or living in Tahiti. **3** *n.* the Polynesian language of Tahiti.

Ta·hoe (tä′hō), *n.* **Lake,** mountain lake in NE California and W Nevada. [**Tahoe** comes from an American Indian word meaning "lake." So its full name means "Lake Lake."]

tai·ga (tï′gə), *n.* the swampy evergreen forest land bordering on the arctic tundra. ❑ *n., pl.* **tai·gas.**

tail (tāl), **1** *n.* the part of an animal's body that sticks out beyond the back of the main part. **2** *n.* something like an animal's tail: *the tail of a kite.* **3** *n.* part at the rear of an airplane. **4** *n.* the rear part of anything; back: *A crowd of children formed the tail of the procession.* **5** *n.pl.* **tails, a** the reverse side of a coin. **b** coat with bottom parts, worn on formal occasions. **6** *adj.* at the back or rear: *tail feathers.* **7** *adj.* coming from behind: *a tail wind.* **8** *v.* to follow closely and secretly, especially in order to watch or prevent escaping: *Police tailed the suspected killer.* ■ Another word that sounds like this is **tale. –tail′less,** *adj.* **–tail′like′,** *adj.*

turn tail, to run away from danger, trouble, etc.

with your tail between your legs, afraid, shamed, or discouraged.

tail·gate (tāl′gāt′), **1** *n.* board at the back end of a wagon, truck, station wagon, etc., that can be let down or removed when loading or unloading. **2** *v.* to drive a vehicle too close to the one ahead of it. **3** *adj.* of or about a picnic set up on a tailgate, especially in a stadium parking lot. ❑ *v.* **tail·gat·ed, tail·gat·ing.**

tail·light (tāl′līt′), *n.* a warning light, usually red, at the rear end of a vehicle.

tai·lor (tā′lər), **1** *n.* person whose business is making, altering, or mending clothes. **2** *v.* to make by tailor's work: *The suit was well tailored.* **3** *v.* to make or mend clothes. **4** *v.* to make specially to fit; adjust; adapt: *tailor a speech to fit the audience.* [See Word Stories at **detail** and **tally.**]

tai·lor·ing (tā′lər ing), *n.* business or work of a tailor.

tail·piece (tāl′pēs′), *n.* piece added at or forming the end.

tail·pipe (tāl′pīp′), *n.* **1** the exhaust pipe of a motor vehicle or airplane. **2** the intake pipe of a suction pump.

tail·spin (tāl′spin′), *n.* a downward movement of an airplane with the nose first and the tail spinning in a circle above.

tail·wind (tāl′wind′), *n.* wind blowing toward the direction in which a ship or aircraft is moving.

Tai·no (tī′nō), *n.* **1** member of an American Indian tribe that lived on the Caribbean Islands. ❑ *n., pl.* **Tai·no** or **Tai·nos.** [**Taino** comes from a word in this tribe's language meaning "noble lord."]

taint (tānt), **1** *n.* a stain or spot; trace of decay, corruption, or disgrace: *No taint of scandal ever touched the mayor.* **2** *n.* a cause of any such condition. **3** *v.* to give a taint to; spoil: *Flies sometimes taint what they touch. Rumors about taking bribes tainted the judge's reputation.* **4** *v.* to become tainted; decay: *Meat will taint if it is left too long in a warm place.* **–taint′less,** *adj.*

WORD STORY **Taint** comes from two old English words that were pronounced the same. One meant "to dye," and the other meant "to convict of a crime." The two ideas combined in the idea of a stain on someone's reputation.

Tai·pei (tī′pā′), *n.* capital of Taiwan. [**Taipei** comes from Chinese words meaning "northern Taiwan."]

Tai·wan (tī′wän′), *n.* island country off SE China. Since 1949 it has been the seat of the Chinese nationalist government. *Capital:* Taipei.

WORD STORY **Taiwan** comes from Chinese words meaning "bay of terraces." The mountain slopes near the island coast have been shaped into level terraces for farms and buildings.

Taiwan Strait, a strait between the South China and East China Seas.

Ta·jik·i·stan (tä jē′kə stän), *n.* country in central Asia. *Capital:* Dushanbe.

Taj Ma·hal (täj′ mə häl′), a famous and beautiful white marble building in northern India, built in the 1600s as a tomb for the ruler's wife.

take (tāk), **1** *v.* to get hold of; hold onto: *I took her hand when we crossed the street.* **2** *v.* to seize; catch; capture: *take a wild animal in a trap.* **3** *v.* to accept: *Take my advice. The man won't take a cent less for the car.* **4** *v.* to get; receive: *She took the gifts and opened them.* **5** *v.* to win: *He took first prize.* **6** *v.* to get; have: *take a seat.* **7** *v.* to obtain from a source: *It takes its name from the inventor.* **8** *v.* to absorb: *Wool takes dye well.* **9** *v.* to use; make use of: *We took a train to Boston.* **10** *v.* to receive into the body; swallow: *take food.* **11** *v.* to let yourself have; indulge in: *take a nap, take a vacation.* **12** *v.* to put up with; stand: *People from the south often find it hard to take the cold weather when they move north.* **13** *v.* to study: *She plans to take art next year.* **14** *v.* to need; require: *It takes time and patience to learn how to play the guitar.* **15** *v.* to choose; select: *Take the shortest way home.* **16** *v.* to remove: *Please take the wastebasket away and empty it.* **17** *v.* to subtract: *If you take 2 from 7, you have 5.* **18** *v.* to go with; escort: *Take them home.* **19** *v.* to lead: *Where will this road take me?* **20** *v.* to carry: *Take your lunch along.* ■ See Usage Note at **bring. 21** *v.* to do; make; obtain by some special method: *Please take my photograph.* **22** *v.* to write down; record: *take minutes at a meeting.* **23** *v.* to form and hold in mind; feel: *She takes pride in her schoolwork.* **24** *v.* to find out: *The doctor took my temperature.* **25** *v.* to understand or suppose: *I take it the train was late.* **26** *v.* to regard; consider: *Let us take an example.* **27** *v.* to engage; hire; lease: *We have taken a cottage for the summer.* **28** *v.* to receive and pay for regularly; subscribe for: *take a newspaper.* **29** *v.* to become affected by: *take cold.* **30** *v.* (in grammar) to be used with: *A plural noun takes a plural verb.* **31** *v.* to catch hold; have effect: *The fire has taken. The medicine seems to be taking; the fever is going away.* **32** *v.* to please; attract; charm: *The song took our fancy.* **33** *v.* to become: *He took sick.* **34** *v.* to swindle; cheat. **35** *n.* amount taken: *a great take of fish.* **36** *n.* profits: *What was the week's take?* **37** *n.* scene photographed or televised at one time. ❑ *v.* **took, tak·en, tak·ing. –tak′er,** *n.*

on the take, INFORMAL. willing to be bribed: *a politician on the take.*

take after, be like; resemble: *She takes after her mother.*

take apart, **1** to separate into parts: *We learned to take apart small engines last week.* **2** to criticize at length; attack: *The newspaper review really took the young novelist apart.* **3** to defeat completely: *The champion boxer took the inexperienced challenger apart in three rounds.*

take back, to withdraw; retract: *I apologized and took back my rude remark.*

take down, to write down: *take down a speech.*

take for, to suppose to be: *be taken for someone else.*

take in, **1** to receive; admit: *take in foster children.* **2** to make smaller: *Please take in the waist of my pants.* **3** to understand. **4** to deceive; trick; cheat. **5** to visit: *take in a show.*

take it out on, INFORMAL. to relieve anger by scolding or hurting someone or something other than the person or thing that caused you to be angry or annoyed.

take off, **1** to leave the ground or water: *Three airplanes took off at the same time.* **2** to rush away: *I took off at the first sign of trouble.* **3** to increase suddenly in popularity: *The new comedy took off.*

take on, **1** to employ; hire. **2** to undertake to deal with: *take on an opponent.* **3** to acquire; assume: *At holiday time, the city took on a festive air.* **4** INFORMAL. to show great excitement, grief, etc. **5** to agree to do; take upon yourself: *I plan to take on more chores this summer.*

take out, **1** to remove: *How can I take this ink stain out?* **2** to borrow a book from a library. **3** to apply for and get a license, patent, etc. **4** to go out with: *He took my sister out to dinner.* **5** SLANG. to kill or destroy.

take over, to take the ownership or control of.

take to, **1** to form a liking for; become fond of: *We took to one another right away.* **2** to go to: *The cat took to the woods and became wild.*

take up, **1** to soak up; absorb: *A sponge takes up liquid.* **2** to make shorter: *The tailor took up the hem of the dress.* **3** to begin; undertake: *He took up piano lessons.* **4** to lift.

take up with, to begin to be friendly with.

take·down (tāk′doun′), **1** *n.* a move in wrestling in which a standing opponent is forced to the floor. **2** *adj.* able to be easily taken down or apart: *takedown seating.* **3** *n.* the act of taking something down.

take-home pay (tāk′hōm′), wages remaining after taxes, insurance fees, and the like have been deducted.

tak·en (tā′kən), *v.* past participle of **take:** *I have taken this toy from the shelf.*

take·off (tāk′ôf′), *n.* **1** act of rising from the ground or water into the air, as in an aircraft; taking off. **2** the place or point at which you take off. **3** INFORMAL. an amusing imitation.

takeoff (def. 1)

take·out (tāk′out′), *adj., n.* carry-out.

take·o·ver (tāk′ō′vər), *n.* act of taking over; seizure of ownership or control: *a takeover of a small business by a larger one.*

tak·ing (tā′king), **1** *adj.* attractive or pleasing; winning: *a taking smile.* **2** *n.* act of someone who takes or condition of being tak-

en. **3** *n.* something that is taken. **4** *n.pl.* **takings,** money taken in; receipts: *The clubs divided the takings from the school bake sale.*

talc (talk), *n.* a soft, smooth mineral, used in making face powder, chalk, etc.

tal·cum (tal′kəm), *n.* **1** talcum powder. **2** talc.

talcum powder, powder made of purified white talc, for use on the face and body.

tale (tāl), *n.* **1** story, especially a made-up story: *a fairy tale.* ■ See Synonym Study at **story**[1]. **2** falsehood; lie. **3** piece of gossip or scandal. ■ Another word that sounds like this is **tail**.

tell tales, to spread gossip or scandal.

tale·bear·er (tāl′bâr′ər), *n.* person who spreads gossip or scandal.

tale·bear·ing (tāl′bâr′ing), *n.* act of spreading gossip or scandal.

tal·ent (tal′ənt), *n.* **1** a special natural ability: *She has a talent for music.* **2** person or persons with talent: *That young singer is a real talent.* **3** an ancient unit of weight or money, varying with time and place.

WORD STORY **Talent** (defs. 1 and 2) comes from definition 3, used in a Bible story. Jesus tells a parable of servants entrusted with money. Some use it for profit, but one only hides it for safekeeping, and he is scolded. The parable is often interpreted as a lesson about the duty to develop natural abilities. In the Middle Ages, people borrowed the word from the Bible and called a natural ability "a talent."

tal·ent·ed (tal′ən tid), *adj.* having natural ability; gifted: *a talented musician.*

tal·is·man (tal′i smən), *n.* **1** stone, ring, etc., engraved with figures or characters supposed to have magic power; charm. **2** anything that acts as a charm. ❑ *n., pl.* **tal·is·mans.**

talk (tôk), **1** *v.* to use words to express feelings or ideas; speak: *The baby is learning to talk.* ■ See Synonym Study at **speak**. **2** *v.* to use a language in speaking; speak: *Can you talk French?* **3** *v.* to exchange words; converse: *They talked for an hour.* **4** *n.* the use of words; spoken words; speech; conversation: *The old friends met for a good talk.* **5** *n.* an informal speech: *The coach gave the team a talk about the need for more team spirit.* **6** *n.* a way of talking: *baby talk.* **7** *v.* to discuss: *They talked politics all evening.* **8** *v.* to consult; confer: *talk with your doctor.* **9** *n.* conference; council: *summit talks.* **10** *v.* to spread ideas by other means than speech: *Some people talk by signing.* **11** *v.* to spread rumors; gossip: *talk behind someone's back.* **12** *n.* gossip or rumor: *There is talk of a quarrel between them.* **13** *n.* a subject for talk or gossip: *be the talk of the town.* —**talk′a·ble,** *adj.*

talk back, to answer rudely or disrespectfully.

talk down to, to speak to in a superior tone.

talk into, to persuade someone to do something: *They talked us into going bowling with them.*

talk out, to discuss thoroughly: *We need to talk this whole problem out before we decide anything.*

talk out of, to persuade someone not to do something: *We talked them out of ordering ten pizzas.*

talk over, to speak about; discuss: *We need to talk things over before deciding how to use this money.*

talk·a·tive (tô′kə tiv), *adj.* having the habit of talking a great deal; fond of talking. —**talk′a·tive·ly,** *adv.* —**talk′a·tive·ness,** *n.*

talk·er (tô′kər), *n.* **1** person who talks. **2** a talkative person.

talk·ing-to (tô′king tü′), *n.* INFORMAL. act of criticizing or scolding someone. ❑ *n., pl.* **talk·ing-tos.**

talk show, a TV or radio show that is mostly conversation between a host and a guest or guests.

tall (tôl), *adj.* **1** higher than the average; having great height: *a tall building.* ■ See Synonym Study at **high**. **2** of a stated height: *two meters tall.* **3** high or large in amount; extravagant: *a tall price, a tall order.* **4** hard to believe; exaggerated: *a tall tale.* —**tall′ness,** *n.*

a	hat	ė	term	ô	order	ch	child		a in about
ā	age	i	it	oi	oil	ng	long		e in taken
ä	far	ī	ice	ou	out	sh	she	ə	i in pencil
â	care	o	hot	u	cup	th	thin		o in lemon
e	let	ō	open	u̇	put	ŦH	then		u in circus
ē	equal	ȯ	saw	ü	rule	zh	measure		

Tal·la·has·see (tal′ə has′ē), *n.* capital of Florida, in the N part. [Tallahassee comes from a Creek word meaning "old town."]

Tal·linn (tä′lin), *n.* capital of Estonia, on the Gulf of Finland.

tall·ish (tȯ′lish), *adj.* rather tall.

tal·low (tal′ō), *n.* the hard fat from sheep, cows, etc., after it has been melted. It is used for making candles, soap, etc. —**tal′low·like′,** *adj.*

tal·ly (tal′ē), **1** *n.* anything, such as a pad, on which a score or account is kept. **2** *v.* to mark on a tally; count: *to tally sales figures.* **3** *n.* account; count: *a tally of deliveries.* **4** *n.* score: *a tally of a game.* **5** *v.* (in sports) to make scoring points; score: *The hockey team tallied seven goals in their last game.* **6** *v.* to agree; correspond: *Your account tallies with mine.* ❑ *n., pl.* **tal·lies;** *v.* **tal·lied, tal·ly·ing.** —**tal′li·er,** *n.*

tal·ly·ho (tal′ē hō′), *interj., n.* a hunter's cry on catching sight of the fox. ❑ *n., pl.* **tal·ly·hos.**

Tal·mud (tal′məd), *n.* a collection of sixty-three volumes containing the Jewish civil and canonical law in the form of interpretation and expansion of the teachings of the Hebrew Scriptures.

tal·on (tal′ən), *n.* claw of an animal, especially a bird of prey: *The eagle seized a rabbit in its talons.*

ta·lus (tā′ləs), *n.* the main bone of the ankle. ❑ *n., pl.* **ta·li** (tā′lī).

tam (tam), *n.* tam-o'-shanter.

ta·ma·le (tə mä′lē), *n.* a Mexican food made of cornmeal and minced meat, seasoned with red peppers, wrapped in cornhusks, and roasted or steamed.

tam·a·rack (tam′ə rak′), *n.* a North American larch that yields strong, heavy timber.

tamarin—up to 17 in. (44 cm) long with the tail

tam·a·rin (tam′ə rin), *n.* any of several kinds of very small monkeys that live in Central and South America. They have long tails and silky fur, and they are related to marmosets.

tam·a·rind (tam′ə rind′), *n.* **1** a tropical tree grown for its wood and fruit. **2** its fruit, a brown pod with juicy, acid pulp, used in foods, drinks, and medicine.

tam·a·risk (tam′ə risk′), *n.* any of numerous ornamental bushes or small trees with slender, feathery branches.

Ta·mau·li·pas (tä′mou′lē′päs), *n.* a state in NE Mexico.

tam·bou·rine (tam′bə rēn′), *n.* a small, shallow drum with jingling metal disks around the side, played by striking it with the knuckles or by shaking it.

tame (tām), **1** *adj.* taken from the wild state and made obedient: *a tame bear.* **2** *adj.* without fear; not wild; gentle: *The birds are so tame that they will eat from our hands.* **3** *v.* to make or become tame; break in: *The lion was tamed for the circus.* **4** *v.* to tone down; subdue: *tame your temper.* **5** *adj.* without spirit; dull: *The party was tame because we were sleepy.* ❑ *adj.* **tam·er, tam·est;** *v.* **tamed, tam·ing.** —**tame′a·ble,** *adj.* —**tame′ly,** *adv.* —**tame′ness,** *n.* —**tam′er,** *n.*

tame·less (tām′lis), *adj.* never tamed; not able to be tamed.

tam-o'-shan·ter (tam′ə shan′tər), *n.* a soft, woolen cap, originally of Scotland, with a flat, round crown and often with a tassel. Also, **tam.**

tamp (tamp), *v.* to pack down: *tamp the earth around a newly planted tree.* —**tamp′er,** *n.*

Tam·pa (tam′pə), *n.* **1** port in W Florida. **2 Tampa Bay,** a bay of the Gulf of Mexico, in W Florida.

tam·per (tam′pər), *v.* to meddle improperly; meddle: *tamper with a lock.* ∎ See Synonym Study at **meddle.** —**tam′per·er,** *n.*

tam·pon (tam′pon), *n.* plug of cotton inserted in a body cavity to absorb bleeding.

tan (tan), **1** *adj.* yellowish brown: *tan shoes.* **2** *n.* the brown color of someone's skin resulting from being in the sun and air: *His arms and legs had a dark tan.* **3** *v.* to make or become brown by exposure to sun and air: *Sun and wind had tanned her face.* **4** *v.* to make a hide into leather by soaking it in a special liquid, especially one containing tannin. **5** *v.* to thrash or spank in punishment. ❑ *adj.* **tan·ner, tan·nest;** *v.* **tanned, tan·ning.** —**tan′na·ble,** *adj.*

tan or **tan.,** tangent.

tan·a·ger (tan′ə jər), *n.* any of numerous small songbirds living mostly in tropical American regions. The males are usually brilliantly colored.

Ta·nan·a·rive (tə nan′ə rēv′), *n.* former name of Antananarivo.

tan·dem (tan′dəm), **1** *adv.* one behind the other: *drive horses tandem.* **2** *adj.* having animals, seats, parts, etc., arranged one behind the other. **3** *n.* two horses harnessed tandem. **4** *n.* carriage drawn by two horses so harnessed. **5** *n.* Also, **tandem bicycle,** bicycle with two seats, one behind the other.

tang (tang), *n.* **1** a strong taste, flavor, or odor: *the tang of mustard, the salt tang of sea air.* **2** a slight touch or suggestion; trace.

Tan·gan·yi·ka (tang′gə nyē′kə), *n.* **1** former country in E Africa, now part of Tanzania. **2 Lake,** lake in central Africa. —**Tan′gan·yi′kan,** *adj., n.*

tan·ge·lo (tan′jə lō), *n.* a crossbreed of a tangerine and a grapefruit. ❑ *n., pl.* **tan·ge·los.**

tan·gent (tan′jənt), **1** *adj.* (in geometry) touching a curve or surface at one point but not intersecting. These circles are tangent: ∞. **2** *n.* a tangent line, curve, or surface. **3** *n.* the ratio of the length of the side opposite an acute angle in a right triangle to the length of the shorter of the other sides. **4** *adj.* in contact; touching.

fly off at a tangent or **go off on a tangent,** to change suddenly from one course of action or thought to another.

tan·gen·tial (tan jen′shəl), *adj.* **1** only indirectly related to something being considered or discussed: *tangential matters.* **2** of or like a tangent. —**tan·gen′tial·ly,** *adv.*

tan·ge·rine (tan′jə rēn′), *n.* a reddish orange citrus fruit with a very loose peel and segments that separate easily. It looks like a small orange and is widely grown in the United States.

tan·gi·ble (tan′jə bəl), *adj.* **1** capable of being touched or felt by touch: *A chair is a tangible object.* **2** real; actual; definite: *The detective sought tangible evidence, not opinion.* —**tan′gi·bil′i·ty, tan′gi·ble·ness,** *n.* —**tan′gi·bly,** *adv.*

Tan·gier (tan jir′), *n.* port in Morocco, on the Strait of Gibraltar. [See Word Story at **tangerine.**]

Tan·giers (tan jirz′), *n.* Tangier.

tan·gle (tang′gəl), **1** *v.* to twist and twine together in a confused mass: *The kitten had tangled the ball of twine.* **2** *n.* a confused or twisted mass: *The climbing vines are all one tangle and need to be pruned and tied up.* **3** *v.* to involve in something that hampers or obstructs; entrap. **4** *n.* a bewildering confusion; mess: *a tangle of contradictory statements.* **5** *v.* to quarrel: *We tangled over who should be team captain.* ❑ *v.* **tan·gled, tan·gling. –tan′gle·ment,** *n.* **–tan′gler,** *n.*

tan·go (tang′gō), **1** *n.* a Spanish American dance with long, gliding steps and many figures and poses. **2** *n.* music for it. **3** *v.* to dance the tango. ❑ *n., pl.* **tan·gos;** *v.* **tan·goed, tan·go·ing.**

tango (def. 3)

tang·y (tang′ē), *adj.* having a tang. ❑ *adj.* **tang·i·er, tang·i·est.**

tank (tangk), **1** *n.* a large container for liquid or gas: *the gasoline tank of a car.* **2** *v.* to put or store in a tank: *The plane tanked up on gas.* **3** *n.* a heavily armored combat vehicle carrying machine guns and usually a cannon, moving on an endless track on each side. Tanks can travel over rough ground, fallen trees, and other obstacles. **–tank′like,** *adj.*

WORD STORY Tank (def. 3) comes from a code word. Tanks were invented during World War I, and for a long time they were a secret weapon. They were called "tanks" so that the enemy would not find out about them. When they were finally used, the name stuck.

tank·ard (tang′kərd), *n.* a large drinking mug with a handle and a hinged cover.

tank car, a railroad car with a tank for carrying liquids or gases.

tank·er (tang′kər), *n.* ship, airplane, or truck with tanks for carrying oil or other liquid freight.

tank·ful (tangk′fúl), *n.* as much as a tank will hold. ❑ *n., pl.* **tank·fuls.**

tank suit, a simple one-piece swimsuit for women that has shoulder straps.

tank top, clothing for the upper body with wide straps for the shoulders. It is similar to a tank suit.

tan·ner (tan′ər), *n.* person whose work is tanning hides.

tan·ner·y (tan′ər ē), *n.* place where hides are tanned. ❑ *n., pl.* **tan·ner·ies.**

tan·nic acid (tan′ik), tannin.

tan·nin (tan′ən), *n.* acid obtained from the bark or galls of oaks, etc., and from certain other plants. It is used in tanning, dyeing, making ink, and in medicine.

tan·ning (tan′ing), *n.* act of converting hides or skins into leather.

tan·sy (tan′zē), *n.* any of several strong-smelling plants with clusters of small yellow flowers, especially one bitter-tasting kind with notched leaves. ❑ *n., pl.* **tan·sies.**

tan·ta·lize (tan′tl īz), *v.* to torment or tease by keeping something desired in sight but out of reach, or by holding out hopes that are repeatedly disappointed: *They tantalized the hungry dog by pretending to feed it.* ❑ *v.* **tan·ta·lized, tan·ta·liz·ing. –tan′ta·liz′er,** *n.* **–tan′ta·liz′ing·ly,** *adv.*

WORD STORY Tantalize comes from Tantalus (tan′tə ləs), a king in Greek mythology. After he died, he was punished for his crimes by being made to stand in water under branches filled with fruit. Whether he reached up for the fruit or down for the water, whatever he wanted moved out of his reach.

tan·ta·lum (tan′tl əm), *n.* a hard, shiny, grayish white metallic element occurring with niobium in certain rare minerals. It is very resistant to corrosion and is used as an alloy in nuclear reactors and in surgical and dental equipment. *Symbol:* Ta

tan·ta·mount (tan′tə mount), *adj.* equivalent: *The withdrawal of his statement is tantamount to an apology.*

tan·trum (tan′trəm), *n.* a sudden, childish outburst of bad temper or ill humor.

Tan·za·ni·a (tan′zə nē′ə), *n.* country in E Africa. It was formed in 1964 by the union of Tanganyika and the adjacent islands of Zanzibar and Pemba. *Capital:* Dodoma. [Tanzania comes from Tanganyika and Zanzibar. When they joined to form a new country, they combined names.] **–Tan′za·ni′an,** *adj., n.*

Tao·ism (tou′iz′əm), *n.* one of the main religions of China. It teaches natural simplicity and humility as a way to peace and harmony in life.

Tao·ist (tou′ist), **1** *n.* believer in Taoism. **2** *adj.* of or belonging to Taoists or Taoism.

tap[1] (tap), **1** *v.* to strike lightly: *Tap him on the shoulder.* **2** *v.* to cause to strike lightly: *She tapped her foot to the music.* **3** *n.* a light blow: *There was a tap at the door.* **4** *n.* sound of a light blow. **5** *v.* to make, put, etc., by light blows: *tap a rhythm, tap time, tap the ashes out of a pipe.* **6** *n.* a small steel plate on a shoe to reduce wear or to make a louder sound in tap-dancing. **7** *n.* tap dance. ❑ *v.* **tapped, tap·ping. –tap′per,** *n.*

tap[2] (tap), **1** *n.* stopper or plug to close a hole in a cask containing liquid. **2** *n.* faucet. **3** *v.* to make a hole in to let out liquid: *tap sugar maples.* **4** *v.* to draw the plug from: *tap a cask.* **5** *v.* to let out liquid by piercing or by drawing a plug. **6** *v.* to make resources, reserves, etc., accessible; penetrate; open up: *This highway taps a large district.* **7** *n.* point in an electric circuit where a connection is or can be made. **8** *v.* to wiretap. **9** *n.* a wiretap. ❑ *v.* **tapped, tap·ping. –tap′per,** *n.*

on tap, 1 ready to be let out of a keg or barrel and served. **2** ready for use; on hand: *I keep extra money on tap for an emergency.*

tap into, to use or arrange to use; make a connection to; draw from: *tap into resources, tap into popular opinion.*

tap dance, dance in which the steps are accented by loud taps of the foot, toe, or heel; tap.

tap-dance (tap′dans′), *v.* to do a tap dance. ❑ *v.* **tap-danced, tap-danc·ing. –tap′-danc·er,** *n.*

tape (tāp), **1** *n.* a long, narrow strip of cloth, paper, plastic, etc.: *adhesive tape.* **2** *n.* a plastic tape on which sounds or images can be recorded; magnetic tape. **3** *v.* to record on such a tape: *The parade was taped to show on TV in the evening.* **4** *v.* to fasten with tape; wrap with tape: *The players taped their ankles for support.* **5** *n.* a long, narrow strip of other material. Surveyors measure with a steel tape. **6** *v.* to measure with a tape measure. **7** *n.* strip, string, etc., stretched across a race track at the finish line. ❑ *v.* **taped, tap·ing. –tape′less,** *adj.* **–tape′like′,** *adj.* **–tap′er,** *n.*

tape deck, the mechanical section of a tape recorder. It may be used with a separate amplifier and speaker system or in connection with a computer.

tape measure, a long strip of cloth or steel marked in inches, feet, etc., for measuring.

ta·per (tā′pər), **1** *v.* to make or become gradually smaller toward one end: *A church spire tapers to a point.* **2** *v.* to grow less gradually; diminish: *Their business tapered off as people moved away.* **3** *n.* a gradual decrease of force, capacity, etc. **4** *n.* a very slender candle. ■ Another word that sounds like this is **tapir.**

tape-re·cord (tāp′ri kôrd′), *v.* to record on a tape recorder.

tape recorder, machine that records sound magnetically on plastic tape and plays the sound back after it is recorded.

tape recording, 1 the recording of sound on a tape. **2** a tape on which sound has been recorded.

tap·es·try (tap′ə strē), *n.* fabric with pictures or designs woven in it, used to hang on walls, cover furniture, etc. ❑ *n., pl.* **tap·es·tries.**

tape·worm (tāp′wėrm′), *n.* any of numerous long, flat worms that live during their adult stage as parasites in the intestines of human beings and other animals.

tap·i·o·ca (tap′ē ō′kə), *n.* a starchy food obtained from the root of the cassava plant. It is used for puddings.

a	hat	ė	term	ô	order	ch	child		
ā	age	i	it	oi	oil	ng	long		a in about
ä	far	ī	ice	ou	out	sh	she		e in taken
â	care	o	hot	u	cup	th	thin	ə	i in pencil
e	let	ō	open	ù	put	ᴛʜ	then		o in lemon
ē	equal	ò	saw	ü	rule	zh	measure		u in circus

T

ta·pir (tā′pər), *n.* any of several large mammals of tropical America and southern Asia, with hoofs and flexible snouts. Tapirs resemble pigs but are related to horses and rhinoceroses. ❑ *n., pl.* **ta·pir** or **ta·pirs.** ■ Another word that sounds like this is **taper.**

tap·root (tap′rüt′), *n.* a main root growing downward.

taps (taps), *n.sing. or pl.* signal on a bugle or drum to put out lights at night. Taps is also sounded at military funerals.

tar[1] (tär), **1** *n.* a thick, black, sticky substance obtained by the distillation of wood or coal. Tar is used to cover and patch roads, roofs, etc. **2** *v.* to cover with tar: *tar a roof.* **3** *n.* the brownish black residue from the smoke of cigarettes, cigars, etc., containing by-products produced by the burning of tobacco. ❑ *v.* **tarred, tar·ring.** —**tar′like′,** *adj.*

tar and feather, to pour heated tar on and cover with feathers as a punishment.

tar[2] (tär), *n.* sailor.

ta·ra·ma·sa·la·ta (tä′rä mä sä·lä′tä), *n.* a Greek spread made of olive oil, fish roe, lemon juice, and bread crumbs or mashed potatoes. ❑ *n., pl.* **ta·ra·ma·sa·la·tas.**

tar·an·tel·la (tar′ən tel′ə), *n.* **1** a rapid, whirling southern Italian dance with a very quick rhythm. **2** music for this dance ❑ *n., pl.* **tar·an·tel·las.** [See Word Story at tarantula.]

ta·ran·tu·la (tə ran′chə lə), *n.* **1** any of various large, hairy spiders living in warm regions, with a painful but usually not serious bite. **2** a large spider of southern Europe with a slightly poisonous bite. ❑ *n., pl.* **ta·ran·tu·las.**

tarantula (def. 2)—up to 2 in. (5 cm) long

> **WORD STORY**   Tarantula and **tarantella** both come from the name of a port in Italy where the European tarantula is common. It was once believed that the bite of this spider caused people to dance uncontrollably, and so a popular dance was named for it.

Ta·ra·wa (tə rä′wə), *n.* capital of Kiribati. It is an atoll in the central Pacific.

tar·dy (tär′dē), *adj.* **1** behind time; late. **2** slow: *a tardy answer.* ❑ *adj.* **tar·di·er, tar·di·est.** —**tar′di·ly,** *adv.* —**tar′di·ness,** *n.*

tar·get (tär′git), **1** *n.* mark for shooting at; thing aimed at. A target is often a circle, but anything may be used as a target. **2** *n.* person or thing that is laughed at or criticized: *Their plan was the target of jokes.* **3** *n.* any aim you try to achieve; goal; objective: *The city championship is our team's target.* **4** *v.* to specify something as a problem or goal; single out: *He targeted my spelling as needing improvement.*

on target, striking the target; to the point; precise: *Criticism of bad planning for new schools was on target.*

> **WORD STORY**   Target comes from a French word meaning "a shield." Soldiers defended themselves from arrows with their shields, so the shields got a lot of arrows stuck in them. Targets used by people practicing shooting arrows had the same look and got the same name.

tar·iff (tar′if), *n.* **1** list of duties or taxes on imports or exports. **2** system of duties or taxes on imports or exports. **3** any duty or tax in such a list or system: *There is a very high tariff on imported jewelry.* **4** any table or scale of prices.

tar·mac (tär′mak′), *n.* **1** surface, such as a road or runway, paved with crushed rock in a tar and creosote binder. **2** Tarmac, trademark for this paving material.

tar·nish (tär′nish), **1** *v.* to dull the luster or brightness of: *Salt will tarnish silver.* **2** *v.* to lose luster or brightness: *The brass doorknobs tarnished.* **3** *n.* loss of luster or brightness. **4** *n.* a discolored coating, especially on silver: *Silver polish will remove the tarnish from those spoons.* **5** *v.* to bring disgrace upon your reputation, honor, etc.; sully; taint. —**tar′nish·a·ble,** *adj.*

ta·ro (tär′ō), *n.* the starchy root of a plant grown in the Pacific islands and other tropical regions, used as food. ❑ *n., pl.* **ta·ros.**

tarp (tärp), *n.* INFORMAL. tarpaulin.

tar paper, heavy paper coated with tar, used for waterproofing and windproofing buildings.

tar·pau·lin (tär pȯ′lən *or* tär′pə lin), *n.* sheet of canvas, plastic, or other strong waterproof material, used as a protective covering.

tar·pon (tär′pən), *n.* any of several large sea fishes, especially a silver-colored game fish found in the warmer parts of the Atlantic Ocean. ❑ *n., pl.* **tar·pon** or **tar·pons.**

tar·ra·gon (tar′ə gon), *n.* a plant with spicy, fragrant leaves, used to flavor vinegar, salads, soups, and other foods.

tar·ry[1] (tar′ē), *v.* **1** to delay leaving; remain; stay: *We tarried another day to see all the sights.* **2** to be tardy; hesitate: *Why do you tarry so long?* ❑ *v.* **tar·ried, tar·ry·ing.**

tar·ry[2] (tär′ē), *adj.* **1** of tar; like tar: *a tarry smell.* **2** covered with tar: *a tarry road.* ❑ *adj.* **tar·ri·er, tar·ri·est.** —**tar′ri·ness,** *n.*

tar·sal (tär′səl), **1** *adj.* of or about the tarsus. **2** *n.* one of the bones or cartilages in the ankle.

tar sand, sand or sandstone containing heavy, thick petroleum deposits.

tar·si·er (tär′sē ər), *n.* any of several kinds of small tree-dwelling primates of Indonesia and the Philippines. Tarsiers have large eyes and long, bare tails.

tar·sus (tär′səs), *n.* the group of seven small bones that make up the ankle joint. ❑ *n., pl.* **tar·si** (tär′sī).

tart[1] (tärt), *adj.* **1** having a sour but agreeable taste: *tart apples.* ■ See Synonym Study at **sour.** **2** sharp; sarcastic: *a tart reply.* —**tart′ly,** *adv.* —**tart′ness,** *n.*

tart[2] (tärt), *n.* pastry filled with cooked fruit, jam, etc.

tar·tan (tärt′n), **1** *n.* a plaid woolen cloth. Each Scottish Highland clan has its own pattern of tartan. **2** *n.* the pattern or design itself. **3** *n.* any similar plaid design or fabric of silk, cotton, etc. **4** *adj.* made of tartan. **5** *adj.* of or like tartan.

tar·tar (tär′tər), *n.* **1** a hard substance, produced by the action of saliva on food, that forms a crust on the teeth. **2** an acid substance in grape juice that forms a reddish crust on the inside of wine casks. After it is purified, this substance is called cream of tartar and is used with sodium bicarbonate to make baking powder.

Tar·tar (tär′tər), **1** *n.* member of a group of Mongolians and Turks who invaded Asia and eastern Europe during the Middle Ages. **2** *n.* **tartar,** person who has a bad temper. **3** *adj.* of or about a Tartar or Tartars. Also, **Tatar** for 1 and 3.

tartar sauce, sauce, usually for fish, made of mayonnaise with chopped pickles, onions, olives, herbs, etc.

Tar·ta·rus (tär′tər əs), *n.* in Greek myths: **1** a place of punishment in the underworld; part of Hades. **2** the underworld; Hades.

Tash·kent (tash kent′), *n.* capital of Uzbekistan.

task (task), **1** *n.* work to be done; piece of work; duty: *His task is to set the table.* **2** *v.* to assign a task to: *Mom tasked us with cleaning out the garage.* **3** *v.* to burden or strain: *Lifting that trunk tasked me beyond my strength.*

take to task, to blame; scold; reprove: *The teacher took the student to task for not studying.*

task force, 1 a temporary group of military units, especially naval units, assigned to one commander for carrying out a specific operation. **2** any group temporarily organized for a specific task.

task·mas·ter (task′mas′tər), *n.* person who sets tasks for others to do, especially tasks that are hard.

Tas·ma·ni·a (taz mā′nē ə), *n.* island off SE Australia. It is a state of Australia. —**Tas·ma′ni·an,** *adj., n.*

Tass or **TASS** (tas *or* täs), *n.* formerly, the government news agency of the Soviet Union.

tas·sel (tas′əl), **1** *n.* a hanging bunch of threads, small cords, beads, etc., fastened together at one end. **2** *n.* something that looks like this. Corn has tassels. **3** *v.* to put tassels on. **4** *v.* to grow tassels: *Corn tassels just before the ears form.* ❑ *v.* **tas·seled, tas·sel·ing** or **tas·selled, tas·sel·ling.** —**tas′sel·er** or **tas′sel·ler,** *n.*

taste (tāst), **1** *n.* what is special about something to the sense organs of the mouth; flavor. Sweet, sour, salt, and bitter are four important tastes. **2** *v.* to try the flavor of something by taking a little into the mouth: *The cook tastes everything to see if it is right.* **3** *n.* the sense by which the flavor of things is perceived. **4**

v. to get the flavor of by the sense of taste: *She tasted almond in the cake.* **5** *v.* to have a particular flavor: *The soup tastes of onion.* **6** *v.* to eat or drink a little bit of: *The children barely tasted their breakfast the day they went to the circus.* **7** *n.* a little bit; sample: *Take a taste of this cake. The snowstorm will give you a taste of northern winter.* **8** *v.* to experience; have: *taste freedom.* **9** *n.* a liking: *Suit your own taste.* **10** *n.* ability to perceive and enjoy what is beautiful and excellent: *My friend has taste in art.* **11** *n.* manner or style that shows such ability: *That collection shows good taste.* ❑ *v.* **tast·ed, tast·ing.** —**tast′a·ble** or **taste′a·ble,** *adj.*

taste bud, any of numerous groups of cells, mostly in the outer layer of the tongue, that sense whether something is sweet, sour, salty, or bitter.

taste·ful (tāst′fəl), *adj.* **1** having good taste; refined. **2** showing or done in good taste: *The room had tasteful furnishings that went well together.* —**taste′ful·ly,** *adv.* —**taste′ful·ness,** *n.*

taste·less (tāst′lis), *adj.* **1** without taste: *Overcooked vegetables are tasteless.* **2** without good taste; in poor taste: *tasteless decorations.* —**taste′less·ly,** *adv.* —**taste′less·ness,** *n.*

tast·er (tā′stər), *n.* person who tastes, especially someone whose work is judging the quality of wine, tea, coffee, etc., by the taste.

tast·y (tā′stē), *adj.* tasting good; pleasing to the taste. ❑ *adj.* **tast·i·er, tast·i·est.** —**tast′i·ly,** *adv.* —**tast′i·ness,** *n.*

> **SYNONYM STUDY** **Tasty, flavorful,** and **appetizing** all mean tasting good. **Tasty** is an informal word: *This soup is mighty tasty.* **Flavorful** suggests a strong, pleasant taste. It is used mostly in writing: *This article will discuss the flavorful foods of India.* **Appetizing** means tasting good enough to make people want more: *Lunch was an appetizing fruit salad.*

tat (tat), *v.* to make a kind of lace by looping and knotting threads with a shuttle. ❑ *v.* **tat·ted, tat·ting.** —**tat′ter,** *n.*

ta·ta·mi (tä tä′mē), *n.* a thick, woven straw floor mat traditionally used in Japanese homes. ❑ *n., pl.* **ta·ta·mi** or **ta·ta·mis.**

Ta·tar (tä′tər), **1** *n.* a descendant of the Tartars, now living in parts of Russia, Uzbekistan, Kyrgyzstan, and central and western Asia. **2** *adj.* of or about a Tatar or Tatars. Also, **Tartar.**

tat·ter (tat′ər), **1** *n.* a torn piece; rag: *After the storm the flag hung in tatters against the flagpole.* **2** *n.pl.* **tatters,** torn or ragged clothing. **3** *v.* to tear or wear to pieces; make ragged.

tat·tered (tat′ərd), *adj.* **1** full of tatters; torn; ragged: *a tattered dress.* **2** wearing torn or ragged clothes.

tat·ting (tat′ing), *n.* **1** process or work of making a kind of lace by looping and knotting thread with a shuttle. **2** lace made in this way.

tat·tle (tat′l), **1** *v.* to tell tales or secrets. **2** *v.* to talk or utter foolishly; gossip. **3** *n.* idle or foolish talk; gossip; telling tales or secrets. ❑ *v.* **tat·tled, tat·tling.** —**tat′tler,** *n.* —**tat′tling·ly,** *adv.*

tat·tle·tale (tat′l tāl′), **1** *n.* person who tells tales on others; telltale. **2** *adj.* revealing; telltale.

tat·too (ta tü′), **1** *v.* to mark the skin with designs or patterns by putting colors into punctures in the skin made by a needle: *An artist tattooed the sailor's arm with the design of a ship.* **2** *n.* the design or pattern made by tattooing. ❑ *v.* **tat·tooed, tat·too·ing;** *n., pl.* **tat·toos.** —**tat·too′er,** *n.*

taught (tot), *v.* past tense and past participle of **teach:** *That professor taught my brother. She has taught arithmetic for many years.* ■ Another word that sounds like this is **taut.**

taunt (tont), **1** *v.* to jeer at; mock; reproach: *My classmates taunted me for being teacher's pet.* **2** *n.* a mocking or insulting remark; jeer. —**taunt′er,** *n.* —**taunt′ing·ly,** *adv.*

taupe (tōp), **1** *n.* a dark, brownish gray. **2** *adj.* dark brownish gray.

Tau·rus (tôr′əs), *n.* **1** a group of stars shaped something like a bull. **2** the second sign of the zodiac, associated with the period from mid-April to mid-May.

taut (tot), *adj.* **1** tightly stretched; tense: *a taut rope.* **2** showing strain; tense: *The shock strained his taut nerves to the breaking point.* **3** in neat condition; tidy: *a taut ship.* ■ Another word that sounds like this is **taught.** —**taut′ly,** *adv.* —**taut′ness,** *n.*

tau·tog (to tog′), *n.* a dark food fish, common along the north Atlantic coast of the United States.

tau·tol·o·gy (to tol′ə jē), *n.* act or example of saying something

over again in other words; useless repetition. EXAMPLE: the *modern* students *of today.* ❑ *n., pl.* **tau·tol·o·gies.**

tav·ern (tav′ərn), *n.* **1** place where alcoholic drinks are sold and drunk; saloon. **2** OLD USE. inn.

taw (to), *n.* **1** a fancy marble used for shooting. **2** the line from which the players shoot their marbles.

taw·dry (to′drē), *adj.* showy and cheap; gaudy. ❑ *adj.* **taw·dri·er, taw·dri·est.** —**taw′dri·ly,** *adv.* —**taw′dri·ness,** *n.*

taw·ny (to′nē), *adj.* brownish yellow: *A lion has a tawny coat.* ❑ *adj.* **taw·ni·er, taw·ni·est.** —**taw′ni·ly,** *adv.* —**taw′ni·ness,** *n.*

tax (taks), **1** *n.* money paid by people for the support of the government and the cost of public works and services; money regularly collected from citizens by their rulers. **2** *v.* to put a tax on. People who own property are taxed in order to provide clean streets, good roads, protection against crime, and free education. **3** *n.* a burden, duty, or demand that oppresses; strain: *Climbing stairs is a tax on a weak heart.* **4** *v.* to lay a heavy burden on; be hard for: *The work taxed my strength.* ❑ *n., pl.* **tax·es** for 1. —**tax′er,** *n.* —**tax′ing·ly,** *adv.* —**tax′less,** *adj.*

tax·a·ble (tak′sə bəl), *adj.* liable to be taxed; subject to taxation: *a taxable income.* —**tax′a·ble·ness,** *n.*

tax·a·tion (tak sā′shən), *n.* **1** act or practice of taxing: *Taxation is necessary to provide roads, schools, and police.* **2** amount people pay for the support of the government; taxes.

tax·i (tak′sē), **1** *n.* car for hire, usually with an automatic meter to record the fare. **2** *v.* to ride in a taxi. **3** *v.* (of an aircraft) to move slowly on the ground or water. An airplane taxis into position before takeoff. ❑ *n., pl.* **tax·is** or **tax·ies;** *v.* **tax·ied, tax·i·ing** or **tax·y·ing.**

taxi (def. 1)

tax·i·cab (tak′sē kab′), *n.* taxi.

tax·i·der·my (tak′sə dèr′mē), *n.* art of preparing the skins of animals and stuffing and mounting them so that they look alive. —**tax′i·der·mist,** *n.*

tax·on·o·my (tak son′ə mē), *n.* **1** classification, especially of biological species. **2** branch of science dealing with classification. —**tax′o·nom′ic,** *adj.* —**tax′o·nom′i·cal·ly,** *adv.* —**tax·on′o·mist,** *n.*

tax·pay·er (taks′pā′ər), *n.* person who pays a tax or is required by law to do so.

Tay·lor (tā′lər), *n.* **1 Elizabeth,** born 1932, American movie star. She has won two Academy Awards as best actress, for the movies *Butterfield 8* and *Who's Afraid of Virginia Woolf?* **2 Zach·a·ry** (zak′ə rē), 1784-1850, the 12th president of the United States, from 1849 to 1850. He died after only 16 months in office.

Tb, symbol for terbium.

TB, T.B., or **t.b.,** tuberculosis.

T-ball (tē′bol′), *n.* baseball for very young children. The ball is hit from a tee, rather than being pitched.

T-bar (tē′bär′), *n.* a ski lift with upside-down T-shaped bars that skiers lean against while being towed uphill.

Tbi·li·si (tə bə lē′sē), *n.* capital of the country of Georgia, in the S part.

tbs. or **tbsp.,** tablespoon or tablespoons.

T

a	hat	ė	term	ô	order	ch	child		
ā	age	i	it	oi	oil	ng	long		a in about
ä	far	ī	ice	ou	out	sh	she		e in taken
â	care	o	hot	u	cup	th	thin	ə	i in pencil
e	let	ō	open	ù	put	ŦH	then		o in lemon
ē	equal	ò	saw	ü	rule	zh	measure		u in circus

Tc, symbol for technetium.

T cell, any of various kinds of white blood cells. Some control immune system reactions to diseases, and others destroy diseased cells or germs.

Tchai·kov·sky (chī kȯf′skē), *n.* Peter Il·ich (il′ich), 1840-1893, Russian composer. His romantic, tuneful compositions include six symphonies, the ballets *Swan Lake* and *The Nutcracker,* and the *1812 Overture.*

TD, (in football) touchdown.

T.D., Treasury Department.

Te, symbol for tellurium.

tea (tē), *n.* **1** a dark brown drink made by pouring boiling water over the dried and prepared leaves of a certain bush. **2** the dried and prepared leaves from which this drink is made. **3** the bush on which these leaves grow. Tea is raised mainly in China, Japan, and India. **4** a light meal in the late afternoon or early evening, at which tea is commonly served. **5** an afternoon reception at which tea is served. **6** any drink prepared from some plant or other substance. **Beef tea** is a strong broth made from beef. ❑ *n., pl.* **teas** for 4,5,6. ■ Other words that sound like this are **tee** and **ti.**

tea bag, tea leaves in a little bag of thin cloth or paper for easy removal from the cup or pot after use.

teach (tēch), *v.* **1** to help to learn; show how to do; make understand: *He is teaching his dog tricks.* **2** to give instruction to: *She teaches her classes well.* **3** to give lessons in: *He teaches mathematics.* **4** to give instruction; act as teacher: *She teaches for a living.* ❑ *v.* **taught, teach·ing.**

teach·a·ble (tē′chǝ bǝl), *adj.* capable of being taught. —**teach′·a·bil′i·ty,** *n.*

teach·er (tē′chǝr), *n.* person who teaches, especially someone who teaches in a school. —**teach′er·like′,** *adj.*

teach·ing (tē′ching), *n.* **1** work or profession of a teacher. **2** act of someone who teaches. **3** what is taught; instruction; precept.

tea·cup (tē′kup′), *n.* cup for drinking tea.

tea·cup·ful (tē′kup′ful), *n.* as much as a teacup holds, usually four fluid ounces. ❑ *n., pl.* **tea·cup·fuls.**

tea·house (tē′hous′), *n.* place where tea and other light refreshments are served. There are many teahouses in Japan and China. ❑ *n., pl.* **tea·hous·es** (tē′hou′ziz).

teak (tēk), *n.* a large tree of the East Indies with hard, durable, yellowish brown wood that is used for furniture, shipbuilding, etc.

tea·ket·tle (tē′ket′l), *n.* kettle for boiling water.

teak·wood (tēk′wud′), *n.* wood of the teak.

teal (tēl), *n.* any of several small wild ducks related to the mallard. ❑ *n., pl.* **teal** or **teals.**

team (tēm), **1** *n.* number of people working or acting together, especially one of the sides in a game, sport, competition, etc.: *a football team, a debating team.* **2** *n.* two or more horses or other animals harnessed together to work. **3** *v.* to join together in a team: *Everybody teamed up to clean the classroom after the party.* ■ Another word that sounds like this is **teem.**

team·mate (tēm′māt′), *n.* a fellow member of a team.

team·ster (tēm′stǝr), *n.* person whose work is hauling things with a truck or driving a team of horses.

team·work (tēm′wėrk′), *n.* the combined action of a number of people that makes the work of the group successful and effective: *Football requires teamwork.*

tea·pot (tē′pot′), *n.* container with a handle and a spout for making and serving tea.

tear¹ (tir), **1** *n.* drop of salty liquid from the eye. **2** *v.* to fill with tears; shed tears. ■ Another word that sounds like this is **tier.**

in tears, shedding tears; crying: *The baby is in tears because he is hungry.*

teamwork

tear² (târ), **1** *v.* to pull apart by force: *tear a box open. I tore the letter into tiny pieces.* **2** *v.* to make by pulling apart: *She tore a hole in her jeans.* **3** *n.* a torn place: *She has a tear in her jeans.* **4** *v.* to pull hard; pull violently: *Tear out the page.* **5** *v.* to cut badly; wound: *The jagged stone tore his skin.* **6** *v.* to divide; split; rend: *The party was torn by two factions.* **7** *v.* to remove by effort; force away: *I couldn't tear myself away from the exciting book I was reading.* **8** *v.* to make miserable; distress: *torn by grief.* **9** *v.* to become torn: *Lace tears easily.* **10** *n.* a torn place; hole: *a tear in my shirt.* **11** *v.* to move with great force or haste: *A car came tearing down the road.* ❑ *v.* **tore, torn, tear·ing.** —**tear′a·ble,** *adj.* —**tear′er,** *n.*

tear down, 1 to pull down; raze; destroy: *to tear down an old building.* **2** to bring about the wreck of; discredit; ruin: *tear down her opponent's reputation.*

tear into, to attack or criticize severely.

tear·drop (tir′drop′), *n.* tear¹ (def. 1).

tear·ful (tir′fǝl), *adj.* **1** full of tears; weeping. **2** causing tears; sad. —**tear′ful·ly,** *adv.* —**tear′ful·ness,** *n.*

tear gas (tir), gas that irritates the eyes and temporarily blinds them with tears. —**tear′-gas′,** *v.*

tea·room (tē′rüm′), *n.* room or shop where tea, coffee, and light meals are served.

tease (tēz), **1** *v.* to pester or upset by jokes, questions, requests, etc.; annoy: *The children teased the dog until it snapped at them.* **2** *v.* to beg: *The child teases for everything he sees.* **3** *n.* person who teases. **4** *v.* to comb out wool, flax, etc. **5** *v.* to comb hair toward the head to produce fullness. **6** *v.* to raise nap on cloth. ❑ *v.* **teased, teas·ing.** —**teas′ing·ly,** *adv.*

teas·er (tē′zǝr), *n.* **1** person or thing that teases. **2** an annoying problem; puzzling task.

tea·spoon (tē′spün′), *n.* **1** a small spoon often used to stir tea or coffee. **2** unit of measure in cooking equal to ⅓ tablespoon.

tea·spoon·ful (tē′spün′fül), *n.* as much as a teaspoon holds. 1 teaspoon = ⅓ tablespoonful. ❑ *n., pl.* **tea·spoon·fuls.**

teat (tēt), *n.* nipple of a breast or udder, from which the young suck milk.

tech., **1** technical. **2** technician. **3** technology.

tech·ne·ti·um (tek nē′shē ǝm), *n.* a radioactive metallic element produced artificially from uranium or molybdenum. *Symbol:* Tc

tech·ni·cal (tek′nǝ kǝl), *adj.* **1** of or about a mechanical or industrial art or applied science: *This technical school trains engineers, chemists, and architects.* **2** of or about the special facts of a science or art: *"Electrolysis" and "ulna" are technical words.* **3** of or about technique: *Her singing showed technical skill, but her voice was weak.* **4** by the rules of a certain science, art, game, etc.: *When the boxer was so badly hurt that the fight was stopped, his opponent won by a technical knockout.* —**tech′ni·cal·ly,** *adv.* —**tech′ni·cal·ness,** *n.*

tech·ni·cal·i·ty (tek′nǝ kal′ǝ tē), *n.* **1** a technical matter, point, detail, term, expression, etc.: *Books on engineering contain many technicalities which the ordinary reader may find difficult.* **2** technical quality or character. ❑ *n., pl.* **tech·ni·cal·i·ties** for 1.

technical sergeant, a military rank. See chart on page 712.

tech·ni·cian (tek nish′ǝn), *n.* **1** person experienced in the technical details of a subject. **2** person skilled in the technique of an art.

Tech·ni·col·or (tek′nǝ kul′ǝr), *n.* trademark for a process of making movies in color.

tech·nique (tek nēk′), *n.* **1** a special method or system used to accomplish something. **2** method or ability of an artist's performance, execution, etc.; technical skill: *The pianist's technique was excellent.*

tech·no·log·i·cal (tek′nə loj′ə kəl), *adj.* of, about, or used in technology. **—tech′no·log′i·cal·ly,** *adv.*

tech·nol·o·gy (tek nol′ə jē), *n.* **1** the use of scientific knowledge to control physical objects and forces: *overcome problems by technology.* **2** any method for carrying out a process involving physical objects and forces: *the technology of weaving.* **—tech·nol′o·gist,** *n.*

tech·no·phobe (tek′nə fōb), *n.* someone who is afraid of using technology or of the effects of technology: *He's such a technophobe he doesn't even have a VCR.* **—tech′no·pho′bic,** *adj.*

tech·no·speak (tek′nō spēk′), *n.* vocabulary used to talk about technology, especially new technology, especially by people interested in technology: *Her explanation was pure technospeak.*

tec·ton·ics (tek ton′iks), *n.* **1** the study of the structure of the earth's crust and of the forces that produce such changes in it as folding, faulting, and the like. **2** plate tectonics.

Te·cum·seh (tə kum′sə), *n.* 1768?-1813, American Indian leader, chief of the Shawnee. He was a British ally in the War of 1812.

teddy bear

ted·dy bear or **Ted·dy bear** (ted′ē), a child's furry toy bear.

WORD STORY **Teddy bear** comes from President Theodore Roosevelt's nickname, Teddy. A cartoon showed him refusing to shoot a bear cub while hunting. A clever toy maker promptly began to sell a stuffed animal labeled the Teddy bear, and it was an immediate and lasting success.

Te De·um (tā dā′əm), **1** a hymn of praise and thanksgiving sung in Roman Catholic and Anglican churches at morning prayers or on special occasions. **2** music for this hymn.

te·di·ous (tē′dē əs *or* tē′jəs), *adj.* long and tiring; boring: *A long, involved talk that you cannot understand is tedious.* **—te′di·ous·ly,** *adv.* **—te′di·ous·ness,** *n.*

te·di·um (tē′dē əm), *n.* state of being tedious; boredom.

tee (tē), **1** *n.* a short wooden or plastic peg with a concave top on which a golf ball is placed when a player drives. **2** *n.* a raised place from which a player starts in playing each hole in golf. **3** *v.* to put a golf ball on a tee. **4** *n.* INFORMAL. T-shirt. ❑ *v.* **teed, tee·ing.** ■ Other words that sound like this are **tea** and **ti.**
tee off, to drive a golf ball from a tee.

teem (tēm), *v.* to be full of; abound; swarm: *The swamp teemed with mosquitoes.* ■ Another word that sounds like this is **team.**

teem·ing (tē′ming), *adj.* **1** full of; alive with: *ponds teeming with fish.* **2** fruitful: *teeming colonies of bacteria.* **—teem′ing·ly,** *adv.* **—teem′ing·ness,** *n.*

teen (tēn), **1** *adj.* teenage: *teen fashions.* **2** *n.* teenager.

teen·age (tēn′āj′), *adj.* **1** of or for a teenager or teenagers: *This store has all the latest teenage fashions.* **2** in your teens; being a teenager: *They have two teenage daughters.*

teen·aged (tēn′ājd′), *adj.* in your teens; being a teenager: *a teenaged athlete.*

teen·ag·er (tēn′ā′jər), *n.* person in his or her teens.

teens (tēnz), *n.pl.* the years of life from 13 to 19 inclusive.

teen·sy (tēn′sē), *adj.* tiny. ❑ *adj.* **teen·si·er, teen·si·est.**

teent·sy (tēnt′sē), *adj.* tiny. ❑ *adj.* **teent·si·er, teent·si·est.**

tee·ny (tē′nē), *adj.* tiny. ❑ *adj.* **tee·ni·er, tee·ni·est.**

tee·pee (tē′pē), *n.* tepee. ❑ *n., pl.* **tee·pees.**

tee shirt, T-shirt.

tee·ter (tē′tər), **1** *v.* to rock unsteadily; sway. **2** *v.* to balance on a seesaw. **3** *n.* seesaw.

tee·ter-tot·ter (tē′tər tot′ər), *n.* seesaw.

teeth (tēth), *n.* plural of **tooth.**
cut your teeth on, to get experience from doing something.
in the teeth of, 1 straight against; in the face of: *We advanced in the teeth of the wind.* **2** in defiance of; in spite of.

teethe (tēŧH), *v.* to grow teeth; cut teeth; have teeth grow through the gums: *Babies teethe.* ❑ *v.* **teethed, teeth·ing.**

tee·to·tal·er (tē tō′tl ər), *n.* person who never takes alcoholic liquor.

Tef·lon (tef′lon), *n.* trademark for a slippery plastic used for coating kitchen utensils, as a dry lubricant, and in electric insulation.

Te·gu·ci·gal·pa (tə gü′sē gal′pə), *n.* capital of Honduras, in the S part.

Teh·ran (te ran′), *n.* capital of Iran, in the N part.

tek·tite (tek′tīt), *n.* any of various rounded, black, glassy objects of different sizes, found in many parts of the world. Tektites are thought to be the result of meteorites striking the earth.

tel., **1** telegram. **2** telegraph. **3** telephone.

Tel A·viv (tel′ ə vēv′), largest city of Israel, in the W part.

tele-, *prefix.* **1** over a long distance: *telescope = device for looking over a long distance.* **2** television: *telecast = broadcast over television.*

tel·e·cast (tel′ə kast′), **1** *v.* to broadcast by television. **2** *n.* a TV broadcast. ❑ *v.* **tel·e·cast** or **tel·e·cast·ed, tel·e·cast·ing. —tel′e·cast′er,** *n.*

tel·e·com·mu·ni·ca·tion (tel′ə kə myü′nə kā′shən), *n.* Often, **telecommunications,** transmission of messages by radio, telephone, satellite, etc.

tel·e·com·mute (tel′ə kə′myüt), *v.* to work for a business while at home, by using telecommunication devices, especially a computer with a modem, to communicate with your office: *She telecommutes on Thursdays but is in the office the rest of the week.* ❑ *v.* **tel·e·com·mut·ed, tel·e·com·mut·ing. —tel′e·com·mut′er,** *n.*

tel·e·con·fer·ence (tel′ə kon′fər əns), *n.* conference among a group of people in different places that are linked by telecommunication.

tel·e·gram (tel′ə gram), *n.* message sent by telegraph: *receive a telegram.*

tel·e·graph (tel′ə graf), **1** *n.* way of sending coded messages over wires by means of electrical signals. **2** *n.* device used for sending these messages. **3** *v.* to send a message by telegraph. **—te·leg·ra·pher** (tə leg′rə fər), *n.*

tel·e·graph·ic (tel′ə graf′ik), *adj.* of or about the telegraph; sent as a telegram. **—tel′e·graph′i·cal·ly,** *adv.*

tel·e·mar·ket·ing (tel′ə mär′kə ting), *n.* the business of selling things by telephone.

tel·e·me·ter (tə lem′ə tər), **1** *n.* device for measuring heat, radiation, etc., and transmitting the measurements to a distant receiving station. **2** *v.* to measure and transmit by telemeter.

tel·e·me·try (tə lem′ə trē), *n.* the use of telemeters for measuring and transmitting information.

tel·e·path·ic (tel′ə path′ik), *adj.* of or by telepathy. **—tel′e·path′i·cal·ly,** *adv.*

te·lep·a·thy (tə lep′ə thē), *n.* communication of one mind with another without using speech, hearing, sight, or any other sense used normally to communicate.

tel·e·phone (tel′ə fōn), **1** *n.* device or system for sending sound or speech to a distant point by means of electrical impulses transmitted by wire. **2** *v.* to talk through a telephone; send a message by telephone. **3** *v.* to make a telephone call to. ❑ *v.* **tel·e·phoned, tel·e·phon·ing. —tel′e·phon′er,** *n.*

telephone book or **telephone directory,** list of names, addresses, and telephone numbers of people or businesses with telephones in a certain area.

tel·e·phon·ic (tel′ə fon′ik), *adj.* of or by the telephone: *telephonic communication.* **—tel′e·phon′i·cal·ly,** *adv.*

tel·e·pho·to lens (tel′ə fō′tō), camera lens for producing an enlarged image of a distant object.

tel·e·print·er (tel′ə prin′tər), *n.* teletypewriter.

Tel·e·Promp·Ter (tel′ə promp′tər), *n.* trademark for a device that shows a speech in large form, a bit at a time, for use by speakers who are being televised.

a	hat	ė	term	ô	order	ch	child		a in about
ā	age	i	it	oi	oil	ng	long		e in taken
ä	far	ī	ice	ou	out	sh	she	ə	i in pencil
â	care	o	hot	u	cup	th	thin		o in lemon
e	let	ō	open	ů	put	ŧH	then		u in circus
ē	equal	ò	saw	ü	rule	zh	measure		

T

tel·e·scope (tel′ə skōp), **1** *n.* device for making distant objects appear nearer and larger. Objects in space are studied by means of telescopes. **2** *n.* device for studying objects in space, using a form of energy other than visible light: *radio telescope.* **3** *v.* to force or be forced together, one inside another like the sliding tubes of some telescopes: *When the trains crashed into each other, the cars were telescoped.* **4** *v.* to shorten; condense: *a telescoped summary.* ❑ *v.* **tel·e·scoped, tel·e·scop·ing.**

tel·e·scop·ic (tel′ə skop′ik), *adj.* **1** obtained or seen by means of a telescope: *a telescopic view of the moon.* **2** visible only through a telescope. **3** far-seeing. **4** consisting of parts that slide one inside another like the tubes of some telescopes.

tel·e·text (tel′ə tekst), *n.* system of delivering information, such as stock-market listings, weather reports, etc., by televising it to viewers.

tel·e·thon (tel′ə thon), *n.* a TV show lasting many hours, especially one seeking contributions for a charity.

tel·e·type (tel′ə tīp), **1** *n.* **Teletype,** trademark for a teletypewriter. **2** *n.* system of sending signals by Teletype. **3** *v.* to send a message by Teletype. ❑ *v.* **tel·e·typed, tel·e·typ·ing.**

tel·e·type·writ·er (tel′ə tīp′rī′tər), *n.* a telegraphic device which resembles a typewriter, used in sending, receiving, and automatically printing out messages.

tel·e·view·er (tel′ə vyü′ər), *n.* person who watches TV.

tel·e·vise (tel′ə vīz), *v.* to send by television: *Will they televise today's game?* ❑ *v.* **tel·e·vised, tel·e·vis·ing.**

tel·e·vi·sion (tel′ə vizh′ən), **1** *n.* system of sending and receiving images and sounds over wires or through the air by means of electrical impulses. In television, waves of light and sound are changed into electric waves and transmitted to a receiver where they are changed back into waves of light and sound so that the images can be seen and the sounds heard. **2** *n.* the device on which these pictures may be seen. **3** *n.* the business of television broadcasting; the television industry. **4** *adj.* of, used in, or sent by television.

tel·ex (tel′eks), **1** *n.* system of communications for transmitting messages between teletypewriters, using telephone and telegraph lines. **2** *n.* a message sent by this system. **3** *v.* to send a message by this system. ❑ *n., pl.* **tel·ex·es** for 2.

tell (tel), *v.* **1** to put in words; say: *Tell the truth.* **2** to tell to; inform: *Tell us about it.* **3** to make known; reveal: *Don't tell where the money is.* **4** to be a telltale: *Promise not to tell.* **5** to recognize; know; distinguish: *He couldn't tell which house it was.* **6** to say to; order; command: *Tell her to stop!* **7** to say to with force: *I don't like it, I tell you.* **8** to have effect or force: *Every blow told.* ❑ *v.* **told, tell·ing.**

tell off, to strike back sharply in words; scold: *She really told me off when she found out I took her book.*

tell on, 1 to inform on; tell tales about: *Please don't tell on me.* **2** to have a harmful effect on; break down: *The strain told on the man's health.*

Tell (tel), *n.* **William,** legendary hero in the Swiss struggle for independence against Austria. He was forced to shoot an apple from his son's head.

tell·er (tel′ər), *n.* **1** a bank cashier who takes in and gives out money. **2** person who tells: *a teller of tales.*

Tel·ler (tel′ər), *n.* **Ed·ward** (ed′wərd), born 1908, American physicist, born in Hungary. He led efforts to develop the hydrogen bomb.

tell·ing (tel′ing), *adj.* having effect or force; striking: *a telling blow.* —**tell′ing·ly,** *adv.*

tell·tale (tel′tāl′), **1** *n.* person who tells tales on others; tattletale. **2** *adj.* serving to identify; revealing: *a telltale fingerprint.*

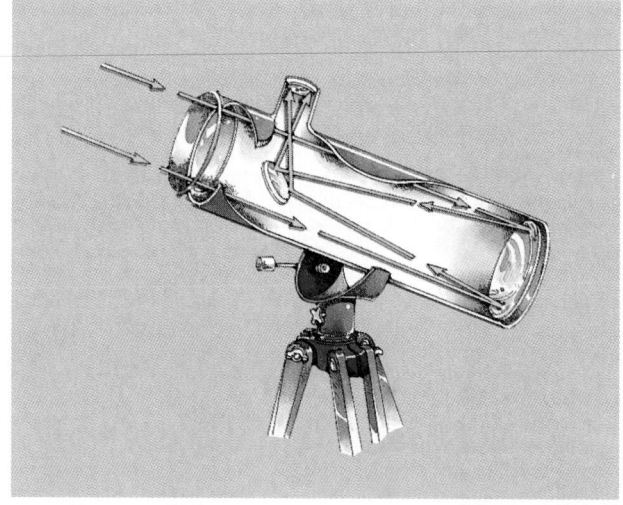

telescope (def. 1)

tel·lur·i·um (te lúr′ē əm), *n.* a silver-white nonmetallic element with some metallic properties, used in alloys. It usually occurs in nature combined with various metals. *Symbol:* Te

tel·o·phase (tel′ə fāz′), *n.* the final stage of cell division.

te·mer·i·ty (tə mer′ə tē), *n.* reckless boldness; rashness.

temp., 1 temperature. **2** temporary.

temp (temp), *n.* someone hired to do a temporary job.

tem·per (tem′pər), **1** *n.* angry state of mind: *In a temper he slammed the door.* **2** *n.* calm state of mind: *I became angry and lost my temper.* **3** *n.* state of mind; disposition; condition: *She was in no temper to be kept waiting.* **4** *v.* to soften; make less severe: *"Temper justice with mercy."* **5** *v.* to bring or be brought to a proper or desired condition of hardness, toughness, flexibility, etc., by mixing or preparing. A painter tempers colors by mixing them with oil. Steel is tempered by heating it and cooling it under controlled conditions until it has the proper degree of hardness and flexibility. **6** *n.* the degree of hardness, toughness, flexibility, etc., of a substance given by tempering: *The temper of the clay was right for shaping.* —**tem′per·a·ble,** *adj.* —**tem′per·er,** *n.*

tem·per·a (tem′pər ə), *n.* **1** method of painting in which colors are mixed with egg white, egg yolk, or other substances instead of oil. **2** poster paint. ❑ *n., pl.* **tem·per·as.**

tem·per·a·ment (tem′pər ə mənt), *n.* **1** someone's nature or disposition: *a shy temperament.* **2** an easily irritated, sensitive nature: *an artist's display of temperament.*

tem·per·a·men·tal (tem′pər ə men′tl), *adj.* **1** likely to have sudden changes of mood; easily irritated; sensitive: *A temperamental person can be hard to live with.* **2** showing a strongly marked individual temperament: *Cats have a temperamental dislike for water.* —**tem′per·a·men′tal·ly,** *adv.*

tem·per·ance (tem′pər əns), *n.* **1** moderation in your actions, speech, habits, etc.; self-control. **2** moderation in the use of alcoholic drinks. **3** the principle and practice of not using alcoholic drinks at all.

tem·per·ate (tem′pər it), *adj.* **1** not very hot and not very cold: *a temperate climate.* **2** moderate; using self-control: *She spoke in a temperate manner, not showing strong feelings.* **3** moderate in using alcoholic drinks. —**tem′per·ate·ly,** *adv.* —**tem′per·ate·ness,** *n.*

Temperate Zone, the part of the earth's surface between the tropic of Cancer and the arctic circle in the Northern Hemisphere, or between the tropic of Capricorn and the antarctic circle in the Southern Hemisphere.

tem·per·a·ture (tem′pər ə chər), *n.* **1** degree of heat or cold. The temperature of freezing water is 32 degrees Fahrenheit (0 degrees Celsius). **2** form of energy found in the motion of an object's molecules; internal energy. When heat flows into an object, temperature increases. **3** a body temperature higher than normal (98.6 degrees Fahrenheit or 37.0 degrees Celsius); fever: *A sick person may have a temperature.*

tem·pered (tem′pərd), *adj.* **1** softened; made less severe: *justice tempered with mercy.* **2** treated so as to become hard but not too brittle: *The sword was made of tempered steel.*

tem·pest (tem′pist), *n.* **1** a violent windstorm, usually with rain, hail, or snow: *The tempest drove the ship onto the rocks.* **2** a violent disturbance; uproar: *a tempest of anger.*

tem·pes·tu·ous (tem pes′chü əs), *adj.* **1** stormy: *It was a tempestuous night.* **2** violent: *a tempestuous fit of anger.* —**tem·pes′tu·ous·ly,** *adv.* —**tem·pes′tu·ous·ness,** *n.*

tem·plate (tem′plit), *n.* **1** a thin, flat piece of wood, metal, etc., used as a pattern when cutting something out of cloth, metal, etc. **2** any model or pattern on which something is formed.

tem·ple[1] (tem′pəl), *n.* **1** building used for the service or worship of a god or gods. **2** synagogue. **3** building set apart for Christian worship; church. **4** Temple, any of three temples in ancient Jerusalem built at different times by the Jews. Solomon built the first Temple. —**tem′ple·like′,** *adj.*

temple[1] (def. 1)

tem·ple[2] (tem′pəl), *n.* the flat part on each side of the forehead.

Temple, *n.* Shirley. See **Black, Shirley Temple.**

tem·po (tem′pō), *n.* **1** the rate of speed at which a piece of music is played: *Composers usually indicate the correct tempo for their music.* **2** rhythm; characteristic rhythm: *the fast tempo of modern life.* ❑ *n., pl.* **tem·pos, tem·pi** (tem′pē).

tem·po·ral[1] (tem′pər əl), *adj.* **1** not religious or sacred; secular. **2** of this life only. **3** of or about time. **4** lasting for a time only; temporary. —**tem′por·al·ly,** *adv.* —**tem′por·al·ness,** *n.*

tem·po·ral[2] (tem′pər əl), *adj.* of the temples or sides of the forehead.

tem·po·rar·y (tem′pə rer′ē), *adj.* lasting for a short time only; used for the time being; not permanent: *This is just a temporary job.* —**tem′po·rar′i·ly,** *adv.* —**tem′po·rar′i·ness,** *n.*

tem·po·rize (tem′pə rīz′), *v.* **1** to avoid doing or deciding something in order to gain time, avoid trouble, etc. **2** to fit your acts to the time or occasion. ❑ *v.* **tem·po·rized, tem·po·riz·ing.** —**tem′por·i·za′tion,** *n.* —**tem′po·riz′er,** *n.* —**tem′po·riz′ing·ly,** *adv.*

tempt (tempt), *v.* **1** to make or try to make someone do something: *Extreme hunger can tempt a person to steal food.* ■ See Synonym Study at **urge. 2** to appeal strongly to; attract: *That candy tempts me.* **3** to provoke: *It is tempting fate to try to cross the lake in that old boat.* —**tempt′a·ble,** *adj.* —**tempt′er,** *n.*

temp·ta·tion (temp tā′shən), *n.* **1** thing that tempts: *Money left carelessly about is a temptation.* **2** act of tempting: *No temptation could make her break her promise.* **3** condition of being tempted: *"Lead us not into temptation."*

tempt·ing (temp′ting), *adj.* apt to tempt; alluring; inviting: *a tempting suggestion.* —**tempt′ing·ly,** *adv.* —**tempt′ing·ness,** *n.*

tem·pur·a (tem pùr′ə), *n.* a Japanese food made by dipping seafood or vegetables in batter and frying in deep fat.

ten (ten), **1** *adj., n.* one more than nine; 10. **2** *n.* set of ten persons or things.

ten·a·ble (ten′ə bəl), *adj.* able to be held or defended: *a tenable position, a tenable theory.* —**ten′a·bil′i·ty, ten′a·ble·ness,** *n.* —**ten′a·bly,** *adv.*

te·na·cious (ti nā′shəs), *adj.* **1** stubborn; persistent: *a tenacious salesman.* **2** holding fast: *the tenacious jaws of a bulldog.* **3** holding fast together; not easily pulled apart. —**te·na′cious·ly,** *adv.* —**te·na′cious·ness,** *n.*

WORD FAMILY

Tenacious and the words below are related. They all come from a Latin word meaning "to hold."

abstain	continue	obtain	tenant
abstinence	detain	pertain	tenement
contain	detention	retainer[1]	tenet
content[1]	entertain	retainer[2]	tennis
content[2]	impertinent	sustain	tenon
continent[1]	maintain	sustenance	tenor
continent[2]	maintenance	tenable	tenure

te·nac·i·ty (ti nas′ə tē), *n.* **1** stubbornness; persistence. **2** firmness in holding fast. **3** firmness in holding together; toughness.

ten·an·cy (ten′ən sē), *n.* **1** condition of being a tenant; occupancy and payment of rent for land or buildings. **2** length of time a tenant occupies a property. ❑ *n., pl.* **ten·an·cies** for 2.

ten·ant (ten′ənt), **1** *n.* person paying rent for the use of land, a building, or space in a building belonging to another person: *That building has apartments for one hundred tenants.* **2** *n.* person or thing that occupies: *Wild animals were the only tenants of the forest.* **3** *v.* to hold or occupy as a tenant; inhabit: *That old house has not been tenanted for many years.* —**ten′ant·less,** *adj.*

tenant farmer, person who lives on and farms land belonging to someone else. The owner receives cash or a share of the crops as rent.

Ten Commandments, (in the Bible) the ten rules for living and for worship that God gave to Moses on Mount Sinai.

tend[1] (tend), *v.* **1** to be apt; be likely; incline to: *Fruit tends to decay. They tend to take a long vacation every other year.* **2** to lead: *The coastline tends to the south here.*

tend[2] (tend), *v.* to care for; look after: *Paramedics tended the accident victims. Landscapers tended the lawns, hedges, and gardens.*

tend·en·cy (ten′dən sē), *n.* a natural inclination to do something: *a tendency to oversleep. Wood has a tendency to swell if it gets wet.* ❑ *n., pl.* **tend·en·cies.**

ten·der[1] (ten′dər), *adj.* **1** not hard or tough; soft: *The meat is tender.* **2** not strong and hardy; delicate: *The leaves in spring are green and tender.* **3** kind; affectionate; loving: *She spoke tender words to the baby.* **4** not rough or crude; gentle: *These young plants need tender care.* **5** young: *She came to live here at the tender age of five.* **6** sensitive; painful; sore: *a tender wound.* **7** feeling pain or grief easily: *a tender heart.* —**ten′der·ly,** *adv.* —**ten′der·ness,** *n.*

ten·der[2] (ten′dər), **1** *v.* to offer formally: *She tendered her resignation.* **2** *n.* a formal offer: *She refused his tender of marriage.* **3** *n.* something offered as payment, especially money. **4** *v.* to offer money, goods, etc., in payment of a debt. —**ten′der·a·ble,** *adj.* —**ten′der·er,** *n.*

tend·er[3] (ten′dər), *n.* **1** person or thing that tends another: *a machine tender.* **2** a small boat carried or towed by a ship and used for landing passengers. **3** the car that carries coal and water, attached behind a steam locomotive.

ten·der·foot (ten′dər fùt′), *n.* **1** newcomer to the pioneer life of the western United States. **2** person not used to rough living and hardships. **3** INFORMAL. an inexperienced person; beginner. ❑ *n., pl.* **ten·der·foots, ten·der·feet** (ten′dər fēt′).

ten·der·heart·ed (ten′dər här′tid), *adj.* kindly; sympathetic. —**ten′der·heart′ed·ly,** *adv.* —**ten′der·heart′ed·ness,** *n.*

a	hat	ė	term	ô	order	ch	child		
ā	age	i	it	oi	oil	ng	long		a in about
ä	far	ī	ice	ou	out	sh	she		e in taken
â	care	o	hot	u	cup	th	thin	ə	i in pencil
e	let	ō	open	ù	put	ŦH	then		o in lemon
ē	equal	ò	saw	ü	rule	zh	measure		u in circus

T

ten·der·ize (ten′də riz′), *v.* to make meat tender by soaking in a solution that breaks down its connective tissue. ❏ *v.* **ten·der·ized, ten·der·iz·ing.** —**ten′der·i·za′tion,** *n.* —**ten′der·iz′er,** *n.*

ten·der·loin (ten′dər loin′), *n.* a tender part of the loin of beef or pork.

ten·di·ni·tis (ten′də ni′tis), *n.* inflammation of a tendon. Also, **tendonitis.**

ten·don (ten′dən), *n.* a tough, strong band or cord of tissue that joins a muscle to a bone or some other body part.

ten·don·i·tis (ten′də ni′tis), *n.* tendinitis.

ten·dril (ten′drəl), *n.* **1** a threadlike part of a climbing plant that attaches itself to something and helps support the plant. **2** something like this part of a plant: *curly tendrils of hair.*

ten·e·ment (ten′ə mənt), *n.* a building, especially in a poor section of a city, divided into sets of rooms occupied by separate families.

ten·et (ten′it), *n.* doctrine, principle, belief, or opinion believed to be true.

ten·fold (ten′fōld′), *adj., adv.* ten times as much or as many.

ten-gal·lon hat (ten′gal′ən), a large hat with a broad brim, usually worn by cowboys.

Tenn., Tennessee.

Ten·nes·see (ten′ə sē′), *n.* **1** one of the south central states of the United States. *Abbreviation:* TN or Tenn. *Capital:* Nashville. **2** river flowing from E Tennessee into the Ohio River. —**Ten′nes·se′an** or **Ten′nes·see′an,** *n.*

Tennessee Valley Authority, TVA.

ten·nis (ten′is), *n.* game played by two or four players on a rectangular court, in which a ball is hit back and forth over a net with a racket.

tennis shoes, sneakers.

Ten·ny·son (ten′ə sən), *n.* **Alfred, Lord,** 1809-1892, English poet. He became the poet laureate of Great Britain in 1850. —**Ten·ny·so·ni·an** (ten′ə sō′nē ən), *adj.*

Te·noch·ti·tlan (tā nòch′tē tlän′), *n.* capital of the Aztec empire, on the site of modern Mexico City.

ten·on (ten′ən), *n.* the end of a piece of wood cut so as to fit into the mortise in another piece and so form a joint.

ten·or (ten′ər), **1** *n.* the highest male voice in music. **2** *n.* singer with such a voice. **3** *n.* part to be sung by such a voice. **4** *adj.* of or for a tenor. **5** *n.* the general tendency; course: *He found he enjoyed the even tenor of country life.* **6** *n.* the general meaning or drift: *I understand French well enough to get the tenor of her speech.*

tenor clef, the C clef when the clef symbol is placed on the fourth line of the staff. See picture at **clef.**

ten·pin (ten′pin′), *n.* **1** a wooden pin used in bowling. **2 tenpins,** the game of bowling.

tense[1] (tens), **1** *adj.* having, showing, or causing strain: *tense nerves, a tense moment.* **2** *adj.* stretched tight; strained to stiffness: *a tense rope, a face tense with pain.* **3** *v.* to stretch tight; stiffen: *She tensed her muscles for the leap.* ❏ *adj.* **tens·er, tens·est;** *v.* **tensed, tens·ing.** —**tense′ly,** *adv.* —**tense′ness,** *n.*

WORD FAMILY Tense[1] and the words below are related. They all come from a Latin word meaning "to stretch."

attend	extensive	ostensible	tend
attention	extent	ostentatious	tendency
contend	inattentive	portend	tender[2]
contentious	intend	pretend	tensile
distend	intense	pretense	tension
extend	intent	superintend	tent

tense[2] (tens), *n.* **1** form of a verb that shows the time of the action or state expressed by the verb. *I dance* is in the present tense. *I danced* is in the past tense. *I will dance* is in the future tense. **2** set of such forms for the first, second, and third persons.

The present tense of *dance* is: *I dance; you dance; he, she, or it dances; we dance; you dance; they dance.* —**tense′less,** *adj.*

ten·sile (ten′səl), *adj.* **1** of or about tension: *Steel has great tensile strength.* **2** able to be stretched; ductile.

ten·sion (ten′shən), *n.* **1** mental strain: *Tension is sometimes brought on by overwork.* **2** situation in which people or groups are nervous or hostile toward each other: *political tension.* **3** a stretched condition: *The tension of the bow gives speed to the arrow.* **4** act of stretching. —**ten′sion·al,** *adj.* —**ten′sion·less,** *adj.*

ten·sor (ten′sər), *n.* muscle that stretches or tightens some part of the body.

ten-speed (ten′spēd′), *n.* a lightweight bicycle with ten gears.

tent (tent), *n.* a movable shelter made of canvas or nylon supported by a pole or poles. —**tent′like′,** *adj.*

ten·ta·cle (ten′tə kəl), *n.* **1** a long, slender, flexible growth on the head or around the mouth of an animal, used to touch, hold, or move; feeler. **2** a sensitive, hairlike growth on a plant.

tentacles (def. 1)

ten·ta·tive (ten′tə tiv), *adj.* **1** done as a trial or experiment; experimental: *They formulated a tentative plan.* **2** uncertain; hesitant: *a tentative laugh.* —**ten′ta·tive·ly,** *adv.* —**ten′ta·tive·ness,** *n.*

tent caterpillar, any of several caterpillars that spin tentlike, silken webs on trees where they live. Tent caterpillars feed on leaves and can do great damage to fruit and forest trees.

ten·ter·hook (ten′tər hùk′), *n.* **on tenterhooks,** in suspense; anxious.

tenth (tenth), *adj., n.* **1** next after the ninth; last in a series of 10. **2** one of 10 equal parts: *A dime is a tenth of a dollar.*

ten·u·ous (ten′yü əs), *adj.* **1** having slight importance; not substantial: *She has only a tenuous claim to the property.* **2** thin or slight; slender: *the tenuous thread of a spider's web.* **3** not dense: *The air ten miles above the earth is very tenuous.* —**ten′u·ous·ly,** *adv.* —**ten′u·ous·ness,** *n.*

ten·ure (ten′yər), *n.* **1** length of time of holding or possessing something: *The tenure of office of the president of our club is one year.* **2** permanent status as a faculty member, granted after a trial period.

Ten·zing Nor·gay (ten′zing nôr′gā), 1914-1986, Tibetan explorer. He and Sir Edmund Hillary were the first people to reach the top of Mount Everest.

te·pee (tē′pē), *n.* tent used by American Indians of the Great Plains, made of hides sewn together and stretched over poles arranged in a cone. Also, **teepee, tipi.** ❏ *n., pl.* **te·pees.**

tep·id (tep′id), *adj.* slightly warm; lukewarm. —**tep′id·ly,** *adv.* —**tep′id·ness,** *n.*

te·qui·la (tə kē′lə), *n.* an alcoholic drink made by distilling the juices obtained from the roasted stems of the agave plant.

ter·a·byte (ter′ə bīt′), *n.* one trillion bytes, used as a measurement of computer storage capacity.

ter·bi·um (ter′bē əm), *n.* a metallic element that occurs in certain minerals with yttrium and ytterbium. *Symbol:* Tb

Te·re·sa (tə rē′sə), *n.* **1 Saint,** 1515-1582, Spanish nun and mystic. **2 Mother,** born 1910, Indian missionary, born in Albania. She won the 1979 Nobel Peace Prize. [**Teresa** comes from a Greek word meaning "harvester."]

ter·i·ya·ki (ter′i yä′kē), *n.* a Japanese meal made of meat, chicken, or shrimp soaked in soy sauce, then broiled or grilled.

term (tèrm), **1** *n.* word or phrase used in connection with some special subject, science, art, or business: *medical terms.* "Acid," "base," and "salt" are terms commonly used in chemistry. **2** *n.* any particular word or expression: *a foreign term.* **3** *v.* to apply a term to; name; call: *The suggestion was termed ridiculous.* **4** *n.* a set period of time; length of time that a thing lasts: *The President's term of office is four years.* **5** *n.* one of the periods into which the school year is divided: *Most schools have a fall term and a spring term.* **6** *n.pl.* **terms, a** conditions: *The terms of the peace were very hard for the defeated nation.* **b** agreement: *The company and the union could not come to terms.* **c** way of speaking: *She talked about you in very flattering terms.* **d** personal relations: *on good terms with our neighbors.* **7** *n.* numerator or denominator in a fraction. For example, $\frac{4}{12}$ reduced to lowest terms is $\frac{1}{3}$. **8** *n.* any part of an algebraic expression separated from the other parts by a plus or minus sign. In $13ax^2 - 2bxy + y$, $13ax^2$, $2bxy$, and y are the terms.
in terms of, in regard to.

WORD STORY   **Term** comes from a Latin word meaning "end" or "boundary line." **Terminal** and **terminate** come from the same Latin word. It is easy to see that a terminal is where a line terminates, but how is a word an end? When it is carefully defined, there is a boundary around the meaning of a word, limiting its meaning. In fact, **define** comes from another Latin word that also means "end" or "limit." And **limit** comes from a Latin word meaning "boundary." So a definition of **term limit** is sort of the end of the end of the end.

ter·mi·nal (tèr′mə nəl), **1** *n.* the end; the end part. A terminal is either end of a railroad line, bus line, airline, or shipping route. At a terminal are sheds, hangars, garages, stations, etc., to handle freight and passengers. **2** *adj.* at the end; forming the end part: *a branch's terminal flower.* **3** *adj.* resulting in death; fatal: *a terminal disease.* **4** *n.* device by which a person and a computer may communicate, usually with a keyboard and a screen. **5** *n.* device or part for making an electrical connection: *the terminals of a battery.* [See Word Story at **term**.] —**ter′mi·nal·ly,** *adv.*

terminal moraine, ridge of rocks, dirt, sand, etc., formed at the point where the glacier carrying them stopped growing and began to melt.

ter·mi·nate (tèr′mə nāt), *v.* **1** to bring to an end; put an end to: *The two lawyers terminated their partnership and each opened a separate office.* **2** to come to an end: *The contract terminates soon.* **3** to dismiss from a job; fire. ❑ *v.* **ter·mi·nat·ed, ter·mi·nat·ing.** [See Word Story at **term**.] —**ter′mi·na′tion,** *n.* —**ter′mi·na′tor,** *n.*

ter·mi·nol·o·gy (tèr′mə nol′ə jē), *n.* the special words or terms used in a science, art, business, etc.: *medical terminology.* ❑ *n., pl.* **ter·mi·nol·o·gies.**

ter·mi·nus (tèr′mə nəs), *n.* **1** terminal (def. 1). **2** any farthest point or stage; boundary; goal; end. ❑ *n., pl.* **ter·mi·nus·es.**

ter·mite (tèr′mīt), *n.* any of many insects with soft, pale bodies; white ant. Termites live in colonies like ants and eat wood, paper, and other materials containing cellulose. They are very destructive to wooden buildings, furniture, books, etc.

term limit, a legal limit to the number of terms that someone can serve in a particular public office. [See Word Story at **term**.]

term paper, an assigned essay written for a course in a school or college, usually due near the end of the term.

tern (tèrn), *n.* any of several seabirds related to gulls but with more slender bodies and bills and usually long, forked tails.
■ Another word that sounds like this is **turn.**

ter·race (ter′is), **1** *n.* a flat, raised level of land with straight or sloping sides. Terraces are often made one above the other in hilly areas to create more space for raising crops. **2** *v.* to form into a terrace or terraces; furnish with terraces: *to terrace a hillside.* **3** *n.* a row of houses or a short street running along the side or top of a slope: *She lives at 7 Oak Terrace.* **4** *n.* a paved outdoor space adjoining a house, used for lounging, dining, etc. **5** *n.* the flat roof of a house. ❑ *v.* **ter·raced, ter·rac·ing.**

ter·ra cot·ta (ter′ə kot′ə), **1** kind of hard, often unglazed,

brownish red earthenware, used for vases, statuettes, building decorations, etc. **2** a dull brownish red. ❑ *pl.* **terra cottas.**

ter·ra fir·ma (ter′ə fèr′mə), solid earth; dry land.

ter·rain (tə rān′), *n.* region of land that is thought of as having particular natural features: *The hilly, rocky terrain of the island made farming difficult.*

Ter·ra·my·cin (ter′ə mī′sn), *n.* trademark for an antibiotic used to treat many bacterial infections.

ter·ra·pin (ter′ə pin), *n.* any of several turtles used for food, such as the diamondback. They live in fresh water or tidewater, such as salt marshes.

ter·rar·i·um (tə rer′ē əm), *n.* a glass enclosure in which plants or small land animals are kept. ❑ *n., pl.* **ter·rar·i·ums, ter·rar·i·a** (tə rer′ē ə).

ter·raz·zo (tə raz′ō *or* tə rät′sō), *n.* a kind of flooring made of marble fragments set in cement.

ter·res·tri·al (tə res′trē əl), *adj.* **1** living on the ground, not in the air or water or in trees: *Cows, lions, and elephants are terrestrial animals.* **2** growing on land; growing in the ground: *terrestrial plants.* **3** of land, not water: *Islands and continents make up the terrestrial parts of the earth.* **4** of or about the earth; not of the heavens: *this terrestrial globe.* —**ter·res′tri·al·ly,** *adv.*

ter·ri·ble (ter′ə bəl), *adj.* **1** causing great fear; dreadful; awful: *a terrible storm.* **2** causing great pain; severe: *terrible suffering.* **3** extremely bad; unpleasant: *a terrible temper, a terrible experience.* —**ter′ri·ble·ness,** *n.*

ter·ri·bly (ter′ə blē), *adv.* **1** in a terrible manner; dreadfully: *The shipwreck survivors suffered terribly before their rescue.* **2** extremely: *I am terribly sorry I stepped on your toes. I was terribly angry when I heard the news.*

ter·ri·er (ter′ē ər), *n.* a small, active dog, formerly used to chase prey into its burrow. Breeds of terriers include **Boston terriers, fox terriers, Irish terriers, Scottish terriers,** and **Yorkshire terriers.**

ter·rif·ic (tə rif′ik), *adj.* **1** causing great fear; terrifying: *A terrific earthquake shook Japan.* **2** very unusual; remarkable; extraordinary: *A terrific hot spell ruined many of the crops.* **3** very good; wonderful: *She is a terrific tennis player.* —**ter·rif′i·cal·ly,** *adv.*

ter·ri·fy (ter′ə fī), *v.* to fill with great fear; frighten very much: *The sight of a large bear terrified the campers.* ❑ *v.* **ter·ri·fied, ter·ri·fy·ing.** —**ter′ri·fy′ing·ly,** *adv.*

ter·ri·to·ri·al (ter′ə tôr′ē əl), *adj.* **1** of or restricted to a particular territory or district: *a territorial government.* **2** of or about territory: *The purchase of Louisiana was a valuable territorial addition to the United States.* **3** defensive with regard to its territory: *Many animals are territorial. He is very territorial about his desk.* —**ter′ri·to′ri·al·ly,** *adv.*

terrace (def. 1)

T

a	hat	è	term	ô	order	ch	child		
ā	age	i	it	oi	oil	ng	long		a in about
ä	far	ī	ice	ou	out	sh	she		e in taken
â	care	o	hot	u	cup	th	thin	ə	i in pencil
e	let	ō	open	ù	put	ŦH	then		o in lemon
ē	equal	ò	saw	ü	rule	zh	measure		u in circus

ter·ri·to·ry (ter′ə tôr′ē), *n.* **1** land belonging to a government; land under the rule of a distant government: *Gibraltar is British territory.* **2** a district not admitted as a state but having its own lawmaking group. Alaska was a territory of the United States until 1958. **3** land; region: *Much territory in northern Africa is desert.* **4** region assigned to a salesman or agent. **5** area, such as a nesting ground, where an animal lives, and which it defends from others of its kind. ❑ *n., pl.* **ter·ri·to·ries** for 1,2,4,5.

WORD FAMILY **Territory** and the words below are related. They all come from a Latin word meaning "earth."

extraterrestrial	terrace	terrarium
inter	terra cotta	terrier
Mediterranean	terra firma	territorial
subterranean	terrain	tureen

ter·ror (ter′ər), *n.* **1** great fear: *The child has a terror of thunder.* **2** cause of great fear: *Pirates were once the terror of the sea.* **3** deliberate violence against people or groups, carried out by another group, a government, etc.

ter·ror·ism (ter′ə riz′əm), *n.* use of terror or violence.

ter·ror·ist (ter′ər ist), *n.* person who uses or favors terrorism.

ter·ror·ize (ter′ə rīz′), *v.* **1** to fill with terror: *The sight of the growling dog terrorized the little child.* **2** to rule or subdue by causing terror. ❑ *v.* **ter·ror·ized, ter·ror·iz·ing.** —**ter′ror·i·za′tion,** *n.*

ter·ry cloth (ter′ē), a rough cloth made of uncut looped yarn.

terse (tèrs), *adj.* brief and to the point: *"No" was her terse reply when I asked her to help me with my homework.* ❑ *adj.* **ters·er, ters·est.** —**terse′ly,** *adv.* —**terse′ness,** *n.*

Ter·ti·ar·y (tèr′shē er′ē), *n.* (in geology) time between about 70 million and 2 million years ago, divided into the Paleocene, Eocene, Oligocene, Miocene, and Pliocene.

test (test), **1** *n.* a list of questions to find out how much someone knows about something; examination: *a test in arithmetic.* **2** *v.* to put to a test of any kind; try out: *The doctor tested my eyes.* **3** *n.* means of trial: *Trouble is a test of character.* **4** *n.* examination of a substance to see what it is or what it contains: *A test showed that the water was pure.* ■ See Synonym Study at **trial.** —**test′a·ble,** *adj.* —**test′er,** *n.*

WORD STORY **Test** comes from a Latin word meaning "clay pot." In the Middle Ages, one kind of clay pot was used to melt and purify gold and silver. People knew the value of something that had been through a test, and they began to use the word for any way of checking quality.

tes·ta·ment (tes′tə mənt), *n.* **1** written instructions telling what to do with someone's property after he or she dies; will. **2 Testament,** one of the two parts into which the Christian Bible is divided; the Old Testament or the New Testament.

tes·tate (tes′tāt), *adj.* having made and left a will.

tes·ta·tor (tes′tā tər), *n.* **1** person who makes a will. **2** person who has died leaving a will.

test ban, international ban on testing of nuclear weapons or other military devices.

tes·ti·cle (tes′ti kəl), *n.* gland in a male human being or animal that produces sperm; testis.

tes·ti·fy (tes′tə fī), *v.* **1** to declare or give evidence under oath in a court of law. **2** to give evidence; bear witness: *The excellence of Shakespeare's plays testifies to his genius.* ❑ *v.* **tes·ti·fied, tes·ti·fy·ing.**

tes·ti·mo·ni·al (tes′tə mō′nē əl), **1** *n.* certificate of character, conduct, qualifications, value, etc.; recommendation: *She received a testimonial from her former employer.* **2** *n.* something given or done to show esteem, admiration, gratitude, etc.: *They collected money for a testimonial to the retiring pastor.* **3** *adj.* given or done as a testimonial.

tes·ti·mo·ny (tes′tə mō′nē), *n.* **1** statement used for evidence or proof: *A witness gave testimony that the defendant was at home all day Sunday.* **2** evidence: *The dry, brown grass was testimony to a hot summer with very little rain.* **3** an open declaration or profession of your faith. ❑ *n., pl.* **tes·ti·mo·nies** for 1,3. [See Word Story at **detest.**]

tes·tis (tes′tis), *n.* testicle. ❑ *n., pl.* **tes·tes** (tes′tēz).

tes·tos·te·rone (te stos′tə rōn′), *n.* hormone produced by the testicles, which causes and maintains male sexual characteristics.

test pilot, pilot that tests new or experimental aircraft by subjecting them to greater than normal stress.

test tube, a thin glass tube closed at one end, used in making laboratory tests.

test-tube (test′tüb′), *adj.* **1** of or about a test tube: *a test-tube experiment.* **2** conceived in a test tube for later implantation in a uterus: *a test-tube baby.*

tes·ty (tes′tē), *adj.* easily irritated; impatient. ❑ *adj.* **tes·ti·er, tes·ti·est.** —**test′i·ly,** *adv.* —**test′i·ness,** *n.*

tet·a·nus (tet′n əs), *n.* disease caused by specific bacteria usually entering the body through wounds, in which the symptoms are violent spasms and stiffness of many muscles, sometimes resulting in death. Tetanus of the jaw muscles is called lockjaw. You can be protected against it by a series of shots.

tête-à-tête (tāt′ə tāt′), **1** *adv.* two together in private; privately: *They dined tête-à-tête.* **2** *adj.* of or for two people in private: *a tête-à-tête conversation.* **3** *n.* a private conversation between two people.

teth·er (teᴛʜ′ər), **1** *n.* rope or chain for fastening an animal so that it can move only within a certain limit. **2** *v.* to fasten with a tether: *tether a horse to a stake.*

at the end of your tether, at the end of your resources or endurance.

teth·er·ball (teᴛʜ′ər bôl′), *n.* game played by two people with a ball fastened by a cord to the top of a tall post. The object of the game is to hit the ball so as to wind the cord around the post, in one direction or the other.

tet·ra (tet′rə), *n.* any of several small, brightly colored tropical freshwater fishes related to piranhas, often kept in aquariums. ❑ *n., pl.* **tet·ras.**

tetra-, *prefix.* four: *tetrahedron = shape with four surfaces.*

tet·ra·he·dron (tet′rə hē′drən), *n.* a solid shape with four surfaces. ❑ *n., pl.* **tet·ra·he·drons, tet·ra·he·dra** (tet′rə hē′drə).

Teu·ton (tüt′n), **1** *n.* a German. **2** *n.* person belonging to the group of northern Europeans that speak Germanic languages. **3** *n.* member of an ancient Germanic tribe that threatened the Roman republic in the 100s B.C. **4** *adj.* German.

tetra—up to 3 in. (8 cm) long

Teu·ton·ic (tü ton′ik), *adj.* **1** of or about the ancient Teutons or their language. **2** Germanic. **3** German.

Tex., Texas.

Tex·an (tek′sən), **1** *adj.* of or about Texas or its people. **2** *n.* person born or living in Texas.

Tex·as (tek′səs), *n.* one of the southwestern states of the United States. *Abbreviation:* TX or Tex. *Capital:* Austin.

WORD STORY **Texas** comes from an American Indian word meaning "friends" or "allies." Spanish explorers in this area used the word about the Indians they met there.

Tex-Mex (teks′meks′), *adj.* combining elements of both Texas and Mexico, or of Texan and Mexican life: *Tex-Mex cooking, Tex-Mex music.*

text (tekst), *n.* **1** the main part of reading matter in a book: *This history book contains 300 pages of text and about 50 pages of maps and pictures.* **2** the original words of a writer. **3** topic; subject: *Town improvement was the speaker's text.* **4** a short passage in the Bible: *The minister preached on the text "Judge not, that ye be not judged."* **5** textbook. **6** computer data in textual form.

WORD STORY **Text** comes from a Latin word meaning "to weave." A text is woven of words. **Tissue** comes from the same Latin word. Its first English meaning is "cloth," and later it was used for things like cloth, such as living membranes.

text-based (tekst′bāst′), *adj.* using only or mainly written words; without graphics or pictures: *a text-based interface.*

text·book (tekst′bük′), *n.* book for regular study by pupils. Most books used in schools are textbooks.

tex·tile (tek′stil *or* tek′stəl), **1** *n.* a woven fabric; cloth: *Beautiful textiles are sold in Paris.* **2** *adj.* suitable for weaving: *Linen, cotton, silk, nylon, and wool are common textile materials.* **3** *adj.* of or about the making, selling, etc., of textiles: *the textile industry.*

tex·tu·al (teks′chü əl), *adj.* of the text: *A misprint is a textual error.*

tex·ture (teks′chər), *n.* **1** the feel that cloth or other things have because of their structure: *Velvet has a soft texture.* **2** arrangement of threads in a woven fabric: *Burlap has a much coarser texture than linen.*

textured vegetable protein, a food product made from soybeans processed to look like ground meat.

Tez·cat·li·po·ca (tez kat lip′ō kä), *n.* the Aztec god of the night sky, known as the god of the smoking mirror.

TGIF, INFORMAL. thank God it's Friday.

-th[1], *suffix.* number ___ in order or position in a series: *sixth = number six in order or position in a series.*

-th[2], *suffix.* **1** act or process of ___ing: *growth = process of growing.* **2** quality or condition of being ___: *truth = quality of being true.*

Th, symbol for thorium.

Thai (tī), **1** *adj.* of or about Thailand, its people, or their language. **2** *n.* person born or living in Thailand. **3** *n.* language of Thailand. ❑ *n., pl.* **Thais** for 2. [See Word Story at **Thailand**.]

Thai·land (tī′land), *n.* country in SE Asia. *Capital:* Bangkok.

thal·a·mus (thal′ə məs), *n.* a part of the brain, at the top of the brain stem, that receives information from nerves and passes it to the parts of the brain that understand it. The thalamus also passes information between various parts of the brain. ❑ *n., pl.* **thal·a·mi** (thal′ə mī),

thal·li·um (thal′ē əm), *n.* a soft, bluish white metallic element that occurs in iron and zinc ores and in various minerals. It is highly poisonous, and its compounds are used to kill insects, rodents, etc. *Symbol:* Tl

thal·lo·phyte (thal′ə fīt), *n.* any plant, such as many seaweeds, with a body that is not divided into leaves, stems, or roots. Thallophytes were formerly considered a division of the plant kingdom, but most of the living things contained in this division, such as bacteria and fungi, have been reclassified into other kingdoms, and this category is now rarely used in classification.

Thames (temz), *n.* river flowing from S England into the North Sea. London is on the Thames. See **Rhine** for map.

than (ŦHan), **1** *conj., prep.* in comparison with: *She is taller than her sister.* **2** *conj.* compared to that which: *You know better than I do.* **3** *prep.* except; besides: *How else can we come than by train?*

thank (thangk), **1** *v.* to say that you are pleased and grateful for something given or done; express gratitude to: *She thanked her teacher for helping her.* **2** *n.pl.* **thanks, a** I thank you: *Thanks for your good wishes.* **b** act of thanking; expression of gratitude and pleasure. **c** feeling of kindness received; gratitude: *You have our thanks for everything you have done.* **3** *v.* to blame: *You have yourself to thank if you eat too much.*

thanks to, owing to; because of: *Thanks to his efforts, the garden is a great success.*

thank·ful (thangk′fəl), *adj.* feeling or expressing thanks; grateful: *He is thankful for good health.* **—thank′ful·ly,** *adv.* **—thank′ful·ness,** *n.*

thank·less (thangk′lis), *adj.* **1** not feeling or expressing thanks;

ungrateful: *The thankless child did not appreciate our gift.* **2** not likely to get thanks; not appreciated: *Giving advice can be a thankless act.* **—thank′less·ly,** *adv.* **—thank′less·ness,** *n.*

thanks·giv·ing (thangks′giv′ing), *n.* **1** expression of thanks: *They offered thanksgiving to God for their escape.* **2** act of giving thanks. **3** **Thanksgiving,** Thanksgiving Day.

Thanksgiving Day, day set apart as a holiday on which to give thanks for past blessings. In the United States, Thanksgiving Day is the fourth Thursday in November. In Canada, it is the second Monday in October.

thank-you (thangk′yü′), **1** *n.* an expression of thanks: *I said thank-you as I left the party.* **2** *adj.* showing thanks: *a thank-you card.*

Thar Desert (tär), desert in NW India.

Tharp (tharp), *n.* **Twy·la** (twī′lə), born 1941, American choreographer and dancer. Her works have used a wide variety of music, including rock and jazz, and of dance styles, including jazz and ballet.

that (ŦHat), **1** *adj., pron. That* is used to point out some person or thing or idea. We use *this* for the thing nearer us, and *that* for the thing farther away from us. *Do you know that boy? Shall we buy this book or that one? I like that better.* **2** *conj. That* is also used to connect a group of words. *I know that 6 and 4 are 10.* **3** *conj. That* is used to show purpose. *Study that you may learn.* **4** *conj. That* is used to show result. *She ran so fast that she was five minutes early.* **5** *pron.* who; whom; which: *Is he the man that sells dogs? She is the girl that you saw in school. Bring the box that will hold most.* **6** *pron.* when; at or in which: *It was the day that school began. The year that we went to England was 1964.* **7** *adv.* to such an extent; to such a degree; so: *The baby cannot stay up that long.* ❑ *pron., pl.* **those** for def. 1.

that's that, that is settled or decided.

thatch (thach), **1** *n.* straw, palm leaves, etc., used as a roof or covering. **2** *v.* to roof or cover with thatch. **—thatch′er,** *n.*

thatch

Thatch·er (thach′ər), *n.* Lady **Mar·ga·ret** (mär′gə rit), born 1925, British political leader, prime minister of Great Britain from 1979 to 1990. She was the first woman to serve as that country's prime minister.

a	hat	ė	term	ô	order	ch	child		a in about
ā	age	i	it	oi	oil	ng	long		e in taken
ä	far	ī	ice	ou	out	sh	she	ə	i in pencil
â	care	o	hot	u	cup	th	thin		o in lemon
e	let	ō	open	ů	put	ŦH	then		u in circus
ē	equal	ò	saw	ü	rule	zh	measure		

T

that'll (т̄нat′l), **1** that will. **2** that shall.

that's (т̄нats), that is.

thaw (thȯ), **1** *v.* to melt ice, snow, or anything frozen; free from frost: *The sun will thaw the ice on the streets.* **2** *n.* weather above the freezing point (32 degrees Fahrenheit or 0 degrees Celsius): *In January we usually have a thaw.* **3** *v.* to become free of frost, ice, etc.: *The pond freezes in November and thaws in April.* **4** *v.* to make or become less cold: *After shoveling snow, I thawed my hands and feet in front of the fire.* **5** *v.* to make or become less stiff and formal in manner; soften: *His shyness thawed under the teacher's kindness.*

THC, the active hallucinogenic chemical in marijuana.

the[1] (т̄нə *or* т̄нi; *stressed* т̄нē), *definite article.* **1** that or those and no others; a certain; a particular: *The dog I saw had no tail. The girl driving the car is my sister.* **2** the well-known; the only: *the Alps.* **3** any one of its kind; any: *The dog is a quadruped.* **4** that which is; those which are: *visit the sick, a love of the beautiful.* **5** the best or most important: *the place to dine.* ■ Another word that can sound like this is **thee.**

the[2] (т̄нə *or* т̄нē), *adv.* in that degree; to that degree: *The later I sit up, the sleepier I become.* ■ Another word that can sound like this is **thee.**

the·a·ter or **the·a·tre** (thē′ə tər), *n.* **1** place where plays are acted or movies are shown. **2** plays; writing, acting in, or producing plays; the drama: *She was interested in the theater and tried to write plays herself.* **3** place of action: *France has been the theater for many wars.* **4** place that looks like a theater in its arrangement of seats: *The surgeon performed an operation before the medical students in the operating theater.*

the·at·ri·cal (thē at′rə kəl), **1** *adj.* of or about the theater or actors: *theatrical performances, a theatrical company.* **2** *adj.* suggesting a theater or acting; for display or effect; artificial. **3** *n.pl.* **theatricals,** dramatic performances, especially as given by amateurs.. **—the·at′ri·cal·ly,** *adv.*

Thebes (thēbz), *n.* **1** important city in ancient Greece. See **Sparta** for map. **2** city in ancient Egypt, on the Nile, formerly a center of Egyptian civilization.

thee (т̄нē), *pron.* OLD USE. you. ■ Another word that can sound like this is **the.**

theft (theft), *n.* act of stealing: *The prisoner was jailed for theft.*

their (т̄нâr), *adj.* of or belonging to them: *I like their house.* ■ See Usage Note at **every.** ■ Other words that sound like this are **there** and **they're.**

theirs (т̄нârz), *pron.* the one or ones belonging to them: *Our house is white; theirs is brown.* ■ Another word that sounds like this is **there's.**

them (т̄нem; *unstressed* т̄нəm), *pron.* the persons, animals, things, or ideas spoken about: *The books are new; take care of them.*

the·mat·ic (thē mat′ik), *adj.* of or about a theme or themes.

theme (thēm), *n.* **1** a short written composition: *Our school themes must be written in ink and on white paper.* **2** topic; subject: *The theme of her speech was human rights.* **3** the principal melody in a piece of music; short melody repeated in different forms. **4** melody used to identify a particular radio or TV show.

theme park, an amusement park in which all or most of the attractions relate to a theme, stated in the name of the park, such as western history or marine wildlife.

theme park

them·selves (т̄нem selvz′ *or* т̄нəm selvz′), *pron.* **1** form of *they* or *them* used to make a statement stronger: *The teachers themselves said the test was too hard.* **2** form used instead of *them* in cases like: *They speak for themselves. They hurt themselves sledding down the hill.* **3** their normal or usual selves: *They are ill and are not themselves today.*

then (т̄нen), **1** *adv.* at that time: *Father talked of his childhood, and recalled that prices were lower then.* **2** *n.* that time: *By then we shall know the result of the election.* **3** *adj.* being at that time; existing then: *The then chairperson was the first to be informed of the budget deficit.* **4** *adv.* soon afterwards: *The noise stopped, and then began again.* **5** *adv.* next in time or place: *First comes spring, then summer.* **6** *adv.* at another time: *Now one team was ahead and then the other.* **7** *adv.* also; besides: *The circus is too good to miss, and then it costs very little.* **8** *adv.* in that case; therefore: *If she painted the best picture, then she should receive the first prize.*

thence (т̄нens), *adv.* from that place; from there: *We went to Italy; thence we went to France.*

thence·forth (т̄нens′fôrth′), *adv.* from then on; from that time forward: *I bought an old guitar and thenceforth I have followed a musical career.*

thence·for·ward (т̄нens′fôr′wərd), *adv.* thenceforth.

the·oc·ra·cy (thē ok′rə sē), *n.* **1** government in which God is recognized as the supreme civil ruler and in which religious authorities rule the state as God's representatives. **2** country or state governed by a theocracy. ❑ *n., pl.* **the·oc·ra·cies. —the·o·crat·ic** (thē′ə krat′ik), *adj.*

the·od·o·lite (thē od′l īt), *n.* a surveying device for measuring horizontal and vertical angles.

Theodore Roosevelt National Park, a national park in W North Dakota, including scenic badlands and buildings from Roosevelt's cattle ranches.

the·o·lo·gian (thē′ə lō′jən), *n.* an expert in theology.

the·o·log·i·cal (thē′ə loj′ə kəl), *adj.* of or about theology. A theological school trains people for the ministry. **—the′o·log′i·cal·ly,** *adv.*

the·ol·o·gy (thē ol′ə jē), *n.* **1** doctrines concerning God and His relations to human beings and the universe. **2** study of religion and religious beliefs. **3** system of religious beliefs. ❑ *n., pl.* **the·ol·o·gies** for 3.

the·o·rem (thē′ər əm *or* thir′əm), *n.* **1** statement or rule in mathematics that has been or is to be proved. EXAMPLE: In any isosceles triangle, the angles opposite the equal sides are equal angles. **2** any statement or rule that can be proved to be true.

the·o·ret·ic (thē′ə ret′ik), *adj.* theoretical.

the·o·ret·i·cal (thē′ə ret′ə kəl), *adj.* **1** planned or worked out in the mind, not from experience; based on theory, not on fact; limited to theory: *We have a theoretical solution to the problem; we can try it and see if it works.* **2** dealing with theory only; not practical: *City students can get a theoretical knowledge of farming from textbooks.* **—the′o·ret′i·cal·ly,** *adv.*

the·or·e·ti·cian (thē′ər ə tish′ən), *n.* an expert in the theory of an art, science, etc.

the·or·ist (thē′ər ist), *n.* person who theorizes.

the·o·rize (thē′ə rīz′), *v.* to form or propose a theory or theories; speculate: *Scientists have theorized about how life began on Earth.* ❑ *v.* **the·o·rized, the·o·riz·ing. —the′o·ri·za′tion,** *n.* **—the′o·riz′er,** *n.*

the·o·ry (thē′ər ē *or* thir′ē), *n.* **1** an explanation based on observation and reasoning: *Darwin's theory of evolution.* **2** the principles or methods of a science or art rather than its practice: *Before she began to compose, she studied music theory.* **3** opinion or idea about something: *I think the fire was started by a careless smoker. What is your theory?* ❑ *n., pl.* **the·o·ries.**

WORD STORY **Theory** comes from a Greek word meaning "a view." English today uses **view** to mean "opinion." If you are explaining your opinions, you may say, "That's how I see things."

ther·a·peu·tic (ther′ə pyü′tik), *adj.* of or about curing or therapy; curative: *Heat has therapeutic value.* **—ther′a·peu′ti·cal·ly,** *adv.*

ther·a·peu·tics (ther′ə pyü′tiks), *n.* branch of medicine that deals with the treating or curing of disease.

ther·a·pist (ther′ə pist), *n.* person who specializes in some form of therapy.

ther·a·py (ther′ə pē), *n.* treatment of diseases, injuries, or disorders: *She goes to physical therapy twice a week to help strengthen her injured muscles.* ❑ *n., pl.* **ther·a·pies.**

there (ᴛʜâr), **1** *adv.* in or at that place: *Sit there. Finish reading the page and stop there.* **2** *adv.* to or into that place: *We are going there tomorrow.* **3** *n.* that place: *We go to New York first and from there to Boston.* **4** *adv.* in that matter: *You are mistaken there.* **5** *adv. There* is also used in sentences in which the verb comes before its subject. *There are three new houses on our street. Is there a drugstore near here?* **6** *adv. There* is used to call attention to some person or thing. *There goes the bell.* **7** *interj. There* is also used to express comfort, encouragement, and so forth. *There, there! don't cry.* ■ Other words that sound like this are **their** and **they're.**

there·a·bout (ᴛʜâr′ə bout′), *adv.* thereabouts.

there·a·bouts (ᴛʜâr′ə bouts′), *adv.* **1** near that place: *She lives downtown, on Main Street or thereabouts.* **2** near that time: *He went home from work late that day, at 5 o'clock or thereabouts.* **3** near that number or amount: *The temperature quickly fell to zero or thereabouts.*

there·af·ter (ᴛʜâr af′tər), *adv.* after that; afterward: *He was very ill as a child and was considered sickly thereafter.*

there·by (ᴛʜâr bī′), *adv.* by means of that; in that way: *He wished to travel and thereby study the customs of other countries.*

there'd (ᴛʜârd), **1** there had. **2** there would.

there·fore (ᴛʜâr′fôr), *adv.* for that reason; as a result of that: *She had to work last night and therefore had little time to study.*

there·in (ᴛʜâr in′), *adv.* **1** in that place; in it: *the oceans and all the creatures therein.* **2** in that matter; in that way: *He is a good worker, but he can't get along with people. Therein lay the problem.*

there'll (ᴛʜârl), **1** there will. **2** there shall.

there·of (ᴛʜâr ov′ *or* ᴛʜâr uv′), *adv.* **1** of or about that or it. **2** from it; from that source.

there·on (ᴛʜâr on′), *adv.* on that; on it: *Next to the window was a table, and a huge book lay thereon.*

there's (ᴛʜârz), there is. ■ Another word that sounds like this is **theirs.**

there·to (ᴛʜâr tü′), *adv.* **1** to that; to it: *The castle stands on a hill, and the road thereto is steep and rough.* **2** in addition to that; also: *The queen gave her faithful servant rich garments and added thereto a bag of gold.*

there·to·fore (ᴛʜâr′tə fôr′), *adv.* before that time; until then.

there·un·der (ᴛʜâr un′dər), *adv.* **1** under that; under it. **2** under the authority of that; according to that.

there·un·to (ᴛʜâr un′tü), *adv.* to that; to it.

there·up·on (ᴛʜâr′ə pon′), *adv.* **1** immediately after that: *The clown appeared; thereupon the people clapped.* **2** because of that; therefore: *They planned to rent the old, abandoned house and thereupon remodeled it.* **3** on that; on it: *The knight carried a shield with a cross painted thereupon.*

there·with (ᴛʜâr wiᴛʜ′ *or* ᴛʜâr with′), *adv.* with that; with it: *She gave him a rose and a smile therewith.*

ther·mal (ᴛʜèr′məl), **1** *adj.* of or about heat. **2** *n.* a rising current of warm air. **—ther′mal·ly,** *adv.*

thermal pollution, the release of heated liquid or gas into a natural environment, raising normal temperature levels and harming things that live there.

thermo-, *prefix.* heat: *thermoelectricity = electricity produced by heat.*

ther·mo·cline (ᴛʜèr′mō klīn), *n.* a horizontal layer separating parts of a lake or sea that are sharply different in temperature.

ther·mo·dy·nam·ic (ᴛʜèr′mō dī nam′ik), *adj.* of or about thermodynamics; using force due to heat or to the conversion of heat into other forms of energy.

ther·mo·dy·nam·ics (ᴛʜèr′mō dī nam′iks), *n.* branch of physics that deals with the relations of heat, other forms of energy, and work.

ther·mo·e·lec·tric (ᴛʜèr′mō i lek′trik), *adj.* of or about thermoelectricity: *a thermoelectric generator.*

ther·mo·e·lec·tric·i·ty (ᴛʜèr′mō i lek tris′ə tē), *n.* electricity produced directly by heat, especially by a temperature difference between two different metals used as conductors in a circuit.

ther·mom·e·ter (thər mom′ə tər), *n.* device for measuring temperature. Most thermometers contain mercury or alcohol in a narrow tube. When the temperature outside the tube goes up, the liquid rises by expanding; when the temperature outside the tube goes down, the liquid drops by contracting.

ther·mo·nu·cle·ar (ᴛʜèr′mō nü′klē ər), *adj.* of or about the fusion of atoms at very high temperature, as in a hydrogen bomb: *a thermonuclear reaction.*

ther·mo·plas·tic (ᴛʜèr′mō plas′tik), **1** *n.* any material that becomes soft and easy to mold when heated, especially certain synthetic resins. **2** *adj.* like such materials.

Ther·mop·y·lae (thər mop′ə lē), *n.* mountain pass in ancient Greece. In 480 B.C., a small force of Greeks defended it against an army of Persians until most of the Greeks were killed. See **Sparta** for map.

ther·mos (ᴛʜèr′məs), *n.* container made with a vacuum between its inner and outer walls so that its contents remain hot or cold for a long time.

thermos bottle, thermos.

ther·mo·sphere (ᴛʜèr′mə sfir), *n.* the highest and hottest region of the atmosphere, extending from about 50 miles (80 kilometers) above the earth's surface out to the edge of the atmosphere; ionosphere.

ther·mo·stat (ᴛʜèr′mə stat), *n.* an automatic device for controlling temperature. In most thermostats, the expansion and contraction of a metal, liquid, or gas opens and closes an electric circuit connected to a furnace, air conditioner, etc.

the·sau·rus (thi sôr′əs), *n.* dictionary in which synonyms, antonyms, and other related words are listed. ❑ *n., pl.* **the·sau·rus·es, the·sau·ri** (thi sôr′ī).

these (ᴛʜēz), *adj., pron.pl. These* is used to point out persons, things, or ideas close to a speaker. *These girls helped me. These are my books.*

The·se·us (thē′sē əs), *n.* (in Greek legends) the chief hero of Athens. He killed the Minotaur and escaped from the Labyrinth with the help of Ariadne.

the·sis (thē′sis), *n.* **1** proposition or statement to be proved or to be supported against objections. **2** a long essay presented by a candidate for a diploma or degree: *His thesis discusses the changing nature of work since 1700.* ❑ *n., pl.* **the·ses** (thē′sēz′).

Thes·pi·an (thes′pē ən), **1** *adj.* of or about drama or tragedy. **2** *n.* **thespian,** actor or actress.

Thes·sa·lo·ni·ans (thes′ə lō′nē ənz), *n.* either of two books of the New Testament written by Saint Paul.

Thes·sa·ly (thes′ə lē), *n.* district in E Greece. **—Thes·sa·li·an** (the sā′lē ən), *adj., n.*

The·tis (thē′tis), *n.* (in Greek legends) a sea nymph who was the mother of Achilles.

they (ᴛʜā), *pron.pl.* **1** the persons, animals, things, or ideas spoken about: *I had three books yesterday. Do you know where they are? They are on the table.* **2** some people; any people; persons: *They say we should have a new school.*

they'd (ᴛʜād), **1** they had. **2** they would.

they'll (ᴛʜāl), **1** they will. **2** they shall.

they're (ᴛʜâr), they are. ■ Other words that sound like this are **their** and **there.**

they've (ᴛʜāv), they have.

thi·a·mine (thī′ə min), *n.* vitamin that promotes growth and prevents and cures beriberi; vitamin B_1. It is found in yeast, meats, whole-grain cereals, and certain vegetables.

thick (thik), **1** *adj.* with much space from one side to the opposite side; not thin: *The castle has thick stone walls.* **2** *adj.* measuring between two opposite sides: *A dime is about one millimeter thick.* **3** *adj.* dense: *The travelers entered a thick forest.* **4** *adj.* filled: *The air was thick with insects.* **5** *adj.* like glue or syrup, not like water: *Thick liquids pour slowly.* **6** *adj.* hard to see through: *Thick smoke hampered the rescue efforts.* **7** *adj.* not

a	hat	ė	term	ô	order	ch	child
ā	age	i	it	oi	oil	ng	long
ä	far	ī	ice	ou	out	sh	she
â	care	o	hot	u	cup	th	thin
e	let	ō	open	ů	put	ᴛʜ	then
ē	equal	ò	saw	ü	rule	zh	measure

ə { a in about, e in taken, i in pencil, o in lemon, u in circus } clear in sound; hoarse: *He had a thick voice because of a cold.* **8** *adj.* stupid; dull: *I couldn't get the lesson through my thick head.* **9** *adv.* thickly: *The field was planted so thick with corn that you could hide among the stalks.* **10** *n.* hardest part; place where there is the most danger, activity, etc.: *They were in the thick of the fight.* **11** *adj.* very friendly; intimate.

through thick and thin, in good times and bad.

> **SYNONYM STUDY** **Thick, dense,** and **compact**[1] all mean close together. **Thick** is a general word: *The weeds are thick here.* **Dense** suggests a lot in a small space: *The dense, wet snow is hard to shovel away.* **Compact** means closely packed: *Put old newspapers in a compact pile.*

thick·en (thik′ən), *v.* **1** to make or become thick or thicker: *You thicken gravy with flour.* **2** to become more involved or complicated: *Later on in the play the plot thickens.* **—thick′en·er,** *n.*

thick·et (thik′it), *n.* bushes or small trees growing close together: *We crawled into the thicket and hid.*

thick·head·ed (thik′hed′id), *adj.* stupid; dull: *Whose thick-headed idea was it to leave without checking to see if we had the theater tickets?* **—thick′head′ed·ness,** *n.*

thick·ly (thik′lē), *adv.* **1** in a thick manner; closely; densely: *Most of New York City is thickly settled.* **2** in great numbers; in abundance: *Weeds grow thickly in the rich soil.* **3** in tones that are hoarse or hard to understand.

thick·ness (thik′nis), *n.* **1** quality of being thick: *The thickness of the walls shuts out all sounds.* **2** distance between two opposite sides; the third measurement of a solid, not length nor breadth: *The length of the board is 10 feet, the width 6 inches, the thickness 2 inches.* **3** layer: *The pad was made up of three thicknesses of cloth.* ❑ *n., pl.* **thick·ness·es** for 3.

thick·set (thik′set′), *adj.* **1** thick in form or build; stocky: *a thickset person.* **2** thickly set: *a thickset hedge.*

thick-skinned (thik′skind′), *adj.* **1** not sensitive to criticism or insults. **2** having a thick skin.

thief (thēf), *n.* person who steals, especially someone who steals secretly and usually without using force: *A thief stole my bicycle from the yard.* ❑ *n., pl.* **thieves.**

thieve (thēv), *v.* to steal. ❑ *v.* **thieved, thiev·ing.**

thiev·er·y (thē′vər ē), *n.* act of stealing; theft.

thieves (thēvz), *n.* plural of **thief.**

thiev·ish (thē′vish), *adj.* **1** having the habit of stealing; likely to steal. **2** like a thief; sly: *a thievish look.* **—thiev′ish·ly,** *adv.* **—thiev′ish·ness,** *n.*

thigh (thī), *n.* part of the leg between the hip and the knee.

thigh·bone (thī′bōn′), *n.* bone of the leg between the hip and the knee; femur.

thim·ble (thim′bəl), *n.* a small metal or plastic cap worn on the finger to protect it when pushing a needle in sewing.

Thim·phu (tim′pü) *n.* capital of Bhutan, in the W part. Also, **Thim·bu** (tim′bü).

thin (thin), **1** *adj.* with little space from one side to the opposite side; not thick: *thin paper, thin wire, thin ice.* **2** *adj.* having little flesh; slender; lean: *a thin person.* **3** *adj.* not closely packed together; scanty: *He has thin hair.* **4** *adj.* not dense: *The air on the top of high mountains is thin.* **5** *adj.* like water; not like glue or syrup: *This gravy is too thin.* **6** *adj.* not deep or strong; having little depth, fullness, or intensity: *a thin color. The sickly child had a shrill, thin voice.* **7** *adj.* easily seen through; flimsy: *It was a thin excuse that satisfied no one.* **8** *v.* to make or become thin: *Traffic thinned out after 6 P.M.* ❑ *adj.* **thin·ner, thin·nest;** *v.* **thinned, thin·ning. —thin′ly,** *adv.* **—thin′ness,** *n.*

thimble

> **SYNONYM STUDY** **Thin, slender,** and **skinny** all mean not having much flesh. **Thin** is a general word: *She is tall and thin.* **Slender** means pleasingly thin: *Runners are often slender and muscular.* **Skinny** means too thin: *A skinny stray dog trotted down the alley.*

thine (ₜHīn), OLD USE. **1** *pron.* yours. "It is thine" means "it is yours." **2** *adj.* your (used only before a vowel or *h*). "Thine eyes" means "your eyes."

thing (thing), *n.* **1** any object or substance; what you can see or hear or touch or taste or smell: *Put these things away.* **2 things,** *pl.* **a** personal belongings. **b** clothes: *I packed my things and took the train.* **3** whatever is spoken of, thought of, or done; act; deed; fact; event; idea: *It was a good thing to do. A strange thing happened.* **4** matter; affair: *Let's settle this thing between us. How are things going?* **5** person or creature: *I felt sorry for the poor thing.*

do your thing, INFORMAL. to do the thing that you want to do, or the thing that you do best.

know a thing or two, be experienced or wise.

make a good thing of, to profit from.

see things, to have hallucinations.

thing·am·a·jig (thing′ə mə jig), *n.* something whose name you have forgotten or do not bother to mention: *Could you hand me that thingamajig over there?*

think (thingk), *v.* **1** to form an idea in the mind: *You must learn to think clearly.* **2** to have in the mind: *He thought that he would go.* **3** to have an opinion; believe: *Do you think it will rain? Do what you think fit.* **4** to reflect: *I want to think before answering that question.* **5** to consider: *They think their teacher a genius.* **6** to imagine: *You can't think how surprised I was.* **7** to expect: *I did not think to find you here.* ❑ *v.* **thought, think·ing. —think′a·ble,** *adj.* **—think′er,** *n.*

think aloud or **think out loud,** to say what you are thinking: *Don't pay any attention to me, I was just thinking out loud.*

think of, 1 to have in mind: *I think of you often.* **2** to imagine: *She doesn't like apple pie. Think of that!* **3** to remember: *I can't think of his name.*

think out, 1 to plan or discover by thinking. **2** to solve or understand by thinking. **3** to think through to the end.

think over, to consider carefully.

think through, to think about something thoroughly, until reaching an understanding or conclusion.

think twice, to think again before acting; hesitate.

think up, to plan or discover by thinking.

> **SYNONYM STUDY** **Think, reason,** and **concentrate** all mean to use the mind in order to form ideas or understand something. **Think** is a general word: *What are you thinking about?* **Reason** means to think carefully in order to form a judgment or solve a problem: *She reasoned that it was better to save her money for a jacket she really liked.* **Concentrate** means to pay close attention and think hard: *I've been concentrating on this geometry problem for an hour.*

think tank, a research institute organized to investigate complicated problems and suggest possible solutions.

thin-skinned (thin′skind′), *adj.* **1** sensitive to criticism, reproach, insults, etc. **2** having a thin skin.

third (thėrd), *adj., n.* **1** next after the second; last in a series of three: *C is the third letter of the alphabet.* **2** one of three equal parts: *We divided the cake into thirds.*

third degree, use of severe treatment by the police to force someone to give information or make a confession.

third-de·gree burn (thėrd′di grē′), a very severe burn where the skin and the deeper tissues are destroyed.

third·ly (thėrd′lē), *adv.* in the third place.

third person, form of a pronoun or verb used to refer to the person spoken of. *He, she, it,* and *they* are pronouns of the third person.

third rail, rail that carries a powerful electric current, paralleling the ordinary rails of a subway or railroad. It powers the car or engine.

third-rate (thėrd′rāt′), *adj.* distinctly inferior.

Third World, the developing nations of the world, especially those in Africa, Asia, and Latin America.

thirst (thėrst), **1** *n.* a dry, uncomfortable feeling in the mouth or throat caused by having had nothing to drink. **2** *n.* desire or need for drink: *She satisfied her thirst with a glass of water.* **3** *v.* to feel thirst; be thirsty. **4** *n.* a strong desire: *a thirst for adventure.* **5** *v.* to have a strong desire.

thirst·i·ly (thėr′stə lē), *adv.* because of thirst: *to drink thirstily.*

thirst·y (thėr′stē), *adj.* **1** feeling thirst; having thirst: *He was very thirsty and wanted a cold soda* **2** without water or moisture; dry: *The land was as thirsty as a desert.* ❑ *adj.* **thirst·i·er, thirst·i·est.** —**thirst′i·ness,** *n.*

thirsty

thir·teen (thėr′tēn′), *n., adj.* three more than ten; 13.

thir·teenth (thėr′tēnth′), *adj., n.* **1** next after the 12th; last in a series of 13. **2** one of 13 equal parts.

thir·ti·eth (thėr′tē ith), *adj., n.* **1** next after the 29th; last in a series of 30. **2** one of 30 equal parts: *A day is about one thirtieth of a month.*

thir·ty (thėr′tē), *adj., n.* three times ten; 30. ❑ *n., pl.* **thir·ties.**

thir·ty-sec·ond note (thėr′tē sek′ənd), (in music) a note played for one thirty-second (1/32) as long a time as a whole note.

this (THis), **1** *adj., pron. This* is used to point out some person, thing, or idea as present, near, or spoken of before. We use *that* for the thing farther away from us and *this* for the thing nearer us. *Shall we get this or that?* **2** *adj.* present; near; spoken of: *this minute, this child.* **3** *adv.* to such an extent or degree; so: *You can have this much.* ❑ *adj., pron., pl.* **these.**

this′ll (THis′əl), this will.

this·tle (this′əl), *n.* any of various plants with prickly stalks and leaves and usually purple flowers. —**this′tle·like′,** *adj.*

this·tle·down (this′əl doun′), *n.* downy growth that forms on ripe thistle seeds.

thith·er (thiTH′ər), *adv.* to or toward that place; there.

tho′ (THō), *conj., adv.* INFORMAL. though.

Tho·hoy·an·dou (tō hoi′an dü′), *n.* capital of Venda.

Thom·as (tom′əs), *n.* one of Jesus' twelve apostles. He at first doubted the Resurrection. [**Thomas** comes from an Aramaic word meaning "twin."]

Thom·as (tom′əs), *n.* **1 Clar·ence** (clâr′əns), born 1948, U.S. Supreme Court Justice, appointed in 1991. **2 Dylan,** 1914-1953, Welsh writer, known for melodic, extravagant language. His works include several books of poetry and the play *Under Milk Wood.*

thong (thong), *n.* **1** a narrow strip of leather, especially one used as a fastening. **2** lash of a whip. **3 thongs,** *pl.* light rubber sandals held onto the feet by a narrow strip of rubber between the toes, with another strip around the side of the foot.

Thor (thôr), *n.* (in Scandinavian myths) the god of thunder. [See Word Story at **Thursday.**]

tho·rac·ic (thô râs′ik), *adj.* of or in the thorax. The thoracic cavity contains the heart and lungs.

tho·rax (thôr′aks), *n.* **1** the part of the body between the neck and the abdomen; chest. **2** the second division of an insect's body, between the head and the abdomen. ❑ *n., pl.* **tho·rax·es.**

Tho·reau (thə rō′), *n.* **Henry David,** 1817-1862, American writer and naturalist, author of *Walden.* ▪ **Thoreau** believed that people should refuse to obey laws they thought were wrong. He went to jail for refusing to pay tax as a protest against slavery.

tho·ri·um (thôr′ē əm), *n.* a dark gray, radioactive, metallic element found in some rare minerals. When thorium is bombarded with neutrons, it changes into a form of uranium that is used as an atomic fuel. *Symbol:* Th

thorn (thôrn), *n.* **1** a stiff, sharp-pointed growth on a stem or branch of a tree or other plant: *Roses have thorns.* **2** tree or other plant with thorns. —**thorn′less,** *adj.*

thorn in the flesh or **thorn in the side,** a cause of annoyance.

thorn·y (thôr′nē), *adj.* **1** full of thorns: *a thorny bush.* **2** troublesome; annoying: *a thorny problem.* ❑ *adj.* **thorn·i·er, thorn·i·est.** —**thorn′i·ness,** *n.*

thor·ough (thėr′ō *or* thėr′ə), *adj.* **1** being all that is needed; complete: *a thorough search for the lost money.* **2** doing all that should be done; very careful: *The doctor was very thorough in examining the patient.* —**thor′ough·ly,** *adv.* —**thor′ough·ness,** *n.*

thor·ough·bred (thėr′ə bred′), **1** *adj.* bred from pure stock; purebred: *The farmer had a fine herd of thoroughbred Holstein cattle.* **2** *n.* a thoroughbred animal, most often a horse. **3** *n.* **Thoroughbred,** any race horse of a breed descended from a crossing of domestic English stock with Arabian stock. **4** *n.* a well-bred or thoroughly trained person.

thor·ough·fare (thėr′ə fâr′), *n.* **1** passage, road, or street open at both ends: *A city street is a public thoroughfare.* **2** a main road.

thor·ough·go·ing (thėr′ə gō′ing), *adj.* thorough; complete.

Thorpe (thôrp), *n.* **Jim** (jim), 1887-1953, American Olympic athlete, baseball and football player. ▪ **Jim Thorpe** became famous while playing for an American Indian school in Pennsylvania. He won gold medals in the decathlon and pentathlon in the 1912 Olympic Games. Because he had earlier played baseball for pay, Olympic officials decided he was a professional athlete and took away his medals. This decision was overturned and his medals were returned in 1982.

those (THōz), *adj., pron.pl. Those* is used to point out persons, things, or ideas some distance from a speaker. *Those girls helped me. Those two problems are hard. Those are my books.*

Thoth (thōth *or* tōt), *n.* Egyptian god of wisdom, speech, and magic, the inventor of letters and numbers, shown as a man with the head of an ibis, or sometimes a baboon.

thou (THou), *pron.sing.* OLD USE. you.

though (THō), **1** *conj.* in spite of the fact that: *Though it was pouring, no one went indoors.* **2** *conj.* yet; still; nevertheless: *He is better, though not yet cured.* **3** *conj.* even if: *Though I fail, I shall try again.* **4** *adv.* however: *I am sorry about our quarrel; you began it, though.* Also, **tho′.**

as though, as if; as it would be if: *You look as though you were tired.*

thought (thôt), **1** *n.* what you think; idea; notion: *I would like your thoughts on the subject.* **2** *n.* the process of thinking: *Thought helps us solve problems.* **3** *n.* care; attention; regard: *Show some thought for others.* **4** *n.* intention: *His thought was to avoid controversy.* **5** *n.* the characteristic thinking of a particular person, time, or place: *twentieth-century scientific thought.* **6** *v.* past tense and past participle of **think:** *We thought it would snow yesterday.* [See Word Story at **batch.**]

thought·ful (thôt′fəl), *adj.* **1** full of thought; thinking: *He was thoughtful for a while and then replied, "No."* **2** careful of others; considerate: *She is always thoughtful of her parents.* **3** indicating thought: *a thoughtful, somewhat puzzled expression.* —**thought′ful·ly,** *adv.* —**thought′ful·ness,** *n.*

thoughtful

SYNONYM STUDY **Thoughtful, considerate,** and **sympathetic** all mean careful of other people's feelings. **Thoughtful** is a general word: *It was thoughtful of you to remember my birthday.* **Considerate** suggests thinking of people's feelings without having to be told: *Be considerate of the neighbors and turn your radio down, please.* **Sympathetic** suggests thoughtful understanding of how others feel: *I have a sympathetic dentist who makes me as comfortable as she can.*

thought·less (thôt′lis), *adj.* **1** without thought; doing things without thinking; careless: *Thoughtless drivers cause many car accidents.* **2** showing little or no care or regard for others; inconsiderate: *It is thoughtless of them to keep us waiting so long.* —**thought′less·ly,** *adv.* —**thought′less·ness,** *n.*

thou·sand (thou′znd), *n., adj.* ten hundred; 1000.

a	hat	ė	term	ô	order	ch	child		a in about
ā	age	i	it	oi	oil	ng	long		e in taken
ä	far	ī	ice	ou	out	sh	she	ə	i in pencil
â	care	o	hot	u	cup	th	thin		o in lemon
e	let	ō	open	ù	put	ŦH	then		u in circus
ē	equal	ò	saw	ü	rule	zh	measure		

T

thou·sandth (thou′zndth), *adj., n.* **1** next after the 999th; last in a series of 1000. **2** one of 1000 equal parts.

Thrace (thrās), *n.* region in the E part of the Balkan Peninsula. In ancient times it was first an independent country and later a Roman province. See **Troy** for map. —**Thra·cian** (thrā′shən), *adj., n.*

thrall (thrôl), *n.* **1** bondage; slavery: *The witch's spell kept the princess in thrall.* **2** person in bondage; enslaved person.

thrall·dom (thrôl′dəm), *n.* bondage; slavery: *A sorcerer held the knight in thralldom.*

thrash (thrash), *v.* **1** to beat as punishment; flog. **2** to move violently; toss: *Unable to sleep, I thrashed about in bed.* **3** to thresh. **thrash out**, to settle by thorough discussion.

thrash·er (thrash′ər), *n.* any of several long-tailed North American songbirds related to the mockingbird and resembling thrushes.

thread (thred), **1** *n.* a very thin cord made of strands of cotton, silk, nylon, etc., spun and twisted together. You sew with thread. **2** *v.* to pass a thread through: *thread a needle.* **3** *v.* to string on a thread: *thread beads onto a string.* **4** *n.* something long and slender like a thread: *The spider hung by a thread.* **5** *n.* the main thought that connects the parts of a story, speech, etc.: *Something distracted her and she lost the thread of their conversation.* **6** *v.* to pass tape or film into a recording device. **7** *v.* to make your way through; make your way carefully: *He threaded his way through the crowd.* **8** *n.* the sloping ridge that winds around a bolt, screw, pipe joint, etc. The thread of a nut interlocks with the thread of a bolt. **9** *v.* to form a thread on a bolt, screw, pipe joint, etc. —**thread′er**, *n.* —**thread′like′**, *adj.*

thread·bare (thred′bâr′), *adj.* **1** worn thin; worn so much that the threads show: *a threadbare coat.* ■ See Synonym Study at **worn**. **2** wearing clothes worn to the threads; shabby: *a threadbare beggar.* **3** old and worn; stale: *Saying "I forgot" is a threadbare excuse.*

thread·y (thred′ē), *adj.* **1** thin and feeble: *a thready pulse.* **2** lacking in fullness: *a thready voice.* **3** made of or resembling a thread. **4** fibrous; stringy or viscid. ❑ *adj.* **thread·i·er, thread·i·est.** —**thread′i·ness**, *n.*

threat (thret), *n.* **1** statement of what will be done to hurt or punish someone: *The teacher's threat to keep us after school stopped our noise.* **2** sign or cause of possible harm or worry: *Pollution is a threat to our health.*

threat·en (thret′n), *v.* **1** to make a threat against; say what will be done to hurt or punish: *The teacher threatened to give a failing grade to students that did no homework.* **2** to utter threats: *They threaten and scold too much.* **3** to be a sign or warning of coming trouble: *Black clouds threaten rain.* **4** to be a cause of possible harm or worry to: *A flood threatened the city.* —**threat′en·er**, *n.* —**threat′en·ing·ly**, *adv.*

three (thrē), *n., adj.* one more than two; 3.

three-di·men·sion·al (thrē′də men′shə nəl), *adj.* **1** having three dimensions, height, depth, and width. **2** seeming to have depth as well as height and width; appearing to exist in three dimensions: *a three-dimensional photograph.*

three·fold (thrē′fōld′), **1** *adj., adv.* three times as much or as many. **2** *adj.* having three parts.

three·pence (thrip′əns), *n.* three British pennies; three pence.

three·pen·ny (thrip′ə nē), *adj.* **1** worth three pence. **2** of little worth; cheap; paltry.

three·score (thrē′skôr′), *adj.* three times twenty; 60.

three·some (thrē′səm), *n.* group of three people.

Three Wise Men, the Magi.

thresh (thresh), *v.* **1** to separate the grain or seeds from wheat, etc., with a machine or by hand with a flail. **2** to toss about; thrash. **thresh out**, to settle by thorough discussion.

thresh·er (thresh′ər), *n.* **1** machine used for separating grain or seeds from the stalks and other parts of wheat, oats, etc. **2** person or thing that threshes. **3** a large shark with a very long tail.

thresh·old (thresh′ōld), *n.* **1** doorway. **2** point of entering; beginning point: *The scientist was on the threshold of a great discovery.* **3** piece of wood or stone placed horizontally under a door. **4** point at which a stimulus begins to be felt: *pain threshold.*

threw (thrü), *v.* past tense of **throw**: *She threw the ball to me.* ■ Other words that sound like this are **through** and **thru**.

thrice (thris), *adv.* three times: *He knocked thrice.*

thrift (thrift), *n.* the careful management of money; the habit of saving: *A bank account encourages thrift.* —**thrift′less**, *adj.*

thrift shop, shop in which secondhand items are sold at low prices.

thrift·y (thrif′tē), *adj.* careful in spending; economical; saving: *a thrifty shopper.* ❑ *adj.* **thrift·i·er, thrift·i·est.** —**thrift′i·ly**, *adv.* —**thrift′i·ness**, *n.*

thrill (thril), **1** *n.* a shivering, exciting feeling: *I get a thrill whenever I see a parade.* **2** *v.* to give a shivering, exciting feeling to: *Stories of adventure thrilled him.* **3** *v.* to have a shivering, exciting feeling: *The children thrilled at the sight of their presents.* **4** *v.* to quiver; tremble: *Her voice thrilled with excitement.* [Thrill comes from an old English word meaning "through." A real thrill goes all the way through you.] —**thrill′ing·ly**, *adv.*

thrill·er (thril′ər), *n.* **1** story, play, TV show, or movie filled with excitement, suspense, etc. **2** person or thing that thrills.

thrive (thriv), *v.* to be successful; grow rich; grow strong; prosper: *Flowers will not thrive without sunshine.* ❑ *v.* **thrived** or **throve, thrived** or **thriv·en** (thriv′ən), **thriv·ing.**

throat (thrōt), *n.* **1** the passage from the mouth to the stomach or the lungs. **2** the front of the neck: *The coat was buttoned up to her throat.*

throat·y (thrō′tē), *adj.* **1** produced or modified in the throat; guttural: *She had a throaty voice.* **2** low-pitched and resonant: *The engine started with a throaty roar.* ❑ *adj.* **throat·i·er, throat·i·est.** —**throat′i·ness**, *n.*

throb (throb), **1** *v.* to beat rapidly or strongly: *The long climb up the hill made my heart throb. My injured foot throbbed with pain.* **2** *n.* a rapid or strong beat: *A throb of pain shot through his head.* **3** *v.* to beat steadily. **4** *n.* a steady beat: *the throb of a pulse.* ❑ *v.* **throbbed, throb·bing.** —**throb′bing·ly**, *adv.*

throes (thrōz), *n.pl.* **1** great pain; agony: *an animal in its death throes.* **2** a desperate struggle; violent disturbance: *a nation in the throes of revolution.*

throm·bo·sis (throm bō′sis), *n.* a blood clot in the heart or in a blood vessel that blocks circulation. ❑ *n., pl.* **throm·bo·ses** (throm bō′sēz).

throm·bus (throm′bəs), *n.* a clot that forms in a blood vessel or within the heart and blocks the circulation. ❑ *n., pl.* **throm·bi** (throm′bi).

throne (thrōn), *n.* **1** a raised, decorated chair on which a king, queen, bishop, or other person of high rank sits during ceremonies. **2** ■ power or authority of a king, queen, etc.: *the throne of England.* ■ Another word that sounds like this is **thrown.**

throng (thrông), **1** *n.* a large crowd. ■ See Synonym Study at **crowd**. **2** *v.* to crowd; fill with a crowd: *People thronged the theater to see the famous actress.* **3** *v.* to come together in a crowd; go or press in large numbers: *The people thronged to see the king.*

throt·tle (throt′l), **1** *n.* valve controlling the flow of gasoline, steam, etc., to an engine. **2** *n.* pedal, lever, etc., controlling such a valve. The throttle of a car is called an accelerator. **3** *v.* to stop or slow an engine by closing such a valve: *to throttle a steam engine.* **4** *v.* to stop the breath by pressure on the throat; choke; strangle. **5** *v.* to hinder or stop the flow of; suppress: *creativity throttled by censorship.* ❑ *v.* **throt·tled, throt·tling.** —**throt′tler**, *n.*

through (thrü), **1** *prep.* from end to end of; from side to side of; between the parts of; from beginning to end of: *march through a town, cut a tunnel through a mountain, drive through a snowstorm.* **2** *adv.* from end to end; from side to side; between the parts: *The ball hit the window and went through.* **3** *prep.* here and there in; over; around: *We traveled through New England visiting many old towns.* **4** *prep.* by way of: *We went out through the back door.* **5** *prep.* by means of: *She became rich through her wise investments.* **6** *adv.* completely; thoroughly: *He walked home in the rain and was wet through.* **7** *adv.* from beginning to end: *She read the book all the way through.* **8** *adv.* all the way: *This train goes through to Boston.* **9** *adj.* going all the way without change: *a through train from New York City to Chicago.* **10** *adj.* for the entire trip: *a through ticket.* **11** *prep.* having reached the end of; finished with: *We are through school at three o'clock.* **12** *adj.* having reached the end; finished: *I am almost through.* **13** *adj.* allowing movement or passage through without stopping: *Is this a through street?* ■ Another word that sounds like this is **threw.**

through and through, completely; thoroughly.

through·out (thrü out′), **1** *prep.* all the way through; through all; in every part of: *The Fourth of July is celebrated throughout the United States.* **2** *adv.* in every part: *The house is well built throughout.*

through·way (thrü′wā′), *n.* thruway.

throve (thrōv), *v.* a past tense of **thrive:** *The plants throve in the rich soil.*

throw (thrō), **1** *v.* to send through the air with force; toss; hurl: *throw a ball. I threw water on the fire.* **2** *n.* act of throwing; a toss or hurl: *That was a good throw from left field to the catcher.* **3** *n.* distance a thing is or may be thrown. **4** *v.* to cause to fall or fall off: *The horse tried to throw its rider. The wrestler threw his opponent.* **5** *v.* to put by force: *throw someone into jail.* **6** *v.* to put carelessly or in haste: *I threw a coat over my shoulders.* **7** *n.* a light blanket, scarf, etc. **8** *v.* to turn, direct, or move, especially quickly: *She threw a glance at us.* **9** *v.* to move a lever or switch that connects or disconnects parts of a switch, clutch, or other mechanism. **10** *v.* INFORMAL. to give a party. **11** *v.* INFORMAL. to let an opponent win a race, game, etc., often for money. ❑ *v.* **threw, thrown, throw·ing.** —**throw′er,** *n.*

throw (def. 4)

throw away, **1** to get rid of; discard: *Throw away those old shoes.* **2** to waste: *Don't throw away your opportunities.*

throw in, to add, especially as a bargain.

throw off, **1** to get rid of: *throw off a cold.* **2** to give off; emit: *The burning oil threw off thick smoke.* **3** to cause to lose: *The fox threw the hounds off its trail by doubling back.*

throw out, **1** to get rid of; discard: *Let's throw out all this old junk.* **2** to reject. **3** (in baseball) to put out a base runner by throwing the ball to a baseman.

throw over, to give up; discard; abandon.

throw up, **1** to vomit. **2** to give up; abandon. **3** to build rapidly and usually carelessly.

throw·a·way (thrō′ə wā′), **1** *adj.* able to be thrown away or discarded: *a throwaway bottle.* **2** *n.* bottle, can, etc., intended to be thrown away after use.

throw·back (thrō′bak′), *n.* a return to an ancestral type or character: *The white stallion was a throwback to an albino ancestor.*

thrown (thrōn), *v.* past participle of **throw:** *She has thrown her old toys away.* ■ Another word that sounds like this is **throne.**

throw rug, scatter rug.

thru (thrü), *prep., adv., adj.* INFORMAL. through. ■ Another word that sounds like this is **threw.**

thrum (thrum), *v.* **1** to play on a stringed instrument by plucking the strings, especially in an idle or careless way; strum. **2** to drum or tap idly with the fingers: *thrumming on a table.* ❑ *v.* **thrummed, thrum·ming.**

thrush (thrush), *n.* any of numerous songbirds including robins, bluebirds, wood thrushes, and veeries. ❑ *n., pl.* **thrush·es.** —**thrush′like′,** *adj.*

thrust (thrust), **1** *v.* to push with force: *He thrust his hands into his pockets.* ■ See Synonym Study at **push.** **2** *n.* a push with force: *She hid the book behind the pillow with a quick thrust.* **3** *v.* to stab; pierce: *thrust a knife into an apple.* **4** *n.* a stab: *A thrust with the pin broke the balloon.* **5** *v.* to put forth; extend: *The tree thrust its roots deep into the ground.* **6** *n.* main or essential part or meaning: *The thrust of his speech was greater opportunities for trained workers.* **7** *n.* the push exerted by the rotation of a pro-

peller, that causes a ship, airplane, etc., to move. **8** *n.* the force driving a rocket or a jet engine forward, caused by the rearward discharge of gases, burning fuels, etc., through the exhaust. ❑ *v.* **thrust, thrust·ing.** —**thrust′er,** *n.*

thru·way (thrü′wā′), *n.* an express highway. Also, **throughway.**

thud (thud), **1** *n.* a dull sound. A heavy blow or fall may cause a thud. *The book hit the floor with a thud.* **2** *v.* to hit, move, or strike with a thud: *The heavy box fell and thudded on the floor.* ❑ *v.* **thud·ded, thud·ding.**

thug (thug), *n.* a rough, violent criminal.

thu·li·um (thü′lē əm), *n.* a metallic element found in various minerals. An isotope of thulium is used as the radiating element in portable X-ray units. *Symbol:* Tm

thumb (thum), **1** *n.* the short, thick finger of the hand. It can be moved against any of the other four fingers to grasp things. **2** *n.* part of a glove or mitten that covers the thumb. **3** *v.* to soil or wear by handling with the thumbs: *The book was badly thumbed.* **4** *v.* to turn pages of a book, magazine, etc., rapidly, reading only portions: *He thumbed the book and gave it back to me.* **5** *v.* INFORMAL. to ask for or get a free ride by holding up one's thumb to motorists going in your direction. —**thumb′like′,** *adj.*

be all thumbs, be very clumsy, awkward, etc.

thumbs down, sign of disapproval or rejection.

thumbs up, sign of approval or acceptance.

twiddle your thumbs, to do nothing; be idle.

under someone's thumb, under someone's power or influence: *The younger children were under the bully's thumb.*

thumb index, series of notches cut in the outer edge of the pages of a book to show sections, so that any section may be found by placing the thumb in the section's notch.

thumb·nail (thum′nāl′), **1** *n.* nail of the thumb. **2** *adj.* very small or short: *a thumbnail sketch.*

thumb·print (thum′print′), *n.* mark made by the lines on the skin of the inner surface of the last joint of the thumb.

thumb·tack (thum′tak′), *n.* tack with a broad, flat head, that can be pressed into a wall, board, etc., with the thumb.

thump (thump), **1** *v.* to strike with something thick and heavy; pound: *She thumped the table with her fist.* **2** *n.* a blow with something thick and heavy; heavy knock: *a thump on the head.* **3** *n.* the dull sound made by a blow, knock, or fall: *We heard a thump when the book fell.* **4** *v.* to make a dull sound: *The hammer thumped against the wood.* **5** *v.* to beat violently: *My heart thumped.* —**thump′er,** *n.*

thun·der (thun′dər), **1** *n.* the loud noise that accompanies or follows a flash of lightning. It is caused by a disturbance of the air resulting from the discharge of electricity. **2** *v.* to make this noise: *It thundered, but no rain fell.* **3** *n.* any noise like this: *the thunder of Niagara Falls.* **4** *v.* to make a noise like this: *The freight train thundered past.* **5** *v.* to say or call very loudly; roar: *thunder a reply.* —**thun′der·er,** *n.* —**thun′der·ing·ly,** *adv.*

thun·der·bolt (thun′dər bōlt′), *n.* **1** a flash of lightning and the thunder that accompanies or follows it. **2** something sudden, startling, and terrible: *The news of the accident came as a thunderbolt.*

thun·der·clap (thun′dər klap′), *n.* **1** a loud crash of thunder. **2** something sudden or startling.

thun·der·cloud (thun′dər kloud′), *n.* **1** a dark, electrically charged cloud that brings thunder and lightning. **2** cumulonimbus.

thun·der·head (thun′dər hed′), *n.* cumulonimbus.

thun·der·ous (thun′dər əs), *adj.* **1** producing thunder. **2** making a noise like thunder: *The actors received thunderous applause at the end of the play.* —**thun′der·ous·ly,** *adv.*

thun·der·show·er (thun′dər shou′ər), *n.* shower with thunder and lightning.

thun·der·storm (thun′dər stôrm′), *n.* storm with thunder and lightning.

a	hat	ė	term	ô	order	ch	child		a in about
ā	age	i	it	oi	oil	ng	long		e in taken
ä	far	ī	ice	ou	out	sh	she	ə	i in pencil
â	care	o	hot	u	cup	th	thin		o in lemon
e	let	ō	open	ů	put	ŦH	then		u in circus
ē	equal	ò	saw	ü	rule	zh	measure		

thun·der·struck (thun′dər struk′), *adj.* overcome, as if hit by a thunderbolt; astonished; amazed: *We were thunderstruck by the terrible news.*

Thur·ber (thėr′bər), *n.* **James,** 1894-1961, American humorous writer and illustrator. His most famous story is "The Secret Life of Walter Mitty."

Thurs. or **Thur.,** Thursday.

Thurs·day (thėrz′dā′ *or* thėrz′dē), *n.* the fifth day of the week, following Wednesday.

> **WORD STORY**   **Thursday** comes from **Thor.** The Romans named this day of the week after Jupiter, their god of thunder. The Scandinavians borrowed the idea but used their own god of thunder.

thus (THUS), *adv.* **1** as a result; therefore: *We hurried and thus arrived on time.* **2** in this way; in the way just stated, indicated, etc.; in the following manner: *He spoke thus: "Friends, Romans, Countrymen."* **3** to this extent or degree; so: *Thus far he is winning.*

thwack (thwak), **1** *v.* to strike hard with a stick or something flat. **2** *n.* a sharp blow with a stick or something flat. **−thwack′er,** *n.*

> **WORD STORY**   **Thwack** comes from the sound of something hitting something. At first, it seems to have been spelled without a *w*, with the meaning "to pat" or "to tap." Later, the meaning seems to have become stronger, and the *w* sound was added to give the word more oomph.

thwart (thwôrt), **1** *v.* to prevent from doing something, particularly by blocking the way; oppose and defeat: *Lack of money thwarted her plans for college.* **2** *n.* a seat across a boat, on which a rower sits. **−thwart′er,** *n.*

thy (THĪ), *adj.* OLD USE. your. "Thy name" means "your name."

thyme (tīm), *n.* any of several small plants related to mint, especially one with sweet-smelling leaves used for seasoning. ■ Another word that sounds like this is **time.**

thy·mine (thī′mēn), *n.* substance present in nucleic acid. It is one of the compounds that form the genetic code in DNA.

thy·mus (thī′məs), *n.* a small, ductless glandlike organ found in young human beings and animals near the base of the neck. It is an organ of the immune system. ❑ *n., pl.* **thy·mus·es.**

thy·roid (thī′roid), **1** *n.* thyroid gland. **2** *n.* medicine made from the thyroid glands of animals, used to treat disorders caused by a deficiency in the thyroid gland. **3** *n.* thyroid cartilage. **4** *adj.* of or about the thyroid gland or thyroid cartilage.

thyroid cartilage, the principal cartilage of the larynx, which forms the lump called the Adam's apple.

thyroid gland, an important ductless gland in the neck of human beings and animals that secretes thyroxine.

thy·rox·ine (thī rok′sēn), *n.* hormone produced by the thyroid gland. It affects growth and metabolism.

thy·self (THĪ self′), *pron.* OLD USE. yourself.

ti (tē), *n.* the seventh tone of the musical scale; si. ■ Other words that sound like this are **tea** and **tee.**

Ti, symbol for titanium.

Tian·jin (tē än′jin′), *n.* port in NE China, near Beijing. Formerly called **Tientsin.**

ti·ar·a (tē âr′ə *or* tē är′ə), *n.* **1** band of gold, jewels, flowers, etc., worn around the head as an ornament. **2** the triple crown worn by the pope as a symbol of his position. ❑ *n., pl.* **ti·ar·as.**

Ti·ber (tī′bər), *n.* river flowing from central Italy through Rome into the Tyrrhenian Sea.

Ti·bet (ti bet′), *n.* former country of central Asia, now part of China. Its official Chinese name is **Xizang.** *Capital:* Lhasa.

Ti·bet·an (ti bet′n), **1** *adj.* of or about Tibet, its people, or their language. **2** *n.* person born or living in Tibet. **3** *n.* language of Tibet.

tib·i·a (tib′ē ə), *n.* shinbone. ❑ *n., pl.* **tib·i·ae** (tib′ē ē′), **tib·i·as.**

tic (tik), *n.* a habitual, involuntary twitching of certain muscles, especially those of the face. ■ Another word that sounds like this is **tick.**

tick¹ (tik), **1** *n.* sound made by a clock or watch. **2** *v.* to make such a sound: *The clock ticked.* **3** *v.* to mark off: *The clock ticked away the minutes.* **4** *n.* a small mark. We use ✓ or / as a tick. **5** *v.* to mark with a tick; check: *He ticked off the items one by one.* **6** *v.*

to function, work, or go: *What makes that gadget tick?* ■ Another word that sounds like this is **tic.**

tick² (tik), *n.* any of numerous tiny eight-legged animals, related to spiders, mites, and scorpions, that attach themselves to humans and animals and suck blood. ■ Another word that sounds like this is **tic.**

tick³ (tik), *n.* the cloth covering of a mattress or pillow. ■ Another word that sounds like this is **tic.**

tick·er (tik′ər), *n.* **1** an electronic or telegraphic device that prints stock-market reports or news on a paper tape. **2** INFORMAL. the heart.

ticker tape, a paper tape on which a ticker prints stock-market reports or news.

tick·et (tik′it), **1** *n.* card or piece of paper that gives its holder a right or privilege: *an airline ticket.* **2** *n.* a written order to appear in court, given to someone accused of breaking a traffic law: *a ticket for speeding.* **3** *v.* to give someone a written order to appear in court: *He was ticketed for illegal parking.* **4** *n.* card or piece of paper attached to something to show its price, etc. **5** *v.* to put a ticket on; mark with a ticket: *All articles in the store are ticketed with the price.* **6** *n.* the list of candidates to be voted on that belong to one political party. [See Word Story at **etiquette.**]

tick·ing (tik′ing), *n.* a strong cotton or linen cloth, used to cover mattresses and pillows.

tick·le (tik′əl), **1** *v.* to touch lightly with your fingers, causing little thrills, shivers, or wriggles: *He tickled the baby's feet and made her laugh.* **2** *v.* to have a feeling like this; cause to have such a feeling: *My nose tickles.* **3** *n.* a tingling or itching feeling. **4** *v.* to excite pleasantly; amuse: *The story tickled me. The child was tickled by her new toys.* **5** *n.* act of tickling. ❑ *v.* **tick·led, tick·ling.**

tick·ler (tik′lər), *n.* person or thing that tickles.

tick·lish (tik′lish), *adj.* **1** sensitive to tickling: *The bottoms of the feet are ticklish.* **2** requiring careful handling; delicate; risky: *Telling your friends their faults is a ticklish business.* **3** sensitive; easily offended: *be ticklish about your age.* **−tick′lish·ly,** *adv.* **−tick′lish·ness,** *n.*

tick-tack-toe (tik′tak tō′), *n.* game in which two players alternately put circles or crosses in a figure of nine squares. The object is to be the first to fill three squares in a row with your mark.

Ti·con·de·ro·ga (tī′kon də rō′gə), *n.* village and old fort on Lake Champlain, in NE New York State.

tid·al (tī′dl), *adj.* of or about tides. **−tid′al·ly,** *adv.*

tidal wave, 1 an enormous, destructive ocean wave, caused by an underwater earthquake. **2** a large wave or sudden increase in the level of water along a shore, caused by unusually strong winds. **3** any great expression or change of feeling: *a tidal wave of popular indignation.*

Tibet

tid·bit (tid′bit′), *n.* a very pleasing bit of food, news, etc.

tid·dly·winks (tid′lē wingks′), *n.* game in which the players try to make small colored disks jump from a flat surface into a cup by pressing on their edges with larger disks.

tide (tīd), *n.* **1** the rise and fall of the ocean about every twelve hours, caused by the gravitational pull of the moon and the sun:

We go swimming at high tide; at low tide we dig clams. **2** anything that changes regularly like the tide: *the tide of public opinion.* **—tide′less,** *adj.*

tide over, to help for a time; see through: *Her savings will tide her over her illness.*

turn the tide, to change from one situation to the opposite: *Two home runs in the seventh inning turned the tide against our team.*

WORD STORY **Tide** comes from an old English word meaning "time." **Tidy** comes from the same old English word. The ending **-tide** is sometimes attached to the names of holidays like Christmas and Easter to mean "time." One of the most impressive things about the ocean tide is that it happens at regular times. **Tidy** began with the meaning "right for the time," especially about farm crops and animals growing as they should and looking healthy. The sense of proper appearance became the main meaning.

tide·land (tīd′land′), *n.* land flooded at high tide.

tide·wa·ter (tīd′wô′tər), **1** *n.* water in rivers, streams, etc., raised and lowered by the ocean tides. **2** *n.* low-lying land along a seacoast, through which such water flows. **3** *adj.* of or about such water or land.

ti·dings (tī′dingz), *n.pl.* news; information: *joyful tidings.*

ti·dy (tī′dē), **1** *adj.* neat and in order: *a tidy room.* ■ See Synonym Study at **neat. 2** *v.* to put in order; make neat: *I tidied the room. Be sure to tidy up before going out.* **3** *adj.* fairly large; considerable: *a tidy sum of money.* ❑ *adj.* **ti·di·er, ti·di·est;** *v.* **ti·died, ti·dy·ing.** [See Word Story at **tide.**] **—ti′di·ly,** *adv.* **—ti′di·ness,** *n.*

tie (tī), **1** *v.* to fasten with string or the like; bind: *Please tie this package.* **2** *v.* to arrange to form a bow or knot: *We tied blue and white ribbons on the party favors.* **3** *v.* to tighten and fasten the string or strings of: *tie your shoes.* **4** *n.* string, cord, chain, etc., used for tying. **5** *n.* necktie. **6** *v.* to fasten, join, or connect in any way; make a bond or connection. **7** *n.* anything that unites; obligation: *family ties, ties of friendship.* **8** *v.* to restrain; restrict; limit: *to be tied to a steady job.* **9** *n.* a heavy piece of timber or iron placed crosswise to form a foundation or support. The rails of a railroad track are fastened to ties about a foot apart. **10** *n.* a connecting beam, rod, or the like. **11** *n.* equality in points, votes, etc.: *The game ended in a tie, 3 to 3.* **12** *n.* a match or contest in which this occurs. **13** *v.* to make the same score; be equal in points: *The two teams tied.* **14** *n.* (in music) a curved line (‿ or ⁀) set above or below two notes of the same pitch, indicating that they are to be played or sung as one sustained tone. ❑ *v.* **tied, ty·ing.**

tie down, to limit; confine; restrict: *tied down by responsibilities.*
tie in, to make or have a connection; relate: *How does that statement tie in with what you said yesterday?*
tie into, INFORMAL. to attack someone or something with great force: *He tied into the household chores as soon as he got home.*
tie up, 1 to tie firmly or tightly. **2** to wrap up. **3** to hinder; stop: *The stalled truck tied up traffic for half an hour.* **4** to invest money or to place property in such a way as to make it unavailable for other purposes: *All our money is tied up in stocks, so we can't invest in your business.* **5** to be very busy: *I can't go now; I'm all tied up.*

tie-dye (tī′dī′), *v.* to dye cloth by tying some of the material in knots to prevent the cloth inside from absorbing the dye. ❑ *v.* **tie-dyed, tie-dye·ing.**

Tien·tsin (tin′tsin′), *n.* Former name of **Tianjin.**

tier (tir), *n.* one of a series of rows arranged one above another: *tiers of seats in a football stadium.* ■ Another word that sounds like this is **tear¹.**

Tier·ra del Fue·go (tyer′ə del fwā′gō), group of islands at the S end of South America. Part belongs to Argentina, part to Chile. See **Patagonia** for map.

WORD STORY **Tierra del Fuego** comes from Spanish words meaning "land of fire." The explorer Magellan, who led the first European expedition to this region, saw many large fires as he sailed past. Tierra del Fuego is cold, and people there kept warm with bonfires in those days.

tie-up (tī′up′), *n.* **1** act of stopping action on account of a strike, storm, accident, etc.: *a traffic tie-up.* **2** connection; relation.

tiff (tif), *n.* a little quarrel.

ti·ger (tī′gər), *n.* a large, fierce cat of Asia, with dull yellow fur striped with black. **—ti′ger·like′,** *adj.*

ti·ger·ish (tī′gər ish), *adj.* like a tiger; fierce; cruel. **—ti′ger·ish·ly,** *adv.* **—ti′ger·ish·ness,** *n.*

tiger lily, lily that has dull orange flowers spotted with black.

tiger moth, any of numerous moths having spotted or striped wings.

tiger—about 9 ft. (2.5 m) long with the tail

tight (tīt), **1** *adj.* close; fitting closely or too closely: *tight clothing.* **2** *adj.* not letting water, air, or gas in or out: *The tight roof kept rain from leaking in.* **3** *adv.* closely; securely; firmly: *The rope was tied too tight.* **4** *adj.* packed or put together firmly; held firmly; firm: *a tight knot.* **5** *adj.* drawn; stretched: *a tight canvas.* **6** *adj.* not having enough time; full: *a tight schedule.* **7** *adj.* hard to deal with or manage; difficult: *A lie got her into a tight spot.* **8** *adj.* almost even; close: *It was a tight race.* **9** *adj.* hard to get; scarce: *Money is tight just now.* **10** *adj.* strict; severe: *to keep tight controls on expenses.* **11** *adj.* stingy: *They are tight with their money.* **—tight′ly,** *adv.* **—tight′ness,** *n.*

sit tight, to keep the same position, opinion, etc.

tight·en (tīt′n), *v.* to make or become tight: *He tightened his belt.* **—tight′en·er,** *n.*

tight-fist·ed (tīt′fis′tid), *adj.* stingy. **—tight′fist′ed·ness,** *n.*

tight-lipped (tīt′lipt′), *adj.* **1** saying little or nothing. **2** keeping the lips firmly together.

tight·rope (tīt′rōp′), *n.* rope or wire cable stretched tight on which acrobats perform.

tights (tīts), *n.pl.* a close-fitting garment, usually covering the lower part of the body and the legs, worn by acrobats, dancers, etc.

tight·wad (tīt′wod′), *n.* a stingy person.

ti·gress (tī′gris), *n.* a female tiger. ❑ *n., pl.* **ti·gress·es.**

Ti·gris (tī′gris), *n.* river flowing from SE Turkey through Iraq, where it joins the Euphrates River and empties into the Persian Gulf. See **Euphrates** for map.

til·de (til′də), *n.* a diacritical mark (˜) to indicate a special sound. It is used over *n* in Spanish when it is pronounced *ny,* as in *cañon* (kä nyōn′). It is used over certain vowels in Portuguese to indicate that they are nasal, as in *São Paulo* (soun pou′lù).

tile (tīl), **1** *n.* a thin piece of baked clay, stone, plastic, etc. Tiles are used for covering roofs, paving floors, and ornamenting. **2** *n.* a thin piece of plastic, rubber, linoleum, or the like, used for covering floors or walls. **3** *n.* a baked clay pipe for draining land. **4** *v.* to put tiles on or in: *to tile a bathroom floor.* ❑ *v.* **tiled, til·ing.** **—tile′like′,** *adj.* **—til′er,** *n.*

tiles (def. 1)

a	hat	ė	term	ô	order	ch	child		
ā	age	i	it	oi	oil	ng	long		a in about
ä	far	ī	ice	ou	out	sh	she		e in taken
â	care	o	hot	u	cup	th	thin	ə	i in pencil
e	let	ō	open	ù	put	ᴛʜ	then		o in lemon
ē	equal	ò	saw	ü	rule	zh	measure		u in circus

T

til·ing (tī′ling), *n.* **1** tiles collectively. **2** the work of covering with tiles. **3** anything made of tiles.

till[1] (til), **1** *prep.* up to the time of; until: *The child played till eight.* **2** *conj.* up to the time when; until: *Walk till you come to a white house.*

till[2] (til), *v.* to cultivate; plow: *Farmers till the land.*

till[3] (til), *n.* a small drawer for money under or behind a counter.

till·age (til′ij), *n.* **1** cultivation of land. **2** tilled land.

till·er[1] (til′ər), *n.* bar or handle used to turn the rudder in steering a boat.

till·er[2] (til′ər), *n.* person who tills land; farmer.

tilt (tilt), **1** *v.* to tip or cause to tip; slope; slant; lean: *You tilt your head forward when you bow. This table tilts.* **2** *n.* a slope; sloping position; a slant: *This table is on a tilt.* **3** *v.* (in the Middle Ages) to rush, charge, or fight with lances. Knights used to tilt on horseback. **4** *n.* (in the Middle Ages) a fight on horseback with lances. **5** *n.* any dispute or quarrel. —**tilt′a·ble**, *adj.* —**tilt′er**, *n.*

full tilt, at full speed; with full force: *The car ran full tilt against the tree.*

tilth (tilth), *n.* **1** cultivation of land. **2** tilled land.

tim·ber (tim′bər), *n.* **1** wood used for building and making things. Houses, ships, and furniture are made from timber. **2** a large piece of wood used in building. Beams and rafters are timbers. **3** growing trees, especially when used to provide wood for building. ■ Another word that can sound like this is **timbre**.

tim·bered (tim′bərd), *adj.* **1** made or furnished with timber. **2** covered with growing trees.

tim·ber·land (tim′bər land′), *n.* land with trees that are, or will be, useful for timber.

tim·ber·line (tim′bər lin′), *n.* line on mountains and in polar regions beyond which trees will not grow because of the cold; tree line.

timber wolf, a gray wolf.

tim·bre (tam′bər *or* tim′bər), *n.* the quality in sounds, regardless of their pitch and volume, that distinguishes a certain voice or instrument from another voice or instrument. Because of differences in timbre, identical notes played on a violin, an oboe, and a trumpet can be distinguished from one another. ■ Another word that can sound like this is **timber**.

Tim·buk·tu (tim′buk tü′), *n.* city of W Africa. From the 1200s to the 1500s, it was a center of trade, wealth, and learning.

time (tīm), **1** *n.* all the days there have been or ever will be; the past, present, and future. Time is measured in years, months, weeks, days, hours, minutes, and seconds. **2** *n.* a part of the past, present, or future: *A minute is a short time.* **3** *n.* period of time; epoch: *the time of the dinosaurs.* **4** *n.* some point in time; a particular point in time: *What time is it? The time the game begins is 2 P.M.* **5** *n.* the right part or point of time: *It is time to eat.* **6** *n.* occasion: *This time we will succeed.* **7** *n.* way of reckoning time: *solar time.* **8** *n.* condition of life: *War brings hard times.* **9** *n.* an experience during a certain time: *He had a good time at the party.* **10** *n.* rate of movement in music or poetry; rhythm: *waltz time, to beat time.* **11** *n.* amount of time that you have worked or should work: *Her normal time is 8 hours a day.* **12** *n.* the pay for a period of work. **13** *n.* leisure: *have time to read.* **14** *v.* to measure the time or rate of speed of: *time a race.* **15** *v.* to do at regular times; do in rhythm with; set the time of: *The dancers timed their steps to the music.* **16** *v.* to set, regulate, or adjust: *The clock was timed to ring at 7:00.* **17** *v.* to choose the moment or occasion for: *He timed his request for a raise so as to catch his boss in a good mood.* **18** *adj.* of or about time. **19** *prep.* **times**, multiplied by. The sign for this in arithmetic is ×. *Four times three is twelve. Twenty is five times as much as four.* ❑ *v.* **timed, tim·ing.** ■ Another word that sounds like this is **thyme**.

against time, trying to finish before a certain time: *They were in a race against time in their rescue efforts.*

at one time, 1 at a period in the past: *At one time they used to be friends.* **2** at the same time; together: *Everyone was interrupting, trying to talk at one time.*

at the same time, however; nevertheless.

at times, now and then; once in a while; sometimes: *At times, I wish I were taller.*

behind the times, old-fashioned; out-of-date.

behind time, late: *The school bus was running behind time this morning.*

for the time being, for the present; for now: *The baby is asleep for the time being.*

from time to time, now and then; once in a while: *From time to time we visit my grandparents.*

in good time, at the right time.

in no time, shortly; before long: *We hurried and arrived home in no time.*

in time, 1 after a while. **2** soon enough: *Will she arrive in time to have dinner with us?* **3** in the right rate of movement in music, dancing, marching, etc.: *We clapped in time to the music.*

keep time, 1 (of a watch or clock) to go correctly. **2** to measure or record time, rate of speed, etc.: *I kept time at the race with a stopwatch.* **3** to sound or move at the right rate: *The marchers kept time to the music.*

make time, to go with speed.

mark time, 1 to move the feet as in marching, but without advancing. **2** to suspend progress temporarily. **3** to go through motions without accomplishing anything.

on time, 1 at the right time; not late; punctual. **2** with time in which to pay; on credit: *She bought a car on time.*

take your time, to not be in any hurry: *He took his time coming home from the game.*

tell time, to know what time it is by the clock; be able to read a clock.

time after time or **time and again,** again and again.

time bomb, 1 a bomb that can be set to explode at a certain time. **2** a situation that may have a disastrous outcome in the future.

time clock, clock with a device to record the times when workers arrive and leave.

time exposure, 1 exposure of a photographic film for a certain time, longer than a half second. **2** photograph taken in this way.

time exposure (def. 2)

time-hon·ored (tīm′on′ərd), *adj.* honored because old and established: *Shaking hands is a time-honored custom.*

time·keep·er (tīm′kē′pər), *n.* person or thing that keeps time: *My watch is an excellent timekeeper.*

time-lapse (tīm′laps′), *adj.* of or by photography in which pictures of a slowly changing process are taken at regular, timed intervals. When projected, the pictures are speeded up to suggest motion and quick change.

time·less (tīm′lis), *adj.* **1** never ending; eternal. **2** referring to no special time. —**time′less·ly,** *adv.* —**time′less·ness,** *n.*

time line, a chart consisting of a printed line representing a certain length of time and subdivided into smaller time units, along which historical events are listed in order at the point they occurred. A time line may be either horizontal or vertical.

time·ly (tīm′lē), *adj.* at the right time: *The timely warning about the storm saved many lives.* ❑ *adj.* **time·li·er, time·li·est.** —**time′li·ness,** *n.*

time-out (tīm′out′), *n.* period when play is stopped during a game. ■ See Synonym Study at **intermission.**

time·piece (tīm′pēs′), *n.* clock or watch.

tim·er (tī′mər), *n.* **1** device for indicating or recording intervals of time, such as a stopwatch. **2** a clockwork device for indicating when a certain period of time has elapsed: *Microwave ovens have timers for baking.* **3** any device that automatically turns something on or off at a preset time. Timers can operate many electrical devices.

time·sav·ing (tīm′sā′ving), *adj.* reducing the time previously needed to do something: *a timesaving appliance.*

time-shar·ing (tīm′shâr′ing), *n.* **1** system in which a large computer is used by many people, for many jobs, at the same time. **2** an agreement in which several people share ownership or rental costs for a vacation home that they take turns living in.

time signature, a sign to show the rhythm of a piece of music, placed at the beginning or where the rhythm changes.

time·ta·ble (tīm′tā′bəl), *n.* schedule showing the times when trains, boats, buses, airplanes, etc., arrive and depart.

time warp, an imaginary twist in time that makes it possible for someone to pass suddenly from one period to another.

time·worn (tīm′wôrn′), *adj.* worn by long existence or use.

time zone, a geographical region within which one standard time is used. The world is divided into 24 time zones, beginning and ending at the International Date Line.

tim·id (tim′id), *adj.* easily frightened; shy: *The timid child was afraid of the dark.* ■ See Synonym Study at **shy**[1]. **—ti·mid·i·ty** (tə·mid′ə tē), **tim·id·ness,** *n.* **—tim′id·ly,** *adv.*

tim·ing (tī′ming), *n.* **1** control of the time or speed of anything to get the greatest effect: *the timing of a stroke in tennis, the timing of an actor in responding to a cue, the timing of the release of a new play.* **2** observance and measurement of the time something takes, often using a stopwatch.

Ti·mor (tē′môr *or* tē môr′), *n.* island in Indonesia.

tim·or·ous (tim′ər əs), *adj.* easily frightened; timid: *The timorous rabbit ran away.* **—tim′or·ous·ly,** *adv.* **—tim′or·ous·ness,** *n.*

tim·o·thy (tim′ə thē), *n.* a kind of coarse grass with long, cylindrical flower spikes, often grown for hay.

Tim·o·thy (tim′ə thē), *n.* **1** a disciple of the apostle Paul. **2** either of the two books of the New Testament written as letters by Paul to Timothy. [**Timothy** comes from Greek words meaning "honor" and "God."]

tim·pa·ni (tim′pə nē), *n.pl.* kettledrums.

tim·pa·nist (tim′pə nist), *n.* person who plays the kettledrums.

tin (tin), **1** *n.* a soft, silver-white metallic element used in making alloys such as bronze and pewter and in plating metals to prevent corrosion. *Symbol:* Sn **2** *adj.* made of tin or plated with tin. **3** *n.* any can, box, pan, or other container made of or plated with tin: *a pie tin.* **4** *v.* to plate with tin. ❑ *v.* **tinned, tin·ning. —tin′like′,** *adj.*

tinc·ture (tingk′chər), *n.* **1** solution of medicine in alcohol: *tincture of iodine.* **2** trace; tinge: *a tincture of amusement in someone's eyes.*

tin·der (tin′dər), *n.* **1** anything that catches fire easily. **2** material used to catch fire from a spark.

tin·der·box (tin′dər boks′), *n.* **1** box for holding tinder, flint, and steel for making a fire. **2** a very flammable thing. ❑ *n., pl.* **tin·der·box·es.**

tine (tīn), *n.* a sharp pointed part or prong: *the tines of a fork.*

tin·foil (tin′foil′), *n.* a very thin sheet of aluminum, tin, or tin and lead, used as a wrapping for candy, medicine tablets, etc.

ting (ting), **1** *v.* to make or cause to make a clear, ringing sound. **2** *n.* such a sound.

tinge (tinj), **1** *v.* to color slightly: *The dawn sky was tinged with pink.* **2** *n.* a slight coloring or tint: *There is a tinge of red in those leaves.* **3** *v.* to add a trace of some quality; change slightly: *Sad memories tinged his present joy.* **4** *n.* a very small amount; trace: *She likes just a tinge of lemon in her tea.* ❑ *v.* **tinged, tinge·ing** or **ting·ing.**

tin·gle (ting′gəl), **1** *v.* to have or cause a feeling of thrills or a prickling, stinging feeling: *to tingle with excitement.* **2** *n.* a prickling, stinging feeling: *The cold caused a tingle in my fingers.* ❑ *v.* **tin·gled, tin·gling. —tin′gling·ly,** *adv.*

tin·gly (ting′glē), *adj.* causing a stinging or tingling feeling. ❑ *adj.* **tin·gli·er, tin·gli·est.**

tink·er (ting′kər), **1** *v.* to work or keep busy in a rather useless way: *I was tinkering in my workshop.* **2** *v.* to work or repair in an unskilled or clumsy way: *The children were tinkering with the clock and broke it.* **3** *n.* (earlier) someone who mended pots, pans, etc. **4** *v.* to mend; patch. **—tink′er·er,** *n.*

tin·kle (ting′kəl), **1** *v.* to make short, light, ringing sounds: *Little bells tinkle.* **2** *n.* series of short, light, ringing sounds: *the tinkle of sleigh bells.* ❑ *v.* **tin·kled, tin·kling. —tin′kling·ly,** *adv.*

tin·kly (ting′klē), *adj.* full of tinkles; marked by tinkling. ❑ *adj.* **tin·kli·er, tin·kli·est.**

tin·ny (tin′ē), *adj.* **1** poor in quality: *cheap, tinny toys.* **2** tasting like tin: *These sardines have a tinny flavor.* **3** of tin; containing tin. ❑ *adj.* **tin·ni·er, tin·ni·est. —tin′ni·ly,** *adv.* **—tin′ni·ness,** *n.*

tin·sel (tin′səl), **1** *n.* very thin sheets, strips, or threads of glittering metal or plastic used to trim Christmas trees, costumes, etc. **2** *n.* anything showy but having little value. **3** *adj.* of or like tinsel; showy but not worth much.

WORD STORY   **Tinsel** comes from an old French word meaning "spark," because it looks sparkly. But why an old French word? How old is tinsel? About 500 years ago, threads of gold and silver wire were used to make "tinsel cloth" sparkle. About 400 years ago, people started using just the threads to decorate Christmas trees, as people still do.

tin·smith (tin′smith′), *n.* person who makes or repairs tinware.

tint (tint), **1** *n.* variety of a color: *The picture was painted in several tints of blue.* **2** *n.* a delicate or pale color. **3** *v.* to put a tint on; color slightly: *The walls were tinted gray.* **—tint′er,** *n.*

tin·type (tin′tīp′), *n.* (earlier) photograph taken on a thin sheet of tin or iron.

tin·ware (tin′wâr′), *n.* articles made of tin or tin plate.

ti·ny (tī′nē), *adj.* very small; wee: *a tiny baby.* ❑ *adj.* **ti·ni·er, ti·ni·est. —ti′ni·ly,** *adv.* **—ti′ni·ness,** *n.*

SYNONYM STUDY   **Tiny, miniature,** and **minute**[2] all mean very small. **Tiny** is a general word: *The baby's fingers are tiny.* **Miniature** means very much smaller than usual: *The doll house has miniature furniture.* **Minute** means very tiny: *The minute bugs can hardly be seen.*

-tion, *suffix.* **1** act or process of ___ing: *addition = act or process of adding.* **2** result of ___ing: *reflection = result of reflecting.* **3** condition of being ___ed: *exhaustion = condition of being exhausted.*

tip[1] (tip), **1** *n.* the end part; end; point: *the tips of the fingers.* **2** *n.* a small piece put on the end of something: *rubber tips to put on the legs of a stool.* **3** *v.* to put a tip on; furnish with a tip: *spears tipped with steel.* **4** *v.* to cover or adorn at the tip: *The mountains were tipped with snow.* ❑ *v.* **tipped, tip·ping. —tip′less,** *adj.*

tip[2] (tip), **1** *v.* to slope; slant: *She tipped the table toward her.* **2** *n.* a slope; slant: *There is such a tip to that table that everything slips off it.* **3** *v.* to upset; overturn: *He tipped over his glass of water.* **4** *v.* to take off a hat in greeting: *The old gentleman tipped his hat to a neighbor.* **5** *v.* to empty out; dump: *She tipped the money in her purse onto the table.* ❑ *v.* **tipped, tip·ping. —tip′pa·ble,** *adj.*

tip[3] (tip), **1** *n.* a small amount of money in return for service: *She gave the waiter a tip.* **2** *v.* to give a small present of money to: *Did you tip the waiter?* **3** *n.* piece of secret information: *He had a tip that the black horse would win the race.* **4** *n.* a useful hint; helpful information: *Someone gave me a tip about pitching a tent where the trees would shade it.* **5** *v.* to hit lightly and sharply; tap. **6** *n.* a light, sharp blow; tap. ❑ *v.* **tipped, tip·ping. —tip′less,** *adj.* **—tip′pa·ble,** *adj.* **—tip′per,** *n.*

tip off, 1 to give secret information or advice to: *They tipped me off about a good bargain.* **2** to warn: *Someone tipped off the criminals and they escaped.*

ti·pi (tē′pē), *n.* tepee. ❑ *n., pl.* **ti·pis.**

a	hat	ė	term	ȯ	order	ch	child		a in about
ā	age	i	it	oi	oil	ng	long		e in taken
ä	far	ī	ice	ou	out	sh	she	ə {	i in pencil
â	care	o	hot	u	cup	th	thin		o in lemon
e	let	ō	open	u̇	put	ᵺ	then		u in circus
ē	equal	ȯ	saw	ü	rule	zh	measure		

T

Lake Titicaca—12,508 ft. (3812 m) above sea level

tip-off (tip′ôf′), *n.* INFORMAL. **1** piece of secret information. **2** a warning.

tip·ple (tip′əl), *v.* to drink alcoholic beverages often. ❑ *v.* **tip·pled, tip·pling.** —**tip′pler,** *n.*

tip·sy (tip′sē), *adj.* **1** somewhat intoxicated but not thoroughly drunk. **2** tipping easily; unsteady; tilted. ❑ *adj.* **tip·si·er, tip·si·est.** —**tip′si·ly,** *adv.* —**tip′si·ness,** *n.*

tip·toe (tip′tō′), **1** *v.* to walk on your toes, without using the heels: *She tiptoed quietly up the stairs.* **2** *n.* the tips of the toes: *walk on tiptoe.* ❑ *v.* **tip·toed, tip·toe·ing.**

tip-top (tip′top′), **1** *adj.* INFORMAL. first-rate; excellent: *I'm in tip-top shape.* **2** *n.* the very top; highest point. **3** *adj.* at the very top or highest point.

ti·rade (tī′rād), *n.* a long, violent speech, full of criticism and disapproval.

Ti·ra·na (ti rä′nə), *n.* capital of Albania, in the central part.

tire[1] (tīr), *v.* **1** to make or become weary: *The work tired him. I tire easily.* **2** to wear down the patience or interest of someone; bore: *Too many long speeches tired the listeners.* ❑ *v.* **tired, tir·ing.**

tire[2] (tīr), *n.* a circle of rubber around a wheel. Some tires have inner tubes for holding air; others hold the air in the tire itself or are made of solid rubber. [Tire[2] comes from **attire**. A tire is like clothing for a wheel.]

tired (tīrd), *adj.* weary; fatigued; exhausted: *I am tired, but I must get back to work.* —**tired′ly,** *adv.* —**tired′ness,** *n.*

SYNONYM STUDY **Tired, fatigued,** and **exhausted** all mean with little energy or strength left. **Tired** is a general word: *Mom is tired when she comes home from work.* **Fatigued** means very tired after hard work or effort: *Exercise should not make you fatigued.* **Exhausted** means having no strength or energy left at all: *He became exhausted and had to quit the race.*

---

tire·less (tīr′lis), *adj.* **1** never becoming tired; requiring little rest: *a tireless worker.* **2** never stopping: *tireless efforts.* —**tire′less·ly,** *adv.* —**tire′less·ness,** *n.*

tire·some (tīr′səm), *adj.* not interesting; tiring; boring: *a tiresome speech.* ■ See Synonym Study at **dull.** —**tire′some·ly,** *adv.* —**tire′some·ness,** *n.*

Ti·rol (tə rōl′ *or* ti′rōl), *n.* region in the Alps, partly in Austria and partly in Italy. Also, **Tyrol.**

'tis (tiz), OLD USE. it is.

tis·sue (tish′ü), *n.* **1** mass of similar cells working together to perform particular functions: *brain tissue, muscle tissue, skin tissue.* **2** living matter of any kind: *plant tissue, animal tissue.* **3** a thin, soft paper that absorbs moisture easily. Tissue is used to wipe the face or the nose. **4** tissue paper. **5** web; network: *The whole story was a tissue of lies.* **6** a thin, light cloth: *Her gown was of silk tissue.* [See Word Story at **text.**]

tissue paper, a very thin, soft paper, used for wrapping, covering things, etc.

tit (tit), *n.* any of several European titmice resembling chickadees.

Ti·tan (tīt′n), *n.* **1** (in Greek myths) any of a family of giants who ruled the world before the gods of Mount Olympus. Prometheus and Atlas were Titans. **2** Also, **titan,** person or thing of enormous size, strength, power, etc.; giant.

ti·tan·ic (tī tan′ik), *adj.* having great size, strength, or power; gigantic: *titanic machinery.* —**ti·tan′i·cal·ly,** *adv.*

ti·ta·ni·um (tī tā′nē əm), *n.* a strong, lightweight, silver-gray metallic element, always found combined with other elements. It is highly resistant to corrosion and is used in making steel and other alloys for missiles, jet engines, etc. *Symbol:* Ti

tithe (tīтн), **1** *n.* one tenth of your yearly income, paid for the support of a church. **2** *v.* to make or pledge such a payment. ❑ *v.* **tithed, tith·ing.** —**tith′er,** *n.*

Tit·i·ca·ca (tit′i kä′kə), *n.* **Lake,** lake between Peru and Bolivia. It is the highest large lake in the world.

tit·il·late (tit′l āt), *v.* **1** to excite pleasantly; stimulate agreeably. **2** to tickle. ❑ *v.* **tit·il·lat·ed, tit·il·lat·ing.** —**tit′il·lat′ing·ly,** *adv.* —**tit′il·la′tion,** *n.*

ti·tle (tī′tl), **1** *n.* the name of a book, play, movie, poem, picture, song, etc. **2** *n.* name showing rank, occupation, or condition in life. King, duke, lord, countess, captain, doctor, professor, Madame, and Miss are titles. **3** *v.* to call by a title; name. **4** *n.* a first-place position; championship: *the tennis title.* **5** *n.* a legal right to the possession of property. **6** *n.* evidence, especially a document, showing such a right. When a house is sold, the seller gives title to the buyer. ❑ *v.* **ti·tled, ti·tling.**

ti·tled (tī′tld), *adj.* having a title: *a titled noble.*

title page, page at the beginning of a book that contains the title, the name of the author and publisher, etc.

tit·mouse (tit′mous′), *n.* any of numerous small birds with short bills and dull-colored feathers. Chickadees are titmice. ❑ *n., pl.* **tit·mice** (tit′mīs′).

Ti·to (tē′tō), *n.* Marshal **Jo·sip Broz** (yō′sip brôz), 1892-1980, Yugoslav political leader, president of Yugoslavia from 1953 to 1980.

tit·ter (tit′ər), **1** *v.* to laugh nervously while trying not to giggle: *The students tittered when their teacher stumbled.* **2** *n.* a nervous giggle or laugh. —**tit′ter·er,** *n.* —**tit′ter·ing·ly,** *adv.*

tit·tle (tit′l), *n.* **1** a very little bit; particle. **2** a small stroke or mark over a letter in writing or printing. The dot over an *i* is a tittle.

tit·u·lar (tich′ə lər), *adj.* **1** in title or name only; nominal: *He is a titular prince without any power.* **2** of or having a title. —**tit′u·lar·ly,** *adv.*

tiz·zy (tiz′ē), *n.* INFORMAL. a very excited, confused state. ❑ *n., pl.* **tiz·zies.**

Tl, symbol for thallium.

Tla·loc (tlä′lōk), *n.* the Aztec god of rain, who was believed to control the growth of corn.

Tlax·ca·la (tlä skä′lä), *n.* a state in central Mexico.

Tlin·git (tling′kət *or* tling′gət), *n.* member of a tribe of American Indians living along the southern coast of Alaska. ❑ *n., pl.* **Tlin·git** or **Tlin·gits.**

TM, trademark.

Tm, symbol for thulium.

TN, Tennessee (used with postal Zip Code).

TNT or **T.N.T.,** trinitrotoluene (a pale yellow solid used as an explosive).

to (tü), **1** *prep.* in the direction of: *Go to the right.* **2** *prep.* as far as; until: *rotten to the core, faithful to the end.* **3** *prep.* for the purpose of; for: *She came to the rescue.* **4** *prep.* so as to produce, cause, or result in: *To their horror, the beast approached.* **5** *prep.* into: *She tore the letter to pieces.* **6** *prep.* along with; with: *We danced to the music.* **7** *prep.* compared with: *The score was 9 to 5.* **8** *prep.* in agreement or accordance with: *It is not to my liking.* **9** *prep.* belonging with; of: *The desk clerk gave me the key to my room.* **10** *prep.* on; against: *Fasten it to the wall. They danced cheek to cheek.* **11** *prep.* about; concerning: *What did he say to that?* **12** *prep.* in: *four apples to the pound.* **13** *prep.* To is used to show action toward. *Give the book to me. Speak to her.* **14** *prep.* To is used with the infinitive form of verbs. *I like to read. The birds began to sing. "To err is human; to forgive, divine."* **15** *adv.* forward: *He wore his cap wrong side to.* **16** *adv.* together; touching; closed: *The door slammed to.* **17** *adv.* to action or work: *Af-*

ter a short rest we set to. ■ See Usage Note at **onto**. ■ Other words that sound like this are **too** and **two**.

to and fro, first one way and then back again; back and forth.

toad (tōd), *n*. **1** any of numerous small, tailless animals something like frogs, living most of the time on land, but laying eggs in water. Most toads have rough, dry, brown skin. **2** any animal like these, such as a tree toad. **—toad′like′**, *adj*.

toad·stool (tōd′stül′), *n*. mushroom, especially a poisonous mushroom.

toad·y (tō′dē), **1** *n*. someone who flatters in order to gain favor. **2** *v*. to flatter. ❑ *n., pl.* **toad·ies**; *v*. **toad·ied, toad·y·ing**.

toast[1] (tōst), **1** *n*. slices of bread browned by heat. **2** *v*. to brown by heat: *We toasted the bread*. **3** *v*. to heat thoroughly: *He toasted his feet by the fire*.

> **WORD STORY** Toast[1] comes from a Latin word meaning "dried by heat." Toast[2] comes from a custom of the Middle Ages. A guest was offered bits of toasted bread in heated wine. The guest would lift the wine goblet and offer thanks to the hosts before drinking.

toast[2] (tōst), **1** *v*. to wish good fortune to before drinking; drink to the health of: *We first toasted our hosts*. **2** *n*. act of drinking to the health of someone or something. **3** *n*. person or thing whose health is proposed and drunk: *"The Queen" was the first toast drunk by the officers*. **4** *n*. a popular or celebrated person: *The actor was the toast of the town*. [See Word Story at **toast**[1].]

toast·er (tō′stər), *n*. an electric appliance for toasting bread.

toaster oven, a portable electric cooking appliance, used for toasting and broiling.

toast·mas·ter (tōst′mas′tər), *n*. person who presides at a dinner, proposes toasts, and introduces the speakers.

toast·y (tō′stē), *adj*. pleasantly and comfortably warm. ❑ *adj*. **toast·i·er, toast·i·est**.

to·bac·co (tə bak′ō), *n*. **1** the prepared leaves of certain related plants, used for smoking or chewing or as snuff. **2** the habit of smoking or chewing tobacco: *to give up tobacco*. ❑ *n., pl.* **to·bac·cos** for 1.

to·bac·co·nist (tə bak′ə nist), *n*. dealer in tobacco.

To·ba·go (tə bā′gō), *n*. island in the West Indies, near Venezuela, part of the country of Trinidad and Tobago.

to·bog·gan (tə bog′ən), **1** *n*. a long, narrow, flat sled with its front end curved upward and without runners. **2** *v*. to slide downhill on such a sled. **—to·bog′gan·er**, *n*.

toboggan

to·day (tə dā′), **1** *n*. this day; the present time: *Today is Wednesday*. **2** *adv*. on or during this day: *What are you doing today?* **3** *adv*. at the present time; now: *Pollution is a major problem today*.

tod·dle (tod′l), *v*. to walk with short, unsteady steps, as a baby does. ❑ *v*. **tod·dled, tod·dling**.

tod·dler (tod′lər), *n*. child just learning to walk.

tod·dy (tod′ē), *n*. drink made of whisky, brandy, etc., with hot water and sugar. ❑ *n., pl.* **tod·dies**.

to·do (tə dü′), *n*. fuss; bustle: *to make a great to-do over nothing*. ❑ *n., pl.* **to·dos**.

toe (tō), **1** *n*. one of the five end parts of the foot. **2** *n*. the part of a stocking, shoe, etc., that covers the toes: *have a hole in the toe of a sock*. **3** *n*. the forepart of a foot or hoof. **4** *n*. anything like a toe: *the toe and heel of a golf club*. **5** *v*. to touch or reach with the toes: *toe a line*. ❑ *v*. **toed, toe·ing**. ■ Another word that sounds like this is **tow**. **—toe′less**, *adj*.

on your toes, ready for action; alert.

toe·nail (tō′nāl′), *n*. the nail growing on a toe.

tof·fee (tô′fē), *n*. a hard, brittle, chewy candy made from molasses or brown sugar and butter. ❑ *n., pl.* **tof·fees**.

to·fu (tō′fü), *n*. food somewhat like cheese make from the curds of the milk of ground soybeans, often pressed into squares; bean curd.

tog (tog), INFORMAL. **1** *n.pl.* **togs**, clothes. **2** *v*. to put on clothes; dress: *to be all togged out in fancy clothes*. ❑ *v*. **togged, tog·ging**.

to·ga (tō′gə), *n*. a loose, outer garment worn in public by citizens of ancient Rome. ❑ *n., pl.* **to·gas**.

to·geth·er (tə geᴛʜ′ər), *adv*. **1** with each other; in company: *They were standing together*. **2** with united action; in cooperation: *to work together for peace*. **3** into one gathering, company, mass, or group: *The principal called the school together*. **4** at the same time: *Rain and snow were falling together*. **5** without a stop or break; continuously: *He worked for days together*. **6** taken or considered as a whole: *This one cost more than all the others together*. ■ See Usage Note at **join**.

> **WORD POWER** TOGETHERNESS ■ What do **co-, col-, com-,** and **con-** have in common? They are all forms of a suffix meaning "in common" or "together." Cooperation and collaboration are such common ideas that people often combine this suffix with another word, confident that others will comprehend.

to·geth·er·ness (tə geᴛʜ′ər nis), *n*. condition of being close together, especially in family or social activities.

tog·gle (tog′əl), **1** *n*. pin, bolt, or rod put through a loop in a rope or a link of a chain to keep it in place, to hold two ropes together, to serve as a hold for the fingers, etc. **2** *v*. to furnish or fasten with a toggle. ❑ *v*. **tog·gled, tog·gling**. **—tog′gler**, *n*.

toggle bolt, fastener make of a bolt and two crosspieces that can open sideways. Toggle bolts are used to attach objects to thin or hollow walls.

To·go (tō′gō), *n*. country in W Africa. *Capital:* Lomé.

toil (toil), **1** *n*. hard work; labor: *They finally succeeded after years of toil*. **2** *v*. to work hard: *to toil with your hands for a living*. ■ See Synonym Study at **work**. **3** *v*. to move with difficulty, pain, or weariness: *Carrying heavy loads, they toiled up the mountain*. [Toil comes from a Latin word meaning "olive oil machine." Someone had to stir the olives in the machine to make sure they all got squeezed, and it must have been a very hard job.] **—toil′er**, *n*.

toi·let (toi′lit), **1** *n*. bathroom; washroom. **2** *n*. a porcelain bowl with a seat attached and with a drain at the bottom connected to a water tank to flush the bowl clean. Waste matter from the body is disposed of in a toilet. **3** *n*. process of dressing. Bathing, combing your hair, and putting on your clothes are all part of your toilet: *I made a hurried toilet*. **4** *adj*. of or for the toilet. Combs and brushes are toilet articles.

> **WORD STORY** Toilet comes from a Latin word meaning "spiderweb." The Romans called a kind of fine cloth after webs, and the French used a similar cloth to wrap clothes in. In English, 300 years ago, toilet was used to mean "putting clothes on," and so it became the name for a dressing room, and then for the room next to the dressing room.

toilet paper, soft, thin, absorbent paper, usually in a roll, for cleaning yourself after using the toilet.

a	hat	ė	term	ô	order	ch	child		
ā	age	i	it	oi	oil	ng	long		a in about
ä	far	ī	ice	ou	out	sh	she		e in taken
â	care	o	hot	u	cup	th	thin	ə	i in pencil
e	let	ō	open	u̇	put	ᴛʜ	then		o in lemon
ē	equal	ò	saw	ü	rule	zh	measure		u in circus

toi·let·ry (toi/lə trē), *n.* Usually, **toiletries**, *pl.* articles for the toilet, including soap, cosmetics, toothpaste, cologne, etc.

toilet water, a fragrant liquid not so strong as perfume, used after bathing, as a cologne in grooming, etc.

toil·some (toil/səm), *adj.* requiring hard work; laborious; wearisome: *a long, toilsome climb up the mountain.*

to·ken (tō/kən), **1** *n.* a mark or sign of something; symbol: *His actions are a token of his sincerity.* **2** *n.* sign of friendship; keepsake: *She received many birthday tokens.* **3** *n.* piece of metal stamped for a higher value than the metal is worth and used for some special purpose, such as bus or subway fare. **4** *n.* piece of metal, plastic, etc., indicating a right or privilege: *This token will admit you to the pool.* **5** *adj.* having only the appearance of; serving as a symbol; nominal; partial: *a token payment, token resistance.*

by the same token, for the same reason; in the same way; moreover.

To·kyo (tō/kē ō), *n.* capital of Japan, in the central part. [Tokyo comes from Japanese words meaning "eastern capital." Which way from Tokyo do you think the previous capital was?]

told (tōld), *v.* past tense and past participle of **tell**: *You told me that last week. We were told to wait.*

To·le·do (tə lē/dō), *n.* **1** city in NW Ohio. **2** city in central Spain.

tol·er·a·ble (tol/ər ə bəl), *adj.* **1** able to be endured; bearable: *The pain has become tolerable.* **2** fairly good: *She is in tolerable health.* —**tol/er·a·bil/i·ty**, *n.* —**tol/er·a·bly,** *adv.*

tol·er·ance (tol/ər əns), *n.* **1** a willingness to be tolerant; a putting up with people whose opinions or ways differ from your own. **2** the power of enduring or resisting the action of a drug, poison, etc. **3** action of allowing or permitting: *The principal's tolerance of their bad behavior surprised us.*

tol·er·ant (tol/ər ənt), *adj.* **1** willing to let other people do as they think best; willing to tolerate beliefs and actions of which you do not approve: *to be tolerant toward all religious beliefs.* ■ See Synonym Study at **patient. 2** able to endure or resist the action of a drug, poison, etc. —**tol/er·ant·ly,** *adv.*

tol·e·rate (tol/ə rāt/), *v.* **1** to allow or permit: *The teacher won't tolerate any disorder.* **2** to bear; endure; put up with: *I cannot tolerate loud noises.* **3** to endure or resist the action of a drug, poison, etc. ❑ *v.* **tol·e·rat·ed, tol·e·rat·ing.** —**tol/e·ra/tor,** *n.*

tol·e·ra·tion (tol/ə rā/shən), *n.* **1** willingness to put up with beliefs and actions of which you do not approve: *Toleration of dishonest officials encourages corruption.* **2** recognition of the right to worship as you think best without loss of civil rights or social privileges; freedom of worship.

Tol·kien (tol/kēn), *n.* **J. R. R.,** 1892-1973, English writer. He wrote *The Hobbit* and *The Lord of the Rings* trilogy.

toll¹ (tōl), **1** *v.* to sound with single strokes slowly and regularly repeated. **2** *n.* stroke or sound of a bell being tolled. **3** *v.* to call, announce, etc., by tolling: *The church bells tolled the President's death.*

toll² (tōl), *n.* **1** tax or fee paid for some right or privilege: *We pay a toll when we use the bridge.* **2** charge for a certain service. There is a toll on long-distance telephone calls. **3** something paid, lost, suffered, etc.: *Accidents take a heavy toll of human lives.*

toll·booth (tōl/büth/), *n.* booth or gate at which tolls are collected before or after going over a bridge, along a highway, etc. ❑ *n., pl.* **toll·booths** (tōl/büthz/ *or* tōl/büths/).

toll·gate (tōl/gāt/), *n.* tollbooth.

toll road, road on which tolls are charged; turnpike.

toll·way (tōl/wā/), *n.* toll road; turnpike.

Tol·stoy (tol/stoi), *n.* **Leo,** 1828-1910, Russian writer. ■ **Leo Tolstoy** wrote the novels *War and Peace* and *Anna Karenina.* Late in his life he had a religious conversion, and he gave away his property and declared his earlier novels were vain.

Tol·tec (tol/tek), *n.* member of an American Indian tribe that lived in central Mexico from about A.D. 900 to about A.D. 1200. The Toltec influenced the culture of the Aztec. ❑ *n., pl.* **Tol·tec** or **Tol·tecs.**

tol·u·ene (tol/yü ēn), *n.* a colorless, flammable liquid obtained from coal tar and petroleum. It is used for making perfumes, dyes, and other chemicals.

tom (tom), *n.* **1** tomcat. **2** the male of various other animals: *Our Thanksgiving turkey was a tom.*

tom·a·hawk (tom/ə hôk), *n.* a light ax used by North American Indians as a weapon and a tool.

to·ma·to (tə mā/tō *or* tə mä/tō), *n.* a juicy, slightly acid, red or yellow fruit, eaten as a vegetable. Tomatoes grow on a spreading, strong-smelling plant with hairy leaves and stems and yellow flowers. ❑ *n., pl.* **to·ma·toes.**

tomb (tüm), *n.* grave, vault, mausoleum, etc., for a dead body, often above ground. —**tomb/like/,** *adj.*

tomato

tom·boy (tom/boi/), *n.* girl who likes to play games supposedly suited to boys; boisterous, romping girl.

tom·boy·ish (tom/boi/ish), *adj.* like or resembling a tomboy. —**tom/boy/ish·ly,** *adv.* —**tom/boy/ish·ness,** *n.*

tomb·stone (tüm/stōn/), *n.* gravestone.

tom·cat (tom/kat/), *n.* a male cat.

tome (tōm), *n.* a book, especially a large, heavy book.

tom·fool·er·y (tom/fü/lər ē), *n.* silly behavior; nonsense.

to·mor·row (tə mor/ō), **1** *n.* the day after today: *Today is Tuesday; tomorrow will be Wednesday.* **2** *n.* the near future: *tomorrow's developments in communications.* **3** *adv.* on the day after today: *I'll see you tomorrow.* **4** *adv.* very soon.

tom-tom (tom/tom/), *n.* a drum, usually beaten with the hands, originally used in the East Indies.

ton (tun), *n.* **1** unit of weight equal to 2000 pounds (**short ton**) in the United States and Canada, and 2240 pounds (**long ton**) in Great Britain. A metric ton is 1000 kilograms. **2** any very large amount or number: *I have a ton of homework. She has a ton of friends.* ■ Another word that sounds like this is **tun.**

ton·al (tō/nl), *adj.* of or about tone or tonality. —**to/nal·ly,** *adv.*

to·nal·i·ty (tō nal/ə tē), *n.* in music: **1** sum of relations existing between the tones of a scale or musical system. **2** a key or system of tones. ❑ *n., pl.* **to·nal·i·ties.**

To·nant·zin (tō/nan tsēn/), *n.* an Aztec mother goddess, sometimes identified with Coatlicue.

tone (tōn), **1** *n.* any sound considered with reference to its quality, pitch, strength, source, etc.: *angry tones, gentle tones, the deep tone of an organ.* **2** *n.* quality of sound: *a voice that is soft in tone.* **3** *n.* in music: **a** a sound of definite pitch and character. **b** whole step. C and D are one tone apart. **4** *n.* manner of speaking or writing: *We disliked their disrespectful tone.* **5** *n.* spirit; character; style: *A tone of quiet elegance prevails in their home.* **6** *n.* normal, healthy condition; vigor: *Regular exercise will keep your body in tone.* **7** *n.* effect of color and of light and shade in a picture: *I like the soft green tone of that painting.* **8** *n.* shade of color: *The room is furnished in tones of brown.* **9** *v.* to restore physical tone to: *Exercise helps tone muscles.* **10** *v.* to harmonize: *This rug tones in well with the wallpaper and furniture.* ❑ *v.* **toned, ton·ing.** —**ton/er,** *n.*

tone down, to soften: *Tone down your voice.*

tone up, to give more sound, color, or vigor to; strengthen: *Bright curtains would tone up this dull room.*

tone arm, the movable arm of a phonograph, holding the needle and cartridge.

tone-deaf (tōn/def/), *adj.* not able to tell the differences among musical tones. —**tone deafness.**

tone·less (tōn/lis), *adj.* **1** without tone; without expression: *a toneless voice, a toneless reading.* **2** (of color) dull. —**tone/less·ly,** *adv.* —**tone/less·ness,** *n.*

Ton·ga (tong/gə), *n.* island country in the S Pacific, northeast of New Zealand. *Capital:* Nukualofa.

tongs (tongz), *n.pl.* tool with two arms that are joined by a hinge, pivot, or spring, used for holding or lifting.

tongue (tung), **1** *n.* the movable fleshy organ in the mouth. The tongue is used in tasting and, by people, for talking. **2** power of speech: *Have you lost your tongue?* **3** way of speaking; speech; talk: *a flattering tongue.* **4** a language: *the English tongue.* ■ See

Synonym Study at **language**. **5** an animal's tongue, usually a cow's, used as food: *We ate cold tongue and salad.* **6** something shaped or used like a tongue: *Tongues of flame leaped from the fire.* **7** the leather or cloth flap under the laces of a shoe. **8** pole of a wagon or other vehicle that extends between the animals pulling the vehicle. —**tongue′like**′, *adj.*

hold your tongue, to keep quiet: *"Hold your tongue while I'm speaking!" he demanded.*

on the tip of your tongue, 1 almost spoken. **2** ready to be spoken. **3** almost remembered or thought of for saying.

with tongue in cheek, with sly humor; not to be taken seriously; in a mocking manner: *I spoke with tongue in cheek when I said I enjoyed doing all that yard work.*

tongue-tied (tung′tīd′), *adj.* **1** unable to speak because of shyness, embarrassment, etc. **2** having the motion of the tongue hindered.

tongue twister, phrase or sentence that is difficult to say quickly without a mistake.

ton·ic (ton′ik), **1** *n.* something that improves health or strength: *Fresh air and exercise are splendid tonics.* **2** *adj.* restoring to health and vigor; giving strength; bracing: *The mountain air is tonic.* **3** in music: **a** *n.* the first note of a scale; keynote. **b** *adj.* of or based on a keynote: *a tonic chord.* —**ton′i·cal·ly,** *adv.*

to·night (tə nīt′), **1** *n.* the night of this day; this night: *I am going to bed early tonight.* **2** *adv.* on or during this night: *Do you think it will snow tonight?*

ton·nage (tun′ij), *n.* **1** the carrying capacity of a ship, expressed in units of 100 cubic feet per ton. A ship with 50,000 cubic feet of space has a tonnage of 500 tons. **2** total amount of shipping, measured in tons. **3** tax on ships at so much a ton. **4** weight in tons.

ton·sil (ton′səl), *n.* either of the two oval masses of tissue on the sides of the throat, just back of the mouth.

ton·sil·lec·to·my (ton′sə lek′tə mē), *n.* the surgical removal of the tonsils. ❑ *n., pl.* **ton·sil·lec·to·mies.**

ton·sil·li·tis (ton′sə lī′tis), *n.* inflammation of the tonsils.

ton·sure (ton′shər), *n.* **1** the shaved part of the head of a priest or monk. **2** act or process of clipping the hair or shaving a part or the whole of the head, formerly required of someone entering the priesthood or an order of monks.

too (tü), *adv.* **1** in addition; also; besides: *The dog is hungry, and thirsty too. We, too, are going away.* **2** beyond what is desirable, proper, or right; more than enough: *I ate too much.* **3** very: *I am only too glad to help.* ■ Other words that sound like this are **to** and **two.**

took (tuk), *v.* past tense of **take:** *She took the car an hour ago.*

tool (tül), **1** *n.* a knife, hammer, wrench, saw, shovel, or any device used in doing work: *Plumbers, mechanics, carpenters, and shoemakers need tools.* **2** *n.* person or thing used by another like a tool: *He is a tool of the party boss. Books are a scholar's tools.* **3** *n.* a part of a machine that cuts, bores, smooths, etc. **4** *v.* to use a tool on; work or shape with a tool: *She tooled beautiful designs in the leather with a knife.* **5** *v.* to provide or equip a factory with tools. ■ Another word that sounds like this is **tulle.**

SYNONYM STUDY **Tool, device,** and **instrument** all mean something used to make work easier. **Tool** is a general word: *We keep a chest with a hammer, screwdrivers, wrenches, and other tools.* **Device** means a tool used for a special job: *The cotton gin was a device to remove seeds from cotton fibers.* **Instrument** means a tool used for a special job that requires exactness: *Surgical instruments must be sterilized.*

tool·box (tül′boks′), *n.* box in which tools and sometimes small parts, accessories, etc., are kept. ❑ *n., pl.* **tool·box·es.**

tool·mak·er (tül′mā′kər), *n.* **1** machinist who makes, repairs, and maintains machine tools. **2** any maker of tools: *Prehistoric people were the first toolmakers.*

toot (tüt), **1** *n.* sound of a horn, whistle, etc. **2** *v.* to give forth a short blast: *He heard the train whistle toot three times.* **3** *v.* to sound a horn, whistle, etc., in short blasts. —**toot′er,** *n.*

tooth (tüth), *n.* **1** one of the hard, bonelike parts in the mouth, used for biting and chewing. **2** something like a tooth. Each one of the projecting parts of a comb, rake, or saw is a tooth. **3** one

of the parts that stick out from the rim of a gearwheel; cog. ❑ *n., pl.* **teeth. —tooth′like**′, *adj.*

fight tooth and nail, to fight fiercely, with all your force.

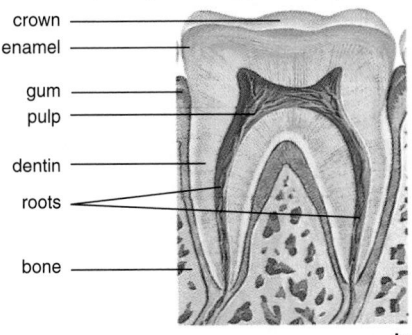

crown
enamel
gum
pulp
dentin
roots
bone

tooth (def. 1)

tooth·ache (tüth′āk′), *n.* pain in a tooth or the teeth.

tooth·brush (tüth′brush′), *n.* a small brush for cleaning the teeth. ❑ *n., pl.* **tooth·brush·es.**

toothed (tütht), *adj.* **1** having teeth. **2** notched: *the toothed surface of a gear.*

toothed whale, any of several whales having many cone-shaped teeth, including dolphins, killer whales, and sperm whales.

tooth·less (tüth′lis), *adj.* without teeth. —**tooth′less·ly,** *adv.* —**tooth′less·ness,** *n.*

tooth·paste (tüth′pāst′), *n.* paste used in cleaning the teeth.

tooth·pick (tüth′pik′), *n.* a small, pointed piece of wood, plastic, etc., for removing bits of food from between the teeth.

tooth·some (tüth′səm), *adj.* pleasing to the taste; tasting good. —**tooth′some·ly,** *adv.* —**tooth′some·ness,** *n.*

tooth·y (tü′thē), *adj.* showing many teeth clearly: *a toothy smile.* ❑ *adj.* **tooth·i·er, tooth·i·est.** —**tooth′i·ly,** *adv.*

top¹ (top), **1** *n.* the highest point or part: *the top of a mountain.* **2** *n.* the upper part, end, or surface: *the top of a table, a shoe top.* **3** *n.* the highest or leading place, rank, etc.: *She is at the top of her class.* **4** *n.* the highest point, pitch, or degree: *They were yelling at the top of their voices.* **5** *n.* the best or most important part: *top of the morning.* **6** *n.* the cover of a bottle, can, etc. **7** *n.* article of clothing worn on the upper body: *a pajama top. She wore a blue top yesterday.* **8** *adj.* of, situated at, or forming the top: *the top shelf of a cupboard.* **9** *adj.* highest or greatest: *He received top honors at school.* **10** *v.* to furnish or decorate with a top: *I will top the cake with icing.* **11** *v.* to be on top of; be the top of: *A church tops the hill.* **12** *v.* to reach the top of: *They topped the mountain.* **13** *v.* to rise high; rise above: *The sun topped the horizon.* **14** *v.* to be higher or greater than: *This week's sales figures top the former record.* **15** *v.* to do better than; outdo; surpass: *His story topped all the rest.* **16** *n.* part of a plant that grows above ground: *Beet tops are somewhat like spinach.* **17** *v.* to remove the top of a plant, tree, etc. ❑ *v.* **topped, top·ping.**

off the top of your head, without previous thought or preparation; in a spontaneous way: *He answered them off the top of his head.*

on top, with success; with victory: *We have the best players, so our team will come out on top.*

on top of, 1 in complete control of: *Firefighters were on top of the dangerous situation.* **2** in addition to; along with: *On top of all the rain, there were severe winds.* **3** following right after: *On top of yesterday's bad news comes today's report of an earthquake.*

top off, to complete; finish; end, especially in a satisfactory way.

top² (top), *n.* toy that spins on a point.

sleep like a top, to sleep soundly.

to·paz (tō′paz), *n.* a hard mineral that occurs in crystals of various forms and colors. Transparent yellow topaz is used as a gem. ❑ *n., pl.* **to·paz·es.**

a	hat	ė	term	ô	order	ch	child		a in about
ā	age	i	it	oi	oil	ng	long		e in taken
ä	far	ī	ice	ou	out	sh	she	ə	i in pencil
â	care	o	hot	u	cup	th	thin		o in lemon
e	let	ō	open	ů	put	ⱦH	then		u in circus
ē	equal	ȯ	saw	ü	rule	zh	measure		

top·coat (top′kōt′), *n.* a lightweight overcoat.

To·pe·ka (tə pē′kə), *n.* capital of Kansas, in the NE part. [**Topeka** comes from a Sioux word meaning "good place for tubers." People knew they could find food fast here.]

top·flight (top′flīt′), *adj.* excellent; very good.

top·gal·lant (top′gal′ənt *or* tə gal′ənt), **1** *n.* the mast or sail above the topmast; the third section of a mast above the deck. **2** *adj.* next above the topmast.

top hat, a tall, black silk hat worn by men in formal clothes; high hat.

top-heav·y (top′hev′ē), *adj.* too heavy at the top. **—top′-heav′i·ness,** *n.*

to·pi·ar·y (tō′pē er′ē), **1** *n.* bushes trimmed into ornamental shapes. **2** *adj.* of or containing such bushes: *a topiary garden.*

top·ic (top′ik), *n.* subject that people think, write, or talk about: *Newspapers discuss the topics of the day.*

top·i·cal (top′ə kəl), *adj.* **1** of or about topics of the day; of current or local interest: *topical issues.* **2** arranged by topics: *Some books have topical outlines for each chapter.* **—top′i·cal·ly,** *adv.*

topic sentence, sentence that expresses the main idea in a paragraph.

top·knot (top′not′), *n.* a knot of hair or a tuft of feathers on the top of the head.

top·mast (top′mast′ *or* top′məst), *n.* the second section of a mast above the deck.

top·most (top′mōst), *adj.* highest: *the topmost branches.*

top-notch (top′noch′), *adj.* first-rate; best possible: *a top-notch designer.*

to·pog·ra·pher (tə pog′rə fər), *n.* an expert in topography.

top·o·graph·ic (top′ə graf′ik), *adj.* topographical.

top·o·graph·i·cal (top′ə graf′ə kəl), *adj.* of or about topography. A topographical map shows mountains, rivers, etc. **—top′o·graph′i·cal·ly,** *adv.*

to·pog·ra·phy (tə pog′rə fē), *n.* **1** the surface features of a place or region, such as hills, valleys, streams, lakes, bridges, tunnels, roads, etc. **2** act or process of preparing an accurate and detailed description or drawing of a region's or place's surface features.

top·ping (top′ing), *n.* something put on top, especially a sauce put on food.

top·ple (top′əl), *v.* **1** to fall forward; tumble down: *The chimney toppled over on the roof.* **2** to throw over or down; overturn: *The wrestler toppled his opponent.* ❑ *v.* **top·pled, top·pling.**

tops (tops), *adj.* of the highest degree in quality, excellence, etc.: *tops in his field.*

top·sail (top′sāl′ *or* top′səl), *n.* the second sail above the deck on a mast.

top-se·cret (top′sē′krit), *adj.* of the greatest secrecy; highly confidential: *top-secret codes.*

top·side (top′sīd′), *adv.* to or on the upper deck: *The crew were all topside.*

top·soil (top′soil′), *n.* the upper part of the soil; soil at or near the surface: *Rich topsoil helps produce good crops.*

top·sy-tur·vy (top′sē tèr′vē), *adv., adj.* **1** upside down. **2** in confusion or disorder: *On moving day everything in the house was topsy-turvy.* **—top′sy-tur′vi·ly,** *adv.* **—top′sy-tur′vi·ness,** *n.*

toque (tōk), *n.* a woman's hat, close-fitting and having no brim or a very small brim.

To·rah (tôr′ə), *n.* **1** the first five books of the Hebrew Scriptures; the Pentateuch. **2** scroll on which the Pentateuch is written. **3** the entire collection of Jewish law and tradition. [**Torah** comes from a Hebrew word meaning "instruction."]

torch (tôrch), *n.* **1** light to be carried around or stuck in a holder on a wall. A piece of pine wood or anything that burns easily makes a good torch. **2** device for producing a very hot flame, used especially to burn off paint and to solder or melt metal. **3** BRITISH. flashlight. ❑ *n., pl.* **torch·es.**

torch·bear·er (tôrch′bâr′ər), *n.* person who carries a torch.

torch·light (tôrch′līt′), *n.* light of a torch or torches.

tore (tôr), *v.* past tense of **tear**²: *She tore her jeans on a nail yesterday.*

to·re·a·dor (tôr′ē ə dôr′), *n.* bullfighter.

to·re·ro (tə râr′ō), *n.* bullfighter. ❑ *n., pl.* **to·re·ros.**

tor·ment (tôr ment′ *or* tôr′ment *for verb;* tôr′ment *for noun*), **1** *v.* to cause very great pain to: *Headaches tormented him.* **2** *n.* a cause of very great pain: *A bad burn can be a torment.* **3** *n.* very great pain: *She suffered torments from her toothache.* **4** *n.* a cause of very much worry or annoyance. **5** *v.* to worry or annoy very much: *Don't torment me with silly questions.* [See Word Story at **torch.**] **—tor·ment′ing·ly,** *adv.* **—tor·men′tor** *or* **tor·ment′er,** *n.*

torn (tôrn), *v.* past participle of **tear**²: *He has torn up the plant by the roots.*

tor·na·do (tôr nā′dō), *n.* an extremely violent and destructive windstorm with winds as high as 300 miles (480 kilometers) per hour. A tornado extends down from a mass of dark clouds as a twisting funnel and moves over the land in a narrow path. ❑ *n., pl.* **tor·na·does** *or* **tor·na·dos.** **—tor·na′do·like′,** *adj.*

tornado

To·ron·to (tə ron′tō), *n.* capital of Ontario, Canada, on Lake Ontario.

tor·pe·do (tôr pē′dō), **1** *n.* a large, cylinder-shaped metal tube that contains explosives and travels under water by its own power. Torpedoes may be fired from submarines or torpedo boats or launched from aircraft to blow up enemy ships. **2** *v.* to attack or destroy with a torpedo. **3** *n.* a firework consisting of an explosive and gravel wrapped in tissue paper. It explodes when it is thrown against something hard. ❑ *n., pl.* **tor·pe·does;** *v.* **tor·pe·doed, tor·pe·do·ing.** **—tor·pe′do·like′,** *adj.*

torpedo boat, a small, fast warship used for attacking with torpedoes.

tor·pid (tôr′pid), *adj.* **1** dull, inactive, or sluggish. **2** not moving or feeling. Animals that hibernate become torpid in winter. [See Word Story at **torpedo.**] **—tor·pid′i·ty,** *n.* **—tor′pid·ly,** *adv.*

tor·por (tôr′pər), *n.* torpid condition.

torque (tôrk), *n.* any force that causes something to rotate.

tor·rent (tôr′ənt), *n.* **1** a violent, rushing stream of water: *The mountain torrent dashed over the rock.* **2** a heavy downpour: *The rain came down in torrents during the thunderstorm.* **3** any violent, rushing stream; flood: *a torrent of questions.*

tor·ren·tial (tô ren′shəl), *adj.* of, caused by, or like a torrent: *torrential rains, a torrential flow of words.* **—tor·ren′tial·ly,** *adv.*

tor·rid (tôr′id), *adj.* very hot: *In this area, July is usually quite torrid.* —**tor′rid′i·ty, tor′rid·ness,** *n.* —**tor′rid·ly,** *adv.*

Torrid Zone, the very warm region between the tropic of Cancer and the tropic of Capricorn; the tropics. The equator divides the Torrid Zone in half.

tor·sion (tôr′shən), *n.* **1** act or process of twisting. **2** condition of being twisted. **3** act or process of twisting an object by two equal and opposite forces.

tor·so (tôr′sō), *n.* **1** the trunk of the human body. **2** the trunk or body of a statue without any head, arms, or legs. ❑ *n., pl.* **tor·sos.**

torte (tôrt), *n.* a rich cake made with beaten egg whites, nuts, fruit, and little flour.

tor·til·la (tôr tē′yə), *n.* a thin, flat, round cake made of corn meal, commonly eaten in Spanish America. It is baked on a flat surface and served hot. ❑ *n., pl.* **tor·til·las.**

tor·toise (tôr′təs), *n.* **1** any of several turtles living only on land, especially in dry regions. Tortoises have short legs and a high, arched shell. **2** any turtle. ❑ *n., pl.* **tor·tois·es** or **tor·toise.**

tor·toise·shell (tôr′təs shel′), **1** *n.* the mottled yellow and brown shell of some turtles. It is much used for combs and ornaments. **2** *adj.* made of tortoiseshell. **3** *adj.* mottled or colored like a tortoiseshell.

tor·tu·ous (tôr′chü əs), *adj.* **1** full of twists, turns, or bends; twisting; winding; crooked: *We found the river's course very tortuous.* **2** mentally or morally crooked; not straightforward: *tortuous reasoning.* —**tor′tu·ous·ly,** *adv.* —**tor′tu·ous·ness,** *n.*

tor·ture (tôr′chər), **1** *n.* act of causing very severe pain to a person or an animal. Torture has been used to make people give evidence about crimes, or to make them confess. **2** *n.* very severe pain; agony: *suffer tortures from rheumatism.* **3** *v.* to cause very severe pain to; torment: *It is cruel to torture animals.* ❑ *v.* **tor·tured, tor·tur·ing.** [See Word Story at **torch.**] —**tor′tur·er,** *n.* —**tor′tur·ing·ly,** *adv.*

tor·tur·ous (tôr′chər əs), *adj.* of, involving, or causing torture. —**tor′tur·ous·ly,** *adv.*

To·ry (tôr′ē), **1** *n.* member of the British political party that favored royal power and the established church and opposed change. The Tory party was renamed the Conservative party in 1832. **2** *n.* member of the Conservative party of Canada. **3** *n.* an American who favored British rule over the colonies at the time of the Revolutionary War. **4** *n.* Also, **tory,** a very conservative person. **5** *adj.* of or about Tories. ❑ *n., pl.* **To·ries** (or **tories** for 4).

Tos·ca·ni·ni (tos′kə nē′nē), *n.* **Ar·tur·o** (ar tür′ō), 1867-1957, American conductor, born in Italy. After leaving Italy to protest its Fascist government, he became famous in the United States leading the New York and NBC orchestras.

toss (tòs), **1** *v.* to throw softly with the palm upward; cast; fling: *She tossed the ball to me.* **2** *v.* to throw about; roll or pitch about: *The ship was tossed by the waves. He tossed in bed all night.* **3** *v.* to lift quickly; throw upward: *She tossed her head.* **4** *v.* to shake up or about, especially to mix the ingredients: *toss a salad.* **5** *v.* to throw a coin to decide something by the side that lands upward. **6** *n.* a throw; act of tossing: *A toss of a coin decided who should play first.* ❑ *n., pl.* **toss·es.** —**toss′er,** *n.*

toss off, 1 to do or make quickly and easily: *She tossed off a poem.* **2** to drink all at once: *He tossed off a glass of milk.*

toss·up (tòs′up′), *n.* **1** an even chance: *It's a tossup as to who will win.* **2** act of tossing a coin to decide something.

tos·ta·da (tō stä′də), *n.* a tortilla fried until crisp and then topped with refried beans, meat, cheese, etc. ❑ *n., pl.* **tos·ta·das.**

tot (tot), *n.* a little child.

to·tal (tō′tl), **1** *n.* the whole amount; sum: *Her expenses reached a total of $108.* **2** *adj.* whole; entire: *The total cost of the house and land will be $250,000.* **3** *v.* to find the sum of; add up: *Total that column of figures.* **4** *v.* to reach an amount of; amount to; equal: *The money spent yearly on chewing gum totals millions of dollars.* **5** *adj.* complete; absolute; utter: *We were in total darkness.* **6** *v.* INFORMAL. to wreck completely: *The collision totaled both cars.* ❑ *v.* **to·taled, to·tal·ing.**

to·tal·i·tar·i·an (to tal′ə ter′ē ən), **1** *adj.* of or about a government controlled by one political group which suppresses all op-

position, often with force, and which controls many aspects of people's lives. A totalitarian government usually regulates what goods are produced by industry, what radio or TV shows are broadcast, what books the people may read, etc. **2** *n.* person in favor of totalitarian principles.

to·tal·i·tar·i·an·ism (to tal′ə ter′ē ə niz′əm), *n.* system, principles, or methods of a totalitarian government.

to·tal·i·ty (tō tal′ə tē), *n.* the total amount; entirety.

to·tal·ly (tō′tl ē), *adv.* completely; entirely; wholly: *I was totally unprepared.*

tote (tōt), *v.* to carry; haul. ❑ *v.* **tot·ed, tot·ing.** —**tot′a·ble,** *adj.* —**tot′er,** *n.*

tote bag, a large handbag similar to a shopping bag, for carrying somewhat bulky objects.

to·tem (tō′təm), *n.* **1** an animal, plant, or other natural object, chosen as the emblem of a tribe, clan, or family. **2** image of such an object. Totems are often carved and painted on poles. —**to·tem·ic** (tō tem′ik), *adj.*

totem pole, pole carved and painted with representations of totems, erected by the American Indians of the northwestern coast of North America, especially in front of their houses.

tot·ter (tot′ər), *v.* **1** to walk with shaky, unsteady steps: *The baby came tottering across the room.* **2** to be unsteady; shake as if about to fall: *The old wall tottered in the gale and fell.* —**tot′ter·er,** *n.* —**tot′ter·ing·ly,** *adv.*

tou·can (tü′kan), *n.* any of several bright-colored, fruit-eating birds of the American tropics, with very large beaks.

toucan—25 in. (64 cm) long

touch (tuch), **1** *v.* to put the hand or some other part of the body on or against: *She touched the soft, furry kitten.* **2** *v.* to put one thing against another; make contact with: *I touched the post with my umbrella.* **3** *v.* to be against; come against: *Your sleeve is touching the butter.* **4** *v.* to be in contact: *Our hands touched.* **5** *n.* act of touching or condition of being touched: *A bubble bursts at a touch.* **6** *n.* the sense by which things are perceived by feeling, handling, or coming against them: *The blind develop a keen touch.* **7** *n.* the feeling caused by touching something; feel: *Worms and fish have a slimy touch.* **8** *n.* communication or connection: *He always kept in touch with his family while he was overseas.* **9** *n.* a slight amount; little bit: *The child has a touch of fever.* **10** *n.* a light, delicate stroke with a brush, pencil, pen, etc.: *The artist finished the picture with a few touches.* **11** *n.* a detail in any artistic work: *a story with charming poetic touches.* **12** *v.* to strike lightly or gently: *touch the strings of a harp.* **13** *v.* to affect with some feeling: *The sad story touched us.* **14** *v.* to relate to; concern: *The matter touches your interest.* **15** *v.* to speak of; deal with; refer to; treat lightly: *Our conversation touched many subjects.* **16** *v.* to handle; use: *He won't touch liquor or tobacco.* **17** *v.* to reach; come up to: *His head almost touches the ceiling.* **18** *v.* to compare with; rival: *Nobody in our class can touch her in science.* **19** *n.* act or manner of playing a musical instrument, especially an instrument with a keyboard: *The piano player had an excellent touch.* **20** *n.* a distinctive manner or quality: *The work showed an expert's touch.* ❑ *n., pl.* **touch·es** for 9-11,19,20. —**touch′a·ble,** *adj.* —**touch′er,** *n.*

touch down, to land an aircraft: *The pilot touched down at a small airfield.*

a	hat	ė	term	ô	order	ch	child		a in about
ā	age	i	it	oi	oil	ng	long		e in taken
ä	far	ī	ice	ou	out	sh	she	ə	i in pencil
â	care	o	hot	u	cup	th	thin		o in lemon
e	let	ō	open	ù	put	ᵮн	then		u in circus
ē	equal	ò	saw	ü	rule	zh	measure		

T

touch off, 1 to cause to go off; fire. **2** to cause to happen.

touch on or **touch upon, 1** to mention; treat lightly: *Our conversation touched on many subjects.* **2** to come close to.

touch up, to change a little; improve: *touch up a photograph.*

touch-and-go (tuch′ən gō′), *adj.* uncertain; risky.

touch·back (tuch′bak′), *n.* a football play in which the ball is downed by the defensive team behind its goal line after the ball has been kicked or passed there by the offensive team. No points are scored.

touch·down (tuch′doun′), *n.* **1** (in football) a score of six points made by crossing the opponent's goal line with the ball. **2** the landing of an aircraft, especially the moment of first contact with the ground.

touched (tucht), *adj.* stirred emotionally: *She was touched by our concern for her welfare.*

touch football, game with rules similar to those of football except that the player carrying the ball is touched rather than tackled, and players wear no protective equipment.

touch·ing (tuch′ing), **1** *adj.* arousing tender feeling: *"A Christmas Carol" is a touching story.* **2** *prep.* concerning; about: *The interviewer asked questions touching my home and school life.* —**touch′ing·ly,** *adv.*

touch-me-not (tuch′mē not′), *n.* either of two impatiens plants that grow in North America.

touch·stone (tuch′stōn′), *n.* **1** any means of testing; a test: *Adversity is the touchstone of friendship.* **2** a black stone, formerly used to test the purity of gold or silver by the color of the streak made on the stone by rubbing it with the metal.

Touch-Tone (tuch′tōn′), *n.* trademark for a telephone dialing system using buttons to produce tones of different pitch. Each tone matches a number.

touch·y (tuch′ē), *adj.* **1** easily hurt or offended; apt to take offense at trifles; too sensitive: *He is tired and very touchy this afternoon.* **2** requiring skill in handling; ticklish; precarious: *a very touchy situation.* ❑ *adj.* **touch·i·er, touch·i·est.** —**touch′i·ly,** *adv.* —**touch′i·ness,** *n.*

tough (tuf), **1** *adj.* bending without breaking: *Leather is tough; cardboard is not.* **2** *adj.* hard to cut, tear, or chew: *The steak was so tough I couldn't eat it.* **3** *adj.* strong; hardy; determined: *tough pioneers.* **4** *adj.* hard; difficult: *Dragging the load uphill was tough work.* ■ See Synonym Study at **hard. 5** *adj.* hard to influence; stubborn: *a tough customer.* **6** *adj.* rough; disorderly: *a tough neighborhood.* **7** *n.* a rough person: *A big gang of toughs attacked them.* ■ Another word that sounds like this is **tuff.** —**tough′ly,** *adv.* —**tough′ness,** *n.*

tough·en (tuf′ən), *v.* to make or become tough: *I toughened my muscles by doing exercises.* —**tough′en·er,** *n.*

Tou·louse-Lau·trec (tü lüz′lō trek′), *n.* **Hen·ri de** (on′rē də), 1864-1901, French painter. Many of his paintings, posters, and prints show scenes of Paris nightclubs and theaters and the city's underworld.

tou·pee (tü pā′), *n.* wig or patch of false hair worn by men to cover a bald spot. ❑ *n., pl.* **tou·pees.**

tour (tur), **1** *v.* to travel through, or from place to place: *Last year they toured Europe. We toured by bus for a week.* **2** *n.* a long journey: *They made a European tour.* **3** *n.* a short journey; a walk around: *Our class made a tour of the old boat.* **4** *v.* to walk around in: *Our class will tour the museum.* **5** *n.* period or turn of military or other activity at a certain place or station: *a soldier on a tour of duty overseas.*

on tour, touring. A show on tour travels around the country giving performances in various places.

Toulouse-Lautrec painting

tour·ism (tur′iz′əm), *n.* **1** act or process of touring or traveling for pleasure. **2** the business of serving tourists.

tour·ist (tur′ist), **1** *n.* person traveling for pleasure. **2** *adj.* of or for tourists: *tourist accommodations.*

tour·ma·line (tur′mə lēn′), *n.* a semiprecious mineral, usually black but sometimes red, pink, green, blue, or yellow. Tourmaline contains silicon, oxygen, aluminum, and boron. The transparent varieties are used in jewelry.

tour·na·ment (tėr′nə mənt *or* tur′nə mənt), *n.* **1** series of contests testing the skill of many persons in some sport: *a golf tournament.* **2** (in the Middle Ages) a contest between two groups of knights on horseback who fought for a prize.

tour·ney (tėr′nē *or* tur′nē), **1** *n.* tournament. **2** *v.* to take part in a tournament. ❑ *n., pl.* **tour·neys;** *v.* **tour·neyed, tour·ney·ing.**

tour·ni·quet (tur′nə ket *or* tėr′nə ket), *n.* device for stopping bleeding by compressing a blood vessel, such as a bandage tightened by twisting with a stick, or a pad held down tightly.

tou·sle (tou′zəl), *v.* to put into disorder; make untidy; muss: *tousled hair.* ❑ *v.* **tou·sled, tou·sling.**

Tous·saint L'Ou·ver·ture (tü′san lü′vər tur), **Pierre** (pyer), 1743-1803, Haitian revolutionary and ruler. ■ **Toussaint L'Ouverture** was born into slavery and lived enslaved until he was 50 years old. He led a revolt of black Haitians and eventually became the ruler of Haiti.

tout (tout), *v.* **1** to try to get customers, jobs, votes, etc. **2** to praise highly and insistently.

tow[1] (tō), **1** *v.* to pull by a rope, chain, etc.: *The tug is towing three barges.* **2** *n.* act of towing: *We called for a tow when our car broke down.* **3** *n.* something being towed: *Each tug had a tow of three barges.* **4** *n.* the rope, chain, etc., used for towing. ■ Another word that sounds like this is **toe.** —**tow′a·ble,** *adj.*

in tow, 1 being pulled by a rope or chain: *The motorboat had the sailboat in tow.* **2** under someone's guidance: *New campers were taken in tow by experienced campers.*

tow[2] (tō), *n.* the coarse, broken fibers of flax, hemp, etc., prepared for spinning. ■ Another word that sounds like this is **toe.**

to·ward (tôrd *or* tə wôrd′), *prep.* **1** in the direction of: *She walked toward the north.* **2** turned or directed to; facing: *to lie with your face toward the wall.* **3** with regard to; regarding; about; concerning: *What is his attitude toward foreign aid?* **4** shortly before; near: *Toward morning the storm ended.* **5** as a help to; for: *Will you give something toward our new hospital?*

to·wards (tôrdz *or* tə wôrdz′), *prep.* toward.

tow·boat (tō′bōt′), *n.* a powerful boat with a flat bottom used to tow or push barges on rivers.

tow·el (tou′əl), *n.* piece of cloth or paper for wiping and drying something wet. We have hand towels, face towels, and bath towels.

throw in the towel, INFORMAL. to admit defeat; surrender.

tow·er (tou′ər), **1** *n.* a high structure, standing alone or forming part of a church, castle, or other buildings. Some towers are forts or prisons. **2** *n.* defense; protection. **3** *v.* to rise high: *The new skyscraper towers over the older buildings.* —**tow′er·like′,** *adj.*

tow·er·ing (tou′ər ing), *adj.* **1** very high: *a towering mountain peak.* **2** very great: *Developing a polio vaccine was a towering achievement.* **3** very violent: *a towering rage.*

Tower of London, an ancient palace-fortress of London. The present building dates back to William I. It has been used as a palace, prison, mint, and arsenal.

tow·head (tō′hed′), *n.* person having very light or pale yellow hair.

tow·head·ed (tō′hed′id), *adj.* having very light or pale yellow hair.

tow·hee (tou′hē *or* tō′hē), *n.* any of several birds of North America with stout bills and long tails, something like sparrows, having calls like their name. ❑ *n., pl.* **tow·hees.**

tow·line (tō′līn′), *n.* rope, chain, or the like, used for towing.

town (toun), *n.* **1** a large group of houses and buildings, smaller than a city but larger than a village: *Do you live in a town or in the country?* **2** any large place with many people living in it: *I hear that Boston is a fine town.* **3** the people of a town: *The whole town was having a holiday.* **4** the part of a town or city where the stores and office buildings are: *Let's go into town to see a show.*

town crier, (long ago) person who called out the news and made announcements in the streets of a city or town.

town hall, a building used for a town's business.

town house, 1 row house. **2** house in town, belonging to someone who has a house in the country.

town·ie (tou′nē), *n.* INFORMAL. someone living in a town or city, especially someone of college age who does not attend a local college.

town meeting, 1 a general meeting of the people who live in a town. **2** (in New England) a meeting of the qualified voters of a town for carrying out public business.

towns·folk (tounz′fōk′), *n.pl.* the people of a town.

town·ship (toun′ship), *n.* **1** a part of a county in the United States and Canada having certain powers of government. **2** (in U.S. surveys of public land) a region or district six miles square, made up of 36 sections.

towns·peo·ple (tounz′pē′pəl), *n.pl.* the people of a town.

tow·path (tō′path′), *n.* (earlier) path along the bank of a canal or river for use in towing boats. ❑ *n., pl.* **tow·paths** (tō′paᴛʜz′ or tō′paths′).

tow·rope (tō′rōp′), *n.* rope used for towing.

tow truck, a truck with the equipment needed to tow away cars.

tox·e·mi·a (tok sē′mē ə), *n.* blood poisoning caused by poisonous substances in the blood.

tox·ic (tok′sik), *adj.* **1** of or caused by poison: *a toxic illness.* **2** poisonous: *toxic plants.* [Toxic comes from a Greek word meaning "a bow." The ancient Greeks sometimes used poisoned arrows.] —**tox′i·cal·ly,** *adv.*

tox·i·cant (tok′sə kənt), *n.* a poison. Many pesticides are toxicants.

tox·ic·i·ty (tok sis′ə tē), *n.* toxic or poisonous quality.

tox·i·col·o·gy (tok′sə kol′ə jē), *n.* science that deals with poisons, their effects, antidotes, detection, etc. —**tox′i·col′o·gist,** *n.*

toxic shock syndrome, a serious, sometimes fatal bacterial disease. Symptoms of toxic shock syndrome are fever, vomiting, diarrhea, and a drop in blood pressure.

tox·in (tok′sən), *n.* any poison formed by a living thing as a product of its metabolism. Snake venom and spider venom are toxins. Toxins formed by bacteria cause diseases such as diphtheria and scarlet fever. The body protects itself against some toxins by producing antitoxins.

tox·oid (tok′soid), *n.* toxin medically treated so that it is no longer poisonous but will still cause antitoxins to be produced when it is injected into the body.

toy (toi), **1** *n.* something for a child to play with; plaything. **2** *n.* thing that has little value or importance. **3** *adj.* of, made as, or like a toy. **4** *adj.* small or miniature in size: *a toy poodle.* **5** *v.* to amuse yourself; play; trifle: *I toyed with my pencil.* —**toy′like′,** *adj.*

trace¹ (trās), **1** *n.* a mark, sign, or evidence of the former existence of something: *Explorers found traces of an ancient city.* **2** *n.* footprint or other mark left; track; trail: *We saw traces of rabbits on the snow.* **3** *v.* to follow by means of marks, tracks, or clues: *The police trace missing persons.* **4** *v.* to follow the course of: *We traced the river to its source. The Aldens trace their family back to John Alden, one of the Pilgrims.* **5** *n.* a very small amount; little bit: *There was a trace of gray in his hair.* **6** *v.* to mark out; draw: *She traced the plan of our new house.* **7** *v.* to copy by following the lines of with a pencil or pen: *I put thin paper over the map and traced it.* ❑ *v.* **traced, trac·ing.** —**trace′a·ble,** *adj.*

WORD FAMILY Trace¹ and the words below are related. They all come from a Latin word meaning "to draw" or "to drag."

abstract	entreat	retract	tract¹
attract	extract	retreat	traction
contract	intractable	subtract	trait
detract	maltreat	tractor¹	treat
distract	portrait	trace²	treaty
distraught	protractor		

trace² (trās), *n.* either of two straps, ropes, or chains by which an animal pulls a wagon, carriage, etc.

trace element, any chemical element necessary in small amounts for health.

trac·er (trā′sər), *n.* **1** someone whose business is tracing missing persons or property. **2** inquiry sent from place to place to locate a missing person, letter, parcel, etc. **3** bullet with a substance in it that burns when the bullet is fired, leaving a visible trail used for aiming. **4** substance, such as a radioactive isotope, that can be observed as it passes through a body, plant, or other system in order to study biological processes or chemical reactions within the system.

trac·er·y (trā′sər ē), *n.* ornamental work or designs consisting of lines. Stonework, carving, and embroidery often have tracery.

tra·che·a (trā′kē ə), *n.* windpipe. ❑ *n., pl.* **tra·che·ae** (trā′kē ē′), **tra·che·as.**

tra·che·ot·o·my (trā′kē ot′ə mē), *n.* a surgical cutting into the trachea. ❑ *n., pl.* **tra·che·ot·o·mies.**

tra·cho·ma (trə kō′mə), *n.* a contagious inflammation of the eyelids and the outer surface of the eyeball.

trac·ing (trā′sing), *n.* copy of something made by marking or drawing over it.

track (trak), **1** *n.* pair of parallel metal rails for cars to run on: *railroad tracks.* **2** *n.* a mark or pattern left: *The dirt road showed many tire tracks.* **3** *n.* footprint: *She investigated the tracks to see what she could learn about the intruder.* **4** *v.* to follow by means of footprints, marks, smell, etc.: *We tracked the deer and photographed it.* **5** *v.* to trace in any way: *I will track down her new address.* **6** *v.* to make footprints or other marks on: *Don't track up the floor.* **7** *v.* to bring snow, mud, etc., into a place on your feet: *He tracked mud into the house.* **8** *n.* path; trail; road: *A track runs through the woods to the cabin.* **9** *n.* an area, usually oval, for running or racing. **10** *n.* track and field. **11** *n.* one of the endless belts of linked steel plates on which a tank, bulldozer, etc., moves. **12** *n.* a band or strip of a phonograph record, movie film, or magnetic tape on which sound has been recorded. **13** *n.* a selection from an album. —**track′a·ble,** *adj.* —**track′er,** *n.*

in your tracks, right where you are: *The squirrel froze in its tracks when it saw us.*

jump the track, to leave the rails suddenly; derail without warning.

keep track of, to keep within your sight or attention: *The interruptions made it difficult to keep track of the story.*

lose track of, to fail to keep in mind or sight: *Working with the computer, I often lose track of what time it is.*

make tracks, INFORMAL. to go very fast; run off: *She saw it was dinnertime and made tracks for home.*

off the track or **off track,** off the subject; wrong.

on the track or **on track,** on the subject; right.

track (def. 3)

track and field, the sports or events of races around a track and the pole vault, shot-put, high jump, etc., on a field in the center of the track.

a	hat	ė	term	ô	order	ch	child		
ā	age	i	it	oi	oil	ng	long		a in about
ä	far	ī	ice	ou	out	sh	she	ə	e in taken
â	care	o	hot	u	cup	th	thin		i in pencil
e	let	ō	open	ù	put	ᴛʜ	then		o in lemon
ē	equal	ò	saw	ü	rule	zh	measure		u in circus

track·ball (trak′bȯl′), *n.* a small ball that can be turned in order to move a cursor on a computer screen. Trackballs are usually built into keyboards and are often used with portable computers.

track·less (trak′lis), *adj.* 1 without a track. 2 without paths or trails: *a trackless wilderness.*

track meet, series of contests in running, jumping, throwing, and similar sports.

tract[1] (trakt), *n.* 1 area of land, buildings, etc.; district: *a tract of desert land.* 2 system of related parts or organs in the body. The stomach and intestines are part of the digestive tract.

tract[2] (trakt), *n.* a little book or pamphlet on a religious or political subject.

trac·ta·ble (trak′tə bəl), *adj.* 1 easily managed or controlled; easy to deal with; docile: *Dogs are more tractable than mules.* 2 easily handled or worked: *Gold is a tractable metal that can be hammered into thin sheets.* **–trac′ta·bil′i·ty, trac′ta·ble·ness,** *n.* **–trac′ta·bly,** *adv.*

trac·tion (trak′shən), *n.* 1 ability to push against a surface without skidding: *Deep treads improve a car tire's traction in snow or rain.* 2 a steady pull on an injured bone that helps it heal properly, supplied by a system of weights and pulleys. 3 act of pulling or condition of being pulled.

trac·tor (trak′tər), *n.* 1 a heavy motor vehicle that moves on wheels or on two endless tracks, used for pulling wagons, plows, etc., along roads or over fields. 2 a powerful short truck used to pull an attached freight trailer along a highway.

trac·tor-trail·er (trak′tər trā′lər), *n.* a freight truck made of a tractor attached to a trailer.

Tra·cy (trā′sē), *n.* **Spen·cer** (spen′ser), 1900-1967, American movie star. He won two Academy Awards as best actor, for *Captains Courageous* in 1937 and *Boys Town* in 1938. He was nominated seven other times.

tractor (def. 1)

trade (trād), 1 *n.* process of buying and selling; exchange of goods; commerce: *The United States has much trade with foreign countries.* 2 *v.* to buy and sell; exchange goods; be in commerce: *Many American companies trade all over the world.* 3 *n.* a purchase or sale: *a grain trade worth millions.* 4 *n.* an exchange: *an even trade of baseball cards.* 5 *v.* to exchange; make an exchange: *If you don't like your lunch, I'll trade with you.* 6 *n.* a kind of work; business, especially one requiring skilled mechanical work: *the carpenter's trade.* 7 *n.* people in the same kind of work or business: *clothes for the building trade.* 8 *n.* customers: *That store has a lot of trade.* 9 *v.* to be a customer: *I have traded at that store for years.* 10 *n.* **the trades,** the trade winds. ❏ *v.* **trad·ed, trad·ing. –trad′a·ble** or **trade′a·ble,** *adj.*

trade in, to give a car, stereo, etc., as payment or part payment for something, especially for a newer model.

trade on, to take advantage of: *He traded on his wealth to gain political influence.*

trade deficit, the amount by which the value of a country's imports exceeds the value of its exports.

trade-in (trād′in′), *n.* car, refrigerator, etc., given or accepted as payment or part payment for something, especially for a newer model.

trade·mark (trād′märk′), 1 *n.* a mark, picture, name, word, symbol, design, or letters, used to identify and distinguish a product or merchandise as belonging to a specific manufacturer or seller. A registered trademark is legally protected, and may be used only by the owner. 2 *v.* to register the trademark of.

trade name, 1 name by which a product is normally called in business or trade. 2 name used by a company to identify a product that it makes or sells, which may be registered as a trademark. 3 name under which a company does business.

trade-off or **trade·off** (trād′ȯf′), *n.* an exchange made in order to gain a compromise: *In a trade-off, the union accepted an increase in pension benefits but no increase in wages.*

trad·er (trā′dər), *n.* 1 person who trades: *The trappers sold furs to traders.* 2 ship used in trading.

trade school, school where mechanical trades are taught.

trades·man (trādz′mən), *n.* storekeeper; shopkeeper. ❏ *n., pl.* **trades·men.**

trades·peo·ple (trādz′pē′pəl), *n.pl.* storekeepers; shopkeepers.

trade union, 1 association of workers in a trade or craft to protect and promote their interests. 2 any labor union.

trade wind, wind blowing steadily toward the equator from about 30 degrees north latitude or about 30 degrees south latitude. North of the equator, it blows from the northeast; south of the equator, from the southeast.

trading post, store or station of a trader, especially on the frontier. Trading posts used to trade food, weapons, clothes, and other articles in exchange for hides and furs.

trading stamp, (earlier) a stamplike piece of paper given to customers as a bonus, to be exchanged for goods.

tra·di·tion (trə dish′ən), *n.* 1 process of handing down beliefs, opinions, customs, stories, etc., from parents to children. 2 custom or belief handed down in this way: *According to tradition, Betsy Ross made the first American flag.* [See Word Story at **treason.**]

tra·di·tion·al (trə dish′ə nəl), *adj.* 1 handed down by tradition: *Shaking hands upon meeting is a traditional custom.* 2 according to tradition: *traditional furniture.* 3 customary: *A July the Fourth parade is traditional in almost every town.* **–tra·di′tion·al·ly,** *adv.*

Tra·fal·gar (trə fal′gər), *n.* **Cape,** cape in SW Spain, on the Atlantic. In a naval battle near this cape in 1805, Napoleon's fleet was defeated by a British fleet under Nelson. [Trafalgar comes from Arabic words meaning "white cape," perhaps because of its sparkling sand.]

traf·fic (traf′ik), 1 *n.* people, motor vehicles, ships, etc., coming and going along a way of travel: *Police stopped traffic on streets near the parade.* 2 *n.* the total business done by a truck line, railroad line, airline, etc.; number of passengers, amount of information, or amount of freight carried: *That bulletin board has heavy traffic—over 150 messages a day.* 3 *n.* process of buying and selling; commerce; trade. 4 *v.* to carry on trade; buy; sell; exchange: *traders trafficking in soybeans.* 5 *n.* dealings; contact; association: *Traffic with criminals is dangerous.* ❏ *v.* **traf·ficked, traf·fick·ing. –traf′fick·er.**

traffic circle, a meeting point of several roads where the merging traffic goes around a central circle in one direction only; rotary.

traffic light, a set of electric lights used for signaling to control traffic at a corner or intersection; stoplight.

tra·ge·di·an (trə jē′dē ən), *n.* 1 actor in tragedies. 2 writer of tragedies.

trag·e·dy (traj′ə dē), *n.* 1 a serious play having an unhappy ending. Shakespeare's *Hamlet* is a tragedy. 2 a very sad or terrible happening: *Her sudden death was a tragedy to her friends.* ❏ *n., pl.* **trag·e·dies.**

trag·ic (traj′ik), *adj.* 1 of or about tragedy: *a tragic poem.* 2 very sad; dreadful: *a tragic event.* **–trag′i·cal·ly,** *adv.*

trag·i·cal (traj′ə kəl), *adj.* tragic.

trail (trāl), 1 *n.* path across a wild or unsettled region: *The hikers followed mountain trails for days.* 2 *n.* a track or smell: *The dogs found the trail of the rabbit.* 3 *v.* to hunt by track or smell: *The dogs trailed the rabbit.* 4 *n.* anything that follows along behind: *The car left a trail of dust behind it.* 5 *v.* to follow along behind; follow: *The dog trailed its master constantly.* 6 *v.* to pull or be pulled along behind: *The child trailed a toy horse.* 7 *v.* to grow along: *Poison ivy trailed by the road.* 8 *v.* to go along slowly: *The children trailed to school.* 9 *v.* to pass little by little: *Her voice trailed off into silence.* 10 *v.* to follow, fall, or lag behind, as in a race, game, etc.: *Our team trailed by three runs with one inning left.*

trail·blaz·er (trāl′blā′zər), *n.* person or thing that pioneers or prepares the way to something new.

trail·er (trā′lər), *n.* 1 a large vehicle used for hauling freight, pulled by a truck. 2 a small two-wheeled or four-wheeled vehicle used for hauling something behind a car or truck: *a boat trailer.* **3** vehicle designed for use as a house or office, usually pulled to a site by a truck; mobile home. **4** person or animal that follows a trail.

trailing arbutus, arbutus. It is the provincial flower of Nova Scotia.

Trail of Tears, 1 the westward trail to present-day Oklahoma that the Cherokee were forced to take in 1838 when Georgia took over their lands. Many Cherokee died on this trip or as a result. **2** similar forced journeys during the 1830s by other American Indian tribes of the Southeast.

train (trān), **1** *n.* a connected line of railroad cars moving along together: *A very long freight train of 100 cars rolled by.* **2** *n.* line of people, animals, wagons, trucks, etc., moving along together: *Her ancestors came to Oregon by wagon train.* **3** *n.* a part that hangs down and drags along: *the train of a gown.* **4** *n.* group of followers; entourage: *the king and his train.* **5** *n.* a continuous series of events or ideas: *A long train of misfortunes overcame them.* **6** *n.* an order of succession; sequence: *I lost my train of thought when I was interrupted.* **7** *v.* to make skillful by teaching and practice: *Saint Bernard dogs were trained to hunt for travelers lost in the snow.* **8** *v.* to teach so as to form character; to bring up; rear: *They trained their child to be considerate of others.* **9** *v.* to make or become fit by exercise and diet: *Runners train for races.* **10** *v.* to point; aim: *train cannon upon a fort.* **11** *v.* to bring into a particular position: *Train the vine around this post.* **–train′a·ble,** *adj.*

train·ee (trā nē′), *n.* person who is receiving training. ❑ *n., pl.* **train·ees.**

train·er (trā′nər), *n.* **1** person who trains horses or other animals to take part in competition or other kinds of performances. **2** person who trains athletes. **3** person who treats minor injuries to members of sports teams.

train·ing (trā′ning), *n.* **1** practical education in some art, profession, etc.: *training for teachers.* **2** development of strength and endurance: *physical training.* ■ See Synonym Study at **exercise.** **3** good condition maintained by exercise, diet, etc.: *The athlete kept in training by not overeating and not smoking.*

training school, a reformatory for the reeducation of young criminal offenders.

train·load (trān′lōd′), *n.* as much as a train can hold or carry.

train·man (trān′mən), *n.* brakeman or other railroad worker in a train crew, who helps the conductor. ❑ *n., pl.* **train·men.**

traipse (trāps), *v.* to walk about aimlessly, carelessly, or needlessly: *The children traipsed about, looking for something to do.* ❑ *v.* **traipsed, traips·ing.**

trait (trāt), *n.* quality of mind, character, etc.; distinguishing feature; characteristic: *Courage, love of fair play, and common sense are desirable traits.*

trai·tor (trā′tər), *n.* **1** person who betrays his or her country or ruler: *Benedict Arnold became a traitor by helping the British during the Revolutionary War.* **2** person who betrays a trust, duty, friend, etc. [See Word Story at **treason.**]

trai·tor·ous (trā′tər əs), *adj.* like a traitor; faithless. **–trai′tor·ous·ly,** *adv.* **–trai′tor·ous·ness,** *n.*

tra·jec·to·ry (trə jek′tər ē), *n.* **1** the curved path of something thrown, shot, or launched into the air. **2** orbit (def. 1). ❑ *n., pl.* **tra·jec·to·ries.**

tram (tram), *n.* **1** truck or car on which loads are carried in mines. **2** BRITISH. streetcar.

tramp (tramp), **1** *v.* to walk heavily: *She tramped across the room in her heavy boots.* **2** *v.* to step heavily on: *He tramped on the flowers.* **3** *n.* sound of a heavy step: *the tramp of marching feet.* **4** *v.* to go on foot; walk: *The hikers tramped through the mountains.* **5** *n.* a long, steady walk; hike: *The children went on a tramp through the woods.* **6** *n.* person who travels from place to place on foot, living by doing odd jobs, begging, etc. **7** *n.* freighter that takes a cargo when and where it can. **–tramp′er,** *n.*

tram·ple (tram′pəl), *v.* **1** to walk or step heavily on; crush: *The cattle trampled the farmer's crops.* **2** to step or tread heavily; tramp: *Don't trample on the flowers.* **3** to treat cruelly, harshly,

or scornfully: *The tyrant trampled his subjects and deprived them of all their rights.* ❑ *v.* **tram·pled, tram·pling. –tram′pler,** *n.* **trample on** or **trample upon,** to treat with scorn, harshness, or cruelty: *to trample on someone's rights.*

tram·po·line (tram′pə lēn′), *n.* piece of canvas or other sturdy fabric stretched on a metal frame, used for tumbling, acrobatics, etc.

trance (trans), *n.* **1** state of unconsciousness somewhat like sleep. A person may be in a trance from illness or from hypnosis. Some people can even put themselves into a trance. **2** condition like daydreaming or a trance: *She sat in a trance, watching the flames in the fireplace.* **–trance′like,** *adj.*

WORD STORY **Trance** comes from a Latin word meaning "across." **Trans-,** the prefix meaning "across," comes from the same Latin word. Romans thought that a person in a trance had crossed the boundary between this world and the next, and might not come back.

tran·quil (trang′kwəl), *adj.* calm; peaceful; quiet: *the tranquil morning air.* **–tran′quil·ly,** *adv.* **–tran′quil·ness,** *n.*

tran·quil·ize (trang′kwə līz), *v.* **1** to make calm, peaceful, or quiet. **2** to become tranquil. ❑ *v.* **tran·quil·ized, tran·quil·iz·ing. –tran′quil·i·za′tion,** *n.*

tran·quil·iz·er (trang′kwə lī′zər), *n.* any of several drugs that relax muscles, reduce nervous tension, lower blood pressure, etc.

tran·quil·li·ty or **tran·quil·i·ty** (trang kwil′ə tē), *n.* tranquil condition; calmness; peacefulness; quiet: *The people wanted only to live in peace and tranquillity.*

tranquil—tranquil waters

trans-, *prefix.* **1** across; through; beyond: *transcontinental = across the continent.* **2** in or to a different place, condition, etc.: *transplant = plant in another place.* [See Word Story at **trance.**]

trans·act (tran zakt′), *v.* to attend to; manage; do; carry on business: *We transact business with stores all over the country.* **–trans·ac′tor,** *n.*

trans·ac·tion (tran zak′shən), *n.* **1** piece of business: *A record was kept of the firm's latest transaction with the bank.* **2** act of carrying on business: *She attends to the transaction of important matters herself.* **3 transactions,** *pl.* record of what was done at the meetings of a society, club, etc.

trans·at·lan·tic (tran′sat lan′tik), *adj.* **1** crossing the Atlantic: *a transatlantic liner, a transatlantic cable.* **2** on the other side of the Atlantic.

trans·ax·le (tran zak′səl), *n.* a part of a car combining the transmission and a section of the front axle. Transaxles are used on cars with front-wheel drive.

trans·Can·a·da (trans′kan′ə də), **1** *adj.* going or extending across Canada, from the Atlantic to the Pacific. **2** *n.* **Trans-Canada,** a highway connecting all the provinces of Canada.

trans·cend (tran send′), *v.* **1** to go beyond the limits or powers of; exceed; be above: *The grandeur of Niagara Falls transcends words.* **2** to be higher or greater than; surpass; excel: *The speed of airplanes transcends that of any previous form of transportation.*

trans·cend·ence (tran sen′dəns), *n.* condition of being transcendent.

trans·cend·ent (tran sen′dənt), *adj.* surpassing ordinary limits; excelling; superior; extraordinary.

tran·scen·den·tal (tran′sen den′tl), *adj.* going beyond ordinary experience or limits.

a	hat	ė	term	ô	order	ch	child		
ā	age	i	it	oi	oil	ng	long	a	in about
ä	far	ī	ice	ou	out	sh	she	e	in taken
â	care	o	hot	u	cup	th	thin	ə { i	in pencil
e	let	ō	open	u̇	put	ŦH	then	o	in lemon
ē	equal	ò	saw	ü	rule	zh	measure	u	in circus

trans·con·ti·nen·tal (tran/skon tə nen/tl), *adj.* crossing a continent: *transcontinental flights.*

tran·scribe (tran skrib/), *v.* **1** to copy in writing or in typewriting: *The minutes of the meeting were transcribed from the secretary's shorthand notes.* **2** to make a recording, usually on tape, for broadcasting at a later time. ❑ *v.* **tran·scribed, tran·scrib·ing.** —**tran·scrib/er,** *n.*

tran·script (tran/skript), *n.* **1** a written or typewritten copy: *The secretary prepared a transcript of the minutes of the meeting.* **2** copy or reproduction of anything: *The college wanted a transcript of my high school record.*

tran·scrip·tion (tran skrip/shən), *n.* **1** act of transcribing; copying. **2** a copy; transcript of a program for use in broadcasting at a later time.

tran·sept (tran/sept), *n.* **1** the shorter part of a cross-shaped church. **2** either end of this part.

trans·fer (tran sfėr/ *or* tran/sfėr/ *for verb;* tran/sfėr/ *for noun*), **1** *v.* to change or move from one person or place to another; shift; hand over: *The engineer was transferred to another department.* **2** *v.* to change from one bus, train, etc., to another: *On our way into the city we transferred from a train to a bus.* **3** *n.* ticket allowing a passenger to change from one bus, train, etc., to another. **4** *n.* point or place for transferring. **5** *v.* to pass a drawing, design, pattern, etc., from one surface to another: *You transfer the embroidery design from the paper to cloth by pressing it with a warm iron.* **6** *n.* thing transferred; a drawing, pattern, etc., passed from one surface onto another. **7** *n.* act of transferring or process of being transferred. ❑ *v.* **trans·ferred, trans·fer·ring.** —**trans·fer/a·ble** *or* **trans·fer/ra·ble,** *adj.*

trans·fer·ence (tran sfėr/əns), *n.* act of transferring or condition of being transferred.

transfer RNA, a form of RNA that delivers amino acids to cell ribosomes for protein formation.

trans·fig·u·ra·tion (tran sfig/yə rā/shən), *n.* a change in form or appearance; transformation.

trans·fig·ure (tran sfig/yər), *v.* **1** to change in form or appearance; transform: *New paint had transfigured the old house.* **2** to change so as to glorify; exalt. ❑ *v.* **trans·fig·ured, trans·fig·ur·ing.** —**trans·fig/ure·ment,** *n.*

trans·fix (tran sfiks/), *v.* **1** to make motionless with amazement, terror, etc. **2** to pierce through; impale: *The hunter transfixed the warthog with a spear.* —**trans·fix·ion** (tran sfik/shən), *n.*

trans·form (tran sfôrm/), *v.* **1** to change in form or appearance: *The blizzard transformed the bushes into mounds of white.* **2** to change in condition, nature, or character: *A tadpole becomes transformed into a frog.* **3** to change an electric current to a higher or lower voltage, from alternating to direct current, or from direct to alternating current. —**trans·form/a·ble,** *adj.*

trans·for·ma·tion (tran/sfôr mā/shən), *n.* act of transforming or condition of being transformed: *the transformation of a caterpillar into a butterfly.*

trans·form·er (tran sfôr/mər), *n.* device for changing an alternating current into one of higher or lower voltage.

trans·fuse (tran sfyüz/), *v.* to transfer blood from one person or animal to another. ❑ *v.* **trans·fused, trans·fus·ing.**

trans·fu·sion (tran sfyü/zhən), *n.* transfer of blood from one person or animal to another: *The injured driver was bleeding badly and needed a transfusion.*

trans·gress (trans gres/ *or* tranz gres/), *v.* **1** to break a law, command, etc.; sin. **2** to go beyond a limit: *Their manners transgress the bounds of good taste.* —**trans·gres/sor,** *n.*

trans·gres·sion (trans gresh/ən *or* tranz gresh/ən), *n.* act of transgressing: *to commit a grave transgression.*

tran·sient (tran/shənt), **1** *adj.* passing swiftly; fleeting; not lasting: *Joy and sorrow are often transient.* **2** *adj.* passing through and not staying long: *a transient guest in a hotel.* **3** *n.* visitor or boarder who stays for a short time. —**tran/sient·ly,** *adv.*

tran·sis·tor (tran zis/tər), *n.* a tiny electronic device, made of a semiconductor, that controls or amplifies the flow of electrons in an electric circuit. Transistors are used in radios, TV sets, computers, and other electronic equipment.

transistor radio, a usually small, battery-powered radio equipped with transistors.

tran·sit (tran/sit *or* tran/zit), *n.* **1** transportation by trains, buses, etc.: *All systems of transit are crowded during the rush hour.* **2** act of carrying or process of being carried across or through a distance: *The goods were damaged in transit.* **3** act or process of passing across or through. **4** device used in surveying to measure angles.

tran·si·tion (tran zish/ən), *n.* a change from one condition, place, thing, activity, topic, etc., to another: *a transition from poverty to power.*

tran·si·tion·al (tran zish/ə nəl), *adj.* marked by change from one more or less fixed condition to another. —**tran·si/tion·al·ly,** *adv.*

tran·si·tive (tran/sə tiv *or* tran/zə tiv), *adj.* taking a direct object. In "Bring me my coat" and "Raise the window," *bring* and *raise* are transitive verbs. —**tran/si·tive·ly,** *adv.* —**tran/si·tive·ness,** *n.*

tran·si·to·ry (tran/sə tôr/ē), *adj.* passing soon or quickly; lasting only a short time: *My distress was transitory; I was soon happy again.* —**tran/si·to/ri·ly,** *adv.* —**tran/si·to/ri·ness,** *n.*

trans·late (tran slāt/ *or* tranz lāt/), *v.* **1** to change from one language into another: *translate a book from French into English.* **2** to express one thing in terms of another: *translate words into action.* ❑ *v.* **trans·lat·ed, trans·lat·ing.** —**trans·lat/a·ble,** *adj.*

trans·la·tion (tran slā/shən *or* tranz lā/shən), *n.* **1** result of translating; version: *a Spanish translation of a book.* **2** act or process of changing into another language: *the translation of the Bible from Hebrew into Latin.*

trans·la·tor (tran slā/tər *or* tranz lā/ tər), *n.* person who translates.

trans·lu·cent (tran slü/snt *or* tranz lü/snt), *adj.* letting light through, but not easily seen through: *Frosted glass is translucent.* —**trans·lu/cent·ly,** *adv.*

trans·mi·gra·tion (tran/smī grā/shən *or* tranz/mī grā/shən), *n.* (in certain religious beliefs) the passing of a soul at death into another body.

trans·mis·si·ble (tran smis/ə bəl *or* tranz mis/ə bəl), *adj.* able to be transmitted: *a transmissible disease.*

trans·mis·sion (tran smish/ən *or* tranz mish/ən), *n.* **1** the part of a car or other motor vehicle that transmits power from the engine to the rear or front axle by the use of gears. **2** act or process of sending or passing something from one person, thing, or place to another: *Mosquitoes are the only means of transmission of malaria.* **3** passage of electromagnetic waves from a transmitter to a receiver: *When transmission is good, even foreign radio stations can be heard.* **4** something transmitted: *a coded radio transmission from headquarters.*

transmission electron microscope, an electron microscope that forms images by passing a beam of electrons through the object being viewed.

trans·mit (tran smit/ *or* tranz mit/), *v.* **1** to send along; pass along: *I will transmit the money by special messenger. Rats transmit disease.* **2** to cause light, heat, sound, etc., to pass through a medium. **3** to convey force or movement from one part of a body or mechanism to another. **4** to send out signals by means of electromagnetic waves or by wire: *Some station is transmitting every hour of the day.* **5** to pass on through inheritance: *Your physical characteristics may be transmitted to your children.* ❑ *v.* **trans·mit·ted, trans·mit·ting.** —**trans·mit/ta·ble,** *adj.*

trans·mit·tal (tran smit/l *or* tranz mit/l), *n.* **1** something that is transmitted; a transmission. **2** act of transmitting.

trans·mit·ter (tran smit/ər *or* tranz mit/ər), *n.* **1** device that sends out signals by electromagnetic waves: *Radio and TV stations have transmitters.* **2** any device that sends information by electric current, such as the microphone in a telephone.

trans·mu·ta·tion (tran/smyə tā/shən *or* tranz/myə tā/shən), *n.* a change from one nature, substance, or form into another.

trans·mute (tran smyüt/ *or* tranz myüt/), *v.* to change from one nature, substance, or form into another: *We can transmute water power into electrical power.* ❑ *v.* **trans·mut·ed, trans·mut·ing.** —**trans·mut/a·ble,** *adj.* —**trans·mut/a·bly,** *adv.* —**trans·mut/er,** *n.*

tran·som (tran/səm), *n.* **1** window or panel over a door or other window, usually hinged for opening. **2** a horizontal bar across a window; crossbar separating a door from the window over it.

trans·pa·cif·ic (tran/spə sif/ik), *adj.* **1** crossing the Pacific. **2** on the other side of the Pacific.

trans·par·en·cy (tran spâr/ən sē), *n.* **1** picture, design, or the like, made visible by light shining through from behind. **2** transparent quality or condition. ❑ *n., pl.* **trans·par·en·cies** for 1.

trans·par·ent (tran spâr/ənt), *adj.* **1** letting light through so that things on the other side can be distinctly seen: *Window glass is transparent.* **2** easily seen through or detected; obvious: *a transparent excuse.* **3** frank; free from pretense or deceit: *a person of transparent honesty.* **–trans·par/ent·ly,** *adv.* **–trans·par/ent·ness,** *n.*

tran·spire (tran spīr/), *v.* **1** to take place; happen: *I heard later what transpired at the meeting.* **2** to leak out; become known. **3** to give off moisture in the form of vapor through the surface of leaves. ❑ *v.* **tran·spired, tran·spir·ing.** **–tran·spir/a·ble,** *adj.* **–tran/spi·ra/tion,** *n.*

trans·plant (tran splant/ *for verb;* tran/splant *for noun*), **1** *v.* to plant again in a different place: *We start the seedlings indoors and then transplant them to the garden.* **2** *v.* to transfer skin, an organ, etc., from one person, animal, or part of the body to another: *transplant a kidney.* **3** *n.* the transfer of skin, an organ, etc., from one person, animal, or part of the body to another: *a heart transplant.* **4** *v.* to remove from one place to another: *a research project transplanted by its director to another university.* **5** *n.* something that has been transplanted. **–trans·plant/a·ble,** *adj.* **–trans/plan·ta/tion,** *n.* **–trans·plant/er,** *n.*

trans·port (tran spôrt/ *for verb;* tran/spôrt *for noun*), **1** *v.* to carry from one place to another: *Wheat is transported from the farms to the mills.* ■ See Synonym Study at **carry. 2** *n.* act or process of carrying from one place to another: *Trucks are much used for transport.* **3** *n.* a ship used to carry troops and supplies. **4** *n.* aircraft that carries passengers, mail, freight, etc. **5** *v.* to arouse by strong feeling; make very emotional: *She was transported with joy by the good news.* **6** *v.* (earlier) to send away to a colony as a punishment: *Years ago, England transported many of its criminals to Australia.* **–trans·port/a·ble,** *adj.* **–trans·port/er,** *n.*

trans·ship (tran ship/), *v.* to transfer from one ship, train, car, etc., to another. ❑ *v.* **trans·shipped, trans·ship·ping.**

tran·sub·stan·ti·a·tion (tran/səb stan/shē ā/shən), *n.* (in Christian theology) the doctrine that the bread and wine of the Holy Communion are changed into the body and blood of Christ.

Trans·vaal (trans väl/ *or* tranz väl/), *n.* province of the Republic of South Africa, in the NE part.

trans·ver·sal (trans vėr/səl *or* tranz vėr/səl), *n.* line intersecting two or more other lines. **–trans·ver/sal·ly,** *adv.*

trans·verse (trans vėrs/ *or* tranz vėrs/), *adj.* lying across; placed crosswise; crossing from side to side: *transverse beams.* **–trans·verse/ly,** *adv.*

Tran·syl·van·ia (tran/səl vā/nyə), *n.* region in central and W Romania, formerly part of Hungary. **–Tran/syl·van/ian,** *adj., n.*

trap (trap), **1** *n.* device for catching animals: *a mouse trap.* **2** *n.* trick for catching someone off guard: *The lawyer set traps to make the witness contradict herself.* **3** *v.* to catch in a device or trick: *to trap a mouse.* **4** *v.* to set traps for animals. **5** *n.* trapdoor. **6** *n.* a bend in a drainpipe that holds a small amount of water to prevent the escape of air, sewer gas, etc. **7** *n.* device to throw clay pigeons or other targets into the air to be shot at. **8** *n.pl.* **traps,** drums, cymbals, bells, gongs, etc., used in a small band or orchestra. ❑ *v.* **trapped, trap·ping.** **–trap/like/,** *adj.*

trap·door (trap/dôr/), *n.* door in a floor or roof.

tra·peze (trə pēz/), *n.* a short horizontal bar hung by ropes like a swing, used by gymnasts and acrobats.

WORD STORY **Trapeze** comes from Greek words meaning "four feet." This was the Greek name for a kind of little table and for the shape of its top. In old times, the ropes and bar of a trapeze were arranged to form this shape.

tra·pe·zi·um (trə pē/zē əm), *n.* a four-sided plane figure having no sides parallel. ❑ *n., pl.* **tra·pe·zi·ums, tra·pe·zi·a** (trə pē/zē ə).

trap·e·zoid (trap/ə zoid), *n.* a four-sided plane figure having two sides parallel and two sides not parallel.

transportation (def. 2)

trans·por·ta·tion (tran/spər tā/shən), *n.* **1** the business of transporting people or goods: *Railroads, trucks, bus lines, and airlines are all engaged in transportation.* **2** means of transport: *When the bus broke down, we had no other transportation to school.* **3** act of transporting: *The transportation for our trip was arranged by the travel bureau.* **4** condition of being transported. **5** cost of transport; ticket for transport. **6** (earlier) act of sending away to another country as a punishment.

trans·pose (tran spōz/), *v.* **1** to change the usual order of letters, words, or numbers: *I transposed the numbers and mistakenly wrote 19 for 91.* **2** (in music) to change the key of. **3** to transfer a term to the other side of an algebraic equation, changing plus to minus or minus to plus. ❑ *v.* **trans·posed, trans·pos·ing.** **–trans·pos/a·ble,** *adj.* **–trans·pos/er,** *n.*

trans·po·si·tion (tran/spə zish/ən), *n.* **1** act of transposing or condition of being transposed. **2** piece of music transposed into a different key.

trans·po·son (trans pō/zon), *n.* section of DNA able to change position and actitivity.

trans·pro·vin·cial (trans/prə vin/shəl), *adj.* stretching across a province: *transprovincial communications.*

trap·per (trap/ər), *n.* person who traps wild animals for fur.

trap·pings (trap/ingz), *n.pl.* things worn; ornaments: *He had all the trappings of a cowboy, but he couldn't even ride a horse.*

trap·shoot·ing (trap/shü/ting), *n.* sport of shooting at targets thrown or released from traps into the air. **–trap/shoot/er,** *n.*

trash (trash), **1** *n.* anything of little or no worth; refuse: *Rake up the trash in the yard.* **2** *n.* worthless stuff; rubbish: *That magazine is trash.* **3** *n.* disreputable people; riffraff. ■ This meaning of **trash** is considered offensive. **4** *v.* to destroy or damage something, often in a cruel, careless way: *The rock star trashed his hotel room. The jealous girls trashed her reputation.*

trash·y (trash/ē), *adj.* like or containing trash; worthless. ❑ *adj.* **trash·i·er, trash·i·est. –trash/i·ly,** *adv.* **–trash/i·ness,** *n.*

trau·ma (trô/mə *or* trou/mə), *n.* **1** a physical wound; injury. **2** the psychological condition produced by wounds or emotional shock. ❑ *n., pl.* **trau·mas, trau·ma·ta** (trô/mə tə *or* trou/mə tə).

a	hat	ė	term	ô	order	ch	child		a in about
ā	age	i	it	oi	oil	ng	long		e in taken
ä	far	ī	ice	ou	out	sh	she	ə	i in pencil
â	care	o	hot	u	cup	th	thin		o in lemon
e	let	ō	open	ů	put	ŦH	then		u in circus
ē	equal	ò	saw	ü	rule	zh	measure		

T

trau·mat·ic (trò mat′ik *or* trou mat′ik), *adj.* of or produced by a wound, injury, or shock: *a traumatic experience.* —**trau·mat′i·cal·ly,** *adv.*

trau·ma·tize (trô′mə tīz *or* trou′mə tīz), *v.* to cause trauma in; injure; shock. ❏ *v.* **trau·ma·tized, trau·ma·tiz·ing.** —**trau′ma·ti·za′tion,** *n.*

tra·vail (trə vāl′ *or* trav′āl), **1** *n.* toil; labor. **2** *v.* to toil; labor. **3** *n.* trouble; hardship: *It was a time of great travail.*

trav·el (trav′əl), **1** *v.* to go from one place to another; journey: *She is traveling to Europe this summer.* **2** *n.* act of going in planes, ships, cars, trains, etc., from one place to another; journeying: *She loves travel.* **3** *n.pl.* **travels,** journeys: *"Gulliver's Travels."* **4** *v.* to move; proceed; pass: *Sound travels in waves.* ❏ *v.* **trav·eled, trav·el·ing** *or* **trav·elled, trav·el·ling.**

travel agent, person whose business is arranging trips, tickets, hotel reservations, and the like for travelers.

trav·eled *or* **trav·elled** (trav′əld), *adj.* **1** having done much traveling: *a well-traveled friend.* **2** much used by travelers: *a heavily traveled road.*

trav·el·er *or* **trav·el·ler** (trav′ə lər), *n.* person or thing that travels.

traveler's check, check issued by a bank for a specific amount and signed by the buyer. A traveler can use it as cash by signing it again when buying or paying for something.

trav·e·logue *or* **trav·e·log** (trav′ə lòg), *n.* **1** movie about travel to a particular place or area. **2** lecture describing travel, usually accompanied by pictures or films.

trav·erse (trə vèrs′ *or* trav′ərs *for verb;* trav′ərs *or* trə vèrs′ *for adj., noun*), **1** *v.* to pass across, over, or through: *Explorers traversed the desert by truck.* **2** *adj.* lying across; being across; transverse. **3** *n.* something put or lying across: *We walked over the traverse that lay across the gully.* ❏ *v.* **trav·ersed, trav·ers·ing.** —**trav·ers′a·ble,** *adj.* —**trav·ers′er,** *n.*

trav·es·ty (trav′ə stē), **1** *n.* an imitation of a serious literary work or subject, done in such a way as to make it seem ridiculous. **2** *n.* any treatment or imitation that makes a serious thing seem ridiculous: *A prejudiced judge made the trial a travesty of justice.* **3** *v.* to make a serious subject or matter ridiculous; imitate in an absurd or grotesque way; parody. ❏ *n., pl.* **trav·es·ties;** *v.* **trav·es·tied, trav·es·ty·ing.**

tra·vois (trə voi′), *n.* a wheelless vehicle used by North American Indians, made of two rods joined by a platform or net for holding the load, pulled by a dog or a horse. ❏ *n., pl.* **tra·vois** (trə voiz′).

trawl (tròl), **1** *n.* a strong net dragged along the bottom of the sea. **2** *v.* to fish or catch fish with a net by dragging it along the bottom of the sea. **3** *n.* line supported by buoys and having many short lines with baited hooks attached to it. **4** *v.* to fish or catch fish with lines supported by buoys.

trawl·er (trò′lər), *n.* boat used in trawling.

tray (trā), *n.* **1** a flat, shallow holder or container with a low rim around it: *I carried the dishes on a tray.* **2** tray with dishes of food on it: *a breakfast tray.* **3** a shallow box that fits into a trunk, cabinet, etc.: *Carpenters keep many of their tools in trays.* ■ Another word that sounds like this is **trey.**

treach·er·ous (trech′ər əs), *adj.* **1** not to be trusted; not faithful; disloyal: *The king was betrayed by treacherous advisers.* ■ See Synonym Study at **disloyal.** **2** having a false appearance of strength, security, etc.; not reliable; deceiving: *Thin ice is treacherous.* —**treach′er·ous·ly,** *adv.* —**treach′er·ous·ness,** *n.*

treach·er·y (trech′ər ē), *n.* **1** treacherous behavior; deceit. **2** treason.

tread (tred), **1** *v.* to set a foot down; walk; step: *Don't tread on the flower beds.* **2** *v.* to walk on or through; step on: *tread the streets.* **3** *v.* to press under the feet; trample on; crush: *tread grapes.* **4** *v.* to make, form, or do by walking: *Cattle had trodden a path to the pond.* **5** *n.* act or sound of stepping: *We heard the tread of marching feet.* **6** *n.* way of walking: *He returned with a heavy tread.* **7** *n.* the part of stairs or of a ladder that someone steps on: *The stair treads were covered with rubber to prevent slipping.* **8** *n.* the part of a tire or wheel that presses against the ground, rail, etc. **9** *n.* pattern of grooves on the contact surface of rubber tires, to improve traction. ❏ *v.* **trod, trod·den** *or* **trod, tread·ing.** —**tread′less,** *adj.*

trea·dle (tred′l), **1** *n.* lever or pedal worked by the foot to make a machine operate: *the treadle of a sewing machine.* **2** *v.* to work a treadle. ❏ *v.* **trea·dled, trea·dling.** —**trea′dler,** *n.*

tread·mill (tred′mil′), *n.* **1** device used for exercise or to power a machine by having a person or animal walk or run on a sloping, endless belt. **2** any wearisome or monotonous routine of work or of life.

trea·son (trē′zn), *n.* betrayal of your country or ruler. Helping the enemies of your country is treason.

WORD STORY **Treason** comes from a Latin word meaning "to hand over." **Traitor** comes from the same Latin word, and so does **tradition.** When a traitor hands over plans to the enemy, that's treason. When parents or teachers hand over customs to young people, that's tradition.

trea·son·a·ble (trē′zn ə bəl), *adj.* involving treason; traitorous: *a treasonable conspiracy.* —**trea′son·a·ble·ness,** *n.* —**trea′son·a·bly,** *adv.*

trea·son·ous (trē′zn əs), *adj.* treasonable. —**trea′son·ous·ly,** *adv.*

treas·ure (trezh′ər), **1** *n.* wealth or riches stored up; valuable things: *The pirates buried their treasure along the coast.* **2** *n.* any thing or person that is much loved or valued: *The silver teapot was my parents' chief treasure.* **3** *v.* to value highly: *treasure good health.* **4** *v.* to put away for future use; store up. ❏ *v.* **treas·ured, treas·ur·ing.** —**treas′ur·a·ble,** *adj.* —**treas′ure·less,** *adj.*

treas·ur·er (trezh′ər ər), *n.* person in charge of money. The treasurer of a club pays its bills.

treas·ure-trove (trezh′ər trōv′), *n.* **1** money, jewels, or other treasure that someone finds, especially if the owner is not known. **2** any valuable discovery or source of valuable items: *a treasure-trove of research material.*

treas·ur·y (trezh′ər ē), *n.* **1** (earlier) a place where money was kept. **2** money owned; funds: *We voted to pay for the party out of the club treasury.* **3** Also, **Treasury,** department of the government that has charge of the income and expenses of a country. The Treasury of the United States collects federal taxes, mints money, supervises national banks, and prevents counterfeiting. ❏ *n., pl.* **treas·ur·ies** for 1.

treat (trēt), **1** *v.* to act toward: *The children treated the puppy with care.* **2** *v.* to think of; consider; regard: *He treated his mistake as a joke.* **3** *v.* to deal with to relieve or cure: *The dentist is treating my toothache.* **4** *v.* to act upon or add something to in order to bring about some special result: *treat drinking water to remove impurities.* **5** *v.* to deal with; discuss: *The article treated the subject thoroughly.* **6** *v.* to express in literature or art: *The author of these books always treats his themes realistically.* **7** *v.* to pay the cost of a treat or entertainment: *treat some friends to ice cream.* **8** *n.* gift of food, drink, or amusement: *"This is my treat,"* she said. **9** *n.* anything that gives pleasure: *Being in the country is a treat to her.* —**treat′a·ble,** *adj.* —**treat′er,** *n.*

trea·tise (trē′tis), *n.* a formal and systematic book or writing dealing with some subject.

treat·ment (trēt′mənt), *n.* **1** act or process of treating: *My cold won't respond to treatment.* **2** way of treating: *This cat has suffered from bad treatment.* **3** thing done or used to treat a disease, condition, etc.: *new treatments for cancer.*

trea·ty (trē′tē), *n.* a formal agreement, especially one between nations, signed and approved by each nation. ❏ *n., pl.* **trea·ties.**

treaty Indian, (in Canada) member of an American Indian tribe or band living on a reserve, who receives money and other rights according to treaty.

treaty money, (in Canada) money paid to treaty Indians.

tre·ble (treb′əl), **1** *adj.* three times: *Her salary is treble mine.* **2** *v.* to make or become three times as much: *He trebled his money by buying property for $20,000 and selling it for $60,000.* **3** *n.* the highest part in music; soprano. **4** *n.* voice or instrument that takes this part. **5** *adj.* of or for the treble. **6** *adj.* shrill; high-pitched. ❏ *v.* **tre·bled, tre·bling.**

WORD STORY **Treble** (defs. 3-6) may come from music in the Middle Ages. At that time, tenor voices sang the melody, and alto voices sang the main harmony. Another harmony part was sometimes given to the highest voices, and that made three times as many voices.

treble clef, symbol in music indicating that the pitch of the notes on a staff is above middle C; G clef. See picture at **clef.**

tre·bly (treb′lē), *adv.* three times.

tree (trē), **1** *n.* a large plant with a woody trunk and usually having branches and leaves at some distance from the ground. **2** *n.* any plant that resembles a tree in form or size. **3** *n.* piece or structure often made of wood or resembling a tree, used for some special purpose: *a clothes tree.* **4** *n.* anything branched like a tree. A family tree is a diagram with branches showing how the members of a family are related. **5** *v.* to chase up a tree: *The cat was treed by a dog.* ❑ *v.* **treed, tree·ing. —tree′like′,** *adj.*

bark up the wrong tree, to pursue the wrong object or use the wrong means to get it.

up a tree, INFORMAL. in a difficult position.

tree farm, place where trees are grown as a business: *Their tree farm grows fruit trees and Christmas trees.*

tree fern, any of various ferns of tropical regions that grow to the size of a tree, with woody, trunklike stems and fronds at the top.

tree frog, any of numerous tree-dwelling frogs, most with adhesive disks on their feet and the ability to change color.

tree·house (trē′hous′), *n.* a small house or platform built in the branches of a tree, usually for children to play in. ❑ *n., pl.* **tree·hous·es** (trē′hou′ziz).

treehouse

tree·less (trē′lis), *adj.* without trees: *They trekked across the treeless plain.* **—tree′less·ness,** *n.*

tree line, timberline.

tree surgery, the treatment of diseased or damaged trees by filling holes, cutting away parts, etc.

tree toad, tree frog.

tree·top (trē′top′), *n.* the top or uppermost part of a tree.

tre·foil (trē′foil), *n.* **1** any of various plants with threefold leaves. Clover is a trefoil. **2** ornament like a threefold leaf.

trek (trek), **1** *v.* to travel slowly by any means: *The soldiers forced the Cherokee to trek from their homes in Georgia to Oklahoma.* **2** *n.* a journey: *Many died on the long trek.* ❑ *v.* **trekked, trek·king. —trek·ker,** *n.*

trel·lis (trel′is), *n.* a frame of light strips of wood or metal crossing one another with open spaces in between, especially one supporting growing vines. ❑ *n., pl.* **trel·lis·es. —trel′lis·like′,** *adj.*

trem·a·tode (trem′ə tōd), *n.* any of numerous parasitic flatworms with suckers and sometimes hooks; fluke.

trem·ble (trem′bəl), **1** *v.* to shake because of fear, excitement, weakness, cold, etc.: *The child's voice trembled with fear.* ■ See Synonym Study at **shake. 2** *v.* to feel fear, anxiety, etc.: *We trembled for the safety of the trapped miners.* **3** *v.* to move gently: *The leaves trembled in the breeze.* **4** *n.* act of trembling: *There was a tremble in her voice as she began to recite.* ❑ *v.* **trem·bled, trem· bling. —trem′bler,** *n.* **—trem′bling·ly,** *adv.*

trem·bly (trem′blē), *adj.* trembling; tremulous. ❑ *adj.* **trem·bli·er, trem·bli·est.**

tre·men·dous (tri men′dəs), *adj.* **1** very great; enormous: *That is a tremendous house for a family of three.* **2** very good; extraordinary: *We had a tremendous time at the party.* **—tre·men′- dous·ly,** *adv.* **—tre·men′dous·ness,** *n.*

trem·o·lo (trem′ə lō), *n.* **1** a rapid repetition of musical tones or a rapid alternation of tones, causing a trembling or vibrating effect. **2** device used to produce this effect. ❑ *n., pl.* **trem·o·los.**

trem·or (trem′ər), *n.* **1** a shaking or trembling movement which you cannot control: *a nervous tremor in the voice.* **2** thrill of emotion or excitement. **3** a shaking or vibrating movement. An earthquake is sometimes called an earth tremor.

trem·u·lous (trem′yə ləs), *adj.* **1** trembling; quivering: *The child's voice was tremulous with sobs.* **2** timid; fearful: *He was*

shy and tremulous in the presence of strangers. **—trem′u·lous·ly,** *adv.* **—trem′u·lous·ness,** *n.*

trench (trench), **1** *n.* any ditch; deep furrow: *to dig a trench for a sewer pipe.* **2** *n.* a long, narrow ditch with earth thrown up in front to protect soldiers. **3** *n.* a long, narrow valley in the ocean floor: *The deepest trenches of the Pacific are much deeper than the Grand Canyon.* **4** *v.* to dig a trench in. ❑ *n., pl.* **trench·es.**

WORD STORY **Trench** comes from a Latin word meaning "to cut." A trench looks like a slice cut in the earth. **Trench coats** date back to World War I, when soldiers spent years in wet trenches and needed good coats.

trench coat, kind of belted raincoat with straps on the shoulders and cuffs. [See Word Story at **trench.**]

trench foot, a foot disease like frostbite, caused by prolonged exposure to cold and wet.

trench mouth, a contagious, painful bacterial infection of the mouth, causing sores on the gums, cheeks, and tongue.

trend (trend), **1** *n.* the general direction; course; tendency: *The trend in electronics is towards tiny components.* **2** *v.* to have a general direction; tend; run: *Modern life trends toward less formal customs.*

trend·y (tren′dē), *adj.* fashionable; stylish: *a trendy design.* ❑ *adj.* **trend·i·er, trend·i·est. —tren′di·ness,** *n.*

Tren·ton (trent′n), *n.* capital of New Jersey, in the W part, on the Delaware River. [Trenton is named for a man named Trent, who founded it.]

trep·i·da·tion (trep′ə dā′shən), *n.* nervous dread; fear; fright.

tres·pass (tres′pəs), **1** *v.* to go on somebody's property without any right: *We put up "No Trespassing" signs on our land.* ■ See Synonym Study at **enter. 2** *v.* to go beyond the limits of what is right, proper, or polite: *I won't trespass on your time any longer.* **3** *n.* act or fact of trespassing. **4** *v.* to do wrong; sin. **5** *n.* a wrong; a sin. **6** *n.* an unlawful act done by force against the person, property, or rights of another. ❑ *n., pl.* **tres·pass·es. —tres′pass·er,** *n.*

tress (tres), *n.* **1** a lock, curl, or braid of hair. **2 tresses,** *pl.* long, flowing hair: *golden tresses.*

tres·tle (tres′əl), *n.* **1** framework similar to a sawhorse, used as a support for a table top, platform, etc. **2** a braced framework of timber, steel, etc., used as a bridge to support a road or railroad tracks.

trey (trā), *n.* card, die, or domino with three spots. ❑ *n., pl.* **treys.** ■ Another word that sounds like this is **tray.**

tri-, *prefix.* **1** having three ___: *triangle = a shape having three angles.* **2** into three ___: *trisect = divide into three parts.* **3** once every three ___: *trimonthly = once every three months.*

tri·ad (trī′ad), *n.* **1** group of three, especially of three closely related persons or things. **2** (in music) a chord of three tones.

tri·al (trī′əl), **1** *n.* a formal examination and deciding of a case in court: *The suspect was brought to trial.* **2** *n.* process of trying or testing the fitness, truth, strength, or other quality of anything: *the trial of a new software program.* **3** *adj.* for a try or test: *a trial run, a trial model.* **4** *n.* trouble; hardship: *The pioneers faced many trials.* **5** *n.* cause of trouble or hardship: *to be a trial to your parents.* **6** *n.* an attempt or effort to do something.

on trial, 1 being tried or tested: *He is here for two weeks on trial.* **2** being tried in a court of law: *The suspect goes on trial next Monday.*

SYNONYM STUDY **Trial, experiment,** and **test** all mean the process of learning about something by trying to do it or use it. **Trial** is a general word: *After repeated trials, we learned how to make fudge.* **Experiment** suggests a carefully planned trial, especially to learn scientific facts: *Her experiment involves growing radishes without light.* **Test** suggests a thorough trial, often an official one: *Government tests make sure that food is safe to eat.*

trial and error, method of arriving at a desired result by repeated experiments until errors are eliminated.

a	hat	ė	term	ô	order	ch	child		
ā	age	i	it	oi	oil	ng	long	⎧	a in about
ä	far	ī	ice	ou	out	sh	she		e in taken
â	care	o	hot	u	cup	th	thin	ə ⎨	i in pencil
e	let	ō	open	u̇	put	ŦH	then		o in lemon
ē	equal	ô	saw	ü	rule	zh	measure	⎩	u in circus

T

tri·an·gle (trī/ang/gəl), *n.* **1** a plane figure having three sides and three angles. **2** something shaped like a triangle. **3** a musical instrument consisting of a steel bar bent into this shape, open at one corner, that is struck with a steel rod.

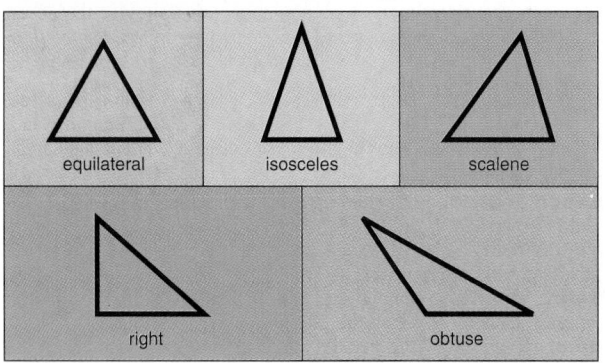

equilateral   isosceles   scalene

right   obtuse

triangles (def. 1)

tri·an·gu·lar (trī ang/gyə lər), *adj.* shaped like a triangle; three-cornered. —**tri·an/gu·lar·ly,** *adv.*

Tri·as·sic (trī as/ik), *n.* (in geology) time between about 230 million and 180 million years ago. During this time, dinosaurs and primitive mammals first appeared, and reptiles dominated the earth.

tri·ath·lete (trī ath/lēt), *n.* one who takes part in a triathlon.

tri·ath·lon (trī ath/lon), *n.* an athletic contest combining a lengthy swim, bicycle ride, and run.

trib·al (trī/bəl), *adj.* of or like a tribe: *tribal customs.*

tribe (trīb), *n.* **1** group of people sharing the same customs, language, and ancestors, forming a community under one leader or group of leaders. **2** class or set of people: *a tribe of hungry children.*

> **USAGE NOTE**   Tribe is a word that some people object to, while other people don't. It is wise to consider your sources and your audience in choosing whether to use this word. If in doubt, ask. Other words you can use instead include *community, people,* and sometimes *nation.*

tribes·man (trībz/mən), *n.* member of a tribe. ❑ *n., pl.* **tribes·men.**

trib·u·la·tion (trib/yə lā/shən), *n.* great trouble; severe trial; affliction: *The castaways on the desert island suffered many tribulations.*

tri·bu·nal (trī byü/nl *or* trī byü/nl), *n.* **1** court of justice; place of judgment: *They were brought before the tribunal of seven judges for trial.* **2** something by or in which judgment is given; deciding authority: *the tribunal of the polls, the tribunal of the press.*

trib·une (trib/yün), *n.* **1** official in ancient Rome chosen by the plebeians to protect their rights and interests. **2** defender of the people.

trib·u·tar·y (trib/yə ter/ē), **1** *n.* stream or river that flows into a larger one: *The Ohio River is one of the tributaries of the Mississippi River.* **2** *adj.* flowing into a larger stream or river. **3** *adj.* paying tribute; required to pay tribute. **4** *n.* a person or country that pays tribute. ❑ *n., pl.* **trib·u·tar·ies.**

trib·ute (trib/yüt), *n.* **1** something done or given to show thanks or respect; compliment: *Labor Day is a tribute to workers.* **2** money paid by one nation to another for peace or protection or because of some agreement. **3** any forced payment: *The pirates demanded tribute from passing ships.*

trice (trīs), *n.* **in a trice,** in a very short time; in a moment: *I'll open the gate in a trice.* [**Trice** comes from a Dutch word meaning "pulley." In old English, **trice** meant "a pull," and **in a trice** meant "with one tug."]

tri·ceps (trī/seps), *n.* the large muscle at the back of the upper arm. It extends or straightens the arm. See picture at **biceps.** ❑ *n., pl.* **tri·ceps.**

tri·cer·a·tops (trī ser/ə tops), *n.* a plant-eating dinosaur with a large horn above each eye, a smaller horn on the nose, a bony shield over the back of the neck, and a long and powerful tail. ❑ *n., pl.* **tri·cer·a·tops·es.**

tri·chi·na (trī kī/nə), *n.* a small roundworm that lives in the bodies of human beings, pigs, and some other animals, in the in-testines as an adult but throughout the body as a larva, causing trichinosis. Trichinae usually get into the human body from pork infected with the larvae and not cooked long enough to destroy them. ❑ *n., pl.* **tri·chi·nae** (trī kī/nē), **tri·chi·nas.**

trich·i·no·sis (trik/ə nō/sis), *n.* disease due to the presence of trichinae, in which the symptoms are headache, chills, fever, and soreness of muscles.

trick (trik), **1** *n.* something done to deceive or cheat: *The false message was a trick to get her to leave the house.* **2** *v.* to deceive; cheat: *We were tricked into buying a stolen sailboat.* ■ See Synonym Study at **cheat. 3** *n.* demonstration of skill, as in juggling or sleight of hand; clever act: *We enjoyed the tricks of the trained animals.* **4** *n.* the best way of doing or dealing with something: *She knows the trick of restoring old furniture.* **5** *n.* piece of mischief; prank; joke: *Hiding my lunch was a mean trick.* **6** *adj.* of, like, or done as a trick or stunt: *trick riding.* **7** *n.* a peculiar habit or way of acting: *He has a trick of pulling at his collar.* **8** *n.* the cards played in one round of a card game. **9** *n.* a turn or period of duty on a job, especially at steering a ship. **10** *v.* to dress: *The guests were all tricked up in fancy clothes.* —**trick/er,** *n.*
do the trick or **turn the trick,** to do what you want done.

trick·er·y (trik/ər ē), *n.* use of tricks; deception; cheating: *He tried to sell me a bike with a broken chain, but I saw through his trickery.*

trick·le (trik/əl), **1** *v.* to flow or cause to flow in drops or in a small stream: *Tears trickled down their cheeks. He trickled water over the flowers.* **2** *n.* a small flow or stream. **3** *v.* to come, go, pass, etc., slowly and unevenly: *An hour before the show people began to trickle into the theater.* ❑ *v.* **trick·led, trick·ling.** —**trick/-ling·ly,** *adv.*

trick or treat, a children's custom of going from door to door on Halloween dressed in costume and asking for gifts of candy, fruit, and the like, by saying "trick or treat."

trick·ster (trik/stər), *n.* **1** a cheat; deceiver. **2** character, especially in myth or legend, known for cleverness and for deceiving or outwitting others. Coyote, Loki, and Mercury are tricksters.

trick·y (trik/ē), *adj.* **1** not doing what is expected; dangerous or difficult to handle: *The back door has a tricky lock.* **2** full of tricks; deceiving: *a tricky person.* ❑ *adj.* **trick·i·er, trick·i·est.** —**trick/i·ly,** *adv.* —**trick/i·ness,** *n.*

tri·col·or (trī/kul/ər), **1** *adj.* having three colors. **2** *n.* flag having three colors. The tricolor of France has three equal vertical sections of blue, white, and red.

tri·col·ored (trī/kul/ərd), *adj.* having three colors: *a tricolored flag.*

tri·cot (trē/kō), *n.* **1** a knitted fabric made by hand or machine. **2** a kind of woolen cloth.

tricolor (def. 2)

tri·cus·pid (trī kus/pid), **1** *n.* a tooth having three points. **2** *adj.* having three points.

tri·cy·cle (trī/sə kəl *or* trī/sik/əl), *n.* vehicle with three wheels, propelled by pedals.

tri·dent (trīd/nt), *n.* a three-pronged spear, especially the spear carried by Neptune, or Poseidon, god of the sea.

tried (trīd), **1** *adj.* tested by experience or examination; proven: *a person of tried abilities.* **2** *v.* past tense and past participle of **try:** *I tried to call you. Have you tried calling again?*

tri·en·ni·al (trī en/ē əl), **1** *adj.* lasting three years. **2** *adj.* occurring every three years. **3** *n.* event that occurs every three years.

tries (trīz), **1** *n.* plural of **try:** *After several tries, I gave up.* **2** *v.* present tense of **try:** *She always tries to do her best.*

tri·fle (trī/fəl), **1** *n.* a small amount; little bit: *He was a trifle late.* **2** *n.* thing having little value or importance. **3** *n.* a small amount of money: *The picture cost only a trifle.* **4** *v.* to talk or act lightly, not seriously: *Don't trifle with serious matters.* **5** *v.* to handle a thing idly; play or toy with: *She trifled with her pencil.* **6** *v.* to spend time, effort, money, etc., on things having little value: *They trifled away the whole morning.* ❑ *v.* **tri·fled, tri·fling.** —**tri/fler,** *n.*

tri·fling (trī′fling), *adj.* **1** having little value; not important; small: *The friends treated their quarrel as only a trifling matter.* ■ See Synonym Study at **unimportant**. **2** frivolous; shallow. —**tri′-fling·ly**, *adv.*

trig·ger (trig′ər), **1** *n.* the small lever pulled back by the finger in firing a gun. **2** *n.* lever pulled or pressed to release a spring or catch and set some mechanism in action. **3** *v.* to set off an explosion: *A spark triggered the explosion.* **4** *v.* to initiate; start: *trigger an outburst of violence.* **5** *n.* anything that sets off or initiates something else.

trig·o·no·met·ric (trig′ə nə met′rik), *adj.* of or about trigonometry. —**trig′o·no·met′ri·cal·ly**, *adv.*

trig·o·nom·e·try (trig′ə nom′ə trē), *n.* branch of mathematics that deals with the relations between the sides and angles of triangles and the calculations based on these.

trill (tril), **1** *v.* to sing, play, sound, or speak with a tremulous, vibrating sound: *Some birds trill their songs.* **2** *n.* act or sound of trilling. **3** *n.* a quick alternation of two musical notes either a tone or a half tone apart. **4** *n.* in phonetics: **a** a rapid vibration of the lips, the tip of the tongue, or the uvula. **b** sound produced by such a vibration.

tril·lion (tril′yən), *n., adj.* **1** (in the United States and Canada) 1 followed by 12 zeros; one thousand billions. **2** (in Great Britain, France, and Germany) 1 followed by 18 zeros; one million billions.

tril·lionth (tril′yənth), *adj., n.* **1** last in a series of a trillion. **2** one of a trillion equal parts.

tril·li·um (tril′ē əm), *n.* any of several plants with three leaves in a whorl from the center of which rises a single flower. The white trillium is the provincial flower of Ontario.

tri·lo·bite (trī′lə bīt), *n.* any of a great many small sea animals that lived hundreds of millions of years ago. A trilobite had a body divided into three lobes, the middle one with many segments. Fossil trilobites are widely found in various rocks.

tril·o·gy (tril′ə jē), *n.* group of three plays, operas, novels, etc., which together form a related series, although each is a complete work in itself. ❑ *n., pl.* **tril·o·gies**.

trim (trim), **1** *v.* to put in good order; make neat by cutting away parts: *The gardener trimmed the hedge. Would you trim my hair?* **2** *v.* to remove parts that are not needed or not neat: *trim dead leaves off plants.* **3** *adj.* neat; in good condition or order: *a trim uniform, a trim athlete.* ■ See Synonym Study at **neat**. **4** *adj.* well designed and maintained: *We saw a trim little sailboat out on the lake.* **5** *n.* good condition or order: *get in trim for a race.* **6** *n.* condition; order: *That ship is in poor trim for a voyage.* **7** *n.* anything used to trim or decorate: *the trim on a coat.* **8** *v.* to decorate: *The children trimmed the Christmas tree.* **9** *v.* to balance a boat, aircraft, etc., by arranging the load carried. **10** *n.* such balance. **11** *v.* to arrange the sails to fit wind and direction. **12** *n.* the visible woodwork inside a building, especially that around doors, windows, and other openings. **13** *v.* INFORMAL. to defeat; beat. ❑ *v.* **trimmed, trim·ming;** *adj.* **trim·mer, trim·mest.** —**trim′ly**, *adv.* —**trim′mer**, *n.* —**trim′ness**, *n.*

tri·mes·ter (trī mes′tər *or* trī′mes′tər), *n.* one third of a school year or of a pregnancy.

trim·ming (trim′ing), *n.* **1** anything used to trim or decorate; decoration; ornament: *trimming for a shirt.* **2** INFORMAL. a defeat; beating. **3** act of someone or something that trims. **4 trimmings,** *pl.* **a** parts cut away in trimming: *hedge trimmings.* **b** everything needed to make something complete and festive: *turkey with all the trimmings.*

tri·month·ly (trī munth′lē), *adj.* occurring every three months.

Trin·i·dad (trin′ə dad), *n.* island in the West Indies, near Venezuela, part of the country of Trinidad and Tobago.

WORD STORY   Trinidad comes from a Spanish word meaning "trinity." In 1498, Columbus named the island for three high mountains that a member of his crew saw there.

Trinidad and Tobago, country composed of two islands in the West Indies. *Capital:* Port-of-Spain.

tri·ni·tro·tol·u·ene (trī nī′trō tol′yü ēn′), *n.* See **TNT**.

trin·i·ty (trin′ə tē), *n.* **1 Trinity,** (in Christian religious use) the union of Father, Son, and Holy Spirit in one divine nature. **2** group of three. ❑ *n., pl.* **trin·i·ties** for 2.

trin·ket (tring′kit), *n.* any small fancy article, bit of jewelry, or the like.

tri·no·mi·al (trī nō′mē əl), **1** *n.* expression in algebra containing three terms connected by plus or minus signs. The expression $a + bx^2 - 2$ is a trinomial. **2** *n.* the scientific name of a living thing, containing three terms, to show a subspecies or variety. **3** *adj.* containing three terms.

tri·o (trē′ō), *n.* **1** group of three singers or players performing together. **2** piece of music for three voices or instruments. **3** any group of three. ❑ *n., pl.* **tri·os**.

tri·ode (trī′ōd), *n.* a vacuum tube that contains a cathode, an anode, and a control grid.

trip (trip), **1** *n.* act of traveling about; journey; voyage: *We took a trip to Europe.* **2** *v.* to stumble: *He tripped on the stairs.* **3** *n.* a loss of footing; stumble; slip. **4** *v.* to cause to stumble and fall: *The loose board on the stairs tripped her.* **5** *v.* to make a mistake; do something wrong: *She tripped on that difficult question.* **6** *v.* to cause to make a mistake or blunder: *The difficult question tripped him.* **7** *v.* to take light, quick steps: *The children came tripping down the path to meet us.* **8** *n.* a light, quick tread; nimble step. **9** *v.* to release or operate a catch, clutch, etc., suddenly; operate, start, or set free a mechanism, weight, etc. **10** *n.* a projecting part, catch, or the like for starting or checking some movement. **11** *n.* SLANG. period of time when a person is under the influence of LSD or another psychedelic drug, during which she or he may experience intense, heightened perception and hallucinations. **12** *v.* SLANG. to take LSD or another hallucinogenic drug. **13** *n.* SLANG. an exciting experience of any kind. ❑ *v.* **tripped, trip·ping.**

SYNONYM STUDY   Trip, journey, and voyage all mean the act of going some distance. **Trip** is a general word: *Our class trip was to Washington.* **Journey** means a long trip: *The journey took several weeks.* **Voyage** means a long trip, especially by ship: *I was seasick on the voyage out.*

tri·par·tite (trī pär′tīt), *adj.* **1** divided into three parts. **2** made or shared by three parties: *a tripartite treaty between Great Britain, the United States, and France.*

tripe (trip), *n.* **1** the walls of the first and second stomachs of an ox, steer, or cow, used as food. **2** something foolish, worthless, or offensive.

trip·ham·mer (trip′ham′ər), *n.* a heavy iron or steel block raised by machinery and then tripped by a mechanism and allowed to drop.

tri·ple (trip′əl), **1** *adj.* having three parts: *a triple crown.* **2** *v.* to make or become three times as much or as many: *The number of club members has tripled this year.* **3** *adj.* three times as much or as many: *a triple portion of cake, to get triple pay.* **4** *n.* number or amount that is three times as large: *Nine is the triple of three.* **5** *n.* hit by which a batter gets to third base in baseball. **6** *v.* to make such a hit: *The batter tripled in the third inning.* ❑ *v.* **tri·pled, tri·pling.**

triple play, play in baseball in which three base runners are put out.

trip·let (trip′lit), *n.* **1** one of three children born at the same time of the same mother. **2** group of three. **3** (in music) group of three notes of equal value to be performed in the time of two. **4** three successive lines of poetry, usually rhyming and equal in length.

trip·li·cate (trip′lə kit *for adj., noun;* trip′lə kāt *for verb*), **1** *adj.* triple; threefold. **2** *n.* one of three things exactly alike. **3** *v.* to make threefold; triple. ❑ *v.* **trip·li·cat·ed, trip·li·cat·ing.** —**trip′li·ca′tion**, *n.*

in triplicate, in three copies exactly alike.

tri·ply (trip′lē), *adv.* in a triple manner; three times.

tri·pod (trī′pod), *n.* **1** a three-legged support or stand for a camera, telescope, etc. **2** stool or other article having three legs.

a	hat	ė	term	ȯ	order	ch	child		
ā	age	i	it	oi	oil	ng	long		a in about
ä	far	ī	ice	ou	out	sh	she		e in taken
â	care	o	hot	u	cup	th	thin	ə	i in pencil
e	let	ō	open	u̇	put	ŦH	then		o in lemon
ē	equal	ȯ	saw	ü	rule	zh	measure		u in circus

Trip·o·li (trip′ə lē), *n.* **1** region in N Africa. It was a Turkish province and later an Italian colony; it is now part of Libya. **2** port and capital of Libya, in the NW part.

trip·ping·ly (trip′ing lē), *adv.* lightly, easily, or quickly.

trip·tych (trip′tik), *n.* set of three panels side by side, having pictures, carvings, or the like, on them. ❑ *n., pl.* **trip·tychs.**

tri·sect (trī sekt′), *v.* to divide into three usually equal parts. —**tri·sec′tion,** *n.* —**tri·sec′tor,** *n.*

tri·ser·vice (trī sėr′vis), *adj.* CANADIAN. of or about the three elements of the Canadian armed forces: air element, land element, sea element.

trite (trīt), *adj.* worn out by use; no longer interesting; commonplace: *"Busy as a bee" is a trite expression.* ❑ *adj.* **trit·er, trit·est.** —**trite′ly,** *adv.* —**trite′ness,** *n.*

trit·i·um (trit′ē əm), *n.* a radioactive isotope of hydrogen, three times as heavy as ordinary hydrogen. It is the explosive used in a hydrogen bomb.

tri·ton (trīt′n), *n.* **1** any of various sea animals that are like large snails with brightly colored, spiral, trumpet-shaped shells. **2** shell of such an animal. **3 Triton,** a Greek sea god with the head and body of a man and the tail of a fish.

tri·umph (trī′umf), **1** *n.* victory; success: *final triumph over the enemy. The exploration of outer space is a great triumph of modern science.* ■ See Synonym Study at **victory. 2** *v.* to gain victory; win success: *Our team triumphed over theirs.* **3** *n.* joy because of victory or success: *We welcomed the team home with cheers of triumph.* [See word history information at **trump**[1].]

tri·um·phal (trī um′fəl), *adj.* of or for a triumph; celebrating a victory: *a triumphal march.*

triumphant (def. 2)

tri·um·phant (trī um′fənt), *adj.* **1** victorious or successful: *a triumphant army.* **2** rejoicing because of victory or success: *The winners spoke in triumphant tones about their skillful play.* —**tri·um′phant·ly,** *adv.*

tri·um·vir (trī um′vər), *n.* (in ancient Rome) one of three men who shared the same public office. ❑ *n., pl.* **tri·um·virs, tri·um·vi·ri** (trī um′və rī′).

tri·um·vir·ate (trī um′vər it), *n.* **1** any association of three in office or authority. **2** any group of three. **3** government by three persons together.

triv·et (triv′it), *n.* a stand or support with three legs or feet. Trivets are used over fires and under hot platters.

triv·i·a (triv′ē ə), *n.pl.* things of little or no importance; trifles; trivialities.

triv·i·al (triv′ē əl), *adj.* not important; trifling; insignificant: *Your composition had only a few trivial mistakes.* —**triv′i·al·ly,** *adv.* —**triv′i·al·ness,** *n.*

WORD STORY Trivial comes from Latin words meaning "three roads." Where big roads meet today, there are motels, gas stations, and restaurants, and often not much else. In ancient times, there were stables and taverns, and often not much else. So the Romans used "crossroads town" as a symbol of little, unimportant things.

triv·i·al·i·ty (triv′ē al′ə tē), *n.* **1** trivial quality. **2** a trivial thing, remark, affair, etc.; trifle. ❑ *n., pl.* **triv·i·al·i·ties** for 2.

triv·i·al·ize (triv′ē ə līz), *v.* to cause to seem trivial, unimportant, etc. ❑ *v.* **triv·i·al·ized, triv·i·al·iz·ing.** —**triv′i·al·i·za′tion,** *n.*

tri·week·ly (trī wēk′lē), **1** *adv.* once every three weeks. **2** *adv.* three times a week. **3** *n.* newspaper or magazine published triweekly. **4** *adj.* occurring or appearing triweekly.

tRNA, transfer RNA.

tro·chee (trō′kē), *n.* a foot or measure in poetry consisting of two syllables, the first accented and the second unaccented. EXAMPLE: "Man′y | peo′ple | won′der | how′ the | clouds′ make | thun′der." ❑ *n., pl.* **tro·chees.**

trod (trod), *v.* past tense and a past participle of **tread:** *He just trod on my toe. The path has been trod by many feet.*

trod·den (trod′n), *v.* a past participle of **tread:** *The cattle had trodden down the corn.*

Troi·lus (troi′ləs), *n.* (in Greek legends) a son of King Priam of Troy. He was killed by Achilles.

Tro·jan (trō′jən), **1** *adj.* of or about Troy or its people. **2** *n.* person who was born or lived in Troy. **3** *n.* person who shows courage or energy: *They worked like Trojans.*

Trojan horse, (in Greek legends) a huge wooden horse in which the Greeks concealed soldiers. Trojans brought the horse into Troy, believing it to be a sacrifice. At night the Greeks crept out of the horse and opened the gates of Troy to the Greek army, ending the Trojan War.

Trojan War, (in Greek legends) a ten years' war fought by the Greeks against Troy to get back Helen, wife of King Menelaus of Sparta, who was carried off by Paris, son of King Priam of Troy.

troll[1] (trōl), *v.* **1** to fish with a moving line, usually by trailing the line behind the boat near the surface: *I trolled for bass.* **2** to sing in succession the parts of a song: *troll a round.* —**troll′er,** *n.*

troll[2] (trōl), *n.* (in Scandinavian folklore) an ugly dwarf or giant living underground or in a cave.

trol·ley (trol′ē), *n.* **1** a grooved wheel at the end of a pole that moves along a wire and carries electricity to a streetcar or an electric engine. A **trolley car** or **trolley bus** is a streetcar or bus with such a wheel. **2** basket, carriage, etc., hung from a grooved wheel that runs along an overhead track. ❑ *n., pl.* **trol·leys.**

trom·bone (trom′bōn *or* trom bōn′), *n.* a large brass wind instrument with a loud tone, with a long, sliding piece for changing the length of the tube to produce various tones.

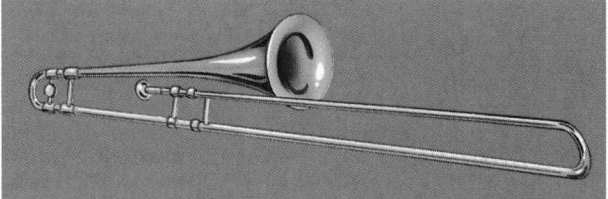

trombone

trom·bon·ist (trom′bō nist), *n.* person who plays the trombone.

troop (trüp), **1** *n.pl.* **troops,** soldiers: *The government sent troops to put down the revolt.* **2** *n.* group or band of persons: *a troop of children.* **3** *n.* a herd, flock, or swarm: *a troop of deer.* **4** *n.* a military unit of cavalry, especially an armored cavalry unit, usually commanded by a captain. **5** *n.* unit of Boy Scouts, Girl Scouts, or Girl Guides made up of two to four patrols or 16 to 32 members. **6** *v.* to gather in a group; move together: *The children trooped around the teacher.* **7** *v.* to walk; go; go away: *The younger children trooped off after the older ones.* ■ Another word that sounds like this is **troupe.**

troop·er (trü′pər), *n.* **1** soldier in the cavalry. **2** a mounted police officer. The state police of some states are called troopers, because they formerly rode horses. **3** a cavalry horse. ■ Another word that sounds like this is **trouper.**

troop·ship (trüp′ship′), *n.* ship used to carry soldiers; transport.

tro·phy (trō′fē), *n.* **1** any prize, cup, etc., awarded to a victorious person or team: *The champion kept her tennis trophies on the mantel.* ■ See Synonym Study at **prize**[1]. **2** a spoil or prize of war, hunting, etc.: *The hunter kept the deer's antlers as a trophy.* **3** anything serving as a remembrance. ❑ *n., pl.* **tro·phies.**

trop·ic (trop′ik), **1** *n.* either of two imaginary circles around the earth at the points farthest north and south where the sun can shine directly overhead. The **tropic of Cancer** is 23.45 degrees north of the equator; the **tropic of Capricorn** is 23.45 degrees south of the equator. **2** *n.pl.* **tropics** or **Tropics,** the regions between and near these circles; the Torrid Zone. The hottest part of the earth is in the tropics. **3** *adj.* of or about the tropics; belonging to the Torrid Zone.

trop·i·cal (trop′ə kəl), *adj.* of or like the tropics: *tropical heat. Bananas are tropical fruit.* **—trop′i·cal·ly,** *adv.*

tropical fish, any of various small, usually brightly colored fishes found in the tropics, commonly kept in home aquariums.

tro·pism (trō′piz əm), *n.* tendency of a living thing to turn or move in response to a stimulus, such as light or gravity.

trop·o·pause (trop′ə pòz), *n.* the region of the atmosphere that is the boundary between the troposphere and the stratosphere.

trop·o·sphere (trop′ə sfir), *n.* region of the atmosphere between the earth and the stratosphere, extending to about 10 miles (16 kilometers) above the earth's surface. Within the troposphere, there is a steady fall of temperature with increasing altitude. Most cloud formations and weather systems occur in the troposphere.

trot (trot), **1** *v.* to go at a gait between a walk and a run by lifting the right forefoot and the left hind foot at about the same time and then the other two feet in the same way. Horses and some other four-legged animals trot. **2** *n.* the motion or gait of trotting. **3** *v.* to ride or drive at a trot: *The riders trotted home.* **4** *v.* to run, but not fast: *The child trotted after me.* **5** *n.* a brisk, steady movement; a slow running. ❑ *v.* **trot·ted, trot·ting.**

Trot·sky (trot′skē), *n.* **Le·on** (lē′on), 1879-1940, leader in the Russian Revolution and Soviet minister of war from 1918 to 1925. He was later exiled and was assassinated in Mexico.

trot·ter (trot′ər), *n.* horse that trots, especially one bred and trained to trot in a race.

trou·ba·dour (trü′bə dôr), *n.* one of the lyric poets and composers of southern France, eastern Spain, and northern Italy from the 1000s to the 1200s. The troubadours wrote mainly about love and chivalry.

trou·ble (trub′əl), **1** *n.* pain and sorrow; distress; worry; difficulty: *The unruly students made trouble for their teacher.* **2** *v.* to cause trouble to; disturb: *The lack of business troubled the grocer.* **3** *n.* something that causes worry or distress; problem: *His troubles began when his car broke down in a rainstorm.* **4** *n.* extra work; bother; effort: *Take the trouble to do careful work.* **5** *v.* to require extra work or effort of: *May I trouble you to pass the sugar?* **6** *v.* to cause yourself inconvenience: *Don't trouble to come to the door; I can let myself in.* **7** *n.* a cause of inconvenience: *Is helping me a trouble to you?* **8** *n.* illness; disease: *heart trouble.* **9** *v.* to cause pain to; hurt; pain: *A toothache troubled me.* ❑ *v.* **trou·bled, trou·bling.** **—trou′bler,** *n.* **—trou′bling·ly,** *adv.*

trou·ble·mak·er (trub′əl mā′kər), *n.* person who often causes trouble for others.

trou·ble·shoot·er (trub′əl shü′tər), *n.* person who discovers and gets rid of causes of trouble for a company, government, etc.

trou·ble·some (trub′əl səm), *adj.* **1** causing trouble; disturbing; annoying: *noisy, troublesome neighbors.* **2** tiresome; difficult: *a troublesome process.* **—trou′ble·some·ly,** *adv.* **—trou′ble·some·ness,** *n.*

trough (trôf), *n.* **1** a long, narrow container for holding food or water: *We led our horses to the watering trough.* **2** channel for carrying water; gutter: *The wooden trough under the eaves of the house carries off rainwater.* **3** a long hollow between two ridges, etc.: *the trough between two waves.* **—trough′like,** *adj.*

trounce (trouns), *v.* **1** to defeat in a contest or match: *We trounced their team.* **2** to beat or thrash. ❑ *v.* **trounced, trounc·ing.**

troupe (trüp), *n.* troop, band, or company, especially a group of performers. ■ Another word that sounds like this is **troop.**

troup·er (trü′pər), *n.* **1** member of a theatrical troupe. **2** an experienced actor. **3** person who can be counted on in spite of difficulties. ■ Another word that sounds like this is **trooper.**

trou·ser (trou′zər), *adj.* of or in trousers: *a trouser leg.*

trou·sers (trou′zərz), *n.pl.* a two-legged outer article of clothing reaching from the waist to the ankles; pants.

trous·seau (trü′sō *or* trü sō′), *n.* a bride's outfit of clothes, linen, etc. ❑ *n., pl.* **trous·seaus** or **trous·seaux** (trü′sōz *or* trü sōz′).

trout (trout), *n.* any of various freshwater food and sport fishes related to salmon. ❑ *n., pl.* **trout** or **trouts.**

trow·el (trou′əl), **1** *n.* tool with a curved blade, used for taking up plants, loosening dirt, etc. **2** *n.* tool with a broad, flat blade, used for spreading or smoothing plaster or mortar. **3** *v.* to spread, smooth, or form with or as if with a trowel. ❑ *v.* **trow·eled, trow·el·ing** or **trow·elled, trow·el·ling.**

troy (troi), **1** *adj.* in or by troy weight. **2** *n.* troy weight.

Troy (troi), *n.* **1** city in the NW part of ancient Asia Minor, scene of the Trojan War. **2** city in E New York State, on the Hudson River.

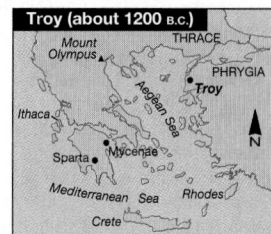
Troy (about 1200 B.C.)

troy weight, system of weights used for gems and precious metals. One pound troy equals a little more than four fifths of an ordinary pound. 12 troy ounces = 1 troy pound.

tru·an·cy (trü′ən sē), *n.* act or habit of playing truant; truant behavior.

tru·ant (trü′ənt), **1** *n.* student who stays away from school without permission. **2** *adj.* staying away from school without permission. **3** *n.* person who neglects duty. **4** *adj.* guilty of neglecting duty: *The truant factory worker left the machine running without watching it.* **5** *adj.* of or for a truant or truants: *a truant officer.*

play truant, 1 to stay away from school without permission. **2** to stay away from work or duties.

truce (trüs), *n.* a stop in fighting; temporary peace: *A truce was declared between the two armies for a week.*

truck[1] (truk), **1** *n.* a strongly built motor vehicle for carrying heavy loads. **2** *v.* to carry on a truck: *truck freight to the warehouse.* **3** *v.* to drive a truck. **4** *n.* frame on small wheels for moving trunks, etc. **5** *n.* frame with two or more pairs of wheels for supporting each end of a railroad car.

truck[2] (truk), *n.* **1** vegetables raised for market. **2** small articles of little value; odds and ends. **3** INFORMAL. rubbish; trash. **4** INFORMAL. dealings: *She has no truck with peddlers.*

truck·er (truk′ər), *n.* **1** person who drives a truck. **2** person whose business is carrying goods or other freight by trucks.

truck farm, farm where vegetables are raised for market.

truck·ing (truk′ing), *n.* act or business of carrying freight on a truck or trucks.

truck·le (truk′əl), *v.* to give up or submit tamely; yield: *Some workers got promoted by truckling to superiors and flattering them.* ❑ *v.* **truck·led, truck·ling.** **—truck′ler,** *n.*

truc·u·lence (truk′yə ləns), *n.* condition of being truculent; fierceness; brutal harshness.

truc·u·lent (truk′yə lənt), *adj.* **1** fierce, savage, or violent: *a truculent villain, a truculent defense of your rights.* **2** brutally harsh or scathing: *a truculent remark.* **—truc′u·lent·ly,** *adv.*

trudge (truj), **1** *v.* to walk wearily or with effort. **2** *n.* a hard or weary walk: *a long trudge up the hill.* ❑ *v.* **trudged, trudg·ing.** **—trudg′er,** *n.*

a	hat	ė	term	ô	order	ch	child		
ā	age	i	it	oi	oil	ng	long		a in about
ä	far	ī	ice	ou	out	sh	she		e in taken
â	care	o	hot	u	cup	th	thin	ə	i in pencil
e	let	ō	open	u̇	put	ŦH	then		o in lemon
ē	equal	ò	saw	ü	rule	zh	measure		u in circus

true (trü), **1** *adj.* correct; right; accurate; not false: *It is true that 6 and 4 are 10. The story I told is true; I did not make it up.* **2** *adj.* real; genuine: *true courage, true kindness.* **3** *adj.* faithful; loyal: *a true friend.* **4** *adj.* agreeing with a standard; right; proper; correct; exact; accurate: *a true copy.* **5** *adj.* representative of the class named: *A sweet potato is not a true potato.* **6** *adj.* rightful; lawful: *the true heir to the property.* **7** *adj.* accurately formed, fitted, or placed: *a true angle.* **8** *v.* to make true; shape, place, or make in the exact position, form, etc., required: *True up that slanting door.* **9** *adj.* steady in direction, force, etc.; unchanging: *The arrow made a true course through the air.* **10** *adv.* in a true manner; truly; exactly: *Your words ring true.* □ *adj.* **tru·er, tru·est;** *v.* **trued, tru·ing** or **true·ing.** [See Word Story at **truce.**] —**true′ness,** *n.*

come true, to happen as expected; become real.

true-blue (trü′blü′), *adj.* constant in your faith, beliefs, etc.; unchanging; loyal: *a true-blue friend.*

true-false test (trü′fôls′), a test that has statements that are to be marked either true or false.

truf·fle (truf′əl), *n.* any of several fungi of central and southern Europe that grow underground and are valued as food. A truffle resembles a potato in appearance.

tru·ism (trü′iz′əm), *n.* statement that almost everybody knows is true, such as "Good health is a blessing."

tru·ly (trü′lē), *adv.* **1** in a true manner; exactly; rightly; faithfully: *Tell me truly what you think.* **2** in fact; really: *It was truly a beautiful sight.*

Tru·man (trü′mən), *n.* **Har·ry S.** (har′ē), 1884-1972, the 33rd president of the United States, from 1945 to 1953. ■ The "S" in **Harry S. Truman** doesn't stand for anything, but Truman was famous for saying what he stood for.

trump[1] (trump), **1** *n.* any playing card of a suit that during the play of a hand ranks higher than the other suits. **2** *n.* Often, **trumps,** *pl.* the suit itself. **3** *v.* to take a trick or card with a trump. **4** *v.* to play a card of the suit that is trump. [**Trump**[1] comes from **triumph.** If a trump card is played against a card of another suit, it wins a victory.]

trump[2] (trump), *v.* to make up in order to deceive: *trump up false charges against a person.*

trump·er·y (trump′ər ē), *n.* something showy but without value; worthless ornaments; useless stuff; rubbish; nonsense.

trum·pet (trum′pit), **1** *n.* a brass wind instrument that has a powerful tone, commonly a curved tube with a flaring bell at one end. **2** *n.* thing shaped like a trumpet. Ear trumpets were once used to help people who were not able to hear well. **3** *v.* to blow a trumpet. **4** *n.* a sound like that of a trumpet. **5** *v.* to make a sound like that of a trumpet: *The elephant trumpeted in fright.* **6** *v.* to proclaim loudly or widely: *trumpet a story all over town.* —**trum′pet·er,** *n.* —**trum′pet·like′,** *adj.*

trumpet creeper, bignonia.

trum·pet·er swan (trum′pi tər), the largest kind of swan, found in the northwestern United States and western Canada. Trumpeter swans have a deep, trumpeting call.

trumpet vine, bignonia.

trun·cate (trung′kāt), **1** *v.* to cut off a part of. **2** *adj.* cut off; blunt, as if cut off: *the truncate leaf of the tulip tree.* □ *v.* **trun·cat·ed, trun·cat·ing.** —**trun′cate·ly,** *adv.* —**trun·ca′tion,** *n.*

trun·cheon (trun′chən), *n.* a short stick used as a weapon by police officers; nightstick.

trun·dle (trun′dl), **1** *v.* to roll along; push along: *The worker trundled a wheelbarrow up a ramp.* **2** *n.* trundle bed. □ *v.* **trun·dled, trun·dling.** —**trun′dler,** *n.*

trundle bed, a low bed on small wheels. It can be pushed under a regular bed when not in use.

trunk (trungk), **1** *n.* the main stem of a tree, from which the branches and roots grow. **2** *n.* a big, sturdy box with a hinged lid, for holding clothes. **3** *n.* the long, flexible snout of an elephant. **4** *n.* an enclosed compartment in the rear of a car for storing baggage, a spare tire, etc. **5** *n.* the main part of anything: *the trunk of a column.* **6** *adj.* main; chief: *a railroad trunk line.* **7** *n.* a human or animal body, not including the head, arms, and legs. **8**

n.pl. **trunks,** very short pants worn by men and boys for swimming, boxing, etc. —**trunk′less,** *adj.* —**trunk′like′,** *adj.*

truss (trus), **1** *v.* to tie or fasten; bind: *truss up a prisoner hand and foot.* **2** *v.* to fasten the wings or legs of a fowl with twine or skewers before cooking it. **3** *n.* framework of beams or other supports, usually connected in a series of triangles and used to support a roof, bridge, etc. **4** *v.* to support a roof, bridge, etc., with trusses. **5** *n.* pad attached to a belt, used to support a hernia. □ *n., pl.* **truss·es.** —**truss′er,** *n.*

trust (trust), **1** *v.* to believe firmly in the honesty, truth, justice, or power of; have faith in: *a person you can trust.* **2** *n.* firm belief in the honesty, truthfulness, justice, or power of someone or something; faith: *The children put trust in their parents.* **3** *v.* to have faith; believe; rely: *Trust in me.* **4** *v.* to rely on; depend on: *If you can't trust your memory, write things down.* **5** *n.* confident expectation or hope: *Our trust is that she will soon be well.* **6** *v.* to hope; believe: *I trust you will soon feel better.* **7** *n.* something managed for the benefit of another; something committed to your care: *The house is a trust which she holds for her dead brother's children.* **8** *n.* duty or responsibility that someone takes on when given confidence or authority: *Congress has a public trust.* **9** *n.* keeping; care: *The will was left in an attorney's trust.* **10** *adj.* managing for an owner. A trust company undertakes to manage property for anyone. **11** *v.* to commit to the care of; leave without fear: *Can I trust the keys to them?* **12** *n.* confidence in the ability or intention of someone to pay at some future time for goods, etc.; business credit: *to sell on trust.* **13** *v.* to give business credit to: *They trusted us for the balance of the payments on the refrigerator.* **14** *n.* an illegal combination of companies to control the production and price of some commodity and to eliminate or reduce competition. **15** *adj.* of or about a trust or trusts; held in trust. —**trust′a·ble,** *adj.* —**trust′er,** *n.*

in trust, as a thing taken charge of for another.

trust to, to rely on; depend on: *trust to luck.*

SYNONYM STUDY **Trust, rely,** and **depend** all mean to believe firmly that a person will do exactly what he or she says. **Trust** is a general word: *I trust you to keep my secret.* **Rely** and **depend** suggest belief that another person will take care of a need: *She relies on her guide dog when she crosses a street. They depend on him to help with the younger children.*

trus·tee (tru stē′), *n.* person responsible for the property or affairs of another person, a company, or an institution: *A trustee will manage his property until he grows up.* □ *n., pl.* **trus·tees.**

trus·tee·ship (tru stē′ship), *n.* **1** position of trustee. **2** administration by a country of a trust territory. **3** trust territory.

trust·ful (trust′fəl), *adj.* ready to have faith; trusting; believing: *The trustful child would lend money to anyone.* —**trust′ful·ly,** *adv.* —**trust′ful·ness,** *n.*

trust fund, money, property, or other valuables held in trust by one person for the benefit of another.

trust·ing (trus′ting), *adj.* trustful. —**trust′ing·ly,** *adv.* —**trust′ing·ness,** *n.*

trust territory, a territory or region administered by a country or countries on behalf of the United Nations.

trust·wor·thy (trust′wėr′ᴛʜē), *adj.* able to be depended on; reliable: *a trustworthy person.* —**trust′wor′thi·ness,** *n.*

trust·y (trus′tē), **1** *adj.* able to be depended on; reliable: *a trusty friend.* **2** *n.* a convict who is given special privileges because of good behavior. □ *adj.* **trust·i·er, trust·i·est;** *n., pl.* **trust·ies.** —**trust′i·ness,** *n.*

truth (trüth), *n.* **1** that which is true: *Tell the truth.* **2** a fixed or established principle, law, etc.; proven doctrine: *a basic scientific truth.* **3** quality or nature of being true, exact, honest, sincere, or loyal: *The jury doubted the truth of the witness's statements.* □ *n., pl.* **truths** (trǖᴛʜz or trüths).

in truth, truly; really; in fact: *It was in truth a beautiful scene.*

Truth (trüth), *n.* **So·journ·er** (sō′jėr′nər), 1797?-1883, American abolitionist. She was the first African American woman to speak publicly against slavery.

truth·ful (trüth′fəl), *adj.* **1** telling the truth: *He is a truthful boy and will tell exactly what happened.* ■ See Synonym Study at **honest. 2** conforming to truth; agreeing with the facts: *You can count on her for a truthful report.* **−truth′ful·ly,** *adv.* **−truth′ful·ness,** *n.*

try (trī), **1** *v.* to make an effort; attempt: *I tried to do the work.* **2** *v.* to attempt to do or accomplish: *It seems easy until you try it.* **3** *v.* to find out about by using; to experiment on or with: *Try this candy and see if you like it.* **4** *n.* an attempt; test; experiment: *Each girl had three tries at the high jump.* **5** *v.* to judge in a court of law: *They were tried and found guilty.* **6** *v.* to put to a severe test; strain: *Her carelessness tries my patience.* **7** *v.* to make pure by melting or boiling: *The lard was tried in a big kettle.* □ *v.* **tried, try·ing;** *n., pl.* **tries.**

try on, to put on to test the fit, looks, etc.: *I tried on several coats.*
try out, 1 to test or sample: *Try out this new recipe for apple pie.* **2** to undergo a test or trial to determine fitness: *He tried out for the baseball team.*

try·ing (trī′ing), *adj.* hard to put up with; annoying: *a long, hot, trying drive.* **−try′ing·ly,** *adv.*

try·out (trī′out′), *n.* test made to determine fitness for a specific purpose: *Tryouts for the swimming team will start tomorrow.*

tryp·a·no·some (tri pan′ə sōm), *n.* any of several microscopic parasites living in the blood of humans and other vertebrates. Trypanosomes are usually transmitted by bloodsucking insects and cause serious diseases, such as sleeping sickness.

tryp·sin (trip′sən), *n.* enzyme in the pancreatic juice that aids in the digestion of proteins.

try square, tool for drawing right angles and testing the squareness of anything. It is formed from two straight pieces joined at right angles.

tryst (trist), *n.* **1** appointment to meet at a certain time and place, especially one made by lovers. **2** place of meeting.

tsar (zär), *n.* czar.

tsa·ri·na (zä rē′nə), *n.* czarina. □ *n., pl.* **tsa·ri·nas.**

tset·se fly (tset′sē *or* tsē′tsē), any of several African flies that suck the blood of mammals and transmit sleeping sickness.

T-shirt (tē′shėrt′), *n.* **1** a light, close-fitting knitted shirt with short sleeves and no collar. **2** an undershirt resembling this. Also, **tee shirt.**

Tsim·shi·an (tsim′shē ən), *n.* member of a tribe of American Indians living in northwestern British Columbia and southern Alaska.

tsp., teaspoon or teaspoons.

T square, a T-shaped ruler used for making parallel lines, etc. The shorter arm slides along the edge of the drawing board, which serves as a guide.

tsu·na·mi (sü nä′mē *or* tsü nä′mē), *n.* a very large and destructive ocean wave caused by an underwater earthquake. □ *n., pl.* **tsu·na·mis** *or* **tsu·na·mi.**

Tu., Tuesday.

Tua·reg (twär′eg), *n.* member of a nomadic Muslim people living in the Sahara. □ *n., pl.* **Tua·reg** *or* **Tua·regs.**

tu·a·ta·ra (tü′ə tär′ə), *n.* a large lizardlike reptile of New Zealand. It is the only modern member of a group of reptiles that lived at the same time as the dinosaurs. □ *n., pl.* **tu·a·ta·ras.**

tub (tub), *n.* **1** a large, open container for washing or bathing. **2** bathtub. **3** bath: *He takes a cold tub every morning.* **4** as much as a tub can hold. **−tub′like,** *adj.*

tu·ba (tü′bə), *n.* a large brass wind instrument of low pitch. □ *n., pl.* **tu·bas.**

tub·by (tub′ē), *adj.* shaped like a tub; short and fat. ■ **Tubby** is sometimes considered offensive. □ *adj.* **tub·bi·er, tub·bi·est. −tub′bi·ness,** *n.*

tube (tüb), *n.* **1** a long pipe of metal, glass, rubber, etc., mostly used to hold or carry liquids or gases. **2** a small cylinder of plastic or thin, easily bent metal with a cap that screws on the open end, used for holding toothpaste, paint, etc. **3** inner tube. **4** pipe or tunnel through which something travels: *The railroad runs under the river in a tube.* **5** anything like a tube: *the bronchial tubes.* **6** an electron or vacuum tube. **7** **the tube,** INFORMAL. television. **−tube′like′,** *adj.*

tube foot, any of many small hollow organs on the arms of a starfish. They act as suckers and are used in moving and in getting food.

tube·less (tüb′lis), *adj.* having no inner tube or tubes: *a tubeless tire.*

tu·ber (tü′bər), *n.* the thick part of an underground stem. A potato is a tuber.

tu·ber·cu·lar (tü bėr′kyə lər), *adj.* **1** having tuberculosis. **2** of or about tuberculosis: *tubercular symptoms.*

tu·ber·cu·lin (tü bėr′kyə lən), *n.* a liquid substance prepared from the germ that causes tuberculosis, used to diagnose tuberculosis.

tu·ber·cu·lo·sis (tü bėr′kyə lō′sis), *n.* an infectious disease affecting various tissues of the body, but most often the lungs.

tube·rose (tüb′rōz′), *n.* a plant with a spike of creamy white, funnel-shaped flowers with a very strong, sweet smell. It is related to the agave.

tu·ber·ous (tü′bər əs), *adj.* **1** bearing tubers. **2** of or like tubers: *a tuberous root.* **3** covered with rounded knobs or swellings.

tube sock, sock that is not shaped at the heel.

tub·ing (tü′bing), *n.* **1** material in the form of a tube: *rubber tubing.* **2** tubes collectively. **3** a piece of tube.

Tub·man (tub′mən), *n.* Harriet (har′ē ət), 1820?-1913, American leader of the underground railroad. ■ **Harriet Tubman,** after escaping from slavery, made 19 trips to help others escape to freedom. Neither she nor anyone with her was ever caught.

tu·bu·lar (tü′byə lər), *adj.* **1** shaped like a tube; round and hollow. **2** of or like a tube or tubes. **3** constructed with or consisting of a number of tubes: *a tubular boiler.* **−tu′bu·lar·ly,** *adv.*

tu·bule (tü′byül), *n.* a small tube.

tuck (tuk), **1** *v.* to thrust into some narrow space or into some out-of-the-way place: *I tucked the letter into my pocket.* **2** *v.* to thrust the edge or end of something closely into place: *Tuck your shirt in.* **3** *v.* to cover snugly: *Tuck the children in bed.* **4** *v.* to pull or gather in a fold or folds: *She tucked up her sleeves before washing her hands.* **5** *n.* a fold sewed in an article of clothing: *The pants were too big, so I put a tuck in them.* **6** *v.* to sew a fold in a garment for trimming or to make it shorter or tighter: *The baby's dress was beautifully tucked with tiny stitches.*

tuck·er (tuk′ər), *v.* INFORMAL. to tire; weary; exhaust: *He was all tuckered out after the long trip.*

Tuc·son (tü′son), *n.* city in S Arizona, famous as a health resort. [**Tucson** comes from an American Indian word meaning "black bottom." It described a nearby mountain.]

Tu·dor (tü′dər), **1** *n.* the royal family that ruled England from 1485 to 1603. Henry VIII belonged to the house of Tudor. **2** *adj.* of or about the English Gothic style of architecture prevailing during the reign of the Tudor family. Tudor architecture often featured flat arches, shallow moldings, and elaborate paneling.

Tues., Tuesday.

Tues·day (tüz′dā′ *or* tüz′dē), *n.* the third day of the week, following Monday. [**Tuesday** comes from the name of the old English god of war and the old English word meaning "day."]

tu·fa (tü′fə), *n.* any of various porous rocks, especially a form of limestone deposited by springs. □ *n., pl.* **tu·fas.**

tuff (tuf), *n.* a kind of rock made of volcanic ash and other small volcanic fragments, all pressed together. ■ Another word that sounds like this is **tough.**

tuf·fet (tuf′ət), *n.* **1** clump of grass; tuft. **2** a low stool.

a	hat	ė	term	ô	order	ch	child		
ā	age	i	it	oi	oil	ng	long	ə	a in about
ä	far	ī	ice	ou	out	sh	she		e in taken
â	care	o	hot	u	cup	th	thin		i in pencil
e	let	ō	open	ù	put	ᴛʜ	then		o in lemon
ē	equal	ò	saw	ü	rule	zh	measure		u in circus

T

tuft (tuft), **1** *n.* bunch of feathers, hair, grass, etc., held together at one end: *The goat had a tuft of hair on its chin.* **2** *n.* cluster of threads sewn tightly through a mattress, comforter, etc., so as to keep the padding in place. **3** *v.* to put tufts on.

tuft·ed (tuf′tid), *adj.* **1** furnished with a tuft or tufts. **2** formed into a tuft or tufts.

tug (tug), **1** *v.* to pull with force or effort; pull hard: *We tugged the boat in to shore. The dog tugged at the rope.* ■ See Synonym Study at **pull. 2** *n.* a hard pull: *The baby gave a tug at my hair.* **3** *n.* tugboat. **4** *v.* to tow by a tugboat. ❑ *v.* **tugged, tug·ging.** —**tug′ger,** *n.*

tug·boat (tug′bōt′), *n.* a small, powerful boat used to tow or push other boats.

tug-of-war (tug′əv wôr′ *or* tug′ə wôr′), *n.* **1** contest between two teams pulling at the ends of a rope, each trying to drag the other over a line marked between them. **2** any hard struggle: *The rival politicians waged a long tug-of-war for the leadership of their party.* ❑ *n., pl.* **tugs-of-war.**

tu·i·tion (tü ish′ən), *n.* **1** money paid for instruction: *a $300 increase in college tuition.* **2** teaching or instruction. —**tu·i′tion·al,** *adj.*

tu·la·re·mi·a (tü′lə rē′mē ə), *n.* an infectious disease of rabbits and other rodents, caused by a bacterium; rabbit fever. It is sometimes transmitted to people by insect bites or by the handling of infected animals.

tu·lip (tü′lip), *n.* any of several plants with long, narrow leaves and cup-shaped flowers of various bright colors. Tulips grow from bulbs and bloom in the spring. [Tulip comes from a Persian word meaning "turban." People thought that the flower looked like a colorful turban.]

tulips

tulip poplar or **tulip tree,** a tall North American tree with greenish yellow flowers like large tulips and soft, white wood, often used in making furniture.

tulle (tül), *n.* a thin, fine net, usually of silk, used for veils, etc. ■ Another word that sounds like this is **tool.**

Tul·sa (tul′sə), *n.* city in NE Oklahoma, on the Arkansas River.

WORD STORY Tulsa comes from a Creek word meaning "old town." This was the name of a Creek town in Alabama, from which the Creek were forced to move to Oklahoma. They gave the same name to their new settlement.

tum·ble (tum′bəl), **1** *v.* to fall headfirst or in a helpless way: *The child tumbled down the stairs.* **2** *n.* a fall by tumbling: *The tumble only bruised the child.* **3** *v.* to throw over or down; cause to fall: *The strong winds tumbled a tree in our yard.* **4** *v.* to roll or toss about: *The patient tumbled restlessly in the bed.* **5** *v.* to move in a hurried or awkward way: *I tumbled out of bed.* **6** *v.* to perform leaps, springs, somersaults, or other acrobatic tricks. **7** *v.* to turn over; rumple; muss: *to tumble bedclothes.* **8** *n.* confusion; disorder: *Her desk was a tumble of papers.* ❑ *v.* **tum·bled, tum·bling.**

tum·ble·down (tum′bəl doun′), *adj.* ready to fall down; not in good condition; dilapidated: *a tumbledown shack in the mountains.*

tum·bler (tum′blər), *n.* **1** a drinking glass without a stem and with a heavy, flat bottom. **2** the contents of such a glass. **3** person who performs leaps, springs, etc.; acrobat. **4** part in the lock that must be moved from a certain position in order to release the bolt.

tum·ble·weed (tum′bəl wēd′), *n.* any of various plants growing in the western United States that break off from their roots and are blown about by the wind.

tum·brel or **tum·bril** (tum′brəl), *n.* **1** cart that carried prisoners to be executed during the French Revolution. **2** a two-wheeled cart, especially one used on a farm for hauling and dumping manure.

tum·my (tum′ē), *n.* INFORMAL. stomach. ❑ *n., pl.* **tum·mies.**

tu·mor (tü′mər), *n.* an abnormal growth of cells or tissue in or on some part of the body. —**tu′mor·like′,** *adj.*

tump·line (tump′lin′), *n.* a strap across the forehead and over the shoulders, used to help carry loads on the back, especially by American Indians.

tu·mult (tü′mult), *n.* **1** a violent disturbance or disorder; uproar: *The cry of "Fire!" caused a tumult.* **2** a violent disturbance of mind or feeling; confusion or excitement: *The fight left her in a tumult.*

tu·mul·tu·ous (tü mul′chü əs), *adj.* **1** marked by tumult; very noisy or disorderly; violent: *a tumultuous celebration.* **2** greatly disturbed: *tumultuous emotion.* —**tu·mul′tu·ous·ly,** *adv.* —**tu·mul′tu·ous·ness,** *n.*

tun (tun), *n.* **1** a large cask for holding liquids. **2** (earlier) unit of capacity for measuring liquor, equal to 252 gallons. ■ Another word that sounds like this is **ton.**

tu·na (tü′nə), *n.* any of several kinds of large sea fishes closely related to mackerel, with coarse, oily flesh that is widely used as food; tunny. ❑ *n., pl.* **tu·na** or **tu·nas.**

tun·a·ble (tü′nə bəl), *adj.* **1** able to be tuned. **2** in tune. —**tun′a·ble·ness,** *n.*

tuna fish, tuna.

tun·dra (tun′drə), *n.* **1** a vast, level, treeless plain in the arctic regions. The ground beneath its surface is frozen even in summer. Much of Alaska, northern Canada, Greenland, and northern Russia is tundra. **2** similar land high on mountains. ❑ *n., pl.* **tun·dras.**

tuna—up to 10 ft. (3 m) long

tune (tün), **1** *n.* piece of music; an air or melody: *popular tunes.* **2** *n.* the proper pitch: *The piano is out of tune.* **3** *n.* mood or manner; tone: *They'll soon change their tune.* **4** *n.* agreement; harmony: *ideas in tune with the times.* **5** *v.* to be in tune; be in harmony. **6** *v.* to adjust to the proper pitch; put in tune: *tune a piano.* ❑ *v.* **tuned, tun·ing.** —**tune′like′,** *adj.*

call the tune, dictate what will be done; be in command: *He thinks because he was the first one on the field that he can call the tune for the game.*

change your tune, to change your mind or what you say.

to the tune of, to the amount or extent of.

tune in, 1 to adjust a radio or TV set to hear or see what is wanted: *tune in an out-of-town radio station.* **2** to pay attention to what other people are saying, feeling, etc.

tune out, 1 adjust a radio or TV set to get rid of a signal or interference that is unwanted. **2** to ignore what other people are saying, feeling, etc.

tune up, 1 to bring musical instruments to the same pitch; put in tune. **2** to put a motor or engine into the best working order.

tune·ful (tün′fəl), *adj.* musical; melodious: *a tuneful song.* —**tune′ful·ly,** *adv.* —**tune′ful·ness,** *n.*

tune·less (tün′lis), *adj.* without tune; not musical. —**tune′less·ly,** *adv.*

tun·er (tü′nər), *n.* **1** device for adjusting a radio to receive a particular frequency. **2** person who tunes pianos, organs, or other musical instruments.

tune-up (tün′up′), *n.* series of checks and adjustments and replacement of certain parts of an engine or motor to keep it running well.

tung·sten (tung′stən), *n.* a heavy, hard, steel-gray, metallic element found only in certain rare minerals. Tungsten has the highest melting point of all metals. It is used in making steel, electric light bulb filaments, drills, etc. *Symbol:* W

tu·nic (tü′nik), *n.* **1** article of clothing like a long shirt, worn by the ancient Greeks and Romans. **2** any article of clothing like this. **3** a short, close-fitting coat worn by soldiers, policemen, etc.

tuning fork, a small, two-pronged steel tool used in tuning musical instruments. When struck it vibrates at a fixed, constant, known rate and so makes a musical tone of a certain pitch that can be used to tune musical instruments.

Tu·nis (tü′nis), *n.* port and capital of Tunisia, in the NE part.

Tu·ni·sia (tü nē′zhə), *n.* country in N Africa. *Capital:* Tunis. —**Tu·ni′sian,** *adj., n.*

tun·nel (tun′l), **1** *n.* an underground passage: *Traffic passes under the river through a tunnel.* **2** *v.* to make an underground passage: *The mole tunneled in the ground.* ❑ *v.* **tun·neled, tun·nel·ing** or **tun·nelled, tun·nel·ling.** —**tun′nel·er,** *n.* —**tun′nel·like′,** *adj.*

WORD STORY **Tunnel** comes from a French word meaning "big barrel." If you put a lot of barrels on their sides and took their tops and bottoms off, you'd have a tunnel shape.

tunnel vision, 1 an eye disorder in which the visual field is narrowed so that only things viewed straight ahead can be seen clearly. **2** extreme narrow-mindedness.

tun·ny (tun′ē), *n.* tuna. ❑ *n., pl.* **tun·ny** or **tun·nies.**

tu·pe·lo (tü′pə lō), *n.* any of several large North American trees growing in swampy regions, with soft, pale wood used in making furniture, crates, and paper pulp. ❑ *n., pl.* **tu·pe·los.**

Tu·pi (tü pē′ or tü′pē), *n.* member of a group of American Indian tribes of Brazil, Paraguay, and Uruguay. Forms of their language are spoken in a large region of South America. ❑ *n., pl.* **Tu·pi** or **Tu·pis.**

WORD SOURCE The **Tupi** language has given many words to the English language. The words below are some of them.

agouti	coati	manioc	tapioca
buccaneer	cougar	maraca	tapir
capybara	jacaranda	piranha	toucan
cashew	jaguar	tanager	

tu·pik (tü′pək), *n.* (in Canada) an Inuit tent made of skins, used as a summer dwelling.

tup·pence (tup′əns), *n.* twopence.

tu·que (tük), *n.* **1** a knitted cap shaped like a stocking, usually knotted at the end, worn especially in Canada. **2** CANADIAN. a tight-fitting knitted cap with a round tassel.

tur·ban (tėr′bən), *n.* **1** scarf wound around the head or around a cap, worn especially by Muslim and Sikh men in parts of India and in some other countries. **2** any hat or headdress like this. ■ Another word that can sound like this is **turbine.**

tur·bid (tėr′bid), *adj.* **1** not clear; muddy; thick: *a turbid river.* **2** confused; disordered: *a turbid imagination.* —**tur·bid′i·ty,** *n.* —**tur′bid·ly,** *adv.*

tur·bine (tėr′bən or tėr′bīn), *n.* engine containing a wheel with paddles or blades, caused to rotate by the pressure of rapidly flowing water, steam, or air. Turbines are often used to turn generators that produce electric power. ■ Another word that can sound like this is **turban.**

tur·bo·charge (tėr′bō chärj′), *v.* **1** to equip with a turbocharger. **2** INFORMAL. to speed up; make faster: *He turbocharged his model car with a bigger battery.* ❑ *v.* **tur·bo·charged, tur·bo·charg·ing.**

tur·bo·charg·er (tėr′bō chär′jər), *n.* a supercharger that is driven by a turbine powered by exhaust gases from the engine. —**tur′bo·charged,** *adj.*

tur·bo·jet (tėr′bō jet′), *n.* **1** jet engine with a turbine-driven air compressor that supplies a continuous, high-pressure flow of air to the burners. **2** aircraft with such an engine.

tur·bo·prop (tėr′bō prop′), *n.* **1** engine adapted from the turbojet, in which a propeller, driven by a shaft from the turbine, provides most of the thrust. Some additional thrust is provided by the ejection of exhaust gases. **2** aircraft with such an engine.

tur·bot (tėr′bət), *n.* a large European flatfish, much valued as food. ❑ *n., pl.* **tur·bot** or **tur·bots.**

tur·bu·lence (tėr′byə ləns), *n.* turbulent condition; disorder: tumult; commotion: *Air turbulence can cause discomfort for passengers.*

tur·bu·lent (tėr′byə lənt), *adj.* **1** causing disturbance; disorderly; unruly; violent: *a turbulent mob.* **2** stormy; tempestuous: *turbulent weather.* —**tur′bu·lent·ly,** *adv.*

tu·reen (tə rēn′), *n.* a deep, covered dish for serving soup, etc.

turf (tėrf), **1** *n.* the upper surface of the soil covered with grass and other small plants, including their roots and the soil clinging to roots; sod. **2** *n.* piece of this. **3** *v.* to cover with turf. **4** *n.* Usually, **the turf, a** a racetrack for horses. **b** horse racing. **5** *n.* INFORMAL. area thought of as your exclusive territory: *They stumbled into a rival gang's turf.* ❑ *n., pl.* **turfs** for 2,5.

tur·gid (tėr′jid), *adj.* **1** puffed out; swollen; bloated. **2** using big words and elaborate comparisons; pompous. —**tur·gid′i·ty,** *n.* —**tur′gid·ly,** *adv.*

Turk (tėrk), *n.* person born or living in Turkey.

Tur·ke·stan (tėr′kə stan′), *n.* a large region in W and central Asia.

tur·key (tėr′kē), *n.* **1** a large North American bird with brown or white feathers and a bare head and neck. It is related to chickens and pheasants. **2** its flesh, used for food. ❑ *n., pl.* **tur·keys.**
talk turkey, to speak in a frank, blunt way: *Let's talk turkey—how much do you want for your bike?*

turkeys (def. 1)—up to 4 ft. (1.2 m) long

WORD STORY **Turkey,** as a name for a bird, comes from a mistake. Actually, two mistakes. When people in Europe first saw turkeys from America, they thought they were seeing other birds, guinea fowl. And they thought that guinea fowl came from Turkey. (They come from Africa.) So people called the wrong birds after the wrong place, but the name stuck.

Tur·key (tėr′kē), *n.* country in W Asia and SE Europe. *Capital:* Ankara. [**Turkey** comes from a Turkish word meaning "strong," the Turks' name for themselves.]

turkey vulture or **turkey buzzard,** American vulture with a bare, reddish head and dark plumage.

Turk·ish (tėr′kish), **1** *adj.* of or about Turkey, its people, or their language. **2** *n.* language of the Turks.

WORD SOURCE **Turkish** has given many words to the English language. The words below are some of them.

bosh	divan	jackal	seraglio
bulgur	halvah	khan	sherbet
caftan	horde	kiosk	vizier
caviar	hummus	pasha	yogurt

Turkish Empire, Ottoman Empire.

turkish towel, a thick, cotton towel with a long nap made of uncut loops.

Turk·men·i·stan (tėrk men′ə stän), *n.* country in W Asia, E of the Caspian Sea. *Capital:* Ashkhabad.

tur·mer·ic (tėr′mər ik), *n.* the yellow root of an East Indian plant, used in powdered form as a seasoning or dye.

tur·moil (tėr′moil), *n.* commotion; disturbance; disorder: *Unexpected guests put us in a turmoil.*

turn (tėrn), **1** *v.* to face in a new direction: *She turned to the blackboard and wrote directions for taking the test.* **2** *v.* to give a new direction to: *He turned his flashlight towards the noise in the corner.* **3** *v.* to move around as a wheel does; rotate: *The merry-go-round turned.* **4** *n.* a change of direction: *a turn to the left.* **5** *v.* to cause to move around as a wheel does: *I turned the crank twice.* **6** *n.* a motion like that of a wheel: *At each turn the screw goes in further.* **7** *v.* to move part way around; change from one side to the other: *Turn over on your back.* **8** *v.* to do by turning; open, close, make lower, higher, tighter, looser, etc., by moving around: *Turn the key in the lock. Turn the oven up to full heat.* **9** *n.* time or chance to do something; opportunity: *My turn comes after yours.* **10** *v.* to take a new direction: *The road turns to the north here.* **11** *n.* place where there is a change in direction: *a turn in the road.* **12** *v.* to change in direction or position; invert; reverse: *turn a page.* **13** *v.* to change or transform so as to be; become: *She turned pale.* **14** *v.* to make or become sour or spoiled: *Warm weather turns milk.* **15** *n.* a change in affairs, conditions,

a	hat	ė	term	ô	order	ch	child		ə	a in about
ā	age	i	it	oi	oil	ng	long			e in taken
ä	far	ī	ice	ou	out	sh	she			i in pencil
â	care	o	hot	u	cup	th	thin			o in lemon
e	let	ō	open	ù	put	ŦH	then			u in circus
ē	equal	ò	saw	ü	rule	zh	measure			

or circumstances: *Matters have taken a turn for the worse. The sick child took a turn for the better.* **16** *v.* to change from one language into another: *Turn this sentence into Latin.* **17** *n.* a form; style: *a scholarly turn of mind.* **18** *v.* to change the attitudes of; unsettle: *Too much praise turns his head.* **19** *v.* to direct your thoughts or attention: *He turned his thoughts toward home.* **20** *v.* to direct thought, eyes, etc.: *turn to God for help.* **21** *v.* to move to the other side of; go around; get beyond: *She turned the corner.* **22** *v.* to pass or get beyond a particular age, time, or amount: *She just turned thirty.* **23** *n.* a twist, bend: *Give that rope a few more turns around the tree.* **24** *n.* deed; act: *One good turn deserves another.* **25** *n.* time or period of work or action: *Take a turn at the oars.* **26** *v.* to make antagonistic; prejudice: *turn friends against friends.* **27** *n.* a walk, drive, or ride: *a turn in the park.* **28** *v.* to form, work, or make by means of a lathe. **29** *v.* to make or become sick: *The sight of blood turns my stomach.* **30** *v.* to become dizzy: *The height made my head turn.* ■ Another word that sounds like this is **tern**. **–turn′a·ble,** *adj.*

at every turn, on every occasion; constantly.

by turns, one after another.

in turn, in proper order.

out of turn, 1 not in proper order. **2** without thinking; inappropriately.

take turns, to act one after another in proper order.

to a turn, to just the right degree: *meat done to a turn.*

turn about or **turn and turn about,** one after another in proper order.

turn down, 1 to fold down: *turn down the covers on the bed.* **2** to bend downward. **3** to place with face downward. **4** to refuse: *turn down a plan.* **5** to reduce the amount, volume, or brightness of something by turning a control switch: *Turn down the gas. Please turn down the sound on the radio.*

turn in, 1 to go to bed: *It's late and I'm going to turn in now.* **2** to give or give back. **3** to exchange: *turn in an old appliance for a new model.*

turn off, 1 to stop the operation, flow, etc., of; shut off: *Is the water tap turned off? Turn off the TV.* **2** to turn aside. **3** INFORMAL. to cause someone to feel displeasure or dislike: *She turns me off with her bragging.*

turn on, 1 to start the operation, flow, etc., of; put on: *Turn on the porch lights.* **2** to attack; resist; oppose: *The dog turned on its pursuer.* **3** to depend on: *The success of the picnic turns on the weather.* **4 a** SLANG. to take or use an intoxicating drug. **b** INFORMAL. to cause someone to feel pleasure or liking: *That music turns me on.*

turn out, 1 to put out; shut off: *Turn out the lights.* **2** to drive out. **3** to come or go out: *Everyone turned out for the circus.* **4** to make; produce. **5** to result; end: *How did the game turn out?* **6** to equip; fit out: *be smartly turned out in a new suit.* **7** be found or known: *The rumor turned out to be true.*

turn over, 1 to give; hand over; transfer: *turn over a job to someone.* **2** to think carefully about; consider in different ways: *turn over an idea in the mind.*

turn to, 1 to go to for help. **2** to get busy; set to work.

turn up, 1 to fold up or over, especially so as to shorten. **2** to increase the amount, volume, or brightness of something by turning a control switch: *Turn up the gas. Turn up the sound on the TV.* **3** to appear; arrive: *An old friend has turned up.* **4** be found; reappear.

turn·a·bout (tèrn′ə bout′), *n.* a change to an opposite position, opinion, etc.

turn·a·round (tèrn′ə round′), *n.* **1** place for a vehicle to turn around. **2** time that it takes for a vehicle to be unloaded and prepared for its next journey. **3** amount of time it takes for a specific service to be completed and the result ready for the purchaser: *The turnaround for an oil change is 15 minutes.* **4** turnabout.

turn·buck·le (tèrn′buk′əl), *n.* a short, hollow piece turning on screws at each end, used to unite and tighten two parts.

turn·coat (tèrn′kōt′), *n.* person who changes to another set of beliefs or political party. ■ **Turncoat** is often considered offensive.

Tur·ner (tèr′nər), *n.* **1 J. M. W.,** 1775-1851, English landscape painter. His paintings treated atmosphere and light in imaginative ways that influenced many of the impressionists. **2 Nat** (nat), 1800-1831, American preacher and rebel leader. ■ **Nat Turner** led

a rebellion in 1831, in which he and more than 60 other enslaved people killed about 60 whites. The whites hanged Turner and 20 other rebels, and killed more than 100 innocent people.

turning point, time or stage in a process at which an important change takes place.

tur·nip (tèr′nəp), *n.* the large, fleshy, roundish root of a garden plant, eaten as a vegetable.

turn·off (tèrn′ôf′), *n.* **1** a place where a road, path, etc., turns off to another. **2** INFORMAL. thing that causes displeasure or dislike: *A boring horror movie is a real turnoff.*

turn·on (tèrn′on′), *n.* INFORMAL. thing that is pleasurably exciting: *Music can be a real turn-on.*

turn·out (tèrn′out′), *n.* **1** a gathering of people: *a large turnout at the outdoor concert.* **2** number of people voting in an election. **3** a wide place in the road, where vehicles can pass.

turn·o·ver (tèrn′ō′vər), *n.* **1** the amount of changing from one job to another: *Employers wish to reduce labor turnover.* **2** act or process of paying out and getting back the money involved in a business transaction: *The store reduced prices to make a quick turnover.* **3** the total amount of business done in a given time: *She made a profit of $6000 on a turnover of $90,000.* **4** a small pie made by folding half the crust over the filling and attaching it to the other half. **5** (in basketball or football) loss of the ball to an opponent because of a misplay or a rule violation. **6** act of turning upside down; an overturn; upset.

turn·pike (tèrn′pik′), *n.* **1** toll road. **2** road that has, or used to have, a gate where toll is paid. **3** any main highway.

turn·stile (tèrn′stil′), *n.* gate with bars that turn, set in an entrance or an exit. A turnstile allows one person through at a time.

turn·ta·ble (tèrn′tā′bəl), *n.* **1** the round, rotating platform of a phonograph upon which records are placed. **2** a rotating platform with a track, for turning locomotives around.

tur·pen·tine (tèr′pən tin), *n.* **1** mixture of oil and resin obtained from various cone-bearing trees. **2** an oil distilled from this mixture. Turpentine is used in mixing paints and varnishes, in medicine, etc.

tur·quoise (tèr′koiz *or* tèr′kwoiz), **1** *n.* a sky blue or greenish blue mineral often used as a gem. **2** *n.* a sky blue or greenish blue, like that of the mineral. **3** *adj.* sky blue; greenish blue.

WORD STORY **Turquoise** comes from **Turkey,** because in old times turquoise came from Turkey. It was called "Turkish stone." Large amounts of turquoise were discovered later in parts of America, but the old name stuck.

tur·ret (tèr′it), *n.* **1** a small tower, often on the corner of a building. **2** any of various low, rotating armored structures that have guns mounted in them, as in a warship or tank. **3** a plastic bubble on the fuselage of some bombers, for machine guns and a gunner. **4** an attachment on a lathe, drill, etc., to hold cutting tools.

tur·ret·ed (tèr′ə tid), *adj.* having a turret or turrets.

J. M. W. Turner painting

tur·tle (tèr′tl), *n.* **1** any of numerous reptiles with soft, rounded bodies enclosed in hard shells into which many kinds can draw the head, legs, and tail. Turtles live in fresh water, in salt water, or on land; those living on land are often called tortoises. **2 Turtle,** a character in African myths and folktales. He is often described as the victim of a trick who finds a way to get even, or as a clever solver of problems. **3** a mark that can be moved about on a computer screen by instructions in LOGO and certain other computer languages.

tur·tle·dove (tėr′tl duv′), *n.* any of several small, slender doves. Turtledoves are noted for their soft cooing and the affection that the mates show for each other.

tur·tle·neck (tėr′tl nek′), *n.* a knitted article of clothing with a high, closely fitting collar, usually worn turned down over itself.

Tus·can (tus′kən), **1** *adj.* of or about Tuscany or its people. **2** *n.* person born or living in Tuscany. **3** *n.* dialect of Tuscany, regarded as the standard form of Italian.

Tus·ca·ny (tus′kə nē), *n.* district in central Italy.

Tus·ca·ro·ra (tus′kə rôr′ə), *n.* member of a tribe of American Indians living formerly in North Carolina, then in New York, now in New York and Ontario. ❑ *n., pl.* **Tus·ca·ro·ra** or **Tus·ca·ro·ras.**

tusk (tusk), *n.* a very long, pointed, projecting tooth. Elephants, walruses, and wild boars have two tusks.

tus·sle (tus′əl), **1** *v.* to struggle or wrestle; scuffle: *The boys tussled over the ball.* **2** *n.* a vigorous or disorderly conflict; severe struggle or hard contest: *The game should have been easy, but it turned into a long, hard tussle.* ❑ *v.* **tus·sled, tus·sling.**

tus·sock (tus′ək), *n.* a tuft of growing grass or the like.

tut (tut), *interj., n.* exclamation of impatience, contempt, or rebuke.

Tut·ankh·a·mun (tü′tängk ä′mən), *n.* died 1350? B.C., king of Egypt from 1358? to 1350? B.C. His tomb, discovered in 1922, contained many treasures.

tu·te·lage (tü′tl ij), *n.* **1** the office or function of a guardian; guardianship; protection. **2** instruction.

tu·tor (tü′tər), **1** *n.* a private teacher: *A tutor comes once a week to help me with mathematics.* **2** *v.* to teach; instruct, especially individually or privately: *She was tutored at home during her long illness.* **3** *v.* to be taught by a tutor: *He is tutoring in algebra.*

tu·to·ri·al (tü tôr′ē əl), *adj.* **1** of or about a tutor: *tutorial authority.* **2** using tutors: *the tutorial system.*

tut·ti-frut·ti (tü′tē frü′tē), **1** *n.* a preserve of mixed fruits. **2** *n.* ice cream containing a variety of fruits or fruit flavorings. **3** *adj.* flavored by mixed fruits.

Tu·tu (tü′tü), *n.* **Des·mond** (dez′mənd), born 1931, South African Anglican bishop. He won the Nobel Peace Prize in 1984 for his work against apartheid.

tu·tu (tü′tü), *n.* a very short, stiff, full skirt worn by a ballet dancer. ❑ *n., pl.* **tu·tus.**

Tu·va·lu (tü vä′lü), *n.* country made up of small islands in the central Pacific. *Capital:* Funafuti.

tux (tuks), *n.* INFORMAL. tuxedo. ❑ *n., pl.* **tux·es.**

tux·e·do (tuk sē′dō), *n.* **1** a man's coat for evening wear, made without tails, usually black with satin lapels. **2** the suit to which such a coat belongs. ❑ *n., pl.* **tux·e·dos** or **tux·e·does.**

WORD STORY **Tuxedo** comes from an Algonquian word meaning "round feet," which was the name for a wolf. The word was used in the name of a town in New York. The first tuxedo jacket was worn at a country club there.

TV, television.

TVA, Tennessee Valley Authority (a U.S. government organization for developing the resources of the Tennessee River valley, started in 1933).

TV dinner, a frozen, precooked meal on a tray of aluminum foil, that is heated in an oven before it is served.

TVP, textured vegetable protein.

twad·dle (twäd′l), **1** *n.* silly, feeble, tiresome talk or writing. **2** *v.* to talk or write in a silly, feeble, tiresome way. ❑ *v.* **twad·dled, twad·dling. —twad′dler,** *n.*

twain (twān), *n., adj.* OLD USE. two.

Twain (twān), *n.* **Mark,** 1835-1910, American humorous writer, author of *Tom Sawyer* and *Huckleberry Finn.* His real name was Samuel Langhorne Clemens.

twang (twang), **1** *n.* a sharp, ringing sound: *The bow made a twang when she shot the arrow.* **2** *v.* to make or cause to make a sharp, ringing sound: *The banjos twanged.* **3** *n.* a sharp, nasal tone: *the twang of a Maine farmer.* **4** *v.* to speak with a sharp, nasal tone.

twang·y (twang′ē), *adj.* having a twang. ❑ *adj.* **twang·i·er, twang·i·est.**

'twas (twäz *or* twuz), it was: *"'Twas the night before Christmas."*

tweak (twēk), **1** *v.* to seize and pull with a sharp jerk and twist: *tweak a person's ear.* **2** *n.* a sharp pull and twist.

tweed (twēd), *n.* **1** cloth with a rough surface, woven in raised diagonal lines. Tweed is sometimes made of wool and cotton or synthetic fibers, and usually has two or more colors woven together. **2** suit, etc., made of this cloth. **3 tweeds,** *pl.* clothes made of tweed.

tweed·y (twē′dē), *adj.* **1** made of or like tweed. **2** given to wearing tweeds. ❑ *adj.* **tweed·i·er, tweed·i·est. —tweed′i·ness,** *n.*

tweet (twēt), **1** *n., interj.* the sound made by a bird. **2** *v.* to make a tweet or tweets: *Birds tweeted softly.*

tweet·er (twē′tər), *n.* a high-fidelity speaker for reproducing sounds of higher frequencies.

tweez·ers (twē′zərz), *n.pl.* small pincers for pulling out hairs, picking up small objects, etc.

twelfth (twelfth), *adj., n.* **1** next after the 11th; last in a series of 12. **2** one of 12 equal parts.

twelve (twelv), *n., adj.* one more than 11; 12. A year has twelve months. [See Word Story at **eleven.**]

twelve·month (twelv′munth′), *n.* twelve months; a year.

twen·ti·eth (twen′tē ith), *adj., n.* **1** next after the 19th; last in a series of 20. **2** one of 20 equal parts.

twen·ty (twen′tē), *adj., n.* two times ten; 20. ❑ *n., pl.* **twen·ties.**

twerp (twėrp), *n.* SLANG. a stupid, silly, unlikable person.

twice (twīs), *adv.* **1** two times: *twice a day.* **2** doubly: *This story is twice as long as the last one.*

twice-told (twīs′tōld′), *adj.* **1** told twice. **2** told many times before; trite.

twid·dle (twid′l), **1** *v.* to twirl: *twiddle your pencil.* **2** *v.* to play with idly. **3** *n.* a twirl. ❑ *v.* **twid·dled, twid·dling.**

twig (twig), *n.* very small branch of a tree or bush: *Dry twigs are good to start a fire with.* **—twig′like′,** *adj.*

twi·light (twī′līt′), **1** *n.* the faint light reflected from the sky before the sun rises and after it sets. **2** *n.* the time during which this light is seen, especially from sunset to dark night. **3** *n.* condition or time after or before full development, glory, etc.: *the twilight of a person's career.* **4** *adj.* of or like faint light: *the twilight hour.*

twilight (def. 1)

twill (twil), *n.* **1** cloth woven in raised diagonal lines. **2** a diagonal line or pattern formed by such weaving.

'twill (twil), it will.

twilled (twild), *adj.* woven in raised diagonal lines.

a	hat	ė	term	ô	order	ch	child		
ā	age	i	it	oi	oil	ng	long		a in about
ä	far	ī	ice	ou	out	sh	she		e in taken
â	care	o	hot	u	cup	th	thin	ə	i in pencil
e	let	ō	open	u̇	put	ŦH	then		o in lemon
ē	equal	ȯ	saw	ü	rule	zh	measure		u in circus

T

twin (twin), **1** *n.* one of two offspring born at the same time of the same mother. Twins sometimes look exactly alike. **2** *adj.* being a twin: *Have you met my twin sister?* **3** *n.* one of two persons or things exactly alike. **4** *adj.* being one of two things very much or exactly alike: *twin beds.* **5** *adj.* having two like parts.

twine (twīn), **1** *n.* a strong thread or string made of two or more strands twisted together. **2** *v.* to twist together: *She twined holly into wreaths.* **3** *v.* to wind or wrap around: *The vine twines around the tree.* **4** *v.* to follow a twisting course; meander. ❑ *v.* **twined, twin·ing.** —**twine′a·ble,** *adj.* —**twin′er,** *n.*

twinge (twinj), **1** *n.* a sudden, sharp pain: *a twinge of rheumatism, a twinge of remorse.* **2** *v.* to feel or affect with such a pain. ❑ *v.* **twinged, twing·ing.** [**Twinge** comes from an old English word meaning "to pinch." A twinge feels as if someone has pinched you.]

twin·kle (twing′kəl), **1** *v.* to shine with quick little gleams: *The stars twinkled.* **2** *v.* to show amusement or merriment: *His eyes twinkled when he laughed.* **3** *n.* sparkle; gleam; shine: *She has a merry twinkle in her eye.* **4** *n.* a quick motion of the eye; wink; blink. **5** *n.* time required for a wink: *in the twinkle of an eye.* ❑ *v.* **twin·kled, twin·kling.** —**twin′kler,** *n.*

twin·kling (twing′kling), *n.* **1** a little, quick gleam. **2** a very brief period; an instant: *The mouse vanished in a twinkling.*

twirl (twėrl), **1** *v.* to revolve rapidly; spin; whirl: *The skater twirled like a top.* ■ See Synonym Study at **spin.** **2** *v.* to turn round and round idly: *He twirled his umbrella as he walked.* **3** *n.* a twirling; spin; whirl; turn: *a twirl in a dance.* [See Word Story at **swirl.**] —**twirl′er,** *n.*

twist (twist), **1** *v.* to turn with a winding motion; wind: *I twisted the cap off the jar.* **2** *v.* to wind together: *This rope is twisted from many threads.* **3** *v.* to turn around: *He twisted in his seat to see what was happening behind him.* **4** *v.* to give a spiral form to. **5** *v.* to bend; curve; turn: *to twist a piece of wire into a loop.* **6** *n.* a curve; bend; turn: *The path is full of twists.* **7** *v.* to force out of shape or place: *twist an ankle.* **8** *v.* to give a wrong meaning to; distort the meaning of: *twist an opposing candidate's words to get votes.* **9** *n.* act of twisting or condition of being twisted: *She locked the door with a twist of her wrist.* **10** *n.* anything made by twisting: *a twist of bread.* **11** *n.* a thread, cord, or rope made of two or more strands twisted together. **12** *n.* a peculiar bias or inclination: *a strange twist of character.* **13** *n.* an unexpected variation: *A new twist in the plot kept the audience in suspense.* —**twist′a·ble,** *adj.* —**twist′ing·ly,** *adv.*

twist·er (twis′tər), *n.* whirlwind; tornado; cyclone.

twitch (twich), **1** *v.* to move with a quick jerk: *The cat's paw twitched when I touched it.* **2** *n.* a quick, jerky movement of some part of the body. **3** *v.* to pull with a sudden tug or jerk; pull at: *She twitched the curtain aside.* ■ See Synonym Study at **jerk**[1]. **4** *n.* a short, sudden pull or jerk: *I felt a twitch at my shirttail.* ❑ *n., pl.* **twitch·es.** —**twitch′er,** *n.*

twit·ter (twit′ər), **1** *n.* sound made by birds; chirping. **2** *v.* to make such a sound: *Birds begin to twitter just before sunrise.* **3** *v.* to titter; giggle. **4** *n.* a brief or muffled giggle; titter. **5** *n.* an excited condition: *My nerves are in a twitter when I have to speak in public.* **6** *v.* to tremble with excitement. —**twit′ter·er,** *n.*

two (tü), *adj., n.* one more than one; 2. ❑ *n., pl.* **twos.** ■ Other words that sound like this are **to** and **too.**

in two, in two parts or pieces.

two-bit (tü′bit′), *adj.* INFORMAL. **1** worth a quarter of a dollar. **2** cheap; worthless: *a two-bit detective.*

two bits, INFORMAL. a quarter of a dollar.

two-by-four (tü′bə fôr′), *n.* piece of lumber measuring about four inches wide and two inches thick. Two-by-fours are much used in building.

two-di·men·sion·al (tü′də men′shə nəl), *adj.* **1** having only two dimensions, height and width. **2** lacking depth; superficial: *a two-dimensional character.*

two-edged (tü′ejd′), *adj.* **1** having two edges; cutting both ways: *a two-edged sword.* **2** able to be effective either way: *a two-edged argument.*

two-faced (tü′fāst′), *adj.* deceitful; hypocritical.

two-fist·ed (tü′fis′tid), *adj.* INFORMAL. strong; vigorous.

two·fold (tü′fōld′), **1** *adj., adv.* two times as much or as many; double. **2** *adj.* having two parts: *We expected a twofold shipment, part coming now and the rest later.*

two·pence (tup′əns), *n.* two British pennies; two pence. Also, **tuppence.**

two·pen·ny (tup′ə nē), *adj.* **1** worth twopence. **2** trifling; worthless.

two-ply (tü′plī′), *adj.* having two thicknesses, folds, layers, or strands.

two·some (tü′səm), *n.* group of two people.

two-step (tü′step′), **1** *n.* a dance in march or polka rhythm, performed with sliding steps. **2** *n.* music for it. **3** *v.* to dance the two-step. ❑ *v.* **two-stepped, two-step·ping.**

two-time (tü′tīm′), *v.* INFORMAL. to betray or be disloyal to; double-cross. ❑ *v.* **two-timed, two-tim·ing.** —**two′tim′er,** *n.*

two-way (tü′wā′), *adj.* **1** moving or allowing movement in two directions: *a two-way street.* **2** used in two ways or for two purposes: *A two-way radio receives and transmits messages.*

twp., township.

TX, Texas (used with postal Zip Code).

-ty[1], *suffix.* ___ tens; ___ times ten: *seventy = seven tens, that is, seven times ten.*

-ty[2], *suffix.* quality, condition, or fact of being ___: *safety = condition or quality of being safe.*

ty·coon (tī kün′), *n.* a rich businessman.

ty·ing (tī′ing), *v.* present participle of **tie:** *He is tying his shoes.*

tyke (tīk), *n.* a small child.

Ty·ler (tī′lər), *n.* **John,** 1790-1862, tenth president of the United States, from 1841 to 1845. ■ **John Tyler** was the first vice president to become president after the death of the previous president. He followed William Henry Harrison.

tym·pan·ic (tim pan′ik), *adj.* of or about the tympanum.

tympanic membrane, eardrum.

tym·pa·num (tim′pə nəm), *n.* **1** the eardrum. **2** the middle ear. ❑ *n., pl.* **tym·pa·nums, tym·pa·na** (tim′pə nə).

type (tīp), **1** *n.* a kind, class, or group having common features: *three types of local government. She is the type of person I like, kind and considerate of others.* **2** *n.* person or thing having the features of a kind, class, or group; example; illustration; model; representative; symbol: *The skyscraper is the type of modern buildings.* **3** *n.* the general form, style, or character of some kind, class, or group: *He is an outdoor type of person.* **4** *n.* piece of metal or wood having on its upper surface a raised letter, figure, or other character for use in printing. **5** *n.* collection of such pieces: *set the manuscript for a book in type.* **6** *n.* printed letters; typewritten letters: *small or large type.* **7** *v.* to write with a typewriter; typewrite: *type a letter asking for a job.* **8** *v.* to find out the type of; classify: *type a person's blood.* ❑ *v.* **typed, typ·ing.**

type·face (tīp′fās′), *n.* **1** style of type: *an italic typeface.* **2** surface of type that receives ink and transfers it to paper.

type·script (tīp′skript′), *n.* a typewritten manuscript.

type·set (tīp′set′), *v.* to set in type. ❑ *v.* **type·set, type·set·ting.**

type·set·ter (tīp′set′ər), *n.* person or machine that sets type for printing.

type·set·ting (tīp′set′ing), **1** *n.* act of setting type for printing. **2** *adj.* used or adapted for setting type: *a typesetting machine.*

type·write (tīp′rīt′), *v.* to write with a typewriter; type: *to typewrite a letter.* ❑ *v.* **type·wrote** (tīp′rōt′), **type·writ·ten, type·writ·ing.**

type·writ·er (tīp′rī′tər), *n.* **1** machine for writing which makes letters, numbers, and other symbols that are similar to printed ones. When the keys of a typewriter keyboard are touched or struck, they are pressed against an inked ribbon onto a sheet of paper. **2** (earlier) typist.

type·writ·ing (tīp′rī′ting), *n.* **1** act or art of using a typewriter: *to study typewriting.* **2** work done on a typewriter: *Your typewriting is very accurate.*

type·writ·ten (tīp′rit′n), **1** *adj.* written with a typewriter: *a typewritten letter.* **2** *v.* past participle of **typewrite:** *Your letter was typewritten and mailed yesterday.*

ty·phoid fever (tī′foid), an infectious, often fatal, bacterial disease in which the symptoms are a high fever and intestinal inflammation. People can be inoculated against typhoid fever.

ty·phoon (tī fün′), *n.* storm with violent wind, and usually with very heavy rain. Typhoons occur in the western Pacific Ocean.

ty·phus (tī′fəs), *n.* an acute, infectious disease in which the symptoms are a high fever, extreme weakness, and dark red spots on the skin. It is caused by a microscopic living thing carried by fleas, lice, ticks, or mites.

typ·i·cal (tip′ə kəl), *adj.* **1** showing the features of a group or kind: *The typical Thanksgiving dinner consists of turkey, cranberry sauce, several vegetables, and mince or pumpkin pie.* **2** of or descriptive of a type; characteristic: *the hospitality typical of frontier people.*

typ·i·cal·ly (tip′ik lē), *adv.* **1** in a typical manner. **2** to a typical degree. **3** ordinarily.

typ·i·fy (tip′ə fī), *v.* **1** to be a symbol of: *The Statue of Liberty typifies the American tradition of freedom.* **2** to have the common features of: *Daniel Boone typifies the pioneer.* ❑ *v.* **typ·i·fied, typ·i·fy·ing. —typ′i·fi·ca′tion,** *n.*

typ·ist (tī′pist), *n.* person who types on a typewriter or a computer keyboard.

ty·po (tī′pō), *n.* INFORMAL. a typographical error. ❑ *n., pl.* **ty·pos.**

ty·pog·ra·pher (tī pog′rə fər), *n.* printer.

ty·po·graph·ic (tī′pə graf′ik), *adj.* typographical.

ty·po·graph·i·cal (tī′pə graf′ə kəl), *adj.* of or about printing or typing: *"Catt" and "cOw" contain typographical errors.* **—ty′po·graph′i·cal·ly,** *adv.*

ty·pog·ra·phy (tī pog′rə fē), *n.* **1** art or process of printing with type; work of setting and arranging type and of printing from it. **2** arrangement, appearance, or style of printed matter.

Tyr (tir), *n.* (in Scandinavian myths) the god of war and victory, son of Odin.

ty·ran·nic (tə ran′ik), *adj.* tyrannical.

ty·ran·ni·cal (tə ran′ə kəl), *adj.* of or like a tyrant; cruel; unjust: *a tyrannical queen.* **—ty·ran′ni·cal·ly,** *adv.*

tyr·an·nize (tir′ə nīz), *v.* **1** to use power cruelly or unjustly; oppress: *The feudal lord tyrannized the peasants who farmed his land.* **2** to rule as a tyrant. ❑ *v.* **tyr·an·nized, tyr·an·niz·ing. —tyr′an·niz′er,** *n.* **—tyr′an·niz′ing·ly,** *adv.*

ty·ran·no·saur (ti ran′ə sôr), *n.* a huge, flesh-eating dinosaur that lived in North America. It walked upright on its hind legs. Also, **tyrannosaurus.**

ty·ran·no·sau·rus (ti ran′ə sôr′əs), *n.* tyrannosaur. ❑ *n., pl.* **ty·ran·no·sau·rus·es.**

tyr·an·nous (tir′ə nəs), *adj.* acting like a tyrant; cruel or unjust; tyrannical: *The Stamp Act seemed tyrannous to the colonists.* **—tyr′an·nous·ly,** *adv.*

tyr·an·ny (tir′ə nē), *n.* **1** cruel or unjust use of power: *Cinderella escaped the tyranny of her stepmother.* **2** a tyrannical act: *The colonists rebelled against the king's tyrannies.* **3** government by an absolute ruler. ❑ *n., pl.* **tyr·an·nies** for 2,3.

ty·rant (tī′rənt), *n.* **1** person who uses power cruelly or unjustly: *A good teacher is never a tyrant.* **2** a cruel or unjust ruler. **3** an absolute ruler, as in ancient Greece. Some tyrants of Greek cities were mild and just rulers.

Tyre (tīr), *n.* ancient port in S Phoenicia. It was noted for its seagoing traders who founded colonies in Spain, Italy, and N Africa. See **Phoenicia** for map.

Tyr·i·an (tir′ē ən), **1** *adj.* of or about Tyre. **2** *n.* person who was born or lived in Tyre.

ty·ro (tī′rō), *n.* beginner in learning anything; novice: *Much practice changed the tyro into an expert.* ❑ *n., pl.* **ty·ros.**

Ty·rol (tə rōl′ *or* ti′rōl), *n.* Tirol.

Tyr·rhe·ni·an Sea (tə rē′nē ən), part of the Mediterranean Sea lying between Italy and Sicily, Sardinia, and Corsica.

tzar (zär), *n.* czar.

tza·ri·na (zä rē′nə), *n.* czarina. ❑ *n., pl.* **tza·ri·nas.**

tyrannosaur—about 19 ft. (6 m) tall

a	hat	ė	term	ô	order	ch	child		
ā	age	i	it	oi	oil	ng	long		a in about
ä	far	ī	ice	ou	out	sh	she	ə	e in taken
â	care	o	hot	u	cup	th	thin		i in pencil
e	let	ō	open	u̇	put	ᴛʜ	then		o in lemon
ē	equal	ȯ	saw	ü	rule	zh	measure		u in circus

927

U or **u** (yü), *n.* **1** the 21st letter of the English alphabet. **2** anything shaped like a U. ❑ *n., pl.* **U's** or **u's.**

U, symbol for uranium.

U., University.

u·biq·ui·tous (yü bik′wə təs), *adj.* being or apparently being everywhere at the same time; present everywhere. **—u·biq′ui·tous·ness,** *n.*

u·biq·ui·ty (yü bik′wə tē), *n.* presence or apparent presence everywhere at the same time.

U-boat (yü′bōt′), *n.* a German submarine.

ud·der (ud′ər), *n.* the baglike part that hangs down from the belly of a cow, female goat, etc. It contains the milk-producing glands and has teats through which milk can flow.

UFO (yü′ef ō′ *or* yü′fō), *n.* an unidentified flying object, reported seen in the sky over many different parts of the world; flying saucer. ❑ *n., pl.* **UFOs** or **UFO's.**

u·fol·o·gist (yü fol′ə jist), *n.* person engaged in or devoted to ufology.

u·fol·o·gy (yü fol′ə jē), *n.* practice or hobby of tracking unidentified flying objects.

U·gan·da (ü gän′də *or* yü gan′də), *n.* country in E Africa. *Capital:* Kampala. **—U·gan′dan,** *adj., n.*

ugh (ug *or* u), *interj.* exclamation of disgust or horror.

Ug·li (ug′lē), *n.* trademark for a crossbreed of a grapefruit and a tangerine. It has a very rough rind.

ug·li·fy (ug′lə fi), *v.* to make ugly; disfigure. ❑ *v.* **ug·li·fied, ug·li·fy·ing. —ug′li·fi·ca′tion,** *n.*

ug·ly (ug′lē), *adj.* **1** very unpleasant to look at: *an ugly house.* **2** bad; disagreeable; offensive: *an ugly smell.* **3** threatening; dangerous: *an ugly wound, ugly clouds.* **4** bad-tempered; quarrelsome; cross: *an ugly mood.* ❑ *adj.* **ug·li·er, ug·li·est. —ug′li·ness,** *n.*

uh (u), *interj.* a sound indicating hesitation, confusion, etc.

UHF or **uhf,** ultrahigh frequency.

uh-huh (u hu′), *interj.* a sound indicating that you are listening or that you agree with what is said.

uh-uh (u′u′), *interj.* a sound indicating disagreement or a negative answer.

U.K., United Kingdom.

U·kraine (yü krān′), *n.* a country in E Europe. It was formerly part of the Soviet Union. *Capital:* Kiev. [**Ukraine** comes from a Slavic word meaning "borderland." The country lies between Poland and Russia.] **—U·krain′i·an,** *adj., n.*

u·ku·le·le (yü′kə lā′lē), *n.* a small guitar having four strings.

U·laan Baa·tar (ü′län bä′tär), capital of Mongolia, in the NE part.

ul·cer (ul′sər), *n.* **1** an open sore on the skin or, within the body, on a mucous membrane. It sometimes discharges pus. **2** a moral sore spot; corrupting influence.

ul·ce·rate (ul′sə rāt′), *v.* **1** to affect or be affected with an ulcer. **2** to form or be formed into an ulcer. ❑ *v.* **ul·ce·rat·ed, ul·ce·rat·ing.**

ul·ce·ra·tion (ul′sə rā′shən), *n.* **1** process of ulcerating or condition of being ulcerated. **2** an ulcer.

ul·cer·ous (ul′sər əs), *adj.* having or affected with an ulcer or ulcers; like an ulcer.

ul·na (ul′nə), *n.* the bone in the forearm on the side opposite the thumb, across from the radius. ❑ *n., pl.* **ul·nas.**

ul·ster (ul′stər), *n.* a long, loose overcoat, often belted.

Ul·ster (ul′stər), *n.* former province of Ireland, now forming Northern Ireland and part of the Republic of Ireland.

ul·ter·i·or (ul tir′ē ər), *adj.* **1** beyond what is stated or expressed; hidden: *an ulterior motive, an ulterior purpose.* **2** more distant; on the farther side. **3** further; later.

ul·ti·mate (ul′tə mit), **1** *adj.* coming at the end; last; final: *The ultimate result of driving too fast might be a serious accident.* **2** *adj.* greatest possible: *To give your life is to pay the ultimate price.* **3** *adj.* fundamental; basic: *The brain is the ultimate source of ideas.* **4** *adj.* beyond which there is nothing at all; extreme: *the ultimate limits of the universe.* **5** *n.* the best or most outstanding example of something: *the ultimate in comfort.*

ul·ti·mate·ly (ul′tə mit lē), *adv.* in the end; finally.

ul·ti·ma·tum (ul′tə mā′təm), *n.* a final offer or demand, given with the threat of severe penalties if refused. ❑ *n., pl.* **ul·ti·ma·tums, ul·ti·ma·ta** (ul′tə mā′tə).

ul·tra (ul′trə), *adj.* beyond what is usual; very; extreme.

ultra-, *prefix.* **1** beyond ___: *ultrasound = sound beyond human hearing.* **2** extremely ___: *ultramodern = extremely modern.*

ul·tra·high frequency (ul′trə hī′), the band of radio frequencies between 300 and 3000 megahertz.

ul·tra·light (ul′trə līt′), **1** *adj.* very light in weight. **2** *n.* a very lightweight airplane made of aluminum tubing and sailcloth, powered by a small engine, and designed to fly at speeds below 64 miles per hour.

ultralight (def. 2)

ul·tra·ma·rine (ul′trə mə rēn′), **1** *n.* a deep blue. **2** *adj.* deep blue. **3** *n.* a blue pigment made from powdered lapis lazuli.

ul·tra·mod·ern (ul′trə mod′ərn), *adj.* extremely modern: *ultramodern furniture.*

ul·tra·son·ic (ul′trə son′ik), *adj.* of or about sound waves beyond the limit of human hearing. **—ul′tra·son′i·cal·ly,** *adv.*

ul·tra·son·ics (ul′trə son′iks), *n.* branch of physics or medicine dealing with ultrasonic waves.

ul·tra·sound (ul′trə sound′), *n.* ultrasonic sound, used in medicine to form images of parts inside the body.

ul·tra·vi·o·let (ul′trə vī′ə lit), *adj.* of or about the invisible rays with wavelengths shorter than those of violet light. Ultraviolet rays in sunlight are important to forming vitamin D, but can cause sunburn.

u·lu (ü′lü), *n.* CANADIAN. an Inuit knife with a crescent-shaped blade, used especially by women to cut blubber. ❑ *n., pl.* **u·lus.**

U·lys·ses (yü lis′ēz), *n.* (in Greek legends) a king of Ithaca and hero of the Trojan War, known for his wisdom and shrewdness. Ulysses was his Latin name. The Greeks called him Odysseus. Homer's *Odyssey* tells about his adventures.

um·bel (um′bəl), *n.* a flower cluster with stalks nearly equal in length springing from a common center, as in Queen Anne's lace.

um·ber (um′bər), **1** *n.* mixture of clay and iron oxide. In its natural state it is a brown pigment called **raw umber.** After heating it becomes dark reddish brown and is called **burnt umber. 2** *n.* a brown or reddish brown. **3** *adj.* brown or reddish brown.

um·bil·i·cal cord (um bil′ə kəl), a cordlike structure that connects the navel of an embryo or fetus with the placenta of the mother. It carries nourishment to the fetus and carries away waste.

um·bil·i·cus (um bil′ə kəs), *n.* **1** navel. **2** a small pit like a navel. ❑ *n., pl.* **um·bil·i·cus·es, um·bi·li·ci** (um bil′ə sī).

um·bra (um′brə), *n.* the completely dark cone of shadow cast by a planet or moon. Umbras cause all total eclipses. ❑ *n., pl.* **um·bras.**

um·brage (um′brij), *n.* **take umbrage,** to take offense; feel insulted or offended: *He takes umbrage at the slightest criticism.*

um·brel·la (um brel′ə), *n.* a light, folding frame covered with cloth or plastic, used as a protection against rain or sun. ❑ *n., pl.* **um·brel·las.** [**Umbrella** comes from a Latin word meaning "shade." So you know that umbrellas were invented to keep off the sun, not the rain.] **—um·brel′la·like′,** *adj.*

umbrella tree, **1** a magnolia tree of the southeastern United States with long leaves in clusters at the ends of branches that look like umbrellas. **2** any tree that resembles an open umbrella.

u·mi·ak (ü′mē ak′), *n.* an open Eskimo boat made of skins covering a wooden frame, propelled by paddles. It is bigger than a kayak.

ump (ump), INFORMAL. **1** *n.* umpire. **2** *v.* to be an umpire for: *He umped both games of the doubleheader.*

um·pire (um′pīr), **1** *n.* person who rules on the plays in a game: *The umpire called the ball a foul.* **2** *n.* person chosen to settle a dispute. **3** *v.* to act as an umpire in a game, dispute, etc. ❑ *v.* **um·pired, um·pir·ing.**

ump·teen (ump′tēn′), *adj.* INFORMAL. a very large number of; countless: *It seemed as if I had umpteen errands to do last weekend.*

Um·ta·ta (üm tä′tə), *n.* capital of Transkei.

un-, *prefix.* **1** not ___: *unjust = not just.* **2** do the opposite of ___: *uncover = do the opposite of cover.*

UN or **U.N.,** United Nations.

un·a·bashed (un′ə basht′), *adj.* not embarrassed, ashamed, or awed. **—un·a·bash·ed·ly** (un′əbash′id lē), *adv.*

un·a·ble (un ā′bəl), *adj.* not able: *A newborn baby is unable to talk.*

un·a·bridged (un′ə brijd′), *adj.* not shortened or condensed; complete: *an unabridged book.*

un·ac·cent·ed (un ak′sen tid), *adj.* not pronounced with force; not accented.

un·ac·com·pa·nied (un′ə kum′pə nēd), *adj.* **1** not accompanied; alone. **2** (in music) without instrumental accompaniment.

un·ac·count·a·ble (un′ə koun′tə bəl), *adj.* **1** not able to be accounted for or explained. **2** not responsible: *A wild animal is unaccountable for its actions.* **—un′ac·count′a·bly,** *adv.*

un·ac·count·ed-for (un′ə koun′tid fôr′), *adj.* not accounted for or explained.

un·ac·cus·tomed (un′ə kus′təmd), *adj.* **1** not accustomed: *Polar bears are unaccustomed to hot weather.* **2** not familiar; unusual; strange: *unaccustomed surroundings.* **—un′ac·cus′tomed·ly,** *adv.* **—un′ac·cus′tomed·ness,** *n.*

un·ac·quaint·ed (un′ə kwān′tid), *adj.* not acquainted.

un′a·bat′ed	un′ac·a·dem′ic	un′ac·cli′ma·tized	un′ac·cred′it·ed	un′a·dapt′ed
un′ab·solved′	un′ac·cept′a·ble	un′ac·com′mo·dat′ing	un′ac·knowl′edged	un′ad·just′a·ble
un′ab·sorbed′	un·ac′cli·mat′ed	un′ac·com′plished	un′a·dapt′a·ble	un′ad·just′ed

U

un·a·dul·te·rat·ed (un′ə dul′tə rā′tid), *adj.* not adulterated; pure: *unadulterated flour.*

un·ad·vis·ed·ly (un′əd vī′zid lē), *adv.* in an indiscreet manner; without careful consideration; rashly.

un·af·fect·ed[1] (un′ə fek′tid), *adj.* not affected; not influenced.

un·af·fect·ed[2] (un′ə fek′tid), *adj.* simple and natural; straightforward; sincere. **–un′af·fect′ed·ly,** *adv.* **–un′af·fect′ed·ness,** *n.*

un·a·fraid (un′ə frād′), *adj.* not afraid; fearless: *In spite of the danger, we were unafraid.*

un·aid·ed (un ā′did), *adj.* not aided; without help.

un·al·ien·a·ble (un ā′lyə nə bəl), *adj.* inalienable.

un·a·ligned (un′ə līnd′), *adj.* nonaligned.

un·al·ter·a·ble (un ôl′tər ə bəl), *adj.* not able to be altered; not changeable. **–un·al′ter·a·bil′i·ty, un·al′ter·a·ble·ness,** *n.* **–un·al′ter·a·bly,** *adv.*

un·al·tered (un ôl′tərd), *adj.* not altered; unchanged.

un·A·mer·i·can (un′ə mer′ə kən), *adj.* not typical of or proper to American traditions, customs, or ideals.

u·na·nim·i·ty (yü′nə nim′ə tē), *n.* complete accord or agreement.

u·nan·i·mous (yü nan′ə məs), *adj.* **1** in complete agreement; agreed: *The children were unanimous in their wish to go to the beach.* **2** marked by or showing complete agreement: *She was elected by a unanimous vote.* [**Unanimous** comes from Latin words meaning "one" and "mind." The idiom **be of one mind** also means "in complete agreement."] **–u·nan′i·mous·ly,** *adv.* **–u·nan′i·mous·ness,** *n.*

un·an·swer·a·ble (un an′sər ə bəl), *adj.* **1** not able to be answered. **2** not able to be disproved. **–un·an′swer·a·bly,** *adv.*

un·ap·proach·a·ble (un′ə prō′chə bəl), *adj.* **1** very hard to approach; distant. **2** without an equal; unrivaled. **–un′ap·proach′a·bil′i·ty, un′ap·proach′a·ble·ness,** *n.* **–un′ap·proach′a·bly,** *adv.*

un·armed (un ärmd′), *adj.* without weapons: *an unarmed robber.*

un·as·sum·ing (un′ə sü′ming), *adj.* modest; not arrogant or boastful: *an unassuming manner.* **–un′as·sum′ing·ness,** *n.*

un·at·tached (un′ə tacht′), *adj.* **1** not attached. **2** not engaged or married.

un·at·tend·ed (un′ə ten′did), *adj.* **1** without attendants; alone: *The king arrived unattended.* **2** not accompanied. **3** not taken care of; not attended to: *The baby was left unattended.*

un·a·vail·ing (un′ə vā′ling), *adj.* not successful; useless: *The dog's efforts to jump the high fence were unavailing.* **–un′a·vail′ing·ly,** *adv.*

un·a·void·a·ble (un′ə voi′də bəl), *adj.* not able to be avoided: *an unavoidable delay.* **–un′a·void′a·bil′i·ty, un′a·void′a·ble·ness,** *n.* **–un′a·void′a·bly,** *adv.*

un·a·ware (un′ə wâr′), **1** *adj.* not aware; unconscious: *We were unaware of the approaching storm.* **2** *adv.* unawares. **–un′a·ware′ly,** *adv.* **–un′a·ware′ness,** *n.*

un·a·wares (un′ə wârz′), *adv.* **1** without being expected; by surprise: *They caught the burglar unawares.* **2** without knowing; unintentionally: *approach danger unawares.*

un·bal·anced (un bal′ənst), *adj.* **1** not entirely sane: *an unbalanced mind.* **2** not balanced.

un·bar (un bär′), *v.* to remove the bars from; unlock. □ *v.* **unbarred, un·bar·ring.**

un·bear·a·ble (un bâr′ə bəl), *adj.* not able to be endured; intolerable: *The pain from a severe toothache is almost unbearable.* **–un·bear′a·ble·ness,** *n.* **–un·bear′a·bly,** *adv.*

un·beat·a·ble (un bē′tə bəl), *adj.* not able to be beaten, overcome, or surpassed: *With the tallest and fastest players in the city, our basketball team was unbeatable.*

un·beat·en (un bēt′n), *adj.* **1** not defeated or surpassed: *Our team was still unbeaten after 14 games.* **2** not trodden; not traveled: *unbeaten paths.* **3** not struck, pounded, or whipped: *unbeaten metal, unbeaten eggs.*

un·be·com·ing (un′bi kum′ing), *adj.* **1** not becoming; not flattering: *unbecoming clothes.* **2** not fitting; not proper: *unbecoming behavior.* **–un′be·com′ing·ly,** *adv.* **–un′be·com′ing·ness,** *n.*

un·be·known (un′bi nōn′), *adj.* not known: *He arrived unbeknown to anyone.*

un·be·knownst (un′bi nōnst′), *adj.* unbeknown.

un·be·lief (un′bi lēf′), *n.* lack of belief; lack of faith.

un·be·liev·a·ble (un′bi lē′və bəl), *adj.* not believable; incredible: *an unbelievable lie.* **–un′be·liev′a·bly,** *adv.*

un·be·liev·er (un′bi lē′vər), *n.* **1** person who does not believe. **2** person who does not believe in a particular religion.

un·be·liev·ing (un′bi lē′ving), *adj.* not believing; doubting. **–un′be·liev′ing·ly,** *adv.*

un·bend (un bend′), *v.* **1** to make or become straight; straighten: *unbend the fingers. The wire was hard and would not unbend.* **2** to release from strain: *unbend a bow.* **3** to relax: *Music helps me unbend after a hard day.* □ *v.* **un·bent, un·bend·ing.** **–un·bend′a·ble,** *adj.*

un·bend·ing (un ben′ding), *adj.* **1** not bending or curving; rigid. **2** not yielding; stubborn; firm: *an unbending will.* **–un·bend′ing·ly,** *adv.*

un·bent (un bent′), *v.* past tense and a past participle of **unbend.**

un·bi·ased (un bī′əst), *adj.* not prejudiced; impartial; fair: *Each member of a jury should be unbiased.* **–un·bi′ased·ly,** *adv.* **–un·bi′ased·ness,** *n.*

unbelievable

un·bid·den (un bid′n), *adj.* **1** not invited: *an unbidden guest.* **2** not commanded.

un·bind (un bīnd′), *v.* to release from bonds or restraint; let loose; untie; unfasten. □ *v.* **un·bound, un·bind·ing.**

un·bleached (un blēcht′), *adj.* not bleached; not made white by bleaching: *unbleached linen.*

un·blem·ished (un blem′isht), *adj.* not blemished; spotless; flawless: *The principal gave him an award for his unblemished attendance record.*

un·blessed or **un·blest** (un blest′), *adj.* **1** not blessed. **2** unhappy.

un′a·dorned′	un′an·nounced′	un′ar·rest′ed	un′at·trac′tive	un′bap·tized′
un′ad·vis′a·ble	un′an·swered′	un′ar·tis′tic	un′au·then′tic	un′barbed′
un′al·lied′	un′ap·peal′ing	un′a·shamed′	un′au·then′ti·cat′ed	un′be·fit′ting
un′al·low′a·ble	un′ap·peased′	un·asked′	un′au·thor·ized′	un′be·hold′en
un′al·loyed′	un′ap·pe·tiz′ing	un′as·sail′a·ble	un′a·vail′a·ble	un′be·trothed′
un′am·big′u·ous	un′ap·pre′ci·at′ed	un′as·signed′	un′a·venged′	un′blam′a·ble
un′am·bi′tious	un′ap·pre′ci·a·tive	un′as·sist′ed	un′a·vowed′	un′blamed′
un·amp′li·fied	un′ap·proved′	un′at·tain′a·ble	un·awed′	un′blink′ing
un·an′i·mat′ed		un′at·tempt′ed′	un·ban′daged	un′blurred′

un·blush·ing (un blush′ing), *adj.* **1** not blushing. **2** unabashed; shameless. —**un·blush′ing·ly**, *adv.*

un·bolt (un bōlt′), *v.* to pull back the bolts of a door, etc.

un·bolt·ed (un bōl′tid), *adj.* not bolted or fastened: *an unbolted door.*

un·born (un bôrn′), *adj.* not yet born; still to come; of the future: *an unborn child, unborn generations.*

un·bos·om (un bŭz′əm), *v.* to reveal; disclose: *unbosomed his fears.*
unbosom yourself, to tell or reveal your thoughts, secrets, etc.

un·bound (un bound′), **1** *adj.* not bound: *Unbound sheets of music were scattered about the room.* **2** *v.* past tense and past participle of **unbind.**

un·bound·ed (un boun′did), *adj.* **1** not kept within limits; not controlled: *unbounded enthusiasm.* **2** not limited; very great; boundless: *the unbounded reaches of the universe.* —**un·bound′ed·ly**, *adv.* —**un·bound′ed·ness**, *n.*

un·bowed (un boud′), *adj.* **1** not bowed or bent. **2** not forced to yield or surrender.

un·break·a·ble (un brā′kə bəl), *adj.* not breakable; not easily broken: *an unbreakable plate.* —**un·break′a·ble·ness**, *n.* —**un·break′a·bly**, *adv.*

un·bri·dled (un brī′dld), *adj.* **1** not controlled; not restrained: *unbridled anger.* **2** not having a bridle on.

un·bro·ken (un brō′kən), *adj.* **1** not interrupted; continuous: *unbroken sleep.* **2** not tamed: *an unbroken colt.* **3** not broken; whole: *an unbroken dish.* —**un·bro′ken·ly**, *adv.* —**un·bro′ken·ness**, *n.*

un·buck·le (un buk′əl), *v.* **1** to unfasten the buckle or buckles of. **2** to unfasten; detach. ❑ *v.* **un·buck′led, un·buck′ling.**

un·bur·den (un bėrd′n), *v.* **1** to relieve your mind or heart by talking. **2** to free from a burden.

un·busi·ness·like (un biz′nis līk′), *adj.* without system and method; not efficient: *unbusinesslike procedures.*

un·but·ton (un but′n), *v.* **1** to unfasten the button or buttons of. **2** to reveal your thoughts, feelings, etc., especially after a long silence.

un·called-for (un kȯld′fôr′), *adj.* **1** unnecessary and improper: *an uncalled-for remark.* **2** not called for; not requested.

un·can·ny (un kan′ē), *adj.* **1** strange and mysterious; weird: *The trees took uncanny shapes in the mist.* **2** so far beyond what is normal or expected as to suggest some special power: *an uncanny sense of direction.* —**un·can′ni·ly**, *adv.* —**un·can′ni·ness**, *n.*

un·cap (un kap′), *v.* to take the cap, top, or covering off of: *uncap a bottle.* ❑ *v.* **un·capped, un·cap·ping.**

un·cared-for (un kârd′fôr′), *adj.* not cared for; neglected.

un·cer·e·mo·ni·ous (un′ser ə mō′nē əs), *adj.* **1** not ceremonious; informal. **2** not as courteous as would be expected. —**un′cer·e·mo·ni·ous·ly**, *adv.* —**un′cer·e·mo·ni·ous·ness**, *n.*

un·cer·tain (un sėrt′n), *adj.* **1** not certain; doubtful: *I came so late that I was uncertain of my welcome.* **2** likely to change; not to be depended on: *This dog has an uncertain temper.* **3** vague; indefinite: *an uncertain shape.* —**un·cer′tain·ly**, *adv.*

SYNONYM STUDY **Uncertain** and **unsettled** both mean not known for sure. **Uncertain** is a general word: *The outcome of the election is still uncertain.* **Unsettled** suggests possible change: *Conditions remain unsettled after the rebellion.*

un·cer·tain·ty (un sėrt′n tē), *n.* **1** uncertain condition; doubt: *There was some uncertainty as to our plans.* **2** something uncertain: *When we'll be coming is still an uncertainty.* ❑ *n., pl.* **un·cer·tain·ties** for 2.

uncertainty principle, 1 (in physics) principle that it is impossible to measure at the same time two related quantities, such as position and velocity, without a predictable inaccuracy. **2** principle that the act of observation changes the nature or condition of the thing that is being observed.

un·chain (un chān′), *v.* to let loose; set free.

un·change·a·ble (un chān′jə bəl), *adj.* not changeable; not able to be changed. —**un·change′a·ble·ness**, *n.* —**un·change′a·bly**, *adv.*

un·changed (un chānjd′), *adj.* not changed; the same: *unchanged tradition.*

un·char·i·ta·ble (un char′ə tə bəl), *adj.* not generous; not charitable; severe; harsh. —**un·char′i·ta·ble·ness**, *n.* —**un·char′i·ta·bly**, *adv.*

un·chart·ed (un chär′tid), *adj.* not mapped; not marked on a chart.

un·chaste (un chāst′), *adj.* not chaste; not virtuous. —**un·chaste′ly**, *adv.* —**un·chaste′ness**, *n.*

un·checked (un chekt′), *adj.* not checked; not restrained.

un·chris·tian (un kris′chən), *adj.* **1** not Christian. **2** unworthy of Christians. —**un·chris′tian·ly**, *adv.*

un·church (un chėrch′), *v.* **1** to expel or excommunicate from church membership. **2** to deprive of church rights and privileges.

un·churched (un chėrchd′), *adj.* not a member of any church; not attending church services.

un·civ·il (un siv′əl), *adj.* not civil; rude; impolite. —**un′ci·vil′i·ty, un·civ′il·ness**, *n.* —**un·civ′il·ly**, *adv.*

un·civ·i·lized (un siv′ə līzd), *adj.* not civilized; barbarian.

un·clad (un klad′), *adj.* not dressed; not clothed; naked.

un·clasp (un klasp′), *v.* **1** to unfasten. **2** to release or be released from a clasp or grasp.

un·cle (ung′kəl), *n.* **1** brother of your father or mother. **2** husband of your aunt.

un·clean (un klēn′), *adj.* **1** not clean; dirty; filthy. **2** not pure morally; evil. **3** not ceremonially clean. —**un·clean′ness**, *n.*

un·clean·ly[1] (un klen′lē), *adj.* not cleanly; unclean. —**un·clean′li·ness**, *n.*

un·clean·ly[2] (un klēn′lē), *adv.* in an unclean manner.

un·clear (un klir′), *adj.* **1** not clear; confusing; vague: *Your directions were unclear and we got lost.* **2** uncertain: *We were unclear about what we were supposed to do.* —**un·clear′ly**, *adv.*

un·clench (un klench′), *v.* to open or become opened from a clenched state: *unclench your fists.*

Uncle Sam (sam), the government or people of the United States. Uncle Sam is usually drawn in pictures as a tall, thin man with white chin whiskers, wearing a high hat, a blue swallow-tailed coat, and red and white striped pants.

un·cloak (un klōk′), *v.* **1** to remove the coat from. **2** to reveal; expose.

un·clothed (un klōᴛʜd′), *adj.* not clothed; naked; bare.

un·coil (un koil′), *v.* to unwind.

un·com·fort·a·ble (un kum′fər tə bəl), *adj.* **1** not comfortable. **2** uneasy. **3** causing discomfort; disagreeable. —**un·com′fort·a·ble·ness**, *n.* —**un·com′fort·a·bly**, *adv.*

un·com·mon (un kom′ən), *adj.* **1** rare; unusual: *Snow is uncommon in Florida.* **2** remarkable: *uncommon skill.* —**un·com′mon·ly**, *adv.* —**un·com′mon·ness**, *n.*

un·com·mu·ni·ca·tive (un′kə myü′nə kə tiv), *adj.* not giving out any information, opinions, etc.; talking little; reserved. —**un′com·mu′ni·ca′tive·ly**, *adv.* —**un′com·mu′ni·ca′tive·ness**, *n.*

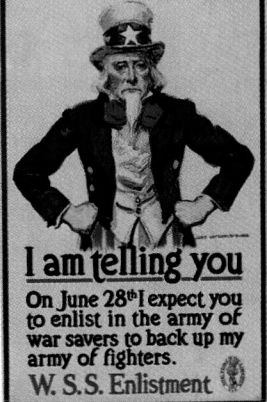

I am telling you
On June 28th I expect you to enlist in the army of war savers to back up my army of fighters.
W. S. S. Enlistment

Uncle Sam

U

un·bought′	un·burnt′	un·chap′e·roned′	un·closed′	un′com·mit′ted
un·braced′	un·can′celed	un·charged′	un·cloud′ed	un′com·pan′ion·a·ble
un·branched′	un·cap′i·tal·ized	un·chas′tened	un·clut′tered	un′com·plain′ing
un·brand′ed	un·cashed′	un·chiv′al·rous	un·col·lect′ed	un′com·plai′sant
un·broth′er·ly	un·caught′	un·chris′tened	un·col′ored	un′com·plet′ed
un·bruised′	un·ceas′ing	un·claimed′	un·combed′	un′com·pli·cat′ed
un·brushed′	un·cen′sored	un·clas′si·fied	un′com·bined′	un′com·pli·men′tar·y
un·bur′ied	un·chal′lenged	un·cleaned′	un·come′ly	un′com·pound′ed
un·burned′	un·chang′ing	un·cleared′	un′com·fort′ed	un′com·pre·hend′ing

un·com·pro·mis·ing (un kom′prə mī′zing), *adj.* unyielding; firm: *An uncompromising person can be hard to deal with.* —**un·com′pro·mis′ing·ly,** *adv.* —**un·com′pro·mis′ing·ness,** *n.*

un·con·cern (un′kən sėrn′), *n.* lack of concern; lack of interest; freedom from care or anxiety; indifference.

un·con·cerned (un′kən sėrnd′), *adj.* **1** free from care or anxiety: *She seemed quite unconcerned about the cut on her finger.* **2** not interested; indifferent: *They were unconcerned with the election next week.* —**un′con·cern′ed·ly,** *adv.*

un·con·di·tion·al (un′kən dish′ə nəl), *adj.* without conditions; absolute: *The victorious general demanded the unconditional surrender of the enemy.* —**un′con·di′tion·al·ly,** *adv.*

un·con·nect·ed (un′kə nek′tid), *adj.* separated; disconnected. —**un′con·nect′ed·ness,** *n.*

un·con·quer·a·ble (un′kong′kər ə bəl), *adj.* not able to be conquered. —**un′con′quer·a·bly,** *adv.*

un·con·scion·a·ble (un kon′shə nə bəl), *adj.* **1** not influenced or guided by conscience: *an unconscionable liar.* **2** very great; unreasonable: *an unconscionable delay.* —**un·con′scion·a·bly,** *adv.*

un·con·scious (un kon′shəs), **1** *adj.* not conscious; not able to feel or think: *knock unconscious, unconscious from anesthetic.* **2** *adj.* not aware: *unconscious of being followed, unconscious of the time.* **3** *adj.* not done or felt consciously; not purposeful: *Her rude remark was unconscious.* **4** *n.* thoughts, feelings, etc., that are present in the mind but that you are not directly or fully aware of; subconscious. —**un·con′scious·ly,** *adv.* —**un·con′scious·ness,** *n.*

un·con·sti·tu·tion·al (un′kon stə tü′shə nəl), *adj.* contrary to the constitution; not constitutional. —**un′con·sti·tu′tion·al·ly,** *adv.*

un·con·sti·tu·tion·al·i·ty (un′kon stə tü′shə nal′ə tē), *n.* condition of being contrary to the constitution.

un·con·trol·la·ble (un′kən trō′lə bəl), *adj.* not able to be controlled; beyond control: *I had an uncontrollable urge to laugh.* —**un′con·trol′la·bly,** *adv.*

un·con·trolled (un′kən trōld′), *adj.* not controlled; not restrained.

un·con·ven·tion·al (un′kən ven′shə nəl), *adj.* not bound by or conforming to convention, rule, or precedent; free from conventionality. —**un·con·ven·tion·al·i·ty** (un′kən ven′shə nal′ə tē), *n.* —**un′con·ven′tion·al·ly,** *adv.*

un·cork (un kôrk′), *v.* to pull the cork from.

un·count·a·ble (un koun′tə bəl), *adj.* not able to be counted; innumerable: *an uncountable number of stars.*

un·count·ed (un koun′tid), *adj.* **1** not counted; not reckoned. **2** very many; innumerable.

un·cou·ple (un kup′əl), *v.* to disconnect; unfasten: *They uncoupled two freight cars.* ❏ *v.* **un·cou·pled, un·cou·pling.** —**un·cou′pler,** *n.*

un·couth (un küth′), *adj.* not refined; awkward; clumsy; crude: *uncouth manners, an uncouth person.* —**un·couth′ly,** *adv.* —**un·couth′ness,** *n.*

un·cov·er (un kuv′ər), *v.* **1** to remove the cover from: *I uncovered the pot.* **2** to make known; reveal; expose: *The reporter uncovered a scandal.*

un·crowned (un kround′), *adj.* **1** not crowned; not having yet assumed the crown. **2** having royal power without being king, queen, etc.

unc·tion (ungk′shən), *n.* **1** act or process of anointing with oil, ointment, etc., for medical purposes or as a religious rite. **2** the oil, ointment, or the like, used for anointing. **3** something soothing or comforting: *the unction of flattery.*

unc·tu·ous (ungk′chü əs), *adj.* **1** too smooth; insincere: *the hypocrite's unctuous manner.* **2** like an oil or ointment in texture; oily; greasy. —**unc′tu·ous·ly,** *adv.* —**unc′tu·ous·ness,** *n.*

un·cul·ti·vat·ed (un kul′tə vā′tid), *adj.* not cultivated; wild; undeveloped.

un·curl (un kėrl′), *v.* to straighten out.

un·cut (un kut′), *adj.* **1** not cut, gashed, or wounded; not having received a cut: *They were fortunate to walk away from the accident uncut, only bruised.* **2** not shortened: *an uncut version of a movie.* **3** not fashioned or shaped by cutting: *an uncut diamond.*

un·daunt·ed (un dôn′tid), *adj.* not afraid; not discouraged; fearless: *The skier was undaunted by the bad fall she suffered in the first race.* —**un·daunt′ed·ly,** *adv.* —**un·daunt′ed·ness,** *n.*

un·de·ceive (un′di sēv′), *v.* to free someone from error, mistake, or deception. ❏ *v.* **un·de·ceived, un·de·ceiv·ing.**

un·de·cid·ed (un′di sī′did), *adj.* **1** not having your mind made up: *I am undecided about which book to buy.* **2** not decided; not settled: *Our schedule is still undecided.* —**un′de·cid′ed·ly,** *adv.* —**un′de·cid′ed·ness,** *n.*

un·de·fined (un′di find′), *adj.* **1** not defined or explained. **2** indefinite.

un·de·mon·stra·tive (un′di mon′strə tiv), *adj.* not expressing feelings freely and openly. —**un′de·mon′stra·tive·ly,** *adv.* —**un′de·mon′stra·tive·ness,** *n.*

un·de·ni·a·ble (un′di nī′ə bəl), *adj.* not able to be denied or disputed; certain. —**un′de·ni′a·bly,** *adv.*

un·der (un′dər), **1** *adv., prep.* below; beneath: *The swimmer went under. The book fell under the table.* **2** *prep.* below the surface of: *under the sea.* **3** *adv.* in or to a lower place or condition. **4** *adj.* lower in position, rank, degree, amount, price, etc.: *the under lip.* **5** *prep.* lower than; lower down than; not so high as: *There is a bruise under your eye.* **6** *prep.* less than: *It will cost under ten dollars.* **7** *prep.* during the rule or time of: *England under King John.* **8** *prep.* according to; because of: *under the law. We cannot join your club under these conditions.* **9** *prep.* represented by: *under a new name.* **10** *prep.* required or bound by: *You are not under any obligation to pay for damaged merchandise.* **11** *prep.* included in a particular group, category, or class: *In this library, books on stamp collecting are listed under philately.*

SYNONYM STUDY **Under, below,** and **beneath** all mean with something else over or on top. **Under** is a general word: *Look under the piano.* **Below** is used to describe something lower than something else: *Far below the building top, the people in the street looked like ants.* **Beneath** suggests that something is covered: *He hid beneath the bed.*

under-, *prefix.* **1** below; beneath: *underline = draw a line below; underground = beneath the ground.* **2** lower: *undersecretary = secretary that is lower in rank; underbid = bid lower than.* **3** not enough: *undernourished = not sufficiently nourished; underweight = not having enough weight.*

un·der·a·chieve (un′dər ə chēv′), *v.* (of a student) to fail to work at the level of your ability. ❏ *v.* **un·der·a·chieved, un·der·a·chiev′ment,** *n.* —**un′der·a·chiev′er,** *n.*

un·der·age (un′dər āj′), *adj.* below the legal or required age.

un·der·arm (un′dər ärm′), **1** *adj.* situated or placed under the arm; found in or near the armpit: *an underarm deodorant.* **2** *n.* armpit. **3** *adj., adv.* underhand: *an underarm pitcher. In softball a pitcher must throw underarm.*

un·der·bid (un′dər bid′), *v.* to make a lower bid than another: *to underbid a competitor in seeking a contract.* ❏ *v.* **un·der·bid, un·der·bid·ding.** —**un′der·bid′der,** *n.*

un·der·brush (un′dər brush′), *n.* bushes and small trees growing under large trees in woods or forests; undergrowth; understory.

un·der·car·riage (un′dər kar′ij), *n.* **1** the supporting framework of a carriage, car, etc. **2** landing gear.

un·com′pro·mised′	un·con·gest′ed	un·con·tam′i·nat′ed	un·cooked′	un·cor·rob′o·rat′ed
un′con·cealed′	un·con′quered	un·con·test′ed	un′co·op′er·a·tive	un′cor·rupt′ed
un′con·fined′	un·con′se·crat′ed	un·con·tra·dict′ed	un′co·or′di·nat′ed	un·cre·at′ed
un′con·firmed′	un·con·sid′ered	un·con·vert′ed	un·cor′dial	un·cred′it·ed
un′con·gealed′	un·con·strained′	un·con·vinced′	un·corked′	un·crit′i·cal
un′con·gen′ial	un·con·sumed′	un·con·vinc′ing	un·cor·rect′ed	un·crowd′ed

un·der·charge (un′dər chärj′), *v.* to charge less than the set or fair price; charge too low a price. ❑ *v.* **un·der·charged, un·der·charg·ing.**

un·der·class (un′dər klas′), *n.* part of the lower class thought to be unable to improve its economic or social situation.

un·der·clothes (un′dər klōz′ *or* un′dər klō̄ᴛʜz′), *n.pl.* underwear.

un·der·cloth·ing (un′dər klō′ᴛʜing), *n.* underwear.

un·der·coat (un′dər kōt′), *n.* **1** coat of paint, varnish, etc., applied before the finishing coats. **2** growth of short, fine hair under an animal's outer coat. **3** undercoating.

un·der·coat·ing (un′dər kō′ting), *n.* a heavy, tarlike substance sprayed on the underside of a car to protect it from water, dirt, salt, etc., on the road.

un·der·cov·er (un′dər kuv′ər), *adj.* working or done in secret: *The jeweler was an undercover agent of the police.*

un·der·cur·rent (un′dər kėr′ənt), *n.* **1** an underlying tendency: *There was an undercurrent of sadness in her laugh.* **2** current below the upper currents, or below the surface, of water, air, etc.

un·der·cut (un′dər kut′ *for verb;* un′dər kut′ *for noun*), **1** *v.* to cut under or beneath; cut away material from so as to leave a portion overhanging. **2** *n.* action of cutting away something underneath. **3** *v.* to reduce the effect or impact of; weaken: *undercut your efforts.* **4** *v.* to sell or work for less than another: *The big chain bookstore undercut the neighborhood bookstore's prices.* ❑ *v.* **un·der·cut, un·der·cut·ting.**

un·der·de·vel·oped (un′dər di- vel′əpt), *adj.* **1** poorly or insufficiently developed in production, technology, medicine, standard of living, etc.: *an underdeveloped country.* **2** not normally developed: *underdeveloped muscles.*

un·der·dog (un′dər dȯg′), *n.* **1** person or group having the worst of any struggle: *His early experience of poverty made him a champion of the underdog.* **2** contestant considered unlikely to win.

underdog (def. 2)

un·der·done (un′dər dun′), *adj.* not cooked enough; cooked very little.

un·der·es·ti·mate (un′dər es′tə māt *for verb;* un′dər es′tə mit *for noun*), **1** *v.* to estimate at too low a value, amount, rate, etc. **2** *n.* an estimate that is too low. ❑ *v.* **un·der·es·ti·mat·ed, un·der·es·ti·mat·ing.**

un·der·ex·pose (un′dər ekspōz′), *v.* to expose a film or negative for too short a time. ❑ *v.* **un·der·ex·posed, un·der·ex·pos·ing.**

un·der·ex·po·sure (un′dər ek spō′zhər), *n.* an exposure for too short a time. Underexposure to light makes a photograph look dim.

un·der·feed (un′dər fēd′), *v.* to feed too little. ❑ *v.* **un·der·fed** (un′dər fed′), **un·der·feed·ing.**

un·der·foot (un′dər fu̇t′), **1** *adv.* under your foot or feet; on the ground; underneath: *The leaves crunched underfoot.* **2** *adj.* in the way: *The cat is always underfoot when I'm cooking a meal.*

un·der·gar·ment (un′dər gär′mənt), *n.* an article of underwear.

un·der·go (un′dər gō′), *v.* **1** to go through; experience; be subjected to: *The town is undergoing many changes as it grows.* **2** to endure; suffer: *The pioneers underwent many hardships.* ❑ *v.* **un·der·went, un·der·gone, un·der·go·ing.**

un·der·gone (un′dər gȯn′), *v.* past participle of **undergo:** *The town has undergone many changes.*

un·der·grad·u·ate (un′dər graj′ü it), **1** *n.* student in a college or university who has not yet received a degree. **2** *adj.* of or for undergraduates.

un·der·ground (un′dər ground′ *for adv.;* un′dər ground′ *for adj., noun*), **1** *adv.* beneath the surface of the ground: *Moles burrow underground.* **2** *adj.* being, working, or used beneath the surface of the ground: *an underground passage.* **3** *n.* ʙʀɪᴛɪsʜ. subway. **4** *adv.* in or into secrecy or concealment: *The thief went underground after the robbery.* **5** *adj.* secret: *an underground plot.* **6** *n.* a secret organization working against an unpopular government, especially during military occupation: *the French underground during World War II.*

Underground Railroad, system by which people secretly helped fugitives from slavery escape to the free states or Canada before the Civil War.

Underground Railroad

un·der·growth (un′dər grōth′), *n.* underbrush.

un·der·hand (un′dər hand′), **1** *adj.* not open or honest; secret; sly. **2** *adv.* secretly; slyly. **3** *adj., adv.* with the hand below the level of the shoulder: *an underhand pitch, throw a ball underhand.*

un·der·hand·ed (un′dər han′did), *adj.* not open or honest; secret; sly: *an underhanded trick.* **–un′der·hand′ed·ly,** *adv.*

un·der·lie (un′dər lī′), *v.* **1** to be at the basis of; form the foundation of. **2** to lie under; be beneath. ❑ *v.* **un·der·lay** (un′dər lā′), **un·der·lain** (un′dər lān′), **un·der·ly·ing.**

un·der·line (un′dər lin′ *or* un′dər lin′), *v.* **1** to draw a line or lines under: *In writing, we underline titles of books.* **2** to make emphatic or more emphatic; emphasize: *to underline the importance of education.* ❑ *v.* **un·der·lined, un·der·lin·ing.**

un·der·ling (un′dər ling), *n.* person of lower rank or position; inferior.

un·der·ly·ing (un′dər li′ing), **1** *adj.* lying under or beneath. **2** *adj.* fundamental; basic; essential: *underlying causes.* **3** *v.* present participle of **underlie.**

un·der·mine (un′dər min′ *or* un′dər min′), *v.* **1** to weaken by secret or unfair means: *Nasty rumors undermined his reputation.* **2** to weaken or destroy gradually: *Many severe colds had undermined her health.* **3** to make a passage or hole under; dig under: *Burrowing animals had undermined the wall.* **4** to wear away the foundations of. ❑ *v.* **un·der·mined, un·der·min·ing.**

un·der·most (un′dər mōst), *adj., adv.* lowest.

un·der·neath (un′dər nēth′), *prep., adv.* beneath; below; under: *They sat underneath a tree. Someone was pushing underneath.*

un·der·nour·ished (un′dər nėr′isht), *adj.* not getting enough good food: *an undernourished child.*

un·crys′tal·lized	un·dam′aged	un′de·ceived′	un′de·fend′ed	un′de·liv′ered
un·cul′tured	un·damped′	un′de·ci′pher·a·ble	un′de·fen′si·ble	un′de·mand′ing
un·curbed′	un·dat′ed	un′de·ci′phered	un′de·filed′	un′dem·o·crat′ic
un·cured′	un·daz′zled	un′de·clared′	un′de·layed′	un′de·mon′stra·ble
un·cur′i·ous	un·de·bat′a·ble	un′dec·o·rat′ed	un′de·let′ed	un′dent′ed
un·cur′tained	un·de·cayed′	un′de·feat′ed	un′de·liv′er·a·ble	un′de·pend′a·ble

U

un·der·nour·ish·ment (un′dər nėr′ish mənt), *n.* lack of nourishment; not having enough food.

un·der·pants (un′dər pants′), *n.pl.* shorts, panties, etc., worn as underwear; drawers.

un·der·part (un′dər pärt′), *n.* the part of an object, animal, etc., that lies below or underneath.

un·der·pass (un′dər pas′), *n.* passageway underneath; walkway or road under railroad tracks or under another road. □ *n., pl.* **un·der·pass·es.**

un·der·pay (un′dər pā′), *v.* to pay too little. □ *v.* **un·der·paid** (un′dər pād′), **un·der·pay·ing.** —**un′der·pay′ment,** *n.*

un·der·pin·ning (un′dər pin′ing), *n.* **1** the materials or structure that give support from beneath to a building, wall, etc. **2** a support; prop.

un·der·priv·i·leged (un′dər priv′ə lijd), *adj.* having fewer advantages than most have, especially because of poverty: *underprivileged children.*

un·der·rate (un′dər rāt′), *v.* to rate or estimate too low; put too low a value on: *Don't underrate this team; it usually wins.* □ *v.* **un·der·rat·ed, un·der·rat·ing.**

un·der·score (un′dər skôr′ *or* un′dər skôr′), *v.* **1** to emphasize. **2** to underline. □ *v.* **un·der·scored, un·der·scor·ing.**

un·der·sea (un′dər sē′ *for adj.;* un′dər sē′ *for adv.*), **1** *adj.* being, working, or used beneath the surface of the sea: *an undersea cable, undersea exploration.* **2** *adv.* underseas.

undersea—undersea life

un·der·seas (un′dər sēz′), *adv.* beneath the surface of the sea: *Submarines go underseas.*

un·der·sec·re·tar·y (un′dər- sek′rə ter′ē), *n.* official ranking just below the secretary in charge of a department of the government. □ *n., pl.* **un·der·sec·re·tar·ies.**

un·der·sell (un′dər sel′), *v.* to sell things at a lower price than another: *This store undersells other local stores.* □ *v.* **un·der·sold, un·der·sell·ing.** —**un′der·sell′er,** *n.*

un·der·shirt (un′dər shėrt′), *n.* shirt worn next to the skin under other clothing.

un·der·shot (un′dər shot′), *adj.* **1** driven by water passing beneath: *an undershot water wheel.* **2** having the lower jaw projecting beyond the upper.

un·der·side (un′dər sīd′), *n.* surface lying underneath; bottom side.

un·der·signed (un′dər sīnd′), **1** *adj.* signed, or having signed, at the end of a letter or document. **2** *n.sing.* or *pl.* **the undersigned,** person or persons signing a letter or document.

un·der·sized (un′dər sīzd′), *adj.* smaller than the usual size: *an undersized fish.*

un·der·skirt (un′dər skėrt′), *n.* skirt worn under an outer skirt.

un·der·sold (un′dər sōld′), *v.* past tense and past participle of **undersell.**

un·der·staffed (un′dər staft′), *adj.* having too small a staff: *an understaffed school.*

un·der·stand (un′dər stand′), *v.* **1** to get the meaning of something: *Now I understand the teacher's question.* **2** to know well; know: *My parents understand local politics.* **3** to be sympathetic; show patience toward: *When I have a problem, I know my friend will understand.* **4** to be informed; learn: *I understand that she bought a house.* **5** to take as a fact; believe: *It is understood that you will come.* **6** to take as meaning; interpret: *I understood your comment as approval of the plan.* **7** to supply in the mind. In "He hit the tree harder than I," the word *did* is understood after *I.* □ *v.* **un·der·stood, un·der·stand·ing.** —**un′der·stand′a·ble,** *adj.* —**un′der·stand′a·bly,** *adv.*

SYNONYM STUDY **Understand** and **know** both mean to have knowledge. **Understand** means to be familiar with the meaning or method of something: *She understands math a lot better than I do.* **Know** means to have ready in the memory: *My dad knows some great recipes.*

un·der·stand·ing (un′dər stan′ding), **1** *n.* comprehension; knowledge: *a clear understanding of the problem.* **2** *n.* ability to learn and know; intelligence: *a person with limited understanding.* **3** *adj.* that understands; intelligent and sympathetic: *an understanding reply.* **4** *n.* knowledge of each other's meaning and wishes: *True friendship is based on understanding.* **5** *n.* a mutual arrangement or agreement: *We have an understanding about the use of the car on Saturdays.* —**un′der·stand′ing·ly,** *adv.*

un·der·state (un′dər stāt′), *v.* to state something with less than the complete facts about it: *The mayor understated the current deficit.* □ *v.* **un·der·stat·ed, un·der·stat·ing.** —**un′der·state′ment,** *n.*

un·der·stat·ed (un′dər stā′tid), *adj.* kept mild or made simple, for greater effect; restrained; played down: *an understated decor.*

un·der·stood (un′dər stůd′), *v.* past tense and past participle of **understand:** *I understood what she said. Have all of you understood today's lesson?*

un·der·sto·ry (un′dər stôr′ē), *n.* underbrush. □ *n., pl.* **un·der·sto·ries.**

un·der·stud·y (un′dər stud′ē), **1** *n.* person who can act as a substitute for an actor, actress, or any other regular performer. **2** *v.* to learn a part in order to replace the regular performer when necessary. **3** *v.* to act as an understudy to. □ *n., pl.* **un·der·stud·ies;** *v.* **un·der·stud·ied, un·der·stud·y·ing.**

un·der·sur·face (un′dər sėr′fis), *n.* underside: *the undersurface of a leaf.*

un·der·take (un′dər tāk′), *v.* **1** to agree to do; take upon yourself: *I will undertake the feeding of your dogs while you are away.* **2** to promise; guarantee. **3** to set about; try; attempt: *undertake to reach home before dark.* □ *v.* **un·der·took, un·der·tak·en, un·der·tak·ing.**

un·der·tak·en (un′dər tā′kən), *v.* past participle of **undertake:** *She has undertaken more than she can do.*

un·der·tak·er (un′dər tā′kər), *n.* funeral director; mortician.

un·der·tak·ing (un′dər tā′king *for 1,2;* un′dər tā′king *for 3*), *n.* **1** something undertaken; task; enterprise: *Starting your own business is a large undertaking.* **2** a promise; guarantee. **3** business of a funeral director.

un·der·the·count·er (un′dər т͟нə koun′tər), *adj.* hidden and stealthy; unauthorized; illegal.

un·der·tone (un′dər tōn′), *n.* **1** a low or very quiet tone: *talk in undertones.* **2** a subdued color; color seen through other colors: *There was an undertone of brown beneath all the gold and crimson of autumn.* **3** something beneath the surface; an underlying quality, condition, or element: *an undertone of sadness in their gaiety.*

---

un′de·served′	un′de·tach′a·ble	un′di·gest′ed	un′dip·lo·mat′ic	un′dis·cour′aged
un′de·serv′ing	un′de·tect′ed	un′dig′ni·fied	un′dis·cern′i·ble	un′dis·cov′ered
un′des·ig·nat′ed	un′de·ter′mined	un′di·lut′ed	un′dis·cern′ing	un′dis·crim′i·nat′ing
un′de·sired′	un′de·terred′	un′di·min′ished	un′dis·charged′	un′dis·so·ci·at′ed
un′de·spair′ing	un′dif·fe·ren′ti·at′ed	un′dimmed′	un′dis·closed′	un′dis·solved′

un·der·took (un/dər tùk/), *v.* past tense of **undertake**: *He failed because he undertook more than he could do.*

un·der·tow (un/dər tō/), *n.* **1** the backward flow from waves breaking on a beach. **2** any strong current below the surface of the water, moving in a direction different from that of the surface current.

un·der·val·ue (un/dər val/yü), *v.* to put too low a value on. ❑ *v.* **un·der·val·ued, un·der·val·u·ing.** —**un/der·val/u·a/tion,** *n.*

un·der·wa·ter (un/dər wò/tər), **1** *adj., adv.* below the surface of the water: *an underwater current, to swim underwater.* **2** *adj.* made for use under the water: *Submarines are underwater boats.*

un·der·way (un/dər wā/), *adv.* going on; in motion; in progress: *The construction of the new library is now underway.*

un·der·wear (un/dər wâr/), *n.* clothing worn under your outer clothes, especially next to the skin; underclothes; underclothing.

un·der·weight (un/dər wāt/), **1** *adj.* having too little weight; below the normal or required weight. **2** *n.* weight that is not up to standard.

un·der·went (un/dər went/), *v.* past tense of **undergo**: *Transportation underwent a great change with the development of the car.*

un·der·world (un/dər wèrld/), *n.* **1** the criminal part of human society. **2** (in Greek myths) the world of the dead; Hades.

un·der·write (un/dər rīt/ *or* un/dər rit/), *v.* **1** to agree to meet the expense of; finance: *underwrite someone's college education.* **2** to sign an insurance policy, thereby accepting the risk of insuring something against loss. **3** to agree to buy all the stocks or bonds of a certain issue that are not bought by the public: *The bankers underwrote the steel company's bonds.* **4** to write under other written matter; sign your name to a document, etc. ❑ *v.* **un·der·wrote** (un/dər rōt/ *or* un/dər rōt/), **un·der·writ·ten** (un/dər rit/n *or* un/dər rit/n), **un·der·writ·ing.**

un·der·writ·er (un/dər rī/tər), *n.* **1** person who underwrites an insurance policy or carries on an insurance business. **2** person who underwrites (usually with others) an issue or issues of stocks or bonds.

un·de·sir·a·ble (un/di zī/rə bəl), **1** *adj.* objectionable; disagreeable: *undesirable side effects.* **2** *n.* an undesirable person or thing. —**un/de·sir·a·bil/i·ty, un/de·sir·a·ble·ness,** *n.* —**un/de·sir·a·bly,** *adv.*

un·de·vel·oped (un/di vel/əpt), *adj.* **1** not put to full use: *undeveloped natural resources of a country.* **2** not developed. **3** not fully grown; immature.

un·did (un did/), *v.* past tense of **undo**: *The fire in the artist's studio undid many years of work.*

un·dis·ci·plined (un dis/ə plind), *adj.* not disciplined; without proper control; untrained.

un·dis·guised (un/dis gīzd/), *adj.* **1** unconcealed; open; plain; frank: *undisguised delight.* **2** not disguised.

un·dis·put·ed (un/dis pyü/tid), *adj.* not disputed; not doubted. —**un/dis·put·ed·ly,** *adv.*

un·dis·tin·guished (un/dis ting/gwisht), *adj.* not distinguished; commonplace.

un·dis·turbed (un/dis tèrbd/), *adj.* not disturbed; not troubled; calm: *The sleeping children were undisturbed by the noise.*

un·di·vid·ed (un/də vī/did), *adj.* not divided; not separated into parts; complete: *Give me your undivided attention.*

un·do (un dü/), *v.* **1** to unfasten; untie: *Please undo the package.* **2** to do away with the effect of; cancel or reverse: *The workers fixed the road, but a heavy storm undid their work.* **3** to bring to ruin; spoil; destroy. ■ Another word that sounds like this is **undue.** ❑ *v.* **un·did, un·done, un·do·ing. —un·do/er,** *n.*

un·do·ing (un dü/ing), *n.* **1** cause of destruction or ruin: *Gambling was their undoing.* **2** act of canceling or reversing the effect of something. **3** act of untying; unfastening.

un·done (un dun/), **1** *adj.* not done; not finished. **2** *adj.* ruined. **3** *adj.* untied; unfastened. **4** *v.* past participle of **undo.**

un·doubt·ed (un dou/tid), *adj.* not doubted; accepted as true: *She is the undoubted winner.* —**un·doubt/ed·ly,** *adv.*

un·draw (un drò/), *v.* to draw back or aside: *She undrew the curtain.* ❑ *v.* **un·drew** (un drü/), **un·drawn** (un dròn/), **un·draw·ing.**

un·dreamed-of (un drēmd/uv/ *or* un drēmd/ov/), *adj.* never thought of, even in the imagination: *undreamed-of advances in medicine.*

un·dress (un dres/), **1** *v.* to take the clothes off; strip. **2** *v.* to take off your clothes. **3** *n.* nakedness; nudity: *be caught in a state of undress.*

un·due (un dü/), *adj.* **1** not fitting; not right; improper: *make rude, undue remarks.* **2** too great; too much; excessive: *Some people give undue importance to money.* ■ Another word that sounds like this is **undo.**

un·du·lant (un/jə lənt), *adj.* waving; wavy.

undulant fever, disease with fever that comes and goes, disorder of the intestines, weakness, and pain in the joints. It is caused by bacterial infection, usually transmitted by contact with infected cattle, goats, or hogs, or by eating untreated milk or milk products.

un·du·late (un/jə lāt), *v.* **1** to move or cause to move in waves: *undulating water.* **2** to have a wavy form or surface: *undulating hair, an undulating prairie.* ❑ *v.* **un·du·lat·ed, un·du·lat·ing.**

undulate—bridge undulating in a high wind

WORD FAMILY Undulate and the following words are related: **abound, abundant, inundate, redound, redundant,** and **surround.** They all come from a Latin word meaning "a wave."

un·du·la·tion (un/jə lā/shən), *n.* **1** a wavelike motion; undulating. **2** a wavy form. **3** one of a series of wavelike bends, curves, swellings, etc.

un·du·ly (un dü/lē), *adv.* **1** in an undue manner; improperly. **2** too much; excessively: *Treatment of the prisoners was unduly harsh.*

un·dy·ing (un dī/ing), *adj.* never dying; deathless; immortal; eternal: *undying fame, undying beauty.*

un·earned (un èrnd/), *adj.* **1** not earned; not gained by labor or service: *unearned income.* **2** not deserved: *unearned punishment.*

un·earth (un èrth/), *v.* **1** to dig up: *unearth a buried city.* **2** to find out; discover: *unearth a plot.*

un·earth·ly (un èrth/lē), *adj.* **1** not of this world; supernatural. **2** strange; weird; ghostly: *We heard an unearthly howling.* —**un·earth/li·ness,** *n.*

un·eas·y (un ē/zē), *adj.* **1** restless; disturbed; anxious: *They became uneasy when the children didn't come home for dinner.* **2** not easy in manner; awkward: *The speaker seemed nervous and uneasy.* **3** not comfortable. ❑ *adj.* **un·eas·i·er, un·eas·i·est.** —**un·eas/i·ly,** *adv.* —**un·eas/i·ness,** *n.*

un·ed·u·cat·ed (un ej/ə kā/tid), *adj.* not educated; not taught or trained. See Synonym Study at **ignorant.**

un·em·ploy·a·ble (un/em ploi/ə bəl), *adj.* not able to be employed, especially because of a disability.

un·em·ployed (un/em ploid/), **1** *adj.* not having a job; having no work: *an unemployed person.* **2** *n.pl.* **the unemployed,** people out of work. **3** *adj.* not employed; not in use: *an unemployed skill.*

un·em·ploy·ment (un/em ploi/mənt), *n.* **1** lack of employment; condition of being out of work. **2** number or percentage of workers that are unemployed: *Unemployment was up last month.*

U

---

un/dis·tin/guish·ing	un/do·mes/ti·cat/ed	un·draped/	un·dyed/	un/e·lim/i·nat/ed
un/dis·tort/ed	un·dou/bled	un·dreamed/	un·eat/en	un/em·bar/rassed
un/dis·tract/ed	un·doubt/ing	un·dreamt/	un/e·co·nom/ic	un/em·bel/lished
un/di·ver/si·fied	un·drained/	un·dressed/	un/e·co·nom/i·cal	un/e·mo/tion·al
un/di·vulged/	un/dra·mat/ic	un·du/ti·ful	un·ed/i·fy/ing	un/em·phat/ic

un·end·ing (un en′ding), *adj.* never ending; endless; continuous: *an unending struggle, the unending change of the seasons.*

un·e·qual (un ē′kwəl), *adj.* **1** not fair; one-sided: *an unequal contest.* **2** not enough; not adequate: *Their strength was unequal to the task.* **3** not the same in amount, size, number, value, degree, or rank: *unequal sums of money.* **4** not regular; not even: *unequal vibrations.* **−un·e′qual·ly,** *adv.*

un·e·qualed or **un·e·qualled** (un ē′kwəld), *adj.* having no equal or superior; matchless: *unequaled beauty, unequaled speed.*

un·e·quiv·o·cal (un′i kwiv′ə kəl), *adj.* clear; plain: *an unequivocal refusal.* **−un′e·quiv·o·cal·ly,** *adv.*

un·err·ing (un ėr′ing *or* un er′ing), *adj.* making no mistakes; exactly right: *unerring aim.* **−un·err′ing·ly,** *adv.*

UNESCO or **U·nes·co** (yü nes′kō), *n.* United Nations Educational, Scientific, and Cultural Organization.

un·e·ven (un ē′vən), *adj.* **1** not level, flat, or smooth: *uneven ground.* ■ See Synonym Study at **rough. 2** not equal: *It was an uneven contest.* **3** not the same or regular; changeable; inconsistent: *Her work is of uneven quality.* **4** leaving a remainder of 1 when divided by 2; odd: *1, 3, 5, 7, and 9 are uneven numbers.* **−un·e′ven·ly,** *adv.* **−un·e′ven·ness,** *n.*

un·e·vent·ful (un′i vent′fəl), *adj.* without important or noticeable occurrences: *an uneventful day.* **−un′e·vent·ful·ly,** *adv.*

un·ex·am·pled (un′eg zam′pəld), *adj.* having no equal or like; like nothing ever before.

un·ex·cep·tion·a·ble (un′ek sep′shə nə bəl), *adj.* beyond criticism; wholly admirable. **−un′ex·cep·tion·a·bly,** *adv.*

un·ex·pect·ed (un′ek spek′tid), *adj.* not expected: *an unexpected difficulty, an unexpected change in the weather.* **−un′ex·pect′ed·ly,** *adv.* **−un′ex·pect′ed·ness,** *n.*

un·fail·ing (un fā′ling), *adj.* **1** never failing; always ready when needed; loyal: *an unfailing friend.* **2** never running short; endless: *an unfailing supply of water.* **3** sure; certain: *unfailing proof of guilt.* **−un·fail′ing·ly,** *adv.* **−un·fail′ing·ness,** *n.*

un·fair (un fâr′), *adj.* not fair; unjust: *an unfair decision. It was unfair of you to trick him.* **−un·fair′ly,** *adv.* **−un·fair′ness,** *n.*

un·faith·ful (un fāth′fəl), *adj.* **1** not faithful; not true to duty or your promises; faithless. **2** not accurate; not exact: *an unfaithful translation.* **−un·faith′ful·ly,** *adv.* **−un·faith′ful·ness,** *n.*

un·fal·ter·ing (un fôl′tər ing), *adj.* not hesitating; firm; steadfast. **−un·fal′ter·ing·ly,** *adv.*

un·fa·mil·iar (un′fə mil′yər), *adj.* **1** not well known; unusual; strange: *That face is unfamiliar to me.* **2** not acquainted: *She is unfamiliar with the Greek language.* **−un′fa·mil′iar′i·ty,** *n.*

un·fas·ten (un fas′n), *v.* to undo; untie; loosen; open: *Don't unfasten your seat belt yet.*

un·fath·om·a·ble (un faтн′ə mə bəl), *adj.* **1** too mysterious to be understood. **2** too deep to be measured.

un·fath·omed (un faтн′əmd), *adj.* **1** not understood. **2** not measured.

un·fa·vor·a·ble (un fā′vər ə bəl), *adj.* not favorable; adverse; harmful: *The forecast for tomorrow is for unfavorable weather.* **−un·fa′vor·a·ble·ness,** *n.* **−un·fa′vor·a·bly,** *adv.*

un·feel·ing (un fē′ling), *adj.* **1** hardhearted; cruel: *a cold, unfeeling person.* **2** not able to feel; numb. **−un·feel′ing·ly,** *adv.* **−un·feel′ing·ness,** *n.*

un·feigned (un fānd′), *adj.* not feigned; sincere; real: *unfeigned joy.* **−un·feign·ed·ly** (un fā′nid lē), *adv.*

un·fin·ished (un fin′isht), *adj.* **1** not finished; not complete: *un-* finished *homework, an unfinished symphony.* **2** without some special finish; not polished or painted: *unfinished furniture.*

un·fit (un fit′), **1** *adj.* not fit; not suitable: *This moldy bread is un-fit to eat.* **2** *adj.* not healthy and strong; in poor physical condition: *He was unfit for the hard work.* **3** *v.* to make unfit; spoil. ❏ *v.* **un·fit·ted, un·fit·ting. −un·fit′ly,** *adv.* **−un·fit′ness,** *n.*

un·flag·ging (un flag′ing), *adj.* not weakening or failing: *unflagging strength, unflagging efforts.* **−un·flag′ging·ly,** *adv.*

un·flap·pa·ble (un flap′ə bəl), *adj.* not easily excited, confused, or alarmed. **−un·flap′pa·bil′i·ty,** *n.*

un·fledged (un flejd′), *adj.* **1** too young to fly; not having full-grown feathers: *an unfledged crow.* **2** undeveloped; immature; inexperienced.

un·flinch·ing (un flin′ching), *adj.* not drawing back from difficulty, danger, or pain; firm: *unflinching courage.* **−un·flinch′ing·ly,** *adv.*

un·fold (un fōld′), *v.* **1** to open the folds of; open up; spread out: *unfold a napkin.* **2** to reveal; show; explain: *unfold a plot.* **3** to open; develop: *Buds unfold into flowers.* **−un·fold′ment,** *n.*

un·forced (un fôrst′), *adj.* **1** not forced; not compelled; willing. **2** natural; spontaneous.

un·fore·seen (un′fôr sēn′), *adj.* not known beforehand; unexpected: *There was an unforeseen delay.*

un·for·get·ta·ble (un′fər get′ə bəl), *adj.* unable to be forgotten: *It was an unforgettable experience.* **−un′for·get·ta·bly,** *adv.*

un·for·giv·a·ble (un′fər giv′ə bəl), *adj.* not to be forgiven; inexcusable: *Such cruelty is unforgivable.*

un·formed (un fôrmd′), *adj.* **1** without definite or regular form; shapeless: *unformed clay.* **2** undeveloped: *an unformed mind.*

un·for·tu·nate (un fôr′chə nit), **1** *adj.* not lucky; having bad luck: *She had an unfortunate accident.* **2** *adj.* not suitable; not fitting: *an unfortunate choice of words.* **3** *n.* an unfortunate person. **−un·for′tu·nate·ly,** *adv.*

un·found·ed (un foun′did), *adj.* without foundation; without reason; baseless: *an unfounded complaint.*

un·freeze (un frēz′), *v.* **1** to thaw; loosen. **2** to free from control or restrictions. **3** to release money for spending. ❏ *v.* **un·froze, un·fro·zen, un·freez·ing.**

un·fre·quent·ed (un′frē kwent′id), *adj.* not frequented; seldom visited; rarely used.

un·friend·ly (un frend′lē), *adj.* **1** not friendly; hostile: *The unfriendly dog barked at me.* **2** not favorable: *unfriendly reviews.* ❏ *adj.* **un·friend·li·er, un·friend·li·est. −un·friend′li·ness,** *n.*

un·froze (un frōz′), *v.* past tense of **unfreeze.**

un·fro·zen (un frō′zn), *v.* past participle of **unfreeze.**

un·fruit·ful (un früt′fəl), *adj.* producing nothing worthwhile; unproductive: *an unfruitful effort.* **−un·fruit′ful·ly,** *adv.* **−un·fruit′-ful·ness,** *n.*

un·furl (un fėrl′), *v.* to spread out; shake out; unfold: *Unfurl the sail.*

un·fur·nished (un fėr′nisht), *adj.* not furnished; without furniture: *an unfurnished apartment.*

un·gain·ly (un gān′lē), *adj.* awkward; clumsy: *Long arms and large hands can give a person an ungainly appearance.* ❏ *adj.* **un·gain·li·er, un·gain·li·est. −un·gain′li·ness,** *n.*

un·gen·er·ous (un jen′ər əs), *adj.* not generous; mean. **−un·gen′er·ous·ly,** *adv.*

un·god·ly (un god′lē), *adj.* **1** not devout; not religious; impious. **2** wicked; sinful. **3** very annoying; outrageous; shocking: *an ungodly noise, pay an ungodly price.* **−un·god′li·ness,** *n.*

---

un′en·closed′	un′en·ter·pris′ing	un′ex·celled′	un′ex·plod′ed	un·fazed′
un′en·cum′bered	un′en·ter·tain′ing	un′ex·cep′tion·al	un′ex·plored′	un·fea′si·ble
un′en·dan′gered	un′en·thu′si·as′tic	un·ex·cit′ed	un′ex·posed′	un·fed′
un′en·dorsed′	un′en·vi·a·ble	un·ex·cit′ing	un′ex·pressed′	un·fed′e·rat′ed
un′en·dur′a·ble	un·en′vied	un′ex·cused′	un′ex·pres′sive	un·felt′
un′en·dur′ing	un·en′vi·ous	un·ex′e·cut′ed	un·ex′pur·gat′ed	un·fem′i·nine
un′en·force′a·ble	un′e·quipped′	un′ex·haust′ed	un′ex·tin′guished	un·fenced′
un′en·forced′	un·es·sen′tial	un′ex·pend′ed	un·fad′ed	un′fer·ment′ed
un′en·gaged′	un·es′ti·mat′ed	un′ex·pired′	un·fad′ing	un′fer·ti·lized
un′en·joy′a·ble	un·eth′i·cal	un′ex·plain′a·ble	un·fash′ion·a·ble	un·fet′tered
un′en·light′ened	un′ex·ag′ger·at′ed	un′ex·plained′	un·fas′tened	un·fil′i·al

un·gov·ern·a·ble (un guv′ər nə bəl), *adj.* impossible to control; very hard to control or rule; unruly. —**un·gov′ern·a·ble·ness**, *n.* —**un·gov′ern·a·bly**, *adv.*

un·grace·ful (un grās′fəl), *adj.* not graceful; not elegant or beautiful; clumsy; awkward. —**un·grace′ful·ly**, *adv.*

un·gra·cious (un grā′shəs), *adj.* **1** not polite; discourteous; rude. **2** unpleasant; disagreeable; displeasing. —**un·gra′cious·ly**, *adv.* —**un·gra′cious·ness**, *n.*

un·grate·ful (un grāt′fəl), *adj.* **1** not grateful; not thankful: *I'm sorry to seem ungrateful, but I don't need your help.* **2** unpleasant; disagreeable: *an ungrateful task.* —**un·grate′ful·ly**, *adv.* —**un·grate′ful·ness**, *n.*

un·ground·ed (un groun′did), *adj.* without foundation; without reasons; unfounded. —**un·ground′ed·ness**, *n.*

un·grudg·ing (un gruj′ing), *adj.* not grudging; willing; hearty; liberal. —**un·grudg′ing·ly**, *adv.*

un·guard·ed (un gär′did), *adj.* **1** not protected: *an unguarded camp.* **2** careless: *In an unguarded moment she gave away the secret.* —**un·guard′ed·ly**, *adv.* —**un·guard′ed·ness**, *n.*

un·guent (ung′gwənt), *n.* ointment for sores, burns, etc.; salve.

un·gu·late (ung′gyə lit), **1** *adj.* having hoofs; belonging to the group of animals having hoofs. **2** *n.* animal that has hoofs. Horses, cows, sheep, and deer are ungulates.

un·hal·lowed (un hal′ōd), *adj.* not made holy; not sacred.

un·hand (un hand′), *v.* OLD USE. to let go; take the hands from; release: *Unhand me at once!*

un·hand·y (un han′dē), *adj.* **1** not easy to handle: *an unhandy tool.* **2** not skillful: *an unhandy worker.*

un·hap·pi·ly (un hap′ə lē), *adv.* **1** not happily: *to live unhappily.* **2** unfortunately: *Unhappily, I missed seeing him.* **3** unsuitably.

un·hap·py (un hap′ē), *adj.* **1** not happy; sad; sorrowful: *an unhappy face.* **2** unlucky: *an unhappy accident.* **3** not suitable: *an unhappy selection of colors.* ❑ *adj.* **un·hap·pi·er, un·hap·pi·est.** —**un·hap′pi·ness**, *n.*

un·harmed (un härmd′), *adj.* not harmed; not injured.

un·health·ful (un helth′fəl), *adj.* bad for the health. —**un·health′ful·ly**, *adv.* —**un·health′ful·ness**, *n.*

un·health·y (un hel′thē), *adj.* **1** hurtful to health; not healthful: *an unhealthy climate.* **2** not possessing good health; not well: *an unhealthy person.* **3** coming from or showing poor health: *an unhealthy paleness.* **4** morally or mentally harmful: *an unhealthy attitude.* ❑ *adj.* **un·health·i·er, un·health·i·est.** —**un·health′i·ly**, *adv.* —**un·health′i·ness**, *n.*

un·heard (un hèrd′), *adj.* **1** not listened to; not heard: *My advice went unheard.* **2** not given a hearing: *condemn a person unheard.*

un·heard-of (un hèrd′uv′ *or* un hèrd′ov′), *adj.* **1** never heard of; unknown: *Electric stoves were unheard-of 200 years ago.* **2** such as was never known before; unprecedented: *unheard-of prices.*

un·heed·ed (un hē′did), *adj.* not heeded; disregarded; unnoticed: *My warning went unheeded.*

un·hes·i·tat·ing (un hez′ə tā′ting), *adj.* prompt; ready. —**un·hes′i·tat·ing·ly**, *adv.*

un·hinge (un hinj′), *v.* **1** to unsettle; upset: *a mind unhinged by shock.* **2** to take a door, etc., off its hinges. **3** to remove the hinges from. **4** to separate from something; detach. ❑ *v.* **un·hinged, un·hing·ing.**

un·hitch (un hich′), *v.* to free from being hitched; unfasten: *We unhitched the trailer from the car.*

un·ho·ly (un hō′lē), *adj.* not holy; wicked; sinful. ❑ *adj.* **un·ho·li·er, un·ho·li·est.** —**un·ho′li·ness**, *n.*

un·hook (un húk′), *v.* **1** to undo by loosening a hook or hooks. **2** to loosen from a hook. **3** to become unhooked; become undone.

un·horse (un hôrs′), *v.* to throw from a horse's back; cause to fall from a horse: *The unknown knight unhorsed all challengers in the tournament.* ❑ *v.* **un·horsed, un·hors·ing.**

un·hur·ried (un hèr′ēd), *adj.* not hurried; without haste; leisurely. —**un·hur′ried·ly**, *adv.*

un·hurt (un hèrt′), *adj.* not hurt; not harmed: *Despite his fall, he was unhurt.*

uni-, *prefix.* one; single: *unicellular = having one cell.*

u·ni·cam·er·al (yü′nə kam′ər əl), *adj.* having only one house in a lawmaking group. Nebraska has a unicameral legislature.

UNICEF or **U·ni·cef** (yü′nə sef), *n.* United Nations Children's Fund.

u·ni·cel·lu·lar (yü′nə sel′yə lər), *adj.* having only one cell. The amoeba is a unicellular animal.

u·ni·corn (yü′nə kôrn), *n.* an imaginary animal like a horse, but with a single, long horn in the middle of its forehead.

u·ni·cy·cle (yü′nə sī′kəl), *n.* vehicle with a single wheel, pedaled like a bicycle, used especially by acrobats and circus performers.

u·ni·fi·ca·tion (yü′nə fə kā′shən), *n.* **1** process of forming into one unit; union: *the unification of many states into one nation.* **2** act of making or condition of being made more alike: *The traffic laws of the different states need unification.*

u·ni·form (yü′nə fôrm), **1** *n.* the distinctive clothes worn by members of a group when on duty, by which they may be recognized as belonging to that group. Soldiers, police officers, and nurses wear uniforms. **2** *adj.* always the same; not changing: *The earth turns at a uniform rate.* **3** *adj.* all alike; not varying: *All the bricks have a uniform size.* **4** *v.* to clothe or furnish with a uniform. —**u′ni·form′ly**, *adv.* —**u′ni·form′ness**, *n.*

unicorn—as imagined by an artist

u·ni·formed (yü′nə fôrmd), *adj.* wearing a uniform; in uniform: *a uniformed soldier, a uniformed schoolgirl.*

u·ni·form·i·ty (yü′nə fôr′mə tē), *n.* uniform condition or character; sameness throughout.

u·ni·fy (yü′nə fī), *v.* to make or form into one; unite: *Several small states were unified into one nation.* ❑ *v.* **u·ni·fied, u·ni·fy·ing.** —**u′ni·fi′a·ble**, *adj.* —**u′ni·fi′er**, *n.*

u·ni·lat·er·al (yü′nə lat′ər əl), *adj.* of, on, or affecting one side only: *unilateral disarmament.* —**u′ni·lat′er·al·ly**, *adv.*

un·filled′	un·for′mu·lat′ed	un·gift′ed	un·hanged′	un·her′ald·ed
un·fil′tered	un·for′ti·fied	un·glam′or·ous	un·har′assed	un′he·ro′ic
un·fil′tered	un·framed′	un·glazed′	un·hard′ened	un·hes′i·tant
un·fired′	un·ful·filled′	un·gov′erned	un·har·mo′ni·ous	un·hin′dered
un·fixed′	un·fun′ny	un·grad′ed	un·har′nessed	un·hon′ored
un·flat′ter·ing	un·gal′lant	un′gram·mat′i·cal	un·hatched′	un·housed′
un·fla′vored	un·gar′nished	un·grat′i·fied	un·healed′	un·hur′ry·ing
un′for·get′ting	un·gath′ered	un′guar·an·teed′	un·heat′ed	un′hy·gien′ic
un′for·giv′en	un·gen·teel′	un·guid′ed	un·heed′ful	un′i·den′ti·fied
un′for·giv′ing	un·gen′tle	un·ham′pered	un·heed′ing	un′id·i·o·mat′ic
un′for·got′ten	un·gen′tle·man·ly	un·hand′i·capped	un·help′ful	un′il·lu′mi·nat′ed

U

un·i·mag·i·na·ble (un′i maj′ə nə bəl), *adj.* not able to be imagined or thought of; inconceivable: *Three hundred years ago, CD-ROMs, VCRs, and cellular phones were unimaginable.* —**un′i·mag′i·na·bly,** *adv.*

un·im·peach·a·ble (un′im pē′chə bəl), *adj.* free from fault, flaw, or error; not to be doubted or questioned: *an unimpeachable fact.* —**un′im·peach′a·bly,** *adv.*

un·im·por·tance (un′im pôrt′ns), *n.* unimportant nature or quality.

un·im·por·tant (un′im pôrt′nt), *adj.* not important; insignificant; trifling: *unimportant details.*

un·in·hab·it·ed (un′in hab′ə tid), *adj.* not lived in; without inhabitants: *an uninhabited wilderness.*

un·in·jured (un in′jərd), *adj.* not hurt; not damaged.

un·in·spired (un′in spīrd′), *adj.* not inspired; dull; tiresome: *uninspired writing.*

un·in·tel·li·gi·ble (un′in tel′ə jə bəl), *adj.* not intelligible; not able to be understood: *unintelligible handwriting.* —**un′in·tel′li·gi·ble·ness,** *n.* —**un′in·tel′li·gi·bly,** *adv.*

un·in·ten·tion·al (un′in ten′shə nəl), *adj.* not intentional; not done purposely. —**un′in·ten′tion·al·ly,** *adv.*

un·in·ter·est·ed (un in′tər ə stid *or* un in′tə res′tid), *adj.* not interested; paying no attention. ■ See Usage Note at **disinterested.**

un·in·ter·est·ing (un in′tər ə sting *or* un in′tə res′ting), *adj.* not interesting: *I didn't finish the book because it was uninteresting.*

un·in·ter·rupt·ed (un′in tə rup′tid), *adj.* without interruption; continuous. —**un′in·ter·rupt′ed·ly,** *adv.*

un·in·vit·ed (un′in vī′tid), *adj.* not invited; without an invitation.

union (def. 4)

un·ion (yü′nyən), *n.* **1** act of uniting or condition of being united: *The United States was formed by the union of thirteen former British colonies.* **2** a group of people, states, etc., united for some special purpose: *Many European countries have joined in a union for defense, foreign policy, and law enforcement.* **3 the Union, a** the United States of America. **b** those states that supported the federal government of the United States during the Civil War. **4** any of many groups of workers joined to protect and promote their common good; labor union or trade union. **5** marriage. **6** device for connecting parts of equipment or machinery, especially a piece to join pipes or tubes together; coupling. **7** (in mathematics) a set including all the members that belong to one or both of two other sets. EXAMPLE: If set A = {1,2,3,4} and set B = {4,5,6}, then the union of the two sets = {1,2,3,4,5,6}.

un·ion·ism (yü′nyə niz′əm), *n.* **1** principle of union. **2** system, principles, or methods of labor unions.

un·ion·ist (yü′nyə nist), *n.* **1** person who favors the uniting of certain groups, states, etc. **2 Unionist,** supporter of the federal government of the United States during the Civil War. **3** member of a labor union.

un·ion·ize (yü′nyə nīz), *v.* **1** to form into a labor union. **2** to organize under a labor union. ❑ *v.* **un·ion·ized, un·ion·iz·ing.** —**un′ion·i·za′tion,** *n.* —**un′ion·iz′er,** *n.*

Union Jack, the flag of the United Kingdom.

Union of South Africa, former name of **Republic of South Africa.**

Union of Soviet Socialist Republics, Soviet Union.

union shop, business establishment that employs only members of a labor union, but may hire other workers provided they join the union within a specified period.

u·nique (yü nēk′), *adj.* **1** having no like or equal; being the only one of its kind: *a unique specimen of rock, a unique experience.* **2** INFORMAL. very uncommon or unusual; rare; remarkable: *Making a vest out of your father's old ties is a rather unique idea.* —**u·nique′ly,** *adv.* —**u·nique′ness,** *n.*

u·ni·sex (yü′nə seks′), *adj.* suitable for use by either sex, especially clothing and hairstyles.

u·ni·son (yü′nə sən), *n.* **1** agreement: *The marchers' feet moved in unison. We spoke in unison.* **2** agreement in pitch of two or more tones, voices, etc.; a sounding together at the same pitch. [Unison comes from Latin words meaning "one" and "sound." People who say the same thing in the same way must really agree.]

u·nit (yü′nit), *n.* **1** a single thing or person. **2** any group of things or persons considered as one: *The family is a social unit.* **3** one of the individuals or groups forming a whole: *The body consists of units called cells.* **4** a standard amount, used for measuring: *A meter is a unit of length; a liter is a unit of volume.* **5** a particular part or section: *the beginning unit of a book.* **6** a part of a machine or other apparatus that has one specific purpose: *the storage unit in a computer.* **7** the smallest whole number; one.

U·ni·tar·i·an (yü′nə ter′ē ən), **1** *n.* Christian who does not accept the doctrine of the Trinity. A Unitarian may follow the moral teachings of Jesus, but does not believe that He was divine. **2** *adj.* of Unitarians.

u·ni·tar·y (yü′nə ter′ē), *adj.* **1** one in nature or process; single; whole: *a unitary government.* **2** of or about a unit or units: *unitary conversion tables.*

u·nite (yü nīt′), *v.* to join together; make one; become one; combine: *The businesses united to form one company.* ❑ *v.* **u·nit·ed, u·nit·ing.** —**u·nit′er,** *n.*

u·nit·ed (yü nī′tid), *adj.* **1** made one; joined; combined. **2** having to do with or produced by two or more. **3** in agreement; in concord: *The neighbors were united in their disapproval of the new housing development.* —**u·nit′ed·ly,** *adv.*

United Arab E·mir·ates (em′ər its), country in E Arabia. *Capital:* Abu Dhabi.

United Arab Republic, former name of Egypt and Syria, from 1958 to 1961, and of Egypt, from 1961 to 1971.

United Empire Loyalist, CANADIAN. **1** Loyalist. **2** descendant of a Loyalist.

united front, a group united to oppose something that threatens the interests of all its members: *Our PTA was a united front against school funding cuts.*

un′i·mag′i·na·tive	un′im·pos′ing	un′im·proved′	un·in′flu·enced	un′i·ni′ti·at′ed
un′im·paired′	un′im·pressed′	un′in·cor′po·rat′ed	un·in·formed′	un′in·struct′ed
un′im·pas′sioned	un′im·pres′sion·a·ble	un′in·fect′ed	un′in·hab′it·a·ble	un′in·struc′tive
un′im·ped′ed	un′im·pres′sive	un′in·flect′ed	un′in·hib′it·ed	un′in·sured′

United Kingdom, 1 country in NW Europe composed of Great Britain and Northern Ireland. *Capital:* London. **2** Great Britain and Ireland from 1801 to 1922.

United Nations, 1 a worldwide organization established in 1945 to promote world peace and economic and social welfare. It has over 170 members. Its headquarters are in New York City. **2** the nations that belong to this organization.

United Kingdom

Shetland Islands

ATLANTIC OCEAN

Orkney Islands

Scotland

North Sea

Northern Ireland **UNITED KINGDOM**

IRELAND *Irish Sea*

Wales England

FRANCE

United States, country in North America composed of 50 states and the District of Columbia. It extends from the Atlantic to the Pacific and from Mexico and the Gulf of Mexico to Canada. Alaska, the 49th state, lies west and northwest of Canada, and Hawaii, the 50th state, is an island group in the Pacific. *Capital:* Washington, D.C.

United States of America, United States.

unit pricing, method of pricing food or other products by showing both the total price and the price per unit of measure (pound, ounce, etc.).

u·ni·ty (yü′nə tē), *n.* **1** condition of being united; oneness: *The group's unity of purpose helped it get results.* **2** harmony: *work together in unity.* **3** oneness of effect; choice and arrangement of material for a composition, book, picture, statue, etc., to secure a single effect.

WORD FAMILY Unity and the words below are related. They all come from a Latin word meaning "one."

unanimous	unify	unison	univalve
unicellular	unilateral	unit	universe
unicorn	union	unite	university
uniform	unique		

univ., 1 universal. **2** university.

u·ni·valve (yü′nə valv′), *n.* any mollusk with a one-piece shell. Snails are univalves.

u·ni·ver·sal (yü′nə vėr′səl), *adj.* **1** of or belonging to all; concerning all: *Food is a universal need.* **2** existing everywhere: *The law of gravity is universal.* ■ See Synonym Study at **general.** —u′ni·ver′sal·ly, *adv.*

U·ni·ver·sal·ist (yü′nə vėr′sə list), *n.* member of a Christian church holding the belief that all people will finally be saved.

u·ni·ver·sal·i·ty (yü′nə vər sal′ə tē), *n.* condition of being universal.

universal joint, joint or coupling between two shafts that transmits or permits rotation in almost any direction. In a motor vehicle, power is transferred from the transmission to the drive shaft through a universal joint so that drive shaft motions do not strain the transmission.

Universal Product Code, a series of short black and white lines that appears on merchandise. At checkout counters, a scanner reads this bar code, and a computer reports the price.

u·ni·verse (yü′nə vėrs′), *n.* **1** the whole of existing things; everything there is, including all space and matter; the cosmos. Our world is a very tiny part of the universe. **2** (in mathematics and logic) the set of all objects being considered at one time. The universe might be the numbers from 0 through 10, all animals, etc.

u·ni·ver·si·ty (yü′nə vėr′sə tē), *n.* institution of learning of the highest grade. A university usually has schools of law, medicine, teaching, business, etc., as well as a college of liberal arts and a graduate school. □ *n., pl.* **u·ni·ver·si·ties.**

un·just (un just′), *adj.* not just; not fair: *Punishing someone for no reason would be unjust.* —un·just′ly, *adv.* —un·just′ness, *n.*

un·jus·ti·fi·a·ble (un jus′tə fī′ə bəl), *adj.* not able to be justified. —un·jus′ti·fi′a·bly, *adv.*

un·kempt (un kempt′), *adj.* **1** not combed. **2** not properly cared for; neglected; untidy: *unkempt clothes.*

un·kind (un kīnd′), *adj.* not kind; harsh; cruel: *I resented their unkind remarks about my friend.* —un·kind′ness, *n.*

SYNONYM STUDY Unkind, mean[2], and nasty all mean hurting others' feelings. **Unkind** is a general word: *Her remarks were true, but unkind.* **Mean** suggests deliberate, selfish efforts: *His practical jokes are just plain mean.* **Nasty** suggests a desire to cause pain: *The nasty villain planned to cheat older people out of their savings.*

un·kind·ly (un kīnd′lē), **1** *adj.* harsh; unkind. **2** *adv.* in an unkind way; harshly: *They spoke unkindly of my friend.* —un·kind′li·ness, *n.*

un·know·a·ble (un nō′ə bəl), *adj.* not able to be known.

un·known (un nōn′), **1** *adj.* not known; not familiar; strange: *Most of Antarctica was once unknown land.* **2** *n.* person or thing that is unknown: *a political unknown. The diver descended into the unknown.*

un·lace (un lās′), *v.* to undo the laces of. □ *v.* **un·laced, un·lac·ing.**

un·latch (un lach′), *v.* to unfasten or open by lifting a latch.

un·law·ful (un lô′fəl), *adj.* contrary to the law; against the law; forbidden; illegal: *Littering is unlawful.* —un·law′ful·ly, *adv.* —un·law′ful·ness, *n.*

un·lead·ed (un led′id), *adj.* without the addition of a lead compound that reduces engine noise: *unleaded gasoline.*

un·learn (un lėrn′), *v.* to get rid of ideas, habits, or tendencies; give up knowledge of; forget.

un·learn·ed (un lėr′nid *for 1;* un lėrnd′ *for 2*), *adj.* **1** not educated; ignorant: *They were unlearned and could not read or write.* **2** not learned; known without being learned: *Swallowing is unlearned behavior.*

un·leash (un lēsh′), *v.* **1** to release from a leash: *She unleashed the dog.* **2** to let loose: *unleash your temper.*

un·leav·ened (un lev′ənd), *adj.* not leavened. Unleavened bread is made without yeast.

un·less (ən les′ *or* un les′), *conj.* if it were not that; if not: *We shall go unless it rains.*

un·let·tered (un let′ərd), *adj.* **1** not educated. **2** not able to read or write; illiterate.

un·like (un līk′), **1** *adj.* not like; different: *The two problems are quite unlike.* **2** *prep.* different from: *to act unlike others.* **3** *prep.* not characteristic or typical of: *Giving up so easily is unlike her.* —un·like′ness, *n.*

un·like·li·hood (un līk′lē hùd), *n.* improbability.

un·like·ly (un līk′lē), *adj.* **1** not likely; not probable: *He is unlikely to win the race.* **2** not likely to succeed: *an unlikely undertaking.* □ *adj.* **un·like·li·er, un·like·li·est.** —un·like′li·ness, *n.*

un·lim·it·ed (un lim′ə tid), *adj.* **1** without limits; boundless. **2** not restrained; not restricted: *a government of unlimited power.* —un·lim′it·ed·ly, *adv.* —un·lim′it·ed·ness, *n.*

un·load (un lōd′), *v.* **1** to remove a load: *They unloaded boxes from the truck.* **2** to take the load from: *They unloaded the car.* **3** to get rid of: *They tried to unload their problems on us.* **4** to remove powder, shot, bullets, or shells from a gun. **5** to discharge a cargo: *The ship is unloading.* —un·load′er, *n.*

un·lock (un lok′), *v.* **1** to open the lock of; open anything firmly closed. **2** to disclose; reveal: *Science has unlocked the mystery of the atom.* **3** to become open or unfastened.

un·looked-for (un lùkt′fôr′), *adj.* unexpected; unforeseen.

un·loose (un lüs′), *v.* to let loose; set free; release. □ *v.* **un·loosed, un·loos·ing.**

un·loos·en (un lü′sn), *v.* to unloose; loosen.

U

un·in′te·grat′ed	**un′in·vit′ing**	**un·know′ing·ly**	**un·li′censed**	**un·list′ed**
un′in·tel′li·gent	**un′in·volved′**	**un·la′beled**	**un·light′ed**	**un·lit′**
un′in·tend′ed	**un·jus′ti·fi′a·bly**	**un·la′dy-like′**	**un·lik′a·ble**	**un·lov′a·ble**
un′in·ven′tive	**un·know′ing**	**un′la·ment′ed**	**un·lined′**	**un·loved′**

un·love·ly (un luv′lē), *adj.* without beauty or charm; not pleasing in appearance; unpleasant; disagreeable: *This new design for a parking garage is unlovely but practical.* —**un·love′li·ness,** *n.*

un·luck·y (un luk′ē), *adj.* not lucky; bringing bad luck; unfortunate. □ *adj.* **un·luck·i·er, un·luck·i·est.** —**un·luck′i·ly,** *adv.* —**un·luck′i·ness,** *n.*

un·made (un mād′), *adj.* **1** not made: *an unmade bed.* **1** past tense of **unmake:** *When Mom came home we unmade our fort.*

un·make (un′māk′), *v.* **1** to undo; destroy; cause to be as if it never existed. **2** to make lower in rank; to remove from office or authority. **3** to change the personality, character, etc., of: *A terrible accident can unmake a person.* □ *v.* **un·made, un·mak·ing.**

un·manned (un mand′), *adj.* without a crew: *an unmanned spaceflight.*

un·man·ner·ly (un man′ər lē), *adj.* having bad manners; rude; discourteous: *It was unmannerly of him to complain that the cake was stale.* —**un·man′ner·li·ness,** *n.*

un·mar·ried (un mar′ēd), *adj.* not married; single.

un·mask (un mask′), *v.* **1** to remove a mask or disguise: *The guests unmasked at midnight.* **2** to take off a mask or disguise from. **3** to expose the true character of: *unmask a coward.*

un·mean·ing (un mē′ning), *adj.* **1** without meaning or significance; meaningless: *unmeaning words.* **2** empty of feeling or thought; without sense or expression; vacant: *an unmeaning stare.* —**un·mean′ing·ly,** *adv.*

un·men·tion·a·ble (un men′shə nə bəl), **1** *adj.* not able to be mentioned; not fit to be spoken about. **2** *n.pl.* **unmentionables,** underwear. —**un·men′tion·a·ble·ness,** *n.* —**un·men′tion·a·bly,** *adv.*

un·mer·ci·ful (un mèr′si fəl), *adj.* having or showing no mercy; cruel. —**un·mer′ci·ful·ly,** *adv.* —**un·mer′ci·ful·ness,** *n.*

un·mind·ful (un mīnd′fəl), *adj.* not mindful; heedless; careless: *He went ahead despite our warning and unmindful of the results.* —**un·mind′ful·ly,** *adv.*

un·mis·tak·a·ble (un′mə stā′kə bəl), *adj.* not able to be mistaken or misunderstood; clear; plain; evident: *The artist's talent was unmistakable.* —**un′mis·tak′a·bly,** *adv.*

un·mit·i·gat·ed (un mit′ə gā′tid), *adj.* **1** unqualified or absolute: *an unmitigated fraud.* **2** not softened or lessened: *unmitigated harshness.* —**un·mit′i·gat′ed·ly,** *adv.*

un·mo·lest·ed (un′mə les′tid), *adj.* not molested; undisturbed.

un·mo·ral (un môr′əl), *adj.* neither moral nor immoral; not perceiving or involving right and wrong.

un·moved (un müvd′), *adj.* **1** not moved; firm: *They tried to convince me, but I was unmoved by their arguments.* **2** not disturbed; indifferent: *Their sad tale left me unmoved.*

un·named (un nāmd′), *adj.* **1** having no name; nameless. **2** not mentioned by name.

un·nat·ur·al (un nach′ər əl), *adj.* **1** not natural; not normal. **2** shocking; horrible. **3** artificial. —**un·nat′ur·al·ly,** *adv.* —**un·nat′ur·al·ness,** *n.*

un·nec·es·sar·y (un nes′ə ser′ē), *adj.* not necessary; needless: *A coat is unnecessary on such a warm day.* —**un·nec′es·sar′i·ly,** *adv.*

un·nerve (un nèrv′), *v.* to deprive of courage, firmness, or self-control: *The sight of blood unnerves some people.* □ *v.* **un·nerved, un·nerv·ing.** —**un·nerv′ing·ly,** *adv.*

un·no·ticed (un nō′tist), *adj.* not noticed; not observed; not receiving any attention: *I slipped into the room unnoticed.*

un·num·bered (un num′bərd), *adj.* **1** not numbered; not counted: *The theater seats were unnumbered.* **2** too many to count; innumerable: *There are unnumbered fish in the ocean.*

un·ob·served (un′əb zèrvd′), *adj.* not observed; not noticed; disregarded: *The thief was unobserved as he left the building.*

un·ob·tru·sive (un′əb trü′siv), *adj.* not overly noticeable; modest; inconspicuous. —**un′ob·tru′sive·ly,** *adv.* —**un′ob·tru′sive·ness,** *n.*

un·oc·cu·pied (un ok′yə pīd), *adj.* **1** not occupied; vacant: *an unoccupied room.* **2** not busy; not in use; idle: *I enjoy being busy; I don't like being unoccupied.*

un·of·fi·cial (un′ə fish′əl), *adj.* not official: *That's the unofficial report, but we are waiting for further facts.* —**un′of·fi′cial·ly,** *adv.*

un·or·gan·ized (un ôr′gə nīzd), *adj.* **1** not formed into an organized or systematized whole. **2** not organized into labor unions.

un·pack (un pak′), *v.* **1** to take out things packed in a box, trunk, etc.: *I unpacked my clothes. She unpacked the groceries.* **2** to take things out of: *unpack a trunk.*

un·paid (un pād′), *adj.* not paid: *unpaid bills for $200.*

un·pal·at·a·ble (un pal′ə tə bəl), *adj.* not agreeable to the taste; unpleasant. —**un·pal′at·a·bil′i·ty,** *n.*

un·par·al·leled (un par′ə leld), *adj.* having no parallel; unequaled; matchless: *an unparalleled achievement.*

un·peg (un peg′), *v.* to loosen or detach. □ *v.* **un·pegged, un·peg·ging.**

un·pin (un pin′), *v.* to take out a pin or pins from; unfasten: *unpin a scarf.* □ *v.* **un·pinned, un·pin·ning.**

un·pleas·ant (un plez′nt), *adj.* not pleasant; disagreeable: *an unpleasant odor.* —**un·pleas′ant·ly,** *adv.*

un·pleas·ant·ness (un plez′nt nis), *n.* **1** unpleasant quality. **2** something unpleasant. **3** a quarrel: *They regretted the unpleasantness about the missing skate.*

un·plug (un plug′), *v.* **1** to remove the plug or stopper from. **2** to disconnect by removing the plug from an electric outlet. □ *v.* **un·plugged, un·plug·ging.**

un·pop·u·lar (un pop′yə lər), *adj.* not popular; not generally liked; disliked: *Creamed cauliflower is the most unpopular thing the cafeteria serves.* —**un·pop·u·lar·i·ty** (un′pop yə lar′ə tē), *n.*

un·prac·ticed (un prak′tist), *adj.* **1** not skilled; not expert. **2** not put into practice; not used.

un·prec·e·dent·ed (un pres′ə den′tid), *adj.* having no precedent; never done before; never known before: *An unprecedented event took place in 1961, when a human being traveled for the first time in outer space.* —**un·prec′e·dent·ed·ly,** *adv.*

un·pre·dict·a·ble (un′pri dik′tə bəl), *adj.* not able to be predicted; uncertain: *How a game would turn out between such evenly matched teams is unpredictable.* —**un′pre·dict′a·bly,** *adv.*

un·prej·u·diced (un prej′ə dist), *adj.* without prejudice; fair; impartial.

un·lov′ing	un·min′gled	un′ob·jec′tion·a·ble	un·paired′	un·picked′
un·mag′ni·fied	un′mis·tak′en	un′o·blig′ing	un·par′don·a·ble	un·pierced′
un·mal′le·a·ble	un·mod′i·fied	un′ob·scured′	un·par′doned	un·pit′ied
un·man′age·a·ble	un·mod′u·lat′ed	un′ob·serv′a·ble	un·par′lia·men′tar·y	un·pit′y·ing
un·man′ly	un·mo′ti·vat′ed	un′ob·serv′ant	un·pas′teur·ized	un·placed′
un′man·u·fac′tured	un·mount′ed	un′ob·serv′ing	un′pa·tri·ot′ic	un·plagued′
un·marked′	un·mourned′	un′ob·struct′ed	un·paved′	un·planned′
un·mar′ket·a·ble	un·mov′a·ble	un′ob·tain′a·ble	un·peace′a·ble	un·plant′ed
un·mar′riage·a·ble	un·mov′ing	un·of′fered	un·peo′pled	un·played′
un·mas′tered	un·mu′si·cal	un·o′pened	un′per·ceived′	un·pleased′
un·matched′	un·muz′zled	un′op·posed′	un′per·ceiv′ing	un·pleas′ing
un·meant′	un·nat′ur·al·ized	un′or·dained′	un·per fect′ed	un·pledged′
un′me·chan′i·cal	un·nav′i·ga·ble	un·or′dered	un′per·plexed′	un·pli′ant
un·melt′ed	un·need′ed	un′o·rig′i·nal	un′per·suad′ed	un·plowed′
un·men′tioned	un·neigh′bor·ly	un·or′tho·dox	un′per·sua′sive	un·plumbed′
un·mer′it·ed	un·not′ed	un′os·ten·ta′tious	un′per·turbed′	un′po·et′ic
un′me·thod′i·cal	un·no′tice·a·ble	un·owned′	un′phil·o·soph′ic	un′po·et′i·cal
un·mil′i·tar′y	un′o·beyed′	un·paint′ed	un′phil·o·soph′i·cal	un·poised′

un·pre·med·i·tat·ed (un′prē med′ə tā′tid), *adj.* not premeditated; not planned in advance.

un·pre·pared (un′pri pârd′), *adj.* **1** not ready: *I was unprepared to go.* **2** not made ready; not worked out ahead: *an unprepared speech.* —**un′pre·par′ed·ness,** *n.*

un·pre·ten·tious (un′pri ten′shəs), *adj.* not given to or marked by pretension; modest: *Despite his vast wealth, he lives in an unpretentious house and drives a small car.* —**un′pre·ten′tious·ly,** *adv.* —**un′pre·ten′tious·ness,** *n.*

un·prin·ci·pled (un prin′sə pəld), *adj.* lacking good moral principles; bad..

un·print·a·ble (un prin′tə bəl), *adj.* not fit or proper to be printed: *When he hit his thumb with the hammer he said an unprintable word, and then apologized immediately.*

un·pro·fes·sion·al (un′prə fesh′ə nəl), *adj.* contrary to professional etiquette; unbecoming in members of a profession: *It would be unprofessional for doctors to speak publicly of their patients' personal problems.* —**un′pro·fes′sion·al·ly,** *adv.*

un·prof·it·a·ble (un prof′ə tə bəl), *adj.* not profitable; producing no gain or advantage. —**un·prof′it·a·ble·ness,** *n.* —**un·prof′it·a·bly,** *adv.*

un·pro·nounce·a·ble (un′prə noun′sə bəl), *adj.* not able to be pronounced.

un·pro·voked (un′prə vōkt′), *adj.* not provoked; without provocation: *an unprovoked outburst.*

un·qual·i·fied (un kwol′ə fid), *adj.* **1** not qualified; not fitted: *They are unqualified for this job.* **2** complete; absolute: *an unqualified failure.* **3** not modified, limited, or restricted in any way: *unqualified praise.* —**un·qual′i·fied′ly,** *adv.*

un·quench·a·ble (un kwen′chə bəl), *adj.* not able to be quenched or extinguished: *an unquenchable thirst, unquenchable zeal.*

un·ques·tion·a·ble (un kwes′chə nə bəl), *adj.* beyond dispute or doubt; certain: *Being tall is an unquestionable advantage to a basketball player.* —**un·ques′tion·a·ble·ness,** *n.* —**un·ques′tion·a·bly,** *adv.*

un·ques·tioned (un kwes′chənd), *adj.* not questioned; not disputed.

un·qui·et (un kwi′ət), *adj.* **1** not at rest; restless: *unquiet sleep.* **2** disturbed; uneasy: *an unquiet mind.* **3** causing or likely to cause trouble: *an unquiet crowd.*

un·rav·el (un rav′əl), *v.* **1** to separate the threads of; pull apart: *Can you unravel this tangle of yarn?* **2** to come apart: *This sweater is unraveling at the elbow.* **3** to bring or come out of a tangled state: *The detective unraveled the mystery.* ❑ *v.* **un·rav·eled, un·rav·el·ing** or **un·rav·elled, un·rav·el·ling.**

un·read (un red′), *adj.* **1** not read: *an unread book.* **2** not having read much: *an unread person.*

un·read·a·ble (un rē′də bəl), *adj.* **1** not able to be read: *an unreadable road sign.* **2** not suitable or fit for reading; not worth reading: *a dull, unreadable book.*

un·read·y (un red′ē), *adj.* **1** not ready; not prepared: *Since the class felt so unready for the test, the teacher put it off until the* following week. **2** not prompt or quick; slow. —**un·read′i·ly,** *adv.* —**un·read′i·ness,** *n.*

un·re·al (un rē′əl), *adj.* **1** not real; imaginary; fanciful: *In the bright morning sunlight, our fears of last night's storm seemed unreal.* See Synonym Study at **imaginary.** **2** so very strange as to be incredible: *an unreal, last-minute victory.*

un·re·al·i·ty (un′rē al′ə tē), *n.* **1** lack of reality; imaginary or fanciful quality. **2** impractical or visionary character or tendency; impracticality. **3** something without reality; something unreal. ❑ *n., pl.* **un·re·al·i·ties** for 3.

un·rea·son·a·ble (un rē′zn ə bəl), *adj.* **1** not reasonable: *an unreasonable fear of the dark.* **2** not moderate; excessive: *They spend an unreasonable amount of money on clothes.* —**un·rea′son·a·ble·ness,** *n.* —**un·rea′son·a·bly,** *adv.*

un·rea·son·ing (un rē′zn ing), *adj.* not reasoning; irrational. —**un·rea′son·ing·ly,** *adv.*

un·re·lent·ing (un′ri len′ting), *adj.* **1** not slackening or relaxing: *She worked at an unrelenting pace.* **2** not yielding to feelings of kindness or compassion; merciless; cruel: *an unrelenting enemy.* —**un′re·lent′ing·ly,** *adv.*

un·re·li·a·ble (un′ri li′ə bəl), *adj.* not reliable; not to be depended on; irresponsible: *Don't count on them to help—they're unreliable.* —**un·re·li·a·bil′i·ty** (un′ri li′ə bil′ə tē), *n.* —**un′re·li′a·bly,** *adv.*

un·re·mit·ting (un′ri mit′ing), *adj.* never stopping; maintained steadily: *unremitting enthusiasm.* —**un′re·mit′ting·ly,** *adv.*

un·re·served (un′ri zėrvd′), *adj.* **1** not restrained in action or speech; frank; open. **2** not restricted, limited, or qualified; without reservation: *She gave him an unreserved recommendation.* —**un·re·serv·ed·ly** (un′ri zėr′vid lē), *adv.*

un·rest (un rest′), *n.* **1** agitation or disturbance amounting almost to rebellion: *The government's injustices caused political unrest among the people.* **2** lack of ease and quiet; restlessness.

un·re·strained (un′ri strānd′), *adj.* not restrained; not held back; not checked: *unrestrained laughter.* —**un′re·strain′ed·ly,** *adv.*

un·right·eous (un ri′chəs), *adj.* not righteous; wicked; sinful; unjust. —**un·right′eous·ly,** *adv.* —**un·right′eous·ness,** *n.*

un·ripe (un rip′), *adj.* not ripe; not fully developed; immature. —**un·ripe′ness,** *n.*

un·ri·valed or **un·ri·valled** (un ri′vəld), *adj.* having no rival; without an equal: *She is the unrivaled champion.*

un·roll (un rōl′), *v.* **1** to open or spread out: *I unrolled my sleeping bag.* **2** to become opened or spread out. **3** to lay open; display: *She unrolled the fabric so that we could see the pattern.*

un·ruf·fled (un ruf′əld), *adj.* **1** not disturbed; calm. **2** not ruffled; smooth.

un·ruled (un rüld′), *adj.* **1** not marked with lines: *unruled paper.* **2** not kept under control; not governed.

un·rul·y (un rü′lē), *adj.* hard to rule or control; disorderly: *The unruly horse threw its rider. The unruly mob stormed the palace.* ❑ *adj.* **un·ru·li·er, un·ru·li·est.** —**un·rul′i·ness,** *n.*

un·sad·dle (un sad′l), *v.* to take the saddle off a horse. ❑ *v.* **un·sad·dled, un·sad·dling.**

un′po·liced′	un′pro·tect′ed	un′re·al·is′tic	un′re·lieved′	un′re·signed′
un·pol′ished	un′pro·test′ed	un·re′al·ized	un′re·mem′bered	un′re·sist′ed
un·pol′lut′ed	un′proved′	un·rea′soned	un′re·mit′ted	un′re·sist′ing
un·pop′u·lat′ed	un·prov′en	un′re·ceived′	un′re·mu′ne·ra·tive	un′re·solved′
un′pre·pos·sess′ing	un′pro·vid′ed	un′re·claimed′	un′re·nowned′	un′re·spon′sive
un·pressed′	un′pro·vok′ing	un·rec′og·niz′a·ble	un·rent′ed	un′re·strict′ed
un′pre·vail′ing	un′pruned′	un·rec′og·nized	un′re·paid′	un′re·ten′tive
un′pre·vent′a·ble	un·pub′li·cized	un′rec·om·pensed	un′re·paired′	un′re·turn′a·ble
un·print′ed	un·pub′lished	un′rec′on·ciled	un′re·pealed′	un′re·turned′
un·priv′i·leged	un·pun′ished	un′re·cord′ed	un·re·pent′ant	un′re·vealed′
un′pro·duc′tive	un′pur·chas·a·ble	un′re·deemed′	un′re·pent′ing	un′re·venged′
un′pro·faned′	un′quail′ing	un′re·fined′	un′re·port′ed	un′re·voked′
un′pro·gres′sive	un·quenched′	un′re·formed′	un′rep·re·sent′a·tive	un′re·ward′ed
un·prom′is·ing	un·ques′tion·ing	un·reg′is·tered	un′rep·re·sent′ed	un′re·ward′ing
un·prompt′ed	un·quot′a·ble	un·reg′u·lat′ed	un′re·pressed′	un′rhymed′
un′pro·nounced′	un·raised′	un′re·lat′ed	un′re·pressed′	un′right′ful
un′pro·pi′tious	un·ran′somed	un′re·laxed′	un′re·proached′	un·rip′ened
un′pro·por′tioned	un·rat′i·fied	un′re·lax′ing	un′re·quit′ed	un′ro·man′tic

U

un·safe (un sāf′), *adj.* not safe; dangerous: *Swimming where there are sharks is unsafe.* —**un·safe′ly,** *adv.* —**un·safe′ness,** *n.*

un·said (un sed′), **1** *adj.* not said: *All the things I had meant to say to him remained unsaid.* **2** *v.* past tense and past participle of **unsay.**

un·san·i·tar·y (un san′ə ter′ē), *adj.* not sanitary; bad for the health; unhealthful: *The cafeteria was closed because of unsanitary conditions.* —**un·san′i·tar′i·ness,** *n.*

un·sat·is·fac·tor·y (un′sat i sfak′tər ē), *adj.* not satisfactory; not good enough to satisfy; inadequate: *Your homework is unsatisfactory because there are too many mistakes.* —**un′sat·is·fac′tor·i·ly,** *adv.*

un·sat·is·fied (un sat′i sfīd), *adj.* not satisfied; not contented: *The tiny meal left me unsatisfied. Her explanation of the events left us unsatisfied*

un·sat·u·rat·ed (un sach′ə rā′tid), *adj.* **1** not soaked thoroughly. **2** able to absorb or dissolve more of something. An unsaturated solution of sugar is one that can dissolve more sugar.

un·sa·vor·y (un sā′vər ē), *adj.* **1** morally unpleasant; offensive: *an unsavory act.* **2** tasteless. **3** unpleasant in taste or smell; distasteful: *an unsavory medicine.* —**un·sa′vor·i·ly,** *adv.* —**un·sa′vor·i·ness,** *n.*

un·say (un sā′), *v.* to take back something said; retract. ❑ *v.* **un·said, un·say·ing.**

un·scathed (un skāᴛн′d), *adj.* not harmed; uninjured: *She escaped unscathed from the car wreck.*

un·schooled (un sküld′), *adj.* not schooled; not taught; not disciplined.

un·sci·en·tif·ic (un′sī ən tif′ik), *adj.* not in accordance with the facts or principles of science: *an unscientific notion.* —**un′sci·en·tif′i·cal·ly,** *adv.*

un·scram·ble (un skram′bəl), *v.* to change from confusion to order; bring out of a scrambled condition: *After the wind died down, we unscrambled the papers that had blown on the floor.* ❑ *v.* **un·scram·bled, un·scram·bling.**

un·screw (un skrü′), *v.* **1** to take out the screw or screws from. **2** to loosen or take off by turning: *unscrew an electric light bulb, Can you help me unscrew this tight lid?*

un·scru·pu·lous (un skrü′pyə ləs), *adj.* not careful about right and wrong; without principles or conscience: *The unscrupulous student cheated on the test.* —**un·scru′pu·lous·ly,** *adv.* —**un·scru′pu·lous·ness,** *n.*

un·seal (un sēl′), *v.* **1** to break or remove the seal of: *unseal a letter.* **2** to open: *The threat of punishment unsealed their lips.*

un·search·a·ble (un sėr′chə bəl), *adj.* not to be searched into; not able to be understood by searching; mysterious. —**un·search′a·bly,** *adv.*

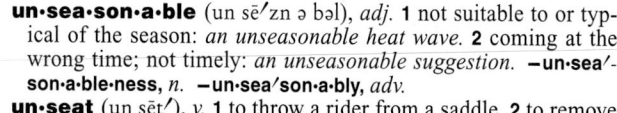

unsafe

un·sea·son·a·ble (un sē′zn ə bəl), *adj.* **1** not suitable to or typical of the season: *an unseasonable heat wave.* **2** coming at the wrong time; not timely: *an unseasonable suggestion.* —**un·sea′son·a·ble·ness,** *n.* —**un·sea′so·na·bly,** *adv.*

un·seat (un sēt′), *v.* **1** to throw a rider from a saddle. **2** to remove from office: *unseat a member of Congress.*

un·seem·ly (un sēm′lē), *adj.* not seemly; not suitable; improper: *Laughter is often unseemly in a courtroom.* ❑ *adj.* **un·seem·li·er, un·seem·li·est.** —**un·seem′li·ness,** *n.*

un·seen (un sēn′), *adj.* **1** not seen; unnoticed: *an unseen error.* **2** not able to be seen; invisible: *an unseen spirit.*

un·self·ish (un sel′fish), *adj.* not selfish; considerate; generous: *an unselfish person, an unselfish act.* —**un·self′ish·ly,** *adv.* —**un·self′ish·ness,** *n.*

un·set·tle (un set′l), *v.* to make or become unstable; disturb; shake; weaken: *The shock unsettled his nerves.* ❑ *v.* **un·set·tled, un·set·tling.**

un·set·tled (un set′ld), *adj.* **1** not in proper condition or order; disordered; disturbed: *We've just moved in, so the house is still unsettled.* **2** liable to change; uncertain: *The weather is unsettled.* ■ See Synonym Study at **uncertain. 3** not paid; not adjusted: *He was out of work and worried about unsettled bills.* **4** not determined or decided: *an unsettled question.* **5** not populated; uninhabited: *Some parts of the world are still unsettled.* —**un·set′tled·ness,** *n.*

un·shak·a·ble (un shā′kə bəl), *adj.* not able to be shaken; firm: *unshakable faith.* —**un·shak′a·bly,** *adv.*

un·shak·en (un shā′kən), *adj.* not shaken; firm: *an unshaken belief.*

un·sheathe (un shēᴛн′), *v.* to draw a sword, knife, etc., from a sheath. ❑ *v.* **un·sheathed, un·sheath·ing.**

un·shod (un shod′), *adj.* without shoes.

un·sight·ly (un sīt′lē), *adj.* ugly or unpleasant to look at: *an unsightly old shack.* —**un·sight′li·ness,** *n.*

un·skilled (un skild′), *adj.* **1** not skilled; not trained; not expert: *They aren't hiring unskilled workers at the factory.* **2** not requiring special skills or training: *unskilled labor.*

un·skill·ful or **un·skil·ful** (un skil′fəl), *adj.* not skillful; lacking in skill; awkward; clumsy: *His unskillful attempt to ski ended in a broken leg.* —**un·skill′ful·ly** or **un·skil′ful·ly,** *adv.* —**un·skill′ful·ness** or **un·skil′ful·ness,** *n.*

un·smil·ing (un smī′ling), *adj.* not smiling; grave; serious: *The school superintendent was unsmiling when he announced the school closings.* —**un·smil′ing·ly,** *adv.*

unsmiling

un·snap (un snap′), *v.* to unfasten the snap or snaps of. ❑ *v.* **un·snapped, un·snap·ping.**

un·snarl (un snärl′), *v.* to remove the snarls from; untangle.

un·so·cia·ble (un sō′shə bəl), *adj.* not sociable; not associating easily with others: *unsociable behavior.* —**un·so′cia·bil′i·ty, un·so′cia·ble·ness,** *n.* —**un·so′cia·bly,** *adv.*

un·saint′ly	un·scorched′	un′se·lec′tive	un·shel′tered	un′sol′dier·ly
un·sal′a·ble	un·scratched′	un′self-con′scious	un·shield′ed	un′so·lic′it·ed
un·sal′ar·ied	un·screened′	un′sen·ti·men′tal	un·shorn′	un·solv′a·ble
un·salt′ed	un·scrip′tur·al	un·serv′ice·a·ble	un·shrink′ing	un·sort′ed
un·sanc′ti·fied	un·sealed′	un·set′	un·sift′ed	un·sound′ed
un·sat′ed	un·sea′soned	un·shad′ed	un·sight′ed	un·sown′
un·sa′ti·at·ed	un·sea′wor′thy	un·shad′owed	un·signed′	un·spe′cial·ized
un·sat′is·fy′ing	un·sec′ond·ed	un·shaped′	un·sized′	un′spe·cif′ic
un·scaled′	un′se·cured′	un·shape′ly	un·slacked′	un·spec′i·fied
un·scarred′	un·seed′ed	un·sharp′ened	un·slaked′	un′spec·tac′u·lar
un·scent′ed	un·see′ing	un·shav′en	un·so′cial	un·spec′u·la·tive
un·sched′uled	un·seg′ment·ed	un·shed′	un·soiled′	un·spent′
un·schol′ar·ly	un·seg′re·gat′ed	un·shelled′	un·sold′	un′spir′i·tu·al

un·solved (un solvd′), *adj.* not solved; not explained: *an unsolved mystery.*

un·so·phis·ti·cat·ed (un′sə fis′tə kā′tid), *adj.* not sophisticated; simple; natural; artless.

un·sought (un sòt′), *adj.* not sought; not looked for; not asked for: *unsought advice, an unsought compliment.*

un·sound (un sound′), *adj.* 1 not based on truth or fact; not valid: *an unsound theory.* 2 not in good condition; not sound: *unsound walls, an unsound business.* 3 not deep; not restful; disturbed: *an unsound sleep.* **—un·sound′ly,** *adv.* **—un·sound′ness,** *n.*

un·spar·ing (un spâr′ing), *adj.* 1 not sparing; very generous; liberal. 2 not merciful; severe. **—un·spar′ing·ly,** *adv.*

un·speak·a·ble (un spē′kə bəl), *adj.* 1 extremely bad; bad or objectionable beyond description. 2 not able to be expressed in words; beyond description; indescribable: *unspeakable joy, an unspeakable loss.* **—un·speak′a·bly,** *adv.*

un·spot·ted (un spot′id), *adj.* not spotted; without spot or stain; pure: *an unspotted reputation.*

un·sta·ble (un stā′bəl), *adj.* 1 not stable; unsteady; shaky: *That stool with a short leg is very unstable.* 2 easily overthrown: *an unstable government.* 3 tending to sudden emotional changes; emotionally unsettled: *an unstable person.* 4 not constant; variable: *an unstable economy.* 5 (of a chemical compound) readily changed into other compounds. **—un·sta′ble·ness,** *n.* **—un·sta′bly,** *adv.*

un·stead·y (un sted′ē), *adj.* 1 not steady; shaky: *an unsteady voice.* 2 likely to change; not reliable; variable: *unsteady winds.* ❑ *adj.* **un·stead·i·er, un·stead·i·est.** **—un·stead′i·ly,** *adv.* **—un·stead′i·ness,** *n.*

un·strap (un strap′), *v.* to take off or loosen the strap or straps of a trunk, box, etc. ❑ *v.* **un·strapped, un·strap·ping.**

un·stressed (un strest′), *adj.* not stressed; unaccented. In *upward,* the second syllable is unstressed.

un·string (un string′), *v.* to take off or loosen the string or strings of: *unstring a guitar.* ❑ *v.* **un·string·ing, un·strung.**

un·strung (un strung′), *adj.* 1 upset or nervous. 2 with strings loose, broken, or missing: *an unstrung guitar.*

un·stud·ied (un stud′ēd), *adj.* 1 not artificial; natural: *unstudied kindness.* 2 not an object of study; not studied.

un·sub·stan·tial (un′səb stan′shəl), *adj.* not substantial; flimsy; slight. **—un′sub·stan′tial·ly,** *adv.*

un·suit·a·ble (un sü′tə bəl), *adj.* not suitable; unfit: *an unsuitable remark, unsuitable behavior.* **—un·suit′a·bly,** *adv.*

un·suit·ed (un sü′tid), *adj.* not suited; unfit.

un·sul·lied (un sul′ēd), *adj.* not sullied; spotless; pure.

un·sung (un sung′), *adj.* 1 not honored or celebrated, especially by song or poetry: *unsung heroes.* 2 not sung: *an unsung note.*

un·su·per·vised (un sü′pər vīzd), *adj.* without supervision; alone: *He's not old enough to stay at home unsupervised.*

un·sup·port·ed (un sə pôrt′əd), *adj.* without basis; without proof: *His accusations are unsupported.*

un·sure (un shùr′), *adj.* not sure; uncertain: *I was unsure about how to spell the word.*

un·sus·pect·ed (un′sə spek′tid), *adj.* 1 not suspected. 2 not thought of: *an unsuspected danger.*

un·sus·pect·ing (un′sə spek′ting), *adj.* not suspecting; not suspicious: *an unsuspecting victim.*

un·tan·gle (un tang′gəl), *v.* 1 to take the tangles out of; disentangle: *Combing will untangle your hair.* 2 to straighten out or clear up: *We untangled the mystery.* ❑ *v.* **un·tan·gled, un·tan·gling.**

un·tapped (un tapt′), *adj.* (of resources, reserves, etc.) not yet available for use; not used: *untapped mineral wealth.*

un·taught (un tòt′), *adj.* 1 not taught; not educated: *an untaught child.* 2 known without being taught; learned naturally: *untaught wisdom.*

un·thank·ful (un thangk′fəl), *adj.* 1 ungrateful. 2 not appreciated; thankless. **—un·thank′ful·ly,** *adv.*

un·think·a·ble (un thing′kə bəl), *adj.* not able to be imagined; inconceivable. **—un·think′a·bly,** *adv.*

un·think·ing (un thing′king), *adj.* 1 thoughtless; careless. 2 showing little or no thought: *blind, unthinking anger.* **—un·think′ing·ly,** *adv.*

un·thought-of (un thòt′uv′ *or* un thòt′ov′), *adj.* not imagined or considered.

un·ti·dy (un tī′dē), *adj.* not in order; not neat: *an untidy house.* ❑ *adj.* **un·ti·di·er, un·ti·di·est.** **—un·ti′di·ly,** *adv.* **—un·ti′di·ness,** *n.*

un·tie (un tī′), *v.* 1 to loosen; unfasten; undo: *untie a knot.* 2 to make free; release: *untie a horse.* ❑ *v.* **un·tied, un·ty·ing.**

un·til (un til′), 1 *prep.* up to the time of: *It was cold from December until April.* 2 *conj.* up to the time when: *We waited until the sun had set.* 3 *prep., conj.* before: *She did not leave until morning. He did not come until the meeting was almost over.* 4 *conj.* to the degree or place that: *She worked until she was tired.*

un·time·ly (un tīm′lē), 1 *adj., adv.* too early; too soon: *an untimely death at the age of 18.* 2 *adj.* at a wrong time or season; unseasonable: *Snow in May is untimely.* **—un·time′li·ness,** *n.*

un·tir·ing (un tī′ring), *adj.* that does not tire; tireless: *an untiring runner, untiring efforts to succeed.* **—un·tir′ing·ly,** *adv.*

un·to (un′tü), *prep.* to: *be faithful unto death.*

un·told (un tōld′), *adj.* 1 very great; immense: *untold wealth.* 2 too many to be counted or numbered; countless: *There are untold stars in the sky.* 3 not told; not revealed: *an untold secret.*

un·touch·a·ble (un tuch′ə bəl), 1 *adj.* not able to be touched; out of reach. 2 *adj.* not to be touched. 3 *n.* person of the lowest caste in India, whose touch supposedly defiled members of higher castes. **—un·touch′a·bil′i·ty,** *n.*

un·touched (un tucht′), *adj.* not touched: *The cat left the milk untouched. The miser was untouched by the poor man's story.*

un·to·ward (un tôrd′ *or* un′tə wôrd′), *adj.* 1 unfavorable; unfortunate: *an untoward wind, an untoward accident.* 2 not proper: *untoward actions.* **—un·to·ward′ly,** *adv.* **—un·to·ward′ness,** *n.*

un·trained (un trānd′), *adj.* not trained; without discipline or education: *The new recruits were completely untrained.*

un·treat·ed (un trē′tid), *adj.* not put through a process or form of treatment; raw: *untreated sewage.*

un·tried (un trīd′), *adj.* not tried; not tested: *an untried plan.*

un·trod (un trod′), *adj.* not trodden: *an untrod wasteland.*

un·true (un trü′), *adj.* 1 not true to the facts; false: *The story was untrue.* 2 not faithful; disloyal: *His friend was untrue.* 3 not true to a standard or rule; not exact; inaccurate. **—un·tru′ly,** *adv.*

un·truth (un trüth′), *n.* 1 lack of truth; falsity; a lie; falsehood. ❑ *n., pl.* **un·truths** (un trüᴛʜz′ *or* un trüths′) for 2.

un·truth·ful (un trüth′fəl), *adj.* 1 not truthful; contrary to the truth: *an untruthful rumor.* 2 not telling the truth: *an untruthful person.* **—un·truth′ful·ly,** *adv.* **—un·truth′ful·ness,** *n.*

U

un·spoiled′	un·strat′i·fied	un·sym·met′ri·cal	un·teach′a·ble	un·trace′a·ble
un·spoilt′	un·sub·dued′	un·sym·pa·thet′ic	un·tech′ni·cal	un·traced′
un·spo′ken	un·sub·mis′sive	un·sym·pa·thiz′ing	un·tem′pered	un·tracked′
un·sports′man·like′	un·sub·stan′ti·at·ed	un·sys·tem·at′ic	un·ten′a·ble	un·trans·fer′a·ble
un·stamped′	un·sug·ges′tive	un·tact′ful	un·ten′ant·ed	un·trans·lat′ed
un·stat′ed	un·sup·pressed′	un·taint′ed	un·tend′ed	un·trav′eled
un·states′man·like′	un·sur·passed′	un·tak′en	un·ter′ri·fied	un·trav′elled
un·ster′i·lized	un·sus·pi′cious	un·tal′ent·ed	un·test′ed	un·trav′ersed
un·stint′ed	un·sus·tained′	un·tamed′	un·thanked′	un·trimmed′
un·stint′ing	un·swayed′	un·tanned′	un·thought′	un·trod′den
un·stitched′	un·sweet′ened	un·tar′nished	un·thought′ful	un·trou′bled
un·stopped′	un·swept′	un·tast′ed	un·thrift′y	un·trust′wor′thy
un·strained′	un·swerv′ing	un·taxed′	un·tilled′	un·turned′

un·tu·tored (un tü′tərd), *adj.* not tutored; not educated; untaught.

un·twine (un twīn′), *v.* to untwist. ❑ *v.* **un·twined, un·twin·ing.**

un·twist (un twist′), *v.* **1** to undo or loosen something twisted; unravel. **2** to become untwisted.

un·used (un yüzd′ *for 1,2;* un yüst′ *for 3*), *adj.* **1** not in use; not being used: *an unused room.* **2** never having been used: *unused drinking cups.* **3** not accustomed: *The actor's hands were unused to labor.*

un·u·su·al (un yü′zhü əl), *adj.* not usual; not ordinary; not in common use; uncommon; rare: *an unusual rock formation, an unusual adventure.* **—un·u′su·al·ly,** *adv.* **—un·u′su·al·ness,** *n.*

un·ut·ter·a·ble (un ut′ər ə bəl), *adj.* not able to be expressed in words; unspeakable. **—un·ut′ter·a·bly,** *adv.*

un·var·nished (un vär′nisht), *adj.* **1** not varnished. **2** plain; unadorned: *the unvarnished truth.*

un·veil (un vāl′), *v.* **1** to remove a veil from: *She unveiled her face.* **2** to remove any cover or covering from; uncover: *The statue was unveiled the day the graduating class presented it to the school.* **3** to make known; reveal; disclose: *unveil a secret.*

unusual

un·veil·ing (un vā′ling), *n.* **1** the act of uncovering or revealing: *the unveiling of a statue.* **2** the act of showing to the public for the first time: *the unveiling of the new budget proposal.*

un·voiced (un voist′), *adj.* **1** not spoken; not expressed in words: *unvoiced gratitude.* **2** (in phonetics) voiceless.

un·want·ed (un wän′tid), *adj.* not wanted: *unwanted advice.*

un·war·rant·ed (un wôr′ən tid), *adj.* not authorized or justified: *unwarranted interference.*

un·war·y (un wâr′ē), *adj.* not wary; not cautious; careless; unguarded. ❑ *adj.* **un·war·i·er, un·war·i·est.** **—un·war′i·ly,** *adv.* **—un·war′i·ness,** *n.*

un·wel·come (un wel′kəm), *adj.* not welcome; not wanted: *The bees were unwelcome guests at our picnic.*

un·well (un wel′), *adj.* not in good health; ailing; ill; sick.

un·wept (un wept′), *adj.* **1** not wept for; not mourned. **2** not shed: *unwept tears.*

un·whole·some (un hōl′səm), *adj.* not wholesome; bad for the body or the mind; unhealthy: *a damp, unwholesome climate. A diet consisting mainly of candy is unwholesome.* **—un·whole′some·ly,** *adv.* **—un·whole′some·ness,** *n.*

un·wield·y (un wēl′dē), *adj.* hard to handle or manage because of size, shape, or weight; bulky and clumsy: *a large, unwieldy package.* **—un·wield′i·ness,** *n.*

un·will·ing (un wil′ing), *adj.* **1** not willing; not consenting: *They were unwilling to help.* **2** not freely or willingly granted or done: *an unwilling acceptance of more responsibilities.* **—un·will′ing·ly,** *adv.* **—un·will′ing·ness,** *n.*

un·wind (un wīnd′), *v.* **1** to relax: *After working all day, she needed to unwind.* **2** to unroll; uncoil: *unwind a ball of string.* **3** to become unrolled or uncoiled. ❑ *v.* **un·wound, un·wind·ing.**

un·wise (un wīz′), *adj.* not wise; not showing good judgment; foolish: *It is unwise to delay going to the doctor if you are sick.* **—un·wise′ly,** *adv.*

un·wit·ting (un wit′ing), *adj.* not knowing; unaware; unconscious; unintentional. **—un·wit′ting·ly,** *adv.*

un·wont·ed (un wôn′tid, un wōn′tid *or* un wun′tid), *adj.* not customary; not usual: *unwonted anger.* **—un·wont′ed·ly,** *adv.* **—un·wont′ed·ness,** *n.*

un·world·ly (un wėrld′lē), *adj.* **1** not caring much for the things of this world, such as money, pleasure, and power. **2** inexperienced; naive. **—un·world′li·ness,** *n.*

un·wor·thy (un wėr′ᴛʜē), *adj.* **1** not worthy; not deserving: *Such a silly story is unworthy of belief.* **2** unsuitable; unfit; unbecoming: *a remark unworthy of a friend.* **3** base; shameful: *unworthy conduct.* ❑ *adj.* **un·wor·thi·er, un·wor·thi·est.** **—un·wor′thi·ly,** *adv.* **—un·wor′thi·ness,** *n.*

un·wound (un wound′), *v.* past tense and past participle of **unwind.**

un·wrap (un rap′), *v.* **1** to remove the wrapping from; open. **2** to become opened. ❑ *v.* **un·wrapped, un·wrap·ping.**

un·writ·ten (un rit′n), *adj.* **1** not written: *an unwritten order.* **2** understood or customary, but not actually expressed in writing: *an unwritten law.*

un·yield·ing (un yēl′ding), *adj.* not yielding; not giving way; firm: *She will succeed because of her unyielding determination.* **—un·yield′ing·ly,** *adv.*

un·yoke (un yōk′), *v.* **1** to free from or remove a yoke: *Unyoke the oxen.* **2** to separate; disconnect. ❑ *v.* **un·yoked, un·yok·ing.**

un·zip (un zip′), *v.* to unfasten a zipper or something held by a zipper. ❑ *v.* **un·zipped, un·zip·ping.**

up (up), **1** *adv.* from a lower to a higher place or condition: *The bird flew up. Prices have gone up.* **2** *adj., adv.* in a higher place or condition: *We stayed up in the mountains several days. The sun is up.* **3** *prep.* to a higher place on; at a higher place in: *The cat ran up the tree.* **4** *prep.* along: *They walked up the street.* **5** *prep.* to, near, or at the upper part of: *We sailed up the river.* **6** *adj.* going or pointed upward: *an up trend.* **7** *n.* piece of good luck: *Life has its ups and downs.* **8** *adj., adv.* out of bed: *The children were up at dawn.* **9** *adv.* thoroughly; completely; entirely: *The house burned up.* **10** *adv.* at an end; over: *The time is up now.* **11** *adv.* in or into being or action: *Don't stir up trouble.* **12** *adv.* to or in an even position; not behind: *catch up in a race, keep up with the times.* **13** *adv.* into storage or a safe place: *Squirrels lay up nuts for the winter.* **14** *adj.* at bat in baseball: *She was up four times in the game.* **15** *adj.* offered or proposed: *Our house is up for sale.* **16** *adv.* for each one; apiece; each: *The score at the half was ten up.* **17** *v.* to put, lift, or get up. **18** *v.* to increase: *They upped the price of eggs.* ❑ *v.* **upped, up·ping.**

on the up and up, honest; legitimate: *Since all the arrangements were carefully explained, we knew everything was on the up and up.*

up against, facing as a thing to be dealt with.

up for, 1 a candidate for: *be up for reelection.* **2** on trial in a court of law for: *be up for robbery.*

up till or **up until,** till; until.

up to, 1 about to do; doing: *She is up to some mischief.* **2** equal to; capable of doing: *Do you feel up to going out so soon after being sick?* **3** before someone as a duty or task to be done: *It's up to the judge to decide if he is guilty.*

up-, *prefix.* **1** higher: *uphill = higher on the hill.* **2** better; more: *upscale = with more income than average.*

up-and-com·ing (up′ən kum′ing), *adj.* on the way to prominence or success; promising: *an up-and-coming young scientist.*

up·beat (up′bēt′), **1** *n.* (in music) an unaccented beat in a measure, especially one preceding a downbeat. **2** *adj.* hopeful; buoyant: *a movie with an upbeat ending.*

up·braid (up brād′), *v.* to find fault with; blame; reprove: *The captain upbraided the guards for falling asleep.*

un·twist′ed	un·veiled′	un·war′like′	un·weath′ered	un·work′a·ble
un·typ′i·cal	un·ven′ti·lat′ed	un·washed′	un·wed′	un·work′man·like′
un·us′a·ble	un·ver′i·fied	un·wast′ed	un·wed′ded	un·worn′
un·ut′tered	un·versed′	un·watched′	un·weed′ed	un·wor′ried
un·vac′ci·nat′ed	un·vexed′	un·wa′tered	un·wife′ly	un·wound′ed
un·val′ued	un·vis′it·ed	un·wa′ver·ing	un·wink′ing	un·wo′ven
un·van′quished	un·vo′cal	un·weaned′	un·wit′nessed	un·wrin′kled
un·var′ied	un·walled′	un·wear′y·ing	un·wom′an·ly	un·wrought′

up·bring·ing (up′bring′ing), *n.* care and training given to a child while growing up; bringing-up.

UPC, Universal Product Code.

up·chuck (up′chuk′), *v.* INFORMAL. to vomit.

up·com·ing (up′kum′ing), *adj.* forthcoming: *an upcoming trial.*

up·coun·try (up′kun′trē), *adj., adv.* in the interior of a country: *an upcountry village. We went fishing upcountry.*

up·date (up dāt′ *for verb;* up′dāt′ *for noun*), **1** *v.* to bring up to date. **2** *n.* the newest, most up-to-date information or data: *a news update, a computer update.* ❑ *v.* **up·dat·ed, up·dat·ing.**

up·draft (up′draft′), *n.* an upward movement of air, wind, gas, etc.

up·end (up end′), *v.* to set on end; stand on end: *If you upend the box it will take up less space.*

up·front or **up-front** (up′frunt′), *adj.* **1** INFORMAL. outspoken; straightforward; direct; candid: *an upfront statement.* **2** in advance: *upfront payments.*

up·grade (up′grād′), **1** *v.* to raise to a higher position, status, rating, etc.: *upgrade a job, upgrade an employee.* **2** *n.* an upward slope or incline. ❑ *v.* **up·grad·ed, up·grad·ing.**
  on the upgrade, increasing in strength, power, value, etc.; improving: *Sales have been on the upgrade since the new ad was shown.*

up·heav·al (up hē′vəl), *n.* **1** a sudden or violent agitation; great turmoil: *a flood, earthquake, or other upheaval.* **2** act of heaving up or condition of being heaved up.

up·heave (up hēv′), *v.* to heave up; lift up: *land upheaved by continental collisions.* ❑ *v.* **up·heaved, up·heav·ing.**

up·held (up held′), *v.* past tense and past participle of **uphold:** *The higher court upheld the lower court's decision.*

up·hill (up′hil′ *for adj.;* up′hil′ *for adv.*), **1** *adj.* up the slope of a hill; upward: *an uphill road.* **2** *adv.* upward: *We walked a mile uphill.* **3** *adj.* difficult: *an uphill fight.*

up·hold (up hōld′), *v.* **1** to give support to; confirm: *The principal upheld the teacher's decision.* **2** to hold up; not let down; support: *We uphold the good name of our school.* **3** to sustain on appeal; approve: *The higher court upheld the decision of the lower court.* ❑ *v.* **up·held, up·hold·ing.** —**up·hold′er,** *n.*

up·hol·ster (up hōl′stər), *v.* to provide furniture with coverings, cushions, springs, stuffing, etc. —**up·hol′ster·er,** *n.*

> **WORD STORY** **Upholster** comes from **uphold.** A person who repairs things keeps them working, the way a person who upholds a decision keeps it in force. So furniture repair workers were called "upholders." Gradually, their work changed to making new furniture, and gradually their name changed too.

up·hol·ster·y (up hōl′stər ē), *n.* **1** coverings for furniture. **2** business of upholstering.

up·keep (up′kēp′), *n.* **1** the act of keeping in good condition; maintenance: *the upkeep of a house.* **2** cost of operating and repair: *The upkeep of a yacht is very expensive.*

up·land (up′lənd), **1** *n.* high land. **2** *adj.* of or about high land; living or growing on high land: *upland meadows.*

up·lift (up lift′ *for verb;* up′lift′ *for noun*), **1** *v.* to raise socially or morally: *I was uplifted by his encouraging words.* **2** *v.* to lift up; raise; elevate. **3** *n.* act of lifting up. **4** *n.* social or moral improvement or effort toward it. —**up·lift′er,** *n.*

up·link (up′lingk′), *n.* the communications connection for transmission of signals from an earth station to a spacecraft or satellite.

up·load (up′lōd′), *v.* to transfer data or programs to a central computer or network.

up·most (up′mōst), *adj.* uppermost.

up·on (ə pon′), *prep.* on.

up·per (up′ər), *adj.* **1** higher: *the upper lip, the upper floors of a building.* **2** farther from the sea: *the upper reaches of a river.*

Upper Canada, Ontario, especially before 1841, when Upper Canada and Lower Canada formed the Province of Canada.

up·per·case (up′ər kās′), in printing: **1** *n.* capital letters. **2** *adj.* in capital letters. **3** *v.* to print in capital letters. ❑ *v.* **up·per·cased, up·per·cas·ing.**

upper chamber or **Upper Chamber,** upper house.

upper class, class of people who are socially and above the middle class. —**up′per-class′,** *adj.*

up·per·cut (up′ər kut′), *n.* (in boxing) a swinging blow directed upward from beneath.

upper hand, advantage; control: *Do what the doctor says or that cold may get the upper hand.*

upper house or **Upper House,** the higher and less representative house of a lawmaking group that has two branches. The Senate is the upper house in the U.S. Congress and in the Canadian Parliament.

Upper Lakes, Lakes Superior, Huron, and sometimes Michigan.

up·per·most (up′ər mōst), **1** *adj.* highest; topmost: *She climbed to the uppermost branch.* **2** *adj.* having the most force or influence; most prominent. **3** *adv.* in, at, or near the top. **4** *adv.* first: *The safety of the passengers was uppermost in the pilot's mind.*

Upper Vol·ta (vol′tə), former name of **Burkina Faso.**

up·pi·ty (up′ə tē), *adj.* INFORMAL. arrogant, self-assertive, or conceited. —**up′pi·ti·ness** or **up′pi·ty·ness,** *n.*

up·raise (up rāz′), *v.* to lift up; raise. ❑ *v.* **up·raised, up·rais·ing.**

up·rate (up′rāt′), *v.* to increase, as in power or efficiency; improve. ❑ *v.* **up·rat·ed, up·rat·ing.**

up·right (up′rīt′), **1** *adv.* straight up; in a vertical position: *Hold yourself upright.* **2** *adj.* standing up straight; erect: *an upright post.* **3** *n.* something standing erect; vertical part or piece. **4** *n.* an upright piano. **5** *adj.* good; honest; righteous: *an upright citizen.* **6** *v.* to raise to an upright position: *to upright a rowboat.* —**up′right′ly,** *adv.* —**up′right′ness,** *n.*

upright piano, a rectangular piano having vertical strings behind the keyboard.

up·rise (up rīz′), *v.* **1** to rise up. **2** to slope upward; ascend. ❑ *v.* **up·rose, up·ris·en, up·ris·ing.**

up·ris·en (up riz′n), *v.* past participle of **uprise.**

up·ris·ing (up′rī′zing), *n.* a revolt; rebellion: *an uprising in a prison.*

up·riv·er (up′riv′ər), *adv., adj.* toward or in the direction of the source of a river: *to swim upriver, upriver rapids.*

up·roar (up′rôr′), *n.* **1** loud or confused noise: *the uproar following a last-minute touchdown.* **2** a confused, disturbed, or excited state: *There was an uproar over the large tax increase.*

up·roar·i·ous (up rôr′ē əs), *adj.* **1** making an uproar; noisy and disorderly: *an uproarious crowd.* **2** loud and confused: *uproarious laughter.* —**up·roar′i·ous·ly,** *adv.* —**up·roar′i·ous·ness,** *n.*

up·root (up rüt′), *v.* **1** to tear up by the roots: *The storm uprooted many trees.* **2** to tear away, remove, or displace completely: *families uprooted from their homes by the flood.*

uproot—an uprooted tree

up·rose (up rōz′), *v.* past tense of **uprise.**

ups and downs, changes in fortunes; successes and failures: *Her career has had many ups and downs.*

up·scale (up′skāl′), *adj.* **1** above average in income and education. **2** of, about, or intended for upscale people: *upscale advertising.*

a	hat	ė	term	ô	order	ch	child		
ā	age	i	it	oi	oil	ng	long		a in about
ä	far	ī	ice	ou	out	sh	she	ə {	e in taken
â	care	o	hot	u	cup	th	thin		i in pencil
e	let	ō	open	ù	put	ŦH	then		o in lemon
ē	equal	ò	saw	ü	rule	zh	measure		u in circus

up·set (up set′ *for verb;* up′set′ *for noun;* up set′or up′set′ *for adj.*), **1** *v.* to tip over; overturn: *He upset his glass of milk. Moving about in a boat may upset it.* **2** *n.* a tipping over; overturn. **3** *adj.* tipped over; overturned: *The upset glass rolled off the table.* **4** *v.* to disturb greatly; disorder: *Rain upset our plans for a picnic. The shock upset my nerves.* **5** *n.* a great disturbance; disorder. **6** *adj.* greatly disturbed; disordered: *an upset stomach.* **7** *v.* to defeat unexpectedly in a contest: *Our candidate upset the mayor in the election.* **8** *n.* an unexpected defeat: *The hockey team suffered an upset.* ❑ *v.* **up·set, up·set·ting.**

up·shot (up′shot′), *n.* conclusion; result: *The upshot of our discussion was a better understanding of one another.*

up·side (up′sīd′), *n.* **1** a favorable situation or way of thinking about a situation, especially in business: *The upside of the long ride to school is the time to talk to my friends.* **2** the upper side.

upside down, 1 having what should be on top at the bottom: *The pie fell upside down.* **2** in or into complete disorder: *The children turned the house upside down.*

up·side-down cake (up′sīd′doun′), a cake made of batter poured over fruit, baked, and served bottom up.

up·stage (up′stāj′), **1** *adv., adj.* toward or at the back of the stage: *walk upstage, upstage furniture.* **2** *v.* to draw attention away from an actor, especially by forcing the actor to face away from the audience. ❑ *v.* **up·staged, up·stag·ing.**

up·stairs (up′stârz′), **1** *adv.* up the stairs: *The boy ran upstairs.* **2** *adj., adv.* on or to an upper floor: *He is waiting in an upstairs hall. She lives upstairs.* **3** *n.* the upper floor or floors: *That small cottage has no upstairs.* **4** *adv.* INFORMAL. in the mind; mentally: *Something's wrong with him upstairs.*

kick upstairs, to promote someone to a higher but less powerful or important position.

up·stand·ing (up stan′ding), *adj.* **1** honorable: *a fine, upstanding young woman.* **2** standing up; erect: *short, upstanding hair.* **—up·stand′ing·ness,** *n.*

up·start (up′stärt′), *n.* **1** person who has suddenly risen from a humble position to wealth, power, or importance. **2** a bold, unpleasant, and conceited person.

up·state (up′stāt′), *adj.* of the part of a state away from and usually north of the principal city: *upstate New York.*

up·stream (up′strēm′), *adv., adj.* against the current of a stream; up a stream: *He swam upstream. We had an upstream campsite.*

up·surge (up′sėrj′), *n.* a rapid rise; upturn: *an upsurge in retail prices.*

up·sweep (up swēp′ *for verb;* up′swēp′ *for noun*), **1** *v.* to sweep or brush upward. **2** *n.* an upswept hairdo: *She arranged her hair in an upsweep for the party.* ❑ *v.* **up·swept, up·sweep·ing.**

up·swept (up′swept′), **1** *adj.* curving or slanting upward: *That dog has an upswept jaw.* **2** *adj.* brushed upward: *an upswept hairdo.* **3** *v.* past tense and past participle of **upsweep.**

up·swing (up′swing′), *n.* **1** an upward swing; movement upward. **2** a marked improvement; strong advance.

up·take (up′tāk′), *n.* **on the uptake,** in understanding and perception: *quick on the uptake.*

up·tight (up′tīt′), *adj.* **1** very upset, angry, or worried: *be uptight over losing a job.* **2** having very old-fashioned, traditional, or conventional ideas: *an uptight neighborhood.* **—up′tight′ness,** *n.*

up-to-date (up′tə dāt′), *adj.* **1** extending to the present time: *an up-to-date record of sales.* **2** keeping up with the times in style, ideas, etc.; modern: *an up-to-date store.*

up·town (up′toun′), *adv., adj.* to or in the upper or higher part of a town or city; away from the main business section of a town or city: *to go uptown. We shopped at an uptown store.*

up·turn (up tėrn′ *for verb;* up′tėrn′ *for noun*), **1** *v.* to turn up. **2** *n.* an improvement: *As the weather improved, there was an upturn in everyone's spirit.*

up·turned (up tėrnd′), *adj.* turned upward: *The rain fell on their upturned faces.*

up·ward (up′wərd), **1** *adv.* toward a higher place: *I climbed upward until I reached the apple.* **2** *adj.* directed or moving toward a higher place; in a higher position: *an upward course, an upward flight.* **3** *adv.* toward a higher or greater rank, amount, age, etc.: *From ten years of age upward, she had studied French.* **4** *adv.* toward the source: *We traced the brook upward.* **—up′ward·ly,** *adv.* **—up′ward·ness,** *n.*

upward of or **upwards of,** more than: *He looked at skates costing upwards of $50.*

up·well·ing (up′wel′ing), *n.* an event or process in which cold water rises, rich in nutrients, from deeper regions of an ocean to the surface.

up·wind (up′wind′), *adj., adv.* against the wind; in the direction from which the wind is blowing: *upwind flight, to fly upwind.*

Ur (ėr), *n.* city in ancient Sumer, on the Euphrates River.

ur·a·cil (yùr′ə səl), *n.* substance present in nucleic acid. It is one of the compounds that form the genetic code in RNA.

U·ral Mountains (yùr′əl), mountain range in W Russia, between Europe and Asia.

Ural River, river flowing south from the Ural Mountains into the Caspian Sea.

u·ra·ni·um (yù rā′nē əm), *n.* a very heavy, white, radioactive metallic element. Some forms of uranium are used in nuclear reactors and nuclear bombs. *Symbol:* U

uranium 235, a rare, unstable form of uranium, used in nuclear reactors and nuclear bombs.

uranium 238, a stable form of uranium not used in nuclear reactors or nuclear bombs. About 99 percent of natural uranium is uranium 238.

U·ra·nus (yùr′ə nəs *or* yù rā′nəs), *n.* **1** the third largest planet in the solar system and the seventh in distance from the sun. **2** a Greek god of heaven. Uranus was the father of the Titans and the Cyclopes.

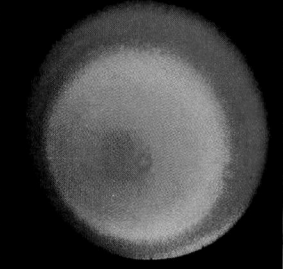
Uranus through color filters

ur·ban (ėr′bən), *adj.* **1** of or about cities or towns: *an urban district, urban planning.* **2** living in a city or cities: *the urban population, urban dwellers.* **3** typical of cities: *urban life.*

ur·bane (ėr bān′), *adj.* courteous, refined, or elegant: *urbane manners.* **—ur′bane′ly,** *adv.*

ur·ban·ite (ėr′bə nīt), *n.* person who lives in a city.

ur·ban·i·ty (ėr′ban′ə tē), *n.* courtesy, refinement, or elegance.

ur·ban·ize (ėr′bə nīz), *v.* to make or become urban: *urbanize an area.* ❑ *v.* **ur·ban·ized, ur·ban·iz·ing.** **—ur′ban·i·za′tion,** *n.*

ur·chin (ėr′chən), *n.* **1** a poor, ragged child. **2** a small or mischievous child. **3** sea urchin.

-ure, *suffix.* **1** act or process of ___ing: *failure = act of failing.* **2** condition of being ___ed: *pleasure = condition of being pleased.* **3** result of being ___ed: *exposure = result of being exposed.* **4** something that ___s: *legislature = something that legislates.* **5** thing that is ___ed: *disclosure = thing that is disclosed.*

u·re·a (yù rē′ə), *n.* substance present in the urine of mammals. Urea produced synthetically is used in making plastics and fertilizers.

u·re·ter (yù rē′tər), *n.* duct that carries urine from a kidney to the bladder.

u·re·thra (yu̇ rē′thrə), *n.* duct through which urine is discharged from the bladder. ❏ *n., pl.* **u·re·thras.** **−u·re′thral,** *adj.*

urge (ėrj), **1** *v.* to try to persuade with arguments; ask earnestly: *We urged them to stay.* **2** *n.* a driving force or impulse: *I had an urge to see my old friends again.* **3** *v.* to push, force, or drive forward or onward: *The rider urged on his horse with whip and spurs. Hunger urged her to find food.* **4** *v.* to plead or argue earnestly for; recommend strongly: *The doctor urged a change of climate.* ❏ *v.* **urged, urg·ing.** **−urg′er,** *n.*

ur·gen·cy (ėr′jən sē), *n.* **1** urgent character; need for immediate action or attention: *Conserving fuel became a matter of great urgency.* **2** insistence: *There was urgency in her voice.*

ur·gent (ėr′jənt), *adj.* **1** demanding immediate action or attention; pressing; important: *an urgent duty, an urgent message.* **2** insistent. **−ur′gent·ly,** *adv.*

ur·i·nal (yu̇r′ə nəl), *n.* **1** place for urinating. **2** container for urine.

ur·i·nal·y·sis (yu̇r′ə nal′ə sis), *n.* a chemical analysis of a sample of urine. By means of urinalysis doctors can detect certain diseases, such as diabetes, or the presence of certain drugs. ❏ *n., pl.* **ur·i·nal·y·ses** (yu̇r′ə nal′ə sēz′).

ur·i·nar·y (yu̇r′ə når′ē), *adj.* **1** of or about urine. **2** of the organs that produce and discharge urine.

ur·i·nate (yu̇r′ə nāt), *v.* to discharge urine from the body. ❏ *v.* **ur·i·nat·ed, ur·i·nat·ing.** **−ur′i·na′tion,** *n.*

ur·ine (yu̇r′ən), *n.* the liquid waste product that is produced by the kidneys. Urine passes through the ureters into the bladder, and is then discharged from the body through the urethra.

urn (ėrn), *n.* **1** vase with a base. Urns have been used since ancient times to hold the ashes of the dead. **2** a coffeepot or teapot with a faucet, used for making or serving coffee or tea at the table. ■ Another word that sounds like this is **earn.**

ur·o·gen·i·tal (yu̇r′ō jen′ə təl), *adj.* of or about the urinary and genital organs.

u·rol·o·gy (yu̇ rol′ə jē), *n.* branch of medicine dealing with the urogenital tract in males or the urinary tract in females. **−u·rol′o·gist,** *n.*

Ur·sa Major (ėr′sə), the most visible northern constellation, shaped something like a bear, and including the stars of the Big Dipper; Great Bear; Big Bear.

urn (def. 1)

Ur·sa Minor (ėr′sə), a northern constellation, shaped something like a bear, that includes the stars of the Little Dipper; Little Bear.

Ur·u·guay (yu̇r′ə gwā *or* yu̇r′ə gwī), *n.* country in the SE part of South America. *Capital:* Montevideo. **−Ur′u·guay′an,** *adj., n.*

us (us), *pron.* We and us mean the person speaking plus the person or persons addressed or spoken about: *They often help us. He came with us to the movie.*

U.S., the United States.

U.S.A. or **USA, 1** the United States of America. **2** U.S. Army.

us·a·ble (yü′zə bəl), *adj.* able to be used; fit for use: *The broken toy was no longer usable.* **−us′a·bil′i·ty, us′a·ble·ness,** *n.* **−us′a·bly,** *adv.*

USAF or **U.S.A.F.,** U.S. Air Force.

us·age (yü′sij), *n.* **1** the customary way of using words: *The actual usage of speakers and writers of English determines what standard English is.* **2** way or manner of using or of being used;

treatment: *The car has had rough usage.* **3** a long-continued practice; customary use; habit; custom.

USCG or **U.S.C.G.,** U.S. Coast Guard.

use (yüz *for verb;* yüs *for noun*), **1** *v.* to put into action or service: *use a knife to cut meat. We use our legs in walking.* **2** *v.* to finish or consume: *We have used most of the money.* **3** *v.* to avail oneself of; put to your own purposes: *May I use your telephone?* **4** *v.* to take advantage of someone for your own benefit: *He tends to use people.* **5** *n.* act of using: *the use of tools.* **6** *n.* condition of being used: *methods long out of use.* **7** *n.* usefulness: *a thing of no practical use.* **8** *n.* purpose that a thing is used for: *find a new use for something.* **9** *n.* way of using: *a proper use of your time, poor use of a material.* **10** *n.* need or occasion for using; necessity; demand: *A camper has use for a hatchet.* **11** *n.* power or capacity of using; ability to use: *lose the use of an arm.* **12** *n.* right or privilege of using: *have the use of a friend's boat for the summer.* ❏ *v.* **used, us·ing.**

have no use for, 1 to not need or want. **2** to dislike.

in use, being used.

make use of, to use; utilize: *She made use of her Spanish while in Mexico.*

put to use, to use: *If you can put that old bicycle to use, you may have it.*

used to (yüst′tü), **1** accustomed to: *I'm not used to cold weather.* **2** formerly did: *I used to have a bicycle, but I don't anymore.*

use up, to consume or expend entirely: *We have used up nearly all of our sugar.*

used (yüzd), *adj.* not new; that has belonged to another or others: *a used car.*

use·ful (yüs′fəl), *adj.* of use; giving service; helpful: *a useful suggestion. He made himself useful around the house.* **−use′ful·ly,** *adv.* **−use′ful·ness,** *n.*

use·less (yüs′lis), *adj.* not usable; worthless: *A TV set would be useless in a house without electricity.* **−use′less·ly,** *adv.* **−use′less·ness,** *n.*

us·er (yü′zər), *n.* one that uses.

us·er-friend·ly (yü′zər frend′lē), *adj.* designed to be easy to use, even by people without training or experience: *The program is so user-friendly, it fixes your mistakes.*

ush·er (ush′ər), **1** *n.* person who shows people to their seats in a theater, church, etc. **2** *v.* to conduct; escort; show: *We ushered the visitors to the door.*

usher in, to inaugurate; introduce: *a winter ushered in by cold rains.*

USMC or **U.S.M.C.,** U.S. Marine Corps.

USN or **U.S.N.,** U.S. Navy.

U.S. Open, 1 a major annual golf tournament, open to both amateur and professional golfers. **2 U.S. Women's Open,** a similar tournament for women golfers. **3** a major annual tennis tourna-

a	hat	ė	term	ô	order	ch	child		a in about
ā	age	i	it	oi	oil	ng	long		e in taken
ä	far	ī	ice	ou	out	sh	she	ə	i in pencil
â	care	o	hot	u	cup	th	thin		o in lemon
e	let	ō	open	u̇	put	ᴛʜ	then		u in circus
ē	equal	ò	saw	ü	rule	zh	measure		

U

ment, open to both amateur and professional women and men players. **4** a major annual bowling tournament, open to both amateur and professional bowlers. **5 Women's U.S. Open,** a similar tournament for women bowlers.

U.S.S.R. or **USSR,** Union of Soviet Socialist Republics.

u·su·al (yü′zhü əl), *adj.* commonly seen, found, or happening; ordinary; customary: *This is our usual spring weather. My usual bedtime is 10 P.M.* **−u′su·al·ly,** *adv.* **−u′su·al·ness,** *n.*

as usual, in the usual manner; as is customary: *My friend and I met, as usual, on the way to school.*

u·sur·er (yü′zhər ər), *n.* person who lends money at an extremely high or unlawful rate of interest.

u·sur·i·ous (yü zhúr′ē əs), *adj.* **1** taking extremely high or unlawful interest for the use of money. **2** of or about usury: *Fifty percent is a usurious rate of interest.* **−u·sur′i·ous·ly,** *adv.* **−u·sur′i·ous·ness,** *n.*

u·surp (yü sėrp′ *or* yü zėrp′), *v.* to seize and hold power, position, or authority by force or without right: *The queen's younger sister tried to usurp the throne.* **−u·surp′er,** *n.*

u·sur·pa·tion (yü′sėr pā′shən *or* yü′zər pā′shən), *n.* act of usurping; the seizing and holding of the place or power of another by force or without right.

u·sur·y (yü′zhər ē), *n.* **1** the lending of money at an extremely high or unlawful rate of interest. **2** an extremely high or unlawful interest.

UT, Utah (used with postal Zip Code).

Ut., Utah.

U·tah (yü′tò *or* yü′tä), *n.* one of the western states of the United States. *Abbreviation:* UT or Ut. *Capital:* Salt Lake City. [Utah comes from **Ute,** which comes from a word in the Ute language. The word may mean "person" or "people."] **−U′tah·an,** *n.*

Ute (yüt), *n.* member of a tribe of American Indians living mostly in Utah and Colorado. □ *n., pl.* **Ute** or **Utes.**

u·ten·sil (yü ten′səl), *n.* **1** container or implement used for practical purposes. Pots and pans are kitchen utensils. **2** device or tool used for some special purpose. Pens and pencils are writing utensils.

u·ter·us (yü′tər əs), *n.* the part of the body in female mammals that holds and nourishes the young till birth; womb. □ *n., pl.* **u·ter·us·es, u·ter·i** (yü′tər ī).

u·til·i·dor (yü til′ə dôr), *n.* CANADIAN. a raised, insulated system of utility pipes containing water, steam, and sewage lines, for communities built on permafrost.

u·til·i·tar·i·an (yü til′ə târ′ē ən), *adj.* **1** of or about utility. **2** aiming at usefulness rather than beauty, style, etc.

u·til·i·ty (yü til′ə tē), **1** *n.* power to satisfy people's needs; usefulness: *They appreciated the utility of their dishwasher.* **2** *n.* company that performs a public service; public utility. Railroads, bus lines, and gas and electric companies are utilities. **3** *n.* a useful thing. **4** *adj.* capable of playing more than one role or position: *a utility infielder.* □ *n., pl.* **u·til·i·ties** for 2,3.

utility room, a room in a house for a furnace, water heater, or other major appliances.

u·ti·lize (yü′tl īz), *v.* to make use of; put to some practical use: *The cook utilized the bones to make soup.* □ *v.* **u·ti·lized, u·ti·liz·ing. −u′ti·liz′a·ble,** *adj.* **−u′ti·li·za′tion,** *n.* **−u′ti·liz′er,** *n.*

ut·most (ut′mōst), **1** *adj.* greatest possible; greatest; highest: *A balanced diet is of the utmost importance to health.* **2** *adj.* most distant; farthest; extreme: *She walked to the utmost edge of the cliff.* **3** *n.* the most that is possible; extreme limit: *He enjoyed himself to the utmost.*

u·to·pi·a or **U·to·pi·a** (yü tō′pē ə), *n.* **1** an ideal place or condition; a perfect place or way to live. **2** an idealistic system or plan of government with ideal laws and social conditions, that is impractical in actual use.

u·to·pi·an or **U·to·pi·an** (yü tō′pē ən), **1** *adj.* of or like a utopia. **2** *adj.* idealistic but impractical. **3** *n.* an idealistic but not always practical reformer; idealist.

ut·ter¹ (ut′ər), *adj.* complete; total; absolute: *When the lights went out, we were in utter darkness.* **−ut′ter·ly,** *adv.*

ut·ter² (ut′ər), *v.* **1** to make known; speak; express: *"Good-by" was the last word he uttered.* **2** to give forth; give out: *He uttered a cry of pain.* [See Word Story at **utter**¹.] **−ut′ter·a·ble,** *adj.*

ut·ter·ance (ut′ər əns), *n.* **1** act of uttering; expression in words or sounds: *The child gave utterance to her grief.* **2** way or manner of speaking. **3** something uttered; a spoken word or words.

ut·ter·most (ut′ər mōst), *adj., n.* utmost.

U-turn (yü′tėrn′), *n.* a U-shaped turn made by a motor vehicle in order to reverse its direction.

UV, ultraviolet.

u·vu·la (yü′vyə lə), *n.* the small piece of flesh hanging down from the soft palate in the back of the mouth. □ *n., pl.* **u·vu·las, u·vu·lae** (yü′vyə lē′). [Uvula comes from a Latin word meaning "little grape." The Romans thought that the uvula looked like a bunch of grapes.]

Uz·bek·i·stan (üz bek′ə stän), *n.* country in central Asia, formerly part of the Soviet Union. *Capital:* Tashkent.

V or **v** (vē), *n.* **1** the 22nd letter of the English alphabet. **2** anything shaped like a V. **3** the Roman numeral for 5. ❑ *n., pl.* **V's** or **v's.**

V, symbol for vanadium.

V, V., or **v,** volt.

v., **1** verb. **2** verse. **3** versus.

VA, Virginia (used with postal Zip Code).

Va., Virginia.

va·can·cy (vā′kən sē), *n.* **1** an unoccupied position: *The retirement of two bookkeepers made two vacancies in our office.* **2** a room, space, or apartment for rent; empty space: *a vacancy in the motel, a vacancy in the parking lot.* **3** condition of being vacant; emptiness. **4** emptiness of mind. ❑ *n., pl.* **va·can·cies** for 1,2.

va·cant (vā′kənt), *adj.* **1** not occupied: *a vacant chair, a vacant house.* **2** empty; not filled: *a vacant space.* **3** empty of thought or intelligence: *When I asked her a question, she just gave me a vacant smile.* **—va′cant·ly,** *adv.*

va·cate (vā′kāt), *v.* to go away from and leave empty or unoccupied; make vacant: *They will vacate the house on May 1.* ❑ *v.* **va·cat·ed, va·cat·ing.**

va·ca·tion (vā kā′shən), **1** *n.* freedom from school, business, or other duties: *There is a vacation from school every summer.* **2** *v.* to take a vacation. **—va·ca′tion·er,** *n.*

vac·ci·nate (vak′sə nāt), *v.* to give someone a vaccine by a shot or other means to protect against a disease. People who are vaccinated against whooping cough, measles, tetanus, polio, etc.,

are made immune to these diseases for several years or longer. ❑ *v.* **vac·ci·nat·ed, vac·ci·nat·ing.**

vac·ci·na·tion (vak′sə nā′shən), *n.* **1** act or process of vaccinating: *Vaccination has eliminated the danger of smallpox.* **2** scar where vaccine was injected.

vac·cine (vak sēn′), *n.* a preparation of dead or weakened bacteria of a particular disease. A vaccine is given by a shot or other means to prevent or lessen the effects of a disease. Vaccines work by causing the body to develop antibodies against the disease germs. Vaccines are used against polio, mumps, measles, and other diseases.

WORD STORY **Vaccine** comes from a Latin word meaning "a cow." The first vaccine was used to give people a mild disease that cows get. This protected people against the related deadly disease, smallpox.

vac·il·late (vas′ə lāt), *v.* **1** to be unable to decide about something: *I was vacillating between two possible choices.* **2** to move first one way and then another; waver. ❑ *v.* **vac·il·lat·ed, vac·il·lat·ing.** **—vac′il·lat′ing·ly,** *adv.* **—vac′il·la′tion,** *n.*

a	hat	ė	term	ô	order	ch	child		⟨ a in about
ā	age	i	it	oi	oil	ng	long		e in taken
ä	far	ī	ice	ou	out	sh	she	ə ⟨	i in pencil
â	care	o	hot	u	cup	th	thin		o in lemon
e	let	ō	open	u̇	put	ŦH	then		u in circus
ē	equal	ȯ	saw	ü	rule	zh	measure		

V

va·cu·i·ty (va kyü′ə tē), *n.* **1** emptiness. **2** an empty space; vacuum. **3** emptiness of mind; lack of ideas or intelligence.

vac·u·ole (vak′yü ōl), *n.* a tiny cavity inside a living cell, containing fluid.

vac·u·ous (vak′yü əs), *adj.* **1** showing no intelligence; stupid. **2** empty. —**vac′u·ous·ly,** *adv.* —**vac′u·ous·ness,** *n.*

vac·u·um (vak′yü əm *or* vak′yüm), **1** *n.* an empty space without even air in it. A perfect vacuum has not yet been created. **2** *n.* a space that has almost no air or other matter in it. Outer space is a vacuum of this sort. **3** *n.* an emptiness; void: *Their child's death left a vacuum in their lives.* **4** *n.* vacuum cleaner. **5** *v.* to clean with a vacuum cleaner: *We vacuum the rugs every week or two.*

vacuum bottle, thermos.

vacuum cleaner, apparatus for cleaning carpets, floors, curtains, etc., by suction.

vac·u·um-packed (vak′yü əm pakt′ *or* vak′yüm pakt′), *adj.* **1** packed in an airtight container to keep fresh: *vacuum-packed coffee.* **2** having had all or most of the air removed before sealing: *vacuum-packed cans.*

vacuum tube, a sealed tube with most air removed, formerly used to control the flow of electric current in radios, TV sets, and other electronic devices. In most of these, transistors are now used instead of vacuum tubes.

Va·duz (vä′düts), *n.* capital of Liechtenstein.

vag·a·bond (vag′ə bond), **1** *n.* an idle wanderer; wanderer; tramp. **2** *adj.* wandering: *The gypsies lead a vagabond life.*

va·gar·y (və ger′ē *or* vā′gər ē), *n.* **1** an odd fancy; extravagant notion: *the vagaries of a dream.* **2** odd action; caprice: *the vagaries of fashion.* ❑ *n., pl.* **va·gar·ies.**

va·gi·na (və jī′nə), *n.* the passage in female mammals that leads from the uterus to the outer sex organs. ❑ *n., pl.* **va·gi·nas.**

vag·i·nal (vaj′ə nəl), *adj.* of, in, or about the vagina.

va·gran·cy (vā′grən sē), *n.* condition of wandering idly from place to place without proper means or ability to earn a living: *The tramp was arrested for vagrancy.*

va·grant (vā′grənt), **1** *n.* an idle wanderer without a home, money, or a job. **2** *adj.* moving in no definite direction or course; wandering: *vagrant thoughts.* **3** *adj.* wandering without a home, money, or a job. —**va′grant·ly,** *adv.*

vague (vāg), *adj.* not definite; not clear; not distinct: *In a fog everything looks vague. His vague directions confused them.* ■ See Synonym Study at **obscure.** ❑ *adj.* **va·guer, va·guest.**
[**Vague** comes from a Latin word meaning "to wander." When you wander, you have only a vague idea of where you are going.] —**vague′ly,** *adv.* —**vague′ness,** *n.*

vain (vān), *adj.* **1** having too much pride in your looks, ability, etc.: *a good-looking but vain person.* **2** of no use; unsuccessful: *I made vain attempts to reach her by telephone.* **3** of no value; empty; worthless: *a vain boast.* ■ Other words that sound like this are **vane** and **vein.** —**vain′ly,** *adv.* —**vain′ness,** *n.*

in vain, 1 without effect or success: *My shout for help was in vain, for no one could hear me.* **2** in a disrespectful manner; lightly or irreverently: *The Bible says that you must not take God's name in vain.*

vain·glo·ri·ous (vān′glôr′ē əs), *adj.* excessively proud or boastful; extremely vain. —**vain′glo′ri·ous·ly,** *adv.* —**vain′glo′ri·ous·ness,** *n.*

vain·glo·ry (vān′glôr′ē), *n.* **1** an extreme pride in yourself; boastful vanity. **2** worthless pomp or show.

val·ance (val′əns), *n.* **1** a short drapery over the top of a window. **2** a short curtain hanging from the frame or canopy of a bed.

Val·dez (val dēz′), *n.* seaport in S Alaska. The Alaska Pipeline ends there.

vale (vāl), *n.* valley. ■ Another word that sounds like this is **veil.**

val·e·dic·to·ri·an (val′ə dik tôr′ē ən), *n.* student who gives the farewell address at the graduating exercises. The valedictorian is usually the student who ranks highest in the class.

val·e·dic·tor·y (val′ə dik′tər ē), **1** *n.* a farewell address, especially at the graduating exercises of a school or college. **2** *adj.* bidding farewell. ❑ *n., pl.* **val·e·dic·tor·ies.**

va·lence (vā′ləns), *n.* ability of an atom or radical to combine with others, determined by the number of electrons lost, added, or shared. Elements with atoms that lose electrons, such as hydrogen and the metals, have a positive valence. Elements with atoms that add electrons, such as oxygen and other nonmetals, have a negative valence. Oxygen has a negative valence of 2; hydrogen has a positive valence of 1; one atom of oxygen combines with two atoms of hydrogen to form a molecule of water.

Va·len·cia (və len′shə), *n.* port in E Spain, on the Mediterranean.

val·en·tine (val′ən tīn), *n.* **1** a greeting card or small gift sent on Saint Valentine's Day, February 14. **2** a sweetheart chosen on this day: *Will you be my valentine?*

Val·en·tine (val′ən tīn), *n.* **Saint,** Christian martyr of the A.D. 200s. He was beheaded by the Romans on February 14.

Valentine's Day, Saint Valentine's Day, February 14.

Val·en·ti·no (val′ən tē′nō), *n.* **Ru·dolph** (rü′dolf), 1895-1926, American silent movie star, born in Italy. ■ **Rudolph Valentino** was wildly popular. He died very young, and thousands of women attended his funeral.

va·ler·i·an (və lir′ē ən), *n.* **1** a garden plant with small pinkish or white flowers. **2** strong-smelling oil of this plant, used in medicine. **3** any of numerous related plants.

val·et (val′it *or* val′ā), *n.* **1** servant who takes care of a man's clothes and gives him personal service. **2** worker in a hotel who cleans or presses clothes.

Val·hal·la (val hal′ə), *n.* (in Scandinavian myths) the hall where the souls of heroes slain in battle feast with the god Odin.

val·iant (val′yənt), *adj.* brave; courageous: *A neighbor's valiant efforts saved the children from the burning building.* —**val′iant·ly,** *adv.* —**val′iant·ness,** *n.*

val·id (val′id), *adj.* **1** supported by facts or authority; sound or true: *She had valid reasons for her objections to the plan.* **2** having legal force; legally binding: *A contract made by a minor child is not valid.* **3** having force; holding good; effective: *Illness is a valid excuse for being absent from school.* —**val′id·ly,** *adv.*

val·i·date (val′ə dāt), *v.* **1** to make valid; give legal force to: *The farmer's deed validated his claim to the land.* **2** to support by facts or authority; confirm. ❑ *v.* **val·i·dat·ed, val·i·dat·ing.** —**val′i·da′tion,** *n.*

va·lid·i·ty (və lid′ə tē), *n.* **1** truth or soundness: *the validity of an argument, the validity of an excuse.* **2** legal soundness or force: *the validity of a contract.*

va·lise (və lēs′), *n.* a small suitcase to hold clothes, etc.

Val·kyr·ie (val′kir ē), *n.* (in Scandinavian myths) one of the goddesses sent by Odin to ride through the air and hover over battlefields, choosing the heroes who would die in battle and afterward leading them to Valhalla.

Val·let·ta (və let′ə), *n.* capital of Malta.

valley (def. 1)

val·ley (val′ē), *n.* **1** region of low land between hills or mountains: *Most large valleys have rivers running through them.* **2** a large region drained by a great river system: *the Mississippi valley.* ❑ *n., pl.* **val·leys.**

Valley Forge, village in SE Pennsylvania, in which Washington and his army spent the winter of 1777-1778.

val·or (val′ər), *n.* bravery; courage: *The soldier received a medal for valor in battle.*

Valor and the words below are related. They all come from a Latin word meaning "to be strong."

avail	evaluate	prevalent	valid
convalescent	invalid[1]	valedictorian	valuable
devalue	invalid[2]	valence	value
equivalent	prevail	valiant	

val·or·ous (val′ər əs), *adj.* valiant; brave; courageous. —**val′or·ous·ly,** *adv.* —**val′or·ous·ness,** *n.*

Val·pa·rai·so (val′pə rī′zō), *n.* port in W central Chile, on the Pacific. [Valparaiso comes from Spanish words meaning "valley of paradise." It is in a pretty part of Chile.]

val·u·a·ble (val′yü ə bəl *or* val′yə bəl), **1** *adj.* having value; being worth something: *valuable information, a valuable friend.* **2** *adj.* worth much money: *a valuable ring.* ■ See Synonym Study at **precious. 3** *n.* Usually, **valuables,** *pl.* articles of value: *She keeps her jewelry and other valuables in a safe.* —**val′u·a·bly,** *adv.*

USAGE NOTE **Valuable** and **invaluable** look as if they should be opposites, but in fact they both mean that something is worth a lot. Why? Because **value** has two meanings as a verb: "to estimate the worth of" and "to think highly of." If you think highly of something, it may be difficult to estimate its worth; it may seem priceless. So what is valuable by the second meaning may be invaluable by the first.

val·u·a·tion (val′yü ā′shən), *n.* **1** estimated or determined value: *The jeweler's valuation of the necklace was $10,000.* **2** act or process of estimating or determining the value of something.

val·ue (val′yü), **1** *n.* the real worth; proper price: *We bought the house for less than its value.* **2** *n.* high worth; excellence, usefulness, or importance: *She appreciated the value of a good education.* **3** *n.* power to buy: *The value of the dollar lessened from 1980 to 1990.* **4** *v.* to estimate the worth of: *The land is valued at $5000 per acre.* **5** *n.* estimated worth: *We placed a value of $3000 on our furniture.* **6** *v.* to think highly of; regard highly: *Since he was an expert, his opinion was valued.* **7** *n.pl.* **values,** things or ideas believed to be important and desirable in your life. **8** *n.* meaning, effect, or force: *the value of a symbol.* **9** *n.* number or amount represented by a symbol: *The value of XIV is fourteen.* **10** *n.* the relative length of a tone in music indicated by a note. ❑ *v.* **val·ued, val·u·ing.** —**val′u·er,** *n.*

val·ue-add·ed tax (val′yü ad′id), a national sales tax added to the price of goods and services at each stage of production and distribution, based on the increase in value at each stage.

val·ued (val′yüd), *adj.* **1** having its value estimated or determined. **2** regarded highly.

val·ue·less (val′yə lis), *adj.* without value; worthless. —**val′ue·less·ness,** *n.*

valve (valv), *n.* **1** a movable part that controls the flow of a liquid or gas through a pipe by opening and closing the pipe. A faucet contains a valve. **2** a part of the body that works like a valve. The valves of the heart are membranes that control the flow of blood into and out of the heart. **3** one of the parts of hinged shells like those of oysters and clams. **4** device in certain brass instruments, such as trumpets and French horns, for changing pitch by changing the direction and length of the column of air. —**valve′less,** *adj.*

va·moose (va müs′), *v.* SLANG. to go away quickly: *They vamoosed when they saw me coming.* ❑ *v.* **va·moosed, va·moos·ing.** [Vamoose comes from a Spanish word meaning "let's go."]

vamp (vamp), *n.* the upper front part of a shoe or boot.

vam·pire (vam′pīr), *n.* **1** (in stories) a corpse supposed to come to life at night and suck the blood of people while they sleep. **2** person who preys ruthlessly on others. **3** vampire bat.

vampire bat, **1** any of several bats of South and Central America that pierce the skin of animals with their sharp teeth and drink the blood. **2** any of various other bats incorrectly supposed to drink blood.

van[1] (van), *n.* **1** a small, enclosed truck designed for light hauling or for recreational use. **2** a large, enclosed truck for moving household goods or animals: *The workers loaded our furniture into the moving van.*

van[2] (van), *n.* the front part of an army or other advancing group; vanguard.

va·na·di·um (və nā′dē əm), *n.* a very hard, silver-white metallic element used in making strong steel alloys. *Symbol:* V

Van Al·len belt (van al′ən), either of two large regions surrounding the earth in nearby outer space, containing many electrically charged subatomic particles held there by the earth's magnetic field.

Van Bur·en (van byür′ən), **Mar·tin** (mär′tən), 1782-1862, the eighth president of the United States, from 1837 to 1841. ■ When **Van Buren** was Vice President, there were rumors of a plot to assassinate him. He carried loaded guns while he presided in the Senate.

Van·cou·ver (van kü′vər), *n.* **1** port in SW Canada. **2** island in the Pacific Ocean, just off the SW coast of Canada. It is part of British Columbia. [Vancouver comes from the name of a British explorer who visited this area before 1800.]

van·dal (van′dl), *n.* **1** person who destroys or damages beautiful or valuable things on purpose: *Vandals had thrown paint on the statues in the park.* **2** Vandal, member of a Germanic tribe that ravaged Gaul, Spain, and northern Africa. In A.D. 455 the Vandals took Rome.

van·dal·ism (van′dl iz′əm), *n.* act of destroying or damaging beautiful or valuable things on purpose: *They were arrested for breaking windows and other acts of vandalism.*

van·dal·ize (van′dl īz), *v.* to destroy or damage on purpose. ❑ *v.* **van·dal·ized, van·dal·iz·ing.** —**van′dal·i·za′tion,** *n.*

vane (vān), *n.* **1** a flat piece of metal, wood, etc., turning on a rod to indicate the direction of the wind; weather vane; weathercock. **2** a flat piece turned on an axis, wheel, etc., by a current of air or liquid, or producing such a current by turning: *the vanes of a windmill.* **3** the flat, soft part of a feather. ■ Other words that sound like this are **vain** and **vein.**

Van Gogh (van gō′ *or* van gŏk′), **Vin·cent** (vin′sənt), 1853-1890, Dutch painter. ■ **Vincent Van Gogh** sold only one painting during his unhappy life. He had epilepsy and cut off one of his ears during a seizure in 1888. His paintings are now worth millions of dollars, each.

Van Gogh painting

van·guard (van′gärd′), *n.* **1** the front part of an army; soldiers marching ahead of the main part of an army to clear the way and guard against surprise; van. **2** leaders of a movement. **3** the foremost or leading position.

a	hat	ė	term	ô	order	ch	child		a	in about
ā	age	i	it	oi	oil	ng	long		e	in taken
ä	far	ī	ice	ou	out	sh	she	ə	i	in pencil
â	care	o	hot	u	cup	th	thin		o	in lemon
e	let	ō	open	ů	put	ŦH	then		u	in circus
ē	equal	ò	saw	ü	rule	zh	measure			

V

va·nil·la (və nil′ə), *n.* a flavoring extract made from the beans of several tropical climbing plants. It is used in candy, ice cream, cakes, and cookies. ❑ *n., pl.* **va·nil·las.**

van·ish (van′ish), *v.* **1** to disappear, especially suddenly: *The sun vanished behind a cloud.* ■ See Synonym Study at **disappear. 2** to pass away; cease to be: *Dinosaurs have vanished from the earth.* **—van′ish·er,** *n.*

vanishing point, 1 a point where parallel lines seem to come together in the distance. **2** a point where anything disappears or comes to an end.

vanishing point

van·i·ty (van′ə tē), *n.* **1** too much pride in your looks, ability, etc. **2** lack of real value: *the vanity of wealth.* **3** worthless pleasure or display. **4** dressing table. **5** a small case containing face powder and rouge. ❑ *n., pl.* **van·i·ties** for 3,4,5.

vanity plate, license plate for a motor vehicle with letters and numbers chosen by the owner.

van pool, a car pool that uses employer-owned vans.

van·quish (vang′kwish), *v.* to conquer; defeat; overcome: *The champion had vanquished all challengers.* **—van′quish·a·ble,** *adj.* **—van′quish·er,** *n.*

van·tage (van′tij), *n.* a better position or condition; advantage.

vantage point, position from which to see, understand, or judge something; point of view: *The hill is a vantage point over the valley. From a modern vantage point, early science seems limited.*

Va·nu·a·tu (vä′nü ä′tü *or* van′wä′tü), *n.* country made up of a group of islands east of Australia. *Capital:* Vila.

vap·id (vap′id), *adj.* without much life or flavor; tasteless; dull. **—vap′id·ly,** *adv.* **—vap′id·ness,** *n.*

va·por (vā′pər), *n.* **1** moisture that can be seen in the air, such as fog or mist. It is usually due to the effect of heat on a liquid: *I could see the vapor from my tea in the cool morning air.* **2** gas formed from a substance that is usually a liquid or a solid; the gaseous form of a liquid or solid: *We could smell the gasoline vapor as Mom filled the car's gas tank.*

va·por·ize (vā′pə riz′), *v.* to change into vapor: *Heat vaporizes water.* ❑ *v.* **va·por·ized, va·por·iz·ing.** **—va·por·i·za′tion,** *n.*

va·por·iz·er (vā′pə ri′zər), *n.* device for converting a liquid into vapor. One kind of vaporizer releases steam into a room for medicinal purposes.

vapor lock, a block in the flow of gasoline to an engine, occurring when heat causes bubbles in the fuel line or carburetor.

va·por·ous (vā′pər əs), *adj.* **1** full of vapor; misty. **2** like vapor. **3** soon passing; worthless. **—va′por·ous·ly,** *adv.*

vapor trail, contrail.

va·quer·o (vä ker′ō), *n.* (in the southwestern United States) a cowboy, herdsman, or cattle driver. ❑ *n., pl.* **va·quer·os.**

var., variant.

var·i·a·bil·i·ty (vâr′ē ə bil′ə tē), *n.* **1** changeableness. **2** tendency to vary.

var·i·a·ble (vâr′ē bəl), **1** *adj.* apt to change; changeable; uncertain: *variable winds. The weather is more variable in New York than it is in California.* **2** *adj.* able to be changed: *The speed of that electric fan is variable.* **3** *n.* thing or quality that varies. **4** *n.* in mathematics: **a** quantity that can assume any of a given set of values. **b** symbol representing this quantity. **—var′i·a·ble·ness,** *n.* **—var′i·a·bly,** *adv.*

var·i·ance (vâr′ē əns), *n.* **1** difference; disagreement. **2** act of varying; change.
at variance, in disagreement: *His deeds are at variance with his words.*

var·i·ant (vâr′ē ənt), **1** *adj.* varying; different: *"Rime" is a variant spelling of "rhyme."* **2** *n.* a different form; a different pronunciation or spelling of the same word.

var·i·a·tion (vâr′ē ā′shən), *n.* **1** act or process of varying; change: *variations in color.* **2** amount of change: *There was a variation of 30 degrees in the temperature yesterday.* **3** a changed or different form: *Which variation of this wallpaper pattern do you like best?* **4** (in music) a tune or theme repeated with changes in rhythm, harmony, etc. **—var′i·a′tion·al,** *adj.*

var·i·cel·la (var′ə sel′ə), *n.* chicken pox.

var·i·col·ored (vâr′i kul′ərd), *adj.* having various colors.

var·i·cose (var′ə kōs), *adj.* abnormally swollen or enlarged: *legs covered with varicose veins.*

var·ied (vâr′ēd), *adj.* of different kinds; having variety: *a varied assortment of candies.* ■ See Usage Note at **various.**

var·i·e·gat·ed (vâr′ē ə gā′tid), *adj.* **1** varied in appearance; marked with different colors: *variegated pansies.* **2** varied. **—var′i·e·gat′ed·ly,** *adv.*

va·ri·e·ty (və ri′ə tē), *n.* **1** difference; change; novelty: *Variety prevents boredom.* **2** several different kinds: *This shop has a variety of toys.* **3** one kind; type; sort: *Which varieties of cake did you buy?* **4** a set of living things, all of one species, somehow like each other and different from others of that species: *fancy varieties of goldfish.* ❑ *n., pl.* **va·ri·e·ties** for 3,4.

variety show, entertainment featuring different kinds of acts, such as songs, dances, acrobatics, and comic skits.

var·i·ous (vâr′ē əs), *adj.* **1** differing from one another; different: *There have been various opinions as to the best way to raise children.* **2** several; many: *We looked at various houses but decided to buy this one.* **—var′i·ous·ly,** *adv.* **—var′i·ous·ness,** *n.*

USAGE NOTE **Various** and **varied** look alike and have related meanings, but they are used differently. **Various** is used about things that are different to begin with, such as trees in a forest. **Varied** is used when someone has deliberately made things different, such as flowers in a garden.

var·mint (vär′mənt), *n.* DIALECT. **1** vermin. **2** an objectionable animal or person. [See Word Story at **vermin.**]

var·nish (vär′nish), **1** *n.* a liquid that gives a smooth, glossy appearance to wood, metal, etc. Varnish is often made from substances like resin dissolved in oil or alcohol. **2** *n.* the smooth, hard surface made by this liquid when it dries: *The varnish on the table was scratched.* **3** *v.* to put varnish on: *They varnished the wood floors of the house.* **4** *n.* a glossy appearance. **5** *n.* a false or deceiving appearance; pretense: *He covered his greed and selfishness with a varnish of good manners.* **6** *v.* to give a false or deceiving appearance to: *to varnish the truth with a lie.* ❑ *n., pl.* **var·nish·es** for 1. **—var′nish·er,** *n.*

var·si·ty (vär′sə tē), *n.* the most important team in a given sport in a university, college, or school. ❑ *n., pl.* **var·si·ties.**

var·y (vâr′ē), *v.* **1** to make or become different; change: *The driver can vary the speed of a car.* **2** to be different; differ: *Stars vary in brightness.* ❑ *v.* **var·ied, var·y·ing.** **—var′y·ing·ly,** *adv.*

vas·cu·lar (vas′kyə lər), *adj.* of, made of, or having vessels that carry blood, sap, etc.

vas def·er·ens (vas def′ər enz), either of a pair of tubes that carry semen from the testicles. ❑ *pl.* **va·sa def·er·en·ti·a** (vā′sə def′ə ren′shē ə).

vase (vās *or* vāz), *n.* holder or container used for ornament or to hold flowers. A vase is usually round, narrowing at the top and bottom. **—vase′like′,** *adj.*

vas·ec·to·my (va sek′tə mē), *n.* the surgical removal of a section of the vas deferens, usually for birth control. ❑ *n., pl.* **vas·ec·to·mies.**

Vas·e·line (vas′ə lēn′), *n.* trademark for a soft, greasy, yellow or whitish substance made from petroleum, used as a healing ointment or as a lubricant.

vas·sal (vas′əl), **1** *n.* (in the feudal system) someone who received land from a lord or superior, to whom in return he gave help in war or some other service. A great noble could be a vassal of the king and have many other men as his vassals. **2** *adj.* like a vassal; like that of a vassal; subordinate: *a vassal nation.* **3** *n.* servant.

> **WORD STORY** **Vassal** comes from a Celtic word meaning "one who stands under." A vassal in the feudal system was required to be under his lord's command in times of war in return for the land the vassal used in times of peace.

vas·sal·age (vas′ə lij), *n.* **1** condition of being a vassal. **2** the homage or service due from a vassal to his lord or superior. **3** dependence; servitude.

vast (vast), *adj.* very great; immense: *Texas and Alaska cover vast territories. A billion dollars is a vast amount of money.* **–vast′ly,** *adv.* **–vast′ness,** *n.*

> **WORD STORY** **Vast** comes from a Latin word meaning "empty." A vast space often seems empty because it is so big. **Waste** comes from the same Latin word. Empty land is called wasteland by farmers because it is not used for crops.

vat (vat), *n.* a large container for liquids; tank: *a vat of dye.*

VAT, (vat *or* vē′ā′tē′), value-added tax.

Vatican (def. 1)

Vat·i·can (vat′ə kən), *n.* **1** the collection of buildings grouped around the palace of the pope in Rome. **2** the government, office, or authority of the pope.

> **WORD STORY** **Vatican** comes from a Latin word meaning "fortuneteller." In old days, people who foretold the future gathered on a hill in Rome. Tradition says that St. Peter was buried on that hill, and popes have lived there for 1500 years.

Vatican City, an independent state inside the city of Rome. It is ruled by the pope and includes Saint Peter's Church and the Vatican.

vaude·ville (vȯd′vil *or* vō′də vil), *n.* theatrical entertainment featuring a variety of acts. Vaudeville consists of songs, dances, acrobatic feats, short plays, trained animals, etc.

> **WORD STORY** **Vaudeville** may come from French words meaning "to go" and "to turn." A song with a chorus goes through each verse and then turns back to repeat the chorus. Songs with a funny chorus were part of some vaudeville acts.

vault[1] (vȯlt), **1** *n.* place for storing valuable things and keeping them safe. Vaults are often made of steel. **2** *n.* place for burial. **3** *n.* an arched roof or ceiling; series of arches. **4** *n.* an arched space or passage. **5** *v.* to make in the form of a vault: *The roof was vaulted.* **6** *v.* to cover with a vault. **7** *n.* an underground cellar or storehouse.

vault[2] (vȯlt), **1** *v.* to jump or leap, especially to jump over something using the hands or a pole: *She vaulted the fence.* **2** *n.* act of vaulting: *His specialty in track is the pole vault.* **–vault′er,** *n.*

vaunt (vȯnt), *v., n.* boast. **–vaunt′er,** *n.* **–vaunt′ing·ly,** *adv.*

vb., **1** verb. **2** verbal.

V.C., Victoria Cross.

VCR, videocassette recorder (a recorder that uses videotape to record and play programs, movies, etc., through a TV set).

VD or **V.D.,** venereal disease.

VDT, video display terminal.

veal (vēl), *n.* flesh of a calf, used for food. [See Word Story at **meat.**]

vec·tor (vek′tər), *n.* quantity involving direction as well as magnitude, represented by an arrow which shows the direction of the force. The length of the arrow indicates the magnitude of the force.

vee·jay (vē′jā′), *n.* SLANG. host of a TV program that is mostly popular music performances recorded on videotape.

veer (vir), **1** *v.* to change in direction; shift; turn: *The wind veered to the south. The talk veered to ghosts.* **2** *v.* to change the direction of: *We veered our boat.* **3** *n.* a shift; turn: *The car made a sudden veer to the left.* **–veer′ing·ly,** *adv.*

veer·y (vir′ē), *n.* a North American thrush with a tawny head, back, and tail and a faintly spotted white breast. ❑ *n., pl.* **veer·ies.**

veg (vej), *v.* Also, **veg out,** to relax; do nothing: *After this difficult week, she wants to veg all weekend.* ❑ *v.* **vegged, veg·ging.**

Ve·ga (vē′gə *or* vā′gə), *n.* a bluish white star, the brightest star in the constellation Lyra.

> **WORD STORY** **Vega** comes from an Arabic word meaning "falling." Middle Eastern astronomers thought of the star as part of a constellation that looked like a vulture descending from the sky.

veg·an (vē′gən *or* vej′an), *n.* a strict vegetarian, especially someone who eats no animal products, avoiding eggs and dairy products.

veg·e·ta·ble (vej′tə bəl *or* vej′ə tə bəl), **1** *n.* plant with fruit, seeds, leaves, roots, or other parts used for food. Peas, corn, lettuce, tomatoes, and beets are vegetables. **2** *n.* the part of such a plant that is used for food: *Shall we have broccoli or spinach as a vegetable for dinner tonight?* **3** *n.* any plant: *Does this substance come from a vegetable or a mineral?* **4** *adj.* of or like plants: *the vegetable kingdom.*

veg·e·tar·i·an (vej′ə ter′ē ən), **1** *n.* person who eats only vegetables but no meat, fish, or other animal products. **2** *adj.* eating vegetable foods only. **3** *adj.* containing no meat: *a vegetarian diet.* **4** *adj.* serving no meat: *a vegetarian restaurant.*

veg·e·tar·i·an·ism (vej′ə ter′ē ə niz′əm), *n.* practice of eating vegetable foods and not eating meat, fish, or poultry. Some vegetarians eat eggs, milk, and cheese.

veg·e·tate (vej′ə tāt), *v.* **1** to live a dull life with very little action or thought. **2** to grow as plants do. ❑ *v.* **veg·e·tat·ed, veg·e·tat·ing.**

veg·e·ta·tion (vej′ə tā′shən), *n.* **1** plant life; growing plants: *There is not much vegetation in deserts.* **2** act or process of vegetating.

veg·e·ta·tive (vej′ə tā′tiv), *adj.* **1** of or about plants or plant life. **2** growing as plants do. **3** having very little action, thought, or feeling. **–veg′e·ta·tive·ly,** *adv.*

veg·gie (vej′ē), INFORMAL. **1** *n.pl.* **veggies,** vegetables: *Eat your veggies.* **2** *n.* vegetarian. **3** *adj.* vegetarian: *a veggie restaurant.*

ve·he·mence (vē′ə məns), *n.* vehement quality or nature; strong feeling; forcefulness; intensity: *The two cousins argued loudly and with vehemence.*

ve·he·ment (vē′ə mənt), *adj.* **1** having or showing strong feeling; caused by strong feeling; eager; passionate: *vehement quarrels.* **2** forceful; vigorous: *a vehement burst of energy.* **–ve′he·ment·ly,** *adv.*

ve·hi·cle (vē′ə kəl), *n.* **1** device for carrying people or things, such as a car, bus, airplane, etc. Cars and trucks are motor vehicles. Rockets are space vehicles. **2** a means by which something

V

a	hat	ė	term	ȯ	order	ch	child		ə	a in about
ā	age	i	it	oi	oil	ng	long			e in taken
ä	far	ī	ice	ou	out	sh	she			i in pencil
â	care	o	hot	u	cup	th	thin			o in lemon
e	let	ō	open	u̇	put	ŦH	then			u in circus
ē	equal	ȯ	saw	ü	rule	zh	measure			

is communicated, shown, or done: *Language is a vehicle of ideas.* **3** (in painting) a liquid into which pigment is mixed for applying color to a surface: *Linseed oil is a vehicle for paint.*

ve·hic·u·lar (vi hik′yə lər), *adj.* of or about vehicles: *vehicular traffic.*

veil (vāl), **1** *n.* piece of very thin material worn to protect or hide the face, or as an ornament. **2** *n.* piece of material worn so as to fall over the head and shoulders. **3** *v.* to cover with a veil: *They veiled their faces.* **4** *n.* anything that screens or hides: *a veil of clouds, a veil of deception.* **5** *v.* to cover, screen, or hide: *Fog veiled the shore. They veiled their plans in secrecy.* ■ Another word that sounds like this is **vale.** —**veil′like′,** *adj.*

vein (vān), **1** *n.* one of the blood vessels that carry blood to the heart from all parts of the body. **2** *n.* one of the vessels forming the framework of a leaf. **3** *n.* one of the ribs that strengthen the wing of an insect. **4** *n.* a crack or layer in rock filled with a deposit, especially of metallic ore: *a vein of copper.* **5** *n.* any streak or marking of a different shade or color in wood, marble, etc. **6** *n.* a state of mind; mood: *The guests chatted in a relaxed vein.* **7** *v.* to cover with veins; mark with veins: *Age had veined his hands.* ■ Other words that sound like this are **vain** and **vane.**

Ve·láz·quez (və las′kəs), *n.* **Die·go** (dyā′gō), 1599-1660, Spanish painter. He painted many portraits of Spanish nobles and royalty with exceptional realism.

Velázquez painting

Vel·cro (vel′krō), *n.* trademark for a kind of fastener, especially for clothing, consisting of two nylon strips. Tiny nylon hooks in one strip attach tightly to tiny loops in the other strip.

veld or **veldt** (velt), *n.* open country in South Africa, with grass or bushes but few trees.

vel·lum (vel′əm), *n.* **1** the finest kind of parchment, usually prepared from the skins of calves and lambs, once used instead of paper for books. **2** paper or cloth imitating such parchment.

ve·loc·i·rap·tor (və los′i rap′tər), *n.* a small, very fast, flesh-eating dinosaur with huge claws, like a deinonychus.

ve·loc·i·ty (və los′ə tē), *n.* **1** swiftness; quickness: *The car sped by with such velocity that the driver's face was just a blur.* **2** rate of motion; speed: *The velocity of light is about 186,000 miles per second.* ❑ *n., pl.* **ve·loc·i·ties** for 2.

ve·lour (və lür′), *n.* fabric like velvet, usually made of silk, wool, cotton, or rayon. Velour is used for clothing, upholstery, etc.

vel·vet (vel′vit), **1** *n.* a very soft cloth with short raised threads on one side, made of silk, rayon, nylon, etc. **2** *adj.* made of velvet: *a velvet jacket.* **3** *adj.* like velvet: *Our kitten has soft, velvet paws.* —**vel′vet·like′,** *adj.*

vel·vet·een (vel′və tēn′), *n.* a cotton fabric resembling velvet.

vel·vet·y (vel′və tē), *adj.* smooth and soft like velvet.

ve·na ca·va (vē′nə kā′və), either of two large veins that empty blood from the upper and lower halves of the body into the right atrium of the heart. ❑ *pl.* **ve·nae ca·vae** (vē′nē kā′vē).

ve·nal (vē′nl), *adj.* **1** willing to sell your services or influence for illegal purposes; open to bribes; corrupt: *Venal judges are a disgrace to a country.* **2** influenced or obtained by bribery: *venal conduct.* —**ve·nal·i·ty** (vē nal′ə tē), *n.* —**ve′nal·ly,** *adv.*

vend (vend), *v.* to sell; peddle: *They were vending popcorn.* —**ven′dor** or **vend′er,** *n.*

Ven·da (ven′də), *n.* country in S Africa, formerly part of the Republic of South Africa. *Capital:* Thohoyandou.

ven·det·ta (ven det′ə), *n.* feud in which a murdered person's relatives try to kill the slayer or the slayer's relatives. ❑ *n., pl.* **ven·det·tas.**

vending machine, machine from which snacks, stamps, etc., are delivered when coins or bills are inserted.

ve·neer (və nir′), **1** *v.* to cover wood with a thin layer of finer wood or other material: *The pine desk is veneered with mahogany.* **2** *n.* a thin layer of wood or other material used in veneering: *The panel had a veneer of gold and ivory.* **3** *v.* to cover anything with a layer of something else to give an appearance of superior quality. **4** *n.* surface appearance or show: *Their treachery was hidden by a veneer of friendship.* —**ve·neer′er,** *n.*

ven·er·a·ble (ven′ər ə bəl), *adj.* worthy of reverence; deserving respect because of age, character, or importance: *venerable customs.* —**ven′er·a·bly,** *adv.*

ven·e·rate (ven′ə rāt′), *v.* to regard with deep respect; revere. ❑ *v.* **ven·e·rat·ed, ven·e·rat·ing.** —**ven′e·ra′tor,** *n.*

ven·e·ra·tion (ven′ə rā′shən), *n.* deep respect; reverence.

ve·ner·e·al (və nir′ē əl), *adj.* of or transmitted by sexual intercourse. Genital herpes, chlamydia, gonorrhea, and syphilis are venereal diseases.

Ve·ne·tian (və nē′shən), **1** *adj.* of or about Venice or its people. **2** *n.* person born or living in Venice.

Venetian blind, a window blind made of many horizontal wooden, steel, or aluminum slats. The blind can be raised and lowered, or the slats can be tilted so that they overlap, to regulate the light that is let in.

Ven·e·zue·la (ven′ə zwā′lə), *n.* country in the N part of South America. *Capital:* Caracas. —**Ven′e·zue′lan,** *adj., n.*

venge·ance (ven′jəns), *n.* punishment in return for a wrong; revenge: *She swore vengeance against her hateful enemies.*
with a vengeance, 1 with great force or violence: *By six o'clock it was raining with a vengeance.* **2** much more than expected.

venge·ful (venj′fəl), *adj.* feeling or showing a strong desire for vengeance. —**venge′ful·ly,** *adv.* —**venge′ful·ness,** *n.*

ve·ni·al (vē′nē əl), *adj.* able to be forgiven; wrong but pardonable. —**ve′ni·al·ly,** *adv.*

Ven·ice (ven′is), *n.* port in NE Italy, on the Adriatic. Venice has many canals in place of streets.

ven·i·son (ven′ə sən), *n.* the flesh of a deer, used for food; deer meat.

ven·om (ven′əm), *n.* **1** the poison of snakes, spiders, etc. **2** hatred; spite; malice: *They spoke of their enemies with venom.*

ven·om·ous (ven′ə məs), *adj.* **1** poisonous: *a venomous snake.* **2** spiteful; malicious: *venomous gossip.* —**ven′om·ous·ly,** *adv.* —**ven′om·ous·ness,** *n.*

ve·nous (vē′nəs), *adj.* of or in veins: *venous blood.*

vent¹ (vent), **1** *n.* hole that lets something in and out: *He used a pencil to make air vents in the box so that the frog could breathe.* **2** *n.* a way out; means of free expression; release: *We gave vent to our grief in tears.* **3** *v.* to let out; express freely: *Don't vent your anger on the dog.* **4** *v.* to make an opening in something. **5** *n.* opening in the earth through which gases and other materials shoot out during a volcanic eruption. **6** *n.* opening on the ocean floor from which flow hot water and dissolved minerals.

vent² (vent), *n.* slit in a garment.

ven·ti·late (ven′tl āt), v. **1** to let fresh air into: *We ventilate a room by opening windows.* **2** to make known publicly; discuss openly. □ v. **ven·ti·lat·ed, ven·ti·lat·ing.**

ven·ti·la·tion (ven′tl ā′shən), n. **1** act or process of supplying with fresh air. **2** means of supplying fresh air: *Air conditioning provides ventilation in summer.*

ven·ti·la·tor (ven′tl ā′tər), n. **1** any device or other means for changing the air in a room, vehicle, or other space. Ventilators may be fans or air conditioners. **2** respirator (def. 2).

ven·tral (ven′trəl), adj. of or on the same side of the body as the belly; abdominal.

ven·tri·cle (ven′trə kəl), n. one of the two lower chambers of the heart. A ventricle receives blood from the atrium and forces it into the arteries. See picture at **heart.**

ven·tril·o·quism (ven tril′ə kwiz′əm), n. art or practice of speaking with the lips shut or nearly shut so that the voice may seem to come from some source other than the speaker.

WORD STORY **Ventriloquism** comes from Latin words meaning "stomach" and "to speak." In ancient times, some ventriloquists claimed to have supernatural beings talking in their stomachs. People would pay for advice from these spirits.

ven·tril·o·quist (ven tril′ə kwist), n. person skilled in ventriloquism.

ven·ture (ven′chər), **1** n. a risky or daring act, project, or the like: *Our courage was equal to any venture. A lucky venture in oil stock made him rich.* **2** v. to expose to risk or danger: *She ventured her life to rescue me.* **3** v. to dare: *No one ventured to interrupt the speaker.* **4** v. to dare to come or go: *We ventured out on the thin ice and fell through.* **5** v. to dare to say or make: *He ventured an objection.* □ v. **ven·tured, ven·tur·ing.**

ven·ture·some (ven′chər səm), adj. **1** inclined to take risks; rash; daring. **2** risky: *a venturesome expedition.* —**ven′ture·some·ly,** adv. —**ven′ture·some·ness,** n.

ven·tur·ous (ven′chər əs), adj. **1** bold; daring; adventurous. **2** risky. —**ven′tur·ous·ly,** adv. —**ven′tur·ous·ness,** n.

ven·ue (ven′yü), n. place where people gather for some activity, such as a sports stadium: *the venue for the Olympic games.*

Ve·nus (vē′nəs), n. **1** the sixth largest planet in the solar system and the second in distance from the sun. It is the planet that comes closest to Earth and from Earth, it is the brightest planet. **2** the Roman goddess of love and beauty. The Greeks called her Aphrodite. **3** any very beautiful woman.

Ve·nus's-fly·trap (vē′nə siz flī′trap′), n. plant with hairy leaves that can fold together to trap and digest insects.

ve·ra·cious (və rā′shəs), adj. **1** truthful. **2** true. ■ Another word that sounds like this is **voracious.** —**ve·ra′cious·ly,** adv. —**ve·ra′cious·ness,** n.

ve·rac·i·ty (və ras′ə tē), n. **1** truthfulness. **2** truth. **3** correctness; accuracy. ■ Another word that sounds like this is **voracity.**

Ve·ra·cruz (ver′ə krüz′), n. a state in E Mexico.

ve·ran·da (və ran′də), n. a large porch along one or more sides of a house or other building. □ n., pl. **ve·ran·das.**

Venus's-flytrap

verb (verb), n. word that tells what is or what is done; the part of speech that expresses action or being. *Do, go, come, be, think, sit, know,* and *eat* are verbs.

WORD POWER **VERBS** ■ **Finalize** and **prioritize** are words that some people dislike. They are examples, however, of a familiar pattern in English. Adjectives and nouns often become **verbs** by adding suffixes. Perhaps the problem with those two verbs is that they were not commonly used until recently. People still notice the suffix-adding process, and this awareness may bother them. With time, the words are likely to become familiar. Suffixes that form verbs include **-ate, -en, -ify,** and **-ize.**

ver·bal (ver′bəl), **1** adj. of or made up of words: *A description is a verbal picture.* ■ See Usage Note at **oral. 2** adj. expressed in spoken words; oral: *a verbal message, a verbal promise.* **3** adj. word for word; literal: *a verbal translation from the French.* **4** adj. having to do with a verb. Two common verbal endings are *-ed* and *-ing.* **5** adj. derived from a verb: *a verbal noun.* **6** n. a noun, adjective, or other word derived from a verb.

ver·bal·ize (ver′bə līz), v. **1** to express in words. **2** to be wordy. □ v. **ver·bal·ized, ver·bal·iz·ing.** —**ver′bal·i·za′tion,** n. —**ver′bal·iz′er,** n.

ver·bal·ly (ver′bə lē), adv. **1** in spoken words; orally: *Instead of replying verbally, I answered with a nod of my head.* **2** word for word: *The witness reported the conversation verbally.* **3** as a verb: *"Veil" is used verbally in "Fog veiled the shore."*

ver·ba·tim (vər bā′tim), adv., adj. word for word; in exactly the same words: *His speech was printed verbatim in the newspaper. The newspaper gave a verbatim report of the speech.*

ver·be·na (vər bē′nə), n. any of numerous garden plants with very long or flattened spikes of flowers in various colors. □ n., pl. **ver·be·nas.**

ver·bi·age (ver′bē ij), n. use of too many words; abundance of useless words.

ver·bose (vər bōs′), adj. using too many words; wordy. —**ver·bose′ly,** adv. —**ver·bose′ness, ver·bos·i·ty** (vər bos′ə tē), n.

ver·dant (verd′nt), adj. green: *The fields are covered with verdant grass.* —**ver′dant·ly,** adv.

Verde (verd), n. Cape. See **Cape Verde.**

Ver·di (ver′dē), n. **Giu·sep·pe** (jü zep′ā), 1813-1901, Italian composer of operas. His works include *Rigoletto* and *Aida.*

ver·dict (ver′dikt), n. **1** the decision of a jury: *The jury returned a verdict of "Not guilty."* **2** any decision or judgment: *the verdict of history.*

ver·di·gris (ver′də grēs′), n. **1** a green or bluish coating that forms on brass, copper, or bronze that is exposed to the air for a long time. **2** a green or bluish green poisonous compound used in paints and insecticides.

ver·dure (ver′jər), n. **1** fresh greenness. **2** a fresh growth of green grass, plants, or leaves.

verge¹ (verj), **1** n. the point at which something begins or happens; brink: *Their business is on the verge of ruin.* **2** v. to be on the verge; border: *The speech was so poorly prepared that it verged on the ridiculous.* □ v. **verged, verg·ing.**

verge² (verj), v. to tend; incline: *The cook was plump, verging toward fatness.* □ v. **verged, verg·ing.**

Ver·gil (ver′jəl), n. Virgil.

ver·i·fi·ca·tion (ver′ə fə kā′shən), n. proof by evidence or testimony; confirmation.

ver·i·fy (ver′ə fī), v. **1** to prove to be true; confirm: *The driver's report of the accident was verified by two witnesses.* **2** to test the correctness of; check the accuracy of: *You can verify the spelling of a word by looking in a dictionary.* □ v. **ver·i·fied, ver·i·fy·ing.** —**ver′i·fi·a·ble,** adj. —**ver′i·fi·a·bly,** adv. —**ver′i·fi′er,** n.

ver·i·ly (ver′ə lē), adv. OLD USE. in truth; truly; really.

ver·i·ta·ble (ver′ə tə bəl), adj. true; real; actual. —**ver′i·ta·ble·ness,** n. —**ver′i·ta·bly,** adv.

ver·i·ty (ver′ə tē), n. **1** truth. **2** a true statement or fact. **3** reality. □ n., pl. **ver·i·ties** for 2.

ver·mi·cel·li (ver′mə sel′ē or ver′mə chel′ē), n. a mixture of flour and water like spaghetti but thinner. [See Word Story at **vermin.**]

ver·mi·form (ver′mə fôrm), adj. shaped like a worm.

vermiform appendix, a slender tube, closed at one end, growing out of the large intestine in the lower right-hand part of the abdomen; appendix. Appendicitis is inflammation of the vermiform appendix.

ver·mil·ion (vər mil′yən), **1** n. a bright red. **2** adj. bright red. **3** n. a bright red coloring matter. [See Word Story at **vermin.**]

V

a	hat	ė	term	ô	order	ch	child		
ā	age	i	it	oi	oil	ng	long		a in about
ä	far	ī	ice	ou	out	sh	she	ə	e in taken
â	care	o	hot	u	cup	th	thin		i in pencil
e	let	ō	open	u̇	put	ᴛʜ	then		o in lemon
ē	equal	ȯ	saw	ü	rule	zh	measure		u in circus

ver·min (vėr′mən), **1** *n.pl.* small animals that are troublesome or destructive. Fleas, lice, bedbugs, rats, and mice are vermin. **2** *n.pl. or sing.* very unpleasant or vile person or persons.

WORD STORY Vermin comes from a Latin word meaning "worm." So does **vermilion**, a color named for a little red worm. **Vermicelli** comes from an Italian word meaning "little worms." And **varmint** comes from **vermin**. Now you know worlds about words and worms.

Ver·mont (vər mont′), *n.* one of the northeastern states of the United States. *Abbreviation:* VT or Vt. *Capital:* Montpelier. [Vermont comes from French words meaning "green mountain." These forested mountains are the state's main geographical feature.] —**Ver·mont′er,** *n.*

ver·mouth (vər müth′), *n.* a white wine flavored with wormwood or other herbs and used as a liqueur or in cocktails.

ver·nac·u·lar (vər nak′yə lər), **1** *n.* a native language; language used by the people of a certain country or place. **2** *adj.* of or in the native language, rather than a literary or learned language. **3** *n.* everyday language; informal speech. **4** *n.* language of a profession, trade, etc.: *There are many technical words in the vernacular of lawyers.*

ver·nal (vėr′nl), *adj.* **1** of or coming in spring: *vernal flowers, vernal equinox.* **2** youthful: *memories from your vernal days.* —**ver′nal·ly,** *adv.*

Verne (vėrn), *n.* **Jules** (jülz), 1828-1905, French writer of science fiction and adventure stories. ■ **Jules Verne** predicted the invention of the airplane, the submarine, television, space travel, and artificial satellites.

Ve·ro·na (və rō′nə), *n.* city in N Italy. The story of *Romeo and Juliet* takes place in Verona.

Ver·sailles (ver sī′), *n.* **1** city in N France, near Paris. A treaty of peace between the Allies and Germany was signed there after World War I, on June 28, 1919. **2** a large palace there.

ver·sa·tile (vėr′sə təl), *adj.* able to do many things well: *She is a versatile student who is skilled at science, art, mathematics, English, German, and history.* —**ver′sa·tile·ly,** *adv.* —**ver′sa·tile·ness, ver′sa·til′i·ty,** *n.*

WORD FAMILY Versatile and the words below are related. They all come from a Latin word meaning "to turn."

adversary	convertible	revert	version
advertise	diversion	subversive	versus
controversy	invert	universe	vertebra
conversation	pervert	varsity	vertical
convert	reverse	verse	

verse (vėrs), *n.* **1** lines of words with a regularly repeated accent and often with rhyme; poetry. **2** a single line of poetry. **3** group of such lines: *Sing the first verse of "America."* **4** type of verse; meter: *blank verse.* **5** a short division of a chapter in the Bible.

versed (vėrst), *adj.* experienced; practiced; skilled: *Our doctor is well versed in the latest medical research.*

ver·si·fi·ca·tion (vėr′sə fə kā′shən), *n.* **1** act or practice of making verses. **2** art or theory of making verses. **3** form or style of poetry; metrical structure.

ver·si·fy (vėr′sə fi), *v.* **1** to write verses. **2** to tell in verse. **3** to turn prose into poetry. ◻ *v.* **ver·si·fied, ver·si·fy·ing.** —**ver′si·fi′er,** *n.*

ver·sion (vėr′zhən), *n.* **1** one particular statement, account, or description: *Each of the three boys gave his own version of the quarrel.* **2** a translation from one language to another: *Though the story was originally written in Japanese, I read an English version.* **3** a special form or variant of something: *I liked the movie version better than the book.*

ver·sus (vėr′səs), *prep.* against: *The most exciting game last week was Los Angeles versus Montreal.*

WORD FAMILY Versus and the following words are related: **versatile, verse, version, vertebra, vertex, vertical,** and **vertigo.** They all come from a Latin word meaning "to turn."

vert., vertical.

ver·te·bra (vėr′tə brə), *n.* any of the bones that form the backbone. ◻ *n., pl.* **ver·te·brae** (vėr′tə brē), **ver·te·bras.**

ver·te·bral (vėr′tə brəl), *adj.* of or about a vertebra or the vertebrae.

ver·te·brate (vėr′tə brit *or* vėr′tə brāt), **1** *n.* animal with a backbone. Fishes, amphibians, reptiles, birds, and mammals are vertebrates. **2** *adj.* having a backbone: *a vertebrate animal.*

ver·tex (vėr′teks), *n.* **1** the highest point; top. **2 a** point opposite the base of a triangle, pyramid, etc. **b** the point where the two sides of an angle meet. ◻ *n., pl.* **ver·tex·es, ver·ti·ces** (vėr′tə sēz).

ver·ti·cal (vėr′tə kəl), **1** *adj.* straight up and down; perpendicular to a level surface; upright. **2** *n.* a vertical line, plane, direction, position, etc. —**ver′ti·cal·ly,** *adv.*

vertical angle, either of the angles on opposite sides of the intersection of two lines; opposite angle.

ver·ti·go (vėr′tə gō), *n.* dizziness; giddiness.

verve (vėrv), *n.* enthusiasm; energy; vigor; spirit; liveliness.

ver·y (ver′ē), **1** *adv.* much; greatly; extremely: *The sunshine is very hot in July.* **2** *adv.* absolutely; exactly: *I stood in the very same place for an hour.* **3** *adj.* same; identical: *The very people who supported the plan are against it now.* **4** *adj.* nothing else than; mere: *The very thought of summer vacation makes her happy.* **5** *adj.* absolute; complete: *The storm meant the very end of our hopes for a picnic.* **6** *adj.* real; true; genuine: *The shrine was said to contain the very bones of the saint.* **7** *adj.* actual: *caught in the very act of stealing.*

SYNONYM STUDY Very, extremely, and highly all mean more than usual. **Very** is a general word: *She is very good at math.* **Extremely** means much more than usual: *He is extremely interested in butterflies.* **Highly** means fully and actively: *The band members are highly excited about their trip.*

very high frequency, the band of radio frequencies between 30 and 300 megahertz.

very low frequency, the band of radio frequencies between 10 and 30 kilohertz.

ves·i·cle (ves′ə kəl), *n.* a small bladder, cavity, sac, or cyst. A blister is a vesicle in the skin.

ves·per (ves′pər), **1** *n.pl.* **vespers** or **Vespers,** a church service held in the late afternoon or in the evening; evensong. **2** *n.* OLD USE. evening. **3** *n.* an evening prayer, hymn, or service. **4** *adj.* of or about vespers or evening.

Ves·puc·ci (ve spü′chē), *n.* **Am·er·i·go** (ə mer′ə gō), 1454-1512, Italian merchant, adventurer, and explorer. America is named for him.

ves·sel (ves′əl), *n.* **1** a large boat; ship: *Ocean liners and other vessels are usually docked by tugboats.* **2** a container or hollow holder. Cups, bowls, pitchers, bottles, barrels, and tubs are vessels. **3** tube carrying blood or other fluid. Veins and arteries are blood vessels.

vest (vest), **1** *n.* a short, sleeveless piece of clothing worn over a shirt or blouse. **2** *v.* to clothe or robe. **3** *v.* to furnish with powers, authority, rights, etc.: *Congress is vested with the power to make laws.* **4** *v.* to put in the possession or control of a person or persons: *The management of the hospital is vested in a board of trustees.* —**vest′like′,** *adj.*

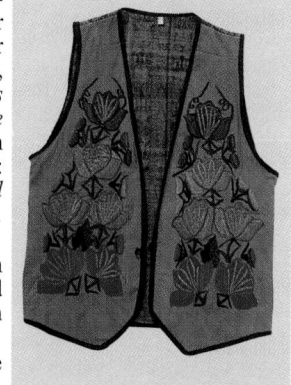

Guatemalan **vest**

Ves·ta (ves′tə), *n.* the Roman goddess of the hearth. A sacred fire was always kept burning in the temple of Vesta.

ves·tal (ves′tl), **1** *n.* one of the vestal virgins. **2** *n.* virgin. **3** *adj.* pure; chaste.

vestal virgin, priestess of the Roman goddess Vesta. Six vestal virgins tended an undying fire in honor of Vesta at her temple in Rome.

vest·ed (ves′tid), *adj.* **1** placed in the possession or control of a person or persons; fixed: *vested rights.* **2** clothed or robed, especially in church garments.

ves·ti·bule (ves′tə byül), *n.* **1** passage or hall between the outer door and the inside of a building. **2** an enclosed space at the end of a railroad passenger car.

ves·tige (ves′tij), *n.* a slight remnant; trace; mark: *The explorers discovered vestiges of an ancient civilization.*

ves·tig·i·al (ve stij′ē əl), *adj.* remaining as a vestige of something that has disappeared. —**ves·tig′i·al·ly,** *adv.*

vest·ment (vest′mənt), *n.* **1** article of clothing worn by a member of the clergy while performing sacred duties. **2** article of clothing, especially a robe or gown, worn by an official on a ceremonial occasion.

ves·try (ves′trē), *n.* **1** room in a church where vestments are kept. **2** room in a church or an attached building, used for Sunday school, prayer meetings, etc. **3** a committee that helps manage church business. ❑ *n., pl.* **ves·tries.**

ves·try·man (ves′trē mən), *n.* member of a committee that helps manage church business. ❑ *n., pl.* **ves·try·men.**

Ve·su·vi·us (və sü′vē əs), *n.* Mount, an active volcano near Naples, Italy. During an eruption in A.D. 79 its lava buried the ancient city of Pompeii. 4000 feet (1220 meters) high.

vet[1] (vet), *n.* veterinarian.

vet[2] (vet), *n.* veteran.

vetch (vech), *n.* any of numerous vines related to the pea, grown as food for cattle and sheep. ❑ *n., pl.* **vetch·es.**

vet·er·an (vet′ər ən), **1** *n.* person who has served in the armed forces. **2** *adj.* having had much experience in war: *Veteran troops fought side by side with the young soldiers.* **3** *n.* person who has had much experience in some position, occupation, etc. **4** *adj.* having had much experience: *veteran troops, a veteran teacher.*

Veterans Day, November 11, a legal holiday honoring all veterans of the armed forces and commemorating the end of World War I and World War II. It was formerly known as Armistice Day.

vet·er·i·nar·i·an (vet′ər ə ner′ē ən), *n.* doctor or surgeon who treats animals.

veterinarian

vet·er·i·nar·y (vet′ər ə ner′ē), **1** *adj.* of or about the medical or surgical treatment of animals. **2** *n.* veterinarian. ❑ *n., pl.* **vet·er·i·nar·ies.**

ve·to (vē′tō), **1** *n.* the right of the president, governor, etc., to reject bills passed by a lawmaking group: *The President has the power of veto over most bills passed in Congress.* **2** *adj.* of or about a veto: *veto power.* **3** *n.* the use of this right: *The governor's veto kept the bill from becoming a law.* **4** *v.* to reject by a veto. **5** *n.* refusal of consent; prohibition: *Our plan met with a veto from the boss.* **6** *v.* to refuse to consent to: *Her parents vetoed her plan to buy a car.* ❑ *n., pl.* **ve·toes** for 3,5; *v.* **ve·toed, ve·to·ing.**

WORD STORY Veto comes from a Latin word meaning "I forbid." In ancient Rome, the common people were represented in government by officials who could not make laws, but who could forbid new laws by this one word.

vex (veks), *v.* **1** to anger by trifles; annoy; provoke: *It is vexing to have to wait for somebody.* **2** to puzzle; frustrate; baffle: *The difficult riddle vexed him all day.* —**vex′er,** *n.* —**vex′ing·ly,** *adv.*

vex·a·tion (vek sā′shən), *n.* **1** annoyance; a being made angry by trifles: *His faced showed his vexation at the delay.* **2** thing that annoys: *Rain on Saturday was a vexation to the children.*

vex·a·tious (vek sā′shəs), *adj.* vexing; annoying. —**vex·a′tious·ly,** *adv.* —**vex·a′tious·ness,** *n.*

V.F.W. or **VFW,** Veterans of Foreign Wars.

VHF, V.H.F., or **vhf,** very high frequency.

VI, Virgin Islands (used with postal Zip Code).

V.I., Virgin Islands.

vi·a (vī′ə *or* vē′ə), *prep.* by way of; by a route that passes through: *She is going from New York to Paris via London.*

vi·a·ble (vī′ə bəl), *adj.* **1** able to keep alive: *a viable animal or plant.* **2** fit to live in; livable: *a viable community.* **3** able to be put to use; workable: *a viable program, a viable economy.* —**vi·a·bil·i·ty** (vī′ə bil′ə tē), *n.* —**vi′a·bly,** *adv.*

vi·a·duct (vī′ə dukt), *n.* bridge for carrying a road or railroad over a valley, a part of a city, etc.

vi·al (vī′əl), *n.* a small glass or plastic bottle for holding medicines or the like.

vi·and (vī′ənd), *n.* **1** article of food. **2 viands,** *pl.* articles of choice food.

vibes (vībz), *n.pl.* **1** SLANG. feelings about a person or event; impression: *She got bad vibes from the stranger.* **2** INFORMAL. vibraphone.

vi·bra·harp (vī′brə härp′), *n.* vibraphone.

vi·bran·cy (vī′brən sē), *n.* quality or condition of being vibrant.

vi·brant (vī′brənt), *adj.* **1** throbbing with vitality, enthusiasm, etc.: *a vibrant personality.* **2** vibrating. **3** resounding; resonant. —**vi′brant·ly,** *adv.*

vi·bra·phone (vī′brə fōn), *n.* musical instrument similar to the xylophone, with metal bars and artificially increased vibration; vibraharp.

vi·brate (vī′brāt), *v.* **1** to move rapidly to and fro: *A piano string vibrates and makes a sound when a key is struck.* **2** to cause to swing to and fro; set in motion. **3** to be moved; quiver. **4** to resound: *The clanging vibrated in her ears.* ❑ *v.* **vi·brat·ed, vi·brat·ing.**

vi·bra·tion (vī brā′shən), *n.* **1** a rapid movement to and fro; quivering motion; vibrating: *The buses shake the house so much that we feel the vibration.* **2** motion back and forth across a position of equilibrium. —**vi·bra′tion·less,** *adj.*

vi·bra·to (vi brä′tō), **1** *n.* a vibrating or pulsating effect produced by a wavering in the pitch of a musical tone. **2** *adv.* with much vibration of tone. ❑ *n., pl.* **vi·bra·tos.**

vi·bra·tor (vī′brā tər), *n.* **1** device causing a vibrating motion or action, such as an electrical device used to massage the body. **2** thing that vibrates.

vi·bra·to·ry (vī′brə tôr′ē), *adj.* of or causing vibration.

vi·bur·num (vī bėr′nəm), *n.* any of numerous bushes or small trees related to the honeysuckle, with showy clusters of white or pinkish flowers.

vic·ar (vik′ər), *n.* **1** the minister of a parish or a member of the clergy who has charge of one chapel in a parish. **2** (in the Roman Catholic Church) a member of the clergy who represents the pope or a bishop. **3** person acting in place of another; representative.

vic·ar·age (vik′ər ij), *n.* **1** residence of a vicar. **2** position or duties of a vicar. **3** salary paid to a vicar.

vi·car·i·ous (vī ker′ē əs), *adj.* felt by sharing in others' experience: *The invalid received vicarious pleasure from reading travel stories.* —**vi·car′i·ous·ly,** *adv.* —**vi·car′i·ous·ness,** *n.*

vice (vīs), *n.* **1** an evil habit or tendency: *Lying and cruelty are vices.* **2** evil; wickedness. **3** bad habit; character flaw: *They believe that gambling is a vice.* ■ Another word that sounds like this is **vise.**

vice-, *prefix.* substitute; deputy; assistant: *vice-president = substitute for the president.*

vice ad·mir·al (vīs′ad′mər əl), a military rank. See chart on page 712.

a	hat	ė	term	ô	order	ch	child		a in about
ā	age	i	it	oi	oil	ng	long		e in taken
ä	far	ī	ice	ou	out	sh	she	ə	i in pencil
â	care	o	hot	u	cup	th	thin		o in lemon
e	let	ō	open	u̇	put	ᴛʜ	then		u in circus
ē	equal	ȯ	saw	ü	rule	zh	measure		

V

957

vice-pres·i·den·cy (vīs/prez/ə dən sē), *n.* position of vice-president. ❑ *n., pl.* **vice-pres·i·den·cies.**

vice-pres·i·dent (vīs/prez/ə dənt), *n.* officer next in rank to the president, who takes the president's place when necessary. If the President of the United States dies or resigns, the Vice-President becomes President. ■ See Usage Note at **capital letter.**

vice-pres·i·den·tial (vīs/prez/ə den/shəl), *adj.* of or about the vice-president.

vice·roy (vīs/roi), *n.* person who rules a country or province, acting as the king's or queen's representative.

vice squad, squad of police who enforce laws against drugs, prostitution, gambling, etc.

vi·ce ver·sa (vī/sə vėr/sə *or* vīs/ vėr/sə), the other way around: *John blamed Mary, and vice versa (Mary blamed John).*

vi·chys·soise (vish/ē swäz/), *n.* a creamy potato and leek soup, sprinkled with chives and served cold.

vi·cin·i·ty (və sin/ə tē), *n.* **1** region near or about a place; neighborhood; surrounding district: *New York and vicinity.* **2** nearness in place; being close; proximity. ❑ *n., pl.* **vi·cin·i·ties** for 1.

vi·cious (vish/əs), *adj.* **1** very violent or cruel: *They were accused of a vicious crime.* ■ See Synonym Study at **cruel.** **2** likely to attack; dangerous: *a vicious animal.* **3** showing a strong desire to harm someone; spiteful: *I won't listen to such vicious gossip.* **4** unpleasantly severe: *a vicious headache.* **—vi′cious·ly,** *adv.* **—vi′cious·ness,** *n.*

vicious circle, two or more undesirable things each of which keeps causing the other.

vi·cis·si·tude (və sis/ə tüd), *n.* change in circumstances, fortune, etc.: *The vicissitudes of life may suddenly make a person poor.*

Vicks·burg (viks/bərg), *n.* city in W Mississippi, on the Mississippi River. Confederate forces there underwent a Union siege before surrendering in 1863.

vic·tim (vik/təm), *n.* **1** person or animal sacrificed, injured, or destroyed: *victims of war, accident victims.* **2** person badly treated or taken advantage of; dupe: *The swindlers had tricked their victims into giving them large sums of money.* **—vic′tim·less,** *adj.*

vic·tim·ize (vik/tə mīz), *v.* **1** to make a victim of; cause to suffer. **2** to cheat; swindle. ❑ *v.* **vic·tim·ized, vic·tim·iz·ing. —vic′tim·i·za′tion,** *n.* **—vic′tim·iz′er,** *n.*

victimless crime, crime that violates an existing law but is not believed to harm another person. Gambling and prostitution are sometimes considered victimless crimes.

vic·tor (vik/tər), *n.* winner; conqueror.

Vic·to·ri·a (vik tôr/ē ə), *n.* **1** 1819-1901, queen of Great Britain from 1837 to 1901. She reigned longer than any other British monarch and was the first empress of the British Empire. **2** capital of British Columbia, Canada. **3** capital of Seychelles. **4** state in SE Australia. *Capital:* Melbourne. **5 Lake,** lake in E Africa, bordered by Kenya, Tanzania, and Uganda. See **Nile** for map.

Victoria Cross, a medal awarded to armed forces personnel of the Commonwealth of Nations for outstanding bravery in the presence of the enemy.

Victoria Day, (in Canada) May 24, a holiday to celebrate Queen Victoria's birthday, since 1952 observed on the Monday just before May 25, also celebrating the birthday of Queen Elizabeth II (April 21).

Vic·to·ri·an (vik tôr/ē ən), **1** *adj.* of or about the time of Queen Victoria. **2** *n.* person, especially an author, who lived during the reign of Queen Victoria. **3** *adj.* typical of Victorians: *Victorian ideals.*

vic·to·ri·ous (vik tôr/ē əs), *adj.* **1** having won a victory; conquering: *a victorious team.* **2** of or showing victory; ending in victory: *The team gave a victorious shout as the winning run scored.* **—vic·to′ri·ous·ly,** *adv.*

victorious (def. 1)

vic·tor·y (vik/tər ē), *n.* defeat of an enemy or opponent; success in a contest: *The game ended in a victory for our school.* ❑ *n., pl.* **vic·tor·ies.**

vict·uals (vit/lz), *n.pl.* food or provisions.

vi·cu·ña (vi kü/nyə *or* vi kü/nə), *n.* **1** a wild mammal of South America, related to and resembling a llama, with a soft, delicate wool. **2** cloth made from this wool. ❑ *n., pl.* **vi·cu·ñas** *or* **vi·cu·ña.**

vid·e·o (vid/ē ō), **1** *adj.* of or about the picture in television: *The video part of the program was off for several minutes because of problems at the TV station.* **2** *n.* television broadcasting or the television industry. **3** *n.* videotape or videocassette. **4** *adj.* having or using a television screen or screen like that of a television: *a video display of computer information.* ❑ *n., pl.* **vid·e·os.**

vid·e·o·cas·sette (vid/ē ō kə set/), *n.* a recording on videotape, housed in a cassette.

videocassette recorder. See **VCR.**

vid·e·o·disc (vid/ē ō disk/), *n.* disk like a phonograph record on which pictures and sounds can be recorded for playing back through a TV set. Videodiscs are also used to store computer data and in video games.

video display terminal, device for communicating with a computer. It has a screen like a TV and often a keyboard.

video game, an electronic game that produces images on a TV or display screen, is accompanied by sound, and permits the player to control the action by means of mechanical devices.

vid·e·o·tape (vid/ē ō tāp/), **1** *n.* a magnetic tape that records and reproduces both sound and picture for TV. **2** *v.* to record on videotape: *The game was videotaped and shown on TV later the same day.* ❑ *v.* **vid·e·o·taped, vid·e·o·tap·ing.**

vie (vī), *v.* to strive for superiority; contend in rivalry; compete. ❑ *v.* **vied, vy·ing. —vi′er,** *n.*

Vi·en·na (vē en/ə), *n.* capital of Austria, in the NE part, on the Danube River.

Vi·en·nese (vē/ə nēz/), **1** *adj.* of or about Vienna or its people. **2** *n.* person born or living in Vienna. ❑ *n., pl.* **Vi·en·nese.**

Vien·tiane (vyen tyän/), *n.* capital of Laos, in the NW part.

Vi·et·cong (vē et/kong/), *n.* **1** the Communist guerrilla force in South Vietnam during the Vietnam War. **2** member of this force. ❑ *n., pl.* **Vi·et·cong** for 2.

Vi·et·minh (vē et/min/), *n.* a Communist group in Vietnam formed during World War II to promote independence.

Vi·et·nam (vē et/näm/), *n.* country in SE Asia. From 1954 to 1976 it was divided into two countries, North Vietnam and South Vietnam. *Capital:* Hanoi. [Vietnam comes from Chinese words meaning "far south." From China, that is where Vietnam is.]

Vi·et Nam (vē et/näm/), Vietnam.

Vi·et·nam·ese (vē et/nə mēz/), **1** *adj.* of or about Vietnam, its people, or their language. **2** *n.* person born or living in Vietnam. **3** *n.* language of Vietnam. ❑ *n., pl.* **Vi·et·nam·ese** for 2.

Vietnam War, war between South Vietnam, the United States, and their allies on the one side, and the Vietcong, North Vietnam, and their allies on the other side. The war began about 1957. The United States withdrew from the war in 1973.

view (vyü), **1** *n.* thing seen; scene: *The view from the top of the hill is beautiful.* **2** *n.* act of seeing; sight: *It was our first view of the ocean.* **3** *n.* the range at which the eye can see something: *A*

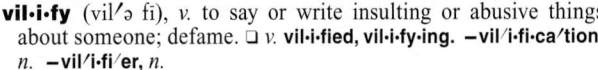

ship came into view. **4** *n.* way of looking at or considering a matter; opinion: *What are your views on the subject?* ■ See Synonym Study at **opinion. 5** *v.* to see; look at: *They viewed the scene with pleasure.* **6** *v.* to look at carefully; inspect. **7** *n.* picture of some scene: *Various views of the coast hung on the walls.* **8** *n.* a mental picture; an idea: *This book will give you a general view of the way the pioneers lived.* **9** *v.* to consider; regard: *The plan was viewed favorably.* **−view′a·ble,** *adj.*

in view, 1 in sight: *As the noise grew louder, the airplane came in view.* **2** under consideration: *Keep the teacher's advice in view as you work.* **3** as a purpose or intention. **4** as a hope; as an expectation.

in view of, considering; because of.

on view, to be seen; open for people to see: *The exhibit is on view from 9 A.M. to 5 P.M.*

with a view to, with the purpose or intention of: *She worked hard after school with a view to earning money for a new bicycle.*

SYNONYM STUDY **View, sight,** and **scene** all mean something to see. **View** means what can be seen from a place: *The apartment has a view of the park.* **Sight** means something worth seeing: *The bus tour goes to all the famous sights of the city.* **Scene** suggests that several parts combine to make a pleasant view: *The painting shows a mountain scene with a waterfall.*

view·er (vyü′ər), *n.* person who views, especially a person who watches TV.

view·find·er (vyü′fīn′dər), *n.* a small lens on the back of a camera that shows how much of a scene is being photographed or televised.

view·less (vyü′lis), *adj.* **1** without a view: *a viewless window.* **2** without views or opinions. **−view′less·ly,** *adv.*

view·point (vyü′point′), *n.* way of thinking about something; attitude of mind; point of view: *A rain that is good from the viewpoint of farmers may be bad from the viewpoint of tourists.*

vig·il (vij′əl), *n.* **1** act of staying awake for some purpose; act of watching; watch: *All night the parents kept vigil over the sick child.* **2** vigils, *pl.* prayers, services, etc., on the night before a religious festival. **3** the day and night before a solemn religious festival.

vig·i·lance (vij′ə ləns), *n.* watchfulness; alertness; caution: *Constant vigilance is necessary in order to avoid accidents in driving.*

vig·i·lant (vij′ə lənt), *adj.* watchful; alert; wide-awake: *The dog kept vigilant guard over the flock of sheep.* **−vig′i·lant·ly,** *adv.*

vig·i·lan·te (vij′ə lan′tē), *n.* member of an unauthorized group of citizens organized to maintain order and punish criminals. In the 1800s, committees of vigilantes were common in frontier territories of the United States.

vig·or (vig′ər), *n.* **1** active strength or force: *The principal argued with vigor that the new school should have a library.* **2** healthy energy or power: *After a long sleep, we felt full of vigor.*

vig·or·ous (vig′ər əs), *adj.* full of vigor; strong and active; energetic; forceful: *a vigorous and lively man. Doctors wage a vigorous war against disease.* **−vig′or·ous·ly,** *adv.* **−vig′or·ous·ness,** *n.*

Vi·king or **vi·king** (vī′king), *n.* one of the Scandinavian seafarers who raided the coasts of Europe during the 700s, 800s, and 900s A.D. The Vikings conquered parts of England, France, Russia, and other countries and explored distant lands that may have included North America.

Vi·la (vē′lə), *n.* capital of Vanuatu.

vile (vīl), *adj.* **1** very bad; wretched: *The weather was vile—rainy and cold.* **2** foul; disgusting: *A vile smell hung in the air around the garbage dump.* **3** evil; immoral: *a vile crime.* ■ See Synonym Study at **base²**. ❑ *adj.* **vil·er, vil·est. −vile′ly,** *adv.* **−vile′ness,** *n.*

Viking

vil·i·fy (vil′ə fī), *v.* to say or write insulting or abusive things about someone; defame. ❑ *v.* **vil·i·fied, vil·i·fy·ing. −vil′i·fi·ca′tion,** *n.* **−vil′i·fi′er,** *n.*

vil·la (vil′ə), *n.* a house in the country or suburbs, or sometimes at the seashore. A villa is usually a large and elegant residence. ❑ *n., pl.* **vil·las.**

Vil·la (vē′yə), *n.* **Pan·cho** (pän′chō), 1877-1923, Mexican revolutionary leader. ■ **Pancho Villa** had the support of the United States at first, but it was withdrawn after reports of brutalities. Villa then attacked Americans traveling in Mexico and burned a town in New Mexico.

vil·lage (vil′ij), *n.* **1** group of houses, usually smaller than a town. **2** the people of a village: *The whole village was at the parade.*

WORD STORY **Village** comes from a Latin word meaning "a country house." **Villain** and **villein** both come from the same word. In ancient times, country houses had villages nearby where the servants lived. The people who owned the houses often thought that the servants were trying to cheat them or steal from them.

vil·lag·er (vil′i jər), *n.* person who lives in a village.

vil·lain (vil′ən), *n.* **1** a very wicked person: *At the end of the story, the villain was caught and punished.* **2** villein. [See Word Story at **village**.]

vil·lain·ous (vil′ə nəs), *adj.* **1** very wicked: *a villainous betrayal.* **2** extremely bad; vile. **−vil′lain·ous·ly,** *adv.* **−vil′lain·ous·ness,** *n.*

vil·lain·y (vil′ə nē), *n.* **1** great wickedness. **2** a wicked act; a crime. ❑ *n., pl.* **vil·lain·ies** for 2.

-ville, *suffix.* INFORMAL. **1** a large amount of a particular thing or activity at one place or time: *Her party was boresville.* **2** condition or situation: *Those two are splitsville.*

vil·lein (vil′ən), *n.* one of a class of half-free peasants in the Middle Ages; villain. A villein was under the control of a lord, but was free in relations with other people.

vil·li (vil′ī), *n.pl.* tiny, hairlike parts growing on the membrane of the small intestine. The villi aid in absorbing certain nutrients from food. ❑ *n., sing.* **vil·lus** (vil′əs).

Vil·ni·us (vil′nē əs), *n.* capital of Lithuania, in the SE part.

vim (vim), *n.* force; energy; vigor: *The campers were full of vim after a good night's sleep.*

Vinci, Leonardo da. See **Leonardo da Vinci.**

vin·di·cate (vin′də kāt), *v.* **1** to clear from suspicion, dishonor, or any charge of wrongdoing: *The verdict of "Not guilty" vindicated them.* **2** to defend successfully against opposition; uphold; justify: *The heir vindicated her claim to the fortune.* ❑ *v.* **vin·di·cat·ed, vin·di·cat·ing. −vin′di·ca′tion,** *n.*

vin·dic·tive (vin dik′tiv), *adj.* **1** bearing a grudge; wanting revenge: *A vindictive person is unforgiving.* **2** showing a strong tendency toward revenge: *a vindictive act.* **−vin·dic′tive·ly,** *adv.* **−vin·dic′tive·ness,** *n.*

vine (vīn), *n.* **1** any plant with a long, slender stem, growing along the ground or climbing by attaching itself to a wall, tree, etc. Melons and pumpkins grow on vines. Ivy is a vine. **2** grapevine. **−vine′like′,** *adj.*

vin·e·gar (vin′ə gər), *n.* a sour liquid produced by the fermentation of cider, wine, malt, etc. Vinegar is used in salad dressing and in flavoring or preserving food. **−vin′e·gar·like′,** *adj.*

vin·e·gar·y (vin′ə gər ē), *adj.* of or like vinegar; sour: *a vinegary taste, a vinegary disposition.*

vine·yard (vin′yərd), *n.* a place planted with grapevines.

vin·tage (vin′tij), **1** *n.* the wine from a certain crop of grapes: *The finest vintages cost much more than others.* **2** *n.* a year's crop of grapes. **3** *n.* the season of gathering grapes and making wine. **4** *adj.* of outstanding quality; choice: *vintage wines.* **5** *n.* type of thing fashionable or popular during an earlier era: *a hat of 1940s vintage.* **6** *adj.* dating from long ago; old-fashioned: *vintage cars.*

a	hat	e̊	term	ô	order	ch	child		
ā	age	i	it	oi	oil	ng	long		a in about
ä	far	ī	ice	ou	out	sh	she		e in taken
â	care	o	hot	u	cup	th	thin	ə	i in pencil
e	let	ō	open	u̇	put	ŦH	then		o in lemon
ē	equal	ȯ	saw	ü	rule	zh	measure		u in circus

vint·ner (vint′nər), *n.* dealer in wine; wine merchant.

vi·nyl (vī′nl), *n.* any of various tough synthetic plastics or resins used in floor coverings, toys, molded articles, phonograph records, etc.

vi·ol (vī′əl), *n.* **1** any of several stringed musical instruments played with a bow and usually held either on or between the knees while they are played. Viols were used mostly in the 1500s and 1600s. **2** double bass.

vi·o·la (vē ō′lə), *n.* a stringed musical instrument like a violin, but somewhat larger and lower in pitch. ❑ *n., pl.* **vi·o·las.**

vi·o·late (vī′ə lāt), *v.* **1** to break a law, rule, agreement, promise, etc.; act contrary to; fail to perform: *Speeding violates the traffic laws.* **2** to break in upon; disturb: *The sound of car horns violated the usual calm of Sunday morning.* **3** to treat with disrespect or contempt: *Vandals violated several grave sites by overturning the tombstones.* ❑ *v.* **vi·o·lat·ed, vi·o·lat·ing.** **–vi′o·la·tive,** *adj.* **–vi′o·lat′or,** *n.*

vi·o·la·tion (vī′ə lā′shən), *n.* **1** act of breaking a law, rule, agreement, promise, etc.: *He was fined $50 for his violation of the traffic law.* **2** act of breaking in upon; interruption or disturbance. **3** treatment of a holy thing with disrespect or contempt.

vi·o·lence (vī′ə ləns), *n.* **1** physical force used to cause injury or destruction to a person or thing. **2** strong force; great force: *She slammed the door with violence.* **3** harm; injury: *It would do violence to her principles to work on Sunday.* **4** strength of action, feeling, etc.

vi·o·lent (vī′ə lənt), *adj.* **1** acting or done with strong, rough force: *a violent blow.* **2** caused by strong, rough force: *a violent death.* **3** showing or caused by very strong feeling, action, etc.: *violent language, a violent rage.* **4** very great; extreme; severe: *a violent pain, violent heat.* **–vi′o·lent·ly,** *adv.*

vi·o·let (vī′ə lit), **1** *n.* any of numerous small plants with purple, blue, yellow, or white flowers. Many common violets grow wild and bloom in the early spring. The purple violet is the provincial flower of New Brunswick. **2** *n.* a bluish purple. **3** *adj.* bluish purple.

vi·o·lin (vī′ə lin′), *n.* a musical instrument with four strings played with a bow. The violin has the highest pitch of the stringed instruments.

vi·o·lin·ist (vī′ə lin′ist), *n.* person who plays the violin.

vi·ol·ist (vē ō′list), *n.* person who plays the viola.

vi·o·lon·cel·list (vī′ə lən chel′ist), *n.* cellist.

vi·o·lon·cel·lo (vī′ə lən chel′ō), *n.* cello. ❑ *n., pl.* **vi·o·lon·cel·los.**

VIP or **V.I.P.,** INFORMAL. very important person.

vi·per (vī′pər), *n.* **1** any of various poisonous snakes with large, hollow fangs and often thick, heavy bodies. **2** a spiteful, treacherous person.

vi·per·ous (vī′pər əs), *adj.* **1** of or like a viper or vipers. **2** spiteful; treacherous. **–vi′per·ous·ly,** *adv.*

vi·ra·go (vi rä′gō *or* və rā′gō), *n.* a violent, bad-tempered, or scolding woman. ❑ *n., pl.* **vi·ra·goes** *or* **vi·ra·gos.** ■ Virago is sometimes considered offensive.

vi·ral (vī′rəl), *adj.* of or caused by a virus. **–vi′ral·ly,** *adv.*

vir·e·o (vir′ē ō), *n.* any of several small, olive-green, North American songbirds that eat insects. ❑ *n., pl.* **vir·e·os.**

Vir·gil (vėr′jəl), *n.* 70-19 B.C., Roman poet, author of the *Aeneid.* Also, **Vergil.**

vir·gin (vėr′jən), **1** *n.* person who has not had sexual intercourse. **2** *n.* **the Virgin,** Virgin Mary. **3** *adj.* of a virgin; suitable for a virgin: *virgin modesty.* **4** *adj.* pure; spotless. Virgin snow is newly fallen snow. **5** *adj.* not yet used: *virgin soil, a virgin forest.*

vir·gin·al (vėr′jə nəl), **1** *adj.* of or suitable for a virgin. **2** *n.* a small harpsichord set in a rectangular box without legs. It was much used in the 1500s and 1600s. **–vir′gin·al·ly,** *adv.*

Vir·gin·ia (vər jin′yə), *n.* one of the southeastern states of the United States. *Abbreviation:* VA or Va. *Capital:* Richmond. **–Vir·gin′ian,** *n.*

WORD STORY **Virginia** comes from the phrase, *the Virgin Queen,* used to describe Elizabeth I of England, who never married. She gave the name when English settlers first came to this area.

Virginia Beach, port in SE Virginia.

Virginia creeper, an American climbing plant having leaves with five leaflets and bluish black berries that are not good to eat; woodbine.

Virginia reel, a U.S. folk dance in which the partners form two lines facing each other and perform a number of dance steps.

Virgin Islands, group of islands in the West Indies, east of Puerto Rico. Several of these islands belong to the United States and the rest (**British Virgin Islands**) are a British territory. *Abbreviation:* VI or V.I.

Virgin Islands National Park, a national park on and around St. John, U.S. Virgin Islands, containing tropical forests and coasts.

Virgin Islands National Park

vir·gin·i·ty (vər jin′ə tē), *n.* condition of being a virgin.

Virgin Mary, the mother of Jesus.

Vir·go (vėr′gō), *n.* **1** group of stars shaped something like a young woman. **2** the sixth sign of the zodiac, associated with the period from mid-August to mid-September.

vir·ile (vir′əl), *adj.* **1** of or typical of a man; manly; masculine. **2** full of strength or vigor; vigorous; forceful.

vi·ril·i·ty (və ril′ə tē), *n.* **1** manhood. **2** strength; vigor; forcefulness.

vi·rol·o·gy (vī rol′ə jē), *n.* science that deals with viruses and virus diseases. **–vi·rol′o·gist,** *n.*

vir·tu·al (vėr′chü əl), *adj.* being something in effect, though not so in name; for all practical purposes; actual; real: *The battle was won with so great a loss of soldiers that it was a virtual defeat.*

virtual image, image formed by a lens and visible only through the lens. It cannot be shown on a screen.

vir·tu·al·ly (vėr′chü ə lē), *adv.* in effect, though not in name; practically: *If you travel by jet plane, New York and London are virtually neighbors.*

virtual reality, computer images created by interactive software to seem like a real environment to the senses of the user.

vir·tue (vėr′chü), *n.* **1** moral excellence; goodness: *a person of the highest virtue.* **2** a particular kind of moral excellence: *Kindness is a virtue.* **3** a good quality: *She praised the virtues of her small car.* **4** chastity; purity. **5** power to produce good results: *There is little virtue in that medicine.*
by virtue of or **in virtue of,** because of; on account of.

vir·tu·os·i·ty (vėr′chü os′ə tē), *n.* skill of a virtuoso.

vir·tu·o·so (vėr′chü ō′sō), *n.* person skilled in the techniques of an art, especially in playing a musical instrument. ❑ *n., pl.* **vir·tu·o·sos, vir·tu·o·si** (vėr′chü ō′sē).

vir·tu·ous (vėr′chü əs), *adj.* **1** having or showing virtue; good; honest; just: *virtuous conduct, a virtuous life.* **2** chaste; pure: *a virtuous maiden.* **–vir′tu·ous·ly,** *adv.* **–vir′tu·ous·ness,** *n.*

vir·u·lence (vir′yə ləns), *n.* **1** quality of being very poisonous or harmful; deadliness: *the virulence of a rattlesnake's bite.* **2** intense bitterness or spite; violent hostility.

vir·u·lent (vir′yə lənt), *adj.* **1** very poisonous or harmful; deadly: *a virulent form of a disease.* **2** intensely bitter or spiteful; violently hostile: *virulent abuse.* **—vir′u·lent·ly,** *adv.*

vi·rus (vī′rəs), *n.* a very small germ formed of protein and nucleic acid. Viruses are smaller than any known bacteria and cannot be seen through most microscopes. They can reproduce only inside the cells of living things. Viruses cause rabies, polio, chicken pox, the common cold, and many other diseases. ❑ *n., pl.* **vi·rus·es.**

WORD STORY　　*Virus* comes from a Latin word meaning "poison." For a long time, people had no idea what viruses were, so they thought that many diseases were caused by some sort of poison. After viruses were discovered, the name was too familiar to change.

vi·sa (vē′zə), *n.* an official signature or endorsement upon a passport, showing that it has been examined and approved. A visa is granted by the consul or other representative of the country to which a person wishes to travel. ❑ *n., pl.* **vi·sas.**

vis·age (viz′ij), *n.* face or appearance: *a grim visage.*

vis·cer·a (vis′ər ə), *n.pl.* the soft internal organs of the body. The heart, stomach, liver, intestines, kidneys, etc., are viscera.

vis·cer·al (vis′ər əl), *adj.* **1** arising from the instinct or from strong feelings: *visceral reactions.* **2** of or in the region of the viscera.

vis·cid (vis′id), *adj.* thick like heavy syrup or glue; sticky.

vis·cos·i·ty (vi skos′ə tē), *n.* condition or quality of being viscous.

vis·count (vī′kount), *n.* nobleman ranking next below an earl or count and next above a baron.

vis·count·ess (vī′koun tis), *n.* **1** wife or widow of a viscount. **2** woman whose rank is equal to that of a viscount. ❑ *n., pl.* **vis·count·ess·es.**

vis·cous (vis′kəs), *adj.* thick like heavy syrup or glue; sticky. **—vis′cous·ly,** *adv.* **—vis′cous·ness,** *n.*

vise (vīs), *n.* tool having two jaws opened and closed by a screw, used to hold an object firmly while work is being done on it. ■ Another word that sounds like this is **vice. —vise′like′,** *adj.*

Vish·nu (vish′nü), *n.* Hindu god of preservation and of well-being.

vis·i·bil·i·ty (viz′ə bil′ə tē), *n.* **1** condition or quality of being visible: *I put lights and reflectors on my bicycle to increase its visibility.* **2** distance at which things are visible: *Fog and rain decreased visibility to about 50 feet.*

vis·i·ble (viz′ə bəl), *adj.* **1** able to be seen: *The shore was barely visible through the fog.* **2** readily evident; apparent; obvious: *There has been visible improvement in his work since he changed schools.* **—vis′i·ble·ness,** *n.* **—vis′i·bly,** *adv.*

Vis·i·goth (viz′ə goth), *n.* member of the western division of the Goths. The Visigoths sacked Rome in A.D. 410 and eventually settled in France and Spain.

vi·sion (vizh′ən), *n.* **1** power of seeing; sense of sight: *I have to wear glasses because my vision is poor.* **2** something that is seen: *The vision of the table loaded with food made our mouths water.* **3** power of seeing with the imagination or by clear thinking, especially seeing what the future may bring: *The founder of this company was a person of great vision.* **4** something seen with the imagination, in a dream, in your thoughts, etc.: *The gambler had visions of great wealth.* **5** a very beautiful person, scene, etc.

vi·sion·ar·y (vizh′ə ner′ē), **1** *n.* person given to imagining or dreaming; person whose ideas seem impractical; dreamer: *Many great scientists have been visionaries.* **2** *adj.* not practical; dreamy: *He is a visionary child; he spends hours daydreaming.* **3** *adj.* not practicable; fanciful: *Fifty years ago people would have regarded plans for an atomic power plant as visionary.* **4** *adj.* of or belonging to a vision; seen in a vision; imaginary: *The visionary scene faded, and she awoke.* **5** *n.* person who sees visions. ❑ *n., pl.* **vi·sion·ar·ies. —vi′sion·ar′i·ness,** *n.*

vis·it (viz′it), **1** *v.* to go to see; come to see: *He visited New York.* **2** *v.* to make a call on or stay with; be a guest of: *She is visiting her aunt.* **3** *v.* to go or come to see in order to inspect, examine officially, give professional service or treatment to, etc.: *The doctor visited her patients at the hospital. The inspector visits the factory once a month.* **4** *n.* act of visiting; a call as a friend, or for the pur-

pose of inspection, examination, professional treatment, etc.: *pay a visit to a friend, a visit to the dentist.* **5** *v.* to come upon; afflict: *They were visited by many troubles.* **6** *v.* to inflict: *She visited her anger at the boss on his assistant.* **7** *v.* to talk or chat.

vis·it·ant (viz′ə tənt), *n.* visitor; guest.

vis·i·ta·tion (viz′ə tā′shən), *n.* **1** act of visiting. **2** a visit for the purpose of making an official inspection or examination. A nation at war has the right of visitation of neutral ships; that is, the right to inspect their cargoes. **3** punishment or reward sent by God.

vis·i·tor (viz′ə tər), *n.* person who visits or is visiting; guest.

SYNONYM STUDY　　*Visitor* and *guest* both mean someone who goes to be with some person, thing, or place. *Visitor* suggests someone who spends time: *This little museum has more than 10,000 visitors a year.* *Guest* suggests someone who is invited and entertained: *She was our guest for a week.*

vi·sor (vī′zər), *n.* **1** the movable front part of a helmet, covering the face. **2** the brim of a cap, projecting in front to shade the eyes. **3** shade above a windshield, that can be lowered to shield the eyes from the sun. **—vi′sor·less,** *adj.*

vis·ta (vis′tə), *n.* **1** view seen through a narrow opening or passage: *The opening between the two rows of trees afforded a vista of the lake.* **2** such an opening or passage itself: *a shady vista of elms.* **3** a mental view: *Education should open up new vistas.* ❑ *n., pl.* **vis·tas.**

VISTA (vis′tə), *n.* Volunteers in Service to America.

Vis·tu·la (vis′chə lə), *n.* river flowing through Poland to the Baltic Sea.

vis·u·al (vizh′ü əl), **1** *adj.* of, for, or by sight: *Nearsightedness is a visual defect.* **2** *adj.* received through the sense of sight: *visual impressions.* **3** *adj.* able to be seen; visible: *the visual parts of the spectrum.* **4** *n.pl.* **visuals, a** the picture portion of movie or television film, not including the sound track. **b** visual aids. **—vis′u·al·ly,** *adv.*

visual aid, device for aiding the learning process through the sense of sight, such as a chart, diagram, movie, video, or filmstrip.

vis·u·al·ize (vizh′ü ə līz), *v.* **1** to form a mental picture of: *visualize the face of an old friend.* **2** to make visible. ❑ *v.* **vis·u·al·ized, vis·u·al·iz·ing. —vis′u·al·i·za′tion,** *n.* **—vis′u·al·iz′er,** *n.*

vi·tal (vī′tl), **1** *adj.* very important; basic; very necessary: *Good government is vital to the welfare of a community.* **2** *adj.* of or about life. Vital statistics give facts about births, deaths, marriages, etc. *Growth and decay are vital processes.* **3** *adj.* necessary to life: *The heart is a vital organ.* ■ See Synonym Study at **necessary. 4** *n.pl.* **vitals, a** parts or organs necessary to life. The brain, heart, lungs, and stomach are vitals. **b** essential parts or features. **5** *adj.* causing death, failure, or ruin: *a vital blow to an industry.* **6** *adj.* full of life and spirit; lively: *What a vital person she is—never idle, never dull!* [*Vital* comes from a Latin word meaning "life." When something is truly vital, people call it "a matter of life and death."] **—vi′tal·ly,** *adv.*

vi·tal·i·ty (vī tal′ə tē), *n.* **1** vital force; power to live: *A person's vitality can be lessened by illness.* **2** power to endure and be active: *Poetry of great vitality is read centuries after it was written.* **3** strength; energy; vigor: *Exercise helps maintain vitality.*

vi·tal·ize (vī′tl īz), *v.* **1** to give life to. **2** to put vitality into; make more energetic, lively, or enterprising. ❑ *v.* **vi·tal·ized, vi·tal·iz·ing. —vi′tal·i·za′tion,** *n.* **—vi′tal·iz′er,** *n.*

vi·ta·min (vī′tə mən), **1** *n.* any of certain special substances necessary in small amounts for the normal growth and proper nourishment of the body, found especially in milk, butter, raw fruits and vegetables, cod-liver oil, and the outside part of wheat and other grains. Lack of essential vitamins causes such diseases as rickets and scurvy, as well as generally poor health. **2** *adj.* of or containing vitamins: *a vitamin tablet, a vitamin deficiency.*

a	hat	ė	term	ô	order	ch	child		a in about
ā	age	i	it	oi	oil	ng	long		e in taken
ä	far	ī	ice	ou	out	sh	she	ə	i in pencil
â	care	o	hot	u	cup	th	thin		o in lemon
e	let	ō	open	u̇	put	ŦH	then		u in circus
ē	equal	ȯ	saw	ü	rule	zh	measure		

V

vitamin A, vitamin found in milk, butter, cod-liver oil, egg yolk, liver, and green and yellow vegetables. Vitamin A increases the resistance of the body to infection and prevents night blindness.

vitamin B, 1 vitamin B complex. **2** thiamine.

vitamin B₁, thiamine.

vitamin B₂, riboflavin.

vitamin B₆, pyridoxine.

vitamin B₁₂, vitamin found especially in liver, milk, and eggs. Lack of vitamin B₁₂ causes anemia and damage to the nervous system.

vitamin B complex, group of vitamins including thiamine, riboflavin, pyridoxine, etc., found in high concentration in yeast and liver.

vitamin C, vitamin found in citrus fruits, tomatoes, leafy green vegetables, etc.; ascorbic acid. Vitamin C prevents and cures scurvy. It cannot be stored in the body and must be regularly replaced.

vitamin D, vitamin found in cod-liver oil, milk, and egg yolk, necessary for the growth and health of bones and teeth. Vitamin D prevents rickets.

vitamin E, vitamin found in wheat germ oil, whole-grain cereals, and lettuce, important to the health of cell membranes.

vitamin G, riboflavin.

vitamin K, vitamin found in leafy green vegetables that promotes clotting of the blood.

vi·ti·ate (vish′ē āt), *v.* to destroy the legal force or authority of: *The contract was vitiated because one person signed under compulsion.* ❑ *v.* **vi·ti·at·ed, vi·ti·at·ing.** —**vi′ti·a′tion,** *n.*

vit·re·ous (vit′rē əs), *adj.* of or like glass; glassy. —**vit′re·ous·ness,** *n.*

vitreous humor, the transparent, jellylike substance that fills the eyeball.

vit·ri·fy (vit′rə fī), *v.* to change into glass or something like glass, especially by fusion through heat. ❑ *v.* **vit·ri·fied, vit·ri·fy·ing.** —**vit′ri·fi′a·ble,** *adj.* —**vit′ri·fi·ca′tion,** *n.*

vit·ri·ol (vit′rē əl), *n.* **1** sulfuric acid. **2** any of certain sulfates of metals, such as **blue vitriol,** a sulfate of copper, **green vitriol,** a sulfate of iron, or **white vitriol,** a sulfate of zinc. Vitriols have a glassy appearance. **3** very sharp speech or severe criticism.

vit·ri·ol·ic (vit′rē ol′ik), *adj.* **1** bitterly severe; sharp: *vitriolic criticism.* **2** of or containing vitriol.

vi·tu·pe·rate (vī tü′pə rāt′), *v.* to scold very severely; find fault with in abusive words; revile. ❑ *v.* **vi·tu·pe·rat·ed, vi·tu·pe·rat·ing.** —**vi·tu′pe·ra′tor,** *n.*

vi·tu·pe·ra·tion (vī tü′pə rā′shən), *n.* bitter abuse in words; very severe scolding.

vi·tu·pe·ra·tive (vī tü′pə rə′tiv), *adj.* abusive; reviling. —**vi·tu′pe·ra·tive·ly,** *adv.*

vi·va (vē′və), *interj.* an exclamation of approval, meaning (long) live (the person or thing named).

vi·va·cious (vī vā′shəs *or* vi va′shəs), *adj.* lively; sprightly; animated; merry: *a vivacious manner.* —**vi·va′cious·ly,** *adv.* —**vi·va′cious·ness,** *n.*

vi·vac·i·ty (vī vas′ə tē *or* vi vas′ə tē), *n.* liveliness; sprightliness; animation; gaiety.

Vi·val·di (vi väl′dē), *n.* **An·to·ni·o** (an tō′nē ō), 1678-1741, Italian composer and violinist. ■ **Vivaldi** composed works for every instrument of his time, but his most important works were for the violin, including *The Four Seasons* concertos.

vive (vēv), *interj.* a French exclamation of approval, meaning (long) live (the person or thing named).

viv·id (viv′id), *adj.* **1** strikingly bright; strong and clear; brilliant: *Dandelions are a vivid yellow.* **2** like life; giving clear ideas of life: *Her description of the party was so vivid that I almost felt I had been there.* **3** strong and distinct: *I have a vivid memory of the fire.* **4** very active; lively: *a vivid imagination.* —**viv′id·ly,** *adv.* —**viv′id·ness,** *n.*

viv·i·fy (viv′ə fī), *v.* **1** to give life or vigor to: *vivify the desert by irrigation.* **2** to make vivid; enliven: *vivify an idea with wit.* ❑ *v.* **viv·i·fied, viv·i·fy·ing.** —**viv′i·fi·ca′tion,** *n.* —**viv′i·fi′er,** *n.*

vi·vip·ar·ous (vī vip′ər əs), *adj.* bringing forth uncovered young, not eggs. Dogs, cats, cows, and human beings are viviparous. —**vi·vip′ar·ous·ly,** *adv.* —**vi·vip′ar·ous·ness,** *n.*

viv·i·sect (viv′ə sekt), *v.* to dissect a living body.

viv·i·sec·tion (viv′ə sek′shən), *n.* act or practice of dissecting or operating on living animals for scientific study.

viv·i·sec·tion·ist (viv′ə sek′shə nist), *n.* person who performs or favors vivisection.

vix·en (vik′sən), *n.* **1** a female fox. **2** a quarrelsome or malicious woman. ■ This meaning of **vixen** is often considered offensive.

> **WORD STORY** **Vixen** comes from **fox.** It used to be spelled with an *f* instead of a *v.* People began to pronounce it as we do now, and the spelling changed. This is unusual in English; usually the spelling stays the same even though the pronunciation has changed.

viz., that is to say; namely: *There are four seasons, viz., spring, summer, fall, and winter.*

vi·zier (vi zir′), *n.* (in Islamic countries) a high official, such as a minister of state.

Vlad·i·vos·tok (vlad′ə vos′tok), *n.* port in SE Russia, on the Sea of Japan.

vocab., vocabulary.

vo·cab·u·lar·y (vō kab′yə ler′ē), *n.* **1** the number of words known or used by a person or group of people: *the vocabulary of science. Reading will increase your vocabulary.* **2** all the words of a language. **3** collection or list of words, usually in alphabetical order, with their translations or meanings: *There is a vocabulary in the back of our French book.* ❑ *n., pl.* **vo·cab·u·lar·ies.**

> **WORD FAMILY** **Vocabulary** and the words below are related. They all come from a Latin word meaning "to call."
>
> | advocate | equivocal | irrevocable | revoke |
> | avocation | evoke | provocation | vocation |
> | convoke | invoke | provoke | |

vo·cal (vō′kəl), *adj.* **1** of or for the voice: *The tongue is a vocal organ.* **2** made with the voice: *I like vocal music better than instrumental.* **3** having a voice; giving forth sound: *Humans are vocal beings. The zoo was vocal with the roar of the lions.* **4** aroused to speech; inclined to talk freely: *become vocal with indignation.* —**vo′cal·ly,** *adv.*

vocal cords, two folds of elastic membrane in the throats of humans and many other animals. When they are pulled tight, the passage of breath between them causes them to vibrate, producing the sound of the voice.

vo·cal·ic (vō kal′ik), *adj.* **1** of or like a vowel sound. **2** having many vowel sounds.

vo·cal·ist (vō′kə list), *n.* singer.

vo·cal·ize (vō′kə līz), *v.* **1** to use the voice; speak, sing, shout, etc. **2** to make vocal; utter: *The dog vocalized its pain in a series of long howls.* ❑ *v.* **vo·cal·ized, vo·cal·iz·ing.** —**vo′cal·i·za′tion,** *n.* —**vo′cal·iz′er,** *n.*

vo·ca·tion (vō kā′shən), *n.* **1** occupation, business, profession, or trade: *Architecture is her vocation.* **2** a strong feeling about, or inclination toward, a certain kind of work, especially religious work.

vivid (def. 1)—flowers in vivid shades of red and blue

vo·ca·tion·al (vō kā′shə nəl), *adj.* of or about some occupation, business, profession, or trade. A vocational school provides training in special trades, such as graphic arts, carpentry, cosmetology, etc. —**vo·ca′tion·al·ly,** *adv.*

vo·cif·er·ous (vō sif′ər əs), *adj.* loud and noisy; shouting; clamoring: *a vociferous person, vociferous cheers.* **—vo·cif′er·ous·ly,** *adv.* **—vo·cif′er·ous·ness,** *n.*

vod·ka (vod′kə), *n.* an alcoholic drink distilled from potatoes, rye, barley, or corn.

vogue (vōg), *n.* **1** the fashion: *Hoop skirts were in vogue more than 100 years ago.* **2** popularity or acceptance: *That song had a great vogue at one time.*

voice (vois), **1** *n.* sound made through the mouth, especially by people in speaking, singing, shouting, etc.: *The voices of the children could be heard coming from the playground.* **2** *n.* power to make sounds through the mouth: *His voice was gone because of a sore throat.* **3** *n.* anything like speech or song: *the voice of the wind.* **4** *n.* ability as a singer: *She knew she had no voice.* **5** *n.* singer: *a choir of fifty voices.* **6** *n.* part of a piece of music for one kind of singer or instrument. **7** *v.* to express; utter: *They voiced their approval of the plan.* **8** *n.* expression: *They gave voice to their joy.* **9** *n.* the right to express an opinion or choice: *We have no voice in the matter.* **10** *n.* form of a verb that shows whether its subject is active or passive. **11** *v.* to utter with a sound made by vibration of the vocal cords. ❑ *v.* **voiced, voic·ing.**
with one voice, unanimously.

voice-ac·ti·vat·ed (vois′ak′tə vā tid), *adj.* put into operation by the sound of a voice: *a voice-activated telephone.*

voice box, larynx.

voiced (voist), *adj.* spoken with a sound made by vibration of the vocal cords. *B* and *d* are voiced sounds.

voice·less (vois′lis), *adj.* **1** having no voice; dumb; silent. **2** not voiced. The consonants *p, t,* and *k* are voiceless. **—voice′less·ly,** *adv.* **—voice′less·ness,** *n.*

voice mail, a computer system for recording telephone messages to be played back later. People use their telephones to call the central computer and hear their messages.

voice-o·ver (vois′ō′vər), *n.* (in movies or TV) words spoken by someone who is not shown, talking about what is being shown.

voice recognition, the process of analyzing human speech with a computer, either to understand speech or to reproduce it; speech recognition: *a program to take dictation by voice recognition.*

void (void), **1** *n.* feeling of emptiness or great loss: *The death of his dog left a void in the boy's life.* **2** *adj.* without legal force or effect; not binding in law: *A contract made by a twelve-year-old is void.* **3** *n.* an empty space. **4** *adj.* empty; vacant: *a void space.* **5** *v.* to make of no force or effect in law. **6** *v.* to empty out.

void·a·ble (voi′də bəl), *adj.* capable of being voided or given up: *The contract was voidable by either party.*

voile (voil), *n.* a very thin cloth with an open weave, used for dresses.

vol., volume.

vol·a·tile (vol′ə təl), *adj.* **1** tending to sudden anger or violence: *a volatile temper, volatile political conditions.* **2** changing rapidly from one mood or interest to another; fickle: *a volatile disposition.* **3** evaporating rapidly; changing into vapor easily: *Gasoline is volatile.* **—vol·a·til·i·ty** (vol′ə til′ə tē), **vol′a·tile·ness,** *n.*

vol·can·ic (vol kan′ik), *adj.* **1** of or caused by a volcano; about volcanoes: *a volcanic eruption.* **2** like a volcano; likely to break out violently: *a volcanic temper.* **—vol·can′i·cal·ly,** *adv.*

vol·can·ism (vol′kə niz′əm), *n.* volcanic activity.

vol·ca·no (vol kā′nō), *n.* **1** an opening in the earth's crust through which steam, ashes, and lava are forced out in periods of activity. **2** an opening like this on the surface of another planet: *Martian volcanoes.* **3** a cone-shaped hill or mountain, built up of the material that is forced out of a volcano. ❑ *n., pl.* **vol·ca·noes** or **vol·ca·nos.**

WORD STORY **Volcano** comes from **Vulcan,** the Roman god of fire. The ancient Romans believed that he lived at the top of the volcano Mount Etna.

vole (vōl), *n.* any of several rodents related to rats, mice, and lemmings, usually with plump bodies and short legs and tails.

Vol·ga (vol′gə), *n.* river in W Russia, flowing into the Caspian Sea.

Vol·go·grad (vol′gə grad), *n.* city in W Russia, on the Volga River. Formerly, **Stalingrad.**

vo·li·tion (vō lish′ən), *n.* act of willing; decision: *She took on extra work of her own volition.*

vol·ley (vol′ē), **1** *n.* shower of stones, bullets, words, oaths, etc.: *A volley of arrows rained down upon the attacking knights.* **2** *n.* the discharge of a number of guns at once. **3** *v.* to discharge or be discharged in a volley: *Cannon volleyed on all sides.* **4** in tennis, volleyball, etc.: **a** *n.* act of hitting a ball while it is still in the air. **b** *v.* to hit or return a ball while it is still in the air. **5** *v.* to hit a tennis ball back and forth over the net until someone misses or faults. ❑ *n., pl.* **vol·leys;** *v.* **vol·leyed, vol·ley·ing. —vol′ley·er,** *n.*

vol·ley·ball (vol′ē bol′), *n.* **1** game played by two teams of players with a large ball and a high net. The players on each side have three hits using only their hands or forearms to return the ball to the other side. **2** ball used in this game.

volleyball (def. 1)

volt (vōlt), *n.* unit for measuring electrical force, equal to the amount of force needed to cause a current of one ampere to flow through a resistance of one ohm.

volt·age (vōl′tij), *n.* strength of electrical force, measured in volts. A current of high voltage is used in transmitting electric power over long distances.

vol·ta·ic cell (vol tā′ik), an electric cell containing two electrodes immersed in an electrolyte and connected by a wire. An electric current is produced in the wire by a chemical reaction between the electrolyte and the electrodes.

Vol·taire (vol târ′), *n.* 1694-1778, French writer and philosopher. ■ **Voltaire** was a powerful critic of traditional beliefs, and his writings contributed to the discontent that caused the French Revolution.

volt·me·ter (vōlt′mē′tər), *n.* device for measuring in volts the force between two points in an electric circuit.

vol·u·ble (vol′yə bəl), *adj.* tending to talk much; fond of talking; talkative: *a voluble speaker.* **—vol·u·bil′i·ty, vol′u·ble·ness,** *n.* **—vol′u·bly,** *adv.*

vol·ume (vol′yəm), *n.* **1** amount of space anything contains or fills: *The storeroom has a volume of 800 cubic feet.* **2** amount; quantity: *the volume of business at a store.* **3** amount of sound; loudness: *Please turn the volume down on the stereo.* **4** book: *We own a library of five hundred volumes.* **5** book forming part of a set or series: *You can find what you want to know in the ninth volume of this encyclopedia.* [**Volume** comes from a Latin word meaning "to roll." Ancient Roman books were rolled scrolls. Big scrolls took up a lot of space, so the space was named for them.]

vol·u·met·ric (vol′yə met′rik), *adj.* of or about measurement by volume. **—vol′u·met′ri·cal·ly,** *adv.*

vo·lu·mi·nous (və lü′mə nəs), *adj.* **1** of great size; very bulky; large: *a voluminous cloak.* **2** forming or filling a large book or

V

a	hat	ė	term	ô	order	ch	child	ə	a in about
ā	age	i	it	oi	oil	ng	long		e in taken
ä	far	ī	ice	ou	out	sh	she		i in pencil
â	care	o	hot	u	cup	th	thin		o in lemon
e	let	ō	open	u̇	put	ᴛʜ	then		u in circus
ē	equal	ȯ	saw	ü	rule	zh	measure		

Volcanoes

Hot rock called magma rises from deep inside the earth. As it nears the surface, magma becomes cooler and sinks back. If magma finds a weak part in the earth's crust, it may break through, causing volcanoes and even splitting the crust. Luckily, this often happens underwater.

Lava is any hot melted rock on the earth's surface. Sometimes it spurts and flows down a mountain almost like water. Sometimes it is so sticky that it flows only a little distance before hardening again. When lava first reaches the surface, it may be as hot as 2000° F (1100°C).

Down the middle of the Atlantic Ocean runs a long line of active volcanoes. Some are tall enough to rise above the water as islands with names, but most are known only to scientists. The earth's crust is dividing here, and every day the United States is a tiny bit farther from Europe.

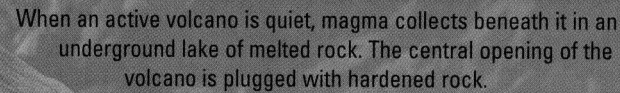

When an active volcano is quiet, magma collects beneath it in an underground lake of melted rock. The central opening of the volcano is plugged with hardened rock.

If more magma enters the underground lake, the magma rises. Or it may be pushed upward by the pressure of gases in the melted rock. Gradually magma works its way past the plug in the central opening. Then the volcano erupts.

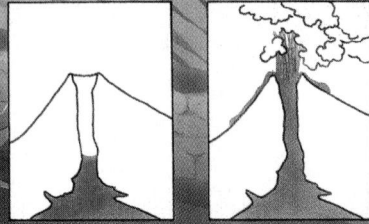

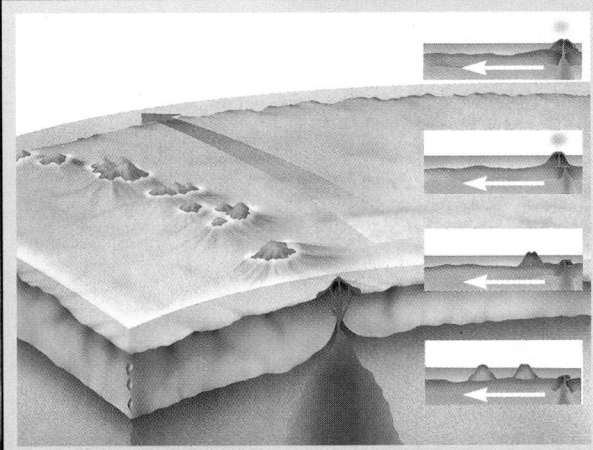

Far out in the Pacific Ocean, the volcanic Hawaiian Islands were formed by a hot spot. Here magma broke through the earth's crust but failed to split it. The crust moved slowly over the stationary hot spot, and eruptions raised a huge mountain.

Finally the moving crust carried the mountain away from the hot spot, and this volcano became extinct. Meanwhile, another volcano came to life and the hot spot began to build another mountain. This process happened many times.

The Hawaiian Islands form a line, with the oldest in the northwest and the youngest in the southeast, where volcanoes are still active. So we can tell that the crust here has moved from southeast to northwest.

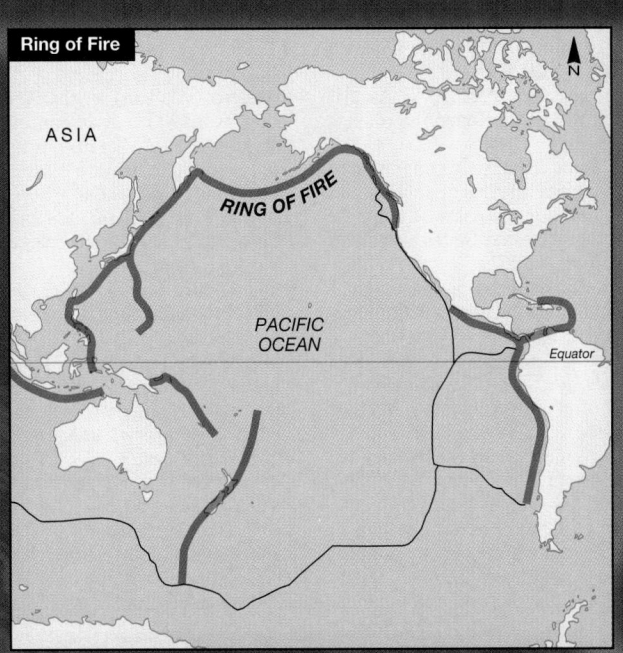

Ring of Fire

ASIA

RING OF FIRE

PACIFIC OCEAN

Equator

N

A "ring of fire" almost completely surrounds the Pacific Ocean. From the tip of South America to Alaska, from Alaska to New Zealand, dozens of volcanoes are found in a line thousands of miles long. Volcanoes are not the only signs of the earth's active interior. Great earthquakes also shake this region. The ocean's name means "peaceful," but its coasts are never peaceful for long.

On August 24, A.D. 79, Mount Vesuvius erupted and buried the Roman city of Pompeii in cinders and ash.

This lightweight material fell so thickly that it preserved many of the city's buildings in great detail.

The bodies of the volcano's victims formed hollows in the ash. These have been filled with plaster to show how people looked as they lay down for the last time.

Volcano	Location	Significance
Mauna Loa	Hawaii, U.S.A.	World's largest volcano; active
Aconcagua	Argentina	Highest American mountain; extinct
Mount Fuji	Japan	Japan's highest mountain; inactive
Mount St. Helens	Washington, U.S.A.	Erupted, 1980; active
Vesuvius	Italy	Buried Pompeii; 79 A.D.; active
Krakatoa	Indonesia	1883 eruption destroyed island; inactive
Kilimanjaro	Tanzania	Highest mountain in Africa; extinct

many books: *a voluminous report.* **3** writing much: *a voluminous author.* **–vo·lu′mi·nous·ly,** *adv.* **–vo·lu′mi·nous·ness,** *n.*

vol·un·tar·y (vol′ən ter′ē), *adj.* **1** acting, done, made, or given of your own free will; not forced or required: *a voluntary confession, a voluntary worker.* **2** done on purpose; intended: *voluntary manslaughter.* **3** controlled by the will: *Talking is voluntary; hiccupping is not voluntary.* **–vol′un·tar′i·ly,** *adv.* **–vol′un·tar′i·ness,** *n.*

voluntary muscle, striated muscle.

vol·un·teer (vol′ən tir′), **1** *n.* person who works without pay. In some towns, the fire department is made up of volunteers. **2** *v.* to offer your services: *She volunteered for the Peace Corps.* **3** *v.* to offer of your own free will: *He volunteered to help.* **4** *adj.* of or made up of volunteers: *Our village has a volunteer fire department.* **5** *adj.* serving as a volunteer: *a volunteer firefighter.* **6** *n.* person who enters any branch of the armed forces by choice; someone who is not drafted. Some soldiers are volunteers. **7** *v.* to tell or say voluntarily: *He volunteered the information.*

vo·lup·tu·ar·y (və lup′chü er′ē), *n.* person who cares a great deal for luxurious or sensual pleasures. ❑ *n., pl.* **vo·lup·tu·ar·ies.**

vo·lup·tu·ous (və lup′chü əs), *adj.* **1** caring a great deal for the pleasures of the senses. **2** giving pleasure to the senses: *voluptuous music.* **–vo·lup′tu·ous·ly,** *adv.* **–vo·lup′tu·ous·ness,** *n.*

vol·vox (vol′voks), *n.* any of several freshwater green algae that form rolling hollow balls containing thousands of individual cells. ❑ *n., pl.* **vol·vox·es.**

vom·it (vom′it), **1** *v.* to expel the contents of the stomach through the mouth; throw up what has been eaten. **2** *n.* the substance thrown up from the stomach. **3** *v.* to throw out or come out with force: *The chimneys vomited smoke.* **–vom′it·er,** *n.*

Von Braun (von brön′), **Wern·her** (wer′nər), 1912-1977, American rocket scientist, born in Germany. He developed the rockets that were used in the first moon landing.

voo·doo (vü′dü), *n.* **1** religion that came from Africa, made up of mysterious rites and practices that include the use of sorcery and magic. Belief in voodoo still prevails in many parts of the West Indies and some parts of the southern United States. **2** person who practices voodoo. ❑ *n., pl.* **voo·doos** for 2.

voo·doo·ism (vü′dü iz′əm), *n.* voodoo rites or practices.

vo·ra·cious (və rā′shəs), *adj.* **1** eating much; greedy in eating; ravenous: *voracious sharks.* **2** very eager; unable to be satisfied: *My sister is a voracious reader of history.* ■ Another word that sounds like this is **veracious.** **–vo·ra′cious·ly,** *adv.* **–vo·ra′cious·ness,** *n.*

vo·rac·i·ty (və ras′ə tē), *n.* quality of being voracious. ■ Another word that sounds like this is **veracity.**

vor·tex (vôr′teks), *n.* a whirling movement or mass of water, air, etc., that pulls everything near it toward its center; whirlpool; whirlwind. ❑ *n., pl.* **vor·tex·es, vor·ti·ces** (vôr′tə sēz).

vote (vōt), **1** *n.* a formal expression of a choice about a proposal, motion, candidate for office, etc. A vote can be cast by a ballot or indicated by saying "aye" or "nay," holding up the hand, standing up, or otherwise. In an election the person receiving the most votes is elected. **2** *n.* the right to cast or indicate a vote: *In this club, senior members have the vote.* **3** *n.* ballot or other means by which a vote is cast or indicated: *A million votes were counted.* **4** *n.* what is expressed or granted by a majority of voters: *receive a vote of confidence.* **5** *n.* votes considered together: *the labor vote, the vote of the people.* **6** *v.* to give or cast a vote: *I voted for that senator.* **7** *v.* to support by your vote: *vote the Republican ticket.* **8** *v.* to pass, determine, or grant by a vote: *Money for a new school was voted by the board.* **9** *v.* to declare: *The children all voted the trip a great success.* ❑ *v.* **vot·ed, vot·ing.**

vote down, to defeat by voting against.

vote in, to elect.

vot·er (vō′tər), *n.* **1** person who votes. **2** person who has the right to vote.

voting machine, machine which records and counts votes in political elections.

vo·tive (vō′tiv), *adj.* promised by a vow; done, given, etc., because of a vow: *He lighted a votive candle.*

vouch (vouch), *v.* to be responsible; give a guarantee for: *I can vouch for the truth of the story.*

vouch·er (vou′chər), *n.* **1** certificate that can be used as payment or to obtain money: *tuition vouchers.* **2** written evidence of payment; receipt. Canceled checks returned from your bank are vouchers.

vouch·safe (vouch sāf′), *v.* to be willing to grant or give; deign to do or give: *She vouchsafed no reply to their rude, prying questions.* ❑ *v.* **vouch·safed, vouch·saf·ing.**

vow (vou), **1** *n.* a solemn promise: *marriage vows.* **2** *n.* a promise made to God: *a nun's vows.* **3** *v.* to make a vow: *He vowed loyalty to the king.* **4** *v.* to make a vow to do, get, etc.: *vow revenge.* **–vow′er,** *n.*

vow·el (vou′əl), **1** *n.* a voiced speech sound produced by not blocking the breath with the lips, teeth, or tongue. A vowel can form a syllable by itself, such as the first syllable of *awful* (ô′-fəl). **2** *n.* letter that stands for such a sound. *A, e, i, o,* and *u* are vowels. *Y* is sometimes a vowel, as in *bicycle.* **–vow′el·less,** *adj.* **–vow′el·like′,** *adj.*

voy·age (voi′ij), **1** *n.* a journey by water; cruise: *We had a pleasant voyage to England.* ■ See Synonym Study at **trip.** **2** *n.* a journey through the air or through space: *the earth's voyage around the sun.* **3** *v.* to make or take a voyage; go by sea or air: *We voyaged across the Atlantic.* ❑ *v.* **voy·aged, voy·ag·ing.** **–voy′ag·er,** *n.*

vo·ya·geur (vwä yä zhėr′), *n.* a French Canadian worker for the early fur-trading companies who transported people and supplies, especially by boat. ❑ *n., pl.* **vo·ya·geurs** (vwä yä zhėrz′).

Voy·a·geurs National Park (voi′ə jәrz), a national park in N Minnesota, containing many lakes and northern woodlands.

VP, V.P., or **V.Pres.,** Vice-President.

vs. or **vs, 1** verse. **2** versus.

VT, Vermont (used with postal Zip Code).

Vt., Vermont.

Vul·can (vul′kən), *n.* the Roman god of fire and metalworking. [See Word Story at **volcano.**]

vul·can·ize (vul′kə nīz), *v.* to treat rubber with sulfur and heat in order to make it more elastic and durable. ❑ *v.* **vul·can·ized, vul·can·iz·ing.** **–vul′can·i·za′tion,** *n.* **–vul′can·iz′er,** *n.*

vul·gar (vul′gər), *adj.* showing a lack of good breeding, manners, taste, etc.; not refined; coarse: *vulgar language.* **–vul′gar·ly,** *adv.* **–vul′gar·ness,** *n.*

vul·gar·ism (vul′gə riz′əm), *n.* word, phrase, or expression used only by uneducated speakers. In "I disrecollect his name," *disrecollect* is a vulgarism.

vul·gar·i·ty (vul gar′ə tē), *n.* **1** lack of refinement; lack of good breeding, manners, taste, etc.; coarseness. **2** thing done or said that shows vulgarity; vulgar act or word: *Their vulgarities annoyed me.* ❑ *n., pl.* **vul·gar·i·ties** for 2.

vul·gar·ize (vul′gə rīz′), *v.* to make vulgar or common; degrade or debase. ❑ *v.* **vul·gar·ized, vul·gar·iz·ing.** **–vul′gar·i·za′tion,** *n.* **–vul′gar·iz′er,** *n.*

Vul·gate (vul′gāt), *n.* the Latin translation of the Bible, made about A.D. 405 by Saint Jerome. It is the Bible used by the Roman Catholic Church.

vul·ner·a·ble (vul′nər ə bəl), *adj.* **1** capable of being wounded or injured; open to attack: *The army's retreat left the city vulnerable.* **2** sensitive to criticism, temptations, influences, etc.: *Most people are vulnerable to ridicule.* **–vul′ner·a·bil′i·ty, vul′ner·a·ble·ness,** *n.* **–vul′ner·a·bly,** *adv.*

vul·pine (vul′pīn), *adj.* of or like a fox.

vul·ture (vul′chər), *n.* **1** any of various large birds of prey related to eagles and hawks, but eating mainly the flesh of dead animals. Vultures usually lack feathers on their heads and necks. **2** a greedy, ruthless person.

vul·va (vul′və), *n.* the external sex organs of a female mammal. ❑ *n., pl.* **vul·vae** (vul′vē), **vul·vas.**

vy·ing (vī′ing), *v.* present participle of **vie:** *Members of the class were vying with each other for a position on the student council.*

vulture (def. 1)

W or **w** (dubʹəl yü), *n.* the 23rd letter of the English alphabet. ❑ *n., pl.* **W's** or **w's.**

w, watt or watts.

W, 1 west. **2** western. **3** symbol for tungsten.

w., 1 watt or watts. **2** week or weeks. **3** weight. **4** west. **5** western. **6** width.

W., 1 Wednesday. **2** west. **3** western.

WA, Washington (used with postal Zip Code).

Wa·bash (wȯʹbash), *n.* river flowing from W Ohio southwest across Indiana into the Ohio River.

WAC or **Wac** (wak), *n.* formerly, woman in the U.S. Army other than a nurse. ■ Another word that sounds like this is **whack.**

wack·o (wakʹō), SLANG. **1** *adj.* wacky. **2** *n.* a very odd or unreasonable person. **3** *n.* person with mental illness. ■ This meaning of **wacko** is often considered offensive. ❑ *n., pl.* **wack·os.**

wack·y (wakʹē), *adj.* SLANG. odd; silly; unconventional. ❑ *adj.* **wack·i·er, wack·i·est. —wackʹi·ly,** *adv.* **—wackʹi·ness,** *n.*

wad (wäd), **1** *n.* a small, soft mass: *I plugged my ears with wads of cotton.* **2** *n.* a tight ball or lump of something: *a wad of chewing gum.* **3** *v.* to make into a wad; press into a wad: *I wadded up the paper and threw it away.* **4** *n.* a round plug of felt, cardboard, etc., used to hold powder and shot in place in a gun or cartridge. **5** *n.* a large, rolled bundle of paper money. **6** *v.* to stuff with a wad. ❑ *v.* **wad·ded, wad·ding.**

wad·dle (wädʹl), **1** *v.* to walk with short steps and an awkward, swaying motion, as a duck does: *The toddler waddled from the house bundled in his snowsuit.* **2** *n.* an awkward, swaying way of walking: *It made us laugh to see his waddle.* ❑ *v.* **wad·dled, wad·dling. —wadʹdler,** *n.*

wade (wād), *v.* **1** to walk through water, snow, sand, mud, or anything that hinders free motion. **2** to make your way with difficulty: *Must I wade through that dull book?* **3** to cross or pass through by wading: *wade a stream.* ❑ *v.* **wad·ed, wad·ing.**

wade into, to attack or go to work upon vigorously.

wad·er (wāʹdər), *n.* **1** person or thing that wades. **2 waders,** *pl.* high, waterproof boots. **3** a wading bird.

wa·di (wäʹdē), *n.* **1** in northern Africa and the Middle East, a valley through which a stream flows during heavy rainfall, but which is dry the rest of the time. **2** stream running through such a valley. ❑ *n., pl.* **wa·dis.**

wading bird, any of various birds with long legs, long necks, and long bills. They wade in shallow water, searching for fishes, frogs and insects to eat. Herons, egrets, and cranes are wading birds.

WAF or **Waf** (waf), *n.* formerly, woman in the U.S. Air Force other than a nurse. ❑ *n., pl.* **WAFs** or **Wafs.**

a	hat	ė	term	ô	order	ch	child		
ā	age	i	it	oi	oil	ng	long	ə {	a in about
ä	far	ī	ice	ou	out	sh	she		e in taken
â	care	o	hot	u	cup	th	thin		i in pencil
e	let	ō	open	u̇	put	ŦH	then		o in lemon
ē	equal	ȯ	saw	ü	rule	zh	measure		u in circus

waf·er (wā′fər), *n.* **1** a flat, dry food made of water and flour baked together, sometimes flavored or sweetened. **2** the thin, round piece of unleavened bread used in Holy Communion in certain churches. **3** a thin piece of candy, chocolate, medicine, etc. **4** a thin slice of silicon crystal from which computer chips can be manufactured. [See Word Story at **waffle**¹.] **—waf′er·like′,** *adj.*

waf·fle¹ (wäf′əl), *n.* a batter cake cooked in a waffle iron until brown and crisp, usually eaten while hot with butter, syrup, etc.

> **WORD STORY** **Waffle**¹ may come from a Germanic word meaning "honeycomb." With its pattern of dents and ridges, a waffle looks something like a piece of honeycomb. **Wafer** comes from the same old German word. Baked thinner, wafers are spelled smaller.

waf·fle² (wäf′əl), *v.* to talk or write about something vaguely or inconsistently, without taking a clear stand on the issue. ◻ *v.* **waf·fled, waf·fling. —waf′fler,** *n.*

waffle iron, utensil consisting of two hinged parts having projections on the heating surfaces that form indentations in waffle batter while cooking it.

waft (wäft *or* waft), **1** *v.* to carry over water or through air: *The waves wafted the boat to shore.* **2** *n.* a breath or puff of air, wind, scent, etc.: *A waft of fresh air came through the window.* **—waft′er,** *n.*

> **WORD STORY** **Waft** comes from a Dutch word meaning "to guard." Ships with valuable cargoes used to sail with other ships that guarded them from attack. These guard ships were called *wafters* and so **waft** changed to mean floating or carrying like a sailboat, on water or even in air.

wag (wag), **1** *v.* to move from side to side or up and down, especially rapidly and repeatedly: *The dog wagged its tail.* **2** *n.* a wagging motion: *My dog greeted me with a wag of its tail.* **3** *n.* person who is fond of making jokes. ◻ *v.* **wagged, wag·ging. —wag′ger,** *n.*

wage (wāj), **1** *n.* Usually, **wages,** *pl. or sing.* the money paid for work done, especially work paid for by the hour: *His wages averaged $450 a week.* **2** *v.* to carry on: *Doctors wage war against disease.* ◻ *v.* **waged, wag·ing. —wage′less,** *adj.*

wage earner, person who works for wages.

wa·ger (wā′jər), **1** *v.* to make a bet; bet; gamble: *I'll wager the black horse will win the race.* **2** *n.* act of betting; bet: *The wager of $10 was promptly paid.* **—wa′ger·er,** *n.*

wag·ish (wag′ish), *adj.* **1** fond of making jokes. **2** typical of a wag; funny; humorous: *a waggish remark.* **—wag′gish·ly,** *adv.* **—wag′gish·ness,** *n.*

wag·gle (wag′əl), **1** *v.* to move quickly and repeatedly from side to side; wag. **2** *n.* a waggling motion. ◻ *v.* **wag·gled, wag·gling.**

Wag·ner (wag′nər *for 1;* väg′nər *for 2*), *n.* **1 Ho·nus** (hō′nəs), 1874-1955, American baseball player. ■ **Honus Wagner** led the National League in batting eight times, including four years in a row. **2 Richard,** 1813-1883, German composer of legendary and mythological operas.

wag·on (wag′ən), *n.* **1** a four-wheeled vehicle, especially one for carrying loads, usually pulled by an animal or animals: *a milk wagon.* **2** a child's four-wheeled toy cart. **3** station wagon.

wag·on·er (wag′ə nər), *n.* person who drives a wagon.

wag·on·load (wag′ən lōd′), *n.* amount that a wagon can hold or carry.

wagon train, (earlier) line of wagons moving along one after another, especially one carrying settlers westward in the 1800s.

waif (wāf), *n.* **1** a homeless or neglected child. **2** anything without an owner; stray thing, animal, etc.

wail (wāl), **1** *v.* to cry loud and long because of grief or pain: *The baby wailed.* **2** *n.* a long cry of grief or pain: *The baby awoke with a wail.* **3** *n.* a sound like such a cry: *the wail of a hungry coyote.* **4** *v.* to make a mournful sound: *The wind wailed around the old house.* **5** *v.* to lament; mourn. ■ Other words that sound like this are **wale** and **whale. —wail′er,** *n.*

wain·scot (wān′skət *or* wān′skŏt), **1** *n.* a lining of wood, usually in panels, on the walls of a room. **2** *v.* to line with wood: *a room wainscoted in oak.* **3** *n.* the lower part of the wall of a room when it is decorated differently from the upper part.

wain·scot·ing (wān′skə ting *or* wān′skō ting), *n.* **1** wainscot. **2** material used for wainscots.

waist (wāst), *n.* **1** the part of the human body between the ribs and the hips. **2** waistline. **3** clothing covering the body from the neck or shoulders to the waistline; blouse or bodice. **4** a narrow middle part: *the waist of a violin.* [**Waist** comes from an old English word meaning "growth." Waists tend to grow.] ■ Another word that sounds like this is **waste.**

waist·band (wāst′band′), *n.* a band around the waist: *the waistband of a skirt or of a pair of trousers.*

waist·coat (wes′kət *or* wāst′kōt′), *n.* BRITISH. a man's vest.

waist·line (wāst′līn′), *n.* **1** line around the body at the smallest part of the waist. **2** place of smallest width in a woman's dress between the arms and the knees. **3** line where the waist and skirt of a dress join.

wait (wāt), **1** *v.* to stay somewhere or stop doing something until someone comes or something happens: *Let's wait in the shade.* **2** *n.* act or time of waiting: *I had a long wait at the doctor's office.* **3** *v.* to look forward; be expecting or ready: *The children wait impatiently for vacation.* **4** *v.* to be left undone; be put off: *That matter can wait until tomorrow.* **5** *v.* to delay or put off: *Wait dinner for me.* **6** *v.* to work as a waiter or waitress: *She waits tables in a little café.* [**Wait** comes from a French word that originally meant "to watch." If you are watching for something, you have to wait until it comes in sight.] ■ Another word that sounds like this is **weight.**

lie in wait, to stay hidden ready to attack: *Robbers lay in wait for the caravan.*

wait on *or* **wait upon, 1** to be a servant to; serve: *wait on hotel guests.* **2** to serve as a waiter or waitress: *to wait on several tables of diners.* **3** to wait for: *to wait on a decision.* **4** to call upon a superior: *The victorious general waited upon the king.*

wait·er (wā′tər), *n.* person who serves or brings food to people in a restaurant; server.

wait·ing (wā′ting), **1** *adj.* that waits: *The waiting crowd rushed to get on the bus.* **2** *n.* time that you wait.

in waiting, in attendance on a king, queen, prince, princess, etc.

waiting list, a list of people who want something, in the order of their chances of getting it.

waiting room, room in a doctor's office, railroad station, etc., for people to wait in.

wagon (def. 1)

wai·tress (wā′tris), *n.* woman who serves or brings food to people in a restaurant. ◻ *n., pl.* **wai·tress·es.**

waive (wāv), *v.* **1** to give up a right, claim, etc.; refrain from claiming or pressing; do without; relinquish: *The lawyer waived the privilege of cross-examining the witness.* **2** to set aside or not enforce: *Admission is waived for senior citizens.* ◻ *v.* **waived, waiv·ing.** ■ Another word that sounds like this is **wave.**

waiv·er (wā′vər), *n.* **1** act of giving up a right, claim, etc.; a waiving. **2** a written statement of this: *The injured man signed a waiver of all claims against the railroad.* ■ Another word that sounds like this is **waver.**

wake¹ (wāk), **1** *v.* to stop sleeping: *I usually wake at dawn. She wakes up at seven every morning.* **2** *v.* to cause to stop sleeping: *The noise of the traffic always wakes the baby. Wake me up early.* **3** *v.* to be awake; stay awake: *Waking or sleeping, we were all excited about our vacation trip.* **4** *v.* to become alive or active: *The flowers wake in the spring.* **5** *v.* to make alive or active: *He needs some interest to wake him up.* **6** *n.* a watch kept beside the body of a dead person before its burial. ❑ *v.* **woke** or **waked, wo·ken** or **waked, wak·ing.**

wake² (wāk), *n.* **1** track left behind a moving ship. **2** track left behind any moving thing.
in the wake of, behind; after: *floods in the wake of a hurricane.*

wake·ful (wāk′fəl), *adj.* **1** not able to sleep: *a wakeful baby.* **2** without sleep: *a wakeful night.* —**wake′ful·ly,** *adv.* —**wake′ful·ness,** *n.*

Wake Island, small island in the N Pacific, about 2000 miles west of Hawaii, belonging to the United States.

wak·en (wā′kən), *v.* to wake.

Wal·cott (wol′cot), *n.* **Der·ek** (der′ək), born 1930, West Indian writer. He won the 1992 Nobel Prize for literature.

Wald·heim (vält′hīm), *n.* **Kurt** (kürt), born 1918, Austrian diplomat. He was the secretary-general of the United Nations from 1972 to 1982. Later he was accused of having committed and concealed war crimes during World War II.

wale (wāl), **1** *n.* a streak or ridge made on the skin by a stick or whip; welt. **2** *v.* to mark with wales; raise wales on. **3** *n.* a ridge in the weave of cloth. ❑ *v.* **waled, wal·ing.** ■ Other words that sound like this are **wail** and **whale.**

Wales (wālz), *n.* division of Great Britain west of England; the land of the Welsh. *Capital:* Cardiff. See **United Kingdom** for map. [See Word Story at **walnut.**]

Wa·le·sa (və wen′sə), *n.* **Lech** (lek), born 1943, president of Poland from 1990 to 1995. He won the 1983 Nobel Peace Prize.

walk (wok), **1** *v.* to go on foot. In walking, a person always has one foot on the ground. *Walk down to the post office with me.* **2** *n.* act of walking, especially for pleasure or exercise: *We went for a walk in the country.* **3** *n.* distance to walk: *The library is a twenty-minute walk from our house.* **4** *v.* to go over, on, or through: *walk the length of a trail.* **5** *v.* to cause to walk; make go slowly: *The rider walked the horse up the hill.* **6** *n.* the slowest gait of a four-legged animal, in which at least two feet are always on the ground. **7** *v.* to accompany or escort in walking; conduct on foot: *walk a guest to the door.* **8** *n.* manner or way of walking; gait: *We could tell she was happy from her lively walk.* **9** *n.* place for walking; path: *There are many pretty walks in the park.* **10** *n.* social position; rank; occupation: *Your walk of life is different from mine.* **11** in baseball: **a** *v.* to go to first base after the pitcher has thrown four balls. **b** *n.* act of going to first base after the pitcher has thrown four balls; base on balls. **c** *v.* to allow a batter to reach first base by pitching four balls.
walk away with or **walk off with, 1** to win or get something with ease: *walk off with first prize.* **2** to steal.
walk out on, to go away and leave; desert.

> **SYNONYM STUDY** **Walk, march,** and **stroll** all mean to move on foot. **Walk** is a general word: *Is the park close enough to walk to?* **March** means to walk steadily, with a regular step: *The band marched down the street.* **Stroll** means to walk at an easy, slow speed: *We strolled through the mall.*

walk·er (wo′kər), *n.* **1** a lightweight four-legged frame used for support while walking. **2** a small framework with wheels in which children support themselves while learning to walk; go-cart. **3** person who walks.

Walk·er (wo′kər), *n.* **1 Alice** (al′is), born 1944, American writer. Her best-known novel is *The Color Purple,* which won the 1983 Pulitzer Prize for fiction. **2 Mary Ed·wards** (ed′wərdz), 1832-1919, American doctor. ■ **Mary Edwards Walker** was the only woman to receive the Medal of Honor. She served as a surgeon in the Union Army during the Civil War.

walk·ie-talk·ie (wo′kē to′kē), *n.* a small, portable receiving and transmitting radio set. It is powered by a battery and has an antenna.

walk-in (wok′in′), *adj.* **1** large enough to walk into: *a walk-in closet.* **2** of or for someone who arrives off the street without an appointment: *a walk-in clinic.*

walking stick, 1 cane. **2** any of several insects with a body like a stick or twig.

walk-on (wok′on′), *n.* **1** part in a play, movie, or TV show in which the actor does little or no speaking. **2** actor having such a part.

walk·out (wok′out′), *n.* **1** strike of workers. **2** a sudden departure from a room, meeting, etc., usually as a form of protest.

walk·o·ver (wok′ō′vər), *n.* an easy victory.

walk-up (wok′up′), *n.* an apartment house or building having no elevator.

walk·way (wok′wā′), *n.* **1** structure for walking on: *an overhead steel walkway.* **2** path; walk.

wall (wol), **1** *n.* side of a room or building: *to wallpaper a bedroom wall, the brick wall of a house.* **2** *n.* the side part of any hollow thing: *the wall of the stomach.* **3** *n.* structure of stone, brick, or other material built up to enclose, divide, support, or protect. Cities used to be surrounded by high walls to keep out enemies. **4** *n.* something like a wall in looks or use: *a wall of water ten feet high, a wall of ignorance. The mayor met a solid wall of protesters.* **5** *v.* to enclose, divide, protect, or fill with or as if with a wall: *wall a garden, wall out the noise of the city.* —**wall′-less,** *adj.* —**wall′-like′,** *adj.*
drive someone up the wall, to greatly annoy or irritate: *His singing really drives me up the wall.*
off the wall, INFORMAL. odd; very unusual.

wal·la·by (wäl′ə bē), *n.* any of various small kangaroos. Some wallabies are no larger than rabbits. ❑ *n., pl.* **wal·la·bies** or **wal·la·by.**

Wal·lace (wol′is), *n.* **George,** born 1919, American political leader. ■ **George Wallace** was the governor of Alabama and ran for president three times. He was a vocal opponent of integration.

wall·board (wol′bôrd′), *n.* any building material, such as plasterboard or fiberboard, made by pressing wood pulp, plaster, etc., into large, flat sheets. Wallboard is used instead of wood or plaster to make or cover inside walls and ceilings.

wallaby—2 ft. 6 in. (76 cm) tall

Wal·len·berg (wol′ən berg), *n.* **Ra·oul** (rä′ül), 1912-?, Swedish businessman and diplomat. ■ **Raoul Wallenberg** helped save about 100,000 Hungarian Jews from being killed by the Nazis by issuing them Swedish passports. He was seized by Soviet forces in 1945. A Soviet report that he had died of a heart attack while in prison in 1947 has been disputed.

Wal·ler (wol′ər), *n.* **Fats** (fats), 1904-1943, American jazz pianist and songwriter. His original name was Thomas Wright Waller.

wal·let (wäl′it), *n.* a small, flat case for carrying paper money, cards, etc., in your pocket; folding pocketbook; billfold.

wall·eye (wol′ī), *n.* a walleyed pike.

wall·eyed (wol′īd′), *adj.* **1** having eyes that show much white and little color. **2** having one or both eyes turned away from the nose, so as to show much white. **3** having large, staring eyes, as some fish do.

walleyed pike, a large North American freshwater game and food fish with large, staring eyes.

wall·flow·er (wol′flou′ər), *n.* **1** INFORMAL. person who sits by the wall at a dance instead of dancing. **2** a plant with sweet-smelling yellow, orange, or red flowers, found growing on walls, cliffs, etc.

a	hat	ė	term	ô	order	ch	child		a in about
ā	age	i	it	oi	oil	ng	long		e in taken
ä	far	ī	ice	ou	out	sh	she	ə	i in pencil
â	care	o	hot	u	cup	th	thin		o in lemon
e	let	ō	open	u̇	put	₮H	then		u in circus
ē	equal	ȯ	saw	ü	rule	zh	measure		

W

wal·lop (wäl′əp), INFORMAL. **1** *v.* to beat soundly; thrash. **2** *v.* to hit something very hard: *The batter walloped a home run over the fence.* **3** *n.* a very hard blow: *The wallop knocked me down.* **4** *n.* power to hit very hard blows. **5** *v.* to defeat thoroughly, as in a game. **—wal′lop·er,** *n.*

wal·low (wäl′ō), **1** *v.* to roll about; flounder: *The pigs wallowed in the mud. The boat wallowed helplessly in the stormy sea.* **2** *v.* to live contentedly in filth, wickedness, etc. **3** *v.* to live or delight self-indulgently or luxuriously in some form of pleasure, manner of life, etc.: *wallow in wealth, wallow in sentimentality.* **4** *n.* act of wallowing. **5** *n.* place where an animal wallows. **—wal′low·er,** *n.*

wall·pa·per (wòl′pā′pər), **1** *n.* paper, usually printed with a pattern in color, for pasting on and covering walls. **2** *v.* to put wallpaper on: *wallpaper a bedroom.*

Wall Street, **1** street in downtown New York City that is the chief financial center of the United States. **2** the money market or the financiers of the United States.

wal·nut (wòl′nut), *n.* **1** a rather large, almost round nut with a hard, ridged shell and a division between its two halves. The meat of the walnut is eaten by itself, used in cakes and candy, etc. **2** the tree that it grows on. **3** the wood of this tree. Some kinds of walnut are used in making furniture.

> **WORD STORY** **Walnut** comes from old English words meaning "foreign" and "nut." The walnut came to England from southern Europe in the Middle Ages. **Wales** comes from the same old English word meaning "foreign." Anglo-Saxons thought of people living in Wales as foreigners, although it was actually the Anglo-Saxons who had invaded England from Europe.

wal·rus (wòl′rəs), *n.* a large sea mammal of arctic regions, like a seal but with long tusks. Walruses are hunted for their hides, tusks, and oil. ❑ *n., pl.* **wal·rus** or **wal·rus·es.** [**Walrus** comes from Dutch words meaning "whale" and "horse." It looks a bit like each.]

walrus—up to 11 ft. (3.4 m) long

waltz (wòlts), **1** *n.* a smooth, even, gliding dance with three beats to a measure. **2** *n.* music for it. **3** *v.* to dance a waltz. **4** *v.* to move lightly or quickly: *She waltzed over to the newcomers with a big smile.* ❑ *n., pl.* **waltz·es.** [**Waltz** comes from a German word meaning "to roll." Waltzing dancers often turn in circles.]

wam·pum (wäm′pəm), *n.* **1** beads made from shells, formerly used by North American Indians as money and for ornament. **2** SLANG. money.

wan (wän), *adj.* **1** lacking natural color; pale: *Her face looked wan after her long illness.* **2** looking worn or tired; faint; weak: *The sick boy gave the doctor a wan smile.* ❑ *adj.* **wan·ner, wan·nest. —wan′ly,** *adv.* **—wan′ness,** *n.*

wand (wänd), *n.* a slender stick or rod: *a magic wand.*

wan·der (wän′dər), *v.* **1** to move here and there without any special purpose: *We wandered around the fair, looking at exhibits.* **2** to follow an uncertain or irregular course; meander: *a driver who wanders all over the road.* **3** to leave the right way; stray: *The dog wandered off and got lost. The speaker wandered away from the subject.* **4** to not be able to think sensibly; be delirious or incoherent: *A high fever can make a person's mind wander.* **—wan′derer,** *n.*

wan·der·lust (wän′dər lust′), *n.* a strong desire to wander: *Her wanderlust led her all over the world.*

wane (wān), **1** *v.* (of the moon) to go through its regular reduction in the amount of its visible portion. The moon wanes when the side facing the earth moves gradually out of the sun's light. **2** *v.* to lose power, influence, or importance: *Many great empires have waned.* **3** *v.* to lose strength or intensity: *The light of day wanes in the evening.* **4** *v.* to draw to a close: *Summer wanes as autumn approaches.* **5** *n.* act or process of waning. ❑ *v.* **waned, wan·ing.**
on the wane, growing less; waning.

wan·gle (wang′gəl), *v.* to manage to get by schemes, tricks, persuasion, etc.: *wangle an interview with a TV star.* ❑ *v.* **wan·gled, wan·gling. —wan′gler,** *n.*

wan·na·be (wän′ə bē′), *n.* INFORMAL. person who hopes, often in vain, to become famous.

want (wänt), **1** *v.* to wish for; wish: *We want a new car. I want to become an engineer.* **2** *n.* thing desired or needed; desire: *someone having few wants.* **3** *v.* to be without; lack: *The fund wants half of the sum needed.* **4** *n.* condition of being without something desired or needed; a lack: *The plant died from want of water.* **5** *v.* to need; require: *Plants want water.* **6** *n.* a need: *supply a long-felt want.* **7** *n.* a lack of food, clothing, or shelter; great poverty: *Those people are in want.* **8** *v.* to need food, clothing, and shelter; be very poor. **9** *v.* to wish to see, speak to, or use someone: *Call me if you want me. You are the one we want for the job.* **10** *v.* to seek after to catch or arrest: *wanted by the police.*

> **SYNONYM STUDY** **Want, desire,** and **crave** all mean to feel an urge to have something or do something. **Want** is a general word: *He wants a pair of skates.* **Desire,** a formal word, means to want something very seriously and very much: *The ambassador said that her country desired peace but would defend its borders.* **Crave** means to want badly, in a way that is hard to bear: *The apples are all eaten and I really crave one.*

want ad, a small notice in a newspaper stating that an employee, an apartment, etc., is wanted.

want·ing (wän′ting), **1** *adj.* not satisfactory; not coming up to a standard or need: *The vegetables were weighed and found wanting.* **2** *adj.* not found or in evidence; lacking; missing: *One volume of the set is wanting.* **3** *prep.* without; less; minus: *a year wanting three days.*

wan·ton (wän′tən), **1** *adj.* done in a reckless, heartless, or malicious way; done without reason or excuse: *a wanton attack, wanton mischief, wanton cruelty.* **2** *adj.* immoral; lewd. **3** *adj.* not restrained; frolicsome; playful: *a wanton breeze, a wanton mood.* **4** *n.* a wanton person. **—wan′ton·ly,** *adv.* **—wan′ton·ness,** *n.*

wap·i·ti (wäp′i tē), *n.* elk (def. 1). ❑ *n., pl.* **wap·i·ti** or **wap·i·tis.**

> **WORD STORY** **Wapiti** comes from a Shawnee word meaning "white rump." It is easy to tell an elk from a moose if they are coming toward you, but if you were a hunter stalking one from behind, this is the difference you would notice. A moose has a dark rump.

war (wôr), **1** *n.* fighting carried on by armed force between nations or parts of a nation. **2** *n.* any fighting or struggle; strife; conflict: *Doctors carry on war against disease.* **3** *n.* the occupation or art of fighting with weapons: *Soldiers are trained for war.* **4** *v.* to make war; fight: *to war with an aggressor, to war against poverty.* **5** *adj.* of or used in war; caused by war: *war weapons, war crimes, war casualties.* ❑ *v.* **warred, war·ring.** ■ Another word that sounds like this is **wore.**

War Between the States, the American Civil War.

war·ble (wôr′bəl), **1** *v.* to sing with trills, repeated notes, or melodious turns: *Birds warbled in the trees.* **2** *v.* to make a sound like that of a bird singing: *The brook warbled over its rocky bed.* **3** *n.* a bird's song or a sound like it: *a canary's warble.* ❑ *v.* **war·bled, war·bling.**

war·bler (wôr′blər), *n.* **1** any of numerous small songbirds, often brightly colored. **2** person, animal, or thing that warbles; singer.

war·bon·net (wôr′bon′it), *n.* a ceremonial headdress set with feathers and often a long trailing piece with feathers, worn by certain North American Indians.

war crime, any brutal act against civilians, prisoners, etc., in time of war.

war cry, battle cry.

ward (wôrd), *n.* **1** a division of a hospital or prison: *a maternity ward.* **2** one of the parts or districts into which a city or town is divided for purposes of government. **3** person under the care of a guardian or of a court.

ward off, to keep away; turn aside: *ward off a blow, ward off an illness.*

-ward, *suffix.* in the direction of ___; toward ___: *homeward = in the direction of home; backward = toward the back.* Also, **-wards.**

ward·en (wôrd′n), *n.* **1** the official in charge of a prison. **2** any official who enforces certain laws and regulations: *a game warden, a fire warden.*

ward·er (wôr′dər), *n.* guard or watchman.

ward·robe (wôrd′rōb′), *n.* **1** a supply of clothes: *a spring wardrobe.* **2** room, closet, or piece of furniture for holding clothes.

WORD STORY Wardrobe comes from French words meaning "guard" and "garment." A wardrobe that holds clothes keeps them safe from dust and moths. Soon the word came to mean the clothes themselves, perhaps from sentences like, "There's nothing in my whole wardrobe that goes with this hat!"

-wards, *suffix.* form of **-ward.**

ware (wâr), *n.* **1** Usually, **wares,** *pl.* a manufactured thing; article for sale: *Household wares are on the third floor at this store.* **2** kind of manufactured thing or article for sale: *copper ware.* **3** earthenware; pottery: *porcelain ware.* ■ Other words that sound like this are **wear** and **where.**

ware·house (wâr′hous′), *n.* place where goods are kept; storehouse. ❑ *n., pl.* **ware·hous·es** (wâr′hou′ziz).

war·fare (wôr′fâr′), *n.* war; fighting.

war·head (wôr′hed′), *n.* the forward part of a torpedo, missile, etc., containing the explosive.

War·hol (wôr′hōl), *n.* **An·dy** (an′dē), 1930?-1987, American artist. His work often showed the same familiar face or image repeated many times. He was one of the creators of pop art.

war·horse (wôr′hôrs′), *n.* **1** INFORMAL. person who has taken part in many battles, struggles, etc.; veteran. **2** horse used in war; charger.

war·like (wôr′līk′), *adj.* **1** fit for war; ready for war; fond of war: *a warlike nation.* **2** threatening war; hostile: *a warlike speech.* ■ See Synonym Study at **hostile.**

war·lock (wôr′lok), *n.* a male witch; wizard.

war·lord (wôr′lôrd′), *n.* **1** a military commander or commander in chief, especially one who is also head of the government. **2** a military leader who has taken control of a region of a country.

warm (wôrm), **1** *adj.* more hot than cold; having some heat; giving forth moderate or gentle heat: *a warm fire. She sat in the warm sunshine.* **2** *adj.* having a feeling of heat: *be warm from running.* **3** *adj.* able to keep in body heat: *a warm coat.* **4** *adj.* having or showing affection, enthusiasm, or zeal: *a warm welcome, a warm heart.* **5** *adj.* exciting; lively: *a warm dispute.* **6** *adj.* fresh and strong: *a warm scent.* **7** *adj.* (in games, treasure hunts, etc.) getting close to what you are looking for. **8** *adj.* suggesting heat. Red, orange, and yellow are called warm colors. **9** *v.* to make or become warm: *warm a room.* **10** *v.* to make or become cheered, interested, friendly, or sympathetic: *The speaker warmed to his subject.* **—warm′ly,** *adv.* **—warm′ness,** *n.*

warm up, **1** to heat or cook again. **2** to make or become more interested, friendly, etc. **3** to practice or exercise for a few minutes before entering a game, contest, etc. **4** to run a machine before using it until it reaches its normal working condition.

warm-blood·ed (wôrm′blud′id), *adj.* **1** having blood that stays about the same temperature regardless of the air or water around the animal. Birds and mammals are warm-blooded; reptiles, fishes, and insects are cold-blooded. **2** with much feeling; eager. **—warm′-blood′ed·ness,** *n.*

warm front, the advancing edge of a warm air mass as it passes over and displaces a cooler one.

warm-heart·ed (wôrm′här′tid), *adj.* kind; sympathetic; friendly. **—warm′heart′ed·ness,** *n.*

warming pan, a covered pan with a long handle for holding hot coals, formerly used to warm beds.

war·mon·ger (wôr′mung′gər), *n.* person who is in favor of war or attempts to bring about war.

warmth (wôrmth), *n.* **1** condition of being warm: *the warmth of the open fire.* **2** warm or friendly feeling: *the warmth of our host's welcome.* **3** liveliness of feelings or emotions; fervor: *She spoke with warmth of the natural beauty of the country.*

warm-up (wôrm′up′), *n.* **1** practice or exercise taken for a few minutes before entering a game, contest, etc. **2** period of running required for a machine to reach normal working condition before use.

warn (wôrn), *v.* **1** to give notice to in advance about possible danger, evil, or harm; put on guard; caution: *The children were warned not to speak to strangers.* **2** to give notice to; inform: *The whistle warned visitors that the ship was ready to sail.* ■ Another word that sounds like this is **worn.**

warn·ing (wôr′ning), *n.* something that warns; notice given in advance: *Let this experience be a warning for you to be more careful in the future.* **—warn′ing·ly,** *adv.*

War of 1812, war between the United States and Great Britain. It lasted from 1812 to 1815.

War of Independence, Revolutionary War.

warp (wôrp), **1** *v.* to bend or twist out of shape: *This floor has warped so that it is not level.* **2** *v.* to mislead; pervert: *Suspicions can warp our judgment.* **3** *n.* a bend or twist; distortion. **4** *v.* to move a ship, etc., by ropes fastened to something fixed. **5** *n.* the threads running lengthwise in a fabric. The warp is crossed by the woof. [Warp comes from an old English word meaning "to throw." It is hard to throw something and make it go straight.] **—warp′er,** *n.*

war·path (wôr′path′), *n.* the way taken by a fighting expedition of North American Indians. ❑ *n., pl.* **war·paths** (wôr′paᵗHz′ or wôr′paths′).

on the warpath, **1** ready for war. **2** looking for a fight; angry.

war·plane (wôr′plān′), *n.* airplane used in war.

warplanes

war·rant (wôr′ənt), **1** *n.* that which gives a right; authority: *He had no warrant to tell us how to behave.* **2** *n.* a written order giving authority for something: *a warrant to search the house.* **3** *v.* to authorize: *The law warrants their arrest.* **4** *v.* to give a good reason for; justify: *Nothing warrants such rudeness.* **5** *v.* to give your word for; guarantee; promise: *The company warranted the quality of their cameras.* **6** *v.* to declare positively; certify: *I'll warrant they won't try that again.*

warrant officer, (in the armed forces) an officer who has received a certificate of appointment, but not a commission, ranking between commissioned officers and enlisted men. See chart on page 712.

W

a	hat	ė	term	ô	order	ch	child		a in about
ā	age	i	it	oi	oil	ng	long		e in taken
ä	far	ī	ice	ou	out	sh	she	ə	i in pencil
â	care	o	hot	u	cup	th	thin		o in lemon
e	let	ō	open	u̇	put	ᵗH	then		u in circus
ē	equal	ò	saw	ü	rule	zh	measure		

war·ran·ty (wôr′ən tē), *n.* **1** a promise or pledge that something is what it is claimed to be; guarantee: *a warranty of the quality of the goods sold.* **2** warrant or authorization. ❑ *n., pl.* **war·ran·ties.**

war·ren (wôr′ən), *n.* **1** piece of ground filled with burrows, where rabbits live or are raised. **2** a crowded district or building.

War·ren (wôr′ən), *n.* **1 Earl** (érl), 1891-1974, chief justice of the U.S. Supreme Court from 1953 to 1969. **2** city in SE Michigan.

war·ri·or (wôr′yər *or* wôr′ē ər), *n.* person experienced in fighting battles. **—war′ri·or·like′,** *adj.*

War·saw (wôr′sô), *n.* capital and largest city of Poland, in the E part.

war·ship (wôr′ship′), *n.* ship armed for war.

wart (wôrt), *n.* **1** a small, hard lump on the skin, caused by a virus. **2** a similar lump on a plant. **—wart′like′,** *adj.*

wart·hog (wôrt′hog′), *n.* a wild hog of Africa that has two large tusks and large, wartlike growths on each side of its face.

war·time (wôr′tīm′), **1** *n.* a time of war. **2** *adj.* of or about a time of war.

War·wick (wôr′wik *or* wôr′ik), *n.* city in E Rhode Island.

war·y (wâr′ē), *adj.* **1** cautious or careful: *They gave wary answers to the stranger's peculiar questions.* ■ See Synonym Study at **careful.** ❑ *adj.* **war·i·er, war·i·est. —war′i·ly,** *adv.* **—war′i·ness,** *n.*

wary of, cautious or careful about: *Be wary of gossip.*

warthog—up to 2 ft. 6 in. (76 cm) high at the shoulder

was (wuz *or* wäz), *v.* form of the verb **be** used with *I, he, she, it,* or any singular noun to indicate the past tense: *I was late.*

wash (wäsh), **1** *v.* to clean with water or other liquid: *wash your face, wash clothes, wash dishes.* **2** *v.* to remove dirt, stains, paint, etc., by or as if by scrubbing with soap and water: *Can you wash that spot out?* **3** *v.* to wash yourself: *I washed before eating dinner.* **4** *v.* to wash clothes: *I have to wash today.* **5** *n.* act of washing or condition of being washed: *This floor needs a good wash.* **6** *n.* quantity of clothes washed or to be washed: *Take the wash from the dryer.* **7** *v.* to undergo washing without damage: *That cloth washes well.* **8** *v.* to carry or be carried along or away by water or other liquid: *Wood is often washed ashore by the waves.* **9** *n.* material carried along by moving water and then deposited as sediment. A delta is formed by the wash of a river. **10** *v.* to wear by water or any liquid: *The cliffs are being washed away by the waves.* **11** *v.* to flow or beat with a lapping sound: *The waves washed upon the rocks.* **12** *n.* motion, rush, or sound of water: *We listened to the wash of the waves against the boat.* **13** *n.* liquid for a special use: *an eye wash.* **14** *n.* a thin coating of color or metal. **15** *v.* to cover with a thin coating of color or of metal: *silver washed with gold.* **16** *v.* to sift earth, ore, etc., by action of water to separate. **17** *n.* the rough or broken water left behind a moving ship. **18** *n.* disturbance in air made by an airplane or any of its parts. ❑ *n., pl.* **wash·es** for 5,13,14.

wash down, **1** to wash from top to bottom or from end to end: *wash down the walls of a kitchen.* **2** to drink some liquid along with or after solid food to help in swallowing.

wash out, **1** to remove by or as if by water. **2** to fail and be released from a school or course of study; flunk out.

wash up, to wash your hands and face.

Wash., the state of Washington.

wash·a·ble (wäsh′ə bəl), *adj.* able to be washed without damage: *washable fabrics.*

Wash·a·kie (wäsh′ə kē), *n.* 1804?-1900, a leader of the Shoshoni Indians. He aided settlers traveling west over the Oregon Trail and sent scouts to help U.S. soldiers against the Sioux who defeated Custer.

wash-and-wear (wäsh′ən wâr′), *adj.* specially treated to require little or no ironing after washing and drying: *wash-and-wear fabrics.*

wash·ba·sin (wäsh′bā′sn), *n.* washbowl.

wash·board (wäsh′bôrd′), *n.* a board with ridges on it, formerly used for rubbing the dirt out of clothes.

wash·bowl (wäsh′bōl′), *n.* bowl for holding water to wash your hands and face; washbasin.

wash·cloth (wäsh′klôth′), *n.* a small cloth for washing yourself. ❑ *n., pl.* **wash·cloths** (wäsh′klôᴛʜz′ *or* wäsh′klôths′).

washed-out (wäsht′out′), *adj.* **1** lacking color; faded. **2** lacking life, spirit, etc.

washed-up (wäsht′up′), *adj.* INFORMAL. at the end of your career; through, especially after having failed: *Washed-up as a writer after two bad books, he became a respectable teacher.*

wash·er (wäsh′ər), *n.* **1** machine that washes. **2** a flat ring of metal, rubber, leather, etc., used to provide tightness or to avoid friction at joints, especially with nuts and bolts. **3** person who washes.

wash·ing (wäsh′ing), *n.* **1** clothes, etc., washed or to be washed: *send washing to the laundry.* **2** act of cleaning with water.

washing machine, machine that washes clothes.

Wash·ing·ton (wäsh′ing tən), *n.* **1 Book·er T.** (búk′ər), 1856-1915, American writer and educator. Born in slavery, he worked for the economic and social advancement of African Americans. **2 George,** 1732-1799, commander in chief of the American army in the Revolutionary War and the first president of the United States, from 1789 to 1797. **3 Mar·tha** (mär′thə), 1731-1802, wife of George Washington. **4** capital of the United States, covering the entire District of Columbia. Washington is situated along the Potomac River between Maryland and Virginia. **5** one of the Pacific states of the United States. *Abbreviation:* WA or Wash. *Capital:* Olympia. [The city and state of **Washington** were named for George Washington, the first president of the United States.] **—Wash·ing·to·ni·an** (wäsh′ing tō′nē ən), *n.*

Washington's Birthday, **1** February 22, the anniversary of George Washington's birthday. **2** Presidents' Day.

wash·out (wäsh′out′), *n.* **1** act of washing away earth, a road, etc., by water. **2** the hole caused by this. **3** failure; disappointment: *The party was a complete washout.*

wash·rag (wäsh′rag′), *n.* washcloth.

wash·room (wäsh′rüm′), *n.* room where toilet facilities are provided; lavatory.

wash·stand (wäsh′stand′), *n.* **1** bowl with pipes and faucets for running water to wash your hands and face. **2** stand for holding a basin, pitcher, etc., for washing.

wash·tub (wäsh′tub′), *n.* tub used to wash or soak clothes in.

was·n't (wuz′nt *or* wäz′nt), was not.

wasp (wäsp), *n.* any of a great many insects related to the ants and the bees, with slender bodies, two pairs of wings, and powerful stings. Hornets and yellow jackets are kinds of wasps. **—wasp′like′,** *adj.*

WASP (wäsp), *n.* a white Anglo-Saxon Protestant. ■ **WASP** is often considered offensive.

wasp·ish (wäs′pish), *adj.* **1** like a wasp; like that of a wasp. **2** bad-tempered; irritable: *a waspish reply.* **—wasp′ish·ly,** *adv.* **—wasp′ish·ness,** *n.*

was·sail (wäs′əl), **1** *n.* a drinking party; revelry with drinking of healths. **2** *v.* to take part in a wassail; revel. **3** *n.* spiced ale or other liquor drunk at a wassail. **4** *v.* to drink to the health of.

wast (wäst *or* wəst), *v.* OLD USE. were. "Thou wast" means "you were."

wast·age (wā′stij), *n.* **1** loss by use, wear, decay, leakage, etc.; waste. **2** amount wasted.

waste (wāst), **1** *v.* to make poor use of; spend uselessly; fail to get full value or benefit from: *Though I had much work to do, I wasted my time doing nothing.* **2** *n.* poor use; useless spending; failure to get the most out of something: *Buying that suit was a waste of money; it is already starting to wear out.* **3** *adj.* thrown away as useless or worthless: *waste products, a pile of waste lumber.* **4** *n.* useless or worthless material; stuff to be thrown away; refuse: *Garbage or sewage is waste.* **5** *n.* material which the body gets rid of because it cannot be digested or used. **6** *adj.* carrying off or holding refuse: *a waste pipe.* **7** *adj.* left over; not used: *waste food.* **8** *n.* bare or wild land; desert; wilderness: *We traveled through treeless wastes.* **9** *adj.* not cultivated; like a desert or wilderness; bare; wild. **10** *v.* to wear down little by lit-

tle; destroy or lose gradually: *The patient was wasted by disease.*
11 *v.* to become weak or thin, especially because of disease: *to waste away.* **12** *v.* to damage greatly; destroy; spoil; ruin: *The soldiers wasted the enemy's fields.* ❑ *v.* **wast·ed, wast·ing.** [See Word Story at **vast.**] ■ Another word that sounds like this is **waist.**

go to waste, be wasted.

lay waste, to damage greatly; destroy; ravage.

waste·bas·ket (wāst′bas′kit), *n.* basket or other container for wastepaper or other trash.

waste·ful (wāst′fəl), *adj.* using or spending too much: *be wasteful of water.* **—waste′ful·ly,** *adv.* **—waste′ful·ness,** *n.*

waste·land (wāst′land′), *n.* barren, uncultivated land.

waste·pa·per (wāst′pā′pər), *n.* paper thrown away or to be thrown away as useless or worthless.

was·trel (wā′strəl), *n.* **1** spendthrift. **2** good-for-nothing.

watch (wäch), **1** *v.* to look attentively or carefully: *The medical students watched while the surgeon performed the operation.* **2** *v.* to look at; observe; view: *Let's watch TV.* **3** *v.* to look or wait with care and attention; be very careful: *I watched for a chance to cross the street.* **4** *n.* device for telling time, small enough to be carried in a pocket or worn on the wrist. **5** *n.* act of careful looking; attitude of attention: *a tornado watch.* **6** *v.* to keep guard: *The sentry watched throughout the night.* **7** *v.* to keep guard over: *The police watched the prisoner.* **8** *n.* person or persons kept to guard and protect: *A call for help aroused the night watch.* **9** *n.* period of time for guarding: *a watch in the night.* **10** *n.* the time of duty of one part of a ship's crew. A watch usually lasts four hours. **11** *n.* the part of a ship's crew on duty at the same time. ❑ *n., pl.* **watch·es.** **—watch′er,** *n.*

watch out, be careful; be on guard: *Watch out for cars!*

watch·band (wäch′band′), *n.* a strip of leather, metal, or plastic to fasten a watch on a wrist.

watch·dog (wäch′dȯg′), *n.* **1** dog kept to guard property. **2** a watchful guardian: *a watchdog of public spending.*

watch·ful (wäch′fəl), *adj.* watching carefully; on the lookout; wide-awake: *You should always be watchful for cars when you cross the street.* **—watch′ful·ly,** *adv.* **—watch′ful·ness,** *n.*

watch·mak·er (wäch′mā′kər), *n.* person who makes and repairs watches.

watch·man (wäch′mən), *n.* person who keeps watch; guard. ❑ *n., pl.* **watch·men.**

watch·tow·er (wäch′tou′ər), *n.* tower from which a watch is kept for enemies, fires, ships, etc.

watch·word (wäch′werd′), *n.* **1** password: *Tonight's watchword is "turnip."* **2** motto; slogan: *"Forward" is our watchword.*

wa·ter (wȯ′tər), **1** *n.* the liquid that fills the oceans, rivers, lakes, and ponds, and falls from the sky as rain. Pure water is a colorless, tasteless, and odorless compound of hydrogen and oxygen. It freezes at 32 degrees Fahrenheit (0 degrees Celsius) and boils at 212 degrees Fahrenheit (100 degrees Celsius). **2** *n.* a liquid like water, occurring in or discharged from the body, such as tears, sweat, saliva, urine, serum, etc. **3** *n.* any liquid preparation that suggests water: *lavender water.* **4** *n.* body of water; sea, lake, river, etc.: *cross the water on a ferry.* **5** *v.* to sprinkle or wet with water: *water a lawn.* **6** *v.* to give water to; supply with water: *After the ride, we fed and watered the horses.* **7** *v.* to weaken by adding water: *It is against the law to sell milk that has been watered.* **8** *v.* to fill with water; discharge water: *Her eyes watered. The cake made my mouth water.* **9** *adj.* holding, storing, or conveying water: *a water jug, a water pipe, a water system.* **10** *adj.* done or used in or on water: *water sports.* **11** *adj.* growing or living in or near water: *water plants.* **12** *n.pl.* **waters,** a flowing water. **b** water moving in waves; the sea; the high sea. **c** mineral water. **—wa′ter·er,** *n.*

by water, on a ship or boat: *travel by water.*

hold water, to stand the test; be true, dependable, effective, etc.

keep your head above water, to stay out of trouble or difficulty, especially out of financial trouble or difficulty.

make your mouth water, to stir up your appetite or desire.

throw cold water on, to discourage: *My parents threw cold water on my plan to camp alone in the woods.*

tread water, to keep yourself from sinking by moving your feet up and down.

water down, 1 to reduce the strength of something by adding water to it. **2** to reduce the strength or effectiveness of a proposal, law, etc.

wa·ter·bed (wȯ′tər bed′), *n.* bed with a mattress consisting of a vinyl bag filled with water.

water bird, bird that swims or wades in water.

wa·ter·borne (wȯ′tər bôrn′), *adj.* **1** carried by a boat, ship, etc.; transported by water. **2** held up by water; floating.

wa·ter·buck (wȯ′tər buk′), *n.* an African antelope often found near rivers, marshes, etc. ❑ *n., pl.* **wa·ter·buck** or **wa·ter·bucks.**

water buffalo, any of several buffalo of Asia, commonly used in farming and to pull loads.

water bug, 1 Croton bug. **2** any of various insects that live in, on, or near water.

Wa·ter·bur·y (wȯ′tər ber′ē), *n.* city in W central Connecticut.

water chestnut, a kind of water plant with a nutlike fruit containing a single large seed that is eaten with vegetables.

water clock, device for measuring time by the dripping or flow of water.

water closet, toilet flushed by water.

wa·ter·col·or (wȯ′tər kul′ər), *n.* **1** paint mixed with water instead of oil. **2** art of painting with watercolors. **3** picture made with watercolors.

water cooler, any device for cooling water, or for cooling something by means of water.

wa·ter·course (wȯ′tər kôrs′), *n.* **1** stream of water; river; brook. **2** channel or bed of a stream of water: *In the summer many watercourses dry up.*

wa·ter·craft (wȯ′tər kraft′), *n.* **1** ship or ships; boat or boats. **2** skill with a boat or ship.

wa·ter·cress (wȯ′tər kres′), *n.* plant that grows in water and has crisp leaves which are used for salad and as a garnish.

water cycle, cycle in nature by which water evaporates from lakes and oceans, condenses in the atmosphere, falls as rain or snow, and flows back into lakes and oceans.

wa·ter·fall (wȯ′tər fȯl′), *n.* fall of water from a high place; cascade or cataract.

waterfall

W

wa·ter·fowl (wȯ′tər foul′), *n.* a water bird, especially one that swims. ❑ *n., pl.* **wa·ter·fowl** or **wa·ter·fowls.**

wa·ter·front (wȯ′tər frunt′), *n.* land at the water's edge, especially the part of a city beside a river, lake, or harbor.

water gap, opening in a mountain ridge through which a stream flows.

Wa·ter·gate (wȯ′tər gāt), *n.* a political scandal involving the 1972 presidential campaign of Richard M. Nixon. It caused President Nixon's resignation in 1974, and resulted in prison terms for many of his aides. [See word history information at **-gate.**]

water hole, hole in the ground where water collects; small pond; pool.

water hyacinth, a water plant with purple or blue flowers and oval leaves, found in tropical South America and grown elsewhere. In Florida and Louisiana, it has become a problem because it grows thickly and interferes with travel by boat.

watering place, 1 resort with springs of mineral water. **2** place where water may be obtained.

wa·ter·less (wȯ′tər lis), *adj.* **1** containing little or no water. **2** needing no water: *waterless cooking.*

water level, the surface level of a body of water: *The water level of the pond rose after the heavy rains.*

water lily, any of several water plants with flat, floating leaves and showy, fragrant flowers. The flowers of the common American water lily are white, or sometimes pink.

wa·ter·line (wȯ′tər lin′), *n.* **1** line where the surface of the water touches the side of a ship or boat. **2** any of several lines marked on a ship's hull to show the depth to which it sinks when unloaded, partly loaded, or fully loaded.

wa·ter·logged (wȯ′tər lȯgd′), *adj.* so full of water that it will barely float.

Wa·ter·loo (wȯ′tər lü), *n.* **1** small town in Belgium, near Brussels, the site of the battle in which Napoleon I was finally defeated in 1815. **2** any decisive or crushing defeat. ❑ *n., pl.* **Wa·ter·loos** for 2.

water main, a large or main pipe for carrying water.

wa·ter·mark (wȯ′tər märk′), *n.* **1** a mark showing how high water has risen or how low it has fallen: *the high watermark of a river.* **2** a faint distinguishing design made in some kinds of paper.

wa·ter·mel·on (wȯ′tər mel′ən), *n.* a large, juicy melon with red, pink, or yellow pulp and a hard, green rind. It grows on a vine.

water moccasin, a large, poisonous snake of the southern United States that lives in swamps and along streams; cottonmouth.

water pistol, a toy pistol that shoots water; squirt gun.

water polo, game played in a swimming pool by two teams of seven swimmers who try to throw or push an inflated ball into the opponent's goal.

wa·ter·pow·er (wȯ′tər pou′ər), *n.* the power from flowing or falling water. It can be used to drive machinery and generate electricity.

wa·ter·proof (wȯ′tər prüf′), **1** *adj.* able to keep water from coming through; resistant to water: *An umbrella should be waterproof.* **2** *v.* to make waterproof: *These hiking shoes have been waterproofed.*

water rat, 1 any rodent that lives on the banks of streams or lakes. **2** muskrat.

wa·ter·re·pel·lent (wȯ′tər ri pel′ənt), *adj.* able to keep out moisture but not entirely waterproof.

wa·ter·shed (wȯ′tər shed′), *n.* **1** ridge between the regions drained by two different river systems; height of land. On one side of a watershed, rivers and streams flow in one direction; on the other side, they flow in another direction. **2** the region drained by one river system.

water ski, one of a pair of skis for gliding over water while being towed at the end of a rope by a motorboat.

wa·ter·ski (wȯ′tər skē′), *v.* to glide over the water on water skis. ❑ *v.* **wa·ter·skied, wa·ter·ski·ing.** **—wa′ter·ski′er,** *n.*

water snake, any of several nonpoisonous snakes living in or around water.

water softener, any chemical substance added to water to remove dissolved minerals that prevent soap from forming suds.

wa·ter·spout (wȯ′tər spout′), *n.* **1** a rapidly spinning column or cone of mist, spray, and water, produced by the action of a whirlwind over the ocean or a lake. **2** pipe that drains water from a roof.

water strider, any of several bugs with long, slender legs, able to walk across the surfaces of ponds and streams.

water table, the level below which the ground is soaked with water.

wa·ter·tight (wȯ′tər tit′), *adj.* **1** so tight that no water can get in or out. Large ships are often divided into watertight compartments by watertight partitions. **2** leaving no opening for misunderstanding, criticism, etc.; perfect: *a watertight argument.*

water tower, 1 structure for the storage of water, tall enough to provide pressure for a water system. **2** fire-fighting equipment used to spray water on the upper parts of tall buildings.

water vapor, water in a gaseous state and below boiling temperature, as distinct from steam.

wa·ter·way (wȯ′tər wā′), *n.* **1** river, canal, or other water that ships can travel. **2** channel for water.

wa·ter·wheel (wȯ′tər wēl′), *n.* wheel turned by water and used to drive machinery. The grindstones of grain mills used to be run by waterwheels.

water wings, two waterproof bags filled with air, put under your arms to hold you afloat while you are learning to swim.

wa·ter·works (wȯ′tər wėrks′), **1** *n.pl.* system of pipes, reservoirs, pumps, etc., for supplying a city or town with water. **2** *n.sing.* building with machinery for pumping water.

wa·ter·y (wȯ′tər ē), *adj.* **1** full of tears; tearful: *watery eyes.* **2** containing too much water: *watery soup.* **3** of water; like water: *A blister is filled with watery fluid.* **4** weak; thin; poor; pale: *a watery blue.* **5** full of water; wet: *watery soil.* **—wa′ter·i·ness,** *n.*

Wat·son (wät′sən), *n.* James, born 1928, American biologist. ■ **James Watson** shared the 1962 Nobel Prize in physiology or medicine with Francis Crick and Maurice Wilkins for creating the double helix model of DNA.

watt (wät), *n.* unit for measuring electrical power, equal to the amount done by a current of one ampere moved by a force of one volt: *My lamp uses a 60-watt bulb.*

WORD STORY The **watt** was named for James Watt. It may seem odd that an electrical unit is named for a steam inventor, but the link is power. Steam engines provided power for most machinery until electrical motors became common. Scientists studying power thought of Watt as a past master.

Watt (wät), *n.* James, 1736-1819, Scottish engineer and inventor who perfected the steam engine.

watt·age (wät′ij), *n.* any amount of electrical power measured in watts, especially in kilowatts.

watt-hour (wät′our′), *n.* unit for measuring electrical energy, equal to the work done by one watt in one hour.

water-skiing

wat·tle¹ (wät′l), **1** *n.* Also, **wattles,** *pl.* sticks interwoven with twigs or branches; framework of wicker: *a hut built of wattle.* **2** *v.* to twist or weave together twigs, branches, etc. ❑ *v.* **wat·tled, wat·tling.**

wat·tle² (wät′l), *n.* the red flesh hanging down from the throat of a chicken, turkey, etc.

Watts (wäts), *n.* district of Los Angeles. In 1965, African Americans rioted here for five days, with loss of life and much property damage.

wave (wāv), **1** *n.* a moving ridge or swell of water: *The raft rose and fell on the waves.* **2** *n.* any movement like this, especially a movement by which energy is transferred from one place to another. Light, heat, and sound travel in waves. Waves are usually measured by their length, amplitude, velocity, and frequency. **3** *n.* a swell or sudden increase in some condition, emotion, etc.; flood or rush of anything: *A wave of cold weather is sweeping over the country.* **4** *v.* to move as waves do; move up and down or back and forth; sway: *The tall grass waved in the breeze.* **5** *v.* to cause to move or sway back and forth or up and down: *wave a flag. Wave your hand.* **6** *v.* to signal or direct by moving the hand or an object back and forth: *The stranded motorist waved a passing driver to the side of the road.* **7** *n.* act of waving: *a wave of the hand.* **8** *n.* a curve or series of curves: *waves in a person's hair.* **9** *v.* to have a wavelike form: *Her hair waves naturally.* **10** *v.* to give a wavelike form to: *wave your hair.* ❑ *v.* **waved, wav·ing.** ■ Another word that sounds like this is **waive.** —**wave′like′,** *adj.*

WAVE or **Wave** (wāv), *n.* formerly, woman in the U.S. Navy other than a nurse. ❑ *n., pl.* **WAVEs** or **Waves.**

wave·length (wāv′lengkth′ *or* wāv′length′), *n.* distance between a point on one wave of water, light, sound, etc., and the point in the same position on the next wave.

wave·let (wāv′lit), *n.* a little wave.

wa·ver (wā′vər), **1** *v.* to be undecided; hesitate: *We are still wavering between a picnic and a trip to the zoo.* **2** *v.* to become unsteady; begin to give way: *His determination began to waver.* **3** *v.* to move back and forth, especially in an unsteady way; flutter: *Butterflies hovered and wavered among the flower blossoms.* **4** *v.* to vary in intensity; flicker: *a wavering light.* **5** *n.* act of wavering. ■ Another word that sounds like this is **waiver.** —**wa′ver·er,** *n.* —**wa′ver·ing·ly,** *adv.*

wav·y (wā′vē), *adj.* having waves or curves: *wavy hair, a wavy line.* ❑ *adj.* **wav·i·er, wav·i·est.** —**wav′i·ness,** *n.*

wax¹ (waks), **1** *n.* a yellowish substance made by bees for constructing their honeycomb. Wax is hard when cold, but can be easily shaped when warm. **2** *n.* any substance like this. Most of the wax used for candles, for keeping air from jelly, etc., is really paraffin. **3** *n.* substance containing wax for polishing floors, furniture, cars, or the like. **4** *v.* to rub, stiffen, polish, etc., with wax or something like wax: *We wax the floor once a month.* ❑ *n., pl.* **wax·es** for 2,3. —**wax′like′,** *adj.*

wax² (waks), *v.* **1** (of the moon) to go through its regular increase in the amount of its visible portion. The moon waxes when the side facing the earth moves gradually into the sun's light. **2** to become: *The party waxed merry.*

wax bean, a yellow string bean.

waxed paper, wax paper.

wax·en (wak′sən), *adj.* **1** made of wax. **2** like wax; smooth, soft, and pale: *Her skin was waxen.*

wax myrtle, bush or tree of eastern North America, related to the bayberry, with small berries coated with wax.

wax paper, paper coated with paraffin.

wax·wing (waks′wing′), *n.* any of several small birds with a crest, grayish brown feathers, and red markings at the tips of the wings. Two kinds are found in North America, the **cedar waxwing** and the **Bohemian waxwing.**

wax·works (waks′wėrks′), *n.* an exhibition of figures made of wax. ❑ *n., pl.* **wax·works.**

wax·y (wak′sē), *adj.* **1** like wax: *The floor had a smooth, waxy surface.* **2** made of wax; containing wax: *a waxy solution.* ❑ *adj.* **wax·i·er, wax·i·est.** —**wax′i·ness,** *n.*

way (wā), **1** *n.* form or mode of doing; manner; style: *a new way of wearing your hair.* **2** *n.* method; means: *Scientists are finding new ways of preventing disease.* **3** *n.* point; feature; respect; detail: *His plan is bad in several ways.* **4** *n.* direction: *Look this way.* **5** *n.* act of coming or going; moving along a course: *Our guide led the way through the museum.* **6** *n.* distance: *The sun is a long way off.* **7** *n.* path; road; means of moving along a course: *The children found a way through the forest.* **8** *n.* space for passing or going ahead: *Please clear a way for us to get through.* **9** *n.* habit; custom: *She's always on time; it's her way.* **10** *n.* one's wish; will: *Just once I'd like to have my own way.* **11** *n.* condition; state: *The patient was in a bad way.* **12** *n.* district; area; region: *They live out our way.* **13** *adv.* at or to a great distance; far: *The cloud of smoke stretched way out to the pier.* ■ Other words that sound like this are **weigh** and **whey.**

by the way, in that connection; incidentally: *By the way, the school library has several interesting new books.*

by way of, 1 by the route of; through. **2** as; for: *By way of an answer he just nodded.*

give way, 1 to make way; retreat; yield. **2** to break down or fall: *The old bridge gave way.* **3** to abandon yourself to emotion: *give way to despair.*

go out of your way, to make a special effort to do something.

have a way with, to have a natural ability with: *She has a way with animals.*

in a way, to a certain extent.

in the way, being an obstacle, hindrance, etc.

lead the way, 1 to go ahead as a guide. **2** to be the first and most successful: *to lead the way in computer education.*

make way, to give space for passing or going ahead; make room: *Cars must make way for a fire engine.*

make your way, 1 to go. **2** to get ahead; succeed.

out of the way, 1 so as not to be an obstacle, hindrance, etc. **2** far from where most people live or go. **3** unusual; strange. **4** not as it should be; worrisome; wrong: *We knew something was out of the way when no one opened the store.*

see your way, to be willing or able.

under way, going on; in motion; in progress: *The ship is under way.*

SYNONYM STUDY **Way, system,** and **method** all mean how something is done. **Way** is a general word: *One way to succeed is through hard work.* **System** means an orderly, logical way of getting things done: *There are two main systems of organizing library books.* **Method** suggests a careful step-by-step action: *His method of cleaning his room is: dust, vacuum, sponge, replace.*

---

way·far·er (wā′fâr′ər), *n.* traveler, especially someone who travels on foot.

way·far·ing (wā′fâr′ing), *adj.* traveling.

way·laid (wā′lād′), *v.* past tense and past participle of **waylay:** *I waylaid her when she entered the meeting.*

way·lay (wā′lā′), *v.* **1** to lie in wait for and attack someone: *Bandits waylaid travelers and robbed them.* **2** to stop a person going somewhere: *Newspaper reporters waylaid the mayor and asked many questions.* ❑ *v.* **way·laid, way·lay·ing.** —**way′lay′er,** *n.*

Wayne (wān), *n.* **John,** 1907-1979, American movie star. He won an Academy Award as Best Actor for the movie *True Grit* in 1969.

way-out (wā′out′), *adj.* INFORMAL. far-out.

-ways, *suffix.* in the direction or position of the ___: *lengthways* = in the direction of the length.

way·side (wā′sīd′), **1** *adj.* along the edge of a road or path: *a wayside inn.* **2** *n.* edge of a road or path: *park on the wayside.*

way station, station between main stations on a railroad or bus line.

way·ward (wā′wərd), *adj.* **1** difficult to control; disobedient; willful: *The wayward student never did any homework.* **2** irregular; unsteady. —**way′ward·ly,** *adv.* —**way′ward·ness,** *n.*

we (wē), *pron.pl.* **1** the persons speaking: *We are glad to see you.* **2** the person speaking. An author, a ruler, or a judge sometimes uses *we* to mean *I.* ■ Another word that sounds like this is **wee.**

weak (wēk), *adj.* **1** lacking bodily strength: *He was too weak to lift the chair.* **2** easily broken or torn: *My foot went through a*

W

a	hat	ė	term	ô	order	ch	child		
ā	age	i	it	oi	oil	ng	long	ə	a in about
ä	far	ī	ice	ou	out	sh	she		e in taken
â	care	o	hot	u	cup	th	thin		i in pencil
e	let	ō	open	u̇	put	ŧн	then		o in lemon
ē	equal	ȯ	saw	ü	rule	zh	measure		u in circus

weak board in the floor. **3** lacking great mental force; easily influenced: *A person with a weak character is easily influenced by others.* **4** lacking force or effectiveness: *a weak law.* **5** not having much of a particular quality: *Weak tea has less flavor than strong tea.* **6** lacking or poor in something specified: *She is still a little weak in spelling.* [**Weak** comes from a Norse word meaning "easy to bend." A weak person bends easily to another person's will.] ■ Another word that sounds like this is **week**.

weak·en (wē′kən), *v.* to make or become weak or weaker: *You can weaken tea by adding water. We are almost to the top of the mountain; let's not weaken now.*

weak·fish (wēk′fish′), *n.* any of four kinds of Atlantic saltwater food fishes with tender mouths and fins supported by sharp stiff spines. □ *n., pl.* **weak·fish** or **weak·fish·es.**

weak·ling (wēk′ling), *n.* a weak person or animal.

weak·ly (wēk′lē), **1** *adv.* in a weak manner. **2** *adj.* weak; feeble; sickly. □ *adj.* **weak·li·er, weak·li·est.** ■ Another word that sounds like this is **weekly.**

weak-mind·ed (wēk′mīn′did), *adj.* **1** having or showing little intelligence; feeble-minded. ■ This meaning of **weak-minded** is often considered offensive. **2** lacking firmness of mind. —**weak′mind′ed·ness,** *n.*

weak·ness (wēk′nis), *n.* **1** condition of being weak; lack of power, force, or vigor: *Weakness kept him in bed.* **2** a weak point; slight fault: *Putting things off is her weakness.* **3** a fondness or liking: *a weakness for sweets.* □ *n., pl.* **weak·ness·es** for 2,3.

wealth (welth), *n.* **1** many valuable possessions; property; riches: *people of wealth, the wealth of a city.* **2** all things that have money value; resources: *The wealth of our country includes its mines and forests as well as its factories.* **3** a large quantity; abundance: *a wealth of words.*

wealth·y (wel′thē), *adj.* **1** having wealth; rich: *a wealthy family.* ■ See Synonym Study at **rich. 2** having a lot of; richly supplied with: *a region wealthy in natural resources.* □ *adj.* **wealth·i·er, wealth·i·est.** —**wealth′i·ly,** *adv.* —**wealth′i·ness,** *n.*

wean (wēn), *v.* **1** to accustom (a child or young animal) to food other than its mother's milk. **2** to accustom someone to do without something; cause to turn away: *wean someone from a bad habit.*

weap·on (wep′ən), *n.* **1** any object or tool used to injure, disable, or kill. Swords, spears, arrows, clubs, guns, knives, artillery, and rockets are weapons. Animals use claws, horns, teeth, and stings as weapons. **2** any means of attack or defense: *Drugs are effective weapons against many diseases.* —**weap′on·less,** *adj.*

wear (wâr), **1** *v.* to have on the body: *wear a coat, wear a beard, wear black, wear a ring.* **2** *v.* to have or show: *The empty old house wore an air of sadness.* **3** *n.* act of wearing or condition of being worn: *Clothing for summer wear is being shown in stores.* **4** *n.* things worn or to be worn; clothing: *The store sells children's wear.* **5** *v.* to last long; give good service: *This material wears well.* **6** *n.* lasting quality; good service: *There is still much wear in these shoes.* **7** *v.* to use up; be used up: *The pencil is worn to a stub.* **8** *v.* to damage or become damaged by use, weather, etc.: *The waves are wearing the beach away.* **9** *n.* damage from use, exposure, etc.: *The rug shows wear.* **10** *v.* to make by rubbing, scraping, washing away, etc.: *Walking wore a hole in my shoe.* **11** *v.* to tire; weary: *They were worn with toil and care.* **12** *v.* to pass or go gradually: *It became hotter as the day wore on.* □ *v.* **wore, worn, wear·ing.** ■ Other words that sound like this are **ware** and **where.** —**wear′a·ble,** *adj.* —**wear′er,** *n.*

wear and tear, damage or loss caused by use.

wear down, 1 to overcome by persistent effort. **2** to reduce in height. **3** to reduce or wear away by use, exposure, etc.

wear off, to become less, slowly and gradually: *The excitement of playing with the new toys soon wore off.*

wear out, 1 to wear or use until no longer fit for use. **2** to tire out; weary: *She was worn out by too much work.*

wear·ing (wâr′ing), *adj.* exhausting; tiring: *a very wearing trip.*

wear·i·some (wir′ē səm), *adj.* wearying; tiring; tiresome: *a wearisome tale.*

wear·y (wir′ē), **1** *adj.* worn out; tired: *weary feet, a weary brain.* **2** *adj.* causing tiredness; tiring: *a weary wait.* **3** *adj.* having your

patience, tolerance, or liking exhausted: *weary of endless speeches.* **4** *v.* to make or become tired: *Walking all day wearied the sightseers.* □ *adj.* **wear·i·er, wear·i·est;** *v.* **wear·ied, wear·y·ing.** —**wear′i·ly,** *adv.* —**wear′i·ness,** *n.*

wea·sel (wē′zəl), *n.* **1** any of several small, flesh-eating mammals related to minks and skunks, with long, slender, furry bodies and short legs. Weasels are very quick and have keen sight and smell. **2** a cunning, sneaky person. —**wea′sel·like′,** *adj.*

weasel word, word lacking force or exact meaning, used to avoid making a clear statement; word with more than one possible meaning or with no specific meaning. In "Certain concerns led the mayor to resign suddenly," *certain concerns* are weasel words.

weath·er (weṮH′ər), **1** *n.* condition of the atmosphere with respect to temperature, moisture, wind, cloudiness, etc.: *hot weather. The weather is very windy today in Chicago.* **2** *n.* windy, rainy, or stormy weather: *damage done by the weather.* **3** *v.* to expose to the weather; wear or discolor by sun, rain, frost, etc.: *Wood turns gray if weathered for a long time.* **4** *v.* to become discolored or worn by air, rain, sun, frost, etc. **5** *v.* to go or come through safely: *The ship weathered the storm.* ■ Another word that sounds like this is **whether.**

weather (def. 4)
weathered wood

under the weather, sick; ailing.

weath·er-beat·en (weṮH′ər bēt′n), *adj.* worn or hardened by the wind, rain, and other forces of the weather: *a seaman's weather-beaten face, a weather-beaten barn.*

weath·er·cock (weṮH′ər kok′), *n.* vane to show which way the wind is blowing, especially one in the shape of a rooster.

weath·er·ing (weṮH′ər ing), *n.* destructive or discoloring action of air, water, frost, etc., especially on rocks.

weath·er·man (weṮH′ər man′), *n.* person who forecasts the weather, especially on TV. □ *n., pl.* **weath·er·men.**

weath·er·proof (weṮH′ər prüf′), **1** *adj.* protected against rain, snow, or wind; able to stand exposure to all kinds of weather. **2** *v.* to protect something from rain, snow, or wind.

weather strip, a narrow strip of cloth or metal to fill or cover the space between the door or window and the casing, so as to keep out rain, snow, and wind.

weather stripping, a weather strip or weather strips: *keep the cold out with weather stripping.*

weather vane, vane (def. 1).

weave (wēv), **1** *v.* to form threads or strips into an object or fabric. People weave thread into cloth, straw into hats, and reeds into baskets. **2** *v.* to make out of thread, strips, or strands of the same material. A spider weaves a web. *She is weaving a rug.* **3** *v.* to work with a loom. **4** *n.* method or pattern of weaving: *Homespun is a cloth of coarse weave.* **5** *v.* to combine into a whole: *The author wove three plots together into one story.* **6** *v.* to make by combining parts: *The author wove a story from three plots.* **7** *v.* to go by twisting and turning; move with a rocking or swaying motion: *The car ahead was weaving in and out of traffic.* □ *v.* **wove** (or **weaved** for 7), **wo·ven** (or **weaved** for 7), **weav·ing.** ■ Another word that sounds like this is **we've.**

weav·er (wē′vər), *n.* **1** person who weaves. **2** person whose work is weaving.

web (web), *n.* **1** a net of very tiny silklike threads spun by a spider. **2** anything like a spiderweb, especially something that ensnares or entangles: *a web of lies.* **3** the skin joining the toes of swimming birds such as ducks and the toes of other water animals such as frogs and beavers. **4** a whole piece of cloth while being woven or after being taken from the loom. **5** Web, the World Wide Web. —**web′like′,** *adj*

webbed (webd), *adj.* **1** formed like a web or with a web. **2** having the toes joined by a web. Ducks have webbed feet.

web·bing (web'ing), *n.* **1** cloth woven into strong strips, used in upholstery and for belts. **2** skin joining the toes, as in a duck's feet.

web-foot·ed (web'füt'id), *adj.* having the toes joined by a web. Geese are web-footed birds.

web page or **Web page,** a World Wide Web document.

web site or **Web site,** **1** a place or an address on the Internet where a World Wide Web document can be found. **2** a World Wide Web document.

Web·ster (web'stər), *n.* **1 Daniel,** 1782-1852, American political leader and orator. He believed the United States should have a strong central government and spoke stirringly in support of that cause. **2 Noah,** 1758-1843, American author who wrote the first well-known American dictionary.

wed (wed), *v.* **1** to marry. **2** to unite. ❑ *v.* **wed·ded, wed·ded** or **wed, wed·ding.**

we'd (wēd), **1** we had. **2** we should. **3** we would. ■ Another word that sounds like this is **weed.**

Wed., Wednesday.

wed·ded (wed'id), *adj.* **1** married. **2** of marriage: *wedded bliss.* **3** united. **4** devoted.

wed·ding (wed'ing), *n.* **1** the marriage ceremony. **2** an anniversary of it. A golden wedding is the fiftieth anniversary of a marriage.

wedge (wej), **1** *n.* piece of wood or metal in the form of an inclined plane, thick at one end and tapering to a thin edge at the other, used in splitting logs, etc. It is a simple machine. **2** *n.* something shaped like a wedge: *a wedge of pie. Wild geese fly in a wedge.* **3** *n.* something that is used, or acts like, a wedge: *The quarrel drove a wedge between him and his relatives.* **4** *v.* to split or separate with a wedge: *He wedged the log apart with a sledge-hammer.* **5** *v.* to fasten or tighten with a wedge: *We wedged the door open with a piece of wood.* **6** *v.* to thrust or pack in tightly; squeeze: *He wedged himself through the window. The child's foot was wedged between the rocks.* **7** *v.* to force a way or opening: *wedge your way into a conversation.* ❑ *v.* **wedged, wedg·ing.**

wed·lock (wed'lok), *n.* married life; marriage.

Wednes·day (wenz'dē), *n.* the fourth day of the week, following Tuesday. [**Wednesday** is named for **Woden.**]

wee (wē), *adj.* very small; tiny: *the wee infant in the crib.* ❑ *adj.* **we·er, we·est.** [**Wee** comes from an old English word meaning "weight." It must have been a tiny weight, used to measure wee things.] ■ Another word that sounds like this is **we.**

weed (wēd), **1** *n.* any plant that tends to grow in great numbers where it is not wanted: *Weeds choked out the vegetables and flowers in the garden.* **2** *v.* to take weeds out of: *Please weed the garden now.* **3** *v.* to take out weeds. ■ Another word that sounds like this is **we'd.** —**weed'less,** *adj.* —**weed'like',** *adj.*

weed out, to remove because not wanted.

weed·er (wē'dər), *n.* **1** person who weeds. **2** tool or machine for digging up weeds.

weeds (wēdz), *n.pl.* black mourning garments: *a widow's weeds.*

weed·y (wē'dē), *adj.* **1** full of weeds: *a weedy garden.* **2** of or like weeds: *weedy growth.* **3** thin and lanky; weak. ❑ *adj.* **weed·i·er, weed·i·est.** —**weed'i·ness,** *n.*

wee hours, the early morning hours.

week (wēk), *n.* **1** seven days, one after another: *My mother has left on a business trip and will be gone a week.* **2** time from Sunday through Saturday: *I am away most of the week but come home on Sunday.* **3** the working days of a seven-day period: *A school week is usually five days.* ■ Another word that sounds like this is **weak.**

week·day (wēk'dā'), *n.* any day of the week except Sunday or (now often) Saturday.

week·end (wēk'end'), **1** *n.* Saturday and Sunday as a time for recreation, visiting, etc.: *We plan to spend this weekend in the country.* **2** *v.* to spend a weekend.

week·ly (wēk'lē), **1** *adj.* of or for a week; lasting a week: *a weekly wage of $400.* **2** *adj.* done, happening, or published once a week: *I subscribe to several weekly magazines.* **3** *adv.* once each week; every week: *I play tennis weekly.* **4** *n.* newspaper or magazine published once a week. ■ Another word that sounds like this is **weakly.** ❑ *n., pl.* **week·lies.**

ween·y (wē'nē), *adj.* INFORMAL. very small; little; tiny. ❑ *adj.* **ween·i·er, ween·i·est.**

weep (wēp), *v.* **1** to shed tears; cry: *They wept for joy when they won the award.* ■ See Synonym Study at **cry. 2** to show sorrow; grieve; mourn. **3** to let fall or flow in drops; shed: *weep bitter tears.* **4** to give off moisture, especially in drops; ooze. ❑ *v.* **wept, weep·ing.**

weeping willow, a large willow tree, with long, slender, drooping branches, originally from eastern Asia, widely grown in Europe and America.

wee·vil (wē'vəl), *n.* any of numerous small beetles that have long snouts and feed on plants. The larvae of weevils feed on and destroy grain, nuts, cotton, fruit, etc.

weevil

weft (weft), *n.* woof[1] (def. 1).

weigh (wā), *v.* **1** to have as a measure by weight: *I weigh 110 pounds.* **2** to find out how heavy a thing is: *weigh yourself, weigh a bag of potatoes.* **3** to measure by weight: *The grocer weighed out five pounds of potatoes.* **4** to bend by weight; burden: *The boughs of the apple tree are weighed down with fruit. They are weighed down with many troubles.* **5** to bear down; be a burden: *Don't let the mistake weigh on your mind.* **6** to have importance or influence; count: *Several factors weighed in the jury's decision to acquit.* **7** to balance in the mind; consider carefully: *weigh both sides of an argument.* ■ See Synonym Study at **consider. 8** to lift up an anchor: *The ship weighed anchor and sailed away.* ■ Other words that sound like this are **way** and **whey.**

weigh in, to find out your weight before a contest.

weight (wāt), **1** *n.* how heavy a thing is: the amount a thing weighs: *The dog's weight is 50 pounds.* **2** *n.* force with which an object is attracted to the earth or some other astronomical object. This force is felt as heaviness. *An astronaut who weighs 180 pounds on earth has a weight of only 30 pounds on the moon, because the moon attracts matter with only ⅙ as much force as the earth does.* **3** *n.* system of units for expressing weight: *avoirdupois weight.* See table on page 975A. **4** *n.* unit of such a system, such as a pound, or a kilogram. **5** *n.* piece of metal used in weighing things: *a pound weight.* **6** *n.* quantity that has a certain weight: *a half-ounce weight of gold dust.* **7** *n.* a heavy object used to hold something in place: *A weight keeps the papers in one place on his desk.* **8** *n.* load; burden: *The pillars support the weight of the roof. Your good news has taken a weight off my mind.* **9** *v.* to load down; burden: *to be weighted with troubles.* **10** *v.* to add weight to; put weight on: *They weighted the elevator too heavily.* **11** *n.* influence; importance; value: *the weight of public opinion.* ■ Another word that sounds like this is **wait.**

pull your weight, to do your part or share.

throw your weight around, to take advantage of your rank or position.

weight·less (wāt'lis), *adj.* **1** having little or no weight: *weightless snow.* **2** being free from the pull of gravity: *weightless travelers in space.* —**weight'less·ly,** *adv.* —**weight'less·ness,** *n.*

weight·lift·ing (wāt'lif'ting), *n.* act or sport of lifting weights to develop muscles or in competition. —**weight'lift'er,** *n.*

weight·y (wā'tē), *adj.* **1** important; serious: *This is indeed a weighty problem.* **2** too heavy; burdensome: *weighty responsibilities.* **3** heavy. ❑ *adj.* **weight·i·er, weight·i·est.** —**weight'i·ly,** *adv.* —**weight'i·ness,** *n.*

Wei·ma·ra·ner (vī'mə rä'nər *or* wī'mə rä'nər), *n.* a medium-sized gray dog with a clipped tail, first bred in Germany as a hunting dog.

a	hat	ė	term	ô	order	ch	child		
ā	age	i	it	oi	oil	ng	long		a in about
ä	far	ī	ice	ou	out	sh	she		e in taken
â	care	o	hot	u	cup	th	thin	ə	i in pencil
e	let	ō	open	ü	put	ᴛʜ	then		o in lemon
ē	equal	ȯ	saw	ü	rule	zh	measure		u in circus

W

Weights and Measures

Metric System

Linear Measure

1/1000 meter	=	1 millimeter
1/100 meter	=	1 centimeter
1/10 meter	=	1 decimeter
10 meters	=	1 decameter
100 meters	=	1 hectometer
1000 meters	=	1 kilometer

Square Measure

1 square centimeter	=	100 square millimeters
1 square meter	=	100 square decimeters
	=	10,000 square centimeters

Cubic Measure

1000 cubic centimeters	=	1 cubic decimeter
1000 cubic decimeters	=	1 cubic meter

Liquid and Dry Measure

1/1000 liter	=	1 milliliter
1/100 liter	=	1 centiliter
1/10 liter	=	1 deciliter
10 liters	=	1 decaliter
100 liters	=	1 hectoliter
1000 liters	=	1 kiloliter

Weight

1/1000 gram	=	1 milligram
1/100 gram	=	1 centigram
1/10 gram	=	1 decigram
10 grams	=	1 decagram
100 grams	=	1 hectogram
1000 grams	=	1 kilogram
1000 kilograms	=	1 metric ton

Customary System

Linear Measure

12 inches	=	1 foot
3 feet	=	1 yard
5 1/2 yards	=	1 rod
40 rods	=	1 furlong
8 furlongs	=	1 mile
1760 yards	=	1 mile
5280 feet	=	1 mile

Square Measure

144 square inches	=	1 square foot
9 square feet	=	1 square yard
30 1/4 square yards	=	1 square rod
160 square rods	=	1 acre
640 acres	=	1 square mile

Cubic Measure

1728 cubic inches	=	1 cubic foot
27 cubic feet	=	1 cubic yard

Liquid Measure

2 cups	=	1 pint
2 pints	=	1 quart
4 quarts	=	1 gallon

Dry Measure

2 pints	=	1 quart
8 quarts	=	1 peck
4 pecks	=	1 bushel

Weight

27 $^{11}/_{32}$ grains	=	1 dram
16 drams	=	1 ounce
16 ounces	=	1 pound
2000 pounds	=	1 short ton
2240 pounds	=	1 long ton

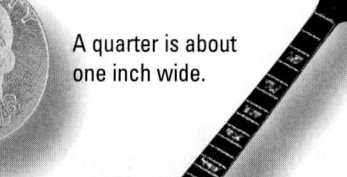

A quarter is about one inch wide.

A guitar is about one meter tall.

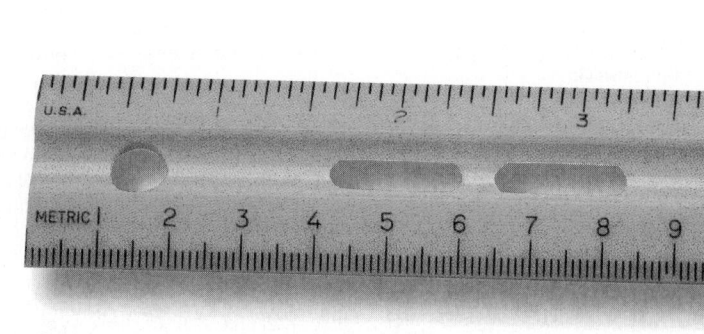

Metric Conversion Table

To Convert	To	Multiply By
Linear Measure		
centimeters	inches	0.394
meters	feet	3.281
meters	yards	1.0936
kilometers	miles	0.62
Linear Measure		
inches	centimeters	2.54
feet	meters	0.3048
yards	meters	0.914
miles	kilometers	1.609
Square Measure		
square centimeters	square inches	0.155
square meters	square feet	10.76
square meters	square yards	1.196
hectares	acres	2.471
square kilometers	square miles	0.386
Square Measure		
square inches	square centimeters	6.45
square feet	square meters	0.093
square yards	square meters	0.836
acres	hectares	0.405
square miles	square kilometers	2.59
Cubic Measure		
cubic centimeters	cubic inches	0.061
cubic meters	cubic yards	1.31
cubic meters	cubic feet	35.32
Cubic Measure		
cubic inches	cubic centimeters	16.387
cubic yards	cubic meters	0.7636
cubic feet	cubic meters	0.028
Liquid Measure		
milliliters	fluid ounces	0.0338
liters	fluid ounces	33.814
liters	quarts	1.057
liters	gallons	0.26

To Convert	To	Multiply By
Liquid Measure		
fluid ounces	milliliters	29.57
fluid ounces	liters	0.03
quarts	liters	0.946
gallons	liters	3.785
Dry Measure		
liters	dry quarts	0.908
liters	pecks	0.114
liters	bushels	0.028
Dry Measure		
dry quarts	liters	1.101
pecks	liters	8.810
bushels	liters	35.24
Weight		
grams	grains	15.43
grams	ounces	0.0353
kilograms	pounds	2.2046
kilograms	tons	0.001
metric tons	tons	1.102
Weight		
grains	grams	0.0648
ounces	grams	28.35
pounds	kilograms	0.4536
tons	kilograms	907.18
tons	metric tons	0.907
Temperature		
Celsius	Fahrenheit	1.8 then add 32
Temperature		
Fahrenheit	Celsius	subtract 32; then divide by 1.8

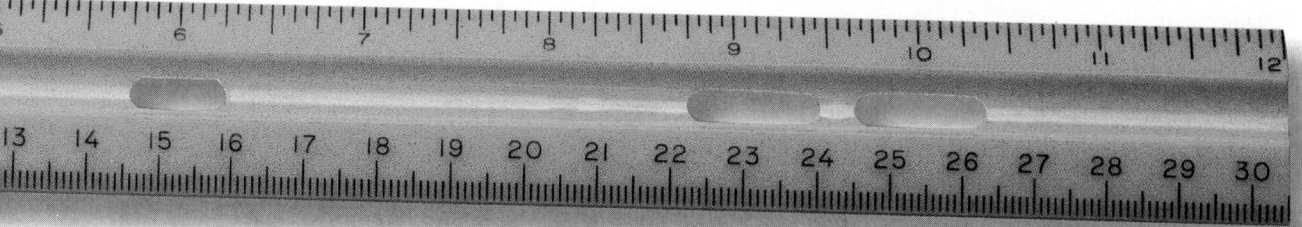

This ruler measures 12 inches (about 30.5 cm) long.

weir (wir), *n.* **1** dam in a river. **2** fence of stakes or broken branches put in a stream or channel to catch fish. ■ Another word that sounds like this is **we're.**

weird—a weird alien in a movie

weird (wird), *adj.* **1** frightening; mysterious; wild: *They were awakened by a weird shriek.* **2** odd; fantastic; of strange appearance: *The shadows made weird figures on the wall.* ■ See Synonym Study at **peculiar.** —**weird′ly,** *adv.* —**weird′ness,** *n.*

WORD STORY   Weird comes from an old English word meaning "fate" or "destiny." Later it was used to mean something that happened by fate, or something that showed what fate would be. A woman who claimed to tell fortunes was called a "weird sister." Shakespeare uses this phrase about the witches in his play *Macbeth.* Because those witches are so strange and mysterious, people began to use **weird** with that meaning. Today the older meaning is gone. Only Shakespeare's use remains.

weird·o (wir′dō), *n.* SLANG. an odd, bizarre, or peculiar person. ❑ *n., pl.* **weird·os.**

welch (welch *or* welsh), *v.* SLANG. to welsh.

wel·come (wel′kəm), **1** *v.* to greet kindly; give a friendly reception to: *We always welcome guests at our house.* **2** *n.* a kind or friendly reception: *You will always have a welcome here.* **3** *v.* to receive gladly: *We welcome new ideas and suggestions.* **4** *adj.* gladly received: *a welcome letter, a welcome visitor, a welcome rest.* **5** *adj.* gladly or freely permitted: *You are welcome to pick the flowers.* **6** *adj.* free to enjoy courtesies, etc., without obligation (said in response to thanks): *You are quite welcome.* **7** *interj.* exclamation of friendly greeting: *Welcome, everyone!* ❑ *v.* **wel·comed, wel·com·ing.** —**wel′come·ly,** *adv.* —**wel′come·ness,** *n.* —**wel′com·er,** *n.*

wear out your welcome, to visit someone too often or too long.

weld (weld), **1** *v.* to join pieces of metal or plastic together by heating the parts that touch to the melting point, so that they can be hammered or pressed together or flow together and become one piece: *She welded the broken rod.* **2** *n.* a welded joint. **3** *n.* act of welding. **4** *v.* to unite closely: *Working together welded them into a strong team.* **5** *v.* to be welded or be capable of being welded: *Steel welds; wood does not.* —**weld′a·ble,** *adj.* —**weld′er,** *n.*

wel·fare (wel′fâr′), *n.* **1** health, happiness, and prosperity; condition of being or doing well: *My uncle asked about the welfare of everyone in our family.* **2** aid provided by the government to poor or needy people.

on welfare, receiving aid from the government because of hardship or need.

welfare state, state whose government provides for the welfare of its citizens through social security, unemployment insurance, free medical treatment, etc.

welfare work, work done to improve the conditions of people who need help, carried on by government, private organizations, or individuals. —**welfare worker.**

well¹ (wel), **1** *adv.* in a satisfactory, favorable, or good manner; all right: *The job was well done. Is everything going well at school?* **2** *adj.* satisfactory; good; right: *It is well you came along.* **3** *adv.*

thoroughly: *Shake the medicine well before taking it. He knew the lesson well.* **4** *adv.* to a considerable degree; much: *The fair brought in well over a hundred dollars.* **5** *adv.* fairly; reasonably: *I couldn't very well refuse their request.* **6** *adj.* healthy: in good health: *I am very well.* ■ See Synonym Study at **healthy.** **7** *adj.* desirable; advisable: *It is always well to start a little early.* **8** *interj.* expression used to show mild surprise or merely to fill in: *Well! Well! Here they are. Well, I'm not sure.* ❑ *adv.* **bet·ter, best.** ■ See Usage Note at **good.**

as well, 1 also; besides. **2** equally.

SYNONYM STUDY   **Well¹, satisfactorily,** and **properly** all mean in a good way. **Well** is a general word: *The story is well written.* **Satisfactorily** means in a good enough way: *The suspect answered questions satisfactorily and was released.* **Properly** suggests something done as it should be: *Your bike now works properly.*

well² (wel), **1** *n.* hole dug or bored in the ground to get water, oil, gas, etc.: *I pumped a bucket of water from the well.* **2** *n.* spring; fountain; source: *This book is a well of ideas.* **3** *n.* shaft for stairs or elevator, extending vertically through the floors of a building. **4** *v.* to spring, rise, or gush: *Tears welled up in the child's eyes. Water welled from a spring beneath the rock.*

we'll (wēl), **1** we shall. **2** we will. ■ Another word that sounds like this is **wheel.**

well-ad·vised (wel′ad vizd′), *adj.* careful; prudent; based on wise advice or thought: *a well-advised silence.*

Wel·land Ship Canal (wel′ənd), canal between Lake Erie and Lake Ontario, enabling ships to pass between the two lakes, bypassing Niagara Falls.

well-ap·point·ed (wel′ə poin′tid), *adj.* having good furniture or equipment: *a well-appointed office.*

well-bal·anced (wel′bal′ənst), *adj.* **1** rightly balanced, adjusted, or regulated: *A well-balanced diet includes plenty of fruit, vegetables, and grains.* **2** sensible; sane: *She has a well-balanced outlook on life.*

well-be·haved (wel′bi hāvd′), *adj.* showing good manners or conduct.

well-be·ing (wel′bē′ing), *n.* health and happiness; welfare: *Our mayor and city council have concern for the well-being of the citizens.*

well-born (wel′bôrn′), *adj.* belonging to a noble or wealthy family.

well-bred (wel′bred′), *adj.* well brought up; having or showing good manners.

well-de·fined (wel′di find′), *adj.* rightly, properly, or definitely marked.

well-de·vel·oped (wel′di vel′əpt), *adj.* **1** developed or worked out well: *a well-developed plan.* **2** showing good development: *The athlete had a well-developed body.*

well-done (wel′dun′), *adj.* **1** performed well; skillfully done: *a well-done job.* **2** (of meat) thoroughly cooked: *well-done pork.*

Welles (welz), *n.* **Or·son** (ôr′sən), 1915-1985, American actor and movie director. ■ Before **Orson Welles** began directing movies, he directed a radio production of H. G. Wells's *War of The Worlds.* The production sounded so real that many people believed that New Jersey was actually being invaded by Martians.

well-fed (wel′fed′), *adj.* showing the result of good feeding; fat; plump.

well-fixed (wel′fikst′), *adj.* well-to-do.

well-groomed (wel′grümd′), *adj.* well cared for; neat and trim.

well-ground·ed (wel′groun′did), *adj.* **1** thoroughly instructed in the fundamental principles of a subject. **2** based on good reasons.

well-heeled (wel′hēld′), *adj.* INFORMAL. well-to-do; prosperous.

well-in·formed (wel′in fôrmd′), *adj.* **1** having reliable or full information on a subject. **2** having information on a wide variety of subjects.

Wel·ling·ton (wel′ing tən), *n.* **1** first **Duke of,** 1769-1852, British general who defeated Napoleon I at Waterloo in 1815. **2** capital of New Zealand, on the S coast of North Island.

well-kept (wel′kept′), *adj.* well cared for; carefully tended.

well-known (wel′nōn′), *adj.* **1** generally or widely known; famous: *a well-known actor.* **2** clearly known; familiar: *a well-known fact.*

well-made (wel′mād′), *adj.* skillfully made; sturdily built: *a well-made old desk.*

well-man·nered (wel′man′ərd), *adj.* having good manners; polite; courteous: *A well-mannered person always remembers to say "please."*

well-mean·ing (wel′mē′ning), *adj.* **1** having good intentions. **2** caused by good intentions.

well·ness (wel′nis), *n.* state of being well or in good health: *Good nutrition promotes wellness.*

well-nigh (wel′nī′), *adv.* very nearly; almost: *It was well-nigh midnight before we arrived home.*

well-off (wel′ôf′), *adj.* **1** in a good condition or position. **2** fairly rich.

well-pre·served (wel′pri zėrvd′), *adj.* showing few signs of age.

well-read (wel′red′), *adj.* having read much; knowing a great deal about books and literature.

well-round·ed (wel′roun′did), *adj.* complete; extensive; wide-ranging: *a well-rounded education.*

Wells (welz), *n.* **H. G.,** 1866-1946, English writer of science fiction, history, and essays. H. G. stands for Herbert George.

Wells-Bar·nett (welz′ bär′net′), *n.* **I·da B.** (ī′də), 1862-1931, American journalist and reformer. Born into slavery, she worked to stop lynchings and helped found the NAACP.

well-spo·ken (wel′spō′kən), *adj.* speaking well, properly, and pleasingly; polite in speech.

well·spring (wel′spring′), *n.* **1** source of a stream or spring; fountainhead. **2** source of supply that never fails; source.

well-thought-of (wel′thôt′uv′ *or* wel′thôt′ov′), *adj.* highly respected; esteemed.

well-timed (wel′timd′), *adj.* at the right time; timely.

well-to-do (wel′tə dü′), *adj.* having enough money to live well; prosperous.

well-wish·er (wel′wish′ər), *n.* person who wishes well to a person, cause, etc.

well-worn (wel′wôrn′), *adj.* **1** much worn by use. **2** used too much; trite; stale.

welsh (welsh *or* welch), *v.* SLANG. **1** to cheat by failing to pay a bet. **2** to avoid carrying out an agreement: *welsh on a promise.* Also, **welch.** ■ Although there is no evidence that **welsh** comes from **Welsh, welsh** may be considered offensive. —**welsh′er,** *n.*

Welsh (welsh *or* welch), **1** *adj.* of or about Wales, its people, or their Celtic language. **2** *n.pl.* the people of Wales. **3** *n.* their language.

Welsh cor·gi (kôr′gē), either of two kinds of Welsh working dogs, both with long bodies, short legs, and foxlike heads. [**Corgi** comes from Welsh words meaning "dwarf" and "dog."]

Welsh·man (welsh′mən *or* welch′mən), *n.* person born or living in Wales. ❑ *n., pl.* **Welsh·men.**

Welsh rabbit or **Welsh rarebit,** melted cheese cooked with milk, egg, etc., and poured over toast or crackers; rarebit.

Welsh·wom·an (welsh′wùm′ən *or* welch′wùm′ən), *n.* woman born or living in Wales. ❑ *n., pl.* **Welsh·wom·en.**

welt (welt), *n.* a raised streak or ridge made on the skin by a blow from a stick or whip.

wel·ter (wel′tər), **1** *n.* a surging or confused mass: *All we saw was a welter of arms, legs, and bodies.* **2** *v.* to roll or tumble about; wallow. **3** *n.* act of rolling or tumbling about. **4** *n.* confusion; commotion. **5** *v.* to be drenched.

wel·ter·weight (wel′tər wāt′), *n.* boxer who weighs more than 135 pounds (61 kilograms) and less than 147 pounds (67 kilograms).

wen (wen), *n.* a harmless saclike growth of the skin, especially on the scalp. ■ Another word that sounds like this is **when.**

wench (wench), *n.* OLD USE. **1** girl or young woman. **2** a woman servant. ❑ *n., pl.* **wench·es.** ■ **Wench** is often considered offensive if used today.

wend (wend), *v.* **1** to direct your way: *We wended our way home.* **2** to go. ❑ *v.* **wend·ed, wend·ing.**

Wen·di·go (wen′di gō′), *n.* (in Algonquian myths) an evil spirit that is cannibalistic in nature.

went (went), *v.* past tense of **go:** *I went home promptly after school.*

wept (wept), *v.* past tense and past participle of **weep:** *The children wept over the loss of their dog.*

were (wėr), *v.* **1** form of the verb **be** used with *you, we, they* or any plural noun to indicate the past tense: *The officer's orders were obeyed.* **2** form of the verb **be** used to express something as possible or as a condition but not as an actual thing: *If I were rich, I would help the poor.* ■ Another word that sounds like this is **whir.**

we're (wir), we are. ■ Another word that sounds like this is **weir.**

weren't (wėrnt), were not.

were·wolf (wer′wùlf′ *or* wir′wùlf′), *n.* (in stories) someone who changes into a wolf at certain times. ❑ *n., pl.* **were·wolves** (wer′wùlvz′ *or* wir′wùlvz).

wert (wėrt), *v.* OLD USE. were. "Thou wert" means "you were."

Wes·ley (wes′lē), *n.* **1 John,** 1703-1791, English clergyman who founded the Methodist Church. **2** his brother, **Charles,** 1707-1788, English clergyman and colleague of John. He wrote many hymns.

Wes·ley·an (wes′lē ən), *n.* member of the church founded by John Wesley; Methodist.

werewolf in a movie

west (west), **1** *n.* direction of the sunset. **2** *adj., adv.* toward the west; farther toward the west: *We took the west road. Walk west three blocks.* **3** *adj.* from the west: *a warm, west wind.* **4** *n.* Also, **West,** the part of any country toward the west. **5** *n.* **West, a** the western part of the United States. **b** the countries in Europe and the Americas as distinguished from those in Asia.

west of, farther west than: *Kansas is west of Pennsylvania.*

West Bank, region west of the Jordan River, formerly held by Jordan, occupied by Israel since 1967.

West Berlin, formerly, the W part of Berlin belonging to West Germany. It was separated from East Berlin by a wall.

west·bound (west′bound′), *adj.* going west.

west·er·ly (wes′tər lē), **1** *adj., adv.* toward the west: *They were heading in a westerly direction.* **2** *adj., adv.* from the west: *a westerly wind.* **3** *n.* wind that blows from the west. ❑ *n., pl.* **west·er·lies.**

west·ern (wes′tərn), **1** *adj.* toward the west: *We sailed to the western shore of the island.* **2** *adj.* from the west: *western breezes.* **3** *adj.* of or in the west: *Wyoming is a western state.* **4** *n.* story, movie, or TV show dealing with life in the western part of the United States, especially cowboy life. **5** *adj.* **Western, a** of or in the western part of the United States. **b** of or in the countries of Europe and America.

west·ern·er (wes′tər nər), *n.* **1** person born or living in the west. **2** Westerner, person born or living in the western part of the United States.

Western Hemisphere, the half of the world that includes North and South America.

west·ern·ize (wes′tər nīz), *v.* to make western in character, ideas, ways, etc.: *Many formerly communist countries are in the process of westernizing.* ❑ *v.* **west·ern·ized, west·ern·iz·ing.** —**west′ern·i·za′tion,** *n.*

west·ern·most (wes′tərn mōst), *adj.* farthest west.

Western Sahara, country in NW Africa, south of Morocco. *Capital:* El Aaiún.

Western Samoa, country made up of several islands in the S Pacific. *Capital:* Apia.

W

a	hat	ė	term	ô	order	ch	child		
ā	age	i	it	oi	oil	ng	long		a in about
ä	far	ī	ice	ou	out	sh	she		e in taken
â	care	o	hot	u	cup	th	thin	ə	i in pencil
e	let	ō	open	ù	put	ŦH	then		o in lemon
ē	equal	ò	saw	ü	rule	zh	measure		u in circus

western yew, (in Canada) Pacific yew.

West Germany, a former country in central Europe, from 1949 to 1990. It is now part of Germany.

West Indian, 1 of, for, or from the West Indies. **2** person born or living in the West Indies.

West Indies, long chain of islands between Florida and South America; Greater Antilles, Lesser Antilles, and Bahamas.

West Ir·i·an (ir′ē än), Irian Jaya.

West·min·ster Abbey (west′min′stər), church in London where the kings and queens of Great Britain are crowned and in which many English monarchs and famous people are buried.

West Point, college for training cadets to become officers in the U.S. Army. It is located on the Hudson River in SE New York State.

West Virginia, one of the southeastern states of the United States. *Abbreviation:* WV or W.Va. *Capital:* Charleston. **—West Virginian.**

WORD STORY West Virginia got its name from the state of Virginia. When the Civil War began, the western part of the state withdrew from Virginia because it did not want to withdraw from the United States, as Virginia had. It became a separate state in 1863.

west·ward (west′wərd), **1** *adv., adj.* toward the west; west: *We walked westward. The orchard is on the westward slope of the hill.* **2** *n.* a westward part, direction, or point.

west·wards (west′wərdz), *adv.* westward.

wet (wet), **1** *adj.* covered or soaked with water or other liquid: *wet hands, a wet sponge.* **2** *adj.* watery: *eyes wet with tears.* **3** *adj.* not yet dry: *The paint is wet: don't touch it.* **4** *v.* to make or become wet: *Wet the cloth before you wipe off the window.* **5** *n.* water or other liquid. **6** *adj.* rainy: *wet weather.* **7** *n.* wetness; rain: *Come in out of the wet.* **8** *adj.* permitting the sale of alcoholic drinks: *a wet town or district.* ❑ *adj.* **wet·ter, wet·test;** *v.* **wet** or **wet·ted, wet·ting.** ■ Another word that sounds like this is **whet.** **—wet′ly,** *adv.* **—wet′ness,** *n.* **—wet′ta·ble,** *adj.* **—wet′ter,** *n.*

SYNONYM STUDY Wet, soggy, and drenched all mean covered with or full of liquid. Wet is a general word: *Don't go out with wet hair.* Soggy means heavy with liquid: *This cereal gets soggy.* Drenched means completely wet: *She was drenched after walking through the downpour.*

wet bar, a small bar with a sink and running water in a home, hotel room, etc.

wet blanket, person or thing that has a discouraging or depressing effect.

wet cell, an electric cell in which the chemical substances producing the current are liquid.

wet·land (wet′land′), *n.* Often, **wetlands,** *pl.* swamp, marsh, or other land that is soaked with water sometimes or always, but where plants continue to grow.

wet suit, a skintight rubber suit worn by skin divers, surfers, sailors, etc.

wet·ting agent (wet′ing), any additive used with a liquid to increase its ability to penetrate or spread over the surface of a material such as cloth, paper, etc.

we've (wēv), we have. ■ Another word that sounds like this is **weave.**

whack (wak), **1** *n.* a sharp, noisy blow: *She hit the ball with a loud whack.* **2** *v.* to strike with such a blow: *The batter whacked the ball out of the park.* **3** *n.* trial or attempt: *I'd like to have a whack at parachuting.* ■ Another word that sounds like this is **WAC.** **—whack′er,** *n.*

WORD STORY Many words beginning with **wh-** were spelled in old English beginning **hw-.** In old English, both letters were pronounced very clearly, but this is not an easy sound to make, so it gradually changed. Many people today pronounce only the *w;* other people say both letters but don't separate them clearly. Probably because of the sound change, the spelling changed, hundreds of years ago. Some words spelled with *wh-* are not pronounced with *w* at all. **Whole,** for instance, was originally spelled and pronounced with only an *h.* Its spelling changed when people got used to writing many other words with *wh-.*

whack·y (wak′ē), *adj.* SLANG. wacky. ❑ *adj.* **whack·i·er, whack·i·est.** **—whack′i·ly,** *adv.* **—whack′i·ness,** *n.*

whale[1] (wāl), **1** *n.* any of various large mammals that spend their whole lives in the sea and are shaped something like fish. Whales are related to dolphins and porpoises. **2** *v.* to hunt and kill whales. ❑ *v.* **whaled, whaling.** ■ Other words that sound like this are **wail** and **wale.** **—whale′like′,** *adj.*

a whale of, INFORMAL. a very excellent, big, or impressive kind of: *a whale of a good time.*

whale[2] (wāl), *v.* to whip severely; beat; thrash. ❑ *v.* **whaled, whaling.** ■ Other words that sound like this are **wail** and **wale.**

whale[1] (def. 1)

whale·boat (wāl′bōt′), *n.* a long, narrow rowboat, pointed at both ends, formerly much used in whaling.

whale·bone (wāl′bōn′), *n.* an elastic, horny substance growing as thin, parallel plates instead of teeth in the upper jaws of some kinds of whales; baleen. Thin strips of whalebone were formerly used for stiffening corsets and dresses.

whal·er (wā′lər), *n.* **1** hunter of whales. **2** ship used for hunting and catching whales.

whal·ing (wā′ling), *n.* the hunting and catching of whales.

wham (wam), **1** *n., interj.* exclamation or sound as of one thing striking hard against another. **2** *v.* to hit with a hard, striking sound. ❑ *v.* **whammed, wham·ming.**

wharf (wôrf), *n.* platform built on the shore or out from the shore, beside which ships can load and unload. ❑ *n., pl.* **wharves** (wôrvz), **wharfs.**

what (wät *or* wut), **1** *pron., adj. What* is used in asking questions about persons or things. *What is your name? What time is it?* **2** *adv.* how much; how: *What does it matter?* **3** *pron., adj.* that which: *I know what you mean. Put back what money is left.* **4** *pron., adj.* whatever; anything that; any that: *Do what you please. Take what supplies you will need.* **5** *adv.* partly: *What with the wind and rain, our walk was spoiled.* **6** *adj., adv., interj. What* is often used to show surprise, doubt, anger, liking, etc., or to add emphasis. *What a pity! What happy times! What! Are you late again?*

and what not, and all kinds of other things: *a collection of buttons, beads, and what not.*

what if, what would happen if: *What if it rains on the day of the game?*

what's what, the true state of affairs: *to know what's what.*

what·ev·er (wät ev′ər *or* wut ev′ər), **1** *pron.* anything that: *Do whatever you like.* **2** *adj.* any that: *Take whatever books you need.* **3** *adj.* no matter who; at all: *Any person whatever can tell you the way.* **4** *pron., adj.* no matter what: *Whatever happens, they are safe. Whatever excuse he makes will not be believed.* **5** *pron. Whatever* is used for emphasis instead of *what. Whatever do you mean?*

what·not (wät′not′ *or* wut′not′), *n.* a stand with several shelves for books, ornaments, etc.

what's (wäts *or* wuts), **1** what is: *What's the latest news?* **2** what has: *What's been going on here lately?*

what·so·ev·er (wät′sō ev′ər *or* wut′sō ev′ər), *pron., adj.* whatever.

wheat (wēt), *n.* **1** the grain of a common cereal grass, used to make flour, pasta, and so on. **2** the plant yielding this grain.

wheat·en (wēt′n), *adj.* made of wheat: *wheaten flour.*

wheat germ, the tiny germ or embryo of the wheat kernel, separated in the milling of flour and used as a cereal, etc. It is rich in vitamins.

whee·dle (wē′dl), *v.* **1** to persuade by flattery, smooth words, caresses, etc.; coax: *The children wheedled their parents into letting them go to the picnic.* **2** to get by wheedling: *They finally wheedled the secret out of me.* ❑ *v.* **whee·dled, whee·dling.** **—whee′dler,** *n.* **—whee′dling·ly,** *adv.*

wheel (wēl), **1** *n.* a round frame or disk turning on an axle or shaft in the center: *bicycle wheels, truck wheels.* **2** *n.* any device, machine, apparatus, etc., shaped or moving like a wheel: *a steering wheel, a potter's wheel.* **3** *n.* any force thought of as moving or propelling: *the wheels of government.* **4** *n.pl.* **wheels,** INFORMAL. car. **5** *v.* to turn: *The rider wheeled her horse about. I wheeled around suddenly when I heard my name called.* **6** *v.* to move on wheels: *I wheeled the load of bricks on a wheelbarrow.* ▪ Another word that sounds like this is **we'll.** —**wheel′less,** *adj.*

at the wheel, 1 at the steering wheel of a car. **2** at the wheel of a ship. **3** in control.

wheel and deal, INFORMAL. to make deals in business, politics, etc., in a bold, cunning way.

wheel and axle, axle on which a wheel is fastened, used to lift weights by winding a rope onto the axle as the wheel is turned. It is a simple machine.

wheel·bar·row (wēl′bar′ō), *n.* a small vehicle with a wheel at the front and two handles at the back, used for carrying loads.

wheel·base (wēl′bās′), *n.* the distance between the front and rear axles of a motor vehicle.

wheel·chair (wēl′châr′), *n.* chair on wheels, used especially by people who are sick or unable to walk. It can be moved by the person who is sitting in the chair.

wheeled (wēld), *adj.* having a wheel or wheels. ▪ Another word that sounds like this is **wield.**

wheel·house (wēl′hous′), *n.* pilothouse. ❏ *n., pl.* **wheel·hous·es** (wēl′hou′ziz).

wheel·ie (wē′lē), *n.* a stunt in which a moving bicycle, motorcycle, or car is balanced only on its back wheel or wheels.

wheelie

Wheel·ing (wē′ling), *n.* city in NW West Virginia, on the Ohio River. [**Wheeling** probably comes from a Delaware Indian word meaning "head place." Historians believe that a prisoner was executed near here by decapitation.]

wheel·wright (wēl′rit′), *n.* (earlier) person whose work was making or repairing wheels, carriages, and wagons.

wheeze (wēz), **1** *v.* to breathe with difficulty and a whistling sound. **2** *n.* a whistling sound caused by difficult breathing. **3** *v.* to make a sound like this: *The old engine wheezed.* ❏ *v.* **wheezed, wheez·ing.** —**wheez′ing·ly,** *adv.*

wheez·y (wē′zē), *adj.* wheezing: *Their old dog had become fat and wheezy.* ❏ *adj.* **wheez·i·er, wheez·i·est.** —**wheez′i·ly,** *adv.* —**wheez′i·ness,** *n.*

whelk (welk), *n.* any of various large sea snails with spiral shells, used for food in Europe.

whelp (welp), **1** *n.* puppy or cub; young dog, wolf, bear, lion, tiger, or seal. **2** *v.* to give birth. **3** *n.* an impudent young person.

when (wen), **1** *adv.* at what time: *When does school close?* **2** *conj.* at the time that: *Stand up when your name is called.* **3** *conj.* at any time that: *The dog comes when it is called.* **4** *conj.* at which time; and then: *We had just decided to go out for a walk, when it began to rain.* **5** *conj.* although: *We have only three books when we need five.* **6** *pron.* what time; which time: *Since when have they had a new car?* **7** *n.* the time or occasion: *the when and where of an act.* ▪ Another word that sounds like this is **wen.**

whence (wens), *adv., conj.* from what place, source, or cause; from where: *Whence do you come? They returned to the country whence they came.*

whence·so·ev·er (wens′sō ev′ər), *conj.* from whatever place, source, or cause.

when·ev·er (wen ev′ər), *conj., adv.* when; at whatever time; at any time that: *Come whenever you wish. I'll come whenever possible.*

when·so·ev·er (wen′sō ev′ər), *conj., adv.* whenever; at whatever time.

where (wâr), **1** *adv.* in what place; at what place: *Where do you live? Where is he?* **2** *adv.* to what place: *Where are you going?* **3** *adv.* from what place: *Where did you get that story?* **4** *n.* what place: *Where did it come from?* **5** *conj.* in which; at which: *That is the house where I was born.* **6** *conj.* to which: *I know the place where he is going.* **7** *adv.* in what way; in what respect: *Where is the harm in trying?* **8** *conj.* in the place in which; at the place at which: *Your coat is where you left it.* **9** *conj.* to the place to which: *I will go where you go.* **10** *n.* place or scene: *the when and where of an act.* ▪ Other words that sound like this are **ware** and **wear.**

where·a·bouts (wâr′ə bouts′), **1** *n.* place where someone or something is: *Do you know the whereabouts of the cottage?* **2** *adv., conj.* where; near what place: *Whereabouts are my books? We did not know whereabouts we were.*

where·as (wâr az′), *conj.* **1** on the contrary; but; while: *Some children like school, whereas others do not.* **2** considering that; since: *"Whereas the people of the colonies have been grieved and burdened with taxes...."*

where·at (wâr at′), *adv., conj.* at what; at which.

where·by (wâr bī′), *adv., conj.* by what; by which: *There is no other way whereby she can do it.*

where·fore (wâr′fôr), **1** *adv.* for what reason? why? **2** *adv.* for which reason; therefore; so. **3** *conj.* for what reason; why. **4** *n.* reason: *I don't want to hear all the whys and wherefores.*

where·in (wâr in′), *adv., conj.* in what; in which; how.

where·of (wâr uv′ *or* wâr ov′), *adv., conj.* of what; of which; of whom: *I know whereof I speak.*

where·on (wâr ȯn′ *or* wâr on′), *adv., conj.* on which; on what: *Cottages occupy the land whereon the old farmhouse stood.*

where·so·ev·er (wâr′sō ev′ər), *conj., adv.* wherever.

where·to (wâr tü′), *adv., conj.* **1** to what; to which; where: *They went to the place whereto they had been sent.* **2** for what purpose; why: *Whereto do you mock me?*

where·up·on (wâr′ə pȯn′), *adv., conj.* **1** upon what; upon which. **2** at which; after which: *He handed me a box, whereupon I opened it.*

wher·ev·er (wâr ev′ər), *conj., adv.* where; to whatever place; in whatever place: *Sit wherever you like. Wherever are you going?*

where·with (wâr wiᴛʜ′ *or* wâr with′), *adv., conj.* with what; with which: *Wherewith shall we be fed?*

where·with·al (wâr′wi ᴛʜȯl), *n.* means, supplies, or money needed: *Has she the wherewithal to pay for the trip?*

wher·ry (wâr′ē), *n.* a light, shallow rowboat for carrying passengers and goods on rivers. ❏ *n., pl.* **wher·ries.**

whet (wet), **1** *v.* to make keen or eager; stimulate: *The smell of food whetted my appetite.* **2** *v.* to sharpen by rubbing: *whet a knife.* ❏ *v.* **whet·ted, whet·ting.** ▪ Another word that sounds like this is **wet.** —**whet′ter,** *n.*

wheth·er (weᴛʜ′ər), *conj.* **1** *Whether* is used in expressing a choice or an alternative. *It matters little whether we go or stay. I do not know whether to work or rest.* **2** either: *Whether sick or well, she is always cheerful.* **3** if: *I asked whether I should finish the work.* ▪ Another word that sounds like this is **weather.**

whet·stone (wet′stōn′), *n.* stone for sharpening knives or tools.

whew (hwyü), *interj., n.* exclamation of surprise, dismay, etc.: *Whew! it's cold!*

a	hat	ė	term	ô	order	ch	child		a in about
ā	age	i	it	oi	oil	ng	long		e in taken
ä	far	ī	ice	ou	out	sh	she	ə	i in pencil
â	care	o	hot	u	cup	th	thin		o in lemon
e	let	ō	open	ů	put	ᴛʜ	then		u in circus
ē	equal	ȯ	saw	ü	rule	zh	measure		

W

whey (wā), *n.* the watery part of milk that separates from the curd when milk sours or when cheese is made. ▪ Other words that sound like this are **way** and **weigh.**

which (wich), **1** *adj., pron.* Which is used in asking questions about persons or things. *Which is the best plan? Which book do you want to read?* ▪ See Usage Note at **that. 2** *adj., pron.* Which is also used in connecting a group of words with some word in the sentence. *Read the book which you have. Be careful which way you turn.* **3** *pron.* the one that; any that: *Here are three boxes. Choose which you like best.* ▪ Another word that sounds like this is **witch.**

which·ev·er (wich ev′ər), *pron., adj.* **1** any one; any that: *Take whichever you want. Buy whichever hat you like.* **2** no matter which: *Whichever you choose will be fine. Whichever side wins I shall be satisfied.*

whiff (wif), **1** *n.* a breathing in of an odor, smoke, or gas: *I took a whiff of the rose.* **2** *n.* a slight gust; puff; breath: *A whiff of smoke blew in my face.* **3** *v.* to blow or puff.

whif·fle·tree (wif′əl trē′), *n.* the horizontal crossbar of a carriage or wagon, to which the traces of a harness are fastened; singletree. Also, **whippletree.** ❑ *n., pl.* **whif·fle·trees.**

Whig (wig), *n.* **1** member of a British political party of the late 1600s to early 1800s that favored reforms and opposed the Tory party. The Whig party became the Liberal party. **2** an American who opposed British rule over the colonies at the time of the Revolutionary War. **3** member of a political party in the United States that was formed about 1834 in opposition to the Democratic Party. It was succeeded by the Republican Party about 1855.

while (wīl), **1** *n.* time; space of time: *He kept us waiting a long while. The mail came a while ago.* ▪ See Usage Note at **awhile. 2** *conj.* during the time that; in the time that: *While I was speaking he said nothing. Summer is pleasant while it lasts.* **3** *conj.* although: *While I like the color of the hat, I do not like its shape.* **4** *v.* to pass or spend in some easy, pleasant manner: *The children while away many afternoons on the beach.* ❑ *v.* **whiled, whil·ing.** ▪ Another word that sounds like this is **wile.**

worth your while, worth your time, attention, or effort: *If you help me with the painting, I'll make it worth your while—I'll pay you $50.*

whim (wim), *n.* a sudden fancy or notion: *I went to the amusement park on a whim.*

whim·per (wim′pər), **1** *v.* to cry with low, broken sounds, in the way that a sick child or dog does: *She heard an animal whimpering in the bushes.* **2** *n.* a whimpering cry. —**whim′per·er,** *n.* —**whim′per·ing·ly,** *adv.*

whim·si·cal (wim′zə kəl), *adj.* having many odd notions or fancies; fanciful; odd: *Her latest whimsical idea is to have us perform the play in frog costumes.* —**whim′si·cal·ly,** *adv.*

whim·sy (wim′zē), *n.* **1** an odd or fanciful notion. **2** odd or fanciful humor; quaintness: *"Alice in Wonderland" is full of whimsy.* ❑ *n., pl.* **whim·sies** for 1.

whine (wīn), **1** *v.* to make a low, complaining cry or sound: *The dog whined to go out with us.* **2** *n.* a low, complaining cry or sound. **3** *v.* to complain in an annoying, childish way: *Some people are always whining about trifles.* **4** *v.* to say with a whine. ❑ *v.* **whined, whin·ing.** ▪ Another word that sounds like this is **wine.** —**whin′er,** *n.* —**whin′ing·ly,** *adv.*

WORD STORY **Whine** comes from an old English word meaning "to whiz," used about arrows. It seems that the high whining of dogs sounded to people like an arrow in flight.

whin·ny (win′ē), **1** *n.* the sound that a horse makes. **2** *v.* to make such a sound. ❑ *n., pl.* **whin·nies;** *v.* **whin·nied, whin·ny·ing.**

whin·y (wī′nē), *adj.* marked by whining; apt to whine; fretful: *Her whiny friend complained about the food at the party.* ❑ *adj.* **whin·i·er, whin·i·est.** —**whin′i·ness,** *n.*

whip (wip), **1** *n.* thing to strike or beat with, usually a stick or handle with a flexible cord at the end. **2** *v.* to strike or beat with or as if with a whip; lash: *whip a horse to make it gallop. Rain whipped the pavement.* **3** *n.* member of a political party who controls the other party members in a <u>lawmaking group</u>, especially their voting. **4** *n.* a whipping motion. **5** *v.* to move, put, or pull

quickly and suddenly: *whip off a coat, whip out a knife. The child whipped behind the tree to hide from us.* **6** *v.* to defeat in a fight, contest, etc.: *The mayor whipped his opponent in the election.* **7** *v.* to beat cream, eggs, etc., to a froth. **8** *n.* dessert made by beating cream, eggs, etc., into a froth: *prune whip.* **9** *v.* to rouse; incite: *The cheerleaders tried to whip up some enthusiasm in the crowd during the final minutes of the game.* ❑ *v.* **whipped, whip·ping.** —**whip′like′,** *adj.* —**whip′per,** *n.*

whip·cord (wip′kôrd′), *n.* **1** a thin, tough, tightly twisted cord, sometimes used for whips. **2** a strong, closely woven woolen cloth with diagonal ridges on it.

whip hand, **1** position of control; advantage: *A clever person often gets the whip hand over others.* **2** the hand that holds the whip when driving a horse-drawn vehicle.

whip·lash (wip′lash′), *n.* **1** injury to the neck caused by a sudden jolt that snaps the head backward and then forward. A driver whose car is struck with force from the rear may suffer whiplash. **2** lash of a whip. ❑ *n., pl.* **whip·lash·es.**

whip·per·snap·per (wip′ər snap′ər), *n.* OLD USE. an impudent young person.

whip·pet (wip′it), *n.* a very swift dog that looks something like a small greyhound, often used in racing.

whip·ple·tree (wip′əl trē′), *n.* whiffletree. ❑ *n., pl.* **whip·ple·trees.**

whip·poor·will (wip′ər wil′ or wip′ər wil), *n.* a North American bird with a call like its name. It is active at night or twilight.

whir (wėr), **1** *n.* noise that sounds like whir-r-r: *the whir of machinery.* **2** *v.* to operate or move with such a noise: *The motor whirs.* ❑ *v.* **whirred, whir·ring.** ▪ Another word that sounds like this is **were.**

whippoorwill

whirl (wėrl), **1** *v.* to turn or swing round and round; spin: *The leaves whirled in the wind.* ▪ See Synonym Study at **spin. 2** *v.* to move round and round: *We whirled about the room.* **3** *v.* to move or carry quickly: *The contest winners were whirled away in a limo.* **4** *n.* a whirling movement: *the whirl of a top.* **5** *v.* to feel dizzy or confused. **6** *n.* dizzy or confused condition: *My thoughts are in a whirl.* **7** *n.* a rapid round of happenings, parties, etc.

▪ Another word that can sound like this is **whorl.** [See Word Story at **swirl.**] —**whirl′er,** *n.*

whirl·i·gig (wėr′li gig′), *n.* **1** toy that whirls or spins. **2** merry-go-round. **3** anything that whirls.

whirl·pool (wėrl′pül′), *n.* **1** current of water whirling around and around rapidly and violently. **2** whirlpool bath.

whirlpool bath, a type of bath, used to treat injuries or for relaxation, with a device that causes water to whirl around inside.

whirl·wind (wėrl′wind′), **1** *n.* current of air whirling violently round and round; whirling windstorm. **2** *adj.* very fast; at great speed: *Our history class went on a whirlwind tour of several foreign countries.*

whisk (wisk), **1** *v.* to sweep or brush from a surface: *After breakfast she whisked the crumbs off the table.* **2** *n.* a quick sweep: *She got rid of the dirt with a few whisks of a brush.* **3** *v.* to move quickly: *I whisked the letter out of sight.* **4** *v.* to beat or whip to a froth: *She whisked the egg whites in a copper bowl.* **5** *n.* a wire beater for eggs, cream, etc.

whisk broom, a small broom for brushing clothes, etc.

whisk·er (wis′kər), *n.* **1** one of the hairs growing on a man's face. **2** whiskers, *pl.* the hair or part of a beard that grows on a man's cheeks. **3** a long, stiff hair growing near the mouth of an animal.

whisk·ered (wis′kərd), *adj.* having whiskers.

whis·key (wis′kē), *n.* a strong alcoholic drink made from such grains as rye, barley, or corn. ❑ *n., pl.* **whis·keys.**

whis·ky (wis′kē), *n.* whiskey. ❑ *n., pl.* **whis·kies.**

whis·ky-jack (wis′kē jak′), *n.* gray jay.

whis·per (wis′pər), **1** *v.* to speak very softly and low. **2** *n.* a very soft, low, spoken sound. **3** *v.* to speak to in a whisper. **4** *v.* to tell secretly or privately: *It is whispered that the business is failing.* **5** *n.* something told secretly or privately: *We have heard a few whispers of scandal.* **6** *v.* to make a soft, rustling sound: *The wind whispered in the pines.* **7** *n.* a soft, rustling sound: *the faint whisper of the leaves.* —**whis′per·er,** *n.*

whist (wist), *n.* a card game something like bridge.

whis·tle (wis′əl), **1** *v.* to make a clear, shrill sound by forcing breath through your teeth or through rounded lips: *The girl whistled and her dog ran to her quickly.* **2** *n.* the sound made by whistling. **3** *n.* instrument for making whistling sounds, usually consisting of a tube through which air or steam is blown. **4** *v.* to blow a whistle: *The traffic officer whistled for the cars to stop.* **5** *v.* to produce or utter by whistling: *whistle a tune.* **6** *v.* to move with a shrill sound: *The wind whistled around the house.* ❑ *v.* **whis·tled, whis·tling.** —**whis′tle·a·ble,** *adj.* —**whis′tler,** *n.*

Whis·tler (wis′lər), *n.* **James Ab·bott Mc·Neill** (ab′ət mək nēl′), 1834-1903, American painter. He felt that pictures need not describe things or tell stories, but should be representations of the imagination of the artist.

whit (wit), *n.* a very small bit: *I don't care a whit what they do.* ■ Another word that sounds like this is **wit.**

white (wit), **1** *n.* the color of snow, salt, or the paper on which this book is printed. **2** *adj.* having or approaching this color: *a white sheet.* **3** *n.* white coloring matter. **4** *n.* white clothing. **5** *n.* part that is white or whitish, such as the albumen surrounding the yolk of an egg or the white part of the eyeball. **6** *adj.* pale: *They all turned white with fear.* **7** *adj.* light-colored: *white meat, a white wine.* **8** *adj.* having a light-colored skin; Caucasian. **9** *n.* person who has light-colored skin; Caucasian. **10** *adj.* silvery; gray: *Grandmother has white hair.* **11** *adj.* snowy: *a white Christmas.* ❑ *adj.* **whit·er, whit·est.** —**white′ness,** *n.*

White (wit), *n.* **E. B.,** 1899-1985, American writer of essays and children's stories. He is best known for his novel *Charlotte's Web.*

white ant, termite.

white blood cell, any colorless blood cell; white corpuscle; leucocyte. White cells destroy disease germs and control immunity.

white·cap (wit′kap′), *n.* wave with a foaming white crest.

white cell, white blood cell.

white-col·lar (wit′kol′ər), *adj.* of or about clerical, professional, or business work or workers.

white corpuscle, white blood cell.

white dwarf, a small, dim star, very dense and cool.

white elephant, anything that is expensive and troublesome to keep and take care of.

white·fish (wit′fish′), *n.* any of various food fishes with white or silvery sides, related to trout, found in lakes and streams. ❑ *n., pl.* **white·fish** or **white·fish·es.**

white flag, a plain white flag displayed as a sign of truce or surrender.

white gold, alloy of gold and nickel or platinum, sometimes with copper and zinc. White gold looks much like platinum and is used for jewelry.

White·hall (wit′hôl′), *n.* **1** street in London, where many government offices are located. **2** the British government or its policies.

white heat, 1 very great heat at which some metals produce a dazzling white light. **2** very great activity, excitement, or feeling.

White·horse (wit′hôrs′), *n.* capital of Yukon Territory, Canada.

white-hot (wit′hot′), *adj.* **1** white with heat; extremely hot: *white-hot molten steel.* **2** very angry; passionate, violent, etc.

White House, 1 the official residence of the President of the United States, in Washington, D.C. **2** office, authority, opinion, etc., of the President of the United States.

the **White House**

white lie, a lie about some small matter; polite or harmless lie: *I told a white lie about liking his painting.*

white matter, the tissue in the brain and spinal cord that consists mostly of nerve cell axons.

White Mountains, range of the Appalachian Mountains in New Hampshire.

whit·en (wit′n), *v.* to make or become white: *Sunshine helps to whiten clothes. A person's hair whitens with age.*

white noise, noise containing all audible frequencies, used to block out other noise and to soothe.

white oak, an oak tree of eastern North America with light gray or whitish bark and hard wood.

white·out (wit′out′), *n.* **1** a weather condition in arctic and antarctic regions in which the sky, horizon, and snow-covered ground all become a single area of dazzling light, without shadows or boundaries. **2** a temporary loss of vision that results from looking at such weather. **3** a blizzard condition in which blowing snow blocks all vision. **4** a thick white liquid used to cover mistakes in typing or writing on paper.

white paper, an official report on some subject.

White Russia, Belarus. —**White Russian.**

White Sea, arm of the Arctic Ocean, located in NW Russia.

white-tailed deer (wit′tāld′), a common North American deer that has reddish fur in the summer, tan fur in the winter, and a tail that is white on the underside.

white·wash (wit′wäsh′), **1** *n.* liquid for whitening walls, woodwork, etc. Whitewash is usually made of lime and water. **2** *v.* to whiten with whitewash. **3** *v.* to cover up the faults or mistakes of: *They tried to whitewash the crime.* **4** *n.* a covering up of faults or mistakes. **5** *v.* INFORMAL. to defeat in a game without a score for the loser. ❑ *n., pl.* **white·wash·es** for 4.

white water, any foaming water, especially in rapids. —**white′wa·ter,** *adj.*

whith·er (wiᴛʜ′ər), *adv., conj.* to what place; to which place; where. ■ Another word that sounds like this is **wither.**

whit·ing[1] (wi′ting), *n.* any of various Atlantic food fishes. ❑ *n., pl.* **whit·ing** or **whit·ings.**

whit·ing[2] (wi′ting), *n.* a powdered white chalk. Whiting is used in making putty, whitewash, and silver polish.

whit·ish (wi′tish), *adj.* somewhat white.

a	hat	ė	term	ô	order	ch	child		
ā	age	i	it	oi	oil	ng	long		a in about
ä	far	ī	ice	ou	out	sh	she	ə	e in taken
â	care	o	hot	u	cup	th	thin		i in pencil
e	let	ō	open	ů	put	ᴛʜ	then		o in lemon
ē	equal	ȯ	saw	ü	rule	zh	measure		u in circus

W

Whit·man (wit′mən), *n.* Walt (wolt), 1819-1892, American poet. His poems praise democracy and the United States, especially in his collection *Leaves of Grass.*

Whit·ney (wit′nē), *n.* **1 Mount,** peak of the Sierra Nevada mountains, in E California, 14,495 feet (4418 meters) high. It is the highest mountain in the United States outside Alaska. **2 E·li** (ē′li), 1765-1825, American who perfected the cotton gin. [Mount Whitney was named by the first surveyors to sight it, after their boss.]

Whit·sun·day (wit′sun′dē), *n.* the seventh Sunday after Easter; Pentecost.

Whit·sun·tide (wit′sən tid′), *n.* the week beginning with Whitsunday, especially the first three days.

whit·tle (wit′l), *v.* **1** to cut shavings or chips from wood, soap, etc., with a knife, usually for fun. **2** to shape by whittling; carve: *The students learned how to whittle animals from wood.* ❑ *v.* **whit·tled, whit·tling. —whit′tler,** *n.*

whittle down, to cut down little by little: *whittle down expenses.*

whiz or **whizz** (wiz), **1** *n.* a humming or hissing sound. **2** *v.* to move or rush with such a sound: *An arrow whizzed past his head.* **3** INFORMAL. *n.* a very clever person; expert: *a computer whiz.* ❑ *n., pl.* **whiz·zes;** *v.* **whizzed, whiz·zing. —whiz′zer,** *n.*

who (hü), *pron.* **1** *Who* is used in asking questions about a person or persons. *Who goes there? Who is your friend? Who told you?* **2** *Who* is also used in connecting a group of words with some previous word that refers to a person or persons in the sentence. *The girl who spoke is my best friend. We saw people who were working in the fields.* **3** the person that; any person that; someone that: *Who is not for us is against us.*

whoa (wō), *interj.* stop! *"Whoa there!" she said to her horse.* ■ Another word that sounds like this is **woe.**

who'd (hüd), **1** who would. **2** who had.

who·dun·it (hü dun′it), *n.* INFORMAL. story, movie, etc., about crime, especially murder, and detectives.

who·ev·er (hü ev′ər), *pron.* **1** who; any person that: *Whoever wants the book may have it.* **2** no matter who: *Whoever else leaves you, I won't.*

whole (hōl), **1** *adj.* having all its parts; complete: *They gave us a whole set of dishes.* **2** *adj.* full; entire: *We worked the whole day. He ate the whole melon.* **3** *n.* all of a thing; the total: *Three thirds make a whole.* **4** *n.* thing complete in itself; a system: *the complex whole of civilization.* **5** *adj.* not injured, broken, or defective: *I came out of the fight with a whole skin.* **6** *adj.* in one piece; undivided: *The dog swallowed the meat whole.* **7** *adj.* well; healthy. [See Word Story at *whack.*] ■ Another word that sounds like this is **hole. —whole′ness,** *n.*

as a whole, as one complete thing; altogether: *The group as a whole protested.*

on the whole, 1 considering everything. **2** for the most part.

whole-grain (hōl′grān′), *adj.* made of grain from which the germ and bran have not been removed: *whole-grain muffins.*

whole·heart·ed (hōl′här′tid), *adj.* enthusiastic; earnest; hearty; devoted: *The school gave the team its wholehearted support.* **—whole′heart′ed·ly,** *adv.*

whole note, (in music) note to be played four times as long as one quarter note.

whole number, a number such as 1, 2, 3, 4, 5, etc., which is not a fraction or a mixed number; integer. 15 and 106 are whole numbers; ½ and ⅞ are fractions; 1⅜ and 23⅔ are mixed numbers.

whole·sale (hōl′sāl′), **1** *n.* sale of goods in large quantities at a time, usually to storekeepers or others who will in turn sell them to users: *Our grocer buys at wholesale and sells at retail.* **2** *adv., adj.* in large lots or quantities: *buy something wholesale. The wholesale price of this coat is $40; the retail price is $99.* **3** *adj.* selling in large quantities: *a wholesale fruit business.* **4** *v.* to sell or be sold in large quantities: *They wholesale these jackets at $25 each.* **5** *adj.* general; extensive: *Avoid wholesale criticism.* ❑ *v.* **whole·saled, whole·sal·ing.**

whole·sal·er (hōl′sā′lər), *n.* a wholesale merchant.

whole·some (hōl′səm), *adj.* **1** good for the health; healthful: *Bananas are a wholesome food.* **2** healthy-looking; suggesting health: *a clean, wholesome face.* **3** good for the mind or morals;

beneficial: *The students had a wholesome interest in learning.* **—whole′some·ly,** *adv.* **—whole′some·ness,** *n.*

whole step, (in music) an interval of two half steps, such as D to E, or F to G.

whole tone, whole step.

whole-wheat (hōl′wēt′), *adj.* **1** made of the entire wheat kernel: *whole-wheat flour.* **2** made from whole-wheat flour: *whole-wheat bread.*

who'll (hül), **1** who will. **2** who shall.

whol·ly (hō′lē), *adv.* to the whole amount or extent; completely; entirely; totally: *The patient was wholly cured.* ■ Other words that sound like this are **holey** and **holy.**

whom (hüm), *pron.* what person; which person. *Whom* is a form of *who. Whom do you like best? He does not know whom to believe. The girl to whom I spoke is my cousin.*

whom·ev·er (hüm′ev′ər), *pron.* **1** whom; any person whom. **2** no matter whom.

whom·so·ev·er (hüm′sō ev′ər), *pron.* any person whom.

whoop (hüp *or* wüp), **1** *n.* a loud cry or shout: *The winner gave a whoop of joy.* **2** *v.* to shout loudly. **3** *n.* the loud, gasping sound someone with whooping cough makes after a fit of coughing. **4** *v.* to make this noise. ■ Another word that can sound like this is **hoop.**

whooping cough, an infectious disease of children, and rarely of adults, that causes fits of coughing that end with a loud, gasping sound.

whooping crane, a large, white, North American crane with a loud, raucous cry. It is nearly extinct.

whoops (hwüps, hwüps, wüps, *or* wüps), *interj.* word used to express surprise, embarrassment, or apology for a mistake.

whoosh (wüsh *or* wüsh), **1** *n.* a soft hissing sound like something rushing through the air. **2** *v.* to move with such a sound: *The arrow whooshed by.* ❑ *n., pl.* **whoosh·es.**

whop·per (wop′ər), *n.* INFORMAL. **1** something very large: *The fish I caught was a whopper.* **2** a big lie: *She was punished for telling such a whopper.*

whooping cranes—up to 5 ft. (1.5 m) tall

whore (hôr), *n.* prostitute. ■ Another word that sounds like this is **hoar.**

whorl (wôrl *or* wèrl), *n.* **1** circle of leaves or flowers around a stem of a plant. **2** one of the turns of the spiral shell of a univalve. **3** anything that circles or turns. People can be identified by the whorls of their fingerprints. ■ Another word that can sound like this is **whirl.**

who's (hüz), **1** who is. **2** who has.

whose (hüz), *pron.* of whom; of which: *The girl whose work got the prize is very talented. Whose book is this?*

who·so·ev·er (hü′sō ev′ər), *pron.* whoever.

why (wi), **1** *adv., conj.* for what reason: *Why did the baby cry? He does not know why he lost.* **2** *conj.* for which; because of which: *That is the reason why I left.* **3** *conj.* the reason for which: *That is why she raised the question.* **4** *n.* reason: *I tried to find out the whys and wherefores of their strange behavior.* **5** *interj.* Why is sometimes used to show surprise, doubt, etc., or just to fill in, without adding any important meaning to what is said. *Why it's all gone! Why, yes, I will if you wish.* ❑ *n., pl.* **whys.**

WI, Wisconsin (used with postal Zip Code).

W.I., West Indies.

Wich·i·ta (wich′ə tò), *n.* city in S Kansas, on the Arkansas River.

Wichita Falls, city in N Texas.

wick (wik), *n.* cord of twisted thread on an oil lamp or candle. When the wick is lit, it draws the oil or melted wax up to be burned. **—wick′less,** *adj.*

wick·ed (wik′id), *adj.* **1** bad; evil; sinful: *a wicked person, wicked deeds.* **2** mischievous; playfully sly: *a wicked smile.* **3** unpleasant; severe: *A wicked snowstorm swept through the state.* **—wick′ed·ly,** *adv.*

SYNONYM STUDY **Wicked, evil,** and **sinful** all mean doing wrong things on purpose. **Wicked** is a general word: *The actor playing the wicked king laughs when he wrongs people.* **Evil** means wicked and causing great harm: *Terrorist bombing is an evil deed.* **Sinful** means doing things judged wrong by the laws of religion: *The Koran says it is sinful to murder or steal.*

wick·ed·ness (wik′id nis), *n.* **1** quality of being wicked. **2** a wicked thing or act. ❑ *n., pl.* **wick·ed·ness·es** for 2.

wick·er (wik′ər), **1** *n.* twigs, or any slender, easily bent material, woven together. Wicker is used in making baskets and furniture. **2** *adj.* made of wicker: *a wicker chair.* **3** *n.* a slender, easily bent branch or twig. [**Wicker** comes from a Scandinavian word meaning "willow branch." Willow branches are often used to make wicker furniture.]

wick·er·work (wik′ər werk′), *n.* objects made of wicker.

wick·et (wik′it), *n.* **1** (in croquet) a wire arch stuck in the ground to knock the ball through. **2** (in cricket) either of the two sets of sticks that one side tries to hit with the ball. **3** a small window: *Buy your tickets at this wicket.* **4** a small door or gate: *The big door has a wicket in it.*

wick·i·up (wik′ē up′), *n.* a hut made of branches covered with mats or grass. Nomadic tribes in the western and southwestern United States used to live in wickiups.

wide (wīd), **1** *adj.* filling much space from side to side; not narrow; broad: *a wide street. The ship sailed across the wide ocean. They went forth into the wide world.* **2** *adj.* extending a certain distance from side to side: *The door is three feet wide.* **3** *adv.* over an extensive space or region: *travel far and wide.* **4** *adj.* having great range; including many different things: *A trip around the world gives wide experience.* **5** *adj.* far open: *He stared with wide eyes.* **6** *adv.* to the full extent; fully: *Open your mouth wide. The gates stand wide open.* **7** *adj.* far from a named point or object: *The shot was wide of the mark.* ❑ *adj.* **wid·er, wid·est.** **—wide′ly,** *adv.* **—wide′ness,** *n.*

wide-an·gle (wīd′ang′gəl), *adj.* using or needing a lens that forms an image across a wide angle of a scene: *a wide-angle shot.*

wide-a·wake (wīd′ə wāk′), *adj.* **1** with the eyes wide open; fully awake. **2** alert; knowing: *The mountain climber was wide-awake to the dangers of the climb.* **—wide′-a·wake′ness,** *n.*

wide-bod·y (wīd′bod′ē), *n.* a type of jet plane with a wide body, able to carry more than 250 passengers. ❑ *n., pl.* **wide·bod·ies.**

wide-eyed (wīd′īd′), *adj.* with the eyes wide open: *The children watched the rabbits with wide-eyed interest.*

wid·en (wīd′n), *v.* to make or become wide or wider: *We widened the path through the forest. The river widens as it flows.* **—wid′en·er,** *n.*

wide·spread (wīd′spred′), *adj.* **1** spread widely: *widespread wings.* **2** spread over a wide space: *a widespread flood.* **3** occurring in many places or among many persons far apart: *a widespread belief.*

widg·eon (wij′ən), *n.* wigeon. ❑ *n., pl.* **widg·eon** or **widg·eons.**

widg·et (wij′it), *n.* gadget.

wid·ow (wid′ō), **1** *n.* woman whose husband is dead and who has not married again. **2** *v.* to make a widow of: *She was widowed last year.*

wid·ow·er (wid′ō ər), *n.* man whose wife is dead and who has not married again.

wid·ow·hood (wid′ō hùd), *n.* condition or time of being a widow.

width (width), *n.* **1** how wide a thing is; distance across; breadth: *The room is 12 feet in width.* **2** piece of a certain width: *Two widths of cloth will make the curtains.*

wield (wēld), *v.* to hold and use; manage; control: *The worker wielded a hammer. A writer wields the pen. The people wield the power in a democracy.* ■ Another word that sounds like this is **wheeled.** **—wield′a·ble,** *adj.* **—wield′er,** *n.*

wield·y (wēl′dē), *adj.* easily controlled or handled; manageable. ❑ *adj.* **wield·i·er, wield·i·est.**

wie·ner (wē′nər), *n.* frankfurter.

Wie·sel (wē zel′), *n.* **El·ie** (el′ē), born 1928, American writer, born in Romania. His writings describe the horrible things he saw and endured as a prisoner in Nazi concentration camps. He won the 1986 Nobel Peace Prize.

wife (wīf), *n.* woman who has a husband; a married woman. ❑ *n., pl.* **wives.** **—wife′hood,** *n.* **—wife′less,** *adj.*

wife·ly (wīf′lē), *adj.* of a wife; like a wife. **—wife′li·ness,** *n.*

wig (wig), *n.* an artificial covering of natural or false hair for the head.

wig·eon (wij′ən), *n.* either of two wild freshwater ducks. Also, **widgeon.** ❑ *n., pl.* **wig·eon** or **wig·eons.**

wig·gle (wig′əl), **1** *v.* to move with short, quick movements from side to side; wriggle: *The puppy wiggled out of my arms.* **2** *n.* such a movement. ❑ *v.* **wig·gled, wig·gling.**

wig·gler (wig′lər), *n.* **1** person or thing that wiggles. **2** the larva or pupa of a mosquito.

wig·gly (wig′lē), *adj.* **1** moving from side to side with quick, short movements: *I couldn't hold the wiggly puppy.* **2** having curves or waves; wavy: *There were wiggly lines on the wallpaper.* ❑ *adj.* **wig·gli·er, wig·gli·est.**

wig·wag (wig′wag′), **1** *v.* to move back and forth. **2** *v.* to signal by movements of arms, flags, or lights, according to a code. **3** *n.* such signaling. ❑ *v.* **wig·wagged, wig·wag·ging.** **—wig′wag′ger,** *n.*

wig·wam (wig′wäm), *n.* hut made of bark, mats, or skins laid over a dome-shaped frame of poles, used by certain North American Indians.

wigwam

wild (wīld), **1** *adj.* living or growing naturally; not grown, tamed, or cultivated by people: *wild strawberries. The tiger is a wild animal.* **2** *adj.* with no people living in it: *the wild region of the far north.* **3** *n.pl.* **wilds,** wild country. **4** *adj.* not civilized; savage: *He is reading about the wild tribes of ancient times in Europe.* **5** *adj.* not held back; not restrained: *a wild rush for the ball.* **6** *adj.* not in proper control or order; uncontrolled; undisciplined: *The children were wild during the teacher's absence.* **7** *adj.* violently excited; frantic: *wild with pain.* **8** *adj.* violent: *a wild snowstorm. Wild waves came roaring onto the shore.* **9** *adj.* unreasonable; silly; senseless: *The child had the wild idea that horses could fly.* **10** *adj.* very eager; enthusiastic: *They were wild about animals.* **11** *adj.* far from the mark: *The shortstop made a wild throw to third base.* **12** *adv.* in a wild manner; to a wild degree: *Daisies grow wild in the field.* **—wild′ly,** *adv.* **—wild′ness,** *n.*

run wild, to live or grow without restraint.

wild and woolly, rough and uncivilized.

SYNONYM STUDY **Wild, frenzied,** and **frantic** all mean extremely excited and out of control. **Wild** is the general word: *The fans went wild when they saw the rock star.* **Frenzied** means too wild to think: *They made a frenzied dash for the train and forgot their suitcases.* **Frantic** means wild with rage, fear, pain, or grief: *In spite of frantic efforts, they could not save their house from the flood.*

wild boar, a wild hog of Europe, southern Asia, and northern Africa. It is the ancestor of all modern domesticated swine.

wild·cat (wīld′kat′), **1** *n.* any of several wild animals related to the common cat and similar to it in appearance, but larger. A lynx is one kind of wildcat. **2** *adj.* not authorized by union officials; begun by small groups or local unions: *a wildcat strike.* **3** *n.* a well drilled for oil or gas in a region where none has been found before. **4** *adj.* not safe; reckless: *He lost all of his money by investing in wildcat stocks.* **5** *n.* a fierce fighter.

W

a	hat	ė	term	ô	order	ch	child		
ā	age	i	it	oi	oil	ng	long	ə	a in about
ä	far	ī	ice	ou	out	sh	she		e in taken
â	care	o	hot	u	cup	th	thin		i in pencil
e	let	ō	open	ù	put	ŦH	then		o in lemon
ē	equal	ò	saw	ü	rule	zh	measure		u in circus

Wilde (wīld), *n.* **Os·car** (os′kər), 1854-1900, British playwright, poet, and novelist, born in Ireland. ■ **Wilde** was famous as a wit and public figure. "There is only one thing in the world worse than being talked about," he remarked, "and that is not being talked about."

wil·de·beest (wil′də bēst′), *n.* gnu. ❑ *n., pl.* **wil·de·beest** or **wil·de·beests.**

Wil·der (wil′dər), *n.* **1 Lau·ra In·galls** (lôr′ə ing′gəlz), 1867-1957, American writer. She wrote the "Little House" series of books for children based on her experiences growing up. **2 Thorn·ton** (thôrn′tən), 1897-1975, American playwright and novelist.

wil·der·ness (wil′dər nis), *n.* **1** a wild, uncultivated, or desolate region with few or no people living in it. **2 the Wilderness,** a wooded region in N Virginia. Several battles took place here during the Civil War, especially in May 1864, as Lee's Confederates fought to keep Grant's Union troops from Richmond. ❑ *n., pl.* **wil·der·ness·es.**

Wilderness Road, road from E Virginia, through the Cumberland Mountains to the Ohio River. An early trail was blazed along this route by Daniel Boone as far as Boonesborough in 1775.

wild-eyed (wīld′īd′), *adj.* **1** staring wildly or angrily. **2** senseless; irrational: *wild-eyed notions.*

wild·fire (wīld′fīr′), *n.* a fire that spreads quickly and is hard to put out.
like wildfire, very rapidly: *The news spread like wildfire.*

wild·flow·er (wīld′flou′ər), *n.* any flowering plant that grows wild in the woods or fields.

wild fowl, birds ordinarily hunted, such as wild ducks or geese, partridges, quails, and pheasants.

wild-goose chase (wīld′gūs′), a useless search or attempt; foolish or hopeless quest.

wild·life (wīld′līf′), *n.* wild animals and plants: *The campers saw many kinds of wildlife.*

wild pitch, a baseball pitch that the catcher cannot catch, allowing one or more base runners to advance.

wild rice, a North American water grass, with grain that is used for food.

Wild West, the western United States during pioneer days.

wile (wīl), **1** *n.* a trick to deceive; cunning trick: *The dishonest antiques dealer used many wiles to make a sale.* **2** *v.* to coax; lure; entice: *The sunshine wiled him away from his work.* ❑ *v.* **wiled, wil·ing.** ■ Another word that sounds like this is **while.**

wil·ful (wil′fəl), *adj.* willful. **—wil′ful·ly,** *adv.* **—wil′ful·ness,** *n.*

Wil·kins (wil′kənz), *n.* **Maur·ice** (môr′is), born 1916, British biologist, born in New Zealand. ■ **Maurice Wilkins** shared the 1962 Nobel Prize in physiology or medicine with Francis Crick and James Watson for creating the double helix model of DNA.

will[1] (wil), *v.* **1** am going to; is going to; are going to: *I will go shopping tomorrow.* **2** am willing to; is willing to; are willing to: *I will help clean the house if he does.* **3** to be able to; can: *The pail will hold four gallons.* **4** must: *Don't argue; you will do it at once!* **5** to do often or usually: *She will read for hours at a time.* **6** to wish; desire: *We cannot always do as we will.* ❑ *v., past tense* **would.**

will[2] (wil), **1** *n.* power of the mind to decide and do: *A good leader must have a strong will.* **2** *n.* purpose or determination: *Although very ill, the patient had the will to live.* **3** *n.* wish; desire: *Elections express the will of the people.* **4** *n.* a legal statement or document telling what you want to be done with your property after you are dead. **5** *v.* to give by such a statement: *They willed all their property to their children.* **6** *n.* feeling toward another: *Most of us feel good will toward people we like.* **7** *v.* to decide by using this power; use the will: *I willed to keep awake.* **8** *v.* to influence or try to influence by deliberate control over thought and action: *She willed the person in front of her to turn around.* **9** *v.* to determine; decide: *Fate has willed it otherwise.*
at will, whenever you wish.

Wil·lem·stad (vil′əm stät), *n.* capital of the Netherlands Antilles.

will·ful (wil′fəl), *adj.* **1** wanting or taking your own way; stubborn: *The willful child would not obey.* **2** done on purpose; intended: *willful murder.* Also, **wilful. —will′ful·ness,** *n.*

will·ful·ly (wil′fə lē), *adv.* **1** by choice; voluntarily. **2** by design; intentionally. **3** selfishly; stubbornly. Also, **wilfully.**

Wil·liam I (wil′yəm), 1027?-1087, duke of Normandy who conquered England at the battle of Hastings in 1066 and was king of England from 1066 to 1087. He was called "William the Conqueror."

Wil·liams (wil′yəmz), *n.* **1 Hank** (hangk), 1923-1953, American country and western singer and composer. **2 Ro·ger** (roj′ər), 1604?-1683, English clergyman who founded Rhode Island. **3 Ted** (ted), born 1918, American baseball player. He was the last player to bat .400 in the major leagues. **4 Tennessee,** 1911-1983, American playwright. His plays include *The Glass Menagerie* and *A Streetcar Named Desire.* **5 William Car·los** (kär′lōs), 1883-1963, American poet and doctor. He won the 1963 Pulitzer Prize for poetry.

Wil·liams·burg (wil′yəmz bėrg′), *n.* city in SE Virginia. It has been restored to look as it did before the Revolutionary War.

wil·lies (wil′ēz), *n.pl.* spell of nervousness.

will·ing (wil′ing), *adj.* **1** ready; consenting: *He is willing to wait.* **2** cheerfully ready: *She is a willing helper.* **—will′ing·ly,** *adv.* **—will′ing·ness,** *n.*

will-o'-the-wisp (wil′ə тнə wisp′), *n.* **1** anything that deceives or misleads by luring someone on: *Most schemes to get rich quickly are likely to be will-o'-the-wisps.* **2** a flickering light appearing at night over marshy places. It is thought to be caused by burning marsh gas.

wil·low (wil′ō), *n.* any of numerous trees or bushes with tough, slender branches and narrow leaves. The branches of most willows bend easily and are used to make furniture, baskets, etc. **—wil′low·like′,** *adj.*

wil·low·y (wil′ō ē), *adj.* **1** like a willow; slender; supple; graceful. **2** having many willows. ❑ *adj.* **wil·low·i·er, wil·low·i·est.**

will·pow·er (wil′pou′ər), *n.* strength of will; determination: *She had the willpower not to go along with silly suggestions.*

wil·ly-nil·ly (wil′ē nil′ē), *adv.* willingly or not; with or against your wishes.

willow

Wil·ming·ton (wil′ming tən), *n.* city in N Delaware, on the Delaware River.

Wil·son (wil′sən), *n.* **1 Wood·row** (wůd′rō), 1856-1924, the 28th president of the United States, from 1913 to 1921. He won the 1919 Nobel Peace Prize. **2 Mount,** peak in SW California, 5710 feet (1740 meters) high. One of the largest telescopes in the world is in the observatory on top of Mount Wilson.

wilt[1] (wilt), *v.* **1** to become limp and bend down; wither: *Flowers wilt when they don't get enough water.* **2** to lose strength, vigor, assurance, etc.: *The hikers wilted after walking 15 miles.* **3** to cause to wilt.

wilt[2] (wilt), *v.* OLD USE. will[1]. "Thou wilt" means "you will."

wil·y (wī′lē), *adj.* using subtle tricks to deceive; crafty; cunning; sly: *The wily thief got away.* ❑ *adj.* **wil·i·er, wil·i·est. —wil′i·ly,** *adv.* **—wil′i·ness,** *n.*

wimp (wimp), *n.* INFORMAL. a weak person. [See Word Source at folk etymology.]

wim·ple (wim′pəl), *n.* cloth for the head arranged in folds about the head, cheeks, chin, and neck, worn sometimes by nuns and formerly by other women.

wimp·y (wim′pē) *adj.* INFORMAL. weak; ineffectual. ❑ *adj.* **wimp·i·er, wimp·i·est.** **—wimp′i·ness,** *n.*

win (win), **1** *v.* to be successful over others; get victory or success: *We all hope our team will win.* **2** *v.* to get victory or success in: *He won the race.* **3** *n.* success; victory: *We had four wins and no defeats.* **4** *v.* to get by effort, ability, or skill; gain: *win fame, win a prize.* **5** *v.* to gain the favor of; persuade: *The speaker soon won the audience. She has completely won the other scientists over to her opinion.* **6** *v.* to get to; reach, often by effort: *win the summit of a mountain.* ❑ *v.* **won, win·ning. —win′less,** *adj.* **—win′na·ble,** *adj.*

wince (wins), **1** *v.* to draw back suddenly; flinch slightly: *I winced when the dentist's drill touched my tooth.* **2** *n.* act of wincing: *Seeing the wince, the dentist stopped drilling for a moment.* ❑ *v.* **winced, winc·ing. —winc′er,** *n.*

winch (winch), **1** *n.* machine for lifting or pulling things, powered either by a hand crank or by an engine attached to a rotating bar. A rope or cable wound on the bar raises or pulls the load. **2** *v.* to lift or pull by using a winch. ❑ *n., pl.* **winch·es.**

wind¹ (wind), **1** *n.* air in motion. The wind varies in force from a slight breeze to a strong gale. **2** *n.* a strong wind; gale: *Winds blowing at ninety miles an hour toppled a tree onto our roof.* **3** *n.* power of breathing; breath: *A runner needs good wind.* **4** *n.* air filled with some smell: *The deer caught wind of us and ran off.* **5** *v.* to put out of breath; cause difficulty in breathing: *Walking up the steep hill winded me.* **6** *v.* to let an animal recover its breath. **7** *n.pl.* **winds,** wind instruments. ❑ *v.* **wind·ed, wind·ing. —wind′less,** *adj.*

get wind of, to find out about; get a hint of: *Don't let Mother get wind of our plans.*

in the wind, happening; about to happen.

take the wind out of someone's sails, to take away someone's advantage, argument, etc., suddenly or unexpectedly.

wind² (wind), **1** *v.* to move this way and that; go in a crooked way; change direction; turn: *A brook winds through the woods. We wound our way through the narrow streets.* **2** *v.* to fold, wrap, or place about something: *She wound her arms around her new puppy.* **3** *v.* to cover with something put, wrapped, or folded around: *The patient's arm is wound with bandages.* **4** *v.* to roll into a ball or on a spool: *We took turns winding yarn. Thread comes wound on spools.* **5** *n.* a bend; turn; twist. **6** *v.* to twist or turn around something: *The vine winds around a pole.* **7** *v.* to make a machine go by turning some part of it: *wind a clock.* **8** *v.* to be wound: *This clock winds easily.* ❑ *v.* **wound, wind·ing.**

wind down, 1 come to an end; finish: *We waited for the music box to wind down.* **2** to relax: *I find that a hot bath helps me wind down.*

wind up, 1 to end; settle; conclude. **2** (in baseball) to make a swinging movement of the arms while twisting the body just before pitching the ball.

wind·bag (wind′bag′), *n.* INFORMAL. person who talks a great deal but does not say much that is interesting or important.

wind·blown (wind′blōn′), *adj.* blown by the wind.

wind·break (wind′brāk′), *n.* a shelter from the wind: *The campers pitched their tent next to the stone wall, so the wall would serve as a windbreak.*

Wind·break·er (wind′brā′kər), *n.* trademark for a short jacket of nylon, wool, etc., with a tight-fitting band at the waist and cuffs. It is worn outdoors.

wind·burn (wind′bėrn′), *n.* roughening or reddening of the skin, caused by being exposed to strong wind.

Wind Cave National Park, a national park in SW South Dakota, containing a cave with unusual crystal formations.

wind chill factor or **wind chill,** the estimated cooling effect on exposed human skin of air temperature and wind speed combined. If the air temperature is 10 degrees Fahrenheit (−12° C) and the wind speed is 20 miles (32 km) per hour, the wind chill is −24 degrees Fahrenheit (−31° C).

wind chimes, small pieces of bamboo, metal, glass, etc., hung so that they tinkle or chime when moved by the wind.

wind·fall (wind′fȯl′), *n.* **1** an unexpected piece of good luck: *Finding this job was a windfall.* **2** fruit blown down by the wind.

wind·flow·er (wind′flou′ər), *n.* anemone.

Wind·hoek (vint′hük), *n.* capital of Namibia, in the central part.

wind·ing (wīn′ding), **1** *n.* something that is wound or coiled. **2** *n.* act of something that winds. **3** *n.* a bend; turn. **4** *adj.* bending; turning. **—wind′ing·ly,** *adv.*

wind instrument (wind), a musical instrument sounded by blowing air into it. French horns, flutes, and trombones are wind instruments.

wind·jam·mer (wind′jam′ər), *n.* a sailing ship.

wind·lass (wind′ləs), *n.* winch used to hoist water from a well or an anchor out of the water. ❑ *n., pl.* **wind·lass·es.**

wind·mill (wind′mil′), *n.* machine powered by the action of the wind upon a wheel of vanes or sails mounted on a tower. Windmills have been used to pump water, grind grain, and produce electricity.

windmill

win·dow (win′dō), *n.* **1** an opening in an outer wall or roof of a building, or in a vehicle, that lets in air or light. **2** structure set in such an opening, with glass or plastic panes and a wooden or metal frame. **3** period of time available or favorable for doing something: *a window of opportunity, a two-day launch window.* **4** a framed area on a computer screen showing information different from that on the rest of the screen. A computer may have several windows open at once, showing several different programs. **—win′dow·less,** *adj.*

WORD STORY **Window** comes from Norse words meaning "wind" and "eye." Since eyes and windows both let in light, why name it for the wind? In ancient times, buildings were heated by open fires, and the smoke got thick. Fresh air was important.

window box, container of wood, metal, or plastic, set on or fastened to a windowsill, in which small plants may be grown.

win·dow·pane (win′dō pān′), *n.* piece of glass or plastic in a window.

win·dow-shop (win′dō shop′), *v.* to look at articles in store windows without going in to buy anything. ❑ *v.* **win·dow-shopped, win·dow-shop·ping.**

win·dow·sill (win′dō sil′), *n.* piece of wood or stone across the bottom of a window.

wind·pipe (wind′pīp′), *n.* the passage by which air is carried from the throat to the lungs; trachea.

wind·row (wind′rō′), *n.* row of hay raked together to dry before being made into heaps.

wind·shear (wind′shir′), *n.* a sudden, powerful shift in wind direction. It is a threat to aircraft that are taking off or landing.

wind·shield (wind′shēld′), *n.* sheet of glass or plastic on the front of a motor vehicle to keep the wind off the driver or passengers.

a	hat	ė	term	ȯ	order	ch	child		a in about
ā	age	i	it	oi	oil	ng	long		e in taken
ä	far	ī	ice	ou	out	sh	she	ə	i in pencil
â	care	o	hot	u	cup	th	thin		o in lemon
e	let	ō	open	ù	put	ŦH	then		u in circus
ē	equal	ȯ	saw	ü	rule	zh	measure		

W

wind·sock (wind′sok′), *n.* device something like a large sock, mounted on a pole and open at one end to catch the wind and show its direction.

Wind·sor (win′zər), *n.* **1** town in S England, where **Windsor Castle,** chief residence of the British sovereign, is located. **2** the family name of the royal house of Great Britain since 1917.

wind·storm (wind′stôrm′), *n.* storm with much wind but little or no rain.

wind·surf·ing (wind′sėr′fing), *n.* surfing on a sailboard; boardsailing.

wind·swept (wind′swept′), *adj.* exposed to the full force of the wind: *a windswept hillside.*

wind tunnel (wind), tunnel for testing the effects of wind and air pressure on aircraft, cars, etc., by blowing air past models or full-sized vehicles at high speeds.

wind·up (wind′up′), *n.* **1** act of winding up; end; close; conclusion: *The windup of the movie was very exciting.* **2** (in baseball) a swinging movement of the arms while twisting the body just before pitching the ball.

wind·ward (wind′wərd), **1** *adj., adv.* on the side toward the wind. **2** *n.* the side toward the wind. **3** *adj., adv.* in the direction from which the wind is blowing.

Wind·ward Islands (wind′wərd), the S part of the Lesser Antilles in the West Indies.

wind·y (win′dē), *adj.* **1** having much wind: *windy weather.* **2** made of wind; empty: *windy talk.* **3** talking a great deal; voluble. ❑ *adj.* **wind·i·er, wind·i·est. —wind′i·ly,** *adv.* **—wind′i·ness,** *n.*

wine (wīn), **1** *n.* an alcoholic drink made from the fermented juice of grapes. **2** *n.* the fermented juice of other fruits or plants: *dandelion wine.* **3** *n.* color of red wine. **4** *v.* to entertain with wine. ❑ *v.* **wined, win·ing.** ■ Another word that sounds like this is **whine.**

wine·press (wīn′pres′), *n.* **1** machine for pressing the juice from grapes. **2** vat in which grapes are crushed underfoot in the process of making wine. ❑ *n., pl.* **wine·press·es.**

wing (wing), **1** *n.* one of the movable parts of a bird, insect, or bat used in flying, or a corresponding part of a bird or insect that does not fly. Birds have one pair of wings; insects usually have two pairs. **2** *n.* anything like a wing in shape or use: *the wings of an airplane.* **3** *n.* part that sticks out from the main part of a building: *The house has a wing at each side.* **4** *n.* either of the side portions of an army or fleet ready for battle. **5** *n.* either of the spaces to the right or left of the stage in a theater. **6** *n.* part of an organization; faction. The liberals of a political group are often called the left wing. **7** *n.* an air force unit composed of two or more groups. **8** *n.* player on either side of the center in hockey, soccer, etc. **9** *v.* to fly: *Modern airliners wing from continent to continent.* **10** *v.* to send or throw something fast: *wing the ball to first base.* **11** *v.* to give speed to: *Terror winged our steps as the bear came closer.* **12** *v.* to wound in the wing or arm: *The bullet winged the bird but did not kill it.* **—wing′less,** *adj.* **—wing′like′,** *adj.*
on the wing, in flight.
take wing, to fly away: *The bird took wing when the cat came near.*
under the wing of, under the protection of.

winged (wingd *or* wing′id), *adj.* **1** having wings: *A gnat is a winged insect.* **2** swift; rapid: *winged messenger.*

wing·span (wing′span′), *n.* distance between the wing tips of an airplane.

wing·spread (wing′spred′), *n.* distance between the outspread tips of the wings, especially of a bird.

wink (wingk), **1** *v.* to close the eyes and open them again quickly: *The bright light made him wink.* **2** *v.* to close and open one eye on purpose as a hint or signal: *I winked at my sister to keep still.* **3** *n.* act of winking: *I gave them a friendly wink.* **4** *n.* a hint or signal given by winking. **5** *v.* to twinkle: *The stars winked.* **6** *n.* a very short time: *quick as a wink.* **—wink′ing·ly,** *adv.*
wink at, to pretend not to see: *My parents knew I came home past my bedtime last night, but they winked at it.*

win·ner (win′ər), *n.* person or thing that wins: *The winner of the contest got a prize.*

win·ning (win′ing), **1** *adj.* that wins: *a winning team.* **2** *adj.* charming; attractive: *a very winning smile.* **3** *n.pl.* **winnings,** what is won; money won: *to pocket your winnings.* **—win′ning·ly,** *adv.*

Win·ni·peg (win′ə peg), *n.* **1** capital of Manitoba, Canada. **2 Lake,** lake in S Canada. [**Winnipeg** comes from a Cree word meaning "muddy water." The name was given first to the lake, later to the city.]

win·now (win′ō), *v.* **1** to blow off the chaff from grain; drive or blow away chaff. **2** to sort out; separate; sift: *winnow truth from lies.*

win·some (win′səm), *adj.* charming; attractive; pleasing: *a winsome young couple, a winsome smile.* **—win′some·ly,** *adv.* **—win′some·ness,** *n.*

Win·ston-Sa·lem (win′stən sā′ləm), *n.* city in N central North Carolina.

win·ter (win′tər), **1** *n.* the coldest of the four seasons; time of the year between autumn and spring. **2** *adj.* of or for winter: *winter clothes, winter weather.* **3** *v.* to pass the winter: *Robins winter in the south.* **4** *v.* to keep or feed during winter: *We wintered our cattle in the warm valley.*

winter—a winter scene

win·ter·green (win′tər grēn′), *n.* a small evergreen plant of North America with bright red berries and aromatic leaves. An oil made from its leaves is used in medicine and as a flavoring.

win·ter·ize (win′tə rīz′), *v.* to make a car, truck, etc., ready for operation or use during the winter. ❑ *v.* **win·ter·ized, win·ter·iz·ing.** **—win′ter·i·za′tion,** *n.*

win·ter·time (win′tər tīm′), *n.* the season of winter.

win·try (win′trē), *adj.* **1** of or like that of winter: *wintry weather, a wintry sky.* **2** not warm or friendly; chilly: *a wintry manner, a wintry smile, a wintry greeting.* ❑ *adj.* **win·tri·er, win·tri·est. —win′tri·ness,** *n.*

wingspread

wipe (wīp), **1** *v.* to rub in order to clean or dry: *Wipe your shoes on the mat.* **2** *v.* to take away, off, or out by rubbing: *Wipe away your tears.* **3** *v.* to remove: *The rain wiped away all the footprints.* **4** *v.* to rub or draw something over a surface. **5** *n.* act of wiping: *He gave his face a hasty wipe.* ❑ *v.* **wiped, wip·ing.**

wipe out, 1 to destroy completely: *Whole cities have been wiped out by volcanoes.* **2** to kill. **3** SLANG. to fall or cause to fall off a surfboard or other sports equipment.

wipe·out (wīp′out′), *n.* **1** complete destruction. **2** SLANG. a fall from a surfboard or other sports equipment.

wip·er (wī′pər), *n.* thing used for wiping: *windshield wipers.*

wire (wīr), **1** *n.* metal drawn out into a thin, flexible rod or fine thread. **2** *n.* a long piece of such metal to carry electric current, as in electric lighting, telephones, and telegraphs. **3** *adj.* made of or consisting of wire: *a wire fence.* **4** *v.* to furnish with wire: *wire a house for electricity.* **5** *v.* to fasten with wire: *She wired the two pieces together.* **6** *n.* telegraph: *He sent a message by wire.* **7** *v.* to telegraph: *I wired a reply.* **8** *n.* telegram: *The news came in a wire.* ❑ *v.* **wired, wir·ing.** **—wire′a·ble,** *adj.* **—wire′like′,** *adj.*

pull wires, to use secret influence to accomplish your purposes: *She pulled wires to get her son a job.*

under the wire, just before it is too late.

wire·haired (wīr′hârd′), *adj.* having coarse, stiff hair: *a wire-haired fox terrier.*

wire·less (wīr′lis), **1** *adj.* using no wires; transmitting by radio waves instead of by electric wires: *wireless communications.* **2** *n.* (earlier) system of transmission by radio waves without the use of wires.

wire·tap (wīr′tap′), **1** *v.* to make a secret connection with a telephone or telegraph line to hear or record messages sent over it: *They wiretapped the embassy phones.* **2** *n.* a secret connection with a telephone or telegraph line. ❑ *v.* **wire·tapped, wire·tap·ping. —wire′tap′per,** *n.*

wire·worm (wīr′wèrm′), *n.* the slender, hard-bodied larva of some kinds of beetles. Wireworms feed on the roots of plants and do much damage to crops.

wir·ing (wī′ring), *n.* system of wires to carry an electric current.

wir·y (wī′rē), *adj.* **1** like wire: *Our terrier has a wiry coat.* **2** lean, strong, and tough: *The gymnast has a small, wiry body.* ❑ *adj.* **wir·i·er, wir·i·est. —wir′i·ly,** *adv.* **—wir′i·ness,** *n.*

Wis. or Wisc., Wisconsin.

Wis·con·sin (wi skon′sən), *n.* one of the north central states of the United States. *Abbreviation:* WI, Wis., or Wisc. *Capital:* Madison. [**Wisconsin** may have come from an American Indian name for the state's central river. No one is sure what the original name meant.] **—Wis·con′sin·ite,** *n.*

wis·dom (wiz′dəm), *n.* **1** knowledge and good judgment based on experience; being wise. **2** wise conduct; wise words: *Her wisdom guided us.* **3** scholarly knowledge.

wisdom tooth, the back tooth on either side of each jaw, ordinarily appearing between the ages of 17 and 25.

wise[1] (wīz), *adj.* **1** having or showing knowledge and good judgment: *a wise judge, wise plans.* **2** having knowledge or information: *The old senator was wise in the ways of politics.* **3** INFORMAL. disrespectfully clever; fresh; pert: *Don't get wise with me, young man.* ❑ *adj.* **wis·er, wis·est. —wise′ly,** *adv.* **—wise′ness,** *n.*

wise up, SLANG. to make or become aware of; learn about: *I wish he would wise up about studying.*

be wise to or get wise to, SLANG. know about or learn about: *I am wise to all his tricks.*

put someone wise or set someone wise, SLANG. to tell someone something, especially something secret: *I put him wise to the plans for the surprise party.*

wise[2] (wīz), *n.* way; manner: *I am in no wise interested.*

-wise, *suffix.* **1** in a particular way or direction: *clockwise = in the way the hands of a clock go; lengthwise = in the direction of the length.* **2** in connection with; about; concerning: *publicity-wise = about publicity.*

wise·a·cre (wī′zā′kər), *n.* wise guy.

wise·crack (wiz′krak′), **1** *n.* a witty and sometimes insulting remark or reply. ■ See Synonym Study at **joke. 2** *v.* to make wisecracks. **—wise′crack′er,** *n.*

wise guy, INFORMAL. person who pretends to know everything; impudent or conceited person.

wish (wish), **1** *v.* to have a need or longing for; want; desire: *What is it that you wish? They wish to see you urgently.* **2** *v.* to have a desire; express a hope: *She wished for a telescope.* **3** *n.* act of wishing or wanting; desire; longing: *I have no wish to be rich.* **4** *n.* expression of a wish: *Please give them my best wishes for a happy New Year.* **5** *v.* to desire something for someone; have or express a hope for: *I wish you a happy New Year.* **6** *v.* to request or command: *Do you wish me to come over now?* **7** *n.* a request or command: *grant someone's slightest wish.* **8** *n.* thing wished for: *She got her wish.* ❑ *n., pl.* **wish·es. —wish′er,** *n.*

wish·bone (wish′bōn′), *n.* the forked bone in the front of the breastbone in most birds.

WORD STORY **Wishbone** comes from the custom of two people's making wishes while breaking the bone by pulling on the two ends. It is said that the person left with the longer piece of bone will get his or her wish. The custom may not be as old as many others, because the word first appeared about 150 years ago.

wish·ful (wish′fəl), *adj.* having or expressing a wish; desiring; desirous: *His boast was only wishful thinking.* **—wish′ful·ly,** *adv.* **—wish′ful·ness,** *n.*

wish·y-wash·y (wish′ē wäsh′ē), *adj.* **1** lacking strength of character; indecisive: *a wishy-washy person.* **2** thin and weak: *wishy-washy soup with no flavor.* **—wish′y-wash′i·ness,** *n.*

wisp (wisp), *n.* **1** bit or bunch of something: *a wisp of fluff, a wisp of hair.* **2** a tiny puff of smoke, steam, etc.: *Wisps of steam rose from the pot.* **3** a little thing: *a wisp of a child.* **—wisp′like′,** *adj.*

wisp·y (wis′pē), *adj.* like a wisp; thin; slight: *wispy feathers.* ❑ *adj.* **wisp·i·er, wisp·i·est. —wisp′i·ly,** *adv.* **—wisp′i·ness,** *n.*

wis·ter·i·a (wi stir′ē ə), *n.* any of several climbing bushes with large, drooping clusters of purple, blue, or white flowers. ❑ *n., pl.* **wis·ter·i·as.**

wist·ful (wist′fəl), *adj.* longing; yearning: *He looked with wistful eyes at the cookies.* **—wist′ful·ly,** *adv.* **—wist′ful·ness,** *n.*

wit (wit), *n.* **1** the power to perceive quickly and express cleverly ideas that are unusual, striking, and amusing: *Her wit made even troubles seem amusing.* **2** person with such power: *Mark Twain was a famous wit.* **3** Usually, **wits,** *pl.* power of understanding; mind or sense: *People with quick wits learn easily. I was out of my wits with fright.* [See Word Story at **witness.**] ■ Another word that sounds like this is **whit.**

to wit, that is to say; namely: *To my daughter I leave all I own— to wit: my house, what is in it, and the land on which it stands.*

witch (wich), *n.* **1** woman believed to have magic powers which she generally used to do evil. **2** an ugly old woman. ■ This meaning of **witch** is offensive. ❑ *n., pl.* **witch·es.** ■ Another word that sounds like this is **which.**

wisteria

W

a	hat	ė	term	ô	order	ch	child		
ā	age	i	it	oi	oil	ng	long		a in about
â	far	ī	ice	ou	out	sh	she	ə	e in taken
â	care	o	hot	u	cup	th	thin		i in pencil
e	let	ō	open	ù	put	ŦH	then		o in lemon
ē	equal	ȯ	saw	ü	rule	zh	measure		u in circus

witch·craft (wich′kraft′), *n.* what a witch does or is believed to be able to do; magic power or influence.

witch doctor, shaman, especially in certain tribal societies.

witch·er·y (wich′ər ē), *n.* **1** witchcraft; magic. **2** charm; fascination.

witch hazel, 1 bush or small tree of eastern North America that has yellow flowers in the fall or winter after the leaves have fallen. **2** lotion for cooling and soothing the skin, made from the bark and leaves of this bush.

witch hunt, 1 persecution or attack on the reputation of someone for political advantage. **2** persecution of people suspected of witchcraft. There were famous witch hunts in Massachusetts in the 1600s.

witch·ing (wich′ing), *adj.* bewitching; magical; enchanting. **—witch′ing·ly,** *adv.*

with (wiᴛʜ *or* with), *prep.* With shows that persons or things are taken together in some way. **1** in the company of: *Come with me.* **2** among: *They will mix with the crowd.* **3** having, wearing, carrying, etc.: *He is a man with brains. She received a telegram with good news.* **4** by means of: *The man cut the meat with a knife.* **5** using; showing: *Work with care.* **6** added to: *Do you want sugar with your tea?* **7** in relation to: *They are friendly with us.* **8** in regard to: *We are pleased with the house.* **9** in proportion to: *Her pay increased with her responsibilities.* **10** because of: *The child is shaking with cold.* **11** in the keeping or service of: *Leave the dog with me.* **12** in the region, sphere, experience, opinion, or view of: *High taxes are unpopular with many people.* **13** at the same time as: *With this battle the war ended.* **14** in the same direction as: *The boat floated along with the current.* **15** on the side of; for: *They are with us in our plan.* **16** against: *The English fought with the Germans.* **17** receiving; having received: *I went with his permission.* **18** in spite of: *With all his weight he was not a strong man.*

with it, INFORMAL. knowing; up-to-date.

with·al (wi ᴛʜȯl′ *or* wi ᴛʜȯl′), *adv.* OLD USE. with it all; as well; besides; also: *I am tired and hungry and hurt withal.*

with·draw (wiᴛʜ drȯ′ *or* with drȯ′), *v.* **1** to pull back; pull away: *The child quickly withdrew his hand from the hot stove. I withdrew from the discussion before it became an argument.* **2** to take back; remove: *The owner of the store agreed to withdraw the charge of theft if the robbers returned the money. She withdrew all of her savings from the bank.* **3** to go away: *She withdrew from the room.* ❑ *v.* **with·drew, with·drawn, with·draw·ing. —with·draw′·a·ble,** *adj.* **—with·draw′er,** *n.*

with·draw·al (wiᴛʜ drȯ′əl *or* with drȯ′əl), *n.* **1** act of withdrawing or condition of being withdrawn. **2** condition of physical distress in an addict who suddenly has no drugs.

with·drawn (wiᴛʜ drȯn′ *or* with drȯn′), **1** *v.* past participle of **withdraw:** *She has withdrawn all her savings from the bank.* **2** *adj.* shy; retiring; reserved. **3** *adj.* isolated; secluded.

with·drew (wiᴛʜ drü′ *or* with drü′), *v.* past tense of **withdraw:** *The coach withdrew the player from the game when he was hurt.*

with·er (wiᴛʜ′ər), *v.* **1** to lose or cause to lose freshness; make or become dry and lifeless; dry up; fade; shrivel: *The hot sun withers the grass. Flowers wither after they are cut. Age had withered the old woman's face.* **2** to humiliate with a harsh look; abash. ■ Another word that sounds like this is **whither.**

with·ers (wiᴛʜ′ərz), *n.pl.* the highest part of a horse's or other four-footed animal's back, between the shoulder blades.

with·held (with held′ *or* wiᴛʜ held′), *v.* past tense and past participle of **withhold:** *The witness withheld information from the police. Because information had been withheld, the wrong person was charged with the crime.*

with·hold (with hōld′ *or* wiᴛʜ hōld′), *v.* **1** to refrain from giving or granting: *There will be no school play if the principal withholds consent.* **2** to hold back; keep back: *Tell the whole story; don't withhold anything.* ❑ *v.* **with·held, with·hold·ing. —with·hold′er,** *n.*

withholding tax, the part of someone's salary or wages deducted for income tax by an employer on behalf of the government.

with·in (wiᴛʜ in′ *or* with in′), **1** *prep.* inside the limits of; not beyond: *The task was within my power. I will guess your weight within five pounds.* **2** *prep.* in or into the inner part of; inside of: *By the use of X rays, doctors can see within the body.* **3** *adv.* in or into the inner part; inside: *The house has been painted within and without.*

with·out (wiᴛʜ out′ *or* with out′), **1** *prep.* with no; not having; free from; lacking: *I drink tea without sugar.* **2** *prep.* so as to leave out, avoid, or neglect: *She walked past without noticing us.* **3** *prep.* outside of; beyond: *Children were playing within and without the house.* **4** *adv.* on the outside; outside: *The house is painted without and within.*

with·stand (with stand′ *or* wiᴛʜ stand′), *v.* to stand against; hold out against; resist; oppose, especially successfully; endure: *These heavy shoes will withstand much hard wear.* ■ See Synonym Study at **oppose.** ❑ *v.* **with·stood, with·stand·ing. —with·stand′er,** *n.*

with·stood (with stůd′ *or* wiᴛʜ stůd′), *v.* past tense and past participle of **withstand:** *The family withstood many hardships. These shoes have withstood three years of hard wear.*

wit·less (wit′lis), *adj.* lacking sense; stupid; foolish: *Crossing the street without looking is a witless thing to do.* **—wit′less·ly,** *adv.* **—wit′less·ness,** *n.*

wit·ness (wit′nis), **1** *n.* person who saw something happen; spectator; eyewitness: *There were several witnesses to the accident.* **2** *v.* to be a witness of; see: *He witnessed the accident.* **3** *n.* person who gives evidence or testifies under oath in a court of law. **4** *n.* evidence; testimony: *A person who gives false witness in court is guilty of perjury.* **5** *v.* to testify to; give evidence of: *Her whole manner witnessed her surprise.* **6** *n.* person who signs a document to show that he or she saw the maker sign it. **7** *v.* to sign a document as a witness: *witness a will.* ❑ *n., pl.* **wit·ness·es. —wit′ness·er,** *n.*

bear witness, to give evidence; testify; be evidence: *The woman's fingerprints bore witness to her guilt. His blushes bore witness to his great embarrassment.*

WORD STORY Witness comes from an old English word that is spelled the same way, meaning "knowledge." The old English word came from **wit** and **-ness,** and **wit** comes from an old English word meaning "to know." So a person with knowness is the right one to bear witness. We still use **knowing** to mean "clever," like **witty.**

witness box, CANADIAN. witness stand.

witness stand, place where a witness stands or sits to give evidence in a court of law.

wit·ti·cism (wit′ə siz′əm), *n.* a witty remark.

wit·ting·ly (wit′ing lē), *adv.* knowingly; intentionally.

wit·ty (wit′ē), *adj.* full of wit; clever and amusing: *A witty person makes witty remarks.* ■ See Synonym Study at **humorous.** ❑ *adj.* **wit·ti·er, wit·ti·est. —wit′ti·ly,** *adv.* **—wit′ti·ness,** *n.*

wives (wīvz), *n.* plural of **wife.**

wiz·ard (wiz′ərd), *n.* **1** man believed to have magic power; magician; sorcerer. **2** a very clever person; expert: *She is a wizard at mathematics.*

wiz·ard·ry (wiz′ər drē), *n.* magic skill; magic.

wiz·ened (wiz′nd), *adj.* dried up; withered; shriveled: *a wizened apple, a wizened face.*

wk., week. ❑ *pl.* **wks.**

wob·ble (wob′əl), **1** *v.* to move unsteadily from side to side; shake; tremble: *A baby wobbles when it begins to walk alone.* **2** *v.* to be uncertain, unsteady, or inconstant; waver. **3** *n.* a wobbling motion. ❑ *v.* **wob·bled, wob·bling. —wob′bler,** *n.*

wob·bly (wob′lē), *adj.* unsteady; shaky; wavering. ❑ *adj.* **wob·bli·er, wob·bli·est. —wob′bli·ness,** *n.*

Wo·den (wōd′n), *n.* Odin.

woe (wō), **1** *n.* great grief, trouble, or distress: *the woes of sickness and poverty.* **2** *interj.* an exclamation of grief, trouble, or distress: *"Woe! woe is me!"* ■ Another word that sounds like this is **whoa.**

woe·be·gone (wō′bi gòn′), *adj.* looking sad or unhappy.

woe·ful (wō′fəl), *adj.* **1** full of woe; sad; sorrowful; wretched: *The lost child had a woeful expression.* **2** pitiful: *a woeful mistake.* **—woe′ful·ly,** *adv.* **—woe′ful·ness,** *n.*

wok (wok), *n.* a metal cooking bowl, used for stir-frying.

woke (wōk), *v.* a past tense of **wake**[1]: *She woke before we did.*

wo·ken (wō′kən), *v.* a past participle of **wake**[1]: *I was woken by the sound of bells.*

wold (wōld), *n.* high, rolling country, bare of woods.

wolf (wůlf), **1** *n.* a flesh-eating mammal related to and resembling dogs, with a long muzzle, high pointed ears, and a bushy tail. Wolves usually hunt in packs. **2** *n.* a cruel, greedy person. **3** *v.* to eat greedily: *The hungry man wolfed down the food.* ❑ *n., pl.* **wolves.** —**wolf′like**′, *adj.*

cry wolf, to give a false alarm.

keep the wolf from the door, to avoid hunger or poverty.

wolves—2 ft. 6 in. (76 cm) high at the shoulder

Wolf Cub, (in Canada) Cub Scout.

Wolfe (wůlf), *n.* **James,** 1727-1759, British general who was killed at the battle of Quebec, in which he defeated the French, gaining Canada for Great Britain.

wolf·hound (wůlf′hound′), *n.* any of three kinds of large dog once used in hunting wolves.

wolf·ish (wůl′fish), *adj.* **1** as a wolf is thought to be; savage: *wolfish cruelty.* **2** greedy: *a wolfish appetite.* —**wolf′ish·ly,** *adv.* —**wolf′ish·ness,** *n.*

wolf·ram (wůl′frəm), *n.* tungsten.

wol·ve·rine (wůl′və rēn′), *n.* a heavily built, flesh-eating mammal living in northern North America, Europe, and Asia. It is related to weasels and badgers.

wolverine—3 ft. 6 in. (1.1 m) long with the tail

wolves (wůlvz), *n.* plural of **wolf.**

wom·an (wům′ən), *n.* **1** an adult female person. When a girl grows up, she becomes a woman. **2** women as a group; womankind. ❑ *n., pl.* **wom·en** for 1.

-woman, *suffix.* **1** woman from a certain place: *Irishwoman = woman from Ireland; Frenchwoman = woman from France.* **2** woman who deals with ___ or is part of ___: *policewoman = woman who is part of the police.*

wom·an·hood (wům′ən hůd), *n.* **1** condition or time of being a woman: *The girl was entering womanhood.* **2** character or qualities of a woman. **3** women as a group: *the womanhood of America.*

wom·an·ish (wům′ə nish), *adj.* (of a man) having qualities or characteristics traditionally thought of as belonging to a woman. ■ Because it has been considered unsuitable for a man to have such qualities, **womanish** has been considered offensive. —**wom′an·ish·ly,** *adv.* —**wom′an·ish·ness,** *n.*

wom·an·kind (wům′ən kind′), *n.* women as a group.

wom·an·like (wům′ən līk′), *adj.* **1** like a woman. **2** suitable for a woman.

wom·an·ly (wům′ən lē), *adj.* **1** having qualities traditionally thought of as belonging to a woman: *a womanly expression of sympathy.* **2** suitable for a woman: *Tennis is as much a womanly as it is a manly sport.* —**wom′an·li·ness,** *n.*

woman's rights, social, political, and legal rights for women, equal to those of men.

woman suffrage, **1** the political right of women to vote. **2** women's votes.

womb (wüm), *n.* **1** the part of the body in female mammals that holds and nourishes the young till birth; uterus. **2** place producing or containing anything.

wom·bat (wom′bat), *n.* either of two kinds of burrowing Australian mammal like a small bear. A female wombat has a pouch for carrying her young.

wom·en (wim′ən), *n.* plural of **woman.**

wom·en·folk (wim′ən fōk′), *n.pl.* INFORMAL. **1** women. **2** a particular group of women, especially those present: *The womenfolk are ready to leave.*

wom·en·folks (wim′ən fōks′), *n.pl.* INFORMAL. women.

Women's Liberation, the efforts of women to achieve equality for women in all areas of life.

women's rights, woman's rights.

won (wun), *v.* past tense and past participle of **win:** *Which side won yesterday? We have won four games.* ■ Another word that sounds like this is **one.**

won·der (wun′dər), **1** *n.* a strange and surprising thing or event: *The Grand Canyon is one of the wonders of the world. It is a wonder that he refused such a good offer.* **2** *n.* the feeling caused by what is strange and surprising: *The baby looked with wonder at the snow.* **3** *v.* to feel wonder: *We wonder at the splendor of the stars.* **4** *v.* to be surprised or astonished: *I shouldn't wonder if she wins the prize.* **5** *v.* to be curious; be curious about; wish to know: *I wonder where she has gone.* —**won′der·er,** *n.* —**won′der·ing·ly,** *adv.*

won·der·ful (wun′dər fəl), *adj.* **1** causing wonder; marvelous; remarkable: *a wonderful adventure.* **2** excellent; splendid; fine: *We had a wonderful time at the party.* —**won′der·ful·ly,** *adv.* —**won′der·ful·ness,** *n.*

SYNONYM STUDY **Wonderful, marvelous,** and **fabulous** all mean surprising and very good. **Wonderful** suggests great pleasure: *We had a wonderful trip.* **Marvelous** suggests something unusual and hard to believe: *She made a marvelous catch and saved the game for our team.* **Fabulous** suggests something very attractive and exciting: *Win fabulous prizes!*

won·der·land (wun′dər land′), *n.* a land or place full of wonders.

won·der·ment (wun′dər mənt), *n.* wonder; surprise: *He stared at the huge bear in wonderment.*

won·drous (wun′drəs), *adj.* wonderful. —**won′drous·ly,** *adv.* —**won′drous·ness,** *n.*

wont (wônt, wōnt, *or* wunt), **1** *adj.* accustomed: *He was wont to read the paper at breakfast.* **2** *n.* custom; habit: *He rose early, as was his wont.*

won't (wōnt), will not.

wont·ed (wôn′tid, wōn′tid, *or* wun′tid), *adj.* accustomed; customary; usual: *The cat was in its wonted place by the stove.* —**wont′ed·ly,** *adv.* —**wont′ed·ness,** *n.*

woo (wü), *v.* **1** to make love to; seek to marry. **2** to seek to win; try to get: *Some people woo fame; some woo wealth.* **3** to try to persuade; urge. ❑ *v.* **wooed, woo·ing.** —**woo′er,** *n.*

W

a	hat	ė	term	ô	order	ch	child		
ā	age	i	it	oi	oil	ng	long		a in about
ä	far	ī	ice	ou	out	sh	she		e in taken
â	care	o	hot	u	cup	th	thin	ə {	i in pencil
e	let	ō	open	ů	put	ŦH	then		o in lemon
ē	equal	ȯ	saw	ü	rule	zh	measure		u in circus

wood (wud), **1** *n.* the hard substance that makes up the trunk and branches beneath the bark of trees and bushes. **2** *n.* trees or parts of trees cut up for use in building houses, making boats, furniture, etc., or as fuel: *We bought wood to build a playhouse. Put some wood on the fire.* **3** *n.* Often, **woods,** *pl.* **a** a large number of growing trees; small forest: *We walked through the woods behind the farm.* **b** area covered by a forest or forests: *Many campers go to the Maine woods.* ■ Another word that sounds like this is **would.** —**wood′less,** *adj.*

out of the woods, out of danger or difficulty.

wood alcohol, methanol.

wood·bine (wud′bīn), *n.* **1** honeysuckle. **2** Virginia creeper.

wood·carv·er (wud′kär′vər), *n.* person who carves figures or other objects from wood.

wood·carv·ing (wud′kär′ving), *n.* **1** an object carved from wood. **2** art or process of carving from wood.

wood·chuck (wud′chuk′), *n.* a small, thick-bodied North American mammal related to squirrels, with short legs and a bushy tail; groundhog. Woodchucks grow fat in summer and sleep in their holes in the ground all winter.

WORD STORY Woodchuck comes from an Algonquian word that English people first spelled *otchek.* So how much wood would an *otchek* have chucked? We would never have asked that question. Gradually, however, people began spelling the word so that it looked more like English words.

wood·cock (wud′kok′), *n.* any of several small game birds with short legs, and long bills used to probe the ground for worms. ❑ *n., pl.* **wood·cock** or **wood·cocks.**

wood·craft (wud′kraft′), *n.* **1** skill in working with wood. **2** knowledge about how to get food and shelter in the woods; skill in hunting, trapping, finding your way, etc.

wood·cut (wud′kut′), *n.* **1** an engraved block of wood to print from. **2** a print from such a block.

wood·cut·ter (wud′kut′ər), *n.* person who cuts down trees or chops wood.

wood·ed (wud′id), *adj.* covered with trees: *The house stood on a wooded hill.*

wood·en (wud′n), *adj.* **1** made of wood. **2** stiff as wood; awkward. **3** dull; stupid. —**wood′en·ly,** *adv.* —**wood′en·ness,** *n.*

Wood·hull (wud′hul′), *n.* **Victoria,** 1838-1927, first woman candidate for President of the United States, in 1872. She also ran a brokerage house and a newspaper.

wood·land (wud′lənd), **1** *n.* land covered with trees. **2** *adj.* of or living in the woods: *woodland animals.*

wood louse, any of several very small animals with flat, oval bodies that live in decaying wood, damp soil, etc.; sow bug. Wood lice are crustaceans, related to crabs.

wood·man (wud′mən), *n.* woodsman. ❑ *n., pl.* **wood·men.**

wood nymph, dryad.

wood·peck·er (wud′pek′ər), *n.* any of numerous birds with hard, pointed bills for pecking holes in trees to get insects.

wood·pile (wud′pīl′), *n.* pile of wood, especially wood for fuel.

wood pulp, pulp made from wood, used in making paper.

wood rat, any of several kinds of rats with large ears and furry tails, found in western North America.

wood·shed (wud′shed′), *n.* shed for storing wood.

woods·man (wudz′mən), *n.* **1** person used to life in the woods and skilled in hunting, fishing, trapping, etc. **2** lumberjack. ❑ *n., pl.* **woods·men.**

woods·y (wud′zē), *adj.* of or like the woods. ❑ *adj.* **woods·i·er, woods·i·est.**

wood thrush, thrush with a white, spotted breast, common in the thickets and woods of eastern North America.

wood·wind (wud′wind′), **1** *n.* any of a group of wind instruments which were originally made of wood, but are now often made of metal or plastic. Clarinets, flutes, oboes, and bassoons are woodwinds. **2** *adj.* of, for, or about woodwinds: *Flutes are in the woodwind section of an orchestra.*

wood·work (wud′werk′), *n.* things made of wood; wooden parts inside a house, such as doors, stairs, moldings, and the like.

wood·work·ing (wud′wer′king), **1** *n.* making or shaping things of wood: *She is skilled in woodworking.* **2** *adj.* of or for woodworking: *woodworking tools.*

wood·y (wud′ē), *adj.* **1** having many trees; covered with trees: *a woody hillside.* **2** consisting of wood: *the woody parts of a bush.* **3** like wood: *Turnips become woody when they are old.* ❑ *adj.* **wood·i·er, wood·i·est.** —**wood′i·ness,** *n.*

woof[1] (wuf), *n.* **1** the threads running from side to side across a woven fabric; weft. The woof crosses the warp. **2** fabric; cloth; texture.

woof[2] (wuf), *n.* **1** a dog's bark in a deep voice. **2** to make this sound.

woof·er (wuf′ər), *n.* a high-fidelity speaker for producing low sounds.

wool (wul), **1** *n.* the soft curly hair or fur of sheep and some other animals. **2** *n.* short, thick, curly hair. **3** *n.* something like wool. **4** *n.* yarn, cloth, or garments made of wool: *wear wool in winter.* **5** *adj.* made of wool. —**wool′like′,** *adj.*

pull the wool over someone's eyes, to deceive or trick someone.

wool (def. 1)—trimming wool from a sheep

wool·en (wul′ən), **1** *adj.* made of wool: *a woolen suit.* **2** *n.* yarn or cloth made of wool. **3** *n.pl.* **woolens,** cloth or clothing made of wool: *I put my woolens in a plastic bag to protect them against moths.* **4** *adj.* of or about wool or cloth made of wool: *a woolen mill.*

Woolf (wulf), *n.* **Virginia,** 1882-1941, British writer. She wrote criticism, essays, and novels concentrating on the internal experience of characters and how they perceive it.

wool·gath·er·ing (wul′gaŦH′ər ing), **1** *n.* absorption in thinking or daydreaming; absent-mindedness. **2** *adj.* inattentive; absent-minded; dreamy.

wool·ly (wul′ē), *adj.* **1** consisting of wool: *the woolly coat of a sheep.* **2** like wool. **3** covered with wool or something like it. **4** not clear; confused; muddled: *woolly thinking.* ❑ *adj.* **wool·li·er, wool·li·est.** Also, **wooly.** —**wool′li·ness,** *n.*

woolly bear, the hair-covered caterpillar of a tiger moth.

wool·y (wul′ē), *adj.* woolly. ❑ *adj.* **wool·i·er, wool·i·est.** —**wool′i·ness,** *n.*

wooz·y (wü′zē), *adj.* muddled; confused. ❑ *adj.* **wooz·i·er, wooz·i·est.** —**wooz′i·ly,** *adv.* —**wooz′i·ness,** *n.*

Worces·ter (wus′tər), *n.* city in central Massachusetts.

word (werd), **1** *n.* a sound or a group of sounds that has meaning and is a unit of speech. We speak words when we talk. **2** *n.* the writing or printing that stands for a word: *This page is filled with words.* **3** *n.* a short talk: *May I have a word with you?* **4** *n.* speech: *He is honest in word and deed.* **5** *n.* a brief expression: *The teacher gave us word of advice.* **6** *n.* command; order: *The tyrant's word was law.* **7** *n.* **the Word,** the Bible. **8** *n.* promise: *She kept her word. He is a man of his word.* **9** *n.* news: *No word has come from the battle front.* **10** *n.pl.* **words,** angry talk; quarrel; dispute. **11** *n.* unit of computer information equal to the number of bits of data that a particular computer can store or process as a unit. **12** *v.* to put into words: *She worded her message clearly.*

be as good as your word, to keep your promise.

by word of mouth, by spoken words; orally.

eat your words, to take back what you have said; retract.

get a word in edgeways, to find a chance to make a remark when someone else is doing all the talking.

in a word, briefly.

in so many words, literally; in those very words.

on my word, I promise.

take the words out of someone's mouth, to say exactly what another person was just going to say.

take you at your word, to take what you say seriously and act accordingly.

upon my word, 1 I promise. 2 expression of surprise.

word for word, in the exact words.

WORD POWER ■ **FROM WORD TO WORD PART** ■ Many prefixes and suffixes in English come from whole words in Latin or Greek. Because those whole words were used so often combined with other words, they gradually changed form and turned into word parts. You can see the same process in English:

-driven	-handed	-less	-proof
extra-	-headed	-like	self-
-footed	-hearted	out-	under-
-free	-legged	over-	

word·book (wėrd′bůk′), *n.* list of words, usually with explanations, etc.; dictionary.

word·ing (wėr′ding), *n.* way of saying something; choice and use of words: *Careful wording is needed for clearness.*

word·less (wėrd′lis), *adj.* 1 without words; speechless. 2 not put into words; unexpressed: *wordless joy.* —**word′less·ly,** *adv.* —**word′less·ness,** *n.*

word of honor, a solemn promise.

word processing, the editing, storage, and reproduction of documents and texts by means of computers, printers, and other complex machines. —**word processor.**

word story, account or explanation of the origin and history of a word; etymology.

Words·worth (wėrdz′wėrth′), *n.* **William,** 1770-1850, English poet. He believed that poetry should use ordinary language and describe actual life.

word·y (wėr′dē), *adj.* using too many words; verbose. ❏ *adj.* **word·i·er, word·i·est.** —**word′i·ly,** *adv.* —**word′i·ness,** *n.*

wore (wôr), *v.* past tense of **wear:** *He wore out his shoes in two months.* ■ Another word that sounds like this is **war.**

work (wėrk), 1 *n.* effort in doing or making something: *Some people like hard work.* 2 *n.* something to do; occupation; employment: *My friend is looking for work.* 3 *n.* place of employment: *still at work.* 4 *n.* something made or done; result of effort: *The artist considers that picture to be her greatest work.* 5 *n.* that on which effort is put: *We carried our work out onto the front porch.* 6 *n.pl.* **works, a** factory or other place for doing some kind of work. **b** the moving parts of a machine: *the works of a watch.* **c** buildings, bridges, docks, etc. **d** actions: *good works.* 7 *v.* to do work; labor: *Most people must work to earn money.* 8 *v.* to work for pay; be employed: *She works at an airplane factory.* 9 *v.* to put effort on: *They worked their pumps by hand.* 10 *v.* to act; operate: *The plan worked well.* 11 *v.* to cause to do work: *That company works its employees hard.* 12 *v.* to make, get, do or bring about by effort: *I worked my way across the room in the dark. She worked her way through college.* 13 *v.* to move as if with effort: *His face worked as he tried to keep back the tears.* 14 *v.* to bring about; cause; do: *The plan worked harm.* 15 *v.* to go slowly or with effort: *We worked our way slowly through the bushes.* 16 *v.* to become up, round, loose, etc.: *The window catch has worked loose.* 17 *v.* to form; shape: *He worked a piece of copper into a tray.* 18 *v.* to move; stir; excite: *Don't work yourself into a temper.* 19 *n.* the result of a force moving an object through a distance. In science, work is done only if something moves. Pushing against a wall does no work, but lifting your hand does. ❏ *v.* **worked** or (OLD USE) **wrought, work·ing.** —**work′a·ble,** *adj.*

at work, 1 at a job. 2 working; busy.

have your work cut out, to have a large amount of work to do in a certain amount of time: *With the deadline so near, she really has her work cut out for her.*

in the works, happening soon: *A new car design is in the works.*

make short work of, to deal with quickly: *The new principal made short work of the overcrowding problems at our school.*

out of work, having no job.

work in, to put in.

work off, to get rid of: *work off a debt.*

work on or work upon, to try to persuade or influence: *We're working on mom to choose Yosemite for vacation this year.*

work out, 1 to plan; develop. 2 to solve; find out. 3 to give exercise to; practice. 4 to result.

work up, 1 to plan; develop: *work up a proposal.* 2 to stir up; excite: *a crowd worked up by speeches.*

SYNONYM STUDY Work, labor, and toil all mean effort in doing or making something. **Work** is a general word: *The students put a great deal of work into their projects.* **Labor** means work that takes bodily strength: *Many fruits are harvested by human labor.* **Toil** means long, tiring work: *After weeks of toil, the vacant lot is now a garden.*

work·a·day (wėr′kə dā′), *adj.* of or about working days; practical; commonplace; ordinary.

work·a·hol·ic (wėr′kə hô′lik), *n.* person who feels a need to work constantly.

work·bench (wėrk′bench′), *n.* a strong, heavy table used by a carpenter, or by anyone who uses tools and materials. ❏ *n., pl.* **work·bench·es.**

work·book (wėrk′bůk′), *n.* 1 book containing outlines for the study of some subject, questions to be answered, etc. 2 book in which a student does written work.

work·day (wėrk′dā′), *n.* 1 day for work; day that is not Sunday or a holiday. 2 part of a day during which work is done.

work·er (wėr′kər), *n.* 1 someone or something that works: *a hard worker.* 2 bee, ant, termite, or other insect that works for its community and usually does not produce offspring.

workers' compensation, insurance that pays a worker who is injured or becomes sick as a result of work; workmen's compensation.

work·fare (wėrk′fâr′), *n.* a welfare program under which those receiving aid must do assigned work or enlist in a job-training program.

work·force (wėrk′fôrs′), *n.* all the workers employed in an area, industry, factory, etc.

work·horse (wėrk′hôrs′), *n.* 1 horse used for labor, and not for showing, racing, or hunting. 2 a very hard worker.

work·house (wėrk′hous′), *n.* 1 house of correction where petty criminals are kept and made to work. 2 (formerly, in Great Britain) a house where very poor people were lodged and set to work. ❏ *n., pl.* **work·hous·es** (wėrk′hou′ziz).

work·ing (wėr′king), 1 *n.* method or manner of work; operation; action: *Do you understand the working of this machine?* 2 *adj.* that works: *The class constructed a working model of a helicopter.* 3 *adj.* of, for, or used in working: *working hours, working clothes.* 4 *adj.* used to operate with or by: *a working majority.*

working class, people who work for wages, especially manual and industrial workers.

work·ing·man (wėr′king man′), *n.* workman. ❏ *n., pl.* **work·ing·men.**

working papers, documents that permit a young person to leave school and go to work.

work·load (wėrk′lōd′), *n.* amount of work done by or assigned to a worker.

work·man (wėrk′mən), *n.* 1 worker. 2 person who works with his or her hands or with machines. ❏ *n., pl.* **work·men.**

work·man·like (wėrk′mən lik′), *adj.* skillful; well-done: *a workmanlike job.*

work·man·ship (wėrk′mən ship), *n.* 1 the art or skill in a worker or the work done: *Good workmanship requires long practice.* 2 quality or manner of work.

workmen's compensation, workers' compensation.

work·out (wėrk′out′), *n.* 1 exercise; practice: *She had a good workout running around the track before breakfast.* 2 trial; test: *The mechanic gave the car a thorough workout after repairing it.*

work·place (wėrk′plās′), *n.* a place where people work, such as a factory or an office building.

work·room (wėrk′rüm′), *n.* room where work is done.

a	hat	ė	term	ô	order	ch	child	
ā	age	i	it	oi	oil	ng	long	a in about
ä	far	ī	ice	ou	out	sh	she	e in taken
â	care	o	hot	u	cup	th	thin	ə ⎨ i in pencil
e	let	ō	open	ů	put	ŦH	then	o in lemon
ē	equal	ȯ	saw	ü	rule	zh	measure	u in circus

W

work·shop (wėrk′shop′), *n.* **1** shop or building where work is done. **2** group of people working on or studying a special project.

work·sta·tion (wėrk′stā′shən), *n.* **1** someone's work area, usually containing a computer terminal. **2** microcomputer or computer terminal, connected to another computer or computer network.

work·ta·ble (wėrk′tā′bəl), *n.* table to work at.

work·week (wėrk′wēk′), *n.* the part of the week in which work is done, usually Monday through Friday.

world (wėrld), *n.* **1** the earth: *Ships can sail around the world.* **2** all of certain parts, people, or things of the earth: *the insect world, the world of fashion.* **3** all people; the public: *The whole world knows it.* **4** the things of this life and the people devoted to them: *Some monks and nuns live apart from the world.* **5** any planet, especially when considered as inhabited: *alien creatures from another world.* **6** any time, condition, or place of life: *the next world, a better world.* **7** all things; everything; the universe. **8** Also, **worlds,** a great deal; very much; large amount: *Sunshine does children a world of good. She knows worlds about frogs.*

for all the world, 1 for any reason, no matter how great. **2** in every respect; exactly.

in the world, 1 anywhere: *the tallest building in the world.* **2** at all; ever: *How in the world did you finish that long assignment?*

out of this world, INFORMAL. great; wonderful: *The science fair was out of this world.*

world-beat·er (wėrld′bē′tər), *n.* a champion.

world-class (wėrld′klas′), *adj.* **1** of the highest rank or ability in the world: *world-class competition, world-class runners.* **2** excellent; outstanding: *a world-class exhibition, a world-class scientist.*

World Cup, an international soccer tournament held every four years, in which 24 nations compete. Qualifying tournaments held during the two years before the World Cup determine the competitors. The previous champion and the host country's team automatically qualify to compete.

world·ly (wėrld′lē), *adj.* **1** of this world; not of heaven: *worldly wealth.* **2** caring much for the interests and pleasures of this world. **3** worldly-wise. ❑ *adj.* **world·li·er, world·li·est.** —**world′li·ness,** *n.*

world·ly-wise (wėrld′lē wīz′), *adj.* wise about the ways and affairs of this world.

World Series, series of baseball games played each fall between the winners of the two major league championships, to decide the professional championship of the United States.

World War I, war fought mainly in Europe and the Middle East, from 1914 to 1918. The United States, Great Britain, France, Russia, and their allies were on one side; Germany, Austria-Hungary, and their allies were on the other side.

World War II, war fought in Europe, Asia, Africa, and elsewhere, from 1939 to 1945. The chief conflict was between Great Britain, the United States, France, and the Soviet Union on one side and Germany, Italy, and Japan on the other.

world-wear·y (wėrld′wir′ē), *adj.* weary of this world; tired of living.

world·wide (wėrld′wīd′), **1** *adj.* spread throughout the world: *Pollution is becoming a worldwide problem.* **2** *adv.* throughout the world: *The depression spread worldwide.*

World Wide Web, a system for finding and presenting information files, called documents, over the Internet. World Wide Web documents can include text, images, sound, animation, and hypertext links to other information.

worm (wėrm), **1** *n.* any of a great many small, slender, crawling or creeping animals. Most worms have soft bodies and no legs. **2** *n.* animal like a worm, such as a grub, caterpillar, or maggot. **3** *n.* something like a worm in shape or movement, such as the thread of a screw. **4** *v.* to move like a worm; crawl or creep like a worm: *worm under a fence.* **5** *v.* to get by persistent, deceitful effort: *He wormed the story out of me.* **6** *n.* a weak, disgusting, or pitiful person. **7** *n.pl.* **worms,** disease caused by parasitic worms in the body, especially in the intestines. —**worm′like′,** *adj.*

worm-eat·en (wėrm′ēt′n), *adj.* **1** eaten into by worms: *worm-eaten timbers.* **2** worn-out; worthless; out-of-date.

worm·wood (wėrm′wud′), *n.* **1** any of numerous bitter plants used in certain liquors and in medicines. **2** something bitter or extremely unpleasant.

worm·y (wėr′mē), *adj.* **1** having worms; containing many worms: *wormy apples.* **2** damaged by worms: *wormy wood.* ❑ *adj.* **worm·i·er, worm·i·est.** —**worm′i·ness,** *n.*

worn (wôrn), **1** *v.* past participle of **wear:** *I have worn these jeans for two years.* **2** *adj.* damaged by use: *worn rugs.* **3** *adj.* tired; wearied: *a worn face.* ■ Another word that sounds like this is **warn.**

SYNONYM STUDY **Worn, shabby,** and **threadbare** all mean damaged from being used a long time. **Worn** is used to describe clothing, tools, books, and furniture: *This jacket is worn at the elbows.* **Shabby** suggests something unattractive and not well cared for: *The cheap hotel had shabby furniture.* **Threadbare** means so worn that threads show through: *The basement rug is threadbare.*

worn-out (wôrn′out′), *adj.* **1** very worn from long, hard use; worn or used until useless or in poor condition: *a worn-out lawnmower, worn-out shoes.* **2** very tired; exhausted.

wor·ri·some (wėr′ē səm), *adj.* **1** causing worry: *a worrisome problem.* **2** inclined to worry. —**wor′ri·some·ly,** *adv.* —**wor′ri·some·ness,** *n.*

wor·ry (wėr′ē), **1** *v.* to feel anxious; be uneasy: *Don't worry about little things. They will worry if we are late.* **2** *v.* to make anxious; trouble: *The problem worried me.* **3** *n.* anxiety; uneasiness; trouble; care: *Worry kept me awake.* **4** *n.* cause of trouble or care: *Parents of a sick child have many worries.* **5** *v.* to annoy; bother; vex: *worry someone with questions.* **6** *v.* to seize and shake with the teeth; bite at; snap at: *The cat worried the mouse.* ❑ *v.* **ried, wor·ry·ing;** *n., pl.* **wor·ries.** —**wor′ried·ly,** *adv.* —**wor′ri·er,** *n.*

wor·ry·wart (wėr′ē wôrt′), *n.* INFORMAL. person who worries too much.

worse (wėrs), **1** *adj.* less well; more ill: *The patient seems even worse today.* **2** *adj.* less good; more evil: *Disobedience is bad enough, but lying about it is worse.* **3** *adv.* in a more severe or evil manner or degree: *It is raining worse than ever today.* **4** *n.* that which is worse: *The loss of their home was terrible, but worse followed.* ❑ *adj., adv.* comparative of **bad, ill.**

wors·en (wėr′sən), *v.* to make or become worse.

wor·ship (wėr′ship), **1** *n.* great honor and reverence paid to someone or something regarded as sacred: *the worship of God.* **2** *v.* to pay great honor and reverence to: *to worship God.* **3** *n.* religious ceremonies or services in which you express such honor and reverence. Prayers and hymns are part of worship. **4** *v.* to take part in a religious service. **5** *n.* great love and admiration; adoration: *hero worship, the worship of wealth.* **6** *v.* to consider extremely precious; hold very dear; adore: *She worships her mother. A miser worships money.* ❑ *v.* **wor·shiped, wor·ship·ing** or **wor·shipped, wor·ship·ping.** —**wor′ship·er** or **wor′ship·per,** *n.*

worship

wor·ship·ful (wėr′ship fəl), *adj.* worshiping: *a worshipful dog with its master.* —**wor′ship·ful·ly,** *adv.* —**wor′ship·ful·ness,** *n.*

worst (wėrst), **1** *adj.* least well; most ill: *This is the worst I've been since I got sick.* **2** *adj.* least good; most evil: *It is the worst movie I've seen.* **3** *adv.* in the worst manner or degree: *He acts worst when he's tired.* **4** *n.* that which is worst: *Yesterday was bad, but the worst is yet to come.* **5** *v.* to beat; defeat: *worst your enemies.* ❑ *adj.* superlative of **bad, ill;** *adv.* superlative of **bad, ill.**

at worst, under the least favorable circumstances.

if worst comes to worst, if the very worst thing happens.

wor·sted (wús′tid *or* wėr′stid), **1** *n.* a firmly twisted woolen thread or yarn. **2** *adj.* made of worsted. **3** *n.* cloth made from such thread or yarn.

worth (wėrth), **1** *adj.* equal in value to: *That book is worth $5.* **2** *n.* quantity that a certain amount will buy: *I bought a dollar's worth of stamps.* **3** *n.* value: *I got my money's worth out of this coat.* **4** *prep.* good or important enough for; deserving of: *That book is worth reading. New York is a city worth visiting.* **5** *prep.* having property that amounts to: *That man is worth millions.* **6** *n.* merit; usefulness; importance: *We should read books of real worth.*

for all you are worth, with all your effort; as hard as possible.

worth·less (wėrth′lis), *adj.* without worth; good-for-nothing; useless: *Throw those worthless, broken toys away.* —**worth′less·ly,** *adv.* —**worth′less·ness,** *n.*

worth·while (wėrth′wīl′), *adj.* worth time, attention, or effort; having real merit: *This is a worthwhile book; you should read it.* —**worth′while′ness,** *n.*

wor·thy (wėr′ᴛʜē), **1** *adj.* deserving; meriting: *Her courage was worthy of high praise.* **2** *adj.* having worth or merit: *Helping the poor is a worthy cause.* **3** *n.* person of great merit; admirable person: *The Wright brothers stand high among American worthies.* ❑ *adj.* **wor·thi·er, wor·thi·est;** *n., pl.* **wor·thies.** —**wor′thi·ly,** *adv.* —**wor′thi·ness,** *n.*

would (wu̇d), *v.* **1** past tense of **will¹:** *She said that she would come. They would go in spite of our warning.* **2** *Would* is used to express future time: *Would they never go?* **3** *Would* is used to express action done again and again in the past time: *The children would play for hours on the beach.* **4** *Would* is used to express a wish: *I would I were rich.* **5** *Would* is used to make a statement or question sound more polite than *will* sounds: *Would you help us, please?* **6** *Would* is used to express conditions: *If you would only try, you could do it.* ■ Another word that sounds like this is **wood.**

would-be (wu̇d′bē′), *adj.* **1** wishing or pretending to be. **2** intended to be.

would·n't (wu̇d′nt), would not.

wouldst (wu̇dst), *v.* ᴏʟᴅ ᴜsᴇ. would. "Thou wouldst" means "you would."

wound¹ (wünd), **1** *n.* a hurt or injury caused by cutting, stabbing, shooting, etc.: *a knife wound, a bullet wound.* **2** *v.* to injure by cutting, stabbing, shooting, etc.; hurt: *The hunter wounded the deer.* **3** *n.* any hurt or injury to feelings, reputation, etc.: *The loss of his job was a wound to his pride.* **4** *v.* to injure in feelings, reputation, etc.: *Her unkind words wounded me.* —**wound′ing·ly,** *adv.*

wound² (wound), *v.* past tense and past participle of **wind²:** *I wound the yarn into a ball. The yarn is wound too tightly.*

wove (wōv), *v.* past tense and a past participle of **weave:** *The spider wove a new web after the first was destroyed.*

wo·ven (wō′vən), *v.* a past participle of **weave:** *This cloth is closely woven.*

wow (wou), **1** *interj.* exclamation of surprise, joy, etc. **2** *v.* sʟᴀɴɢ. to overwhelm with delight and amazement: *The magician wowed the audience.*

wpm, words per minute.

wrack (rak), **1** *n.* ruin; destruction. **2** *v.* to wreck or be wrecked. **3** *n.* seaweed cast ashore. ■ Another word that sounds like this is **rack.**

wrack and ruin, ruin; destruction: *go to wrack and ruin.*

WORD STORY Many words beginning with **wr-** come from old English, in which both letters were pronounced in such words. This is not an easy sound to make, and people gradually stopped making it. By about 400 years ago, the *w* had become silent in *wr-,* but the spelling had become familiar, so it lasted.

wraith (rāth), *n.* specter; ghost.

Wran·gell-St. E·li·as National Park (rang′gəl sānt′i li′əs), a national park in SE Alaska, containing many very tall mountains and many glaciers. It is bigger than Vermont.

wran·gle (rang′gəl), **1** *v.* to argue or dispute in a noisy or angry way: *The children wrangled about who should wash the dog.* **2** *n.*

a noisy dispute; angry quarrel. **3** *v.* to herd or tend horses, cattle, etc., on the range. ❑ *v.* **wran·gled, wran·gling.**

wran·gler (rang′glər), *n.* **1** (in the western United States and Canada) a herder in charge of horses, cattle, etc. **2** person who wrangles.

wrap (rap), **1** *v.* to cover with paper and tie up or fasten: *Have you wrapped his birthday present yet?* **2** *v.* to cover by winding or folding something around: *She wrapped herself in a shawl.* **3** *v.* to wind or fold as a covering: *Wrap a shawl around yourself.* **4** *v.* to envelop; veil: *The mountain peak is wrapped in clouds. She sat wrapped in thought.* **5** *n.* an outer covering. Shawls, scarfs, coats, and furs are wraps. ❑ *v.* **wrapped, wrap·ping.** ■ Another word that sounds like this is **rap.**

wrapped up in, devoted to; thinking mainly of: *She is so wrapped up in her work that we never see her any more.*

wrap up, 1 to put on warm outer clothes. **2** to finish; conclude: *Let's wrap up this meeting; it's getting late.*

wrap·a·round (rap′ə round′), **1** *adj.* worn by pulling around the body: *a wraparound coat.* **2** *n.* piece of clothing worn this way. **3** *adj.* very broad and curving: *a wraparound windshield.*

wrap·per (rap′ər), *n.* **1** a covering or cover: *Some magazines are mailed in plastic wrappers.* **2** person or thing that wraps. **3** a woman's long, loose garment to wear in the house.

wrap·ping (rap′ing), *n.* paper, cloth, etc., in which something is wrapped.

wrap-up (rap′up′), *n.* the final item or summary of a news report.

wrath (rath), *n.* very great anger; rage.

wrath·ful (rath′fəl), *adj.* very angry; showing wrath: *The wrathful lion turned on the hunters. Its wrathful eyes flashed.* —**wrath′ful·ly,** *adv.* —**wrath′ful·ness,** *n.*

wreak (rēk), *v.* **1** to give expression to strong feelings: *I wreaked my anger on my sister by screaming at her.* **2** to inflict vengeance, punishment, etc. ■ Another word that sounds like this is **reek.**

wreath (rēth), *n.* **1** a ring of flowers or leaves twisted together: *There were wreaths in the windows at Christmas.* **2** something suggesting a wreath: *a wreath of smoke.* ❑ *n., pl.* **wreaths** (rēᴛʜz *or* rēths).

wreathe (rēᴛʜ), *v.* **1** to make into a wreath: *The children wreathed a chain of daisies.* **2** to decorate or adorn with wreaths: *The doors of the houses were wreathed with greens.* **3** to make a ring around; encircle: *Mist wreathed the hills.* ❑ *v.* **wreathed, wreath·ing.** —**wreath′er,** *n.*

wreathed in smiles, smiling greatly.

wreck (rek), **1** *n.* destruction of a motor vehicle, ship, building, train, or aircraft: *The hurricane caused many wrecks. Reckless driving causes many wrecks on the highway.* **2** *n.* any destruction or serious injury: *Heavy rains caused the wreck of many crops.* **3** *n.* what is left of anything that has been destroyed or much injured: *The waves cast the wreck of a ship upon the shore.* ■ See Synonym Study at **ruin. 4** *v.* to cause the wreck of; destroy; ruin: *Raccoons wrecked our campsite looking for food.* **5** *n.* person who has lost his or her health or money: *She is a wreck from overwork.*

wreck·age (rek′ij), *n.* **1** what is left by a wreck or wrecks: *The shore was covered with the wreckage of ships.* **2** act of wrecking or condition of being wrecked: *They felt defeated by the wreckage of their hopes.*

wreck·er (rek′ər), *n.* **1** person, truck, train, or machine that removes wrecks. **2** person whose work is tearing down buildings. **3** person or ship that recovers wrecked or disabled ships or their cargoes.

W

wren (ren), *n.* any of more than 60 kinds of small songbirds with slender bills and short tails. One kind often builds nests near houses.

a	hat	ė	term	ô	order	ch	child		
ā	age	i	it	oi	oil	ng	long	ə	a in about
ä	far	ī	ice	ou	out	sh	she		e in taken
â	care	o	hot	u	cup	th	thin		i in pencil
e	let	ō	open	u̇	put	ᴛʜ	then		o in lemon
ē	equal	ò	saw	ü	rule	zh	measure		u in circus

Wren (ren), *n.* Sir **Christopher,** 1632-1723, English architect. He designed many London churches, royal palaces, and university buildings in a vigorous neoclassic and baroque style.

Wren building

wrench (rench), **1** *v.* to twist or pull violently: *He wrenched the knob off the door.* ■ See Synonym Study at **jerk**[1]. **2** *v.* to injure by twisting: *She wrenched her back doing acrobatics.* **3** *n.* tool for turning nuts, bolts, etc. **4** *n.* a violent twist or twisting pull: *He broke the branch off with a sudden wrench.* **5** *v.* to twist or distort something's meaning; misinterpret. **6** *n.* injury caused by twisting. **7** *n.* source of grief or sorrow: *It was a wrench to leave our old home.* ❏ *n., pl.* **wrench·es.** —**wrench′er,** *n.* —**wrench′ing·ly,** *adv.*

wrest (rest), *v.* **1** to twist, pull, or tear away with force; wrench away: *She wrested the knife from her attacker.* **2** to take by force: *An enemy wrested the power from the duke.* **3** to obtain by persistence or persuasion; wring: *wrest a secret from someone.* ■ Another word that sounds like this is **rest.** —**wrest′er,** *n.*

wres·tle (res′əl), **1** *v.* to try to throw or force an opponent to the ground. **2** *v.* to contend with in wrestling, or as if in wrestling. **3** *v.* to struggle: *I have been wrestling with this problem for over an hour.* **4** *n.* a wrestling match. ❏ *v.* **wres·tled, wres·tling.** —**wres′tler,** *n.*

wres·tling (res′ling), *n.* sport or contest in which two opponents try to throw or force each other to the ground. The rules for wrestling do not allow using the fists or certain holds on the body.

wretch (rech), *n.* **1** a very unfortunate or unhappy person. **2** a very bad person. ❏ *n., pl.* **wretch·es.** ■ Another word that sounds like this is **retch.**

wretch·ed (rech′id), *adj.* **1** very unfortunate or unhappy. **2** very unsatisfactory; miserable: *a wretched hut.* **3** very bad: *a wretched traitor.* —**wretch′ed·ly,** *adv.* —**wretch′ed·ness,** *n.*

wrig·gle (rig′əl), **1** *v.* to twist and turn: *Children wriggle when they are restless.* **2** *v.* to move by twisting and turning: *The worm wriggled when I tried to put it on the hook.* **3** *v.* to make your way by shifts and tricks: *wriggle out of a difficulty.* **4** *n.* a wriggling motion. ❏ *v.* **wrig·gled, wrig·gling.** —**wrig′gling·ly,** *adv.*

wrig·gler (rig′lər), *n.* **1** person who wriggles. **2** larva of a mosquito.

wrig·gly (rig′lē), *adj.* twisting and turning. ❏ *adj.* **wrig·gli·er, wrig·gli·est.**

Wright (rīt), *n.* **1** Frank Lloyd, 1867-1959, American architect who created a modern style for American houses. **2** Or·ville (ôr′vəl), 1871-1948, and his brother Wil·bur (wil′bər), 1867-1912, American inventors. ■ The **Wright brothers** invented the motor-powered airplane and made the world's first powered flight in 1903. **3 Richard,** 1908-1960, American writer. His books about African American experiences include *Native Son* and *Black Boy.*

wring (ring), **1** *v.* to twist with force; squeeze hard: *wring out a wet swimsuit.* **2** *v.* to get by twisting or squeezing; force out: *wring water from a wet rag.* **3** *v.* to get by force, effort, or persuasion: *wring a secret from someone.* **4** *v.* to clasp and hold firmly; press: *She wrung her old friend's hand.* **5** *v.* to cause pain or pity in: *Their poverty wrung our hearts.* **6** *v.* to twist violently; wrench: *He was so angry he threatened to wring my neck.* **7** *n.* a twist or squeeze. ❏ *v.* **wrung, wring·ing.** ■ Another word that sounds like this is **ring.**

wring·er (ring′ər), *n.* machine for squeezing water from wet clothes. ■ Another word that sounds like this is **ringer.**

wrin·kle (ring′kəl), **1** *n.* an irregular ridge or fold; crease: *a smooth forehead, without wrinkles. I must press out the wrinkles in this shirt.* **2** *v.* to make a wrinkle or wrinkles in: *She wrinkled her forehead.* **3** *v.* to have wrinkles; acquire wrinkles: *This shirt will not wrinkle.* **4** *n.* useful hint or idea; clever trick: *He knows all the latest wrinkles in style.* ❏ *v.* **wrin·kled, wrin·kling.**

wrin·kly (ring′klē), *adj.* wrinkled. ❏ *adj.* **wrin·kli·er, wrin·kli·est.**

wrist (rist), *n.* the joint connecting hand and arm.

wrist·band (rist′band′), *n.* **1** band worn around the wrist to soak up sweat during exercise. **2** watchband. **3** part of a sleeve fitting around the wrist.

wrist·watch (rist′woch′), *n.* a small watch worn on the wrist. ❏ *n., pl.* **wrist·watch·es.**

writ (rit), *n.* **1** formal order directing someone to do or not to do something: *A writ from the judge ordered the prisoner's release from jail.* **2** something written; piece of writing. The Bible is sometimes called Holy Writ.

write (rīt), *v.* **1** to make letters or words with pen, pencil, chalk, etc.: *Please write on both sides of the paper.* **2** to put down the letters or words of: *Write your name and address.* **3** to make up stories, books, etc.; compose: *He writes mysteries.* **4** to be a writer: *Her ambition was to write.* **5** to write a letter: *I write to my family every week.* **6** to write a letter to: *She wrote her parents that she would be home for New Year's.* **7** to show plainly: *Amusement was written on her face.* **8** to record information in a computer memory, on a disk, etc. ❏ *v.* **wrote, writ·ten, writ·ing.** ■ Other words that sound like this are **right** and **rite.** —**writ′a·ble,** *adj.*

write down, to put into writing.

write off, 1 to cancel officially: *to write off a debt.* **2** to state that something now has no value: *After the storm, the insurance company wrote off the boat as a total loss.* **3** to regard as a complete failure: *After months of disagreement, they wrote off the partnership.*

write out, 1 to put into writing. **2** to write in full.

write up, to write a description or report of something, especially a full and detailed one.

WORD STORY **Write** comes from an old English word meaning "to scratch." Long ago, Germanic peoples used runes, letters carved into stone or wood, or scratched into coins, jewelry, and weapons. When they began to use the alphabet and ink, their pens were sharpened feathers that made a scratchy sound. If you have an itch to create, writing is a good way to scratch it.

write-in (rīt′in′), **1** *adj.* of or for a candidate who is not listed on the ballot but who can be voted for by writing the candidate's name. **2** *n.* such a candidate or vote.

writ·er (rī′tər), *n.* **1** person who writes. **2** person whose occupation is writing; author.

write-up (rīt′up′), *n.* a written description or account.

Frank Lloyd Wright building

writhe (rī<small>TH</small>), *v.* **1** to twist and turn; twist about: *She writhed in pain. The snake writhed along the branch.* **2** to suffer mentally; be very uncomfortable. ❏ *v.* **writhed, writh·ing.** —**writh′er,** *n.* —**writh′ing·ly,** *adv.*

writ·ing (rī′ting), *n.* **1** act of making letters or words with pen, pencil, chalk, etc. **2** written form: *Put your ideas in writing.* **3** handwriting: *Your writing is hard to read.* **4** something written; a letter, paper, document, etc. **5** literary work; a book or other literary production: *the writings of Benjamin Franklin.* **6** profession or business of someone who writes.

writ·ten (rit′n), *v.* past participle of **write:** *He has written a letter.*

wrong (rȯng), **1** *adv.* not right; bad: *Stealing is wrong.* **2** *adv.* not true; not correct; not what it should be: *give a wrong answer.* **3** *adv.* not proper; not fit; unsuitable: *Heavy boots would be the wrong thing to wear for tennis.* **4** *adv.* out of order: *Something is wrong with the car.* **5** *adv.* in an incorrect way; badly: *They did their homework wrong and had to do it over.* **6** *n.* anything not right; wrong thing or action: *Two wrongs do not make a right.* **7** *n.* injustice; injury; harm: *You can do an innocent person a wrong by spreading false rumors.* **8** *v.* to do harm to; treat unfairly; injure: *forgive someone who has wronged you.* **9** *adv.* not meant to be seen; least important: *the wrong side of cloth.* **—wrong′·ly,** *adv.* **—wrong′ness,** *n.*

go wrong, **1** to turn out badly: *Everything went wrong today.* **2** to stop being good and become bad.

in the wrong, at fault; guilty.

wrong·do·er (rȯng′dü′ər), *n.* person who does wrong.

wrong·do·ing (rȯng′dü′ing), *n.* act of doing wrong; bad acts: *The thief was guilty of wrongdoing.*

wrong·ful (rȯng′fəl), *adj.* **1** wrong. **2** unlawful. **—wrong′ful·ly,** *adv.* **—wrong′ful·ness,** *n.*

wrong·head·ed (rȯng′hed′id), *adj.* **1** wrong in judgment or opinion. **2** stubborn even when wrong. **—wrong′head′ed·ly,** *adv.* **—wrong′head′ed·ness,** *n.*

wrote (rōt), *v.* past tense of **write:** *He wrote his parents a long letter.* ■ Another word that sounds like this is **rote.**

wroth (rȯth), *adj.* OLD USE. angry.

wrought (rȯt), **1** *adj.* made: *a skillfully wrought piece of pottery.* **2** *adj.* (of metals) formed by hammering. **3** *v.* OLD USE. worked; a past tense and a past participle of **work.**

wrought iron, a tough, durable form of iron with little carbon in it. Wrought iron will not break as easily as cast iron.

wrung (rung), *v.* past tense and past participle of **wring:** *I wrung out the wet cloth and hung it up. His heart is wrung with pity for the poor.* ■ Another word that sounds like this is **rung.**

wry (rī), *adj.* **1** turned to one side; twisted: *She made a wry face to show her disgust.* **2** ironic: *wry humor.* ❑ *adj.* **wri·er, wri·est.** ■ Another word that sounds like this is **rye.** **—wry′·ly,** *adv.* **—wry′ness,** *n.*

wt., weight.

WV, West Virginia (used with postal Zip Code).

W.Va., West Virginia.

WWW, World Wide Web.

WY, Wyoming (used with postal Zip Code).

Wy·eth (wī′əth), *n.* **Andrew,** born 1917, American painter. His paintings show detailed rural scenes.

Wyo., Wyoming.

Wy·o·ming (wī ō′ming), *n.* one of the western states of the United States. *Abbreviation:* WY or Wyo. *Capital:* Cheyenne. **—Wy·o′ming·ite,** *n.*

WORD STORY **Wyoming** got its name from Wyoming Valley, Pennsylvania. The name *Wyoming* comes from a Delaware Indian word meaning "upon the great plain." It became popular after a poem called "Gertrude of Wyoming" was published. A member of Congress proposed it as the name of the western land that became the state of Wyoming.

a	hat	ė	term	ô	order	ch	child		a in about
ā	age	i	it	oi	oil	ng	long		e in taken
ä	far	ī	ice	ou	out	sh	she	ə	i in pencil
â	care	o	hot	u	cup	th	thin		o in lemon
e	let	ō	open	u̇	put	ʈʜ	then		u in circus
ē	equal	ȯ	saw	ü	rule	zh	measure		

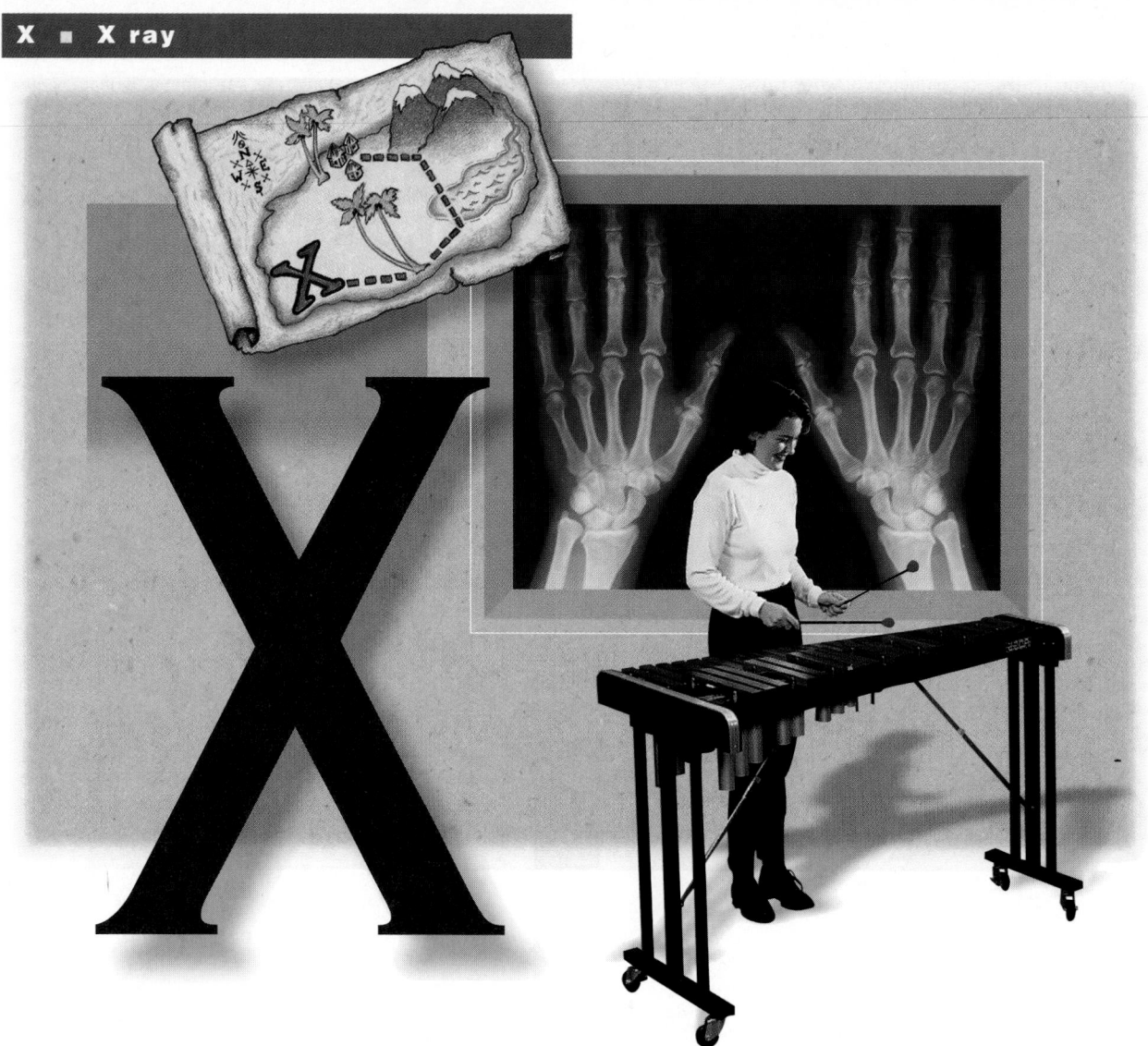

X or **x** (eks), *n.* **1** the 24th letter of the English alphabet. **2** (in mathematics) an unknown quantity. **3** a mark in the shape of an X, made instead of a signature by someone who cannot write. **4** a mark that shows a particular place on a map or diagram: *X marks the spot where the gold is supposed to be buried.* **5** the Roman numeral for 10. ❑ *n., pl.* **X's** or **x's.**

X, a former rating for a movie that was restricted to people over the age of 17.

x-ax·is (eks′ak′sis), *n.* the horizontal line on a chart or graph where the horizontal axis and vertical axis meet at 0.

X chromosome, one of the two chromosomes that determine sex. A fertilized egg cell containing two X chromosomes, one from each parent, develops into a female.

Xe, symbol for xenon.

xe·bec (zē′bek), *n.* a small, three-masted boat of the Mediterranean.

WORD STORY Words beginning with **x** are pronounced to begin with *z*. If *x*, why *z*? Originally, people pronounced them with a *gz* sound, like *x* in *exactly*. But this sound is hard to make, and gradually people gave up.

xe·non (zē′non), *n.* a colorless, odorless element that is a gas forming a very small part of the air. Xenon is used in filling flashbulbs. It forms compounds with fluorine and oxygen. *Symbol:* Xe

xen·o·pho·bi·a (zen′ə fō′bē ə), *n.* fear of foreigners. —**xen·o·pho′bic,** *adj.* —**xen′o·pho′bi·cal·ly,** *adv.*

xer·i·scap·ing (zēr′i skāp′ing), *n.* landscape design that minimizes the need for or the use of water, used for homes, parks, and public spaces.

xe·rog·ra·phy (zi rog′rə fē), *n.* a dry process for making copies of letters, pictures, etc., by using electrically charged particles to form a photographic print. —**xe′ro·graph′ic,** *adj.* —**xe′ro·graph′i·cal·ly,** *adv.*

xer·o·phyte (zir′ə fīt), *n.* any plant that loses very little water and can grow in deserts or other very dry ground. Cactuses, sagebrush, and century plants are xerophytes.

Xer·ox (zir′oks), **1** *n.* trademark for a process of making copies of letters, pictures, etc., by xerography. **2** *v.* to make a copy or copies using a Xerox copying machine.

Xerx·es (zėrk′sēz′), *n.* 519?-465 B.C., king of ancient Persia from 486? to 465 B.C. He tried to conquer Greece but was defeated in 480 B.C. [**Xerxes** comes from a Persian word meaning "king."]

Xi·zang (shē′zäng′), *n.* Chinese name of **Tibet.**

XL, extra large.

X·mas (kris′məs *or* ek′sməs), *n.* Christmas. [See Word Story at **character.**]

X ray, 1 an electromagnetic wave with very high energy and very short wavelength, able to go through substances that ordinary light cannot penetrate. X rays can make pictures on photographic film or sensing devices, showing the interior of the body, of luggage, etc. **2** picture made by X rays.

X-ray (eks′rā′), **1** *v.* to examine, photograph, or treat with X rays: *The doctor X-rayed my hand to find out if any bones had been broken by my fall.* **2** *adj.* of, by, or about X rays: *an X-ray examination of one's teeth.*

xy·lem (zī′lem), *n.* the woody part of plants. Water and dissolved minerals pass upward from the roots through its tissue.

xy·li·tol (zī′li tol), *n.* a natural sweetener found in many plants. Xylitol obtained from birch trees is used as a sugar substitute.

xy·lo·phone (zī′lə fōn), *n.* a musical instrument consisting of two rows of wooden bars of varying lengths, which are sounded by striking with wooden hammers.

xy·lo·phon·ist (zī′lə fō′nist), *n.* person who plays on a xylophone.

X ray

xylophone

X

Y or **y** (wī), *n.* **1** the 25th letter of the English alphabet. **2** anything shaped like a Y. ❑ *n., pl.* **Y's** or **y's.**

Y, symbol for yttrium.

y., **1** yard or yards. **2** year.

-y¹, *suffix.* **1** having; containing ___: *bumpy = having bumps; salty = containing salt.* **2** like ___: *dreamy = like a dream.* **3** somewhat ___: *chilly = somewhat chill.* **4** ready to; tending to ___: *sleepy = ready to sleep.*

-y², *suffix.* **1** condition or quality: *jealousy = jealous quality; victory = condition of being a victor.* **2** activity of ___ing: *delivery = activity of delivering.*

yacht (yät), **1** *n.* boat equipped with sails or an engine, or both, used for pleasure trips or for racing. **2** *v.* to sail or race on a yacht. [**Yacht** comes from an old Dutch word meaning "a chasing ship." The kind of light, fast ship used for chasing other ships, especially pirates, was also good for pleasure sailing and racing.]

yacht·ing (yät′ing), *n.* **1** art of racing or sailing a yacht. **2** pastime of sailing or racing on a yacht.

yachts·man (yäts′mən), *n.* person who owns, races, or sails a yacht. ❑ *n., pl.* **yachts·men.**

yack (yak), *v.* INFORMAL. yak².

ya·hoo (yä′hü *or* yā′hü), *n.* a rough, coarse, or crude person. ❑ *n., pl.* **ya·hoos.**

yak¹ (yak), *n.* a long-haired ox of Tibet and central Asia. Yaks are raised for meat, milk, and hair and for carrying loads.

yak² (yak), *v.* INFORMAL. to talk endlessly and foolishly. ❑ *v.* **yakked, yak·king.** Also, **yack.**

ya·ku·za (yä′kü′zä), *n.* a Japanese gangster. ❑ *n., pl.* **ya·ku·za.**

Yal·ta (yôl′tə), *n.* port and winter resort in S Crimea, on the Black Sea.

Ya·lu (yä′lü), *n.* river in E Asia, between Manchuria and Korea.

yam (yam), *n.* **1** the thick, starchy, orange root of a vine of warm regions, eaten as a vegetable. **2** the sweet potato. [**Yam** comes from a Bantu word meaning "to eat."]

yam·mer (yam′ər), **1** *v.* to whine; whimper. **2** *v.* to talk loudly and constantly; chatter. **3** *n.* sound of whining or chattering.

Ya·mous·sou·kro (yä′mə sü′krō), *n.* capital of Côte d'Ivoire.

Yan·gon (yän′gōn′), *n.* capital and chief port of Burma, in the S part.

Yang·tze (yang′sē′), *n.* former name of **Chang Jiang.**

WORD STORY **Yangtze** may come from Chinese words meaning "twin river." It has two major branches. The modern Chinese name, **Chang Jiang,** means "long river."

yank (yangk), **1** *v.* to pull with a sudden motion; jerk; tug: *She yanked the weeds out of the garden.* **2** *n.* a sudden pull; tug.

Yank (yangk), *n., adj.* INFORMAL. Yankee.

Yan·kee (yang′kē), **1** *n.* person born or living in New England. **2** *n.* person born or living in the North, especially during the Civil War. **3** *n.* person born or living in the United States; American. **4** *adj.* of, for, or about Yankees. ❑ *n., pl.* **Yan·kees.**

Yankee Doo·dle (dü′dl), an American song, probably of English origin and taken over by the American soldiers in the Revolutionary War.

Yaoun·dé (youn dā′), *n.* capital of Cameroon.

yap (yap), **1** *v.* to bark in a quick, sharp way; yelp: *The little dog yapped at every strange person who came to the door.* **2** *n.* a quick, sharp bark; yelp. **3** *v.* SLANG. to talk sharply, noisily, or foolishly. **4** *n.* SLANG. sharp, noisy, or foolish talk. ❑ *v.* **yapped, yap·ping.** —**yap′per,** *n.*

Ya·qui (yä′kē), *n.* member of a tribe of American Indians living in northwestern Mexico and now in southern Arizona. ❑ *n., pl.* **Ya·qui** or **Ya·quis.**

yard[1] (yärd), *n.* **1** piece of ground near or around a house, barn, school, etc.: *You can play outside in the yard.* **2** piece of enclosed ground for some special purpose or business: *a chicken yard.* **3** space with tracks where railroad cars are stored, maintained, shifted around, and rearranged into trains.

yard[2] (yärd), *n.* **1** unit of length equal to 36 inches; 3 feet: *buy six yards of cloth, run 50 yards.* **2** a pole or beam fastened across a mast, used to support a sail.

yard·age (yär′dij), *n.* any amount of length measured in yards.

yard·arm (yärd′ärm′), *n.* either end of the beam or pole used to support a square sail.

yard goods, cloth cut to measure and sold by the yard.

yard·mas·ter (yärd′mas′tər), *n.* person in charge of a railroad yard.

yard sale, garage sale.

yard·stick (yärd′stik′), *n.* **1** a stick one yard long, used for measuring. **2** standard of judgment or comparison.

Ya·ren (yä′rən), *n.* capital of Nauru.

yar·mul·ke (yär′məl kə), *n.* skullcap worn by Orthodox and Conservative Jewish males, especially for prayer and ceremonial occasions.

yarn (yärn), *n.* **1** any spun thread, especially thread prepared for weaving or knitting: *I'm knitting a scarf from this yarn.* **2** tale; story: *We took turns making up yarns and telling them.*

yar·row (yar′ō), *n.* any of several common plants with finely divided leaves and flat clusters of white, pink, or yellow flowers.

yaw (yô), **1** *v.* (of a boat or ship) to turn from a straight course; go unsteadily. **2** *v.* (of an aircraft) to turn from a straight course by a motion about its vertical axis. **3** *n.* movement from a straight course.

yawl (yôl), *n.* boat with a large mast near the bow and a small mast near the stern.

yawn (yôn), **1** *v.* to open the mouth wide because you are sleepy, tired, or bored. **2** *n.* act of doing so. **3** *v.* to open wide: *The canyon yawned in front of us.*

yaws (yôz), *n.* a contagious disease of the tropics that produces sores on the skin.

y-ax·is (wī′ak′sis), *n.* the vertical line on a chart or graph where the horizontal axis and vertical axis meet at 0.

Yb, symbol for ytterbium.

Y chromosome, one of the two chromosomes that determine sex. A fertilized egg cell containing a Y chromosome develops into a male.

yd., yard. ❑ *pl.* **yd.** or **yds.**

ye[1] (yē), *pron.* OLD USE. you.

ye[2] (ᴛнē *or* yē), *definite article.* an old way of writing the definite article "the."

yea (yā), **1** *adv.* yes (used in agreeing with or assenting to something). **2** *adv.* indeed; truly (used to introduce a sentence or clause). **3** *n.* a vote or voter in favor of something: *The yeas outnumber the nays, so the plan is approved.* **4** *interj.* exclamation expressing approval or support for a person, team, etc.

Yea·ger (yā′gər), *n.* **Charles,** born 1923, American pilot. He was the first person to fly faster than the speed of sound, in 1947.

yeah (ye, ya, *or* ye′ə), *adv.* INFORMAL. yes.

year (yir), *n.* **1** 12 months or 365 days; January 1 to December 31. A leap year has 366 days. **2** 12 months counted from any time: *a year from today.* **3** the part of a year spent in a particular activity: *Our school year is about nine months.* **4** amount of time it takes any planet to go once around the sun: *The Martian year is longer than Earth's, but shorter than Saturn's.* **5** solar year.

6 sidereal year. **7 years,** *pl.* age: *young in years but old in wisdom.*
year after year, every year.
year by year, with each succeeding year; as years go by.
year in, year out, always; continuously.

year·book (yir′bůk′), *n.* book or report published every year. Yearbooks often report facts of the year. The graduating class of a school or college usually publishes a yearbook, with pictures of its members.

year·ling (yir′ling), **1** *n.* animal one year old. **2** *adj.* one year old: *a yearling colt.*

year·long (yir′lông′), *adj.* lasting for a year.

year·ly (yir′lē), **1** *adj., adv.* once a year; in every year: *He takes a yearly trip to New York. That company sends out new calendars to its customers yearly.* **2** *adj.* for a year: *a yearly salary of $40,000.* **3** *adj.* lasting a year: *The earth makes a yearly revolution around the sun.*

yearn (yèrn), *v.* **1** to feel a longing or desire; desire earnestly: *I yearned for home.* **2** to feel pity; have tender feelings: *Our hearts yearned for the homeless victims of the flood.* —**yearn′ing·ly,** *adv.*

yearn·ing (yèr′ning), *n.* earnest or strong desire; longing: *a yearning to be popular.*

year-round (yir′round′), *adj., adv.* throughout the year: *She is a year-round resident. She lives here year-round.*

yeast (yēst), *n.* **1** substance that causes bread dough to rise and beer to ferment. Yeast contains many tiny one-celled fungi that grow quickly in any material containing sugar. **2** any of the fungi that form yeast. **3** yeast cake. **4** foam; froth. —**yeast′less,** *adj.* —**yeast′like′,** *adj.*

yeast cake, a small block or cake of compressed yeast.

yeast·y (yē′stē), *adj.* **1** of, containing, or resembling yeast. **2** frothy or foamy: *yeasty waves.* ❑ *adj.* **yeast·i·er, yeast·i·est.** —**yeast′i·ly,** *adv.* —**yeast′i·ness,** *n.*

Yeats (yāts), *n.* **William But·ler** (but′lər), 1865-1939, Irish writer of poems, plays, and essays. He won the 1923 Nobel Prize for literature.

yell (yel), **1** *v.* to cry out with a strong, loud sound: *I yelled with pain.* **2** *n.* a strong, loud cry. **3** *v.* to say with a yell: *We yelled our good-bys as the bus pulled away.* ▪ See Synonym Study at **shout.** **4** *n.* a special shout or cheer used by a school or college to encourage its sports teams. —**yell′er,** *n.*

yel·low (yel′ō), **1** *n.* the color of gold, butter, or ripe lemons. **2** *adj.* having this color. **3** *v.* to make or become yellow: *Paper yellows with age.* **4** *n.* the yolk of an egg, or other thing that is yellow. **5** *adj.* cowardly. ▪ This meaning of **yellow** is sometimes considered offensive. —**yel′low·ness,** *n.*

yellow fever, a dangerous, infectious, viral disease of warm climates, carried by the bite of a certain mosquito; yellow jack. It causes high fever and turns the skin yellow. It was once common in some southern states.

yel·low·ham·mer (yel′ō ham′ər), *n.* yellow-shafted flicker. See **flicker**[2].

yel·low·ish (yel′ō ish), *adj.* somewhat yellow.

yellow jack, **1** yellow fever. **2** a yellow flag used as a signal of quarantine.

yellow jacket, wasp marked with bright yellow.

yellow journalism, journalism that reports stories of crimes, scandal, warfare, etc., in a sensational, often one-sided way, intended to excite readers or viewers.

Yel·low·knife (yəl′ə nif′), *n.* capital of Northwest Territories, Canada.

Yellow Pages, a section of a telephone directory or a separate directory printed on yellow paper, that lists business services and professional people. Within each classification of business or profession, the names are alphabetized.

Yellow River, former name of **Huang He.**

Yellow Sea, part of Pacific Ocean between NE China and Korea.

a	hat	ė	term	ô	order	ch	child		
ā	age	i	it	oi	oil	ng	long	ə	a in about
ä	far	ī	ice	ou	out	sh	she		e in taken
â	care	o	hot	u	cup	th	thin		i in pencil
e	let	ō	open	ů	put	ᴛн	then		o in lemon
ē	equal	ô	saw	ü	rule	zh	measure		u in circus

Y

999

Yel·low·stone (yel′ə stōn′), *n.* Yellowstone National Park.
Yellowstone National Park, a large national park, mostly in NW Wyoming, containing geysers, hot springs, and waterfalls in a scenic canyon.

Yellowstone National Park

yellow warbler, a small American warbler. The male is bright yellow with a darker back.

yelp (yelp), **1** *n.* the quick, sharp bark or cry of a dog, fox, etc. **2** *v.* to make such a bark or cry. **3** *v.* to utter with a yelp. [Yelp comes from an old English word meaning "to boast." Someone who brags a lot is like a dog that barks all the time—annoying.] **—yelp′er,** *n.*

Yelt·sin (yelt′sin), *n.* **Bor·is** (bôr′is), born 1931, president of Russia since 1991.

Yem·en (yem′ən), *n.* country in SW Arabia. *Capital:* Sanaa.

WORD STORY Yemen comes from an Arabic word meaning "right hand." If a person faces Mecca from the West, Yemen is on the right-hand side, to the south.

Yem·e·ni (yem′ə nē), *n.* person born or living in Yemen. ❑ *n., pl.* **Yem·e·ni** or **Yem·e·nis.**

yen¹ (yen), *n.* unit of money of Japan. ❑ *n., pl.* **yen.**

yen² (yen), **1** *n.* a sharp desire or hunger; urgent fancy: *a yen for ice cream.* **2** *v.* to have a yen; desire sharply or urgently. ❑ *v.* **yenned, yen·ning.**

yeo·man (yō′mən), *n.* **1** (in the U.S. Navy) a petty officer who performs clerical duties. **2** (formerly, in Great Britain) an owner of land, but not a large amount, who usually farmed it himself. **3** OLD USE. servant or attendant in a royal or noble household. ❑ *n., pl.* **yeo·men.**

yeo·man·ry (yō′mən rē), *n.* yeomen.

yer·ba maté (yâr′bə *or* yėr′bə), maté.

Yer·e·van (yer′ə vän′), *n.* capital of Armenia.

yes (yes), **1** *adv.* word used to indicate that you can or will, or that something is so; word used to show agreement, acceptance, or consent: *Yes, five and two are seven. When he asked me if I'd go, I said, "Yes."* **2** *n.* agreement; acceptance; consent: *I gave a yes to his invitation.* **3** *adv.* and what is more; in addition to that: *"Your work is good, yes, very good," he said.* **4** *n.* a vote for; person voting in favor of something: *The yeses won.* ❑ *n., pl.* **yes·es.**

ye·shi·va (yə shē′və), *n.* **1** a Jewish school for higher studies, often a rabbinical seminary. **2** a Jewish elementary or high school in which both religious and secular subjects are taught. ❑ *n., pl.* **ye·shi·vas, ye·shi·voth** (ye shē′vōt′).

yes-man (yes′man′), *n.* INFORMAL. person who constantly agrees with an employer, superior officer, political party, etc., without criticism. ❑ *n., pl.* **yes-men.**

yes·ter·day (yes′tər dē), **1** *n.* the day before today: *Yesterday was cold and rainy.* **2** *adv.* on the day before today. **3** *n.* the recent past: *We are often amused by the fashions of yesterday.* **4** *adv.* recently.

yes·ter·year (yes′tər yir′), *n., adv.* OLD USE. last year; the year before this.

yet (yet), **1** *adv.* up to the present time; thus far: *The work is not yet finished.* **2** *adv.* at this time; now: *Don't go yet.* **3** *adv.* at that time; then: *It was not yet dark.* **4** *adv.* even now; still: *She is doing her homework yet.* **5** *adv.* sometime: *I may yet get rich.* **6** *adv.* additionally; again: *Let us try yet one more time.* **7** *adv.* moreover: *They won't do it for you nor yet for me.* **8** *adv.* even: *The judge spoke yet more harshly to the lawbreaker.* **9** *adv., conj.* but: *The story was strange, yet true. The work is good, yet it could be better.*
as yet, up to now.

ye·ti (ye′tē), *n.* Abominable Snowman. ❑ *n., pl.* **ye·tis.**

yew (yū), *n.* **1** any of several evergreen trees and bushes of Europe, Asia, and North America, with bright red seeds. **2** the wood of these trees. Bows for archery used to be made of a kind of yew that grows in England. ■ Other words that sound like this are **ewe** and **you.**

Yid·dish (yid′ish), **1** *n.* language which originally developed from a dialect of German. Yiddish contains many Hebrew expressions and is written in Hebrew characters. It is spoken mainly by Jews of eastern and central Europe, and their descendants. **2** *adj.* of, in, or about Yiddish.

WORD SOURCE Yiddish has given many words to the English language. The words below are some of them.

bagel	chutzpah	lox¹	nosh
blintz	halvah	maven	shtick

yield (yēld), **1** *v.* to produce: *This land yields good crops. Mines yield ore.* **2** *n.* amount yielded; product: *This year's yield from the silver mine was very large.* **3** *n.* income produced by an investment; profit. **4** *v.* to give in return; bring in: *an investment which yielded a large profit.* **5** *v.* to give; grant: *Her parents yielded their consent to the plan.* **6** *v.* to give up; surrender: *The enemy yielded to our soldiers.* **7** *v.* to give way: *Traffic on a side street should yield to traffic on a highway.* **8** *v.* to give place: *We yield to nobody in love of freedom.* **—yield′er,** *n.*

yield·ing (yēl′ding), *adj.* not resisting; submissive: *a person with a humble and yielding nature.* ■ See Synonym Study at **soft.** **—yield′ing·ly,** *adv.* **—yield′ing·ness,** *n.*

yip (yip), **1** *v.* (especially of dogs) to bark or yelp sharply. **2** *n.* a sharp, barking sound. ❑ *v.* **yipped, yip·ping.**

yipe (yīp), *interj.* word used to express fear, pain, surprise, etc.

yip·pee (yip′ē), *interj.* shout of great joy.

YMCA or **Y.M.C.A.,** Young Men's Christian Association.

YMHA or **Y.M.H.A.,** Young Men's Hebrew Association.

yo·del (yō′dl), **1** *v.* to sing with frequent changes from the ordinary voice to a forced shrill voice or falsetto and back again, in the manner of mountaineers of Switzerland and the Tirol. **2** *n.* act or sound of yodeling. ❑ *v.* **yo·deled, yo·del·ing** or **yo·delled, yo·del·ling. —yo′del·er** or **yo′del·ler,** *n.*

yo·ga (yō′gə), *n.* **1 Yoga,** system of Hindu religious philosophy that requires intense mental and physical discipline as a means of attaining a state of union with the universal spirit. **2** system of physical exercises and positions used in Yoga.

yo·gi (yō′gē), *n.* person who practices or follows yoga. ❑ *n., pl.* **yo·gis.**

yo·gurt (yō′gərt), *n.* kind of liquid food made from milk thickened by the action of bacteria. Yogurt is often sweetened and flavored.

yoke (yōk), **1** *n.* a wooden frame which fits around the necks of two work animals to fasten them together for pulling a plow or vehicle. **2** *n.* a pair of animals fastened together by a yoke: *The plow was drawn by a yoke of oxen.* **3** *n.* frame that fits across someone's shoulders for carrying two more or less equal loads. **4** *v.* to put a yoke on; fasten with a yoke. **5** *v.* to harness or fasten a work animal or animals to: *The farmer yoked the plow.* **6** *n.* part of a garment fitting the neck and shoulders closely. **7** *n.* a top piece to a skirt, fitting the hips. **8** *n.* something that binds together; bond; tie: *the yoke of marriage.* **9** *v.* to join; unite: *They are yoked in marriage.* **10** *n.* something that enslaves people or holds them in submission: *Throw off your yoke and be free.* **11** *n.* rule; dominion: *The country was under the yoke of a dictator.* ❑ *v.* **yoked, yok·ing.** ■ Another word that sounds like this is **yolk.**

yo·kel (yō′kəl), *n.* an awkward or unsophisticated person from the country.

Yo·ko·ha·ma (yō′kə hä′mə), *n.* port in central Japan, near Tokyo.

yolk (yōk), *n.* the yellow part of an egg. ■ Another word that sounds like this is **yoke.** [Yolk comes from an old English word meaning "yellow." So egg white and egg yolk are both named for colors.]

Yom Kip·pur (yom kip′ər *or* yom ki pür′), a Jewish fast day of atonement for sins; Day of Atonement. It occurs ten days after Rosh Hashanah, the Jewish New Year.

yon (yon), *adj., adv.* OLD USE. yonder.

yon·der (yon′dər), **1** *adv.* over there; within sight, but not near: *Look at that wild duck yonder! The sky is getting black yonder in the west.* **2** *adj.* being within sight, but not near; situated over there: *On yonder hill stands a ruined castle.*

Yon·kers (yong′kərz), *n.* city just north of New York City.

WORD STORY Yonkers comes from a Dutch word meaning "squire." It was a title given to the man who owned a farm here before there was a city. His farm was known as "the squire's," and the name stuck.

yore (yôr), *n.* **of yore,** now long since gone; long past: *She told us an old tale about days of yore.*

York (yôrk), *n.* **1** the royal house of England from 1461 to 1485. Its emblem was a white rose. **2** city in NE England. **3** Yorkshire.

WORD STORY York may come from a Celtic word meaning "yew tree." The English kings of the house of York had the family name **Plantagenet,** which means "broom branch" in Latin. Despite these names, their fortunes did not grow, and they were soon swept out of power.

York·shire (yôrk′shər), *n.* county in NE England.

Yorkshire pudding, a batter cake often served with roast beef.

Yorkshire terrier, a small, shaggy dog with a steel-blue coat, first bred in northern England to kill rats.

York·town (yôrk′toun′), *n.* village in SE Virginia, where Lord Cornwallis surrendered to George Washington in 1781.

Yo·sem·i·te (yō sem′ə tē), *n.* **1** Yosemite National Park. **2** a very deep valley in this park, famous for its waterfalls. [Yosemite comes from an American Indian word meaning "grizzly bear."]

Yosemite National Park, large national park in E central California, containing a very deep valley famous for its cliffs, peaks, and waterfalls.

Yosemite National Park

you (yü), *pron. sing. or pl.* **1** the person or persons spoken to: *Are you ready? Then you may go.* **2** one; anybody: *You never can tell. You push this button to get a light.* ■ Other words that sound like this are **ewe** and **yew.**

you-all (yü′ól′ *or* yól), *pron.pl.* DIALECT. you: *You-all come and see us real soon.*

you'd (yüd), **1** you had. **2** you would.

you'll (yül), **1** you will. **2** you shall.

young (yung), **1** *adj.* in the early part of life or growth; not old: *A puppy is a young dog.* **2** *n.* young offspring: *An animal will fight to protect its young.* **3** *n.pl.* **the young,** young people. **4** *adj.* having the looks or qualities of youth or a young person: *She looks and acts young for her age.* **5** *adj.* not so old as another or the other: *Young Mr. Jones worked for his father.* **6** *adj.* without much experience or practice: *I was too young in the business to be successful.* **7** *adj.* in an early stage; not far advanced: *The night was still young when they left the party.* ❑ *adj.* **young·er** (yung′gər), **young·est** (yung′gist).
with young, pregnant.

Young (yung), *n.* **1** **Brig·ham** (brig′əm), 1801-1877, American Mormon leader, who led the Mormons to Utah. **2 Cy** (sī), 1867-1955, American baseball player. ■ **Cy Young** pitched 7356 innings and won 511 games, more than any other pitcher. The Cy Young Award is given each year to the best pitchers in the American and the National Leagues.

young·ish (yung′ish), *adj.* rather young.

young·ster (yung′stər), *n.* **1** child: *Those youngsters are still in kindergarten.* **2** a young person.

Youngs·town (yungz′toun′), *n.* city in NE Ohio.

your (yür), *adj.* **1** belonging to you: *Wash your hands.* **2** having to do with you: *We enjoyed your visit.* **3** well-known; that you speak of; that is spoken of: *your real lover of music, your average voter.* **4** *Your* is used as part of a title. *Your Lordship, Your Ladyship, Your Highness, Your Honor.*

you're (yür), you are.

yours (yürz), *pron. sing. or pl.* **1** the one or ones belonging to you: *This pencil is yours. My hands are clean; yours are dirty.* **2** at your service: *I am yours to command.* **3** *Yours* is used in closing a letter, just before the signature: *Yours truly, Sincerely yours.*

your·self (yür self′ *or* yər self′), *pron.* **1** form of *you* used to make a statement stronger: *You yourself know the story is not true.* **2** form used instead of *you* in cases like: *Did you hurt yourself? Can you teach yourself this song?* **3** your real or true self: *Now that your cold is better, you'll feel like yourself again.* ❑ *pron., pl.* **your·selves.** ■ See Usage Note at **myself.**

your·selves (yür selvz′ *or* yər selvz′), *pron.* plural of **yourself:** *You can all see for yourselves that the jar is full.*

youth (yüth), *n.* **1** fact or quality of being young: *In spite of her youth, she has already traveled widely.* **2** the time between childhood and adulthood. **3** a young man. **4** *sing. or pl.* young people. ❑ *n., pl.* **youths** (yüths *or* yüᴛнz), **youth** for 3.

youth·ful (yüth′fəl), *adj.* **1** having the looks or qualities of youth; fresh; lively: *a youthful spirit.* **2** young. **3** of or suitable for youth: *youthful clothing.* —**youth′ful·ly,** *adv.* —**youth′ful·ness,** *n.*

youth hostel, a supervised lodging place for young people on bicycle trips, hikes, etc.; hostel.

you've (yüv), you have.

yowl (youl), **1** *n.* a long, loud, wailing cry; howl. **2** *v.* to howl: *That dog is always yowling.*

yo-yo (yō′yō), *n.* a small wheel-shaped toy made of two wooden or plastic disks joined by a peg. A yo-yo can be spun out and reeled back to the hand by means of a string that is wound around the peg. ❑ *n., pl.* **yo-yos.**

yo-yo

a	hat	ė	term	ô	order	ch	child		a in about
ā	age	i	it	oi	oil	ng	long		e in taken
ä	far	ī	ice	ou	out	sh	she	ə	i in pencil
â	care	o	hot	u	cup	th	thin		o in lemon
e	let	ō	open	ù	put	ᴛн	then		u in circus
ē	equal	ò	saw	ü	rule	zh	measure		

Y

yr., year. ❏ *pl.* **yr.** or **yrs.**

yt·ter·bi·um (i tėr′bē əm), *n.* a metallic rare-earth element, used in experiments. *Symbol:* Yb

yt·tri·um (it′rē əm), *n.* a dark gray metallic element, used in television sets, lasers, and electronic equipment. *Symbol:* Y

yu·an (yü än′), *n.* unit of money in the People's Republic of China. ❏ *n., pl.* **yu·an.**

Yu·ca·tán (yü′kə tan′), *n.* **1** peninsula of SE Mexico and N Central America. **2** state in SE Mexico.

yuc·ca (yuk′ə), *n.* any of several plants and trees found in dry, warm regions of North and Central America, with stiff, narrow, pointed leaves and bell-shaped flowers. ❏ *n., pl.* **yuc·cas.**

yuck (yuk), *interj.* word used to express disgust, strong dislike, etc.

yuck·y (yuk′ē), *adj.* SLANG. disgusting; very unpleasant; distasteful: *yucky old wet rags.* ❏ *adj.* **yuck·i·er, yuck·i·est.**

Yu·go·slav (yü′gō släv′), **1** *n.* person born or living in Yugoslavia. **2** *adj.* of or about Yugoslavia or its people.

yucca

Yu·go·sla·vi·a (yü′gō slä′vē ə), *n.* a former country in SE Europe. —**Yu′go·sla′vi·an,** *adj., n.*

WORD STORY **Yugoslavia** comes from Slavic words meaning "south" and "Slav." You can guess which part means "south." Most of the people of Yugoslavia were Slavs, and most Slavs lived farther north.

Yu·kon (yü′kon), *n.* **1** river flowing from NW Canada through Alaska into the Bering Sea. **2 Yukon Territory,** territory in NW Canada. *Capital:* Whitehorse.

WORD STORY **Yukon** comes from an American Indian word meaning "big river." The territory was named for the river. If this story sounds familiar, see the Word Story at **Mississippi.**

yule or **Yule** (yül), *n.* **1** Christmas. **2** yuletide.

Yule log, a large log burned at Christmas.

yule·tide or **Yule·tide** (yül′tīd′), *n.* the Christmas season.

yum (yum), *interj.* word used to express pleasure or delight, especially about food.

yum·my (yum′ē), *adj.* very pleasing to the senses; delicious; delightful. ❏ *adj.* **yum·mi·er, yum·mi·est.**

Yup·pie or **yup·pie** (yup′ē), *n.* SLANG. member of the young, professional middle class.

yurt (yürt), *n.* a portable, tentlike dwelling made of a framework of branches covered with felt, used by nomadic Mongols in central Asia.

YWCA or **Y.W.C.A.,** Young Women's Christian Association.

YWHA or **Y.W.H.A.,** Young Women's Hebrew Association.

Z or **z** (zē), *n.* the 26th and last letter of the English alphabet. ❑ *n., pl.* **Z's** or **z's**.

Za·ca·te·cas (sä′kä tä′käs), *n.* a state in N central Mexico.

Za·greb (zä′greb) *n.* capital of Croatia.

Za·har·i·as (zə har′ē əs), *n.* **Babe Did·rik·son** (bāb did′rik sən), 1911?-1956, American athlete. ∎ **Babe Didrikson Zaharias** was an all-around athlete who set three track and field world records in the 1932 Olympic Games. She also competed in swimming, basketball, baseball, tennis, and diving, and helped found the Ladies Professional Golf Association. In 1946 and 1947 she won 17 straight golf tournaments.

Za·ïre (zä ir′), *n.* **1** country in central Africa. *Capital:* Kinshasa. **2** Congo (def. 2). —**Za·ïr·e·an** or **Za·ïr·i·an** (zä ir′ē ən), *adj., n.*

Zam·be·zi (zam bē′zē), *n.* river flowing through S Africa into the Indian Ocean.

Zam·bi·a (zam′bē ə), *n.* country in S Africa. *Capital:* Lusaka. [**Zambia** is named for the Zambezi River, which got its name from a local word meaning "river."] —**Zam′bi·an**, *adj., n.*

za·ny (zā′nē), **1** *n.* a fool. **2** *n.* a clown. **3** *adj.* clownish; foolish; idiotic. ❑ *n., pl.* **za·nies**; *adj.* **za·ni·er, za·ni·est.** —**za′ni·ly**, *adv.* —**za′ni·ness**, *n.*

WORD STORY **Zany** comes from *Giovanni* (jō vän′nē), the name of a famous Italian clown character in plays. As a nickname, the clown Giovanni was called Zanni. And people who acted clownishly were called zanies.

Zan·zi·bar (zan′zə bär), *n.* island near the E coast of Africa. It is part of Tanzania. [**Zanzibar** comes from an Arabic word meaning "black."]

zap (zap), INFORMAL. **1** *interj.* exclamation of surprise, shock, dismay, etc.: *Zap! A home run beat us.* **2** *v.* to hit hard; beat; defeat; kill. **3** *v.* to go quickly past a commercial or undesired parts of a taped TV program by using a remote control or by speeding up VCR tape. **4** *v.* to cook in a microwave oven. ❑ *v.* **zapped, zap·ping.**

Za·pa·ta (sə pä′tə), *n.* **Em·il·i·a·no** (ā′mē lyä′nō), 1879-1919, Mexican revolutionary of Indian descent. He fought for redistribution of land in Mexico.

zeal (zēl), *n.* eager desire or effort; earnest enthusiasm.

zeal·ot (zel′ət), *n.* person who shows too much zeal; fanatic.

zeal·ous (zel′əs), *adj.* full of zeal; eager; earnest; enthusiastic: *We made zealous efforts to clean up the house for the party.* [See Word Story at **jealous**.] —**zeal′ous·ly**, *adv.* —**zeal′ous·ness**, *n.*

ze·bra (zē′brə), *n.* any of three kinds of wild mammals of Africa, related to horses and donkeys but with dark and white stripes. ❑ *n., pl.* **ze·bras** or **ze·bra.**

a	hat	ė	term	ô	order	ch	child		a in about
ā	age	i	it	oi	oil	ng	long		e in taken
ä	far	ī	ice	ou	out	sh	she	ə	i in pencil
â	care	o	hot	u	cup	th	thin		o in lemon
e	let	ō	open	ù	put	∓H	then		u in circus
ē	equal	ò	saw	ü	rule	zh	measure		

zebra mussel, a shellfish of Europe and Asia accidentally brought to the Great Lakes where it is rapidly increasing in numbers. Zebra mussels clog equipment and compete with native species.

ze·bu (zē′bü), *n.* an ox of Asia and eastern Africa with a large hump over the shoulders. The zebu has been domesticated as a farm animal. ❑ *n., pl.* **ze·bus** or **ze·bu.**

Zech·a·ri·ah (zek′ə rī′ə), *n.* **1** (in the Bible) a Hebrew prophet. **2** a book of the Bible. [Zechariah comes from Hebrew words meaning "remembrance of God."]

Ze·dil·lo (sā dē′yō), *n.* **Ponce de Le·ón** (pȯn′sā dā lā ōn′), born 1951, Mexican political leader, president of Mexico since 1994.

Zen Buddhism (zen), a Japanese form of Buddhism that emphasizes meditation and introspection.

ze·nith (zē′nith), *n.* **1** the point in the sky directly overhead. **2** the highest point: *At the zenith of its power, Rome ruled all of Europe.*

Zeph·a·ni·ah (zef′ə nī′ə), *n.* **1** (in the Bible) a Hebrew prophet. **2** a book of the Old Testament.

zeph·yr (zef′ər), *n.* **1** the west wind. **2** any soft, gentle wind; mild breeze. **3** a fine, soft yarn or worsted.

Zep·pe·lin or **zep·pe·lin** (zep′ə lən), *n.* a large, rigid, cylinder-shaped airship with separate compartments filled with gas. Zeppelins were mostly used from 1914 to 1937.

zeppelin

ze·ro (zir′ō), **1** *n.* the figure or digit 0; naught. **2** *n.* point marked with a zero on the scale of a thermometer, etc. **3** *n.* temperature that corresponds to zero on the scale of a thermometer. **4** *adj.* of or at nothing: *The other team's score was zero.* **5** *n.* complete absence of quantity; nothing: *One minus zero is one.* **6** *adj.* not any; none at all: *zero visibility in dense fog.* **7** *n.* a very low point: *The losing team's spirit sank to zero.* ❑ *n., pl.* **zer·os** or **zer·oes.**
zero in on, 1 to get the range of a target by adjusting the sights of a firearm, etc. **2** to aim with precision toward a target. **3** to come near from all sides; close in on; surround: *zero in on a target.*

WORD STORY Zero comes from an Arabic word meaning "empty." **Cipher** comes from the same Arabic word. A zero shows that a place in a number has no value, and so is empty.

zero gravity or **zero g,** condition in which the effects of gravity are not felt. In spacecraft, zero gravity is experienced as weightlessness.

zero hour, 1 time set for beginning an attack or other military operation. **2** time set for any important action to begin; crucial moment.

zero population growth, the condition in which a population has stabilized in number, because the birthrate and death rate have become equal.

zest (zest), *n.* **1** keen enjoyment; great pleasure: *The hungry children ate with zest.* **2** a pleasant or exciting quality: *Wit gives zest to conversation.* **—zest′less,** *adj.*

WORD STORY Zest comes from a French word meaning "peel of an orange or lemon." This part of the fruit has a very strong flavor, used to make food and drink more appetizing. **Zest** and **relish** are both words from eating that are now used about many other activities. In old days, a good meal was probably many people's idea of a good time.

zest·ful (zest′fəl), *adj.* marked by zest. **—zest′ful·ly,** *adv.* **—zest′ful·ness,** *n.*

Zeus (züs), *n.* Jupiter (def. 2).

Zhou En·lai. See **Chou En·lai.**

zig·gu·rat (zig′ù rat), *n.* an ancient Assyrian and Babylonian temple shaped like a pyramid with separate levels, each smaller than the one under it, so as to have a terrace at each level.

zig·zag (zig′zag′), **1** *adj., adv.* with short, sharp turns from one side to the other: *to go in a zigzag direction. The path ran zigzag up the hill.* **2** *v.* to move in a zigzag way: *Lightning zigzagged across the sky.* **3** *n.* a zigzag line or course. **4** *n.* one of the short, sharp turns of a zigzag. ❑ *v.* **zig·zagged, zig·zag·ging.**

zilch (zilch), *n.* INFORMAL. zero; nothing.

zil·lion (zil′yən), INFORMAL. **1** *n.* any very large, indefinite number. **2** *adj.* very many; a great many: *He knows a zillion jokes.*

Zim·ba·bwe (zim bä′bwä or zim bä′bwē), *n.* country in SE Africa. *Capital:* Harare. Formerly called **Rhodesia. —Zim·ba′·bwe·an,** *adj., n.*

zinc (zingk), *n.* a bluish white metallic element that is not much affected by air or moisture at ordinary temperatures. At high temperatures it burns with a bright, blue-green flame. Zinc is used in alloys such as brass, as a rustproof coating for iron, as a roofing material, in electric batteries, in paint, and in medicine. *Symbol:* Zn

zinc oxide, compound of zinc and oxygen, used in making paint, rubber, glass, cosmetics, and ointments.

zine (zēn), *n.* INFORMAL. magazine, especially a small or amateur one.

zing (zing), **1** *interj., n.* a sharp, humming sound. **2** *n.* liveliness; spirit; zest: *a story without zing.*

zin·ni·a (zin′ē ə), *n.* any of several garden plants like large daisies, grown for their showy flowers of many colors. ❑ *n., pl.* **zin·ni·as.**

zinnia

Zi·on (zī′ən), *n.* **1** hill in Jerusalem on which the royal palace and the Temple were built. **2** Israel or the Israelites; the people of Israel. **3** heaven, as the final home of those who are virtuous. **4** home of the Christian church of God.

Zi·on·ism (zī′ə niz′əm), *n.* movement that started in the 1800s to set up a Jewish national state in Palestine and that now seeks to help maintain and develop the state of Israel.

Zi·on·ist (zī′ə nist), *n.* person who supports or favors Zionism.

Zion National Park, a national park in SW Utah.

zip¹ (zip), **1** *n.* a sudden, brief, hissing sound, as of a flying bullet. **2** *v.* to make such a sound. **3** *n.* energy or vim. **4** *v.* to move or act quickly or with much energy or power: *Cars were zipping along the highway.* ❑ *v.* **zipped, zip·ping.**

zip² (zip), *v.* to fasten or close with a zipper: *zip up your jacket before going out.* ❑ *v.* **zipped, zip·ping.**

zip³ (zip), *n.* SLANG. zero, especially as the score of a game.

Zip Code, 1 ZIP Code, system of numbers, each of which identifies one of the postal delivery areas into which the United States has been divided. **2** a number in this system. [Zip Code comes from Zone Improvement Plan Code.]

zip·per (zip′ər), *n.* **1** a fastener in which two rows of metal or plastic teeth can be made to hook together or come apart by pulling on a sliding tab. Zippers are used on clothing, boots, luggage, etc. **2** *v.* to fasten or close with a zipper: *Zipper your jacket before you go out.*

zip·py (zip′ē), *adj.* full of energy; lively. ❑ *adj.* **zip·pi·er, zip·pi·est.**

zir·con (zėr′kon), *n.* a crystalline mineral that occurs in various forms and colors. Transparent zircon is used as a gem.

zir·co·ni·um (zėr kō′nē əm), *n.* a white metallic element obtained from zircon. Zirconium is used in alloys for coating parts of nuclear reactors. *Symbol:* Zr

zit (zit), *n.* SLANG. pimple.

zith·er (zith′ər *or* ziᴛʜ′ər), *n.* a musical instrument having 30 to 40 strings, played with the fingers and a plectrum.

zi·ti (zē′tē), *n.pl.* short tubes of pasta, often cooked in tomato sauce.

zlo·ty (zlô′tē), *n.* unit of money in Poland. ❑ *n., pl.* **zlo·tys** or **zlo·ty.**

Zn, symbol for zinc.

zo·di·ac (zō′dē ak), *n.* **1** the section of the sky through which the location of sunrise moves north and south each year. It is divided into 12 equal parts called signs, named for 12 constellations found in them. **2** diagram representing the zodiac, used in astrology. —**zo·di·a·cal** (zō dī′ə kəl), *adj.*

zither

WORD STORY Zodiac comes from a Greek word meaning "animal." Because so many signs of the zodiac are constellations named for animals, ancient Greeks called this part of the sky the circle of the animals.

zom·bie (zom′bē), *n.* **1** corpse supposedly brought to a trancelike condition resembling life by a supernatural power. People who practice voodoo believe in zombies. **2** a supernatural power or force that supposedly makes the dead move and act.

zon·al (zō′nl), *adj.* **1** of or about a zone or zones. **2** divided into zones. —**zon′al·ly,** *adv.*

zone (zōn), **1** *n.* any of the five great regions of the earth's surface, bounded by imaginary lines going around the earth parallel to the equator. Zones differ from each other in climate. The Frigid Zones are coldest, and the Torrid Zone is warmest. **2** *n.* any region or area treated or thought of as different from others. A combat zone is an area where fighting is going on. **3** *n.* area or district in a city or town under special restrictions on building or the use of buildings: *a residential zone.* **4** *v.* to divide into or be formed into zones: *The neighborhood is zoned partly for factories, partly for residences.* **5** *n.* one of the numbered sections into which a large city or metropolitan area is divided for delivery of mail. **6** *n.* an area within which the same rate is charged for parcel post shipments. ❑ *v.* **zoned, zon·ing.**

SYNONYM STUDY **Zone, region,** and **district** all mean a particular place, large or small, that has something special about it. **Zone** usually suggests a part of the world: *Bananas grow in the tropical zone.* **Region** means a place that can be described in some way so as to tell it from other places: *In the northern region of the state, the land is good for farming.* **District** means a part of a larger place, suggesting a special activity: *The city's large banks all have buildings in the downtown financial district.*

zoo (zü), *n.* place where wild animals are kept and shown; zoological garden. ❑ *n., pl.* **zoos.**

zoo-, *prefix.* animal or animals: *zoology = the science of animals.*

zoo·keep·er (zü′kē′pər), *n.* person who works in a zoo.

zo·o·log·i·cal (zō′ə loj′ə kəl), *adj.* **1** of or about animals and animal life. **2** of or about zoology. —**zo′o·log′i·cal·ly,** *adv.*

zoological garden, zoo.

zo·ol·o·gy (zō ol′ə jē), *n.* the science of animals; the study of animals and animal life. Zoology is a branch of biology. —**zo·ol′o·gist,** *n.*

zoom (züm), *v.* **1** to move rapidly upward or downward: *The airplane zoomed up out of sight.* **2** to move very rapidly: *The car zoomed past us, going 80 miles an hour.* **3** to move or travel with a humming or buzzing sound: *The bumblebee zoomed from flower to flower.*

zoom in on, 1 to adjust a zoom lens to take a close-up shot. **2** to examine closely; concentrate attention: *She was able to zoom in on the cause of our problem and solve it.*

zoom lens, type of movie, TV, or video camera lens which can be adjusted quickly to take either wide-angle distance shots or close-up shots.

zo·o·plank·ton (zō′ō plangk′tən), *n.* the animals in plankton.

Zo·ro·as·ter (zôr′ō as′tər), *n.* Persian religious prophet who lived about 600 B.C. He taught that life is a battle between forces of good and evil.

Zo·ro·as·tri·an (zôr′ō as′trē ən), **1** *adj.* of or about Zoroaster or the religion founded by him. **2** *n.* person believing in the teachings of Zoroaster.

Zo·ro·as·tri·an·ism (zôr′ō as′trē ə niz′əm), *n.* religion founded by Zoroaster and practiced in ancient Persia. Zoroastrianism taught that there is an eternal struggle between the powers of light and of darkness.

zounds (zoundz), *interj.* OLD USE. oath expressing surprise or anger.

Zr, symbol for zirconium.

zuc·chi·ni (zü kē′nē), *n.* a dark green squash shaped like a cucumber. It is eaten as a vegetable. ❑ *n., pl.* **zuc·chi·ni** or **zuc·chi·nis.**

Zui·der Zee (zī′dər zē′), a shallow gulf in central Netherlands. It is now closed off from the North Sea by a dike.

Zu·lu (zü′lü), **1** *n.* member of a Bantu people of SE Africa. **2** *n.* their language. **3** *adj.* of or about this people or their language. ❑ *n., pl.* **Zu·lu** or **Zu·lus** for 1.

Zu·lu·land (zü′lü land), *n.* territory in NE Natal, in the Republic of South Africa. Zululand is the home of the Zulu.

Zu·ñi (zü′nyē), *n.* member of a tribe of American Indians living in western New Mexico. ❑ *n., pl.* **Zu·ñi** or **Zu·ñis.**

Zur·ich (zur′ik), *n.* city in N Switzerland.

zwie·back (swī′bak′ *or* zwī′bak′), *n.* kind of bread or cake cut into slices and toasted dry in an oven.

zy·de·co (zī′də kō′), *n.* a kind of dance music influenced by the blues, played mostly in Louisiana and Texas. Zydeco music is played on the accordion, guitar, and violin.

zy·gote (zī′gōt), *n.* the cell formed by the union of two reproductive cells. A fertilized egg is a zygote.

zoo

a	hat	ė	term	ô	order	ch	child	ə	a in about
ā	age	i	it	oi	oil	ng	long		e in taken
ä	far	ī	ice	ou	out	sh	she		i in pencil
â	care	o	hot	u	cup	th	thin		o in lemon
e	let	ō	open	ù	put	ᴛʜ	then		u in circus
ē	equal	ò	saw	ü	rule	zh	measure		

Art and Photo Credits

Unless otherwise acknowledged, all photographs are the property of Scott, Foresman and Company. Page abbreviations are as follow: (T) top, (C) center, (B) bottom, (R) right, (BG) background.

Frontmatter Tom Murphy/Superstock, Inc.

Dictionary

A Opener page (T) Superstock, Inc. (B) Tom Murphy/Superstock, Inc. **abbey, aborigine** Cynthia Clampitt **abstract** Stadtische Galerie im Lenbachaus **abyss** Wiley Wales/ProFiles West, Inc. **accentuate** Sylvain Grandadam/Photo Researchers **accordion** Richard Heinz/Superstock **adventure** Wiley Wales/ProFiles West, Inc. **aflutter** Superstock, Inc. **agile** LIFE Nature Library/THE PRIMATES, Published by Time Life Books, Inc. **aikido** Ron Bailey/ © Chicago Tribune, 1980, World Rights Reserved. **air bag** Courtesy Ford Motor Company **airplane** Courtesy Concorde **albino** Jessica Ehlers/Bruce Coleman Inc. **allegiance** Bob Daemmrich **alluvial** NASA **altar** Cathy Wilson **American eagle** (R)Leo Keeler/Animals Animals (L) Public Domain **amphibian** Dr. Paul Zahl/Photo Researchers **Anasazi** John Moore **Angora rabbit** Leonard Lee Rue III/Photo Researchers **annual ring** Gilbert Grant/Photo Researchers **anticline** Robert Nonnemacher **antique** Cynthia Clampitt **ape** (CL) Tom McHugh/Photo Researchers, (CR) C. K. Lorenz/Photo Researchers (R) S. R. Maglione/Photo Researchers **Appaloosa** Walter D. Osborne/Photo Researchers **aqueduct** Michelle E. Ryan **archaeopteryx** Peabody Museum **arid** John Moore **artifact** Museum of the American Indian, Smithsonian Institution **ascension** Scala/Art Resource, NY **assembly line** Courtesy Ford Motor Company **astronaut** NASA **athlete** Robert Amft/Superstock, Inc. **ATMOSPHERE** (spread) all photos Superstock, Inc. **attention** Leon Dishman/Superstock, Inc. **attire** Lemoine/Sygma **Audubon** Courtesy The New York Historical Society, NYC **avalanche** Art Twomey/Photo Researchers **autumn** Don and Pat Valenti/fStop Pictures Inc. **award** Focus on Sports, Inc.

B Opener page (BL) Don Dixon **Badlands National Park** Alain Thomas/Photo Researchers **balance** Bob Daemmrich **Baltimore oriole** Anthony Mercieca/Photo Researchers **banyan** Beatrice Neff/Photo Researchers **Barcelona** Superstock, Inc. **basalt** Ken M. Johns/Photo Researchers**batik** Superstock, Inc. **bedeck** Private Collection **beetle** Superstock, Inc. **beginning** Bob Daemmrich **Belgium** Will & Deni McIntyre/Photo Researchers **beluga** Richard Kolar/Animals Animals **bermuda shorts** Superstock, Inc. **bilateral symmetry** ProFiles West, Inc. **billow** David Weintraub /Photo Researchers **biodiversity** Superstock, Inc. **biplane** Cynthia Clampitt **bird of paradise** Baiyer River Sanctuary, New Guinea/Tom McHugh/Photo Researchers **black-eyed susan** Cynthia Clampitt **black hole** Don Dixon **blowhole** Tom McHugh/Photo Researchers**boardsailing, bobsled** Superstock, Inc. **Bolivar** Corbis-Bettmann Archive **booby** G. C. Kelley/Photo Researchers **boomerang** Superstock, Inc. **booster** NASA **border** Superstock, Inc. **borzoi** Margot Conte/Animals Animals **botanical garden** Cynthia Clampitt **Bourke-White** Margaret Bourke-White/Life Magazine © Time Warner, Inc. **bracelets** Karen Koblik **breakwater** Cynthia Clampitt **breathtaking** E. Hugo **bridge** Cynthia Clampitt **Bryce Canyon National Park** Douglas Faulkner/Photo Researchers **Buckingham Palace** 113 Superstock, Inc. **bulge** Jeff Lepore/Photo Researchers **bust** "Sioux Indian Man". Courtesy Field Museum of Natural History, Chicago and the Superstock, Inc.

C Opener page (C) Superstock, Inc. **cactus** E. Hugo **Calder, camouflage** Superstock, Inc. **canyon** John Moore **Carlsbad Caverns National Park** John Pontier/Animals Animals/Earth Scenes **Cassatt** Superstock, Inc. **celebrate** Lawrence Migdale **Cezanne** Hermitage Museum, St Petersburg, Russia/Superstock, Inc. **chairlift** Superstock, Inc. **chamois** Peter Weimann/Animals Animals **Charlie Chaplin** University of Texas at Austin, Austin, Texas. **charge, Chartres, Chicago** Superstock, Inc. **chihuahua** Robert Pearcy/Animals Animals **CHINA AND THE SILK ROAD** (spread) 153a (b) Superstock, 153a-153b Inc. Superstock, Inc. 153b(b) James L. Amos (t) Superstock, Inc. **chrysanthemums** Superstock, Inc. **cirrus** John Lemker/Animals Animals/Earth Scenes **city hall** Robert Frerck/Odyssey Productions **cleaner** Superstock, Inc. **clear-cut** David Thompson/Earth Scenes **climber** Superstock, Inc. **closed captioning** Robert Amft **clown** Superstock, Inc. **collapse** J. de Selliers/Superstock, Inc. **color-blind** MacMillan Science Company, Inc. **Columbia Plateau** Thane/Earth Scenes **comet** National Optical Astronomy Observatories **commencement, computer graphics, concentric circles, congestion, conning tower, consequence** Superstock, Inc. **controller** NASA **Copenhagen, costume, countryside, courthouse** Superstock, Inc. **cowgirl** Allen Russell/ProFiles West, Inc. **crater** Meteor Crater Enterprise **cricket** Donald Specker/Animals Animals **crop-dusting, crude, crutch** Superstock, Inc. **cumulus** Cy Furlan **curtsy** Musee D'Orsay, Paris/Bridgeman CollectionSuperstock, Inc. **cyclone** Superstock, Inc. **cygnet** Margot Conte/Animals Animals

D Opener page (TR) Howard Hall/Oxford Scientific Films/Animals Animals **Dali** Dali, Salvador, "THE PERSISTENCE OF MEMORY." 1931. Oil on canvas, 9-1/2 x 13". Collection, The Museum of Modern Art, New York. Given anonymously. Photograph © The Museum of Modern Art, New York. **Day of the Dead** Superstock, Inc. **dead heat** AP/Wide World **deep** Richard Bready **delicate** Superstock, Inc. **demagogue** ACME/Corbis-Bettmann **depict** Superstock, Inc. **derail** Library of Congress **derby** UPI/Corbis-Bettmann **desert** Cecil W. Stoughton/Eastern National Parks & Monuments Association **desperadoes** Museum of Modern Art, Film Stills Archive **development** Superstock, Inc. **devastate** Bob Daemmrich **dig** John Gebhardt **dingo** Cynthia Clampitt **dirty** Focus on Sports, Inc. **discount** Superstock, Inc. **Disney** Kobal Collection **dispute** Brian Drake/Sports Chrome West, Inc. **diversity** Ulrike Welsch **dolphin** Howard Hall/Oxford Scientific Films/Animals Animals **double-decker, downhill,** Superstock, Inc. **drama** Photographed by Keith Hamshere © Lucasfilm Ltd. (LFL) 1984, All Rights Reserved. **drawbridge, dressy** Superstock, Inc. **drums** Robert Fried **dunes** Don and Pat Valenti **dust bowl** Library of Congress **dye** Jason Laure/Laure Communications

E Opener page (TL) Leo Keeler/Animals Animals (B) Superstock, Inc. (TR) Superstock, Inc. **eclipse** NASA **ECOSYSTEMS** (spread) (L) Jack Wilburn/Animals Animals (R) Runk/Schoenberg/Grant Heilman Photography **efface** Superstock, Inc. **elated** Bob Daemmrich **El Greco** Superstock, Inc. **emblem** Courtesy UNICEF **endurance** Robert Amft **enormous** Los Angeles County Museum of Natural History **entertainer** Brooks Kraft/Sygma **envelop** J. H. Robinson/Earth Scenes **epitaph, equestrian** Superstock, Inc. **erosion** Trevor Barrett/Earth Scenes **eskimo dog** Superstock, Inc. **Everglades National Park** Ted Levin/Earth Scenes **excavate** Breck P. Kent/Earth Scenes **excursion** Robert Frerck/Odyssey Productions **exert** Superstock, Inc. **experiment** Bob Daemmrich **explore** NASA **exquisite** Planet Art **extravaganza** Bob Daemmrich

F Opener page (L) Superstock, Inc. (R) Kobal Collection **facet** Superstock, Inc. **farmyard** Superstock, Inc. **feast** Ca Rezzonico, Venice/e.t. Archives, London/Superstock, Inc. **fellowship** Bob Daemmrich **ferris wheel** Courtesy Navy Pier, Chicago **fiber optics** Superstock, Inc. **fingering** Bob Daemmrich **fire tower** Breck P. Kent/Earth Scenes **fish-eye** Dan Morrill **fjord** E. R. Degginger/Earth Scenes **flamingo, flashy, flood, Florence, fluffy, folk dance** Superstock, Inc. **following** R. Maiman/Sygma **ford** Tim Brown/ProFiles West, Inc. **foreshorten** National Archives **formation** Superstock, Inc. **fountain** Barry Durand/Odyssey Productions **Frankenstein** Kobal Collection **free fall** Tom Sanders/Photri/Stock Market **freeze-dry** NASA **fresco** Knossos, Crete/Superstock, Inc. **Fijiyama** Superstock, Inc. **fungus** Peter Weimann/Earth Scenes **fury** Orsula Markus/Photo Researchers **futuristic** Courtesy Universidad Nacional Antonoma de Mexico, Instituto de Ingeniera, Sunrayce '95, Proyecto Tonatiah.

G Opener page (TR) Bernard Desestres/Vandystadt/Photo Researchers **galaxy** U.S. Naval Observatory **ganesha** Gian Berto Vanni/Art Resource **Gauguin** Norton Simon Foundation San Marino, Califorina/Bridgeman Collection/Superstock, Inc. **Genghis Kahn** Granger Collection **geodesic domes** Todd S. Dacquisto/Third Coast Stock Source, Inc. **geyser** B. G. Murray, Jr./Earth Scenes **giant sequoia** L. L. T. Rhodes/Earth Scenes **Glacier Bay National Park** Alan Fortune/Earth Scenes **glider** Bernard Desestres/Vandystadt/Photo Rsearchers **glitter** Harvey Schwartz/ProFiles West, Inc. **gnarl** Cynthia Clampitt **gondola** Superstock, Inc. **goose** Vito Palmisano **Goya** Giraudon/Art Resource

Granada Superstock, Inc.　**Great Wall of China** Warwick Johnson/Oxford Scientific Films/Earth Scenes　**grindstone** Bob Daemmrich　**griot** Robert Caputo/Aurora　**ground crew** Will & Deni McIntyre/Photo Re searchers　**gyrfalcon** Superstock, Inc.

H　**Opener page**　Bruce Watkins/Animals Animals　(B) Ralph A. Reinhold/Animals Animals　(T)Superstock, Inc.　**hammerhead** Bruce Watkins/Animals Animals　**handicraft** Elizabeth Harris/Tony Stone Images　**hang glider** Superstock, Inc.　**harbor** Michael P. Gadomski/Earth Scenes　**harp** Cynthia Clampitt　**haystack** Superstock, Inc.　**headdress** Cynthia Clampitt　**hedgehog** Reed Williams/Animals Animals　**herd** Superstock, Inc.　**heron** Bob Daemmrich　**hieroglyphics** Cynthia Clampitt　**high wire** Edward C. Cohen/Superstock, Inc.　**hippopotamus** Animals Animals　**hog** Superstock, Inc.　**hologram** Philippe Plailly/Photo Researchers, Inc.　**honor** Bob Daemmrich　**hornbill** Martyn F. Chillmaid/Oxford Scientific Films/Animals Animals　**hose** Superstock, Inc.　**hot spring** David J. Boyle/Earth Scenes　**houseboat** J. D. Barnell/Superstock, Inc.　**Hubble Space Telescope** NASA　**hurricane** NASA　**husky** Zig Leszczynski/Animals Animals　**hyena** Ralph A. Reinhold/Animals Animals

I　**Opener page**　(TL) Jeff Schultz/AlaskaStock　(TR,BR) Superstock, Inc.　**ice skater** Focus on Sports, Inc.　**immigrants** Library of Congress　**impala** Peter Weimann/Animals Animals　**impersonator** Barry King/Gamma-Liaison　**imprint, impure** Superstock, Inc.　**incrustation** Richard Bready　**Independence Day** Paul Gelsobello/Gamma-Liaison　**indigenous** Elizabeth Posner　**inflate** Evan Agostini/Gamma-Liaison　**ingot** Superstock, Inc.　**inlet** Bob Nonnemacher　**inoculation** Bob Daemmrich　**insignia** U.S. Army photo　**instability, interchange** Superstock, Inc.　**interrogation** Kobal Collection　**invasion** U.S. Coast Guard　**invention** Smithsonian Institution　**inviting scene, ivied** Superstock, Inc.　**Iwo Jima** Defense Dept. Photo

J　**Opener page**　(CL, CR) Superstock, Inc.　(T) JPL/NASA　**jaguar** Michael Fogden/Animals Animals　**Joshua tree** Patti Murray/Earth Scenes　**jump** Bob Daemmrich　**Jupiter** JPL/NASA

K　**Opener page**　(L) Mickey Gibson/Animals Animals　(R) Fred Felleman/Tony Stone Images　**kayak** Wiley Wales/ProFiles West, Inc.　**Kilimanjaro** Zig Leszczynski/Earth Scenes　**killer whale** Mickey Gibson/Animals Animals　**knight** Fernando DaSilva on horseback in front of castle　**koala** Mickey Gibson/Animals Animals　**KNIGHTS AND CASTLES** (spread) (BG) Superstock, Inc.　pg. 485a (BC, BR) Victoria & Albert Museum, London/Superstock, Inc.　(BL) British Library, London/Superstock, Inc.　(C) Bibliotheque Nationale, Paris/Superstock, Inc.　pg. 485b (B) Bibliotheque Nationale, Paris/Superstock, Inc. (T) Art Resource　**Kremlin** Superstock, Inc.

L　**Opener page**　(BL) Gerard Lacz/Animals Animals　(TR) E. R. Degginger/Earth Scenes　(BR) Superstock, Inc.　**labyrinth** M. B. Duda/Photo Researchers　**Lange photograph** Library of Congress　**lava** E. R. Degginger/Earth Scenes　**Le Corbusier** Giraudon/Art Resource　**leopard** Gerard Lacz/Animals Animals　**levee** Gregory Foster/Gamma-Liaison　**Liberty Bell** Superstock, Inc.　**lifelike** AP/Wide World　**light** Bob Daemmrich　**lily** Bob Nonnemacher　**line** Bob Daemmrich　**lion** David J. Boyle/Animals Animals　**litter** Fritz Prenzel/Animals Animals　**loon** Johnny Johnson/Animals Animals　**lost** Bob Daemmrich　**low tide** Robert Maier/Earth Scenes Accademia Venezia/Art Resource　**lynx** Joe McDonald/Animals Animals

M　**Opener page**　(B) American Museum of Natural History, New York/Superstock, Inc.　(C) Superstock, Inc.　(T) John A. Anderson/Animals Animals　**majestic** T.P.I./ProFiles West, Inc.　**Manet** Musee d'Orsay, Paris/A.G.E Spain/Superstock, Inc.　**march** UPI/Corbis-Bettmann　**market** Bill Bachmann/ProFiles West, Inc.　**Mars** U.S. Geological Survey, Flagstaff, AZ.　**MARINE LIFE** (spread) (BG) Superstock, Inc.　(L) Marty Snyderman/Ocean Environment　(R) John Gerlach/Animals Animals　(B) Howard Hall/Oxford Scientific Films/Animals Animals　**mask** (L) British Museum, London/Superstock, Inc.　(CL) Christie's, London/Superstock, Inc.　(CR) Werner Forman Archive/Noh Theatre Collection, Kongo School, Kyoto/Art Resource　(R) American Museum of Natural History, New York/Superstock, Inc.　**mass-produce** Superstock, Inc.　**Matisse** Hermitage Museum, St Petersburg, Russia/Bridgeman Collection/Superstock, Inc.　**maypole** Superstock, Inc.　**mechanic** Bob Daemmrich　**megalith** Jerome Wyckoff/Earth Scenes　**merry-go-round, Mesa Verde National Park** Superstock, Inc.　**migration** Wiley Wales/ProFiles West, Inc.　**mine** Superstock, Inc.　**minuteman** Library of Congress　**moat** Superstock, Inc.　**mollusk** G.J. Bernard/Animals Animals　**monorail** Superstock, Inc.　**monument** Rob Crandall/Stock Connection　**moray** Alison Kuiter/Oxford Scientific Films/Animals Animals　**Moscow** Superstock, Inc.　**mountain goat** Ray Richardson/Animals Animals　**mouse** Marty Cardano　**mural** Superstock, Inc.　**musk ox** Johnny Johnson/Animals Animals　**mutualism** Joe McDonald/Animals Animals　**mysterious** Wiley Wales/ProFiles West, Inc.　**mystify** Gamma Liaison

N　**Opener page**　(CR) Smithsonian Institution　(T) Superstock, Inc.　**narcissus, narrow** Michelle E. Ryan　**nautilus** Gregory Brown/Animals Animals　**nebula** © 1959 by California Institute of Technology & Carnegie Institute of Washington　**Nefertiti** Vanni/Berlin/Art Resource　**neon sign** Smithsonian Institution　**newlywed** Leslye Borden/PhotoEdit　**newt** Robert Maier/Animals Animals　**Niagara Falls** John R. Raup/Earth Scenes　**nonviolent** UPI/Corbis-Bettmann　**nova** John Sanford/SPL/Photo Researchers　**nurse** Mary Kate Denny/PhotoEdit

O　**Opener page**　(TR) Superstock, Inc.　(TL) Stouffer Prod. Ltd/Animals Animals　**obelisk, oddity, officiate** Superstock, Inc.　**oil well** ProFiles West, Inc.　**old-fashioned** Bob Winsett/ProFiles West, Inc.　**Olympic Games** Focus on Sports, Inc.　**open-air** Elizabeth Posner　**opossum** Stouffer Prod. Ltd/Animals Animals　**organize** Bob Daemmrich　**origami** David R. Frazier　**osprey** Cliff Hollis/ProFiles West, Inc.　**outdoors** Wiley Wales/ProFiles West, Inc.　**outrigger** Carl Roessler/Earth Scenes　**ovation** Focus on Sports, Inc.　**overbite** Archive Photos　**overhead** Bob Daemmrich

P　**Opener page**　(B, C) Superstock, Inc.　(L) Nancy Rotenberg/Animals Animals　**paddy** Allen Russell/ProFiles West, Inc.　**pagoda** Superstock, Inc.　**PAINTING** (spread) (T) Van Hoorick Fine Art/Superstock, Inc.　(BR) Private Collection/Lerner Fine Art Gallery/Superstock, Inc.　(BG) Superstock, Inc.　(C) Digital reconstruction by Doug Stern based on photography by Enrico Ferorelli and David W. Woodell/National Geographic Society Image Collection.　(BL) Christie's, London/Superstock, Inc.　**panda** Gerard Lacz/Animals Animals　**pantomine** Express Newspapers/Archive Photos　**parachute, Paris, Parthenon** Superstock, Inc.　**path** Richard Bready　**pattern** Allen Russell/ProFiles West, Inc.　**pentagon** Superstock, Inc.　**periscope** Official U.S. Navy Photograph　**perspective** Janet Hill　**petroglyphs** John Moore　**pheasant** Ken Cole/Animals Animals　**Picasso** Solomon R. Guggenheim Museum, New York/Superstock, Inc.　**pig** Tom Pollak/Superstock, Inc.　**pitcher** Focus on Sports, Inc.　**placid** Superstock, Inc.　**plantarium** Courtesy Adler Planetarium and Astronomy Museum, Chicago.　**plesiosaur** Superstock, Inc.　**plunge** David Stoecklein　**plumage** Herb Segars/Animals Animals　**pogo stick** Superstock, Inc.　**police** Michelle E. Ryan　**pollution** Phil Lauro/ProFiles West, Inc.　**Ponce de Leon** Public Domain　**pop art** Richard Pettibone/Private Collection/Superstock, Inc.　**pose** Bob Daemmrich　**posse** Corbis-Bettmann Archive　**pothole** Alex S. MarcLean/Landslides　**pouch** Fritz Prenzel/Animals Animals　**praying mantis** Nancy Rotenberg/Animals Animals　**prehensile** Zig Leszczynski/Animals Animals　**prepare** Bob Daemmrich　**preserve** Harry Taylor/Oxford Scientific Films/Earth Scenes　**pride** Bob Daemmrich　**prism** Runk/Schoenberger/Grant Heilman Photography　**proboscis** Superstock, Inc.　**procession** Bob Daemmrich　**profile** John W. Warden/West Stock　**pronghorn** Len Rue Jr./Animals Animals　**proportion** Don Pitcher/AlaskaStock Images　**pueblo** Thame/Earth Scenes　**punch** Focus on Sports, Inc.　**punt** Chuck Solomon/Focus on Sports, Inc.　**puppet** Robert Frerck/Odyssey Productions　**pyramid** Michael J. Howell/Superstock, Inc.　**pyramid** Superstock, Inc.　**python** M. Krishnan/Animals Animals

Q　**Opener page**　(BL) George Whiteley/Photo Researchers　(C) Joe McDonald/Animals Animals　**quail** Joe McDonald/Animals Animals　**quartz** Sinclair Stammers/Science Photo Library/Photo Researchers　**quintuplets, quiz program** Archive Photos

R　**Opener page**　(BL) Archive Photos　(TR) Allen Russell/ProFiles West, Inc.　(BR, TL) Superstock, Inc.　**racquetball** Superstock, Inc.　**radiology** Bob Daemmrich　**rainbow** Kevin Alexander/ProFiles West, Inc.　**ram** Leonard Lee Rue III/Animals Animals　**ray** Superstock, Inc.　**realistic** Christie's London/Superstock, Inc.　**reception** Anthony Neste/Focus on Sports, Inc.　**red line** Joe Patronite/Allsport USA　**reflection** Janet Hill regatta, rehabilitate Superstock, Inc.   remembrance Michelle E. Ryan   replica Instituto Nacional de Anthropologiae Historia   restoration Bob Daemmrich   reticulate Superstock, Inc.   Revere Art Resource   Revolutionary War Lexington Historcial Society   rigging Superstock, Inc.   Rivera Schalwijk/Art Resource   robot Archive Photos/Archive Films   Rodin Christie's, London/Superstock, Inc.   rose window George Ranalli/Photo Researchers   roundhouse Corbis-Bettmann Archive   row house Robert Brenner/PhotoEdit   ruin Michelle E. Ryan   rumble seat Corbis-Bettmann Archive   run-down Superstock, Inc.   Rushmore Allen Russell/ProFiles West, Inc.

S   Opener page   (B) Henry Augloos/Animals Animals   (C) Superstock, Inc.   (TR) Bob Daemmrich   (TL) NASA   safe Bill Kunkel/Focus on Sports, Inc.   saguaro Janet Hill   salmon Johnny Johnson/Animals Animals   San Francisco, sari Superstock, Inc.   sapphire Gemmedia   satellite NASA   scaly anteater Bruce Watkins/Animals Animals   scarlet tanager Tom Edwards/Animals Animals   scepter Erich Lessing/Art Resource   school house John Neubauer/PhotoEdit   scoreboard Superstock, Inc.   scorpion Zig Leszczynski/Animals Animals   scrimshaw Lee Boltin/Boltin Picture Library   SCULPTURE (spread) pg. 773a (BR) Gala/Superstock, Inc.   (BL) Jacksonville Art Museum, Florida/Superstock, Inc.   (C) Christie's, London/Superstock, Inc. (T) Sculpture by Joe Poodlat/Taloyoak   (BG) Allen Russell/ProFiles West, Inc.   pg. 773b (BL) Metropolitan Museum of Art, The Michael C. Rockefeller Memorial Collection, Gift of Nelson A. Rockefeller, 1972. 1978.412.310)   (TL) Hirshhorn Museum, Washington, D.C./SuperStock   (R) Superstock, Inc.   sea horse Herb Segars/Animals Animals   Seattle Superstock, Inc.   sego lily Rod Planck/Superstock, Inc.   semaphore U.S. Navy from Robert A. Carlisle, Elsilrac Enterprises.   send-off, sentry Superstock, Inc.   serape Beryl Goldberg   series Leo Castelli Gallery, New York City/Lerner Fine Art Gallery/Superstock, Inc.   Seuss Rob Schoenbaum/Black Star   shaggy Mickey Gibson/Animals Animals   shadow Richard Bready   sheepdog Henry Augloos/Animals Animals   Shenandoah National Park Michael P. Gadomski/Earth Scenes   Shih Tzu George F. Godfrey/Animals Animals   shore Superstock, Inc.   shotput Focus on Sports, Inc.   shrine Superstock, Inc.   show window Richard Palsey/Stock Boston   siamese cat Mike & Moppet Reed/Animals Animals   sidesaddle Corbis-Bettmann   sign language Bob Daemmrich   silhouette Janet Hill   single file John W. Warden/Superstock, Inc.   sinkhole St Petersburg Times/Gamma Liaison   ski jump Superstock, Inc.   skywriting Lowell Georgia/Photo Researchers   sled dogs Harry Cutting/Animals Animals   slime Breck P. Kent/Animals Animals   sluice Library of Congress   smog Superstock, Inc.   smokejumper Ferry/Gamma Liaison   snapdragon Richard Shiell/Animals Animals   snow leopard Michael Dick/Animals Animals   soccer Bob Daemmrich   sod Corbis-Bettmann Archive   solar panel Bob Daemmrich   soothsayer Superstock, Inc.   Spanish moss B.F. Head/Earth Scenes   space shuttle NASA   SPACE (spread) pg. 827a (BG, B, T,) NASA   (C) Kitt Peak National Observatory   pg. 827b (T, B) JPL/NASA   spectrum Runk/Schoenberger/Grant Heilman Photography   spice Carl Scofield/ProFiles West, Inc.   spire Michelle E. Ryan   splash Comstock Inc.   sponge Mickey Gibson/Animals Animals   spotlight Roger Tully/Tony Stone Images   square Superstock, Inc.   stalactite Mickey Gibson/Earth Scenes   stampede Kathi Lamm/Tony Stone Images   station Robert Nonnemacher   Statue of Liberty Superstock, Inc.   steel band Superstock, Inc.   Stieglitz Philadelphia Museum of Art, Given by Carl Zigrosser   Stockholm Superstock, Inc.   stratum Don & Pat Valenti   stretcher Superstock, Inc.   streetcar Richard Bready   striped, stunt Superstock, Inc.   sturgeon Gerard Lacz/Animals Animals   submarine, subway Superstock, Inc.   suffragette Corbis-Bettmann Archive   Sullivan Art Resource   sunflower Metropolitan Museum of Art, New York/Superstock, Inc.   support Michelle E. Ryan   Supreme Court Mary D. Browning/Uniphoto   surrealism e.t. archives, London/Superstock, Inc.   suspension bridge Superstock, Inc.   swan dive Gary Bigham/Adventure Photo   switchboard Superstock, Inc.   swordtail Oxford Scientific Films/Animals Animals   symphony orchestra Oliver Benn/Tony Stone Images

T   Opener page   (TR) Superstock, Inc.   (TR) John Chellman/Animals Animals   Taj Mahal Superstock, Inc.   takeoff Fred J. Maroon/Photo Researchers   tamarin Shane Moore/Animals Animals   tango Paul Chesley/Tony Stone Images   teamwork Bob Daemmrich   temple Mike Kirkpatrick/ProFiles West, Inc.   tentacle G. J. Bernard/Oxford Scientific Films/Animals Animals   terrace Tim Brown/ProFiles West, Inc.   tetra Gerard Lacz/Animals Animals   thatch, theme park Superstock, Inc.   throw Bob Daemmrich   Tibet Superstock, Inc.   tile Victoria & Albert Museum, London/Art Resource   time exposure Superstock, Inc.   Titicaca Elizabeth Posner   toboggan Superstock, Inc.   tornado E. R. Degginger/Earth Scenes   toucan John Chellman/Animals Animals   Toulouse-Lautrec Pushkin Museum of Fine Arts, Moscow, Russia/A.K.G. Berlin/Superstock, Inc.   tractor Superstock, Inc.   tranquil Tim Brown/ProFiles West, Inc.   treehouse J.R. Williams/Earth Scenes   triumphant Bob Daemmrich   tulip Richard Bready   turkey, Turner Superstock, Inc.   twilight Rocky Fry

U   Opener page   (TL) National Archives   (TR) Erich Lessing/Art Resource   ultralight Steven Burr WIlliams/Liaison Interntional   Uncle Sam The American Legion National Headquarters   underdog Focus on Sports, Inc.   Underground Railroad Cincinnati Art Museum   undulate UPI/Corbis-Bettmann   unicorn Erich Lessing/Art Resource   union Robert Kusel/Tony Stone Images   unsmiling Grant Wood, "American Gothic," (detail), © 1996 Grant Wood/VAGA/Superstock, Inc.   unsafe Ken Biggs/Tony Stone Images   unusual Leen Van Der Slik/Earth Scenes   uproot L. L. Rhodes/Earth Scenes   Uranus JPL/NASA

V   Opener page   (TL) Superstock, Inc.   (C) J. A. L. Cooke/Oxford Scientific Films/Animals Animals   valley, Vatican City Superstock, Inc.   Velazquez Museo del Prado, Madrid, Spain/A.K.G. Berlin/Superstock, Inc.   Venus's-flytrap J. A. L. Cooke/Oxford ScientificFilms/Animals Animals   Virgin Islands National Park Michael Fredericks/Earth Scenes   vivid John Lemker/Earth Scenes   volleyball David R. Frazier   Volcano (spread) E. R. Degginger/Earth Scenes   (BG) David Weintraub /Photo Researchers   (B) Mike Andrews/Earth Scenes   (R) Superstock, Inc.

W   Opener page   (L) Peter Meimann/Animals Animals   (R) Dagmar/Focus on Sports, Inc.   wagon Allen Russell/ProFiles West, Inc.   wallaby Ken Cole/Animals Animals   walrus Leo Keller/Animals Animals   warplane Frank Wootton   warthog Leonard Lee Rue III/Animals Animals   water-ski Superstock, Inc.   weather Janet Hill   weird Kobal Collection   werewolf Film Stills Archive, Museum of Modern Art, New York, Courtesy Universal Pictures   wheelie Dagmar/Focus on Sports, Inc.   White House Superstock, Inc.   whooping crane Ray Richardson/Animals Animals   willow Michelle E. Ryan   windmill Tim Brown/ProFiles West, Inc.   winter Carl Scofield/ProFiles West, Inc.   wingspread E. R. Degginger/Animals Animals   wisteria Richard Shiell/Animals Animals   wolf Peter Meimann/Animals Animals   wolverine Leonard Lee Rue III/Animals Animals   wool Cynthia Clampitt   worship Paul Chesley/Tony Stone Images   Wren Superstock, Inc.   Wright Western Pennsylvania Conservancy/Art Resource

X   Opener page   (TL) Robert Nonnemacher

Y   Opener page   (TL) Superstock, Inc.   (BL) Michael Dick/Animals Animals   (BR) Superstock, Inc.   Yellowstone National Park Richard Bready   Yosemite National Park Michael Fogden/Oxford Scientific Films/Earth Scenes   yucca Hans & Judy Beste/Earth Scenes Wide World

Z   Opener page   (TL) Wide World   (BL) Robert Nonnemacher   zeppelin Wide World   zinnia Robert Nonnemacher

End Matter   p. 1019 (cr) Michael Evans/The White House   (bl) The White House   (bc) The Governor's Office, Arkansas

All maps thoughout were created by Mapping Specialists Limited.

Student Reference

Table of Contents

World: Focus on the Atlantic   1010

Physical Features of the World   1012

These United States   1014

Presidents   1016

Table of Chemical Elements   1020

Geological Time   1021

Mathematical Formulas   1022

Proofreader's Marks   1024

We the people ...

The World
Focus on the Atlantic

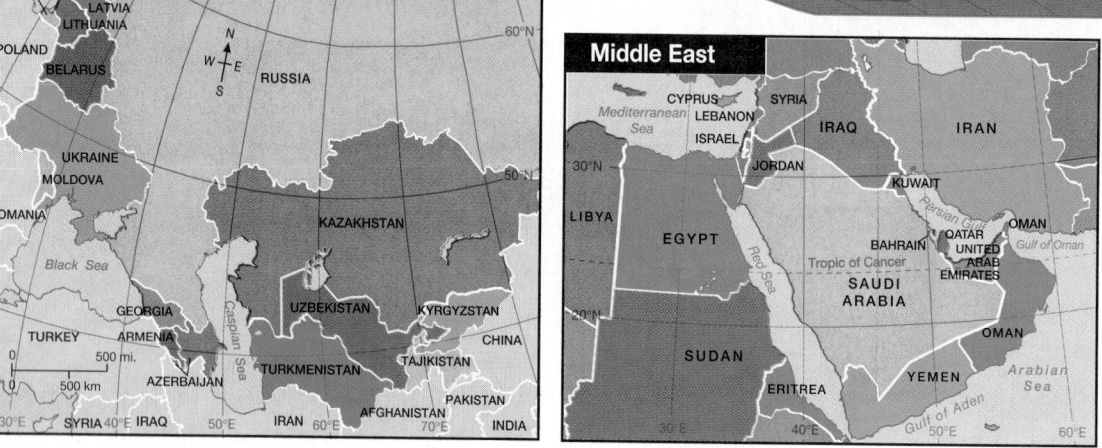

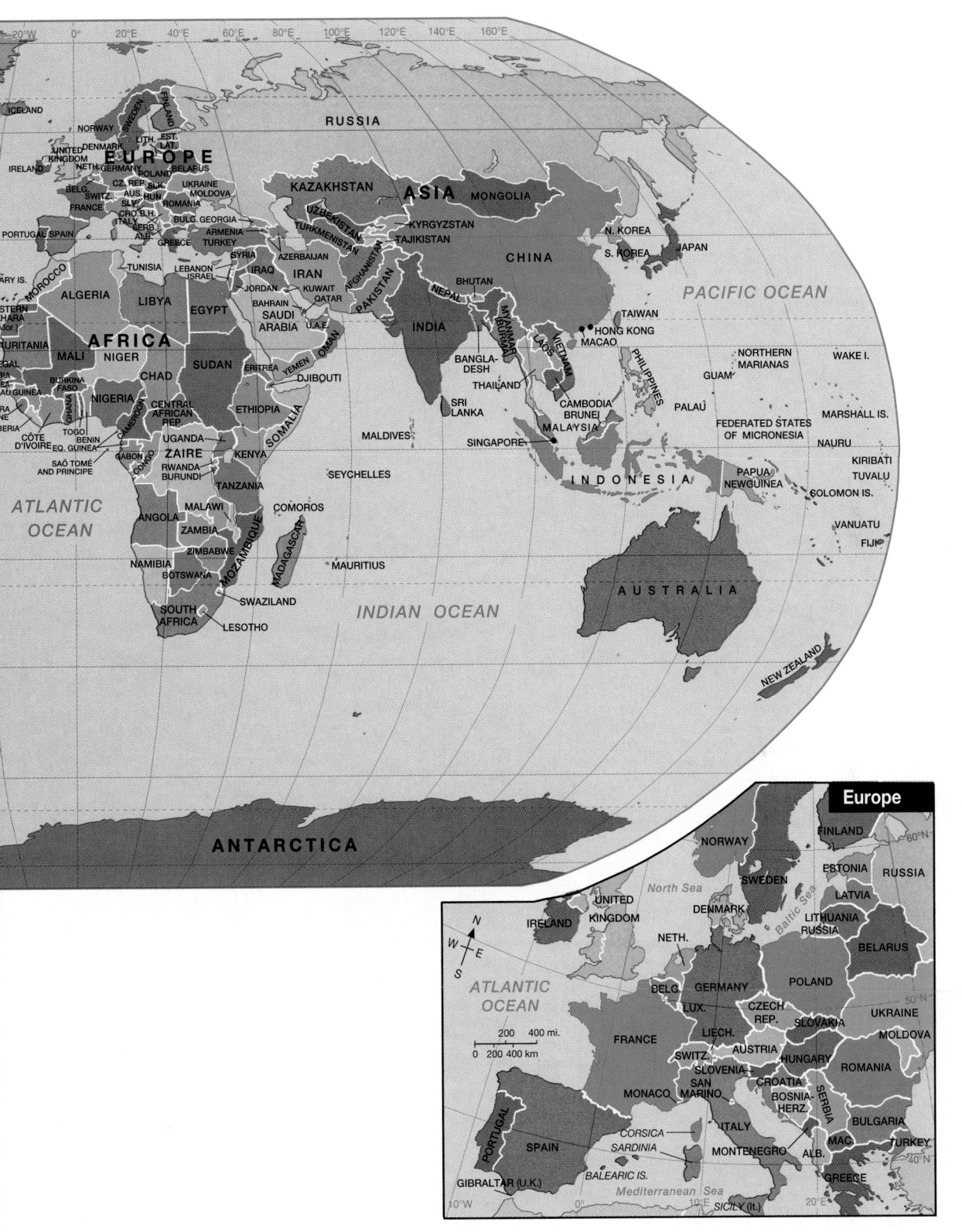

20°W   0°   20°E   40°E   60°E   80°E   100°E   120°E   140°E   160°E

ICELAND

NORWAY

UNITED
KINGDOM

IRELAND

DENMARK

NETH. GERMANY

EUROPE

SWEDEN

FINLAND

LITH. EST.
LAT.

RUSSIA

BELG.
SWITZ.
FRANCE

CZ. REP.
AUS. SLK.
SLV.
CRO. B.H.
ITALY
SERB.
ALB.

POLAND
BELARUS

UKRAINE
MOLDOVA
ROMANIA
BULG. GEORGIA

KAZAKHSTAN

ASIA

MONGOLIA

PORTUGAL SPAIN

ARY IS.

MOROCCO

GREECE
ARMENIA
TURKEY

AZERBAIJAN

UZBEKISTAN

TURKMENISTAN

KYRGYZSTAN
TAJIKISTAN

TUNISIA
LEBANON
ISRAEL

SYRIA

IRAQ

JORDAN

IRAN

CHINA

N. KOREA

S. KOREA

JAPAN

PACIFIC OCEAN

ALGERIA

LIBYA

EGYPT

KUWAIT
QATAR
BAHRAIN

SAUDI
ARABIA

U.A.E.

AFGHANISTAN

PAKISTAN

NEPAL

BHUTAN

TAIWAN

HONG KONG
MACAO

WESTERN
SAHARA

Mor.

MAURITANIA

AFRICA

NIGER

CHAD

SUDAN

YEMEN

DJIBOUTI

OMAN

INDIA

BANGLA-
DESH

MYANMAR
BURMA

LAOS

VIETNAM

NORTHERN
MARIANAS

WAKE I.

EGAL

BURKINA
FASO

MALI

NIGERIA

CENTRAL
AFRICAN
REP.

ERITREA

ETHIOPIA

THAILAND

SRI
LANKA

CAMBODIA
BRUNEI

GUAM

PALAU

PHILIPPINES

MARSHALL IS.

GUINEA

IBERIA

CÔTE
D'IVOIRE

GHANA

TOGO
BENIN
EQ. GUINEA

CAMEROON

GABON

SAO TOMÉ
AND PRINCIPE

CONGO

ZAIRE

UGANDA

RWANDA
BURUNDI

KENYA

SOMALIA

MALAYSIA

SINGAPORE

MALDIVES

FEDERATED STATES
OF MICRONESIA

NAURU

KIRIBATI

TUVALU

ATLANTIC
OCEAN

ANGOLA

ZAMBIA

MALAWI

TANZANIA

SEYCHELLES

INDONESIA

PAPUA
NEWGUINEA

SOLOMON IS.

VANUATU

FIJI

NAMIBIA

BOTSWANA

ZIMBABWE

MOZAMBIQUE

MADAGASCAR

COMOROS

MAURITIUS

AUSTRALIA

SOUTH
AFRICA

SWAZILAND

LESOTHO

INDIAN OCEAN

NEW ZEALAND

ANTARCTICA

Physical Features of the World

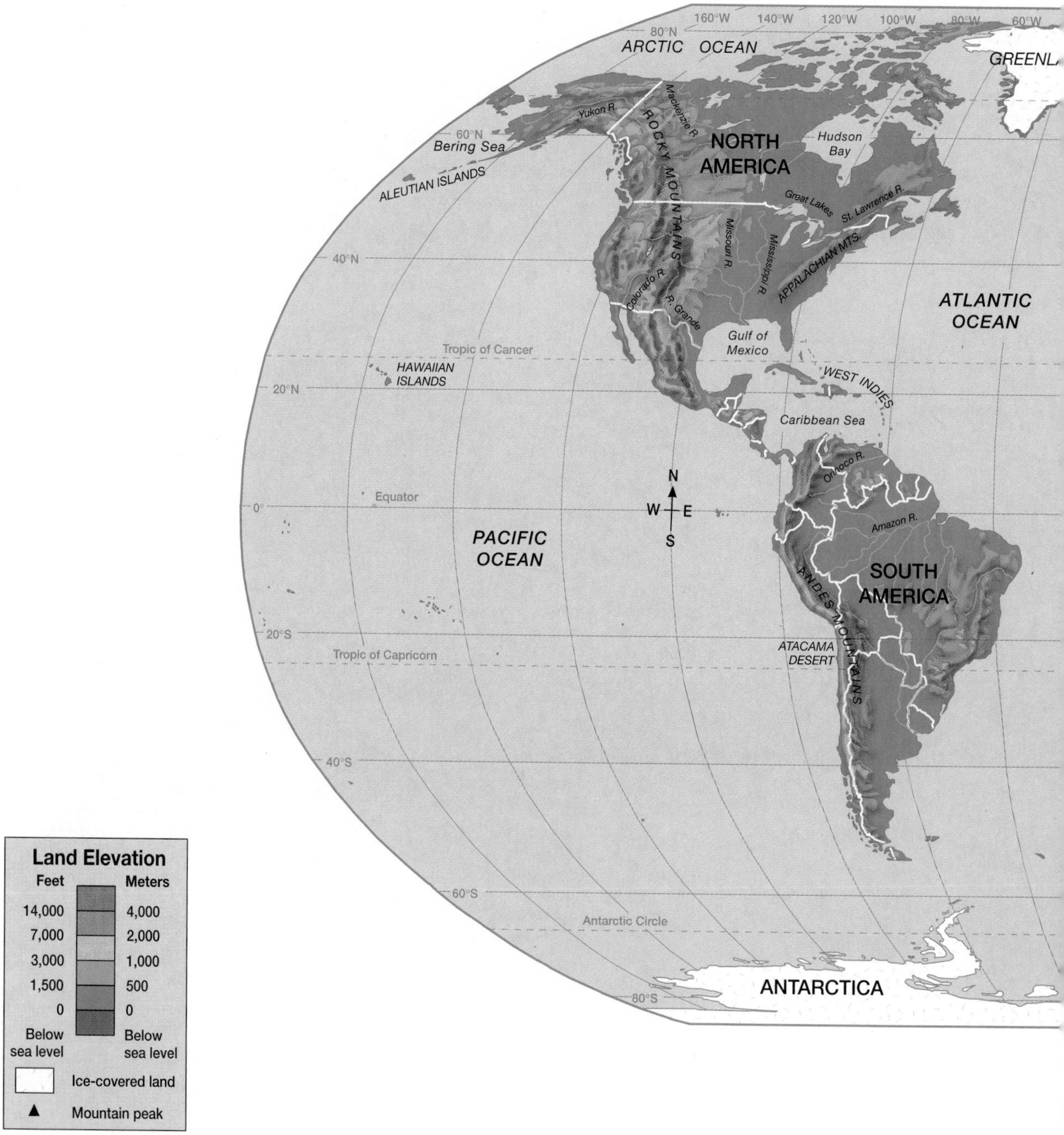

ARCTIC OCEAN

GREENLA

NORTH AMERICA

Bering Sea

ALEUTIAN ISLANDS

Yukon R.

Mackenzie R.

ROCKY MOUNTAINS

Hudson Bay

Great Lakes

St. Lawrence R.

Missouri R.

Mississippi R.

APPALACHIAN MTS.

Colorado R.

R. Grande

ATLANTIC OCEAN

Gulf of Mexico

Tropic of Cancer

HAWAIIAN ISLANDS

WEST INDIES

Caribbean Sea

Orinoco R.

Equator

Amazon R.

PACIFIC OCEAN

SOUTH AMERICA

ANDES MOUNTAINS

ATACAMA DESERT

Tropic of Capricorn

Antarctic Circle

ANTARCTICA

N W E S

160°W 140°W 120°W 100°W 80°W 60°W
80°N
60°N
40°N
20°N
0°
20°S
40°S
60°S
80°S

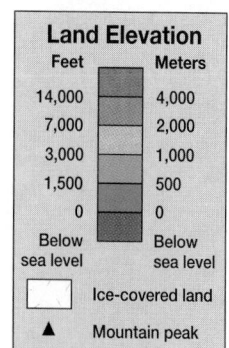

Land Elevation

Feet		Meters
14,000		4,000
7,000		2,000
3,000		1,000
1,500		500
0		0
Below sea level		Below sea level

☐ Ice-covered land

▲ Mountain peak

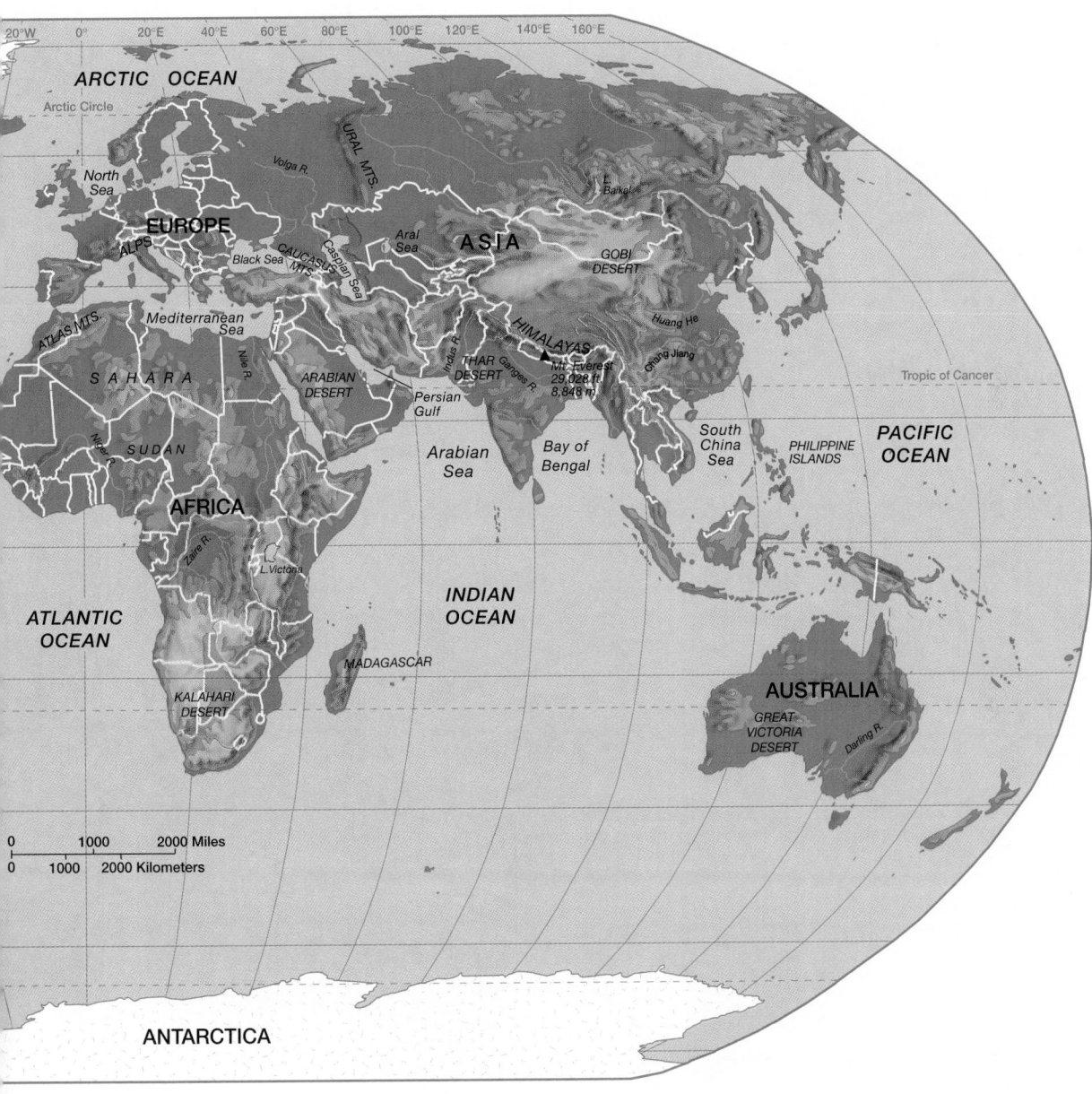

20°W 0° 20°E 40°E 60°E 80°E 100°E 120°E 140°E 160°E

ARCTIC OCEAN

Arctic Circle

North
Sea

EUROPE

ALPS

ATLAS MTS.

Volga R.

URAL MTS.

Black Sea

CAUCASUS
MTS.

Caspian Sea

Aral
Sea

ASIA

*L.
Baikal*

*GOBI
DESERT*

*Mediterranean
Sea*

Nile R.

S A H A R A

Niger R.

S U D A N

AFRICA

ARABIAN
DESERT

Persian
Gulf

Indus R.

THAR
DESERT

Ganges R.

HIMALAYAS

▲ Mt. Everest
29,028 ft
8,848 m)

Huang He

Chang Jiang

Tropic of Cancer

Arabian
Sea

Bay of
Bengal

South
China
Sea

PHILIPPINE
ISLANDS

**PACIFIC
OCEAN**

Zaire R.

L. Victoria

**ATLANTIC
OCEAN**

MADAGASCAR

**INDIAN
OCEAN**

KALAHARI
DESERT

AUSTRALIA

GREAT
VICTORIA
DESERT

Darling R.

0   1000   2000 Miles
0   1000   2000 Kilometers

ANTARCTICA

These United States

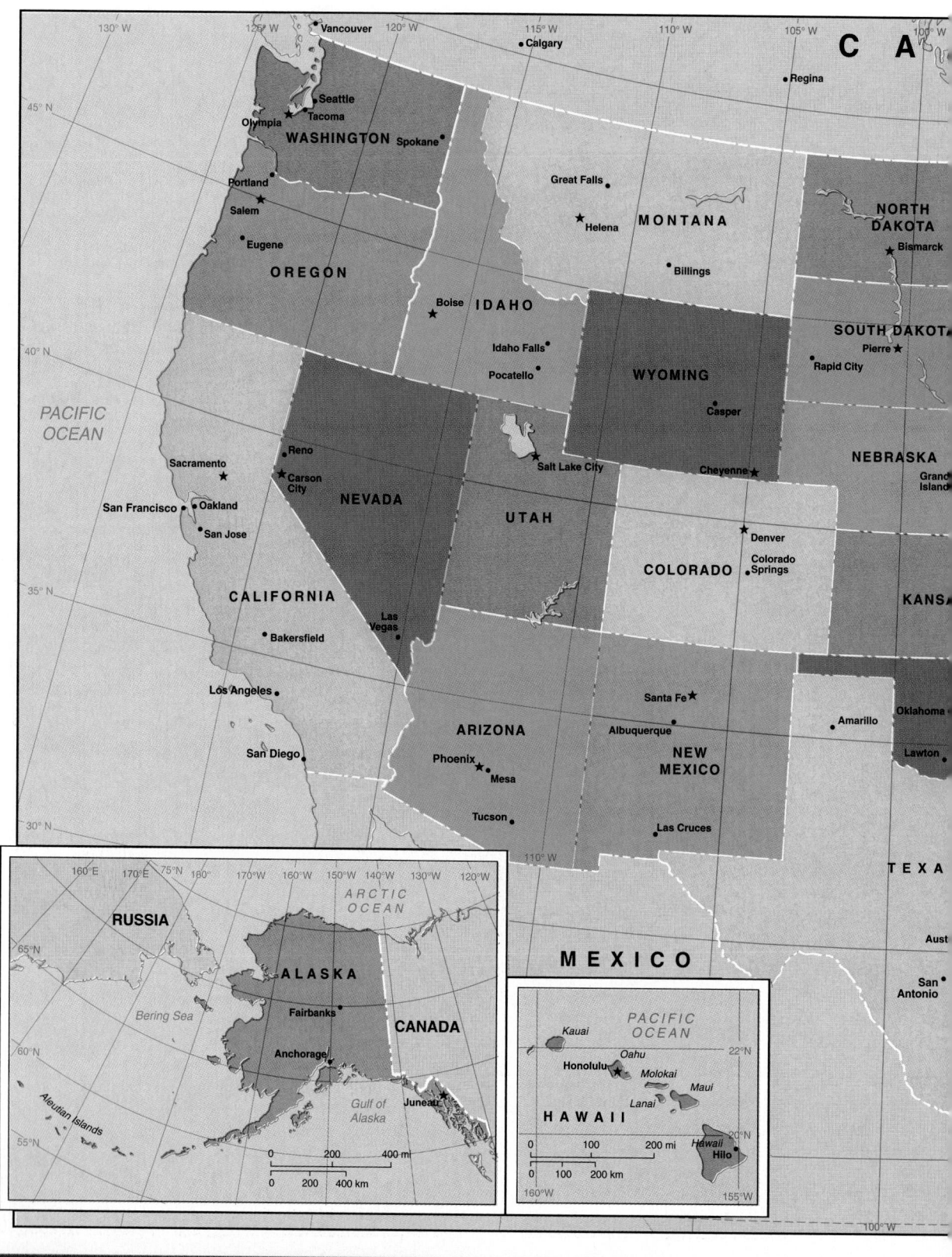

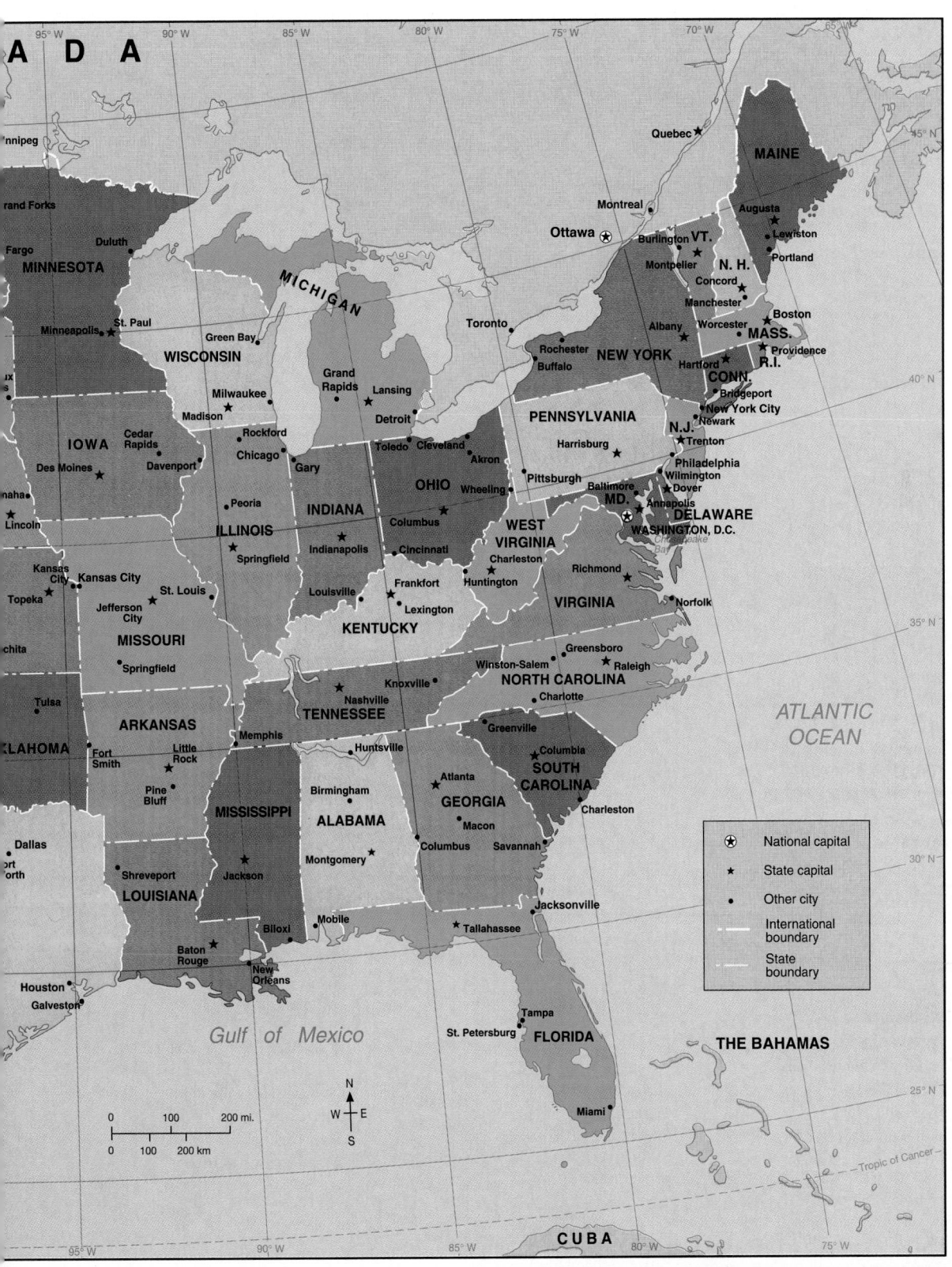

CANADA

95° W   90° W   85° W   80° W   75° W   70° W   65° W

45° N

Winnipeg

Grand Forks

Fargo

Duluth

MINNESOTA

Minneapolis   St. Paul

Sioux

IOWA   Cedar Rapids

Des Moines   Davenport

Omaha

Lincoln

WISCONSIN

Green Bay

Milwaukee

Madison   Rockford

Chicago   Gary

Peoria

ILLINOIS   Springfield

Kansas City   Kansas City

Topeka   Jefferson City

MISSOURI

Springfield

Wichita

OKLAHOMA   Fort Smith   Little Rock

Tulsa   Pine Bluff

MICHIGAN

Grand Rapids   Lansing

Detroit

Toledo   Cleveland   Akron

INDIANA

Columbus

Indianapolis   Cincinnati

OHIO   Wheeling

Pittsburgh

Louisville   Frankfort   Huntington

Lexington   Charleston

KENTUCKY

WEST VIRGINIA

TENNESSEE

Nashville   Knoxville

Memphis   Huntsville

ARKANSAS

MISSISSIPPI   **ALABAMA**

Birmingham

Jackson   Montgomery

Dallas   Fort Worth

Shreveport

LOUISIANA

Baton Rouge   Biloxi   Mobile

New Orleans

Houston

Galveston

Gulf of Mexico

Toronto

Rochester   Buffalo

NEW YORK

PENNSYLVANIA

Harrisburg

Baltimore

VIRGINIA

Richmond   Norfolk

Winston-Salem   Greensboro   Raleigh

NORTH CAROLINA   Charlotte

Greenville

Columbia   **SOUTH CAROLINA**

GEORGIA   Charleston

Atlanta

Macon

Columbus   Savannah

Jacksonville

Tallahassee

Tampa

St. Petersburg   **FLORIDA**

Miami

Quebec

Montreal

Ottawa   Burlington   **VT.**   **MAINE**

Montpelier   Augusta   Lewiston

Concord   **N. H.**   Portland

Manchester

Albany   Worcester   Boston

MASS.

Hartford   Providence

CONN.   **R.I.**

Bridgeport

New York City

N.J.   Newark

Trenton

Philadelphia

Wilmington

MD.   Dover

Annapolis   **DELAWARE**

WASHINGTON, D.C.

Chesapeake Bay

ATLANTIC OCEAN

THE BAHAMAS

Tropic of Cancer

CUBA

45° N
40° N
35° N
30° N
25° N

Symbol	Legend
⊛	National capital
★	State capital
•	Other city
— — —	International boundary
— — —	State boundary

N
W — E
S

0   100   200 mi.

0   100   200 km

1015

Presidents of the United States

Beneath each president's picture are his name, his age on becoming president, the state where he was born, his birth and death dates, his years in office, his political party, the name of his vice-president, and the name of his first lady.

George Washington, 57
Virginia (1732-1799)
In office: 1789-1797
No political party
John Adams
Martha Dandridge Washington

John Adams, 61
Massachusetts (1735-1826)
In office: 1797-1801
Federalist Party
Thomas Jefferson
Abigail Smith Adams

Thomas Jefferson, 57
Virginia (1743-1826)
In office: 1801-1809
Democratic-Republican Party
Aaron Burr; George Clinton
widower

James Madison, 57
Virginia (1751-1836)
In office: 1809-1817
Democratic-Republican Party
George Clinton; Elbridge Gerry
Dolley Payne Madison

James Monroe, 58
Virginia (1758-1831)
In office: 1817-1825
Democratic-Republican Party
Daniel D. Tompkins
Elizabeth Kortright Monroe

John Quincy Adams, 57
Massachusetts (1767-1848)
In office: 1825-1829
Democratic-Republican Party
John C. Calhoun
Louisa Johnson Adams

Andrew Jackson, 61
South Carolina (1767-1845)
In office: 1829-1837
Democratic Party
John C. Calhoun; Martin Van Buren
widower

Martin Van Buren, 54
New York (1782-1862)
In office: 1837-1841
Democratic Party
Richard M. Johnson
widower

William Henry Harrison, 68
Virginia (1773-1841)
In office: 1841 (one month)*
Whig Party
John Tyler
Anna Symmes Harrison

* died in office

John Tyler, 51
Virginia (1790-1862)
In office: 1841-1845
Whig Party
(No vice-president)
Letitia Tyler (died in 1842);
Julia Tyler

James K. Polk, 49
North Carolina (1795-1849)
In office: 1845-1849
Democratic Party
George M. Dallas
Sarah Childress Polk

Zachary Taylor, 64
Virginia (1784-1850)
In office: 1849-1850*
Whig Party
Millard Fillmore
Margaret Smith Taylor

Millard Fillmore, 50
New York (1800-1874)
In office: 1850-1853
Whig Party
(No vice-president)
Abigail Powers Fillmore

Franklin Pierce, 48
New Hampshire (1804-1869)
In office: 1853-1857
Democratic Party
William R. King
Jane Appleton Pierce

James Buchanan, 65
Pennsylvania (1791-1868)
In office: 1857-1861
Democratic Party
John C. Breckinridge
Unmarried

Abraham Lincoln, 52
Kentucky (1809-1865)
In office: 1861-1865 †
Republican Party
Hannibal Hamlin; Andrew Johnson
Mary Todd Lincoln

Andrew Johnson, 56
North Carolina (1808-1875)
In office: 1865-1869
Democratic Party
(No vice-president)
Eliza McCardle Johnson

Ulysses S. Grant, 46
Ohio (1822-1885)
In office: 1869-1877
Republican Party
Schuyler Colfax; Henry Wilson
Julia Dent Grant

Rutherford B. Hayes, 54
Ohio (1822-1893)
In office: 1877-1881
Republican Party
William A. Wheeler
Lucy Webb Hayes

James A. Garfield, 49
Ohio (1831-1881)
In office: 1881 (6 1/2 months) †
Republican Party
Chester A. Arthur
Lucretia Rudolph Garfield

Chester A. Arthur, 51
Vermont (1829-1886)
In office: 1881-1885
Republican Party
(No vice-president)
Ellen Herndon Arthur

† assassinated   * died in office

Grover Cleveland, 47 and 55
New Jersey (1837-1908)
In office: 1885-1889; 1893-1897
Democratic Party
Thomas Hendricks;
Adlai E. Stevenson
Frances Folsom Cleveland

Benjamin Harrison, 55
Ohio (1833-1901)
In office: 1889-1893
Republican Party
Levi P. Morton
Caroline Scott Harrison

William McKinley, 54
Ohio (1843-1901)
In office: 1897-1901 †
Republican Party
Garret A. Hobart; Theodore Roosevelt
Ida Saxton McKinley

Theodore Roosevelt, 42
New York (1858-1919)
In office: 1901-1909
Republican Party
Charles Warren Fairbanks
Edith Carow Roosevelt

William Howard Taft, 51
Ohio (1857-1930)
In office: 1909-1913
Republican Party
James S. Sherman
Helen Herron Taft

Woodrow Wilson, 56
Virginia (1856-1924)
In office: 1913-1921
Democratic Party
Thomas A. Marshall
Ellen Wilson (died 1914);
Edith Wilson

Warren G. Harding, 55
Ohio (1865-1923)
In office: 1921-1923*
Republican Party
Calvin Coolidge
Florence Kling Harding

Calvin Coolidge, 51
Vermont (1872-1933)
In office: 1923-1929
Republican Party
Charles G. Dawes
Grace Goodhue Coolidge

Herbert C. Hoover, 54
Iowa (1874-1964)
In office: 1929-1933
Republican Party
Charles Curtis
Lou Henry Hoover

Franklin Delano Roosevelt,
51
New York (1882-1945)
In office: 1933-1945*
Democratic Party
John Garner; Henry Wallace;
Harry S. Truman
Anna Eleanor Roosevelt

Harry S. Truman, 60
Missouri (1884-1972)
In office: 1945-1953
Democratic Party
Alben W. Barkley
Elizabeth (Bess) Wallace Truman

Dwight D. Eisenhower, 62
Texas (1890-1969)
In office: 1953-1961
Republican Party
Richard M. Nixon
Mamie Doud Eisenhower

* died in office

† assassinated

John F. Kennedy, 43
Massachusetts (1917-1963)
In office: 1961-1963 †
Democratic Party
Lyndon Baines Johnson
Jacqueline Bouvier Kennedy

Lyndon Baines Johnson, 55
Texas (1908-1973)
In office: 1963-1969
Democratic Party
Hubert H. Humphrey
Claudia (Lady Bird) Taylor Johnson

Richard M. Nixon, 56
California (1913-1994)
In office: 1969-1974 ‡
Republican Party
Spiro T. Agnew; Gerald R. Ford
Thelma (Pat) Ryan Nixon

Gerald R. Ford, 61
Nebraska (1913-)
In office: 1974-1977
Republican Party
Nelson Rockefeller
Elizabeth (Betty) Bloomer Ford

Jimmy (James E.) Carter, 52
Georgia (1924-)
In office: 1977-1981
Democratic Party
Walter F. Mondale
Rosalynn Smith Carter

Ronald Reagan, 69
Illinois (1911-)
In office: 1981-1989
Republican Party
George H. W. Bush
Nancy Davis Reagan

George H. W. Bush, 64
Massachusetts (1924-)
In office: 1989-1993
Republican Party
Dan (James Danforth) Quayle
Barbara Pierce Bush

Bill (William) Clinton, 46
Arkansas, (1946-)
In office: 1993-
Democratic Party
Albert Gore
Hillary Rodham Clinton

Facts About the Presidency

Qualifications
at least 35 years old
born a citizen of the United States
lived in the United States 14 years

Term of Office
four years, and not more than twice (since 1951)

Inauguration
January 20 after election (since 1933; formerly March 4)

Oath of Office
"I do solemnly swear (or affirm) that I will faithfully execute
the office of President of the United States, and will to the
best of my ability, preserve, protect, and defend the
Constitution of the United States."

† assassinated   ‡ resigned

Table of Chemical Elements

A scientific law of grouping chemical elements by the number of their protons and by their chemical similarities was proposed in 1869 by Russian chemist Dmitri Mendeleev. It is said that the idea came to him in a dream. Using this law, Mendeleev was able to predict the chemical qualities of three elements that scientists had not yet discovered. The accuracy of his predictions led chemists to accept his law and to create this table summarizing the results.

More than 40 chemical elements have been discovered since Mendeleev proposed his law, and each new element follows the same patterns as those before. Today, scientists create new elements artificially, using huge machines that slam atoms together. The atoms of the new elements are so unstable that they quickly break apart. As a result, scientists are not sure who first discovered many of these elements, or who should give them names. Officially, for now, they have numbers.

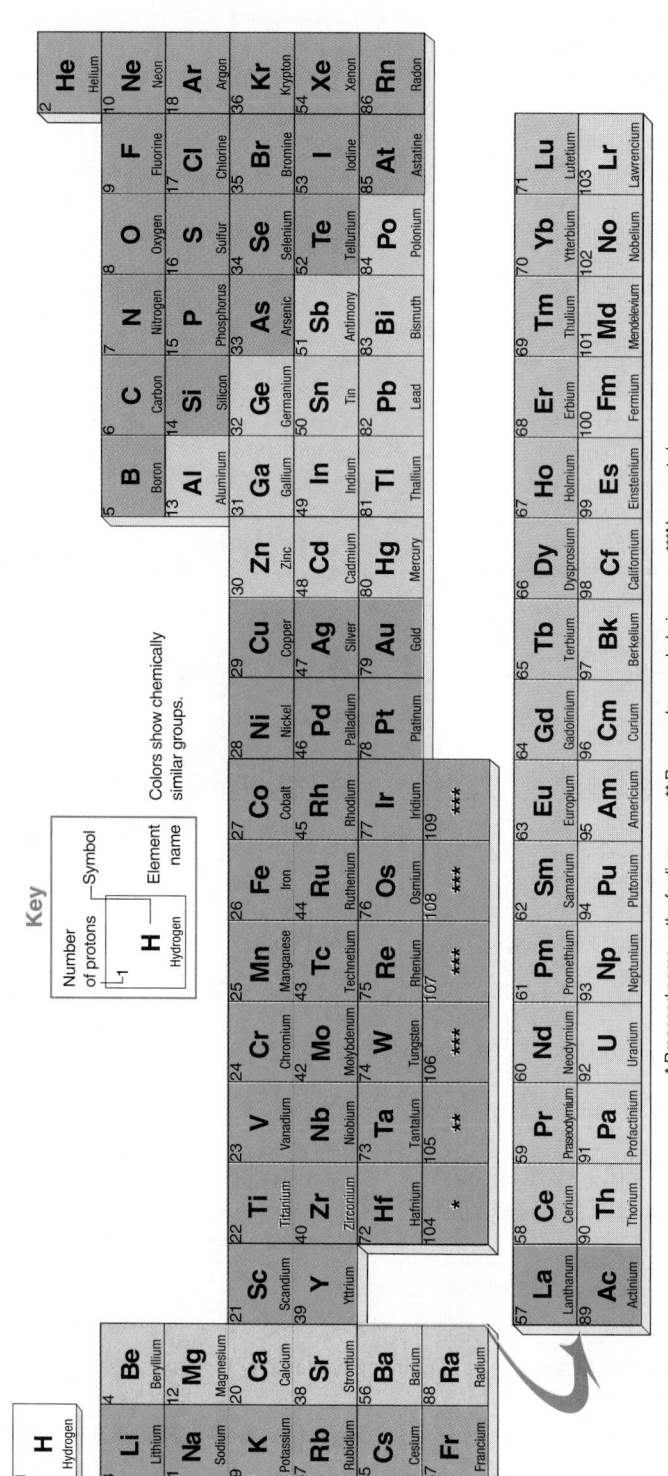

Key

Number of protons → 1
Symbol → **H**
Element name → Hydrogen

Colors show chemically similar groups.

* Proposed name, rutherfordium   ** Proposed name, hahnium   *** Name not chosen

Geological Time

CENOZOIC ERA	QUATERNARY PERIOD	*Recent Epoch*	Begins 11,000 years ago. Glaciers recede and Ice Age ends. Modern human beings live throughout the world. Climate mild to warm.
		Pleistocene Epoch	Begins 2,000,000 years ago. Massive glaciers erode the land and form many lake basins, including the Great Lakes. Human beings appear. Many large mammals become extinct. Climate cold to mild.
	TERTIARY PERIOD	*Pliocene Epoch*	Begins 12,000,000 years ago. Land bridge emerges between North and South America. Mammals continue development, migrate between continents, and remain dominant. Primates appear with some specifically human characteristics. Climate cooler.
		Miocene Epoch	Begins 25,000,000 years ago. First anthropoid apes appear. Mastodons appear in North America. Forests decrease while grasses develop and cover vast plains. Grazing mammals appear and flourish as a result. Climate mild to cool.
		Oligocene Epoch	Begins 40,000,000 years ago. Alps and Himalayas begin to rise. Modern mammals develop and become dominant. First apes appear. Forests widespread. Climate mild.
		Eocene Epoch	Begins 60,000,000 years ago. Mammals flourish; small ancestors of many modern mammals appear (cats, elephants). Flowering plants widespread. Tropical and subtropical forests. Climate mild to warm.
		Paleocene Epoch	Begins 70,000,000 years ago. Small, primitive mammals abundant. Modern toothless birds develop. First primates appear. Flowering plants dominant. Climate mild.
MESOZOIC ERA	CRETACEOUS PERIOD		Begins 135,000,000 years ago. Chalk deposited. Coal swamps formed in W North America. Mammals still insignificant in size and number compared to reptiles. Flowering plants and hardwood trees develop, become abundant. Dinosaurs and flying reptiles become extinct. Climate cool.
	JURASSIC PERIOD		Begins 180,000,000 years ago. Land is low with swampy areas and inland seas. Birds and flying reptiles appear. Dinosaurs are abundant. Small mammals and modern insects (bees, ants) develop. Climate mild and moist.
	TRIASSIC PERIOD		Begins 230,000,000 years ago. First dinosaurs and primitive mammals appear. Land and marine reptiles abundant. Cone-bearing plants grow in thick forests. Climate mild and dry.
PALEOZOIC ERA	PERMIAN PERIOD		Begins 260,000,000 years ago. Inland seas drain. Deserts and salt basins are common in Northern Hemisphere. Glaciation in Southern Hemisphere. Marine invertebrates and amphibians decrease. Reptiles increase. Many swamp plants become extinct. Climate warm and dry.
	CARBONIFEROUS PERIOD — PENNSYLVANIAN PERIOD		Begins 310,000,000 years ago. Large inland seas. Amphibians abundant. Reptiles appear. Large insects common. Thick fernlike vegetation in coal-forming, swampy forests. Climate warm and very moist.
	CARBONIFEROUS PERIOD — MISSISSIPPIAN PERIOD		Begins 350,000,000 years ago. Shallow seas and swampy lowlands widespread. Amphibians, sharks, and bony fishes abundant. Winged insects appear. Climate warm and moist.
	DEVONIAN PERIOD		Begins 400,000,000 years ago. Shallow seas widespread. Europe and North America probably part of same continent. Fishes increase in size and diversity. Seed-bearing plants appear. Climate hot and moist.
	SILURIAN PERIOD		Begins 425,000,000 years ago. Air-breathing animals appear. Primitive fishes highest form of life. First land plants (mosses) appear. Climate mild and dry.
	ORDOVICIAN PERIOD		Begins 500,000,000 years ago. Much of the land is covered by seas. First appearance of corals, clams, and cephalopods. First vertebrates (primitive fishes) appear. Climate mild.
	CAMBRIAN PERIOD		Begins 600,000,000 years ago. Living things become much more complex. First hard shells, legs, joints, and jaws appear. Common fossils are trilobites (insectlike sea animals), brachiopods, and snails. Climate mild.
PRECAMBRIAN ERA	**PROTEROZOIC ERA**		Begins about 2 billion years ago. Simple marine life (algae, fungi, and bacteria) develops. Evidence of some simple marine animals (sponges and wormlike animals). Climate warm to cool.
	ARCHEOZOIC ERA		Rocks about 3½ billion years old preserve a record of volcanic activity, mountain building, and erosion. First known life exists. Climate variable, but temperatures are such that water is a liquid rather than a solid or gas.

Mathematical Formulas

Perimeter (P) of a:

rectangle $=$ 2 × the length + 2 × the width
$P = 2l + 2w$

square $=$ 4 × the side
$P = 4s$

polygon $=$ the sum of the sides
$P = a + b + c + d$

Circumference (C) of a:

circle $=$ π × the diameter
$=$ π × twice the radius
$C = \pi d = 2\pi r$

Area (A) of a:

rectangle $=$ the length × the width
$A = lw$

square $=$ a side × a side
$A = s \times s = s^2$

triangle $=$ ½ × the base × the height
$A = \frac{1}{2}bh$

circle $=$ π × the radius × the radius
$A = \pi r^2$

parallelogram $=$ the base × the height
$A = bh$

trapezoid $=$ ½ × the height × the sum of the bases
$A = \frac{1}{2}h(a + b)$

Surface Area (S) of a:

cylinder $=$ 2π × the radius × (the radius + the height)
$S = 2\pi r(r + h)$

sphere $=$ 4π × the radius × the radius
$S = 4\pi r^2$

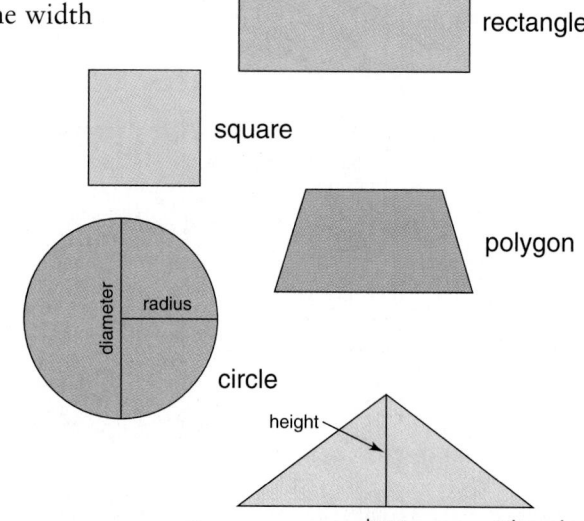

rectangle

square

polygon

circle

triangle

parallelogram

trapezoid

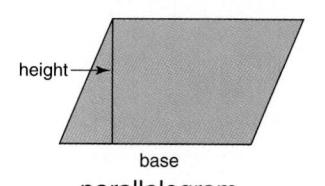

cylinder

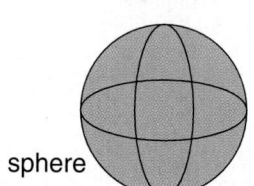

sphere

$$\text{cone} = \text{area of base} + \pi \times \text{radius} \times \text{slant height}$$
$$S = \pi r^2 + \pi r l = \pi r (r + l)$$

pyramid = the area of the base + ½ × the slant height × the perimeter of the base
$$S = \text{the area of the base} + \tfrac{1}{2} lP$$

rectangular prism = the sum of the area of its faces

cube = the sum of the area of its faces
$$S = 6s^2$$

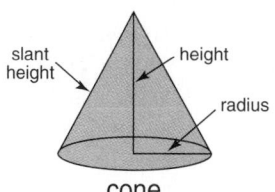

cone

Volume (V) of a:

cylinder = the area of the base × the height
$$V = Bh = \pi r^2 h$$

sphere = ⅓ × π × radius cubed
$$V = \tfrac{4}{3}\pi r^3$$

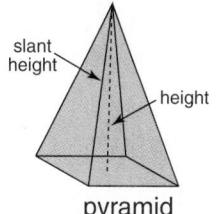

pyramid

cone = ⅓ × the area of the base × the height
$$V = \tfrac{1}{3} Bh = \tfrac{1}{3}\pi r^2 h$$

pyramid = ⅓ × the area of the base × the height
$$V = \tfrac{1}{3} Bh$$

rectangular prism = the length × the width × the height
$$V = lwh$$

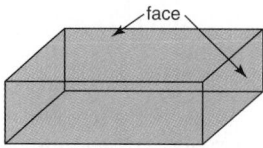

rectangular prism

cube = a side × a side × a side = side cubed
$$V = s^3$$

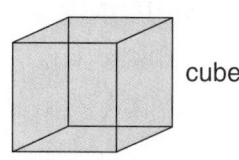

cube

Baseball Formulas:

$$\text{Batting Average} = \frac{\text{hits}}{\text{times at bat}}$$
$$BA = H \div AB$$

$$\text{Earned Run Average} = 9 \times \frac{\text{earned runs}}{\text{innings pitched}}$$
$$ERA = 9(R \div I)$$

Proofreader's Marks

Proofreader's Marks

the ⊘enator	*lc*	lowercase the capital letter
s̲e̲nator Watkins	*cap*	capitalize the lowercase letter
A̲TLANTIC	*c̲/lc*	initial capital with lowercase letters
Time̲	*ital*	indicate italics by underlining
motor cycle	◡	close up
She jumped off of the wall.	ℒ	delete
Paul called me Big Brover	*stet*	let it stand
in ㉕ years	(sp)	spell it out
I want ⌄talk to you.	∧	something left out
Mrs⌄ Maddox	⊙	insert period
my teacher⌄ Mr. Steiner	⋏	insert comma
groceries⌄ milk, butter, and jam	(:)	insert colon
We seldom see each other⌄ however, we are still friends.	;/	insert semicolon
Why did you say that⌄	?/	insert question mark
Mr. Lupas⌄ smile	⋎	insert apostrophe
Kevin said,⌄If you go . . .	⁌⁌	insert open quotation marks
"We should begin,⌄ she said.	⁍⁍	insert close quotation marks
high⌄school classes	/=/	insert hyphen
the following chart⌄see page 1⌄	(/)	insert parentheses
fre͡ind	∿	transpose
	⁋	new paragraph
	no ⁋	no new paragraph
All⌄right	#	insert space

Full pronunciation key

The pronunciation of each word is shown just after the word, in this way: **ab·bre·vi·ate** (ə brē′vē āt).

The letters and signs used are pronounced as in the words below.

The mark ′ is placed after a syllable with primary or heavy accent, as in the example above.

The mark ′ after a syllable shows a secondary or lighter accent, as in **ab·bre·vi·a·tion** (ə brē′vē ā′shən).

a	hat, cap		**p**	paper, cup
ā	age, face		**r**	run, try
â	care, fair		**s**	say, yes
ä	father, far		**sh**	she, rush
			t	tell, it
b	bad, rob		**th**	thin, both
ch	child, much		**ᴛʜ**	then, smooth
d	did, red			
			u	cup, butter
e	let, best		**u̇**	full, put
ē	equal, be		**ü**	rule, move
ėr	term, learn			
			v	very, save
f	fat, if		**w**	will, woman
g	go, bag		**y**	young, yet
h	he, how		**z**	zero, breeze
			zh	measure, seizure
i	it, pin			
ī	ice, five		**ə**	represents:
				a in about
j	jam, enjoy			e in taken
k	kind, seek			i in pencil
l	land, coal			o in lemon
m	me, am			u in circus
n	no, in			
ng	long, bring			
o	hot, rock			
ō	open, go			
ȯ	all, caught			
ô	order, all			
oi	oil, voice			
ou	house, out			